NOT … **典注解**

(abbreviat … **为缩略形式)**

abbreviation [abbr]	
aerospace	
algebra	
anatomy	
appendix [app]	
approving [approv]	褒义[褒]
archaic [arch]	古语[古]
architecture	建筑[建]
art	美术
astronomy	天文学[天]
attributive [attrib]	用作定语[作定语]
Australian [Austral]	澳大利亚英语[澳]
becoming dated	逐渐陈旧[渐旧]
bible	圣经
biology	生物学[生]
botany	植物学[植]
British (spelling, pronunciation, etc) [Brit]	英式英语
broadcasting	广播[播]
catchphrase	警语
chemistry	化学[化]
cinema	电影[影]
combining form [comb form]	构词成分
commerce	商业, 贸易[商]
comparative (form of an adjective, adverb) [compar]	比较级(形容词或副词形式)
computing	电子计算机技术[计]
contracted form	缩约式
dated	陈旧[旧]
derogatory [derog]	贬义[贬]
dialect	方言[方]
economics	经济[经]
education	教育[教]
electronics	电子学[电子]
emphatic [emph]	强调式[强调]
engineering	工程[工]
especially [esp]	尤指, 尤作, 尤为, 尤称, 尤用于
euphemistic [euph]	委婉语[婉]
feminine [fem]	阴性
figurative [fig]	比喻用法[比喻]
finance	财政, 金融[财]
formal [fml]	文雅语, 书面语, 郑重语, 庄重语, 正规用语[文]
formerly	旧时
French	法语[法]
geography	地理学[地理]
geology	地质学[地质]
geometry	几何[几]
German	德语[德]
Greek	希腊语[希腊]
heraldry	纹章[纹]
history	历史[史]
idiom(s) [idm]	习语
illustration [illus]	插图
in compounds	用以构成复合词
informal [infml]	口语, 通俗语, 俗(读)作[口]
Irish	爱尔兰英语[爱尔兰]

ironic	反语
Italian	意大利语[意]
jocular [joc]	戏谑语[谑]
journalism	新闻学[新闻]
Latin	拉丁语[拉]
law	法律[律]
linguistics	语言学[语言]
literature	文学
masculine [masc]	阳性
mathematics	数学[数]
medical	医学[医]
medicine	药物(学)[药]
military	军事[军]
music	音乐[音]
nautical	航海[海]
negative [neg]	否定(词),否定式
New Zealand [NZ]	新西兰英语[新西兰]
non-standard	不规范
offensive	轻蔑语[蔑]
often	常作
personal pronoun [pers pron]	人称代词
philosophy	哲学[哲]
phonetics	语音学[语音]
photography	摄影[摄]
physics	物理学[物]
plural unchanged [pl unchanged]	复数不变
politics	政治[政]
predicative [pred]	用作表语[作表语]
prefix [pref]	前缀
proprietary [propr]	专利名称[专利名]
psychology	心理学[心]
radio	无线电技术[无]
rare	罕
reflexive [reflex]	反身
relative [rel]	关系词[关系]
religion	宗教[宗]
rhetorical [rhet]	修辞学[修辞]
Russian	俄语[俄]
saying	谚语[谚]
Scottish [Scot]	苏格兰英语[苏格兰]
sexist	性别偏见
slang [sl]	俚语[俚]
sociology	社会学[社]
sometimes	有时作
South African [S African]	南非英语[南非]
Spanish	西班牙语[西]
sport	体育[体]
strong form	强读式
suffix [suff]	后缀
superlative (form of an adjective, adverb) [superl]	最高级(形容词或副词形式)
symbol [symb]	符号
taboo [⚠]	避讳语[讳]
television [TV]	电视[视]
theatre	戏剧[戏]
United States (spelling, pronunciation, etc) [US]	美式英语
usually [usu]	通常作
zoology	动物学[动]

牛津高阶
英汉双解词典

OXFORD
ADVANCED LEARNER'S
ENGLISH-CHINESE
DICTIONARY

第四版　增补本

Extended fourth edition

正文原著：霍恩比 (AS Hornby)
正文编译：李北达

商务印书馆
The Commercial Press

牛津大学出版社
Oxford University Press

OXFORD
UNIVERSITY PRESS

牛津大学出版社隶属牛津大学，出版业务遍布全球，致力弘扬牛津大学推动优质研究、学术和教育的宗旨。

牛津　纽约
奥克兰　曼谷　布宜诺斯艾利斯　开普敦　马德拉斯
达累斯萨拉姆　德里　香港　伊斯坦布尔　卡拉奇　加尔各答
吉隆坡　马德里　墨尔本　墨西哥城　孟买　奈罗比
圣保罗　上海　新加坡　台北　东京　多伦多

联营公司：柏林

OXFORD 为牛津大学出版社之注册商标

牛津高阶英汉双解词典（第四版）
英语原版 Oxford Advanced Learner's Dictionary of Current English (Fourth edition)

印次（即最小之数字）29 28 27 26

ISBN 7-100-03415-9/H·869（简体字本）

出版：　商务印书馆
北京王府井大街36号（邮政编码 100710）
牛津大学出版社（中国）有限公司
香港鲗鱼涌英皇道979号太古坊和域大厦东翼18楼
印刷：　中国
国内总发行：商务印书馆
国外以及香港、澳门、台湾地区总发行：牛津大学出版社（中国）有限公司

牛津高阶英汉双解词典(第四版)
(简化汉字本)

增补本出版说明

本书是《牛津高阶英汉双解词典》第四版的简化汉字本,自1997年问世以来,颇受读者青睐,连年再版,印数已达百万册,并多次荣登畅销书榜首。

目前,人类已进入信息化的21世纪,随着各个领域的飞速发展,大量的新词新语涌进我们的生活。为了更快地进入新世纪全球化的信息通道,牛津大学出版社于1999年推出该词典的《增补本》,增加了100页的"新词补编"(置于词典正文之后),亦即增收了近年来在物理、化学、天文学、医学、生物工程、电子计算机等高科技领域以及政治、经济、社会生活、文学艺术、大众传媒等方面出现的约3000个英语新词(或具有了新义的旧词)。这些新词因频繁地出现在当今英语图书和报刊之中而成为我们阅读的拦路虎。从这个意义上讲,《增补本》的出版可谓与时俱进。此外,《增补本》中还增加了餐厅、卧室、厨房、卫生间和浴室这四个与生活密切相关的插图附录,以满足读者各个方面的需求。

经牛津大学出版社授权,我馆推出该词典简化汉字版的《增补本》,相信这部《增补本》一定会受到广大读者的欢迎。

商务印书馆编辑部

2002年1月

牛津高阶英汉双解词典（第四版）
（简化汉字本）

出版说明

本书原称*Oxford Advanced Learner's Dictionary of Current English*（简称*OALD*），其英文本自问世以来历经三次修订，在本世纪下半叶40多年中一直风行全世界，受到广大读者的热烈欢迎。1988年，我馆经牛津大学出版社准许，在内地出版发行《牛津现代高级英汉双解词典》（简化汉字本），其英文本即本词典的第三版。1989年，牛津大学出版社推出词典英文本的第四版，由著名语言学家A.P.Cowie主持，对第三版又作了全面的修订，使词典的篇幅比第三版增加了50%以上，在选词、注音、释义、例证、用法说明、句型符号以及习语的收录等各个方面都作了更新，因而内容更丰富、更实用、更切合非英语国家广大英语学习者的需求，堪称当今英语词典之佼佼者。1994年，词典的英汉双解本问世，书名改称《牛津高阶英汉双解词典》（李北达编译，英汉双解繁体汉字本，牛津大学出版社，1994，香港）。经牛津大学出版社惠允，我馆可在内地出版发行上述英汉双解版的简化汉字本，也就是摆在读者面前的这一本书。

本书出版前，经牛津大学出版社同意，我们对原书在文字上作了一些技术处理，使之更符合内地读者的习惯。如有不妥之处，敬请读者指正。

商务印书馆编辑部

1997年7月

CONTENTS 目录

序言一 —— 金圣华

学习外语，就好比闯入一个文化隔阂、风光迥异的国度，举目所见，全是陌生的事物，漠然的脸孔。如何在这毫不熟悉的环境中生活求存、立足植根？这就想起了一句老话："在家靠父母，出外靠朋友。"

对了，必须靠朋友。朋友在哪里？各式各类的词典、词汇，就是学习外语必备的良伴。然而初学者往往不知就里，毫无头绪，最喜欢把坊间一大堆词典，不管有用没用，照搬回家，陈列案头，以备不时之需。谁知道一旦在学习中碰到难题，需要有人指点迷津时，却发觉尽管翻破多少词典，也往往不得要领。这就悟出相识满天下，知己无一人的道理。原来，徒有泛泛之交，并不济事。自以为朋友众多，到了紧要关头，却一个也唤不来。因此，择书如择友，选择适当的词典，更应小心翼翼、慎于分辨。

《牛津高阶英汉双解词典》(《OALECD》) 第4版编排严谨，释义详尽，处处为用者着想，因此自1994年出版以来，广受欢迎。然而，目前科技发达，资讯频繁，自1994年至今，仅仅五、六年间，英语世界中又衍生出成千上万的新字新词。这些词汇字组，涵盖极广，举凡西方社会日常生活的每一层面，均有所涉，真可谓五花八门、洋洋大观，例如 software piracy（涉及电脑）、superbug（涉及医药）、stage-diving（涉及流行音乐）、sound bite（涉及媒体）、veg out（涉及电视）等字眼，触目可见。语言文字，是思想文化的媒介，要了解今日西方文明的演变，促进中外文化的交流，英语新词，不可不学。牛津词典出版组有鉴及此，乃从各类资料文献如《Oxford Advanced Learner's Dictionary》第5版、《The Oxford Dictionary of New Words》，以及电视电台、报章刊物中，将目前最为流行的新字新词，按中国读者所需，精挑细选，去芜存菁，筛出新词约3000个，编译成册，这就是第4版《新词补编》的由来。

一如既往，《新词补编》的体例编排，跟正文一般，亦以中英对照、例句详尽为特色。《OALECD》的编者，一向矢志以"原文要懂、译文要通"为原则，这原则，看似简单，实则不然。仅以"译文要通"来说，坊间许多双语词典就做不到。词典中的词条，既要释义，又要举例，若能释义正确无误，例句扼要实用，而又没有"译文腔"佶屈聱牙，生硬死板的弊病，诚非易事。在《新词补编》中，喜见译文精简恰当，畅顺可读，例如 bird-strike 一词，意指飞鸟与飞机相撞引致的空难，例句中提到 several wild geese 时，译为"几只野雁"，而非如一般粗心大意的译者般译成"几只野鹅"；shoebox 一词译为"斗室、小屋、蜗居"；trophy wife 一词的例句中，谈到年老丈夫携年轻妻子亮相时，The old man was clearly thrilled ...，译为"那老头儿……兴奋之情溢于言表"等，都一再表现出编译者的苦心与功力。

翻译新词，有时可以套用旧语，赋予新义，但一不留神，就会似是而非，多生误会。万一英语新词所代表的内涵意念，复杂抽象，无法在中文已有词汇中找到意义对等的字眼，就必须译制新词。在《新词补编》中，trophy wife 译为"门面夫人"、courtesy car 译为"迎宾车"等，都是可取的例子。但译制时应严格遵守汉语的规范，以免产生非驴非马、不中不西的表达方式，变成污染中文的始作俑者。

《牛津高阶英汉双解词典》增补本中，旧词新字，兼集一书，恰似人生道上，旧雨新知，欢聚一堂。增补本内容翔实，包罗万有，在吾人学习英语的漫漫长途中，不啻为足以信赖的良朋益友。

金圣华
香港中文大学

金圣华，香港中文大学翻译系讲座教授；1990至1992年任香港翻译学会会长。金教授曾出版多本创作及翻译论著，如《桥畔闲眺》、《打开一扇门》、《一道清流》；《英译中：英汉翻译概论》、《英语新辞辞汇》、《桥畔译谈：翻译散论八十篇》、《傅雷与他的世界》等；并翻译出版多部文学作品，如麦克勒丝的《小酒馆的悲歌》、康拉德的《海隅逐客》、厄戴克的《约翰·厄戴克小说选集》、布迈恪的《石与影》和《黑娃的故事》等。1997年6月因对推动香港翻译工作贡献良多而获OBE（英帝国官佐）勋衔。

序言二 —— 余光中

享誉五百多年的牛津大学出版社，即使英语词典之编印，也已超过百年。在系衍族繁的牛津词典世家之中，最适合非英语国家的学生查用的一种，首推这部《Oxford Advanced Learner's Dictionary》(简称《OALD》)。

本书初版于 1948 年，由霍恩比 (A.S. Hornby) 主编。其后在 1963年与 1974年历经增订，读者日众，先后印刷59次。1989年由考伊 (A.P. Cowie) 主持增订，推出这广受欢迎的第4版。编者在序言里开宗明义就指出：《OALD》旨在解决外国学生研习英语所面临的特殊困难，若能善用，无论对其阅读或写作，均必大有裨益。第4版在前三版的坚实基础上精益求精，在语法、句型、例句各方面更为加强，并彻底修订了动词的分类，而且简化了成语、派生词、复合词等等的检寻。参与第4版编写工作的各行专家，多达40余人；词典学者有17人之众，已称鼎盛，甚至插图绘制也动员了十多位行家，可见专业之谨严，规模之庞大。

我使用本书的第4版已有年余，觉其编排紧凑，解析详尽，查阅省时，而例句之多，尤便于解惑释疑。要了解一字一词，与其个别释义，不如置于句中，用上下文的呼应来衬托，更加明了。这一点，林语堂先生最为强调。一般人常说查词典，如果有谁主张读词典，人必笑其迂阔。其实，好的词典不但要勤查，也应细读。当然不是整页整本地阅读，而是在查某字某词之际，应该把它所属的标题仔细读完，包括例句。英文往往一词数解，常用词的定义尤为繁复，初习者必须逐条耐心细读，若是只查了前面的一两条说明，便含糊接受，就会文不对题。像《OALD》这么精编详析的词典，每一则注释、每一个符号都有作用，不可草草放过。查词典，是学习英语必下的基本功夫。老师所教的毕竟有限，但词典所教的，却是无穷。

除了正文之外，本书前后的附录与图表等等多达百页，至为丰富，足见编辑小组为了方便读者，真是煞费苦心。这些附录都是“入境问俗”所必具，并非锦上添花、聊备一格。

初用本书的读者，至少应该先将前面的音标、注解二表和简要的实用说明，细细阅读，并且时时重温。后面的图表也应常加参考，标点的用法尤应熟悉。

研究最为深入而设计最具匠心、最有条理的一大附录，是全书之末的详细说明。其中语法指南的部分尤为透彻，动词的句型更是条分缕析，32型的变化逐一道来，并详加举例，真是洋洋大观。读者真要善用此书，就应该耐心细看一遍，以后也应常常查阅，好在后衬页附有32型的动词模式表，可以一索即得。本书编者对读者的照顾体贴，已经无微不至，只等读者善加利用，努力自修了。

不过，使用本书的读者首应了解，这本词典针对的是当代英语，如果他要解决的疑难，不属当代而是古代的英文，例如莎士比亚的剧本或是米尔顿的史诗，那他就应去查别种词典。专就当代英语的解释与示范而言，则本书之规模与品质确乎出类拔萃。正如众多学者一样，我也深受其益，所以乐于推荐给广大读者。

《牛津高阶英汉双解词典》第4版中译详实，对于初习者最为方便。读者如能英汉同时并比参阅，当可左右逢源，深入了解，则在查词典之余尚可兼学翻译，又添一种收获了。

余光中
台湾中山大学

余光中，福建永春人，1928年生于南京。先后肄业于金陵大学及厦门大学，1952年台湾大学外文系毕业，1959年美国爱奥华大学文艺硕士。曾任教于台湾师范大学、政治大学之外文系及香港中文大学之中文系，1985年任台湾中山大学文学院长、外文研究所长，现任中山大学讲座教授。

余教授出版专书40多种，包括诗集《莲的联想》、《白玉苦瓜》、《与永恒拔河》、《安石榴》；散文集《听听那冷雨》、《记忆和铁轨一样长》、《隔水呼渡》；翻译《梵谷传》、《老人和大海》、《英美现代诗选》等。所译王尔德喜剧《不可儿戏》、《温夫人的扇子》、《理想丈夫》屡在台港上演。评论集《从徐霞客到梵谷》与《井然有序》曾获1994及1996之联合报年度最佳书奖。

余光中的诗文先后收入中学及大专课本，近年亦为大陆及香港课本采用。《乡愁》等诗谱成歌曲，对现代民歌运动颇有影响。为他谱曲的音乐家包括吕泉生、戴金泉、周蓝萍、杨弦、李泰祥、罗大佑、应广仪等多人。

序言三——郑仰平

翻词典是件乐事。我们每天都会碰到一些新字新词，要是能养成习惯，每天晚上睡觉之前都要去查一查，总会学到些新知识，这一天也没有白过。法国巴黎大学高级翻译学院前院长 Danica Seleskovitch 女士说过，从事口译工作的人，绝不能放过一个生字，遇到不认识的字就要查个明白。

语文其实同其他学问一样，我们穷一生的努力，也只能学到一部分，而且常常是一小部分而已。忘了是谁说的，“语言是活的，像人，像河，总是改变。”

所以，我们用的词典不论怎样完善，也只能用来参考，绝不能代替我们思考。而我们常常看到，从事语文工作的人，总会有几十本词典，原因就是：每一本词典固然都有其优点，但也会有其不足之处。

《牛津高阶英汉双解词典》是一本比较完善的词典，兼有英英和英汉词典之长，对中学生和大学生，甚至做翻译工作的人也足够了。

但是，对语文有兴趣的读者，千万不要吝惜在词典上所花的钱。不同的词典，可以在不同方面满足你对语文的好奇心。这些收获，不是金钱可以买到的。

郑仰平
香港城市大学

郑仰平，原籍广东，1929年出生于香港，早年于上海及广州接受教育。郑氏于1950年到香港，任职香港电台，后于1961年往印度，于印度电台中文台主持新闻专辑，开始从事翻译及广播工作。于1964年回港后不久，郑氏随即赴伦敦，在英国广播电台继续翻译及广播事业。

郑先生于1972年返港，出任香港政府的即时传译总主任，并于同年的立法局会议上提供即时传译服务。

1983年中国及英国政府就香港前途问题进行谈判期间，郑先生为英方首席传译员。1984年中英政府签署联合声明后，郑氏在联合联络小组担任传译员，至1986年获擢升为会议传译总主任，负责培训普通话传译人才。

1987年，郑氏到美国加州蒙特雷国际研究学院出任翻译系副教授。1989年转往台湾辅仁大学任翻译学研究所副教授。1990年返港后加入《明报》，并曾于香港城市大学任教。

郑氏为国际传译员协会会员，于1989年获香港翻译学会颁授荣誉会士衔。

序言四 —— 王佐良

我在50年代在北京教英语之初，用过不少词典，发现它们多数只利于阅读英文书刊，唯有一部新出版的《Oxford Advanced Learner's Dictionary》(简称《OALD》) 对外国人学习使用英语最有帮助。常用词的用法处理特别细致，例句语言地道，处处考虑到外国学生的特殊困难。动词按照用法归纳成若干类型尤为一大特色，这也正是编者霍恩比 (A.S. Hornby) 先生对词典学的贡献。

在日常教学的实际使用中，《OALD》能够帮忙帮到点子上。正是你感到困惑的地方，它能给你清楚的指点。因此师生都喜欢用它。它一再重版，后来又配上高质量的汉语译文而出版了双解本 (《Oxford Advanced Learner's English-Chinese Dictionary》《牛津高阶英汉双解词典》)。本双解版英汉并重，中译符合汉语规范。中国学生定能从中获得更大的益处。

现在这个新版保持了以前各版的优点，而又作了改进。本书文字处理更精当，例句更丰富，动词类型划分得更科学；此外还增加了用法说明，加上印刷清楚，排版醒目，是一部美观实用的工具书。

我自己现在仍在经常用它，除了查词的用法，也通过它来加深我对词义的了解。上面说了，这本词典的优点之一是能帮助人弄清英语的用法。但是用法是根据意义而变的，只有通过不同的用法才能掌握一个词的确切含义。特别在"短语动词" (phrasal verb) 方面，搭配上的小小不同就能引起意义上的巨大差别。这时候《牛津高阶英汉双解词典》对它们的细致处理和大量例句就起了很好的辨析作用。因此多查这本词典，不仅能帮助人说好写好英语，还能使他更确切地听懂读懂英语，收获是双重的。我对此有切身体会，所以乐于把它推荐给广大的英语学生。

王佐良
北京外国语大学

王佐良（1916–1995），浙江上虞人，清华大学毕业，牛津大学研究生。历任北京外国语学院英语系主任、副院长、顾问，院学术委员会主任，博士生导师，北京外国语大学外国文学研究所所长、国务院学位委员会学科评议组外国文学组组长、中国外国文学学会副会长、中国莎士比亚研究会副会长、中国作家协会外国文学委员会委员、国家教委高等学校专业外语编审委员会主任、国家教委高等学校专业外语教学指导委员会顾问、中华文学基金会中英文学交流奖评议委员会主任、中国外语教学研究会副会长、中国英语教学研究会会长、《外国文学》和《文苑》主编。

王佐良的著（译）作计30余部。主要译作有：培根的《随笔》、《彭斯诗选》、《苏格兰诗选》、《英国诗选》，以及《雷雨》的英译本。代表作有：《英国诗史》、《英国散文的流变》、《莎士比亚绪论》、《论契合——比较文学研究集》、《翻译：思考与试笔》、《心智的风景线》、《论新开端》和《照澜集》。他还是《英国二十世纪文学史》、《英国文学名篇选注》、《欧洲文化入门》和《英语文体学引论》等书的主编和《汉英词典》的副主编。由于他在外国文学研究领域所作的开创性贡献，曾先后获得北京市哲学社会科学优秀成果荣誉奖、一等奖、全国高校优秀教材奖和高校出版社优秀学术专著奖。

序言五 —— 董乐山

原名《牛津现代高级英汉双解词典》去年出了第4版，改名为《牛津高阶英汉双解词典》，并有在内地发行汉语简体字本的计划，这是英汉词典界值得称道的一件事。

我从事英语翻译工作快50年了，接触到的英汉词典不少，但真正得心应手的却不多。这大概是由于本人翻译工作的性质所决定，而一般词典或者过于一般化，或者过于专业化，都不能满足有综合化这个特殊要求的翻译工作的需要。而《OALD》是一本供高年级学生学习英语使用的词典，针对性很强，对于从事英语教学者很有用，因此，我在50年代最初见这本词典时，由于它对我的用途不大，没有怎么在意。

到了60年代我改行做了一段时间的英语教学工作，这才发现《OALD》可以说是英语教员所必备的一本工具书。我尤其欣赏它的两大优点：一是用英语释义，不但便于教学，而且有利于帮助学生确切掌握词义；二是它归纳了多种基本句型，便于启发和提高学生的造句能力。这两者对于打好学生英语基础都有很大帮助，不是一般词典所能及的。后来《OALD》又出了英汉双解版，我又担心添了汉语解释，是否会画蛇添足，或者“扬短避长”，反而失去了原来用英语解释的特色？

最近有机会读到《OALD》的英汉双解第四版，颇有耳目一新之感，发现它的汉语注释和例句翻译不但没有减弱原来英语注释的作用，反而进一步增强了使用者对词义的理解，而且由于有例句翻译，对于翻译工作者寻找适当的汉语表达方式也提供了启迪，这是十分难能可贵的。特别是由于词条的增添，例句、插图、附录等等的丰富，它已不是一部learner’s dictionary，而是user’s dictionary了。

最后要提一下的是：它的汉语名称中“高级”一词改为“高阶”，仅此一端，可以看出主其事者确是高手，因为原来的名称不免有misnomer之疵。

董乐山
中国社会科学院
美国研究所

董乐山（1924–1999），1946年毕业于上海圣约翰大学英国文学系，国内著名翻译家和美国学学者。曾任中国社会科学院美国研究所研究员及研究生院美国学系主任。

董氏的著名译作有《第三帝国的兴亡》、《西行漫记》、《1984》、《中午的黑暗》、《基督的最后诱惑》、《苏格拉底的审判》、《西方人文主义传统》、《奥威尔文集》、《古典学》等。撰写和编纂的作品有《译余废墨》、《边缘人语》、《文化的休闲》、《文化的误读》、《美国的罪与罚》、《英汉美国社会知识小辞典》等。

社会职务方面，董氏为中国作家协会会员、国际笔会中国中心会员、中国翻译工作者协会理事、中国美国文学研究会常务理事、中华美国学会第一届常务理事、前三S研究会副会长等。董氏曾获上海文汇报短篇小说一等奖、广东地区文学翻译一等奖、中美文学交流奖等。

编译者序 —— 李北达

翻译词典是件苦事，越认真越苦。回想20年前参与翻译《An English Reader's Dictionary》(《牛津英汉双解词典》后易名《牛津进阶英汉双解词典》)，译者多凭自己的语言知识参考其他英汉词典进行翻译，不免产生一些错误，如将 suet 译作“板油（羊牛腰子上的硬脂肪，可作烹调用）”，又如将 gear“排挡”误作“排档”，校订时也未察不妥。后来知道只有猪的体腔内才有“板油”，而“挡”与“档”二字的形、音、义皆不同。英汉词典中似是而非的“混血词”和“混血句”不胜枚举，且以讹传讹、为虎作伥，愧对莘莘学子。

此次翻译《Oxford Advanced Learner's Dictionary》，要求原文要懂，译文要通。原文要懂，就是要求译者充分理解原文，先将原文定义准确译出，帮助使用词典的人理解原文，然后再将汉语对应词置于定义之后。对应词力求贴切，宁缺勿滥。在定义之后的示例中，选用适合示例中的词语而不机械地套用定义译文中的对应词。这样既丰富了定义的对应词，也可避免初学者误将词典奉为圭臬，从而可进一步扩大思路，达到本词典抛砖引玉的目的。译文要通，就是力求汉语词句规范，在汉语工具书中有据可查，包括人名和地名用字、数字用法等。根据原文需要，译文也相应或文或俗，不避讳粗鄙词语，但尽力避免使用方言词语。英语习语 (idioms) 的翻译也和一般词条一样大多只译定义，但有些则仿照汉语谚语形式译出原文习语词组而不取貌合神离的汉语成语。原文示例词组甚多，一般均译成对应的汉语词组而不译成句子，这就难免出现一些拖泥带水的词组，算是无可奈何的遗憾。使用本词典的人在组词成句时，幸勿照搬这类译文词组示例。有连接号的词条中的示例多为表明构词方式或另有独立词条，一般不译。英语中新的词语或表达方法，在译文需作创新处理时，均经反复推敲使之符合汉语词法和句法规律。英汉词典中的汉语要达到汉语词典的水平，编译出名副其实的英汉词典，这是我多年的夙愿也是工作中的努力方向。

本词典翻译过程中，喜见《汉语大词典》前几卷相继出版，《汉语大字典》、《简明不列颠百科全书》、新版《Oxford English Dictionary》等汉、英、科技等工具书先后问世。感谢众多无声老师相助，本词典的译文有了可靠的依据，减少了许多错误。通过学习得知汉语中的“肉豆蔻”(nutmeg) 是木本，“小豆蔻”(cardamom) 是草本；英语中的 stepbrother（既不同父又不同母）与 half-brother（同父异母或同母异父）不同。又如 except 若只译作“除了”，容易产生歧义。因为“除了”可用于“除了他，我们也去”（包括式），也可用于“除了他，我们都不去”（排除式），还可用于“除了吃就是睡”（非此即彼）。本词典处理为“除了（某人 *[* 某事物 *]*）之外（表示所说的不包括在内）”，从而排除了另外两种歧义。本词典的译者和编辑在工作中不少时间都是用于反复翻查汉语工具书，以确保译文准确。

本词典是根据《Oxford Advanced Learner's Dictionary》1989年第4版，1990年第4次印刷至1991年第6次印刷的版本翻译的。1974年出版的第3版至今已20年，其英汉译本《牛津现代高级英汉双解词典》于1984年出版，至今也已10年。现在的第4版是全面修订的新版，内容比第3版增加50%以上。英汉译本定名《牛津高阶英汉双解词典》，共收词语57100条，其中有4000新条目；示例共81500项，绝大部分都是新增加的。本版重新编排简明的动词模式、增添大量副词示例，更为实用。形容词区分为作定语或作表语的两种用法；作表语用的形容词不译“的”字，以示这一区别。新设立200项专题处理的语法或困难词语用法说明，辨析清楚。全新插图共1820项，均有译文对照。习语和短语动词共12720项，均设有互相参照条目，便于查找。另外增添了3项新附录和两种使用本词典的说明，列于词典前的是简要实用说明，列于词典后的是供进一步研修的详细说明。本词典译文忠实于英语原版，不作任何删节；但经原编者同意修订了原版疏漏、欠妥或近几年因时移世异而必须更改的词语300余处。为使分类合理，调整了个别示例的位置，如将Monday week 从 Monday 项下移至 week 项下，并增加一 Friday week 示例。为使译文重点突出，有时需将修饰部分用括号括起置于需说明部分之前，有时需将解释部分用括号括起置于需说明部分之后。定义中并列各项一般用分号隔开，但与括号中内容有关各项用逗号隔开。英语中的斜线号表示其后为可用以替换的词语；但汉语词界 (word boundary) 不能一目了然，无法清楚表明替换部分。本词典试用斜方括号（*[ ]*）作为“替换号”，将可替换部分置于斜方括号中，若其中有几项并列的可替换部分，其间用斜线号隔开。为节省篇幅，译文中省略号使用3个圆点；为便于排版，引号一般用单引号。

本词典的主要译者还有赵志云、吕振飞、王式训、张家巽、李竹、季晨等各位先生。他们从事英汉翻译经验丰富、工作认真，在人手少、任务重的情况下为翻译本词典做出了巨大贡献。李沙沙女士校阅了中文部分。在此向各位致以衷心的谢意。本词典的英语顾问是 Harry Simon（西门华教授），因是多年好友，所以即使经常彻夜长谈也仍不厌其烦，协助解决了很多翻译难题，深为感谢。

我要特别感谢的是牛津大学出版社英汉词典组的编辑主任谭柏山先生和编辑文逢参、黄勉之、陈颂、刘慧萍、黄雪孟、古韶贞各位小姐。他们一丝不苟逐字查证、反复校对，改正了各种错误，增加了 KK 音标和缩略语等多项译文。感谢台湾林茂松教授协助审订 KK 音标。感谢 Richard Barnard 先生、 Jenny McKirdy 小姐、 Sophie Kersey 小姐等各位编辑和第4版原版编辑主理人 Jonathan Crowther 先生，他们在百忙之中兼任我们的英语顾问。感谢前总编辑张煌昌先生。感谢牛津大学出版社主持本词典工作的董事兼总编辑王伟文先生。他统筹全局、事必躬亲，使本词典得以顺利出版。

因工作习惯通宵达旦，算是上了几年“夜大学”。但囿于学识浅陋，本词典译文中的错误或不妥之处，均由我个人负责。本词典的出版不是译者学习的结束，而是重新学习的开始。敬希使用本词典的各位专家、读者诸君不吝赐教，以便再版时纠正。

李北达
香港大学

李北达，1941年生，北京市人。1963年毕业于河北大学外语系英语专业，同年留校任外语系英语教师至1974年（移居香港）。1975年受聘于香港大学教授对外汉语至今。现任香港大学中文系中国语文学部高级语文导师，亚洲辞书学会会员。自1974年起从事翻译工作，参与编译的著作主要有《二十世纪世界大事实录》1980；《第二次世界大战实录》1982；参与或主持编译的英汉词典主要有《英文字用法指南》1981；《牛津英汉双解词典》繁体字版1981，简体字版1982，易名《牛津进阶英汉双解词典》1987；《牛津高阶英汉双解词典》第4版，繁体字版1994，简体字版1997，唯读光碟版1995；《牛津初阶英汉双解词典》第2版1996。

Preface to Oxford Advanced Learner's Dictionary of Current English fourth edition

It is just over forty years since OUP published its first edition of the late A S Hornby's *Advanced Learner's Dictionary*. This was a remarkable pioneering work, based on detailed research into aspects of English usage (including construction patterns and collocations) known to cause difficulties for foreign students, and reflecting a clear understanding of their needs as readers and writers of the language. Hornby perceived that proficiency in English implied the ability to compose as well as to understand, and that the learner's dictionary must be designed to develop both kinds of skill.

In planning the present edition I have built on the strengths of the Hornby tradition, giving close attention to grammatical words and patterns and even greater prominence than before to illustrative examples. But there are some major innovations, including a completely revised verb pattern scheme and a redesigned entry structure, facilitating access to idioms, derivatives and compounds, as well as to the individual senses of polysemous words. The dictionary has benefited from a four-year programme of basic research carried out by the OUP Lexical Research Unit at the University of Leeds, especially in its thematic treatment of verbs and nouns in the new Notes on Usage. It has profited greatly, too, from access to the very rich resources of the Oxford English Dictionary archive.

The fourth edition has drawn on the expert knowledge of several specialists. The late Professor A C Gimson was among the first to be involved in planning, but his untimely death deprived us of his guidance as work proceeded. The job of Phonetics Editor was taken on and very ably carried out by a close colleague, Dr Susan Ramsaran. She has provided, as a new feature, a full treatment of variant pronunciations and of stress in idioms and illustrative phrases.

This comprehensive revision has also called for collaborative effort by a large group of specialist editors and computer staff at Oxford. The result testifies to the commitment and professional skill of the whole team; but particular thanks are due to Moira Hardcastle, Richard Milbank and Ann Watson for carrying the responsibility for specific aspects of the revision over very long periods.

To the OALD Unit Manager, Jonathan Crowther, an additional measure of thanks is due. He has played a key role at every stage of the project and I pay tribute to him, in particular for his co-ordination of a complex computer program, his meticulous attention to the detail of dictionary organization and his exemplary editing.

A P Cowie
University of Leeds

英语原版序言译文

由已故 AS 霍恩比编纂的《Advanced Learner's Dictionary》自从牛津大学出版社发行第一版以来刚过了四十个年头. 这部词典是卓越的拓荒之作. 作者详尽研究了英语的各种用法(包括结构模式和搭配关系), 从而为外国学生编纂出解决这些困难的词典, 反映出作者清楚了解他们读英语和写英语的需要. 霍恩比体察到精通英语不仅在于正确理解, 还要善于运用, 他为学习英语的人编纂的词典就是要培养这两种技能.

在规划本版时, 我在霍恩比一向致力的基础上密切注重虚词和语法模式, 比以前更加突出了解释性示例. 然而也有些重大更新, 包括完全修订了动词模式系统和重新设计了词条结构, 这样不仅便于查找多义词的各个义项, 也便于查找习语、派生词、复合词.

本词典编纂过程中获益于牛津大学出版社词典研究组的科研成果, 这是在利兹大学进行为时四年的一项基础研究. 我们获益尤深的是在"用法说明"方面的动词和名词的专题处理. 本词典另一受益巨大之处是有幸获得《Oxford English Dictionary》(《牛津英语词典》)档案的极为丰富的资料.

第四版深获几位资深专家襄助. 已故 AC 吉姆森教授是首位参与计划中的专家之一, 但他不幸早逝, 致使我们工作进行之中痛失指导. 本词典的语音编辑工作是由我的亲密同事苏珊·拉姆萨拉博士承担而独当一面. 她提供了一个新项目, 就是对异读词和习语及其示例的重音做了完整处理.

这次全面修订获得牛津各学科众多专门编辑和计算机工作人员的通力协助. 本版顺利完成是群策群力的结果, 是全体专家造诣的证明; 但要特别感谢的是莫里亚·哈德卡尔、理查德·米尔班克和安·沃森, 他们经年累月承担着各有关方面的修订工作.

我要向《OALD》的编辑主理人乔纳森·克劳瑟再次致谢. 他在此项工作的各个阶段举足轻重, 特别感谢他在复杂的计算机程序上的协调工作, 他在词典的组织工作方面一丝不苟、编辑能力卓尔不群.

AP 考伊
利兹大学

KEY TO ENTRIES 词条用法

headword 首词

definition of the headword 首词的定义

car·di·gan /ˈkɑːdɪɡən; ˋkɑrdɪɡən/ *n* knitted woollen jacket, usu with no collar and with buttons at the front 毛衣(通常指无领有扣前对襟的).

---

examples of different uses of the headword 首词的不同用法举例

pur·sue /pəˈsjuː; *US* -ˈsuː; pɚˋsu/ *v* [Tn] (*fml* 文) **1** follow (sb/sth), esp in order to catch or kill; chase 追赶,追逐(某人[某物]); (尤指)追捕,追杀;追寻;追求: *pursue a wild animal, one's prey, a thief* 追捕野兽、被捕食的动物、窃贼 ○ *The police pursued the stolen vehicle along the motorway.* 警察在高速公路上追赶被盗的车辆.

---

alternative spelling of the headword 首词的不同拼法

fa·cia (also **fas·cia**) /ˈfeɪʃə; ˋfeʃə/ *n* **1** = DASHBOARD (DASH[1]). **2** board, etc with a name on it, put above the front entrance of a shop 商店入口处的店主名牌;店号;招牌.

---

different word used with the same meaning 等义词

lime[1] /laɪm; laɪm/ *n* [U] **1** (also **'quicklime**) white substance (calcium oxide) obtained by heating limestone, used in making cement and mortar and as a fertilizer 石灰. **2** = BIRDLIME (BIRD).

---

number of the definition 义项编号

letters to show closely related meanings 词义紧密相关的字母编号

start of the idioms section 习语部分开始

idioms shown in bold print 用黑体表示习语

march[1] /mɑːtʃ; mɑrtʃ/ *v* **1** **(a)** [I, Ipr, Ip] walk as soldiers do, with regular steps of equal length 齐步走;行进;前进: *Quick march!* ie a military command to start marching 快步走! ○ *Demonstrators marched through the streets.* 示威者在街道中行进. ○ *They marched in and took over the town.* 他们进占了这一市镇. ○ *march by, past, in, out, off, away, etc* 经过、走过、开进、出发、离开、开走 ○ *The army has marched thirty miles today.* 部队今天已行军三十英里. **(b)** [I, Ipr, Ip] walk purposefully and determinedly (含有某目的和决心)走: *She marched in and demanded an apology.* 她毅然地走进来要求向她道歉. **(c)** [Tn·pr, Tn·p] cause (sb) to march 使(某人)行进: *march the troops up and down* 让部队来回练习走步 ○ *They marched the prisoner away.* 他们令监犯齐步走. ○ *She was marched into a cell.* 她被押进一间囚室. **2** (idm 习语) **get one's marching orders; give sb his/her marching orders** (*infml or joc* 口或谑) be told/tell sb to go; be dismissed/dismiss sb 被通知[告诉某人]离去;被解雇[解雇某人]: *She was totally unreliable, so she got/was given her marching orders.* 她完全不可靠,所以给解雇了. **3** (phr v) **march past (sb)** (of troops) march ceremonially past (an honoured guest, a high-ranking officer, etc), eg in a parade (指部队)作分列式在(贵宾、首长等)面前经过(如受检阅). ▷ **marcher** *n*: *freedom marchers* 争取自由的示威者 ○ *civil-rights marchers* 争取民权的游行者.

la·bor·at·ory /ləˈbɒrətrɪ; *US* ˈlæbrətɔːrɪ; ˈlæbrəˌtorɪ/ *n* room or building used for (esp scientific) research, experiments, testing, etc 实验室.

pronunciation of the headword with the different pronunciation used by speakers of American English 首词的读音及美式英语异读音

---

pi·geon /ˈpɪdʒɪn; ˈpɪdʒən/ *n* **1** (**a**) [C] any of several types of wild or tame bird of the dove family 鸽子: *a ˈcarrier-/ˈhoming-pigeon*, ie one trained to carry messages or to race as a sport 信鸽. ⇨illus at App 1 见附录 1 插图, page iv. (**b**) [U] flesh of a wild pigeon eaten as food 野鸽肉: [attrib 作定语] *pigeon pie* 鸽肉排. **2** (idm 习语) **ˈone's pigeon** (*infml* 口) one's responsibility or business 自己的责任或事情: *I don't care where the money comes from: that's not ˈmy pigeon.* 我不管钱从哪儿来,那不是我的事. **put/set the cat among the pigeons** ⇨CAT¹.

stress marks in idioms and examples 习语和示例中的重音标志

reference to the headword where an idiom is defined 相关参照,指示该习语所在的首词词条

---

champ¹ /tʃæmp; tʃæmp/ *v* **1** [I, Tn] (esp of horses) chew (food) noisily (尤指马)大声嚼(食物). **2** [Ipr, Tn] **~ (at/on) sth** (of horses) bite at sth nervously or impatiently (指马) 急躁地或不耐烦地咬某物: *horses champing at the bit* 咬着嚼子的马. **3** [I, Ipr, It] **~ (at sth)** (used esp in the continuous tenses 尤用于进行时态) be eager or impatient, esp to begin sth 急切或不耐烦 (尤指开始做某事物): *He was champing with rage at the delay.* 他对这一延误着急上火. ○ *The boys were champing to start.* 男孩儿们恨不得马上就出发. **4** (idm 习语) **ˌchamp at the ˈbit** (*infml* 口) be restlessly impatient to start doing sth 迫不及待要做某事.

champ² /tʃæmp; tʃæmp/ *n* (*infml* 口)= CHAMPION 2.

headwords with the same spelling separated by different numbers 拼法相同的首词,以不同号码列出

information about which preposition to use after the headword 首词后的连用介词用法说明

special note on grammar or usage 语法或用法的特殊说明

part of speech label 词类标志

headword and definition number where the meaning is given 提供词义的首词和义项号码

---

shake¹ /ʃeɪk; ʃek/ *v* (*pt* **shook** /ʃʊk; ʃʊk/, *pp* **shaken** /ˈʃeɪkən; ˈʃekən/) **1** (**a**) [La, I, Tn, Tn·p, Cn·a] **~ sb/sth (about/around)** (cause sb/sth to) move quickly and often jerkily from side to side or up and down (使某人[某物])急速摇动或颠簸(常指猛然产生或停止): *a bolt shaking loose in an engine* 发动机上震松的螺栓

irregular forms of a verb with pronunciation 动词不规则变化及其读音

codes showing the verb patterns 动词模式代码

safe[1] /seɪf; sef/ *adj* (-r,-st) 1 [pred 作表语] ~(from sth/sb) protected from danger and harm; secure 安全;平安;无危险: *You'll be safe here.* 你在这里很安全. ○ *safe from attack/attackers* 免受攻击[他人攻击]. 2 [pred 作表语]...

comparative and superlative forms of the adjective 形容词的比较级和最高级

grammatical information about adjectives 形容词在语法上的用法说明

---

mouse /maʊs; maʊs/ *n* (*pl* **mice** /maɪs; maɪs/) 1 (often in compounds 常用以构成复合词) (any of several kinds of) small rodent with a long thin tail 鼠: *a 'house mouse* 家鼠 ○ *a 'field-mouse* 田鼠 ○ *a 'harvest-mouse* 收割鼠. ⇨illus 见插图. 2 (*fig esp joc or derog* 比喻,尤作戏谑语或作贬义) shy, timid person 羞怯、胆小的人: *His wife, a strange little mouse, never said anything.* 他的妻子竟然胆小如鼠,一句话都没说. ○ *Are you a man or a mouse* (ie brave or cowardly)? 你是男子汉还是胆小鬼? 3 (*computing* 计) small hand-held device that is moved across a desk-top, etc to produce a corresponding movement of the cursor, with buttons for entering commands 鼠标; 滑鼠. ⇨illus at COMPUTER 见 COMPUTER 插图.

irregular plural form of a noun with pronunciation 名词的不规则复数形式及其读音

reference to an illustration on the page 参看本页插图

labels giving information about usage 用法说明的标志

label showing specialist subject area 专门知识领域说明的标志

reference to an illustration at another entry 参看另一词条插图

---

ash[1] /æʃ; æʃ/ *n* (a) [C] tree commonly found in forests, with silver-grey bark and hard close-grained wood 梣(即白蜡树). ⇨illus at App 1 见附录1之插图, page i. (b) [U] its wood, used for tool handles, etc 梣木(用作工具的把柄等).

grammatical information about nouns 名词在语法上的用法说明

reference to an illustration in the Appendices 参看附录插图

---

ring[2] /rɪŋ; rɪŋ/ *v* (*pt* **rang** /ræŋ; ræŋ/, *pp* **rung** /rʌŋ; rʌŋ/) 1 [I] make a clear resonant sound, usu like that of a bell being struck 发出清晰响亮的声音(通常指似铃声): *Will you answer the telephone if it rings?* 电话铃声响时请你接电话好吗? ○ *The metal door rang as it slammed shut.* 金属门猛一关上时发出咣的响声. ○ *The buzzer rang when the meal was ready.* 饭做好时蜂鸣器发出嗞嗞的响声. 2 [Tn, Tn·pr] cause (a bell, etc) to sound 使(钟铃等)发声: *ring the fire alarm* 鸣响火警警报 ○ *ring the bell for school assembly* 敲钟通知全校集合. 3 [La] produce a certain effect when heard 产生某种声音效果; 听起来: *Her words rang hollow,...* 她的话听起来很虚... 10 (phr v) **ring off** (*Brit*) end a telephone conversation 挂断电话: *He rang off before I could explain.* 我还没来得及解释,他就把电话挂上了. **ring out** sound loudly and clearly 发出响亮而清晰的声音: *A pistol shot rang out.* 响起了手枪的声音. **ring sth up** record (an amount, etc) on a cash register 将(款额等)记入现金出纳机: *ring up all the items, the total, £6.99* 把所有款项、总额、6.99英镑的一笔钱记入现金出纳机.

start of the phrasal verbs section 短语动词部分开始

phrasal verbs (special uses of a verb with a particle or preposition) shown in bold print 短语动词(动词与小词或介词连用的特殊用法),用黑体表示

sad /sæd; sæd/ *adj* **(-dder, -ddest)** **1** showing or causing sorrow; unhappy 悲哀的;忧愁的;难过的: *a sad look, event, story* 忧愁的表情、伤心的事件、悲惨的故事 ○ *John is sad because his dog has died.* 约翰因为自己的狗死了非常伤心. ○ *I'm sad you're leaving.* 你要走了,我很难过. ○ *It was a sad day for us all when the school closed down.* 学校关闭那天,我们都很悲痛. ○ *Why is she looking so sad?* 她为什么愁容满面?

doubling of consonants in the comparative and superlative forms of the adjective 形容词比较级和最高级形式中的辅音字母重复

---

chat /tʃæt; tʃæt/ *n* [C, U] friendly informal conversation 聊天; 闲谈: *I had a long chat with her (about her job).* (关于她的工作)我和她聊了很久. ○ *That's enough chat – get back to work.* 别再聊了——回去工作吧. ⇨Usage at TALK[1] 用法见 TALK[1].

▷**chat** *v* **(-tt-)** **1** [I, Ipr, Ip] **~ (away); ~ (to/with sb) (about sth)** have a chat 聊天;闲谈: *They were chatting (away) in the corner.* 他们在角落里闲谈. ○

reference to a usage note where words with similar meanings are compared 参看该词条所附近义词语用法说明

doubling of consonants before adding -ed and -ing to the verb 动词加-ed 和-ing 前的辅音字母重复

NOTE ON USAGE 用法: Both **long** and **a long time** are used as adverbial expressions of time. ☆ **long** 和 **a long time** 都用作表示时间的状语. **1 Long** is not used in positive sentences unless it is modified by another adverb, eg *too, enough, ago* ☆ **long** 只在受另一副词如 too、enough、ago 修饰时才用于肯定句: *You've been sleeping too long/long enough.* 你睡得太久了[你睡的时间够长了]. ○ *She waited there (for) a long time.* 她在那里等了很长时间. **2** Both can be used in questions 这两者均可用于疑问句: *Have you been here long/a long time?* 你在这里呆了很久[很长时间]了吗? **3** In negative sentences there can be a difference in meaning. 在否定句中二者意义有别. Compare 试比较: *I haven't been here for a long time* (ie It is a long time since I was last here) and *I haven't been here long* (ie I arrived here only a short time ago). '我已很久没到这里来了(即离上次我来此已很长时间了)'和'我到这里没多久(即我刚到不久)'.

special paragraph explaining the differences between similar words and phrases 近义词语用法说明

---

re·ject /rɪˈdʒekt; rɪˋdʒɛkt/ *v* **1** [Tn, Cn·n/a] refuse to accept (sb/sth) 拒绝接受(某人[某事物]): *reject a gift, a possibility, an opinion, a suggestion* 拒绝接受一件礼物、一种可能性、一条意见、一项建议 ○ *a rejected candidate, applicant, etc* 遭到拒绝的候选人、申请人等 ○ ... **3** [Tn] not give due affection to (sb/sth); rebuff 不给予(某人[某事物])应有的爱;慢待: *The child was rejected by its parents.* 这孩子未受到父母的疼爱.

▷ **re·ject** /ˈriːdʒekt; ˋridʒɛkt/ *n* rejected person or thing 被拒绝或被抛弃的人或事物: *rejects from an officers' training course* 军官培训课程的不合格者 ○ *export rejects*, ie damaged or imperfect goods 被拒收的出口货物 ○ [attrib 作定语] *reject china, earthenware, etc* 不合格的瓷器、陶器等.

re·jec·tion /rɪˈdʒekʃn; rɪˋdʒɛkʃən/ *n* **(a)** [U] rejecting or being rejected 拒绝;抛弃. **(b)** [C] instance of this 拒绝;抛弃: *Her proposal met with continual rejections.* 她的建议一再遭到拒绝.

□ **reˈjection slip** formal note from an editor or a publisher accompanying a rejected article, book, etc 退稿通知单(编辑或出版者附在退稿等上的).

start of the derivative section 派生词部分开始

derivatives of the headword with pronunciation 首词的派生词及其读音

start of the compound section 复合词部分开始

compound of the headword with a mark showing where the main stress falls 首词复合词及表示主重音的标志

pa·tho·lo·gical /ˌpæθəˈlɒdʒɪkl; ˌpæθəˈlɑdʒɪkl/ *adj* **1** of or relating to pathology 病理学的;与病理学有关的. **2** of or caused by a physical or mental illness 疾病的;由疾病引起的. **3** (*infml* 口) unreasonable; irrational 无道理的;非理智的;病态的: *a pathological fear of spiders, obsession with death, hatred of sb* 对蜘蛛无端的恐惧、受死亡强迫观念的困扰、对某人病态的憎恨 ○ *a pathological* (ie compulsive) *liar* 病态说谎者.
▷ **pa·tho·lo·gic·ally** /-klɪ; -klɪ/ *adv*: *pathologically jealous, mean, etc* 忌妒狂的、吝啬狂的.

dots showing where a word can be divided when writing or typing 圆点表示书写或打字时可断开的位置

gloss in example to make clear the meaning of the headword in a particular case 示例中说明首词词义的特殊注释

---

inch /ɪntʃ; ɪntʃ/ *n* **1** (*abbr* 缩写 **in**) measure of length equal to 2.54 cm or one twelfth of a foot 英寸 (1 英尺等于 12 英寸,1 英寸等于 2.54 厘米) : *a pile of books 12 inches high* 一摞厚达 12 英寸的书. ⇨App 4,5 见附录 4、5. **2** small amount or distance 少量;短距离:

reference to sections of the appendices 参看附录部分

---

jo·vial /ˈdʒəʊvɪəl; ˈdʒovɪəl/ *adj* very cheerful and good-humoured; merry 愉快的;快乐的: *a friendly jovial fellow* 和蔼而快乐的人○ *in a jovial mood* 以愉快的心情. ▷ **jo·vi·al·ity** /ˌdʒəʊvɪˈælətɪ; ˌdʒovɪˈælətɪ/ *n* [U]. **jo·vi·ally** /-ɪəlɪ; -ɪəlɪ/ *adv*.

derivatives that are close in meaning to the headword and are undefined 与首词词义紧密相关的派生词,不提供定义

---

au·tumn /ˈɔːtəm; ˈɔtəm/ (*US* **fall**) *n* [U, C] the third season of the year, coming between summer and winter 秋;秋天;秋季.

different word used in American English 美式英语用词

---

col·our[1] (*US* **color**) /ˈkʌlə(r); ˈkʌlɚ/ *n* **1 (a)** [U] visible quality that objects have, produced by rays of light of different wavelengths being reflected by them 颜色:

different spelling used in American English 美式英语拼法

---

joiner /ˈdʒɔɪnə(r); ˈdʒɔɪnɚ/ *n* (*Brit*) skilled workman who makes the wooden fittings of a building, eg window frames and doors 细木工. Cf 参看 CARPENTER.

reference to another headword with a related meaning 参看词义相关的另一个首词

USING THE DICTIONARY – A PRACTICAL GUIDE
本词典用法 —— 实用说明

This practical user's guide to the *Oxford Advanced Learner's Dictionary* has been written especially for students.《牛津高阶英汉双解词典》的这一使用者说明，是专为学生编写的. The Guide does not try to provide a full explanation of all the kinds of information that are given, or how they are arranged. 这一"说明"并不着眼于全面解释词典中的各种资料及其编排方法. (If you need a detailed description you should turn to the section headed *Using the Dictionary – A Detailed Guide to the Entries* at the back. 若需详细说明，可参阅书末"本词典用法 —— 词条使用详细说明".) Instead, it is written from the point of view of a student (ie you) wishing to find answers to the problems that you meet when trying to understand or use English. 编写这部分是从学生(你)的角度出发，希望在理解或使用英语的过程中找到问题的答案. Generally, these problems are of two kinds 一般来说，这些问题有两类:

A You need to know **how to look up words and their meanings** in the dictionary. 你想知道怎样在本词典中查阅词语和词义.

B You need to know **how to use words in speech or writing** correctly and appropriately. 你想知道在口语或书面语中怎样正确恰当地使用词语.

You should try following the steps in this guide and looking up the examples shown before you start using the dictionary regularly. 你应该尽量按照这个"说明"的步骤先查阅这里的示例，然后再正式使用本词典. In this way you will begin to develop the reference skills needed to become a successful dictionary user. 这样你就逐步培养了必备的技巧，使用本词典就得心应手了.

A FINDING WORDS AND MEANINGS 查阅词语和词义

SIMPLE WORDS 单纯词

1 What is a simple word? 什么是单纯词?

A SIMPLE WORD (sometimes called a ROOT) is a word like *perhaps*, *read* or *police*. 单纯词(有时称作"词根")是像 perhaps、read 或 police 之类的词. Roots cannot be broken down into smaller meaningful parts – unlike *reader* (a DERIVATIVE), which consists of *read* and *-er*, or *policeman* (a COMPOUND), which consists of *police* and *man*. 词根不能再分成更小的有意义的部分 —— 不同于 reader(派生词)包括 read 和 -er 两部分，也不同于 policeman(复合词)包括 police 和 man 两个单纯词.

2 How to look up simple words 怎样查阅单纯词?

Let us suppose that you've met this sentence 假设你遇到这样一个句子:

Perhaps your student will win a prize next year.

This sentence consists entirely of simple words – there are no derivatives or compounds. 这个句子完全是由单纯词构成的 —— 没有派生词或复合词. Each word has its own special section (its own ENTRY) in the dictionary, and each appears at the top of its entry (in **bold** print) in the same spelling as in the sentence. 每个词在本词典中均有其各自的一个项目(词条)，每个词都在词条之首(用**黑体**印刷)，与上述句中拼法相同. Here are two entries which show this 下面的两个词条可以说明这一点:

per·haps /pəˈhæps, *also* præps; pɚˈhæps, præps/ *adv* it may be (that); possibly . . .

stu·dent /ˈstjuːdnt; *US* ˈstuː-; ˈstudn̩t/ *n* **1 (a)** person who is studying for a degree, diploma, etc at a university or some other place of higher education or technical training: *a BA student* ○ *a medical student* . . .

3 Simple words in the plural form, in the past tense, etc 单纯词的复数、过去时态形式等

Simple words, and derivatives and compounds too, take special endings (called INFLECTIONS) when they are being used in the plural or in a different tense, etc. 单纯词(派生词和复合词亦然)用作复数或在不同的时态等中，要有某种词尾(称为屈折变化). Look at this example 请看这一例句:

Perhaps your students will win prizes next year.

Here, *students* and *prizes* are the PLURAL forms of *student* and *prize.* 这里的 students 和 prizes 是 student 和 prize 的复数形式. But the entries you should refer to are those for **student** and **prize** (SINGULAR forms), as before. 但是要查找的词条仍然是 **student** 和 **prize**(单数形式)的词条. Now look at this 再看看这一句子:

Your students won prizes last year.

Here, *won* is the PAST TENSE form of *win*, and **win** is the entry you need to turn to. 句中 won 是 win 的过去时态形式, 你需要查找的是 **win** 这一词条. However, just in case you don't know that *win* and *won* are related, a special entry is provided at **won** to direct you to **win** 但是惟恐你不知道 win 与 won 相关, 特为 **won** 立一词条指示你去查阅 **win**:

won *pt, pp of* WIN.

4 Different spellings of the same simple word 单纯词的异体字(同一词的不同拼法)

Sometimes a word has different spellings. 有时一个字有不同的拼法. Compare *banian* and *banyan* (the name of a kind of fig-tree). 试比较 banian 和 banyan(榕树). Now suppose that you meet *banyan* for the first time, and want to find out its meaning. 假设你第一次遇到 banyan 这个词, 想知道是什么意思. This spelling is given as an alternative at the entry for **banian**, like this 这种拼法是在 **banian** 词条中, 像下面这样列为异体字:

ban·ian (also **ban·yan**) ... *n* Indian fig-tree ...

However **banian** and **banyan** are quite a long way from each other in alphabetical order (*banish, banjo, bank* and *banquet* all come in between). 但是, 按照字母顺序排列 **banian** 和 **banyan** 两字之间相隔颇远(banish、banjo、bank、banquet 等都在两者之间). It is unlikely you would find the above entry if all you had was the spelling *banyan*. 假设你只知道 banyan 这一拼法, 就不大可能找到这个词. So a special entry is given at **banyan** to redirect you 因此在 **banyan** 处特设一指示词条:

ban·yan = BANIAN.

5 Different words which have the same form 同形异义词(拼法相同而词义不同的词)

Sometimes, the same spelling of a word can be used in two or more different ways. 有时同一个拼法的词可用于不止一种用法. *Fine*, for instance, can be a noun, a verb, an adjective or an adverb. 例如 fine 可为名词、动词、形容词或副词. In order to check its meaning you must know which entry to look at. 为查找其词义, 你须先知道查哪个词条. Now suppose that you are faced with this sentence 假如你遇到这样一个句子:

Everyone thought that the fine was too heavy.

You refer to **fine** in the dictionary and you find three numbered entries, including four part of speech labels (*n, v, adj, adv*) 你在本词典中查找 **fine**, 却发现有三个带号码的词条, 包含四种词类(n、v、adj、adv):

fine[1] ... *n* ... *Offenders may be liable to a heavy fine.*
▷ **fine** *v* ... *The court fined him £500* ...
fine[2] ... *adj* ... a very fine performance ...
fine[3] ... *adv* ... *That suits me fine* ...

Which of these entries will explain the meaning of *fine* as it is used in the sentence? 这些词条中哪个是句中 fine 的意思呢? Here are two strategies you can use 你可有两种方法: (a) Try to work out the part of speech of *fine* from clues in the sentence itself. 设法从句子本身的线索找出 fine 所属的词类. Since *fine* is preceded by *the* and described by *heavy*, it is a noun. 由于 fine 之前有个冠词 the 和形容词 heavy, 可见它是个名词. Or you can try 另一方法可以是: (b) Compare the words of your sentence with those of the examples. 把你句中的词与示例中的词比较一下. You will notice that *heavy* appears in your sentence and in an example in the noun section of the first entry (where it describes *fine*). 你能注意到你句中有 heavy 这个词, 在第一个词条中名词部分的示例中也有这个词(描述 fine 的). So *fine* in your sentence is a noun meaning 'a sum of money that must be paid as a punishment'. 由此可知你句中的 fine 是名词, 意为 "a sum of money that must be paid as a punishment 罚款".

6 Looking for a meaning when a word has several meanings 从多义词中查找所需的词义

Suppose that you read or hear the following sentences 假设你看到或听到如下的句子:

Have you checked all the details of the report?

The attack has been checked on the central front.

In both sentences *check* is used as a verb, not as a noun, so you need to refer to **check**¹, not **check**² or **check**³. 在这两句中 check 都是动词而不是名词, 所以你要查看的是 **check**¹ 而不是 **check**² 或 **check**³. But the verb entry has several meanings. 但是这个动词词条中有几项词义. How do you decide which one is being used in each sentence? 怎样决定哪句中用哪个词义呢? A helpful approach is to compare the words which accompany *check* in each sentence with those which accompany it in the various examples. 有个好办法, 就是把句中 check 前后的词与示例中 check 前后的词比较一下. Here is part of the entry 下面是该词条的部分内容:

check¹ ... *v* **1** ... **(b)** [Tn] examine (sth) in order to make sure that it is correct, safe, satisfactory ... *check the items against the list* ... *He must check his work more carefully* ... **2 (a)** cause (sb/sth) to stop or go more slowly ... *check the enemy's advance* ...

If you now look back at your first sentence, you will notice that *details* (the object of *check*) is close in meaning to *items* in the first of the dictionary examples given here. 回过头来再看看你的第一个句子, 你能注意到 details(check 的宾语)与本词典这里的第一个示例中的 items 在意思上相近. You may notice too that if you turn round the second sentence (*We have checked the attack*...) it is very like *check the enemy's advance* (the last example). 你也可能注意到若把第二个句子转换一下(We have checked the attack...)就很像 check the enemy's advance ... (最后一个示例). From this, it is not hard to work out that in the first sentence *check* means 'examine in order to make sure ...', while in the second it means 'cause to stop or go more slowly'. 由此不难确定在第一句中 check 意为 "examine in order to make sure ... 检查; 检验; 核对; 核实", 在第二句中其意为 "cause to stop or go more slowly 停止或缓慢进行".

IDIOMS 习语

1 What is an idiom? 什么是习语?

An IDIOM is a phrase which has a special meaning of its own. 习语本身是有特殊含义的短语. (It is difficult to work out the meaning of the whole phrase from the meanings of the individual words. 很难从其中各部分的意思琢磨出整个短语的意思.) Examples are 举例如下: as a matter of fact (= in reality; to tell the truth 实际上; 说实话), 又如 with a vengeance (= with unusual speed or enthusiasm 以异常的速度或劲头儿). Idioms are often unchangeable 习语中的词往往不可变动: we don't say *as a matter of truth* or *with a retaliation*. 不可说 "as a matter of truth", 也不可说 "with a retaliation".

2 How to find idioms in the dictionary 怎样在本词典中查找习语

Let's suppose that you read or hear the following sentences 假设你看到或听到以下的句子:

Of course it's important – it's a matter of life and death.

I managed to get these shirts on the cheap.

Perhaps you are puzzled by the phrases at the ends of these sentences 也许你对这两句末尾中的短语不太明白: you sense that *life and death* does not literally mean 'living or dying' and you have never seen *cheap* used after *the* (ie as a noun). 你意识到 life and death 并非是字面上"生和死"的意思, 你也从未见过 cheap 用于冠词 the 之后(即用作名词). So what should you do? 那怎么办呢? (a) Turn to the entry for the first important word (the first noun, verb, adjective or adverb) that puzzles you. 找出你不明白的短语中第一个重要的词(第一个名词、动词、形容词或副词), 找到这个词所在的词条. In the first sentence this is probably *matter*. 在第一句中这个词可能是 matter. (b) Look through the numbered sections of that entry till you find '(idm)' (= IDIOMS), like this 查阅该词条中的各义项号码, 找到号码后有(idm)字样(即 idioms)处, 像下面这样:

matter[1] ... **5** (idm) **as a matter of fact** ... **be no laughing matter** ... **for ˈthat matter** ...

(c) Then read through the list of phrases in bold print till you find **a matter of life and death** in its alphabetical place. 然后在黑体字的短语中按字母顺序找到 **a matter of life and death**.

a ˌmatter of ˌlife and ˈdeath an issue that is crucial to survival, success, etc: *Of course this must have priority – it's a matter of life and death.* **a matter of opinion** ...

What happens if you decide to look up **life**? 倘若你以为应该查阅的是 **life** 词条, 又如何呢? Again, look for the numbered section labelled '(idm)'. 同样, 还是查找义项号码后有(idm)标志处. You will find 你就看到下面内容:

life ... **15** (idm) ... **a matter of life and death** ⇨ MATTER[1].

(This takes you to **matter**[1], which as we have seen is the first important word in the idiom and is the entry where the idiom is explained. 这里的符号指示你查阅 **matter**[1], 就是在这一习语中我们看到的第一个重要的词, 也就是解释这一习语的词条.)

Next you want to find the meaning of *on the cheap*. 下一步你想找出 on the cheap 的含义. You may perhaps look in the entry for **on**, but the idiom is not there. 你也许查看 **on** 的词条, 却没有这一习语. (This is because *on* is a preposition, not a noun, a verb, an adjective or an adverb. 因为 on 是介词, 不是名词、动词、形容词或副词.) So you turn to **cheap**, follow the procedure already explained, and find 那么你又查到 **cheap**, 按照上述方法找到以下部分:

cheap ... **7** (idm) ... **ˌhold sth ˈcheap** ... **ˌmake oneself ˈcheap** ... **on the ˈcheap** (*infml*) without paying the usual, or a fair, price: *buy, sell, get sth on the cheap.*

PHRASAL VERBS 短语动词

1 What is a phrasal verb? 什么是短语动词?

In English, verbs often combine with prepositions (eg *into, from, of, out of*) or adverbs (eg *away, back, up, out*) of position or direction. 英语中, 动词常与介词(如 into、from、of、out of)或表示位置或方向的副词(如 away、back、up、out)结合使用. Some combinations have meanings which are not easy to understand from those of the individual words. 这类结合表达的意思, 有的不容易从各个词的意思中看出来. Those combinations are called PHRASAL VERBS. 这类的结合叫做短语动词. Examples are *make (something) up* (= invent), *come across (somebody or something)* (= discover), *break down* (= collapse). 例如 make (something) up (= invent 发明)、come across (somebody or something) (= discover 发现)、break down (= collapse 崩溃; 垮). Some phrasal verbs consist of three words, e.g. *put up with (somebody or something)* (= tolerate). 有些短语动词包含三个词, 如 put up with (somebody or something) (= tolerate 容忍; 忍受).

2 How to find phrasal verbs in the dictionary 怎样在本词典中查找短语动词

First it is important to be able to tell whether *go over*, *walk out*, *run on*, etc are phrasal verbs or not. 首先, 重要的一点是要能辨认出 go over、walk out、run on 等是不是短语动词. Look at this sentence 请看下面这个句子:

The waiter went over to a cupboard and took some glasses out.

Here, *went over* and *took ... out* are not phrasal verbs, because they express ordinary 'movement' meanings of the verbs and ordinary 'direction' meanings of the adverbs. 这里的 went over 和 took ... out 并非短语动词, 因为所表达的是这两个动词普通的"动作"之义, 及这两个副词普通的"方向"之义. Those meanings can be referred to in the numbered sections of the entries for **go**, **over**, **take** and **out**. 这些词义可从 **go**、**over**、**take**、**out** 词条中带有编号的义项中找到. But suppose you meet this sentence 但是假设你遇到这样一个句子:

Do you mind going over my maths homework?

Here, *going over* obviously has nothing to do with movement; it is a phrasal verb and has a special meaning of its own. 这里的 going over 显然与动作无关; 这是个短语动词,

本身有特殊的含义. Locating phrasal verbs in the dictionary is simple. 在本词典中查找短语动词方法很简单: (a) Find the entry for the first word (here, the verb **go**). 找出第一个词(此处为动词 **go**)所在的词条. (b) Read through the numbered sections till you find the heading '(phr v)'. 查阅有编号的各义项, 找到号码后有(phr v)字样之处 (c) Individual phrasal verbs are listed alphabetically. 各短语动词均按字母顺序排列. You will find *go over sth* between *go over* and *go over (to ...)*. 你可以找到 go over sth 就在 go over 和 go over(to ...)之间. There you will see it is defined as 'examine the details of sth; check sth' as the second of its definitions. 你在那里能看到其后的第二个义项: "examine the details of sth; check sth 检查某事物的细节; 核对某事物".

DERIVATIVES 派生词

1 What is a derivative? 什么是派生词?

A DERIVATIVE is a word that is formed from a simple word (or root) by adding a SUFFIX, like this 派生词是由单纯词(或词根)加上后缀构成的词, 如 : *embarrass* + *-ment* = *embarrassment, dirt* + *-y* = *dirty*. Sometimes the form of the simple word does not change, as when *shoulder* (noun) becomes *shoulder* (verb), or *poor* (adjective) becomes *the poor* (noun). 有时单纯词的词形并无变化, 如 shoulder(名词)变为 shoulder (动词)或 poor(形容词)变为 the poor(名词).

2 How to look up derivatives 怎样查阅派生词

Suppose that you want to look up *wavy* and *packer*. 假设你想查阅 wavy 和 packer 这两个词. (a) First, find out if there are separate entries for these words. 首先, 看看这两个词有没有独立的词条. (There aren't. 没有.) This tells you that *wavy* and *packer* don't have special meanings of their own, but are closely related in meaning (and in spelling) to simple words. 这表明 wavy 和 packer 并没有特殊的词义, 而是与单纯词的词义(及拼法)密切相关. (b) Try to guess what these simple words are (*wave* and *pack*). 设法猜出是哪两个单纯词(wave 和 pack). (c) Search towards the end of the **wave** entry and the two **pack** entries for a triangle 查找 **wave** 词条和 **pack** 两个词条后部的三角符号: ▷. The derivatives are listed after the triangle. 派生词均排列在三角符号之后.

3 Derivatives which have entries of their own 有独立词条的派生词

You meet the adverb *scarcely* in the sentence 你在下面句中遇到了 scarcely 这个副词:

> *I've scarcely had time to look at the report yet.*

(a) You start by guessing that *scarcely* is a derivative (it looks like *quickly* and *roughly*), and that it is formed from *scarce* (adjective). 你起初猜想 scarcely 是个派生词(看起来与 quickly 和 roughly 相似), 以为是由 scarce(形容词)派生的.
(b) So you look in the entry for **scarce**, but the adverb is not there. 于是你查阅 **scarce** 词条, 但并没有这个副词.
(c) What is the reason for this? 这是什么原因呢? *Scarcely* is quite unrelated in meaning to *scarce*, so it has an entry of its own. 因为 scarcely 与 scarce 的意思完全无关, 因此 scarcely 本身有独立的词条.

Now take the noun *explosion*. 再来看看 explosion 这个名词. (a) You think that this may be close in meaning to the verb *explode*. 你可能认为这个词和动词 expode 意思上紧密相关. (It is. 确实如此.) (b) So you look for the noun in the verb entry. 于是你查阅该动词词条, 想找其中的这个名词. (It is not there. 并不在该处.) (c) Why? 为什么呢? *Explosion* is so different in spelling from *explode* that some people might not look for it at the entry **explode**. 因为 explosion 和 explode 的拼法差别很大, 有的人可能不去在 **explode** 词条中查找. So it has its own separate entry. 所以 explosion 也有其独立的词条. (You have now learnt an important rule of arrangement 你现在知道了一条重要的规则: a derivative is included in the same entry as its root unless they are very different in meaning, or spelling, or both. 派生词排列在其词根所属的词条中; 但若在词义上或拼法上或这两方面与词根差别很大时, 则派生词自立一词条.)

4 Derivatives formed without adding a suffix 不增加后缀构成的派生词

Suppose that you meet the word *boost*, used like this 假设你遇到了 boost 这个词, 是

这样使用的:

The government's policies will give trade a boost.

In the dictionary *boost* is a verb, but in the sentence it is a noun. 在本词典中 boost 是动词, 但在这个句子里却是名词. Now, where do you look for the noun? 那么, 你到哪儿去查找这个名词呢? (a) You wonder if the noun is related to the verb or not, and you look for a separate entry for **boost** (noun). 你不清楚这个名词是否和这个动词相关, 你就去查 **boost** (noun)想找这样一个独立词条. (There isn't one. 并没有这个词条.) (b) You now look for the noun in the SAME entry as the verb, and find it there. 你又在动词同一词条中去找这个名词, 在该处找到了. (c) You can now see that they are together because the words are close in meaning, as well as being identical in spelling. 你现在明白了, 这两个词编排在一起是因为其拼法相同而且词义紧密相关.

COMPOUNDS 复合词

1 What is a compound? 什么是复合词?

A COMPOUND is made up of two or more simple words. 复合词是由至少两个单纯词构成的. So *swim-suit (swim + suit)* is a compound, and so are *footpath (foot + path)* and *headache (head + ache)*. 因此 swim-suit (swim + suit) 是复合词, footpath (foot + path) 和 headache (head + ache) 也是复合词. A compound can be a noun (*policeman*), an adjective (*easygoing*), a verb (*baby-sit*) or an adverb (*helter-skelter*). 复合词的词类可为名词 (policeman)、形容词 (easygoing)、动词 (baby-sit) 或副词 (helter-skelter). Some compounds are written as one single unit and some with a hyphen (as in the examples above). 有些复合词写成一个整体, 有些带有连字号(如上述示例). But some appear as two separate words (*money order, town hall*). 但是有些是两个独立的词 (money order、town hall).

2 How to look up compounds 怎样查阅复合词

Imagine you have just met *chicken-run*, and wish to look up its meaning. 设想你刚遇到 chicken-run 这个词, 想查一下词义. (a) First you check to see whether the compound has a separate entry. 首先, 你查看这个复合词是否有独立的词条. (It hasn't, so you now know that *chicken-run* doesn't have a special meaning of its own, but is related to a meaning of *chicken* and of *run*. 没有, 于是你知道了 chicken-run 本身并没有特殊词义, 而是与 chicken 和 run 的词义有关.) (b) You expect that the compound is listed in the entry for *chicken*, becasue this is the first part, and you look down that entry. 你料到这个复合词编排在 chicken 词条中, 因为 chicken 是这个复合词的第一部分, 于是你查阅该词条. (c) At the bottom you find a box 在该词条末尾处你看到一个方形符号: □. Below that, the compounds are listed alphabetically 在方形符号下, 就是按字母顺序排列的复合词:

□ **chicken-feed ...**
chicken-hearted ...
chicken-pox ...
chicken-run ...
chicken-wire ...

3 Compounds with entries of their own 有独立词条的复合词

You have met the word *chickweed*. 你遇到了 chickweed 这个词. (a) You assume this is a compound because you have met *chick* and *weed* as separate words. 你猜想这是个复合词, 因为你见过 chick 和 weed 都是独立的词. (b) You look up the entry for **chick**, but *chickweed* is not there. 你查阅 **chick** 这个词条, 并没有 chickweed 这个词. (c) You assume then that *chickweed* has a special meaning unconnected with **chick** (= a young bird). 你于是估计到 chickweed 的词义与 **chick**(= a young bird 幼鸟)无关, 而是有其特殊的词义. (It has. 确实有特殊词义.) (d) You look for a separate entry for **chickweed**, and find it. 你查阅 **chickweed** 独立词条, 结果找到了.

B WRITING AND SPEAKING ENGLISH 写英文和说英语

SPELLING 拼法

1 Where to divide a word 怎样把字断开

You may need to know where to divide a long word at the end of a line of writing. You can find out by using the dictionary. 写英文时在一行末尾处碰上个较长的字, 在这个字

的什么地方断开. 你使用本词典就可解决这个问题. (a) Let us suppose that the word is *imperialism*. 我们假设遇到的是 imperialism 这个字. Does this divide after *imper-*, after *imperi-*, or in another place? 可断开处是在 imper- 之后、在 imperi- 之后, 还是在其他地方呢? (b) You refer to the entry for the word and notice a number of a raised dots 你查找这个字的词条, 注意到这个字的中间有几个黑点:

im·peri·al·ism

(c) These dots indicate that, at the end of a line, the word may be broken as in *im-perialism, imperi-alism, imperial-ism*. 这些黑点表示在一行的末尾处这个字可以断开为 im-perialism、imperi-alism、imperial-ism.

2 Irregular forms of nouns 名词的不规则形式

You suspect that the plural of the noun *phenomenon* is irregular (ie that it is NOT *phenomenons*). 你猜想到 phenomenon 这个名词的复数形式是不规则的(即其复数形式不是"phenomenons"). (a) Turn to the entry for **phenomenon** and look for the part of speech label 翻查 **phenomenon** 这个词条, 查找词类标志: *n.* (b) In round brackets just after it you will find the plural ending **-ena** and its pronunciation 紧接在这个名词标志后有个圆括号, 你可看到其中有其复数结尾 **-ena** 及其读音:

phe·nom·enon /fəˈnɒmɪnən ...; fəˈnɒmə-ˌnɒn/ *n* (*pl* **-ena** /-ɪnə; -ənə/) ...

You also want to check whether the form of a particular noun, eg *grouse*, remains the same when it refers to several birds. 你还想查一下某个名词(如 grouse)其复数形式是否与单数同形. Again you look for round brackets 同样, 你要查看圆括号:

grouse /graʊs; graʊs/ *n* ... (*pl* unchanged)

3 Irregular forms of verbs 动词的不规则形式

You are not sure whether verbs ending in *-t* double the *t* in the past tense. 以 -t 结尾的动词用于过去时态是否要重复 t 字母, 你或许没有把握. (Is *transmitted* or *transmited* correct? 是 transmitted 正确, 还是 transmited 正确? And which of *debitted* and *debited* is right? debitted 和 debited 哪个对呢?) (a) Look up the entires for **transmit** and **debit**. 查阅 **transmit** 和 **debit** 的词条. (b) Look for round brackets after the *v* label. 查阅 *v* 标志后的圆括号. You find this 你看到如下内容:

transmit /trænzˈmɪt; trænzˋmɪt/ *v* **(-tt-)** ...
debit /ˈdebɪt; ˋdɛbɪt/ ... *v* ...

(c) The bold **-tt-** at **transmit** means that you double the *t*, as in *transmitted*. 在 **transmit** 词条中用黑体印刷的 **-tt-** 意为要重复 t 字母, 如 transmitted. The absence of the **-tt-** from the **debit** entry means that *debited* (single *t*) is right. 在 **debit** 词条中没有 **-tt-** 字样, 意为 debited(单个的 t)正确. *Debit* forms a regular past tense, just adding *ed*; so NO extra information is given. ☆ debit 用于过去时态时仅加 -ed 即可构成规则变化; 所以词典中不提供额外信息.

Suppose you're aware that the verb *drink* is irregular, and you want to check the spellings of the irregular forms. 假设你知道 drink 是不规则动词, 你想查看这个不规则形式的拼法. Again, you look in the entry for round brackets after the *v* label 你还得查阅该词条, 找到在 *v* 标志后的圆括号:

drink /drɪŋk; drɪŋk/ *v* (*pt* **drank** /dræŋk; dræŋk/, *pp* **drunk** /drʌŋk; drʌŋk/) ...

4 Irregular forms of adjectives 形容词的不规则形式

You know that some adjectives take a final *-er* or *-est* to express the ideas of 'more' or 'most'. 你知道某些形容词后面加上 -er 或 -est 可表示"更"或"最"之意. You want to check that a particular adjective does this (eg *high*) 你想查阅某形容词是否符合这一规则 (如 high 字). (a) You look up the entry for **high**. 你查阅 **high** 这个词条. (b) You search for round brackets after the label *adj.* 你寻找在 *adj* 标志后的圆括号. There you find the two endings in bold print 你看到其中有两个黑体印刷的词尾:

high /haɪ; haɪ/ *adj* **(-er, -est)**

You are not sure whether an adjective ending in *-y* (eg *pretty*) changes the *-y* to *-i-* before adding *-er* or *-est*. 你不清楚 -y 结尾的形容词(如 pretty)是否需要将 -y 改为 -i- 然后再加上 -er 或 -est. Again you look for round brackets after the label *adj*, and find an **-i-** shown as part of the endings 你再看看 *adj* 标志后的圆括号, 看到词尾部分中有 **-i-**:

pretty /ˈprɪtɪ; ˋprɪtɪ/ *adj* **(-ier, -iest)**.

PRONUNCIATION 读音

1 Alternative pronunciations 异读

You have heard the word *against* pronounced in two ways by British speakers. 你听到过 against 这个字英国人有两种读音. Are both equally acceptable? 这两种都同样算是规范的读音吗? Look up the entry for *against*, and you will find two pronunciations, with no comment added. 查看一下 against 词条, 你看到有两种读音, 没有评注. Both can be safely used. 这两种都可使用.

against /ə'genst, ə'geɪnst/ ...

You have also met *amenity* pronounced in two ways. 你还遇到过 amenity 有两种读音. Are both of these acceptable? 这两种都合标准吗? Look up the entry 查查词条:

amen·ity /ə'mi:nətɪ, *also* ə'menətɪ/ ...

Here, the use of *also* means that the second form is less often used, but it is not incorrect. 此处的 also 意为第二种读音用得较少, 但并非不正确.

2 British and American pronunciation 英式和美式读音

You known that British speakers pronounce *tomato* in one way, but have heard that Americans use another pronunciation. 你知道英国人说 tomato 时有一种发音形式, 但听到过美国人用另一种读音形式. You turn to the entry 你查阅该词条:

to·mato /tə'mɑ:təʊ; *US* tə'meɪtəʊ; tə'meto/ ...

Here, the normal British pronunciation has no label, while the normal American one is marked *US*. 此处英式读音没有标志, 美式读音标示 *US*.

CHOOSING THE RIGHT WORD 选用恰当的词

1 Words which differ slightly in meaning or use 词义或用法稍有差别的词

You wonder whether it is appropriate to use the word *trader* in the sentence 你想知道在下面句中用 trader 一词是否恰当:

He's a trader in rare stamps.

or whether *dealer* or *merchant* might be better choices in this context. 还是用 dealer 或 merchant 更适合上述情况. (a) If you look up **trader** (in the entry at **trade**[2]) you will notice an arrow referring you to a USAGE note at **dealer**. 你若查阅 **trader**(在 **trade**[2] 词条中)就会注意到有个箭头指示你查阅 **dealer** 词条所附"用法"说明. (b) Now compare carefully the definitions and examples in this note, and notice that a dealer sells 'individual objects and has a specialized knowledge of these'. 仔细比较一下说明中的定义和示例就会注意到 dealer 出售的是"individual objects and has a specialized knowledge of these 某类物品, 并对之有专业知识". (c) It is clear that *rare stamps* fits this definition (and also matches the example *antique dealer*). 很清楚, rare stamps 适用于这一定义(而且还与 antique dealer 这一示例相仿). *Dealer*, then, is the best choice. 因此, dealer 最为恰当.

2 Words which are opposite in meaning 意思相反的词语

You have met the word *down* used in this sentence 你遇到过 down 这个词用于下面这一句中:

She has just come down from Oxford.

(a) You turn to the entry for **down**[1] (adverbial particle) and find the numbered definition which explains the meaning of *down* in your sentence: 'away from a university'. 你翻阅 **down**[1](副词小词)词条, 看到有编号的义项中解释你句中的这一词义: "away from a university 离开大学". (b) You wonder if *up* can be used in the opposite meaning and at the end of that section there is a cross-reference to the corresponding meaning of *up* 你想知道是否 up 可用于相反的意思, 在该义项末尾有个关于 up 词义的相互参照注释:

down[1] ... *adv part* ... Cf UP.

(c) You turn to **up** and find that meaning 你翻阅到 **up** 词条, 找到这一词义: "to or in a university 朝着大学或在大学."

3 Words which are different in style 修辞格不同的词

You have met the word *galore*, meaning 'in plenty' and wonder if it reflects a special attitude on the part of the writer. 你遇到 galore 这个词, 意为 "in plenty 很多", 不知道

是否反映出用这个词的人有某种态度. (a) You look up the entry, and search for a note in *italics* in front of the definition 你查阅该词条,在定义前找到圆括号中用斜体印刷的说明:

> **ga·lore ...** (*usu approv*) (following *ns*) in plenty: *to have books, food, friends, money galore ...*

(b) You see from this note that *He has money galore* is usually used approvingly of a person, his position, etc. 你从这一说明得知 He has money galore 通常用于褒扬某人、其地位等.

CHOOSING THE RIGHT PATTERN OR STRUCTURE 选择适当的模式或结构

1 Composing sentences according to the correct patterns 按照正确模式造句

You already know that it is correct to use a 'that' clause after the verb *imagine* – like this 你已经知道应该在 imagine 这一动词后用 that 从句 —— 像下面这样:

> *I always imagined that she was taller than her sister.*

Now you wonder whether it is also possible to use *her* (or *him*) plus *to be, to have,* etc 你想知道是否也可使用 her(或 him)加上 to be、to have 等这种形式:

> *I always imagined her to be taller than her sister.*

To check, you refer to the entry for **imagine** and the meaning 'form a mental image of (sth)', and search for an example which is like your sentence. 为弄清这一点,你查阅 **imagine** 词条及词义 "form a mental image of (sth) 想像,设想(某事物)"并寻找像你的句子的示例. You find this 你找到这一句:

> *Imagine yourself (to be) rich and famous.*

This shows your guess is right. 这表明你猜想得对. But you notice *'to be'* in BRACKETS after *imagine yourself*. 但是你注意到在 imagine yourself 之后的 to be 是在括号中. This means you can correctly place an adjective DIRECTLY after *imagine her* 这表示在 imagine her 之后可直接用个形容词:

> *I always imagined her taller than her sister.*

When you have been using the dictionary for some time, you will find it quicker to find out what the patterns are by referring to the CODES – [Tn], [Tf], etc – just above the definition. 本词典你用过一段时间之后,只要看一下定义前的代码([Tn]、[Tf]等)就知道是什么动词模式了. (➪ DETAILED GUIDE, 10.1.4. 见"详细说明", 10.1.4)

2 Choosing the correct preposition after a noun, a verb or an adjective 在名词、动词或形容词之后选用适当的介词

You know that the preposition *to* is sometimes used after the verb *relate*, as in this sentence 你知道介词 to 有时用于动词 relate 之后,如这一句中的:

> *The enquiry relates inflation to high wage demands.*

You wonder if *with* can also be used after *relate* in this meaning. 你想知道要表达同样的意思在 relate 之后是否也可以用 with. (a) You look up **relate** and find the appropriate meaning 你查阅 **relate** 找到恰当的词义: **2(a)** ... 'connect (two things) in thought or meaning'. (在思想上或意义上)将(两事物)联系起来. (b) Just above this definition, in bold print, you will see: **~ sth to/with sth** which means 'relate something to or with something'. 就在这一定义前,你看到有黑体字: **~ sth to/with sth**, 意为 relate something to or with something. So *either* preposition is correct for this meaning of the verb. 由此可知这个动词表达的这个意思,这两个介词用哪个都对. (c) Look again at the pattern in bold print. 再看以下用黑体印刷的动词模式. There are no brackets around 'to/with sth'. ☆ to/with sth 两端没有括号. This means that, in this meaning, *relate* must ALWAYS be used with a preposition. 这表示在这一词义上, relate 一定要与介词连用.

But suppose you choose a different meaning of the verb. 但是假设你选用的是该动词的另一词义. Look at this 看看这一句:

> *She related these events to her audience.*

Here, the verb means 'tell' or 'give an account of'. 这个动词在这里意为 "tell 告诉" 或 "give an account of 叙述". (a) Find this definition (at number **1**). 找出这一定义(在第一义项). (b) Just above is this: **~ sth (to sb)**, which means 'relate something (to somebody)'. 就在这一义项之前有: **~ sth (to sb)**, 意为 relate something (to somebody). (c) Note that 'to somebody' is in brackets. 注意 "to somebody" 是在括号中. This means that you CAN leave these words out of a sentence, as in this example 这表示句中可以不用的词, 如以下示例:

She related these events.

3 Knowing which nouns to use with verbs, which adjectives to use with nouns, etc 了解名词与动词、形容词与名词等的搭配关系

You have met the rather formal phrase *imbued with religious fervour*, and you wish to know what other nouns are normally used after this verb. 你遇到个很文的词组 imbued with religious fervour, 想知道在这个动词后一般还可用哪些名词. (a) You look up the entry and find this definition and this example 你查阅该词条, 看见如下的定义和示例:

im·bue ... fill or inspire (sb/sth) with (feelings, etc): *imbued with patriotism, ambition, love, etc*

(b) You see that nouns referring to emotions or feelings are used with this verb: 'etc' tells you that other similar nouns could be added. 你看到指情绪与感觉的名词可与这一动词连用; "etc 等" 表示其他类似的名词也可使用.

You are aware that you can say *a mature man* or *a mature woman*. 你知道可以说 a mature man 或 a mature woman. But can you use nouns of DIFFERENT kinds with this adjective? 但是不同种类的名词可以不可以和这个形容词连用呢? What about *a mature eagle* (one that is fully grown)? ☆ a mature eagle(已经长大的)这种搭配行吗? (a) You turn to the entry and find this list 你翻阅该词条找到以下内容:

mature ... *mature person, oak, starling*

(b) You know from seeing *starling* that *eagle* is possible (and that names of trees are possible too). 你看到 starling 而知道 eagle 可以用(而且树名也可用). (c) You note that there is no *etc* here. 你注意到此处没有 "etc 等" 字样. This is because the nouns are so different in meaning. 这是因为示例中几个名词的意思差别很大.

By now you are familiar with the types of information you can find in the dictionary. 到现在你已经熟悉了本词典中的各类内容. You will be able to use it to help you every time you are speaking or writing English. 你在说英语或写英文的时候就可以借助这本词典了. There is also the section at the back of the dictionary, called *A Detailed Guide to the Entries*, where you will find a full description of the content of an entry. 在本词典后部还附有一篇 "词条使用详细说明", 是对词条内容的全面解释.

A a

A, a[1] /eɪ; e/ *n* (*pl* **A's, a's** /eɪz; ez/) **1** the first letter of the English alphabet 英语字母表的第一个字母: *'Ann' begins with (an) A/'A'.* Ann一字以A字母开始. **2** (*music* 音) the sixth note in the scale of C major C大调音阶中的第六音或音符. **3** academic mark indicating the highest standard of work 学业成绩达最高标准的评价符号: *get (an) A/'A' in biology* 生物(学科)得A. **4** (used to designate a range of standard paper sizes 用以标明一系列标准纸张的规格): [attrib 作定语] *an A4 folder* A4纸张大小的文件夹, 即297×210 mm. **5** (idm 习语) **A1** /ˌeɪ ˈwʌn; ˈeˈwʌn/ (*infml* 口) excellent; first rate 极好的; 头等的; 第一流的: *an ˌA1 ˈdinner* 一顿美餐 ○ *I'm feeling A1,* ie very well. 我身体好极了. **from A to B** from one place to another 从一处到另一处: *I don't care what a car looks like as long as it gets me from A to B.* 我倒不在乎汽车的样子, 只要能把我从一处载到另一处就行了. **from A to Z** from beginning to end; thoroughly 从头到尾; 彻底地: *know a subject from A to Z* 精通一科目.

□ **A-OK** /ˌeɪ əʊˈkeɪ; ˌe oˈke/ *adj* [usu pred 通常作表语] (*US infml* 口) emphatically OK 极佳; 顶呱呱. Cf 参看 OKAY.

A-road /ˈeɪ rəʊd; ˈe ˌrod/ *n* (*Brit*) major road, less important than a motorway but usu wider and straighter than a B-road A级公路(重要性次于高速公路的主干公路, 但通常比B级公路宽且直): *There's a good A-road going North — the A1.* 有一条良好的A级公路通往北方——A级1号公路.

ˈ**A-side** *n* (music recorded on the) first or main side of a single-play gramophone record (单曲唱片的)A面, 正面(上的乐曲).

a[2] /ə; ə; *strong form* 强读式 eɪ; e/ (also **an** /ən; ən; *strong form* 强读式 æn; æn/) *indef art* (The form *a* is used before consonant sounds and the form *an* before vowel sounds. Both are used before [C], [Cgp] or [sing] *ns* that have not previously been made specific. a用于辅音前, an用于元音前. 两者均用于前文未曾确指的可数单数名词或集合名词之前.) **1** one 一(个): *a man, hotel, girl, committee, unit, U-turn* (一个)男人、旅馆、姑娘、委员会、单位、U形转弯 (Cf 参看 *some men, hotels, girls, etc*) ○ *an egg, aunt, uncle, hour, X-ray, MP, L-plate* (一个)蛋、姑姑、叔叔、小时、X光照片、下院议员、L字牌 (Cf 参看 *some eggs, aunts, uncles, hours, etc*) ○ *I can only carry two at a time.* 我一次只能携带两个. ○ *There's a book on the table — is that the one you want?* 桌子上有一本书——是不是你要的那一本? **2** (used with an abstract *n* that is restricted by the phrase which follows it 与抽象名词连用时, 该名词后须有限定性词组): *There was still an abundance of food when we arrived.* 我们抵达时还有很多食物. ○ *We're looking for someone with a good knowledge of German.* 我们正在找一个精通德语的人. **3** any; every 任何; 每一(个): *A horse is a quadruped.* 马是四足动物. (Cf 参看 *Horses are quadrupeds.*) ○ *An owl can see in the dark.* 猫头鹰在黑暗中能看见东西. (Cf 参看 *Owls can see*...). **4** one single 单一的: *He didn't tell us a thing about his holiday.* 他度假的事对我们只字未提. **5** (used with *ns* followed by *of + possess det + n + 's* 与名词+ of +所有格限定词+名词+ 's连用): *a friend of my father's,* ie one of my father's friends 我父亲的一个朋友 ○ *a habit of Sally's,* ie one of Sally's habits 萨莉的一种习惯. **6** (used in front of two *ns* seen as a unit 用于可视为一体的两个名词之前): *a cup and saucer* 一副杯碟 ○ *a knife and fork* 一副刀叉. **7** to or for each; per 每一; 每: *£2 a gallon* 每加仑2英镑 ○ *800 words a day* 每天800字 ○ *50p a pound* 每磅50便士. **8** (*often derog* 常作贬义) person like (sb) 像(某人)的人: *My boss is a little Napoleon.* 我的老板是个小拿破仑. **9** (used with sb's name to show that the speaker does not know the person 与某人姓名连用, 表示说话者不认识此人): *Do we know a Tim Smith?* 咱们认识一个叫蒂姆·史密斯的人吗? ○ *A Mrs Green is waiting to see you.* 有一位格林太太正等着见你. ○ *A Doctor Simpson telephoned.* 有一位辛普森医生来过电话. **10** (used to show membership of a class 用以表示一群体中的成员): *My mother is a solicitor.* 我母亲是律师. ○ *My father is a Fulham supporter.* 我父亲是富勒姆足球队的球迷. **11** painting, sculpture, etc by 由...作的绘画、雕刻等: *The painting my grandfather gave me turned out to be a Constable.* 我祖父给我的那幅画原来是康斯塔伯的作品.

NOTE ON USAGE 用法: Note that the sound of the first letter of an abbreviation, not its spelling, determines the form and pronunciation of the article before it 注意用于缩写字前面的冠词, 其词形和读音取决于该缩写字的第一个字母的读音, 而不取决于其书写形式: *an MP* ○ *an SRN* ○ *a UHF radio* ○ *the* /ðɪ; ðɪ/ *NSPCC* ○ *the* /ðə; ðə/ *USA*.

a- *pref* 前缀 **1** (with *ns, adjs* and *advs* 与名词、形容词、副词结合) not; without 不; 无; 非: *atheist* ○ *atypical* ○ *asexually.* ⇨Usage at UN- 用法见UN-. **2** (with *vs* forming *adjs* 与动词结合构成形容词) in the state or process of 处于...状态或过程中: *awake* ○ *asleep* ○ *ablaze* ○ *adrift*.

A *abbr* 缩写 = **1** ampere(s): *13A*, eg on a fuse 13安(如标于保险丝上者). **2** answer. Cf 参看 Q. **3** (in academic degrees 在学位方面) Associate of: *ARCM*, ie Associate of the Royal College of Music 皇家音乐学院副研究员. Cf 参看 F2.

A /eɪ; e/ *symb* 符号 (*Brit*) (of roads) major (指公路)A级(主干公路): *the A40 to Oxford* 通往牛津的A级40号公路 ○ *an A-road* 一条A级公路. Cf 参看 B.

AA /ˌeɪ ˈeɪ; ˌe ˈe/ *abbr* 缩写 = **1** (*US*) Alcoholics Anonymous 嗜酒者互诫协会. **2** (*Brit*) Automobile Association 汽车协会: *members of the AA* 汽车协会会员.

AAA /ˌeɪ eɪ ˈeɪ; ˌe e ˈe/ *abbr* 缩写 = **1** (also **the three A's**) (*Brit*) Amateur Athletic Association 业余体育协会. **2** (*US*) American Automobile Association 美国汽车协会.

AB /ˌeɪ ˈbiː; ˌe ˈbi/ *abbr* 缩写 = **1** (*Brit*) able-bodied seaman. **2** (*US*) Bachelor of Arts.

aback /əˈbæk; əˈbæk/ *adv* (phr v) **take sb aback** ⇨ TAKE.

aba·cus /ˈæbəkəs; ˈæbəkəs/ *n* (*pl* **-cuses** /-kəsɪz; -kə,sɪz/) frame with beads that slide along parallel rods, used for teaching numbers to children, and (in some countries) for counting 算盘.

ab·aft /əˈbɑːft; *US* əˈbæft; əˈbæft/ *adv* (*nautical* 海) in or towards the stern half of a ship 在船尾; 向船尾.

▷ **ab·aft** *prep* (*nautical* 海) nearer to the stern than (sth); behind 比(某物)更接近船尾; 在...后面: *abaft the mainmast* 在船的主桅后面.

aban·don /əˈbændən; əˈbændən/ *v* **1** (**a**) [Tn] go away from (a person or thing or place) not intending to return; forsake; desert 离开(某人、某物或某地)而不返回; 遗弃; 抛弃; 离弃: *a baby abandoned by its parents* 被父母遗弃的婴儿 ○ *an abandoned car, dwelling, fort, village* 被抛弃的汽车、被离弃的住所、被遗弃的堡垒、被离弃的村庄 ○ *give orders to abandon ship,* ie to leave a sinking ship 下令弃船(离开正在下沉的船). (**b**) [Tn, Dn·pr] **~ sth/sb (to sb)** leave sth/sb to be taken (by sb) 舍弃某物[某人]而被(别人)取得: *They abandoned their lands to the invading forces.* 他们丢下了土地,遭侵略军占领. **2** [Tn] give up completely (esp sth begun) 完全放弃(尤指已开始的某事物): *abandon a project, plan, scheme, etc* 放弃一项方案、计划、设计等 ○ *urge people who smoke to abandon the habit* 敦促吸烟的人戒烟 ○ *He abandoned all hope,* ie stopped hoping. 他放弃了一切希望. ○ *The match was abandoned because of bad weather.* 比赛因天气恶劣而取消. **3** [Tn·pr] **~ oneself to sth** (*fml* 文) yield completely to (an emotion or impulse) 完全屈从于(某种情感或冲动): *He abandoned* *himself to despair.* 他陷入绝望中.

▷ **aban·don** (also **aban·don·ment**) *n* [U] freedom from worry or inhibitions 放任; 纵情: *dance with wild/gay abandon* 狂放地[尽情地]跳舞.

aban·doned *adj* [usu attrib 通常作定语] (of people or behaviour) wild or immoral (指人或行为)放荡的, 堕落的.

aban·don·ment *n* [U] **1** abandoning 遗弃; 抛弃; 离弃; 放弃; 舍弃: *Her abandonment of the idea upset him.* 她放弃了这一意见, 他很不高兴. **2** = ABANDON *n*.

abase /əˈbeɪs; əˈbes/ *v* [Tn] **~ oneself/sb** lower oneself/sb in dignity; degrade oneself/sb 降低自己[某人]的身分; 屈辱自己[某人]. ▷ **abase·ment** *n* [U].

abashed /əˈbæʃt; əˈbæʃt/ *adj* [pred 作表语] **~ (at/by sth)** embarrassed; ashamed 尴尬; 羞愧: *His boss's criticism left him feeling rather abashed.* 老板批评了他, 他感到有些难为情.

abate /əˈbeɪt; əˈbet/ *v* [I, Tn] (of wind, noise, pain, etc) make or become less (指风力、声音、痛苦等)减小, 减少, 减轻: *The ship sailed when the storm had abated.* 那船在暴风雨减弱后起航了. ○ *People are campaigning to abate the noise in our cities.* 大家正在进行一场减低城市噪音的运动. ▷ **abate·ment** *n* [U].

ab·at·toir /ˈæbətwɑ:(r); *US* ˌæbəˈtwɑ:r; ˌæbəˈtwɑr/ *n* = SLAUGHTERHOUSE (SLAUGHTER).

ab·bess /ˈæbes; ˋæbɛs/ *n* woman who is head of a convent or nunnery 女修道院院长.

ab·bey /ˈæbɪ; ˋæbɪ/ *n* **1** [C] building(s) in which monks or nuns live as a community under an abbot or abbess 修道院. **2** [CGp] the whole number of monks or nuns in an abbey 修道院中全体修士或修女. **3** [C] church or house that was formerly an abbey 曾为修道院的大教堂或房屋: *Westminster Abbey* 威斯敏斯特大教堂.

ab·bot /ˈæbət; ˋæbət/ *n* man who is head of a monastery or abbey 男修道院院长; 大寺院住持.

abbr (also **abbrev**) *abbr* 缩写 = abbreviated; abbreviation.

ab·bre·vi·ate /əˈbri:vɪeɪt; əˋbrivɪˌet/ *v* [Tn, Tn·pr] **~ sth (to sth)** shorten (a word, phrase, etc), esp by omitting letters 缩短(字、词组等, 尤指省略字母); 缩写: *In writing, the title 'Doctor' is abbreviated to 'Dr'.* 在书写时, Doctor 头衔的缩写是 Dr.

▷ **ab·bre·vi·ation** /əˌbri:vɪˈeɪʃn; əˌbrivɪˋeʃən/ *n* **1** [U] abbreviating or being abbreviated 缩短; 缩写. **2** [C] shortened form of a word, phrase, etc 缩写词; 略语: *'Sept' is an abbreviation for 'September'.* Sept 是 September 的缩写. ○ *'GB' is the abbreviation of/for 'Great Britain'.* GB 是 Great Britain 的缩写.

ABC /ˌeɪ bi: ˈsi:; ˋeˋbiˋsi/ *n* [sing] **1** (Roman) alphabet, ie all the letters from A to Z (罗马)字母表, 即由 A 至 Z 所有字母: *Does the boy know his ABC?* 这个男孩儿认识字母了吗? **2** simplest and most basic facts about a subject 一门学科的最简单、最基本的要点; 基础知识: *the ABC of gardening* 园艺入门. **3** (idm 习语) **easy as ABC** ⇨ EASY[1].

ABC /ˌeɪ bi: ˈsi:; ˋeˋbiˋsi/ *abbr* 缩写 = **1** American Broadcasting Company 美国广播公司: *watch ABC* 收看美国广播公司的节目. **2** Australian Broadcasting Commission 澳大利亚广播公司.

ab·dic·ate /ˈæbdɪkeɪt; ˋæbdəˌket/ *v* **1** [I] resign from or formally renounce the throne 退位; 逊位: *King Edward VIII abdicated in 1936.* 英王爱德华八世于1936年退位. **2** [Tn] (*fml* 文) formally relinquish (power, a high official position, etc) 正式放弃(权力、高位等): *He's abdicated all responsibility in the affair.* 他已经放弃了这件事中的一切职责. ▷ **ab·dica·tion** /ˌæbdɪˈkeɪʃn; ˌæbdəˋkeʃən/ *n* [C, U].

ab·do·men /ˈæbdəmən; ˋæbdəmən/ *n* **1** part of the body below the chest and diaphragm, containing the stomach, bowels and digestive organs 腹部. Cf 参看 INTESTINE. **2** rearmost section of an insect, a spider or a crustacean 昆虫、蜘蛛或甲壳类动物的腹部: *head, thorax and abdomen* 头部、胸部及腹部. ⇨illus at INSECT 见 INSECT 之插图.

▷ **ab·dom·inal** /æbˈdɒmɪnl; æbˋdɑmən!/ *adj* in, of or for the abdomen 腹部中的; 腹部的: *abdominal pains* 腹痛 ○ *an abdominal operation* 腹部手术. **ab·dom·in·ally** /æbˈdɒmɪnəlɪ; æbˋdɑmɪnlɪ/ *adv*.

ab·duct /əbˈdʌkt, æb-; əbˋdʌkt, æb-/ *v* [Tn] take (sb) away illegally, using force or deception; kidnap 诱拐; 绑架. ▷ **ab·duc·tion** /əbˈdʌkʃn, æb-; əbˋdʌkʃən, æb-/ *n* [U, C]. **ab·ductor** *n*.

abeam /əˈbi:m; əˋbim/ *adv* (*nautical* 海) on a line at right angles to the length of a ship or an aircraft 正横(在与船身[机身]成直角的线上): *The lighthouse was abeam of the ship.* 灯塔在船的正横方向.

ab·er·rant /æˈberənt; æbˋɛrənt/ *adj* not following the normal or correct way 不循常轨的; 不走正路的: *aberrant behaviour* 越轨行为.

ab·er·ra·tion /ˌæbəˈreɪʃn; ˌæbəˋreʃən/ *n* **1** (**a**) [U] deviation from what is accepted as normal or right 偏差; 越轨: *steal sth in a moment of aberration* 一时糊涂而偷东西. (**b**) [C] moral or mental lapse; temporary loss of memory 失检或失常; 一时失去记忆力: *Owing to a strange mental aberration he forgot his own name.* 由于一种莫名的精神错乱, 他把自己的名字忘了. **2** [C] fault or defect 毛病; 差错: *an aberration in the computer* 计算机的差错.

abet /əˈbet; əˋbɛt/ *v* (**-tt-**) **1** (**a**) [Tn, Tn·pr] **~ sb (in sth)** help or encourage sb to commit an offence or do sth wrong 唆使; 怂恿: *He was abetted in these illegal activities by his wife.* 他受妻子怂恿进行这些非法活动. (**b**) [Tn] encourage (a crime, etc) 教唆, 鼓动(犯罪等): *You are abetting theft.* 你在教唆偷窃. **2** (idm 习语) **aid and abet** ⇨ AID. ▷ **abet·ter**, (*esp law* 尤用于法律) **abet·tor** *ns*.

abey·ance /əˈbeɪəns; əˋbeəns/ *n* [U] (idm 习语) **be in abeyance; fall/go into abeyance** (of a right, rule, problem, etc) be suspended temporarily; not be in force or use for a time (指权利、规则等)暂时中止; (指问题等)缓议; 暂时无效或停用: *The question is in abeyance*, ie left unanswered, eg until more information is obtained. 这个问题暂时搁置(如待获得更多资料时再行解决). ○ *This law falls into abeyance when the country's security is threatened.* 当国家安全受到威胁时, 这项法规暂停实施.

ab·hor /əbˈhɔ:(r); əbˋhɔr/ *v* (**-rr-**) [Tn] feel hatred and disgust for (sb/sth); detest 憎恨(某人[某事物]); 厌恶; 讨厌: *abhor terrorism, terrorists* 憎恨恐怖活动、恐怖分子.

▷ **ab·hor·rence** /əbˈhɒrəns; *US* -ˈhɔ:r-; əbˋhɔrəns/ *n* [U] hatred and disgust 憎恨; 厌恶: *have an abhorrence of war* 憎恶战争.

ab·hor·rent /əbˈhɒrənt; *US* -ˈhɔ:r-; əbˋhɔrənt/ *adj* **~ (to sb)** disgusting; hateful 讨厌的; 可恶的; 可恨的: *Violence is abhorrent to his gentle nature.* 他性情温和, 讨厌暴力.

abide /əˈbaɪd; əˋbaɪd/ *v* (*pt, pp* **abided**; in sense 3 用于下述第3义时作 **abode** /əˈbəʊd; əˋbod/) **1** [Tn] (esp with *can/could*, in negative sentences or questions 尤于否定句或疑问句中与 can/could 连用) tolerate (sb/sth); endure; bear 容忍(某人[某事物]); 忍受; 忍耐: *I can't abide that man.* 我对那个人忍无可忍. ○ *How could you abide such conditions?* 这种环境你怎么受得了呢? **2** [Ipr] **~ by sth** act in accordance with sth; be faithful to sth 遵守某事物; 忠于某事物: *abide by* (ie keep) *a promise* 遵守诺言 ○ *abide by* (ie observe) *an agreement, verdict, ruling, etc* 履行协议、服从裁决、遵从裁定 ○ *You'll have to abide by* (ie accept) *the referee's decision.* 你得遵从裁判的决定. **3** [Ipr] (*arch* 古) remain; continue; stay 逗留; 延续; 居留; 停留: *abide at a place* 住在某地 ○ *abide with sb* 和某人同住.

▷ **abid·ing** *adj* enduring; permanent 持久的; 永久的: *an abiding friendship, hatred, mistrust, etc* 永恒的友谊、永世的仇恨、积久的疑忌.

abil·ity /əˈbɪlətɪ; əˋbɪlətɪ/ *n* **1** [U] capacity or power to do sth physical or mental 做体力、脑力或机械工作的能力或力量: *a machine with the ability to cope with large loads* 能处理大负荷量的机器 ○ *He has the ability to do the work.* 他有做这项工作的能力. **2** (**a**) [U] cleverness; intelligence 智慧; 才智: *a woman of great ability* 很有才能的女子. (**b**) [U, C] talent 天资; 天分: *have a great musical ability* 很有音乐天才 ○ *We found him work more suited to his abilities.* 我们给他找到了更适合他的能力的工作. **3** (idm 习语) **to the best of one's ability** ⇨ BEST[3].

ab·ject /ˈæbdʒekt; ˋæbdʒɛkt/ *adj* **1** (of conditions) wretched; hopeless (指境况)凄惨的, 绝望的: *living in* *abject poverty/misery* 过着极穷困［悲惨］的生活. **2** (of people, their actions or behaviour) lacking all pride; contemptible; despicable (指人、动作或行为)无耻的, 下贱的, 卑鄙的: *an abject coward* 可鄙的胆小鬼 ○ *an abject* (ie very humble) *apology* 低声下气的道歉. ▷ **ab·jectly** *adv*.

ab·jure /əbˈdʒʊə(r); əbˈdʒʊr/ *v* [Tn] (*fml* 文) promise or swear to give up (a claim, an opinion, a belief, etc); renounce formally 承诺或发誓放弃(要求、意见、信仰等); 正式放弃: *abjure one's religion* 发誓放弃其宗教信仰. ▷ **ab·jura·tion** /ˌæbdʒʊəˈreɪʃn; ˌæbdʒʊˈreʃən/ *n* [U, C].

ab·lat·ive /ˈæblətɪv; ˈæblətɪv/ *n* (usu *sing* 通常作单数) (*grammar*) special form of a noun, a pronoun or an adjective used (in some inflected languages) to indicate or describe esp the agent or instrument of an action 夺格(某些屈折语中的名词、代词或形容词的一种格, 尤其表示动作的主动者或动作赖以进行的工具).
▷ **ab·lat·ive** *adj* of or in the ablative 夺格的.

ab·laut /ˈæblaʊt; ˈæblaʊt/ *n* [U] (*linguistics* 语言) systematic way in which vowels change in related forms of a word, esp in Indo-European languages (eg *drive, drove, driven*) 元音交替(尤指在印欧语系中, 一个词的相关形式中有规律的变化, 如 drive、drove、driven).

ablaze /əˈbleɪz; əˈblez/ *adj* [pred 作表语] **1** burning; on fire 燃烧; 着火: *set sth ablaze* 点火烧某物 ○ *The whole building was soon ablaze.* 整座建筑物很快就烧起来了. **2 ~ (with sth)** (*fig* 比喻) (**a**) very bright; glittering 明亮; 灿烂: *The palace was ablaze with lights.* 那座宫殿灯火辉煌. (**b**) very excited 非常激动: *His face was ablaze with anger.* 他满面怒容.

able[1] /ˈeɪbl; ˈebl̩/ *adj* **be ~ to do sth** (used as a *modal v* 用作情态动词) have the power, means or opportunity to do sth 有能力、办法或机会做某事; 能: *The child is not yet able to write.* 这个孩子还不会写字. ○ *Will you be able to come?* 你能来吗? ○ *You are better able to do it than I (am).* 你比我更有能力做这件事.

able[2] /ˈeɪbl; ˈebl̩/ *adj* (**-r**, **-st** /ˈeɪblɪst; ˈeblɪst/) having knowledge or skill; competent; capable 有知识或技能的; 有能力的; 有本事的: *an able worker* 有才干的工作者 ○ *the ablest/most able student in the class* 班上最有才华的学生.
▷ **ably** /ˈeɪblɪ; ˈeblɪ/ *adv* in an able manner 能干地: *They have done their work very ably.* 他们胜任愉快地做完了工作.
□ ˌ**able-ˈbodied** /-ˈbɒdɪd; -ˈbɑdɪd/ *adj* healthy, fit and strong 健康的; 强壮的.
ˌ**able(-ˌbodied) ˈseaman** (*abbr* 缩写 **AB**) sailor who is trained and fit for all duties (受过训练能承担各种任务的)一等水兵. ⇨App 9 见附录 9.

-able, -ible /əbl; əbl̩/ *suff* 后缀 **1** (with *ns* forming *adjs* 与名词结合构成形容词) having or showing the quality of 具有或显示…性质或特点的: *fashionable* ○ *comfortable*. **2** (with *vs* forming *adjs* 与动词结合构成形容词) (**a**) that may or must be 可以…的; 必须…的: *eatable* ○ *payable* ○ *reducible*. (**b**) apt to 有…倾向的: *changeable* ○ *perishable*. ▷ **-ability**, **-ibility** (forming uncountable *ns* 用以构成不可数名词): *profitability* ○ *reversibility*. **-ably**, **-ibly** (forming *advs* 用以构成副词): *noticeably* ○ *incredibly*.

ab·lu·tion /əˈbluːʃn; əbˈluʃən/ *n* (usu *pl* 通常作复数) (*fml or joc* 文或谑) ceremonial washing of the body, hands, sacred vessels, etc (对身体、手、圣器等的)洁净礼: *perform one's ablutions*, ie wash oneself 沐浴.

ABM /ˌeɪ biː ˈem; ˌe bi ˈɛm/ *abbr* 缩写 = anti-ballistic missile 反弹道导弹.

ab·nega·tion /ˌæbnɪˈgeɪʃn; ˌæbnɪˈgeʃən/ *n* [U] (*fml* 文) **1** denial or renunciation (of a doctrine) 否定或放弃(某主义或学说). **2** (also ˌ**self-abneˈgation**) self-sacrifice 克己; 自制; 自我牺牲.

ab·nor·mal /æbˈnɔːml; æbˈnɔrml̩/ *adj* different, esp in an undesirable way, from what is normal, ordinary or expected 反常的; 不正常的; 变态的: *abnormal specimens, weather conditions, behaviour* 异常的样品、反常的天气、变态行为 ○ *be physically/mentally abnormal* 身体上［精神上］不正常. ▷ **ab·nor·mal·ity** /ˌæbnɔːˈmælətɪ; ˌæbnɔrˈmælətɪ/ *n* [U, C]. **ab·nor·mally** /æbˈnɔːməlɪ; æbˈnɔrml̩ɪ/ *adv*: *abnormally large feet* 异常巨大的脚.

Abo /ˈæbəʊ; ˈæbo/ *n* (*pl* **~s**) (⚠ *Austral sl offensive* 讳, 澳, 俚, 蔑) = ABORIGINAL.

aboard /əˈbɔːd; əˈbɔrd/ *adv part, prep* on or into a ship, an aircraft, a train or (*esp US*) a bus 在船、飞机、火车或公共汽车上(在美式英语中尤指公共汽车); 上船、飞机、火车或公共汽车: *We went/climbed aboard.* 我们上了船(或飞机、车等). ○ *Welcome aboard!* 欢迎乘坐这船(或飞机、车等)! ○ *All aboard!* ie The ship, etc is about to depart. 请各位上船(或飞机、车等)! ○ *He was already aboard the ship.* 他已经上船了.

abode[1] /əˈbəʊd; əˈbod/ *n* [sing] (*fml or rhet or joc* 文或修辞或谑) **1** house; home 房屋; 家: *one's place of abode*, ie where one lives 居住处(住所) ○ *Welcome to our humble abode!* 欢迎光临寒舍! **2** (idm 习语) **no fixed abode/address** ⇨ FIX[1].

abode[2] *pt, pp* of ABIDE 3.

ab·ol·ish /əˈbɒlɪʃ; əˈbɑlɪʃ/ *v* [Tn] end the existence of (a custom, an institution, etc) 废除, 废止(习俗、制度等): *Should the death penalty be abolished?* 应该废除死刑吗?
▷ **ab·oli·tion** /ˌæbəˈlɪʃn; ˌæbəˈlɪʃən/ *n* [U] abolishing or being abolished 废除; 废止: *the abolition of slavery, hanging* 奴隶制度、绞刑的废除. **ab·oli·tion·ist** /ˌæbəˈlɪʃənɪst; ˌæbəˈlɪʃənɪst/ *n* person who favours abolition, esp of capital punishment 废除论者; (尤指)主张废除死刑者.

A-bomb /ˈeɪ bɒm; ˈe ˌbɑm/ *n* = ATOMIC BOMB (ATOMIC).

ab·om·in·able /əˈbɒmɪnəbl; *US* -mən-; əˈbɑmənəbl̩/ *adj* **1 ~ (to sb)** (*fml* 文) causing disgust; detestable 讨厌的; 可恶的: *Your behaviour is abominable to me.* 我讨厌你的行为. **2** (*infml* 口) very unpleasant 令人很不愉快的: *abominable weather, food, music* 糟糕的天气、食物、音乐. ▷ **ab·om·in·ably** /əˈbɒmɪnəblɪ; *US* -mən-; əˈbɑmənəblɪ/ *adv*.
□ **Abominable Snowman** = YETI.

ab·om·in·ate /əˈbɒmɪneɪt; *US* -mən-; əˈbɑməˌnet/ *v* [Tn] feel hatred or disgust for (sth/sb); detest; loathe 憎恨; 厌恶; 讨厌; 憎恶: *I abominate fascism.* 我憎恨法西斯主义.
▷ **ab·om·ina·tion** /əˌbɒmɪˈneɪʃn; *US* -mən-; əˌbɑməˈneʃən/ *n* **1** [U] feeling of disgust and extreme hatred 深恶痛绝: *hold sth in abomination* 憎恶某事物. **2** [C] act, habit, person or thing that is hated 令人憎恶的行为、习惯、人或事物: *That new concrete building is an abomination.* 那座新的混凝土建筑物是个讨厌的东西.

ab·ori·gin·al /ˌæbəˈrɪdʒənl; ˌæbəˈrɪdʒənl̩/ *adj* (esp of people) inhabiting a land from a very early period, esp before the arrival of colonists (尤指人)从很早的时期(尤指殖民者到来之前)就居住于某地的; 土著的: *aboriginal inhabitants, plants* 土著居民、土生植物.
▷ **ab·ori·ginal** *n* **1** aboriginal inhabitant 土著; 土人. **2** (also **Aboriginal**) aboriginal inhabitant of Australia 澳大利亚土人.

ab·ori·gines /ˌæbəˈrɪdʒəniːz; ˌæbəˈrɪdʒəˌniz/ *n* [pl] aboriginal inhabitants, esp (**Aborigines**) those of Australia (尤指澳大利亚的)土著居民.
▷ **ab·ori·gine** /ˌæbəˈrɪdʒənɪ; ˌæbəˈrɪdʒəˌnɪ/ *n* (*infml* 口) aboriginal inhabitant 土著; 土人.

abort /əˈbɔːt; əˈbɔrt/ *v* **1** (*medical* 医) (**a**) [Tn] cause (sb/sth) to undergo abortion 使流产; 使堕胎: *abort an expectant mother, a deformed foetus, the pregnancy* 为孕妇、因为胎儿畸形、为终止妊娠做人工流产. (**b**) [I] undergo abortion; miscarry 流产; 小产: *She aborted after four months.* 她怀孕四个月后流产了. **2** [I, Tn] (cause sth to) end prematurely and unsuccessfully (使某事物)中止, 夭折: *abort a space mission*, ie cancel it in space, usu because of mechanical trouble 中止一次航天任务(通常因机械故障而在太空中取消该任务) ○ *abort a computer program* 中止计算机的程序.
▷ **aborted** *adj* **1** undeveloped 未发育的. **2** (*biology* 生) rudimentary 发育不全的; 退化的: *Thorns are aborted branches.* 植物的刺是退化的枝.

abor·tion /əˈbɔːʃn; əˈbɔrʃən/ *n* **1** (**a**) [U] (esp deliberately induced) expulsion of a foetus from the womb before it is able to survive, esp in the first 28 weeks of pregnancy 人工流产; 堕胎; 打胎: *Many people are anti-abortion.* 很多人反对人工流产. (**b**) [C]: *operation to terminate a pregnancy* 人工流产手术 ○ *She had an abortion.* 她做了人工流产. Cf 参看 MISCARRIAGE 1. **2** [C] project or action that has failed completely 已经完全失败的计划或行动.

A

▷ **abor·tion·ist** /əˈbɔːʃənɪst; əˈbɔrʃənɪst/ *n* person who performs abortions, esp illegally 为人堕胎者(尤指非法者).

abort·ive /əˈbɔːtɪv; əˈbɔrtɪv/ *adj* coming to nothing; unsuccessful 落空的; 失败的: *an abortive attempt, coup, mission* 落空的尝试、政变、任务 ○ *plans that proved abortive* 终归失败了的计划. ▷ **abort·ively** *adv*.

abound /əˈbaʊnd; əˈbaʊnd/ *v* **1** [I] be very plentiful; exist in great numbers 非常多; 大量存在: *Oranges abound here all the year round.* 这里一年到头都有很多橙子. **2** [Ipr] **~ in/with sth** have sth in great numbers or quantities 有大量某物: *The river abounds in/with fish.* 这条河里有很多鱼.

about[1] /əˈbaʊt; əˈbaʊt/ *adv* **1** (also *esp US* **around**) a little more or less than; a little before or after; approximately 比…稍多或稍少; 在…稍前或稍后; 大约; 左右: *It costs about £10.* 这需10英镑左右. ○ *He's about the same height as you.* 他大约像你那么高. ○ *She drove for about ten miles.* 她开车行驶了大约十英里. ○ *They waited for about an hour.* 他们等了大约一个小时. **2** (*infml* 口) nearly 将近: *I'm (just) about ready.* 我(就)快准备好了. **3** (*infml* 口) (in understatements 用于含蓄的言语): *I've had just about enough*, ie quite enough. 我已经差不多够了(十分够了). ○ *He's been promoted, and about time too*, ie it ought to have happened earlier. 他获提升了, 也差不多到时候了(早就该提升了). **4** (idm 习语) **that's about ˈit/the ˈsize of it** (*infml* 口) that is how I see it or assess it 大致如此[大小差不多] (据我所看到或估计到的).

about[2] /əˈbaʊt; əˈbaʊt/ *adv part* (in senses 1, 2 and 3 *esp Brit*; in these senses also, *esp US*, **around** 1、2、3义尤用于英式英语; 这些词义, 尤于美式英语, 也可用 **around**) **1** (**a**) (indicating movement) here and there, in many directions; all around (表示动向)到处, 各处, 处处: *The children were rushing aˈbout.* 孩子们到处乱闯. ○ *The boys were climbing about on the rocks.* 男孩子都在岩石上乱爬呢. (**b**) (indicating position) here and there (in a place) (表示位置)(在某一地方)到处; 各处: *books lying about on the ˈfloor* 散置地上的书 ○ *people sitting about on the ˈgrass* 在草地上各处坐着的人们. **2** in circulation; moving around 在传播中; 在流动中; 在周围活动: *There was nobody aˈbout*, ie Nobody was to be seen. 周围没有人. ○ *There's a lot of ˈflu about*, ie Many people have flu. 有许多人患流感. ○ *He'll soon be aˈbout again*, eg after an illness. 他不久就又能四处走动了(如病愈后). **3** somewhere near; not far off 附近; 不远: *She's ˈsomewhere about.* 她就在附近. **4** facing around 向后转: *put the ship aˈbout*, ie so as to face in the opposite direction 使船掉头(转成相反的方向) ○ *It's the wrong way aˈbout.* 刚好相反了. ○ *Aˌbout ˈturn!* ie Turn to face the opposite way (as a military command). 向后转! (军事口令).

□ **aˌbout-ˈturn** (*US* **aˌbout-ˈface**) *n* **1** turn made so as to face the opposite direction 向后转. **2** (*fig* 比喻) complete change of opinion, policy, etc 意见、政策等完全改变: *These new measures indicate an about-turn in government policy.* 这些新措施表明政府的政策彻底改变了.

about[3] /əˈbaʊt; əˈbaʊt/ *prep* (in senses 1, 2 and 5 *US* **around**; *Brit* also **around** in these senses 1、2、5义, 美式英语用 **around**; 这些词义, 英式英语也可用 **around**) **1** (**a**) (indicating movement) here and there in (a place); in many directions in (表示动向)在…到处, 在…各处: *walking about the town* 在城里到处走 ○ *travelling about the world* 环游世界 ○ *Look aˈbout you.* 看看你的周围. (**b**) (indicating position, state, etc) here and there in (a place); at points throughout (表示位置、状况等)在(某地)到处; 在所有各点: *papers strewn about the room* 散置于室内各处的文件. **2** near to (a place); not far off from 在…附近; 离…不远: *She's somewhere about the place.* 她就在附近. ○ *I dropped the key somewhere about here.* 我把钥匙掉在这儿附近了. **3** on the subject of (sb/sth); in connection with; concerning or regarding 关于; 对于; 有关: *a book about flowers* 关于花卉的书 ○ *Tell me about it.* 把这件事告诉我. ○ *What is he so angry about?* 他对什么事这么生气? ○ *He is careless about his personal appearance.* 他对自己的仪表毫不在意. ⇨Usage 见所附用法. **4** concerned or occupied with (sth) 从事于; 忙于: *And while you're aˈbout it…*, ie while you're doing that… 在你做那件事的时候… ○ *Mind what you're about*, ie Be careful. 注意你正在做的事(小心). **5** at a time near to; at approximately 将近…的时候; 大约在…: *He arrived (at) about ten o'clock.* 他大约(在)十点钟到的. **6** (idm 习语) **be about to do sth** intend to do sth immediately; be on the point of doing sth 即将; 正要: *As I was about to say when you interrupted me…* 我正要说的时候, 你插嘴了… ○ *We're about to start.* 我们即将动身. ○ *I'm not about to admit defeat*, ie I have no intention of doing so. 我还不想认输. **how/what about…?** (**a**) (used when asking for information or to get sb's opinion 用以询问消息或征求意见): *What about his qualifications* (ie Is he qualified) *for the job?* 他有资格做这件工作吗? (**b**) (used when making a suggestion 用以提出建议): *How about going to France for our holidays?* 咱们到法国去度假好吗?

NOTE ON USAGE 用法: Both **about** and **on** can mean 'on the subject of'. ☆ **about** 和 **on** 均意为 '关于'. A book, film or lecture **on** Chinese art, education or prehistory suggests a serious, academic presentation. 在关于中国的艺术、教育或史前时期的书、电影或演讲中, 用 **on** 意味着具有严肃的学术性的内容. A book, discussion or TV programme **about** China, schools or dinosaurs is of more general interest and more informal. 在关于中国、学校或恐龙的书、讨论会或电视节目中, 用 **about** 则更具一般性和通俗性.

above[1] /əˈbʌv; əˈbʌv/ *adv* **1** at or to a higher point; overhead 在较高处; 到较高处; 在头顶上方: *My bedroom is immediately above.* 我的卧室就在上面. ○ *Put the biscuits on the shelf above.* 把饼干放到上面的架子上. ○ *Seen from above, the fields looked like a geometrical pattern.* 从高处往下看, 那些农田像是几何图案. ○ *A voice called down to us from above.* 从上面传来叫我们的声音. **2** earlier or further back (in a book, an article, etc) (书、文章等的)前文, 上文: *in the above paragraph* 在上一段 ○ *As was stated above…* 如上所述… ○ *See above, page 97* 见前文, 第97页. **3** (*rhet* 修辞) in or to heaven 在天上; 到天上: *the powers above* 上天神明 ○ *blessings from above* 上天的祝福 ○ *gone above* 上天堂了. Cf 参看 BELOW, UNDER, UNDERNEATH.

□ **ˌabove-ˈmentioned**, **ˌabove-ˈnamed** *adjs* mentioned or named earlier (in this book, article, etc) (在本书中、在本文中等)上述的. Cf 参看 UNDERMENTIONED.

above[2] /əˈbʌv; əˈbʌv/ *prep* **1** (**a**) higher than (sth) 高于; 在…之上: *The sun rose above the horizon.* 太阳已升到地平线之上. ○ *The water came above our knees.* 水没过了我们的膝部. ○ *We were flying above the clouds.* 我们在云层上面飞行. (Cf 参看 *We were flying over/across the Sahara.*) (**b**) higher in rank, position, importance, etc than (sb/sth) 级别、地位、重要性等高于…: *A captain in the Navy ranks above a captain in the Army.* 海军的 captain (上校)军阶高于陆军的 captain (上尉). ○ *She married above her*, ie married sb from a higher social class than herself. 她嫁给了社会地位比她高的人. **2** greater in number, price, weight, etc than (sth) 数目、价钱、重量等超过…: *The temperature has been above the average recently.* 近来的气温一直比平均温度高. ○ *There's nothing in this shop above/over a dollar.* 这个店里没有一样东西价钱超过一元. ○ *It weighs above/over ten tons.* 这东西的重量超过十吨. ○ *Applicants must be above/over the age of 18.* 申请人年龄必须超过18岁. **3** (*fml* 文) more than (sb/sth) 超过; 胜过: *Should a soldier value honour above life?* 军人应视荣誉重于生命吗? **4** beyond the reach of (sth) because too good, great, etc (因优良、出色等)超出…的范围: *He is above suspicion*, ie is not suspected because he is completely trusted. 他无可怀疑(因为他是可以完全信赖的人, 所以不受怀疑). ○ *Her behaviour was above/beyond reproach.* 她的行为是无可指责的. **5** too good, etc for (sth) (因好、优越等)不做, 不为, 不屑: *She wouldn't lie — she's above that.* 她不至于说谎 —— 她不屑做那种事. ○ *She is above deceit*, ie is not deceitful. 她不会骗人的. ○ *Although she's the manager, she's not above asking* (ie she isn't too proud to ask) *for advice from her staff.* 她虽身为经理, 却并不耻于向下属请教.

6 upstream from (a place) 在(一处)的上游: *the waterfall above the bridge* 在桥的上游的瀑布. **7** (idm 习语) **above ˈall** most important of all; especially 最重要的; 尤其: *He longs above all (else) to see his family again.* 他尤其渴望再见到家里的人. **aˈbove oneself** too pleased with oneself; conceited; arrogant 兴高采烈; 得意忘形; 自高自大; 趾高气扬. Cf 参看 BELOW, UNDER, UNDERNEATH.

□ **above-board** *adv, adj* ⇨ ABOVE BOARD (BOARD[1]).

NOTE ON USAGE 用法: **1** When they indicate a position higher than something, **above** and **over** can often be used in the same way ☆ **above** 和 **over** 表示'在比某物高的位置'时, 用法往往相同: *They built a new room above/over the garage.* 他们在车房上面加盖了一个房间. **2** When there is movement across something, only **over** can be used 在表示一动作越过某物时, 只能用 **over**: *She threw the ball over the fence.* 她把球扔过了篱笆. ○ *jump over the stream* 跳过小溪. **3** **Over** can also mean 'covering' ☆ **over** 还可表示'盖着'的意思: *Pull the sheet over the body.* 拉起被单盖住身体. ○ *Throw the water over the flames.* 把水泼在火焰上. **4** **Over** and **above** can mean 'more than' in number, measurement, etc. ☆ **over** 和 **above** 可以表示在数目或量度上等等'多于'的意思. **Above** is generally used in relation to a minimum or standard ☆ **above** 一般用于表示与'最低限度'或'标准'有关的事物: *2 000 ft above sea-level* 海拔 2 000 英尺 ○ *above average intelligence/height* 在一般智力[高度]以上 ○ *two degrees above zero* 零上二度 ○ *He's over fifty.* 他已年过半百. ○ *She's been here over two hours.* 她在这里已超过两小时了.

ab·ra·ca·dabra /ˌæbrəkəˈdæbrə; ˌæbrəkəˈdæbrə/ *n, interj* meaningless word said as a supposedly magic formula esp by conjurors while performing magic tricks 咒语(尤指魔术师表演魔术时所说的): *'Abracadabra,' said the conjuror as he pulled the rabbit from the hat.* 魔术师口中念念有词, 把兔子从礼帽中掏了出来.

ab·rade /əˈbreɪd; əˈbred/ *v* [Tn] wear away (skin, fabric, rock, etc) by rubbing; scrape off 磨损(表皮、织物、岩石等); 刮除.

ab·ra·sion /əˈbreɪʒn; əˈbreʒən/ *n* **1** [U] scraping or wearing away; rubbing off 刮除; 磨损; 擦掉. **2** [C] damaged area, esp of the skin, caused by rubbing, etc 擦伤处(尤指皮肤因磨擦等造成者).

ab·ras·ive /əˈbreɪsɪv; əˈbresɪv/ *adj* **1** that scrapes or rubs sth away; rough 有研磨作用的; 粗糙的: *abrasive substances, surfaces, materials* 研磨剂、研磨面、研磨材料. **2** (*fig* 比喻) tending to hurt other people's feelings; harsh and offensive 伤人感情的; 粗鲁的; 粗暴的: *an abrasive person, personality, tone of voice* 粗鲁的人、粗暴的个性、粗俗的语气.

▷ **ab·ras·ive** *n* [U, C] substance used for grinding or polishing surfaces (用以研磨或抛光表面的)磨料.

abreast /əˈbrest; əˈbrɛst/ *adv* **1** ~ **(of sb/sth)** side by side (with sb/sth) and facing the same way 并列; 并排: *cycling two abreast* 两辆自行车并行 ○ *The boat came abreast of us and signalled us to stop.* 小船开过来与我们并排, 发出讯号要我们停下. **2** (idm 习语) **be/keep abreast of sth** be or remain up to date with or well-informed about sth 跟上某事物: *You should read the newspapers to keep abreast of current affairs.* 应该看报以便了解时事.

abridge /əˈbrɪdʒ; əˈbrɪdʒ/ *v* [Tn] make (a book, etc) shorter, esp by using fewer words; condense 删节, 节略(书等): *an abridged edition/version of 'War and Peace'* 《战争与和平》的节略版[节本].

▷ **abridge·ment** (also **abridg·ment**) *n* **1** [U] shortening of a book, etc (书等的)删节, 节略. **2** [C] book, etc that has been abridged 节本; 摘要.

abroad /əˈbrɔːd; əˈbrɔd/ *adv* **1** in or to a foreign country or countries; away from one's own country 在国外; 到国外; 出国: *be, go, live, travel abroad* 在外国[出国/旅居外国/到外国] ○ *visitors (who have come) from abroad*, ie from another country 外国(来的)游客. **2** being circulated widely 广泛流传: *There's a rumour abroad that...*, ie People are saying that.... 谣言盛传, 说是.... **3** (*arch or rhet* 古或修辞) out of doors 户外; 室外: *Have you ventured abroad yet today?* 你今天敢出门了吗?

ab·rog·ate /ˈæbrəgeɪt; ˈæbrəˌget/ *v* [Tn] (*fml* 文) cancel, repeal or annul (sth) 废止; 废除; 取消; 宣告无效: *abrogate a law, custom, treaty* 废除一法例、习俗、条约. ▷ **ab·roga·tion** /ˌæbrəˈgeɪʃn; ˌæbrəˈgeʃən/ *n* [U, C].

ab·rupt /əˈbrʌpt; əˈbrʌpt/ *adj* **1** sudden and unexpected 突然的; 意外的: *a road with many abrupt turns* 一条有很多急转弯的路 ○ *an abrupt ending, change, departure* 突如其来的终止、骤然的变化、突然的离去. **2** (**a**) (of speech, etc) not smooth; disconnected; disjointed (指言语等)不流畅的, 不连贯的, 支离的: *short abrupt sentences* 短小而不连贯的句子 ○ *an abrupt style of writing* 不流畅的文体. (**b**) (of behaviour) rough; curt (指行为)粗鲁的, 唐突的: *He has an abrupt manner*, ie makes no attempt to be polite. 他举止粗鲁. **3** (of a slope) very steep (指斜坡)陡峭的. ▷ **ab·ruptly** *adv*. **ab·rupt·ness** *n* [U].

abs·cess /ˈæbsɪs; ˈæbˌsɪs/ *n* swollen part of the body in which a thick yellowish liquid (called *pus*) has collected 脓肿: *abscesses on the gums* 齿龈脓肿.

ab·scond /əbˈskɒnd; əbˈskɑnd/ *v* **1** [I, Ipr] **~(from...)** go away suddenly and secretly, esp in order to avoid arrest 潜逃; 逃亡: *He absconded from the country.* 他已潜逃出境. **2** [Ipr] **~ with sth** go away taking sth to which one has no right 携赃潜逃: *He absconded with £8 000 stolen from his employer.* 他偷了雇主 8 000 英镑, 携赃潜逃了.

ab·seil /ˈæbseɪl; ˈæbsel/ *v* [I, Ipr, Ip] (in mountaineering) descend a steep slope or vertical rock face by using a double rope that is fixed at a higher point (在登山运动中, 使用固定于高处的双折绳沿悬崖峭壁)缘绳下降: *abseil down the mountain* 从山坡上缘绳下降.

▷ **ab·seil** *n* act of abseiling 缘绳下降.

ab·sence /ˈæbsəns; ˈæbsn̩s/ *n* **1** ~ **(from...)** (**a**) [U] being away 缺席; 离开; 不在某处: *His repeated absence (from school) is worrying.* 他一再缺课使人担忧. ○ *It happened during/in your absence.* 那是当你不在的时候发生的. ○ *In the absence of the manager* (ie While he is away) *I shall be in charge.* 经理不在的时候, 由我负责. ○ *during his absence in America*, ie while he was there 当他不在此地而在美国的期间. (**b**) [C] occasion or time of being away 不在某处的次数或时间: *numerous absences from school* 无数次的缺课 ○ *throughout his long absence* 在他长期不在(某处)的期间 ○ *after an absence of three months* 在离开三个月之后. Cf 参看 PRESENCE. **2** [U] lack; non-existence 缺乏; 不存在: *the absence of definite proof* 缺乏确凿的证据. **3** (idm 习语) ˌ**absence of ˈmind** failure to think about what one is doing; absent-mindedness 心不在焉; 神不守舍. **conspicuous by one's absence** ⇨ CONSPICUOUS. **leave of absence** ⇨ LEAVE[2].

ab·sent[1] /ˈæbsənt; ˈæbsn̩t/ *adj* **1** ~ **(from sth)** (**a**) not present (at sth); at another place (than...) 不在场的; 在别处的: *be absent from school, a meeting, work* 不上学、不到会、缺勤 ○ *absent friends* 不在场的朋友们. (**b**) not existing; lacking 不存在的; 缺少的; 无: *Love was totally absent from his childhood.* 他童年时代没受到丝毫的疼爱. **2** showing that one is not really thinking about what is being said or done around one 茫然的; 恍惚的: *an absent expression, look, etc* 茫然的表情、样子等.

□ ˌ**absent-ˈminded** *adj* with one's mind on other things; forgetful 心不在焉的; 健忘的: *become absent-minded with age* 因上了年纪而变得丢三落四. ˌ**absent-ˈmindedly** *adv*. ˌ**absent-ˈmindedness** *n* [U].

ab·sent[2] /əbˈsent; əbˈsɛnt/ *v* [Tn, Tn·pr] **~ oneself (from sth)** (*fml* 文) not be present (at sth); stay away (from sth) 不在; 不参与: *He deliberately absented himself from the meeting.* 他故意不到会.

ab·sent·ee /ˌæbsənˈtiː; ˌæbsn̩ˈti/ *n* person who is absent 不在者; 缺席者; 缺勤者.

▷ **ab·sent·ee·ism** /ˌæbsənˈtiːɪzəm; ˌæbsn̩ˈtiˌɪzəm/ *n* [U] frequent absence from school or work, esp without good reason (经常性的)旷课, 旷工, 旷职(尤指无正当理由者).

□ ˌ**absentee ˈballot** (*US*) voting in advance by people (**absentee voters**) who will be away on the day of an election 缺席选举人票(选举人将于选举日缺席而提前投的选票).

A

ˌ**absentee ˈlandlord** person who does not live at and rarely visits the property he lets (不居于产权所在地也很少到该地的)遥领地主、房主或业主.

ab·sinthe (also **ab·sinth**) /ˈæbsɪnθ; ˋæbsɪnθ/ *n* [U] bitter green alcoholic drink made with wormwood and other herbs 苦艾酒(一种苦味绿色的含酒精饮料, 由苦艾及其它芳香植物调制而成).

ab·so·lute /ˈæbsəlu:t; ˋæbsəˌlut/ *adj* **1 (a)** complete; total 绝对的; 完全的; 全部的: *have absolute trust in a person* 对一个人绝对的信任 ○ *tell the absolute truth* 绝对说实话 ○ *absolute ignorance, silence* 全然无知、寂然无声 ○ *You're an absolute fool!* 你是个十足的傻瓜! **(b)** certain; undoubted 肯定的; 无疑的: *have absolute proof* 有确凿的证据 ○ *It's an absolute fact.* 这是千真万确的事实. **2** unlimited; unrestricted; unqualified 无限制的; 不受约束的; 无条件的: *absolute power* 绝对的权力. **3** having unlimited power; despotic 有无限权力的; 专制的: *an absolute ruler* 专制统治者. **4** not relative; independent 非相对的; 独立的: *There is no absolute standard for beauty.* 美是没有绝对的标准的.

▷ **the ab·so·lute** *n* [sing] (*philosophy* 哲) that which is regarded as existing independently of anything else 绝对(不依赖任何其它条件而存在).

□ ˌ**absolute maˈjority** majority over all rivals combined; more than half 绝对多数; 超过半数.

ˌ**absolute ˈzero** lowest temperature that is theoretically possible 绝对零度(理论上的最低温度). ⇨App 5 见附录5.

ab·so·lutely /ˈæbsəlu:tlɪ; ˌæbsəˋlutlɪ/ *adv* **1** completely 绝对地; 完全地: *It's absolutely impossible.* 这是绝对不可能的. ○ *You're absolutely right.* 你完全正确. **2** unreservedly; unconditionally 无保留地; 无条件地: *I absolutely refuse.* 我全然拒绝. ○ *He believes absolutely that....* 他完全相信.... **3** not relatively; in an absolute (4) sense 非相对地; 独立地: *The term is being used absolutely.* 这个词语是独立使用的. **4** (used to give emphasis 用以加强语气) positively 确实地; 全然地: *It's absolutely pouring down.* 大雨真是倾盆而下. ○ *He did absolutely no work*, ie no work at all. 他简直什么都没干. **5** /ˌæbsəˈlu:tlɪ; ˌæbsəˋlutlɪ/ (*infml* 口) (used in answer to a question or as a comment 用于回答问题或用作评语) yes; certainly; quite so 正是; 当然; 对极了: *'Don't you agree?' 'Oh, absolutely!'* '你同意吧?' '噢, 当然!'

ab·so·lu·tion /ˌæbsəˈlu:ʃn; ˌæbsəˋluʃən/ *n* [U] (esp in the Christian Church) formal declaration by a priest that a person's sins have been forgiven (尤指基督教中, 由教士对某人)宣布赦罪, 解罪: *grant sb absolution* 赦免某人的罪 ○ *pronounce absolution* 宣读赦罪文.

ab·so·lut·ism /ˈæbsəlu:tɪzəm; ˋæbsəlutˌɪzəm/ *n* [U] (*politics* 政) **(a)** principle that those responsible for government should have unlimited power 专制主义. **(b)** government with unlimited power 专制统治. ▷ **ab·so·lut·ist** *n*.

ab·solve /əbˈzɒlv; əbˋzɑlv/ *v* [Tn, Tn·pr] **~ sb (from/of sth) 1** (*fml esp law* 文, 尤用于法律) clear sb (of guilt); declare sb free (from blame, a promise, a duty, etc) 开脱某人(的罪责); 宣布免除某人(所受的责难、要履行的诺言、要负的责任等): *The court absolved the accused man (from all responsibility for her death).* 法官判决被告无罪(对她的死亡不必负任何责任). **2** give absolution to sb 赦免某人的罪责: *absolve repentant sinners* 赦免悔改的罪人.

ab·sorb /əbˈsɔ:b; əbˋsɔrb/ *v* [Tn] **1 (a)** take (sth) in; suck up 吸收(某事物); 吸进: *absorb heat* 吸热 ○ *Plants absorb oxygen.* 植物吸收氧气. ○ *Dry sand absorbs water.* 干沙吸水. ○ *Aspirin is quickly absorbed by/into the body.* 阿司匹林很快被身体吸收了. ○ (*fig* 比喻) *Clever children absorb knowledge easily.* 聪明孩子容易吸收知识. **(b)** include (sth/sb) as part of itself or oneself; incorporate; merge with 将(某物[某人])合并; 并吞; 同化: *The larger firm absorbed the smaller one.* 那大公司并吞了那小公司. ○ *The surrounding villages have been absorbed by/into the growing city.* 周围的村庄已经并入了那不断扩展的城市. **2** reduce the effect of (an impact, a difficulty, etc) 减轻(冲击、困难等的)作用或影响: *Buffers absorbed most of the shock.* 缓冲器使震动减少了许多. **3** hold the attention or interest of (sb) fully 完全吸引住(某人)的注意力或兴趣: *His business absorbs him.* 他专心致志地处理业务.

▷ **ab·sorbed** *adj* with one's attention fully held 精神集中的: *absorbed in her book* 埋头读她的书.

ab·sorb·ent /-ənt; -ənt/ *n, adj* (substance) that is able to take in moisture, etc 能吸收水分等的(物质): *absorbent cotton wool* 脱脂棉.

ab·sorb·ing *adj* holding the attention fully 十分吸引人的: *an absorbing film* 引人入胜的影片.

ab·sorp·tion /əbˈsɔ:pʃn; əbˋsɔrpʃən/ *n* [U] **~ (by/in sth)** absorbing or being absorbed 吸收; 专心致志; 全神贯注: *His work suffered because of his total absorption in sport.* 他热中于运动而影响了工作.

ab·stain /əbˈsteɪn; əbˋsten/ *v* [I, Ipr] **~ (from sth) 1** keep oneself from doing or enjoying sth, esp from taking alcoholic drinks; refrain 戒(尤指酒); 戒除. **2** decline to use one's vote 弃权(不投票): *At the last election he abstained (from voting/the vote).* 上次选举时他弃权了(没投票).

▷ **ab·stain·er** *n* person who abstains 戒酒者; (投票)弃权者: *a total abstainer*, ie one who never takes alcoholic drinks 绝对戒酒的人.

ab·ste·mi·ous /əbˈsti:mɪəs; əbˋstimɪəs/ *adj* not taking much food or drink; not self-indulgent; moderate 饮食有度的; 有节制的; 适度的: *an abstemious person, meal* 饮食有度的人、节俭的一餐 ○ *abstemious habits* 节制饮食的习惯. ▷ **ab·ste·mi·ously** *adv*. **ab·ste·mi·ous·ness** *n* [U].

ab·sten·tion /əbˈstenʃn; əbˋstenʃən/ *n* **(a)** [U] **~ (from sth)** abstaining, esp not using one's vote at an election 弃权(尤指不投选票). **(b)** [C] instance of this 弃权票: *five votes in favour of the proposal, three against and two abstentions* 五票赞成该项提议, 三票反对, 两票弃权.

ab·stin·ence /ˈæbstɪnəns; ˋæbstənəns/ *n* [U] **~ (from sth)** abstaining, esp from food or alcoholic drinks 禁绝(尤指食物或酒): *total abstinence* 完全戒酒. ▷ **ab·stin·ent** /ˈæbstɪnənt; ˋæbstənənt/ *adj* [usu pred 通常作表语].

ab·stract[1] /ˈæbstrækt; ˋæbstrækt/ *adj* **1** existing in thought or as an idea but not having a physical or practical existence 抽象的: *We may talk of beautiful things, but beauty itself is abstract.* 我们尽可谈论美的事物, 然而美本身却是抽象的. ○ *He has some abstract* (ie vague, impractical) *notion of wanting to change the world.* 他有一种要改造世界的空想. **2** (of art) not representing objects in a realistic way but expressing the artist's ideas and feelings about certain aspects of them (指艺术)抽象派的: *an abstract painting, painter* 抽象画、抽象派画家. Cf 参看 CONCRETE[1] 1.

□ ˌ**abstract ˈnoun** noun that refers to an abstract quality or state, eg *goodness* or *freedom* 抽象名词(如goodness或freedom).

ab·stract[2] /ˈæbstrækt; æbˋstrækt/ *n* **1** abstract idea or quality 抽象; 抽象的概念; 抽象性. **2** example of abstract art 抽象派艺术品: *a painter of abstracts* 抽象画的画家. **3** short account of the contents of a book, etc; summary (书籍等的)摘要; 概括: *an abstract of a lecture* 讲演的摘要. **4** (idm 习语) **in the ˈabstract** in a theoretical way 抽象地; 在理论上: *Consider the problem in the abstract*, ie as if it had no relation to any specific object, person, fact, etc. 就事论事地考虑一下这一问题(假定不涉及任何具体对象、个人、事实等).

ab·stract[3] /əbˈstrækt; əbˋstrækt/ *v* **1** [Tn, Tn·pr] **~ sth (from sth)** remove sth; separate sth (from sth) 除去某物; (从某物中)提取, 抽取或分离出某物: *abstract metal from ore* 从矿砂中提取金属. **2** [Tn] make a written summary of (a book, etc) 写出(书等的)要点.

ab·strac·ted /æbˈstræktɪd; æbˋstræktɪd/ *adj* thinking of other things; not paying attention 心不在焉的; 走神儿的. ▷ **ab·strac·tedly** *adv*.

ab·strac·tion /əbˈstrækʃn; əbˋstrækʃən/ *n* **1** [U] **~ of sth (from sth)** removing; taking away 除掉; 去掉; 拿走; 提取; 抽取. **2** [C] abstract idea 抽象概念: *lose oneself in abstractions*, ie become unrealistic in one's thinking 沉迷在幻想中. **3** [U] absent-mindedness 心不在焉; 走神儿.

ab·struse /əbˈstru:s; æbˋstrus/ *adj* difficult to understand 难解的; 深奥的. ▷ **ab·strusely** *adv*. **ab·struse·ness** *n* [U].

ab·surd /əbˈsɜ:d; əbˋsɝd/ *adj* **1** unreasonable; not sensible 不合理的; 荒谬的; 荒唐的: *What an absurd* *suggestion!* 多么荒唐的建议! ○ *It was absurd of you to suggest such a thing.* 你竟提出这种事, 真荒唐. **2** foolish in a funny way; ridiculous 愚蠢得可笑的; 怪诞不经的: *That uniform makes them look absurd.* 他们穿着那种制服看起来怪模怪样的. ▷ **ab·surd·ity** *n* [U, C]. **ab·surdly** *adv*.

abund·ance /əˈbʌndəns; əˋbʌndəns/ *n* [U, sing] quantity that is more than enough; plenty 丰富; 充裕: *There was good food in abundance/an abundance of good food at the party.* 宴会上有丰美的食物.

abund·ant /əˈbʌndənt; əˋbʌndənt/ *adj* **1** more than enough; plentiful 丰富的; 充裕的: *an abundant supply of fruit* 水果的充足供应 ○ *We have abundant proof of his guilt.* 我们有充分的证据证明他有罪. **2** [pred 作表语] **~ in sth** having plenty of sth; rich in sth 富有某事物; 富于某事物: *a land abundant in minerals* 矿产丰富的土地.

▷ **abund·antly** *adv* plentifully 丰富地; 充裕地: *be abundantly supplied with fruit* 水果供应充足 ○ *He's made his views abundantly* (ie very) *clear.* 他已经充分表明了自己的观点.

ab·use¹ /əˈbjuːz; əˋbjuz/ *v* [Tn] **1** make bad or wrong use of (sth) 滥用、妄用(某事物): *abuse one's authority, sb's hospitality, the confidence placed in one* 滥用权威、辜负某人的热情招待、辜负对自己的信任. **2** treat (sb) badly; exploit 虐待某人; 剥削: *a much abused wife* 备受虐待的妻子. Cf 参看 MISUSE. **3** speak insultingly to or about (sb); attack in words 说(某人的)坏话; 辱骂; 诋毁.

ab·use² /əˈbjuːs; əˋbjus/ *n* **1** (**a**) [U] wrong or bad use or treatment of sth/sb 对某事物[某人]的滥用、妄用或虐待: *drug abuse* 滥用麻醉药品 ○ *child abuse* 虐待儿童. (**b**) [C] **~ of sth** wrong or bad use of sth 对某事物的滥用、妄用: *an abuse of trust, privilege, authority* 辜负别人的信任、滥用特权、滥用权力. **2** [C] unjust or corrupt practice 恶习; 弊端; 不正之风: *put a stop to political abuses* 煞住政治上的不正之风. **3** [U] insulting words; offensive or coarse language 恶言; 辱骂; 粗话: *hurl (a stream of) abuse at sb* 破口(滔滔不绝)大骂某人 ○ *The word 'bastard' is often used as a term of abuse.* '杂种'一词常用作咒骂用语.

ab·us·ive /əˈbjuːsɪv; əˋbjusɪv/ *adj* (of speech or a person) criticizing harshly and rudely; insulting (指言语或人)责骂的, 辱骂的: *abusive language, remarks, etc* 骂人的语言、话等 ○ *He became abusive*, ie began uttering angry insults, curses, etc. 他骂起来了. ▷ **ab·us·ively** *adv*.

abut /əˈbʌt; əˋbʌt/ *v* (**-tt-**) [Ipr] **~ on/against sth** (of land or a building) have a common boundary or side with sth; adjoin sth (指土地或建筑物)邻接或毗连某物, 与某物接界: *His land abuts on the motorway.* 他的土地和高速公路毗连. ○ *Their house abuts against ours.* 他们的房子紧挨着我们的房子.

abut·ment /əˈbʌtmənt; əˋbʌtmənt/ *n* (*engineering* 工) structure that bears the weight of a bridge or an arch 桥台, 拱座(用以支承桥或拱的建筑物).

abys·mal /əˈbɪzməl; əˋbɪzml̩/ *adj* **1** (*infml* 口) extremely bad 极坏的: *live in abysmal conditions* 在极恶劣的情况下生活 ○ *His manners are abysmal.* 他态度极其恶劣. **2** extreme; utter 极端的; 完全的: *abysmal ignorance* 极端的无知. ▷ **abys·mally** *adv*.

abyss /əˈbɪs; əˋbɪs/ *n* hole so deep that it seems to have no bottom 深渊: (*fig* 比喻) *an abyss of ignorance, despair, loneliness, etc* 无知的、绝望的、寂寞的...深渊.

AC (also **ac**) /ˌeɪ ˈsiː; ˌe ˋsi/ *abbr* 缩写 = alternating current. Cf 参看 DC3.

a/c *abbr* 缩写 = (*commerce* 商) account (current) (往来)帐户: *charge to a/c 319054* 记入 319054 号帐户 ○ *a/c payee only*, ie on cheques 限入受款人帐户(支票上的用语).

aca·cia /əˈkeɪʃə; əˋkeʃə/ *n* any of several trees with yellow or white flowers, esp one from which gum arabic is obtained 金合欢树(任何一种金合欢属的树, 开黄花或白花, 尤指可提取阿拉伯树胶者).

aca·demic /ˌækəˈdemɪk; ˌækəˋdɛmɪk/ *adj* **1** [attrib 作定语] of (teaching or learning in) schools, colleges, etc 学校的; 学院的: *the ˌacademic ˈyear*, ie the total time within a year when teaching is done in schools, etc, usu starting in September or October 学年 ○ *ˌacademic ˈfreedom*, ie liberty to teach and discuss educational matters without interference from politicians, etc 学术自由. **2** [attrib 作定语] scholarly; not technical or practical 学者式的; 非技术的或实用的: *academic subjects* 学科. **3** of theoretical interest only 仅注重理论的; 学术的: *a matter of academic concern* 学术方面的事 ○ *The question is purely academic*, ie not relevant to practical affairs but still interesting. 这是一个纯学术性的问题(与实际事务无关, 但仍使人感兴趣).

▷ **aca·demic** *n* teacher at a university, college, etc; professional scholar 大专院校的教师; 专业学者.

aca·dem·ic·ally /-klɪ; -klɪ/ *adv*.

aca·demi·cian /əˌkædəˈmɪʃn; *US* ˌækədəˈmɪʃn; ˌækədəˋmɪʃən/ *n* member of an academy(3) 院士; 学会会员.

acad·emy /əˈkædəmɪ; əˋkædəmɪ/ *n* **1** school for special training 专科院校: *an aˌcademy of ˈmusic* 音乐学院 ○ *a ˈnaval/ˈmilitary academy* 海军[陆军]军官学校. **2** (in Scotland) secondary school (苏格兰的)中等学校. **3** (usu 通常作 **Academy**) society of distinguished scholars or artists; society for cultivating art, literature, etc, of which membership is an honour 高等学术团体; 学会: *The Royal Academy (of Arts)* 皇家(艺术)学会.

□ **Aˌcademy Aˈward** one of the annual awards for achievement in the cinema given by the US Academy of Motion Picture Arts and Sciences 金像奖(由美国电影艺术科学院颁发的电影艺术年度奖). Cf 参看 OSCAR.

ACAS /ˈeɪkæs; ˋekæs/ *abbr* 缩写 = (*Brit*) Advisory, Conciliation and Arbitration Service, for helping with negotiation during industrial disputes (在有工业纠纷期间协助谈判的)咨询调解仲裁处.

ac·cede /əkˈsiːd; əkˋsid/ *v* [I, Ipr] **~ (to sth)** (*fml* 文) **1** (**a**) take office 就职: *accede to the chancellorship* 就任大臣、大学名誉校长等. (**b**) become monarch 即位: *Queen Victoria acceded to the throne in 1837.* 维多利亚女王于1837年即位. **2** agree (to a request, proposal, etc) 同意(一请求、建议等).

ac·cel·er·ando /ækˌseləˈrændəʊ; ækˌsɛləˋrændo/ *adv, adj, n* (*pl* **-dos** or **-di**) (*music* 音) with gradually increasing speed 渐快(的).

▷ **ac·cel·er·ando** *n* (*pl* **~s**) piece of music (to be) played in this way (演奏)渐快的音乐. Cf 参看 RALLENTANDO.

ac·cel·er·ate /əkˈseləreɪt; əkˋsɛləˌret/ *v* **1** [Tn] make (sth) move faster or happen earlier; increase the speed of 使(某事物)加快; 促进(某事物); 加速: *accelerating the rate of growth* 提高生长率. **2** [I] move or happen more quickly 加速; 加快: *The car accelerated as it overtook me.* 那辆汽车一加速就超越了我. Cf 参看 DECELERATE.

▷ **ac·cel·era·tion** /əkˌseləˈreɪʃn; əkˌsɛləˋreʃən/ *n* [U] **1** making or being made quicker; increase in speed 加快; 促进; 加速: *an acceleration in the rate of economic growth* 经济发展速率的增长. **2** (of a vehicle) ability to gain speed (指车辆)加速性能: *a car with good acceleration* 加速性能良好的汽车.

ac·cel·er·ator /əkˈseləreɪtə(r); əkˋsɛləˌretɚ/ *n* **1** device for increasing speed, esp the pedal in a car, etc that controls the speed of the engine 加速器; 加速装置(尤指汽车等的油门踏板). ⇨illus at App 1 见附录1之插图, page xii. **2** (*physics* 物) apparatus for causing charged particles to move at high speeds 粒子加速器. **3** (*chemistry* 化) substance that causes a chemical reaction to happen more quickly 加速剂; 促进剂.

ac·cent /ˈæksent, ˈæksənt; ˋæksɛnt/ *n* **1** [C] emphasis given to a syllable or word by means of stress or pitch 重音(用重读或提高音调的方法使一音节或词突出): *In the word 'today' the accent is on the second syllable.* today 一字的重音在第二个音节上. **2** [C] mark or symbol, usu above a letter, used in writing and printing to indicate such emphasis or the quality of a vowel sound 重音符号(用于书写印刷中, 表示一元音的重音或音值的符号, 通常标在字母上方). **3** [C, U] national, local or individual way of pronouncing words (民族、地方或个人的)口音, 腔调, 土腔: *speak English with a foreign accent* 说英语带外国腔 ○ *have an American accent* 有美国口音 ○ *a voice without (a trace of) accent* 不带(丝毫)地方口音的声音. Cf 参看 BROGUE, DIALECT. **4** [C usu *sing*, U 作可数名词时通常作单数, 亦作不可数名词] special emphasis given to sth (对某事物的)强调; 重点:

A

In all our products the accent is on quality. 在我们一切产品中,最重视的就是质量.

▷ **ac·cent** /æk'sent; ˋæksɛnt/ *v* [Tn] **1** pronounce (a word or syllable) with emphasis 重读(一词或音节). **2** write accents on (words, etc) 把重音符号加在(词等)上.

ac·cen·tu·ate /ək'sentʃʊeɪt; əkˋsɛntʃʊˌet/ *v* [Tn] make (sth) very noticeable or prominent; emphasize 突出(某事物); 强调: *The tight jumper only accentuated his fat stomach.* 那件紧身套头毛衣反更突出了他那肥胖的肚子. ▷ **ac·cen·tu·ation** /əkˌsentʃʊ'eɪʃn; əkˌsɛntʃʊˋeʃən/ *n* [U].

ac·cept /ək'sept; əkˋsɛpt/ *v* **1** (**a**) [Tn] take (sth offered) willingly 欣然接受(他人提供的事物): *accept a gift, a piece of advice, an apology* 接受礼物、劝告、道歉. (**b**) [I, Tn] say yes to (an offer, invitation, etc) 接受(提议、邀请等): *She offered him a lift and he accepted (it).* 她请他坐她的车, 他就领情了. ○ *He proposed marriage and she accepted (him).* 他向她求婚, 她就同意了. (**c**) [Tn] receive (sth/sb) as adequate or suitable 接收, 收取(某事物); 接受(某事物[某人]): *Will you accept a cheque?* 你收支票吗? ○ *The machine only accepts 10p coins.* 这机器只收10便士的硬币. ○ *The college I applied to has accepted me.* 我报了名的学院已经录取我了. **2** [Tn] be willing to agree to (sth) 同意, 认可, 赞同(某事物): *accept the judge's decision* 同意法官的判决 ○ *I accept the proposed changes.* 我赞成所提出的变动. **3** [Tn] take upon oneself (a responsibility, etc) 承担(责任等): *He accepts blame for the accident*, ie agrees that it was his fault. 他承认那事故是他的错. ○ *You must accept the consequences of your action.* 你必须对你行动的后果负责. **4** [Tn, Tf, Tw, Cn·n/a] **~ sth (as sth)** take sth as true; believe sth 认为某事物属实; 相信某事物: *I cannot accept that he is to blame.* 我认为不能责怪他. ○ *We do not accept your explanation/what you have said.* 我们不相信你的解释[你所说的话]. ○ *Can we accept his account as the true version?* 我们能够相信他说的是实情吗? ○ *It is an accepted fact*, ie sth that everyone thinks is true. 这是公认的事实. **5** [Tn] treat (sb/sth) as welcome 欢迎(某人[某事物]): *He was never really accepted by his classmates.* 他同班同学从未真正把他当作自己人.

ac·cept·able /ək'septəbl; əkˋsɛptəbḷ/ *adj* **~ (to sb) 1** (**a**) worth accepting 值得接受的: *Is the proposal acceptable to you?* 这个建议你认为可以接受吗? (**b**) welcome 受欢迎的: *A cup of tea would be most acceptable.* 来一杯茶就最好不过了. **2** tolerable 可容忍的: *an acceptable risk, sacrifice, profit margin* 可冒的险、可作的牺牲、可容许的利润幅度. ▷ **ac·cept·ab·il·ity** /əkˌseptə'bɪlətɪ; əkˌsɛptəˋbɪlətɪ/ *n* [U]. **ac·cept·ably** /-blɪ; -blɪ/ *adv*.

ac·cept·ance /ək'septəns; əkˋsɛptəns/ *n* **1** [C, U] (act of) accepting or being accepted 接受; 答应; 同意; 认可: *Since we sent out the invitations we've received five acceptances and one refusal.* 我们发出请帖以后, 收到的回复是五位接受, 一位推辞. **2** [U] favourable reception; approval 赞成; 赞同: *The new laws gained widespread acceptance.* 新法例广获赞同. **3** [C] (*commerce* 商) (**a**) agreement to pay a bill 承兑, 认付(票据). (**b**) bill accepted in this way 承兑汇票.

ac·ceptor /ək'septə(r); əkˋsɛptɚ/ *n* (*physics* 物) atom or molecule able to receive an extra electron 能够接受额外电子的原子或分子; 接受体.

ac·cess /'ækses; ˋæksɛs/ *n* [U] **1 ~ (to sth)** means of approaching or entering (a place); way in (接近或进入某地的)方法; 通路: *The only access to the farmhouse is across the fields.* 要到那农舍去唯有穿过田地. ○ *The village is easy/difficult of access*, ie easy/difficult to reach. 到那个村子的路很容易[很难]走. **2 ~ (to sth/sb)** opportunity or right to use sth or approach sb (使用某物或接近某人的)机会或权利: *get access to classified information* 得到接触秘密情报的机会 ○ *Students must have access to a good library.* 学生要有使用好图书馆的便利条件. ○ *Only high officials had access to the president.* 只有高级官员才可以接近总统.

▷ **ac·cess** *v* [Tn] (*computing* 计) get information from or put information into (a computer file) 存取(计算机文件): *She accessed three different files to find the correct information.* 她存取了三个文件以找寻所要的信息. ○ *The files were accessed every day to keep them up to date.* 文件每日存取, 使之不断更新.

□ **'access road 1** (*esp US*) = SLIP-ROAD (SLIP). **2** road giving access to a place, site, etc (到一地方、场所等的)通路.

'access time (*computing* 计) time taken to obtain information stored in a computer 存取时间(取出计算机中储存的信息所用的时间).

ac·cess·ible /ək'sesəbl; əkˋsɛsəbḷ/ *adj* **~ (to sb)** that can be reached, used, etc 可接近的; 可进入的; 可使用的: *a beach accessible only from the sea* 只能从海上到达的沙滩 ○ *documents not accessible to the public* 公众无法接触到的文件. ▷ **ac·cess·ib·il·ity** /əkˌsesə'bɪlətɪ; əkˌsɛsəˋbɪlətɪ/ *n* [U].

ac·ces·sion /æk'seʃn; ækˋsɛʃən/ *n* **~ (to sth) 1** [U] reaching a rank or position 达到某一级别或地位: *celebrating the queen's accession (to the throne)* 庆祝女王登基. **2** (**a**) [C] thing added, esp a new item in a library, museum, etc 增添物(尤指图书馆、博物馆等的新书或展品): *recent accessions to the art gallery* 美术馆最近增添的展品. (**b**) [U] action of being added 增添; 增加: *the accession of new members to the party* 新党员的增加.

▷ **ac·ces·sion** *v* [Tn] record the addition of (a new item) to a library, museum, etc 将(图书馆、博物馆等的新书、新展品)登记入册.

ac·cess·ory /ək'sesərɪ; əkˋsɛsərɪ/ *n* **1** (usu *pl* 通常作复数) (**a**) thing that is a useful or decorative extra but that is not essential; minor fitting or attachment 附属品; 配件; 附件: *bicycle accessories*, eg lamp, pump, etc 自行车附件(如车灯、打气筒等). (**b**) small article of (esp women's) dress, eg a belt, handbag, etc (尤指妇女的)服装配搭物(如皮带、手提包等). **2** (also **ac·cess·ary**) **~ (to sth)** (*law* 律) person who helps another in a crime 从犯; 帮凶; 同谋: *He was charged with being an accessory to murder.* 他被控为谋杀罪的从犯. **3** (idm 习语) **accessory before/after the fact** (*law* 律) person who, although not present when a crime is committed, helps the person committing it beforehand/afterwards 事前[事后]从犯(犯罪时不在场, 但于事前[事后]协助犯罪者).

▷ **ac·cess·ory** *adj* additional; extra 附加的; 额外的.

ac·ci·dent /'æksɪdənt; ˋæksədənt/ *n* **1** [C] event that happens unexpectedly and causes damage, injury, etc 事故; 故障; 横祸; 不幸; 不测; 意外: *be killed in a car/road accident* 在车祸[交通事故]中遇难 ○ *I had a slight accident at home and broke some crockery.* 我在家出了点儿小事, 打碎了些陶器. ○ *He's very late — I do hope he hasn't met with an accident.* 他这么晚还没来——我真希望他别出事. ○ [attrib 作定语] *accident insurance* 事故保险. **2** [U] chance; fortune 机遇; 命运; 造化: *By accident of birth* (ie Because of where he happened to be born) *he is entitled to British citizenship.* 因出生的造化, 他成为英国公民(因有缘生于该地). **3** (idm 习语) **ˌaccidents ˌwill 'happen** (*saying* 谚) some unfortunate events must be accepted as inevitable 意外事故在所难免. **by accident** as a result of chance or mishap 偶然; 意外地: *I only found it by accident.* 我只是碰巧找到的. **a chapter of accidents** ⇨ CHAPTER. **without 'accident** safely 安全地; 平安地.

□ **'accident-prone** *adj* [usu pred 通常作表语] more than usually likely to have accidents 易出事故.

ac·ci·dental /ˌæksɪ'dentl; ˌæksəˋdɛntḷ/ *adj* happening unexpectedly or by chance 意外的; 偶然的: *a verdict of accidental death* 意外死亡的裁决 ○ *an accidental meeting with a friend* 偶然遇到一位朋友. ▷ **ac·ci·dent·ally** /-təlɪ; -tḷɪ/ *adv*.

ac·claim /ə'kleɪm; əˋklem/ *v* **1** (**a**) [Tn] welcome (sb/sth) with shouts of approval; applaud loudly 向(某人[某事物])欢呼; 喝彩: *acclaim the winner of a race* 向赛跑得胜者喝彩. (**b**) [esp passive 尤用于被动语态: Tn, Cn·n/a] **~ sb/sth (as sth)** acknowledge the greatness of sb/sth 称赞某人[某事物]: *a much acclaimed performance* 备受称赞的表演 ○ *It was acclaimed as a great discovery.* 那被赞誉为伟大的发现. **2** [Cn·n] (*fml* 文) hail or salute (sb) as sth 欢呼或拥戴(某人)为某事物: *They acclaimed him king.* 大家拥立他为国王.

▷ **ac·claim** *n* [U] enthusiastic welcome or approval; praise 热烈欢迎或赞同; 称赞: *The book received great critical acclaim.* 这本书大获评论界的赞扬.

ac·clama·tion /ˌæklə'meɪʃn; ˌæklə'meʃən/ *n* **1** [U] loud and enthusiastic approval (of a proposal, etc) (对提议等)高声而热烈的赞同: *elected by acclamation,* ie without voting 以欢呼声通过而选出的(不经投票表决). **2** [C usu *pl* 通常作复数] shouting to honour or welcome sb (向某人)欢呼, 喝彩: *the acclamations of the crowd* 群众的欢呼.

ac·cli·mat·ize, -ise /ə'klaɪmətaɪz; ə'klaɪməˌtaɪz/ *v* [I, Ipr, Tn, Tn·pr] **~ (oneself/sb/sth) (to sth)** get (oneself, animals, plants, etc) used to a new climate or a new environment, new conditions, etc; become or make accustomed (to sth) 使(自己、动物、植物等)习惯于新的气候或新的环境、新的形势等; 使适应(某事物); 服水土: *It takes many months to acclimatize/become acclimatized to life in a tropical climate.* 要用许多月的时间才能适应热带的生活. ▷ **ac·cli·mat·iza·tion, -isation** /əˌklaɪmətaɪ'zeɪʃn; *US* -tɪ'z-; əˌklaɪmətə'zeʃən/ *n* [U].

ac·cliv·ity /ə'klɪvətɪ; ə'klɪvətɪ/ *n* (*fml* 文) upward slope 向上的斜坡或斜面. Cf 参看 DECLIVITY.

ac·col·ade /'ækəleɪd; *US* ˌækə'leɪd; ˌækə'led/ *n* **1** praise; approval 嘉奖; 赞许: *To be chosen to represent their country is the highest accolade for most athletes.* 能被选拔出来代表国家参赛, 是多数运动员的最高荣誉. **2** ceremonial tap on the shoulder with the flat part of a sword, given when a knighthood is conferred 册封爵士的仪式(用剑面在肩上轻拍一下).

ac·com·mod·ate /ə'kɒmədeɪt; ə'kɑməˌdet/ *v* **1** [Tn] provide lodging or room for (sb) 供给(某人)住宿或房间: *This hotel can accommodate up to 500 guests.* 这旅馆可供达500位来宾住宿. **2** [Tn·pr] **~ sth to sth** change or adjust sth so that it fits or harmonizes with sth else 适应; 迁就; 迎合: *I will accommodate my plans to yours.* 我修改一下计划以便和你的计划相适应. **3** (*fml* 文) **(a)** [Tn, Tn·pr] **~ sb (with sth)** grant or supply (sth) to sb 准予或提供某人(某事物): *The bank will accommodate you with a loan.* 银行将贷给你一笔款. **(b)** [Tn] do (sb) a favour; oblige 帮(某人的)忙; 施恩惠于: *I shall endeavour to accommodate you whenever possible.* 只要有可能, 我将尽力帮你. **4** [Tn] (*fml* 文) cater for (sth/sb); take into consideration 顺应(某事物[某人]); 考虑到: *accommodate the special needs of minority groups* 照顾少数团体的特殊需要.

▷ **ac·com·mod·at·ing** *adj* (of a person) easy to deal with; willing to help; obliging (指人)随和的, 乐于助人的, 施恩惠的.

ac·com·moda·tion /əˌkɒmə'deɪʃn; əˌkɑmə'deʃən/ *n* **1** **(a)** [U] (*Brit*) room(s), esp for living in; lodgings 房间(尤指作居住用者); 住所: *find suitable, cheap, temporary, permanent, etc accommodation* 找合适的、便宜的、临时的、永久的等住宿处 ○ *Hotel accommodation is scarce.* 旅馆的房间不足. ○ *Wanted, accommodation for a young married couple.* 征租, 供年轻夫妇的住房. **(b)** **accommodations** [pl] (*US*) lodgings; room(s) and food 住宿; 膳宿. **2** [U] **~ (of sth to sth)** (*fml* 文) process of adapting; adjustment 适应; 调节: *arrange the accommodation of my plans to yours* 调整我的计划以便和你的相适应. **3** [C] (*fml* 文) convenient arrangement; compromise 调解; 和解: *The two sides failed to agree on every point but came to an accommodation.* 双方并非在每一点上意见都一致, 但已达成和解.

□ **accommo'dation address** address often used on letters to or by sb who is unable or unwilling to give a permanent address 寄宿地址(常用于信件上, 因不愿或不能告以永久地址).

accommo'dation ladder ladder hung from the side of a ship to reach small boats (悬于船舷, 用以连接小船的)舷梯.

ac·com·pani·ment /ə'kʌmpənɪmənt; ə'kʌmpənɪmənt/ *n* **1** thing that naturally or often goes with another thing 伴随物; 与之俱来的事物: *White wine provided the perfect accompaniment to the meal.* 白葡萄酒是这顿饭的最佳佐餐酒. **2** (*music* 音) part played by an instrument or orchestra to support a solo instrument or voice or a choir 伴奏: *singing with (a) piano accompaniment* 由钢琴伴奏的演唱.

ac·com·pan·ist /ə'kʌmpənɪst; ə'kʌmpənɪst/ *n* person who plays a musical accompaniment 伴奏者.

ac·com·pany /ə'kʌmpənɪ; ə'kʌmpənɪ/ *v* (*pt, pp* **-nied**) **1** [Tn] walk or travel with (sb) as a companion or helper; escort 伴随或跟随(某人); 陪伴: *I must ask you to accompany me to the police station.* 我得要求你陪我去一趟警察分局. ○ *He was accompanied on the expedition by his wife.* 他那次远行有妻子陪同. ○ *Warships will accompany the convoy.* 军舰将护送船队. **2** [esp passive 尤用于被动语态: Tn, Tn·pr] **~ sth (by/with sth)** **(a)** be present or occur with sth 与某事物同时存在或发生: *fever accompanied with delirium* 发烧而说胡话 ○ *strong winds accompanied by heavy rain* 狂风夹着暴雨. **(b)** provide sth in addition to sth else; supplement sth 兼带; 附有: *Each application should be accompanied by a stamped addressed envelope.* 每份申请书均须附回邮信封、贴上邮票、写好地址. **3** [Tn, Tn·pr] **~ sb (at/on sth)** (*music* 音) play an accompaniment for sb 给某人伴奏: *The singer was accompanied at/on the piano by her sister.* 那位演唱者的姐姐用钢琴给她伴奏.

ac·com·plice /ə'kʌmplɪs; *US* ə'kɒm-; ə'kɑmplɪs/ *n* person who helps another to do sth wicked or illegal 从犯; 帮凶; 同谋: *The police arrested him and his two accomplices.* 警方逮捕了他和他的两个同谋.

ac·com·plish /ə'kʌmplɪʃ; *US* ə'kɒm-; ə'kɑmplɪʃ/ *v* [Tn] **1** succeed in doing (sth); complete successfully; achieve 完成(某事物); 做成功; 实现: *accomplish one's aim, a task* 达到目的、完成任务 ○ *a man who will never accomplish anything* 永远一事无成的人. **2** (idm 习语) **an accomplished 'fact** thing that has been done and is no longer worth arguing about because it cannot be changed 既成事实.

▷ **ac·comp·lished** *adj* **1 ~ (in sth)** skilled 有技巧的; 熟练的: *an accomplished dancer, cook, poet, etc* 有才艺的舞蹈家、厨师、诗人等 ○ *be accomplished in music* 擅长音乐. **2** well trained or educated in social skills such as conversation, art, music, etc 在谈吐、美术、音乐等方面受过良好训练或教育的: *an accomplished young lady* 年轻的才女.

ac·com·plish·ment /ə'kʌmplɪʃmənt; *US* ə'kɒm-; ə'kɑmplɪʃmənt/ *n* **1** [U] successful completion 完成; 成功: *celebrate the accomplishment of one's objectives* 庆祝大功告成. **2** [C] thing achieved 成就; 成绩. **3** [C] skill that can be learnt, esp in the social arts 才艺, 技艺, 教养(尤指在社交方面): *Dancing and singing were among her many accomplishments.* 她多才多艺, 能歌善舞.

ac·cord[1] /ə'kɔːd; ə'kɔrd/ *n* **1** peace treaty; agreement 和平条约; 协议: *an accord between countries/with another country* 国与国之间的[与另一国的]条约. **2** (idm 习语) **in accord (with sth/sb)** agreeing (with sth/sb); in harmony 与(某事物[某人])一致; 融洽: *Such an act would not be in accord with our policy.* 这种做法不符合我们的政策. ○ *They live in perfect accord with each other.* 他们生活在一起十分融洽. **of one's own ac'cord** without being asked or forced; voluntarily 主动地; 自愿地: *He joined the army of his own accord.* 他自愿地参了军. **with ˌone ac'cord** everybody agreeing; unanimously 全体一致; 一致地: *With one accord they all stood up and cheered.* 他们全体一致起立欢呼.

ac·cord[2] /ə'kɔːd; ə'kɔrd/ *v* **1** [Ipr] **~ with sth** (*fml* 文) (of a thing) agree or be in harmony with sth; correspond with sth (指事物)与某事物一致或相配合, 与某事物相符: *His behaviour does not accord with his principles.* 他的行为与他的原则不符. ○ *What you say does not accord with the previous evidence.* 你所说的与以前的证词不一致. **2** [Dn·n, Dn·pr] **~ sth to sb** (*fml* 文) give or grant sth to sb 给与或赠与某人某事物: *accord sb permission/accord permission to sb* 允许某人 ○ *The tribute accorded him was fully deserved.* 对他的赞扬他完全当之无愧.

ac·cord·ance /ə'kɔːdns; ə'kɔrdn̩s/ *n* (idm 习语) **in accordance with sth** in agreement or harmony with sth 按照或依据某事物: *in accordance with sb's wishes* 按照某人的愿望 ○ *act in accordance with custom, the regulations, the law* 依照惯例、规章、法律.

ac·cord·ing /ə'kɔːdɪŋ; ə'kɔrdɪŋ/ **1 according to** *prep* **(a)** as stated by (sb) or in (sth) 据(某人)所述; 根据(某事物): *According to John you were in Edinburgh last week.* 据约翰说, 你上星期在爱丁堡. ○ *You've been in prison six times according to our records.* 根据我们的记录, 你曾入狱六次. **(b)** in a manner that is consistent

A

with (sth) 按照，依照(某事物): *act according to one's principles* 按照自己的原则行事 ○ *Everything went according to plan.* 一切都是按照计划进行的. ○ *The work was done according to her instructions.* 那工作是依照她的指示做的. **(c)** in a manner or degree that is in proportion to (sth) 视或依(某事物)而定: *salary according to qualifications and experience* 视资历和经验而定的薪水 ○ *Arrange the exhibits according to size.* 将展品按大小排列. **2 according as** *conj* (*fml* 文) in a manner or to a degree that varies as 取决于: *Everyone contributes according as he is able.* 每个人根据自己的能力作出贡献.

▷ **ac·cord·ingly** *adv* **1** in a manner that is suggested by what is known or has been said 按照已知的或所说的情形: *I've told you what the situation is; you must act accordingly.* 我已经把情况告诉你了，你得采取相应的行动. **2** for that reason; therefore 因此；所以；于是.

ac·cor·dion /əˈkɔːdɪən; əˈkɔrdɪən/ *n* (also **piano accordion**) portable musical instrument with a bellows, metal reeds and a keyboard 手风琴. ⇨illus at CONCERTINA 见CONCERTINA之插图.

ac·cost /əˈkɒst; *US* əˈkɔːst; əˈkɔst/ *v* [Tn] **(a)** approach and speak to (sb) boldly 贸然上前与(某人)搭讪或攀谈: *She was accosted by a complete stranger.* 有一个她完全不认识的人过来跟她搭讪. **(b)** (of a prostitute) solicit (sb) (指妓女)勾搭，勾引(某人).

ac·count[1] /əˈkaʊnt; əˈkaunt/ *n* **1** (*abbr* 缩写 **a/c**) statement of money paid or owed for goods or services 帐目；帐单: *send in/render an account* 报帐[开送帐单] ○ *keep the accounts*, ie keep a detailed record of money spent and received 记帐 ○ *The accounts show a profit of £9 000.* 帐上显示盈利9 000英镑. **2** (*abbr* 缩写 **a/c**) arrangement made with a bank, firm, etc allowing credit for financial or commercial transactions (used esp as in the expressions shown) 帐户，户头(与银行、商店等在财务或商务交易上的约定，尤用于以下示例): *have an account at/with that bank*, ie keep money there and use its facilities 在那个银行有帐户 ○ *open/close an account* 开[结束]户头 ○ *pay money into/draw money out of an account* 在一帐户中存[取]钱 ○ *I have £200 in my account.* 我的户头里有200英镑. ○ *Will you pay cash or shall I charge it to your account* (eg at a shop or restaurant)? 您愿意付现金还是记入您的帐里？(如在商店或饭馆里) **3** report; description 报告；叙述: *She gave the police a full account of the incident.* 她把事件向警方作了详细叙述. ○ *Don't believe the newspaper account (of what happened).* 不要相信报纸上(对所发生的事情)的报道. ○ *Keep an account of your daily activities.* 把你每天的活动都记下来. **4** (idm 习语) **by/from all accounts** according to what has been said or reported 据说；根据报道: *I've never been there but it is, by all accounts, a lovely place.* 我从来没去过那个地方，人家都说那地方很好. **by one's own account** according to what one says oneself 据某人自己所说. **call sb to account** ⇨ CALL[2]. **give a good, poor, etc account of oneself** do or perform well, badly, etc esp in a contest 表现好、不好等(尤指于竞赛中): *Our team gave a splendid account of themselves to win the match.* 我们队表现出色，赢了那场比赛. **leave sth out of account/consideration** ⇨ LEAVE[1]. **of great, small, no, some, etc acˈcount** of great, small, etc importance 很重要、不大重要等: *a man of no account* 无足轻重的人. **on account (a)** as a payment in advance of a larger one 作为先付的部分款项: *I'll give you £20 on account.* 我先付你20英镑. **(b)** to be paid for later 以后付款；赊帐: *buy sth on account* 赊购某物. **on account of sth; on this/that account** because of sth; for this/that reason 因为、由于、为了某事物；为此: *We delayed our departure on account of the bad weather.* 由于天气不好，我们将启程的时间推迟了. **on no account; not on any account** not for any reason 决不可以；切莫: *Don't on any account leave the prisoner unguarded.* 这个囚犯决不能没人看守. **on one's own acˈcount (a)** for one's own benefit and at one's own risk 为自己的利益甘冒风险: *work on one's own account* 自行负责地工作. **(b)** on one's own behalf 为了自己: *I was worried on my own account, not yours.* 我担心是为我自己，而不是为了你. **on sb's account** for sb's sake 为了某人的缘故: *Don't change your plans on my account.* 不要为了我而改变你的计划. **put/turn sth to good acˈcount** use (money, talents, etc) well and profitably 善用(钱、才智等)；利用: *He turned his artistic gifts to good account by becoming a sculptor.* 他发挥艺术天才，成了雕刻家. **render an account of oneself, etc** ⇨ RENDER. **settle one's/an account (with sb)** ⇨ SETTLE. **square one's account/accounts with sb** ⇨ SQUARE. **take account of sth; take sth into account** include sth in one's assessment, etc; make allowances for sth; consider sth 计及；斟酌；体谅；考虑: *When judging his performance, don't take his age into account.* 评定他的表现时，不必考虑他的年龄.

ac·count[2] /əˈkaʊnt; əˈkaunt/ *v* **1** [Cn·a] regard (sb/sth) as; consider 将(某人[某事物])看做；视为: *In English law a man is accounted innocent until he is proved guilty.* 根据英国法律，一个人未经证实有罪仍视为无罪. **2** [Ipr] **~ (to sb) for sth** give a satisfactory record of (money, etc in one's care) (对自己掌管的钱等)作令人满意的交代: *We must account (to our employer) for every penny we spend during a business trip.* 我们得把我们出差时所花的每一分钱(向雇主)交代清楚. **3** (idm 习语) **there's no accounting for taste** (*saying* 谚) it is impossible to explain why people have different likes and dislikes 人各有所好(人的好恶是无可理喻的). **4** (phr v) **account for sth** be the explanation of sth; explain the cause of sth 作某事物的解释；解释某事物的原因: *His illness accounts for his absence.* 他因病缺席. ○ *Please account for your disgraceful conduct.* 对你的可耻行为请作解释. **account for sth/sb** destroy sth or kill sb 摧毁某事物；杀死某人: *Our anti-aircraft guns accounted for five enemy bombers.* 我军高射炮击落五架敌军轰炸机.

ac·count·able /əˈkaʊntəbl; əˈkauntəbl̩/ *adj* [pred 作表语] **~ (to sb) (for sth)** required or expected to give an explanation for one's actions, etc; responsible (对自己的行为等)应作解说；负责: *Who are you accountable to in the organization?* 你在这个组织里向谁负责？○ *He is mentally ill and cannot be held accountable for his actions.* 他有精神病，不能对自己的行为负责.

ac·count·ant /əˈkaʊntənt; əˈkauntənt/ *n* person whose profession is to keep or inspect financial accounts 会计师；会计员.

▷ **ac·count·ancy** /əˈkaʊntənsɪ; əˈkauntənsɪ/ *n* [U] profession of an accountant 会计职业.

ac·cou·tre·ments /əˈkuːtəmənts; əˈkutɚmənts/ (*US* **ac·cou·ter·ments** /*US* əˈkuːtərmənts; əˈkutɚmənts/) *n* [pl] **1** equipment; trappings 装备；服饰. **2** soldier's equipment other than weapons and clothes 士兵(除武器及军服以外)的装备.

ac·credit /əˈkredɪt; əˈkrɛdɪt/ *v* **1** [Tn·pr usu passive 通常用于被动语态] **~ sth to sb/~ sb with sth** attribute (a saying, etc) to sb; credit sb with (a saying, etc) 认为(某说法等)出自某人；认为某人所(说等): *He is accredited with having first introduced this word into the language.* 是他在这个语言中首先使用这个词的. **2** [Tn·pr] **~ sb to/at...; ~ sb to sb** (*fml* 文) send or appoint sb (esp an ambassador) as the official representative to (a foreign government, etc) 委派或任命某人(到外国政府等)任官方代表(尤指大使等): *He was accredited to/at Madrid/accredited to the Spanish king.* 他被委任为驻马德里[被委任为谒见西班牙国王]的大使. **3** [Tn] gain belief or influence for (advice, an adviser, a statement, etc) 因(提建议、作顾问、提出主张等而)获得信赖或有影响力.

▷ **ac·cred·ited** *adj* [usu attrib 通常作定语] **1** officially recognized 官方认可的: *our accredited representative* 我们的官方认可的代表. **2** generally accepted or believed 普遍接受的；公认的: *the accredited theories* 普遍接受的理论. **3** certified as being of a prescribed quality 质量鉴定合格的.

ac·cre·tion /əˈkriːʃn; əˈkriʃən/ *n* **1** [U] **(a)** growth or increase by means of gradual additions (逐渐地)生长，增大. **(b)** the growing of separate things into one 连生；合生. **2** [C] **(a)** added matter that causes such growth 增添物. **(b)** thing formed by the addition of such matter 积累而成的东西: *a chimney blocked by an accretion of soot* 被聚积的煤烟子所堵塞的烟囱.

ac·crue /əˈkruː; əˈkru/ *v* [I, Ipr] **~ (to sb) (from sth)** come as a natural increase or advantage, esp financial;

accumulate 自然增长或利益增加(尤指财务); 积累: *the power and wealth which accrued to the prince* 王子的权力和财产的增加 ○ *Interest will accrue if you keep your money in a savings account.* 把钱存在储蓄帐户里就会生息. ▷ **ac·crual** *n* [U, C].

ac·cu·mu·late /əˈkjuːmjʊleɪt; əˈkjumjəˌlet/ *v* **1** [Tn] gradually get or gather together an increasing number or quantity of (sth); get (sth) in this way 积累, 聚积(某物); 聚集而成(某事物): *accumulate books, a library* 收藏书籍、集成书库 ○ *accumulate enough evidence to ensure his conviction* 搜集足够的证据以给他定罪 ○ *By investing wisely she accumulated a fortune.* 她由于投资精明而积蓄了一笔财产. ○ *My savings are accumulating interest.* 我的储蓄不断生息. **2** [I] increase in number or quantity 增加: *Dust and dirt soon accumulate if a house is not cleaned regularly.* 房屋不经常打扫, 尘土很快就越积越多. ▷ **ac·cu·mu·la·tion** /əˌkjuːmjʊˈleɪʃn; əˌkjumjəˈleʃən/ *n* [U, C]: *the accumulation of money, knowledge, experience* 金钱、知识、经验的积累 ○ *an accumulation of unwanted rubbish* 多余的废物成堆.

ac·cu·mu·lat·ive /əˈkjuːmjʊlətɪv; *US* -leɪtɪv; əˈkjumjəˈletɪv/ *adj* growing steadily by a series of additions; resulting from accumulation; cumulative 积累的; 聚积的; 累积的: *accumulative interest* 累积的利息 ○ *the accumulative effects of eating too much* 长期饮食过量造成的后果.

ac·cu·mu·lator /əˈkjuːmjʊleɪtə(r); əˈkjumjəˌletɚ/ *n* **1** (*Brit*) storage battery that can be recharged, eg for a motor vehicle 蓄电池(如用于机动车辆者). **2** (*esp Brit*) bet placed on a series of sporting events, esp horse races, with the winnings from each being staked on the next 累积赌注(尤指在赛马等连续赌博项目中, 将前次所赢的钱加在下一次之上者). **3** device in a computer that stores and progressively adds numbers 累加器(计算机中储存并累积数目的装置).

ac·cur·acy /ˈækjərəsɪ; ˈækjərəsɪ/ *n* [U] precision or exactness, esp resulting from careful effort 精确, 准确(尤指用心的结果): *predict sth with great accuracy* 极准确地预言某事物 ○ *It is impossible to say with any (degree of) accuracy how many are affected.* 无论如何也说不准受影响的有多少.

ac·cur·ate /ˈækjərət; ˈækjərɪt/ *adj* **1** free from error 正确无误的: *an accurate clock, map, weighing machine* 准确的钟、地图、衡器 ○ *accurate statistics, measurements, calculations, etc* 准确的统计、测量、计算等 ○ *His description was accurate.* 他的叙述很正确. **2** careful and exact 精确的; 准确的: *take accurate aim* 瞄得准 ○ *Journalists are not always accurate (in what they write).* 新闻工作者(的报道)并非一贯准确. ▷ **ac·cur·ately** *adv*.

ac·cur·sed /əˈkɜːsɪd; əˈkɝsɪd/ *adj* **1** [usu attrib 通常作定语] (*infml* 口) hateful; detestable; annoying 可恨的; 可恶的; 讨厌的: *those accursed neighbours of ours* 我们那些可恶的邻居 ○ *this accursed weather* 这讨厌的天气. **2** (*dated* 旧) under a curse 被诅咒的.

ac·cusa·tion /ˌækjuːˈzeɪʃn; ˌækjəˈzeʃən/ *n* **1** [U] accusing or being accused 指责; 谴责; 控告: *prevent the accusation of an innocent person* 防止指控无辜. **2** [C] statement accusing a person of a fault, wrongdoing or crime (控告某人的)罪状: *Accusations of corruption have been made/brought/laid against him.* 对他贪污的控告已经提出.

ac·cus·at·ive /əˈkjuːzətɪv; əˈkjuzətɪv/ *n* (usu *sing* 通常作单数) (*grammar*) special form of a noun, a pronoun or an adjective used (in some inflected languages) when it is the direct object of a verb 宾格(某些屈折语中名词、代词或形容词作动词直接宾语时的一种格).
▷ **ac·cus·at·ive** *adj* of or in the accusative 宾格的: *The accusative forms of the pronouns 'I', 'we' and 'she' are 'me', 'us' and 'her'.* 代词I、we、she的宾格形式是me、us、her.

ac·cuse /əˈkjuːz; əˈkjuz/ *v* [Tn, Tn·pr] **~ sb (of sth)** say that sb has done wrong, is guilty (of sth) or has broken the law 指责某人有错、犯(某)罪或犯法; 指控; 控告; 谴责: *accuse sb of cheating, cowardice, theft* 谴责某人欺诈、指责某人怯懦、控告某人偷窃.
▷ **ac·cus·at·ory** /əˈkjuːzətərɪ; *US* -tɔːrɪ; əˈkjuzəˌtɔrɪ/ *adj* of or indicating an accusation 指责的; 谴责的; 控告的: *accusatory remarks, glances* 责备的言语、目光.
the ac·cused *n* (*pl* unchanged 复数不变) person charged in a criminal case 刑事被告: *The accused was/were acquitted of the charge.* 被告被宣告无罪.
ac·cuser *n*.
ac·cus·ingly /əˈkjuːzɪŋlɪ; əˈkjuzɪŋlɪ/ *adv* in an accusing manner 以谴责或控告的态度: *look, point, etc accusingly at sb* 以责备的态度看着、指着…某人.

ac·cus·tom /əˈkʌstəm; əˈkʌstəm/ *v* [Tn·pr] **~ oneself/sb/sth to sth** make oneself, etc used to sth 使自己等习惯于某事物: *He quickly accustomed himself to this new way of life.* 他很快就习惯了这种新的生活方式.
▷ **ac·cus·tomed** *adj* **1** [attrib 作定语] usual; habitual 通常的; 惯常的: *He took his accustomed seat by the fire.* 他坐在火炉旁他常坐的座位上. **2** [pred 作表语] **~ to sth** used to sth 习惯于某事物: *I soon got accustomed to his strange ways.* 我不久就习惯了他那些奇怪的做法. ○ *He quickly became accustomed to the local food.* 他很快就习惯了当地的食物. ○ *My eyes slowly grew accustomed to the gloom.* 我的眼睛对黑暗慢慢适应了. ○ *This is not the kind of treatment I am accustomed to,* ie not the kind I usually receive. 这不是我惯常受到的那种待遇.

ace /eɪs; es/ *n* **1** playing-card with a large single spot, usu having the highest or lowest value in card games 幺点的纸牌(通常在纸牌游戏中点数最高或最低): *the ace of spades* 黑桃幺. **2** (*infml* 口) person who is an expert at some activity 某些活动中的能手: [attrib 作定语] *an ace pilot, footballer, marksman, etc* 王牌驾驶员、足球健将、神射手. **3** (in tennis) stroke, esp a service, that is too good for the opponent to return (网球赛中, 尤指发球)得分的一击. **4** (idm 习语) **(have) an ace up one's sleeve**; *US* **(have) an ace in the hole** (*infml* 口) (have) sth effective kept secretly in reserve 暗中保留的王牌. **play one's ace** use one's best resource 使出绝招. **within an ace of sth/doing sth** very near to (doing) sth 差一点儿, 几乎(做)某事: *He was within an ace of death/being killed.* 他险些丧了命.

acerbic /əˈsɜːbɪk; əˈsɝbɪk/ *adj* (*fml* 文) (esp of speech or manner) harsh and sharp (尤指说话或态度)严厉的, 尖刻的: *an acerbic remark, tone, etc* 尖刻的话、腔调等.
▷ **acerb·ity** /əˈsɜːbətɪ; əˈsɝbətɪ/ *n* [U, C].

acet·ate /ˈæsɪteɪt; ˈæsəˌtet/ *n* **1** [U, C] (*chemistry* 化) compound derived from acetic acid 醋酸盐. **2** [C] (also **acetate silk**) fabric made from cellulose acetate (用醋酸纤维素制成的)人造丝.

acetic /əˈsiːtɪk; əˈsitɪk/ *adj* of or like vinegar 醋的; 酸的.
□ **aˌcetic ˈacid** acid in vinegar that gives it its characteristic taste and smell 醋酸.

acet·one /ˈæsɪtəʊn; ˈæsəˌton/ *n* [U] (*chemistry* 化) colourless liquid with a strong smell used to dilute paints and varnishes and to make certain chemicals 丙酮.

acet·yl·ene /əˈsetɪliːn; əˈsɛtˌin/ *n* [U] (*chemistry* 化) colourless gas that burns with a bright flame, used in cutting and welding metal 乙炔; 电石气.

ache /eɪk; ek/ *n* (often in compounds 常用以构成复合词) continuous dull pain (持续而隐约的)疼痛: *ˈbackache* ○ *ˈearache* ○ *a ˈheadache* ○ *ˈstomach-ache* ○ *ˈtoothache* ○ *a ˈtummy-ache* ○ *My body was all aches and pains.* 我浑身疼痛. ○ *He has an ache in his/the chest.* 他胸部疼痛.
▷ **ache** *v* **1** [I] suffer from a continuous dull pain 持续地隐隐作痛: *My head aches/is aching.* 我头痛. ○ *I'm aching all over.* 我浑身疼痛. ○ (*fig* 比喻) *It makes my heart ache* (ie makes me sad) *to see her suffer.* 看到她受罪使我痛心. **2** [Ipr, It] **~ for sb/sth** have a longing for sb/sth or to do sth 渴望得到某人[某事物]或做某事: *He was aching for home/to go home.* 他渴望回家.
achy /ˈeɪkɪ; ˈekɪ/ *adj* (*infml* 口) full of or suffering from aches 疼痛的.

achieve /əˈtʃiːv; əˈtʃiv/ *v* [Tn] **1** gain or reach (sth), usu by effort, skill, courage, etc (通常藉努力、技巧、勇气等)获得或达到(某事物): *achieve success, one's ambition, notoriety, peace of mind* 获得成功、实现抱负、落得个臭名、得到心情的平静. **2** get (sth) done; accomplish or complete 做成(某事物); 实现; 完成: *I've achieved only half of what I'd hoped to do.* 我希望做到的, 我仅完成了一半.
▷ **achiev·able** *adj* (of an objective) that can be achieved (指目的)可完成的, 可达到的.
achieve·ment *n* **1** [U] action of achieving 完成; 达到:

celebrate the achievement of one's aims 庆祝愿望的实现. **2** [C] thing done successfully, esp with effort and skill 成就, 成绩(尤指藉努力和技巧而得到者): *the greatest scientific achievement of the decade* 这十年的最伟大的科学成就. ⇨Usage at ACT[1] 用法见 ACT[1].

Achil·les /əˈkɪliːz; əˋkɪliz/ *n* (idm 习语) **an/one's Achilles' ˈheel** weak or vulnerable point; fault, esp in sb's character, which can lead to his downfall 致命弱点; (尤指某人个性中可导致一败涂地的)缺陷: *Vanity is his Achilles' heel.* 虚荣自负是他的致命伤.

□ **Achilles' ˈtendon** tendon attaching the calf muscles to the heel 跟腱(连接小腿三头肌与足跟的腱).

achy ⇨ ACHE.

acid[1] /ˈæsɪd; ˋæsɪd/ *n* **1** [U, C] (*chemistry* 化) substance that contains hydrogen, which can be replaced by a metal to form a salt 酸(能被金属置换出氢而成为盐的物质): *Vinegar contains acetic acid.* 醋中含有醋酸. ○ *Some acids burn holes in wood.* 有些酸能把木头烧成洞. Cf 参看 ALKALI. **2** [C] any sour substance 酸味物质. **3** [U] (*sl* 俚) = LSD. **4** (idm 习语) **the ˈacid test** test that gives conclusive proof of the value or worth of sth/sb 决定性考验: *The acid test of a good driver is whether he remains calm in an emergency.* 衡量驾驶员水平的决定性考验, 就是看他在紧急关头能否保持镇静.

▷ **acid·ic** /əˈsɪdɪk; əˋsɪdɪk/ *adj* of or like an acid 酸性的; 酸味的.

acid·osis /ˌæsɪˈdəʊsɪs; ˌæsɪˋdosɪs/ *n* [U] condition of having too much acid in the blood or body tissues 酸中毒.

□ ˌ**acid ˈrain** rainwater that is made acid by chemical substances (esp from factories) becoming dissolved in it, and that damages trees, crops, etc 酸雨.

acid[2] /ˈæsɪd; ˋæsɪd/ *adj* **1** having a bitter sharp taste; sour 酸味的; 酸的: *A lemon is an acid fruit.* 柠檬是一种酸的水果. ○ *Vinegar has an acid taste.* 醋有酸味. **2** (*fig* 比喻) severe; sarcastic 尖酸刻薄的; 讥讽的: *an acid wit* 讥讽的才智 ○ *His remarks were rather acid.* 他的话有些尖酸刻薄. **3** (*chemistry* 化) having the essential properties of an acid 酸性的. Cf 参看 ALKALINE (ALKALI).

▷ **acid·ify** /əˈsɪdɪfaɪ; əˋsɪdəˌfaɪ/ *v* (*pt*, *pp* **-ied**) [I, Tn] (cause sth to) become acid (使)变酸.

acid·ity /əˈsɪdətɪ; əˋsɪdətɪ/ *n* [U] state or quality of being acid 酸味; 酸性: *suffer from acidity of the stomach* 患胃酸过多.

acidly *adv* sarcastically 讥讽地.

acid·ulous /əˈsɪdjʊləs; *US* -ɪdʒʊl-; əˋsɪdʒələs/ *adj* rather sharp or bitter in taste or manner (味)酸的; (态度)尖酸刻薄的.

▷ **acid·ulated** /əˈsɪdjʊleɪtɪd; *US* -ɪdʒʊl-; əˋsɪdʒəˌletɪd/ *adj* made slightly acid 带酸味的; 微酸的.

ac·know·ledge /əkˈnɒlɪdʒ; əkˋnɑlɪdʒ/ *v* **1** [Tn, Tf, Tw, Cn·a, Cn·t] accept the truth of (sth); admit (sth) 承认(某事物)属实; 供认(某事物): *acknowledge the need for reform* 承认改革的需要 ○ *a generally acknowledged fact* 公认的事实 ○ *He acknowledged it to be true/that it was true.* 他供认那是事实. ○ *They refused to acknowledge defeat/that they were defeated/themselves beaten.* 他们拒不承认失败[他们被打败/自己被击败]. **2** [Tn] report that one has received (sth) 告知已收到(某物): *acknowledge (receipt of) a letter* 告知已收到一封信. **3** [Tn] express thanks for (sth) 为(某事物)表示感谢: *acknowledge help* 对相助表示感谢 ○ *His services to the country were never officially acknowledged.* 他对国家所作的贡献从未受到过正式的表彰. **4** [Tn] show that one has noticed or recognized (sb) by a smile, nod of the head, greeting, etc 以微笑、点头、打招呼等表示注意到或认出(某人): *I was standing right next to her, but she didn't even acknowledge me/my presence.* 我就站在她旁边, 可是她连个招呼都不跟我打. **5** (**a**) [Cn·n/a, Cn·t] **~ sb (as sth)** accept sb (as sth) 承认某人(为某事物): *Stephen acknowledged Henry as* (ie recognized his claim to be) *his heir.* 斯蒂芬接受亨利为他的继承人. ○ *He was generally acknowledged to be the finest poet in the land.* 他是公认的全国最优秀的诗人. (**b**) [Tn] accept or recognize (sth) 接受或承认(某事物): *The country acknowledged his claim to the throne.* 全国人民确认了他的王权.

▷ **ac·know·ledge·ment** (also **ac·know·ledg·ment**) *n* **1** [U] act of acknowledging 承认; 致谢; 感谢: *We are sending you some money in acknowledgement of your valuable help.* 我们谨奉薄酬, 对您的大力协助聊表谢忱. **2** [C] (**a**) letter, etc stating that sth has been received (表示收到某物的)回信, 收条, 回帖等: *I didn't receive an acknowledgement of my application.* 对我的申请, 我还没收到回信. (**b**) thing given or done in return for a service, etc 回敬之物; 答谢: *These flowers are a small acknowledgement of your great kindness.* 这些花是用来对您的恩惠略表谢意的. **3** [C, U] statement (in a book, etc) of an author's thanks to other people or writings that have helped him (于书籍等中, 作者对曾借助的人或作品的)志谢, 感谢: *Her theory was quoted without (an) acknowledgement.* 她的理论被人引用而未向她致谢.

acme /ˈækmɪ; ˋækmɪ/ *n* (usu *sing* 通常作单数) highest stage of development; point of perfection (发展的)顶点; (尽善尽美的)极点: *reach the acme of success* 达到成功的顶点.

acne /ˈæknɪ; ˋæknɪ/ *n* [U] inflammation of the oil-glands of the skin, producing red pimples on the face and neck 痤疮; 粉刺: *Many adolescents suffer from/have acne.* 很多青少年患有痤疮[长粉刺].

aco·lyte /ˈækəlaɪt; ˋækəˌlaɪt/ *n* **1** person who helps a priest in certain church services (教士或僧侣等在举行宗教仪式时的)助手; 侍僧. **2** assistant; apprentice; faithful follower 助手; 徒弟; 信徒.

acon·ite /ˈækənaɪt; ˋækəˌnaɪt/ *n* **1** [C, U] perennial plant with yellow or blue flowers and a poisonous root 乌头(一种开黄花或蓝花, 根有毒的植物, 又称狼毒). **2** [U] drug made from this plant 用乌头制的药物.

acorn /ˈeɪkɔːn; ˋeˌkɔrn/ *n* **1** fruit of the oak-tree, with a cup-like base 橡子, 栎实(栎树的果实). ⇨illus at App 1 见附录1之插图, page i. **2** (idm 习语) **big, etc oaks from little acorns grow** ⇨ OAK.

acous·tic /əˈkuːstɪk; əˋkustɪk/ *adj* **1** (**a**) of sound or the sense of hearing 声音的; 听觉的. (**b**) of acoustics 1 传音效果的; 声学的. **2** [usu attrib 通常作定语] (of a musical instrument) not electric (指乐器)原声的(不是电的): *an acoustic guitar* 原声吉他. ⇨illus at App 1 见附录1之插图, page xi.

▷ **acous·tic** *n* [sing] = ACOUSTICS 1: *The hall has a fine acoustic.* 这个大厅的传音效果很好.

acous·tic·ally *adv*: *The hall is excellent acoustically.* 这个大厅在传音方面极好.

acous·tics *n* **1** [pl] (also **acoustic** [sing]) qualities of a room, hall, etc that make it good or bad for carrying sound (房间、大厅等的)传音效果, 音响效果: *The acoustics of this concert hall are excellent.* 这个音乐厅的传音效果极好. **2** [sing *v*] scientific study of sound 声学; 音响学.

ac·quaint /əˈkweɪnt; əˋkwent/ *v* [Tn·pr] **~ sb/oneself with sth** make sb/oneself familiar with or aware of sth 使某人[自己]熟悉或了解某事物: *Please acquaint me with the facts of the case.* 请把这事的情况告诉我. ○ *The lawyer acquainted himself with the details of his client's business affairs.* 那位律师了解委托人生意上的详情.

▷ **ac·quain·ted** *adj* [pred 作表语] **1 ~ with sth** familiar with sth 对某事物熟悉: *Are you acquainted with the works of Shakespeare?* 你对莎士比亚的作品熟悉吗? ○ *You will soon become fully acquainted with the procedures.* 你很快就会对这些程序完全熟悉了. **2 ~ (with sb)** knowing sb personally 对某人认识的: *I am not acquainted with the lady.* 我不认识那位女士. ○ *We are/became acquainted.* 我们认识[已经认识了]. ○ *Let's get better acquainted.* 让我们进一步相互了解吧.

ac·quaint·ance /əˈkweɪntəns; əˋkwentəns/ *n* **1** [U] **~ with sth/sb** (often slight) knowledge of sth/sb 对某事物[某人](常为略微的)了解: *He has some little acquaintance with the Japanese language.* 他稍微会一点儿日语. **2** [C] person whom one knows but who is not a close friend 相识而非密友者; 泛泛之交: *He has a wide circle of acquaintances.* 他交游甚广. ○ *She's an old acquaintance*, ie I've known her for a long time. 她是个老相识(我早就认识她). **3** (idm 习语) **have a nodding acquaintance with sb/sth** ⇨ NOD. **make sb's acquaintance/make the acquaintance of sb** get to know sb; meet sb personally 结识某人; 与某人相见: *I made his acquaintance at a party.* 我是在一个聚会

上认识他的. **on (further) acˈquaintance** when known for a (longer) period of time 认识了一段(较长)时间以后: *His manner seemed unpleasant at first, but he improved on further acquaintance.* 他的举止起初让人很不愉快, 但是经过进一步接触他改了许多. **scrape an acquaintance with sb** ⇨ SCRAPE[1].

ac·qui·esce /ˌækwɪˈes; ˌækwɪˋɛs/ *v* [I, Ipr] **~ (in sth)** (*fml* 文) accept sth without protest; offer no opposition (to a plan, conclusion, etc) 默认; 顺从; 默许(一计划、结论等): *Her parents will never acquiesce in such an unsuitable marriage.* 她的父母决不会答应这门不相宜的婚事.

▷ **ac·qui·es·cence** /ˌækwɪˈesns; ˌækwɪˋɛsns/ *n* [U].

ac·qui·es·cent /-ˈesnt; -ˋɛsn̩t/ *adj* ready to acquiesce 默认的; 顺从的: *an acquiescent nature* 和顺的性情 ○ *She is too acquiescent*, ie too ready to comply. 她太百依百顺了.

ac·quire /əˈkwaɪə(r); əˋkwaɪr/ *v* **1** [Tn] (**a**) gain (sth) by one's own ability, efforts or behaviour (靠自己的能力、努力或行为而)获得, 得到(某事物): *acquire a good knowledge of English, an antique painting, a taste for brandy, a reputation for dishonesty* 学好英语、得到一幅古画、学会喝白兰地酒、得到不诚实的名声. (**b**) obtain (sth); be given (sth) 取得(某事物); 收到(某事物): *My sister couldn't take her desk with her to the new house: that's how I came to acquire it.* 我妹妹无法把她的书桌搬入新居, 我就是这样才得到它的. ○ *We've just acquired a dog.* 我们刚得到一只狗. **2** (idm 习语) **an acquired ˈtaste** thing that one learns to like gradually 逐渐培养的爱好: *Abstract art is an acquired taste.* 抽象派艺术要慢慢才会欣赏.

ac·quisi·tion /ˌækwɪˈzɪʃn; ˌækwəˋzɪʃən/ *n* **1** [U] action of acquiring 获得; 得到: *the acquisition of antiques, knowledge, a fortune* 获得古董、知识、财富. **2** [C] thing acquired, esp sth useful 获得物(尤指有用的): *the library's most recent acquisitions*, ie books it has obtained recently 图书馆最近增添的书籍 ○ *The school has a valuable new acquisition* (ie a valuable new teacher) *in Mr Smith.* 学校里来了个生力军(很好的新教师)史密斯先生.

ac·quis·it·ive /əˈkwɪzətɪv; əˋkwɪzətɪv/ *adj* (*often derog* 常作贬义) keen to acquire things, esp material possessions 渴望得到的; 贪得无厌的, 一味追求的(尤指物质占有方面): *an acquisitive collector* 贪多务得的收藏家. ▷ **ac·quis·it·ively** *adv*. **ac·quis·it·ive·ness** *n* [U].

ac·quit /əˈkwɪt; əˋkwɪt/ *v* (**-tt-**) **1** [Tn, Tn·pr] **~ sb (of sth)** declare sb to be not guilty (of a crime, etc); free or clear sb (of blame, responsibility, etc) 宣告某人无罪; 给某人平反, 免除责任: *The jury acquitted him of (the charge of) murder.* 陪审团宣告他谋杀罪(的罪名)不成立. Cf 参看 CONVICT. **2** [Tn] **~ oneself well, badly, etc** behave or perform in a specified way (以某种方式)活动或表现: *He acquitted himself bravely in the battle.* 他在战斗中表现得很勇敢.

▷ **ac·quit·tal** /əˈkwɪtl; əˋkwɪtl̩/ *n* (*law* 律) **1** [C] judgement that a person is not guilty of the crime with which he has been charged 无罪的判决: *There were three convictions and two acquittals in court today.* 今日法庭宣判三人有罪、两人无罪. **2** [U] being acquitted 被宣判无罪: *Lack of evidence resulted in their acquittal.* 因证据不足而宣判他们无罪.

acre /ˈeɪkə(r); ˋekɚ/ *n* **1** measure of land, 4 840 square yards or about 4 050 square metres 英亩(等于 4 840 平方码或约 4 050 平方米): *a three-acre wood* 三英亩的树林. ⇨App 4, 5 见附录 4、5. **2** field; piece of land 耕地; 土地: *rolling acres of farm land* 起伏不平的广阔田地.

▷ **acre·age** /ˈeɪkərɪdʒ; ˋekərɪdʒ/ *n* [U] area of land measured in acres 以英亩量度的土地面积; 英亩数: *What is the acreage of the farm?* 这个农场有多少英亩?

ac·rid /ˈækrɪd; ˋækrɪd/ *adj* **1** having a strongly bitter smell or taste 呛人的; 辛辣的; 苦的: *acrid fumes from burning rubber* 燃烧橡胶的刺鼻浓烟 ○ *Vinegar smells acrid.* 醋味呛人. **2** bitter in temper or manner; caustic (性情或态度)刻薄的, 讥刺的: *an acrid dispute* 一场激烈的争论. ▷ **ac·rid·ity** /əˈkrɪdətɪ; əˋkrɪdətɪ/ *n* [U].

ac·ri·mony /ˈækrɪmənɪ; *US* -məʊnɪ; ˋækrəˌmonɪ/ *n* [U] bitterness of manner or words (态度或言语的)尖刻, 刻薄: *The dispute was settled without acrimony.* 这场争论未剑拔弩张而获解决.

▷ **ac·ri·mo·ni·ous** /ˌækrɪˈməʊnɪəs; ˌækrəˋmonɪəs/ *adj* (esp of quarrels) bitter (尤指争吵)尖酸刻薄的: *an acrimonious meeting, discussion, atmosphere* 争吵激烈的会议、讨论、气氛. **ac·ri·mo·ni·ously** *adv*.

ac·ro·bat /ˈækrəbæt; ˋækrəˌbæt/ *n* person, esp at a circus, who performs difficult or unusual physical acts (eg somersaults, walking on the hands or walking on a rope) 杂技演员.

▷ **ac·ro·batic** /ˌækrəˈbætɪk; ˌækrəˋbætɪk/ *adj* of or like an acrobat 杂技的; 像杂技表演的: *acrobatic feats, skills* 杂技、杂技技艺. **ac·ro·bat·ic·ally** *adv*.

ac·ro·bat·ics *n* **1** [pl] acrobatic acts 杂技动作; 杂技: *perform/do acrobatics* 表演杂技 ○ *Her acrobatics were greeted with loud applause.* 她的杂技表演赢得了热烈的掌声. **2** [sing *v*] art of performing these 杂技表演艺术: *Acrobatics takes a long time to learn.* 杂技要用很长时间学习.

ac·ro·nym /ˈækrənɪm; ˋækrənɪm/ *n* word formed from the initial letters of a group of words, eg *UNESCO* /juːˈneskəʊ; juˋnɛsko/, ie United Nations Educational, Scientific and Cultural Organization 首字母缩略词(由一组词中各词的首字母组合而成的词, 如 UNESCO 是由 United Nations Educational, Scientific and Cultural Organization 各词的首字母组成的词).

ac·ro·polis /əˈkrɒpəlɪs; əˋkrɑpəlɪs/ *n* citadel or upper fortified part of an ancient Greek city (古希腊城市的)卫城: *Many tourists visit the Acropolis in Athens.* 有很多游客参观雅典的卫城.

across[1] /əˈkrɒs; *US* əˈkrɔːs; əˋkrɔs/ *adv part* **1** from one side to the other side 从一边到另一边; 横过: *Can you swim across?* 你能游过去吗? ○ *Will you row me across?* 你划船把我送过去行吗? ○ *I helped the blind man across.* 我帮助那个盲人过去了. ○ *Come across to my office this afternoon.* 你今天下午到我办公室来一趟. **2** on the other side 在另一边: *We leave Dover at ten and we should be across in France by midnight.* 我们十点钟离开多佛, 午夜时应能抵达法国那边. **3** from side to side 从这边到那边之间; 宽: *The river is half a mile across*, ie wide. 这条河有半英里宽.

□ **across from** *prep* (*esp US*) opposite (sth) 在...的对面: *Just across from our house there's a school.* 就在我们房子的对面有一所学校.

across[2] /əˈkrɒs; *US* əˈkrɔːs; əˋkrɔs/ *prep* **1** from one side to the other side of (sth) 从(某物)的一边到另一边; 横过(某物): *walk across the street* 走过这条街 ○ *row sb across a lake* 划船送某人过湖. **2** on the other side of (sth) 在(某物)的另一边: *We shall soon be across the Channel.* 我们不久即将渡过英吉利海峡了. ○ *He shouted to me from across the room.* 他从房间的另一边向我喊. ○ *My house is just across the street.* 我的房子就在马路对面. **3** extending from one side to the other side of (sth) 从(某物)的一边向另一边伸展: *a bridge across the river* 横跨河上的一座桥 ○ *Draw a line across the page.* 在这页上画一条横线. **4** so as to cross or intersect (sth) 交叉; 与(某物)相交叉: *He sat with his arms across his chest.* 他两臂在胸前交叉坐着.

ac·ros·tic /əˈkrɒstɪk; *US* -ˈkrɔːs-; əˋkrɔstɪk/ *n* poem or word-puzzle in which the first, or the first and last, letters of the lines form a word or words 离合诗; 离合字谜(数行诗句或文字的首字母或首尾字母能组合成词或词组者).

ac·rylic /əˈkrɪlɪk; əˋkrɪlɪk/ *adj* of a synthetic material made from an organic acid and used for making dress fabrics, etc 丙烯酸的.

▷ **ac·rylic** *n* [U, C] acrylic fibre, plastic or resin 丙烯酸的纤维、塑料或树脂.

act[1] /ækt; ækt/ *n* **1** (**a**) [C] thing done; deed 行为; 举动: *It is an act of kindness/a kind act to help a blind man across the street.* 帮助盲人过马路是做好事. ○ *This dreadful murder is surely the act of a madman.* 这种令人惊骇的谋杀纯粹是疯子的行为. (**b**) **(the) Acts (of the Apostles)** [pl] (in the Bible) accounts of the missionary work of the Apostles《使徒行传》(《圣经》中对使徒传道的记述). ⇨Usage 见所附用法. **2** [C] any of the main divisions of a play or an opera (戏剧中的)一幕: *a play in five acts* 一出五幕剧 ○ *The hero dies in Act 4, Scene 3.* 男主角在第4幕第3场中死去. **3** [C] any of a series of short performances in a programme; piece of entertainment 简短的节目; 一段表演: *a circus*

A

act 马戏表演 ○ *a song and dance act* 歌舞表演. **4** [C] decree or law made by a legislative body (立法机构所立的)法案, 法令: *an Act of Parliament* (英国议会的)法例 ○ *Parliament has passed an act which makes such sports illegal.* 议会通过了一项法例, 规定这些娱乐是非法的. **5** [C] (*infml* 口) way of behaving which is not genuine, but which is adopted for the effect it will have on others; pretence (used esp as in the expressions shown 假装(尤用于以下示例)): *Don't take her seriously — it's all an act.* 别跟她认真——完全是装腔作势. ○ *She's just putting on an act,* ie only pretending. 她只是装模作样罢了. **6** (idm 习语) **an ˌact of ˈGod** (*law* 律) event caused by uncontrollable natural forces, eg a storm, a flood, an earthquake or a volcanic eruption 天灾, 自然灾害(如暴风雨、水灾、地震或火山爆发): *insure against all loss or damage excluding that caused by an act of God* 承保一切损失或毁坏, 不包括天灾造成的. **be/get in on the act** (*infml* 口) be/become involved in a particular activity, esp for one's own benefit or profit (尤指为自己得到好处或利益而)参与某种活动: *She has made a lot of money from her business and now her family want to get in on the act too.* 她在生意上赚了大钱, 现在她家里的人也要插手了. **do a disappearing act** ⇨ DISAPPEAR. **(catch sb) in the (very) act (of doing sth)** (discover sb) while he is doing sth, esp sth wrong (发现某人)正做某事(尤指坏事); 当场: *I caught her in the act (of reading my letters).* 我当场发现了她(正在看我的信). ○ *In the act of bending down, he slipped and hurt his back.* 他一弯腰滑倒了, 跌伤了背. **read the Riot Act** ⇨ READ.

NOTE ON USAGE 用法: **1** An **act** or **action** can be good or bad. ☆ **act** 或 **action** 用于指好事或坏事均可. The words are close in meaning and sometimes identical 这两个词词义相近, 有时完全相同: *a generous act/action* 慷慨之举 ○ *the acts/actions of a monster* 妖怪的举动. When speaking about general behaviour, **actions** is used 凡指一般的行动或行为, 可用 **actions**: *He is impulsive in his actions.* 他凭一时冲动行事. An **act** is often specified ☆ **act** 一词常伴有具体说明: *Helping the homeless is an act of mercy.* 帮助无家可归者是慈善行为. **Deed** is more formal and often refers to major acts ☆ **deed** 一词较文雅, 常指重大的举动: *be guilty of many foul deeds* 有多项恶行 ○ *He spent his whole life doing good deeds.* 他一生行善. **2** **Exploit**, **feat** and **achievement** are all desirable or noteworthy actions. ☆ **exploit**、**feat**、**achievement** 三词均指令人向往的或值得注目的举动或行为. Both **feat** and **achievement** emphasize the difficulty of accomplishing something mental or physical ☆ **feat** 和 **achievement** 均着重指在脑力或体力方面完成某事物的艰巨性: *Coming top in the exam was quite an achievement.* 考第一是很了不起的成绩. ○ *The new bridge is a feat of engineering.* 这座新桥是建筑工程的壮举. **Exploit** relates to the performance of a physical action or series of actions which are often brave or daring ☆ **exploit** 指体力的行为表现, 常为敢闯敢干的举动: *The travellers wrote an account of their dangerous exploits in the Andes.* 旅行者写了一篇叙述他们在安第斯山历险的文章.

act[2] /ækt; ækt/ *v* **1** [I] (**a**) do sth; perform actions 做某事; 采取行动: *The time for talking is past; we must act at once.* 没有时间再说了, 我们必须立刻行动. ○ *The girl's life was saved because the doctors acted so promptly.* 由于医生们行动迅速, 那个女孩子得救了. ○ *You acted* (ie behaved) *wisely by/in ignoring such bad advice.* 你没理会那些坏主意, 做得聪明. (**b**) do what is expected of one as a professional or an official person 以专业人员的身分去做; 尽职: *The police refused to act without more evidence.* 因为没有更多的证据, 警方拒绝受理. **2** (**a**) [I] perform a part in a play or film; be an actor or actress (在戏剧或电影中)演出; 当演员: *Have you ever acted?* 你当过演员吗? ○ *She acts well.* 她演得很好. (**b**) [Ln, Tn] take the part of (a character in a play or film) 扮演(戏剧或电影中的角色): *Who is acting (the part of) Hamlet?* 谁扮演哈姆雷特(这个角色)? (**c**) [Ln, I] pretend by one's behaviour to be a certain person or type of person 装作, 仿效(某人或某种人的行为): *He's not really angry — he's just acting (the stern father).* 他倒不是真生气——只是装装(严父的)样子罢了. **3** (idm 习语) **act/play the fool** ⇨ FOOL[1]. **act/play the goat** ⇨ GOAT. **4** (phr v) **act as sb/sth** perform the role or function of sb/sth 充任某角色; 担任某工作: *I don't understand their language; you'll have to act as interpreter.* 我不懂他们的语言, 你得当翻译了. **act for/on behalf of sb** perform sb's duties, etc on his behalf; represent sb 代理某人的职务; 代表某人: *During her illness her solicitor has been acting for her in her business affairs.* 在她患病期间, 她的律师一直代理她的业务. **act on sth** (**a**) take action in accordance with or as a result of sth 奉行; 根据某事物: *Acting on information received, the police raided the club.* 警方根据所获情报, 突然搜查了那个俱乐部. (**b**) have an effect on sth 对某事物起作用: *Alcohol acts on the brain.* 酒精对大脑有影响. **act sth out** act a part, usu in a real-life situation and for some purpose 扮演一角色(通常于现实生活中为某种目的): *She acted out the role of wronged lover to make him feel guilty.* 她扮作受了冤枉的情人, 好让他感到内疚. **act up** (*infml* 口) cause pain or annoyance by functioning badly 出毛病; 犯病: *My sprained ankle has been acting up badly all week.* 我的脚扭伤了, 整整难受了一个星期. ○ *The car's acting up again.* 这辆汽车又出毛病了.

▷ **act·ing** *n* [U] (art or occupation of) performing parts in plays, films, TV, etc (在戏剧、电影、电视等中的)表演(的艺术或职业); 演技: *She did a lot of acting while she was at college.* 她在念大学时演过很多次戏剧.

act·ing /ˈæktɪŋ; ˋæktɪŋ/ *adj* [attrib 作定语] doing the duties of another person for a time 代理的: *the acting manager, headmistress, etc* 代理的经理、(女)校长等.

ac·tin·ism /ˈæktɪnɪzəm; ˋæktɪnˌɪzəm/ *n* [U] property of short-wave radiation that produces chemical changes, as in photography 光化性(光波的辐射性能, 可产生化学变化, 如摄影术中者).

ac·tion /ˈækʃn; ˋækʃən/ *n* **1** [U] (**a**) process of doing sth; using energy or influence; activity 行动; 作用; 活动: *I only like films that have got plenty of action.* 我只喜欢有很多惊险动作的电影. ○ *The time has come for action.* 行动的时候到了. ○ *a man of action,* ie one who achieves much by being decisive and energetic 实干家(靠果敢和干劲而取得成就的人). (**b**) [C]thing done; deed; act 所作之事; 行为; 行动: *Her quick action saved his life.* 她动作迅速因而救了他一命. ○ *You must judge a person by his actions, not by what he says.* 判断一个人, 要看他的所作所为, 而不是看他所说的话. ⇨Usage at ACT[1] 用法见 ACT[1]. **2** [U] events in a story or play (故事或戏剧中的)情节: *The action is set in France.* 事情发生在法国. **3** [sing] **~ on sth** effect that one substance has on another (一物质对另一物质所起的)作用: *The action of salt on ice causes it to melt.* 盐作用于冰而使其融化. **4** [U] fighting in battle between troops, warships, etc (军队、军舰等之间的)战斗, 战事: *killed in action* 阵亡 ○ *the destruction caused by enemy action* 敌军在战斗中造成的破坏 ○ *He saw* (ie was involved in) *action in North Africa.* 他曾经历了北非的战事. **5** [C] legal process; lawsuit 诉讼: *He brought an action against her,* ie sought judgement against her in a lawcourt. 他起诉她了. **6** [C] (**a**) way of functioning, esp of a part of the body 功能(尤指身体某部的): *study the action of the liver* 研究肝功能. (**b**) way of moving, eg of an athlete, or of a horse when jumping 动作的姿势(如运动员或马跳时): *a fast bowler with a fine action* 姿势优美而动作敏捷的滚木球运动员. (**c**) mechanism of an instrument, esp of a gun, piano or clock 机械装置(尤指枪炮、钢琴、钟表等者). **7** (idm 习语) **ˌactions speak ˌlouder than ˈwords** (*saying* 谚) what a person actually does means more than what he says he will do 行动胜于语言. **course of action** ⇨ COURSE. **in ˈaction** in operation or engaging in a typical activity 在运转; 在操作; 在某项活动中: *I've heard she's a marvellous player but I've never seen her in action.* 我听说她是位高手, 但是我从未实地见过. **into ˈaction** into operation or a typical activity 实施; 进行其活动: *put a plan into action* 将计划付诸实施 ○ *At daybreak the troops went into action,* ie started fighting. 拂晓时部队投入战斗. **out of ˈaction** no longer able to operate or function; not working 不能再运转; 失去效用; 不工作: *This machine is out of action.* 这台机器出了故障. ○ *The enemy guns put many of our tanks out of action.* 敌军炮火击毁我军很多坦克. ○ *I've been out of* *action for several weeks with a broken leg.* 我的腿折了，已经几个星期没工作了. **a piece/slice of the 'action** (*infml* 口) involvement in some enterprise, esp in order to get a share of the profits 参与某事(尤指为获得利益的): *I'm only putting money into this scheme if I get a slice of the action.* 我若能分一杯羹，才出钱参与这一计划. **swing into action** ⇨ SWING[1]. **take 'action** do sth in response to what has happened 采取行动; 行动起来: *Immediate action must be taken to stop the fire spreading.* 必须立即采取行动阻止火势蔓延. **take evasive action** ⇨ EVASIVE. **where the 'action is** (*infml* 口) any place where life is thought to be busy, enjoyable, profitable, etc 热闹、享乐、有利可图等的地方: *Life in the country can be dull — London is where all the action is.* 乡下的生活有时是很枯燥的——伦敦才是最热闹的地方.

▷ **ac·tion·able** *adj* giving sufficient cause for a lawsuit 可提起诉讼的: *Be careful what you say — your remarks may be actionable.* 你说话要小心——你的话是可用来控告你的.

□ **'action group** group formed to take active measures, esp in politics 行动小组(尤指政治方面).

'action painting type of abstract painting in which the artist puts the paint on randomly, eg by throwing or splashing it 行动绘画(抽象派作画的一种，画家任意泼洒颜料而成).

,action 'replay running again, often in slow motion, of part of a film showing a specific incident, esp in a sports match 动作重放(常为缓慢重放影片中某细节，尤用于运动比赛中).

'action stations positions to which soldiers, etc go when fighting is expected to begin (即将开始作战时，士兵等所应就的)战斗岗位: (*fig* 比喻) *Action stations, I can hear the boss coming!* 各就各位，我已经听见老板来了!

ac·tiv·ate /'æktɪveɪt; 'æktə,vet/ *v* [Tn] **1** make (sth) active 使(某事物)活动: *The burglar alarm was activated by mistake.* 防盗铃误响了. **2** (*physics* 物) make (sth) radioactive 使(某物)产生放射性. **3** (*chemistry* 化) make (a reaction) happen more quickly, eg by heat 使(反应)加快(如通过加热); 使活化. ▷ **ac·tiva·tion** /,æktɪ'veɪʃn; ,æktə'veʃən/ *n* [U].

act·ive /'æktɪv; 'æktɪv/ *adj* **1** (**a**) (in the habit of) doing things; energetic (惯于)做事的; 精力旺盛的; 积极的; 活跃的: *Although he's quite old he's still very active.* 他虽然老了，可仍闲不住. ○ *lead an active life*, ie one full of activity 过着活跃的生活 ○ *She takes an active part* (ie is energetically involved) *in local politics.* 她积极参加本地的政治活动. (**b**) quick; lively 迅速的; 活跃的: *have an active brain* 头脑灵活. **2** functioning; in operation 起作用的; 操作中的: *an active volcano*, ie one that erupts occasionally 活火山. **3** having an effect; not merely passive 有效的; 主动的: *the active ingredients* 有效成分 ○ *active resistance* 积极抵抗. **4** radioactive 放射性的. **5** (*grammar*) of the form of a verb whose grammatical subject is the person or thing that performs the action, as in *He was driving the car* and *The children ate the cake* 主动语态的(动词的一种形态，其语法上的主语为施动的人或物，如 He was driving the car 及 The children ate the cake 等句). Cf 参看 PASSIVE.

▷ **act·ive** *n* [sing] (also **active voice**) (*grammar*) active(5) forms of a verb 动词的主动语态形式: *In the sentence 'She cleaned the car' the verb is in the active.* 在 She cleaned the car 句中，动词是主动式. Cf 参看 PASSIVE VOICE (PASSIVE).

act·ively *adv*: *actively involved in the project* 积极参与该计划 ○ *Your proposal is being actively considered.* 你的建议正获积极考虑.

ac·tive·ness *n* [U].

□ **active 'service** (*US* also **active 'duty**) full-time service in the armed forces, esp during a war 现役; (尤指)战时服役: *be on active service* 服现役.

active voice = ACTIVE *n*.

act·iv·ist /'æktɪvɪst; 'æktɪvɪst/ *n* person who takes or supports vigorous action, esp for a political cause 积极分子(参与或支持激烈活动的人，尤指政治方面).

act·iv·ity /æk'tɪvətɪ; æk'tɪvətɪ/ *n* **1** [U] (**a**) being active or lively 活动性; 活力. (**b**) busy or energetic action 繁忙的或充满活力的活动: *The house has been full of activity all day.* 房子里整天都很热闹. **2** [C esp *pl* 尤作复数] specific thing or things done; action; occupation 所做的事情; 活动; 工作; 消遣: *outdoor, recreational, sporting, classroom activities* 户外、娱乐、体育、课堂活动 ○ *Her activities include tennis and painting.* 她的活动包括打网球和绘画. ○ *Sailing is an activity I much enjoy.* 帆船运动是我非常喜爱的活动.

actor /'æktə(r); 'æktɚ/ *n* person who acts on the stage, on TV or in films 演员.

act·ress /'æktrɪs; 'æktrɪs/ *n* woman actor 女演员.

ac·tual /'æktʃuəl; 'æktʃuəl/ *adj* existing in fact; real 实在的; 真实的; 实际的; 确实的: *What were his actual words?* 他到底是怎么说的? ○ *The actual cost was much higher than we had expected.* 实际成本比我们预料的高得多. ○ *He looks younger than his wife, but in actual fact he's a lot older.* 他看上去比他妻子年轻，可是实际上他大得多. ⇨Usage at NEW 用法见 NEW.

▷ **ac·tu·ally** /'æktʃuəlɪ; 'æktʃuəlɪ/ *adv* **1** really; in fact 实际地; 实在地: *What did he 'actually say?* 他实际上说了些什么? ○ *Actually, I'm busy at the moment — can I phone you back?* 说实在的，我现在正忙着——我给你回电话行吗? ○ *the political party actually in power* 实际掌权的政党. **2** though it may seem strange; even 居然; 竟然: *He actually expected me to pay for his ticket.* 他竟然指望我给他付票钱. ○ *She not only entered the competition — she actually won it!* 她不但参加了竞赛——而且居然获胜了!

ac·tu·al·ity /,æktʃʊ'ælətɪ; ,æktʃʊ'ælətɪ/ *n* **1** [U] actual existence; reality 实际; 真实. **2 actualities** [pl] existing conditions; facts 实际情况; 现状; 事实.

ac·tu·ary /'æktʃuərɪ; *US* -tʃuerɪ; 'æktʃu,ɛrɪ/ *n* expert who calculates insurance risks and premiums (by studying rates of mortality and frequency of accidents, fires, thefts, etc) 精算师(保险业的专业人员，以研究死亡率及事故、火灾、窃案等的频率为依据来估算风险和保险费者). ▷ **ac·tu·ar·ial** /,æktʃʊ'eərɪəl; ,æktʃʊ'ɛrɪəl/ *adj*.

ac·tu·ate /'æktʃueɪt; 'æktʃu,et/ *v* [Tn] (*fml* 文) **1** make (a machine, an electrical device, etc) move or work; make (a process) begin 使(机器、电器等)开动，发动; 使(一过程)开始. **2** cause (sb) to act; motivate 使(某人)行动; 促使: *He was actuated solely by greed.* 他完全是受了贪欲的驱使.

acu·ity /ə'kju:ətɪ; ə'kjuətɪ/ *n* [U] (*fml* 文) (esp of thought or the senses) sharpness; acuteness (尤指思想或感官)敏锐，尖锐.

acu·men /'ækjʊmen, *also* ə'kju:mən; ə'kjumən/ *n* [U] ability to understand and judge things quickly and clearly; shrewdness 敏锐; 精明; 聪明: *business acumen* 善理业务的才智 ○ *have/show/display great political acumen* 有[显示/展现]极大的政治才干.

acu·punc·ture /'ækjʊpʌŋktʃə(r); 'ækju,pʌŋktʃɚ/ *n* [U] (*medical* 医) method of pricking the tissues of the human body with fine needles in order to cure disease, to relieve pain or as a local anaesthetic 针刺疗法; 针刺.

▷ **acu·punc·tur·ist** *n* expert in acupuncture 针疗医师.

acute /ə'kju:t; ə'kjut/ *adj* (**-r**, **-st**) **1** very great; severe 极大的; 严重的: *suffer acute hardship* 遭受极大的苦难 ○ *There's an acute shortage of water.* 严重缺水. **2** (**a**) (of feelings or the senses) keen; sharp; penetrating (指感觉或感官)敏锐的，深刻的，剧烈的: *suffer acute pain, embarrassment, remorse, etc* 感到剧烈的疼痛、极度的尴尬、深深的懊悔等 ○ *Dogs have an acute sense of smell.* 狗的嗅觉很敏锐. (**b**) shrewd; perceptive 精明的; 有观察力的: *He is an acute observer.* 他是个敏锐的观察家. ○ *Her judgement is acute.* 她的判断力很强. **3** (of an illness) coming quickly to the most severe or critical stage (指疾病)急性的: *acute appendicitis* 急性阑尾炎 ○ *an acute patient*, ie one whose illness has reached this stage 患急性病的病人. Cf 参看 CHRONIC. ▷ **acutely** *adv*: *I am acutely aware of the difficulty we face.* 我深切地了解我们所面临的困难. **acute·ness** *n* [U].

□ **acute 'accent** mark over a vowel (´) as over *e* in *café* 锐音符，锐重音(标在元音上方的变音符号，如 café 一字中 e 上方的´).

acute 'angle angle of less than 90° 锐角(小于 90° 的角). ⇨illus at ANGLE 见 ANGLE 之插图.

-acy ⇨ -CY.

AD /,eɪ 'di:; ,e 'di/ *abbr* 缩写 = in the year of Our Lord; of the Christian era (Latin *anno domini*) 公元(源自拉

丁文 *anno domini*): *in (the year)* ˌ*55 A'D*/ˌ*AD 5'5* 公元55年. Cf 参看 BC 1.

A

ad /æd; æd/ *n* (*infml* 口) =ADVERTISEMENT (ADVERTISE): *put an ad in the local paper* 在本地报纸上刊登广告.

adage /ˈædɪdʒ; ˋædɪdʒ/ *n* traditional saying; proverb 格言; 箴言; 谚语.

ada·gio /əˈdɑːdʒɪəʊ; əˋdɑdʒo/ *adj, adv* (*music* 音) in slow time; slowly and gracefully 缓慢(的); 缓慢而优美(的).

▷ **ada·gio** *n* (*pl* **-gios**) (part of a) piece of music (to be) played in this way 缓慢速度的乐曲(的乐章).

Adam /ˈædəm; ˋædəm/ *n* **1** (in the Bible) the first man 亚当(《圣经》中的第一个男人). **2** (idm 习语) **not know sb from Adam** ⇨ KNOW.

□ ˌ**Adam's** ˈ**apple** part at the front of the neck, especially prominent in men, that moves up and down when one speaks 喉结. ⇨illus at THROAT 见 THROAT 之插图.

ad·am·ant /ˈædəmənt; ˋædəˌmɑnt/ *adj* (esp of a person or his manner) firmly or stubbornly determined; unwilling to be persuaded (尤指人或态度)坚决的, 坚强的, 倔强的, 坚定不移的: *an adamant refusal* 断然拒绝 ○ *She was quite adamant that she would not come.* 她坚决不来. ○ *On this point I am adamant*, ie my decision will not change. 在这一点上我是坚定不移的. ▷ **ad·am·antly** *adv*.

ad·apt /əˈdæpt; əˋdæpt/ *v* **1** (**a**) [Tn, Tn·pr, Tnt] **~ sth (for sth)** make sth suitable for a new use, situation, etc; modify sth 使某事物适合于新的用途、情况等; 修改某事物: *This machine has been specially adapted for use underwater.* 这机器是为水下使用而特别改装的. ○ *These styles can be adapted to suit individual tastes.* 这些式样均可改动以适应个人不同的爱好. (**b**) [Tn, Tn·pr] **~ sth (for sth) (from sth)** alter or modify (a text) for television, the stage, etc (为电视、舞台等)改编或改写(稿本): *This novel has been adapted for radio* (ie translated and changed so that it can be presented on the radio) *from the Russian original.* 这部小说已由俄文原著改编成无线电广播节目(经翻译及改写后可于无线电中播放). **2** [I, Ipr, Tn·pr] **~ (oneself) (to sth)** become adjusted to new conditions, etc 适应(新环境等): *Our eyes slowly adapted to the dark.* 我们的眼睛慢慢地适应了黑暗的环境. ○ *She adapted (herself) quickly to the new climate.* 她很快地适应了这种新的气候.

▷ **ad·apt·able** *adj* (**a**) (*approv* 褒) able to adapt oneself/itself 能适应的; 适应性强的: *He is not very adaptable*, ie does not adapt easily to new circumstances, etc. 他的适应性不强. (**b**) able to be adapted 可改编的; 可改写的. **ad·apt·ab·il·ity** /əˌdæptəˈbɪlətɪ; əˌdæptəˋbɪlətɪ/ *n* [U].

ad·apta·tion /ˌædæpˈteɪʃn; ˌædæpˋteʃən/ *n* **~ (of sth) (for/to sth) 1** [U] (*esp biology* 尤用于生物学) action or process of adapting or being adapted 适应; 适应性; 适应性变化. **2** [C] thing made by adapting sth else, esp a text for production on the stage, radio, etc 改制物; (尤指为舞台演出、无线电广播等而源自其它材料的)改编本: *an adaptation for children of a play by Shakespeare* 为儿童改编的莎士比亚剧本.

ad·aptor *n* **1** device that connects pieces of equipment that were not originally designed to be connected 适配器, 转接器(用以转接不可直接连接的器材). **2** type of plug that enables several electrical appliances to be connected to one socket 转接器(可使几个用电器连接于同一插座上的一种插头). **3** (also **ad·apter**) person who adapts sth 改编者.

ADC /ˌeɪ diː ˈsiː; ˌe di ˋsi/ *abbr* 缩写 = aide-de-camp.

add /æd; æd/ *v* **1** [Tn, Tn·pr] **~ sth (to sth)** put sth together with sth else so as to increase the size, number, amount, etc 加; 添; 增加: *Whisk the egg and then add the flour.* 打好鸡蛋以后再加面粉. ○ *He added his signature (to the petition).* 他(在请愿书上)签上了自己的名字. ○ *If the tea is too strong, add some more water.* 若茶太酽, 就再加些水. ○ *Many words have been added to this edition of the dictionary.* 本词典的这一版里新增加了很多词. ○ *This was an added* (ie an extra, a further) *disappointment.* 这又是一件失望的事. **2** [Tn, Tn·pr, Tn·p] **~ A to B; ~ A and B (together)** put (numbers or amounts) together to get a total 加: *If you add 5 and 5 (together), you get 10.* 5加5得10. ○ *Add 9 to the total.* 在总数上再加9. Cf 参看 SUBTRACT. **3** [Tn, Tn·pr, Tf] **~ sth (to sth)** continue to say sth; make (a further remark) 继续说; 又说; 补充说: *I have nothing to add to my earlier statement.* 我对我先前说的话, 没有什么补充的. ○ *'And don't be late,' she added.* 她又加上一句: '可别迟到.' ○ *As a postscript to his letter he added that he loved her.* 他在信中加上附言, 写上了他爱她. **4** (idm 习语) **add** ˌ**fuel to the** ˈ**flames** do or say sth that makes people react more strongly or fiercely 火上加油(做的或说的使人反应更强烈或激烈). **add** ˌ**insult to** ˈ**injury** make a relationship with another person even worse by offending him as well as actually harming him 伤害之外又加侮辱(使关系更糟). **5** (phr v) **add sth in** include sth; put or pour sth in 包括某事物; 把某物加进去. **add sth on (to sth)** include or attach sth 包括或附加某事物: *add on a 10% service charge* 加上10%服务费. **add to sth** increase sth 增加某事物: *The bad weather only added to our difficulties.* 这种坏天气更增加了我们的困难. ○ *The house has been added to* (ie New rooms, etc have been built on to it) *from time to time.* 这所房子不时进行扩建. **add up** (*infml* 口) seem reasonable or consistent; make sense 前后一致; 合理: *His story just doesn't add up — he must be lying.* 他说的前后不一致——一定撒谎了. **add (sth) up** calculate the total of (two or more numbers or amounts) (两个或两个以上的数或量)加起来: *The waiter can't add up.* 这个服务员不会算帐. ○ *Add up all the money I owe you.* 把我应付你的钱都加在一起. **add up to sth** (**a**) amount to sth 总计共达: *These numbers add up to 100.* 这些数目合计为100. (**b**) (*infml* 口) be equivalent to sth; indicate sth 相等于某事物; 意为某事物: *These clues don't really add up to very much*, ie give us very little information. 这些线索没什么实际意义.

ad·den·dum /əˈdendəm; əˋdɛndəm/ *n* (*pl* **-da** /-də; -də/) **1** [C] thing that is to be added 附加物. **2 ad·denda** [sing or pl *v*] material added at the end of a book 补遗; 补编; 附录.

ad·der /ˈædə(r); ˋædɚ/ *n* small poisonous snake; viper 小毒蛇; 蝰蛇.

ad·dict /ˈædɪkt; ˋædɪkt/ *n* **1** person who is unable to stop taking drugs, alcohol, etc 离不开麻醉药、酒类等的人; 有瘾的人: *a heroin addict* 有海洛因毒瘾的人. **2** person who is strongly interested in sth 对某事物有强烈兴趣的人: *a chess, TV, football addict* 棋迷、电视迷、足球迷.

▷ **ad·dic·ted** /əˈdɪktɪd; əˋdɪktɪd/ *adj* [pred 作表语] **~ (to sth) 1** unable to stop taking or using sth as a habit 成习惯而离不开某事物; 对某事物有瘾: *become addicted to drugs, alcohol, tobacco, etc* 对麻醉药、酒、烟等上瘾了. **2** strongly interested in sth as a hobby or pastime 对某事物有强烈兴趣而成为嗜好或消遣的: *be addicted to TV soap operas* 沉迷于电视连续剧.

ad·dic·tion /əˈdɪkʃn; əˋdɪkʃən/ *n* [U, C] **~ (to sth)** condition of taking drugs, etc habitually and being unable to stop doing so without suffering adverse effects 瘾; 沉溺: *heroin addiction* 海洛因毒瘾 ○ *overcome one's addiction to alcohol* 克制酒瘾.

ad·dict·ive /əˈdɪktɪv; əˋdɪktɪv/ *adj* causing addiction 使人上瘾的: *addictive drugs* 使人上瘾的麻醉药物 ○ *Coffee is addictive in a mild way.* 咖啡能稍微使人上瘾.

ad·di·tion /əˈdɪʃn; əˋdɪʃən/ *n* **1** [U] adding, esp calculating the total of two or more numbers 加(尤指计算两个或两个以上数目的总和). **2** [C] **~ (to sth)** person or thing added or joined 增加的人或事物: *Such an outfit would be a useful addition to my wardrobe.* 在我的服装中添置这一套会有用的. ○ *They've just had an addition to the family*, ie another child. 他们家里刚刚又添了一口人(另一个孩子). ○ *Ann will be a very useful addition to our team.* 安来到我们队给我们增加了一员干将. **3** (idm 习语) **in addition (to sb/sth)** as an extra person, thing or circumstance 加之; 除...之外: *In addition (to the names on the list) there are six other applicants.* 除此(名单上的名字)之外, 还有六个申请人.

▷ **ad·di·tional** /-ʃənl; -ʃənl/ *adj* added; extra; supplementary 附加的; 另外的; 外加的: *additional charges, candidates, supplies* 外加的费用、候选人、供应. **ad·di·tion·ally** /-ʃənəlɪ; -ʃənlɪ/ *adv*.

ad·dit·ive /ˈædɪtɪv; ˋædətɪv/ *n* substance added in small amounts for a special purpose 为某目的而加进的少量

物质; 添加剂: *chemical additives in food* 食品中的化学添加剂 ○ *food additives*, ie to add colour or flavour to the food or to preserve it 食品添加剂(用以增加食物的颜色或味道或使之防腐).
▷ **ad·dit·ive** *adj* involving addition 添加的; 附加的.

addle /ˈædl; ˋædl/ *v* **1** [Tn] confuse (sth/sb); muddle 将(某事物)弄乱; 将(某人)弄糊涂; 使混乱: *My brain feels addled.* 我感到昏头昏脑的. **2** (**a**) [I] (of an egg) become rotten and not produce a chick (指蛋)变坏而不能孵化. (**b**) [Tn] cause (an egg) to become rotten 使(蛋)变坏: *addled eggs* 变坏了的蛋.

ad·dress[1] /əˈdres; *US* ˈædres; ˋædrɛs/ *n* **1** details of where a person lives, works or can be found, and where letters, etc may be delivered 住址; 地址; 通讯处: *Tell me if you change your address.* 如果你的地址改变了, 请告诉我. ○ *My home/business address is 3 West St, Oxford.* 我家[办公处]的地址是牛津西街3号. **2** speech made to an audience 演说; 演讲. **3** (*computing* 计) part of a computer instruction that specifies where a piece of information is stored (计算机指令中标明某信息储存于何处的)位址. **4** (idm 习语) **a form of address** ⇨ FORM[1].

ad·dress[2] /əˈdres; əˋdrɛs/ *v* **1** [Tn, Tn·pr] **~ sth (to sb/sth)** write on (a letter, parcel, etc) the name and address of the person, firm, etc that it is to be delivered to (在信件、包裹等上)写收件人或公司等的名字及地址: *The card was wrongly addressed to (us at) our old home.* 那张(给我们的)明信片误写了我们的旧地址. **2** [Tn] make a speech to (a person or an audience), esp formally 向(某人或听众)讲话(尤指正式地): *The chairman will now address the meeting.* 现在由主席向与会者讲话. **3** [Tn·pr] **~ sth to sb/sth** direct (a remark or written statement) to sb/sth 对某人[某事物]提出(意见或书面陈述): *Please address all complaints to the manager.* 一切意见均请向经理提出. **4** [Cn·n/a] **~ sb as sth** use (a particular name or title) in speaking or writing to sb 用(某姓名或头衔)称呼某人: *Don't address me as 'Colonel': I'm only a major.* 不要称我'上校', 我只是少校. **5** [Tn·pr] **~ oneself to sth** (*fml* 文) direct one's attention to (a problem); tackle sth 把注意力集中于(某问题); 致力于某事: *It is time we addressed ourselves to the main item on the agenda.* 现在我们该把注意力集中到议事日程上的主要项目上来了. **6** [Tn] take aim at (the ball) in golf (高尔夫球戏中)瞄准(球). **7** [Tn] (*computing* 计) store or retrieve (a piece of information) by using an address[1](3) (用计算机中的位址指令)存人或取出(信息).
▷ **ad·dressee** /ˌædreˈsiː; ˌædrɛsˋi/ *n* person to whom a letter, etc is addressed 收信人; 收件人.

ad·duce /əˈdjuːs; *US* əˈduːs; əˋdus/ *v* [Tn] (*fml* 文) put (sth) forward as an example or as proof 提出、举出(某事物)为例或为证; 引证: *I could adduce several reasons for his strange behaviour.* 对他的奇怪行为, 我能提出几点原因.

-ade *suff* 后缀 (with countable *ns* forming uncountable *ns* 与可数名词结合构成不可数名词) drink made from or tasting of the specified fruit 由某种水果制成的或有某种水果味道的饮料: *orangeade*.

ad·en·oids /ˈædɪnɔɪdz; *US* -dən-; ˋædn̩ˌɔɪdz/ *n* [pl] (*anatomy* 解) pieces of spongy tissue between the back of the nose and the throat, often making breathing and speaking difficult 腺样增殖体(鼻后与喉之间的海绵状组织, 常可造成呼吸及说话困难): *have one's adenoids out*, ie by a surgical operation 摘除某人的腺样增殖体(施外科手术) ○ (*infml* 口) *She's got adenoids*, ie is suffering from an inflammation of the adenoids. 她患腺样增殖症.
▷ **ad·en·oidal** /ˌædɪˈnɔɪdl; ˌædn̩ˋɔɪdl/ *adj* **1** of the adenoids 腺样增殖的. **2** affected by diseased adenoids 患腺样增殖症的: *an adenoidal child, voice* 患腺样增殖症的儿童、嗓音.

adept /ˈædept, əˈdept; ˋædɛpt, əˋdɛpt/ *adj* **~ (in sth); ~ (at/in doing sth)** expert or skilful in (doing) sth 对(做)某事物内行的, 熟练的: *She's adept at growing roses.* 她善于种玫瑰花.
▷ **adept** *n* **~ (at/in sth)** person who is skilful (in sth) (某事物的)行家; 内行; 熟手: *He's an adept in carpentry.* 他是木工行家.

ad·equate /ˈædɪkwət; ˋædəkwɪt/ *adj* **~ (to/for sth)** satisfactory in quantity or quality; sufficient (数量或质量)令人满意的; 足够的; 充分的; 适当的: *take adequate precautions* 采取适当的预防措施 ○ *Our accommodation is barely adequate.* 我们的住房不太够用. ○ *Their earnings are adequate (to their needs).* 他们挣的钱足够(需要). ○ *Your work is adequate but I'm sure you could do better.* 你的工作做得不错, 但是我肯定你还能做得更好. ○ *She has adequate grounds for a divorce.* 她离婚有充分的理由. ▷ **ad·equacy** /ˈædɪkwəsɪ; ˋædəkwəsɪ/ *n* [U]. **ad·equately** *adv*: *Are you adequately insured?* 你买的保险够不够?

ad·here /ədˈhɪə(r); ədˋhɪr/ *v* (*fml* 文) **1** [I, Ipr] **~ (to sth)** remain attached (to sth); stick (as if) by means of glue or suction 固着(于某物); 胶着; 黏着; 附着: *Paste is used to make one surface adhere to another.* 浆糊是用以使一个接触面粘住另一个接触面的. **2** [Ipr] **~ to sth** (**a**) give support to sth; remain faithful to sth 坚持某事物; 忠于某事物: *adhere to one's opinions, a promise, a political party* 坚持自己的意见、坚守诺言、忠于一政党. (**b**) act in accordance with sth; follow sth 依照某事物; 遵循某事物: *adhere to one's principles, a treaty, a schedule, the rules* 坚持自己的原则、遵守一条约、遵照一时间表、依照规则.

ad·her·ent /ədˈhɪərənt; ədˋhɪrənt/ *n* supporter of a party or doctrine (一政党或主义的)支持者, 拥护者: *The movement is gaining more and more adherents.* 支持这个运动的人越来越多了.
▷ **ad·her·ent** *adj* **~ (to sth)** sticking; adhering 黏着的; 附着的: *an adherent surface* 黏着面. **ad·her·ence** /-rəns; -rəns/ *n* [U] **~ (to sth)**: *their strict adherence to their religion* 他们对其宗教虔诚的信奉.

ad·he·sion /ədˈhiːʒn; ədˋhiʒən/ *n* **1** [U] **~ (to sth)** being or becoming attached (to sth) (与某物)黏合; 黏附, 附着(于某物). **2** [U] **~ (to sth)** (*fml* 文) support (for a plan, an ideology, a political party, etc) 支持, 拥护(一计划、思想、政党等). **3** (*medical* 医) (**a**) [U] unnatural growing together of body tissues that are normally separate, as a result of inflammation or injury 粘连(因炎症病变或损伤而使体内组织粘在一起). (**b**) [C] tissue formed in this way 粘连的组织: *painful adhesions caused by a wound that is slow to heal* 愈合缓慢的伤口引起的粘连疼痛.

ad·hes·ive /ədˈhiːsɪv; ədˋhisɪv/ *adj* that can adhere; causing things to adhere; sticky 可黏着的; 黏性的: *adhesive side of a stamp* 邮票[印花]有胶粘的一面 ○ *adhesive tape/plaster* 黏胶带[橡皮膏].
▷ **ad·hes·ive** *n* [C, U] substance that makes things stick 胶粘剂: *quick-drying adhesives* 快干胶(合剂). Cf 参看 CEMENT 2, GLUE.

ad hoc /ˌæd ˈhɒk; ˋædˋhɑk/ *adj, adv* (*Latin* 拉) **1** (made or arranged) for a particular purpose only; special(ly) 仅为某一目的(而做或安排)(的); 特别(的): *appoint an ad hoc committee to deal with the affair* 指定一特别委员会处理此事. **2** (in a way that is) not planned in advance; informal(ly) 非事先计划(的); 非正式(的): *Problems were solved on an ad hoc basis.* 做了一些变通问题便解决了. ○ *Points of policy are decided ad hoc.* 政策的条款是临时决定的.

adieu /əˈdjuː; *US* əˈduː; əˋdu/ *interj, n* (*pl* **adieus** or **adieux** /əˈdjuːz; *US* əˈduːz; əˋduz/) (*arch or fml* 古或文) **1** goodbye 再见: *Bidding them adieu we departed.* 我们向他们告别后就离开了. **2** (idm 习语) **make one's aˈdieus** say goodbye 告别; 辞行.

ad in·fin·itum /ˌæd ˌɪnfɪˈnaɪtəm; ˋædˌɪnfəˋnaɪtəm/ (*Latin* 拉) without limit; for ever 无限地; 永远地: *I don't want to go on working here ad infinitum.* 我不愿意永远在这里干下去.

ad·ip·ose /ˈædɪpəʊs; ˋædəˌpos/ *adj* [usu attrib 通常作定语] of animal fat; fatty 脂肪的; 多脂肪的: *a layer of adipose tissue under the skin* 皮下的一层脂肪组织. ▷ **ad·ip·os·ity** /ˌædɪˈpɒsətɪ; ˌædəˋpɑsətɪ/ *n* [U].

Adj *abbr* 缩写 = Adjutant.

ad·ja·cent /əˈdʒeɪsnt; əˋdʒesn̩t/ *adj* **~ (to sth)** situated near or next to sth; close or touching 与某物邻近的; 毗连的; 接近的; 相接触的: *We work in adjacent rooms.* 我们在邻接的房间里工作. ○ *My room is adjacent to his.* 我的房间与他的相连接. ▷ **ad·ja·cency** /-snsɪ; -sn̩sɪ/ *n* [U]. **ad·ja·cently** *adv*.
□ **adjacent ˈangles** (*geometry* 几) angles that share a

common line 邻角(有一条公共边的角). ⇨illus at ANGLE 见ANGLE之插图.

A

ad·ject·ive /ˈædʒɪktɪv; ˋædʒɪktɪv/ *n* (*grammar*) word that indicates a quality of the person or thing referred to by a noun, eg *old, rotten, foreign* in *an old house, rotten apples, foreign names* 形容词(表示作为名词的人或事物的性质的词, 如在 an old house、rotten apples、foreign names 中的 old、rotten、foreign).
▷ **ad·ject·ival** /ˌædʒekˈtaɪvl; ˌædʒɪkˋtaɪvl/ *adj* of or like an adjective 形容词的; 像形容词的: *an adjectival phrase/clause* 形容词短语 [从句]. **ad·ject·ivally** /ˌædʒekˈtaɪvəlɪ; ˌædʒɪkˋtaɪvl̩ɪ/ *adv*.

ad·join /əˈdʒɔɪn; əˋdʒɔɪn/ *v* [I, Tn] be next or nearest to and joined with (sth) 临近; 邻近; 接近; 毗连: *We heard laughter in the adjoining room.* 我们听到了邻屋的笑声. ○ *The playing-field adjoins the school.* 运动场紧靠着学校.

ad·journ /əˈdʒɜːn; əˋdʒɝn/ *v* **1 (a)** [Tn usu passive 通常用于被动语态] stop (a meeting, etc) for a time; postpone 停止(会议等)一段时间; 休(会); 使延期: *The trial was adjourned for a week/until the following week.* 审讯暂停一星期 [下星期继续进行]. **(b)** [I] (of people at a meeting, in court, etc) stop proceedings and separate (指会议、法庭等的人)休会、休庭: *The court will adjourn for lunch.* 法庭午餐时间休庭. ○ *Let's adjourn until tomorrow.* 咱们休会, 明天继续进行. **2** [Ipr] **~to...** (of people who have come together) go to another place (指聚集的人)到另一处去: *After dinner we all adjourned to the lounge.* 饭后我们都到休息室去了. ▷ **ad·journment** *n* [C, U]: *The judge granted us a short adjournment.* 法官准予我们短期休庭.

ad·judge /əˈdʒʌdʒ; əˋdʒʌdʒ/ *v* (*fml* 文) **1** (also **adjudicate**) [Tf, Cn·a, Cn·t] declare officially or decide by law 审判; 裁决; 依法判处: *The court adjudged that she was guilty.* 法院宣判她有罪. ○ *The court adjudged her (to be) guilty.* 法院判定她有罪. **2** [Tn·pr] **~ sth to sb** award sth to sb 将某事物判给、断与某人: *The court adjudged legal damages to her.* 法院将法定损害赔偿金判给了她.

ad·ju·dic·ate /əˈdʒuːdɪkeɪt; əˋdʒudɪˌket/ *v* **1 (a)** [I, Ipr] act as judge in a court, tribunal, contest, etc 判决; 裁决; 裁判: *Would you please adjudicate on who should get the prize?* 请你评判谁应该得奖好吗? **(b)** [Tn] judge and give a decision on (sth) 裁断, 裁定(某事物): *adjudicate sb's claim for damages* 裁定某人提出的对损害赔偿金的要求. **2** [Tf, Cn·a, Cn·t] = ADJUDGE 1.
▷ **ad·ju·dica·tion** /əˌdʒuːdɪˈkeɪʃn; əˌdʒudɪˋkeʃən/ *n* [U]. **ad·ju·dic·ator** *n* judge, esp in a competition 裁判, 评判员(尤指竞赛中者).

ad·junct /ˈædʒʌŋkt; ˋædʒʌŋkt/ *n* **1 ~ (to/of sth)** thing that is added or attached to sth else but is less important and not essential 附加物; 附属品; 附件. **2** (*grammar*) adverb or adverbial phrase added to a clause or sentence to modify the meaning of the verb 附加语, 修饰语(从句或句子中修饰或限定动词的副词或副词短语).

ad·jure /əˈdʒʊə(r); əˋdʒʊr/ *v* [Dn·t] (*fml* 文) command or request (sb) earnestly or solemnly 恳切地或郑重地命令或要求(某人): *I adjure you to tell the truth before this court.* 我要求你对本庭说实话. ▷ **ad·jura·tion** /ˌædʒʊəˈreɪʃn; ˌædʒʊˋreʃən/ *n* [U, C].

ad·just /əˈdʒʌst; əˋdʒʌst/ *v* **1** [Tn] **(a)** put (sth) into the correct order or position; arrange 整理; 整顿; 安排: *She carefully adjusted her clothes and her hair before going out.* 她出门之前仔细地整了整衣服和头发. **(b)** alter (sth) by a small amount so that it will fit or be right for use; regulate 校准; 调准; 校正: *adjust the rear mirror, the focus of a camera, the sights of a gun* 调准后视镜、照相机的焦距、枪炮的瞄准器 ○ *The brakes need adjusting.* 制动器需要调节了. ○ *Please do not adjust your set*, eg as a warning on a TV screen that the controls do not need to be changed. 请勿自行调节(如电视机屏幕上的警告语句, 意为各项操作装置无需更动). **2** [I, Ipr, Tn, Tn·pr] **~ (sth/oneself) (to sth)** become or make suited (to new conditions); adapt 使适合(新环境等); 适应: *former soldiers who have difficulty in adjusting to civilian life* 很难适应平民生活的退伍军人 ○ *The body quickly adjusts (itself) to changes in temperature.* 身体迅速(自行)调节以适应气温的变化. **3** [Tn] decide (the amount to be paid out for loss or damages) when settling an insurance claim (结算保险赔偿金时)评定(对损失应付的款额或损害赔偿).
▷ **ad·just·able** *adj* that can be adjusted 可调节的; 可调整的: *adjustable seat-belts* 可调节的座位安全带.
ad·just·ment *n* [C, U] (act of) adjusting 调节; 调整; (保险赔偿款额的)评定: *I've made a few minor adjustments to the seating plan.* 我对座次表作了小小的调整. ○ *Some adjustment of the lens may be necessary.* 可能有必要调节一下镜头.

ad·jut·ant /ˈædʒʊtənt; ˋædʒətənt/ *n* army officer responsible for administrative work in a battalion 副官.
□ ˌ**Adjutant** ˈ**General** high-ranking administrative officer in the army 副官处长.
ˈ**adjutant bird** type of large Indian stork 秃鹳(一种印度大鹳).

ad lib /ˌæd ˈlɪb; ædˈlɪb/ *adj* (*infml* 口) (esp of speaking and performing in public) without preparation; spontaneous (尤指当众讲话及表演)未经事先准备的, 即兴的, 即席的: *give an ad lib* (ie improvised) *performance* 作即兴表演.
▷ **ad lib** *adv* (*infml* 口) **1** without preparation; spontaneously 即兴地; 即席地; 临时地: *I had forgotten to bring my notes and had to speak ad lib.* 我忘记带讲稿了, 只好临时讲几句. **2** as one pleases; without restraint; freely 随便地; 无拘束地; 自由地: *We were told to help ourselves to the food ad lib.* 这些食物让我们随便吃.
ad lib *v* (**-bb-**) [I] (*infml* 口) speak or act without preparation, esp when performing in public; improvise 临时讲话或表演(尤指当众); 即席表演: *The actress often forgot her lines but was very good at ad libbing.* 那个女演员常忘台词, 却极擅长临时拼凑.

Adm *abbr* 缩写 = Admiral: *Adm (Richard) Hill* 海军上将(理查)希尔.

ad·man /ˈædmæn; ˋædˌmæn/ *n* (*pl* **admen** /ˈædmen; ˋædmɛn/) (*infml* 口) person who produces commercial advertisements 制作商业广告的人.

ad·mass /ˈædmæs; ˋædmæs/ *n* [sing] (*dated* 旧 *Brit*) section of the public that is thought to be easily influenced by advertising and the media 易受广告及传播媒介影响的大众.

ad·min·is·ter /ədˈmɪnɪstə(r); ədˋmɪnəstɚ/ *v* **1 (a)** [Tn, Dn·pr] **~ sth (to sb)** (*fml* 文) hand out or give sth formally; provide 正式发给或给予某事物; 供给: *administer punishment, justice, comfort* 予以惩罚、主持正义、给予安慰 ○ *administer relief to famine victims* 向饥民发放救济品 ○ *administer the last rites to a dying man* 为临死的人主持临终仪式 ○ *administer an oath to sb*, ie hear him swear it officially 使某人宣誓. **(b)** [Tn] put (sth) into operation; apply 执行; 施行; 实施: *administer the law* 执法. **2** [Tn] control the affairs of (a business, etc); manage 管理(业务等); 治理: *administer a charity, a trust fund, an estate* 经管慈善事业、信托基金、地产 ○ *administer* (ie govern) *a country* 治理国家.

ad·min·is·tra·tion /ədˌmɪnɪˈstreɪʃn; ədˌmɪnəˋstreʃən/ *n* **1** [U] **~ (of sth)** administering; giving 实施; 执行; 给予; 供给: *be responsible for the administration of justice, the law, charitable aid, an oath, a remedy* 负责赏罚、执法、慈善救济、主持宣誓、用药. **2** [U] management of public or business affairs 公共事务的管理; 经营; 行政: *He works in hospital administration.* 他从事医院管理工作. ○ *Head teachers are more involved in administration than in teaching.* 校长的行政工作比教学工作多. **3** (often 常作 **the Administration**) [C] (part of the Government that manages public affairs during the) period of office of a US President 美国总统任期; 美国总统任期内的政府: *during the Kennedy Administration* 在肯尼迪总统任期内 ○ *Successive administrations have failed to solve the country's economic problems.* 历届政府均未能解决国家的经济问题.

ad·min·is·trat·ive /ədˈmɪnɪstrətɪv; *US* -streɪtɪv; ədˋmɪnəˌstretɪv/ *adj* of or involving the management of public or business affairs 管理公共事务的; 经营的; 行政的: *an administrative post, problem* 行政职位、问题 ○ *Her duties are purely administrative.* 她的职责纯粹是行政方面的. ▷ **ad·min·is·trat·ively** *adv*: *administratively complicated* 行政上复杂的.

ad·min·is·trator /ədˈmɪnɪstreɪtə(r); ədˋmɪnəˌstretɚ/ *n*

1 (a) person responsible for managing (esp business) affairs 管理人; 行政人员. (b) person able to manage well 有管理能力的人; 有行政才能的人: *She's an excellent administrator.* 她是个优秀的管理人员. 2 (*law* 律) person appointed to manage the property of others 被指定管理他人财产的人.

ad·mir·able /ˈædmərəbl; ˋædmərəbl̩/ *adj* deserving or causing admiration; excellent 令人钦佩的; 极好的: *an admirable performance* 优美的表演 ○ *His handling of the situation was admirable.* 他对这情况的处理令人钦佩. ▷ **ad·mir·ably** /-əblɪ; -əblɪ/ *adv*.

ad·miral /ˈædmərəl; ˋædmərəl/ *n* (a) naval officer of high rank; officer commanding a fleet or squadron 海军将官; 舰队司令: *rear-admiral* 海军少将 ○ *vice-admiral* 海军中将 ○ *The admiral visits the ships under his command by helicopter.* 舰队司令乘直升机视察他所指挥的军舰. (b) **Admiral** naval officer of the second highest rank 海军上将. ⇨ App 9 见附录 9.
▷ **ad·mir·alty** /-əltɪ; -əltɪ/ *n* [Gp] **the Admiralty** (*Brit*) (formerly) Government department controlling the Navy (旧时)海军部.
□ ˌ**Admiral of the** ˈ**Fleet** (*US* ˌ**Fleet** ˈ**Admiral**) commander-in-chief of the Navy 海军元帅.

ad·mira·tion /ˌædməˈreɪʃn; ˏædməˋreʃən/ *n* 1 [U] feeling of respect, warm approval or pleasure 钦佩; 赞赏; 羡慕: *Her handling of the crisis fills me with admiration.* 她对这一危机的处理使我赞叹不已. ○ *I have great admiration for his courage.* 我十分佩服他的勇气. ○ *They looked in silent admiration at the painting.* 他们默默地欣赏着那幅画. 2 [sing] person or thing that is admired 受到赞赏的人或事物: *He was the admiration of his whole family.* 他受到全家人的敬重. 3 (idm 习语) **a mutual admiration society** ⇨ MUTUAL.

ad·mire /ədˈmaɪə(r); ədˋmaɪr/ *v* 1 [Tn, Tn·pr, Tsg] ~ **sb/sth (for sth)** regard sb/sth with respect, pleasure, satisfaction, etc 钦佩、赞赏、羡慕某人[某事物]: *They admired our garden.* 他们称赞我们的花园. ○ *I admire him for his success in business.* 我佩服他事业有成. 2 [Tn] express admiration of (sb/sth) 表示赞美, 夸奖(某人[某事物]): *Aren't you going to admire my new hat?* 你难道不想夸夸我的新帽子吗? ▷ **ad·mirer** *n* (a) person who admires sb/sth 赞赏者; 羡慕者: *I am not a great admirer of her work.* 我对她的工作不太欣赏. (b) man who admires and is attracted to a woman 爱慕某女子的男子: *She has many admirers.* 她有许多追求者.
ad·mir·ing *adj* showing or feeling admiration 赞赏的; 赞美的; 羡慕的: *give sb/receive admiring glances* 投以[赢得]赞赏的目光 ○ *be welcomed by admiring fans* 受到崇拜者的欢迎. **ad·mir·ingly** *adv*.

ad·miss·ible /ədˈmɪsəbl; ədˋmɪsəbl̩/ *adj* 1 (*law* 律) that can be allowed 可容许的; 可采纳的: *admissible evidence* 可采纳的证据. 2 (*fml* 文) worthy of being accepted or considered 值得接受的; 值得考虑的: *Such behaviour is not admissible among our staff.* 这种行为在我们职员中是不允许的. ▷ **ad·miss·ib·il·ity** /ədˌmɪsəˈbɪlətɪ; ədˏmɪsəˋbɪlətɪ/ *n* [U]. **ad·miss·ibly** /-blɪ; -blɪ/ *adv*.

ad·mis·sion /ədˈmɪʃn; ədˋmɪʃən/ *n* 1 [U] ~ **(to/into sth)** entering or being allowed to enter a building, society, school, etc 进入或获准进入某建筑物、社团、学校等: *Admission (to the club) is restricted to members only.* 只准会员进入(俱乐部). ○ *Admission to British universities depends on examination results.* 英国大学入学以考试成绩为凭. ○ *A week after his admission into the army, he fell ill.* 他入伍后一星期就病了. ○ *Do they charge for admission?* 入场要收费吗? ○ *How does one gain admission to the Buckingham Palace?* 怎样才能获准进入白金汉宫? 2 [U] money charged for being admitted to a public place 公众场所入场费; 门票钱: *You have to pay £2 admission.* 你须付2英镑入场费. 3 [U] ~ **(of sth)**; ~ **(that...)** statement acknowledging the truth of sth; confession 承认; 招认; 供认; 坦白: *an admission that one has lied* 对自己说了谎的供认 ○ *Her resignation amounts to an admission of failure.* 她的辞职等于承认失败. 4 (idm 习语) **by/on one's own adˈmission** as one has oneself admitted 如其自己所承认的: *He is a coward by his own admission.* 他自己承认是个胆小鬼.

ad·mit /ədˈmɪt; ədˋmɪt/ *v* **(-tt-)** 1 [Tn, Tn·pr] ~ **sb/sth (into/to sth)** (a) allow sb/sth to enter 许可某人[某物]进入: *That man is not to be admitted.* 不准那个人进来. ○ *Each ticket admits two people to the party.* 每张票可供两人入场参加聚会. ○ *The small window admitted very little light.* 那扇小窗户只能透进一点光线. (b) accept sb into a hospital as a patient, or into a school, etc as a pupil 接受某人(入院或入学等): *The school admits sixty new boys and girls every year.* 这所学校每年招收六十名男女新生. ○ *He was admitted to hospital with minor burns.* 他因轻度烧伤而入院. 2 [Tn] (of an enclosed space) have room for (sb/sth) (指一范围内)可容纳(某人[某事物]): *The theatre admits only 250 people.* 这家戏院只能容纳250人. 3 [Ipr, Tn, Tf, Tnt, Tg] ~ **to sth/doing sth** recognize or acknowledge sth as true, often reluctantly; confess sth 承认, 供认, 招认(常为不情愿地); 坦白某事物: *George would never admit to being wrong.* 乔治从不认错. ○ *The prisoner has admitted his guilt.* 犯人认罪了. ○ *I admit my mistake/that I was wrong.* 我承认是我的错[我错了]. ○ *I admit (that) you have a point.* 我承认你有理. ○ *He admitted having stolen the car.* 他招认偷了那辆汽车. ○ *It is now generally admitted to have been* (ie Most people agree and accept that it was) *a mistake.* 如今人们公认这是个错误. 4 [Ipr] ~ **of sth** (*fml* 文) allow the possibility of sth; leave room for sth 容许某事物; 对某事物留有余地: *His conduct admits of no excuse.* 他的行为无可宽恕. ○ *The plan does not admit of improvement*, ie cannot be improved. 这项计划已无改进余地了(已尽善尽美). 5 (idm 习语) **be admitted to sb's presence** (*fml* 文) be allowed to enter the room, etc where sb (esp sb important) is 获准会见某人(尤指要人).
▷ **ad·mit·ted** *adj* [attrib 作定语] as one has admitted oneself to be 自己承认的: *an admitted liar* 直认不讳的说谎者. **ad·mit·tedly** *adv* (esp in initial position 尤用于句首) as is or must be admitted 无可否认地; 诚然: *Admittedly, he didn't know that at the time.* 无可否认, 他当时并不知道. ○ *Admittedly, I've never actually been there.* 说实在的, 我从未去过那里.

ad·mit·tance /ədˈmɪtns; ədˋmɪtn̩s/ *n* [U] allowing sb or being allowed to enter (esp a private place); right of entry 准许某人或某人获准进入(尤指私人场所); 进入的权利: *No admittance — keep out!* 严禁入内! ○ *I was refused admittance to the house.* 我被拒之门外.

ad·mix·ture /ædˈmɪkstʃə(r); ædˋmɪkstʃɚ/ *n* (*fml* 文) (a) [C] thing added, esp as a minor ingredient 混合物, 搀合物(尤指次要成分). (b) [U] process of adding this 混合; 搀合.

ad·mon·ish /ədˈmɒnɪʃ; ədˋmɑnɪʃ/ *v* (*fml* 文) 1 [Tn, Tn·pr] ~ **sb (for/against sth)** give a mild but firm warning or scolding to sb 温和而严正地警告或责备某人: *The teacher admonished the boys for being lazy.* 老师责备男学生懒惰. 2 [Dn·t] advise or urge (sb) seriously 劝告或告诫(某人): *She admonished us to seek professional help.* 她劝我们向专业人士求助.
▷ **ad·mon·ish·ment, ad·moni·tion** /ˌædməˈnɪʃn; ˏædməˋnɪʃən/ *ns* [U, C] (*fml* 文) warning 警告.
ad·mon·it·ory /ədˈmɒnɪtrɪ; *US* -tɔːrɪ; ədˋmɑnəˏtɔrɪ/ *adj* (*fml* 文) admonishing 劝告的; 轻责的: *an admonitory letter, tone of voice* 劝告的信、语气.

ad nau·seam /ˌæd ˈnɔːzɪæm; ˋædˋnɔzɪˏæm/ (*Latin* 拉) to an excessive or sickening extent 达到过分或厌烦的程度: *play the same four records ad nauseam*, ie again and again so that it becomes irritating 没完没了地播放那四张唱片(一遍又一遍而使人生厌).

ado /əˈduː; əˋdu/ *n* [U] trouble; fuss; unnecessary activity (used esp as in the expressions shown) 麻烦, 忙乱, 无谓的纷扰(尤用于以下示例): *Without more/much/further ado, we set off.* 我们出发的时候没有更多的[什么/进一步的]麻烦. ○ *It was all much ado about nothing.* 完全是庸人自扰.

adobe /əˈdəʊbɪ; əˋdobɪ/ *n* [U] 1 brick made of clay and straw and dried in the sun 土坯(用黏土与草所制, 晒干而成): [attrib 作定语] *adobe houses* 土坯砌成的房子. 2 clay from which this type of brick is made 制土坯的黏土.

ado·les·cence /ˌædəˈlesns; ˏædl̩ˋɛsn̩s/ *n* [U] time in a person's life between childhood and mature adulthood 青春, 青春期(童年与成年之间的时期): *during (one's) adolescence* 在(某人的)青春期间.
▷ **ado·les·cent** /ˌædəˈlesnt; ˏædl̩ˋɛsn̩t/ *adj* of or typical

of adolescence 青春期的；青春期特有的：*adolescent boys, crises, attitudes* 青春期的男子、易出现的问题、心态. — *n* young person between childhood and adulthood (ie roughly between the ages of 13 and 17) 青少年(介于儿童与成人之间的年轻人，大约13至17岁之间者).

ad·opt /əˈdɒpt; əˈdɑpt/ *v* **1** [Tn, Tn·pr] **~ sb (as sth)** take sb into one's family, esp as one's child or heir 收养某人(尤指作为儿女或继承人)；过继：*Having no children of their own they decided to adopt an orphan.* 他们因没有亲生儿女，所以决定领养一个孤儿. ○ *Paul's mother had him adopted because she couldn't look after him herself.* 保罗的母亲因为自己无力抚养他，便将他送给别人收养了. ○ *He is their adopted son.* 他是他们的养子. Cf 参看 FOSTER 2. **2** [Tn·pr] **~ sb as sth** choose sb as a candidate or representative 挑选某人作候选人或代表：*She has been adopted as Labour candidate for York.* 她被提名为约克郡的工党候选人. **3** [Tn] take over and have or use (sth) as one's own 采纳；采取；采用：*adopt a name, a custom, an idea, a style of dress* 取名、随俗、采纳一意见、采用一服装式样 ○ *adopt a hard line towards terrorists* 对恐怖分子采取强硬态度 ○ *her adopted country*, ie not her native country but the one in which she has chosen to live 她所选择居留的国家(非其祖国而由其自择居留的国家). **4** [Tn] accept (eg a report or recommendation); approve 接受，通过(如报告或建议)；批准：*Congress has adopted the new measures.* 国会通过了新的议案.

▷ **ad·op·tion** /əˈdɒpʃn; əˈdɑpʃən/ *n* [C, U] (act of) adopting or being adopted 收养；过继；挑选；采纳；采取；采用；接受：*offer a child for adoption* 将孩子送给他人收养 ○ *her adoption as Labour candidate for York* 她作为约克郡工党候选人的提名 ○ *the country of her adoption* 她所选择居留的国家 ○ *This textbook has had adoptions* (ie been officially chosen for special study) *in many countries.* 这本教科书已被很多国家采用.

ad·op·tive *adj* [usu attrib 通常作定语] related by adoption 有收养关系的；过继的；采纳的；接受的：*his adoptive parents* 他的养父养母.

ad·or·able /əˈdɔːrəbl; əˈdorəbl̩/ *adj* very attractive; delightful; lovable 迷人的；讨人喜欢的；可爱的：*What an adorable child!* 多可爱的孩子！○ *Your dress is absolutely adorable.* 你的衣服太漂亮了. ○ *My darling, you are adorable.* 亲爱的，你真迷人. ▷ **ad·or·ably** /-əblɪ; -əblɪ/ *adv*.

ad·ore /əˈdɔː(r); əˈdor/ *v* **1** [Tn] (**a**) love deeply and respect (sb) highly 热爱；爱慕；敬爱；崇敬；敬仰：*He adores his wife and children.* 他深爱妻儿. (**b**) worship (God) 崇拜(上帝). **2** [Tn, Tg] (*infml* 口) (not used in the continuous tenses 不用于进行时态) like (sth) very much 非常喜爱(某事物)：*adore ice-cream, Paris, skiing* 非常喜欢冰激凌、巴黎、滑雪 ○ *I simply adore that dress!* 我简直太喜欢那件连衣裙了.

▷ **ad·ora·tion** /ˌædəˈreɪʃn; ˌædəˈreʃən/ *n* [U] great love or worship 热爱；爱慕；敬爱；崇敬；崇拜：*be filled with adoration* 充满敬意 ○ *They knelt in adoration of their gods.* 他们跪拜诸神.

ad·or·ing *adj* [usu attrib 通常作定语] showing great love 表示爱慕的：*his adoring grandmother* 他慈爱的祖母 ○ *give sb an adoring look* 向某人投以爱慕的目光.

ad·or·ingly *adv*.

ad·orn /əˈdɔːn; əˈdorn/ *v* [Tn, Tn·pr] **~ sth/sb/oneself (with sth)** add beauty or ornament to sth/sb/oneself 装饰某物[某人/自己]；装点；佩带；装扮：*admire the paintings that adorn the walls* 欣赏那些装点四壁的绘画 ○ *The dancer was adorned with flowers.* 跳舞的人戴着很多花.

▷ **ad·orn·ment** *n* **1** [U] act of adorning 装饰；装点；佩带；装扮：*a simple dress without adornment* 朴素而无装饰的连衣裙. **2** [C] thing that adorns; ornament 装饰物；装饰品：*Many adornments were carved on the temple walls.* 寺院的墙壁上刻着很多装饰物.

ad·renal /əˈdriːnl; əˈdrinl̩/ *adj* (*anatomy* 解) close to the kidneys 肾旁的；肾上的.

□ **aˈdrenal gland** (*anatomy* 解) either of the two ductless glands above the kidney that produce adrenalin 肾上腺.

ad·ren·alin /əˈdrenəlɪn; ædˈrɛnl̩ɪn/ *n* [U] (*medical* 医) (**a**) hormone produced by the adrenal glands that increases the heart rate and stimulates the nervous system, causing a feeling of excitement 肾上腺素. (**b**) this substance prepared synthetically for medical use (药用)合成肾上腺素.

adrift /əˈdrɪft; əˈdrɪft/ *adj* [pred 作表语] **1** (**a**) (esp of a boat) driven by wind and water and out of control; drifting (尤指船)随风及水流漂浮而失去控制；漂浮：*cut a boat adrift from its moorings* 割断系索使小船漂离系泊处 ○ *The survivors were adrift on a raft for six days.* 幸存者在筏子上漂浮了六天. (**b**) (*fig* 比喻) having no purpose; aimless 没有目的；无目标：*young people adrift in our big cities* 在我们大城市里四处游荡的年轻人 ○ *turn sb adrift*, ie send sb away without help or support 逐出某人(使其漂泊流浪). **2** (*infml* 口) (**a**) unfastened; loose 脱开；松开：*Part of the car's bumper had come adrift.* 汽车的保险杠有一处松动了. (**b**) out of order; wrong 有故障；出错；有毛病：*Our plans went badly adrift.* 我们的计划严重受挫.

adroit /əˈdrɔɪt; əˈdrɔɪt/ *adj* **~ (at/in sth)** skilful; clever 熟练的；机敏的；灵巧的：*the minister's adroit handling of the crisis* 部长应付难关的巧妙手段 ○ *He soon became adroit at steering the boat.* 他很快就熟练掌握了驾船技术. Cf 参看 MALADROIT. ▷ **adroitly** *adv* **adroit·ness** *n* [U].

ad·sorb /ædˈsɔːb; ædˈsorb/ *v* [Tn] (usu of a solid) attract and hold (a gas or liquid) to its surface (常指固体)吸附(气体或液体)至其表面：*Iron adsorbs oxygen.* 铁能吸附氧. ▷ **ad·sorb·ent** /-ənt; -ənt/ *adj*. **ad·sorp·tion** /ədˈsɔːpʃn; ædˈsorpʃən/ *n* [U].

ADT /ˌeɪ diː ˈtiː; ˌe di ˈti/ *abbr* 缩写 = (in Canada, Puerto Rico and Bermuda) Atlantic Daylight Time (用于加拿大、波多黎各、百慕大的)大西洋夏令时间.

adu·la·tion /ˌædjʊˈleɪʃn; *US* ˌædʒʊˈl-; ˌædʒəˈleʃən/ *n* [U] excessive admiration or praise; flattery 谄媚；奉承；吹捧；恭维：*the fans' adulation of their favourite pop stars* 歌迷们对他们所喜爱的流行曲歌手的吹捧. ▷ **adu·lat·ory** *adj*.

ad·ult /ˈædʌlt, *also* əˈdʌlt; ˈædʌlt, əˈdʌlt/ *adj* **1** (**a**) grown to full size or strength 发育成熟的：*adult monkeys* 发育成熟的猴子. (**b**) intellectually and emotionally mature 智力及情感上已成熟的：*His behaviour is not particularly adult.* 他的举止行为还不太成熟. **2** (*law* 律) old enough to vote, marry, etc 已成人的(已达投票、结婚等年龄的).

▷ **ad·ult** *n* adult person or animal 成年的人或动物：*These films are suitable for adults only.* 这些电影只适宜成人观看. ○ *The bear was a fully grown adult.* 那只熊已完全发育成熟. ○ [attrib 作定语] *adult education*, ie for those over the usual school age 成人教育(为超过学龄的人而设).

adult·hood *n* [U] state of being adult 成年：*reach adulthood* 已到成年.

adul·ter·ate /əˈdʌltəreɪt; əˈdʌltəˌret/ *v* [Tn] make (sth) poorer in quality by adding another substance 使(某物)质量因掺入它物而变劣；掺假；掺杂：*adulterated milk*, eg with water added 掺假的奶(如加水的). ▷ **adul·tera·tion** /əˌdʌltəˈreɪʃn; əˌdʌltəˈreʃən/ *n* [U].

adul·tery /əˈdʌltərɪ; əˈdʌltərɪ/ *n* [U] voluntary sexual intercourse between a married person and sb who is not that person's husband or wife 通奸：*commit adultery* 犯通奸.

▷ **adul·terer** /əˈdʌltərə(r); əˈdʌltərɚ/ (*fem* 阴性作 **adul·ter·ess** /əˈdʌltərɪs; əˈdʌltərɪs/) *n* person who commits adultery 通奸者.

adul·ter·ous /əˈdʌltərəs; əˈdʌltərəs/ *adj* of or involving adultery 通奸的：*have an adulterous affair with sb* 与某人有奸情.

ad·um·brate /ˈædʌmbreɪt; ædˈʌmbret/ *v* [Tn] (*fml* 文) **1** indicate (sth) faintly or in outline 略微地或概括地暗示(某事物). **2** suggest (esp a coming event) in advance; foreshadow 预示，预告(尤指即将发生的事)；预兆. ▷ **ad·um·bra·tion** /ˌædʌmˈbreɪʃn; ˌædʌmˈbreʃən/ *n* [U, C].

ad·vance[1] /ədˈvɑːns; *US* -ˈvæns; ədˈvæns/ *n* **1** [C usu *sing* 通常作单数] forward movement 前进；推进；前移：*The enemy's advance was halted.* 敌军的推进遭到了遏止. **2** (**a**) [U] progress 进步；发展：*the continued advance of civilization* 文明的不断进步. (**b**) [C] **~ (in sth)** improvement 改进；进展；改善：*recent advances in* *medical science* 医学上的新进展. **3** [C] **~ (on sth)** increase in price or amount 价格或数量的增加: *'Any advance on* (ie Who will offer more than) *£20?' called the auctioneer.* 拍卖人喊道：'20英镑, 还有增加的吗?' ○ *Share prices showed significant advances today.* 今日股票价格大幅上涨. **4** [C] money paid before it is due, or for work only partially completed; loan 预付; 预支; 借贷: *The bank gave/made her an advance of £500.* 银行贷给她500英镑. ○ *She asked for an advance on her salary.* 她请求预支薪水. **5 advances** [pl] **~ (to sb)** attempts to establish a friendly or an amorous relationship or a business agreement 亲近; 套交情; 求爱; 拉关系: *He made advances to her.* 他向她示爱. ○ *She rejected his advances.* 她拒绝了他的追求. **6** (idm 习语) **in advance (of sth)** beforehand; ahead in time 预先; 事先; 事前: *The rent must be paid in advance.* 租金须预付. ○ *Send your luggage on in advance.* 请把行李预先送出. ○ *It's impossible to know in advance what will happen.* 预知未来发生的事是不可能的. ○ *Galileo's ideas were well in advance of the age in which he lived.* 伽利略的思想远远超越了他所生活的时代.

▷ **ad·vance** *adj* [attrib 作定语] **1** going before others 先行的; 先头的: *the advance party*, ie a group (of explorers, soldiers, etc) sent on ahead 先遣队; 先头部队. **2** done or provided in advance 预先做好的; 预先供给的: *give sb advance warning/notice of sth* 对某事物给某人预先警告[通知] ○ *make an advance booking*, ie reserve a hotel room, a seat in a theatre, etc before the time when it is needed 预定(旅馆房间、戏票等) ○ *an advance copy of a new book*, ie one supplied before publication 新书样本(出版前提供者).

ad·vance² /əd'vɑːns; US -'væns; əd'væns/ *v* **1** **(a)** [I, Ipr, In/pr] **~ (on/towards sb/sth)** come or go forward 前进: *The mob advanced towards/on us shouting angrily.* 暴徒们怒吼着向我们涌来. ○ *Our troops have advanced two miles.* 我们的部队已经前进了两英里. **(b)** [I] (*fig* 比喻) make progress 进步: *advance in one's career* 在事业上进步 ○ *Has civilization advanced during this century?* 本世纪文明有所进步吗? **2** [Tn] move or put (sb/sth) forward 向前移动或推进(某人[某事物]): *The general advanced his troops at night.* 将军夜晚将部队向前推进. ○ *He advanced his queen to threaten his opponent's king*, ie in a game of chess. 他向前走后棋, 直逼对方的王棋(于国际象棋棋局中). Cf 参看 RETREAT 1. **3** [Tn] help the progress of (sth); promote (a person, plan, etc) 促进(某事物); 推动(某人、计划等): *Such conduct is unlikely to advance your interests.* 这种行为对你可不大有利. **4** [Tn] (*fml* 文) make or present (a claim, suggestion, etc) 作出, 提出(要求、建议等): *Scientists have advanced a new theory to explain this phenomenon.* 科学家已提出一种新理论来解释这一现象. **5** [Dn·n, Dn·pr] **~ sth (to sb)** pay (money) before it is due to be paid; lend (money) 预付(钱); 借(钱): *The bank advanced me £2 000.* 银行借给我2 000英镑. ○ *He asked his employer to advance him a month's salary.* 他请求雇主先预支一个月的薪水. **6** [Tn, Tn·pr] bring (an event) to an earlier date 提前; 提早: *The date of the meeting was advanced from 10 to 3 June.* 会议日期已由6月10日提前到6月3日. Cf 参看 POSTPONE 1. **7** **(a)** [Tn] increase (a price) 提高(价格); 涨(价). **(b)** [I] (of prices, costs, etc) rise (指价格、成本、费用等)上涨: *Property values continue to advance rapidly.* 房地产价值继续急速上涨.

▷ **ad·vanced** *adj* **1** far on in life or progress 在生命或进程中远远在前的: *be advanced in years* 年事已高 ○ *She died at an advanced age.* 她活到高龄才去世. **2** not elementary 非初步的; 高深的; 高等的: *advanced studies* 高深的研究. **3** new and not yet generally accepted 新的而尚未被普遍接受的; 先进的; 先驱的; 超前的: *have advanced ideas* 有先进的思想.

□ **advanced 'credit** (also **advanced 'standing**) (*US*) credit given by one college for courses taken at another 跨校学分(大专院校对学生在其它院校所学课程给予的学分).

Ad'vanced level (also **A level** /'eɪ levl; 'e lɛvl/) (in Britain) higher level in the General Certificate of Education examinations (英国普通教育文凭考试中的)高级程度. Cf 参看 A/S LEVEL, ORDINARY LEVEL (ORDINARY), GENERAL CERTIFICATE OF SECONDARY EDUCATION (GENERAL).

ad·vance·ment /əd'vɑːnsmənt; US -'vænsmənt; əd'vænsmənt/ *n* [U] **1** act of advancing; furthering 前进; 进步; 促进; 推进; 提出; 预付; 提前; (价格)上涨: *the advancement of learning* 学问的进展. **2** promotion in rank or status 级别或地位的晋升; 升级: *The job offers good opportunities for advancement.* 这份工作有很好的晋升机会.

ad·vant·age /əd'vɑːntɪdʒ; US -'væn-; əd'væntɪdʒ/ *n* **1** **(a)** [C] **~ (over sb)** condition or circumstance that gives one superiority or success (esp when competing with others) (尤指与他人竞争时)优越的或成功的条件或环境; 优势: *gain an advantage over an opponent* 获得超越对手的优势 ○ *He has the advantage of a steady job.* 他有工作稳定的有利条件. ○ *Her French upbringing gives her certain advantages over other students in her class.* 她有法国式的教养, 使她比班上其他同学略胜一筹. **(b)** [U] benefit; profit 益处; 利益: *There is little advantage in buying a dictionary if you can't read.* 如果不识字, 买字典就没有什么用了. **2** [sing] (in tennis) first point scored after deuce (网球中)局末或盘末平分后所得的第一分: [attrib 作定语] *Becker reached advantage point several times before losing the game.* 贝克于打平局后曾有几次先得分, 后来才输的. **3** (idm 习语) **have the advantage of sb** be in a better position than sb, esp in knowing sth that he does not know 比某人强, 占上风(尤指知其所不知): *You have the advantage of me, I'm afraid*, eg said when a stranger addresses one by name. 您认识我, 我还不认识您, 失敬得很(如被陌生人直呼姓名时所说的话). **take advantage of sth/sb** **(a)** make use of sth well, properly, etc 充分利用: *They took full advantage of the hotel's facilities.* 他们充分利用旅馆的设备. **(b)** make use of sb/sth unfairly or deceitfully to get what one wants; exploit sb/sth (为达到个人目的而不正当地或不老实地)利用某人或某事: *She took advantage of my generosity*, ie took more than I had intended to give. 她利用了我的慷慨(取得比我想给的多). ○ *He's using his charm to try to take advantage of her*, ie seduce her. 他用魅力企图占她的便宜(诱奸她). **to ad'vantage** in a way that shows the best aspects of sth 用某种方法使优点突出: *The picture may be seen to (its best) advantage against a plain wall.* 这幅画衬在素墙上就更加(格外)好看了. **to sb's advantage** with results which are profitable or helpful to sb 其结果对某人有利或有帮助: *The agreement is/works to our advantage.* 协议对我们有利. **turn sth to one's (own) ad'vantage** cause (a situation or an event) to lead to personal profit; make the most of sth 使(情况或事情)导致个人获利; 充分利用某事物.

▷ **ad·vant·age** *v* [Tn] (*fml* 文) be beneficial to (sb); profit 有益于(某人); 有利于.

ad·vant·age·ous /ˌædvən'teɪdʒəs; ˌædvən'tedʒəs/ *adj* **~ (to sb)** profitable; beneficial 有利的; 有益的. **ad·vant·age·ously** *adv*.

ad·vent /'ædvənt; 'ædvɛnt/ *n* [sing] **1 the ~ of sth/sb** the approach or arrival of (an important person, event, etc) (重要人物、事件等的)来临, 到来: *With the advent of the new chairman, the company began to prosper.* 随着新主席的到来, 公司也开始有了起色. **2 Advent** **(a)** the period (with four Sundays) before Christmas 基督降临节(圣诞节前包括四个星期日的期间): [attrib 作定语] *Advent hymns* 基督降临节圣歌. **(b)** (*Bible* 圣经) the coming of Christ 基督降临.

▷ **Ad·vent·ist** /'ædvəntɪst, *also* əd'ventɪst; 'ædvɛntɪst/ *n* member of a religious group believing that Christ's second coming is very near 基督复临论者(相信基督即将复临的教徒).

ad·ven·ti·tious /ˌædven'tɪʃəs; ˌædvɛn'tɪʃəs/ *adj* (*fml* 文) not planned; accidental 未经计划的; 偶然的: *an adventitious occurrence* 偶发事件.

ad·ven·ture /əd'ventʃə(r); əd'ventʃɚ/ *n* **1** [C] unusual, exciting or dangerous experience or undertaking 不寻常的, 有刺激性的或危险的经历或工作; 奇遇; 冒险: *have an adventure* 有一次奇遇 ○ *her adventures in Africa* 她在非洲的冒险经历. **2** [U] excitement associated with danger, taking risks, etc 涉及危险、冒险等的刺激: *a love/spirit/sense of adventure* 对冒险的爱好[冒险的精神/冒险的意识] ○ *a life full of adventure* 充满惊险刺激的生活 ○ [attrib 作定语] *adventure stories* 惊险故事.

A

▷ **ad·ven·turer** /əd'ventʃərə(r); əd'ventʃərə/ (*fem* 阴性作 **ad·ven·tur·ess** /əd'ventʃərɪs; əd'ventʃərɪs/) *n* **1** person who seeks adventures 冒险家. **2** (*often derog* 常作贬义) person who is ready to take risks or act dishonestly, immorally, etc in seeking personal gain 投机分子(为谋私利甘冒风险或做不诚实、不道德的事的人).

ad·ven·tur·ous *adj* **1** eager for or fond of adventure 渴望冒险的; 喜欢冒险的: *adventurous children* 喜欢冒险的儿童. **2** full of danger and excitement 充满危险和刺激的; 惊险的: *an adventurous holiday* 惊险刺激的假日. **ad·ven·tur·ously** *adv*.

□ **ad'venture playground** playground containing objects and structures of wood, metal, etc for children to play with, in or on 惊险乐园(内有木制、铁制等物体或构架供儿童玩耍或攀登).

ad·verb /'ædvɜ:b; 'ædvɝb/ *n* (*grammar*) word that adds more information about place, time, circumstance, manner, cause, degree, etc to a verb, an adjective, a phrase or another adverb 副词(对动词、形容词、短语或另一副词增加地点、时间、环境、方式、原因、程度等信息的词): *In 'speak kindly', 'incredibly deep', 'just in time' and 'too quickly', 'kindly', 'incredibly', 'just' and 'too' are all adverbs.* 在 speak kindly、incredibly deep、just in time、too quickly 中, kindly、incredibly、just、too 都是副词.

▷ **ad·ver·bial** /əd'vɜ:bɪəl; əd'vɝbɪəl/ *adj* of, like or containing an adverb 副词或状语的; 像副词或状语的; 含有副词或状语的: *'Very quickly indeed' is an adverbial phrase.* very quickly indeed 是副词短语. **ad·ver·bi·ally** /æd'vɜ:bɪəlɪ; æd'vɝbɪəlɪ/ *adv*.

ad·vers·ary /'ædvəsərɪ; US -serɪ; 'ædvɚ,serɪ/ *n* opponent in a contest; enemy 竞赛中的对手; 敌手: *He defeated his old adversary.* 他击败了他的老对手.

ad·verse /'ædvɜ:s; æd'vɝs/ *adj* [usu attrib 通常作定语] **1** (**a**) not favourable; contrary 不利的; 相反的: *adverse winds, weather conditions, circumstances* 逆风、恶劣的天气、逆境. (**b**) hostile; opposing 敌对的; 反对的: *adverse criticism* 非难 ○ *an adverse reaction to the proposals* 对那些建议的异议. **2** harmful 有害的: *the adverse effects of drugs* 药物的有害的副作用. ▷ **ad·versely** *adv*: *His health was adversely affected by the climate.* 他的健康因气候影响而严重受损.

ad·vers·ity /əd'vɜ:sətɪ; əd'vɝsətɪ/ *n* **1** [U] unfavourable conditions; trouble 逆境; 不幸; 厄运: *remain cheerful in adversity* 处于逆境而仍乐观 ○ *face adversity with courage* 有勇气面对厄运. **2** [C] unfortunate event or circumstances 不幸的事件或遭遇; 祸事; 苦难: *She overcame many adversities.* 她饱经祸患而百折不挠.

ad·vert /'ædvɜ:t; æd'vɝt/ *n* (*Brit infml* 口) = ADVERTISEMENT 2 (ADVERTISE).

ad·vert·ise /'ædvətaɪz; 'ædvɚ,taɪz/ *v* **1** [Tn] make (sth) generally or publicly known 使(某事物)尽人皆知; 公布; 宣传: *advertise a meeting, a concert, a job* 公布[宣传]一次会议、一次音乐会、一项工作 ○ *It may be safer not to advertise your presence.* 不把你出席的事声张出去也许更为安全. **2** [I, Tn] praise (sth) publicly in order to encourage people to buy or use it 公开赞扬(某事物)以鼓动别人购买或使用; 做广告宣传; 登广告宣传: *advertise on TV, in a newspaper* 在电视上做广告、在报纸上登广告 ○ *advertise soap, one's house, one's services* 做广告宣传肥皂、自己的房子、自己的服务. **3** [Ipr] ~ **for sb/sth** ask for sb/sth by placing a notice in a newspaper, etc 在报刊等上面登征求某人或某事物的广告: *I must advertise for a new secretary.* 我得刊登广告聘请一位新秘书.

▷ **ad·vert·ise·ment** /əd'vɜ:tɪsmənt; US ,ædvər'taɪzmənt; ,ædvɚ'taɪzmənt/ *n* **1** [U] action of advertising 出公告; 做广告; 登广告: [attrib 作定语] *the advertisement page* 广告专页. **2** [C] (also **advert, ad**) ~ **(for sb/sth)** public notice offering or asking for goods, services, etc 广告(推销或征求货物、服务等): *If you want to sell your old sofa, why not put an advertisement in the local paper?* 你若打算卖掉旧沙发, 何不在本地报纸上登个广告呢? **ad·vert·iser** *n* person who advertises 登广告的人.

ad·vert·ising *n* [U] **1** action of advertising 广告宣传; 做广告; 登广告: [attrib 作定语] *a national advertising campaign* 一场全国性的广告宣传攻势. **2** business that deals with the publicizing of goods, esp to increase sales 广告业; 广告事务: *He works in advertising.* 他从事广告业. ○ *Cigarette advertising should be banned.* 应该禁止香烟的广告业务. ○ [attrib 作定语] *advertising revenue* 广告收入.

ad·vice /əd'vaɪs; əd'vaɪs/ *n* [U] **1** opinion given about what to do or how to behave 劝告; 忠告; 建议: *act on/follow/take sb's advice*, ie do what sb suggests 听从[遵从/接受]某人的劝告 ○ *You should take legal advice*, ie consult a lawyer. 你应该征询律师的意见. ○ *My advice to you would be to wait.* 我劝你等着. ○ *If you take my advice you'll see a doctor.* 如果你听我的话, 就去看病. ○ *Let me give you a piece/a bit/a few words/a word of advice....* 让我给你一项[一点/几句话的/一句话的]忠告.... **2** (*esp commerce* 尤用于商业) formal note giving information about a transaction, etc (关于交易等资料的)通知: *We received advice that the goods had been dispatched.* 我们收到了关于货物已发出的通知. ○ [attrib 作定语] *an advice note* 通知单.

ad·vis·able /əd'vaɪzəbl; əd'vaɪzəbl/ *adj* [usu pred 通常作表语] worth recommending as a course of action; sensible 可取; 明智: *Do you think it advisable to wait?* 你认为等着好不好?

▷ **ad·vis·ab·il·ity** /əd,vaɪzə'bɪlətɪ; əd,vaɪzə'bɪlətɪ/ *n* [U].

ad·vise /əd'vaɪz; əd'vaɪz/ *v* **1** [Ipr, Tn, Tn·pr, Tf, Tw, Tg, Dn·f, Dn·w, Dn·t] ~ **(sb) against sth/doing sth; ~ sb (on sth)** give advice to sb; recommend 劝告; 忠告; 建议: *The doctor advised (me to take) a complete rest.* 医生让(我)完全休息. ○ *They advised her against marrying quickly.* 他们劝她不要太快结婚. ○ *She advises the Government on economic affairs.* 她向政府提出经济方面的建议. ○ *We advised that they should start early/advised them to start early.* 我们建议他们应该及早开始. [我们建议他们及早开始.] ○ *I'd advise taking a different approach.* 我建议换个方式. ○ *You would be well advised* (ie sensible) *to stay indoors.* 你最好待在屋里. ○ *Can you advise (me) what to do next?* 你看(我)下一步怎么办? **2** [Tn, Tn·pr, Dn·f, Dn·w] ~ **sb (of sth)** (*esp commerce* 尤用于商业) inform or notify sb 通知或告知某人: *Please advise us of the dispatch of the goods/when the goods are dispatched.* 货物发出[货物发出时]请通知我们.

▷ **ad·visedly** /əd'vaɪzɪdlɪ; əd'vaɪzɪdlɪ/ *adv* (*fml* 文) after careful thought; deliberately 深思熟虑的; 故意的: *I use these words advisedly.* 我是特意用这些字的.

ad·viser (also *esp US* **ad·visor**) *n* ~ **(to sb) (on sth)** person who gives advice, esp sb who is regularly consulted 顾问: *serve as special adviser to the President* 作总统的特别顾问.

ad·vis·ory /əd'vaɪzərɪ; əd'vaɪzərɪ/ *adj* having the power to advise; giving advice 有权进言的; 顾问的; 咨询的: *an advisory committee, body, role* 咨询委员会、机关、任务.

ad·vo·cacy /'ædvəkəsɪ; 'ædvəkəsɪ/ *n* [U] **1** ~ **(of sth)** giving of support (to a cause, etc) 拥护(一事业等); 鼓吹; 提倡; 主张: *She is well known for her advocacy of women's rights.* 她因鼓吹妇权运动而甚为知名. **2** (*law* 律) profession or work of an advocate(2) 律师的职业或工作.

ad·voc·ate /'ædvəkeɪt; 'ædvə,ket/ *v* [Tn, Tf, Tg, Tsg] speak publicly in favour of (sth); recommend; support 拥护; 提倡; 支持: *I advocate a policy of gradual reform.* 我拥护逐步改革的政策. ○ *Do you advocate banning cars in the city centre?* 你支持禁止汽车在市中心通行这一主张吗?

▷ **ad·voc·ate** /'ædvəkət; 'ædvəkɪt/ *n* **1** ~ **(of sth)** person who supports or speaks in favour of a cause, policy, etc (对一事业、方针、政策等的)支持者, 拥护者, 鼓吹者, 提倡者: *a lifelong advocate of disarmament* 为裁军奋斗终生的人. **2** person who pleads on behalf of another, esp a lawyer who presents a client's case in a lawcourt 律师. Cf 参看 BARRISTER, SOLICITOR. **3** (idm 习语) **devil's advocate** ⇨ DEVIL.

advt *abbr* 缩写 = advertisement.

adze (*US* **adz**) /ædz; ædz/ *n* tool like an axe with a blade at right angles to the handle used for cutting or shaping large pieces of wood 锛子.

ae·gis /'i:dʒɪs; 'idʒɪs/ *n* (idm 习语) **under the aegis of sb/sth** with the protection or support of sb/sth, esp a public institution 在某人或某事物(尤指公共机构)的保护或支持下: *Medical supplies are being flown in under the aegis of the Red Cross.* 在红十字会的保护下, 正在空运进医药用品.

aeon (also **eon**) /ˈi:ən; ˋiən/ *n* period of time so long that it cannot be measured 极长而无法计算的时期; 万古: *The earth was formed aeons ago.* 地球形成于亿万年前.

aer·ate /ˈeəreɪt; ˋeə,ret/ *v* [Tn] **1** add carbon dioxide to (a liquid) under pressure 加压充注二氧化碳于(液体): *aerated water* 汽水. **2** expose (sth) to the chemical action of air 将(某物)置于空气中使其起化学作用: *aerate the soil by digging it* 翻地使土壤通气. ▷ **aera·tion** /eəˈreɪʃn; ,eəˋreʃən/ *n* [U].

aer·ial¹ /ˈeərɪəl; ˋɛrɪəl/ (*US* **antenna**) *n* one or more wires or rods for sending or receiving radio waves 天线. ⇨illus at App 1 见附录1之插图, page vii.

aer·ial² /ˈeərɪəl; ˋɛrɪəl/ *adj* **1** from aircraft or the air 从飞行器上的; 从空中的: *aerial bombardment, photography, reconnaissance* 轰炸、空中摄影术、空中侦察. **2** existing or suspended in the air 存在或悬浮于空中的: *an aerial railway* 架空铁道; 高架铁道. **3** (*arch* 古) of or like air (似)空气的.

aerie = EYRIE.

aero- *comb form* 构词成分 of air or aircraft 空气的; 飞行器的: *aerodynamic* ○ *aerospace*.

aero·batics /,eərəˈbætɪks; ,ɛrəˋbætɪks/ *n* **1** [pl] spectacular feats performed with aircraft, esp as part of a display, eg flying upside-down or in loops 特技飞行(尤指表演项目, 如翻身或翻筋斗飞行): *The aerobatics were the best part of the show.* 表演中最精彩的节目是特技飞行. **2** [sing *v*] art of performing these 特技飞行术: *Aerobatics is a dangerous sport.* 特技飞行是危险的运动. ▷ **aero·batic** *adj*.

aer·obics /eəˈrəubɪks; ɛˋrobɪks/ *n* [pl] energetic physical exercises done in order to increase the amount of oxygen taken into the body 有氧运动(为增加体内氧气的健身运动); 健美操; 健身操.

aero·drome /ˈeərədrəum; ˋɛrə,drom/ *n* (*dated* 旧 esp *Brit*) small airport or airfield, used mainly by private aircraft (主要为私人飞机使用的)小飞机场.

aero·dy·nam·ics /,eərəudaɪˈnæmɪks; ,ɛrodaɪˋnæmɪks/ *n* [pl, usu sing *v* 通常与单数动词连用] science dealing with the forces acting on solid bodies (eg aircraft or bullets) moving through air 空气动力学; 气体动力学. ▷ **aero·dy·namic** *adj*.

aero·naut·ics /,eərəˈnɔ:tɪks; ,ɛrəˋnɔtɪks/ *n* [pl, usu sing *v* 通常与单数动词连用] scientific study or practice of flying and navigating aircraft 航空学; 航空术. ▷ **aero·nautic, aero·naut·ical** /-ˈnɔ:tɪkl; -ˋnɔtɪkl/ *adjs*: *aeronautical engineering, skills* 航空工程的; 航空技术的.

aero·plane /ˈeərəpleɪn; ˋɛrə,plen/ (*US* **air·plane** /ˈeər-pleɪn; ˋɛr,plen/) *n* aircraft that is heavier than air, with wings and one or more engines 飞机.

aero·sol /ˈeərəsɒl; *US* -sɔ:l; ˋɛrə,sɔl/ *n* (**a**) [U] substance (eg scent, paint, insecticide) sealed in a container under pressure, with a device for releasing it as a fine spray 加压密封于容器中用喷雾装置释放出来的物质(如香水、颜料、杀虫剂); 喷雾剂: [attrib 作定语] *an aerosol can* 喷雾罐. ⇨illus at CAN 见CAN之插图. (**b**) [C] such a container 喷雾器; 雾化器: *Deodorants are available as aerosols or roll-ons.* 除臭剂有喷雾装或滚抹装.

aero·space /ˈeərəuspeɪs; ˋɛro,spes/ *n* [U] **1** the earth's atmosphere and the space beyond it 地球大气层及其外面的宇宙空间; 航空航天空间. **2** technology of aircraft, spacecraft, etc that operate in this 航空航天技术: [attrib 作定语] *the aerospace industry* 航空航天工业.

aes·thete /ˈi:sθi:t; ˋɛsθit/ (*US* also **es·thete** /ˈesθi:t; ˋɛs-θit/) *n* (*sometimes derog* 有时作贬义) person who has or claims to have a fine appreciation of art and beauty 审美家.

aes·thetic /i:sˈθetɪk; ɛsˋθɛtɪk/ (*US* also **es·thetic** /es-ˈθetɪk; ɛsˋθɛtɪk/) *adj* [usu attrib 通常作定语] **1** (**a**) concerned with beauty and the appreciation of beauty 有关美的; 美学的: *aesthetic standards* 美学标准 ○ *an aesthetic sense* 美感. (**b**) appreciating beauty and beautiful things 对美和美的事物欣赏的; 审美的: *an aesthetic person* 有美感的人. **2** pleasing to look at; artistic; tasteful 悦目的; 艺术的; 雅致的: *aesthetic design* 美观的设计 ○ *Their furniture was more aesthetic than practical.* 他们的家具华而不实.
▷ **aes·thet·ic·ally** (*US* also **es-**) /-klɪ; -klɪ/ *adv*: *aesthetically pleasing* 美观可爱的.
aes·theti·cism /i:sˈθetɪsɪzəm; ɛsˋθɛtɪ,sɪzəm/ (*US* also **es-**) *n* [U].
aes·thet·ics (*US* also **es-**) *n* [sing *v*] branch of philosophy dealing with the principles of beauty and artistic taste 美学(哲学中的一门学科, 研究美和艺术鉴赏的原理).

ae·ti·ology (*US* also **eti·ology**) /,i:tɪˈɒlədʒɪ; ,ɪtɪˋɑlədʒɪ/ *n* [U] **1** study of causes and reasons 原因论(对原因及成因的研究). **2** (*medicine* 药) study of the causes of disease 病原学; 病因学: *the aetiology of malaria* 疟疾的病因研究.

afar /əˈfɑ:(r); əˋfɑr/ *adv* **1** at or to a distance 在远处; 到远处: *lights visible afar off* 远处能见到的光. **2** (idm 习语) **from a'far** from a long distance away 从远处: *news from afar* 远方来的消息.

af·fable /ˈæfəbl; ˋæfəbl/ *adj* **1** polite and friendly 谦恭有礼的; 和蔼可亲的: *affable to everybody* 对每个人都彬彬有礼的 ○ *an affable reply* 谦恭的回答. **2** easy to talk to 易于交谈的: *He found her parents very affable.* 他觉得她父母很好说话. ▷ **af·fa·bil·ity** /,æfəˈbɪlətɪ; ,æfəˋbɪlə-tɪ/ *n* [U]. **af·fably** /-əblɪ; -əblɪ/ *adv*.

af·fair /əˈfeə(r); əˋfɛr/ *n* **1** [sing] thing (to be) done; concern; matter 事; 事务; 事情: *It's not my affair*, ie I am not interested in or responsible for it. 那不是我的事. **2** **affairs** [pl] (**a**) personal business matters 个人的业务: *put one's affairs in order* 料理自己的业务. (**b**) matters of public interest 公共的事务: *current/foreign/world affairs* 时事[外交事务/世界事务] ○ *affairs of state* 国事; 国务; 政务. **3** [C esp *sing* 尤作单数] (**a**) event; happening 事件; 事情: *We must try to forget this sad affair.* 我们要尽量把这件难过的事忘掉. ○ *The press exaggerated the whole affair wildly.* 新闻报道肆意夸大了整个事件. (**b**) event or series of events connected with a particular person, thing or place 与某人、某物或某地有关的事件: *the Suez affair* 苏伊士事件. (**c**) organized social event 有组织的社交活动: *The wedding was a very grand affair.* 那婚礼是件盛事. **4** [C] (*infml* 口) (following an *adj* 用于形容词之后) thing described in a specified way (具体描述的)东西, 物件: *Her hat was an amazing affair of ribbons and feathers.* 她那顶帽子是个有丝带和羽毛的绝妙物件. **5** [C] sexual relationship between people who are not married to each other 与配偶以外的人发生的性关系: *She's having an affair with her boss.* 她和老板有暧昧关系. **6** (idm 习语) **a state of affairs** ⇨ STATE.

af·fect¹ /əˈfekt; əˋfɛkt/ *v* [Tn] **1** have an influence on (sb/sth); produce an effect on 影响: *The tax increases have affected us all.* 加税已经影响了我们大家. ○ *The change in climate may affect your health*, ie be bad for you. 气候的变化可能影响你的健康. ○ *Their opinion will not affect my decision.* 他们的意见不会影响我的决定. **2** (of disease) attack (sb/sth); infect (指疾病)侵袭(某人[某物]); 感染: *Cancer had affected his lungs.* 癌已侵及他的肺脏. **3** cause (sb) to have feelings of sadness or sympathy; touch 使(某人)有悲伤或同情的感觉; 感动: *We were deeply affected by the news of her death.* 她死亡的噩耗使我们深为感伤.
▷ **af·fect·ing** moving or touching 动人的; 感人的: *an affecting appeal for help* 感人的求助. **af·fect·ingly** *adv*.

NOTE ON USAGE 用法: **Affect** is a verb meaning 'have an influence on' ☆ **affect**是动词, 意为'影响': *Alcohol affects drivers' concentration.* 酒精能影响司机的注意力. **Effect** is a noun meaning 'result or influence' ☆ **effect**是名词, 意为'效果'或'影响': *Alcohol has a very bad effect on drivers.* 酒精对司机的影响很大. It is also a (formal) verb meaning 'accomplish' ☆ **effect**这个词还是个(文雅的)动词, 意为'完成': *They effected their escape in the middle of the night.* 他们半夜逃脱了.

af·fect² /əˈfekt; əˋfɛkt/ *v* **1** [Tn] (*often derog* 常作贬义) make an obvious show of using, wearing or liking (sth) 炫耀(所使用、穿戴或爱好的事物): *affect bright colours, bow ties* 炫耀鲜艳的颜色、蝶形领结 ○ *He affects a pretentious use of language*, ie tries to impress people by using obscure words, etc. 他爱卖弄词藻. **2** (**a**) [Tn, Tt] pretend to have or feel (sth) 装作; 假装: *affect not to know sth/affect ignorance of sth* 装作不知道某事[装作对某事物一无所知] ○ *She affected a foreign accent.* 她装出外国腔调. (**b**) [Ln] (*fml* 文) pretend to be (sth); pose as 装成; 扮成: *She affects the helpless female.* 她装成柔弱女性.

▷ **af·fec·ted** /əˈfektɪd; əˈfɛktɪd/ *adj* not natural or genuine; pretended; artificial 不自然的; 不真实的; 装扮的; 做作的: *an affected politeness, cheerfulness, etc* 虚伪的礼貌、强作欢颜 ○ *a highly affected style of writing* 极为矫揉造作的写作风格 ○ *Do try not to be so affected.* 千万别这么装模作样的.

af·fec·ta·tion /ˌæfekˈteɪʃn; ˌæfɛkˋteʃən/ *n* **1** [C, U] (instance of) unnatural behaviour, manner of speaking, etc, intended to impress others 为给人留有印象而作出不自然的样子; 做作: *His little affectations irritated her.* 他做作的小动作激怒了她. ○ *I detest all affectation.* 我厌恶一切矫揉造作的行为. **2** [C] **~ (of sth)** pretence; deliberate display (of sth that is not truly felt) 假装; 故意表现(不是真正感觉的事物): *an affectation of interest, indifference, etc* 装作有兴趣、假装不在乎.

af·fec·tion /əˈfekʃn; əˈfɛkʃən/ *n* **1** [U, C usu *pl* 通常作复数] **~ (for/towards sb/sth)** feeling of fondness; love 喜爱; 爱: *He felt great affection for his sister.* 他很疼他的妹妹. ○ *The old king was held in great affection.* 年老的国王极受爱戴. ○ *I tried to win her affection(s).* 我尽力讨她的欢心. **2** [C] (*dated* 旧) disease or diseased condition 疾病; 病情: *an affection of the throat* 咽喉疾患.

af·fec·tion·ate /əˈfekʃənət; əˈfɛkʃənət/ *adj* **~ (towards sb)** showing fondness (for sb); loving (向某人)示爱的; 爱的: *an affectionate child* 有爱心的孩子 ○ *affectionate kisses, words, smiles* 示爱的吻、话、微笑 ○ *He is very affectionate towards his children.* 他很爱他的孩子. ▷ **af·fec·tion·ately** *adv*: *He patted her affectionately on the head.* 他疼爱地拍拍她的头. ○ *Yours affectionately*, ie used at the end of a letter to a close relative or friend. 你亲爱的(用于给至亲好友的书信末尾).

af·fi·ance /əˈfaɪəns; əˈfaɪəns/ *v* [usu passive 通常用于被动语态: Tn, Tn·pr] **~ sb (to sb)** (*dated or fml* 旧或文) promise sb in marriage 和某人订婚: *He is affianced to the princess*, ie engaged to marry her. 他和公主订婚了.

af·fi·da·vit /ˌæfɪˈdeɪvɪt; ˌæfəˈdevɪt/ *n* (*law* 律) written statement that can be used as evidence in court, made by sb who swears that it is true (宣誓属实可用作法庭证据的)书面证词; 宣誓书: *swear/make/take/sign an affidavit* 订立[签署]宣誓书.

af·fili·ate /əˈfɪlɪeɪt; əˈfɪlɪˌet/ *v* [usu passive 通常用于被动语态: Tn, Tn·pr] **~ sb/sth (to/with sb/sth)** attach (a person, a society, an institution, etc) to a larger organization 使(个人、社团、机构等)隶属于一较大组织; 使接纳为成员: *We are affiliated with the national group.* 我们隶属于国营组织. ○ *The College is affiliated to the University.* 这所学院附属于这所大学.

▷ **af·fili·ate** /əˈfɪlɪət; əˈfɪlɪət/ *n* affiliated person, institution, etc 被接纳的人、隶属的机构等: [attrib 作定语] *affiliate members* 会员.

af·fili·ation /əˌfɪlɪˈeɪʃn; əˌfɪlɪˋeʃən/ *n* **1** [U] affiliating or being affiliated 加入; 附属. **2** [C] link or connection made by affiliating (因加入而有的)联系或关系: *The society has many affiliations throughout the country.* 这个社团在全国有很多关系.

□ **affili'ation order** (*law* 律) order compelling the father of an illegitimate child to help to support it 父子关系确认令(令非婚生子之父协助抚养).

af·fin·ity /əˈfɪnətɪ; əˈfɪnətɪ/ *n* **1** [U, C] **~ (with sb/sth); ~ (between A and B)** structural resemblance or similarity of character; relationship 构造相似; 特点相近; 关系: *There is (a) close affinity between Italian and Spanish.* 意大利语和西班牙语很近似. ○ *Early man shows certain affinities with the ape.* 早期的人类和猿有某些相似之处. **2** [C] **~ (to/for sb/sth); ~ (between A and B)** strong liking for or attraction to sb/sth 强烈喜爱(某人[某事物]): *They share a special affinity.* 他们有共同的特殊爱好. ○ *She has a strong affinity for Beethoven.* 她酷爱贝多芬的乐曲. **3** [C] **~ (with sb)** (*law* 律) relationship, esp by marriage (尤指姻亲)关系: *He was not an impartial witness because of his affinity with the accused.* 他不是公正的见证人, 因为他与被告有姻亲关系. **4** [C] **~ (for sth)** (*chemistry* 化) tendency of certain substances to combine with others 亲和性; 亲和力: *the affinity of salt for water* 盐对水的亲和力.

af·firm /əˈfɜːm; əˈfɝm/ *v* **1** [Tn, Tf, Dn·pr, Dpr·f] **~ sth (to sb)** state sth as the truth; assert sth 肯定某事物属实; 断言某事物: *She affirmed her innocence.* 她坚称自己无罪. ○ *He affirmed that he was responsible.* 他肯定是他负责. Cf 参看 DENY. **2** [I] (*law* 律) make a solemn declaration in court instead of swearing an oath (在法庭上不经宣誓而)郑重陈词.

▷ **af·firma·tion** /ˌæfəˈmeɪʃn; ˌæfɚˋmeʃən/ *n* **1** [C, U] (act of) affirming 肯定; 断言: *The poem is a joyous affirmation of the power of love.* 这首诗以欢快的笔触肯定了爱情的力量. **2** [C] (**a**) thing that is affirmed 肯定的事物. (**b**) (*law* 律) solemn declaration made in court instead of an oath (在法庭上不经宣誓而作的)郑重陈词.

af·firm·at·ive /əˈfɜːmətɪv; əˈfɝmətɪv/ *adj* (of words, etc) expressing agreement; indicating 'yes' (指言语等)表示同意的; 意为'是的'; 肯定的: *an affirmative reply, nod, reaction* 表示同意的回答、点头、反应. Cf 参看 NEGATIVE.

▷ **af·firm·at·ive** *n* **1** word or statement that expresses agreement 表示同意的词语或陈述. **2** (idm 习语) **in the af'firmative** (*fml* 文) expressing agreement 表示同意: *He answered in the affirmative*, ie said 'yes'. 他作了肯定的回答.

af·firm·at·ively *adv*.

af·fix1 /əˈfɪks; əˈfɪks/ *v* [Tn, Tn·pr] **~ sth (to/on sth)** (*fml* 文) **1** stick, fasten or attach sth 粘上、贴上、系住、附上、固定住某物: *affix a stamp to an envelope* 在信封上贴邮票 ○ *affix a seal on a document* 在文件上盖印. **2** add sth in writing 添写上某事物: *affix one's signature to a contract* 在合同上签字.

af·fix2 /ˈæfɪks; ˋæfɪks/ *n* (*grammar*) letter or group of letters added to the beginning or the end of a word to change its meaning or the way it is used; prefix or suffix, eg *un-*, *-esque* and *-less* in *unkind*, *picturesque* and *hopeless* 词缀(加在一词的词首或词尾的字母, 以改变其含义或用法); 前缀或后缀(如unkind、picturesque和hopeless中的un-、-esque和-less).

af·flict /əˈflɪkt; əˈflɪkt/ *v* [usu passive 通常用于被动语态: Tn, Tn·pr] **~ sb/sth (with sth)** cause trouble, pain or distress to sb/sth 使某人[某物]苦恼、疼痛或悲痛: *She is afflicted with* (ie suffers from) *arthritis.* 她患关节炎. ○ *Severe drought has afflicted the countryside.* 严重的干旱使乡村深受其害.

▷ **af·flic·tion** /əˈflɪkʃn; əˈflɪkʃən/ *n* (*fml* 文) **1** [U] pain; suffering; distress 疼痛; 折磨; 悲痛: *help people in affliction* 帮助受苦的人. **2** [C] thing that causes suffering 造成痛苦的事物: *Blindness can be a terrible affliction.* 失明有时极为痛苦.

af·flu·ence /ˈæflʊəns; ˋæfluəns/ *n* [U] abundance of money, goods or property; wealth 丰富; 富裕: *live in/live a life of affluence* 生活优裕[过富裕的日子] ○ *He quickly rose to affluence*, ie became wealthy. 他很快就富起来了.

af·flu·ent /ˈæflʊənt; ˋæfluənt/ *adj* rich; prosperous 富裕的; 丰富的; 繁荣的: *affluent circumstances* 富裕的环境 ○ *an affluent lifestyle* 富足的生活方式 ○ *His parents were very affluent.* 他的父母很富裕. ○ *the affluent society*, ie one in which most people have a high standard of living 富足的社会(多数人生活水平很高的社会).

af·ford /əˈfɔːd; əˈfɔrd/ *v* **1** [no passive 不用于被动语态: Tn, Tt] (usu with *can*, *could* or *be able to* 通常与can、could或be able to连用) have enough money, time, space, etc for (a specified purpose) 为(某目的)有足够的钱、时间、地方等: *They walked because they couldn't afford (to take) a taxi.* 他们因为坐不起计程车而步行. ○ *You can't afford* (ie are not in a position to spend) *£90.* 你可不能花90英镑. ○ *I'd love to go on holiday but I can't afford the time.* 我倒想去度假, 可是抽不出时间来. ○ *We would give more examples if we could afford the space.* 假如我们能匀出篇幅来, 就可以多举些例子了. **2** [no passive 不用于被动语态: Tn, Tt] (usu with *can* or *could* 通常与can或could连用) be able to do sth without risk to oneself 能不冒风险而做某事物: *I mustn't* *annoy my boss because I can't afford to lose my job*, ie must not take the risk of losing my job. 我可得罪不起老板，因为我舍不得丢掉这份工作. ○ *You can ill afford to criticize others when you behave so badly yourself.* 本身行为不正，则不宜批评别人. **3** [Tn, Dn·n, Dn·pr] **~ sth (to sb)** (*fml* 文) provide sth; give sth 供给某事物; 给予某事物: *The tree afforded (us) welcome shade.* 这棵树下好乘凉. ○ *Television affords pleasure to many.* 电视给很多人带来乐趣.

af·for·est /əˈfɒrɪst; *US* əˈfɔːr-; əˈfɔrɪst/ *v* [Tn] plant (areas of land) with trees to form a forest 造林于(某地). ▷ **af·for·est·ation** /əˌfɒrɪˈsteɪʃn; *US* əˌfɔːr-; əˌfɔrəsˈteʃən/ *n* [U].

af·fray /əˈfreɪ; əˈfre/ *n* (usu *sing* 通常作单数) (*fml or law* 文或律) disturbance of the peace caused by fighting or rioting in a public place 在公共场所扰乱治安、吵架、打架、闹事、滋事: *The men were charged with causing an affray.* 那些人被控扰乱治安.

af·front /əˈfrʌnt; əˈfrʌnt/ *n* (usu *sing* 通常作单数) **~ (to sb/sth)** deliberately insulting or disrespectful remark, action, etc, esp in public (尤指当众)故意侮辱, 有意冒犯: *His speech was an affront to all decent members of the community.* 他的话对社区所有体面的成员是故意的侮辱.

▷ **af·front** /əˈfrʌnt; əˈfrʌnt/ *v* [Tn usu passive 通常用于被动语态] insult (sb) deliberately and openly; offend 故意而公然地侮辱(某人); 冒犯. **af·fronted** *adj* **~ (at/by sth)** offended 被冒犯的; 被得罪的: *He felt deeply affronted at her rudeness.* 他深为她的粗野所触怒.

Af·ghan /ˈæfgæn; ˈæfgæn/ *n* **1** (**a**) [C] native or inhabitant of Afghanistan 阿富汗人. (**b**) [U] language of Afghanistan 阿富汗语. **2 afghan** [C] type of loose sheepskin coat 一种宽松的羊皮外衣.

□ ˌ**Afghan** ˈ**hound** tall breed of dog with long silky hair 阿富汗猎狗.

afi·cion·ado /əˌfɪsjəˈnɑːdəʊ, *also* əˌfɪʃj-; əˌfisjəˈnɑdo, əˌfɪʃ-/ *n* (*pl* **~s**) (*Spanish* 西) person who is very enthusiastic about a particular sport or pastime 非常热中于某项运动或消遣的人; 狂热爱好者; 迷: *an aficionado of bullfighting* 斗牛迷.

afield /əˈfiːld; əˈfild/ *adv* (idm 习语) **far/farther/further aˈfield** far, etc away, esp from home; to or at a distance 远离(尤指家乡); 到远方; 在远处: *Some villagers have never been further afield than the neighbouring town.* 有些村民从未远离过附近的市镇. ○ *To find the causes of the problem we need look no further afield than our own department.* 要找出问题所在, 不必超出我们本部门的范围.

aflame /əˈfleɪm; əˈflem/ *adj* [pred 作表语] **1** (red as if) in flames; burning (红似)着火; 燃烧: *The whole building was soon aflame.* 整个建筑物不久就燃烧起来了. ○ *Her cheeks were aflame.* 她的两颊绯红. ○ *The autumn woods were aflame with colour.* 那片秋林红似火. **2** very excited 非常激动: *aflame with desire* 欲火如焚.

AFL-CIO /ˌeɪ ef ˈel ˌsiː aɪ ˈəʊ; ˌe ɛf ˈɛl ˌsi aɪ ˈo/ *abbr* 缩写 = (*US*) American Federation of Labor and Congress of Industrial Organizations 美国劳工联合会及产业工会联合会.

afloat /əˈfləʊt; əˈflot/ *adj* [pred 作表语] **1** floating in water or air (在水中或空中)漂浮着: *The boat stuck on a sandbank but we soon got it afloat again.* 小船在沙丘搁浅, 没过多久我们就又使它航行自如了. ○ *The ship was listing badly but still kept afloat.* 船倾侧得很厉害, 但却仍然漂浮不沉. **2** at sea; on board ship 在海上; 在船上: *enjoy life afloat* 喜欢海上生活. **3** out of debt or difficulties 无债; 无困难: *The firm managed to stay afloat during the recession.* 在经济衰退期间, 公司设法渡过了难关. **4** functioning 起作用: *get a new business afloat*, ie start it 创办新的企业. **5** (of rumours) being generally talked about; circulating (指谣言)传播; 流传: *There's a story afloat that he'll resign.* 有个传闻说他要辞职.

afoot /əˈfʊt; əˈfut/ *adj* [pred 作表语] being prepared or progressing 在准备中; 在进行中: *There's mischief afoot*, ie being planned. 有人准备捣鬼. ○ *There's a scheme afoot to put a motorway through the park.* 现在正酝酿着一个计划, 要修一条穿过公园的高速公路.

afore·men·tioned /əˌfɔːˈmenʃənd; əˈfɔrˌmɛnʃənd/ (also **afore·said** /əˈfɔːsed; əˈfɔrˌsɛd/, **said**) *adj* [usu attrib 通常作定语] (*fml* 文) (esp in legal documents) mentioned or referred to earlier (尤用于法律文件)前面所述的, 上述的: *The aforementioned (ˈperson/ˈpersons) was/were acting suspiciously.* 前面所述的人行动可疑.

afore·thought /əˈfɔːθɔːt; əˈfɔrˌθɔt/ *adj* (idm 习语) **with malice aforethought** ⇨ MALICE.

a for·ti·ori /ˌeɪ ˌfɔːtɪˈɔːraɪ; ˈeˌfɔrʃɪˈoraɪ/ (*Latin* 拉) for this stronger reason 因为这一更充分理由; 更加: *If he can afford a luxury yacht, then a fortiori he can afford to pay his debts.* 他若能买得起豪华的快艇, 就更能匀出钱来还债了.

afraid /əˈfreɪd; əˈfred/ *adj* [pred 作表语] **1** (**a**) **~ (of sb/sth); ~ (of doing sth/to do sth)** frightened 畏惧; 害怕: *Don't be afraid.* 不要怕. ○ *There's nothing to be afraid of.* 没有什么可害怕的. ○ *Are you afraid of snakes?* 你怕蛇吗? ○ *He's afraid of going out/to go out alone at night.* 他害怕夜晚独自出去. ○ *Don't be afraid* (ie Don't hesitate) *to ask for help if you need it.* 倘若需要帮忙的话, 尽管提出来(不必犹豫). (**b**) **~ of doing sth/~ that...** worried or anxious about (the possible result of sth) 担忧或忧虑(某事物可能产生的后果); 恐怕: *I didn't mention it because I was afraid of upsetting him/afraid (that) I might upset him.* 我没有提起那件事, 因为我怕他心烦意乱. ○ *He's afraid of losing customers/that he might lose customers.* 他怕失去顾客[可能失去顾客]. (**c**) **~ for sth/sb** frightened or worried about things that may put sth/sb in danger 担心(某事物[某人]会遇到危险): *parents afraid for (the safety of) their children* 为儿女(的安全)担忧的父母. **2** (idm 习语) **be afraid of one's own shadow** be very timid 很胆小; 非常胆怯. **I'm afraid (that...)** (usu without *that*, used to express politely a piece of information that may be unwelcome 通常不用 that, 用以有礼貌地表达可能令人不快的信息) I am sorry to say 我很抱歉地说: *I'm afraid we can't come.* 很抱歉, 我们不能来. ○ *I can't help you, I'm afraid.* 我帮不了你的忙, 对不起. ○ *'Have we missed the train?' 'I'm afraid so.'* '我们误了火车了吗?' '很遗憾, 是误了.' ○ *'Have you any milk?' 'I'm afraid not.'* '你有牛奶吗?' '对不起, 没有.'

afresh /əˈfreʃ; əˈfrɛʃ/ *adv* again, esp from the very beginning (尤指从头)再; 重新: *Let's start afresh.* 咱们重新开始吧. ○ *The work will have to be done afresh.* 这工作得重新再做了.

Af·rican /ˈæfrɪkən; ˈæfrɪkən/ *adj* of Africa or its people or languages 非洲的; 非洲人的; 非洲语言的.

▷ **Af·rican** *n* native of Africa, esp a dark-skinned person 非洲土人(尤指黑皮肤的人).

□ ˌ**African** ˈ**violet** E African plant with purple, pink or white flowers, usu grown indoors 非洲紫罗兰.

Af·ri·kaans /ˌæfrɪˈkɑːns; ˌæfrɪˈkɑns/ *n* [U] language developed from Dutch, spoken in S Africa 南非荷兰语(源自荷兰语, 用于南非).

Af·ri·kaner /ˌæfrɪˈkɑːnə (r); ˌæfrɪˈkɑnɚ/ *n* white S African, usu of Dutch descent, whose native language is Afrikaans 南非白人(通常为荷兰人后裔, 母语为南非荷兰语).

Afro /ˈæfrəʊ; ˈæfro/ *adj* (of hair-style) very curly, thick and long, like the hair of some Blacks (指发型, 像某些黑人的头发, 鬈曲、浓密而长的)非洲式的. ⇨illus at HAIR 见 HAIR 之插图.

Afro- *comb form* 构词成分 African; of Africa 非洲的: *Afro-Asian*, ie of Africa and Asia.

Afro-American /ˌæfrəʊ əˈmerɪkən; ˈæfroəˈmɛrɪkən/ *adj* of American Blacks or their culture 美国黑人的; 美国黑人文化的.

▷ ˌ**Afro-Aˈmerican** *n* American of African descent 美国黑人.

aft /ɑːft; *US* æft; æft/ *adv* **1** in, near or towards the stern of a ship or the tail of an aircraft 在、近或向(船或飞行器)尾部. **2** (idm 习语) **fore and aft** ⇨ FORE[1].

after[1] /ˈɑːftə(r); *US* ˈæf-; ˈæftɚ/ *adv* **1** later (in time) (在时间上)以后, 之后, 后来: *The day after, he apologized.* 次日, 他道歉了. ○ *It reappeared long/soon after.* 过后很久[不久]又出现了. ○ *They lived happily ever after.* 他们后来一直生活得很幸福. **2** behind (in place) (在位置上)在后: *She followed on after.* 她在后面跟着. Cf 参看 BEFORE[1]. ⇨Usage at BEFORE[2] 用法见 BEFORE[2].

□ ˈ**afterglow** *n* [U] glow in the sky after sunset (日落后天空中的)余晖; 夕照; 晚霞.

after[2] /ˈɑːftə(r); *US* ˈæf-; ˋæftɚ/ *prep* **1** (**a**) later than (sth) 比…更晚: *leave after lunch, shortly after six, the day after tomorrow, the week after next* 午餐后、刚过六点钟、后天、下下星期离去 ○ (*US*) *half after seven in the morning*, ie 7.30 am 上午七点半. (**b**) **sth ~ sth** (indicating much repetition 表示多次重复): *day after day/week after week/year after year/time after time*, ie very often 日复一日[一星期一星期地/一年一年地/一次又一次地] ○ *He fired shot after shot*, ie many shots. 他一枪一枪地发射. Cf 参看 BEFORE[2] 1. ➪Usage at BEFORE[2] 用法见 BEFORE[2]. **2** behind (sb/sth) 在…后面: *Shut the door after you when you go out.* 出去时请随手关门. **3** next to and following (sb/sth) in order, arrangement or importance (在顺序、排列或重要性上)在…之后, 跟在…后面, 仅次于: *C comes after B in the alphabet.* 在字母表中C接在B后面. ○ *Your name comes after mine on the list.* 在名单上你的名字在我的名字之后. ○ *His book is the best on the subject after mine.* 他的书对这一问题的论述是最好的, 仅次于我的书. ○ *After you,* ie Please enter before me, serve yourself first, etc. 您先请(然后再轮到我). ○ *After you with the salt.* 您先用盐, 然后给我. ➪Usage at BEFORE[2] 用法见 BEFORE[2]. **4** because of (sth); following 因为; 由于; 在…以后: *After what he did to my family, I hate him.* 由于他对我家的所作所为, 我才恨他. ○ *After your conduct last time, did you expect to be invited again?* 有了你上次的行为, 你以为还会邀请你吗? **5** in pursuit of or in search of (sb/sth) 追赶; 寻找; 探求: *We ran after the thief.* 我们追赶窃贼. ○ *The police are after him.* 警方正在追捕他. ○ *She's after* (ie She wants) *a job in publishing.* 她正在找一份出版业的工作. **6** about (sb/sth); concerning 关于: *They inquired after you*, ie asked how you were. 他们问候你. **7** in spite of (sth) 尽管; 虽然: *After everything I've done for him, he still ignores me.* 尽管我什么都为他做了, 他还是不理我. **8** in the style of (sb/sth); in imitation of 依照; 仿照: *a painting after Rubens* 一幅仿鲁本斯的画 ○ *draw up a constitution after the American model* 仿照美国模式起草宪法 ○ *We've named the baby after you*, ie given him your first name in honour of you. 我们是用你的名字给这个婴儿取名的. **9** (idm 习语) ˌ**after** ˈ**all** (**a**) in spite of what has been said, done or expected 毕竟; 终究; 归根结底: *So you've come after all!* 你到底还是来了! ○ *After all, what does it matter?* 归根结底, 那有什么关系呢? (**b**) it should be remembered 应该记住: *He should have offered to pay — he has plenty of money, after all.* 他应该主动提出付款 —— 他有的是钱, 别忘了.

□ ˈ**afterbirth** *n* [sing] placenta and foetal membrane discharged from the womb after childbirth 胞衣; 胎盘和胎膜.

ˈ**after-damp** *n* [U] poisonous mixture of gases after the explosion of firedamp in a coal-mine (煤矿沼气)爆炸后的毒气.

ˈ**afterlife** *n* [sing] existence that is thought by some to follow death 来生; 来世: *Do you believe in an afterlife?* 你相信有来生吗?

ˈ**aftershave** *n* [U, C] lotion used on the face after shaving (剃须后搽的)润肤液: [attrib 作定语] *aftershave lotion* 剃须后搽的润肤液.

after[3] /ˈɑːftə(r); *US* ˈæf-; ˋæftɚ/ *conj* at or during a time later than (sth) 在…以后的时间或期间: *I arrived after he (had) left.* 我在他走后到的. ○ *We'll arrive after you've left.* 我们将在你走以后到达. Cf 参看 BEFORE[3].

after[4] /ˈɑːftə(r); *US* ˈæf-; ˋæftɚ/ *adj* [attrib 作定语] **1** later; following 以后的; 后来的: *in after years* 在以后的年月里. **2** nearer the stern of a ship 靠近船的后部的: *the* ˈ*after cabins* 后舱.

▷ ˈ**after·most** *adj* furthest aft 最后面的.

□ ˈ**after-care** *n* [U] attention or treatment given to a person who has just left hospital, prison, etc (对出院、出狱等的人给予的)事后护理或安置: [attrib 作定语] ˌ*after-care* ˈ*services* 事后服务.

ˈ**after-effect** *n* effect that occurs afterwards, eg a delayed effect of a drug used medically 后效(如用药后延迟的效应); effect that occurs after its cause has gone 后遗效应; 副作用: *suffer from/feel no unpleasant after-effects* 感到[未感到]有不良的副作用.

ˈ**after-image** *n* sensation retained by one of the senses, esp the eye, after the original stimulus has stopped 后遗感觉; (尤指)残留影像, 后像, 余像; 余音; 余味; 余感色.

ˈ**after-taste** *n* [sing] **1** taste that stays after eating or drinking sth 余味: *wine which leaves an unpleasant aftertaste (in the mouth)* (在口中)留有不良余味的酒. **2** (*fig* 比喻) impression or feeling that stays in the mind 回味.

ˈ**afterthought** *n* thing that is thought of or added later 事后想到或添加的事物: *Just as an afterthought — why not ask Jim?* 这是事后想起的 —— 为什么不问问吉姆呢? ○ *The film was made first and the music was added as an afterthought.* 这部电影是先拍摄画面的, 音乐是后加上的. ○ *Mary was a bit of an afterthought — her brothers and sisters are all much older than her.* 玛丽算是后添的 —— 她哥哥姐姐都比她大得多.

af·ter·math /ˈɑːftəmæθ; *Brit also* -mɑːθ; ˋæftɚˌmæθ/ *n* (usu *sing* 通常作单数) circumstances that follow and are a consequence of an event, etc (esp an unpleasant one) (尤指不幸的)事件的余波, 余殃, 后果: *the rebuilding which took place in the aftermath of the war* 在战后余殃中的重建.

af·ter·noon /ˌɑːftəˈnuːn; *US* ˌæf-; ˌæftɚˋnun/ *n* [U, C] time from midday or lunch-time to about 6 pm or sunset (if this is earlier) 下午: *in/during the afternoon* 在下午 ○ *this/yesterday/tomorrow afternoon* 今天[昨天/明天]下午 ○ *every afternoon* 每天下午 ○ *on Sunday afternoon* 在星期日下午 ○ *on the afternoon of 12 May* 在5月12日下午 ○ *one afternoon last week* 上星期的一个下午 ○ *She goes there two afternoons a week.* 她每星期有两天下午到那里去. ○ [attrib 作定语] *an afternoon sleep, performance, train* 午觉、午后表演、下午班火车 ○ *afternoon tea* 下午茶点. ➪Usage at MORNING 用法见 MORNING.

▷ **af·ter·noons** *adv* in the afternoons as a practice or habit (通常或习惯)在下午: *Afternoons, he works at home.* 下午他都在家工作.

af·ters /ˈɑːftəz; *US* ˈæf-; ˋæftɚz/ *n* [pl] (*Brit infml* 口) (usu sweet) course following the main course of a meal 后盘(一顿饭的主菜后的一道菜, 通常为甜品): *What's for afters?* 后盘是什么? ○ *We had fruit salad for afters.* 我们后盘吃的是水果色拉. Cf 参看 DESSERT, PUDDING 1.

af·ter·wards /ˈɑːftəwədz; *US* ˈæf-; ˋæftɚwɚdz/ (*US* also **af·ter·ward**) *adv* at a later time 后来; 然后; 以后: *Let's go to the theatre first and eat afterwards.* 咱们先去看戏, 然后再吃吧. Cf 参看 BEFORE[1]. ➪Usage at BEFORE[2] 用法见 BEFORE[2].

again /əˈgen, əˈgeɪn; əˋgɛn, əˋgen/ *adv* **1** once more; another time 再一次; 又; 再: *Try again.* 再试一次. ○ *Say that again, please.* 请再说一遍. ○ *Here comes Joe, drunk again.* 乔来了, 又喝醉了. ○ *Do call again.* 一定再来电话啊. ○ *Don't do that again.* 别再做那种事了. ○ *This must never happen again.* 这样的事决不可以再发生了. **2** as before; to or in the original place or condition 如前; 恢复原状: *He was glad to be home again.* 他又回到家里, 感到很高兴. ○ *Back again already?* 已经又回来了? ○ *You'll never get the money back again.* 那笔钱你再也弄不回来了. ○ *You'll soon be well again.* 你不久就会康复. ○ *I'm glad he's himself/his old self again*, ie that he has returned to his normal state again after a shock, an illness, etc. 他又恢复正常[老样子]了, 我感到很高兴. **3** (**a**) likewise; furthermore 同样地; 也; 此外; 而且; 再者: *Again, we have to consider the legal implications.* 再者, 我们还要考虑到法律方面的含义. (**b**) on the other hand 另一方面: *I might, and (there/then) again I might not.* 我可能, 可也不一定. **4** in addition 增加: *I'd like as many/much again*, ie twice as many/much. 我愿再增加一倍. ○ *half as much again*, ie one-and-a-half times as much 增加一半. **5** (idm 习语) **aˌgain and aˈgain** repeatedly 反复地; 屡次地; 一再地; 再三地: *I've told you again and again not to do that.* 我三番五次地告诉过你, 不要做那种事.

against /əˈgenst, əˈgeɪnst; əˋgɛnst, əˋgenst/ *prep* **1** in opposition to (sb/sth) 逆着; 反对; 违反; 与…相反: *We were rowing against the current.* 我们逆水划船. ○ *Are most people against the proposal?* 是多数人都反对这项提议吗? ○ *That's against the law.* 那是违法的. ○ *She was married against her will.* 她结婚是有违本意的. ○ *His age is against him*, ie is a disadvantage to him. 他的年龄于他不利. **2** in contact with (sb/sth); into collision with 触; 碰; 倚; 靠; 撞: *Put the piano there, with its back*

A

against the wall. 把钢琴放在那里，背靠着墙. ○ *He was leaning against a tree.* 他倚着一棵树. ○ *The rain beat against the car windscreen.* 雨点打在汽车挡风玻璃上. **3** in contrast to (sth) 衬托; 相映; 对照; 对比: *silhouetted against the sky* 以天空为背景显出轮廓的 ○ *The skier's red clothes stood out clearly against the snow.* 滑雪者的红衣服在雪的衬托下显得分外醒目. ○ (*fig* 比喻) *The salaries here are low (as) against the rates elsewhere.* 这里的薪水与别处相比是很低的. **4** in preparation for (sth); in anticipation of 防备; 预防: *protect plants against frost* 保护植物以防霜冻 ○ *take precautions against fire* 采取防火措施 ○ *an injection against rabies* 狂犬病预防针. **5** opposite (sth), so as to cancel or lessen 抵消; 抵偿; 抵补: *allowances to be set against income* 用以抵补总收入的津贴. **6** in return for (sth) 作为…的交换: *What's the rate of exchange against the dollar?* 美元的兑换率是多少? ○ *Tickets are issued only against payment of the full fee.* 只有付讫全费才可将票发出. **7** (idm 习语) **as against sth** ⇨ AS.

agape /əˈgeɪp; əˋgep/ *adj* [pred 作表语] **~ (with sth)** (of the mouth) wide open, esp with wonder (指嘴)大张着(尤指因惊奇): *He watched with mouth agape.* 他张着大嘴注视着.

ag·ate /ˈægət; ˋægət/ *n* [U, C] type of very hard semi-precious stone with bands or patches of colour 玛瑙: *a brooch made of agate* 玛瑙做的饰针 ○ [attrib 作定语] *an agate ring* 玛瑙戒指.

age[1] /eɪdʒ; edʒ/ *n* **1** [C, U] length of time that a person has lived or a thing has existed 人所生活的或事物所存在的期间; 年龄; 年岁; 年纪; 寿命: *What age is he?* 他多大年纪? ○ *He's six years of age/six years old.* 他六岁. ○ *Their ages are two and ten.* 他们的年龄是一个两岁，一个十岁. ○ *At what age did she retire?* 她多少岁退休的? ○ *I left school at the age of 18.* 我中学毕业时18岁. ○ *When I was your age...* 当我像你这样年纪时… ○ *We have a son your age.* 我们有个儿子和你同岁. ○ *He lived to a great age.* 他活到很大年纪. ○ *Geologists have calculated the age of the earth.* 地质学家已经计算出了地球的年龄. ○ [attrib 作定语] *Anyone can enter the contest — there's no age limit*, ie no one will be regarded as too old or too young. 任何人均可参加竞赛——无年龄限制. ⇨App 4 见附录4. **2** [U] latter part of life; old age 生命的后期; 老年; 晚年: *the wisdom that comes with age* 因年老而积累的智慧 ○ *His face was wrinkled with age.* 他的脸因苍老而起皱. ○ *Fine wine improves with age.* 美酒陈年味更醇. Cf 参看 YOUTH 1, 2. **3** [C] period of history with special characteristics or events (具有某种特征或特殊事件的)历史时期; 时代: *the Elizabethan Age*, ie the time of Queen Elizabeth I of England 伊丽莎白时代(英国女王伊丽莎白一世的时代) ○ *the modern age, the nuclear age, the age of the microchip* 现代、核子时代、微晶片时代. **4** [C usu *pl* 通常作复数] (*infml* 口) very long time 极长的时间; 很久: *I waited (for) ages/an age.* 我等候很久了. ○ *It took (us) ages to find a place to park.* (我们)找了好半天才找到个停车的地方. **5** (idm 习语) **the age/years of discretion** ⇨ DISCRETION. **at a tender age/of tender age** ⇨ TENDER[1]. **the awkward age** ⇨ AWKWARD. **ˌbe/ˌcome of ˈage** reach the age at which one has an adult's legal rights and obligations 成年; 达到法定年龄. **ˌbe your ˈage** (*infml* 口) (esp imperative 尤用于祈使语气) behave as sb of your age should and not as though you were much younger 年纪不小了(举止应与你年纪相称，不要装成更小的样子). **feel one's age** ⇨ FEEL. **in this day and age** ⇨ DAY. **ˌlook one's ˈage** seem as old as one really is 容貌与年龄相称: *She doesn't look her age at all*, ie appears much younger than she really is. 她一点儿也不像那么大年纪(显得年轻得多). **(be) of an ˈage** having reached an age when one should do sth 达到该做某事的年龄: *He's of an age when he ought to settle down.* 他已经到了应该安顿下来的年龄了. **of an ˈage with sb** of the same age as sb 与某人同岁; 同庚. **ˌover ˈage** too old 超龄. **ˌunder ˈage** not old enough; not yet adult 未到规定年龄; 未成年: *You shouldn't sell cigarettes to teenagers who are under age/to under-age teenagers.* 你不应该把香烟卖给没到岁数的青少年.

□ **ˈage-group** (also **ˈage-bracket**) *n* (people in a) period of life between two (often specified) ages 某组年龄范围(内的人们): *mix with (people in) one's own age-group* 与自己年龄范围的人混在一起 ○ *Only people in the age-bracket 20-30 need apply.* 只有年龄在20-30岁之间的人才可以申请.

ˈagelong *adj* [usu attrib 通常作定语] existing for a very long time 长久存在着的: *man's agelong struggle for freedom* 人类为自由而进行的长期奋斗.

ˌage of conˈsent age at which sb, esp a girl, is considered old enough to consent to sexual intercourse 承诺年龄(尤指女子，已到对性行为可以自主的年龄).

ˌage-ˈold *adj* [usu attrib 通常作定语] having existed for a very long time 存在已久的; 古老的: *ˌage-old ˈcustoms, ˈceremonies, etc* 古老的习俗、礼仪等.

age[2] /eɪdʒ; edʒ/ *v* (*pres p* **ageing** or **aging**, *pp* **aged** /eɪdʒd; edʒd/) **1 (a)** [I] grow old; show signs of growing old 变老; 显老; 见老: *He's aged a lot recently.* 他最近很见老. ○ *She's aging gracefully.* 她老得有风韵. **(b)** [Tn] cause (sb) to become old 使(某人)变老: *Worry aged him rapidly.* 忧虑使他老得很快. ○ *I found her greatly aged.* 我发现她老得多了. **2 (a)** [I] become mature 变成熟; 变陈: *allow wine to age* 使酒变陈. **(b)** [Tn] cause or allow (sth) to mature 使(某事物)成熟.

▷ **aged** *adj* **1** /eɪdʒd; edʒd/ [pred 作表语] of the age of 年龄在…岁: *The boy was aged ten.* 那个男孩十岁. **2** /ˈeɪdʒɪd; ˋedʒɪd/ [attrib 作定语] very old 极老的; 年老的: *an aged man* 一位老人. ⇨Usage at OLD 用法见 OLD. **the aged** /ˈeɪdʒɪd; ˋedʒɪd/ *n* [pl] very old people 老年人: *caring for the sick and the aged* 照顾病人和老人.

age·ing (also **aging**) *n* [U] **1** process of growing old 变老的过程. **2** changes that occur as the result of time passing 随时间流逝而发生的变化.

-age *suff* 后缀 (with *ns* and *vs* forming *ns* 与名词及动词结合构成名词) **1** state or condition of ... 的状态或情况: *bondage.* **2** set or group of ... 的组合或群体: *baggage* ○ *a/the peerage.* **3** action or result of ... 的动作或结果: *breakage* ○ *wastage.* **4** cost of ... 的费用: *postage* ○ *porterage.* **5** place where ... 的地方: *anchorage* ○ *orphanage.* **6** quantity or measure of ... 的数量或计量: *mileage* ○ *dosage.*

age·ism (also **agism**) /ˈeɪdʒɪzəm; ˋedʒɪzəm/ *n* [U] (*derog* 贬) (practice of) treating people unfairly or unjustly because of their age 年龄歧视(的习气).

age·less /ˈeɪdʒlɪs; ˋedʒlɪs/ *adj* **1** never growing old or appearing to grow old 不变老的; 不显老的: *Her beauty seems ageless.* 她驻颜有术. **2** eternal 永久的; 永恒的; 永存的: *the ageless mystery of the universe* 宇宙的永恒的奥秘.

agency /ˈeɪdʒənsɪ; ˋedʒənsɪ/ *n* **1 (a)** business or place of business providing a (usu specified) service 经销; 代办; 代理; 经销处; 代理处: *an employment, a travel, an advertising, a secretarial, etc agency* 职业介绍所、旅行社、广告社、秘书介绍所 ○ *Our company has agencies all over the world.* 本公司在全世界都设有代办处. **(b)** (*esp US*) government office providing a specific service 政府的特种机构: *Central Intelligence Agency* 中央情报局. **2** (idm 习语) **by/through the agency of sth/sb** (*fml* 文) as a result of the action of sb/sth 由于或通过某人[某事物]的作用: *rocks worn smooth through the agency of water* 被水冲得光滑的岩石 ○ *He obtained his position by/through the agency of friends.* 他通过朋友的帮助得到了一个职位.

agenda /əˈdʒendə; əˋdʒɛndə/ *n* (list of) matters of business to be discussed at a meeting, etc 在会议上要讨论的事项(单); 议事单; 议程表: *What is the next item on the agenda?* 议程表上的下一项是什么? ○ *The agenda for the meeting is as follows....* 这次会议的议程如下….

agent /ˈeɪdʒənt; ˋedʒənt/ *n* **1** person who acts for, or manages the affairs of, other people in business, politics, etc (商业、政治等方面的)代理人，经纪人: *an insurance agent* 保险业经纪人 ○ *a travel agent* 旅行社经纪人 ○ *our agents in the Middle East* 我们在中东的代理人. **2 (a)** person who does sth or causes sth to happen (做某事或使某事发生的)施动者: *the agent of his own ruin* 他自我毁灭的根源. **(b)** force or substance that produces an effect or change 产生某种效果或变化的力量或物质; 动因; 作用物; 剂: *cleaning, oxidizing agents* 除垢剂、氧化剂 ○ *Yeast is the raising agent in bread.* 酵母是面包的发酵剂. **3** = SECRET AGENT (SECRET): *an enemy agent* 敌探.

agent pro·vo·ca·teur /ˌæʒɒn prəˌvɒkəˈtɜː(r); ˋɑʒˌɑn

A

pro,vɑkə'tɜ:/ (*pl* **agents provocateurs** /ˌæʒɒn prəˌvɒkə'tɜ:(r); 'ɑʒ,ɑn pro,vɑkə'tɜ:/) (*French* 法) person employed to help in catching suspected criminals by tempting them to act illegally (受雇诱使嫌疑犯触犯刑律以便将之逮捕的)密探, 坐探.

ag·glom·er·ate /ə'glɒməreɪt; ə'glɑmə,ret/ *v* [I, Tn] (cause sth to) become collected into a mass (使某物)成团, 结块, 凝聚.
▷ **ag·glom·er·ate** /ə'glɒmərət; ə'glɑmərɪt/ *n* [U] (*geology* 地质) fragments of (esp volcanic) rock fused together in a mass (尤指火山岩的)集块石.
ag·glom·er·ate *adj* formed or growing into a mass 成团的; 结块的; 凝聚的.
ag·glom·era·tion /əˌglɒmə'reɪʃn; əˌglɑmə'reʃən/ *n* **1** [U] action of agglomerating 成团; 结块; 凝聚. **2** [C] (esp untidy) collection of objects (尤指不整齐的)聚集; 堆: *an ugly agglomeration of new buildings* 一大片杂乱难看的新建筑物.

ag·glu·tin·ate /ə'glu:tɪneɪt; *US* -tən-; ə'glutn,et/ *v* [I, Tn] join together as with glue; combine (使)黏结; (使)黏着; (使)结合. ▷ **ag·glu·tina·tion** /əˌglu:tɪ'neɪʃn; *US* -tə'n-; əˌglutn̩'eʃən/ *n* [U]. **ag·glu·tin·at·ive** /ə'glu:tɪnətɪv; *US* -təneɪtɪv; ə'glutn̩,etɪv/ *adj*: *Agglutinative languages* 黏着型语言.

ag·grand·ize, -ise /ə'grændaɪz; ə'græn,daɪz/ *v* [Tn] (*fml* 文) increase the power, rank, wealth or importance of (a person or country) 加大, 扩张, 增加(个人或国家的权力、力量、级别、财富或重要性). ▷ **ag·grand·ize·ment, -isement** /ə'grændɪzmənt; ə'grændɪzmənt/ *n* [U]: *His sole aim is personal aggrandizement.* 他唯一的目标就是要扩充个人的权势.

ag·grav·ate /'ægrəveɪt; 'ægrə,vet/ *v* [Tn] **1** make (a disease, a situation, an offence, etc) worse or more serious 使(疾病、情况、罪过等)恶化, 更坏, 加重, 加剧: *He aggravated his condition by leaving hospital too soon.* 他因过早出院而使病情恶化. **2** (*infml* 口) irritate (sb); annoy 激怒; 惹恼: *He aggravates her just by looking at her.* 他只是看着她就把她惹恼了.
▷ **ag·grav·at·ing** *adj* (*infml* 口) irritating; annoying 激怒的; 惹恼的: *Constant interruptions are very aggravating when you're trying to work.* 要工作的时候, 接连不断的干扰就使人非常恼火.
ag·grava·tion /ˌægrə'veɪʃn; ˌægrə'veʃən/ *n* **1** [U] making more serious; irritation 恶化; 激怒. **2** [C] thing that annoys 恼人的事物: *minor aggravations* 小别扭.

ag·greg·ate[1] /'ægrɪgeɪt; 'ægrɪ,get/ *v* **1** [I, Tn, Tn·pr] ~ **sb (to sth)** (*fml* 文) be formed or bring sb into an assembled group or amount (使)聚集; (使)集合: *aggregating riches* 聚集财富 ○ *aggregate sb to a political party* 吸收某人加入一政党. **2** [Tn] (*infml* 口) amount to (a total) 总计; 合计: *The television audience aggregated 30 millions.* 电视观众合计达3 000万人. ▷ **ag·grega·tion** /ˌægrɪ'geɪʃn; ˌægrɪ'geʃən/ *n* [U, C].

ag·greg·ate[2] /'ægrɪgət; 'ægrɪgɪt/ *n* **1** [C] total amount; mass or amount brought together 总计; 合计; 总量: *the complete aggregate of unemployment figures* 失业人数总计. **2** [U] (*geology* 地质) mass of minerals formed into one type of rock 聚成岩; 聚合体. **3** [U] materials (sand, gravel, etc) that are mixed with cement and water to make concrete 骨料(沙、碎石等, 可与水泥、水混合而成混凝土). **4** (idm 习语) **in the 'aggregate** added together; collectively 总计; 合计; 归结起来: *The tax increases will, in the aggregate, cause much hardship.* 增加税收归结起来将造成很多困难. **on 'aggregate** taken as a whole 整个来说; 总体上: *Our team scored the most goals on aggregate.* 整个来说, 我们队得分最多.
▷ **ag·greg·ate** *adj* [attrib 作定语] total; combined 总的; 合计的; 结合的: *the aggregate sum, amount, profit, etc* 总计、总量、总利润.

ag·gres·sion /ə'greʃn; ə'grɛʃən/ *n* **1** [C, U] (instance of) unprovoked attacking or hostility by one country against another 侵略: *an act of open aggression* 公然的侵略行动. **2** [U] (*psychology* 心) hostile feelings or behaviour 敌对的情绪或行为; 攻击行动: *She was always full of aggression as a child.* 她自幼心中就充满了敌对情绪.

ag·gress·ive /ə'gresɪv; ə'grɛsɪv/ *adj* **1** (**a**) (of people or animals) apt or ready to attack; offensive; quarrelsome (指人或动物)侵略的, 好攻击的, 好寻衅的, 好争吵的: *dogs trained to be aggressive* 训练成攻击型的狗 ○ *Aggressive nations threaten world peace.* 侵略成性的国家威胁世界和平. (**b**) (of things or actions) for or of an attack; offensive (指事物或行动)攻击性的: *aggressive weapons* 攻击性的武器. **2** (*often approv* 常作褒义) forceful; self-assertive 强有力的; 坚持己见的: *A good salesman must be aggressive if he wants to succeed.* 要做个好推销员一定要有闯劲才能成功. ▷ **ag·gress·ively** *adv*. **ag·gress·ive·ness** *n* [U].

ag·gressor /ə'gresə(r); ə'grɛsɚ/ *n* person or country that attacks first, without being provoked (无故而首先发动攻击的)个人或国家; 寻衅攻击者; 侵略者; 侵略国: *armed aggressors* 武装的侵略者 ○ [attrib 作定语] *the aggressor nation* 侵略国.

ag·grieved /ə'gri:vd; ə'grivd/ *adj* ~ **(at/over sth)** made to feel resentful (because of unfair treatment, etc) (因受到不公平对待等而感到)愤恨的; 愤愤不平的; 受屈的: *feel much aggrieved at losing one's job* 对失去工作感到极大怨恨 ○ *I was aggrieved to find that someone had used my toothbrush.* 我发现有人用过我的牙刷, 我很不高兴. ○ *the aggrieved party*, eg in a legal case 受冤屈的一方(如案件中).

ag·gro /'ægrəʊ; 'ægro/ *n* [U] (*Brit sl* 俚) violent aggressive behaviour intended to cause trouble 闹事; 滋事; 寻衅: *Don't give me any aggro or I'll call the police!* 你别找茬儿闹事, 要不然我就叫警察了!

aghast /ə'gɑ:st; *US* ə'gæst; ə'gæst/ *adj* [pred 作表语] ~ **(at sth)** filled with horror or amazement 惊恐; 惊奇: *He stood aghast at the terrible sight.* 他被那可怕的景象吓呆了.

agile /'ædʒaɪl; *US* 'ædʒl; 'ædʒəl/ *adj* able to move quickly and easily; active; nimble 敏捷的; 灵活的; 活泼的; 机敏的: *as agile as a monkey* 像猴子那么敏捷 ○ (*fig* 比喻) *an agile mind/brain* 敏捷的才思[机敏的头脑]. ▷ **agilely** *adv*. **agil·ity** /ə'dʒɪlətɪ; ə'dʒɪlətɪ/ *n* [U].

aging ⇨ AGE[2].

agit·ate /'ædʒɪteɪt; 'ædʒə,tet/ *v* **1** [Tn] cause anxiety to (a person, his feelings, etc); disturb; excite 使(人、感情等)产生忧虑; 搅乱; 激动: *She was agitated by his sudden appearance at the party.* 他在聚会中突然出现, 使她心烦意乱. **2** [Ipr] ~ **for/against sth** argue publicly or campaign for/against sth 煽动; 鼓动; 鼓吹: *agitate for tax reform* 鼓吹税制改革 ○ *agitate against nuclear weapons* 鼓动反对核武器. **3** [Tn] stir or shake (a liquid) briskly 搅动或摇动(液体): *Agitate the mixture to dissolve the powder.* 搅动混合物而使粉末溶化.
▷ **agit·ated** *adj* troubled or excited 焦虑的; 激动的: *Don't get all agitated!* 不要那么激动! **agita·tion** /ˌædʒɪ'teɪʃn; ˌædʒə'teʃən/ *n* **1** [U] disturbed state of mind or feelings; anxiety 烦乱; 心焦; 忧虑: *She was in a state of great agitation.* 她极度心慌意乱. **2** (**a**) [C, U] public discussion for or against sth 公开辩论; 大辩论: *women leading the agitation for equal rights* 为争取男女平等而带头辩论的妇女们. (**b**) [U] serious public concern or unrest connected with such discussion (因受鼓动而引起公众的)关注, 不安, 骚动.
agit·ator *n* **1** person who stirs up public opinion, esp on a political matter 鼓动者, 煽动者(尤指在政治方面). **2** device for shaking or mixing a liquid 液体搅拌器.

agit·prop /'ædʒɪtprɒp; 'ædʒɪt,prɑp/ *n* [U] Former Russian Communist propaganda, usu in the form of literature, music or art 前苏联共产党的宣传鼓动(通常为寓于文学、音乐或艺术中者).

aglow /ə'gləʊ; ə'glo/ *adv, adj* [pred 作表语] glowing; shining with warmth and colour 发红光; 发热; 发光彩: *Christmas trees aglow with coloured lights* 张灯结彩的圣诞树. ○ (*fig* 比喻) *happy children's faces all aglow* 快乐的儿童满面红光.

AGM /ˌeɪ dʒi: 'em; ˌe dʒi 'ɛm/ *abbr* 缩写 = (*esp Brit*) annual general meeting 年会.

ag·nail /'ægneɪl; 'æg,nel/ *n* = HANGNAIL.

ag·nostic /æg'nɒstɪk; æg'nɑstɪk/ *n* person who believes that nothing can be known about the existence of God or of anything except material things 不可知论者(对于上帝或除物质以外的任何事物是否存在, 认为不可能知道的人).
▷ **ag·nostic** *adj* holding this belief 不可知论的.
ag·nos·ti·cism /æg'nɒstɪsɪzəm; æg'nɑstə,sɪzəm/ *n* [U].

ago /əˈɡəʊ; əˋɡo/ *adv* (used after the word or phrase it modifies, esp with the simple past tense, not with the perfect tense 用于其所修饰的词语之后, 尤与简单过去时态连用而不与完成时态连用) gone by; in the past 前; 以前: *ten years ago* 十年前 ○ *not long ago* 不久以前 ○ *It happened a few minutes ago.* 那是几分钟以前发生的事. ○ *How long ago is it that you last saw her?* 你上一次看见她是多久以前的事? ○ *It was seven years ago that my brother died.* 我哥哥是七年前死的. ⇨Usage at RECENT 用法见 RECENT.

agog /əˈɡɒɡ; əˋɡɑɡ/ *adj* [pred 作表语] eager; excited 渴望; 急切; 兴奋; 激动: *agog with curiosity* 因好奇而兴奋的 ○ *be agog for news/to hear the news* 亟待得到[听到]消息 ○ *He was all agog at the surprise announcement.* 他听到那突如其来的宣布, 大为激动.

ag·on·ize, -ise /ˈæɡənaɪz; ˋæɡə,naɪz/ *v* [I, Ipr] **~ (about/over sth)** suffer great anxiety or worry intensely (about sth) (对某事物)极度忧虑或担心: *We agonized for hours about which wallpaper to buy.* 对买哪种壁纸, 我们伤了几小时的脑筋.

▷ **ag·on·ized, -ised** *adj* expressing agony 表示痛苦的: *an agonized look, scream* 痛苦的表情、尖叫声.

ag·on·iz·ing, -ising *adj* causing agony 使人痛苦的: *an agonizing pain, delay, decision* 折磨人的疼痛、恼人的耽搁、痛苦的决定. **ag·on·izingly, -isingly** *adv: agonizingly slow* 折磨人地缓慢.

ag·ony /ˈæɡənɪ; ˋæɡənɪ/ *n* **1** [U, C] extreme mental or physical suffering (精神或肉体的)极大痛苦: *The wounded man was in agony.* 那受伤的人痛苦已极. ○ *They suffered the agony of watching him burn to death.* 他们眼巴巴见他活活烧死而五内如焚. ○ *She was in an agony of indecision.* 她陷于犹豫不决的痛苦之中. ○ *He suffered agonies of remorse.* 他饱受悔恨的煎熬. **2** (idm 习语) **pile on the agony** ⇨ PILE[3]. **prolong the agony** ⇨ PROLONG.

□ **ˈagony aunt** (*Brit infml or joc* 口或谑) person who writes replies to letters printed in an agony column(2) 读者来信专栏主持人. 参看下条 agony column(2).

ˈagony column (*Brit infml or joc* 口或谑) **1** = PERSONAL COLUMN (PERSONAL). **2** part of a newspaper or magazine for letters from readers writing for advice about personal problems (报刊中关于个人疑难问题征询意见的)读者来信专栏.

ago·ra·phobia /ˌæɡərəˈfəʊbɪə; ˌæɡərəˋfobɪə/ *n* [U] abnormal fear of being in open spaces 广场恐怖; 空旷恐惧; 恐旷症.

▷ **ago·ra·phobic** /-ˈfəʊbɪk; -ˋfobɪk/ *n, adj* (person) suffering from this fear 患恐旷症的(人).

ag·rar·ian /əˈɡreərɪən; əˋɡrɛrɪən/ *adj* [usu attrib 通常作定语] (of the cultivation or ownership) of land (指耕种或所有权)土地的: *agrarian laws, problems, reforms* 土地法、问题、改革.

agree /əˈɡriː; əˋɡri/ *v* **1** [I, Ipr, It] **~ (to sth)** say 'yes'; say that one is willing; consent (to sth) 同意; 愿意; 答应(某事物): *I asked for a pay rise and she agreed.* 我请求加薪, 她就答应了. ○ *Is he going to agree to our suggestion?* 他会同意我们的建议吗? ○ *He agreed to let me go home early.* 他同意让我早些回家. Cf 参看 REFUSE[2]. **2 (a)** [I, Ipr, It, Tf, Tw] **~ (with sb) (about/on sth); ~ (with sb) (about sb); ~ (with sth)** be in harmony (with sb); have or form a similar opinion (as sb) 同意; 赞成; (与某人)意见一致: *When he said that, I had to agree.* 他既然说出那样的话了, 我也只好同意了. ○ *Do you agree with me about the need for more schools?* 关于多建一些学校一事, 你同意我的意见吗? ○ *We couldn't agree on a date/when to meet.* 关于日期[什么时候见面], 我们未能取得一致意见. ○ *I agree with his analysis of the situation.* 我同意他对情况的分析. ○ *We agreed to start early.* 我们赞成早些开始. ○ *Do we all agree that the proposal is a good one?* 我们是不是都一致认为这个建议很好? Cf 参看 DISAGREE. **(b)** [Tn] reach the same opinion on (sth) 在(某事物)上取得一致的意见; 商定; 约定: *Can we agree a price?* 我们能不能商定一个价格? ○ *They met at the agreed time.* 他们在约好的时间相见了. **3** [Tn] accept (sth) as correct; approve 认为(某事物)正确无误; 认可: *The tax inspector agreed the figures.* 税务稽查员核准了这些数字. ○ *Next year's budget has been agreed.* 明年的预算已获通过. **4** [I, Ipr] **~ (with sth)** be consistent (with sth); match (与某事物)相一致; 相符合; 相吻合: *The two accounts do not agree.* 这两个帐目不相符. ○ *Your account of the affair does not agree with mine.* 这件事你的说法和我的说法不一致. Cf 参看 DISAGREE. **5** [I, Ip] **~ (together)** be happy together; enjoy each other's company 合得来; 相投: *Brothers and sisters never seem to agree.* 兄弟姐妹好像总是合不来. Cf 参看 DISAGREE. **6** [I, Ipr] **~ (with sth)** (*grammar*) correspond (with a word or phrase) in number, person, etc (与一个词或词组在数、人称等上)一致: *The verb agrees with its subject in number and person.* 动词在数和人称上与主语一致. Cf 参看 DISAGREE. **7** (idm 习语) **aˌgree to ˈdiffer** accept differences of opinion, esp in order to avoid further argument 承认有分歧, 保留不同意见(尤用于为避免进一步争论): *We must agree to differ on this.* 我们得承认在这一问题上有分歧. **be agreed (on/about sth); be agreed (that...)** (with *it* or a plural subject 与 it 或复数主语连用) have reached an agreement 达成协议; 意见一致: *Are we all agreed on the best course of action?* 我们是否都一致同意这一最佳措施? ○ *It was agreed that another meeting was necessary.* 大家一致认为有必要再开一次会. **ˌcouldn't agree (with sb) ˈmore** agree completely with sb 与某人意见完全一致: *'The scheme's bound to fail.' 'I couldn't agree more!'* '这项计划注定要失败.' '你说得太对了!' **8** (phr v) **agree with sb** (esp in negative sentences or questions 尤用于否定句或疑问句) suit sb's health or digestion (对某人的健康或胃口)适合: *The humid climate didn't agree with him.* 那潮湿的气候对他不合适. ○ *I like mushrooms but unfortunately they don't agree with me*, ie they make me ill if I eat them. 我喜欢吃蘑菇, 可惜吃了难受(我吃了以后不舒服).

agree·able /əˈɡriːəbl; əˋɡriəbl/ *adj* **1** pleasing; giving pleasure 令人喜悦的; 令人愉快的; 宜人的: *agreeable weather* 宜人的天气 ○ *agreeable company* 合得来的同伴 ○ *I found him most agreeable.* 我觉得他极易相处. **2** [pred 作表语] **~ (to sth)** ready to agree 准备同意; 欣然同意: *If you're agreeable to our proposal, we'll go ahead.* 如果你同意我们的建议, 我们就进行了. ○ *I'll invite her, if you're agreeable to her coming.* 如果你乐意她来的话, 我就请她.

▷ **agree·ably** /-əblɪ; -əblɪ/ *adv* pleasantly 愉快地; 欣然: *agreeably surprised* 惊喜交加.

agree·ment /əˈɡriːmənt; əˋɡrimənt/ *n* **1** [C] arrangement, promise or contract made with sb 协定; 协议; 承诺; 合约: *Please sign the agreement.* 请签协议. ○ *An agreement with the employers was finally worked out.* 与雇主们的协议终于达成了. ○ *They have broken the agreement between us.* 他们撕毁了与我们的协议. **2** [U] harmony in opinion or feeling (意见或感情)协调, 相合, 一致: *The two sides failed to reach agreement.* 双方未能取得一致意见. ○ *There is little agreement as to what our policy should be.* 我们的方针政策应该怎样, 几乎没有一致的意见. ○ *Are we in agreement about the price?* 我们对价格的意见一致吗? **3** [U] (*grammar*) having the same number, gender, case or person (数、性、格或人称)一致: *agreement between subject and verb* 主语与动词一致. **4** (idm 习语) **a gentleman's agreement** ⇨ GENTLEMAN.

ag·ri·cul·ture /ˈæɡrɪkʌltʃə(r); ˋæɡrɪ,kʌltʃɚ/ *n* [U] science or practice of cultivating the land and rearing animals; farming 农学; 农业. ▷ **ag·ri·cul·tural** /ˌæɡrɪˈkʌltʃərəl; ˌæɡrɪˋkʌltʃərəl/ *adj: agricultural land, workers, machinery* 农业用地、工作者、机械. **ag·ri·cul·tur·ally** *adv.* **ag·ri·cul·tur·ist** /ˌæɡrɪˈkʌltʃərɪst; ˌæɡrɪˋkʌltʃərɪst/ *n.*

agr(o)- *comb form* 构词成分 of soil 泥土的; 土壤的: *agriculture* ○ *agronomy.*

ag·ro·no·my /əˈɡrɒnəmɪ; əˋɡrɑnəmɪ/ *n* [U] science of controlling the soil to produce crops 农学; 农艺学; 作物学. ▷ **ag·ro·nom·ist** /əˈɡrɒnəmɪst; əˋɡrɑnəmɪst/ *n.*

aground /əˈɡraʊnd; əˋɡraʊnd/ *adv, adj* [pred 作表语] (of ships) touching the bottom in shallow water (指船)搁浅: *The tanker was/went/ran aground.* 油船搁浅了.

ah /ɑː; ɑ/ *interj* (used to express surprise, delight, admiration, sympathy, etc 用以表示惊奇、喜悦、赞美、同情等): *Ah, ˈthere you are.* 啊, 原来你在这儿. ○ *Ah, good, here's the bus.* 啊, 太好了, 公共汽车来了. ○ *Ah, what a lovely baby!* 啊, 多可爱的小孩儿! ○ *Ah well, never mind.* 啊, 好啦, 没什么.

aha /ɑːˈhɑː; ɑˋhɑ/ *interj* (used esp to express surprise or triumph 尤用以表示惊奇或胜利): *Aha, so that's where she hides her money!* 啊哈, 原来她把钱藏在这儿了!

ahead /əˈhed; əˋhɛd/ *adv* **~ (of sb/sth)** further forward in space or time (在空间或时间上)向前, 往前, 朝前; 在前: *He ran ahead.* 他跑在前面. ○ *The way ahead was blocked by fallen trees.* 前面的路被倒下的树挡住了. ○ *The time to relax is when we're ahead*, eg in advance of our working schedule. 我们提前完成, 才是休息的时候(如提前完成工作计划).

□ **aˈhead of** *prep* **1** further forward in space or time than (sb/sth); in front of (在空间或时间上比某人[某事物])更前, 更早: *Directly ahead of us is the royal palace.* 我们正前方就是皇宫. ○ *London is about five hours ahead of New York.* 伦敦时间比纽约早五小时左右. ○ *Ahead of us lay ten days of intensive training.* 我们当前有十天的强化训练. **2** in the lead over (sb/sth); further advanced than 处于(某人[某事物])的领先地位; 比...更先进; 领先: *She was always well ahead of the rest of the class.* 她在班上总是遥遥领先. ○ *His ideas were (way) ahead of his time.* 他的思想比他所处的时代先进(得多).

ahem /əˈhəm; əˋhɛm/ *interj* (used in writing to indicate the noise made when clearing the throat, esp to get sb's attention, express disapproval or gain time 书面语中用以表示清嗓子的声音, 尤用以引人注意、表示不以为然或用以赢得时间): *Ahem, might I make a suggestion?* 啊哼, 我可以提个建议吗?

ahoy /əˈhɔɪ; əˋhɔɪ/ *interj* (cry used by seamen to call attention 船员们用以引人注意的呼喊声): *Ahoy there!* 啊嗬! ○ *Land/Ship ahoy!* ie There is land/a ship in sight. 啊, 看到陆地[船]了!

AI /ˌeɪ ˈaɪ; ˌe ˋaɪ/ *abbr* 缩写 = (*computing* 计) artificial intelligence.

aid /eɪd; ed/ *n* **1** [U] help 帮助; 援助: *with the aid of a friend* 在朋友的帮助下 ○ *legal aid* 法律援助 ○ *She came quickly to his aid*, ie to help him. 她急忙来帮助他. **2** [C] thing or person that helps 有助之物或人: *a ˈhearing aid* 助听器 ○ *ˈteaching aids* 教具 ○ *visual ˈaids*, eg pictures, films, etc used in teaching 视觉教具(如用于教学中的图片、影片等). **3** [U] food, money, etc sent to a country to help it (帮助某国的食物、金钱等)援助: *How much overseas/foreign aid does Britain give?* 英国在援外方面做出多少贡献? ○ [attrib 作定语] *medical ˈaid programmes* 医疗援助计划. **4** (idm 习语) **in aid of sth/sb** in support of sth/sb 以支援或帮助某事物[某人]: *collect money in aid of charity* 为资助慈善事业募捐. **what's (all) this, etc in aid of?** (*infml* 口) what is the purpose of this, etc? 这个(等)有什么用(意)?: *Now then, what's all this crying in aid of?* 得啦, 还有什么好哭的?

▷ **aid** *v* **1** [Tn, Tn·pr, Tnt] **~ sb (in/with sth)** (*fml* 文) help sb 帮助某人. **2** (idm 习语) **ˌaid and aˈbet** (*esp law* 尤用于法律) encourage or help (sb) in some criminal activity 怂恿或协助(某人)犯罪.

aide /eɪd; ed/ *n* **1** = AIDE-DE-CAMP. **2** (*esp US*) assistant 助手: *the chief aides to the President* 总统的主要助手们.

aide-de-camp /ˌeɪd də ˈkɒm; *US* ˈkæmp; ˋeddəˋkæmp/ (also **aide**) *n* (*pl* **aides-de-camp** /ˌeɪd də ˈkɒm; ˋeddəˋkæmp/) (*abbr* 缩写 **ADC**) naval or military officer who acts as assistant to a senior officer (海军或陆军的高级长官的)副官.

aide-mémoire /ˌeɪd memˈwɑː(r); ˌed,memˋwɑr/ *n* (*pl* **aides-mémoire** /ˌeɪd memˈwɑː(r); ˌed,memˋwɑr/) document, book, etc used to remind sb of sth 备忘录.

AIDS (also **Aids**) /eɪdz; edz/ *abbr* 缩写 = (*medical* 医) Acquired Immune Deficiency Syndrome 艾滋病, 爱滋病(后天免疫缺损综合征): *an Aids victim* 艾滋病患者 ○ *Aids is a fatal disease.* 艾滋病是绝症.

ail /eɪl; el/ *v* [Tn] (*arch* 古) trouble (sb) in body or mind (used esp as in the expression shown) 使(某人)痛苦或烦恼(尤用于以下示例): *What ails you?* 你有什么烦恼?

▷ **ail·ing** *adj* unwell; ill 不舒服; 生病; 有病: *My wife is ailing.* 我的妻子病了. ○ (*fig* 比喻) *the ailing economy* 病态的经济.

ail·eron /ˈeɪlərɒn; ˋeləˌrɑn/ *n* hinged part of the wing of an aircraft, used to control its balance while it is flying 副翼(飞机的机翼上控制飞行平衡的活动辅助翼). ⇨ illus at AIRCRAFT 见 AIRCRAFT 之插图.

ail·ment /ˈeɪlmənt; ˋelmənt/ *n* illness, esp a slight one 疾病(尤指轻病); 小病: *He's prone to minor ailments.* 他动不动就生点儿病.

aim[1] /eɪm; em/ *v* **1** (**a**) [I, Ipr, Tn, Tn·pr] **~ (sth) (at sth/sb)** point or direct (a weapon, blow, missile, etc) towards an object 瞄准; 对准: *You're not aiming straight.* 你瞄得不准. ○ *He aimed (his gun) at the target, fired and missed it.* 他(用枪)瞄准目标开火, 却未打中. ○ *The punch was aimed at his opponent's head.* 那一拳是冲着对手的头打去的. (**b**) [I, Ipr] **~ (at/for sth)** direct one's efforts (in the specified direction) (向某方向)努力; 力争: *He has always aimed high*, ie been ambitious. 他总是志气很高. ○ *She's aiming at* (ie trying to win) *a scholarship.* 她争取获得奖学金. (**c**) [Tn·pr] **~ sth at sb** direct (a comment, criticism, etc) at sb (评论、批评等)针对某人: *My remarks were not aimed at you.* 我的话并非针对你说的. **2** [Ipr, It] **~ at doing sth** intend or try to do sth 意欲、企图、力求做某事物: *We must aim at increasing/to increase exports.* 我们要力求增加出口货物.

aim[2] /eɪm; em/ *n* **1** [U] action of pointing or directing a weapon or missile at a target (武器或投射物向目标的)瞄准, 对准, 瞄: *My aim was accurate.* 我瞄得很准. ○ *Take careful aim (at the target) before firing.* 开火之前仔细瞄准(目标). ○ *He missed his aim*, ie did not hit the target. 他瞄准失误(未打中目标). **2** [C] purpose; intention 目的; 意图: *He has only one aim in life — to become rich.* 他活着只有一个目的 —— 发财.

aim·less /ˈeɪmlɪs; ˋemlɪs/ *adj* having no purpose 无目的的; 无目标的: *aimless wanderings* 无目的地四处流浪 ○ *lead an aimless life* 过着没有目标的生活. ▷ **aim·lessly** *adv*: *drift aimlessly from job to job* 漫无目标地不断更换工作. **aim·less·ness** *n* [U].

ain't /eɪnt; ent/ *contracted form* 缩约式 (*non-standard or joc* 不规范或谑) **1** am/is/are not: *Things ain't what they used to be.* 情况不像过去那样了. **2** has/have not: *You ain't seen nothing yet.* 你什么也没看见.

air[1] /eə(r); ɛr/ *n* **1** [U] mixture of gases surrounding the earth and breathed by all land animals and plants 空气: *Let's go out for some fresh air.* 咱们出去呼吸点儿新鲜空气吧. **2** [U] (**a**) the earth's atmosphere; open space in this 大气; 天空: *the birds of the air* 天空的鸟 ○ *be in the open air* 露天. (**b**) the earth's atmosphere as the place where aircraft fly 空中: *send goods by air* 空运货物 ○ *travel by air*, ie in an aircraft 乘飞机 ○ *The site of the old fort is clearly visible from the air.* 古堡的遗址在空中看得很清楚. ○ [attrib 作定语] *air travel, transport, traffic, freight* 航空旅行、运输、交通、货运. **3** [C] impression given; appearance or manner 给人的印象; 外貌; 态度: *smile with a triumphant air* 带着胜利神情的微笑 ○ *do things with an air*, ie confidently 很神气地(有信心地)做事情 ○ *The place has an air of mystery (about it)*, ie looks mysterious. 那地方有一种神秘的气氛(环绕着). **4** [C] (*dated* 旧) melody; tune 旋律; 曲调: *Bach's Air on a G String* 巴赫的G弦之歌. **5** [C] (*dated* 旧) light wind; breeze 微风; 和风. **6** (idm 习语) **ˌairs and ˈgraces** (*derog* 贬) affected manner intended (usu unsuccessfully) to make one appear a very refined person 矫揉造作; 惺惺作态. **a breath of fresh air** ⇨ BREATH. **castles in the air** ⇨ CASTLE. **a change of air/climate** ⇨ CHANGE[2]. **clear the air** ⇨ CLEAR[3]. **give oneself/put on ˈairs** behave in an unnatural or affected way in order to impress others 装模作样; 装腔作势. **hot air** ⇨ HOT. **in the ˈair** (**a**) in circulation; current 在流传中; 流行的: *There's (a feeling of) unrest in the air.* 四处充满了不安(的感觉). (**b**) uncertain; undecided 未确定的; 悬而未决的: *Our plans are still (up) in the air.* 我们的计划仍悬而未决. **in the open air** ⇨ OPEN[1]. **light as air/as a feather** ⇨ LIGHT[3]. **ˌon/ˌoff the ˈair** broadcast(ing)/not broadcast(ing) on radio or television (无线电或电视)广播[停播]: *This channel comes on the air every morning at 7 am.* 这个频道每天早晨7点钟开始播放. ○ *We'll be off the air for the summer and returning for a new series in the autumn.* 我们将于夏季停播而于秋季开始播放一套新节目. **ˌtake the ˈair** (*dated or fml* 旧或文) go out of doors in order to enjoy the fresh air 到户外呼吸新鲜空气. **tread on air** ⇨ TREAD. **vanish, etc into thin air** ⇨ THIN. **with one's nose in the air** ⇨ NOSE[1].

□ **ˈair base** place from which military aircraft operate

空军基地.
ˈ**air-bed** *n* mattress that can be filled with air 充气床垫.
ˈ**air-bladder** *n* (in animals and plants) bladder filled with air (动植物的)充有气体的囊, 鳔, 气囊.
ˈ**air brake** brake worked by air pressure 气闸; 气压制动器.
ˈ**airbrush** *n* device for spraying paint by means of compressed air (喷颜料的)气笔; 喷枪.
ˈ**Airbus** *n* (*propr* 专利名) aircraft operating regularly and often over short or medium distances 中短程班机.
ˌ**Air Chief** ˈ**Marshal** (*Brit*) second highest rank in the Royal Air Force (皇家空军)空军上将.
ˌ**air** ˈ**commodore** (*Brit*) officer of the Royal Air Force next below Air Vice-Marshal (皇家空军)空军准将.
ˈ**air-conditioning** *n* [U] system controlling the humidity and temperature of the air in a room or building 空气调节系统(控制室内或建筑物内空气湿度和温度的系统). ˈ**air-conditioned** *adj*: *an air-conditioned office* 有空气调节设备的办公室 ○ *Is the house air-conditioned?* 这所房子是空气调节的吗? **air·conditioner** *n*.
ˌ**air-**ˈ**cooled** *adj* cooled by a current of air 空气冷却的: *an* ˌ*air-cooled* ˈ*engine* 空气冷却的发动机.
ˈ**aircrew** *n* [CGp] crew of an aircraft 空勤人员; 空勤组.
ˈ**air-cushion** *n* **1** cushion that can be filled with air 气垫(可充气的垫子). **2** layer of air supporting eg a hovercraft 气垫(支撑如气垫船的空气层).
ˈ**airfield** *n* area of open level ground equipped with hangars and runways for (esp military) aircraft (尤指军用)飞机场.
ˈ**air force** [CGp] branch of the armed forces that uses aircraft for attack and defence 空军: *the Royal Air Force* 皇家空军 ○ [attrib 作定语] *air force officers* 空军军官.
ˈ**airgun** *n* (also ˈ**air rifle**) gun that fires pellets by means of compressed air 气枪.
ˈ**air hostess** stewardess in a passenger aircraft (客机上的)女服务员, 空中小姐.
ˈ**air letter** single sheet of light paper folded to form a letter that may be sent cheaply by airmail 航空邮笺(单页薄纸折成的航空信件, 邮资较廉).
ˈ**airlift** *n* transport of supplies, troops, etc by aircraft, esp in an emergency or when other routes are blocked 空运(尤指于紧急时期或其它通路封闭时, 运送补给、军队等): *an emergency airlift of food to the famine-stricken areas* 紧急空运食物至饥荒灾区. — *v* [Tn] transport (people, supplies, etc) in this way (此种)空运(人, 物资等): *Civilians trapped in the beleaguered city have been airlifted to safety.* 被围困在城里的老百姓已空运到安全地区.
ˈ**airline** *n* [CGp] company or service providing regular flights for public use (有定期班机为民众使用的)航空公司, 航空服务: [attrib 作定语] *an airline pilot* 民航飞机驾驶员. ˈ**airliner** *n* large passenger aircraft (大型民航)班机.
ˈ**airlock** *n* **1** stoppage in the flow of liquid in a pump or pipe, caused by a bubble of air 气塞(液泵或液管中阻止液体流动的气泡堵塞). **2** compartment with an airtight door at each end, providing access to a pressurized chamber 气闸室(两端有密闭门可通往增压室).
ˈ**airmail** *n* [U] mail carried by air 航空邮件: *send a letter (by) airmail* 寄航空信 ○ [attrib 作定语] *an airmail envelope* 航空信封 ○ *an airmail edition*, eg of a newspaper or magazine, printed on special light paper 航空版(如用特种薄纸印的报刊). — *v* [Tn] send (sth) by airmail 用航空邮寄(某物).
ˈ**airman** /-mən; -mən/ *n* (*pl* ˈ**airmen** /-mən; -mən/) **1** pilot or member of the crew of an aircraft 飞机驾驶员或乘务员. **2** (*Brit*) member of the Royal Air Force, esp below the rank of a commissioned officer 皇家空军人员(尤指军阶低于少尉者). ⇨App 9 见附录 9.
ˌ**Air** ˈ**Marshal** (*Brit*) third highest rank in the Royal Air Force (皇家空军)空军中将. ⇨App 9 见附录 9.
ˈ**airplane** *n* (*US*) = AEROPLANE.
ˈ**air pocket** partial vacuum in the air causing aircraft in flight to drop suddenly 气阱(大气中的半真空状态, 可造成飞行中的飞机突然下坠).
ˈ**airport** *n* large area where civil aircraft land and take off, usu with facilities for passengers and goods, and customs (民航)飞机场; 航空站.
ˈ**air pump** device for pumping air into or out of sth 气泵.
ˈ**air raid** attack by aircraft dropping bombs 空袭: *Many civilians were killed in the air raids on London.* 在伦敦遭空袭时, 有很多老百姓遇难. ○ [attrib 作定语] *an air-raid warning, shelter* 空袭警报、防空洞.
air rifle = AIRGUN.
ˌ**air-sea** ˈ**rescue** (organization for the) rescue of people from the sea using aircraft 海空救援, 海空救护队(用飞行器从海中救人).
ˈ**airship** *n* aircraft filled with gas and driven by engines 飞艇; 飞船.
ˈ**airsick** *adj* feeling sick as a result of travelling in an aircraft 晕机的. ˈ**airsickness** *n* [U].
ˈ**airspace** *n* [U] part of the earth's atmosphere above a country and legally controlled by that country 空域; 领空: *a violation of British airspace by foreign aircraft*, ie flying over Britain without permission 外国飞机对英国领空的侵犯.
ˈ**air speed** speed of an aircraft relative to the air through which it is moving 空速(飞行器与其所穿过的空气的相对速度). Cf 参看 GROUND SPEED (GROUND[1]).
ˈ**airstrip** (also **landing-field, landing-strip**) *n* strip of ground cleared for aircraft to land and take off (为飞机起落而开辟的)简易跑道.
ˈ**air terminal** building in a town providing transport to and from an airport 航空终点站(为往返于机场提供交通工具的市内集散处).
ˈ**airtight** *adj* not allowing air to enter or escape 不透气的; 密闭的; 密封的.
ˌ**air-to-**ˈ**air** *adj* [usu attrib 通常作定语] from one aircraft to another in flight 空对空的(在飞行中从一飞行器到另一飞行器的): *an air-to-air missile* 空对空导弹.
air traffic controller person at an airport who gives radio instructions to pilots wishing to take off or land 空中交通管制员, 航空调度员(在飞机场向要起飞或降落的飞行员发出无线电指示的人员). **air traffic control** organization within which such a person works 空中交通管制.
ˌ**Air Vice** ˈ**Marshal** (*Brit*) fourth highest rank in the Royal Air Force (皇家空军)空军少将. ⇨App 9 见附录 9.
ˈ**air-waves** *n* [pl] radio waves 无线电波.
ˈ**airway** *n* **1** ventilating passage (eg in a mine) 通气道(如矿井中者). **2** route regularly taken by aircraft 航线(飞机航行所循的固定路线).
ˈ**airwoman** *n* (*pl* **-women**) **1** woman pilot or member of the crew of an aircraft 女飞行员; 女空勤人员. **2** (*Brit*) member of the Women's Royal Air Force, esp below the rank of commissioned officer (女)皇家空军人员(尤指军阶低于少尉者).
ˈ**airworthy** *adj* (of aircraft) fit to fly; in good working order (指飞行器)适航的; 飞行性能良好的. **airworthiness** *n* [U].

air[2] /eə(r); ɛr/ *v* [Tn] **1** (**a**) put (clothing, etc) in a warm place or the open air in order to make it quite dry 晾(衣物等); 晾干. (**b**) let air into (a room, etc) to cool or freshen it 通风; 透风. **2** express (an idea, a complaint, etc) publicly 公开表示(意见、不满等): *air one's views, opinions, grievances, etc* 述说自己的看法、意见、冤情等 ○ *He likes to air his knowledge*, ie let others see how much he knows. 他喜欢炫耀自己的知识. ▷ **air·ing** /ˈeərɪŋ; ˋɛrɪŋ/ *n* [sing]: *give the blanket a good airing*, ie expose it to fresh air or warmth 把毯子好好过一下风 ○ (*fig* 比喻) *give one's views an airing*, ie express them to others 表明自己的观点.
□ ˈ**airing cupboard** heated cupboard in which to keep sheets, towels, etc (储藏被单、毛巾等的)暖橱, 烘柜.

air·borne /ˈeəbɔːn; ˋɛrˌbɔrn/ *adj* (**a**) [attrib 作定语] transported by the air 空运的; 空中传播的; 空气传播的; 风媒的: *airborne seeds* 空气传播的种子. (**b**) [pred 作表语] (of aircraft) in the air after taking off (指飞行器)起飞后在飞行中: *Smoking is forbidden until the plane is airborne.* 飞机升空时禁止吸烟. (**c**) [attrib 作定语] (of troops) specially trained for operations using aircraft (指部队)受过空战训练的: *an airborne division* 空降师.

air·craft /ˈeəkrɑːft; ˋɛrˌkræft/ *n* (*pl* unchanged 复数不变) any machine or structure that can fly in the air and is regarded as a vehicle or carrier 飞行器(可在空中飞行作运载用的任何机器或建造物); 航空器; 飞机; 飞艇;

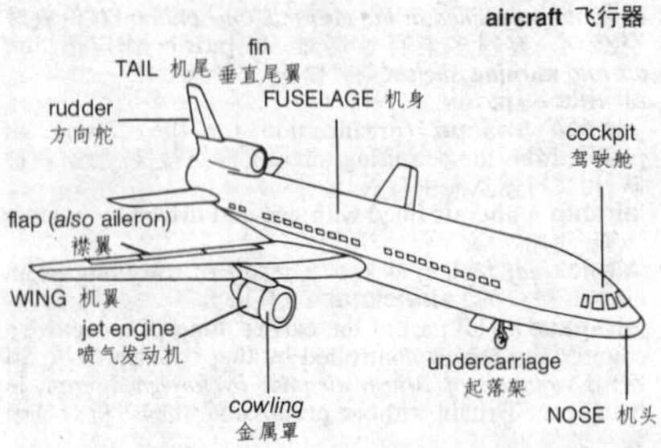

飞船. ⇨illus 见插图.

□ ˈ**aircraft-carrier** *n* ship that carries aircraft and is used as a base for landing and taking off 航空母舰.

ˈ**aircraftman** /-mən; -mən/ *n* (*pl* **-men** /-mən; -mən/) (*Brit*) lowest rank in the Royal Air Force (皇家空军)空军士兵.

ˈ**aircraftwoman** *n* (*pl* **-women** /-wɪmɪn; -wɪmɪn/) (*Brit*) lowest rank in the Women's Royal Air Force (皇家空军)空军女兵.

air·less /ˈeəlɪs; ˋɛrlɪs/ *adj* **1** not having enough fresh air; stuffy 缺少新鲜空气的; 不通风的: *an airless room* 空气不流通的房间. **2** without a breeze; calm and still 无风的; 平静的: *It was a hot, airless evening.* 那是一个闷热的晚上.

airy /ˈeərɪ; ˋɛrɪ/ *adj* (**-ier, -iest**) **1** having plenty of fresh air moving about; well-ventilated 空气流通的; 通风的: *The office was light and airy.* 那间办公室又明亮又通风. **2** [usu attrib 通常作定语] (**a**) light as air 像空气一样轻的; 轻飘飘的: *an airy silk gauze* 轻飘飘的丝质薄纱. (**b**) (*fig* 比喻) without substance; not sincere 无实质的; 不诚恳的: *an airy promise*, ie one that is unlikely to be kept 轻诺. (**c**) carefree and light-hearted 无忧无虑的; 轻松的; 漫不经心的: *an airy manner* 轻松的样子 ○ *an airy disregard for the law* 对法律满不在乎.

▷ **air·ily** /ˈeərəlɪ; ˋɛrəlɪ/ *adv* in a carefree light-hearted manner 无忧无虑地; 轻松地; 漫不经心地: *'I don't care,' he said airily.* '我才不在乎呢,'他漫不经心地说.

□ ˌ**airy-ˈfairy** *adj* (*infml derog* 口, 贬) not practical or realistic 不实际的; 不现实的: *airy-fairy notions* 异想天开的想法 ○ *The scheme seems a bit airy-fairy to me.* 这个计划我看有些不着边际.

aisle /aɪl; aɪl/ *n* **1** side passage in a church that is divided by a row of pillars from the nave (教堂内用列柱与中堂分隔的)侧廊, 走道. ⇨illus at App 1 见附录1之插图, page viii. **2** passage between rows of seats in a church, theatre, railway carriage, etc (教堂、剧院、客车车厢等内座位间的)通道, 走道. ⇨illus at App 1 见附录1之插图, page ix. **3** (idm 习语) **knock them in the aisles** ⇨ KNOCK². **rolling in the aisles** ⇨ ROLL.

aitch /eɪtʃ; etʃ/ *n* **1** the letter H H字母. **2** (idm 习语) **drop one's aitches** ⇨ DROP².

aitch·bone /ˈeɪtʃbəʊn; ˋetʃˌbon/ *n* (**a**) rump-bone of an animal 动物的臀骨. (**b**) piece of beef cut from the part above this bone (牛的)臀骨肉.

ajar /əˈdʒɑː(r); əˋdʒɑr/ *adj* [pred 作表语] (of a door) slightly open (指门)微开着, 半开着: *The door was/stood ajar.* 那扇门半开着. ○ *leave the door ajar* 让门半开着.

aka *abbr* 缩写 = (*esp US*) also known as 又名; 亦称: *Antonio Fratelli, aka 'Big Tony'* 安东尼奥·弗拉特里, 又叫'大托尼'.

akimbo /əˈkɪmbəʊ; əˋkɪmbo/ *adv* (idm 习语) **with arms akimbo** ⇨ ARM. ⇨illus at ARM 见 ARM 之插图.

akin /əˈkɪn; əˋkɪn/ *adj* [pred 作表语] **~ (to sth)** similar; related 近似; 有关系: *He felt something akin to pity.* 他感到有一种近于怜悯的感情. ○ *Pity and love are closely akin.* 怜悯近乎爱.

-al *suff* 后缀 **1** (with *ns* forming *adjs* 与名词结合构成形容词) of or concerning ...的; 关于...的: *magical* ○ *verbal*. **2** (with *vs* forming *ns* 与动词结合构成名词) process or state of... 的过程或状态: *recital* ○ *survival*.
▷ **-ally** (with sense 1 forming *advs* 与上述第1义的词结合构成副词): *sensationally*.

ala·bas·ter /ˈæləbɑːstə(r); *US* -bæs-; ˋæləˌbæstɚ/ *n* [U] soft (usu white) stone, like marble in appearance, often carved to make ornaments 雪花石膏(一种质软而通常为白色的石料, 貌似大理石, 常用以雕刻成装饰品).

▷ **ala·bas·ter** *adj* [usu attrib 通常作定语] (**a**) of alabaster 雪花石膏的: *an alabaster vase* 雪花石膏花瓶. (**b**) white or smooth like alabaster (像雪花石膏一样)白润光滑的: *her alabaster complexion* 她那白润光滑的肌肤.

à la carte /ˌɑː lɑː ˈkɑːt; ˌɑləˋkɑrt/ (of a restaurant meal) ordered as separate items from a menu, not at a fixed price for the complete meal (指饭馆的饭菜)按菜单分别点菜的(而非定价套餐): *We only have an à la carte menu.* 我们只有分类菜单. Cf 参看 TABLE D'HÔTE.

alac·rity /əˈlækrətɪ; əˋlækrətɪ/ *n* [U] (*fml or rhet* 文或修辞) prompt and eager readiness 爽快; 乐意: *He accepted her offer with alacrity.* 他欣然接受了她的建议.

à la mode /ˌɑː lɑː ˈməʊd; ˌɑləˋmod/ **1** fashionable 时髦的; 流行的. **2** (*US*) (of food) served with ice-cream (指食物)加上冰激凌的: *apple pie à la mode* 苹果饼加冰激凌.

alarm /əˈlɑːm; əˋlɑrm/ *n* **1** [C] (**a**) warning sound or signal 警报的声音或信号: *give/raise/sound the alarm* 发出警报. (**b**) apparatus that gives such a warning 警报器; 警报装置: *Where's the fire alarm?* 火警的警铃在哪里? **2** [C] = ALARM CLOCK. **3** [U] fear and excitement caused by the expectation of danger 惊慌; 恐慌: *This news fills me with alarm.* 这消息使我大为惊慌. ○ *He jumped up in alarm.* 他惊慌地跳了起来. ○ *There's no cause for alarm.* 不必惊慌. **4** (idm 习语) **a false alarm** ⇨ FALSE.

▷ **alarm** *v* [Tn] give a warning or feeling of danger to (a person or an animal); frighten; disturb 警告或惊吓(人或动物); 使惊觉; 惊动: *I don't want to alarm you, but there's a strange man in your garden.* 我并不想吓着你, 不过你的花园里可有个生人. ○ *Alarmed by the noise, the birds flew away.* 那声音把鸟吓飞了. **alarmed** *adj* [pred 作表语] **~ (at/by sth)** anxious or afraid 担心; 害怕: *I'm rather alarmed (to hear) that you're planning to leave the company.* (听说)你打算脱离这个公司, 我有些担心. **alarm·ing** *adj* causing fear; disturbing 使人害怕的; 吓人的; 扰乱人心的: *an alarming increase in the number of burglaries* 窃案惊人的增多 ○ *The report is most alarming.* 这个报告最为扰乱人心. **alarm·ingly** *adv*: *Prices have increased alarmingly.* 价格惊人地增长.

alarm·ist *n* (*derog* 贬) person who alarms others unnecessarily or excessively 不必要地或过分地使他人惊慌的人. — *adj*: *alarmist warnings, forecasts, etc* 危言耸听的警告、预告等 ○ *We mustn't be alarmist.* 我们不要危言耸听.

□ **aˈlarm clock** (also **alarm**) clock with a device that can be set to ring at a particular time, esp to wake sleepers 闹钟: *set the alarm (clock) for six o'clock* 把闹钟定在六点钟响.

alas /əˈlæs; əˋlæs/ *interj* (*dated or rhet* 旧或修辞) (expressing sorrow or regret 表示悲哀或懊悔): *Alas, they've all sold out, madam.* 哎呀, 都卖光了, 小姐.

al·ba·tross /ˈælbətrɒs; *US also* -trɔːs; ˋælbəˌtrɔs, -trɑs/ *n* large white sea-bird with long wings, common in the Pacific and Southern Oceans 信天翁(白色长翼大海鸟, 常见于太平洋及南半球各海洋).

al·beit /ˌɔːlˈbiːɪt; ɔlˋbiɪt/ *conj* (*dated or fml* 旧或文) although 虽然; 尽管: *I tried, albeit unsuccessfully, to contact him.* 尽管并未与他联系上, 可是我已经尽力而为了. ⇨Usage at ALTHOUGH 用法见 ALTHOUGH.

al·bino /ælˈbiːnəʊ; *US* -ˈbaɪ-; ælˋbaɪno/ *n* (*pl* **~s**) person or animal born with no colouring pigment in the skin and hair (which are white) and the eyes (which are pink) 患白化病的人或动物(先天色素缺乏患者, 皮肤毛发呈白色, 眼呈粉红色): [attrib 作定语] *an albino rabbit* 患白化病的兔子.

al·bum /ˈælbəm; ˋælbəm/ *n* **1** book in which a collection of photographs, autographs, postage stamps, etc can be kept 收存照片、签名手迹、邮票等的册子. **2** long-playing record with several items by the same performer

(有同一人的几项演唱或演奏的)歌集唱片: *This is one of the songs from/on her latest album.* 这是她的最新歌集唱片里的一首歌. Cf 参看 SINGLE *n* 5.

al·bu·men /ˈælbjʊmɪn; *US* ælˈbju:mən; ælˋbjumən/ *n* [U] **1** white of egg 蛋白; 蛋清. ⇨illus at EGG 见 EGG 之插图. **2** (*botany* 植) substance found in many seeds, esp the eatable part 胚乳.

al·bu·min /ˈælbjʊmɪn; *US* ælˈbju:mɪn; ælˋbjumɪn/ *n* [U] protein found in egg-white, milk, blood and some plants 白蛋白.

al·chemy /ˈælkəmɪ; ˋælkəmɪ/ *n* [U] medieval form of chemistry, the chief aim of which was to discover how to turn ordinary metals into gold 炼金术(中世纪化学, 其主要目的是寻求将普通金属转变成黄金的方法).
▷ **al·chem·ist** /ˈælkəmɪst; ˋælkəmɪst/ *n* person who studied or practised alchemy 炼金术士.

al·co·hol /ˈælkəhɒl; *US* -hɔ:l; ˋælkə,hɔl/ *n* **1** [U] (**a**) colourless liquid that can cause drunkenness, contained in drinks such as beer, wine, brandy and whisky 酒精. (**b**) this liquid used as a solvent and fuel 乙醇. **2** [U] drinks containing this 含酒精的饮料; 酒: *prohibit the sale of alcohol* 禁止售酒 ○ *I never touch* (ie drink drinks that contain) *alcohol.* 我从不喝酒. **3** [U, C] chemical compound of the same type as alcohol 醇.
▷ **al·co·holic** /ˌælkəˈhɒlɪk; *US* -ˈhɔ:l-; ˌælkəˋhɔlɪk/ *adj* **1** of or containing alcohol 酒精的; 含酒精的: *ˌalcoholic ˈdrinks* 含酒精的饮料 ○ *Home-made wine can be very alcoholic.* 自制的酒有的酒性很烈. **2** [attrib 作定语] caused by drinking alcohol 由喝酒引起的: *be in an ˌalcoholic ˈstupor* 醉得不省人事. — *n* person who drinks too much alcohol or suffers from alcoholism 饮酒过度的人; 酒鬼; 酒精中毒的人.
al·co·hol·ism /-ɪzəm; -ˌɪzəm/ *n* [U] (disease caused by) continual heavy drinking of alcohol 酒精中毒(症).

al·cove /ˈælkəʊv; ˋælkov/ *n* small space in a room, etc formed by part of the wall being set back; recess 壁凹(墙壁凹进处); 凹室; 壁龛: *The bed fits neatly into the alcove.* 床正好放进壁凹里.

al·der /ˈɔ:ldə(r); ˋɔldɚ/ *n* tree of the birch family, usu growing in marshy places 桤木(桦木科, 通常生长于沼泽地带).

al·der·man /ˈɔ:ldəmən; ˋɔldɚmən/ *n* (*pl* **-men** /-mən; -mən/) **1** (*Brit*) (esp formerly) member of a county or borough council, next in rank below the mayor (尤指旧时地位仅次于市长的)高级市政官. **2** (*US*) (in some cities) member of the city council, representing a particular part of the city (某些城市中的)市参议员. ▷ **al·der·manic** /ˌɔ:ldəˈmænɪk; ˌɔldɚˋmænɪk/ *adj*.

ale /eɪl; el/ *n* **1** (**a**) [U, C] (used esp in compounds and phrases 尤用于复合词及词组中) (type of) strong beer, usu sold in bottles 浓啤酒(酒精浓度高、通常为瓶装的啤酒): *We sell a wide range of ales and stouts.* 我们出售种类繁多的浓啤酒和黑啤酒. (**b**) [C] glass of ale 一杯浓啤酒: *Two light ales, please.* 请来两杯淡的啤酒. **2** [U] (*dated or dialect* 旧或方) beer 啤酒: *a pint of ale* 一品脱啤酒. **3** (idm 习语) **cakes and ale** ⇨ CAKE.
□ **ˈalehouse** *n* (*pl* **-houses** /-haʊzɪz; -haʊzɪz/) (*arch* 古) inn or tavern 客栈; 酒馆.

alert /əˈlɜ:t; əˋlɝt/ *adj* **~ (to sth)** attentive and quick to think or act 警惕的; 警觉的; 机警的: *be alert to possible dangers* 对可能发生的危险有警觉 ○ *The alert listener will have noticed the error.* 耳朵尖的人能听出这个错. ○ *Although he's over eighty his mind is still remarkably alert.* 他虽已年逾八十, 但头脑仍十分机敏.
▷ **alert** *n* **1** (usu *sing* 通常作单数) (time of) special watchfulness before or during an attack 警戒(期间): *The troops were placed on full alert.* 部队处于全面戒备状态. **2** warning given to prepare for danger or an attack 警报: *give/receive the alert* 发出[收到]警报. **3** (idm 习语) **on the aˈlert (against/for sth)** watchful and prepared 警惕; 提防: *Police warned the public to be on the alert for suspected terrorists.* 警方警告群众警惕涉嫌的恐怖分子.
alert *v* **1** [Tn] warn (soldiers, etc) to watch for danger and be ready to act 使(士兵等)警戒, 戒备: *Why weren't the police alerted?* 为什么警方没戒备起来? **2** [Tn·pr] **~ sb to sth** make sb aware of sth 提醒某人注意某事: *alert staff to the crisis facing the company* 提醒职员注意公司面临的危局.
alertly *adv*.
alert·ness *n* [U].

A level /ˈeɪ levl; ˋe lɛvl/ (*infml* 口) = ADVANCED LEVEL (ADVANCE): *When are you taking A level/your A levels?* 你什么时候参加(英国普通教育文凭的)高级考试? ○ *How many A levels have you got?* 你在(英国普通教育文凭的)高级考试中有几项及格? Cf 参看 O LEVEL, GCSE.

al·falfa /ælˈfælfə; ælˋfælfə/ *n* [U] (US) = LUCERNE.

al·fresco /ælˈfreskəʊ; ælˋfrɛsko/ *adj, adv* in the open air 露天(的); 在户外(的): *an alfresco lunch* 露天午餐 ○ *lunching alfresco* 在户外吃午饭.

al·gae /ˈældʒi:, *also* ˈælgaɪ; ˋældʒi/ *n* [pl] (*sing* **alga** /ˈælgə; ˋælgə/) very simple plants with no true stems or leaves, found chiefly in water 藻; 藻类.

al·ge·bra /ˈældʒɪbrə; ˋældʒəbrə/ *n* [U] branch of mathematics in which letters and symbols are used to represent quantities 代数学; 代数. ▷ **al·geb·raic** /ˌældʒɪˈbreɪɪk; ˌældʒəˋbre·ɪk/ *adj*. **al·geb·ra·ic·ally** /-klɪ; -klɪ/ *adv*.

ALGOL (also **Algol**) /ˈælgɒl; ˋælgɑl/ *abbr* 缩写 = (*computing* 计) algorithmic oriented language, a high-level programming language 算法语言.

al·go·rithm /ˈælgərɪðəm; ˋælgəˌrɪðəm/ *n* (*esp computing* 尤作计算机术语) set of rules or procedures that must be followed in solving a problem 算法; 计算程序.

alias /ˈeɪlɪəs; ˋelɪəs/ *n* name by which a person is called at other times or in other places; false name 别名; 化名; 假名: *The criminal Mick Clark has/uses several aliases.* 那个叫米克·克拉克的罪犯有[使用]好几个化名.
▷ **alias** *adv* also (falsely) called 又名; 化名: *Mick Clark, alias Sid Brown, is wanted for questioning by the police.* 米克·克拉克, 又名锡德·布朗, 被警方通缉审问.

alibi /ˈælɪbaɪ; ˋæləˌbaɪ/ *n* **1** (*law* 律) formal statement or evidence that a person was in another place at the time of a crime 某人当时不在犯罪现场的申辩或证明: *The suspects all had good alibis for the day of the robbery.* 所有疑犯都有在抢劫案发当天不在犯罪现场的充足证明. **2** (*infml* 口) excuse of any kind 借口; 托辞: *Late again, Richard? What's your alibi this time?* 理查德, 又迟到了? 这次你有什么借口呢?

alien /ˈeɪlɪən; ˋelɪən/ *n* **1** (*fml or law* 文或律) person who is not a naturalized citizen of the country in which he is living 外侨; 侨民; 外国人. **2** being from another world 从另一世界来的生物.
▷ **alien** *adj* **1** (**a**) foreign 外国的: *an alien land* 外国. (**b**) unfamiliar; strange 不熟悉的; 陌生的: *an alien environment* 陌生的环境 ○ *alien customs* 陌生的风俗习惯. **2** [pred 作表语] **~ to sth/sb** contrary to sth; hateful to sb 与某事物相反; 使某人憎恨: *Such principles are alien to our religion.* 这些原则与我们的宗教信仰相抵触. ○ *Cruelty was quite alien to his nature/to him.* 残忍的行为与他的本性[与他]格格不入.

alien·ate /ˈeɪlɪəneɪt; ˋelɪənˌet/ *v* **1** [Tn, Tn·pr] **~ sb (from sb/sth)** cause sb to become unfriendly or indifferent; estrange sb 使某人疏远或冷淡; 离间某人: *The Prime Minister's policy alienated many of her followers.* 首相的政策使很多拥护她的人疏远了她. ○ *Many artists feel alienated from society,* ie feel they do not belong to it or have been rejected by it. 很多艺术家都感到与社会脱节. **2** [Tn] (*law* 律) transfer the ownership of (property) from one person to another 转让(财产)所有权; 让渡.
▷ **ali·ena·tion** /ˌeɪlɪəˈneɪʃn; ˌelɪənˋeʃən/ *n* [U] **~ (from sb/sth)** alienating or being alienated; estrangement 疏远; 离间: *His criminal activities led to complete alienation from his family.* 他的犯罪活动导致了他与家庭完全隔绝. ○ *Mental illness can create a sense of alienation from the real world.* 精神病能产生一种与现实世界脱离的感觉.

alight[1] /əˈlaɪt; əˋlaɪt/ *adj* [pred 作表语] on fire; lit 烧着; 点着: *A cigarette set the dry grass alight.* 香烟把干草点着了. ○ *Her dress caught alight in the gas fire.* 她的衣服让煤气炉烧着了. ○ (*fig* 比喻) *Their faces were alight with joy.* 他们因喜悦而容光焕发.

alight[2] /əˈlaɪt; əˋlaɪt/ *v* (*fml* 文) **1** [I, Ipr] **~ (from sth)** get down from a horse or vehicle (从马上或车上)下来: *Passengers should never alight from a moving bus.* 公共汽车未停稳时, 乘客万勿下车. Cf 参看 DISMOUNT 1. **2** [I, Ipr] **~ (on sth)** (of a bird) come down from the air

A

and settle (指鸟)飞落: *The sparrow alighted on a nearby branch.* 那只麻雀飞落在附近的树枝上. **3** [Ipr] **~ on sth** find sth by chance 偶然发现、碰见某事物: *My eye alighted on a dusty old book at the back of the shelf.* 我偶然发现在书架后面有一本满是灰尘的旧书.

align /əˈlaɪn; əˈlaɪn/ *v* **1 (a)** [Tn, Tn·pr] **~ sth (with sth)** place or arrange (a thing or things) in a straight line 将(某物)放置或排列在一条直线上: *a row of trees aligned with the edge of the road* 与路边成一直线的一排树. **(b)** [Tn] put (the parts of a machine) into the correct position in relation to each other 将(机器的部件)安装到相互间正确的位置上: *align the wheels of a car* 校准汽车的轮子. **2** [Tn·pr] **~ oneself with sb** join sb as an ally; come into agreement with sb 与某人结盟; 与某人一致: *The Communist Party has aligned itself with the Socialists.* 共产党与社会党结成了联盟.

▷ **align·ment** *n* [U, C] **1** arrangement in a straight line 排成直线: *The sights of the gun must be in alignment with the target.* 枪的瞄准器必须与射击目标对准成一线. **2** (esp political) arrangement in groups (尤指政治上的)联盟: *the alignment of Japan with the West* 日本与西方的联盟. **3** (idm 习语) **out of alignment** not in line 不成一直线.

alike /əˈlaɪk; əˈlaɪk/ *adj* [pred 作表语] like one another; similar 相同; 一样; 相似: *These two photographs are almost alike.* 这两张照片几乎一样. ○ *The twins don't look at all alike.* 这对双胞胎一点儿都不像. ○ *All music is alike to him*, ie He cannot tell one kind from another. 各种音乐在他听来全都一样(他辨别不出音乐的种类).

▷ **alike** *adv* in the same way 同样地: *treat everybody exactly alike* 一视同仁 ○ *The climate here is always hot, summer and winter alike.* 这里的气候总是那么热, 夏季和冬季都一样.

ali·ment·ary /ˌælɪˈmentərɪ; ˌæləˈmɛntərɪ/ *adj* of food and digestion 食物及消化的.

□ **ˌalimentary caˈnal** tubular passage between the mouth and the anus through which food passes as it is digested 消化道.

ali·mony /ˈælɪmənɪ; *US* -məʊnɪ; ˈæləˌmonɪ/ *n* [U] allowance that a court may order a man to pay to his wife or former wife before or after a legal separation or divorce (经法院判决在分居或离婚以前或以后男方付给妻子或前妻的)赡养费. Cf 参看 MAINTENANCE 2.

alive /əˈlaɪv; əˈlaɪv/ *adj* [pred 作表语] **1** living; not dead 活着; 没死: *She was still alive when I reached the hospital.* 当我赶到医院的时候, 她还活着呢. ○ *Many people are still buried alive after the earthquake.* 在地震过后, 仍有很多人被活生生埋着. **2** active; lively 活泼; 活动; 有活力: *You seem very much alive today.* 你今天好像非常活跃. **3** in existence; continuing 存在着; 继续不断: *Newspaper reports kept interest in the story alive.* 报纸报道的这件事一直很吸引人. **4** (idm 习语) **aˌlive and ˈkicking** (*infml* 口) still living, in good health and active 生气勃勃; 精神饱满; 活泼; 活跃: *You'll be glad to hear that Bill is alive and kicking.* 比尔现在精神饱满, 你听了一定很高兴. **(be) alive to sth** aware of or responsive to sth 对某事物注意到的或敏感的: *He is fully alive to the possible dangers.* 他充分注意到会有危险. **(be) alive with sth** full of (living or moving things) 充满(活的或动的东西): *The lake was alive with fish.* 湖里满是游来游去的鱼. **ˌlook aˈlive** hurry up; be brisk 赶快; 快些: *Look alive! You'll miss the bus.* 快点儿啊! 你要赶不上公共汽车了.

al·kali /ˈælkəlaɪ; ˈælkəˌlaɪ/ *n* [C, U] (*chemistry* 化) any of a class of substances (eg caustic soda and ammonia) that neutralize acids and form caustic or corrosive solutions in water 碱. Cf 参看 ACID[1] 1. ▷ **al·kal·ine** *adj*: *alkaline soil* 碱性土壤. Cf 参看 ACID[2] 3. **al·ka·lin·ity** /ælkəˈlɪnɪtɪ; ˌælkəˈlɪnətɪ/ *n* [U].

all[1] /ɔːl; ɔl/ *indef det* **1** (used with plural *ns*; the *n* may be preceded by *the, this/that/these/those, my, his, her,* etc or a cardinal number 与复数名词连用, 在名词前可用 the、this[that/these/those]my、his、her等, 也可用基数词) the whole number of 全部; 全数; 全体; 所有; 一切: *All horses are animals, but not all animals are horses.* 所有的马都是动物, 但并非所有的动物都是马. ○ *All the people you invited are coming.* 你所邀请的人全都来. ○ *All my plants have died.* 我的花草全都死了. ○ *All five men are hard workers.* 他们五个人都很努力. **2** (used with uncountable *ns*; the *n* may be preceded by *the, this/that* or *my, his, her,* etc 与不可数名词连用, 在名词前可用 the, this[that]或 my、his、her等) the whole amount of 全部; 全数; 所有; 一切: *All wood tends to shrink.* 所有木头都会缩一些. ○ *You've had all the fun and I've had all the hard work.* 所有美事儿都是你的, 所有苦事儿都是我的. ○ *All this mail must be answered.* 这批信件都得回复. **3** (used with singular *ns* denoting a period of time 与表示一段时间的单数名词连用) (for) the whole duration of 全; 整; 整个: *He's worked hard all year/month/week/day*, ie throughout the year, etc. 他全年[整月/整星期/全天]都很努力. ○ *She was abroad all last summer.* 她去年整个夏天都在国外. ○ *We were unemployed (for) all that time.* 在整整那段时期我们都失业了. ○ *He has lived all his life in London.* 他一生都住在伦敦. ⇨Usage 见所附用法. **4** the greatest possible 极大限度的: *with all speed/haste/dispatch* 全速[尽快/尽速] ○ *in all honesty/frankness/sincerity*, ie speaking with the greatest honesty, etc 最诚实地[坦白地/真诚地]. **5** any whatever 无论什么; 任何: *Beyond all doubt* (ie There can't be any doubt that) *changes are coming.* 毫无疑问, 要有变化了. ○ *He denied all knowledge of the crime.* 他声称对那罪行一无所知. **6** (idm 习语) **and all ˈthat (jazz, rubbish, etc)** (*infml* 口) and other similar things 诸如此类的: *I'm bored by history — dates and battles and all that stuff.* 我让历史科给烦透了——那些日期、战争之类的事. **for all** ⇨ FOR[1]. **not all that good, well, etc** not particularly good, well, etc 不那么美好、完美等: *He doesn't sing all that well.* 他唱得并不那么好. **not as bad(ly), etc as all ˈthat** not to the extent implied 不到那种程度; 不至于: *They're not as rich as all that.* 他们并非那么富有.

□ **ˌAll ˈFools' Day** = APRIL FOOL'S DAY (APRIL).

ˈall-night *adj* [attrib 作定语] lasting, functioning, etc throughout the night 通宵的: *an all-night party, café, vigil* 通宵的聚会、咖啡馆、熬夜.

ˌAll ˈSaints' Day (also **ˌAll ˈHallows' Day**) 1 November 万圣节(11月1日).

ˌAll ˈSouls' Day 2 November 万灵节(11月2日).

ˈall-time *adj* [attrib 作定语] of all recorded time 有纪录以来的; 历来的; 空前的: *one of the all-time great tennis players* 历来最好的网球健将 ○ *an all-time* (ie unsurpassed) *record* 空前的纪录 ○ *Profits are at an all-time low*, ie lower than they have ever been. 利润空前地低.

NOTE ON USAGE 用法: **All** and **half** can be used with countable and uncountable nouns. ☆ **all** 和 **half** 与可数名词和不可数名词连用均可. **Both** is used only with plural countable nouns and refers to two in number. ☆ **both** 只与复数的可数名词连用, 所指数目为二. **1** All three can come before a noun, often with a determiner (eg *the, this, my*). 这三个词都可用于名词之前, 常与限定词(如 the、this、my)连用. **Half** must be followed by a determiner ☆ **half** 若用于名词之前, 其后必接一限定词: *He's been here all (the) week.* 他整个儿星期都在这里. ○ *Half this money is yours.* 这笔钱有一半是你的. ○ *Both (our) cars are Fords.* (我们的)两辆汽车都是福特牌的. ○ *Both (the/his) parents are teachers.* (他的)父母都是教师. **2 All** and **both** can come after a noun or pronoun ☆ **all** 和 **both** 均可用于名词或代词之后: *The spectators all booed the teams.* 全体观众都向两队喝倒彩. ○ *His parents are both teachers.* 他父母都是教师. ○ *We all/both arrived late.* 我们都[俩]来晚了. **3 All, both** and **half** are used with **of** followed by a noun or a pronoun ☆ **all**、**both** 和 **half** 都可与 **of** 连用, 其后接名词或代词: *All/Half (of) the milk had been drunk.* 所有的[有一半]奶已喝完. ○ *Both (of) his brothers are lawyers.* 他的两个哥哥都是律师. ○ *All/Both/Half of us wanted to leave early.* 我们大家[我们俩/有一半人]都想早些走.

all[2] /ɔːl; ɔl/ *indef pron* **1** the whole number or amount 全部; 全数; 所有; 一切. **(a) ~ (of sb/sth)** (referring back 用以复指前文): *We had several bottles of beer left — all (of them) have disappeared.* 我们剩下几瓶啤酒来着——全不见了. ○ *I invited my five sisters but not all (of them) can come.* 我邀请了我的五个姐妹, 但(她们)却不能都来. ○ *Some of the food has been eaten, but not all* (*of it*). 有些食物吃了, 倒不是所有的(食物)都吃了. (**b**) **~ of sb/sth** (referring forward 用以预指后文): *All of the mourners were dressed in black/They were all dressed in black.* 所有哀悼的人都穿着黑衣服[他们全穿着黑衣服]. ○ *All of the toys were broken/They were all broken.* 所有玩具都坏了[那些都坏了]. ○ *Take all of the wine/Take it all.* 把所有的酒都喝光[把酒都喝光]. ○ *All of this is yours/This is all yours.* 所有这些都是你的[这些都是你的]. **2** (followed by a relative clause, often without *that* 后接关系从句, 常不用 that) the only thing; everything 唯一的事或物; 每件事或物; 所有的一切: *All I want is peace and quiet.* 我所要的只是安宁. ○ *He took all there was/all that I had.* 他把所有的都拿去了[我所有的都拿去了]. **3** (idm 习语) **all in 'all** when everything is considered 从各方面考虑; 从各方面来说: *All in all it had been a great success.* 从各方面来说, 那都是极大的成功. **all or 'nothing** (of a course of action) requiring all one's efforts (指行动过程)需竭尽全力: *It's all or nothing — if we don't score now we've lost the match.* 一定要全力以赴——如果现在得不到分, 我们就输定了. **and·'all** also; included; in addition 也; 包括; 而且: *The wind blew everything off the table, tablecloth and all.* 风把桌子上的所有东西连桌布都吹掉了. **(not) at all** in any way; to any extent 根本; 丝毫: *I didn't enjoy it at all.* 我一点儿都不喜欢. ○ *There was nothing at all to eat.* 根本没有东西吃. ○ *Are you at all worried about the forecast?* 对这项预报你不担点儿心吗? **in all** altogether; as a total 一共; 总计: *There were twelve of us in all for dinner.* 我们一共十二个人吃饭. ○ *That's £5.40 in all.* 总共5.40英镑. **,not at 'all** (used as a polite reply to an expression of thanks 回答对方道谢的客套话). **one's 'all** everything one has; life 自己所有的一切; 生命: *They gave their all* (ie fought and died) *in the war.* 他们在战争中牺牲了.

all³ /ɔ:l; ɔl/ *indef adv* **1** completely 全; 完全: *She was dressed all in white*, ie All the clothes she was wearing were white. 她全身都穿着白的. ○ *She lives all alone/all by herself.* 她独自[一个人]生活. ○ *The coffee went all over my trousers.* 咖啡全洒在我裤子上了. **2** (*infml* 口) very 很; 非常: *She was all excited.* 她非常兴奋. ○ *Now don't get all upset about it.* 别为那件事太烦恼了. **3** (used with *too* and *adjs* or *advs* 与too及形容词或副词连用) more than is desirable 过于: *The end of the holiday came all too soon.* 假期结束得未免太快了. **4** (in sports and games) to each side (在运动与比赛中)各方: *The score was four all.* 比分是四平. **5** (idm 习语) **all a'long** (*infml* 口) all the time; from the beginning 一直; 始终; 从开始起就: *I realized I had had it in my pocket all along.* 我发觉原来这一直就在我口袋里. **all but** almost 几乎; 差不多: *The party was all but over when we arrived.* 我们到达时, 聚会已近尾声. ○ *It was all but impossible to climb back into the boat.* 再回到小船上已几乎不可能了. **all 'in** physically tired; exhausted 疲劳的; 筋疲力尽的: *At the end of the race he felt all in.* 他在赛跑结束时感到筋疲力尽. **all of sth** (of size, height, distance, etc) probably more than; fully (指体积、高度、距离等)可能超过; 足足: *It was all of two miles to the beach.* 离沙滩足足有两英里. **all 'one** forming a complete unit 成一整体; 合一: *We don't have a separate dining-room — the living area is all one.* 我们没有单独的饭厅——活动空间都在一处. **all over** (**a**) everywhere 到处; 各处: *We looked all over for the ring.* 我们到处找那只指环. ○ *I'm aching all over after the match.* 比赛后我浑身疼痛. (**b**) what one would expect of the person specified 正像所说的人一样: *That sounds like my sister all over.* 听起来跟我姐姐一模一样. **all 'right** (also *infml* 口语亦作 **al'right**) (**a**) as desired; satisfactor(il)y 如愿; 满意(的): *Is the coffee all right?* 这咖啡行吗? ○ *Are you getting along all right in your new job?* 你的新工作还行吗? (**b**) safe and well 安全而健康: *I hope the children are all right.* 我希望孩子们平安而健康. (**c**) only just good enough 尚可: *This homework is all right but you could do better.* 这份家庭作业还算可以, 其实你可以做得更好. (**d**) (expressing agreement to do what sb has asked 表示同意做某人所要求的事): *'Will you post this for me?' 'Yes, all right.'* '你把这个给我寄去可以吗?' '好吧.' (**e**) (expressing absolute certainty 表示绝对肯定): *That's the man I saw in the car all right.* 那就是我看见的那个在汽车里的人, 错不了. **all the better, harder, etc** so much better, harder, etc 更好、更努力等: *We'll have to work all the harder with two members of staff away ill.* 有两个职员因病缺勤, 我们只好加把劲儿了. **,all 'there** (*infml* 口) completely sane; mentally alert 十分清醒的; 机敏的: *He behaves very oddly at times — I don't think he's quite all there.* 他有时很怪——我觉得他头脑不太正常. **be all about sb/sth** have sb/sth as its subject matter or main point of interest 把某人[某事物]当作议题或重点: *The news is all about the latest summit meeting.* 这条消息是关于最近的首脑级会议的. **be all for sth/doing sth** believe strongly that sth is desirable 坚信某事物是想望的: *She's all for more nursery schools being built.* 她坚持主张多建托儿所. **be all 'one to sb** (of two or more choices) be a matter of indifference to sb (指有所选择时)对某人来说无所谓: *It's all one to me whether we eat now or later.* 现在吃或是等一会儿再吃对我来说都一样. **be all over ...** become known by everyone in (a place) 在(某处)为人人皆知: *News of the holiday was all over the school within minutes.* 放假的消息几分钟内全校就人人皆知了. **be all 'over sb** (*infml* 口) show excessive affection for or enthusiasm about sb when in his company 巴结某人; 讨好某人: *You can see he's infatuated by her — he was all over her at the party.* 你能看出来他被她迷住了——在聚会上他一直向她献殷勤. **be all up (with sb)** (*infml* 口) be the end (for sb) (对某人来说)全完了: *It looks as though it's all up with us now*, ie we're ruined, have no further chances, etc. 看来我们现在算全完了(我们垮了, 没有希望了等).

□ **,all-'clear** *n* **the all-clear** (usu *sing* 通常作单数) signal that danger is over 解除警报的信号; 解除危险的信号.

,all-'in *adj* including everything 包括一切的: *an ,all-in 'price*, ie with no extras 包括一切的价格(无额外费用).

'all-in wrestling type of wrestling in which there are few or no restrictions 自由式摔跤(无甚限制或全无限制的一种摔跤方式).

'all out using all possible strength and resources 全力以赴的: *The team is going all out to win the championship.* 这个队为了争取冠军而全力以赴. ○ [attrib 作定语] *make an all-out attempt to meet a deadline* 竭尽全力设法不逾期.

,all-'purpose *adj* having many different uses 有多种用途的; 通用的: *an ,all-purpose 'workroom* 通用工作室.

,all-'round *adj* [attrib 作定语] **1** not specialized; general 多方面的; 全面的: *a good all-'round education* 良好的全面发展的教育. **2** (of a person) with a wide range of abilities (指人)全能的; 多面手的: *an ,all-round 'sportsman* 全能运动员. **all-rounder** *n* person with a wide range of abilities 全能的人; 多面手.

'all-star *adj* [attrib 作定语] including many famous actors 包括很多著名演员的; 明星云集的: *an all-star cast* 有很多明星的演员阵容.

all- *pref* 前缀 (forming compound *adjs* and *advs* 用以构成复合形容词及副词) **1** entirely 完全; 全部; 全: *an all-electric kitchen* ○ *an all-American show.* **2** in the highest degree 最高程度; 最; 极: *all-important* ○ *all-powerful* ○ *all-merciful.*

Allah /'ælə; 'ælə/ *n* name of God among Muslims and among Arabs of all faiths 安拉, 真主(穆斯林及有各种不同信仰的阿拉伯人所信奉的神).

al·lay /ə'leɪ; ə'le/ *v* [Tn] (*fml* 文) make (sth) less; relieve 减轻; 缓和: *allay trouble, fears, suffering, doubt, suspicion* 减轻烦恼、恐惧、苦难、疑惑、嫌疑.

al·lega·tion /,ælɪ'geɪʃn; ,ælə'geʃən/ *n* **1** act of alleging 陈述; 宣称; 声称; 辩解. **2** statement made without proof (无证据的)陈词: *These are serious allegations.* 这是很严重的提法.

al·lege /ə'ledʒ; ə'lɛdʒ/ *v* [Tf, Cn·n/a, Cn·t only passive 只用于被动语态] (*fml* 文) state (sth) as a fact but without proof; give as an argument or excuse (无证据地)陈述, 宣称, 声称(某事); 辩解: *The prisoner alleges that he was at home on the night of the crime.* 囚犯辩称案发当晚他在家中. ○ *He alleged illness as the reason for his absence.* 他称病缺席. ○ *We were alleged to have brought goods into the country illegally.* 我们被指控非法携带货物入境.

▷ **al·leged** *adj* [attrib 作定语] stated without being proved (未经证实而)陈述的: *the alleged culprit*, ie the person said to be the culprit 被控的疑犯. **al·legedly** /əˈledʒɪdlɪ; əˈlɛdʒɪdlɪ/ *adv*: *The novel was allegedly written by a computer.* 那部小说据称是电脑写的.

al·le·gi·ance /əˈliːdʒəns; əˈlidʒəns/ *n* [U] (*fml* 文) **~ (to sb/sth)** support of or loyalty to a government, ruler, cause, etc (对政府、统治者、事业等的)拥护, 忠诚: *swear (an oath of) allegiance to the Queen* 宣誓效忠女王.

al·leg·ory /ˈælɪgərɪ; *US* ˈælɪgɔːrɪ; ˈæləˌgɔrɪ/ *n* [U, C] (style of a) story, painting or description in which the characters and events are meant as symbols of purity, truth, patience, etc 寓言(体), 讽喻(风格)(以人物和事件象征纯洁、真理、耐心等的故事、绘画或叙述). ▷ **al·leg·or·ical** /ˌælɪˈgɒrɪkl; *US* ˌælɪˈgɔːrəkl; ˌæləˈgɔrɪkəl/ *adj*. **al·leg·or·ic·ally** *adv*.

al·leg·retto /ˌælɪˈgretəʊ; ˌæləˈgrɛto/ *adj*, *adv* (*music* 音) fairly fast and lively 稍快而活泼(的).

▷ **al·leg·retto** *n* (*pl* **~s**) piece of music (to be) played in this way 小快板的乐曲.

al·legro /əˈleɪgrəʊ; əˈlegro/ *adj*, *adv* (*music* 音) in quick time; fast and lively 快速(的); 快速而活泼(的).

▷ **al·legro** *n* (*pl* **~s**) piece of music (to be) played in this way 快板的乐曲.

al·le·luia /ˌælɪˈluːjə; ˌæləˈlujə/ (also **hal·le·lu·jah**) *n*, *interj* (song or shout expressing) praise to God 哈利路亚(表达赞美上帝的歌或欢呼).

al·lergy /ˈælədʒɪ; ˈæləˑdʒɪ/ *n* **~ (to sth)** medical condition that produces an unfavourable reaction to certain foods, pollens, insect bites, etc (对某些食物、花粉、虫咬等的)变态反应性; 过敏症: *have an allergy to certain milk products* 对某些奶制品有过敏反应.

▷ **al·ler·gic** /əˈlɜːdʒɪk; əˈlɝdʒɪk/ *adj* **1** [pred 作表语] **~ (to sth)** having an allergy 有变应性; 过敏性: *I like cats but unfortunately I'm allergic to them.* 我很喜欢猫, 但可惜我对猫过敏. **2** caused by an allergy 由变态反应引起的; 由过敏引起的: *an allergic rash* 变应疹. **3** [pred 作表语] **~ to sth** (*joc infml* 谑, 口) having a strong dislike of sth (对某事物)有强烈反感: *I'm allergic to hard work!* 我最讨厌累活儿!

al·le·vi·ate /əˈliːvɪeɪt; əˈliviˌet/ *v* [Tn] make (sth) less severe; ease 减轻; 缓和: *The doctor gave her an injection to alleviate the pain.* 医生给她注射以减轻疼痛. ○ *They alleviated the boredom of waiting by singing songs.* 他们以唱歌来减轻等候的厌烦. ▷ **al·le·vi·ation** /əˌliːvɪˈeɪʃn; əˌliviˈeʃən/ *n* [U].

al·ley /ˈælɪ; ˈælɪ/ *n* **1** (also ˈ**alley-way**) narrow passage, esp between or behind houses or other buildings, usu for pedestrians only 胡同; 小巷. **2** path bordered by trees or hedges in a garden or park (花园或公园中由树木或树篱间成的)小径. ⇨Usage at ROAD 用法见 ROAD. **3** long narrow area in which games like tenpin bowling and skittles are played (十柱及九柱滚木球戏[保龄球]等的长而窄的)滚道, 球道.

al·li·ance /əˈlaɪəns; əˈlaɪəns/ *n* **1** [U] action or state of being joined or associated 结合; 结盟: *States seek to become stronger through alliance.* 各国力求通过结盟而更加强大. **2** [C] union or association formed for mutual benefit, esp between families (by marriage), countries or organizations 联姻; 联盟; 联合: *enter into/break off an alliance with a neighbouring state* 与邻国结成[解除]联盟. **3** (idm 习语) **in alliance (with sb/sth)** united; joined together 与…联合; 与…结合: *We are working in alliance with our foreign partners.* 我们与外国合伙人联合一道工作.

al·lied ⇨ ALLY.

al·li·ga·tor /ˈælɪgeɪtə(r); ˈæləˌgetɚ/ *n* **1** [C] reptile of the crocodile family found esp in the rivers and lakes of tropical America and China 短吻鳄(鳄科爬行动物, 产于热带的美洲及中国的江河湖泊). **2** [U] its skin made into leather 短吻鳄皮革: [attrib 作定语] *an alligator handbag* 鳄鱼皮手提包.

al·lit·era·tion /əˌlɪtəˈreɪʃn; əˌlɪtəˈreʃən/ *n* [U] occurrence of the same letter or sound at the beginning of two or more words in succession, as in *sing a song of sixpence* or *as thick as thieves* 头韵(连续的词语中出现的开头相同的字母或语音, 如在sing a song of sixpence或在as thick as thieves中者). ▷ **al·lit·er·at·ive** /əˈlɪtrətɪv; *US* əˈlɪtəreɪtɪv; əˈlɪtəˌretɪv/ *adj*. **al·lit·er·at·ively** *adv*.

al·loc·ate /ˈæləkeɪt; ˈæləˌket/ *v* [Tn, Dn·n, Dn·pr] **~ sth (to sb/sth)** allot or assign sth (to sb/sth) for a special purpose (为某目的)配给, 分配某事物(给某人[某事物]): *allocate funds for repair work* 拨出经费作维修用 ○ *He allocated each of us our tasks/allocated tasks to each of us.* 他给我们每个人都分配了工作.

▷ **al·loca·tion** /ˌæləˈkeɪʃn; ˌæləˈkeʃən/ *n* **1** [U] action of allocating 配给; 分配; 拨出. **2** [C] amount (of money, space, etc) allocated (钱、地方等的)配给量: *We've spent our entire allocation for the year.* 我们已经把今年拨给我们的全部经费都花光了.

al·lot /əˈlɒt; əˈlɑt/ *v* (**-tt-**) [Tn, Dn·n, Dn·pr] **~ sth (to sb/sth)** give (time, money, duties, etc) as a share of what is available; apportion sth (按现有份额)分配, 拨给, 摊派(时间、钱、任务等): *How much cash has been allotted?* 拨给多少现款? ○ *We did the work within the time they'd allotted (to) us.* 我们在指定的时间内把工作做完了. ○ *Who will she allot the easy jobs to?* 她把轻活儿分给谁呢?

▷ **al·lot·ment** *n* **1** [U] action of allotting 分配; 分派; 摊派; 拨款. **2** [C] amount or portion allotted 份额. **3** [C] (*esp Brit*) small area of public land rented for growing vegetables or flowers (作种菜或种花之用而出租的)小片公地.

al·low /əˈlaʊ; əˈlaʊ/ *v* **1** (**a**) [Tnt] permit (sb/sth) to do sth 允许, 许可, 准许(某人[某事物])做某事物: *My boss doesn't allow me to use the telephone.* 老板不许我使用电话. ○ *Passengers are not allowed to smoke.* 乘客不得吸烟. ○ (*fig* 比喻) *She allowed her mind to wander.* 她任由思绪徘徊. (**b**) [Tn] let (sth) be done or happen 容许(某事物)发生: *Photography is not allowed in this theatre.* 本剧院内不准摄影. ○ *We don't allow smoking in our house.* 在我们家里不容许吸烟. (**c**) [Tn esp passive 尤用于被动语态] (usu negative 通常作否定式) permit (sb/sth) to go in 准予(某人[某物])进入: *Dogs not allowed/No dogs allowed*, ie It is not permitted to bring dogs into this park, building, etc. 不准携狗入内. **2** [Dn·n, Dn·pr] **~ sth to sb** let sb have sth 让某人得到某事物: *This diet allows you one glass of wine a day.* 这种规定饮食可让你每天喝一杯酒. ○ *How much holiday are you allowed?* 你有多少天假? ○ *I'm not allowed visitors.* 不准我有访客. ○ *The garage allowed me £500 on my old car*, ie as a discount on the price of a new one. 汽车修理厂给我的旧汽车作价500英镑. ○ (*fig* 比喻) *He allows his imagination full play*, ie does not try to control it. 他任自己的想像力充分发挥(不想控制它). **3** [Tn, Tn·pr] **~ sth (for sb/sth)** provide sth or set sth aside for a purpose or in estimating sth (为某目的或作估计)留出, 打出某事物: *allow four sandwiches each/per head* 给每人准备四块三明治 ○ *You must allow three metres for a long-sleeved dress.* 做长袖的衣服你得打出三米来. ○ *I should allow an hour to get to London.* 到伦敦去我得留出一小时来. **4** (**a**) [Tn, Tf] (*law* 律) agree that (sth) is true or correct 同意(某事物)属实或正确: *The judge allowed my claim.* 法官同意了我的要求. ○ *He allowed that I had the right to appeal.* 他同意我有权上诉. (**b**) [Tf, Tnt] (*fml* 文) accept (sth); admit 接受(某事物); 承认: *Even if we allow that the poet was mad…* 即使我们承认那位诗人是疯子… ○ *Many allow him to be the leading artist in his field.* 很多人都认为他在这一艺术领域首屈一指. **5** (phr v) **allow for sb/sth** include sb/sth in one's calculations 在计算、估计、考虑时包括某人[某事物]: *It will take you half an hour to get to the station, allowing for traffic delays.* 把路上的耽搁算进去, 你要用半小时才能到车站. **allow sb in, out, up, etc** permit sb to enter, leave, get up, etc 允许某人进入、离开、起来等: *She won't allow the children in(to the house) until they've wiped their shoes.* 孩子们不把鞋擦干净, 她就不让他们进(屋). ○ *The patient was allowed up* (ie permitted to get out of bed) *after 10 days.* 病人十天以后才允许起来(准予离床下地). **allow of sth** (*fml* 文) permit sth; leave room for sth 容许某事物; 对某事物留有余地: *The facts allow of only one explanation.* 这些事实只能有一种解释.

▷ **al·low·able** *adj* that is or can be allowed by law, the rules, etc (法律、规则等)可容许的; 可承认的: *allowable expenses* 许可支出.

al·low·ance /əˈlaʊəns; əˈlaʊəns/ *n* **1** [C, U] amount of sth, esp money, allowed or given regularly 津贴; 补助: *an allowance of £15 per day* 每天15英镑的津贴 ○ *be paid*

A

a clothing/subsistence/travel allowance, ie money to be spent on clothes, etc 付给治装[生活/旅途]津贴 ○ *I didn't receive any allowance from my father.* 我没有收到父亲给的零用钱. ○ *a luggage allowance*, ie amount of luggage a passenger can take free, esp on an aeroplane 免费携带行李额(尤指在飞机上). **2** [C] sum of money deducted; discount 折价; 折扣: *get an allowance for your old car, fridge, cooker* 获得你的旧汽车、冰箱、炉具的折价 ○ *tax allowance*, ie money deducted from income before the current rate of tax is imposed 免税额(征收本年度税款前从总收入中减除的款额). **3** (idm 习语) **make (an) allowance for sth** consider sth when making a decision, etc (在做决定等时)考虑到某事物. **make allowances for sb** regard sb as deserving to be treated differently from others for some reason (因某原因需区别对待而)体谅、照顾某人: *You must make allowances for him because he has been ill.* 你应该体谅他, 因为他一直病着.

al·loy[1] /ˈælɔɪ; ˈælɔɪ/ *n* [C, U] **1** metal formed of a mixture of metals or of metal and another substance 合金; 齐: *Brass is an alloy of copper and zinc.* 黄铜是铜和锌的合金. ○ [attrib 作定语] *alloy steel* 合金钢. **2** inferior metal mixed with one of greater value, esp gold or silver (与一种贵金属, 尤指金或银熔合的)贱金属.

al·loy[2] /əˈlɔɪ; əˈlɔɪ/ *v* [Tn] **1** mix (sth) with metal(s) of lower value 将(某贵金属)与贱金属熔合. **2** (*fig fml* 比喻, 文) weaken or spoil (sth) by sth that reduces value or pleasure (因有减低价值或乐趣的事物而)使(某事物)减弱或受损: *happiness that no fear could alloy* 不受恐惧影响的幸福.

all·spice /ˈɔːlspaɪs; ˈɔlˌspaɪs/ (also **pimento**) *n* [U] spice made from the dried berries of the pimento, a West Indian tree 多香果香料(取自西印度多香果树的浆果干).

al·lude /əˈluːd; əˈlud/ *v* [Ipr] **~ to sb/sth** (*fml* 文) mention sb/sth briefly or indirectly 提及、暗指或暗示某人[某事物]: *You alluded to certain developments in your speech — what exactly did you mean?* 你在讲话中提到某些发展——确切的意思是什么呢?

al·lure /əˈlʊə(r); əˈlʊr/ *v* [Tn, Tnt] (*fml or rhet* 文或修辞) tempt or attract (sb) by the expectation of gaining sth (以可获得某事物)诱惑、引诱或吸引(某人): *Many settlers were allured by promises of easy wealth.* 很多安家落户的人都是受了诱惑, 以为转眼就能发财而来的.

▷ **al·lure** *n* [C, U] attractiveness; charm 诱惑力; 魅力: *the false allure of big-city life* 大城市生活的虚幻的诱惑力.

al·lure·ment *n* [C, U].

al·lur·ing *adj* attractive; charming 吸引人的; 迷人的; 诱惑人的: *an alluring smile, prospect, promise* 迷人的微笑、前景、承诺.

al·lu·sion /əˈluːʒn; əˈluʒən/ *n* **~ (to sb/sth)** indirect reference 间接提及; 暗指; 典故: *Her poetry is full of obscure literary allusions.* 他的诗里用了很多晦涩的文学典故. ○ *He resents any allusion to his baldness.* 他讨厌人家影射他秃顶.

▷ **al·lus·ive** *adj* /əˈluːsɪv; əˈlusɪv/ containing allusions 含暗示的; 暗指的; 含典故的: *Her allusive style is difficult to follow.* 她引经据典的风格晦涩难懂.

al·lu·vial /əˈluːvɪəl; əˈluvɪəl/ *adj* [usu attrib 通常作定语] made of sand, earth, etc left by rivers or floods, esp in a delta 冲积的; 淤积的: *alluvial deposits/soil/plains* 冲积物[土/平原].

ally /əˈlaɪ; əˈlaɪ/ *v* (*pt, pp* **allied**) [Ipr, Tn·pr] **~ (sb/oneself) with/to sb/sth** join or become joined with sb/sth by treaty, marriage, etc 与某人[某事物]结盟、联盟或联姻: *Britain has allied itself with other western powers for trade and defence.* 英国与其他西方强国结成了贸易及防御联盟.

▷ **al·lied** /æˈlaɪd, *also* ˈælaɪd; ˈælˌaɪd/ *adj* **~ (to sth)** connected; similar 有关联的; 类似的: *a union of ˈallied trades* 一个同业工会 ○ *The increase in violent crimes is alˈlied to the rise in unemployment.* 暴力罪案的增加与失业的增加有关.

ally /ˈælaɪ; ˈælaɪ/ *n* **1** [C] person, country, etc joined with another in order to give help and support 同盟者; 同盟国. **2 the Allies** [pl] those countries which fought with Britain in World War I and II (第一次世界大战中的)协约国; (第二次世界大战中的)同盟国.

Alma Ma·ter /ˌælmə ˈmɑːtə(r); ˈɑlməˈmɑtɚ/ **1** (*fml or joc* 文或谑) university or school at which one was or is being taught 母校. **2** (*US*) school song or anthem 校歌.

al·manac (also **al·manack**) /ˈɔːlmənæk; *US also* ˈæl-; ˈɔlməˌnæk, ˈæl-/ *n* **1** annual book or calendar of months and days, giving information about the sun, moon, tides, anniversaries, etc 历书, 年历, 天文历(有月份、日期及有关日、月、潮汐、纪念日等资料). **2** book published annually giving statistical information on various subjects, eg sport, the theatre, etc 年鉴(逐年出版的载有各项如运动、戏剧等统计资料的书).

al·mighty /ɔːlˈmaɪtɪ; ɔlˈmaɪtɪ/ *adj* **1** having all power; powerful beyond measure 全能的; 有无限权力的: *God Almighty/Almighty God* 全能的上帝. **2** [attrib 作定语] (*infml* 口) very great 极大的: *an almighty crash, nuisance, row* 极大的碰撞、讨厌事、吵嚷.

▷ **the Al·mighty** *n* [sing] God 上帝.

al·mond /ˈɑːmənd; ˈɑmənd/ *n* **1** type of tree related to the plum and peach 扁桃树. **2** nut inside the stone-fruit of this tree 扁桃仁; 杏仁: [attrib 作定语] *almond essence* 扁桃香精. ⇨illus at NUT 见 NUT 之插图.

□ **ˌalmond-ˈeyed** *adj* having narrow oval eyes 杏眼的(眼睛呈扁椭圆形的).

ˌalmond ˈpaste edible paste made from finely ground almonds 杏仁糊.

al·moner /ˈɑːmənə(r); *US* ˈælm-; ˈælmənɚ/ *n* **1** (formerly) official who distributed money and gave help to the poor 施赈员(旧时负责发放救济金赈济贫民的官员). **2** (*Brit* also **medical social worker**) social worker attached to a hospital 医院中的社会工作者.

al·most /ˈɔːlməʊst; ˈɔlˌmost/ *adv* **1** (used before *advs, ns, adjs, vs, dets* and *prons* 用于副词、名词、形容词、动词、限定词及代词之前) nearly; not quite 几乎; 差不多; 不十分: *It's a mistake they almost always make.* 那是他们几乎总要犯的错误. ○ *It's almost time to go.* 差不多是该走的时候了. ○ *Dinner's almost ready.* 饭差不多准备好了. ○ *He slipped and almost fell.* 他脚下一滑, 险些跌倒. ○ *He's almost six feet tall.* 他差不多有六英尺高. ○ *Almost anything will do.* 几乎什么都行. **2** (used before *no, nobody, none, nothing, never* 用于 no、nobody、none、nothing、never 之前) virtually; practically 实质上; 实际上; 简直: *Almost no one* (ie Hardly anyone) *believed him.* 实际上没有一个人相信他. ○ *The speaker said almost nothing* (ie scarcely anything) *worth listening to.* 那个发言人说的话简直没有一句值得听.

NOTE ON USAGE 用法: **Almost, nearly, scarcely** and **hardly** are adverbs and can be used with verbs, adverbs, adjectives and nouns. ☆ **almost**、**nearly**、**scarcely** 和 **hardly** 都是副词, 均可与动词、副词、形容词和名词连用. **1 Almost** and **nearly** are usually used in positive sentences ☆ **almost** 和 **nearly** 通常用于肯定句: *She fell and almost/nearly broke her neck.* 她跌倒了, 险些跌断了脖子. ○ *He nearly/almost always arrives late.* 他差不多总是迟到. **2 Almost** can be used with negative words. ☆ **almost** 可与否定词连用. In these cases it can be replaced with **hardly** or **scarcely** ☆ **almost** 和否定词的组合可与 **hardly** 或 **scarcely** 互换: *He ate almost nothing* (= *He ate hardly anything*). 他几乎什么也没吃. ○ *There's almost no space to sit* (= *There's hardly any space to sit*). 差不多没地方坐了. **3 Hardly** is generally preferred to **almost** + a negative verb 用 **hardly** 一般比用 **almost** + 动词否定式为宜: *She sang so quietly that I could hardly hear her* (not *I almost couldn't hear*). 她唱的声音很小, 我几乎听不见(不说 I almost couldn't hear). **4** In sentences indicating one thing happening immediately after another, **hardly** and **scarcely** can be placed at the beginning of the sentence and then subject and verb are inverted 表示一件事紧接另一件事发生的句中, 可将 **hardly** 和 **scarcely** 置于句首, 然后将主语和动词的位置互换: *Hardly/Scarcely had we arrived, when it began to rain.* 我们刚一到就下起雨来了.

alms /ɑːmz; ɑmz/ *n* [pl] (*dated* 旧) money, clothes, food, etc given to poor people 救济金; 施舍物: *He gave alms to beggars in the street.* 他给街上的乞丐一些施舍. ○ *They had to beg alms (of others) in order to feed their children.* 他们得(向别人)乞求救济来养活孩子.

□ **'almshouse** *n* (*Brit*) house, founded by gifts of charity, where poor (usu old) people may live without paying rent 救济院(由慈善机关捐赠所设, 收容贫民, 通常为老人, 免房租).

aloe /'æləʊ; 'ælo/ *n* **1** [C] type of plant with thick pointed leaves that grows in Southern Africa 芦荟(产于南非的一种植物, 叶厚而尖). **2 aloes** [sing *v*] (also **bitter aloes**) juice of the aloe plant used in medicine 芦荟苷(得自芦荟叶汁, 用作药物).

aloft /ə'lɒft; *US* ə'lɔ:ft; ə'lɔft/ *adv* **1** up in the air; overhead 在空中; 在头顶上: *flags flying aloft* 旗子高高飘扬 ○ *The balloons were already aloft.* 气球已经升空了. **2** above the deck or in the rigging of a ship 在甲板上空; 在帆索上: *He went aloft to check the sails.* 他上去检查船帆.

alone /ə'ləʊn; ə'lon/ *adj* [pred 作表语], *adv* **1** (**a**) without any companions 无伴; 独自; 孤单; 孤独: *I don't like going out alone after dark.* 我不愿意天黑后独自外出. ○ *She lives all alone in that large house.* 她独自一人住在那所大房子里. ○ (*fig* 比喻) *She stands alone* (ie is without equal) *among modern sculptors.* 她在现代雕塑家中是独一无二的. (**b**) without the help of other people or things 无他人或事物相助; 单独(的); 独力(的): *It will be difficult for one person alone.* 单独一个人很困难. ○ *She raised her family quite alone.* 她独力养家. ○ *I prefer to work on it alone.* 我愿意独力做这件事. Cf 参看 LONE, LONELY 1. ⇨Usage 见所附用法. **2** (following a *n* or *pron* 用于名词或代词之后) only; exclusively 只有; 仅仅: *The shoes alone cost £100.* 光是鞋就花了100英镑. ○ (*saying* 谚) *Time alone will tell.* 日久自明. ○ *He will be remembered for that one book alone.* 仅仅那一本书就可以使他留名于世了. ○ *You alone can help me.* 只有你才能帮助我. **3** (idm 习语) **go it a'lone** (attempt to) carry out a task or start a difficult project without help from anyone (试图)独力执行一任务或开始一艰难工作; 单干: *He decided to go it alone and start his own business.* 他决定单干创业. **leave/let sb/sth alone** not take, touch or interfere with sb/sth; not try to influence or change sb/sth 不带走、不触摸、不干涉某人[某事物]; 不想左右或改变某人[某事物]: *She's asked to be left alone but the press keep pestering her.* 她要求不要打扰她, 但报界总是缠着她不放. ○ *I've told you before — leave my things alone!* 我早已告诉过你——不要动我的东西! **leave/let well alone** ⇨ WELL[3]. **let alone** without considering 不必考虑: *There isn't enough room for 'us, let alone six dogs and a cat.* 连我们的地方都不够, 更不必说六条狗和一只猫了. ○ *I haven't decided on the 'menu yet, let alone bought the food.* 我还没决定吃什么菜呢, 更不必说买好了. **not be alone in doing sth** be one of several people who think, feel, etc sth 不单一个人这样想、感觉等某事物: *He is not alone in believing* (ie Other people agree with him) *that it may lead to war.* 不单他一个人认为那会引起战争.

NOTE ON USAGE 用法: **1 Alone** and **solitary** describe a person or thing that is separate from others. ☆ **alone**和**solitary**都用以形容一人或一事物与他人或他事物相分离. A person may prefer to be **alone/solitary** and these words do not suggest unhappiness. 用 **alone/solitary** 形容的人可能是其本人愿意如此, 这两个词并无不愉快的含义. **Alone** is not used before a noun ☆ **alone**不可用于名词之前: *I look forward to being alone in the house.* 我盼望着能自己一人在这所房子里. ○ *Our house stands alone at the end of the lane.* 我们的房子坐落在这条小巷的尽头, 没有左邻右舍. ○ *She goes for long solitary walks.* 她独自漫步, 走了很长的路. In this sense **on my, our, etc own** or **by myself, ourselves, etc** are often used in informal speech instead of **alone** 在口语中表达这种含义常用 **on my**、**our ...own**或**by myself**、**ourselves**等, 而不用 **alone**: *She's going on holiday on her own this year.* 她今年独自一人去度假. **2 Lonely** and, in US English, **lonesome** suggests that someone does not want to be alone and is unhappy ☆ **lonely**及在美式英语中用的**lonesome**, 指并非本人愿意如此, 含有不愉快之意: *He was very lonely at first when he moved to London.* 他当初刚到伦敦时很孤单. ○ *She led a solitary existence but was seldom lonely.* 她独自生活却很少感到孤单. **3 Lonely** and **solitary** can describe out-of-the-way places where people rarely go ☆ **lonely**和**solitary**可用以形容很少有人到的偏僻地方: *a lonely/solitary cottage on the moors* 荒野中孤零零的农舍.

along /ə'lɒŋ; *US* ə'lɔ:ŋ; ə'lɔŋ/ *prep* **1** from one end to or towards the other end of (sth) 沿着; 顺着: *walk along the street* 沿着街道走 ○ *go along the corridor* 顺着走廊走. **2** close to or parallel with the length of (sth) 与(某事物)的长边接近或平行: *Flowers grow along the side of the wall.* 花贴着墙生长. ○ *You can picnic along the river bank.* 你们可以靠河沿野餐.

▷ **along** *adv part* **1** onward; forward 向前; 往前: *The policeman told the crowds to move along.* 警察叫人群向前走动. ○ *Come along or we'll be late.* 快点儿吧, 要不然就迟到了. **2** in one's or sb's company: 随同; 陪同 (*infml* 口) *Come to the party and bring some friends along.* 请来参加聚会并带些朋友来. ○ *He took his dog along (with him) to work.* 他带着狗(与他)一起上班. ○ *I'll be along* (ie I will come and join you) *in a few minutes.* 我马上就来. **3** (idm 习语) **along with sth** in addition to sth 除某事物以外: *Tobacco is taxed in most countries, along with alcohol.* 除酒之外, 烟草在多数国家都要征税.

□ **alongside** /ə'lɒŋsaɪd; *US* əlɔ:ŋ'saɪd; ə'lɔŋ'saɪd/ *adv* close to the side of a ship, pier, etc 靠着(轮船、码头等的)边: *a boat moored alongside* 靠着码头停泊的船. — *prep* beside (sth) 在...旁边: *The car drew up alongside the kerb.* 小汽车在路边停下来.

aloof /ə'lu:f; ə'luf/ *adj* [usu pred 通常作表语] **~ (from sb/sth) 1** cool and remote in character; unconcerned 冷淡; 疏远; 淡漠: *I find her very aloof and unfriendly.* 我觉得她非常冷淡, 不好相处. ○ *Throughout the conversation he remained silent and aloof.* 在谈话过程中他始终一言不发、无动于衷. **2** (idm 习语) **keep/hold/stand aloof from sb/sth** take no part in sth; show no friendship towards sb 不参与某事物; 对某人无友好表示: *He stood aloof from the crowd.* 他远离人群. ▷ **aloof·ness** *n* [U].

aloud /ə'laʊd; ə'laud/ *adv* **1** in a voice loud enough to be heard, not silently or in a whisper 出声地(用足以使人听得到的声音, 既非默不作声地亦非悄悄声地): *He read his sister's letter aloud.* 他喃喃地读他妹妹的信. **2** loudly, so as to be heard at a distance 大声地, 高声地(使得在远处也听得见): *She called aloud for help.* 她高声呼救. **3** (idm 习语) **think aloud** ⇨ THINK[1].

alp /ælp; ælp/ *n* **1** (**a**) [C] high mountain, esp in Switzerland and neighbouring countries (尤指瑞士及其邻国间的)高山, 高峰. (**b**) **the Alps** [pl] group of these mountains, mostly in Switzerland, France and Italy 阿尔卑斯山脉(大部分在瑞士、法国及意大利境内). **3** [C] pasture-land on mountains in Switzerland (瑞士境内的)山区牧场.

al·paca /æl'pækə; æl'pækə/ *n* (**a**) [C] type of S American llama with long wool (南美一种体毛长的)羊驼. (**b**) [U] (cloth made from) its wool 羊驼毛织物: [attrib 作定语] *an alpaca coat* 羊驼呢外衣.

al·pen·stock /'ælpənstɒk; 'ælpən,stɑk/ *n* long stick with an iron tip, used in climbing mountains (带铁头的长的)登山杖.

al·pha /'ælfə; 'ælfə/ *n* **1** the first letter in the Greek alphabet (A, α) 希腊语字母表的第一个字母(A, α). **2** (idm 习语) **ˌAlpha and 'Omega** the beginning and the end 始终; 首尾.

□ **'alpha particle** any of the positively charged particles emitted in radioactivity or other nuclear reactions α粒子.

ˌalpha radi'ation emission of alpha rays α辐射.

'alpha ray stream of alpha particles α射线.

al·pha·bet /'ælfəbet; 'ælfə,bɛt/ *n* set of letters or symbols in a fixed order, used when writing a language 字母表: *There are 26 letters in the English alphabet.* 英语字母表中有26个字母.

▷ **al·pha·bet·ical** /ˌælfə'betɪkl; ˌælfə'bɛtɪkḷ/ *adj* in the order of the alphabet 按字母表顺序的: *Put these words in alphabetical order.* 把这些字按字母表顺序排列起来.

al·pha·bet·ic·ally /-klɪ; -klɪ/ *adv*: *books arranged alphabetically by author* 按作者姓名的字母顺序排列的书.

alp·ine /ˈælpaɪn; ˋælpaɪn/ *adj* of or found in high mountains, esp the Alps 高山的, 高山上的(尤指阿尔卑斯山): *alpine flowers* 高山上的花.
▷ **alp·ine** *n* plant that grows best in mountain regions 高山植物.

al·ready /ɔːlˈredɪ; ɔlˋrɛdɪ/ *adv* **1** (used esp with perfect tenses of a *v* 尤与动词完成时态连用) before now or before a stated or suggested time in the past 已经, 早已(在此之前或在所指的过去某时间之前): *I've already seen that film, so I'd rather see another one.* 我已经看过那部电影了, 所以还是看部别的吧. ○ *The teacher was already in the room when I arrived.* 我到的时候, 老师已经在屋里了. ○ *She had already left when I phoned.* 我打电话时, 她早已走了. **2** (used in negative sentences or questions, to show surprise 用于否定句或疑问句, 表示惊奇) as soon or as early as this 已经(如此之快或如此之早): *Have your children started school already?* 你的孩子们已经上学了? ○ *Is it 10 o'clock already?* 已经10点钟了吗? ○ *You're not leaving us already, are you?* 你已经决定要离开我们了, 是吧?

NOTE ON USAGE 用法: **Yet** and **already** are both used when talking about the possible completion of an action by or before a particular time. They are mostly used with the perfect tenses (in US usage also with the simple past). ☆ **yet** 和 **already** 均用以表示到某时或某时前可能完成的动作. 两者多与完成时态连用(在美式英语中还与简单过去时态连用). **Yet** is only used in negative statements and in questions ☆ **yet** 只用于否定的陈述句及疑问句: *'It's time to go.' 'I'm not ready yet.'* '该走了.' '我还没准备好呢.' ○ *Are you out of bed yet?* 你已经起床了吗? **Already** emphasizes the completion of an action. It is usually used in positive statements ☆ **already** 强调动作的完成, 常与肯定的陈述句连用: *By midday they had already travelled 200 miles.* 到中午为止, 他们已经走了200英里了. **Already** can be used in questions to express surprise ☆ **already** 可用于疑问句, 表示惊奇: *Have you finished lunch already? It's only 12 o'clock!* 你已经吃过午饭了吗? 现在才12点钟啊!

alright /ɔːlˈraɪt; ɔlˋraɪt/ *adv* (*non-standard or infml* 不规范或口) = ALL RIGHT (ALL[3]).

Al·sa·tian /ælˈseɪʃn; ælˋseʃən/ *n* (*US* **German shepherd**) type of large smooth-haired dog like a wolf, often trained to help the police 德国种狼狗(体大、毛光滑, 常训练作警犬). ⇨illus at App 1 见附录1之插图, page iii.

also /ˈɔːlsəʊ; ˋɔlso/ *adv* (not used with negative *vs* 不与否定式动词连用) in addition; besides; too 而且; 还; 也: *She speaks French and German and also a little Russian.* 她会说法语、德语, 还会说一点儿俄语. ○ *He is young and good-looking, and also very rich.* 他又年轻又漂亮, 而且还很富有. ○ *I teach five days a week and I also teach evening classes.* 我每星期教五天, 而且还教晚上的课. ○ *She not only plays well, but also writes music.* 她不仅很会演奏, 而且还会作曲.
□ ˈ**also-ran** *n* **1** (in racing) horse or dog not among the first three to finish (赛马或赛狗中不在前三名以内的)落选的马或狗. **2** (*fig* 比喻) person who fails to gain success or distinction 没有成功或无成就的人: *I'm afraid John is one of life's also-rans.* 很遗憾, 约翰是人间的庸才.

NOTE ON USAGE 用法: **Also, too** and **as well** indicate that the word or part of the sentence that they are specially linked to has been added to something previously mentioned. ☆ **also**、**too**、**as well** 均指句中有关词语与前面提到的事物相结合或相一致. They differ in degree of formality and position in the sentence. 这三个词语的雅俗程度和在句中的位置有所不同. **Also** is more formal and usually comes before the main verb (but after 'be' if this is the main verb) ☆ **also** 含较庄重色彩, 通常用于主要动词之前(但若主要动词是be, 则置于其后): *I've met Jane and I've also met her mother.* 我已见到简, 我也见到了她的母亲. ○ *He speaks French and he also writes it.* 他会说法语也会写法文. ○ *She was rich. She was also selfish.* 她很富. 她也很自私. **Too** and **as well** are less formal and usually come at the end of the clause ☆ **too** 和 **as well** 较为通俗, 通常用于从句的句尾: *I've read the book and I've seen the film as well/too.* 我看过这本书, 也看过这部电影. In negative sentences, **not...either** is used to indicate addition 在否定句中, 用 **not...either** 表示这种增加的成分: *They haven't phoned and they haven't written either.* 他们没来过电话, 而且也没来过信.

al·tar /ˈɔːltə(r); ˋɔltɚ/ *n* **1** (in Christian churches) table on which bread and wine are consecrated in the Communion service (基督教教堂内的)圣餐桌. ⇨illus at App 1 见附录1之插图, page viii. **2** table or raised flat-topped platform on which offerings are made to a god (供奉神时用以放置供品的)供桌, 祭坛. **3** (idm 习语) **lead sb to the altar** ⇨LEAD[3].
□ ˈ**altar-piece** *n* painting or sculpture placed behind an altar 祭坛后面的绘画或雕刻.

al·ter /ˈɔːltə(r); ˋɔltɚ/ *v* **1** [I, Tn] (cause sth/sb to) become different; change in character, position, size, shape, etc (使某事物[某人])改变; 更改, 变更, 修改, 改(性质、位置, 大小、形状等): *I didn't recognize him because he had altered so much.* 我没认出他来, 因为他变了许多. ○ *She had to alter her clothes after losing weight.* 她瘦了以后, 衣服也得修改了. ○ *The plane altered course.* 飞机更改了航线. ○ *That alters things,* ie makes the situation different. 那就使情况发生变化. ⇨ Usage at CHANGE[1] 用法见CHANGE[1]. **2** [Tn] (*euph* 婉 *esp US*) remove the testicles or ovaries of (an animal) 阉割; 给(雄性动物)去势; 给(雌性动物)割去卵巢.
▷ **al·ter·able** /ˈɔːltərəbl; ˋɔltɚəbl/ *adj* that can be altered 可改变的; 可修改的.
al·tera·tion /ˌɔːltəˈreɪʃn; ˌɔltəˋreʃən/ *n* **1** [U] changing; making a change 改变; 更改; 变更; 修改: *How much alteration will be necessary?* 需要改多少? **2** [C] act or result of changing 改变; 更改; 变更; 修改: *We are making a few alterations to the house.* 我们对房子进行了一些改建.

al·ter·ca·tion /ˌɔːltəˈkeɪʃn; ˌɔltɚˋkeʃən/ *n* [C, U] (*fml* 文) (act of) quarrelling or arguing noisily 口角; 争论; 争辩; 争吵. ⇨Usage at ARGUMENT 用法见ARGUMENT.

al·ter ego /ˌæltər ˈegəʊ; *US* ˈiːgəʊ; ˋæltɚˋigo/ (*pl* **alter egos**) (*Latin* 拉) intimate friend; person very like oneself 知己; 至友; 挚友; 至交; 极像自己的人: *He's my alter ego — we go everywhere together.* 他是我的知己——彼此形影不离.

al·tern·ate[1] /ɔːlˈtɜːnət; *US* ˈɔːltərnət; ˋɔltɚnət/ *adj* [usu attrib 通常作定语] **1** (of two things) happening or following one after the other (指两种事物)交替的, 轮流的: *a pattern of alternate circles and squares* 圆形与方形相间的图案 ○ *alternate triumph and despair* 交替而来的得意与失意. **2** every second 间隔的; 每隔一个的: *on alternate days,* eg on Monday, Wednesday, Friday, etc 每隔一日(如星期一、三、五等). **3** (of leaves growing on both sides of a stem) not opposite each other 互生的(指叶在梗两边非对生的). ▷ **al·tern·ately** *adv*.
□ **alˌternate ˈangles** (*mathematics* 数) angles like those in the Z shape formed when one line intersects two others 错角(一直线截另外两直线所成的如Z字形中的角).

al·tern·ate[2] /ˈɔːltəneɪt; ˋɔltɚˌnet/ *v* **1** [Tn, Tn·pr] **~ A and B/~ A with B** cause (things or people) to occur or appear one after the other; arrange by turns 使(事物或人)交替发生或出现; 轮流安排: *Most farmers alternate their crops.* 多数农民实行轮作. ○ *He alternated kindness with cruelty,* ie was kind, then cruel, then kind again, etc. 他恩威并行(时而和蔼可亲, 时而凶狠残暴). ○ *She alternated boys and girls round the table.* 她让男女相间围成一桌. **2** [Ipr] **~ with sth; ~ between A and B** occur in turn; consist of two different things in turn 轮流; 交替: *Rainy days alternated with dry ones.* 雨天与晴天交替更迭. ○ *The weather alternated between rain and sunshine.* 时而下雨, 时而放晴. ○ *Their work alternates between London and New York,* ie is first in London, then in New York, then back in London, etc. 他们的工作轮流在伦敦和纽约两地进行.
▷ **al·terna·tion** /ˌɔːltəˈneɪʃn; ˌɔltɚˋneʃən/ *n* [U, C].
al·tern·ator /ˈɔːltəneɪtə(r); ˋɔltɚˌnetɚ/ *n* dynamo that produces an alternating current 交流发电机.
□ ˌ**alternating ˈcurrent** (*abbr* 缩写 **AC**) electric current that reverses its direction at regular intervals 交

A

流电; 交变电流. Cf 参看 DIRECT CURRENT (DIRECT[1]).

al·tern·at·ive /ɔːlˈtɜːnətɪv; ɔlˈtɝnətɪv/ *adj* [attrib 作定语] **1** available in place of sth else; other 可用以代替其它事物的; 另一可选用的; 其他的: *find alternative means of transport* 另找一个运输方法 ○ *Have you got an alternative suggestion?* 你有没有其它的建议? ○ *The alternative book to study for the examination is 'War and Peace'.* 可供应考选读的另一本书是《战争与和平》. **2** (idm 习语) **the alˌternative soˈciety** people who prefer not to live according to the conventional standards of social behaviour 另择群体(不循传统的社会行为准则而生活的人们).

▷ **al·tern·at·ive** *n* **1** choice of two or more possibilities 可能性中的选择: *You have the alternative of marrying or remaining a bachelor.* 你可以结婚也可以仍做单身汉, 任你选择. ○ *Caught in the act, he had no alternative but to confess.* 他被当场抓住, 除了招供别无出路. **2** one of two or more possibilities 可能性之一: *One of the alternatives open to you is to resign.* 你辞职也是个办法.

al·tern·at·ively *adv* as an alternative 作为一种选择: *We could take the train or alternatively go by car.* 我们可以坐火车去, 也可以坐汽车去.

al·though (*US* also **altho**) /ɔːlˈðəʊ; ɔlˈðo/ *conj* **1** in spite of the fact that; even if 虽然; 尽管; 即使: *Although he had only entered the contest for fun, he won first prize.* 尽管他参加这次竞赛只不过是闹着玩儿而已, 却赢得了头奖. **2** and yet; nevertheless; but 然而; 可是: *He said they were married, although I'm sure they aren't.* 他说他们已经结婚了, 可是我肯定他们没结婚.

NOTE ON USAGE 用法: **1 Although** and **(even) though** can be used at the beginning of a sentence or a clause with a verb. ☆ **although** 和 **(even) though** 均可用于句首或从句之首, 与动词连用. **Though** is less formal ☆ **though** 较为通俗: *Although/Though/Even though we all tried our best, we lost the game.* 虽然我们已尽了最大的力量, 但还是输了. ○ *We lost the game although/though/even though we tried our best.* 我们输了, 然而我们已尽了最大的力量. **2 However** can be used to give a similar meaning, but must begin a new sentence ☆ **however** 也可用以表达相同的意思, 但必须用于另起一句的句首: *We all tried our best. However, we lost the game.* 我们都已尽了最大的力量. 但我们还是输了. **3 Though** and **however** can come at the end of a sentence ☆ **though** 和 **however** 可用于句尾: *We all tried our best. We lost the game, though/however.* 我们都已尽了最大的力量. 不过我们还是输了. **4 (Al)though** (or more formal **albeit**) can come before an adjective, adverb or adverbial phrase ☆ **(al)though** (更文雅的词是 **albeit**) 可用于形容词、副词或副词词组之前: *Her appointment was a significant, (al)though/albeit temporary success.* 她受聘虽说是临时性的, 但却是一大成功. ○ *He performed the task well, (al)though/albeit slowly.* 他把任务完成得很好, 只是有些慢.

al·ti·meter /ˈæltɪmiːtə(r); *US* ˌælˈtɪmətər; ælˈtɪmətɚ/ *n* instrument used esp in aircraft for showing the height above sea-level (尤指用于飞行器的)高度表; 测高计.

al·ti·tude /ˈæltɪtjuːd; *US* -tuːd; ˋæltəˌtud/ *n* **1** height above sea-level 海拔; 高度: *What is the altitude of this village?* 这个村子海拔多少? ○ *We are flying at an altitude of 20 000 feet.* 我们的飞行高度是20 000英尺. ○ [attrib 作定语] *altitude sickness* 高原病. **2** (often *pl* 常作复数) place or area high above sea-level 海拔甚高的地方: *It is difficult to breathe at these altitudes.* 在这些高的地方很难呼吸. **3** (*astronomy* 天) distance of a star or planet above the horizon, measured as an angle 地平纬度.

alto /ˈæltəʊ; ˋælto/ *n* (*pl* **~s**) (*music* 音) **1** (singer with a) voice of the highest adult male pitch 男声最高音(歌手). **2** = CONTRALTO. **3** part written for the alto voice 中音部. **4** musical instrument with the second highest pitch in its group 中音乐器: *an alto-saxophone* 中音萨克斯管.

al·to·gether /ˌɔːltəˈgeðə(r); ˌɔltəˋgɛðɚ/ *adv* **1** entirely, completely 完全地; 全部地: *I don't altogether agree with you.* 我并不完全同意你的意见. ○ *I am not altogether happy about the decision.* 我对这一决定不十分满意. **2** including everything 总共; 一共: *You owe me £68.03 altogether.* 你一共欠我68.03英镑. **3** considering everything; on the whole 总起来说; 总而言之: *The weather was bad and the food dreadful. Altogether the holiday was very disappointing.* 天气又坏, 吃的又糟. 总而言之, 这次假日很扫兴.

▷ **al·to·gether** *n* (idm 习语) **in the altoˈgether** (*infml* 口) without clothes on; naked 一丝不挂; 裸体.

al·tru·ism /ˈæltruːɪzəm; ˋæltrʊˌɪzəm/ *n* [U] principle of considering the welfare and happiness of others before one's own; unselfishness 利他主义; 无私. Cf 参看 EGOISM 2.

▷ **al·tru·ist** /ˈæltruːɪst; ˋæltrʊɪst/ *n* unselfish person 利他主义者; 无私的人.

al·tru·istic /ˌæltruːˈɪstɪk; ˌæltrʊˋɪstɪk/ *adj*. **al·tru·ist·ic·ally** /-klɪ; -klɪ/ *adv*.

alum /ˈæləm; ˋæləm/ *n* [U] white mineral salt used in medicine and in dyeing 明矾, 白矾(用于医药及染色).

alu·mi·nium /ˌæljʊˈmɪnɪəm; ˌæljəˋmɪnɪəm/ (*US* **alu·mi·num** /əˈluːmɪnəm; əˋlumɪnəm/) *n* [U] chemical element, a light silvery metal, not tarnished by air, used either pure or as an alloy for making cooking utensils, electrical apparatus, etc 铝: [attrib 作定语] *aluminium foil*, eg for wrapping food 铝箔(如用以包食物的). ⇨ App 10 见附录10.

alumna /əˈlʌmnə; əˋlʌmnə/ *n* (*pl* **-nae** /-niː; -ni/) (*US*) female former student of a school, college or university 女校友; 女毕业生.

alum·nus /əˈlʌmnəs; əˋlʌmnəs/ *n* (*pl* **-ni** /-naɪ; -naɪ/) (*US*) male former student of a school, college or university 男校友; 男毕业生.

al·ve·olar /ælˈvɪələ(r), ˌælvɪˈəʊlə(r); ælˋviəlɚ/ *adj*, *n* (*phonetics* 语音) (of a) consonant made with the tongue touching the bony ridge behind the upper front teeth, eg /t/ or /d/ 齿龈音(的)(用舌抵住上齿后面的隆骨而发出的辅音, 如 /t/ 或 /d/). ⇨ illus at THROAT 见 THROAT 之插图.

al·ways /ˈɔːlweɪz; ˋɔlwez/ *adv* **1** at all times; without exception 永远地; 无例外地; 总是; 一直: *I always think of her in that dress.* 我总是想着她穿着那件连衣裙的样子. ○ *He nearly always wears a bow tie.* 他差不多总是系着蝴蝶领结. ○ *She has always loved gardening.* 她一直喜爱园艺. **2** repeatedly; regularly 重复地; 有规律地; 一贯地: *The postman always calls at 7.30.* 邮递员一贯7时30分来. ○ *We're nearly always at church on Sundays.* 我们星期日几乎都在教堂做礼拜. **3** (usu with the continuous tenses 常与进行时态连用) again and again; persistently 一次又一次地; 持续地; 老是: *He was always asking for money.* 他老是要钱. ○ *Why are you always biting your nails?* 你为什么老是咬指甲? **4** (with *can*/*could* 与 can/could 连用) if everything else fails; whatever the circumstances may be 实在不行的话; 无论如何: *You could always use a dictionary.* 你无论如何还可以使用词典嘛. ○ *They can always go to a bank if they need more money.* 他们如果需要更多的钱, 反正还可以到银行去取. **5** (idm 习语) **always supposing (that)...** if a specified condition is fulfilled 如果某条件得到满足: *I'm going to university, always supposing I pass my exams.* 我若考试及格就要上大学了. **as ˈalways** in a way that is expected because it usu happens like that 料想与平时一样地: *As always he was late and had to run to catch the bus.* 他像平时一样又晚了, 得跑着去赶公共汽车了.

am ⇨ BE.

AM /ˌeɪ ˈem; ˋe ˋɛm/ *abbr* 缩写 = **1** (*radio* 无) amplitude modulation 振幅调制; 调幅. Cf 参看 FM 2. **2** (*US*) Master of Arts 文学硕士. Cf 参看 MA.

am (*US* **AM**) /ˌeɪ ˈem; ˋe ˋɛm/ *abbr* 缩写 = before noon (Latin *ante meridiem*) 午前, 上午(源自拉丁文 *ante meridiem*): *at 10 am*, ie in the morning 上午10时. Cf 参看 PM.

am·al·gam /əˈmælgəm; əˋmælgəm/ *n* **1** [U] alloy of mercury with another metal 汞合金; 汞齐: *The dentist used amalgam to fill my teeth.* 牙医用汞合金给我补牙. **2** [C] mixture or blend 混合物: *a subtle amalgam of spices* 适中的混合香料.

am·al·gam·ate /əˈmælgəmeɪt; əˋmælgəˌmet/ *v* [I, Ipr, Tn, Tn·pr] **~ (sb/sth) (with sb/sth)** (cause people or things to) combine or unite (使人或事物)合并, 联合, 结合: *Our local brewery has amalgamated with another* *firm.* 我们本地的酿酒厂与另一个公司合并了. ○ *The boys' and girls' schools have (been) amalgamated to form a new comprehensive.* 男校和女校联合而组成了一所新的综合中学.

▷ **am·al·gama·tion** /əˌmælgə'meɪʃn; əˌmælgə`meʃən/ *n* (**a**) [U] mixing or uniting 混合; 合并; 联合; 结合: *Amalgamation was the only alternative to going bankrupt.* 联合起来是避免破产的唯一途径. (**b**) [C] instance of this 混合; 合并; 联合; 结合: *We've seen two amalgamations in one week.* 我们在一个星期内已经见到两件合并的事了.

am·anu·en·sis /əˌmænju'ensɪs; əˌmænju`ɛnsɪs/ *n* (*pl* **-ses** /-si:z; -siz/) (*dated or fml* 旧或文) person who writes from dictation or copies what sb else has written 听写员; 誊写员.

amass /ə'mæs; ə`mæs/ *v* [Tn] gather together or collect (sth), esp in large quantities (尤指大量地)积累, 积聚, 收集(某事物): *amass a fortune* 积累财富 ○ *They amassed enough evidence to convict him on six charges.* 他们搜集了足够的证据, 宣判他有六条罪状.

ama·teur /'æmətə(r); `æməˌtɝ/ *n* **1** person who practises a sport or artistic skill without receiving money for it 业余爱好者(不为金钱而从事体育或艺术活动的人): *The tournament is open to amateurs as well as professionals.* 这次比赛不仅职业运动员可以参加, 而且业余运动员也可以参加. ○ *Although he's only an amateur he's a first-class player.* 虽然他只是个业余爱好者, 但却是一流的高手. ○ [attrib 作定语] *an amateur photographer, golfer, boxer, etc* 业余摄影、高尔夫球、拳击等爱好者 ○ *amateur dramatics, wrestling, etc* 业余演剧、摔跤等. Cf 参看 PROFESSIONAL *n.* **2** (*usu derog* 通常作贬义) person who is unskilled or inexperienced in an activity 技术不熟练的人; 无经验的人: *I shouldn't employ them — they're just a bunch of amateurs.* 我不应该雇用他们 —— 简直是一群外行.

▷ **ama·teur·ish** /'æmətərɪʃ; `æməˌtɝɪʃ/ *adj* (*often derog* 常作贬义) inexpert; unskilled 外行的; 不熟练的. **ama·teur·ishly** /'æmətərɪʃlɪ; `æməˌtɝɪʃlɪ/ *adv.* **ama·teur·ism** /'æmətərɪzəm; `æməˌtɝɪzm̩/ *n* [U].

am·at·ory /'æmətərɪ; *US* -tɔ:rɪ; `æməˌtorɪ/ *adj* (*fml or joc* 文或谑) relating to or inspired by sexual love 性爱的; 爱情的; 色情的: *amatory literature, adventures* 艳情文学、艳遇.

am·aze /ə'meɪz; ə`mez/ *v* [Tn esp passive 尤用于被动语态] fill (sb) with great surprise or wonder 使(某人)惊异或惊奇: *He amazed everyone by passing his driving test.* 他驾驶考试合格使大家很惊奇. ○ *We were amazed at/by the change in his appearance.* 他的样子变得使我们大为惊讶. ○ *She was amazed/It amazed her that he was still alive.* 他居然还活着使她感到惊异. ▷ **amaze·ment** *n* [U]: *He looked at me in amazement.* 他惊愕地看着我. ○ *I heard with amazement that....* 我听到...大为吃惊. **amaz·ing** *adj* (*usu approv* 通常作褒义): *an amazing speed, player, feat* 令人惊异的速度、表演者、事迹 ○ *I find it amazing that you can't swim.* 你不会游泳可使我大吃一惊. **amaz·ingly** *adv*: *She's amazingly clever.* 她出奇地聪明.

am·azon /'æməzən; *US* -zɒn; `æməˌzɑn/ *n* **1** tall strong athletic woman 魁梧健壮的女人. **2 Amazon** (in Greek mythology) member of a race of female warriors (希腊神话中的)亚马孙族女战士. ▷ **ama·zo·nian** /ˌæmə'zəʊnɪən; ˌæmə`zonɪən/ *adj.*

am·bas·sador /æm'bæsədə(r); æm`bæsədɚ/ *n* **1** diplomat sent from one country to another either as a permanent representative or on a special mission 大使; 使节: *the British Ambassador to Greece* 英国驻希腊大使. Cf 参看 CONSUL 1, HIGH COMMISSIONER (HIGH[1]). **2** authorized representative or messenger 经授权的代表或使者.

▷ **am·bas·sad·orial** /æmˌbæsə'dɔ:rɪəl; æmˌbæsə`dorɪəl/ *adj.*

am·bas·sad·ress /æm'bæsədrɪs; æm`bæsədrɪs/ *n* **1** female ambassador 女大使. **2** ambassador's wife 大使夫人.

□ **ambassador-at-large** *n* (*pl* **-dors-at-large**) (*esp US*) ambassador to more than one country, often on a specific mission 无任所大使; 巡回大使.

am·ber /'æmbə(r); `æmbɚ/ *n* **1** [U] (**a**) hard clear yellowish-brown gum used for making ornaments or jewellery 琥珀: [attrib 作定语] *an amber necklace* 琥珀项链. (**b**) its colour 琥珀色(黄褐色). **2** [C] yellow traffic-light seen between red and green 黄色交通信号灯(显示于红色与绿色交通信号灯之间).

am·ber·gris /'æmbəgri:s; *US* -grɪs; `æmbɚˌgrɪs/ *n* [U] wax-like substance present in the intestines of sperm-whales and found floating in tropical seas, used as a fixative in perfumes 龙涎香(抹香鲸肠道内的蜡状物质, 见于热带海洋中漂浮, 可用作香精的定香剂).

ambi- *comb form* 构词成分 referring to both of two 两者: *ambidextrous* ○ *ambivalent.*

am·bi·dex·trous /ˌæmbɪ'dekstrəs; ˌæmbə`dɛkstrəs/ *adj* able to use the left hand or the right hand equally well 左右手都很灵巧的.

am·bi·ence (also **am·bi·ance**) /'æmbɪəns; `æmbɪəns/ *n* environment; atmosphere of a place 环境; 气氛: *We've tried to create the ambience of a French bistro.* 我们想尽量创造出法国小餐馆的气氛.

am·bi·ent /'æmbɪənt; `æmbɪənt/ *adj* [attrib 作定语] (*fml* 文) (of air, etc) on all sides; surrounding (指空气等)环绕四周的, 周围的.

am·bi·gu·ity /ˌæmbɪ'gju:ətɪ; ˌæmbɪ`gjuətɪ/ *n* (**a**) [U] presence of more than one meaning 不止一种意思; 歧义: *Much British humour depends on ambiguity.* 英国幽默有很多是靠一语双关而得. (**b**) [C] instance of this 模棱两可的意思: *She was quick to notice the ambiguities in the article.* 她很快就察觉出了文中的那些模棱两可的意思.

am·bigu·ous /æm'bɪgjʊəs; æm`bɪgjuəs/ *adj* **1** having more than one possible meaning 有不止一种意思的; 有歧义的: *'Look at those pretty little girls' dresses' is ambiguous, because it is not clear whether the girls or the dresses are 'pretty'.* '看看那些漂亮的小女孩儿的连衣裙'这句话有歧义, 因为不清楚是'小女孩儿'还是'连衣裙'是'漂亮的'. **2** uncertain in meaning or intention 意向不明的; 暧昧的: *an ambiguous smile, glance, gesture, etc* 用意含糊的微笑、一瞥、手势等. ▷ **am·bigu·ously** *adv.* **am·bigu·ous·ness** *n* [U].

am·bit /'æmbɪt; `æmbɪt/ *n* [sing] bounds, scope or extent (of power, authority, etc) (权势等的)范围, 界限, 限度.

am·bi·tion /æm'bɪʃn; æm`bɪʃən/ *n* **~ (to be/do sth)** **1** (**a**) [U, C] strong desire to achieve sth 雄心; 野心; 志气; 抱负; 志向: *filled with ambition to become famous, rich, powerful, etc* 立志要成名、发财、有权势等. (**b**) [C] particular desire of this kind 雄心; 野心; 志气; 抱负; 志向: *have great ambitions* 有远大的志向. **2** [C] object of this desire 目标; 夙愿: *achieve/realize/fulfil one's ambitions* 达到目标[实现抱负/得偿夙愿].

am·bi·tious /æm'bɪʃəs; æm`bɪʃəs/ *adj* **1 ~ (to be/do sth); ~ (for sth)** full of ambition, esp for success or money (尤指为获得成功或金钱)有雄心的, 野心勃勃的: *an ambitious young manager* 有雄心壮志的年轻的经理 ○ *ambitious to succeed in life* 立志要有所成就 ○ *ambitious for one's children* 望子成龙. **2** showing or requiring ambition 显示或需要有雄心的或野心的: *ambitious plans to complete the project ahead of schedule* 要提前完成这一项目的宏伟计划. ▷ **am·bi·tiously** *adv.*

am·bi·val·ent /æm'bɪvələnt; æm`bɪvələnt/ *adj* having or showing mixed feelings about a certain object, person or situation 对某物、某人或某境况具有或显示矛盾情感的: *an ambivalent attitude towards one's best friend's wife* 对至友的妻子有矛盾的心态. ▷ **am·bi·val·ence** *n* [U]. **am·bi·val·ently** *adv.*

amble /'æmbl; `æmbl̩/ *v* [I, Ipr, Ip] **1** (of a person) ride or walk at a slow, leisurely pace (指人)乘骑缓行或漫步, 徐行: *He came ambling down the road.* 他沿路溜溜达达地来了. ○ *We ambled along for miles.* 我们缓缓而行达数英里. **2** (of a horse) move slowly, lifting the two feet on one side together (指马)溜花蹄(同侧两蹄同时离地行走).

▷ **amble** *n* [sing] slow, leisurely pace 缓步; 徐步; 漫步: *walk at an amble* 徐步而行.

am·bro·sia /æm'brəʊzɪə; *US* -əʊʒə; æm`broʒə/ *n* [U] **1** (in Greek mythology) food of the gods (希腊神话中)神仙的食物. Cf 参看 NECTAR 2. **2** thing that tastes or smells delicious 好吃或好闻的东西.

am·bu·lance /'æmbjʊləns; `æmbjələns/ *n* vehicle equipped to carry sick or injured people to hospital, etc

救护车.

am·bush /ˈæmbʊʃ; ˋæmbʊʃ/ *n* **1** [U] (of troops, police, etc) waiting in a hidden position to make a surprise attack (指部队、警察等)在隐蔽位置等待突然袭击; 埋伏: *lie/wait in ambush* 打埋伏. **2** [C] **(a)** surprise attack from a hidden position 从隐蔽位置突然袭击; 伏击: *They laid an ambush for the enemy patrol.* 他们埋伏起来准备伏击巡逻的敌人. **(b)** people making such an attack 埋伏着的人; 伏兵. **(c)** place from which it is made 设伏地点; 伏击处.

▷ **am·bush** *v* [Tn] make a surprise attack on (sb) from a hidden position 从隐蔽位置突然袭击(某人); 伏击: *ambush an enemy patrol* 伏击巡逻的敌人.

ameba (*US*) = AMOEBA.

ameli·or·ate /əˈmiːlɪəreɪt; əˈmiljəˌret/ *v* [I, Tn] (*fml* 文) (cause sth to) become better (使某事物)变得更好, 改善, 改良: *ameliorate conditions, circumstances, living standards, etc* 改进情况、改善环境、提高生活水平. ▷ **ameli·ora·tion** /əˌmiːlɪəˈreɪʃn; əˌmiljəˈreʃən/ *n* [U].

amen /ɑːˈmen, eɪˈmen; ˋɑˈmɛn, ˋeˈmɛn/ *interj, n* (used esp at the end of a prayer or hymn 尤用于祈祷或圣歌结束时) so be it; may it be so 阿门; 但愿如此; 诚心所愿: *The choir sang the amens beautifully.* 唱诗班唱的阿门非常优美. ○ *Amen to that,* ie I certainly agree with that. 我当然同意.

amen·able /əˈmiːnəbl; əˈminəbl̩/ *adj* **1 ~ (to sth)** (of people) willing to be influenced or controlled (by sth) (指人)(对某事物)顺从的, 服帖的: *amenable to kindness, advice, reason* 对好话、劝告、道理顺从的 ○ *I find him amenable to argument.* 我觉得他是个讲理的人. **2 ~ to sth (a)** (of people) subject to the authority of sth (指人)(对某事物的权威)服从的: *amenable to the law* 守法. **(b)** (of cases, situations, etc) that can be tested by sth (指事情, 情况等)经得起某事物检验的: *This case is not amenable to the normal rules.* 这件事经不起常规的检验.

amend /əˈmend; əˋmɛnd/ *v* **1** [Tn] correct an error in (sth); make minor improvements in; change slightly 改正; 略改进; 稍改动: *amend a document, proposal, law* 修改文件、建议、法律. **2** [I, Tn] (*fml* 文) (cause sth to) become better; improve (使某事物)变得更好; 改善; 改进: *You must amend your behaviour.* 你的行为得改一改.

▷ **amend·ment** *n* **1** [C] **~ (to sth)** minor alteration or addition to a document, etc 对文件等所作的次要的修改或增添: *Parliament debated several amendments to the bill.* 议会对议案的数份修正案进行了辩论. **2** [U] amending 修改; 改动: *passed without amendment* 未经改动而获通过.

amends /əˈmendz; əˋmɛndz/ *n* [pl] (idm 习语) **make amends (to sb) (for sth)** compensate sb (for an insult or injury given in the past) (对所施加的侮辱或损害)赔偿某人: *How can I ever make amends for ruining their party?* 我把他们的聚会弄糟了, 这个罪可怎么赔得起呀?

amen·ity /əˈmiːnətɪ, *also* əˈmenətɪ; əˈmɛnətɪ/ *n* **1** [C often *pl* 常作复数] feature or facility of a place that makes life there easy or pleasant 生活福利设施; 文娱康乐场所; 方便设施: *People who retire to the country often miss the amenities of a town*, eg libraries, cinemas, etc. 退居到乡村的人们时常怀念城市舒适的生活(如图书馆、电影院等). ○ *A sauna in the hotel would be a useful amenity.* 旅馆中的芬兰蒸汽浴室倒是个有益的好设施. **2** [U] (*fml* 文) pleasantness 愉快; 适意: *He immediately noticed the amenity of his new surroundings.* 他立刻觉察到了新环境的宜人之处.

Am·er·ican /əˈmerɪkən; əˋmɛrɪkən/ *adj* of N or S America, esp the USA 北美洲或南美洲的; (尤指)美国的.

▷ **Am·er·ican** *n* **1** native of America 美洲人. **2** citizen of the USA 美国公民; 美国人. **3** (also **American English**) the English language as spoken in the USA 美式英语.

Am·er·ic·an·ism *n* word or phrase used in American English but not in standard English in Britain 美式词语(用于美式英语中而不用于英式规范英语中的词语).

Am·er·ic·an·ize, -ise *v* [Tn] make (sb/sth) American in character 使(某人[某事物])美国化.

□ **American ˈfootball** American game of football like Rugby, played by two teams of 11 players who advance

American Football 美式橄榄球

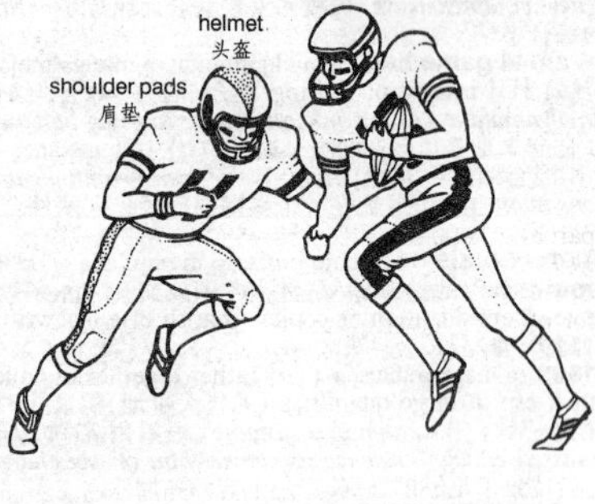

by running with and passing an oval-shaped ball 美式橄榄球; 美式足球. ⇨App 4 见附录4. ⇨illus 见插图.

American ˈIndian (also **Amerindian**) (one) of the original inhabitants of America 美洲印第安人.

Aˈmerican plan (*US*) system of hotel charges including room, meals and service 美式旅馆收费制(旅馆膳宿及服务费合并计算制).

Am·er·in·dian /ˌæmˈrɪndɪən; ˌæməˈrɪndɪən/ *n* = AMERICAN INDIAN (AMERICAN).

ameth·yst /ˈæmɪθɪst; ˋæməθɪst/ *n* [C, U] purple or violet precious stone 紫晶; 紫水晶: [attrib 作定语] *an amethyst bracelet* 紫晶手镯.

ami·able /ˈeɪmɪəbl; ˋemɪəbl̩/ *adj* showing and inspiring friendliness; pleasant and good-tempered 友好的; 和蔼可亲的; 好脾气的: *an amiable character, mood, conversation* 温柔的性格、欢快的心情、亲切的交谈. ▷ **ami·ab·il·ity** /ˌeɪmɪəˈbɪlətɪ; ˌemɪəˈbɪlətɪ/ *n* [U]. **ami·ably** *adv*.

am·ic·able /ˈæmɪkəbl; ˋæmɪkəbl̩/ *adj* showing friendliness; without hostility 友好的; 无敌意的: *An amicable settlement was reached.* 已达成和解. ▷ **am·ic·ab·il·ity** /ˌæmɪkəˈbɪlətɪ; ˌæmɪkəˈbɪlətɪ/ *n* [U]. **am·ic·ably** *adv*: *They lived together amicably for several years.* 他们在一起和睦地生活了好几年.

amid /əˈmɪd; əˈmɪd/ (also **amidst** /əˈmɪdst; əˈmɪdst/) *prep* (*dated or fml* 旧或文) in the middle of (sth); among 在...当中; 在...中: *Amid all the rush and confusion she forgot to say goodbye.* 她在忙乱中忘记了告辞.

amid·ships /əˈmɪdʃɪps; əˈmɪdʃɪps/ (also **mid·ships**) *adv* half-way between the bows and stern of a ship 在船中部: *go/stand amidships* 走向[站在]船中部 ○ *You'll find your cabin amidships.* 你的舱位在船中部.

amino acid /əˌmiːnəʊ ˈæsɪd; əˌmino ˋæsɪd/ (*chemistry* 化) any of several organic compounds found in protein 氨基酸.

amir = EMIR.

amiss /əˈmɪs; əˈmɪs/ *adj* [pred 作表语], *adv* (*dated* 旧) **1** wrong(ly); inappropriate(ly) 错误; 不恰当: *Something seems to be amiss — can I help?* 好像有点儿不对头——要我帮忙吗? **2** (idm 习语) **(not) come/go aˈmiss** (not) be unwelcome or unsuitable (并非)不称心或不顺当: *A new pair of shoes wouldn't come amiss.* 新鞋不会不称心的. **take sth aˈmiss** be offended by sth 被某事物冒犯: *Would she take it amiss if I offered to help?* 如果我冒昧相助, 她会见怪吗?

am·ity /ˈæmətɪ; ˋæmətɪ/ *n* [U] friendly relationship between people or countries (人与人或国与国之间的)友好关系: *live in amity with one's neighbours* 与四邻和睦相处.

am·meter /ˈæmɪtə(r); ˋæmˌɪtɚ/ *n* instrument that measures electric current in amperes 安培计; 电流表.

ammo·nia /əˈməʊnɪə; əˈmonɪə/ *n* [U] **1** colourless gas with a strong smell, used in refrigerators and for making explosives 氨; 阿摩尼亚. **2** (also **liquid ammonia**) solution of this gas in water, used in cleaning 氨水; 阿摩尼亚水.

am·mon·ite /ˈæmənaɪt; ˋæməˌnaɪt/ *n* fossil of a shell, with a coiled shape 菊石(一种甲壳类动物化石, 壳呈旋

卷盘状).

am·mu·ni·tion /ˌæmjʊˈnɪʃn; ˌæmjəˈnɪʃən/ *n* [U] **1** supply of bullets, bombs, grenades, etc fired from weapons or thrown 弹药: *They had to meet the attack with very little ammunition.* 他们不得不以极少的弹药应战. **2** (*fig* 比喻) facts and reasoning used in trying to win an argument 用于争论中的事实和论据: *This letter gave her all the ammunition she needed.* 这封信给她提供了她所需要的一切论据.

am·ne·sia /æmˈniːzɪə; *US* -ˈniːʒə; æmˈniʒə/ *n* [U] partial or total loss of memory 遗忘症(部分或全部记忆缺失).

am·nesty /ˈæmnəstɪ; ˋæmnəstɪ/ *n* general pardon, esp for offences against the State 大赦(尤指对国家所犯的罪行): *An amnesty has been declared.* 已经宣布大赦了 ○ *The rebels returned home under a general amnesty.* 造反的人经大赦释放回家.

amoeba (*US* **ameba**) /əˈmiːbə; əˋmibə/ *n* (*pl* **~s** or **~e** /-biː; -bi/) microscopic organism consisting of a single cell, found in water and soil, which changes shape constantly 阿米巴; 变形虫.

▷ **amoebic** /əˈmiːbɪk; əˋmibɪk/ *adj* of or caused by amoebae 阿米巴的; 由阿米巴引起的: *amoebic dysentery* 阿米巴痢疾.

amok /əˈmɒk; əˋmɑk/ (also **amuck** /əˈmʌk; əˋmʌk/) *adv* (idm 习语) **run amok** rush about in a wild and angry frenzy 横冲直撞; 乱窜: *The tiger escaped from the zoo and ran amok for hours.* 老虎逃出了动物园, 张牙舞爪乱窜了几小时.

among /əˈmʌŋ; əˋmʌŋ/ (also **amongst** /əˈmʌŋst; əˋmʌŋst/) *prep* (followed by a plural *n* or *pron* or a group *n* 后接复数名词或代词或集合名词) **1** surrounded by (sb/sth) 被…所围绕; 在…中间: *work among the poor, the sick, the elderly, etc* 在穷人、病人、老人等中工作 ○ *He found it amongst a pile of old books.* 他是在一堆旧书中找到它的. **2** in the number of (sth); included in 其中; 包括在内: *I was among the last to leave.* 我是最后离去者之一. ○ *Among those present were the Prime Minister and her husband.* 那些出席者中有首相及其丈夫. ○ *He was only one amongst many who needed help.* 他只是众多需要帮助者之一. **3** (in parts) to each member of (a group) 把(部分)…分给每一成员: *distribute the books among the class* 把书发给全班. **4** between 在…相互之间: *Politicians are always arguing amongst themselves.* 政客们总是彼此争论不休. ○ (*saying* 谚) *There is honour among thieves.* 盗亦有道.

NOTE ON USAGE 用法: **1 Among** is used of people or things considered as a group ☆ **among** 用于指作为一整体的人或事物: *Share out the books among the class.* 把书分发给全班. ○ *They talked among themselves while they waited.* 他们一边等着一边互相谈话. ○ *standing among the crowd at the football match* 在人群中站着看足球比赛. **2 Between** is used of people or things, either two in number or more than two considered individually ☆ **between** 用于指两个或两个以上各自独立的人或事物: *one book between two (pupils)* 两个人(小学生)一本书 ○ *She divided her possessions equally between her four children.* 她把自己的财物平均分给了她的四个孩子. ○ *They hung flags across the street between the houses.* 他们把旗子横跨街道悬挂在两边房子中间. ○ *There's a lot of disagreement between the two main political parties on this issue.* 对这一问题, 两大政党间有很大分歧. (Compare 试比较: *There's a lot of disagreement among politicians on this issue.* 对这一问题, 政治家们有很大分歧.)

amoral /ˌeɪˈmɒrəl; *US* ˌeɪˈmɔːrəl; eˋmɔrəl/ *adj* not based on moral standards; not following any moral rules 不基于道德标准的; 不遵守道德准则的. Cf 参看 IMMORAL.

am·or·ous /ˈæmərəs; ˋæmərəs/ *adj* readily showing or feeling love; relating to (esp sexual) love 表示爱情的; 多情的; 有关(尤指性)爱的; 色情的: *amorous looks, letters, poetry, experiences* 脉脉含情的样子、情书、情诗、性爱的体验 ○ *He became quite amorous at the office party.* 在职员聚会上他已春心荡漾了. ▷ **am·or·ously** *adv*: *gazing amorously into her eyes* 含情脉脉地凝视着她的眼睛. **am·or·ous·ness** *n* [U]: *a reputation for amorousness* 好色的名声.

amorph·ous /əˈmɔːfəs; əˋmɔrfəs/ *adj* [usu attrib 通常作定语] having no definite shape or form; not organized 无定形的; 无组织的; 杂乱的: *amorphous blobs of paint* 乱七八糟的颜料 ○ *an amorphous collection of jumpers and socks* 一堆套头毛衣和袜子.

amor·tize, -ise /əˈmɔːtaɪz; *US* ˈæmərtaɪz; ˋæmɚˌtaɪz/ *v* [Tn] (*law* 律) end (a debt) by making regular payments into a special fund 向某基金管理机构分期偿还, 摊还(债款). ▷ **amort·iza·tion, -isation** /əˌmɔːtɪˈzeɪʃn; *US* ˌæmərtɪ-; ˌæmɚtəˋzeʃən/ *n* [U].

amount /əˈmaʊnt; əˋmaʊnt/ *v* [Ipr] **~ to sth 1** add up to or total sth 总计; 共达: *The cost amounted to £250.* 费用共达250英镑. ○ *Our information doesn't amount to much*, ie We have very little information. 我们的资料有限. **2** be equal to or the equivalent of sth 等于或相当于某事物: *It all amounts to a lot of hard work.* 这一切就相当于很多繁重的工作. ○ *What you say amounts to a direct accusation.* 你所说的话等于直接的指责. **3** (idm 习语) **amount to/come to/be the same thing** ⇨ SAME[1].

▷ **amount** *n* **~ (of sth)** (used esp with [U] *ns* 尤与不可数名词连用) **1** total sum or value 总数; 总额; 总值: *a bill for the full amount* 全部金额的帐单 ○ *Can you really afford this amount?* 你真付得起这个总数吗? **2** quantity 数量: *a large amount of work, money, furniture* 大量的工作、钱、家具 ○ *Food was provided in varying amounts.* 食物供应多少不等. ○ *No amount of encouragement would make him jump*, ie Despite much encouragement he refused to jump. 无论怎么鼓励他, 他也不跳. **3** (idm 习语) **any amount of sth** a large quantity of sth 大量: *He can get any amount of help.* 他能得到大量的帮助.

amour /əˈmʊə(r); əˋmʊr/ *n* (*joc or rhet* 谑或修辞) (esp secret) love affair (尤指秘密的)恋情; 偷情: *Have you heard about his latest amour?* 你听说他最近偷情的事了吗?

amour propre /ˌæmʊə ˈprɒprə; ˌæmʊrˋprɔprə/ (*French* 法) self-respect; self-esteem 自尊; 自重; 自负: *Try not to offend his amour propre.* 尽量别伤他自尊心.

amp /æmp; æmp/ *n* (*infml* 口) = AMPERE.

am·pere /ˈæmpeə(r); *US* ˈæmpɪər; ˋæmpɪr/ (also **amp**) *n* (*abbr* 缩写 **A**) unit for measuring electric current 安培. ⇨App 11 见附录11.

▷ **am·per·age** /ˈæmpərɪdʒ; ˋæmpərɪdʒ/ *n* [U] strength of electric current measured in amperes 安培数; 电流强度.

am·per·sand /ˈæmpəsænd; ˋæmpɚsˌænd/ *n* sign (&) meaning 'and' '&' 号, 意为 'and': *Ampersands are often used in names of companies, eg Brown, Brown & Watkins.* '&' 号常用于公司名称中, 如Brown, Brown & Watkins.

am·phet·amine /æmˈfetəmiːn; æmˋfɛtəˌmin/ *n* [C, U] (*medical* 医) (any of several types of) synthetic drug used esp as a stimulant 苯异丙胺; 安非他明.

amphi- *comb form* 构词成分 **1** both; of both kinds 两; 两类: *amphibian*. **2** around 圆形的: *amphitheatre*.

am·phi·bian /æmˈfɪbɪən; æmˋfɪbɪən/ *n* **1** animal able to live both on land and in water 两栖动物: *Frogs and newts are amphibians.* 青蛙和蝾螈都是两栖动物. **2** aircraft that can take off from or alight on either land or water 水陆两用飞行器. **3** vehicle that can move over land or water 水陆两用车.

am·phi·bi·ous /æmˈfɪbɪəs; æmˋfɪbɪəs/ *adj* **1** living or operating both on land and in water 两栖的; 水陆两用的: *amphibious vehicles* 水陆两用车辆. **2** [usu attrib 通常作定语] involving both sea and land forces 两栖作战的: *amphibious operations* 两栖作战.

am·phi·theatre (*US* **-ter**) /ˈæmfɪθɪətə(r); ˋæmfəˌθiətɚ/ *n* **1** oval or circular unroofed building with rows of seats rising in steps all round an open space, used for presenting entertainments 圆形剧场, 竞技场(椭圆形或圆形露天建筑物, 四周有阶梯式座位, 中央有表演场地): *Some famous amphitheatres were built by the Romans.* 一些著名的竞技场都是罗马人修建的. **2** similar but semi-circular arrangement of seats inside a building used for eg lectures 内有半周阶梯式座位的建筑物(如阶梯教室). **3** level area surrounded by hills 四周有小山环绕的平地.

ample /ˈæmpl; ˋæmpl̩/ *adj* **1** (more than) enough 足够的: *ample time to get to the station* 到车站时间充足 ○ *A*

A

small piece of cake will be ample, thank you. 一小块蛋糕就足够了,谢谢你. ○ *£5 will be ample for my needs.* 5英镑就足够我用的了. **2** abundant; plentiful 充足的; 富裕的: *a man of ample strength* 力气大的人 ○ *The director of the company receives an ample salary.* 公司的董事薪水很高. **3** large in size; spacious; extensive 大的; 宽敞的; 广泛的: *an ample bosom* 丰满的胸部 ○ *There's ample room for the children on the back seat.* 后座很宽敞足容得下孩子们. ○ *The election was given ample coverage on TV.* 电视上对选举作了广泛的报道. ▷ **am·ply** /ˈæmplɪ; ˋæmplɪ/ *adv*: *amply fed, furnished, provided for, rewarded* 有足够的食物、家具、供应、报酬.

amp·lify /ˈæmplɪfaɪ; ˋæmplə,faɪ/ *v* (*pt, pp* **-fied**) [Tn] **1** increase (sth) in size or strength 放大或增强(某事物): *amplify the sound, electric current, signal* 增强声音、电流、信号. **2** add details to (a story, etc); make fuller 补充叙述(故事、事件等); 详述: *We must ask you to amplify your statement.* 我们得请你对你的说法作进一步的说明.

▷ **amp·li·fica·tion** /ˌæmplɪfɪˈkeɪʃn; ˌæmpləfəˋkeʃən/ *n* [U].

amp·li·fier *n* device for amplifying (esp sounds or radio signals) 放大器; (尤指)扩音器, 扩大器, 扬声器.

am·pli·tude /ˈæmplɪtjuːd; *US* -tuːd; ˋæmplə,tud/ *n* [U] **1** (*fml* 文) breadth; largeness; abundance 广阔; 广大; 丰富. **2** (*physics* 物) maximum extent to which a particular vibration, oscilation, radio wave, etc differ from the average 振幅; 波幅; 幅度: *Sound waves are measured by their amplitude.* 声波是根据其振幅来测量的.

am·poule (*US* also **am·pule**) /ˈæmpuːl; ˋæmpul/ *n* (*medical* 医) small sealed container holding a liquid, esp for injections 安瓿(装液体的密封小瓶, 尤指注射针剂).

am·pu·tate /ˈæmpjʊteɪt; ˋæmpjʊ,tet/ *v* [I, Tn] cut off (a diseased or an injured limb) by surgical operation (用外科手术)切除(患病或受伤的肢体); 截(肢); 施截肢术: *Her arm is so badly injured they will have to amputate (it).* 她的胳膊伤势严重, 他们不得不锯掉(它). ▷ **am·pu·ta·tion** /ˌæmpjʊˈteɪʃn; ˌæmpjʊˋteʃən/ *n* [U, C].

amuck = AMOK.

amu·let /ˈæmjʊlɪt; ˋæmjəlɪt/ *n* piece of jewellery, etc worn as a charm[1](2) against evil 护身符(为避邪而佩带的珠宝等物).

amuse /əˈmjuːz; əˋmjuz/ *v* [Tn] **1** make (sb) laugh or smile 逗(某人)笑: *Everyone was amused at/by the story about the dog.* 大家听了关于那只狗的故事都笑起来了. ○ *My funny drawings amused the children.* 我的滑稽的图画把孩子们给逗乐了. ○ *We were amused to learn that...* 我们得知...都笑了起来. **2** make time pass pleasantly for (sb) 使(某人)消遣: *These toys will help to keep the baby amused.* 这些玩具能让这个婴儿一直很快乐. ○ *They amused themselves by looking at old photographs.* 他们以看旧照片消遣.

▷ **amuse·ment 1** [C] thing that makes time pass pleasantly 娱乐品; 娱乐活动; 消遣: *I would never choose to watch cricket as an amusement.* 我决不会把看板球当作消遣. ○ *The hotel offers its guests a wide variety of amusements.* 这个旅馆为住客提供了各种各样的娱乐活动. **2** [U] state of being amused 娱乐; 快乐: *She could not disguise her amusement at his mistake.* 她对他的错误忍俊不禁. ○ *To my great amusement his false beard fell off.* 使我感到极其好笑的是他的假胡子掉下来了. ○ *I only do it for amusement*, ie not for any serious purpose. 我只不过是做着玩而已(并无正经目的). **aˈmusement arcade** room or hall containing coin-operated machines for playing games 游戏机室, 游戏机厅(设有以硬币开动的机器). **aˈmusement park** open area with swings, roundabouts, shooting galleries, etc where one can amuse oneself 娱乐园(设有秋千、旋转木马、打靶场等).

amus·ing *adj* causing laughter or smiles; enjoyable 好笑的; 有趣的; 引人发笑的: *an amusing story, story-teller* 好笑的故事、讲故事的人 ○ *Our visits to the theatre made the holiday more amusing.* 我们因看了几场戏而使假日倍添情趣.

an ⇨ A[2].

-an ⇨ -IAN.

-ana ⇨ -IANA.

ana·chron·ism /əˈnækrənɪzəm; əˋnækrə,nɪzəm/ *n* **1** mistake of placing sth in the wrong historical period 时代上的错误, 弄错年代(将某事物置错历史时期的错误): *It would be an anachronism to talk of Queen Victoria watching television.* 谈到维多利亚女王看电视是时代上的错误. **2** thing dated wrongly in this way 被置错时代或年代的事物: *Modern dress is an anachronism in productions of Shakespeare's plays.* 在莎士比亚剧作演出中出现的现代服装, 是弄错年代的东西. **3** person, custom or idea regarded as out of date 被视为过时的人、习俗、思想: *The monarchy is seen by some as an anachronism in present-day society.* 君主政体在当今社会中被一些人视为是过时的制度. ▷ **ana·chron·istic** /əˌnækrəˈnɪstɪk; əˌnækrəˋnɪstɪk/ *adj*.

ana·conda /ˌænəˈkɒndə; ˌænəˋkɑndə/ *n* large snake of tropical S America that crushes its victims to death 森蚺(产于热带南美洲的大蟒蛇, 可用身体绞死猎物, 亦称大水蟒).

an·ae·mia (*US* **ane·mia**) /əˈniːmɪə; əˋnimɪə/ *n* [U] (*medical* 医) condition of the blood caused by a lack of red corpuscles, making the person look pale 贫血症.

▷ **an·aemic** (*US* **an·emic**) /əˈniːmɪk; əˋnimɪk/ *adj* **1** suffering from or showing the symptoms of anaemia 患贫血症的; 显示贫血症的: *She looks anaemic in my opinion.* 我看她像有贫血症. **2** (*fig* 比喻) lacking vigour; weak 缺少活力的; 虚弱的: *an anaemic performance* 有气无力的表演.

an·aes·the·sia /ˌænɪsˈθiːzɪə; ˌænəsˋθiʒə/ (*US* **an·es·thesia** /-ˈθiːʒə; -ˋθiʒə/) *n* [U] state of being unable to feel (pain, heat, cold, etc) (对疼痛、热、冷等)感觉缺失; 麻木; 麻醉.

▷ **an·aes·thetic** (*US* **an·es·thetic**) /ˌænɪsˈθetɪk; ˌænəsˋθɛtɪk/ *n* [C, U] substance or process that produces anaesthesia 麻醉剂; 麻醉术: *be under (an) anaesthetic* 处于麻醉状态 ○ *give sb a general anaesthetic*, ie cause sb to lose consciousness 给某人全身麻醉 ○ *a local anaesthetic* (ie one affecting part of the body) *for the removal of a tooth* 为拔牙而施的局部麻醉. — *adj* producing anaesthesia 产生麻醉的.

an·aes·thet·ist (*US* **an·es·thet·ist**) /əˈniːsθətɪst; əˋnɛsθətɪst/ *n* person trained to administer anaesthetics 麻醉师.

an·aes·thet·ize, -ise (*US* **an·es·thet·ize**) /əˈniːsθətaɪz; əˋnɛsθə,taɪz/ *v* [Tn] administer an anaesthetic to (sb); deprive of sensation 使麻醉; 使麻木. **an·aes·thet·iza·tion, -isation** (*US* **an·es·thet·iza·tion**) /əˌniːsθətaɪˈzeɪʃn; əˌnɛsθətəˋzeʃən/ *n* [U].

ana·gram /ˈænəgræm; ˋænə,græm/ *n* word or phrase made by rearranging the letters of another word or phrase 变形词; 变形词组(将一词或一词组的字母位置变换而组成的新词或新词组): *'Cart-horse' is an anagram of 'orchestra'.* 'Cart-horse' 是 'orchestra' 的变形词. ○ *This crossword is full of anagrams.* 这个纵横填字字谜里有很多变形词.

anal /ˈeɪnl; ˋenḷ/ *adj* of the anus 肛门的: *the anal region* 肛门部位.

an·al·gesia /ˌænælˈdʒiːzɪə; *US* -ʒə; ˌænælˋdʒiʒə/ *n* [U] (*medical* 医) loss of ability to feel pain while still conscious 痛觉缺失.

▷ **an·al·gesic** /ˌænælˈdʒiːsɪk; ˌænælˋdʒisɪk/ *adj, n* (having the effects of a) substance that relieves pain 止痛的; 止痛药: *Aspirin is a mild analgesic.* 阿司匹林是药性平和的止痛药.

ana·log·ous /əˈnæləgəs; əˋnæləgəs/ *adj* **~ (to/with sth)** partially similar or parallel; offering an analogy 类似的; 相似的: *The two processes are not analogous.* 这两种过程不相似. ○ *The present crisis is analogous with the situation immediately before the war.* 目前的危机与大战前夕的形势类似. ▷ **ana·log·ously** *adv*.

ana·logue (*US* **ana·log**) /ˈænəlɒg; *US* -lɔːg; ˋænḷ,ɔg/ *n* thing that is similar to another thing 类似物: *A vegetarian gets protein not from meat but from its analogues.* 素食者所摄取的蛋白质不是来自肉类而是来自近似肉类的食物.

□ ˌ**analogue comˈputer** computer using physical quantities, eg voltage, weight, length, etc, to represent numbers 模拟计算机(用物理量如电压、重量、长度等来表示数量的计算机): *A slide-rule is a simple analogue computer.* 计算尺是简单的模拟计算机. Cf 参看

DIGITAL COMPUTER (DIGIT).

ana·logy /əˈnælədʒɪ; əˋnælədʒɪ/ *n* **1** [C] **~ (between sth and sth)** partial similarity between two things that are compared 类似; 相似: *point to analogies between the two events* 指出两起事件的相似之处 ○ *The teacher drew an analogy between the human heart and a pump.* 教师打了一个比喻, 把人的心脏比作唧筒. **2** [U] **~ (with sth)** process of reasoning based on such similarity 类推: *My theory applies to you and by analogy to others like you.* 我的理论适用于你, 照此类推, 也适用于像你这样的其他人. **3** [U] way in which words change their form because of their similarity to other words 类推法(因某些词与其它词相似而类推出其词形变化的方法).

ana·lyse (*US* **ana·lyze**) /ˈænəlaɪz; ˋænḷ,aɪz/ *v* [Tn] **1** separate (sth) into its parts in order to study its nature or structure 分析(将事物分解成各部分以研究其性质或结构): *analyse the sample and identify it* 分析样品进行鉴定 ○ *By analysing the parts of the sentence we learn more about English grammar.* 分析句子成分就能多了解一些英语语法. **2** examine and explain (sth) 观察并解释(某事物); 研究: *We must try to analyse the causes of the strike.* 我们得研究一下罢工的原因. **3** = PSYCHO-ANALYSE.

ana·lysis /əˈnæləsɪs; əˋnæləsɪs/ *n* (*pl* **-yses** /-əsi:z; -ə,siz/) **1** [U, C] study of sth by examining its parts and their relationship 分析(对事物的各个部分及其相互关系的研究): *Textual analysis identified the author as Shakespeare.* 对原文的分析研究鉴定出作者是莎士比亚. ○ *Close analysis of sales figures shows clear regional variations.* 对销售额的仔细分析显示出明显的地区差别. **2** [C] statement of the result of this 分析结果的报告: *present a detailed analysis of the situation* 对形势提出一份详细的分析报告. **3** [U] = PSYCHO-ANALYSIS. **4** (idm 习语) **in the ˌlast/ˌfinal aˈnalysis** after all due consideration 总之; 归根结底: *In the final analysis I think our sympathy lies with the heroine of the play.* 总之, 我认为我们都同情剧中的女主人公.

▷ **ana·lytic** /ˌænəˈlɪtɪk; ˌænḷˋɪtɪk/, **ana·lyt·ical** /-kl; -kḷ/ *adjs* of or using analysis 分析的; 用分析方法的. **ana·lytic·ally** /-klɪ; -klɪ/ *adv*.

ana·lyst /ˈænəlɪst; ˋænḷɪst/ *n* **1** person skilled in making (esp chemical) analyses 分析家; (尤指)化验员. **2** = PSYCHO-ANALYST.

ana·paest /ˈænəpi:st; ˋænə,pɛst/ (*US* **ana·pest** /-pest; -,pɛst/) *n* metrical foot in poetry consisting of two short or unstressed syllables followed by one long or stressed syllable 抑抑扬格(有两个短音节或非重音音节, 其后跟有一个长音节或重音音节的一种音步). ▷ **ana·paestic** /ˌænəˈpi:stɪk; ˌænəˋpɛstɪk/ (*US* **ana·pestic** /-ˈpestɪk; -ˋpɛstɪk/) *adj*: *'Like the 'leaves of the 'forest when 'summer is 'green' has an anapaestic rhythm.* 'Like the 'leaves of the 'forest when 'summer is 'green' 的韵律属于抑抑扬格.

ana·phora /əˈnæfərə; əˋnæfərə/ *n* [U] (*grammar*) use of a word to refer back to or replace a word previously used, eg *do* in *If you don't want to iron my shirt I'll do it.* 前指替代法(用一个词来复指或替代前面用过的词, 如在If you don't want to iron my shirt I' ll do it句中do的用法). ▷ **ana·phoric** /ˌænəˈfɒrɪk; ˌænəˋfɔrɪk/ *adj*.

an·ar·chy /ˈænəkɪ; ˋænɚkɪ/ *n* [U] **1** absence of government or control in society; lawlessness 无政府状态; 无法无天: *The overthrow of the regime was followed by a period of anarchy.* 那政权被推翻以后, 有一段时期是无政府状态. **2** disorder; confusion 无秩序; 混乱: *In the absence of their teacher the class was in a state of anarchy.* 教师不在, 班上一片混乱.

▷ **an·archic** /əˈnɑ:kɪk; ənˋɑrkɪk/, **an·arch·ical** /-ɪkl; -ɪkḷ/ *adjs*.

an·arch·ism /ˈænəkɪzəm; ˋænɚkɪzəm/ *n* [U] political theory that laws and government should be abolished 无政府主义(主张法律和政府都应取消的一种政治理论). **an·arch·ist** *n* person who believes in anarchism 无政府主义者.

ana·thema /əˈnæθəmə; əˋnæθəmə/ *n* **1** [U, C] detested person or thing 极讨厌的人或事物: *Racial prejudice is (an) anathema to me.* 我对种族偏见深恶痛绝. **2** [C] formal declaration of the Christian Church, excommunicating sb or condemning sth as evil (基督教把某人逐出教会或谴责某事物为邪恶的)咒诅.

▷ **ana·them·at·ize, -ise** /əˈnæθəmətaɪz; əˋnæθəmə,taɪz/ *v* [I, Tn] curse (sb/sth) 诅咒(某人[某事物]).

ana·tomy /əˈnætəmɪ; əˋnætəmɪ/ *n* **1** [U] scientific study of the structure of animal bodies 解剖学: *We have to do anatomy next term.* 我们下学期得学解剖学了. **2** [C] bodily structure of an animal or plant (动植物的)解剖构造: *the anatomy of the frog* 青蛙的解剖构造. **3** [C] (*joc* 谑) human body 人体: *Various parts of his anatomy were clearly visible.* 他身体的各个部分都看得很清楚.

▷ **ana·tom·ical** /ˌænəˈtɒmɪkl; ˌænəˋtɑmɪkḷ/ *adj*. **ana·tom·ic·ally** /-klɪ; -klɪ/ *adv*.

ana·tom·ist /əˈnætəmɪst; əˋnætəmɪst/ *n* person who studies anatomy 解剖学者.

-ance, -ence *suff* 后缀 (with *vs* forming *ns* 与动词结合构成名词) action or state of ...的动作或状态: *assistance* ○ *resemblance* ○ *confidence*.

an·cestor /ˈænsestə(r); ˋænsɛstɚ/ *n* **1** (*fem* 阴性作 **an·ces·tress** /-trɪs; -trɪs/) any of the people from whom sb is descended, esp those more remote than his grandparents; forefather 祖先; 祖宗: *His ancestors had come to England as refugees.* 他的祖先来到英国的时候是难民. Cf 参看 DESCENDANT (DESCEND). **2** (*fig* 比喻) early form of a machine or structure which later became more developed; forerunner 原型(某机器或结构的早期形式); 先驱: *The ancestor of the modern bicycle was called a penny farthing.* 现代自行车的原型叫做'前轮大后轮小的自行车'.

▷ **an·ces·tral** /ænˈsestrəl; ænˋsɛstrəl/ *adj* belonging to or inherited from one's ancestors 祖先的; 祖传的: *her ancestral home* 她的祖居.

an·ces·try /ˈænsestrɪ; ˋænsɛstrɪ/ *n* line of ancestors 世系: *a distinguished ancestry* 名门望族.

an·chor /ˈæŋkə(r); ˋæŋkɚ/ *n* **1** heavy metal device attached to a rope, chain, etc and used to moor a ship or boat to the sea-bottom or a balloon to the ground 锚, 锚固装置(用缆、链等连接着的金属设备, 用以将船舶固定于海底或将气球固定在地面上): *They brought the boat into the harbour and dropped (the) anchor.* 他们把船开进海港下锚停泊. **2** (*fig* 比喻) person or thing that gives stability or security 可以依靠的人或事物; 靠山; 后盾. **3** (idm 习语) **at ˈanchor** moored by the anchor 抛锚停泊: *We lay at anchor outside the harbour.* 我们在港外抛锚停泊. **bring (a ship)/come to ˈanchor** stop sailing and lower the anchor 停航抛锚. **cast anchor** ⇨ CAST. **ride at anchor** ⇨ RIDE². **slip anchor** ⇨ SLIP². **weigh anchor** ⇨ WEIGH.

▷ **an·chor** *v* [I, Tn] lower an anchor; make (sth) secure with an anchor 抛锚; 用锚固装置固定(某物): *We anchored (our boat) close to the shore.* 我们近岸抛锚停泊(船).

an·chor·age /ˈæŋkərɪdʒ; ˋæŋkərɪdʒ/ *n* **1** [C] place where ships, etc may anchor safely (船只等安全的)停泊处, 锚地. **2** [U] money charged for anchoring 停泊税.

□ **ˈanchor man** /mæn; mæn/ **1** person who co-ordinates the work of a group, esp that of interviewers and reporters in a radio or television broadcast (尤指无线电或电视采访的)主持人. **2** strong member of a sports team who has a vital part to play (运动队员中的)主力: *The anchor man in a relay team runs last.* 接力队中的主力跑最后一棒.

an·chor·ite /ˈæŋkəraɪt; ˋæŋkə,raɪt/ *n* hermit or religious recluse 隐士; 隐居修道者.

an·chovy /ˈæntʃəvɪ; *US* ˈæntʃəuvɪ; ˋæn,tʃovɪ/ *n* small fish of the herring family with a strong flavour : [attrib 作定语] ˌ*anchovy* ˈ*paste* 鱼酱.

an·cient /ˈeɪnʃənt; ˋenʃənt/ *adj* **1** belonging to times long past 古代的; 远古的: *ancient civilizations* 古代的文明. **2** (*usu joc* 通常作戏谑语) very old 极老的: *I feel pretty ancient when I see how the younger generation behaves.* 看到年轻一代的举止行为, 我觉得我太老了. ⇨Usage at OLD 用法见OLD.

▷ **the an·cients** *n* [pl] people who lived in ancient times, esp the Greeks and Romans (尤指希腊及罗马的)古人.

□ **ˌancient ˈhistory** history of the Greek and Roman civilizations 古代史(希腊及罗马文明史).

ˌancient ˈmonument (*Brit*) old building, etc recognized by the Government as worth preserving 古迹

(尤指英国政府认为值得保存的古代建筑物).

an·cil·lary /æn'sɪlərɪ; US 'ænsəlerɪ; ˋænsə,lɛrɪ/ *adj* ~ **(to sth)** helping in a subsidiary way 辅助的: *ancillary staff, duties, roads, industries* 辅助职员、任务、道路、工业.

-ancy, -ency *suff* 后缀 (with *ns, adjs* and *vs* forming *ns* 与名词、形容词、动词结合构成名词) state or quality of ...的状态或性质: *complacency* ○ *irrelevancy* ○ *presidency*.

and /ənd, ən, *also* n; ənd, ən, n, *esp after* t, d; *strong form* 强读式 ænd; ænd/ *conj* (used to connect words of the same part of speech, phrases or clauses) **1** also; in addition to 和; 与; 及; 同; 又; 并; 亦; 且; 兼; 而: *bread and butter* 面包和黄油 ○ *slowly and carefully* 缓慢而仔细地 ○ *able to read and write* 能读又能写 ○ *one woman, two men and three children* 一个女人、两个男人及三个孩子 ○ *shutting doors and opening windows* 关门及开窗 (When *and* connects two *ns* standing for things or people that are closely linked, a determiner is not normally repeated before the second *n* 若and所连接的两个名词为紧密相关的人或物, 第二个名词前一般不必再用限定词, 如 *a knife and fork* 一副刀叉, *my father and mother* 我的父母, 否则就要重复限定词, 如 *a knife and a spoon* 一把刀和一个勺, *my father and my uncle* 我的父亲和我的叔父.) **2** added to; plus 加: *5 and 5 makes 10.* 5加5等于10. (When numbers are said, *and* is used between the hundreds and any digits that follow 说到数目时, 百位和其后任何位数之间要用and, 如 *two thousand, two hundred and sixty four* 二千二百六十四, 即2 264. The use of *and* in expressions of time is now dated 表示时间的词语中使用 and, 这一用法现已过时, 如 *five and twenty past two*, 现作 twenty-five past two 两点二十五.) **3** then; following this 然后; 其后; 接着; 就: *She came in and sat down.* 她进来以后就坐下了. ○ *I pulled the trigger and the gun went off.* 我一扣扳机, 枪就响了. **4** as a result of this 因此; 那么; 就: *Work hard and* (ie If you work hard) *you will pass your examinations.* 你若用功, 考试就能及格. ○ *Arrive late once more and* (ie If you arrive late once more) *you're fired.* 你再迟到一次, 就把你开除. **5** then again; repeatedly; increasingly 一再地; 重复地; 继续增加地: *We walked for miles and miles.* 我们走了很长很长的路. ○ *They talked for hours and hours.* 他们谈了很长很长时间. ○ *Your work is getting better and better.* 你干得越来越好了. ○ *He tried and tried but without success.* 他试了又试却未成功. **6** contrasting with (different kinds of the same thing) 与(同一事物的不同种类)相对照: *Don't worry — there are rules and rules*, ie Some rules are more important, more easy to ignore, etc than others. 别担心——规则跟规则不一样(有的规则比其他规则重要、容易疏忽等).

□ **and/or** (*infml* 口) together with or as an alternative to ...和...或者...或...: *Bring wine and/or chocolates.* 把酒和[或]巧克力拿来.

NOTE ON USAGE 用法: In informal English **and** can be used after a few verbs (eg **go, come**) instead of **to.** It indicates purpose 在口语中, **and**可代替**to**用于少数几个动词如**go**、**come**之后, 表示目的: *Will you go and fetch me a screwdriver, please?* 请你去给我拿把改锥来, 好吗? ○ *Can I come and look at your work?* 我能来看看你的作品吗? ○ *We stayed and had a drink.* 我们留下来喝了点酒. ○ *He stopped and bought some flowers.* 他停下来买了些花. When used with **try** and in the phrase *wait and see* only the base form of the verb is possible 在与**try**连用时及在wait and see这一词组中, 动词只可用原形: *Try and improve.* 尽量改进. ○ *We'll try and get one tomorrow.* 我们明天设法弄一个来. ○ *'What's for dinner?' 'Wait and see.'* '吃什么饭?' '等着瞧吧.'

an·dante /æn'dæntɪ; æn'dæntɪ/ *adj, adv* (*music* 音) (to be played) in moderately slow time 行板速度(的); 用行板速度(演奏)(的).

▷ **an·dante** *n* piece of music (to be) played thus 行板速度演奏的乐曲.

and·iron /'ændaɪən; 'ænd,aɪɚn/ (also **firedog**) *n* iron support (usu one of a pair) for holding logs in a fireplace 柴架(壁炉中盛木柴的铁架, 常为一对).

an·dro·gyn·ous /æn'drɒdʒɪnəs; æn'drɑdʒənəs/ *adj* **1** having both male and female characteristics; hermaphrodite 兼有雌雄两性特征的; 兼有男女两性的: *pop-stars dressing up in androgynous styles* 穿着半男半女式服装的流行歌手. **2** (*botany* 植) (of a plant) having both stamens and pistils in the same flower (指植物)一朵花中兼有雄蕊和雌蕊的; 雌雄同序的.

an·ec·dote /'ænɪkdəʊt; ˋænɪk,dot/ *n* short, interesting or amusing story about a real person or event 轶事, 逸闻(关于真人真事的短小有趣的事). ▷ **an·ec·dotal** /,ænek'dəʊtl; ,ænɪkˋdotl/ *adj*: *anecdotal memoirs* 轶事录.

an·emia, an·emic (*US*) = ANAEMIA, ANAEMIC.

an·emo·meter /,ænɪ'mɒmɪtə(r); ,ænəˋmɑmətɚ/ (also **wind·gauge**) *n* instrument for measuring the force of the wind 风速表.

anemone /ə'nemənɪ; əˋnɛmə,ni/ *n* small wild or garden plant with white, red or purple star-shaped flowers 银莲花(野生或园栽短小植物, 开白、红或紫色星状花).

an·er·oid ba·ro·meter /,ænərɔɪd bə'rɒmɪtə(r); ,ænə,rɔɪd bəˋrɑmətɚ/ instrument that measures air-pressure by the action of air on the outside of a box containing a vacuum 空盒气压计; 无液气压计.

an·es·the·sia, an·es·thetic (*US*) = ANAESTHESIA, ANAESTHETIC.

anew /ə'nju:; US ə'nu:; əˋnu/ *adv* (*usu rhet* 通常作修辞) in a new or different way; again 重新; 再: *Our efforts must begin anew.* 我们得从头再来.

angel 天使

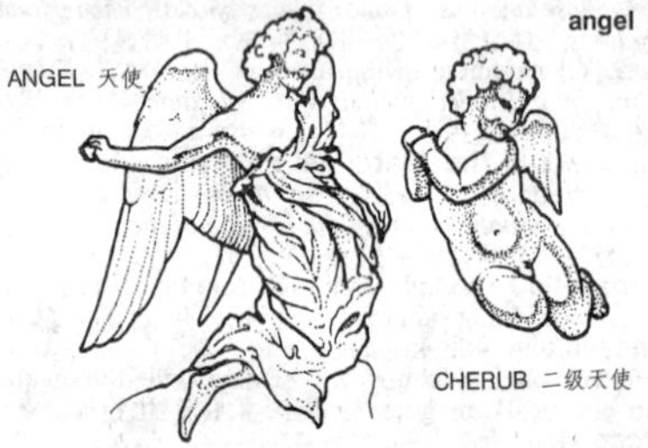

an·gel /'eɪndʒl; ˋendʒəl/ *n* **1** (esp in Christian belief) messenger or attendant of God 天使(尤指基督教信仰中上帝的使者或侍者): *Angels are usually shown in pictures dressed in white, with wings.* 在图画中的天使通常是身穿白衣, 生有翅膀. ⇨illus 见插图. **2** beautiful, innocent or kind person 安琪儿(美丽、纯真或善良的人): *Mary's three children are all angels — not like mine.* 玛丽的三个孩子都像安琪儿一样可爱——跟我的孩子可不一样. ○ *Be an angel and make me a cup of tea.* 你做做好事, 给我沏杯茶吧. ○ *He sings like an angel*, ie very sweetly. 他唱得婉转动听. **3** (idm 习语) **a ministering angel** ⇨ MINISTER[2].

▷ **an·gelic** /æn'dʒelɪk; ænˋdʒɛlɪk/ *adj* of or like an angel 天使的; 天使般的; 美丽、纯真或善良的: *an angelic smile, voice, face* 天使般的微笑、声音、面孔. **an·gel·ic·ally** /-klɪ; -klɪ/ *adv*: *The children behaved angelically.* 孩子们乖得像天使一样.

□ **'angel cake** light sponge cake 蛋糕.

'angel-fish *n* (*pl* unchanged 复数不变) fish with wing-like fins 神仙鱼.

an·gel·ica /æn'dʒelɪkə; ænˋdʒɛlɪkə/ *n* [U] (**a**) sweet-smelling plant used in cooking and in medicine 白芷(一种有香味的植物, 用于烹调及医药). (**b**) stalks of this plant that have been boiled in sugar 蜜饯的白芷茎.

an·gelus /'ændʒɪləs; ˋændʒələs/ *n* [sing] (also **Angelus**) **1** (in the Roman Catholic Church) prayer to the Virgin Mary (天主教中)对圣母玛利亚的祈祷. **2** bell rung at morning, noon and sunset, calling people to say this prayer (为招唤人们作此祈祷而于早晨、中午、日落时敲的)祈祷钟.

an·ger /'æŋgə(r); ˋæŋgɚ/ *n* [U] **1** strong feeling of displeasure and hostility 怒气; 怒火: *filled with anger at the way he had been tricked* 对于他这样被骗而怒火中烧 ○ *speak in anger about the plight of poor people* 含怒讲述穷人的苦难处境 ○ *It was said in a moment of anger.* 那

是一时的气话. **2** (idm 习语) **more in sorrow than in anger** ⇨ SORROW.

▷ **an·ger** *v* [Tn] fill (sb) with anger; make angry 使(某人)发怒; 激怒: *He was angered by the selfishness of the others.* 他因为别人的自私而发怒.

an·gina pec·toris /æn,dʒaɪnə 'pektərɪs; æn'dʒaɪnə 'pɛktərɪs/ (also **angina**) *n* [U] (*medical* 医) disease of the heart which results in sharp pains in the chest after exertion 心绞痛.

angle 角

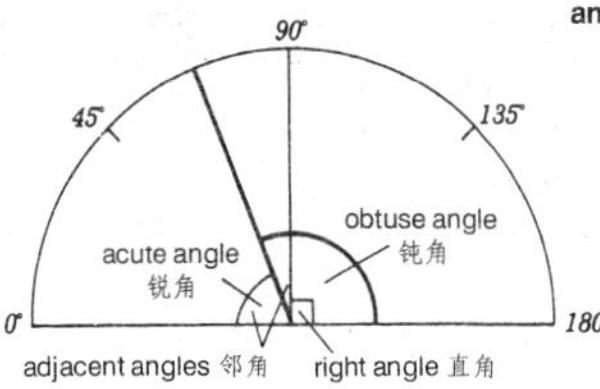

angle[1] /'æŋgl; 'æŋgl/ *n* **1** space between two lines or surfaces that meet 角(两线或面相交所形成的空间): *an angle of 45°* 45°的角. ⇨illus 见插图. **2** point of view 角度; 观点: *Seen from this angle the woman in the picture is smiling.* 从这个角度来看, 画中的女子面带微笑. ○ (*fig* 比喻) *Try looking at the affair from a different angle.* 试从另一角度来看这件事. **3** corner (of a building or an object) (建筑物或物体的)角: *She hit her knee against the angle of the bed.* 她的膝盖撞到床角上了. **4** (idm 习语) **at an 'angle** not straight up; sloping 不是直上直下的; 倾斜的: *The famous tower of Pisa leans at an angle.* 有名的比萨塔是斜的.

▷ **angle** *v* **1** [Tn] move or place (sth) in a slanting position 斜移或斜置(某物): *Try angling the camera for a more interesting picture.* 试用照相机斜着照, 照出来的相片更有意思. **2** [Tn, Tn·pr] **~ sth (at/to/towards sb)** present (information, etc) from a particular point of view 从某一角度传达(信息等): *This programme is angled at young viewers.* 这个节目是针对年轻观众的.

angle[2] /'æŋgl; 'æŋgl/ *v* **1** [I] (usu 通常作 **go angling**) fish with line and hook 钓鱼: *angling for trout* 钓鳟鱼. **2** [Ipr] **~ for sth** (*infml* 口) try and obtain sth by hinting 使用暗示手段以期获得某事物: *angle for compliments, an invitation, a free ticket* 诱使别人夸奖、婉转地使别人提出邀请、转弯抹角想要一张免费票.

▷ **ang·ler** /'æŋglə(r); 'æŋglɚ/ *n* person who goes angling 钓鱼者. Cf 参看 FISHERMAN.

ang·ling *n* [U] art or sport of fishing with a line and hook 钓鱼术: *Angling is his main hobby.* 钓鱼是他的主要爱好.

An·glican /'æŋglɪkən; 'æŋglɪkən/ *n, adj* (member) of the Church of England or of another Church with the same beliefs and forms of worship 英国国教的, 英国圣公会等的(教徒): *the Anglican prayer-book* 英国国教的祈祷书.

An·gli·cize, -ise /'æŋglɪsaɪz; 'æŋglə,saɪz/ *v* [Tn] make (sb/sth) English or like English 使(某人[某事物])英国化或英语化: *Anglicized pronunciation* 英语化的发音.

▷ **An·gli·cism** /'æŋglɪsɪzəm; 'æŋglə,sɪzəm/ *n* typically English way of saying sth; English word or phrase used by speakers of another language 典型的英国说法; (说另一语言的人所使用的)英语词语: *The French language contains many Anglicisms, such as 'le weekend'.* 法语中含有很多英语词语如 'le weekend'.

Anglo- *comb form* 构词成分 English or British 英国的; 不列颠的: *Anglo-American* ○ *Anglophobia*.

Anglo-American /,æŋgləʊ ə'merɪkən; 'æŋglo ə'mɛrɪkən/ *n* American person descended from an English family 英裔美国人.

▷ **Anglo-American** *adj* of or concerning England and America 英美的; 关于英美的: *the Anglo-American agreement* 英美协议.

Anglo-Catholic /,æŋgləʊ 'kæθəlɪk; 'æŋglo 'kæθəlɪk/ *n, adj* (member) of the section of the Church of England that stresses its unbroken connection with the early Christian Church and objects to being called Protestant 英国国教高教会派的(教徒)(坚称其与早期基督教会一脉相承的关系, 并拒被称为新教派者).

Anglo-French /,æŋgləʊ 'frentʃ; 'æŋglo 'frɛntʃ/ *adj* English and French 英法的: *a joint Anglo-French project* 英法联合项目.

Anglo-Indian /,æŋgləʊ 'ɪndɪən; 'æŋglo 'ɪndɪən/ *n, adj* **1** (person) of mixed British and Indian blood 英印混血的(人). **2** (*dated* 旧) (person) of British birth but having lived for a long time in India 长期侨居印度的英国的(人).

Ang·lo·phile /'æŋgləʊfaɪl; 'æŋglo,faɪl/ *n* person who loves England or English things 亲英者(喜爱英国或英国事物的人).

Ang·lo·phobe /'æŋgləʊfəʊb; 'æŋglo,fob/ *n* person who hates or fears England or English things 仇英者, 恐英者(对英国或英国事物憎恶或恐惧的人).

Ang·lo·pho·bia /,æŋgləʊ'fəʊbɪə; ,æŋglo'fobɪə/ *n* [U] (esp excessive) hatred or fear of England or English things 仇英, 恐英(对英国或英国事物极度的憎恶或恐惧).

ang·lo·phone /'æŋgləʊfəʊn; 'æŋglo,fon/ *n, adj* (person) speaking English, esp where English is not the only language spoken 说英语的(人)(尤指在英语并非唯一通行的语言地区).

Anglo-Saxon /,æŋgləʊ 'sæksn; 'æŋglo 'sæksn̩/ *n* **1** person of English descent 盎格鲁撒克逊人(英国血统的人). **2** English person of the period before the Norman Conquest (在诺曼人征服以前的时期的)英国人. **3** (also **Old English**) the English language of this period 古英语(该时期的英语). ▷ **Anglo-Saxon** *adj*.

an·gora /æŋ'gɔːrə; æŋ'gɔrə/ *n* **1** [C] long-haired breed of cat, goat or rabbit 安哥拉猫、山羊或兔. **2** [U] yarn or material made from the hair of angora goats or rabbits 安哥拉毛纱或呢(用安哥拉山羊或兔的毛纺成的毛纱或制成的毛呢).

angry /'æŋgrɪ; 'æŋgrɪ/ *adj* **(-ier, -iest) 1 ~ (with sb) (at/about sth)** filled with anger 生气的; 愤怒的; 发怒的: *angry at being delayed/about the delay* 因被耽搁[因耽搁]而生气 ○ *I was angry with myself for making such a stupid mistake.* 我因为犯了这么愚蠢的错误而在生自己的气. ○ (*fig* 比喻) *The sea/sky looks angry*, ie stormy, threatening. 海上怒涛澎湃[天空乌云滚滚、风雨交加]. **2** (of a wound) painful; inflamed (指伤口)疼痛的, 发炎的. **3** (idm 习语) **an angry young man** young man, esp an intellectual, who disagrees strongly with the existing moral, social and political attitudes and tries to change them by means of public protest, through his writings, etc 愤怒的青年(尤指知识分子, 因强烈不满现实的道德、社会、政治等观念, 力图通过写作等方式鼓动人民大众奋起反抗进行改革). ▷ **an·grily** /-əlɪ; -əlɪ/ *adv*.

angst /æŋst; æŋst/ *n* [U] (*German* 德) feeling of anxiety, guilt or remorse, esp about the state of the world 忧虑, 负疚, 懊恼(尤指对于世界局势).

an·guish /'æŋgwɪʃ; 'æŋgwɪʃ/ *n* [U] severe physical or mental pain (肉体的或精神的)极度痛苦: *I was in anguish until I knew she was still alive.* 我以前不知道她还活着, 所以一直万分痛苦.

▷ **an·guished** *adj* feeling or expressing anguish 感到痛苦的; 表现痛苦的: *an anguished heart* 痛苦的心情 ○ *anguished cries* 痛苦的叫喊.

an·gu·lar /'æŋgjʊlə(r); 'æŋgjəlɚ/ *adj* **1** having angles or sharp corners 有角的; 有尖角的. **2** (of people) thin and bony (指人)瘦削的, 骨瘦如柴的. **3** (of a person's character or manner) stiff and awkward (指性格或举止)死板的, 生硬的, 不灵活的: *an angular posture, gait, stride* 僵挺的姿势、步法、大步. **4** measured by the angle 用角度量的: *angular distance*, ie the distance between two objects measured as an angle from a given point 角距离(由一定点到两物体之间所量度的夹角).

▷ **an·gu·lar·ity** /,æŋgjʊ'lærətɪ; ,æŋgjə'lærətɪ/ *n* [U, C].

an·il·ine /'ænɪliːn; *US* 'ænəlɪn; 'ænl̩,ɪn/ *n* [U] oily liquid obtained chemically from coal tar, used in making dyes, drugs, etc 苯胺(用化学方法自煤焦油中提炼出的油状液体, 用于制造染料、药品等).

an·im·ad·vert /,ænɪmæd'vɜːt; ,ænəmæd'vɝt/ *v* [Ipr] **~ (on sb/sth)** (*fml* 文) make (esp critical) remarks

about sb/sth 评论、(尤指)批评、谴责某人[某事物].
▷ **an·im·ad·ver·sion** /-ˈvɜːʃn; *US* -ʒn; -ˋvɝʒən/ *n* [C, U] criticism 评论; 批评; 谴责.

an·imal /ˈænɪml; ˋænəml/ *n* **1** living thing that can feel and move voluntarily 动物(能有感觉并能自行移动的生物): *Men, dogs, birds, flies, fish and snakes are all animals.* 人、狗、鸟、蝇、鱼、蛇都是动物. ○ [attrib 作定语] *the ˈanimal kingdom* 动物界. Cf 参看 VEGETABLE, MINERAL. **2** any such creature other than a human being 动物(除人以外的此类任何生物). **3** four-footed creature as distinct from a bird, a fish or an insect 四足动物, 兽, 牲畜(有别于鸟、鱼、虫). **4** wild or brutish person 粗野残暴的人; 兽性的人; 衣冠禽兽.
▷ **an·imal** *adj* [attrib 作定语] characteristic of animals 有动物特性的: *animal needs*, eg food and drink 肉体上的需要(如食物和饮料) ○ *animal desires*, ie sexual desires 肉欲.
□ ˌ**animal** ˈ**husbandry** the care and management of cattle, sheep, horses, etc 畜牧业(对牛、羊、马等的饲养和管理).
ˌ**animal** ˈ**magnetism** **1** (formerly) hypnotism (旧时)动物磁性(催眠术). **2** physical attraction in animals 动物间的肉体吸引.
ˌ**animal** ˈ**spirits** natural enjoyment of life 生趣; 生气.

an·im·al·cule /ˌænɪˈmælkjuːl; ˌænəˋmælkjul/ *n* microscopically small animal 微小动物.

an·im·ate[1] /ˈænɪmət; ˋænəmɪt/ *adj* living; having life 活的; 有生命的: *The dog lay so still it scarcely seemed animate.* 那条狗卧着一动也不动, 简直不像活的.

an·im·ate[2] /ˈænɪmeɪt; ˋænəˌmet/ *v* **1** [Tn] give life to (sth/sb); make lively 赋予(某事物[某人])以生命; 使活泼; 使有生气: *A smile animated her face.* 一丝笑容使她脸上平添了生气. **2** [Tn, Tn·pr] **~ sb (to/with sth)** inspire or motivate sb 激励或鼓舞某人: *animate sb to greater efforts, with a desire to succeed* 激励某人更加努力、争取胜利 ○ *Animated by fresh hope, he started again.* 他在新希望的激励之下, 又从头做起. **3** [Tn] produce (sth) as an animated cartoon 绘制(动画片).
▷ **an·im·ated** *adj* **1** lively 活跃的; 活泼的: *an animated discussion* 热烈的讨论 ○ *I had rarely seen him so animated.* 我很少见到他这么活跃. **2** given the appearance of movement 看起来活动的: *animated drawings* 动画. **an·im·atedly** *adv.* ˌ**animated car**ˈ**toon** = CARTOON 2.
an·imat·ion /ˌænɪˈmeɪʃn; ˌænəˋmeʃən/ *n* [U] **1** liveliness; vivacity 生气; 活力: *We could see how excited he was by the animation in his face.* 我们从他脸上的神气就能看出他多么兴奋. **2** technique of making animated cartoons 动画片制作技术. Cf 参看 SUSPENDED ANIMATION (SUSPEND).
an·im·ator *n* person who makes animated cartoons 动画片制作者.

an·im·ism /ˈænɪmɪzəm; ˋænəˌmɪzəm/ *n* [U] belief that all natural objects and phenomena (eg trees, stones, the wind, etc) have souls 泛灵论, 万物有灵论(相信一切自然的物体及现象, 如树、石、风等都有灵魂).

an·im·os·ity /ˌænɪˈmɒsətɪ; ˌænəˋmɑsətɪ/ *n* [C, U] **~ (against/towards sb/sth); ~ (between A and B)** (instance of) strong dislike or of hostility 憎恶; 敌意; 仇恨: *He felt no animosity towards his critics.* 他对批评他的人并不怀恨在心. ○ *I could sense the animosity between them.* 我能觉察出他们彼此间的敌意.

an·imus /ˈænɪməs; ˋænəməs/ *n* [U] **1** animosity shown in speech or action (表现在语言或行动中的)敌意, 恶意, 仇恨. **2** (*psychology* 心) masculine part of a woman's personality (女性人格中的)男性基质.

an·ise /ˈænɪs; ˋænɪs/ *n* plant with sweet-smelling seeds 茴芹.

ani·seed /ˈænɪsiːd; ˋænɪˌsid/ *n* [U] seed of anise, used for flavouring liqueurs and sweets 茴芹籽(用于酒类及糖果调味).

ankle /ˈæŋkl; ˋæŋkl/ *n* **1** joint connecting the foot with the leg 踝; 踝关节. **2** thin part of the leg between this joint and the calf 踝节部; 脚腕子: [attrib 作定语] *ˈankle socks*, ie short socks covering the ankles but no higher (只到踝节部的)短袜. ⇨illus at FOOT 见 FOOT 之插图.
▷ **ank·let** /ˈæŋklɪt; ˋæŋklɪt/ ornamental chain, ring or band worn round the ankle 脚镯(戴在脚腕子上作装饰用的链、环或箍).

an·nals /ˈænlz; ˋænl̩z/ *n* [pl] story of events year by year; historical records 编年史; 历史记载; 年鉴: *a name that will go down in the annals*, ie be recorded in history 将载入编年史的名字(载入史册) ○ *the Annals of the Society* 社会年刊.
▷ **an·nal·ist** /ˈænəlɪst; ˋænl̩ɪst/ *n* person who writes annals 编年史作者.

an·neal /əˈniːl; əˋnil/ *v* [Tn] make (metals, glass, etc) tough by cooling slowly after heating 使(金属、玻璃等)退火、焖火(将金属或玻璃加热, 然后缓慢冷却, 以增强其韧性).

an·nex /əˈneks; əˋnɛks/ *v* **1** [Tn] take possession of (a territory, etc) 兼并, 并吞(领土等): *annex a neighbouring state* 兼并邻国. **2** [Tn, Tn·pr] **~ sth (to sth)** add or join sth to a larger thing 附加; 添加: *A new wing has been annexed to the hospital.* 医院已经增建了一个新侧楼.
▷ **an·nexa·tion** /ˌænekˈseɪʃn; ˌænɛksˋeʃən/ *n* **(a)** [U] act of annexing 并吞; 附加. **(b)** [C] instance of this; that which is annexed 并吞; 附加; 附加物.

an·nexe (also *esp US* **annex**) /ˈæneks; ˋænɛks/ *n* **~ (to sth)** **1** building added to a larger one; building providing additional accommodation 增建部分; 添加的建筑; 附属建筑: *The hotel was full so we had to sleep in the annexe.* 旅馆已经客满, 我们只好到附属部去睡. **2** addition, eg to a document 附录, 附件(如附加于文件者).

an·ni·hil·ate /əˈnaɪəleɪt; əˋnaɪəˌlet/ *v* [Tn] destroy (sb/sth) completely 完全消灭, 歼灭(某人[某事物]): *The enemy was annihilated.* 敌人被歼灭了.
▷ **an·ni·hila·tion** /əˌnaɪəˈleɪʃn; əˌnaɪəˋleʃən/ *n* [U] complete destruction 全部毁灭; 灭绝: *A full-scale nuclear war could lead to the annihilation of the human race.* 全面的核子战争能导致人类的灭绝.

an·ni·vers·ary /ˌænɪˈvɜːsərɪ; ˌænəˋvɝsərɪ/ *n* yearly return of the date of an event; celebration of this 周年纪念日; 周年纪念: *the hundredth anniversary of the composer's death* 作曲家逝世一百周年纪念 ○ *our wedding anniversary* 我们的结婚周年纪念 ○ [attrib 作定语] *an anniversary dinner* 周年纪念餐.

an·not·ate /ˈænəteɪt; ˋænəˌtet/ *v* [Tn] add notes to (a book, manuscript, text, etc) giving explanation or comment 给(书、稿、文字等)作注释或评注: *annotated by the author* 由作者加注释的.
▷ **an·nota·tion** /ˌænəˈteɪʃn; ˌænəˋteʃən/ *n* **1** [U] action or process of annotating (作)注释; (作)评注. **2** [C] note or comment added to a text 注释; 评注: *annotations in the margin* 页边上的评注.

an·nounce /əˈnaʊns; əˋnaʊns/ *v* **1** [Tn, Tf, Tw, Dn·pr, Dpr·f, Dpr·w] make (sth) known publicly 宣布; 宣告; 发表: *They announced their engagement to the family.* 他们向家里宣布他们已经订婚了. ○ *The Prime Minister announced that she would resign.* 首相宣布她将辞职. ○ *Have they announced when the race will begin?* 宣布比赛什么时候开始了吗? **2** [Tn] make known the presence or arrival of (sb/sth) 通报(某人[某事物])的出席或到来: *Would you announce the guests as they come in?* 客人来时你通报一声好吗? **3** [Tn] introduce (a speaker, singer, etc) on radio, TV, etc (在无线电、电视等上)主持介绍(演讲者、演唱者等).
▷ **an·nounce·ment** *n* statement in spoken or written form that makes sth known 宣布; 宣告; 通告: *The announcement of the royal birth was broadcast to the nation.* 王室成员降生的通告已向全国广播. ○ *Announcements of births, marriages and deaths appear in some newspapers.* 有些报纸刊登出生、婚姻、死亡的通告.
an·noun·cer *n* person who announces speakers, singers, programmes, etc, esp on radio or TV 播音员, 广播员(尤指无线电或电视节目主持人).

an·noy /əˈnɔɪ; əˋnɔɪ/ *v* [Tn] **1** cause slight anger to (sb); irritate 使(某人)不悦; 惹恼: *His constant sniffing annoys me.* 他不停地抽鼻子使我心烦. ○ *It annoys me when people forget to say thank you.* 遇到有人忘记道谢的时候, 我就不痛快. ○ *I was annoyed by his insensitive remarks.* 我听了他那些没分寸的话, 心里很不痛快. **2** cause trouble or discomfort to (sb); harass 打搅, 骚扰(某人): *Stop annoying your mother.* 别再烦你母亲了. ○ *The mosquitoes annoyed me so much I couldn't sleep.* 蚊

子搅得我无法入睡.

▷ **an·noy·ance** /-əns; -əns/ *n* **1** [U] being annoyed 烦恼: *a look of annoyance* 烦恼的表情 ○ *much to our annoyance* 使我们十分烦恼地. **2** [C] thing that annoys 烦恼的事物: *One of the annoyances of working here is the difficulty of parking near the office.* 在这里工作有一件伤脑筋的事, 就是在办公处附近很难停车.

an·noyed *adj* **~ (with sb) (at/about sth); ~ (that.../to do sth)** rather angry 颇为生气的: *He got very annoyed with me about my carelessness.* 我太粗心大意, 使他很生气. ○ *I'm extremely annoyed at the way he always stares at me in the office.* 他在办公室里老是目不转睛地盯着我, 真把我气坏了. ○ *Will she be annoyed that you forgot to phone?* 你忘记打电话了, 她会生气吗? ○ *I was annoyed to find they had left without me.* 他们撇下我走了, 使我很不痛快.

an·noy·ing *adj* causing slight anger or irritation 使人颇为生气或烦恼的: *This interruption is very annoying.* 这种打扰真讨厌. ○ *How annoying, I've left my wallet at home!* 多讨厌, 我把钱包落在家里了.

an·nual /ˈænjʊəl; ˋænjuəl/ *adj* [usu attrib 通常作定语] **1** happening every year 每年的; 年度的; 一年一次的: *annual event, meeting, report, show, visit* 一年一次的大事、会议、报告、演出、访问. **2** calculated for the year 按年度计算的: *an annual income, production, rainfall, subscription* 年收入、产量、雨量、(预订)费. **3** lasting for one year 持续一年的: *the annual course of the sun* 太阳在一年期间的运行.

▷ **an·nual** *n* **1** plant that lives for one year or season 一年生植物; 一季生植物. **2** book or periodical that is published once a year, having the same title each time but different contents 年鉴; 年刊; 年报.

an·nu·ally *adv*: *The exhibition is held annually.* 这种展览每年举行一次.

an·nu·ity /əˈnju:ətɪ; *US* -ˈnu:-; əˋnuətɪ/ *n* **1** fixed sum of money paid to sb yearly, usu for the remaining part of his lifetime 年金; 养老金: *receiving a modest annuity* 获得些微的年金. **2** form of insurance that provides such a regular annual income 年金保险.

▷ **an·nu·it·ant** /əˈnju:ɪtənt; *US* -ˈnu:-; əˋnuətənt/ *n* person who receives an annuity 接受年金的人; 领取养老金的人.

an·nul /əˈnʌl; əˋnʌl/ *v* [Tn] **(-ll-)** declare (sth) no longer valid; abolish; cancel 宣告(某事物)无效; 废止; 取消: *annul an agreement/a contract/a law/a marriage* 宣告协议[合同/法令/婚姻]无效. ▷ **an·nul·ment** *n* [C, U].

an·nu·lar /ˈænjʊlə(r); ˋænjələ˞/ *adj* shaped like a ring 环形的; 有环纹的: *The annular markings on a tree indicate its age.* 树的环形纹理显示其年龄.

□ ˌ**annular eˈclipse** eclipse of the sun by the moon when a ring of sunlight can be seen round the moon 环蚀(在月球周围可见到一圈阳光的日蚀).

an·nun·ci·ation /əˌnʌnsɪˈeɪʃn; əˌnʌnsɪˋeʃən/ *n* **the Annunciation** [sing] (*religion* 宗) (festival held on 25 March to commemorate) the announcement to Mary that she was to be the mother of Christ 圣母领报(天使预告圣母马利亚, 她将生育耶稣); 圣母领报节(3月25日).

an·ode /ˈænəʊd; ˋænod/ *n* **1** positive electrode by which an electric current enters a device 阳极; 正极. Cf 参看 CATHODE. **2** positive terminal of a battery 电池的阳极接头.

ano·dyne /ˈænədaɪn; ˋænəˌdaɪn/ *n, adj* **1** (drug) that can relieve pain 止痛的(药). **2** (thing) that can relieve or soothe mental distress 能解除或减轻忧愁的(事物).

anoint /əˈnɔɪnt; əˋnɔɪnt/ *v* **1** [Tn, Tn·pr] **~ sb (with sth)** apply oil or ointment to sb (esp as a religious ceremony) 涂油或膏于某人; (尤指作为一种宗教仪式)为某人施涂油礼: *The priest anointed the baby's forehead.* 神父在婴儿的前额上施涂油礼. **2** [Cn·n] show that (sb) has taken high office by doing this 施涂油礼以示(某人)已就高职: *The high priest anointed him king.* 大祭司施涂油礼, 以示他已成为国王.

an·om·al·ous /əˈnɒmələs; əˋnɑmələs/ *adj* different from what is normal; irregular 异常的; 不规则的: *He is in an anomalous position as the only part-time worker in the firm.* 他与众不同, 是公司里唯一的兼职人员.

▷ **an·om·al·ously** *adv*.

an·om·aly /əˈnɒməlɪ; əˋnɑməlɪ/ *n* anomalous thing; irregularity 异常的事物; 不合规则: *the many anomalies in the tax system* 税务制度中的多种异常现象.

anon /əˈnɒn; əˋnɑn/ *adv* (*dated or joc* 旧或谑) **1** soon 不久: *See you anon.* 再会. **2** (idm 习语) **ever and anon** ⇨ EVER.

anon /əˈnɒn; əˋnɑn/ *abbr* 缩写 = (usu at the end of a piece of writing, etc 常用于一篇文字等的末端) (by an) anonymous (author) (作者为)无名氏.

an·onym·ity /ˌænəˈnɪmətɪ; ˌænəˋnɪmətɪ/ *n* [U] state of being anonymous 无名; 匿名; 作者不明.

an·onym·ous /əˈnɒnɪməs; əˋnɑnəməs/ *adj* **1** with a name that is not known or not made public 不知姓名的; 名字不公开的: *an anonymous donor, buyer, benefactor, etc* 不透露姓名的捐赠者、购买者、捐助者等 ○ *The author wishes to remain anonymous.* 作者希望姓名不公开. **2** written or given by sb who does not reveal his name 匿名的; 不具名的: *an anonymous letter, message, gift, phone call* 匿名信、不具名的信息、无名氏的礼物、未留名的电话. ▷ **an·onym·ously** *adv*.

an·oph·eles /əˈnɒfɪli:z; əˋnɑfəˌliz/ *n* mosquito of the type that spreads malaria 疟蚊.

an·orak /ˈænəræk; ˋænəˌræk/ *n* (usu waterproof) hooded jacket worn as a protection against rain, wind and cold (通常为防水的)带风帽外套(可挡雨、挡风、御寒的).

an·or·exia /ˌænəˈreksɪə; ˌænəˋrɛksɪə/ *n* [U] (*medical* 医) **1** loss of the wish to eat 厌食; 食欲丧失. **2** (also **an·or·exia ner·vosa** /nɜ:ˈvəʊsə; nɚˋvosə/) mental illness that causes abnormal fear of eating and thus leads to dangerous loss of weight 神经性厌食症.

▷ **an·or·exic** /ˌænəˈreksɪk; ˌænəˋrɛksɪk/ (also **an·or·ectic**) /-ˈrektɪk; -ˋrɛktɪk/ *n, adj* (person who is) suffering from anorexia nervosa 神经性厌食症的(患者).

an·other /əˈnʌðə(r); əˋnʌðɚ/ *indef det* **1** an additional (person or thing) 再加上一个的(人或事物); 又一; 再一: *Would you like another cup of tea?* 你要再来一杯茶吗? ○ *She's going to have another baby.* 她又快有孩子了. ○ *In another two weeks it'll be finished.* 再过两个星期就完了. **2** a different (person or thing) 不是同一个的(人或事物); 另一: *We can do it another time.* 我们可以下次再做. ○ *She's got another boy-friend.* 她又有了一个男朋友. ○ *That's quite another matter.* 那完全是另一回事. ○ *This pen doesn't work — can you give me another one?* 这枝钢笔不行——你能另给我一枝吗? **3** a similar (person or thing) 类似的(人或事物): *Can he be another Einstein?* 他能成为另一个爱因斯坦吗?

▷ **an·other** *indef pron* **1** an additional person or thing 另一个人或事物: *Can I have another?* 我能再来一个吗? ○ *Not another!* 别再来一个! ○ *Suddenly the letters started arriving — another of them came today.* 突然信件都来了——今天又来了一封. **2** a different person or thing 不是同一个人或事物: *I don't like this room — let's ask for another.* 我不喜欢这间屋子——咱们另要一间吧. **3** a similar person or thing 类似的人或事物: *Shakespeare is the greatest English writer — will there ever be such another?* 莎士比亚是最伟大的英国文豪——还能有这样的人物吗?

ans *abbr* 缩写 = answer.

an·swer[1] /ˈɑ:nsə(r); *US* ˈænsər; ˋænsɚ/ *n* **~ (to sb/sth)** **1** thing said, written or done as a response or reaction; reply 回答; 应答; 答复: *The answer he gave was quite surprising.* 他的回答出人意外. ○ *Have you had an answer to your letter?* 你那封信有回音了没有? ○ *I rang the bell but there was no answer.* 我按了铃, 却没有人应门. **2** solution to a problem, difficulty, etc (难题、困难等的)解决办法, 答案: *This could be the answer to all our problems.* 这或许就是我们全部问题的解决办法. ○ *Who knows the answer to this question?* 谁知道这个问题的答案? ○ *The answer to 3 × 17 is 51.* 3 × 17的答案是51. **3** (idm 习语) **a dusty answer** ⇨ DUSTY. **have/know all the answers** (*often derog* 常作贬义) know a great deal about sth 对某事物所知甚详: *He thinks he knows all the answers.* 他自以为什么都懂. **in answer (to sth)** as a reply 作为回应: *The doctor came at once in answer to my phone call.* 医生一接到我的电话立刻就来了.

an·swer[2] /ˈɑ:nsə(r); *US* ˈænsər; ˋænsɚ/ *v* **1** [I, Tn, Tf, Dn·n] say, write or do sth in response to (sb/sth) 回答; 答复: *Think carefully before you answer.* 先仔细想一想再回答. ○ *answer the question, the teacher, the invitation* 回

答问题、老师、邀请 ○ *answer the door*, ie open the door after sb has knocked or rung the bell 应门(有人敲门或按门铃后去开门) ○ *answer the telephone*, ie pick up the receiver and speak to the person who is calling 接电话; 听电话 ○ *My prayers have been answered*, ie I have got what I wanted. 我的祈祷已经应验了(我已得偿所愿). ○ *Nobody answered my call for help.* 没有人理会我的呼救. ○ (*fml* 文) *How do you answer the charge?* 你怎样答辩? ○ *She answered that she preferred to eat alone.* 她回答说她愿意独自吃. ○ *Can you answer me this?* 你能回答我这一点吗? Cf 参看 REPLY. **2** [Tn] be suitable for (sth); satisfy 适合, 符合(某事物); 满意: *answer sb's purpose/needs/requirements* 符合某人的目的[需要/要求]. **3** (idm 习语) **answer to the description (of sb/sth)** correspond to or match the description (of sb/sth) 与描述的(人或事物)相符合: *The photograph answers to the description of the wanted man.* 这张照片与通缉人相符. **answer to the name of sth** (*infml or joc* 口或谑) (esp of a pet animal) have the name of sth; be called sth (尤指宠爱的动物)名叫, 叫作: *My dog answers to the name of Spot.* 我的狗的名字叫小花. **4** (phr v) **answer back** defend oneself against sth written or said about one 为自己辩护; 辩白: *It's wrong of the press to publish articles attacking the Queen when she can't answer back.* 新闻界发表文章抨击女王是不对的, 因为她不能辩白. **answer (sb) back** speak rudely or cheekily (to sb), esp when being criticized oneself 反驳; 回嘴; 顶嘴; 还口: *He's a rude little boy, always answering his mother back.* 他是个没礼貌的孩子, 总和母亲顶嘴. **answer for sb/sth** (**a**) be responsible for or blamed for sth 对某事物负责; 为某事物受责: *He has a lot to answer for.* 他要负责很多事情. ○ *You will have to answer for your crimes one day.* 你总有一天要因为你的罪行而得到报应的. (**b**) speak on behalf of sb or in support of sth 代表某人或支持某事物而讲话: *I agree but I can't answer for my colleagues.* 我同意, 但是我不能代表我的同事们. ○ *Knowing her well I can certainly answer for her honesty*, ie can guarantee that she is honest. 我很了解她, 当然能担保她诚实. **answer to sb (for sth)** be responsible to sb 向某人负责; 对某人承担责任: *Who do you answer to in your new job?* 你做的新工作要向谁负责? ○ *You will answer to me for any damage to the car.* 这辆汽车有任何损坏, 你要对我承担责任. **answer to sth** be controlled by sth 由某事物控制: *The plane answered smoothly to the controls.* 这架飞机操纵自如.

▷ **an·swer·able** /ˈɑːnsərəbl; ˋænsərəbl/ *adj* **1** that can be answered 可回答的; 可答复的. **2** [pred 作表语] ~ **to sb (for sth)** responsible to sb 向某人承担责任; 向某人负责; 对某人承担后果: *I am answerable to the company for the use of this equipment.* 我要向公司承担使用这一设备的责任.

an·swer·phone /ˈɑːnsəfəʊn; *US* ˈæns-; ˋænsɚˌfon/ *n* device that automatically answers telephone calls and records any message left by the caller 电话录音机.

ant /ænt; ænt/ *n* **1** any of several types of very small insect that live in highly organized groups and work very hard 蚂蚁. **2** (idm 习语) **have ants in one's pants** (*infml* 口) be very restless or excited about sth 坐立不安.

□ ˈ**ant-eater** *n* any of various types of animal that feed on ants 食蚁兽.

ˈ**anthill** *n* mound of earth, etc formed by ants over their nest 蚁塚; 蚁丘.

-ant, -ent *suff* 后缀 **1** (with *vs* forming *adjs* 与动词结合构成形容词) that is or does (sth) 处于...状态的; 进行...动作的: *significant* ○ *different.* **2** (with *vs* forming *ns* 与动词结合构成名词) person or thing that ...的人或事物: *inhabitant* ○ *deterrent.*

ant·acid /æntˈæsɪd; æntˋæsɪd/ *n* [C, U], *adj* (substance) that prevents or reduces acidity in the stomach 解酸的(药剂); 抗酸的(药剂): *I need an/some antacid to cure my indigestion.* 我需要一种[一些]解酸药医治消化不良.

ant·ag·on·ism /ænˈtægənɪzəm; ænˋtægəˌnɪzəm/ *n* [C, U] ~ **(against/for/to/towards sb/sth)**; ~ **(between A and B)** (instance of) active opposition or hostility, esp between two people 对立, 对抗, 敌对(尤指两人之间): *The antagonism he felt towards his old enemy was still very strong.* 他对旧冤家的敌对情绪仍然很大. ○ *You could sense the antagonism between them.* 你能觉察出他们之间有对立情绪.

ant·ag·on·ist /ænˈtægənɪst; ænˋtægəˌnɪst/ *n* person who actively opposes sb/sth; adversary 对抗者; 对手; 敌手.

ant·ag·on·istic /ænˌtægəˈnɪstɪk; ænˌtægəˋnɪstɪk/ *adj* ~ **(to/towards sb/sth)** showing or feeling antagonism; hostile 对抗的; 敌对的: *He's always antagonistic towards new ideas.* 他总是抗拒新思想. ▷ **ant·ag·on·ist·ic·ally** /-klɪ; -klɪ/ *adv*.

ant·ag·on·ize, -ise /ænˈtægənaɪz; ænˋtægəˌnaɪz/ *v* [Tn] arouse hostility in (sb); annoy 引起(某人)的对抗; 骚扰: *It would be dangerous to antagonize him.* 招惹他可危险.

Ant·arc·tic /ænˈtɑːktɪk; æntˋɑrktɪk/ *adj* of the regions around the South Pole 南极的. ⇨illus at GLOBE 见 GLOBE 之插图.

▷ **the Ant·arc·tic** *n* [sing] the regions around the South Pole 南极洲.

□ **the Antarctic** ˈ**Circle** the line of latitude 66° 30′S. 南极圈(南半球66° 30′ 的纬线所形成的圈). ⇨illus at GLOBE 见 GLOBE 之插图.

ante /ˈæntɪ; ˋæntɪ/ *n* stake in poker[2], etc that a player must make before receiving new cards (打扑克等再要牌前所下的)赌注: *raise/up the ante*, ie increase one's stake 加大赌注.

▷ **ante** *v* **1** [Tn] make (sth) as an ante 下(赌注). **2** (phr v) **ante up** (*esp US*) make a stake or payment 下赌注; 付款.

ante- *pref* 前缀 (with *ns*, *adjs* and *vs* 加于名词、形容词、动词前) (of time or position) before; in front of (指时间或位置)在...之前; 在...的前面: *ante-room* ○ *antenatal* ○ *antedate*. Cf 参看 POST-, PRE-.

ante·cedent /ˌæntɪˈsiːdnt; ˌæntəˋsidn̩t/ *n* **1** [C] (*fml* 文) thing or circumstance that is or comes before another 前事; 前情. **2** [C] (*grammar*) word or phrase to which a following word, esp a relative pronoun, refers 先行词: *'Which proves I'm right' is not clear unless we know the antecedent of 'which'.* 'Which proves I'm right' 意思不清楚, 必须要知道which这一先行词所指为何才行. **3** **antecedents** [pl] person's ancestors or past life 祖先; 身世; 经历.

▷ **ante·cedence** *n* [U] (*fml* 文) priority 居先; 在先.

ante·cedent *adj* ~ **(to sb/sth)** (*fml* 文) previous 先前的.

ante·cham·ber /ˈæntɪtʃeɪmbə(r); ˋæntɪˌtʃembɚ/ *n* (*fml* 文) = ANTE-ROOM.

ante·date /ˌæntɪˈdeɪt; ˌæntɪˋdet/ (also **pre-date**) *v* [Tn] **1** put an earlier date on (a document, letter, etc) than the one at the time of writing (在文件、信件等上面)写上比实际书写日期早的日期: *an antedated cheque* 填有比实际日期早的支票. **2** be before (sth/sb) in time 先于, 早于(某事物[某人]): *This event antedates the discovery of America by several centuries.* 这件事比发现美洲早几个世纪. Cf 参看 POST-DATE.

ante·di·lu·vian /ˌæntɪdɪˈluːvɪən; ˌæntɪdɪˋluvɪən/ *adj* **1** of the time before Noah's Flood 挪亚洪水以前的. **2** (*infml or joc* 口或谑) completely out of date; old-fashioned 完全过时的; 旧式的: *His ideas are positively antediluvian!* 他的思想是纯粹的老古董!

ante·lope /ˈæntɪləʊp; ˋæntl̩ˌop/ *n* (*pl* unchanged or ~**s** 复数或不变或作 **antelopes**) any of various types of animal resembling a deer, with thin legs and able to run very fast, found esp in Africa 羚羊.

ante·natal /ˌæntɪˈneɪtl; ˌæntɪˋnetl̩/ *adj* [usu attrib 通常作定语] (**a**) existing or occurring before birth; pre-natal 出生前的; 胎儿期的: *Antenatal complications can affect a baby's health.* 胎儿期并发症能影响婴儿的健康. (**b**) for pregnant women 为孕妇的: *antenatal clinics* 产前检查所. Cf 参看 POSTNATAL.

▷ **ante·natal** *n* medical examination of a pregnant woman 产前检查.

an·tenna /ænˈtenə; ænˋtɛnə/ *n* **1** (*pl* **-nae** /-niː; -ni/) either of a pair of flexible sensitive organs on the heads of insects, crustaceans, etc; feeler 触角; 触须. ⇨illus at BUTTERFLY 见 BUTTERFLY 之插图. **2** (*pl* ~**s**) (*US*) = AERIAL[1] (无线电或电视的)天线.

ante·pen·ul·tim·ate /ˌæntɪpɪˈnʌltɪmət; ˌæntɪpɪˋnʌltəmət/ *adj* third from last 倒数第三的: *The main stress in 'photography' falls on the antepenultimate syllable.*

photography 一字的主重音在倒数第三个音节上.

an·terior /æn'tɪərɪə(r); æn'tɪrɪɚ/ *adj* [usu attrib 通常作定语] (*fml* 文) coming before in position or time; nearer the front 前面的; 先前的; 较靠近前方的. Cf 参看 POSTERIOR.

ante-room /'æntɪrʊm, -ru:m; 'æntɪ,rum/ (also **ante·chamber**) *n* room leading into a larger or more important room; waiting-room (通人大厅或正室的)前厅, 前室, 接待室.

an·them /'ænθəm; 'ænθəm/ *n* short musical composition, usu for a choir and an organ, to be sung in religious services, often with words taken from the Bible 圣歌(通常为短小的合唱曲, 用管风琴伴奏, 于宗教礼拜时演唱, 歌词多取自《圣经》词句). Cf 参看 MOTET.

an·ther /'ænθə(r); 'ænθɚ/ *n* (*botany* 植) part of the stamen of a flower that contains the pollen 花药(花的雄蕊上带花粉的部分).

an·tho·logy /æn'θɒlədʒɪ; æn'θɑlədʒɪ/ *n* collection of poems or pieces of prose on the same subject or by the same writer (同一主题或同一作者的)诗集, 文集, 选集: *an anthology of love poetry* 情诗集.

▷ **an·tho·lo·gist** /æn'θɒlədʒɪst; æn'θɑlədʒɪst/ *n* person who compiles an anthology 选集的编选者.

an·thra·cite /'ænθrəsaɪt; 'ænθrə,saɪt/ *n* [U] very hard form of coal that burns with little smoke or flame 无烟煤.

an·thrax /'ænθræks; 'ænθræks/ *n* [U] infectious, often fatal, disease of sheep and cattle that can be transmitted to people 炭疽(牛羊的传染病, 常可致命, 也可传给人).

anthrop(o)- *comb form* 构词成分 of human beings 人; 人类: *anthropomorphic* ○ *anthropology*.

an·throp·oid /'ænθrəpɔɪd; 'ænθrə,pɔɪd/ *adj* man-like in form (形体)似人的: *anthropoid ancestors of modern man* 现代人的类人祖先.

▷ **an·throp·oid** *n* any of a group of apes that have no tails and resemble man, eg the chimpanzee or the gorilla 类人猿(如黑猩猩或大猩猩).

an·thro·po·logy /,ænθrə'pɒlədʒɪ; ,ænθrə'pɑlədʒɪ/ *n* [U] study of mankind, esp of its origins, development, customs and beliefs 人类学(对人类的研究, 尤指研究其起源、发展、风俗、信仰). Cf 参看 ETHNOLOGY, SOCIOLOGY.

▷ **an·thro·po·lo·gical** /,ænθrəpə'lɒdʒɪkl; ,ænθrəpə'lɑdʒɪkl/ *adj*.

an·thro·po·lo·gist /,ænθrə'pɒlədʒɪst; ,ænθrə'pɑlədʒɪst/ *n* student of or expert in anthropology 人类学者; 人类学家.

an·thro·po·morphic /,ænθrəpə'mɔ:fɪk; ,ænθrəpə'mɔrfɪk/ *adj* treating gods, animals, etc as human in form and personality 拟人化的(把神、动物等看作具有人的形体及人格的). ▷ **an·thro·po·morph·ism** /,ænθrəpə'mɔ:fɪzəm; ,ænθrəpə'mɔrfɪzəm/ *n* [U].

anti /'æntɪ; 'æntɪ/ *prep* in opposition to (sb/sth); against 反对(某人[某事物]); 反: *They're completely anti the new proposals.* 他们完全反对新的提议. Cf 参看 PRO[1].

anti- (also **ant-**) *pref* 前缀 (used widely with *ns* and *adjs* 可与很多名词和形容词结合) **1** opposed to; against 反对; 反: *anti-aircraft* ○ *anti-personnel*. Cf 参看 PRO-. **2** opposite of ...的对立面: *anti-hero* ○ *anticlimactic*. **3** preventing 防止; 阻止; 抗: *antiseptic* ○ *antifreeze* ○ *antacid*.

NOTE ON USAGE 用法: **Anti-** and **counter-** both have the meaning of 'opposed to'. ☆ **anti-** 和 **counter-** 都有'反...'之意. **Anti-** suggests an attitude of opposition ☆ **anti-** 指反对的态度: *anti-war literature* 反战文学 ○ *the anti-nuclear campaign* 反核子运动; while **counter-** refers to an action taken to prevent or respond to something ☆ **counter-** 指为防止某事物或针对某事物而采取的行动: *counter-espionage activities* 反间谍而进行的活动 ○ *counter-revolution* 反革命.

anti-aircraft /,æntɪ 'eəkrɑ:ft; *US* -kræft; ,æntɪ'ɛr,kræft/ *adj* designed to destroy enemy aircraft 歼击敌机的; 防空的: *anti-aircraft guns, missiles, etc* 高射炮、对空导弹等.

an·ti·bal·listic mis·sile /,æntɪbəlɪstɪk 'mɪsaɪl; *US* 'mɪsl; ,æntɪbə'lɪstɪk 'mɪsl/ rocket designed to destroy another in the air 反弹道导弹.

an·ti·bi·otic /,æntɪbaɪ'ɒtɪk; ,æntɪbaɪ'ɑtɪk/ *n*, *adj* (substance, eg penicillin) that can destroy or prevent the growth of bacteria 抗菌素, 抗生素(如青霉素); 抗菌的; 抗生的.

an·ti·body /'æntɪbɒdɪ; 'æntɪ,bɑdɪ/ *n* substance formed in the blood in response to harmful bacteria, etc, which it then attacks and destroys 抗体(血液中形成的抵抗并杀死病菌的物质): *Our bodies produce antibodies to counteract disease.* 我们的身体能产生抗体以抵抗疾病.

an·tic /'æntɪk; 'æntɪk/ *n* (usu *pl* 通常作复数) absurd or exaggerated movement or behaviour intended to amuse people (为引起观众发笑而作出的)滑稽的或夸张的动作: *laughing at the clown's silly antics* 因小丑笨拙的动作而发笑.

an·ti·cip·ate /æn'tɪsɪpeɪt; æn'tɪsə,pet/ *v* **1** [Tn, Tf, Tg, Tsg] expect (sth) 期望, 预料(某事物): *Do you anticipate (meeting) any trouble?* 你预料会有麻烦吗? ○ *We anticipate that demand is likely to increase.* 我们预料需求可能增加. **2** [Tn, Tf, Tw] see (what is going to happen or what needs to be done) and act accordingly 预见到(要发生的事或需要做的事)而采取措施: *She anticipates all her mother's needs.* 她预见到母亲的一切需要而事先做好安排. ○ *Anticipating that it would soon be dark, they all took torches.* 他们预见到天快黑了, 就都带上了手电筒. ○ *A good general can anticipate what the enemy will do.* 善战的将领能预知敌军动向而作好战斗部署. **3** [Tn, Tsg] (*fml* 文) do (sth) before it can be done by sb else; forestall (sb/sth) 先(于别人而)做(某事); 抢先于(某人[某事物]): *When Scott reached the South Pole he found Amundsen had anticipated him.* 当斯科特抵达南极的时候, 发现阿蒙森比他到得更早. ○ *Earlier explorers probably anticipated Columbus's discovery of America.* 早期的探险家可能在哥伦布之前已发现美洲. ○ *We anticipated their (making a) complaint by writing a full report.* 我们没等他们(提出)投诉而抢先写好了一份详尽的报告. **4** [Tn, Tsg] (*fml* 文) deal with or use (sth) before the right or natural time 预先处理或提前使用(某事物): *anticipate one's income*, ie spend money before receiving it 提前使用进款. ▷ **an·ti·cip·at·ory** /æn'tɪsɪpeɪtərɪ; æn'tɪsəpə,torɪ/ *adj* (*fml* 文): *anticipatory precautions* 预先的防范.

an·ti·cipa·tion /æn,tɪsɪ'peɪʃn; æn,tɪsə'peʃən/ *n* [U] action or state of anticipating 预料; 预期; 预测: *A tennis player shows good anticipation by moving quickly into position.* 网球运动员能迅速进人适当位置, 显示其预测准确. ○ *In anticipation of bad weather they took plenty of warm clothes.* 他们预料到会变天而带了很多厚衣服.

an·ti·cli·max /,æntɪ'klaɪmæks; ,æntɪ'klaɪmæks/ *n* disappointing end to a series of events which had seemed likely to become more interesting, exciting or impressive 令人扫兴的结局: *The holiday itself was rather an anticlimax after all the excitement of planning it.* 尽管计划度假时兴致勃勃, 而到头来假日本身却颇为扫兴. ▷ **an·ti·cli·mac·tic** /,æntɪklaɪ'mæktɪk; ,æntɪklaɪ'mæktɪk/ *adj* (*fml* 文).

an·ti·clock·wise /,æntɪ'klɒkwaɪz; ,æntɪ'klɑkwaɪz/ (also *esp US* **coun·ter·clock·wise**) *adv*, *adj* in the direction opposite to the movements of the hands of a clock 逆时针方向(的): *Turn the key anti'clockwise/in an ,anticlockwise di'rection.* 逆时针方向转动钥匙. Cf 参看 CLOCKWISE (CLOCK[1]).

an·ti·cyc·lone /,æntɪ'saɪkləʊn; ,æntɪ'saɪklon/ *n* area in which atmospheric pressure is high, producing fine and settled weather, with an outward flow of air 反气旋; 高气压区. Cf 参看 DEPRESSION.

anti-depressant /,æntɪdɪ'presnt; ,æntɪdɪ'prɛsənt/ *n*, *adj* (drug) that reduces depression (1) 抗抑郁的(药物): *She's been taking/on anti-depressants since her baby died.* 从她的婴儿死亡以后, 她就一直服用抗抑郁药.

an·ti·dote /'æntɪdəʊt; 'æntɪ,dot/ *n* ~ **(against/for/to sth)** **1** substance that acts against the effects of a poison or disease 解毒药; 解毒剂: *an antidote against snake-bites, malaria, food poisoning* 蛇咬、疟疾、食物中毒的解毒药. **2** (*fig* 比喻) anything that counteracts sth unpleasant 抵消不愉快事物的任何事物: *The holiday was a marvellous antidote to the pressures of office work.* 那个假日是消除上班工作压力的灵丹妙药.

an·ti·freeze /'æntɪfri:z; ,æntɪ'friz/ *n* [U] substance

A

added to water to lower its freezing point, eg as used in the radiator of a motor vehicle 防冻剂, 抗凝剂(加于水中以降低其冰点, 如用于机动车辆的散热器中者).

an·ti·gen /ˈæntɪdʒən; ˋæntədʒən/ *n* [U] (*medical* 医) substance which, when it is put into the body, causes it to produce antibodies 抗原(进入机体后能诱发机体产生抗体的物质).

anti-hero /ˈæntɪ hɪərəʊ; ,æntɪˋhɪro/ *n* (*pl* **~es**) central character in a story or drama who lacks the qualities usu associated with a hero, such as courage and dignity 反主角(小说或戏剧中缺乏主角通常所具有的气质的主角, 如缺乏勇气与尊严).

an·ti·his·tam·ine /ˌæntɪˈhɪstəmiːn; ,æntɪˋhɪstəmin/ *n* [C, U] (*medical* 医) any of a variety of drugs used to treat allergies 抗组胺剂, 抗组织胺药(用于医治变应性反应的多种药物).

an·ti·knock /ˌæntɪˈnɒk; ,æntɪˋnɑk/ *n* [U] substance added to motor fuel to prevent or reduce knock[2](4) in the engine 抗震剂, 防震剂(加于内燃机燃料中以防止或减低爆震的物质).

an·ti·log·ar·ithm /ˌæntɪˈlɒgərɪðəm; *US* -ˈlɔːg-; ,æntɪˋlɔgə,rɪðəm/ (also **an·ti·log** /ˈæntɪlɒg; *US* -lɔːg; ˋæntɪlɔg/) *n* (*mathematics* 数) number to which a logarithm belongs 反对数; 逆对数: *1 000, 100 and 10 are the antilogarithms of 3, 2 and 1.* 1 000、100、10 是3、2、1的反对数.

an·ti·mony /ˈæntɪmənɪ; *US* ˈæntɪməʊnɪ; ˋæntə,monɪ/ *n* [U] chemical element, a brittle silvery-white metal used esp in alloys 锑. ⇨App 10 见附录10.

an·ti·pathy /ænˈtɪpəθɪ; ænˋtɪpəθɪ/ *n* **~ (to/towards/ against sb/sth)**; **~ (between A and B)** **(a)** [U] strong or deep dislike 反感; 厌恶; 憎恶: *She felt no antipathy towards younger women.* 她对比她年轻的妇女没有反感. **(b)** [C] instance or object of this 反感; 厌恶; 憎恶; 厌恶的对象: *He showed a marked antipathy to foreigners.* 他对外国人流露出明显的反感.
▷ **an·ti·path·etic** /ˌæntɪpəˈθetɪk; æn,tɪpəˋθɛtɪk/ *adj* **~ (to/towards sb/sth)** showing or feeling antipathy 流露出反感的; 感到厌恶的.

anti-personnel /ˌæntɪ ˌpɜːsəˈnel; ,æntɪ,pɝsəˋnɛl/ *adj* (of bombs, explosives, etc) designed to kill or injure people, not to destroy property, vehicles, etc (指炸弹、炸药等)杀伤性的(旨在杀伤人而不在摧毁物资、车辆等).

an·ti·per·spir·ant /ˌæntɪˈpɜːspərənt; ,æntɪˋpɝspərənt/ *n* [C, U] substance that prevents or reduces perspiration, esp under the arms 防汗剂, 止汗剂(尤指对于腋下的汗).

an·ti·podes /ænˈtɪpədiːz; ænˋtɪpə,diz/ *n* [pl] **1** places on opposite sides of the earth to each other 对蹠地(地球两边正相反的地区). **2 the Antipodes** the Australasian regions in relation to Europe 澳大拉西亚地区(与欧洲相反).

an·ti·quar·ian /ˌæntɪˈkweərɪən; ,æntɪˋkwɛrɪən/ *adj* [usu attrib 通常作定语] of, for or concerning the study, collection or sale of antiques, esp old or rare books 研究、搜集或出售古物的(尤指古籍或珍本书): *an antiquarian bookseller* 古籍商. ▷ **an·ti·quar·ian** *n* = ANTIQUARY.

an·ti·quary /ˈæntɪkwərɪ; *US* ˈæntɪkwerɪ; ˋæntɪ,kwɛrɪ/ (also **antiquarian**) *n* person who studies, collects or sells antiques 研究、搜集或出售古物的人.

an·ti·quated /ˈæntɪkweɪtɪd; ˋæntə,kwetɪd/ *adj* **1** (*usu derog* 通常作贬义) (of things) out of date, obsolete (指事物)过时的, 废弃的. **2** (of people, ideas, etc) old-fashioned (指人、思想等)旧式的.

an·tique /ænˈtiːk; ænˋtik/ *adj* **1** **(a)** belonging to the distant past 古时的. **(b)** existing since old times 自古就有的. **2** valuable because of age and rarity (因古老和稀少而)珍贵的. ⇨Usage at OLD 用法见OLD.
▷ **an·tique** *n* object, eg a piece of furniture or a work of art, that is old and valuable, esp one that is of interest to collectors 文物; 古董; 古玩: [attrib 作定语] *an antique shop*, ie one that sells antiques 古玩店.

an·tiquity /ænˈtɪkwətɪ; ænˋtɪkwətɪ/ *n* **1** [U] ancient times, esp before the Middle Ages 古代(尤指中世纪前): *the heroes of antiquity* 古代的英雄. **2** [U] great age 久远的年代: *Athens is a city of great antiquity.* 雅典是一座古城. **3** [C usu *pl* 通常作复数] object that dates from ancient times 古物; 古迹: *a museum full of Greek and Roman antiquities*, eg coins, pottery, sculptures 有很多希腊和罗马古物的博物馆.

an·tir·rhinum /ˌæntɪˈraɪnəm; ,æntɪˋraɪnəm/ (also **snap·dragon**) *n* (*botany* 植) type of garden flower with bag-shaped petals which open when pressed 金鱼草(一种园圃花, 有袋形花瓣, 受压而张开, 俗称龙头花).

anti-Semite /ˌæntɪ ˈsiːmaɪt; *US* ˈsem-; ,æntɪˋsɛmaɪt/ *n* person who hates Jews 反对犹太人的人. ▷ **anti-Semitic** /ˌæntɪ sɪˈmɪtɪk; ,æntɪsəˋmɪtɪk/ *adj.* **anti-Semitism** /ˌæntɪ ˈsemɪtɪzəm; ,æntɪˋsɛmə,tɪzəm/ *n* [U].

an·ti·sep·tic /ˌæntɪˈseptɪk; ,æntəˋsɛptɪk/ *n* [C, U] substance that prevents a wound, etc from becoming septic, esp by destroying bacteria 防腐剂; 消毒剂; 抗菌剂: *Have you got any antiseptic for this cut?* 这个伤口你消毒了吗? ▷ **an·ti·sep·tic** *adj* **1** preventing infection by destroying bacteria 防腐的; 消毒的; 抗菌的. **2** thoroughly clean and free from bacteria 消过毒的; 无菌的: *an ˌantiseptic ˈbandage* 消毒绷带.

an·ti·so·cial /ˌæntɪˈsəʊʃl; ,æntɪˋsoʃəl/ *adj* **1** opposed or harmful to the laws and customs of an organized community 反社会的(反对或妨害法律与风俗习惯的): *It is antisocial to leave one's litter in public places.* 在公众场所遗弃杂物是妨害公众利益的. **2** avoiding the company of others; unsociable 避免社交的; 不合群的: *ˌantisocial beˈhaviour* 不爱交际的行为 ○ *It's rather antisocial of you not to come to the party.* 你不参加这个聚会就有些不合群了.

anti-tank /ˌæntɪˈtæŋk; ,æntɪˋtæŋk/ *adj* [attrib 作定语] designed to destroy enemy tanks 反坦克的: *ˌanti-tank ˈmissiles* 反坦克导弹.

an·ti·thesis /ænˈtɪθəsɪs; ænˋtɪθəsɪs/ *n* (*pl* **-ses** /ænˈtɪθəsiːz; ænˋtɪθə,siz/) **1** **(a)** [C usu *sing* 通常作单数] **~ (of/ to sth/sb)** direct opposite 正相反; 对立: *Slavery is the antithesis of freedom.* 奴役与自由是对立的. **(b)** [U] **~ (of sth to sth)**; **~ (between A and B)** contrast; opposition 对照; 相反: *The style of his speech was in complete antithesis to mine.* 他和我的讲话方式完全相反. **2** [C, U] contrast of ideas marked by the choice and arrangement of words 对语; 对句; 对偶; 对照: *'Give me liberty, or give me death' is an example of antithesis.* '不自由, 毋宁死' 是对语的一个例子. ▷ **an·tithetic** /ˌæntɪˈθetɪk; æntɪˋθɛtɪk/, **an·ti·thet·ical** /-ɪkl; -ɪkḷ/ *adjs.* **an·ti·thet·ic·ally** /-klɪ; -klɪ/ *adv.*

an·ti·toxin /ˌæntɪˈtɒksɪn; ,æntɪˋtɑksɪn/ *n* [C, U] substance that acts against a poisonous substance and prevents it from having a harmful effect 抗毒素(抵抗有毒物质并防止其产生有害作用的物质).

ant·ler /ˈæntlə(r); ˋæntlɚ/ *n* branched horn of a stag or of some other deer 鹿角: *a fine pair of antlers* 一对完美的鹿角. ⇨illus at DEER 见DEER之插图. ▷ **ant·lered** *adj.*

ant·onym /ˈæntənɪm; ˋæntə,nɪm/ *n* word that is opposite in meaning to another 反义词: *'Old' has two possible antonyms: 'young' and 'new'.* 'Old' 有两个反义词: 'young' 和 'new'. Cf 参看 SYNONYM.

anus /ˈeɪnəs; ˋenəs/ *n* (*pl* **~es**) (*anatomy* 解) opening at the end of the alimentary canal, through which waste matter passes out of the body 肛门. ⇨illus at DIGESTIVE SYSTEM 见DIGESTIVE SYSTEM之插图. ▷ **anal** /ˈeɪnl; ˋenḷ/ *adj.*

an·vil /ˈænvɪl; ˋænvɪl/ *n* **1** iron block on which a smith shapes heated metal by hammering it 铁砧. **2** (*anatomy* 解) one of the bones in the ear 砧骨. ⇨illus at EAR 见EAR之插图.

an·xi·ety /æŋˈzaɪətɪ; æŋˋzaɪətɪ/ *n* **1** **(a)** [U] troubled feeling in the mind caused by fear and uncertainty about the future 忧虑; 担心; 焦虑: *We waited for news with a growing sense of anxiety.* 我们等待着消息, 越来越焦急. ○ *He caused his parents great anxiety by cycling long distances alone.* 他独自骑自行车远行, 父母非常担心. **(b)** [C] instance of such a feeling 忧虑; 担心; 焦虑: *The anxieties of the past week had left her exhausted.* 上星期把她愁得没精打采. ○ *The doctor's report removed all their anxieties.* 医生的报告消除了他们的一切忧虑. **2** [U] **~ for sth/to do sth** strong desire or eagerness for sth/to do sth 渴望; 热望: *anxiety to please* 急于讨好.

anxious /ˈæŋkʃəs; ˋæŋkʃəs/ *adj* **1** **~ (about/for sb/ sth)** feeling anxiety; worried; uneasy 忧虑的; 担忧的; 不安的: *an anxious mother* 焦虑不安的母亲 ○ *I am very* *anxious about my son's health.* 我非常担心儿子的健康. ○ *He was anxious for his family, who were travelling abroad.* 他担心在国外旅行的家眷. **2** [attrib 作定语] causing anxiety 引起忧虑的; 令人担心的: *We had a few anxious moments before landing safely.* 我们在安全着陆以前, 感到阵阵忧虑. **3 ~ for sth/(for sb) to do sth/that...** strongly wishing sth; eager for sth 渴望某事物; 急切想要某事物: *anxious for their safety* 悬望他们平安无事 ○ *anxious to meet you/for his brother to meet you* 渴望见到你[他的弟弟见到你] ○ *They were anxious that aid should be sent promptly.* 他们盼望援助物品迅速送到. ▷ **anxiously** *adv*.

any[1] /ˈenɪ; ˋɛnɪ/ *indef det* **1** (used in negative sentences and in questions; after *if/whether*; after *hardly, never, without*, etc; and after such *vs* as *prevent, ban, avoid, forbid* 用于否定句及疑问句; 用于 if/whether 之后; 用于 hardly、never、without 等之后; 用于 prevent、ban、avoid、forbid 一类动词之后) **(a)** (used with [U] *ns* 与不可数名词连用) an unspecified amount of 任何量的: *I didn't eat any meat.* 我一点儿肉都没吃. ○ *Do you know any French?* 你会法语吗? ○ *There was hardly any free time.* 简直没有什么空闲时间. ○ *We did the job without any difficulty.* 我们毫不费力就做完了工作. ○ *To avoid any delay please phone your order direct.* 为免延误, 请直接打电话预订. ○ *It didn't seem to be any distance* (ie It seemed a very short distance) *to the road.* 那条路似乎没多远. **(b)** (used with plural [C] *ns* 与复数可数名词连用) an unspecified number of (people or things) 任何数目的(人或物): *I haven't read any books by Tolstoy.* 我没看过托尔斯泰的书. ○ *Are there any stamps in that drawer?* 那抽屉里有邮票吗? ○ *I wonder whether Mr Black has any roses in his garden.* 我不知道布莱克先生的花园里有没有玫瑰. ○ *You can't go out without any shoes.* 不穿鞋就不能出去. ○ *They bought a dog to prevent any burglaries.* 他们买了条狗以防盗贼. Cf 参看 SOME[1]. **2 (a)** (used with singular [C] *ns* 与单数可数名词连用) one out of a number, (the particular choice being unimportant) 任一(哪一个并不重要): *Take any book you like.* 你喜欢哪本书就拿哪本. ○ *Give me a pen — any pen will do.* 给我一枝钢笔——哪枝都行. ○ *Phone me any day next week.* 下星期的任何一天给我打个电话. **(b)** (used with singular [C] *ns* in negative sentences or sentences implying doubt or negation; also used after *if/whether* 用于否定句或有疑问或否定含义的句中, 与单数可数名词连用; 亦用于 if/whether 之后) a; one 一个: *Hasn't it got any tail?* 它有尾巴吗? ○ *I can't see any door in this room.* 我看不到这房间有门. **3** every; no matter which 每一个; 无论哪个: *Any fool could tell you that.* 连傻瓜都知道. ○ *You'll find me here at any hour of the day.* 你可以看到我整天任何时候都在这里. ○ *Any train from this platform stops at Gatwick.* 从这一月台开出的火车都在盖特威克停. ○ *They want any money you can spare.* 你有多少闲钱他们都要. **4** (used in negative sentences and after *if/whether* 用于否定句及 if/whether 之后) a normal; an ordinary 平常的; 普通的; 一般的: *This isn't any old bed — it belonged to Shakespeare.* 这可不是一般的旧床——是莎士比亚的. ○ *If it were any ordinary paint you would need two coats.* 若是普通颜料就要涂两层. ○ *She isn't just any woman — she's the Queen.* 她并非寻常妇女——她是女王.

□ **ˈany time** whatever time you like 随便什么时候: *Come round any time.* 什么时候来都可以.

any[2] /ˈenɪ; ˋɛnɪ/ *indef pron* **1** (used in negative sentences and in questions; after *if/whether*; and after *hardly, never, without*, etc 用于否定句及疑问句; 用于 if/whether 之后; 用于 hardly、never、without 等词之后) an unspecified amount or number 任何的数量. **(a)** (referring back 用以复指前文): *I can't give you any.* 我一点儿也不能给你. ○ *Have you got any?* 你有吗? **(b)** (referring forward 用以预指后文): *She didn't spend any of the money.* 这钱她一点儿都没花. ○ *If he had read any of those books he would have known the answer.* 他假若看了这些书中的任何一本, 就知道答案了. ○ *He returned home without any of the others.* 没有任何人和他一起回家. **2** one single example 一例: *If you recognize 'any of the people in the photograph, tell us.* 你若能认出照片中的任何人, 就告诉我们. Cf 参看 SOME[3]. **3** (idm 习语) **sb isn't ˈhaving any** (*infml* 口) sb isn't interested or does not agree 某人不感兴趣或不同意: *I tried to get her to talk about her divorce but she wasn't having any.* 我想引她谈谈她离婚的事, 但她不愿意说.

any[3] /ˈenɪ; ˋɛnɪ/ *indef adv* (used with *faster, slower, better*, etc, in questions and after *if/whether* 用于疑问句中, 与 faster、slower、better 等连用; 用于 if/whether 之后) to any degree; at all 在任何程度上; 丝毫: *I can't run any faster.* 我无法跑得更快了. ○ *Is your father any better at all?* 你父亲有些好转吗? ○ *If it were any further we wouldn't be able to get there.* 假使再远一些, 我们就到不了了. ○ *I can't afford to spend any more on food.* 用在食物上的钱, 再多一点儿我也花不起了. ○ *The children didn't behave any too well*, ie They behaved rather badly. 孩子们的表现并未见好.

□ **any ˈmore** (*US* **anymore**) any further; now, or any longer starting from now 再; 更; 还; 目前; 现在; 今后: *She doesn't live here any more.* 她已不在这里住了.

any·body /ˈenɪbɒdɪ; ˋɛnɪ,bɑdɪ/ (also **anyone**) *indef pron* **1** any person 任何人: *Did anybody see you?* 有人看见你了吗? ○ *Hardly anybody came.* 几乎没有人来. ○ *Anybody who saw the accident should phone the police.* 见到这一事故的人应打电话通知警方. ○ *He left without speaking to anyone else.* 他未和任何人打招呼就离开了. **2** one person out of many (the choice being unimportant) 其中任何一人(是谁并不重要): *Anybody will tell you where the bus stop is.* 谁都能告诉你公共汽车站在哪里. ○ *Ask anyone in your class.* 问问你们同班的人. **3** (in negative sentences 用于否定句) any person of importance 任何重要的人: *She wasn't anybody before she got that job.* 她得到那份工作以前并非重要人物.

any·how /ˈenɪhaʊ; ˋɛnɪ,haʊ/ *indef adv* **1** carelessly; unsystematically 随随便便地; 杂乱无章地: *The books were lying on the shelves just/all anyhow.* 书都乱放在书架上. ○ *He made notes anyhow across the page.* 他在那页上胡乱作了些笔记. **2** (also **anyway**) whatever the facts may be; in spite of this; at least 无论如何; 即使如此; 至少: *It's too late now, anyhow.* 无论如何现在已经太迟了. ○ *Anyhow, you can try.* 至少你可以试试.

any·one /ˈenɪwʌn; ˋɛnɪ,wʌn/ *indef pron* = ANYBODY.

any·place (*US*) = ANYWHERE.

any·thing /ˈenɪθɪŋ; ˋɛnɪ,θɪŋ/ *indef pron* **1** any thing 任何事物: *Did she tell you anything interesting?* 她跟你说过什么有趣的事吗? ○ *There's never anything worth watching on TV.* 电视上从来没有值得看的节目. ○ *If you remember anything at all, please let us know.* 你要是想起什么来, 就告诉我们. **2** any thing of importance 任何重要的事物: *Is there anything* (ie any truth) *in these rumours?* 这些谣传中有真事吗? **3** something (its exact nature being unimportant) 某事物(其确切性质并不重要): *I'm very hungry — I'll eat anything.* 我饿极了——什么都能吃. ○ *Anything will do to sleep on.* 什么东西都可以, 只要能在上面睡觉就行. **4** (idm 习语) **anything but** definitely not 绝对不: *The hotel was anything but satisfactory.* 这家旅馆太不让人满意了. **anything like sb/sth** (*infml* 口) in any way similar(ly) 有些像: *He isn't anything like my first boss.* 他一点也不像我第一个老板. ○ *The film wasn't anything like as good as ET.* 这部电影一点都不如《外星人》那么好. **like ˈanything** (*infml* 口) very much; very quickly, loudly, successfully, etc 非常; 十分迅速、响亮、成功等: *The thief ran like anything when he heard the alarm.* 那贼听到警铃声就飞快逃走了. **or anything** (*infml* 口) (used to refer to similar examples 用以指相似的例子) or another thing similar to that mentioned (与所提到的)相似的另一事物: *If you want to call a meeting or anything, put up a notice.* 要想召集会议什么的, 就要出个通知.

any·way /ˈenɪweɪ; ˋɛnɪ,we/ *indef adv* = ANYHOW 2.

any·where /ˈenɪweə(r); *US* -hweər; ˋɛnɪ,hwɛr/ (*US* also **anyplace**) *indef adv* **1** in, at or to any place 在、向或到任何地方: *I can't see it anywhere.* 我在什么地方都见不到它. ○ *If you want to go anywhere else, let me know.* 你要到别的地方去, 就要告诉我. **2** one place out of many (the choice being unimportant) 任何一处(何处并不重要): *Put the box down anywhere.* 把箱子放在哪里都行. ○ *We can go anywhere you like.* 你喜欢去哪里我们都可以去.

▷ **any·where** *indef pron* any place 任何地方: *I haven't anywhere to stay.* 我没有地方待. ○ *Do you know anywhere (where) I can buy a second-hand typewriter?* 你知道哪里能买到旧打字机吗?

A

aorta /eɪˈɔːtə; eˈɔrtə/ *n* main artery through which blood is carried from the left side of the heart 主动脉; 大动脉.

apace /əˈpeɪs; əˈpes/ *adv* (*dated or rhet* 旧或修辞) quickly 飞快地; 迅速地: *Work is proceeding apace.* 工作进展迅速.

apart /əˈpɑːt; əˈpɑrt/ *adv* **1** to or at a distance 相距; 相隔: *The two houses stood 500 metres apart.* 这两所房子相距500米. ○ *The employers and the unions are still miles apart*, ie are far from agreement. 雇主与工会之间仍有很大距离(远不能取得一致意见). **2** to or on one side; aside 向一边; 在一边: *She keeps herself apart from* (ie does not mix with) *other people.* 她与别人保持距离(不与别人混在一起). **3** separate(ly) 分开; 分离: *You never see them apart these days.* 他们近来形影不离. ○ *He was standing with his feet wide apart.* 他站在那儿, 两脚分开的距离很大. ○ *These pages are stuck together — I can't pull them apart.* 这几页都粘在一起了——我揭不开. **4** into pieces 成碎片: *I'm sorry, the cup just came/fell apart in my hands.* 很遗憾, 这个杯子竟在我手上碎了. **5** (idm 习语) **be poles apart** ⇨ POLE[1]. **joking apart** ⇨ JOKE. **put/set sb/sth apart (from sb/sth)** make sb/sth appear superior or unique 使某人[某事物]显得优越或独特: *His use of language sets him apart from most other modern writers.* 他对语言的运用在现代作家中别具一格. **a race apart** ⇨ RACE. **take sb/sth apart** criticize sb/sth severely 严厉批评某人[某事物]: *He took my essay apart but I found his criticism helpful.* 他把我的文章狠狠地批评了一顿, 但我认为他的批评有好处. **take sth apart** separate sth into pieces 拆开某物: *John enjoys taking old clocks apart.* 约翰喜欢拆卸旧钟. **tell/know A and B apart** distinguish two people or things; recognize the difference between two people or things 能分辨两个人或两种事物; 能看出两个人或两种事物之间的区别. **worlds apart** ⇨ WORLD.

□ **apart from** (also *esp US* **aside from**) *prep* **1** independently of (sth); except for 除了(某事物)以外…都、全、没、没有等; 除去: *Apart from his nose* (Cf 参看 *His nose apart*) *he's quite good-looking.* 他除了鼻子以外, 哪儿都很好看. **2** in addition to (sth) 除了(某事物)以外…也、还、只等; 不止: *Apart from the injuries to his face and hands, he broke both legs.* 他除了脸部和双手受伤以外, 两条腿也断了.

apart·heid /əˈpɑːthaɪt, -heɪt; əˈpɑrthaɪt, -het/ *n* [U] (in S Africa) (official government policy of) racial segregation, separating Europeans and non-Europeans (南非)欧洲人与非欧洲人的种族隔离(的政府政策).

apart·ment /əˈpɑːtmənt; əˈpɑrtmənt/ *n* (*abbr* 缩写 **apt**) **1** (*US*) = FLAT[1]. **2** set of rooms, usu furnished and rented, esp for a holiday 一套房间(通常设有家具供出租, 尤指为度假用的). **3** (often *pl* 常作复数) single room in a house, esp a large or famous one 厅堂; 殿堂: *You can visit the whole palace except for the private apartments.* 整个宫殿都可以参观, 只有内殿不开放.

□ **aˈpartment block** (*Brit*) (*US* **aˈpartment house**) block of flats 公寓.

ap·athy /ˈæpəθɪ; ˈæpəθɪ/ *n* [U] **~ (towards sb/sth)** lack of interest, enthusiasm or concern; indifference 缺乏兴趣; 无积极性; 漠不关心; 无动于衷: *Extreme poverty had reduced them to a state of apathy.* 极端的贫困使他们万念俱灰.

▷ **apa·thetic** /ˌæpəˈθetɪk; ˌæpəˈθɛtɪk/ *adj* showing or feeling apathy 缺乏兴趣的; 无积极性的; 漠不关心的; 无动于衷的. **apa·thet·ic·ally** /-klɪ; -klɪ/ *adv*.

ape /eɪp; ep/ *n* **1** any of the four (usu tailless) primates (gorilla, chimpanzee, orang-utan, gibbon) most closely related to man 猿(通常指无尾猿, 即大猩猩、黑猩猩、猩猩或长臂猿). ⇨illus 见插图. **2** (idm 习语) **go ape** (*sl* 俚) start behaving crazily 变得狂热; 发疯似的.

▷ **ape** *v* [Tn] imitate (sb/sth); mimic 学(某人[某事物])的样; 模仿.

□ **ˈape-man** *n* extinct creature intermediate between ape and man 猿人.

aperi·ent /əˈpɪərɪənt; əˈpɪrɪənt/ *n* [C, U], *adj* (*fml* 文) (medicine that is) laxative 轻泻的(药); 通便的(药).

aper·itif /əˈperətɪf; *US* əˌperəˈtiːf; əˈpɛrəˌtif/ *n* alcoholic drink taken as an appetizer before a meal 开胃酒; 饭前酒.

aper·ture /ˈæpətʃə(r); ˈæpɚˌtʃɚ/ *n* **1** narrow opening 窄孔; 隙缝. **2** (size of an) adjustable opening for

apes 猿

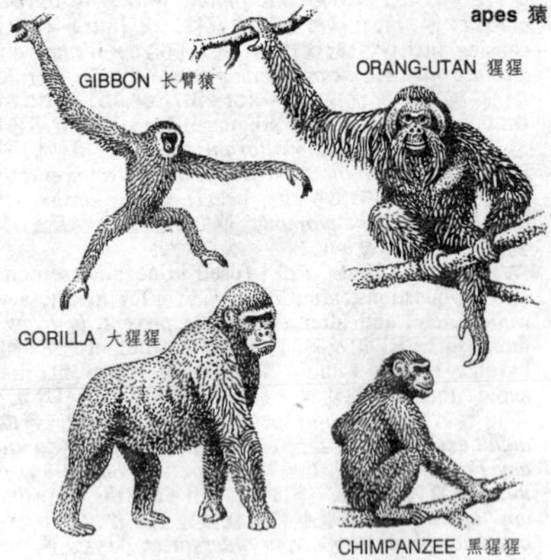

admitting light into a camera (照相机的)光圈孔径(大小): *What aperture are you using?* 你使用多大的光圈?

apex /ˈeɪpeks; ˈepɛks/ *n* (*pl* **~es** or **apices** /ˈeɪpɪsiːz; ˈepɪˌsiz/) top or highest point 顶点; 最高点: *the apex of a triangle* 三角形的顶点 ○ (*fig* 比喻) *At 41 he'd reached the apex of his career.* 他41岁时到达事业的顶峰.

apha·sia /əˈfeɪzɪə; *US* -ʒə; əˈfeʒə/ *n* [U] (*medical* 医) partial or total loss of ability to speak or understand spoken language, caused by damage to the brain 失语症(因脑部受损而部分或全部失去口语表达或理解的能力).

▷ **apha·sic** *n*, *adj* (person) suffering from aphasia 患失语症的(人).

aphid /ˈeɪfɪd; ˈefɪd/ *n* = APHIS.

aphis /ˈeɪfɪs; ˈefɪs/ (also **aphid**) *n* (*pl* **aphides** /ˈeɪfɪdiːz; ˈefəˌdiz/) very small insect, eg greenfly, that is harmful to plants 蚜虫.

aph·or·ism /ˈæfərɪzəm; ˈæfəˌrɪzəm/ *n* short wise saying; maxim 格言; 警句. ▷ **aph·or·istic** /ˌæfəˈrɪstɪk; ˌæfəˈrɪstɪk/ *adj*.

aph·ro·dis·iac /ˌæfrəˈdɪzɪæk; ˌæfrəˈdɪzɪˌæk/ *n* [C, U], *adj* (substance or drug) arousing sexual desire 激发性欲的(药物); 催欲剂; 春药.

api·ary /ˈeɪpɪərɪ; *US* -ɪerɪ; ˈepɪˌɛrɪ/ *n* place with a number of hives where bees are kept 养蜂场; 蜂房.

▷ **api·ar·ist** /ˈeɪpɪərɪst; ˈepɪərɪst/ *n* person who keeps bees 养蜂者.

apiece /əˈpiːs; əˈpis/ *adv* to, for or by each one of a group 每个; 每人; 各: *three cakes apiece* 每人三块蛋糕 ○ *costing 50p apiece* 每个50便士 ○ *We wrote it together, a page apiece.* 我们一起写的, 每人一页.

apish /ˈeɪpɪʃ; ˈepɪʃ/ *adj* (*usu derog* 通常作贬义) **1** of or like an ape; stupid 猿的; 像猿的; 愚蠢的. **2** imitating sb in a foolish way 傻里傻气地模仿某人的: *His apish devotion irritated her.* 他那惺惺作态的愚忠使她恼火.

aplomb /əˈplɒm; əˈplɑm/ *n* [U] confidence and self-control; poise 自信; 沉着: *She performs the duties of a princess with great aplomb.* 她泰然自若地履行王妃的职责.

apo·ca·lypse /əˈpɒkəlɪps; əˈpɑkəˌlɪps/ *n* **1** [C] revelation, esp about the future of the world (尤指关于世界未来的)启示. **2 the Apocalypse** [sing] the last book in the Bible, recording the revelation of St John about the end of the world 启示录(《圣经》中最后一卷, 记录圣约翰关于世界末日的启示). **3** [sing] event of great significance or violence similar to events in the Apocalypse 巨大事件(具有重大意义的事件或大动乱, 类似《启示录》中者).

▷ **apo·ca·lyp·tic** /əˌpɒkəˈlɪptɪk; əˌpɑkəˈlɪptɪk/ *adj* prophesying great and dramatic events like those in the Apocalypse (像《启示录》中一样, 对巨大事件)有启示的. **apo·ca·lyp·tic·ally** /-klɪ; -klɪ/ *adv*.

Apo·cry·pha /əˈpɒkrɪfə; əˈpɑkrəfə/ *n* [sing *v*] those

books of the Old Testament that were not accepted by Jews as part of the Hebrew Scriptures and were not included in the Protestant Bible at the Reformation 伪经(《旧约全书》中犹太人不予承认为希伯来《圣经》的经籍, 在宗教改革运动中也不予收入新教《圣经》中).

▷ **apo·cry·phal** /əˈpɒkrɪfl; əˈpɑkrəfəl/ *adj* not likely to be genuine; untrue or invented 不足凭信的; 伪的; 虚构的: *Most of the stories about his private life are probably apocryphal.* 有关他私生活的事可能大部分都是虚构的.

apo·gee /ˈæpədʒiː; ˈæpəˌdʒi/ *n* **1** (*astronomy* 天) position in the orbit of the moon, a planet or a satellite when it is at its greatest distance from the earth 远地点(月球、行星或卫星轨道上距离地球最远的点). **2** (*fig* 比喻) highest or furthest point; climax 最高点; 最远点; 极点.

apol·it·ical /ˌeɪpəˈlɪtɪkl; ˌepəˈlɪtɪkl/ *adj* not interested or involved in politics 不关心政治的; 不涉及政治的.

apo·lo·getic /əˌpɒləˈdʒetɪk; əˌpɑləˈdʒɛtɪk/ *adj* **~ (about/for sth)** feeling or expressing regret; making an apology 表示歉意的; 道歉的: *an apologetic letter, voice* 道歉信、语气 ○ *He was deeply apologetic about his late arrival.* 他对迟到深表歉意.

▷ **apo·lo·get·ic·ally** /-klɪ; -klɪ/ *adv*.

apo·lo·get·ics *n* [sing *v*] art or practice of defending ideas or beliefs (esp those of Christianity) by logical argument (尤指为捍卫基督教教义或信仰的)辩护; 护教学. Cf 参看 APOLOGY 2.

apo·lo·gist /əˈpɒlədʒɪst; əˈpɑlədʒɪst/ *n* person who defends a doctrine by logical argument (为某主义的)辩护者.

apo·lo·gize, -ise /əˈpɒlədʒaɪz; əˈpɑləˌdʒaɪz/ *v* [I, Ipr] **~ (to sb) (for sth)** make an apology; say one is sorry 道歉; 赔不是: *I must apologize for not being able to meet you.* 我因为没能接你而向你道歉. ○ *Apologize to your sister!* 给你姐姐赔个不是!

apo·logy /əˈpɒlədʒɪ; əˈpɑlədʒɪ/ *n* **1 ~ (to sb) (for sth)** statement to say one is sorry for having done wrong or hurt sb's feelings 道歉; 谢罪; 认错: *offer/make/accept an apology* 道歉[致歉/接受道歉] ○ *I made my apologies (to my host) and left early.* 我(向主人)道过歉后提早离去. **2** (*fml* 文) explanation or defence (of beliefs, etc) (为信仰等的)辩解, 辩护. Cf 参看 APOLOGETICS (APOLOGETIC). **3** (idm 习语) **an apology for sth** inferior type of sth; poor replacement 低劣的某事物; 勉强的代用物: *Please excuse this wretched apology for a meal.* 请包涵这顿不像样的饭菜.

apoph·thegm (also **apo·thegm**) /ˈæpəθem; ˈæpəˌθɛm/ *n* short forceful saying expressing a general principle; maxim 格言; 箴言; 警句.

apo·plexy /ˈæpəpleksɪ; ˈæpəˌplɛksɪ/ *n* [U] sudden inability to feel or move, caused by the blockage or rupture of an artery in the brain 中风, 卒中(由脑血管栓塞或破裂而引起的突然失去知觉或瘫痪). Cf 参看 STROKE[1] 7.

▷ **apo·plectic** /ˌæpəˈplektɪk; ˌæpəˈplɛktɪk/ *adj* **1** of or suffering from apoplexy (患)中风的; (患)卒中的: *an apoplectic stroke/fit* 中风的发作. **2** (*infml* 口) red in the face; easily made angry; very angry 脸红的; 易怒的; 大怒的: *apoplectic with fury* 勃然大怒.

apos·tasy /əˈpɒstəsɪ; əˈpɑstəsɪ/ *n* (**a**) [U] abandoning one's religious beliefs, principles, political party, etc 放弃宗教信仰; 背教; 变节; 脱党. (**b**) [C] instance of this 背教; 变节; 脱党.

▷ **apos·tate** /əˈpɒsteɪt; əˈpɑstet/ *n* person who renounces his former beliefs, etc 背教者; 变节者; 脱党者.

a pos·teri·ori /ˌeɪ ˌpɒsterɪˈɔːraɪ; ˈepɑsˌtɛrɪˈɔraɪ/ (using reasoning that proceeds) from known facts to probable causes, eg saying '*The boys are very tired so they must have walked a long way.*' (用推理方法)由已知事实推测出原因(如说'孩子们很疲倦, 那么他们一定走了很长的路.') Cf 参看 A PRIORI.

apostle /əˈpɒsl; əˈpɑsl̩/ *n* **1** (also **Apostle**) any of the twelve men sent out by Christ to spread his teaching 使徒(基督为宣传他的教导而派出的十二位门徒之一). **2** leader or teacher of a new faith or movement (新信仰或运动的)倡导者, 导师.

▷ **apo·stolic** /ˌæpəˈstɒlɪk; ˌæpəsˈtɑlɪk/ *adj* **1** of the Apostles or their teaching 使徒的; 使徒教导的. **2** of the Pope 教皇的. ˌ**apostolic sucˈcession** the passing of spiritual authority from the Apostles through successive popes and other bishops 使徒统绪(神权自使徒传至教皇及其他主教的一脉相承).

apo·strophe[1] /əˈpɒstrəfɪ; əˈpɑstrəfɪ/ *n* sign (') used to show that one or more letters or numbers have been omitted (as in *can't* for *cannot*, *I'm* for *I am*, *'76* for *1976*, etc), the possessive form of nouns (as in *the boy's/boys'* meaning *of the boy/boys*), and the plural of letters (as in *There are two l's in 'bell'*) 撇号(')(可作省字符, 用以表示字母或数字的省略, 如can't为cannot之略, I'm为I am之略, '76为1976之略; 亦可作名词所有格符号, 如The boy's/boys'意为of the boy/boys; 也可用以构成字母的复数形式, 如在there are two l's in 'bell'一句中的bell一字有两个l). ⇨App 3 见附录3.

apo·strophe[2] /əˈpɒstrəfɪ; əˈpɑstrəfɪ/ *n* (*fml* 文) passage in a public speech, poem, etc, addressed to a person (often dead or absent) or to a thing as if it were a person 呼语(在演说或诗歌等中对某人, 常为死者或不在场者, 或对拟人的事物所说的话).

▷ **apo·stroph·ize, -ise** /əˈpɒstrəfaɪz; əˈpɑstrəˌfaɪz/ *v* [Tn] (*fml* 文) make an apostrophe to (sb/sth) 对(某人[某事物])发出呼语.

apo·thec·ary /əˈpɒθəkərɪ; *US* -kerɪ; əˈpɑθəˌkɛrɪ/ *n* (*arch* 古) person who prepares and sells medicines and medical goods 药剂师; 药商.

□ **apothecaries' weight** system of units formerly used in weighing drugs (旧时用于称量药物重量的)药衡制.

apo·thegm = APOPHTHEGM.

apo·the·osis /əˌpɒθɪˈəʊsɪs; əˌpɑθɪˈosɪs/ *n* (*pl* **-ses** /-siːz; -siz/) **1** (of a human being) making or becoming a god or a saint (指人)封为神或尊为神, 神化: *the apotheosis of a Roman Emperor* 对罗马皇帝的神化. **2** glorified ideal; highest development of sth 尊崇的理想; 某事物发展的顶峰: *The legends of King Arthur represent the apotheosis of chivalry.* 亚瑟王的传说代表骑士精神的顶峰.

ap·pal (*US* also **ap·pall**) /əˈpɔːl; əˈpɔl/ *v* (**-ll-**) [Tn] fill (sb) with horror or dismay; shock deeply 使(某人)惊骇或沮丧; 使大吃一惊: *The newspaper reports of starving children appalled me.* 报纸对饥饿儿童的报道使我大为震惊. ○ *We were appalled at the prospect of having to miss our holiday.* 我们为失去这一假日而感到大失所望.

▷ **ap·pal·ling** *adj* (*infml* 口) shocking; extremely bad 骇人的; 极恶劣的: *I've never seen such appalling behaviour.* 我从来没见过这么恶劣的行为. ○ *I find much modern architecture quite appalling.* 我觉得很多现代建筑十分糟糕. **ap·pal·lingly** *adv*: *appallingly thin* 极其薄的.

ap·par·atus /ˌæpəˈreɪtəs; *US* -ˈrætəs; ˌæpəˈrætəs/ *n* [U, C] (*rare pl* **~es** 复数作 **apparatuses**, 罕用) **1** (**a**) set of instruments, etc used esp in scientific experiments 仪器; 设备; 装置: *laboratory apparatus* 实验室设备. (**b**) equipment used for doing sth, esp in gymnastics 器械(尤指体操的): *The vaulting horse is a difficult piece of apparatus to master.* 鞍马是很难掌握的器械. ○ *Firemen needed breathing apparatus to enter the burning house.* 消防队员需用呼吸器械才能进入燃烧着的房屋. ⇨Usage at MACHINE 用法见 MACHINE. **2** complex structure of an organization 机构; 机关; 组织: *the whole apparatus of government* 整个政府机构. **3** system of bodily organs 器官: *the respiratory apparatus* 呼吸器官.

ap·parel /əˈpærəl; əˈpærəl/ *n* [U] (*dated or fml* 旧或文) clothing; dress 衣服; 服装: *lords and ladies in rich apparel* 服饰华丽的王公贵妇.

ap·par·ent /əˈpærənt; əˈpærənt/ *adj* **1** [pred 作表语] clearly seen or understood; obvious 清楚易见或易懂; 明显; 显然: *Certain problems were apparent from the outset.* 有些问题从一开始就是显而易见的. ○ *It became apparent that she was going to die.* 很明显她快要死了. ○ *Their motives, as will soon become apparent* (ie as you will soon see), *are completely selfish.* 他们的动机很快就能看出, 完全是自私自利. **2** seeming; unreal 表面上的; 假的: *Her apparent indifference made him even more nervous.* 她表面上若无其事反而使他更加紧张. ○ *Their affluence is more apparent than real,* ie They are not as rich as they seem to be. 他们的富有是虚有其表(并非像看上去的那么阔).

▷ **ap·par·ently** *adv* according to appearances; as it

A

seems 看来; 似乎: *He had apparently escaped by bribing a guard.* 他看来是贿赂了守卫而逃跑的. ○ *Apparently* (ie I have heard that) *they're getting divorced.* 看样子(听说)他们要离婚了.

ap·pari·tion /ˌæpəˈrɪʃn; ˌæpəˋrɪʃən/ *n* **1** (**a**) appearance, esp of sth startling, strange or unexpected 出现(尤指惊人的、不寻常的或未料到的事物). (**b**) person or thing that appears thus 突如其来的人或事物: *a weird apparition in fancy dress* 身穿奇装异服而突然出现的古怪人物. **2** ghost or phantom 鬼怪; 幽灵: *You look as though you've seen an apparition.* 你好像撞见了鬼似的.

ap·peal /əˈpi:l; əˋpil/ *v* **1** [Ipr, Dpr·t] **~ to sb (for sth); ~ for sth** make an earnest request 恳求; 呼吁: *I am appealing on behalf of the famine victims.* 我代表饥民恳求援助. ○ *The police appealed to the crowd not to panic.* 警方向群众呼吁不要惊慌. **2** [I, Ipr] **~ (to sb)** be attractive or interesting (to sb) (对某人)有吸引力; (使某人)感兴趣: *The idea of camping has never appealed (to me).* 对露营这种想法(我)从来就不感兴趣. ○ *Do these paintings appeal to you?* 你对这些画感兴趣吗? ○ *Her sense of humour appealed to him enormously.* 她的幽默感把他强烈地吸引住了. **3** [I, Ipr] **~ (to sth) (against sth)** (*law* 律) take a question to a higher court where it can be heard again and a new decision given (向上级法院)上诉: *I've decided not to appeal.* 我决定不上诉. ○ *She appealed to the high court against her sentence.* 她不服判决而向高等法院上诉. **4** [I, Ipr] **~ (to sb) (for/against sth)** (in cricket) ask (the umpire) to declare a batsman out or to give some other decision (板球赛中)提请(裁判员)宣布击球员出局或作出其它裁判: *The whole side appealed for a catch.* 全队提请裁判员判接球得分. ○ *The captain appealed against the light,* ie said that the light was not good enough for the game to continue. 队长对光线提出异议(认为光线不好不宜继续比赛).

▷ **ap·peal** *n* **1** (**a**) [C] **~ (to sb) (for sth)** earnest request 恳求; 呼吁: *an appeal for help, food, extra staff* 恳求援助、食物、增添职员 ○ *a charity appeal* 慈善募捐呼吁. (**b**) [U] request for help or sympathy 吁请援助或同情: *Her eyes held a look of silent appeal.* 她眼中流露着无声的求助神情. **2** [U] attractiveness; interest 吸引力; 兴趣: *Does jazz hold any appeal for you?* 你对爵士乐有兴趣吗? ○ *The new fashion soon lost its appeal.* 那种新式样不久就失去了吸引力. **3** [C] (*law* 律) act of appealing (APPEAL 3) 上诉: *lodge an appeal* 提出上诉 ○ *have the right of appeal* 有上诉权 ○ [attrib 作定语] *an appeal court* 上诉法庭. **4** [C] (in cricket) act of asking the umpire for a decision (板球赛中)提请裁判员裁判.

ap·peal·ing *adj* **1** attractive; charming 动人的; 媚人的: *I don't find small boys very appealing.* 我觉得小男孩儿不太讨人喜欢. ○ *The idea of a holiday abroad is certainly appealing.* 到外国度假的主意肯定大受欢迎. **2** causing sb to feel pity or sympathy 令人怜悯或同情的: *an appealing glance* 惹人怜的眼神. **ap·peal·ingly** *adv*.

ap·pear /əˈpɪə(r); əˋpɪr/ *v* **1** [I] (**a**) come into view; become visible 出现; 显现; 呈现: *A ship appeared on the horizon.* 船出现在水平线上. ○ *A light appeared at the end of the tunnel.* 隧道的尽头露出了亮光. ○ *A rash has appeared on his body.* 他身上出现了丘疹. (**b**) arrive 来到: *He promised to be here at four o'clock but didn't appear until six.* 他答应四点钟来, 可是六点钟才到. **2** [I] (**a**) present oneself publicly or formally 公开或正式露面: *The tenor soloist is unable to appear tonight because of illness.* 男高音独唱者因病今晚不能演出. ○ *I have to appear in court on a charge of drunken driving.* 我被控告醉酒驾驶而要出庭受审. (**b**) act as a counsel in a lawcourt (作为辩护人)出庭: *appear for the defendant/prosecution* 为被告[原告]出庭辩护. **3** [I] (of a book or an article) be published or printed (指书或文章)发表或出版: *His new book will be appearing in the spring.* 他的新著将于春季问世. ○ *The news appeared next day on the front page.* 那则消息次日刊登在头版上了. **4** [La, Ln, I, It] give the impression of being or doing sth; seem 显得; 好像; 似乎: *The streets appeared deserted.* 街上似乎行人绝迹. ○ *Don't make him appear a fool.* 别把他弄得像个傻子似的. ○ *She appears to have many friends.* 她好像有很多朋友. ○ *There appears to have been/It appears that there has been a mistake.* 看来一直就有错. ○ *You appear to have made/It appears that you have made a mistake.* 似乎你弄错了. ○ *'Has he been found guilty?' 'It appears so/not.'* '是他被判有罪吗?' '好像是[不是].' **5** (idm 习语) **it appears/appeared as if.../as though...** the impression is/was given that... 看来; 似乎: *It appears as if she's lost interest in her job.* 看来她对自己的工作已失去兴趣.

NOTE ON USAGE 用法: The two pairs of synonyms **appear/seem** and **happen/chance** are intransitive verbs and are not generally used in the continuous tenses. ☆ **appear/seem** 和 **happen/chance** 这两对同义词都是不及物动词, 一般不用于进行时态. They are commonly used in these two patterns 这四个词通常用于以下两种句型: **1** *It appears/seems that he's resigned.* 好像他已经辞职了. ○ *It happened/chanced that she spoke fluent Swahili.* 偏巧她很会说斯瓦希里语. **2** *He appears/seems to have resigned.* 他好像已经辞职了. ○ *She happened/chanced to speak fluent Swahili.* 她偏巧很会说斯瓦希里语. **Chance** is more formal than **happen.** ☆ **happen** 比 **chance** 更多用于口语. **Appear** and **seem** are used in a variety of other patterns ☆ **appear** 和 **seem** 还可用于其它多种句型: *She appeared/seemed very confident.* 她显得很自信. ○ *'Are they reliable?' 'It appears/seems not.'* '他们可靠吗?' '似乎不太可靠.' ○ *'It's going to rain.' 'So it appears/seems.'* '要下雨了.' '看样子像.' **So** is often used for emphasis with **happen/chance** 为加强语气, **so** 常与 **happen/chance** 连用: *It so happened/chanced that I'd met her a few years before.* 碰巧我几年前见过她.

ap·pear·ance /əˈpɪərəns; əˋpɪrəns/ *n* **1** [C] coming into view; arrival 出现; 来到: *The sudden appearance of a policeman caused the thief to run away.* 警察突然出现, 小偷就逃跑了. ○ *They finally made their appearance* (ie appeared, arrived) *at 11.30.* 他们终于在11时30分来到. **2** [C] act of appearing in public as a performer, etc 露面; 出场: *His first appearance on stage was at the age of three.* 他三岁时初次登台. **3** [C, U] that which shows; what sb/sth appears to be 外表; 外貌; 外观: *Fine clothes added to his strikingly handsome appearance.* 华丽的服装使他那极其英俊的外貌更为增色. ○ *She gave every appearance of being extremely rich.* 她处处表现得极为阔气. ○ *Don't judge by appearances — appearances can be misleading.* 勿以外貌取人——外貌不可靠. ○ *The building was like a prison in appearance.* 这座建筑的外观像监狱. **4** (idm 习语) **ˌkeep up apˈpearances** maintain an outward show, esp of prosperity, in order to hide what one does not want others to see 维持体面; 装门面; 虚饰外表: *There's no point in keeping up appearances when everyone knows we're nearly bankrupt.* 人家都知道我们快破产了, 何必还打肿脸充胖子. **ˌput in an apˈpearance** show oneself at or attend a meeting, party, etc, esp for a short time 露一下面: *I don't want to go to the party but I'd better put in an appearance, I suppose.* 我不想参加那个聚会, 可是我最好还是要露一下面. **to all apˈpearances** so far as can be seen; outwardly 看来; 显然; 外表上: *He was to all outward appearances dead.* 他显然已经死了.

ap·pease /əˈpi:z; əˋpiz/ *v* [Tn] make (sb/sth) quiet or calm, usu by making concessions or by satisfying demands 使(某人[某事物])安静或平息(通常为作出让步或满足要求): *appease sb's anger/hunger/curiosity* 平息某人的怒气[使某人充饥/满足某人的好奇心].

▷ **ap·pease·ment** *n* [U] act or policy of appeasing, esp by making concessions to a possible enemy in order to avoid war 平息的行动或政策(尤指为避免战争而对潜在的敌人作出让步); 安抚; 姑息; 绥靖.

ap·pel·lant /əˈpelənt; əˋpɛlənt/ *adj* (*law* 律) concerned with appeals 上诉的.

▷ **ap·pel·lant** *n* (*law* 律) person who appeals to a higher court 上诉人.

ap·pel·la·tion /ˌæpəˈleɪʃn; ˌæpəˋleʃən/ *n* (*fml* 文) name or title; system of naming 名称; 称呼; 称号; 命名的编排.

ap·pend /əˈpend; əˋpɛnd/ *v* [Tn, Tn·pr] **~ sth (to sth)** (*fml* 文) attach or add sth (esp in writing) 附加, 添上或增补某事物(尤指文字): *append one's signature to a document* 在文件上加上署名 ○ *append an extra clause to the contract* 在合同上增加一项条款.

ap·pend·age /ə'pendɪdʒ; ə`pɛndɪdʒ/ *n* thing that is added to, or that forms a natural part of, sth larger 附加物; 附属物; 组成部分: *The elephant's trunk is a unique form of appendage.* 象的鼻子是一种独特的附肢.

ap·pend·ec·tomy /ˌæpen'dektəmɪ; ˌæpɛn`dɛktəmɪ/ (also **ap·pendic·ec·tomy** /əˌpendɪ'sektəmɪ; əˌpɛndə`sɛktəmɪ/) *n* (*medical* 医) surgical removal of the appendix(2) 阑尾切除术.

ap·pen·di·citis /əˌpendɪ'saɪtɪs; əˌpɛndə`saɪtɪs/ *n* [U] inflammation of the appendix(2) 阑尾炎.

ap·pendix /ə'pendɪks; ə`pɛndɪks/ *n* **1** (*pl* **-dices** /-dɪsi:z; -dəˌsiz/) section that gives extra information at the end of a book or document 附录: *This dictionary has several appendices, including one on irregular verbs.* 这部词典有几项附录, 包括不规则动词附录. **2** (*pl* **-dixes**) (also ˌ**vermiform ap'pendix**) small tube-shaped bag of tissue attached to the intestine 阑尾. ⇨illus at DIGESTIVE SYSTEM 见 DIGESTIVE SYSTEM 之插图.

ap·per·tain /ˌæpə'teɪn; ˌæpɚ`ten/ *v* [Ipr] **~ to sb/sth** (*fml* 文) belong or relate to sb/sth as a right; be appropriate to sb/sth (作为权利)属于或关于某人[某事物]; 适合于某人[某事物]: *the duties and privileges appertaining to one's high office* 居于高职位所具有的职责和特权.

ap·pet·ite /'æpɪtaɪt; `æpəˌtaɪt/ *n* **1** [U] physical desire, esp for food or pleasure 肉体的欲望(尤指对食物或享乐); 食欲; 胃口: *When I was ill I completely lost my appetite.* 我生病时完全没有食欲. ○ *Don't spoil your appetite by eating sweets before meals.* 饭前不要吃糖以免影响食欲. ○ (*fig* 比喻) *He had no appetite for the fight.* 他毫无斗志. **2** [C] instance of a natural desire for sth (对某事物的)自然的欲望: *The long walk has given me a good appetite.* 走了长路使我食欲大振. ○ *He has an amazing appetite for hard work.* 他出奇地喜爱艰巨的工作. ○ *a person of gross sexual appetites* 性欲旺盛的人.

ap·pet·izer, -iser /'æpɪtaɪzə(r); `æpəˌtaɪzɚ/ *n* thing that is eaten or drunk before a meal to stimulate the appetite 正餐前的开胃食物或饮料; 开胃品: *Small savoury biscuits provide a simple appetizer.* 可口的小饼干就是简单的开胃品.

ap·pet·iz·ing, -ising /'æpɪtaɪzɪŋ; `æpəˌtaɪzɪŋ/ *adj* (of food, etc) stimulating the appetite (指食物等)促进食欲的, 开胃的, 刺激欲望的: *an appetizing smell from the kitchen* 来自厨房的令人垂涎的香味 ○ *The list of ingredients sounds very appetizing.* 这张单子上列的配料听起来使人馋涎欲滴. ▷ **ap·pet·iz·ingly, -isingly** *adv.*

ap·plaud /ə'plɔ:d; ə`plɔd/ *v* **1** [I, Tn] show approval of (sb/sth) by clapping the hands 向(某人[某事物])鼓掌表示欢迎或赞赏: *The crowd applauded (him/the perfomance) for five minutes.* 群众(为他[演出])鼓掌五分钟. **2** [Tn] praise (sb/sth); approve 称赞; 赞成: *I applaud your decision.* 我赞成你的决定.

ap·plause /ə'plɔ:z; ə`plɔz/ *n* [U] **1** approval expressed by clapping the hands 鼓掌欢迎: *He sat down amid deafening applause.* 他在震耳欲聋的掌声中就坐. **2** warm approval 热情称赞: *Her new novel was greeted by reviewers with rapturous applause.* 她的新小说备受书评家推崇.

apple /'æpl; `æpḷ/ *n* **1** (**a**) round fruit with firm juicy flesh and green, red or yellow skin when ripe 苹果: [attrib 作定语] *an apple pie* 苹果馅饼 ○ *apple sauce* 苹果酱. ⇨illus at FRUIT 见 FRUIT 之插图. (**b**) (also **'apple tree**) tree bearing this fruit 苹果树. **2** (idm 习语) **an/the ˌapple of 'discord** (*fml* 文) cause of an argument or a quarrel 争端; 祸根. **the ˌapple of sb's 'eye** person or thing that is loved more than any other 心爱的人或物; 掌上明珠: *She is the apple of her father's eye.* 她是父亲的掌上明珠. **in ˌapple-pie 'order** very neatly arranged 井然有序.

□ **'applecart** *n* (idm 习语) **upset the/sb's applecart** ⇨ UPSET.

'applejack *n* [U] (*US*) strong alcoholic drink distilled from fermented cider 苹果白兰地(由发酵的苹果汁蒸馏而成的烈性酒).

ap·pli·ance /ə'plaɪəns; ə`plaɪəns/ *n* **1** instrument or device for a specific purpose 工具; 用具; 器具; 器械: *a kitchen full of electrical appliances,* eg a washing-machine, dish washer, liquidizer, etc 有各种电器用具的厨房(如洗衣机、洗碗机、果汁机等). ⇨Usage at MACHINE 用法见 MACHINE. **2** = FIRE-ENGINE (FIRE).

ap·plic·able /'æplɪkəbl, *also* ə'plɪkəbl; `æplɪkəbḷ, ə`plɪkəbḷ/ *adj* [pred 作表语] **~ (to sb/sth)** that can be applied (APPLY 7); appropriate or suitable 可适用; 合适; 适当: *This part of the form is not applicable* (ie does not apply) *to foreign students.* 表格中的这一部分不适用于外国学生. ▷ **ap·plic·ab·il·ity** /ˌæplɪkə'bɪlətɪ; ˌæplɪkə`bɪlətɪ/ *n* [U].

ap·plic·ant /'æplɪkənt; `æpləkənt/ *n* **~ (for sth)** person who applies, esp for a job, etc 申请人(尤指为求职等): *As the wages were low, there were few applicants for the job.* 因为工资低, 没有什么人申请这份工作.

ap·plica·tion /ˌæplɪ'keɪʃn; ˌæplə`keʃən/ *n* **1** (**a**) [U] **~ (to sb) (for sth)** formal request 申请; 请求: *Keys are available on application to the principal.* 向校长申请就可得到钥匙. (**b**) [C] instance of this 申请; 请求: *We received 400 applications for the job.* 对这份工作, 我们接到400人的申请. ○ [attrib 作定语] *an application form,* ie a form on which to make an application 申请表. **2** (**a**) [U, C] **~ (of sth) (to sth)** act of applying one thing to another 敷用; 施用: *lotion for external application only,* ie to be put on the skin, not swallowed 只限外用的敷剂(用于皮肤, 不可内服) ○ *three applications per day* 每日敷用三次. (**b**) [C] substance applied 敷用的物质: *an application to relieve muscle pain* 减轻肌肉疼痛的敷剂. **3** [U] making a rule, etc take effect (使规则等)生效; 实施: *the strict application of the law* 严明执法. **4** [U] concentrated effort; hard work 专心; 努力: *Success as a writer demands great application.* 要成为作家就得狠下功夫. **5** [U, C] **~ (to sth)** act of putting a theory, discovery, etc to practical use 应用; 运用: *a new invention that will have application / a variety of applications in industry* 工业上可应用的[有多种用途的]新发明.

ap·plic·ator /'æplɪkeɪtə(r); `æplɪˌketɚ/ *n* thing used to apply (APPLY 2) sth 涂敷器: *Use the applicator provided to spread the glue.* 使用所附涂敷器涂用胶水.

ap·plied ⇨ APPLY.

ap·pli·qué /æ'pli:keɪ; *US* ˌæplɪ'keɪ; ˌæplɪ`ke/ *n* [U] decorative needlework in which pieces of one type of material are cut out and attached to another 缝饰; 镶饰; 贴花; 补花.

▷ **ap·pli·qué** *v* (*pt, pp* **appliquéd**) [Tn] decorate (sth) in this way 在(某物上)缝饰; 以补花镶饰(某物).

ap·ply /ə'plaɪ; ə`plaɪ/ *v* (*pt, pp* **applied**) **1** [I, Ipr] **~ (to sb) (for sth)** make a formal request 申请; 请求: *You should apply immediately, in person or by letter.* 你应该立即申请, 亲自去也好, 写信也好. ○ *apply to the publishers for permission to reprint an extract* 向出版者请求准予转印节录 ○ *apply for a job, post, passport, visa* 申请工作、职位、护照、签证. **2** [Tn, Tn·pr] **~ sth (to sth)** put or spread sth (onto sth) 贴; 敷; 涂; 搽: *apply the ointment sparingly* 涂搽少许油膏 ○ *apply the glue to both surfaces* 两面都涂上胶水 ○ (*fig* 比喻) *I'd never apply the word 'readable' to any of his books.* 我决不会把他的任何一本书称为是'可以一读的'. **3** [Tn] make (a law, etc) operate or become effective 使(法律等)实施或生效; 应用; 运用: *apply a law/rule/precept* 执行法律[规则/规程] ○ *apply economic sanctions* 施行经济制裁. **4** [I, Ipr] **~ (to sb/sth)** be relevant (to sb/sth); have an effect (与某人[某物])有关; 有效; 适用: *These rules don't always apply.* 这些规则并非总能行得通. ○ *What I have said applies only to some of you.* 我所说的只适用于你们当中的一部分人. **5** [Tn, Tn·pr] **~ sth (to sth)** cause (a force, etc) to affect sth 使用(力量等)对某事物起作用: *apply force, pressure, heat, etc* 用力、压力、热力等 ○ *apply the brakes hard* 用力刹车. **6** [Tn, Tn·pr] **~ oneself/sth (to sth/doing sth)** concentrate one's thought and energy (on a task) 集中精力(做事); 专心: *You will only pass your exams if you really apply yourself (to your work).* 你只有真正专心致志(用功), 考试才能及格. ○ *We must apply our minds to finding a solution.* 我们要动动脑筋找出解决的办法来. **7** [Tn, Tn·pr] **~ sth (to sth)** make practical use of sth 运用, 应用某事物: *The results of this research can be applied to new developments in technology.* 这项研究成果能应用于新的技术开发方面.

▷ **ap·plied** /ə'plaɪd; ə`plaɪd/ *adj* [usu attrib 通常作定语] used in a practical way; not merely theoretical 应用

A

的; 实用的: *applied mathematics*, eg as used in engineering 应用数学(如用于工程学中者) ○ *applied linguistics* 应用语言学. Cf 参看 PURE 5.

ap·point /əˈpɔɪnt; əˈpɔɪnt/ *v* **1** [Tn, Tn·pr, Cn·n, Cn·n/a, Cn·t] **~ sb (to sth); ~ sb (as sth)** choose sb for a job or position of responsibility 挑选(某人)做某工作或任某职位; 任命; 委派: *They have appointed Smith/a new manager.* 他们已经任用了史密斯[一位新经理]. ○ *He was appointed to the vacant post.* 他被委派填补那空缺. ○ *Who shall we appoint (as) chairperson?* 我们选派谁担任主席呢? ○ *We must appoint sb to act as secretary.* 我们得指定一个人当秘书. **2** [Tn] create (sth) by choosing members 挑选人员以组成(某事物): *appoint a committee* 挑选人员组成委员会. **3** [Tn, Tn·pr] **~ sth (for sth)** (*fml* 文) fix or decide on sth 确定或决定某事物: *appoint a date to meet/for a meeting* 约定一个日期见面[开会] ○ *The time appointed for the meeting was 10.30.* 规定开会的时间是10时30分.

▷ **ap·pointee** /əpɔɪnˈtiː; ə,pɔɪnˈti/ *n* person appointed to a job or position 被任命者; 被委派者; 被指定者.

ap·point·ment /əˈpɔɪntmənt; əˈpɔɪntmənt/ *n* **1** (**a**) [C, U] **~ (to sth)** (act of) appointing a person to a job 任命; 任用; 委派: *His promotion to manager was a popular appointment.* 他升任经理是众望所归的. (**b**) [C] job to which sb is appointed (被任用的)工作, 职位: *I'm looking for a permanent appointment.* 我正在寻找固定的工作. **2** [C, U] **~ (with sb)** arrangement to meet or visit sb at a particular time 约会; 预约: *make/fix an appointment with sb* 与某人约会 ○ *keep/break an appointment* 践[失]约 ○ *I have a dental appointment at 3 pm.* 我下午3时有个牙科的预约. ○ *Interviews are by appointment only.* 会晤需经预约. **3 appointments** [pl] equipment; furniture 设备; 家具.

ap·por·tion /əˈpɔːʃn; əˈpɔrʃən/ *v* [Tn, Tn·pr, Dn·n] **~ sth (among/to sb)** give sth as a share; allot sth 分配某事物; 分派某事物: *I don't wish to apportion blame among you/to any of you.* 我不愿意怪罪你们大家[你们任何人]. ○ *He apportioned the members of the team their various tasks.* 他已把各项任务分配给队员们. Cf 参看 PORTION *v*. ▷ **ap·por·tion·ment** *n* [U].

ap·pos·ite /ˈæpəzɪt; ˈæpəzɪt/ *adj* **~ (to sth)** (of a remark, etc) very appropriate (for a purpose or an occasion)(指言辞等)适当的, 合适的, 恰当的 : *an apposite comment, illustration, example, etc* 恰当的评论、说明、例子等 ○ *I found his speech wholly apposite to the current debate.* 我认为他的讲话对当前的辩论是恰到好处的. ▷ **ap·pos·itely** *adv*. **ap·pos·ite·ness** *n* [U].

ap·posi·tion /,æpəˈzɪʃn; ,æpəˈzɪʃən/ *n* [U] (*grammar*) addition of one word or phrase to another word or phrase as an explanation 同位; 同格: *In 'Queen Elizabeth, the Queen Mother' 'the Queen Mother' is in apposition to 'Queen Elizabeth'.* 在'Queen Elizabeth, the Queen Mother'一语中'the Queen Mother'是'Queen Elizabeth'的同位语.

ap·praise /əˈpreɪz; əˈprez/ *v* [Tn] assess the value or quality of (sb/sth) 评价; 估价; 鉴定; 评定: *appraise a student's work* 评定学生的作业 ○ *an appraising glance* 估量的眼光 ○ *It would be unwise to buy the house before having it appraised.* 买房子不事先估价是不明智的.

▷ **ap·praisal** /əˈpreɪzl; əˈprezl̩/ *n* [C, U] (act of) appraising sb/sth; valuation 评价; 估价; 鉴定; 评定.

ap·pre·ciable /əˈpriːʃəbl; əˈpriʃəbl̩/ *adj* that can be seen or felt; considerable 可察觉到的; 可观的: *an appreciable drop in temperature* 气温些微的下降 ○ *The increase in salary will be appreciable.* 薪水的增加将很可观. ▷ **ap·pre·ciably** /-əblɪ; -əblɪ/ *adv*: *He's looking appreciably thinner.* 看得出来他消瘦了.

ap·preci·ate /əˈpriːʃɪeɪt; əˈpriʃɪ,et/ *v* **1** [Tn] understand and enjoy (sth); value highly 理解并欣赏(某事物); 赏识; 高度评价: *You can't fully appreciate foreign literature in translation.* 看翻译作品很难欣赏到外国文学的精髓. ○ *I really appreciate a good cup of tea.* 有好茶一杯, 我就真乐在其中了. ○ *Your help was greatly appreciated*, ie We were grateful for it. 非常感谢你的帮助. **2** [Tn, Tf, Tw] understand (sth) with sympathy 体恤, 体念, 体谅(某事物): *I appreciate your problem, but I don't think I can help you.* 我理解你的困难, 但却爱莫能助. ○ *I appreciate that you may have prior commitments.* 我体谅你可能事先已另有承诺. ○ *You don't seem to appreciate how busy I am.* 你似乎不能体念我多么忙. **3** [I] increase in value 增值; 涨价: *Local property has appreciated (in value) since they built the motorway nearby.* 自从附近修建了高速公路, 本地的地产(价值)已经增值.

▷ **ap·pre·ci·at·ive** /əˈpriːʃətɪv; əˈpriʃɪ,etɪv/ *adj* **~ (of sth)** feeling or showing understanding or gratitude 有欣赏力的; 表示赏识的; 感激的: *an appreciative letter, audience, look* 感谢信、表示欣赏的观众(或听众)、赏识的神情 ○ *I'm most appreciative of your generosity.* 我对你的慷慨感激之至. **ap·pre·ci·at·ively** *adv*.

ap·pre·ci·ation /ə,priːʃɪˈeɪʃn; ə,priʃɪˈeʃən/ *n* **1** [U] understanding and enjoyment 欣赏: *She shows little or no appreciation of good music.* 她对于好音乐鲜有或没有欣赏的能力. **2** [U] grateful recognition of an action 感激; 感谢: *Please accept this gift in appreciation of all you've done for us.* 多蒙鼎力协助, 无任感谢. 谨备薄礼, 敬请哂纳. **3** [C] (*fml* 文) (esp written) statement of the qualities of a work of art, person's life, etc (尤指书面的)鉴定, 鉴别, 评价, 评论: *an appreciation of the poet's work* 对诗人作品的评论. **4** [U] increase in value 增值; 涨价: *The pound's rapid appreciation is creating problems for exporters.* 英镑急速升值给出口商造成困难.

ap·pre·hend /,æprɪˈhend; ,æprɪˈhɛnd/ *v* **1** [Tn] (*fml* 文) seize (sb); arrest 逮捕; 拘押: *The thief was apprehended (by the police) in the act of stealing a car.* 窃贼在偷汽车时当场被(警察)抓住. **2** [Tn, Tf] (*dated* or *rhet* 旧或修辞) grasp the meaning of (sb/sth); understand 领悟; 理解: *Do I apprehend you aright*, ie Do you mean what I think you mean? 你的意思我领会得对吗? Cf 参看 COMPREHEND.

ap·pre·hen·sion /,æprɪˈhenʃn; ,æprɪˈhɛnʃən/ *n* **1** [U, C] anxiety about the future; fear 忧虑; 担心; 恐惧: *filled with apprehension* 忧心忡忡 ○ *I feel a certain apprehension about my interview tomorrow.* 我对明天的面试感到有些担心. **2** [U] understanding 理解; 领悟. Cf 参看 COMPREHENSION. **3** [U] seizing; arrest 逮捕; 拘押: *the apprehension of the robbers, escaped prisoners, etc* 逮捕强盗、逃犯等.

ap·pre·hen·sive /,æprɪˈhensɪv; ,æprɪˈhɛnsɪv/ *adj* **~ (about/of sth); ~ (that.../for sb/sth)** feeling anxiety; fearful; uneasy 忧虑的; 害怕的; 不安的: *apprehensive about the results of the exams* 为考试成绩担忧 ○ *apprehensive that he would be beaten* 害怕他会挨打 ○ *apprehensive for sb's safety* 担心某人的安全. ▷ **ap·pre·hen·sively** *adv*.

ap·pren·tice /əˈprentɪs; əˈprɛntɪs/ *n* **1** person who has agreed to work for a skilled employer for a fixed period in return for being taught his trade or craft 学徒; 徒弟: [attrib 作定语] *an apprentice plumber* 见习铅管工人. **2** beginner or novice 生手; 新手.

▷ **ap·pren·tice** *v* [esp passive 尤用于被动语态: Tn, Tn·pr] **~ sb (to sb)** make sb work as an apprentice (for sb) 使某人(给某人)当学徒.

ap·pren·tice·ship /-tɪʃɪp; -tɪ,ʃɪp/ *n* (time of) being an apprentice 学徒身分(的期限): *serve an/one's apprenticeship with a carpenter* 跟木匠当学徒.

ap·prise /əˈpraɪz; əˈpraɪz/ *v* [Tn·pr esp passive 尤用于被动语态] **~ sb of sth** (*fml* 文) inform sb of sth 将某事通知某人: *I was apprised of the committee's decision.* 我已获悉委员会的决定.

ap·pro /ˈæprəʊ; ˈæpro/ *n* (idm 习语) **on appro** (*Brit infml* 口) = ON APPROVAL (APPROVAL).

ap·proach /əˈprəʊtʃ; əˈprotʃ/ *v* **1** [I, Tn] come near or nearer to (sb/sth) in space or time (在空间或时间上)接近, 靠近(某人[某事物]): *The time is approaching when we must think about buying a new house.* 我们要想一想买新房子的事了, 时机即将来临. ○ *As you approach the town the first building you see is the church.* 接近那座城镇的时候, 首先看到的就是教堂. **2** [Tn] be similar in quality or character to (sb/sth) (在性质或特点上)接近(某人[某事物]): *Few writers even begin to approach Shakespeare's greatness.* 莎士比亚的伟大, 鲜有作家能望其项背. **3** [Tn] go to (sb) for help or support or in order to offer sth (为求助或提供某事物)接近(某人): *approach one's bank manager for a loan* 找银行经理寻求贷款 ○ *approach a witness with a bribe* 前去贿赂目击者 ○ *I find him difficult to approach*, ie not easy to talk to in a friendly way. 我觉得他很难接近(不好谈话). **4** [Tn] begin to tackle (a task, problem, etc) 着手处理(事务、难题等): *Before trying to solve the puzzle, let us consider the best way to approach it.* 要想解决这一难题, 咱们先来考虑一下如何着手方为上策.

▷ **ap·proach** *n* **1** [sing] act of approaching 接近: *Heavy footsteps signalled the teacher's approach.* 沉重的脚步声显示教师已经走近了. ○ *At her approach the children ran off.* 她走近的时候, 孩子们都跑了. **2** [C] **~ to sth** thing resembling sth in quality or character 性质或特点相似的事物: *That's the nearest approach to a smile he ever makes.* 那已算是他能做出的最近乎微笑的表示了. **3** [C] way leading to sth; path; road 通路; 进路; 道路: *All the approaches to the palace were guarded by troops.* 通往宫殿的所有道路都有部队把守. ○ [attrib 作定语] *Police are patrolling the major approach roads to the stadium.* 警察正在通往运动场的主要通路上巡逻. **4** [C] way of dealing with a person or thing 方法; 手段: *a new approach to language teaching* 语言教学的新方法. **5** [C] attempt to reach agreement or become friendly with sb (想与某人商议或亲近的)尝试, 意图: *The club has made an approach to a local business firm for sponsorship.* 俱乐部已试探向本地一家公司寻求资助. ○ *She resented his persistent approaches.* 他一再地表示亲近使她很反感. **6** [C] final part of an aircraft's flight before landing 进场(飞机着陆前的最后飞行阶段): *the approach to the runway* 进入跑道的进场飞行. **7** [C] (in golf) stroke from the fairway to the green (高尔夫球赛中)从外野击向球穴区草地. **8** (idm 习语) **easy/difficult of approach** (*fml* 文) easy/difficult to talk to in a friendly way 平易近人的[难于接近的].

ap·proach·able *adj* **1** (of people or things) that can be approached (指人或物)可接近的: *The village is only approachable from the south.* 这个村子只有从南边才能到达. **2** friendly and easy to talk to 和蔼可亲的. **ap·proach·ab·il·ity** /əˌprəʊtʃəˈbɪlətɪ; əˌprotʃəˈbɪlətɪ/ *n* [U].

ap·proba·tion /ˌæprəˈbeɪʃn; ˌæprəˋbeʃən/ *n* [U] (*fml* 文) approval; consent 认可; 批准: *awaiting the approbation of the court* 等候法院批准.

ap·pro·pri·ate[1] /əˈprəʊprɪət; əˋproprɪɪt/ *adj* **~ (for/to sth)** suitable; right and proper 适当的; 合适的; 正当的: *Sports clothes are not appropriate for a formal wedding.* 运动服用于正式婚礼中是不适当的. ○ *His formal style of speaking was appropriate to the occasion.* 他郑重其事的讲话方式适合于那个场合. ○ *You will be informed of the details at the appropriate time.* 在适当的时候将把详情告诉你. ▷ **ap·pro·pri·ately** *adv*. **ap·pro·pri·ate·ness** *n* [U].

ap·pro·pri·ate[2] /əˈprəʊprɪeɪt; əˋproprɪˌet/ *v* **1** [Tn] take (sth) for one's own use, esp without permission or illegally 拿(某事物)为己所用(尤指未经获准或非法者); 擅用; 挪用; 窃用: *He was accused of appropriating club funds.* 他被控告挪用俱乐部基金. **2** [Tn·pr] **~ sth for sth** put (esp money) on one side for a special purpose 拨出(尤指款项): *£5 000 has been appropriated for a new training scheme.* 为新的训练计划已经拨款5 000英镑.

▷ **ap·pro·pri·ation** /əˌprəʊprɪˈeɪʃn; əˌproprɪˋeʃən/ *n* **1** (a) [U] appropriating or being appropriated 擅用; 挪用; 窃用; 拨款. (b) [C] instance of this 擅用; 挪用; 窃用; 拨款. **2** [C] thing, esp a sum of money, that is appropriated 擅用; 挪用; 窃用或拨用的物品(尤指款项): *make an appropriation of £20 000 for payment of debts* 挪用20 000英镑还债. ○ *the US Senate Appropriations Committee*, ie dealing with funds for defence, welfare, etc 美国参议院拨款委员会(负责国防、福利等的拨款).

ap·proval /əˈpruːvl; əˋpruvḷ/ *n* [U] **1** feeling or showing or saying that one thinks sth is good or acceptable or satisfactory 赞成; 认可; 满意; 同意: *give one's approval* 表示同意 ○ *Do the plans meet with your approval?* 这些计划你赞成吗? ○ *a nod of approval* 首肯. **2** (idm 习语) **on apˈproval** (of goods) supplied to a customer on condition that they may be returned if they are not satisfactory (指货物)不满意可以退的. **seal of approval** ⇨ SEAL[2].

ap·prove /əˈpruːv; əˋpruv/ *v* **1** [I, Ipr] **~ (of sb/sth)** say, show or feel that sth is good or acceptable or satisfactory 赞成; 认可; 满意; 同意: *She doesn't want to take her new boy-friend home in case her parents don't approve (of him).* 她不愿把新男朋友带回家, 怕父母看不中(他). ○ *I approve of your trying to earn some money, but please don't neglect your studies.* 我同意你去挣一些钱, 可是请不要误了功课. **2** [Tn] confirm (sth); accept 批准(某事物); 通过: *The minutes of the last meeting were approved.* 上次会议记录已获得通过. ○ *The auditors approved the company's accounts.* 审计员核准了公司的帐目. ▷ **ap·prov·ing** *adj*: *She received many approving glances.* 很多赞许的目光向她投来. **ap·prov·ingly** *adv*.

□ **apˈproved school** (formerly) place for housing, training and educating young offenders (旧时)少年感化院. Cf 参看 BORSTAL, REFORMATORY.

approx *abbr* 缩写 = approximate; approximately.

ap·prox·im·ate[1] /əˈprɒksɪmət; əˋprɑksəmɪt/ *adj* almost correct or exact but not completely so 近乎正确或精确的; 大约的; 大概的: *an approximate price, figure, amount, etc* 大约的价格、数字、数量等 ○ *What is the approximate size of this room?* 这间屋子大概有多大? ▷ **ap·prox·im·ately** *adv*: *It cost approximately £300 — I can't remember exactly.* 价钱大约是300英镑——我记不清了.

ap·prox·im·ate[2] /əˈprɒksɪmeɪt; əˋprɑksəˌmet/ *v* [Ipr] **~ to sth** be almost the same as sth 与某事物几乎相同; 接近: *Your story approximates to the facts we already know.* 你所说的与我们已经了解的事实很接近.

▷ **ap·prox·ima·tion** /əˌprɒksɪˈmeɪʃn; əˌprɑksəˋmeʃən/ *n* **1** [C] amount or estimate that is not exactly right but nearly so 近乎准确的量或估计; 近似值: *3 000 students each year would be an approximation.* 每年3 000名学生, 这是个大约的数字. **2** [U] process of being or getting near (in number, quality, etc) 概算; 近似法.

ap·pur·ten·ance /əˈpɜːtɪnəns; əˋpɝtṇəns/ *n* (usu *pl* 通常作复数) (*law* 律) **1** minor piece of property; accessory 小片地产; 附属物. **2** privilege or right that goes with the ownership of property 附属于财产所有权的特权或权利: *He inherited the manor and all its appurtenances.* 他继承了那片庄园及其一切特权.

Apr *abbr* 缩写 = April: *14 Apr 1986* 1986年4月14日.

après-ski /ˌæpreɪ ˈskiː; ˌæpreˋski/ *n* (*French* 法) time of leisure after a day's skiing in a resort (在度假胜地滑雪一天后的)闲暇时间: *I enjoyed the après-ski more than the skiing itself.* 我喜欢滑雪, 更喜欢滑雪后的闲暇时间. ○ [attrib 作定语] *après-ski clothes, activities* 滑雪后穿的衣服、进行的活动.

ap·ri·cot /ˈeɪprɪkɒt; ˋeprɪˌkɑt/ *n* **1** [C] (a) round stone-fruit with soft flesh, related to the plum and peach and orange-yellow when ripe 杏: [attrib 作定语] *ˌapricot ˈjam* 杏酱. (b) tree bearing this fruit 杏树. **2** [U] colour of a ripe apricot 杏黄色.

Ap·ril /ˈeɪprəl; ˋeprəl/ *n* [U, C] (*abbr* 缩写 **Apr**) the fourth month of the year, next after March 四月: *She was born in April.* 她是四月出生的. ○ *When were you born? The first of April/April the first/(US) April first.* 你是什么时候出生的? 四月一日. ○ [attrib 作定语] *April showers*, ie short periods of rain alternating with fine weather. 忽下忽停的春雨.

□ **ˌApril ˈFool** victim of a practical joke traditionally played on 1 April (4月1日愚人节)受愚弄的人. **ˌApril ˈFool's Day** (also **ˌAll ˈFools' Day**) 1 April 愚人节(4月1日).

a pri·ori /ˌeɪ praɪˈɔːraɪ; ˋepraɪˋoraɪ/ (using reasoning that proceeds) from known causes to imagined effects, eg saying *'They've been walking all day so they must be hungry.'* (用推理方法)由已知原因推测出结果(如说: '他们走了一整天, 那么他们一定饿了.') Cf 参看 A POSTERIORI.

ap·ron /ˈeɪprən; ˋeprən/ *n* **1** (a) garment worn over the front part of the body to keep the wearer's clothes clean while working 围裙. ⇨illus 见插图. (b) any similar covering worn as part of ceremonial dress 礼服中的像围裙的部分. **2** hard-surfaced area on an airfield, where aircraft are manoeuvred, loaded or unloaded 停机坪(飞机场上为调动飞机、装卸货物、乘客上下等用的坚实平地). **3** (also **ˌapron ˈstage**) (in the theatre) part of the stage that extends into the auditorium in front of the curtain 台口(舞台幕前的突出部分). **4** (idm 习语)

(tied to) one's mother's, wife's, etc apron strings (too much under) the influence and control of one's mother, etc (深受)母亲、妻子等的影响及控制.

apro·pos /ˌæprəˈpəʊ; ˌæprəˈpo/ *adv, adj* [pred 作表语] (in a way that is) appropriate or relevant to what is being said or done (与正在说的或做的)适宜或有关, 恰好, 及时: *You'll find the last paragraph extremely apropos.* 你会觉得最后一段文字极为中肯.

□ **apropos of** *prep* with reference to (sth); concerning 至于; 关于: *Apropos of what you were just saying....* 关于你刚才所说的话....

apse /æps; æps/ *n* semicircular or many-sided recess with an arched or domed roof, esp at the east end of a church 半圆室(尤指教堂东端的半圆形或多边形凹室, 顶为拱形或圆形).

apt /æpt; æpt/ *adj* **(-er, -est)** **1** suitable; appropriate 适当的; 恰当的: *an apt quotation* 恰当的引语. **2 ~ (at doing sth)** quick at learning 学得快的; 聪明的: *She's one of my aptest students.* 她是我的最聪明的一个学生. ○ *very apt at programming a computer* 非常善于编电脑程序. **3** [pred 作表语] **~ to do sth** likely or having a tendency to do sth 易于做某事物; 有做某事物的倾向: *apt to be forgetful, careless, quick-tempered, etc* 健忘、总是粗心大意、动不动就发脾气 ○ *My pen is rather apt to leak.* 我的钢笔爱漏墨水.

▷ **aptly** *adv* suitably; appropriately 适当地; 恰当地: *aptly punished for one's misdeeds* 因行为不检而受到适当惩罚.

apt·ness *n* [U].

APT /ˌeɪ piː ˈtiː; ˌe pi ˈti/ *abbr* 缩写 = (*Brit*) Advanced Passenger Train 高级客车.

apt *abbr* 缩写 = apartment.

ap·ti·tude /ˈæptɪtjuːd; *US* -tuːd; ˈæptəˌtud/ *n* [U, C] **~ (for sth/doing sth)** natural ability or skill 天生的才能或技巧; 天资; 天赋: *Does she show any aptitude for games?* 能看得出她有体育方面的天赋吗? ○ *He has an unfortunate aptitude for saying the wrong thing.* 他有失言的倒霉本事.

□ **ˈaptitude test** test to find if sb is suitable for a particular type of work or course of training 能力倾向测验, 性向测验(用以确定某人是否适宜从事某种工作或参加某种训练课程). Cf 参看 INTELLIGENCE TEST (INTELLIGENCE).

Aqua·lung /ˈækwəlʌŋ; ˈækwəˌlʌŋ/ *n* (*propr* 专利名) portable underwater breathing apparatus used by divers 水肺; 潜水呼吸器.

aqua·mar·ine /ˌækwəməˈriːn; ˌækwəməˈrin/ *n* **1** [C] bluish-green precious stone 海蓝宝石; 蓝晶. **2** [U] its colour 海蓝色.

aqua·plane /ˈækwəpleɪn; ˈækwəˌplen/ *n* board on which a person stands while being towed across water by a speedboat 滑水板(人站立其上, 由快艇牵引在水上滑行的板).

▷ **aqua·plane** *v* [I] **1** ride on an aquaplane 滑水(站在滑水板上作水上滑行运动). **2** (of a vehicle) skid or glide forward uncontrollably on the wet surface of a road (指车辆)在潮湿路面上失去控制向前滑动.

aquar·ium /əˈkweərɪəm; əˈkwɛrɪəm/ *n* (*pl* **~s** or **-ria**) (building containing an) artificial pond or glass tank where live fish and other water creatures and plants are kept 水族馆; 水族箱; 养鱼缸.

Aquar·ius /əˈkweərɪəs; əˈkwɛrɪəs/ *n* **1** [U] the eleventh sign of the zodiac, the Water-carrier 宝瓶宫(黄道第十一宫). **2** [C] person born under the influence of this sign 属宝瓶宫星座的人. ▷ **Aquar·ian** *n, adj.* ⇨Usage at ZODIAC 用法见 ZODIAC. ⇨illus at ZODIAC 见 ZODIAC 之插图.

aquatic /əˈkwætɪk; əˈkwætɪk/ *adj* [usu attrib 通常作定语] **1** (of plants, animals, etc) growing or living in or near water (指植物、动物等)生长于水中或水边的, 水生的: *Many forms of aquatic life inhabit ponds.* 有很多种水生动植物均栖居于池塘. **2** (of sports) taking place on or in water (指运动)水上的, 水中的: *Swimming and water-skiing are both aquatic sports.* 游泳和滑水都是水上运动.

aqua·tint /ˈækwətɪnt; ˈækwəˌtɪnt/ *n* **1** [U] process of etching on copper using nitric acid 铜版画飞尘腐蚀法; 凹版腐蚀制版法. **2** [C] picture made in this way 用飞尘腐蚀法印制的图画.

aque·duct /ˈækwɪdʌkt; ˈækwɪˌdʌkt/ *n* structure for carrying water across country, esp one built like a bridge over a valley or low ground 输水道(跨越地域的输送水的结构, 尤指通过河谷或低地的桥状高架水道).

aque·ous /ˈeɪkwɪəs; ˈekwɪəs/ *adj* of or like water; produced by water 水的; 像水的; 水成的: *chemicals dissolved in an aqueous solution* 溶于水溶液的化学药品.

aquil·ine /ˈækwɪlaɪn; ˈækwəˌlaɪn/ *adj* of or like an eagle 鹰的; 像鹰的: *an aquiline nose*, ie one curved like an eagle's beak 鹰钩鼻.

Arab /ˈærəb; ˈærəb/ *n* **1** any of the Semitic people descended from the original inhabitants of the Arabian Peninsula, now inhabiting the Middle East and N Africa generally 阿拉伯人. **2** type of horse originally bred in Arabia 阿拉伯马.

▷ **Arab** *adj* of Arabia or the Arabs 阿拉伯的; 阿拉伯人的: *the Arab countries* 阿拉伯国家.

ar·ab·esque /ˌærəˈbesk; ˌærəˈbɛsk/ *n* **1** (in art) elaborate design of intertwined leaves, branches, scrolls, etc (艺术上)阿拉伯装饰风格(由树叶、树枝、涡卷等形状交织的精细图案). **2** (in ballet) position of a dancer balanced on one leg with the other stretched horizontally backwards 阿拉贝斯克舞姿(芭蕾舞中的一种舞姿, 单腿直立, 另一腿向后平伸).

Ara·bian /əˈreɪbɪən; əˈrebɪən/ *adj* of Arabia or the Arabs 阿拉伯的; 阿拉伯人的: *the Arabian Sea* 阿拉伯海.

▷ **Ara·bian** *n* (*dated* 旧) Arab(1) 阿拉伯人.

Ar·abic /ˈærəbɪk; ˈærəbɪk/ *adj* of the Arabs, esp their language or literature 阿拉伯人的(尤指其语言或文学). ▷ **Ar·abic** *n* [U] language of the Arabs 阿拉伯语.

□ **ˌarabic ˈnumerals** (also **ˌarabic ˈfigures**) the symbols 0, 1, 2, 3, 4, etc 阿拉伯数字(0、1、2、3、4等). ⇨App 4 见附录 4. Cf 参看 ROMAN NUMERALS (ROMAN).

Ar·ab·ist /ˈærəbɪst; ˈærəbɪst/ *n* student of or expert in Arabic culture, language, history, etc 研究阿拉伯文化、语言、历史等的学者或专家.

ar·able /ˈærəbl; ˈærəbl̩/ *n* [U], *adj* (land that is) suitable for ploughing and for growing crops 适于耕作的(土地); 可耕的(土地).

arach·nid /əˈræknɪd; əˈræknɪd/ *n* any of the class of animals including spiders, scorpions, ticks and mites 蛛形纲动物(包括蜘蛛、蝎子、蜱、螨).

ar·biter /ˈɑːbɪtə(r); ˈɑrbɪtɚ/ *n* **1 ~ (of sth)** person who has power to decide what will be done, accepted, etc with regard to sth (对某事物有权决定处理、认可等的)仲裁人; 裁决人; 权威人士: *the arbiters of fashion* 时装的权威. **2** (*dated or Scot* 旧或苏格兰) = ARBITRATOR.

ar·bit·rary /ˈɑːbɪtrərɪ; *US* ˈɑːrbɪtrerɪ; ˈɑrbəˌtrɛrɪ/ *adj* **1** based on personal opinion or impulse, not on reason 任意的; 任性的; 主观的: *The choice of players for the team seems completely arbitrary.* 队员的挑选似乎完全是主观决定的. **2** using uncontrolled power without considering others; dictatorial 霸道的; 专横的; 独断独行的: *an arbitrary ruler* 专横的统治者 ○ *arbitrary powers* 霸权. ▷ **ar·bit·rar·ily** *adv.* **ar·bit·rari·ness** *n* [U].

ar·bit·rate /ˈɑːbɪtreɪt; ˈɑrbəˌtret/ *v* [I, Ipr, Tn, Tn·pr] **~ (sth) (between A and B)** make a judgement about or settle (a dispute) between two parties (usu when asked by them to do so) 仲裁, 公断(通常为经双方要求解决争端): *He was asked to arbitrate (a serious dispute) between management and the unions.* 他被邀请在资方与工会之间(对一严重争端)作出仲裁.

ar·bit·ra·tion /ˌɑːbɪˈtreɪʃn; ˌɑrbəˋtreʃən/ *n* **1** [U] settling of a dispute by a person or people chosen to do this by both sides in the dispute (由争执双方挑选的人所作的)仲裁, 公断: *take/refer the matter to arbitration* 将此事交付公断. **2** (idm 习语) ˌ**go to arbiˈtration** ask sb to settle a dispute by arbitrating 提请仲裁: *The union finally agreed to go to arbitration as a way of ending the strike.* 工会最后同意提请仲裁以结束罢工.

ar·bit·rator /ˈɑːbɪtreɪtə(r); ˋɑrbəˌtretɚ/ (also **arbiter**) *n* person chosen to settle a dispute between two parties 仲裁人; 公断人.

ar·bor·eal /ɑːˈbɔːrɪəl; ɑrˋbɔrɪəl/ *adj* (*fml* 文) of or living in trees 树木的; 栖于树木的: *Squirrels are arboreal creatures.* 松鼠是栖于树上的动物.

ar·bor·etum /ˌɑːbəˈriːtəm; ˌɑrbəˋritəm/ *n* (*pl* **-tums** or **-ta**) place where trees are grown for scientific study or for display (供科学研究或展览用的)树木园, 植物园.

ar·bour (*US* **ar·bor**) /ˈɑːbə(r); ˋɑrbɚ/ *n* shady place among trees or climbing plants, esp one made in a garden for people to sit in (树木或攀缘植物构成的)树阴处; (尤指公园中的凉亭, 棚架).

arc /ɑːk; ɑrk/ *n* **1** part of the circumference of a circle or some other curved line 弧(圆周或其它曲线的一部分). ⇨illus at CIRCLE 见CIRCLE之插图. **2** thing with this shape 弧形物: *the arc of a rainbow* 虹的弧形. **3** luminous electric current passing across a gap between two terminals 电弧; 弧光.

▷ **arc** *v* (*pt, pp* **arced** /ɑːkt; ɑrkt/, *pres p* **arcing** /ˈɑːkɪŋ; ˋɑrkɪŋ/) [I] form an electric arc 形成电弧; 产生弧光.

□ ˈ**arc lamp** (also ˈ**arc light**) lamp giving light produced by an electric arc 弧光灯.

ˌ**arc ˈwelding** welding by means of an electric arc (电)弧焊.

ar·cade /ɑːˈkeɪd; ɑrˋked/ *n* covered passage or area, esp one with an arched roof and shops along one or both sides 拱廊(尤指有拱形顶盖, 一侧或两侧有商店的通道): *a shopping arcade* 拱廊市场.

ar·cane /ɑːˈkeɪn; ɑrˋken/ *adj* secret; mysterious 秘密的; 神秘的: *arcane rituals, ceremonies, customs, etc* 秘密的仪式、典礼、习俗等.

arch[1] /ɑːtʃ; ɑrtʃ/ *n* **1** curved structure supporting the weight of sth above it, eg a bridge or the upper storey of a building 拱(用以支撑如桥梁或上层建筑重量的弧形结构): *a bridge with three arches* 有三个拱的桥. ⇨illus at App 1 见附录1之插图, page viii. **2** (also **archway**) similar structure forming a passageway or an ornamental gateway 拱道; 拱门; 拱形牌坊: *Go through the arch and follow the path.* 穿过拱门, 沿着那条路走. ○ *Marble Arch is a famous London landmark.* 大理石拱门是著名的伦敦标志. **3** thing shaped like an arch, esp the raised part of the foot between the sole and the heel 拱形物; (尤指)足底弓. ⇨illus at FOOT 见FOOT之插图.

▷ **arch** *v* **1** [Tn] form (sth) into an arch 将(某物)构成拱形; 拱起: *The cat arched its back when it saw the dog.* 那猫看见狗时就拱起了背. **2** [Ipr] ~ **across/over sth** form an arch across sth; span sth 形成拱形跨越某物; 用拱连接: *Tall trees arched across the river.* 高大的树木成拱形横跨过那条河.

arch[2] /ɑːtʃ; ɑrtʃ/ *adj* [attrib 作定语] playful in a deliberate or an affected way 调皮的; 淘气的: *an arch smile, glance, look, etc* 淘气的微笑、目光、神情等.

arch- *comb form* 构词成分 **1** chief; most important 为首的; 最重要的: *archangel* ○ *archbishop*. **2** extremely bad 极坏的: *arch-enemy*.

archae·ology /ˌɑːkɪˈɒlədʒɪ; ˌɑrkɪˋɑlədʒɪ/ *n* [U] study of ancient civilizations by scientific analysis of physical remains found in the ground 考古学.

▷ **archae·olo·gical** /ˌɑːkɪəˈlɒdʒɪkl; ˌɑrkɪəˋlɑdʒɪkl/ *adj* of or related to archaeology 考古学的; 与考古学有关的: *archaeological finds* 考古发现.

archae·olo·gist /ˌɑːkɪˈɒlədʒɪst; ˌɑrkɪˋɑlədʒɪst/ *n* expert in archaeology 考古学家.

ar·chaic /ɑːˈkeɪɪk; ɑrˋke·ɪk/ *adj* **1** of a much earlier or an ancient period in history 古代的. **2** (esp of words, etc in a language) no longer in current use (尤指词语)已不通用的, 古体的, 陈旧的: *'Thou art' is an archaic form of 'you are'.* 'Thou art' 是 'you are' 的古体.

▷ **archa·ism** /ˈɑːkeɪɪzəm; ˋɑrkeˌɪzəm/ *n* **1** [C] archaic word or expression 古字; 古词; 古语. **2** [U] use or imitation of what is archaic, esp in language and art 拟古, 拟古主义(尤指在语言及艺术上).

arch·an·gel /ˈɑːkˌeɪndʒl; ˋɑrkˋendʒəl/ *n* angel of the highest rank 天使长; 大天使.

arch·bishop /ˌɑːtʃˈbɪʃəp; ˋɑrtʃˋbɪʃəp/ *n* bishop of the highest rank, responsible for a large church district 大主教.

▷ **arch·bish·op·ric** /ˌɑːtʃˈbɪʃəprɪk; ˌɑrtʃˋbɪʃəprɪk/ *n* **1** position of archbishop 大主教的职位. **2** district under the care of an archbishop 大主教的管区.

arch·deacon /ˌɑːtʃˈdiːkən; ˋɑrtʃˋdikən/ *n* (in the Anglican Church) priest next below the rank of bishop (英国国教的)副主教.

▷ **arch·deac·onry** *n* position, rank or house of an archdeacon 副主教的职位、级别或住所.

arch·di·ocese /ˌɑːtʃˈdaɪəsɪs; ˋɑrtʃˋdaɪəˌsɪs/ *n* district under the care of an archbishop; archbishopric 大主教管区.

arch·duke /ˌɑːtʃˈdjuːk; *US* -ˈduːk; ˋɑrtʃˋduk/ *n* (*fem* 阴性作 **arch·duch·ess** /ˌɑːtʃˈdʌtʃɪs; ˋɑrtʃˋdʌtʃɪs/) duke of the highest rank, esp (formerly) the son of the Austrian Emperor 大公(尤指旧时奥国皇太子).

arch-enemy /ˌɑːtʃ ˈenəmɪ; ˋɑrtʃˋɛnəmɪ/ *n* **1** [C] chief enemy 大敌; 主要敌人. **2 the Arch-enemy** [sing] the Devil 魔王; 撒旦.

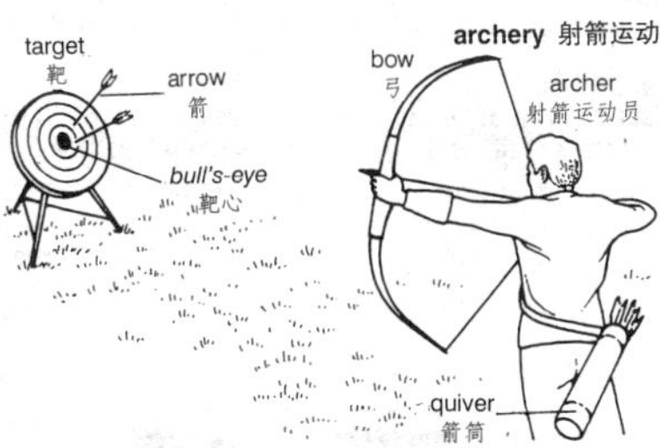

archer /ˈɑːtʃə(r); ˋɑrtʃɚ/ *n* person who shoots with a bow and arrows, esp as a sport or (formerly) in battle 射箭运动员; (旧时)弓箭手. ⇨illus 见插图.

▷ **arch·ery** /ˈɑːtʃərɪ; ˋɑrtʃərɪ/ *n* [U] skill or sport of shooting with a bow and arrows 射箭术; 射箭运动. ⇨ illus 见插图.

arche·type /ˈɑːkɪtaɪp; ˋɑrkəˌtaɪp/ *n* **1** original or ideal model from which others are copied; prototype 原始模型; 原型. **2** typical example of sth 某事物的典型. ▷ **arche·typal** /ˈɑːkɪtaɪpl, ˌɑːkɪˈtaɪpl; ˋɑrkɪˋtaɪpl/ *adj*.

archi·pe·lago /ˌɑːkɪˈpeləgəʊ; ˌɑrkəˋpɛləˌgo/ *n* (*pl* **~s** or **~es**) (sea surrounding a) group of many islands 群岛; 群岛周围的海.

archi·tect /ˈɑːkɪtekt; ˋɑrkəˌtɛkt/ *n* person who designs buildings and supervises their construction 建筑师; 设计师: *the architect's plans for the new theatre* 建筑师兴建新剧院的设计图 ○ (*fig* 比喻) *He was one of the principal architects of the revolution.* 他是那次革命的一位发动者.

archi·tec·ture /ˈɑːkɪtektʃə(r); ˋɑrkəˌtɛktʃɚ/ *n* [U] **1** art and science of designing and constructing buildings 建筑学. **2** design or style of a building or buildings 建筑设计; 建筑风格: *the architecture of the eighteenth century* 十八世纪的建筑风格 ○ *Modern architecture depresses me.* 现代的建筑设计使我感到很憋闷.

▷ **archi·tec·tural** /ˌɑːkɪˈtektʃərəl; ˌɑrkəˋtɛktʃərəl/ *adj* of or related to architecture 建筑学的; 建筑上的: *an architectural triumph* 建筑学的成就. **archi·tec·tur·ally** *adv*: *The house is of little interest architecturally.* 这所房子在建筑学上无足轻重.

arch·ives /ˈɑːkaɪvz; ˋɑrkaɪvz/ *n* [pl] **1** (collection of)

A

historical documents or records of a government, town, etc (政府或城镇等的)档案, 案卷: *I found this old map in the family archives.* 我在家谱中发现了这幅旧地图. **2** place where such records are kept 档案保管处; 档案馆.
▷ **arch·iv·ist** /ˈɑːkɪvɪst; ˋɑrkəvɪst/ *n* person who is trained to keep archives 档案保管员.

arch·way /ˈɑːtʃweɪ; ˋɑrtʃˌwe/ *n* = ARCH[1] 2.

Arc·tic /ˈɑːktɪk; ˋɑrktɪk/ *adj* **1** [attrib 作定语] of the regions around the North Pole 北极的; 北极区的. ⇨ illus at GLOBE 见 GLOBE之插图. **2 arctic (a)** very cold 极冷的; 严寒的: *arctic weather* 严寒的天气 ○ *The conditions were arctic.* 周围环境极冷. (**b**) [attrib 作定语] suitable for such conditions 适于寒冷的: *arctic clothing* 寒衣.
▷ **the Arc·tic** *n* [sing] the regions around the North Pole 北极; 北极区.
□ **the ˌArctic ˈCircle** the line of latitude 66° 30'N 北极圈(北纬66° 30'的线). ⇨illus at GLOBE 见 GLOBE 之插图.

-ard *suff* 后缀 (with *adjs* forming *ns* 与形容词结合构成名词) having the specified (usu negative) quality 具有某种(通常为否定的)品质: *drunkard* ○ *dullard.*

ar·dent /ˈɑːdnt; ˋɑrdn̩t/ *adj* full of ardour; enthusiastic 热心的; 热情的: *an ardent supporter of the local football team* 本地足球队的球迷 ○ *ardent in her admiration of the artist* 她对那位艺术家的倾慕. ▷ **ar·dently** *adv.*

ar·dour (*US* **ar·dor**) /ˈɑːdə(r); ˋɑrdɚ/ *n* [U] **~ (for sb/sth)** great warmth of feeling; enthusiasm; zeal 热情; 热心: *His ardour for the cause inspired his followers.* 他对事业的热情激励着他的追随者.

ar·du·ous /ˈɑːdjʊəs; *US* -dʒʊ-; ˋɑrdʒʊəs/ *adj* needing much effort or energy; laborious 艰巨的; 费力的: *an arduous task* 艰巨的任务 ○ *The work is arduous and the hours are long.* 工作吃力, 时间又长. ▷ **ar·du·ously** *adv.*

are[1] ⇨ BE.

are[2] /ɑː(r); ɑr/ *n* metric unit of area, equal to 100 square metres 公亩(等于100平方米). ⇨App 5 见附录 5.

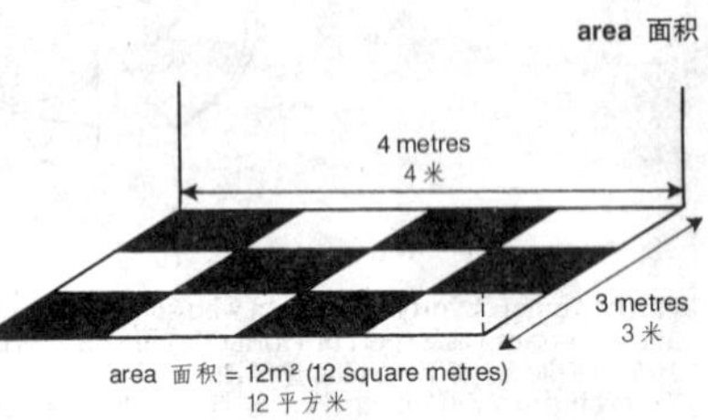

area /ˈeərɪə; ˋɛrɪə/ *n* **1** (**a**) [U] extent or measurement of a surface 面积(表面的范围或量度): *The area of the office is 35 square metres.* 办公室的面积是35平方米. ○ *The kitchen is 12 square metres in area/has an area of 12 square metres.* 厨房的面积是12平方米. ⇨App 4 见附录 4. (**b**) [C] particular measured surface 面积(某一量度的表面): *Compare the areas of these triangles.* 比较一下这些三角形的面积. ⇨illus 见插图. Cf 参看 VOLUME 2. **2** [C] (**a**) part of a surface 表面的一部分: *Clean the area round the cooker.* 把炊具周围弄干净. (**b**) region of the earth's surface; district of a city, etc (地球表面的)地域; (城市等的)地区: *mountainous, uninhabited, desert, etc areas of the world* 世界上的山脉的、无人居住的、沙漠的地域 ○ *Do you like the area* (ie neighbourhood) *where you're living?* 你喜欢你居住的地区吗? (**c**) space reserved for a specific use 留作某种用途的空间: *a ˈpicnic area* 野餐区 ○ *the reˈception area* 接待处. **3** [C] range of activity or interest 领域; 方面: *the area of finance, training, development, etc* 财政、训练、发展方面 ○ *The meeting revealed certain areas of disagreement,* ie matters on which those present did not agree. 会议上暴露出某些分歧之处(出席者意见不一致的事项). **4** [C] small courtyard in front of the basement of a house, usu with access to the street 地下室前的小庭院(通常可通往街道): [attrib 作定语] *sitting on the area steps* 坐在地下室前小庭院的台阶上.
□ **ˈarea code** (*US*) dialling code identifying an area or region, used before the local telephone number 电话分区代号(用于当地电话号码之前). ⇨App 4 见附录 4.

areca /ˈærɪkə, əˈriːkə; ˋærɪkə, əˈrikə/ *n* tropical Asiatic palm-tree bearing white flowers and orange or red nuts 槟榔树.
□ **areca nut** (also **betel-nut**) seed of this tree 槟榔果.

arena /əˈriːnə; əˈrinə/ *n* **1** level area in the centre of an amphitheatre or a sports stadium 圆形剧场或运动场中心的平地. **2** (*fig* 比喻) place or scene of activity or conflict 活动或斗争的场所或场面: *the political arena* 政治舞台.

aren't /ɑːnt; ɑrnt/ *contracted form* 缩约式 (*infml* 口) **1** are not: *They aren't here.* 他们不在这里. **2** (in questions 用于问句) am not: *Aren't I clever?* 难道我不聪明吗? ⇨ BE.

ar·ête /æˈreɪt; æˋret/ *n* sharp mountain ridge, esp in Switzerland 陡峭的山脊(尤指瑞士的).

ar·gon /ˈɑːɡɒn; ˋɑrɡɑn/ *n* [U] chemical element, an almost inert gas present in the atmosphere 氩. ⇨App 10 见附录 10.

ar·got /ˈɑːɡəʊ; ˋɑrɡo/ *n* [U] words and phrases used by a particular group (esp thieves) and not intended to be understood by others; cant 某集体(尤指盗贼)不欲人知而使用的词语; 黑话; 切口; 隐语; 暗语; 行话.

ar·gue /ˈɑːɡjuː; ˋɑrɡju/ *v* **1** [I, Ipr] **~ (with sb) (about/over sth)** express an opposite opinion; exchange angry words; quarrel 争论; 争辩; 争吵: *The couple next door are always arguing.* 邻居的夫妇总吵架. ○ *Don't argue with your mother.* 不要和母亲争辩. ○ *We argued with the waiter about the price of the meal.* 我们跟服务员争执那顿饭的价钱. **2** [I, Ipr, Tf] **~ (for/against sth)** give reasons for or against sth, esp with the aim of persuading sb 说理; 争辩; 辩论: *He argues convincingly.* 他的辩解很有说服力. ○ *argue for the right to strike* 为争取罢工权利而辩论 ○ *I argued that we needed a larger office.* 我据理力争我们需要大些的办公室. **3** [Tn] (*fml* 文) discuss (sth); debate 讨论; 辩论: *The lawyers argued the case for hours.* 律师们对那个案件辩论了几小时. **4** (idm 习语) **ˌargue the ˈtoss** say that one disagrees about a decision 反对某项决定: *Let's not argue the toss — we have to accept his choice.* 我们不必争论已经决定的事——只好听他的. **5** (phr v) **argue sb into/out of doing sth** persuade sb to do/not to do sth by giving reasons 说服、劝说某人做[不做]某事: *They argued him into withdrawing his complaint.* 他们说服他撤回了投诉.
▷ **ar·gu·able** /ˈɑːɡjʊəbl; ˋɑrɡjʊəbl̩/ *adj* **1** that can be argued or asserted 可论证的; 可断言的: *It is arguable that we would be just as efficient with fewer staff.* 我们的职员少一些也能发挥同样效率, 这是言之成理的. **2** not certain; questionable 可疑的; 有问题的: *This account contains many arguable statements.* 这种说法含有很多疑点. **ar·gu·ably** /-əblɪ; -əblɪ/ *adv* one can argue (2) that 可争辩地; 按理; 按说: *John sings very well though Peter is arguably the better actor.* 约翰唱得很好, 不过按理说彼得演得更好.

ar·gu·ment /ˈɑːɡjʊmənt; ˋɑrɡjəmənt/ *n* **1** [C] **~ (with sb) (about/over sth)** disagreement; quarrel 争论; 争辩; 争吵: *get into/have an argument with the referee (about his decision)* 与裁判员争辩(他所做的裁判). **2** [U] discussion based on reasoning 争论; 辩论: *We agreed without much further argument.* 我们没怎么进一步争论就达成了一致意见. **3** [C] **~ (for/against sth); ~ (that...)** reason or reasons put forward 论据; 论点; 理由: *There are strong arguments for and against capital punishment.* 对于执行死刑, 赞成与反对的双方都有强有力的论据. ○ *The Government's argument is that they must first aim to beat inflation.* 政府的论点是必须首先着眼于抑制通货膨胀. **4** [C] summary of the subject matter of a book, etc; theme 概要; 梗概; 主题. **5** (idm 习语) **for the sake of argument** ⇨ SAKE.

NOTE ON USAGE 用法: **1** An **argument** (over/about sth) is a strong verbal disagreement between people ☆ **argument**一词(后可接over/about某事物)指人与人之间用激烈言语表达的分歧: *Most families have arguments over money.* 大多数家庭都有金钱方面

的争执. ○ *I had an argument with my neighbour about a tree in his garden.* 我和邻人因其花园里一棵树的事而争了起来. **2** A **quarrel** is a sharp, often angry, exchange of words between people ☆ **quarrel** 指尖锐的, 常为气愤的言语交锋: *The whole thing turned into a bitter quarrel.* 整件事酿成了激烈的争吵. **3** A **row** is angry and may involve shouting, usually for a short time ☆ **row** 一词意含愤怒, 可能夹杂着喊叫, 通常为时短暂: *She had a dreadful row with her parents and left home.* 她和父母大吵一场就离开了家. A **row** can also take place between public figures or organizations ☆ **row** 还可发生于头面人物之间或组织机构之间: *There was a huge row in Parliament and the minister resigned.* 议会上举座哗然, 部长旋即辞职. **4 Altercation** is a formal word and indicates a noisy argument. ☆ **altercation** 是个文雅的词, 意为吵吵嚷嚷的争辩. **5** A **fight** generally involves force or weapons rather than words ☆ **fight** 一般涉及使用暴力或凶器而不限于言语: *The argument turned into a fight when knives were produced.* 一亮出刀来, 那场争论就演变成武斗了.

ar·gu·men·ta·tion /ˌɑ:gjʊmenˈteɪʃn; ˌɑrgjəmɛnˋteʃən/ *n* [U] (*fml* 文) process of arguing; debate 立论; 论证; 辩论; 争论.

ar·gu·ment·at·ive /ˌɑ:gjʊˈmentətɪv; ˌɑrgjəˋmɛntətɪv/ *adj* fond of arguing (ARGUE 1) 爱争论的; 好辩论的. ▷ **ar·gu·ment·at·ively** *adj*.

argy-bargy /ˌɑ:dʒɪ ˈbɑ:dʒɪ; ˋɑrdʒɪ ˋbɑrdʒɪ/ *n* [U] (*Brit infml* 口) noisy but usu not serious quarrelling 嘈杂的但常为不严重的争吵; 吵嘴; 拌嘴; 抬杠; 吵闹: *What's all this argy-bargy?* 怎么回事, 这么吵吵嚷嚷的?

aria /ˈɑ:rɪə; ˋɑrɪə/ *n* song for one voice, esp in an opera or oratorio 咏叹调(尤指歌剧或清唱剧中者).

-arian *suff* 后缀 (forming *ns* and *adjs* 用以构成名词和形容词) believing in; practising 相信…的(人); 实行…的(人): *humanitarian* ○ *disciplinarian*.

arid /ˈærɪd; ˋærɪd/ *adj* **1** (of land or climate) having little or no rainfall; dry (指土壤或气候)干旱的, 干燥的: *the arid deserts of Africa* 非洲的干旱沙漠 ○ *Nothing grows in these arid conditions.* 在这些干旱环境中, 寸草不生. **2** dull; uninteresting 枯燥的; 无趣味的: *have long, arid discussions about unimportant matters* 对鸡毛蒜皮的事进行的冗长而枯燥的讨论. ▷ **arid·ity** /əˈrɪdətɪ; əˋrɪdətɪ/ *n* [U]. **aridly** *adv*. **arid·ness** *n* [U].

Ar·ies /ˈeəri:z; ˋɛriz/ *n* **1** [U] the first sign of the zodiac, the Ram 白羊宫(黄道第一宫). **2** [C] (*pl* unchanged 复数不变) person born under the influence of this sign 属白羊宫星座的人. ⇨Usage at ZODIAC 用法见 ZODIAC. ⇨ illus at ZODIAC 见 ZODIAC 之插图.

aright /əˈraɪt; əˋraɪt/ *adv* (*arch or rhet* 古或修辞) (never used in front of the *v* 不可用于动词之前) rightly 正确; 对: *Do I hear you aright?* 你的意思我理解得对吗?

arise /əˈraɪz; əˋraɪz/ *v* (*pt* **arose** /əˈrəʊz; əˋroz/, *pp* **arisen** /əˈrɪzn; əˋrɪzn̩/) **1** [I] become evident; appear; originate 呈现; 出现; 发生: *A new difficulty has arisen.* 出现了新困难. ○ *Use this money when the need arises.* 有需要时就使用这笔钱. ○ *A storm arose during the night.* 夜间起风暴了. **2** [Ipr] **~ out of/from sth** follow as a result of sth 因某事物而产生、造成、引起: *problems arising out of the lack of communication* 由于缺乏交流而产生的问题 ○ *Are there any matters arising from the minutes of the last meeting?* 关于上次会议的记录有没有问题? **3** [I] (*arch* 古) get up or stand up 起身; 起来; 起立.

ar·is·to·cracy /ˌærɪˈstɒkrəsɪ; ˌærəˋstɑkrəsɪ/ *n* **1** [CGp] highest social class; the nobility 贵族阶级; 贵族: *members of the aristocracy* 贵族成员. **2** (**a**) [U] government by people of the highest social class 贵族政府; 贵族统治. (**b**) [C] country or state with such a government 贵族统治的国家或政体. **3** [C] most able or gifted members of any class (任何阶级或阶层的)最优秀的人物: *an aristocracy of talent* 人杰.

ar·is·to·crat /ˈærɪstəkræt; *US* əˈrɪst-; əˋrɪstəˌkræt/ *n* member of the aristocracy; nobleman or noblewoman 贵族的成员; 贵族. Cf 参看 COMMONER.

▷ **ar·is·to·cratic** /ˌærɪstəˈkrætɪk; *US* əˌrɪstə-; əˌrɪstəˋkrætɪk/ *adj* belonging to or typical of the aristocracy 贵族的; 贵族统治的; 有贵族气派的: *an aristocratic name, family, bearing, life-style* 贵族的名字、家庭、仪态、生活方式. **ar·is·to·crat·ic·ally** /-klɪ; -klɪ/ *adv*.

arith·metic /əˈrɪθmətɪk; əˋrɪθməˌtɪk/ *n* [U] (**a**) branch of mathematics that deals with calculations using numbers 算术. (**b**) these calculations 算术的计算.

▷ **ar·ith·metic** /ˌærɪθˈmetɪk; ˌærɪθˋmɛtɪk/, **ar·ith·met·ical** *adjs* of or concerning arithmetic 算术的; 关于算术的. **ˌarithmetic proˈgression** (also **arithˌmetical proˈgression**) series of numbers that increase or decrease by the same amount each time, eg 1, 2, 3, etc or 8, 6, 4, etc 算数级数, 等差级数(如1、2、3等或8、6、4等). Cf 参看 GEOMETRIC PROGRESSION (GEOMETRY). **ar·ith·met·ic·ally** /-klɪ; -klɪ/ *adv*.

ar·ith·meti·cian /əˌrɪθməˈtɪʃn; əˌrɪθməˋtɪʃən/ *n* expert in arithmetic 算术家.

ark /ɑ:k; ɑrk/ *n* (in the Bible) ship in which Noah, his family and animals were saved from the Flood 方舟(《圣经》中挪亚及其家人和动物为避洪水而乘的大船).

□ **the ˌArk of the ˈCovenant** wooden chest in which the writings of Jewish law were originally kept 约柜(保藏犹太法约的木柜).

ARM IN ARM 臂挽着臂 HAND IN HAND 手拉着手

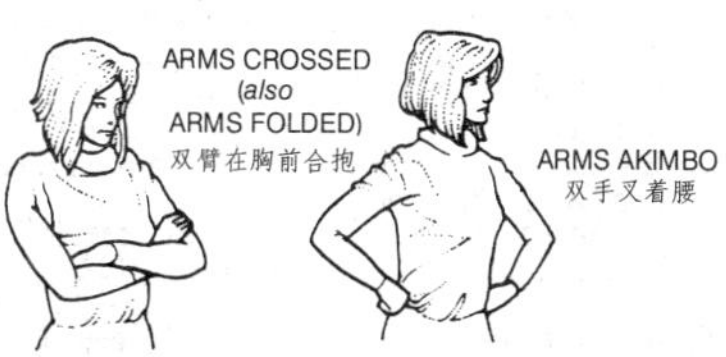

arm[1] /ɑ:m; ɑrm/ *n* **1** either of the two upper limbs of the human body, from the shoulder to the hand 上肢(肩到手的部分); 手臂: *She held the baby in her arms.* 她抱着那个婴儿. ○ *He gave her his arm* (ie let her hold it for support) *as they crossed the road.* 他们横过马路的时候, 他向她伸出手臂(让她挽住). ○ *She was carrying a book under her arm*, ie between her arm and her body. 她腋下挟着一本书. ○ *He rushed into her arms*, ie to be embraced by her. 他投入她的怀抱中. ⇨illus at HUMAN 见 HUMAN 之插图. **2** sleeve 袖子: *There's a tear in the arm of my jacket.* 我上衣袖子上有个破口. **3** thing that is shaped like or operates like an arm 臂状物: *the arms of a chair*, ie parts on which the arms can rest 椅子的扶手 ○ *an arm of the sea*, ie a long inlet 海湾 ○ *an arm of a tree*, ie a large branch 大树枝 ○ *the (pick-up) arm of a record-player* 电唱头(拾音器)臂. ⇨illus at App 1 见附录1之插图, page xvi. **4** (idm 习语) **ˌarm in ˈarm** (of two people) with the arm of one linked with the arm of the other (指两人)挎着胳膊, 臂挽着臂: *strolling happily arm in arm* 臂挽着臂愉快地散步. ⇨illus 见插图. **the (long) arm of the ˈlaw** (extent of) the authority or power of the law 法律的权威或力量(的限度): *He fled to Brazil trying to escape the long arm of the law.* 他逃到巴西, 企图逃避恢恢法网. **at arm's ˈlength** with the arm fully extended away from the body 以一臂之距: *holding one's hand out at arm's length* 伸直手臂. **a babe in arms** ⇨ BABE. **chance one's arm** ⇨ CHANCE[2]. **fold one's arms** ⇨ FOLD[1]. **fold sb/sth in one's arms** ⇨ FOLD[1]. **have a long arm** ⇨ LONG[1]. **keep sb at arm's**

length not allow oneself to become too friendly with sb 与某人保持距离; 不使自己太亲近某人. **a shot in the arm** ⇨ SHOT[1]. **twist sb's arm** ⇨ TWIST. **with arms akimbo** with one's hands on one's hips and one's elbows pointed outwards 双手叉着腰. ⇨illus 见插图. **with open 'arms** ⇨ OPEN[1].

□ **'arm-band** (also **'armlet**) *n* band of material worn round the arm or sleeve 臂环; 袖箍; 臂章; 袖章: *Many people at the funeral were wearing black arm-bands.* 在丧礼上, 很多人臂戴黑纱.

'armchair *n* chair with supports for the arms (单座的)沙发. ⇨illus at App 1 见附录1之插图, page xvi. — *adj* [attrib 作定语] without having or providing practical experience of sth 对某事物没有实际经验的: *armchair critics* 空谈的批评家 ○ *an armchair traveller*, ie sb who reads or hears about travel but does not travel himself 神游旅行者(只阅读或听说关于旅游的事而不亲身旅行的人) ○ *armchair theatre*, eg plays on radio or TV 广播剧(如无线电或电视广播的戏剧).

'armful /'ɑ:mfʊl; 'ɑrm,fʊl/ *n* quantity that can be carried by one or both arms 单臂或双臂围住的量: *armfuls of flowers* 一抱一抱的花 ○ *carrying books by the armful* 携带着成抱的书.

'armhole *n* opening in a garment through which the arm is put 袖孔.

armlet /'ɑ:mlɪt; 'ɑrmlɪt/ *n* = ARM-BAND.

'armpit *n* hollow under the arm at the shoulder 腋窝; 夹肢窝; 胳肢窝. ⇨illus at HUMAN 见 HUMAN 之插图.

arm[2] /ɑ:m; ɑrm/ *n* branch or division of a country's military forces 兵种: *troops supported by the air arm* 有空军支援的部队.

arm[3] /ɑ:m; ɑrm/ *v* **1** [I, Tn, Tn·pr] **~ oneself/sb (with sth)** supply or equip oneself/sb with weapons; prepare for war or fighting 供给自己[某人]武器; 武装; 装备; 备战: *The enemy is arming.* 敌人正在备战. ○ *The mob armed themselves with sticks and stones.* 暴乱的群众用棍子和石块作武器. ○ *Police say the man is armed and dangerous.* 警方称该男子携有武器, 十分危险. ○ *warships armed with nuclear weapons* 有核武器装备的军舰 ○ (*fig* 比喻) *She arrived at the interview armed with lists of statistics.* 她带着统计资料前往面试. **2** [Tn] make (a bomb, etc) ready to explode 使(炸弹等)准备爆炸. **3** (idm 习语) **,armed to the 'teeth** having many weapons 武装到牙齿(全副武装).

□ **the ,armed 'forces, the ,armed 'services** a country's army, navy and air force 武装力量(一国的陆海空三军).

,armed neu'trality policy of remaining neutral but prepared for defence against attack 武装中立(保持中立但准备自卫的政策).

ar·mada /ɑ:'mɑ:də; ɑr'mɑdə/ *n* **1** [C] large fleet of ships 舰队. **2 the Armada** [sing] the Spanish fleet sent to attack England in 1588 无敌舰队(1588年被派遣进攻英国的西班牙舰队).

ar·ma·dillo /,ɑ:mə'dɪləʊ; ,ɑrmə'dɪlo/ *n* (*pl* **~s**) small burrowing animal of S America with a shell of bony plates around its body which allow it to roll up into a ball when attacked 犰狳(产于南美洲的穴居小动物, 身体覆盖有骨质板甲胄, 遇敌时全身可缩成一团).

Ar·ma·ged·don /,ɑ:mə'gedn; ,ɑrmə'gedn/ *n* [sing] **1** (in the Bible) scene of the final conflict between good and evil at the end of the world (《圣经》中)世界末日善与恶决战的战场. **2** (*fig* 比喻) any similar dramatic conflict (任何类似的)大决战.

ar·ma·ment /'ɑ:məmənt; 'ɑrməmənt/ *n* **1** [C often *pl* 常作复数] weapons, esp the guns on a tank, an aircraft, etc 武器; (尤指坦克、飞机等配备的)大炮: [attrib 作定语] *the armaments industry* 军火工业. **2** [C usu *pl* 通常作复数] military forces equipped for war 武装力量; 军事力量. **3** [U] process of equipping military forces for war 武装(过程).

ar·ma·ture /'ɑ:mətʃə(r); 'ɑrmətʃɚ/ *n* part of a dynamo that rotates in a magnetic field to produce an electric current; rotating coil(s) in an electric motor 电枢; 转子; 电枢线圈; 衔铁线圈.

ar·mis·tice /'ɑ:mɪstɪs; 'ɑrməstɪs/ *n* agreement during a war to stop fighting for a certain time; truce 休战; 停战; 休战条约; 停战条约.

□ **'Armistice Day** (*US* **'Veterans' Day**) 11 November, the anniversary of the armistice that ended fighting in World War I (第一次世界大战的)停战纪念日(11月11日). Cf 参看 REMEMBRANCE SUNDAY (REMEMBRANCE).

ar·mor·ial /ɑ:'mɔ:rɪəl; ɑr'mɔrɪəl/ *adj* of heraldry or coats of arms (COAT OF ARMS (COAT)) 纹章的; 盾徽的: *armorial bearings* 盾形纹章.

ar·mour (*US* **ar·mor**) /'ɑ:mə(r); 'ɑrmɚ/ *n* [U] **1** (formerly) protective, usu metal, covering for the body, worn when fighting (旧时)甲胄; 盔甲; 铁甲: *a suit of armour* 一套盔甲. **2** metal plates covering warships, tanks, etc to protect them from shells, missiles, etc (军舰、坦克等的防炮弹、导弹等的)装甲(板). **3** group of vehicles protected in this way 装甲车辆, 装甲部队: *an attack by infantry and armour* 步兵和装甲兵的进攻. **4** (idm 习语) **a chink in sb's armour** ⇨ CHINK[1].

▷ **ar·moured** (*US* **ar·mored**) *adj* **1** covered or protected with armour (2)装甲的: *an armoured car* 装甲车 ○ *The cruiser was heavily armoured.* 那艘巡洋舰有坚固的装甲. **2** equipped with armoured vehicles 配备有装甲车辆的: *an armoured column, division, etc* 装甲纵队、师等.

ar·mourer (*US* **ar·morer**) *n* **1** person who makes or repairs weapons and armour 武器和甲胄的制造或维修者. **2** person in charge of firearms 军械士.

ar·moury (*US* **ar·mory**) /'ɑ:mərɪ; 'ɑrmərɪ/ *n* place where arms and armour are kept; arsenal 军械库; 兵工厂.

□ **'armour-plate** (*US* **'armor-**) *n* sheet of metal used as armour(2) 装甲板.

arms /ɑ:mz; ɑrmz/ *n* [pl] **1** weapons, eg guns, rifles, explosives, etc 武器(如枪、炮、炸药等): *arms and ammunition* 武器和弹药 ○ *Policemen on special duties may carry arms.* 执行特种任务的警察可以携带武器. ○ [attrib 作定语] *an arms depot* 军火库. **2** =COAT OF ARMS (COAT). **3** (idm 习语) **bear arms** ⇨ BEAR[2]. **brothers in arms** ⇨ BROTHER. **ground arms** ⇨ GROUND[2]. **take up arms (against sb)** (*fml* 文) (prepare to) go to war; begin to fight 拿起武器; (准备)作战. **under 'arms** equipped with weapons and ready to fight 配备武器, 严阵以待: *a force of 300 000 already under arms* 30万军队严阵以待. **(be) up in 'arms (about/over sth)** protesting strongly about sth 强烈反对: *The whole village is up in arms about the proposal to build an airport nearby.* 全村强烈反对在附近修建机场的计划.

□ **'arms race** competition among nations in which each tries to become militarily stronger than the others 军备竞赛.

army /'ɑ:mɪ; 'ɑrmɪ/ *n* **1** (**a**) [CGp] part of a country's military forces that is organized and equipped for fighting on land 陆军: *The two armies fought for control of the bridge.* 两军为占据那座桥而战. (**b**) **the army** [sing] profession of being a soldier 当兵的职业: *go into, be in, join, leave, etc the army* 参军[当兵/入伍/退伍] ○ [attrib 作定语] *army life* 部队的生活. **2** [CGp] large number (of people, animals, etc) (人、动物等的)大军, 大群: *an army of workmen, officials, ants* 大群工人、官员、蚂蚁. **3** [CGp] organized group of people formed for a purpose 集团; 团体: *an army of volunteers* 自愿者组成的团体; 志愿军 ○ *the Salvation Army* 救世军.

aroma /ə'rəʊmə; ə'romə/ *n* (esp pleasant) distinctive smell; fragrance 芳香; 香气: *the aroma of coffee, cigars, hot chestnuts* 咖啡、雪茄、热栗子的香味.

▷ **aro·matic** /,ærə'mætɪk; ,ærə'mætɪk/ *adj* having a pleasant, distinctive smell; fragrant 芳香的; 有香味的: *aromatic spices* 香料.

arose *pt* of ARISE.

around[1] /ə'raʊnd; ə'raʊnd/ *adv* **1** on every side; in every direction 在四周; 在周围: *hear laughter all around* 听到四周的笑声. **2** (*infml* 口 *esp US*) approximately; about[1] (1) 大约; 大概: *around 100 people* 大约100人 ○ *at around five o'clock* 5点钟左右. **3** (in measurements) following the circumference (度量)周长: *an old tree that was six feet around* 一棵周长6英尺的老树.

around[2] /ə'raʊnd; ə'raʊnd/ *adv part* (*esp US*) **1** (**a**) here and there; in many directions 到处; 四面八方: *run, drive, walk, look, etc around* 到处跑、驾驶、走、看等 ○ *children playing around on the sand* 在沙地上各处玩耍的孩子们 ○ *travel around in Europe for six weeks* 在欧洲各地旅行6个星期. (**b**) here and there within a particular area (在某一范围内)四处: *Several young girls were sitting around looking bored.* 有几个女孩儿没精打采地随处坐着. ○ *books left around on the floor* 满地放着书. **2** in circulation; available 流通; 可得到的: *There was a lot of money around in those days.* 那年月有很多富裕钱. ○ *There will be new potatoes around in the shops soon.* 新下来的马铃薯不久就要上市了. ○ *Cable television has been around for some time now.* 有线电视面世已有些时日了. **3 (a)** in the surrounding area; near 在附近; 在近处: *I can't see anyone around.* 我看见附近一个人都没有. ○ *See you soon, I expect — I'll be around.* 希望不久能见到你——我就在附近. **(b)** throughout the surrounding area or building 遍及周围的地区或建筑物: *I'll send someone to show you around.* 我派人带你到周围转转. ○ *You have 15 minutes to look around.* 你有15分钟的时间到周围看看. **4** through an angle of 180° 经过180°角; 向相反的方向: *Turn around*, ie so as to face in the opposite direction. 向后转. Cf 参看 ABOUT[2]. **5** (idm 习语) **be around** be active and prominent in a particular field or profession 在某一领域或行业中活跃而突出: *a new tennis champion who could be around for the next few years* 以后几年能大显身手的新网球冠军 ○ *She's been around as a film director since the 1960's.* 从六十年代起, 她就一直是个很活跃的电影导演. **have been around** have gained knowledge and experience of the world, esp in sexual matters 有见识; 有阅历(尤指性事): *He pretends he's been around but he's really very immature.* 他装作老于世故, 而实际上却很不成熟. ○ *You won't fool her — she's been around, you know.* 你骗不到她的——你要知道她是情场老手.

around[3] /əˈraʊnd; əˋraund/ *prep* (*esp US*) **1 (a)** here and there in; to many places within (a larger area) 到处; (在较大范围内)向各处: *running around the playground* 在运动场上到处跑 ○ *travel around the world* 环球旅行. **(b)** here and there in; at many points within (a particular area) 到处; (在某范围内)在各点: *Chairs were left untidily around the room.* 屋里到处乱放着椅子. ○ *Blobs of paint were dotted around the canvas.* 油画布上满是涂抹的颜料. **2** near (a place) 在近处; 在附近: *It's around here somewhere.* 它就在附近某处. ○ *I saw him around the place this morning.* 今天早晨我看见他就在那儿附近. **3 (a)** forming a circle round (sth); following (such a route) 围绕; 环绕: *He put his arms around her shoulders.* 他搂抱着她的双肩. ○ *run around the block* 围绕着大楼跑 ○ *The earth moves around the sun.* 地球围绕着太阳运转. **(b)** follow the curve of (sth) 沿着某物的曲线: *going around the corner at 80 mph* 以每小时80英里的速度转弯. **4** (at) approximately (a time or date) (在)大约(某时或某日): *See you around 7.30.* 7点30分左右见. ○ *It'll be finished around Christmas.* 这事将在圣诞节前后完成. ○ *fashionable around the turn of the century* 在世纪之交时流行的 ○ *It happened around 10 years ago.* 那是大约在十年前发生的事. Cf 参看 ABOUT[3].

arouse /əˈraʊz; əˋrauz/ *v* **1** [Tn, Tn·pr] **~ sb (from sth)** wake sb from sleep 唤醒某人: *He was aroused from his nap by the doorbell.* 他午睡时被门铃吵醒. **2** [Tn] cause (sth) to appear; awaken 引起(某事物); 激发: *Her strange behaviour aroused our suspicions.* 她不寻常的举动引起我们的猜疑. ○ *He succeeded in arousing the nation's sympathy.* 他已经激发了全民的同情. **3 (a)** [Tn, Tn·pr] **~ sb (from/out of sth)** cause sb to become active 鼓动、鼓励、激励某人: *arouse sb from apathy, inactivity, etc* 鼓励某人活跃起来、活动起来等. **(b)** [Tn] stimulate (sb) sexually (在性欲方面)刺激(某人). Cf 参看 ROUSE. ▷ **arousal** /əˈraʊzl; əˋrauzl̩/ *n.*

ar·peg·gio /ɑːˈpedʒɪəʊ; ɑrˋpɛdʒɪ,o/ *n* (*pl* **~s**) (*music* 音) **(a)** notes of a chord[1] played quickly one after the other, not simultaneously 琶音; 急速和弦. **(b)** playing or singing of a chord in this way 琶音的演唱; 急速和弦的演奏: *practising arpeggios* 练习演奏急速和弦.

arr *abbr* 缩写 = **1** (*music* 音) arranged (by): *English folk song, arr Percy Grainger* 由格兰杰改编的英国民歌. **2** arrival; arrive(s); arrived; arriving: *arr London 06.00* 早晨6时整抵达伦敦. Cf 参看 DEP 1.

ar·rack /ˈærək; ˋærək/ *n* [U] strong alcoholic drink made in Eastern countries (东方国家所酿制的)阿拉克烧酒.

ar·raign /əˈreɪn; əˋren/ *v* **1** [Tn, Tn·pr] **~ sb (for sth)** (*law* 律) bring a criminal charge against sb; bring sb to court for trial 控告某人; 提讯, 传讯某人: *arraign sb on a charge of murder* 控告某人犯谋杀罪 ○ *He was arraigned for theft.* 他因偷窃罪被传讯. **2** [Tn] (*fml* 文) criticize (sth) strongly 强烈谴责(某事物). ▷ **ar·raign·ment** *n* [U, C].

ar·range /əˈreɪndʒ; əˋrendʒ/ *v* **1** [Tn] put (sth) in order; make tidy, neat or attractive 安排; 整理; 布置; 排列: *arrange the books on the shelves* 整理书架上的书 ○ *arrange some flowers in a vase* 插好花瓶里的花 ○ *She arranged all her business affairs before going on holiday.* 她在度假前把业务都安排好了. **2 (a)** [Tn] plan the details of (a future event); organize in advance 筹备; 安排: *arrange a dinner to celebrate their anniversary* 筹备庆祝他们周年纪念的聚餐 ○ *arrange a programme, a timetable, an itinerary, etc* 安排节目、时间表、旅行计划等 ○ *Her marriage was arranged by her parents*, ie They chose her future husband. 她的婚姻是父母包办的. **(b)** [Ipr, Tt] **~ for sb/sth (to do sth)** make sth happen; ensure that sth happens 使某事物发生; 确保某事物发生; 准备; 设法: *I've arranged for a car (to meet you at the airport).* 我已经准备了一辆汽车(到机场接你). ○ *I'll arrange to be in when you call.* 你来电话的时候, 我一定在屋里等着. **3** [Ipr, Tn, Tn·pr, Tf, Tw, Tt] **~ with sb about sth; ~ (with sb) to do sth** agree with sb about sth or to do sth 约定; 商定: *I've arranged with the neighbours about feeding the cats.* 我已和邻居商量妥喂猫的事. ○ *Let's arrange a time and place for our next meeting.* 咱们定好下次会议的时间和地点吧. ○ *I arranged with my parents that we could borrow their car.* 我和父母说好我们可以用他们的汽车. ○ *They arranged to meet at 7 o'clock.* 他们约好7点钟见. **4** [Tn, Tn·pr] **~ sth (for sth)** adapt (a piece of music) for a particular instrument, voice, etc 改编(乐曲): *He arranged many traditional folk songs (for the piano).* 他(为钢琴演奏)改编了很多传统民歌.

NOTE ON USAGE 用法: The verbs **arrange, organize** and **plan** all have two main meanings. ☆ **arrange**、**organize**、**plan** 这三个动词都含有两层主要意思. The first is connected with putting things in order, the second with making preparations in advance. 一是把事物按顺序排好, 二是事先作好准备. **1 Arrange** is to put in a pleasing or correct order ☆ **arrange** 指的是排成合意的或正确的顺序: *You must arrange these books in alphabetical order.* 你要把这些书按字母顺序排好. **Organize** is to put into a working system ☆ **organize** 是指理成便于工作的次序: *To write a good essay you must first organize your ideas logically.* 要写出好文章, 必须先从逻辑上理顺思绪. **Plan** is to draw a diagram of a place, project, etc ☆ **plan** 是指勾画出一地方或工程等的图样: *Before we buy anything, let's plan the kitchen on paper.* 咱们先在纸上画出厨房的图样再买东西. **2** When we **arrange** a meeting we invite all the necessary people 我们 **arrange** 一会议, 意思是邀请必要到会的人: *Could you arrange a meeting with Mrs Wilson for Monday, please?* 是否能请你安排星期一和威尔逊夫人见面? To **organize** a meeting we need to make all the necessary provisions, eg book a room, provide equipment and refreshments, etc 要 **organize** 一会议, 我们需要作好一切必要的准备, 如预定房间, 提供设施和茶点等: *Who's going to organize the sandwiches for Monday's meeting?* 谁来准备星期一会议上的三明治? When we **plan** a meeting, we decide in detail on its length, on the agenda, etc 我们 **plan** 一会议, 就要确定会议的长短、议事程序等细节: *If we don't plan this meeting properly, we'll get side-tracked into discussing unimportant issues.* 倘若我们计划不好这一会议, 就会使讨论扯到枝节问题上去了.

ar·range·ment /əˈreɪndʒmənt; əˋrendʒmənt/ *n* **1 (a)** [U] putting in order; arranging 安排; 整理; 布置; 排列: *Can I leave the arrangement of the tables to you?* 我把安排这些桌子的事交给你办行吗? **(b)** [C] result of this; thing arranged 安排; 整理; 布置; 排列: *a plan of the seating arrangements* 座次安排计划 ○ *Her flower arrangement won first prize.* 她的插花赢得头奖. **2** [C usu *pl* 通常作复数] **~ (about/for sth)** plan; preparation 计划; 筹备; 准备; 安排: *He's responsible for all the travel arrangements.* 他负责旅行的一切安排. ○

A

Please make your own arrangements for accommodation. 请自行安排食宿. ○ *I'll make arrangements for you to be met at the airport.* 我将安排到机场接你的事. **3** [U, C] **~ (with sb) to do sth; ~ (with sb) (about/over sth)** agreement; settlement 同意; 约定; 解决: *Appointments can be made by arrangement (with my secretary).* 约见时间可以(与我的秘书)商定解决. ○ *We can come to some arrangement over the price.* 价钱方面, 我们可以商议解决. ○ *I have an arrangement with your bank to cash cheques here.* 我已和贵方银行商妥, 支票可以在此兑现. **4** [C] adaptation of a piece of music 改编的乐曲: *a new arrangement of a popular dance tune* 新改编的流行舞曲.

ar·rant /ˈærənt; ˋærənt/ *adj* [attrib 作定语] (of a bad person or thing) to the highest degree; utter (指坏人或坏事)绝顶的, 十足的, 完全的: *an arrant fool, hypocrite, liar, rogue, etc* 十足的傻瓜、伪君子、说谎者、流氓等 ○ *He's talking arrant nonsense.* 他完全胡说八道.

ar·ray /əˈreɪ; əˋre/ *v* [Tn esp passive 尤用于被动语态] (*fml* 文) **1** place (esp armed forces, troops, etc) in battle order 部署(尤指兵力等): *His soldiers were arrayed along the river bank.* 他的士兵沿着河岸摆开阵势. **2** dress or clothe (sb/oneself) 穿着: *arrayed in ceremonial robes* 穿着长袍礼服.

▷ **ar·ray** *n* **1** [C] impressive display or series 展示; 显示; 陈列; 一系列: *an array of facts, information, statistics, etc* 一连串的事实、信息、统计数字等 ○ *an array of bottles of different shapes and sizes* 各式各样大小不一的瓶子. **2** [U] (*fml* 文) clothes; clothing 衣服; 服装: *The royal couple appeared in splendid array.* 王室伉俪身穿盛装出现. **3** [C] (*computing* 计) collection of data arranged so that it can be extracted by means of a special program 数组, 阵列(可经某种程序取出的一系列数据).

ar·rears /əˈrɪəz; əˋrɪrz/ *n* [pl] **1** money that is owed and should have been paid earlier (过时未付的)欠款: *arrears of salary* 欠薪 ○ *rent arrears* 欠租. **2** work that has not yet been done 未做完的工作: *arrears of correspondence*, ie letters waiting to be answered 待复的信件. **3** (idm 习语) **be in/fall into arrears (with sth)** (**a**) be late in paying money that is owed 拖欠: *I have fallen into arrears with my rent.* 我已经拖欠租金了. ○ *Payment is made in arrears*, ie at the end of the period in which eg the work was done. 后行付款(在最后的一段时间付款, 例如工作完成后). (**b**) be late in doing work that is necessary 拖延(应做的事): *I'm in arrears with the housework.* 我的家务事还拖着呢.

ar·rest /əˈrest; əˋrɛst/ *v* [Tn] **1** seize (sb) with the authority of the law 依法逮捕, 拘留, 扣留(某人): *After the match three youths were arrested.* 比赛过后有三个青年被捕. **2** (*fml* 文) stop or check (a process or movement) 阻止或抑制(进展或运动): *Attempts are being made to arrest the spread of the disease.* 现正设法遏止这种疾病的蔓延. **3** attract (sth) 吸引(某事物): *An unusual painting arrested his attention.* 一幅异乎寻常的画引起了他的注意.

▷ **ar·rest** *n* **1** act of arresting (ARREST 1) 逮捕; 拘留: *The police made several arrests.* 警方逮捕了好几个人. **2** stoppage 停止: *The patient died after suffering a cardiac arrest*, ie when his heart stopped functioning properly. 病人患心搏停止而死亡(心脏停止跳动). **3** (idm 习语) **be/place sb/put sb under arrest** be/be made a prisoner 被逮捕; 被拘留; 成为囚犯: *I am placing you under arrest for attempted burglary.* 我按企图盗窃罪逮捕你. ○ *You are under arrest.* 你被捕了.

ar·rest·ing *adj* attracting attention; striking 引人注意的; 显著的: *an arresting smile* 引人注目的微笑.

ar·rival /əˈraɪvl; əˋraɪvḷ/ *n* **1** [U] act of arriving 到达; 抵达: *Cheers greeted the arrival of the Queen.* 一片欢呼声欢迎女王莅临. ○ *On (your) arrival at the hotel please wait for further instructions.* (你)抵达旅馆后, 请听候进一步指示. ○ *to await arrival*, ie (on a letter, parcel, etc) to be kept until the person to whom it is addressed arrives 待领(写在信件、包裹等上面的字样, 意为等候收件人前来领取). **2** [C] person or thing that arrives 到达的人或物: *Late arrivals must wait in the foyer.* 来晚的人要在门厅等候. ○ *We're expecting a new arrival* (ie a new baby) *in the family soon.* 我们期待着家中不久将添一个新生儿.

ar·rive /əˈraɪv; əˋraɪv/ *v* **1** [I, Ipr] **~ (at/in...)** reach (a place), esp at the end of a journey 到达, 抵达(某地)(尤指旅途的终点): *arrive home* 到家 ○ *What time did you arrive?* 你几点钟到的? ○ *We arrived at the station five minutes late.* 我们到车站晚了五分钟. ○ *They will arrive in New York at noon.* 他们将于中午到达纽约. **2** [I] (of an event in time) come (指有时间性的事件)到来: *The great day has arrived.* 伟大的日子已经到来. ○ *The baby finally arrived* (ie was born) *just after midnight.* 婴儿终于在刚过午夜时候降生了. **3** [I] (*infml* 口) become well known or successful 成名; 成功: *You know you've arrived when you're asked to appear on TV.* 邀请你在电视上亮相的时候, 你就知道你已经名声在外了. **4** (phr v) **arrive at sth** reach sth 达成或得出某事物: *arrive at an agreement, a decision, a conclusion, etc* 达成协议、作出决定、得出结论.

ar·rog·ant /ˈærəgənt; ˋærəgənt/ *adj* behaving in a proud and superior manner; showing too much pride in oneself and too little consideration for others 傲慢的; 自大的: *an arrogant tone of voice* 傲慢的口气 ○ *It's arrogant of you to assume you'll win every time.* 你自以为每次都能赢, 未免太自大了. ▷ **ar·rog·ance** /ˈærəgəns; ˋærəgəns/ *n* [U]. **ar·rog·antly** *adv*.

ar·rog·ate /ˈærəgeɪt; ˋærə,get/ *v* [Tn·pr] (*fml* 文) **1 ~ sth to oneself** claim or take sth to which one has no right 冒称; 妄取: *arrogating all the credit to himself* 把一切功劳都归于他自己. **2 ~ sth to sb** say unjustly that sb thinks or acts wrongly 不公平地说某人错: *arrogate evil motives to a rival* 硬说对手居心不良.

ar·row /ˈærəʊ; ˋæro/ *n* **1** thin pointed stick designed to be shot from a bow[1](1) 箭; 矢. ⇨illus at ARCHERY 见ARCHERY之插图. **2** mark or sign resembling this →, used to show direction or position 箭号, 箭头(即 →, 用以指示方位): *Follow the arrows on the map.* 跟着地图上的箭头走. **3** (idm 习语) **straight as an arrow/die** ⇨ STRAIGHT[1].

□ ˈ**arrowhead** *n* pointed end of an arrow 箭头; 箭镞.

ar·row·root /ˈærəʊruːt; ˋæro,rut/ *n* (**a**) [U] edible starch prepared from the root of an American plant 竹芋粉. (**b**) [U, C] this plant 竹芋.

arse /ɑːs; ɑrs/ *n* (⚠ *sl* 讳, 俚) **1** (*US* **ass** /æs; æs/) buttocks; anus 屁股; 肛门. **2** (usu following an *adj* 通常用于形容词之后) person 人: *You stupid arse!* 你这个笨蛋! **3** (idm 习语) **lick sb's arse** ⇨ LICK. **not know one's arse from one's elbow** ⇨ KNOW.

▷ **arse** *v* (phr v) **arse about/around** (⚠ *Brit sl* 讳, 俚) behave in a silly manner 举动愚笨: *Stop arsing about and give me back my shoes.* 别傻里傻气的, 快把鞋还给我.

□ ˈ**arse-hole** (*US* ˈ**ass-hole**) *n* (⚠ *sl* 讳, 俚) (often used as a term of abuse 常用作辱骂语) anus 肛门.

ˈ**arse-licker** *n* (⚠ *sl* 讳, 俚) person who tries to win favours by flattering people 马屁精.

ar·senal /ˈɑːsənl; ˋɑrsṇəl/ *n* **1** place where weapons and ammunition are made or stored 军械场; 军火库. **2** store of weapons 储藏的武器; 武库: (*fig* 比喻) *The speaker made full use of his arsenal of invective.* 演讲者振振有词地大张挞伐.

ar·senic /ˈɑːsnɪk; ˋɑrsṇɪk/ *n* [U] (*chemistry* 化) **1** brittle steel-grey element 砷. ⇨App 10 见附录10. **2** violently poisonous white compound of this 砒霜; 信石.

ar·son /ˈɑːsn; ˋɑrsṇ/ *n* [U] criminal and deliberate act of setting fire to a house or other building, either from malice or in order to claim insurance money 放火; 纵火.

▷ **ar·son·ist** /ˈɑːsənɪst; ˋɑrsənɪst/ *n* person who is guilty of arson 放火犯; 纵火犯.

art[1] /ɑːt; ɑrt/ *n* **1** [U] (**a**) creation or expression of sth beautiful, esp in a visual form, eg painting, sculpture, etc 美的事物的创造或表现(尤指用视觉形式, 如绘画、雕刻等); 艺术; 美术: *the art of the Renaissance* 文艺复兴时期的艺术 ○ *children's art* 儿童的艺术 ○ [attrib 作定语] *an art critic, historian, lover, etc* 艺术批评家、艺术史家、艺术爱好者. (**b**) skill in such creation 艺术技巧: *Her performance displayed great art.* 她的表演表现了高度的艺术技巧. ○ *This tapestry is a work of art.* 这张挂毯是件艺术品. (**c**) instances of this 艺术; 美术: [attrib 作定语] *an* ˈ*art exhibition/gallery* 艺术展览[馆]. **2 the arts** [pl] = FINE ART (FINE). **3 arts** [pl] subjects of study (eg languages, literature, history) in which imaginative and creative skills are more important than the exact measurement and calculation needed in science 文科: [attrib 作定语] *an arts degree with honours in sociology* 他持有社会学的文科(荣誉)学位. **4** [C, U] any skill or ability that can be learnt by practice, esp contrasted with scientific technique; knack (尤指与科学技术相对而言的, 经过实践获得的)技能, 技巧: *the art of appearing confident at interviews* 在面试时表现自信的技巧 ○ *Threading a needle is an art in itself.* 穿针引线本身就是一种技巧. ○ *The art of letter-writing is fast disappearing.* 尺牍技巧行将消失. **5** (**a**) [U] cunning; trickery 狡诈; 欺诈. (**b**) [C] trick; wile 奸计; 诡计: *well-practised in the arts of seduction* 惯用诱骗诡计. **6** (idm 习语) **get sth down to a fine art** ⇨ FINE².

□ ˈ**art-form** *n* type of artistic activity involving special materials or techniques 艺术形式: *Film-making is now accepted as an art-form.* 电影制片现已公认是一种艺术形式.

ˌ**arts and** ˈ**crafts** decorative design and handicraft 工艺美术; 手工艺.

ˈ**artwork** *n* photographs and illustrations in books, newspapers and magazines 书籍和报刊上的图片.

art² /ɑːt; ɑrt/ *v* (*arch* 古) (*2nd pers sing pres t* form of *be*, used with *thou* be 的单数第二人称现在时态, 与 thou 连用): *'O rose, thou art sick.'* '玫瑰, 汝病矣.'

arte·fact (also **arti·fact**) /ˈɑːtɪfækt; ˋɑrtɪˌfækt/ *n* thing made by man, esp a tool or weapon of archaeological interest 人工制品(尤指有考古价值的工具或武器): *prehistoric artefacts made of bone and pottery* 史前的骨制及陶制器具.

ar·ter·ial /ɑːˈtɪərɪəl; ɑrˋtɪrɪəl/ *adj* of or like an artery 动脉的; 像动脉的: *the arterial system*, ie of the body 动脉网 ○ *arterial roads*, ie important main roads (道路的)干线.

ar·terio·scler·osis /ɑːˌtɪərɪəʊskləˈrəʊsɪs; ɑrˋtɪrɪˌosklɪˋrosɪs/ *n* [U] diseased condition in which the walls of the arteries become harder and hinder the circulation of the blood 动脉硬化.

ar·tery /ˈɑːtərɪ; ˋɑrtərɪ/ *n* **1** any of the tubes carrying blood from the heart to all parts of the body 动脉. Cf 参看 VEIN. **2** important route for traffic or transport, eg a road, railway line or river 干线(交通或运输的重要路线, 如公路、铁路线或河流).

ar·te·sian well /ɑːˌtiːzɪən ˈwel; *US* ɑːrˈtiːʒn; ɑrˋtiʒənˋwɛl/ vertically drilled hole in the ground through which a steady supply of water rises to the surface by natural pressure 自流井; 喷水井.

art·ful /ˈɑːtfl; ˋɑrtfəl/ *adj* [usu attrib 通常作定语] **1** (of people) cunningly clever at getting what one wants; crafty (指人)狡猾的; 诡诈的: *He's an artful devil!* 他诡计多端! **2** (of things or actions) cleverly made or contrived (指事物或行动)巧妙作出或设计的: *an artful deception, trick, etc* 骗局、诡计 ○ *an artful little gadget for opening tins* 小巧玲珑的开罐头工具. ▷ **art·fully** /ˈɑːtfəlɪ; ˋɑrtfəlɪ/ *adv*. **art·ful·ness** *n* [U]. Cf 参看 ARTLESS.

arth·ritis /ɑːˈθraɪtɪs; ɑrˋθraɪtɪs/ *n* [U] inflammation of a joint or joints of the body, causing pain and stiffness 关节炎. Cf 参看 FIBROSITIS, RHEUMATISM.

▷ **arth·ritic** /ɑːˈθrɪtɪk; ɑrˋθrɪtɪk/ *adj* suffering from or caused by arthritis 患关节炎的; 关节炎造成的: *arthritic hands, pains* 患关节炎的手、疼痛. — *n* person suffering from arthritis 关节炎患者.

ar·ti·choke /ˈɑːtɪtʃəʊk; ˋɑrtɪˌtʃok/ *n* **1** (also **globe artichoke**) plant like a large thistle with a flowering head of thick leaf-like scales used as a vegetable 洋蓟(一种大型蓟状植物, 有厚叶状苞片的花头, 可作蔬菜). **2** (also **Jerusalem artichoke** /dʒəˌruːsələm ˈɑːtɪtʃəʊk; dʒəˌruzələm ˋɑrtɪˌtʃok/) type of sunflower with tuberous roots used as a vegetable 菊芋(向日葵属植物, 其块根可作蔬菜, 亦称洋姜).

art·icle /ˈɑːtɪkl; ˋɑrtɪkl/ *n* **1** particular or separate thing, esp one of a set 物件; 物品(尤指一套中之一): *articles of clothing*, eg shirts, socks, hats, coats 衣物(如衬衫、袜子、帽子、外衣) ○ *toilet articles*, eg soap, toothpaste, shaving-cream 梳妆用品(如肥皂、牙膏、刮胡膏) ○ *The articles found in the car helped the police identify the body.* 警方根据从汽车里找到的物品认出了尸体的身分. **2** piece of writing, complete in itself, in a newspaper, magazine, etc (报刊上的)文章: *an interesting article on/about education* 一篇关于教育的使人感兴趣的文章. **3** (*law* 律) separate clause or item in an agreement or a contract (协议或合同的)项目, 条款: *articles of apprenticeship*, ie the formal agreement between an apprentice and his employer 师徒合约. **4** (*grammar*) either of the determiners 'a/an' (*the indefinite article*) or 'the' (*the definite article*) 冠词(不定冠词 a/an 或定冠词 the).

▷ **art·icle** *v* [usu passive 通常用于被动语态: Tn, Tn·pr] **~ sb (to sb)** employ sb under contract as a trainee 雇用某人为受合同约束的受训者: *an articled clerk* 订有见习合同的店员 ○ *articled to a solicitor* 受律师实习条款约束的.

□ ˌ**article of** ˈ**faith 1** basic point of sb's religious belief (宗教信仰的)信条. **2** any firmly held belief 信念; 信条.

ar·ticu·late¹ /ɑːˈtɪkjʊlət; ɑrˋtɪkjəlɪt/ *adj* **1** (of a person) able to express one's ideas clearly in words (指人)能用词语把意思表达清楚的: *She's unusually articulate for a ten-year-old.* 对一个十岁的孩子来说, 她异乎寻常地能说会道. **2** (of speech) clearly pronounced (指讲话)发音清晰的. **3** having joints 有关节的. ▷ **ar·ticu·lately** *adv*. **ar·ticu·late·ness** *n* [U].

ar·ticu·late² /ɑːˈtɪkjʊleɪt; ɑrˋtɪkjəˌlet/ *v* **1** [I, Tn] speak (sth) clearly and distinctly 清楚明白地说(某事): *I'm a little deaf — please articulate (your words) carefully.* 我有些耳背——请(把话)仔细说清楚. **2** [Ipr, Tn·pr usu passive 通常用于被动语态] **~ (sth) with sth** form a joint or connect (sth) by joints with sth 形成关节; (用关节)连接: *bones that articulate/are articulated with others* 以关节与其它骨骼相连的骨骼.

□ arˌticulated ˈ**vehicle**, arˌ**ticulated** ˈ**lorry** (*US* **tractor-trailer**) vehicle with sections connected by flexible joints so that it can turn more easily 铰接车(带有用铰链连接其它部分的车辆, 转弯较易). ⇨illus at LORRY 见 LORRY 之插图.

ar·ticu·la·tion /ɑːˌtɪkjʊˈleɪʃn; ɑrˌtɪkjəˋleʃən/ *n* **1** [U] making of speech sounds 发音: *As he drank more wine his articulation became worse.* 他又多喝了些酒, 口齿也就更不清楚了. **2** [U, C] (connection by means of a) joint (用关节)连接; 关节.

arti·fact = ARTEFACT.

ar·ti·fice /ˈɑːtɪfɪs; ˋɑrtəfɪs/ *n* [C, U] (instance of) clever trickery; deception 诡计; 欺骗: *Pretending to faint was merely (an) artifice.* 假装昏迷只不过是个诡计.

ar·ti·fi·cer /ɑːˈtɪfɪsə(r); ɑrˋtɪfəsɚ/ *n* skilled workman or mechanic, esp one in the army or navy 技工; 工匠; (尤指陆军或海军中的)技术兵.

ar·ti·fi·cial /ˌɑːtɪˈfɪʃl; ˌɑrtəˋfɪʃəl/ *adj* **1** made or produced by man in imitation of sth natural; not real 人造的; 人工的; 假的: *artificial flowers, light, limbs, pearls* 假花、人造光、义肢、假珍珠. **2** affected; insincere; not genuine 做作的; 虚假的; 假的: *Her artificial gaiety disguised an inner sadness.* 她以矫揉造作的快乐掩饰着内心的悲痛.

▷ **ar·ti·fi·ci·al·ity** /ˌɑːtɪfɪʃɪˈælətɪ; ˌɑrtɪˌfɪʃɪˋælətɪ/ *n* [U]. **ar·ti·fi·cially** /ˌɑːtɪˈfɪʃəlɪ; ˌɑrtəˋfɪʃəlɪ/ *adv*.

□ ˌ**artificial insemi**ˈ**nation** injection of semen into the womb (esp of animals) artificially, so that conception can occur without sexual intercourse 人工授精(尤指施于动物的).

ˌ**artificial in**ˈ**telligence** (*abbr* 缩写 **AI**) (study of) the capacity of machines to simulate intelligent human behaviour 人工智能(的研究).

ˌ**artificial respi**ˈ**ration** process of forcing air into and out of the lungs to stimulate natural breathing again when it has failed, eg in a person who has almost drowned 人工呼吸.

ar·til·lery /ɑːˈtɪlərɪ; ɑrˋtɪlərɪ/ *n* [U] **1** heavy guns (often mounted on wheels) used in fighting on land 大炮: [attrib 作定语] *an artillery regiment* 炮兵团. **2** branch of an army that uses these 炮兵部队: *a captain in the artillery* 炮兵部队的上尉.

ar·tisan /ˌɑːtɪˈzæn; *US* ˈɑːrtɪzn; ˋɑrtəzn̩/ *n* (*fml* 文) skilled workman or craftsman 技工; 工匠: *an artisan in leatherwork* 皮匠.

art·ist /ˈɑːtɪst; ˋɑrtɪst/ *n* **1** person who practises any of the fine arts, esp painting 搞艺术的人; 艺术家; (尤指)画画儿的人, 画家: *Constable was a great English artist.* 康斯太布尔是伟大的英国画家. **2** person who does sth with great skill 能手; 大师: *The carpenter has made this*

A

cupboard beautifully — he's a real artist. 那个木匠做的这个柜子很漂亮——他真是个能工巧匠. **3** = ARTISTE.

ar·tiste /ɑːˈtiːst; ɑrˋtist/ *n* professional entertainer, eg a singer, a dancer, an actor, etc 职业表演者; 艺人: *Among the artistes appearing on our show tonight we have....* 今晚为我们演出的(表演者)有....

art·istic /ɑːˈtɪstɪk; ɑrˋtɪstɪk/ *adj* **1** (**a**) having natural skill in any of the fine arts 有艺术才能的. (**b**) showing a sensitive appreciation of and liking for the fine arts 有审美能力的; 爱好艺术的: *She comes from a very artistic family.* 她出身于很有艺术修养的家庭. **2** done with skill and good taste; beautiful 有艺术技巧的; 有美感的: *The decor is so artistic.* 全部装饰很有艺术性. **3** of art and artists 艺术的; 艺术家的: *an artistic temperament*, ie impulsive and eccentric behaviour thought to be typical of artists 艺术家的气质(感情冲动, 行为古怪被视为艺术家的特征). ▷ **art·ist·ic·ally** /ɑːˈtɪstɪklɪ; ɑrˋtɪstɪklɪ/ *adv*.

art·istry /ˈɑːtɪstrɪ; ˋɑrtɪstrɪ/ *n* [U] skill or work of an artist 艺术技巧; 艺术作品; 艺术工作: *admire the artistry of the painter's use of colour* 钦佩这位画家使用颜色的技巧.

art·less /ˈɑːtlɪs; ˋɑrtlɪs/ *adj* simple and natural; without deceit 单纯而自然的; 无虚饰的: *as artless as a child of five* 像五岁孩子那样天真烂漫 ○ *My artless comment was mistaken for rudeness.* 我直言不讳的评论被误会为粗暴无礼. Cf 参看 ARTFUL.

arty /ˈɑːtɪ; ˋɑrtɪ/ *adj* (*infml derog* 口, 贬) showing a pretentious artistic style or a false or exaggerated interest in art 附庸风雅的; 冒充有艺术修养的: *His arty clothes look out of place in the office.* 他的奇装异服, 在办公室里很不顺眼.

□ ˌ**arty-ˈcrafty** *adj* (*joc or derog infml* 谑或贬, 口) (of furniture and household objects) appearing to be made by hand and designed for artistic effect rather than for usefulness or comfort (指家具及家庭用品)显示出是手工制作的, 设计华而不实的.

arum lily /ˌeərəm ˈlɪlɪ; ˌɛrəm ˋlɪlɪ/ type of tall cultivated lily with a long white funnel-shaped flower 白星海芋.

-ary *suff* 后缀 (with *ns* forming *adjs* and *ns* 与名词结合构成形容词及名词) concerned with; of 有关...的; ...的: *planetary* ○ *reactionary* ○ *budgetary* ○ *commentary*.

Aryan /ˈeərɪən; ˋɛrɪən/ *adj* **1** of the Indo-European group of languages 雅利安语系的. **2** of speakers of these languages 说雅利安语的人.

▷ **Aryan** *n* **1** person who speaks an Indo-European language 雅利安人. **2** (formerly used in Germany under Nazi rule) person with non-Jewish Germanic ancestors (旧时用于纳粹统治下的德国)非犹太日尔曼民族的后裔.

as /əz; əz; *strong form* 强读式 æz; æz/ *prep* **1** so as to appear to be (sb) 好像(某人): *dressed as a policeman* 打扮得像个警察 ○ *They entered the building disguised as cleaners.* 他们化装成清洁工人的模样进入大楼. **2** having the function or character of (sb) 有(某人)的身分或特性; 作为; 当作: *a job as a packer* 包装者的工作 ○ *work as a courier* 当导游 ○ *I'm speaking as your employer.* 我以雇主的身分和你说话. ○ *Treat me as a friend.* 把我当作朋友. ○ *accept sb as an equal* 把某人视为同等的人 ○ *I respect him as a writer and as a man.* 我尊重他这位作家, 也尊重他这个人. ⇨Usage 见所附用法. **3** (**a**) since sb is (sth) 因某人是(某身分): *As her private secretary he has access to all her correspondence.* 他是她的私人秘书, 能接触到她所有的信件. (**b**) when or while sb is (sth) 当某人是(某身分)时: *As a child she was sent to six different schools.* 她儿时前后上过六所学校.

▷ **as** *adv* **1 as...as** (used before *advs* and *adjs* in order to make a comparison 用于副词和形容词之前, 以构成比较句型) (**a**) (with the second *as* a *prep* 第二个as用作介词) to the same extent...; equally...as 达到与...相同的程度; 与...等同: *as tall as his father* 和他父亲一样高 ○ *This dress is twice as expensive as that.* 这件连衣裙比那件贵一倍. ○ *He doesn't play half as well as his sister.* 他演奏的水平不及他姐姐的一半. ○ *I haven't known him as long as you.* 我没有你认识他的时间长. ○ *As likely as not* (ie Very probably), *it will rain.* 很有可能要下雨. (**b**) (with the second *as* a *conj* 第二个as用作连词) to the same extent...as; equally...as 同...一样达到某种程度; 与...等同: *He looks as ill as he sounded on the phone.* 他的样子和他在电话中说话的声音反映的病情是一样的. ○ *His eyes aren't quite as blue as they look in the film.* 他的眼睛不像在电影里见到的那么蓝. ○ *Run as fast as you can.* 你能跑多快就跑多快. ○ *He recited as much of the poem as he could remember.* 他把诗中记得住的都背诵出来了. ○ *She's as good an actress as she is a singer.* 她当演员和当歌手都一样出色. **2** not differently from; like 和...无不同; 像; 如: *As before he remained unmoved.* 他和以往一样无动于衷. ○ *The 'h' is silent as in 'hour'.* 在 hour 这个字中, h 不发音.

as *conj* **1** during the time when; while 在...期间; 当...的时候: *I watched her as she combed her hair.* 她梳头的时候我一直看着她. ○ *As he grew older he lost interest in everything except gardening.* 他年纪越来越大, 除了喜欢园艺以外, 对一切都失去了兴趣. **2** (usu placed at the beginning of the sentence 通常置于句首) since; because 由于; 因为: *As you weren't there I left a message.* 因为你不在那里, 我留了个信儿. ○ *As she's been ill perhaps she'll need some help.* 她由于生病可能需要些帮助. **3** (used after an *adj* or *adv* to introduce a clause of concession 用于形容词或副词之后, 引导让步从句) although 尽管; 即使; 虽然: *Young as I am, I already know what career I want to follow.* 我虽然还小, 可是对要从事的职业已胸有成竹了. ○ *Talented as he is, he is not yet ready to turn professional.* 别看他有天分, 他还没把心用到专业上去. ○ *Much as I like you, I couldn't live with you.* 我尽管很喜欢你, 却不能和你在一起生活. ○ *Try as he would/might, he couldn't open the door.* 他试过多次了, 却仍打不开那门. **4** in the way in which 以...方式: *Do as I say and sit down.* 照我说的, 坐下. ○ *Leave the table as it is*, ie Do not disturb the things on it. 那桌子就那样吧(不要动上面的东西). ○ *Why didn't you catch the last bus as I told you to?* 你怎么不听我的话赶乘末班公共汽车呢? **5** a fact which 为...之事实: *Cyprus, as you know, is an island in the Mediterranean.* 如你所知, 塞浦路斯是地中海的岛国. ○ *The Beatles, as many of you are old enough to remember, came from Liverpool.* 你们这样年纪的人大多还记得披头士乐队吧, 他们都是利物浦人. **6** (usu followed by *be* or *do* + subject 通常后接be或do + 主语) and so too 也一样: *She's unusually tall, as are both her parents.* 她特别高, 她父母也都那么高. ○ *He's a doctor, as was his wife before she had children.* 他是医生, 他妻子生儿育女之前也当过医生. ⇨Usage 见所附用法. **7** (idm 习语) **as against sth** in contrast with sth 与...对照; 与...相比: *She gets Saturdays off in her new job as against working alternate weekends in her last one.* 她新找的这份工作星期六放假, 而原来的那份工作周末是隔周放假. ○ *We had twelve hours of sunshine yesterday, as against a forecast of continuous rain.* 昨日有十二小时的晴天, 预报却说仍有雨. ˌ**as and ˈwhen** (**a**) (referring to an uncertain future event or action 指将来的某一未定的事或行动) when 到时候: *We'll decide on our team as and when we qualify for the competition.* 我们等到有资格参加比赛时, 再来决定本队参赛人员. Cf 参看 IF AND WHEN (IF). (**b**) (*infml* 口) when possible; eventually 可能时; 终于; 最终: *I'll tell you more as and when*, ie as soon as I can. 有可能时我再多跟你说. **as for sb/sth** with regard to sb/sth 至于某人[某事物]: *As for the hotel, it was very uncomfortable and miles from the sea.* 至于旅馆呢, 非常不舒服, 而且离海边有好几里地. ○ *As for you, you ought to be ashamed of yourself.* 至于你, 你应该感到惭愧. **as from**; *esp US* **as of** (indicating the time or date from which sth starts 指某事物开始的时间或日期): *As from next Monday you can use my office.* 从下星期一起, 你可以使用我的办公室. ○ *We shall have a new address as of 12 May.* 我们自5月12日起将用新地址. **as if**; **as though** with the appearance of; apparently 好像; 似乎; 仿佛: *He behaved as if nothing had happened.* 他装作若无其事的样子. ○ *As if unsure of where she was, she hesitated and looked round.* 她仿佛茫然不知身在何处, 犹犹豫豫向四周打量. ○ *He rubbed his eyes and yawned as though waking up after a long sleep.* 他又揉眼睛又打哈欠, 好像睡了一大觉刚醒似的. ˌ**as it ˈis** taking present circumstances into account; as things are 照现状看; 看样子: *We were hoping to have a holiday next week — as it is, we may not be able to get away.* 我们原来盼望着下星期放假——看样子走不了了. ○ *I* *thought I might be transferred but as it is I shall have to look for a new job.* 我以为我可能调动工作, 照目前情况看我得另找工作了. ˌ**as it ˈwere** (used to comment on the speaker's own choice of words, which may give only an approximate meaning 用以评断自己用词是否恰当, 指词义接近而已): *She seemed very relaxed — in her natural setting as it were.* 她似乎十分悠然自得 —— 可以说是有自己随遇而安的天地. ○ *He'd been watching the water rising for two hours — preparing to meet his destiny, as it were — before help arrived.* 他在获救前的两小时中, 一直眼看着水在上涨 —— 可谓准备听天由命了. **as to sth; as regards sth** with regard to sth; regarding sth 至于某事物; 提到某事物: *As to correcting our homework, the teacher always makes us do it ourselves.* 谈到批改我们的作业, 老师总是让我们自己改. ○ *There are no special rules as regards what clothes you should wear.* 至于应该穿什么衣服, 并没有硬性规定. **as yet** ⇨ YET. ˌ**as you ˈwere** (used as an order to soldiers, etc to return to their previous positions, activities, etc 用作口令, 意为恢复到原来的位置、姿势、活动等).

NOTE ON USAGE 用法: **1** When referring to the similarity between people, things and actions, both **as** and **like** are used 在谈到人、事物或动作彼此有相同点或共同点时, 使用 **as** 和 **like** 均可. **Like** is a preposition and is used before nouns and pronouns ☆ **like** 是介词, 用于名词和代词之前: *Like me, she enjoys all kinds of music.* 她和我一样, 各种音乐都喜爱. **As** is a conjunction and is used before a clause ☆ **as** 是连词, 用于分句之前: *She enjoys all kinds of music, as I do.* 她各种音乐都喜爱, 和我一样. In informal speech **like** is frequently used as a conjunction, replacing both **as** and **as if** 在口语中, **like** 往往用作连词, 当作 **as** 和 **as if** 使用: *Nobody understands him like/as I do.* 没有人能像我这样理解他. ○ *It looks like/as if he won't arrive in time.* 看来他好像不能按时到达了. **2** Compare the use of **as** and **like** indicating occupations or functions 试比较 **as** 和 **like** 用于职业或作用方面的用法: *She worked as a teacher* (ie was a teacher) *for many years.* 她当了许多年的教师. *Our doctor always talks to me like a teacher talking to a child,* ie He is not a teacher but he has the manner of one. 给我们看病的医生对我说话总是像教师对小学生说话一样.

ASA /ˌeɪ es ˈeɪ; ˌe ɛs ˋe/ *abbr* 缩写 = **1** Advertising Standards Authority 广告标准局. **2** (also **ASA/BS**) (of a scale of film speeds) American Standards Association (/British Standard) (指底片度数)美国标准(〔英国标准〕): *ASA/BS 100* 美国标准〔英国标准〕100 度. Cf 参看 BS, BSI, DIN, ISO.

asap /ˌeɪ es eɪ ˈpi:; ˌe ɛs e ˋpi/ *abbr* 缩写 = as soon as possible 尽快.

as·bes·tos /æsˈbestɒs, *also* əzˈbestəs; æsˋbɛstəs/ *n* [U] soft fibrous grey mineral substance that can be made into fireproof material or used for heat insulation 石棉 (柔软的灰色纤维状矿物, 可用以制造耐火材料或用以隔热).

▷ **as·bes·tosis** /ˌæsbesˈtəʊsɪs; ˌæsbɛsˋtosɪs/ *n* [U] disease of the lungs caused by inhaling asbestos particles 石棉沉着病.

as·cend /əˈsend; əˋsɛnd/ *v* [I, Tn] (*fml* 文) go or come up (sth) 上升; 升高: *The path started to ascend more steeply at this point.* 这条路从这里向上就更陡了. ○ *We watched the mists ascending from the valley below.* 我们看着薄雾从下面的山谷中升起. ○ *notes ascending and descending the scale* 上升及下降音阶的音符 ○ (*fig* 比喻) *ascend the throne*, ie become king or queen 登基(帝王即位).

as·cend·ancy (also **as·cend·ency**) /əˈsendənsɪ; əˋsɛndənsɪ/ *n* [U] ~ **(over sb/sth)** (position of) having dominant power or control 有支配的力量或控制力(的地位): *He has (gained) the ascendancy over all his main rivals.* 他(获)有压倒一切主要对手的优势.

as·cend·ant (also **as·cend·ent**) /əˈsendənt; əˋsɛndənt/ *n* (idm 习语) **in the ascendant** rising in power and influence 权势日益增强: *Though he is still a young man his political career is already in the ascendant.* 他虽然年纪轻轻, 可是他在政坛上已青云直上了.

as·cen·sion /əˈsenʃn; əˋsɛnʃən/ *n* **1** [U] act of ascending 上升; 升高. **2 the Ascension** [sing] (in the Bible) departure of Jesus from the earth into heaven (《圣经》中)耶稣升天.

□ **Asˈcension Day** day on which the Ascension is commemorated in the Christian Church, ie the Thursday that is the fortieth day after Easter 耶稣升天节(复活节后的第四十天, 星期四).

as·cent /əˈsent; əˋsɛnt/ *n* **1** act of ascending 上升; 升高: *the ascent of Mount Everest* 登埃佛勒斯峰(即珠穆朗玛峰) ○ *Who was the first man to make an ascent in a balloon?* 第一个乘气球升空的人是谁? **2** upward path or slope 上坡路; 爬坡: *The last part of the ascent is very steep.* 最后一段上坡路很陡.

as·cer·tain /ˌæsəˈteɪn; ˌæsɚˋten/ *v* [Tn, Tf, Tw] (*fml* 文) discover (sth) so that one is certain; get to know 查明; 弄清; 确定: *ascertain the true facts* 查明事实真相 ○ *ascertain that the report is accurate* 弄清报告准确无误 ○ *ascertain who is likely to come to the meeting* 确定谁有可能来开会 ○ *The police are trying to ascertain what really happened.* 警方正设法查个水落石出. ▷ **as·cer·tain·able** *adj*. **as·cer·tain·ment** *n* [U].

as·cetic /əˈsetɪk; əˋsɛtɪk/ *adj* [usu attrib 通常作定语] not allowing oneself pleasures and comforts; having or involving a very austere life 不让自己快乐和舒服的; 苦行的; 过极简朴生活的: *the ascetic existence of monks and hermits* 僧侣隐士的清苦生活.

▷ **as·cetic** *n* person who leads a very simple life without basic comforts, esp for religious reasons 苦行者; 苦行修道者.

as·cet·ic·ally /-klɪ; -klɪ/ *adv*.

as·cet·icism /əˈsetɪsɪzəm; əˋsɛtəˌsɪzəm/ *n* [U].

as·cor·bic acid /əˌskɔ:bɪk ˈæsɪd; əˋskɔrbɪk ˋæsɪd/ vitamin found esp in citrus fruits and vegetables; vitamin C 抗坏血酸(即维生素 C).

ascribe /əˈskraɪb; əˋskraɪb/ *v* [Tn·pr] ~ **sth to sb/sth** consider sth to be caused by, written by or belonging to sb/sth 认为某事物是由某人〔某事物〕所造成或写成; 归功于、归咎于某人〔某事物〕: *He ascribed his failure to bad luck.* 他把失败归咎于运气不好. ○ *This play is usually ascribed to Shakespeare.* 这个剧本一般认为是莎士比亚所作. ○ *You can't ascribe the same meaning to both words.* 不要认为这两个词的意思是相同的.

▷ **ascrib·able** *adj* [pred 作表语] ~ **to sb/sth** that can be ascribed to sb/sth 可归于、起因于某人〔某事物〕: *His success is ascribable simply to hard work.* 他的成功就是由于勤奋.

ascrip·tion /əˈskrɪpʃn; əsˋkrɪpʃən/ *n* [C, U] ~ **(to sb/sth)** (*fml* 文) (act of) ascribing sth (to sb/sth) 归因; 归功; 归咎.

ASEAN /ˈæzɪæn; ˋæzɪæn/ *abbr* 缩写 = Association of South-East Asian Nations 东南亚国家联盟.

asep·sis /ˌeɪˈsepsɪs; *US* əˈsep-; əˋsɛpsɪs/ *n* [U] state of being free from harmful bacteria 无菌; 无毒.

aseptic /ˌeɪˈseptɪk; *US* əˈsep-; əˋsɛptɪk/ *adj* (of wounds, dressings, etc) free from bacteria that cause a thing to become septic; surgically clean (指伤口、敷料等)无菌的; (外科医疗上)无感染的.

asex·ual /ˌeɪˈsekʃʊəl; eˋsɛkʃʊəl/ *adj* **1** without sex or sex organs 无性的; 无性器官的: *asexual reproduction* 无性生殖. **2** having or showing no interest in sexual relations 对两性关系(显示)无兴趣的: *an asexual relationship* 没有性关系的关系. ▷ **asexu·al·ity** /eɪˌsekʃʊˈælətɪ; eˌsɛkʃʊˋælətɪ/ *n* [U].

ash[1] /æʃ; æʃ/ *n* **(a)** [C] tree commonly found in forests, with silver-grey bark and hard close-grained wood (即白蜡树). ⇨illus at App 1 见附录1之插图, page i. **(b)** [U] its wood, used for tool handles, etc 木(用作工具的把柄等).

□ **ˈash plant** *n* strong walking-stick made from the stem of a young ash tree 白蜡杆手杖.

ash[2] /æʃ; æʃ/ *n* [U] powder that remains after sth (esp tobacco, coal, etc) has burnt 灰末; 灰: *cigarette ash* 香烟灰 ○ *volcanic ash* 火山灰 ○ *Coke is an economical fuel but it leaves a lot of ash.* 焦炭是一种很经济的燃料, 可是燃烧后剩下很多灰. Cf 参看 ASHES.

□ ˌ**ash ˈblonde (a)** (of hair) very light greyish-blond in colour (指头发)略呈浅灰的金黄色. **(b)** woman with hair of this colour 有这种颜色头发的女子.

ˈashpan *n* tray (placed underneath a fireplace, stove,

etc) into which the ashes drop from a fire (壁炉、火炉等下面的)炉灰盘.

ˈ**ashtray** *n* small dish or container into which smokers put tobacco ash, cigarette ends, etc 烟灰缸.

ˌ**Ash ˈWednesday** first day of Lent 圣灰星期三(大斋首日). Cf 参看 SHROVE TUESDAY.

ashamed /əˈʃeɪmd; əˋʃemd/ *adj* [pred 作表语] **1 ~ (of sth/sb/oneself); ~ (that...)** feeling shame, embarrassment, etc about sth/sb or because of one's own actions 感到羞耻; 感到惭愧: *ashamed of her behaviour at the party* 对她在聚会上的行为感到羞耻 ○ *You should be ashamed of yourself for telling such lies.* 你应该为说这些谎话而感到羞耻. ○ *He felt ashamed of having done so little work.* 他因只做了这么一点儿工作而感到惭愧. ○ *I feel ashamed that I haven't written for so long.* 我很久未曾写信, 甚为惭愧. **2 ~ to do sth** reluctant to do sth because of shame or embarrassment 因为羞耻或惭愧而勉强作某事: *I'm ashamed to say I haven't been to church for three years.* 我真不好意思说我已经三年没上教堂了. ○ *He felt too ashamed to ask for help.* 他不好意思请求帮助. ○ *I'm ashamed to let you see my paintings.* 让你看我的画, 很难为情.

ash·en /ˈæʃn; ˋæʃən/ *adj* like ashes in colour; very pale 灰色的; 苍白的: *She listened to the tragic news ashen-faced.* 她听到这一悲惨消息, 脸都白了.

ashes /ˈæʃɪz; ˋæʃɪz/ *n* [pl] **1** powder that remains after sth has been destroyed by burning 灰烬: *Ashes were all that remained of her books after the fire.* 大火过后, 她的书已全部化为灰烬. ○ *The house was burnt to ashes overnight.* 那所房子一夜之间烧成灰烬. Cf 参看 ASH. **2** remains of a human body after cremation 骨灰: *His ashes were buried next to those of his wife.* 他的骨灰埋葬在妻子骨灰的旁边. **3 the Ashes** symbolic trophy won by the winning team after a series of cricket test matches between England and Australia (英国与澳大利亚板球决赛连续获胜队所赢得的象征性的)锦标. **4** (idm 习语) **rake over old ashes** ⇨ RAKE[1]. **sackcloth and ashes** ⇨ SACKCLOTH (SACK[1]).

ashore /əˈʃɔː(r); əˋʃɔr/ *adv* to or on the shore or land 上岸; 上陆; 在岸上; 在陆上: *We went ashore when the boat reached the port.* 船一靠港我们就上岸了. ○ *The ship was driven ashore* (ie forced onto the shore) *by the bad weather.* 天气十分恶劣, 轮船被迫靠岸.

ashy /ˈæʃɪ; ˋæʃɪ/ *adj* of or like ashes; covered with ashes 灰的; 像灰的; 覆盖着灰的: *His face was ashy grey.* 他面如土色.

Asian /ˈeɪʃn; *US* ˈeɪʒn; ˋeʒən/ *n* (person descended from a) native or inhabitant of Asia 亚洲人.

▷ **Asian** *adj* of Asia 亚洲的.

Asi·atic /ˌeɪʃɪˈætɪk; *US* ˌeɪʒɪ-; ˌeʒɪˋætɪk/ *adj* of Asia 亚洲的: *the Asiatic plains* 亚洲的平原.

▷ **Asi·atic** *n* (*offensive* 蔑) Asian person 亚洲人.

aside /əˈsaɪd; əˋsaɪd/ *adv* **1** on or to one side of the main position, direction, etc 在一边; 向一边: *pull the curtain aside* 把帘子拉向一边 ○ *Stand aside and let these people pass.* 靠边站, 让这些人过去. ○ *He took me aside to tell me of his wife's illness.* 他把我拉到一边, 告诉我他妻子病的事. ○ (*fig* 比喻) *You must put aside* (ie out of your thoughts) *any idea of a holiday this year.* 你得把今年要度假的想法撇开. **2** in reserve 留着: *set aside some money for one's retirement* 为退休而存些钱 ○ *Please put this jumper aside* (ie reserve it) *for me.* 请给我留着这件毛衣.

▷ **aside** *n* **1** (in the theatre) words spoken by an actor on stage that are intended to be heard by the audience but not by the other characters on stage 旁白(戏剧角色背着台上其他剧中人对观众所说的话). **2** incidental remark 顺便说的话: *I mention it only as an aside.* 我只是顺便提及此事.

□ **aside from** *prep* (*esp US*) = APART FROM (APART).

as·in·ine /ˈæsɪnaɪn; ˋæsṇˌaɪn/ *adj* stupid or stubborn 愚蠢的; 固执的: *What an asinine thing to say!* 说的话多蠢!

ask /ɑːsk; æsk/ *v* **1** [I, Ipr, Tn, Tn·pr, Tw, Dn·n, Dn·w] **~ (sb) (about sb/sth); ~ sth of sb** request information (about sb/sth) (from sb) 问; 询问: *Ask (him) about the ring you lost — he may have found it.* 问问(他)你丢的戒指——也许他捡到了. ○ *Don't be afraid of asking questions.* 不要怕提问题. ○ *Did you ask the price?* 你问价钱了吗? ○ (*fml* 文) *No questions were asked of us.* 没有人问我们问题. ○ *He asked if I could drive.* 他问我会不会开车. ○ *She asked them their names.* 她问他们的姓名. ○ *I had to ask the teacher what to do next.* 我得问问老师下一步做什么. **2** [Ipr, Tn, Tn·pr, Tw, Dn·w, Dn·t] **~ (sb) for sth; ~ sth (of sb)** request that sb gives sth or does sth 要求某人给某事物或做某事物: *Did you ask (your boss) for a pay increase?* 你请求(老板)加薪了吗? ○ *ask sb's advice, opinion, views, etc* 征询某人的高见、意见、看法等 ○ *If you want to camp in this field you must ask the farmer's permission.* 在这块地上露营要征求农民的许可. ○ *May I ask a favour (of you)?* 能不能(请你)帮我一个忙? ○ *It's asking rather a lot of you to have my whole family to stay.* 我全家在此逗留要打搅您, 未免有些过分了. ○ *She asked (me) if I would drive her home.* 她请求我开车送她回家. ○ *I asked James to buy some bread.* 我叫詹姆斯去买些面包. **3** [Tw, Tt, Dn·w, Dn·t] request permission to do sth 请求准许做某事: *ask to use the car* 请求准许使用汽车 ○ *ask to speak to sb*, eg on the phone 请求准许与某人谈话(如打电话时) ○ *I asked (the doctor) whether/if I could get up.* 我请求(医生)让我下床. ○ *I must ask you to excuse me.* 我得请你原谅. **4** [Tn·pr, Tn·p, Dn·t] **~ sb (to sth)** invite sb 邀请, 请某人: *ask them to dinner* 请他们吃饭 ○ *He's asked me out several times already.* 他已经几次邀请我外出. ○ *Shall we ask the neighbours in/round* (ie to our house)? 咱们把邻居请(到咱家)来好吗? ○ *She's asked him to come to the party.* 她邀请他来参加聚会. **5** [Tn, Tn·pr] **~ sth (for sth)** request sth as a price 要价; 讨价: *You're asking too much.* 你要价太高. ○ *What are they asking for their house?* 他们那所房子要多少钱? ○ *He's asking £80 a month rent for that flat.* 那套房间月租他要80英镑. **6** (idm 习语) ˈ**ask for trouble/it** (*infml* 口) behave in a way that is likely to result in trouble 自找麻烦; 自讨苦吃: *Driving after drinking alcohol is asking for trouble.* 酒后开车是自讨苦吃. **for the ˈasking** if one merely asks 只需开口; 只要索取: *The job is yours for the asking*, ie If you say you want it, it will be given to you. 你一开口就能得到那份工作. **I ˈask you** (*infml* 口) (expressing disbelief, surprise, annoyance, etc 表示怀疑、惊奇、烦恼等): *They're thinking of taxing textbooks — I ask you, we'll have to pay to go to bed next!* 教科书也快要上税了——好傢伙, 眼看连睡觉都得付钱了! **if you ask ˈme** if you would like to know my opinion 如果你想知道我的看法; 恕我直言; 不瞒你说: *If you ask me, he hasn't got long to live.* 恕我直言, 他活不长了. **7** (phr v) **ask after sb** request information about sb's health 问候某人的健康; 问候; 问安: *He always asks after you in his letters.* 他每次来信都向你问候. **ask for sb/sth** say that one wants to see or speak to sb or to be given or directed to sth 要求见某人; 要求与某人谈话; 要某事物; 要求指点: *ask for the manager, the tickets, the bar* 要求见经理; 要票; 询问酒吧地点.

□ ˈ**asking price** price at which sth is offered for sale 要价; 开价; 叫价: *They refused to accept less than the asking price.* 他们言无二价.

NOTE ON USAGE 用法: When making a request for somebody to do something, **ask** is the most usual and informal word 若要某人做某事, **ask**是最通俗、最口语化的词: *I asked her to shut the window.* 我让她关上窗户. ○ *He asked me for a light.* 他向我借个火. The verb **request** is mainly used in formal speech and writing, often in public notices and commonly in the passive form ☆ **request**这一动词主要用于庄重的讲话和文字中, 常用于通告中, 多用于被动式: *Dear Sir, I have been requested to inform you that ...* 敬启者: 兹通知阁下 ... ○ *Passengers are kindly requested not to smoke at the buffet counter.* 乘客请勿在自助餐台附近吸烟. **Beg** suggests the asking of a great favour in a humble manner ☆ **beg** 指以谦恭的姿态要求给予巨大的帮助: *He knew he had hurt her and begged her to forgive him.* 他自知伤了她的心而央求她原谅. **Entreat, implore** and **beseech** are stronger and more formal than **beg** ☆ **entreat**、**implore**、**beseech**三词均比**beg**的词义强而文雅: *He entreated/implored/beseeched her not to desert him.* 他恳求她不要抛弃他.

askance /əˈskæns; əˋskæns/ *adv* (idm 习语) **look**

askance (at sb/sth) look (usu sideways) at sb/sth with distrust or disapproval (因怀疑或不满而)斜着眼睛看某人[某事物]; 侧目而视; 瞟: *look askance at the price* 对那个价钱侧目而视 ○ *She looked at me rather askance when I suggested a swim in the nude.* 我提议裸体游泳, 她就瞟了我一眼.

askew /əˈskjuː; əˋskju/ *adj* [pred 作表语], *adv* not in a straight or level position; crooked(ly) 歪; 斜; 歪斜: *The picture is hanging askew.* 这张画挂歪了. ○ *He's got his hat on askew.* 他歪戴着帽子. ○ *The line is drawn all askew.* 这条线都画斜了.

aslant /əˈslɑːnt; *US* əˈslænt; əˋslænt/ *adv*, *prep* in a slanting direction or obliquely (across) 斜; 倾斜地(跨过): *The evening sunlight shone aslant through the window.* 夕照斜穿入窗. ○ *The wrecked train lay aslant the track.* 失事的火车横在铁轨上.

asleep /əˈsliːp; əˋslip/ *adj* [pred 作表语] **1** not awake; sleeping 睡着; 睡熟: *Don't wake her up — she's fast/sound asleep.* 别吵醒她——她睡得很熟[很香]. ○ *He fell asleep during the sermon.* 他在听讲道时睡着了. **2** (of limbs) having no feeling; numb (指四肢)麻木, 发麻, 麻痹: *I've been sitting on my leg and now it's asleep.* 我把腿坐麻了.

A/S level /eɪ ˈes levl; e ˌɛs lɛvḷ/ (in Britain) GCE examination of a standard between GCSE and Advanced level, allowing students to study more subjects than at Advanced level (英国)程度在普通中等教育证书与高级程度之间的一种普通教育证书考试, 及格者所学科目多于高级程度者.

asp /æsp; æsp/ *n* small poisonous snake found esp in N Africa (尤指北非产的)小毒蛇.

as·par·agus /əˈspærəgəs; əˋspærəgəs/ *n* [U] **(a)** plant with feathery leaves whose young shoots are cooked and eaten as a vegetable 芦笋(石刁柏的通称, 也称龙须菜). **(b)** these shoots 芦笋的嫩茎: *have (some) asparagus for lunch* 午饭有(些)芦笋 ○ [attrib 作定语] *asparagus soup* 芦笋汤.

as·pect /ˈæspekt; ˋæspɛkt/ *n* **1** [C] particular part or feature of sth being considered 方面: *look at every aspect of the problem* 看这问题的各个方面. **2** [sing] (*fml* 文) (esp of people) appearance or look (尤指人)样子, 容貌, 神态: *a man of enormous size and terrifying aspect* 面目狰狞的彪形大汉. **3** [C usu *sing* 通常作单数] side of a building that faces a particular direction (建筑物的)方向, 方位: *The house has a southern aspect.* 这所房子朝南. **4** [C] (in astrology) relative position of stars and planets, thought to influence events on earth 星位(占星术中命星与行星间的相对位置, 认为可影响人间事物). **5** [C] (*grammar*) range of meanings expressed by the verb forms *have* + past participle (eg *has worked*) or *be* + present participle (eg *is working*) 体(动词的语法范畴, 以 have + 过去分词表示, 如 has worked, 或以 be + 现在分词表示, 如 is working).

▷ **as·pect·ual** /æˈspektʃʊəl; æˋspɛktʃuəl/ *adj* (*grammar*) concerned with aspect(5) (动词)体的: *There is an aspectual difference between 'He crossed the road' and 'He was crossing the road'.* He crossed the road 和 He was crossing the road 两句中动词的体是不同的.

as·pen /ˈæspən; ˋæspən/ *n* tree of the poplar family with leaves that flutter even in the slightest wind 白杨.

as·per·ity /æˈsperətɪ; æsˋpɛrətɪ/ *n* (*fml* 文) **1** [U] harshness or severity, esp of manner 粗暴, 粗鲁(尤指态度、举止): *reply with asperity* 粗鲁地回答. **2** [C usu *pl*, U 作可数名词时通常作复数, 亦作不可数名词] (instance of) very cold or severe weather 严寒的天气: *suffer the asperities of winter near the North Pole* 遭受近北极严冬之苦.

as·per·sions /əˈspɜːʃnz; *US* -ʒnz; əˋspɝʒənz/ *n* [pl] (*fml or rhet* 文或修辞) **1** damaging or derogatory remarks 诽谤; 诬蔑: *I strongly resent such unwarranted aspersions.* 我对这种莫须有的诽谤深恶痛绝. **2** (idm 习语) **cast aspersions** ⇨ CAST[1].

as·phalt /ˈæsfælt; *US* -fɔːlt; ˋæsfɔlt/ *n* [U] black sticky substance like coal tar, mixed with sand or gravel for making road surfaces, or used to make roofs, etc waterproof 沥青(通称柏油).

▷ **as·phalt** *v* [Tn] cover (esp a road) with asphalt 以沥青铺(尤指道路).

as·phyxia /əsˈfɪksɪə; *US* æsˈf-; æsˋfɪksɪə/ *n* [U] condition caused by lack of air in the lungs; suffocation 窒息.

▷ **as·phyxi·ate** /əsˈfɪksɪeɪt; əsˋfɪksɪˌet/ *v* [Tn usu passive 通常用于被动语态] cause (sb) to become ill or to die by preventing enough air from reaching the lungs; suffocate 使(某人)窒息而病或死: *asphyxiated by the smoke and poisonous fumes* 被烟和毒气窒息. **as·phyxi·ation** /əsˌfɪksɪˈeɪʃn; əsˌfɪksɪˋeʃən/ *n* [U].

as·pic /ˈæspɪk; ˋæspɪk/ *n* [U] clear meat jelly served with or around meat, fish, eggs, etc (肉类的)冻子: *chicken in aspic* 鸡肉冻子.

as·pi·dis·tra /ˌæspɪˈdɪstrə; ˌæspɪˋdɪstrə/ *n* tall plant with broad pointed leaves, usu grown indoors 蜘蛛抱蛋(一种高大植物, 叶宽而尖, 常为室内盆栽, 别称'一叶').

as·pir·ant /əˈspaɪərənt; əˋspaɪrənt/ *n* **~ (to/after/for sth)** (*fml* 文) person who is ambitious (for fame, promotion, success, etc) 有抱负的人; 有进取心的人: *an aspirant to the presidency* 争当总统的人.

as·pir·ate /ˈæspərət; ˋæspərɪt/ *n* (*phonetics* 语音) sound of 'h' or of a consonant containing it 送气音; 吐气音: *The word 'hour' is pronounced without an initial aspirate.* hour 一字的开头字母 h 不发送气音.

▷ **as·pir·ate** /ˈæspəreɪt; ˋæspəˌret/ *v* [Tn] pronounce (sth) with an 'h' sound 将(某字)发成送气音: *The initial 'h' in 'hour' is not aspirated.* hour 一字中起首的 h 不发送气音.

as·pira·tion /ˌæspəˈreɪʃn; ˌæspəˋreʃən/ *n* **1** [U, C often *pl* 常作复数] **~ (for/after sth); ~ (to do sth)** strong desire or ambition 渴望; 抱负; 志气: *She was filled with the aspiration to succeed in life.* 她渴望有所成就. ○ *He has serious aspirations to a career in politics.* 他有从政的雄心壮志. **2** [U] aspirating 发送气音.

as·pire /əˈspaɪə(r); əˋspaɪr/ *v* [Ipr, It] **~ after/to sth** desire strongly to achieve sth; have ambition for sth 渴望成就某事物; 对某事物有雄心或野心: *aspire after knowledge* 渴求知识 ○ *aspire to become an author* 热望成为作家 ○ *Aspiring musicians must practise many hours a day.* 有抱负的音乐家每天要练习很多小时.

as·pirin /ˈæsprɪn, ˈæspərɪn; ˋæspərɪn/ *n* **(a)** [U] medicine used to relieve pain and reduce fever 阿司匹林(镇痛解热药): *Have you got any aspirin?* 你有阿司匹林吗? **(b)** [C] tablet(2) of this 阿司匹林药片: *Take two aspirins for your headache.* 你头疼吃两片阿司匹林吧.

ass[1] /æs; æs/ *n* **1** (also **donkey**) animal related to the horse, with long ears and a tuft at the end of its tail 驴. **2** (*infml* 口) stupid person 傻瓜; 笨蛋: *Don't be such an ass!* 别这么傻了! **3** (idm 习语) **make an ˈass of oneself** behave stupidly so that one appears ridiculous 出洋相; 干傻事: *I made a real ass of myself at the meeting — standing up and then forgetting the question.* 我在会上真出了洋相了——一站起来就把问题忘了.

ass[2] /æs; æs/ *n* (⚠ *US sl* 讳, 俚) **1** [C] = ARSE. **2** [U] sexual intercourse 性交.

as·sail /əˈseɪl; əˋsel/ *v* [Tn, Tn·pr] **~ sb (with sth)** (*fml* 文) attack sb violently or repeatedly 猛击, 痛打, 攻击某人: *assailed with fierce blows to the head* 殴打头部 ○ *assail sb with questions, insults, etc* 对某人质问、侮辱等 ○ *assailed by worries, doubts, fears, etc* 饱受烦恼、疑惑、恐惧等折磨.

▷ **as·sail·ant** *n* (*fml* 文) person who attacks 攻击者: *He was unable to recognize his assailant in the dark.* 他在黑暗中认不出殴打他的人.

as·sas·sin /əˈsæsɪn; *US* -sn; əˋsæsṇ/ *n* killer, esp one who kills an important or famous person for money or for political reasons 暗杀者, 行刺者(尤指为金钱或政治目的而杀害要人或名人者).

as·sas·sin·ate /əˈsæsɪneɪt; *US* -sən-; əˋsæsṇˌet/ *v* [Tn] kill (esp an important or famous person) for money or for political reasons 暗杀, 行刺(尤指为金钱或政治目的而杀害要人或名人).

▷ **as·sas·sina·tion** /əˌsæsɪˈneɪʃn; *US* -səˈneɪʃn; əˌsæsṇˋeʃən/ *n* **(a)** [U] murder of this kind 暗杀; 行刺. **(b)** [C] instance of this 暗杀; 行刺.

as·sault /əˈsɔːlt; əˋsɔlt/ *n* [C, U] **~ (on sth)** sudden violent attack 突然而猛烈的攻击; 突袭; 突击: *make an assault on the enemy lines* 突袭敌军阵线 ○ *The roar of city traffic is a steady assault on one's nerves.* 市区车辆的喧嚣声不停地刺激着神经. ○ *an alarming increase in cases of indecent assault*, eg rape 强奸猥亵案件惊人的增加.

A

▷ **as·sault** *v* [Tn] make an assault on (sb) 突袭; 突击: *He got two years' imprisonment for assaulting a police officer.* 他因袭击警察而遭两年监禁. ○ *Six women have been sexually assaulted in the area recently.* 最近这一带有六个女子遭受强奸猥亵.

□ **as,sault and 'battery** (*law* 律) violent physical attack on sb 殴打.

as'sault craft portable boat with an outboard motor, used for making attacks across rivers, etc 突击艇(发动机装于船外的一种轻便船, 在渡河等突击时使用).

as·say /əˈseɪ; əˋse/ *n* testing of esp metals for quality 试验、测定、鉴定(尤指对金属质量): *make an assay of an ore* 对一矿石作试验鉴定.

▷ **as·say** *v* **1** [Tn] test the quality of (a metal); analyse (eg an ore) 测定(金属)的质量; 分析(如矿石). **2** [Tn, Tt] (*arch* 古) attempt (esp sth difficult) 尝试(尤指困难事物).

as·se·gai /ˈæsəgaɪ; ˋæsə,gaɪ/ *n* light iron-tipped throwing-spear used by S African tribes (南非部族使用的)铁尖轻标枪.

as·sem·blage /əˈsemblɪdʒ; əˋsɛmblɪdʒ/ *n* **1** [U] (*fml* 文) act of bringing or coming together; assembly 集合; 组合; 装配. **2** [C] (*often joc* 常作戏谑语) collection of things or people 聚集的物或人: *an odd assemblage of broken bits of furniture* 一堆奇形怪状的破烂家具.

as·semble /əˈsembl; əˋsɛmbl̩/ *v* **1** [I, Tn] (cause people or things to) come together; collect 集合; 聚集; 收集: *The whole school (was) assembled in the main hall.* 全校在大礼堂集合. ○ *assemble evidence, material, equipment, a collection of objects* 收集证据、材料、设备、物品. **2** [Tn] fit together (the parts of sth) 装配; 安装: *assemble the parts of a watch* 装配表的零件 ○ *The bookcase can easily be assembled with a screwdriver.* 这书柜用一把螺丝刀就可以很容易地安装起来.

as·sem·bly /əˈsemblɪ; əˋsɛmblɪ/ *n* **1** (**a**) [U] coming together of a group of people for a specific purpose 集合; 集会: *Morning assembly is held in the school hall.* 晨会在学校礼堂举行. ○ *deny sb the right of assembly* 不予某人集会的权利 ○ [attrib 作定语] *assembly rooms* 会议室. (**b**) [CGp] group of people in such a meeting 集合的人们; 参加集会的人们: *The motion was put to the assembly.* 这项动议已提交给大会了. ○ *The national assembly has/have met to discuss the crisis.* 国民大会已对这一危机进行了讨论. ○ *the legislative assemblies of the USA* 美国各州的两院制议会. **2** (**a**) [U] act or process of fitting together the parts of sth 装配; 安装: *The assembly of cars is often done by machines.* 汽车常由机器装配. ○ *Each component is carefully checked before assembly.* 每个零件在装配前都经过仔细检查. ○ [attrib 作定语] *an assembly plant*, eg in a factory 装配车间(如工厂中者). (**b**) [C] unit consisting of smaller manufactured parts that have been fitted together 装配组件: *the tail assembly of an aircraft* 飞机的机尾装配组件. **3** [C] sound of a drum or bugle calling soldiers to assemble (军队的)集合鼓, 集合号.

□ **as'sembly line** sequence of machines and workers along which a product moves as it is assembled in stages 装配线: *He works on the assembly line at the local car factory.* 他在本地汽车制造厂装配线上工作.

as·sent /əˈsent; əˋsɛnt/ *n* [U] **~ (to sth)** (*fml* 文) agreement; approval 同意; 赞成: *give one's assent to a proposal* 对建议表示同意 ○ *by common assent*, ie with everybody's agreement 一致同意 ○ *The new bill passed by Parliament has received the royal assent*, ie been approved by the monarch. 议会所通过的新法案已获国王批准.

▷ **as·sent** *v* [I, Ipr] **~ (to sth)** express agreement; consent 同意; 赞成: *I can never assent to such a request.* 我决不能同意这种要求.

as·sert /əˈsɜːt; əˋsɝt/ *v* **1** [Tn] (**a**) make others recognize (sth) by behaving firmly and confidently 坚定而有信心地使别人认识到(某事物); 坚持: *assert one's authority, independence, rights* 坚持自己的权威性、独立性、权利. (**b**) **~ oneself** behave in a confident manner that attracts attention and respect 表现出自信而受到注意和尊重: *You're too timid — you must try to assert yourself more.* 你太畏缩了——要尽量增强自信心. **2** [Tn, Tf] state (sth) clearly and forcefully as the truth 清楚而有力地表明(某事物)为事实; 声称; 断言: *She asserted her innocence/that she was innocent.* 她坚称自己很清白[她是无辜的].

as·ser·tion /əˈsɜːʃn; əˋsɝʃən/ *n* **1** [U] action of claiming or stating forcefully; insistence 有力的声言或陈词; 坚持: *assertion of one's authority* 对自己权威的维护 ○ *an air of self-assertion* 坚持己见的姿态 ○ *speak with assertion* 坚定地说. **2** [C] strong statement claiming the truth of sth (声称某事物属实的)强硬陈词; 断言: *I seriously question a number of your assertions.* 对你所坚持的说法, 有几点我甚为怀疑.

as·sert·ive /əˈsɜːtɪv; əˋsɝtɪv/ *adj* showing a strong and confident personality; asserting oneself 表现出刚毅与自信性格的; 坚定而自信的: *an assertive young man* 有自信心的年轻人 ○ *state one's opinions in an assertive tone of voice* 以坚定自信的语气表达自己的意见. ▷ **as·sert·ively** *adv*. **as·sert·ive·ness** *n* [U].

as·sess /əˈses; əˋsɛs/ *v* **1** [Tn, Tn·pr] **~ sth (at sth)** decide or fix the amount of sth 确定, 评定(某数额): *assess sb's taxes/income* 评定某人的税额[总收入] ○ *assess the damage at £350* 评定损害赔偿金为350英镑. **2** [Tn] decide or fix the value of (sth); evaluate 确定, 评定(某事物)的价值; 估价: *have a house assessed by a valuer* 由估价者给房子估价. **3** [Tn, Cn·n/a] **~ sth (as sth)** estimate the quality of sth 估计、评定某事物的质量: *It's difficult to assess the impact of the President's speech.* 总统讲话的巨大影响很难估计. ○ *I'd assess your chances as extremely low.* 我估计你成功的机会极微.

▷ **as·sess·ment** *n* **1** (**a**) [U] action of assessing 确定; 评定: *Continuous assessment is made of all students' work.* 对全体学生的功课作出连贯性的评定. (**b**) [C] evaluation or opinion 评价; 看法: *What is your assessment of the situation?* 你对这一情况有什么看法? **2** [C] amount fixed for payment 核定的付款额: *a tax assessment* 税款核定额.

as·ses·sor *n* **1** person who assesses taxes or the value of property, etc (评定税款或财产价值等的)评税员, 估价员. **2** person who advises a judge in court on technical matters 陪审法官(法庭技术顾问).

as·set /ˈæset; ˋæsɛt/ *n* **1 ~ (to sb/sth)** (**a**) valuable or useful quality or skill 有价值的或有用的特性或技能: *Good health is a great asset.* 健康就是莫大的财富. (**b**) valuable or useful person 有价值的或有用的人: *He's an enormous asset to the team.* 他是队里的骨干. **2** (usu *pl* 通常作复数) thing, esp property, owned by a person, company, etc that has value and can be used or sold to pay debts (属于个人或公司所有, 可用以抵偿债务或变卖后支付债务的)财产, 资产: *His assets included shares in the company and a house in London.* 他的财产包括公司的股票和位于伦敦的房子. Cf 参看 LIABILITY.

□ **'asset-stripping** *n* [U] (*commerce* 商) practice of buying at a cheap price a company with financial difficulties and then selling its assets individually to make a profit 资产倒卖(廉价收买经济上有困难的公司, 然后将其资产逐一变卖获利的做法).

as·sev·er·ate /əˈsevəreɪt; əˋsɛvə,ret/ *v* [Tn, Tf] (*fml* 文) state (sth) firmly and solemnly (坚定而郑重地)宣称, 陈词, 断言: *asseverate one's innocence/that one is innocent* 坚称自己很清白[自己是无辜的]. ▷ **as·sev·era·tion** /ə,sevəˈreɪʃn; ə,sɛvəˋreʃən/ *n* [U, C].

as·si·du·ity /,æsɪˈdjuːətɪ; *US* -duː-; ,æsəˋduətɪ/ *n* [U] (*fml* 文) constant and careful attention to a task 专心致志; 勤勉: *He shows great assiduity in all his work.* 他对所有工作都兢兢业业.

as·sidu·ous /əˈsɪdjʊəs; *US* -dʒʊəs; əˋsɪdʒʊəs/ *adj* (*fml* 文) showing constant and careful attention 专心致志的; 勤勉的: *be assiduous in one's duties* 认真执行任务 ○ *The book was the result of ten years' assiduous research.* 那本书是十年苦心钻研的成果. ▷ **as·sidu·ously** *adv*.

as·sign /əˈsaɪn; əˋsaɪn/ *v* **1** [Dn·n, Dn·pr] **~ sth to sb** give sth to sb as a share of work to be done or of things to be used 分配给某人一部分工作去做或一份东西去使用: *The teacher has assigned each of us a holiday task.* 教师给我们每个人都分配了假日的工作. ○ *The two large classrooms have been assigned to us.* 这两间大教室已经分配给我们了. **2** [Tn·pr, Tnt] **~ sb to sth** name sb for a task or position; appoint sb 指定某人做一工作或任一职务; 委派, 选派某人: *They've assigned their best man to the job.* 他们选派了最合适的人做那项工作. ○ *One of the members was assigned to take the minutes.* 其

中的一个成员被指定作记录. **3** [Tn·pr, Cn·n/a] name or fix (a time, place, reason, etc for sth) 指定(时间、地点); 确定(原因): *Shall we assign Thursdays for our weekly meetings?* 我们把每周例会定在星期四好吗? ○ *It is impossible to assign an exact date to this building.* 确定这座建筑物的确切年代是不可能的. ○ *Can we assign jealousy as the motive for the crime?* 我们能否确定这一犯罪动机是出于嫉妒? **4** [Tn·pr] **~ sth to sb** (*law* 律) transfer (property, rights, etc) to sb 将(财产、权利等)转让予某人; 过户予某人.

▷ **as·sign·able** *adj* that can be assigned 可指定的; 可委派的; 可归因的; 可转让的.

as·sign·ment *n* **1** [C] task or duty that is assigned to sb 指定给某人的任务或职责: *Your next assignment will be to find these missing persons.* 你的下一项任务是寻找这些失踪的人. ○ *She was sent abroad on a difficult assignment.* 她被派出国执行一项艰巨任务. **2** [U] act of assigning (esp property, rights, etc) 转让(尤指财产、权利等): *a deed of assignment* 转让契约.

as·sig·na·tion /ˌæsɪɡˈneɪʃn; ˌæsɪɡˈneʃən/ *n* (*fml or rhet* 文或修辞) arrangement to meet sb, esp secretly or illicitly 约会, 幽会(尤指秘密的或不正当的): *an assignation with a lover* 与情人的幽会.

as·sim·il·ate /əˈsɪməleɪt; əˈsɪmlˌet/ *v* **1** [I, Tn] (**a**) (cause sth to) become absorbed into the body after digestion (使某物)经消化而吸收: *Some foods assimilate/are assimilated more easily than others.* 有些食物比另一些食物容易吸收. (**b**) (allow sb/sth to) become part of another social group or state (让某人[某事物])同化: *The USA has assimilated people from many different countries.* 美国同化了来自许多国家的人. **2** [Tn] absorb (ideas, knowledge, etc) in the mind 吸收(思想、知识等): *Children in school are expected to assimilate what they have been taught.* 希望在学的儿童能吸收教给他们的知识. **3** [Tn·pr esp passive 尤用于被动语态] **~ sth to sth** make sth similar to sth 使某事物与另一事物相似.

▷ **as·sim·ila·tion** /əˌsɪməˈleɪʃn; əˌsɪmlˈeʃən/ *n* [U] **1** process of assimilating or being assimilated (被)吸收或同化的过程. **2** (*phonetics* 语音) change in a speech sound when it becomes similar to another speech sound next to it 同化(一个语音受相邻语音影响而产生与之相同或相似的变化).

as·sist /əˈsɪst; əˈsɪst/ *v* **1** [I, Ipr, Tn, Tn·pr, Tnt] **~ (sb) in/with sth; ~ (sb) in doing sth** (*fml* 文) help 帮助; 援助; 协助: *The head teacher's deputy assists with many of his duties.* 副校长帮助校长做很多工作. ○ *Two men are assisting the police in their enquiries*, ie are answering questions which may lead to their arrest as suspected criminals or help the police find other suspects. 有两个人正在协助警方进行对他们的询问(回答涉嫌犯罪的问题从而将之逮捕或协助警方追查其他疑犯). ○ *You will be required to assist Mrs Smith in preparing a report.* 你将要协助史密斯夫人准备一份报告. **2** [Ipr] **~ at/in sth** (*fml* 文) be present at or take part in sth 在某场合出席; 参加某事物: *assist at the ceremony* 参加仪式.

▷ **as·sist·ance** *n* [U] (*fml* 文) help 帮助; 援助; 帮忙: *Please call if you require assistance.* 如果需要帮忙, 请打电话. ○ *Can I be of any assistance, sir?* 我能帮点儿忙吗, 先生? ○ *Despite his cries no one came to his assistance.* 尽管他大声喊叫, 却没有人来帮助他. ○ *I can't move this piano without assistance.* 没有人帮忙, 我可挪不动这架钢琴.

as·sist·ant *n* **1** person who helps 助手; 助理: *My assistant will operate the tape-recorder.* 我的助手将操纵录音机. **2** person who serves customers in a shop 店员. — *adj* [attrib 作定语] (*abbr* 缩写 **asst**) helping, and ranking next below, a senior person 助理的: *the assistant manager* 协理; 襄理; 副经理 ○ *a senior assistant master*, ie in a school (男)高级助理教师.

as·size /əˈsaɪz; əˈsaɪz/ *n* [C usu *pl*, U 作可数名词时通常作复数, 亦作不可数名词] (formerly) lawcourt session held periodically in each county of England and Wales for trying civil and criminal cases 巡回审判(旧时英国高等法院在英格兰和威尔士各郡举行的定期庭审, 审理民事与刑事案件): *courts of assize* 巡回审判法庭.

Assoc (also **assoc**) *abbr* 缩写 = associate(d); association.

as·so·ci·ate[1] /əˈsəʊʃɪət; əˈsoʃɪət/ *adj* [attrib 作定语] **1** joined or allied with a profession or organization (与某职业或组织)联合的, 联盟的, 合伙的: *an associate judge* 陪审法官 ○ *the associate producer of a film* 联合制片人. **2** having a lower level of membership than full members 准的(会员): *Associate members do not have the right to vote.* 准会员没有选举权.

▷ **as·so·ci·ate** *n* **1** partner; colleague; companion 合伙人; 同事; 伙伴: *one's business associates* 业务合伙人 ○ *They are associates in crime.* 他们是共犯. **2** associate member 准会员.

as·so·ci·ate[2] /əˈsəʊʃɪeɪt; əˈsoʃɪˌet/ *v* **1** [Tn, Tn·pr] **~ sb/sth (with sb/sth)** join (people or things) together; connect (ideas, etc) in one's mind 将(人或事物)联系起来; 在头脑中联想(主意等): *You wouldn't normally associate these two writers — their styles are completely different.* 通常不会把这两位作家相提并论——他们两人的风格完全不同. ○ *Whisky is usually associated with Scotland.* 人们常把威士忌同苏格兰联系起来. ○ *I always associate him with fast cars.* 我总是由他联想到高速汽车. **2** [Ipr] **~ with sb** act together with or often deal with sb 与某人交往或常打交道: *I don't like you associating with such people.* 我不喜欢你和那些人混在一起. **3** [Tn·pr] **~ oneself with sth** declare or show that one is in agreement with sth 声称或表示自己赞同某事物: *I have never associated myself with political extremism.* 我从来不赞同政治上的极端主义.

as·so·ci·ation /əˌsəʊsɪˈeɪʃn; əˌsosɪˈeʃən/ *n* **1** [U] (**a**) **~ (with sb/sth)** action of associating or being associated 联合; 联系; 联盟; 合伙: *His English improved enormously because of his association with British people.* 因为他和英国人有来往, 所以他的英语突飞猛进. ○ *There has always been a close association between these two schools.* 这两所学校一向有密切联系. ○ *We are working in association with a number of local companies to raise money for the homeless.* 我们与本地一些公司联合为无家可归的人筹款. (**b**) being in sb's company; friendship 与某人为伍; 友谊; 友情; 交往: *She became famous through her association with several poets.* 她通过与几位诗人的交往而出名了. **2** [C] mental connection between ideas 联想: *What associations does the sea have for you?* 你从大海能联想到什么? **3** [C] group of people joined together for a common purpose; organization 社团; 协会; 学会: *Do you belong to any professional associations?* 你是哪个专业学会的?

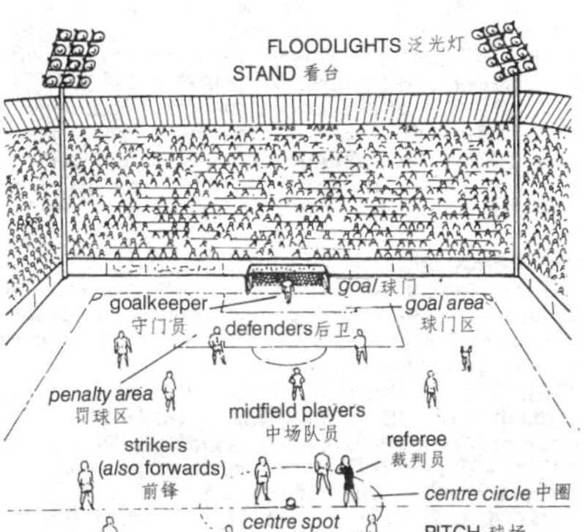

Association football 英式足球

□ **Asˌsociation ˈfootball** (also **football, soccer**) form of football played by two teams of eleven players, using a round ball that must not be handled during play except by the goalkeeper (英式)足球.

as·son·ance /ˈæsənəns; ˈæsənəns/ *n* [U] (rhyme that depends on the) similarity between the vowel sounds only or the consonant sounds only of two words or syllables, as in *sharper* and *garter* or *killed* and *cold* 半谐音(两个词或音节的元音类似或辅音类似, 如 sharper

和 garter 或 killed 和 cold).

A

as·sort·ed /əˈsɔːtɪd; əˈsɔrtɪd/ *adj* of different sorts; mixed 各种各样的; 混杂的; 什锦的: *a tin of assorted biscuits* 一罐什锦饼干.

▷ **as·sort·ment** /əˈsɔːtmənt; əˈsɔrtmənt/ *n* collection of different things or of different types of the same thing; mixture 各类物品或同类各种物品的聚集; 混合物: *a wide assortment of gifts to choose from* 各式各样的礼品可供选择 ○ *wearing an odd assortment of clothes* 穿着奇装异服.

Asst (also **asst**) *abbr* 缩写 = assistant: *Asst Sec* 部长助理.

as·suage /əˈsweɪdʒ; əˈswedʒ/ *v* [Tn] (*fml* 文) make (sth) less severe; soothe 减轻; 缓和; 平息: *assuage one's hunger, thirst, grief, longing, etc* 充饥、解渴、减轻悲痛、抑制欲念.

as·sume /əˈsjuːm; *US* əˈsuːm; əˈsum/ *v* **1** [Tn, Tf, Tnt] accept (sth) as true before there is proof 假定; 假设; 设想; 以为: *We cannot assume anything in this case.* 在这种情形下我们无法作任何揣测. ○ *I am assuming that the present situation is going to continue.* 我认为目前的情况将会继续下去. ○ *We must assume him to be innocent until he is proved guilty.* 尚未证实他有罪, 就得假定他是清白的. ○ *We can all leave together — assuming (that) the others aren't late.* 我们大家可以一起走——假定其他人不耽搁的话. **2** [Tn] put on or display (sth) falsely; pretend 装作; 装出; 假装: *assume ignorance, indifference, an air of concern, etc* 假装不知情、装作不在乎、假意关心等 ○ *The look of innocence she assumed had us all fooled.* 她装出清白无辜的样子把我们都愚弄了. **3** [Tn] begin to act in or exercise (sth); undertake; take on 开始从事; 承担; 担任; 呈: *assume office* 就职 ○ *He assumes his new responsibilities next month.* 他下月承担新任务. ○ *The problem is beginning to assume massive proportions*, ie become very great. 问题越来越大了.

▷ **as·sumed** *adj* [attrib 作定语] pretended; false 假装的; 假的: *living under an assumed name* 使用假名字活着.

as·sump·tion /əˈsʌmpʃn; əˈsʌmpʃən/ *n* **1** [C] thing accepted as true or as sure to happen, but not proved 假定; 假设; 设想: *The theory is based on a series of wrong assumptions.* 这一理论是以一系列错误的设想为根据的. ○ *We are working on the assumption that the rate of inflation will not increase next year.* 我们在假定明年通货膨胀率不增加的情况下工作. **2** [U] **~ of sth** act of displaying (insincere feelings, etc) 显示出(假情假意等)的行动; 假装: *Their assumption of an air of confidence fooled nobody.* 他们装出信心十足的样子却欺骗不了任何人. **3** [C] **~ of sth** act of taking on (a position, etc) 承担, 担任(职务等): *her assumption of supreme power* 她掌大权. **4 the Assumption** [sing] **(a)** the taking of the Virgin Mary into Heaven in bodily form 圣母升天. **(b)** festival on 15 August celebrating this 圣母升天节(8月15日).

as·sur·ance /əˈʃɔːrəns; *US* əˈʃʊərəns; əˈʃurəns/ *n* **1** (also **self-assurance**) [U] confident belief in one's own abilities and powers 自信; 把握: *act with, display, possess assurance* 有把握、有信心、胸有成竹 ○ *She shows remarkable assurance on stage for one so young.* 她小小年纪, 在台上却泰然自若. **2** [C] statement expressing certainty about sth; promise 保证; 担保: *He gave me an assurance that it would be ready by Friday.* 他向我保证星期五一定准备好. ○ *Despite repeated assurances he failed to repay the money he had borrowed.* 他尽管再三保证, 但是借去的钱却始终没还. **3** [U] (*esp Brit*) insurance, esp on sb's life 保险(尤指人寿): *a life assurance policy* 人寿保险单.

as·sure /əˈʃɔː(r); *US* əˈʃʊər; əˈʃur/ *v* **1 (a)** [Dn·f] tell (sb) positively or confidently 明确地或有信心地告诉(某人); 向(某人)保证: *I assure you they'll be perfectly safe with us.* 我向你保证, 他们和我们在一起十分安全. ○ *They were assured that everything possible was being done.* 已经向他们保证, 凡是可能做的都做到了. **(b)** [Tn·pr, Dn·f] **~ sb/oneself (of sth)** cause sb/oneself to be sure or feel certain about sth 使某人[自己]对某事物确信不疑或觉得肯定无误: *They tried to assure him of their willingness to work.* 他们尽力使他相信他们乐意工作. ○ *She was able to assure herself that nothing had been taken from her purse.* 她确信钱包里什么东西都没被拿走. **2** [Tn] make (sth) certain; ensure 使(某事物)确定; 确保: *Her success as an actress was now assured.* 她当演员很成功, 已毋庸置疑了. **3** [Tn] insure (sth), esp against sb's death 给(某事物)保险(尤指寿险): *What is the sum assured?* 人寿保险额是多少? **4** (idm 习语) **rest assured** ⇨ REST[1].

▷ **as·sured** (also **self-assured**) *adj* confident 自信的; 有把握的: *His public speaking manner is still not very assured.* 他演讲的神态还显出有点缺乏自信.

as·suredly /əˈʃɔːrɪdlɪ; *US* əˈʃʊərədlɪ; əˈʃurɪdlɪ/ *adv* (*arch* 古) certainly 确定地; 肯定地.

the as·sured *n* (*pl* unchanged 复数不变) person who has an assurance policy on his life 已保寿险的人.

AST /ˌeɪ es ˈtiː; ˌe ɛs ˈti/ *abbr* 缩写 = (in Canada) Atlantic Standard Time (用于加拿大)大西洋标准时间.

astat·ine /ˈæstətiːn; ˈæstəˌtin/ *n* [U] (*chemistry* 化) artificial radioactive element 砹(人工放射性元素). ⇨ App 10 见附录 10.

as·ter /ˈæstə(r); ˈæstɚ/ *n* garden plant similar to the daisy with flowers that have a yellow centre and white, pink or purple petals 紫菀(雏菊状园艺植物, 花中央呈黄色, 花瓣为白色、粉红色或紫色).

as·ter·isk /ˈæstərɪsk; ˈæstəˌrɪsk/ *n* star-shaped symbol (*) used in writing and printing to call attention to sth, eg a footnote, or to show that letters are omitted, as in *Mr J*n*s* for *Mr Jones* 星号(即 *, 用于书写及印刷中以引起注意, 例如有脚注或有省略的字母, 如以 Mr J*n*s 代表 Mr Jones).

▷ **as·ter·isk** *v* [Tn] mark (a word, phrase, etc) with an asterisk 用星号标出(词语等): *The asterisked questions may be omitted.* 带星号的问题可以略去.

astern /əˈstɜːn; əˈstɝn/ *adv* **1** in, at or towards the stern of a ship or the tail of an aircraft 在或向船或飞行器的尾部. **2** (of a ship) backwards (指船)向后: *Full speed astern!* 全速后退!

□ **astern of** *prep* behind (another ship) 在(另一船)的后面: *They fell astern of us*, ie moved into position behind us. 他们落在我们船的后面.

as·ter·oid /ˈæstərɔɪd; ˈæstəˌrɔɪd/ *n* any of many small planets revolving round the sun, esp between the orbits of Mars and Jupiter (尤指火星和木星轨道间运行的)小行星.

asthma /ˈæsmə; *US* ˈæzmə; ˈæzmə/ *n* [U] chronic chest illness causing wheezing and difficulty in breathing 气喘; 哮喘.

▷ **asth·matic** /æsˈmætɪk; *US* æz-; æzˈmætɪk/ *adj* of or suffering from asthma 气喘的; 患气喘病的: *asthmatic pains* 气喘疼痛 ○ *an asthmatic child* 患气喘病的儿童. — *n* person suffering from asthma 气喘病患者.

astig·mat·ism /əˈstɪgmətɪzəm; əˈstɪgməˌtɪzəm/ *n* [U] defect in an eye or a lens that prevents correct focusing (眼睛)散光, 乱视; (透镜)象散性, 象散现象. ▷ **astig·matic** /ˌæstɪgˈmætɪk; ˌæstɪgˈmætɪk/ *adj*.

astir /əˈstɜː(r); əˈstɝ/ *adv, adj* [pred 作表语] **1** in a state of excited movement 处于激动状态: *News of the Queen's visit set the whole town astir.* 女王到访的消息轰动全城. **2** (*dated* 旧) out of bed 起床: *He's never astir before 10 o'clock.* 他从不在 10 点钟以前起床.

as·ton·ish /əˈstɒnɪʃ; əˈstɑnɪʃ/ *v* [Tn] surprise (sb) greatly 使(某人)惊讶, 吃惊, 震惊: *The news astonished everyone.* 这消息使大家感到惊讶. ○ *It astonishes me that no one has thought of this before.* 以前谁也没想到这一点, 使我感到惊讶. ○ *He was astonished to hear he had got the job.* 他听到获得了那份工作而感到惊讶.

▷ **as·ton·ished** *adj* [usu pred 通常作表语] very surprised 感到惊讶; 吃惊: *She looked astonished when she heard the news.* 她听到那消息显得很吃惊.

as·ton·ish·ing *adj* very surprising 使人惊讶的; 惊人的: *I find it quite astonishing that none of you liked the play.* 我感到惊讶的是你们谁都不喜欢那个剧. ○ *There were an astonishing number of applicants for the job.* 申请这份工作的人数多得惊人. **as·ton·ish·ingly** *adv*.

as·ton·ish·ment *n* [U] great surprise 惊讶; 惊奇: *Imagine my astonishment when Peter walked in!* 你可以想像, 当彼得进来的时候, 我是多么惊奇. ○ *To my astonishment it had completely disappeared.* 使我惊讶的是, 它消失得无影无踪了. ○ *He looked at me in astonishment.* 他惊奇地看着我.

astound /əˈstaʊnd; əˈstaund/ *v* [Tn usu passive 通常用

于被动语态] overcome (sb) with surprise or shock; amaze 使震惊; 使大吃一惊; 使惊奇: *We were astounded to read your letter.* 我们看了你的信大吃一惊.

▷ **astound·ing** *adj* amazing 使人震惊的: *The figures revealed by the report are astounding.* 这份报告透露的数字使人震惊.

as·tra·khan /ˌæstrəˈkæn; *US* ˈæstrəkən; ˋæstrəkən/ *n* [U] (**a**) skin of young lambs with tightly-curled wool 阿斯特拉罕羔皮; 俄国羔皮 (**b**) material imitating this 仿羔皮的织物: [attrib 作定语] *an astrakhan hat* 阿斯特拉罕羔皮帽.

as·tral /ˈæstrəl; ˋæstrəl/ *adj* [usu attrib 通常作定语] of or from the stars 星的; 从星球来的: *an astral body* 星星 ○ *astral beams* 星光.

astray /əˈstreɪ; əˋstre/ *adv* **1** away from the right path or direction 歧途; 迷路: *The misleading sign led me astray.* 那个标志误人使我迷了路. ○ (*fig* 比喻) *He had been led astray by undesirable friends.* 他被损友引入歧途. **2** (idm 习语) **go aˈstray** become mislaid 误置; 被放错地方: *Have you seen my book? It seems to have gone astray.* 你看见我的书了吗? 不知道搁哪儿了.

astride /əˈstraɪd; əˋstraɪd/ *adv* **1** with one leg on each side 跨着地; 骑着地: *Ladies ride horses by sitting astride or side-saddle.* 女子骑马可以跨骑也可以坐横鞍. **2** with legs wide apart 双腿劈得很大.

▷ **astride** *prep* with one leg on each side of (sth) 跨着; 骑着: *sitting astride a horse, a gate, sb's knee* 骑在马上、大门上、某人的膝上.

astrin·gent /əˈstrɪndʒənt; əˋstrɪndʒənt/ *n* substance, used medically or in cosmetics, that makes skin or body tissue contract and so stops bleeding 收敛剂; 止血药.

▷ **astrin·gent** *adj* **1** of or having the effect of an astringent; styptic 收敛的; 止血的. **2** (*fig* 比喻) harsh; severe 严厉的; 严酷的: *astringent criticism* 严厉的批评. **astrin·gency** /əˈstrɪndʒənsɪ; əˋstrɪndʒənsɪ/ *n* [U].

astro- *comb form* 构词成分 of the stars or outer space 星的; 外太空的: *astronaut* ○ *astrology.*

as·tro·labe /ˈæstrəleɪb; ˋæstrə,leb/ *n* (formerly) instrument used for measuring the altitude of the sun, stars, etc 星盘(旧时用以测量太阳、星星等的高度的仪器).

as·tro·logy /əˈstrɒlədʒɪ; əˋstrɑlədʒɪ/ *n* [U] study of the positions of the stars and movements of the planets in the belief that they influence human affairs 占星术(对命星位置和行星运行的研究, 认为可影响人类事务). Cf 参看 HOROSCOPE, ZODIAC.

▷ **as·tro·lo·ger** /-dʒə(r); -dʒɚ/ *n* person who is an expert in astrology 占星家.

as·tro·lo·gical /ˌæstrəˈlɒdʒɪkl; ,æstrəˋlɑdʒɪkḷ/ *adj.*

as·tro·naut /ˈæstrənɔːt; ˋæstrə,nɔt/ *n* person who travels in a spacecraft 宇航员; 航天员; 太空人: *a rocket manned by trained astronauts* 载有受过训练的宇航员的火箭.

▷ **as·tro·naut·ics** /ˌæstrəˈnɔːtɪks; ,æstrəˋnɔtɪks/ *n* [sing *v*] science and technology of space travel 航天学; 太空飞行学.

as·tro·nomy /əˈstrɒnəmɪ; əˋstrɑnəmɪ/ *n* [U] scientific study of the sun, moon, stars, planets, etc 天文学.

▷ **as·tro·nomer** /-nəmə(r); -nəmɚ/ *n* person who studies or is an expert in astronomy 天文学者; 天文学家.

as·tro·nom·ical /ˌæstrəˈnɒmɪkl; ,æstrəˋnɑmɪkḷ/ *adj* **1** of astronomy 天文学的. **2** (*infml* 口) very large in amount, size, etc 极大的; 庞大的: *He's been offered an astronomical salary.* 有人出巨额薪水聘请他.

as·tro·phys·ics /ˌæstrəʊˈfɪzɪks; ,æstroˋfɪzɪks/ *n* [sing *v*] branch of astronomy dealing with the physics and chemistry of the stars, planets, etc 天体物理学.

as·tute /əˈstjuːt; *US* əˈstuːt; əˋstut/ *adj* clever and quick at seeing how to gain an advantage; shrewd 精明的; 机敏的; 狡诈的: *an astute lawyer, businessman, judge of character, etc* 干练的律师、精明的商人、知人之明 ○ *It was an astute move to sell just before prices went down.* 正好在价格下跌前脱手, 真是精明之举. ▷ **as·tutely** *adv.* **as·tute·ness** *n* [U].

asun·der /əˈsʌndə(r); əˋsʌndɚ/ *adv* (*dated or fml* 旧或文) into pieces; apart 碎; 散: *families torn asunder by the war* 被这场战争拆散的家庭 ○ *The house was ripped asunder by the explosion.* 房子被炸得粉碎.

asy·lum /əˈsaɪləm; əˋsaɪləm/ *n* **1** (**a**) [U] safety; refuge 安全; 庇护: *ask for/be granted political asylum,* ie protection given to a political refugee by a foreign country 请求[准予]政治避难(外国给予政治难民的保护). (**b**) [C] place of safety or refuge 庇护所; 避难所. **2** [C] (*dated* 旧) hospital for the care of mentally ill or destitute people 精神病院; 收容所.

asym·met·ric /ˌeɪsɪˈmetrɪk; ,esɪˋmɛtrɪk/ (also **asym·met·rical** /-ɪkl; -ɪkḷ/) *adj* not having parts that correspond to each other in size, shape, etc; lacking symmetry 不对称的: *Most people's faces are asymmetrical.* 多数人的脸并不对称.

at /ət; ət; *strong form* 强读式 æt; æt/ *prep* **1** (**a**) (indicating a point in space 指空间的某一点): *at the end of the runway* 在跑道的尽头 ○ *at the corner of the street* 在街道的拐角 ○ *go in at the side door* 从旁门进入 ○ *change at Didcot* 在迪德考特转换 ○ *arrive at the airport* 到达飞机场 ○ *At the roundabout take the third exit.* 在环状交叉路口从第三条出路驶出. ○ *I'll be at home* (ie not at work, school, church, etc) *all morning.* 我一上午都在家. (**b**) (used with the name of a building, esp with reference to the activities going on inside 与建筑物名称连用, 尤指其中进行的活动): *She's at the theatre, cinema, etc,* ie watching a play, film, etc. 她在戏院里、电影院里等(看戏、看电影等) ○ *She works at the hospital.* 她在医院工作. ○ *He's at* (ie staying at) *the Grand Hotel.* 他住在格兰德大旅馆. (**c**) among those who attend 在参加者中: *at a concert, conference, match, etc* 参加音乐会、会议、比赛等. (**d**) (used with the name of a person + *'s* to refer to that person's home or place of work 与人名+'s连用, 指其家或工作处): *They're at Keith's.* 他们在基思家. ○ *I was at my father's.* 我先前在我父亲处. ○ *They didn't have any bread at the baker's.* 面包店里那时没有面包. (**e**) (indicating place of employment or study 指受雇的或学习的处所): *He's been at the bank longer than anyone else.* 他在银行工作时期比别人都长. ○ *I'm at the head office.* 我在总公司工作. ○ *her three years at Oxford* 她在牛津三年求学期间 (Cf 参看 *spend three days in Oxford as a tourist*). **2** (**a**) (indicating a point in time 指时间的某一点): *start, meet, leave, etc at 2 o'clock* 在2时开始、会见、离开等 ○ *at 3.15/a quarter past 3* 在3点15分[3时1刻] ○ *He is to be shot at dawn.* 定于黎明将他枪决. ○ *I didn't know he was dead at the time of speaking,* ie when I spoke. 我讲话时不知道他已死亡. ○ *At the moment you called I was in the garden shed.* 你来电话时我正在花园的小屋里. ○ *at the end of the holiday* 假日的终结. (**b**) (indicating a period of time 指一段时间): *At night you can see the stars.* 夜晚可以看到星星. ○ *What are you doing at* (*US on*) *the weekend?* 你在周末做什么? ○ *take a few days' holiday at Christmas, Easter, Whitsun, etc* 在圣诞节、复活节、圣灵降临节等休几天假. (**c**) (used to indicate the age at which sb does sth 用以指某人做某事时的年龄): *She got married at 55.* 她55岁时结婚. ○ *You can retire at 60.* 60岁时可以退休. ○ *He left school at (the age of) 16.* 他16(岁)时中学毕业. ⇨Usage at TIME[1] 用法见 TIME[1]. **3** (**a**) in the direction of or towards (sb/sth) 向或朝(某人[某物])的方向: *aim the ball at the hole* 将球对准那个洞 ○ *direct one's advertising at a wider audience* 将宣传面向范围更大的群众 ○ *smile, grin, stare, wave, etc at sb* 对着某人微笑、咧着嘴笑、凝视、挥手等 ○ *A man with a gun was shooting at the crowd.* 有一持枪男子向人群射击. ○ *The dog rushed at me, wagging its tail.* 那狗摇晃着尾巴朝我奔来. ○ *She shouted at me but I couldn't hear.* 她冲着我喊叫, 可是我并没听见. ○ *throw stones at the can in the water,* ie trying to hit it 用石块向水中的罐扔去(想打中它). (**b**) (used to show that sb tries to do sth but does not succeed or complete it 用以表示某人尽力做某事物却未做成或未做完): *clutch at a rope* 去抓绳索 ○ *guess at the meaning* 猜测意思 ○ *She nibbled at a sandwich,* ie ate only tiny portions. 她咬了几口三明治. **4** (indicating the distance away from sth 指离某事物的距离): *Can you read a car number-plate at fifty metres?* 你能在离汽车五十米远处看清车牌号码吗? ○ *hold sth at arm's length* 伸直胳膊握住某物. **5** (indicating a state, condition or continuous activity 指某状态、情形或持续的活动): *at war with their neighbours* 与他们的邻国交战 ○ *stand at ease,* ie in a relaxed position 稍息(休息的姿势) ○ *put sb at risk* 置某人于危险地位 ○ *children at play* 玩耍着的儿童 ○ *She's at work in the garden.* 她正在花园

A

里干活儿. **6** (**a**) (indicating a rate, price, speed, etc 指比率、价格、速度等): *House prices are rising at a higher rate than inflation.* 房价比通货膨胀上涨的比率高. ○ *I bought this coat at half-price/at 50% discount.* 我用半价[5折]买的这件外衣. ○ *driving at 70 mph* 以每小时70英里的速度驾驶. (**b**) (indicating order or frequency 指顺序或频率): *at the first attempt* 初次尝试 ○ *at two-minute intervals*, ie once every two minutes 每隔两分钟. **7** in response to (sth) 对(某事物)回应: *attend the dinner at the chairman's invitation* 应主席之邀赴宴 ○ *at the king's command* 奉国王之命. **8** (used with *his, her, our*, etc and a superlative *adj* 与 his、her、our 等及形容词的最高级连用): *This was Torvill and Dean at their best.* 这是托维尔和迪安的最佳表现. ○ *The garden's at its most beautiful in June.* 花园在六月份最美丽. ○ *an example of British craftsmanship at its finest* 英国手工艺的瑰宝. **9** (used after many *adjs* and *ns* 用于许多形容词和名词之后): *good, clever, skilled, etc at restoring furniture, etc* 善于、精于、长于翻修家具等 ○ *hopeless at (playing) chess* 对(下)国际象棋不堪造就 ○ *She's a genius at doing crossword puzzles.* 她做纵横填字游戏是一绝. ○ *busy at their homework* 都在忙着做功课 ○ *impatient at the delay* 因耽搁而不耐烦 ○ *amused at the cartoons* 对着连环画乐不可支 ○ *delighted at the result* 对结果满心欢喜 ○ *puzzled at her silence* 对她的缄默大惑不解 ○ *his anger at being beaten* 他被击败时的气恼. **10** (idm 习语) ˌ**where it's** ˈ**at** (*infml* 口) place or activity that is very popular or fashionable 热闹的或时髦的场所或活动: *Judging by the crowds waiting to get in this seems to be where it's at.* 从争先恐后等待进去的人群来看, 这似乎是个热闹去处. (For idioms such as **at hand**, **at once**, **at a low ebb**, etc see entries at **hand**[1], **once**, **low**[1], etc. 查阅 **at hand**、**at once**、**at a low ebb** 等习语, 见 **hand**[1]、**once**、**low**[1] 等词条.)

at·av·ism /ˈætəvɪzəm; ˋætəˌvɪzəm/ *n* [U] reappearance in a person of a characteristic or quality that has not been seen in his family for many generations 返祖现象. Cf 参看 THROW-BACK (THROW[1]). ▷ **at·av·istic** /ˌætəˈvɪstɪk; ˌætəˋvɪstɪk/ *adj*: *an atavistic urge* 返祖倾向.

ate *pt* of EAT.

-ate *suff* 后缀 **1** (with *ns* forming *adjs* 与名词结合构成形容词) full of or showing a specified quality 富于或显示某性质: *affectionate* ○ *passionate* ○ *Italianate*. **2** (forming *ns* 用以构成名词) (**a**) (group of people with a) status or function (有某种)身分或职务(的团体): *electorate* ○ *doctorate*. (**b**) (*chemistry* 化) salt formed by the action of a particular acid 由某种酸的作用而形成的盐: *sulphate* ○ *nitrate*. **3** (with *ns* and *adjs* forming *vs* 与名词和形容词结合构成动词) give (to sth) the specified thing or quality 给予(某事物)某物或某性质: *hyphenate* ○ *chlorinate* ○ *activate*. ▷ **-ately** (forming *advs* 用以构成副词): *affectionately*.

atel·ier /əˈtelɪeɪ; *US* ˌætlˈjeɪ; ˋætḷˌje/ *n* artist's studio or workshop (艺术家的)工作室或制作室.

athe·ism /ˈeɪθɪɪzəm; ˋeθɪˌɪzəm/ *n* [U] belief that there is no God 无神论.

▷ **athe·ist** /ˈeɪθɪɪst; ˋeθɪɪst/ *n* person who believes that there is no God 无神论者. Cf 参看 HEATHEN, PAGAN.

athe·istic /ˌeɪθɪˈɪstɪk; ˌeθɪˋɪstɪk/ *adj*.

ath·lete /ˈæθli:t; ˋæθlit/ *n* **1** person who trains to compete in physical exercises and sports, esp running and jumping 运动员, 体育家(尤指跑和跳项目). **2** person who has the strength and skill to perform well at sports 在运动方面有体力和技巧的人; 健儿: *Most first-class footballers are natural athletes.* 多数一流的足球运动员都是天生的健将.

□ ˌ**athlete's** ˈ**foot** (*infml* 口) fungous disease of the feet 脚癣.

ath·letic /æθˈletɪk; æθˋlɛtɪk/ *adj* **1** [attrib 作定语] of athletes or athletics 运动员的; 运动的: *an athletic club* 运动员俱乐部 ○ *athletic sports* 体育运动. **2** physically strong, healthy and active 体格健壮而活跃的: *an athletic figure* 健壮的体格 ○ *She looks very athletic.* 她看起来很健美.

ath·let·ics /æθˈletɪks; æθˋlɛtɪks/ *n* [sing *v*] physical exercises and competitive sports, esp running and jumping 体育运动(尤指跑和跳): [attrib 作定语] *an athletics meeting* 运动会. ⇨App 4 见附录4.

at-home /ət ˈhəʊm; ətˋhom/ *n* (*dated* 旧) informal party in sb's home, to which guests may come at any time within certain hours 家庭招待会(在家庭内举行的非正式的聚会, 客人可在规定的若干小时内随时光临).

athwart /əˈθwɔ:t; əˋθwɔrt/ *adv, prep* (*esp nautical* 尤用于航海) obliquely across (sth); from one side to the other side (of) 横跨着; 横穿过; 从一边到另一边: *The ship was anchored athwart the harbour mouth.* 轮船横着停泊在港口里.

-ation ⇨ -ION.

atishoo /əˈtɪʃu:; əˋtɪʃu/ *interj* (indicating the sound made by sb sneezing) 阿嚏(打喷嚏的声音).

-ative *suff* 后缀 (with *vs* forming *adjs* 与动词结合构成形容词) doing or tending to do (sth) 与做(某事物)有...关系的; 有...倾向的; 有...性质的: *illustrative* ○ *imitative* ○ *talkative*. ▷ **-atively** (forming *advs* 用以构成副词): *quantitatively*.

at·las /ˈætləs; ˋætləs/ *n* book of maps 地图集; 地图册.

at·mo·sphere /ˈætməsfɪə(r); ˋætməsˌfɪr/ *n* **1** (**a**) **the atmosphere** [sing] the mixture of gases that surrounds the earth 大气, 大气层(包围地球的气体). (**b**) [C] mixture of gases that surrounds any planet or star 包围任何星球的气体: *the moon's atmosphere* 月球周围的气体 ○ *an atmosphere that supports life* 可以维持生命的气体. **2** [sing] air in or around a place 某一地方的空气: *The atmosphere is very stuffy in here — can we open a window?* 这里的空气很闷 —— 咱们能把窗户打开吗? **3** [sing] feeling in the mind that is created by a group of people or a place; mood 气氛; 情绪: *An atmosphere of tension filled the room.* 屋子里笼罩着紧张的气氛. ○ *The atmosphere changed as soon as she walked in.* 她一进来气氛就变了. ○ *The atmosphere over dinner was warm and friendly.* 用餐时洋溢着热情友好的气氛.

at·mo·spheric /ˌætməsˈferɪk; ˌætməsˋfɛrɪk/ *adj* **1** of or related to the atmosphere 大气的; 大气层的: *unusual atmospheric conditions* 异常的大气状态. **2** creating an atmosphere(3) 制造气氛的: *atmospheric lighting* 制造气氛的灯光.

▷ **at·mo·spher·ics** *n* [pl] (**a**) electrical disturbances in the atmosphere 天电. (**b**) interference or crackling sounds on radios, etc caused by these 天电干扰(由天电造成的对无线电等的干扰或杂音).

□ ˌ**atmospheric** ˈ**pressure** pressure at a point due to the weight of the column of air above it 大气压力.

atoll /ˈætɒl; ˋætɑl/ *n* ring-shaped coral reef enclosing a lagoon 环状珊瑚岛; 环礁.

atom /ˈætəm; ˋætəm/ *n* **1** (**a**) [C] smallest part of an element that can exist chemically 原子: *Two atoms of hydrogen combine with one atom of oxygen to form a molecule of water.* 两个氢原子和一个氧原子结合而形成一个水分子. (**b**) [sing] this as a source of energy 原子能: *the power of the atom* 原子动力 ○ [attrib 作定语] *an atom scientist* 原子能专家. **2** [C] very small quantity or thing 极微小的量或事物: *The tower was blown to atoms by the force of the explosion.* 爆炸的力量把塔炸得粉碎. ○ *There isn't an atom of truth in the rumour.* 谣言中没有丝毫的真实性.

□ ˈ**atom bomb** = ATOMIC BOMB (ATOMIC).

atomic /əˈtɒmɪk; əˋtɑmɪk/ *adj* [usu attrib 通常作定语] of an atom or atoms 原子的: *atomic physics* 原子物理学 ○ *atomic warfare*, ie using atomic bombs 原子战争(即使用原子弹的).

□ **aˌtomic** ˈ**bomb** (also **A-bomb**, **atom bomb**) bomb whose explosive power comes from the rapid release of nuclear energy 原子弹.

aˌtomic ˈ**energy** energy obtained as the result of nuclear fission 原子能.

aˌtomic ˈ**number** number of protons in the nucleus of an atom 原子序数.

aˌtomic ˈ**pile** early type of nuclear reactor 原子反应堆.

aˌtomic ˈ**weight** (also **relative atomic mass**) ratio between the mass of one atom of an element and one-twelfth of the weight of an atom of carbon 12 原子量(某元素的一个原子的质量与十二分之一的碳12原子量的比值).

at·om·ize, -ise /ˈætəmaɪz; ˋætəmˌaɪz/ *v* [Tn] reduce (sth) to atoms or fine particles 使(某物)分裂成原子或微粒; 使雾化.

▷ **at·om·izer, -iser** *n* device for producing a fine spray from a liquid, eg perfume 喷雾器(如喷香水的器具).

A

atonal /eɪˈtəʊnl; eˋtonl̩/ *adj* (*music* 音) not written in any key or system of scales (SCALE[2] 6) 无调的; 不成调的. ▷ **aton·al·ity** /ˌeɪtəʊˈnælətɪ; ˌetoˋnælətɪ/ *n* [U].

atone /əˈtəʊn; əˋton/ *v* [I, Ipr] **~ (for sth)** (*fml* 文) act in a way that compensates for a previous wrong, error, etc 补(过); 赎(罪): *atone for a crime, a sin, one's mistakes, one's bad behaviour, etc* 抵罪、赎罪、弥补过错、补救不良行为等 ○ *I have treated you unkindly — how can I atone (for it)?* 我一向待你很刻薄——我怎么才能赔罪呢?

▷ **atone·ment** *n* **1** [C, U] (*fml* 文) act of atoning 补偿(过失); 赔礼; 赔罪; 谢罪: *He sent her some flowers in atonement for his earlier rudeness.* 他因自己先前的粗鲁而向她献花赔罪. **2 the Atonement** [sing] the suffering and death of Christ to atone for the sins of mankind 耶稣为替世人赎罪而承受的苦难及其死亡.

atop /əˈtɒp; əˋtɑp/ *prep* (*dated or rhet* 旧或修辞) at or on the top of (sth) 在…顶上: *a seagull perched atop the mast* 停歇在桅杆顶上的海鸥.

-ator *suff* 后缀 (with *vs* forming *ns* 与动词结合构成名词) person or thing that performs the specified action 做某动作的人或事物: *creator* ○ *percolator*.

at·ro·cious /əˈtrəʊʃəs; əˋtroʃəs/ *adj* **1** very wicked, cruel or shocking 恶毒的; 残忍的; 残暴的: *atrocious crimes, injuries, acts of brutality, etc* 残暴的罪行、伤害、兽行等. **2** (*infml* 口) very bad or unpleasant 恶劣的; 讨厌的: *speak English with an atrocious accent* 用难听的口音说英语 ○ *Isn't the weather atrocious?* 天气真糟透了, 是吧?
▷ **at·ro·ciously** *adv*. **at·ro·cious·ness** *n* [U].

at·ro·city /əˈtrɒsətɪ; əˋtrɑsətɪ/ *n* **(a)** [U] great wickedness or cruelty 恶毒; 残忍; 残暴: *I am shocked by the atrocity of this man's crimes.* 这个人行凶手段残忍狠毒使我震惊. **(b)** [C esp *pl* 尤作复数] very wicked or cruel act 暴行: *Many atrocities are committed on innocent people in wartime.* 战争期间无辜百姓横遭蹂躏.

at·rophy /ˈætrəfɪ; ˋætrəfɪ/ *n* [U] wasting away of the body or part of it through lack of nourishment or use (身体或身体某部因缺乏营养或不常使用而)萎缩: (*fig* 比喻) *The cultural life of the country will sink into atrophy unless more writers and artists emerge.* 除非能多涌现出一些作家和艺术家, 否则这个国家的文化生活将枯萎衰退.

▷ **at·rophy** *v* (*pt, pp* **-ied**) [I, Tn] (cause sth to) suffer atrophy (使某事物)萎缩: *atrophied limbs, muscles* 萎缩的肢体、肌肉.

at·tach /əˈtætʃ; əˋtætʃ/ *v* **1** [Tn, Tn·pr] **~ sth (to sth)** fasten or join sth (to sth) 将某物系在、缚在或附在(另一物)上: *a house with a garage attached* 带有车房的房子 ○ *attach a label to each piece of luggage* 每件行李上都加上标签 ○ *a document attached to a letter (with a pin)* 信中(用别针)附一文件 ○ *Attached* (ie Attached to this letter) *you will find....* 随信附上…. Cf 参看 DETACH 1. **2** [Tn·pr] **(a) ~ oneself to sb/sth** join sb/sth as a (sometimes unwelcome or uninvited) companion or member (有时指不受欢迎或未受邀请而)依附某人[参加某事]: *A young man attached himself to me at the party and I couldn't get rid of him.* 聚会中有个小青年总缠着我, 我也甩不开他. ○ *I attached myself to a group of tourists entering the museum.* 我随着一队游客混入了博物馆. **(b) ~ sb to sb/sth** (esp passive 尤用于被动语态) assign sb to (a person or group) for special duties 将某人派给(一人或一组织)去执行某任务; 使隶属于: *You'll be attached to this department until the end of the year.* 你在年底前将暂属于这一部门. **3 (a)** [Tn·pr] **~ sth to sth** connect sth with sth; attribute sth to sth 将某事物与另一事物相联系; 将某事物归于另一事物: *Do you attach any importance to what he said?* 你认为他说的话重要吗? **(b)** [Ipr] **~ to sb** (*fml* 文) be connected with or attributable to sb 与某人相关联; 归于某人: *No blame attaches to you in this affair.* 这件事不怪你. **4** [Tn] (*law* 律) take or seize (sb or sb's property) by legal authority 逮捕(某人); 扣押, 查封(某人的财物). **5** (idm 习语) **no strings attached/without strings** ⇨ STRING[1].

▷ **at·tached** *adj* [pred 作表语] **~ (to sb/sth)** full of affection for sb/sth 依恋、爱慕、留恋某人[某事物]: *I've never seen two people so attached (to each other).* 我从没见过两个人(彼此)这样如胶似漆. ○ *We've grown very attached to this house and would hate to move.* 我们十分留恋这所房子, 真舍不得搬家.

at·tach·ment *n* **1** [U] action of attaching; being attached 附着; 附属; 附带: *She's on attachment to* (ie temporarily working in) *the Ministry of Defence.* 她暂时隶属于国防部. **2** [C] thing that is or can be attached 附属物; 附件: *an electric drill with a range of different attachments* 带有各种配件的电钻. **3** [U] **~ (to/for sb/sth)** affection; devotion 依恋; 眷恋; 留恋: *feel a strong attachment to one's family* 十分恋家. **4** [U] (*law* 律) seizing sb's property, etc with legal authority 扣押或查封某人的财物.

at·taché /əˈtæʃeɪ; *US* ˌætəˈʃeɪ; ˌætəˋʃe/ *n* person attached to an ambassador's staff with a particular responsibility 使馆随员; 使馆职员: *the naval/military/air/press attaché* 海军武官[陆军武官/空军武官/新闻参事].

□ **atˈtaché case** small rectangular case for carrying documents, etc 公文包.

at·tack /əˈtæk; əˋtæk/ *n* **1** [C, U] **~ (on sb/sth)** violent attempt to hurt, overcome or defeat sb/sth 伤害; 攻击; 进攻; 攻打: *make an attack on the enemy, bridge, town* 向敌人、桥梁、城镇进攻 ○ *the victim of a terrorist attack* 恐怖分子攻击的受害者 ○ *Our troops are now on the attack.* 我们的部队正在进攻. ○ *The patrol came under attack from all sides.* 巡逻队遭到来自四面八方的攻击. ○ (*saying* 谚) *Attack is the best form of defence.* 进攻是最好的防御. **2** [C, U] **~ (on sb/sth)** strong criticism in speech or writing 抨击; 非难: *an attack on the Government's policies* 对政府政策的抨击. **3** [C] **~ (on sth)** vigorous attempt to deal with sth 对某事物奋力着手处理; 动手: *an all-out attack on poverty, unemployment, etc* 全力着手解决贫困、失业等问题. **4** [C] sudden start of an illness, etc (疾病等突然的)侵袭, 发作: *an attack of asthma, flu, malaria, hiccups, nerves, etc* 气喘、流感、疟疾、呃逆、神经质等发作 ○ *a ˈheart attack* 心脏病发作 ○ (*fig* 比喻) *an attack of the giggles* 一阵咯咯的傻笑. **5** [U] (esp vigorous) way of beginning sth (尤指强有力的)开始某事物: *This piece of music needs to be played with more attack.* 这段乐曲的开始部分要演奏得更加雄壮有力. **6** [C usu *sing* 通常作单数] (*sport* 体) (players who are in the) position of trying to score in a game, eg of football or cricket (在如足球或板球比赛中处于可得分的)进攻位置(的运动员): *England's attack has been weakened by the injury of certain key players.* 英格兰队某些主力运动员受伤而使攻球削弱. ○ *We must move more players into the attack.* 我们要多调配运动员到攻球区.

▷ **at·tack** *v* **1** [I, Tn] make an attack on (sb/sth) 攻击; 进攻; 袭击: *They decided to attack at night.* 他们决定夜晚进攻. ○ *attack a neighbouring country* 攻击邻国 ○ *A woman was attacked and robbed by a gang of youths.* 有一妇女遭到一群青年的袭击和抢劫. **2** [Tn] criticize (sb/sth) severely 抨击: *a newspaper article attacking the Prime Minister* 报纸上抨击首相的文章. **3** [Tn] begin to deal with (sth) vigorously; tackle 奋力着手处理(某事物); 对付: *The Government is making no attempt to attack unemployment.* 政府无意解决失业问题. ○ *Shall we attack the washing-up?* 咱们动手洗碗碟好吗? ○ *They attacked their meal with gusto.* 他们大吃大喝. **4** [Tn] act harmfully on (sth/sb) 侵袭, 腐蚀(某事物[某人]): *a disease that attacks the brain* 侵袭大脑的疾病 ○ *Rust attacks metals.* 锈能腐蚀金属. **at·tacker** *n* person who attacks 攻击者; 进攻者; 抨击者.

at·tain /əˈteɪn; əˋten/ *v* **1** [Tn] succeed in getting (sth); achieve 获得(某事物); 达到; 实现: *attain a position of power* 获得权位 ○ *attain one's goal, objective, ambition, etc* 实现目的、目标、抱负等 ○ *attain our target of £50 000* 达到我们的50 000英镑的目标. **2** [Ipr, Tn] **~ (to) sth** (*usu fml* 通常作文雅语) reach or arrive at sth, esp with effort 达到, 到达某事物(尤指经过努力): *He attained the age of 25 before marrying.* 他年届廿五始完婚.

▷ **at·tain·able** *adj* that can be attained 可获得; 可达到的; 可实现的: *These objectives are certainly attainable.* 这些目标一定可以达到.

at·tain·ment *n* **1** [U] success in reaching 达到; 到达: *The attainment of her ambitions was still a dream.* 她要实现抱负仍是一种梦想. **2** [C usu *pl* 通常作复数] thing attained, esp skill or knowledge 成就; 造诣: *a scholar of the highest attainments* 造诣极高的学者.

A

at·tar /ˈætə(r); ˋætɚ/ *n* [U] fragrant oil obtained from flowers 香精: *attar of roses* 玫瑰油.

at·tempt /əˈtempt; əˋtɛmpt/ *v* [Tn, Tt] make an effort to accomplish (sth); try (to do sth) 尝试; 努力; 试图: *The prisoners attempted an escape/to escape, but failed.* 囚犯企图逃跑, 但是失败了. ○ *Don't attempt the impossible.* 不要试图做不可能的事. ○ *He was charged with attempted robbery.* 他被控以意图抢劫罪. ○ *All candidates must attempt Questions 1-5.* 所有考生均须回答第1–5题. ○ *They are attempting (to climb) the steepest part of the mountain.* 他们努力攀登这座山的最陡的部分. ○ *She will attempt to beat the world record.* 她决心要打破世界纪录.

▷ **at·tempt** *n* **1 ~ (to do sth/at doing sth)** act of attempting sth 试图; 企图; 尝试: *They made no attempt to escape/at escaping.* 他们并未图谋逃跑. ○ *My early attempts at learning to drive were unsuccessful.* 我曾经几次打算学开车, 却都没有学成. ○ *They failed in all their attempts to climb the mountain.* 他们攀登那座山的一切尝试都失败了. **2 ~ (at sth)** thing produced by sb trying to do or make sth 试图做某事物而得到的产物: *My first attempt at a chocolate cake tasted horrible.* 我首次试做的巧克力蛋糕难吃极了. **3 ~ (on sth)** effort to improve on or end sth; attack 对改进或结束某事物所做的努力; 攻击; 袭击: *the latest attempt on the world land speed record* 为创造世界陆上速度纪录所做的最新尝试 ○ *An attempt was made on the Pope's life.* 有人策划杀害教皇.

at·tend /əˈtend; əˋtɛnd/ *v* **1** [I, Ipr] **~ (to sb/sth)** apply one's mind steadily; give careful thought 专心; 仔细考虑: *Why weren't you attending when I explained before?* 我以前解释的时候, 你怎么不注意听呢? ○ *Attend to your work and stop talking.* 专心工作, 不要说话. **2** [Ipr] **~ to sb/sth** give practical consideration to sb/sth 照顾、关照某人[某事物]: *A nurse attends to his needs.* 有个护士照顾他. ○ *Are you being attended to* (eg said by an assistant to a customer in a shop)? 有人接待您吗(如店员问顾客)? ○ *Could you attend to* (ie deal with) *this matter immediately?* 你能不能立刻处理这件事? **3** [Tn] take care of (sb); look after 照看(某人); 照料; 看护: *Dr Smith attended her in hospital.* 史密斯医生在医院中给她治病. **4** [Tn] go regularly to (a place); be present at 照例去(某处); 出席: *attend school, church, etc* 上学、上教堂等 ○ *They had a quiet wedding — only a few friends attended (it).* 他们的婚礼静悄悄的——只有几个朋友参加. ○ *The meeting was well attended*, ie Many people were there. 有很多人出席会议. **5** [Tn] (*fml* 文) be with (sb/sth); accompany 伴随(某人[某事物]); 陪伴: *The Queen was attended by her ladies-in-waiting.* 女王由宫廷女侍陪伴. ○ (*fig* 比喻) *May good fortune attend you!* 祝你红运当头!

▷ **at·tender** *n* person who attends (ATTEND 4) 参加者; 出席者: *She's a regular attender at evening classes.* 她上夜校一贯按时出席.

at·tend·ance /əˈtendəns; əˋtɛndəns/ *n* **1** [U, C] action or time of being present 出席; 到场; 参加: *Attendance at evening prayers is not compulsory.* 参加晚祷并非硬性规定. ○ *You have missed several attendances this term.* 这学期你有几次缺席. **2** [C] number of people present 出席人数: *They're expecting a large attendance at the meeting.* 他们希望有很多人出席这次会议. ○ *Attendances have increased since we reduced the price of tickets.* 我们降低了票价, 到场的人就多起来了. **3** (idm 习语) **dance attendance on sb** ⇨ DANCE². **in attendance (on sb)** present in order to look after, protect or serve sb 护理; 卫护; 服侍: *A nurse was in constant attendance.* 有个护士随时护理. ○ *The President always has six bodyguards in close attendance.* 总统有六名警卫员时时刻刻在左右保卫.

□ **atˈtendance allowance** (*Brit*) money paid by the state to sb who cares for a severely disabled relative, etc (国家付给因护理严重伤残的亲友的)护理津贴.

atˈtendance centre (*Brit*) place where young offenders must go regularly for supervision, as an alternative to being sent to prison 少年教导所.

at·tend·ant /əˈtendənt; əˋtɛndənt/ *n* **1** person whose job is to provide a service in a public place 服务员; 侍者: *a cloakroom, swimming-pool, museum, etc attendant* 衣帽间、游泳池、博物馆等处的服务员. **2** (esp *pl* 尤作复数) servant or companion 随员; 陪侍: *the queen's attendants* 女王的侍从.

▷ **at·tend·ant** *adj* [attrib 作定语] accompanying 伴随的; 陪从的: *an attendant nurse* 专责护士 ○ *attendant circumstances* 附带情况 ○ *famine and its attendant diseases* 饥荒及随之而来的疾病.

at·ten·tion /əˈtenʃn; əˋtɛnʃən/ *n* **1** [U] action of applying one's mind to sth/sb or noticing sth/sb 注意; 专心; 留心: *call sb's attention to sth* 叫[引起]某人注意某事 ○ *Please pay attention* (ie listen carefully) *(to what I am saying).* 请注意(我说的话). ○ *She turned her attention to a new problem.* 她把注意力转移到一个新问题上. ○ *Our attention was held throughout his long talk.* 我们始终专心听着他的长篇大论. ○ *You must give your full attention to what you are doing.* 你必须全神贯注地做你所做的事. ○ *I keep trying to attract the waiter's attention.* 我不断示意招呼服务员. ○ *It has been brought to my attention* (ie I have been informed) *that....* 我已获悉.... **2** [U] special care or action; practical consideration 特别的照顾或处理; 实际的考虑: *He gives all his attention to his car.* 他十分关心他的汽车. ○ *This letter is for the attention of the manager.* 这封信是要经理亲自处理的. ○ *The roof needs attention*, ie to be repaired. 屋顶需要修理了. **3** [C usu *pl* 通常作复数] (*fml* 文) kind or thoughtful act 厚待; 殷勤: *He showed his concern for his sick mother by his many little attentions.* 他对病中的母亲表现了无微不至的关心. **4** [U] soldier's drill position, standing upright with feet together and arms stretched downwards (used esp in the expressions shown) 立正的姿势(尤用于以下示例): *come to/stand at attention* 立正. Cf 参看 EASE¹ 2. **5** (idm 习语) **catch sb's attention/eye** ⇨ CATCH¹. **draw attention to sth** ⇨ DRAW². **give one's undivided attention; get/have sb's undivided attention** ⇨ UNDIVIDED. **snap to attention** ⇨ SNAP. ▷ **at·ten·tion** *interj* **1** (calling people to listen to an announcement, etc 招唤人们注意听通告等): *Attention, please! The bus will leave in ten minutes.* 请注意! 公共汽车十分钟后开. ○ *Attention all shipping, motorists, housewives....* 所有船舶、机动车驾驶员、家庭主妇请注意.... **2** (also *infml* 口语亦作 **shun** /ʃʌn; ʃʌn/) (ordering soldiers to come to attention (4) 命令士兵立正.)

at·tent·ive /əˈtentɪv; əˋtɛntɪv/ *adj* **~ (to sb/sth)** giving attention (to sb/sth); alert and watchful (对某人[某事物])注意的; 留心的; 警惕的: *an attentive audience* 聚精会神的听众[观众] ○ *A good hostess is always attentive to the needs of her guests.* 好客的女主人能随时留心客人的需要. ▷ **at·tent·ively** *adv*: *listening attentively to the speaker* 专心地听着演讲人的话.

at·tenu·ate /əˈtenjʊeɪt; əˋtɛnjʊˌet/ *v* [Tn] (*fml* 文) **1** make (sth/sb) thin or slender 使(某事物[某人])变细或变瘦: *attenuated limbs* 枯瘦如柴的四肢. **2** (*esp law* 尤用于法律) reduce the force or value of (sth); weaken 减弱(某事物)的力量; 降低(某事物)的价值; 弱化: *attenuating circumstances*, ie facts that weaken the strength of an argument 情有可原的情形(可使辩论的强度减轻的事实). ▷ **at·tenu·ation** /əˌtenjʊˈeɪʃn; əˌtɛnjʊˋeʃən/ *n* [U].

at·test /əˈtest; əˋtɛst/ *v* (*fml* 文) **1** [Ipr, Tn] **~ (to) sth** be or give clear proof of sth 作为或提供某事物的明证: *His handling of the crisis attested to his strength of character.* 他对危机的处理证明了他性格坚强. ○ *Her outstanding abilities were attested by her rapid promotion.* 她杰出的才干已经由她获得迅速提升而得到证明. ○ *These papers attest the fact that....* 这些文件证明了这一事实.... **2** [Tn] declare (sth) to be true or genuine; be a witness to (sth) 声称(某事物)属实或是真的; 作为(某事物)的见证: *attest a signature* 对签字作见证.

▷ **at·testa·tion** /ˌæteˈsteɪʃn; ˌætɛsˋteʃən/ *n* [U, C].

at·tested *adj* (*Brit*) certified to be free from disease, esp tuberculosis 证明无病的(尤指结核病): *attested cattle/milk* 证明无病的牛[不含病菌的奶].

at·tic /ˈætɪk; ˋætɪk/ *n* space or room immediately below the roof of a house 阁楼; 顶楼: *furniture stored in the attic* 在阁楼里存放的家具 ○ [attrib 作定语] *an attic bedroom* 顶楼卧室. Cf 参看 GARRET.

at·tire /əˈtaɪə(r); əˋtaɪr/ *n* [U] (*dated or fml* 旧或文) clothes; dress 衣服; 服装: *wearing formal attire* 穿着礼服.

▷ **at·tire** *v* [Tn usu passive 通常用于被动语态] (*dated* 旧) dress (sb) 穿着: *attired in robes of silk and fur* 穿着丝织的和毛皮的长袍.

at·ti·tude /ˈætɪtju:d; *US* -tu:d; ˋætəˏtud/ *n* **1** ~ **(to/towards sb/sth)** way of thinking or behaving 看法; 态度: *What is your attitude to abortion?* 你对堕胎有什么看法? ○ *She shows a very positive attitude to her work.* 她工作态度非常积极. ○ *Don't take that attitude with me, young man!* 别用这种态度对我, 小伙子! **2** (*fml* 文) way of positioning the body 姿势: *The photographer has caught him in the attitude of prayer*, eg kneeling. 摄影者捕捉住他祈祷的姿势(如跪着). **3** (idm 习语) **strike an attitude/a pose** ⇨ STRIKE².

▷ **at·ti·tu·din·ize, -ise** /ˌætɪˈtju:dɪnaɪz; *US* -ˈtu:dən-; ˏætəˋtudṇˏaɪz/ *v* [I] speak, write or behave in an affected way in order to impress others (在说话、书写或行动中)装腔作势.

attn *abbr* 缩写 = (*commerce* 商) (for the) attention of: *Publicity Dept, attn Mr C Biggs* 宣传部, 送交西·比格兹先生.

at·tor·ney /əˈtɜ:nɪ; əˋtɝnɪ/ *n* **1** person appointed to act for another in business or legal matters (业务或法律事务上的)代理人: *power of attorney*, ie authority to act as attorney 代理权 ○ *a letter of attorney*, ie one giving sb this authority 授权书. **2** (*US*) lawyer, esp one qualified to act for clients in court 律师(尤指有资格代表当事人出庭者): *a district attorney*, ie the public prosecutor for a particular region 地方检察官.

□ **Atˌtorney-ˈGeneral** *n* (*abbr* 缩写 **Atty-Gen**) (in certain countries) chief legal officer, appointed by the Government (某些国家的)司法部长. Cf 参看 SOLICITOR-GENERAL (SOLICITOR).

at·tract /əˈtrækt; əˋtrækt/ *v* [Tn] **1** pull (sth) towards itself/oneself by unseen force 吸引: *A magnet attracts steel.* 磁石能吸钢铁. **2** (**a**) arouse interest or pleasure in (sb/sth) 引起(某人[某事物]的兴趣或快感; 激发; 引诱: *The light attracted a lot of insects.* 亮光招引了很多昆虫. ○ *The dog was attracted by the smell of the meat.* 狗受到肉味的引诱. ○ *Babies are attracted to bright colours.* 婴儿喜欢鲜艳的颜色. ○ *Do any of these designs attract you?* 这些设计中有使你感兴趣的吗? ○ *I'm very attracted to her*, ie I feel I would like to become more friendly with her. 我对她产生了好感. (**b**) arouse (sth); prompt 引起; 激起: *attract sb's attention, interest, etc* 引起某人的注意、兴趣等 ○ *The new play has attracted a good deal of criticism.* 这出新剧招致很多批评.

at·trac·tion /əˈtrækʃn; əˋtrækʃən/ *n* **1** [U] action or power of attracting 吸引; 吸引力: *I can't see the attraction of sitting on the beach all day.* 我看不出整天坐在沙滩上有什么意思. ○ *She felt an immediate attraction to him.* 她对他一见钟情. ○ *The television has little attraction for me.* 电视对我没有什么吸引力. **2** [C] thing that attracts (ATTRACT 2a) 有吸引力的事物: *One of the main attractions of the job is the high salary.* 这份工作最吸引人的是薪水高. ○ *City life holds few attractions for me.* 城市生活中没有什么吸引我的东西. Cf 参看 REPULSION.

at·tract·ive /əˈtræktɪv; əˋtræktɪv/ *adj* having the power to attract(2a); pleasing or interesting 有吸引力的; 诱人的; 使人愉快的; 引起兴趣的: *I don't find him at all attractive.* 我觉得他一点儿也不讨人喜欢. ○ *Your proposal sounds very attractive.* 你的建议很动听. ○ *goods for sale at attractive prices* 价钱低廉诱人的货物. ⇨ Usage at BEAUTIFUL 用法见 BEAUTIFUL. ▷ **at·tract·ively** *adv*: *attractively arranged, displayed, presented, etc* 诱人地摆着、陈列着、展示着等. **at·tract·ive·ness** *n* [U].

at·trib·ute¹ /əˈtrɪbju:t; əˋtrɪbjut/ *v* [Tn·pr] ~ **sth to sb/sth** regard sth as belonging to, caused by or produced by sb/sth 认为某事物属于某人[某事物]; 认为某事物由某人[某事物]引起或产生: *This play is usually attributed to Shakespeare.* 这个剧本通常认为是莎士比亚作的. ○ *She attributes her success to hard work and a bit of luck.* 她认为她的成功是由于勤奋加上一点儿运气而得来的.

▷ **at·trib·ut·able** /əˈtrɪbjʊtəbl; əˋtrɪbjutəbḷ/ *adj* [pred 作表语] ~ **to sb/sth** that can be attributed to sb/sth 可归属或归因于某人[某事物]: *Is this painting attributable to Michelangelo?* 这幅画是米开朗琪罗画的吗?

at·tri·bu·tion /ˌætrɪˈbju:ʃn; ˏætrəˋbjuʃən/ *n* **1** [U] attributing sth to sb/sth 将某事物归属或归因于某人[某事物]. **2** [C] thing or quality attributed to sb/sth 所归属或归因于某人[某事物]的事物或特性.

at·tri·bute² /ˈætrɪbju:t; ˋætrəˏbjut/ *n* **1** quality regarded as a natural or typical part of sb/sth 属性; 特质; 性质: *Her greatest attribute was her kindness.* 她最大的特点是为人厚道. ○ *Patience is one of the most important attributes in a teacher.* 当教师最重要的一个品性就是要有耐心. **2** object recognized as a symbol of a person or his position 人物或其职位的标志; 象征: *The sceptre is an attribute of kingly power.* 节杖是国王权力的象征.

at·trib·ut·ive /əˈtrɪbjʊtɪv; əˋtrɪbjətɪv/ *adj* (*grammar*) (of adjectives or nouns) used directly before a noun, to describe it (指形容词或名词)定语的. Cf 参看 PREDICATIVE. ▷ **at·trib·ut·ively** *adv*.

at·tri·tion /əˈtrɪʃn; əˋtrɪʃən/ *n* [U] **1** process of gradually weakening sb's strength and confidence by continuous harassment (used esp in the expression shown) 消耗, 消损(尤用于以下示例): *a war of attrition* 消耗战. **2** wearing sth away by rubbing; friction 磨损; 摩擦.

at·tune /əˈtju:n; *US* əˈtu:n; əˋtun/ *v* [Tn·pr usu passive 通常用于被动语态] ~ **sth/sb to sth** bring sth/sb into harmony or agreement with sth; make sth/sb familiar with sth 使某事物[某人]与另一事物调合或一致; 使某事物[某人]熟悉另一事物: *We/Our ears are becoming attuned to the noise of the new factory nearby.* 我们[我们的耳朵]逐渐适应了附近新工厂的噪声.

Atty-Gen *abbr* 缩写 = (*esp US*) Attorney-General.

atyp·ical /ˌeɪˈtɪpɪkl; eˋtɪpɪkḷ/ *adj* not representative or characteristic of its type; not typical 不具代表性或同类特性的; 非典型的: *a creature that is atypical of its species* 没有其同类特性的生物. ▷ **atyp·ic·ally** /-klɪ; -klɪ/ *adv*.

au·ber·gine /ˈəʊbəʒi:n; ˋobɚˏʒin/ (also *esp US* **egg-plant**) *n* [C, U] (**a**) large (almost egg-shaped) dark purple fruit, used as a vegetable 茄子(果实). (**b**) plant producing this fruit 茄子(植物).

au·brie·tia /ɔ:ˈbri:ʃə; ɔˋbriʃə/ *n* small perennial plant that flowers in spring and is often grown on stone walls, rockeries, etc 紫花芥(矮小的多年生植物, 春季开花, 常生长于石壁、假山等上面).

au·burn /ˈɔ:bən; ˋɔbɚn/ *adj* (esp of hair) reddish-brown (尤指毛发)红褐色的.

auc·tion /ˈɔ:kʃn, *also* ˈɒkʃn; ˋɔkʃən/ *n* **1** [U] method of selling things in which each item is sold to the person who offers the most money for it 拍卖(方式): *The house is up for auction/will be sold by auction.* 这所房子将要拍卖. ○ *It should fetch* (ie be sold for) *£100 000 at auction.* 拍卖它可得100 000英镑. **2** [C] (also ˈ**auction sale**) public event when this takes place 拍卖: *attend all the local auctions* 参加本地所有的拍卖活动.

▷ **auc·tion** *v* **1** [Tn] sell (sth) by auction 拍卖. **2** (phr v) **auction sth off** sell (esp surplus or unwanted goods) by auction 拍卖掉(尤指剩余的或多余的物资): *The Army is auctioning off a lot of old equipment.* 军队正在把大量旧装备拍卖掉.

auc·tion·eer /ˌɔ:kʃəˈnɪə(r); ˏɔkʃənˋɪr/ *n* person whose job is conducting auctions 拍卖人.

□ ˈ**auction bridge** form of bridge² in which players bid for the right to name trumps 竞叫桥牌(桥牌戏的一种, 谁叫牌最高就由谁定王牌).

au·da·cious /ɔ:ˈdeɪʃəs; ɔˋdeʃəs/ *adj* **1** showing a willingness to take risks; daring; fearless 有冒险精神的; 大胆的; 无畏的: *an audacious plan, scheme, etc* 大胆的计划、设计等. **2** impudent; recklessly bold 厚颜无耻的; 鲁莽的: *an audacious remark* 放肆的话. ▷ **au·da·ciously** *adv*. **au·da·city** /ɔ:ˈdæsətɪ; ɔˋdæsətɪ/ *n* [U]: *He had the audacity to tell me I was too fat.* 他竟然胆敢对我说我太肥胖.

aud·ible /ˈɔ:dəbl; ˋɔdəbḷ/ *adj* that can be heard clearly 听得见的: *Her voice was scarcely audible above the noise of the wind.* 在风声中, 她的声音几乎听不见. ▷ **aud·ib·il·ity** /ˌɔ:dəˈbɪlətɪ; ˏɔdəˋbɪlətɪ/ *n* [U]. **aud·ibly** /-əblɪ; -əblɪ/ *adv*.

au·di·ence /ˈɔ:dɪəns; ˋɔdɪəns/ *n* **1** [CGp] group of people who have gathered together to hear or watch sb/sth 听众; 观众: *The audience was/were enthusiastic on the opening night of the play.* 那出戏首次公演之夜观众非常热情. ○ *She has addressed audiences all over the*

A

country. 她曾向全国各地的听众演讲. **2** [C] number of people who watch, read or listen to the same thing 看着或听着同一事物的人们: *An audience of millions watched the royal wedding on TV.* 数以百万计的人们在电视上观看皇家婚礼. ○ *His book reached an even wider audience when it was filmed for television.* 他的书拍成电视以后, 使读者范围扩大到观众了. **3** [C] formal interview with a ruler or an important person 与统治者或要人的正式会见; 觐见; 谒见: *request an audience with the Queen* 请求觐见女王 ○ *grant a private audience to a foreign ambassador* 准予外国大使私人谒见.

audio- *comb form* 构词成分 of hearing or sound 听觉的; 声音的: *audio-visual*.

au·dio fre·quency /ˌɔːdɪəʊ ˈfriːkwənsɪ; ˌɔdɪo ˈfrikwənsɪ/ (radio) frequency that can be heard when converted into sound waves by a loudspeaker 成音频率; 音频.

au·dio typ·ist /ˈɔːdɪəʊ taɪpɪst; ˈɔdɪo ˌtaɪpɪst/ person who listens to a tape recording and types what is heard 录音打字员(听录音打字的人员).

audio-visual /ˌɔːdɪəʊ ˈvɪʒʊəl; ˌɔdɪo ˈvɪʒʊəl/ *adj* (*abbr* 缩写 **AV**) using both sight and sound 视觉听觉的; 视听的: *ˌaudio-visual ˈaids for the classroom*, eg cassette recorders, video recorders, pictures, etc 课堂视听教具(如盒式录音机、录像机、图片等).

audit /ˈɔːdɪt; ˈɔdɪt/ *n* official (usu yearly) examination of accounts to see that they are in order (政府的)审计, 查帐(通常为一年一度的).

▷ **audit** *v* [Tn] examine (accounts, etc) officially 审计, 查核(帐目等).

au·di·tion /ɔːˈdɪʃn; ɔˈdɪʃən/ *n* trial hearing of a person who wants to perform as an actor, a singer, a musician, etc (对拟做演员、歌手、乐师等人的)试听, 试音: *I'm going to the audition but I don't expect I'll get a part.* 我去试音, 可并不指望会给我个角色演出.

▷ **au·di·tion** *v* **1** [I] take part in an audition 试音: *Which part are you auditioning for?* 你扮什么角色试音? **2** [Tn] give an audition to (sb) 试听: *None of the actresses we've auditioned is suitable.* 我们试听的这些女演员都不合适.

aud·itor /ˈɔːdɪtə(r); ˈɔdɪtɚ/ *n* person who audits accounts 审计员; 查帐人.

aud·it·or·ium /ˌɔːdɪˈtɔːrɪəm; ˌɔdəˈtɔrɪəm/ *n* part of a theatre, concert hall, etc in which an audience sits 观众席; 听众席.

aud·it·ory /ˈɔːdɪtrɪ; *US* -tɔːrɪ; ˈɔdəˌtɔrɪ/ *adj* of or concerned with hearing 听觉的; 关于听觉的: *the auditory nerve* 听觉神经.

au fait /ˌəʊ ˈfeɪ; oˈfe/ *adj* [pred 作表语] (*French* 法) ~ **(with sth)** fully acquainted (with sth) (对某事物)熟悉; 通晓: *It's my first week here so I'm not yet au fait with the system.* 我刚来不到一个星期, 对这里的制度还不太熟悉.

au fond /ˌəʊ ˈfɒn; ˌoˈfɔ̃/ *adv* (*French* 法) basically 基本上; 根本地: *The problem is that, au fond, he's very lazy.* 问题是他根本就很懒.

Aug *abbr* 缩写 = August: *31 Aug 1908* 1908年8月31日.

auger /ˈɔːɡə(r); ˈɔɡɚ/ *n* tool for boring holes in wood, like a gimlet but larger 螺旋钻; 麻花钻.

aught /ɔːt; ɔt/ *pron* (*arch* 古) **1** anything 任何事物. **2** (idm 习语) **for aught/all sb knows** ⇨ KNOW.

aug·ment /ɔːɡˈment; ɔɡˈmɛnt/ *v* [Tn] (*fml* 文) make (sth) larger in number or size; increase 增多; 增大; 增加: *augment one's income by writing reviews* 藉写书评而增加收入.

▷ **aug·men·ta·tion** /ˌɔːɡmenˈteɪʃn; ˌɔɡmɛnˈteʃən/ *n* (*fml* 文) **1** [U] action of augmenting or being augmented 增多; 增大; 增加. **2** [C] thing that is added to sth 增加物.

au gra·tin /ˌəʊ ˈɡrætæn; oˈɡrætn̩/ *adv* (*French* 法) cooked with a crisp coating of breadcrumbs or grated cheese 烤制成带有一层松脆的面包屑或干酪末: *cauliflower au gratin* 脆皮菜花.

au·gur /ˈɔːɡə(r); ˈɔɡɚ/ *n* (in ancient Rome) religious official who foretold future events by watching the behaviour of birds, etc (古罗马教会中观察鸟类等动态而预卜吉凶的)占卜官.

▷ **au·gur** *v* **1** [Tn] be a sign of (sth); foretell 预兆; 预示: *Does this augur disaster for our team?* 这是否预兆我们队大难临头? **2** (idm 习语) **augur well/ill for sb/sth** (*fml* 文) be a good/bad sign for sb/sth in the future 预示某人[某事物]的吉[凶]: *The quality of your work augurs well for the examinations next month.* 你的功课做得这么好预示下月准考得好.

au·gury /ˈɔːɡjʊrɪ; ˈɔɡjərɪ/ *n* omen; sign 征兆; 预兆.

au·gust /ɔːˈɡʌst; ɔˈɡʌst/ *adj* [usu attrib 通常作定语] inspiring feelings of respect and awe; majestic and imposing 令人敬畏的; 威严的; 堂皇的: *an august body of elder statesmen* 德高望重的政界元老们.

Au·gust /ˈɔːɡəst; ˈɔɡəst/ *n* [U, C] (*abbr* 缩写 **Aug**) the eighth month of the year, next after July 八月.

For the uses of *August* see the examples at *April.* 关于August的用法见April词条中的示例.

Au·gustan /ɔːˈɡʌstən; ɔˈɡʌstən/ *adj* **1** of the reign of Augustus Caesar, when Latin literature flourished (拉丁文学全盛时期的)奥古斯都·恺撒统治时期的. **2** (of any literature) classical(1); stylish (指任何文学)经典的, 典雅的: *The Augustan age of English literature includes the writers Dryden, Swift and Pope.* 在英国文学的全盛时期里有德莱顿、斯威夫特和蒲柏等文豪.

auk /ɔːk; ɔk/ *n* northern sea-bird with short narrow wings 海雀(北方海鸟, 翅短而窄).

auld lang syne /ˌɔːld læŋ ˈsaɪn; ˌɔld læŋ ˈsaɪn/ (*Scot* 苏格兰) (title of a popular song sung esp at the beginning of each new year and expressing feelings of friendship for the sake of) good times long ago 美好的往日(歌曲名, 尤于新年时及抒发对往日友谊之情时唱的).

aunt /ɑːnt; *US* ænt; ænt/ **1 (a)** *n* sister of one's father or mother; wife of one's uncle 姑母; 姨母; 伯母; 婶母; 舅母: *Aunt Mary is my mother's sister.* 玛丽姨母是我母亲的妹妹. ⇨App 8 见附录8. **(b)** woman whose brother or sister has a child 身为姑母或姨母的女子. **2** (*infml* 口) (used by children, usu in front of a first name 儿童用语, 通常用于被称呼者名前, 不与姓同称) unrelated woman friend, esp of one's parents 阿姨, 姑姑(尤指父母的朋友).

▷ **auntie** (also **aunty**) /ˈɑːntɪ; *US* ˈæntɪ; ˈæntɪ/ *n* (*infml* 口) = aunt.

□ **ˌAunt ˈSally 1** wooden figure used as a target in a throwing-game at fairs, etc 在游乐场等处用作投掷游戏目标的木偶. **2** (*fig* 比喻) person or thing that is subjected to general abuse and criticism, often undeserved 广为人指责的人或事物(常为代人受过者); 替罪羊; 替死鬼: *Any public figure risks being made an Aunt Sally by the popular press.* 任何知名人士都要冒风险, 会成为通俗刊物的众矢之的.

au pair /ˌəʊ ˈpeə(r); oˈpɛr/ person (usu from overseas) who receives board and lodging with a family in return for helping with the housework, etc 以帮做家务事等换取食宿(通常为来自海外)的人; 换工: *We've got a German au pair for six months.* 我们找到了一个可以干六个月的德国换工. ○ [attrib 作定语] *an au pair girl* 做换工的姑娘.

aura /ˈɔːrə; ˈɔrə/ *n* distinctive atmosphere that seems to surround and be caused by a person or thing (发自某人或某物而环绕其周围的)特殊气氛; 氛围: *She always seems to have an aura of happiness about her.* 她好像总是喜气洋洋的.

aural /ˈɔːrəl *or, rarely,* 罕读作 ˈaʊrəl; ˈɔrəl/ *adj* of or concerning the ear or hearing 耳的或听觉的; 关于耳的或听觉的: *an aural surgeon* 耳科外科医师 ○ *aural comprehension tests* 听力测验. ▷ **aur·ally** *adv*.

au·re·ola /ɔːˈrɪələ; ɔˈriələ/ (also **au·re·ole** /ˈɔːrɪəʊl; ˈɔrɪˌol/) *n* (*pl* **~s**) **1** = HALO. **2** = CORONA.

au re·voir /ˌəʊ rəˈvwɑː(r); ˌorəvˈwɑr/ (*French* 法) goodbye until we meet again 再见: *Au revoir, see you again next year!* 再见, 明年见!

aur·icle /ˈɔːrɪkl; ˈɔrɪkl̩/ *n* **1** external part of the ear 耳郭; 耳廓. ⇨illus at EAR 见EAR之插图. **2** small pouch in each of the two upper parts of the heart 心房; 心耳. Cf 参看 VENTRICLE 2.

au·ri·cu·lar /ɔːˈrɪkjʊlə(r); ɔˈrɪkjəlɚ/ *adj* of or like the ear 耳的; 耳状的: *an auricular confession*, ie one spoken privately into the ear of a priest 秘密忏悔(向神父秘密耳语忏悔).

au·ri·fer·ous /ɔːˈrɪfərəs; ɔˈrɪfərəs/ *adj* (of rock) yielding gold (指岩石)含金的, 产金的.

au·rora /ɔːˈrɔːrə; ɔˈrɔrə/ *n* **1 auˌrora boreˈalis** /bɔːrɪˈeɪlɪs; ˌbɔrɪˈelɪs/ (also **the northern lights**) bands of coloured light, mainly red and green, seen in the sky at night near the North Pole and caused by electrical radiation 北极光(在北极上空夜晚可见由电辐射产生的带状彩色光, 以红绿为主). **2 auˌrora auˈstralis** /ɒˈstreɪlɪs; ɔsˋtrelɪs/ similar lights seen in the southern hemisphere 南极光(在南半球可见的类似的光).

aus·pi·ces /ˈɔːspɪsɪz; ˋɔspɪsɪz/ *n* [pl] (idm 习语) **under the auspices of sb/sth** helped and supported by sb/sth; having sb/sth as a patron 在某人[某事物]的帮助或支持下; 有某人[某事物]赞助的: *set up a business under the auspices of a government aid scheme* 在政府援助计划资助下创办公司. **under favourable, etc auspices** with favourable, etc prospects 有吉利等的希望: *The committee began its work under unfavourable auspices.* 委员会工作伊始即十分不利.

aus·pi·cious /ɔːˈspɪʃəs; ɔˋspɪʃəs/ *adj* showing signs of future success; favourable; promising 吉利的; 吉祥的; 有前途的: *I'm pleased that you've made such an auspicious start to the new term.* 你新学期开门红使我很高兴.

Aus·sie /ˈɒzɪ; ˋɔsɪ/ *n, adj* (*infml* 口) (native or inhabitant) of Australia 澳大利亚的(土著或居民).

aus·tere /ɒˈstɪə(r), *also* ɔːˈstɪə(r); ɔˋstɪr/ *adj* **1** (of a person or his behaviour) severely and strictly moral; having no pleasures or comforts (指人或行为)束身自修的, 苦行的: *monks leading simple, austere lives* 过着清苦生活的僧侣. **2** (of a building or place) very simple and plain; without ornament or comfort (指建筑物或地方)简朴的, 无装饰的, 简陋的: *The room was furnished in austere style.* 这间屋子的陈设都很简单朴素.

▷ **aus·terely** *adv*.

aus·ter·ity /ɒˈsterətɪ, *also* ɔːˈsterətɪ; ɔˋstɛrətɪ/ *n* **1** [U] quality of being austere 简朴; 紧缩: *the austerity of the Government's economic measures* 政府经济措施方面的紧缩 ○ *War was followed by many years of austerity.* 战争结束后还要过多年的紧日子. **2** [C usu *pl* 通常作复数] condition, activity or practice that is part of an austere way of life 节衣缩食; 艰苦朴素: *Wartime austerities included food rationing and shortage of fuel.* 战时的艰苦包括食物配给和燃料短缺.

Aus·tra·lian /ɒˈstreɪlɪən, *also* ɔːˈstreɪlɪən; ɔˋstreljən/ *n, adj* (native or inhabitant) of Australia 澳大利亚的(土著或居民).

□ **ˌAustralian ˈRules** Australian game, similar to Rugby and played by two teams of 18 players 澳大利亚规则(澳大利亚式足球运动, 类似橄榄球, 由两队各18人参赛).

Austro- *comb form* 构词成分 Austrian; of Austria 奥地利的: *the Austro-Hungarian empire*.

au·then·tic /ɔːˈθentɪk; ɔˋθɛntɪk/ *adj* **1** known to be true or genuine 真实的; 真正的: *an authentic document, signature, painting* 正式文件、亲笔签字、原作绘画. **2** trustworthy; reliable 可信的; 可靠的: *an authentic statement* 可靠的陈述.

▷ **au·then·tic·ally** /-klɪ; -klɪ/ *adv*.

au·then·ti·city /ˌɔːθenˈtɪsətɪ; ˌɔθənˋtɪsətɪ/ *n* [U] quality of being authentic 真实性; 可靠性; 确实性: *The authenticity of the manuscript is beyond doubt.* 手稿的真实性是毋庸置疑的.

au·then·tic·ate /ɔːˈθentɪkeɪt; ɔˋθɛntɪˌket/ *v* [Tn] prove (sth) to be valid or genuine or true 证明(某事物)有效或是真的或属实: *authenticate a claim* 证实索求合理 ○ *Experts have authenticated the writing as that of Shakespeare himself.* 专家们已经鉴定出这是莎士比亚的手迹. ▷ **au·then·tica·tion** /ɔːˌθentɪˈkeɪʃn; ɔˌθɛntɪˋkeʃən/ *n* [U].

au·thor /ˈɔːθə(r); ˋɔθɚ/ *n* **1** writer of a book, play, etc (书、剧本等的)著者, 作家: *Dickens is my favourite author.* 狄更斯是我最喜爱的作家. **2** person who creates or begins sth, esp a plan or an idea 创造者; 创始者; 发起人: *As the author of the scheme I can't really comment.* 我作为这一计划的创始人是不便置评的.

▷ **au·thor·ess** /ˈɔːθərɪs; ˋɔθɚɪs/ *n* woman author 女作家.

au·thor·ship *n* [U] **1** origin of a book, etc (书等的)来源、出处、作者: *The authorship of this poem is not known.* 这首诗出处不详. **2** state of being an author 作家或创始者的身分.

au·thor·it·ar·ian /ɔːˌθɒrɪˈteərɪən; ɔˌθɑrəˋtɛrɪən/ *adj* favouring complete obedience to authority (esp that of the State) before personal freedom 权力主义的(主张绝对服从权威, 尤指政权, 高于个人自由): *an authoritarian government, regime, doctrine* 权力主义的政府、政体、教义等 ○ *The school is run on authoritarian lines.* 这所学校走的是权力主义路线.

▷ **au·thor·it·ar·ian** *n* person who believes in complete obedience to authority 权力主义者: *My father was a strict authoritarian.* 我父亲是绝对的权力主义者.

au·thor·it·ar·ian·ism *n* [U].

au·thor·it·at·ive /ɔːˈθɒrətətɪv; *US* -teɪtɪv; ɔˋθɑrəˌtetɪv/ *adj* **1** having authority; that can be trusted; reliable 有权力的; 有权威的; 可相信的; 可靠的: *information from an authoritative source* 来自权威方面的消息. **2** given with authority; official 权威的; 官方的; 当局的: *authoritative instructions, orders, etc* 官方的指示、命令等. **3** showing or seeming to show authority 显示权力的; 好像显示权威的: *an authoritative tone of voice* 权威式的口吻. ▷ **au·thor·it·at·ively** *adv*.

au·thor·ity /ɔːˈθɒrətɪ; ɔˋθɑrətɪ/ *n* **1** [U] **(a)** power to give orders and make others obey 权力; 权威: *The leader must be a person of authority.* 领袖必须是有权威的人. ○ *She now has authority over the people she used to take orders from.* 她现在有权力支配那些一贯向她发号施令的人. ○ *Who is in authority* (ie holds the position of command) *now?* 现在谁掌权? ○ *I am acting under her authority*, ie following her orders. 我受她支配. **(b)** **~ (to do sth)** right to act in a specific way 职权; 权限: *Only the treasurer has authority to sign cheques.* 只有司库有权签署支票. ○ *We have the authority to search this building.* 我们有权搜查这座建筑物. **2** [C often *pl* 常作复数] person or group having the power to give orders or take action 有权力发号施令的人或团体; 当局; 官方: *He's in the care of the local authority.* 他归地方当局管. ○ *The health authorities are investigating the matter.* 卫生当局正调查这件事. ○ *I shall have to report this to the authorities.* 我得把这事向当局报告. **3** [C] **(a)** person with special knowledge 具有专门知识的人; 权威: *She's an authority on phonetics.* 她是语音学权威. **(b)** book, etc that can supply reliable information or evidence 可提供可靠资料或证据的书籍等; 权威著作: *What is your authority for that statement?* 你的说法出处何在? ○ *Always quote your authorities*, ie give the names of books, people, etc used as sources for facts. 引用资料一定要注明出处(即注明书名、人名等, 用作论据的出处).

au·thor·ize, -ise /ˈɔːθəraɪz; ˋɔθəˌraɪz/ *v* **1** [Tn, Dn·t] give authority to (sb) 授权; 委任; 委托: *I have authorized him to act for me while I am away.* 我已经委托他当我不在的时候代我处理. **2** [Tn] give authority for (sth); sanction 批准; 认可: *authorize a payment* 批准付款 ○ *Has this visit been authorized?* 这次访问获准了吗?

▷ **auth·or·iz·ation, -isation** /ˌɔːθəraɪˈzeɪʃn; *US* -rɪˈz-; ˌɔθərəˋzeʃən/ *n* **1** [U] action of authorizing 授权; 委任; 委托. **2 ~ (for sth/to do sth)** **(a)** [U] power given to sb to do sth 授予某人做某事的权力. **(b)** [C] document, etc giving this 授权书; 委任状; 委托书: *May I see your authorization for this?* 我可以看看你做这件事的授权书吗?

□ **the ˌAuthorized ˈVersion** (*abbr* 缩写 **AV**) the English translation of the Bible first published in 1611 and authorized by King James I for use in churches 钦定英译本(《圣经》的英译本, 首次出版于1611年, 由英王詹姆士一世钦定用于宗教仪式中).

aut·ism /ˈɔːtɪzəm; ˋɔtɪzəm/ *n* [U] (*psychology* 心) serious mental illness, esp of children, in which one becomes unable to communicate or form relationships with others 自向症, 孤独症(严重的精神病, 尤见于儿童, 患者无法与他人交往).

▷ **aut·istic** /ɔːˈtɪstɪk; ɔˋtɪstɪk/ *adj* (*psychology* 心) suffering from autism 患自向症的.

auto /ˈɔːtəʊ; ˋɔto/ *n* (*pl* **~s**) (*infml* 口 *esp US*) car 汽车.

aut(o)- *comb form* 构词成分 **1** of oneself 自己的: *autobiography* ○ *autograph*. **2** by oneself or itself; independent(ly) 靠自己的; 由本身的; 独自的(地): *autocracy* ○ *automobile*.

auto·bahn /ˈɔːtəbɑːn; ˋɔtəˌbɑn/ *n* motorway in Germany, Austria or Switzerland (德国、奥地利或瑞士的)高速公路.

A

auto·bio·graphy /ˌɔːtəbaɪˈɒɡrəfɪ; ˌɔtəbaɪˈɑɡrəfɪ/ *n* **1** [C] story of a person's life written by that person 自传: *She has just written her autobiography.* 她刚写完自传. **2** [U] this type of writing 自传写作.
▷ **auto·bio·graphic** /ˌɔːtəˌbaɪəˈɡræfɪk; ˌɔtəˌbaɪəˈɡræfɪk/, **auto·bio·graph·ical** /-ɪkl; -ɪkḷ/ *adjs* of or concerning autobiography 自传的; 有关自传的: *His novels are largely autobiographical*, ie though fictional they describe many of his own experiences. 他的小说大多是自传式的(即虽属虚构, 但却描述许多亲身经历).

auto·cracy /ɔːˈtɒkrəsɪ; ɔˈtɑkrəsɪ/ *n* (**a**) [U] government by one person with unlimited power; despotism 独裁政体; 专制政治. (**b**) [C] country governed in this way 独裁国家; 专制国家.

auto·crat /ˈɔːtəkræt; ˈɔtəˌkræt/ *n* **1** ruler of an autocracy 独裁者; 专制君主. **2** person who gives orders without consulting others and expects to be obeyed at all times 专横霸道的人. ▷ **auto·cratic** /ˌɔːtəˈkrætɪk; ˌɔtəˈkrætɪk/ *adj*. **auto·crati·cally** /-klɪ; -klɪ/ *adv*.

auto·cross /ˈɔːtəʊkrɒs; ˈɔtokrɔs/ *n* [U] sport of motor-racing across country 汽车越野比赛.

Auto·cue /ˈɔːtəʊkjuː; ˈɔtokju/ *n* (*propr* 专利名) device next to the camera from which a person speaking on TV can read the script without having to learn it 自动提示器(电视摄像机旁的一种装置, 电视上的讲话者可从中读出讲稿或台词而不必死记硬背). Cf 参看 TELEPROMPTER.

auto·graph /ˈɔːtəɡrɑːf; *US* -ɡræf; ˈɔtəˌɡræf/ *n* person's signature or handwriting, esp when kept as a souvenir 亲笔签名, 手迹(尤指为留作纪念者): *I've got lots of famous footballers' autographs.* 我有许多著名足球运动员的亲笔签名. ○ [attrib 作定语] *an autograph book/album* 签名簿[册].
▷ **auto·graph** *v* [Tn] write one's name on or in (sth) 在(某物)上签名; 签名于(某物): *an autographed copy* 签过名的一份.

auto·mat /ˈɔːtəmæt; ˈɔtəˌmæt/ *n* (*US*) restaurant in which customers get their own food from closed compartments by putting coins in slots to open them 自助餐馆(一种饭馆, 顾客在投币孔中投入硬币便可打开食品分隔柜门而自行取出食品).

auto·mate /ˈɔːtəmeɪt; ˈɔtəˌmet/ *v* [Tn esp passive 尤用于被动语态] cause (sth) to operate by automation 使(某事物)自动操作: *This part of the assembly process is now fully automated.* 装配过程的这一部分现在是全自动的.

auto·matic /ˌɔːtəˈmætɪk; ˌɔtəˈmætɪk/ *adj* **1** (of a machine) working by itself without direct human control; self-regulating (指机器)自动的; 自动调整的: *an automatic washing-machine* 自动洗衣机 ○ *automatic gears*, ie in a motor vehicle 自动排挡(机动车辆中的自动变速装置) ○ *an automatic rifle*, ie one that continues firing as long as the trigger is pressed 自动步枪(只要一直扣住扳机便可连续射击的步枪). **2** (of actions) done without thinking, esp from habit or routine; unconscious (指动作)未加思索而做出的(尤指基于习惯或因袭陈规者); 无意识的: *For most of us breathing is automatic.* 我们大多数人的呼吸都是无意识的. **3** following necessarily 必然随之而来的: *A fine for this offence is automatic.* 对于这种过失, 罚款是必然的.
▷ **auto·matic** *n* **1** automatic machine or gun or tool 自动的机器或枪炮或工具. **2** car with automatic transmission 自动汽车(有自动变速器的汽车).
au·to·mat·ic·ally /-klɪ; -klɪ/ *adv*.
□ ˌ**automatic** ˈ**pilot** device in an aircraft or a ship to keep it on a set course without human control (飞行器或轮船上的)自动驾驶仪.
ˌ**automatic trans**ˈ**mission** system in a motor vehicle that changes the gears automatically 自动变速器(机动车辆中的自动换挡系统).

auto·ma·tion /ˌɔːtəˈmeɪʃn; ˌɔtəˈmeʃən/ *n* [U] use of automatic equipment and machines to do work previously done by people 自动化(用自动设备和机器做以前需要人来做的工作): *Automation will mean the loss of many jobs in this factory.* 自动化将意味着这个工厂要减少许多工作职位.

au·to·maton /ɔːˈtɒmətən; *US* -tɒn; ɔˈtɑməˌtɑn/ *n* (*pl* **~s** or **-ta** /-tə; -tə/) **1** = ROBOT 1. **2** (*fig* 比喻) person who seems to act mechanically and without thinking 看上去动作呆板而又不动脑筋的人. Cf 参看 ROBOT 2.

auto·mo·bile /ˈɔːtəməbiːl, *also* ˌɔːtəməˈbiːl; ˈɔtəməˌbil/ *n* (*esp US*) = CAR 1 汽车.

auto·nom·ous /ɔːˈtɒnəməs; ɔˈtɑnəməs/ *adj* self-governing; acting independently 自治的; 自主的; 独立的: *an alliance of autonomous states* 自治州联盟.
▷ **auto·nomy** /ɔːˈtɒnəmɪ; ɔˈtɑnəmɪ/ *n* [U] self-government; independence 自治; 自主; 独立: *Branch managers have full autonomy in their own areas.* 分支机构的经理在其管辖范围内有充分的自主权.

aut·opsy /ˈɔːtɒpsɪ; ˈɔtɑpsɪ/ *n* examination of a dead body to learn the cause of death; post-mortem (为了解死亡原因而做的)尸体剖检; 验尸: [attrib 作定语] *an autopsy report* 尸检报告. Cf 参看 BIOPSY.

auto·strada /ˈɔːtəʊstrɑːdə; ˌɔtoˈstrɑdə/ *n* (*Italian* 意) motorway in Italy (意大利的)高速公路.

auto-suggestion /ˌɔːtəʊ səˈdʒestʃən; ˌɔtosəˈdʒɛstʃən/ *n* [U] (*psychology* 心) process by which a person under hypnosis or subconsciously suggests to himself a way of changing his own behaviour 自我暗示(处于催眠状态中或下意识地暗示自己改变行为).

au·tumn /ˈɔːtəm; ˈɔtəm/ (*US* **fall**) *n* [U, C] the third season of the year, coming between summer and winter, ie from September to November in the northern hemisphere 秋, 秋天, 秋季(一年的第三季, 在北半球为从九月至十一月): *The leaves turn brown in autumn.* 秋天树叶变黄. ○ *in the autumn of 1980* 在1980年的秋天 ○ *in (the) early/late autumn* 在初[晚]秋 ○ *It's been one of the coldest autumns for years.* 这是多年来最冷的秋天. ○ [attrib 作定语] *autumn colours, weather, fashions* 秋季的色彩、天气、流行式样 ○ (*fig* 比喻) *in the autumn of* (ie the later part of) *one's life* 在暮年(晚年).
▷ **au·tum·nal** /ɔːˈtʌmnəl; ɔˈtʌmnḷ/ *adj* [usu pred 通常作表语] of or like autumn 秋天; 像秋天: *The weather in June was positively autumnal.* 那六月的天气真像秋天似的.

aux·ili·ary /ɔːɡˈzɪlɪərɪ; ɔɡˈzɪlərɪ/ *adj* giving help or support; additional 帮助的; 辅助的; 附加的; 副的: *auxiliary troops* 辅助部队 ○ *an auxiliary nurse* 助理护士 ○ *an auxiliary generator in case of power cuts* 万一断电时使用的备用发电机.
▷ **aux·ili·ary** *n* **1** [C] person or thing that helps 辅助的人或事物; 辅助者: *medical auxiliaries* 医疗辅助人员[设备]. **2 auxiliaries** [pl] additional (esp foreign or allied) troops used by a country at war (尤指战时外国或同盟国的)援军. **3** [C] (also **au**ˌ**xiliary** ˈ**verb**) verb used with main verbs to show tense, mood, etc, and to form questions, eg *do* and *has* in *Do you know where he has gone?* 助动词(与主要动词连用表示时态、语气等, 也用以构成问句, 如在 Do you know where he has gone? 句中的 do 和 has).

AV /ˌeɪ ˈviː; ˌeˈvi/ *abbr* 缩写 = **1** audio-visual. **2** Authorized Version (of the Bible).

avail /əˈveɪl; əˈvel/ *v* **1** [Tn·pr] **~ oneself of sth** (*fml* 文) make use of sth; take advantage of sth 使用某事物; 利用某事物: *You must avail yourself of every opportunity to speak English.* 你要利用一切机会说英语. **2** [I, Ipr] (*dated* 旧) be of value or help 有价值; 有帮助; 有用: *What can avail against the storm?* 用什么来抵挡风暴? **3** (idm 习语) **a**ˌ**vail sb** ˈ**nothing** (*dated* 旧) be of no use to sb 对某人无用.
▷ **avail** *n* (idm 习语) **of little/no a**ˈ**vail** not very/not at all helpful or effective 没有多大[一点儿]帮助、用处或效果: *The advice we got was of no avail.* 我们得到的建议完全没用. **to little/no a**ˈ**vail**; **without a**ˈ**vail** with little/no success 没有什么成果[没有成果]: *The doctors tried everything to keep him alive but to no avail.* 医生们曾竭尽全力抢救他的生命, 但却徒劳无功.

avail·able /əˈveɪləbl; əˈveləbl/ *adj* **1** (of things) that can be used or obtained (指物)可用的或可得到的: *Tickets are available at the box office.* 票房有票. ○ *You will be informed when the book becomes available.* 这本书有货时就通知你. ○ *This was the only available room.* 只剩下那个房间可用了. **2** (of people) free to be seen, talked to, etc (指人)可会见的, 可与之交谈的等: *I'm available in the afternoon.* 我下午有空. ○ *The Prime Minister was not available for comment.* 首相无暇作出评论. ▷ **avail·ab·il·ity** /əˌveɪləˈbɪlətɪ; əˌveləˈbɪlətɪ/ *n* [U].

ava·lanche /ˈævəlɑːnʃ; *US* -læntʃ; ˈævḷˌæntʃ/ *n* mass of snow, ice and rock that slides rapidly down the side of a mountain 雪崩; 山崩: *Yesterday's avalanche killed a party of skiers and destroyed several trees.* 昨天的雪崩造成一批滑雪者死亡, 并毁坏了一些树木. ○ (*fig* 比喻) *We received an avalanche of letters in reply to our advertisement.* 广告登出后, 我们收到雪片般涌来的大批信件.

avant-garde /ˌævɒŋ ˈgɑːd; ˌævɑnˋgɑrd/ *adj* favouring new and progressive ideas, esp in art and literature 先锋的, 先驱的(尤指在文学艺术方面): *avant-garde writers, artists, etc* 先锋作家、艺术家等 ○ *the avant-garde movement* 先驱运动.

▷ **avant-garde** *n* [CGp] group of people introducing such ideas 先锋派: *a member of the avant-garde* 先锋派成员.

av·ar·ice /ˈævərɪs; ˋævərɪs/ *n* [U] (*fml* 文) greed for wealth or gain 贪婪; 贪心: *Avarice makes rich people want to become even richer.* 贪婪使富人想要更富. ▷ **av·ari·cious** /ˌævəˈrɪʃəs; ˌævəˋrɪʃəs/ *adj*. **av·ari·cious·ly** *adv*.

avdp *abbr* 缩写 = avoirdupois.

Ave *abbr* 缩写 = Avenue: *5 St George's Ave* 圣乔治大街5号.

avenge /əˈvendʒ; əˋvɛndʒ/ *v* **1** [Tn] take or get revenge for (a wrong done to sb/oneself) 为(某人[自己])的冤屈)报仇, 伸冤, 雪耻: *She avenged her father's murder.* 她为其父被谋杀而复了仇. **2** [Tn·pr] **~ oneself on sb/sth** take or get revenge on sb/sth for such a wrong 向某人[某事物]报仇、报复: *She avenged herself on her father's killers.* 她向杀父之人报了仇. ▷ **aven·ger** *n*.

av·enue /ˈævənjuː; *US* -nuː; ˋævəˌnu/ *n* **1** wide road or path, often lined with trees, esp one that leads to a large house (常为两旁有树的)大道, 林阴道(尤指通往一宅门者). **2** (*abbr* 缩写 **Ave**) wide street lined with trees or tall buildings (两旁有树木或高楼的)大街. ⇨Usage at ROAD 用法见 ROAD. **3** way of approaching or making progress towards sth 途径; 手段: *an avenue to success, fame, etc* 成功、成名等之路 ○ *Several avenues are open to us.* 我们面前有几条可行之路. ○ *We have explored every avenue.* 我们已经探索过了各种途径.

aver /əˈvɜː(r); əˋvɝ/ *v* (**-rr-**) [Tn, Tf] (*fml* 文) state (sth) firmly and positively; assert 断言; 主张; 坚称.

av·er·age /ˈævərɪdʒ; ˋævərɪdʒ/ *n* **1** [C] result of adding several amounts together and dividing the total by the number of amounts 平均; 平均数: *The average of 4, 5 and 9 is 6.* 4、5、9三个数的平均数是6. **2** [U] standard or level regarded as usual 一般水平; 平均水准: *These marks are well above/below average.* 这些分数远在一般水平以上[以下]. **3** (idm 习语) **the law of averages** ⇨ LAW. **on (the) ˈaverage** taking account of use, performance, etc over a period 按平均数计算: *We fail one student per year on average.* 我们平均每年有一个学生不及格.

▷ **av·er·age** *adj* **1** [attrib 作定语] found by calculating the average 平均的: *The average age of the students is 19.* 学生的平均年龄是19岁. ○ *The average temperature in Oxford last month was 18°C.* 牛津上月的平均气温是18°C. **2** of the ordinary or usual standard 一般标准的; 普通的; 平常的: *children of average intelligence* 智力一般的儿童 ○ *Rainfall is about average for the time of year.* 对一年中的这个时候来说, 降雨量还算普通.

av·er·age *v* **1** [I, Tn] find the average of (sth) 求(某事物)的平均数; 平均: *I've done some averaging to reach these figures.* 我平均以后得出这些数. **2** [Tn no passive 不用于被动语态] do or amount to (sth) as an average measure or rate 平均值为; 平均为: *This car averages 40 miles to the gallon.* 这辆汽车平均每加仑可行40英里. ○ *The rainfall averages 36 inches a year.* 年降雨量平均为36英寸. **3** (phr v) **average ˈout (at sth)** result in an average (of sth) 达到(某事物的)平均数; 以(某事物)的平均数为结果: *Meals average out at £5 per head.* 膳食平均每人5英镑. ○ *Sometimes I pay, sometimes he pays — it seems to average out* (ie result in a fair balance) *in the end.* 有时我付钱, 有时他付钱——到头来似乎两相抵消. **average sth out (at sth)** calculate the average of sth 算出某事物的平均数: *The tax authorities averaged his profit out at £3 000 a year over 5 years.* 税务局算出他5年的平均利润为每年3 000英镑.

averse /əˈvɜːs; əˋvɝs/ *adj* [pred 作表语] **~ to sth** (*fml or rhet* 文或修辞) not liking sth; opposed to sth 不喜欢某事物; 反对某事物: *He seems to be averse to hard work.* 看来他不愿做艰苦的工作. ○ *I'm not averse to a drop of whisky after dinner.* 我倒不反对饭后喝点儿威士忌.

aver·sion /əˈvɜːʃn; *US* əˈvɜːrʒn; əˋvɝʒən/ *n* **1** [C, U] **~ (to sb/sth)** strong dislike 厌恶; 嫌恶: *I've always had an aversion to getting up early.* 我从来就厌恶早起. ○ *He took an immediate aversion to his new boss.* 他对新老板一见就反感. **2** [C] thing that is disliked 讨厌的事物: *Smoking is one of my pet* (ie particular, personal) *aversions.* 吸烟是我特别讨厌的事.

avert /əˈvɜːt; əˋvɝt/ *v* **1** [Tn, Tn·pr] **~ sth (from sth)** turn sth away 将(某事物)移开: *avert one's eyes/gaze/glance from the terrible sight* 转移目光, 不看那可怕的情景. **2** [Tn] prevent (sth); avoid 防止(某事物); 避免: *avert an accident, a crisis, a disaster, etc by prompt action* 迅速采取行动以避免事故、危险、灾祸等 ○ *He managed to avert suspicion.* 他设法避嫌.

avi·ary /ˈeɪvɪərɪ; *US* -vɪerɪ; ˋevɪˌɛrɪ/ *n* large cage or building for keeping birds in, eg in a zoo 大鸟笼, 鸟舍(如动物园中者).

avi·ation /ˌeɪvɪˈeɪʃn; ˌevɪˋeʃən/ *n* [U] **1** science or practice of flying aircraft 航空学; 航空. **2** design and manufacture of aircraft 飞行器的设计与制造: [attrib 作定语] *the aviation business/industry* 飞机制造业.

▷ **avi·ator** /ˈeɪvɪeɪtə(r); ˋevɪˌetɚ/ *n* (*dated* 旧) person who flies an aircraft as the pilot or one of the crew 飞行器驾驶员; 空勤人员.

avid /ˈævɪd; ˋævɪd/ *adj* **~ (for sth)** eager; greedy 渴望的; 贪婪的: *an avid collector of old coins* 对旧钱币求之若渴的收藏家 ○ *avid for news of her son* 渴望得到她儿子的消息.

▷ **avid·ity** /əˈvɪdətɪ; əˋvɪdətɪ/ *n* [U] (*fml* 文) eagerness 热望; 贪婪.

avidly *adv*: *She reads avidly.* 她如饥似渴地读书.

avi·on·ics /ˌeɪvɪˈɒnɪks; ˌevɪˋɑnɪks/ *n* [sing *v*] science of electronics applied to aviation 航空电子学.

avo·cado /ˌævəˈkɑːdəʊ; ˌævəˋkɑdo/ *n* (*pl* **~s**) pear-shaped tropical fruit 鳄梨(一种梨形的热带水果, 又名油梨).

avoid /əˈvɔɪd; əˋvɔɪd/ *v* **1** [Tn, Tg] (**a**) keep oneself away from (sb/sth) 避开, 躲避(某人[某事物]): *avoid (driving in) the centre of town* 避开市中心(行驶) ○ *I think he's avoiding me.* 我觉得他躲着我. (**b**) stop (sth) happening; prevent 防止发生(某事物); 预防: *Try to avoid accidents.* 尽量防止发生事故. ○ *I just avoided running over the cat.* 我差一点儿轧着猫. **2** (idm 习语) **avoid sb/sth like the ˈplague** (*infml* 口) try very hard not to meet sb/sth 极力回避, 尽量躲开某人[某事物]: *He's been avoiding me like the plague since our quarrel.* 我们吵架以后, 他一直如避蛇蝎似的躲着我.

▷ **avoid·able** *adj* that can be avoided 可避免的.

avoid·ance *n* [U] act of avoiding 回避; 躲避: *tax avoidance*, ie managing to pay the minimum amount of tax required by law 逃税.

avoir·du·pois /ˌævədəˈpɔɪz; ˌævɚdəˋpɔɪz/ *n* [U] (*abbr* 缩写 **avdp**) non-metric system of weights based on the pound, equal to 16 ounces or 7 000 grains 常衡(非公制的衡制, 基于1磅等于16盎司或7 000谷). ⇨App 5 见附录5.

avow /əˈvaʊ; əˋvaʊ/ *v* [Tn, Cn·n, Cn·t] (*fml* 文) declare (sth) openly; admit 公开宣称(某事物); 承认: *avow one's belief, faith, conviction, etc* 公开表示相信、信仰、服理等 ○ *avow oneself (to be) a socialist* 公开宣布自己是社会主义者 ○ *The avowed aim of this Government is to reduce taxation.* 这届政府所宣称的目标是减少税收.

▷ **avowal** *n* (*fml* 文) (**a**) [U] open declaration 公开宣称; 公开表示. (**b**) [C] instance of this 公开宣称; 公开表示: *make an avowal of his love* 公开表示他的爱情.

avow·edly /əˈvaʊɪdlɪ; əˋvaʊɪdlɪ/ *adv* (*fml* 文) admittedly; openly 公开承认地; 公开地: *avowedly responsible for an error* 公开承认错误.

avun·cu·lar /əˈvʌŋkjʊlə(r); əˋvʌŋkjəlɚ/ *adj* (*fml* 文) of or like an uncle, esp in manner 叔伯的, 像叔伯的(尤指举止态度): *He adopts an avuncular tone of voice when giving advice to junior colleagues.* 他用长辈的口气劝告年轻的同事.

AWACS /ˈeɪwæks; ˋewæks/ *abbr* 缩写 = airborne warning and control system 机载警报和控制系统: *planes fitted with AWACS* 装有机载警报和控制系统的

飞机.

await /əˈweɪt; əˈwet/ *v* [Tn] (*fml* 文) **1** (of a person) wait for (sb/sth) (指人)等候, 等待(某人[某事物]): *awaiting instructions, results, a reply* 等候指示、结果、答复. **2** be ready or waiting for (sb/sth) 准备以待, 期待(某人[某事物]): *A warm welcome awaits all our customers.* 对我们所有的顾客准备好了热烈的欢迎. ○ *A surprise awaited us on our arrival.* 我们到达的时候, 等待着我们的是一件出乎意料的事.

awake[1] /əˈweɪk; əˈwek/ *v* (*pt* **awoke** /əˈwəʊk; əˈwok/, *pp* **awoken** /əˈwəʊkən; əˈwokən/) [I, Tn] **1** (cause a person or an animal to) stop sleeping; wake (使人或动物)醒; 弄醒: *She awoke when the nurse entered the room.* 护士进屋的时候, 她就醒了. ○ *He awoke the sleeping child.* 他把那个睡着的孩子弄醒了. **2** (*fig* 比喻) (cause sth to) become active (使某事物)活动; 引起; 激起: *The letter awoke old fears.* 那封信又勾起了往日的恐惧. **3** (phr v) **awake to sth** become aware of sth; realize sth 对某事物觉醒、觉悟、醒悟; 觉察到、领悟到、意识到某事物: *awake to the dangers, the opportunities, one's surroundings* 觉察到有危险、有机会、意识到自己所处的环境.

awake[2] /əˈweɪk; əˈwek/ *adj* [pred 作表语] **1** not asleep, esp immediately before and after sleeping 醒着(尤指刚要睡觉和刚睡完觉): *They aren't awake yet.* 他们还没醒呢. ○ *Are the children still awake?* 孩子们还没睡着吗? ○ *They're wide* (ie fully) *awake.* 他们精神着呢(毫无睡意). **2 ~ to sth** conscious or aware of sth 对某事物觉察到的、意识到的、警觉的: *Are you fully awake to the danger you're in?* 你充分意识到自己所处的危险了吗?

awaken /əˈweɪkən; əˈwekən/ *v* **1** [I, Tn] (cause a person or an animal to) stop sleeping; waken (使人或动物)醒; 弄醒; 醒来; 醒着: *We awakened to find the others had gone.* 我们醒来发觉其他人已经走了. ○ *I was awakened by the sound of church bells.* 我被教堂的钟声吵醒. ○ (*fig* 比喻) *They were making enough noise to awaken the dead.* 他们发出的声音大得能把死人吵醒. **2** [Tn] cause (sth) to become active 使(某事物)活动, 活跃; 引起; 激起: *Her story awakened our interest.* 她说的事引起了我们的兴趣. **3** (phr v) **awaken sb to sth** cause sb to become aware of sth 使某人意识到某事; 唤醒某人警惕某事: *awaken society to the dangers of drugs* 唤醒社会警惕毒品的危害.

▷ **awaken·ing** /əˈweɪkənɪŋ; əˈwekənɪŋ/ *n* [sing] act of realizing 觉醒; 醒悟: *The discovery that her husband was unfaithful to her was a rude* (ie shocking) *awakening.* 她发觉丈夫对自己不忠而猛醒.

award /əˈwɔːd; əˈwɔrd/ *v* [Tn, Dn·n, Dn·pr] **~ sth (to sb)** make an official decision to give sth to sb as a prize, as payment or as a punishment 颁发; 授予; 给与; 判定: *The judges awarded both finalists equal points.* 裁判员判定决赛双方分数相同. ○ *The court awarded (him) damages of £50 000.* 法庭判给(他)50 000英镑损害赔偿费. ○ *She was awarded a medal for bravery.* 她因勇敢而获得奖章.

▷ **award** *n* **1** [U] decision to give sth, made by a judge, etc 裁定; 决定: *the award of a scholarship* 奖学金颁发决定. **2** [C] thing or amount awarded 奖品; 奖状; 奖金: *She showed us the athletics awards she had won.* 她给我们看她赢得的体育运动奖. ○ [attrib 作定语] *an award presentation/ceremony* 奖品的颁发[颁奖仪式]. **3** [C] (*Brit*) money paid to a student at university, etc to help meet living costs; grant 助学金: *Mary is not eligible for an award.* 玛丽没有申请助学金的资格.

aware /əˈweə(r); əˈwɛr/ *adj* **1** [pred 作表语] **~ of sb/sth; ~ that...** having knowledge or realization of sb/sth 对某人[某事物]知道、明白、觉察到、意识到: *aware of the risk, danger, threat, etc* 觉察到风险、危险、威胁等 ○ *Are you aware of the time?* 你知道是什么时候了吗? ○ *It happened without my being aware of it.* 事情在我不知不觉中发生了. ○ *I'm (well) aware that very few jobs are available.* 我(很)清楚工作职位非常少. ○ *She became aware that something was burning.* 她发觉有东西烧着了. ○ *I don't think you're aware (of) how much this means to me.* 我想你还不知道这对我多么重要. **2** well-informed; interested, esp in current events 见闻广博的, 感兴趣的(尤指对时事): *She's always been a politically aware person.* 她一直非常关心政治. ▷ **aware·ness** *n* [U].

awash /əˈwɒʃ; əˈwɑʃ/ *adj* [pred 作表语] covered or flooded with sea water, being at or near the level of the waves (因与海浪高度相当而)被海水漫过的或淹没: *These rocks are awash at high tide.* 这些礁石在涨潮时被海水淹没. ○ *The ship's deck was awash in the storm.* 在暴风中轮船的甲板被海水漫过. ○ (*fig* 比喻) *The sink had overflowed and the kitchen floor was awash.* 洗涤槽的水溢出来了, 厨房里满地都是水.

away /əˈweɪ; əˈwe/ *adv part* (For special uses with *vs*, see the *v* entries. 与动词搭配的特殊用法见有关动词词条.) **1 ~ (from sb/sth)** to or at a distance in space or time (from sb/sth) (在空间或时间上)向或在离(某人[某事物])某距离处: *The sea is 2 miles away from the hotel.* 大海距旅馆2英里. ○ *The shops are a few minutes' walk away.* 商店离此有几分钟的步行路程. ○ *Christmas is only a week away.* 圣诞节只有一个星期就到了. ○ *They're away on holiday for 2 weeks.* 他们外出度假两星期. ○ *Don't go away.* 不要走开. ○ *Have you cleared away your books from the table?* 你把你的书都从桌上拿开了吗? ○ *The bright light made her look away.* 这光太强, 她把脸转开了. **2** continuously 继续不断地: *She was still writing away furiously when the bell went.* 铃响时她仍拼命地写个不停. ○ *They worked away for two days to get it finished.* 他们连续两天不停地工作才做完. ○ *After five minutes they were talking away like old friends.* 五分钟后他们就像老朋友一样谈起来了. **3** until it disappears completely 直至完全消失: *The water boiled away.* 水已烧干. ○ *The picture faded away.* 图画已完全褪了色. ○ *The hut was swept away by the flood.* 茅屋已被洪水卷走. ○ (*fig* 比喻) *They danced the night away*, ie all night. 他们跳舞跳个通宵. **4** (of a football, cricket, etc team) at the opponents' ground (指足球、板球等球队)在对方场地上, 在客队场地上: *They're playing away tomorrow.* 他们明天在客队场地比赛. ○ [attrib 作定语] *We lost all our away matches.* 我们外出比赛全输了. Cf 参看 HOME[2] 3. **5** (idm 习语) **away with sb/sth** (used in exclamations 用于感叹句) remove sb/sth; make sb/sth leave 除掉某人[某事物]; 使某人[某事物]离开: *Away with all these petty restrictions!* 废除一切繁琐限制! **right/straight away/off** ⇨ RIGHT[2].

awe /ɔː; ɔ/ *n* [U] feeling of respect combined with fear or wonder 敬畏; 惊惧: *Her first view of the pyramids filled her with awe.* 她初见金字塔时, 敬畏之感油然而生. ○ *I was/lived in awe of my father until I was at least fifteen.* 我至少在十五岁以前一直惧怕父亲. ○ *My brother was much older and cleverer than me so I always held him in awe.* 我哥哥比我大得多也比我聪明得多, 所以我始终对他怀有敬畏之心.

▷ **awe** *v* [usu passive 通常用于被动语态: Tn, Tn·pr] **~ sb (into sth)** fill sb with awe 使某人敬畏或惊惧: *awed by the solemnity of the occasion* 那场合严肃得怕人 ○ *They were awed into silence by the sternness of her voice.* 她严厉的声音把他们吓得鸦雀无声了.

awe·some /-səm; -səm/ *adj* causing awe 使人敬畏的; 使人惊惧的: *His strength was awesome.* 他的力量大得怕人.

□ ˈ**awe-inspiring** *adj* causing awe 使人敬畏的; 使人惊惧的: *an awe-inspiring sight* 使人望而生畏的情景.

ˈ**awestricken**, ˈ**awestruck** *adjs* suddenly filled with awe 顿生敬畏的; 惊惧的.

aweigh /əˈweɪ; əˈwe/ *adv* (*nautical* 海) (of an anchor) hanging just above the bottom of the sea (指锚)在刚离海底处悬着: *Anchors aweigh!* 起锚喽!

aw·ful /ˈɔːfl; ˈɔfl/ *adj* **1** extremely bad or unpleasant; terrible 极坏的; 极讨厌的; 可怕的: *an awful accident, experience, shock, etc* 可怕的事故、经历、打击等 ○ *The plight of starving people is too awful to think about.* 饥民的苦境糟得不敢去想. **2** (*infml* 口) very bad; dreadful 很坏的; 糟透的: *What awful weather!* 多么坏的天气! ○ *I feel awful.* 我觉得难受极了. ○ *It's an awful nuisance?* 讨厌透了! ○ *The film was awful.* 那个电影糟透了. **3** [attrib 作定语] (*infml* 口) very great 极度的: *That's an awful lot of money.* 那是很多很多钱哪. ○ *I'm in an awful hurry to get to the bank.* 我正急着去银行.

▷ **aw·fully** /ˈɔːflɪ; ˈɔflɪ/ *adv* (*infml* 口) very; very much 很; 非常: *awfully hot* 热极了 ○ *awfully sorry* 非常抱歉 ○ *It's awfully kind of you.* 多谢、多谢. ○ *I'm afraid I'm awfully late.* 我实在太迟了. ○ *Thanks awfully for the present.* 万分感谢您的厚礼.

awhile /əˈwaɪl; *US* əˈhwaɪl; əˋhwaɪl/ *adv* for a short time 一会儿; 片刻; 暂时: *Stay awhile.* 呆一会儿. ○ *We won't be leaving yet awhile*, ie not for a short time. 我们暂时还不走.

awk·ward /ˈɔ:kwəd; ˋɔkwɚd/ *adj* **1** badly designed; difficult to use 设计不当的; 使用不便的; 别扭的: *The handle of this teapot has an awkward shape.* 这茶壶把儿的形状真别扭. ○ *It's an awkward door — you have to bend down to go through it.* 这扇门很不方便——得弯着腰才能过去. **2** causing difficulty, embarrassment or inconvenience 造成困难、尴尬或不便的: *an awkward series of bends in the road* 路上一连串难走的弯 ○ *You've put me in a very awkward position.* 你把我弄得很狼狈. ○ *Please arrange the next meeting at a less awkward time.* 请把下次会议时间安排得方便些. ○ *It's very awkward of you not to play for the team tomorrow.* 你明天不为本队参加比赛可太不像话了. ○ *Stop being so awkward!* 别这么别别扭扭的! **3** lacking skill or grace; clumsy 无技巧的; 不熟练的; 不灵活的; 笨拙的: *Swans are surprisingly awkward on land.* 天鹅在陆地上笨得出奇. ○ *I was always an awkward dancer.* 我跳舞一向是笨手笨脚的. **4** embarrassed 尴尬的; 难为情的; 不好意思的; 狼狈的: *I realized they wanted to be alone together so I felt very awkward.* 我意识到了他们想要单独在一起, 所以觉得很尴尬. **5** (idm 习语) **the ˈawkward age** period of adolescence when young people lack confidence and have difficulty preparing for adult life 尴尬年龄(青春期的一段时期, 青少年在此期间缺乏自信心, 难以适应成人生活). **an ˌawkward ˈcustomer** person or animal that is difficult or dangerous to deal with 难对付的傢伙(难以应付的或危险的人或动物). ▷ **awk·wardly** *adv.* **awk·ward·ness** *n* [U].

awl /ɔ:l; ɔl/ *n* small pointed tool for making holes, esp in leather or wood 锥子.

awn·ing /ˈɔ:nɪŋ; ˋɔnɪŋ/ *n* canvas or plastic sheet fixed to a wall above a door or window and stretched out as a protection against rain or sun 遮篷(固定于外墙门窗上方向外伸延的帆布或塑料篷, 作防雨或遮阳用).

awoke *pt* of AWAKE.

AWOL /ˈeɪwɒl; ˋewɔl/ *abbr* 缩写 = absent without leave 擅离职守; 开小差.

awry /əˈraɪ; əˋraɪ/ *adv* **1** crookedly; out of position; askew 曲; 歪; 斜. **2** wrongly; amiss 出错; 失误: *Our plans went awry.* 我们的计划出岔子了.
▷ **awry** *adj* [pred 作表语] crooked 扭曲; 歪; 斜: *Her clothes were all awry.* 她的衣服全都歪歪扭扭的.

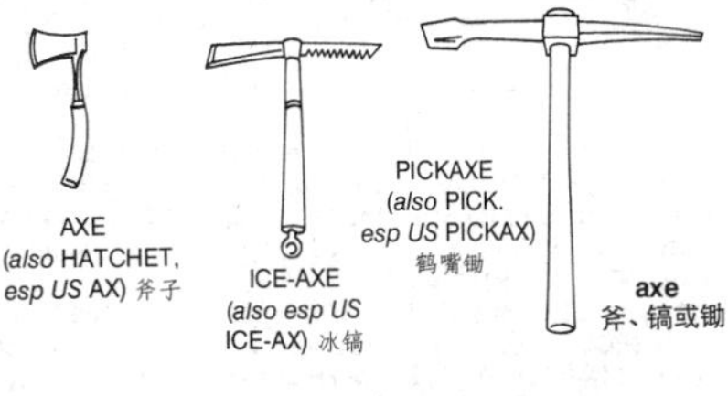

axe (also *esp US* **ax**) /æks; æks/ *n* **1** tool with a handle and a heavy metal blade used for chopping wood, cutting down trees, etc 斧; 斧子: (*fig* 比喻) *apply the axe to* (ie drastically reduce) *local government spending* 大刀阔斧削减地方政府的开支. ⇨illus 见插图. **2** (idm 习语) **get the ˈaxe** (*infml* 口) be removed or dismissed, esp from a job 被解雇; 被开除: *A lot of people in shipbuilding will get the axe.* 造船业的很多人将被解雇. **ˌhave an ˈaxe to grind** have private reasons for being involved in sth 有私心; 有个人打算; 另有企图: *She's only doing it out of kindness — she's got no particular axe to grind.* 她只是出于好心——倒不是别有用心.
▷ **axe** (also *esp US* **ax**) *v* [Tn] **1** remove (sb/sth) or dismiss (sb) 削除(某人[某事物]); 解雇; 开除(某人): *He/His job has been axed.* 他[他的工作]已经裁减掉了. **2** greatly reduce (costs, services, etc) 大刀阔斧地削减(成本), 精简(机构等): *School grants are to be axed next year.* 学校补助金明年将大大削减.

ax·iom /ˈæksɪəm; ˋæksɪəm/ *n* statement that is accepted as true without further proof or argument 公理.
▷ **ax·io·matic** /ˌæksɪəˈmætɪk; ˌæksɪəˋmætɪk/ *adj* of or like an axiom; clear and evident without needing to be proved 公理的; 像公理的; 无需证明就清楚明白的: *It is axiomatic (to say) that a whole is greater than any of its parts.* 整体大于其任何一部分是公理.

axis /ˈæksɪs; ˋæksɪs/ *n* (*pl* **axes** /ˈæksi:z ˋæksiz/) **1** [C] imaginary line through the centre of a rotating object 轴(穿过旋转物体中心的假想的线): *The earth's axis is the line between the North and South Poles.* 地轴是南北极之间的线. ⇨illus at GLOBE 见 GLOBE 之插图. **2** [C] line that divides a regular figure into two symmetrical parts 轴线(将一匀称的图形分成两个对称部分的线): *The axis of a circle is its diameter.* 圆的轴线是其直径. **3** [C] fixed reference line for measurement, eg on a graph (为量度用的)固定参照线: *the horizontal and vertical axes* 横竖坐标轴. **4** [C] agreement or alliance between two or more countries 轴心(国与国之间的协定或联盟). **5 the Axis** [sing] the alliance of Germany, Italy and Japan in World War II 轴心国(第二次世界大战中德、意、日三国的联盟).

axle /ˈæksl; ˋæksl/ *n* **1** rod on which or with which a wheel turns 轮轴. **2** rod that connects a pair of wheels on a vehicle 车轴: *The back axle is broken.* 后车轴断了. ⇨illus at App 1 见附录1之插图, page xii.

aya·tol·lah /ˌaɪəˈtɒlə; ˌaɪəˋtɑlə/ *n* senior Muslim religious leader in Iran 伊朗穆斯林宗教领袖.

aye (also **ay**) /aɪ; aɪ/ *interj* (*arch or dialect* 古或方) yes 是; 对: *ˌAye, ˈaye, sir!* eg in reply to an order by a naval officer 是, 长官! (如回答海军军官的命令).
▷ **aye** (also **ay**) *n* **1** (usu *pl* 通常作复数) vote in support of a motion at a meeting (会议中支持某动议的)赞成票. **2** (idm 习语) **the ayes ˈhave it** more people have voted for the motion than against it 赞成者占多数.

aza·lea /əˈzeɪlɪə; əˋzeljə/ *n* flowering shrub of the rhododendron family 杜鹃花.

azi·muth /ˈæzɪməθ; ˋæzəməθ/ *n* **1** (*astronomy* 天) arc of the sky from the zenith to the horizon 地平经度(从天顶到地平圈在天空的弧度). **2** (in surveying) angle between this arc and the meridian (测量中)方位角(此弧与子午圈之间的夹角).

azure /ˈæʒə(r), *also* ˈæzjʊə(r); ˋæʒɚ/ *n* [U], *adj* bright blue, as of the sky 天蓝色(的); 浅蓝色(的); 蔚蓝色(的): *a lake reflecting the azure of the sky* 反射着蔚蓝色天空的湖面 ○ *a dress of azure silk* 天蓝色的丝绸连衣裙.

B b

B, b /bi:; bi/ *n* (*pl* **B's, b's** /bi:z; biz/) **1** the second letter of the English alphabet 英语字母表的第二个字母: *There are three b's in bubble.* 在 bubble 这个字中有三个 b. **2** (*music* 音) the seventh note in the scale of C major C大调音阶中的第七音或音符. **3** academic mark of second highest standard 学业成绩达次高标准的评价符号: *get (a) B/'B' in English* 英语(学科)得B.
□ **'B-road** *n* (in Britain) less important road than a motorway or an A-road, often narrow and winding (英国)B级公路(重要性次于高速公路或A级公路, 常较狭窄而曲折).

B /bi:; bi/ *abbr* 缩写 = (of lead used in pencils) black, because soft (指铅笔心)黑色色重的(因质软之故): *a B/BB/2B pencil* 一个B[两个B/2B]的铅笔. Cf 参看 H, HB.

B /bi:; bi/ *symb* 符号 (*Brit*) (of roads) secondary (指公路)B级: the B1224 to York 通往约克郡的B级1224号公路 ○ *a 'B-road* 一条B级公路. Cf 参看 A.

b *abbr* 缩写 = born: *Emily Jane Clifton b 1800.* 埃米莉·简·克利夫顿, 生于1800年. Cf 参看 D 2.

BA /ˌbi: 'eɪ; ˌbi 'e/ *abbr* 缩写 = **1** (*US* **AB**) Bachelor of Arts 文学士: *have/be a BA in history* 有历史学学士学位[为历史学学士] ○ *Jim Fox BA (Hons)* 吉姆·福克斯(荣誉)文学士. **2** British Airways 英国航空公司: *flight BA430 to Rome* 乘英航430号班机飞往罗马.

baa /bɑ:; bɑ/ *n* cry of a sheep or lamb 咩(羊叫声).
▷ **baa** *v* (*pres p* **baaing**, *pt* **baaed** or **baa'd** /bɑ:d; bɑd/) [I] make this cry; bleat 发咩声; (羊或小牛)叫.

babble /'bæbl; 'bæbl̩/ *v* **1** [I, Ipr, Ip] (**a**) talk in a way that is difficult or impossible to understand 含糊不清地说; 作咿呀声: *Stop babbling and speak more slowly.* 别老是咿咿呀呀的, 说慢点儿. ○ *tourists babbling (away) in a foreign language* 叽哩咕噜地说着外国话的游客. (**b**) chatter in a thoughtless or confused way 唠唠叨叨; 喋喋不休; 信口胡说; 胡言乱语: *What is he babbling (on) about?* 他在唠叨什么? **2** [I] (of streams, etc) make a continuous murmuring sound (指流水等)作潺潺声: *a babbling brook* 潺潺的小溪.
▷ **babble** *n* [U] **1** (**a**) talk that is difficult or impossible to understand 含糊不清的话: *hear the babble of many voices* 听见许多人在唧唧喳喳地说话. (**b**) foolish talk 蠢话; 胡话. **2** gentle sound of water flowing over stones, etc (流水经过石子等的)潺潺声.
bab·bler /'bæblə(r); 'bæblɚ/ *n* person who babbles 说话含糊不清的人; 唠唠叨叨的人.

babe /beɪb; beb/ *n* **1** (*arch* 古) baby 婴儿. **2** (*US sl* 俚) young woman 姑娘; 少女; 妞儿. **3** (idm 习语) **a ˌbabe in 'arms** (**a**) very young baby not able to walk or crawl 襁褓中的婴儿. (**b**) innocent or helpless person 单纯的或不能自助的人. **out of the mouths of babes and sucklings** ⇨ MOUTH[1].

ba·bel /'beɪbl; 'bebl̩/ *n* [sing] scene of noisy talking and confusion 人声嘈杂、乱糟糟的场面: *a babel of voices in the busy market* 繁忙的市场上嘈杂的声音.

ba·boon /bə'bu:n; *US* bæ-; bæ'bun/ *n* large African or Arabian monkey with a dog-like face 狒狒. ⇨illus at MONKEY 见 MONKEY 之插图.

baby /'beɪbɪ; 'bebɪ/ *n* **1** (**a**) very young child or animal 婴儿; 幼小的动物: *Both mother and baby are doing well.* 母子均平安. ○ [attrib 作定语] *a ˌbaby 'boy/'girl* 男婴[女婴] ○ *a baby thrush, monkey, crocodile* 幼小的鸫、猴子、鳄鱼. (**b**) (*infml* 口) youngest member of a family or group 家庭或团体中最年幼的成员: *He's the baby of the team.* 他在队里最年轻. (**c**) childish or timid person 孩子气的人; 胆怯的人: *Stop crying and don't be such a baby.* 别哭了, 不要这样孩子气. **2** (**a**) (*sl* 俚 *esp US*) young woman, esp a man's girl-friend 姑娘; (尤指男子的)女友. (**b**) (*US sl* 俚) person 人. **3** [attrib 作定语] very small of its kind 小型的: *a baby car* 小型汽车. **4** (idm 习语) **be ˌone's 'baby** (*infml* 口) be sth that one has created or has in one's care 由某人造成的事物; 归某人管的事物: *It's your baby,* ie You must deal with it. 这是你干的(应由你来处理). **leave sb holding the baby** ⇨ LEAVE[1]. **smooth as a baby's bottom** ⇨ SMOOTH[1]. **start a baby** ⇨ START[2]. **throw the baby out with the bath water** foolishly discard a valuable idea, plan, etc at the same time as one is getting rid of sth unpleasant or undesirable 把婴儿和洗澡水一齐倒掉(在把不想要或不需要的东西扔掉的同时, 也愚蠢地抛弃了有价值的意见、计划等); 在去其糟粕的同时, 也丢掉了精华.
▷ **baby** *v* (*pt, pp* **babied**) [Tn] treat (sb) like a baby; pamper 把(某人)当成小孩; 纵容: *Don't baby him.* 不要纵容他.
ba·by·hood *n* [sing] (**a**) state of being a baby 婴儿期. (**b**) time when one is a baby 婴儿时代.
ba·by·ish *adj* of, like or suitable for a baby 婴儿的; 婴儿般的; 适于婴儿的: *Now that Ned can read he finds his early picture books too babyish.* 由于内德已经识字, 他觉得他以前的那些画册都太浅了.
□ **'baby carriage** (*US*) = PRAM.
'baby-faced *adj* having a smooth round babyish face 娃娃脸的.
ˌbaby 'grand small grand piano 小型三角钢琴.
'baby-minder *n* person paid to look after a baby for long periods (eg while the parents are working) 受雇长期照看婴儿者(如婴儿父母上班时); 保姆.
'baby-sit *v* (**-tt-**; *pt* **-sat**) [I] be a baby-sitter 代人临时照看婴儿: *She regularly baby-sits for us.* 她定期前来为我们照看婴儿. **'baby-sitter** *n* (*infml* 口) (also **sitter**) person who looks after a child for a short time while the parents are out 小孩父母外出时临时照看孩子的人; 临时保姆. **'baby-sitting** *n* [U].
'baby-snatcher *n* woman who steals a baby, esp from its pram 窃婴女人(尤指自婴儿车内偷窃的).
'baby-talk *n* unnatural or simplified language used by or to babies before they can speak properly 儿语(婴儿牙牙学语阶段所用或对其使用的一种不合规则的或简单语言).
'baby tooth (*esp US*) = MILK TOOTH (MILK).

bac·ca·laur·eate /ˌbækə'lɔ:rɪət; ˌbækə'lɔrɪɪt/ *n* last secondary school examination in France and in many international schools (法国和许多国际学校的)中学毕业考试: *sit, take, pass, fail, etc one's baccalaureate* 参加、接受、通过、未通过…中学毕业考试.

bac·carat /'bækərɑ:; ˌbækə'rɑ/ *n* [U] card-game played by gamblers 巴卡拉纸牌戏(赌博者玩的).

bac·chanal /'bækənl; 'bækənl̩/ *n* (*pl* **~s** or **~ia** /ˌbækə'neɪlɪə; ˌbækə'nelɪə/) (*dated or fml* 旧或文) bout of noisy, drunken merrymaking 狂饮作乐. ▷ **bac·chan·a·lian** /ˌbækə'neɪlɪən; ˌbækə'nelɪən/ *adj*: *bacchanalian revels* 狂欢作乐的饮宴.

baccy /'bækɪ; 'bækɪ/ *n* [U] (*Brit infml* 口) tobacco 烟草.

bach·elor /'bætʃələ(r); 'bætʃəlɚ/ *n* **1** (**a**) unmarried man 未婚男子; 单身汉: *He remained a bachelor all his life.* 他终生未娶. ○ *a confirmed bachelor*, ie one who has decided never to marry 抱独身主义的男子(决心终身不娶的人) ○ [attrib 作定语] *a bachelor girl*, ie an unmarried woman who lives independently 独立生活的未婚女子. Cf 参看 SPINSTER. (**b**) [attrib 作定语] of or suitable for an unmarried person 单身者的; 适宜于单身者的: *a bachelor flat* 单身公寓. **2** person who holds a first university degree 获学士学位的人: *a bachelor's degree* 学士学位 ○ *Bachelor of Arts/Science* 文[理]学士.

ba·cil·lus /bə'sɪləs; bə'sɪləs/ *n* (*pl* **-cilli** /bə'sɪlaɪ; bə'sɪlaɪ/) rod-like bacterium, esp one of the types that cause disease 杆菌(尤指病菌).

back[1] /bæk; bæk/ *n* **1** part or surface of an object that is furthest from the front; part that is less used, less visible or less important 后部; 后面; 背面; 反面: *If you use mirrors you can see the back of your head.* 使用两个镜子能看见自己的头的后部. ○ *The index is at the back (of the book).* 索引在(书的)末尾. ○ *The child sat in the back (of the car) behind the driver.* 那孩子坐在(汽车的)

后部，司机身后的位置上. ○ *I was at the back (of the cinema) and couldn't see well.* 我坐在(电影院的)后排，所以看不好. ○ *Write your address on the back (of the cheque).* 把你的地址写在(支票的)背面. ○ *a room at the back of the house* 房屋内靠后面的一个房间 ○ *a house with a garden at the back* 有后花园的房屋 ○ *You can't cut with the back of the knife.* 用刀背就无法切割. ○ *the back of one's hand*, ie the side with the nails and the knuckles 手背. Cf 参看 FRONT 1. **2 (a)** rear part of the human body from the neck to the buttocks; spine 人体的背部; 脊椎骨: *He lay on his back and looked up at the sky.* 他仰卧着观看天空. ○ *She broke her back in a climbing accident.* 她在一次攀登事故中折断了脊梁骨. **(b)** part of an animal's body that corresponds to this 动物的脊背: *Fasten the saddle on the horse's back.* 把鞍子系在马背上. ⇨illus at HORSE 见 HORSE 之插图. **3** part of a garment covering the back 后襟. **4** part of a chair against which a seated person's back rests 椅子的靠背; 椅背. ⇨illus at App 1 见附录1之插图, page xvi. **5** (in football, etc) defensive player whose position is near the goal (足球等)后卫. **6** (idm 习语) **at the back of one's mind** in one's thoughts, but without being of immediate or central concern 在内心中(但并非急事或要事): *At the back of his mind was the vague idea that he had met her before.* 他隐隐约约地觉得以前曾经见过她. **the ˌback of beyˈond** an isolated place, far from a centre of social and cultural activity 与外界隔绝的地方; 远离闹市的地方: *They live somewhere at the back of beyond.* 他们住的地方远离闹市. **ˌback to ˈback** with back against back 背靠背: *Stand back to back and let's see who's taller.* 背靠背站好, 看看谁的个子高. **ˌback to ˈfront** with the back placed where the front should be

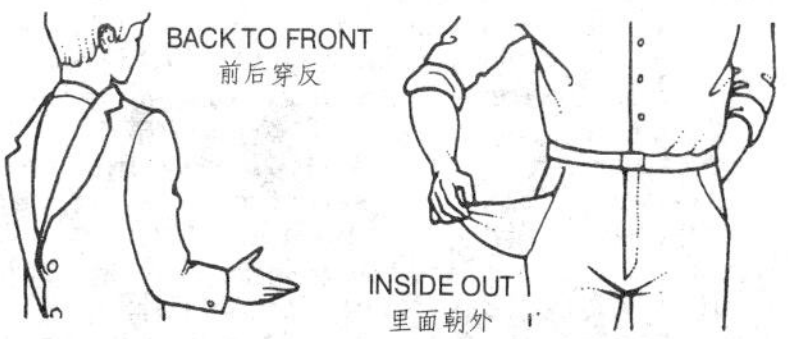

前后颠倒: *Your pullover is on back to front.* 你的套头毛衣前后穿反了. ⇨illus 见插图. **be glad, etc to see the back of sb/sth** be pleased, etc that one will not see sb/sth again 因不再见到某人[某事物]而高兴等. **behind sb's ˈback** without sb's knowledge or consent 不让某人知道或不经某人同意; 背着某人: *They say nasty things about him behind his back.* 他们在背后说他的坏话. Cf 参看 TO SB'S FACE (FACE[1]). **be on sb's ˈback** annoy, hinder or persecute sb 惹恼某人; 妨碍某人; 找某人麻烦. **break one's ˈback (to do sth)** work very hard (to achieve sth) 拼命工作(以实现某目的). **break the back of sth** finish the larger or more difficult part of (a task) 完成(某项任务的)大部分或较艰难的部分. **get/put sb's ˈback up** make sb angry 使某人生气: *His offhand manner put my back up.* 他那随随便便的样子我看着很生气. **get off sb's ˈback** (*infml* 口) stop annoying, hindering or persecuting sb 不再惹恼某人; 不再妨碍某人; 不再找某人麻烦. **have eyes in the back of one's head** ⇨ EYE[1]. **have one's ˌback to the ˈwall** be in a difficult position and forced to defend oneself 陷于必须背水一战的困境. **know sth like the back of one's hand** ⇨ KNOW. **make a rod for one's own back** ⇨ ROD. **a pat on the back** ⇨ PAT[2] *n*. **pat sb/oneself on the back** ⇨ PAT[2] *v*. **put one's ˈback into sth** work at sth with all one's energy 不遗余力地从事某工作; 全力以赴. **a stab in the back** ⇨ STAB *n*. **stab sb in the back** ⇨ STAB *v*. **turn one's back on sb/sth** avoid or reject sb/sth 避开或拒绝接受某人[某事物]: *He turned his back on his family when he became famous.* 他成名以后对自己家里的人连理都不理. **water off a duck's back** ⇨ WATER. **you scratch my back and I'll scratch yours** ⇨ SCRATCH[1].

▷ **back·less** *adj* (of dress) cut low at the back[1](2a) (指连衣裙)露出后背的.

□ **ˈbackache** *n* [U, C] ache or pain in the back[1](2a) 背痛; 腰痛.

ˈbackbone *n* **1** [C] line of bones down the middle of the back from the skull to the hips; spine; spinal column 脊柱; 脊椎. ⇨illus at SKELETON 见 SKELETON 之插图. **2** [sing] (*fig* 比喻) chief support 中坚; 栋梁: *Such people are the backbone of the country.* 这样的人是国家的栋梁. **3** [U] (*fig* 比喻) strength; firmness 力气; 坚定性: *He has no backbone*, ie lacks stamina, perseverance, strength of character, etc. 他没有脊梁骨(缺少体力、毅力、坚强的性格等). **4** (idm 习语) **to the ˈbackbone** thoroughly 彻底地.

ˈback-breaking *adj* exhausting 使人筋疲力尽的: *back-breaking work, effort, etc* 使人筋疲力尽的工作、努力等.

ˈbackpack *n* (*esp US*) = RUCKSACK. **ˈbackpacker** *n*. **ˈbackpacking** *n* [U].

ˈbackrest *n* support for the back[1](2a) 靠背.

ˈbackscratcher *n* device with claws on a long handle for scratching one's own back[1](2a) 搔背扒子(带爪的长柄用具, 用以自己搔背, 俗称痒痒挠儿、不求人).

ˈbackstroke *n* [U] swimming stroke done on one's back in the water 仰泳.

back[2] /bæk; bæk/ *adj* (esp attrib and in compounds; no comparative or superlative 尤用于定语及复合词中; 无比较级或最高级) **1** situated behind 位置在后的: *a back garden* 后花园 ○ *the back door* 后门 ○ *back teeth* 槽牙 ○ *ˈback streets*, ie usu narrow streets in a poor part of a town 后街(通常指城镇贫民区中狭窄的街道). **2 (a)** of or for a past time 以前的; 过去的: *back issues of a magazine* 过期的杂志. **(b)** owed for a time in the past; overdue 拖欠的; 逾期的: *back pay/taxes/rent* 积欠的工资[税款/租金]. **3** (*phonetics* 语音) (of a vowel) formed at the back of the mouth (指元音)后元音的. **4** (idm 习语) **put sth on the back burner** (*infml* 口) put work, etc aside to be dealt with later 将工作等暂时搁置留待以后处理. **by/through the back door** in an unfair illegal way 走后门(采取不正当不合法的手段): *He used his influential friends to help him get into the civil service by the back door.* 他利用那些有权有势的朋友帮助他走后门, 到政府行政部门任职.

□ **ˌback-ˈbench** *n* (usu *pl* 通常作复数) (*Brit*) seat in the House of Commons for a back-bencher 后座议员席(英国下议院中后座议员的席位): *sit on the back-benches* 坐后座议员席 ○ [attrib 作定语] *ˌback-bench MˈPs* 后座议员. **ˌback-ˈbencher** *n* (*Brit*) member of Parliament who does not hold an important position in the government or opposition 后座议员(在政府或反对党中均不担任重要职务的国会议员).

ˈbackcloth *n* (*Brit*) printed cloth hung at the back of a stage in a theatre, as part of the scenery 背景幕布.

ˈbackdrop *n* = BACKCLOTH.

ˈbackhand *n* [sing] (in tennis, etc) stroke or blow made with the back of the hand turned towards the opponent (网球等)反手抽击: *He has a good backhand*, ie can make good backhand shots. 他反手击球很棒. ○ [attrib 作定语] *a backhand stroke, shot, drive, etc* 反手击球、抽球、打球等. Cf 参看 FOREHAND.

ˌbackˈhanded *adj* [usu attrib 通常作定语] **1** played as a backhand 反手击球的. **2** indirect 间接的; 转弯抹角的: *a ˌbackhanded ˈcompliment*, ie one made in a sarcastic way so that it is not a compliment at all 挖苦人的恭维话(表面上恭维, 实则挖苦).

ˈbackhander *n* (*sl* 俚) bribe 贿赂.

ˈbacklist *n* publisher's list of books still in print (出版商的)重版书目录.

ˈbacklog *n* (usu *sing* 通常作单数) accumulation of work or business not yet attended to 积压的工作; 待办的业务: *a backlog of work, unanswered letters* 积压的工作[待复信件] ○ *After the postal strike there was a huge backlog of undelivered mail.* 邮政部门罢工以后, 大量邮件积压下来.

ˌback ˈnumber issue of a periodical of an earlier date, not now on sale 过期的、现已不出售的期刊.

ˈback road (*esp US*) = BY-ROAD.

ˌback ˈroom *n* **1** (esp unimportant) room at the back of a building 后室(位于建筑物后部的房间, 尤指无重要用途的). **2** (idm 习语) **ˌback-room ˈboys** (*infml* 口 *esp Brit*) scientists, engineers, research workers, etc who receive little public attention 在幕后默默工作的科学家、工程师、研究人员等.

ˌ**back ˈseat 1** seat at the back of a car, etc 后座(位于汽车等后部的座位). **2** (idm 习语) **a ˌback-seat ˈdriver** (*derog* 贬) passenger in a car who gives unwanted advice to the driver 对司机胡乱指点的乘客. **take a back seat** (*fig* 比喻) behave as if one were unimportant; take a less prominent part in sth 装扮成不重要的角色; 在某事物中起较次要的作用.

B

ˈ**backside** *n* (*infml* 口) buttocks 屁股: *Get off your backside and do some work!* 别老坐着, 干点儿实事!

ˈ**backstage** *adv* **1** behind the stage in a theatre 在后台; 向后台: *I was taken backstage to meet the actors.* 我被带到后台去会见演员. **2** (*fig* 比喻) unseen by the public 幕后: *I'd like to know what really goes on backstage in government.* 我很想知道政府在幕后到底在干些什么.

ˈ**backwater** *n* (usu *sing* 通常作单数) **1** part of a river not reached by the current, where the water does not flow 死水. **2** (*fig* 比喻) place that remains unaffected by events, progress, new ideas, etc 不受外界的变化、进步、新观念等影响的地方; 闭塞地区: *I find this town too much of a backwater.* 我觉得这个城镇太闭塞.

ˈ**backwoods** *n* [pl] **1** uncleared forest land 未开拓的丛林地区. **2** remote or sparsely inhabited region 人烟稀少的边远地区. **3** culturally backward area 文化落后的地区. ˈ**backwoodsman** /-mən; -mən/ *n* (*pl* **-men** /-mən; -mən/) person who lives in the backwoods 居住在未开拓的丛林地区[人烟稀少的边远地区/文化落后地区]的人.

ˌ**backˈyard** *n* (also **yard**) **1** **(a)** (*Brit*) (esp of terraced houses) usu paved area at the back of a house (尤指成排房屋)(位于房屋后部通常为铺砌的)后院. **(b)** (*US*) whole area behind and belonging to a house, including the lawn, garden, etc 后院(房屋后面并属于该房屋, 包括草地、花园等在内的一整块地). **2** (*fig* 比喻) area that is very close (used esp in the expression shown) 很近的区域(尤用于以下示例): *in one's own backyard*, ie within one's own organization 在自己的后院(在自己的组织内).

back[3] /bæk; bæk/ *adv part* **1** **(a)** towards or at the rear; away from the front or centre 往后; 在后; 在背面: *Stand back to allow the procession to pass.* 往后站, 让队伍通过. ○ *Sit well back in your chair.* 靠着椅背坐好. ○ *You've combed your hair back.* 你已把头发梳到后面. ○ *The house stands back* (ie at some distance) *from the road.* 那房屋离公路有一段距离. ○ *We passed a garage, about a mile back.* 我们经过了一个汽车服务站, 大约有一英里远了. Cf 参看 FORWARD[1] 1. **(b)** under control 控制住; 忍住: *He could no longer hold back his tears.* 他再也忍不住自己的眼泪. ○ *The barriers failed to hold/keep the crowds back.* 那些障碍物未能拦住群众. **2** **(a)** in(to) an earlier position, condition or stage 在(回到)以前的位置、状况或阶段: *Put the book back on the shelf.* 把书放回到书架上. ○ *Please give me my ball back.* 请把球还给我. ○ *My aunt is just back* (ie has just returned) *from Paris.* 我姨妈刚从巴黎回来. ○ *It takes me an hour to walk there and back.* 我步行一个来回用一小时. ○ *We shall be back* (ie home again) *by six o'clock.* 我们六点钟回来. ○ *The party expects to be back in power after the election.* 该党希望大选以后能重新掌权. **(b)** (of time) ago; into the past (指时间)以前, 上溯: *(way) back in the Middle Ages* 上溯到中世纪 ○ *That was a few years back.* 那是几年以前的事. **3** in return 回报: *If he kicks me, I'll kick him back.* 他若踢我, 我就踢他. ○ *Jane wrote him a long letter, but he never wrote back.* 简给他写了封长信, 然而他一直没有回信. ○ *She smiled at him, and he smiled back.* 她向他微笑, 他也向她微笑. **4** (idm 习语) ˌ**back and ˈforth** from one place to another and back again repeatedly 来回地: *ferries sailing back and forth between Dover and Calais* 往返于多佛港和加来港之间的渡船. **(in) back of sth** (*US infml* 口) behind sth 在某物的后面: *the houses back of the church* 位于教堂后面的房屋.

□ ˈ**backbite** *v* (*pt, pp* ˈ**backbitten**) [I] (esp in the continuous tenses 尤用于进行时态) slander the reputation of sb who is not present 背后中伤他人. ˈ**backbiter** *n* person who backbites 背后中伤他人的人. ˈ**backbiting** *n* [U].

ˈ**backchat** *n* [U] (*US* **back talk**) (*infml* 口) answering back cheekily 顶嘴; 强嘴: *I want none of your backchat!* 我不许你顶嘴!

ˈ**backcomb** (also **tease**) *v* [Tn] comb (hair) from the ends back towards the scalp to give it a fuller appearance 逆梳(头发)(从发梢梳向头皮以使头发蓬松).

ˈ**backdate** *v* [Tn] declare that (sth) is to be regarded as valid from some date in the past 宣布(某事物)自过去某日起即为有效: *a pay increase awarded in June and backdated to 1 May* 6月份发放的从5月1日算起的增薪.

ˈ**backfire** *v* **1** [I] ignite or explode too early, esp in an internal combustion engine 过早点火或爆燃(尤指内燃机); 回火; 逆火: *The car/engine backfired noisily.* 那汽车[发动机]发生逆火引起爆鸣. **2** [I, Ipr] **~ (on sb)** (*fig* 比喻) produce an unexpected and unwanted result esp for the people responsible for the action 产生出乎意料及事与愿违的结果(尤指对于该行为的责任者而言): *The plot backfired (on the terrorist) when the bomb exploded too soon.* 由于炸弹过早爆炸, (恐怖分子的)阴谋未能得逞. Cf 参看 MISFIRE. — *n* early explosion, esp in an internal combustion engine 过早爆燃(尤指内燃机); 回火; 逆火.

ˈ**back-formation** *n* [U, C] (process of making a) word that appears to be the root of a longer word, eg *televise* from *television* 逆构词(该词看来像是某一较长单词的词根, 如由television逆造出 televise); 逆序造词法.

ˈ**backlash** *n* [sing] extreme and usu violent reaction to some event 对某些事情的激烈的、通常诉诸暴力的反应: *The fall of the fascist dictatorship was followed by a left-wing backlash.* 法西斯专政的垮台引起左翼运动的高涨.

back-ˈpedal *v* (**-ll-**; *US* **-l-**) **1** [I] pedal backwards on a bicycle, etc 倒蹬(自行车等). **2** [I, Ipr] **~ (on sth)** (*fig* 比喻) withdraw from an earlier statement or policy; reverse one's previous action 背弃以前的言论或政策; 变卦: *The Government are back-pedalling on their election promises.* 内阁正在背弃它竞选时的诺言.

ˈ**backslide** *v* (*pt, pp* ˈ**backslid**) [I] lapse from good ways into one's former bad ways of living (从良好的生活方式)倒退(到以往不良的生活方式): *He's a reformed criminal who may yet backslide.* 他是个经过改造的罪犯, 然而仍有可能故态复萌. ˈ**backsliding** *n* [U].

ˈ**backspace** *v* [I] move the carriage of a typewriter backwards one or more spaces by pressing the special key for this 按退格键(使打字机滚筒退格).

ˈ**back talk** (*US*) = BACKCHAT.

ˈ**backtrack** *v* [I] **1** return by the way that one came 由原路返回; 走回头路. **2** (*fig* 比喻) withdraw from an earlier argument or policy 背弃已往的言论或政策.

ˈ**backwash** *n* **1** backward movement of water in waves, esp behind a moving ship 回浪. **2** (*fig* 比喻) (usu unpleasant) results of an action, a policy or an event (行为、政策或事件的)后果, 余波(通常为不愉快者): [attrib 作定语] *the backwash effect of the war years* 战争年代的遗祸.

back[4] /bæk; bæk/ *v* **1** [I, Ipr, Ip, Tn, Tn·pr, Tn·p] (cause sth to) move backwards (使某物)后退: *back (a car) out of/into the garage, onto the road, into* (ie hitting) *a tree* 开倒车驶出[驶入]车房、驶上公路、撞着一棵树. **2** [Ipr, Tn] **~ (on/onto) sth** face sth at the back 背对着某物: *Our house backs on(to) the river.* 我们的房子背靠着河. **3** [Tn] **(a)** give help or support to (sb/sth) 帮助, 支持(某人[某事]): *She's the candidate who is backed by the Labour Party.* 她是工党支持的候选人. **(b)** give financial support to (sb/sth) 给(某人[某事物])以财务上的支持: *Who is backing the film?* 谁是那影片的赞助人? **4** [Tn] bet money on (a horse, greyhound, etc) 下赌注于(赛马、赛狗等): *I backed four horses but won nothing.* 我在四匹马上下了注, 但全都输了. ○ *Did anyone back the winner?* 有人下注下在最后胜出的这匹马上了吗? ○ *The favourite was heavily backed*, ie Much money was bet on its winning the race. 在那匹热门马上下了重注. **5** [Tn, Tn·pr esp passive 尤用于被动语态] **~ sth (with sth)** cover the back of sth; be a lining to sth 覆盖某物的背面; 作某物的衬里: *The photograph was backed with cardboard.* 照片背面衬上了一层纸板. **6** [Tn] sign (sth) on the back as a promise to pay if necessary; endorse 在背面签字作为可根据需要随时付

款的担保; 背书: *back a bill, note, etc* 在单据、票据等上背书. **7** [I] (of wind) change gradually in an anti-clockwise direction (eg from E to NE to N) (指风向)循反时针方向逐渐改变(如由东风转为东北风再转为北风). Cf 参看 VEER 2. **8** (idm 习语) **ˌback the wrong ˈhorse** support the loser (in a contest) 下错了赌注; 支持(竞赛中的)输家. **9** (phr v) **back away (from sb/sth)** move backwards in fear or dislike 因害怕或厌恶而后退: *The child backed away from the big dog.* 那个孩子看见大狗就向后退了. **back ˈdown**; *US* **back ˈoff** give up a claim to sth; yield 放弃对某事物的要求; 屈服: *He proved that he was right and his critics had to back down.* 他证明了他是正确的, 而那些非难他的人不得不收起他们那一套. **back out (of sth)** withdraw from (an agreement, a promise, etc) 不履行(协议、承诺等): *It's too late to back out (of the deal) now.* 现在要(在这笔交易上)打退堂鼓为时已晚. **back up** (*US*) = BACK[4] 1: *You can back up another two yards.* 你可以再后退两码. **back sb/sth up** give support or encouragement to sb/sth 支持或鼓励某人[某事物]: *If I tell the police I was with you that day, will you back up my ˈstory/back me ˈup?* 假若我对警方说那天我和你在一起, 你肯为我这个说法作证[为我作证]吗? **back sth up** (*computing* 计) make a copy of (a file, program, etc) in case the original is lost or damaged 制作(文件、程序等的)复制件(以防原件丢失或损坏).

▷ **backer** *n* **1** person who gives (esp financial) support to another person, an undertaking, etc 赞助人; (尤指)资助人. **2** person who bets money on a horse, etc (赛马等中的)下赌注者.

back·ing *n* **1** (**a**) [U] help; support 帮助; 支持. (**b**) [sing] group of supporters 一群支持者: *The new leader has a large backing.* 那位新领导人有大批的支持者. **2** [U] material used to form the back of sth or to support sth 用作某物的背衬材料; 用作支撑某物的材料: *cloth, rubber, cardboard, etc backing* 布、橡胶、纸板等做的背衬. **3** [U, C usu *sing* 通常作单数] (esp in pop music) musical accompaniment to a singer (尤指流行音乐)为歌手的伴奏: *vocal/instrumental backing* 和音[伴奏] ○ [attrib 作定语] *a backing group* 和音小组.

□ **ˈback-up** *n* **1** [U] support; reserve 支持; 支援; 后备: *The police had military back-up.* 警方有军队作后盾. ○ [attrib 作定语] *back-up services* 善后服务 ○ *the back-up team of a racing driver* 赛车手的后勤队. **2** [U, C] (*computing* 计) (making a) copy of a file, program, etc for use in case the original is lost or damaged (制作)(文件、程序等的)复制件(以备原件丢失或损坏时使用): [attrib 作定语] *a back-up disc* 复制件磁盘.

back·gam·mon /ˌbækˈgæmən, ˈbækgæmən; ˈbæk-ˌgæmən/ *n* [U] game for two players played on a double board with draughts and dice 西洋双陆棋(供两人玩, 使用对折棋盘、棋子、色子).

back·ground /ˈbækgraʊnd; ˈbækˌgraʊnd/ *n* **1** [sing] part of a view, scene or description that forms a setting for the chief objects, people, etc 背景. Cf 参看 FOREGROUND. **2** [sing] (**a**) inconspicuous position (used esp in the expressions shown) 不显著的位置; 幕后(尤用于以下示例): *be/be kept/stay in the background*, ie not in the centre of public attention 在[保持在/留在]幕后(避开公众的注意). (**b**) [attrib 作定语] unobtrusive 不明显的: *background music* 背景音乐; 配乐. Cf 参看 FOREGROUND. **3** (**a**) [sing] conditions and events surrounding and influencing sth 围绕并影响某事物的情况和事件: *These political developments should be seen against a background of increasing East-West tension.* 分析这些政治形势时, 应考虑到东西方关系正日趋紧张. ○ [attrib 作定语] *background information* 背景资料. (**b**) [C] person's social class, education, training, etc 人的社会阶层、学历、资历等: *He has a working-class background.* 他是工人阶级出身. (**c**) [U] information that is needed to understand a problem, etc (为了解某问题等所需的)资料: *Can you give me more background on the company's financial position?* 你能向我多提供一些有关该公司财务状况的资料吗?

back·ward /ˈbækwəd; ˈbækwɚd/ *adj* **1** directed towards the back or the starting point 向后的; 向原出发点的: *a backward glance, somersault* 向后一瞥、翻一个筋斗. **2** having made or making less than normal progress 落后的; 后进的: *a very backward part of the country, with no proper roads and no electricity* 这个国家中极其落后的地区, 既没有像样的公路也没有电力供应 ○ *John was rather backward as a child; he was nearly three before he could walk.* 约翰小时候有点迟钝, 差不多三岁才学会走路. **3** [pred 作表语] **~ (in sth)** shy; reluctant; hesitant 害羞; 怯生生; 迟疑: *Sheila is very clever but rather backward in expressing her ideas.* 希拉很聪明, 然而在表达思想时却有些腼腆. Cf 参看 FORWARD.

▷ **back·wards** (also **back·ward**) *adv* **1** away from one's front; towards the back 向后: *He looked backwards over his shoulder.* 他回头向后看. **2** with the back or the end first 倒着; 颠倒: *It's not easy to run backwards.* 倒着跑不容易. ○ *The word 'star' is 'rats' backwards.* star 这个字是倒着拼的 rats. **3** toward a worse or a previous state 回到更坏的或先前的状况: *Let's take a journey backwards through time*, ie imagine we are going back to an earlier period in history. 让我们作一次逆着时间的旅行(想像我们回到过去的历史时期里). ○ *Instead of making progress, my work actually seems to be going backwards.* 我的工作不但没有进步, 实际上像是在倒退. ⇨Usage at FORWARD[2] 用法见 FORWARD[2]. **4** (idm 习语) **ˌbackward(s) and ˈforward(s)** first in one direction and then in the other 来回地: *travelling backwards and forwards between London and the south coast* 往返于伦敦和南海岸之间 ○ [attrib 作定语] *a backward and forward movement* 往复运动. **bend/lean over ˈbackwards (to do sth)** (*infml* 口) make a great effort 努力; 竭力: *Although we bent over backwards to please her, our new manager was still very critical of our work.* 尽管我们竭力讨好新经理, 但她仍然对我们的工作百般挑剔. **know sth backwards** ⇨ KNOW.

back·ward·ness *n* [U].

ba·con /ˈbeɪkən; ˈbekən/ *n* [U] **1** salted or smoked meat from the back or sides of a pig 腌猪肉, 熏猪肉(猪的背部或肋部的肉): *a rasher of bacon* 一片腌猪肉. Cf 参看 GAMMON, HAM 1, PORK. **2** (idm 习语) **bring home the bacon** ⇨ HOME[3]. **save one's bacon** ⇨ SAVE[1].

bac·teria /bækˈtɪərɪə; bækˈtɪrɪə/ *n* [pl] (*sing* **-ium** /-ɪəm; -ɪəm/) simplest and smallest forms of plant life, microscopic organisms that exist in large numbers in air, water and soil, and also in living and dead creatures and plants, and are often a cause of disease 细菌.

▷ **bac·terial** /-rɪəl; -rɪəl/ *adj* of or caused by bacteria 细菌的; 由细菌引起的: *bacterial contamination* 细菌感染.

bac·teri·ology /bækˌtɪərɪˈɒlədʒɪ; ˈbækˌtɪrɪˈɑlədʒɪ/ *n* [U] scientific study of bacteria 细菌学. **bac·teri·olo·gist** /-dʒɪst; -dʒɪst/ *n* person specializing in bacteriology 细菌学家.

bad[1] /bæd; bæd/ *adj* (**worse** /wɜːs; wɝs/, **worst** /wɜːst; wɝst/) **1** (**a**) of poor quality; below an acceptable standard; faulty 坏的; 劣质的; 不合格的; 有错的: *a bad lecture, harvest* 很糟的演讲、收成 ○ *bad pronunciation, eyesight* 很差的发音、视力 ○ *You can't take photographs if the light is bad.* 光线不足, 就无法拍照. (**b**) (used with names of occupations or with *ns* derived from *vs* 与职业名称连用或与动词派生的名词连用) not competent; not able to perform satisfactorily 不能胜任的; 表现不能令人满意的: *a bad teacher, hairdresser, poet, etc* 滥竽充数的教师、理发师、诗人等 ○ *a bad liar, listener, etc* 很差劲的说谎者、听者等 ○ *a bad loser*, ie one who complains when he loses 没出息的失败者(失败后怨天尤人的人). **2** not morally acceptable; wicked 不道德的; 邪恶的: *It's bad to steal.* 偷窃真缺德. ○ *He led a bad life.* 他曾经过着邪恶的生活. **3** unpleasant; disagreeable; unwelcome 令人不快的; 使人讨厌的; 不受欢迎的: *In the recession, our firm went through a bad time.* 我们公司在经济衰退时期历尽艰辛. ○ *What bad weather we're having!* 多讨厌的天气! ○ *He's had some bad news: his father has died suddenly.* 他得悉噩耗: 父亲突然去世. ○ *These rotting bananas are giving off a bad smell.* 这些腐烂的香蕉发出难闻的气味. **4** [usu attrib 通常作定语] (of things that are in themselves undesirable) serious; noticeable (指那些本身就要不得的东西)严重的, 显著的: *a bad mistake, accident, fracture, headache* 严重的错误、事故、骨折、头痛. **5** (of food) not fit to be eaten because of decay; rotting or rotten (指食物)因变质而不能食用的, 正在腐烂或已经腐烂的: *bad eggs, meat, etc* 腐坏的蛋、肉等 ○ *The fish will go bad if you don't put it in the fridge.* 这鱼不放入冰箱内就会腐坏. **6** [usu attrib 通常作定语]

unhealthy or diseased 不健康的; 有病的: *bad teeth* 蛀牙 ○ *a bad back*, ie one that causes pain 背部疼痛. **7** [pred 作表语] **~ for sb/sth** hurtful or injurious to sb/sth 有害于某人[某事物]: *Smoking is bad for you/bad for your health.* 吸烟有害于你[有害于你的健康]. ○ *Too much rain is bad for the crops.* 雨量过多对庄稼不利. **8 ~ (for sth/to do sth)** unsuitable; difficult 不适宜的; 困难的: *a bad time for buying a house/to buy a house* 不宜于购置房产的时期 ○ *This beach is good for swimming but bad for surfing.* 这片海滩宜于游泳而不适合作冲浪运动. **9** (idm 习语) **go from ˌbad to ˈworse** (of a bad condition, situation, etc) become even worse (指坏的状态、情况等)越来越坏: *We were hoping for an improvement but things have gone from bad to worse.* 我们但愿有所改善, 然而事情却每况愈下. **(be/get) in bad (with sb)** (*US infml* 口) (be/become) disapproved of or out of favour 不被赏识; 失宠: *If you get in bad with the boss, you'll have problems.* 要是上司不喜欢你, 你就该有麻烦了. **not ˈbad** (*infml* 口) quite good; better than expected 不错; 比预料的要好: *That was not bad for a first attempt.* 按初次尝试来说, 那就算不错了. ○ *'How are you feeling?' 'Not too bad!'* '你觉得怎么样?' '还可以!' **too bad** (**a**) regrettable (used sympathetically) 遗憾的(用以表示同情): *It's too bad you can't come to the party.* 你不能来参加宴会真遗憾. (**b**) (*infml ironic* 口, 反语) unfortunate (used dismissively)不幸的(用作轻蔑回绝): *'My share's too small.' 'Too bad! It's all you're going to get.'* '我这份太少了.' '你将就点儿吧! 你能得到的就是这些.' (For other idioms containing **bad**, see entries for other major words in each idiom 查阅其他含有 **bad** 一词的习语, 见该习语中含有其他主要词的词条, 如 **turn up like a bad penny** ⇨ PENNY.)

▷ **bad** *adv* (*US infml* 口) badly(2) 非常; 在很大程度上: *That's what I want, and I want it bad.* 这就是我想要的, 而且是迫不及待要得到的. ○ *Are you hurt bad?* 你伤得厉害吗?

baddy *n* (*infml* 口) villain in a film, novel, etc (电影、小说等中的)反面人物, 坏人: *In real life, it's not so easy to divide people into goodies and baddies.* 在现实生活中, 要划分好人和坏人并非易事.

badly *adv* (**worse**, **worst**) **1** in an inadequate or unsatisfactory manner 不好; 以不适当的或不能令人满意的方式: *play, work, sing, etc badly* 玩得、干得、唱得...不好 ○ *badly made, dressed, etc* 做得、穿得...不像样子的 ○ *I'm afraid our team's doing rather badly.* 我看我们队的表现不太好. **2** (with expressions indicating a want, need, etc or undesirable conditions 与表示匮乏、需要等用语连用或与表示不良情况的用语连用) very much; to a great extent 非常; 在很大程度上: *badly in need of repair* 亟须修理 ○ *badly wounded* 伤情严重 ○ *badly beaten at football* 在足球赛中惨败 ○ *They want to see her very badly.* 他们很想见到她. **3** (idm 习语) **badly off** in a poor position, esp financially 潦倒; (尤指)穷困: *We shouldn't complain about being poor — many families are much worse off (than we are).* 我们不应该因为穷而叫苦连天——许多人的家境(比起我们来)还要糟得多呢. **be badly off for sth** be in need (of sth); be inadequately supplied (with sth) 需要(某物); 供应(某物)不足: *The refugees are badly off for blankets, and even worse off for food.* 难民需要毯子, 更需要食物.

bad·ness *n* [U].

□ ˌ**bad ˈdebt** debt that is unlikely to be paid 坏帐.

ˈ**bad lands** *n* [pl] (*US*) barren regions 不毛之地.

ˌ**bad ˈlanguage** obscene or profane words used insultingly or to add emphasis; swear-words 脏话; 骂人的话.

ˈ**bad-mouth** *v* [Tn] (*US infml* 口) talk maliciously about (sb); slander 恶意中伤(某人); 诽谤.

ˌ**bad-ˈtempered** *adj* usually cross 脾气坏的.

bad[2] /bæd; bæd/ *n* **the bad** [U] **1** that which is wicked, unpleasant, etc 坏的事物. **2** (idm 习语) **go to the ˈbad** become completely immoral 道德败坏; 堕落. **take the ˌbad with the ˈgood** accept the unwelcome aspects (of life, a situation, etc) as well as the welcome ones 好坏都看得开. **to the ˈbad** (used to describe a financial position) in debit (用以形容财务状况)亏损, 负债: *I am £500 to the bad*, ie I have £500 less than I had. 我负债500英镑.

bade ⇨ BID.

badge /bædʒ; bædʒ/ *n* (**a**) thing worn (usu a design on cloth or sth made of metal) to show a person's occupation, rank, membership of a society, etc 徽章: *a cap badge*, eg of a schoolboy or soldier 帽徽. ⇨illus at HAT 见HAT之插图. (**b**) (*fig* 比喻) thing that shows a quality or condition 象征; 标志: *Chains are a badge of slavery.* 锁链是奴隶制度的标志.

badger[1] /ˈbædʒə(r); ˈbædʒɚ/ *n* animal of the weasel family, grey with black and white stripes on its head, living in holes in the ground and moving about at night. ⇨illus at App 1 见附录1之插图, page iii.

badger[2] /ˈbædʒə(r); ˈbædʒɚ/ *v* [Tn, Tn·pr, Dn·t] **~ sb (with/for sth)**; **~ sb (into doing sth)** pester sb; nag sb persistently 纠缠某人; 烦扰某人: *Stop badgering your father with questions!* 别老拿问题去烦你父亲了! ○ *She badgered me into doing what she wanted.* 她闹着要我照她要求的做. ○ *Tom has been badgering his uncle to buy him a camera.* 汤姆一直缠着他叔叔给他买照相机.

bad·in·age /ˈbædɪnɑːʒ; *US* ˌbædənˈɑːʒ; ˌbædnˈɑʒ/ *n* [U] (*French* 法) playful teasing; banter 开玩笑; 打趣.

bad·min·ton /ˈbædmɪntən; ˈbædmɪntən/ *n* [U] game for two or four people played with rackets and shuttlecocks on a court with a high net 羽毛球运动.

baffle[1] /ˈbæfl; ˈbæfl̩/ *v* [Tn] **1** be too difficult for (sb) to understand; puzzle 使(某人)困惑; 难倒: *One of the exam questions baffled me completely.* 有一道试题把我完全难住了. ○ *Police are baffled as to the identity of the killer.* 警方不解凶手是谁. **2** prevent (sb) from doing sth; frustrate 阻止(某人)做某事; 使受挫: *She baffled all our attempts to find her.* 她千方百计不让我们找到她.

▷ **baf·fle·ment** *n* [U]. **baf·fling** *adj*: *a baffling crime* 难于侦破的罪案.

baffle[2] /ˈbæfl; ˈbæfl̩/ *n* screen used to hinder or control the flow of sound, light or liquid (阻碍或控制声音传播、光线照射或液体流动的)屏蔽, 挡板, 隔板, 遮护物.

BAFTA /ˈbæftə; ˈbæftə/ *abbr* 缩写 = British Academy of Film and Television Arts 英国影视艺术学会: *BAFTA awards* 英国影视艺术学会奖.

bag[1] /bæg; bæg/ *n* **1** (**a**) container made of flexible material (eg paper, cloth or leather) with an opening at the top, used for carrying things from place to place 袋; 包; 提包: *a ˈshopping-bag* 购物袋 ○ *a ˈhandbag* 手提包 ○ *a ˈkitbag* 旅行袋 ○ *a ˈtoolbag* 工具袋 ○ *a ˈmailbag* 邮袋. (**b**) such a container with its contents; the amount it contains 一袋或一包的物品; 一袋或一包的量: *two bags of coal* 两袋煤. **2** thing resembling a bag 袋状物: *bags under the eyes*, ie loose folds of skin under the eyes, eg from lack of sleep 眼下肿包. **3** all the birds, animals, etc shot or caught 猎获物: *We got a good bag today.* 我们今天猎获甚丰. **4** (*infml derog* 口, 贬) fussy, unattractive or bad-tempered (usu older) woman 爱挑剔的、令人厌烦或脾气坏的(通常为较年长的)女人: *She's an awful old bag.* 她是个爱挑剔的老太婆. **5** (idm 习语) ˌ**bag and ˈbaggage** with all one's belongings, often suddenly or secretly 带着全部财物(常为突然地或秘密地): *Her tenant left, bag and baggage, without paying the rent.* 她的房客未付房租就带着全部财物离去了. **a ˌbag of ˈbones** a very thin person or animal 骨瘦如柴的人或动物: *The cat had not been fed for weeks and was just a bag of bones.* 那只猫已有几个星期没喂食了, 简直成了皮包骨. **be in the ˈbag** (*infml* 口) (of a result, an outcome, etc) be as desired (指结果、结局等)不成问题, 如探囊取物: *Her re-election is in the bag.* 她在改选中已稳操胜券. **let the cat out of the bag** ⇨ CAT[1]. **pack one's bags** ⇨ PACK[2]. **the whole bag of tricks** ⇨ WHOLE.

bag[2] /bæg; bæg/ *v* (**-gg-**) **1** [Tn, Tn·p] **~ sth (up)** put into a bag or bags 装进袋里: *bag (up) wheat* 把小麦装进袋里. **2** [Tn] (of hunters) kill or catch (sth) (指猎人)打死或捕获(某物): *They bagged nothing except a couple of rabbits.* 他们除猎到两只兔子以外, 一无所获. **3** [Tn] (*infml* 口) take (sth) without permission but without intending to steal 未经准许而拿走(某物)(但无偷盗之意): *Who's bagged my matches?* 谁把我的火柴拿走了? ○ *She bagged* (ie occupied, sat in) *the most comfortable chair.* 她占了最舒适的椅子. ○ *try to bag an empty table*, ie to secure one, eg in a crowded restaurant 设法占住一张空桌子(如在拥挤的餐馆中). **4** [I, Ipr] sag or hang loosely, looking like a cloth bag 宽松地下垂或悬吊(如布袋状): *trousers that bag at the knee* 膝盖部分宽松的裤子. **5** (idm 习语) **bags (I)...** (*infml* 口) I claim... 我要求...: *Bags I go first.* 我要第一个去.

ba·ga·telle /ˌbægəˈtel; ˌbægəˋtɛl/ *n* **1** [U] game played on a board with small balls that are hit into holes 小型台球游戏. **2** [C] something small and unimportant 小玩意儿; 无足轻重的东西: *a mere bagatelle* 小事一桩. **3** [C] short piece of music 小曲; 音乐小品.

ba·gel /ˈbeɪgl; ˋbegəl/ *n* hard ring-shaped bread roll 一种圈状硬面包.

bag·gage /ˈbægɪdʒ; ˋbægɪdʒ/ *n* **1** [U] = LUGGAGE. **2** [U] equipment carried by an army 辎重. **3** [C] (*dated infml joc* 旧, 口, 谑) lively or mischievous girl 活泼或调皮的女孩儿: *Come here, you little baggage!* 过来, 你这小丫头! **4** (idm 习语) **bag and baggage** ⇨ BAG[1].

□ ˈ**baggage car** (*US*) = ˋLUGGAGE VAN (LUGGAGE).

ˈ**baggage room** (*US*) = LEFT-LUGGAGE OFFICE (LEFT[1]).

baggy /ˈbægɪ; ˋbægɪ/ *adj* (**-ier, -iest**) hanging loosely 宽松地下垂的: *baggy trousers* 宽松的裤子. ▷ **bag·gily** *adv*. **bag·gi·ness** *n* [U].

bagpipes 风笛

bag·pipes /ˈbægpaɪps; ˋbæg,paɪps/ (also **pipes**) *n* [pl] musical instrument played by storing air in a bag held under the arm, which is then pressed out through pipes 风笛: *Scottish bagpipes* 苏格兰风笛.

bags[1] /bægz; bægz/ *n* [pl] (*infml* 口) trousers 裤子: *Oxford bags* 牛津裤.

bags[2] /bægz; bægz/ *n* [pl] **~ (of sth)** (*infml* 口) plenty (of sth) (某物的)大量: *There's bags of room.* 有许多地方. ○ *Don't worry about money: I've got bags.* 别为钱发愁: 我有的是.

bah /bɑ:; bɑ/ *interj* (expressing disgust or contempt 表示厌恶或轻蔑).

bail[1] /beɪl; bel/ *n* [U] **1** money paid by or for a person accused of a crime, as security that he will return for his trial if he is allowed to go free until then 保释金. **2** permission for a person to be released on such security 准许保释: *The magistrate granted/refused him bail.* 地方法官准许[不准]他保释. **3** (idm 习语) **go/stand** ˈ**bail (for sb)** give bail (to secure sb's freedom) 交保释金(保释某人). **jump bail** ⇨ JUMP[2]. **(out) on** ˈ**bail** free after payment of bail 交保释金后获释: *The accused was released on bail (of £1 000) pending trial.* 那被告在交纳(1000英镑)保释金后, 在开庭前暂时获释.

▷ **bail** *v* (phr v) **bail sb out (a)** obtain or allow the release of sb on bail 保释某人. **(b)** (*fig infml* 比喻, 口) rescue sb from (esp financial) difficulties 救助某人摆脱困境(尤指财务方面): *The club faced bankruptcy until a wealthy local businessman bailed them out.* 俱乐部那时眼看就要破产, 后来本地有位富商鼎力相助, 才摆脱困境.

bail[2] (also **bale**) /beɪl; bel/ *v* [I, Ip, Tn, Tn·p] **~ (out)/ sth (out)** throw (water) out of a boat with buckets, etc; clear (a boat) in this way 用桶将(水)从船内舀出; 以这种方式给(船)清除积水: *bailing water (out)* 舀水往船外泼 ○ *bailing (out) the boat* 清除船中积水 ○ *The boat will sink unless we bail (out).* 我们不把积水清除掉, 船就要沉了.

bail[3] /beɪl; bel/ *n* (in cricket) either of the two cross-pieces resting on each set of three stumps (板球)三柱门上的横木.

bailey /ˈbeɪlɪ; ˋbelɪ/ *n* **1** outer wall of a castle (城堡的)郭. **2** courtyard enclosed by this wall (城堡外郭所围绕的)堡场.

Bailey bridge /ˈbeɪlɪ brɪdʒ; ˋbelɪ brɪdʒ/ portable military bridge made of prefabricated sections that can be fitted together quickly 贝利桥(军用便桥, 由可迅速安装的预制件组成).

bail·iff /ˈbeɪlɪf; ˋbelɪf/ *n* **1** law officer who helps a sheriff in issuing writs and making arrests (协助郡长发布令状及执行逮捕使命的)执行官. **2** (*Brit*) landlord's agent or steward; manager of an estate or farm (地主的)代理人或管家; (房地产或农场的)看守人. **3** (*US*) official in a lawcourt, esp one who takes people to their seats and announces the arrival of the judge 法警(尤指负责带位并宣布法官出庭的).

B

bairn /beən; bɛrn/ *n* (*Scot* 苏格兰) child 小孩儿.

bait /beɪt; bet/ *n* [U] **1** food or imitation food put on a hook to catch fish or placed in nets, traps, etc to attract prey 鱼饵; 诱饵: *The fish nibbled at/rose to/took/swallowed the bait.* 那鱼轻咬[浮向/咬着了/吞下了]鱼饵. ○ *live bait*, ie small fish used to catch larger fish 活饵(用作鱼饵引诱大鱼上钩的小鱼). **2** (*fig* 比喻) thing that is used to attract or tempt 引诱物; 诱惑物. **3** (idm 习语) **rise to the bait** ⇨ RISE[2]. **swallow the bait** ⇨ SWALLOW[2].

▷ **bait** *v* **1** [Tn, Tn·pr] **~ sth (with sth)** put (real or imitation food) on or in sth to catch fish, animals, etc 置(饵)于某物之上或之内(以捕鱼、兽等): *bait a trap* 把饵放入陷阱里 ○ *bait a hook with a worm* 把鱼虫放在钩上作鱼饵. **2** [Tn] **(a)** torment (a chained animal) by making dogs attack it, often as a form of entertainment 纵犬撕咬(被链锁住的动物)(通常作为娱乐): ˈ*bear-baiting* 纵犬斗熊. **(b)** torment (sb) by making cruel or insulting remarks 以侮辱性言辞折磨(某人).

baize /beɪz; bez/ *n* [U] thick (usu green) woollen cloth used for covering billiard-tables, card-tables, doors, etc 台面呢(一种厚毛呢, 通常为绿色, 用作台球台、牌桌、门等的衬垫).

bake /beɪk; bek/ *v* **1** [I, Tn, Dn·n, Dn·pr] **~ sth (for sb)** (cause sth to) be cooked by dry heat in an oven (使某物)在烤箱烘烤: *bake bread, cakes, etc* 烘面包、糕饼等 ○ *The bread is baking/being baked.* 面包正在烘烤. ○ *I'm baking Alex a birthday cake/baking a birthday cake for Alex.* 我正在给阿列克斯烤生日蛋糕. ○ *baked potatoes* 烤的马铃薯 ○ *baked beans*, ie haricot beans baked and tinned with tomato sauce 烘豆(经烘烤后加入番茄汁做成罐头的菜豆). ⇨Usage at COOK 用法见 COOK. **2** [I, Tn, Cn·a] (cause sth to) become hard by heating (使某物)烤硬: *The sun baked the ground hard.* 太阳把地晒得硬帮帮的. ○ *The bricks are baking in the kilns.* 窑里正在烧砖. **3** [I] (*fig infml* 比喻, 口) be or become very hot 灼热; 炎热: *It's baking today!* 今天天气炎热! ○ *We are baking in the sun.* 我们让太阳晒熟了.

▷ **baker** *n* **1** person who bakes and sells bread, etc 烘制并出售面包等的人; 面包师傅: *buy some rolls at the baker's* 在面包店里买些圆面包. **2** (idm 习语) **a baker's** ˈ**dozen** thirteen 十三.

bakery /ˈbeɪkərɪ; ˋbekərɪ/ *n* place where bread is baked for sale 面包房; 面包厂.

□ ˌ**baking-**ˈ**hot** *adj* (*infml* 口) very hot 灼热的; 炎热的: *a* ˌ*baking-hot* ˈ*day* 炎热的一天.

ˈ**baking-powder** *n* [U] mixture of powders used to make cakes, etc rise and become light during baking 发酵粉.

bake·lite /ˈbeɪkəlaɪt; ˋbekə,laɪt/ *n* [U] type of plastic 电木; 胶木.

bak·sheesh /bækˈʃi:ʃ, *also* ˈbækʃi:ʃ; bækˋʃiʃ, ˋbækʃiʃ/ *n* [U] (in the Middle East) money given as a tip or to help the poor (中东地区的)小费, 赏钱.

ba·la·clava /ˌbæləˈklɑ:və; ˌbæləˋklɑvə/ *n* (also ˌ**Balaclava** ˈ**helmet**) closely-fitting hat that covers the head and neck but not the face 巴拉克拉瓦帽(紧紧罩住头部和颈部而只露出脸部的帽子).

ba·la·laika /ˌbæləˈlaɪkə; ˌbæləˋlaɪkə/ *n* musical instrument like a guitar with a triangular body and three strings, popular in Slav countries 巴拉莱卡琴(类似吉他的乐器, 琴身为三角形, 有三根弦, 流行于斯拉夫国家).

bal·ance[1] /ˈbæləns; ˋbæləns/ *n* **1** [C] instrument used for weighing, with a central pivot, a beam and two scales or pans 天平; 秤. ⇨ illus at SCALE[3] 见 SCALE[3] 之插图. **2** [U] **(a)** even distribution of weight; steadiness 平衡; 平稳: *Riders need a good sense of balance.* 骑车的人必须善

于保持平衡. (**b**) steadiness of mind; sanity 心境的平稳; 心智健全: *His wife's sudden death upset the balance of his mind.* 他妻子突然去世, 他感到六神无主. **3** [U, sing] (**a**) **~ (in sth/between A and B)** condition that exists when two opposites are equal or in correct proportions 均衡状态; 均势: *Try to achieve a better balance between work and play.* 争取把工作和娱乐更好地结合起来. ○ *This newspaper maintains a good balance in its presentation of different opinions.* 这家报纸刊登不同意见始终做到不偏不倚. (**b**) pleasing proportion of parts in a whole 谐调; 匀称: *All the parts of the building are in perfect balance.* 建筑物的各部分都显得非常匀称. ○ *This painting has a pleasing balance of shapes and colours.* 这幅画在构图和色彩方面都十分谐调. **4** [C usu *sing* 通常作单数] (*finance* 财) difference between two columns of an account, ie money received or owing and money spent or owed 收支差额; 余额: *I must check my bank balance*, ie find out how much money I have in my account. 我要核对一下我在银行的余额(看我的帐户上有多少钱). **5** (**a**) [C usu *sing* 通常作单数] amount (of money) still owed after some payment has been made 余欠之(钱)数: *The balance (of £500) will be paid within one week.* 余欠之数(500英镑)将于一周内付清. (**b**) **the balance** [sing] remainder of sth after part has already been used, taken, etc 剩余: *The balance of your order will be supplied when we receive fresh stock.* 贵方所订购货物之其余部分, 一俟我方进货即可供应. ○ *When will you take the balance of your annual leave?* 你打算什么时候使用剩余的年假? ⇨Usage at REST[3] 用法见 REST[3]. **6** (idm 习语) **(be/hang) in the balance** (of a decision, result, sb's future, etc) (be) uncertain or undecided (指决定、结果、某人的未来等)不能确定的, 尚未决定的: *The future of this project is (hanging) in the balance.* 这项目的下一步仍然悬而未决. **keep/lose one's 'balance** keep steady/become unsteady; remain upright/fall 保持[失去]平衡; 立稳[倒下]: *It is difficult to keep one's balance on an icy pavement.* 人行道上结了冰, 要想不摔倒可不容易. ○ *She cycled too fast round the corner, lost her balance and fell off.* 她骑车因拐弯太快, 失去平衡而摔倒了. **(catch/throw sb) off balance** (find/cause sb to be) in danger of falling because his steadiness is disturbed (发现[使]某人)摇摇欲坠: *I was caught off balance by the sudden wind and nearly fell.* 突然一阵风吹得我东摇西晃险些摔倒. **on 'balance** (*infml* 口) having considered every aspect, argument, etc 考虑周全; 总的来看: *Despite some failures, our firm has had quite a good year on balance.* 我们公司尽管存在某些不足之处, 总的来看这一年还是相当不错的. **redress the balance** ⇨ REDRESS *v*. **strike a balance** ⇨ STRIKE[2]. **tip the balance** ⇨ TIP[2] 3.

□ ˌ**balance of 'payments** difference between the amount paid to foreign countries for imports and services and the amount received from them for exports, etc in a given period 国际收支差额: [attrib 作定语] *a healthy balance-of-payments position* 良好的国际收支状况.

ˌ**balance of 'power 1** situation in which power is equally divided among rival states or groups of states 均势(对立的国家或国家集团之间势均力敌的状况). **2** (*politics* 政) power held by a small group when rival larger groups are equal or almost equal in strength (当处于对立状态的较大团体力量均衡或接近均衡时)小团体所具有的举足轻重的力量: *Since the two main parties each won the same number of seats, the minority party holds the balance of power.* 由于两个主要政党都赢得了相同数量的席位, 因此作为少数派的政党居于举足轻重的地位.

ˌ**balance of 'trade** difference in value between exports and imports 进出口贸易差额: [attrib 作定语] *a balance-of-trade deficit*, ie when a country's exports are worth less than its imports 贸易赤字(进口多于出口).

'**balance sheet** written record of money received and paid out, showing the difference between the two total amounts 资产负债表, 资金平衡表(显示收支总差额的记录).

bal·ance[2] /ˈbæləns; ˋbæləns/ *v* **1** (**a**) [Tn, Tn·pr] keep or put (sth) in a state of balance[1](2a) 使(某物)保持平衡: *a clown balancing a stick on the end of his nose* 在鼻尖上立着棍子使之保持平衡的丑角. (**b**) [I, Ipr] be or put oneself in a state of balance 使自己保持平衡: *He balanced precariously on the narrow window-ledge.* 他在狭窄的窗台上很难保持平衡. ○ *How long can you balance on one foot?* 你能单脚站立多久? **2** (*finance* 财) (**a**) [Tn] compare the total debits and credits in (an account) and record the sum needed to make them equal 结算: *balance an account/one's books* 结帐 ○ *balance the budget*, ie arrange for income and expenditure to be equal 平衡预算(使收支相抵). (**b**) [I] (of an account, a balance sheet, etc) show equal totals of debits and credits (指帐目、资产负债表等)显示借贷相抵(收支平衡): *Do the firm's accounts balance?* 这家公司的帐目收支是否平衡? (**c**) [Tn] be of the same value as (sth opposite); offset 与(某对比事物)等价; 抵消: *This year's profits will balance our previous losses.* 本年度的盈利将与上一年度的亏损相抵. ○ (*fig* 比喻) *His lack of experience was balanced by his willingness to learn.* 他悉心好学弥补了经验不足. **3** [Tn·pr] **~ A against B** compare the value of one plan, argument, etc with that of another 将此一计划、主张等与彼一计划、主张等作价值上的比较; 权衡二者之利弊: *She balanced the attractions of a high salary against the prospect of working long hours.* 她对高薪和长工时两者的利弊作了权衡比较. **4** [Tn] give equal importance to (different parts of sth) 对(某事物的不同部分)给予同等的重视; 等量齐观: *This school aims to balance the amount of time spent on arts and science subjects.* 这所学校在时间安排上努力做到文理并重. ○ *Try to balance your diet by eating more fruit and less protein.* 多吃些水果, 少摄入些蛋白质, 使饮食均衡合理.

▷ **bal·anced** *adj* [usu attrib 通常作定语] keeping or showing a balance 保持平衡的; 显示平衡的: *a balanced state of mind*, ie a stable one, in which no single emotion is too strong 内心的平衡(无过激情绪的稳定心态) ○ *a balanced decision*, ie one reached after comparing all the arguments 折衷的决定(比较所有意见之后作出的决定) ○ *a balanced diet*, ie one with the quantity and variety of food needed for good health 均衡饮食(按照增进健康所需之食物数量及品种进行调配的饮食).

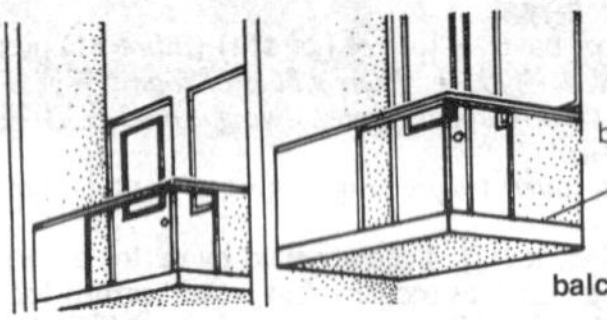

balcony 阳台

bal·cony /ˈbælkənɪ; ˋbælkənɪ/ *n* **1** platform with a wall or rail built onto the outside wall of a building and reached from an upstairs room 阳台. ⇨illus 见插图. **2** (*US*) = CIRCLE 3.

bald /bɔːld; bɔld/ *adj* **1** (**a**) (of people) having little or no hair on the scalp (指人)秃头的, 无发或少发的. (**b**) without the expected covering 缺少应有的覆盖物的: *Our dog has a bald patch* (ie a patch with no hair) *on its leg.* 我们的狗的腿上秃了一块. ○ *bald* (ie badly worn) *tyres* 光秃的(严重磨损的)轮胎 ○ (*fig* 比喻) *a bald landscape*, ie one with no trees, bushes, etc 光秃秃的景象(没有树木等). **2** without elaboration; plain or dull 不刻意修饰的; 简单的; 单调的: *bald facts* 简单的事实 ○ *a bald statement of the facts* 对事实的直截了当的陈述. **3** (idm 习语) **(as) bald as a coot** (*infml* 口) completely bald 头顶全秃的.

▷ **bald·ing** *adj* becoming bald 变秃的: *He was already balding at the age of 25.* 他25岁就秃顶了.

baldly *adv* in plain words; with no elaboration 直截了当地; 不加修饰地: *To put it baldly…*, ie If I may speak plainly, without trying to soften what I am saying… 直截了当地说吧….

bald·ness *n* [U].

□ ˌ**bald 'eagle** N American eagle with a white head and white tail feathers, used as an emblem of the USA 白头雕, 秃雕(产于北美洲的雕, 头部和尾部羽毛为白色, 是象征美国的国鸟).

bal·der·dash /ˈbɔːldədæʃ; ˈbɔldɚˌdæʃ/ *n* [U] (*dated infml* 旧, 口) nonsense 胡话: *He's talking balderdash.* 他胡说八道.

bale[1] /beɪl; bel/ *n* large bundle of paper, straw, goods, etc pressed together and tied with rope or wire ready to be moved, sold, etc 大包; 大捆: *bales of hay* 干草捆 ○ *The cloth was packed in bales.* 布已打成包.

▷ **bale** *v* [Tn, Tn·p] **~ sth (up)** make sth into or pack sth in bales 将某物打成包或包装成捆: *baling hay* 捆干草.

bale[2] /beɪl; bel/ *v* **1** [I, Ip, Tn, Tn·p] = BAIL[2]. **2** (phr v) **bale out (of sth)** jump out using a parachute (from an aircraft that is damaged or out of control) (从损坏或失控的飞机中)跳伞.

bale·ful /ˈbeɪlfʊl; ˈbelfəl/ *adj* threatening evil or harm; menacing 凶恶的; 有害的; 险恶的: *a baleful look, influence, presence* 凶恶的样子、势力、态度. ▷ **bale·fully** /ˈbeɪlfʊlɪ; ˈbelfəlɪ/ *adv*.

balk[1] (also **baulk**) /bɔːk; bɔk/ *n* thick, roughly-squared wooden beam (粗加工的)大方木料.

balk[2] (also **baulk**) /bɔːk; bɔk/ *v* **1** [I, Ipr] **~ (at sth)** be reluctant to tackle sth because it is difficult, dangerous, unpleasant, etc (因困难、危险、乏味等)不愿从事某事: *The horse balked at* (ie refused to jump) *the high hedge.* 马在高高的树篱面前逡巡不前(不愿跳越). ○ *His parents balked at the cost of the guitar he wanted.* 他想要那个吉他, 但他父母看到吉他的价格却踌躇不决. **2** (*dated* 旧) **(a)** [Tn] deliberately obstruct or prevent (sth) 故意妨碍或阻止(某事物): *balk sb's plans* 使某人的计划受挫. **(b)** [Tn·pr] **~ sb of sth** prevent sb from getting sth 阻止某人获得某事物: *They were balked of their prey.* 他们受阻捕不到猎物.

ball[1] /bɔːl; bɔl/ *n* **1 (a)** solid or hollow sphere used in games (各种游戏所用的实心或空心的)球: *a ˈfootball* 足球 ○ *a ˈtennis-ball* 网球 ○ *a ˈcricket-ball* 板球. ⇨illus at BASKETBALL, HOCKEY 见 BASKETBALL, HOCKEY 之插图. **(b)** any similar sphere 任何球状物: *Signs with three balls hang outside pawnbrokers' shops.* 当铺外面悬挂着三个球的标记. **2 (a)** (in cricket) single delivery of the ball by the bowler (板球)投球手投出的一个球. **(b)** (in baseball) any strike or throw (棒球)一击或一投: *a foul ball* 界外球. **(c)** (in football, hockey, etc) movement of the ball by a player (足球、曲棍球等的)传球: *send over a high ball* 高吊传球. **3** round mass of material that has been pressed together, rolled or wound into shape 挤压、旋滚或缠绕成团的球状物: *a ˈmeat ball* 肉丸子 ○ *a ˈsnowball* 雪球 ○ *a ball of ˈwool/ˈstring* 绒线[线]团. **4** rounded part 圆形部分: *the ball of the thumb*, ie the part near the palm 大拇指下面近掌心的球形部分. ⇨illus at HAND 见 HAND 之插图. ○ *the ball of the foot*, ie the part near the base of the big toe 脚掌下面近拇趾根的球形部分. **5** (usu *pl* 通常作复数) (*infml* 口) testicle 睾丸. **6** (idm 习语) **the ball is in one's/sb's ˈcourt** one/sb must make the next move (in a negotiation, etc) (谈判等)下一个轮到自己[某人]. **a ball of ˈfire** (*infml* 口) person full of energy and enthusiasm 精力充沛热情洋溢的人. **have the ball at one's ˈfeet** have a good chance of succeeding 有成功的好机会. **keep/start the ˈball rolling** continue/start a conversation or an activity 继续[开始]谈话或活动. **(be) on the ˈball** (*infml* 口) be alert and aware of new ideas, trends, etc 对新的思想、动向等敏感而熟悉: *The new publicity manager is really on the ball.* 新的宣传部主任确实很内行. **play ˈball** (*infml* 口) co-operate 合作: *They're refusing to play ball (with us).* 他们拒绝(与我们)合作.

▷ **ball** *v* [Tn] form (sth) into a ball by winding, squeezing, etc 以缠绕、挤压等方法使(某物)成为一团: *ball one's fist* 攥拳.

□ ˌ**ball-ˈbearing** *n* **(a)** type of bearing(5) in which small steel balls are used to reduce friction 滚珠轴承. **(b)** (usu *pl* 通常作复数) any of these balls (滚珠轴承的)滚珠.

ˈ**ballboy**, ˈ**ballgirl** *ns* young person who retrieves balls for the players in a tennis match 网球场上捡球的年轻人.

ˈ**ballcock** *n* device with a floating ball that controls the water level in a cistern 浮球旋塞; 浮球阀.

ˈ**ball game 1 (a)** any game played with a ball 球类运动. **(b)** (*US*) game of baseball 棒球戏. **2** (*sl* 俚) state of affairs 局面: *We're into a whole new ball game.* 我们正处于一种全新的局面.

ˈ**ballpark** *n* **1** (*US*) place where baseball is played 棒球场. **2** (*sl* 俚) area; range 区域; 范围: *a guess that's just not in the right ballpark*, ie one that is wildly inaccurate 不着边际的瞎猜 ○ [attrib 作定语] *a ballpark figure*, ie a rough estimate 约略的数字.

ˈ**ball-point** *n* (also ˌ**ball-point ˈpen**) pen that writes with a tiny ball at its point which rolls ink onto the paper 圆珠笔. Cf 参看 BIRO.

ball[2] /bɔːl; bɔl/ *n* **1** formal social gathering for dancing (正式举办的)舞会. **2** (idm 习语) **have (oneself) a ˈball** (*infml* 口 *esp US*) have a very good time 过得非常愉快.

□ ˈ**ballroom** *n* large room used for dancing 跳舞厅. Cf 参看 DANCE-HALL (DANCE[1]). ˌ**ballroom ˈdancing** formal type of dancing to conventional rhythms 交际舞; 交谊舞.

bal·lad /ˈbæləd; ˈbæləd/ *n* simple song or poem, esp one that tells a story 歌谣; 诗歌; 谣曲; (尤指)叙事歌谣.

bal·lade /bæˈlɑːd; bæˈlɑd/ *n* **1** poem with one or more verses, each having 7, 8 or 10 lines, and a short final verse 联韵诗(全诗有一个或数个诗节, 每节7行、8行或10行, 另有一个短小的尾节). **2** romantic piece of music 叙事曲; 浪漫曲.

bal·last /ˈbæləst; ˈbæləst/ *n* **1** [U] heavy material placed in a ship's hold to keep it steady 压舱物, 压载物(船中用以保持平稳的). **2** [U] sand or other material carried in a balloon, that can be thrown out to make the balloon go higher 气球所装载的沙子或其他物质(可将其抛掉以使气球升得更高). **3** [U] stones, etc used to make a foundation for a railway, road, etc (铺筑铁路、公路等之路基所用的)石块, 道砟. **4** [C] device used for stabilizing current in an electric circuit 镇流器. **5** (idm 习语) **in ballast** (of a ship) carrying only ballast (指船)仅装有压舱物的.

▷ **bal·last** *v* [Tn, Tn·pr] **~ sth (with sth)** supply sth with ballast 给某物装上压载物.

bal·ler·ina /ˌbæləˈriːnə; ˌbæləˈrinə/ *n* female ballet dancer, esp one who takes leading parts 芭蕾舞女演员(尤指扮演主角的).

bal·let /ˈbæleɪ; ˈbæle/ *n* **1 (a)** (sometimes 有时作 **the ballet**) [U] style of dancing used to tell a story in a dramatic performance with music but without speech or singing 芭蕾舞: *enjoy (the) classical ballet* 欣赏古典芭蕾舞 ○ [attrib 作定语] *ballet music* 芭蕾舞音乐. **(b)** [C] story performed in this way 芭蕾舞剧: *Have you seen this ballet before?* 你从前看过这出芭蕾舞剧吗? **2** [CGp] group of dancers who regularly perform ballet together 芭蕾舞的演出团体: *members of the Bolshoi Ballet* 大剧院芭蕾舞团的演员.

□ ˈ**ballet-dancer** *n* person who dances in ballets 芭蕾舞演员.

bal·list·ics /bəˈlɪstɪks; bəˈlɪstɪks/ *n* [sing *v*] study of things that are shot or fired through the air, eg bullets, missiles, etc 弹道学(对射击或发射之物如子弹、导弹等的研究): [attrib 作定语] *a ballistics expert* 弹道学专家.

□ balˌ**listic ˈmissile** missile that is initially powered and guided and thereafter controlled by gravity 弹道导弹.

bal·locks (also **bol·locks**) /ˈbɒləks; ˈbɑləks/ *n* (⚠ *infml* 讳, 口) **1** [pl] testicles 睾丸. **2** [U] nonsense 胡说: *What a load of ballocks!* 一派胡言!

▷ **bal·locks** *interj* (⚠ *infml* 讳, 口) nonsense 胡说.

bal·loon /bəˈluːn; bəˈlun/ *n* **1** brightly-coloured rubber bag that is filled with air, used as a child's toy or a decoration (用作玩具或装饰品的)气球. **2** (also **hot-ˈair balloon**) large flexible bag filled with hot air or gas to make it rise in the air, often carrying a basket, etc for passengers 热气气球(常悬有吊篮等以载人). **3** (in strip cartoons, etc) shape like a balloon (ie round with a narrow neck) in which speech is shown (连环画等)供写对白的气球状线条圈(即带狭颈的圆圈). **4** (idm 习语) **when the balˈloon goes up** (*infml* 口) when expected trouble begins 当意料中的麻烦到来时: *I don't want to be around when the balloon goes up.* 要出事了, 我趁早离开是非之地.

▷ **bal·loon** *v* [I] **1** swell out like a balloon 膨胀如气球: *Her skirt ballooned in the wind.* 她的裙子让风吹得鼓起

来了. **2** (usu 通常作 **go ballooning**) travel in a balloon as a sport 乘气球(作为运动): *They like to go ballooning at weekends.* 他们周末喜欢乘气球玩.

bal·loon·ist *n* person who travels by balloon, esp as a sport 乘气球的人(尤指作为运动).

bal·lot /ˈbælət; ˋbælət/ *n* **1** (**a**) (also ˈ**ballot-paper**) [C] piece of paper used in secret voting (无记名投票所用的)选票. (**b**) [U] system of secret voting 无记名投票制度: *elected by ballot* 无记名投票选举的. (**c**) [C] instance of this 无记名投票: *hold a ballot of members* 成员举行的无记名投票 ○ *We should put it to a ballot.* 我们应该对此进行无记名投票. **2** [C] number of votes recorded in a ballot 无记名投票所得的票数.

▷ **bal·lot** *v* **1** [I, Ipr] **~ (for sb/sth)** vote by ballot (for sb/sth) 以无记名投票方式(对某人[某事物])进行表决. **2** [Tn, Tn·pr] **~ sb (about/on sth)** cause sb to vote (on sth) secretly 使某人以无记名方式投票表决(某事物): *The union balloted its members on the proposed changes.* 工会让会员们以无记名方式就所建议的改革进行表决.

□ ˈ**ballot-box** *n* box in which voters place their ballot-papers 投票箱.

balls /bɔːlz; bɔlz/ *n* (⚠ *infml* 讳, 口) **1** [sing *v*] mess 杂乱: *What a balls you've made of it!* 你把它搞得多乱哪! **2** [U] nonsense 胡说: *That's a load of balls!* 那全是胡说八道! ○ *What he said was all balls.* 他说的净是废话.

▷ **balls** *interj* (⚠ *infml* 讳, 口) nonsense 胡说: *Absolute balls!* 纯粹胡说八道!

balls *v* (phr v) **balls sth up**; *US* also **ball sth up** (⚠ *infml* 讳, 口) make a mess of sth 把某事物搞糟: *He ballsed up all my plans by being so late.* 他来得很晚, 把我的计划全打乱了. Cf 参看 BALL[1] 5.

balls-up /ˈbɔːlz ʌp; ˋbɔlz ˏʌp/ (*US* also **ball-up** /ˈbɔːl ʌp; ˋbɔl ˏʌp/) *n* (⚠ *infml* 讳, 口) mess; botched job 杂乱; 拙劣的工作: *I made a proper balls-up of that exam.* 那次考试我考得一塌糊涂.

bally /ˈbælɪ; ˋbælɪ/ *adj, adv* (*dated Brit sl* 旧, 俚) bloody[2](1) 非常; 极端: *It's a bally nuisance!* 讨厌极了!

bal·ly·hoo /ˌbælɪˈhuː; *US* ˈbælɪhuː; ˋbælɪˏhu/ *n* [U] (*infml derog* 口, 贬) **1** noisy publicity or advertising 大吹大擂; 大肆宣扬. **2** unnecessary noise or fuss 咋咋呼呼; 大惊小怪.

balm /bɑːm; bɑm/ *n* [U, C] **1** (also **balsam**) sweet-smelling oil or ointment obtained from certain types of tree, used for soothing pain or for healing (从某些树中提取的可止痛或疗伤的)芳香油, 香脂. **2** (*fig* 比喻) thing that soothes the mind 安慰物: *The gentle music was (a) balm to his ears.* 那柔和的音乐对他是一种安慰.

▷ **balmy** *adj* (**-ier**, **-iest**) **1** (of air) gentle and pleasantly warm (指空气)温暖的, 暖和的. **2** fragrant and soothing; like balm 芳香的; 能止痛的; 如香脂的. **3** (*esp US*) = BARMY. **balm·ily** *adv*. **balmi·ness** *n* [U].

ba·lo·ney = BOLONEY.

balsa /ˈbɔːlsə; ˋbɔlsə/ *n* (**a**) [U] lightweight wood used for making models, rafts, etc 轻木(轻质木材, 用以制作模型、木筏等). (**b**) [C] tropical American tree from which this comes 轻木树(生长于热带美洲).

bal·sam /ˈbɔːlsəm; ˋbɔlsəm/ *n* **1** [C] flowering plant grown in gardens 凤仙花. **2** (**a**) [C] tree yielding balm 产芳香油的树. (**b**) [U, C] = BALM.

bal·us·ter /ˈbæləstə(r); ˋbæləstɚ/ *n* any of the short pillars in a balustrade 栏杆柱.

bal·us·trade /ˌbæləˈstreɪd; ˏbæləˋstred/ *n* row of upright posts or small pillars joined along the top by a rail or stonework, and placed round a balcony, terrace, flat roof, etc (阳台、平台、平屋顶等的)栏杆.

bam·boo /bæmˈbuː; bæmˋbu/ *n* [C, U] tall plant of the grass family with hard hollow jointed stems that are used for making canes, furniture, etc 竹; 竹子: *the bamboos growing by the river* 生长于河边的竹子 ○ *a house of bamboo* 竹屋 ○ [attrib 作定语] *a bamboo chair* 竹椅.

bam·boozle /bæmˈbuːzl; bæmˋbuzl̩/ *v* (*infml* 口) **1** [Tn] mystify (sb); puzzle 使(某人)迷惑; 使为难: *You've completely bamboozled me.* 你完全把我搞糊涂了. **2** (phr v) **bamboozle sb into (doing) sth** trick sb into (doing) sth 哄骗某人做某事: *He bamboozled me into believing that he'd lost all his money.* 他欺骗我让我相信他把钱全丢光了. **bamboozle sb out of sth** cheat sb out of sth 骗取某人的某物.

ban /bæn; bæn/ *v* (**-nn-**) **1** [Tn] officially forbid (sth) 明令禁止(某事物): *The play was banned (by the censor).* 该剧本遭(审查员)查禁. ○ *The Government has banned the use of chemical weapons.* 政府已经禁止使用化学武器. ○ *a ban-the-bomb demonstration*, ie one protesting against the use of nuclear weapons 要求禁止使用核武器的示威活动. **2 ~ sb (from sth/from doing sth)** officially forbid sb (to do sth) 明令禁止某人(做某事): *He was banned from (attending) the meeting.* 不准他出席该会议. ○ *She's been banned from driving for six months.* 已禁止她开车, 为期六个月.

▷ **ban** *n* **~ (on sth/sb)** order that bans; prohibition 禁令; 禁止: *put a ban on the import of alcohol* 宣布禁止酒类进口.

banal /bəˈnɑːl; *US* ˈbeɪnl; ˋbenl̩/ *adj* commonplace; uninteresting 平常的; 乏味的: *banal remarks, thoughts, sentiments, etc* 平平常常的话语、思想、感情等.

▷ **ba·nal·ity** /bəˈnælətɪ; bəˋnælətɪ/ *n* **1** [U] quality of being banal 平常; 乏味. **2** [C] banal remark 平常话; 陈词滥调: *a speech consisting mainly of banalities* 有很多陈词滥调的讲话.

ba·nana /bəˈnɑːnə; *US* bəˈnænə; bəˋnænə/ *n* **1** (**a**) long thick-skinned edible fruit that is yellow when ripe 香蕉. ⇨illus at FRUIT 见FRUIT之插图. (**b**) tropical or semi-tropical tree bearing this fruit 香蕉树(生长于热带或亚热带). **2** (idm 习语) **go baˈnanas** (*sl* 俚) become mad or angry; act very foolishly 发疯; 发怒; 傻里傻气.

□ **baˈnana republic** (*derog* 贬) small, often unstable, country whose economy depends on the export of fruit 香蕉共和国(以水果输出为经济命脉的, 常为不稳定的小国).

baˈnana skin (*infml* 口) source of difficulty or embarrassment, esp to a public figure, an organization, etc 造成困难或麻烦的根源(尤对某知名人物、组织等而言): *The proposed tax changes are likely to prove a banana skin for the Government.* 建议中的税务变动很可能给政府带来无穷后患.

band /bænd; bænd/ *n* **1** [C] (**a**) thin flat strip, hoop or loop used for fastening things together or for placing round an object to strengthen it 带; 箍; 条: *iron bands round a barrel* 桶外的铁箍 ○ *papers kept together with a rubber band* 用橡皮筋套在一起的文件 ○ *the waistband of a dress* 连衣裙上的腰带. (**b**) strip or line on sth, different in colour or design from the rest (颜色或图案异于其他部分的)条纹, 条饰: *a white plate with a blue band round the edge* 带蓝边的白盘子. **2** [CGp] organized group of people doing sth together with a common purpose 一队; 一伙; 一组; 一帮: *a band of robbers, fugitives, revellers, etc* 一帮强盗、逃亡者、寻欢作乐的人等. **3** [CGp] (**a**) group of people playing esp wind instruments (尤指管乐)乐队: *a brass* ˈ*band* 铜管乐队 ○ *a military* ˈ*band* 军乐队. (**b**) group of people playing popular music, often for dancing 流行音乐乐队(常为舞蹈作伴奏的): *a* ˈ*dance band* 为舞会作伴奏的乐队 ○ *a* ˈ*jazz band* 爵士乐队. Cf 参看 ORCHESTRA. **4** (also ˈ**waveband**) [C] (*radio* 无) range of wavelengths within specified limits 波段; 频带: *the 19-metre band* 19米的波段.

▷ **band** *v* **1** [Tn] put a band(1a) on or round (sth) 在(某物)上加带或箍. **2** [Ip] **~ together** unite in a group 联合: *band together to protest* 联合抗议 ○ *band together against a common enemy* 联合起来共同对敌.

□ ˈ**bandmaster** *n* person who conducts a band(3a,b) (管)乐队指挥.

ˈ**band-saw** *n* machine-driven saw in the form of an endless belt 带锯(环形带状的机械锯).

ˈ**bandsman** /-zmən; -zmən/ *n* (*pl* **-men** /-zmən; -zmən/) person who plays in a band(3a) (管)乐队队员.

ˈ**bandstand** /ˈbændstænd; ˋbændˏstænd/ *n* covered platform for a band(3a) playing outdoors (室外有顶棚的)演奏台.

ˈ**bandwagon** *n* (idm 习语) **climb/jump on the** ˈ**bandwagon** (*infml* 口) join others in doing sth fashionable or likely to be successful 赶浪头; 赶时髦; 随大溜.

ban·dage /ˈbændɪdʒ; ˋbændɪdʒ/ *n* strip of material used for binding round a wound or an injury 绷带(包扎伤口或患处的纱布带).

▷ **ban·dage** *v* [Tn, Tn·pr, Tn·p] **~ sth/sb (up) (with sth)** wind a bandage round (a part of) sb 用绷带包扎某人(的身体部位): *bandage (up) a wound* 用绷带包扎伤口 ○ *a bandaged hand* 扎了绷带的手.

Band-aid /ˈbændeɪd; ˋbændedˏ/ *n* [C, U] (*US propr* 专利名) type of sticking-plaster 一种橡皮膏.

ban·danna /bænˈdænə; bænˋdænə/ *n* large handkerchief with coloured spots, usu worn round the neck 有彩色斑点的大围巾.

B and B (also **b and b**) /ˌbiː ən ˈbiː; ˌbi ən ˋbi/ *abbr* 缩写 = (*Brit infml* 口) bed and breakfast.

band·box /ˈbændbɒks; ˋbændˌbɑks/ *n* light cardboard box for hats, etc 轻纸板盒(装帽子等).

ban·deau /ˈbændəʊ; *US* bænˈdəʊ; bænˋdo/ *n* (*pl* **-deaux** /-dəʊz; *US* -ˈdəʊz; -ˋdoz/) narrow band worn round the head by a woman to keep her hair in place (女用)束发带.

ban·dit /ˈbændɪt; ˋbændɪt/ *n* member of a gang of armed robbers 土匪; 强盗: *Buses driving through the mountains have been attacked by bandits.* 驶经山区的公共汽车遭到匪徒袭击.

▷ **ban·ditry** *n* [U] activity of bandits 盗匪行径.

ban·do·leer (also **ban·do·lier**) /ˌbændəˈlɪə(r); ˌbændəˋlɪr/ *n* shoulder-belt with pockets for bullets or cartridges (挎在肩上的)子弹带.

bandy¹ /ˈbændɪ; ˋbændɪ/ *v* (*pt, pp* **bandied**) **1** (idm 习语) **bandy ˈwords (with sb)** (*dated* 旧) exchange words, etc, esp when quarrelling 吵嘴; 顶嘴: *Don't bandy words with me, young man!* 别跟我强嘴, 小伙子! **2** (phr v) **bandy sth about** (usu passive 通常用于被动语态) pass on (a rumour, information, etc), often in a thoughtless way 传播(谣言、消息等)(常为漫不经心地): *The stories being bandied about are completely false.* 这些道听途说的事全属子虚. ○ *Her name is being bandied about as the next chairperson.* 到处传说她将作下届主席.

bandy² /ˈbændɪ; ˋbændɪ/ *adj* (**-ier, -iest**) (*usu derog* 通常作贬义) (of the legs) curving outwards at the knees (指腿部)膝向外弯曲的.

□ ˈ**bandy-legged** *adj* (of people or animals) having bandy legs (指人或动物)两腿向外弯曲, 罗圈腿的.

bane /beɪn; ben/ *n* (idm 习语) **the bane of sb's existence/life** cause of sb's ruin or trouble 某人罹祸或不幸的原因; 祸根: *Those noisy neighbours are the bane of my life.* 那些吵吵闹闹的邻居成了我生活中的一大忧患. ○ *Drink was the bane of his existence.* 他喝酒把自己毁了.

▷ **bane·ful** /-fʊl; -fəl/ *adj* evil or causing evil 有害的; 有毒的: *a baneful influence* 有害的影响. **bane·fully** /-fʊlɪ; -fəlɪ/ *adv*.

bang¹ /bæŋ; bæŋ/ *v* **1** (a) [Ipr, Tn, Tn·pr, Tn·p] strike (sth) deliberately and violently, often in order to make a loud noise 故意猛砸(常为产生巨响): *He was banging on the door with his fist.* 他用拳头砸门. ○ *I banged the door.* 我砰的一声关上了门. ○ *She banged her fist on the table.* 她用拳头猛捶桌子. ○ *I banged the box down on the floor.* 我砰的一声把盒子摔在地板上. **(b)** [I, Ip, Tn, Tn·p] **~ (sth) (down, to, etc)** close with a loud noise 砰的一声关上: *A door was banging somewhere,* ie opening and closing noisily. 不知哪里有扇门砰砰作响(开门和关门的响声). ○ *Don't bang the door!* 不要砰砰地关门! ○ *He banged the lid down.* 他把盖子砰的一声关上了. **2 (a)** [Tn, Tn·pr] hit violently and often unintentionally 猛击(常为无心地): *She tripped and banged her knee on the desk.* 她绊倒了, 膝盖猛磕在书桌上. **(b)** [Ipr] **~ into sb/sth** collide with sb/sth violently 猛撞着某人[某物]: *He ran round the corner and banged straight into a lamp-post.* 他跑过拐角处时迎面撞在灯柱上. **3** [I, Ip] make a loud noise 发巨响: *The fireworks banged impressively.* 烟火响声震天. **4** (phr v) **bang about/around** move around noisily 发出响声地动来动去: *We could hear the children banging about upstairs.* 我们可以听见孩子们在楼上乒乒乓乓地跑来跑去. **bang away (a)** (*infml* 口) work hard, esp using a typewriter 努力工作(尤指打字). **(b)** (*sl* 俚) have vigorous sexual intercourse 纵情性交. **(c)** (*infml* 口) fire continuously 不断射击: *We were banging away at the enemy.* 我们乒乒乓乓向敌人射击. ○ *The guns banged away all day.* 枪炮声整天响个不停.

NOTE ON USAGE 用法: **1 Knock** means hitting something with a clear, sharp sound. ☆ **knock** 意为敲击某物而发出清脆的声音. One may knock to signal one's presence to others 可用敲击发出的声音向别人表示有人在此: *Can you go to the door? Someone's knocking.* 你到门那儿去看看好吗? 有人敲门. ○ *He knocked at the window to be let in.* 他敲敲窗户要进来. **Knock** can denote an accidental action which hurts or breaks something ☆ **knock** 可指意外的动作, 可造成伤痛或毁坏东西: *I knocked my hand against the table.* 我的手碰到桌子上了. ○ *I knocked the plate off the table with my elbow.* 我的胳膊肘把盘子从桌上碰掉了. **2 Bump** means hitting something by accident and with a dull sound ☆ **bump** 的意思是偶然地碰撞某物并发出低沉的声音: *The bus bumped into the back of the car.* 公共汽车砰的一声撞上了一辆汽车的后部. ○ *He ran round the corner and bumped into an old lady.* 他跑过拐角处, 撞着了一个老太太. ○ *I bumped my head on the low beam.* 我的头撞到低梁上了. **3 Bang** suggests a harder blow and a louder sound. ☆ **bang** 指撞击更重, 声音也更大. Banging may be intentional hitting, expressing anger or urgency 这种撞击可以是有意的, 表示气愤或着急: *He banged his fist on the table to emphasize his argument.* 他用拳头敲着桌子为自己的辩驳助威. ○ *He banged on the door until it was opened.* 他砰砰地敲门, 直到把门敲开为止. Banging may also be accidental and painful 这种撞击也可以是意外的及产生痛苦的: *I banged my elbow on the corner of the table.* 我的胳膊肘撞着桌子角了. **4 Bash** is informal and means breaking or injuring something or somebody by hitting hard ☆ **bash** 是口语用词, 意为猛力地撞毁某物或撞伤某人: *The thieves bashed the woman over the head.* 强盗猛击那女子的头部. ○ *The car bashed into the tree.* 汽车猛力撞着一棵树.

B

bang² /bæŋ; bæŋ/ *n* **1** violent blow 猛击; 猛撞: *He fell and got a nasty bang on the head.* 他摔了一跤, 头部磕得很重. **2** sudden loud noise 突然的巨响: *She always shuts the door with a bang.* 她关门时总是砰的一声. ○ *The firework exploded with a loud bang.* 烟火砰的一声爆开了. **3** (*sl* 俚) act of sexual intercourse 性交: *have a quick bang* 速决性交. **4** (idm 习语) **go (off) with a ˈbang**; *US* **go over with a ˈbang** (*infml* 口) (of a performance, etc) be successful (指演出等)取得成功.

▷ **bang** *interj* (used to imitate a loud noise 用作模仿巨响的象声词): *'Bang! Bang! You're dead!' shouted the small boy.* '砰! 砰! 打死你了!' 那小男孩嚷道.

bang³ /bæŋ; bæŋ/ *adv* (*infml* 口) **1** suddenly, violently or noisily; abruptly 突然地; 猛烈地; 发出响声地; 粗暴地: *I tripped and fell bang on the floor.* 我绊倒了, 重重地摔在地板上. **2 (a)** exactly; precisely 恰好; 正好: *bang in the middle of the performance* 演出正进行到一半 ○ *Your guess was bang on target.* 你猜得对极了. **(b)** completely 完全地; 彻底地: *This film is bang up to date.* 这部影片是全新的. **3** (idm 习语) **bang goes sth** (*infml* 口) that is the (sudden) end of sth 为某事物的(突然的)结尾: *Bang went his hopes of promotion.* 他获得晋升的希望突然破灭了. **be bang ˈon** (*sl* 俚) be exactly right 恰到好处: *Her criticisms were bang on every time.* 她的批评每次都非常中肯. ○ *Your budget figures were bang on this year.* 你今年的预算数字十分准确. **go ˈbang** (*infml* 口) burst or explode with a loud noise 在一声巨响中爆裂或爆炸.

bang⁴ /bæŋ; bæŋ/ *n* (usu *pl* 通常作复数) (*US*) = FRINGE¹.

banger /ˈbæŋə(r); ˋbæŋɚ/ *n* (*Brit infml* 口) **1** sausage 香肠. **2** firework made to explode with a loud noise 爆竹; 鞭炮. **3** noisy old car 噪声大的旧汽车.

bangle /ˈbæŋgl; ˋbæŋgḷ/ *n* large decorative ring worn round the arm or ankle 手镯; 脚镯.

ban·ian (also **ban·yan**) /ˈbænɪən; ˋbænjən/ (also ˈ**banyan-tree**) *n* Indian fig-tree whose branches come down to the ground and take root 榕树.

ban·ish /ˈbænɪʃ; ˋbænɪʃ/ *v* [Tn, Tn·pr] **1 ~ sb (from sth)** send sb away, esp out of the country, as a punishment 放逐某人(尤指驱逐出境, 作为惩罚): *He was banished (from his homeland) for life.* 他被终生流放(他乡). **2 ~ sth (from sth)** drive (thoughts, etc) out (of the mind) (自心中)排除(想法等): *banish fear* 消除恐惧 ○ *She banished all thoughts of a restful holiday (from her mind).* 她(从心里)打消了过一个宁静假日的

想法.
▷ **ban·ish·ment** *n* [U] state or process of being banished 流放: *lifelong banishment* 终身流放.

ban·is·ter /ˈbænɪstə(r); ˈbænɪstɚ/ *n* (usu *pl* 通常作复数) handrail of a stair and the upright poles supporting it 楼梯的扶手及其支柱: *children sliding down the banister(s)* 沿楼梯扶手往下滑的孩子们. ⇨illus at STAIRCASE 见STAIRCASE之插图.

B

banjo /ˈbændʒəʊ; ˈbændʒo/ *n* (*pl* **~s**) stringed musical instrument with a long neck and a round body, played by plucking with the fingers 班卓琴(一种弦乐器, 长颈、圆身, 用手指弹拨).

bank[1] /bæŋk; bæŋk/ *n* **1** land sloping up along each side of a river or canal; ground near a river 河边的斜坡; 河边的土地; 河岸; 河畔: *Can you jump over to the opposite bank?* 你能跳到对岸吗? ○ *My house is on the south bank (of the river).* 我家坐落在(河的)南岸. ⇨Usage at COAST[1] 用法见 COAST[1]. **2** sloping ground, often forming a border or division (通常为形成边界或分界线的)坡地: *low banks of earth between rice-fields* 稻田之间的地埂; 田埂 ○ *flowers growing on the banks on each side of the country lanes* 乡间小路两旁斜坡上长的花. **3** = SANDBANK (SAND). **4** flat-topped mass of cloud, snow, etc, esp one formed by the wind 顶部平坦的云堆、雪堆等(尤指由风吹成的): *The sun went behind a bank of clouds.* 太阳钻到云堆里去了.

bank[2] /bæŋk; bæŋk/ *v* **1** [I] (of an aircraft, etc) travel with one side higher than the other, usu when turning (指飞机等)倾斜飞行(通常于转弯时): *The plane banked steeply to the left.* 飞机陡然向左侧倾斜飞行. **2** (phr v) **bank up** rise in the form of banks[1](4) 聚积成平顶状: *The snow has banked up against the shed.* 雪在小屋旁聚积起来. **bank sth up** (**a**) make sth into banks 使某物成堤状. (**b**) stop water of (a river, etc) from flowing by making a bank of earth, mud, etc (用泥土等)筑堤以堵截(河等的)流水: *bank up a stream* 筑堤以堵截水流. (**c**) heap coal-dust, etc on (the fire in a fireplace or furnace) so that the fire burns slowly for a long time (用煤灰等)封炉火.

bank[3] /bæŋk; bæŋk/ *n* **1** establishment for keeping money, valuables, etc safely, the money being paid out on the customer's order (by means of cheques) 银行: *have money in the bank*, ie have savings 在银行中有存款 ○ [attrib 作定语] *a ˈbank manager* 银行经理 ○ *a ˈbank account* 银行帐户 ○ *a ˈbank loan*, ie money borrowed from a bank 银行贷款. **2** (in gambling) sum of money held by the keeper of a gaming table, from which he pays his losses (赌博)庄家的赌本. **3** store (of valuable things, information, etc) (贵重物品、信息等的)储库: *build up a bank of useful addresses, references, information, etc* 建立一个有用的地址、参考书目、信息等的储存库 ○ *a ˈblood bank* 血库 ○ *a ˈdata bank* 数据库. **4** (idm 习语) **ˌbreak the ˈbank** (**a**) (in gambling) win more money than is in the bank[3](2) (赌博)赢的钱比庄家的赌本还要多. (**b**) (*infml* 口) cost more than one can afford 花费不起: *Come on! One evening at the theatre won't break the bank.* 得啦! 看一晚上戏不会倾家荡产的.

□ **ˈbank balance** amount of money credited to or owed by an individual bank account 银行存款余额.

ˈbank-book (also **passbook**) *n* book containing a record of a customer's bank account 银行存折.

ˈbank card = CHEQUE CARD (CHEQUE).

ˈbank draft (document used for) the transferring of money from one bank to another 银行汇票; 银行之间的汇兑.

ˌbank ˈholiday 1 (*Brit*) day (not a Saturday or a Sunday) on which banks are officially closed, usu a public holiday (eg Easter Monday, Christmas Day, etc) (星期六和星期日以外的)银行假日(通常为公众假日, 如复活节后的星期一、圣诞节等). **2** (*US*) any weekday on which banks are closed, usu on special instructions from the Government (星期日以外的任何的)银行假日(通常为奉政府命令停止营业的).

ˈbanknote = NOTE[1].

ˈbank rate minimum rate of interest in a country as fixed by a central bank or banks 银行贴现率(中央银行规定的全国最低利率).

ˈbank statement printed record showing all the money paid into and out of a customer's bank account within a certain period 银行结单(显示某时期内储户存取款项的清单).

bank[4] /bæŋk; bæŋk/ *v* **1** [Tn] place (money) in a bank 将(钱)存入银行: *bank one's savings, takings, etc* 把余钱、收入等存入银行. **2** [I, Ipr] **~ (with sb/sth)** have an account (at a particular bank) (在某银行中)有帐户: *Who do you bank with?* 你在哪家银行存款? ○ *Where do you bank?* 你的钱存在哪家银行? **3** (phr v) **bank on sb/sth** base one's hopes on sb/sth 寄希望于某人[某事物]: *I'm banking on your help/on you to help me.* 我指望你的帮助[你来帮助我]. ○ *He was banking on the train being on time.* 他指望火车能正点.

▷ **banker** *n* **1** owner, director or manager of a bank[3](1) 银行的老板、董事长或经理. **2** (in gambling) person who holds the bank[3](2) (赌博中的)庄家.

ˌbanker's ˈorder = STANDING ORDER (STANDING).

bank·ing *n* [U] business of running a bank[3](1) 银行业: *choose banking as a career* 选择银行业为职业 ○ *She's in banking.* 她在银行界任职.

bank[5] /bæŋk; bæŋk/ *n* row or series of similar objects, eg in a machine (类似物件的)一排或一系列(如机器中的): *a bank of lights, switches, etc* 一列灯、开关等 ○ *a bank of cylinders in an engine* 发动机中的一排汽缸 ○ *a bank of oars* 一排桨.

bank·rupt /ˈbæŋkrʌpt; ˈbæŋkrʌpt/ *n* (*law* 律) person judged by a lawcourt to be unable to pay his debts in full, whose property is then taken by the court and used to repay his creditors 破产者.

▷ **bank·rupt** *adj* **1** (**a**) (*law* 律) declared by a court to be a bankrupt 经法院宣判为破产的. (**b**) unable to pay one's debts 无力还债的: *go/be bankrupt* 破产. **2 ~ (of sth)** (*derog* 贬) completely lacking (in sth that is good) 完全缺乏(某种良好事物): *bankrupt of ideas, moral scruples* 毫无主意、道德上的约束 ○ *a society that is morally bankrupt* 道德沦丧的社会.

bank·rupt *v* [Tn] make (sb) bankrupt 使(某人)破产.

bank·ruptcy /ˈbæŋkrəpsɪ; ˈbæŋkrəpsɪ/ *n* (**a**) [U] state of being bankrupt 破产(的状况): [attrib 作定语] *in the bankruptcy court* 在破产审理法庭上. (**b**) [C] instance of this 破产: *Ten bankruptcies were recorded in this town last year.* 去年这个城镇有十起破产事件.

ban·ner /ˈbænə(r); ˈbænɚ/ *n* **1** large strip of cloth showing an emblem or slogan, which is displayed or carried, usu on two poles, during eg political or religious processions (显示某种标志或口号的布制的)横幅(通常用两根竿子撑开或握举, 见于如政治或宗教的游行行列中): *The marchers carried banners with the words 'No Nuclear Weapons' in large letters.* 游行者打着横幅, 上有大字'禁止使用核武器'. ⇨illus at FLAG 见 FLAG 之插图. **2** (*dated* 旧) flag 旗帜: *the banner of freedom* 自由的旗帜. **3** [attrib 作定语] (*US*) excellent 极佳的: *a banner year for exports* 出口情况最好的一年. **4** (idm 习语) **under the banner (of sth)** claiming to support (a particular set of ideas) 声称拥护(某套主张): *She fought the election under the banner of equal rights.* 她打着平等的旗号参加了竞选.

□ **ˌbanner ˈheadline** (also **streamer**) large newspaper headline, often printed across a whole page (报纸的)大标题(常为通栏的).

banns /bænz; bænz/ *n* [pl] public announcement in church that two people intend to marry each other (教堂里的)结婚预告: *read/publish the banns* 阅读[公布]结婚预告 ○ *have one's banns called*, ie have one's forthcoming marriage announced 公布结婚预告.

ban·quet /ˈbæŋkwɪt; ˈbæŋkwɪt/ *n* elaborate formal meal, usu for a special event, at which speeches are often made 宴会, 盛宴(通常指为某事, 常有致辞): *a ˈwedding banquet* 婚宴.

▷ **ban·quet** *v* **1** [Tn] give a banquet for (sb) 宴请(某人). **2** [I] take part in a banquet 参加宴会.

ban·shee /bænˈʃiː; *US* ˈbænʃiː; ˈbænʃi/ *n* (*esp Irish* 尤用于爱尔兰) female spirit with a distinctive wail, thought by some to warn of death in a house 报丧女妖(以特有的哭声预示某家有丧事).

ban·tam /ˈbæntəm; ˈbæntəm/ *n* type of small domestic fowl 矮脚鸡: [attrib 作定语] *bantam cocks* 矮脚公鸡.

ban·tam·weight /ˈbæntəmweɪt; ˈbæntəm,wet/ *n* **1** boxer weighing between 51 and 53.5 kilograms, next above flyweight 最轻量级拳击手(体重在51和53.5公斤之间, 仅高于特轻量级). **2** wrestler weighing between 52 and 57 kilograms 次轻量级摔跤运动员(体重在52和57公斤之间).

ban·ter /ˈbæntə(r); ˋbæntɚ/ *n* [U] playful, good-humoured teasing 打趣; 戏谑; 玩笑: *players exchanging light-hearted banter with the crowd* 跟观众开轻松玩笑的演员.

▷ **ban·ter** *v* [I] speak playfully or jokingly 打趣; 戏谑; 开玩笑. **ban·ter·ing** *adj* playfully teasing 开玩笑的: *a bantering tone of voice* 开玩笑的口气. **ban·ter·ingly** *adv*.

Bantu /ˌbænˈtuː; *US also* ˈbɑːntuː; ˋbænˋtu, ˋbɑnˋtu/ *n* **the Bantu** (also **the Ban·tus**) [pl] large group of related Negroid peoples of central and S Africa 班图人(非洲中部和南部人数众多的黑人部族).

▷ **Bantu** *adj* of these peoples or their languages 班图人的; 班图语的.

ban·yan = BANIAN.

bao·bab /ˈbeɪəbæb; *US* ˈbaʊbæb; ˋbaoˌbæb/ *n* African tree with a very thick trunk and large fruit with edible pulp 猴面包树(产于非洲, 树干极粗, 果大, 果肉可供食用).

bap·tism /ˈbæptɪzəm; ˋbæptɪzəm/ *n* **1** (**a**) [U] ceremony marking a person's admission into the Christian Church either by dipping him in water or by sprinkling him with water, and often giving him a name or names 洗礼, 浸礼(基督教的入教仪式). (**b**) [C] instance of this 洗礼; 浸礼: *There were six baptisms at this church last week.* 上星期这个教堂为六个人施行了洗礼. **2** (idm 习语) **a ˌbaptism of ˈfire** (**a**) soldier's first experience of warfare 战火的洗礼(指士兵初次上阵). (**b**) introduction to an unpleasant experience 初次的不愉快经历: *a young teacher facing her baptism of fire* 面对初登讲台考验的年轻女教师.

▷ **bap·tis·mal** /bæpˈtɪzməl; bæpˋtɪzml̩/ *adj* [attrib 作定语] of or related to baptism 洗礼的; 与洗礼有关的: *a baptismal name, font* 洗礼名、洗礼盆 ○ *baptismal water* 洗礼水.

Bap·tist /ˈbæptɪst; ˋbæptɪst/ *n, adj* (member) of a Protestant Church that believes in baptism by immersion at an age when a person is old enough to understand what the ceremony means 浸礼会的; 浸礼会教徒.

bap·tize, -ise /bæpˈtaɪz; bæpˋtaɪz/ *v* [Tn, Cn·n esp passive 尤用于被动语态] **1** give baptism to (sb); christen 为(某人)施洗礼; 洗礼时命名: *She was baptized Mary.* 她受洗礼时被命名为玛丽. **2** admit into a specified church by baptism 以洗礼方式使加入某教会: *I was baptized a Catholic.* 我曾受洗礼成为天主教徒. Cf 参看 CHRISTEN.

bar[1] /bɑː(r); bɑr/ *n* **1** [C] (**a**) piece of solid material 棒; 条: *a long iron bar* 长铁条 ○ *a bar of chocolate, soap* 一条巧克力、肥皂. (**b**) narrow piece of wood or metal placed (often parallel to others in a grid) as an obstacle in a doorway, window, etc, or to act as a grate in a fire, furnace, etc (门窗等的)闩或杠; (炉灶等的)格栅: *There's a strong bar on the door.* 门上有一个很坚固的闩. ○ *They fitted bars to their windows to stop burglars getting in.* 他们在窗户上加了窗条以防盗贼进入. **2** [C] narrow band (of colour, light, etc) (色、光等的)带, 条: *At sunset, there was a bar of red across the western sky.* 日落时, 西边天空有一道红晖. **3** [C] strip of metal across the ribbon of a military medal to show service in a particular area or an additional award of that medal 军功奖章绶带上面的金属横条, 表示曾在某地区服役或曾再次获得该奖章. **4** [C] (**a**) vertical line dividing printed music into sections of equal value in time 乐谱上划分各小节的垂直线; 小节线. (**b**) one of these sections and the notes in it 乐谱的一个小节: *Hum the opening bars of your favourite tune.* 哼一哼你喜爱的曲子的开头几个小节. ⇨illus at MUSICAL 见MUSICAL之插图. **5** [C] (**a**) bank or ridge of sand, etc across the mouth of a river or the entrance to a bay (河口或海湾入口处的)沙洲: *The ship stuck fast on the bar.* 那船牢牢地搁浅在沙洲上. (**b**) (usu *sing* 通常作单数) (*fig* 比喻) thing that hinders or stops progress; barrier 影响或阻碍进步的事物; 障碍: *Poor health may be a bar to success in life.* 健康不佳可能成为人一生中取得成功的障碍. **6** [sing] barrier in a lawcourt separating the judge, prisoner, lawyers, etc from the spectators (法庭上将法官、囚犯、律师等与听众隔开的)围栏: *the prisoner at the bar* 受审讯的刑事被告 ○ (*fig* 比喻) *She will be judged at the bar of public opinion.* 她将受到舆论的制裁. **7** [sing] (**a**) (*Brit*) railing where non-members of Parliament stand when answering or addressing members (国会中非议员在接受议员的咨询时立于其后的)栏杆. (**b**) (*US*) similar place in the US Senate, House of Representatives, and State Legislatures (美国参议院、众议院以及州议会中的)非议员席. **8 the bar** [Gp, sing] (**a**) (*Brit*) (all those who belong to) the profession of barrister 律师的职业; 律师界: *She's training for the bar.* 她正在接受当律师的培训. ○ *be called to the bar*, ie be received into the profession of barrister 获得律师资格. (**b**) (*US*) (all those who belong to) the legal profession 法律专业(人士); 法律界. **9** [C] (**a**) counter where (esp alcoholic) drinks are served 卖饮料(尤指酒类)的柜台; 酒吧: *sitting on a stool by the bar* 坐在卖酒柜台前的凳子上. (**b**) room in a hotel, public house, etc in which such drinks are served (旅馆、客栈等的)酒吧间: *They walked into the bar.* 他们走进了酒吧间. **10** [C] (esp in compounds 尤用以构成复合词) (**a**) place where certain types of food and drink are served across a counter 通过柜台出售某类食品和饮料的处所: *a ˈsandwich bar* ○ *a ˈcoffee bar* ○ *a ˈwine bar.* (**b**) counter offering certain services 提供某些服务的柜台: *a ˈheel bar*, ie where the heels, etc of shoes are repaired. **11** (idm 习语) **beˌhind ˈbars** (*infml* 口) in prison 被关押; 坐牢: *The murderer is now safely behind bars.* 杀人犯现在已被关押, 不能为害了.

□ **ˌbar ˈbilliards** indoor game like billiards in which balls are aimed at holes in the table 一种类似弹子戏的室内游戏(玩时将台上的球击入孔内).

ˈbar chart (also **histogram**) graph on which bars of equal width but varying height are used to represent quantities 条形图(一种统计图表, 系以等宽而不等高的竖条表示数量). ⇨illus at CHART 见CHART之插图.

ˈbar code pattern of thick and thin parallel lines printed on goods in shops, etc and containing coded information for a computer 条形码(印在商品上的粗细不同的平行线条, 含有计算机使用的代码信息).

ˈbarmaid *n* woman who serves drinks, etc at a bar 酒吧间女服务员.

ˈbarman /-mən; -mən/ *n* (*pl* **-men** /-mən; -mən/) man who serves drinks, etc at a bar 酒吧间男服务员.

ˈbartender *n* (*esp US*) = BARMAN.

bar[2] /bɑː(r); bɑr/ *v* (**-rr-**) **1** [Tn] fasten (a door, gate, etc) with a bar[1](1b) or bars 闩上(门等). **2** [Tn] obstruct (sth) so as to prevent progress 阻碍(某事物): *Soldiers barred the road so we had to turn back.* 士兵挡住了去路, 我们只好折回. ○ (*fig* 比喻) *Poverty bars the way to progress.* 贫穷妨碍了进步. **3** [Tn·pr] **~ sb from sth/doing sth** prevent sb from using sth or from doing sth 阻止某人用某物; 阻止某人做某事: *She was barred from (entering) the competition because of her age.* 她因年龄的关系而被禁止(参加)比赛. **4** [usu passive 通常用于被动语态: Tn, Tn·pr] **~ sth (with sth)** mark sth (with a stripe or stripes) 加条纹于某物: *a sky barred with clouds* 有一条条浮云的天空. **5** (phr v) **bar sb in (sth)/out (of sth)** keep sb from leaving or entering (a building, etc) by fastening the door, windows, etc with a bar or bars 把门、窗等闩上使某人无法出入于(建筑物等): *He barred himself in (the house).* 他把自己关在屋里.

bar[3] /bɑː(r); bɑr/ *prep* **1** except; not counting 除外; 不计: *The whole class is here bar two that are ill.* 除两人生病外, 全班都到齐了. Cf 参看 BARRING. **2** (idm 习语) **bar none** with no exception 无例外: *That's the best meal I've ever had, bar none.* 那是我吃过的最好的一顿饭菜, 无与伦比.

bar[4] /bɑː(r); bɑr/ *n* unit of pressure used in meteorology 巴(气象学所用的压强单位).

barb /bɑːb; bɑrb/ *n* **1** point of an arrow, a fish-hook, etc curved backwards to make it difficult to pull out (箭、鱼钩等的)倒钩. ⇨illus at HOOK 见HOOK之插图. **2** (*fig* 比喻) hurtful remark 伤人的话: *cruel barbs of ridicule* 挖苦人的刺耳言语.

▷ **barbed** *adj* having a barb or barbs 有倒钩的; 有倒刺的: *a barbed hook* 带倒钩的钩子 ○ (*fig* 比喻) *barbed*

B

comments 刺人的话. **barbed wire** wire with short sharp points along it, used for fences, etc 刺钢丝(用作铁丝网等): *The barbed wire fence round the perimeter discouraged intruders.* 周围有铁丝网阻止了外人闯入.

bar·bar·ian /bɑːˈbeərɪən; bɑrˋbɛrɪən/ *n, adj* (*often derog* 常作贬义) (person who is) primitive, coarse or cruel 野蛮的, 粗鲁的或残忍的(人): *barbarian tribes* 原始部落 ○ *football supporters acting like barbarians* 足球场上举止粗野的呐喊助威者.

bar·baric /bɑːˈbærɪk; bɑrˋbærɪk/ *adj* (*often derog* 常作贬义) of or like barbarians; extremely wild, rough, cruel or rude 野蛮人的; 野蛮的; 极其粗野、粗鲁、残忍或残暴的: *barbaric splendour, cruelty, taste* 野蛮人的奇观、残忍、趣味. ▷ **bar·bar·ic·ally** /-klɪ; -klɪ/ *adv*.

bar·bar·ism /ˈbɑːbərɪzəm; ˋbɑrbə,rɪzəm/ *n* **1** [U] (*derog* 贬) state of being uncivilized, ignorant, or rude 未开化的、愚昧的或粗野的状态. **2** [U, C] (use of a) word or expression that is unacceptable, usu because it is foreign or vulgar 不规范的词语(通常因是外来语或鄙俗语); 不规范词语的运用: *teaching students to rid their writing of barbarisms* 教学生在写作中避免使用不规范的词语.

bar·bar·ity /bɑːˈbærətɪ; bɑrˋbærətɪ/ *n* (**a**) [U] savage cruelty 残酷; 残暴. (**b**) [C] instance of this 暴行: *the barbarities of modern warfare* 现代战争之残酷.

bar·bar·ize, -ise /ˈbɑːbəraɪz; ˋbɑrbə,raɪz/ *v* [Tn] make (sb) barbarous 使(某人)野蛮; 使(某人)粗野.

bar·bar·ous /ˈbɑːbərəs; ˋbɑrbərəs/ *adj* (*derog* 贬) **1** unrefined in taste, habits, etc (趣味、习惯等)粗俗的: *barbarous sounds* 粗声粗气. **2** cruel or savage 残忍的; 残暴的: *barbarous cruelty, treatment* 残暴的行为、对待 ○ *barbarous soldiers* 残暴的士兵. ▷ **bar·bar·ously** *adv*. **bar·bar·ous·ness** *n* [U].

bar·be·cue /ˈbɑːbɪkjuː; ˋbɑrbɪ,kju/ *n* **1** [C] metal frame for cooking meat, etc over an open fire (在篝火上烤肉等用的)金属烤架. **2** [C] outdoor party at which food is cooked in this way and eaten (吃烤肉等的)野餐. **3** [U] food cooked in this way 烤的食物.

▷ **bar·be·cue** *v* [Tn] cook (meat, etc) on a barbecue 在烤架上烤(肉等): *barbecued chicken* 烤鸡.

barber /ˈbɑːbə(r); ˋbɑrbɚ/ *n* person whose trade is cutting men's hair and shaving them (给男子剪发和刮胡子的)理发师: *I'm going to the barber's (shop) to get my hair cut.* 我要去理发店理发. Cf 参看 HAIRDRESSER (HAIR).

□ ˈ**barber-shop** *n* (*US*) place where a barber works 理发店. — *adj* [attrib 作定语] (*US*) of a type of music for four unaccompanied male voices singing in close harmony 男声四重唱的: *a barber-shop quartet* 男声四重唱.

ˌ**barber's** ˈ**pole** pole with red and white spiral stripes, used as a barber's sign 理发店旋转立柱(上有红白螺旋条纹, 用作理发店的标志).

bar·bit·ur·ate /bɑːˈbɪtjʊrət; ,bɑrˋbɪtjʊrət/ *n* any of a group of sedative drugs 巴比土酸盐(一种镇静剂): *He died from an overdose of barbiturates.* 他因服用过量巴比土而死亡. ○ [attrib 作定语] *barbiturate poisoning* 巴比土中毒.

bar·car·ole /ˌbɑːkəˈrəʊl, -ˈrɒl; ˋbɑrkə,rol/ *n* piece of music, esp for the piano, with a steady lilting rhythm 船歌(一种乐曲, 尤指一种节奏徐缓轻快活泼的钢琴曲).

bard /bɑːd; bɑrd/ *n* **1** (esp Celtic) minstrel (尤指凯尔特民族的)吟游诗人. **2** (*arch* 古) poet 诗人: *the Bard (of Avon)*, ie Shakespeare 莎士比亚的别称. ▷ **bardic** *adj*.

bare[1] /beə(r); bɛr/ *adj* (**-r, -st**) **1** (**a**) without clothing 裸露的: *bare legs* 光腿 ○ *bare to the waist*, ie wearing no clothes above the waist 裸露上身. (**b**) without the usual covering or protection 缺少遮盖的; 没有保护的: *bare floors*, ie without carpets, rugs, etc 光地板(无地毯等的) ○ *a bare hillside*, ie one without shrubs or trees 光秃的山坡(没有树木的山坡) ○ *trees that are already bare*, ie that have already lost their leaves 光秃了的树木(树叶已落光的) ○ *with his head bare*, ie not wearing a hat 他光着头(未戴帽) ○ *with one's bare hands*, ie without tools or weapons 赤手(未带工具或武器). **2** ~ (**of sth**) empty or almost empty (of the expected contents) (指不该空者)空的, 几乎空了的: *a room bare of furniture* 空无家具的房间 ○ *a larder bare of food* 空空如也的食品柜 ○ *bare shelves* 空无一物的架子. **3** [attrib 作定语] only just sufficient; basic 仅够的; 基本的: *the bare necessities of life*, ie things needed merely to stay alive 最低限度的生活必需品 ○ *a bare majority*, ie a very small one 勉强超过半数 ○ *the bare facts*, ie without any additional comment or detail 事实真相(无评论或细节). **4** (idm 习语) **the bare** ˈ**bones (of sth)** main or basic facts (of some matter or situation) (某事或某情况的)梗概, 概要. **lay sth** ˈ**bare** expose or make known sth secret or hidden 揭露; 揭发: *lay bare the truth, sb's treachery, a plot* 揭露真相、某人的背叛行为、阴谋.

▷ **barely** *adv* **1** only just; scarcely 仅够; 几乎没有: *We barely had time to catch the train.* 我们几乎来不及赶火车. ○ *He can barely read or write.* 他勉强识字. **2** in a bare way 赤裸裸地; 光秃秃地; 空空地: *The room was barely furnished*, ie had little furniture in it. 室内几乎没有陈设可言.

bare·ness *n* [U].

□ ˈ**bareback** *adj, adv* on a horse without a saddle 不用马鞍(的): *a bareback rider* 不用马鞍的骑手 ○ *ride bareback* 骑马不用马鞍.

ˈ**barefaced** *adj* [attrib 作定语] impudent; shameless 厚颜无耻的; 不要脸的: *a barefaced lie* 无耻的谎言 ○ *It's barefaced robbery asking such a high price for that old bicycle!* 那辆旧自行车要价如此之高真是无耻的敲诈.

ˈ**barefoot** (also ˌ**bare**ˈ**footed**) *adj, adv* without shoes or stockings 赤脚(的): *children running barefoot in the sand* 光着脚在沙地上跑的孩子们.

ˌ**bare**ˈ**headed** *adj, adv* not wearing a hat 光着头(的); 不戴帽(的).

ˌ**bare**ˈ**legged** /-ˈlegd, -ˈlegɪd; -ˋlɛgd/ *adj, adv* wearing nothing on one's legs 光着腿(的).

bare[2] /beə(r); bɛr/ *v* **1** [Tn] uncover (sth); reveal 使(某物)裸露出来; 揭开: *bare one's chest* 袒胸 ○ *He bared his head* (ie took off his hat to show respect) *as the funeral procession passed.* 送葬行列走过时他脱帽致敬. ○ *bare the end of a wire*, ie strip off the covering of rubber, etc before making an electrical connection 剥开电线的端部(剥去包覆的橡皮等以便接线). **2** (idm 习语) **bare its** ˈ**teeth** (of an animal) show its teeth when angry (指动物)龇牙咧嘴(发怒时). **bare one's** ˈ**heart**/ˈ**soul (to sb)** (*rhet or joc* 修辞或谑) make known one's deepest feelings 披露心事; 诉说衷肠.

bar·gain[1] /ˈbɑːgɪn; ˋbɑrgɪn/ *n* **1** agreement in which both or all sides promise to do sth for each other 协议(双方或各方约定彼此要为对方做的事项): *If you promote our goods, we will give you a good discount as our part of the bargain.* 若你方经销我们的货物, 我方愿给予你相当大的优惠作为回报. ○ *The bargain they reached with their employers was to reduce their wage claim in return for a shorter working week.* 他们与雇主达成的协议是他们在工资方面降低要求, 但每周工时要缩短. **2** thing bought or sold for less than its usual price 廉价购买或廉价出售之物: *It's a bargain*, ie It is very good value for money. 这可是便宜货 ○ [attrib 作定语] *a bargain price*, ie a low price 廉价. **3** (idm 习语) **a bad** ˈ**bargain** (**a**) agreement that is more beneficial to the other side(s) than to oneself 对方占便宜的协议; 吃亏的交易. (**b**) thing bought because it was thought cheap but which one later regrets buying 后悔当初不该买的便宜货. **drive a hard bargain** ⇨ DRIVE[1]. **a good** ˈ**bargain** (**a**) agreement that is more beneficial to oneself than to the other side(s) 自己占便宜的协议; 上算的交易: *You've got a good bargain there.* 你做了一笔很上算的交易. (**b**) thing, usu valuable, bought at a very low price 以极其便宜的价格购得之物(通常指值钱的物品). **into the** ˈ**bargain**; *US* also **in the** ˈ**bargain** (*infml* 口) in addition; moreover 加之; 此外: *She was a distinguished scientist — and a gifted painter into the bargain.* 她是一位杰出的科学家——同时还是一位很有才华的画家呢. **strike a bargain** ⇨ STRIKE[2].

□ ˈ**bargain counter** part of a store where goods are offered for sale at reduced prices (商店的)廉价品柜台, 廉价部.

ˈ**bargain-hunter** *n* person looking for goods at very low prices 专拣便宜货的人.

bar·gain[2] /ˈbɑːgɪn; ˋbɑrgɪn/ *v* **1** [I, Ipr] ~ (**with sb**) (**about/over/for sth**) discuss (with sb) prices, terms of trade, etc with the aim of buying or selling goods, or changing conditions, on terms that are favourable to oneself (与某人)讨价还价; 洽谈成交条件; 谈判: *Never* *pay the advertised price for a car; always try to bargain.* 千万不要照牌价购买汽车，总得讲讲价才是. ○ *Dealers bargain with growers over the price of coffee.* 商人与种植者就咖啡的价格进行商洽. ○ *The unions bargained (with management) for a shorter working week.* 工会为缩短工作周而(与资方)讨价还价. **2** (phr v) **bargain sth away** give sth away (esp sth valuable in exchange for sth less so) 牺牲某物(尤指以贵物交换贱物): *The leaders bargained away the freedom of their people.* 领导人拿人民的自由来做交易. **bargain for sth; bargain on sth** (*infml* 口) (often negative 常用于否定式) expect; be prepared for 预料; 有备于: *The exam was more difficult than I had bargained for.* 这次考试之难出乎我的意料之外. ○ *Tom didn't bargain on his wife returning so soon.* 汤姆没有想到他妻子会回来得这么快. ○ *When the politician agreed to answer questions on television, he got more than he had bargained for*, ie was unpleasantly surprised at the consequences. 这个政客同意在电视上公开回答问题, 不料竟弄巧成拙(其后果使他感到愕然).

bar·gain·ing /ˈbɑːɡɪnɪŋ; ˋbɑrɡɪnɪŋ/ *n* [U] discussion of prices, terms of trade, etc 讨价还价; 洽谈成交条件等: *After much hard bargaining we reached an agreement.* 经过激烈的讨价还价, 我们终于达成了协议.

□ ˈ**bargaining counter** special advantage that can be used to outweigh an advantage possessed by an opponent 特殊的、足以压倒对方的优势: *Ownership of the land gives us a strong bargaining counter.* 领有这片土地使我们在谈判中处于优势.

ˈ**bargaining position** position, favourable or unfavourable, reached when bargaining 讨价还价时所达到的有利或不利的地位: *We're now in a rather poor bargaining position.* 我们现在所处的谈判地位不太有利.

barge[1] /bɑːdʒ; bɑrdʒ/ *n* **1** large flat-bottomed boat for carrying goods and people on rivers, canals, etc 驳船(河流、运河等中载运客货的大型平底船). **2** large ornamental rowing-boat for ceremonial occasions (举行庆典时使用的)大型彩饰划艇, 画舫.

▷ **bar·gee** /bɑːˈdʒiː; ˌbɑrˋdʒi/ *n* (*Brit*) (*US* **barge·man**) (**a**) person in charge of a barge 驳船或大划艇上撑船的人. (**b**) member of a barge's crew 驳船或大划艇的船夫.

□ ˈ**barge-pole** *n* **1** long pole used for guiding a barge 驳船上用的撑篙. **2** (idm 习语) **not touch sb/sth with a barge-pole** ⇨ TOUCH[2].

barge[2] /bɑːdʒ; bɑrdʒ/ *v* (*infml* 口) **1** [I, Ipr, Ip] rush or bump heavily and clumsily 鲁莽而大力地冲撞: *Stop barging (into people)!* 别撞(人)! ○ *He barged past me in the queue.* 我在排队时他在我面前硬挤过去了. **2** (phr v) **barge about** move about heavily and clumsily 到处乱闯. **barge in/into sth** enter or interrupt sth rudely or clumsily 蛮不讲理地闯入或打扰某事物: *I tried to stop him coming through the door but he just barged (his way) in.* 我想拦住他, 不让他进门, 可是他硬闯进来了. ○ *Don't barge into the conversation.* 别插嘴.

ba·ri·tone /ˈbærɪtəʊn; ˋbærəˌton/ *n* (*music* 音) **1** male voice between tenor and bass 男中音. **2** singer with such a voice 男中音歌手: [attrib 作定语] *a baritone aria* 男中音独唱曲.

bar·ium /ˈbeərɪəm; ˋbɛrɪəm/ *n* [U] chemical element, a soft silvery-white metal the compounds of which are used in industry 钡. ⇨App 10 见附录10.

□ ˌ**barium** ˈ**meal** chemical substance, opaque to X-rays, that is taken in to a patient's digestive tract, usu by swallowing, before the tract is X-rayed 钡餐.

bark[1] /bɑːk; bɑrk/ *n* [U, C] tough outer covering of tree trunks and branches 树皮.

▷ **bark** *v* [Tn] **1** remove the bark from (a tree) 剥去(某棵树的)树皮. **2** accidentally scrape the skin off (one's knuckles, knees, etc) 不慎擦破(指节、膝盖等的)皮肤: *He barked his shins (by falling) against some stone steps.* 他在石头台阶上(跌倒了,)擦破了小腿的皮.

bark[2] /bɑːk; bɑrk/ *n* **1** (**a**) sharp harsh sound made by dogs and foxes 犬吠声; 狐狸的嗥叫声. (**b**) (*fig* 比喻) any similar sound, eg the sound of gunfire or of a cough 任何似犬狐叫的声音(如枪击声或咳嗽声). **2** (idm 习语) **sb's bark is worse than his bite** (*infml* 口) though sb often sounds angry, fierce, etc, in fact he rarely carries out his threats 虽然某人嘴很厉害, 但心并不坏.

▷ **bark** *v* **1** (**a**) [I, Ipr] **~ (at sb/sth)** (of dogs, etc) give a bark or barks (指狗等)吠叫: *Our dog always barks at strangers.* 我们的狗一见生人就叫. (**b**) [I] (*fig* 比喻) (of people coughing, guns, etc) make a similar sound (指人的咳嗽、枪击等)发出似犬吠的声音. **2** [I, Ipr, Tn, Tn·p] **~ (at sb); ~ sth (out)** say (sth) in a sharp harsh voice 以尖锐或咆哮的声音说出(某事): *When she's angry, she often barks at the children.* 她生气时, 常呵斥孩子. ○ *The sergeant barked (out) an order.* 那个士官大声发出命令. **3** (idm 习语) **bark up the wrong** ˈ**tree** (esp in the continuous tenses 尤用于进行时态) be mistaken about sth 把某事物搞错了; 错怪了人: *If you think that, you're barking up the wrong tree altogether.* 你要是那样想, 你就大错特错了.

barker /ˈbɑːkə(r); ˋbɑrkɚ/ *n* (*infml* 口) person who stands by a stall at a fair, a market, an auction, etc and shouts loudly to attract customers (在集市、市场、拍卖场所等处站在货摊旁)大声叫卖的贩子.

bar·ley /ˈbɑːlɪ; ˋbɑrlɪ/ *n* [U] (grass-like plant producing) grain used for food and for making beer and whisky 大麦; 大麦粒. ⇨illus at CEREAL 见 CEREAL 之插图.

□ ˈ**barleycorn** *n* [U] grain of barley 大麦粒.

ˈ**barley sugar** hard clear sweet[2](1) made from boiled sugar 大麦糖(糖溶化后制成的一种硬而透明的糖果).

ˈ**barley water** (*Brit*) drink, sometimes flavoured, made by boiling barley in water and then straining it 大麦汁(将大麦用水煮后过滤而制成的饮料, 有时加入调料): *lemon barley water* 柠檬大麦汁.

bar mitz·vah /ˌbɑː ˈmɪtsvə; ˌbɑr ˋmɪtsvə/ **1** Jewish boy who has reached the age of 13, when he assumes the religious responsibilities of an adult 年满13岁开始尽成年人之宗教义务的犹太男子. **2** ceremony at which he does this 犹太男子的成年礼.

barmy /ˈbɑːmɪ; ˋbɑrmɪ/ (also *esp US* **balmy**) *adj* (**-ier**, **-iest**) (*infml* 口) foolish; crazy 愚蠢的; 疯狂的.

barn /bɑːn; bɑrn/ *n* **1** simple building for storing hay, grain, etc on a farm (农场里储存干草、谷物等的)仓房. **2** (*fig derog* 比喻, 贬) any unattractive large building 不顺眼的大建筑物: *They live in that great barn of a house.* 他们住在那所简陋的大房子里. **3** (*US*) (**a**) building for sheltering farm animals, eg cows or horses 牲口棚舍(如牛栏或马厩). (**b**) building for a fleet of buses, vans, etc (公共汽车、货车等的)车库.

□ ˈ**barn dance** **1** type of traditional country dance 谷仓舞(一种传统的乡村舞蹈). **2** informal social occasion at which such dances are performed 谷仓舞会.

barn-ˈ**owl** *n* type of owl that often nests in barns and other buildings 仓鸮(一种常在谷仓及其他建筑物上筑巢的猫头鹰). ⇨illus at App 1 见附录1之插图, page iv.

ˈ**barnyard** *n* area on a farm around a barn 农场谷仓周围的空地.

barn·acle /ˈbɑːnəkl; ˋbɑrnəkḷ/ *n* small shellfish that attaches itself to objects under water, eg rocks or the bottoms of ships 藤壶(附着于水下物体如岩石或船底的小甲壳动物): (*fig* 比喻) *He clung to his mother like a barnacle*, ie followed her closely everywhere. 他形影不离地跟着母亲.

barn·storm /ˈbɑːnstɔːm; ˋbɑrnˌstɔrm/ *v* [I] (*US*) travel quickly through rural areas making political speeches, presenting plays, etc 下乡作巡回政治演说; 下乡作巡回演出. ▷ ˈ**barn·stormer** *n*.

ba·ro·meter /bəˈrɒmɪtə(r); bəˋrɑmətɚ/ *n* **1** instrument for measuring atmospheric pressure, used esp for forecasting the weather 气压计, 晴雨表(尤用以预报天气): *The barometer is falling*, ie Wet weather is indicated. 气压计在下降(表示天气潮湿). **2** (*fig* 比喻) thing that indicates changes (in public opinion, market prices, sb's mood, etc) 显示(舆论、物价、人的情绪等的)变化的事物: *a reliable barometer of public feeling* 反映公众情绪的可靠的标志. ▷ **ba·ro·met·ric** /ˌbærəˈmetrɪk; ˌbærəˋmɛtrɪk/ *adj*: *barometric pressure* 大气压.

baron /ˈbærən; ˋbærən/ *n* **1** member of the lowest rank of the British peerage (called *Lord X*) or of non-British nobility (called *Baron Y*) 男爵(英国贵族的最低一级成员, 称为 Lord X; 非英国贵族的此一级成员, 称为 Baron Y). **2** powerful and wealthy leader of industry 工业巨头: *a* ˈ*press baron* 报业大王 ○ ˈ*oil barons* 石油大王.

▷ **bar·on·ess** /ˈbærənɪs, *also* ˌbærəˈnes; ˋbærənɪs/ *n* **1** woman holding the rank of baron in her own right 女男

爵. **2** wife of a baron 男爵夫人.

ba·ro·nial /bəˈrəʊnɪəl; bəˈronɪəl/ *adj* [usu attrib 通常作定语] of or suitable for a baron 男爵的; 适合男爵身分的.

bar·onet /ˈbærənɪt; ˈbærənɪt/ *n* (*abbrs* 缩写 **Bart, Bt**) member of the lowest hereditary titled order in Britain below a baron but above a knight 准男爵(英国世袭爵位中最低等级的受勋者, 地位在男爵之下爵士之上): *Sir John Williams, Bart* 约翰·威廉斯准男爵.

▷ **bar·on·etcy** /ˈbærənɪtsɪ; ˈbærənɪtsɪ/ *n* rank or title of a baronet 准男爵的爵位或头衔.

B

ba·roque /bəˈrɒk; *US* bəˈrəʊk; bəˈrok/ *adj*, *n* (of the) highly ornate style fashionable in the arts (esp architecture) in Europe in the 17th and 18th centuries 巴罗克风格, 巴罗克风格的(十七八世纪欧洲时兴的高度华丽的艺术风格, 尤指建筑方面).

barque /bɑːk; bɑrk/ *n* sailing-ship with 3, 4 or 5 masts and sails (三桅、四桅或五桅的)帆船.

bar·rack /ˈbærək; ˈbærək/ *v* [I, Tn] (*Brit or Austral infml* 英或澳, 口) shout protests or jeer at (players in a game, speakers, performers, etc) 向(比赛者、演讲者、表演者等)喝倒彩, 发出嘘声: *The crowd started barracking (the slow rate of play).* 群众(对比赛的速度之慢)喝起了倒彩.

▷ **bar·rack·ing** *n* [C, U] noisy protest by an audience or spectators 听众或观众的鼓噪抗议: *The crowd gave the visiting politician quite a barracking.* 群众对这位来访的政客鼓噪抗议.

bar·racks /ˈbærəks; ˈbærəks/ *n* **1** [sing or pl *v*] large building or group of buildings for soldiers to live in 兵营; 营房: *As punishment, the men were confined to barracks.* 士兵受罚, 不准离开营房. ○ *There used to be a barracks in this town.* 这个城里过去曾设有兵营. **2** [sing *v*] (*fig infml* 比喻, 口) any large ugly building 不雅观的大建筑物: *Their house was a great barracks of a place.* 他们住的是个简陋的大房子.

▷ **barrack-** (in compounds 用以构成复合词) of a barracks 兵营的: *barrack-square*, ie ground near a barracks where soldiers are drilled.

bar·ra·cuda /ˌbærəˈkuːdə; ˌbærəˈkudə/ *n* large fierce Caribbean fish 魣(产于加勒比海的凶猛大鱼).

bar·rage /ˈbærɑːʒ; *US* bəˈrɑːʒ; bəˈrɑʒ/ *n* **1** barrier built across a river to store water for irrigation, prevent flooding, etc 堰; 拦河坝. **2** (**a**) heavy continuous gunfire directed onto a particular area to restrict enemy movement 弹幕; 火力网: *lay down a barrage* 布设火力网. (**b**) (*fig* 比喻) large number (of questions, criticisms, etc) delivered quickly, one after the other 连珠炮似的一大堆(问题、批评等): *face a barrage of angry complaints* 面对一连串愤怒的投诉.

bar·rel /ˈbærəl; ˈbærəl/ *n* **1** (**a**) large round container with flat ends and bulging in the middle, made of wood, metal or plastic 桶; 琵琶桶. ⇨illus 见插图. (**b**) amount that a barrel contains 一桶的量. **2** long metal tube forming part of sth, esp a gun or a pen (物体某部的)金属管(尤指枪管或笔管). ⇨illus at GUN 见GUN之插图. **3** (idm 习语) **lock, stock and barrel** ⇨ LOCK². **(get/have sb) over a barrel** (*infml* 口) (have sb) at one's mercy; in a helpless position (使某人)听从摆布; 束手无策. **scrape the barrel** ⇨ SCRAPE¹.

▷ **bar·rel** *v* (**-ll-**; *US* **-l-**) [Tn] put (sth) in a barrel or barrels 将(某物)装入桶中.

□ **ˈbarrel-organ** *n* mechanical instrument from which music is produced by turning a handle, usu played in the streets for money 手摇风琴.

bar·ren /ˈbærən; ˈbærən/ *adj* **1** (of land) not good enough to produce crops (指土地)贫瘠的. **2** (of plants or trees) not producing fruit or seeds (指花草或树木)不结果的, 不结实的. **3** (*dated or fml* 旧或文) (of women or female animals) unable to bear young (指妇女或雌性动物)不能生育的, 不妊的. **4** [usu attrib 通常作定语] (*fig* 比喻) without value, interest or result 无价值、趣味或结果的: *a barren discussion* 毫无意义的讨论. ▷ **bar·ren·ness** /ˈbærənnɪs; ˈbærənnɪs/ *n* [U].

bar·ri·cade /ˌbærɪˈkeɪd; ˌbærəˈked/ *n* barrier hastily built as a defence or an obstacle 匆匆设置的壁垒或路障: *The soldiers stormed the barricades erected by the rioting crowd.* 士兵们向暴乱分子设置的街垒发起了猛攻.

▷ **bar·ri·cade** *v* (phr v) **barricade sb in (sth)/out (of sth)** keep sb in/out by making a barricade 设障碍物使某人不得进入[外出]: *They barricaded themselves in (their rooms).* 他们把自己关在(自己的屋子)里面. **barricade sth off** block (eg a street) with a barricade 用障碍物封锁(例如一条街): *The police barricaded off the entrance to the square.* 警方在广场的入口处设置了路障.

bar·rier /ˈbærɪə(r); ˈbærɪɚ/ *n* **1** (**a**) thing that prevents or controls progress or movement 阻碍进步或控制活动的事物: *The Sahara Desert is a natural barrier between North and Central Africa.* 撒哈拉沙漠是北非与中非之间的天然屏障. ○ *Show your ticket at the barrier.* 请在检票处出示票以备查验. (**b**) (*fig* 比喻) hindrance 障碍; 妨碍: *Poor health may be a barrier to success.* 健康欠佳可能成为取得成功的障碍. **2** thing that keeps people apart 使人隔离的事物: *barriers of race and religion* 种族和宗教的鸿沟 ○ *the language barrier* 语言的隔阂.

□ **barrier ˈcream** cream used for protecting skin from damage or infection 护肤脂(用以防止皮肤受损伤或受感染).

barrier ˈreef coral reef separated from land by a channel 堡礁, 堤礁.

bar·ring /ˈbɑːrɪŋ; ˈbɑrɪŋ/ *prep* not including or allowing for (sth); if there is/are not 如果没有(某事物): *Barring accidents, we should arrive on time.* 倘无意外, 我们应准时到达. Cf 参看 BAR³ 1.

bar·ris·ter /ˈbærɪstə(r); ˈbærɪstɚ/ *n* (in English law) lawyer who has the right to speak and argue as an advocate in higher lawcourts (英国法律中)(有权在高等法院出庭辩论的)律师; 讼务律师. Cf 参看 ADVOCATE *n* 2, SOLICITOR 1.

bar·row¹ /ˈbærəʊ; ˈbæro/ *n* **1** = WHEELBARROW (WHEEL). **2** small cart with two wheels, pulled or pushed by hand 两轮手推车.

□ **ˈbarrow boy** person who sells things from a barrow in the street 街头推车小贩.

bar·row² /ˈbærəʊ; ˈbæro/ *n* mound built over a burial place in prehistoric times 史前时期的古坟; 古墓. Cf 参看 TUMULUS.

Bart /bɑːt; bɑrt/ *abbr* 缩写 = Baronet.

bar·ter /ˈbɑːtə(r); ˈbɑrtɚ/ *v* **1** [Tn, Tn·pr, Tn·p] **~ sth (for sth); ~ sth (away)** exchange (goods, property, etc) for other goods, etc without using money 以(货物、财产等)交换其他货物等(不使用货币): *barter wheat for machinery* 以小麦换机器 ○ (*fig* 比喻) *barter away one's rights, honour, freedom* 出卖自己的权利、荣誉、自由. **2** [I, Ipr] **~ (with sb) (for sth)** trade by exchanging sth for sth else without using money 进行易货贸易; 以货易货; 作物物交换: *The prisoners tried to barter with the guards for their freedom.* 囚犯企图跟看守做换取自由的交易.

▷ **bar·ter** *n* [U] exchange of goods for other goods without using money 易货贸易; 以货易货; 物物交换: *On these islands a system of barter is used.* 在这些岛上仍然实行着物物交换的制度.

bas·alt /ˈbæsɔːlt; *US* ˈbeɪsɔːlt, bəˈsɔːlt; ˈbesɔlt, bəˈsɔlt/ *n* [U] type of dark rock of volcanic origin 玄武岩.

base¹ /beɪs; bes/ *n* **1** (**a**) lowest part of sth, esp the part on which it rests or is supported (某物的)底部; (尤指)底座, 基底: *the base of a pillar, column, etc* 柱基等. (**b**) (*geometry* 几) line or surface on which a figure stands 底边; 底面: *the base of a triangle, pyramid, etc* 三角形的底边、角锥体的底面等. **(c)** (*fig* 比喻) starting-point; underlying principle 起点; 基本原则: *She used her family's history as a base for her novel.* 她把她一家人的经历作为她小说的素材. ○ *His arguments had a sound economic base.* 他的立论在经济方面是有充分根据的. **2** (*chemistry* 化) substance (eg an alkali) capable of combining with an acid to form a salt 可与酸化合成盐的物质(如碱); 盐基. **3** main part or ingredient to which other things are added 混合配料的主要成分: *a drink with a rum base* 以朗姆酒为主要成分的饮料 ○ *Some paints have an oil base.* 有些颜料是以油脂作为主要成分. ○ *Put some moisturizer on as a base before applying your make-up.* 使用化妆品之前先用点润肤脂打底. **4** place at which armed forces, expeditions, etc have their stores (军队、探险队等的)基地, 根据地: *a ˈnaval base* 海军基地 ○ *an ˈair base* 空军基地 ○ [attrib 作定语] *a base camp*, eg for a mountaineering expedition 大本营(如为登山队所建者) ○ *establish, set up a base* 建立、设立根据地. **5** (*mathematics* 数) number on which a numerical system is built up, eg 10 in the decimal system, 2 in the binary system 基数(如十进制系统以10为基数, 二进制系统以2为基数). **6** (in baseball) each of the four positions to be reached by a runner (棒球)垒. ⇨illus at BASEBALL 见 BASEBALL 之插图. **7** (idm 习语) **not get to first base** ⇨ FIRST BASE (FIRST[1]). **off base** (*US infml* 口) **(a)** mistaken 错误的: *You're a bit off base there.* 你在那个地方有点不对头. **(b)** unprepared 毫无准备的: *Her reply caught him off base.* 她的答复使他不知所措.

▷ **base·less** *adj* without cause or foundation 无原因的; 无根据的: *baseless fears, rumours, suspicions* 无根据的恐慌、谣言、怀疑.

□ ˈ**baseboard** *n* (*US*) = SKIRTING-BOARD (SKIRT). ˈ**base hit** (also **single**) (in baseball) hit that enables a batter to reach first base (棒球)安全打(使击球手能上第一垒的击球).

ˈ**baseline** *n* (*sport* 体) line marking each end of the court in tennis or the boundary of the running track in baseball (网球场的)底线; (棒球场的)垒线. ⇨illus at TENNIS 见 TENNIS 之插图.

ˈ**base rate** (*finance* 财) interest rate used by individual banks as a basis for fixing their interest rates for borrowers and investors 基本利率(银行各自使用的利率, 据此而定出适用于贷款者和投资者的利率).

base[2] /beɪs; bes/ *v* **1** [Tn·pr] **~ sth on sth** use sth as grounds, evidence, etc for sth else 以某事物为另一事物的根据、证据等: *I base my hopes on the good news we had yesterday.* 我把希望寄托在我们昨天得到的好消息上. ○ *This novel is based on historical facts.* 这部小说是以历史事实为根据的. ○ *Direct taxation is usually based on income*, ie A person's income is used to calculate the amount of tax he has to pay. 直接税通常以收入为依据(根据个人收入计算出应交税款的数额). **2** [esp passive 尤用于被动语态: Tn·pr, Tn·p] **~ sb in/at...** place sb in (a place from which to work and travel) 把某人安置在(某地进行工作和活动): *Where are you based now?* 现在把你安置在哪里工作了? ○ *Most of our staff are based in Cairo.* 我们大部分工作人员都驻在开罗.

base[3] /beɪs; bes/ *adj* **(-r, -st)** **1** (*fml derog* 文, 贬) dishonourable; despicable 不光彩的; 卑鄙的: *acting from base motives* 从卑鄙动机出发的行动. **2** not pure 不纯的: *base coin* 搀有贱金属的硬币. **3** low in value 不值钱的: *base metal* 贱金属.

▷ **basely** *adv* in a base[3](1) manner 卑鄙地. **base·ness** *n* [U] state of being base[3](1) 卑鄙.

base·ball /ˈbeɪsbɔːl; ˈbesˌbɔl/ *n* [U] game popular in the USA, played with a bat and ball by two teams of nine players each on a field with four bases (BASE[1] 6) 棒球运动: [attrib 作定语] *a baseball pitch* 棒球投掷. ⇨App 4 见附录4. ⇨illus 见插图. Cf 参看 ROUNDERS.

base·ment /ˈbeɪsmənt; ˈbesmənt/ *n* lowest room or rooms in a building, partly or wholly below ground level 地下室.

ba·ses **1** *pl* of BASIS. **2** *pl* of BASE[1].

bash /bæʃ; bæʃ/ *v* (*infml* 口) **1** [Tn, Tn·pr] strike (sb/sth) heavily so as to break or injure 猛击(某人[某物]): *bash sb on the head with a club* 用棍棒猛击某人头部. **2**

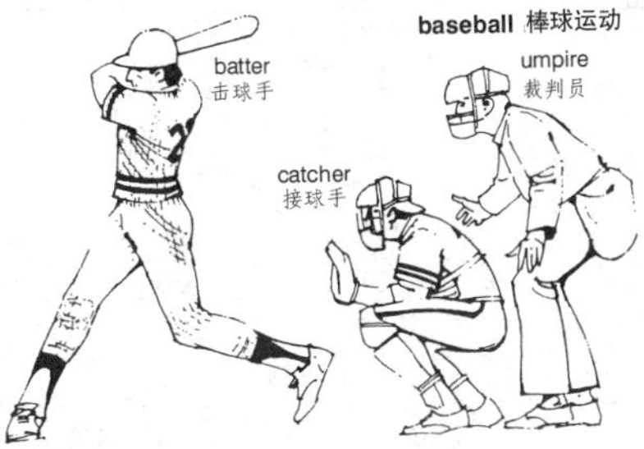

[Ipr, Tn·pr] **~ (sth) against/into sb/sth** (cause sth to) collide violently with sb/sth (使某物)猛撞某人[某物]: *He tripped and bashed his head against the railing.* 他跌了一跤, 头部撞在栏杆上了. **3** (phr v) **bash ahead/away/on (with sth)** continue doing sth quickly and enthusiastically, but not carefully 勤快地做着某事(但不细心). **bash sth in/down** cause sth to collapse inwards by striking it violently 猛击某物使之向内塌陷: *bash in the lid of a box* 砸瘪盒盖 ○ *They bashed the door down.* 他们砸倒了房门. **bash sb up** (*Brit infml* 口) treat sb violently 以暴力对待某人: *He was bashed up in the playground by some older boys.* 有几个年龄较大的男孩子在操场上对他动武.

▷ **bash** *n* **1** (*infml* 口) violent blow 猛烈的打击: *give sb a bash on the nose* 照着某人的鼻子狠狠一击. **2** (idm 习语) **have a bash (at sth)** (*infml* 口) attempt sth (usu sth previously untried) 尝试做某事(通常为以往不曾试过的): *I've never tried water-skiing before, but I'd love to have a bash at it.* 我以前从未做过滑水运动, 但是我倒愿意试一试.

bash·ing *n* [U, C] (often in compounds 常用以构成复合词) violent attack (often on members of specific groups) 猛烈的攻击(通常施加于一定团体的成员): *union-bashing*, ie the practice of trying to discredit a trade union by fierce criticism, etc 对工会的猛烈攻击(指企图以激烈的攻击性言论等破坏工会名声的行动) ○ *give sb a bashing* 给某人一顿痛打. ⇨Usage at BANG[1] 用法见 BANG[1].

bash·ful /ˈbæʃfl; ˈbæʃfəl/ *adj* shy and self-conscious 害羞的; 难为情的. ▷ **bash·fully** /-fəlɪ; -fəlɪ/ *adv*. **bash·ful·ness** *n* [U].

ba·sic /ˈbeɪsɪk; ˈbesɪk/ *adj* **1 ~ (to sth)** forming a base or starting-point; fundamental 基本的; 根本的; 基础的: *argue from basic principles* 从基本原则出发的争论 ○ *the basic vocabulary of a language*, ie those words that must be learnt 一种语言的基本词汇(即必须掌握的语词) ○ *These facts are basic to an understanding of the case.* 这些事实是了解这一案件的重要依据. **2** simplest or lowest in level; standard 初级的; 基本的; 标准的: *basic pay*, ie without extras such as overtime payments 基本工资(不包括超时费等额外收入) ○ *our basic requirements* 我们的基本需求 ○ *My knowledge of physics is pretty basic*, ie is only at the elementary level. 我的物理知识相当浮浅.

▷ **ba·sic·ally** /-klɪ; -klɪ/ *adv* with reference to essential matters (which are often seen as different from what is superficially apparent); fundamentally 基本上; 根本上; 本质上: *Despite her criticisms, she is basically very fond of you.* 别看她批评你, 她其实很喜欢你. ○ *Basically I agree with your proposals, but there are a few small points I'd like to discuss.* 我基本上同意你的建议, 但是有几个小问题有待商榷.

ba·sics *n* [pl] essential matters 实质性的东西: *Let's stop chatting and get down to basics*, ie concentrate on important matters. 我们别再闲聊了, 静下心来干些要紧的事吧.

□ **basic** ˈ**slag** fertilizer containing phosphates obtained during the manufacture of steel 碱性炉渣(一种含磷酸盐的肥料, 为炼钢的副产品).

BASIC (also **Basic**) /ˈbeɪsɪk; ˈbesɪk/ *abbr* 缩写 = (*computing* 计) beginners' all-purpose symbolic instruction code, a simple programming language 初学者通用符号指令代码(一种简单的程序设计语言).

basil /ˈbæzl; ˋbæzl̩/ *n* [U] sweet-smelling herb used in cooking 罗勒(芳香的草本植物, 用于烹调).

ba·sil·ica /bəˈzɪlɪkə; bəˋzɪlɪkə/ *n* (*architecture* 建) large oblong-shaped church or hall with a double row of columns inside and an apse at one end 长方形的大教堂或大会堂(内有两行圆柱, 一端有半圆形殿堂): *the Basilica of St Peter's in Rome* 罗马的圣彼得大教堂.

ba·si·lisk /ˈbæzɪlɪsk; ˋbæsəˌlɪsk/ *n* **1** small tropical American lizard (热带美洲的)小蜥蜴. **2** mythical reptile said to be able to cause death by its look or breath (神话中的)蛇怪(传说其目光或气息可致命).

ba·sin /ˈbeɪsn; ˋbesn̩/ *n* **1** = WASH-BASIN (WASH). **2** round open bowl for holding liquids or for preparing food in 盆. ⇨illus at BUCKET 见BUCKET之插图. **3** hollow place where water collects (eg a stone structure at the base of a fountain) 水洼; 水槽; 水池(如喷泉下方之石结构盛水池). **4** deep, almost land-locked, harbour 几乎全部被陆地围绕的深港; 内湾: *a yacht basin* 游艇的小港湾. **5** depression in the earth's surface; round valley 洼地; 盆地: *The village lay in a peaceful basin surrounded by hills.* 那村庄坐落在平静的山坳里. **6** area of land drained by a river 流域: *the Thames basin* 泰晤士河流域.

▷ **ba·sin·ful** /-fʊl; -ful/ *n* amount that a basin contains 一盆的量: *two basinfuls of water* 两盆水.

ba·sis /ˈbeɪsɪs; ˋbesɪs/ *n* (*pl* **bases** /ˈbeɪsiːz; ˋbesiz/) **1** main principle that underlies sth; foundation 构成某事物的主要原则; 基础: *the basis of morality, friendship, etc* 道德、友谊等的基础 ○ *arguments that have a firm basis*, ie that are founded on facts 有坚实基础(有事实根据)的论据 ○ *Rates of work are calculated on a weekly basis.* 工资是以周为计算基准的. **2** starting-point for a discussion 讨论的出发点: *No basis for negotiations has been agreed upon.* 谈判以什么为中心议题尚未取得一致意见. ○ *This agenda will form the basis of our next meeting.* 本议程将成为下次会议的中心议题.

bask /bɑːsk; *US* bæsk; bæsk/ *v* [I, Ipr] ~ **(in sth)** sit or lie enjoying warmth 坐着或躺着取暖: *basking in the sunshine, by the fire, on the beach* 在阳光下、火炉旁、海滩上取暖 ○ (*fig* 比喻) *basking in sb's favour, approval, etc* 受某人的恩惠、嘉许等.

bas·ket /ˈbɑːskɪt; *US* ˈbæskɪt; ˋbæskɪt/ *n* **1** (**a**) container, usu made of material that bends and twists easily (eg reed, cane, wire), with or without a handle 篮, 篓, 筐(通常用易于编织的材料如芦苇秆、藤子、金属丝等制成, 可有柄或无柄): *a* ˈ*shopping basket* 购物篮子 ○ *a* ˈ*clothes basket* 衣筐 ○ *a* ˌ*waste-*ˈ*paper basket* 字纸篓. (**b**) amount that a basket contains 一篮、篓或筐的量: *They picked three baskets of apples.* 他们摘了三筐苹果. **2** (idm 习语) **put all one's eggs in/into one basket** ⇨ EGG[1]. ▷ **bas·ket·ful** /-fʊl; -ˌfʊl/ *n* = BASKET 1b.

basketball 篮球运动

□ **basketball** /ˈbɑːskɪtbɔːl; *US* ˈbæs-; ˋbæskɪtˌbɔl/ *n* [U] game played by two teams of five players in which goals are scored by throwing a large ball into an open-ended net fixed high on a hoop at the opponents' end of the court 篮球赛. ⇨App 4 见附录4.

ˈ**basketwork** *n* [U] (**a**) art of weaving material in the style of a basket 编篮筐的技艺. (**b**) material woven in this way 编成篮筐的材料: *a fine piece of basketwork* 精美的篮筐编织品.

bas-relief /ˌbæs rɪˈliːf, *also* ˈbɑː rɪliːf; ˌbæsrɪˋlif/ *n* (**a**) [U] form of sculpture or carving in which a figure or design projects only slightly from its background (人像或图样略微凸出于平面的)半浮雕, 浅浮雕. (**b**) [C] example of this 浅浮雕品.

bass[1] /bæs; bæs/ *n* (*pl* unchanged or ~**es** 复数或不变或作 **basses**) any of several freshwater or sea fish of the perch family used as food 鲈鱼(淡水或海洋中产, 可食): *a shoal of bass* 鲈鱼群 ○ *They caught three basses.* 他们捉到三条鲈鱼.

bass[2] /beɪs; bes/ *n* **1** (**a**) lowest male voice 男低音: *Is he a bass or a baritone?* 他是男低音还是男中音? (**b**) singer with such a voice 男低音歌手: *He is a very fine bass.* 他是非常优秀的男低音歌手. **2** lowest part in music (for voice or instruments) (声乐或器乐的)低音部: *He sings bass.* 他唱低音. **3** = DOUBLE-BASS (DOUBLE). **4** (also **bass guitar**) electric guitar producing very low notes 低音电吉他.

▷ **bass** *adj* [attrib 作定语] low in tone 低音的: *a bass* ˈ*voice* 低音的嗓子 ○ *a bass clari*ˈ*net* 低音竖笛 ○ *the* ˌ*bass* ˈ*clef*, ie symbol in music showing that the notes following in it are low in pitch 低音谱号(乐谱上表明其后的音符为低音的符号). Cf 参看 TREBLE[2].

bas·set /ˈbæsɪt; ˋbæsɪt/ (also ˈ**basset-hound**) *n* short-legged dog used in hunting 矮腿猎犬.

bas·sinet /ˌbæsɪˈnet; ˌbæsəˋnɛt/ *n* baby's wicker cradle with a hood 有篷罩的柳条摇篮.

bas·soon /bəˈsuːn; bəˋsun/ *n* low-pitched woodwind instrument with a double reed 低音管, 巴松管(低音的双簧木管乐器). ⇨illus at App 1 见附录1之插图, page x.

bast /bæst; bæst/ *n* fibre from the inner bark of (esp lime) trees, used for tying and weaving baskets, mats, etc (得自树木的, 尤指菩提树的)内皮纤维(用于编结篮筐、席子等).

bas·tard /ˈbɑːstəd; *US* ˈbæs-; ˋbæstɚd/ *n* **1** illegitimate child 私生子: [attrib 作定语] *a bastard child/daughter/son* 私生儿[女/子]. **2** (*sl derog* 俚, 贬) (**a**) (usu male) person regarded with contempt; ruthless or cruel person (通常指男性)被人瞧不起的人, 冷酷无情的人, 残忍的人: *You rotten bastard!* 你这下流坯! ○ *He's a real bastard, leaving his wife in that way.* 他真狠心, 弃妻子于不顾. (**b**) thing that causes difficulty, pain, etc 使人感到为难、疼痛等的事物: *It's a bastard of a problem, this one.* 这个问题真使人伤脑筋. ○ *My headache's a real bastard.* 我的头疼得真要命. **3** (*sl* 俚) (**a**) (used to address sb, usu a male friend, informally 用于称呼某人, 通常为男性朋友, 用于口语): *Harry, you old bastard! Fancy meeting you here!* 哈利, 你这老傢伙! 真没想到在这里遇见你! (**b**) (used for showing sympathy, usu about a man 用以表示同情, 通常用于男子) unfortunate fellow 不幸的人: *The poor bastard! He's just lost his job.* 那可怜的傢伙! 他刚失去了工作. **4** [usu attrib 通常作定语] not genuine or authentic; showing an odd mixture 不纯的; 不实的; 杂乱的: *a bastard style, language* 混杂的文体、语言.

▷ **bas·tard·ize, -ise** *v* [Tn] (used esp in the past participle 尤作过去分词) make (sth) less pure or authentic 使(某事物)不纯或失真: *a bastardized form of English* 英语的不规范的形式. **bas·tard·iza·tion, -isation** *n* [U].

bas·tardy *n* [U] (*law* 律) state of being a bastard(1) 私生子地位.

baste[1] /beɪst; best/ *v* [Tn] sew (pieces of material) together with long temporary stitches 疏缝, 假缝, 绷(用长针脚暂时缝合).

baste[2] /beɪst; best/ *v* [Tn] pour fat, juices, etc over (meat, etc) to keep it moist during cooking (烹调时往肉等上)浇油脂、汁液等(以保持滋润).

bas·ti·nado /ˌbæstɪˈnɑːdəʊ, -ˈneɪd-; ˌbæstəˋnedo/ *n* (*pl* ~**s**) beating with a stick on the soles of the feet 笞蹠刑(用棍棒打脚掌).

▷ **bas·ti·nado** *v* [Tn] punish or torture (sb) by beating in this way (对某人)施以笞蹠刑.

bas·tion /ˈbæstɪən; ˋbæstɪən/ *n* **1** part of a fortification that projects from the rest 棱堡(防御工事的凸出部分). **2** military stronghold near enemy territory 临近敌区的军事据点. **3** (*fig* 比喻) person or thing defending or protecting sth that is threatened 堡垒; 保护者; 保卫者; 捍卫者: *a bastion of democracy, freedom, etc* 捍卫民主、

自由等的堡垒 ○ *'The last bastions of privilege are crumbling,' announced the speaker.* 演讲者宣称: '特权制度的最后一个堡垒正在崩溃.'

bat[1] /bæt; bæt/ *n* **1** small mouse-like animal that flies at night and feeds on fruit and insects 蝙蝠. ⇨illus at App 1 见附录1之插图, page iii. **2** (idm 习语) **blind as a bat** ⇨ BLIND[1]. **have ˌbats in the ˈbelfry** (*infml* 口) be crazy; have strange ideas 古里古怪; 异想天开. **like a ˌbat out of ˈhell** (*infml* 口) quickly; at top speed 迅速地; 以最高的速度: *He dashed around like a bat out of hell.* 他发疯似的横冲直撞.

bat[2] /bæt; bæt/ *n* **1** (usu wooden) implement of a specified size and shape, and with a handle, used for hitting the ball in games such as cricket, baseball and table tennis (板球、棒球、乒乓球等的)球板、球棒或球拍. ⇨illus at CRICKET 见 CRICKET 之插图. **2** = BATSMAN: *He's a useful bat.* 他是优秀的击球员. **3** (idm 习语) **ˌoff one's own ˈbat** (*infml* 口) without help or encouragement from anyone else; unaided 靠自己的力量; 独力的: *She made the suggestions off her own bat,* ie without being asked for them. 她提这些建议完全是她自己的意思.

▷ **bat** *v* (**-tt-**) **1** [I] (**a**) use a bat 用球板、球棒、球拍等击球: *He bats well.* 他是击球能手.(**b**) have a turn with a bat 轮到执板(或棒、拍)上阵; 轮到击球: *Green batted for two hours.* 格林执棒两小时. **2** [Tn, Tn·p] hit (sth) with a bat 用板(或棒、拍)击(某物): *batting a ball about* 跑来跑去击球. **ˈbat·ter** *n* (*US*) (esp in baseball) person who bats (尤指于棒球赛中)击球手. ⇨illus at BASEBALL 见 BASEBALL 之插图.

□ **ˈbatsman** /-smən; -smən/ *n* (*pl* **-men**) player who bats in cricket 板球的击球手: *He's a good batsman but a poor bowler.* 他击球不错, 但投球不太好. ⇨illus at CRICKET 见 CRICKET 之插图.

bat[3] /bæt; bæt/ *n* (idm 习语) **at a rare, surprising, terrific, etc ˈbat** (*infml* 口) at a fast, etc speed 以极快的、惊人的、吓人的速度.

bat[4] /bæt; bæt/ *v* (**-tt-**) (idm 习语) **not bat an ˈeyelid** (*infml* 口) not show any surprise or feelings 不露声色; 处之泰然: *The condemned man listened to his sentence without batting an eyelid.* 那被定罪的人木无表情地听着对他的宣判.

batch /bætʃ; bætʃ/ *n* **1** number of loaves, cakes, etc baked together (面包、糕饼等的)一炉: *baked in batches of twenty* 以二十个为一炉烘烤的. **2** number of people or things dealt with as a group (人或物的)一批: *a new batch of recruits for the army* 一批新兵 ○ *a batch of letters to be answered* 待复的一批信件. **3** (*computing* 计) set of jobs that are processed together by a computer with no input from individual terminals (计算机在终端停止输入的情况下汇集处理的)成批作业: [attrib 作定语] *a batch run* 成批处理.

□ **ˌbatch ˈprocessing** (*computing* 计) system of processing a batch of jobs as a group 成批处理的程序.

bated /ˈbeɪtɪd; ˋbetɪd/ *adj* (idm 习语) **with ˌbated ˈbreath** holding one's breath anxiously or excitedly 因焦急或兴奋而屏住气息: *We waited with bated breath for the winner to be announced.* 我们屏住呼吸等待宣布获胜者的姓名.

bath /bɑ:θ; *US* bæθ; bæθ/ *n* (*pl* **~s** /bɑ:ðz; *US* bæðz; bæðz/) **1** [C] washing of the whole body, esp when sitting or lying in water 洗澡; 沐浴: *I shall have a hot bath and go to bed.* 我要去洗个热水澡, 然后睡觉. ○ *He takes a cold bath every morning.* 他每天早晨都洗冷水澡. **2** [C] (**a**) (also **ˈbath-tub, tub**) large, usu oblong, container for water in which a person sits to have a bath 澡盆; 浴缸. (**b**) water placed in this ready for use 洗澡水: *Please run a bath for me.* 请给我放一盆洗澡水. ○ *Your bath is ready.* 洗澡水给你准备好了. **3** [C] (container for) liquid in which sth is washed or dipped in chemical and industrial processes 化学及工业生产过程中用以洗涤或浸泡某物的液体; 盛此液体的容器: *an ˈoil bath,* eg for parts of machinery 油槽(如用于浸洗机器零件的) ○ *a bath of red dye* 红染缸. **4 baths** [pl] (**a**) (*Brit*) an indoor public swimming-pool 室内公共游泳池: *heated swimming-baths* 加温的室内公共游泳池. (**b**) building where baths may be taken 澡堂; 浴室: *Turkish ˈbaths* 土耳其式浴室. **5** (idm 习语) **throw the baby out with the bath water** ⇨ BABY.

▷ **bath** *v* (*Brit*) **1** [Tn] give a bath to (sb/sth) 给(某人)洗澡; 清洗(某物): *bath the baby* 给婴儿洗澡. **2** [I] take a bath 洗澡: *I bath every night.* 我每晚洗澡.

□ **ˈbath mat** small absorbent mat for a person to stand on after getting out of a bath 浴室脚垫(出浴后使用的有吸水性能的小脚垫).

ˈbathrobe (also **robe**) *n* **1** loose, usu towelling, garment worn before and after taking a bath 浴衣(浴前浴后穿用的宽松服装, 通常用毛巾布料缝制). **2** (*US*) = DRESSING-GOWN (DRESSING).

ˈbathroom *n* 1 (*Brit sometimes euph* 有时作委婉语) room in which there is a bath (and also usu a wash-basin and sometimes a toilet) 浴室; 盥洗室; 洗手间: *Go and wash your hands in the bathroom.* 去盥洗室把手洗干净. **2** (*US*) (room with a) toilet 抽水马桶; (有抽水马桶的)厕所: *I need to go to the bathroom.* 我要上厕所. ⇨ Usage at TOILET 用法见 TOILET.

ˈbath-tub *n* = BATH 2.

bath chair /ˌbɑ:θ ˈtʃeə(r); ˋbæθ,tʃɛr/ type of wheelchair for an invalid 伤残人使用的一种轮椅.

bathe /beɪð; beð/ *v* **1** [Tn] apply water to (sth); soak in water 用水洗(某物); 用水浸泡: *The doctor told him to bathe his eyes twice a day.* 医生叫他每天洗眼两次. ○ *The nurse bathed the wound.* 护士冲洗伤口. **2** [I] (*esp Brit*) go swimming in the sea, a river, a lake, etc for enjoyment 去海里、河里、湖里等游泳以娱情: *On hot days we often bathe/go bathing in the river.* 天热时我们常在河里[去河里]游泳.

▷ **bathe** *n* (esp *sing* 尤作单数) (*esp Brit*) action of swimming in the sea, etc (在海里等)游泳: *It's a sunny day. Let's go for a bathe.* 今天天气晴朗, 咱们游泳去吧.

bathed *adj* [pred 作表语] **~ in/with sth** wet or bright all over with sth 全被某物弄湿; 全被某物照亮: *Her face was bathed in tears.* 她泪流满面. ○ *After the match, I was bathed with sweat.* 比赛之后我汗流浃背. ○ *The countryside was bathed in brilliant sunshine.* 这一带乡村沐浴在阳光里.

bather /ˈbeɪðə(r); ˋbeðɚ/ *n*.

bath·ing /ˈbeɪðɪŋ; ˋbeðɪŋ/ *n* [U] (*esp Brit*) action of going into the sea, etc to bathe (到江河湖海等处)游泳: *She's fond of bathing.* 她喜欢游泳. ○ *Bathing prohibited!* ie Swimming, etc is not allowed here, eg because it would be unsafe. 禁止游泳(因不安全)!

□ **ˈbathing-cap** *n* close-fitting rubber cap worn over the hair while swimming 游泳帽.

ˈbathing-costume (also **ˈbathing-suit**) *n* (*Brit becoming dated* 渐旧) = SWIMMING-COSTUME (SWIM).

bathos /ˈbeɪθɒs; ˋbeθas/ *n* [U] sudden change (in writing or speech) from what is deeply moving or important to what is foolish or trivial; anticlimax 突降(指在文章或讲话中, 从精彩动人或意义重大的内容突然转入荒谬或平淡的内容); 突降法(从高潮突然降为低潮的修辞法).

bathy·sphere /ˈbæθɪsfɪə(r); ˋbæθɪ,sfɪr/ *n* large, strongly built, hollow sphere that can be lowered deep into the sea (usu for observing marine life) 探海球, 潜水球(为一坚固的大型球形结构, 可潜人深海中, 通常用于观察海洋生物).

batik /bəˈti:k, *also* ˈbætɪk; ˋbətik, ˋbætɪk/ *n* **1** [U] method of printing coloured designs on cloth by waxing the parts that are not to be dyed 蜡防印花法. **2** [C] material dyed in this way 用蜡防印花法印染的花布: [attrib 作定语] *a batik dress* 用蜡防印花布做的连衣裙.

ba·tiste /bæˈti:st, *also* bəˈt-; bæˋtist, bəˋt-/ *n* [U] fine thin linen or cotton cloth 上等细亚麻布或细薄棉布.

bat·man /ˈbætmən; ˋbætmən/ *n* (*pl* **-men** /-mən; -mən/) (*Brit*) soldier who acts as an army officer's personal servant 勤务兵; 传令兵.

baton /ˈbætn, ˈbætɒn; *US* bəˈtɒn; bæˋtan/ *n* **1** = TRUNCHEON: [attrib 作定语] *a baton charge,* ie one made by police, etc armed with batons to drive a crowd back 持警棍出击(警察等用警棍驱退群众). **2** short thin stick used by the conductor of a band or orchestra (乐队指挥所用的)指挥棒. **3** short stick that indicates a certain rank (表示官阶的)权杖: *a Field-Marshal's baton* 陆军元帅的司令杖. **4** short stick carried and handed on in a relay race (接力赛跑用的)接力棒. **5** decorative stick held and twirled by drum majors, etc (军乐队指挥所用的装饰性的)指挥棒.

bats /bæts; bæts/ *adj* [pred 作表语] (*infml* 口) (esp of people) mad; eccentric (尤指人)发疯, 反常. Cf 参看 BATTY.

bat·tal·ion /bəˈtælɪən; bəˈtæljən/ *n* (*abbr* 缩写 **Bn**) army unit composed of several companies and forming part of a regiment or brigade 营(陆军单位).

B

bat·ten[1] /ˈbætn; ˈbætn̩/ *n* **1** long board, esp one used to keep other boards in place, or to which other boards are nailed 板条(尤指用以固定其他板材或将其他板材钉于其上者). **2** (on a ship) strip of wood or metal used to fasten down covers or tarpaulins over a hatch 压条(船上用以扣紧舱口盖或舱盖布的木条或金属条).

▷ **bat·ten** *v* [Tn, Tn·p] **~ sth (down)** (esp on a ship) fasten sth securely with battens (尤指船上)用压条固定住某物: *batten down the hatches*, eg when a storm is expected 封住舱口(如风暴快来时).

bat·ten[2] /ˈbætn; ˈbætn̩/ *v* (phr v) **batten on sb/sth** (*esp derog* 尤作贬义) thrive or live well at the expense of sb/sth, or so as to injure sb/sth 损及某人[某事物]以自肥: *She avoided having to work by battening on her rich relatives.* 她仗着她那些有钱的亲戚而不必工作, 得以坐享清福.

bat·ter[1] /ˈbætə(r); ˈbætɚ/ *v* **1** [Ipr, Ip, Tn] **~ at/on sth** hit (sb/sth) hard and often 接连猛击(某人[某物]): *He kept battering (away) at the door.* 他接连不断地砸门. ○ *battered babies/wives*, ie ones that suffer repeated violence from parents/husbands 受虐的幼儿[妻子]. **2** (phr v) **batter sth down** flatten sth by hitting it repeatedly 不断打击某物使之倒下: *Let's batter the door down.* 咱们把这门砸掉吧. **batter sth to sth** cause sth to become a specified shape by hitting it hard and often 经常猛力打击使某物变成某状: *The huge waves battered the wrecked ship to pieces.* 巨浪将那艘失事的船只冲击得支离破碎. ○ *The victim's face was battered to a pulp.* 受害者的脸打得血肉模糊.

▷ **bat·tered** *adj* out of shape because of age, regular use or frequent accidents 由于年久、经常使用或事故频仍等原因而走样的: *a battered old hat* 一顶破旧不堪的帽子 ○ *Your car looks rather battered.* 你的汽车看上去破破烂烂的.

□ **ˈbattering-ram** *n* large heavy log with an iron head formerly used in war for breaking down walls, etc 攻城槌(为一端带有铁头的巨型沉重圆木, 旧时于战争中用以撞破城墙等).

bat·ter[2] /ˈbætə(r); ˈbætɚ/ *n* [U] beaten mixture of flour, eggs, milk, etc for cooking (为烹调而将面粉、蛋、奶等搅拌成的)糊状物: *fish fried in batter* 蘸面糊煎的鱼 ○ *pancake batter* 做薄煎饼的面糊.

bat·tery /ˈbætərɪ; ˈbætərɪ/ *n* **1** [C] portable container of a cell or cells for supplying electricity 电池; 电池组; 电瓶: *a ˈcar battery* 汽车用的蓄电池 ○ *a ˈtorch battery* 手电筒用的电池 ○ *This pocket calculator needs two batteries.* 这个袖珍计算器需用两节干电池. ⇨illus at App 1 见附录1之插图, page xii. **2** [C] (**a**) group of big guns on a warship or on land 军舰上的炮组; 陆地上的炮台. (**b**) army unit consisting of big guns, with men and vehicles 炮兵连(由大炮、炮兵及车辆组成). **3** [C] large and often confusing set of similar tools, instruments, etc used together (同类用具、器物等的)一套, 一组: *a battery of lights* 一组灯 ○ (*fig* 比喻) *She faced a battery of questions.* 她面临一连串的问题. **4** [C] series of cages in which hens, etc are kept (to make them lay more eggs or grow fatter) 养鸡房(养鸡等用的成排鸡笼, 可使母鸡多产蛋或育肥): [attrib 作定语] *a battery hen* 养鸡房饲养的母鸡 ○ *battery eggs* 养鸡场产的蛋. Cf 参看 FREE-RANGE (FREE[1]). **5** [U] (*law* 律) unlawfully hitting sb or touching him or his clothes threateningly 殴打. **6** (idm 习语) **recharge one's batteries** ⇨ RECHARGE.

□ ˌ**battery ˈfarm** farm where large numbers of hens are kept in batteries 养鸡场. ˌ**battery ˈfarming**.

battle /ˈbætl; ˈbætl̩/ *n* **1** [C, U] fight, esp between organized armed forces 战斗; 战役; 交战: *a fierce battle* 激烈的战斗 ○ *the battle of Waterloo* 滑铁卢战役 ○ *go out to battle* 奔赴战场 ○ *die in battle* 阵亡. **2** [C] (*fig* 比喻) any contest or struggle 争斗; 斗争: *a battle of words, wits* 一场舌战、智斗 ○ *Their whole life was a constant battle against poverty.* 他们一生都在不断地与贫穷作斗争. **3** (idm 习语) **do battle (with sb) (about sth)** fight or argue fiercely (with sb) (about sth) (为某事)(与某人)激烈斗争或争论. **fight a losing battle** ⇨ FIGHT[1]. **give ˈbattle** (*dated* 旧) show that one is ready to fight 挑战. **half the battle** an important or the most important part of achieving sth 实现某目的至关重要的部分: *When you're ill, wanting to get well again is often half the battle.* 生病时, 有决心把病治好往往是最为重要的. **join battle** ⇨ JOIN.

▷ **battle** *v* [I, Ipr, Ip] **~ (with/against sb/sth) (for sth)**; **~ (on)** struggle 斗争; 搏斗; 奋斗: *battling against ill health* 与病魔作斗争 ○ *They battled with the wind and the waves.* 他们与风浪搏斗. ○ *I'm battling with my employers for a pay-rise.* 我正向雇主力争增加工资. ○ *Progress is slow but we keep battling on.* 进展虽慢, 但是我们在继续奋斗.

□ **ˈbattleaxe** *n* (**a**) (formerly) heavy axe with a long handle, used as a weapon 战斧(旧时用作武器的长柄重斧). (**b**) (*infml derog* 口, 贬) unpleasantly domineering (usu older) woman (通常指较年长的)悍妇, 母老虎.

ˈbattle-cruiser *n* large warship, faster and lighter than a battleship 战列巡洋舰(一种比战列舰速度快、吨位轻的大军舰).

ˈbattle-cry *n* (**a**) (esp formerly) rallying cry used in battle (尤指旧时)战斗呐喊. (**b**) (*fig* 比喻) slogan or rallying cry of a group of people fighting for the same cause (为共同事业而斗争的人们所用的)标语或口号.

ˈbattledress *n* [U] soldier's uniform of blouse and trousers 野战服装.

ˈbattlefield, **ˈbattleground** *ns* place where a battle is or was fought 战场.

ˈbattleship *n* large warship with big guns and heavy armour 战列舰.

bat·tle·ments /ˈbætlmənts; ˈbætl̩mənts/ *n* [pl] (flat roof of a tower or castle surrounded by) low walls with openings at intervals made for shooting through 雉堞; 城垛. ⇨illus at CASTLE 见 CASTLE 之插图.

batty /ˈbætɪ; ˈbætɪ/ *adj* (**-ier**, **-iest**) (*infml* 口) (of people, ideas, etc) crazy; slightly mad (指人、思想等)疯狂的, 稍反常的. Cf 参看 BATS.

bauble /ˈbɔ:bl; ˈbɔbl̩/ *n* (*usu derog* 通常作贬义) showy ornament of little value 华而不实的装饰品.

baulk = BALK.

baux·ite /ˈbɔ:ksaɪt; ˈbɔksaɪt/ *n* [U] clay-like substance from which aluminium is obtained 铝土岩, 铝矾土(炼铝的原料).

bawdy /ˈbɔ:dɪ; ˈbɔdɪ/ *adj* (**-ier**, **-iest**) amusing in a coarse or indecent way (以粗俗或下流的方式)娱人的: *bawdy jokes, stories, etc* 淫猥的笑话、故事等.

▷ **bawd·ily** *adv*. **bawdi·ness** *n* [U].

bawdy *n* [U] (*dated* 旧) bawdy talk or stories 淫猥的话或故事.

bawl /bɔ:l; bɔl/ *v* **1** [I, Ipr, Ip, Tn, Tn·pr, Tn·p] **~ (sth) (out)** shout or cry loudly 大叫; 大喊: *That baby has been bawling for hours.* 那婴儿已经大声哭叫了几小时. ○ *He bawled at me across the street.* 他在街道的另一边冲着我大喊. ○ *We bawled for help but no one heard us.* 我们大声求援可是无人听见. ○ *The sergeant bawled (out) a command (to his men).* 那个中士(向士兵)大声发令. **2** (phr v) ˌ**bawl sb ˈout** (*esp US infml* 口) scold sb severely 严厉呵责某人.

bay[1] /beɪ; be/ (also **ˈbay-tree**) *n* laurel with dark green leaves and purple berries 月桂树(长有深绿色树叶和紫色浆果).

□ **ˈbay-leaf** *n* (*pl* **-leaves**) dried leaf of the bay-tree, spicy when crushed, used as seasoning in cooking 月桂树的干树叶(压榨时有香味, 可作烹饪的调味品).

bay[2] /beɪ; be/ *n* part of the sea, or of a large lake, enclosed by a wide curve of the shore 海湾; 湖湾: *the Bay of Bengal* 孟加拉湾 ○ *Hudson Bay* 哈得孙湾.

bay[3] /beɪ; be/ *n* **1** (**a**) one of a series of compartments in a building, a structure or an area, esp one designed for storing things, parking vehicles, etc 建筑物、构架或区域内的分隔空间(尤指用于贮物、停放车辆等的): *a ˈparking bay* 停车房 ○ *Put the equipment in No 3 bay.* 把这设备放在第三号储藏间里. (**b**) (esp in compounds 尤用以构成复合词) any special compartment or area 任何有专门用途的隔间或区域: *the ˈbomb-bay*, ie the compartment in the fuselage of an aircraft where bombs are carried ○ *the ˈsick-bay*, ie part of a ship, building, school, etc set aside for the care of the sick or the injured. **2** recess in a room or building（房间或其他建筑物的）凹进处.

□ ˌ**bay** ˈ**window** window, usu with glass on three sides, projecting from an outside wall 凸窗（向墙外突出, 通常三面有玻璃的窗户）. ⇨illus at App 1 见附录1之插图, page vi.

bay[4] /beɪ; be/ *n* **1** deep bark, esp of hounds while hunting 低沉的吠声（尤指猎犬行猎时发出的）. **2** (idm 习语) **at** ˈ**bay** (esp of a hunted animal) forced to face its attackers and show defiance because unable to escape （尤指被追猎的动物）被迫作困兽之斗; 狗急跳墙. **bring sb/sth to** ˈ**bay** force (a fleeing enemy, a hunted animal, etc) into a position from which escape is impossible （将逃跑的敌人、追猎的动物等）逼到绝路上. **hold/keep sb at** ˈ**bay** prevent (an enemy, pursuers, etc) from coming near 不让（敌人、追逐者等）逼近: *I'm trying to keep my creditors at bay.* 我竭力躲避债主.

▷ **bay** *v* [I] (esp of hounds, etc) bark with a deep note （尤指猎犬等）低沉地吠叫: *the baying cry of a wolf* 狼的低沉嗥叫声.

bay[5] /beɪ; be/ *n, adj* (horse) of a reddish-brown colour 红棕色的（马）: *riding a big bay (mare)* 骑着红棕色的大（母）马.

bay·onet /ˈbeɪənɪt; ˈbeənɪt/ *n* dagger-like blade that can be fixed to the muzzle of a rifle and used in hand-to-hand fighting 枪刺; 刺刀.

▷ **bay·onet** /ˈbeɪənɪt, *also* ˌbeɪəˈnet; ˈbeənɪt/ *v* [Tn] stab (sb/sth) with a bayonet 用枪刺刺（某人［某物］）: *bayoneted to death* 被枪刺刺死.

bayou /ˈbaɪuː; ˈbaɪu/ *n* (in the southern USA) slow-moving marshy part of a river away from the main stream （美国南部的）长沼.

ba·zaar /bəˈzɑː(r); bəˈzɑr/ *n* **1** (in eastern countries) group of shops or stalls or part of a town where these are （东方国家的）市场, 城市的商业区. **2** (in Britain, USA, etc) (place where there is a) sale of goods to raise money for charitable purposes （英、美等国）（为慈善事业筹集款项的）义卖, 义卖市场: *a church bazaar* 教会主持的义卖.

ba·zooka /bəˈzuːkə; bəˈzukə/ *n* portable weapon used for launching anti-tank rockets （便携式）反坦克火箭筒.

BBC /ˌbiː biː ˈsiː; ˌbi bi ˈsi/ *abbr* 缩写 = British Broadcasting Corporation 英国广播公司: *listen to the BBC* 收听英国广播公司的节目 ○ *BBC English*, ie a form of English with a high standard of correctness BBC英语（高度纯正的英语）. Cf 参看 IBA, ITV.

BBFC /ˌbiː biː ef ˈsiː; ˌbi bi ɛf ˈsi/ *abbr* 缩写 = British Board of Film Censors 英国电影审查局.

BC /ˌbiː ˈsiː; ˌbi ˈsi/ *abbr* 缩写 = **1** Before Christ 公元前: *in (the year) 2000 BC* 在公元前2000年. Cf 参看 AD. **2** British Council (a government-sponsored organization for the promotion of English language and culture in other countries) 英国文化协会.

be[1] /bɪ; bɪ; *strong form* 强读式 biː; bi/ *v* ⇨Usage at BE[2] 用法见BE[2]. **1** (used after *there* and before *a/an, no, some,* ETC + *n* 用于there之后及a/an、no、some等+名词之前) **(a)** exist; occur; live 有; 存在; 生存: *Is there a God?* 有上帝吗? ○ *For there to be life there must be air and water.* 一定要有空气和水才有生命. ○ *There are no easy answers.* 现成的答案是没有的. ○ *There are many such people.* 这样的人多的是. ○ *Once upon a time there was a princess.* 从前有一个公主. ○ *There have been cows in that field since my grandfather's time.* 从我祖父那时候起, 那片地上就养着牛. **(b)** be present; stand 在; 在场: *There's a bus-stop down the road* 路的前方有一个公共汽车站. (Cf 参看 *The bus-stop is down the road.*) *There were no books on the shelf.* 书架上没有书. ○ *There are some good photographs in this exhibition.* 这一展览会上有些好照片. **2** (with an *adv* or a prepositional phrase indicating position in space or time 与表示地点或时间的副词或介词短语连用) **(a)** be situated 位于; 处于: *The lamp is on the table.* 灯在桌子上. ○ *The stable is a mile away.* 马房距此一英里远. ○ *Mary's upstairs.* 玛丽在楼上. ○ *John's out in the garden.* 约翰在外面花园里. ○ *They are on holiday in the Lake District.* 他们在英格兰湖区度假. **(b)** happen; occur; take place 发生; 产生; 举行: *The party is after work.* 聚会在下班后举行. ○ *The election was on Monday.* 选举是在星期一进行的. ○ *The concert will be in the school hall.* 音乐会将在学校的礼堂内举行. ○ *The meetings are on Tuesdays and Thursdays in the main hall.* 会议在星期二和星期四于大礼堂举行. **(c)** remain 停留; 逗留; 待: *She has been in her room for hours.* 她在自己的房间里待了几个小时. ○ *They're here till Christmas.* 他们在这里要一直逗留到圣诞节. **(d)** attend; be present 出席; 到场: *Were you at church yesterday?* 昨天你去过教堂吗? ○ *I'll be at the party.* 我参加这个聚会. **3** (with an *adv* or a prepositional phrase indicating direction, a starting point, etc 与副词或介词短语连用表示方向、起点等) leave; arrive 离开; 到达: *I'll be on my way very soon.* 我很快就要上路. ○ *She's from Italy*, ie Her native country is Italy. 她是意大利人（她的原籍是意大利）. **4** (usu with an *adv* or a prepositional phrase indicating destination; in the perfect tenses only 通常与副词或介词短语连用表示目的; 仅用于完成时态) visit or call 到某地; 访问; 拜访: *I've never been to Spain.* 我从未到过西班牙. ○ *She had been abroad many times.* 她多次出国. ○ *Has the plumber been* (ie called) *yet?* 管子工来过了吗? **5** [La, Ln] (indicating a quality or a state 表示性质或状况): *Life is unfair.* 生活就是不公平的. ○ *The world is round.* 地球是圆的. ○ *He is ten years old.* 他十岁了. ○ *I am of average height.* 我中等身材. ○ *Be quick!* 赶快! ○ *She's a great beauty.* 她是个大美人. ○ *'How are you?' 'I'm quite well, thanks.'* '你好吗?' '很好, 谢谢.' **6** [La, Ln] (in exclamations 用于感叹句): *Were ˈthey surprised to see us!* 他们哪里想到会见到我们! ○ *Aren't you a great cook!* 你做的菜真好吃! ○ *Wasn't that a good film!* 那部影片真棒! **7** [Ln] (indicating the name, profession, pastime, etc of the subject 表示所谈论的话题的名称、职业、消遣等): *Today is Monday.* 今天星期一. ○ *You are the man I want.* 你是我需要的人. ○ *'Who is that?' 'It's the postman.'* '那是什么人?' '是邮递员.' ○ *Susan is a doctor.* 苏姗是医生. ○ *Peter is a keen footballer in his spare time.* 彼得在业余时间里很喜欢踢足球. ○ *He wants to be* (ie become) *a fireman when he grows up.* 他希望长大以后当（成为）消防队员. **8** [Ln] (indicating possession, actual or intended 表示实际所有或意欲得到): *The money's not yours, it's John's*, ie It belongs to John and not to you. 这笔钱不是你的, 是约翰的. ○ *This parcel is for you.* 这个包裹是给你的. **9** [Ln] (showing equivalence in value, number, etc 表示价值、数目等相等) **(a)** cost 价值; 花费: *'How much is that dress?' 'It's £50.'* '那件连衣裙多少钱?' '50英镑.' **(b)** amount to; equal 合计; 等于: *Twice two is four.* 二二得四. ○ *Three and three is six.* 三加三等于六. ○ *Four threes are twelve.* 四乘三等于十二. **(c)** constitute 组成: *London is not England*, ie Don't think that all of England is like London. 伦敦并不等于英国（勿以为整个英格兰都像伦敦一样）. **(d)** represent 代表: *Let x be the sum of a and b.* 设x为a与b之和. **(e)** mean; signify 意味; 表示: *It is nothing to me.* 这对我来说不算什么. ○ *A thousand pounds is nothing to a rich man.* 一千镑对富翁来说算不上什么. **10** (idm 习语) **the** ˌ**be-all and** ˈ**end-all (of sth)** (*infml* 口) the most important part; all that matters 最重要的部分; 最要紧的事: *Her boy-friend is the be-all and end-all of her existence.* 她的男朋友就是她生活中最重要的内容. **(he, etc has) been and** ˈ**done sth** (*infml* 口) (expressing protest and surprise 表示抗议和惊奇): *Someone's been (and gone) and eaten my porridge!* 有人来过（又走了）, 竟把我的麦片粥给喝了! **be one'self** act naturally 自然地行事: *Don't try to act sophisticated — just be yourself.* 不要装得老成持重——你是怎么样就怎么样. ˌ**be that as it** ˈ**may** despite that; nevertheless 不顾; 尽管: *I accept that he's old and frail; be that as it may, he's still a good politician.* 我承认他年老体衰, 然而尽管如此, 他仍是优秀的政治家. **it is/was as if.../as though...** it seems/seemed that... 似乎...; 好像...: *It's as if he never listens to a word I say.* 我说的话似乎他从来都不听. **...that was** ...as sb used to be called 如人们过去对某人常用的称呼: *Miss Brown that was*, ie before her marriage. 布朗小姐, 即她婚前的称呼. **-to-**ˈ**be** (in compounds 用以构成复合词) future 未来; 将来: *his* ˌ*bride-to-*ˈ*be*, ie his future bride ○ ˌ*mothers-to-*ˈ*be*, ie pregnant women. (For other idioms containing **be**, see entries for *ns, adjs,* etc 与**be**搭配的其他习语见有关名词、形容词等的词条, 如 **be the death of sb** ⇨DEATH.)

B

B

be² /bɪ; bɪ; *strong form* 强读式 bi:; bi/ *aux v* ⇨Usage 见所附用法 **1** (used with a past participle to form the passive 与过去分词连用构成被动语态): *He was killed in the war.* 他阵亡了. ○ *Where were they made?* 这些东西是在哪里制造的? ○ *The thief was caught.* 窃贼被捉住了. ○ *The house is/was being built.* 那房屋正在[那时正在]建造. ○ *You will be severely punished if you do not obey.* 你不服从, 就会受到严惩. **2** (used with present participles to form continuous tenses 与现在分词连用构成进行时态): *They are/were reading.* 他们正在[那时正在]阅读. ○ *I am studying Chinese.* 我正在学习汉语. ○ *I shall be seeing him soon.* 我不久就会见到他了. ○ *What have you been doing this week?* 你这星期以来在干什么? ○ *I'm always being criticized.* 我总是挨批. **3** (with *to* + infinitive 与to+不定式连用) **(a)** (expressing duty, necessity, etc 表示责任、需要等): *I am to* (ie I have been told to) *inform you that*... 我有义务(我受人之托)通知你... ○ *You are to report* (ie must, should report) *to the police.* 你应该报警. **(b)** (expressing arrangement, intention or purpose 表示安排、意向或目的): *They are to be married,* ie will be married. 他们打算结婚. ○ *Each participant was to pay his own expenses.* 每个参加者都必须自费. ○ *The telegram was to say that she'd be late.* 电报说她可能晚到. **(c)** (expressing possibility 表示可能性): *The book was not to be* (ie could not be) *found.* 那本书找不到了. **(d)** (expressing destiny 表示注定): *He was never to see his wife again,* ie Although he did not know it at the time, he did not see her again. 他从那以后就再也见不到他的妻子了. ○ *The celebrations were not to be,* ie They did not, in fact, take place. 庆祝活动结果未能举行. **(e)** (only in the form *were*, expressing supposition 仅用were这一形式, 表示假设): *If I were to tell you/ Were I to tell you that I killed him, would you believe me?* 假如我对你说是我杀死了他, 你相信吗? ○ *If it were to rain, we would have to cancel the match tomorrow.* 假如下雨, 我们只好取消明天的比赛.

NOTE ON USAGE 用法: **Be** is used as a main verb (**be**¹) and as an auxiliary verb (**be**²). ☆ **be**可用作主要动词 (**be**¹), 也可作助动词 (**be**²). The various written and spoken forms are the same for both verbs 两者的各种书面语和口语形式均相同: **am** (*pres t* with *I*) /əm, m; m/, *strong form* /æm; æm/; written contraction **I'm** /aɪm; aɪm/; negative question **aren't I?** /ˈɑ:ntaɪ; *US* ˈɑ:rəntaɪ; ɑrnt aɪ/. ☆ **am** (现在时态与 *I* 连用)/əm, m; m/, 强读式 /æm; æm/; 书写缩约式 **I'm** /aɪm; aɪm/; 否定疑问式 **aren't I?** /ˈɑ:ntaɪ; 美式 ˈɑ:rəntaɪ; ɑrnt aɪ/. ☆ **is** (*pres t* with *he, she, it*) /s, z; s, z/, *strong form* /ɪz; ɪz/; written contractions **it's** /ɪts; ɪts/, **Jack's** /dʒæks; dʒæks/, **he's** /hi:z, hɪz; hɪz/, **she's** /ʃi:z, ʃɪz; ʃɪz/, **the cow's** /ðə kaʊz; ðə ˈkaʊz/; negative **isn't** /ˈɪznt; ˈɪznt/. ☆ **is** (现在时态与 *he*、*she*、*it* 连用)/s, z; s, z/, 强读式 /ɪz; ɪz/; 书写缩约式 **it's** /ɪts; ɪts/, **Jack's** /dʒæks; dʒæks/, **he's** /hi:z, hɪz; hɪz/, **she's** /ʃi:z, ʃɪz; ʃɪz/, **the cow's** /ðə kaʊz; ðə ˈkaʊz/; 否定式 **isn't** /ˈɪznt; ˈɪznt/. ☆ **are** (*pres t* with *you, we, they*) /ə(r); ɚ/, *strong form* /ɑ:(r); ɑr/; written contractions **we're** /wɪə(r); wɪr/, **you're** /jʊə(r), jɔ:(r); jʊr/, **they're** /ðeə(r); ðer/; negative **aren't** /ɑ:nt; *US* ˈɑ:rənt; ɑrnt/. ☆ **are** (现在时态与*you*、*we*、*they* 连用)/ə(r); ɚ/, 强读式 /ɑ:(r); ɑr/; 书写缩约式 **we're** /wɪə(r); wɪr/, **you're** /jʊə(r), jɔ:(r); jʊr/, **they're** /ðeə(r); ðer/; 否定式 **aren't** /ɑ:nt; 美式 ˈɑ:rənt; ɑrnt/. ☆ **was** (*pt* with *I, he, she, it*) /wəz; wəz/, *strong form* /wɒz; *US* wʌz; wʌz/; negative **wasn't** /ˈwɒznt; *US* ˈwʌznt; ˈwʌznt/. ☆ **was** (过去时态与*I*、*he*、*she*、*it* 连用)/wəz; wəz/, 强读式 /wɒz; 美式 wʌz; wʌz/; 否定式 **wasn't** /ˈwɒznt; 美式 ˈwʌznt; ˈwʌznt/. ☆ **were** (*pt* with *you, we, they*) /wə(r); wɚ/, *strong form* /wɜ:(r); wɝ/; negative **weren't** /wɜ:nt; *US* ˈwɜ:rənt; wɝnt/. ☆ **were** (过去时态与 *you*、*we*、*they*连用)/wə(r); wɚ/, 强读式 /wɜ:(r); wɝ/; 否定式 **weren't** /wɜ:nt; 美式 ˈwɜ:rənt; wɝnt/. ☆ **being** (*pres p*) /ˈbi:ɪŋ; ˈbiɪŋ/. ☆ **being**(现在分词) /ˈbi:ɪŋ; ˈbiɪŋ/. ☆ **been** (*pp*) /bi:n; *US also* bɪn; bɪn/. ☆ **been**(过去分词)/bi:n; 美式 bɪn; bɪn/.

be- *pref* 前缀 **1** (with *vs* and *adjs* ending in *-ed* 与动词和以 -ed 结尾的形容词结合) all around; all over 全面; 到处: *besmear* ○ *bedeck* ○ *bejewelled.* **2** (with *ns* and *adjs* forming transitive *vs* 与名词和形容词结合, 构成及物动词) make or treat as 使; 视为: *befriend* ○ *belittle.* **3** (with intransitive *vs* forming transitive *vs* 与不及物动词结合, 构成及物动词): *bemoan* ○ *bewail.*

beach /bi:tʃ; bitʃ/ *n* **1** stretch of sand or pebbles along the edge of the sea or a lake; shore between high and low water mark 海滩; 湖滩; 滩地: *holiday-makers sunbathing on the beach* 在沙滩上作日光浴的度假者. ⇨illus at COAST 见COAST之插图. **2** (idm 习语) **not the only pebble on the beach** ⇨ PEBBLE. ⇨Usage at COAST¹ 用法见 COAST¹.

▷ **beach** *v* [Tn] bring (esp a boat or ship) on shore from out of the water (尤指船只)从水中推或拖至岸上.

□ ˈ**beach-ball** *n* large lightweight inflated ball for games on the beach 沙滩球(供海滩游戏用的大而轻的充气球).

ˈ**beach buggy** small motor vehicle used for racing on beaches, waste ground, etc 沙滩车(在海滩、荒地等处使用的小型机动赛车).

ˈ**beachcomber** /-ˌkəʊmə(r); -ˌkomɚ/ *n* **1** person without a regular job who lives by selling whatever he can find on beaches 海滩游民(无固定工作, 以在海滩捡破烂为生的人). **2** long wave rolling in from the sea (涌向海滩的)长形巨浪.

ˈ**beach-head** *n* strong position on a beach established by an army which has just landed and is preparing to advance and attack (部队登陆后准备进攻时所建的)滩头阵地. Cf 参看 BRIDGEHEAD (BRIDGE¹).

ˈ**beachwear** *n* [U] clothes for swimming, sunbathing, playing games, etc on the beach 海滩装(在海滩游泳、进行日光浴、游戏等时穿的服装).

beacon /ˈbi:kən; ˈbikən/ *n* **1** fire lit on a hilltop as a signal 烽火. **2** **(a)** light fixed on rocks or on the coast to warn or guide ships, or on a mountain, tall building, etc to warn aircraft 灯塔; 灯标. **(b)** flashing light on an airfield for the guidance of pilots (飞机场上指示飞机起降的)闪光灯. **3** signal station such as a lighthouse (灯塔之类的)信号站. **4** radio station or transmitter whose signal helps ships and aircraft to discover their position (帮助航船和飞行器确定位置的)无线电台或发射台. **5** (*Brit*) = BELISHA BEACON.

bead /bi:d; bid/ *n* **1** **(a)** [C] small piece of (usu hard) material with a hole through it, for threading with others on a string, or for sewing onto material (有孔可穿连成串或缝在衣物上的)小珠子: *a string of glass beads* 一串玻璃珠子. **(b)** **beads** [pl] necklace made of beads 珠子项链. **2** [C] drop of liquid 滴: *beads of sweat on his forehead* 他额头上的汗珠. **3** (idm 习语) **draw a bead** ⇨ DRAW².

▷ **bead·ing** *n* [U, C] strip of wood or stone, rounded or with a pattern of beads, used as decorative edging 有串珠花样的木条或石条(用作缘饰).

beadle /ˈbi:dl; ˈbidl̩/ *n* (*Brit*) **1** officer helping in certain church or college ceremonies (某些教会或学校的礼仪活动的)助理员. **2** (formerly) parish officer who helped the priest by keeping order in church, giving money to the poor, etc (旧时教区中协助牧师维持教堂秩序、向穷人发放赈济款等的)助理员.

beady /ˈbi:dɪ; ˈbidɪ/ *adj* (of eyes) small, round and bright like beads (指眼睛)小而圆, 晶亮如珠子的: *Not much escapes our teacher's beady eye,* ie Our teacher sees almost everything. 任何事都很难逃过我们老师那明亮的眼睛.

beagle /ˈbi:gl; ˈbigl̩/ *n* small short-legged dog used for hunting hares 猎兔狗(猎兔用的一种短腿小猎狗).

▷ **beag·ling** /ˈbi:glɪŋ; ˈbiglɪŋ/ *n* [U] hunting on foot with beagles 带着猎兔狗徒步行猎.

beak¹ /bi:k; bik/ *n* **1** hard horny part of a bird's mouth 鸟喙. ⇨illus at App 1 见附录1之插图, page iv. **2** anything shaped like this, esp a hooked nose 鸟喙形状的任何物体; (尤指)鹰钩鼻子.

▷ **beaked** /bi:kt; bikt/ *adj* (usu in compounds 通常用以构成复合词) having a beak (of the specified type) (鸟嘴或鸟嘴形物)有某种嘴的: *long-beaked.*

beak² /bi:k; bik/ *n* (*Brit sl* 俚) magistrate 地方执法官: *brought up before the beak* 被告到官府.

beaker /ˈbi:kə(r); ˈbikɚ/ *n* **1** open glass container with a lip for pouring, used in chemistry laboratories 烧杯. **2** tall narrow cup for drinking, often without a handle 细高的杯(常无柄): *a beaker of coffee from the drinks machine* 取自饮料机的一杯咖啡.

beam /biːm; bim/ *n* **1** long piece of wood, metal, concrete, etc, usu horizontal and supported at both ends, that carries the weight of part of a building or some other structure 梁. **2** (**a**) any of the horizontal cross-timbers of a ship, joining the sides and supporting the deck 船梁(船上连接两舷并支撑甲板的横木). (**b**) breadth of a ship at its widest part 船宽(船身最宽部分的距离). **3** horizontal bar of weighing-scales from which the pans hang 衡器上悬吊秤盘的横杆. ⇨illus at SCALE 见SCALE之插图. **4** ray or stream of light or other radiation (eg from a lamp or a lighthouse, the sun or the moon) (灯、灯塔、日月等的)光线、光束或其他射线: *the beam of the torch, searchlight, etc* 手电筒、探照灯等的光束 ○ *The car's headlights were on full beam*, ie not dipped to avoid dazzling other drivers. 那辆汽车的前大灯都开着(未能为防止将其他司机眼睛照花而放低前大灯). **5** bright and happy look or smile 欢快的表情; 微笑: *a beam of pleasure* 一丝笑容. **6** series of radio or radar signals used to guide ships or aircraft (为船只或飞行器导航的无线电或雷达的)信号流. **7** (idm 习语) **broad in the beam** ⇨ BROAD[1]. **off (the) ˈbeam** (*infml* 口) mistaken; wrong 错误的; 不对: *Your calculation is way off beam.* 你的计算大错特错. **on the ˈbeam** (*infml* 口) on the right track; correct 正确的; 对.

▷ **beam** *v* **1** (**a**) [I] (of the sun, etc) send out light and warmth (指太阳等)发光, 发热. (**b**) [I, Ipr] **~ (at sb)** smile happily and cheerfully 愉快地微笑: *The winner beamed with satisfaction.* 获胜者满意地笑了. **2** [Tn, Tn·pr] **~ sth (to...) (from...)** broadcast (a message, television programme, etc) 播送(消息、电视节目等): *The World Cup Final was beamed live from Britain to Japan.* 世界杯决赛从英国向日本作了实况转播.

□ **beam-ˈends** *n* [pl] (idm 习语) **on her beam-ends** (of a ship) lying over to one side; almost capsizing (指船)向一边倾斜; 几乎翻船. **on one's beam-ends** (of a person) with very little money left; almost destitute (指人)经济拮据; 几乎一无所有.

bean /biːn; bin/ *n* **1** (**a**) smooth, usu kidney-shaped, seed, used as a vegetable 豆子: ˌ*broad* ˈ*beans* 蚕豆 ○ ˈ*kidney beans* 菜豆 ○ ˈ*soya beans* 大豆 ○ ˌ*haricot* ˈ*beans* 扁豆. (**b**) any of the various plants that bear these seeds in long pods 豆科植物. (**c**) pod containing such seeds, which is itself eaten as a vegetable 豆荚(可食用): ˌ*runner* ˈ*beans* 红花菜豆. **2** similar seed of other plants, eg cocoa or coffee 其他植物的豆状果实(如可可豆或咖啡豆). **3** (idm 习语) **full of beans/life** ⇨ FULL. **a hill of beans** ⇨ HILL. **know how many beans make five** ⇨ KNOW. **not have a ˈbean** (*infml* 口) have no money 不名一文. **spill the beans** ⇨ SPILL[1].

□ ˈ**beanfeast** (also **beano**) *n* (*dated Brit infml* 旧, 口) merry celebration or party 喜庆; 喜宴.

ˈ**beanpole** *n* (*infml* 口) tall thin person 瘦高个子.

ˈ**bean sprouts** sprouts of young bean seeds often eaten uncooked, esp in Chinese dishes 豆芽.

beano /ˈbiːnəʊ; ˈbino/ *n* (*pl* **~s**) (*dated Brit infml* 旧, 口) = BEANFEAST (BEAN).

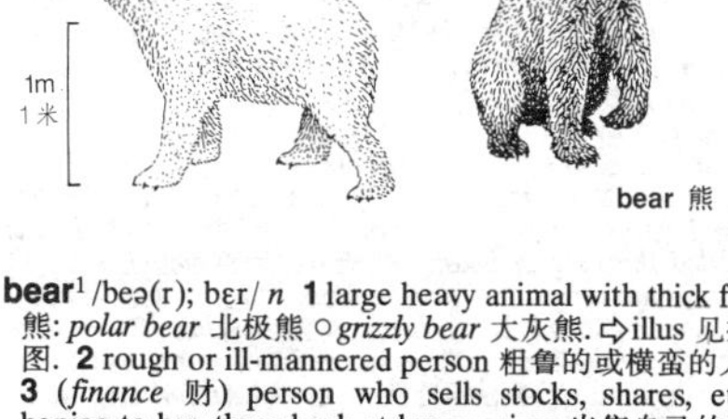

bear 熊

bear[1] /beə(r); bɛr/ *n* **1** large heavy animal with thick fur 熊: *polar bear* 北极熊 ○ *grizzly bear* 大灰熊. ⇨illus 见插图. **2** rough or ill-mannered person 粗鲁的或横蛮的人. **3** (*finance* 财) person who sells stocks, shares, etc, hoping to buy them back at lower prices 出售自己的证券、股票等, 希望以较低价格购回的人; 股票看跌的人: [attrib 作定语] *a* ˈ*bear market*, ie a situation in which share prices are falling rapidly 卖空的市场(股票价格急剧跌落的行情). Cf 参看 BULL[1] 3. **4** (idm 习语) **a bear garden** place or meeting at which there is much rough or noisy behaviour 嘈杂喧闹的场所或会议. **like a ˌbear with a sore ˈhead** (*infml* 口) irritable; bad-tempered 易怒的; 脾气坏的: *When he's just woken up he's like a bear with a sore head.* 他刚睡醒时, 非常暴躁.

▷ **bear·ish** /ˈbeərɪʃ; ˈbɛrɪʃ/ *adj* **1** rough or bad-tempered 粗暴的; 脾气坏的. **2** (*finance* 财) characterized by or causing a fall in the price of stocks 以证券价格下跌为特征的; 引起证券价格下跌的: *a bearish market* 刮跌风的证券交易市场. Cf 参看 BULLISH (BULL[1]).

□ ˈ**bear-hug** *n* powerful tight embrace 紧紧的搂抱.

ˈ**bearskin** *n* **1** fur of a bear 熊皮: [attrib 作定语] *a bearskin rug* 熊皮地毯. **2** tall hat of black fur worn by British guardsmen (英国卫兵戴的)黑皮高帽.

bear[2] /beə(r); bɛr/ *v* (*pt* **bore** /bɔː(r); bɔr/, *pp* **borne** /bɔːn; bɔrn/) **1** [Tn] show (sth); carry visibly; display 显示(某事物); 明显地带有; 表现: *The document bore his signature.* 这分文件有他的签字. ○ *The ring bears an inscription.* 这个戒指上刻有字. ○ *The coach bears the royal coat of arms.* 这辆大马车上有王室的盾形纹章. ○ *I saw a tombstone bearing the date 1602.* 我见到一块刻有1602年字样的墓碑. ○ *He was badly wounded in the war and still bears the scars.* 他在战争中受了重伤, 现在仍有伤疤. ○ *She bears little resemblance to* (ie is not much like) *her mother.* 她长得不太像她的母亲. ○ *The title of the essay bore little relation to the contents*, ie was not much connected with them. 这篇文章的题目和内容不大相符. **2** [Tn] be known by (sth); have 以(某事物)为人所知; 具有: *a family that bore an ancient and honoured name* 名门世家 ○ *A married woman usually bears her husband's surname.* 女子出嫁以后通常随夫姓. **3** [Tn, Tn·pr, Tn·p] (*dated or fml* 旧或文) carry (sb/sth), esp while moving 携带(某人[某物])(尤指于移动中): *bear a heavy load* 负重 ○ *three kings bearing gifts* 进贡的三位国王 ○ *They bore his body to the tomb.* 他们把他的遗体抬到墓地. ○ *The canoe was borne along by the current.* 那独木舟顺流而下. ⇨Usage at CARRY 用法见 CARRY. **4** [Tn] (**a**) support (sb/sth); sustain 支撑(某人[某事物]); 支持: *The ice is too thin to bear your weight.* 冰太薄, 承受不住你的重量. (**b**) take (responsibility, etc) on oneself; shoulder 负起(责任等); 肩负: *Do the bride's parents have to bear the cost of the wedding?* 要由新娘的父母来负担婚礼所需的费用吗? ○ *The President has to bear the blame.* 总统难辞其咎. ○ *He's a carefree fellow who bears his responsibilities lightly.* 他是个满不在意不大负责的人. **5** (**a**) [Tn, Tt, Tg, Tsg] (more informal, with *can/could*, in negative sentences or questions 多用于口语, 在否定句或疑问句中与 can [could]连用) endure (sth); tolerate; stand 忍受; 忍耐; 承受: *The pain was almost more than he could bear.* 这样的痛苦几乎使他受不了. ○ *She bore her sorrow without complaint.* 她毫无怨言地忍受着悲痛. ○ *I can't bear (having) cats in the house.* 屋里有猫我可真受不了. ○ *How can you bear to eat that stuff?* 你怎么能吃得下那样的东西? ○ *He can't bear to be laughed at/bear being laughed at.* 他禁不住拿他取笑. (**b**) [Tn, Tg] (in negative sentences, esp with the direct objects shown 用于否定句, 尤与下列所示直接宾语连用) be fit for (sth); allow 适宜于(某事物); 允许: *Modern paintings don't bear comparison with those of the old masters*, ie because they are greatly inferior. 现代的绘画是不能与已往大师的作品相提并论的(因为这些绘画过于拙劣). ○ *The plan won't bear close inspection*, ie It will be found to be unsatisfactory when carefully examined. 那计划经不起仔细的推敲(若仔细推敲, 就会发现并不尽如人意). ○ *Her joke doesn't bear repeating*, ie because it is not funny or may offend. 她的笑话不宜说第二遍(因为没意思或可能得罪人). ○ *His sufferings don't bear thinking about*, ie because they are or were so terrible. 他受的苦难简直不堪回首(因苦不胜言). **6** [Tn, Tn·pr, Dn·n] **~ sth (against/towards sb)** keep (feelings, etc) in the mind (used esp as in the expressions shown 心怀(感情等)(尤用于以下示例)): *bear a grudge against sb/bear sb a grudge* 对某人怀恨在心 ○ *He bears no resentment towards them.* 他对他们并无怨恨. ○ *She bore him no ill will.* 她对他毫无恶意. **7** [Tn, Tn·pr] **~ oneself well, etc** move, behave or conduct oneself in a specified way 举止; 表现; 持身: *He bears himself* (ie stands, walks, etc) *like a soldier.* 他的一

B

举一动(站立、行走等)有如军人. ○ *He bore himself with dignity at a difficult time.* 他在困难的时候仍保持原有的尊严. **8** [Tn, Dn·n] (*fml* 文) give birth to (sb) 生育: *bear a child* 生孩子 ○ *She has borne him six sons.* 她给他生了六个儿子. ⇨Usage 见所附用法. **9** [Tn] produce (sth); yield 生产(某事物); 出产: *trees bearing pink blossom* 开粉红色花朵的树木 ○ *land which bears no crops* 不毛之地 ○ (*fig* 比喻) *His efforts bore no result*, ie were unsuccessful. 他的努力毫无结果(不成功). **10** [Ipr] **~ (to the) north, left, etc** go or turn in the specified direction 向某方向行进或转弯: *The road bears (to the) west.* 这条道路通往西部. ○ *When you get to the fork in the road, bear (to the) right.* 你走到这条路的分岔口时, 就向右拐. **11** (idm 习语) **bear 'arms** (*arch* 古) serve as a soldier; fight 从军; 战斗. **bear the brunt of sth** receive the main force, shock or impact of sth 承受某事物的主要压力或正面的冲撞: *bear the full brunt of the attack* 面对攻击首当其冲 ○ *His secretary has to bear the brunt of his temper.* 他的秘书成了他的出气筒. **bear/stand comparison with sb/sth** ⇨ COMPARISON. **bear 'fruit** have (usu the desired) results 产生(通常为所期望的)结果: *His efforts finally bore fruit and permission was granted.* 他的努力终于有了结果, 请求得到了批准. **bear hard, heavily, severely, etc on sb** be a burden on sb; oppress sb 成为某人的沉重负担; 压迫某人: *Taxation bears heavily on us all.* 交税成了我们大家的沉重负担. **bear/have some/no reference to sth** ⇨ REFERENCE. **bear in mind (that)...** remember that... 记住...: *Stay in the foyer if you wish, but bear in mind (that) the performance begins in two minutes.* 要是你愿意, 就在休息室里待一会儿吧, 可是别忘了, 还有两分钟就要开演了. **bear/keep sb/sth in mind** ⇨ mind[1]. **bear witness (to sth)** provide evidence of the truth (of sth); speak in support (of sth) 证明(某事物); (为某事物)作证: *He/His evidence bore witness to my testimony.* 他[他的证据]可以印证我的证词. ○ (*fig* 比喻) *The new housing bears witness to the energy of the Council.* 这些新建的住宅是议会具有能力的证明. **be borne 'in on sb** come to be realized by sb 使某人认清: *The terrible truth was borne in on him*, ie He became fully aware of it. 他完全了解到了这可怕的真相. ○ *It was gradually borne in on us that defeat was inevitable.* 我们渐渐地认识到失败是不可避免的. **bring pressure to bear on sb** ⇨ PRESSURE. **bring sth to bear (on sb/sth)** apply sth (to sb/sth) 把某事物应用于(某人[某事物]): *We must bring all our energies to bear upon the task.* 我们应把全副精力用于此项工作上. ○ *Pressure was brought to bear on us to finish the work on time.* 我们受到压力, 必须如期完成这项工作. **grin and bear it** ⇨ GRIN. **12** (phr v) **bear sth/sb away/off** (*dated or fml* 旧或文) seize and carry away 捉走; 夺走; 拿走: *They bore off several captives.* 他们抓走了几个俘虏. ○ *He bore away* (ie won) *the first prize.* 他夺得(赢得)了头奖. **bear down sb/sth** overcome or defeat sb/sth 战胜或击败某人[某事物]: *bear down the enemy, all resistance* 击垮敌人; 镇压一切反抗. **bear 'down on sb/sth** move quickly and threateningly towards sb/sth 向某人[某事物]迅速逼近: *The angry farmer was bearing down on us.* 那个怒气冲冲的农民迅速地向我们逼来. **'bear on sth** relate to sth; affect sth 与某事物有关; 对某事物有影响: *These are matters that bear on the welfare of the community.* 这些都是涉及社会福利的问题. **bear sb/sth 'out** support (sb); confirm (sth) 为(某人)作证; 证实(某事物): *The other witnesses will bear me out/bear out what I say.* 其他证人会为我[为我所说的话]作证. **bear 'up (against/under sth)** be strong enough not to despair; cope; manage 不气馁; 对付; 处理: *He's bearing up well against all his misfortunes.* 他以坚强的意志对待他所有的不幸. **'bear with sb/sth** tolerate sb/sth patiently 耐心地忍受某人[某事物]: *We must bear with her* (ie treat her with sympathy) *during this difficult period.* 在此困难时期, 我们对她一定要忍让(对待她要有同情心). ○ *If you will bear with me* (ie listen patiently to me) *a little longer...* 请耐心容我把话说完....

NOTE ON USAGE 用法: The verb **bear** (past participle **borne**) in the sense of 'give birth to' is formal ☆ **bear**(过去分词为 **borne**)这一动词作'生育'解时较文雅: *bear a child* 生孩子 ○ *She's borne him six children.* 她给他生育了六个孩子. Less formal is 较通俗的说法是: *She's had six children.* 她生了六个孩子. The past participle **borne** is not used in the passive in this sense. 过去分词 **borne** 作'生育'解时不用被动语态. There is another past participle **born,** which is used only in the passive voice 另有一过去分词 **born,** 仅用于被动语态: *She was born in 1954.* 她生于1954年. ○ *Ten children are born in this hospital every day.* 这所医院每天有十个孩子出生. ○ *He was born to/of wealthy parents.* 他出生于有钱人家.

bear·able /ˈbeərəbl; ˋbɛrəbl̩/ *adj* that can be endured; tolerable 可忍受的; 经得住的: *The climate is bearable.* 这种气候尚可忍受.

beard[1] /bɪəd; bɪrd/ *n* (**a**) [U, C] hair growing on the chin and the lower cheeks of a man's face (下巴和面颊下部的)胡须; 络腮胡子: *a week's growth of beard* 一星期未刮的胡子 ○ *Who's that man with the beard?* 那个留着大胡子的人是谁? ○ *He has (grown) a beard.* 他留着大胡子. ⇨illus at HEAD 见 HEAD 之插图. Cf 参看 MOUSTACHE1, WHISKER 1. (**b**) [C] similar hairy growth on an animal or plant (动物的)颔毛; (植物的)芒: *a goat's beard* 山羊的胡子.

▷ **bear·ded** *adj* having a beard 有胡须的; 有颔毛的; 有芒刺的.

beard·less *adj* having no beard 无胡须的; 无颔毛的; 无芒刺的: *a beardless youth*, ie an immature young man 嘴下没毛的青年(少不更事的年轻人).

beard[2] /bɪəd; bɪrd/ *v* **1** [Tn] defy (sb/sth) openly; oppose bravely 公然反对(某人[某事物]); 勇敢地对抗. **2** (idm 习语) **beard the lion in his 'den** visit sb important in order to challenge him, obtain a favour, etc 入狮穴捋狮须(走访某要人以向其提出质询、获得某种好处等).

bearer /ˈbeərə(r); ˋbɛrɚ/ *n* **1** person who brings a letter or message 送信人; 捎信人: *I'm the bearer of good news.* 我带来了好消息. **2** (**a**) person employed to carry things, eg equipment on an expedition; porter 脚夫; 搬运工人: *A team of African bearers came with us on safari.* 有一队非洲脚夫和我们一起进行狩猎旅行. (**b**) person who helps to carry a coffin, stretcher, etc (棺材、担架等的)抬送者. **3** person who has a cheque for payment on demand (即期支票的)持票人: *This cheque is payable to the bearer*, ie to the person who presents it at a bank. 本支票可兑付给持票人.

bear·ing /ˈbeərɪŋ; ˋbɛrɪŋ/ *n* **1** [sing] (**a**) way of standing, walking, etc; deportment (站立、步行等的)姿态: *a man of soldierly bearing* 有军人仪态的人. (**b**) behaviour 行为; 举止: *her dignified bearing throughout the trial* 在整个审讯过程中, 她那端庄的举止. **2** [U] **~ on sth** relevance to sth 与某事物的关系: *What he said had not much bearing on the problem.* 他说的话跟这个问题没有多大关系. **3 bearings** [pl] aspects 方面: *We must consider the question in all its bearings.* 我们应该考虑到问题的各个方面. **4** [C] direction in degrees as measured from a known position (从一已知位置测出的)方位(度数): *take a (compass) bearing on the lighthouse* (用罗盘)测定灯塔的方位. **5** [C] device reducing friction in part of a machine where another part turns 轴承: *ball-'bearings* 滚珠轴承. **6** [C] heraldic emblem 纹章. **7** (idm 习语) **get/take one's 'bearings** find out where one is by recognizing landmarks, etc (藉可辨认的陆标等)确定自己的位置. **lose one's bearings** ⇨ LOSE. **past (all) 'bearing** no longer to be tolerated 忍无可忍.

bear·ish ⇨ BEAR[1].

beast /biːst; bist/ *n* **1** (*dated or fml* 旧或文) animal, esp a large four-footed one 动物(尤指大的、有四条腿的): *all the beasts of the earth* 地球上的一切走兽 ○ *The lion is called the king of beasts.* 狮子被称为百兽之王. **2** (**a**) brutal or disgusting person 野蛮的人; 令人生厌的人: *When he's drunk he's a beast.* 他喝醉时很野蛮. ○ *Drink brings out the beast in him*, ie emphasizes the brutal part of his nature. 他酒后兽性大发. (**b**) (*infml* 口) (used playfully or reproachfully 用以打趣或斥责) unpleasant person 令人不快的人: *Stop tickling me, you beast!* 别胳肢我了, 你这讨厌鬼! ○ *Don't be such a beast!* 别那么讨人嫌!

▷ **beastly** *adj* **1** like a beast; brutal 野兽般的; 凶残的.

2 (*infml* 口 *esp Brit*) unpleasant; nasty 使人不愉快的; 恶劣的: *What beastly weather!* 多么恶劣的天气! ○ *That's absolutely beastly of him.* 那他可太可恶了. — *adv* (*infml* 口 *esp Brit*) very; extremely 很; 极其: *It's beastly cold outside!* 外边冷极了!

□ **beast of 'burden** animal, such as a donkey, used for carrying heavy loads on its back 力畜, 役畜, 牲口(如驴).

beat[1] /bi:t; bit/ *v* (*pt* **beat**, *pp* **beaten** /'bi:tn; 'bitn/) **1** [Ipr, Tn, Tn·pr] hit (sb/sth) repeatedly, esp with a stick (接连地)打(某人[某物])(尤指棒打): *Somebody was beating at the door.* 有人不停地敲门. ○ *Who's beating the drum?* 谁在敲鼓? ○ *She was beating the carpet/beating the dust out of the carpet*, ie removing dust from the carpet by beating it. 她正在敲打地毯[敲打地毯上的灰尘](以敲打的方式除尘). **2** [Cn·a] reduce (sb) to a specified state by hitting repeatedly 把(某人)直打成某种状况: *They beat the prisoner unconscious.* 他们把那囚犯打得不省人事. ⇨Usage at HIT[1] 用法见 HIT[1]. **3** [Tn, Tn·pr, Tn·p, Cn·a] change the shape of (esp metal) by blows; hammer 锤打使(尤指金属)变形; 用锤敲打: *beaten silver* 银箔 ○ *The gold was beaten (out) into fine strips.* 金子被锤成了细条形. ○ *beat metal flat* 把金属锤平. **4** [I, Tn] strike (bushes, undergrowth, etc) to raise game for shooting 击打(灌木、下层林木等)使猎物暴露出来以便射杀之. **5** [Tn, Tn·pr] make (a path, etc) by pressing branches down and walking over them 披荆斩棘开辟(路等); 踏出(一条路): *a well-beaten path*, ie one worn hard by much use 久经践踏的路 ○ *The hunters beat a path through the undergrowth.* 猎人们开了一条路穿过小树丛. **6** [Ipr] ~ **against/on sth/sb** (of the rain, sun, wind, etc) strike sth/sb (指雨、日、风等)袭及某物[某人]: *Hailstones beat against the window.* 冰雹落在窗户上. ○ *The waves were beating on the shore.* 波涛拍岸. **7** [Tn, Tn·pr, Tn·p] ~ **sth (up)** mix sth vigorously using a fork, whisk, etc (用叉子、打蛋器等)用力搅拌某物: *beat the eggs (up) (to a frothy consistency)* 打蛋(至起泡的浓度) ○ *beat the flour and milk together* 把面粉和牛奶搅拌一起. **8** (**a**) [I] (of the heart) expand and contract rhythmically (指心脏)有节奏地舒张与收缩, 跳动: *He's alive — his heart is still beating.* 他还活着——心脏还在跳. (**b**) [I] give a rhythmical sound; pulsate 发出有节奏的响声; 脉动: *We heard the drums beating.* 我们听到了敲鼓的声音. (**c**) [I, Tn] (cause sth to) move up and down repeatedly; flap (使某物)不停地上下动; 拍动: *The birds wings were beating frantically.* 那些鸟儿的翅膀在使劲地拍打着. ○ *It was beating its wings.* 它鼓动着翅膀. **9** (**a**) [Tn, Tn·pr] ~ **sb (at sth)** defeat sb; win against sb; do better than sb 打败某人; 打赢某人; 胜过某人: *Our team was easily beaten.* 我队被对方轻易打败了. ○ *He beat me (at chess, squash, etc).* 他(下棋、打壁球等)赢了我. (**b**) [Tn] be better than (sth); defeat 胜于(某事物); 击败: *Nothing beats home cooking.* 什么也不如家里做的好吃. ○ *You can't beat Italian clothes.* 意大利的服装无与伦比. ○ *The Government's main aim is to beat inflation.* 政府的主要目标是减低通货膨胀. ○ *beat the speed record*, ie go faster than anyone before 打破速度纪录. (**c**) [Tn] (*infml* 口) be too difficult for (sb); puzzle 难倒(某人); 使困惑: *a problem that beats even the experts* 连行家也感到棘手的问题 ○ *It beats me* (ie I don't know) *how/why he did it.* 他如何[为何]做的, 这问题算是把我难住了(我不知道). **10** (idm 习语) ˌ**beat about the 'bush** talk about sth without coming to the main point 拐弯抹角地说; 东拉西扯: *Stop beating about the bush and tell us who won.* 不要东拉西扯了, 告诉我们是谁赢了吧. **beat sb at his own game** defeat or do better than sb in an activity which he has chosen or in which he thinks that he is strong 在某人自选的或拿手的方面击败或胜过某人. **beat one's breast** show that one knows one has done wrong and is sorry, often with an excessive display of grief, remorse, etc 捶胸顿足(表示自己知错而痛惜, 常伴有极度的伤心、悔恨等). **beat the clock** finish a task, race, etc before a particular time 在特定的时间以前结束工作、竞赛等. **beat/knock the daylights out of sb** ⇨ DAYLIGHTS. **beat the drum (for sb/sth)** speak enthusiastically in support of sb/sth (为某人[某事物])敲边鼓. **beat/knock hell out of sb/sth** ⇨ HELL. **beat sb 'hollow** beat sb decisively 给某人以致命打击: *Our team was beaten hollow.* 我们这个队被打得落花流水. '**beat it** (*sl* 俚) go away 走开: *This is private land, so beat it!* 这里是私人地产, 请走开! **beat a (hasty) re'treat** go away or back hurriedly 匆匆走开; 仓皇撤退: *The poacher beat a hasty retreat when he saw the police coming.* 偷猎者见有警察来到立刻仓皇逃走. **beat, etc sense into sb** ⇨ SENSE. **beat the rap** (*US sl* 俚) escape without being punished 逃避惩罚; 逍遥法外. **beat 'time (to sth)** mark or follow the rhythm (of music) by waving a stick or by tapping one's foot, etc (按照音乐节奏, 用挥棍或踏脚等方式)打拍子: *He beat time (to the music) with his fingers.* 他用手指(随着这支乐曲)打拍子. ˌ**can you 'beat it** (expressing surprise or shocked amusement 表示惊奇或喜出望外). **if you can't beat them, join them** (*catchphrase* 警语) if a rival group, firm, etc continues to be more successful than one's own, it is better to go over to their side and get any advantages one can by doing so 若竞争对手(团体、商号等)占了上风, 那就最好站到他们一边亦从中获益. ˌ**off the** ˌ**beaten 'track** in an isolated place where people rarely go 在人迹罕至之处: *They live miles off the beaten track.* 他们住的地方远离人烟. **a rod/stick to beat sb with** fact, argument, event, etc that is used in order to blame or punish sb 用以怪罪或惩罚某人的事实、理由、事情等. **11** (phr v) **beat sth down** (**a**) force an entry by hitting (a door, etc) repeatedly 破(门等)而入: *The thieves had beaten the door down.* 那小偷破门而入. (**b**) flatten sth 使某物变平; 使某物倒下: *The wheat had been beaten down by the rain.* 麦子被雨打倒了. **beat down (on sb/sth)** (of the sun) shine with great heat (指太阳)曝晒: *The sun beat down (on the desert sand).* 太阳曝晒着(沙漠). **beat sb/sth down (to sth)** persuade (the seller) to reduce (the price of sth) 劝说(卖方)降低(某物价格): *He wanted £800 for the car but I beat him down (to £600).* 他那辆汽车要价 800 英镑, 而我杀低了价(到 600 英镑). ○ *I beat down the price (to £600).* 我把价格压低(到 600 英镑)了.

beat sb into/to sth bring sb to a specified state by hitting repeatedly 把某人[某物]直打成某种状况: *The children were beaten into submission.* 孩子们被打得服服帖帖. ○ *The dog was beaten to death.* 那狗被打得一命呜呼. **beat sb/sth off** drive sb/sth away by fighting 以战斗驱除某人[某事物]: *The attacker/attack was beaten off.* 进攻者[进攻]被打退了. **beat sth out** (**a**) produce (a rhythm, etc) by drumming 敲击出(节奏等): *He beat out a tune on a tin can.* 他在洋铁罐上敲奏出一支曲子来. (**b**) extinguish (a fire) by beating 扑灭(火): *We beat the flames out.* 我们把火扑灭了. (**c**) remove sth by striking with a hammer, etc 以锤打等方法除去: *beat out the dent in the car's wing* 锤平汽车挡泥板上的凹痕. **beat sb to...** arrive at (a place) before sb 先于某人到达(某处): *I'll beat you to the top of the hill*, ie I'll race you and get there first. 我能比你先到山顶. **beat sb to it** achieve, reach or take sth before sb else 抢先一步; 捷足先登: *Scott aimed to get to the South Pole first, but Amundsen beat him to it.* 斯科特原打算第一个到达南极, 但是阿蒙森却已捷足先登. ○ *I was about to take the last cake, but he beat me to it.* 我正要去拿那最后一块蛋糕, 而他却抢先拿走了. **beat sb up** hit, kick or thrash sb severely 狠打、踢或揍某人: *He was badly beaten up by a gang of thugs.* 他被一帮暴徒打得死去活来.

▷ **beat** *adj* [pred 作表语] tired out; exhausted 筋疲力尽; 疲惫不堪: *I'm (dead) beat.* 我已筋疲力尽.

beat·ing *n* **1** hitting repeatedly with a stick, etc, usu as punishment (用棍棒等)接连打(通常作为惩罚): *give sb/get a good beating* 给某人[挨了]一顿痛打. **2** (*infml* 口) defeat 失败: *Our team got a sound beating.* 我们队遭到惨败. **3** (idm 习语) **take a lot of/some 'beating** be difficult to surpass 难以超越: *She will take some beating*, ie It will be difficult to do better than her. 超越她是不易的(要做得比她好绝非易事). ○ *His record will take a lot of beating.* 他创的纪录很难打破.

□ ˌ**beat-'up** *adj* (*infml* 口 *esp US*) worn out; battered 穿破的; 用坏的: *a* ˌ*beat-up old 'car* 破旧的汽车.

beat[2] /bi:t; bit/ *n* **1** stroke (eg on a drum) or regular sequence of strokes; sound of this 敲击(声)(如击鼓); 有规律的一连串敲打(声): *We heard the beat of a drum.* 我们听见敲鼓的声音. **2** emphasis repeated regularly, marking rhythm in music or poetry; strongly marked rhythm of pop or rock music (音乐或诗歌中形成节奏的)强音拍; (流行音乐或摇滚音乐的)强节奏: *The song has a good beat.* 这歌曲节奏很强. **3** route along which sb goes regularly; area allocated to a policeman, watchman, etc (某人日常行经的)路线; (警察、看守人等执行任务的)区域: *a policeman out on the/his beat* 外出到辖区执行巡逻任务的警察. **4** (idm 习语) **out of/off one's 'beat** (*infml* 口) different from what one usually does; unfamiliar 非自己本行的; 非自己所擅长的. **pound the beat** ⇨ POUND³.

B

beater /ˈbiːtə(r); ˋbitɚ/ *n* **1** (often in compounds 常用以构成复合词) utensil for beating things 打东西用的器具: *a 'carpet-beater* ○ *an 'egg-beater.* **2** person employed to drive birds and animals out of the undergrowth towards huntsmen with guns 助猎者(受雇将鸟兽从矮树丛中驱赶至猎人处的人).

be·atif·ic /bɪəˈtɪfɪk; ˌbiəˋtɪfɪk/ *adj* (*fml* 文) showing or giving great joy and serenity; blissful 快乐而安详的; 赐福的; 有福的: *a beatific smile* 慈祥的笑容. ▷ **be·atif·ic·ally** /-klɪ; -klɪ/ *adv*.

be·atify /bɪˈætɪfaɪ; bɪˋætəˌfaɪ/ *v* (*pt, pp* **-fied**) [Tn] (of the Pope) honour (a dead person) by stating officially that he or she is in heaven (指教皇)为(死者)行宣福礼(宣布死者已升天).
▷ **be·ati·fica·tion** /bɪˌætɪfɪˈkeɪʃn; bɪˌætəfəˋkeʃən/ *n* (**a**) [C] such an official statement 宣福礼. (**b**) [U] honouring or being honoured in this way 宣福或被宣福.

be·ati·tude /bɪˈætɪtjuːd; *US* -tuːd; bɪˋætəˌtud/ *n* **1** [U] (*fml* 文) great happiness; blessedness 至福; 天福. **2 the Beatitudes** [pl] (in the Bible) series of eight statements by Christ on blessedness, each beginning 'Blessed are...' (《圣经》中)(耶稣所论的)八福(每论的开始都是'这样的人有福了...').

beat·nik /ˈbiːtnɪk; ˋbitnɪk/ *n* (*dated* 旧) (in the 1950's and early 1960's) person behaving and dressing unconventionally as a defiant protest against Western morality and as a means of self-expression '垮掉的一代'的成员(二十世纪五十年代及六十年代初期, 以怪僻的行为和奇特的装束表示蔑视西方道德并藉以表现自我的人). Cf 参看 HIPPIE.

beau /bəʊ; bo/ *n* (*pl* **~x** /bəʊz; boz/) **1** (*US*) boy-friend; lover 男友; 情郎. **2** (*dated* 旧) dandy; fop 花花公子; 纨袴子弟.
□ **the beau monde** /ˌbəʊ ˈmɔːnd; boˋmɑnd/ fashionable society 上流社会; 时髦的社交界.

Beau·fort scale /ˌbəʊfət ˈskeɪl; ˌbofɚt ˋskel/ scale for measuring wind speed ranging originally from 0 (calm) to 12 (hurricane) 蒲福风级(最初将风速划分为由0-12即由无风到飓风的等级): *registering 8 on the Beaufort scale* 风力为8级.

Beau·jo·lais /ˈbəʊʒəleɪ; *US* ˌbəʊʒəˈleɪ; ˌboʒəˋle/ *n* (*pl* unchanged 复数不变) [C, U] (type of) light, usu red, wine from the Beaujolais district of France 博若莱酒(法国博若莱地区产的淡葡萄酒, 通常为红色).

beaut /bjuːt; bjut/ *n* (*US and Austral sl* 美, 澳, 俚) beautiful person or thing 美人; 美好的东西.
▷ **beaut** *adj, interj* (*sl esp Austral* 俚, 尤用于澳大利亚) excellent; fine 了不起的; 绝妙的.

beau·te·ous /ˈbjuːtɪəs; ˋbjutɪəs/ *adj* (*arch* 古) beautiful 美丽的; 美好的.

beau·ti·cian /bjuːˈtɪʃn; bjuˋtɪʃən/ *n* person whose job is to give beautifying treatments to the face or body 美容师.

beau·ti·ful /ˈbjuːtɪfl; ˋbjutəfəl/ *adj* **1** having beauty; giving pleasure to the senses or the mind 美丽的; 美观的; 美好的: *a beautiful face, baby, flower, view, voice, poem, smell, morning* 美妙的脸庞、婴儿、花朵、景物、声音、诗歌、气味、早晨 ○ *beautiful weather, music, chocolate* 极好的天气、音乐、巧克力. **2** very satisfactory 极其满意的: *The organization was beautiful.* 组织工作极佳. ○ *What beautiful timing!* 时间正合适!
▷ **beau·ti·fully** /-flɪ; -fəlɪ/ *adv* **1** in a lovely manner 美妙地: *She sings beautifully.* 她唱得美极了. **2** most satisfactorily 极其满意地: *That will do beautifully.* 那样好极了. ○ *The car is running beautifully.* 这辆汽车性能好极了.

NOTE ON USAGE 用法: When describing people, **beautiful** and **pretty** are generally used of women and children, and **handsome** of men. 形容人的时候, **beautiful** 和 **pretty** 一般用于妇女儿童, 而 **handsome** 则用于男子. They all relate to the pleasing appearance of the face. 这些词都可指容貌悦目. **Beautiful** is a serious and approving description, suggesting elegance and perfection. ☆ **beautiful** 是个有分量的、表示赞许的形容词, 含有高雅和完美的意思. **Pretty** may suggest a delicate feminine appearance and can be used disapprovingly of men. ☆ **pretty** 可指娇媚温柔的容貌, 但也可用于男子, 含贬义. **Handsome** may be applied to women and suggest dignity and maturity. ☆ **handsome** 可用于指妇女, 含有端庄和成熟的意思. **Good-looking** and **attractive** are used of both men and women. ☆ **good-looking** 和 **attractive** 用于男女均可. **Fair** (meaning 'beautiful') is archaic. ☆ **fair**(作beautiful解的词义)已不通用. All these adjectives except **attractive** can be used of animals and all except **good-looking** with inanimate and abstract nouns 所有这些形容词, 除 **attractive** 外, 均可用于动物, 而除 **good-looking** 外, 均可与指无生命的和抽象的名词连用: *a beautiful/an attractive voice* 优美的[动人的]嗓子 ○ *a handsome/good-looking horse* 漂亮的[好看的]马 ○ *a beautiful/pretty village* 美丽的[漂亮的]村庄 ○ *a handsome/an attractive offer* 优厚的[吸引人的]条件.

beau·tify /ˈbjuːtɪfaɪ; ˋbjutəˌfaɪ/ *v* (*pt, pp* **-fied**) [Tn] make (sb/sth) beautiful; adorn 使(某人[某事物])变美; 美化; 装饰. Cf 参看 PRETTIFY. ▷ **beau·ti·fi·ca·tion** /ˌbjuːtɪfɪˈkeɪʃn; ˌbjutəfəˋkeʃən/ *n* [U].

beauty /ˈbjuːtɪ; ˋbjutɪ/ *n* **1** [U] combination of qualities that give pleasure to the senses (esp to the eye or ear) or to the mind 美: *the beauty of the sunset, of her singing, of poetry* 日落、她的歌喉、诗作之美 ○ *She was a woman of great beauty.* 她曾经是个大美人. ○ [attrib 作定语] *a beauty competition/contest*, ie one in which judges decide on the most beautiful competitor 选美会. **2** [C] (**a**) person or thing that is beautiful 美丽的人或事物: *She was a famous beauty in her youth.* 她年轻时是个有名的美人. ○ *That new car is an absolute beauty.* 那辆新车漂亮极了. (**b**) fine specimen; excellent example 极好的样品; 范例: *Look at these moths: here's a beauty.* 请看这些蛾子: 这是一个珍品. ○ *That last goal was a beauty.* 最后进去的那个球真漂亮. (**c**) pleasing or attractive feature 极具魅力或吸引力的特色: *The beauty of living in California is that the weather is so good.* 在加利福尼亚居住的好处就在于气候宜人. ○ *The machine needs very little attention — that's the beauty of it.* 那机器不用怎样看管——好就好在这里. **3** (idm 习语) **beauty is only skin 'deep** (*saying* 谚) outward appearance is less important than hidden or inner qualities 美貌只是一层皮(外表没有隐蔽的或内在的素质那么重要).
□ **'beauty queen** woman judged to be the most beautiful in a beauty contest (选美会上评选出的)最美的女子.
'beauty salon (also **'beauty parlour**) place where customers receive treatment (eg face-massage, hairdressing, manicuring) to increase their beauty 美容院.
'beauty sleep (*joc* 谑) sleep before midnight, light-heartedly regarded as important for a person's beauty 美容觉(午夜前的睡眠, 戏称关乎美容): *Good night, I must get my beauty sleep.* 再见吧, 我得去睡个美容觉.
'beauty spot 1 place famous for its beautiful scenery 风景点; 名胜. **2** mole or artificial spot on a woman's face, once thought to add to her beauty 美人斑(妇女面部天生的或人为的、曾被视为一种美的痣或斑).

beaux *pl* of BEAU.

bea·ver /ˈbiːvə(r); ˋbivɚ/ *n* **1** [C] fur-coated animal with strong teeth that lives both on land and in water and gnaws down trees to build dams 海狸. **2** [U] its brown fur 海狸的褐色皮毛: [attrib 作定语] *a beaver hat* 海狸皮帽子. **3** (idm 习语) **an eager beaver** ⇨ EAGER.
▷ **bea·ver** *v* (phr v) **beaver away (at sth)** (*infml* 口 *esp Brit*) work hard 勤奋工作: *I've been beavering away at this job for hours.* 我几小时一直在全力做这件事.

be·bop /ˈbiːbɒp; ˋbibɑp/ (also **bop**) *n* [U] type of jazz music with complex rhythms and harmonies 比博普(一

种具有复杂的节律与和声的爵士音乐).

be·calmed /bɪˈkɑːmd; bɪˈkɑmd/ *adj* [usu pred 通常作表语] (of a sailing-ship) unable to move because there is no wind (指帆船)(因无风)不能航行.

be·came *pt* of BECOME.

be·cause /bɪˈkɒz; *US also* -kɔːz; bɪˈkɔz/ *conj* for the reason that 因为: *I did it because he told me to.* 我做这事是因为他叫我做的. ○ *Just because I don't complain, people think I'm satisfied.* 因为我没发牢骚, 人们就以为我心满意足了.

□ **beˈcause of** *prep* by reason of (sb/sth); on account of 因为(某人[某事物]); 由于: *They are here because of us.* 他们是为了我们而来到这里的. ○ *He walked slowly because of his bad leg.* 他走得慢是因为腿有毛病. ○ *Because of his wife('s) being there, I said nothing about it.* 因为他妻子在场, 我对此事一字未提.

beck[1] /bek; bɛk/ *n* (*Brit dialect* 方) mountain stream; brook 山涧; 溪流.

beck[2] /bek; bɛk/ *n* (idm 习语) **at one's/sb's ˌbeck and ˈcall** always ready to obey one's/sb's orders immediately 听命于人; 唯某人之命是从: *The king has always had servants at his beck and call.* 国王有奴仆们随时听他使唤. ○ *I'm not at your beck and call, you know.* 你要知道, 我是不会听你指使的.

beckon /ˈbekən; ˈbɛkən/ *v* **1** [I, Ipr, Tn, Dn·t, Dpr·t] ~ **(to) sb (to do sth)** make a gesture to sb with the hand, arm or head, usu to make him come nearer or to follow (以手、臂或头部的动作)召唤某人(通常为使之走近或跟随自己): *She beckoned (to) me (to follow).* 她招手要我跟着她. ○ (*fig* 比喻) *City life beckons* (ie attracts) *many a country boy.* 都市生活吸引着许许多多的乡村子弟. **2** (phr v) **beckon sb in, on, over, etc** gesture to sb to move in a specified direction 示意某人按指定的方向行动: *The policeman beckoned us over.* 警察打手势让我们通过. ○ *A girl standing at the mouth of the cave beckoned him in.* 站在洞口的一个姑娘摆手叫他进去. ○ *They beckoned me into the room.* 他们示意我进入房间.

be·come /bɪˈkʌm; bɪˈkʌm/ *v* (*pt* **became** /bɪˈkeɪm; bɪˈkem/, *pp* **become**) **1** [La, Ln] (**a**) come to be; grow to be 变为; 成为: *They soon became angry.* 他们过了一会就生气了. ○ *He has become accustomed to his new duties.* 他已经适应了新的职务. ○ *That child was to become a great leader.* 那孩子长大后必定成为伟大领袖. ○ *They became great friends.* 他们成了莫逆之交. ○ *She became a doctor.* 她成了医生. ○ *It has become a rule that we sing during our tea-break.* 我们在吃茶点的休息时间里唱歌已成惯例. (**b**) begin to be 开始成为: *It's becoming dangerous to go out alone at night.* 夜间独自外出已经越来越危险了. ○ *The noise of traffic is becoming a cause for concern.* 交通噪音已经开始引起人们的关注. ○ *Those boys are becoming a nuisance.* 那些男孩子越来越惹人讨厌了. ⇨Usage 见所附用法. **2** [Tn] (*fml* 文) (**a**) be suitable for (sb); suit 适于(某人); 适合: *Her new hat certainly becomes her.* 她的新帽子十分适合她戴. (**b**) be fitting or appropriate for (sb); befit 适合于(某人身分); 适宜: *Such language* (eg vulgar or insulting words) *does not become a lady like you.* 这样的语言(如粗俗或无礼的言辞)与你这样一位女士的身分很不相称. ○ *It ill becomes you to complain.* 发牢骚可与你的身分不相称. **3** (idm 习语) **what becomes of sb/sth** what is happening to sb/sth 某人[某事物]情况如何: *What will become of my child if I die?* 假如我死了, 我的孩子会怎样呢? ○ *I wonder what became of the people who lived next door?* 不知道以前住在隔壁的人怎么样了? ○ *What became of the dreams of our youth?* ie What we hoped for did not actually happen. 我们年轻时的理想今何在?

▷ **be·com·ing** *adj* (*fml* 文) **1** (*approv* 褒) (of dress, etc) well suited to the wearer (指衣服等)合身的, 适于穿戴者的: *a becoming hat, hair-style, etc* 合适的帽子、发型等 ○ *Your outfit is most becoming.* 你的服装太合适了. **2** suitable; appropriate; fitting 适合的; 适当的; 适宜的: *He behaved with a becoming modesty/with a modesty becoming his junior position.* 他举止间有一种颇为适度的谦恭[有一种适合于其下级地位的谦恭]. **be·com·ingly** *adv*.

NOTE ON USAGE 用法: When talking about a change in the state, appearance, etc of a person or thing, we often use **become, get, turn** and **go** followed by an adjective. 谈到人或物的状态、外貌等的变化时, 常用 **become**、**get**、**turn**、**go**, 后接形容词. In general, **become** and **turn** are more formal than **get** and **go.** 总的来说, **become** 和 **turn** 比 **get** 和 **go** 更文雅. **1** When referring to temporary changes in a person's emotional or physical state or to permanent natural changes, we use **become** or **get** (less formal) 指一个人的暂时性的身心变化或永久性的自然变化, 可用 **become** 或 **get** (后者较通俗): *become/get angry, famous, fat, ill, old, etc* 生气、成名、发胖、得病、见老等. **2 Become** and **get** are also used of changes in the weather and of social developments ☆ **become** 和 **get** 还都可用于指天气的变化和社会的趋势: *It's becoming/getting cold, dark, cloudy, etc.* 天渐渐冷了、黑了、多云了等. ○ *Divorce is becoming/getting more common.* 离婚现象越来越常见了. **3** When indicating a worsening of someone's physical or mental powers, we use **go** 指某人肉体上或精神上由强转弱时, 用 **go** 字: *go bald, deaf, insane, etc* 发秃、聋、疯等. It is used similarly of things 这个字还可用于指事物由强转弱: *The meat's gone off/bad.* 肉变味了[坏了]. ○ *The radio's gone wrong.* 收音机出毛病了. **4 Go** and **turn** are used when people or things change colour ☆ **go** 和 **turn** 可用于指人或事物的颜色变化: *She went/turned blue with cold.* 她冻得脸色发[变]青了. ○ *The rotten meat went/turned green.* 这块腐烂的肉发[变]绿了.

bec·querel /ˈbekərel; bɛkˈrɛl/ *n* (*physics* 物) SI unit of radioactivity 贝克勒尔(放射性强度的标准国际单位).

bed[1] /bed; bɛd/ *n* **1** (**a**) [C, U] thing to sleep or rest on, esp a piece of furniture with a mattress and coverings 床: *go to bed* 去睡; 就寝 ○ *be in bed* 卧床; 睡觉 ○ *get out of/into bed* 起[上]床 ○ *sit on the bed* 坐在床上 ○ *a room with two single beds/a double bed* 有两张单人床[一张双人床]的房间 ○ *The tramp's bed was a park bench.* 公园里的长凳就是这个流浪汉的床. ○ *Can you give me a bed for the night?* 你能留我过夜吗? (**b**) [U] being in bed; use of a bed; sleep or rest 睡觉; 卧床休息: *I've put the children to bed.* 我安置孩子们去睡觉了. ○ *He has a mug of cocoa before bed.* 他临睡前喝一缸子可可. ○ *It's time for bed.* 该睡觉了. (**c**) [C] mattress 床垫: *a feather bed* 羽绒床垫 ○ *a spring bed* 弹簧床垫. (**d**) [U] (*fig infml* 比喻, 口) sexual intercourse 性交: *They think of nothing but bed!* 他们不想别的, 光想着行房! **2** [C] bottom of the sea, a river, a lake, etc (海、河、湖等的)底部: *explore the ocean bed* 探测海底. **3** layer of clay, rock, etc below the surface soil; stratum (地表下由黏土、岩石等构成的)分层; 地层: *a bed of clay, limestone, sand, etc* 一层黏土、石灰石、沙子等. **4** [C] (**a**) flat base on which sth rests; foundation 基座; 基础: *The machine rests on a bed of concrete.* 机器安装在混凝土基座上. (**b**) layer of rock, stone, etc as a foundation for a road or railway (公路或铁路的)路基. **5** garden plot; piece of ground for growing flowers, vegetables, etc 园圃里的小块种植地; 种植花草、菜蔬等的地块: *a ˈseed-bed* 苗床 ○ *ˈflower-beds* 花坛 ○ *a bed of herbs* 一片药草地. **6** (idm 习语) **as one ˌmakes one's bed, so one must ˈlie on it** (*saying* 谚) one must accept the consequences of one's own actions 自作自受; 自食其果. **ˌbed and ˈboard** overnight accommodation and meals (过夜的)膳宿. **ˌbed and ˈbreakfast** (*abbrs* 缩写 **B and B, b and b**) sleeping accommodation and a meal the next morning, in hotels, etc (旅馆之类的)夜宿兼包次日早餐: *Bed and breakfast costs £15 a night.* 留宿一夜兼包次日早餐费用为15英镑. **a bed of ˈroses** pleasant carefree living 快乐人生; 优哉游哉的生活: *Life isn't a bed of roses.* 人生并非事事称心如意. **die in one's bed** ⇨ DIE[2]. **early to bed and early to rise** ⇨ EARLY. **go to bed with sb** (*infml* 口) have sexual intercourse with sb 与某人性交. **have got out of bed on the wrong side** be bad-tempered for the whole day 整天情绪不好. **make the ˈbed** arrange the sheets, blankets, etc so that the bed is ready for somebody to sleep in 铺床. **take to one's ˈbed** go to one's bed because of illness and stay there 卧病在床. **wet the/one's bed** ⇨ WET *v*.

□ **ˈbedbug** *n* wingless blood-sucking insect that lives in beds, etc 臭虫.

ˈbedclothes *n* [pl] sheets, blankets, pillows, etc 床上用

品(床单、毯子、枕头等).

ˈ**bedfellow** *n* **(a)** person with whom one shares a bed 同床者. **(b)** (*fig* 比喻) associate; companion 同事; 伙伴: *The fortunes of war create strange bedfellows*, ie unexpected alliances. 战乱使人萍水相逢(意料之外的结合).

ˈ**bed-linen** *n* [U] sheets and pillowcases 床单及枕头套.

ˈ**bedpan** *n* container for use as a lavatory by a person who is ill and in bed (卧床病人用的)便盆.

ˈ**bedpost** *n* each of the upright supports at the corners of a bedstead (esp the old-fashioned type) (尤指旧式床的)床柱.

ˈ**bedridden** *adj* confined to bed, esp permanently, because of illness or weakness (因患病或体弱)卧床不起的(尤指长期的).

ˈ**bedrock** *n* [U] **(a)** solid rock beneath loose soil, sand, etc 松土、沙子等下面的坚固的岩石: *reach/get down to bedrock* 深及基岩. **(b)** (*fig* 比喻) basic facts or principles 基本的事实或原则: *the bedrock of one's beliefs* 基本信念.

ˈ**bedroll** *n* (*esp US and NZ* 尤用于美国及新西兰) portable bedding that can be rolled into a bundle (as used by campers) 铺盖卷(如露营者所用的).

ˈ**bedroom** *n* room for sleeping in 卧室.

ˈ**bedside** *n* [usu sing 通常作单数] **1** area beside a bed 床边: [attrib 作定语] *a bedside table* 床头小几. **2** (idm 习语) ˌ**bedside** ˈ**manner** doctor's way of dealing with a patient 医疗服务态度: *Dr Green has a good bedside manner*, ie He is tactful and pleasant. 格林医生对病人的态度很好(他讲究方式方法, 使人愉快).

ˌ**bed-**ˈ**sitting-room** (also *infml* 口语亦作 ˌ**bed-**ˈ**sitter**, ˈ**bed-sit**) *n* (*Brit*) room used for both living and sleeping in 卧室兼起居室.

ˈ**bedsore** *n* sore on an invalid caused by lying in bed for a long time 褥疮.

ˈ**bedspread** *n* top cover spread over a bed 床罩.

ˈ**bedstead** *n* framework of wood or metal supporting the springs and mattress of a bed (木质或金属的)床架.

ˈ**bedtime** *n* [U] time for going to bed 就寝时间: *His bedtime is eight o'clock.* 他的就寝时间是八点钟. ○ *It's long past your bedtime.* 你的就寝时间早就过了. ○ [attrib 作定语] *a bedtime story*, ie one read to a child at bedtime 睡前故事(给孩子临睡前讲的故事).

ˈ**bed-wetting** *n* [U] urinating in bed while asleep 尿床.

bed[2] /bed; bɛd/ *v* **(-dd-)** **1** [Tn, Tn·pr] **~ sth (in sth)** place or fix sth firmly; embed sth 使某物固定或安置稳固; 嵌入某物中: *The bricks are bedded in concrete.* 用混凝土砌砖. ○ *The bullet bedded itself in* (ie went deeply into) *the wall.* 子弹嵌入(射入)墙中. **2** [Tn, Tn·pr] plant (sth) 种植(某物): *Bed the roots in the compost.* 把植物的根插入混合肥料中. **3** [Tn, Tn·pr] accommodate (sb); provide with a bed 向(某人)提供住宿; 供给床位: *The wounded were bedded in the farmhouse.* 把伤员安置在农家住宿. **4** [Tn] (*infml* 口) have casual sexual intercourse with (sb) 随便地与(某人)发生性关系: *He's bedded more girls than he can remember.* 他和多少姑娘上过床, 多得连他自己也记不清了. **5** (phr v) **bed down** settle for the night 安排过夜: *The soldiers bedded down in a barn.* 士兵们在谷仓里打铺过夜. **bed sth down** provide (an animal) with straw, etc to rest on for the night (铺稻草等)供(动物)夜间歇息. **bed sth out** transfer (young plants) from a greenhouse, etc to a garden bed 将(幼小的植物)从温室等中移栽到园地里: *bed out the seedlings, young cabbages, etc* 移栽幼苗、幼小的洋白菜等.

▷ **-bedded** (forming compound *adjs* 用以构成复合形容词) having the specified type or number of beds 有某种类型床的或床数的: *a single-/double-/twin-bedded room.*

bed·ding *n* [U] **1** bedclothes and mattresses 铺盖. **2** straw, etc for animals to sleep on (供动物歇息的)垫草. ˈ**bedding plant** one suitable for planting in a garden bed 适于在园地里种植的植物.

B Ed /ˌbiː ˈed; ˌbi ˋɛd/ *abbr* 缩写 = Bachelor of Education 教育学士: *have/be a B Ed* 有教育学士学位 [为教育学士] ○ *Dilip Patel B Ed* 迪利普·帕特尔教育学士.

be·daub /bɪˈdɔːb; bɪˋdɔb/ *v* [esp passive 尤用于被动语态: Tn, Tn·pr] **~ sth/sb (with sth)** smear sth/sb (with sth dirty, sticky, etc) (用脏物、黏物等)涂抹某物 [某人]: *faces bedaubed with grease-paint* 用油彩抹过的脸.

be·deck /bɪˈdek; bɪˋdɛk/ *v* [esp passive 尤用于被动语态: Tn, Tn·pr] **~ sth/sb (with sth)** adorn or decorate sth/sb 装饰, 打扮某物 [某人]: *streets bedecked with flags* 饰以旗帜的街道.

be·devil /bɪˈdevl; bɪˋdɛvl̩/ *v* **(-ll-;** *US* **-l-)** [Tn esp passive 尤用于被动语态] trouble (sb/sth) greatly; torment; afflict 使(某人 [某物])大为困扰, 烦恼; 折磨: *an industry bedevilled with strikes* 为罢工所困扰的企业 ○ *a family bedevilled by misfortune* 遭遇到不幸的家庭 ○ *Bad weather bedevilled our plans.* 因为天气恶劣我们的计划大受影响.

bed·lam /ˈbedləm; ˋbɛdləm/ *n* [U] scene of noisy confusion; uproar 乱哄哄的场面; 喧嚣: *What's happening in that room? It's (like) bedlam in there.* 那个房间里怎么了? 乱哄哄的.

bed·ouin (also **Bed·ouin**) /ˈbeduɪn; ˋbɛduɪn/ *n* (*pl* unchanged 复数不变) member of a nomadic Arab people living in tents in the desert 贝都因人(在沙漠中居住于帐篷里的阿拉伯游牧部落中的人): [attrib 作定语] *a bedouin tribe* 阿拉伯游牧部落.

be·drag·gled /bɪˈdrægld; bɪˋdrægl̩d/ (also **drag·gled**) *adj* made wet or dirty by rain, mud, etc; untidy (被雨、泥等)弄湿或弄脏的; 不整齐的: *bedraggled appearance, clothes, hair* 邋遢的样子、衣服、头发 ○ *The tents looked very bedraggled after the storm.* 暴风雨过后帐篷又湿又脏.

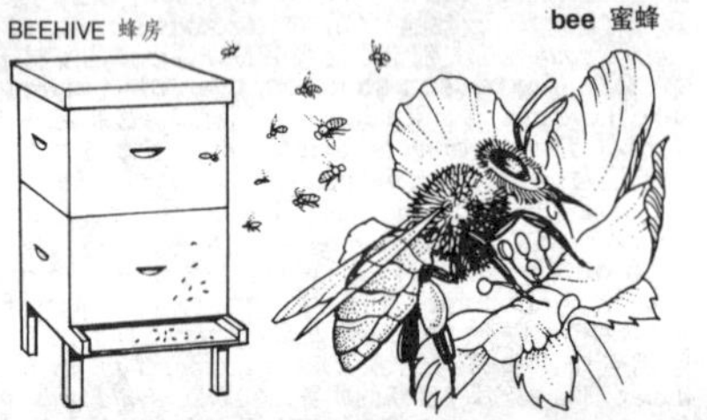
BEEHIVE 蜂房 bee 蜜蜂

bee[1] /biː; bi/ *n* **1** four-winged insect with a sting, that lives in a colony and collects nectar and pollen from flowers to produce wax and honey 蜜蜂. ⇨illus 见插图. **2** (idm 习语) **the** ˌ**bee's** ˈ**knees** (*infml* 口) thing that is outstandingly good 出类拔萃之物: *She thinks she's the bee's knees*, ie has a very high opinion of herself. 她自视甚高. **the birds and the bees** ⇨ BIRD. **busy as a bee** ⇨ BUSY. **have a** ˈ**bee in one's bonnet (about sth)** (*infml* 口) have a particular idea which occupies one's thoughts continually 头脑中总是不断地想着某一件事: *Our teacher has a bee in his bonnet about punctuation.* 我们的老师没完没了地琢磨着标点符号.

□ ˈ**beehive** *n* container made for bees to live in 蜂房.

ˈ**bee-keeper** person who keeps honey bees 养蜂人.

bee[2] /biː; bi/ *n* (*US*) meeting in a group, esp of neighbours and friends, for work or pleasure (尤指邻居和朋友间为工作或娱乐而举行的)聚会: *a* ˈ*sewing bee* 缝纫会 ○ *a* ˈ*spelling bee* 拼字比赛.

Beeb /biːb; bib/ *n* **the Beeb** [sing] (*infml* 口) the British Broadcasting Corporation (BBC) 英国广播公司.

beech /biːtʃ; bitʃ/ *n* **(a)** [C] (also ˈ**beech tree**) type of tree with smooth bark, shiny leaves and small triangular nuts 山毛榉. ⇨illus at App 1 见附录1之插图, page i. **(b)** [U] its wood 其木材.

beef /biːf; bif/ *n* **1 (a)** [U] flesh of an ox, a bull or a cow, used as meat (食用)牛肉: [attrib 作定语] *beef cattle*, ie those bred and reared for their meat 菜牛(饲养以供肉食的牛). **(b)** [C] (*pl* **beeves** /biːvz; bivz/) ox, etc bred for meat 菜牛. **2** [U] (*infml* 口) muscular strength 体力: *He's got plenty of beef.* 他力气很大. **3** [C] (*pl* **beefs**) (*sl* 俚) grumble; complaint 怨言; 牢骚.

▷ **beef** *v* (*sl* 俚) **1** [I, Ipr] **~ (about sth/sb)** grumble; complain 抱怨; 发牢骚: *What are you beefing about now?* 你在发什么牢骚? **2** (phr v) **beef sth up** (*infml* 口 *esp US*) add force or weight to sth 加强; 加重: *The new* *evidence beefed up their case.* 有了新的证据，他们的理由更充足了.

beefy *adj* (**-ier, -iest**) (*infml* 口) having a strong muscular body 身强体壮的; 肌肉发达的: *He's big and beefy.* 他身材魁梧，肌肉发达. **beefi·ness** *n* [U].

□ **beefburger** /ˈbi:fbɜ:gə(r); ˈbif,bɝgɚ/ *n* hamburger 汉堡包.

ˈ**beefsteak** *n* thick piece of beef for grilling, etc 牛排.

beef ˈ**tea** drink, usu for people who are ill, made by boiling beef in water 牛肉汁(通常作病人进补用).

beef·eater /ˈbi:fi:tə(r); ˈbif,itɚ/ *n* (*Brit*) guard at the Tower of London; Yeoman of the Guard 伦敦塔的卫兵; 英王仪仗卫士.

bee-line /ˈbi:ˌlaɪn; ˈbiˈlaɪn/ *n* (idm 习语) **make a** ˈ**bee-line for sth/sb** (*infml* 口) go directly towards sth/sb 直奔至某事物[某人]处: *As soon as he arrived he made a bee-line for the bar.* 他一来到就直奔向酒吧柜台.

been *pp* of BE.

NOTE ON USAGE 用法: **Been** is used as the past participle of both 'be' and 'go' ☆ **been** 用作 'be' 和 'go' 两字的过去分词: *I've never been seriously ill* (be). 我从未得过大病(动词原形为 be). ○ *I've never been to London* (go). 我从未去过伦敦(动词原形为 go). **Gone** is also a past participle of 'go' ☆ **gone** 也是 'go' 的过去分词: *They've been to the cinema* means that they went and have returned. '他们去过电影院'意思是他们去了而且已回来了. *They've gone to the cinema* means that they went and are not back yet. '他们去电影院了'意思是他们去了但是还没回来.

beep /bi:p; bip/ *n* short high-pitched sound, as made by a car horn or by electronic equipment (汽车喇叭或电子设备所发出的)嘟嘟声, 哔哔声.

▷ **beep** *v* [I] make this sound 发嘟嘟声; 发哔哔声: *The computer beeps regularly.* 计算机发出有规律的哔哔声.

beer /bɪə(r); bɪr/ *n* **1** (**a**) [U] alcoholic drink made from malt and flavoured with hops, etc 啤酒: *a barrel, bottle, glass of beer* 一桶、瓶、杯啤酒 ○ [attrib 作定语] *a* ˈ*beer glass* 啤酒杯. (**b**) [C] type of beer 啤酒的一种: *beers brewed in Germany* 产于德国的啤酒. (**c**) [C] glass of beer 一杯啤酒: *Two beers, please.* 劳驾，来两杯啤酒. **2** [U, C] (esp in compounds 尤用以构成复合词) other fermented drink made from roots, etc 用植物的根等经过发酵制成的其他饮料: ˌ*ginger-*ˈ*beer.* **3** (idm 习语) ˌ**beer and** ˈ**skittles** pleasure; amusement 欢乐; 吃喝玩乐: *Marriage isn't all beer and skittles,* ie isn't always free of trouble. 婚姻生活并不尽是吃喝玩乐(有时也免不了有些烦恼). **small beer** ⇨ SMALL.

▷ **beery** /ˈbɪərɪ; ˈbɪrɪ/ *adj* like or smelling of beer 似啤酒的; 啤酒味的: *a beery taste, smell* 啤酒的味道、气味 ○ *beery men* 身上有啤酒味的人.

□ ˈ**beer-mat** *n* small, usu cardboard, table-mat for a beer glass 啤酒杯垫(通常由硬纸板制成).

bees·wax /ˈbi:zwæks; ˈbiz,wæks/ *n* [U] yellowish wax made by bees for building honeycombs, also used for making wood polish 蜂蜡; 黄蜡.

beet /bi:t; bit/ *n* [U, C] **1** type of plant with a fleshy root which is used as a vegetable or for making sugar 甜菜. **2** (*US*) = BEETROOT.

beetle[1] /ˈbi:tl; ˈbitl̩/ *n* any of several types of insect, often large and black, with hard wing-cases 甲虫.

▷ **beetle** *v* (phr v) **beetle along, about, away, off, etc** (*infml* 口) move along, etc quickly, either on foot or in a car; hurry 急速移动(步行或乘车); 急急忙忙: *The kids beetled off home.* 孩子们急急忙忙回家去了.

beetle[2] /ˈbi:tl; ˈbitl̩/ *n* tool like a hammer, with a heavy head for beating, crushing, etc 槌子; 夯.

beet·ling /ˈbi:tlɪŋ; ˈbitlɪŋ/ *adj* [attrib 作定语] overhanging; jutting out 悬垂的; 突出的: *beetling cliffs* 悬崖.

beet·root /ˈbi:tru:t; ˈbit,rut/ (*US* **beet**) *n* **1** [U, C] dark red fleshy root of the beet plant, eaten as a vegetable when cooked 甜菜根. **2** (idm 习语) **red as a beetroot** ⇨ RED.

beeves *pl* of BEEF 2.

be·fall /bɪˈfɔ:l; bɪˈfɔl/ *v* (*pt* **befell** /bɪˈfel; bɪˈfɛl/, *pp* **befallen** /bɪˈfɔ:lən; bɪˈfɔlən/) [I, Tn] (used only in the 3rd person 只用于第三人称) (*arch* 古) happen to (sb) 降临到(某人)头上; 发生: *We shall never leave you, whatever befalls.* 不管发生什么事情，我们永远也不会离开你. ○ *A great misfortune befell him.* 一场大难降临到他的头上.

be·fit /bɪˈfɪt; bɪˈfɪt/ *v* (**-tt-**) [Tn] (used only in the 3rd person 只用于第三人称) (*fml* 文) be right and suitable for (sb); be appropriate for 适合于(某人); 合适: *You should dress in a way that befits a woman of your position.* 你的衣着应与你这种地位的妇女相称. ○ *It ill befits a priest to act uncharitably.* 当牧师而不以慈悲为怀是不合适的.

▷ **be·fit·ting** *adj* appropriate 适当的: *act with befitting modesty* 谦恭得体. **be·fit·tingly** *adv*.

be·fog /bɪˈfɒg; bɪˈfag/ *v* (**-gg-**) [Tn] confuse (sb/sth); make unclear or obscure 把(某人[某事物])弄糊涂; 使模糊: *Old age had befogged his mind.* 他老糊涂了.

be·fore[1] /bɪˈfɔ:(r); bɪˈfɔr/ *adv* at an earlier time; in the past; already 以前; 过去; 已经: *You should have told me so before.* 你早就应该告诉我. ○ *It had been fine the day/week before,* ie the previous day/week. 前一天[一周]天气很好(以过去某时为准的前一天[一周]). ○ *That had happened long before,* ie a long time earlier. 那事老早就发生了(比过去某时早得多). ○ *I've seen that film before.* 我以前看过那部影片. ⇨Usage at BEFORE[2] 用法见 BEFORE[2]. Cf 参看 AFTER[1], AFTERWARDS.

be·fore[2] /bɪˈfɔ:(r); bɪˈfɔr/ *prep* **1** earlier than (sb/sth) 早于(某人[某事物]); 在(某人[某事物])以前: *before lunch* 午餐前 ○ *the day before yesterday* 前天 ○ *two days before Christmas* 圣诞节的前两天 ○ *The year before last he won a gold medal, and the year before that he won the silver.* 他前年赢得一枚金牌，大前年赢得一枚银牌. ○ *She's lived there since before the war.* 她从战前就一直住在那里. ○ *He arrived before me.* 他在我之前到达. ○ *He taught English as his father had before him.* 他教过英语，他父亲以前也教过英语. ○ *Something ought to have been done before now.* 早就该采取措施了. ○ *We'll know before long,* ie soon. 我们不久就会知道. ○ *Turn left just before* (ie before you reach) *the cinema.* 在快要到电影院时向左拐. Cf 参看 AFTER[2] 1. **2** (**a**) (with reference to position) in front of (sb/sth) (指位置)在(某人[某物])前面: *We knelt before the throne.* 我们在御座前跪下. ○ (*fig* 比喻) *The task before us is not an easy one.* 我们面临的任务可不轻. Cf 参看 BEHIND[2] 1. (**b**) (with reference to order or arrangement) in front of (sb/sth); ahead of (指顺序或排列)在(某人[某事物])之前; 先于(某人[某事物]): *B comes before C in the alphabet.* B 在字母表里排在 C 之前. ○ *Your name comes before mine on the list.* 名单上你的名字在我之前. ○ *ladies before gentlemen* 女士优先于先生 ○ *He puts his work before everything,* ie regards it as more important than anything else. 他把工作放在第一位(看得比任何事都重要). Cf 参看 AFTER[2] 3. **3** in the presence of (sb) 在(某人)面前: *He was brought before the judge.* 他被带到法官面前. ○ *She said it before witnesses.* 她是当着证人的面说的. ○ *He made a statement before the House of Commons.* 他在下议院当众发表了一个声明. **4** (*fml* 文) rather than (sth); in preference to 与其…，不如…; 宁可: *death before dishonour* 宁死不受辱. **5** (*fml* 文) under pressure from (sb/sth) 被(某人[某事物])所迫: *Our troops recoiled before the attack.* 我部队迫于敌人的进攻而后撤. ○ *They retreated before the enemy.* 他们迫于敌方压力而退却. ○ *The ship sailed before the wind,* ie with the wind blowing from behind. 轮船顺风航行.

NOTE ON USAGE 用法: **1 In front of** and **behind** are prepositions and opposite in meaning ☆ **in front of** 和 **behind** 均用作介词，但意思相反. They indicate the relative position of people or things 这两个词语都指人或事物的相对位置: *Johnny is in front of me in the photo.* 照片中约翰尼在我的前面. ○ *The garage is behind the house.* 车房在房子的后面. ○ *The dog ran in front of the bus.* 狗在公共汽车前面跑. ○ *The mouse ran behind the cupboard.* 老鼠在柜子后面跑. **2 In front** and **behind** are also adverbs ☆ **in front** 和 **behind** 还可作副词: *I'd like to sit in front.* 我愿意坐在前面. ○ *The taxi followed on behind.* 计程车在后面跟着. **3 Before** and **after** relate to time and can be ☆ **before** 和 **after** 可指时间，可作 (**a**) adverbs 副词: *the day after/before* 次

日[前一日] ○ *I had met him before.* 我在那事之前就见过他. ○ *I'll see you after.* (Here **afterwards** is more common.) 我以后再见你. (此处用**afterwards**更普通.) **(b)** prepositions 介词: *the day after/before my birthday* 我生日的次日[前一日] ○ *I'll see you after the meeting.* 散会后我再见你. **(c)** conjunctions 连词: *We had dinner after/before they arrived.* 他们到达之后[之前]我们吃的饭. **4 Before** and **after** can suggest place, especially when this is closely associated with time or order in a se-quence. ☆ **before** 和 **after** 亦可指地点, 尤其用于所指的地点是与时间或先后顺序有密切关系时. *I was before/after you in the queue.* 我排队排在你前面[后面]. ○ *C comes before E in the alphabet.* 在字母表里C排在E之前.

B

be·fore[3] /bɪˈfɔ:(r); bɪˈfɔr/ *conj* **1** earlier than the time when (指时间)在...以前: *Do it before you forget.* 趁早动手, 免得忘了. ○ *It may be many years before we meet again.* 大概要过许多年我们才能再见. ○ *Before the week was out* (ie had ended), *they were dead.* 那个星期还没过完他们就死了. ○ *It will be a long time before we finish this dictionary.* 我们需要很长的时间才能把这部词典编译完. Cf 参看 AFTER[3]. **2** rather than 不愿: *I'd shoot myself before I apologized to him!* 我宁死也不向他道歉!

be·fore·hand /bɪˈfɔ:hænd; bɪˈfɔr,hænd/ *adv* **1** in advance; in readiness; earlier 预先; 有准备地; 较早: *I had made preparations beforehand.* 我预先作了准备. ○ *He warned me beforehand what to expect.* 他预先提醒过我这件事. ○ *We were aware of the problem beforehand.* 我们事先就知道有这个问题. **2 ~ (with sth)** early or too early 早; 过早: *She is always beforehand with the rent,* ie is ready to pay it before it is due. 她总是提前把租金准备好. Cf 参看 BEHINDHAND.

be·friend /bɪˈfrend; bɪˈfrɛnd/ *v* [Tn] act as a friend to (sb); be kind to (esp sb needing help) 对(某人)尽朋友之道; 对(某人, 尤指需要帮助者)照顾: *They befriended the young girl, providing her with food and shelter.* 他们热心地照顾这个年轻的姑娘, 给她吃的、给她住处. ○ *We were befriended by a stray dog.* 有一只失散的狗倒和我们很好.

be·fuddled /bɪˈfʌdld; bɪˈfʌdḷd/ *adj* made stupid; confused 搞糊涂的; 迷迷糊糊的: *his befuddled mind* 他那糊涂的头脑 ○ *be befuddled by drink, old age* 因喝酒、年老而迷迷糊糊.

beg /beg; bɛg/ *v* **(-gg-)** **1** [I, Ipr, Tn, Tn·pr] **~ (from sb); ~ (for) sth (from/of sb)** ask for (money, food, clothes, etc) as a gift or as charity; make a living in this way 乞求(金钱、食物、衣服等); 行乞: *There are hundreds begging in the streets.* 街上有数以百计的乞丐. ○ *a begging letter,* ie one that asks for help, esp money 求援信(尤指要求金钱资助的) ○ *He was so poor he had to beg (for) money from passers-by.* 他穷得要向行人乞求布施. **2** [Ipr, Tn, Tn·pr, Tf, Tt, Cn·t] **~ sth (of sb)/~ (sb) for sth** ask earnestly or humbly (for sth) 恳求, 祈求(某事物): *Set him free, I beg (of) you!* 放开他吧, 我求求你! ○ *May I beg a favour (of you)?* 可以(请你)帮个忙吗? ○ *He begged mercy (of the king).* 他祈求(国王)宽恕. ○ *He begged (her) for forgiveness.* 他请求(她)原谅. ○ *The boy begged that he might be allowed/begged to be allowed to come with us.* 这男孩子恳求允许他和我们一道来. ○ *I beg (of) you not to take any risks.* 我恳求你不要冒险. ⇨Usage at ASK 用法见 ASK. **3** [I, Ipr] **~ (for sth)** (of a dog) stand on the hind legs with the front paws raised expectantly (指狗)用后腿站立前爪抬起作乞求状: *teach one's dog to beg (for its food)* 教狗乞食. **4** (idm 习语) **beg leave to do sth** (*fml* 文) ask for permission to do sth 请求准许干某事: *I beg leave to address the Council.* 我请求允许向议会发表演说. **beg sb's ˈpardon** apologize to sb for sth one had done or said, or intends to do or say, that is inconvenient for others or is considered rude in polite society 请原谅, 很抱歉(言行失当或失礼时常作此语). **beg the ˈquestion** not deal properly with the matter being discussed by assuming that a question needing an answer has been answered (假定需解决的问题已解决, 用以)回避正题: *Your proposal begs the question whether a change is needed at all.* 到底是否需要改革, 你的提议回避了问题的实质. **I beg to differ** (used to express disagreement with sb 用以表示与某人意见不一致): *'He's clearly the best candidate.' 'I beg to differ.'* '他显然是最合适的候选人了.' '恕我不能赞同.' **go ˈbegging** (of things) be unwanted (指物)不想要的; 没人要的: *If that sandwich is going begging, I'll have it.* 这份三明治没人要, 我就要了. **I beg your pardon** **(a)** I am sorry; please excuse me 对不起; 请原谅: *'You've taken my seat.' 'Oh I beg your pardon!'* '你占了我的座位了.' '噢, 真对不起!' **(b)** please repeat that 请重复一遍: *I beg your pardon — I didn't hear what you said.* 请再说一遍——我没听见你刚才说的话. **(c)** (expressing anger 表示气愤) I must object; I am offended 我可不依; 得罪了我: *I beg your pardon but the woman you're insulting happens to be my wife.* 请你尊重些, 你侮辱的这个女人正是我的妻子. **5** (phr v) **beg off** ask to be excused from doing sth 请求不做某事: *He promised to attend but then begged off.* 他本来答应出席的, 但后来却推辞了. **beg sb off** ask that sb be excused or released, esp from a punishment 为某人说情, 请求原谅某人(尤指免于处罚).

be·gan *pt* of BEGIN.

be·get /bɪˈget; bɪˈgɛt/ *v* (**-tt-**; *pt* **begot** /bɪˈgɒt; bɪˈgɑt/ or, in archaic use, 古语拼作 **begat** /bɪˈgæt; bɪˈgæt/, *pp* **begotten** /bɪˈgɒtn; bɪˈgɑtn̩/) [Tn] **1** (*arch* 古) be the father of (sb) 为(某人)之父: *Abraham begat Isaac.* 亚伯拉罕生了以撒. **2** (*fml or dated* 文或旧) cause (sth); result in 产生(某事物); 导致: *War begets misery and ruin.* 战争是苦难与毁灭的祸根.

beg·gar /ˈbegə(r); ˈbɛgɚ/ *n* **1** person who lives by begging; very poor person 乞丐; 很穷的人. **2** (*infml* 口) person; fellow 人; 傢伙: *You lucky beggar!* 你这幸运的傢伙! ○ *The cheeky beggar!* 不要脸的傢伙! **3** (idm 习语) **ˌbeggars can't be ˈchoosers** (*infml saying* 口, 谚) when you have no choice, you must be satisfied with what is available 叫花子不能挑肥拣瘦(无选择余地, 只好有什么算什么); 饥不择食: *I would have preferred a bed, but beggars can't be choosers so I slept on the sofa.* 我本想要张床, 但是叫花子不能挑肥拣瘦, 所以我就睡在沙发上了.

▷ **beg·gar** *v* **1** [Tn] make (sb/sth) poor; impoverish; ruin 使(某人[某事物])穷, 贫困; 毁坏: *a nation beggared by crippling taxes* 困于苛捐杂税的国民. **2** (idm 习语) **beggar deˈscription** be too extraordinary to describe adequately 难以形容: *a sunset which beggared description* 妙不可言的日落景象 ○ *His conduct is so bad it beggars (all) description.* 他的品行之坏不可名状.

beg·garly *adj* **1** very poor 赤贫的; 极穷的. **2** mean; ungenerous 刻薄的; 吝啬的: *a beggarly wage* 菲薄的工资.

beg·gary *n* [U] extreme poverty 赤贫: *be reduced to beggary* 陷于极度贫困之中.

be·gin /bɪˈgɪn; bɪˈgɪn/ *v* (**-nn-**; *pt* **began** /bɪˈgæn; bɪˈgæn/, *pp* **begun** /bɪˈgʌn; bɪˈgʌn/) **1 (a)** [Tn] set (sth) in motion; start 使(某物)启动; 开始: *begin work, a meeting* 开始工作、开会 ○ *The building hasn't even been begun.* 这座建筑物还没有动工呢. ○ *I began school* (ie attended it for the first time) *when I was five.* 我五岁入学. ○ *He has begun* (ie started reading or writing) *a new book.* 他已开始读(或写)一本新书. **(b)** [I] be set in motion; start 启动; 开始: *When does the concert begin?* 音乐会什么时候开始? ○ *The meeting will begin at nine.* 会议将在九点开始. ○ *Building began last year.* 建筑工程去年已经开始. **2 (a)** [Tt] (used to indicate states of mind, or mental activities, which are starting 用以指心理状态和思维活动的开始): *She began to feel dizzy.* 她感到头昏眼花. ○ *I'm beginning to understand.* 我逐渐明白了. ○ *I was beginning to think you'd never come.* 我开始意识到你永远不会来了. **(b)** [Tt, Tg] (used to indicate a process that is beginning, the subject being a thing, not a person 用以指一过程的开始, 主语是物而不是人): *The paper was beginning to peel off the walls.* 墙上的纸渐渐脱落了. ○ *The barometer began to fall.* 气压计的读数开始下降. ○ *The water is beginning to boil.* 水逐渐沸腾起来. ⇨ Usage 见所附用法. **3** [I, Ipr] be the first to do sth or take the first step in doing sth (在做某事时)作为起始者或作为第一步: *Shall I begin* (ie take the first step or be the first to speak)? 我可以开始说了吗[可以由我开始吗]? ○ *Let's begin at* (ie start from) *page 9.* 我们从第9页开始吧. ○ *She's begun on* (ie started writing or reading) *a new novel.* 她已开始写(或阅读)一本新小说.

○ *I have to begin with an apology.* 我得首先表示歉意. **4** [I, Ipr] have its starting-point or first element; have its nearest boundary 起始于; 起源于; 最接近的界限为: *When does spring end and summer begin?* 春天在什么时候结束, 夏天从什么时候开始? ○ *The new fare will be £1, beginning (from) next month.* 从下月起, 新车费为1英镑. ○ *The English alphabet begins with 'A' and ends with 'Z'.* 英文字母表以A开始, 以Z结束. **5** [Tt] (*infml* 口) (usu in negative sentences 用于否定句) make an attempt to do sth; show some likelihood of doing sth 意欲做某事物; 显出要做某事物的样子: *The authorities couldn't even begin to assess the damage,* ie because it was so great. 当局简直无从估计其损失. ○ *I can't begin to thank you,* ie I don't know what to say to thank you properly. 我真不知道该怎样感谢你. ○ *He didn't even begin to understand.* 他半点儿也不懂. ⇨Usage 见所附用法. **6** (idm 习语) **charity begins at home** ⇨ CHARITY. **to begin with** (**a**) in the first place; firstly 首先; 第一: *I'm not going. To begin with I haven't a ticket, and secondly I don't like the play.* 我不去. 一来我没票, 二来我不喜欢这出戏. (**b**) at first 起初: *To begin with he had no money, but later he became quite rich.* 他起初没钱, 可是后来相当富有了. ⇨Usage at HOPEFUL 用法见HOPEFUL.

▷ **be·gin·ner** *n* **1** person who is just beginning to learn or do sth 初学者; 新手. **2** (idm 习语) **beginner's 'luck** good luck or accidental success at the start of learning to do sth 初学者的好运气或意外成功.

be·gin·ning *n* **1** (**a**) first part 开始的部分: *I missed the beginning of the film.* 我没能看到这部影片的开头. ○ *You've made a good beginning.* 你已经做出了良好的开端. (**b**) starting-point 起点: *Recite the poem (right) from the (very) beginning.* 从头开始背诵这首诗. ○ *I've read the book from beginning to end.* 我把这本书从头到尾看完了. **2** (often *pl* 常作复数) source; origin 源; 根源: *Did democracy have its beginnings in Athens?* 民主制度是创始于雅典吗? ○ *Many big businesses start from small beginnings.* 许多大企业都是从小企业起步的. **3** (idm 习语) **the ˌbeginning of the 'end** first clear sign of the final (and usu unfavourable) outcome 结局(通常为不利者)的前兆: *Defeat in this important battle was the beginning of the end for us.* 这场重要战役的失利是我们败局已定的前兆.

NOTE ON USAGE 用法: **1** Very often **begin** and **start** can be used in the same way, though **start** is more common in informal speech ☆ **begin**和**start**的用法往往相同, 但**start**多用于口语: *What time do you begin/start work in the morning?* 你上午几点钟开始工作? ○ *The concert begins/starts at 7.30 pm.* 音乐会晚上7时30分开始. **2** After continuous tenses of **begin** and **start** we do not normally use the *-ing* form of a verb 在**begin**和**start**的进行时态之后, 一般不用动词的-ing形式: *He began/started crying/to cry* but *It's starting/beginning to rain* (NOT *raining*). '他哭起来了'(英文句中可用crying/to cry), 但'下起雨来了'(英文句中不可用raining). **3** In some senses only **start** can be used 有些词义只可用**start**: *If we want to get there tonight, we should start* (ie set off) *now.* 假设我们想今天晚上到那里, 现在就得动身. ○ *The car won't start/I can't start the car.* 这辆汽车发动不起来[这辆汽车我发动不起来].

be·gone /bɪˈgɒn; US -ˈgɔːn; bɪˈgɔn/ *interj* (*arch* 古) go away immediately 走开.

be·go·nia /bɪˈgəʊnɪə; bɪˈgonɪə/ *n* garden plant with brightly coloured leaves and flowers 秋海棠.

be·gorra /bɪˈgɒrə; bɪˈgɑrə/ *interj* (*Irish* 爱尔兰) By God! 天哪!

be·got, be·got·ten *pt, pp* of BEGET.

be·grudge /bɪˈgrʌdʒ; bɪˈgrʌdʒ/ *v* **1** [Tn, Tg, Tsg] resent or be dissatisfied with (sth) 对(某事物)感到不快或不满: *I begrudge every penny I pay in tax.* 我交税交的每一便士心里都不痛快. **2** [Dn·n] envy (sb) the possession of (sth) 忌妒(某人)有(某事物): *Nobody begrudges you your success.* 没有人忌妒你的成功. ▷ **be·grudg·ingly** *adv.*

be·guile /bɪˈgaɪl; bɪˈgaɪl/ (*dated or fml* 旧或文) **1** (**a**) [Tn] charm (sb) 迷住(某人): *The travellers were beguiled by the beauty of the landscape.* 游客对这美丽的景色赞叹不已. (**b**) [Tn, Tn·pr] **~ sb (with sth)** win the attention or interest of sb; amuse sb 吸引某人的注意或兴趣; 使某人快乐: *He beguiled us with many a tale of adventure.* 他讲了许多冒险故事, 我们听得津津有味. (**c**) [Tn, Tn·pr] **~ sth (with/by sth)** cause (time, etc) to pass pleasantly 使(时间等)过得愉快: *Our journey was beguiled with spirited talk.* 我们旅行中谈笑风生, 过得很愉快. **2** [Tn, Tn·pr] **~ sb (into doing sth)** deceive sb 欺骗某人: *They were beguiled into giving him large sums of money.* 他们受骗, 给了他一大笔钱. ▷ **be·guile·ment** *n* [U]. **be·guil·ing** *adj.* **be·guil·ingly** *adv.*

B

be·gum /ˈbeɪgəm; ˈbigəm/ *n* Muslim woman of high rank 穆斯林贵妇.

be·gun *pp* of BEGIN.

be·half /bɪˈhɑːf; US -ˈhæf; bɪˈhæf/ *n* (idm 习语) **on behalf of sb/on sb's behalf**; *US* **in behalf of sb/in sb's behalf** as the representative of or spokesman for sb; in the interest of sb 做某人的代表或代言人; 为某人之利益: *On behalf of my colleagues and myself I thank you.* 我代表我的同事以及我自己向你表示谢意. ○ *Ken is not present, so I shall accept the prize on his behalf.* 肯不在场, 所以我代表他领奖. ○ *The legal guardian must act on behalf of the child.* 法定监护人应该维护这个孩子的利益. ○ *Don't be uneasy on my behalf,* ie about me. 不要为我担心.

be·have /bɪˈheɪv; bɪˈhev/ *v* **1** [I, Ipr] **~ well, badly, etc (towards sb)** act or conduct oneself in the specified way (举止或行为)表现: *She behaves (towards me) more like a friend than a mother.* 她像朋友一样(待我), 而不像是我的母亲. ○ *He has behaved shamefully towards his wife.* 他对妻子的态度很可耻. **2** [I, Tn] **~ (oneself)** show good manners; conduct oneself well 表现良好; 行为良好: *Children, please behave (yourselves)!* 孩子们, 规矩些! **3** [I] (of machines, etc) work or function well (or in another specified way) (指机器等)运转或性能良好: *How's your new car behaving?* 你的新汽车好使吗?

▷ **-behaved** (forming compound *adjs* 用以构成复合形容词) behaving in a specified way 有某种表现的: *well-/ill-/badly-behaved children.*

be·ha·vi·our (*US* **be·ha·vior**) /bɪˈheɪvjə(r); bɪˈhevjɚ/ *n* **1** [U] way of treating others; manners 待人态度; 举止: *She was ashamed of her children's (bad) behaviour.* 她因为她的孩子不规矩而感到羞愧. ○ *Their behaviour towards me shows that they do not like me.* 从他们对我的态度可以看出他们不喜欢我. **2** [U] way of acting or functioning 行为方式; 活动方式: *study the behaviour of infants, apes, bees* 研究婴儿、猿猴、蜜蜂的活动习性. **3** (idm 习语) **be on one's best behaviour** ⇨ BEST[1].

▷ **be·ha·vi·oural** (*US* **-oral**) /-jərəl; -jərəl/ *adj* of behaviour 行为的. **beˌhavioural 'science** study of human behaviour 行为科学.

be·ha·vi·our·ism (*US* **-or·ism**) /-jərɪzəm; -jərˌɪzəm/ *n* [U] (*psychology* 心) doctrine that all human actions could, if full knowledge were available, be explained by stimulus and response 行为主义. **be·ha·vi·our·ist** (*US* **-or·ist**) /-jərɪst; -jərɪst/ *n* believer in this doctrine 行为主义者.

be·head /bɪˈhed; bɪˈhɛd/ *v* [Tn] cut off the head of (sb), esp as a punishment 砍(某人)的头(尤指刑罚): *Anne Boleyn was beheaded in 1536.* 安妮·博林于1536年被斩首.

be·held *pt, pp* of BEHOLD.

be·hest /bɪˈhest; bɪˈhɛst/ *n* (idm 习语) **at sb's beˈhest** (*dated or fml* 旧或文) on sb's orders 听命; 遵命: *at the king's behest/at the behest of the king* 奉谕旨.

be·hind[1] /bɪˈhaɪnd; bɪˈhaɪnd/ *prep* **1** (**a**) in or to a position at the back of (sb/sth) 在或向(某人[某事物])的后面: *Who's the girl standing behind Richard?* 站在理查德后面的那个姑娘是谁? ○ *Stay close behind me in the crowd.* 在人群里你要紧紧地跟着我. ○ *The golf course is behind our house.* 高尔夫球场在我们房屋的后面. ○ *a small street behind the station* 车站后面的一条小街 ○ *She glanced behind her.* 她向身后看了一眼. ○ *work behind the counter,* eg as a sales assistant in a shop 站柜台 ○ *Don't forget to lock the door behind you,* ie when you leave. 别忘了出门时把门锁上. ○ (*fig* 比喻) *The accident is behind you now* (ie in the past), *so forget about it.* 事情已经过去了, 别再想它了. (**b**) on the other

B

side of (sb/sth) 在(某人[某事物])的另一面: *hide behind a tree* 躲在树的后面 ○ *Behind the curtain she found a door.* 在帘子的后面她发现了一个门. ○ *The sun disappeared behind the clouds.* 太阳躲到云层里去了. Cf 参看 IN FRONT OF (FRONT). ⇨Usage at BEFORE[2] 用法见 BEFORE[2]. **2** making less progress than (sb/sth) 落后于(某人[某事物]): *He's behind the rest of the class in reading.* 他在阅读方面不如班上的其他同学. ○ *Britain is behind Japan in developing modern technology.* 在发展现代技术方面英国落后于日本. ○ *be behind schedule,* ie late 落后于预定计划. **3** supportive of (sb/sth); in favour of 支持(某人[某事物]); 赞成: *My family is right behind me in my ambition to become a doctor.* 我们家对我立志当医生完全赞同. ○ *He's trying to win the election with only 30% of voters behind him.* 他正争取在选举中取胜, 虽然只有30%的选民支持他. **4** responsible for starting or developing (sth) 作为发生或发展(某事物)的起因: *the thought that was behind the suggestion* 提出这个建议的想法 ○ *the man behind the scheme to build a new hospital* 兴建新医院这一方案的发起人. **5** (idm 习语) **be behind sth** be the reason for sth 是某事物的原因: *What's behind the smart suit and eager smile?* 穿得这样漂亮、笑得这样甜, 究竟是什么原因?

be·hind[2] /bɪˈhaɪnd; bɪˋhaɪnd/ *adv part* **1** in or to a position at the back of sb/sth 在或向(某人[某事物])背后: *I cycled off down the road with the dog running behind.* 我骑着自行车顺着道路行驶, 那只狗在后面跟着跑. ○ *The others are a long way behind.* 其他的人远远地落在后面. ○ *What have we left behind* (ie after going away)? 我们走后留下什么了? ○ *Don't look behind or you may fall.* 别回头看, 不然要跌跤的. ○ *He was shot from behind as he ran away.* 他跑开时, 有人从后面将他射中. ○ *We had fallen so far behind that it seemed pointless continuing.* 我们已经落在后面很远, 继续下去似乎没有什么意义. ○ *I had to stay behind after school,* ie remain in school after lessons were over. 放学以后我还得留在学校. Cf 参看 IN FRONT (FRONT). ⇨Usage at BEFORE[2] 用法见 BEFORE[2]. **2 ~ (in/with sth)** failing to pay (money) or complete (work) by the date when it is due; in arrears (with sth) 拖欠; 积压: *I'm terribly behind (with the rent) this month.* 我这个月(租金)拖欠得太久了. ○ *He's behind in handing in homework.* 他没能按时交家庭作业.

be·hind[3] /bɪˈhaɪnd; bɪˋhaɪnd/ *n* (*infml euph* 口, 婉) buttocks 屁股: *She fell and landed on her behind.* 她摔了个仰八叉. ○ *He kicked the boy's behind.* 他踢这个男孩儿的屁股.

be·hind·hand /bɪˈhaɪndhænd; bɪˋhaɪnd,hænd/ *adj* [pred 作表语] **~ (with/in sth)** in arrears or late (esp in paying a debt) 拖欠; 晚交(尤指欠款): *be behindhand with the rent* 欠租 ○ *get behindhand in one's work* 拖延工作 ○ *He is never behindhand in offering advice,* ie is always eager to advise. 他向别人提出劝告从来都很及时(一向热衷于劝人). Cf 参看 BEFOREHAND.

be·hold /bɪˈhəʊld; bɪˋhold/ *v* (*pt, pp* **beheld** /bɪˈheld; bɪˋhɛld/) **1** [Tn] (*arch or rhet* 古或修辞) (often imperative 常用于祈使语气) see (esp sth unusual) 看(尤指不寻常之物): *The babe was a wonder to behold.* 这个婴孩看上去令人称奇. ○ *Behold the king!* 看, 国王驾到! **2** (idm 习语) **lo and behold** ⇨ LO. ▷ **be·hold·er** *n.*

be·holden /bɪˈhəʊldən; bɪˋholdən/ *adj* [pred 作表语] **~ to sb (for sth)** (*dated or fml* 旧或文) owing thanks or indebted to sb 感激某人; 欠某人人情: *We were much beholden to him for his kindness.* 我们对他的好意感激万分.

be·hove /bɪˈhəʊv; bɪˋhov/ (*US* **be·hoove** /bɪˈhuːv; bɪˋhuv/) *v* [Tnt] (used with *it*; not in the continuous tenses 与it连用, 不用于进行时态) (*dated or fml* 旧或文) be right or necessary for (sb) 对(某人)来说理应或必须: *It behoves you* (ie You ought) *to be courteous at all times.* 你应当时时刻刻注意礼节. ○ *It ill behoves Anne* (ie She ought not) *to speak thus of her benefactor.* 安不应该这样谈论她的恩人.

beige /beɪʒ; beʒ/ *adj, n* [U] (of a) very light yellowish brown 米黄色(的): *a beige carpet* 米色地毯.

be·ing /ˈbiːɪŋ; ˋbiɪŋ/ *n* **1** [U] (**a**) existence 存在: *the richest company in being today* 现今实力最为雄厚的公司 ○ *What is the purpose of our being?* 我们生存的目的是什么? (**b**) one's essence or nature; self 本质; 本性; 本身: *I detest violence with my whole being.* 我从心底里憎恶暴力. **2** [C] living creature 生物: *human beings* 人 ○ *a strange being from another planet* 来自其他星球的奇异生物. **3** (idm 习语) **bring sth into ˈbeing** cause sth to have reality or existence; create sth 使某事物产生或存在; 创造出某物. ˌ**come into ˈbeing** begin to exist 开始存在: *When did the world come into being?* 世界是何时开始存在的?

be·jew·elled (*US* **be·jew·eled**) /bɪˈdʒuːəld; bɪˋdʒuəld/ *adj* decorated or adorned with jewels 饰以珠宝的.

be·la·bour (*US* **be·la·bor**) /bɪˈleɪbə(r); bɪˋlebɚ/ *v* [Tn, Tn·pr] **~ sb/sth (with sth)** (*arch* 古) beat sb/sth hard; attack sb/sth 使劲打某人[某物]; 攻击: *He belaboured the donkey mercilessly.* 他恶狠狠地猛抽那头驴. ○ (*fig* 比喻) *They belaboured us with insults.* 他们对我们肆加凌辱.

be·lated /bɪˈleɪtɪd; bɪˋletɪd/ *adj* coming very late or too late 来得很迟的; 来得太迟的: *a belated apology, Christmas card* 为时已晚的道歉、来迟了的圣诞贺卡. ▷ **be·latedly** *adv.*

be·lay /bɪˈleɪ; bɪˋle/ *v* [Tn] (in mountaineering and sailing) fix (a rope) round a peg, rock, etc in order to secure it (登山和航海时)将(绳索)系绕于(桩子、岩石等)上以固定之.

▷ **be·lay** /bɪˈleɪ; bɪˋle, *also, in mountaineering* 作登山用词时, 亦作 ˈbiːleɪ; ˋbile/ *n* fixing a rope in this way 以上述方法固定绳索.

belch /beltʃ; bɛltʃ/ *v* **1** [I] send out gas from the stomach noisily through the mouth 打嗝. **2** [Tn, Tn·pr, Tn·p] **~ sth (out/forth)** send sth out from an opening or a funnel; gush sth 从洞穴或烟囱中放出(某物); 喷出: *factory chimneys belching smoke (into the sky)* 工厂中(向天上)冒烟的烟囱 ○ *The volcano belched out smoke and ashes.* 火山喷出了烟尘.

▷ **belch** *n* act or sound of belching 嗝; 打嗝声: *give a loud belch* 大声地打了一个嗝.

be·lea·guer /bɪˈliːgə(r); bɪˋligɚ/ *v* [Tn usu passive 通常用于被动语态] **1** besiege (sb/sth) 围住, 围攻(某人[某事物]): *a beleaguered garrison* 被围的要塞. **2** harass (sb) continually 使(某人)苦恼不已: *beleaguered by naughty children* 受顽皮孩子的烦扰.

bel·fry /ˈbelfrɪ; ˋbɛlfrɪ/ *n* **1** tower for bells; part of a church tower in which bells hang 钟楼; 教堂塔楼中悬钟的部分. ⇨illus at App 1 见附录1之插图, page viii. **2** (idm 习语) **have bats in the belfry** ⇨ BAT[1].

be·lie /bɪˈlaɪ; bɪˋlaɪ/ *v* (*pres p* **belying**, *pp* **belied**) [Tn] **1** give a wrong or an untrue idea of (sth) 使人对于(某事物)产生错误的或不符合实际的想法: *His cheerful manner belied his real feelings.* 他那快活的样子掩饰了他的真实感情. **2** fail to justify or fulfil (a hope, promise etc) 不足以证明; 未能实现(希望、诺言等): *Practical experience belies this theory.* 实际经验证明这个理论是错误的.

be·lief /bɪˈliːf; bɪˋlif/ *n* **1** [U] **~ in sth/sb** feeling that sth/sb is real and true; trust or confidence in sth/sb 对某事物[某人]的真实性和正确性所具有的信心; 对某事物[某人]的信仰或信赖: *I haven't much belief in his honesty,* ie cannot feel sure that he is honest. 我对他的诚实缺乏足够的信心. ○ *He has great belief in his doctor,* ie is confident that his doctor can cure him. 他对那位医生无比信赖. ○ *She has lost her belief in God,* ie no longer thinks that God exists. 她已不相信上帝(不相信真有上帝). **2** [C] (**a**) thing accepted as true or real; what one believes 认为正确或确实的事物; 信念; 相信: *It is my belief that...,* ie It is my firm opinion that... 我相信.... ○ *He acted in accordance with his beliefs.* 他按照自己的信念行事. (**b**) religion or sth taught as part of religion 宗教信仰; 教义: *Christian beliefs* 基督教的教义. **3** (idm 习语) **beyond beˈlief** too great, difficult, dreadful, etc to be believed; incredible (因太大、太难、太可怕等)难以置信的; 不可思议的: *I find his behaviour (irresponsible) beyond belief.* 我发觉他的所作所为(不负责任)到了简直令人难以置信的地步. **in the belief that...** feeling confident that... 相信...: *He came to me in the belief that I could help him.* 他到我这里来, 相信我能帮助他. **to the best of one's belief/knowledge** ⇨ BEST[3].

be·lieve /bɪˈliːv; bɪˋliv/ *v* **1** [Tn, Tw] feel sure of the truth of (sth); accept the statement of (sb) as true 相信(某事物)的真实性; 认为(某人)的话属实: *I believe him/what he says.* 我相信他[他的话]. ○ *I'm innocent, please believe me.* 我是无辜的, 请相信我吧. ○ *I'll believe it/that when I see it*, ie Until I have evidence, I remain sceptical. 我亲眼见到才能相信(尚无证据, 我仍有怀疑). ○ *I'm told he's been in prison, and I can well believe it*, ie it doesn't surprise me. 有人对我说他进过监狱, 我完全能够相信这一点. **2** [Tf, Tw, Tnt] think (perhaps mistakenly); suppose 认为, 以为(容或有误); 设想: *People used to believe (that) the world was flat.* 过去人们以为地球是扁的. ○ *Nobody will believe what difficulty we have had/believe how difficult it has been for us.* 谁也想像不到我们遇到了什么样的困难[这对我们来说一直是多么困难]. ○ *They believed him to be insane.* 他们认为他疯了. ○ *I believe it to have been a mistake.* 我认为这一直就是错的. ○ *Mr Smith, I believe*, ie I presume you are Mr Smith. 我想您就是史密斯先生吧. ○ *'Is he coming?' 'I believe so/not.'* '他来吗?' '我想他来[不来].' **3** [I] have religious faith 具有宗教信仰: *He thinks that everyone who believes will go to heaven.* 他认为凡是信神者都将进天堂. **4** (idm 习语) **beˌlieve it or ˈnot** it may sound surprising but it is true 信不信由你: *Believe it or not, we were left waiting in the rain for two hours.* 信不信由你, 我们冒雨一直等了两个小时. **beˌlieve (you) ˈme** I assure you 我向你保证: *Believe you me, the government won't meddle with the tax system.* 我向你保证, 政府绝不会干预税收制度的. **give sb to believe/understand** ⇨ GIVE[1]. **lead sb to believe** ⇨ LEAD[3]. **make believe (that...)** pretend 假装: *The boys made believe (that) they were astronauts.* 男孩儿们假扮成航天员. Cf 参看 MAKE-BELIEVE (MAKE[1]). **not beˌlieve one's ˈears/ˈeyes** be unable to believe that what one hears or sees is real because one is so astonished 惊讶得无法相信所见所闻是事实. **ˌseeing is ˈbelieving** (*saying* 谚) one needs to see sth before one can believe it exists or happens 眼见为实. **ˌwould you beˈlieve (it)?** (expressing astonishment or dismay 表示惊讶或沮丧) although it is hard to believe 尽管难以置信: *Today, would you believe, she came to work in an evening dress!* 说出来你可能不信, 今天她穿了晚礼服来上班! **5** (phr v) **believe in sb/sth** feel sure of the existence of sb/sth 相信某人[某事物]的存在: *I believe in God.* 我信仰上帝. ○ *Do you believe in ghosts?* 你相信有鬼吗? **believe in sth/sb; believe in doing sth** trust sth/sb; feel sure of the worth or truth of sth 相信某事物[某人]; 肯定某事物的价值或正确性: *I believe in his good character.* 我相信他品德良好. ○ *Do you believe in nuclear disarmament?* 你认为真能裁减核军备吗? ○ *He believes in getting plenty of exercise.* 他相信多做运动必有好处. **believe sth of sb** accept that sb is capable of a particular action, etc 相信某人在从事某种特殊活动等方面的才能: *If I hadn't seen him doing it I would never have believed it of him.* 要不是亲眼看见, 我怎么也不会相信他能做这事.

▷ **be·liev·able** *adj* that can be believed 可信的. **be·liev·ably** /-əblɪ; -əblɪ/ *adv*.

be·liever *n* **1** person who believes, esp sb with religious faith 笃信者; (尤指)教徒. **2** (idm 习语) **be a (great/firm) believer in sth** feel sure of the worth of sth 肯定某事物的价值: *I'm not a great believer in (taking) regular physical exercise.* 我对经常锻炼身体的好处有点怀疑.

Beli·sha beacon /bəˈliːʃə; bəˈliʃə/ (also **beacon**) (*Brit*) post with an orange flashing light on top, marking a pedestrian crossing 人行横道指示灯(为橘黄色闪光灯).

be·little /bɪˈlɪtl; bɪˈlɪtl/ *v* [Tn] make (a person or an action) seem unimportant or of little value 轻视; 贬低: *Don't belittle yourself*, ie Don't be too modest about your abilities or achievements. 不要小看你自己.

▷ **be·little·ment** *n* [U].

be·lit·tling *adj* making sb seem unimportant or worthless 轻视某人的; 小看某人的: *I find it belittling to be criticized by someone so much younger than me.* 有个比我年轻许多的人批评了我, 我觉得是小看了我.

bell /bel; bɛl/ *n* **1** hollow metal object, usu shaped like a cup, that makes a ringing sound when struck 钟; 铃: *church bells* 教堂的钟 ○ *a bicycle bell* 自行车的铃. ⇨ illus 见插图. ⇨illus at App 1 见附录1之插图, page xiii.

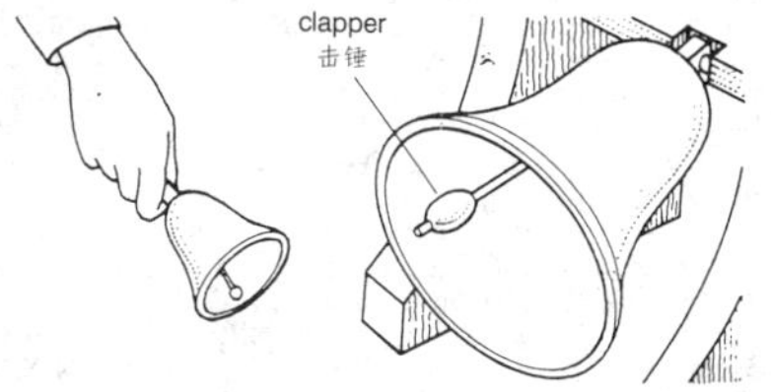

bells 铃或钟

2 sound of this as a time-signal (报时的)钟声或铃声: *There's the bell for the end of the lesson.* 下课铃响了. ○ *The boxer was saved by the bell*, ie He escaped further severe treatment when the bell sounded. 那拳击手因铃响而得救(因铃响而免遭对方进一步的打击). **3** thing shaped like a bell 钟形物. ⇨illus at App 1 见附录1之插图, page x. **4** (idm 习语) **clear as a bell** ⇨ CLEAR[1]. **ring a bell** ⇨ RING[2]. **sound as a bell** ⇨ SOUND[1].

□ **ˈbell-bottoms** *n* [pl] trousers made very wide below the knee 喇叭裤. **ˈbell-bottomed** *adj* (of trousers) made in this way 喇叭式的(指裤).

ˈbellboy *n* (*US*) = PAGE-BOY (PAGE[2]).

ˈbell-buoy *n* buoy with a warning bell that is made to ring by the movement of the waves 钟铃浮标(随波浪运动而发声).

ˈbell captain (*US*) person in charge of bellboys (旅馆男服务员的)领班.

ˈbellhop, **ˈbellman** (*pl* **-men**) *ns* (*US*) = BELLBOY.

ˈbell-pull *n* handle or cord pulled to make a bell ring (钟或铃的)柄或拉索.

ˈbell-push *n* button pressed to operate an electric bell 电铃按钮.

ˈbell-ringer *n* [C], **ˈbell-ringing** *n* [U] (person) ringing church bells 教堂鸣钟(者). Cf 参看 CAMPANOLOGY.

ˈbell-tent *n* tent supported by a central pole and shaped like a bell 钟形帐篷(由中心立柱支撑, 呈钟形).

belle /bel; bɛl/ *n* beautiful woman or the most beautiful woman in a group, etc 美女; 艳压群芳的美人: *the belle of the ball*, ie the most beautiful woman present at a dance 舞会之花(舞会上最美的女子) ○ *the belle of New York* 纽约美人.

belles-lettres /ˌbel ˈletrə; bɛlˈlɛtrə/ *n* [sing or pl *v*] (*French* 法) literary studies and writings (contrasted with those on commercial, technical, scientific, etc subjects) 纯文学.

bel·li·cose /ˈbelɪkəʊs; ˈbɛlə,kos/ *adj* (*fml* 文) eager to fight; warlike; aggressive 好斗的; 好战的; 寻衅的: *a bellicose nation, nature* 好斗的民族、天性. ▷ **bel·li·cos·ity** /ˌbelɪˈkɒsətɪ; ˌbɛləˈkɑsətɪ/ *n* [U].

-bellied ⇨ BELLY.

bel·li·ger·ent /bɪˈlɪdʒərənt; bəˈlɪdʒərənt/ *adj* **1** waging war; engaged in a conflict 交战的; 卷入冲突的: *the belligerent powers*, ie those countries at war 交战国. **2** showing an eagerness to fight or argue; aggressive 好斗或好辩成性的; 寻衅的: *a belligerent person, manner, speech* 寻衅的人、态度、言辞.

▷ **bel·li·ger·ence** /-əns; -əns/, **bel·li·ger·ency** /-ənsɪ; -ənsɪ/ *ns* [U].

bel·li·ger·ent *n* country, group or person engaged in war 交战的国家、群体或个人.

bel·low /ˈbeləʊ; ˈbɛlo/ *v* **1** [I] make a deep loud noise like a bull; roar, esp with pain 发出(像牛的)吼叫声; 咆哮(尤指因痛苦): *The bull bellowed angrily.* 公牛怒吼起来. **2** [I, Ipr, Tn, Tn·pr] **~ (sth) (at sb)** say (sth) loudly or angrily; shout (大声地或愤怒地)说出(某事); 大叫: *The music was so loud we had to bellow at each other to be heard.* 音乐的声音实在太大, 我们只有彼此大声喊叫才能把话听清. ○ *The sergeant bellowed orders at the platoon.* 士官向全排士兵大声地发出命令. ▷ **bel·low** *n*.

bel·lows /ˈbeləʊz; ˈbɛloz/ *n* [pl] apparatus for driving air into or through sth, eg through the pipes of a church organ 风箱: *a pair of bellows*, ie two-handled bellows for blowing air into a fire 手用吹风器(俗称皮老虎).

belly /ˈbelɪ; ˈbɛlɪ/ *n* **1 (a)** part of the body below the chest, containing the stomach, bowels and digestive organs; abdomen 腹部. ⇨illus at HORSE 见HORSE之插图. **(b)** (*infml* 口) front of the human body from the waist to the groin 肚子. **(c)** stomach 胃: *with an empty belly*, ie hungry 空着肚子(饿着). **2** bulging or rounded part of sth 物体鼓出或成弧状的部分: *in the belly of a ship* 在船腹里.

▷ **-bellied** /-belɪd; -bɛlɪd/ (forming compound *adjs* 用以构成复合形容词) having a belly of the specified type 有某种类型肚子的: *ˌbig-ˈbellied* ○ *ˈpot-bellied*.

belly *v* (*pt, pp* **bellied**) (phr v) **belly (sth) out** swell out 鼓胀; 凸出: *The sails bellied out.* 船帆张得满满的. ○ *The wind bellied out the sails.* 大风把帆张得满满的.

□ **ˈbellyache** *n* [C, U] (*infml* 口) stomach pain 胃痛. — *v* [I] (*infml* 口) grumble repeatedly; complain, esp without good reason 怨天尤人, 满腹牢骚(尤指无充分理由): *Stop bellyaching all the time!* 别总是满腹牢骚!

ˈbelly-button *n* (*infml* 口) navel 肚脐.

ˈbelly-dance *n* dance, originating in the Middle East, performed by a woman with erotic movements of the belly 肚皮舞. **ˈbelly-dancer** *n*.

ˈbelly-flop *n* (*infml* 口) clumsy dive in which the body hits the water almost horizontally (身体近乎平着入水的)笨拙跳水.

ˈbelly-laugh *n* (*infml* 口) deep loud unrestrained laugh 捧腹大笑.

belly·ful /ˈbelɪfʊl; ˈbɛlɪˌfʊl/ *n* (idm 习语) **have had a/one's ˈbellyful of sb/sth** (*infml* 口) have had as much as one can tolerate of sb/sth 受够了(某人[某事物]): *I've had a/my bellyful of your complaints.* 我已经听够了你的怨言.

be·long /bɪˈlɒŋ; *US* -lɔːŋ; bəˈlɔŋ/ *v* **1** [Ipr] **(a) ~ to sb** be the property of sb 为某人之财物; 属于: *These books belong to me*, ie are mine. 这些书是我的. ○ *Who(m) does this belong to?* 这是谁的? **(b) ~ to sth** be connected with sth or a place; be correctly assigned to sth 与某事物或某处有关联; 派作某种用场正好: *I belong to Glasgow.* 我是格拉斯哥人. ○ *That lid belongs to this jar.* 那个盖子是配这个瓶子的. **2 ~ to sth** be a member of (a group, a family, an organization, etc) 是(某团体、家庭、组织等中的)一员: *He has never belonged to a trade union.* 他从未加入过工会. ○ *The daffodil belongs to the genus 'Narcissus'.* 黄水仙是水仙属植物. **3 (a)** [Ipr, Ip] **~ (with sb/sth)** have a proper or usual place, as specified 应该在某处; 通常在某处: *Where does this belong?* ie Where is it kept? 这个应该在什么地方? ○ *The hammer belongs (in the shed) with the rest of the tools.* 这把锤子通常和(工具房的)其他工具放在一起. ○ *The vase belongs on this shelf.* 花瓶应该放在这个架子上. ○ *A child belongs with* (ie should live with and be cared for by) *its mother.* 孩子应该和母亲在一起(应和母亲一同生活以便得到照顾). ○ *These items don't belong under this heading*, ie are wrongly classified. 这些项目不该列在这个标题下(不属此类). **(b)** [I] fit a certain environment 适应某种环境: *He doesn't feel he belongs/has no sense of belonging here*, ie He feels an outsider. 他不适应这儿的环境(他觉得自己是外人).

▷ **be·long·ings** *n* [pl] person's movable possessions (ie not land, buildings, etc) 动产(即指除土地、建筑物等之外的财产): *After his death his sister sorted through his (personal) belongings.* 他死后, 他妹妹整理了他的(私人)财物. ○ *The tourists lost all their belongings in the hotel fire.* 因旅馆失火, 游客财物尽失.

be·loved *adj* **(a)** /bɪˈlʌvd; bɪˈlʌvd/ [pred 作表语] **~ (by/of sb)** much loved 深爱: *This man was beloved by/of all who knew him.* 认识他的人都很喜欢他. **(b)** /bɪˈlʌvɪd; bɪˈlʌvɪd/ [attrib 作定语] much loved; darling 深爱的; 亲爱的: *in memory of my beloved husband* 纪念亲爱的丈夫.

▷ **be·loved** /bɪˈlʌvɪd; bɪˈlʌvɪd/ *n* dearly loved person; darling 心爱的人; 爱人: *He wrote a sonnet to his beloved.* 他写了一首十四行诗, 献给他心爱的人.

be·low /bɪˈləʊ; bəˈlo/ *prep* at or to a lower position, level, rank, etc than (sb/sth) 在或向低于(某人[某事物])的位置、平面、等级等: *Please do not write below this line.* 请不要写在这条线的下面. ○ *Skirts must be below* (ie long enough to cover) *the knee.* 裙子要长过膝盖以下. ○ *The body was visible below the surface of the lake.* 尸体在湖水下清晰可见. ○ *The temperature remained below freezing all day.* 温度整天都在冰点以下. ○ *A sergeant in the police force is below an inspector.* 警察中巡佐的职位低于巡官. ○ *The standard of his work is well below the average of his class.* 他的成绩大大低于班上的平均成绩. ○ *You can cross the river a short distance below* (ie downstream from) *the waterfall.* 在瀑布下游附近可以过河. Cf 参看 ABOVE².

▷ **be·low** *adv part* **1** at or to a lower level, position or place 在或向较低处: *the sky above and the sea below* 上面的天, 下面的海 ○ *live on the floor below* 住在下一层楼 ○ *hear the music from below* 听到从下面传来的音乐声 ○ *See below* (eg at the foot of the page) *for references.* 见下面(如本页末)注解. ○ *The passengers who felt seasick stayed below.* 晕船的乘客待在下层. **2** (idm 习语) **down below** ⇨ DOWN. **here below** ⇨ HERE. Cf 参看 ABOVE¹.

belt /belt; bɛlt/ *n* **1** strip of leather, cloth, etc usu worn around the waist 腰带; 裤带: *a coat with a belt attached* 有腰带的外套 ○ *a ˈsword-belt* 佩剑带 ○ *You don't need braces if you're wearing a belt!* 若系着腰带, 就用不着背带了! **2** endless moving strap, used to connect wheels and so drive machinery or carry things along 传动带; 传送带: *a ˈfan belt* 风扇皮带 ○ *a conˈveyor belt* 运输带. **3** distinct area, region or extent; zone 地带; 分区; 地区; 区域: *a country's ˈcotton, ˈforest, inˈdustrial, etc belt* 国家的产棉、森林、工业等地区 ○ *live in the comˈmuter belt* 住在通勤者居住带 ○ *a belt of rain moving across the country* 经该国而移动的降雨带. **4** (*sl* 俚) heavy blow 重击; 痛打. **5** (idm 习语) **(hit sb) below the ˈbelt** (fight) unfairly 用不正当手段(攻击). **tighten one's belt** ⇨ TIGHTEN (TIGHT). **under one's ˈbelt** (*infml* 口) achieved; obtained 达到的; 获得的: *She already has good academic qualifications under her belt.* 她已获得良好学历.

▷ **belt** *v* **1 (a)** [Tn] put or fasten a belt round (sth) 围绕(某物)系上带子: *Your mackintosh looks better belted.* 你的雨衣系上带子更好看. **(b)** [Tn·pr, Tn·p] attach (sth) with a belt 用带子系住(某物): *The officer belted his sword on.* 军官用皮带扣住佩刀. **2** [Tn, Dn·n] (*sl* 俚) thrash (sb); hit 抽打(某人); 打: *If you don't shut up, I'll belt you (one).* 你再不闭嘴, 我就揍你(一顿). **3** (phr v) **belt along, up, down, etc** (*sl* 俚) move very fast in the specified direction 向某方向快速移动: *A car came belting along (the road).* 一辆汽车(沿路)飞速驶来. ○ *He went belting up/down the motorway at 90 mph.* 他在高速公路上以每小时90英里的速度疾驶. **belt sth out** (*sl* 俚) sing or play sth loudly and forcefully 大声地、强有力地唱出或奏出: *a radio belting out pop music* 大声播放流行音乐的收音机. **belt ˈup (a)** (*infml* 口) fasten one's seat-belt (esp in a car) 束紧安全带(尤指乘坐汽车时). **(b)** (*sl* 俚) be quiet 安静: *Belt up, I can't hear what your mother is saying!* 安静点, 我听不见你母亲说的话了.

belt·ing *n* (*sl* 俚) beating 打: *give the boy a good belting*, ie thrash him soundly 给这孩子一顿痛打.

□ **ˈbelt line** (*US*) bus or train service that operates around the edge of a city or city area 环城线(围绕城市外缘或市区行驶的公共汽车或火车服务系统).

be·moan /bɪˈməʊn; bɪˈmon/ *v* [Tn] (*fml* 文) show sorrow for or complain about (sb/sth) 为(某人[某事物])而悲伤, 抱怨: *bemoan one's sad fate* 自叹命苦 ○ *bemoan the shortage of funds for research* 抱怨研究经费不足.

be·mused /bɪˈmjuːzd; bɪˈmjuzd/ *adj* bewildered or confused 困惑的; 茫然的; 不知所措的: *a bemused tone of voice* 含混的声调 ○ *He was totally bemused by the traffic system in the city.* 这城市里的交通制度把他完全弄糊涂了.

ben /ben; bɛn/ *n* (*Scot* 苏格兰) (esp in names) mountain peak (尤用于名称中)山峰: *Ben Nevis* 尼维斯峰.

bench /bentʃ; bɛntʃ/ *n* **1** [C] **(a)** long seat made of wood or stone (木制或石制的)长凳: *a park bench* 公园中的长凳. **(b)** (*Brit*) (in the House of Commons) seat for a certain group of MPs (下议院中)某类议员的席位: *the back-/cross-/front-benches* 后座[中立/前座]议员席 ○ *There was cheering from the Labour benches.* 从工党议员席那边响起一阵欢呼声. **2 the bench (a)** [sing] lawcourt 法院: *the Queen's Bench*, ie a division of the British High Court of Justice 英国高等法院. **(b)** [sing] judge's seat in court (法院中的)法官席位. (**c**) [Gp] judges or magistrates as a group 法官(总称). (**d**) [Gp] judge(s) or magistrate(s) hearing a case (审理案件的)法官. **3** [C] long working-table for a carpenter, mechanic, scientist, etc (木工、机修工人、科研人员等使用的长形的)工作台. **4** (idm 习语) **on the 'bench** appointed as a judge or magistrate 担任法官职务.

□ **'bench-mark** *n* (**a**) mark cut in a rock, concrete post, etc by surveyors for use in measuring comparative levels, etc 基准点(测量人员在岩石、混凝土立柱等上面刻下的标记, 用以测量相对高度等. (**b**) (*fig* 比喻) standard example or point of reference for making comparisons (供比较之用的)样板或参照点.

'bench seat seat (for two or three people) across the whole width of a car (汽车中的)横排长座.

bend[1] /bend; bɛnd/ *v* (*pt, pp* **bent** /bent; bɛnt/) **1** [Tn, Tn·p] force (sth that was straight) into an angle; make crooked or curved 使弯曲: *It's hard to bend an iron bar.* 把铁棒弄弯很不容易. ○ *The mast was bent during the storm.* 桅杆在风暴中变弯了. ○ *The heat of the fire has bent these records.* 火把这些唱片烤翘了. ○ *Touch your toes without bending your knees.* 用手够到你的脚趾, 膝盖别弯曲. ○ *bend the wire up/down/forwards/back* 把金属线弯上去[下去/向前/向后]. **2** (**a**) [I, Ipr, Ip] (of an object) become curved or angular (指物体)弯曲: *The road bends to the right after a few yards.* 这条路在几码远的地方转向右方. (**b**) [I, Ipr, Ip] (of an object) turn downwards in a curve (指物体)向下弯: *The branch bent but didn't break when the boy climbed along it.* 那男孩爬上树枝时, 树枝弯曲了, 但是没有折断. (**c**) [I, Ipr, Ip, Tn, Tn·pr, Tn·p] (cause sb/sth to) bow or stoop (in a specified direction) (使某人)弯腰, 弯身; (使某物沿某方向)弯: *She bent down and picked it up.* 她俯身把它拾起来. ○ *He bent forward to listen to the child.* 他弯下身来听那孩子说话. ○ *The boy bent over to be caned.* 那男孩子撅过屁股来挨藤条打. ○ *They (were) bent double crouching under the table.* 他们蜷着身子蹲在桌子底下. ○ *His head was bent over a book.* 他埋头读书. **3** [Tn·pr, Tn·p] turn (sth) in a new direction 使(某物)转到新的方向: *We bent our steps towards home.* 我们转过脚步朝家走. **4** (idm 习语) **bend the 'rules** change or interpret the rules, laws, etc in a way that suits oneself or the circumstances (根据情况)放宽规定; 变通; 通融. **bend one's mind to sth** direct one's thoughts to sth 专心于某事物: *He couldn't bend his mind to his studies.* 他不能专心学习. **bend/lean over backwards** ⇨ BACKWARDS (BACKWARD). **on bended 'knee(s)** (as if) kneeling to pray or to beg humbly (仿佛)跪下祈祷或卑躬屈膝地哀求. **5** (phr v) **bend (sb) to sth** (force sb to) submit to sth (迫使某人)屈服, 顺从: *bend to sb's will* 顺从某人的意志 ○ *bend sb to one's will* 使某人顺从. **be bent on sth/on doing sth** be determined on (a course of action); have one's mind firmly set on (doing) sth 决心采取(某行动); 专心致志于(做)某事: *be bent on pleasure, mischief, etc* 一心要享乐、捣鬼等 ○ *He is bent on winning at all costs.* 他决心不惜一切去争取胜利.

▷ **bendy** *adj* (*infml* 口) (**a**) having many bends; winding 弯弯曲曲的; 迂回曲折的: *a bendy road* 弯弯曲曲的道路. (**b**) that can be bent easily; flexible 易弯曲的; 柔性的: *bendy material* 柔性材料 ○ *a bendy twig* 易弯曲的嫩枝.

bend[2] /bend; bɛnd/ *n* **1** curve or turn, esp in a road, racecourse, river, etc 弯, 拐角(尤指道路、赛场跑道、河流等): *a slight, gentle, sharp, sudden, etc bend* 一个小小的、平缓的、急转的、突然出现的…弯. **2** sailor's knot for tying rope 绑结(水手打的绳结). **3** (idm 习语) **(drive sb/be/go) round the bend/twist** (*infml* 口) (make sb/be/become) crazy; mad (使某人)发疯, 恼火: *His behaviour is driving me round the bend*, ie annoys me very much. 他的行为使我很恼火.

bender /ˈbendə(r); ˋbɛndɚ/ *n* (*sl* 俚) period of wild drinking 狂饮的一段时间: *go on a drunken bender for three days* 狂饮三天.

bends /bendz; bɛndz/ *n* [pl] **the bends** (*infml* 口) severe pains and difficulty in breathing experienced by deep-sea divers who come to the surface too quickly 潜函病(深海潜水员因浮出水面太快而感到关节剧痛、呼吸困难的症状).

be·neath /bɪˈni:θ; bɪˋniθ/ *prep* (*fml* 文) **1** in or to a lower position than (sb/sth); under 在或向低于(某人[某事物])的位置; 在…下面: *They found the body buried beneath a pile of leaves.* 他们在一堆树叶下面发现了那具尸体. ○ *The boat sank beneath the waves.* 小船淹没在浪涛中. **2** not worthy of (sb) 对(某人)来说不值得: *He considers such jobs beneath him*, ie not suited to his rank or status. 他认为做这样的工作有失身分. ○ *They thought she had married beneath her*, ie married a man of lower social status. 他们认为她下嫁给了社会地位比她低的人. Cf 参看 ABOVE[2].

▷ **be·neath** *adv* (*fml* 文) in or to a lower position; underneath 在或向较低的位置; 在下面: *Her careful make-up hid the signs of age beneath.* 她的精心化妆掩饰了脂粉下面岁月刻下的痕迹.

Bene·dict·ine *n* **1** /ˌbenɪˈdɪktɪn; ˌbɛnəˋdɪktɪn/ [C] monk or nun of the religious order founded by St Benedict 圣本笃修会的修士或修女: [attrib 作定语] *the Benedictine order* 本笃会. **2** /ˌbenɪˈdɪkti:n; ˌbɛnəˋdɪktɪn/ [U, C] (*propr* 专利名) liqueur originally made by monks of this order (本笃会修士创始酿造的)甜露酒.

be·ne·dic·tion /ˌbenɪˈdɪkʃn; ˌbɛnəˋdɪkʃən/ *n* [C, U] blessing, esp one said before a meal or at the end of a church service 祝福(尤指餐前或礼拜结束时的祝祷): *pronounce/say the benediction* 祝福 ○ *confer one's benediction on sb* 祝福某人.

be·ne·fac·tion /ˌbenɪˈfækʃn; ˌbɛnəˋfækʃən/ *n* (*fml* 文) **1** [U] action of giving or doing good 善行; 善举. **2** [C] gift; donation 赠品; 捐赠: *She made many charitable benefactions.* 她作过很多慈善捐赠.

be·ne·factor /ˈbenɪfæktə(r); ˋbɛnə,fæktɚ/ *n* person who gives money or other help to a school, hospital, charity, etc 捐助者; 施主.

▷ **be·ne·fact·ress** /ˈbenɪfæktrɪs; ˋbɛnə,fæktrɪs/ *n* woman benefactor 女捐助人; 女施主.

be·ne·fice /ˈbenɪfɪs; ˋbɛnəfɪs/ *n* position (in charge of a parish) that provides a clergyman with his income (牧区牧师的)有俸圣职.

▷ **be·ne·ficed** /ˈbenɪfɪst; ˋbɛnə,fɪst/ *adj* having a benefice 享有圣俸的: *a beneficed priest* 享有圣俸的牧师.

be·ne·fi·cent /bɪˈnefɪsnt; bəˋnɛfəsn̩t/ *adj* (*fml* 文) showing active kindness; generous; charitable 行善的; 乐善好施的; 慷慨的; 慈善的: *a beneficent patron* 慷慨的赞助人. ▷ **be·ne·fi·cence** /bɪˈnefɪsns; bəˋnɛfəsn̩s/ *n* [U].

be·ne·fi·cial /ˌbenɪˈfɪʃl; ˌbɛnəˋfɪʃəl/ *adj* **~ (to sth/sb)** having a helpful or useful effect; advantageous 有益的; 有用的; 有好处的: *a beneficial result, influence, etc* 有益的结果、影响等 ○ *Fresh air is beneficial to one's health.* 新鲜空气有益于健康. ▷ **be·ne·fi·cially** /-ʃəlɪ; -ʃəlɪ/ *adv*.

be·ne·fi·ciary /ˌbenɪˈfɪʃərɪ; *US* -ˈfɪʃɪerɪ; ˌbɛnəˋfɪʃɪ,ɛrɪ/ *n* person who receives sth, esp one who receives money, property, etc when sb dies 受益者; 受惠者; (尤指)承受遗产者.

be·ne·fit /ˈbenɪfɪt; ˋbɛnəfɪt/ *n* **1** (**a**) [U] profit; gain; future good (used esp with the *vs* and *preps* shown) 利益, 实惠, 未来的好处(尤与以下所示动词及介词连用): *Because of illness she didn't get much benefit from her stay abroad.* 她待在国外因生病而未得到多大好处. ○ *I've had the benefit of a good education.* 我得益于良好的教育. ○ *It was achieved with the benefit* (ie help, aid) *of modern technology.* 借助现代技术, 这个目标已经达到. ○ *The new regulations will be of great benefit to us all.* 新规章对我们大家都会大有好处. ○ *A change in the law would be to everyone's benefit.* 法律中的一项修改将符合所有人的利益. (**b**) [C] thing from which one gains or profits; advantage 优越性; 优良条件: *the benefits of modern medicine, science, higher education* 现代医学、科学、高等教育的优良条件. **2** [U, C] allowance of money, etc to which sb is entitled from an insurance policy or from government funds 保险金; 救济金; 抚恤金; 补助金: *medical, unemployment, sickness, etc benefit(s)* 医疗、失业、疾病等补助. **3** [C, esp attrib 尤作定语] public performance or game held in order to raise money for a particular player, charity, etc (为某运动员或慈善事业等筹款而举行的)义演或义赛: *a 'benefit match, performance, concert, etc* 义赛、义演、慈善音乐会等. **4** (idm 习语) **for sb's benefit** in order to help,

B

B

guide, instruct, etc sb 以对某人进行帮助、指引、指导等: *The warning sign was put there for the benefit of the public.* 那儿设立了警告牌以引起人们的警惕. ○ *Although she didn't mention me by name, I know her remarks were intended for my benefit.* 虽然她没提到我的名字, 但我明白她的话是为我好. **give sb the ˌbenefit of the ˈdoubt** accept that sb is innocent, right, etc because there is no clear evidence to support one's feeling that he may not be 因证据不足而承认某人无罪、无过失等: *By allowing her to go free the judge gave the accused the benefit of the doubt.* 法官对被告作了无罪推定而释放了她.

▷ **be·ne·fit** *v* (*pt, pp* **-fited**; *US also* **-fitted**) **1** [Tn] do good to (sb/sth) 使(某人[某事物])受益: *These facilities have benefited the whole town.* 这些设施使全城受益. **2** [I, Ipr] **~ (from/by sth)** receive benefit or gain 得益: *Who stands to* (ie is likely to) *benefit most by the new tax laws?* 什么人可能从新的税法中得到最大的好处? ○ *He hasn't benefited from* (ie become wiser with) *the experience.* 他虽有体验却无长进.

be·ne·vol·ent /bɪˈnevələnt; bəˋnɛvələnt/ *adj* **~ (to/towards sb) 1** being, or wishing to be, kind, friendly and helpful 好心肠的; 与人为善的; 助人为乐的: *a benevolent air, attitude, manner, etc* 和蔼可亲的神态、态度、样子等 ○ *a benevolent dictator* 发善心的独裁者 ○ *benevolent despotism* 施仁政的专制政体. **2** doing good rather than making profit; charitable 行善的; 慈善的: *a benevolent institution/society/fund* 慈善机构[团体/基金].

▷ **be·ne·vol·ence** /bɪˈnevələns; bəˋnɛvələns/ *n* [U] desire to do good; kindness and generosity 好心肠; 善心; 仁慈.

be·ne·vol·ently *adv*.

B Eng /ˌbiːˈendʒ; ˌbiˋɛndʒ/ *abbr* 缩写 = Bachelor of Engineering 工学士: *have/be a B Eng* 有工学士学位[为工学士] ○ *Greg James B Eng* 工学士格雷格·詹姆斯.

be·nighted /bɪˈnaɪtɪd; bɪˋnaɪtɪd/ *adj* (*dated* 旧) unenlightened morally or intellectually; ignorant; backward 未开化的; 愚昧无知的; 落后的: *benighted savages* 未开化的野人.

be·nign /bɪˈnaɪn; bɪˋnaɪn/ *adj* **1** (of people or actions) kindly; gentle (指人或行为)慈祥的, 和善的. **2** (of climate) mild; pleasant (指气候)温和的, 宜人的. **3** (of a tumour, etc) not likely to spread or recur after treatment; not dangerous (指肿瘤等)良性的, 无危险的. ▷ **be·nignly** *adv*. Cf 参看 MALIGNANT.

bent[1] /bent; bɛnt/ *n* **1** (usu *sing* 通常作单数) **~ (for sth/doing sth)** natural skill (at sth); liking or inclination (for sth/doing sth) (对某事物的)特长; (对某事物[做某事]的)爱好, 嗜好: *She has a (natural) bent for music.* 她(生性)爱好音乐. ○ *He is of a studious bent.* 他天生好学. **2** (idm 习语) **follow one's bent** ➪ FOLLOW.

bent[2] /bent; bɛnt/ *adj* (*sl* 俚 *esp Brit*) **1** dishonest; corrupt 不诚实的; 不正的; 贪污受贿的: *a bent copper,* ie a policeman who can be bribed 贪赃枉法的警察. **2** [usu pred 通常作表语] (*derog* 贬) homosexual 同性恋.

bent[3] *pt, pp* of BEND[1].

be·numbed /bɪˈnʌmd; bɪˋnʌmd/ *adj* (*fml* 文) made numb; with all feeling taken away 麻木的; 失去感觉的: *fingers benumbed with cold* 冻得麻木的手指.

Ben·ze·drine /ˈbenzədriːn; ˋbɛnzədrin/ *n* [U] (*propr* 专利名) type of amphetamine 苯齐巨林; 苯异丙胺; 安非他明.

ben·zene /ˈbenziːn; ˋbɛnzin/ *n* [U] colourless liquid obtained from petroleum and coal tar, used in making plastics and many chemical products 苯.

ben·zine /ˈbenziːn; ˋbɛnzin/ *n* [U] colourless liquid mixture of hydrocarbons obtained from petroleum and used in dry-cleaning 轻质汽油; 挥发油; 石油精.

ben·zol /ˈbenzɒl; *US* -zɔːl; ˋbɛnzɔl/ *n* [U] (esp unrefined) benzene (尤指未经提炼的)苯.

be·queath /bɪˈkwiːð; bɪˋkwið/ *v* (*fml* 文) [Tn, Dn·n, Dn·pr] **~ sth (to sb) 1** arrange, by making a will, to give (property, money etc) (to sb) when one dies 将(财物等)遗赠(给某人): *He bequeathed £1 000 (to charity).* 他遗赠(给慈善事业)1 000英镑. ○ *She has bequeathed me her jewellery.* 她把珠宝遗赠给我了. **2** (*fig* 比喻) pass on (knowledge, etc) (to those who come after) 将(知识等)传给(后人): *discoveries bequeathed to us by scientists of the last century* 上个世纪的科学家留传给我们的发现.

be·quest /bɪˈkwest; bɪˋkwɛst/ *n* (*fml* 文) **1** act of bequeathing 遗赠: *the bequest of one's paintings to a gallery* 把绘画遗赠给美术馆. **2** thing bequeathed; legacy 遗产; 遗物: *leave a bequest of £2 000 each to one's grandchildren* 留给孙儿每人一笔2 000英镑的遗产.

be·rate /bɪˈreɪt; bɪˋret/ *v* [Tn] (*fml* 文) scold sharply 严厉责备; 痛斥.

be·reave /bɪˈriːv; bəˋriv/ *v* [Tn, Tn·pr] **~ sb (of sb)** (*fml* 文) deprive sb (esp of a relative) by death 使某人丧失(尤指亲属): *an accident which bereaved him of his wife and child* 使他丧失妻儿的事故 ○ *the bereaved husband*, ie the man whose wife had died 死了妻子的男人.

▷ **the be·reaved** *n* (*pl* unchanged 复数不变) (*fml* 文) person who is bereaved 丧失亲人的人: *The bereaved is/are still in mourning.* 丧亲者仍在带孝.

be·reave·ment *n* **1** [U] state of being bereaved 丧失亲人; 丧亲之痛: *We all sympathize with you in your bereavement.* 我们对你丧亲之痛表示同情. **2** [C] instance of this 亲人丧亡: *She was absent because of a recent bereavement.* 她因最近丧亲而缺席.

be·reft /bɪˈreft; bəˋrɛft/ *adj* [pred 作表语] **~ (of sth)** (*fml* 文) deprived of (a power or quality) 失去(某种能力或性质): *be bereft of speech*, ie be unable to speak 失去说话的能力 ○ *bereft of hope*, ie without hope 失去希望 ○ *bereft of reason*, ie mad 失去理智.

beret /ˈbereɪ; *US* bəˈreɪ; bəˋre/ *n* round flat cap with no peak, usu made of soft cloth or felt 贝雷帽(扁圆的无檐帽, 通常用柔软的布或毡制成). ➪ illus at HAT 见 HAT 之插图.

beri·beri /ˌberɪˈberɪ; ˋbɛrɪˋbɛrɪ/ *n* [U] mainly tropical disease affecting the nervous system, caused by lack of vitamin B 脚气(由于缺乏维生素B而引起的影响神经系统的热带疾病).

berk /bɜːk; bɝk/ *n* (*Brit sl derog* 俚, 贬) stupid person (esp a man) 笨蛋(尤指男子).

berry /ˈberɪ; ˋbɛrɪ/ *n* **1** small juicy fruit without a stone 聚合果: *blackberry* 黑莓 ○ *raspberry* 悬钩子 ○ *holly berries* 泡叶枸子. **2** (*botany* 植) fruit with seeds enclosed in pulp (eg gooseberry, tomato, banana) 浆果(如醋栗、西红柿、香蕉). **3** egg of a fish or lobster 鱼或龙虾的卵. **4** (idm 习语) **brown as a berry** ➪ BROWN.

ber·serk /bəˈsɜːk; bɚˋsɝk/ *adj* [usu pred 通常作表语] wild with rage 狂怒: *send sb/go/be berserk* 使某人勃然大怒.

berth /bɜːθ; bɝθ/ *n* **1** sleeping-place on a ship, train, etc (船、列车等的)卧铺. **2** place for a ship to be tied up in a harbour, or to be at anchor (船舶的)停泊地或锚位: *find a safe berth*, eg one protected from bad weather 寻找安全的停泊地(如躲避恶劣天气的处所). **3** (*infml* 口) job or position (esp an enjoyable one) 职务或职位(尤指顺心的): *a snug/cosy berth* 舒适的[惬意的]职位. **4** (idm 习语) **give sb/sth a wide berth** ➪ WIDE.

▷ **berth** *v* **1** [Tn usu passive 通常用于被动语态] provide (sb) with a sleeping-place 为(某人)提供卧铺: *Six passengers can be berthed on the lower deck.* 下层舱可为六位乘客提供卧铺. **2 (a)** [Tn] tie up (a ship) in a harbour or at a suitable place; moor 将(船)系泊(在港口或适当地方); 停泊. **(b)** [I] (of a ship) come to a berth; moor (指船)来到停泊地; 停泊: *The liner berthed at midday.* 班轮中午到达停泊地.

beryl /ˈberəl; ˋbɛrəl/ *n* transparent precious stone, usu green 绿宝石; 绿柱石; 绿玉.

be·seech /bɪˈsiːtʃ; bɪˋsitʃ/ *v* (*pt, pp* **besought** /bɪˈsɔːt; bɪˋsɔt/ or **beseeched**) (*fml* 文) **1** [Tn, Tn·pr, Dn·t] **~ sb (for sth)** ask sb earnestly; implore sb; entreat sb 恳求、哀求或祈求某人: *Spare him, I beseech you.* 我恳求你饶了他吧. ○ *The prisoner besought the judge for mercy/to be merciful.* 囚犯恳求法官宽恕[乞求宽大]. **2** [Tn] ask earnestly for (sth); beg for (sth) 企求(某事物); 乞求(某事物): *She besought his forgiveness.* 她乞求他原谅. ➪Usage at ASK 用法见 ASK.

▷ **be·seech·ing** *adj* [attrib 作定语] (of a look, tone of voice, etc) entreating or appealing for sth (指样子、声调等)恳求的, 哀求的. **be·seech·ingly** *adv*.

be·set /bɪˈset; bɪˋsɛt/ *v* (**-tt-**; *pt, pp* **beset**) [Tn esp passive 尤用于被动语态] (*fml* 文) surround (sb/sth) on all sides; trouble constantly; threaten 围绕(某人[某事物]); 镶嵌; 困扰; 威胁: *beset by doubts* 为疑问所困扰 ○ *The voyage was beset with dangers.* 这次航程充满了危险. ○ *the difficulties, pressures, temptations, etc that beset us all* 缠绕着我们的困难, 压力, 诱惑等.

▷ **be·set·ting** *adj* [attrib 作定语] habitually affecting or troubling sb 经常影响着或困扰着某人的: *a besetting difficulty/fear/sin* 重重的困难[经常性的恐惧/易犯的罪恶].

be·side /bɪˈsaɪd; bɪˈsaɪd/ *prep* **1** at the side of (sb/sth); next to 在(某人[某事物])的旁边; 在...附近: *Sit beside your sister.* 坐在你妹妹旁边. ○ *I keep a dictionary beside me when I'm doing crosswords.* 我填纵横字谜的时候, 手边总有一本字典. **2** compared with (sb/sth) 与(某人[某事物])相比: *Beside your earlier work this piece seems rather disappointing.* 这件工作同你早先的工作相比, 有些令人失望. **3** (idm 习语) **beˈside oneself (with sth)** having lost one's self-control because of the intensity of the emotion one is feeling (因过于激动)失去自制力: *He was beside himself with rage when he saw the mess.* 他看到一切都乱七八糟就勃然大怒.

be·sides /bɪˈsaɪdz; bɪˈsaɪdz/ *prep* **1** in addition to (sb/sth) 除(某人[某事物])之外(还有): *There will be five of us for dinner, besides John.* 除约翰外, 还有我们五个人要一起吃饭. ○ *The play was badly acted, besides being far too long.* 这出戏除了太长之外, 演得也不好. **2** (following a negative 用于否定词之后) except (sb/sth); apart from 除(某人[某事物])之外(没有): *She has no relations besides an aged aunt.* 她除了有一个年老的伯母以外, 再没有亲戚了. ○ *No one writes to me besides you.* 除你以外, 没有人给我写信.

▷ **be·sides** *adv* in addition; also 而且; 还有: *I haven't time to see the film — besides, it's had dreadful reviews.* 我没有时间去看这部影片 —— 再说, 影评也诸多贬斥. ○ *Peter is our youngest child, and we have three others besides.* 彼得是我们最小的孩子, 我们另外还有三个孩子.

be·siege /bɪˈsiːdʒ; bɪˈsidʒ/ *v* **1** [Tn] surround (a place) with armed forces in order to make it surrender (用军队)包围(某处)以迫降: *Troy was besieged by the Greeks.* 特洛伊城被希腊人包围了. **2** (*fig* 比喻) **(a)** [Tn] surround (sb/sth) closely; crowd round 围住(某人[某事物]); 团团围住: *The Prime Minister was besieged by reporters.* 首相被记者们团团围住. **(b)** [Tn·pr esp passive 尤用于被动语态] **~ sb with sth** overwhelm sb with (questions, requests, etc) 以(问题, 请求等)使某人应接不暇: *The teacher was besieged with questions from his pupils.* 学生提出的问题很多, 教师应接不暇.

be·smear /bɪˈsmɪə(r); bɪˈsmɪr/ *v* [Tn, Tn·pr] **~ sth/sb (with sth)** (*fml* 文) make sth/sb dirty; smear sth/sb (with greasy or sticky stuff) 将某物[某人]弄脏; (以油性或黏性物质)涂污: *hands besmeared with oil* 被油污弄脏了的手.

be·smirch /bɪˈsmɜːtʃ; bɪˈsmɝtʃ/ (also **smirch**) *v* [Tn] (*fml* 文) dishonour (sb/sth); slander 玷污(某人[某事物]); 诽谤: *besmirch sb's reputation, name, honour, etc* 败坏某人的名誉、名声、荣誉等.

be·som /ˈbiːzəm; ˈbizəm/ *n* broom made by tying a bundle of twigs to a long stick 长柄细枝扫帚.

be·sot·ted /bɪˈsɒtɪd; bɪˈsɑtɪd/ *adj* [pred 作表语] **~ (by/with sb/sth)** made silly or stupid, esp by love 发痴, 变蠢(尤指受爱情驱使): *He is totally besotted with the girl,* ie deeply in love with her. 他一心痴恋着那个姑娘.

be·sought *pt, pp* of BESEECH.

be·spang·led /bɪˈspæŋɡld; bɪˈspæŋɡld/ *adj* [pred 作表语] **~ (with sth)** decorated with (things that shine or sparkle) 用(亮晶晶的东西)装饰: *a sky bespangled with stars* 闪烁着繁星的天空.

be·spat·tered /bɪˈspætəd; bɪˈspætəd/ *adj* [pred 作表语] **~ (with sth)** covered with (spots of dirt, etc) (被泥点等)溅污: *Her clothes were bespattered with mud.* 她的衣服溅上了泥污.

be·speak /bɪˈspiːk; bɪˈspik/ *v* (*pt* **bespoke** /bɪˈspəʊk; bɪˈspok/, *pp* **bespoke** or **bespoken** /bɪˈspəʊkən; bɪˈspokən/) [Tn] (*dated or fml* 旧或文) be evidence of (sth); indicate 证明(某事物); 表示: *His polite manners bespoke the gentleman.* 他那彬彬有礼的举止显出他是个绅士.

be·spec·tacled /bɪˈspektəkld; bɪˈspɛktəkld/ *adj* wearing spectacles 戴眼镜的.

be·spoke /bɪˈspəʊk; bɪˈspok/ *adj* [usu attrib 通常作定语] **1** (of clothes) made according to the customer's specifications (指衣服)定做的: *a bespoke suit* 一套定做的衣服. **2** making such clothes 做定做衣服的: *a bespoke tailor* 做定做衣服的裁缝. **3** (*computing* 计) (of software) specially written to suit the needs of the individual user (指软件)为适应个别使用者的需要特别编写的.

B

best[1] /best; bɛst/ *adj* (*superlative of* GOOD[1] GOOD[1]的最高级) **1** of the most excellent, desirable, suitable, etc kind 最好的; 最优秀的; 最理想的; 最合适的: *my best friend* 我最好的朋友 ○ *the best dinner I've ever had* 我吃过的最好的一顿饭 ○ *The best thing to do would be to apologize.* 最好还是道歉吧. ○ *The best thing about the party was the food.* 在那次聚会中最好的就是食物了. ○ *He's the best man for the job.* 他是最适于做这项工作的人. ○ *What is the best* (ie the shortest, easiest, etc) *way to get there?* 到那里去最好怎么走(最短、最方便等)? ○ *It's best to go by bus.* 最好坐公共汽车去. Cf 参看 GOOD, BETTER. **2** (idm 习语) **be on one's best beˈhaviour** behave as well as possible 竭力循规蹈矩. **one's best bet** (*infml* 口) action most likely to bring success 最好的办法; 最佳措施: *Your best bet would be to call again tomorrow.* 你最好明天再打电话来. **one's best bib and ˈtucker** (*dated or joc* 旧或谑) one's best clothes, worn only on special occasions (只在特殊场合下才穿的)最好的衣服. **one's best/strongest card** ⇨ CARD[1]. **the best/better part of sth** ⇨ PART[1]. **make the best use of sth** use sth as profitably as possible 充分利用某事物: *She's certainly made the best use of her opportunities.* 她确实充分利用了一切机会. **put one's best ˈfoot forward** go as fast as one can 从速行事. **with the ˌbest will in the ˈworld** even when one has made every effort to be fair, etc 尽管已尽心竭力.

□ **ˌbest ˈman** male friend or relative of a bridegroom who supports him at his wedding 男傧相. Cf 参看 BRIDESMAID.

best[2] /best; bɛst/ *adv* (*superlative of* WELL[2] WELL[2]的最高级) **1** (often in compounds 常用以构成复合词) **(a)** in the most excellent manner 最好地: *the best-dressed politician* 穿得最讲究的政治家 ○ *the best kept garden in the street* 这条街上收拾得最漂亮的花园 ○ *He works best in the mornings.* 他早晨工作效率最高. ○ *These insects are best seen through a microscope.* 这些昆虫透过显微镜看得最清楚. ○ *She's the person best able to cope.* 她是个最能妥善处理问题的人. ○ *Do as you think best,* ie as you think should be done. 你认为怎么好, 就怎么办吧. ○ *You know best,* ie You know better than anyone else what should be done, what is correct, etc. 你最清楚不过了. **(b)** to the greatest degree; most 最大程度地; 最: *the best-known/best-loved politician* 最著名的[最受人爱戴的]政治家 ○ *I enjoyed his first novel best (of all).* 我最喜欢他的第一部小说. **2** (idm 习语) **as ˌbest one ˈcan** not perfectly but as well as one is able to 尽自己最大努力; 尽力而为: *The facilities were not ideal but we managed as best we could.* 设备不理想, 但我们已经尽了最大的努力. **for reasons/some reason best known to oneself** ⇨ REASON. **had better/best** ⇨ BETTER[2]. **know best** ⇨ KNOW.

□ **ˌbest ˈseller** product, esp a book, that sells in very large numbers 畅销的产品(尤指书): [attrib 作定语] *the best-seller list* 畅销书目录. **ˌbest-ˈselling** *adj* having very large sales; very popular 畅销的; 流行的: *a ˌbest-selling ˈnovel, ˈauthor, ˈseries* 畅销的小说、畅销书的作者、畅销的丛书.

best[3] /best; bɛst/ *n* [sing] **1** that which is best; the outstanding thing or person among several 最好的东西; 最好的人: *She wants the best of everything,* ie wants her life, possessions, etc to be perfect. 她要的一切都是最好的. ○ *When you pay that much for a meal you expect the best.* 一顿饭花那么多钱是想吃到最好的东西. ○ *He was acting from the best of motives.* 他的动机是好的. ○ *She's the best of the lot/bunch.* 她出类拔萃. ○ *He is among the best of our workers.* 他是我们工作人员中最好的一个. ○ *We're the best of friends,* ie very close friends. 我们是至交(最亲密的朋友). **2** most important advantage or aspect of sth 某事物的最重要的优越性或方面: *That's* *the best of having a car.* 那就是有辆汽车的最大好处. ○ *The best we can hope for is that nobody gets killed.* 我们所能盼望的最好结果就是没有人被害. **3** (idm 习语) **all the 'best** (*infml* 口) (used esp when saying goodbye 尤用于告别时) I hope everything goes well for you 希望你一切顺利: *Goodbye, and all the best!* 再见, 祝你一切顺利! ○ *Here's wishing you all the best in the coming year.* 祝愿你来年一切顺利. **at 'best** taking the most hopeful view 充其量: *We can't arrive before Friday at best.* 我们无论如何星期五以前也到不了. **at its/one's best** in the best state or form 处于最佳状态: *modern architecture at its best* 处于鼎盛时期的现代建筑学 ○ *Chaplin was at his best playing the little tramp.* 卓别林扮演小流浪汉已达登峰造极的境界. ○ *I wasn't feeling at my best at the party so I didn't enjoy it.* 在那次聚会上我身体不太好, 所以兴致不高. **(even) at the 'best of times** even when circumstances are most favourable 即使在最好的情况下: *He's difficult at the best of times — usually he's impossible.* 他即使在情绪最好的时候, 都很难相处——平常就更令人受不了了. **be (all) for the 'best** be good in the end, although not at first seeming to be good 结果总会好的. **the best of both worlds** benefits of two widely differing activities that one can enjoy simultaneously 从两种截然不同的活动中同时获益: *She's a career woman and a mother, so she has the best of both worlds.* 她又当职业妇女, 又当母亲, 两全其美. **the best of British (luck) (to sb)** (*often ironic* 常作反语) (used when wishing sb good luck in some activity, esp when he is thought unlikely to succeed 用以祝某人撞大运, 尤指不太可能成功者). **(play) the best of 'three, etc** play(ing) up to three, five, etc games, the winner being the person who wins most of them 五局三胜, 三局两胜等: *We were playing the best of five but we stopped after three because John won them all.* 我们约定五局三胜, 但到三局就停了, 因为约翰连胜三局. **bring out the 'best/'worst in sb** reveal sb's best/worst qualities 表现出某人优秀[恶劣]的品质: *The family crisis really brought out the best in her.* 她在家庭遇到危难时, 表现出她的优秀品质. **do, try, etc one's (level/very) 'best; do the best one 'can** do all that one can 全力以赴; 竭尽全力: *I did my best to stop her.* 我已尽力阻止她. ○ *It doesn't matter if you don't win — just do your best.* 赢不了也不要紧——只要你尽力而为. **get/have the 'best of it, the deal, etc** win; gain the advantage 获胜; 得益. **look one's/its 'best** look as beautiful, attractive, etc as possible 使人看上去最美, 最吸引人等: *The garden looks its best in the spring.* 这个花园春天看上去最美. **make the best of it/things/a bad deal/a bad job** do what one can and be as contented as possible in spite of misfortune, failure, etc (遭到不幸或失败时)尽力而为, 随遇而安. **make the 'best of oneself** make oneself as attractive as possible 尽量使自己具有吸引力. **one's Sunday best** ⇨ SUNDAY. **to the best of one's a'bility** using all one's ability 尽其所能. **to the best of one's be'lief/'knowledge** so far as one knows (without being certain) 尽其所知(不一定有把握): *To the best of my knowledge she is still living there.* 就我所知, 她还在那里住. **to the best of one's memory** as far as one can remember 记忆所及: *To the best of my memory he always had a beard.* 我记得他总是留着胡子. **with the 'best (of them)** as well as anyone 跟别人一样好: *At sixty he still plays tennis with the best of them.* 他六十岁了, 可网球打得和别人不相上下. **with the 'best of intentions** intending only to help or do good 一心助人; 一片好意: *It was done with the best of intentions.* 是出于一片好心才这样做的.

best[4] /best; bɛst/ *v* [Tn esp passive 尤用于被动语态] defeat (sb); outwit 打败(某人); 智胜.

bes·tial /'bestɪəl; *US* 'bestʃəl; 'bɛstʃəl/ *adj* (*derog* 贬) of or like a beast; brutish; cruel 野兽的; 野兽般的; 野蛮的; 残忍的: *a bestial person, act* 野蛮的人、动作 ○ *bestial violence, lust, fury* 野兽般的凶猛、欲望、狂暴.

▷ **bes·ti·al·ity** /ˌbestɪ'ælətɪ; *US* ˌbestʃɪ-; ˌbɛstʃɪ'ælətɪ/ *n* **1** [U] **(a)** quality of being bestial 兽性; 兽行: *an act of horrifying bestiality* 可怕的兽行. **(b)** sexual activity between a human and an animal 兽奸(人兽之间的性行为). **2** [C] brutal act, esp of a sexually perverted kind 兽性的行为; (尤指)性变态.

bes·ti·ally *adv*.

bes·ti·ary /'bestɪərɪ; *US* -tɪerɪ; 'bɛstɪˌɛrɪ/ *n* medieval collection of stories about animals, including fables and legends (中世纪的)动物寓言集.

be·stir /bɪ'stɜ:(r); bɪ'stɝ/ *v* (**-rr-**) [Tn] **~ oneself** (*fml or joc* 文或谑) become active or busy 发奋; 振作: *He was too lazy to bestir himself even to answer the telephone.* 他懒得甚至不愿接电话.

be·stow /bɪ'stəʊ; bɪ'sto/ *v* [Tn, Tn·pr] **~ sth (on sb)** (*fml* 文) present sth as a gift (to sb); confer (将某事物作为礼物)赠(予某人); 赠与; 授与: *an honour bestowed on her by the king* 国王赐与她的荣誉. ▷ **be·stowal** /bɪ'stəʊəl; bɪ'stoəl/ *n* [U].

be·stride /bɪ'straɪd; bɪ'straɪd/ *v* (*pt* **bestrode** /bɪ'strəʊd; bɪ'strod/, *pp* **bestridden** /bɪ'strɪdn; bɪ'strɪdn̩/) [Tn] (*fml* 文) sit or stand with one leg on each side of (sth) 两腿分开跨着坐或站在(某物)上: *bestride a horse, chair, ditch, fence* 跨在马、椅子、沟渠、围栏上.

bet /bet; bɛt/ *v* (**-tt-**; *pt, pp* **bet** or **betted**) **1** [I, Ipr, Tn·pr, Tf, Dn·n, Dn·f] **~ (sth) (on sth)** risk (money) on a race or on some other event of which the result is doubtful 打赌; 赌博: *I don't enjoy betting.* 我不喜欢赌博. ○ *He spends all his money betting on horses.* 他把所有的钱都用在赌马上. ○ *She bet me £20 that I wouldn't be able to give up smoking.* 她和我打20英镑的赌, 说我戒不了烟. **2** (idm 习语) **bet one's bottom 'dollar (on sth/that...)** (*infml* 口) be absolutely certain about sth 绝对确信某事物; 打包票: *You can bet your bottom dollar he won't have waited for us.* 你可以打包票, 他是绝不会等我们的. **I bet (that)...** (*infml* 口) I am certain 我敢肯定: *I bet he arrives late — he always does.* 我敢肯定他得迟到——他一贯如此. ˌ**you 'bet** (*infml* 口) you may be sure (of it) 你可确信; 的确; 当然: *'Are you going to the match?' 'You bet (I am)!'* '你去看比赛吗?' '当然(我去)!'

▷ **bet** *n* **1 (a)** arrangement to risk money, etc on an event of which the result is doubtful 赌博: *make a bet* 打赌 ○ *have a bet on the Derby* 在德比大赛中赌马 ○ *win/lose a bet* 打赌而赢[输]. **(b)** money, etc risked in this way (金钱等)赌注: *place/put a bet on a horse* 在一匹马上下赌注. **2** (*infml* 口) opinion; prediction 意见; 预言: *My bet is they've got held up in the traffic.* 我想他们一定是在路上因交通拥挤而受阻了. **3** (idm 习语) **one's best bet** ⇨ BEST[1]. **hedge one's bets** ⇨ HEDGE.

beta /'bi:tə; *US* 'beɪtə; 'betə/ *n* the second letter of the Greek alphabet (Β, β) 希腊语字母表中的第二个字母(Β, β).

bet·el /'bi:tl; 'bitl̩/ *n* [U] tropical Asian plant whose leaf is chewed with the betel-nut 槟榔.

□ **'betel-nut** *n* [U, C] = ARECA NUT (ARECA).

bête noire /ˌbeɪt 'nwɑ:(r); ˌbet'nwɑr/ (*pl* **bêtes noires** /ˌbeɪt 'nwɑ:(r); ˌbet'nwɑr/) (*French* 法) person or thing that one particularly dislikes 特别讨厌的人或事物.

be·tide /bɪ'taɪd; bɪ'taɪd/ *v* (idm 习语) **woe betide sb** ⇨ WOE.

be·token /bɪ'təʊkən; bɪ'tokən/ *v* [Tn] (*fml* 文) be a sign of (sth); indicate 预示(某事物); 表示: *milder weather betokening the arrival of spring* 预示春天到来的暖和天气.

be·tray /bɪ'treɪ; bɪ'tre/ *v* **1** [Tn, Tn·pr] **~ sb/sth (to sb)** hand over or show sb/sth disloyally (to an enemy) (向敌人)出卖某人或泄漏某事: *betraying state secrets* 泄漏国家机密 ○ *Judas betrayed Jesus (to the authorities).* 犹大(向当局)出卖了耶稣. **2** [Tn] be disloyal to (sth) 背叛(某事物): *betray one's country, one's principles* 背叛自己的国家、自己的原则 ○ *In failing to return the money he betrayed our trust.* 他未能归还那笔钱而辜负了我们的信任. **3** [Tn] **(a)** show (sth) unintentionally; be a sign of 无意中显示出(某事物); 显露出; 表现出: *She said she was sorry, but her eyes betrayed her secret delight.* 她说她很难过, 但从她的眼神里却流露出她内心的喜悦. ○ *His accent betrayed the fact that he was foreign.* 他的口音显露出他是外国人. **(b) ~ oneself** show what or who one really is 暴露出本来面目: *He had a good disguise, but as soon as he spoke he betrayed himself,* ie he was recognized by his voice. 他伪装得很好, 可是一说话就原形毕露了(听他的声音就能认出他来).

▷ **be·trayal** /bɪ'treɪəl; bɪ'treəl/ *n* **(a)** [U] betraying or being betrayed 背叛或被出卖: *an act of betrayal* 背叛的

行为. **(b)** [C] instance of this 背叛: *a betrayal of trust* 对信任的辜负.

be·trayer *n*.

be·troth /bɪˈtrəʊð; bɪˋtroð/ *v* [usu passive 通常用于被动语态: Tn, Tn·pr] **~ sb (to sb)** (*arch or fml* 古或文) bind sb with a promise to marry; engage sb to marry 将某人许配给; 订婚: *She was betrothed (to the duke).* 她已许配(给公爵)了. ○ *The pair were later betrothed.* 那对男女后来订婚了.

▷ **be·trothal** /bɪˈtrəʊðl; bɪˋtroðəl/ *n* [C, U] (*fml* 文) engagement to be married 许婚; 订婚.

be·trothed *n* [sing], *adj* (*fml* 文) (person) engaged to be married 已订婚的(人): *his betrothed* 他的未婚妻 ○ *the betrothed couple* 未婚夫妻.

bet·ter[1] /ˈbetə(r); ˋbɛtɚ/ *adj* (*comparative of* GOOD[1] GOOD[1]的比较级) **1 (a)** of a more excellent or desirable kind 更好的; 更理想的: *a better worker, job, car* 更好的工作人员、工作、汽车 ○ *You're a better man than I (am).* 你人比我好. ○ *The weather couldn't have been better.* 天气好得不能再好了. ○ *Life was difficult then but things have got better and better over the years.* 那时生活很艰苦, 但情况已一年比一年好了. ○ *He resolved to lead a better life* (ie be more virtuous) *in future.* 他决心以后过较高尚的生活(更有道德的). **(b)** of a more precise or suitable kind 更准确的; 更合适的: *Having talked to the witnesses I now have a better idea (of) what happened.* 我与证人谈过话, 现在对所发生的事情更清楚了. ○ *Can't you think of a better word than 'nice' to describe your holiday?* 你难道不能想出一个比'好'更恰当的字眼来形容你的假日吗? Cf 参看 BEST[1]. **2** partly or fully recovered from an illness 疾病渐愈或痊愈: *The patient is much better today.* 病人今天好多了. ○ *His ankle is getting better.* 他的脚踝渐渐痊愈了. Cf 参看 WELL[2] 1, WORSE. **3** (idm 习语) **against one's better ˈjudgement** even though one feels that it may be unwise 即使感到可能不太好; 明知不可为而为之: *He agreed, but very much against his better judgement.* 他同意了, 但是他对此并不以为然. **be better than one's ˈword** be more generous than one has promised to be 比所许诺的更宽厚. **be no better than she ˈshould be** (*dated euph* 旧, 婉) (of a woman) have casual sexual relationships (指女子)性关系随便, 不正经, 不规矩. **the best/better part of sth** ⇨ PART[1]. **one's better ˈfeelings/ˈnature** more honourable or virtuous part of one's character 个人的优良天性或高尚情操. **one's better ˈhalf** (*infml joc* 口, 谑) one's wife or husband 自己的妻子或丈夫. **ˌbetter luck ˈnext time** (*saying* 谚) (used to encourage sb after a setback 用以鼓励受挫的人) **discretion is the better part of valour** ⇨ DISCRETION. **half a loaf is better than none/than no bread** ⇨ HALF. **have seen/known better ˈdays** be poorer or in a worse state now than formerly 现在比以前穷困或情况恶劣; 曾有过一段好日子: *That coat has seen better days.* 那件大衣曾体面过. **(be) little/no better than** practically; almost the same as 实际上; 简直就是: *He's no better than a common thief.* 他简直就是小偷. **prevention is better than cure** ⇨ PREVENTION. **two heads are better than one** ⇨ TWO.

bet·ter[2] /ˈbetə(r); ˋbɛtɚ/ *adv* (*comparative of* WELL[2] WELL[2]的比较级) **1** in a more pleasant, efficient, desirable, etc way 更愉快地; 更有效地; 更理想地: *You would write better if you had a good pen.* 要是有枝好笔, 就能写得更好. ○ *She sings better than I (do).* 她比我唱得好. **2** to a greater degree; more 较大程度地; 更: *I like him better than her.* 我喜欢他胜过喜欢她. ○ *You'll like it better when you understand it more.* 当你对它更了解时, 你就会更喜欢它. ○ *The better I know her, the more I admire her.* 我对她越了解, 就越爱慕她. **3** more usefully 更有用地: *His advice is better ignored*, ie It should be ignored. 他的话最好别听. ○ *If the roads are icy, you'd be better advised* (ie it would be more prudent) *to delay your departure.* 要是路上结冰了, 你最好考虑延期出发. **4** (idm 习语) **be better off (doing sth)** be wiser (to do sth specified) (对于做某事来说)是较为明智的: *He'd be better off going to the police about it.* 他最好把这件事报告警方. **be better off without sb/sth** be happier or more at ease without sb/sth 若无某人[某事物]会更快乐或更自在: *We'd be better off without them as neighbours.* 要是没有这家邻居, 我们就过得更愉快了. **ˌbetter the ˌdevil you ˈknow (than the ˌdevil you ˈdon't)** (*saying* 谚) it is easier to deal with an undesirable but familiar person, situation, etc than to risk a change which may make things worse 跟认识的魔鬼打交道总比跟不认识的魔鬼打交道好(对付讨厌的但熟悉的人、事情等较容易; 若冒险改变情况, 可能更糟). **ˌbetter ˈlate than ˈnever** (*saying* 谚) **(a)** (used as an excuse or apology for one's lateness 用作表示自己迟延的借口或歉意) **(b)** some success, however delayed or small it is, is better than none at all 迟做总比根本不做好; 有些成绩总比完全没有好. **better ˌsafe than ˈsorry** (*saying* 谚) it is wiser to be over-cautious and take proper care than to be rash and careless (and so do sth which one may regret) 稳妥总比后悔好. **better/worse still** ⇨ STILL[2]. **do better to do sth** be more sensible if one does sth 若做某事则更明智: *Don't buy now — you'd do better to wait for the sales.* 现在先别买——最好等到大减价时再买. **go one ˈbetter (than sb/sth)** do better (than sb/sth); outdo sb/sth 胜过(某人[某事物])一筹: *I bought a small boat, then he went one better and bought a yacht.* 我买了一只小船, 而他胜我一筹, 购置了一艘游艇. **had better/best** would be wise to 最好: *You'd better not say that.* 你最好别说那样的话. ○ *Hadn't we better take an umbrella?* 我们最好带一把伞吧? ○ *I had better* (ie I think I should) *begin by introducing myself.* 我最好(我想我应该)先作一下自我介绍. **know better** ⇨ KNOW. **not know any better** ⇨ KNOW. **old enough to know better** ⇨ OLD. **think better of sth** ⇨ THINK[1].

bet·ter[3] /ˈbetə(r); ˋbɛtɚ/ *n* **1** that which is better 更好者: *We had hoped for better.* 我们曾希望情况好转. ○ *I expected better of him*, ie I thought he would have behaved better. 我原来料想他会更好一些(我以为他能表现得好些). **2** (idm 习语) **one's (elders and) ˈbetters** (older and) wiser, more experienced people 前辈; 长者: *You should show greater respect for your elders and betters.* 你应该对长辈和上级尊重些. **a change for the better/worse** ⇨ CHANGE[2]. **(feel) (all) the better for sth** benefiting physically or mentally from sth 从某事物中获得肉体上或精神上的享受: *You'll feel all the better for (having had) a holiday.* 度(了)一次假你就觉得好多了. **for ˌbetter (or) for ˈworse** in both good and bad fortune 同甘共苦, 祸福与共. **for ˌbetter or ˈworse** whether the result is good or bad 不管是好是坏; 不管结果如何: *It's been done, and, for better or worse, we can't change it now.* 事已至此, 无论是好是坏, 已无法改变. **get the better of sb/sth** defeat sb/sth 胜过某人[某事物]: *You always get the better of me at chess.* 你下国际象棋总是赢我. ○ *His shyness got the better of him*, ie He was overcome by shyness. 他羞得无地自容. **get the better of sth** win in (an argument, etc) (在争论等中)得胜: *She always gets the better of our quarrels.* 我们吵架时她总是占上风. **the less/least said (about sb/sth) the better** (*saying* 谚) that person or thing is an unpleasant subject and it is better not to talk about him/it 少提为妙. **so much the ˈbetter/ˈworse (for sb/sth)** that is even better/worse 甚至更好[更坏]: *The result is not very important to us, but if we do win, (then) so much the better.* 输赢对我们并不十分重要, 但假如我们真赢了, (那)就更好了. **the sooner the better** ⇨ SOON. **think (all) the better of sb** ⇨ THINK[1].

bet·ter[4] /ˈbetə(r); ˋbɛtɚ/ *v* [Tn] **1 (a)** do better than (sth); surpass 胜过(某事物); 超越: *This achievement cannot be bettered.* 这一成就好得不能再好了. **(b)** improve (sth) 改善(某事物): *The government hopes to better the conditions of the workers.* 政府希望改善工作人员的状况. **2 ~ oneself** get a better social position or status 获得更好的社会地位; 高升.

▷ **bet·ter·ment** *n* [U] (*fml* 文) making or becoming better; improvement 改好; 改良; 改善; 改进.

bet·ter[5] /ˈbetə(r); ˋbɛtɚ/ *n* person who bets; punter 打赌者; 下赌注的人.

betting-shop /ˈbetɪŋ ʃɒp; ˋbɛtɪŋ ˌʃɑp/ *n* bookmaker's office (赌赛马等的)赌注登记处, 彩票经理部.

be·tween /bɪˈtwiːn; bəˋtwin/ *prep* **1 (a)** in or into the space separating (two or more points, objects, people, etc) 介于(两者或多者)之间: *Q comes between P and R* *in the English alphabet.* 在英语字母表中，Q位于P与R之间。○ *I lost my keys somewhere between the car and the house.* 我的钥匙失落在汽车与房子之间的什么地方了. ○ *Peter sat between Mary and Jane.* 彼得坐在玛丽和简之间. ○ *Switzerland lies between France, Germany, Austria and Italy.* 瑞士位于法国、德国、奥地利和意大利之间. ○ *The baby crawled between her father's legs.* 婴儿在她父亲的双腿中间爬. ○ (*fig* 比喻) *My job is somewhere between a typist and a personal assistant.* 我的工作介于打字员和私人助理二者之间. (**b**) in the period of time separating (two days, years, events, etc) 在一段时间(两天、两年、两次事件等)之内: *It's cheaper between 6 pm and 8 am.* 下午6时至上午8时之间较为便宜. ○ *I'm usually free between Tuesday and Thursday.* 我通常在星期二至星期四有空. ○ *Children must attend school between 5 and 16.* 5至16岁的孩子必须上学. ○ *Many changes took place between the two world wars.* 两次世界大战之间发生了很多的变化. **2** at some point along a scale from (one amount, weight, distance, etc) to (another) 介于(数量、重量、距离等的)两个量度之间: *cost between one and two pounds* 花费一至二镑 ○ *weigh between nine and ten stones* 重九至十石 ○ *London is between fifty and sixty miles from Oxford.* 伦敦离牛津五十至六十英里. ○ *The temperature remained between 25°C and 30°C all week.* 整整一星期, 温度一直在25°C至30°C之间. **3** (of a line) separating (one place) from another (指一条线)将(一处)与另一处分隔开: *build a wall between my garden and my neighbour's* 在我的花园与邻居花园之间砌一堵墙 ○ *draw a line between sections A and B* 在剖面A与B之间划一条线 ○ *the boundary between Sweden and Norway* 瑞典与挪威的分界线. **4** from (one place) to (another) 从(一处)到(另一处): *fly between London and Paris twice daily* 每天在伦敦与巴黎之间飞行两次 ○ *sail between Dover and Calais* 在多佛与加莱之间航行 ○ *a good road between London and Brighton* 伦敦与布赖顿之间的一条很好的道路. **5** (indicating a connection or relationship 表示有联系或有关系): *an obvious link between unemployment and the crime rate* 失业与犯罪率之间的明显的关系 ○ *the bond between a boy and his dog* 男孩和他的狗之间的亲密关系 ○ *They have settled the dispute between them.* 他们已解决了他们之间的争端. ○ *the affection, friendship, love, etc between people* 人与人之间的感情、友谊、爱情等. **6** (**a**) shared by (two people or things) (两人或两物)共享的; 共有的: *We drank a bottle of wine between us.* 我们俩共喝一瓶酒. ○ *This is just between you and me/between ourselves*, ie It is a secret. 这件事只有你和我[我们俩]知道(这是秘密). ○ *They carried only one rucksack between them.* 他们两人只带一个背包. (**b**) by the actions or contributions of (esp two people or things) 协力做或做出贡献: *They wrote the book between them.* 他们共同写成了这本书. ○ *Between them they raised £500.* 他们共筹得500英镑. ○ *We can afford to buy a house between us.* 我们有能力合买一所房子. ⇨ Usage at AMONG 用法见AMONG.

▷ **be·tween** (also **in be·tween**) *adv* (**a**) in or into the space separating two or more points, objects, people, etc 在(分隔的两个或几个点、物、人等)之间: *One town ends where the next begins and there's a road that runs between.* 一个城镇连接着另一个城镇, 两者之间有一条路. ○ *You'd have a good view of the sea from here except for the block of flats in between.* 要不是隔着这座公寓大楼, 大海的景色就可以从这里一览无遗. (**b**) in the period of time separating two dates, events, etc 在两个分隔的日期、事件等之间: *We have two lessons this morning, but there's some free time in between.* 今天上午我们有两节课, 课间有些休息时间.

be·twixt /bɪˈtwɪkst; bəˋtwɪkst/ *adv, prep* (idm 习语) **betwixt and between** in an intermediate position; neither one thing nor the other 居中; 非此非彼; 模棱两可: *It's difficult buying clothes for ten-year-olds — at that age they're betwixt and between.* 很难给十岁的孩子买衣服 —— 这种年龄说大不大, 说小又不小.

bevel /ˈbevl; ˋbɛvl̩/ *n* **1** sloping edge or surface, eg at the side of a picture frame or a sheet of plate glass 斜边或斜面(如镜框或玻璃板的边缘). ⇨ illus 见插图. **2** (in carpentry and stonework) tool for making such edges (木匠和石匠用的)斜角规.

▷ **bevel** *v* (**-ll-**; *US* **-l-**) [Tn] give a sloping edge to (sth) 把(某物)切成或磨成斜边或斜角: *bevelled edges* 弄成斜面的边.

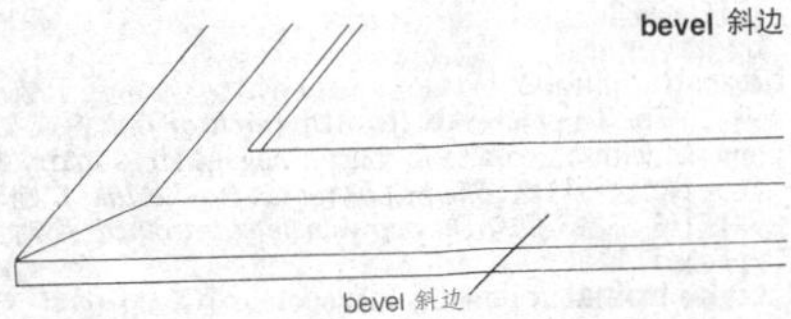

□ ˈ**bevel gear** either of a pair of gears with sloping toothed edges 伞齿轮; 锥齿轮. ⇨ illus at GEAR 见GEAR之插图.

bev·er·age /ˈbevərɪdʒ; ˋbɛvərɪdʒ/ *n* (*fml or joc* 文或谑) any type of drink except water, eg milk, tea, wine, beer (除水以外的)饮料(如牛奶、茶、葡萄酒、啤酒).

bevy /ˈbevɪ; ˋbɛvɪ/ *n* **1** large group 一群: *a bevy of beautiful girls* 一群美丽的姑娘. **2** flock of birds, esp quails 鸟群(尤指鹌鹑).

be·wail /bɪˈweɪl; bɪˋwel/ *v* [Tn] (*fml* 文) express sorrow over (sth); mourn for 因(某事物)而悲愁; 悲哀: *bewailing one's lost youth, innocence, etc* 为失去的青春、天真等而感伤.

be·ware /bɪˈweə(r); bɪˋwɛr/ *v* [I, Ipr] (used only in the infinitive and imperative 仅用于不定式及祈使句) **~ (of sb/sth)** be cautious (of sb/sth); take care (about sb/sth) 谨防(某人[某事物]); 当心(某人[某事物]): *He told us to beware (of pickpockets, the dog, icy roads).* 他告诉我们要当心(小偷、狗、结冰的道路). ○ *Beware — wet paint!* 注意 —— 油漆未干!

be·wil·der /bɪˈwɪldə(r); bɪˋwɪldɚ/ *v* [Tn] puzzle (sb); confuse 迷惑(某人); 混乱: *The child was bewildered by the noise and the crowds.* 孩子让噪声和人群给弄得晕头转向. ○ *I am totally bewildered by the clues to this crossword puzzle.* 这个纵横字谜的提示完全把我弄糊涂了.

▷ **be·wil·der·ing** /bɪˈwɪldərɪŋ; bɪˋwɪldərɪŋ/ *adj* puzzling 令人困惑的; 费解的: *bewildering speed, complexity* 令人晕头转向的速度、复杂性.

be·wil·der·ment *n* [U] state of being bewildered 混乱; 困惑: *watch, listen, gape in bewilderment* 目瞪口呆地看着、听着、愣着.

be·witch /bɪˈwɪtʃ; bɪˋwɪtʃ/ *v* [Tn] **1** put a magic spell on (sb) 对(某人)施魔法; 蛊惑(某人): *The wicked fairy bewitched the prince and turned him into a frog.* 邪恶的女妖对王子施魔法, 将他变成一只青蛙. **2** delight (sb) very much; enchant 令(某人)心醉、入迷; 使喜悦: *He was bewitched by her beauty.* 她生得貌美, 他一见倾心.

▷ **be·witch·ing** *adj* very delightful or attractive 使人心醉的; 使人着迷的: *a bewitching smile* 迷人的微笑. **be·witch·ingly** *adv*.

bey·ond /bɪˈjɒnd; bɪˋjɑnd/ *prep* **1** at or to a more distant point than (sth) 在或向(某物)的远处: *The new housing estate stretches beyond the playing-fields.* 新的住宅区一直延伸到游乐场的那一边. ○ *The road continues beyond the village up into the hills.* 这条路绵延不断越过村子直入山中. **2** later than (a specified time) 迟于或超过(某一时间): *It won't go on beyond midnight.* 这不会持续到午夜以后. ○ *I know what I shall be doing for the next three weeks but I haven't thought beyond that.* 我知道未来的三个星期我要干什么, 但再往后我就没想过. ○ *She carried on teaching well beyond retirement age*, ie when she was older than 60. 她早超过了退休年龄(年逾60)仍教书. **3** not within the range of (sth); surpassing 越出(某事物)范围; 超越: *The bicycle is beyond repair*, ie is too badly damaged to repair. 这辆自行车已不能修理了. ○ *After 25 years the town centre had changed beyond (all) recognition.* 25年过去了, 市中心变得认不出来了. ○ *They're paying £75 000 for a small flat — it's beyond belief!* 他们要以75 000英镑买一套小公寓 —— 简直难以置信. ○ *She's living beyond her means*, ie spending more than she earns. 她入不敷出(花的比挣的多). ○ *Her skill as a musician is beyond praise*, ie of extremely high quality. 她是一个音乐家, 其技巧令人赞叹不已(具有极高的水平). **4** except (sth); apart from 除(某事物)以外; 除了: *He's got nothing beyond his state pension.* 除

了国家发的养老金，他一无所有. ○ *I didn't notice anything beyond his rather strange accent.* 除了他那颇为古怪的口音以外，我没注意到别的. **5** (idm 习语) **be beyond sb** (*infml* 口) be impossible for sb to imagine, understand or calculate 对于某人来说，难以想像、理解或估计: *It's beyond me why she wants to marry Geoff.* 我不能理解她为什么要和杰弗结婚. ○ *How people design computer games is beyond me.* 我不明白电脑游戏是怎么设计的.

▷ **bey·ond** *adv* at or to a distance 在远处；向远方: *Snowdon and the mountains beyond were covered in snow.* 斯诺登那边的山到处都是白雪皑皑. ○ *We must look beyond for signs of change.* 我们应该把目光放远，看到变化的迹象. ○ *The immediate future is clear, but it's hard to tell what lies beyond.* 近期内的情况很清楚，但很难说以后如何.

be·zique /bɪˈziːk; bəˋzik/ *n* [U] card-game for two people played with a double pack of 64 cards 比齐克牌戏(一种两人玩的纸牌戏，用两副牌，共64张).

BFPO /ˌbiː ef piː ˈəʊ; ˌbi ɛf pi ˋo/ *abbr* 缩写 = British Forces Post Office 英国军邮局: *Capt. John Jones, HMS Amazon, BFPO (ships)*, eg on a letter 英国皇家海军舰艇亚马逊号，军邮(舰)约翰·琼斯舰长(如用于信件上).

bi- *pref* 前缀 two; twice 二；两次: *biannual* ○ *bicentenary*. Cf 参看 DI-, TRI-.

NOTE ON USAGE 用法: Note that **bi-** is used with certain expressions of time (eg *bimonthly*) to mean both 'every two' (months) and 'twice a' (month) 注意 **bi-** 附加在某些表示时间的词语前面(如 bimonthly)，兼有'每两'(月)和(每月)'两次'两种含义. There is a distinction between *biennial* (every two years) and *biannual* (twice a year). ☆ biennial 意为'每两年'，biannual 意为'每年两次'，这二者的区别则十分清楚.

bi·an·nual /baɪˈænjʊəl; baɪˋænjuəl/ *adj* occurring twice a year 一年发生两次的: *a biannual meeting* 一年举行两次的会议. ▷ **bi·an·nu·ally** *adv*.

bias /ˈbaɪəs; ˋbaɪəs/ *n* **1** opinion or feeling that strongly favours one side in an argument or one item in a group or series; predisposition; prejudice 偏见；成见；偏心: *The university has a bias towards/in favour of/against the sciences.* 该大学偏重[侧重/歧视]理科. ○ *The committee is of a/has a conservative bias.* 委员会有一种保守的偏见. ○ *He is without bias*, ie is impartial. 他没有成见. **2** slanting direction across threads of woven material (织物的)斜纹: *The skirt is cut on the bias*, ie cut with the threads running diagonally across the weave. 这条裙子是斜裁的(斜开料剪裁). **3** (**a**) (in bowls) tendency of the ball to swerve because of the way it is weighted (滚木球的)偏斜. (**b**) weighting that causes this (滚木球的)偏重心.

▷ **bias** *v* (**-s-**, **-ss-**) [Tn, Tn·pr] **~ sb (towards/in favour of/against sb/sth)** give a bias to sb; prejudice sb; influence sb, esp unfairly 对某人有偏见、成见、影响(尤指不公正者): *a bias(s)ed account/jury*, ie one which is not impartial 有偏见的叙述[陪审团] ○ *The newspaper/He is clearly bias(s)ed (in the government's favour).* 报纸[他]很明显是偏向(政府)的.

□ **bias binding** strip of fabric cut diagonally, used to bind edges (用于包边的)斜裁滚边料.

bib /bɪb; bɪb/ *n* **1** piece of cloth or plastic fixed under a child's chin to protect its clothes while it is eating (小儿用的)围嘴. **2** front part of an apron, above the waist 围裙的上部(腰以上的部分). **3** (idm 习语) **one's best bib and tucker** ⇨ BEST[1].

bible /ˈbaɪbl; ˋbaɪbḷ/ *n* (**a**) (also **the Bible**) sacred writings of the Christian Church, comprising the Old and New Testaments 圣经(包括旧约和新约的基督教圣书). (**b**) copy of these 圣经的文本: *three bibles* 三本圣经. (**c**) (*fig* 比喻) any authoritative book 任何有权威的书: *the stamp-collector's bible* 集邮者的经典.

▷ **bib·lical** /ˈbɪblɪkl; ˋbɪblɪkḷ/ *adj* of or in the Bible 圣经的；圣经中的: *a biblical theme, expression* 有关圣经的题目、言辞 ○ *biblical times, language* 圣经的时代、语言.

□ **bible-bashing**, **bible-punching** *ns* [U] (*infml derog* 口，贬) evangelical preaching 热衷于福音传道的.

biblio- *comb form* 构词成分 (forming *ns* and *adjs* 用以构成名词和形容词) of books 书的: *bibliophile* ○ *bibliographical*.

bib·lio·graphy /ˌbɪblɪˈɒgrəfɪ; ˌbɪblɪˋɑgrəfɪ/ *n* **1** [C] list of books or articles about a particular subject or by a particular author (有关某一专题或某一作者的著作的)书目，索引，文献: *There is a useful bibliography at the end of each chapter.* 在每一章后附有一份有用的参考书目. **2** [U] study of the history of books and their production 书志学；文献学. ▷ **bib·lio·grapher** /-ˈɒgrəfə(r); -ˋɑgrəfɚ/ *n*. **bib·lio·graph·ical** /ˌbɪblɪəˈgræfɪkl; ˌbɪblɪəˋgræfɪkḷ/ *adj*.

bib·lio·phile /ˈbɪblɪəfaɪl; ˋbɪblɪəˌfaɪl/ *n* person who loves or collects books 书籍爱好者；藏书家.

bibu·lous /ˈbɪbjʊləs; ˋbɪbjələs/ *adj* (*joc* 谑) excessively fond of or addicted to alcoholic drink 嗜酒的；有酒瘾的.

bi·cam·er·al /ˌbaɪˈkæmərəl; baɪˋkæmərəl/ *adj* having two legislative chambers (eg in Britain the House of Commons and the House of Lords) 有两个议会的(如英国的上议院和下议院): *a bicameral system of government* 两院制政体.

bi·carb *n* [U] (*infml* 口) = SODIUM BICARBONATE (SODIUM).

bi·car·bon·ate /ˌbaɪˈkɑːbənət; baɪˋkɑrbənɪt/ *n* [U] (*chemistry* 化) salt containing double proportion of carbon dioxide 碳酸氢盐；重碳酸盐.

□ **bicarbonate of soda** = SODIUM BICARBONATE (SODIUM).

bi·cen·ten·ary /ˌbaɪsenˈtiːnərɪ; *US* -ˈsentənerɪ; baɪˋsɛntəˌnɛrɪ/ *n* two-hundredth anniversary; celebration of this 二百周年；二百周年庆祝活动: *1949 was the bicentenary of Goethe's birth.* 1949 年是歌德诞生二百周年. ○ [attrib 作定语] *bicentenary celebrations* 二百周年庆典.

bi·cen·ten·nial /ˌbaɪsenˈtenɪəl; ˌbaɪsɛnˋtɛnɪəl/ *adj* happening once in two hundred years; marking a bicentenary 二百年一次的；二百周年纪念的: *a bicentennial anniversary/celebration* 二百周年纪念活动[庆典].

▷ **bi·cen·ten·nial** *n* = BICENTENARY.

bi·ceps /ˈbaɪseps; ˋbaɪsɛps/ *n* (*pl* unchanged 复数不变) large muscle at the front of the upper arm, which bends the elbow 二头肌: *His biceps is/are impressive.* 他臂力过人. Cf 参看 TRICEPS.

bicker /ˈbɪkə(r); ˋbɪkɚ/ *v* [I] **~ (with sb) (over/about sth)** quarrel about unimportant things (为小事)争吵: *The children are always bickering (with each other) (over their toys).* 孩子们常常(为玩具)争吵.

bi·cycle /ˈbaɪsɪkl; ˋbaɪˌsɪkḷ/ *n* two-wheeled vehicle on which a person rides, using pedals to drive it along 自行车；脚踏车. ⇨ illus at App 1 见附录1之插图, page xiii. Cf 参看 BIKE, CYCLE.

▷ **bi·cycle** *v* [I, Ipr, Ip] ride on a bicycle 骑自行车. **bi·cyc·list** *n*.

□ **bicycle-clip** *n* each of a pair of clips for holding trousers at the ankles while cycling (骑自行车时用的)裤脚夹.

bid[1] /bɪd; bɪd/ *v* (**-dd-**; *pt*, *pp* **bid**; in sense 3, *pt* usu 用于下述第3义时过去式通常作 **bade** /bæd; bæd/, *pp* **bidden** /ˈbɪdn; ˋbɪdṇ/) **1** [I, Ipr, Tn, Tn·pr] **~ (sth) (for sth)**; *esp US* **~ (sth) (on sth)** (**a**) offer (a price) in order to buy sth, esp at an auction (购物时)出价；(尤指拍卖时)喊价: *What am I bid (for this painting)?* (这幅画)给我个价，诸位愿意出多少钱? ○ *She bid £500 (for the painting).* 她喊价500英镑(买这幅画). ○ *We had hoped to get the house but another couple was bidding against us*, ie repeatedly offering a higher price than us. 我们原希望买下这所房子，但另一对夫妇不断抬价与我们竞买. (**b**) offer (a price) for doing work, providing a service, etc 投标: *Several firms have bid for the contract to build the new concert hall.* 有几家公司投标，争取建造新音乐厅的合同. **2** [I, Tn] (in card-games, esp bridge) make a bid[2](4) (纸牌戏中，尤指桥牌)叫(牌): *bid two hearts* 叫2红桃. **3** (*arch or fml* 古或文) (**a**) [Dn·t] order (sb); tell 吩咐(某人)；告诉: *Do as you are bidden.* 按照吩咐你的去做. ○ *She bade me (to) come in.* 她叫我进来. (**b**) [Dn·pr, Dn·t] invite (sb) 邀请(某人): *guests bidden to (attend) the feast* 应邀赴宴的宾客. (**c**) [no passive 不用于被动语态: Dn·n, Dn·pr] **~ sth to sb** say sth as a greeting, etc 说(问候、打招呼等的话): *bid sb good morning* 向某人道早安 ○ *He bade farewell* (ie said goodbye) *to his sweetheart.* 他向他的情人告别. **4** (idm

习语) **bid fair to do sth** (*arch or rhet* 古或修辞) seem likely to do sth 有做某事的可能: *The plan for a new hospital bids fair to succeed.* 兴建新医院的计划有希望成功.

▷ **bid·dable** *adj* ready to obey; docile 听话的; 温顺的.
bid·der *n* person or group that bids at an auction (拍卖时的)喊价者: *The house went to the highest bidder*, ie the person who offered the most money. 房子卖给了出价最高的人.

B

bid·ding *n* [U] **1** (*fml* 文) order; command 吩咐; 命令: *do sb's bidding*, ie obey sb 服从 ○ *At his father's bidding he wrote to his lawyer.* 他遵照父亲的吩咐给律师写信. **2** offering of prices at an auction (拍卖时的)竞买, 喊价, 出价: *Bidding was brisk*, ie Many offers were made one after the other. 出价很踊跃(一个接一个地竞相喊价). **3** (in card-games) process of bidding (BID[1] 2) (纸牌戏中)叫牌: *Can you remind me of the bidding* (ie who bid what)? 请再说一次谁叫了什么牌.

bid[2] /bɪd; bɪd/ *n* **1** price offered in order to buy sth, esp at an auction (为购某物的)出价(尤指拍卖时): *make a bid of £50 for a painting* 为一幅画出价50英镑 ○ *Any higher/further bids?* 还有出更高价的吗? **2** (*esp US*) = TENDER[3]. **3** effort to do, obtain, achieve, etc sth; attempt (做、获得、实现…某事物的)努力; 企图: *He failed in his bid to reach the summit.* 他攀登顶峰未能成功. ○ *make a bid for power/popular support* 争取权力[大众的支持]. **4** statement of the number of tricks a player proposes to win in a card-game (打桥牌时牌手对欲赢墩数的)叫牌: *'It's your bid next.' 'No bid.'* '轮到你叫牌了.' '我不叫.'

bide /baɪd; baɪd/ *v* **1** (*arch lit* 古, 文学) = ABIDE. **2** (idm 习语) **bide one's time** wait for a good opportunity 等待有利时机.

bi·det /ˈbiːdeɪ; *US* biːˈdeɪ; biˋde/ *n* low basin for washing the genitals and bottom (洗生殖器和臀部用的)坐浴盆.

bi·en·nial /baɪˈenɪəl; baɪˋɛnɪəl/ *adj* **1** happening every second year 两年一次的. **2** lasting for two years 持续两年的.

▷ **bi·en·nial** *n* plant that lives for two years, flowering in the second year 两年生植物(两年开一次花).
bi·en·ni·ally *adv*.

bier /bɪə(r); bɪr/ *n* frame on which a coffin or a dead body is carried or placed before burial 棺材架; 停尸架.

biff /bɪf; bɪf/ *n* (*infml* 口) sharp blow, esp with the fist 猛击(尤指用拳).

▷ **biff** *v* [Tn] (*infml* 口) hit or strike (sb) 打, 击(某人): *biff sb on the nose* 打某人的鼻子.

bi·focal /ˌbaɪˈfəʊkl; baɪˋfokl/ *adj* (esp of lenses in spectacles) designed for looking at both distant and close objects (尤指眼镜的镜片)远近两用的.

▷ **bi·foc·als** *n* [pl] spectacles with bifocal lenses 双光眼镜: *a pair of bifocals* 一副双光眼镜.

bi·furc·ate /ˈbaɪfəkeɪt; ˋbaɪfɚˌket/ *v* [I] (*fml* 文) (of roads, rivers, branches of trees, etc) divide into or have two branches (指道路、河流、树枝等)分岔, 分成两支.

▷ **bi·furca·tion** /ˌbaɪfəˈkeɪʃn; ˌbaɪfɚˋkeʃən/ *n*.

big /bɪg; bɪg/ *adj* (**-gger**, **-ggest**) **1** large in size, extent or intensity (在体积、面积、范围、程度或强度方面)大的: *a big garden, man, majority, defeat, explosion, argument* 大花园[高大的人/大多数/大败/大爆炸/大辩论] ○ *the big toe*, ie the largest 大脚趾 ○ *a big 'g'*, ie a capital G 大写的g(大写字母G) ○ (*infml* 口) *big money*, ie a lot of money 大笔的钱 ○ *The bigger* (ie worse) *the crime, the longer the gaol sentence.* 犯的罪越大, 刑期越长. ○ *He's the biggest liar* (ie He tells more lies than anyone else) *I know.* 他是我所知道的最大的骗子. ○ *She's a big eater/spender*, ie She eats/spends a lot. 她是个饭量大[花钱多]的人. Cf 参看 SMALL. **2** (more) grown up 成长(得更)大的: *my big sister*, ie my elder sister 我的姐姐 ○ *He's big enough to go out without his parents.* 他已长大, 不用父母陪着出门了. **3** [attrib 作定语] important 重大的; 重要的: *the big match* 重大的比赛 ○ *a big decision* 重大的决定 ○ *the biggest moment of my life* 我一生中最重要的时刻. **4** (*infml* 口) ambitious; extravagant 有雄心的; 过分的: *have big ideas/plans* 有远大的理想[有庞大的计划]. **5** (*infml* 口 *esp US*) popular with the public 大受欢迎的: *Video games are big this year.* 今年的电视游戏大受欢迎. ⇨ Usage 见所附用法. **6** **~ on sth** (*infml* 口) (*esp US*) keen on sth; enthusiastic about sth 精于某事物; 热衷于某事物: *The firm is big on extravagant promotion drives.* 这家公司正大搞推销运动. **7** (idm 习语) **be/get too big for one's boots** (*infml* 口) be/become very self-important or conceited 自大; 自负. **a ˌbig ˈcheese** (*sl derog* 俚, 贬) very important and powerful person 要人; 大亨. **big deal!** (*infml ironic* 口, 反语) I am not impressed 没什么了不起: *We're getting a wage increase of £40 a year, before tax. Big deal!* 我们工资一年要增加40英镑, 未扣除所得税. 有什么了不起! **a big fish (in a little pond)** an important and influential person (in a small community or restricted situation) (小地方或小范围内的)大人物. **a big noise/shot** (*infml* 口) important person 要人. **the big stick** the threat of using force, esp of great military strength 大棒政策(以实力, 尤指以强大的武力相威胁). **the big three/four, etc** the three, four, etc most important nations, people, companies, things, etc 三个、四个等最具有重要性的国家、人物、公司、事物等: *a meeting of the big five* 五强会议. **the big time** (*infml* 口) highest or most successful level in a profession, etc, esp in show business (某一职业等的)第一流, 最高水平(尤指演艺事业). **sb's eyes are bigger than his belly/stomach** ⇨ EYE[1]. **give sb/get a big ˈhand** applaud sb/be applauded loudly and generously 大声喝彩: *Let's all give her a big hand.* 让我们大家为她热烈鼓掌. **have bigger/other fish to fry** ⇨ FISH[1]. **in a big/small way** ⇨ WAY[1].

▷ **big** *adv* (*sl* 俚) **1** in a big manner; impressively; grandly 宏大地; 予人深刻印象地; 盛大地: *Let's think big*, ie plan ambitiously. 我们要立大志展宏图. ○ *He likes to talk big*, ie is very boastful. 他爱说大话. **2** successfully 成功地: *a band which comes/goes over big with pop fans* 受流行音乐歌迷欢迎而大为成功的乐队.
big·ness *n* [U].

□ **big ˈbang** hypothetical explosion that some scientists suggest caused the creation of the universe (某些科学家假设的导致宇宙起源的)创世大爆炸: [attrib 作定语] *the big bang theory* 大爆炸论.

Big ˈBrother dictator or the forces of a totalitarian state controlling every aspect of people's lives while pretending to be kindly 老大哥(专制国家中假仁假义的独裁者或势力).

big ˈbusiness commerce on a very large financial scale 大企业.

big ˈdipper (*Brit*) narrow railway at fairs with a track that rises and falls steeply 云霄飞车, 过山车(游乐场中沿陡峻铁道滑行的游戏车).

Big ˈDipper (*US*) = PLOUGH[2].

big ˈend (in an engine) end of a connecting-rod encircling the crankshaft (发动机的)连杆大头(环绕曲柄轴的连杆曲轴端).

big ˈgame larger animals hunted for sport 大的猎物.

ˈbig-head *n* (*infml* 口) conceited person 自命不凡的人. **big-ˈheaded** *adj*.

big-ˈhearted *adj* very kind; generous 善良的; 慷慨的.

big ˈtop main tent at a circus (马戏场的)主帐篷.

big ˈwheel huge revolving vertical wheel with passenger cars, used at fairs 大转轮(在垂直转动的巨轮上挂有载人座厢的游乐设施.

ˈbigwig *n* (*infml* 口) important person 要人.

NOTE ON USAGE 用法: **1 Big** and **large** are used when talking about physical size, extent, capacity or number. ☆ **big** 和 **large** 都用于指物质的体积、面积、范围、程度、能量或数量. **Big** is more informal. ☆ **big** 更口语化. **Large** is not normally used to describe people ☆ **large** 一般不用于指人: *They live in a big/large house in the country.* 他们住在乡下的一所大房子里. ○ *Which is the biggest/largest desert in the world?* 世界上最大的沙漠是哪一个? ○ *Her husband is a very big man.* 她丈夫身材很高大. ○ *There was a big/large crowd at the football match.* 有一大群人看足球比赛. **2 Great** is mostly used when talking (usually approvingly) about importance, quality, ability or extent. ☆ **great** 大多用于指重要性、特性、能力或程度(通常含褒义). **Great** can be used with uncountable nouns ☆ **great** 可与不可数名词连用: *He's a great painter, footballer, man, etc.* 他是个伟大的画家、足球健将、人物等. ○ *Peter the Great* *was a Russian ruler.* 彼得大帝曾是俄国的统治者. ○ *She lived to a great age.* 她活到很大年纪. ○ *with great enthusiasm, joy, pleasure, etc* 满腔热情、满怀喜悦、满心欢喜. **3 Large** and **great** are very similar in meaning when used with *amount, quantity* and *number* ☆ **large** 和 **great** 用于指数额、数量或数目时词义非常接近: *They spent a large/great amount of money on their holidays.* 他们度假花了一大笔钱. Note also the phrase 请注意这一词组: *to a large/great extent* 在很大程度上.

bi·gamy /ˈbɪgəmɪ; ˋbɪgəmɪ/ *n* [U] (crime of) marrying a person when still legally married to someone else 重婚; 重婚罪.
▷ **bi·gam·ist** *n* person guilty of bigamy 犯重婚罪者.
bi·gam·ous /ˈbɪgəməs; ˋbɪgəməs/ *adj* guilty of bigamy; involving bigamy 犯重婚罪的; 重婚的: *a bigamous marriage* 重婚. **bi·gam·ously** *adv*.

bight /baɪt; baɪt/ *n* **1** long inward curve in a coast 海湾: *The Great Australian Bight* 澳大利亚大海湾. **2** loop made in a rope 绳环; 绳圈.

bigot /ˈbɪgət; ˋbɪgət/ *n* person who holds strong (esp religious or political) beliefs and opinions, and is intolerant of anyone who disagrees 偏执的人(尤指在宗教信仰或政治方面): *religious bigots* 宗教的卫道士.
▷ **big·oted** *adj* intolerant and narrow-minded 偏执的; 心地狭窄的: *bigoted views* 偏执的观点 ○ *He is so bigoted that it is impossible to argue with him.* 他固执得不可理喻.
big·otry *n* [U] bigoted attitude or behaviour 固执的态度或行为.

bi·jou /ˈbiːʒuː; ˋbiʒu/ *n* (*pl* **bijoux** /ˈbiːʒuː; ˋbiʒu/) (*French* 法) jewel 珠宝; 首饰.
▷ **bi·jou** *adj* [attrib 作定语] small and elegant 小巧玲珑的: *a bijou residence* 小巧别致的住宅.

bike /baɪk; baɪk/ *n* (*infml* 口) **1** bicycle 自行车; 脚踏车. **2** motor cycle 摩托车. Cf 参看 CYCLE.
▷ **bike** *v* [I] (*infml* 口) ride a bicycle or motor cycle 骑自行车或摩托车: *Let's go biking.* 咱们骑车去吧.

bi·kini /bɪˈkiːnɪ; bɪˋkinɪ/ *n* scanty two-piece costume worn by women for swimming and sun-bathing 比基尼泳装(三点式女游泳服): [attrib 作定语] *a bikini top*, ie the top half of a bikini 比基尼泳装的上半部.

bi·labial /ˌbaɪˈleɪbɪəl; baɪˋlebɪəl/ *n* (*phonetics* 语音) speech sound produced by using both lips 双唇音的: *In English, b, p, m and w are bilabials.* 英语中的b、p、m、w为双唇音. ▷ **bi·labial** *adj*.

bi·lat·eral /ˌbaɪˈlætərəl; baɪˋlætərəl/ *adj* having two sides; affecting or involving two parties, countries, etc 有两边的; (两党、两国等)双边的: *a bilateral agreement/treaty* 双边的协议[条约]. Cf 参看 MULTILATERAL, UNILATERAL.
▷ **bi·lat·er·al·ism** *n* [U] principle based on bilateral agreements between countries, esp in trade and finance 根据两国间双边协议的原则(尤指于贸易与金融方面).
bi·lat·er·ally *adv*.

bil·berry /ˈbɪlbrɪ; *US* -berɪ; ˋbɪlˌbɛrɪ/ (also **blaeberry**, **whortleberry**) *n* (**a**) small N European shrub growing on moors and in mountain woods 欧洲越橘(生长在北欧荒原和山林中的一种小灌木). (**b**) its edible dark blue berry 欧洲越橘的浆果(深蓝色, 可食). Cf 参看 BLUEBERRY.

bile /baɪl; baɪl/ *n* [U] **1** bitter yellowish liquid produced by the liver to help the body to digest fats 胆汁. **2** (*fig* 比喻) bad temper; irritability 坏脾气; 暴躁.
□ ˈ**bile-duct** *n* (*anatomy* 解) tube taking bile to the duodenum 胆管. ⇨illus at DIGESTIVE SYSTEM 见 DIGESTIVE SYSTEM 之插图.

bilge /bɪldʒ; bɪldʒ/ *n* **1** [C] almost flat part of the bottom of a ship, inside or outside 舱底, 舭部(船底内部或外部近于平坦的部分). **2** (also ˈ**bilge-water**) [U] dirty water that collects in a ship's bilge 舱底污水. **3** [U] (*sl* 俚) worthless ideas or talk; nonsense 无聊的想法; 无聊的话; 废话: *Don't give me that bilge!* 别跟我说那些废话!

bil·har·zia /ˌbɪlˈhɑːtsɪə; bɪlˋhɑrtsɪə/ *n* [U] (*medical* 医) tropical disease caused by worms in the blood and bladder 血吸虫病.

bi·lin·gual /ˌbaɪˈlɪŋgwəl; baɪˋlɪŋgwəl/ *adj* **1** (**a**) able to speak two languages equally well 会说两种语言的: *He is bilingual (in French and Spanish).* 他操(法语和西班牙语)两种语言. (**b**) having or using two languages 通行或使用两种语言的: *a bilingual community* 通用两种语言的社区. **2** expressed or written in two languages 用两种语言表达或书写的: *a bilingual dictionary* 双语词典. Cf 参看 MONOLINGUAL, MULTILINGUAL.
▷ **bi·lin·gual** *n* bilingual person 通两种语言的人.
bi·lin·gually *adv*.

bi·li·ous /ˈbɪlɪəs; ˋbɪljəs/ *adj* **1** caused by or suffering from too much bile 因胆汁过多而引起的; 患胆病的: *a bilious attack* 胆病发作 ○ *I feel a little bilious after last night's dinner.* 我昨天吃过晚饭后, 感到有点不舒服. **2** bad-tempered; irritable 脾气不好的; 易怒的. **3** of a sickly yellowish colour (similar to bile) 黄疸颜色的: *a bilious (shade of) green* 黄绿色. ▷ **bi·li·ous·ness** *n* [U].

bilk /bɪlk; bɪlk/ *v* [Tn, Tn·pr] **~ sb ((out) of sth)** avoid paying money to sb; cheat sb (out of sth) 躲某人的债; 骗取某人(某物): *He bilked us of all our money.* 他把我们的钱都骗光了.

bill[1] /bɪl; bɪl/ *n* **1** (*esp Brit*) (*US* **check**) written statement of money owed for goods or services supplied 帐单: *telephone, gas, heating bills* 电话、煤气、暖气帐单 ○ *a bill for £5* 一张5英镑的帐单 ○ *Have you paid the bill?* 你付帐了吗? **2** written or printed advertisement; notice; poster, placard 广告; 招贴; 海报; 告示: *Stick no bills!* ie Sticking posters, etc here is forbidden. 禁止招贴! **3** programme of entertainment (at a cinema, theatre, etc) (电影院、剧场等的)节目单: *a horror double bill* (ie programme consisting of two horror films) *on TV* 一张介绍两部恐怖片子的电视节目单. **4** draft of a proposed law, to be discussed by a parliament (提交议会讨论的)法案: *propose, pass, throw out, amend a bill* 提出[通过/否决/修订]一项议案 ○ *The Industrial Relations Bill.* 劳资关系法案. **5** (*US*) = NOTE[1]: *a ten-dollar bill* 一张十元钞票. **6** (idm 习语) **a clean bill of health** ⇨ CLEAN[1]. **fill/fit the ˈbill** be adequate or suitable (for a specific purpose) 适合于(某一目的): *If you're very hungry a double helping of spaghetti should fit the bill!* 要是很饿的话, 吃两份意大利细面条就行了! **foot the bill** ⇨ FOOT[2]. **head/top the ˈbill** be the most important item or person on a list or a programme of entertainments 清单或节目单上最主要的节目或角色: *She topped the bill at the Palace Theatre.* 她在皇宫剧院演主角.
▷ **bill** *v* **1** [Tn, Tn·pr] **~ sb (for sth)** send sb a bill (for sth) 送交某人帐单(要求为某事物付帐): *I can't pay for the books now. Will you bill me (for them) later?* 这些书我现在不能付款, 事后给我寄帐单来好吗? **2** [Tnt esp passive 尤用于被动语态] announce or advertise; put in a programme 宣布; 贴广告; 列入节目单: *He is billed to* (ie It is announced that he will) *appear as Othello.* 已把他列入节目单内, 将扮演奥赛罗.
□ ˈ**billboard** *n* (*US*) large outdoor board for advertisements; hoarding 露天大广告牌; 大招贴板.
ˈ**billfold** *n* (*US*) = WALLET.
bill of exˈchange written order to pay money to a named person on a given date 汇票.
bill of ˈfare list of dishes that can be ordered in a restaurant; menu 菜单.
bill of ˈlading list giving details of a ship's cargo 提货单.
bill of ˈrights statement of basic human rights 权利法案; 人权法案: *the Bill of Rights of the US Constitution* 美国宪法的人权法案.
bill of ˈsale official document recording the sale of personal property 卖据.
ˈ**billposter** (also ˈ**billsticker**) *n* person who sticks posters or advertisements on walls, hoardings, etc 张贴海报或广告的人.

bill[2] /bɪl; bɪl/ *n* **1** bird's beak (鸟的)嘴, 喙. ⇨illus at App 1 见附录1之插图, page v. **2** (esp in geographical names 尤用于地理名称) narrow promontory 岬; 岬角: *Portland Bill* 波特兰海岬.
▷ **bill** *v* **1** [I] (of doves) stroke each other with their beaks (指鸽子)接嘴. **2** (idm 习语) **bill and ˈcoo** (*infml* 口) (of lovers) exchange kisses and loving whispers (指情人间)接吻及谈情.

bil·la·bong /ˈbɪləbɒŋ; ˋbɪləbɑŋ/ *n* (*Austral* 澳) branch of a river that forms a backwater (形成回水的)河的支流.

B

bil·let[1] /ˈbɪlɪt; ˋbɪlɪt/ *n* **1** lodging for soldiers or evacuees, esp in a private house（士兵或被疏散人员的）住宿处（尤指分住于民宅的）: *The troops are all in billets,* ie not in camp or barracks. 部队全部住在民房里（不住在营地或军营里）. **2** (*dated infml* 旧, 口) job; position 工作; 职位: *a cushy billet*, ie an undemanding one 轻松的工作.

▷ **bil·let** *v* [Tn, Tn·pr] **~ sb (on/with sb)** place (soldiers) in lodgings 安置（士兵）住宿: *The soldiers were billeted on an old lady.* 士兵们已安顿在一位老太太家里.

bil·let[2] /ˈbɪlɪt; ˋbɪlɪt/ *n* thick piece of firewood 木柴块.

billet-doux /bɪleɪ ˈdu:; ˋbɪleˋdu/ *n* (*pl* **billets-doux** /ˌbɪleɪ ˈdu:z; ˌbɪleˋduz/) (*joc* 谑) love-letter 情书.

bill·hook /ˈbɪlhʊk; ˋbɪlhʊk/ *n* long-handled tool with a curved blade for pruning trees, etc（修剪树枝等用的）长柄钩刀.

bil·liards /ˈbɪlɪədz; ˋbɪljədz/ *n* [sing *v*] game for two people played with cues and three balls on an oblong cloth-covered table 台球戏; 弹子戏: *have a game of billiards* 打一局台球 ○ *Billiards is played by women as well as men.* 打台球男女皆宜.

▷ **bil·liard-** /ˈbɪlɪəd-; ˋbɪljərd-/ (in compounds 用以构成复合词) of or used for billiards 台球的; 用于打台球的: *a billiard-cue/room/table.*

bil·lion /ˈbɪlɪən; ˋbɪljən/ *pron, det* **1** (*Brit*) 1 000 000 000 000; one million million(s) 万亿; 兆兆. ⇨App 4 见附录 4. **2** (*esp US*) 1 000 000 000; one thousand million(s) 十亿; 千兆. ⇨App 4 见附录 4.

▷ **bil·lion** *n* (*pl* unchanged or **~s** 复数或不变或作 **billions**) **1** (*Brit*) the number 1 000 000 000 000 万亿之数. **2** (*esp US*) the number 1 000 000 000 十亿之数. Cf 参看 MILLIARD. For the uses of *billion* see the examples at *hundred.* 关于 billion 的用法见 hundred 词条中的示例.

bil·low /ˈbɪləʊ; ˋbɪlo/ *n* **1** (*arch* 古) large wave 巨浪. **2** swelling mass (eg of smoke or fog) like a wave 如波涛滚滚之物（如浓烟或浓雾）.

▷ **bil·low** *v* [I, Ipr, Ip] rise or roll like waves 如波涛般起伏或翻滚: *sails billowing (out) in the wind* 在风中扬起的船帆 ○ *Smoke billowed from the burning houses.* 浓烟从着火的房子中滚滚地冒出来.

bil·lowy *adj* rising or moving like waves 如波涛汹涌的.

billy /ˈbɪlɪ; ˋbɪlɪ/ (also ˈ**bil·ly·can**) *n* tin can with a lid and handle used by campers for cooking（露营时烹饪用的有盖和把的）铁罐.

billy-goat /ˈbɪlɪ gəʊt; ˋbɪlɪˌgot/ *n* male goat 公山羊. ⇨ illus at GOAT 见 GOAT 之插图. Cf 参看 NANNY-GOAT.

billy-oh (also ˈ**billy-o**) /ˈbɪlɪ əʊ; ˋbɪlɪ o/ *n* (idm 习语) **like ˈbilly-oh** (*dated infml* 旧, 口) vigorously; fast 猛烈地; 很快地: *go, work, run, etc like billy-oh* 很快地去、工作、跑等.

bil·tong /ˈbɪltɒŋ; ˋbɪlˌtɑŋ/ *n* [U] (in S Africa) strips of lean meat salted and dried in the sun（南非的）晒干的腌瘦肉条.

bi·met·al·lism /ˌbaɪˈmetəlɪzəm; baɪˋmɛtḷˌɪzəm/ *n* [U] use of two metals, esp gold and silver, with a fixed ratio to each other as the monetary standard 复本位制（尤指金银二本位制, 在货币的法定纯度中保持二者的固定比率）.

▷ **bi·met·al·lic** /ˌbaɪmɪˈtælɪk; ˌbaɪməˋtælɪk/ *adj* **1** made of or using two metals 双金属的; 用双金属制造的; 使用双金属的. **2** using the system of bimetallism 复本位制的.

bi·monthly /ˌbaɪˈmʌnθlɪ; baɪˋmʌnθlɪ/ *adj* produced or happening every second month or twice a month 两月一次的; 每月两次的: *a bimonthly journal, event* 双月刊、活动.

bin /bɪn; bɪn/ *n* **1** large container, usu with a lid, for storing bread, flour, coal, wine, etc（贮存面包、面粉、煤、酒等的通常有盖的）大箱子: *a ˈbread bin* 面包箱. **2** (*esp Brit*) = DUSTBIN (DUST).

bin·ary /ˈbaɪnərɪ; ˋbaɪnərɪ/ *adj* of or involving a pair or pairs 成双的.

□ ˌ**binary ˈdigit** either the digit 0 or the digit 1, as used in binary notation 二进制数字（0 或 1, 用于二进制记数法）.

ˌ**binary noˈtation**, ˈ**system** system of numbers, common in computing, using only the two digits 0 and 1 二进制记数法（仅用 0 和 1 的记数方法, 计算机运算中多见）.

ˌ**binary ˈstar** two stars that revolve around a common centre 双星（环绕一共同中心旋转的两颗星）.

bind /baɪnd; baɪnd/ *v* (*pt, pp* **bound** /baʊnd; baʊnd/) **1** [Tn, Tn·pr, Tn·p] **~ A (to B); ~ A and B (together)** (**a**) tie or fasten, eg with rope 捆绑或系紧（如用绳）: *The hostages were bound (with ropes) and gagged.* 人质被（用绳）捆住并塞住了口. ○ *They bound his legs (together) so he couldn't escape.* 他们将他的双腿捆（在一）起使他无法逃跑. ○ *He was bound to a chair and left.* 他被绑在一把椅子上, 就那样待着. (**b**) (*fig* 比喻) hold (people or things) together; unite 将（人或物）合在一起; 结合: *the feelings that bind him to her* 把他与她结合在一起的感情. **2** [Tn, Tn·p] **~ sth (up)** tie a band or strip of material round sth（用带或条）束捆、扎、绑: *bind (up)* (ie bandage) *a wound* 包扎伤口 ○ *hair bound up with ribbon* 扎上丝带的头发. **3** [Tn, Tn·pr] **~ sth (in sth)** fasten (sheets of paper) between covers 装订: *bind a book* 装订书籍 ○ *a well-bound book* 装订精美的书 ○ *two volumes bound in leather* 皮面精装的两卷书. **4** [Tn, Tn·pr] **~ sth (with sth)** cover (the edge of sth) in order to strengthen it or as a decoration 将（某物）封边（加固或作装饰）: *bind the cuffs of a jacket with leather* 给上衣袖口镶皮边 ○ *bind the edge of a carpet*, ie to prevent fraying 给地毯包边（防止磨损）. **5** [I, Tn, Tn·p] **~ sth (up/together)** (cause sth to) stick together in a solid mass（使）粘成硬块: *Add an egg-yolk to the flour and fat to make it bind/to bind the mixture.* 在面粉和油脂中加入蛋黄使之凝结. ○ *Frost binds the soil.* 霜把土壤冻结了. ○ *The earth is ˈfrost-bound*, ie frozen hard. 地面冻硬了. ○ *Some foods bind the bowels/are binding*, ie cause constipation. 有些食物容易引起便秘. **6** [Tn, Tn·pr, Cn·t] **~ sb/oneself (to sth)** impose a duty or legal obligation on sb (to do sth)（用责任或法律义务）约束某人（使之做某事）: *bind sb to secrecy*, ie make him promise to keep sth secret 使某人答应保守秘密 ○ *bind sb to pay a debt* 使某人必须还债. **7** (idm 习语) **bind/tie sb hand and foot** ⇨ HAND[1]. **8** (phr v) **bind sb over (to keep the peace)** (*law* 律) warn sb that he will appear in court again if he breaks the law 令某人具结（遵守治安法令）: *The magistrate bound him over (to keep the peace) for a year.* 法官要他具结一年内不得扰乱治安.

▷ **bind** *n* [sing] (*infml* 口) nuisance 讨厌的事情: *It's a hell of a bind.* 这件事讨厌透了.

binder *n* **1** person who binds books; bookbinder 装订工. **2** machine that binds harvested corn into sheaves, or straw into bales 割捆机. **3** cover for holding sheets of paper, magazines, etc together 活页夹. **4** substance (eg bitumen, cement) that makes things stick together 黏合剂.

bind·ery *n* place where books are bound 书籍装订厂.

bind·ing *n* **1** [C] strong covering holding the pages of a book together（书的）封皮. **2** [U] fabric used for binding edges, eg braid 绲边; 绲条; 滚边. — *adj* **~ (on/upon sb)** imposing a legal obligation (on sb) 对（某人）有法律约束力的: *The agreement is binding on both parties.* 协议对双方具有约束力.

bind·weed /ˈbaɪndwi:d; ˋbaɪndˌwid/ *n* [U, C] type of wild convolvulus 旋花属植物.

bine /baɪn; baɪn/ *n* twisting stem of a climbing plant, esp the hop 攀生植物的蔓（尤指葎草蔓）.

binge /bɪndʒ; bɪndʒ/ *n* (*infml* 口) **1** time of wild or excessive eating and drinking（大吃大喝的）狂欢: *He went on/had a three-day binge.* 他大吃大喝了三天. **2** excessive indulgence in anything; spree 放纵; 纵情: *a ˈshopping binge* 大买特买.

bingo /ˈbɪŋgəʊ; ˋbɪŋgo/ *n* [U] gambling game in which players cover numbers on individual cards as the numbers are called at random 宾戈（一种赌博游戏）: [attrib 作定语] *a ˈbingo hall* 宾戈游戏厅.

bin·nacle /ˈbɪnəkl; ˋbɪnəkḷ/ *n* (*nautical* 海) non-magnetic case for a ship's compass 罗经柜（用于轮船罗盘的无磁性箱柜）.

bin·ocu·lars /bɪˈnɒkjʊləz; bɪˋnɑkjələz/ *n* [pl] instrument with a lens for each eye, making distant objects seem nearer 双筒望远镜: *watch from a distance through (a pair of) binoculars* 用双筒望远镜观看远处.

bi·no·mial /baɪˈnəʊmɪəl; baɪˋnomɪəl/ *n* (*mathematics* 数) algebraic expression consisting of two terms joined by + or − (代数的)二项式. ▷ **bi·no·mi·al** *adj*.

bi(o)- *comb form* 构词成分 of living things; of (esp human) life 生物的; (尤指人的)生命的: *biology* ○ *biodegradable* ○ *biography*.

bio·chem·istry /ˌbaɪəʊˈkemɪstrɪ; ˌbaɪoˋkɛmɪstrɪ/ *n* [U] scientific study of the chemistry of living organisms 生物化学.
▷ **bio·chem·ical** /ˌbaɪəʊˈkemɪkl; ˌbaɪoˋkɛmɪkl/ *adj*.
bio·chem·ist /ˌbaɪəʊˈkemɪst; ˌbaɪoˋkɛmɪst/ *n* expert in biochemistry 生物化学家.

bio·de·grad·able /ˌbaɪəʊdɪˈgreɪdəbl; ˌbaɪo,dɪˋgredəbl/ *adj* (of substances) that can be made to rot by bacteria (指物质)可由生物降解的.

bio·graphy /baɪˈɒgrəfɪ; baɪˋɑgrəfɪ/ *n* (**a**) [C] story of a person's life written by sb else (由其他人撰写的)传记: *Boswell's biography of Johnson*. 博斯威尔撰写的约翰逊传记. (**b**) [U] such writing as a branch of literature 传记文学: *I prefer biography to fiction*. 我喜欢看传记, 不太喜欢看小说.
▷ **bio·grapher** /baɪˈɒgrəfə(r); baɪˋɑgrəfɚ/ *n* person who writes a biography 传记作家.
bio·graphic, -ical /ˌbaɪəˈgræfɪk, -ɪkl; ˌbaɪəˋgræfɪk, -ɪkl/ *adjs*.

bio·lo·gical /ˌbaɪəˈlɒdʒɪkl; ˌbaɪəˋlɑdʒɪkl/ *adj* of or relating to biology 生物学的; 与生物学有关的: *a biological experiment, reaction* 生物学实验[反应] ○ *biological soap-powders*, ie ones that clean by destroying the living organisms contained in dirt 生物制剂皂粉. ▷ **bio·lo·gic·ally** *adv*.
□ **bioˌlogical conˈtrol** control of pests, esp insects, by the introduction of their natural enemy 生物控制(对有害生物, 尤指害虫, 利用其天敌进行控制).
bioˌlogical ˈwarfare (also ˌ**germ ˈwarfare**) use of germs as a weapon in war 生物战; 细菌战.

bio·logy /baɪˈɒlədʒɪ; baɪˋɑlədʒɪ/ *n* [U] scientific study of the life and structure of plants and animals 生物学.
▷ **bio·lo·gist** /-dʒɪst; -dʒɪst/ *n* expert in biology 生物学家. Cf 参看 BOTANY, ZOOLOGY.

bi·onic /baɪˈɒnɪk; baɪˋɑnɪk/ *adj* (in science fiction) having parts of the body that are operated electronically; having superhuman strength as a result of this (在科幻小说中)身体某部受电子操纵的, 有超人力量的.

bi·opsy /ˈbaɪɒpsɪ; ˋbaɪɑpsɪ/ *n* (*medical* 医) examination of fluids or tissue taken from a living body to diagnose a disease 活组织检查. Cf 参看 AUTOPSY.

bio·rhythm /ˈbaɪəʊrɪðəm; ˋbaɪo,rɪðəm/ *n* any of the recurring cycles of physical, emotional and intellectual activity said to affect human behaviour 生物节律(据说可影响人类行为的体力、感情和智力活动的循环).

bio·scope /ˈbaɪəskəʊp; ˋbaɪə,skop/ *n* (*S African* 南非) cinema 电影院.

bio·tech·no·logy /ˌbaɪəʊtekˈnɒlədʒɪ; ˌbaɪotɛkˋnɑlədʒɪ/ *n* [U] branch of technology concerned with the forms of industrial production that use micro-organisms and their biological processes 生物工艺学.

bi·par·tisan /ˌbaɪpɑːtɪˈzæn; *US* ˌbaɪˈpɑːrtɪzn; baɪˋpɑrtəzn̩/ *adj* of or involving two political parties 两党的; 代表两党的: *a bipartisan policy* 获得两党支持的政策 ○ *bipartisan talks* 两党的会谈.

bi·part·ite /baɪˈpɑːtaɪt; baɪˋpɑr,taɪt/ *adj* **1** consisting of two parts 由两部分构成的; 双边的. **2** shared by or involving two groups or parties 双方共有的; 涉及双方的: *a bipartite agreement, treaty, etc* 双边协定、条约等.

bi·ped /ˈbaɪped; ˋbaɪpɛd/ *n* animal with two feet 二足动物.

bi·plane /ˈbaɪpleɪn; ˋbaɪ,plen/ *n* early type of aeroplane with two sets of wings, one above the other 双翼飞机. Cf 参看 MONOPLANE.

birch /bɜːtʃ; bɝtʃ/ *n* **1** [U, C] (wood of a) type of northern forest tree with smooth bark and thin branches 白桦树; 桦木. ⇨illus at App 1 见附录1之插图, page i. **2** [C] birch rod or a bundle of birch twigs, formerly used for flogging schoolboys and young offenders 桦条(旧时用以抽打学童和少年犯): *Should we bring back the birch as a punishment?* 我们应该恢复用桦条抽打的体罚吗?
▷ **birch** *v* [Tn] flog with a birch(2) 用桦条打.

bird /bɜːd; bɝd/ *n* **1** feathered animal with two wings and two legs, usu able to fly 鸟; 禽. ⇨illus at App 1 见附录1之插图, pages iv, v. **2** (*sl* 俚esp *Brit*) young woman 妞; 姑娘: *Terry's got a new bird*, ie girl-friend. 特里有了个新女朋友. **3** (*infml* 口) person 人; 傢伙: *a queer bird* 怪人 ○ *a wise old bird* 聪明老练的人 ○ *The professional footballer who also plays cricket is a rare bird nowadays*, ie There are very few of them. 职业足球员也打板球的现在很少见了. **4** (idm 习语) **the bird has ˈflown** (*catchphrase* 警语) the wanted person has escaped 要捉的人逃走了. **a bird in the ˈhand is worth two in the ˈbush** (*saying* 谚) it is better to be content with what one has than to risk losing everything by being too greedy 一鸟在手, 胜于二鸟在林(最好满足于现有的, 以免因贪心而失去一切). **the birds and the ˈbees** (*euph* 婉) basic facts about sex 基本的性知识: *tell a child about the birds and the bees* 给孩子讲解基本的性知识. **a ˌbird's ˌeye ˈview (of sth)** (**a**) general view from a high position looking down 俯视; 鸟瞰: *From the plane we had a bird's eye view of London*. 我们从飞机上鸟瞰伦敦. (**b**) general summary (of a subject) (某科目的)概观. **birds of a ˈfeather (flock toˈgether)** (*saying* 谚) people of the same sort (are found together) 鸟以群分(同类的人在一起). **an early bird** ⇨ EARLY. **the early bird catches the worm** ⇨ EARLY. **(strictly) for the birds** (*infml derog* 口, 贬) not important; worthless 不重要的; 无价值的. **give sb/get the ˈbird** (*sl* 俚) shout at sb/be shouted at rudely and disapprovingly 用喊声轰某人: *The comedian got the bird*, ie was jeered at by the audience. 那喜剧演员让人喝了倒彩. **a home bird** ⇨ HOME[1]. **kill two birds with one stone** ⇨ KILL. **like a bird** (*infml* 口) without difficulty; smoothly 毫无困难地; 一帆风顺地: *My new car goes like a bird*. 我的新汽车行驶自如. **a little bird told me** ⇨ LITTLE[1].
□ **ˈbird-bath** *n* basin for birds to bathe in (usu in a garden) 鸟浴池(通常设于花园).
ˈbirdbrained (*infml derog* 口, 贬) stupid; silly 愚蠢的; 笨的.
ˈbirdcage wire cage for a domestic bird or birds 鸟笼.
ˈbirdlime (also **lime**) *n* [U] sticky substance spread on branches to catch small birds (涂在树枝上以捕捉小鸟的)粘胶.
ˌ**bird of ˈparadise** New Guinea bird with very bright plumage 极乐鸟(产于新几内亚, 羽毛鲜艳).
ˌ**bird of ˈpassage 1** migratory bird 候鸟. **2** (*fig* 比喻) person who passes through a place without staying there long 经某处而不久留的人.
ˌ**bird of ˈprey** bird that kills other animals for food 猛禽. ⇨illus at App 1 见附录1之插图, page iv.
ˈbird sanctuary area where birds are protected and helped to breed 鸟类保护区.
ˈbirdseed *n* [U] special seeds for feeding caged birds 鸟食.
ˈbird-song *n* [U] musical cry of birds 鸟的婉转啼鸣; 啁啾.
ˈbird-table *n* platform on which food for birds is placed 放置鸟食的平台.
ˈbird-watcher *n* [C], **ˈbird-watching** *n* [U] (person whose hobby is) studying birds in their natural surroundings (在大自然中)对鸟的研究(的爱好者).

birdie /ˈbɜːdɪ; ˋbɝdɪ/ *n* **1** (*infml* 口) little bird 小鸟. **2** score of one stroke under par for a hole at golf 高尔夫球运动中比规定击球次数少一击入穴所得的分数. Cf 参看 EAGLE 2, PAR[1] 3.

bi·retta /bɪˈretə; bəˋrɛtə/ *n* square, usu black, cap worn by Roman Catholic priests 法冠(天主教教士戴的通常为黑色的四角帽).

biro /ˈbaɪərəʊ; ˋbaɪro/ *n* (*pl* **~s**) (*propr* 专利名) type of ball-point pen 一种圆珠笔.

birth /bɜːθ; bɝθ/ *n* **1** (**a**) [U] emergence of young from the mother's body; being born or bearing young 分娩; 出生; 生育: *The father was present at the (moment of) birth*. 婴儿出生时其父亲在场. ○ *The baby weighed seven pounds at birth*. 婴儿出生时重七磅. ○ *He has been blind from birth*, ie all his life. 他自出生时就双目失明. (**b**) [C] instance of this 分娩; 出生; 生育: *There were three births at the hospital yesterday*. 昨天这所医院里有三个婴儿出生. **2** [C] (*fig* 比喻) coming into existence;

beginning 起源；开始：*the birth of capitalism, socialism, a political party, an idea* 资本主义、社会主义、一个政党、一种思想的起源。 **3** [U] family origin; descent 家庭出身；门第：*of noble birth*, ie from an aristocratic family 高贵身世的(出身于贵族家庭) ○ *She is English by birth but French by marriage.* 她是英国血统，但嫁给法国人而入了法国籍。 **4** (idm 习语) **give birth (to sb/sth)** produce young 生孩子；产仔：*She gave birth (to a healthy baby) last night.* 她昨天晚上生了(一个健康的婴儿)。○ (*fig* 比喻) *Marx's ideas gave birth to communism.* 马克思的思想孕育了共产主义。

B

□ ˈ**birth certificate** official document giving the date and place of a person's birth 出生证明书.

ˈ**birth-control** *n* [U] controlling the number of children one has, esp by contraception 节育：*The pill is one method of birth-control.* 服用避孕丸是一种节育措施。

ˈ**birthmark** *n* unusual coloured mark on a person's skin at birth 胎记；胎痣.

ˈ**birthplace** *n* house or district where a person was born 出生处；出生地：*Mozart's birthplace is (in) Salzburg.* 莫扎特的出生地是萨尔茨堡。

ˈ**birth rate** ratio of births in one year to every thousand people 出生率.

ˈ**birthright** *n* privilege or property which a person may claim because of birth or status 由于出身或地位而可以享有的特权或财产；与生俱来的权利：*The estate is the birthright of the eldest son.* 长子对这份地产有继承权。○ (*fig* 比喻) *Freedom is our natural birthright.* 自由是我们的天赋权利。

birth·day /ˈbɜːθdeɪ; ˋbɝθ,de/ *n* **1** (anniversary of the) day of a person's birth 人的出生日期；生日：*Happy birthday!* 生日快乐！○ [attrib 作定语] *a ˈbirthday card, party, present* 生日贺卡、宴会、礼物。 **2** (idm 习语) **in one's ˈbirthday suit** (*infml joc* 口，谑) naked 裸体的.

bis·cuit /ˈbɪskɪt; ˋbɪskɪt/ *n* **1** [C] small flat thin piece of pastry baked crisp 饼干。 **2** [C] (*US*) soft cake like a scone 软烤饼。 **3** [U] light-brown colour 淡褐色。 **4** [U] pottery that has been fired (FIRE[2] 7) but not glazed (经烤焙而未上釉彩的)本色陶器。 **5** (idm 习语) **take the biscuit/cake** (*Brit infml* 口) be extremely or specially amusing, annoying, surprising, etc 极其可笑、讨厌、惊奇等：*He's done stupid things before, but this really takes the biscuit*, ie is the most stupid thing. 他以前倒也干过傻事，但这次实在太离谱了(做了最愚蠢的事)。

bi·sect /baɪˈsekt; baɪˋsɛkt/ *v* [Tn] divide into two (usu equal) parts 分成两个(通常为相等的)部分；二等分。 ▷ **bi·sec·tion** /baɪˈsekʃn; baɪˋsɛkʃən/ *n* [U, C].

bi·sex·ual /ˌbaɪˈsekʃʊəl; baɪˋsɛkʃʊəl/ *adj* **1** sexually attracted to both men and women 对男女两性都有性欲的。Cf 参看 HETEROSEXUAL, HOMOSEXUAL. **2** having both male and female sexual organs; hermaphrodite 具有两性生殖器官的；雌雄同体的.

▷ **bi·sex·ual** *n* person who is bisexual 对男女两性都有性欲的人；具有两性生殖器官的人；阴阳人.

bi·sexu·al·ity /ˌbaɪsekʃʊˈælətɪ; ˌbaɪsɛkʃʊˋælətɪ/ *n* [U].

bishop /ˈbɪʃəp; ˋbɪʃəp/ *n* **1** senior clergyman in charge of the work of the Church in a city or district 主教：*the Bishop of Durham* 达勒姆市主教。 **2** chess piece shaped like a bishop's hat (国际象棋中的)象。⇨illus at CHESS 见 CHESS 之插图.

▷ **bish·op·ric** /ˈbɪʃəprɪk; ˋbɪʃəprɪk/ *n* **1** position of a bishop 主教的职位。 **2** district under a bishop's control; diocese 主教的管区；主教辖区.

bis·muth /ˈbɪzməθ; ˋbɪzməθ/ *n* [U] chemical element, a greyish-white metal used in alloys; compound of this used in medicines 铋。⇨App 10 见附录10.

bi·son /ˈbaɪsn; ˋbaɪsn/ *n* (*pl* unchanged 复数不变) **1** American buffalo 北美野牛。 **2** European wild ox 欧洲野牛.

bis·tro /ˈbiːstrəʊ; ˋbɪstro/ *n* (*pl* **~s**) small restaurant 小餐馆.

bit[1] /bɪt; bɪt/ *n* **1** (**a**) [C] small piece or amount (of sth) 小块；少量：*bits of bread, cheese, paper* 一点面包、干酪、纸张 ○ *a bit of advice, help, luck, news* 一点劝告、帮助、运气、消息 ○ *I've got a bit of* (ie some) *shopping to do.* 我得去买点东西。 (**b**) [sing] **a ~ (of sth)** (*infml ironic* 口，反语) large amount 大量：*'How much money has he got in the bank?' 'A fair bit.'* '他在银行里有多少存款？' '可多啦。' ○ *It takes quite a bit of time to get from London to Glasgow.* 从伦敦到格拉斯哥要花很多时间。○ *This novel will take a bit of reading*, ie a long time to read. 这本小说真够看的(要花很多时间)。 **2** [C] (**a**) (*Brit*) small coin, esp an obsolete one worth three or six old pence 小硬币(尤指已作废的面值三或六便士的旧币)：*a threepenny bit* 三便士硬币。 (**b**) (*US*) (usu *pl* and in phrases 通常用于复数和词组) 12½ cents 十二分半(美元)：*two bits or a quarter (of a dollar)* (美元的)两个十二分半的钱币或一个二十五分的钱币。 **3** [sing] (*sl* 俚) set of actions, attitudes, etc associated with a specific group, person or activity 与某集体、人或活动有关的一系列行动、态度等：*She couldn't accept the whole drug-culture bit.* 她看不惯一切和毒品有关的事。 **4** (idm 习语) **a bit** (**a**) slightly; rather 稍微；有一点儿：*'Are you tired?' 'Yes, I am a bit (tired).'* '你累了吗？' '是的，我有点儿(累)。' ○ *This book costs a bit (too) much.* 这本书(太)贵了一点儿。○ *These trousers are a bit tight.* 这条裤子有点儿紧。 (**b**) short time or distance 短时间；短距离：*Wait a bit!* 稍等一会儿！○ *Move up a bit.* 稍微向上挪一下。 **bit by ˈbit** a piece at a time; gradually 一点儿一点儿地；逐渐地：*He assembled the model aircraft bit by bit.* 他一块一块地装配飞机模型。○ *He saved money bit by bit until he had enough to buy a car.* 他一点儿一点儿攒钱直到够买一辆汽车。 **a bit ˈmuch** (*infml* 口) unwelcome; excessive; unreasonable 不受欢迎；过分；不合理：*The noise from that party is getting a bit much.* 从聚会上传来的喧闹声越发过分了。○ *It's a bit much ringing me up at three o'clock in the morning.* 凌晨三点钟就打电话来，太不像话了。 **a bit of a** (*infml* 口) rather a 有点儿：*He's a bit of a bully, coward, fool, bore, etc.* 他有点儿霸道、胆怯、愚蠢、烦人等。○ *This rail strike is a bit of a nuisance*, ie is rather inconvenient. 这次铁路罢工真有点儿讨厌(不太方便)。 **a bit of all ˈright** (*Brit sl* 俚) very attractive or pleasing person or thing 非常吸引人或讨人喜欢的人或事物：*Dave's girl-friend is a bit of all right.* 戴夫的女朋友很可爱。 **a bit of ˈcrumpet/ˈfluff/ˈskirt/ˈstuff** (*Brit sl sexist* 俚，性别偏见) pretty girl or woman 漂亮的女子。 **a bit ˈthick** (*infml* 口) more than one can or wishes to tolerate; not fair or reasonable 不能或不愿容忍的；不公平或不合理的：*It's a bit thick expecting us to work on Sundays.* 想让我们在星期日工作可真不像话。 **bits and ˈbobs; bits and ˈpieces** (*infml* 口) small objects or items of various kinds 各种各样的小零碎儿：*I always have a lot of bits and pieces in my coat pocket.* 我的大衣口袋里总是装着零七八碎的东西。 **do one's ˈbit** (*infml* 口) do one's share (of a task); make a useful contribution 做自己分内的(事)；作有益的贡献：*We can finish this job on time if everyone does his bit.* 每一个人都尽自己的本分，我们就能按时完成这项工作。 **every bit as good, bad, etc (as sb/sth)** just as; equally 同样；相等：*Rome is every bit as beautiful as Paris.* 罗马和巴黎一样美丽。○ *He's as clever as she is: every bit as.* 他和她一样聪明，完全一样。 **not a ˈbit; not one (little) ˈbit** not at all; not in any way 一点儿也不：*'Are you cold?' 'Not a bit.'* '你冷吗？' '一点儿也不冷。' ○ *It's not a bit of use* (ie There's no point in) *complaining.* 抱怨毫无用处。○ *I don't like that idea one little bit.* 我一点儿也不喜欢那个主意。 **not a ˈbit of it!** (*infml* 口) not at all; on the contrary 一点儿也不；相反：*You'd think she'd be tired after such a long journey, but not a bit of it!* 你以为她在这么长的旅行之后一定会很疲劳，可是她一点儿也不累！ **thrilled to bits** ⇨ THRILL. **to bits** into small pieces 成为碎片：*pull/tear sth to bits* 将某物扯[撕]成碎片 ○ *The parchment came/fell to bits* (ie disintegrated) *in my hands.* 羊皮纸在我手中成了碎片。

▷ **bitty** *adj* (*usu derog* 通常作贬义) made up of bits; lacking unity 拼凑的；零碎的：*a bitty conversation, interview, film* 东拉西扯的对话、电影 ○ *The play is rather bitty.* 这出戏有点儿像拼凑的。

□ ˈ**bit part** small part in a play or film (戏剧或电影中的)小角色.

bit[2] /bɪt; bɪt/ *n* **1** metal part of a bridle put in a horse's mouth as a way of controlling it 嚼子。⇨illus at HARNESS 见 HARNESS 之插图。 **2** part of a tool that cuts or grips when twisted; tool for drilling holes 刀头，钳口(工具的切削或钳夹的部分)；钻头。Cf 参看 DRILL[1], BRACE[1] 1. **3** (idm 习语) **champ at the bit** ⇨ CHAMP[1]. **get/take the bit between one's/the ˈteeth** tackle a problem, task, etc in a determined, independent or headstrong way 全

力以赴; 独力承担; 勇往直前.

bit[3] /bɪt; bɪt/ *n* (*computing* 计) unit of information expressed as a choice between two possibilities; binary digit 比特(信息单位, 以在两种可能性之间的一种选择表示); 二进制数字; 二进制位.

bit[4] *pt* of BITE[1].

bitch /bɪtʃ; bɪtʃ/ *n* **1** female dog, fox, otter or wolf (雌性的)狗、狐、獭或狼: *a greyhound bitch* 雌灵猩. Cf 参看 DOG 1, VIXEN. **2** (**a**) (*sl derog* 俚, 贬) spiteful woman 恶毒的女人; 泼妇: *Don't talk to me like that, you bitch!* 你这个母夜叉, 别跟我这样说话! (**b**) (*sl* 俚) difficult problem or situation 为难的问题或情况. **3** (idm 习语) **son of a ˈbitch** ⇨ SON.

▷ **bitch** *v* [I, Ipr] **~ (about sb/sth)** (*infml* 口) make spiteful comments; complain or grumble 出言不逊; 抱怨; 发牢骚: *She's always bitching about the people at work.* 她总是埋怨正在干活儿的人.

bitchy *adj* spiteful or bad-tempered 不怀好意的; 脾气坏的: *a bitchy remark* 尖酸刻薄的话. **bitchi·ness** *n* [U].

bite[1] /baɪt; baɪt/ *v* (*pt* **bit** /bɪt; bɪt/, *pp* **bitten** /ˈbɪtn; ˋbɪtn̩/) **1** [I, Ipr, Tn] **~ (into sth)** cut into or nip (sth/sb) with the teeth 咬(某物[某人]): *Does your dog bite?* ie Is it in the habit of biting people? 你的狗咬人吗? ○ *She bit into the apple.* 她咬了一口苹果. ○ *That dog just bit me in the leg.* 那条狗刚咬了我的腿. ○ *Stop biting your nails!* 别再咬指甲了! **2** [Tn] (of an insect) sting; (of a snake) pierce (sb's skin) with its teeth (指昆虫)咬、叮、蜇;(指蛇)咬: *badly bitten by mosquitoes* 被蚊子叮得很厉害 ○ (*joc* 谑) *We were bitten to death* (ie bitten a great deal) *by flies while camping.* 露营时我们让飞虫咬得死去活来. **3** [I] (of fish) take or try to take the bait (指鱼)吞饵, 吃饵, 咬饵: *The fish won't bite today.* 今天鱼不上钩. ○ (*fig* 比喻) *I tried to sell him my old car, but he wouldn't bite*, ie he didn't accept the offer. 我打算把我的旧汽车卖给他, 可是他不肯上钩. **4** [I, Tn] (cause sb/sth to) smart or sting (使某人[某物])感觉剧痛或刺痛: *Her fingers were bitten by the frost/were ˈfrost-bitten.* 她的手指冻伤了. **5** [I] take a strong hold; grip sth firmly 紧握; 抓紧, 咬住(某物): *Wheels won't bite on a slippery surface.* 车轮打滑. **6** [I] become effective, usu in an unpleasant way 见效(通常指坏事): *The miners' strike is really starting to bite.* 矿工罢工就要真正显出威力了. **7** (idm 习语) **be bitten by sth** have a strong interest in or enthusiasm for sth 对某事物有强烈的兴趣; 热衷于某事物: *John's taken up stamp-collecting; he seems really bitten by it.* 约翰已经着手集邮, 好像真入迷了. **bite the ˈbullet** accept sth unpleasant in a resigned way 硬着头皮接受不愉快的事物. **bite the ˈdust** (*infml* 口) (**a**) fall down dead 倒地而死. (**b**) be defeated or rejected 被打败; 被拒绝: *Another of my great ideas bites the dust!* 我的一个好主意又碰壁了! **bite the hand that ˈfeeds one** be unfriendly to or harm sb who has been kind to one 对有德于己的人怀恶意或加害; 忘恩负义. **bite sb's head off** (*infml* 口) criticize sb angrily (and often unfairly) 愤怒地批评某人(常为不公正地): *I was only five minutes late but she really bit my head off.* 我仅仅迟到五分钟, 可她就把我狠狠地说了一顿. **bite off ˌmore than one can ˈchew** (*infml* 口) attempt to do too much or sth that is too demanding 试图做过多的事或太费周折的事. **bite one's ˈlip** grip one's lip or lips between the teeth to prevent oneself from saying sth, sobbing, showing emotion, etc 咬住嘴唇, 以忍住话、啜泣或感情宣泄等. **the biter ˈbit** the person that intended to cheat or harm sb was cheated or harmed himself 打算骗人或害人的人反而自己上当受骗或受害. **bite one's tongue** try hard not to say what one thinks or feels; blame oneself for having said sth embarrassing, hurtful, etc 强忍着不说出自己的想法或感觉; 因曾说出令人难堪或伤感情的话等而自责. **(have) sth to bite on** (have) sth definite to do, examine, etc 有确切的事可做可查等. **once bitten, twice shy** ⇨ ONCE. **what's biting him, you, etc?** (*infml* 口) what's worrying him, you, etc? 他、你...愁什么呢? **8** (phr v) **bite at sth** try to bite sth; snap at sth 去咬某物; 突然猛咬某物: *dogs biting at each other's tails* 互相咬住对方尾巴的狗. **bite sth off** cut sth off by biting 咬下某物: *bite off a large chunk of apple* 咬下一大块苹果.

▷ **bit·ing** *adj* **1** causing a smarting pain 引起剧痛的: *a biting wind* 刺骨的寒风. **2** (of remarks) sharply critical; cutting (指言语)尖刻的, 严厉的, 辛辣的: *biting sarcasm* 尖刻的讽刺. **bit·ingly** *adv*.

bite[2] /baɪt; baɪt/ *n* **1** [C] (**a**) act of biting 咬: *eat sth in one bite* 将某物一口吃下去 ○ *The dog gave me a playful bite.* 狗咬着我玩儿. (**b**) piece cut off by biting 咬下来的一块: *A bite had been taken out of my sandwich.* 我的三明治给咬去了一口. **2** [sing] (*infml* 口) food 食物: *I haven't had a bite (to eat) all morning.* 整整一早晨我一口东西都没吃. **3** [C] wound made by a bite or a sting 咬伤; 叮伤; 蜇伤: *insect, mosquito, snake bites* 虫咬伤、蚊子叮伤、蛇咬伤. **4** [C] taking of bait by a fish 鱼吞食诱饵; 上钩: *anglers waiting for a bite* 等着鱼上钩的垂钓者. **5** [sing, U] sharpness; sting 尖刻; 刺痛: *There's a bite in the air*, ie It's cold. 寒风刺骨. ○ *His words had no bite*, ie were harmless or ineffective. 他的话里没有尖刻的意思. ○ *This cheese has a real bite*, ie a strong flavour. 这干酪的味可真厉害. **6** [U] cutting power or firm grip 切割能力; 紧抓; 紧握; 吃住: *This drill has no bite.* 这个钻钻不进去. **7** (idm 习语) **sb's bark is worse than his bite** ⇨ BARK[2]. **have/get two bites at the ˈcherry** have a second opportunity to do sth; make a second attempt at doing sth 有做某事的第二次机会; 作第二次的尝试.

bit·ten *pt* of BITE[1].

bit·ter /ˈbɪtə(r); ˋbɪtɚ/ *adj* **1** having a sharp taste like aspirin or unsweetened coffee; not sweet 苦的; 有苦味的: *Black coffee leaves a bitter taste in the mouth.* 不加奶的咖啡在嘴里留下了一些苦味. **2** difficult to accept; causing sorrow; unwelcome 难以接受的; 引起悲伤的; 不受欢迎的: *learn from bitter experience* 从惨痛教训中吸取教益 ○ *Failing the exam was a bitter disappointment to him.* 他考试不及格很伤心失望. **3** caused by, feeling or showing envy, hatred or disappointment 引起、感觉或显示出嫉妒、憎恶、怨恨或失望的: *bitter quarrels, enemies, words* 剧烈的争吵、死敌、恶毒的言语 ○ *shed bitter tears* 落下伤心泪 ○ *She feels/is bitter about her divorce.* 她对离婚觉得很感伤. **4** piercingly cold 严寒: *a bitter wind* 刺骨的寒风. **5** (idm 习语) **a bitter ˈpill (for sb) (to swallow)** thing that is unpleasant or humiliating to accept 难以忍受的、不愉快的或丢脸的事: *Defeat in the election was a bitter pill for him to swallow.* 在选举中失败是他难以下咽的苦果. **to the bitter ˈend** until all that is possible has been done 拼到底: *fight, struggle, etc to the bitter end* 战斗[斗争]...到底.

▷ **bit·ter** *n* [U] (*Brit*) bitter beer strongly flavoured with hops (用蛇麻子调味的)苦啤酒: *A pint of bitter, please.* 请来一品脱苦啤酒.

bit·terly *adv* in a bitter way 苦苦地; 惨痛地: *be bitterly disappointed* 伤心失望 ○ *She wept bitterly.* 她哭得很伤心. ○ *He is bitterly* (ie very deeply) *opposed to nuclear weapons.* 他强烈地反对核武器.

bit·ter·ness *n* [U].

bit·ters *n* [U, sing or pl *v*] liquor flavoured with bitter herbs, used in cocktails 用苦味药草调味的酒(用于鸡尾酒): *gin and bitters* 苦味杜松子酒 ○ *a dash of bitters* 少许苦味酒.

□ **ˌbitter-ˈsweet** *adj* **1** sweet but with a bitter taste at the end 甜中带苦的. **2** (*fig* 比喻) pleasant but with a hint of sadness 欢乐中带有一丝忧伤: *bitter-sweet experiences/memories* 苦乐交织的经历[回忆].

bit·tern /ˈbɪtən; ˋbɪtɚn/ *n* marsh bird related to the heron, with a characteristic booming call 麻鳽(苍鹭类, 鸣声低沉, 栖息于沼泽).

bitu·men /ˈbɪtjʊmən; *US* bəˈtu:mən; bɪˋtumən/ *n* [U] black sticky substance obtained from petroleum, used for covering roads or roofs 沥青.

▷ **bi·tu·min·ous** /bɪˈtju:mɪnəs; *US* -ˈtu:-; bɪˋtumənəs/ *adj* containing bitumen 含有沥青的: *bituminous coal*, ie coal that burns with smoky yellow flames 烟煤.

bi·valve /ˈbaɪvælv; ˋbaɪˌvælv/ *n* (*zoology* 动) shellfish with a hinged double shell, eg a mussel or clam 双壳贝类(如贻贝或蛤): [attrib 作定语] *a bivalve mollusc* 一种双壳软体动物.

biv·ouac /ˈbɪvʊæk; ˋbɪvʊˌæk/ *n* temporary camp without tents or any other cover, esp used by soldiers or mountaineers (无帐篷或其他遮盖物的)临时营地(尤指

士兵或登山者所用的).

▷ **biv·ouac** *v* [I] (**-ck-**) make or camp in a bivouac 在露天地上宿营: *We bivouacked on the open plain.* 我们在开阔的原野上露营.

bi·zarre /bɪˈzɑː(r); bɪˈzɑr/ *adj* strange in appearance or effect; grotesque; eccentric 奇形怪状的; 古怪的.

bk *abbr* 缩写 = (*pl* **bks**) book: *Streamline Bk 2*《流线》第二册.

B

blab /blæb; blæb/ *v* (**-bb-**) [I] (*infml* 口) **1** give away a secret by indiscreet talk; confess 因不慎的谈吐而泄漏秘密; 认错: *It'll remain a secret unless someone blabs.* 除非有人泄漏出去, 否则这永远是个秘密. **2** = BLABBER.

blab·ber /ˈblæbə(r); ˈblæbɚ/ (also **blab**) *v* [I] (*infml* 口) talk foolishly or too much 胡扯; 瞎说; 饶舌: *What's he blabbering (on) about?* 他胡扯些什么?

▷ **blab·ber** *n* [U] (*infml* 口) foolish or persistent talk 愚蠢的或喋喋不休的话.

□ ˈ**blabbermouth** *n* (*infml* 口) person who blabs 多嘴人, 碎嘴子; 泄密者.

black[1] /blæk; blæk/ *adj* **1** (**a**) of the very darkest colour, like coal or soot; opposite of white; of a colour very similar to this 黑的; 黑色的: *black shoes* 黑鞋 ○ *a black suit* 一套黑衣服 ○ *black coffee*, ie without cream or milk 不加奶油或牛奶的咖啡. Cf 参看 WHITE[1]. (**b**) (almost) without light, completely dark (几乎)没有光亮的, 完全黑暗的: *a black starless night* 一个漆黑没有星星的夜晚. (**c**) (of water, clouds, etc) dark, gloomy (指水、云等)昏黑的, 幽暗的: *a deep, black pool* 又深又黑的水潭 ○ *The sky looks black and threatening*, ie stormy. 天色阴沉可怕. **2** (**a**) of a dark-skinned race 黑肤色人种的: *Many black people emigrated to Britain in the 1950's.* 在二十世纪五十年代许多黑人移民到英国. ○ *Britain's black minority/population* 英国的黑人少数民族[人口]. (**b**) of black people 黑人的: *black culture* 黑人的文化. **3** very dirty; covered with dirt 很脏的; 有污垢的: *hands black with grime* 污黑的手. **4** (*fig* 比喻) without hope; very sad or melancholy 毫无希望的; 感伤的; 忧郁的: *The future looks black.* 前途暗淡. ○ *black news* 坏消息 ○ *black* (ie very great) *despair* 绝望 ○ *a black day, week, etc*, ie one full of sad or unwelcome events 倒霉的一天、一周等. **5** [usu attrib 通常作定语] very angry or resentful 恼怒的; 怨恨的: *a black look/mood* 怒目而视[低落的情绪]. **6** evil or wicked; very harmful 邪恶的; 不义的; 非常有害的: *a black deed/lie* 昧着良心的行为[谎言]. **7** funny but in a cynical or macabre way 荒诞、恐怖而有趣的: *black humour* 黑色幽默(荒诞的或恐怖的幽默) ○ *a black joke* 黑色笑话(荒诞的或恐怖的笑话). **8** (of goods, etc) not to be handled by trade unionists while others are on strike (指货物等)(在罢工时)工会会员不予处理的: *The strikers declared the cargo black.* 罢工者宣布那批货不予处理. **9** (idm 习语) **(beat sb) black and ˈblue** (hit sb until he is) covered with bruises (把某人打得)青一块紫一块. **(as) black as ink/pitch** very dark; completely black 墨黑; 漆黑. **not as black as it/one is ˈpainted** not as bad as it/one is said to be 不像所说的那么坏. **of the blackest/deepest dye** ⇨ DYE[2]. **the pot calling the kettle black** ⇨ POT[1].

▷ **blacken** /ˈblækən; ˈblækən/ *v* [Tn] **1** make or become black or very dark 使黑; 使变黑. **2** [Tn] say unpleasant things about (sth) 诋毁, 诽谤(某事物): *blacken a person's character/name* 诋毁某人的品格[名声].

black·ness *n* [U].

□ **black ˈart** = BLACK MAGIC.

ˌ**black-ˈbeetle** *n* type of cockroach 蟑螂.

ˈ**blackberry** /ˈblækbrɪ, -berɪ; ˈblækˌbɛrɪ/ *n* **1** wild shrub with thorny stems 黑莓(野生灌木, 树干有刺). **2** its small dark edible fruit 黑莓(可供食用的黑色小果子). — *v* [I] (*pt, pp* **-ried**) gather blackberries 采黑莓: *go blackberrying* 去采黑莓.

ˈ**blackbird** *n* European songbird of the thrush family, the male of which is black 黑鹂(欧洲鸫科鸣禽, 雄鸟黑色). ⇨illus at App 1 见附录1之插图, page iv.

ˈ**blackboard** *n* (*US* ˈ**chalkboard**) dark-coloured board used for writing on with chalk, esp in a school classroom 黑板.

ˌ**black ˈbox** automatic device for recording details of the flight of a plane 黑盒(记录飞机飞行详情的自动装置).

ˌ**black ˈcomedy** play, etc that presents the unpleasant or tragic realities of life in a comic way 黑色喜剧(以喜剧形式表现不愉快的或悲剧的人生现实的戏剧等).

the ˈBlack Country smoky industrial area in the West Midlands of England 黑乡(英格兰的西米德兰烟雾弥漫的工业区).

ˌ**blackˈcurrant** *n* **1** common garden shrub 黑醋栗(欧洲常见园栽灌木). **2** its small dark edible berry 黑醋栗(深色可食用的小果子).

the Black ˈDeath widespread epidemic of bubonic plague in the 14th century 黑死病(14世纪广泛传染的淋巴腺鼠疫).

ˌ**black eˈconomy** unofficial system of employing and paying workers without observing legal requirements such as the payment of income tax 黑市经营(对工人雇用及付酬不遵守缴纳所得税等法规的做法): *The growing black economy is beginning to worry the Government.* 黑市经营日益泛滥, 政府已开始担忧.

black ˈeye dark bruised skin around a person's eye, resulting from a blow (被打得)眼圈发青: *give sb a black eye*, ie hit sb in the eye causing a bruise 把某人打得眼圈发青.

ˈ**Black Friar** Dominican monk (多明我会的)修道士.

ˈ**blackhead** *n* small black pimple blocking a pore in the skin 黑头粉刺.

ˌ**black ˈhole** region in outer space from which no matter or radiation can escape 黑洞(任何物质或辐射均无从逃逸的外太空区域).

ˌ**black ˈice** thin transparent layer of ice on a road surface 黑冰, 薄冰(路面上薄而透明的冰层): *The lorry skidded on a stretch of black ice.* 货车在薄冰路面上打滑.

ˈ**blackjack** *n* **1** [C] (*esp US*) type of stick or club used as a weapon, esp a leather-covered metal pipe held by a strap or flexible handle (用作武器的)棍子或棒子(尤指包着皮革的金属管, 有皮带或弹性手柄). **2** [U] = PONTOON[2].

ˌ**blackˈlead** *n* [U] grey-black substance used in lead pencils and for polishing 石墨; 笔铅. — *v* [Tn] polish (sth) with blacklead 用石墨抛光某物.

ˌ**black ˈmagic** type of magic that involves calling on the powers of evil 妖术; 诅咒巫术.

ˌ**Black Maˈria** /məˈraɪə; məˈraɪə/ (*infml* 口) police van for transporting prisoners 囚车.

ˌ**black ˈmark** sign of disapproval or discredit (placed against a person's name) (指人品)污点: (*fig* 比喻) *The public scandal left a black mark on his career.* 这一尽人皆知的丑闻给他的事业留下了污点.

ˌ**black ˈmarket** illegal buying and selling of goods or currencies (esp where there is official rationing) 黑市; 黑市交易: *buy/sell sth on the black market* 在黑市上买[卖]某物 ○ [attrib 作定语] *black market goods* 黑市货物. ˌ**black ˌmarkeˈteer** person who trades on the black market 做黑市交易者.

ˌ**black ˈmass** travesty of the Mass, in which Satan is worshipped instead of God 黑弥撒(渎神弥撒, 所赞颂的是撒旦而非上帝).

ˌ**Black ˈMuslim** member of a militant group of Blacks, esp in the USA, who follow Islam 黑人穆斯林(尤指美国追随伊斯兰教的黑人激进组织成员).

ˈ**black-out** *n* **1** (**a**) period when all lights must be put out or covered, esp as a precaution during an air attack 灯火管制期(尤指为防空袭的): *Curtains must be drawn during the black-out.* 在灯火管制期间必须拉上窗帘. (**b**) period of darkness caused by an electrical power failure 停电. (**c**) (*theatre* 戏) extinguishing of stage lights, eg at the end of a scene 舞台熄灯(如在戏剧中一幕结束时的). **2** temporary loss of consciousness or sight or memory 暂时失去知觉、视力或记忆. **3** prevention of the release of information 封锁消息: *The government imposed a news black-out* (ie stopped the broadcasting and printing of news) *during the crisis.* 政府在那次危机期间实施新闻封锁.

ˌ**black ˈpepper** hot seasoning made by grinding dried unripe berries of the pepper plant 黑胡椒.

ˌ**Black ˈPower** movement supporting civil rights and political power for black people 黑人民权运动.

ˌ**black ˈpudding** type of large dark sausage made from

dried blood, suet and barley 黑香肠(用干血、牛羊脂肪油和大麦制成的).

ˌ**Black ˈSash** women's anti-apartheid organization in S Africa 黑带组织(南非反对种族隔离制度的妇女组织).

ˌ**black ˈsheep** person regarded as a disgrace or a failure by other members of his family or group 害群之马: *My brother is the black sheep of the family.* 我弟弟是我们家的害群之马.

ˈ**blackshirt** *n* member of a fascist organization 黑衫党党员(法西斯组织成员).

ˈ**black spot** place where accidents often happen, esp on a road 黑点地区(常发生事故的地点, 尤指道路某处): *a notorious (accident) black spot* 声名狼藉(常发生事故)的黑点地区.

ˈ**blackthorn** *n* thorny European shrub with white blossom and purple fruit like a small plum 黑刺李(欧洲有刺灌木, 开白花结紫果, 像小李子).

black ˈtie (a) black bow-tie worn with a dinner jacket 黑领结(穿黑色晚礼服上衣时所配的黑色蝴蝶领结). **(b)** [esp attrib 尤作定语] requiring formal dress 要求穿礼服的: *a black tie dinner/affair* 要求穿礼服的宴会[场合] ○ *It's black tie,* ie Dinner-jackets should be worn. 那是要穿晚礼服的.

ˌ**black-water ˈfever** very severe type of malaria with bloody urine 黑尿热, 黑水热(严重的疟疾, 尿液带血).

ˌ**black ˈwidow** poisonous American spider, the female of which often eats its mate 黑寡妇(美洲有毒蜘蛛, 雌蜘蛛常在交配后吃掉雄蜘蛛).

black[2] /blæk; blæk/ *n* **1** [U] black colour 黑色: *Black is not my favourite colour.* 黑色不是我喜爱的颜色. **2** [U] black clothes or material 黑色衣物或材料: *The mourners were dressed in black.* 哀悼者穿黑服. **3** (usu 通常作 **Black**) [C] (*formerly derog, now the preferred word*) person of a dark-skinned race; negro (原含贬意, 现以此词为宜)黑色皮肤种族的人; 黑人: *Discrimination against Blacks is still common.* 歧视黑人仍是普遍现象. **4** (idm 习语) **be in the ˈblack** have money in one's bank account 在银行有存款. Cf 参看 BE IN THE RED (RED[2] 4). **black and ˈwhite** (of television, photographs, etc) showing no colours except black, white and shades of grey (指电视、照片等)黑白: *I changed my black and white television for a colour set.* 我把黑白电视换了一台彩色的. ○ *Most old films were made in black and white.* 多数旧电影片都是黑白的. **in black and white** in writing or in print 白纸黑字(书写的或印刷的): *I want the contract in black and white.* 我要这项合同见诸文字. **(in) black and white** (in) absolute terms, eg of good and bad, right and wrong 黑白分明; 是非分明: *see/view the issue in black and white* 是非分明地看待这一问题. **work like a black/Trojan** work very hard 工作非常努力.

black[3] /blæk; blæk/ *v* **1** [Tn] make (sth) black; put polish on (shoes, etc) 把(某物)弄黑; 把鞋油等涂在(皮鞋等物)上. **2** [Tn] refuse to handle (goods, etc); boycott 拒绝装卸(货物等); 抵制: *The lorry had been blacked by strikers and could not be unloaded.* 那辆货车遭罢工者抵制而无法卸货. **3** (phr v) **black ˈout** lose consciousness or memory temporarily 暂时失去知觉或记忆; 昏厥: *The plane dived suddenly, causing the pilot to black out.* 飞机猛然俯冲致使驾驶员昏厥. **black sth out (a)** extinguish (lights, etc) completely or cover (windows, etc) so that light cannot be seen from outside 完全熄灭(灯火等)或遮住(窗户等)使外面看不到光亮: *houses blacked out during an air raid* 空袭时实行灯火管制的房屋. **(b)** cover (sth written and printed) with black ink, etc so that it cannot be read (在书写或印刷材料上)用墨水涂去.

black·amoor /ˈblækəmɔː(r) *or, rarely,* 罕读作 -mʊə(r); ˋblækəˌmʊr/ *n* (*dated derog offensive* 旧, 贬, 蔑) negro or dark-skinned person 黑人; 黑色皮肤的人.

black·ball /ˈblækbɔːl; ˋblækˌbɔl/ *v* [Tn] prevent (sb) from joining a club or group by voting against him in a ballot 投反对票以阻止(某人)加入某俱乐部或某组织: *blackball a candidate* 投票反对一候选人.

black·guard /ˈblægɑːd; ˋblægɑrd/ *n* (*fml* 文) dishonourable man; scoundrel 无耻之徒; 恶棍; 无赖; 流氓.

▷ **black·guardly** *adj* (*fml* 文) dishonest or immoral 无耻的; 不道德的; 邪恶的; 下流的: *a blackguardly trick* 卑鄙的手段.

black·leg /ˈblækleg; ˋblækˌlɛg/ *n* (*derog* 贬) person who works when his fellow workers are on strike 工贼(在别人罢工时上工的人). Cf 参看 STRIKE-BREAKER (STRIKE[1]).

▷ **black·leg** *v* [I] **(-gg-)** (*derog* 贬) act as a blackleg 当工贼(在别人罢工时去上工).

black·list /ˈblæklɪst; ˋblækˌlɪst/ *n* list of people who are considered dangerous or who are to be punished 黑名单: *The police drew up a blacklist of wanted terrorists.* 警方拟就一份通缉恐怖分子的黑名单.

▷ **black·list** *v* [Tn] put (sb) on a blacklist 把(某人)列入黑名单: *He was blacklisted because of his extremist views.* 他因观点偏激而被列入黑名单.

black·mail /ˈblækmeɪl; ˋblækˌmel/ *n* [U] **1** demanding money (from sb) by threatening to reveal information which could harm him 勒索; 敲诈: *be found guilty of blackmail* 被裁决犯有勒索罪. **2** use of threats to influence a person or group 用威胁来左右别人: *'Increase productivity or lose your jobs.' 'That's blackmail!'* '你们要提高生产率, 不然就把你们解雇!' '这是要挟!'

▷ **black·mail** *v* [Tn, Tn·pr] **~ sb (into doing sth)** force sb to do sth by blackmail 要挟某人做某事: *He was blackmailed by an enemy agent (into passing on state secrets).* 敌特威胁他(要他交出国家机密). ○ *The strikers refused to be blackmailed into returning to work.* 罢工者拒绝了要挟复工的条件.

black·mailer *n* person who commits blackmail 勒索者; 敲诈者.

black·smith /ˈblæksmɪθ; ˋblæksmɪθ/ (also **smith**) *n* person whose job is to make and repair things made of iron, esp horseshoes 铁匠(尤指马蹄铁匠).

blad·der /ˈblædə(r); ˋblædɚ/ *n* **1** bag made of membrane in which urine collects in human and animal bodies 膀胱. **2** similar bag that can be inflated for various uses (eg the rubber lining of a football) (任何可充气的)囊状物(如足球内的橡皮球胆).

blade /bleɪd; bled/ *n* **1 (a)** flat cutting part of a knife, sword, chisel, etc (刀、剑、凿等的)刃: *a penknife with five blades* 五开的折刀. ⇨illus at KNIFE, SWORD 见 KNIFE, SWORD 之插图. **(b)** = RAZOR-BLADE (RAZOR). **2** (*dated* 旧) sword; swordsman 剑; 剑客; 击剑家. **3** flat wide part of an oar, a propeller, a spade, a cricket bat, etc (划水桨、螺旋桨、锹、铲、板球击球板等的)扁宽平面部分. ⇨illus at ROWING-BOAT 见 ROWING-BOAT 之插图. **4 (a)** flat narrow leaf of certain plants, esp grasses and cereals (植物的)叶片(尤指草类与谷类的): *a blade of grass/corn* 一片草叶[禾叶]. **(b)** flat part of a leaf or petal (叶子或花瓣的)扁平部分.

blae·berry /ˈbleɪbrɪ; *US* -berɪ; ˋbleˌbɛrɪ/ *n* = BILBERRY.

blah /blɑː; blɑ/ *n* [U] (*infml* 口) talk that sounds impressive but actually says very little 冠冕堂皇的废话: *That's just a lot of blah.* 那纯粹都是胡扯. ○ *There he goes, blah blah blah, talking nonsense as usual.* 他又来这一套了, 夸夸其谈, 像往常一样谈来谈去都是废话.

blame /bleɪm; blem/ *v* **1** [Tn, Tn·pr] **~ sb (for sth)/~ sth on sb** consider or say that sb is responsible for sth done (badly or wrongly) or not done 责备; 责怪; 指责; 埋怨; 归咎于: *I don't blame you,* ie I think your action was justified. 我不怪你(我认为你做得有道理). ○ (*saying* 谚) *A bad workman blames his tools,* ie refuses to accept the responsibility for his own mistakes. 拙匠埋怨工具差(不承认错在自己). ○ *If you fail the exam you'll only have yourself to blame,* ie it will be your own fault. 你若考试不及格, 只能怪自己. ○ *She blamed him for the failure of their marriage/blamed the failure of their marriage on him.* 她把婚姻的触礁归咎于他. **2** (idm 习语) **be to blame (for sth)** be responsible for sth bad; deserve to be blamed 对某坏事应负责任; 应受责备: *Which driver was to blame for the accident?* 这事故是哪个司机的责任? ○ *She was in no way to blame.* 决不应该责备她.

▷ **blame** *n* [U] **~ (for sth) 1** responsibility for sth done badly or wrongly (对做坏的或做错的事所负的)责任: *bear/take/accept/get the blame (for sth)* (对某事)承担责任 ○ *Where does the blame for our failure lie?* ie Who or what is responsible? 我们失败的症结在哪里? **2** criticism for doing sth wrong 对做错某事的批评: *He incurred much blame for his stubborn attitude.* 他态度顽固而招致许多责难. **3** (idm 习语) **lay/put the blame (for sth) on sb** blame sb for sth 把某事归咎于某人.

B

blame·less *adj* deserving no blame; innocent 无可责备的; 无过失的: *a blameless life* 无可指责的一生 ○ *None of us is blameless in this matter.* 在这件事上, 我们没有一个人是无过错的. **blame·lessly** *adv*. **blame·worthy** *adj* deserving blame 应受责备的.

blanch /blɑːntʃ; *US* blæntʃ; blæntʃ/ *v* **1** [Tn] prepare (food, esp vegetables) by putting briefly in boiling water; scald 焯(食物, 尤指蔬菜); 烫洗: *You blanch almonds to remove their skins.* 你把杏仁焯一下, 烫去表皮. **2** [I, Ipr] **~ (with sth) (at sth)** become pale (with fear, cold, etc) (因害怕、寒冷等而)脸色苍白: *He blanched (with fear) at the sight of the snake.* 他看见蛇(吓得)脸色煞白.

blanc·mange /bləˈmɒnʒ; bləˋmɑnʒ/ *n* [C, U] jelly-like pudding made with milk in a mould 牛奶冻儿(用牛奶调制, 放在模子里成型的胶状点心).

bland /blænd; blænd/ *adj* (**-er**, **-est**) **1** gentle or casual in manner; showing no strong emotions; suave 文雅的; 随和的; 不动感情; 和蔼的. **2** (*sometimes derog* 有时作贬义) (of food) not rich or stimulating; very mild in flavour; tasteless (指食物)不油腻的, 无刺激性的, 清淡的, 无味的: *He eats only bland food because of his ulcer.* 他患溃疡, 只能吃无刺激性的食物. ○ *This cheese is rather bland.* 这干酪没什么味道. **3** without striking features; uninteresting 无显著特征的; 引不起兴趣的: *He has a bland appearance.* 他外表平庸. ▷ **blandly** *adv*. **bland·ness** *n* [U].

bland·ish·ment /ˈblændɪʃmənt; ˋblændɪʃmənt/ *n* (usu *pl* 通常作复数) (*fml* 文) flattering or coaxing words and actions 谄媚或哄骗的言语和行为: *She resisted his blandishments.* 她把他的甜言蜜语顶了回去.

blank /blæŋk; blæŋk/ *adj* (**-er**, **-est**) **1** (**a**) without writing or print; unmarked 空白的; 无痕迹的: *a blank sheet of paper* 一张白纸 ○ *a blank page* 空白的一页 ○ *Write on one side of the page and leave the other side blank.* 在这页的一边写字, 另一边空着. (**b**) (of a document, etc) with empty spaces for writing answers, a signature, etc (指文件等)有空白处的(供填写答复、签字等): *a blank form* 空白的表格. (**c**) bare; empty 光着的; 空的: *a blank wall*, ie without doors, windows, pictures, etc 一堵光秃秃的墙(没有门窗, 没有图画等). **2** without expression, understanding or interest; empty 没表情的; 不理解的; 没兴趣的; 空虚的: *a blank expression/face/gaze* 茫然的表情[面孔/凝视] ○ *He looked blank*, ie puzzled. 他显得不知所措. ○ *Her questions drew blank looks all round*, ie No one seemed to know how to answer them. 她的问题把大家问得目瞪口呆. ○ *Suddenly my mind went blank*, ie I was unable to remember anything or think properly. 猛然间我的脑子里成了一片空白. **3** [attrib 作定语] total; absolute 全部的; 绝对的: *a blank denial/refusal* 全然的否认[拒绝].

▷ **blank** *n* **1** (**a**) empty space in a document, etc for writing answers, a signature, etc (文件之类供作答、签名等所留的)空白: *fill in the blanks on the question paper* 在问卷上填空 ○ *If you can't answer the question, leave a blank.* 如果答不上来就空着. (**b**) printed document with empty spaces 空白表格: *I've filled in this form incorrectly. Can I have another blank?* 我把表格填错了. 再给我一张空白的, 可以吗? **2** empty space; void 空白; 空虚; 空隙: *My mind/memory was a (complete) blank — I couldn't think of a single answer.* 我头脑[记忆]里(完全)是一片空白 —— 连一个答案也想不出. **3** = BLANK CARTRIDGE. **4** (idm 习语) **draw a blank** ⇨ DRAW².

blank *v* (phr v) **blank sth out** obscure or erase sth 掩盖; 删去.

blankly *adv* with a blank expression 茫然若失: *look blankly at sb/sth* 呆呆地看着某人[某物].

blank·ness *n* [U].

□ ˌ**blank** ˈ**cartridge** cartridge that contains powder but no bullet (有弹药而无弹头的)空弹, 空包弹.

ˌ**blank** ˈ**cheque** (**a**) signed cheque with the amount to be paid left blank, for the payee to write in (由受款人自行填写金额的)空白支票. (**b**) (*fig* 比喻) complete authority to do sth 对某事可全权处理: *The architect was given/presented with a blank cheque to design a new city centre.* 设计师被授予全权设计一个新的城市中心区.

ˌ**blank** ˈ**verse** verse written in lines of usu ten syllables, without rhyme 无韵诗(通常为每行十个音节而不押韵的诗歌): *Many Elizabethan plays are written in blank verse.* 伊丽莎白时代的许多戏剧以无韵诗形式写成.

blan·ket /ˈblæŋkɪt; ˋblæŋkɪt/ *n* **1** thick woollen covering used, esp on beds, for keeping people warm 毛毯; 毡子: *It's cold — I need another blanket.* 太冷了 —— 我再要一条毯子. **2** (*fig* 比喻) thick covering mass or layer 覆盖着厚厚的块或层: *a blanket of fog/cloud/smoke/snow* 一层雾[云/烟/雪]. **3** [attrib 作定语] covering all cases or classes; general; comprehensive 包括一切情形或种类的; 总括的; 综合的: *a blanket agreement/term/rule* 一揽子协议[总的条件/总则]. **4** (idm 习语) **be born on the wrong side of the blanket** ⇨ BORN. **a wet blanket** ⇨ WET.

▷ **blan·ket** *v* [Tn, Tn·pr] **~ sth (in/with sth)** cover sth completely 完全覆盖某物: *The countryside was blanketed with snow/fog.* 乡村被雪[雾]覆盖着.

blare /bleə(r); blɛr/ *v* **1** [I, Ip] **~ (out)** make a loud harsh sound like a trumpet 发出像喇叭一样响亮刺耳的声音: *Car horns blared.* 汽车的喇叭响了. ○ *The trumpets blared* ˈ*out.* 喇叭齐鸣. **2** [Tn, Tn·p] **~ sth (out)** produce or utter (such sounds) 发出(上述的声音): *The radio blared out pop music.* 无线电高声播放流行音乐.

▷ **blare** *n* [U] blaring sound 巨大刺耳的声音: *the blare of police sirens, a brass band* 警车警报器的鸣声[铜管乐队的奏鸣声].

blar·ney /ˈblɑːnɪ; ˋblɑrnɪ/ *n* [U] (*infml* 口) smooth talk that flatters and deceives people 奉承话; 花言巧语.

blasé /ˈblɑːzeɪ; *US* blɑːˈzeɪ; blɑˋze/ *adj* **~ (about sth)** bored or not impressed by things because one has already experienced or seen them so often 腻烦的: *a blasé attitude/manner* 一副无所谓的态度[样子] ○ *She's very blasé about parties.* 她非常腻烦聚会.

blas·pheme /blæsˈfiːm; blæsˋfim/ *v* [I, Ipr, Tn] **~ (against sb/sth)** swear or curse using the name of God; speak in an irreverent way about (God or sacred things) 亵渎(神祇或神圣的事物): *blaspheme (against) the name of God* 亵渎神的名 ○ *He always swears and blasphemes when he's drunk.* 他酒醉后总是骂骂咧咧, 亵渎神祇.

▷ **blas·phemer** *n* person who blasphemes 亵渎神者.

blas·phem·ous /ˈblæsfəməs; ˋblæsfɪməs/ *adj* showing contempt or irreverence for God and sacred things 对上帝和神圣事物表示轻蔑或不敬的: *blasphemous words/curses/language* 亵渎神祇的词语[诅咒/言语]. **blas·phem·ously** *adv*.

blas·phemy /ˈblæsfəmɪ; ˋblæsfɪmɪ/ *n* (**a**) [U] blasphemous behaviour or language 亵渎神祇的行为或言语: *the sin of blasphemy* 亵渎神祇的罪恶. (**b**) [C] instance of this 亵渎神祇: *the blasphemies of the heretic* 异教徒对神祇的亵渎.

blast[1] /blɑːst; *US* blæst; blæst/ *n* **1** [C, U] explosion; destructive wave of air from an explosion 爆炸; (由爆炸所引起具有破坏力的)气浪; 冲击波: *a bomb blast* 炸弹的爆炸 ○ *Several passers-by were killed by (the) blast.* 数名路人被炸死. **2** [C] sudden strong gust of air 一阵强烈的气流: *the wind's icy blasts* 阵阵冰冷的风 ○ *a blast of hot air from the furnace* 来自高炉的一股炽热气浪. **3** [C] loud sound made by a brass instrument, car horn, etc (铜管乐器或汽车喇叭等所发出的)响亮声音: *blow a blast on a bugle, trumpet, whistle, etc* 军号、喇叭、哨子等吹出的声音. **4** [C] stream of hot air used to intensify the heat in a furnace 鼓风热气流(用以提高熔炉温度). **5** (idm 习语) **full blast** ⇨ FULL.

□ ˈ**blast-furnace** *n* furnace for melting iron ore using blasts of hot air forced into it 鼓风炉; 高炉.

blast[2] /blɑːst; *US* blæst; blæst/ *v* **1** [I, Tn] destroy or break apart (esp rocks) using explosives 用炸药炸开(尤指石头): *Danger! Blasting in progress!* 危险! 正在爆破! ○ *The village was blasted by enemy bombs.* 村子被敌人炸弹炸毁. **2** [Tn] damage or destroy (esp plants) by blight, cold, heat, etc; cause to wither (使)枯萎, (使)凋谢(尤指植物): *buds/crops blasted by frost/wind* 被霜[风]所毁的幼芽[农作物]. **3** [I] make a loud harsh noise 发出响亮刺耳的噪音. **4** [Tn] (*infml* 口) criticize (sb/sth) severely 严厉地批评, 痛斥(某人[某事物]): *The film was blasted by the critics.* 这部电影遭到影评家的猛烈的抨击. **5** (phr v) **blast sth away, down, in, etc** break something in a specified way by blasting 把某物炸至(某种状况): *The explosion blasted the door open/down/in.* 这爆炸把屋门炸开[炸倒/炸进屋内]. **blast**

ˈ**off** (of spacecraft) be launched by the firing of rockets (指宇宙飞船)被火箭发射出: *Apollo II blasted off at noon.* 阿波罗2号于中午发射升空.
▷ **blast** *interj* (expressing annoyance) how infuriating! (表示烦恼)倒霉! 糟糕!: *Blast! I've burnt the toast.* 真倒霉! 我把面包片烤煳了.
blas·ted *adj* [attrib 作定语] (*infml* 口) very annoying 令人非常烦恼的: *What a blasted nuisance!* 这事多讨厌!
blas·ting *n* (*infml* 口) harsh criticism 严厉的批评: *give his work a terrific blasting* 对他的工作狠批一通.
□ ˈ**blast-off** *n* (time of) launching of a spacecraft 宇宙飞船发射(的时间): *Blast-off is in 30 seconds.* 30秒钟后发射升空.

bla·tant /ˈbleɪtnt; ˋbletn̩t/ *adj* very obvious; unashamed; flagrant 非常明显的; 厚颜无耻的; 明目张胆的: *a blatant lie* 无耻的谎言 ○ *blatant disobedience, disrespect, insolence, etc* 明目张胆的抗拒、怠慢、侮慢等.
▷ **bla·tancy** /ˈbleɪtnsɪ; ˋbletn̩sɪ/ *n* [U] blatant quality 明显; 厚颜无耻; 明目张胆: *the sheer blatancy of the crime* 罪恶昭彰.
bla·tantly *adv*.

blather /ˈblæðə(r); ˋblæðɚ/ (also **blether** /ˈbleðə(r); ˋblɛðɚ/) *v* [I, Ipr, Ip] **~ (on) (about sb/sth)** (*esp Scot* 尤用于苏格兰) talk foolishly 胡说; 瞎扯.
▷ **blather** (also **blether**) *n* [U] foolish talk 胡话; 蠢话.

blaze[1] /bleɪz; blez/ *n* **1** [C] (**a**) bright flame or fire 火焰; 火光: *Dry wood makes a good blaze.* 干木燃起夺目的火焰. (**b**) very large (often dangerous) fire 大火; 火灾: *Five people died in the blaze.* 有五人死于火灾. **2** [sing] **~ of sth** (**a**) very bright display (of light, colour, etc); brightness, brilliance (光、颜色等的)呈现; 明亮; 光辉: *The garden is a blaze of colour*, ie full of colourful flowers. 花园里万紫千红. ○ *The high street is a blaze of lights in the evening.* 晚上大街上灯火辉煌. (**b**) (*fig* 比喻) striking display or show 引人注目的展现或显示: *a blaze of glory/publicity* 荣耀[声名显赫]. (**c**) (*fig* 比喻) sudden outburst (of a violent feeling) (强烈感情的)骤然迸发: *a blaze of anger/passion/temper* 勃然大怒[大动感情/大发雷霆].

blaze[2] /bleɪz; blez/ *v* **1** [I] burn brightly and fiercely 猛烈地燃烧: *A good fire was blazing in the grate.* 炉箅子上的火很旺. ○ *When the firemen arrived the whole building was blazing.* 消防队到达时, 整座建筑物正在熊熊燃烧着. **2** [I, Ipr, Ip] shine brightly 发光; 照耀: *Bright lights blazed all along the street.* 雪亮的灯光照得街道通明. ○ *The sun blazed down on the desert.* 阳光照射在沙漠上. **3** [I, Ipr] **~ (with sth)** (*fig* 比喻) show great feeling, esp anger 表现强烈的感情(尤指愤怒): *She was blazing with indignation*, ie was extremely angry. 她勃然大怒. ○ *a blazing row* 愤怒的吼叫 ○ *His eyes blazed (with anger).* (由于愤怒)他的眼里充满怒火. **4** (phr v) **blaze away** fire continuously with guns 连续地射击: *Our gunners/guns kept blazing away at the enemy.* 我们的炮手[枪炮]一直不停地向敌军射击. **blaze up** (**a**) burst into flames 发出火焰; 燃烧起来: *The fire blazed up when he added paraffin.* 他加了一些煤油, 火就燃烧起来了. (**b**) (*fig* 比喻) suddenly become angry 忽然发怒: *He blazed up without warning.* 他突如其来地勃然大怒.

blaze[3] /bleɪz; blez/ *n* **1** white mark on an animal's face (动物面部上的)白斑. **2** mark cut in the bark of a tree to show sb which way to go (在树皮上割出指示去向的)记号.
▷ **blaze** *v* **1** [Tn] mark (a tree) by cutting off some bark (在树上)(割下一些树皮)作标记. **2** (idm 习语) **blaze a ˈtrail** do sth for the first time and show others how to do it; be a pioneer (in sth) 作模范; (在某事中)作先行者: *blazing a trail in the field of laser surgery* 在激光外科手术领域中开拓新路. Cf 参看 TRAIL-BLAZER (TRAIL).

blaze[4] /bleɪz; blez/ (also **blazon**) *v* [Tn] make (sth) known; proclaim 把(某事)公之于众; 宣布: *The news was blazed all over the daily papers.* 所有日报都刊登了这条消息.

blazer /ˈbleɪzə(r); ˋblezɚ/ *n* jacket, without matching trousers, often showing the colours or badge of a club, school, team, etc (不与裤子配套的)西装上衣(常以其颜色或徽章作某俱乐部、学校、队组等的标记).

blazes /ˈbleɪzɪz; ˋblezɪz/ *n* [pl] (*sl* 俚) **1** (esp in expressions of anger or surprise) hell 地狱(尤作表示愤怒或惊讶用语): *Who/What the blazes is that?* 那究竟是谁[什么]? ○ *What the blazes are you doing?* 你到底在搞什么鬼呢? ○ *Go to blazes!* 该死! 见鬼去吧! **2** (idm 习语) **like blazes** vigorously, fast 精力充沛地, 迅速地: *run/work like blazes* 拼命地跑[干活].

blazon /ˈbleɪzn; ˋblezn̩/ *n* heraldic shield; coat of arms 纹章; 盾徽.
▷ **blazon** *v* [Tn] **1** = EMBLAZON. **2** = BLAZE[4].

bldg *abbr* 缩写 = building: *engineering bldg*, eg on a university campus 工程学大楼(如大学校园内的).

bleach /bli:tʃ; blitʃ/ *v* [I, Tn] (cause sth to) become white or pale (by chemical action or sunlight) (使某物)变白; 漂白: *bones of animals bleaching in the desert* 沙漠里变白的兽骨 ○ *bleach cotton, linen, etc* 漂白棉花、亚麻等 ○ *hair bleached by the sun* 由于日晒而发白的毛发.
▷ **bleach** *n* [U, C] substance or process that bleaches or sterilizes 漂白或消毒; 漂白剂: *soak shirts in bleach to remove the stains* 在漂白剂中浸泡衬衣以清除污垢.
□ ˈ**bleaching-powder** *n* substance used to remove colour from dyed materials, eg chloride of lime 漂白粉.

bleach·ers /ˈbli:tʃəz; ˋblitʃɚz/ *n* [pl] (*US*) cheap seats at a sports ground that are not roofed over (运动场内票价低廉的)露天座位.

bleak /bli:k; blik/ *adj* (**-er, -est**) **1** (**a**) (of a landscape) bare; exposed; wind-swept (指景物)荒凉的, 裸露的, 光秃秃的: *bleak hills, mountains, moors, etc* 荒凉的丘陵、群山、旷野等. (**b**) (of the weather) cold and dreary (指天气)寒冷的, 阴沉的: *a bleak winter day* 冬天的一个阴冷日子. **2** (*fig* 比喻) not hopeful or encouraging; dismal; gloomy 无望的; 阴郁的; 黯淡的: *a bleak outlook/prospect* 黯淡的前景[前途] ○ *The future looks bleak.* 前途黯淡. ▷ **bleakly** *adv*. **bleak·ness** *n* [U].

bleary /ˈblɪərɪ; ˋblɪrɪ/ *adj* (of eyes) blurred, esp because of tiredness; seeing dimly (指视力)模糊的(尤因疲倦所致); 矇矇眬眬的.
▷ **blear·ily** *adv* with bleary eyes 视力模糊地: *look blearily at sb* 矇矇眬眬地看某人.
□ ˌ**bleary-ˈeyed** *adj* having bleary eyes 眼睛迷离的: *He's always bleary-eyed early in the morning.* 早上他总是睡眼惺忪.

bleat /bli:t; blit/ *n* cry of a sheep, goat or calf; any noise like this 羊或牛犊的叫声; 类似羊或牛犊叫的声音.
▷ **bleat** *v* **1** [I] make a bleat 作羊或牛犊叫声. **2** [I, Ip, Tn, Tn·p] **~ (sth) (out)** (*fig* 比喻) say (sth) or speak feebly or plaintively 以微弱或哀伤的声音说(某事物): *What are you bleating about?* 你喃喃地说些什么? ○ *He bleated out a feeble excuse.* 他以微弱的声音作无力的辩解.

bleed /bli:d; blid/ *v* (*pt, pp* **bled** /bled; blɛd/) **1** (**a**) [I] lose or emit blood 流血: *bleed to death* 流血而死. (**b**) [I, Ipr] **~ (for sth)** (*fig* 比喻) suffer wounds or die (for a cause, one's country) (为事业、祖国)负伤或牺牲: *those who bled for the revolution* 为革命而献身的人们. **2** [Tn] draw blood from (sb) 给(某人)放血: *Doctors used to bleed people when they were ill.* 从前医生常常给病人放血. **3** [Tn, Tn·pr] **~ sb (for sth)** (*infml* 口) extort (money) from sb 向某人勒索(钱财): *The blackmailers bled him for every penny he had.* 勒索者把他的钱榨得一干二净. **4** [I] (of a plant, tree, etc) lose sap or juice (指花草、树木等)流浆, 流出汁液. **5** (idm 习语) **bleed sb white** take away all sb's money 榨取某人所有的钱. **one's heart bleeds for sb** ⇨ HEART.

bleeder /ˈbli:də(r); ˋblidɚ/ *n* (*Brit sl usu derog* 俚, 通常作贬义) person 人; 傢伙: *You stupid bleeder!* 你这个蠢才!

bleed·ing /ˈbli:dɪŋ; ˋblidɪŋ/ *adj* [attrib 作定语] (*Brit sl* 俚) = BLOODY[2].

bleep /bli:p; blip/ *n* short high-pitched sound made by an electronic device to attract attention (为引人注意使电子装置发出的)短促高音: *The computer gave a regular bleep.* 计算机发出有一定节律的哔哔声.
▷ **bleep** *v* **1** [I] emit bleeps 发哔哔声. **2** [Tn] call (esp a doctor) with a bleeper 用传呼机找人(尤指找医生): *Please bleep the doctor on duty immediately.* 请立刻用传呼机召值班医生. **bleeper** *n* device that emits bleeps 发出哔哔声的装置; 传呼机.

blem·ish /ˈblemɪʃ; ˋblɛmɪʃ/ *n* **1** mark or stain that spoils the beauty or perfection of sb/sth (有损于人或事物的美观或完美的)污点或痕迹; 瑕疵: *a blemish on a pear,* *carpet, table-cloth* 梨上的烂斑、地毯上的污垢、桌布上的污点 ○ *She has a blemish above her right eye.* 她右眼上方有一个疤. **2** (*fig* 比喻) defect, fault or flaw 缺点; 过错; 毛病: *His character/reputation is without (a) blemish.* 他在品德[名誉]上毫无瑕疵.

▷ **blem·ish** *v* [Tn] spoil the beauty or perfection of (sb/sth); flaw; mar 有损于(某人[某事物])美观或完美; 玷污; 损伤: *a blemished peach* 有烂斑的桃子 ○ *The pianist's performance was blemished by several wrong notes.* 钢琴家的演奏由于弹错了几个音符而使人感到美中不足.

B

blench /blentʃ; blɛntʃ/ *v* [I] make a sudden movement because of fear; flinch 因恐惧而突然一动; 畏缩.

blend /blend; blɛnd/ *v* **1** [Tn] mix (different types of sth) in order to get a certain quality 混合; 搀和: *blended whisky/tea/coffee/tobacco* 混合的威士忌[茶叶/咖啡/烟草]. **2** (**a**) [I, Ipr, Ip] **~ (with sth)/~ (together)** form a mixture; mix 成为混合物; 混合: *Oil does not blend with water.* 油不融于水. ○ *Oil and water do not blend.* 油与水不能混合. (**b**) [Tn, Tn·pr, Tn·p] **~ A with B/~ A and B (together)** mix one thing with another; mix things together 将此物与彼物混合; 把东西搀杂在一起: *Blend the eggs with the milk.* 把蛋搀到奶里. ○ *Blend the eggs and milk (together).* 把蛋和奶搀到一起. **3** (**a**) [I, Ipr, Ip] **~ (with sth)/~ (together)** combine with sth in a harmonious way; look or sound good together 调和; 协调; 融合: *Those cottages blend perfectly with the landscape.* 那些农舍与周围的风景完全融为一体了. ○ *Their voices blend (together) well.* 他们的声音很和谐. (**b**) [I, Ipr] **~ (into sth)** (esp of colours) shade gradually into each other (尤指颜色)逐渐融合在一起: *The sea and the sky seemed to blend into each another.* 大海和蓝天似乎连成了一片. **4** (phr v) **blend in (with sth)** mix harmoniously (with sth) (与某物)十分协调: *The new office block doesn't blend in with its surroundings.* 新的办公大楼与周围的环境很不协调. **blend sth in** (in cooking) add another ingredient to sth and mix the two (烹饪时)在某物中加入其他成分使之混合: *Melt the butter and then blend in the flour.* 先把黄油融化, 然后加入面粉.

▷ **blend** *n* **1** mixture of different sorts 不同种类的混合物: *Which blend of coffee would you like?* 你要哪一种混合咖啡? ○ (*fig* 比喻) *His manner is a blend of charm and politeness.* 他的举止既充满魅力, 又彬彬有礼. **2** = PORTMANTEAU WORD (PORTMANTEAU).

blender *n* = LIQUIDIZER (LIQUIDIZE).

bless /bles; blɛs/ *v* (*pt, pp* **blessed** /blest; blɛst/; in sense 5, *pp* **blest** /blest; blɛst/) [Tn] **1** ask God's favour and protection for (sb/sth) 求神赐福于(某人[某事物]); 求神保佑: *They brought the children to Jesus and he blessed them.* 他们把孩子们领到耶稣跟前, 耶稣就赐福予他们. ○ *The Pope blessed the crowd.* 教皇向人群祝福. ○ *The priest blessed the harvest.* 牧师祈求丰收. **2** (esp in Christian ritual) make (sth) sacred or holy; consecrate (尤用于基督教仪式中)使(某事物)神圣; 奉献: *The priest blessed the bread and wine*, ie before the celebration of the Eucharist. 牧师先将饼和酒圣洁化, 然后开始圣餐仪式. **3** (esp in Christian Church services) call (God) holy; praise; glorify (尤用于基督教教会礼拜仪式中)颂扬(上帝); 赞美: *'We bless Thy Holy Name.'* '我们颂赞您的圣名.' **4** (esp imperative in prayers 尤用于祷文中的祈使句) (*fml* 文) grant health, happiness and success to (sb/sth) 赐与(某人[某事物])健康、幸福及成功: *Bless* (ie We ask God to bless) *all those who are hungry, lonely or sick.* 求神赐福于那些饥饿、孤独或患病的人. **5** (*pp* **blest**) (*dated infml* 旧, 口) (esp in exclamations expressing surprise 尤用于感叹句, 表示惊奇): *Bless me!* 哎呀! ○ *Bless my soul!* 哎呀! ○ *Well, I'm blest!* 哎呀! ○ *I'm blest if I know!* ie I don't know at all. 我要是知道就好了(我一点也不知道). **6** (idm 习语) **be blessed with sth/sb** be fortunate in having sth/sb 在某事物[某人]方面有福: *He is blessed with excellent health.* 他身体好极了, 真有福. ○ (*joc or ironic* 谑或反语) *Mrs Murphy is blessed with twelve children.* 墨菲夫人有十二个孩子, 真有福气. **'bless you** (used as an *interj* to express thanks or affection, or said to sb who has sneezed 用作感叹词, 表示谢意或情意, 或当别人打喷嚏时说): *You've bought me a present? Bless you!* 你给我买来一个礼物是吗? 太感谢你了!

blessed /ˈblesɪd; ˋblɛsɪd/ *adj* **1** holy; sacred 神圣的; 圣洁的: *the Blessed Virgin*, ie the mother of Jesus, the Virgin Mary 圣母马利亚(耶稣之母). **2** (in religious language) fortunate (宗教用语)有福的: *Blessed are the meek.* 温顺的人有福了. **3** [attrib 作定语] giving pleasure; enjoyable 带来欢乐的; 令人愉快的: *a moment of blessed calm* 充满欢乐的太平时刻. **4** (in the Roman Catholic Church) (of a person) beatified by the Pope (天主教)(指人)受教皇宣福礼的. **5** (*euph infml* 婉, 口) (used to express mild anger, surprise, etc 用以表示轻度气愤、惊奇等) damned 该死的; 他妈的: *I can't see a blessed thing without my glasses.* 我不带眼镜他妈的什么也看不清.

▷ **the Blessed** *n* [pl *v*] those who live with God in heaven 与上帝同在天堂中的圣徒们.

blessedly *adv*: *It's so blessedly quiet here.* 这儿多么静啊.

blessed·ness /ˈblesɪdnɪs; ˋblɛsɪdnɪs/ *n* [U].

□ **the ˌBlessed ˈSacrament** = SACRAMENT 2.

bless·ing /ˈblesɪŋ; ˋblɛsɪŋ/ *n* **1** (usu *sing* 通常作单数) (**a**) God's favour and protection 神恩; 神的保佑: *ask for God's blessing* 求神保佑. (**b**) prayer asking for this (求神保佑的)祈祷. (**c**) short prayer of thanks to God before or after a meal (餐前或餐后的)祷告: *say a blessing* 祷告. **2** (usu *sing* 通常作单数) good wishes; approval 祝愿; 认可: *I cannot give my blessing to such a proposal.* 我不能同意这样的提议. **3** thing that one is glad of; thing that brings happiness 令人高兴的事物; 带来幸福的事物: *What a blessing you weren't hurt in the accident!* 你在这次事故中没有受伤, 真是幸运! **4** (idm 习语) **a blessing in disˈguise** thing that seems unfortunate, but is later seen to be fortunate 初看似乎不幸, 然而过后看来却是幸运的事; 祸中福: *Not getting into university may be a blessing in disguise; I don't think you'd have been happy there.* 没能上大学焉知非福, 我想你在大学里是不会觉得快乐的. **count one's blessings** ⇨ COUNT[1].

blether = BLATHER.

blew *pt* of BLOW.

blight /blaɪt; blaɪt/ *n* **1** [U] (**a**) disease that withers plants 植物枯萎病. (**b**) [sing] fungus or insect causing this (引起植物枯萎病的)真菌或昆虫. **2** [C] **~ (on/upon sb/sth)** (*fig* 比喻) destructive or harmful force 破坏或损害之力: *cast/put a blight on sb/sth* 打击某人[某事物] ○ *Unemployment is a blight on our community.* 失业是我们社会的一大祸患. **3** [U] ugly or neglected part (esp of cities) 丑陋的或疏于治理的部分(尤指城市): *the blight of inner-city slums* 丑陋脏乱的旧城区的贫民区.

▷ **blight** *v* [Tn] **1** affect (sth) with blight; wither 使(某物)患枯萎病; 使枯萎: *The apple trees were blighted by frost.* 苹果树因严寒而枯萎. **2** spoil (sth); mar 损坏(某事物); 损害: *a career blighted by ill-health* 因体弱多病所影响的事业.

blighter /ˈblaɪtə(r); ˋblaɪtɚ/ *n* (*dated Brit infml* 旧, 口) **1** person; fellow 人; 傢伙: *You lucky blighter!* 你这幸运的傢伙! **2** contemptible or annoying person 可鄙的或讨厌的人: *The blighter stole my purse!* 坏蛋偷了我的钱包!

Blighty /ˈblaɪtɪ; ˋblaɪtɪ/ *n* (*dated Brit army sl* 旧, 英军俚) (used by soldiers serving abroad 海外服役士兵用语) Britain; home 英国本土; 老家.

bli·mey /ˈblaɪmɪ; ˋblaɪmɪ/ *interj* (*Brit sl* 俚) (expressing surprise or annoyance 表示惊奇或烦恼): *Blimey, that's a funny hat!* 嘿, 这顶帽子真古怪!

blimp /blɪmp; blɪmp/ *n* small airship without a rigid frame (无刚性构架的)小型飞艇.

Blimp /blɪmp; blɪmp/ *n* (also ˌ**Colonel ˈBlimp**) (*Brit infml derog* 口, 贬) pompous and reactionary person (esp an old army officer) 高傲自大、顽固保守的人(尤指老军官). ▷ **blimp·ish** *adj*.

blind[1] /blaɪnd; blaɪnd/ *adj* **1** unable to see 瞎的: *a blind person* 盲人 ○ *be blind from birth, in one eye* 生下来就有一只眼瞎了. **2** [attrib 作定语] of or for blind people 盲人的; 为盲人的: *a ˈblind school* 盲人学校. **3** [pred 作表语] **~ (to sth)** unable or unwilling to understand or notice sth; oblivious (to sth); unaware (of sth) (对某事物)视而不见, 不以为意, 一无所知: *I must have been blind not to realize the danger we were in.* 我一定是瞎了眼, 连我们身临险境也看不出来. ○ *He is completely* *blind to her faults.* 他一点儿也觉察不到她的错误. **4** [usu attrib 通常作定语] (*fig* 比喻) **(a)** without reason or judgement 缺乏理性或判断力的: *blind hatred/obedience/prejudice* 盲目的憎恨[顺从/偏见] ○ *love/faith that is blind* 盲目的爱情[信仰]. **(b)** not ruled by purpose; thoughtless; reckless 没有目的的; 轻率的; 不顾后果的: *the blind forces of nature/destiny* 不可捉摸的自然[命运]之力 ○ *be in a blind fury/panic/rage* 无明火起[无谓惊慌/乱发脾气] ○ *blind haste/speed* 瞎忙[疯狂的速度]. **5** [usu attrib 通常作定语] concealed; hidden 隐蔽的; 暗藏的: *a blind driveway/entrance* 隐蔽的车道[入口] ○ *a blind bend/corner/turning*, ie one that prevents the driver from seeing the road ahead (使司机看不见前面马路的转弯处)隐蔽的弯角[拐角/转弯处]. **6** (of an aircraft manoeuvre in cloud, fog, etc) done with the aid of instruments only, without being able to see (指飞机在云、雾等中飞行时)(被障蔽了视线)仅靠仪器导航的: *blind flying* 仪器导航飞行 ○ *a blind landing* 仪器导航降落. **7** (idm 习语) **(as) blind as a 'bat** unable to see clearly or easily; unable to see what is obvious to others 看不清的; 不易看清的; 看不见的(别人却看得见的): *He's as blind as a bat without his glasses.* 他不戴眼镜时简直跟瞎子一样. **turn a blind 'eye (to sth)** pretend not to notice 假装看不见: *The manager turned a blind eye when his staff were late.* 职员迟到时经理装作没看见.

▷ **the blind** *n* [pl *v*] **1** blind people 盲人: *a school for the blind* 盲人学校. **2** (idm 习语) **the blind leading the 'blind** (*saying* 谚) people without adequate experience or knowledge attempting to guide or advise others like them 瞎子给瞎子引路(自己无经验或学识, 却想指导他人者).

blind *adv* **1** without being able to see; with the aid of instruments only 看不见地; 仅凭仪器导向地: *drive/fly blind* 仪器导向驾驶[仪器导航飞行]. **2** (idm 习语) **blind 'drunk** (*infml* 口) very drunk 酩酊大醉. **swear blind** ⇨ SWEAR.

blindly *adv*.

blind·ness *n* [U].

□ ˌ**blind 'alley 1** alley that is closed at one end; cul-de-sac 仅有一端与外间相通的小巷; 死胡同. **2** (*fig* 比喻) course of action which may seem promising at first but which in the end has no satisfactory result 起初似乎大有希望, 而结果却不能令人满意的做法; 钻死胡同.

ˌ**blind 'date** (*infml* 口) arrangement to meet socially made between a man and a woman who have not met each other before 彼此未见过面的男女的约会.

ˌ**blind-ˌman's 'buff** game in which a player who is blindfolded tries to catch and identify the other players 捉迷藏.

'**blind spot 1** part of the retina in the eye that is not sensitive to light 盲点(视网膜上不能感光的部分). **2** area that a motorist cannot see 车辆驾驶者看不见的区域: *I didn't see the car that was overtaking me — it was in my blind spot.* 我没有看见超越我的那辆汽车——当时正位于我的盲点上. **3** subject about which a person is prejudiced or ignorant 某人不喜欢的或一窍不通的科目: *History is one of his blind spots.* 历史是他一窍不通的科目.

blind[2] /blaɪnd; blaɪnd/ *v* **1** [Tn] make (sb) temporarily or permanently blind 使(某人)(暂时地或永久地)失明: *a blinding flash/light* 令人目眩的闪光[亮光] ○ *He was blinded* (ie dazzled) *by the sunlight.* 他因阳光照射而看不见东西(眼花). ○ *The soldier was blinded in the explosion.* 这个军人在那次爆炸中双目失明. **2** [Tn, Tn·pr] **~ sb (to sth)** (*fig* 比喻) deprive sb of reason, judgement or good sense 使人丧失思考力、判断力或良好的感觉: *Her love for him blinded her (to his faults).* 她非常爱他以至(对他的缺点)丧失了判断力. **3** (idm 习语) **blind sb with science** confuse sb with a display of technical knowledge 炫示科技知识使某人摸不着头脑.

blind[3] /blaɪnd; blaɪnd/ *n* **1** (*US* **shade, window-shade**) screen for a window, esp one made of a roll of cloth fixed on a roller and pulled down 窗帘(尤指固定在卷轴上能够拉下来的布质窗帘): *draw/lower/raise the blinds* 拉[放下/扯起]窗帘. **2** thing or person used in order to deceive or mislead (用以蒙骗或迷误对方的)事物或人: *His job as a diplomat was a blind for his spying.* 他担任外交官的职务是为了给他的间谍身分打掩护. **3** (*US*) = HIDE *n* 1.

blinder /'blaɪndə(r); 'blaɪndɚ/ *n* (*Brit sl* 俚) **1** time of excessive drinking 狂饮时刻: *be/go on a blinder* 出席[赴]狂饮宴会. **2** outstanding performance (in a game) (比赛中的)精彩表演: *play a blinder (of a shot, game, etc)* (射击、比赛等)做精彩表演 ○ *The last goal was a blinder.* 最后那次进球得分真是精彩极了.

blinders /'blaɪndəz; 'blaɪnˌdɚz/ *n* [pl] (*US*) = BLINKERS.

blind·fold /'blaɪndfəʊld; 'blaɪndˌfold/ *v* [Tn] cover the eyes of (sb) with a bandage, cloth, etc so that he cannot see (用布条等)蒙住(某人)双眼: *blindfold a hostage, prisoner, etc* 蒙住人质、囚犯等的双眼.

▷ **blind·fold** *n* such a cover for the eyes (作上述用途的)蒙眼物.

blind·fold *adj, adv* with the eyes blindfolded 蒙住眼睛(的): *I could do that blindfold*, ie easily, regardless of obstacles. 我蒙着眼也能做(不费吹灰之力, 无视任何障碍).

blink /blɪŋk; blɪŋk/ *v* **1** [I, Tn] shut and open the eyes quickly 眨眼: *He blinked in the bright sunlight.* 他在灿烂的阳光照射下眨着眼睛. ○ *How long can you stare without blinking (your eyes)?* 你能瞪着看多长时间不眨眼? **2** [I] (of distant lights) shine unsteadily; flicker (指远处灯光)闪烁: *Harbour lights were blinking on the horizon.* 海港的灯火在水平线上闪烁着. **3** (idm 习语) **blink the fact (that...)** refuse to consider; ignore 不考虑; 不顾及: *You can't blink the fact that the country's economy is suffering.* 不能不考虑国家经济正遇到困难这一事实. **4** (phr v) **blink sth away/back** try to control or hide (esp tears) by blinking 尽力用眨眼来控制或遮掩(尤指眼泪): *Although in pain, she bravely blinked back her tears.* 她虽然很疼痛, 但还是硬把眼泪抑制住了.

▷ **blink** *n* **1** act of blinking 眨眼. **2** sudden quick gleam of light 闪光. **3** (idm 习语) **on the blink** (*infml* 口) (of a machine) not working properly; out of order (指机器)不灵, 出故障: *The washing machine's on the blink again.* 洗衣机又出毛病了.

blinkered /'blɪŋkəd; 'blɪŋkɚd/ *adj* **1** (of a horse) wearing blinkers (指马)带眼罩的. **2** (*fig* 比喻) unable to understand or recognize sth; narrow-minded 不能了解或不能认识某事物的; 心胸狭窄的: *a blinkered attitude* 偏见.

blinkers /'blɪŋkəz; 'blɪŋkɚz/ (*US* **blinders**) *n* [pl] leather pieces fixed on a bridle to prevent a horse from seeing sideways 马眼罩. ⇨illus at HARNESS 见 HARNESS 之插图.

blink·ing /'blɪŋkɪŋ; 'blɪŋkɪŋ/ *adj, adv* (*infml euph* 口, 婉) = BLOODY[2]: *It's a blinking nuisance.* 这真是讨厌极了.

blip /blɪp; blɪp/ *n* **1** spot of light on a radar screen (雷达屏幕上的)光点. **2** quick popping sound 短促而尖锐的声音.

bliss /blɪs; blɪs/ *n* [U] perfect happiness; great joy 洪福; 极乐: *a life of bliss* 幸福的一生 ○ *living in married/wedded bliss*, ie very happily married 过着十分美满的婚姻生活 ○ *What bliss! I don't have to go to work today.* 太高兴了! ——我今天不用去上班.

▷ **bliss·ful** /-fl; -fəl/ *adj* extremely happy; joyful 极幸福的; 极快乐的: (*ironic* 反语) *blissful ignorance*, ie being unaware of sth unpleasant 幸而不知道(对令人不快的事情一无所知). **bliss·fully** /-fəlɪ; -fəlɪ/ *adv*.

blis·ter /'blɪstə(r); 'blɪstɚ/ *n* **1** bubble-like swelling under the skin, filled with watery liquid (caused by rubbing, burning, etc) (因磨擦、烧伤等而起的)水泡: *These tight shoes have given me blisters on my ankles.* 这双鞋太紧, 把我的脚腕儿磨起了泡. **2** similar raised swelling on the surface of metal, painted wood, plants, etc (金属、油漆过的木器、植物等的表面的)气泡.

▷ **blis·ter** *v* [I, Tn] (cause sth to) form blisters (使某物)起泡: *My feet blister easily.* 我的脚容易起泡. ○ *The hot sun blistered the paint.* 炎热的阳光晒得油漆起了泡.

blis·ter·ing /'blɪstərɪŋ; 'blɪstərɪŋ/ *adj* **1** (of heat or speed) very great; extreme (指热度或速度)极高的, 极端的: *The runners set off at a blistering pace.* 赛跑者以极高的速度起跑. **2** (of criticism) severe; sharp (指批评)严厉的, 尖锐的: *blistering sarcasm, scorn, etc* 尖刻的讥讽、嘲弄等. **blis·ter·ingly** *adv*.

□ '**blister pack** package in which goods are sold,

consisting of a transparent domed cover on a backing of cardboard, etc 罩板包装(以硬纸板为衬, 上有凸起透明罩的货物包装).

blithe /blaɪð; blaɪð/ *adj* [usu attrib 通常作定语] happy and carefree; casual 快乐无忧的; 漫不经心的: *a blithe lack of concern* 漠不关心 ○ *a blithe spirit*, ie a happy person 快乐的人.
▷ **blithely** *adv* in a blithe manner 快活地; 无忧无虑地; 漫不经心地: *He was blithely unaware of the trouble he had caused.* 他对他所造成的麻烦毫无所知, 无忧无虑.

B

blith·er·ing /ˈblɪðərɪŋ; ˋblɪðərɪŋ/ *adj* [attrib 作定语] (*infml* 口) absolute; contemptible 绝对的; 可鄙的: *You blithering idiot!* 你这个地地道道的傻瓜!

B Litt /ˌbiː ˈlɪt; ˌbi ˋlɪt/ *abbr* 缩写 = Bachelor of Letters 文学士: *have/be a B Litt in English* 有英国文学士学位[为英国文学士] ○ *Sue Hill B Litt* 休·希尔文学士.

blitz /blɪts; blɪts/ *n* **1** [C] sudden intensive military attack, esp from the air 闪击; (尤指)空袭: *carry out a blitz on enemy targets* 对敌方目标进行闪电式空袭 ○ [attrib 作定语] *blitz bombing* 闪击轰炸. **2 the Blitz** [sing] intensive German air raids on Britain in 1940 1940年德国对英国的猛烈空袭. **3** [C] **~ (on sth)** (*fig infml* 比喻, 口) any sudden or concentrated effort (突击性的或集中性的)工作: *I had a blitz on the kitchen today, and now it's really clean.* 我今天在厨房里做了一阵扫除, 现在确实干净了.
▷ **blitz** *v* [Tn] attack or damage (sth) in a blitz (以闪电式空袭)攻击或破坏(某物): *Many towns were badly blitzed during the war.* 战争中许多城镇毁于空袭.

bliz·zard /ˈblɪzəd; ˋblɪzɚd/ *n* severe snowstorm 暴风雪.

bloated /ˈbləʊtɪd; ˋblotɪd/ *adj* swollen with fat, gas or liquid (因含脂肪、气体或液体)肿胀的: *a bloated face* 臃肿的脸 ○ *I've had so much to eat I feel absolutely bloated.* 我吃得过多, 肚子胀得不得了. ○ (*fig* 比喻) *bloated with pride* 骄傲自大的.

bloater /ˈbləʊtə(r); ˋblotɚ/ *n* salted smoked herring 腌熏的鲱鱼.

blob /blɒb; blɑb/ *n* drop of (esp thick) liquid; small round mass or spot of colour 液体(尤指浓液)的一滴; 颜料的小圆块或小圆点: *a blob of paint, wax, cream* 一滴油漆、蜡油、奶油.

bloc /blɒk; blɑk/ *n* group of countries or parties united by a common interest (国家或政党的)集团: *the Eastern/Western bloc* 东欧[西方]集团.

block[1] /blɒk; blɑk/ *n* **1** (**a**) [C] large solid piece of wood, stone, metal, etc, usu with flat surfaces (木、石、金属等的)大块(通常为有平面的): *a block of concrete, granite, marble, etc* 一块混凝土砌块、花岗石、大理石等. (**b**) [C] piece of wood for chopping or hammering on 木砧: *a ˈchopping-block* 砧板 ○ *a butcher's block* 肉墩. (**c**) **the block** [sing] (formerly) large piece of wood on which a condemned person put his neck to have his head cut off (旧时)垫头砧(受刑人引颈断头用的大木块): *go/be sent to the block* 上[被送上]垫头砧. **2** [C] child's wooden or plastic toy brick 积木: *a set of (building) blocks* 一副(建筑)积木. **3** [C] large building divided into separate flats or offices (有许多相互独立的公寓或办公室的)大建筑物: *blocks of ˈflats* 公寓大楼楼群 ○ *an ˈoffice block* 办公大楼 ○ *a ˈtower block*, ie a skyscraper 高层建筑. **4** [C] (**a**) group of buildings bounded by streets on four sides (四面临街的)建筑群: *go for a walk round the block* 绕楼群散步. (**b**) (*esp US*) length of one side of such a group (此类建筑群)一侧的长度: *He lives three blocks away from here.* 他住的地方与此处相隔三条街. **5** [C] large quantity of things regarded as a single unit (看作一个单一整体的)大量事物: *a block of theatre seats* 戏院的一个座位区 ○ *a block of shares*, ie in a business (某企业的)一大宗股分 ○ [attrib 作定语] *a block booking*, ie the booking at one time of a large number of seats 团体票预订(一次预订大量座位). **6** [C] pad of paper for writing or drawing on 活页本; 拍纸簿. **7** [C] piece of wood or metal with designs engraved on it for printing (刻有图案供印刷用的)木板或金属板; 印板. **8** [C usu *sing* 通常作单数] thing that makes movement or progress difficult or impossible; obstruction; obstacle 妨碍物; 阻碍; 障碍: *a block in the pipe, gutter, drain, etc* 阻塞管道、排水沟、下水道等的污物 ○ (*fig* 比喻) *The government's stubborn attitude was a block to further talks.* 政府的僵硬态度是进一步会谈的障碍. **9** (idm 习语) **a chip off the old block** ⇨ CHIP[1]. **have a block (about sth)** fail to understand, feel, etc because of emotional tension 因情绪紧张而不能了解、感知等: *He has a mental block about maths.* 他一遇到数学问题就糊涂. **knock sb's block/head off** ⇨ KNOCK[2].
□ ˌ**block and ˈtackle** lifting device consisting of ropes and pulleys 滑轮组(有缆绳和滑轮的起重装置).
ˌ**block ˈdiagram** diagram showing the general arrangement of parts of a system 方框图; 框图.
ˌ**block ˈletter** (also ˌ**block ˈcapital**) separate capital letter 正楷大写字母: *fill in a form in block letters* 用正楷大写字母填表.
ˌ**block ˈvote** (also ˈ**card vote**) voting system in which each voter has influence in proportion to the number of people he represents 集团投票(按投票者所代表的人数决定表决权大小的表决制度).

block[2] /blɒk; blɑk/ *v* **1** (**a**) [Tn, Tn·p] **~ sth (up)** make movement or flow difficult or impossible on or in sth; obstruct sth 阻碍; 堵塞: *a drain blocked (up) by mud, dead leaves, etc* 被污泥、枯叶等堵塞的下水道 ○ *Heavy snow is blocking all roads into Scotland.* 大雪阻塞了所有通往苏格兰的道路. ○ *A large crowd blocked the corridors and exits.* 人群把走廊和出口都堵死了. ○ *My nose is blocked (up)*, eg because of a heavy cold. 我鼻子堵了(如因患重感冒). (**b**) [Tn] prevent (sb/sth) from moving or progressing; hinder; obstruct 阻挡(某人[某事物]); 阻碍; 堵塞: *block an opponent's move*, eg in a game of chess 封死对方(如下棋中) ○ *The accident blocked traffic in the town centre.* 事故阻塞了市中心的交通. ○ *Progress in the talks was blocked by the Government's intransigence.* 由于政府拒绝让步使会谈中断. **2** [Tn] limit or prevent the use or expenditure of (currency, assets, etc) 限制或阻止(货币、资产等)使用或花费: *blocked sterling* 冻结英国货币. **3** [Tn] (in cricket) stop (the ball) with the bat held defensively in front of the wicket (板球运动中)(在三柱门前举板)挡住(来球). **4** (phr v) **block sth in/out** make a rough sketch or plan of sth 画某物的草图; 定某事物的计划: *block in the plan of a house* 画房屋的设计草图. **block sth off** separate (one place from another) using a solid barrier (用障碍物)隔开: *Police blocked off the street after the explosion.* 在发生爆炸之后, 警方用路障封锁了那条路.
▷ **block·age** /ˈblɒkɪdʒ; ˋblɑkɪdʒ/ *n* (**a**) thing that blocks; obstruction 障碍物; 阻塞: *a blockage in an artery, drain-pipe, etc* 动脉、排水管道等的堵塞. (**b**) state of being blocked 被阻塞的状态.

block·ade /blɒˈkeɪd; blɑˋked/ *n* **1** surrounding or closing of a place (esp a port) by warships or soldiers to prevent people or goods getting in or out 封锁(以战舰或士兵包围或封闭某地, 尤指港口, 使人或货物不能进出). **2** (idm 习语) **break/run a blockade** (esp of a ship) get through a blockade (尤指船只)越过封锁线; 突破封锁. **lift/raise a blockade** end a blockade 解除封锁.
▷ **block·ade** *v* [Tn] close (a town, port, etc) with a blockade 封锁(城市、港口等): *a harbour blockaded by enemy ships* 海港被敌方舰艇封锁.

block-buster /ˈblɒkbʌste(r); ˋblɑkˌbʌstɚ/ *n* (*infml* 口) **1** very powerful bomb that can destroy many buildings 巨型炸弹. **2** book or film strongly promoted by its producers to increase sales (出版人或制片人为了促进销售额而大力宣传的)书或影片. **3** (*US*) person who persuades people to sell their property quickly and cheaply out of fear of decreasing values 物业唆卖掮客(劝人贱价抛售物业以防贬值的人).
▷ ˈ**block-busting** *n* [U] activity of block-busters (BLOCK-BUSTER 3) 物业唆卖.

block·head /ˈblɒkhed; ˋblɑkˌhɛd/ *n* (*infml* 口) stupid person 笨蛋; 傻瓜.

block·house /ˈblɒkhaʊs; ˋblɑkˌhaʊs/ *n* **1** concrete structure strengthened to give shelter from gun-fire, and with openings for defenders to shoot from 碉堡. **2** (*US*) (formerly) wooden fort with openings in the walls for defenders to shoot from (旧时)木堡(防守者可通过其墙孔向外射击).

bloke /bləʊk; blok/ *n* (*Brit infml* 口) man 人; 傢伙.

blond (also esp of a woman **blonde** 亦作 **blonde**, 尤指

女子) /blɒnd; blɑnd/ *n, adj* (person) having golden or pale-coloured hair 有金黄色或浅色头发的(人): *Who was that blonde I saw you with last night?* 昨晚我看见和你一道的那个金发女郎是谁? Cf 参看 BRUNETTE.

blood[1] /blʌd; blʌd/ *n* **1** [U] red liquid flowing through the bodies of humans and animals 血: *give blood*, eg so that it can be used in a blood transfusion 供血 ○ *He lost a lot of blood in the accident.* 他在事故中流了不少血. ○ *Much blood was shed* (ie Many people were killed) *in the war.* 战争中死了许多人. **2** [U] (*fml* 文) family; descent; race 血统; 家世; 种族: *of noble Scottish blood* 出身于苏格兰名门的 ○ *They are of the same blood.* 他们是同宗. **3** [C] (*dated* 旧 *Brit*) rich and fashionable young man; dandy 纨袴子弟; 花花公子. **4** (idm 习语) **bad blood (between A and B)** feelings of mutual hatred or strong dislike 仇恨; 恶感: *There's a lot of bad blood between those two families.* 这两家人积怨很深. **be after/out for sb's 'blood** (*infml* 口) intend to hurt or humiliate sb, esp as a punishment or as revenge 企图伤害或凌辱某人(尤指作为惩罚或报复者): (*joc* 谑) *I was late for work again this morning — my boss is after my blood.* 今早我上班又迟到了——老板要找我麻烦了. **be/run in one's/the 'blood** be part of one's nature or character because one has inherited it or become used to it (因遗传或环境影响)具有某种禀性或特征: *Most of my family are musicians; it runs in the blood.* 我家里的人大都擅长音乐, 是世传. **blood and 'thunder** (*infml* 口) (in films, novels, etc) violent and melodramatic action (电影、小说等)暴力和刺激性的情节: [attrib 作定语] *a blood-and-thunder story* 充满暴力和刺激性内容的小说. **blood is thicker than 'water** (*saying* 谚) family relationships are the strongest ones 血浓于水(亲属关系最强有力). **sb's 'blood is up** sb is in a fighting mood 某人准备战斗: *After being insulted like that, my blood is really up!* 受到这样的侮辱, 我不禁怒火中烧! **(like getting/trying to get) blood out of/from a 'stone** (of money, sympathy, understanding, etc) almost impossible to obtain from sb (指金钱、同情、谅解等)几乎不可能从某人处得到的: *Getting a pay rise in this firm is like getting blood from a stone.* 在这家商行里想增加工资简直是缘木求鱼. **(have sb's) 'blood on one's hands** (carry) responsibility for the death of a person or people 对他人的死亡负有责任: *a dictator with much blood on his hands* 血债累累的独裁者. **draw blood** ⇨ DRAW[2]. **flesh and blood** ⇨ FLESH. **one's flesh and blood** ⇨ FLESH. **freeze one's blood; make one's blood freeze** ⇨ FREEZE. **in cold blood** ⇨ COLD[1]. **make sb's 'blood boil** make sb very angry 使某人非常生气: *The way he treats his children makes my blood boil.* 他那样对待他的孩子, 我非常气愤. **make sb's blood run cold** fill sb with fear and horror 使人感到惧怕和恐怖: *The sight of the dead body made his blood run cold.* 他看见尸体不禁毛骨悚然. **new/fresh 'blood** (in a group, firm, club, etc) new members, esp young ones, with new ideas, skills or methods (团体、公司、俱乐部等的)新人; (尤指有新的思想、技能或工作方法的)年轻人: *This company is badly in need of new blood.* 这个公司亟需新人. **of the blood ('royal)** related to the royal family 皇族的; 皇家的: *a prince of the blood (royal)* 有皇族血统的王子. **spill blood** ⇨ SPILL[1]. **stir the/one's blood** ⇨ STIR. **sweat blood** ⇨ SWEAT.

□ **'blood bank** place where blood is stored for use in hospitals, etc 血库(储存血液以供医院等使用的处所).

'blood-bath *n* indiscriminate killing of many people; massacre 大屠杀; 杀戮: *The battle was a blood-bath.* 这次战役血流成河.

'blood-brother *n* man who has sworn to treat another man as his brother, usu in a ceremony in which their blood is mixed together 盟兄弟, 把兄弟(通常指歃血为盟的).

'blood count (counting of the) number of red and white corpuscles in a sample of blood 血球(计数).

'blood-curdling *adj* filling one with horror; terrifying 使人恐惧的; 毛骨悚然的: *a blood-curdling cry, scream, story* 令人毛骨悚然的叫喊声、尖叫声、故事.

'blood-donor *n* person who gives his blood for transfusions 供血者; 献血者; 捐血者.

'blood feud continuous quarrel between groups or families, with each murdering members of the other; vendetta 血仇(团体或家族之间互相残杀的持久争斗).

'blood group (also **'blood type**) any of the several distinct classes of human blood 血型: *His blood group is AO.* 他的血是AO型.

'blood-heat *n* [U] normal temperature of human blood (about 37°C, 98.4°F) 人体血液的正常温度(约为37 °C、98.4 °F).

'blood-letting *n* [U] **1** surgical removal of some of a patient's blood 给病人放血的外科手术. **2** (*infml* 口) **(a)** bloodshed 流血. **(b)** (*fig* 比喻) bitter quarrelling 吵架: *This blood-letting is damaging the reputation of the party.* 这场争吵有损于党的名声.

'blood-lust *n* [U] strong desire to kill 嗜杀.

'blood-money *n* [U] **1** money paid to a hired killer (付与受雇杀手的)酬金. **2** money paid to the family of a murdered person as compensation (付与被谋杀者家庭的)抚恤金.

'blood orange type of orange with red streaks in its pulp 血橙(一种果肉带有红色条纹的橙子).

'blood-poisoning (also **toxaemia**) *n* [U] infection of the blood with harmful bacteria, esp through a cut or wound 毒血症.

'blood pressure pressure of the blood on the walls of the arteries (varying with a person's age or health) 血压: *have high/low blood pressure* 血压高[低] ○ (*fig* 比喻) *Politicians always raise his blood pressure*, ie make him extremely angry. 政治家的言行常常把他气得怒发冲冠.

ˌblood-'red *adj* having the colour of blood; bright red 血红色的; 鲜红的: *Her finger-nails were blood-red.* 她指甲鲜红. ○ *ˌblood-red 'nails* 鲜红的指甲.

'blood-relation *n* person related to sb by birth 骨肉; 血亲.

'bloodshed *n* [U] killing or wounding of people (人的)伤亡: *The two sides called a truce to avoid further bloodshed.* 双方宣布停战以避免再有伤亡.

'bloodshot *adj* (of eyes) red because of swollen or broken blood-vessels (指眼睛)(因肿胀或布满血丝)通红的, 充血的: *His eyes were bloodshot from lack of sleep.* 他因缺少睡眠而两眼通红.

'blood sports sports (eg fox-hunting) in which animals or birds are killed 猎杀鸟兽的活动(如猎狐).

'blood-stained *adj* **1** stained with blood 有血污的: *a blood-stained shirt* 沾有血迹的衬衫. **2** (*fig* 比喻) characterized or disgraced by bloodshed 血腥的: *a blood-stained reputation, regime, tyrant* 血腥的名声、政权、暴君.

'bloodstock *n* [U] thoroughbred horses 纯种马.

'bloodstream *n* [sing] blood flowing through the body 在体内循环的血液: *inject drugs into the bloodstream* 把药物注射到血液里.

'bloodsucker *n* **1** animal that sucks blood, esp a leech 吸血动物; (尤指)水蛭. **2** (*fig infml* 比喻, 口) person who tries to take as much money as possible from others 吸血鬼(榨取他人钱财之徒).

'blood test examination of a sample of blood, esp for medical diagnosis 验血(尤指用于医疗诊断的).

'blood transfusion injection of blood into a blood-vessel of a person or an animal 输血.

'blood-vessel *n* any of the tubes (arteries, veins or capillaries) through which blood flows in the body 血管: *burst a blood-vessel* 血管破裂.

blood[2] /blʌd; blʌd/ *v* [Tn] **1** (in hunting) allow (a young hound) to taste the blood of eg a fox for the first time (行猎时)让(初次上阵的猎犬)先尝尝(如狐狸的)血腥味. **2** (*fig* 比喻) give (sb) his first experience of an activity; initiate 给(某人)初试的机会: *This will be her first match for her country; she hasn't yet been blooded.* 她将首次代表国家参赛, 这是破题儿第一遭.

blood·hound /'blʌdhaʊnd; 'blʌdˌhaʊnd/ *n* type of large dog with a good sense of smell, used for tracking (一种嗅觉灵敏、作追踪用的)大猎犬.

blood·less /'blʌdlɪs; 'blʌdlɪs/ *adj* **1** without blood or killing 不流血的; 无伤亡的: *a bloodless coup/revolution/victory* 不流血的政变[革命/胜利]. **2** pale; anaemic 苍白的; 无血色的: *He has bloodless cheeks.* 他面颊苍白. **3** (*fig* 比喻) **(a)** (of a person) lacking energy or enthusiasm; dull; lifeless (指人)无精打采的, 无生气的,

B

无活力的. (**b**) lacking emotion; unfeeling 缺少情感的; 无感情的.

blood·thirsty /ˈblʌdθɜːstɪ; ˋblʌdˏθɝstɪ/ *adj* **1** (**a**) cruel and eager to kill; murderous 嗜杀的; 凶杀的: *a bloodthirsty killer, tribe, warrior* 杀人不眨眼的凶手、嗜杀的部族、喋血的勇士. (**b**) taking pleasure or showing interest in killing and violence 对残杀和暴力感兴趣或以之取乐的: *bloodthirsty spectators* 爱看暴力表演的观众. **2** (of a book, film, etc) describing or showing killing and violence (指书、影片等)描写或表现凶杀和暴力的. ▷ **blood·thirs·tily** *adv*. **blood·thirs·ti·ness** *n* [U].

B

bloody[1] /ˈblʌdɪ; ˋblʌdɪ/ *adj* (**-ier, -iest**) **1** covered with blood; bleeding 血染的; 出血的: *His clothes were torn and bloody.* 他的衣服撕破了并染有血迹. ○ *give sb a bloody nose*, ie hit sb's nose so that it bleeds 把某人打得鼻孔流血. **2** involving much bloodshed 大量流血的; 伤亡惨重的: *a bloody battle* 一场血战. **3** cruel; bloodthirsty 残忍的; 嗜血成性的: *a bloody deed, murder, tyrant* 残忍的行为、血腥的谋杀、嗜杀成性的暴君.
▷ **blood·ily** *adv*.
bloody *v* (*pt, pp* **bloodied**) [Tn] stain (sb/sth) with blood 使(某人[某事物])沾上血迹.

bloody[2] /ˈblʌdɪ; ˋblʌdɪ/ *adj* [attrib 作定语], *adv* (⚠ *Brit infml* 讳, 口) **1** (used to emphasize a judgement or comment 用以加强判断或评论的语气) utter(ly); absolute(ly); extreme(ly) 完全; 绝对; 极端: *bloody nonsense, rubbish, etc* 胡闹、无聊…透顶 ○ *This rail strike is a bloody nuisance.* 这次铁路罢工真讨厌. ○ *What a bloody waste of time!* 多浪费时间哪! ○ *That was a bloody good meal!* 这真是一顿非常丰盛的饭菜! **2** (used to stress anger or annoyance 用以加强愤怒或厌恶的语气): *What the bloody hell are you doing?* 你到底在搞什么鬼? ○ *I don't bloody care.* 我根本就不在乎. **3** (idm 习语) **bloody well** (*Brit infml* 口) (used to emphasize an angry statement, esp an order 用以强调气愤的话, 尤指命令) certainly; definitely 当然; 的确: *'I'm not coming with you.' 'Yes you bloody well are!'* '我不跟你一块儿去.' '不行, 你一定得跟我一块儿去!'
□ ˌ**bloody-ˈminded** *adj* (*Brit infml* 口) deliberately unhelpful or obstructive 故意不予合作的; 存心刁难的: *Everybody else accepts the decision. Why must you be so bloody-minded?* 别人都同意这个决议, 你为什么偏要故意刁难? **bloody-mindedness** *n* [U].

bloom /bluːm; blum/ *n* **1** [C] flower, esp of plants admired chiefly for their flowers (eg roses, tulips, chrysanthemums) 花(尤指主要供观赏的, 如玫瑰、郁金香、菊花): *These roses have beautiful blooms.* 这些玫瑰花开得真美. ⇨illus at App 1 见附录1之插图, page ii. Cf 参看 BLOSSOM. **2** [U] (*fig* 比喻) freshness; perfection 新鲜; 完美: *be in/have lost the bloom of youth* 正值[失去]青春. **3** [U] covering of fine powder that forms on ripe plums, grapes, etc 粉衣, 粉霜(成熟的李子、葡萄等表面所生的一层霜粉). **4** (idm 习语) **in (full) bloom** (of plants, gardens, etc) flowering (指植物、园圃等)开花: *The garden looks lovely when the roses are in bloom.* 玫瑰花开时园内美丽诱人. ○ (*fig* 比喻) *Her genius was in full bloom*, ie at its best or highest point. 她才华横溢(处于最佳状态或颠峰时期). **take the bloom off sth** cause sth to lose its freshness or perfection 使某事物失去新鲜感或失去光彩: *Their frequent rows took the bloom off their marriage.* 他们经常吵架, 使得美满婚姻恶化.
▷ **bloom** *v* **1** [I] (**a**) produce flowers; flower; blossom 开花: *Daffodils and crocuses bloom in the spring.* 水仙花和番红花在春天开放. (**b**) (*fig* 比喻) flourish; prosper 茂盛; 繁荣: *Our friendship is blooming.* 我们之间情长谊深. **2** [I, Ipr] **~ (with sth)** (**a**) (of a garden, etc) be full of plants or flowers in bloom (指花园等)长满茂盛的花木: *The garden is blooming with spring flowers.* 园内春花盛开. (**b**) (*fig* 比喻) be in a healthy or flourishing condition (because of sth) (由于某种原因)处于健康或隆盛状态: *They were blooming with health and happiness.* 他们既健康又快乐.

bloomer /ˈbluːmə(r); ˋblumɚ/ *n* (*Brit infml* 口) serious mistake; blunder (严重的)错误; 大错: *He made a tremendous bloomer.* 他犯了个大错.

bloomers /ˈbluːməz; ˋblumɚz/ *n* [pl] short loose trousers gathered at the knee, formerly worn by women for games, cycling, etc (旧时女子于运动、骑车等时穿的长及膝部的)短灯笼裤: *a pair of bloomers* 一条短灯笼裤.

bloom·ing /ˈbluːmɪŋ; ˋblumɪŋ/ *adj* [attrib 作定语], *adv* (*Brit infml euph* 口, 婉) = BLOODY[2].

blooper /ˈbluːpə(r); ˋblupɚ/ *n* (*infml* 口 *esp US*) embarrassing public blunder or mistake (在大庭广众之中犯的很难堪的)错误; 洋相.

blos·som /ˈblɒsəm; ˋblɑsəm/ *n* **1** [C] flower, esp of a fruit tree or flowering shrub 花(尤指果树或灌木的花). Cf 参看 BLOOM. **2** [U] mass of flowers on a tree or shrub (树木上的)花丛, 花簇: *apple, cherry, etc blossom* 苹果花、樱桃花等的花簇. **3** (idm 习语) **in (full) blossom** (esp of trees and shrubs) bearing blossom (尤指树木)正在开花: *The apple trees are in blossom.* 苹果树正在开花.
▷ **blos·som** *v* **1** [I] (of a tree or shrub) produce blossom (指树木)开花: *The cherry trees blossomed early this year.* 樱桃树今年开花早. **2** [I, Ipr, Ip] **~ (out) (into sth)** (*fig* 比喻) (**a**) develop in a healthy or promising way; grow or develop (into sth); flourish 健康地成长; 长成或发展成(某事物); 兴盛: *a blossoming friendship, partnership, etc* 发展中的友谊、合作等 ○ *Mozart blossomed (as a composer) very early in life.* 莫扎特早在童年时已初露头角(成为作曲家). ○ *She has blossomed (out) into a beautiful young woman.* 她已亭亭玉立, 成了美丽的少女. (**b**) become more lively 变得活跃: *He used to be painfully shy, but now he's started to blossom (out).* 他以前极腼腆, 现在活泼起来了.

blot[1] /blɒt; blɑt/ *n* **1** spot or stain made by ink, etc (墨水等的)污点或污迹: *a page covered in (ink) blots* 染有墨迹的一页. **2 ~ on sth** (*fig derog* 比喻, 贬) act or quality that spoils sb's good character or reputation 有损某人良好品格或名声的行为或品质: *His involvement in the scandal was a blot on his reputation.* 他因卷入丑闻, 在名誉上留下污点. **3** (idm 习语) **a blot on sb's/the eˈscutcheon** (*joc* 谑) act, event, etc that disgraces a family or some other group 使家庭或其他集体丢脸的行为、事件等. **a blot on the ˈlandscape** object (esp an ugly building) that spoils the beauty of a place 损害美好景色的物体(尤指不雅观的建筑物): *That new factory is a blot on the landscape.* 那新建的工厂破坏了此地的景色.

blot[2] /blɒt; blɑt/ *v* (**-tt-**) **1** [Tn] make a blot or blots on (paper); stain (with ink) 在(纸)上留下污点; (用墨水)弄脏: *an exercise book blotted with ink* 被墨水弄脏的练习本. **2** [Tn] soak up or dry (sth) with blotting-paper (用吸墨纸)吸干(某物): *blot spilt ink, one's writing paper* 把洒出的墨水、字迹未干的纸吸干. **3** (idm 习语) **blot one's ˈcopy-book** (*infml* 口) spoil one's (previous) good record or reputation 有损(以往的)好形象或名声: *She blotted her copy-book by being an hour late for work.* 她上班迟到了一小时, 破坏了以往的良好形象. **4** (phr v) **blot sth out** (**a**) cover or hide (writing, etc) with a blot (用墨点)覆盖或遮住(字迹等): *Several words in the letter had been blotted out.* 信中有几个字已涂掉了. (**b**) (esp of mist, fog, etc) hide sth completely (尤指雾等)完全遮住(某物): *Thick cloud blotted out the view.* 云层把风景遮住了. (**c**) (*fig* 比喻) remove or destroy (thoughts, memories, etc) completely 完全消除, 彻底清除(思想、记忆等).
▷ **blot·ter** *n* pad or large piece of blotting-paper 吸墨纸簿; (大张)吸墨纸.
□ ˈ**blotting-paper** *n* [U] absorbent paper for drying wet ink 吸墨纸.

blotch /blɒtʃ; blɑtʃ/ *n* large discoloured mark, usu irregular in shape (on skin, paper, material, etc) (皮肤、纸张、材料等上的)大斑点: *His face was covered in ugly red blotches.* 他脸上有许多难看的红色大斑点.
▷ **blotched, blotchy** *adjs* covered in blotches 有大块大块斑点的: *blotchy skin* 有大块斑点的皮肤.

blotto /ˈblɒtəʊ; ˋblɑto/ *adj* [pred 作表语] (*infml* 口) very drunk 酩酊大醉: *You were completely blotto last night.* 昨晚你烂醉如泥.

blouse /blaʊz; *US* blaʊs; blaʊs/ *n* **1** garment like a shirt, worn by women 女衬衫: *She was wearing a skirt and blouse.* 她穿着裙子和衬衫. **2** type of jacket worn by soldiers as part of their uniform 军服上衣.

blow[1] /bləʊ; blo/ *v* (*pt* **blew** /bluː; blu/, *pp* **blown** /bləʊn; blon/ or, in sense 12 用于下述第12义时作

blowed /bləʊd; blod/) **1** [I, Ipr] (often with *it* as the subject 常与作主语的 it 连用) (of the wind or a current of air) be moving (指风或气流)吹, 刮, 流动: *It was blowing hard/blowing a gale*, ie There was a strong wind. 刮大风[狂风]了. ○ *A cold wind blew across the river.* 河面刮过一股冷风. **2** [I, Ipr, Tn·pr, Tn·p] send out (a current of air, etc) from the mouth 吹, 呼, 吐(气等): *You're not blowing hard enough!* 你吹得劲儿不够. ○ *blow on one's food*, ie to cool it 向食物吹气(使之变凉) ○ *blow on one's fingers*, ie to warm them 向手指呵气(使之暖和) ○ *The policeman asked me to blow into a plastic bag*, ie in order to breathalyse me. 警察要我吹一下塑料袋(以测定我呼吸中的酒精含量). ○ *He drew on his cigarette and blew out a stream of smoke.* 他吸了一口香烟, 吐出来一股烟雾. ⇨ illus 见插图. **3** [I, Ip] be moved by the wind 被风吹动: *hair blowing (about) in the wind* 被风吹拂(吹散)的头发. **4** [Tn] make or shape (sth) by blowing 吹成, 吹出(某物): *blow smoke rings* 吹烟圈 ○ *blow bubbles*, eg by blowing onto a film of soapy water 吹泡泡(如用肥皂水吹泡) ○ *blow glass*, ie send a current of air into molten glass 吹玻璃(将气流吹入熔融的玻璃中使之成形). **5** [Tn] use (sth) to make a current of air 使用(某物)以产生气流: *blow bellows* 拉风箱. **6** (**a**) [Ipr, Tn] produce sound from (a brass instrument, whistle, etc) by blowing into it 吹(铜管乐器、笛哨等): *blow (on) a horn* 吹号 ○ *The referee blew his whistle.* 裁判鸣笛. (**b**) [I] (of an instrument, etc) sound in this way (指乐器等)吹奏出声: *the noise of trumpets blowing* 吹喇叭产生的噪音. **7** [I, Tn] (cause sth to) melt with too strong an electric current (使某物)因电流过强而熔化: *A fuse has blown.* 保险丝烧断了. ○ *I've blown a fuse.* 我把保险丝烧断了. **8** [Tn] break (sth) with explosives 炸坏(某物): *The safe had been blown by the thieves.* 保险箱被窃贼炸开了. **9** [Tn] (*sl* 俚) reveal (sth) 显露, 泄露(某事物): *The spy's cover was blown.* 间谍的伪装被揭穿了. **10** [Tn, Tn·pr] **~ sth (on sth)** (*infml* 口) spend a lot of money (on sth) (在某事物上)花很多钱: *blow £50 on a meal* 一顿饭就花了50英镑. **11** [Tn] spoil or fail to use (an opportunity) 错过(良机): *He blew it/blew his chances by arriving late for the interview.* 他面试迟到了, 错过了机会. **12** (*pp* **blowed** /bləʊd; blod/) [Tn] (*infml* 口) (used esp in the imperative in expressions of anger, surprise, etc 尤用于表示气愤, 惊奇等的祈使句) damn (sb/sth) 该死的(某人[某事物]): *Blow it! We've missed the bus.* 糟糕! 我们没赶上公共汽车. ○ *Well, blow me/I'm blowed! I never thought I'd see you again.* 我的天哪! 我还以为再也见不着你了. ○ *I'm blowed if I'm going to* (ie I certainly will not) *let him treat you like that.* 我要是容许他这样对待你, 我就不是人(我决不允许). **13** [Tn] (*US sl* 俚) leave (a place) suddenly 突然离开(某地). **14** (idm 习语) **blow the 'gaff** (*sl* 俚) reveal a secret 泄露秘密. **blow hot and 'cold (about sth)** (*infml* 口) keep changing one's opinions (about sth); vacillate (对某事)无定见; 优柔寡断: *He blows hot and cold about getting married.* 他对结婚犹豫不决. **blow (sb) a 'kiss** kiss one's hand and then pretend to blow the kiss (towards sb) 送(某人)飞吻. **blow one's/sb's 'brains out** kill oneself/sb by shooting in the head 枪击自己[某人]头部致死. **blow one's/sb's 'mind** (*sl* 俚) produce a pleasant or shocking feeling in one/sb 使自己[某人]感到高兴或惊愕. **blow one's 'nose** clear one's nose of mucus by breathing out strongly through it into a handkerchief 擤鼻涕. **blow off/let off steam** ⇨ STEAM. **blow one's own 'trumpet** (*infml* 口) praise one's own abilities and achievements; boast 自吹自擂; 夸口. **blow one's 'top**; *US* **blow one's 'stack** (*infml* 口) lose one's temper 发脾气; 大发雷霆. **blow the whistle on sb/sth** (*infml* 口) make sb suddenly stop doing sth, esp sth illegal, eg by informing the authorities 使某人立即停止干某事(如向当局告发, 尤指停止其非法勾当). **puff and blow** ⇨ PUFF². **see which way the wind is blowing** ⇨ WAY¹. **15** (phr v) **blow (sb/sth) down, off, over, etc** move or be moved in the specified direction by the force of the wind, sb's breath, etc (借助于风、呼气等之力沿某方向)移动: *My hat blew off.* 我的帽子被风刮掉了. ○ *The door blew open.* 门被风吹开了. ○ *Several chimneys blew down during the storm.* 有几个烟囱在暴风雨中刮倒了. ○ *I was almost blown over by the wind.* 我几乎被风刮倒. ○ *The ship was blown onto the rocks.* 船被风刮到礁石上了. ○ *The bomb blast blew two passers-by across the street.* 炸弹爆炸的强劲气流把两个行人刮到街的另一边去了. ○ *He blew the dust off the book*, ie removed the dust by blowing. 他吹掉书上的灰尘.

blow in/blow into 'sth (*infml* 口) arrive or enter (a place) suddenly 突然来到或进入(某地): *Look who's just blown in!* 瞧瞧谁来了!

blow out (**a**) (of a flame, etc) be extinguished by the wind, etc (指火焰等)被风等熄灭: *Somebody opened the door and the candle blew out.* 有人打开了门, 蜡烛随之被吹灭了. (**b**) (of an oil or gas well) send out oil or gas suddenly in an uncontrolled manner (指油井或气井)井喷. **blow itself out** (of a storm, etc) lose its force; dwindle to nothing (指风暴等)减弱, 停止. **blow sth out** extinguish (a flame, etc) by blowing 吹灭(火焰等).

blow over pass away without having a serious effect 安然过去; 平息: *The storm blew over in the night.* 风暴在夜里停止了. ○ *The scandal will soon blow over.* 这一丑闻不久就会平息.

blow up (**a**) explode; be destroyed by an explosion 爆炸; 被炸坏: *The bomb blew up.* 炸弹爆炸了. ○ *A policeman was killed when his booby-trapped car blew up.* 警察被藏在他汽车里的炸弹炸死了. (**b**) start suddenly and with force 突然开始且来势凶猛: *A storm is blowing up.* 风暴来临. ○ (*fig* 比喻) *A political crisis has blown up over the President's latest speech.* 总统最近的演说触发了政治危机. (**c**) (*infml* 口) lose one's temper 发脾气; 勃然大怒: *I'm sorry I blew up at you.* 很抱歉, 对你发火了. **blow sb up** (*infml* 口) reprimand sb severely 训斥某人: *She got blown up by her boss for being late.* 她因迟到而受到老板严厉训斥. **blow sth up** (**a**) destroy sth by an explosion 炸坏某物: *The police station was blown up by terrorists.* 派出所让恐怖分子炸毁了. (**b**) inflate sth with air or gas 给某物充气: *This tyre's a bit flat; it needs blowing up.* 这个轮胎气不太足, 需要打气. (**c**) make (esp a photograph) bigger; enlarge sth 放大某物(尤指照片): *What a lovely photo! Why don't you have it blown up?* 多美的照片哪! 你怎么不把它放大呢? (**d**) (*infml* 口) exaggerate or inflate sth 夸大某事物: *His abilities as an actor have been greatly blown up by the popular press.* 通俗的报刊过分夸张了他的演技. ○ *The whole affair was blown up out of all proportion.* 整件事夸大得走样了.

▷ **blowy** *adj* windy 多风的: *a blowy day* 刮风天.

□ **'blow-dry** *v* (*pt, pp* **-dried**) [Tn] style (the hair) while drying it with a hand-held drier 用手持吹风机把(头发)吹干并定型. — *n* act of drying and styling the hair in this way 用上述方法将头发吹干并定型的作业: *ask the hairdresser for a wash and blow-dry* 要求理发师洗头并吹干定型.

'blow-hole *n* **1** vent for air, smoke, etc in a tunnel (隧道的)通风口. **2** hole in the ice through which seals, etc breathe (海豹等用以呼吸的)冰窟窿. **3** whale's nostril situated at the back of its skull (鲸鱼的)鼻孔.

ˌblowing-'up *n* scolding 责骂: *get a terrible blowing-up for sth* 为某事挨了一顿大骂.

'blowlamp (*US* **torch**, **'blowtorch**) *n* burner for directing a very hot flame onto part of a surface, eg to remove old paint 喷灯.

'blow-out *n* **1** bursting of a tyre on a motor vehicle (机动车的)轮胎爆裂: *have a blow-out on the motorway* 在高速公路上发生轮胎爆裂事故. **2** melting of an electric fuse 保险丝烧断. **3** sudden uncontrolled escape of oil or gas from a well 井喷. **4** (*sl* 俚) large meal 盛餐.

'blow-up *n* enlargement (of a photograph) (照片)放

大: *Do a blow-up of this corner of the negative.* 把底片的这一角放大.

blow[2] /bləʊ; blo/ *n* **1** act of blowing 吹: *give one's nose a good blow*, ie clear it thoroughly 把鼻子好好地擤一擤. **2** (idm 习语) **go for/have a ˈblow** go for a short walk in the fresh air 到空气新鲜的地方去散步.

blow[3] /bləʊ; blo/ *n* **1** hard stroke (given with the fist, a weapon, etc) (用拳头、武器等的)重击: *He received a severe blow on/to the head.* 他头部受到重重的一击. **2 ~ (to sb/sth)** sudden shock, set-back or disaster (for sb/sth) (对某人[某事物]而言)突然的打击、挫折或灾祸: *a blow to one's pride* 对自尊心的重大打击 ○ *His wife's death was a great blow (to him).* 他妻子去世(对他)是一大打击. **3** (idm 习语) **at one ˈblow; at a (single) ˈblow** with one stroke or effort 一击; 一下子; 一举: *He felled his three attackers at a single blow.* 他一下子撂倒了三个袭击他的人. **a ˌblow-by-ˈblow account, description, etc (of sth)** account giving all the details (of an event) as they occur (对某事的)详尽的报道: *He gave us a blow-by-blow account of the evening's events.* 他给我们详细叙述了晚间的赛事. **come to ˈblows (over sth)** start fighting (because of sth) (为某事)打起来: *We almost came to blows over what colour our new carpet should be.* 我们为了用什么颜色的新地毯险些打了起来. **deal sb/sth a blow** ⇨ DEAL[3]. **get a ˈblow/ˈpunch in** succeed in hitting sb 打中某人. **strike a blow for/against sth** ⇨ STRIKE[2].

blower /ˈbləʊə(r); ˈbloɚ/ *n* **1** device that produces a current of air 吹风机; 鼓风机. **2** (*Brit infml* 口) telephone 电话: *You can always get me on the blower.* 你随时打电话都能找到我.

blow·fly /ˈbləʊflaɪ; ˈbloˌflaɪ/ *n* fly that lays its eggs on meat; bluebottle 丽蝇.

blown *pp* of BLOW[1].

blowzy /ˈblaʊzɪ; ˈblaʊzɪ/ *adj* (*derog* 贬) (of a woman or her appearance) untidy and coarse-looking (指女人或其外表)邋遢的, 不雅观的.

blub·ber[1] /ˈblʌbə(r); ˈblʌbɚ/ *n* [U] fat of whales and other sea animals from which oil is obtained 鲸脂.

blub·ber[2] /ˈblʌbə(r); ˈblʌbɚ/ *v* [I] (*usu derog* 通常作贬义) weep noisily 号啕大哭: *Stop blubbering, you big baby!* 大宝贝, 别哭了!

bludgeon /ˈblʌdʒən; ˈblʌdʒən/ *n* short thick stick with a heavy end, used as a weapon 大头短棒(用作武器).

▷ **bludgeon** *v* **1** [Tn] hit (sb) repeatedly with a bludgeon, or with any heavy object (用大头短棒或其他重物)连击(某人): *He had been bludgeoned to death.* 他被大头短棒连击致死. **2** [Tn, Tn·pr] **~ sb (into doing sth)** (*fig* 比喻) force sb (to do sth) 强迫某人(做某事): *They tried to bludgeon me into telling them, but I refused.* 他们尽力迫使我告诉他们, 但我拒绝了.

blue[1] /bluː; blu/ *adj* **1** having the colour of a clear sky or the sea on a sunny day 蓝色的; 天蓝色的; 蔚蓝的; 青色的: *blue eyes* 蓝眼睛 ○ *a blue dress, shirt, etc* 蓝衣服、衬衫等 ○ *He was blue in the face*, ie His face was a purplish colour because of cold or exertion. 他脸色发青(因寒冷或用力过度而稍泛紫色). ○ *Her hands were blue with cold.* 她的双手都冻青了. ⇨illus at SPECTRUM 见SPECTRUM之插图. **2** [pred 作表语] (*infml* 口) sad; depressed 忧伤; 沮丧: *Don't look so blue — smile!* 别这样愁眉苦脸的——笑一笑吧! **3** indecent; pornographic 下流的; 色情的: *a blue film/movie/joke* 黄色的影片[电影/笑话]. **4** (idm 习语) **black and blue** ⇨ BLACK[1]. **sb's ˌblue-eyed ˈboy** (*infml esp Brit usu derog* 口, 通常作贬义) favourite of a person or group; darling; pet 亲信; 宠儿; 宝贝儿; 宠物: *He's the manager's blue-eyed boy.* 他是经理的亲信. **once in a blue moon** ⇨ ONCE. **scream, etc blue ˈmurder** (*infml* 口) protest wildly and noisily 强烈抗议; 哗然反对: *The union yelled blue murder when one of its members was sacked.* 有一会员遭解雇, 工会表示强烈抗议. **(do sth) till one is blue in the ˈface** (*infml* 口) (work, etc) as hard and as long as one possibly can (usu without success) (工作等)努力和持久到了极点(通常并不成功): *He can write me letters till he's blue in the face, I'm not going to reply.* 任他没完没了地给我写信, 我就是不回信. ▷ **blue·ness** *n* [U].

□ ˌ**blue ˈbaby** baby whose skin is blue at birth because of a heart defect (因心脏有缺陷, 出生时)皮肤发青的婴儿.

ˌ**blue ˈblood** aristocratic descent or birth 贵族出身; 贵族身分. ˌ**blue-ˈblooded** *adj*: *a ˌblue-blooded ˈfamily* 贵族世家.

ˈ**blue book** (*Brit*) parliamentary or Privy Council report 蓝皮书(英国国会或枢密院的报告书).

ˌ**blue ˈcheese** cheese showing lines of blue mould (有蓝色霉样条纹的)蓝干酪.

ˌ**blue-ˈchip** *n, adj* (*commerce* 商) (industrial share) considered to be a safe investment 可靠的(工业股票); 蓝筹(股).

ˌ**blue-ˈcollar** *adj* [attrib 作定语] of or relating to manual workers 体力劳动者的; 蓝领阶级的: *blue-ˈcollar workers, jobs* 蓝领工人、工作 ○ *a blue-ˈcollar union* 蓝领工人的工会. Cf 参看 WHITE-COLLAR (WHITE[1]).

ˌ**blue ˈensign** (*Brit*) flag of government departments 政府部门的旗子.

ˈ**bluejacket** *n* seaman in the navy 水兵.

ˌ**blue-ˈpencil** *v* [Tn] alter or remove (parts of a book, film, play, etc); edit; censor 修改或删除(书、影片、剧本等的部分内容); 编辑; 出版审查.

ˌ**Blue ˈPeter** blue flag with a central white square, used to show that a ship is about to sail 开航旗(蓝底、中间有一白色正方形的信号旗).

ˌ**blue ˈribbon** honour or prize awarded to the winner of a competition 蓝绶带(授予竞赛优胜者的荣誉或奖励).

ˈ**blue tit** type of small bird with a blue head, tail and wings and yellow underparts 蓝山雀. ⇨illus at App 1 见附录1之插图, page iv.

ˌ**blue ˈwhale** type of whale with a dorsal fin, the largest known living animal 蓝鲸.

blue[2] /bluː; blu/ *n* **1** (**a**) [C, U] blue colour 蓝色; 青色: *light/dark blue* 浅[深]蓝色 ○ *material with a lot of blue in it* 蓝色成分多的材料. (**b**) [U] blue clothes 蓝色服装: *dressed in blue* 穿着蓝色衣服. **2** [C] (**a**) (*Brit*) distinction awarded to a sportsman who represents either Oxford or Cambridge University in a match between the two 蓝色荣誉(授予代表牛津或剑桥大学参加两校比赛的运动员的最高荣誉): *get a/one's blue for cricket, football, etc* 参加牛津与剑桥两校板球、足球等比赛而获得蓝色荣誉. (**b**) person who has won a blue 获得蓝色荣誉的人: *an Oxford/a Cambridge (hockey) blue* 牛津[剑桥](曲棍球)蓝色荣誉获得者. **3 the blue** [sing] (*dated infml* 旧, 口) sea or sky 大海; 蓝天: *The boat sailed off into the blue.* 小船已驶出海. **4** [sing or pl *v*] (**a**) **the blues** slow melancholy jazz music originating among Blacks in the southern US 布鲁斯音乐(源自美国南方黑人中情调忧郁的慢速爵士音乐): [attrib 作定语] *a blues singer, melody* 布鲁斯歌手、曲调. (**b**) **blues** song of this type 布鲁斯歌曲: *sing a blues* 唱布鲁斯歌曲. **5 the blues** [pl] (*infml* 口) feelings of deep sadness or depression 极其忧伤或沮丧的情绪: *have (an attack of) the blues* 觉得伤心. **6** (idm 习语) **a bolt from the blue** ⇨ BOLT[1]. **the boys in blue** ⇨ BOY[1]. **out of the ˈblue** unexpected(ly); without warning 意外(的); 未事先告知: *She arrived out of the blue.* 她没有事先告知就来了. ○ *His resignation came (right) out of the blue.* 他突然辞职, 使人感到意外.

blue[3] /bluː; blu/ *v* [Tn] (*infml* 口) spend (money) recklessly 乱花(钱): *He won £500 and then blued the lot in three days.* 他赢了500英镑, 可是才三天就花得精光.

blue·bell /ˈbluːbel; ˈbluˌbɛl/ *n* (**a**) (in S England) plant with blue or white bell-shaped flowers; wood hyacinth (英格兰南部的)风铃草(开蓝色或白色钟形花). ⇨illus at App 1 见附录1之插图, page ii. (**b**) (in Scotland and N England) harebell (苏格兰和英格兰北部的)圆叶风铃草.

blue·berry /ˈbluːbrɪ; *US* -berɪ; ˈbluˌbɛrɪ/ *n* (**a**) small N American shrub 南方越橘(北美的小灌木). (**b**) its edible dark blue berry 南方越橘(上述灌木的深蓝色果实, 可食). Cf 参看 BILBERRY.

blue·bottle /ˈbluːbɒtl; ˈbluˌbɑtl̩/ *n* large buzzing fly with a blue body 青蝇.

blue·print /ˈbluːprɪnt; ˈbluˌprɪnt/ *n* **1** photographic print of building plans, with white lines on a blue background 蓝图. **2** (*fig* 比喻) detailed plan or scheme (详细的)计划, 方案: *a blueprint for success* 争取成功的详细方案 ○ [attrib 作定语] *Plans have reached the blueprint stage.* 计划即将制订出来.

blue·stock·ing /ˈbluːstɒkɪŋ; ˈbluˌstɑkɪŋ/ *n* (*sometimes* *derog* 有时作贬义) woman having, or pretending to have, literary tastes and learning 有(或装成有)文学修养和学识的女性.

bluff[1] /blʌf; blʌf/ *v* **1** [I, Tn] try to deceive (sb) by pretending to be stronger, braver, cleverer, etc than one is 虚张声势; 吓唬(某人): *I don't believe he'd really do what he threatens — he's only bluffing (us).* 我不相信他真会按他威胁的话去做, 他不过吓唬(我们)罢了. **2** (phr v) **bluff sb into doing sth** make sb believe or do sth by deceiving him 骗某人相信某事; 骗某人做某事: *They were bluffed into believing we were not ready for the attack.* 他们上了当, 以为我们还没有作好进攻准备. **bluff it ˈout** survive a difficult situation by deceiving others (借蒙骗别人)摆脱困境, 绝处逢生. **bluff one's way out (of sth)** escape from a difficult situation by deceiving others (借蒙骗别人)逃离困境.

▷ **bluff** *n* **1** [U, C] bluffing; threat intended to influence sb without being carried out 虚张声势; 吓唬: *The company's threat to sack anyone who went on strike was just (a) bluff.* 公司威胁说谁罢工就解雇谁, 那只不过是虚张声势罢了. **2** (idm 习语) **call sb's bluff** ⇨ CALL[2].

bluff[2] /blʌf; blʌf/ *n* cliff or headland with a broad and very steep face (伸向大海的)悬崖峭壁.

bluff[3] /blʌf; blʌf/ *adj* **1** (esp of cliffs) with a broad steep or vertical front (尤指悬崖)前部宽阔陡直的. **2** (of a person, his manner, etc) frank and abrupt, but good-natured (指人、态度等)粗豪坦率的(但为善意的): *He is kind and friendly despite his rather bluff manner.* 他为人厚道, 待人亲切, 虽然态度有些粗鲁. ▷ **bluff·ness** *n* [U].

blu·ish /ˈbluːɪʃ; ˋbluɪʃ/ *adj* tending towards blue; fairly blue 接近蓝色的; 浅蓝的: *eyes of bluish green* 绿中透蓝的眼睛.

blun·der /ˈblʌndə(r); ˋblʌndɚ/ *n* stupid or careless mistake (愚蠢的或粗心的)错误: *I've made an awful blunder.* 我做了一件大错特错的事. ⇨Usage at MISTAKE 用法见 MISTAKE.

▷ **blun·der** *v* **1** [I] make a blunder 犯(愚蠢的或粗心的)错误: *The police blundered badly by arresting the wrong man.* 警方抓错了人, 犯了荒唐的大错. **2** (phr v) **blunder about, around, etc** move about clumsily or uncertainly, as if blind 乱闯; 瞎闯: *He blundered about the room, feeling for the light switch.* 他在房间里磕磕绊绊地摸索电灯的开关. **blunder into sth** walk into or strike sth through clumsiness or inability to see (因笨拙或看不见)碰着某物: *In the darkness, he blundered into the hall table.* 黑暗中他撞着了大厅里的桌子. **blun·derer** /ˈblʌndərə(r); ˋblʌndərɚ/ *n* person who makes blunders 犯粗心错误的人.

blun·der·buss /ˈblʌndəbʌs; ˋblʌndɚˌbʌs/ *n* old type of gun with a wide mouth, firing many bullets or small shot at short range 旧式大口径前膛枪.

blunt /blʌnt; blʌnt/ *adj* (**-er, -est**) **1** without a sharp edge or a point 不锋利的; 不尖的; 钝的: *a blunt knife, razor-blade, saw, pencil, etc* 钝的小刀、不锋利的刀片、不快的锯、秃的铅笔等. **2** (*fig* 比喻) (of a person, remark, etc) frank and straightforward; not trying to be polite or tactful (指人、言语等)坦诚的, 直率的, 不客气的, 欠圆通的: *a blunt refusal* 不客气的拒绝 ○ *Let me be quite blunt (with you) — your work is appalling.* (对你)直说吧 —— 你的工作太差劲.

▷ **blunt** *v* [Tn] make (sth) blunt or less sharp 把(某物)弄钝: *a knife blunted by years of use* 多年用钝了的刀 ○ *a fine mind blunted by boredom* 因厌烦而变得迟钝的头脑.

bluntly *adv* in a blunt(2) manner 坦率地: *To put it bluntly, you're fired!* 直截了当地说吧, 你被解雇了!

blunt·ness *n* [U].

blur /blɜː(r); blɝ/ *n* thing that appears hazy and indistinct 模糊之物; 朦胧的状况: *The town was just a blur on the horizon.* 朝地平线望去, 小城一片朦胧. ○ *Everything is a blur when I take my glasses off.* 我不戴眼镜时, 什么也看不清. ○ (*fig* 比喻) *My memories of childhood are only a blur.* 我对童年的生活已经记不太清了.

▷ **blur** *v* (**-rr-**) [I, Tn] (cause sth to) become unclear or indistinct (使某事物)变得模糊不清: *Her eyes blurred with tears.* 她泪眼迷离. ○ *a blurred photograph* 模糊不清的照片 ○ *blurred writing* 模糊不清的字迹 ○ *Mist blurred the view.* 雾霭障蔽了视线. ○ (*fig* 比喻) *His memory is blurred by his illness.* 他因患病记忆力减退.

blurb /blɜːb; blɝb/ *n* publisher's short description of the contents of a book, usu printed on the jacket or cover (出版者对书的)内容简介(通常印在护封或封底上).

blurt /blɜːt; blɝt/ *v* (phr v) **blurt sth out** say sth suddenly and tactlessly 脱口说出: *He blurted out the bad news before I could stop him.* 我还没来得及阻止他, 他已冲口说出了这个坏消息.

B

blush /blʌʃ; blʌʃ/ *v* **1** [I, Ipr] **~ (with sth) (at sth)** become red in the face (because of sth) (因某事物)脸红: *blush with shame, embarrassment, etc* 因羞愧、难堪等而脸红 ○ *the blushing bride* 羞赧的新娘 ○ *She blushed at (the thought of) her stupid mistake.* 她因(想到)自己干的蠢事而脸红. **2** [It] (*fig* 比喻) be ashamed 羞愧: *I blush to admit/confess that...* 我羞愧地承认[供认]....

▷ **blush** *n* **1** reddening of the face (from shame, embarrassment, etc) (因羞愧、难堪等)脸上泛出的红晕: *She turned away to hide her blushes.* 她转过身去, 不让人看见她两颊绯红. **2** (idm 习语) **spare sb's blushes** ⇨ SPARE[2].

blusher *n* [C, U] cosmetic used to give the cheeks a rosy colour 胭脂.

blush·ingly *adv.*

blus·ter /ˈblʌstə(r); ˋblʌstɚ/ *v* **1** [I] (of the wind) blow fiercely or in strong gusts (指风)猛刮, 阵阵狂吹: *The gale blustered all night.* 刮了一夜狂风. **2** [I] talk in an aggressive, boastful or threatening way (usu with little effect) 咄咄逼人, 口出狂言, 威吓(通常作用不大). **3** (phr v) **bluster one's way out of sth** try to escape from sth by talking aggressively, boastfully, etc (言语尖刻或口出狂言等)冀求摆脱某事物: *He always tries to bluster his way out of difficult situations.* 他总是自吹自擂以摆脱困境.

▷ **blus·ter** *n* [U] **1** noise of a violent wind (狂风的)呼啸声. **2** (*fig* 比喻) blustering talk or behaviour; noisy but empty threats 吓唬人的言语或行为; 虚张声势的恫吓: *I wasn't frightened by what he said — it was just bluster.* 他说的话吓不倒我 —— 不过是雷声大, 雨点小.

blus·tery /ˈblʌstrɪ; ˋblʌstrɪ/ *adj* (of the weather) very windy; gusty (指天气)刮大风的, 刮阵风的: *a blustery day* 刮大风的一天.

BMA /ˌbiː em ˈeɪ; ˌbi ɛm ˋe/ *abbr* 缩写 = British Medical Association 英国医学会: *a member of the BMA* 英国医学会会员.

B Mus /ˌbiː ˈmʌs; ˌbi ˋmʌs/ *abbr* 缩写 = Bachelor of Music 音乐学士: *have/be a B Mus* 有音乐学士学位[为音乐学士] ○ *John Scott B Mus* 约翰·斯科特音乐学士.

Bn *abbr* 缩写 = battalion: *1st Bn Coldstream Guards* 科尔德斯特里姆卫队第一营.

BO (also **bo**) /ˌbiː ˈəʊ; ˌbi ˋo/ (*infml* 口 *esp Brit*) body odour 体臭; 狐臭: *have BO* 有体臭.

boa /ˈbəʊə; ˋboə/ *n* **1** (also ˈ**boa con·strictor**) large non-poisonous S American snake that kills its prey by crushing it 蟒, 蟒蛇(产于南美洲). ⇨illus at SNAKE 见 SNAKE 之插图. **2** long thin type of scarf made of fur or feathers and worn by women (女用)长围巾(毛皮或羽毛制的): *a feather boa* 羽毛围巾.

boar /bɔː(r); bɔr/ *n* (*pl* unchanged or **~s** 复数或不变或作 **boars**) **1** male wild pig 公野猪. **2** uncastrated male domestic pig 未阉的公猪. Cf 参看 HOG 1, SOW[1].

board[1] /bɔːd; bɔrd/ *n* **1** [C] long thin flat piece of cut wood used for building walls, floors, boats, etc (长而薄的)木板(用于建造墙壁、地板、船身等). **2** [U] (esp in compounds 尤用以构成复合词) material made of compressed wood fibres, etc and cut into thin stiff sheets (用压缩木纤维等制成的)硬薄板: ˈ*chipboard*, ˈ*hardboard*. **3** [C usu *pl* 通常作复数] thick stiff paper (sometimes covered with cloth) used for book covers (书籍封面用的)厚硬纸板(有时加有布面): *a book bound in cloth boards* 用布面纸板作封面的书. **4** [C] (esp in compounds 尤用以构成复合词) flat piece of wood or other stiff material used for a specific purpose 板子; 牌子: *a* ˈ*notice-board* ○ *an* ˈ*ironing-board* ○ *a* ˈ*diving-board* ○ *a* ˈ*breadboard*, ie for cutting bread on. **5** [C] flat surface marked with patterns, etc on which certain games are played 棋盘: [attrib 作定语] *Chess, draughts and ludo are* ˈ*board games.* 国际象棋、国际跳

棋及儿童掷色子游戏都是在棋盘上比赛的游戏. ⇨illus at CHESS 见CHESS之插图. **6 the boards** [pl] (*dated or joc* 旧或谑) the theatre; acting as a profession 舞台; 演艺业: *Are you still treading the boards?* 你还在当演员吗? **7** [CGp] group of people controlling a company or some other organization; committee; council (公司或其他机构的)主管人员; 委员会; 理事会; 董事会: *the 'coal/'gas/elec'tricity/'water board* 煤炭[煤气/电力/水务]部 ○ *the board of governors (of a school)* (学校的)董事会 ○ *She has a seat on/is on the board (of directors) of a large company.* 她是某大公司董事会成员之一. ○ *The board is/are unhappy about falling sales.* 董事会对销售额下降很不满. ○ [attrib 作定语] *a 'board meeting* 董事会议. **8** [U] (cost of) daily meals (in rented accommodation) (寄宿时的)膳食(费): *He pays £40 a week (for) board and lodging.* 他每周支付膳宿费40英镑. **9** (idm 习语) **(be) above 'board** (esp of a business transaction) honest and open (尤指商业交易)光明正大的: *The deal was completely above board.* 这笔交易是完全光明正大的. ○ [attrib 作定语] *an a,bove-board 'deal* 光明正大的交易. **a,cross the 'board (a)** involving all members, groups or classes (of a company, an industry, a society, etc) 包括(某公司、行业、社团等的)所有成员、组织或阶层; 全面的: *This firm needs radical changes across the board.* 这家公司需要全面彻底大改组. ○ [attrib 作定语] *an a,cross-the-board 'wage increase* 全部人员的加薪. **(b)** (*US*) (of a bet) placed so that one wins if the horse, etc finishes the race in first, second or third place (指赌注)压于某匹马等, 无论跑第一、第二或第三, 下注者皆赢. **bed and board** ⇨ BED[1]. **free on board/rail** ⇨ FREE[1]. **,go by the 'board** (of plans, etc) be abandoned or rejected; (of principles, etc) be ignored (指计划等)被放弃; (指原则等)被忽视: *I'm afraid the new car will have to go by the board — we can't afford it.* 我看买新汽车的事要告吹——我们买不起. **on 'board** on or in a ship or an aircraft 在船上; 在飞行器上: *Have the passengers gone on board yet?* 旅客已经上船[上飞机]了吗? **sweep the board** ⇨ SWEEP[1]. **take sth on 'board** (*infml* 口) accept (a responsibility, etc); recognize (a problem, etc) 承担(责任等); 承认(问题等): *I'm too busy to take this new job on board at the moment.* 我太忙, 目前不能接受这项新工作.

▷ **board·ing** *n* [U] (structure made of) boards (BOARD[1] 1) 木板(建造之物).

□ **'boardroom** *n* room in which the meetings of the board of directors of a company are held (公司董事会的)会议室.

'boardwalk *n* (*US*) promenade, usu made of planks, along a beach (海滨的)人行道(通常为木板铺设的).

board[2] /bɔːd; bɔrd/ *v* **1** [Tn, Tn·p] **~ sth (up/over)** cover sth with boards (BOARD[1] 1) 用木板覆盖(某物): *a boarded floor* 木板地面 ○ *All the windows were boarded up.* 所有窗户都用木板遮住了. **2 (a)** [I, Ipr] **~ (at.../with sb)** take meals (and usu live) in sb's house 在某人家中寄膳(通常兼寄宿): *He boarded at my house/with me until he found a flat.* 他找到住房之前, 在我家寄膳. **(b)** [Tn] provide (sb) with meals and accommodation 给(某人)提供膳宿: *She usually boards students during the college term.* 她经常在学期中给学生提供膳宿. **3** [Tn] get on or into (a ship, a train, an aircraft, a bus, etc) 上(船、火车、飞机、公共汽车等): *Please board the plane immediately.* 请立刻上飞机. ○ *Flight BA193 for Paris is now boarding,* ie is ready for passengers to board. 乘飞往巴黎的BA193 班机的旅客现在可以登机. **4** (phr v) **board out** have meals away from the place where one lives 在外搭伙. **board sb out** give sb food and lodging away from his place of work, school, etc 供给某人在外膳宿(不在工作地、学校等): *Many students have to be boarded out in the town.* 许多学生得在城里膳宿.

▷ **boarder** *n* **1** person who boards at sb's house 在某人家中寄膳者. **2** pupil who lives at a boarding-school during the term 在学校寄宿的学生: *This school has 300 boarders and 150 day pupils.* 这所学校有寄宿生300人, 走读生150人. **3** person who boards a ship, esp when attacking it 登船的人(尤指攻击该船时).

□ **'boarding card** card allowing a person to board a ship or plane 登船证; 登机证.

'boarding-house *n* house providing meals and accommodation 供膳宿的宿舍.

'boarding-school *n* school where some or all of the pupils live during the term 寄宿学校: *Our son's at boarding-school — we only see him during the holidays.* 我们的儿子在寄宿学校, 所以我们只能在假期见到他. Cf 参看 DAY-SCHOOL (DAY).

boast /bəʊst; bost/ *v* **1** [I, Ipr, Tf] **~ (about/of sth)** talk (about one's own achievements, abilities, etc) with too much pride and satisfaction 自夸; 自吹自擂: *He's always boasting about his children's success at school.* 他总是夸耀他的孩子们学习成绩好. ○ *That's nothing to boast about.* 那没有什么值得自吹的. ○ *He boasted of being/boasted that he was the best player in the team.* 他自夸是队里的最佳队员. **2** [Tn] possess (sth to be proud of) 有(引以为荣的事物): *The town boasts a world-famous art gallery.* 这个镇子引以为荣的是有个闻名于世的美术馆.

▷ **boast** *n* **1 ~ (that...)** (*derog* 贬) boastful statement 自夸的话: *His boast that he could drink ten pints of beer impressed nobody.* 他自吹自擂说能喝十品脱啤酒, 但无人理睬他. **2** thing that one is proud of; cause for satisfaction 引以自豪的事物; 令人满意的原因: *It was his proud boast that he had never missed a day's work because of illness.* 他从未请过一天病假, 这是他引以自豪的事.

boaster *n* person who boasts 自夸者.

boast·ful /-fʊl; -,fəl/ *adj* **(a)** (of a person) often boasting (指人)好自夸的. **(b)** (of a statement, etc) full of self-praise (指言语等)充满自夸的. **boast·fully** /-fəlɪ; -fəlɪ/ *adv*.

boat /bəʊt; bot/ *n* **1** small vessel for travelling in on water, moved by oars, sails or a motor (使用桨、帆或发动机驱动的)小船: *a rowing-/sailing-boat* 用桨划的船[帆船] ○ *motor/fishing boats* 汽艇[渔船] ○ *We crossed the river in a boat/by boat.* 我们乘船渡河. ○ *Boats for hire — £5 an hour.* 游船出租——每小时5英镑. ○ *a ship's boats,* ie lifeboats carried on board a ship 轮船上的救生艇. **2** any ship (任何)船: *'How are you going to France?' 'I'm going by/taking the boat* (eg the ferry).' '你打算怎样去法国?' '我打算乘船去.' **3** dish shaped like a boat for serving sauce or gravy (盛调料或肉汁的)船形碟子. **4** (idm 习语) **be in the same boat** ⇨ SAME[1]. **burn one's boats/bridges** ⇨ BURN[2]. **miss the boat/bus** ⇨ MISS[3]. **push the boat out** ⇨ PUSH[2]. **rock the boat** ⇨ ROCK[2].

▷ **boat** *v* [I] (usu 通常作 **go boating**) travel or go in a boat for pleasure 划船游玩: *We go boating on the lake every weekend.* 我们每个周末都到湖上划船.

□ **'boat-hook** *n* long pole with a hook and a spike at one end, used for pulling or pushing boats (一端有钩的)篙.

'boat-house *n* shed beside a river or lake for keeping boats in 船库(停船的棚屋).

'boatman /-mən; -mən/ *n* (*pl* **-men**) man who hires out small boats; man who transports people in small boats for payment 出租小船的人; 用船摆渡取酬的人.

'boat people refugees leaving a country in boats 船民(乘船离国的难民).

'boat race race between rowing-boats, esp **(the Boat Race)** the annual race between the rowing crews of Oxford and Cambridge Universities 划船比赛(尤指牛津与剑桥大学之间一年一度的比赛).

'boat-train *n* train that takes people to or from a passenger ship (与客轮联运的)火车.

boater /ˈbəʊtə(r); ˈbotɚ/ *n* hard straw hat with a flat top and straight brim (originally worn for boating) 硬草帽(原为划船时戴的).

boat·swain (also **bo'sn**, **bos'n**, **bo'sun**) /ˈbəʊsn; ˈbosn̩/ *n* senior seaman on a ship who supervises the crew and is responsible for the ship's equipment 水手长(管理其他水手并负责船上设备者).

bob[1] /bɒb; bɑb/ *v* (**-bb-**) **1** [I, Ipr, Ip] **~ (up and down)** move quickly up and down (esp on water) 上下疾动(尤指在水上): *toy boats bobbing (up and down) on the waves* 在水波上颠簸的玩具船. **2** (idm 习语) **bob a curtsy (to sb)** curtsy quickly (to sb) (向某人)行屈膝礼: *The ballerina bobbed a curtsy (to the audience) before leaving the stage.* 那个芭蕾舞女演员在下台之前(向观众)行屈膝礼. **3** (phr v) **bob up** come to the surface quickly; (re-)appear suddenly 迅速浮起；突然(再)出现：*She dived below the surface, then bobbed up like a cork again a few seconds later.* 她潜入水中，几秒钟后像软木塞一样又浮了上来. ○ (*fig* 比喻) *He keeps bobbing up in the most unlikely places.* 他总是在极不可能出现的地方突然出现.

▷ **bob** *n* **1** quick movement down and up; jerk 上下的疾动；急动：*a bob of the head* 点头. **2** curtsy 屈膝礼.

bob[2] /bɒb; bɑb/ *v* (**-bb-**) [Tn] cut (a woman's hair) short so that it hangs loosely above the shoulders 将(女子的头发)剪短至肩以上：*have/wear one's hair bobbed* 把头发剪短[留]至肩以上.

▷ **bob** *n* style of bobbed hair (女子)短发型(至肩以上)：*She wears her hair in a bob.* 她留着短发.

bob[3] /bɒb; bɑb/ *n* (*pl* unchanged 复数不变) (*infml* 口) former British coin, the shilling, replaced by the 5p coin 先令(旧时英国硬币，后由5便士硬币所代替).

bob[4] /bɒb; bɑb/ *n* (idm 习语) **bob's your 'uncle** (*infml* 口) (used to express the ease with which a task can be completed successfully 用以表示工作轻而易举)：*To switch the oven on, turn the knob, and bob's your uncle!* 把烤箱的电源接通，转动旋钮，完事大吉！

bob·bin /'bɒbɪn; 'bɑbɪn/ *n* small roller or spool for holding thread, yarn, wire, etc in a machine (机器上缠绕纱线、金属丝等的)小滚筒，小卷轴.

bobble /'bɒbl; 'bɑbl̩/ *n* small woolly ball used as a decoration (esp on a hat) (装饰用的)绒线球(尤指帽子上的).

bobby /'bɒbɪ; 'bɑbɪ/ *n* (*Brit infml* 口) policeman 警察.

bobby pin /'bɒbɪ pɪn; 'bɑbɪ pɪn/ (*US*) small metal hair-grip (金属的)小发夹.

bob-sleigh /'bɒbsleɪ; 'bɑb,sle/ (also **bob-sled** /-sled; -,slɛd/) *n* large racing sledge for two or more people, with brakes, a steering-wheel and two sets of runners 大雪橇(竞赛用，供两人或两人以上乘坐，上面有制动器、方向盘和两组滑橇)：*a two-/four-man bob-sleigh* 两人[四人]雪橇.

▷ **bob-sleigh** *v* [I] ride in a bob-sleigh 乘雪橇.

bob·tail /'bɒbteɪl; 'bɑb,tel/ *n* **1** (horse or dog with a) tail cut short 剪短的尾巴；(尾巴剪短的)马或狗. **2** (idm 习语) **ragtag and bobtail** ⇨ RAGTAG.

bod /bɒd; bɑd/ *n* (*Brit infml* 口) person (esp a man) 人(尤指男子)：*He's an odd bod.* 他是个怪人.

bode /bəʊd; bod/ *v* **1** [Dn·n no passive 不用于被动语态] (*fml or dated* 文或旧) be a sign of (sth coming) 预示：*This bodes us no good.* 这对我们不是吉兆. **2** (idm 习语) **bode 'well/'ill (for sb/sth)** be a good/bad sign (for sb/sth) (对某人[某事物])预示吉[凶]：*The bad trading figures do not bode well for the company's future.* 这些交易数额欠佳，预示公司前景不妙.

bod·ice /'bɒdɪs; 'bɑdɪs/ *n* **1** upper part of a woman's dress, down to the waist 连衣裙的上部(下至腰处). **2** woman's or child's close-fitting undergarment like a vest (妇女或儿童的)紧身胸衣.

-bodied /-'bɒdɪd; -bɑdɪd/ (forming compound *adjs* 用以构成复合形容词) having the specified type of body 有某种躯体的：*big-bodied* ○ *able-bodied* ○ *full-bodied*.

bod·ily /'bɒdɪlɪ; 'bɑdl̩ɪ/ *adj* [attrib 作定语] of the human body; physical 人体的；肉体的：*bodily needs*, eg food, warmth 身体的需要(如食物、温暖) ○ *bodily organs*, eg the heart, the liver 身体的器官(如心脏、肝脏) ○ *bodily harm*, ie physical injury 身体的伤害.

▷ **bod·ily** *adv* **1** as a whole or mass; completely 全部地；整体地；完全地：*The audience rose bodily to cheer the speaker.* 听众全体起立向演讲者欢呼. ○ *The monument was moved bodily to a new site.* 纪念碑整个迁到一个新场址. **2** by taking hold of the body; forcibly 抓住身体；强行地：*The prisoners were thrown bodily into the police van.* 囚犯被揪着推进警车.

bod·kin /'bɒdkɪn; 'bɑdkɪn/ *n* blunt thick needle with a large eye, used for pulling tape, etc through a hem (大眼无尖的)粗针(用以将带子等穿过衣边).

body /'bɒdɪ; 'bɑdɪ/ *n* **1** [C] whole physical structure of a human being or an animal (人或动物的)身体，躯体：*Children's bodies grow steadily.* 儿童的身体不断发育成长. **2** [C] dead body; corpse or carcass 死尸；尸体：*The police found a body at the bottom of the lake.* 警方在湖底发现了一具尸体. ○ *His body was brought back to England for burial.* 他的遗体已运回英国埋葬. **3** [C] main part of a human body, apart from the head and limbs; trunk; torso 躯干：*He has a strong body, but rather thin legs.* 他躯干粗壮，但腿却很瘦. ○ *She was badly burned on the face and body.* 她面部和身上严重烧伤. **4** [sing] **the ~ of sth** main part of sth, esp a vehicle or building 主体(尤指车辆或建筑物)：*the body of a plane, ship, car, etc* 机身、船身、车身等 ○ *the body of a theatre, concert hall, etc*, ie the central part where the seats are 戏院、音乐厅等的主体部分(中央有座位的部分) ○ *The main body of the book deals with the author's political career.* 书中主要部分写的是作者的政治生涯. **5** [CGp] group of people working or acting as a unit 集体；团体；群体：*a body of troops, supporters, people, etc* 一支部队、一群支持者、一批人等 ○ *a legislative, an elected body* 立法团体、当选的团体 ○ *A government body is investigating the problem.* 政府部门正在调查此问题. ○ *The Governing Body of the school is/are concerned about discipline.* 学校当局很关心纪律问题. **6** [C] **~ of sth** large amount of sth; mass or collection of sth (某事物的)大量、片、块、堆等：*a body of evidence, information, etc* 大量证据、信息等 ○ *large bodies of water*, eg lakes or seas 大片水域(如湖泊或海洋) ○ *There is a large body of support for nuclear disarmament.* 拥护裁减核军备的人很多. **7** [C] distinct piece of matter; object 物体：*heavenly bodies*, ie stars, planets, etc 天体 ○ *I've got a foreign body* (eg an insect or a speck of dirt) *in my eye.* 我眼中有异物(如小虫或灰尘). **8** [U] full strong flavour, esp of wine 丰满；浓郁；(尤指酒)酿郁：*a wine with plenty of body* 酿酒. **9** [C] (*dated Brit infml* 旧，口) person 人：*a cheerful old body* 快乐的老人. **10** (idm 习语) **body and 'soul** with all one's energies; completely 全心全意地；完完全全地：*love sb body and soul* 真心实意爱某人 ○ *He fought body and soul for his country.* 他全心全意地为祖国而战斗. **in a 'body** (of a group) all together 全体：*The protesters marched in a body to the town hall.* 全体抗议者向市政厅行进. **keep body and 'soul together** stay alive (though with some difficulty); survive 餬口；勉强维持生活：*He scarcely has enough money to keep body and soul together.* 他几乎无钱维持生活. **over my dead body** ⇨ DEAD.

Often parts of the body are closely linked to particular verbs. The combination of the verb and part of the body expresses emotions or attitudes. 身体部位词语多与某些动词搭配使用. 这种搭配可表达一定的情感或态度.

ACTION 动作	PART OF BODY 身体部位	POSSIBLE EMOTION OR ATTITUDE EXPRESSED 可表达的情感或态度
clench	fist	anger, aggression
crease/furrow/knit	brow	concentration, puzzlement
drum	fingers	impatience
lick	lips	anticipation
purse	lips	disapproval, dislike
raise	eyebrows	inquiry, surprise
shrug	shoulders	doubt, indifference
stick out	tongue	disrespect
wrinkle	nose	dislike, distaste

□ **'body-blow** *n* **1** (in boxing) blow to the body(3) (拳击中)(向对手身体的)打击. **2** (*fig* 比喻) severe disappointment or set-back (极大的)失望，挫折：*The death of its leader was a body-blow to the party.* 领袖的逝世对党是巨大的损失.

'body-building *n* [U] strengthening the muscles of the body through exercise (通过锻炼)增强体质.

'body clock biological mechanism that automatically controls various recurring functions of the human body, eg the need to sleep 生物钟(自动控制人体各种周期性节律的生物机制，如睡眠的需要)：*I only arrived in London yesterday and my body clock is still on New York time.* 我昨天刚到伦敦，而我的生物钟仍然是纽约时间.

'body language expressing how one feels by the way one sits, stands, moves, etc rather than by words 身势语，

身体语言(通过坐、站、移动等动作表达意思).
ˈ**bodyline** *n* [U] (in cricket) type of bowling in which the ball is aimed at the batsman's body rather than at the wicket (板球)瞄准击球员身体(而不瞄准三柱门)的投球.
ˈ**body odour** (*abbr* 缩写 **BO**) smell of the human body, esp when unwashed, often regarded as unpleasant 人体的气味(尤指未沐浴者, 常指难闻的); 体臭; 狐臭.
the ˌ**body** ˈ**politic** the State as an organized group of citizens 国家(政治上组织起来的全体人民).
ˈ**body-snatcher** *n* (formerly) person stealing corpses from graves and selling them for dissection (旧时)掘墓盗尸者(将尸体出卖供解剖用).
ˈ**body stocking** woman's undergarment covering the body(3) and legs (女用)全身内衣.

B

body·guard /ˈbɒdɪɡɑ:d; ˋbɑdɪˌɡɑrd/ *n* [C, CGp] man or group of men whose job is to protect an important person (重要人物的)侍卫, 卫队, 保镖: *The President's bodyguard is/are armed.* 总统的侍卫佩带着武器.

body·work /ˈbɒdɪwɜ:k; ˋbɑdɪˌwɝk/ *n* [U] main outside structure of a motor vehicle (机动车辆的)车身: *paint, repair, damage the bodywork of a car* 给汽车车身喷漆、修理汽车车身、损坏汽车车身.

Boer /bɔ:(r); bɔr/ *n* (formerly) African of Dutch descent; Afrikaner (旧时)荷兰裔非洲人; 布尔人: [attrib 作定语] *The Boer War*, ie the war between the Boers and the British (1899-1902). 布尔战争(布尔人与英国人之间的战争, 1899-1902).

bof·fin /ˈbɒfɪn; ˋbɑfɪn/ *n* (*Brit infml* 口) scientist, esp one doing research 科学家(尤指从事研究工作的人).

bog /bɒɡ; bɑɡ/ *n* **1** [C, U] (area of) wet spongy ground formed of decaying vegetation (地面为腐朽植物的)沼泽(地区): *a peat bog* 泥炭沼 ○ *Keep to the path — parts of the moor are bog.* 沿着这条小路走——荒野上多处是沼泽地. **2** [C] (*Brit sl* 俚) lavatory 厕所.
▷ **bog** *v* (**-gg-**) (phr v) **bog (sth) down** (usu passive 通常用于被动语态) (**a**) (cause sth to) sink into mud or wet ground (使某物)陷入泥沼: *The tank (got) bogged down in the mud.* 坦克陷入泥沼之中. (**b**) (*fig* 比喻) (cause sth to) become stuck and unable to make progress (使某物)陷入困境不能前进: *Our discussions got bogged down in irrelevant detail.* 我们的讨论纠缠在无关紧要的细节上.
boggy /ˈbɒɡɪ; ˋbɑɡɪ/ *adj* (of land) soft and wet (指土地)软而湿的: *boggy ground, moorland, etc* 软而湿的地面、高沼地等.

bo·gey[1] = BOGY.

bo·gey[2] /ˈbəʊɡɪ; ˋboɡɪ/ *n* **1** (*esp Brit*) (in golf) standard score that a good player should make for a hole or course (高尔夫球)(高手于一洞或一场应取的)标准杆数. Cf 参看 PAR[1] 3. **2** (in golf) score of one over the standard for a hole (高尔夫球)超一击(超过标准杆数一杆击入一洞).

boggle /ˈbɒɡl; ˋbɑɡl/ *v* **1** [I, Ipr] **~ (at sth)** (*infml* 口) hesitate (at sth) in alarm or amazement (对某事物)(因惊慌或惊奇)犹豫不决: *He boggled at the thought of swimming in winter.* 他想到要在冬天游泳就有些犹豫. **2** (idm 习语) **the mind/imagination** ˈ**boggles (at sth)** (*infml* 口) one can hardly accept or imagine (an idea, a suggestion, etc) (对某一想法、建议等)难以接受或难以想像: *My neighbour wears his dressing-gown to work. The mind boggles!* 我的邻居穿着晨衣去上班. 真不可思议! **boggle sb's/the** ˈ**mind** (*US infml* 口) amaze or shock sb 使某人惊奇或吃惊: *It boggles my mind!* 这使我大吃一惊! Cf 参看 MIND-BOGGLING (MIND[1]).

bo·gie /ˈbəʊɡɪ; ˋboɡɪ/ *n* undercarriage with wheels fitted below the end of a railway vehicle and pivoted for going round curves (铁路车辆的)转向架.

bo·gus /ˈbəʊɡəs; ˋboɡəs/ *adj* not genuine; false 伪造的; 假的: *a bogus passport, doctor, claim* 伪造的护照、冒充的医生、冒领.

bogy (also **bo·gey**) /ˈbəʊɡɪ; ˋboɡɪ/ *n* **1** (**a**) (also ˈ**bo·gy·man** /-mæn; -mæn/) imaginary evil spirit (used to frighten children) 鬼怪(用以吓唬儿童的). (**b**) thing that causes fear, often without reason; bugbear 使人害怕的事物(常无理由); 吓人的东西: *Inflation is the bogy of many governments.* 通货膨胀是许多政府害怕的事情. **2** (*children's sl* 童俚) small lump of mucus in the nose 鼻涕疙瘩.

bo·he·mian /bəʊˈhi:mɪən; boˋhimɪən/ *n, adj* (person, esp an artist) having or displaying a very informal and unconventional way of life 生活方式不正规和不合习俗的(人, 尤指艺术家).

boil[1] /bɔɪl; bɔɪl/ *n* (usu painful) infected swelling under the skin, producing pus (常为疼痛的)皮下脓肿.

boil[2] /bɔɪl; bɔɪl/ *v* **1** (**a**) [I] (of a liquid) bubble up and change to vapour by being heated (指液体)沸腾; (水)开: *When water boils it turns into steam.* 水沸腾而变成蒸汽. ○ *The kettle* (ie The water in the kettle) *is boiling.* 壶(里的水)开了. ○ *Have the potatoes* (ie Has the water in which the potatoes are being cooked) *boiled yet?* 煮马铃薯的水开了吗? ⇨Usage at WATER[1] 用法见 WATER[1]. (**b**) [I, Ip] **~ (away)** continue to boil 不断沸腾: *There's a saucepan boiling away on the stove.* 炉子上锅里的水一直开着. **2** [Tn] cause (a liquid) to boil 使(液体)沸腾: *boil some water for the rice* 把水煮开做饭. **3** [I, Tn, Dn·n, Dn·pr] **~ sth (for sb)** cook or wash sth in boiling water 用开水煮或洗某物: *boiled cabbage, carrots, potatoes, etc* 煮熟的洋白菜、胡萝卜、马铃薯等 ○ *Please boil me an egg/boil an egg for me.* 请给我煮一个鸡蛋. ⇨ Usage at COOK 用法见 COOK. **4** [I, Ip] be very angry or agitated 愤怒; 激动: *He was boiling (over) with rage.* 他怒火中烧. **5** (idm 习语) **boil** ˈ**dry** (of a liquid) boil until there is none left (指液体)煮干: *Don't let the pan boil dry.* 别把锅里的水煮干了. **keep the pot boiling** ⇨ POT[1]. **make sb's blood boil** ⇨ BLOOD[1]. **6** (phr v) **boil (sth) away** (cause sth to) boil until nothing remains; evaporate (sth) (使某物)烧干; 使(某物)蒸发: *The water in the kettle had all boiled away.* 壶里的水完全烧干了. **boil (sth) down** reduce or be reduced by boiling 煮浓; 熬浓. **boil sth down (to sth)** (*infml* 口) summarize sth; condense sth 归纳(某事物); 浓缩某事物: *Could you boil that article down to 400 words?* 你能把这篇文章缩写成400字吗? **boil down to sth** (be able to) be summarized as sth (能)归结为某事物: *The issue really boils down to a clash between left and right.* 这场争论确实可归结为左派与右派之间的冲突. **boil over** (**a**) (of liquid in a pan, etc) boil and flow over the side of a pan, etc (指锅等容器中的液体)沸腾而溢出: *The milk is boiling over.* 牛奶沸腾得溢出来了. (**b**) (*infml* 口) be very angry 非常恼火. (**c**) (of a situation, quarrel, etc) reach a point of crisis; explode (指形势、争论等)达到危急关头; 爆发: *The crisis is in danger of boiling over into civil war.* 这一危机有触发内战之势.
▷ **boil** *n* **1** act of boiling 沸腾. **2** (idm 习语) **be on the** ˈ**boil** be boiling 沸腾着. **bring sth to the** ˈ**boil** heat sth until it boils 将某物煮至沸腾: *Bring the mixture to the boil, then let it simmer for ten minutes.* 把混合物煮至沸腾, 然后再用文火煮十分钟. **come to the** ˈ**boil** begin to boil 开始沸腾. **off the** ˈ**boil** having just stopped boiling 停止沸腾: (*fig infml* 比喻, 口) *He began by playing brilliantly but he's rather gone off the boil* (ie he has begun playing less well) *in the last few minutes.* 一开始他表现得非常出色, 但最后几分钟就不怎么好了.
boil·ing *adj* = BOILING HOT: *You must be boiling in that thick sweater.* 你穿着那件厚毛衣一定很热吧.
□ **boiled** ˈ**sweet** sweet made of boiled sugar 硬糖.
boiling ˈ**hot** (*infml* 口) very hot 炎热的; 酷热的: *a boiling hot day* 炎热的一天.
ˈ**boiling-point** *n* **1** temperature at which a liquid begins to boil 沸点. ⇨App 5 见附录5. **2** (*infml* 口) condition or state of great excitement 极度兴奋: *The match has reached boiling-point.* 比赛已进入高潮.

boiler /ˈbɔɪlə(r); ˋbɔɪlɚ/ *n* **1** metal container in which water is heated, eg to produce steam in an engine 锅炉. **2** tank in which hot water is stored, esp for central heating and other household needs 热水器(尤指为集中供暖设备及家庭其他用途供热水的). **3** large metal tub for boiling laundry (煮衣服用的)大金属桶. Cf 参看 COPPER[1] 3.
□ ˈ**boiler suit** one-piece garment worn for rough work (干粗活穿的)连衫裤. Cf 参看 OVERALLS.

bois·ter·ous /ˈbɔɪstərəs; ˋbɔɪstərəs/ *adj* **1** (of people or behaviour) noisy, lively and cheerful (指人或行为)喧闹的; 活跃的; 热闹的: *a boisterous party* 热闹的聚会 ○ *The children are very boisterous today.* 今天孩子们非常活泼. **2** (of the wind or sea) stormy; rough (指风)猛烈

的，急遽的；（指海）波涛汹涌的. ▷ **bois·ter·ously** *adv*. **bois·ter·ous·ness** *n* [U].

bold /bəʊld; bold/ *adj* (**-er, -est**) **1** confident and brave; daring; enterprising 自信和勇敢的；大胆的；有进取心的：*a bold warrior* 无畏的战士 ○ *bold plans, tactics, etc* 大胆的计划、战术等 ○ *a bold scheme to rebuild the city centre* 重建城市中心的大胆规划. **2** (*dated* 旧) without feelings of shame; immodest 无耻的；无礼的：*She waited for him to invite her to dance, not wishing to seem bold.* 她等他邀请她跳舞，而不愿显得失慎. **3** clearly visible; distinct; striking; vivid 显而易见的；轮廓清楚的；突出的；生动的：*the bold outline of a mountain against the sky* 天空衬托出山的清楚轮廓 ○ *bold, legible handwriting* 醒目而清楚的字体 ○ *She paints with bold strokes of the brush.* 她用雄健有力的笔触绘画. **4** printed in thick type 用粗体印刷的：*The headwords in this dictionary are in bold type.* 本词典的词条用的是粗体字. **5** (idm 习语) **be/make so bold (as to do sth)** (*fml* 文) (esp in a social situation) dare (to do sth); presume or venture (to do sth) （尤指于社交场合）冒昧地（做某事），擅自（做某事）：*One student made so bold as to argue with the professor.* 有个学生真冒失，竟然和教授争论起来. **(as) bold as ˈbrass** very cheeky; impudent 厚颜无耻的：*He walked in, bold as brass, and asked me to lend him £50!* 他走进来，厚颜无耻地要我借给他50英镑！ **put on, show, etc a bold front** try to appear brave and cheerful in order to hide one's true feelings 竭力表现出勇敢和快乐以掩盖自己的真实感情. ▷ **boldly** *adv*. **bold·ness** *n* [U].

bole /bəʊl; bol/ *n* trunk of a tree 树干.

bo·lero *n* (*pl* **~s**) **1** /bəˈleərəʊ; boˈlɛro/ (music for a) type of Spanish dance 波列罗舞（一种西班牙舞）（曲）. **2** /ˈbɒlərəʊ; boˈlɛro/ woman's short jacket with no front fastening （前襟敞开的）女短外衣.

boll /bəʊl; bol/ *n* seed-case of the cotton plant or flax （棉或亚麻的）圆荚，铃.
□ ˌ**boll-ˈweevil** *n* destructive insect whose larvae eat cotton bolls 棉铃象甲（侵害棉铃的小昆虫）.

bol·lard /ˈbɒlɑːd; ˈbɑlɚd/ *n* **1** short thick post on a quay or ship's deck, to which a ship's mooring ropes are tied （码头或船甲板上的）系缆柱. **2** short post on a kerb or traffic island （路边镶边石或交通安全岛上的）短柱.

bol·locks = BALLOCKS.

bo·lo·ney (also **ba·lo·ney**) /bəˈləʊnɪ; bəˈlonɪ/ *n* [U] (*infml* 口) nonsense; rubbish 胡说八道；胡扯：*Don't talk boloney!* 不要胡说八道！

Bol·shevik /ˈbɒlʃəvɪk; *US also* ˈbəʊl-; ˈbɑlʃəˌvɪk, ˈbol-/ *n* **1** member of the majority socialist group supporting the Russian revolution in 1917 布尔什维克（拥护1917年俄国革命的社会主义者多数派的成员）. **2** (*infml derog* 口，贬) any radical socialist 激进的社会主义者. ▷ **Bol·shev·ism** /ˈbɒlʃəvɪzəm; ˈbɑlʃəˌvɪzəm/ *n* [U]. **Bol·shev·ist** /ˈbɒlʃəvɪst; ˈbɑlʃəvɪst/ *n*.

bol·shie (also **bol·shy**) /ˈbɒlʃɪ; ˈbɑlʃɪ/ *adj* (**-ier, -iest**) (*Brit infml derog* 口，贬) deliberately unco-operative; awkward; stubborn 蓄意不合作的；不灵活的；固执的：*be in a bolshie mood* 有抵触情绪 ○ *be bolshie about sth* 对某事固执己见.

bol·ster /ˈbəʊlstə(r); ˈbolstɚ/ *n* long pillow, usu shaped like a roll, across the head of a bed （床头上的）长垫枕.
▷ **bol·ster** *v* [Tn, Tn·p] **~ sb/sth (up)** give support to sb/sth; strengthen or reinforce sth 支持某人［某事物］；加强某事物：*bolster sb's morale/courage* 提高某人的士气［增加某人的勇气］ ○ *It bolstered my belief that ... ...* 加强了我的信念. ○ *The government borrowed money to bolster up the economy.* 政府借贷以促进经济发展.

bolt 闩或螺栓

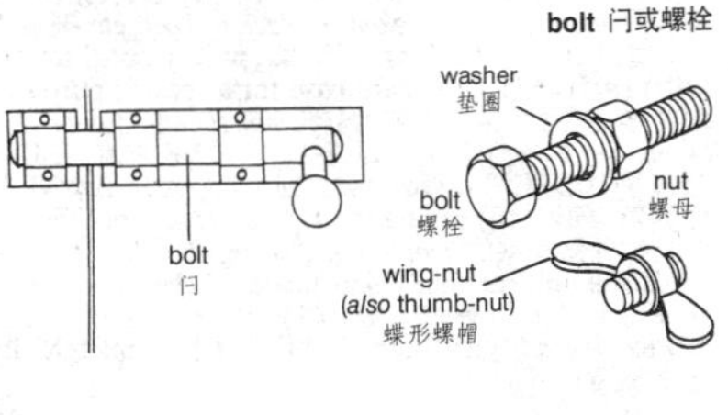

bolt[1] /bəʊlt; bolt/ *n* **1** metal bar that slides into a socket to lock a door, window, etc （门、窗等的）闩. **2** metal pin with a head at one end, and a thread (as on a screw), used with a nut for fastening things together 螺栓. **3** short heavy arrow shot from a crossbow （用弩弓发射的）弩箭. **4** flash of lightning 闪电；霹雳. **5** quantity of cloth, etc wound in a roll （布匹等的量）一匹，一卷. **6** (idm 习语) **a ˌbolt from the ˈblue** unexpected (and usu unwelcome) event; complete surprise 意外的（通常为不受欢迎的）事件；晴天霹雳：*The news of his death was (like) a bolt from the blue.* 他逝世的消息犹如晴天霹雳. **the nuts and bolts** ⇨ NUT. **shoot one's bolt** ⇨ SHOOT[1].
▷ **bolt** *v* **1** (**a**) [I, Tn] fasten (sth) with a bolt[1](1) 将（某物）闩上：*The gate bolts on the inside.* 这大门是从里面闩上的. ○ *Remember to bolt all the doors and windows.* 别忘将所有门窗闩住. (**b**) [Tn, Tn·pr, Tn·p]. **~ A to B; ~ A and B (together)** fasten objects (together) with bolts (BOLT[1] 2) 用螺栓将物体固定住：*The vice is bolted to the work-bench.* 老虎钳是用螺栓拧在工作台上的. ○ *The various parts of the car are bolted together.* 这辆汽车的各种配件是用螺栓装在一起的. **2** (phr v) **bolt sb in/out** prevent sb from leaving/entering a room, house, etc by bolting the doors, etc 将门等闩上不让某人出［入］.

bolt[2] /bəʊlt; bolt/ *v* **1** [I] (**a**) (esp of a horse) run away suddenly out of control （尤指马）惊（突然失控逃跑）：*The horse bolted in terror at the sound of the gun.* 枪声把马吓惊了. (**b**) (of a person) run away quickly （指人）迅速逃跑：*When the police arrived the burglars bolted.* 警察来到时，窃贼立即逃跑了. **2** [Tn, Tn·p] **~ sth (down)** swallow (food) quickly 匆匆吞咽（食物）：*Don't bolt your food — you'll get indigestion!* 别这么狼吞虎咽——你会消化不良的！ **3** [I] (of plants) grow quickly upwards and stop flowering when seeds are produced （指植物）迅速成长结子而不再开花：*My lettuces have bolted.* 我种的莴苣已经结子了. **4** (idm 习语) **lock, etc the stable door after the horse has bolted** ⇨ STABLE[2].
▷ **bolt** *n* **1** [sing] act of bolting (BOLT[2] 1b); sudden dash 逃跑；猛冲. **2** (idm 习语) **make a bolt/dash/run for it** try to escape/to reach sth quickly 试图迅速逃走［抵达某处］：*When the police arrived he made a bolt for it/for the door.* 警方来到时，他慌忙逃走［夺门而逃］了.
□ ˈ**bolt-hole** *n* place to which one can escape 可供逃奔的地方.

bolt[3] /bəʊlt; bolt/ *adv* (idm 习语) **bolt ˈupright** very straight; quite upright 挺直地；直立地：*sit bolt upright* 挺直地坐着.

bomb /bɒm; bɑm/ *n* **1** [C] container filled with explosive or incendiary material, made to explode when dropped or thrown, or by a timing device 炸弹：*Enemy aircraft dropped bombs on the city.* 敌机向这个城市投掷炸弹. ○ *Terrorists placed a 50-pound bomb in the railway station.* 恐怖分子在火车站安放了一枚50磅重的炸弹. **2** [C] (in compounds 用以构成复合词) explosive device placed in or attached to a specified object 装在某物体内或附着在某物体上的爆炸装置：*a letter-bomb* ○ *a parcel/car bomb*. **3 the bomb** [sing] atomic or hydrogen bomb 原子弹或氢弹：*Anti-nuclear organizations want to ban the bomb.* 反核武器组织要求禁止使用核武器. **4 a bomb** [sing] (*infml* 口) a lot of money 大量金钱：*That dress must have cost (her) a bomb!* 那连衣裙一定花了（她）很多钱！ ○ *Some company directors make* (ie earn) *an absolute bomb.* 有些公司董事赚很多钱. **5** (idm 习语) **go like a ˈbomb** (*infml* 口) (**a**) (of a vehicle) go very fast （指车辆）疾驶：*My new car goes like a bomb.* 我的新汽车跑得特别快. (**b**) be very successful 非常成功：*Her party went like a bomb.* 她那个聚会极为成功.
▷ **bomb** *v* **1** [Tn] attack (sb/sth) with bombs; drop bombs on 用炸弹攻击（某人［某物］）；投炸弹于：*London was heavily bombed during the last war.* 上次大战期间伦敦遭到猛烈轰炸. ○ *Terrorists bombed several police stations.* 恐怖分子炸毁了几所警察分局. **2** [I, Ip] **~ (out)** (*infml* 口 *esp US*) fail 惨败：*Her new play bombed after only three nights.* 她的新戏只演出三晚就演不下去. **3** (phr v) **bomb along, down, up, etc** (*Brit infml* 口) move very fast (usu in a vehicle) in the specified direction （通常指乘车）朝某方向疾驶：*bombing down the motorway at ninety miles an hour* 以每

小时九十英里的速度在高速公路上疾驶. **bomb sb out** (esp passive 尤用于被动语态) make sb homeless by destroying his house with bombs 用炸弹摧毁某人的房屋而使其无家可归: *Our parents were bombed out twice during the war.* 我们的父母在战争期间有两次被炸弹炸得无家可归.

B

□ ˈ**bomb-bay** *n* compartment in an aircraft for carrying bombs 飞机上的炸弹舱.

ˈ**bomb-disposal** *n* [U] removal and detonation of unexploded bombs 未爆炸弹处理(移走并引爆): [attrib 作定语] *a bomb-disposal squad/team/officer/unit* 炸弹拆除组[队/官员/部门].

ˈ**bomb-proof** *adj* giving protection against bombs 防炸弹的: *a bomb-proof shelter* 防空避难室.

ˈ**bomb-sight** *n* device in an aircraft for aiming bombs (飞机上的)轰炸瞄准器.

ˈ**bomb-site** *n* area in a town where all the buildings have been destroyed by bombs 炸毁的市区.

bom·bard /bɒmˈbɑːd; bɑmˈbɑrd/ *v* [Tn, Tn·pr] **~ sb/sth (with sth)** **1** (**a**) attack (a place) with bombs or shells (esp from big guns) 轰炸(某地); 炮轰(某地): *Enemy positions were bombarded before our infantry attacked.* 炮轰敌军阵地之后, 我步兵开始进攻. (**b**) (*fig* 比喻) attack sb with persistent questions, abuse, etc (以连珠炮式的问题、辱骂等)攻击某人: *Reporters bombarded the President with questions about his economic policy.* 新闻记者提出许多有关经济政策的问题围攻总统. **2** (*physics* 物) direct a stream of high-speed particles at (an atom, etc) (以一束高速粒子)撞击(原子等). ▷ **bom·bard·ment** *n* [C, U].

bom·bard·ier /ˌbɒmbəˈdɪə(r); ˌbɑmbɚˈdɪr/ *n* **1** (*Brit*) non-commissioned officer in an artillery regiment below a sergeant 炮兵下士. **2** (*US*) member of the crew of a bomber who aims and releases bombs (轰炸机的)投弹手.

bom·bast /ˈbɒmbæst; ˈbɑmbæst/ *n* [U] pompous and meaningless words 浮夸的言语; 高调: *His speech was full of bombast.* 他的讲演通篇是夸夸其谈.

▷ **bom·bastic** /bɒmˈbæstɪk; bɑmˈbæstɪk/ *adj* (of a person or his words) pompous and empty (指人或言词)浮夸的, 空洞的. **bom·bast·ic·ally** /-klɪ; -klɪ/ *adv*.

bomber /ˈbɒmə(r); ˈbɑmɚ/ *n* **1** aircraft that carries and drops bombs 轰炸机. **2** person (esp a terrorist) who throws or plants bombs 投掷或安放炸弹的人(尤指恐怖分子).

bomb·shell /ˈbɒmʃel; ˈbɑmˌʃɛl/ *n* (*infml* 口) shocking and usu unpleasant surprise (令人震惊的, 通常为令人不快的)意外事件: *The news of his death was a bombshell.* 他逝世的消息使人震惊.

bona fide /ˌbəʊnə ˈfaɪdɪ; ˈbonə ˈfaɪdɪ/ *adj* [esp attrib 尤作定语], *adv* genuine(ly); without fraud or deception; legal(ly) 真实(的); 真诚(的); 合法(的): *a bona fide agreement/contract/deal* 真诚的协议[合约/交易].

▷ **bona fides** /-dɪz; -diz/ *n* [U] (*law* 律) honest intention; sincerity 诚意; 真诚: *establish one's bona fides* 证明自己的诚意.

bon·anza /bəˈnænzə; boˈnænzə/ *n* **1** source of sudden great wealth or luck; increase in profits 暴富或幸运之源; 利润的增加: [attrib 作定语] *It's been a bonanza* (ie very profitable) *year for the tourist trade.* 对旅游业来说, 这是财源滚滚的一年. **2** (*US*) rich output from a gold mine, oil well, etc (金矿、油井等的)丰富产量.

bon-bon /ˈbɒnbɒn; ˈbɑnˌbɑn/ *n* sweet, esp one with a fancy shape 糖果(尤指形状别致的).

bond /bɒnd; bɑnd/ *n* **1** [C] (**a**) written agreement or promise that has legal force; covenant (具有法律效力的)书面协定或允诺; 契约; 合同; 票据: *We entered into a solemn bond.* 我们缔结了一项正式协定. (**b**) signed document containing such an agreement 已签署的上述文件. **2** [C] certificate issued by a government or a company acknowledging that money has been lent to it and will be paid back with interest (政府或公司发行的)有息债券: *National Savings bonds* 国家储蓄债券 ○ *Government bonds* 公债. **3** [C] thing that unites people or groups; link or tie 将人或团体联合起来的事物; 联系; 关系: *the bonds of friendship/affection* 友谊[感情]的纽带 ○ *The trade agreement helped to strengthen the bonds between the two countries.* 这项贸易协定有助于加强两国之间的联系. **4** [sing] state of being joined 连接; 接合; 结合: *This glue makes a good firm bond.* 这种胶水粘得很结实. **5 bonds** [pl] ropes or chains binding a prisoner 捆绑囚犯的绳索或锁链: (*fig* 比喻) *the bonds of oppression, tyranny, injustice, etc* 压迫、专制、不公正等桎梏. **6** (idm 习语) **in/out of bond** (*commerce* 商) (of imported goods) in/out of a bonded warehouse (指进口货物)在关栈中(尚未完税)[由关栈提出(已完税)]: *place goods in/take goods out of bond* 将(未完税)货物存入关栈[将(已完税)货物由关栈提出]. **sb's word is as good as his bond** ⇨ WORD.

▷ **bond** *v* **1** [Tn] put (goods) in a bonded warehouse 将(货物)存入关栈: *bonded whisky, cigarettes, etc* 扣存关栈以待完税的威士忌、香烟等. **2** [Tn, Tn·pr, Tn·p] **~ A and B (together); ~ A to B** join two things securely together; unite two things with a bond 将两个物体牢固结合起来; 用黏结剂将两个物体接合起来: *You need a strong adhesive to bond wood to metal.* 需要强力胶才能把木料粘在金属上.

□ ˌ**bonded** ˈ**warehouse** warehouse where goods are stored until Customs duties are paid (存放货物以待完税的)保税仓库; 关栈.

bond·age /ˈbɒndɪdʒ; ˈbɑndɪdʒ/ *n* [U] (*dated or fml* 旧或文) slavery; captivity 奴役; 束缚: *keep sb in bondage* 使某人被奴役.

bone /bəʊn; bon/ *n* **1** [C] any of the hard parts that form the skeleton of an animal's body 骨骼; 骨头: *This fish has a lot of bones in it.* 这种鱼有很多刺. ○ *I've broken a bone in my arm.* 我的臂部骨折了. ○ *Her bones were laid to rest*, ie Her body was buried. 她的尸骨已下葬. **2** [U] hard substance of which bones are made 骨质: *Buttons are sometimes made of bone.* 钮扣有时是用骨头做的. **3** [C] thin strip of metal or plastic used to stiffen a brassiere, shirt collar, etc (使乳罩、衬衣领等坚挺的)金属或塑料薄条. **4** (idm 习语) **a bag of bones** ⇨ BAG[1]. **the bare bones** ⇨ BARE[1]. **a bone of conˈtention** subject about which there is disagreement 有争执的问题: *The border has always been a bone of contention between these two countries.* 这两国之间的边界问题历来是争议的焦点. **chill sb to the bone/marrow** ⇨ CHILL. **close to/near the ˈbone** (*infml* 口) (**a**) (of a remark, question, etc) unkindly or tactlessly revealing the truth about sb/sth (指言语、问题等)不客气或不圆滑地揭露关于某人[某事物]的真相: *Some of his comments about her appearance were a bit close to the bone.* 他对她外貌的一些评论有点太露骨了. (**b**) (of a joke, story, etc) almost indecent; likely to offend some people (指玩笑、故事等)近乎猥亵的, 有可能冒犯某些人的: *Some scenes in the play are rather near the bone.* 这个剧里有些情节相当猥亵. **cut, pare, etc sth to the ˈbone** reduce sth considerably or drastically 大幅度地减少某事物: *Train services have been cut to the bone.* 列车车次已大幅度减少. ○ *Our budget has been pared to the bone.* 我们的预算已削减到最低限度. **dry as a bone** ⇨ DRY[1]. **feel in one's bones** ⇨ FEEL[1]. **have a ˈbone to pick with sb** have sth to argue or quarrel about with sb 就某事跟某人辩论或争吵: *I've got a bone to pick with you. Where's the money I lent you last week?* 我得跟你讲讲理, 上星期我借给你的钱到哪里去了? **make no bones about (doing) sth** be frank about sth; admit sth readily; do not hesitate to do sth 对某事物坦率; 易于接受某事物; 对做某事物不犹豫: *He made no bones about his extreme left-wing views.* 他毫不隐讳自己极左的观点. ○ *She made no bones about telling her husband she wanted a divorce.* 她坦率地告诉她丈夫, 她要离婚. **skin and bone** ⇨ SKIN. **work one's fingers to the bone** ⇨ FINGER.

▷ **bone** *v* **1** [Tn] take bones out of (sth) 剔去(某物)的骨头: *bone a fish, a chicken, a piece of beef, etc* 剔去鱼刺、鸡骨、一块牛肉的骨头等. **2** (phr v) **bone up on (sth)** (*infml* 口) study hard (usu for a specific purpose) 刻苦学习(通常指为某目的): *I must bone up on my French before we go to Paris.* 在我们去巴黎之前, 我必须刻苦学习法语. **-boned** (forming compound *adjs* 用以构成复合形容词) having the type of bones specified 具有某种骨骼类型的: *small-boned* ○ *large-boned*.

□ ˌ**bone** ˈ**china** thin china made of clay mixed with bone ash (以混有骨灰的陶土制成的)骨灰瓷.

ˌ**bone-**ˈ**dry** *adj* [usu pred 通常作表语] completely dry 完全干燥.

ˌ**bone ˈidle** (*derog* 贬) very lazy 极懒惰.
ˈ**bone-meal** *n* [U] crushed animal bones used as fertilizer 骨粉(用作肥料).
ˈ**bone-shaker** *n* (*infml joc* 口, 谑) rickety and uncomfortable old bicycle or car (摇晃而使人难受的)旧自行车或汽车.

bone·head /ˈbəʊnhed; ˈbonˌhɛd/ *n* (*infml derog* 口, 贬) stupid person 蠢人.

boner /ˈbəʊnə(r); ˈbonɚ/ *n* (*US infml* 口) stupid mistake; blunder (愚蠢的)错误; 大错.

bon·fire /ˈbɒnfaɪə(r); ˈbɑnˌfaɪr/ *n* large fire made outdoors for burning rubbish or as a celebration (为烧掉垃圾或为庆祝而在户外燃起的)大火堆, 篝火: *We made a bonfire of dead leaves in the garden.* 我们在花园里点燃火堆把枯叶烧掉.
□ ˈ**Bonfire Night** (in Britain) the night of 5 November when the failure of the Gunpowder Plot is celebrated with bonfires and fireworks (英国)篝火之夜(11月5日晚用篝火和烟火来纪念'火药阴谋'的失败).

bongo /ˈbɒŋgəʊ; ˈbɑŋgo/ *n* (*pl* **~s** or **~ es**) one of a pair of small drums played with the fingers (用手指敲打的一对)小鼓(之一).

bon·homie /ˈbɒnəmɪ; *US* ˌbɒnəˈmiː; ˌbɑnəˈmi/ *n* [U] (*French* 法) hearty cheerfulness of manner 和蔼; 亲切.

bonk·ers /ˈbɒŋkəz; ˈbɑŋkɚz/ *adj* [pred 作表语] (*Brit sl* 俚) completely mad; crazy 疯狂: *You're stark raving bonkers!* 你完全疯了!

bon mot /ˌbɒn ˈməʊ; ˌbɑn ˈmo/ *n* (*pl* **bons mots**) /ˌbɒn ˈməʊz; ˌbɑn ˈmoz/ (*French* 法) witty saying or remark 隽语; 珠玑妙语.

bon·net /ˈbɒnɪt; ˈbɑnɪt/ *n* **1** hat tied with strings under the chin, worn by babies and formerly by women (婴儿和旧时女子戴的)在颏下系带的帽子. **2** (in Scotland) man's round brimless cap (苏格兰)(男用)无檐圆帽. **3** (*US* **hood**) hinged cover over the engine of a motor vehicle (机动车辆的)发动机罩盖. ⇨illus at App 1 见附录1之插图, page xii. **4** (idm 习语) **have a bee in one's bonnet** ⇨ BEE[1].

bonny /ˈbɒnɪ; ˈbɑnɪ/ *adj* (**-ier, -iest**) (*approv esp Scot* 褒, 尤用于苏格兰) attractive or beautiful; healthy-looking 有吸引力的; 美丽的; 健美的: *a bonny lass/baby* 美丽的少女[婴儿]. ▷ **bon·nily** *adv*.

bo·nus /ˈbəʊnəs; ˈbonəs/ *n* (*pl* **~es**) **1** payment added to what is usual or expected, eg an extra dividend paid to shareholders in a company or to holders of an insurance policy 额外津贴; 奖金; 红利: *a productivity bonus*, ie money added to wages when workers produce more goods, etc 生产奖金 ○ *Company employees received a £25 Christmas bonus.* 公司雇员得到25英镑的圣诞节赠金. **2** anything pleasant in addition to what is expected 意外的好处: *The warm weather in winter has been a real bonus.* 冬天有这样暖和的天气真是喜出望外.

bony /ˈbəʊnɪ; ˈbonɪ/ *adj* (**-ier, -iest**) **1** of or like bone 骨的; 似骨的. **2** full of bones 多骨的: *This fish is very bony.* 这种鱼刺多. **3** thin and having prominent bones 瘦的; 皮包骨的: *bony fingers* 纤瘦的手指 ○ *a tall bony man* 高而瘦的男人. ⇨Usage at THIN 用法见 THIN.

boo /buː; bu/ *interj, n* **1** sound made to show disapproval or contempt 呸(表示不赞成或唾弃): *The Prime Minister's speech was greeted with boos and jeers.* 首相的演讲遭喝倒彩. **2** exclamation used to surprise or startle sb 嘘, 哟(使人感到突然或吃惊的喊声). **3** (idm 习语) **not say boo to a goose** ⇨ SAY.
▷ **boo** *v* **1** [I, Tn] show disapproval or contempt for (sb/sth) by shouting 'boo' 用'呸'的声音表示不赞成或唾弃(某人[某事物]): *You can hear the crowd booing.* 你可以听到人群中的一片呸呸声. **2** (phr v) **boo sb off (sth)** force sb to leave by booing 用'呸'声来迫使某人离开: *The actors were booed off the stage.* 演员被倒彩声轰下了台.

boob[1] /buːb; bub/ (also **boo·boo** /ˈbuːbuː; ˈbubu/) *n* (*infml* 口) stupid mistake (愚蠢的)错误.
▷ **boob** *v* [I] make a boob 犯(愚蠢的)错误: *Oh dear, I've boobed again.* 哎呀, 我又犯了愚蠢的错误.

boob[2] /buːb; bub/ *n* (⚠ *sl* 讳, 俚) (usu *pl* 通常作复数) woman's breast (女子的)乳房.

booby /ˈbuːbɪ; ˈbubɪ/ *n* (*dated derog* 旧, 贬) foolish person 笨人: *He's a great booby!* 他是个大笨蛋!
□ ˈ**booby prize** (also **wooden spoon**) prize given as a joke to the person who is last in a race or competition 末名奖(为开玩笑送给竞赛中最后一名的奖品).
ˈ**booby trap 1** hidden trap designed to surprise sb, eg sth balanced on top of a door so that it will fall on the first person opening it (为吓某人而设的)陷阱(如在门顶上放置某物, 有人开门时即落其身上). **2** hidden bomb designed to explode when an apparently harmless object is touched 饵雷; 诡雷: *The police did not go near the abandoned car, fearing it was a booby trap.* 警方没接近那辆弃置的汽车, 怕那里有饵雷. ○ [attrib 作定语] *a booby-trap bomb* 饵雷炸弹. **booby-trap** *v* (**-pp-**) [Tn] place a booby-trap in or on (sth) 将饵雷放在(某物)里面或上面: *The car had been booby-trapped by terrorists.* 恐怖分子在那辆汽车里安放了饵雷.

B

boodle /ˈbuːdl; ˈbudl̩/ *n* [U] (*sl* 俚 *esp US*) money, esp money gained by stealing or bribery 钱(尤指偷盗或受贿的钱).

boogie /ˈbuːgɪ; *US* ˈbʊgɪ; ˈbʊgɪ/ (also ˌ**boogie-ˈwoogie** /-ˈwuːgɪ; *US* -ˈwʊgɪ; -ˈwʊgɪ/) *n* [U] type of blues music, played on the piano, with a strong rhythmical beat 布吉乐(用钢琴演奏的节奏性强的一种布鲁斯音乐): *play boogie* 演奏布吉乐 ○ [attrib 作定语] *a boogie beat* 布吉乐的拍子.

book[1] /bʊk; bʊk/ *n* **1** [C] (**a**) number of printed or written sheets of paper bound together in a cover 书; 书籍: *a leather-bound book* 皮面装订的书. (**b**) written work or composition, eg a novel, a dictionary, an encyclopedia, etc 著作: *writing/reading a book about/on Shakespeare* 写[读]关于莎士比亚的书. **2** [C] number of blank or lined sheets of paper fastened together in a cover and used for writing in 簿; 本子: *Write the essay in your (exercise-)books, not on rough paper.* 把文章写在练习簿里, 不要写在草稿纸上. **3 books** [pl] written records of the finances of a business; accounts 帐簿: *do the books*, ie check the accounts 查帐 ○ *The company's books are audited every year.* 这家公司的帐目每年都核对. **4** [C] number of similar items fastened together in the shape of a book 装订成书本形的同类物品: *a book of stamps/tickets/matches* 一沓邮票[票/火柴]. **5** [C] any of the main divisions of a large written work (大型著作的)卷, 篇, 部: *the books of the Bible* 《圣经》中的记、书. **6** [sing] words of an opera or a musical; libretto (歌剧的)歌词, 脚本. **7** [C] record of bets made, eg on a horse race 赌注登记(如赌马等): *keep/make/open a book (on sth)*, ie take bets (on a match, race, etc) 接受赌注(在比赛、赛马等项目中). **8 the book** [sing] telephone directory 电话号码簿: *Are you in the book?* 电话簿里有你的电话号码吗? **9** (idm 习语) **be in sb's good/bad ˈbooks** (*infml* 口) have/not have sb's favour or approval 得到[得不到]某人的好感或赞许: *You'll be in the boss's bad books if you don't work harder.* 工作不努力, 老板对你就没有好感. **bring sb to ˈbook (for sth)** require sb to give an explanation (of his behaviour) 要求某人(对其行为)作出解释: *bring a criminal to book* 盘问犯人. **by the ˈbook** (*infml* 口) strictly according to the rules 严格按照规章办事: *He's always careful to do things by the book.* 他总是小心翼翼地按规章办事. **a closed book** ⇨ CLOSE[4]. **cook the books** ⇨ COOK. **every/any trick in the book** ⇨ TRICK. **(be) on the books of sth** (be) employed as a player by a football club 受雇于足球俱乐部作运动员: *He's on Everton's books.* 他受雇于埃弗顿足球俱乐部. **an open book** ⇨ OPEN[1]. **read sb like a book** ⇨ READ. **suit one's/sb's books** ⇨ SUIT[2]. **take a leaf out of sb's book** ⇨ LEAF. **throw the book at sb** (*infml* 口) remind sb forcefully of the correct procedure to be followed in some task (and perhaps punish him for not following it) 警告某人须按规定办事(否则可能受处分).
□ ˈ**bookbinder** [C], ˈ**bookbinding** [U] *ns* (person whose job is) putting covers on books 装订(工人).
ˈ**bookcase** *n* piece of furniture with shelves for books 书橱; 书柜.
ˈ**book club** club which sells books at a reduced price to members who agree to buy a minimum number 购书会(会员购书不少于一定数量可获折扣).
ˈ**book-end** *n* (usu *pl* 通常作复数) either of a pair of supports to keep books upright 书立; 书挡; 书靠.

B

ˈ**bookkeeper** [C], ˈ**bookkeeping** [U] *ns* (person whose job is) recording business transactions 簿记(员).
ˈ**bookmaker** (also *infml* 口语亦作 **bookie**) [C], ˈ**book-making** [U] *ns* (person whose job is) taking bets on horse races, etc 接受赛马等赌注(为业者).
ˈ**bookmark** (also ˈ**bookmarker**) *n* strip placed between the pages of a book to mark the reader's place 书签.
ˈ**bookmobile** /-məʊbi:l; -ˋmobil/ *n* (*esp US*) vehicle used as a travelling library 用作流动图书馆的车.
ˈ**book-plate** *n* piece of paper, usu with a printed design, pasted in a book to show who owns it 藏书票(贴在书中作藏书者标志, 通常印有图案).
ˈ**bookseller** *n* person whose job is selling books 书商.
ˈ**bookshop** (*US* also ˈ**bookstore**) *n* shop which sells mainly books 书店.
ˈ**bookstall** *n* (*US* ˈ**news-stand**) stall or stand at which books, newpapers and magazines are sold 书摊.
ˈ**book token** voucher that can be exchanged for books of a given value 书券: *a £10 book token* 一张10英镑的书券.
ˈ**bookworm** *n* **1** grub that eats holes in books 书虫; 蠹鱼. **2** (*fig* 比喻) person who is very fond of reading books 极其喜欢读书的人; 书迷: *She's a bit of a bookworm.* 她可算是个书迷.

book[2] /bʊk; bʊk/ *v* **1** (**a**) [I, Tn, Tn·p] **~ sth (up)** reserve (a place, accommodation, etc); buy (a ticket, etc) in advance 预订(位子, 膳宿等); 预购(票等): *Book early if you want to be sure of a seat.* 要想十拿九稳有个座位, 那就早订座. ○ *book a hotel room, a seat on a plane* 预订旅馆房间、飞机座位 ○ *I'd like to book three seats for tonight's concert.* 我想预订今晚音乐会的三个座位. ○ *The hotel/performance is fully booked (up)*, ie There are no more rooms/tickets available. 这家旅馆的房间[这次演出的票]全预订出去了. (**b**) [Tn·pr] **~ sb on sth** reserve a place, ticket, etc for sb on (a plane, etc) 为某人预订(飞机等的)座位、票等: *We're booked on the next flight.* 我们预订了下一班的机票. (**c**) [Tn] engage or hire (sb) in advance 预约或雇用(某人): *We've booked a conjuror for our Christmas party.* 我们为圣诞节的聚会预约了一位魔术师. **2** [Tn] (*infml* 口) enter the name of (sb) in a book or record, esp when bringing a charge 将(某人)的姓名记在本子上或记录内(尤指控告): *The police booked me for speeding.* 警方因我超速行车把我的姓名记了下来. ○ *He was booked by the referee for foul play.* 他因为动作犯规而被裁判记下姓名. **3** (phr v) **book in** register at a hotel, an airport, etc (在旅馆、机场等处)登记. **book sb in** make a reservation for sb (at a hotel, etc) 为某人预订(旅馆房间等): *We've booked you in at the Plaza for two nights.* 我们为你在普拉扎旅馆预订了两夜的房间.
▷ **book·able** *adj* that can be reserved 可预订的: *All seats are bookable in advance.* 所有的座位都可以预订.
book·ing *n* [C, U] (*esp Brit*) (instance of) reserving seats, etc in advance; reservation 预订; 预定: *a block booking* 集体预订 ○ *We can't accept any more bookings.* 我们不能再接受任何预订了. ○ *She's in charge of booking(s).* 她主管预订业务. ˈ**booking-clerk** *n* (*esp Brit*) person who sells tickets, eg at a railway station 售票员. ˈ**booking-office** *n* (*esp Brit*) office where tickets are sold 售票处.

bookie /ˈbʊkɪ; ˋbʊkɪ/ *n* (*infml* 口) = BOOKMAKER (BOOK[1]).

book·ish /ˈbʊkɪʃ; ˋbʊkɪʃ/ *adj* **1** fond of reading; studious 爱读书的; 好学的: *She was always a bookish child.* 她一直是个爱读书的孩子. **2** having knowledge or ideas gained from reading rather than practical experience 书生气的(只有书本知识而无实际经验). ▷ **book·ish·ness** *n* [U].

book·let /ˈbʊklɪt; ˋbʊklɪt/ *n* thin book, usu in paper covers 小册子.

boom[1] /bu:m; bum/ *v* **1** [I, Ip] make a deep hollow resonant sound 发出深沉、有回响的声音: *waves booming on the seashore* 撞击海岸发出隆隆声的海浪 ○ *We could hear the enemy guns booming (away) in the distance.* 我们能听到远处敌人的大炮轰隆声. ○ *The headmaster's voice boomed (out) across the playground.* 校长瓮声瓮气的声音传遍操场. **2** [I, Ip, Tn, Tn·p] **~ (sth) (out)** utter (sth) in a booming voice 用深沉的嗓音讲(话): *'Get out of my sight!' he boomed.* '走开!'他用低沉的声音说.
▷ **boom** *n* (usu *sing* 通常作单数) deep hollow sound 深沉的声音: *the boom of the guns, the surf* 大炮、波涛拍岸的隆隆声.

boom[2] /bu:m; bum/ *n* sudden increase (in population, trade, etc); period of prosperity (人口、贸易等的)突然增加; 繁荣昌盛时期: *The oil market is enjoying a boom.* 石油市场欣欣向荣. ○ [attrib 作定语] *a boom year (for trade, exports, etc)* (贸易、出口等)繁荣昌盛的一年.
▷ **boom** *v* [I] have a period of rapid economic growth 处于经济迅速发展时期: *Business is booming.* 商业正在迅速发展.
□ ˈ**boom town** town that grows or prospers during a boom (在繁荣时期)兴旺发达起来的城市.

boom[3] /bu:m; bum/ *n* **1** (on a sailing-boat) long pole used to keep the bottom of a sail stretched 帆的下桁; 帆杠. ⇨illus at YACHT 见 YACHT 之插图. **2** (also **derrick boom**) pole attached to a derrick crane, used for loading and unloading a cargo 吊杆. **3** (**a**) barrier (usu of heavy chains) placed across a river or harbour entrance as a defence against enemy ships 横江铁索(用以防御敌舰). (**b**) barrier (usu a mass of logs) placed across a river to prevent logs from floating away 水栅(通常为圆木, 用以防止木材漂走). **4** long movable arm for a microphone 话筒的可移动长臂: [attrib 作定语] *a boom microphone* 有可移动长臂的话筒.

boom·er·ang /ˈbu:məræŋ; ˋbuməˌræŋ/ *n* **1** curved flat wooden missile (used by Australian Aborigines) which can be thrown so that it returns to the thrower if it fails to hit anything 回力棒, 回飞镖(澳大利亚土著的木制飞镖, 呈扁平曲形, 掷出后, 如未击中物体, 能飞回原处). **2** (*fig* 比喻) action or remark that causes unexpected harm to the person responsible for it 自食其果的言行: [attrib 作定语] *a boomerang effect* 自作自受的后果.
▷ **boom·er·ang** *v* [I, Ipr] act as a boomerang 自食其果; 自作自受: *His attempt to discredit his opponent boomeranged (on him) when he was charged with libel.* 他企图败坏对手名声反而自食其果, 被控以诽谤罪.

boon[1] /bu:n; bun/ *n* **1** (*dated* 旧) request or favour (used esp with the *vs* shown) 请求, 恩惠(尤与下列动词连用): *ask a boon of sb* 请求某人赐惠 ○ *grant a boon* 施恩. **2** thing that one is thankful for; benefit; advantage 所感激的事; 好处; 利益: *Parks are a great boon to people in big cities.* 在大城市里, 公园是人们的好去处. ○ *A warm coat is a real boon in cold weather.* 寒衣在天冷时是至宝.

boon[2] /bu:n; bun/ *adj* (idm 习语) **a boon companion** cheerful friend with whom one enjoys spending time 好友: *Bill and Bob are boon companions.* 比尔和鲍勃是很合得来的朋友.

boor /bʊə(r), bɔ:(r); bʊr/ *n* (*derog* 贬) rough, rude or insensitive man 粗鲁、无礼或不灵敏的人: *Don't be such a boor!* 不要这样粗鲁!
▷ **boor·ish** /ˈbʊərɪʃ, ˈbɔ:rɪʃ; ˋbʊrɪʃ/ *adj* of or like a boor 粗鲁的; 粗野的; 笨拙的: *boorish youths, behaviour, remarks* 粗鲁的年轻人、举止、言语. **boor·ishly** *adv*. **boor·ish·ness** *n* [U].

boost /bu:st; bust/ *v* [Tn] increase the strength or value of (sth); help or encourage (sb/sth) 增强(某事物)的力量; 提高(某事物)的价值; 帮助; 鼓励; 促进(某人[某事物]): *boost an electric current* 增强电流 ○ *boost imports, share prices, the dollar, etc* 增加进口、提高股票价格、提高美元汇价 ○ *boost production* 促进生产 ○ *The unexpected win boosted the team's morale.* 意外的胜利鼓舞了全队的士气.
▷ **boost** *n* increase; help; encouragement 增加; 帮助; 鼓励: *a boost in sales, exports, etc* 销售、出口等的增长 ○ *give the economy, the pound, etc a boost* 使经济、英镑等有起色 ○ *give sb's confidence a boost* 增强某人的信心.
booster *n* **1** thing that boosts 令人鼓舞的事物: *a morale booster*, ie sth that makes one feel more confident 精神鼓舞. **2** device for increasing power or voltage 增强动力或电压的装置. **3** (also ˈ**booster rocket**) rocket used to give initial speed to a missile or spacecraft 助推火箭(给予导弹或航天器以初速度的). **4** dose or injection (of a medicine or drug) that increases the effect of an earlier one 辅助药剂, 增效药剂(用以加强前次药剂效力的).

boot[1] /bu:t; but/ *n* **1** outer covering for the foot and ankle, made of eg leather or rubber 靴子: *a pair of*

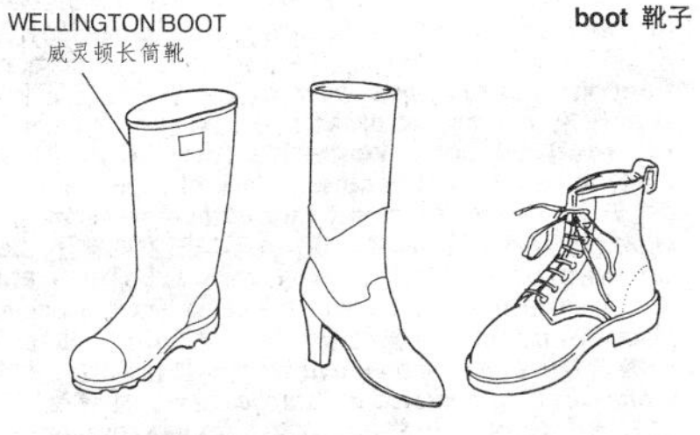

football boots 一双足球靴 ○ *tough boots for walking* 耐穿的轻便靴. ➪illus 见插图. Cf 参看 SANDAL, SHOE 1. **2** (usu *sing* 通常作单数) (*infml* 口) blow with the foot; kick 踢: *He gave the ball a tremendous boot.* 他重重地踢了这球一脚. **3** (*Brit*) (*US* **trunk**) compartment for luggage, usu at the back of a motor car 行李箱(通常在汽车后部): *Put the luggage in the boot.* 把行李放在汽车行李箱里. ➪illus at App 1 见附录1之插图, page xii. **4** (idm 习语) **be/get too big for one's boots** ➪ BIG. **the boot is on the other 'foot** the situation has been reversed 情况变得与原来相反. **die with one's boots on** ➪DIE[2]. **give sb/get the 'boot** (*infml* 口) dismiss sb/be dismissed from a job 解雇某人; 某人被解雇: *If you're late once more you're getting the boot.* 你再迟到一次, 就要把你解雇了. **have one's heart in one's boots** ➪ HEART. **lick sb's boots** ➪ LICK. **put the 'boot in** (*infml* 口 *esp Brit*) kick sb brutally; be ruthless 狠踢某人; 残忍无情. **tough as old boots** ➪ TOUGH.

▷ **boot** *v* **1** [Tn, Tn·pr, Tn·p] kick (sth/sb) 踢(某物[某人]): *boot a ball (about)* 踢球 ○ *boot sb in the face* 踢某人的脸. **2** [I, Ip, Tn, Tn·p] **~ (sth) (up)** (*computing* 计) load (an operating system, a program, etc) into a computer's memory, esp automatically; prepare (a computer) for operation in this way 引导; (尤指自动地)将(操作系统、程序等)写入, 装入, 寄存于计算机、存储器; 以上述方法启动(计算机). **3** (phr v) **boot sb out (of sth)** (*infml* 口) (**a**) throw sb out by force 把某人赶出去: *His father booted him out of the house.* 他父亲把他从家里赶了出去. (**b**) dismiss sb from a job 解雇某人.

□ **'bootlace** *n* string or leather strip for tying boots or shoes 靴带; 鞋带.

'bootstrap *n* (idm 习语) **pull oneself up by one's bootstraps** ➪ PULL[2].

boot[2] /bu:t; but/ *n* (idm 习语) **to boot** (*arch or joc* 古或谑) in addition; as well 除此以外; 再者: *She's an attractive woman, and wealthy to boot.* 她是个很有魅力的女人, 而且很富有.

bootee /bu:'ti:; bu'ti/ *n* **1** baby's woollen boot (婴儿的)毛线鞋. **2** woman's short lined boot (女用)短统靴(有衬里).

booth /bu:ð; *US* bu:θ; buθ/ *n* **1** small, usu temporary, stall where goods are sold or displayed at a market, a fair or an exhibition 售货摊; 摊位. **2** small enclosure or compartment for a specific purpose (有某种用途的)小房间: *a telephone booth*, ie for a public telephone 电话亭 ○ *a polling booth*, ie for voting at elections 投票间.

boot·leg /'bu:tleg; 'but,lɛg/ *v* (**-gg-**) [Tn] **1** smuggle (alcohol) 私运(酒). **2** make and sell (sth) illegally 非法制造及销售(某物). ➪Usage at SMUGGLE 用法见SMUGGLE.

▷ **boot·leg** *adj* [attrib 作定语] (esp of alcohol) smuggled or made and sold illegally (尤指酒)偷运或非法制造并销售的: *bootleg liquor* 私酒 ○ *a bootleg record*, eg one recorded illegally at a concert 非法录制的唱片(如在音乐会上非法录制的).

boot·leg·ger /-legə(r); -,lɛgɚ/ *n*.

booty /'bu:tɪ; 'butɪ/ *n* [U] things taken by thieves or captured from an enemy in war; loot; plunder 赃物; 战利品; 掠夺物.

booze /bu:z; buz/ *v* (*infml* 口) [I] drink alcoholic liquor, esp in large quantities 喝酒(尤指大量): *He likes to go out boozing with his mates.* 他喜欢和朋友到外面喝酒.

▷ **booze** *n* [U] (*infml* 口) **1** alcoholic drink 含酒精的饮料. **2** (idm 习语) **go/be on the booze** (*infml* 口) have a period of heavy drinking 喝很多酒: *Her husband's been on the booze again.* 她丈夫又不停地喝起酒来.

boozer *n* (*infml* 口) **1** person who boozes 酗酒者: *He's always been a bit of a boozer.* 他总是有点醉醺醺的. **2** (*Brit*) pub 酒馆.

boozy *adj* (**-ier, -iest**) (*infml* 口) drinking or involving much alcoholic liquor; drunken 好喝酒的; 酒量大的; 喝醉的: *a boozy old man* 好喝酒的老人 ○ *a boozy party* 狂欢狂饮酒会.

□ **'booze-up** *n* (*Brit infml* 口) time of heavy drinking 痛饮狂欢: *The party was a real booze-up.* 这次聚会大家都开怀畅饮了.

bop /bɒp; bɑp/ *n* **1** [U] = BEBOP. **2** [C, U] (*infml* 口) dance or dancing to pop music 博普舞(伴以流行乐曲的舞蹈): *Let's have a bop.* 让我们来跳博普舞吧.

▷ **bop** *v* (**-pp-**) [I] (*infml* 口) dance to pop music 跳博普舞: *go bopping* 去跳博普舞. **bop·per** *n* (*infml* 口) **1** person who dances to pop music 跳博普舞者. **2** = TEENY-BOPPER (TEENY).

bor·acic /bə'ræsɪk; bə'ræsɪk/ *adj* = BORIC.

bor·age /'bɒrɪdʒ; *US* 'bɔ:rɪdʒ; 'bɔrɪdʒ/ *n* [U] plant with blue flowers and hairy leaves which are used in salads and to flavour drinks 琉璃苣(蓝花毛叶植物, 叶可用于色拉和饮料调味).

borax /'bɔ:ræks; 'bɔrəks/ *n* [U] white powder, a compound of boron, used in making glass, enamels and detergents 硼砂; 月石.

Bor·deaux /bɔ:'dəʊ; bɔr'do/ *n* (*pl* unchanged 复数不变) [U, C] type of red or white wine from the Bordeaux district of SW France 波尔多葡萄酒. Cf 参看 CLARET.

bor·der /'bɔ:də(r); 'bɔrdɚ/ *n* **1** (**a**) [C] (land near the) line dividing two countries or areas; frontier 边界; 边境; 国界; 国境; 边境地区: *The terrorists escaped across/over the border.* 恐怖分子越过边境逃走了. ○ [attrib 作定语] *a border town, guard, patrol* 边境城市、边防卫兵、边防巡逻 ○ *border incidents*, ie small fights between soldiers of two neighbouring countries 边境事件(两邻国士兵之间的小冲突). (**b**) **the Border** [sing] (area near) one particular border, esp that between England and Scotland, or the United States and Mexico 边界(地带)(尤指英格兰与苏格兰之间或美国与墨西哥之间的). ➪Usage 见所附用法. **2** [C] band or strip, usu ornamental, around or along the edge of sth 边(通常作装饰用的): *the border of a picture/photograph* 图画[照片]的装饰边 ○ *a handkerchief, tablecloth, etc with an embroidered border* 有绣花花边的手帕、桌布等. **3** [C] strip of ground along the edge of a lawn or path for planting flowers or shrubs (草地或小路边缘的)狭长花坛: *a herbaceous border* 多年生草本植物花坛 ○ *a border of tulips* 郁金香花坛. ➪illus at App 1 见附录1之插图, page vii.

▷ **bor·der** *v* **1** [Tn] be a border to (sth); be on the border of (sth) 与(某物)接界, 接壤; 在(某物)的边上: *Our garden is bordered on one side by a stream.* 我们的花园有一边以小河为界. ○ *How many countries border Switzerland?* 有多少国家与瑞士接壤? **2** [Tn, Tn·pr] **~ sth (with sth)** put a border(2) on sth 在某物上镶边: *a handkerchief bordered with lace* 镶了花边的手帕. **3** [Ipr] **~ on sth** (**a**) be next to sth; adjoin sth 接近某物; 毗邻某物: *The new housing estate borders on the motorway.* 新住宅区紧接高速公路. (**b**) (*fig* 比喻) be almost the same as sth; verge on sth 几乎与某事物相同; 在某事物的边缘: *The boy's reply to his teacher was bordering on rudeness.* 那男学生回答教师的问话时态度近乎粗鲁. ○ *Our task borders on the impossible.* 我们的任务几乎是不可能完成的.

bor·derer *n* person who lives near a border, esp that between England and Scotland 边界地带的居民(尤指英格兰与苏格兰之间的).

□ **'borderland** /-lænd; -,lænd/ *n* **1** [C] district on either side of a border or boundary 边疆. **2** [sing] (*fig* 比喻) intermediate state or condition 中间状态或情况: *the borderland between sleeping and waking* 睡与醒之间的状态; 半睡半醒.

'borderline *n* line that marks a border 边界线; 国境线; 分界线: (*fig* 比喻) *The borderline between informal* *language and slang is hard to define.* 口语和俚语之间的分界线是很难确定的. — *adj* between two different groups or categories 介乎两种组别或类型之间的: *a borderline case* 难以确定的两可情况 ○ *a borderline candidate*, ie sb who may or may not pass an examination, be suitable for a job, etc 边缘人物(可能及格也可能不及格的考生, 可能胜任也可能不胜任工作等的候选人) ○ *a borderline pass/failure (in an examination)* (考试)在及格与不及格两可的情况下及格[不及格].

B

NOTE ON USAGE 用法: **Border** and **frontier** refer to the dividing line between two countries or states or the land near that line. ☆ **border** 和 **frontier** 均指两国之间的边界线或边界地区. **Border** is more often used when there is a natural division such as a river 有天然分界线(如河流)时多用 **border**: *the border/frontier between Spain and Portugal* 西班牙和葡萄牙之间的边界 ○ *the Italian border/frontier* 意大利的边界 ○ *The Rio Grande marks the border between Mexico and the USA.* 里奥格兰德河是墨西哥和美国之间的界河. ○ *border/frontier villages* 边界地区的村庄. **Frontier** is used of an inhabited region close to wild, unsettled territory, especially in North America in the early days of white settlement. ☆ **frontier** 用于指接近荒野的、无人烟的居民区, 尤指于北美白人定居的初期. **Frontier** is used figuratively, whereas **border** is not ☆ **frontier** 可作比喻用词, 而 **border** 不作比喻用词: *the frontiers of knowledge, science, etc* 知识、科学等有待开发的领域. A **boundary** is a precise line marking the outer limits of an area ☆ **boundary** 是指标明一区域外缘的明确界线: *The lane is the boundary of our land.* 那条小路就是我们这片地的界线. **Boundary** is used with administrative areas smaller than a state or country ☆ **boundary** 用于指行政区域, 范围比国家小: *the county, parish, etc boundary* 郡、牧区等的地界.

bore[1] /bɔ:(r); bɔr/ *v* **1** [I, Ipr, Tn, Tn·pr] make (a hole, well, tunnel, etc) with a revolving tool or by digging 挖, 掘, 钻, 开凿(洞、井、隧道等): *This drill can bore through rock.* 这台钻机能钻透岩石. ○ *bore a hole in wood* 在木头上钻个洞 ○ *bore a tunnel through a mountain* 开凿穿山隧道. **2** [Ipr, Ip, Tn·pr, Tn·p] move by burrowing 掘进: *The mole bored (its way) underground.* 鼹鼠在地下挖掘(路).
▷ **bore** *n* **1** (also ˈ**bore·hole**) deep hole made in the ground (esp to find water or oil) 打进地下的深洞(尤指为寻找水或石油的); 井眼. **2** (esp in compounds 尤用以构成复合词) (diameter of the) hollow part inside a gun barrel 枪膛, 炮膛(的口径): *a twelve-bore shotgun* 十二口径滑膛枪 ○ *small-bore guns* 小口径枪.

bore[2] /bɔ:(r); bɔr/ *vt* **1** [Tn] make (sb) feel tired and uninterested by being dull or tedious 使(某人)感到厌烦(因单调或乏味): *I've heard all his stories before; they bore me/he bores me.* 他的事我以前都听说过了, 那些事[他]真使我厌烦. ○ *I'm bored: let's go to the cinema.* 我闷了, 咱们去看电影吧. ○ *I hope you're not getting bored (by my conversation).* 但愿(我的话)没让你厌烦. **2** (idm 习语) **bore sb to** ˈ**death**/ˈ**tears** bore sb intensely 令某人极度厌烦: *Long novels bore me to tears.* 我觉得长篇小说特别使人厌烦. **a crashing bore** ⇨ CRASH[2].
▷ **bore** *n* person or thing that bores; nuisance 令人讨厌的人或事物; 麻烦: *Don't be such a bore!* 别这么讨厌! ○ *We've run out of petrol. What a bore!* 我们的汽油用完了. 真麻烦! **bore·dom** /-dəm; -dəm/ *n* [U] state of being bored 厌烦; 厌倦.
bor·ing /ˈbɔ:rɪŋ; ˈbɔrɪŋ/ *adj* uninteresting; dull; tedious 无趣的; 单调的; 乏味的: *a boring conversation, job, book, party* 枯燥无味的谈话、工作、书、聚会.

bore[3] /bɔ:(r); bɔr/ *n* high tidal wave that moves along a narrow estuary from the sea 涌潮.

bore[4] *pt* of BEAR[2].

boric /ˈbɔ:rɪk; ˈbɔrɪk/ *adj* of or containing boron 硼的; 含硼的.
□ ˌ**boric** ˈ**acid** (also **boracic acid** /bəˌræsɪk ˈæsɪd; bəˌræsɪk ˈæsɪd/) substance derived from borax and used as an antiseptic 硼酸.

born /bɔ:n; bɔrn/ *v* (used only in the passive without *by* 仅用于被动语态, 不与 by 连用) **1 be born** come into the world by birth 出生; 出世: *She was born in 1950.* 她生于1950年. ○ (*fig* 比喻) *The Trades Union movement was born* (ie founded) *in the early years of the century.* 工会运动创始于本世纪初. ○ *He was born* (ie destined from birth) *to be a great writer.* 他生下来就注定是个伟大的作家. ⇨Usage at BEAR[2] 用法见 BEAR[2]. **2** (idm 习语) **(not) be born** ˈ**yesterday** (not) be foolish or likely to be deceived because of lack of experience (并非)无知: *You can't fool me; I wasn't born yesterday, you know.* 你骗不了我; 你要知道, 我不是三岁的孩子. **be/be born/be made that way** ⇨ WAY[1]. ˌ**born and** ˈ**bred** born, brought up and educated (in a specified place or manner) (在某处或以某种方式)出生、成长及受教育: *He's London born and bred.* 他是在伦敦长大的. ○ *She was born and bred a Catholic.* 她一出生就受到天主教的熏陶. **born in the purple** born in a royal or very aristocratic family 生于王室或显贵的家庭. **born of sb/sth** owing one's existence to sb/sth; originating from sth 由于某人[某事物]而得以存在; 来源于某事物: *He was born of German parents.* 他的父母是德国人. ○ *Her socialist beliefs were born of a hatred of injustice.* 她的社会主义信念来自她对社会上不公平现象的痛恨. **born on the wrong side of the blanket** (*euph* 婉) illegitimate 私生. **born with a silver** ˈ**spoon in one's mouth** (*saying* 谚) having wealthy parents 生于富贵之家. **in all one's born** ˈ**days** (*infml* 口) in one's whole life 一生; 平生: *I've never heard such nonsense in all my born days!* 我一生中从未听到过这种胡言乱语! **there's one born every** ˈ**minute** (*saying* 谚) there are a lot of gullible people 总会有人上当的. **to the manner born** ⇨ MANNER.
▷ **born** *adj* [attrib 作定语] having a specific natural quality or ability 天生的: *be a born leader, loser, writer, athlete, etc* 天生的领袖、庸才、作家、运动员等.
-born (forming compound *ns* and *adjs* 用以构成复合名词和形容词) having a specific order, status or place of birth 按某排行、有某身分或于某地出生的: *first-born* ○ *nobly-born* ○ *French-born*.
□ ˌ**born-a**ˈ**gain** *adj* [usu attrib 通常作定语] having been converted, esp to evangelical Christianity 重生的, 皈依的(尤指皈依福音派基督教): *a* ˌ*born-again* ˈ*Christian* 重生的基督徒.

borne *pp* of BEAR[2]. ⇨Usage at BEAR[2] 用法见 BEAR[2].

boron /ˈbɔ:rɒn; ˈbɔran/ *n* [U] non-metallic chemical element used in metal working and in nuclear reactors 硼. ⇨App 10 见附录10.

bor·ough /ˈbʌrə; *US* -rəʊ; ˈbʌro/ *n* **1** (*Brit*) **(a)** town or district with a corporation and certain rights of self-government granted by royal charter (享有特权的)自治城镇, 自治市. **(b)** any of the administrative areas of Greater London (大伦敦的)行政区(之一). Cf 参看 PARISH 2. **2** (*US*) **(a)** any of the five administrative areas of New York City (纽约城的五个)行政区(之一). **(b)** (in some states) town with a legal corporation (某些州)有法定自治机关的城镇.

bor·row /ˈbɒrəʊ; ˈbɑro/ *v* [I, Ipr, Tn, Tn·pr] **~ (sth) (from sb/sth)** **1** receive or obtain (sth) temporarily (from sb/sth), with the promise or intention of returning it (向某人[从某处])借(某物): *borrow (money) from the bank, a friend* 向银行、朋友借(钱) ○ *I've forgotten my pen. Could I borrow yours?* 我忘了带笔. 可以借用一下你的吗? ○ *borrow a book from the library* 向图书馆借书. Cf 参看 LEND. **2 (a)** take and use (sth) as one's own; copy (sth) 将别人的(某物)当作自己的来使用; 抄袭(某事物): *borrow freely from other writers* 肆意抄袭其他作者的作品 ○ *borrow sb's ideas, methods* 采用某人的想法、方法 ○ *Handel borrowed music from other composers.* 韩德尔的作品借鉴了其他作曲家的乐曲. **(b)** (of a language) adopt (a word or phrase) from another language (指某语言)借用(另一种语言的词语): *The expression 'nouveau riche' is borrowed from French.* 'nouveau riche'(暴发户)这个词是从法语借来的. **3** (idm 习语) **(be living on) borrowed time** period of time for which one continues living after an illness or a crisis which might have caused one to die (大难未死)继续活着的一段时间.
▷ **bor·rower** *n* person who borrows 借东西的人. Cf 参看 LENDER (LEND).
bor·row·ing *n* thing borrowed, esp a word adopted by

one language from another 借用的事物;(尤指)借词: *The company will soon be able to repay its borrowings from the bank.* 这家公司不久就能偿还所借的银行贷款. ○ *English has many borrowings from French.* 英语中有许多词是从法语借来的.

Bor·stal /ˈbɔːstl; ˋbɔrstəl/ *n* [C, U] institution for reforming young offenders 青少年管教所: *be sent to Borstal* 被送到青少年管教所. Cf 参看 APPROVED SCHOOL (APPROVE), REFORMATORY.

bortsch (also **borsch**) /bɔːʃ; bɔrʃ/ *n* [U] Russian or Polish soup made with beetroot and cabbage and served hot or cold 罗宋汤.

bor·zoi /ˈbɔːzɔɪ; ˋbɔrzɔɪ/ *n* type of large dog with long hair and a silky coat; Russian wolfhound 俄国狼狗(有丝光长毛的一种大狗).

bosh /bɒʃ; bɑʃ/ *n* [U], *interj* (*infml* 口) nonsense 废话; 胡说: *You're talking bosh!* 你胡说八道!

bo'sn, bos'n = BOATSWAIN.

bosom /ˈbʊzəm; ˋbuzəm/ *n* **1** [C] person's chest, esp a woman's breasts (人的)胸部;(尤指女子的)乳房: *hold sb to one's bosom* 把某人搂在自己的怀里 ○ *She has a large bosom.* 她的乳房很大. **2** [C] part of a dress covering the bosom (衣服的)胸部. **3** [sing] **the ~ of sth** loving care and protection of sth 对某事物的关怀和保护: *live in the bosom of one's family* 在家庭的关怀中生活 ○ *welcomed into the bosom of the Church* 欢迎投入教会的怀抱.

▷ **bos·omy** *adj* (*infml* 口) (of a woman) having large breasts (指女子)乳房大的.

□ **bosom ˈfriend** very close friend 知心朋友; 知己; 密友.

boss[1] /bɒs; bɑs/ *n* (*infml* 口) person who controls or gives orders to workers; manager; employer 老板; 经理; 上司; 工头; 领班: *ask one's boss for a pay rise* 请求老板增加工资 ○ *Who's (the) boss in this house?* ie Is the wife or the husband in control? 谁是一家之主(是妻子还是丈夫当家)?

▷ **boss** *v* [Tn, Tn·p] **~ sb (about/around)** (*infml derog* 口, 贬) give orders to sb in an overbearing way 向某人发号施令: *He's always bossing his wife about.* 他总是呼来唤去地指使妻子.

bossy *adj* (**-ier, -iest**) (*derog* 贬) fond of giving people orders; domineering 爱发号施令的; 爱指使人的; 专横的; 飞扬跋扈的. **boss·ily** *adv*. **bossi·ness** *n* [U].

boss[2] /bɒs; bɑs/ *n* round projecting knob or stud, esp in the centre of a shield or as a decoration on a church ceiling 圆形凸起物;(尤指)盾的中心或教堂天花板上的突起装饰.

boss-eyed /ˈbɒsaɪd; ˋbɑs,aɪd/ *adj* (*infml* 口) (**a**) blind in one eye 一只眼瞎的; 独眼的. (**b**) cross-eyed 斜眼的.

boss-shot /ˈbɒsʃɒt; ˋbɑs,ʃɑt/ *n* bad shot, guess or attempt 不准确的射击或猜测; 拙劣的尝试: *make a boss-shot at/of sth* 把某事弄得一团糟.

bo'sun = BOATSWAIN.

bot·any /ˈbɒtənɪ; ˋbɑtn̩ɪ/ *n* [U] scientific study of plants and their structure 植物学. Cf 参看 BIOLOGY, ZOOLOGY.

▷ **bo·tan·ical** /bəˈtænɪkl; bəˋtænɪkl̩/ *adj* of or relating to botany 植物学的; 与植物学有关的. **boˌtanical ˈgardens** park where plants and trees are grown for scientific study 植物园.

bot·an·ist /ˈbɒtənɪst; ˋbɑtn̩ɪst/ *n* expert in botany 植物学家.

bot·an·ize, -ise /ˈbɒtənaɪz; ˋbɑtn̩,aɪz/ *v* [I] study and collect wild plants 研究、采集野生植物.

botch /bɒtʃ; bɑtʃ/ *v* [Tn, Tn·p] **~ sth (up)** spoil sth by poor or clumsy work; repair sth badly (笨手笨脚地)弄坏某事物; 把某物修理得很糟: *a botched job*, ie a piece of work that is done badly 笨活儿 ○ *The actor botched* (ie forgot or stumbled over) *his lines.* 那演员把台词念糟了. ○ *The mechanic tried to repair my car, but he really botched it up.* 那个技工想把我的汽车修好, 可是他一修更糟了.

▷ **botch** (also **botch-up**) *n* piece of badly done work 粗制滥造的活儿: *make a botch of sth* 把某事物办糟了.

botcher *n* person who botches work 笨手笨脚的人.

both[1] /bəʊθ; boθ/ *adj* **1** (with *pl ns*; the *n* may be preceded by a *def art*, a *demons det* or a *possess det* 与复数名词连用, 名词前可有定冠词、指示限定词或所有格限定词) the two; the one as well as the other 二者; 两者都: *hold sth in both hands* 双手拿着某物 ○ *Both books/Both the books/Both these books are expensive.* 这两本书都很贵. ○ *He is blind in both eyes.* 他双目失明. ○ *There are shops on both sides of the street.* 街道两边都有商店. ○ *Both (her) children are at university.* (她的)两个孩子都在上大学. **2** (idm 习语) **have/want it/things ˈboth ways** (try to) combine two ways of thinking or behaving, satisfy two demands, obtain two results, etc which are, or might be thought to be, exclusive of each other 二者得兼: *You can't have it both ways*, ie You must decide on one thing or the other. 二者不可得兼(须选择其一). ⇨Usage at ALL[1] 用法见 ALL[1].

both[2] /bəʊθ; boθ/ *pron* (**a**) **~ (of sb/sth)** (referring back to a *pl n* or *pron* 复指前文之复数名词或代词) the two; not only the one but also the other 二者: *He has two brothers: both live in London.* 他有两个兄弟, 都住在伦敦. ○ *His parents are both dead.* 他父母双亡. ○ *We both want to go to the party.* 我们俩都想去参加聚会. ○ *I like these shirts. I'll take both of them.* 我喜欢这种衬衫. 我两件都要. (**b**) **~ of sb/sth** (referring forward to a *pl n* or *pron* 预指后文之复数名词或代词) the two; not only the one but also the other 二者: *Both of us want to go* (Cf 参看 *We both want to go*) *to the party.* 我们俩都想去参加聚会. ○ *Both of her children have* (Cf 参看 *Her children both have*) *blue eyes.* 她的两个孩子都是蓝眼睛. ⇨Usage at ALL[1] 用法见 ALL[1].

both[3] /bəʊθ; boθ/ *adv* **~... and...** not only... but also... 不但...而且...; 既...又...; 又...又...: *be both tired and hungry* 又累又饿 ○ *She spoke both French and English.* 她既会说法语也会说英语. ○ *Both his brother and sister are married.* 他的哥哥和姐姐两人都已婚. ○ *She was a success both as a pianist and as a conductor.* 她是出色的钢琴家和指挥家.

bother /ˈbɒðə(r); ˋbɑðɚ/ *v* **1** (**a**) [Tn, Tn·pr, Dn·t] **~ sb (about/with sth)** cause trouble or annoyance to sb; pester sb 打扰或烦扰某人; 给某人添麻烦: *I'm sorry to bother you, but could you tell me the way to the station?* 对不起打扰一下, 请问去车站怎么走? ○ *Does the pain from your operation bother you much?* 你手术后疼得很难受吗? ○ *Does my smoking bother you?* 我吸烟会不会影响你? ○ *Don't bother your father (about it) now; he's very tired.* 现在别(拿这个)去打搅你父亲, 他很累了. ○ *He's always bothering me to lend him money.* 他老是闹着要我借给他钱. (**b**) [Tn] worry (sb) 使(某人)不安: *What's bothering you?* 你愁什么呢? ○ *Don't let his criticisms bother you.* 别因为他批评你而感到烦恼. ○ *The problem has been bothering me for weeks.* 那问题已经困扰了我几个星期. ○ *It bothers me that he can be so insensitive.* 他这样麻木不仁, 我心里很不痛快. **2** (**a**) [I, Tt] take the time or trouble (to do sth) (为做某事物)费工夫, 添麻烦: *'Shall I help you with the washing up?' 'Don't bother — I'll do it later.'* '要不要我帮你洗碗碟?' '不用麻烦了——我待一会儿洗.' ○ *He didn't even bother to say thank you.* 他甚至连说一声谢谢都不肯. (**b**) [Ipr] **~ about sb/sth** concern oneself about sb/sth 关心某人[某事物]: *Don't bother about us — we'll join you later.* 别惦记我们——我们不久就和你们在一起了. **3** [Tn] (used in the imperative to express annoyance at sth 用于祈使句, 表示对某事物厌烦): *Bother this car! It's always breaking down.* 这辆汽车真讨厌! 老抛锚. **4** (idm 习语) **bother oneself/one's head about sth** be anxious or concerned about sth 为某事物焦虑或操心. **can't be bothered (to do sth)** not do sth because one considers it to be too much trouble 嫌麻烦而不为; 偷懒: *The grass needs cutting but I can't be bothered to do it today.* 草得剪一剪了, 但我今天却懒得去做. ○ *He could produce excellent work but usually he can't be bothered.* 他其实可以把工作做好, 可他往往嫌费事而不干. **hot and bothered** ⇨ HOT.

▷ **bother** *n* **1** [U] trouble; inconvenience 麻烦; 不便: *a spot of bother* 不便之处 ○ *Did you have much bother finding the house?* 你找到这所房子费劲吗? ○ *'Thanks for your help!' 'It was no bother.'* '谢谢你的帮助!' '没什么.' ○ *I'm sorry to have put you to all this bother*, ie to have caused you so much inconvenience. 真抱歉给你添了这么多的麻烦. **2 a bother** [sing] annoying thing; nuisance 恼人的事物; 讨厌的事物: *What a bother! We've missed the bus.* 真恼人! 我们误了公共汽车.

bother *interj* (used to express annoyance 用以表示烦

恼): *Oh bother! I've left my money at home.* 真讨厌! 我把钱落在家里了.

both·era·tion /ˌbɒðəˈreɪʃn; ˌbɑðəˈreʃən/ *interj* (*infml* 口) = BOTHER *interj*.

both·er·some /-səm; -səm/ *adj* causing bother; annoying 引起麻烦的; 令人厌烦的.

bottle /ˈbɒtl; ˈbɑtl̩/ *n* **1** [C] (**a**) glass or plastic container, usu with a narrow neck, used for storing liquids 瓶子: *a ˈwine bottle* 酒瓶 ○ *a ˈmilk bottle* 奶瓶 ○ *Come to my party on Saturday — and remember to bring a bottle*, ie of alcoholic drink. 你来参加我们星期六的聚会吧 —— 还有, 别忘了带瓶酒来. ⇨illus 见插图. (**b**) amount contained in a bottle 一瓶的量: *We drank a (whole) bottle of wine between us.* 我们俩喝了一(整)瓶酒. **2 the bottle** [sing] (*euph* 婉) alcoholic drink 酒精饮料; 酒: *She's a bit too fond of the bottle.* 她有点太爱喝酒了. **3** [C usu *sing* 通常作单数] baby's feeding bottle or milk from this (used instead of mother's milk) 婴儿奶瓶; 奶瓶装的奶(用以代替母乳): *brought up on the bottle* 牛奶喂大的 ○ *give a baby its bottle* 给婴儿喂牛奶. **4** [U] (*Brit sl* 俚) courage; impudence 勇气; 卤莽: *He's got (a lot of) bottle!* 他真是个(大)冒失鬼! **5** (idm 习语) **be on the ˈbottle** (*infml* 口) be an alcoholic 是个酒徒: *He was on the bottle for five years.* 他酗酒已五年. **hit the bottle** ⇨ HIT[1].

▷ **bottle** *v* **1** [Tn] (**a**) put (sth) into bottles 将(某物)装入瓶中: *bottled beer* 瓶装啤酒. (**b**) preserve (sth) by storing in glass jars 将(某物)盛入玻璃罐中贮存: *Do you bottle your fruit or freeze it?* 你是把水果装在罐里保存呢, 还是冷冻起来保存? **2** (phr v) **bottle sth up** not allow (emotions) to be seen; restrain or suppress (feelings) 掩盖(情绪); 抑制(感情): *Instead of discussing their problems, they bottle up all their anger and resentment.* 他们不是把问题提出来讨论, 而是把怒气和怨愤憋在肚子里.

□ ˈ**bottle bank** large container in which empty bottles are placed so that the glass can be reused 贮瓶箱(放置回收空瓶的容器, 以备再生产使用).

ˈ**bottle-feed** *v* [Tn] feed (a baby) with a bottle 用奶瓶喂(婴儿): *Were you bottle-fed or breast-fed as a child?* 你是吃牛奶长大的呢, 还是吃母奶长大的?

ˈ**bottle-green** *adj* dark green 深绿色的.

ˈ**bottle-neck** *n* (**a**) narrow or restricted stretch of road which causes traffic to slow down or stop 瓶颈路段(道路的狭窄或受限制的部分, 交通易受阻). (**b**) anything that slows down production in a manufacturing process, etc (影响生产效率的)障碍.

ˈ**bottle-opener** *n* metal device for opening bottles of beer, etc 开瓶器.

ˈ**bottle-party** *n* party to which each guest brings a bottle of wine, etc 赴宴者各携一瓶酒等的聚会.

bot·tom /ˈbɒtəm; ˈbɑtəm/ *n* **1** [C usu *sing* 通常作单数] lowest part or point of sth 物体最低的部分或最低点: *the bottom of a hill, mountain, slope, valley, etc* 丘、山、坡、谷等的底部 ○ *The telephone is at the bottom of the stairs.* 电话在楼梯下面. ○ *There are tea leaves in the bottom of my cup.* 我的杯底有茶叶. ○ *The book I want is (right) at the bottom of the pile.* 我要的那本书(就)在这堆书底下. ○ *Sign your name at the bottom of the page, please.* 请在这一页的下方签上你的名字. **2** [C usu *sing* 通常作单数] part on which sth rests; underside 物体最低的部位; 底面: *The manufacturer's name is on the bottom of the plate.* 制造厂商的名称在盘子背面. **3** [C] part of the body on which one sits; buttocks 臀部; 屁股: *fall on one's bottom* 摔倒时屁股着地 ○ *smack a child's bottom* 打孩子的屁股. **4** [sing] farthest part or point (of sth); far end (of sth) 最远的部分; 最远点: *There's a pub at the bottom of the road.* 路的尽头有一家酒馆. ○ *The tool shed is at the bottom of the garden*, ie at the end farthest from the house. 工具房在花园的尽里头. **5** [sing] (person or group in the) lowest position in a class, list, etc (处于等级、名单等)最低位置(的人或团体): *He was always bottom of the class in maths.* 他的数学成绩在班上总是垫底. ○ *Our team came/was bottom of the league last season.* 我们队在上季度的联赛中排名最后. ○ *She started at the bottom and worked her way up to become manager of the company.* 她从最低的位置干起, 通过努力终于当上了公司的经理. **6** [sing] ground under a sea, lake or river (海洋、湖泊或河流的)底: *The water is very deep here, I can't touch (the) bottom.* 这儿水很深, 我摸不着底. ○ *The 'Titanic' went to the bottom*, ie sank. '提坦'号客轮沉入海底了. **7** [C] ship's hull; keel 船身; (船的)龙骨. **8** [C usu *pl* 通常作复数] lower part of a two-piece garment (两件一套的服装的)下件: *pyjama bottoms* 睡裤 ○ *track suit bottoms* 运动裤. **9** [U] lowest gear 最低挡: *drive up a steep hill in bottom* 用低挡驶上陡峭的山. **10** (idm 习语) **at bottom** in reality; really; basically 其实; 实际上; 基本上: *He seems aggressive but at bottom he is kind and good-natured.* 他表面上好与人争, 而实际上却很善良厚道. **be at the bottom of sth** be the basic cause or originator of sth 是某事物的起因或根源: *Who is at the bottom of these rumours?* 谁是这些谣言的制造者? **the bottom (of sth) falls out** collapse occurs 崩溃: *The bottom has fallen out of the market*, ie Trade has dropped to a very low level. 市场崩溃了(生意很萧条). ○ *The bottom fell out of his world* (ie His life lost its meaning) *when his wife died.* 他妻子死时, 他的世界陷于崩溃(他的生活失去了意义). **bottoms ˈup!** (*infml* 口) (said as a toast to tell people to finish their drinks 祝酒时请人干杯的用语). **from the bottom of one's ˈheart** with deep feeling; truly; sincerely 深情地; 忠实地; 诚恳地: *love sb, congratulate sb, regret sth from the bottom of one's heart* 由衷地爱某人、祝贺某人、惋惜某事物. **from top to bottom** ⇨ TOP[1]. **get to the bottom of sth** find out the real cause of sth or the truth about sth 弄清某事物的真正原因或真相: *We must get to the bottom of this mystery.* 我们一定要彻底解开这个谜. **knock the bottom out of sth** ⇨ KNOCK[2]. **smooth as a baby's bottom** ⇨ SMOOTH[1]. **touch bottom** ⇨ TOUCH[2].

▷ **bot·tom** *adj* [attrib 作定语] **1** in the lowest or last position 最低的; 最后的: *the bottom line (on a page)* (一页的)最末一行 ○ *the bottom rung (of a ladder)* (梯子的)最下一级 ○ *the bottom step (of a flight of stairs)* (一段阶梯的)最下一级 ○ *Put your books on the bottom shelf.* 把你的书放在最下层的架子上. ○ *go up a hill in bottom gear* 用低挡上山. **2** (idm 习语) **bet one's bottom dollar** ⇨ BET.

bot·tom *v* (phr v) **bottom out** (*commerce* 商) (of prices, shares, etc) reach the lowest level (指物价、股票价格等)跌落最低水平: *There is no sign that the recession has bottomed out yet.* 没有迹象表明萧条已经到了极点.

bot·tom·less *adj* **1** very deep 极深的: *a bottomless pit, gorge, etc* 无底的深坑、峡谷等. **2** (*fig* 比喻) unlimited; inexhaustible 无限的; 无穷尽的: *bottomless reserves of energy* 取之不尽的能源.

bot·tom·most /ˈbɒtəmməʊst; ˈbɑtəmˌmost/ *adj* [attrib 作定语] lowest 最低的: *the bottommost depths of the sea* 海洋的最深处.

□ ˌ**bottom ˈdrawer** (*US* ˈ**hope chest**) store of clothes, linen, cutlery, etc collected by a woman in preparation for marriage 嫁妆.

ˌ**bottom ˈline** (*infml* 口) deciding or crucial factor; essential point (in an argument, etc) 决定性因素; (论辩等的)基本论点: *If you don't make a profit you go out of business: that's the bottom line.* 不盈利, 就停业: 根本问题就在这里.

botu·lism /ˈbɒtjʊlɪzəm; ˈbɑtʃəˌlɪzəm/ *n* [U] type of severe food poisoning caused by bacteria in badly preserved food 肉毒中毒(由变质的腌制食品引起的一种严重的细菌性食物中毒).

bou·doir /ˈbu:dwɑ:(r); buˈdwar/ *n* (esp formerly) woman's bedroom or private sitting-room (尤指旧时)闺房.

bouf·fant /ˈbu:fɑ:n; buˈfɑnt/ *adj* (of a hair-style) made to appear puffed out by being combed back towards the roots (指发型)鼓起的, 蓬松的: *a ˌbouffant ˈhair-do* 蓬松的发式.

bou·gain·vil·laea /ˌbu:gənˈvɪlɪə; ˌbugənˈvɪlɪə/ *n* tropical climbing shrub with large red or purple bracts 叶子花, 九重葛(热带蔓生灌木, 苞片大, 呈红色或紫色).

bough /baʊ; baʊ/ *n* any of the main branches of a tree (树的)主枝.

bought *pt, pp of* BUY.

bouil·lon /ˈbu:jɒn; ˈbuljɑn/ *n* [U] thin clear soup or broth; stock[1] (9) 肉汁清汤; 肉汤.

boul·der /ˈbəʊldə(r); ˈboldɚ/ *n* large rock worn and shaped by water or the weather (经风雨或水侵蚀而成的)巨石.

bou·le·vard /ˈbu:ləvɑ:d; *US* ˈbʊl-;ˈbʊlə,vɑrd/ *n* **1** wide city street, often with trees on each side 大街(两旁常植有树木的); 林阴大道. **2** (*US*) broad main road 干路; 大道.

bounce /ˈbaʊns; baʊns/ *v* **1** [I, Ipr, Tn, Tn·pr] (cause sth to) spring back when sent against sth hard (使某物)(碰到硬物)弹回: *A rubber ball bounces well.* 橡皮球弹力好. ○ *The ball bounced over the wall.* 那球弹过墙去了. ○ *The goalkeeper bounced the ball twice before kicking it.* 守门员先把球拍了两下, 然后一脚踢出. ○ *She bounced the ball against the wall.* 她把球掷到墙上让它弹回. **2** [I, Ip, Tn] (cause sb to) move up and down in a lively manner (in the specified direction) (使某人)活跃地上下跳动: *The child bounced (up and down) on the bed.* 那孩子在床上蹦蹦跳跳. ○ *He bounced his baby on his knee.* 他把婴儿放在膝上颠着玩. ⇨Usage at JUMP[2] 用法见 JUMP[2]. **3** [I] (*infml* 口) (of a cheque) be sent back by a bank as worthless (because there is no money in the account) (指支票)遭银行退票(因帐户中无钱): *I hope this cheque doesn't bounce.* 我希望这张支票别遭退票. Cf 参看 DISHONOUR *v* 2. **4** (phr v) **bounce along, down, into, etc** move in the specified direction with an up and down motion 以上上下下的动作沿某方向移动: *He came bouncing into the room.* 他蹦蹦跳跳地进了房间. ○ *The car bounced along the bumpy mountain road.* 汽车在崎岖的山路上颠簸行驶. **bounce back** (*infml* 口) recover well after a setback 受挫折后恢复原状: *Share prices bounced back this morning.* 股票价格今晨回升了. ○ *She's had many misfortunes in her life but she always bounces back.* 她一生中经历过许多挫折,然而总是能重新振作起来.

▷ **bounce** *n* **1** [C] act of bouncing 弹跳: *catch a ball on the bounce/first bounce*, ie after it has bounced once 球弹起时[一弹起]就把它抓住. **2** [U] (**a**) ability to bounce 弹力. (**b**) (of a person) liveliness; vitality (指人)活力; 生气: *She's got a lot of bounce.* 她浑身都是劲儿.

boun·cer (also **bumper**) *n* **1** (in cricket) bowled ball that bounces high and forcefully (板球)反弹力大的高球: *bowl sb a fast bouncer* 向某人投掷反弹力大的快速高球. **2** (*infml* 口) person employed by a club, restaurant, etc to throw out trouble-makers (俱乐部, 饭店等雇用的)驱逐捣乱者的人.

bounc·ing *adj* ~ **(with sth)** strong and healthy 健壮的; 强健的: *a bouncing baby* 健壮的婴儿 ○ *He was bouncing with energy.* 他身强力壮.

bouncy *adj* (**-ier**, **-iest**) **1** (of a ball) able to bounce (指球)有弹性的. **2** (of a person) lively (指人)活跃的.

bound[1] /baʊnd; baʊnd/ *v* [Tn usu passive 通常用于被动语态] form the boundary of (sth); limit 形成(某事物)的界线; 限制: *Germany is bounded on the west by France and on the south by Switzerland.* 德国西面与法国接壤, 南与瑞士为邻. ○ *The airfield is bounded by woods on all sides.* 飞机场的四周都是树林.

bound[2] /baʊnd; baʊnd/ *v* [Ipr, Ip] jump or spring; run with jumping movements (in a specified direction) 跳; 跃; 蹦着跑(向某方向): *He bounded into the room and announced that he was getting married.* 他蹦蹦跳跳地跑进房间里, 宣布他要结婚了. ○ *The dog came bounding up to its master.* 那狗蹿到主人面前.

▷ **bound** *n* **1** bounding movement; leap; spring 跳; 跳跃: *The dog cleared* (ie jumped over) *the gate in one bound.* 那狗一跳就越过了栅门. **2** (idm 习语) **by/in leaps and bounds** ⇨ LEAP.

bound[3] /baʊnd; baʊnd/ *adj* [pred 作表语] ~ **(for...)** going or ready to go in the direction of 去; 准备去: *Where are you bound (for)?* 你要去哪儿? ○ *We are bound for home.* 我们打算回家. ○ *This ship is outward bound/homeward bound*, ie sailing away from/towards its home port. 这只船是在出航[返航]. ▷ **-bound** (forming compound *adjs* 用以构成复合形容词) heading for a specified place or in a specified direction 向某处的; 向某方向的: *We're London-bound.* 我们是前往伦敦的. ○ *Northbound traffic may be delayed because of an accident on the motorway.* 因高速公路上发生了事故, 北往的交通可能受阻.

bound[4] *pt, pp of* BIND.

bound[5] /baʊnd; baʊnd/ *adj* [pred 作表语] ~ **to do sth** **1** certain to do sth 一定做某事: *The weather is bound to get better tomorrow.* 明天天气一定会变好. ○ *You've done so much work that you're bound to pass the exam.* 你下了这么大工夫, 一定能考及格. **2** obliged by law or duty to do sth 有法律责任或有义务做某事的: *I feel bound to tell you that you're drinking too much.* 我觉得有必要跟你说, 你酒喝得太多了. ○ *I am bound to say I disagree with you on this point.* 我必须声明不同意你这一点. **3** (idm 习语) **bound ˈup in sth** very busy with sth; very interested in sth 忙于某事的; 热衷于某事物的: *He seems very bound up in his work.* 他似乎非常喜欢自己的工作. **bound ˈup with sth** closely connected with sth 与某事物关系密切的: *The welfare of the individual is bound up with the welfare of the community.* 个人的福利与社会的福利有着密切的关系. **honour bound** ⇨ HONOUR[1]. **ˈI'll be bound** (*dated infml* 旧, 口) I feel sure 我确信: *The children are up to some mischief, I'll be bound!* 孩子们在搞恶作剧,我敢肯定!

▷ **-bound** (forming compound *adjs* 用以构成复合形容词) **1** confined to a specified place 限制在某个场所的: *I don't like being desk-bound* (eg in an office) *all day.* 我不喜欢整天拴在办公桌旁(如在办公室里). ○ *His illness has left him completely house-bound.* 他因病完全足不出户. **2** obstructed or hindered by the specified conditions 因某种情况而受阻的: *fogbound/snowbound airports* ○ *Strikebound travellers face long delays this weekend.* 因罢工而受阻的旅客本周末要耽搁很长时间了.

bound·ary /ˈbaʊndrɪ; ˈbaʊndrɪ/ *n* **1** line that marks a limit; dividing line 界限; 分界线: *The fence marks the boundary between my land and hers.* 这道栅栏是我的地和她的地的分界线. ○ *The ball was caught by a fielder standing just inside the boundary.* 那球被正站在边界线内的守场员接住了. ○ (*fig* 比喻) *Scientists continue to push back the boundaries of knowledge.* 科学家不断地把知识领域的边缘向外扩展. ⇨Usage at BORDER 用法见 BORDER. **2** (in cricket) hit to or over the boundary, scoring 4 or 6 runs (板球)击至或击过边线(可得4分或6分): *He scored 26 runs, all in boundaries.* 他得了26分, 都是打边线球获得的.

bounden /ˈbaʊndən; ˈbaʊndən/ *adj* (idm 习语) **one's bounden ˈduty** (*fml* 文) duty dictated by one's conscience 本分.

bounder /ˈbaʊndə(r); ˈbaʊndɚ/ *n* (*dated Brit infml derog* 旧, 口, 贬) man whose behaviour is morally unacceptable 不道德的人.

bound·less /ˈbaʊndlɪs; ˈbaʊndlɪs/ *adj* without limits 无限的: *boundless generosity, enthusiasm* 无比的慷慨、热情. ▷ **bound·lessly** *adv*.

bounds /baʊndz; baʊndz/ *n* [pl] **1** limits 界限: *keep within/go beyond the bounds of reason, sanity, decency, propriety, etc* 有[没]理性、理智、体统、礼貌等 ○ *It is not beyond the bounds of possibility (that...).* (...)不是不可能的. ○ *Are there no bounds to his ambition?* 他的野心难道没有止境吗? ○ *Public spending must be kept within reasonable bounds.* 公共事务的开销必须保持在合理的范围以内. **2** (idm 习语) **know no bounds** ⇨ KNOW. **out of ˈbounds (to sb)** (*US* **off limits**) (of a place) not to be entered or visited (by sb) (指某地方)禁止(某人)入内; 谢绝(某人)参观: *The town's pubs and bars are out of bounds to troops.* 军人不得进入城里的酒馆和酒吧.

boun·teous /ˈbaʊntɪəs; ˈbaʊntɪəs/ *adj* (*dated or rhet* 旧

或修辞) **1** (of a person) generous (指人)慷慨的. **2** freely given; plentiful 丰富的; 充裕的: *God's bounteous blessings.* 上帝的慷慨赐福. ▷ **boun·teously** *adv.* **boun·teous·ness** *n* [U].

boun·ti·ful /ˈbaʊntɪfl; ˋbaʊntəfəl/ *adj* (*dated* 旧) **1** giving generously 慷慨给予的. **2** abundant 丰富的; 充裕的: *a bountiful supply of food* 充足的食物供应. ▷ **boun·ti·fully** /ˈbaʊntɪfəlɪ; ˋbaʊntəflɪ/ *adv.*

B

bounty /ˈbaʊntɪ; ˋbaʊntɪ/ *n* **1** [U] (*dated* 旧) generosity in giving; liberality 慷慨; 大方: *a monarch famous for his bounty* 以好施而闻名的君主. **2** [C] (*dated* 旧) generous gift 慷慨馈赠的礼物. **3** [C] reward or payment offered (usu by a government) to encourage sb to do sth (eg to increase production of goods) 奖金(通常由政府提供, 以鼓励某人作某事, 如提高产量).

bou·quet /bʊˈkeɪ; buˋke/ *n* **1** bunch of flowers for carrying in the hand (often presented as a gift) 花束(常用作礼物): *a bride's bouquet* 新娘的花束 ○ *The soloist received a huge bouquet of roses.* 独唱者得到了很大的一束玫瑰花. **2** (*fig* 比喻) expression of praise; compliment 称赞; 恭维. **3** characteristic aroma of a wine or liqueur 酒的芳香: *This brandy has a fine bouquet.* 这种白兰地酒芳香扑鼻.

□ **bouquet garni** /ˌbu:keɪ ˈgɑ:ni:; buˋke gɑˋni/ bunch of herbs used for flavouring soups, stews, etc 香料束(捆成束的香料, 作汤、炖菜等的作料).

bour·bon /ˈbɜ:bən; ˋbɝbən/ *n* (**a**) [U] type of whisky distilled in the US chiefly from maize 波旁威士忌(产于美国, 多酿自玉米). (**b**) [C] glass of this 一杯波旁威士忌酒.

bour·geois /ˈbɔ:ʒwɑ:; *US* ˌbʊərˈʒwɑ:; bʊrˋʒwɑ/ *adj* **1** of or relating to the property-owning middle class 中产阶级的; 关于中产阶级的. **2** (*derog* 贬) (**a**) concerned with material possessions and social status 耽于名利的: *They've become very bourgeois since they got married.* 他们结婚以后就一味追求物质享受和社会地位了. (**b**) conventionally respectable; conservative 清高的; 保守的: *bourgeois tastes, attitudes, ideas, etc* 高雅的趣味、风度、思想等. (**c**) unimaginative; philistine 缺乏想像力的; 平庸的. **3** (in Marxist thought) of or relating to the bourgeoisie(2); capitalist (马克思学说中)资产阶级的, 关于资产阶级的, 资本家的, 资本主义的.

▷ **bour·geois** *n* (*pl* unchanged 复数不变) [C] (*usu derog* 通常作贬义) bourgeois person 中产阶级分子; 耽于名利的人; 清高的人; 平庸的人; 资产阶级分子.

bour·geoisie /ˌbʊəʒwɑ:ˈzi:; ˌbʊrʒwɑˋzi/ *n* [Gp] (*usu derog* 通常作贬义) **1** middle classes, esp those owning property 中产阶级: *the rise of the bourgeoisie in the 19th century* 19世纪中产阶级的兴起. **2** (in Marxist thought) capitalist ruling class that exploits the working class (马克思学说中)居于统治地位的资产阶级(剥削工人阶级者). Cf 参看 PROLETARIAT.

bourse /bʊəs; bʊrs/ *n* European stock exchange, esp (**the Bourse**) the one in Paris 欧洲证券交易所; (尤指)巴黎证券交易所.

bout /baʊt; baʊt/ *n* **1 ~ (of sth/doing sth)** (**a**) short period of a specified activity 一回; 一次; 一阵: *a ˈdrinking-bout* 一次宴饮 ○ *She has bouts of hard work followed by long periods of inactivity.* 她总是努力干上一阵, 然后一待就是很长时间. (**b**) attack (of an illness) (指疾病)侵袭, 发作: *a bout of flu, bronchitis, rheumatism, etc* 流感、支气管炎、风湿病等的侵袭 ○ *He suffers from frequent bouts of depression.* 他患多发性抑郁症. **2** boxing or wrestling contest 拳击或摔跤比赛.

bou·tique /bu:ˈti:k; buˋtik/ *n* small shop selling clothes and other articles of the latest fashion 精品店(经销时装及时髦用品的小商店).

bo·vine /ˈbəʊvaɪn; ˋbovaɪn/ *adj* **1** (*fml* 文) of or relating to cattle 牛的; 关于牛的. **2** (*derog* 贬) dull and stupid 迟钝的; 笨拙的: *a bovine expression, character, mentality* 鲁钝的表情、性情、头脑 ○ *bovine stupidity* 像牛一样的笨拙.

bow[1] /bəʊ; bo/ *n* **1** piece of wood bent into a curve by a tight string joining its ends, used as a weapon for shooting arrows (射箭用的)弓: *hunt with bows and arrows* 以弓、箭行猎. ⇨illus at ARCHERY 见ARCHERY之插图. **2** wooden rod with strands of horse-hair stretched from end to end, used for playing stringed instruments 琴弓. ⇨illus at App 1 见附录1之插图, page xi. **3** knot made with loops; ribbon tied in this way 蝴蝶结; 打成蝴蝶结的丝带: *tie shoelaces in a bow* 把鞋带打成蝴蝶结 ○ *a dress decorated with bows* 饰有蝴蝶结的连衣裙. ⇨illus 见插图. **4** (idm 习语) **have two strings/a second, etc string to one's bow** have a second person, skill or resource available to one for a particular purpose, as a replacement for or an alternative to a first 有后备人选、技术或资源; 有两手准备: *As both a novelist and a university lecturer, she has two strings to her bow.* 她又是小说家又当大学讲师, 有两手准备.

▷ **bow** *v* [I, Tn] use a bow on (a stringed instrument) 用弓拉(弦乐器). **bow·ing** *n* [U] technique of using the bow to play a violin, etc (拉小提琴等的)弓法: *The cellist's bowing was very sensitive.* 那位大提琴手的弓法十分细腻.

□ ˌ**bow-ˈlegs** *n* [pl] legs that curve outwards at the knees 弓形腿; 罗圈腿. ˌ**bow-ˈlegged** *adj*: *a* ˌ*bow-ˈlegged gait* 罗圈腿的步态.

ˈ**bowman** /-mən; -mən/ *n* (*pl* **-men** /-mən; -mən/) archer 弓箭手.

ˌ**bow-ˈtie** *n* man's necktie tied in a knot with a double loop, worn esp on formal occasions 蝶形领结. ⇨illus 见插图.

ˌ**bow-ˈwindow** *n* type of bay window with curved glass 弓形窗; 凸肚窗.

bow[2] /baʊ; baʊ/ *v* **1** (**a**) [I, Ipr, Ip] **~ (down) (to/before sb/sth)** bend the head or body as a sign of respect or as a greeting 鞠躬; 点头(表示尊敬或打招呼): *The cast bowed as the audience applauded.* 演员们向鼓掌的观众鞠躬. ○ *We all bowed to the Queen.* 我们都向女王鞠躬致敬. ○ *The priest bowed down before the altar.* 牧师在圣坛前行鞠躬礼. (**b**) [Tn] bend (the head or body) as a sign of respect 俯(首)或欠(身)致敬: *The congregation bowed their heads in prayer.* 会众在一起低头祷告. **2** [usu passive 通常用于被动语态: Tn, Tn·p] bend (sb/sth) under or as if under a weight 压弯(某人[某物]); 像被压弯: *His back was bowed with age.* 他因年老而驼背. ○ *branches bowed down by the snow on them* 被积雪压弯的树枝. **3** (idm 习语) ˌ**bow and ˈscrape** (*usu derog* 通常作贬义) behave in an obsequious or a servile manner 点头哈腰; 奴颜婢膝: *The waiter showed us to our table with much bowing and scraping.* 服务员一个劲儿地点头哈腰领我们就座. **4** (phr v) **bow sb in/out** bow to sb as he enters/leaves a room, etc 躬身迎入[送出]某人. **bow out (of sth)** (**a**) withdraw from sth 退出, 离开某事物: *I'm bowing out of this scheme — I don't approve of it.* 我退出这个计划——我不同意它. (**b**) retire from an important position 从要位上离退: *After thirty years in politics, he is finally bowing out.* 他从政三十年之后, 终于决定退出政坛. **bow to sth** submit to sth; accept sth 顺从某事物; 接受某事物: *bow to the inevitable* 顺从命运; 听天由命 ○ *bow to sb's opinion, wishes, greater experience* 尊重某人的意见、意愿、丰富的经验 ○ *We're tired of having to bow to authority.* 我们对必须服从权威这一点感到厌倦.

▷ **bow** *n* **1** bending of the head or body (as a greeting, etc) 点头致意; 鞠躬礼: *acknowledge sb with a bow* 点头招呼某人 ○ *He made a bow and left the room.* 他鞠了一个躬就离开了房间. **2** (idm 习语) **take a/one's ˈbow** (of an actor or actors) acknowledge applause by bowing (BOW[2] 1a) (指演员)鞠躬谢幕.

bow[3] /baʊ; baʊ/ *n* **1** (often *pl* 常作复数) front or forward end of a boat or ship 船头; 船首; 艏: *The yacht hit a rock and damaged her bows.* 游艇碰上了礁石, 撞坏了船头. ⇨illus at YACHT 见YACHT之插图. **2** (in rowing) oarsman nearest the bow (划艇)船头的划桨手. Cf 参看 STROKE[1] 3.

bowd·ler·ize, -ise /ˈbaʊdləraɪz; ˋbaʊdləˌraɪz/ *v* [Tn] (*sometimes derog* 有时作贬义) remove words or scenes considered indecent from (a book, play, etc); expurgate; censor 删除(书刊、剧本等中)有伤风化的词语或场面; 删去; 删改. ▷ **bowd·ler·iza·tion, -isa·tion** /ˌbaʊdləraɪˈzeɪʃn; *US* -rɪˈz-; ˌbaʊdlərəˈzeʃən/ *n* [C, U].

bowel /ˈbaʊəl; ˈbaʊəl/ *n* (usu *pl*, except in medical use and when used attributively 除用作医学名词及修饰语外, 通常作复数) **1** part of the alimentary canal below the stomach; intestine 肠: [attrib 作定语] *a bowel complaint/disorder* 腹泻[肠道疾患] ○ *cancer of the bowel* 肠癌 ○ *move one's bowels*, ie defecate 大便(通便). **2** deepest or innermost part (of a place) (某处的)最深的或最靠里面的部分: *in the bowels of the earth*, ie deep underground 在地下深处.
□ ˈ**bowel movement** (**a**) discharge of waste matter from the bowels 排便. (**b**) waste matter discharged; faeces 粪便; 大便.

bower /ˈbaʊə(r); ˈbaʊɚ/ *n* **1** (**a**) shady place under trees or climbing-plants in a wood or garden; arbour (树林或花园中的)阴凉处; 凉棚. (**b**) summer-house 凉亭. **2** (*dated* 旧) lady's bedroom; boudoir (女子的)卧室; 闺房.
□ ˈ**bower-bird** *n* type of Australian bird of paradise 造园鸟(产于澳大利亚).

bowl[1] /bəʊl; bol/ *n* **1** (**a**) (esp in compounds 尤用以构成复合词) deep round dish, used esp for holding food or liquid 碗; 钵: *a sugar bowl* 糖钵 ○ *a fruit bowl* 果盘 ○ *a washing-up bowl* 洗涤盆. (**b**) amount contained in a bowl 一碗的量: *a bowl of soup, cereal, porridge, etc* 一碗汤、谷类食品、麦片粥等. ⇨illus at BUCKET, PLATE 见 BUCKET、PLATE 之插图. **2** hollow rounded part of certain objects (物体的)圆形凹陷部分: *the bowl of a spoon* 匙子的凹处 ○ *a lavatory bowl* 便池 ○ *He filled the bowl of his pipe with tobacco.* 他往烟斗里装烟丝. **3** (*esp US*) amphitheatre (for open-air concerts, etc) (供音乐会等用的)圆形露天剧场: *the Hollywood Bowl* 好莱坞圆形露天剧场.

bowl[2] /bəʊl; bol/ *n* **1** [C] heavy wooden ball that is weighted so that it rolls in a curve, used in the game of bowls (滚木球戏所用的)木球. **2** [C] heavy ball used in skittles and ten-pin bowling (撞柱戏和十柱保龄球戏所用的)球. **3 bowls** [sing *v*] game played on a smooth lawn, in which two players take turns to roll bowls as near as possible to a small ball 滚木球戏(在平坦草地上进行, 两人轮流滚动木球, 力求接近一小球): *play bowls* 玩滚木球戏.

bowl[3] /bəʊl; bol/ *v* **1** [I] play a game of bowls or bowling 玩滚木球或地滚球(保龄球). **2** [Tn] (in the games of bowls or bowling) roll (a ball) (滚木球或保龄球戏)滚(球). **3** [I, Tn] (in cricket) send (the ball) from one's hand towards the batsman by swinging the arm over the head without bending the elbow (板球)投(球): *bowl fast/slow* 投得快[慢] ○ *Well bowled!* 投得好! **4** [Tn, Tn·p] **~ sb (out)** dismiss (a batsman) by bowling a ball that hits the wicket behind him (因投出的球击中击球员后面的三柱门)使(击球员)出局: *He was bowled for 120*, ie dismissed in this way after scoring 120 runs. 他得到120分之后被判出局. **5** (phr v) **bowl along, down, etc** (of a car or its passengers) move fast and smoothly (in the specified direction) (指汽车或其乘客)快而稳地行进: *We were bowling along (the motorway) at seventy miles per hour.* 我们以每小时七十英里的速度(在高速公路上)飞驰. **bowl sb over** (**a**) knock sb down 击倒某人. (**b**) surprise sb greatly; astound sb 使某人大吃一惊; 令某人惊奇: *We were bowled over by the news of her marriage.* 我们听到她结婚的消息大为惊讶.

bowler[1] /ˈbəʊlə(r); ˈbolɚ/ *n* **1** person who bowls in cricket (板球)投球手: *a fast, slow, etc bowler* 投球快、慢等的投球手 ○ *a left-arm spin bowler* 投左手旋转球的投球手. ⇨illus at CRICKET 见 CRICKET 之插图. **2** person who plays bowls 玩滚木球戏的人.

bowler[2] /ˈbəʊlə(r); ˈbolɚ/ *n* (also ˌ**bowler** ˈ**hat**, *US* **derby**) hard, usu black, felt hat with a curved brim and rounded top 常礼帽(一种卷檐的圆顶硬毡帽, 通常为黑色): *Many London businessmen wear bowlers.* 伦敦的许多商人戴常礼帽. ⇨illus at HAT 见 HAT 之插图.

bow·line /ˈbəʊlɪn; ˈbolɪn/ *n* (also ˈ**bowline knot**) knot forming a secure loop at the end of a rope, used by sailors, climbers, etc 单套结(水手、攀登者等打的一种结实的结).

bowl·ing /ˈbəʊlɪŋ; ˈbolɪŋ/ *n* [U] **1** any of various games (eg skittles, ten-pin bowling) in which heavy balls are rolled along a special track towards a group of wooden pins 地滚球戏(使用重球沿轨道朝木柱滚动的各种游戏, 如撞柱戏、十柱保龄球戏): *a bowling match* 保龄球比赛. **2** the game of bowls 滚木球戏. **3** (in cricket) sending the ball from the hand towards the batsman (板球)朝击球员方向投球: *a good piece of bowling* 投一个好球.
□ ˈ**bowling-alley** *n* (**a**) long narrow track along which balls are rolled in bowling or skittles (保龄球戏或撞柱戏的狭长的)球道. (**b**) building containing several of these 地滚球场.
ˈ**bowling-green** *n* area of grass cut short for playing bowls on 草地滚木球场.

bowls ⇨ BOWL[2] 3.

bow·sprit /ˈbəʊsprɪt; ˈboˌsprɪt/ *n* long pole projecting from the front of a ship, to which the ropes supporting the sails are fasten 船首斜桅.

bow-wow /ˌbaʊ ˈwaʊ; ˈbaʊˈwaʊ/ *interj* (imitating the bark of a dog 模仿狗叫声).
▷ ˈ**bow-wow** *n* (used by or to young children 儿语) dog 狗.

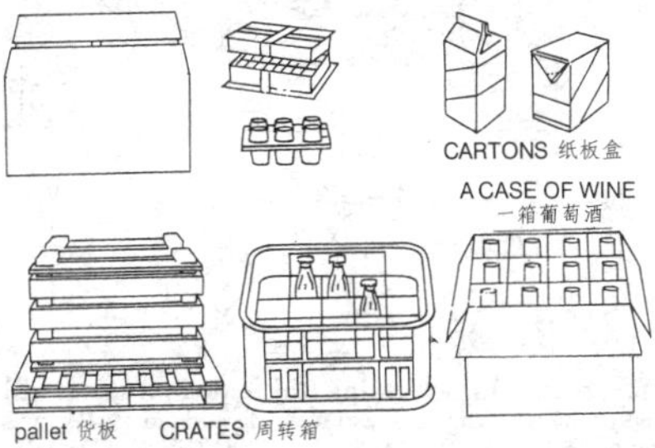

boxes 盒子或箱子

box[1] /bɒks; bɑks/ *n* **1** [C] (**a**) (esp in compounds 尤用以构成复合词) container made of wood, cardboard, metal, etc with a flat base and usu a lid, for holding solids 盒; 匣; 箱: *a tool-box* ○ *a money-box* ○ *a shoe box* ○ *a cigar box* ○ *She packed her books in cardboard boxes.* 她把书装进纸箱里. (**b**) box with its contents 盒或箱及其盛物: *a box of chocolates, matches, cigars* 一盒巧克力、火柴、雪茄烟. **2** [C] (**a**) separate compartment or enclosed area, eg for a group of people in a theatre, stadium, etc, for witnesses in a lawcourt, or for a horse in a stable 分离的隔间或围着的区域(如戏院的包厢、运动场的分区看台、法庭的证人席、马厩中的隔栏): *reserve a box at the theatre* 预订戏院的一个包厢 ○ *the witness box* 证人席 ○ *a horse-box* 马栏. ⇨illus at App 1 见附录1之插图, page ix. (**b**) small hut or shelter for a specific purpose (为某目的而设的)小亭, 岗亭: *a sentry-box* 哨亭 ○ *a signal-box* 信号所 ○ *a telephone-box* 电话间. **3** [C] (in cricket) rounded plastic shield worn by batsmen and wicket-keepers to protect the genitals (板球)护身(击球员和守门员为防止生殖器受伤而戴的圆形塑料护罩). **4 the box** [sing] (*Brit infml* 口) television 电视: *What's on the box tonight?* 今晚电视上有什么节目? **5** [C] = BOX NUMBER.
▷ **box** *v* **1** [Tn] put (sth) into a box 将(某物)装入盒或箱中: *a boxed set of records* 盒装的一套唱片. **2** (phr v) **box sb/sth in** prevent (a runner, horse, car, etc) from moving freely (esp in a race) 妨碍(赛跑者、马、汽车等)自由行动(尤于比赛中): *One of the runners got boxed in on the final bend.* 一个赛跑者在转最后一弯时被人挡住了. **box sb/sth in/up** shut sb/sth in a small space 将某人[某物]禁锢在狭小的空间里: *He feels boxed in, living in that tiny flat.* 他身居斗室, 感到很不自在. ○ *She hates being boxed up in an office all day.* 她讨厌整天关在办公室里.
box·ful *n* full box (of sth) (某物的)整盒, 整箱: *a boxful of books, clothes, toys* 一整箱书、衣服、玩具.

□ ˈ**boxcar** *n* (*US*) enclosed railway goods van（火车的）载货车厢.
ˈ**box junction** (*Brit*) area of road where two roads cross, marked with a criss-cross pattern of yellow stripes on which vehicles must not stop, designed to help the flow of traffic 路口黄格区(绘有黄色斜格的路口, 机动车不得停留其间以利交通疏导).
ˈ**box-kite** *n* kite with an open box-like frame 箱形风筝(有开口的箱形框架).
box ˈ**lunch** (*US*) light meal, usu of sandwiches and fruit, provided in a cardboard box or similar container 盒饭.
ˈ**box number** number given in newspaper advertisements to which replies may be sent（报纸广告中为读者复信而设的）信箱号码.
ˈ**box-office** *n* office at a theatre, cinema, etc where tickets are bought or reserved（戏院、影院等的）售票处, 票房: [attrib 作定语] *The film was a box-office success*, ie It was financially successful because many people went to see it. 这部影片很卖座.

B

box[2] /bɒks; bɑks/ *v* **1** [I, Ipr, Tn] **~ (with/against sb)** fight (sb) with the fists, esp wearing padded gloves, as a sport 拳击(某人)(尤指戴拳击手套的运动): *Did you box at school?* 你在学校时练过拳击吗? **2** (idm 习语) **box sb's ears** hit sb on the ear with the open hand or fist（以掌或拳）打某人耳光: *He boxed the boy's ears for being cheeky.* 他打了这男孩儿耳光以教训其不懂羞耻.
▷ **box** *n* (usu *sing* 通常作单数) blow (usu on sb's ear) with the open hand or fist 掌击或拳击(通常指打耳光).
boxer *n* **1** person who boxes, esp as a sport 拳击者;（尤指）拳击运动员: *a heavyweight boxer* 重量级拳击手. **2** breed of dog like a bulldog but with longer legs 拳师犬（似斗牛狗而腿稍长）. ˈ**boxer shorts** man's loose-fitting underpants（男用宽松的）内裤衩.
box·ing *n* [U] sport of fighting with the fists 拳击(运动). ˈ**boxing-glove** *n* either of a pair of padded gloves worn for boxing 拳击手套. ⇨illus 见插图. ˈ**boxing-match** *n* fight between two boxers 拳击比赛.
box[3] /bɒks; bɑks/ *n* **1** [C, U] small evergreen shrub with thick dark leaves, used esp for garden hedges 黄杨. **2** (also ˈ**box·wood**) [U] hard wood of this shrub 黄杨木.
Box·ing Day /ˈbɒksɪŋ deɪ; ˈbɑksɪŋˌde/ the first weekday after Christmas Day 节礼日(圣诞节之后的第一个周日).
boy[1] /bɔɪ; bɔɪ/ *n* **1** [C] male child; son 男孩; 儿子: *The Joneses have two boys and a girl.* 琼斯一家有两个男孩儿一个女孩儿. ○ *His eldest boy is at university.* 他的长子上大学了. **2** [C] young man; lad; youth 小伙子; 少年; 青年: *He lived in Edinburgh as a boy.* 他年轻时住在爱丁堡. ○ *A group of boys were playing football in the street.* 一帮小伙子当时正在街上踢足球. ○ *How many boys are there in your class at school?* 你们班有多少男同学? **3** [C] (esp in compounds 尤用以构成复合词) boy or young man who does a specified job 从事某种职业的男童或小伙子: *the paper-boy*. **4 the boys** [pl] (*infml* 口) group of men who are friends and go out together 哥儿们: *a night out with the boys*, eg at a public house 与哥儿们在外泡了一夜(如在酒馆里) ○ *He plays football with the boys on Saturday afternoons.* 他星期六下午跟弟兄们踢足球. ○ *He likes to feel that he's one of the boys.* 他乐于把自己当成弟兄们的一分子. **5** [C] (*derog offensive* 贬, 蔑) (in some countries) male servant or labourer（某些国家的）男仆或男性劳工. **6** (idm 习语) **back-room boys** ⇨ BACK-ROOM (BACK[2]). **sb's blue-eyed boy** ⇨ BLUE[1]. **the boys in** ˈ**blue** (*Brit infml* 口) the police or a group of police officers 警方; 一群警察. ˌ**boys** ˌ**will be** ˈ**boys** (*saying* 谚) young boys, and also sometimes grown men, occasionally behave in a childish way, and this may be excused 孩子总归是孩子(男孩子, 甚至有些成年男子, 偶尔现出孩子气, 可以谅解). **jobs for the boys** ⇨ JOB[1]. **man and boy** ⇨ MAN. **sort out the men from the boys** ⇨ SORT[2].
▷ **boy·hood** *n* [U, C usu *sing* 通常作单数] state or time of being a boy（男子的）童年, 少年时期: *a happy, unhappy, lonely, etc boyhood*（指男子）幸福的、不幸的、孤独的...童年时期 ○ [attrib 作定语] *boyhood friends*（指男子）童年时代的朋友们.
boy·ish *adj* (*often approv* 常作褒义) of or like a boy 男孩子的; 男孩子般的: *boyish ambitions, hopes, enthusiasm* 男孩子的志向、愿望、热情 ○ *He/She has boyish good looks.* 他长得稚气可爱[她长得像个好看的男孩儿].
□ ˈ**boy-friend** *n* regular male companion of a girl or woman, with whom she is romantically or sexually involved 男朋友: *She had lots of boy-friends before she got married.* 她婚前有许多男朋友.
Boy ˈ**Scout** = SCOUT 2.
boy[2] /bɔɪ; bɔɪ/ *interj* (*infml* 口 *esp US*) (expressing surprise, pleasure, relief or contempt 表示惊奇、愉快、快慰或轻视): *Boy, am I glad to see you!* 啊, 见到你真高兴!
boy·cott /ˈbɔɪkɒt; ˈbɔɪˌkɑt/ *v* [Tn] (**a**) (usu of a group of people) refuse to have social or commercial relations with (a person, company, country, etc)（通常指一群人）拒绝与(某人、公司、国家等)交往或通商. (**b**) refuse to handle or buy (goods); refuse to take part in (eg a meeting) 拒绝处理或购买(货物); 拒绝参加(如会议); 抵制: *boycotting foreign imports* 抵制外国货物进口 ○ *Athletes from several countries boycotted the Olympic Games.* 有好几国的运动员抵制奥林匹克运动会.
▷ **boy·cott** *n* refusal to deal or trade with (a person, country, etc); refusal to handle (goods)（对与某人、某国等交往或贸易的）抵制;（对处理货物的）抵制: *place/put sth under a boycott* 对某事物实行抵制.
BP /ˌbiː ˈpiː; ˌbi ˈpi/ *abbr* 缩写 = British Petroleum 英国石油公司: *work for BP* 为英国石油公司工作.
BPC /ˌbiː piː ˈsiː; ˌbi pi ˈsi/ *abbr* 缩写 = (esp on labels of chemical products) British Pharmaceutical Codex（尤用于化学产品标签）英国副药典.
B Phil /ˌbiː ˈfɪl; ˌbi ˈfɪl/ *abbr* 缩写 = Bachelor of Philosophy 哲学学士: *have/be a B Phil* 有哲学学士学位[为哲学学士] ○ *Jill Green B Phil* 哲学学士吉尔·格林.
BR /ˌbiː ˈɑː(r); ˌbi ˈɑr/ *abbr* 缩写 = British Rail 英国铁路公司: *BR's Southern Region services* 英国铁路公司南部地区服务段.
Br *abbr* 缩写 = **1** British. **2** (*religion* 宗) Brother: *Br Peter* 彼得修士.
bra /brɑː; brɑ/ *n* = BRASSIÈRE.
brace[1] /breɪs; bres/ *n* **1** [C] device that clamps things together or holds and supports them in position 夹具; 支架; 支撑之物. Cf 参看 BIT[2] 2. **2** [C] wire device worn inside the mouth (esp by children) for straightening the teeth 牙箍(矫正牙齿的钢丝套, 尤为儿童所用): *My daughter has to wear a brace on her teeth.* 我的女儿得戴牙箍以矫正牙齿. **3 braces** [pl] (*US* **suspenders**) straps for holding trousers up, fastened to the waistband at the front and the back and passing over the shoulders 吊裤带; 背带: *a pair of braces* 一副背带. **4** [C] either of the two marks { and } used in printing or writing to show that words, etc between them are connected 大括号({ })之任何一边. Cf 参看 BRACKET.
□ ˌ**brace and** ˈ**bit** hand tool for boring holes, with a revolving handle and a removable drill 手摇曲柄钻.
brace[2] /breɪs; bres/ *n* (*pl* unchanged 复数不变) pair (esp of game birds) 一对, 一双(尤指作猎物的鸟): *two brace of partridge(s)* 两对山鹑.
brace[3] /breɪs; bres/ *v* **1** [Tn] (**a**) support (sth) with a brace[1](1) 用支架支住(某物): *The struts are firmly braced.* 构架的支柱很牢固. (**b**) make (sth) stronger or

firmer; reinforce 使(某物)更为坚固; 增强. **2** [Tn, Tn·pr] place (one's hand or foot) firmly in order to resist an impact or balance oneself 把(手或脚)支撑稳(以防冲撞或以保持身体平衡): *He braced his foot against the wall and jumped.* 他一只脚抵着墙跳. **3** [Tn, Tn·pr] **~ oneself (for sth)** steady or prepare oneself for sth difficult or unpleasant (针对困难的或令人不快的事物)稳住情绪或做好准备: *We braced ourselves for a bumpy landing.* 我们已做好准备, 着陆时会很颠簸. **4** (phr v) **brace up** (*esp US*) not become sad or dispirited, eg after a defeat or disappointment; take heart 振作起来; 打起精神.

▷ **brac·ing** *adj* (esp of weather conditions) invigorating; stimulating (尤指天气情况)令人振奋的, 给人带来活力的: *bracing sea air* 宜人的海滨空气 ○ *a bracing walk* 令人心神爽快的散步.

brace·let /ˈbreɪslɪt; ˋbreslɪt/ *n* ornamental band worn on the wrist or arm 手镯; 臂镯.

bracken /ˈbrækən; ˋbrækən/ *n* [U] (**a**) large fern growing on hillsides and heathland 欧洲蕨(一种大的蕨类植物, 生长在山坡和荒原上). (**b**) mass of such ferns 一簇欧洲蕨.

bracket /ˈbrækɪt; ˋbrækɪt/ *n* **1** (**a**) wooden or metal angle-shaped support fixed to or built into a wall to hold a shelf, etc 托架(木制或金属制, 固定在墙上以托住搁板等). (**b**) support on a wall for a lamp 墙壁上的灯架. **2** (usu *pl* 通常作复数) (in printing or writing) any one of the marks used in pairs for enclosing words, figures, etc to separate them from what precedes or follows, eg ( ) (*round brackets* or *parentheses*), [ ] (*square brackets*), < > (*angle brackets*), { } (*braces*) (印刷或书写中)括号(如圆括号( )、方括号[ ]、尖括号〈 〉、大括号{ }任何一对的一边): *Put your name in brackets at the top of each page.* 把你的名字填在每页上端的括号内. ⇨App 3 见附录3. **3** group or category within specified limits (有一定上下限的)分类, 档次: *be in the lower/higher income bracket* 属于低[高]收入等级 ○ *the 20-30 age bracket*, ie those people between the ages of 20 and 30 20-30岁的年龄组.

▷ **bracket** *v* **1** [Tn] support (sth) with a bracket (用托架)支撑(某物). **2** [Tn] (in printing or writing) enclose (words, figures, etc) in brackets (BRACKET 2) (印刷或书写中)把(词语、数字等)置于括号中. **3** [Tn, Tn·pr, Tn·p] **~ A and B (together); ~ A with B** group things or people in the same category (to suggest that they are similar, equal or connected in some way) 将事物或人置于同一范畴(以示相似、相同或相关): *It's wrong to bracket him with the extremists in his party — his views are very moderate.* 把他跟他们党内的极端分子等同看待是不对的——他的观点其实很温和.

brack·ish /ˈbrækɪʃ; ˋbrækɪʃ/ *adj* (of water) slightly salty (指水)略咸的.

bract /brækt; brækt/ *n* leaf-like and often brightly coloured part of a plant, growing below the flower (eg in bougainvillaea and poinsettia) 苞.

brad /bræd; bræd/ *n* thin flat nail with no head or a very small head 角钉, 无头钉(无头或头很小的).

brad·awl /ˈbrædɔːl; ˋbræd,ɔl/ *n* small hand-tool with a sharp point for boring holes 小锥子.

brae /breɪ; bre/ *n* (*Scot* 苏格兰) steep slope; hillside 陡坡; 山坡.

brag /bræg; bræg/ *v* (**-gg-**) [I, Ipr, Tf] **~ (about/of sth)** talk with too much pride (about sth); boast 吹嘘(某事物); 自夸: *Stop bragging!* 别吹牛! ○ *He's been bragging about his new car.* 他一直夸他的新汽车. ○ *She bragged that she could run faster than me.* 她夸口说她比我跑得快.

▷ **brag** *n* [U, C] boastful talk or statement 大话.

brag·gart /ˈbrægət; ˋbrægɚt/ *n* person who brags 吹牛者; 说大话者.

brah·min /ˈbrɑːmɪn; ˋbrɑmɪn/ (also **brah·man** /-ən; -ən/) *n* member of the highest or priestly Hindu caste 婆罗门(印度种姓制度中最高等级或僧侣阶级).

braid /breɪd; bred/ *n* **1** [U] number of threads of silk, cotton, etc woven together in a narrow band for decorating clothes and material 穗带(由丝线、棉线等编织而成, 用作衣物和料子的装饰): *The general's uniform was trimmed with gold braid.* 将官的制服饰有金色的穗带. **2** [C] (*US*) = PLAIT 发辫; 辫子: *She wears her hair in braids.* 她梳着辫子. ⇨illus at PLAIT 见 PLAIT 之插图.

▷ **braid** *v* [Tn] **1** decorate (clothes or material) with braid 用穗带装饰(衣物或料子): *She braided the neckline, hem and cuffs of the dress.* 她用穗带装饰连衣裙的领口、折边和袖口. **2** (*US*) = PLAIT 编成辫子: *She braids her hair every morning.* 她每天早晨都梳辫子.

B

Braille /breɪl; brel/ *n* [U] system of reading and writing for blind people, using raised dots to represent letters which can be read by touching them 盲文(供盲人阅读和书写用的凸点符号).

brain /breɪn; bren/ *n* **1** [C] organ of the body that controls thought, memory and feeling, consisting of a mass of soft grey matter inside the head 脑: *a disease of the brain* 脑部疾患 ○ *The brain is the centre of the nervous system.* 脑是神经系统的中枢. ○ [attrib 作定语] *brain surgery* 脑外科. **2** [U, C often *pl* 常作复数] mind or intellect; intelligence 头脑; 智力: *He has very little brain.* 他没有什么头脑. ○ *She has an excellent brain.* 她很有头脑. ○ *You need brains to become a university professor.* 当大学教授要有才智. ○ *He has one of the best brains in the university.* 他是这所大学里才智出众的人. **3** (**a**) [C] (*infml* 口) clever person; intellectual 聪明人; 知识分子: *He is one of the leading brains in the country.* 他是国家的知识分子精英. (**b**) **the brains** [sing *v*] (*infml* 口) cleverest person in a group 智力超群的人: *He's the brains of the family.* 他是全家最聪明的人. ○ *She was the brains behind the whole scheme.* 她是整个方案背后的主脑. **4** (idm 习语) **blow one's brains out** ⇨ BLOW[1]. **cudgel one's brains** ⇨ CUDGEL. **have sth on the brain** (*infml* 口) think about sth constantly; be obsessed by sth 一心想着某事物; 对某事物入迷: *I've had this tune on the brain all day but I can't remember what it's called.* 我脑海里整天回荡着这个曲调, 但我想不起来叫什么了. **pick sb's brains** ⇨ PICK[3]. **rack one's brain(s)** ⇨ RACK[2]. **tax one's/sb's brains** ⇨ TAX.

▷ **brain** *v* [Tn] kill (a person or an animal) with a heavy blow on the head (猛击头部)打死(人或动物): (*fig infml* 比喻, 口) *I nearly brained myself on that low beam.* 那低矮的横梁险些把我的头撞碎.

brain·less *adj* stupid; foolish 没有头脑的; 愚蠢的; 傻的: *That was a pretty brainless thing to do.* 那样做很愚蠢.

brainy *adj* (**-ier, -iest**) (*infml* 口) clever; intelligent 聪明的; 有智慧的: *Her children are all very brainy.* 她的孩子个个都很聪明.

□ ˈ**brain-child** *n* [sing] person's original plan, invention or idea 某人的构想、构思、发明或创见: *The new arts centre is the brain-child of a wealthy local businessman.* 这座新艺术馆是根据当地一位富商的构想而修建的.

ˈ**brain-drain** *n* (usu *sing* 通常作单数) (*infml* 口) loss to a country when skilled and clever people emigrate from it to other countries 人才外流.

ˈ**brain fever** inflammation of the brain 脑膜炎.

ˈ**brainpower** *n* [U] ability to think; intelligence 智力; 智能.

ˈ**brain-teaser** *n* difficult problem; puzzle 困难问题; 难题.

ˈ**brains trust** (*US* **brain trust**) group of experts who answer questions and give advice, eg on a radio programme (提供咨询服务的)专家小组(如于电台节目中的); 智囊团.

brain·storm /ˈbreɪnstɔːm; ˋbren,stɔrm/ *n* **1** sudden violent mental disturbance 突发性精神错乱. **2** (*Brit infml* 口) moment of confusion or forgetfulness; sudden mental aberration 一时糊涂、忘记或想不起来; 突然的神智不清: *I must have had a brainstorm — I couldn't remember my own telephone number for a moment.* 我一定是糊涂了——一时想不起自己的电话号码了. **3** (*US infml* 口) = BRAINWAVE.

brain·storm·ing /ˈbreɪnstɔːmɪŋ; ˋbren,stɔrmɪŋ/ *n* [U] (*esp US*) method of solving problems in which all the members of a group suggest ideas which are then discussed 群策群力, 通力攻关(大家献计献策, 通过集体讨论解决问题): [attrib 作定语] *a brainstorming session* 通力攻关会.

brain·wash /ˈbreɪnwɒʃ; ˋbren,wɔʃ/ *v* [Tn, Tn·pr] **~ sb (into doing sth)** force sb to reject old beliefs or ideas and to accept new ones by the use of extreme mental pressure 洗脑(以极大的精神压力迫使某人放弃旧的信念或思想而接受新的一套): (*fig* 比喻) *I refuse to be brainwashed by advertisers into buying something I don't need.* 我可不让广告商给我洗脑, 去买那些我不需要的东西. ▷ **brain·wash·ing** *n* [U].

B

brain·wave /ˈbreɪnweɪv; ˋbrenˌwev/ (*US* **brainstorm**) *n* (*infml* 口) sudden clever idea 灵机; 灵感脑波: *Unless someone has a brainwave we'll never solve this problem.* 除非谁能灵机一动拿出主意, 否则我们永远解决不了这个问题.

braise /breɪz; brez/ *v* [Tn] cook (meat or vegetables) slowly with very little liquid in a closed container 炖(肉或蔬菜); 焖; 煨: *braised beef and onions* 炖洋葱牛肉 ○ *braising steak*, ie steak to be braised 用来炖的肉排.

brake[1] /breɪk; brek/ *n* (**a**) device for reducing the speed of or stopping a car, bicycle, train, etc 制动器; 闸; 刹车: *put on/apply the brake(s)* 使用制动器 ○ *His brakes failed on a steep hill.* 他的车闸在陡峭的山路上失灵了. ○ (*fig* 比喻) *The Government is determined to put a brake on public spending.* 政府决定遏制公共事务的开支. ○ *Ignorance acts as a brake to progress.* 无知阻碍了进步. ⇨illus at App 1 见附录1之插图, page xiii. (**b**) pedal, etc that operates such a device 制动器的踏板等: *The brake (pedal) is between the clutch and the accelerator.* 制动器(踏板)在离合器和加速器之间. ⇨illus at App 1 见附录1之插图, page xii.

▷ **brake** *v* [I, Tn] (cause sth to) slow down using a brake 用制动器(使某物)减速; 刹(车): *The driver braked hard as the child ran onto the road in front of him.* 那孩子跑到汽车前面的路上, 司机猛踩刹车.

□ ˈ**brake fluid** liquid used in hydraulic brakes 制动液(液压制动器所用的液体).

ˈ**brake light** (*US* ˈ**stoplight**) red light at the back of a car, etc which lights up when the brakes are applied 制动灯, 刹车灯(汽车等刹车时尾部亮起的红灯).

brake-ˈhorsepower *n* [U] power of an engine measured by the force needed to brake it 制动马力; 刹车马力.

ˈ**brake-shoe** *n* curved block or plate that presses against a wheel to brake it 闸瓦; 制动片; 刹车片.

brake[2] /breɪk; brek/ *n* area of brushwood, thick undergrowth or bracken; thicket 矮丛林地带; 灌木丛.

bramble /ˈbræmbl; ˋbræmbḷ/ *n* wild shrub with long prickly shoots; blackberry bush 荆棘; 黑莓灌木丛.

bran /bræn; bræn/ *n* [U] outer covering of grain separated from the flour by sifting 糠; 麸. Cf 参看 HUSK 1.

□ ˈ**bran-tub** *n* (*Brit*) tub containing bran or sawdust in which small gifts are hidden; lucky dip 糠桶(装有糠或锯末的摸彩桶, 内藏小件礼物).

branch /brɑːntʃ; *US* bræntʃ; bræntʃ/ *n* **1** arm-like division of a tree, growing from the trunk or from a bough 树枝: *He climbed up the tree and hid among the branches.* 他爬上树, 藏在树枝后面. ⇨illus at App 1 见附录1之插图, page i. **2** similar division of a river, road, railway or mountain range (河流、公路、铁路或山脉的)类似分支: *a branch of the Rhine* 莱茵河的支流 ○ [attrib 作定语] *a branch line*, ie a division of a main railway line, serving country areas 支线(铁路干线通往乡村的分支). **3** subdivision of a family, a subject of knowledge, or a group of languages (家族的)分支; (知识的)分科; (语言的)分系: *His uncle's branch of the family emigrated to Australia.* 他的家族中叔父这一支系已移居澳大利亚. ○ *Gynaecology is a branch of medicine.* 妇科学是医学的一个分科. **4** local office or shop belonging to a large firm or organization (属于某大公司或机构的)地方办事处或分店: *The bank has branches in all parts of the country.* 该银行在全国各地设有分行. ○ [attrib 作定语] *a branch post office* 邮局的分局. **5** (idm 习语) **root and branch** ⇨ ROOT[1].

▷ **branch** *v* [I] **1** (of a tree) send out or divide into branches (指树)长出枝, 分出枝杈. **2** (of a road) divide into branches (指道路)分岔: *The road branches after the level-crossing.* 这条路在经过平面交叉道口后岔开了. **3** (phr v) **branch ˈoff** (of a vehicle or road) turn from one road into a (usu) smaller one (指车辆或大路)转入或转为(通常为)小路: *The car in front of us suddenly branched off to the left.* 我们前面的那辆汽车突然转入左边的小路上去了. ○ *The road to the village branches off on the right.* 通往该村的道路向右转为一条小路. **branch ˈout (into sth)** extend or expand one's activities or interests in a new direction 向新的方向扩展自己的活动或兴趣: *The company began by specializing in radios but has now decided to branch out into computers.* 该公司开始时专营无线电器材, 现在已决定扩展业务经营计算机了. ○ *She's leaving the company to branch out on her own.* 她打算脱离这家公司, 自己开业.

brand /brænd; brænd/ *n* **1** (**a**) particular make of goods or their trade mark 商品的牌子; 商标: *Which brand of toothpaste do you prefer?* 你爱用什么牌子的牙膏? ○ [attrib 作定语] *a ˈbrand name* 商标名称 ○ *brand loyalty*, ie tendency of customers to continue buying the same brand 对某商标的信赖(顾客购买同一牌子商品的倾向). (**b**) particular type or kind 特殊的种类: *a strange brand of humour* 一种古怪的幽默. **2** piece of burning wood 燃烧着的木头. **3** (**a**) mark of identification (esp on cattle and sheep) made with a hot iron 烙印(尤指打在牛羊身上的). (**b**) (also ˈ**branding-iron**) iron used for this (作上述用的)烙铁. ⇨illus at IRON 见 IRON 之插图.

▷ **brand** *v* **1** [Tn, Tn·pr] **~ sth (on sth)** mark sth with or as if with a brand(3a) (似)在某事物上打烙印: *On big farms cattle are usually branded.* 大农场里的牛通常打有烙印. ○ (*fig* 比喻) *The experiences of his unhappy childhood are branded on his memory.* 他童年的不幸遭遇铭刻在他的记忆里. **2** [Tn, Cn·n, Cn·n/a] **~ sb (as sth)** give a bad name to sb; denounce sb 给某人加上污名; 谴责某人: *The scandal branded him for life.* 这件丑事使他终生蒙受耻辱. ○ *He was branded (as) a trouble-maker for taking part in the demonstration.* 他因参加了示威游行而被指责为捣乱分子.

□ ˌ**brand-ˈnew** *adj* completely new 全新的; 崭新的.

ˈ**branding-iron** *n* = BRAND 3b.

bran·dish /ˈbrændɪʃ; ˋbrændɪʃ/ *v* [Tn] wave (sth) in a triumphant or threatening way; display 得意地或威胁地挥动(某物); 显示: *brandish a gun, a knife, an axe, etc* 挥舞枪、刀子、斧头等 ○ *The demonstrators brandished banners and shouted slogans.* 示威者挥舞着旗帜, 呼喊着口号.

brandy /ˈbrændɪ; ˋbrændɪ/ *n* (**a**) [U] strong alcoholic drink distilled from wine or fermented fruit-juice 白兰地. (**b**) [C] type of brandy 一种白兰地: *Cognac and Armagnac are fine brandies.* 科尼亚克和阿马尼亚克是两种优质白兰地. (**c**) [C] glass of brandy 一杯白兰地: *Two brandies and soda, please.* 劳驾, 来两杯白兰地加苏打水.

□ ˈ**brandy-snap** *n* crisp rolled gingerbread wafer, often filled with cream 白兰地小脆饼(常有奶油夹层).

brash /bræʃ; bræʃ/ *adj* (*derog* 贬) **1** (of a person, his manner, etc) confident in a rude or aggressive way; impudently self-assertive (指人、态度等)粗鲁而自信的, 盛气凌人的, 自以为是的: *His brash answers annoyed the interviewers.* 他回答问题自以为是, 面试的人感到很不痛快. **2** (of colours, clothing, etc) loud; garish; showy (指颜色、衣服等)花哨的, 俗气的: *He was wearing a rather brash tie.* 他系着一条颇为显眼的领带. ▷ **brashly** *adv*. **brash·ness** *n* [U].

brass /brɑːs; *US* bræs; bræs/ *n* **1** [U] bright yellow metal made by mixing copper and zinc 黄铜: [attrib 作定语] *brass doorknobs, buttons* 黄铜的门把手、钮扣 ○ *a brass foundry* 黄铜铸造厂. **2** (**a**) [U] objects made of brass, eg candlesticks, ornaments, etc 黄铜制品(如烛台、饰物等): *do/clean/polish the brass* 处理[擦净/擦亮]黄铜器. (**b**) [C] brass ornament worn by a horse 马戴的黄铜饰物. **3 the brass** [Gp] (group of people in an orchestra who play) wind instruments made of brass (乐队中的)铜管乐器(组): *The brass is/are too loud.* 铜管乐的声音过大. ⇨illus at App 1 见附录1之插图, page x. **4** [C] (*esp Brit*) brass memorial tablet fixed to the floor or wall of a church (教堂的地上或墙上的)黄铜纪念牌. **5** [U] (*Brit sl* 俚) money 钱: *He's got plenty of brass.* 他很有钱. **6** [U] (*infml* 口) impudence; cheek 厚颜无耻; 厚脸皮: *He had the brass to ask his boss for a 20% pay rise.* 他厚着脸皮要求老板给他增加20%的工资. **7** (idm 习语) **bold as brass** ⇨ BOLD. **get down to brass ˈtacks** (*infml* 口) start to consider the basic facts or practical details of sth 开始考虑某事物的基本事实

或具体细节. **top brass** ⇨ TOP[1].

▷ **brassy** *adj* (**-ier, -iest**) **1** like brass in colour 黄铜色的. **2** like a brass musical instrument in sound; harsh; blaring 声如铜管乐器的; 刺耳的; 嘹亮的. **3** (esp of a woman, her manner, etc) vulgarly showy and impudent; loud and flashy (尤指女人、其举止等)俗不可耐的, 无耻招摇的, 花里胡哨的. **brass·ily** *adv*. **brassi·ness** *n* [U].

□ ˌ**brass** ˈ**band** band playing brass and percussion instruments only 铜管乐队.

ˌ**brass** ˈ**hat** (*infml* 口 *esp Brit*) high-ranking officer in the army; any important person 高级军官; 要员.

brass ˈ**knuckles** (*US*) = KNUCKLEDUSTER (KNUCKLE).

ˌ**brass** ˈ**plate** plate of brass displayed outside a house or office, giving the name and profession of the occupant 黄铜门牌.

ˈ**brass-rubbing** *n* **1** [U] making a copy of the design on a brass(4) by rubbing a piece of paper placed over it with chalk or wax (用粉笔或蜡笔在覆盖于黄铜纪念牌上的纸上涂画以)拓印图案. **2** [C] copy made in this way (使用上述方法制成的)拓印品.

bras·serie /ˈbræsərɪ; ˌbræsəˈri/ *n* type of restaurant serving esp beer with food (以售啤酒为主的)餐馆.

bras·si·ère /ˈbræsɪə(r); *US* brəˈzɪər; brəˈzɪr/ (also **bra** /brɑː; brɑ/) *n* woman's undergarment worn to support the breasts 乳罩.

brat /bræt; bræt/ *n* (*derog* 贬) child, esp a badly-behaved one 孩子; (尤指)顽童.

bra·vado /brəˈvɑːdəʊ; brəˈvɑdo/ *n* [U] (usu unnecessary or false) display of boldness (通常指无必要的或虚伪的)逞能, 虚张声势: *Take no notice of his threats — they're sheer bravado.* 别理会他的威胁——完全是虚张声势.

brave /breɪv; brev/ *adj* (**-r, -st**) **1** (of a person) ready to face and endure danger, pain or suffering; having no fear; courageous (指人)勇敢的; 无畏的; 有勇气的: *brave men and women* 勇敢的男男女女 ○ *Be brave!* 勇敢些! ○ *It was brave of her to go into the burning building.* 她进入了燃烧着的大楼, 真勇敢. ○ *He was very brave about his operation.* 他对手术毫无惧色. **2** (of an action) requiring or showing courage (指行为)需要勇气的, 表现勇敢的: *a brave act, deed, speech* 有勇气的举动、行为、讲话 ○ *a brave fight against disease* 与疾病进行的毫不畏惧的斗争. **3** (idm 习语) **(a) brave new world** (*catchphrase often ironic* 警语, 常作反语) a new era resulting from revolutionary changes, reforms, etc in society 美好的新世界(社会经历革命、改革等之后的新时期).

▷ **brave** *n* **1** [C] N American Indian warrior 北美洲的印第安战士. **2 the brave** [pl *v*] brave people 勇敢的人: *the brave who died in battle* 阵亡的英勇战士.

brave *v* **1** [Tn] endure or face (sth/sb) without showing fear 以无畏的精神忍受或面对(某事物[某人]): *brave dangers* 冒着危险 ○ *brave one's critics* 勇于面对批评 ○ *We decided to brave* (ie go out in spite of) *the bad weather.* 尽管天气不好, 我们仍决定要出去. **2** (phr v) **brave it** ˈ**out** face hostility, suspicion or blame defiantly 对含敌意、猜疑或责难的言行持对抗态度: *He tried to brave it out when the police questioned him.* 警察盘问他时, 他想硬着头皮顶过去.

bravely *adv*.

bravery /ˈbreɪvərɪ; ˈbrevərɪ/ *n* [U] being brave; courage 勇气; 胆量: *a medal for bravery in battle* 授予在战斗中表现英勇者的奖章.

bravo /ˌbrɑːˈvəʊ; ˈbrɑvo/ *interj*, *n* (*pl* **~s**) shout of approval, esp to an actor or a performer 喝彩声(尤用以称赞演员或表演者): *Bravo! Well played!* 好哇! 演得好哇!

bra·vura /brəˈvʊərə; brəˈvjʊrə/ *n* [U] (in a musical performance) brilliant style or technique (音乐演奏中)优美的风格或精湛的技巧: [attrib 作定语] *a bravura performance* 精彩的演奏.

brawl /brɔːl; brɔl/ *n* noisy quarrel or fight 大声争吵; 打架: *a drunken brawl in a bar* 在酒吧间里醉汉的吵闹.

▷ **brawl** *v* [I] take part in a brawl 打闹: *gangs of youths brawling in the street* 在街上打打闹闹的一帮青年. **brawler** *n*.

brawn /brɔːn; brɔn/ *n* [U] **1** strong muscles; muscular strength 强壮的肌肉; 强健的体力: *a job needing brains* (ie intelligence) *rather than brawn* 需用脑力而非体力的工作. **2** (*Brit*) (*US* **head cheese**) meat, esp from a pig's or calf's head, boiled, chopped and pressed in a mould with jelly 肉冻(尤指猪的或牛犊的头肉, 煮熟切碎加果胶或明胶模压而成).

▷ **brawny** *adj* (**-ier, -iest**) strong and muscular 强壮的; 肌肉发达的: *brawny arms* 肌肉发达的胳膊.

bray /breɪ; bre/ *n* (**a**) cry of a donkey 驴叫声. (**b**) sound like this 似驴叫的声音.

▷ **bray** *v* [I] make this cry or sound (驴)叫; 发出似驴叫的声音: *a braying laugh* 粗声大笑.

brazen /ˈbreɪzn; ˈbreznؚ/ *adj* **1** (*derog* 贬) shameless; insolent 无耻的; 无礼的: *brazen insolence, rudeness, etc* 不知羞耻的无礼举动、粗野举动等 ○ *a brazen hussy* 恬不知耻的荡妇. **2** (**a**) made of brass; like brass 黄铜制的; 黄铜般的. (**b**) having a harsh brassy sound 声音响亮刺耳的: *the brazen notes of a trumpet* 喇叭的响亮的声音.

▷ **brazen** *v* (phr v) **brazen it** ˈ**out** behave, after doing wrong, as if one has nothing to be ashamed of (做错事以后)显出若无其事的样子.

brazenly *adv* shamelessly 厚颜无耻地.

bra·zier /ˈbreɪzɪə(r); ˈbreʒɚ/ *n* open metal framework for holding a charcoal or coal fire (金属的)火盆.

breach /briːtʃ; britʃ/ *n* **1** [C, U] breaking or neglect (of a law, an agreement, a duty, etc) 违犯, 违反(法规、协议、职责等): *a breach of loyalty, trust, protocol, etc* 不忠、背信、背约等 ○ *a breach of confidence*, ie giving away a secret 泄密 ○ *sue sb for breach of contract* 控告某人违反合同 ○ *a breach of security*, ie failure to protect official secrets 破坏安全的行为(泄露政府机密). **2** [C] break in usu friendly relations between people or groups (友好关系的)中断: *a breach of diplomatic relations between two countries* 两国之间外交关系的破裂. **3** [C] opening, eg one made in a wall by attacking forces or the sea 缺口(如墙上或堤上的突破口): *The huge waves made a breach in the sea wall.* 大浪在堤上冲出一个缺口. **4** (idm 习语) **step into the breach** ⇨ STEP[1].

▷ **breach** *v* [Tn] make a gap in (a defensive wall, etc) (在防御工事等上)打开缺口: *Our tanks have breached the enemy defences.* 我方坦克突破了敌人的防线.

□ ˌ**breach of** ˈ**promise** (*law* 律) (formerly) breaking of a promise to marry sb (旧时)悔婚.

ˌ**breach of the** ˈ**peace** (*law* 律) crime of causing a public disturbance, eg by fighting in the street 扰乱治安罪(如在街上斗殴).

bread 面包

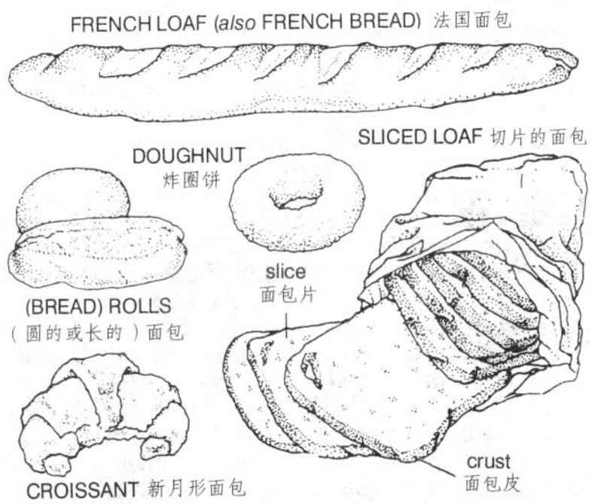

bread /bred; brɛd/ *n* [U] **1** food made of flour, water and usu yeast, kneaded and then baked 面包: *a loaf/slice/piece of bread* 一条[片/块]面包 ○ *brown/white bread* 黑[白]面包. ⇨illus 见插图. **2** (*sl* 俚) money 钱. **3** (idm 习语) ˌ**bread and** ˈ**water** plainest possible food 简单的饮食: *I had to live on bread and water when I was a student.* 我上大学时只能靠粗茶淡饭过活. **cast one's bread upon the water(s)** ⇨ CAST[1]. **one's daily bread** ⇨ DAILY. **half a loaf is better than none/than no bread** ⇨ HALF. **know which side**

one's bread is buttered ⇨ KNOW. **take the bread out of sb's ˈmouth** take away sb's means of earning a living 使某人无以为生; 砸某人的饭碗.
▷ **breaded** *adj* (of meat or fish) sprinkled with breadcrumbs for cooking (指肉或鱼)(为烹饪用)撒上面包屑的.
□ **bread and butter** /ˌbred n ˈbʌtə(r); ˈbrɛdṇˈbʌtɚ/ **1** slices of bread spread with butter 抹黄油的面包片. **2** (*infml* 口) (way of earning) one's living 生活; 生计; 谋生之道: *Acting is his bread and butter.* 演戏就是他的饭碗. ○ *How does he earn his bread and butter?* 他怎样谋生? ○ [attrib 作定语] *Jobs, pensions and housing are the bread-and-butter issues of politics*, ie the basic ones. 就业、养老金和住房问题是和政治有关的基本问题. **3** (idm 习语) **a bread-and-ˈbutter letter** letter thanking a host or hostess for hospitality 感谢款待的信.
ˈ**bread-bin** *n* container for keeping loaves of bread in 面包盒; 面包箱.
ˈ**breadboard** *n* board of wood, etc for cutting bread on 切面包板.
ˈ**breadcrumbs** *n* [pl] tiny pieces of bread, usu from the inner part of a loaf 面包屑(通常得自面包瓤): *fish covered with breadcrumbs and then fried* 裹上面包屑后煎炸的鱼.

bread-fruit /ˈbredfruːt; ˈbrɛdˌfrut/ *n* [C, U] round edible tropical fruit with white starchy pulp 面包果(一种可食的圆形热带水果, 果肉白色, 含淀粉).

bread·line /ˈbredlaɪn; ˈbrɛdˌlaɪn/ *n* **1** queue of people waiting for free food given as charity 等候领救济食品的队伍. **2** (idm 习语) **on the breadline** very poor 极其穷困: *We've been living on the breadline for weeks.* 几个星期以来我们一直吃了上顿没下顿.

breadth /bredθ; brɛdθ/ *n* **1** [U, C] distance or measurement from side to side; width 宽度: *a garden, room, river ten metres in breadth* 十米宽的花园、房间、河流 ○ *pieces of material of different breadths* 宽度不一的料子. ⇨illus at DIMENSION 见 DIMENSION 之插图. **2** [U] wide extent (eg of knowledge); range 宽广的程度(如指知识); 范围: *Her breadth of experience makes her ideal for the job.* 她经验丰富, 最能胜任这项工作. **3** [U] freedom from narrow-mindedness or prejudice 宽宏大量的; 不抱偏见的: *show breadth of mind, outlook, opinions, etc* 在思想、观点、见解等方面表现宽宏大度. **4** (idm 习语) **by a hair/a hair's breadth** ⇨ HAIR. **the length and breadth of sth** ⇨ LENGTH.

bread-winner /ˈbredwɪnə(r); ˈbrɛdˌwɪnɚ/ *n* person whose earnings support his or her family 养家活口者: *Mum's the bread-winner in our family.* 妈妈养活我们全家.

break[1] /breɪk; brek/ *v* (*pt* **broke** /brəʊk; brok/, *pp* **broken** /ˈbrəʊkən; ˈbrokən/) **1** (**a**) [I, Ipr] **~ (in/into sth)** (of a whole object) separate into two or more parts as a result of force or strain (but not by cutting) (指完整物体)破, 碎, 断(非切割所致): *The string broke.* 绳子断了. ○ *Glass breaks easily.* 玻璃容易破碎. ○ *The bag broke under the weight of the shopping inside it.* 买的东西太重, 把袋子撑破了. ○ *She dropped the plate and it broke into pieces/in two.* 她把盘子摔碎[两半]了. (**b**) [Tn, Tn·pr] **~ sth (in/into sth)** cause (a whole object) to do this 弄破, 弄碎, 弄断(完整物体): *break a cup, vase, window, etc* 打破杯子、花瓶、窗户等 ○ *She fell off a ladder and broke her arm.* 她从梯子上摔下来, 跌断了胳膊. ○ *If you pull too hard you will break the rope.* 如果太用力拉, 就会把绳子拉断. ○ *He broke the bar of chocolate into two (pieces).* 他把巧克力掰成两半. **2** [I, Tn] become unusable by being damaged; make (sth) unusable by damaging 已坏; 损坏(某物): *My watch is broken.* 我的表坏了. **3** [Tn] cut the surface of (the skin) so as to cause bleeding 弄破(皮肤)表面以致出血: *The dog bit me but didn't break the skin.* 那狗咬了我一口, 但是没有把皮咬破. **4** [Tn] not follow or obey (sth); fail to observe (a law, promise, etc) 不依从或不服从(某事物); 不遵守(法律、诺言等): *break the law, the rules, the conditions, etc* 违反法律、规则、所定条件等 ○ *break an agreement, a contract, a promise, one's word, etc* 违反协议、合同、诺言、自己说的话等 ○ *break an appointment*, ie fail to come to it 爽约(未能赴约) ○ *He was breaking the speed limit*, ie travelling faster than the law allows. 他违章超速行驶. **5** [I, Ip] **~ (off)** stop doing sth for a while; pause 稍停; 停顿: *Let's break for tea.* 咱们停一停, 喝点儿茶. **6** [Tn] (**a**) destroy the continuity of (sth); interrupt 中断(某事物); 打断: *break sb's concentration* 分散某人的注意力 ○ *We broke our journey (to London) at Oxford*, ie stopped in Oxford on the way to London. 我们在牛津中止了(去伦敦的)行程. ○ *a broken night's sleep*, ie a night during which the sleeper keeps waking 夜间断断续续的睡眠 ○ *He failed to break (his opponent's) service*, ie to win a game (at tennis, etc) when his opponent was serving. 他未能破(对方的)发球局(如网球等). (**b**) interrupt the flow of an electric current in (a circuit) 使(电路)电流中断. (**c**) cause (sth) to be incomplete 使(某事物)不完整: *break a set of books, china, etc*, eg by giving away a part or parts of it 拆散整套的书、瓷器等(如将其中某部分送人而不能成套). (**d**) cause (sth) to end 终止(某事物): *She broke the silence by coughing.* 她的咳嗽声打破了沉寂. (**e**) bring (sth) to an end by force 强行制止(某事物): *break a blockade/siege* 突破封锁[包围] ○ *The employers have not broken the dockers' strike.* 资方未能使码头工人结束罢工. **7** [I] (of the weather) change suddenly after a settled period (指天气)(持续一段时间之后)突然起变化: *The fine weather/The heatwave broke at last.* 好天气[热天气]终于突然转变了. **8** [I] show an opening; disperse 出现缝隙; 消散: *The clouds broke and the sun came out.* 云一散开, 太阳就出来了. **9** [I] (**a**) come into being 形成: *Dawn/The day was breaking*, ie Daylight was beginning. 天已破晓. Cf 参看 DAYBREAK (DAY). (**b**) begin suddenly and violently 突然而激烈地开始: *The storm broke.* 暴风雨突然来临. (**c**) become known; be revealed 传开; 被揭露: *There was a public outcry when the scandal broke.* 丑闻传开后引起了公愤. **10** (**a**) [Tn] weaken or destroy (sth) 减弱或毁坏(某事物): *break sb's morale, resistance, resolve, spirit, etc* 瓦解某人的士气、抵抗力、决心、精神等 ○ *The Government is determined to break the power of the trade unions.* 政府决心摧毁工会的势力. ○ *The scandal broke him*, ie ruined his reputation and destroyed his self-confidence. 这一丑闻把他毁了. (**b**) [I] become weak or be destroyed 减弱; 被毁坏: *Throughout the ordeal his spirit never broke.* 经历了这场苦难, 他的精神并未垮. ○ *He broke under questioning* (ie was no longer able to endure it) *and confessed to everything.* 他经受不住盘问, 精神上垮了下来, 于是供认了一切. (**c**) [Tn] overwhelm (sb) with a strong emotion, eg grief 使(某人)难以承受(强烈感情, 如悲伤): *The death of his wife broke him completely.* 他妻子逝世使他肝肠寸断. **11** [I] (**a**) (of the voice) change its tone because of emotion (指嗓音)(因激动)变调: *Her voice broke as she told the dreadful news.* 她说出这可怕的消息时, 嗓音都变了. (**b**) (of a boy's voice) become deeper at puberty (指男孩的声音)青春期时变低沉: *His voice broke when he was thirteen.* 他十三岁的时候嗓音变粗了. **12** [Tn] do better than or surpass (a record) 打破(纪录): *break the Commonwealth/World/Olympic 100 metres record* 打破英联邦[世界/奥林匹克]100米纪录. **13** [I] (of the ball in cricket) change direction after hitting the ground; spin (指板球)着地后改变方向, 旋转. **14** [I] (of the sea) curl and fall in waves (指海洋)浪涛冲撞: *the sound of waves breaking on the beach* 波涛冲撞着海滩的声音 ○ *The sea was breaking over the wrecked ship.* 海水冲撞着破船的残骸. **15** [Tn] decipher (sth); solve 译解(某事物); 破译: *break a code* 译解密码. **16** (For idioms containing **break**, see entries for *ns, adjs*, etc 习语中有 **break** 者, 见有关名词、形容词等词条, 如 **break even** ⇨ EVEN[1]; **break sb's heart** ⇨ HEART.) **17** (phr v) **break away (from sb/sth)** (**a**) escape suddenly (from captivity) 突然逃脱, 挣脱(束缚): *The prisoner broke away from his guards.* 囚犯从看守者手中逃脱了. (**b**) leave a political party, state, etc, esp to form a new one 脱离某政党、政府等(尤指另建新组织): *Several Labour MPs broke away to join the Social Democrats.* 有些工党下议院议员脱党后加入社会民主党. ○ *A province has broken away to form a new state.* 有一个省脱离了旧政府而另组新政府.
break down (**a**) cease to function because of a mechanical, electrical, etc fault (因机械、电力等故障)停止运转, 失灵, 失效: *The telephone system has broken down.* 电话系统失灵了. ○ *We* (ie Our car) *broke down on the motorway.* 我们(的汽车)在高速公路上抛锚了.

(b) fail; collapse 失败; 崩溃; 瓦解; 垮: *Negotiations between the two sides have broken down.* 双方谈判已经破裂. ○ *If law and order break down, anarchy will result.* 法治一垮, 就会出现无政府状态. **(c)** (of sb's health) become very bad; collapse (指某人健康状况)变得恶劣; 垮: *Her health broke down under the pressure of work.* 工作的压力把她的身体弄垮了. **(d)** lose control of one's feelings 感情失去控制: *He broke down and wept when he heard the news.* 他听到这个消息时不禁痛哭起来.

break (sth) down (esp of money spent) be divided or divide into parts by analysis (尤指金钱花费)分成几部分, 细分: *Expenditure on the project breaks down as follows: wages £10m, plant £4m, raw materials £5m.* 该工程费用开支可分成如下几部分: 工资一千万英镑, 厂房设备四百万英镑, 原料五百万英镑. **break sth down** **(a)** make sth collapse by striking it hard 猛击某物使之毁坏: *Firemen had to break the door down to reach the people trapped inside.* 消防人员须破门而人, 才能抢救困在屋里的人. **(b)** cause sth to collapse; overcome, conquer or destroy sth 使某事物瓦解; 镇压、克服、破坏某事物: *break down resistance, opposition, etc* 镇压抵抗、反抗等 ○ *break down sb's reserve, shyness, etc* 克服某人的沉默、羞怯等心态 ○ *How can we break down the barriers of fear and hostility which divide the two communities?* 怎样才能消除这两地区人民之间的恐惧和仇恨呢? **(c)** change the chemical composition of sth 改变某物的化学成分: *Sugar and starch are broken down in the stomach.* 糖和淀粉在胃里被分解.

break sth from sth remove sth from sth larger by breaking 折断某物以除去其中某部分: *He broke a piece of bread from the loaf.* 他从长条面包中掰下一小块.

break in enter a building by force 强行进入屋内: *Burglars had broken in while we were away on holiday.* 我们假日外出时, 窃贼曾进入屋内. **break sb/sth in** train and discipline sb/sth 训练某人[某物]: *break in new recruits, a young horse* 训练新兵、驯服小马. **break in (on sth)** interrupt or disturb (sth) 打断, 干扰(某事物): *Please don't break in on our conversation.* 请别打断我们的谈话.

break into sth **(a)** enter sth by force 强行进入某处: *His house was broken into* (eg by burglars) *last week.* 上星期有人闯入他的房屋(如窃贼). **(b)** suddenly begin (to laugh, sing, cheer, etc) 突然开始(大笑、唱歌、欢呼等): *As the President's car arrived, the crowd broke into loud applause.* 总统的汽车到达时, 群众中爆发出热烈的掌声. **(c)** suddenly change (from a slower to a faster pace) 突然改变(由慢到快): *break into a trot/canter/gallop* (马)突然改成小跑[慢跑/飞跑] ○ *The man broke into a run when he saw the police.* 那人一见到警察, 拔腿就跑. **(d)** (of an activity) use up (time that would normally be spent doing sth else) (指活动)用去(应做其他事情的时间): *All this extra work I'm doing is breaking into my leisure time.* 我目前的这一切额外工作用去了我的闲暇时间. **(e)** use (a banknote or coin of high value) to buy sth costing less 使用(大面值的钞票或硬币)购买低于该面值的某事物: *I can't pay the 50p I owe you without breaking into a £5 note.* 我得把一张5英镑的钞票破开, 才能把欠你的50便士付给你. **(f)** open and use (sth kept for an emergency) 动用(应急储备物资): *break into emergency supplies of food* 动用应急储备的食物.

break off stop speaking 停止讲话: *He broke off in the middle of a sentence.* 他一句话只说了一半就停住了.

break (sth) off (cause sth to) become separated from sth as a result of force or strain (使某物)折断: *The door handle has broken off.* 门的把手断了. ○ *She broke off a piece of chocolate and gave it to me.* 她掰下一块巧克力给我. **break sth off** end sth suddenly; discontinue sth 突然中止某事物; 中断某事物: *break off diplomatic relations (with a country)* 中断(与某国的)外交关系 ○ *They've broken off their engagement/broken it off.* 他们已经解除了婚约.

break out (of violent events) start suddenly (指激烈事件)突然发生: *Fire broke out during the night.* 夜间突然发生了火灾. ○ *Rioting broke out between rival groups of fans.* 双方球迷之间发生了骚乱. ○ *War broke out in 1939.* 1939年爆发了战争. Cf 参看 OUTBREAK. **break out (of sth)** escape from a place by using force (强行)逃出某处: *Several prisoners broke out of the jail.* 有几名囚犯越狱了. Cf 参看 BREAK-OUT. **break out in sth** **(a)** suddenly become covered in sth 突然布满某物: *His face broke out in a rash.* 他的脸上突然长满了皮疹. ○ *He broke out in a cold sweat*, eg through fear. 他出了一身冷汗(如由于恐惧). **(b)** suddenly begin to show strong feelings 突然流露出强烈的感情: *She broke out in a rage.* 她勃然大怒.

break through make new and important discoveries 有重要创见; 突破: *Scientists say they are beginning to break through in the fight against cancer.* 科学家们说, 他们在防治癌症方面开始有所突破. **break through (sth)** **(a)** make a way through (sth) using force; penetrate (sth) 强行穿过(某事物); 插入(某事物): *Demonstrators broke through the police cordon.* 示威群众突破了警戒线. **(b)** (of the sun or moon) appear from behind (clouds) (指太阳或月亮)从(云层)后面出现: *The sun broke through at last in the afternoon.* 太阳在下午终于从云层后面钻出来了. **break through sth** overcome sth 克服某事物: *break through sb's reserve, shyness, etc* 克服某人的沉默、羞怯等心态.

break up **(a)** (of members of a group) go away in different directions; disperse (指群体中的成员)解散, 散去: *The meeting broke up at eleven o'clock.* 会议在十一点钟散会. **(b)** (*Brit*) (of a school, its staff or its pupils) begin the holidays when school closes at the end of term (指学校、教职员或学生)期末放假: *When do you break up for Christmas?* 你们什么时候放圣诞节假? **(c)** become very weak; collapse 变得衰弱; 瓦解; 崩溃: *He was breaking up under the strain.* 他劳累过度, 身体逐渐衰弱. **(d)** (esp of a period of fine weather) end (尤指一段时期的好天气)结束: *The weather shows signs of breaking up.* 好天气看样子要过去了. **break (sth) up** **(a)** (cause sth to) separate into smaller pieces by cutting, striking, etc (将某物)割碎, 击碎, 打碎, 撞碎: *The ship broke up on the rocks.* 船触礁撞毁了. ○ *The ship was broken up for scrap metal.* 这艘船拆毁了当废铁用. **(b)** (cause sth to) come to an end (使某事物)结束: *Their marriage is breaking up.* 他们的婚姻已破裂. ○ *They decided to break up the partnership.* 他们决定终止合作关系. **break sth up** **(a)** disperse or scatter sth using force 强行驱散某物: *Police were called in to break up the meeting.* 出动了警察将集会驱散. **(b)** divide sth by means of analysis, an administrative decision, etc (通过分析、行政决定等方法)分开某事物: *Sentences can be broken up into clauses.* 句子可分成分句. ○ *The Government has broken up the large private estates.* 政府把大片的私人地产分割开. **break up (with sb)** end a relationship with sb 与某人绝交: *She's just broken up with her boy-friend.* 她刚与男朋友绝交.

break with sb end a relationship with sb 与某人绝交: *break with one's girl-friend* 与女朋友绝交. **break with sth** give up sth; abandon sth 与某事物决裂; 放弃某事物: *break with tradition, old habits, the past, etc* 与传统、旧习惯、过去等决裂.

▷ **break·able** /ˈbreɪkəbl; ˋbrekəbl/ *adj* easily broken 易碎的. **break·ables** *n* [pl] breakable objects, eg glasses and cups 易碎的物品(如玻璃杯和瓷杯).

□ **ˈbreakaway** *n* loss of members from a group by withdrawal; secession 脱离组织; 退出: *a breakaway from the Tory party* 脱离保守党 ○ [attrib 作定语] *a breakaway group on the left of the Labour party* 脱离工党左派的组织.

ˈbreak-dancing *n* [U] energetic and acrobatic style of dancing, often competitive or as a display, esp popular with young Black Americans 霹雳舞.

ˈbreak-in *n* forcible entry into a building 闯入某建筑物: *Police are investigating a break-in at the bank.* 警方正在调查有人闯入银行的事件.

ˈbreak-out *n* escape from prison, esp one involving the use of force (尤指强行)越狱: *a mass break-out of prisoners* 囚犯集体越狱.

ˈbreakthrough *n* **1** act of breaking through an enemy's defences 突破敌人防线. **2** important development or discovery, esp in scientific knowledge 重大的发展, 发现, 突破(尤指科学知识方面): *a major breakthrough in cancer research* 癌症研究方面的重大突破 ○ *a breakthrough in negotiations* 谈判的重大进展.

ˈbreakup *n* end (of a relationship or partnership) (关系或合作的)决裂: *The breakup of their marriage* *surprised no one.* 他们婚姻破裂谁都不觉得奇怪.

break[2] /breɪk; brek/ *n* **1 ~ (in sth)** (**a**) opening made by breaking; broken place 裂缝; 破裂处: *a break in a fence, wall, water-pipe* 篱笆、墙壁、水管的裂口. (**b**) gap; space 空隙; 空间: *a break in the clouds*, ie where blue sky is visible 云层间的空隙(可以看到蓝天) ○ *Wait for a break in the traffic before crossing the road.* 要等到暂无车辆来往时, 再过马路. **2** (**a**) interval, esp between periods of work; pause (时间的)间隙(尤指工作期间的); 停歇: *morning break*, eg between lessons at school 上午的休息(如课间时) ○ *lunch-break*, eg in an office, a school or a factory 午餐时间的休息(如办公室、学校或工厂中的) ○ *have/take an hour's break for lunch* 休息一小时进午餐 ○ *work for five hours without a break* 五小时一直不间断地工作 ○ *a break in a conversation* 谈话中的停顿. (**b**) short holiday 短期假日: *a weekend break in the country* 在乡村过的周末假日. **3 ~ (in sth); ~ (with sb/sth)** (**a**) change or interruption in sth continuous (有连贯性的事物的)改变, 中断: *a break in a child's education* 孩子教育的中断 ○ *a break in the weather*, ie a change from bad to good weather 天气的转变(由坏转好) ○ *a break with tradition*, ie a significant change from what is accepted in art, behaviour, morals, etc 与旧传统决裂(背离公认的艺术、行为、道德等准则). (**b**) discontinuation or end of a relationship 中止或断绝关系: *a break in diplomatic relations* 外交关系的中断 ○ *She's been depressed since the break with her boy-friend.* 她自从与男朋友断绝关系以来一直情绪消沉. **4** (*infml* 口) piece of luck, esp one that leads to further success 机会; 幸运; (尤指)转运, 转机: *a big/lucky break* 难得的[幸运的]机会 ○ *a bad break*, ie a piece of bad luck 坏运气(倒霉) ○ *give sb a break*, ie a chance to show his ability 给某人一次机会(表现才能的时机). **5** (in cricket) change in direction of a bowled ball as it bounces (板球)(投的球)改向反弹: *an off/a leg break*, ie a ball that spins to the right/left on bouncing 球向右的[左的]旋转反弹. **6** (also **break of service**, **service break**) (in tennis) instance of winning a point when one's opponent is serving (网球)接对手发球时得分: *Smith has had two breaks already in this set.* 史密斯在这场比赛中有两次接发球得分. ○ [attrib 作定语] *break point*, eg when the score is 30-40 转折球(如比分为30比40). **7** (in billiards or snooker) series of successful shots by one player; score made by such a series (弹子戏或台球戏)连续击中, 连续得分: *a break of 52* 连续得52分. **8** (idm 习语) **break of day** dawn 破晓; 黎明: *at break of day* 破晓时分. **make a break (for it)** escape, esp from prison 逃跑; (尤指)越狱.

NOTE ON USAGE 用法: **Break** applies especially to a rest during the working day or at school ☆ **break** 尤用作工间或课间的休息: *a lunch, coffee break* 午餐时间的、喝咖啡时间的休息 ○ *the mid-morning break* 上午的中间休息 ○ *10 minutes' break* 10分钟的休息. It also covers the meanings of several other words. 这个词还含有其他几个词的意思. A **pause** is usually short and often applied to speech ☆ **pause** 通常为时很短, 常用于指讲话中的停顿: *a pause for breath* 喘口气的停顿 ○ *a pause/break in the conversation* 谈话中的停顿. **Recess** is the scheduled holiday of Parliament, and in US English it is also the break between school classes. ☆ **recess** 是议会的规定假日, 美式英语中还指学校课间的休息. An **interval** in British English is the break between the parts of a play, etc ☆ **interval** 在英式英语中指戏剧等演出的幕间休息: *We had a quick drink in the interval.* 我们在中间休息时匆匆喝了点东西. This is also called an **intermission**, especially in US English. 这种休息也叫 **intermission**, 尤用于美式英语. An **interlude** may be an interval or a short event during a longer activity, often contrasting with it ☆ **interlude** 可指interval, 也可指在一长期活动中的片段, 往往是相对长期活动而言的: *Her time in Paris was a happy interlude in a difficult career.* 她在巴黎期间是她艰辛的事业中一段愉快的插曲. A **rest** does not indicate a definite length of time, but suggests a necessary period of relaxation after an activity ☆ **rest** 不表示确切的时间长短, 而是指在一活动之后需要松弛的一段时间: *You look tired. You need a good rest.* 你看来累了. 你需要好好休息一下.

break·age /ˈbreɪkɪdʒ; ˈbrekɪdʒ/ *n* **1** [C, U] act of or damage caused by breaking 毁坏; 破损: *a parcel carefully packed to prevent breakage* 防止破损而仔细包好的包裹. **2** [C] broken thing 破损之物. **3** [C usu *pl* 通常作复数] broken objects 破损物件: *The hotel allows £300 a year for breakages*, ie for the cost of replacing broken dishes, etc. 这家旅馆每年打出300英镑的损耗费(盘碟等损坏补充费用).

break·down /ˈbreɪkdaʊn; ˈbrek,daʊn/ *n* **1** mechanical failure 机械的故障: *Our car/We had a breakdown on the motorway.* 我们的汽车[我们]在高速公路上抛锚了. **2** collapse or failure 瓦解; 失败; 破裂: *a breakdown of negotiations on disarmament* 裁军谈判的破裂. **3** weakening or collapse of sb's (esp mental) health 身体(尤指精神)衰弱: *The strain of his job led to the complete breakdown of his health.* 他工作过度, 把身体完全累垮了. ○ *She suffered a nervous breakdown.* 她患神经衰弱. **4** statistical analysis 统计分析: *a breakdown of expenditure* 支出的统计分析.

breaker /ˈbreɪkə(r); ˈbrekɚ/ *n* **1** large wave that breaks into foam as it moves towards the shore 大浪(拍岸而成浪花的). **2** (esp in compounds 尤用以构成复合词) person or thing that breaks 击碎者; 打破者: *a ship-breaker* ○ *a law-breaker* ○ *a record-breaker*.

break·fast /ˈbrekfəst; ˈbrɛkfəst/ *n* [C, U] **1** first meal of the day 一天的第一顿饭; 早餐; 早饭: *a light/big/hearty breakfast* 量少的[量多的/丰富的]早餐 ○ *have bacon and eggs for breakfast* 早餐有腌猪肉和鸡蛋 ○ *They were having breakfast when I arrived.* 我到达时, 他们正在用早餐. ○ *She doesn't eat much breakfast.* 她早点吃得不多. **2** (idm 习语) **bed and breakfast** ⇨ BED[1]. **a dog's breakfast/dinner** ⇨ DOG[1]. **eat sb for breakfast** ⇨ EAT.

▷ **break·fast** *v* [I, Ipr] **~ (on sth)** eat breakfast 用早餐; 吃早饭: *We breakfasted on toast and coffee.* 我们用的早餐是烤面包片和咖啡.

break·neck /ˈbreɪknek; ˈbrek,nɛk/ *adj* [attrib 作定语] dangerously fast 快得危险的: *drive, ride, travel, etc at breakneck speed* 以非常危险的高速度开车、骑马、行进等.

break·wa·ter /ˈbreɪkwɔːtə(r); ˈbrek,wɔtɚ/ *n* wall built out into the sea to protect a coast or harbour from the force of the waves 防波堤.

bream /briːm; brim/ *n* (*pl* unchanged 复数不变) **1** type of freshwater fish of the carp family 欧鳊(一种鲤科的淡水鱼). **2** (also ˈ**sea-bream**) type of salt-water fish similar to this 鲷科的海鱼.

breast /brest; brɛst/ *n* **1** [C] either of the two parts of a woman's body that produce milk (女子的)乳房: *a baby at the breast* 哺乳的婴孩 ○ *cancer of the breast* 乳(腺)癌 ○ *The breasts swell during pregnancy.* 怀孕期乳房发胀. **2** [C] (**a**) (*rhet* 修辞) upper front part of the human body; chest (人体的)胸部, 胸膛: *clasp/hold sb to one's breast* 把某人拥抱在怀里. (**b**) part of a garment covering this (衣服的)胸部: *a soldier with medals pinned to the breast of his coat* 胸前别着许多奖章的士兵. **3** [C, U] part of an animal corresponding to the human breast, eaten as food (动物的)胸脯(作食物用者): *chicken breasts* 鸡胸脯 ○ *breast of lamb* 羔羊胸脯. **4** (*dated* 旧) source of feelings; heart 心情; 思绪: *a troubled breast* 心烦意乱. **5** (idm 习语) **beat one's breast** ⇨ BEAT[1]. **make a clean breast of sth** ⇨ CLEAN[1].

▷ **breast** *v* [Tn] **1** (**a**) touch (sth) with the breast(2a) 以胸部触及(某物): *The runner breasted the tape*, ie to win a race. 赛跑者以胸部触线(赛跑获胜). (**b**) face and move forward against (sth) 挺身冲向(某事物): *breasting the waves* 破浪前进. **2** reach the top of (sth) 抵达(某事物)的顶端: *breast a hill/rise* 抵达山[岗]的顶端.

□ ˈ**breastbone** (also **sternum**) *n* thin flat vertical bone in the chest between the ribs 胸骨. ⇨illus at SKELETON 见 SKELETON 之插图.

ˈ**breast-feed** *v* (*pt, pp* ˈ**breast-fed**) [Tn] feed (a baby) with milk from the breast 用乳房的奶喂(婴儿): *Were her children breast-fed or bottle-fed?* 她的孩子喂的是人奶还是牛奶?

ˌ**breast-**ˈ**high** *adj, adv* high as the breast 齐胸高(的):

The wheat was/stood breast-high. 麦子长得齐胸高.

ˈ**breastplate** *n* piece of armour covering the breast 护胸甲.

ˌ**breast** ˈ**pocket** pocket on the breast of a jacket (上衣)胸前的口袋.

ˈ**breast-stroke** *n* [sing] swimming stroke, with chest downwards, in which the arms are extended in front of the head and then swept back, while the legs move in a corresponding way 蛙泳: *do (the) breast-stroke* 游蛙泳.

ˈ**breastwork** *n* low wall of earth, etc put up as a temporary defence 胸墙.

breath /breθ; brɛθ/ *n* **1** (**a**) [U] (also *infml* 口语亦作 **puff**) air taken into and sent out of the lungs (呼吸的)空气: *You can see people's breath on a cold day.* 冷天能看到人们呼出的空气. ○ *His breath smelt of garlic.* 他呼出的气中有蒜味. (**b**) [C] single act of taking air into the lungs 吸气: *take a deep breath*, ie fill the lungs with air 深吸一口气. **2 ~ of sth** [sing] slight movement of air; gently blowing (空气的)轻微流动; 微风: *There wasn't a breath of air/wind.* 一点儿风都没有. **3 ~ of sth** [sing] (*fig* 比喻) slight suggestion or rumour of sth; hint of sth 迹象; 暗示: *a breath of scandal* 一丝流言蜚语 ○ *the first breath of spring* 早春的气息. **4** (idm 习语) **a breath of fresh air** (**a**) opportunity to breathe clean air, esp out of doors 呼吸新鲜空气的机会(尤指户外). (**b**) person or thing that is a welcome and refreshing change 带来起色的人或事物: *Her smile is a breath of fresh air in this gloomy office.* 她的微笑给沉闷的办公室带来生气. **the breath of** ˈ**life (to/for sb)** thing that stimulates or inspires (sb); thing that is necessary (to sb) (某人的)精神支柱; (某人)必不可少的东西: *Religion is the breath of life to/for her.* 宗教是她不可或缺的精神支柱. **catch one's breath** ⇨ CATCH[1]. **draw breath** ⇨ DRAW[2]. **draw one's first/last breath** ⇨ DRAW[2]. **get one's** ˈ**breath (again/back)** return to one's normal rate of breathing 恢复正常呼吸: *It took us a few minutes to get our breath back after the race.* 赛跑后我们用了好几分钟才恢复了正常呼吸. **hold one's** ˈ**breath** stop breathing for a short time (eg during a medical examination or from fear or excitement) 暂时屏住呼吸(如体检时或因恐惧、激动): *How long can you hold your breath for?* 你能屏住呼吸多久? ○ *The audience held its/their breath as the acrobat walked along the tightrope.* 杂技演员走钢丝时, 观众都屏住了呼吸. **in the same breath** ⇨ SAME. **lose one's breath** ⇨ LOSE. **one's last/dying** ˈ**breath** last moment of one's life 临终. **(be) out of/short of** ˈ**breath** breathing very quickly (eg after running fast); panting hard 呼吸急促(如快跑以后); 喘不过气来; 上气不接下气: *His heart condition makes him short of breath.* 他心脏状况不佳使他呼吸急促. **save one's breath** ⇨ SAVE[1]. **say sth, speak, etc under one's** ˈ**breath** say sth, etc in a whisper 低声地说. **take sb's** ˈ**breath away** startle or surprise sb 使某人吃惊或惊奇. **waste one's breath** ⇨ WASTE[2]. **with bated breath** ⇨ BATED.

▷ **breathy** *adj* (**-ier, -iest**) (of the voice) with a noticeable sound of breathing (指嗓音)带有明显呼吸声音的.

□ ˈ**breath test** test of a driver's breath to measure how much alcohol he has drunk 呼吸测验(对司机的呼吸的测验, 以确定其体内酒精含量).

breath·alyse /ˈbreθəlaɪz; ˋbrɛθəlaɪz/ *v* test (sb) with a breathalyser (用呼吸分析器)检验(某人).

▷ **breath·alyser** *n* (*Brit*) (*US* **breath·alyzer, drunkometer**) device used by the police for measuring the amount of alcohol in a driver's breath 呼吸分析器(警方用以测量司机呼吸中的酒精含量的仪器).

breathe /bri:ð; brið/ *v* **1** [I] take air into the lungs and send it out again 呼吸: *People breathe more slowly when they are asleep.* 人睡觉时呼吸比较缓慢. ○ *She's still breathing*, ie still alive. 她仍在呼吸(还活着). ○ *He was breathing hard/heavily after racing for the train.* 他跑着赶上火车以后, 吃力地喘着气. **2** [Ip, Tn, Tn·p] **~ in/out; ~ sth (in/out)** take (air, etc) into or send (it) out of the lungs 吸入或呼出(空气等): *The doctor told me to breathe in and then breathe out (again) slowly.* 医生叫我吸气然后(再)慢慢地呼出. ○ *It's good to breathe (in) fresh country air instead of city smoke.* 呼吸乡间的新鲜空气而不吸入城市的烟尘是有益的. **3** [Tn] say (sth) softly; whisper 轻声说(某事); 低语: *breathe loving words in sb's ear* 在某人耳边低语情话 ○ *breathe a threat* 低声说出恐吓的话. **4** show that one is full of (a feeling); exude 表示充满(感情); 流露: *The team breathed confidence before the match.* 该队在比赛前显得很有信心. **5** (idm 习语) **(be able to) breathe (easily/freely) again** feel calm or relieved after a period of tension, fear or exertion; relax (在一度紧张、恐惧或努力之后)恢复平静或安下心来; 松口气: *Now my debts are paid I can breathe again.* 现在我已还清欠债, 可以松口气了. **breathe down sb's** ˈ**neck** (*infml* 口) be close behind sb (eg in a race); watch sb (too) closely 随后紧跟某人(如赛跑中); 紧紧盯住(某人): *I can't concentrate with you breathing down my neck.* 你这样紧紧盯着我, 使我精神无法集中. **(not) breathe a** ˈ**word (of/about sth) (to sb)** (not) tell sb sth (esp a secret); (not) reveal sth to sb (不)告诉某人某事(尤指秘密); (不)向某人透露某事: *Promise me you won't breathe a word of this to anyone.* 答应我别将此事泄漏给任何人. **breathe one's** ˈ**last** (*fml euph* 文, 婉) die 断气. **6** (phr v) **breathe sth into sb/sth** fill (a person or group) with (a feeling) 使(某人或团体)充满(某种感情): *The new manager has breathed fresh life into* (ie revitalized) *the company.* 新经理给公司带来了朝气.

▷ **breath·ing** *n* [U] action of breathing 呼吸: *heavy breathing* 深沉的呼吸 ○ [attrib 作定语] *breathing apparatus* 呼吸器.

ˈ**breathing-space** *n* [C, U] time to rest between periods of effort; pause 歇口气的时间; 暂停: *The summer holidays gave us a welcome breathing-space.* 暑假给了我们一段愉快的歇夏时间.

breather /ˈbri:ðə(r); ˋbriðɚ/ *n* (*infml* 口) **1** short pause for rest 短时间的休息: *take/have a breather* 休息一下. **2** short period to refresh oneself in the open air (为提神而到户外的)短暂活动: *I must go out for a quick breather.* 我得出去换换脑子了.

breath·less /ˈbreθlɪs; ˋbrɛθlɪs/ *adj* **1** (**a**) breathing quickly or with difficulty; panting 呼吸急促或困难的; 气喘吁吁的: *breathless after running up the stairs* 跑上楼梯后气喘吁吁的 ○ *Heavy smoking makes him breathless.* 吸烟过多使他气喘. (**b**) causing one to be breathless; strenuous 引起气喘的; 费力的: *breathless haste/hurry/pace/speed* 赶得使人喘不过气来的仓促[匆忙/步子/速度]. **2** (**a**) [pred 作表语] holding one's breath (because of fear, excitement, etc) (因恐惧、激动等)屏住呼吸: *breathless with terror, wonder, amazement, etc* 因恐怖、诧异、惊奇等而屏住呼吸. (**b**) [attrib 作定语] tense; making one hold one's breath 紧张的; 使人屏住呼吸的: *a breathless hush in the concert hall* 音乐厅内屏息无声. **3** with no air or wind 无空气的; 无风的: *a breathless calm* 死寂. ▷ **breath·lessly** *adv*. **breath·less·ness** *n* [U].

breath·tak·ing /ˈbreθteɪkɪŋ; ˋbrɛθˌtekɪŋ/ *adj* very exciting; spectacular 非常激动人心的; 壮观的: *a breathtaking view, mountain-range, waterfall* 壮丽的景色、山脉、瀑布 ○ *Her beauty was breathtaking.* 她艳丽动人. ▷ **breath·tak·ingly** *adv*.

bred *pt, pp* of BREED.

breech /bri:tʃ; britʃ/ *n* back part of a gun barrel where the bullet or shell is placed 枪炮的后膛(装子弹或炮弹的地方): *a breech-loading gun* 由后膛装弹的枪炮. Cf 参看 MUZZLE 2.

□ ˈ**breech birth** birth in which the baby's buttocks or feet appear first 臀位分娩.

ˈ**breech-block** *n* steel block that closes the breech of a gun 枪闩; 炮闩.

breeches /ˈbrɪtʃɪz; ˋbrɪtʃɪz/ *n* [pl] **1** short trousers fastened just below the knee, worn esp for horse-riding or as part of ceremonial dress (膝下束紧的)短裤(尤指马裤或礼裤): *a pair of (*ˈ*knee-)breeches* 一条(膝下束紧的)短裤 ○ ˈ*riding breeches* 马裤. **2** (*joc* 谑) trousers 裤子.

□ **breeches-buoy** *n* /ˈbri:tʃɪz bɔɪ; ˈbritʃɪz bɔɪ/ apparatus for rescuing people at sea, consisting of canvas breeches attached to a lifebuoy that runs along a rope between a ship and the shore or between two ships 短裤形救生器.

breed /bri:d; brid/ *v* (*pt, pp* **bred** /bred; brɛd/) **1** [I] (of animals) produce young (指动物)生育, 繁殖: *How often do lions breed?* 狮子多长时间产一次崽? **2** [Tn]

B

B

keep (animals) for the purpose of producing young, esp by selecting the best parents for mating 饲养(动物)(尤指为选种繁殖的): *breed cattle, dogs, horses, etc* 养牛、狗、马等. **3** [esp passive 尤用于被动语态: Tn, Tn·pr, Cn·n/a, Cn·t] **~ sb (as sth)** bring up; train; educate 养育; 训练; 教育: *a well-bred child* 有教养的孩子 ○ *Spartan youths were bred as warriors.* 斯巴达青年被培养成战士. **4** [Tn] lead to (sth); cause 导致(某事物); 造成: *Dirt breeds disease.* 污秽导致疾病丛生. ○ *Unemployment breeds social unrest.* 失业能造成社会不安定. **5** (idm 习语) **born and bred** ⇨ BORN. **familiarity breeds contempt** ⇨ FAMILIARITY.

▷ **breed** *n* **1** family or variety of animals, etc having a similar appearance and usu developed by deliberate selection (动物等的)品种(通常为特意繁殖的): *a breed of cattle, sheep, etc* 牛、羊等的品种 ○ *What breed is your dog?* 你的狗是什么品种的? **2** type; kind 类型; 种类: *a new breed of politician* 新式的政治家.

breeder *n* person who breeds animals 饲养员: *a dog, horse, cattle, etc breeder* 狗、马、牛等的饲养员 ○ *a breeder of racehorses* 赛马马匹的饲养员.

ˈ**breeder reactor** type of nuclear reactor that produces more radio-active material than is put into it 增殖反应堆.

breed·ing *n* [U] **1** producing of young by animals (动物的)生育, 繁殖, 生殖: [attrib 作定语] *the breeding season* 繁殖季节. **2** keeping of animals for breeding (为繁殖)饲养动物: *the breeding of horses* 马的饲养. **3** (good manners resulting from) training or family background 教养; 有教养的举止: *a man of good breeding* 有良好教养的人.

ˈ**breeding-ground** *n* **1** place where wild animals go to produce their young (野生动物的)繁殖地: *Some birds fly south to find good breeding-grounds.* 有些鸟飞到南方去寻找适合产卵的地方. **2** (*fig* 比喻) place where sth (usu harmful) can develop 某事物(通常指有害事物)的滋生地: *Damp, dirty houses are a breeding ground for disease.* 房屋潮湿、肮脏可滋生疾病.

breeze /bri:z; briz/ *n* **1** [C, U] light wind 微风: *a sea breeze* 海风 ○ *A gentle breeze was blowing.* 微风轻吹. ○ *There's not much breeze today.* 今天没有什么风. **2** [sing] (*infml* 口 *esp US*) thing that is easy to do or enjoy 容易做的事物; 容易享有的事物: *Some people think learning to drive is a breeze.* 有些人认为不费吹灰之力就可学会开车. **3** [C] (*Brit infml* 口) noisy quarrel 争吵. **4** (idm 习语) **shoot the breeze** ⇨ SHOOT[1].

▷ **breeze** *v* (phr v) **breeze along, in, out, etc** (*infml* 口) move in a cheerful carefree way (in the specified direction) (向某方向)飘然移动: *Look who's just breezed in!* 看, 一阵风把谁刮来啦! ○ *He breezes through life, never worrying about anything.* 他生活一帆风顺, 什么事也不用操心.

breezy *adj* (**-ier, -iest**) **1** (**a**) slightly windy 有微风的: *a breezy day* 和风丽日 ○ *breezy weather* 轻风和畅的天气. (**b**) exposed to breezes 微风吹过的: *a breezy corner, beach, hillside* 风凉的拐角处、沙滩、山坡. **2** (of a person, his manner, etc) cheerful; light-hearted (指人、举止等)快活的, 轻松愉快的: *You're very bright and breezy today!* 你今天满面春风啊! **breez·ily** /ˈbri:zɪlɪ; ˈbrizɪlɪ/ *adv*. **breezi·ness** /ˈbri:zɪnɪs; ˈbrizɪnɪs/ *n* [U].

□ ˈ**breezeway** *n* (*US*) covered, often enclosed, passageway between two buildings (两建筑物之间有顶的, 常为有围墙的)过道.

breeze-block /ˈbri:z blɒk; ˈbriz,blɑk/ (*Brit*) *n* lightweight building block made of cinders, sand and cement (煤渣、沙、水泥制成的)一种轻型建筑砌块, 煤渣砌块.

breth·ren /ˈbreðrən; ˈbrɛðrən/ *n* [pl] (*arch* except when used of or by certain religious groups 古用语, 现只用于某些宗教团体) brothers (某些宗教团体的)教友.

breve /bri:v; briv/ *n* (*music* 音) long note equal to two semibreves 倍全音符; 二全音符.

bre·vi·ary /ˈbri:vɪərɪ; *US* -ɪerɪ; ˈbrivɪ,ɛrɪ/ *n* book of prayers to be said daily by Roman Catholic priests 日课经(天主教神甫每日祈祷用的书).

brev·ity /ˈbrevətɪ; ˈbrɛvətɪ/ *n* [U] **1** shortness or briefness (of time) 短暂: *the brevity of Mozart's life* 莫扎特短暂的一生. **2** conciseness (in speaking or writing) (说话或行文的)简洁: *He is famous for the brevity of his speeches.* 他以言词简洁著称.

brew /bru:; bru/ *v* **1** [Tn] make (beer) by mixing, boiling and fermenting malt, hops, etc and water 酿造(啤酒): *He brews his own beer at home.* 他在家自己酿造啤酒. **2** (**a**) [Tn, Tn·p] **~ sth (up)** prepare (a hot drink, esp tea) by mixing leaves, etc with boiling water 调制(热饮料, 尤指沏茶); 冲泡: *We brewed (up) a nice pot of tea.* 我们沏了一壶好茶. (**b**) [I] (esp of tea) become brewed (尤指茶)沏着, 冲泡着: *There's (a pot of) tea brewing in the kitchen.* 厨房里沏了(一壶)茶. **3** (**a**) [Tn, Tn·p] **~ sth (up)** prepare or plan (sth unpleasant) 图谋, 策划(不愉快的事物): *Those boys are brewing mischief.* 那些孩子正在搞恶作剧. ○ *brew (up) a wicked plot* 图谋不轨. (**b**) [I] (of sth unpleasant) grow in force; look likely to happen; develop (指不愉快的事物)形成, 即将发生, 酝酿: *A storm is brewing.* 暴风雨即将来临. ○ *Trouble is brewing in the trade unions.* 工会正酝酿着闹事. ○ *In 1938 war was brewing in Europe.* 1938年欧洲酝酿着一场战争. **4** (phr v) **brew up** (*infml* 口) prepare a drink of tea 沏茶: *campers brewing up outside their tents* 在帐篷外烧火沏茶的露营者.

▷ **brew** *n* **1** (**a**) (amount of) drink made by brewing (esp tea or beer) 酿造或冲泡的饮料(的量)(尤指茶或啤酒): *home brew*, ie beer made at home 家酿的饮料(自制的啤酒) ○ *What's your favourite brew (of beer)?* 你爱喝什么啤酒? ○ *We'll need more than one brew* (eg of tea) *for twenty people.* 我们二十人不能只沏一份(如茶). (**b**) quality or nature of what is brewed (啤酒或茶等的)质量: *I like a good strong brew.* 我喜欢喝浓的. **2** (*fig* 比喻) any mixture of circumstances, ideas, events, etc (环境、思想、事件等的)混合物: *The film is a rich brew of adventure, sex and comedy.* 这部电影是惊险、性爱及幽默的大杂烩.

brewer *n* person whose job is brewing beer 啤酒酿造者.

brew·ery /ˈbrʊərɪ; ˈbruərɪ/ *n* building in which beer is brewed 啤酒厂. Cf 参看 DISTILLERY (DISTILLER).

□ ˈ**brew-up** *n* (*Brit infml* 口) act of making tea 沏茶: *We always have a brew-up at 11 o'clock.* 我们总是在11点钟沏茶.

briar = BRIER.

bribe /braɪb; braɪb/ *n* thing given, offered or promised to sb to influence or persuade him to do sth (often dishonest) for the giver 贿赂: *take/accept bribes* 受贿 ○ *The policeman was offered/given a bribe of £500 to keep his mouth shut.* 向该警察行贿500英镑让他闭口不言.

▷ **bribe** *v* **1** (**a**) [Tn, Tn·pr, Tnt] **~ sb (with sth)** give a bribe (of sth) to sb; try to persuade sb to do sth with a bribe 用(某事物)向某人行贿; 行贿以说通某人做某事: *attempt to bribe a jury with offers of money* 试图以金钱贿赂陪审团 ○ *One of the witnesses was bribed to give false evidence.* 有个证人受贿而提供伪证. (**b**) [I] give bribes; practise bribery 行贿. **2** (idm 习语) **bribe one's way into/out of sth, past sb, etc** get somewhere by using bribery 用行贿手段到达某处或达到某目的: *He bribed his way past the guard and escaped.* 他买通看守而逃之夭夭了. **3** (phr v) **bribe sb into doing sth** make sb do sth with a bribe 贿赂某人做某事. **brib·able** /ˈbraɪbəbl; ˈbraɪbəbl/ *adj* able to be bribed 可受贿的; 可收买的. **bribery** /ˈbraɪbərɪ; ˈbraɪbərɪ/ *n* [U] giving or taking of bribes 行贿; 受贿: *accuse/convict sb of bribery* 指控[宣判]某人贿赂.

bric-à-brac /ˈbrɪkəbræk; ˈbrɪkə,bræk/ *n* [U] ornaments, trinkets and small items of furniture of little value (不大值钱的)饰物, 小摆设: *She collects bric-à-brac.* 她爱好搜集小摆设.

brick /brɪk; brɪk/ *n* **1** [C, U] (usu rectangular block of) baked or dried clay used for building (通常指长方形的)砖, 坯: *a pile of bricks* 一堆砖 ○ *houses built/made of red brick* 红砖造的房屋 ○ [attrib 作定语] *a brick wall* 砖墙. ⇨illus at App 1 见附录1之插图, page vi. **2** [C] child's (usu wooden) toy building block 积木. **3** [C] thing shaped like a brick, esp a block of ice-cream 砖形的东西; (尤指)冰激凌. **4** [C] (*Brit infml* 口) generous or loyal person 慷慨的或忠实的人: *She's been a real brick, looking after me while I've been ill.* 我病中她一直照看我, 真是个大好人. **5** (idm 习语) **bang, etc one's head against a brick wall** ⇨ HEAD[1]. **drop a brick/clanger** ⇨ DROP[2]. **like a cat on hot bricks** ⇨ CAT[1].

like a ton of bricks ⇨ TON. **make bricks without 'straw** try to work without adequate material, money, information, etc 要工作却无充分物力、财力、资料等; 作无米之炊.

▷ **brick** *v* (phr v) **brick sth in/up** fill in, block or seal (an opening) with bricks 用砖堵住(洞口): *brick up a window/doorway/fireplace to prevent draughts* 用砖把窗户[门口/壁炉]堵住以防止进风.

□ **'brickbat** *n* **1** piece of brick, esp one thrown as a weapon 砖头(尤指作武器投掷的). **2** (*fig infml* 比喻, 口) rude or derogatory remark; insult 粗鲁的或贬责的话; 凌辱: *The Minister's speech was greeted with brickbats.* 部长的演说遭到了抨击.

'bricklayer [C], **'bricklaying** [U] *ns* (workman trained or skilled in) building with bricks 砌砖盖房; 砖瓦匠.

'brickwork *n* [U] **1** (part of a) structure built of bricks 用砖造的建筑物(的部分): *The brickwork in this house is in need of repair.* 这所房子的砖造部分需要修理. **2** building with bricks 砌砖工程: *Are you any good at brickwork?* 你擅长瓦工活儿吗?

'brickyard *n* place where bricks are made 砖场; 砖厂.

bri·dal /'braɪdl; 'braɪdl/ *adj* [attrib 作定语] of a bride or wedding 新娘的; 婚礼的: *the bridal party*, ie the bride and her attendants and close friends 新娘一方 ○ *a bridal suite*, ie a suite of rooms in a hotel for a newly married couple 新婚套间(旅馆中的新婚夫妇用房).

bride /braɪd; braɪd/ *n* woman on or just before her wedding-day; newly married woman 新娘; 新婚的妇女.

bride·groom /'braɪdgrʊm, *also* -gru:m; 'braɪd,grʊm, -grum/ (also **groom**) *n* man on or just before his wedding-day; newly married man 新郎; 新婚的男子: *Let's drink (a toast) to the bride and bridegroom!* 让我们举杯向新娘和新郎祝贺!

brides·maid /'braɪdzmeɪd; 'braɪdz,med/ *n* young woman or girl (usu unmarried and often one of several) attending a bride at her wedding 女傧相; 伴娘. Cf 参看 BEST MAN (BEST[1]).

bridge[1] /brɪdʒ; brɪdʒ/ *n* **1** structure of wood, iron, concrete, etc, providing a way across a river, road, railway, etc 桥梁: *a bridge across the stream* 横跨溪流的桥梁 ○ *a railway bridge*, ie one for a railway across a river, etc 铁路桥梁(跨越河流等的). ⇨illus 见插图. **2** (*fig* 比喻) thing that provides a connection or contact between two or more things 借以相互联系或接触的事物: *Cultural exchanges are a way of building bridges between nations.* 文化交流是国与国之间建立联系的桥梁. **3** raised platform across the deck of a ship, from which it is controlled and navigated by the captain and officers 船桥, 舰桥(船长及高级船员操纵及导航之处). **4** (**a**) bony upper part of the nose 鼻梁. (**b**) part of a pair of glasses that rests on the nose 鼻梁架(眼镜上的). ⇨illus at GLASS 见GLASS之插图. **5** movable piece of wood, etc over which the strings of a violin, etc are stretched 琴马(小提琴等上绷弦用的). ⇨illus at App 1 见附录1之插图, page xi. **6** device for keeping false teeth in place, fastened to natural teeth on each side 齿桥(固定假牙用者). **7** (idm 习语) **burn one's boats/bridges** ⇨ BURN[2]. **cross one's bridges when one comes to them** ⇨ CROSS[2]. **a lot of/much water has flowed, etc under the bridge** ⇨ WATER[1]. **water under the bridge** ⇨ WATER[1].

▷ **bridge** *v* **1** [Tn] build or form a bridge over (sth) 在(某事物)上架桥: *bridge a river, canal, ravine, etc* 在河流、运河、深谷等上面架桥. **2** (idm 习语) **bridge a/the 'gap** (**a**) fill an awkward or empty space 填补尴尬的或空白的间隙: *bridge a gap in the conversation* 不使谈话冷场 ○ *A snack in the afternoon bridges the gap between lunch and supper.* 在午餐和晚餐之间, 下午吃些点心补充一下. (**b**) reduce the distance (between widely contrasting groups) 缩短(悬殊的)距离: *How can we bridge the gap between rich and poor?* 怎样才能缩小贫富之间的差距?

□ **'bridgehead** *n* area captured and fortified in enemy territory, esp on the enemy's side of a river (敌占区内的)桥头堡. Cf 参看 BEACH-HEAD (BEACH).

'bridging loan loan given (esp by a bank) for the period between two transactions, eg between buying a new house and selling the old one (尤指银行的)临时贷款(如于买新房卖旧房之间).

bridge[2] /brɪdʒ; brɪdʒ/ *n* [U] card-game for four players developed from whist, in which one player's cards are exposed on the table and played by his partner 桥牌.

bridle /'braɪdl; 'braɪdl/ *n* part of a horse's harness that goes on its head, including the metal bit for the mouth, the straps and the reins 马勒(包括衔铁、笼头、缰绳).

▷ **bridle** *v* **1** [Tn] put a bridle on (a horse) 给(马)装马勒. **2** [Tn] (*fig* 比喻) keep (feelings, etc) under control; restrain 控制(感情等); 约束: *bridle one's emotions/passions/temper/rage* 控制[感情/热情/脾气/怒气] ○ *bridle one's tongue*, ie be careful what one says 说话谨慎. Cf 参看 UNBRIDLED. **3** [I, Ipr] ~ (**at sth**) show anger, resentment, etc (because of sth), esp by drawing one's head up or back (因某事物)表示愤怒、不满等(尤指作昂首或收颔状): *He bridled (with anger) at her offensive remarks.* 他听了她无礼的话(愤怒得)扬起头来.

□ **'bridle-path** (also **'bridle-way**) *n* path suitable for horse-riding, but not for cars, etc 马道(适宜骑马而不通行汽车的路).

Brie /bri:; bri/ *n* [U] type of soft French cheese 布里干酪(一种柔软的法国干酪).

brief[1] /bri:f; brif/ *adj* (**-er, -est**) **1** (**a**) lasting only a short time; short 时间短暂的; 简短的: *a brief conversation, discussion, meeting, visit, delay* 短暂的谈话、讨论、会议、访问、耽搁 ○ *Mozart's life was brief.* 莫扎特的一生是短暂的. (**b**) (of speech or writing) using few words; concise (指说话或写作)简短的; 简洁的: *a brief account, report, description, etc of the accident* 对事故简短的叙述、报道、描述 ○ *Please be brief*, ie say what you want to say quickly. 请简断截说. **2** (of clothes) short; scanty (指衣着)短的, 刚刚够大的: *a brief bikini* 短小的比基尼游泳衣. **3** (idm 习语) **in brief** in a few words 简言之: *In brief, your work is bad.* 总之, 你做得不好.

▷ **briefly** *adv* **1** for a short time 短暂地: *He paused briefly before continuing.* 他停了片刻又继续进行. **2** in a few words 简单地说: *Briefly, you're fired!* 一句话, 你被解雇了!

brief[2] /bri:f; brif/ *n* **1** (**a**) summary of the facts of a legal case prepared for a barrister (为讼务律师准备的)案情摘要. (**b**) case given to a barrister (给讼务律师承办的)案件: *Will you accept this brief?* 你接受这个案件吗? **2** instructions and information relating to a particular situation, job, or task (对某情况、工作或任务的)指示和资料: *stick to one's brief*, ie only do what one is required to do 照章办事(仅做分内的事) ○ *It's not part of my brief to train new employees.* 训练新雇员不是我工作范围以内的事. **3** (idm 习语) **hold no brief for (sb/sth)** not wish to support or be in favour of (sb/sth) 不支持, 不赞成(某人[某事物]): *I hold no brief for those who say that violence can be justified.* 我不赞成人们说有时使用暴力是合乎情理的.

▷ **brief** *v* **1** [Tn, Tnt] give a brief[2](1a) to (sb) 将案件委托(某人): *The company has briefed a top lawyer to defend it.* 公司已将案件委托给最好的律师进行辩护. **2** [Tn, Tn·pr] ~ **sb (on sth)** give sb detailed information or instructions in advance (about sth) 事先给某人详细介绍或指示(某事物): *The Prime Minister was fully briefed before the meeting.* 首相在会议前已掌握了详尽资料. ○ *The Air Commodore briefed the bomber crew on their dangerous mission.* 空军准将向轰炸机机组下达执行危险任务的各项指示. Cf 参看 DEBRIEF. **brief·ing** *n* [C, U] detailed instructions and information given at a meeting (esp before a military operation) (会议上作的)详细指示和介绍; (尤指军事行动前的)会议部署:

receive (a) thorough briefing 听取详细指示 ○ [attrib 作定语] *a briefing session* 任务布置会.

brief·case /ˈbri:fkeɪs; ˋbrif,kes/ *n* flat leather or plastic case for carrying documents (扁平的、皮革或塑料的)公事包. ⇨illus at LUGGAGE 见 LUGGAGE 之插图.

briefs /bri:fs; brifs/ *n* [pl] short close-fitting pants or knickers (贴身的)短内裤: *a new pair of briefs* 一条新的三角裤.

B

brier (also **briar**) /ˈbraɪə(r); ˋbraɪɚ/ *n* **1** thorny bush; wild rose 荆棘; 野玫瑰. **2** bush with a hard woody root used for making tobacco-pipes 欧石南(其坚硬木质根部可制作烟斗). **3** tobacco-pipe made from this (用欧石南根制成的)烟斗.

brig /brɪg; brɪg/ *n* **1** sailing-ship with two masts and square sails 方帆双桅船. **2** (*US*) prison, esp one on a warship for members of the Navy 禁闭室(尤指军舰上关押海军人员的).

Brig *abbr* 缩写 = Brigadier: *Brig (John) West* (约翰)韦斯特准将.

bri·gade /brɪˈgeɪd; brɪˋged/ *n* **1** army unit, usu of three battalions, forming part of a division 旅(陆军的编制单位). **2** group of people, esp one organized for a particular purpose 队, 组(尤指为某特殊目的而组织的): *the fire brigade* 消防队 ○ (*joc* 谑) *He's joined the bowler-hatted brigade working in the City.* 他已跻身于那帮戴常礼帽的人的行列, 在伦敦商业区工作.

▷ **bri·gad·ier** /ˌbrɪgəˈdɪə(r); ˌbrɪgəˋdɪr/ *n* officer in the British Army between the ranks of colonel and major general, commanding a brigade; staff officer having similar status (英国陆军)准将, 旅长; (相当于该地位的)参谋长. ⇨App 9 见附录 9.

brig·and /ˈbrɪgənd; ˋbrɪgənd/ *n* (*dated* 旧) member of a band of robbers, esp one attacking travellers in forests and mountains 强盗, 土匪(尤指在山林中抢劫旅客的).

brig·an·tine /ˈbrɪgənti:n; ˋbrɪgən,tin/ *n* sailing-ship like a brig, but with fewer sails 双桅帆船.

bright /braɪt; braɪt/ *adj* (**-er, -est**) **1** giving out or reflecting much light; shining 发光的; 反光的; 明亮的: *bright sunshine* 灿烂的阳光 ○ *bright eyes* 明亮的眼睛 ○ *Tomorrow's weather will be cloudy with bright periods.* 明天的天气多云、间中有阳光. **2** (of a colour) intense; bold; vivid (指颜色)鲜艳的, 鲜明的, 醒目的: *a bright blue dress* 宝蓝色的连衣裙 ○ *The leaves on the trees are bright green in spring.* 春天树上的叶子是翠绿的. **3** promising; hopeful 光明的; 有希望的: *a child with a bright future* 有前途的孩子 ○ *Prospects for the coming year look bright.* 来年前景看来很有希望. **4** cheerful and lively 愉快的; 活泼的: *She has a bright personality.* 她个性爽朗. **5** clever; intelligent 伶俐的; 聪明的; 有智慧的: *a bright idea/suggestion* 高明的见解[建议] ○ *He is the brightest (child) in the class.* 他是班里最聪明的(孩子). **6** (idm 习语) **(be/get up) bright and ˈearly** very early in the morning 一大早; 大清早: *You're (up) bright and early today!* 你今天真早哇! **(as) bright as a ˈbutton** very clever; quick-witted 聪敏的; 伶俐的; 机灵的. **the bright ˈlights** (excitement of) city life 都市生活(的丰富多彩): *He grew up in the country, but then found he preferred the bright lights.* 他在乡村长大, 但后来觉得很喜欢繁华的都市生活. **a bright ˈspark** (*infml often ironic* 口, 常作反语) lively and intelligent person (esp one who is young and promising) 活泼而聪明的人(尤指有为的年轻人): *Some bright spark has left the tap running all night.* 哪个小淘气干的聪明事, 让水龙头开了一夜. **look on the ˈbright side** find sth to be cheerful or hopeful about in spite of difficulties 在困境中看到事物光明的一面.

▷ **bright** *adv* brightly 光明地: *The stars were shining bright.* 星光灿烂.

brighten /ˈbraɪtn; ˋbraɪtn̩/ *v* [I, Ip, Tn, Tn·p] **~ (sth) (up)** (cause sth/sb to) become brighter, more cheerful or more hopeful (使某人[某事物])焕发光彩, 更愉快, 更有希望: *The sky/weather is brightening.* 天空[天气]转晴. ○ *He brightened (up) when he heard the good news.* 他听到这个好消息时喜形于色. ○ *Flowers brighten (up) a room.* 房间里有了花显得满室生辉.

brightly *adv*: *a brightly lit room* 照得明亮的房间 ○ *brightly coloured curtains* 颜色鲜艳的窗帘.

bright·ness *n* [U].

brill /brɪl; brɪl/ *n* flat-fish like a turbot 菱鲆.

bril·liant /ˈbrɪlɪənt; ˋbrɪljənt/ *adj* **1** very bright; sparkling 非常明亮的; 光辉夺目的: *brilliant sunshine* 灿烂的阳光 ○ *a brilliant diamond* 耀眼的钻石 ○ *a sky of brilliant blue* 蔚蓝色的天空. **2** (**a**) very intelligent; highly skilled or talented 极聪明的; 技艺精湛的; 才华横溢的: *a brilliant scientist, musician, footballer, etc* 卓越的科学家、音乐家、足球运动员等 ○ *She has a brilliant mind.* 她头脑敏锐. (**b**) causing admiration; outstanding; exceptional 令人钦佩的; 杰出的; 非凡的: *a brilliant achievement, exploit, career, performance, etc* 非凡的成就、功绩、事业、表演等 ○ *The play was a brilliant success.* 这出戏是一大成功. ▷ **bril·liance** /ˈbrɪlɪəns; ˋbrɪljəns/, **bril·liancy** /ˈbrɪlɪənsɪ; ˋbrɪljənsɪ/ *ns* [U]. **bril·liantly** *adv*.

bril·liantine /ˈbrɪlɪənti:n; ˋbrɪljən,tin/ *n* [U] oily substance used to make men's hair shiny and smooth (男用)润发油.

brim /brɪm; brɪm/ *n* **1** top edge of a cup, bowl, glass, etc (杯口、碗口等的)边, 边缘: *full to the brim* 满到边缘. **2** projecting edge of a hat, that gives shade and protection against rain 帽檐. ⇨illus at HAT 见 HAT 之插图.

▷ **brim** *v* (**-mm-**) **1** [I, Ipr] **~ (with sth)** be or become full to the brim 注满: *a mug brimming with coffee* 注满咖啡的大缸子 ○ *eyes brimming with tears* 盈盈泪眼 ○ (*fig* 比喻) *The team were brimming with confidence before the match.* 这个队在比赛前充满了信心. **2** (phr v) **brim over (with sth)** overflow 溢出: *a glass brimming over with water* 溢出水的玻璃杯 ○ (*fig* 比喻) *brim over with excitement, happiness, joy, etc* 洋溢着兴奋、幸福、欢乐等.

-brimmed (forming compound *adjs* 用以构成复合形容词) (of a hat) having the type of brim specified (指帽子)有某种檐的: *a broad-/wide-/floppy-brimmed hat.*

brim·ful (also **brim-full**) /ˌbrɪmˈfʊl; ˋbrɪmˋfʊl/ *adj* [pred 作表语] **~ (of/with sth)** full to the brim (with sth) (某物)满到边缘: *The basin was brim-full (of water).* 盆(里的水)已经满到边了. ○ (*fig* 比喻) *Our new manager is ˌbrimful of ˈenergy.* 我们的新经理精力十分充沛.

brim·stone /ˈbrɪmstəʊn; ˋbrɪm,ston/ *n* [U] (*arch* 古) **1** sulphur 硫磺. **2** (idm 习语) **fire and brimstone** ⇨ FIRE[1].

brindled /ˈbrɪndld; ˋbrɪndl̩d/ *adj* (esp of cows, dogs and cats) brown with streaks of another colour (尤指牛、狗、猫)棕色的并夹杂其他颜色之斑纹的.

brine /braɪn; braɪn/ *n* [U] **1** very salty water used esp for pickling 盐水(尤作腌泡用的): *herrings pickled in brine* 盐水腌过的鲱鱼. **2** sea-water 海水.

▷ **briny** *adj* salty 咸的. **the briny** *n* [sing] (*dated joc* 旧, 谑) the sea 海: *take a dip in the briny* 到海里小游片刻.

bring /brɪŋ; brɪŋ/ *v* (*pt, pp* **brought** /brɔ:t; brɔt/) **1** [Tn, Tn·pr, Tn·p, Dn·n, Dn·pr] **~ sb/sth (with one)**; **~ sth (for sb)** come carrying sth or accompanied by sb 带着某物或某人来: *He always brings a bottle of wine (with him) when he comes to dinner.* 他来吃饭时总是(随身)带来一瓶酒. ○ *She brought her boyfriend to the party.* 她带着男朋友来参加聚会. ○ *The secretary brought him into the room/brought him in.* 秘书带着他进入室内. ○ (*fig* 比喻) *The team's new manager brings ten years' experience to the job.* 该队新来的负责人有十年的工作经验. ○ *Take this empty box away and bring me a full one.* 把这个空盒子拿走, 给我拿个满的来. ○ *Bring me a glass of water/Bring a glass of water for me.* 给我拿一杯水来. **2** (**a**) [Tn] result in (sth); cause; produce 导致(某事物); 引起; 产生: *These pills bring relief from pain.* 这些药丸可以止痛. ○ *Spring brings warm weather and flowers.* 随着春天的到来, 天气和暖, 百花盛开. ○ *The revolution brought many changes.* 这场革命带来了许多变化. ○ *The sad news brought tears to his eyes*, ie made him cry. 他得知这一不幸的消息, 眼泪夺眶而出. (**b**) [Tn, Dn·n] produce (sth) as profit or income 产生, 创造(某事物)作为利润或收入: *His writing brings him £10 000 a year.* 他的作品给他带来一年 10 000 英镑的收入. ○ *Her great wealth brought her no happiness.* 她的巨大财富并未给她带来幸福. **3** [Tn·pr] **~ sb/sth to sth** cause sb/sth to be in a certain state or position 使某人[某事物]处于某种情况或境地: *His incompetence has brought the company to the brink of bankruptcy.* 他很无能, 公司已因而濒于破产. **4** [Cn·g] cause (sb) to move in the way specified 使(某人)按某方式移动: *The full-back brought* *him crashing to the ground*, ie caused him to fall heavily. 后卫把他摔倒在地. ○ *Her cries brought the neighbours running*, ie caused them to come running to her. 她大声喊叫, 邻居闻声朝她跑来. **5** [Tn, Tn·pr] **~ sth (against sb)** put forward (charges, etc) in a lawcourt 向法庭提起(诉讼等): *bring a charge/a legal action/an accusation against sb* 指控[起诉/控告]某人. **6** [Cn·t] force or make (oneself) do sth 强迫或促使(自己)做某事: *She could not bring herself to tell him the tragic news.* 她没有勇气把那悲惨消息告诉他. **7** (used with *to* or *into* in many expressions to show that sb/sth is caused to reach the state or condition indicated by the *n* 与 to 或 into 连用可构成许多固定词组, 表示某人[某事物]达到其后的名词所示的情况或境地, 如 *Her intervention brought the meeting to a close*, ie ended the meeting 会议因她干预而中断; *The mild weather will bring the trees into blossom*, ie cause the trees to blossom 天气暖和, 树木就要开花了; for similar expressions, see entries for *ns* 类似固定词组见有关名词词条, 如 *bring sth to an end* ⇨ END.) **8** (For idioms containing **bring**, see entries for *ns*, *adjs*, etc 习语中有 **bring** 者, 见有关名词、形容词等的词条, 如 **bring sb to book** ⇨ BOOK[1]; **bring sth to light** ⇨ LIGHT[1].) **9** (phr v) **bring sth about** (**a**) (*nautical* 海) cause (a sailing-boat) to change direction 使(帆船)改变方向: *The helmsman brought us* (ie our boat) *about.* 那舵手把我们的船掉过头来. (**b**) cause sth to happen 使(某事物)发生; 导致: *bring about reforms, a war, sb's ruin* 导致改革、战争、某人的毁灭 ○ *The Liberals wish to bring about changes in the electoral system.* 自由党人想要改变选举制度. ⇨Usage at CAUSE 用法见 CAUSE.

bring sb/sth back (**a**) return sb/sth 送回某人[某事物]: *Please bring back the book tomorrow.* 请明天把书送回来. ○ *He brought me back* (ie gave me a lift home) *in his car.* 他用汽车把我送回家. **bring sth back** (**a**) restore or reintroduce sth 恢复某事物: *MPs voted against bringing back the death penalty.* 下议院议员投票反对恢复死刑. (**b**) call sth to mind 回想起某事物: *The old photograph brought back many memories.* 这张旧照片引起许多回忆. **bring sb back sth** return with sth for sb 为某人带回某物: *If you're going to the shops, could you bring me back some cigarettes?* 你要是到商店去, 可以给我捎些香烟来吗? **bring sb back to sth** restore sb to sth 使某人恢复某事物: *A week by the sea brought her back to health.* 她待在海滨一周后恢复了健康.

bring sb/sth before sb present sb/sth for discussion, decision or judgement 将某人[某事物]提交讨论或裁决: *The matter will be brought before the committee.* 此事将提交委员会讨论. ○ *He was brought before the court and found guilty.* 他出庭受审并被裁决有罪.

bring sb down (**a**) (in football) cause sb to fall over by fouling him (足球)犯规使某人跌倒: *He was brought down in the penalty area.* 他在罚球区被对方撞倒. (**b**) (in Rugby) tackle sb (橄榄球)挡住对方带球跑的队员. (**c**) cause the defeat of sb; overthrow sb 使某人失败; 打倒某人: *The scandal may bring down the government.* 这一丑闻可能导致政府垮台. **bring sth down** (**a**) cause (an aircraft) to fall out of the sky 使(飞行器)从空中落下: *bring down an enemy fighter* 击落敌人一架战斗机. (**b**) land (an aircraft) 使(飞行器)着陆: *The pilot brought his crippled plane down in a field.* 驾驶员把失灵的飞机降落在田地里. (**c**) cause (an animal or a bird) to fall over or fall out of the sky by killing or wounding it 打死或打伤(禽兽): *He aimed, fired and brought down the antelope.* 他瞄准羚羊射击, 把它打倒了. (**d**) lower or reduce sth 降低或减少某事物: *bring down prices, the rate of inflation, the cost of living, etc* 降低价格、通货膨胀率、生活费用等. (**e**) (*mathematics* 数) transfer (a digit) from one part of a sum to another 将(数字)移下.

bring sth forth (*fml* 文) produce sth 产生某事物: *Trees bring forth fruit.* 树木能结出果实.

bring sth forward (**a**) move sth to an earlier time; advance sth 将某事物提前: *The meeting has been brought forward from 10 May to 3 May.* 会议已由5月10日提前到5月3日召开. (**b**) (in bookkeeping) transfer (the total of a column of figures) to the next column (簿记)将(一列数字的总数)转到下一列: *A credit balance of £50 was brought forward from his September account.* 贷方余额50英镑是从他九月份的帐上转来的. (**c**) propose or present sth for discussion; raise sth 将某事提交讨论; 提出某事: *matters brought forward from the last meeting* 上次会议提出来的事项.

bring sb in (**a**) (of the police) bring sb to a police station to be questioned or charged; arrest sb (指警察)将某人抓进警察局去盘问或起诉; 逮捕某人: *Two suspicious characters were brought in.* 逮捕了两名嫌疑犯. (**b**) introduce sb as an adviser, a helper, etc 介绍某人充当顾问、助手等: *Experts were brought in to advise the Government.* 请来了专家担当政府顾问. **bring sth in** (**a**) pick and gather (crops, fruit, etc) 摘取并收集(作物、水果等): *bring in a good harvest* 获得好收成. (**b**) introduce (legislation) 提出(议案): *bring in a bill to improve road safety* 提出改善道路安全的法案. (**c**) pronounce (a verdict on an accused person) 宣布(对被告的裁决): *The jury brought in a verdict of guilty.* 陪审团裁断被告有罪. **bring (sb) in sth** produce (an amount) as profit or income (for sb) (使某人)获得(某数额)作为利润或收入: *His freelance work brings (him) in £5 000 a year.* 他从事自由职业每年可获5 000英镑. ○ *He does odd jobs that bring him in about £30 a week.* 他做零工每周可赚约30英镑. **bring sb in (on sth)** allow sb to participate in sth 让某人参与某事: *Local residents were angry at not being brought in on* (ie not being consulted about) *the new housing scheme.* 新的房屋计划未征询当地居民的意见, 他们感到非常气愤.

bring sb off rescue sb from a ship 从船上救出某人: *The passengers and crew were brought off by the Dover lifeboat.* 乘客及船员都被多佛尔的救生艇救出. **bring sth off** (*infml* 口) manage to do (sth difficult) successfully 设法把(困难的事情)做成功: *The goalkeeper brought off a superb save.* 守门员漂亮地救出了险球. ○ *It was a difficult task, but we brought it off.* 那工作很困难, 但是我们圆满完成了.

bring sb on help (a learner, etc) to develop or improve 帮助(学习者等)进步或提高: *The coach is bringing on some promising youngsters in the reserve team.* 教练正在帮助后备队中有前途的年轻人提高技术. **bring sth on** (**a**) lead to, result in or cause sth 导致、造成或引起某事物: *He was out in the rain all day and this brought on a bad cold.* 他在外面淋了一天雨, 因此患了重感冒. ○ *nervous tension brought on by overwork* 因劳累过度所造成的神经紧张. (**b**) cause (crops, fruit, etc) to grow rapidly 促使(作物、水果等)迅速生长: *The hot weather is bringing the wheat on nicely.* 因天气热小麦长势良好. **bring sth on oneself/sb** cause sth (usu unpleasant) to happen to oneself/sb else 使(通常为不愉快的)某事发生在自己[别人]身上: *You have brought shame and disgrace on yourself and your family.* 你给你本人和家庭带来了耻辱.

bring sb out (**a**) cause sb to strike 使某人罢工: *The shop-stewards brought out the miners.* 工人代表发动矿工罢工. (**b**) cause sb to lose his shyness 使某人消除羞怯心理: *She's nice — but needs a lot of bringing out.* 她很不错, 但尚需多加克服羞怯心理. **bring sth out** (**a**) cause sth to appear or open 使某事物出现或开放: *The sunshine will bring out the blossom.* 阳光将使花朵开放. (**b**) produce sth; publish sth 生产某物; 出版某物: *The company is bringing out a new sports car.* 公司正在生产一种新跑车. ○ *bring out sb's latest novel* 出版某人最新小说 ○ *New personal computers are brought out almost daily.* 几乎每天都有新型个人计算机推出. (**c**) show sth clearly; reveal sth 清楚地显示出某事物; 揭示出某事物: *The enlargement brings out the details in the photograph.* 照片放大后细微之处都很清楚. (**d**) make sth clear or explicit 使某事物清楚或明白; 说明; 阐明: *bring out the meaning of a poem* 揭示一首诗的意义. (**e**) cause (a quality) to be seen in sb; elicit sth 使某人的(品质)显现; 引出某物: *A crisis brings out the best in her.* 在紧急关头看出了她的优秀品质. **bring sb out in sth** cause sb to be covered in sth 使某人浑身都有某事物: *The heat brought him out in a rash.* 因气温很高, 他浑身长了皮疹.

bring sb over (to...) cause sb to come to a place from overseas 使某人从海外来到某地: *Next summer he hopes to bring his family over from the States.* 他希望明年夏天把他一家人从美国接来. **bring sb over (to sth)** make sb change his way of thinking, loyalties, etc 使某人

B

改变思想方法、信念等: *bring sb over to one's cause* 把某人争取到己方.
bring sb round cause sb to regain consciousness after fainting 使某人恢复知觉: *Three women fainted in the heat but were quickly brought round with brandy.* 有三个女子中暑昏倒, 全靠白兰地使她们很快苏醒过来了.
bring sth round (*nautical* 海) make (a boat) face in the opposite direction 使(船)掉头. **bring sb round/around (to...)** cause sb to come to sb's house 使某人来串门: *Do bring your wife round one evening; we'd love to meet her.* 哪天晚上把你妻子带来, 我们都想见见她.
bring sb round (to sth) convert sb, esp to one's point of view 改变某人的观点(尤指使之与自己一致): *He wasn't keen on the plan, but we managed to bring him round.* 他本来不太喜欢这个计划, 但我们设法把他说服了. **bring sth round to sth** direct (a conversation) to a particular subject 把(话题)转移到某事物上: *He brought the discussion round to football.* 他把讨论的话题转到足球上去了.
bring sb through help sb to recover; save sb 促使某人痊愈; 拯救某人: *He was very ill, but the doctors brought him through.* 他病得很厉害, 但经医生治疗他已转危为安.
bring sb to = BRING SB ROUND. **bring sth to** (*nautical* 海) make (a boat) stop 使(船)停下.
bring A and B together help (two people or groups) to end a quarrel; reconcile 促使(争执双方)和解; 使和好: *The loss of their son brought the parents together.* 夫妻双方因失去儿子而言归于好.
bring sb under bring sb under control; subdue sb 控制某人; 制服某人: *The rebels were quickly brought under.* 叛乱者很快被制服了. **bring sth under sth** include sth within a category 将某事物纳人某一范畴; 归类: *The points to be discussed can be brought under three main headings.* 所论各点可以归为三个主要方面.
bring sb up (**a**) (esp passive 尤用于被动语态) raise, rear or educate sb 培养, 养育或教育某人: *She brought up five children.* 她养育了五个孩子. ○ *Her parents died when she was a baby and she was brought up by her aunt.* 她出生后不久父母双亡, 是由姑母抚养大的. ○ *a well-/badly-brought up child* 有教养的[教养不良的]孩子 ○ *He was brought up to* (ie taught as a child to) *respect authority.* 他从小就受到尊敬师长的教育. Cf 参看 UPBRINGING. (**b**) (*law* 律) cause sb to appear for trial 使某人出庭受审: *He was brought up on a charge of drunken driving.* 他被控醉后开车而出庭受审. (**c**) cause sb to stop moving or speaking suddenly 使某人突然停止移动或谈话: *His remark brought me up short/sharp/with a jerk.* 他的话我听后一下子愣住了. **bring sb/sth up** move or call (soldiers, guns, etc) to the front line 把(士兵、枪炮等)调往前线: *We need to bring up more tanks.* 我们需要多调些坦克到前线. **bring sth up** (**a**) vomit sth 呕吐某物: *bring up one's lunch* 吐出午饭吃的食物. (**b**) call attention to sth; raise sth 使注意某事物; 提出某事物: *These are matters that you can bring up in committee.* 这些事你可以在委员会上提出. **bring sb up against sth** make sb face or confront sth 使某人面临或面对某事物: *Working in the slums brought her up against the realities of poverty.* 她在贫民区工作, 使她正视贫困的现实. **bring sb/sth up to sth** bring sb/sth to (an acceptable level or standard) 使某人[某事物]达到(认可的水平或标准): *His work in maths needs to be brought up to the standard of the others.* 他的数学功课需要赶上别人的水平.
□ ˌ**bring-and-ˈbuy sale** (*Brit*) sale, often for charity, at which people bring items for sale and buy those brought by others 义卖(常为慈善性质, 人们自携物品进行交易).

brink /brɪŋk; brɪŋk/ *n* **1** [C usu *sing* 通常作单数] (**a**) edge at the top of a steep high place, eg a cliff (陡峭处, 如峭壁顶端的)边缘: *the brink of a precipice* 悬崖的边缘. (**b**) edge of a stretch of (usu deep) water 深渊的边缘: *He stood shivering on the brink, waiting to dive in.* 他站在边上等待跳水时浑身发抖. **2** [sing] **the ~ of sth** (*fig* 比喻) point or state very close to sth unknown, dangerous or exciting (未知的、危险的或刺激性事物的)边缘: *on the brink of death, war, disaster, success* 在死亡、战争、灾难、成功的边缘 ○ *Scientists are on the brink of (making) a breakthrough in the treatment of cancer.* 科学家们在治疗癌症方面即将获得重大突破. ○ *His incompetence has brought us to the brink of ruin.* 他很无能已导致我们濒临绝境.

brink·man·ship /ˈbrɪŋkmənʃɪp; ˋbrɪŋkmənˌʃɪp/ *n* [U] art or practice of pursuing a dangerous policy to the limits of safety, eg to the brink of war 边缘政策(将危险的政策推到极限, 如战争的边缘).

briny ⇨ BRINE.

bri·oche /ˈbriːɒʃ; *US* ˈbriːəʊʃ; ˋbrioʃ/ *n* small round sweetened bread roll 奶油圆蛋糕.

bri·quette (also **bri·quet**) /brɪˈket; brɪˋkɛt/ *n* small block of compressed coal-dust used as fuel 煤砖, 煤饼, 煤球(煤末压制成的燃料).

brisk /brɪsk; brɪsk/ *adj* (**-er**, **-est**) **1** quick; active; energetic 敏捷的; 活泼的; 精神饱满的: *a brisk walk, walker* 轻快的散步、走路轻快的人 ○ *at a brisk pace* 以轻快的步伐 ○ *a brisk and efficient manner* 胜任愉快的样子 ○ *Business is brisk today.* 今天生意兴隆. **2** giving a healthy feeling; refreshing 令人爽快的; 清新的: *a brisk breeze* 清新的微风. ▷ **briskly** *adv*. **brisk·ness** *n* [U].

bris·ket /ˈbrɪskɪt; ˋbrɪskɪt/ *n* [U] meat (usu beef) cut from the breast of an animal (动物的)胸肉(通常指牛肉).

bristle /ˈbrɪsl; ˋbrɪsḷ/ *n* **1** short stiff hair 短而硬的毛发: *a face covered with bristles* 满脸胡楂儿. **2** one of the short stiff hairs in a brush 刷子毛: *My toothbrush is losing its bristles.* 我的牙刷掉毛.
▷ **bristle** *v* **1** [I, Ip] **~ (up)** (of an animal's fur) stand up stiffly in fear or anger (指动物的毛)竖起(因惧怕或发怒): *The dog's fur bristled as it sensed danger.* 那狗觉察到危险时, 毛都竖立起来了. **2** [I, Ipr] **~ (with sth)** show anger, indignation, etc 显出愤怒、愤慨等: *bristle with defiance, pride, etc* 充溢着蔑视、傲慢等 ○ *She bristled (with rage) at his rude remarks.* 她听了他粗鲁的话怒不可遏. **3** (phr v) **bristle with sth** be thickly covered with sth; have a large number of sth (usu unpleasant) 覆盖着很厚的或很密的某物; 有大量的某事物(通常指坏的): *trenches bristling with machine-guns* 布满机枪的战壕 ○ *The problem bristles with difficulties.* 此问题困难重重.
bristly /ˈbrɪslɪ; ˋbrɪslɪ/ *adj* like or full of bristles; prickly; rough 如刚毛的; 多硬毛的; 有刺的; 粗糙的: *a bristly chin* 长满胡楂儿的下巴 ○ *She finds his beard too bristly.* 她觉得他的胡须太扎人.

Brit /brɪt; brɪt/ *n* (*esp joc or derog* 尤作戏谑语或作贬义) British person 英国人.

Brit·ain /ˈbrɪtn; ˋbrɪtṇ/ *n* = GREAT BRITAIN (GREAT). ⇨ Usage at GREAT 用法见 GREAT.

Bri·tan·nic /brɪˈtænɪk; brɪˋtænɪk/ *adj* **Her/His Britannic Majesty** (*fml* 文) Queen/King of Britain 英国女王[国王/陛下].

Brit·ish /ˈbrɪtɪʃ; ˋbrɪtɪʃ/ *adj* **1** of the United Kingdom (of Great Britain and Northern Ireland) or its inhabitants (大不列颠及北爱尔兰)联合王国的; 英国人民的: *a British passport* 英国护照 ○ *the British Government* 英国政府 ○ *He was born in France but his parents are British.* 他出生于法国, 但父母是英国人. **2** (idm 习语) **the best of British** ⇨ BEST[3].
▷ **the Brit·ish** *n* [pl *v*] British people 英国人民.
Brit·isher *n* (*US*) native or inhabitant of Britain, esp of England 英国人; (尤指)英格兰人.
□ ˌ**British ˈEnglish** English as spoken in the British Isles 英式英语(不列颠群岛的人说的英语).
the ˌBritish ˈIsles Britain and Ireland with the islands near their coasts 不列颠群岛(包括不列颠和爱尔兰两岛及周围小岛). ⇨illus at App 1 见附录1之插图, pages xiv, xv. ⇨Usage at GREAT 用法见 GREAT.

Briton /ˈbrɪtn; ˋbrɪtṇ/ *n* native or inhabitant of Britain 英国土著或居民. ⇨Usage at GREAT 用法见 GREAT.

brittle /ˈbrɪtl; ˋbrɪtḷ/ *adj* **1** (**a**) hard but easily broken; fragile 硬而易碎的; 脆弱的: *as brittle as thin glass* 如薄玻璃一样容易破碎. (**b**) (*fig* 比喻) easily damaged; insecure 容易损坏的; 不安全的: *He has a brittle temper,* ie loses his temper easily. 他脾气急. ○ *Constant stress has made our nerves brittle.* 我们长期处于紧张状态, 神经已吃不消了. **2** (of a sound) unpleasantly hard and sharp (指声音)尖利的: *a brittle laugh* 尖利的笑声 ○ *The orchestra was brittle in tone.* 管弦乐队演奏的曲调尖利刺耳. **3** (of a person) lacking in warmth; hard (指人)冷

淡的, 难相处的: *a cold, brittle woman* 冷漠、不好接近的女人. ▷ **brittle·ness** *n* [U].

broach /brəʊtʃ; brotʃ/ *v* [Tn] **1** make a hole in (a barrel) to draw off the liquid inside; open (a bottle, etc) to use the contents 在(桶)上打眼放出液体; 打开(瓶子等)以使用其中之物: *Let's broach another bottle of wine.* 我们再打开一瓶酒吧. **2** (*fig* 比喻) begin a discussion of (a topic) 开始商讨(一议题): *He broached the subject of a loan with his bank manager.* 他向银行经理提出贷款问题.

broad[1] /brɔ:d; brɔd/ *adj* (**-er**, **-est**) **1** large in size from one side to the other; wide 宽的; 阔的; 广的: *a broad street, avenue, river, canal, etc* 宽阔的街道、林阴道、河流、运河等 ○ *broad shoulders* 宽肩膀 ○ *He is tall, broad and muscular.* 他身高肩宽, 肌肉发达. Cf 参看 NARROW 1, THIN 1. **2** (after a phrase expressing measurement 用于表示量度的词组之后) from side to side; in breadth 宽: *a river twenty metres broad* 一条二十米宽的河. **3** (of land or sea) covering a wide area; extensive (指陆地或海洋)辽阔的, 宽广的: *a broad expanse of water* 辽阔无际的水面 ○ *The broad plains of the American West.* 美国西部辽阔的平原. ○ (*fig* 比喻) *There is broad support for the Government's policies.* 政府的政策得到广泛的拥护. **4** clear; obvious; unmistakable 清楚的; 明显的; 无误的: *a broad grin/smile* 咧嘴而笑 ○ *The Minister gave a broad hint that she intends to raise taxes.* 首相明白地暗示她打算提高税额. **5** [attrib 作定语] general; not detailed 大概的; 不详细的; 粗略的: *the broad outline of a plan, proposal, etc* 计划、建议等的提纲 ○ *The negotiators reached broad agreement on the main issues.* 谈判者在主要问题上基本达成协议. ○ *She's a feminist, in the broadest sense of the word.* 她大体上算是一个男女平等主义者. **6** (of ideas, opinions, etc) tolerant; liberal (指思想、意见等)宽宏的, 胸怀开阔的: *a man of broad views* 豁达大度的人. **7** (of speech) having many of the sounds typical of a particular region (指言语)方言腔调很重的: *a broad Yorkshire accent* 很重的约克郡口音. **8** indecent; coarse 下流的; 粗俗的: *broad humour* 粗俗的幽默. **9** (idm 习语) **(in) broad 'daylight** (in) the full light of day (在)光天化日; 大白天: *The robbery occurred in broad daylight, in a crowded street.* 在拥挤的街道上, 光天化日之下竟发生了抢劫. **broad in the 'beam** (*infml* 口) (of a person) rather fat round the hips (指人)臀部相当丰满的. **it's as ˌbroad as it's 'long** (*Brit infml* 口) it makes no real difference which of two alternatives one chooses 在两者中选择哪一个并无实际分别; 横竖都一样.

▷ **broaden** /ˈbrɔ:dn; ˋbrɔdn̩/ *v* [I, Ip, Tn] **~ (out)** (cause sth to) become broader (使某物)加宽; 变宽: *He* (ie His body) *broadened out in his twenties.* 他二十多岁时身躯变宽了. ○ *The road broadens (out) after this bend.* 经过这一弯处以后, 路就变宽了. ○ *You should broaden your experience by travelling more.* 你应该多到各地走走以增广见识.

broadly *adv* **1** in a broad[1](4) way 清楚地; 明显地; 无误地: *smile/grin broadly* 开怀地笑. **2** generally 一般地; 大体上; 概括地: *Broadly speaking, I agree with you.* 我大体上同意你的意见.

broad·ness *n* [U] = BREADTH.

the Broads *n* [pl] group of shallow lakes in E Anglia, popular for boating holidays 布罗兹区(英吉利郡东部以度假划船胜地见称的浅湖区): *the Norfolk Broads* 诺福克郡的布罗兹湖区. ⇨illus at App 1 见附录1之插图, pages xiv, xv.

□ **ˌbroad 'bean** (**a**) type of bean with large flat edible seeds 蚕豆(植物). (**b**) one of these seeds 蚕豆(种子).

ˌBroad 'Church group within the Church of England favouring a liberal interpretation of doctrine 广教会派(英国国教中主张不拘泥于教条的派别).

'broad jump (*US*) = LONG JUMP (LONG).

ˌbroad-'minded *adj* willing to listen to opinions different from one's own; not easily shocked; tolerant 愿意听取不同意见的; 心胸开阔的; 度量大的. **ˌbroad-'mindedness** *n* [U].

'broadsword *n* (formerly) large sword with a broad blade, used for cutting rather than stabbing (旧时)(宽刃的)大砍刀.

broad[2] /brɔ:d; brɔd/ *n* (*US sl* 俚) woman 女子.

broad·cast /ˈbrɔ:dkɑ:st; *US* ˈbrɔ:dkæst; ˋbrɔdˌkæst/ *v* (*pt, pp* **broadcast**) **1** (**a**) [Tn] send out (programmes) by radio or television (用无线电或电视)播送(节目): *broadcast the news, a concert, a football match* 播送新闻、音乐演奏、足球比赛. (**b**) [I] send out radio or television programmes 播送(无线电或电视)节目: *The BBC broadcasts all over the world.* 英国广播公司向全世界播送节目. **2** [I] speak or appear on radio or television (在无线电或电视上)讲话或出现: *He broadcasts on current affairs.* 他发表时事广播演说. **3** [Tn] make (sth) widely known 宣布(某事物): *broadcast one's views* 表明自己的观点. **4** [I, Tn] sow (seed) by scattering 撒播(种子).

▷ **broad·cast** *n* radio or television programme (无线电或电视的)广播节目: *a party political broadcast*, eg before an election 某党派的政治广播节目(如选举前) ○ *a broadcast of a football match* 足球比赛的广播节目.

broad·caster *n* person who broadcasts 广播员: *a well-known broadcaster on political/religious affairs* 政治[宗教]事务的著名广播员.

broad·cast·ing *n* [U] sending out programmes on radio or television (无线电或电视节目)广播: *work in broadcasting* 从事广播工作 ○ [attrib 作定语] *the British Broadcasting Corporation*, ie the BBC 英国广播公司.

broad·cloth /ˈbrɔ:dklɒθ; *US* -klɔ:θ; ˋbrɔdˌklɔθ/ *n* [U] fine cloth of cotton, wool or silk (棉、毛或丝织成的)细布.

broad·loom /ˈbrɔ:dlu:m; ˋbrɔdˌlum/ *n, adj* (carpet) woven in broad widths 织成宽幅的(地毯).

broad·sheet /ˈbrɔ:dʃi:t; ˋbrɔdˌʃit/ *n* **1** large sheet of paper printed on one side only with information or an advertisement, etc (单面印有信息、广告等的)大张印刷品. **2** newspaper printed on a large size of paper (大幅的)报纸. Cf 参看 TABLOID.

broad·side /ˈbrɔ:dsaɪd; ˋbrɔdˌsaɪd/ *n* **1** (**a**) firing at the same time of all the guns on one side of a warship (战舰一侧的)舷炮齐发: *fire a broadside* 舷炮轰击. (**b**) (*fig* 比喻) fierce attack in words, either written or spoken (口头或书面的)猛烈抨击: *The Prime Minister delivered a broadside at her critics.* 首相对批评她的人进行了猛烈抨击. **2** side of a ship above the water (水面以上的)舷侧. **3** (idm 习语) **broadside 'on (to sth)** (of a ship) with one side facing (sth); sideways on (指船)以侧面对着(某物): *The ship hit the harbour wall broadside on.* 这条船的侧面碰撞了港口岸壁.

bro·cade /brəˈkeɪd; broˋked/ *n* [C, U] fabric woven with a raised pattern, esp of gold or silver threads 浮花锦缎(尤指有金丝或银丝的): [attrib 作定语] *brocade curtains* 织锦帘子.

▷ **bro·cade** *v* [Tn] decorate (cloth) with raised patterns (织物上)织出浮花: *a dress brocaded with floral designs* 织有花卉图案的连衣裙.

broc·coli /ˈbrɒkəli; ˋbrɑkəlɪ/ *n* [U] type of cauliflower with many small greenish flower-heads, eaten as a vegetable 花椰菜; 花茎甘蓝. ⇨illus at CABBAGE 见 CABBAGE之插图.

bro·chure /ˈbrəʊʃə(r); *US* brəʊˈʃʊər; broˋʃʊr/ *n* booklet or pamphlet containing information about sth or advertising sth (作介绍或宣传用的)小册子: *a travel/holiday brochure* 旅游[度假]指南.

bro·derie ang·laise /ˌbrəʊdrɪ ɒ:ŋˈgleɪz; broˋdrɪ ɑŋˋglez/ *n* [U] open embroidery on white linen, etc; cloth embroidered in this way 英格兰刺绣(在白亚麻布等上的刺绣); 有英格兰刺绣的织物.

brogue[1] /brəʊg; brog/ *n* (usu *pl* 通常作复数) strong outdoor shoe with thick soles and a pattern in the leather (户外穿的结实的厚底)镂花皮鞋: *a pair of brogues* 一双镂花皮鞋.

brogue[2] /brəʊg; brog/ *n* (usu *sing* 通常作单数) strong regional accent, esp the Irish way of speaking English 土腔(尤指爱尔兰人说英语的腔调): *a soft Irish brogue* 柔和的爱尔兰土腔. Cf 参看 ACCENT 3, DIALECT.

broil /brɔɪl; brɔɪl/ *v* **1** (*esp US*) (**a**) [Tn] cook (meat) on a fire or gridiron; grill (在火上或铁架上)烧烤(肉类); 炙: *broil a chicken* 烤鸡. (**b**) [I] be cooked in this way 烧; 烤. **2** [I, Tn] (cause sb to) be or become very hot (使某人感到)极热: *sit broiling in the sun* 坐在阳光下曝晒 ○ *a broiling day* 炎热的一天.

▷ **broiler** *n* young chicken reared for broiling or roasting (适于烧烤的)嫩鸡: [attrib 作定语] *a broiler*

B

house, ie a building in which such chickens are kept and reared (饲养此类鸡的)鸡房. Cf 参看 ROASTER (ROAST).

broke[1] *pt* of BREAK[1].

broke[2] /brəʊk; brok/ *adj* **1** [pred 作表语] (*infml* 口) having no money; penniless; bankrupt 没有钱; 一个子儿也没有; 破产: *Could you lend me £10? I'm completely broke!* 你能借给我10英镑吗? 我一个钱也没有! **2** (idm 习语) **flat/stony broke** (*infml* 口) completely broke 穷到极点. **go for broke** (*infml* 口 *esp US*) risk everything in one determined attempt at sth 孤注一掷.

broken[1] *pp* of BREAK[1].

broken[2] /ˈbrəʊkən; ˋbrokən/ *adj* **1** [usu attrib 通常作定语] not continuous; disturbed or interrupted 中断的; 受打搅的; 受干扰的: *broken sleep* 断断续续的睡眠 ○ *broken sunshine* 时隐时现的阳光. **2** [attrib 作定语] (of a foreign language) spoken imperfectly; not fluent (指外语)蹩脚的, 不流利的: *speak in broken English* 英语说得不流利. **3** (of land) having an uneven surface; rough (指地面)凹凸不平的, 崎岖的: *an area of broken, rocky ground* 凹凸不平的、多岩石的地面. **4** [attrib 作定语] (of a person) weakened and exhausted by illness or misfortune (指人)因病或不幸而身心衰竭: *He was a broken man after the failure of his business.* 他生意失败以后, 整个人一蹶不振. **5** (idm 习语) **a broken ˈreed** person who has become unreliable or ineffective 不再可靠的人; 效率变低的人.

□ ˌ**broken-ˈdown** *adj* in a very bad condition; worn out or sick 状况极坏的; 筋疲力尽的; 有病的: *a ˌbroken-down old ˈcar, ˈman, ˈhorse* 破损的旧汽车、心力交瘁的人、筋疲力尽的马.

ˌ**broken-ˈhearted** *adj* overwhelmed by grief 心碎的; 伤心的; 悲哀的: *He was broken-hearted when his wife died.* 他在妻子死去时, 肝肠寸断.

ˌ**broken ˈhome** family in which the parents have divorced or separated 破裂的家庭(双亲离婚或分居): *He comes from a broken home.* 他来自一个破裂的家庭.

broker /ˈbrəʊkə(r); ˋbrokɚ/ *n* **1** person who buys and sells things (eg shares in a business) for others; middleman 经纪人(如替人买卖股票的); 中间人; 掮客: *insurance broker* 保险业经纪人. **2** = STOCKBROKER (STOCK[1]). **3** official appointed to sell the goods of sb who cannot pay his debts 出售无力偿债者财物的官员.

▷ **broker·age** /ˈbrəʊkərɪdʒ; ˋbrokərɪdʒ/ *n* [U] broker's fee or commission (中间人的)经手费、佣金或回扣.

brolly /ˈbrɒlɪ; ˋbrɑlɪ/ *n* (*infml* 口 *esp Brit*) umbrella 伞.

brom·ide /ˈbrəʊmaɪd; ˋbromaɪd/ *n* **1** [C, U] chemical compound of bromine, used in medicine to calm the nerves 溴化物(用作镇静剂). **2** [C] (*infml* 口) old, stale idea or statement 陈腐的想法或言语.

brom·ine /ˈbrəʊmiːn; ˋbromin/ *n* [U] chemical element, a non-metallic liquid, compounds of which are used in medicine and photography 溴. ⇨App 10 见附录10.

bron·chial /ˈbrɒŋkɪəl; ˋbrɑŋkɪəl/ *adj* [usu attrib 通常作定语] of or affecting the two main branches of the windpipe (**bronchial tubes** or **bronchi**) leading to the lungs 支气管的: *bronchial asthma* 支气管哮喘 ○ *bronchial pneumonia* 支气管肺炎. ⇨illus at RESPIRE 见 RESPIRE 之插图.

bron·chitis /brɒŋˈkaɪtɪs; brɑŋˋkaɪtɪs/ *n* [U] inflammation of the mucous membrane inside the bronchial tubes 支气管炎.

▷ **bron·chitic** /brɒŋˈkɪtɪk; brɑŋˋkɪtɪk/ *adj* suffering from or prone to bronchitis 患支气管炎的; 易患支气管炎的.

bronco /ˈbrɒŋkəʊ; ˋbrɑŋko/ *n* (*pl* **~s**) wild or half-tamed horse of the western US (美国西部的)野马或半驯服的马.

bron·to·saurus /ˌbrɒntəˈsɔːrəs; ˌbrɑntəˋsɔrəs/ *n* (*pl* **~es**) large plant-eating dinosaur 雷龙(一种巨大的食草恐龙).

Bronx cheer /ˌbrɒŋks ˈtʃɪə(r); ˌbrɑŋks ˋtʃɪr/ (*US infml* 口) = RASPBERRY 2.

bronze /brɒnz; brɑnz/ *n* **1** [U] alloy of copper and tin 青铜(铜与锡的合金): *a statue (cast) in bronze* 青铜像. **2** [U] colour of bronze; reddish-brown 青铜色; 赤褐色: *tanned a deep shade of bronze* 晒成了赤褐色. **3** [C] **(a)** work of art, eg a statue, made of bronze 青铜制艺术品(如铜像): *a fine collection of bronzes* 一批珍藏的青铜制品. **(b)** = BRONZE MEDAL.

▷ **bronze** *v* [Tn esp passive 尤用于被动语态] make (sth) bronze in colour 使(某物)变成赤褐色: *a face bronzed by the sun* 被太阳晒成赤褐色的面孔.

bronze *adj* made of or having the colour of bronze 青铜制成的; 青铜色的: *a bronze vase, statue, bowl, axe, etc* 青铜制的花瓶、雕像、碗、斧等 ○ *the bronze tints of autumn leaves* 秋天树叶的赤褐色.

□ **the ˈBronze Age** period when men used tools and weapons made of bronze (between the Stone Age and the Iron Age) 青铜器时代(介于石器时代与铁器时代之间).

bronze ˈmedal medal awarded as third prize in a competition or race (比赛获第三名奖给的)铜牌, 铜质奖章.

brooch /brəʊtʃ; brotʃ/ *n* ornament with a hinged pin and clasp, worn on women's clothes (女子衣物上佩带的)饰针, 胸针.

brood /bruːd; brud/ *n* [C, Gp] **1** all the young birds or other animals produced at one hatching or birth (一窝孵出的)幼鸟; (一次产出的)动物: *a hen and her brood (of chicks)* 母鸡和它的一窝小鸡. **2** (*joc* 谑) family of children 一家的孩子: *There's Mrs O'Brien taking her brood for a walk.* 奥布赖恩太太领着她那群孩子散步呢.

▷ **brood** *v* **1** [I] (of a bird) sit on eggs to hatch them (指鸟)孵雏. **2** [I, Ipr] **~ (on/over sth)** think (about sth) for a long time in a troubled or resentful way 忧闷地沉思(某事物): *When he's depressed he sits brooding for hours.* 他消沉的时候, 就坐着沉思几小时. ○ *It doesn't help to brood on your mistakes.* 对所犯的错误耿耿于怀是无济于事的.

broody *adj* (**-ier**, **-iest**) **1** **(a)** (of a hen) wanting to brood (指母鸡)要孵卵的. **(b)** (*fig* 比喻) (of a woman) badly wanting to have a baby (指妇女)迫切想有个孩子的. **2** (*fig* 比喻) moody; depressed 沮丧的; 抑郁的: *Why are you so broody today?* 你今天为什么这样闷闷不乐? **broodily** *adv*. **broodi·ness** *n* [U].

□ ˈ**brood-mare** *n* mare kept for breeding 传种母马.

brook[1] /brʊk; brʊk/ *n* small stream 小溪.

brook[2] /brʊk; brʊk/ *v* [Tn, Tg, Tsg] (*fml* 文) (usu with a negative 通常与否定词连用) tolerate (sth); allow 忍受(某事物); 容让: *a strict teacher who brooks no nonsense from her pupils* 不容学生胡闹的严格的女教师 ○ *I will not brook anyone interfering with my affairs.* 我决不让任何人干预我的事.

broom[1] /bruːm; brum/ *n* [U] shrub with yellow or white flowers growing esp on sandy ground 金雀花(多生长于沙地).

broom[2] /bruːm, also brʊm; brum/ *n* **1** brush with a long handle for sweeping floors 扫帚. **2** (idm 习语) **a new broom** ⇨ NEW.

□ ˈ**broomstick** *n* handle of a broom (on which witches were said to ride through the air) 扫帚柄(传说巫婆乘之飞行).

Bros *abbr* 缩写 = (*commerce* 商) Brothers: *Hanley Bros Ltd, Architects & Surveyors* 汉利兄弟建筑及测量有限公司.

broth /brɒθ; *US* brɔːθ; brɔθ/ *n* [U] **1** water in which meat, fish or vegetables have been boiled; stock (煮肉、鱼或蔬菜的)清汤; 原汤; 高汤. **2** soup made from this (以上述汤料做的)汤: *Scotch broth* 苏格兰汤. **3** (idm 习语) **too many cooks spoil the broth** ⇨ COOK *n*.

brothel /ˈbrɒθl; ˋbrɑθəl/ *n* house where men pay to have sex with prostitutes 妓院.

brother /ˈbrʌðə(r); ˋbrʌðɚ/ *n* **1** man or boy having the same parents as another person 兄; 弟: *my elder/younger brother* 我的哥哥[弟弟] ○ *Does she have any brothers or sisters?* 她有兄弟姐妹吗? ○ *Have you invited the Smith brothers to the party?* 你邀请史密斯兄弟参加宴会了吗? ○ *He was like a brother to me*, ie very kind. 他待我像兄弟一样. ⇨App 8 见附录8. **2** person united with others by belonging to the same group, society, profession, etc 同志; 同人; 同行; 同业; 同事: *We are all brothers in the same fight against injustice.* 在共同反对非正义行为的斗争中, 我们都是同志. ○ [attrib 作定语] *He was greatly respected by his brother doctors/officers.* 与他共事的医生[军官]对他非常尊敬. **3** (*pl* **brethren** /ˈbreðrən; ˋbrɛðrən/) **(a)** (title of a) member of a religious order, esp a monk (同教会的)教友(的称呼); (尤指)修士: *Brother Luke will say grace.* 卢克修士将做感恩祷告. **(b)**

member of certain evangelical Christian sects (基督教某些福音派的)教友: *The Brethren hold a prayer meeting every Thursday.* 教友每周四举行一次祷告会. **4** (idm 习语) **brothers in 'arms** soldiers serving together, esp in wartime 战友.

▷ **brother** *interj* (*esp US*) (used to express irritation or surprise 用以表示恼怒或惊奇): *Oh, brother!* 嘎，好傢伙!

broth·er·hood /-hʊd; -ˌhʊd/ *n* **1** [U] (**a**) relationship of brothers 兄弟的关系: *the ties of brotherhood* 兄弟间的手足亲情. (**b**) comradeship; friendship between brothers 同志关系; 兄弟情谊: *live in peace and brotherhood* 和睦友好地生活. **2** [C, Gp] members of an association formed for a particular purpose, eg a religious society or socialist organization 全体志同道合者(如宗教社团或社会主义组织中的).

broth·erly *adj* of or like a brother 兄弟的; 兄弟般的: *brotherly love/affection/feelings* 兄弟般的爱[深情/感情]. **broth·er·li·ness** *n* [U].

□ **brother-in-law** /ˈbrʌðər ɪn lɔ:; ˈbrʌðər ɪn ˌlɔ/ (*pl* **-s-in-law** /ˈbrʌðəz ɪn lɔ:; ˈbrʌðərz ɪn ˌlɔ/) **1** brother of one's husband or wife 大伯子; 小叔子; 内兄; 内弟. **2** husband of one's sister 姐夫; 妹夫. **3** husband of the sister of one's wife or husband 姐夫, 妹夫(妻子或丈夫的姐姐或妹妹的丈夫). ⇨App 8 见附录8.

brougham /ˈbru:əm; ˈbruəm/ *n* (formerly) four-wheeled closed carriage drawn by one horse (旧时)(一匹马拉的有车厢的)四轮马车.

brought *pt, pp* of BRING.

brou·haha /ˈbru:hɑ:hɑ:; *US* ˈbru:hɑ:hɑ:; ˈbruhɑhɑ/ *n* [U] (*infml* 口) noisy excitement or commotion 喧嚷; 骚动.

brow /braʊ; braʊ/ *n* **1** (usu *pl* 通常作复数) = EYEBROW. **2** = FOREHEAD: *mop one's brow* 擦前额. ⇨Usage at BODY 用法见 BODY. **3** slope leading to the top (of a hill); edge (of a cliff) (山的)坡顶; (悬崖的)边缘: *Our car stalled on the brow of a steep hill.* 我们的汽车在山顶陡坡处抛锚了. **4** (idm 习语) **knit one's 'brow(s)** ⇨ KNIT.

brow·beat /ˈbraʊbi:t; ˈbraʊˌbit/ *v* (*pt* **browbeat**, *pp* **browbeaten** /ˈbraʊbi:tn; ˈbraʊˌbitn̩/) [Tn, Tn·pr] **~ sb (into doing sth)** frighten sb with stern looks and words; bully; intimidate (以神情或言语)吓唬某人; 欺侮; 威吓: *The judge browbeat the witness.* 那法官威吓证人. ○ *I won't be browbeaten into accepting your proposals.* 我不会在威迫之下接受你的提议.

▷ **brow·beaten** *adj* frightened through constant bullying (因不断受欺侮)害怕的: *a poor, browbeaten little clerk* 可怜的、被吓坏的小职员.

brown /braʊn; braʊn/ *adj* (**-er, -est**) **1** having the colour of toasted bread, or coffee mixed with milk 褐色的; 棕色的: *brown eyes* 棕色的眼睛 ○ *dark brown shoes* 深褐色的皮鞋 ○ *leaves turning brown in the autumn* 秋天枯黄的树叶. **2** having skin of this colour; sun-tanned 棕色皮肤的; 太阳晒黑的: *He's very brown after his summer holiday.* 他一暑假皮肤晒得黝黑. **3** (idm 习语) **(as) brown as a 'berry** having skin tanned brown by the sun or the weather 皮肤晒得黝黑的. **in a brown 'study** in deep thought; in a reverie 沉思; 默想; 出神.

▷ **brown** *n* **1** [C, U] brown colour 棕色: *leaves of various shades of brown* 各种深浅不同的棕色树叶. **2** [U] brown clothes 褐色衣物: *Brown doesn't suit you.* 你不适合穿褐色衣服.

brown *v* [I, Tn] **1** (cause sth to) become brown (使某物)变成褐色: *Heat the butter until it browns.* 把黄油加热, 直到变成褐色为止. ○ *a face browned by the sun* 太阳晒黑了的面孔. **2** (idm 习语) **browned 'off** (*infml* 口 *esp Brit*) bored; fed up; disheartened 厌烦的; 忍受够了的; 气馁的: *He's browned off with his job.* 他厌烦他的工作.

brown·ing *n* [U] substance for colouring gravy (调制肉汁的)棕色着色剂.

brown·ish, browny *adjs* tending towards brown; fairly brown 带褐色的; 近棕色的.

□ ˌ**brown 'bread** bread made with wholemeal flour 黑面包.

ˌ**brown 'paper** strong coarse paper for wrapping parcels, etc (棕色的粗糙的)包装纸.

'**brownstone** *n* [U] reddish-brown sandstone used for building (建筑用的)褐沙石.

ˌ**brown 'sugar** sugar that is only partly refined 红糖; 黄糖.

brownie /ˈbraʊnɪ; ˈbraʊnɪ/ *n* **1** small good-natured fairy 棕仙(性情善良的小精灵). **2 Brownie** (also **Brownie Guide**) member of the junior branch of the Guides (who wear brown uniforms) (身着褐色制服的)幼年童子军. **3** (*esp US*) small rich cake made with chocolate and nuts (带坚果的)巧克力蛋糕.

B

browse /braʊz; braʊz/ *v* **1** (**a**) [I] examine books in a casual, leisurely way 随意翻阅书刊; 浏览: *browse in a library/bookshop* 在图书馆[书店]里浏览书籍. (**b**) [Ipr] **~ through sth** look through (a book, etc) in this way 浏览(书等): *browse through a magazine* 浏览杂志. **2** [I] (of cows, goats, etc) feed by nibbling grass, leaves, etc (指牛、羊等)吃(草、树叶等): *cattle browsing in the fields* 在田间吃草的牛.

▷ **browse** *n* (usu *sing* 通常作单数) (act or period of) browsing 浏览: *have a browse in a bookshop* 在书店浏览一段时间.

bruise /bru:z; bruz/ *n* injury caused by a blow to the body or to a fruit, discolouring the skin but not breaking it 挫伤: *He was covered in bruises after falling off his bicycle.* 他从自行车上摔下来, 满身青一块、紫一块.

▷ **bruise** *v* **1** [Tn] cause a bruise or bruises on (sth/sb) 使(某物[某人])受挫伤: *He fell and bruised himself/his leg.* 他跌倒后身体[腿]受了挫伤. ○ *Her face was badly bruised in the crash.* 她碰得鼻青脸肿. **2** [I] show the effects of a blow or knock 显出击伤或碰伤: *Don't drop the peaches — they bruise easily.* 桃儿容易碰伤——要轻拿轻放. ○ (*fig* 比喻) *Don't hurt her feelings — she bruises very easily.* 别伤害她的感情——她很娇气. **bruiser** *n* (*infml* 口) large strong tough man 彪形大汉: *He looks a real bruiser.* 他真像个彪形大汉.

bruit /bru:t; brut/ *v* (phr v) **~ sth abroad/about** (*fml or joc* 文或谑) spread (a rumour or report) 散布(谣言或传言): *It's been bruited about that...* 到处传播... ○ *The news of the impending marriage was bruited abroad.* 婚期临近的消息传遍了各处.

brunch /brʌntʃ; brʌntʃ/ *n* [C, U] (*infml* 口 *esp US*) late morning meal eaten instead of breakfast and lunch 早午餐(早餐和午餐并作一顿吃).

bru·nette /bru:ˈnet; bruˈnɛt/ *n* white woman with dark-brown hair and (usu) darkish skin (生有深褐色头发和通常为浅黑色皮肤的)白种女子. Cf 参看 BLOND.

brunt /brʌnt; brʌnt/ *n* (idm 习语) **bear the brunt of sth** ⇨ BEAR[2].

brush 刷子

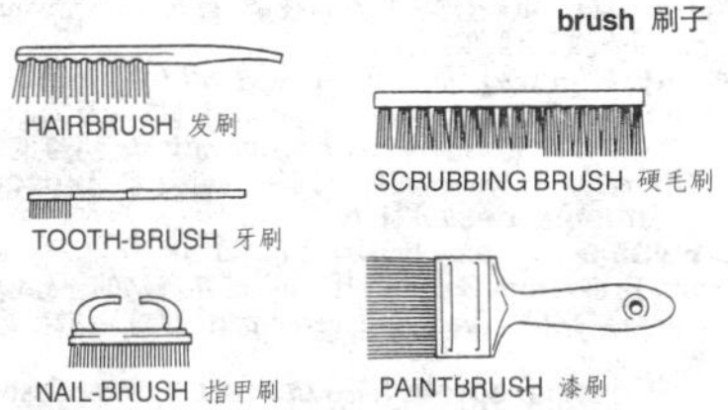

brush[1] /brʌʃ; brʌʃ/ *n* **1** [C] implement with bristles of hair, wire, nylon, etc set in a block of wood, etc and used for scrubbing, sweeping, cleaning, painting, tidying the hair, etc (用鬃毛、金属丝、尼龙等制造的)刷子, 画笔, 毛笔: *a 'clothes-brush* 衣刷 ○ *a 'tooth-brush* 牙刷 ○ *a 'paintbrush* 画笔 ○ *a 'hairbrush* 发刷. ⇨illus 见插图. **2** [sing] act of brushing 刷: *give one's clothes, shoes, teeth, hair a good brush* 把自己的衣服、鞋、牙齿、头发好好刷一刷. **3** [sing] light touch (made in passing) (经过时)轻触: *He knocked a glass off the table with a brush of his coat/arm.* 他的大衣[手臂]把桌上的玻璃杯碰掉了. **4** [C] fox's tail 狐狸尾巴. ⇨illus at App 1 见附录1之插图, page iii. **5** [U] land covered by small trees and shrubs; undergrowth 灌木丛地带; 矮树丛: [attrib 作定语] *a brush fire* 灌木丛火灾. **6** [C] **~ with sb** short unfriendly encounter with sb; quarrel 与某人有小冲突; 争吵: *a brush with the law/police* 轻微的触犯法律[与警方有小冲突] ○ *She had a nasty brush with her boss this* *morning*. 今天早晨她跟老板大吵了一顿. **7** (idm 习语) **tarred with the same brush** ⇨ TAR[1].

□ ˈ**brushwood** *n* [U] **1** broken or cut branches or twigs (折断的或砍下的)树枝. **2** = BRUSH[1] 5.

ˈ**brushwork** *n* [U] particular way in which an artist paints with a brush (画家的)笔法: *Picasso's brushwork is particularly fine*. 毕加索的笔法精妙绝伦.

B

brush[2] /brʌʃ; brʌʃ/ *v* **1** [Tn] use a brush on (sb/sth); clean, polish, make tidy or smooth with a brush 用刷子刷(某人[某物]); 刷干净; 刷亮; 刷整齐; 刷顺: *brush your clothes, shoes, hair, teeth* 刷你的衣服、鞋、头发、牙齿. **2** [Cn·a] put (sth) into a particular state with a brush 把(某物)刷成某种状态: *brush one's teeth clean* 把牙齿刷干净. **3** [Tn] touch (sb) lightly in passing 经过时触及(某人): *leaves brushing one's cheek* 拂着面颊的树叶 ○ *His hand brushed hers.* 他的手碰到她的手. **4** (phr v) **brush against/by/past sb/sth** touch sb/sth lightly while moving close to him/it 接近某人[某物]时轻轻相碰: *She brushed past him without saying a word.* 她经过时碰了他一下, 一句话也没说. ○ *A cat brushed against her leg in the darkness.* 黑暗中, 一只猫蹭着了她的腿. **brush sb/sth aside** push sb/sth to one side; pay little or no attention to sb/sth 把某人[某事物]推在一边; 漠视某人: *The enemy brushed aside our defences.* 敌人冲破了我们的防御工事. ○ *He brushed aside my objections to his plan.* 我反对他的计划, 他不予理会. **brush sth away/off** remove sth (from sth) with or as if with a brush (从某事物上)刷去(或好像刷去)某事物: *brush mud off (one's trousers)* 把(裤子上的)泥土刷掉 ○ *He brushed the fly away (from his face).* 他把苍蝇(从脸上)赶走. **brush oneself/sth down** clean oneself/sth by thorough brushing 把自己[某物]刷干净: *Your coat needs brushing down. It's covered in dust.* 你的大衣需要刷干净, 上面满是灰尘. **brush off** be removed by brushing 被刷掉: *Mud brushes off easily when it's dry.* 泥土干后容易刷掉. **brush sb ˈoff** (*infml* 口) refuse to listen to sb; ignore sb 不理会某人; 漠视某人: *He's very keen on her but she's always brushing him ˈoff.* 他非常喜爱她, 但她总是不理睬他. **brush sth up/brush up on sth** study or practise sth in order to get back a skill that was lost 重温, 重新练习(已荒疏的技巧): *I must brush up (on) my Italian before I go to Rome*. 我去罗马以前必须把意大利语重温一下.

□ ˈ**brush-off** *n* (*pl* **brush-offs**) (*infml* 口) rejection; snub 拒绝; 怠慢: *She gave him the brush-off*. 她给他来个不理睬.

ˈ**brush-up** *n* (*pl* **brush-ups**) **1** act of tidying one's appearance 打扮整洁. **2** act of studying to get back former skill 重新学习过去的技能: *give one's Spanish a brush-up* 重温西班牙语.

brusque /bruːsk; *US* brʌsk; brʌsk/ *adj* (of a person, his manner, etc) rough and abrupt; curt (指人及人的举止等)粗暴和唐突, 无礼的: *a brusque attitude* 粗鲁的举止 ○ *His reply was brusque*. 他的回答很唐突. ▷ **brusquely** *adv*. **brusque·ness** *n* [U].

Brus·sels /ˈbrʌslz; ˋbrʌslz/ *adj* [attrib 作定语] of or from Brussels in Belgium 比利时布鲁塞尔的; 从比利时布鲁塞尔来的: *Brussels lace/carpets* 布鲁塞尔花边[地毯].

□ ˌ**Brussels ˈsprout** (also **sprout**) **1** type of cabbage with edible buds like tiny cabbages growing on its stem 汤菜; 抱子甘蓝. **2** (esp *pl* 尤作复数) one of these buds, eaten as a vegetable 汤菜(可食用的球芽). ⇨ illus at CABBAGE 见 CABBAGE 之插图.

bru·tal /ˈbruːtl; ˋbrutl/ *adj* cruel; savage; merciless 残忍的; 野蛮的; 冷酷无情的: *a brutal tyrant, dictator, murderer, etc* 残忍的暴君、独裁者、谋杀犯等 ○ *a brutal attack, murder, punishment* 野蛮的进攻、谋杀、惩罚.

▷ **bru·tal·ity** /bruːˈtæləti; bruˋtælətɪ/ *n* **1** [U] brutal behaviour; cruelty; savagery 野蛮的行为; 残忍; 野蛮. **2** [C] brutal act 暴行: *the brutalities of war* 战争的暴行.

bru·tal·ize, -ise *v* [Tn usu passive 通常用于被动语态] make (sb) brutal or insensitive 使(某人)变得残酷无情: *soldiers brutalized by a long war* 因长期战争而变得残忍的士兵.

bru·tally /ˈbruːtəlɪ; ˋbrutlɪ/ *adv*.

brute /bruːt; brut/ *n* **1** animal, esp a large or fierce one 野兽(尤指巨大或凶猛的): *That dog looks a real brute.* 那条狗真像一只野兽. **2** (*sometimes joc* 有时作戏谑语) brutal and insensitive person 残忍及冷酷无情的人: *His father was a drunken brute.* 他的父亲是个酗酒成性、冷酷无情的人. ○ *You've forgotten my birthday again, you brute!* 你真没良心, 又把我的生日忘了! **3** unpleasant or difficult thing 令人不快或难办的事情: *a brute of a problem* 棘手的问题 ○ *This lock's a brute — it just won't open*. 这个锁真讨厌——就是打不开.

▷ **brute** *adj* [attrib 作定语] not involving thought or reason; unthinking 无理性的; 无思想的: *brute force/strength* 暴力[蛮力].

bru·tish *adj* of or like a brute 野兽的; 野兽般的: *brutish behaviour, manners, etc* 野兽般的行为[举止].

bru·tishly *adv*.

BS /ˌbiː ˈes; ˌbi ˋɛs/ *abbr* 缩写 = **1** (*US*) Bachelor of Science 理学学士. **2** (*Brit*) Bachelor of Surgery 外科学士: *have/be a BS* 有外科学士学位[为外科学士] ○ *Tom Hunt MB, BS* 汤姆·亨特医学士, 外科学士. **3** (on labels, etc) British Standard (showing the specification number of the British Standards Institution) (标签等上的)英国标准(表明英国标准学会的规格编号): *produced to BS4353* 按照英国标准规格编号 4353 生产的. Cf 参看 ASA 2.

BSc /ˌbiː es ˈsiː; ˌbi ɛs ˋsi/ (*US* **BS**) *abbr* 缩写 = Bachelor of Science 理学学士: *have/be a BSc in Botany* 有植物学理学学士学位[为植物学理学学士] ○ *Jill Ayres BSc* 吉尔·艾尔斯理学学士.

BSI /ˌbiː es ˈaɪ; ˌbi ɛs ˋaɪ/ *abbr* 缩写 = British Standards Institution 英国标准学会.

BST /ˌbiː es ˈtiː; ˌbi ɛs ˋti/ *abbr* 缩写 = British Summer Time 英国夏令时间. Cf 参看 GMT.

Bt *abbr* 缩写 = Baronet: *James Hyde-Stanley Bt* 詹姆士·海德·斯坦利准男爵.

BTA /ˌbiː tiː ˈeɪ; ˌbi ti ˋe/ *abbr* 缩写 = British Tourist Authority 英国旅游管理局.

Bthu (also **Btu**) *abbr* 缩写 = British thermal unit(s) 英国热量单位.

bubble /ˈbʌbl; ˋbʌbl/ *n* **1** floating ball formed of liquid and containing air or gas (液体形成的)气泡: *soap bubbles* 肥皂泡 ○ *Children love blowing bubbles*. 儿童爱吹泡泡. **2** ball of air or gas in a liquid or a solidified liquid such as glass (液体或由液体变成的固体, 如玻璃, 中存留的)气泡: *Champagne is full of bubbles.* 香槟酒有很多气泡. ○ *This glass vase has a bubble in its base*. 这个玻璃花瓶底座里有一个气泡. **3** (idm 习语) **prick the bubble** ⇨ PRICK[2].

▷ **bubble** *v* **1** [I] (of a liquid) rise in or form bubbles; boil (指液体)起泡, 沸腾: *stew bubbling in the pot* 在锅里冒着泡的炖肉. **2** [I] make the sound of bubbles 发出气泡声: *a bubbling stream/fountain* 汩汩的溪流[泉水]. **3** [I, Ipr, Ip] ~ **(over) (with sth)** (*fig* 比喻) be full of (usu happy) feelings 充满(通常指喜悦的)感情: *be bubbling (over) with excitement, enthusiasm, high spirits, etc* 充满激动、兴奋、高昂等情绪. **4** (phr v) **bubble along, out, over, up, etc** move in the specified direction in bubbles or with a bubbling sound 向某方向汩汩地流动: *a spring bubbling out of the ground* 汩汩冒出地面的泉水 ○ *Gases from deep in the earth bubble up through the lake*. 地下深处的气体从湖底冒了出来.

bubbly /ˈbʌblɪ; ˋbʌblɪ/ *adj* (**-ier, -iest**) **1** full of bubbles 充满气泡的: *bubbly lemonade* 泡多的汽水. **2** (*fig approv* 比喻, 褒) (usu of a woman) lively; vivacious; animated (通常指女子)活泼的, 快活的, 生气勃勃的: *a bubbly personality* 活泼的个性. — *n* [U] (*infml* 口) champagne 香槟酒: *Have some more bubbly!* 再喝一些香槟酒吧!

□ ˌ**bubble and ˈsqueak** cooked cabbage and potato mixed and fried 洋白菜煎土豆.

ˈ**bubble bath** liquid, crystals or powder added to a bath to make it foam and smell pleasant (加进浴水中可产生泡沫和香味的)泡沫液, 泡沫粒, 泡沫粉.

ˈ**bubble gum** chewing-gum that can be blown into bubbles 泡泡糖(可吹成泡泡的口香糖).

bu·bonic plague /bjuːˌbɒnɪk ˈpleɪg; bjuˌbɑnɪk ˋpleg/ (also **the plague**) contagious, usu fatal, disease spread by rats, causing swellings in the armpits and groin, fever and delirium 腺鼠疫; 腹股沟淋巴结鼠疫.

buc·can·eer /ˌbʌkəˈnɪə(r); ˌbʌkəˋnɪr/ *n* **1** pirate 海盗. **2** unscrupulous and reckless person 肆无忌惮的人.

buck[1] /bʌk; bʌk/ *n* **1** (*pl* unchanged or **~s** 复数或不变

或作 **bucks**) male deer, hare or rabbit 雄鹿; 雄兔. Cf 参看 STAG 1. **2** (*US sl derog* 俚, 贬) [esp attrib 尤作定语] young Indian or Negro man 年轻的印第安人或黑人.

□ ˈ**buckskin** *n* [U] soft leather made from the skin of deer or goats, used for making gloves, bags, etc (鹿皮或羊皮所制成的)柔软皮革(用以制手套、皮包等).

ˌ**buck-ˈtooth** *n* (*pl* **-teeth**) projecting upper front tooth (突出的)上前牙; 獠牙.

buck² /bʌk; bʌk/ *v* **1** (**a**) [I] (of a horse) jump with the four feet together and the back arched (指马)弓背跳跃. (**b**) [Tn, Tn·p] **~ sb (off)** throw (a rider) to the ground by doing this (马弓背跳跃)将(骑者)摔于地上. **2** [Tn] (*US infml* 口) resist or oppose (sb/sth) 反抗、反对(某人[某事]): *Don't try to buck the system.* 不要反对这个制度. **3** (idm 习语) **buck one's iˈdeas up** (*infml* 口) become more alert; take a more serious and responsible attitude 打起精神; 认真负责. **4** (phr v) **buck ˈup** (*infml* 口) hurry 赶紧; 赶快: *Buck up! We're going to be late.* 快点儿! 我们快要晚了. **buck (sb) up** (*infml* 口) (cause sb to) become more cheerful (使某人)高兴起来, 打起精神来: *The good news bucked us all up.* 大家听了这个好消息都高兴起来. ○ *Buck up! Things aren't as bad as you think.* 打起精神来! 事情并非像你想的那么糟.

▷ **bucked** *adj* [pred 作表语] (*infml* 口 *esp Brit*) pleased and encouraged 高兴; 受鼓舞: *She felt really bucked after passing her driving test.* 她驾驶测验合格后, 感到很高兴.

buck³ /bʌk; bʌk/ *n* (*US infml* 口) US dollar 美元. ⇨App 4 见附录4.

buck⁴ /bʌk; bʌk/ *n* **1** object formerly placed in front of a player whose turn it was to deal in poker (旧时扑克牌戏中, 轮到某牌手做庄时, 置于其前面的)庄家标志. **2** (idm 习语) **the buck stops ˈhere** (*catchphrase* 警语) responsibility or blame is accepted here and cannot be passed on to sb else 责无旁贷(承担责任而不推诿给别人). **pass the buck** ⇨ PASS².

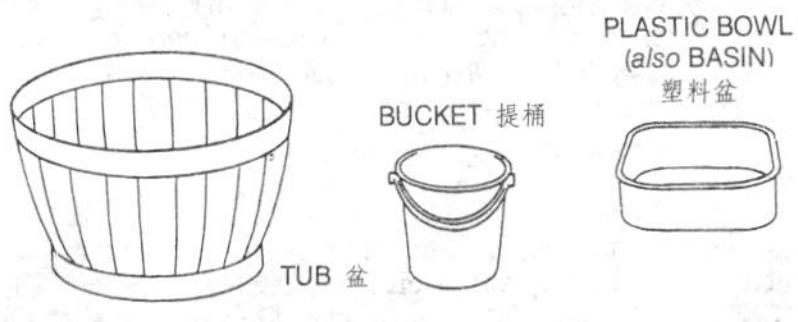

bucket /ˈbʌkɪt; ˋbʌkɪt/ *n* **1** round open container with a handle for carrying or holding liquids, sand, etc (带提梁的)圆桶; 提桶: *build sandcastles with a bucket and spade* 用提桶和铁铲建造沙堆模型城堡. ⇨illus 见插图. **2** (also ˈ**bucket·ful**) amount a bucket contains 一桶的量; 一满桶: *two buckets/bucketfuls of water* 两桶[满桶]水. **3** scoop of a mechanical shovel, dredger, water-wheel, etc (挖土机、挖泥机上的)铲斗; (水轮机上的)戽斗等. **4 buckets** [pl] large amounts (esp of rain or tears) 大量(尤指雨或泪): *The rain came down/fell in buckets.* 大雨倾盆而下. ○ *She wept buckets.* 她泪如雨下. **5** (idm 习语) **a drop in the bucket/ocean** ⇨ DROP¹. **kick the ˈbucket** ⇨ KICK¹.

▷ **bucket** *v* [I, Ip] **~ (down)** (of rain) pour down heavily (指雨)倾盆而下: *It/The rain bucketed down all afternoon.* 瓢泼大雨下了一下午.

□ ˈ**bucket seat** (in a car or an aircraft) seat with a rounded back, for one person (汽车或飞机上的)凹背单人坐具.

ˈ**bucket-shop** *n* (*infml derog* 口, 贬) unregistered business, esp one selling cheap airline tickets 无照商号(尤指卖廉价机票的).

buck·eye /ˈbʌkaɪ; ˋbʌkˌaɪ/ *n* (*US*) **1** horse-chestnut tree 七叶树. **2** its shiny reddish-brown nut (七叶树的)坚果(光滑, 呈红褐色).

buckle /ˈbʌkl; ˋbʌkl/ *n* **1** metal or plastic clasp with a hinged spike for fastening a belt or straps (皮带等的)锁扣, 扣环. **2** ornamental clasp on a shoe (鞋上的)装饰扣.

▷ **buckle** *v* **1** [I, Ip, Tn, Tn·p] **~ (sth) (up)** fasten (sth) or be fastened with a buckle 用锁扣扣紧(某物): *My belt is loose; I didn't buckle it up tightly enough.* 我的腰带松了, 我没扣紧. ○ *These shoes buckle at the side.* 这鞋在侧面系扣. **2** [I, Tn] (cause sb/sth to) crumple or bend (usu because of pressure or heat) (使某人[某事物])屈服, 顺从, 让步, 弄弯, 变形(通常因受力或受热所致): *The metal buckled in the heat.* 金属因受热而变形. ○ *The crash buckled the front of my car.* 我的汽车前部撞瘪了. ○ (*fig* 比喻) *He's beginning to buckle under the pressure of work.* 工作快要把他压垮了. **3** (phr v) **buckle down to sth** (*infml* 口) start sth in a determined way 下定决心做某事: *She's really buckling down to her new job.* 她埋头苦干做新工作. **buckle sb in/into sth** fasten sb in (a seat, etc) with a belt 用皮带把某人扣在(座位等)上: *The parachutist was buckled into his harness.* 跳伞者扣上了背带. **buckle (sth) on** (cause sth to) be attached with a buckle (使某物)被锁扣扣住: *a sword that buckles on* 用锁扣扣住的剑 ○ *buckle on one's belt* 把自己的皮带系紧. **buckle ˈto** (*infml* 口) (esp of a group) make a special effort (usu in the face of difficulties) (尤指集体)特别努力(通常为面对困难时): *The children had to buckle to while their mother was in hospital.* 孩子们因母亲住院只好事事更加努力.

buck·ler /ˈbʌklə(r); ˋbʌklɚ/ *n* small round shield held by a handle or worn on the arm (有柄的或戴在臂上的)小圆盾.

buck·ram /ˈbʌkrəm; ˋbʌkrəm/ *n* [U] stiff cloth used esp for binding books 硬布(尤用于装订书籍).

buck·shee /ˌbʌkˈʃiː; ˋbʌkˌʃi/ *adj, adv* (*Brit sl* 俚) free of charge 免费(的): *buckshee tickets* 免费票 ○ *travel buckshee* 免费旅行.

buck·shot /ˈbʌkʃɒt; ˋbʌkˌʃɑt/ *n* [U] large size of lead shot¹(5) for firing from shotguns (猎枪用的)大号铅弹.

buck·wheat /ˈbʌkwiːt; *US* -hwiːt; ˋbʌkˌhwit/ *n* [U] dark seeds of grain used for feeding horses and poultry 荞麦.

□ ˈ**buckwheat flour** flour made from these seeds, used in US for breakfast pancakes 荞麦粉; 荞麦面.

bu·colic /bjuːˈkɒlɪk; bjuˋkɑlɪk/ *adj* of country life or the countryside; rustic 乡村生活的; 田园生活的.

▷ **bu·colics** *n* [pl] poems about country life 田园诗.

bud /bʌd; bʌd/ *n* **1** small knob from which a flower, branch or cluster of leaves develops 花蕾; (枝叶的)芽: *Buds appear on the trees in spring.* 春天树木发芽了. **2** flower or leaf not fully open 未全开的花; 未长成的叶. ⇨illus at App 1 见附录1之插图, page ii. **3** (idm 习语) **(be) in bud** having or sending out buds 含苞待放中; 萌芽中: *The trees and hedgerows are in bud.* 大树小树都已长出嫩芽. **nip sth in the bud** ⇨ NIP.

▷ **bud** *v* (**-dd-**) [I] produce buds 发芽: *The trees are budding early this year.* 今年树木发芽早. **bud·ding** *adj* beginning to develop well 开始发展的: *a budding novelist, actor, sportsman, etc* 崭露头角的小说家、演员、运动员等.

Bud·dhism /ˈbʊdɪzəm; ˋbʊdɪzəm/ *n* [U] Asian religion based on the teachings of the N Indian philosopher Gautama Siddartha or Buddha 佛教. ▷ **Bud·dhist** /ˈbʊdɪst; ˋbʊdɪst/ *n, adj*: *a devout Buddhist* 虔诚的佛教徒 ○ *Buddhist monks* 佛教徒 ○ *a Buddhist temple* 佛教的寺院.

buddy /ˈbʌdɪ; ˋbʌdɪ/ *n* (*infml* 口 *esp US*) friend 朋友: *Hi there, buddy!* 嘿, 老兄! ○ *He and I were buddies at school.* 他和我求学时期是好朋友.

budge /bʌdʒ; bʌdʒ/ *v* [I, Tn] (usu in negative sentences 通常用于否定句) **1** (cause sth to) move slightly (使某物)稍微移动, 动一动: *My car's stuck in the mud, and it won't budge/I can't budge it.* 我的汽车陷入泥中, 一动也不动[我无法使它移动]. **2** (cause sb to) change an attitude or opinion (使某人)改变态度或意见: *Once he's made up his mind, he never budges/you can never budge him (from his opinion).* 他一旦下了决心就毫不动摇[无法使他改变(意见)].

budger·igar /ˈbʌdʒərɪɡɑː(r); ˋbʌdʒərɪˌɡɑr/ *n* type of Australian parakeet, often kept as a cage-bird 澳洲长尾小鹦鹉; 虎皮鹦鹉.

budget /ˈbʌdʒɪt; ˋbʌdʒɪt/ *n* **1** (**a**) estimate or plan of how money will be spent over a period of time, in relation to the amount of money available 预算: *a weekly budget* 周预算. (**b**) annual government statement of a country's expenditure and how it will be financed 政

府的年度预算: *The Chancellor of the Exchequer is expected to announce tax cuts in this year's budget.* 人们期望财政大臣公布在本年度预算中削减税收. **2** amount of money needed or allotted for a specific purpose 专用开支; 专款: *limit oneself to a daily budget of £10* 限制自己每日零花10英镑. **3** (idm 习语) **on a (tight) budget** having only a small amount of money 缺少钱; 拮据: *A family on a budget can't afford meat every day.* 经济拮据的家庭不能每天享用肉食.

B

▷ **budget** *v* **1** [Tn, Tn·pr] **~ sth (for sth)** plan the spending of or provide (money) in a budget 将(款项)编入预算: *The government has budgeted £10 000 000 for education spending.* 政府将10 000 000英镑编入教育预算. **2** [I, Ipr] **~ (for sth)** save or allocate money (for a particular purpose) (为某目的)存钱, 安排款项, 编预算: *If we budget carefully, we'll be able to afford a new car.* 我们精打细算就能买辆新汽车了. ○ *budget for the coming year, for a holiday abroad, for a drop in sales, etc* 为来年、为去外国度假、为营业额下降时...安排款项.

budget *adj* [attrib 作定语] inexpensive; cheap 不贵的; 便宜的; 廉价的; 贱的: *a budget meal, holiday* 经济实惠的饭菜、假日.

budget·ary /ˈbʌdʒɪtərɪ; *US* -terɪ; ˋbʌdʒɪˌtɛrɪ/ *adj* of a budget 预算的: *budgetary provisions* 预算的拨款.

□ ˈ**budget account** account at a shop, etc into which a customer makes regular payments, receiving credit in proportion to these; similar account at a bank, for paying regularly recurring bills 预算帐户.

budgie /ˈbʌdʒɪ; ˋbʌdʒɪ/ *n* (*infml* 口) = budgerigar.

buff[1] /bʌf; bʌf/ *n* [U] **1** (**a**) strong soft dull-yellow leather 柔韧的暗黄色的皮革. (**b**) colour of this 暗黄色. **2** (idm 习语) **in the** ˈ**buff** (*infml* 口 *esp Brit*) with no clothes on 一丝不挂; 赤身露体. **strip to the buff** ⇨ STRIP.

▷ **buff** *adj* made of or having the colour of buff 用柔韧的暗黄色皮革制的; 暗黄色的: *a buff envelope, uniform* 牛皮纸信封、暗黄色制服.

buff *v* [Tn, Tn·p] **~ sth (up)** polish sth with a soft material (用柔软的材料)擦亮、抛光某物: *buff (up) shoes with a cloth* 用布把鞋擦亮.

buff[2] /bʌf; bʌf/ *n* (preceded by a *n* 前接名词) (*infml* 口) person who is enthusiastic and knowledgeable about a specified subject or activity (某方面或某活动的)爱好者, 行家: *a film, an opera, a tennis buff* 电影、歌剧、网球爱好者.

buf·falo /ˈbʌfələʊ; ˋbʌfḷˌo/ *n* (*pl* unchanged or **~es** 复数或不变或作 **buffaloes**) large ox of various kinds, including the wild S African buffalo, the tame (often domesticated) Asian buffalo and the N American bison 水牛; (南非或北美的)野牛: *fifty buffaloes* 五十头水牛 ○ *a herd of buffalo* 一群野牛.

buf·fer[1] /ˈbʌfə(r); ˋbʌfɚ/ *n* **1** device for lessening the effect of a blow or collision, esp on a railway vehicle or at the end of a railway track 缓冲器, 减震器(尤指设于铁路车辆或铁轨末端的). **2** (*fig* 比喻) person or thing that lessens a shock or protects sb/sth against difficulties 缓冲者; 缓冲物: *His sense of humour was a useful buffer when things were going badly for him.* 他有幽默感, 这使他在逆境中聊以自慰. **3** country or area between two powerful states, lessening the risk of war between them 缓冲国; 缓冲地区: [attrib 作定语] *a buffer state/zone* 缓冲国[地带].

▷ **buf·fer** *v* [Tn] act as a buffer to (sb/sth) (对某人[某事物])起缓冲作用; 缓和; 缓解.

buf·fer[2] /ˈbʌfə(r); ˋbʌfɚ/ *n* (usu 通常作 **old buffer**) (*Brit infml* 口) foolish or incompetent old man 老糊涂; 老朽: *a silly old buffer* 一个老糊涂.

buf·fet[1] /ˈbʊfeɪ; *US* bəˈfeɪ; buˋfe/ *n* **1** counter where food and drink may be bought and consumed, esp in a railway station or on a train 饮食柜台(尤指火车站或火车内的). **2** meal at which guests serve themselves from a number of dishes; food provided for this 自助餐; (自助餐的)食物: *Dinner will be a cold buffet, not a sit-down meal.* 正餐是凉的自助餐, 不是坐着让人侍候的那一种. ○ [attrib 作定语] *a buffet lunch/supper* 自助午餐[晚餐].

□ ˈ**buffet car** railway carriage serving light meals (火车)餐车.

buf·fet[2] /ˈbʌfɪt; ˋbʌfɪt/ *n* blow (esp with the hand) or shock 打(尤指用手); 打击: (*fig* 比喻) *suffer the buffets of a cruel fate* 遭受悲惨命运的打击.

▷ **buf·fet** *v* [Tn, Tn·p] **~ sb/sth (about)** knock or push sb/sth roughly from side to side 把某人[某物]打来打去或推来推去: *flowers buffeted by the rain and wind* 受风吹雨打的花 ○ (*fig* 比喻) *be buffeted by misfortune* 饱受灾祸的蹂躏 ○ *a boat buffeted (about) by the waves* 被大浪冲来冲去的船. **buf·fet·ing** *n*: *The flowers took quite a buffeting in the storm.* 花朵在暴风雨中备受摧残.

buf·foon /bəˈfuːn; bʌˋfun/ *n* ridiculous but amusing person; clown 滑稽有趣的人; 丑角: *play the buffoon* 扮演丑角.

▷ **buf·foon·ery** /-ərɪ; -ərɪ/ *n* [U] ridiculous behaviour; clowning 滑稽可笑的举动; 扮小丑.

bug /bʌg; bʌg/ *n* **1** [C] small flat foul-smelling insect infesting dirty houses and beds 臭虫. **2** [C] (*esp US*) any small insect 小昆虫. **3** [C] (*infml* 口) (illness caused by a) germ or infectious virus 细菌或传染性病毒(引起的疾病): *I think I've caught a bug.* 我看我已经受细菌感染了. ○ *There are a lot of bugs about in winter.* 冬天有很多流行病. **4** (usu 通常作 **the bug**) [sing] (*infml* 口) obsessive interest (in sth specified) (对所指事物的)极大兴趣: *He was never interested in cooking before, but now he's been bitten by/he's got the bug.* 他以前对烹饪从不感兴趣, 但是现在可着迷了. **5** [C] (*infml* 口) defect in a machine, esp a computer 机器故障(尤指计算机的): *There's a bug in the system.* 设备中有故障. **6** [C] (*infml* 口) small hidden microphone placed (eg by intelligence services) so that conversations can be heard at a distance 窃听器: *search a room for bugs* 搜查房间寻找窃听器 ○ *plant a bug in an embassy* 在大使馆内放置窃听器. **7** (idm 习语) **snug as a bug in a rug** ⇨ SNUG.

▷ **bug** *v* (**-gg-**) [Tn] **1** (**a**) fit (a room, telephone, etc) with a hidden microphone for listening to conversations 将窃听器装在(房间、电话等)里: *This office is bugged.* 这个办公室已装上了窃听器. (**b**) listen to (a conversation, etc) with a hidden microphone (用窃听器)窃听(谈话等): *a bugging device* 窃听装置 ○ *Be careful what you say; our conversation may be being bugged.* 说话要当心, 咱们的话可能被窃听了. **2** (*infml* 口 *esp US*) annoy (sb); irritate (使某人)烦恼; 激怒: *What's bugging you?* 你有什么别扭事儿? ○ *That man really bugs me.* 那个人真把我惹火了.

□ ˈ**bug-eyed** *adj* (*infml* 口) with bulging eyes 凸眼的.

bug·bear /ˈbʌgbeə(r); ˋbʌgˌbɛr/ *n* thing that is feared or disliked or causes annoyance 使人畏惧或厌恶的事物; 造成困扰的事物: *Inflation is the Government's main bugbear.* 通货膨胀是政府的主要难题.

bug·ger /ˈbʌgə(r); ˋbʌgɚ/ *n* (⚠ 讳 *esp Brit*) **1** (*law* 律) person who commits buggery; sodomite 鸡奸者. **2** (*infml* 口) (**a**) annoying or contemptible person 讨厌的人; 小人: *You stupid bugger! You could have run me over!* 你这个浑蛋! 你差一点儿把我碾死! (**b**) (in expressions of sympathy or kind feeling) person or animal (用于表示同情或关心的词语)人或动物: *Poor bugger! His wife left him last week.* 可怜的傢伙! 他妻子上星期离开了他. **3** (*infml* 口) thing that causes difficulties 造成困难的事物: *This door's a (real) bugger to open.* 这扇门(真)难开. **4** (idm 习语) **play silly buggers** ⇨ SILLY.

▷ **bug·ger** *v* (⚠ 讳) **1** [Tn] (*law* 律) have anal intercourse with (sb) 与(某人)鸡奸. **2** [Tn] (*infml* 口) (usu imperative, expressing anger or annoyance at sb/sth 通常用于祈使语气, 表示对某人[某事物]愤怒或烦恼): *Bugger it! I've burnt the toast.* 妈的! 我把面包片烤焦了. ○ *You're always late, bugger you.* 你他妈老迟到. **3** [Tn, Tn·p] **~ sth (up)** (*infml* 口) spoil or ruin sth 糟蹋, 毁坏(某事物). **4** (idm 习语) ˌ**bugger** ˈ**me** (*infml* 口) (expressing surprise or amazement 表示惊奇或惊异): *Bugger me! Did you see that?* 好傢伙! 你看到了吗? **5** (phr v) **bugger about/around** (*infml* 口) behave stupidly or irresponsibly (笨拙地或不负责任地)胡闹, 乱来: *Stop buggering about with those matches or you'll set the house on fire.* 别玩火柴了, 不然要把房子烧了. **bugger sb about/around** (*infml* 口) treat sb badly or in a casual way 苛待或慢待某人: *I'm sick of being buggered about by the company.* 我讨厌公司对我这样冷淡. **bugger off** (*infml* 口) (esp imperative 尤用于祈使语气) go away 走开: *Bugger off and leave me alone.* 走

开，别烦我. ○ *I was only two minutes late but they'd all buggered off.* 我只晚了两分钟，可他们全走了.

bug·ger *interj* (⚠ *infml* 讳, 口) (expressing anger or annoyance 表示气愤或烦恼): *Oh bugger! I've left my keys at home.* 他妈的! 我把钥匙落在家里了.

bug·gered *adj* (⚠ *infml* 讳, 口) [pred 作表语] very tired; exhausted 非常疲倦; 筋疲力尽: *I'm completely buggered after that game of tennis.* 这场网球可把我累垮了. **bug·gery** /ˈbʌgərɪ; ˋbʌgərɪ/ *n* [U] (⚠ *law* 讳, 律) anal intercourse; sodomy 鸡奸.

□ ˌ**bugger-ˈall** *n* [U] (⚠ *infml* 讳, 口) nothing 什么也没有; 屁事没有: *There's bugger-all to do in this place.* 这儿没什么屁事可干.

buggy /ˈbʌgɪ; ˋbʌgɪ/ *n* **1** small strongly-built motor vehicle (坚固的)小机动车: *a beach buggy* 沙滩车. **2** (also ˈ**baby buggy**) (*US*) = PRAM. **3** (formerly) light carriage pulled by one horse, for one or two people (旧时)(由一匹马拉的单人或双人的)轻便马车.

bugle /ˈbju:gl; ˋbjugl/ *n* brass musical instrument like a small trumpet but without keys or valves, used for giving military signals 军号. ⇨illus at App 1 见附录1之插图, page x.

▷ **bu·gler** /ˈbju:glə(r); ˋbjuglɚ/ *n* person who blows a bugle 军号手.

build /bɪld; bɪld/ *v* (*pt, pp* **built** /bɪlt; bɪlt/) **1** (**a**) [Tn, Tn·pr, Dn·n, Dn·pr] **~ sth (of/from/out of sth)**; **~ sth (for sb)** make or construct sth by putting parts or material together 修建、建造或建筑某物: *build a house, road, railway* 修建房屋、道路、铁路 ○ *a house built of stone, bricks, etc* 用石、砖等盖的房子 ○ *Birds build their nests out of twigs.* 鸟儿用细树枝筑巢. ○ *His father built him a model aeroplane.* 他父亲给他做了一架模型飞机. (**b**) [I] construct houses, etc 盖房子等: *The local council intends to build on this site.* 地方议会打算在这块地上盖房子. **2** [Tn] develop (sth); establish 开发(某事物); 创建; 兴建: *build a business* 创业 ○ *build a better future, a new career, etc* 创造更好的未来、新事业等. **3** (idm 习语) ˌ**Rome was not** ˌ**built in a** ˈ**day** (*saying* 谚) time and hard work are necessary for a difficult or important task 罗马不是一天建成的(伟业建成非一日之功). **4** (phr v) **build sth in/build sth into sth** (esp passive 尤用于被动语态) (**a**) make sth a fixed and permanent part of sth larger 在某较大物体上建某物: *build a cupboard/bookcase into a wall* 在墙上建造壁橱[书橱] ○ *We're having new wardrobes built in.* 我们嵌加了新的衣橱. (**b**) (*fig* 比喻) make sth a necessary part of sth 将某事物加入另一事物中; 列入; 并入; 插入: *build an extra clause into the contract* 将一项额外条款列入合同中. **build sth into sth** put parts together to form sth 将各部分合在一起变成某事物: *build loose stones into a strong wall* 用石块建成坚固的墙 ○ *build scraps of metal into a work of art* 用金属碎块制成艺术品. **build sth on /build sth onto sth** add sth (eg an extra room) to an existing structure by building (在现有建筑物上)增建某物(如另一房间): *The new wing was built on(to the hospital) last year.* 去年(医院)增建了新侧楼. **build on sth** use sth as a foundation for further progress 用某事物作为进一步发展的基础; 建基于某事物之上: *build on earlier achievements, success, results, etc* 建基于原来的成就、成功、成果等之上. **build sth on sth** base sth on sth 把某事物作另一事物的基础: *build one's hopes on the economic strength of the country* 把自己的希望建立在国家的经济实力上 ○ *an argument built on sound logic* 逻辑性强的论点. **build up** become greater, more numerous or more intense 变得更大、更多或更强: *Traffic is building up on roads into the city.* 来往的车辆在通往市区的道路上越聚越多. ○ *Tension built up as the crisis approached.* 危机越近越紧张. **build oneself/sb up** make oneself/sb healthier or stronger 使自己[某人]健康或强壮: *You need more protein to build you up.* 你需要增加蛋白质以增强体质. **build sb/sth up** (esp passive 尤用于被动语态) speak with great (often undeserved or exaggerated) praise about sb/sth 捧(吹捧)某人[某事物]: *The film was built up to be a masterpiece, but I found it very disappointing.* 这部影片被吹捧为杰作，可是我觉得令人失望. **build sth up** (**a**) acquire, develop, increase or strengthen sth gradually 逐步获得、发展、增加或增强某事物: *build up a big library, a fine reputation, a thriving business* 逐步建起一座大图书馆、逐步赢得好的声誉、逐步建立起兴旺发达的事业 ○ *build up one's strength after an illness* 病后逐渐增强体力. (**b**) (esp passive 尤用于被动语态) cover (an area) with buildings 建筑物遍布(某地区): *The village has been built up since I lived here.* 我在这里住过，从那时起，这个村子已经盖满了房子.

▷ **build** *n* [U, C] shape and size (of the human body) (人体的)体形, 体格: *a man of athletic, powerful, slender, average, etc build* 身体强健、强壮、苗条、一般等的人 ○ *We are (of) the same build.* 我们的体形相同. ○ *Our build is/builds are similar.* 我们的体形相似.

builder *n* **1** person who builds, esp one whose job is building houses, etc 建造者; (尤指)房屋建筑者. **2** (in compounds 用以构成复合词) person or thing that creates or develops sth 创造或开发某事物的人或事物: *an empire-builder* 帝国的缔造者 ○ *a confidence-builder* 助人建立信心的事物.

built (after *advs* and in compound *adjs* 用于副词之后或用以构成复合形容词) having the specified build 有某种体形的: *solidly built* ○ *a well-built man,* ie one who is broad and muscular.

□ ˈ**build-up** *n* **1** (**a**) gradual increase or accumulation 逐渐增加或积累: *a steady build-up of traffic* 来往车辆逐渐增多 ○ *A build-up of enemy forces is reported.* 据悉敌军正在集结. (**b**) **~ (to sth)** gradual approach (to a climax); gradual preparation (for sth) 逐渐达到(高潮); 逐渐准备(某事物): *the build-up to the President's visit* 总统访问的准备工作. **2** favourable description (esp of a performer or spectacle) in advance (尤指为表演者或场面)造舆论, 鸣锣开道: *The press has given the show a tremendous build-up.* 新闻界为这一演出大造声势.

ˌ**built-ˈin** (also **in-built**) *adj* [attrib 作定语] constructed to form part of a structure 与某结构建成一体的; 并入的; 嵌入的: *a bedroom with* ˌ*built-in* ˈ*wardrobes* 有嵌入衣柜的卧室 ○ (*fig* 比喻) *a pay deal with built-in guarantees of employment* 带有雇用担保的工资协议.

ˌ**built-ˈup** *adj* [usu attrib 通常作定语] covered with buildings 布满建筑物的: *a* ˌ*built-up* ˈ*area* 建筑物多的地方.

build·ing /ˈbɪldɪŋ; ˋbɪldɪŋ/ *n* **1** [U] (art, business or profession of) constructing houses, etc 建筑(的艺术或行业): [attrib 作定语] *the building trade* 建筑业 ○ *building materials* 建筑材料. **2** [C] (*abbr* 缩写 **bldg**) structure with a roof and walls (有屋顶和墙的)结构, 建筑物: *Schools, churches, houses and factories are all buildings.* 学校、教堂、住宅、厂房均为建筑物.

□ ˈ**building site** area of land on which a house, etc is being built 建筑工地.

ˈ**building society** (*Brit*) organization that accepts deposits and lends out money to people who wish to buy or build houses 房屋建筑协会(接受买房或建房人的保证金及向其贷款的组织).

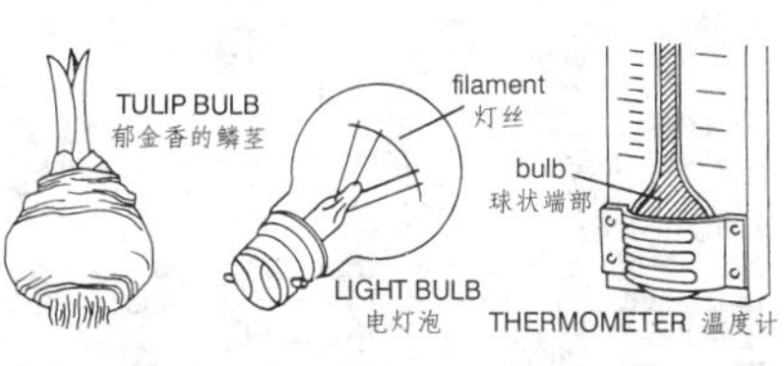

bulb /bʌlb; bʌlb/ *n* ⇨illus 见插图. **1** thick rounded underground stem of certain plants (eg the lily, onion, tulip) sending roots downwards and leaves upwards 鳞茎(如百合、洋葱、郁金香等植物的地下茎). ⇨illus at App 1 见附录1之插图, page ii. **2** (also ˈ**light bulb**) pear-shaped glass container for the filament of an electric light 电灯泡: *change a bulb* 换灯泡 ○ *a 60-watt light bulb* 60瓦的灯泡. **3** object shaped like a bulb, eg the bulging end of a thermometer 鳞茎状物(如温度计球状的一端).

▷ **bulb·ous** /ˈbʌlbəs; ˋbʌlbəs/ *adj* **1** growing from a bulb 由鳞茎长出的. **2** shaped like a bulb; round and fat 鳞茎状的; 又圆又胖的: *a bulbous nose* 圆圆的鼻子.

bulge /bʌldʒ; bʌldʒ/ *n* **1** rounded swelling; outward curve 鼓起; 凸出: *What's that bulge in your pocket?* 你口

袋里鼓鼓囊囊的是什么? **2** (*infml* 口) temporary increase in quantity 暂时增多: *a population bulge* 人口膨胀 ○ *After the war there was a bulge in the birth-rate.* 战后出生率激增.

▷ **bulge** *v* [I, Ipr, Ip] **~ (out) (with sth)** form a bulge: swell outwards 鼓起; 凸起; 膨胀: *I can't eat any more. My stomach's bulging.* 我一点儿也吃不下了, 肚子都鼓起来了. ○ *pockets bulging with apples* 装着苹果而鼓起来的口袋.

bulgy /ˈbʌldʒɪ; ˈbʌldʒɪ/ *adj.*

bulk /bʌlk; bʌlk/ *n* **1** [U] size, quantity or volume, esp when great 体积, 数量, 容量(尤指巨大的): *It's not their weight that makes these sacks hard to carry, it's their bulk.* 这些袋子难于搬运, 倒不是因为重而是体积太大. ○ *The sheer bulk of Mozart's music is extraordinary.* 莫扎特的乐曲, 其数量之巨就已很了不起了. **2** [C] large shape, body or person 巨大的形体或身躯: *He heaved his huge bulk out of the chair.* 他挺起巨大的身躯, 从椅子上站了起来. **3** [U] food that is not digested but is eaten to stimulate the intestine; roughage 仅刺激肠管而不被消化的食物; 纤维性物质; 食用糠: *You need more bulk in your diet.* 你的饮食中需要添点儿纤维素. **4** [sing] **the ~ (of sth)** main part (of sth) (某事物的)主要部分; 大部分: *The bulk of the work has already been done.* 大部分工作已经完成. ○ *The eldest son inherited the bulk of the estate.* 长子继承了遗产的大部分. **5** (idm 习语) **in ˈbulk (a)** in large amounts 大量: *buy (sth) in bulk* 大量购买(某物). **(b)** (of a cargo, etc) not packed in boxes; loose (指货物等)不装箱的, 散装的: *shipped in bulk* 散装货运.

▷ **bulk** *v* 1 (idm 习语) **bulk ˈlarge** seem important; be prominent 显得重要; 突出: *The war still bulks large in the memories of those who fought in it.* 对于那些曾参战的人来说, 那场战争仍记忆犹新. **2** (phr v) **bulk sth out** make sth bigger or thicker 使某事物更大或更厚: *add extra pages to bulk a book out* 增加额外页数使书更厚.

bulky *adj* (**-ier**, **-iest**) taking up much space; awkward to move or carry 庞大的; 巨大的; 笨重的: *the bulky figure of Inspector Jones* 琼斯巡官的庞大身躯 ○ *a bulky parcel, crate, load, etc* 巨大的包裹、包装箱、载荷等.

□ ˌ**bulk ˈbuying** buying in large amounts, esp the buying of most of a producer's output by one purchaser 大量购买; (尤指)包购(一买主购买某生产者的大多数产品).

bulk·head /ˈbʌlkhed; ˈbʌlk,hɛd/ *n* upright watertight partition or wall between compartments in a ship or aircraft (船舱或机舱的)防水隔板, 隔墙.

bull[1] /bʊl; bʊl/ *n* **1** uncastrated male of any animal in the ox family (未阉割的)公牛: [attrib 作定语] *a bull neck*, ie a short thick one, like a bull's 短粗的脖子(像牛的脖子). Cf 参看 BULLOCK, COW[1] 1, OX 1, STEER[2]. **2** male of the elephant, whale and other large animals 雄的(象、鲸等)大动物. Cf 参看 COW[1] 2. **3** (in the Stock Exchange) person who buys shares hoping to sell them soon afterwards at a higher price (证券交易所中)买进股分以期不久可高价卖出的人: [attrib 作定语] *a bull market*, ie a situation in which share prices are rising (股票的)上涨行情. Cf 参看 BEAR[1] 3. **4** (*US sl* 俚) policeman or detective 警察; 侦探. **5** = BULL'S-EYE. **6** (idm 习语) **a bull in a ˈchina shop** person who is rough and clumsy when skill and care are needed (在需要细心和技巧的工作中)莽撞而笨拙的人. **a cock-and-bull story** ⇨ COCK. **a red rag to a bull** ⇨ RED[1]. **take the bull by the ˈhorns** face a difficulty or danger boldly 勇敢地面对困难或危险.

▷ **bull·ish** *adj* (in the Stock Exchange) characterized by or causing a rise in share prices (证券交易所中)看涨的. Cf 参看 BEARISH (BEAR[1]).

□ ˈ**bullfight** *n* traditional public entertainment, esp in Spain and S America, in which bulls are baited and usu killed in the arena 斗牛. ˈ**bullfighter** *n*. ˈ**bullfighting** *n* [U].

ˌ**bull-ˈheaded** *adj* obstinate or stubborn in a clumsy way 又笨又顽固的; 又笨又执拗的.

ˌ**bull-ˈnecked** *adj* having a short thick neck 脖子短粗的.

ˈ**bullring** *n* arena for bullfighting 斗牛场.

bull[2] /bʊl; bʊl/ *n* official order or announcement from the Pope 教皇诏书: *a papal bull* 教皇诏书.

bull[3] /bʊl; bʊl/ *n* [U] **1** (also **Irish bull**) foolish, amusing and illogical use of words (eg 'If you do not receive this letter, please write and tell me') 愚蠢可笑又不合逻辑的措辞(如'你若收不到这封信, 请来信告诉我'). **2** (*sl* 俚) = BULLSHIT: *That's a lot/a load of bull!* 胡说八道! **3** (*Brit army sl* 英军俚) tiresome routine tasks (esp the cleaning of boots, equipment, etc) 令人厌烦的例行工作(尤指擦靴子、擦装备等).

bull·dog /ˈbʊldɒg; ˈbʊl,dɔg/ *n* sturdy, powerful and courageous type of dog with a large head and a short thick neck 斗牛狗; 大头狗. ⇨illus at App 1 见附录1之插图, page iii.

□ ˌ**bulldog ˈclip** clip with a spring that closes tightly and is used for holding papers, etc together (夹纸用的)弹簧夹.

bulldozer 推土机

bull·doze /ˈbʊldəʊz; ˈbʊl,doz/ *v* **1** [Tn] remove or flatten (sth) with a bulldozer (用推土机)推掉或推平(某物): *The area was bulldozed to make way for a new road.* 那片地已被推土机推平用以修筑新路. **2** [Tn, Tn·pr] **~ sb (into doing sth)** (*fig* 比喻) force sb to do sth, esp by frightening him 强迫某人做某事物(尤指用威胁手段); 胁迫: *They bulldozed me into signing the agreement.* 他们胁迫我签约. **3** [Tn·pr] push sth with force in the specified direction (朝某方向)强力推动某事物: (*fig* 比喻) *He bulldozed his way into the room.* 他硬闯进房间里. ○ *She bulldozed her plans past the committee.* 她硬使委员会通过了她的计划.

▷ **bull·dozer** /ˈbʊldəʊzə(r); ˈbʊl,dozɚ/ *n* powerful tractor with a broad steel blade in front, used for moving earth or clearing ground 推土机. ⇨illus 见插图.

bul·let /ˈbʊlɪt; ˈbʊlɪt/ *n* **1** small missile, usu round or cylindrical with a pointed end, fired from a gun or rifle 子弹: *He was killed by a single bullet in the heart.* 他被一颗子弹射中心脏而死亡. **2** (idm 习语) **bite the bullet** ⇨ BITE[1].

□ ˌ**bullet-ˈheaded** /-ˈhedɪd; -ˈhɛdɪd/ *adj* having a small round head 有小圆头的.

ˈ**bullet-proof** *adj* that can stop bullets passing through it 防弹的: *a bullet-proof shirt/vest/jacket* 防弹衬衣[背心/上衣].

bul·letin /ˈbʊlətɪn; ˈbʊlətɪn/ *n* **1** short official statement of news 布告; 公告; 公报: *a news bulletin* 新闻简报. **2** printed newsletter produced by an association, a group or a society (由社团或协会等刊印的)通讯, 会刊.

□ ˈ**bulletin board** (*US*) = NOTICE-BOARD (NOTICE).

bull·finch /ˈbʊlfɪntʃ; ˈbʊl,fɪntʃ/ *n* songbird with a strong rounded beak and a pink breast 红腹灰雀.

bull·frog /ˈbʊlfrɒg; ˈbʊl,frag/ *n* type of large American frog with a loud croak 牛蛙(产于美洲).

bull·horn /ˈbʊlhɔːn; ˈbʊl,hɔrn/ *n* (*US*) = LOUD HAILER (LOUD).

bul·lion /ˈbʊljən; ˈbʊljən/ *n* [U] gold or silver in bulk or bars, before it is made into coins, etc (锭形或条形的)金或银: *The thieves stole £1 000 000 in gold bullion.* 窃贼偷去价值1 000 000英镑的金条.

bul·lock /ˈbʊlək; ˈbʊlək/ *n* bull that has been castrated 阉牛. Cf 参看 BULL[1] 1, OX 1, STEER[2].

bull's-eye /ˈbʊlzaɪ; ˈbʊlz,aɪ/ *n* **1 (a)** centre of a target, having the highest value in archery and darts 靶心; 鹄的. ⇨illus at ARCHERY, DART 见 ARCHERY、DART 之插图. **(b)** shot that hits this 命中靶心的一击: *scoring a bull's-eye* 击中靶心得分. **2** large hard round peppermint sweet 大块圆形硬薄荷糖.

bull·shit /ˈbʊlʃɪt; ˈbʊl,ʃɪt/ (also **bull**) *n* [U], *interj* (⚠ *sl* 讳, 俚) nonsense; rubbish 胡说; 瞎扯: *a load/lot of bullshit* 胡说八道 ○ *He's talking bullshit.* 他在瞎扯.

bull-terrier /,bʊlˈterɪə(r); ,bʊlˈterɪɚ/ *n* dog of a breed produced by crossing (CROSS[2] 7) a bulldog and a terrier 斗牛㹴狗(由斗牛狗与㹴杂交所生的狗).

bully[1] /ˈbʊlɪ; ˈbʊlɪ/ *n* person who uses his strength or power to frighten or hurt weaker people 恃强凌弱的人: *Leave that little girl alone, you big bully!* 离那小姑娘远点儿, 你这个大坏蛋!

▷ **bully** *v* (*pt, pp* **bullied**) **1** [Tn] frighten or hurt (a weaker person) 恐吓, 欺负, 伤害(弱者): *He was bullied by the older boys at school.* 他在学校里受到大孩子的欺负. **2** (phr v) **bully sb into doing sth** (try to) force sb to do sth by frightening him (企图)胁迫某人做某事: *The manager tried to bully his men into working harder by threatening them with dismissal.* 经理企图以解雇相威胁, 迫使职工更卖力气.

□ ˈ**bully-boy** *n* rough violent man, esp one paid to frighten or injure others 打手, 暴徒(尤指受雇对他人进行威胁或伤害的人): [attrib 作定语] (*fig* 比喻) *bully-boy tactics* 暴徒手段.

bully[2] /ˈbʊlɪ; ˈbʊlɪ/ *n* [U] (also ˈ**bully beef**) (*infml* 口) corned beef in tins 罐头牛肉.

bully[3] /ˈbʊlɪ; ˈbʊlɪ/ *interj* (idm 习语) **bully for sb** (*infml esp ironic* 口, 尤作反语) well done 干得好; 干得漂亮: *You've solved the puzzle at last? Well, bully for 'you!* 你最后把这难题解决啦? 哦, 你可真棒!

bully[4] /bʊlɪ; ˈbʊlɪ/ *n* (in hockey) (formerly) way of starting a game in which two opposing players strike their sticks together three times before trying to hit the ball (曲棍球)(旧时)开局方法(双方各一队员互击球棍三次, 然后力争击球).

▷ **bully** *v* (*pt, pp* **bullied**) (phr v) **bully off** start play in this way (按此法)开赛.

bul·rush /ˈbʊlrʌʃ; ˈbʊl,rʌʃ/ *n* type of tall rush(3) with a thick velvety head 藨草; 宽叶香蒲; 灯心草.

bul·wark /ˈbʊlwək; ˈbʊlwɚk/ *n* **1** wall, esp of earth, built as a defence 壁垒(尤指用泥土堆砌者); 防御工事. **2** (*fig* 比喻) person or thing that supports, defends or protects 支持, 防御或保护的人或事物: *Democracy is a bulwark of freedom.* 民主是自由的保障. **3** (usu *pl* 通常作复数) ship's side above the level of the deck 舷墙(甲板线以上的船侧).

bum[1] /bʌm; bʌm/ *n* (*infml* 口 *esp Brit*) part of the body on which one sits; buttocks 屁股.

bum[2] /bʌm; bʌm/ *n* (*infml* 口 *esp US*) **1** wandering beggar; tramp; loafer 流浪乞丐; 游民; 盲流; 闲荡者: *bums sleeping rough in the streets* 横七竖八地睡在街上的无业游民. **2** lazy irresponsible person 懒惰不负责任的人: *You lousy bum!* 你简直是个没用的懒蛋!

▷ **bum** *adj* [attrib 作定语] (*infml* 口) of bad quality; useless 劣质的; 无用的: *a bum film, concert, party* 差劲的影片、音乐会、聚会.

bum *v* (**-mm-**) (*infml* 口) **1** [Tn, Tn·pr] **~ sth (off sb)** get sth (from sb) by begging; cadge sth (从某人处)乞讨某事物; 乞求某事物: *bum a lift* 请求搭便车 ○ *Can I bum a cigarette off you?* 我向你要一枝香烟行吗? **2** (phr v) **bum aˈround** travel around or spend one's time doing nothing in particular (无所事事地)漫游, 闲荡: *I bummed around (in) Europe for a year before university.* 我在欧洲漫游了一年才上大学.

bumble /ˈbʌmbl; ˈbʌmbl̩/ *v* **1** [I, Ipr, Ip] **~ (on) (about sth)** speak in a rambling and clumsy manner 语无伦次地说: *What are you bumbling (on) about?* 你颠三倒四地说些什么呀? **2** (phr v) **bumble about, along, etc** act or move in a specified direction in a clumsy disorganized manner 笨拙而无规则地活动; 跌跌撞撞地行进: *The professor bumbled absent-mindedly along the road.* 教授心不在焉地沿途瞎逛.

▷ **bum·bling** *adj* [attrib 作定语] behaving in a clumsy disorganized way 动作笨拙而无规则的; 笨手笨脚的; 胡乱的: *You bumbling idiot!* 你这个笨蛋!

bumble-bee /ˈbʌmblbi:; ˈbʌmbl̩,bi/ *n* large hairy bee with a loud hum 大黄蜂.

bumf (also **bumph**) /bʌmf; bʌmf/ *n* (*Brit sl joc or derog* 俚, 谑或贬) paper, esp official forms and documents 纸; (尤指)公文, 表格, 文件: *'What's in the post today?' 'Just a lot of bumf from the insurance people.'* '今天的邮件里有什么?' '只有保险公司寄来的一大堆表格.

bump /bʌmp; bʌmp/ *v* **1** [Ipr] **~ against/into sb/sth** knock or strike sth with a dull-sounding blow; collide with sth 碰撞或敲击某物(发出低沉响声); 与某物相撞: *In the dark I bumped into a chair.* 我在黑暗中碰到了椅子. ○ *The car bumped against the kerb.* 汽车撞上了路边石. **2** [Tn, Tn·pr] **~ sth (against/on sth)** hit or knock sth (esp a part of the body) (against sth) (尤指身体的一部分)碰、撞某物: *bump one's head (on the ceiling)* 自己的头碰着了(天花板) ○ *The driver bumped the kerb while reversing.* 司机倒车时撞着了路边石. ⇨Usage at BANG[1] 用法见 BANG[1]. **3** (phr v) **bump along, down, etc** move with a jolting action in the specified direction 颠簸而行: *The old bus bumped along the mountain road.* 旧公共汽车沿着山路颠簸行驶. **bump into sb** (*infml* 口) meet sb by chance 碰见某人; 偶遇; 巧遇: *Guess who I bumped into today?* 你猜我今天碰见谁了? **bump sb off** (*sl* 俚) kill or murder sb 杀死某人; 谋杀某人. **bump sth up** (*infml* 口) increase or raise sth 增加或提高某事物: *bump up prices, salaries, etc* 提高物价、薪金等.

▷ **bump** *n* **1** (dull sound of a) blow, knock or impact; collision (发出低沉响声的)撞击, 碰撞, 冲撞, 相撞: *The two children collided with a bump.* 两个孩子砰的一声撞上了. ○ *The passengers felt a violent bump as the plane landed.* 飞机着陆时, 乘客感到猛烈的冲撞. **2** swelling on the body, esp one caused by a blow; lump or bulge 肿胀, 肿块(尤指因碰撞所致); 隆起; 凸起: *covered in bumps and bruises* 遍布肿块和挫伤 ○ *get a nasty bump on the head* 头上起了一个大包. **3** uneven patch on a surface 物体表面上的隆起物: *a road with a lot of bumps in it* 有一块块隆起的路.

bump *adv* **1** with a bump; suddenly 砰的一声; 突然地: *He fell off the ladder and landed bump on the ground.* 他从梯子上砰的一声跌到地上. **2** (idm 习语) **things that go bump in the night** ⇨ THING.

bumpy *adj* (**-ier, -iest**) **1** with an uneven surface 表面不平的; 崎岖不平的: *a bumpy road, track, etc* 不平的路面、跑道等. **2** causing jolts 引起颠簸的: *a bumpy ride, flight, drive, etc* 颠簸的乘行、飞行、驾驶等. **bump·ily** *adv*. **bum·pi·ness** *n* [U].

bumper[1] /ˈbʌmpə(r); ˈbʌmpɚ/ *n* bar fixed to the front and back of a motor vehicle to lessen the effect of a collision (机动车辆前后的)保险杠. ⇨illus at App 1 见附录1之插图, page xii.

□ ,**bumper-to-ˈbumper** *adj, adv* (of vehicles) in a line, each close behind the one in front (指车辆)首尾相接(的): *We sat bumper-to-bumper in the traffic jam.* 我们遇到交通阻塞, 汽车一辆辆首尾相接动弹不得. ○ *travel bumper-to-bumper* 车一辆紧接一辆行驶.

bumper[2] /ˈbʌmpə(r); ˈbʌmpɚ/ *adj* [attrib 作定语] unusually large or plentiful 异常巨大的; 异常多的: *a bumper crop/harvest* 巨大的收成[特大的丰收] ○ *a bumper edition/issue/number*, eg of a magazine 特大版[刊/号](如杂志的).

bumper[3] /ˈbʌmpə(r); ˈbʌmpɚ/ *n* = BOUNCER 1.

bumph = BUMF.

bump·kin /ˈbʌmpkɪn; ˈbʌmpkɪn/ *n* (*usu derog* 通常作贬义) awkward or simple person from the country 乡巴佬; 土包子; 土老帽儿.

bump·tious /ˈbʌmpʃəs; ˈbʌmpʃəs/ *adj* (*derog* 贬) (of a person, his manner, etc) self-important and conceited (指人、举止等)自负的, 傲慢的, 骄横的: *bumptious officials, behaviour* 骄横的官员、行为. ▷ **bump·tiously** *adv*. **bump·tious·ness** *n* [U].

bun /bʌn; bʌn/ *n* **1** small round sweet cake 小而圆的甜面包或点心: *a currant bun* 带葡萄干的小圆面包. Cf 参看 ROLL[1] 2. **2** (esp woman's) hair twisted into a tight knot at the back of the head (尤指女子的)发髻: *put, wear one's hair in a bun* 把头发盘成发髻. **3** (idm 习语) **have a ˈbun in the oven** (*infml joc* 口, 谑) be pregnant 怀孕.

□ ˈ**bun-fight** *n* (*infml* 口) tea-party 茶会.

bunch /bʌntʃ; bʌntʃ/ *n* **1** [C] number of things (usu of the same kind) growing, fastened or grouped together 串; 束; 卷; 团: *a bunch of bananas, grapes, etc* 一串香蕉、葡萄等 ○ *bunches of flowers* 花束 ○ *a bunch of keys* 一串钥匙. ⇨illus at GRAPE 见 GRAPE 之插图. **2** [CGp] (*infml* 口) group of people; gang; mob 人群; 匪帮; 暴

B

民: *a bunch of thugs* 一群恶棍 ○ *I don't like any of them much, but he's the best of the bunch*, ie the least unpleasant. 这帮人我谁也不喜欢, 但他还算是其中最好的呢.

▷ **bunch** *v* [I, Ip, Tn, Tn·p] ~ **(sth/sb) (up)** (cause sth/sb to) be formed into a bunch or bunches (使某物[某人])成束, 成捆, 成群: *a blouse that bunches at the waist* 束腰女衬衫 ○ *runners all bunched together*, ie closely grouped 挤在一起的赛跑者 ○ *Cross the road one at a time — don't bunch up.* 一次一个地过马路——别都挤在一起.

bundle /ˈbʌndl; ˈbʌndḷ/ *n* **1** [C] collection of things fastened or wrapped together 束、捆、扎或包在一起的东西: *a bundle of sticks, clothes, newspapers* 一捆细棍、一包衣物、一卷报纸 ○ *books tied up in bundles of twenty* 扎成二十本一捆的书. **2** [sing] **a ~ of sth** (*infml* 口) a lot of sth; a mass of sth 大堆的东西; 大量的事物: *That child is a bundle of mischief!* 那孩子是淘气包! ○ *He's not exactly a bundle of fun*, ie an amusing person. 他不算是个十分有趣的人. **3** [sing] (*infml* 口) large amount of money 很多钱; 巨款: *That car must have cost a bundle.* 这辆汽车一定值很多钱. **4** (idm 习语) **a bundle of 'nerves** in a very nervous state 神经极度紧张: *The poor chap was a bundle of nerves at the interview.* 这小子在面试时紧张极了. **go a bundle on sb/sth** (*infml* 口) be very fond of sb/sth 非常喜欢某人[某事物]: *I don't go a bundle on her new husband, do you?* 我不大喜欢她的新婚丈夫, 你呢?

▷ **bundle** *v* **1** [Tn, Tn·p] ~ **sth (up)** make or tie sth into a bundle or bundles 把某物捆成捆: *The firewood was cut and bundled (together).* 木柴已劈好并捆在一起了. ○ *We bundled up some old clothes for the jumble sale.* 我们把一些旧衣物捆起来准备义卖. **2** (phr v) **bundle sth into sth** throw sth or put sth away quickly and untidily in the specified place 把某物随便扔到某处: *She bundled her clothes into the drawer without folding them.* 她把衣服胡乱扔进抽屉里, 连叠都不叠. **bundle (sb) out, off, into, etc** go or send (sb) hastily or roughly in the specified direction 匆忙走向某处; (将某人)匆匆打发到某处: *We all bundled into the tiny car.* 我们全都挤进那辆小汽车里. ○ *I was bundled into a police van.* 我被推进警车. ○ *She bundled her son off to school.* 她匆匆忙忙把儿子打发到学校去了. **bundle (sb) up** dress (sb) in warm clothes 给(某人)穿上暖和的衣服.

bung /bʌŋ; bʌŋ/ *n* stopper for closing the hole in a barrel or jar (桶或罐的)盖子, 塞子.

▷ **bung** *v* **1** [esp passive 尤用于被动语态: Tn, Tn·pr, Tn·p] ~ **sth (up) (with sth)** close or block sth with or as with a bung (用塞盖)塞住; 堵住; 封住: *My nose is (all) bunged up. I must be getting a cold.* 我鼻子(全)堵住了, 一定是着凉了. ○ *The drains are bunged up with dead leaves.* 落叶把下水道堵住了. **2** [Tn·pr, Tn·p] (*Brit infml* 口) throw or toss (sth) 扔, 掷(某物): *Bung the newspaper over here, will you?* 你把报纸扔过来, 行吗?

□ **'bung-hole** *n* hole for filling or emptying a barrel 桶孔.

bun·ga·low /ˈbʌŋgələʊ; ˈbʌŋgə,lo/ *n* small house with one storey 平房. ⇨illus at App 1 见附录1之插图, page vii.

bungle /ˈbʌŋgl; ˈbʌŋgl/ *v* [I, Tn] do (sth) badly or clumsily; spoil (a task) through lack of skill 笨手笨脚地做(某事物); 粗制滥造; (因技术差或不熟练)把(工作)做糟: *It looks as though you've bungled again.* 看来你好像又把事情搞糟了. ○ *Don't let him mend your bike. He's sure to bungle the job.* 别让他修理你的自行车. 他肯定会弄得一团糟的. ○ *The gang spent a year planning the robbery and then bungled it.* 这伙人蓄谋抢劫已有一年之久, 然而到头来却失手了.

▷ **bungle** *n* (usu *sing* 通常作单数) bungled piece of work 拙劣的工作: *The whole job was a gigantic bungle.* 整件工作都糟透了.

bun·gler /ˈbʌŋglə(r); ˈbʌŋglɚ/ *n* person who bungles 笨手笨脚的人: *You incompetent bungler!* 你这个成事不足败事有余的家伙!

bun·ion /ˈbʌnjən; ˈbʌnjən/ *n* painful swelling, esp on the first joint of the big toe 炎肿; (尤指)拇囊炎肿.

bunk[1] /bʌŋk; bʌŋk/ *n* **1** narrow bed built into a wall like a shelf, eg on a ship (架设于壁上的)狭窄铺位(如于船上的). **2** (also **'bunk bed**) one of a pair of single beds, fixed one above the other, esp for children 双层床的上铺或下铺(尤指儿童所用的). ⇨illus at App 1 见附录1之插图, page xvi.

bunk[2] /bʌŋk; bʌŋk/ *n* (idm 习语) **do a 'bunk** (*Brit infml* 口) run away 逃走: *The cashier has done a bunk with the day's takings.* 出纳员携带该日营业收入逃走了.

bunk[3] /bʌŋk; bʌŋk/ *n* [U] (*infml* 口) = BUNKUM: *Don't talk bunk!* 别胡说!

bunker /ˈbʌŋkə(r); ˈbʌŋkɚ/ *n* **1** container for storing fuel, esp on a ship or outside a house 贮存燃料的容器(尤指船上的燃料舱或房屋外的燃料箱). **2** (also *esp US* **'sand trap**) sandy hollow on a golf course, from which it is difficult to hit the ball (高尔夫球场上难于击球的)沙坑. ⇨illus at GOLF 见 GOLF之插图. **3** strongly built underground shelter for soldiers, guns, etc 地下掩体; 地堡.

▷ **bunker** *v* **1** [Tn] fill (a ship's bunker) with fuel 将燃料装进(燃料舱). **2** [Tn usu passive 通常用于被动语态] (in golf) hit (the ball) into a bunker (高尔夫球)把(球)击入沙坑: *He/His ball is bunkered.* 他把球打进了沙坑.

bun·kum /ˈbʌŋkəm; ˈbʌŋkəm/ (also **bunk**) *n* [U] (*infml* 口) nonsense 胡说: *Don't believe what he's saying — it's pure bunkum.* 别相信他的话——纯粹是胡说八道.

bunny /ˈbʌnɪ; ˈbʌnɪ/ *n* **1** (used by and to small children 用作儿语) rabbit 兔子. **2** (also **'bunny girl**) (*often sexist* 常含性别偏见) night-club hostess, esp one wearing a costume that includes false rabbit's ears and a tail 兔儿女郎(夜总会的女招待, 尤指以假的兔子耳朵及尾巴为装饰者).

Bun·sen burner /ˌbʌnsn ˈbɜ:nə(r); ˌbʌnsn̩ ˈbɝnɚ/ *n* gas burner used in chemical laboratories, consisting of a vertical tube with an adjustable air valve 本生灯.

bunt·ing[1] /ˈbʌntɪŋ; ˈbʌntɪŋ/ *n* any of various small songbirds related to the finch family, with short thick bills 鹀(一种雀科鸣鸟, 喙短粗).

bunt·ing[2] /ˈbʌntɪŋ; ˈbʌntɪŋ/ *n* [U] (**a**) coloured flags and streamers used for decorating streets and buildings (用以装饰街道和建筑物的)彩旗和彩带. (**b**) loosely-woven fabric used for making these (做彩旗和彩带用的)粗纺的织物.

buoy /bɔɪ; bɔɪ/ *n* **1** floating object anchored to the bottom of the sea, a river, etc to mark places that are dangerous for boats or to show where boats may go, etc 浮标; 航标. **2** = LIFEBUOY (LIFE).

▷ **buoy** *v* **1** [Tn, Tn·p] ~ **sth (out)** mark the position of sth with a buoy 用浮标指示某位置: *buoy submerged rocks* 用浮标指示暗礁位置. **2** (phr v) **buoy sb/sth up** (esp passive 尤用于被动语态) (**a**) keep sb/sth afloat 使某人[某物]漂浮: *The raft was buoyed up by empty petrol cans.* 这木筏依靠空的汽油桶的浮力漂浮. (**b**) (*fig* 比喻) keep (prices, etc) at a high or satisfactory level 使(价格等)保持在高的或令人满意的水平上: *Share prices were buoyed up by hopes of an end to the recession.* 因经济衰退状况终止有望, 股票价格得以保持高位. (**c**) (*fig* 比喻) raise the hopes or spirits of sb; encourage sb 给某人带来希望; 使某人振作; 鼓舞某人: *We felt buoyed up by the good news.* 我们觉得这个好消息很令人鼓舞.

buoy·ant /ˈbɔɪənt; ˈbɔɪənt/ *adj* **1** (**a**) (of an object) able to float (指物体)能漂浮的: *The raft would be more buoyant if it was less heavy.* 木筏若轻一点, 浮力就更大了. (**b**) (of a liquid) able to keep things floating (指液体)能浮起物体的, 有浮力的: *Salt water is more buoyant than fresh water.* 盐水比淡水浮力大. **2** (of stock-market prices, etc) tending to rise (指证券市场的价格等)看涨的: *Share prices were buoyant today in active trading.* 今日股票交投活跃, 价格看涨. **3** (of a person, his manner, etc) able to recover quickly after a setback; cheerfully resilient (指人、态度等)能从挫折中迅速振作起来的; 乐天的: *a buoyant disposition, personality, etc* 乐天的性情、个性等. ▷ **buoy·ancy** /-ənsɪ; -ənsɪ/ *n* [U]. **buoy·antly** *adv*.

bur (also **burr**) /bɜ:(r); bɝ/ *n* (plant with a) prickly seed-case or flower-head that clings to hair or clothing 刺蒺藜(易附着于毛发或衣服上): (*fig* 比喻) *She tried to get rid of him at the party but he stuck to her like a bur.* 在宴会上她尽力摆脱他, 可他却像刺蒺藜一样钩住她不放.

burble /ˈbɜ:bl; ˈbɝbḷ/ *v* **1** [I] make a gentle murmuring or bubbling sound 发出沙沙声; 发出汩汩声. **2** [I, Ipr, Ip] **~ (on) (about sth)** speak in a rambling manner 东拉西扯地说: *What's he burbling (on) about?* 他在胡扯些什么呀?

bur·den /ˈbɜːdn; ˈbɝdn̩/ *n* **1** [C] thing or person that is carried; heavy load 所负载的事物或人; 重负: *bear/carry/shoulder a heavy burden* 负有[负起/肩负]重担. **2** [C] (*fig* 比喻) duty, obligation, responsibility, etc that is hard to bear (难以承担的)职责、义务、责任等: *the burden of heavy taxation on the tax-payer* 纳税者负担的重税 ○ *the burden of grief, guilt, remorse, etc* 压在心头的悲伤、内疚、悔恨等 ○ *His invalid father is becoming a burden (to him).* 他父亲体弱多病, (对他)渐渐成了累赘. **3** [sing] **the ~ of sth** main theme of a speech, an article, etc (演说、文章等的)主题, 要点: *The burden of his argument was that...* 他论证的要点是.... **4** [U] ship's carrying capacity; tonnage (船的)装载量, 吨位.

▷ **bur·den** *v* [Tn, Tn·pr] **~ sb/oneself (with sth)** put a burden on sb/oneself; load sb/oneself 加负担于某人[自己]: *refugees burdened with all their possessions* 带着沉重家当的难民 ○ (*fig* 比喻) *I don't want to burden you with my problems.* 我不想让我的问题给你增加负担. ○ *Industry is heavily burdened with taxation.* 工业为重税所累.

bur·den·some /-səm; -səm/ *adj* hard to bear; troublesome 难以承担的; 令人困扰的: *burdensome duties, responsibilities, etc* 难以承担的职务、责任等.

□ **the ˌburden of ˈproof** (*law* 律) obligation to prove that what one says is true 举证责任(提供证据的责任).

bur·eau /ˈbjʊərəʊ; *US* ˈbjʊro; ˈbjʊro/ *n* (*pl* **-reaux** or **-reaus** /-rəʊz; -roz/) **1** (*Brit*) writing desk with drawers (有抽屉的)办公桌, 写字台. ⇨illus at App 1 见附录1之插图, page xvi. **2** (*US*) = CHEST OF DRAWERS (CHEST). **3** (*esp US*) government department 政府机关; 局; 司; 处: *Federal Bureau of Investigation* 联邦调查局. **4** office; agency 办公室; 办事处: *a travel bureau* 旅行社 ○ *an information bureau* 询问处.

bur·eau·cracy /bjʊəˈrɒkrəsɪ; bjʊˈrɑkrəsɪ/ *n* (*often derog* 常作贬义) **1** (**a**) [U] system of government through departments managed by State officials, not by elected representatives 官僚制度; 官僚体制. (**b**) [C] country having such a system 实行官僚制度的国家. (**c**) [CGp] officials appointed to manage such a system, as a group 官僚(总称). **2** [U] excessive or complicated official routine, esp because of too many departments and offices 官僚作风.

bur·eau·crat /ˈbjʊərəkræt; ˈbjʊrəˌkræt/ *n* (*often derog* 常作贬义) official working in a government department, esp one who follows administrative routine and the rules of the department very strictly 官员(尤指墨守成规的): *insensitive, bungling, etc bureaucrats* 麻木的、坏事的...官老爷.

▷ **bur·eau·cratic** /ˌbjʊərəˈkrætɪk; ˌbjʊrəˈkrætɪk/ *adj* (*often derog* 常作贬义) of, like or relating to a bureaucracy or bureaucrats 官僚制度的; 官僚的; 官僚般的: *bureaucratic government* 官僚政府 ○ *The report revealed a major bureaucratic muddle.* 这个报告揭示了官僚作风引起的严重混乱. **bur·eau·crat·ic·ally** /-ɪklɪ; -ɪklɪ/ *adv*.

bur·ette /bjʊəˈret; bjʊˈrɛt/ *n* (*chemistry* 化) glass tube with a tap, used for measuring small quantities of liquid let out of it 滴定管; 量管.

bur·geon /ˈbɜːdʒən; ˈbɝdʒən/ *v* [I] **1** (*arch* 古) (of a plant) put out leaves; sprout (指植物)发芽, 萌发. **2** (*fml* 文) begin to grow rapidly; flourish 开始迅速成长; 茂盛: *a burgeoning population* 迅速增长的人口 ○ *a burgeoning talent* 迅速增长的才干.

burger /ˈbɜːgə(r); ˈbɝgɚ/ *n* (*infml* 口) = HAMBURGER.

▷ **-burger** (forming compound *ns* 用以构成复合名词) (*infml* 口) food prepared or cooked like or with a hamburger (汉堡包式)夹馅包: *a ˈsteakburger* ○ *a ˈcheeseburger*.

burgh /ˈbʌrə; ˈbʌrə/ *n* (*Scot* 苏格兰) borough 享有特权的自治城镇; 自治市.

burgher /ˈbɜːgə(r); ˈbɝgɚ/ *n* (*arch or joc* 古或谑) (esp respectable) citizen of a particular town (尤指受尊敬的)(某市的)市民: *The pop festival has shocked the good burghers of Canterbury.* 流行歌曲音乐汇演震动了坎特伯雷有头有脸的市民.

burg·lar /ˈbɜːglə(r); ˈbɝglɚ/ *n* person who enters a building illegally, esp by force, in order to steal 窃贼(尤指强行进入建筑物的): *The burglar got into the house through the bedroom window.* 窃贼是从卧室的窗户潜入这所房子的. Cf 参看 ROBBER (ROB), THIEF.

▷ **burg·lary** /ˈbɜːglərɪ; ˈbɝglərɪ/ *n* [C, U] (instance of the) crime of entering a building in order to steal 入户行窃; 入户盗窃罪: *A number of burglaries have been committed in this area recently.* 这一带最近发生了若干起入户盗窃案. ○ *be accused/convicted of burglary* 被控以[判以]入户盗窃罪.

□ **ˈburglar-alarm** *n* automatic device that rings an alarm bell when a burglar enters a building 防盗铃; 自动警铃.

ˈburglar-proof *adj* (of a building) made so that burglars cannot break into it (指建筑物)防盗的.

burgle /ˈbɜːgl; ˈbɝgl/ (*US* **burg·lar·ize, -ise** /ˈbɜːgləraɪz; ˈbɝgləˌraɪz/) *v* [Tn] steal from (a house or person) after entering a building illegally 入户盗窃: *burgle a shop* 盗窃一家商店 ○ *We were burgled while we were on holiday.* 我们度假期间屋里进贼了. ⇨Usage at ROB 用法见 ROB.

bur·go·mas·ter /ˈbɜːgəmɑːstə (r); ˈbɝgəˌmæstɚ/ *n* mayor of a Dutch or Flemish town 荷兰或佛兰芒城镇的市长或镇长.

Bur·gundy /ˈbɜːgəndɪ; ˈbɝgəndɪ/ *n* **1** [U, C] any of various types of red or white wine from the Burgundy area of eastern France 勃艮第葡萄酒(产于法国东部勃艮第地区的红酒或白酒). **2** [U] dark purplish-red colour 深的紫红色.

burial /ˈberɪəl; ˈbɛrɪəl/ *n* [U, C] burying, esp of a dead body; funeral 埋葬; 葬礼: *Cremation is more common than burial in some countries.* 在某些国家, 火葬比土葬普遍. ○ *The burial took place on Friday.* 葬礼已于星期五举行. ○ [attrib 作定语] *the burial service* 葬礼.

□ **ˈburial-ground** *n* place where dead bodies are buried; cemetery 墓地; 公墓: *a prehistoric burial-ground* 史前时期的墓地.

bur·lesque /bɜːˈlesk; bɝˈlɛsk/ *n* **1** [C, U] (piece of writing that mocks sb/sth by) comic or exaggerated imitation; parody (滑稽或夸张的)模仿; (以此种手法写的)嘲讽性作品: *a burlesque of a novel, poem, etc* 对某小说、某诗等的讽刺性模仿. **2** [U] (*US*) type of bawdy comedy show, often involving striptease 一种低级的诙谐表演(常包括脱衣舞).

▷ **bur·lesque** *adj* [usu attrib 通常作定语] of, relating to or using burlesque(1, 2) (滑稽或夸张性)模仿的; (以此种手法创作的)讽刺性作品的, 低级诙谐表演的: *a burlesque actor* 作低级诙谐表演的演员 ○ *burlesque acting* 滑稽夸张的模仿表演.

bur·lesque *v* [Tn] make a burlesque of (sb/sth); parody (以滑稽或夸张手法)模仿嘲弄(某人[某事物]).

burly /ˈbɜːlɪ; ˈbɝlɪ/ *adj* (**-ier, -iest**) with a strong heavy body; sturdy 身强力壮的; 魁梧的; 结实的; 健壮的: *a burly policeman* 魁梧的警察. ▷ **bur·li·ness** *n* [U].

burn[1] /bɜːn; bɝn/ *n* (*Scot* 苏格兰) small stream 小溪; 小河.

burn[2] /bɜːn; bɝn/ *v* (*pt, pp* **burnt** /bɜːnt; bɝnt/ or **burned** /bɜːnd; bɝnd/) ⇨Usage at DREAM[2] 用法见 DREAM[2]. **1** (**a**) [Tn] destroy, damage, injure or mark (sb/sth) by fire, heat or acid 烧毁, 烧坏, 烧伤, 烧焦, 烫伤, 酸蚀(某人[某物]): *burn dead leaves, waste paper, rubbish, etc* 焚烧枯叶、废纸、垃圾等 ○ *The house was burnt to the ground*, ie completely destroyed by fire. 这所房子已焚为平地. ○ *All his belongings were burnt in the fire.* 他所有的财物都已付之一炬. ○ *Sorry, I've burnt the toast.* 对不起, 我把面包片烤焦了. ○ *His face was badly burnt by the hot sun.* 他的脸被烈日晒伤了. ○ *The soup is very hot. Don't burn your mouth.* 汤很热. 别烫着你的嘴. ○ *The child burnt its fingers/itself while playing with a match.* 那孩子玩火柴时把手指[自己]烧伤了. (**b**) [I] be marked, damaged or spoilt in this way 被烧坏; 被烧毁; 被烧伤; 被烧焦; 被烫着; 被酸蚀: *Her skin burns easily.* 她的皮肤不禁晒. ○ *I can smell something burning.* 我闻到有东西烧焦了. **2** [Tn, Tn·pr] make (a hole or mark) by burning 烧出(窟窿或痕迹): *The cigarette burnt a hole in the carpet.* 香烟在地毯上烧了一个窟窿. **3** [Tn] use (sth) as fuel 使用(某物)为燃料: *Do you burn coal as well as wood on this fire?* 你是不是用煤也用木头

生这炉火? ○ *a central heating boiler that burns gas/oil/coke* 以煤气[石油/焦炭]为燃料的中央供暖锅炉. **4** [I, Tn] (cause a person or an animal to) be killed by fire (使人或动物)被烧死: *Ten people burnt to death in the hotel fire.* 旅馆失火烧死了十人. ○ *Joan of Arc was burnt (alive) at the stake.* 圣女贞德在火刑柱上被(活活)烧死. **5 (a)** [La, I] be on fire or alight; produce heat or light 燃烧; 发光; 发热; 发亮: *a burning building* 燃烧着的建筑物 ○ *The house burned for hours before the blaze was put out.* 那所房子燃烧了数小时火才扑灭. ○ *A fire was burning merrily in the grate.* 壁炉里炉火很旺. ○ *The fire had burnt low*, ie was nearly out. 火快要熄灭了. ○ *A single light burned in the empty house.* 那所空房子里有一盏孤灯亮着. **(b)** [I] be able to catch fire 能点着: *Paper burns easily.* 纸容易点着. ○ *Damp wood doesn't burn well.* 潮湿的木头不好烧. **6** [Tn] make (sth) by burning 烧制(某物); 烤制(某物): *burn charcoal* 烧制木炭. **7** [I, Tn] (cause sb/sth to) feel painfully hot (使某人[某物])发烫: *Your forehead's burning. Have you got a fever?* 你前额很烫. 是不是发烧了? **8** [Ipr] **~ with sth** (usu in the continuous tenses 通常用于进行时态) be full of strong emotion 充满强烈的情感: *be burning with rage, desire, longing, etc* 怒火中烧、欲火焚心、热望如焚. **9** [Ipr, It] **~ for sth** (usu in the continuous tenses 通常用于进行时态) want to do sth very much 极欲做某事: (*rhet* 修辞) *He was burning to avenge the death of his father.* 他心急如焚要报杀父之仇. **10** (idm 习语) **burn one's 'boats/'bridges** do sth that makes it impossible to go back to a previous situation 做事不留退路或后路; 破釜沉舟: *Think carefully before you resign — if you do that you will have burnt your boats.* 你对辞职一事须三思—— 辞了职就断了自己的后路. **burn the candle at both 'ends** exhaust oneself by trying to do too many things 由于超负荷地工作而耗尽精力; 操劳过度. **burn one's 'fingers/get one's 'fingers burnt** suffer (often financially) as a result of foolish behaviour or meddling 由于愚蠢的举动或管闲事而吃苦头(常指破财): *He got his fingers badly burnt dabbling in the stock-market.* 他在证券市场胡乱买卖而大吃苦头. **burn the midnight 'oil** study or work until late at night 挑灯夜战; 开夜车: *She takes her exams next week, so she's burning the midnight oil.* 她下周要考试, 所以在开夜车. **burn sth to a crisp** cook sth too long, so that it becomes burnt 烹得过久而烧焦: (*fig* 比喻) *I lay in the sun all day and got burnt to a crisp.* 我在太阳下躺了一整天, 都快烤焦了. **sb's ears are burning** ⇨ EAR[1]. **feel one's ears burning** ⇨ FEEL[1]. **have money to burn** ⇨ MONEY. **money burns a hole in sb's pocket** ⇨ MONEY.

11 (phr v) **burn away** continue to burn 继续燃烧: *a fire burning away in the grate* 壁炉里继续燃着的炉火. **burn (sth) away (a)** (cause sth to) become less by burning (使某物)逐渐烧掉: *Half the candle had burnt away.* 蜡烛已烧掉一半. **(b)** (cause sth to) be removed by burning (将某物)烧掉: *Most of the skin on his face got burnt away in the fire.* 在火灾中, 他脸上的皮肤大部分烧掉了.

burn down (of a fire) burn less brightly or strongly (指火)渐渐烧完; 火力减弱: *The room grew colder as the fire burnt down.* 随着炉火逐渐减弱, 房间越来越冷. **burn (sth) down** (cause sth to) be destroyed to the foundations by fire (将某物)焚为平地, 烧得精光: *The house burnt down in half an hour.* 那所房子在半小时之内就被焚为平地. ○ *Don't leave the gas on — you might burn the house down.* 别忘了关煤气炉—— 不然会把房子烧掉的.

burn sth off remove sth by burning 烧掉某物: *Burn the old paint off before re-painting the door.* 先把门上的旧漆烧掉再上新漆.

burn (itself) out (a) (of a fire) stop burning because there is no more fuel (指火)因燃料用尽而熄灭: *The fire had burnt (itself) out before the fire brigade arrived.* 在消防队赶到以前, 火已(自行)熄灭. **(b)** (of a rocket) finish its supply of fuel (指火箭)燃料用尽. **burn (sth) out** (cause sth to) stop working because of friction or excessive heat (使某物)因摩擦或过热而不能操作; 烧坏: *The clutch has burnt out.* 离合器因过热而失灵. ○ *burn out a fuse, motor, transformer* 烧坏保险丝、发动机、变压器. **burn oneself out** exhaust oneself or ruin one's health, esp by working too hard 筋疲力尽或损害了自己的健康(尤指因劳累过度): *If he doesn't stop working so hard, he'll burn himself out.* 他继续这样拼命地工作, 就会累垮的. **burn sb out** (esp passive 尤用于被动语态) force sb to leave his house by burning it 放火烧某人的房子迫使其离去: *The family was burnt out (of house and home) and forced to leave the area.* 这家人因为房子被人放火烧了, 不得不离开这个地区. **burn sth out** (esp passive 尤用于被动语态) completely destroy sth by burning; gut sth 烧光某物; 烧空某物: *The hotel was completely burnt out.* 该旅馆毁于大火. ○ *the burnt-out wreck of a car* 汽车焚毁后的残骸.

burn (sth) to sth (cause sth to) be reduced to the specified state by burning (将某物)烧成某种状态: *It burned to ashes.* 它已烧成灰烬了. ○ *You've burnt the toast to a cinder*, ie so that it is hard and black. 你把面包片烤焦了.

burn up (a) (of a fire) produce brighter and stronger flames (指火)燃烧得更旺: *put more wood on a fire to make it burn up* 再往火上续点木柴让它烧旺些. **(b)** (of an object entering the earth's atmosphere) be destroyed by heat (指进入地球大气层的物体)着火烧毁. **burn sb up** (*US infml* 口) make sb very angry 使某人大动肝火. **burn sth up** get rid of sth by burning 把某物烧掉; 焚化: *burn up all the garden rubbish* 把花园里的垃圾都烧掉.

▷ **burn** *n* **1** injury or mark caused by fire, heat or acid 火、热或酸所造成的伤害或伤痕: *He died of the burns he received in the fire.* 他因在火灾中受烧伤而死. **2** firing of the rockets in a spacecraft (to change its course) 宇宙飞船中的火箭的发射(以改变航向).

burner *n* **1** part of a gas lamp, oven, etc from which the light or flame comes (煤气灯的)灯头; (煤气烤箱的)炉膛. **2** person who burns sth or makes sth by burning 烧制或烤制某物的人: *a charcoal-burner* 烧炭工人. **3** (idm 习语) **put sth on the back burner** ⇨ BACK[2].

burn·ing *adj* [attrib 作定语] **1** intense; extreme 强烈的; 极端的: *a burning thirst* 极渴 ○ *a burning desire for sth* 对某事物的强烈的欲望. **2** very important; urgent; crucial 极其重要的; 紧急的; 关键性的: *one of the most burning issues of the day* 当前最重要的问题之一.

burnt *adj* marked, damaged or hurt by burning 有烧痕的; 烧坏的; 烧伤的: *rather burnt toast* 有点焦的面包片 ○ *Your hand looks badly burnt.* 你的手好像受了很重的烫伤.

burnt 'offering thing offered as a sacrifice by burning 燔祭品.

□ **'burn-up** *n* (*Brit sl* 俚) ride on a motor-cycle, etc at high speed (摩托车等)高速行驶.

burn·ish /ˈbɜːnɪʃ; ˈbɝnɪʃ/ *v* [Tn] make (metal) smooth and shiny by rubbing; polish 将(金属)打磨光亮; 抛光: *burnished copper* 经过抛光的铜.

bur·nous /bɜːˈnuːs; bɝˈnus/ *n* type of cloak with a hood, worn by Arabs (阿拉伯人穿的)连有兜帽的斗篷.

burp /bɜːp; bɝp/ *n* (*infml* 口) belch 嗝; 饱嗝.

▷ **burp** *v* (*infml* 口) **1** [I] belch 打嗝. **2** [Tn] cause (a baby) to bring up wind from the stomach, esp by stroking or patting the back 使(婴儿)打嗝(尤指以抚背或拍背的方法).

burr[1] = BUR.

burr[2] /bɜː(r); bɝ/ *n* (usu *sing* 通常作单数) **1** whirring or humming sound made eg by parts of a machine turning quickly or by a telephone 隆隆声(如机器部件快速运转时发出的); 嗡嗡声(如电话机的声音). **2** strong pronunciation of the 'r' sound, typical of certain English accents; accent using this 浓重的 r 音(为英语某些方音); 带有浓重的 r 音的口音: *speak with a soft West Country burr* 用柔和的英国西南部地区的腔调说话.

▷ **burr** *v* [I] make a burr 发浓重的 r 音.

bur·row /ˈbʌrəʊ; ˈbʌro/ *n* hole made in the ground and used as a home or shelter by rabbits, foxes, etc (兔、狐等掘的)地洞.

▷ **bur·row** *v* **1 (a)** [Tn] make (sth) by digging 挖掘成(洞穴等): *Rabbits had burrowed holes in the grassy bank.* 兔子在河岸的草地上掘了些洞. **(b)** [I] dig a hole; tunnel 挖洞; 挖掘地道. **2** (phr v) **burrow (one's way) into, through, under, etc** move in the specified direction by or as if by digging 借挖掘或似挖掘的动作朝某方向移动: *The fox burrowed (its way) under the fence to reach the chickens.* 那狐狸在围栏下面掘(一条

路)到鸡窝处. ○ *The prisoners escaped by burrowing under the wall.* 囚犯们在墙下掘地道逃走了. ○ *The child burrowed under the bedclothes.* 那孩子在被窝里钻来钻去. ○ (*fig* 比喻) *We had to burrow through a mass of files to find the documents we wanted* 我们要在案卷堆里翻来翻去以寻找我们所要的文件.

bur·sar /ˈbɜːsə(r); ˋbɝsɚ/ *n* **1** person who manages the finances of a school or college (学校的)财务主任. **2** person holding a scholarship at a university (大学中)获奖学金的学生.

▷ **burs·ary** /ˈbɜːsərɪ; ˋbɝsərɪ/ *n* **1** college bursar's office (学院的)财务处. **2** scholarship or grant awarded to a student (授予学生的)奖学金或助学金.

burst[1] /bɜːst; bɝst/ *v* (*pt, pp* **burst**) **1** [I, Tn] (cause sth to) break violently open or apart, esp because of pressure from inside; explode (使某物)爆炸; 胀破; 爆破: *If you blow that balloon up any more it will burst.* 那气球再吹就要破了. ○ *The dam burst under the weight of water.* 那水坝在水的压力下决口了. ○ *Water-pipes often burst in cold weather.* 水管在寒冷的天气里经常冻裂. ○ (*fig* 比喻) *I've eaten so much I feel ready to burst!* 我吃得太多, 肚子都要撑破了! ○ *The river burst its banks and flooded the town.* 河水冲决了堤岸, 淹没了城镇. ○ *Don't get so angry! You'll burst a blood-vessel!* 别生这么大的气! 会把血管气崩的! **2** [I, Ipr] **~ (with sth)** (only in the continuous tenses 仅用于进行时态) be full to the point of breaking open 满到要胀破的程度: *'More pudding?' 'No thanks. I'm bursting!'* '再吃点布丁好吗?' '不了, 我肚子已经胀了!' ○ *May I use your lavatory — I'm bursting!* ie I need to urinate urgently. 我可以用用你们的厕所吗——我实在憋不住了. ○ *a bag bursting with shopping* 撑得鼓鼓的购物袋 ○ (*fig* 比喻) *be bursting with happiness, pride, excitement, etc* 充满喜气、骄傲、激情等. **3** (idm 习语) **be bursting at the ˈseams** (*infml* 口) be very full or tight 满满当当: *I've eaten so much I'm bursting at the seams.* 我吃得太多了, 肚子都要撑破了. **be bursting to do sth** be very eager to do sth 极欲干某事: *She was bursting to tell him the good news.* 她迫不及待地要把这个好消息告诉他. **burst (sth) ˈopen** (cause sth to) open suddenly or violently (使某物)突然或猛然打开: *The police burst the door open.* 警察把门撞开了. **4** (phr v) **burst ˈin** enter (a room, etc) suddenly 突然进入(房间等): *The police burst in (through the door) and arrested the gang.* 警察突然闯进(房门)逮捕了那帮人. **burst in on sb/sth** interrupt sb/sth (by arriving suddenly) (因突然来到)阻碍某人[某事物]: *burst in on a meeting* 打断会议 ○ *How dare you burst in on us without knocking!* 你怎么胆敢不敲门就闯进来! **burst into sth** send out or produce sth suddenly and violently 突然而猛烈地发出或产生出某事物: *The aircraft crashed and burst into flames,* ie suddenly began to burn. 飞机坠毁起火. ○ *burst into tears, song, angry speech,* ie suddenly begin to cry, sing, speak angrily 突然哭、唱、吵起来 ○ *trees bursting into leaf/bloom/blossom/flower* 长出新叶[开花]的树木. **burst into, out of, through, etc sth** move suddenly and forcibly in the specified direction; appear suddenly from somewhere 突然而猛力地向某一方向移动; 从某处突然出现: *An angry crowd burst through the lines of police and into the street.* 愤怒的人群突破了警方的封锁线走到街上. ○ *The oil burst out of the ground.* 石油从地下喷发出来. ○ *The sun burst through the clouds.* 太阳突然从云端里露出来. **burst on/upon sb/sth** come suddenly and unexpectedly to sb/sth 突然而意外地出现在某人[某物]面前: *The truth burst upon him,* ie He suddenly realized it. 他突然了解了真相. ○ *A major new talent has burst on the literary scene.* 有个惹人瞩目的新秀突然出现于文坛. **burst out (a)** speak suddenly and with feeling; exclaim 突然激动地说; 叫嚷: *'I hate you!' she burst out.* '我讨厌你!' 她叫嚷道. **(b)** (with the *-ing* form 与 -ing 连用) suddenly begin (doing sth) 突然开始(做某事): *burst out crying/laughing/singing* 突然哭起来[笑起来/唱起来].

burst[2] /bɜːst; bɝst/ *n* **1 (a)** bursting; explosion 爆炸; 爆破: *the burst of a shell, bomb* 炮弹、炸弹的爆炸. **(b)** split caused by this 爆裂; 胀裂: *a burst in a water-pipe* 水管的破裂. **2** brief violent effort; spurt 短暂而巨大的努力; 冲刺: *a burst of energy, speed, etc* 迸发出的能量、速度等 ○ *work in short bursts* 一阵一阵猛干. **3** sudden outbreak of sth 某事物的突然爆发: *a burst of anger, enthusiasm, etc* 怒火、热情等的迸发 ○ *a burst of applause* 一阵欢呼. **4** short series of shots from a gun (枪的)一阵短暂的射击: *a burst of machine-gun fire* 机关枪的一阵扫射.

bur·ton /ˈbɜːtn; ˋbɝtn̩/ *n* (idm 习语) **go for a ˈburton** (*Brit infml* 口) be lost, destroyed or killed 失踪; 被毁; 被杀: *It's pouring with rain, so I'm afraid our picnic's gone for a burton.* 下起了瓢泼大雨, 我们的野餐恐怕要吹了.

B

bury /ˈberɪ; ˋbɛrɪ/ *v* (*pt, pp* **buried**) **1** [Tn] **(a)** place (a dead body) in a grave or in the sea 将(尸体)土葬, 海葬: *He was buried with his wife.* 他和他妻子葬在一起. ○ *Where is Shakespeare buried?* 莎士比亚葬于何处? ○ *He's been dead and buried for years!* 他已死亡并且埋葬多年了! **(b)** (*euph* 婉) lose (sb) by death 丧: *She's eighty-five and has buried three husbands.* 她现年八十五岁, 曾三度丧夫. **2** [Tn, Tn·pr, Cn·a] hide (sb/sth) in the earth; cover with soil, rocks, leaves, etc 将(某人[某物])藏匿于地下; 以土壤、石块、树叶等覆盖: *buried treasure* 埋藏的财宝 ○ *Our dog buries its bones in the garden.* 我们的狗把骨头埋藏在花园里. ○ *The house was buried under ten feet of snow.* 那所房子被掩埋在十英尺厚的雪底下. ○ *The miners were buried alive when the tunnel collapsed.* 矿坑坍塌时, 矿工被活活埋在里面了. **3** [Tn, Tn·pr] hide (sb/sth) from sight; cover up 遮盖(某人[某物]); 覆盖: *Your letter got buried under a pile of papers.* 你的信压在一堆文件下面了. ○ *She buried her face in her hands and wept.* 她双手掩面哭了起来. **4** [Tn] dismiss (sth) from one's mind; completely forget about 从记忆中除去(某事物); 忘记: *It's time to bury our differences and be friends again.* 是我们摈弃分歧重归于好的时候了. **5** [Tn·pr] **~ sth (in sth)** plunge sth (into sth) 使某物陷入(某物之中): *The lion buried its teeth in the antelope's neck.* 那狮子咬住羚羊的脖子. ○ *He walked slowly, his hands buried in his pockets.* 他走得很慢, 两手插在衣袋里. ○ *Her head was buried in the book she was reading.* 她在埋头读书. **6** (idm 习语) **ˌbury the ˈhatchet** stop quarrelling and become friendly 言归于好. **bury/hide one's head in the sand** ⇨ HEAD[1]. **7** (phr v) **bury oneself in sth (a)** go to (a place where one will meet few people) 前往(某隐居处所): *He buried himself (away) in the country to write a book.* 他隐居到乡下去写书. **(b)** involve oneself in or concentrate deeply on sth 埋头于或专心致志于某事物: *In the evenings he buries himself in his books.* 每天晚上他都埋头读书.

bus /bʌs; bʌs/ *n* (*pl* **buses**; *US* also **busses**) **1** large vehicle carrying passengers between stopping-places along a fixed route 公共汽车: *Shall we walk or go by bus?* 我们是步行呢, 还是乘公共汽车呢? ○ [attrib 作定语] *a bus driver/conductor* 公共汽车司机[乘务员] ○ *a bus station* 公共汽车站. **2** (idm 习语) **miss the boat/bus** ⇨ MISS[3].

▷ **bus** *v* (*pres p* **busing**; also *esp US* **bussing**, *pt, pp* **bused**; also *esp US* **bussed**) **1** [I] (also **bus it**) travel by bus 乘公共汽车: *I usually bus (it) to work in the morning.* 我早上通常乘坐公共汽车上班. **2** [Tn] **(a)** transport (sb) by bus 用公共汽车运送(某人). **(b)** (*US*) transport (children) by bus from white areas to schools in black areas and vice versa, to create racially integrated schools 用公共汽车把儿童从白人区送往黑人区就读, 或从黑人区送往白人区就读, 以在学校实现种族融合.

□ ˈ**bus lane** strip of road for use by buses only 公共汽车专用的行车线.

ˈ**busman** /-mən; -mən/ *n* (idm 习语) **a busman's ˈholiday** holiday spent doing the same thing that one does at work 照常工作的假日.

ˈ**bus-shelter** *n* structure at a bus-stop providing shelter for people waiting for a bus (公共汽车停车站为候车乘客设的)候车棚.

ˈ**bus-stop** *n* regular stopping-place for a bus; sign marking this 公共汽车停车站.

busby /ˈbʌzbɪ; ˋbʌzbɪ/ *n* tall fur cap worn by hussars, gunners, etc for ceremonial parades, etc (轻骑兵、枪炮手等在阅兵等场合所戴的)高皮帽.

bush /bʊʃ; bʊʃ/ *n* **1** [C] **(a)** low thickly-growing plant with several woody stems coming up from the root; shrub (有几个茎的)灌木: *a rose bush* 蔷薇丛 ○

gooseberry bushes 醋栗树丛. Cf 参看 TREE. (**b**) thing resembling this, esp a clump of hair or fur 类似灌木之物(尤指蓬乱的毛发或皮毛). **2** (often 常作 **the bush**) [U] wild uncultivated land, esp in Africa, Australia and (with forests) Canada 荒野(尤指非洲、澳洲以及加拿大森林地区未开发的地方). **3** (idm 习语) **beat about the bush** ⇨ BEAT[1]. **a bird in the hand is worth two in the bush** ⇨ BIRD.

B

▷ **bushy** *adj* (**-ier**, **-iest**) **1** covered with bushes 长满灌木的. **2** growing thickly; shaggy 茂密的; 粗而蓬乱的: *a bushy moustache* 粗而密的髭须 ○ *bushy eyebrows* 浓密的眉毛. **bushi·ness** *n* [U].

□ ˈ**bush-baby** *n* small African lemur with large eyes and a long tail 灌丛婴猴(非洲的一种大眼长尾的小狐猴).

ˈ**Bushman** /-mən; -mən/ *n* (*pl* **-men**) member of various S W African tribes living and hunting in the bush 居于西南非洲灌木丛林中以行猎为生的部族的人.

ˌ**bush** ˈ**telegraph** process by which information, rumours, etc spread rapidly (消息、谣言等的)快速传播, 不胫而走.

bushed /bʊʃt; bʊʃt/ *adj* [pred 作表语] (*US infml* 口) very tired 疲惫不堪.

bushel /ˈbʊʃl; ˈbʊʃəl/ *n* **1** measure for grain and fruit (8 gallons or about 36.4 litres) 蒲式耳(计量谷物及水果的单位, 等于8加仑或大约36.4升). **2** (idm 习语) **hide one's light under a bushel** ⇨ HIDE[1].

bus·ier, busi·est, busily ⇨ BUSY.

busi·ness /ˈbɪznɪs; ˈbɪznɪs/ *n* **1** [C, U] one's usual occupation; profession 日常工作; 职业: *He tries not to let (his) business interfere with his home life.* 他尽量不让日常工作妨碍他的家庭生活. **2** [U] (**a**) buying and selling (esp as a profession); commerce; trade 买卖(尤指作为职业); 商业; 贸易: *We don't do (much) business with foreign companies.* 我们跟外国公司没有(多少)生意来往. ○ *He's in* (ie works in) *the oil business.* 他做油类生意. ○ *She has set up in business as a bookseller.* 她已创业成为书商. ○ *He wants to be a doctor or go into business.* 他想当医生或者经商. ○ [attrib 作定语] *a business trip* 商务之行 ○ *a business lunch* 商务午餐 ○ *business sense*, ie knowledge of commercial procedures 商业知识. (**b**) volume or rate of buying and selling 成交额; 成交率: *Business is always brisk before Christmas.* 圣诞节前生意总是很兴隆. **3** [C] commercial establishment; firm; shop 商业机构; 公司; 商店: *have/own one's own business* 有自己的商行 ○ *She runs a thriving grocery business.* 她经营着一家生意兴隆的食品杂货店. ○ *Many small businesses have gone bankrupt recently.* 近来有许多小商店倒闭. **4** [U] thing that one is rightly concerned with or interested in; duty; task 理应关心的事; 职责; 任务: *It is the business of the police to protect the community.* 保障社会的安全是警察的职责. ○ *I shall make it my business to find out who is responsible.* 我要查出是谁的责任. ○ *My private life is none of your business/is no business of yours.* 我的私生活与你毫不相干. **5** [U] things that need to be dealt with; matters to be discussed 需要处理的事; 所讨论的问题: *The main business of this meeting is our wages claim.* 这次会议的主要议题是我们在工资方面的要求. ○ *Unless there is any other business, we can end the meeting.* 如果没有别的事情, 我们的会议可以结束了. **6** [sing] (*often derog* 常作贬义) matter; affair 事情; 事务; 勾当: *an odd, a strange, a disturbing, etc business* 怪事、奇事、乱事等 ○ *What a business it is moving house!* 搬家这件事真够受的! ○ *I'm sick of the whole business.* 我觉得整件事都很讨厌. ○ *That plane crash was an awful business.* 那架飞机坠毁了, 真是件糟糕的事. ○ *What's this business I hear about you losing your job?* 听说你丢掉了工作, 究竟是怎么回事? **7** [U] gestures, facial expressions, etc made by actors on stage to give extra effect to what they are saying 演员的舞台动作、面部表情等(用以增强台词的效果). **8** (idm 习语) **business as** ˈ**usual** (*catchphrase* 警语) things will proceed normally despite difficulties or disturbances (尽管有困难或干扰)照常营业, 一切如常. **the** ˈ**business end (of sth)** (*infml* 口) part of a tool, an instrument, a weapon, etc that performs its particular function (工具、仪器、武器等)发挥效用的部分: *Never hold a gun by the business end.* 拿枪千万别拿枪口那端. ˌ**business is** ˈ**business** (*catchphrase* 警语) in financial and commercial matters one must not be influenced by friendship, pity, etc 公事公办. **funny business** ⇨ FUNNY. **get down to** ˈ**business** start the work that must be done 开始干正事; 言归正传. **go about one's** ˈ**business** occupy oneself with one's own affairs 忙于自己的事情: *The streets were filled with people going about their daily business.* 街上到处都是为日常事务而奔波的人. **go out of** ˈ**business** become bankrupt 破产; 倒闭. **have no business to do sth/doing sth** have no right to do sth 无权做某事: *You've no business to be here — this is private property.* 你无权待在这里——这是私人地方. **like** ˈ**nobody's business** (*infml* 口) very much, fast or well 非常; 多极了; 快极了; 好极了: *My head hurts like nobody's business.* 我的头疼死了. **mean business** ⇨ MEAN[1]. **mind one's own business** ⇨ MIND[2]. **on** ˈ**business** for the purpose of doing business 因公: *I'll be away on business next week.* 下星期我要出差. **send sb about his business** ⇨ SEND.

□ ˈ**business address** address of one's place of work 办公地址; 工作地址.

ˈ**business card** small card printed with sb's name and details of his job and company (业务)名片.

ˈ**business hours** hours during which a shop or an office is open for work 营业时间; 办公时间.

ˈ**businesslike** *adj* efficient; systematic 有效的; 有条不紊的: *Negotiations were conducted in a businesslike manner.* 谈判按部就班地进行.

ˈ**businessman**/-mæn; -ˌmæn/, ˈ**businesswoman** *ns* **1** person working in business, esp the manager of a company 从事工商业的人; (尤指)经理. **2** person who is skilful and alert in financial matters 熟悉并精于财经业务的人: *I ought to have got a better price for the car but I'm not a very good businessman.* 那辆汽车我本该讨个更合适的价钱, 只是我并不大会讨价还价. ⇨Usage at CHAIR 用法见 CHAIR.

ˈ**business studies** study of economics and management 经济与管理的学习或研究.

busk /bʌsk; bʌsk/ *v* [I] (*infml* 口) entertain people in a public place, eg by playing music, for money 在公共场所卖艺(尤指演奏乐曲). ▷ **busker** *n*. **busk·ing** *n* [U].

bust[1] /bʌst; bʌst/ *n* **1** sculpture of a person's head, shoulders and chest 半身雕塑像(包括头、肩、胸). **2** (**a**) woman's breasts; bosom 女子的乳房; 胸部. (**b**) measurement round a woman's chest and back (女子的)胸围: [attrib 作定语] *What is your bust size, madam?* 小姐, 您胸围的尺寸是多少?

▷ **busty** *adj* having large breasts 乳房大的.

bust[2] /bʌst; bʌst/ *v* (*pt*, *pp* **bust** or **busted**) (*infml* 口) **1** [Tn] break (sth); smash 打破(某物); 打碎: *I dropped my camera on the pavement and bust it.* 我把照相机掉在人行道上摔坏了. **2** [Tn, Tn·pr] **~ sth/sb (for sth)** (of the police) raid (a house) or arrest sb (指警方)突击搜查(房屋)或拘捕某人: *Mickey's been busted for drugs.* 米基曾因毒品事而被捕. **3** [Tn] reduce (sb) to a lower military rank; demote 降低(某人)军阶; 使降级: *He was busted (to corporal) for being absent without leave.* 他因擅离职守而被降级(为下士). **4** (phr v) **bust up** (*infml* 口) (esp of a married couple) quarrel and separate (尤指夫妻间)争吵而离异: *They bust up after five years of marriage.* 他们婚后五年离异了. **bust sth up** cause sth to end; disrupt sth 使某事物终止; 破坏某事物: *bust up a meeting* 使会议终止 ○ *It was his drinking that busted up their marriage.* 是他的酗酒行为破坏了他们的婚姻.

▷ **bust** *n* raid or arrest by the police 警方的突击搜查或拘捕.

bust *adj* [pred 作表语] (*infml* 口) **1** broken; not working 毁坏; 不能操作: *My watch is bust.* 我的表坏了. **2** bankrupt 破产; 倒闭. **3** (idm 习语) **go** ˈ**bust** (of a person or a business) become bankrupt; fail financially (指人或企业)破产.

□ ˈ**bust-up** *n* **1** violent quarrel 激烈的争吵. **2** breaking up of a relationship, esp marriage 关系破裂(尤指婚姻).

bus·tard /ˈbʌstəd; ˈbʌstɚd/ *n* large land bird that can run very fast 鸨(一种体大善跑的陆地鸟).

bus·ter /ˈbʌstə(r); ˈbʌstɚ/ *n* (*US infml usu derog* 口, 通常作贬义) (used as a form of address to a man 用作对

男子的称呼): *Get lost, buster!* 走开, 老兄!

bustle[1] /ˈbʌsl; ˋbʌsḷ/ *v* **1** [I, Ipr, Ip, Tn, Tn·pr, Tn·p] (cause sb to) move busily and energetically (in the specified direction) (使某人)急忙而活跃地(向某方向)移动: *bustling about in the kitchen* 在厨房里忙得团团转 ○ *She bustled the children off to school.* 她催促孩子们上学去. **2** [I, Ipr] **~ (with sth)** be full of (noise, activity, etc) 到处是(嘈杂的声音、繁忙的景象等): *bustling streets* 熙熙攘攘的街道 ○ *The city centre was bustling with life.* 城市中心充满了生活的繁忙景象.

▷ **bustle** *n* [U] excited and noisy activity 热闹的活动: *the (hustle and) bustle of city life* 都市生活的(拥挤和)繁忙景象.

bustle[2] /ˈbʌsl; ˋbʌsḷ/ *n* (formerly) frame or padding used to puff out a woman's dress at the back (旧时)(女装后部的)裙撑, 衬垫.

busy /ˈbɪzɪ; ˋbɪzɪ/ *adj* **(-ier, -iest) 1 ~ (at/with sth); ~ (doing sth)** having much to do; working (on sth); occupied (with sth) 忙的; 正做(某事)的; 忙于(某事)的: *Doctors are busy people.* 医生都是大忙人. ○ *Could I have a word with you, if you're not too busy?* 你若不太忙的话, 我跟你说句话行吗? ○ *She's busy at/with her homework.* 她正忙着做家庭作业. ○ *Please go away — can't you see I'm busy?* 请走开吧 —— 你看不见我正忙着吗? ○ *She's busy writing letters.* 她正忙着写信呢. **2** full of activity 繁忙的: *a busy day, life, time of year, etc* 忙碌的一天、一生、一些日子 ○ *a busy office, street, town* 繁忙的事务所、街道、城镇 ○ *Victoria is one of London's busiest stations.* 维多利亚站是伦敦最繁忙的一个车站. ○ *The shops are very busy at Christmas.* 圣诞节期间店铺忙得不可开交. **3 (a)** = ENGAGED (ENGAGE). **(b)** being used (and so not available) 正用着的; 正被占用的: *The (telephone) line is busy.* (电话)占线. ○ *The photocopier has been busy all morning.* 影印机一上午都用着. **4** (of a picture or design) too full of detail (指图画或图样)复杂的: *This wallpaper is too busy for the bedroom.* 这壁纸的图案太乱, 不适合用于卧室. **5** (idm 习语) **(as) busy as a bee** very busy (and happy to be so) 忙个不停(并以此为乐): *The children are busy as bees, helping their mother in the garden.* 孩子们忙个不停地在花园里帮母亲干活儿. **get busy** start working 开始工作: *We've only got an hour to do the job — we'd better get busy.* 我们只有一个小时来做这项工作 —— 最好动手干吧.

▷ **busily** *adv*: *busily engaged on a new project* 忙于新的工作项目. **busy** *v* (*pt, pp* **busied**) [Tn, Tn·pr, Tng] **~ oneself (with sth); ~ oneself (in/with) doing sth** occupy oneself or keep oneself busy (with sth) 使自己忙于(某事): *busy oneself in the garden, with the housework, etc* 忙于园艺、家务等 ○ *He busied himself cooking the dinner.* 他忙着做饭.

busy·body /ˈbɪzɪbɒdɪ; ˋbɪzɪˌbɑdɪ/ *n* (*derog* 贬) person who interferes in other people's affairs 好管闲事的人; 多事的人: *He's an interfering busybody!* 他好管闲事!

but[1] /bʌt, *also* bət; bʌt, bət/ *adv* **1** (*esp dated or fml* 尤作旧或作文雅语) only 只; 仅仅: *He's but a boy.* 他不过是个孩子. ○ *If I had but known she was ill, I would have visited her.* 我倘若知道她病了, 早就去探望她了. ○ *I don't think we'll succeed. Still, we can but try.* 我想我们不会成功. 但是不妨试一试. **2** (idm 习语) **one cannot/could not but...** (*fml* 文) one can only...; one is obliged to... 不得不...; 只好...: *It was a rash thing to do, yet one cannot but admire her courage.* 这事做得过于鲁莽, 然而不能不佩服她的勇气. ○ *I could not but admit that he was right and I was wrong.* 我不得不承认他对了, 我错了.

but[2] /bət; bət; *strong form* 强读式 bʌt; bʌt/ *conj* (often used to introduce a word or phrase contrasting with or qualifying what has gone before 常用以引出与前文相对照或修饰前文的词语) **1** on the contrary 相反地; 而; 却: *You've bought the wrong shirt. It's not the red one I wanted but the blue one.* 你买错了衬衫. 我要的不是红色的; 而是蓝色的. ○ *Tom went to the party, but his brother didn't.* 汤姆去参加聚会了, 他的兄弟却没去. ○ *He doesn't like music but his wife does.* 他不喜欢音乐, 可他的妻子却很喜欢. **2 (a)** yet; however; in spite of this 但; 然而; 尽管如此: *She cut her knee badly, but didn't cry.* 她弄伤了膝盖, 但是并没有哭. ○ *I'd love to go to the theatre tonight, but I'm too busy.* 我倒是很想今晚去看戏的, 只是我太忙了. ○ *This restaurant serves cheap but excellent food.* 这家餐馆价廉物美. ○ *He's hard-working, but not very clever.* 他很努力, 却不大聪明. **(b)** yet also; at the same time 但也; 但又; 同时也; 同时又: *He was tired but happy after the long walk.* 他走了一段很长的路之后, 虽然很累但也很愉快. **3** (*dated or fml* 旧或文) (usu after a negative 通常用于否定词语之后) without the result that...; without it also being the case that... 而不产生...的结果; 而不同时也...: *I never pass my old house but I think of the happy years I spent there.* 每当我路过我的故居时, 都会追忆起我在那儿度过的快乐岁月. ○ *No man is so cruel but he may feel some pity.* 没有人会残忍到连一点同情心都没有. **4** (showing disagreement, surprise or astonishment 表示异议、惊奇或吃惊): *'I'll give you ten pounds to repair the damage.' 'But that's not nearly enough!'* '我给你十英镑赔偿你的损失吧.' '那可远远不够哇!' ○ *'I'm getting married.' 'But that's wonderful!'* '我快要结婚了.' '啊, 那太好了!' **5** (used to emphasize a word 用以加强某词的语气): *Nothing, but nothing will make me change my mind.* 没有任何事情, 绝对没有任何事情可以使我改变主意. **6** (idm 习语) **ˌbut me no ˈbuts** don't argue with me or make excuses 不要跟我争辩或推托. **ˌbut that...** (*dated or fml* 旧或文) **(a)** were it not for the fact that... 要不是...; 若非...: *But that you had seen me in the water, I would have drowned.* 要不是你看见我掉在水里, 我早就淹死了. ○ *He would have come with us but that he had no money.* 他要不是因为缺钱, 就跟我们一起来了. **(b)** (after a negative 用于否定词语之后) that...: *I don't deny/doubt/question but that you're telling the truth.* 我并不否认[猜疑/怀疑]你所说的是事实. **(c)** other than 不同于; 非: *Who knows but that what he says is true? We have no proof that he is lying.* 谁能知道他说的不是真话? 我们没有证据证明他说谎. **but then** on the other hand; moreover; nevertheless 但另一方面; 此外; 不过: *He speaks very good French — but then he did live in Paris for three years.* 他法语说得好极了 —— 但他毕竟在巴黎居住三年了. **not only...but also...** both... and... 不但...而且...: *He is not only arrogant but also selfish.* 他不但傲慢, 而且自私.

but[3] /bət; bət; *strong form* 强读式 bʌt; bʌt/ *prep* **1** (used after the negatives *nobody, none, nowhere,* etc, the question words *who, where,* etc, and also *all, everyone, anyone,* etc 用于否定词 nobody、none、nowhere 等和疑问词 who、where 等之后, 以及 all、everyone、anyone 等之后) except (sb/sth); apart from; other than 除(某人[某事物])以外; 此外; 不同于: *The problem is anything but easy.* 这个问题可绝对不容易. ○ *Everyone was there but him.* 除了他之外, 所有的人都在. ○ *Nobody but you could be so selfish.* 除了你之外, 谁也不会这样自私. ○ *Nothing but trouble will come of this plan.* 这个计划只能带来麻烦. **2** (idm 习语) **but for sb/sth** /ˈbʌt fə; ˋbʌt fɚ/ except for sb/sth; without sb/sth 要不是因为某人[某事物]; 如果没有某人[某事物]: *But for the rain we would have had a nice holiday.* 要不是因为下雨, 我们的假日一定过得很惬意. ○ *But for the safety-belt I wouldn't be alive today.* 假若没有安全带, 我就活不到今天了.

but[4] /bʌt, *also* bət; bʌt, bət/ *rel pron* 关系代词 (*dated or fml* 旧或文) (after a negative 用于否定词语之后) who/that do/does not 无人[事物]不: *There is no man but feels* (ie no man who does not feel) *pity for starving children.* 没有人不同情那些嗷嗷待哺的孩子. ○ *There is not one of us but wishes* (ie not one of us that does not wish) *to help you.* 我们没有一个人不想帮助你.

bu·tane /ˈbju:teɪn; ˋbjuten/ *n* [U] inflammable gas produced from petroleum, used in liquid form as a fuel (for cooking, heating, lighting, etc) 丁烷.

butch /bʊtʃ; bʊtʃ/ *adj* (*infml* 口) **1** (*often derog* 常作贬义) (of a woman) having a masculine appearance and behaviour (指女子)(外貌和行为)男性化的. **2** (*often approv* 常作褒义) (of a man) exaggeratedly or aggressively masculine (指男子)极具男子气的, 雄赳赳的.

but·cher /ˈbʊtʃə(r); ˋbʊtʃɚ/ *n* **1** person whose job is killing animals for food or cutting up and selling meat 屠夫; 肉商: *buy meat at the butcher's (shop)* 在肉铺买肉. **2** (*derog* 贬) person who kills people unnecessarily and brutally 妄杀无辜者; 刽子手: *a mindless butcher of innocent people* 滥杀无辜毫无人性的刽子手.

▷ **but·cher** *v* [Tn] **1** kill and prepare (animals) for meat 屠宰. **2** (*derog* 贬) kill (people or animals) unnecessarily and brutally 屠杀, 滥杀, 残杀(人或动物): *Women and children were butchered by the rebels.* 妇女和儿童遭到叛乱者的屠杀. **3** (*fig* 比喻) make a mess of (sth); ruin 将(某事物)弄得一团糟; 毁坏: *None of the cast can act at all — they're butchering the play.* 这班演员中没有一个人会演戏——他们把这个戏演得一团糟.

B

but·chery *n* [U] **1** butcher's trade 屠宰业. **2** unnecessary or brutal killing 无谓而残忍的杀戮.

but·ler /ˈbʌtlə(r); ˋbʌtlɚ/ *n* chief male servant of a house, usu in charge of the wine-cellar 男管家(通常负责管理酒窖).

butt[1] /bʌt; bʌt/ *n* **1** large cask or barrel for storing wine or beer 大酒桶. **2** large barrel for collecting rainwater, eg from a roof (接雨水用的)大水桶(如接房顶滴下的雨水的).

butt[2] /bʌt; bʌt/ *n* **1** thicker end of a tool or weapon (工具或武器)较粗的一端: *a rifle butt* 步枪的枪托. ⇨illus at GUN 见GUN之插图. **2** short piece at the end of a cigar or cigarette that is left when it has been smoked; stub 烟头; 烟蒂: *an ashtray full of butts* 盛满烟头的烟灰碟. **3** (*infml* 口 *esp US*) buttocks; bottom 屁股; 臀部: *Get off your butts and do some work!* 别老坐着, 干点正经事!

butt[3] /bʌt; bʌt/ *n* **1** (**a**) [C] mound of earth behind the targets on a shooting-range 靶垛. (**b**) **the butts** [pl] shooting-range 靶场. **2** [C] person or thing that is often mocked or teased 笑柄(常被嘲笑或戏弄的人或事物): *be the butt of everyone's jokes* 成为众人取笑的对象.

butt[4] /bʌt; bʌt/ *v* **1** [Tn, Tn·pr] hit or push (sb/sth) with the head (like a goat) 以头撞或顶(某人[某物])(如山羊般): *butt sb in the stomach* 撞某人的腹部. **2** [Tn·pr] hit (one's head) on sth (自己的头部)撞到某物上: *He butted his head against the shelf as he was getting up.* 他起来时一头撞在搁架上了. **3** (phr v) **butt in (on sb/sth)** (*infml* 口) interrupt (sb/sth) or interfere (in sth) 干扰(某人[某事物]); 干涉(某事物): *Don't butt in like that when I'm speaking.* 我讲话时别这样打断我的话. ○ *May I butt in on your conversation?* 我可以插句话吗?

but·ter /ˈbʌtə(r); ˋbʌtɚ/ *n* **1** [U] fatty food substance, made from cream by churning, that is spread on bread, etc or used in cooking 黄油; 奶油: *Would you like some more bread and butter?* 再来一点黄油面包好吗? ○ *Shall I use oil or butter for frying the onions?* 我用普通油还是黄油来炒洋葱呢? **2** [U] (in compounds 用以构成复合词) similar food substance made from the specified material 黄油状的食品: *peanut butter.* **3** (idm 习语) **(look as if/as though) ˌbutter would not ˌmelt in one's ˈmouth** appear innocent, although one is probably not 看起来老老实实(其实并不见得). **like a knife through butter** ⇨ KNIFE.

▷ **but·ter** *v* **1** [Tn] spread or put butter on (esp bread) 将黄油涂于(尤指面包)上: *(hot) buttered toast* 涂了黄油的(热的)烤面包片 ○ *buttered carrots* 胡萝卜蘸黄油. **2** (idm 习语) **know which side one's bread is buttered** ⇨ KNOW. **3** (phr v) **butter sb up** (*infml* 口) flatter sb 讨好某人: *I've seen you buttering up the boss!* 我看见你巴结老板来着!

but·tery *adj* like, containing or covered with butter 似黄油的; 含黄油的; 涂过黄油的.

□ **ˈbuttermilk** *n* [U] liquid that remains after butter has been separated from milk 脱脂乳.

ˈbutterscotch *n* [U] hard toffee made by boiling butter and sugar together 黄油硬糖.

butter-bean /ˈbʌtə bi:n; ˋbʌtɚˌbin/ *n* large white type of bean, often dried before being sold 利马豆.

but·ter·cup /ˈbʌtəkʌp; ˋbʌtɚˌkʌp/ *n* wild plant with bright yellow cup-shaped flowers 毛茛(一种野生植物, 开杯形黄色花). ⇨illus at App 1 见附录1之插图, page ii.

butter-fingers /ˈbʌtəfɪŋgəz; ˋbʌtɚˌfɪŋgɚz/ *n* (*pl* unchanged 复数不变) (*infml* 口) person who is likely to drop things 常拿不住东西的人.

but·ter·fly /ˈbʌtəflaɪ; ˋbʌtɚˌflaɪ/ *n* **1** [C] insect with a long thin body and four (usu brightly coloured) wings 蝴蝶. ⇨illus 见插图. **2** [C] (*fig* 比喻) person who never settles down to one job or activity for long 无恒心的人; 没常性的人: *a social butterfly* 交际花. **3** [sing] (also **ˈbutterfly stroke**) stroke in swimming in which both

the life cycle of a butterfly 蝴蝶的生命周期

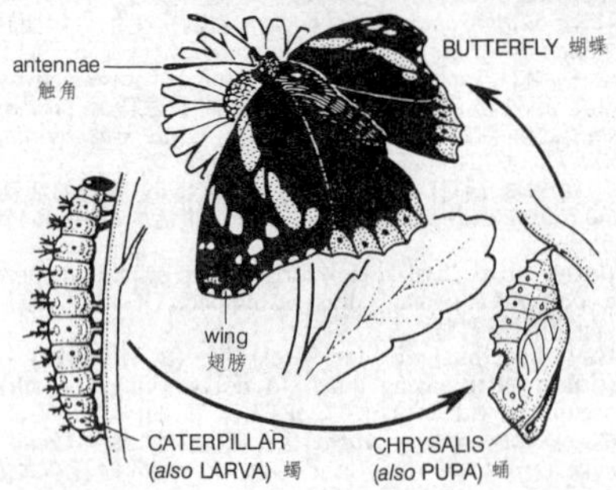

arms are raised and lifted forwards at the same time while the legs move up and down together 蝶泳: *doing (the) butterfly* 游蝶泳. **4** (idm 习语) **have ˈbutterflies (in one's stomach)** (*infml* 口) have a nervous feeling in one's stomach before doing sth (做某事以前)心慌, 紧张.

but·tock /ˈbʌtək; ˋbʌtək/ *n* (esp *pl* 尤作复数) either of the two fleshy rounded parts of the body on which a person sits 臀部的半边; 半边屁股: *the left/right buttock* 左[右]臀 ○ *a smack on the buttocks* 打在屁股上的一巴掌. ⇨illus at HUMAN 见HUMAN之插图.

but·ton /ˈbʌtn; ˋbʌtn̩/ *n* **1** knob or disc made of wood, metal, etc sewn onto a garment as a fastener or as an ornament 钮扣: *a coat, jacket, shirt, trouser button* 大衣、上衣、衬衫、裤子的钮扣 ○ *lose a button* 掉了一个钮扣 ○ *sew on a new button* 缝上一个新钮扣 ○ *do one's buttons up* 扣上钮扣. ⇨illus at JACKET 见JACKET之插图. **2** small knob that is pressed to operate a doorbell, a switch on a machine, etc (操纵门铃、机器开关等的)按钮: *Which button do I press to turn the radio on?* 我该按哪个按钮才能打开收音机? **3** (idm 习语) **bright as a button** ⇨ BRIGHT. **on the ˈbutton** (*US infml* 口) precisely 正好; 精确; 准确: *You've got it on the button!* 你完全正确!

▷ **but·ton** *v* **1** (**a**) [Tn, Tn·p] **~ sth (up)** fasten sth with buttons 扣上某物的钮扣: *button (up) one's coat, jacket, shirt, etc* 扣上大衣、上衣、衬衫等的钮扣. (**b**) [I, Ip] **~ (up)** be fastened with buttons 用钮扣扣上: *This dress buttons at the back.* 这件连衣裙是在背后系扣的. **2** (idm 习语) **button (up) one's lip** (*US sl* 俚) be silent 默不作声; 闭口不谈. **3** (phr v) **button sth up** (*infml* 口) complete sth successfully 顺利完成某事物: *The deal should be buttoned up by tomorrow.* 这笔生意应于明天顺利成交.

□ **ˌbutton-down ˈcollar** collar with ends that are fastened to the shirt with buttons 两端有钮扣扣在衬衫上的衣领.

ˌbuttoned ˈup silent and reserved; shy 沉默寡言的; 羞答答的: *I've never met anyone so buttoned up.* 我从来没有见到过这样不爱讲话的人.

ˈbuttonhole *n* **1** slit through which a button is passed to fasten clothing 钮扣孔; 扣眼. ⇨illus at JACKET 见JACKET之插图. **2** flower worn in the buttonhole of the lapel of a coat or jacket 大衣或上衣翻领的钮扣孔上佩带的花. — *v* [Tn] make (sb) stop and listen, often reluctantly, to what one wants to say 使(某人)停下来(常为勉强地)听着.

ˈbuttonhook *n* hook for pulling a button into place through a buttonhole 钮扣钩(牵引钮扣穿过钮扣孔的钩).

ˌbutton ˈmushroom small unopened mushroom 未长开的小蘑菇.

but·tress /ˈbʌtrɪs; ˋbʌtrɪs/ *n* **1** support built against a wall 扶壁. ⇨illus at App 1 见附录1之插图, page viii. **2** thing or person that supports or reinforces sth, or protects against sth 支撑物; 支柱; 支持力量: *a country* *admired as a buttress of democracy* 作为民主支柱而为人称道的国家 ○ *He was a buttress against extremism in the party.* 他是党内反对极端主义的中坚分子.

▷ **but·tress** *v* [Tn, Tn·p] **~ sth (up)** support or strengthen sth 支持或加强某事物: (*fig* 比喻) *More government spending is needed to buttress industry.* 为加强工业发展需要政府增加拨款. ○ *You need more facts to buttress up your argument.* 你需要有更多的事实来支持你的论据.

buxom /ˈbʌksəm; ˈbʌksəm/ *adj* (*usu approv esp joc* 通常作褒义, 尤作戏谑语) (of women) plump and healthy-looking; having a large bosom (指女子)健美而丰满的; 乳房突出的.

buy /baɪ; baɪ/ *v* (*pt, pp* **bought** /bɔːt; bɔt/) **1** [I, Tn, Tn·pr, Cn·a, Dn·n, Dn·pr] **~ sth (for sb)** obtain (sth) by giving money; purchase 购买(某物); 采购: *House prices are low; it's a good time to buy.* 现在房价很低, 买房子正是时候. ○ *Where did you buy that coat?* 那件大衣你是在哪儿买的? ○ *I bought this watch (from a friend) for £10.* 这个表我是用10英镑(从朋友那里)买的. ○ *Did you buy your car new or second-hand?* 你买的汽车是新的还是旧的? ○ *I must buy myself a new shirt.* 我得买件新衬衫了. ○ *She's buying a present for her boy-friend.* 她在给男朋友购买礼品. **2** [Tn] be the means of obtaining (sth) 换取(某事物)的方法或手段: *He gave his children the best education that money could buy.* 他不惜花费金钱让孩子得到最好的教育. ○ *Money can't buy happiness.* 金钱买不到幸福. ○ *A pound today buys much less than it did a year ago.* 今天一英镑远远买不到一年前能买的那么多东西. **3** [Tn usu passive 通常用于被动语态] obtain (sth) by a sacrifice 作出牺牲以获得(某事物): *His fame was bought at the expense of health and happiness.* 他获得了名声牺牲了健康和幸福. ○ *The victory was dearly bought,* ie Many people were killed to achieve it. 胜利是以昂贵的代价换来的(许多人为之丧命). **4** [Tn] (*infml* 口) accept (sth) as valid; believe 认为合乎情理而接受(某事物); 相信: *No one will buy that excuse.* 谁也不会相信那个借口. **5** [Tn] bribe (sb) 贿赂(某人): *He can't be bought,* ie is too honest to accept a bribe. 收买不了他. **6** (idm 习语) **buy a pig in a ˈpoke** buy sth without seeing it or knowing if it is satisfactory 购买物品不看货色或不知是否合意; 隔山买老牛. **buy ˈtime** delay sth that seems to be about to happen 拖延时间: *The union leaders are trying to buy time by prolonging the negotiations.* 工会的领袖企图以延长谈判过程来拖延时间. **7** (phr v) **buy sth in (a)** buy a stock of sth 大量买进某物: *buy in coal for the winter* 买进大批冬煤. **(b)** (at an auction) buy back (an item for which the bidding has not reached the agreed price) for the owner (在拍卖中)(因出价未达商妥的价钱)为物主买回(原物). **buy sb off** pay sb not to act against one's interests 收买某人: *Unless he drops the charge we'll have to buy him off.* 他若不撤销指控, 我们就得收买他. **buy sb out** pay sb to give up a share in a business (usu in order to become the sole owner of it oneself) 买下某人公司的股分(通常为独占该公司): *Having bought out all his partners he now owns the whole company.* 他买下合伙人的全部股分, 现在整个公司是他的了. **buy sb over** bribe sb 贿赂某人. **buy sth up** buy all or as much as possible of sth 将某物全部买下; 尽量购入某物: *A New York business man has bought up the entire company.* 纽约的一个商人把整个公司收购了.

▷ **buy** *n* act of buying sth; thing bought 购买; 所购的物品: *a good buy,* ie a useful purchase or a bargain 便宜货 ○ *Best buys of the week are carrots and cabbages, which are plentiful and cheap.* 本星期买胡萝卜和洋白菜最合算, 因货源充足, 价格低廉.

buyer *n* **1** person who buys 购买者: *Have you found a buyer for your house?* 你那房子找到买主没有? **2** person employed to choose and buy stock for a large shop (大商店的)进货员, 采购员. **buyer's market** state of affairs when goods are plentiful and prices are low 买方市场(货物充足、价格低廉的市场状况).

buzz /bʌz; bʌz/ *v* **1** [I] **(a)** make a humming sound 作嗡嗡声: *bees, flies and wasps buzzing round a pot of jam* 围着果酱罐子嗡嗡叫的蜜蜂、苍蝇、黄蜂. **(b)** (of the ears) be filled with a humming sound (指耳朵)嗡嗡响: *My ears began buzzing.* 我的耳朵嗡嗡响起来了. **2** [I, Ipr] **~ (with sth)** be full of excited talk, gossip or rumours 充满兴奋的谈话声、闲话或谣言: *The courtroom buzzed as the defendant was led in.* 被告被带进来时, 审判室里发出一阵嘈杂声. ○ *The village was buzzing with excitement at the news of the Queen's visit.* 全村的人都兴奋地谈论着女王莅临的消息. ○ *The office is buzzing with rumours.* 办公室里嘁嘁喳喳地议论着谣言. **3** [Ipr, Tn] **~ (for) sb** summon sb with a buzzer 用蜂响器传唤某人: *The doctor buzzed (for) the next patient.* 医生按蜂鸣器传唤下一个病人. **4** [Tn] (*infml* 口) telephone (sb) 给(某人)打电话: *I'll buzz you at work.* 我上班时将给你打电话. **5** [Tn] fly close to (sb/sth) as a warning 飞近(某人[某物])表示警告: *Two fighters buzzed the convoy as it approached the coast.* 当船队接近海岸时, 两架战斗机飞近示警. **6** (phr v) **buzz about/around (sth)** move quickly and busily 迅速而匆忙地移动: *She buzzed around the kitchen making preparations for the party.* 她在厨房里忙来忙去为这次聚会作准备. **buzz ˈoff** (*Brit infml* 口) (esp imperative 尤用于祈使语气) go away 走开: *Just buzz off and leave me alone!* 走开, 让我清静一下!

▷ **buzz** *n* **1** [C] humming sound (esp one made by an insect) 嗡嗡声(尤指昆虫所发的): *the angry buzz of a bee/wasp* 蜜蜂[黄蜂]很响的嗡嗡声. **2** [sing] **(a)** low confused sound of people talking 乱哄哄的说话声: *the buzz of voices in the crowded room* 挤满人的房间里乱哄哄的声音. **(b)** rumour 谣言: *There's a buzz going round that the boss has resigned.* 有传闻说主管已经辞职了. **3** [C] sound of a buzzer 蜂响器的声音. **4** [sing] (*infml* 口 *esp US*) feeling of pleasure or excitement 愉快或兴奋之情: *Flying gives me a real buzz.* 飞行可真叫我兴奋. **5** (idm 习语) **give sb a ˈbuzz** (*infml* 口) make a telephone call to sb 给某人打电话.

buzzer *n* electrical device that produces a buzzing sound as a signal 蜂响器; 蜂鸣器; 蜂音器.

□ **ˈbuzz-word** *n* specialist or technical word or phrase that becomes fashionable and popular (流行而时髦的)专业词语或技术用语. Cf 参看 VOGUE-WORD (VOGUE).

buz·zard /ˈbʌzəd; ˈbʌzɚd/ *n* type of large hawk 鵟(一种巨鹰). ⇨illus at App 1 见附录1之插图, page iv.

by[1] /baɪ; baɪ/ *adv part* **1** near 靠近: *He stole the money when no one was by.* 他趁旁边无人时把钱偷走了. ○ *He lives close/near by.* 他住在附近. **2** past 经过: *drive, go, run, walk, etc by* 驶过; 经过; 跑过; 走过等 ○ *He hurried by without speaking to me.* 他匆匆经过没有跟我说话. ○ *Excuse me, I can't get by.* 劳驾, 请让我过去. ○ *Time goes by so quickly.* 时间过得真快. **3** aside; in reserve 在旁边; 保留: *lay/put/set sth by* 把某物摆[放/搁]在一边 ○ *I always keep a bottle of wine by in case friends call round.* 我平时总存着一瓶酒以备朋友来时喝. **4** (idm 习语) **by and ˈby** (*dated* 旧) before long; soon 不久; 马上: *They'll be arriving by and by.* 他们不久就要到达. **by the by/bye** = BY THE WAY (WAY[1]). **by and large** ⇨ LARGE.

by[2] /baɪ; baɪ/ *prep* **1** near (sb/sth); at the side of; beside 靠近(某人[某物]); 在…旁边; 在…附近: *a house by the church, river, railway* 教堂、河流、铁路附近的一所房子 ○ *The telephone is by the window.* 电话在窗户那儿. ○ *Come and sit by me.* 来坐在我身旁. ○ *We had a day by the sea.* 我们在海边度过了一天. **2** (showing the route taken) passing through (sth or a place); along; across (表示路线)通过(某物或某地); 顺着; 越过: *He entered by the back door.* 他从后门进入. ○ *We travelled to Rome by Milan and Florence.* 我们途经米兰和佛罗伦萨到达罗马. ○ *We came by country roads, not by the motorway.* 我们是沿着乡间的路来的, 不是从高速公路来的. **3** past (sb/sth) 经过(某人[某物]): *He walked by me without speaking.* 他从我身边走过, 没说一句话. ○ *I go by the church every morning on my way to work.* 我每天早晨上班要经过教堂. **4** not later than (a time); before 不迟于(某时); 在…之前: *Can you finish the work by five o'clock/tomorrow/next Monday?* 你能在五点钟[明天/下星期一]以前做完这工作吗? ○ *By this time next week we shall be in New York.* 下星期的这个时候我们将在纽约. ○ *He ought to have arrived by now/by this time.* 此时此刻他早该到了. ○ *By the time (that) this letter reaches you I will have left the country.* 你接到这封信时, 我已离开这个国家了. **5** (usu without *the* 通常不用 the) (emphasizing the circumstances of an action) during (a period of time) or in (sth) (强调行动的客观情况)在(某时期)内; 在(某情况)下: *travel by day/night*

白天［夜间］旅行 ○ *She sleeps by day and works by night.* 她白天睡觉，夜间工作. ○ *The view is best seen by daylight/moonlight.* 此处风景在日光［月光］下观赏最美. ○ *Reading by* (ie with the use of) *artificial light is bad for the eyes.* 阅读时使用人工照明会损害眼睛. **6** (usu after a passive *v* 通常用于被动式动词之后) (**a**) through the action, power or work of (sb/sth) 借(某人［某事物］)的动作、力量或作品: *a play (written) by Shakespeare* 莎士比亚(写)的剧本 ○ *a church designed by Wren* 雷恩所设计的教堂 ○ *He was arrested by the police.* 他被警方逮捕了. ○ *He was shot by a terrorist with a machine-gun.* 他被恐怖分子用机关枪打死了. ○ *run over by a bus* 被公共汽车碾过 ○ *struck by lightning* 遭闪电击中. (**b**) through the means of (sth/doing sth) 通过(某事物［做某事物］)的方式: *The room is heated by gas/oil.* 这房间是用煤气［油］取暖的. ○ *May I pay by cheque?* 我可以用支票付款吗? ○ *I shall contact you by letter/telephone.* 我将写信［打电话］和你联系. ○ *He earns his living by writing.* 他靠写作为生. ○ *You switch the radio on by pressing this button.* 按这个按钮就能开收音机. ○ *By working hard he gained rapid promotion.* 他工作努力因而晋级很快. **7** (without *the* 不用 the) as a result of (sth); because of; through 因(某事物)所致; 由于; 凭借: *meet by chance* 不期而遇 ○ *achieve sth by skill, determination, etc* 凭技艺、决心等实现某事物 ○ *do sth by mistake/accident* 误做某事［碰巧而做某事］ ○ *The coroner's verdict was 'death by misadventure'.* 验尸官鉴定为意外事故造成的死亡. **8** with the action of (doing sth) 以(做某事)的行动: *Let me begin by saying...* 让我首先说这样一件事, ... ○ *He shocked the whole company by resigning.* 他辞职的消息全公司都感到震惊. **9** (indicating a means of transport or a route taken 表示运输或取道的方式): *travel by boat/bus/car/plane* 乘船［公共汽车/小汽车/飞机］旅行 ○ *travel by air/land/sea* 航空［陆路/航海］旅行. **10** (indicating a part of the body, or an item of clothing touched, held, etc 表示被触及、被持住等的身体或衣物某处): *take sb by the hand* 抓住某人的手 ○ *seize sb by the hair, collar, lapel, etc* 抓住某人的头发、衣领、翻领等 ○ *grab sb by the scruff of the neck* 抓住某人的颈背. **11** (with *the* 与 the 连用) using (sth) as a standard or unit 以(某事物)为标准或单位: *rent a car by the day/week/month* 按日［周/月］租用汽车 ○ *sell eggs by the dozen, material by the yard, coal by the ton* 卖蛋论打、卖布论码、卖煤论吨 ○ *pay sb by the day/hour* 按天［小时］付给某人款 ○ *We sell ice-creams by the thousand in the summer.* 我们在夏天出售的冰激凌数以千计. **12** in successive units, groups or degrees of 以连续的单位、批量或程度计: *improving day by day, little by little, bit by bit, etc* 一天一天地、一些一些地、一点一点地...改善 ○ *The children came in two by two.* 孩子两个两个地进来. **13** (**a**) (showing the dimensions of a rectangle or a cube 表示长方形或立方体的大小): *The room measures fifteen feet by twenty feet.* 这房间十五英尺宽二十英尺长. (**b**) (in multiplication or division 用于乘法或除法运算): *6 (multiplied/divided) by 2 equals 12/3.* 6(乘［除］)以2等于12［3］. **14** to the extent of (sth) 到(某事物)的程度: *The bullet missed him by two inches.* 那子弹差两英寸就打中他了. ○ *The carpet is too short by three feet.* 那地毯短了三英尺. ○ *It would be better by far* (ie much better) *to....* 那比...好多了. **15** according to (sth); from the evidence of 按照(某事物); 根据: *By my watch it is two o'clock.* 我的表现在是两点钟. ○ *Judging by appearances can be misleading.* 凭外表下判断是会误事的. ○ *I could tell by the look on her face that something terrible had happened.* 我一看她的脸色就知道出了大事了. **16** in accordance with (sth); in agreement with 按照(某事物); 符合: *play a game by the rules* 按规则做游戏 ○ *by sb's leave*, ie with sb's permission 得到某人的许可. **17** with respect to (sb/sth); with regard to 涉及(某人［某事物］); 关于: *be German by birth, a solicitor by profession, a joiner by trade* 出生地为德国、职业为律师、行业为细木工 ○ *do one's duty by sb* 尽到自己对某人的责任. **18** (in oaths 用于誓词) in the name of (sb/sth) 以(某人［某事物］)的名义: *By God!* 上帝可以作证! ○ *I swear by Almighty God..., by all that I hold dear..., etc* 我在全能的上帝面前、以我的一切起誓.... **19** (idm 习语) **have/keep sth by one** have sth close to one; have sth within easy reach 将某物放在身边; 使手边有某物: *I keep a dictionary by me when I'm doing crosswords.* 我做纵横填字游戏时，手边总放着一本词典.

by- (also **bye-**) *pref* 前缀 (with *ns* or *vs* 与名词或动词连用) **1** of secondary importance; incidental 次要的; 附带的: *by-product* ○ *bye-law*. **2** near 接近: *bystander* ○ *bypass*.

bye[1] /baɪ; baɪ/ *n* (*sport* 体) **1** (in cricket) run scored from a ball that passes the batsman without being hit by him (板球)漏击得分(球越过击球手未被击中). **2** situation in which a player having no opponent in one round of a tournament proceeds to the next round as if he had won 轮空(运动员在比赛中因无对手而自动进入下一轮的情况).

bye[2] /baɪ; baɪ/ (also **bye-bye** /ˌbaɪˈbaɪ, ˋbaɪˌbaɪ/) *interj* (*infml* 口) goodbye 再见: *Bye(-bye)! See you next week.* 再见! 下星期再会.

bye-byes /ˈbaɪbaɪz; ˋbaɪˌbaɪz/ *n* [U] (used esp when speaking to young children 尤用于儿语) sleep 睡觉: *It's time to go to/time for bye-byes!* 现在该去睡觉了!

by-election /ˈbaɪɪlekʃn; ˋbaɪɪˌlɛkʃən/ *n* election of a new Member of Parliament in a single constituency whose member has died or resigned (单独在某一选区举行的)国会议员的补缺选举. Cf 参看 GENERAL ELECTION (GENERAL).

by·gone /ˈbaɪgɒn; ˋbaɪˌgɑn/ *adj* [attrib 作定语] past 过去的; 以前的; 过时的: *a bygone age* 过去的年代 ○ *in bygone days* 往日.

▷ **by·gones** *n* (idm 习语) **let ˌbygones be ˈbygones** (*saying* 谚) let us forgive and forget past quarrels 过去的事就让它过去吧(让我们互相谅解、捐弃前嫌吧).

by-law /ˈbaɪlɔː; ˋbaɪˌlɔ/ *n* **1** (also ˈ**bye-law**) law or regulation made by a local, not a central, authority (地方)法规. **2** (*US*) regulation of a club or company (俱乐部或公司的)章程.

by·line /ˈbaɪlaɪn; ˋbaɪˌlaɪn/ *n* line at the beginning or end of an article in a newspaper, etc, giving the writer's name (报刊等的文章开头或结尾)标出作者名字的一行.

by·pass /ˈbaɪpɑːs; *US* -pæs; ˋbaɪˌpæs/ *n* **1** road by which traffic can go round a city, busy area, etc instead of through it (绕开城市、闹市区等的)旁道: *If we take the bypass we'll avoid the town centre.* 我们走旁道，就能避开市镇的中心. **2** (*medical* 医) alternative passage for blood to circulate through during a surgical operation, esp on the heart 分路; 旁路; 旁通管; 分流术: [attrib 作定语] *bypass surgery* 使用旁通管的外科手术.

▷ **by·pass** *v* [Tn] **1** provide (a town, etc) with a bypass 在(市镇等)外围辟一条旁道: *a plan to bypass the town centre* 在市镇中心外围开辟旁道的计划. **2** go around or avoid (sth), using a bypass 走旁道以绕过或避开(某物): *We managed to bypass the shopping centre by taking side-streets.* 我们尽量走小路以绕过购物中心区. ○ (*fig* 比喻) *bypass a difficulty, problem, etc* 避开困难、问题等. **3** ignore (a rule, procedure, etc) or fail to consult (sb) in order to act quickly 为图省事而不顾(规则、手续等)或不请教(某人): *He bypassed his colleagues on the board and went ahead with the deal.* 他未征求董事会中同事的意见就做了这笔交易.

by-play /ˈbaɪpleɪ; ˋbaɪˌple/ *n* [U] (*theatre* 戏) action apart from and less important than that of the main story 与主要情节无关的次要动作: (*fig* 比喻) *While the chairman was speaking, two committee members were engaged in heated by-play at the end of the table.* 主席讲话时，有两名委员在桌子的另一边一个劲儿地搞小动作.

by-product /ˈbaɪprɒdʌkt; ˋbaɪˌprɑdʌkt/ *n* **1** substance produced during the making of sth else 副产品: *Ammonia, coal tar and coke are all by-products obtained in the manufacture of coal gas.* 氨气、煤焦油、焦煤都是煤气生产过程中的副产品. **2** secondary result; side effect 连带的结果; 副作用: *An increase in crime is one of the by-products of unemployment.* 犯罪率增加是失业问题造成的一种恶果.

by-road /ˈbaɪrəʊd; ˋbaɪˌrod/ *n* (*US* **back road**) minor road 小路.

by·stander /ˈbaɪstændə(r); ˋbaɪˌstændɚ/ *n* person standing near, but not taking part, when sth happens; onlooker 旁观者: *an innocent bystander* 无辜的旁观者 ○ *Police* *interviewed several bystanders after the accident.* 事故发生后, 警方询问了几个现场旁观者.

byte /baɪt; baɪt/ *n* (*computing* 计) fixed number of binary digits, often representing a single character 字节; 位组.

by·way /ˈbaɪweɪ; ˋbaɪ,we/ *n* **1** [C] = BY-ROAD: *highways and byways* 大路和小路. **2 byways** [pl] (*fig* 比喻) less important or well-known areas (of a subject) (学科中)较次要或较冷僻的方面: *the byways of German literature* 德国文学的冷门部分.

by·word /ˈbaɪwɜːd; ˋbaɪ,wɝd/ *n* **1 ~ for sth** person or thing considered to be a notable or typical example of a quality 代表某种品性的人或事物: *His name has become a byword for cruelty.* 他的名字成了残酷无情的别称. ○ *The firm is a byword for excellence.* 这家商号是优质的保证. **2** common saying or expression 俗语; 谚语.

By·zan·tine /baɪˈzæntaɪn, ˈbɪzəntaɪn; ˋbɪzən,taɪn/ *adj* **1** of Byzantium or the E Roman Empire 拜占庭帝国的; 东罗马帝国的. **2** of or relating to the Byzantine style of architecture (建筑)拜占庭式的, 拜占庭风格的. **3** (*usu derog* 通常作贬义) like Byzantine politics, ie complicated, secretive and difficult to change 似拜占庭政治的; 复杂难解的; 行事诡秘的; 难变更的: *an organization of Byzantine complexity* 像拜占庭复杂诡秘的机构.

C c

C

C, c /si:; si/ *n* (*pl* **C's, c's** /si:z; siz/) **1** the third letter of the English alphabet 英语字母表的第三个字母: *'Cat' starts with (a) C/'C'.* cat一字以c字母开始. **2** (*music* 音) the first note in the scale of C major C大调音阶中的第一音或音符. **3** academic mark indicating the third highest standard 学业成绩达第三等的评价符号: *get (a) C/'C' in physics* 物理(学科)得C.

C *abbr* 缩写 = **1** Cape: *C Horn*, eg on a map 合恩角(如标于地图上者). **2** (degree or degrees) Celsius; centigrade: *Water freezes at 0°C.* 水在0°C时结冰. Cf 参看 F *abbr* 缩写 1. **3** (also **c**) Roman numeral for 100 (Latin *centum*) 罗马数字的100(源自拉丁文*centum*). **4** (also *symb* 符号为 ©) (*commerce* 商) copyright 版权所有: © *Oxford University Press 1986* © 牛津大学出版社1986.

c *abbr* 缩写 = **1** cent(s). **2** century(1b): *in the 19th c* 在19世纪 ○ *a c19 church* 19世纪的教堂. Cf 参看 CENT *abbr* 缩写. **3** (also **ca**) (esp before dates 尤用于年代之前) about; approximately (Latin *circa*) 约, 大约(源自拉丁文*circa*): *c1890* 约1890年.

CAA /ˌsi: eɪ ˈeɪ; ˌsi e ˈe/ *abbr* 缩写 = (*Brit*) Civil Aviation Authority 民用航空局.

cab /kæb; kæb/ *n* **1** = TAXI: *Shall we walk or take a cab/go by cab?* 咱们走着去呢, 还是坐计程车去? **2** driver's compartment in a train, lorry or crane (机车、卡车或起重机的)驾驶室, 司机室. **3** (formerly) horse-drawn carriage for public hire (旧时)出租马车.

□ **ˈcab-driver** *n* driver of a cab 计程车司机.

ˈcabstand *n* (*US*) = TAXI-RANK (TAXI).

CAB /ˌsi: eɪ ˈbi:; ˌsi e ˈbi/ *abbr* 缩写 = (*Brit*) Citizens' Advice Bureau 公民咨询局.

ca·bal /kəˈbæl; kəˈbæl/ *n* [CGp, C] (group of people involved in a) secret political plot 政治阴谋(集团).

cab·a·ret /ˈkæbəreɪ; *US* ˌkæbəˈreɪ; ˌkæbəˈre/ *n* **1** [U, C] entertainment (esp singing or dancing) provided in a restaurant or night-club while the customers are eating or drinking 卡巴莱(餐馆或夜总会中为进食顾客所做的表演, 尤指歌舞): *Have you done any cabaret?* 你做过卡巴莱表演吗? **2** [C] such a restaurant or night-club 卡巴莱餐馆或夜总会: *a singer in a cabaret* 卡巴莱餐馆或夜总会的歌手.

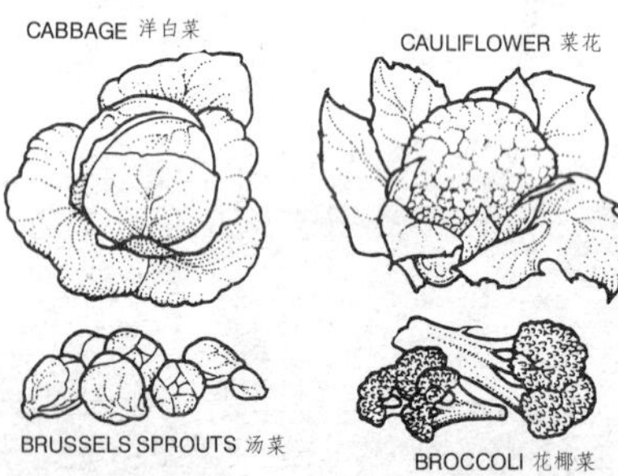

cab·bage /ˈkæbɪdʒ; ˈkæbɪdʒ/ *n* **1** (**a**) [C] any of various types of vegetable with green or purple leaves, usu forming a round head 洋白菜, 卷心菜, 包心菜(结球甘蓝的通称). ⇨illus 见插图. (**b**) [U] these leaves (usu cooked and) eaten as food 洋白菜(通常指熟的). **2** [C] (*Brit infml* 口) (**a**) dull inactive person without interests or ambition 无精打采或无进取心的人. (**b**) person who has lost his mental faculties, eg because of brain damage or illness, and is completely dependent on others 丧失智力的人.

cabby (also **cab·bie**) /ˈkæbɪ; ˈkæbɪ/ *n* (*infml* 口) taxi-driver 计程车司机.

ca·ber /ˈkeɪbə(r); ˈkebɚ/ *n* long heavy wooden pole thrown in the air as a trial of strength in the Scottish sport of tossing the caber (在苏格兰人的运动中为测臂力而投掷使用的)长而重的木杆.

cabin /ˈkæbɪn; ˈkæbɪn/ *n* **1** small room or compartment on a ship, an aircraft or a spacecraft (轮船或飞行器的)舱室: *book a cabin on a boat* 预订船舱 ○ *the pilot's cabin* 飞行员室. **2** small hut or shelter, usu made of wood 小棚屋(通常为木制的).

□ **ˈcabin-boy** *n* boy who works as a waiter on a ship (船上的)(男)服务员.

ˈcabin class second highest standard of accommodation on a ship (轮船)二等舱.

ˈcabin cruiser = CRUISER (CRUISE).

cab·inet /ˈkæbɪnɪt; ˈkæbənɪt/ *n* **1** [C] piece of furniture with drawers or shelves for storing or displaying things 储藏柜: *a filing cabinet* 文件柜 ○ *a medicine cabinet* 药品柜 ○ *a china cabinet* 瓷器柜. **2** [C] case or container for a radio, record-player or television (放收音机、唱机或电视机的)框架或间格. **3** (also **the Cabinet**) [CGp] group of the most important government ministers, responsible for government administration and policy 内阁: *Members of the Cabinet are chosen by the Prime Minister.* 内阁阁员是由首相挑选的. ○ [attrib 作定语] *a cabinet minister, meeting, reshuffle* 内阁阁员、会议、改组.

□ **ˈcabinet-maker** *n* craftsman who makes fine wooden furniture 家具木工; 细木工.

cable /ˈkeɪbl; ˈkebḷ/ *n* **1** [C, U] (length of) thick strong rope made of fibre or wire, used esp for tying up ships 绳缆, 绳索(尤指系船用的). **2** [C] rope or chain of an anchor 锚索; 锚链. **3** [C] (as a nautical measure) one tenth of a nautical mile, about 200 yards 链(海上测距单位, 等于十分之一海里, 约200码). ⇨App 5 见附录5. **4** [C] (**a**) set of insulated wires (esp one laid underground or on the bottom of the sea) for carrying messages by telegraph (用以通电报的)绝缘导线; (尤指)地下电缆, 海底电缆. (**b**) (also **cable·gram**) message sent abroad in this way 电报: *send sb/receive a cable* 拍给某人[接收]电报. Cf 参看 TELEGRAM. **5** [C] set of insulated wires for carrying electricity overhead 架空电缆.

▷ **cable** *v* (**a**) [I, Ipr] **~ (to sb) (from ...)** send a cable to sb abroad 给海外某人拍发电报: *Please write or cable.* 请来信或来电. (**b**) [Tn, Tn·pr, Tf] inform (sb) by cable 给(某人)拍发电报: *Don't forget to cable us as soon as you arrive.* 别忘了一到就给我们打个电报. (**c**) [Tn, Dn·n, Dn·pr] **~ sth (to sb)** send (money, a message, etc) by cable 用电报汇(款); 打电报传送(信息): *News of his death was cabled to his family.* 他的死讯已电告其家属.

□ **ˈcable-car** *n* car supported and drawn by a moving cable, usu carrying passengers up or down a mountain 缆车.

ˈcablegram /ˈkeɪblgræm; ˈkebḷˌgræm/ *n* = CABLE *n* 4.

cable ˈrailway railway on a steep slope along which cars are drawn up and down by a moving cable with power from a stationary engine at the bottom or the top 缆车铁路.

ˈcable stitch stitch in knitting that resembles twisted rope 缆绳状针织法.

cable ˈtelevision (also **ˈcablevision**) system of broadcasting television programmes by cable to subscribers 缆线电视; 有线电视.

ca·boodle /kəˈbu:dl; kəˈbudḷ/ *n* (idm 习语) **the whole caboodle** ⇨ WHOLE.

ca·boose /kəˈbu:s; kəˈbus/ *n* **1** kitchen on a ship's deck (轮船上的)厨房. **2** (*US*) guard's van, esp on a goods train 守车(尤指铁路货车上的).

ca·cao /kəˈkɑ:əʊ, *also* kəˈkeɪəʊ; ˌkəˈkɑo, ˌkəˈkeo/ *n* (*pl* **~s**) (**a**) (also **caˈcao-bean**) seed from which cocoa and chocolate are made 可可豆. (**b**) (also **cacˈao-tree**) tropical tree on which this grows 可可树.

cache /kæʃ; kæʃ/ *n* **(a)** place for hiding food, treasure or weapons 隐藏食物、财宝或武器的地方; 贮藏处. **(b)** hidden store of food, etc (隐藏的食物等的)贮存物: *an arms cache* 贮藏的武器.
▷ **cache** *v* [Tn] place (sth) in a cache 将(某物)藏于贮藏处.

cachet /ˈkæʃeɪ; *US* kæˈʃeɪ; kæˋʃe/ *n* **1** [U] respect or admiration that sb gets because of his reputation or his achievements; prestige 威望; 声望; 威信: *Her success in business had earned her a certain cachet in society.* 她事业有成, 赢得了一定的社会声望. **2** [C] distinguishing mark showing the excellence or authenticity of sth (表明某物优良可靠的)荣誉标志: *Rembrandt's paintings show the cachet of genius.* 伦勃朗的绘画是天才的象征.

cachou /ˈkæʃuː; *US* kəˈʃuː; kəˋʃu/ *n* scented sweet eaten (esp formerly) to make the breath smell pleasant 口香糖(尤指旧时用以使口气芬芳的).

cackle /ˈkækl; ˋkækl/ *n* **1** [U] loud clucking noise that a hen makes after laying an egg (母鸡生蛋后的)咯咯叫声: *the cackle of hens/geese* 母鸡[母鹅]的咯咯叫声. **2** [C] loud raucous or silly laugh 哈哈大笑; 咯咯大笑; 傻笑: *The old woman gave a loud cackle.* 老太太咯咯地笑起来了. **3** [U] noisy chatter 高声谈话. **4** (idm 习语) **cut the ˈcackle** (*infml* 口) stop talking about irrelevant or unimportant matters 少说废话.
▷ **cackle** *v* [I, Ip] **1** (of a hen) make a cackle (指母鸡)咯咯叫. **2** (of a person) laugh or chatter noisily (指人)高声谈笑: *cackling on for hours* 高声谈笑半天.

ca·co·phony /kəˈkɒfənɪ; kəˋkɑfənɪ/ *n* [U, C usu *sing* 通常作单数] loud unpleasant mixture of discordant sounds 响亮而不和谐的声音; 刺耳的声音. ▷ **ca·co·phon·ous** /-nəs; -nəs/ *adj*.

cactus
仙人掌或仙人球

cac·tus /ˈkæktəs; ˋkæktəs/ *n* (*pl* **~es** or **cacti** /ˈkæktaɪ; ˋkæktaɪ/) any of various types of plants growing in hot dry regions, with thick fleshy stems and usu prickles, but no leaves 仙人掌. ⇨illus 见插图.

cad /kæd; kæd/ *n* (*dated derog* 旧, 贬) man who behaves dishonourably 下流男子: *He's no gentleman, he's a cad.* 他可不是正经人, 他是个无赖.
▷ **cad·dish** /ˈkædɪʃ; ˋkædɪʃ/ *adj* of or like a cad 下流人的; 像下流人的: *a caddish trick* 卑鄙的手段.

ca·da·ver /kəˈdɑːvə(r), *also* -ˈdeɪv-; *US* kəˈdævər; kəˋdævɚ/ *n* (*esp medical* 尤用于医学) dead body of a person; corpse 死尸; 尸体.
▷ **ca·da·ver·ous** /kəˈdævərəs; kəˋdævərəs/ *adj* looking like a corpse; very pale and gaunt 像死尸的; 苍白的; 死灰的.

cad·die (also **caddy**) /ˈkædɪ; ˋkædɪ/ *n* person who carries a golfer's clubs for him during a game 球童(为打高尔夫球的人背球棒的人).
▷ **cad·die** *v* [I, Ipr] **~ (for sb)** act as a caddie 当球童: *Would you like me to caddie for you?* 我给你当球童好吗?

caddy /ˈkædɪ; ˋkædɪ/ *n* = TEA-CADDY (TEA).

ca·dence /ˈkeɪdns; ˋkedn̩s/ *n* **1** rhythm in sound 节奏; 韵律. **2** rise and fall of the voice in speaking (说话时语调的)抑扬顿挫: *recite poetry with beautiful cadences* 以优美的韵律朗诵诗歌. **3** end of a musical phrase 乐章的结尾.

ca·denza /kəˈdenzə; kəˋdɛnzə/ *n* (*music* 音) elaborate passage played by the soloist, usu near the end of a movement in a concerto 华彩段(通常在协奏曲近结尾处独奏者发挥技巧的段落).

ca·det /kəˈdet; kəˋdɛt/ *n* young person training to become a policeman or an officer in the armed forces 受训当警察或军官的年轻人: *army/naval/air force cadets* 陆[海/空]军学员 ○ *a police cadet* 见习警察.
□ **caˈdet corps** (in some British schools) organization giving military training to older boys (英国某些学校中)对高年级男生进行军训的组织.

cadge /kædʒ; kædʒ/ *v* [I, Ipr, Tn, Tn·pr] **~ (sth) (from sb)** (*sometimes derog* 有时作贬义) get or try to get (sth) (from sb) by asking, often unreasonably (向某人)索要或要求(某事物)(常为无缘故的); 占便宜: *Could I cadge a lift with you?* 我能顺便坐你的汽车吗? ○ *He's always cadging meals from his friends.* 他总吃朋友的便宜饭. ▷ **cadger** *n*.

cad·mium /ˈkædmɪəm; ˋkædmɪəm/ *n* [U] chemical element, a soft bluish-white metal that looks like tin 镉. ⇨App 10 见附录 10.

cadre /ˈkɑːdə(r); *US* ˈkædrɪ; ˋkædrɪ/ *n* **1** small permanent group of trained workers, soldiers, etc that can be enlarged when necessary 核心小组(受过训练的工作人员、军人等, 必要时可以扩充). **2** a member of such a group 干部.

Cae·sar /ˈsiːzə(r); ˋsizɚ/ *n* title of the Roman Emperors from Augustus to Hadrian 凯撒(古罗马帝国自奥古斯都至哈德良期间皇帝的称号).

Cae·sar·ean /sɪˈzeərɪən; sɪˋzɛrɪən/ *n* (also **Cesarian**, **Caeˌsarean ˈsection**) surgical operation for delivering a baby by cutting the walls of the mother's abdomen and uterus 剖腹产术: *It was a difficult birth: she had to have a Caesarean.* 她因为难产, 要做剖腹产术.

caes·ura /sɪˈzjʊərə; *US* sɪˈʒʊərə; sɪˋʒʊrə/ *n* pause near the middle of a line of poetry 一行诗句近中间处的停顿.

café /ˈkæfeɪ; *US* kæˈfeɪ; kæˋfe/ *n* small inexpensive restaurant serving light meals and (in Britain usu non-alcoholic) drinks 小餐馆(在英国通常不供应酒类).

caf·et·eria /ˌkæfəˈtɪərɪə; ˏkæfəˋtɪrɪə/ *n* restaurant (esp in a factory or college) in which customers collect their meals on trays from a counter 自助食堂(尤指工厂或学校中自己用托盘从柜台领取食物的).

caf·feine /ˈkæfiːn; ˋkæfin/ *n* [U] stimulant drug found in tea leaves and coffee beans 咖啡碱; 咖啡因.

caf·tan (also **kaf·tan**) /ˈkæftæn; ˋkæftæn/ *n* **1** long loose garment, usu with a belt at the waist, worn by men in the Near East (近东男子穿的肥大的)长袍(通常有腰带). **2** woman's long loose dress (女用肥大的)长袍.

cage /keɪdʒ; kedʒ/ *n* **1** structure made of bars or wires in which birds or animals are kept or carried 鸟笼; 兽槛. **2** enclosed platform used to raise and lower people and equipment in the shaft of a mine (矿井中的)升降车.
▷ **cage** *v* **1** [Tn] put or keep (sb/sth) in a cage 将(某人[某物])关入笼中. **2** (phr v) **cage sb in** make sb feel that he is in a cage 使某人觉得身困笼中: *I felt terribly caged in in that office.* 我呆在那个办公室里感觉真像在笼子里一样.

cagey /ˈkeɪdʒɪ; ˋkedʒɪ/ *adj* (**cagier**, **cagiest**) **~ (about sth)** (*infml* 口) cautious about giving information; wary; secretive 秘而不宣的; 谨小慎微的; 讳莫如深的: *He's very cagey about his family.* 他对他家庭的事守口如瓶.
▷ **ca·gily** *adv*. **ca·gi·ness** (also **ca·gey·ness**) *n* [U].

ca·goule /kəˈguːl; kəˋgul/ *n* light long waterproof jacket with a hood 有兜帽的轻便长雨衣.

ca·hoots /kəˈhuːts; kəˋhuts/ *n* (idm 习语) **be in cahoots (with sb)** (*infml* 口 *esp US*) be planning sth (usu dishonest) with sb; be in league (with sb) 与某人合谋某事(通常为坏事); (与某人)结伙: *The two criminals were in cahoots (with each other).* 那两个罪犯(彼此)勾结在一起.

cai·man = CAYMAN.

cairn /keən; kɛrn/ *n* mound of rough stones built as a landmark or as a memorial, eg on a mountain top 堆石标(作路标或纪念用的石堆, 如在山顶上的).

cais·son /ˈkeɪsn; ˋkesn̩/ *n* **1** large watertight box or chamber in which men can work under water (eg when building foundations) 沉箱(工人进行水下作业, 如建底座时所乘的大潜水箱). **2** large box (usu on wheels) in which ammunition is carried 弹药箱; (通常为)弹药车.

ca·jole /kəˈdʒəʊl; kəˋdʒol/ *v* [Tn, Tn·pr] **(a) ~ sb (into/out of sth); ~ sb (into/out of doing sth)** persuade sb (to do sth) by flattery or deceit; coax sb 哄

C

骗某人(作某事); 劝诱某人: *She was cajoled into (accepting) a new contract.* 她受人哄骗而接受了新合同. **(b) ~ sth out of sb** get (information, etc) from sb in this way 以上述手段从某人处得到(信息等): *The confession had to be cajoled out of him.* 连哄带劝他才坦白. ▷ **ca·jolery** *n* [U].

cake /keɪk; kek/ *n* **1** [C, U] sweet food made from a mixture of flour, eggs, butter, sugar, etc baked in a certain shape or size and usu iced or decorated 糕; 蛋糕; 糕饼: *a sponge cake* 海绵状蛋糕 ○ *a chocolate cake* 巧克力蛋糕 ○ *a fruit cake* 水果蛋糕 ○ *a piece/slice of (birthday) cake* 一块[片](生日)蛋糕 ○ *an assortment of fancy cakes* 什锦花蛋糕 ○ *Have some more cake!* 再多吃些蛋糕! **2** [C] other food mixture cooked in a round flat shape 饼: *ˈfish cakes* 鱼肉饼 ○ *poˈtato cakes* 马铃薯饼. **3** [C] shaped or hardened mass of a substance 块状物: *a cake of soap* 一块肥皂. **4** (idm 习语) **cakes and ˈale** pleasurable things in life 生活中的乐事; 吃喝玩乐: *Life isn't all cakes and ale, you know.* 要知道生活并非都是吃喝玩乐. **get, want, etc a slice/share of the ˈcake** get, etc a share of the benefits or profits one is or feels entitled to, eg as an employee of a business or an industry or as a member of a profession 得到应得的一份利益: *As workers in a profit-making industry, miners are demanding a larger slice of the cake.* 矿工们身处赚钱的企业, 要求多分一杯羹. **have one's cake and ˈeat it** (*infml* 口) enjoy the benefits from two alternative courses of action, etc when only one or the other is possible (在两者中只可得其一时)两者兼得: *He wants a regular income but doesn't want to work. He can't have his cake and eat it!* 他又想要有稳定的收入, 又不想工作. 他不能两者兼得. **a piece of cake** ⇨ PIECE[1]. **sell like hot cakes** ⇨ SELL. **take the biscuit/cake** ⇨ BISCUIT.

▷ **cake** *v* **1** [esp passive 尤用于被动语态: Tn, Tn·pr] **~ sth (in/with sth)** cover sth thickly (with sth that becomes hard when dry (以干后可变硬的东西)厚厚地覆盖某物): *His shoes were caked with mud.* 他鞋上粘着厚厚的泥. **2** [I] harden into a compact mass 结成硬块: *Blood from the wound had caked on his face.* 伤口的血在他脸上结成了硬块.

CAL (also **Cal**) /kæl; kæl/ *abbr* 缩写 = computer-aided/-assisted learning 计算机辅助学习; 电脑辅助学习.

cal *abbr* 缩写 = calorie(s).

cala·bash /ˈkæləbæʃ; ˈkæləˌbæʃ/ *n* **1** large fruit or gourd of which the hard outer skin is used as a container for liquids 葫芦. **2** tropical American tree on which this grows 葫芦树(产于热带美洲).

cal·amine /ˈkæləmaɪn; ˈkæləˌmaɪn/ *n* [U] (also **calamine lotion**) pink lotion used to soothe sore or burnt skin 炉甘石洗剂(用作皮肤灼伤止痛的粉红色药液).

ca·lam·ity /kəlˈæmətɪ; kəˈlæmətɪ/ *n* serious misfortune or disaster 灾祸; 灾难: *The earthquake was the worst calamity in the country's history.* 那次地震是全国有史以来最严重的灾难. ○ (*joc* 谑) *There are worse calamities than failing your driving test.* 比起你驾驶考试不合格来说, 更大的灾难还多着呢.

▷ **ca·lam·it·ous** /kəˈlæmɪtəs; kəˈlæmətəs/ *adj* **~ (to sb/sth)** involving or causing a calamity; disastrous 受灾的; 造成灾害的; 灾难的.

cal·cify /ˈkælsɪfaɪ; ˈkælsəˌfaɪ/ *v* (*pt, pp* **-fied**) [I, Tn] (cause sth to) harden by a deposit of calcium salts (使某物)钙化. ▷ **cal·ci·fi·ca·tion** /ˌkælsɪfɪˈkeɪʃn; ˌkælsəfɪˈkeʃən/ *n* [U].

cal·cine /ˈkælsaɪn; ˈkælsaɪn/ *v* [I, Tn] (cause sth to) be reduced to powder by burning; burn to ashes (使某物)烧成粉末; 烧成灰.

▷ **cal·cina·tion** /ˌkælsɪˈneɪʃn; ˌkælsɪˈneʃən/ *n* [U] conversion of a metal into an oxide by burning 煅烧.

cal·cium /ˈkælsɪəm; ˈkælsɪəm/ *n* [U] chemical element, a greyish-white metal found as a compound in bones, teeth and chalk 钙. ⇨App 10 见附录10.

□ **ˌcalcium ˈcarbide** compound of calcium and carbon used in making acetylene gas 碳化钙.

ˌcalcium hyˈdroxide white crystalline compound of calcium; slaked lime 氢氧化钙; 熟石灰.

cal·cul·able /ˈkælkjʊləbl; ˈkælkjələbl̩/ *adj* that can be calculated 可计算的; 可推算的; 可估计的.

cal·cu·late /ˈkælkjʊleɪt; ˈkælkjəˌlet/ *v* **1** [Tn, Tf, Tw] work (sth) out by using numbers or one's judgement; estimate 计算; 推算; 估计: *calculate the cost of sth/how much sth will cost* 计算某事物的费用 ○ *Scientists have calculated that the world's population will double by the end of the century.* 科学家已推算出世界人口在本世纪末将要增加一倍. ○ *I calculate that we will reach London at about 3 pm.* 我估计我们大约在下午3时到达伦敦. **2** [Tn, Tf, Tnt] (*US infml* 口) suppose (sth); believe 认为; 觉得; 相信. **3** (idm 习语) **be calculated to do sth** be intended or designed to do sth 打算或计划做某事: *This advertisement is calculated to appeal to children.* 这个广告是针对儿童设计的. ○ *His speech was calculated to stir up the crowd.* 他讲的话是有意鼓动群众的. **a calculated ˈinsult** deliberate or premeditated insult 故意的或存心的侮辱. **a calculated ˈrisk** risk taken deliberately with full knowledge of the dangers (明知有危险)有意进行的冒险. **4** (phr v) **calculate on sth/doing sth** depend or rely on sth 指望或依靠某事物: *We can't calculate on (having) good weather for the barbecue.* 我们不能指望着(有)好天气才去烧烤.

▷ **cal·cu·lat·ing** *adj* selfishly scheming; shrewd 有私心的; 精明的: *a cold and calculating killer* 冷酷而诡诈的凶手 ○ *a calculating businessman* 精明的生意人.

cal·cu·la·tion /ˌkælkjʊˈleɪʃn; ˌkælkjəˈleʃən/ *n* **1** [C, U] (result of) calculating 计算, 推算, 估计(的结果): *Our calculations show that the firm made a profit of over £1 000 000 last year.* 我们的计算结果表明公司去年赢利超过1 000 000英镑. ○ *You're out* (ie You have made a mistake) *in your calculations.* 你失算了(你犯了个错误). ○ *After much calculation* (ie careful thought) *they offered him the job.* 他们经过慎重考虑以后, 把这项工作交给他了. **2** [U] scheming 计划; 策划.

cal·cu·lator /ˈkælkjʊleɪtə(r); ˈkælkjəˌletɚ/ *n* **1** small electronic device for making mathematical calculations 计算器. **2** person who calculates 计算的人.

cal·cu·lus /ˈkælkjʊləs; ˈkælkjələs/ *n* (*pl* **-li** /-laɪ; -ˌlaɪ/ or **-luses** /-ləsɪz; -ləsɪz/) branch of mathematics, divided into two parts (*differential calculus* and *integral calculus*), that deals with problems involving rates of variation 微积分(学).

cal·dron (*esp US*) = CAULDRON.

cal·en·dar /ˈkælɪndə(r); ˈkæləndɚ/ *n* **1** **(a)** chart showing the days, weeks and months of a particular year 日历: *Do you have next year's calendar?* 你有明年的日历吗? **(b)** device that can be adjusted to show the date each day 日历仪(可校准显示每日日期的装置): *a desk calendar* 座台日历仪. **2** (usu *sing* 通常作单数) list of dates or events of a particular kind 日程表: *The Cup Final is an important date in the sporting calendar.* 足总杯决赛在运动日程表中是个重要日子. **3** system by which time is divided into fixed periods, and of marking the beginning and end of a year 历法: *the Gregorian/Julian/Muslim calendar* 格雷果里[儒略/穆斯林]历.

□ **ˌcalendar ˈmonth** **1** any one of the twelve months of the calendar 历月(日历中十二个月份中的任何一个月). Cf 参看 LUNAR MONTH (LUNAR). **2** period of time from a certain date in one month to the same date in the next one 从某月某日至下月同一日的期间.

ˌcalendar ˈyear (also **year**) period of time from 1 January to 31 December in the same year 历年(从1月1日至同年12月31日的期间).

cal·en·der /ˈkælɪndə(r); ˈkæləndɚ/ *n* machine for pressing and smoothing cloth or paper 研光机, 轮压机(压光布或纸的机器).

▷ **cal·en·der** *v* [Tn] press (sth) in a calender 用研光机压光(某物).

calf[1] /kɑːf; *US* kæf; kæf/ *n* (*pl* **calves** /kɑːvz; *US* kævz; kævz/) **1** [C] **(a)** young of cattle 小牛; 犊. ⇨illus at cow 见cow之插图. Cf 参看 BULL[1] 1, COW[1] 1. **(b)** young of the seal, the whale and certain other animals (海豹、鲸及其他一些动物的)崽, 幼兽. Cf 参看 BULL[1] 2, COW[1] 2. **2** [U] (also **ˈcalf·skin**) leather made from the skin of a calf 小牛皮革. **3** (idm 习语) **(be) in/with ˈcalf** (of a cow) pregnant (指母牛)怀孕的. **kill the fatted calf** ⇨ KILL.

□ **ˈcalf-love** = PUPPY-LOVE (PUPPY).

calf[2] /kɑːf; *US* kæf; kæf/ *n* (*pl* **calves** /kɑːvz; *US* kævz; kævz/) fleshy back part of the leg below the knee

腓(自膝以下的小腿后部多肉的部分); 腿肚子. ⇨illus at HUMAN 见 HUMAN 之插图.

cal·ib·rate /ˈkælɪbreɪt; ˋkæləˌbret/ *v* [Tn] mark or correct the units of measurement on (the scale of a thermometer or some other measuring instrument) 标定或校准(温度计或其他一些计量器刻度)上的计量单位.

▷ **cal·ib·ration** /ˌkælɪˈbreɪʃn; ˌkæləˋbreʃən/ *n* **1** [U] action of calibrating 标定或校准计量单位. **2** [C] units of measurement marked on a thermometer, etc (温度计等的)刻度.

cal·ibre (*US* **cal·iber**) /ˈkælɪbə(r); ˋkæləbɚ/ *n* **1** [C] diameter of the inside of a tube or gun-barrel (管子或枪炮筒的)口径. **2** [U] quality; ability; distinction 质量; 能力; 特性: *His work is of the highest calibre.* 他的工作质量最高. ○ *The firm needs more people of your calibre.* 公司需要多找些有你这种才干的人.

cal·ico /ˈkælɪkəʊ; ˋkæləˌko/ *n* (*pl* **~es**; *US* **~s**) [U, C] **1** (*esp Brit*) type of cotton cloth, esp plain white or unbleached 棉布(尤指素白的或未经漂白的). **2** (*esp US*) printed cotton fabric 印花棉布.

ca·li·per = CALLIPER.

ca·liph /ˈkeɪlɪf; ˋkelɪf/ *n* (**a**) title formerly used by Muslim rulers who were successors of Muhammad 哈里发(旧时用作默罕默德继承者穆斯林统治者的称号). (**b**) chief civil and religious ruler in certain Muslim countries 哈里发(某些穆斯林国家中政教合一的统治者).

▷ **ca·liph·ate** /ˈkælɪfeɪt; ˋkælɪˌfet/ *n* position, reign or territory of a caliph 哈里发的职位、统治或辖区.

ca·lis·then·ics = CALLISTHENICS.

calk (*US*) = CAULK.

call[1] /kɔːl; kɔl/ *n* **1** [C] shout; cry 呼喊; 喊叫: *a call for help* 大声呼救 ○ *They came at my call*, ie when I shouted to them. 我把他们喊来了. **2** [C] characteristic cry of a bird (鸟的)鸣叫, 啼叫. **3** [C] signal sounded on a horn, bugle, etc 喇叭、军号等的号声. **4** [C] short visit (to sb's house) (到某人家)拜访: *pay a call on a friend* 访友 ○ *The doctor has five calls to make this morning.* 今早大夫要去五家出诊. ○ *We must return her call*, ie visit her because she visited us. 我们得到她家回访. **5** [C] (also ˈ**phone call**, **ring**) act of telephoning; conversation on the telephone 打电话; 用电话交谈: *give sb/make/receive/return a call* 给某人打[拨/接/回]电话 ○ *Were there any calls for me while I was out?* 我出去的时候, 有人来过电话吗? **6** (**a**) [C] order, signal or invitation, esp to come or meet; summons 命令, 信号, 邀请(尤指使之前来或相见); 召唤: *The Prime Minister is waiting for a call to the Palace.* 首相待召进宫. ○ *An actor's call tells him when to go on stage.* 有剧务示意让他到时上场. ○ *This is the last call for passengers travelling on flight BA 199 to Rome.* 乘坐英航199号班机飞往罗马的乘客, 这是最后一次通知. ○ (*fig* 比喻) *He answered the call of duty and enlisted in the army.* 他应征入伍. (**b**) [sing] **~ (of sth)** inner urge to follow a course of action or profession; vocation 感召; 神召: *feel the call (of the priesthood)* 感到(教士圣职的)神召. (**c**) [sing] **~ of sth** attraction or fascination of (a particular place or activity) (某处或某活动的)吸引力, 诱惑力: *the call of the sea, of the wild, of faraway places, etc* 大海、荒野、遥远地方等的吸引力. (**d**) [C] **~ for sth** request or demand for sth 对某事物的要求或号召: *The President made a call for national unity.* 总统号召全国人民团结起来. ○ *There were calls for the Prime Minister's resignation from the Opposition parties.* 在反对党中, 有人要求首相辞职. **7** [U] **~ for sth** (esp in negative sentences and questions 尤用于否定句及疑问句中) need or occasion for sth 对某事物的需要, 必要或理由: *There isn't much call for such things these days.* 这种东西近来需求量不大. ○ *There was no call for such rudeness.* 没必要这么粗暴. **8** [C] **~ on sb/sth** demand on sb/sth 对某人[某事物]的需求: *He is a busy man with many calls on his time.* 他很忙, 有很多事需要花时间去做. **9** [C] (in card-games) player's bid or turn to bid (纸牌戏中)叫牌, 轮到叫牌: *It's your call, partner.* 伙伴, 该你叫牌了. **10** (idm 习语) **at one's/sb's beck and call** ⇨ BECK[2]. **a call of ˈnature** (*euph* 婉) need to urinate or defecate 要小便或大便. **a close call** ⇨ CLOSE[1]. **(be) on ˈcall** (esp of a doctor) available for work if necessary (尤指医生)随叫随到: *Who's on call tonight?* 今晚谁值班? **a port of call** ⇨ PORT[1]. **within ˈcall** near enough to hear sb shouting (for help, etc) 在(求救等)喊声能听到的范围内; 附近.

□ ˈ**call-box** *n* = TELEPHONE-BOX (TELEPHONE).

ˈ**call-girl** *n* prostitute who makes appointments by telephone 应召女郎(用电话召唤的妓女).

ˈ**call-in** = PHONE-IN (PHONE[1]).

call[2] /kɔːl; kɔl/ *v* **1** [I, Ipr, Ip, Tn, Tn·p] **~ (out) to sb (for sth); ~ (sth) (out)** say (sth) loudly to attract sb's attention; shout; cry 大声说(某事物)以引起别人注意; 喊; 叫: *I thought I heard sb calling.* 我好像听见有人喊叫. ○ *Why didn't you come when I called (out) (your name)?* 我喊(出)(你名字)的时候, 你为什么不来? ○ *She called to her father for help.* 她向父亲喊叫求救. ○ *The injured soldiers called out in pain.* 受伤的士兵疼得大叫. ○ *The teacher called out the children's names*, eg to check they were all present. 教师大声点名(如考勤). **2** [I] (of a bird or an animal) make its characteristic cry (指禽兽)叫. **3** [Tn, Tn·pr, Tn·p, Dn·n, Dn·pr] order or ask (sb/sth) to come (to a specified place) by shouting, telephoning, writing, etc; summon (通过喊叫、电话、文字等)命令或要求(某人[某物])来(到某处); 召唤: *call the fire brigade, the police, a doctor, an ambulance, etc* 叫消防队、警察、医生、救护车等 ○ *Call the children (in): it's time for tea.* 叫孩子们(进来), 该吃下午茶点了. ○ *Several candidates were called for a second interview.* 有几个候选人被叫来作第二次面试. ○ *The doctor has been called (away) to an urgent case.* 医生被叫去看急症病人了. ○ *The ambassador was called back to London by the Prime Minister.* 大使被首相召回伦敦. ○ *I have to be at the airport in 20 minutes — please call (me) a taxi.* 我20分钟后得到机场——请(给我)叫辆计程车. ○ *call sb's attention to sth*, ie invite sb to examine or think carefully about sth 叫某人注意某事. **4** (**a**) [I, Ipr, Ip] **~ (in/round) (on sb/at...) (for sb/sth)** make a short visit; go to sb's house, etc (to get sth or to go somewhere with him)拜访; 去某人家等(取某物或与他去某处): *Let's call (in) on John/at John's house.* 咱们去拜访约翰吧[去约翰家吧]. ○ *He was out when I called (round) (to see him).* 我去拜访(探望他)的时候, 他不在家. ○ *I'll call for* (ie collect) *you at 7 o'clock.* 我7点钟到你家接你. ○ *Will you call in at the supermarket for some eggs and milk?* 你顺便去超级市场买些鸡蛋和牛奶好吗? ⇨ Usage at VISIT 用法见 VISIT. (**b**) [Ipr] **~ at...** (of a train, etc) stop at (a place) (指火车等)在(某处)停靠: *The train on platform 3 is for London, calling at Didcot and Reading.* 第3站台的火车开往伦敦, 在迪科特和雷丁停车. **5** [I, Tn] telephone (sb) 给(某人)打电话: *I'll call (you) again later.* 我稍后再(给你)打电话. ○ *My brother called me (from Leeds) last night.* 我弟弟昨晚(从利兹)给我打来电话. **6** [Tn] order (sth) to take place; announce 令(某事)举行, 进行; 宣布: *call a meeting, an election, a strike* 举行会议、选举、罢工. **7** [Tn] wake (sb) 叫醒(某人): *Please call me at 7 o'clock tomorrow morning.* 请在明早7点钟把我叫醒. **8** [Cn·a, Cn·n] (**a**) describe or address (sb/sth) as, name 给(某人[某事物])取名; 将(某人[某事物])称为或叫作: *How dare you call me fat!* 你怎么敢叫我胖子! ○ *His name is Richard but we call him Dick.* 他名叫里查, 可是我们都叫他迪克. ○ *What's your dog called?* 你的狗叫什么名字? ○ (*ironic* 反语) *He hasn't had anything published and he calls himself a writer!* 他什么都没发表过, 却自称作家! (**b**) consider (sb/sth) to be; regard as 认为(某人[某事物])是; 看作: *I call his behaviour mean and selfish.* 我认为他的行为卑鄙、自私. ○ *I would never call German an easy language.* 我认为德语可不容易学. ○ *How can you be so unkind and still call yourself my friend?* 你怎么能这么不通人情, 还自称是我的朋友? ○ *You owe me £5.04 — let's call it £5*, ie settle the sum at £5. 你欠我5.04英镑——就算5英镑吧. **9** [I, Tn] (in card-games) declare (a trump suit, etc); bid (纸牌戏中)定(王牌等); 叫牌: *Have you called yet?* 你叫牌了吗? ○ *Who called hearts?* 谁定的红桃? **10** (idm 习语) **be/feel called to (do) sth** be/feel summoned to a particular profession or vocation 被召[感召]任某种职务或使命: *be called to the bar*, ie become a barrister 成为讼务律师 ○ *feel called to the ministry/the priesthood* 被牧师[教士]使命感召. **bring/call sb/sth to mind** ⇨ MIND[1]. **call sb's ˈbluff**

challenge sb to do what he is threatening to do (believing that he will not dare to do it) 要求某人摊牌(迫使某人做他威胁要做的事——认为他不敢做); 向某人挑战. **call a 'halt (to sth)** stop (work, a habit, etc) 停止(工作); 改掉(某习惯): *Let's call a halt (to the meeting) and continue tomorrow.* 咱们暂停(会议), 明天接着开. **call sth into being** (*fml* 文) create sth 创造某事物. **call sth into play** bring sth into operation 发挥; 发扬; 发动; 调动: *Chess is a game that calls into play all one's powers of concentration.* 下国际象棋要全神贯注才行. **call sth in/into 'question** doubt sth or cause sth to be doubted 怀疑某事物; 使某事物受怀疑: *His honesty has never been called in question.* 他的诚实从未有人怀疑过. **call it a 'day** (*infml* 口) decide or agree to stop (doing sth) temporarily or permanently 决定或同意暂时或永久停止(进行某事物): *After forty years in politics he thinks it's time to call it a day*, ie to retire. 他从政四十年, 认为该结束了(退休). **call it 'quits** (*infml* 口) agree to stop a contest, quarrel, etc on even terms (同意不分胜负)停止比赛、争吵等. **call sb 'names** jeer at or insult sb 嘲弄或侮辱某人. **call sth one's 'own** claim sth as one's property 声称某事物归自己所有: *He has nothing he can call his own.* 他一无所有. **call the 'shots/the 'tune** (*infml* 口) be in a position to control a situation 控制; 操纵; 定调子. **call a spade a 'spade** speak plainly and frankly 直言不讳. **call sb to account (for/over sth)** make sb explain (an error, a loss, etc) 使某人解释(错误、损失等): *His boss called him to account for failing to meet the deadline.* 老板叫他解释未能按时完成的原因. **call sb/sth to order** ask (people in a meeting) to be silent so that business may start or continue 要求(与会者)安静(以便开始或继续进行正事). **he who pays the piper calls the tune** ⇨ PAY². **the pot calling the kettle black** ⇨ POT¹. **11** (phr v) **call by** (*infml* 口) visit a place or a person briefly when passing 顺路参观某处或探望某人: *Could you call by on your way home?* 你回家的时候, 能顺路来一下吗?

call sb down (*US infml* 口) reprimand or scold sb severely 严厉申斥或责骂某人. **call sth down on sb** (*fml* 文) invoke (curses, etc) on sb 祈求(降祸…)于某人.

call for sth require, demand or need sth 要求、需求或需要某事物: *The situation calls for prompt action.* 形势所迫, 必须立即采取行动. ○ *'I've been promoted.' 'This calls for a celebration!'* '我已经升职了.' '这可得庆祝一下喽!' ○ *That rude remark was not called for!* 何必说那么难听的话! Cf 参看 UNCALLED-FOR.

call sth forth (*fml* 文) cause sth to appear or be shown; elicit sth 使某事物出现或显出; 引出某事物: *His speech called forth an angry response.* 他的话惹人生气.

call sth in order or request the return of sth 下令或请求收回某物: *The library called in all overdue books.* 图书馆要求把所有逾期未还的书收回. ○ *Cars with serious faults have been called in by the manufacturers.* 有严重故障的汽车原厂要求收回.

call sb/sth off order (dogs, soldiers, etc) to stop attacking, searching, etc 命令(狗、士兵等)停止追击、搜查等: *Please call your dog off — it's frightening the children.* 请把你的狗叫开——已经吓着孩子了. **call sth off** cancel or abandon sth 取消或放弃某事物: *call off a deal, a journey, a picnic, a strike* 取消一交易、旅行、野餐、罢工 ○ *They have called off their engagement*, ie decided not to get married. 他们已经解除了婚约. ○ *The match was called off because of bad weather.* 由于天气不好, 比赛取消了.

call on/upon sb (to do sth) (**a**) formally invite or request sb (to speak, etc) 郑重邀请或要求某人(讲话等): *I now call upon the chairman to address the meeting.* 现在请主席致辞. (**b**) appeal to or urge sb (to do sth) 恳求或促使某人(做某事): *We are calling upon you to help us.* 我们恳求你帮助我们. ○ *I feel called upon* (ie feel that I ought) *to warn you that….* 我觉得我应该提醒你….

call sb out (**a**) summon sb, esp to an emergency 召唤某人(尤指处理紧急事件): *call out the fire brigade, troops, guard, etc* 召(集)消防队、部队、守卫人员等. (**b**) order or advise (workers) to go on strike 命令或建议(工人)罢工: *Miners were called out (on strike) by union leaders.* 矿工遵照工会领袖的指示举行罢工.

call sb/sth up (**a**) (*esp US*) telephone sb 给某人打电话. (**b**) bring sth back to one's mind; recall sth 想起某事物; 回忆某事: *The sound of happy laughter called up memories of his childhood.* 这欢笑声使他回忆起童年时代的情景. (**c**) summon sb for military service; draft sb 征召某人服兵役; 选派某人.

▷ **caller** *n* person who makes a brief visit or a telephone call 访问者; 打电话者.

□ **'calling-card** *n* (*US*) = VISITING-CARD (VISIT).

'call-up *n* (*US* **draft**) [U, C esp *sing* 尤作单数] summons for military service (服兵役的)征集令, 征召令: *receive one's call-up* 收到征集令 ○ [attrib 作定语] *young men of call-up age* 适龄应征的年轻人.

cal·li·graphy /kəˈlɪgrəfɪ; kəˈlɪgrəfɪ/ *n* [U] (art of producing) beautiful handwriting 书法. ▷ **cal·li·grapher** *n*.

call·ing /ˈkɔːlɪŋ; ˈkɔlɪŋ/ *n* **1** profession; trade 职业; 行业. **2** strong urge or feeling of duty to do a particular job; vocation 对做某项工作的强烈欲望或责任感; 使命; 神的感召: *He believes it is his calling to become a priest.* 他认为当教士是自己的使命.

callipers 测径器

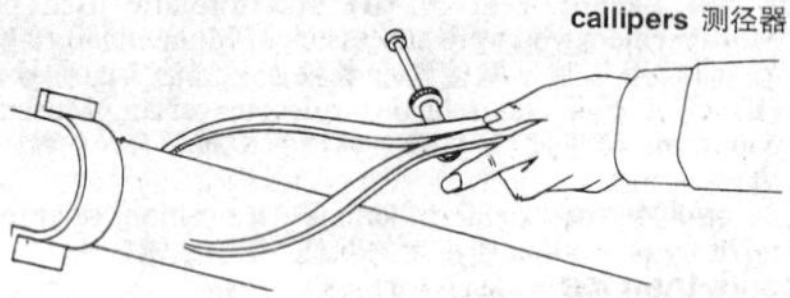

cal·li·per (also **ca·li·per**) /ˈkælɪpə(r); ˈkæləpɚ/ *n* **1** [C usu *pl* 通常作复数] metal support for weak or injured legs 双脚规形夹(因腿部无力或损伤而使用的金属支架). **2 callipers** [pl] instrument for measuring the diameter of tubes or round objects 测径器; 双脚规; 卡钳: *a pair of callipers* 一把测径器. ⇨ illus 见插图.

cal·lis·thenics (also **ca·lis·thenics**) /ˌkælɪsˈθenɪks; ˌkæləsˈθenɪks/ *n* [sing or pl *v*] exercises to develop strong and graceful bodies 柔软体操; 健美运动.

cal·los·ity /kæˈlɒsətɪ; kæˈlɑsətɪ/ *n* (*fml* 文) area of hardened skin; callus 胼胝, 茧子(皮肤硬化的部分).

cal·lous /ˈkæləs; ˈkæləs/ *adj* **1** cruelly insensitive or unsympathetic 冷酷无情的; 无同情心的: *a callous person, attitude, act* 冷酷无情的人、态度、行为. **2** (of the skin) hardened, eg by rough work (指皮肤)硬化的, 起茧子的(如因做粗重活儿所致).

▷ **cal·loused** *adj* (of the skin) hardened; having calluses (指皮肤)硬化的, 有茧子的: *calloused hands* 有茧子的手.

cal·lously *adv* in a callous(1) way 冷酷无情地; 无同情心地.

cal·lous·ness *n* [U] callous(1) behaviour 冷酷无情; 无同情心的行为.

cal·low /ˈkæləʊ; ˈkælo/ *adj* (*derog* 贬) immature and inexperienced 既不成熟又无经验的; 乳臭未干的: *a callow youth* 黄口小儿 ○ *callow thinking* 异想天开. ▷ **cal·low·ness** *n* [U].

cal·lus /ˈkæləs; ˈkæləs/ *n* area of thick hardened skin 胼胝, 茧子(皮肤硬化增厚的部分): *calluses on one's palms* 手掌上的茧子.

calm /kɑːm; *US also* kɑːlm; kɑm, kɑlm/ *adj* (**-er, -est**) **1** (**a**) (of the sea) without large waves; still (指海洋)无浪的, 平静的. (**b**) (of the weather) not windy (指天气)无风的: *a calm, cloudless day* 无风无云的一天. **2** not excited, nervous or agitated; quiet; untroubled 镇定的; 安静的; 无忧虑的: *It is important to keep/stay calm in an emergency.* 在紧急情况下保持镇静是很重要的. ○ *The city is calm again after yesterday's riots.* 这座城市经过昨天的动乱以后又平静下来了. ⇨Usage at QUIET 用法见QUIET.

▷ **calm** *n* [C, U] **1** calm condition or period 平静的状态或时期: *the calm of a summer evening* 夏日夜晚的宁静 ○ *After the storm came a calm.* 风暴过后, 万籁俱寂. **2** (idm 习语) **the calm before the storm** time of unnatural calm immediately before an expected outburst of violent activity, passion, etc 暴风雨前的平静(在预料到激烈的活动、情绪等即将爆发之前的反常的

平静时期).

calm *v* [I, Ip, Tn, Tn·p] ~ **(sb) (down)** (cause sb to) become calm (使某人)平静, 镇静, 安静: *Just calm down a bit!* 你先静一静! ○ *Have a brandy — it'll help to calm you (down).* 来点儿白兰地 —— 能使你静下来.

calmly *adv*: *He walked into the shop and calmly* (ie impudently and self-confidently) *stole a pair of gloves.* 他走进商店若无其事地偷了一副手套.

calm·ness *n* [U].

Calor gas /ˈkælə gæs; ˋkælɚˌgæs/ *n* [U] (*propr* 专利名) liquid butane stored under pressure in containers for domestic use 罐装石油气.

cal·orie /ˈkælərɪ; ˋkælərɪ/ *n* (*abbr* 缩写 **cal**) **1** unit for measuring a quantity of heat 卡路里, 卡(热量单位). **2** unit for measuring the energy value of food 大卡, 千卡(食物含能量的热值单位): *An ounce of sugar has about 100 calories.* 一盎司的糖含约100大卡的热量. ○ *Her diet restricts her to 1 500 calories a day.* 她的规定饮食限制她每天摄入1 500大卡的热量.

▷ **cal·or·ific** /ˌkæləˈrɪfɪk; ˌkæləˋrɪfɪk/ *adj* [usu attrib 通常作定语] of or producing heat 生热的; 发热的: *calorific value*, ie the quantity of heat or energy produced by a given amount of fuel or food 发热值(燃料或食物产生的热量).

cal·umny /ˈkæləmnɪ; ˋkæləmnɪ/ *n* (*fml* 文) **1** [C] false statement about sb, made to damage his character 诬蔑; 中伤: *a victim of vicious calumnies* 恶毒诬蔑的受害者. **2** [U] slander 诽谤: *accuse sb of calumny* 控告某人诽谤.

▷ **ca·lum·ni·ate** /kəˈlʌmnɪeɪt; kəˋlʌmnɪˌet/ *v* [Tn] (*fml* 文) slander (sb) 诬蔑, 中伤, 诽谤(某人).

ca·lum·ni·ous /kəˈlʌmnɪəs; kəˋlʌmnɪəs/ *adj* (*fml* 文) slanderous 诬蔑的; 中伤的; 诽谤的.

calve /kɑːv; *US* kæv; kæv/ *v* [I] give birth to a calf 生小牛: *Our cows will be calving soon.* 我们的牛快生小牛了.

calves *pl of* CALF[1], CALF[2].

Cal·vin·ism /ˈkælvɪnɪzəm; ˋkælvɪnɪzəm/ *n* [U] religious teaching of the French Protestant John Calvin (1509-64) and of his followers 加尔文主义, 加尔文教义(法国新教派加尔文, 1509-1564, 及其追随者的宗教教义).

▷ **Cal·vin·ist** /ˈkælvɪnɪst; ˋkælvɪnɪst/ *n* follower of Calvin's teaching 加尔文派教徒.

ca·lypso /kəˈlɪpsəʊ; kəˋlɪpso/ *n* (*pl* ~**s**) West Indian song about a subject of current interest, having a variable rhythm and often improvised words. 卡利普索小调(西印度群岛歌曲, 以时事为主题, 有多种韵律, 临时填词演唱).

ca·lyx /ˈkeɪlɪks; ˋkelɪks/ *n* (*pl* ~**es** or **calyces** /ˈkeɪlɪsiːz; ˋkelɪˌsiz/) (*botany* 植) ring of leaves (called *sepals*) enclosing an unopened flower-bud 花萼(花瓣外层的一圈小叶, 称为萼片). ⇨illus at App 1 见附录1之插图, page ii.

cam /kæm; kæm/ *n* projecting part on a wheel designed to change the circular motion of the wheel as it turns into up-and-down or backwards-and-forwards motion of another part 凸轮(轮上的凸起部件, 用以使轮的圆周运动转变成另一部件的上下或前后运动).

□ **camshaft** /ˈkæmʃɑːft; *US* -ʃæft; ˋkæmˌʃæft/ *n* shaft with a cam or cams on it, esp in a motor vehicle 凸轮轴(有凸轮的轴, 尤用于机动车辆).

ca·ma·ra·derie /ˌkæməˈrɑːdərɪ; *US* -ˈræd-; ˌkɑməˋrædərɪ/ *n* [U] friendship and mutual trust; comradeship 友谊与互相信任; 同志情谊.

cam·ber /ˈkæmbə(r); ˋkæmbɚ/ *n* slight upward curve on the surface of sth, esp a road 中凸形, 拱势(物体, 尤指道路, 表面略向上弯的曲面).

▷ **cam·ber** *v* [Tn] give a camber to (esp a road) 使(尤指路面)拱起: *The street is quite steeply cambered at this point.* 这条街的这个地方拱起很高.

camb·ric /ˈkeɪmbrɪk; ˋkembrɪk/ *n* [U] fine thin linen or cotton cloth 细麻纱; 细棉布.

cam·corder /ˈkæmkɔːdə(r); ˋkæmˌkɔrdɚ/ *n* portable video camera with a built-in video recorder 摄像录像机.

came *pt of* COME.

camel /ˈkæml; ˋkæml̩/ *n* **1** [C] animal with a long neck and one or two humps on its back, used in desert countries for riding and for carrying goods 骆驼. ⇨illus 见插图. Cf 参看 DROMEDARY. **2** [U] fawn colour 驼色; 浅棕色.

□ ˈ**camel-hair** (also ˈ**camel's-hair**) *n* [U] **1** soft

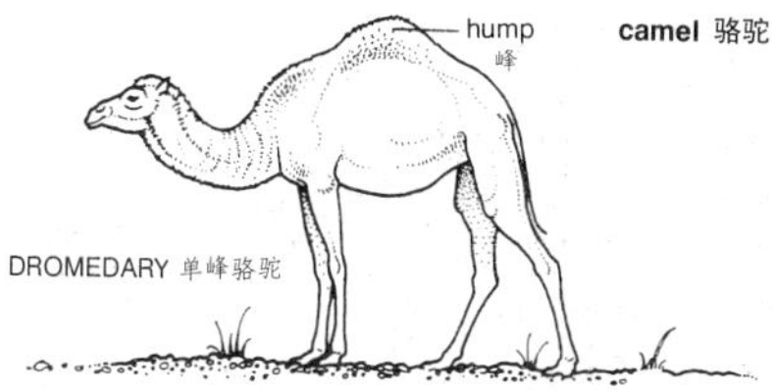

camel 骆驼

heavy yellowish cloth made of camel's hair or a mixture of camel's hair and wool 骆驼毛; 驼绒: [attrib 作定语] *a camel-hair coat* 驼绒外衣. **2** fine soft hair used in artists' brushes 驼毛(用以制画笔).

ca·mel·lia /kəˈmiːlɪə; kəˋmilɪə/ *n* (**a**) evergreen shrub from China and Japan with shiny leaves and white, red or pink flowers 山茶. (**b**) flower of this shrub 山茶花.

Cam·em·bert /ˈkæməmbeə(r); ˋkæməmˌbɛr/ *n* [U, C] type of soft creamy cheese from N France 卡门培尔奶酪(产于法国北部的软干酪).

ca·meo /ˈkæmɪəʊ; ˋkæmɪˌo/ *n* (*pl* ~**s**) **1** small piece of hard stone with a raised design, esp one with two coloured layers so that the background is of a different colour from the design 浮雕宝石(刻有浮雕的小硬宝石, 尤指有两层不同颜色者, 一层为背景另一层为浮雕): [attrib 作定语] *a cameo brooch* 浮雕饰针. **2** (**a**) small but well-acted part in a film or play (电影或戏剧的)小品: [attrib 作定语] *a cameo performance/part/role* 小品演出[台词/角色]. (**b**) short piece of fine descriptive writing 小品文.

camera 照相机

cam·era /ˈkæmərə; ˋkæmərə/ *n* **1** apparatus for taking photographs, moving pictures or television pictures 照相机; (电影)摄影机; (电视)摄像机: *a video camera*, ie one that converts visual images into an electrical signal to produce television pictures 摄像机(可将影像转换成电信号而产生电视画面的). ⇨illus 见插图. **2** (idm 习语) **in** ˈ**camera** in a judge's private room; not in public; privately 在法官的私室里; 不公开地; 私下: *The trial was held/The case was heard in camera.* 那一审讯不公开[那一案件已秘密审讯].

□ ˈ**cameraman** /-mæn; -ˌmæn/ *n* (*pl* **-men**) person whose job is operating a camera for film-making or television (电影或电视)摄影师.

camo·mile (also **chamomile**) /ˈkæməmaɪl; ˋkæməˌmaɪl/ *n* [U] (**a**) sweet-smelling plant with daisy-like flowers 春黄菊(一种有香味的植物, 花状如雏菊). (**b**) its dried leaves and flowers used in medicine as a tonic 春黄菊(其干叶及花可作补药).

cam·ou·flage /ˈkæməflɑːʒ; ˋkæməˌflɑʒ/ *n* **1** [U] way of hiding or disguising soldiers, military equipment, etc, eg with paint, netting or leaves, so that they look like part of their surroundings (军事上的)伪装, 掩饰: *use the branches of trees as camouflage* 用树枝伪装. **2** [C] such a disguise 伪装; 掩饰: *The polar bear's white fur is a natural camouflage*, ie because the bear is hard to see in the snow. 北极熊的白色毛皮是天然的保护色.

▷ **cam·ou·flage** *v* [Tn] hide (sb/sth) by camouflage 用伪装遮掩(某人[某事物]): *The soldiers camouflaged themselves with leaves and branches.* 士兵们用树枝树叶把自己伪装起来.

camp[1] /kæmp; kæmp/ *n* **1** (**a**) place where people (eg holiday-makers, Scouts or explorers) live temporarily in tents or huts 营地: *a holiday camp* 度假营 ○ *leave/return to camp* 离开[回到]营地 ○ *We pitched (our) camp* (ie put up our tents) *by a lake.* 我们在湖边扎营(支起帐篷). (**b**) place where prisoners or refugees are kept, often for long periods 关押囚犯或收容难民的地方(常指长期的): *a prison camp* 战俘营 ○ *a concentration camp* 集中营 ○ *a transit camp* 中转营. **2** place where soldiers are lodged or trained 兵营(士兵住宿或训练的地方): *an army camp* 军营. **3** group of people with the same (esp political or religious) ideas 阵营(尤指政治或宗教观点相同的人所组成的): *the socialist camp* 社会主义阵营 ○ *They belong to different political camps.* 他们属于不同的政治阵营. **4** (idm 习语) **carry the war into the enemy's camp** ⇨ CARRY. **have a foot in both camps** ⇨ FOOT[1]. **strike camp** ⇨ STRIKE[2].

C

▷ **camp** *v* **1** (**a**) [I] put up a tent or tents 设营; 扎营; 宿营: *Where shall we camp tonight?* 我们今晚在哪里宿营? (**b**) [I, Ip] ~ **(out)** live in a tent 在帐篷中住宿: *They camped (out) in the woods for a week.* 他们在树林里搭帐篷住了一个星期. **2** [I] (usu 通常作 **go camping**) spend a holiday living in tents 野营度假: *The boys went camping in Greece last year.* 那些男孩子去年到希腊去露营度假. **3** [I] live temporarily as if in a camp (如宿营般)暂住: *I'm camping on the floor in a friend's flat for two weeks.* 我在朋友家地板上临时寄宿两个星期. **camper** *n* person who camps 宿营者; 露营者. **camping** *n* [U] holiday spent living in tents 野营度假: *Do you like camping?* 你喜欢野营度假吗? ○ [attrib 作定语] *camping equipment* 露营装备.

□ ˌ**camp-ˈbed** (*US* ˈ**campcot**) *n* portable folding bed (not only for use in a camp) 折叠床, 行军床(不仅用于行军宿营).

ˈ**camp-fire** *n* outdoor fire made of logs, etc by campers 营火.

ˈ**camp-follower** *n* **1** non-military person (eg a prostitute) following an army to sell goods or services 随军售货或服务的非军事人员(如营妓). **2** (*often derog* 常作贬义) person who attaches himself to a particular group, party, etc although not a member of it; hanger-on 依附于某一团体而并非其成员者; 跟随者.

ˈ**camp meeting** (*US*) religious meeting held outdoors or in a large tent 野营布道会.

ˈ**campsite** (also ˈ**camping-site**) *n* place for camping, usu specially equipped for holiday-makers 露营区.

camp[2] /kæmp; kæmp/ *adj* (*infml* 口) **1** (of a man, his manner, etc) affected and effeminate; homosexual (指男子及其举止等)扭怩作态的, 女性化的; 同性恋的: *a camp walk, voice, gesture* 扭怩作态的步子、声音、姿势. **2** exaggerated in style, esp for humorous effect; affectedly theatrical 式样或风格过分夸张的(尤指为达到幽默效果); 做作的.

▷ **camp** *n* [U] camp behaviour 做作的举止行为: *Her performance was pure camp.* 她的表现纯粹是演戏.

camp *v* (phr v) **camp it up** (*infml* 口) (**a**) display one's homosexuality through effeminate behaviour (通过女性化的举止行为)显示自己的同性恋特征. (**b**) overact grotesquely 表现得古怪过火.

cam·paign /kæmˈpeɪn; kæmˋpen/ *n* **1** series of military operations with a particular aim, usu in one area 战役: *He fought in the N African campaign during the last war.* 在上次战争中他在北非战役参战. **2** series of planned activities with a particular social, commercial or political aim 运动(为某一社会的、商业的或政治的目的而进行的一系列有计划的活动): *a campaign against nuclear weapons* 反对核武器运动 ○ *an advertising campaign,* ie to promote a particular product 广告宣传运动(以推销某产品) ○ *an election campaign* 竞选运动 ○ *a campaign to raise money for the needy* 为贫苦人筹款的运动.

▷ **cam·paign** *v* [I, Ipr, It] ~ **(for/against sb/sth)** take part in or lead a campaign 参加或领导一战役或运动: *She spent her life campaigning for women's rights.* 她毕生致力于女权运动. ○ *campaign to have sanctions imposed* 发起实施制裁的运动. **cam·paigner** *n* person who campaigns 参加战役或运动的人: *an old campaigner,* ie sb with much experience of a particular activity 老练的人.

cam·pa·nile /ˌkæmpəˈniːlɪ; ˌkæmpəˋnilɪ/ *n* bell-tower, esp one that is not part of another building 钟楼(尤指不依附于其他建筑而独立的).

cam·pano·logy /ˌkæmpəˈnɒlədʒɪ; ˌkæmpəˋnɑlədʒɪ/ *n* [U] (*fml* 文) study of bells and the art of bell-ringing 钟学; 鸣钟术. ▷ **cam·pano·lo·gist** /-ədʒɪst; -ədʒɪst/ *n*.

cam·phor /ˈkæmfə(r); ˋkæmfɚ/ *n* [U] strong-smelling white substance used in medicine and mothballs and in making plastics 樟脑.

▷ **cam·phor·ated** /ˈkæmfəreɪtɪd; ˋkæmfəˌretɪd/ *adj* containing camphor 含樟脑的: *camphorated oil* 樟脑油.

cam·pus /ˈkæmpəs; ˋkæmpəs/ *n* (*pl* **~es**) **1** grounds and buildings of a university or college (大学或学院的)校园: *He lives on (the) campus,* ie in a building within the university grounds. 他在学校里住. **2** (*US*) university or branch of a university 大学或其分校: [attrib 作定语] *campus life* 大学生活.

CAMRA (also **Camra**) /ˈkæmrə; ˋkæmrə/ *abbr* 缩写 = (*Brit*) Campaign for Real Ale (ie beer brewed in the traditional way) 弘扬传统啤酒运动: *Camra pubs* 传统啤酒酒馆.

can 金属的或塑料的容器

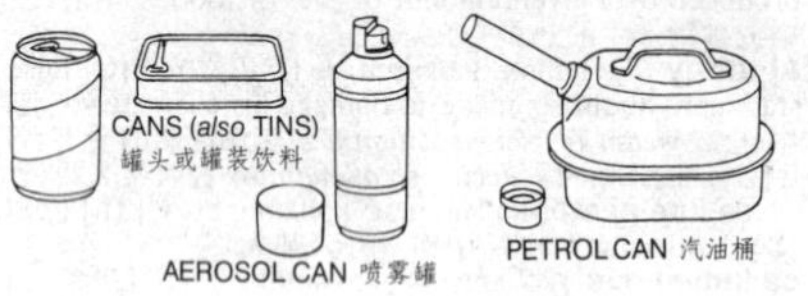

can[1] /kæn; kæn/ *n* ⇨illus 见插图. **1** [C] (often in compounds 常用以构成复合词) metal or plastic container for holding or carrying liquids 装运液体用的金属或塑料的容器: *an* ˈ*oilcan* ○ *a* ˈ*petrol can/a can of* ˈ*petrol* ○ *a* ˈ*watering-can.* **2** [C] (**a**) (also *esp Brit* **tin**) sealed tin in which food or drink is preserved and sold 罐头: *a* ˈ*beer can* 罐装啤酒 ○ [attrib 作定语] *a can opener* 开罐器. (**b**) contents of or amount contained in a can 罐头里容纳的东西或容纳的量: *a can of peaches* 一罐桃 ○ *He drank four cans of beer.* 他喝了四罐啤酒. **3 the can** [sing] (*US sl* 俚) (**a**) prison 监狱; 牢房. (**b**) lavatory 厕所. **4** (idm 习语) **a can of** ˈ**worms** (*infml* 口) complicated problem 复杂的问题. **carry the can** ⇨ CARRY. **(be) in the** ˈ**can** (of a film, video-tape, etc) recorded and edited; completed and ready for use (指影片、录像带等)摄制及剪接完毕的, 完成以备用的.

▷ **can** *v* (**-nn-**) [Tn] preserve (food) by putting it in a sealed can 将(食物)装入密封罐中保存: *canned* ˈ*fruit* 罐装水果 ○ *a* ˈ*canning factory* 罐头食品制造厂.

can·nery /ˈkænərɪ; ˋkænərɪ/ *n* place where food is canned 罐头食品厂.

□ ˌ**canned** ˈ**music** (*infml usu derog* 口, 通常作贬义) music recorded for reproduction 录音音乐: *Restaurants often play canned music.* 饭馆里常播放录音音乐.

can[2] /kən; kən; *strong form* 强读式 kæn; kæn/ *modal v* (*neg* 否定式 **cannot** /ˈkænɒt; ˋkænɑt/, *contracted form* 缩约式 **can't** /kɑːnt; *US* kænt; kænt/; *pt* **could** /kəd; kəd; *strong form* 强读式 kʊd; kʊd/, *neg* 否定式 **could not**, *contracted form* 缩约式 **couldn't** /ˈkʊdnt; ˋkʊdn̩t/) **1** (**a**) (indicating ability 表示能力): *I can run fast.* 我能跑得很快. ○ *Can you call back tomorrow?* 你明天能回个电话吗? ○ *He couldn't answer the question.* 他不能回答那个问题. ○ *The stadium can be emptied in four minutes.* 这个运动场能用四分钟时间清场. (**b**) (indicating acquired knowledge or skill 表示获得的知识或技能): *They can speak French.* 他们会说法语. ○ *Can he cook?* 他会做饭吗? ○ *I could drive a car before I left school.* 我中学毕业前就会开车了. (**c**) (used with verbs of perception 与感官动词连用): *I can hear music.* 我听见有音乐声. ○ *I thought I could smell something burning.* 我好像闻到什么东西烧着了. ○ *He could still taste the garlic they'd had for lunch.* 他嘴里还有他们午饭时吃的蒜的味道. **2** (indicating permission 表示许可): *Can I read your newspaper?* 我能看看你的报纸吗? ○ *Can I take you home?* 我送你回家行吗? ○ *You can take the car, if you want.* 你要用那辆汽车就尽管用. ○ *We can't* *wear jeans at work.* 我们上班时不准穿牛仔裤. ○ *The boys could play football but the girls had to go to the library.* 男孩儿可以踢足球而女孩儿只好到图书馆去. ⇨Usage 1 at MAY[1] 见 MAY[1] 所附用法第1项. **3** (indicating requests 表示要求): *Can you help me with this box?* 你能帮我弄这个箱子吗? ○ *Can you feed the cat?* 你喂喂猫好吗? **4** (**a**) (indicating possibility 表示可能性): *That can't be Mary — she's in hospital.* 那不可能是玛丽——她住院了. ○ *He can't have slept through all that noise.* 那么吵他不可能睡得着觉. ○ *There's someone outside — who can it be?* 外面有人——会是谁呢? ⇨Usage 2 at MAY[1] 见 MAY[1] 所附用法第2项. (**b**) (used to express bewilderment or incredulity 用以表示疑惑或怀疑): *What 'can they be doing?* 他们在干些什么呢? ○ *Can he be serious?* 他当真是这个意思吗? ○ *Where 'can she have put it?* 她能把它放在哪儿呢? **5** (used to describe typical behaviour or state 用以描述特有的行为或情形): *He can be very tactless sometimes.* 他有时很不讲方式方法. ○ *She can be very forgetful.* 她这个人很健忘. ○ *Scotland can be very cold.* 苏格兰要是冷起来还真够冷的. ○ *It can be quite windy on the hills.* 山上的风就是那么大. **6** (used to make suggestions 用以提出建议): *We can eat in a restaurant, if you like.* 你愿意的话, 咱们可以在饭馆吃饭. ○ *I can take the car if necessary.* 必要时我可以开车去. ⇨Usage 3 at SHALL 见 SHALL 所附用法第3项.

Ca·na·dian /kəˈneɪdɪən; kəˋnedɪən/ *n, adj* (native or inhabitant) of Canada 加拿大的(本地人或居民).

ca·nal /kəˈnæl; kəˋnæl/ *n* **1** channel cut through land for boats or ships to travel along, or to carry water for irrigation 运河: *The Suez Canal joins the Mediterranean and the Red Sea.* 苏伊士运河连接着地中海和红海. Cf 参看 RIVER 1. **2** tube through which air or food passes in a plant or an animal's body (植物中或动物体内空气或食物通过的)管道: *the alimentary canal* 消化道.

▷ **can·al·ize, -ise** /ˈkænəlaɪz; ˋkænḷ,aɪz/ *v* [Tn] **1** make a canal through (an area) 开掘运河通过(一区域). **2** convert (a river) into a canal (by straightening it, building locks, etc) 将(河流)改造成运河(如改直河床, 修建闸门等). **3** direct (sth) to achieve a particular aim; channel 引导(某事物)以达到某目的: *canalize one's energies into voluntary work* 把精力放到义务工作上. **can·al·iza·tion, -isation** /ˌkænəlaɪˈzeɪʃn; *US* -nəlɪˈz-; ˌkænḷəˋzeʃən/ *n* [U].

□ **caˈnal boat** long narrow boat used on canals 运河船(用于运河中的长而窄的船).

can·apé /ˈkænəpeɪ; *US* ˌkænəˈpeɪ; ˋkænəpe/ *n* small biscuit or piece of bread, pastry, etc spread with cheese, meat, fish, etc and usu served with drinks at a party 加有乳酪、肉、鱼等的小饼干或面包片、糕饼等(通常用于聚会中佐以饮料).

ca·nard /kæˈnɑːd, ˈkænɑːd; kəˋnɑrd/ *n* false report or rumour 虚报; 谎报; 谣传.

ca·nary /kəˈneərɪ; kəˋnɛrɪ/ *n* small yellow songbird, usu kept in a cage as a pet 加那利雀; 金丝雀.

□ **caˌnary ˈyellow** light yellow colour 浅黄色.

ca·nasta /kəˈnæstə; kəˋnæstə/ *n* [U] card-game similar to rummy and played with two packs of cards 卡纳斯塔(一种用两副纸牌玩的纸牌戏).

can·can /ˈkænkæn; ˋkænkæn/ *n* [sing] lively dance with high kicking, performed by women in long skirts 康康舞(由穿长裙女人跳的活泼的高踢腿舞): *do/dance the cancan* 跳康康舞.

can·cel /ˈkænsl; ˋkænsḷ/ *v* (**-ll-**; *US* **-l-**) **1** [Tn] say that (sth already arranged and decided upon) will not be done or take place; call off 取消; 废除: *cancel a holiday, concert, meeting*, eg because of illness 取消假日[音乐会/会议](如因病) ○ *The match had to be cancelled because of bad weather.* 比赛因天气不好只得取消. Cf 参看 POSTPONE. **2** [Tn] order (sth) to be stopped; make (sth) invalid 命令(某事物)停止; 使(某事物)作废: *cancel an agreement, a contract, a subscription, etc* 取消协议、合同、预订单等 ○ *He cancelled his order*, ie said he no longer wanted to receive the goods he had ordered. 他撤销了订货单. **3** [Tn] cross out (sth written) 删除(所写的内容): *Cancel that last sentence.* 把最后一句删掉. **4** [Tn] mark (a postage stamp or ticket) to prevent further use 注销, 盖销(邮票或其他票证以防再用). **5** [Tn] (*mathematics* 数) remove (a common factor) from the numerator and denominator of a fraction, or from both sides of an equation, usu by crossing it out 约去, 消去(分数中分子和分母的公因数或方程式两端的相等部分). **6** (phr v) **cancel (sth) out** be equal (to sth) in force and effect; counterbalance (sth) 抵消; 对消: *These arguments cancel (each other) out.* 不同的争论(彼此)势均力敌. ○ *Her kindness and generosity cancel out her occasional flashes of temper.* 她为人厚道、慷慨大方, 倒也弥补了她偶尔发点儿脾气.

▷ **can·cel·la·tion** /ˌkænsəˈleɪʃn; ˌkænsḷˋeʃən/ *n* **1** [U] cancelling or being cancelled 取消; 撤销; 删除; 注销; 抵消: *Her cancellation of her trip to Paris upset our plan.* 她取消了巴黎之行打乱了我们的计划. ○ *the cancellation of the match due to fog* 比赛因有雾而取消. **2** [C] instance of this; thing that has been cancelled (CANCEL 1, 2), eg a theatre ticket 取消; 作废的事物(如戏票): *Are there any cancellations for this evening's performance?* 今晚演出的节目有取消的吗? **3** [C] mark used to cancel a postage stamp, etc 注销的印记; (加于邮票上的)盖销戳记.

Can·cer /ˈkænsə(r); ˋkænsɚ/ *n* **1** the fourth sign of the zodiac, the Crab 巨蟹宫(黄道第四宫). **2** [C] person born under the influence of this sign 属巨蟹宫星座的人. ⇨Usage at ZODIAC 用法见 ZODIAC. ⇨illus at ZODIAC 见 ZODIAC 之插图.

can·cer /ˈkænsə(r); ˋkænsɚ/ *n* **1** (**a**) [C, U] diseased growth in the body, often causing death; malignant tumour 癌; 癌瘤; 癌肿: *Doctors found a cancer on her breast.* 医生发现她患乳癌. ○ *The cancer has spread to his stomach.* 癌肿已扩散到他的胃部. (**b**) [U] disease in which such growths form 癌症: *lung cancer* 肺癌 ○ *cancer of the liver* 肝癌. **2** [C] (*fig* 比喻) evil or dangerous thing that spreads quickly 迅速蔓延的恶劣的或危险的事物: *Violence is a cancer in our society.* 暴力行为是我们社会的祸害. Cf 参看 CANKER 3.

▷ **can·cer·ous** /ˈkænsərəs; ˋkænsərəs/ *n* of, like or affected with cancer (似)癌的; 患癌症的: *Is the growth benign or cancerous?* 这个肿瘤是良性的还是癌肿性的?

can·dela /kænˈdelə; kænˋdɛlə/ *n* unit for measuring the intensity of light 坎德拉, 新烛光(发光强度单位). ⇨ App 11 见附录 11.

can·de·lab·rum /ˌkændɪˈlɑːbrəm; ˌkændḷˋebrəm/ *n* (*pl* **-bra** /-brə; -brə/; also *sing* **candelabra**, *pl* **-bras** /-brəz; -brəz/) large ornamental branched holder for candles or lights (装饰性的)枝状大烛台或灯台.

can·did /ˈkændɪd; ˋkændɪd/ *adj* not hiding one's thoughts; frank and honest 率直的; 坦白而诚实的: *a candid opinion, statement, person* 直言、直说、直性人 ○ *Let me be quite candid with you: your work is not good enough.* 不瞒你说, 你的工作不怎么好. ▷ **can·didly** *adv*: *Candidly* (ie Speaking frankly), *David, I think you're being unreasonable.* 大卫, 说实话我认为你不讲道理. **can·did·ness** *n* [U].

can·did·ate /ˈkændɪdət; *US* -deɪt; ˋkændə,det/ *n* **1** person who applies for a job or is nominated for election (esp to Parliament) (求职)申请人; (尤指国会的)候选人: *stand as Labour candidate in a parliamentary election* 国会竞选中作为工党候选人 ○ *offer oneself as a candidate for a post* 自荐为某职位的候选人. **2** person taking an examination 参加考试的人: *Most candidates passed in grammar.* 参加考试的人大多数语法及格. **3** **~ (for sth)** person considered to be suitable for a particular position or likely to get sth 被认为适合任某职位或可能得到某事物的人: *The company is being forced to reduce staff and I fear I'm a likely candidate (for redundancy).* 公司被迫裁员, 恐怕我是其中之一(冗员).

▷ **can·di·da·ture** /ˈkændɪdətʃə(r); ˋkændədətʃɚ/ (also *esp Brit* **can·did·acy** /ˈkændɪdəsɪ; ˋkændɪdəsɪ/) *n* [U] being a candidate(1) 申请人或候选人的资格或身分: *announce one's candidature* 宣布自己为候选人.

can·died ⇨ CANDY.

candle /ˈkændl; ˋkændḷ/ *n* **1** round stick of wax with a wick through it which is lit to give light as it burns 蜡烛. ⇨illus 见插图. **2** (idm 习语) **burn the candle at both ends** ⇨ BURN[2]. **the game is not worth the candle** ⇨ GAME[1]. **not hold a candle to sb/sth** (*infml* 口) be inferior to sb/sth 比不上某人[某事物]: *She writes quite amusing stories but she can't hold a candle to the more serious novelists.* 她能写些很有趣的故事, 但是

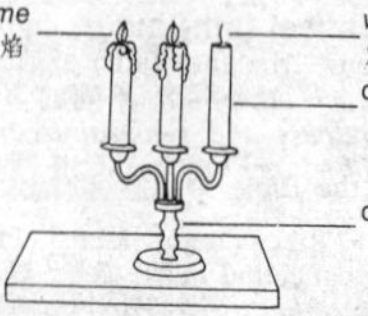

candle 蜡烛

C

比不上那些写出内容能发人深省的小说家.

□ ˈ**candle-light** *n* [U] light produced by candles 烛光: *read, work, etc by candle-light* 在烛光下阅读、工作等.

ˈ**candlepower** *n* [U] unit of measurement of light, expressed in candelas 烛光(量度光的单位, 以坎德拉表示): *a ten candlepower lamp* 十烛光的灯.

ˈ**candlestick** *n* holder for one or more candles 蜡台; 烛台.

can·dle·wick /ˈkændlwɪk; ˋkændḷ,wɪk/ *n* [U] soft cotton fabric with a raised tufted pattern 灯芯纱盘花簇绒(有凸起花纹的软棉布): [attrib 作定语] *a candlewick bedspread* 灯芯纱盘花床单.

cand·our (*US* **can·dor**) /ˈkændə(r); ˋkændɚ/ *n* [U] candid behaviour, speech or quality; frankness 坦白; 率直.

C and W *abbr* 缩写 = (*music* 音) country-and-western.

candy /ˈkændɪ; ˋkændɪ/ *n* **1** [U] sugar hardened by repeated boiling 冰糖. **2** (*esp US*) (**a**) [U] sweets or chocolate 糖果; 巧克力. (**b**) [C] a sweet or a chocolate 糖果; 巧克力.

▷ **candy** *v* (*pt, pp* **candied**) **1** [Tn esp passive 尤用于被动语态] preserve (eg fruit) by boiling in sugar (用糖煮过以)保存(如水果): *candied plums* 蜜饯李子 ○ *candied peel*, eg of lemons or oranges 蜜饯果皮(如柠檬皮或橙皮). **2** [I, Tn] (cause sth to) form into sugar crystals (使某物)成糖的结晶.

□ ˈ**candy-floss** *n* [U] (*US* also ˌ**cotton** ˈ**candy**) type of light fluffy sweet made by spinning melted sugar and eaten on a stick 棉花糖.

candy·tuft /ˈkændɪtʌft; ˋkændɪ,tʌft/ *n* plant with clusters of white, pink or purple flowers 屈曲花.

cane /keɪn; ken/ *n* **1** (**a**) [C] hollow jointed stem of certain plants, eg bamboo or sugar-cane 某些植物的中空而有节的茎(如竹或甘蔗). (**b**) [U] such stems used as a material for making furniture, etc 这类植物的茎(用作家具等的材料): [attrib 作定语] *a cane chair* 藤椅. **2** [C] thin woody stem of a raspberry plant 悬钩子植物的细茎. **3** (**a**) [C] length of cane, or a thin rod, used for supporting plants, as a walking-stick or for beating people as a punishment 竹杖; 藤条; 棍棒. (**b**) **the cane** [sing] (in some schools) the punishment in which children are beaten with a cane (某些学校中)对学生用藤条或棍棒责打的惩罚: *get/be given the cane* 受[挨]藤条鞭打 ○ *Many teachers wish to abolish the cane.* 很多教师希望废除用藤条等的体罚.

▷ **cane** *v* [Tn] **1** punish (sb) by beating with a cane 用藤条或竹棍等责打(某人): *The headmaster caned the boys for disobedience.* 校长用藤条责打不听话的男学生. **2** (*infml* 口 *esp Brit*) defeat (sb) totally 完全打败(某人): *We really caned them in the last match.* 我们最后一场比赛可真把他们打得落花流水. **3** weave cane into (a chair, etc) 用竹或藤等编制成(椅子等). **can·ing** *n* [U, C]: *give sb a good caning* 用藤条给某人一顿好打.

□ ˈ**cane-sugar** *n* [U] sugar obtained from the juice of sugar-cane 蔗糖.

can·ine /ˈkeɪnaɪn; ˋkenaɪn/ *adj* of, like or relating to dogs (似)犬的; 与犬有关的.

▷ **can·ine** *n* **1** (*fml* 文) dog 犬. **2** (also **canine tooth**) (in a human being) any of the four pointed teeth next to the incisors (人的)犬齿. ⇨illus at TOOTH 见TOOTH之插图.

can·is·ter /ˈkænɪstə(r); ˋkænɪstɚ/ *n* **1** small (usu metal) container for holding tea, coffee, etc (通常为金属的)小罐(装茶叶、咖啡等). **2** cylinder, filled with shot or tear-gas, that bursts and releases its contents when fired from a gun or thrown 霰弹筒(内装弹丸或催泪气体, 以枪炮发射或投掷后爆炸).

can·ker /ˈkæŋkə(r); ˋkæŋkɚ/ *n* **1** [U] disease that destroys the wood of plants and trees (植物的)溃疡病. **2** [U] disease causing ulcerous sores on the ears of animals, esp dogs and cats (动物耳部的)溃疡(尤指猫狗). **3** [C] (*fig* 比喻) evil or dangerous influence that spreads and corrupts people (蔓延并腐蚀人们的)祸害, 祸患, 祸根: *Drug addiction is a dangerous canker in society.* 吸毒成瘾是腐蚀社会的一大祸害. Cf 参看 CANCER 2.

▷ **can·ker** *v* [Tn] infect or corrupt (sb) with canker 使(某人)患溃疡; 腐蚀(某人).

can·ker·ous /ˈkæŋkərəs; ˋkæŋkərəs/ *adj* of, like or causing canker 溃疡的; 似溃疡的; 引起溃疡的.

can·na·bis /ˈkænəbɪs; ˋkænəbɪs/ *n* [U] **1** hemp plant 大麻. **2** any of various drugs made from the dried leaves and flowers of the hemp plant that are smoked or chewed for their intoxicating effect 大麻毒品: *arrested for possessing cannabis* 因藏有大麻而被捕. Cf 参看 HASHISH, MARIJUANA.

can·nel·loni /ˌkænəˈləʊnɪ; ˌkænəˋlonɪ/ *n* [U] rolls of pasta filled with meat and seasoning (肉馅的)面卷.

can·nery ⇨ CAN[1].

can·ni·bal /ˈkænɪbl; ˋkænəbḷ/ *n* (**a**) person who eats human flesh 吃人肉的人: [attrib 作定语] *a cannibal tribe* 食人的部落. (**b**) animal that eats its own kind 同类相食的动物.

▷ **can·ni·bal·ism** /ˈkænɪbəlɪzəm; ˋkænəbḷ,ɪzəm/ *n* [U] practice of eating one's own kind 同类相食. **can·nib·al·istic** /ˌkænɪbəˈlɪstɪk; ˌkænəbḷˋɪstɪk/ *adj* of or like cannibals (似)食人者的, 同类相食者的.

can·ni·bal·ize, -ise /ˈkænɪbəlaɪz; ˋkænəbḷ,aɪz/ *v* [Tn] use (a machine, vehicle, etc) to provide spare parts for others 用(机器、车辆等)为其他同类(机器、车辆等)提供备用零件: *cannibalize an old radio to repair one's record-player* 把旧收音机的零件拆下去修配电唱机. **can·ni·bal·iza·tion, -isation** /ˌkænɪbəlaɪˈzeɪʃn; *US* -lɪˈz-; ˌkænəbələˋzeʃən/ *n* [U].

can·non /ˈkænən; ˋkænən/ *n* [C] **1** (*pl* unchanged 复数不变) old type of large heavy gun firing solid metal balls (发射实心金属炮弹的旧式)大炮. **2** (*pl* unchanged 复数不变) automatic gun firing shells (SHELL 3a) from an aircraft, a tank, etc (飞行器、坦克等的)机关炮: *two 20-millimetre cannon* 两个20毫米口径的机关炮. **3** (in billiards) shot in which the player's ball hits two other balls one after the other (台球戏中)主球连撞二球.

▷ **can·non** *v* (phr v) **cannon against/into sb/sth** collide heavily with sb/sth 与某人[某事物]猛撞.

□ ˈ**cannon-ball** *n* large metal ball fired from a cannon (旧式大炮发射的巨大的金属)炮弹.

ˈ**cannon-fodder** *n* [U] soldiers regarded only as material that is expendable in war 炮灰.

can·non·ade /ˌkænəˈneɪd; ˌkænənˋed/ *n* continuous firing of heavy guns 连续炮轰.

can·not /ˈkænɒt; ˋkænɑt/ = CAN NOT (CAN[2]).

canny /ˈkænɪ; ˋkænɪ/ *adj* (**-ier, -iest**) shrewd and careful, esp in business matters 精明仔细的(尤指在生意上). ▷ **can·nily** *adv*. **can·ni·ness** *n* [U].

canoe 独木舟

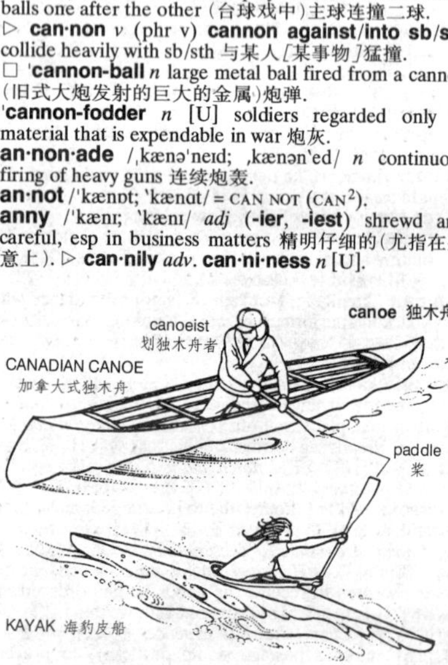

ca·noe /kəˈnuː; kəˋnu/ *n* **1** light narrow boat moved by one or more paddles 狭窄的轻舟; 独木舟. ⇨illus 见插图. **2** (idm 习语) **paddle one's own canoe** ⇨ PADDLE[1].

▷ **ca·noe** *v* (*pt, pp* **canoed**, *pres p* **canoeing**) [I] (usu 通常作 **go canoeing**) travel in a canoe 乘独木舟; 划独木舟.

ca·noe·ist /kəˈnuːɪst; kəˋnuɪst/ *n* person who paddles a canoe 划独木舟者. ⇨illus 见插图.

canon[1] /ˈkænən; ˋkænən/ *n* **1** general rule, standard or principle by which sth is judged 总的规则、标准或原则: *This film offends against all the canons of good taste.* 这部影片违反了审美的一切准则. **2** (**a**) list of sacred books accepted as genuine 真经; 正经: *the canon of Holy Scripture* 《圣经》的真经. (**b**) set of writings, etc accepted as genuinely by a particular author (某作家的)真作: *the Shakespeare canon* 莎士比亚真本.

▷ **can·on·ical** /kəˈnɒnɪkl; kəˋnɑnɪkḷ/ *adj* **1** according to canon law 依照教规的. **2** included in the canon(2a) 被收入真经的. **3** standard; accepted 标准的; 认可的.

ca·non·icals *n* [pl] clothes worn by a priest during a church service (教士在布道时所穿的)法衣.

□ ˌ**canon ˈlaw** church law 教会法规.

canon[2] /ˈkænən; ˋkænən/ *n* priest with special duties in a cathedral 在大教堂中任职的教士: *The Rev Canon Arthur Brown* 阿瑟·布朗教士.

can·on·ize, -ise /ˈkænənaɪz; ˋkænənˌaɪz/ *v* [Tn] officially declare (sb) to be a saint(1a) 正式宣布(某人)为圣徒.

▷ **can·on·iza·tion, -isation** /ˌkænənaɪˈzeɪʃn; *US* -nɪˈz-; ˌkænənəˋzeʃən/ *n* [C, U] (instance of) canonizing or being canonized 正式宣布为圣徒.

can·opy /ˈkænəpɪ; ˋkænəpɪ/ *n* **1** hanging cover forming a shelter above a throne, bed, etc (宝座或床等上面的)华盖, 罩篷. **2** cover for the cockpit of an aircraft (飞行器上的)座舱罩. **3** (*fig* 比喻) any overhanging covering 任何悬于上空的覆盖物: *the grey canopy of the sky* 灰灰的天幕 ○ *a canopy of leaves*, eg in a forest 树冠层(如森林中的).

cant[1] /kænt; kænt/ *n* [U] **1** insincere talk, esp about religion or morality; hypocrisy 虚伪的话(尤指关于宗教或道德的话); 伪善. **2** specialized language of a particular group; jargon 某一团体的专用语; 行话; 术语: *thieves' cant* 盗贼的黑话 ○ [attrib 作定语] *a cant expression* 术语.

cant[2] /kænt; kænt/ *n* **1** sloping surface or position 倾斜的面或位置. **2** sudden movement that tilts or overturns sth 突然一动(可使某物倾斜或翻转).

▷ **cant** *v* [I, Ip, Tn, Tn·p] **~ (sth) (over)** (cause sth to) tilt, overturn (使某物)倾斜, 翻转: *cant a boat to repair it* 把船翻过来修理.

can't contracted form of CANNOT (CAN[2]) CANNOT 之缩约式.

Cantab /ˈkæntæb; ˋkæntæb/ *abbr* 缩写 = (esp in degree titles) of Cambridge (University) (Latin *Cantabrigiensis*) (尤用于学衔)剑桥(大学)的(源自拉丁文 *Cantabrigiensis*): *James Cox MA (Cantab)* 詹姆斯·考克斯文学硕士(剑桥大学). Cf 参看 OXON 2.

can·ta·loup (also **can·ta·loupe**) /ˈkæntəluːp; ˋkæntḷˌop/ *n* [C, U] type of melon 皱皮瓜: *a slice of cantaloup* 一片皱皮瓜.

can·tan·ker·ous /kænˈtæŋkərəs; kænˋtæŋkərəs/ *adj* bad-tempered; quarrelsome 脾气坏的; 好争吵的. ▷ **can·tan·ker·ously** *adv*.

can·tata /kænˈtɑːtə; kənˋtɑtə/ *n* short musical work, often on a religious subject, sung by soloists and usu a choir, accompanied by an orchestra 康塔塔(短小音乐作品, 常为宗教内容的, 由独唱演员演唱, 通常有合唱伴唱, 由管弦乐队伴奏): *Bach's cantatas* 巴赫的康塔塔. Cf 参看 ORATORIO.

can·teen /kænˈtiːn; kænˋtin/ *n* **1** place serving food and drink in a factory, an office, a school, etc (工厂、办事处、学校等的)食堂. **2** (*Brit*) case or box containing a set of knives, forks and spoons (一套刀、叉、勺的)餐具箱. **3** soldier's or camper's water-flask (士兵或露营者的)水壶.

can·ter /ˈkæntə(r); ˋkæntɚ/ *n* (usu *sing* 通常作单数) **1** (of a horse) movement that is faster than a trot but slower than a gallop (指马)慢跑, 小跑. **2** ride on a horse moving at this speed 骑马慢跑: *go for a canter* 去骑马慢跑. **3** (idm 习语) **at a canter** without effort; easily 不费力地; 容易地: *win a race at a canter* 在径赛中轻易获胜.

▷ **can·ter** *v* [I, Tn] (cause a horse to) move at a canter (使马)慢跑: *We cantered our horses for several miles.* 我们骑着马慢跑了几英里.

cant·icle /ˈkæntɪkl; ˋkæntɪkḷ/ *n* hymn or chant with words taken from the Bible 赞美歌(歌词取自《圣经》的短颂歌).

can·ti·lever /ˈkæntɪliːvə(r); ˋkæntḷˌivɚ/ *n* beam or bracket projecting from a wall to support eg a balcony (自墙壁伸出以支撑阳台等的)悬臂或支架.

□ ˈ**cantilever bridge** bridge made of two cantilevers projecting from piers and joined by girders 悬臂桥(由桥墩伸出两根悬臂, 中间以横梁连接而成).

canto /ˈkæntəʊ; ˋkænto/ *n* (*pl* **~s**) any of the main divisions of a long poem 长诗中的篇章.

can·ton /ˈkæntɒn; ˋkæntɑn/ *n* subdivision of a country, esp of Switzerland 州(尤指瑞士的).

Can·ton·ese /ˌkæntəˈniːz; ˌkæntənˋiz/ *n* [U] form of Chinese spoken in southern China and in Hong Kong 粤语; 广州话.

can·ton·ment /kænˈtuːnmənt; *US* -ˈtəʊn-; kænˋtonmənt/ *n* **1** place where soldiers live 士兵的驻地; 军营. **2** permanent military camp, esp in India 永久性兵站(尤指印度的).

can·tor /ˈkæntɔː(r); ˋkæntɚ/ *n* leader of the singing in a church or synagogue (教堂或犹太教会堂唱诗班的)领唱者.

can·vas /ˈkænvəs; ˋkænvəs/ *n* **1** [U] strong coarse cloth used for making tents, sails, etc and by artists for painting on 帆布; 画布: [attrib 作定语] *a canvas bag* 帆布袋. **2** [C] (**a**) piece of canvas for painting on 画布. (**b**) oil-painting 油画: *Turner's canvases* 特纳的油画. **3** (idm 习语) **under canvas** (**a**) (of soldiers, campers, etc) living in tents (指士兵、露营者等)在帐篷里居住: *sleep under canvas* 在帐篷里睡觉. (**b**) (of a ship) with sails spread (指船)张帆.

can·vass /ˈkænvəs; ˋkænvəs/ *v* **1** [I, Ipr, Tn, Tn·pr] **~ (sb) (for sth)** go around an area asking (people) for (political support) (在政治方面)游说: *go out canvassing (for votes)* (为拉选票)出去游说 ○ *The Labour candidate will canvass the constituency next month.* 工党候选人下月将向全体选民游说拉票. **2** [Tn] find out the opinions of (eg voters before an election) 调查(如选举前选民)的意见. **3** [Tn] suggest (an idea, etc) for discussion 为讨论而提出(意见等): *canvass the idea/notion/theory* 为讨论而提出意见[想法/主张].

▷ **can·vass** *n* act of canvassing 游说; 民意调查; 建议.

canvasser *n* person who canvasses 游说者; 民意调查者; 建议者.

can·yon /ˈkænjən; ˋkænjən/ *n* deep gorge, usu with a river flowing through it 峡谷(通常有河流经过其中): *the Grand Canyon, Arizona* (美国)亚利桑那州科罗拉多大峡谷.

cap /kæp; kæp/ *n* **1** soft head-covering without a brim but often with a peak, worn by men and boys (男用无帽檐但常有帽舌的)软帽, 便帽: *an old man in a flat cap* 戴着扁软帽的老人 ○ *British schoolboys sometimes wear caps*, ie as part of their school uniform. 英国男生有时候戴制服帽(校服的一部分). ⇨illus at HAT 见 HAT 之插图. **2** (esp in compounds 尤用以构成复合词) any close-fitting soft head-covering worn for various purposes 软帽: *a ˈbathing-cap* ○ *a ˈbaseball cap* ○ *a ˈnurse's cap* ○ *a ˈshower-cap*. **3** (*sport* 体 *esp Brit*) (**a**) cap given to sb who is chosen to play for a school, county, country, etc, esp at cricket, football or Rugby 选手帽(授予选拔出的校队、县队、国家队等运动员的帽子, 尤指在板球、足球或橄榄球项目中): *He's won three caps* (ie been chosen to play three times) *for England.* 他三次获授英格兰队选手帽(三次被选出参加比赛). (**b**) player chosen for such a team 被选出代表这种球队的选手. **4** academic head-dress with a flat top and a tassel (学位)方帽: *wear cap and gown on graduation day* 毕业典礼那天戴方帽、穿长袍. Cf 参看 MORTAR-BOARD (MORTAR[2]). **5** protective cover or top (for a pen, bottle, camera lens, etc) (钢笔、瓶子、照相机镜头等的)帽, 盖. **6** natural covering shaped like a cap 帽状的天然顶盖: *the polar ˈice-cap* 地极冰冠. **7** (also **Dutch ˈcap**) =

C

DIAPHRAGM 4. **8** (**a**) = PERCUSSION CAP (PERCUSSION). (**b**) small amount of explosive contained in a paper strip, for making a small explosion in a toy gun 砸炮(封于纸条中的少量火药, 用于玩具枪中产生轻微爆炸声). **9** (idm 习语) **cap in 'hand** humbly; in a servile manner 谦卑地; 谦恭地: *go cap in hand to sb, asking for money* 卑躬屈膝地去找某人要钱. **a feather in one's cap** ⇨ FEATHER[1]. **if the cap fits (,wear it)** if sb feels that a remark applies to him (he should act accordingly) 若某人觉得某话适用于他(, 他就知道应怎样做): *I have noticed some employees coming to work an hour late. I shall name no names, but if the cap fits....* 我已经注意到有些雇员上班迟到一个小时. 我不点出名字来, 但是要是你觉得我说的是你.... **set one's cap at sb** (*dated* 旧) (of a girl or woman) try to attract a man as a husband or lover (指女子)诱使某人娶她或做她的情人.

▷ **cap** *v* (**-pp-**) [Tn] **1** (**a**) put a cap(5) on (sth); cover the top or end of 加帽或盖儿于(某物)上; 覆盖: *mountains capped with snow/mist* 被雪覆盖着的[被雾笼罩着的]山峰. (**b**) = CROWN[2] 4. **2** follow (sth) with sth better, bigger, funnier, etc (以更好、更大、更有趣...的事物)继(某事物)之后: *cap a joke, story, etc* 说个更好的笑话、故事等. **3** (*sport* 体 *esp Brit*) award a cap to (a player); select (a player) for a national team 授予(运动员)选手帽; 选拔(运动员)入国家队: *He was capped 36 times for England.* 他已经36次获选入英格兰队. **4** (in Scottish universities) award a degree to (sb) (苏格兰大学)将学位授予(某人). **5** (idm 习语) **to cap it all** as a final piece of bad or good fortune 倒运或走运的最后一件事: *Last week he crashed his car, then he lost his job and now to cap it all his wife has left him!* 上星期他把汽车撞坏了, 接着又失去了工作, 更倒霉的是妻子也离他而去了!

cap·ab·il·ity /ˌkeɪpəˈbɪlətɪ; ˌkepəˋbɪlətɪ/ *n* **1** [U] **~ (to do sth/of doing sth)**; **~ (for sth)** quality of being able to do sth; ability 能做某事的素质; 能力: *You have the capability to do/of doing this job well.* 你有能力把这件工作做好. ○ *nuclear capability*, ie power or capacity to fight a nuclear war 核力量(进行核战争的力量或能力). **2 capabilities** [pl] undeveloped gift or quality 尚未发挥的天资或素质: *He has great capabilities as a writer.* 他极具作家潜质.

cap·able /ˈkeɪpəbl; ˋkepəbl̩/ *adj* **1** having (esp practical) ability; able; competent 有(尤指实际的)能力的; 有能力的; 能胜任的: *a very capable woman* 很能干的女子. **2** [pred 作表语] **~ of (doing) sth** (**a**) having the ability or power necessary for sth 有做某事所必要的能力或力量: *You are capable of better work than this.* 你能做得更好. ○ *Show me what you are capable of*, ie how well you can work. 让我看看你有什么本事. ○ *He is capable of running a mile in four minutes.* 他能用四分钟跑一英里. (**b**) have the character or inclination to do sth 有做某事的特长或倾向: *He's quite capable of lying* (ie It wouldn't be surprising if he lied) *to get out of trouble.* 他很会蒙混过关(他若撒谎亦不足为奇). **3** [pred 作表语] **~ of sth** (*fml* 文) (of situations, remarks, etc) open to or allowing sth (指情况、言语等)可以, 容许: *Our position is capable of improvement.* 我们的地位可以改善.

▷ **cap·ably** *adv* in a capable(1) way 有能力地: *handle a situation, manage a business capably* 有能力应付一情况、处理一事务.

ca·pa·cious /kəˈpeɪʃəs; kəˋpeʃəs/ *adj* (of things) that can hold much; roomy 容量大的; 宽敞的: *capacious pockets* 容量大的口袋 ○ *a capacious memory* 能记住很多事情的记忆力. ▷ **ca·pa·cious·ness** *n* [U].

ca·pa·city /kəˈpæsətɪ; kəˋpæsətɪ/ *n* **1** [U] ability to hold or contain sth 容纳某事物的能力: *a hall with a seating capacity of 2 000* 有2 000个座位的大厅 ○ *filled to capacity*, ie completely full 全满 ○ [attrib 作定语] *a capacity crowd*, ie one that fills a sports ground, etc 挤满的人群(挤满了运动场等地的). **2** [sing] power to produce sth 生产力: *factories working at full capacity* 全力生产的工厂. **3** [sing] **~ (for sth)** ability to produce, experience, understand or learn sth 生产、体会、理解或学习的能力: *She has an enormous capacity for hard work.* 她有苦干的巨大能力. ○ *Some people have a greater capacity for happiness than others.* 有的人享得起福, 有的人享不起福. ○ *This book is within the capacity of* (ie can be understood by) *younger readers.* 这本书年轻的读者也能看懂. **4** (idm 习语) **in one's capacity as sth** in a certain function or position 以某种身分或立场: *act in one's capacity as a po'lice officer/in one's po'lice capacity* 以警察的身分行事.

ca·par·ison /kəˈpærɪsn; kəˋpærəsn̩/ *n* (usu *pl* 通常作复数) (formerly) decorated covering for a horse, or for a horse and knight (旧时)装饰性的马衣或马与武士的盛装.

▷ **ca·par·ison** *v* [Tn] put caparisons on (a horse) 给(马)穿马衣.

cape[1] /keɪp; kep/ *n* loose sleeveless garment like a cloak but usu shorter 披肩; 短斗篷.

cape[2] /keɪp; kep/ *n* (*abbr* 缩写 **C**) **1** [C] (often in geographical names 常用于地理名称) piece of high land sticking out into the sea 海角; 岬: *Cape Horn* 合恩角. **2 the Cape** [sing] (in S Africa) the Cape of Good Hope; Cape Province (南非的)好望角, 好望角省.

□ **Cape 'Coloured** (in S Africa) person of mixed race (南非的)混血儿.

ca·per[1] /ˈkeɪpə(r); ˋkepɚ/ *v* [I, Ip] **~ (about)** jump or run about playfully 蹦蹦跳跳; 跑来跑去: *lambs capering (about) in the fields* 在田野上蹦蹦跳跳的小羊羔.

▷ **ca·per** *n* **1** jump; leap 跳; 跳跃. **2** (*infml* 口) (**a**) mischievous act; prank 恶作剧; 戏弄. (**b**) dishonest or criminal scheme 不诚实的或罪恶的勾当: *What's your little caper?* 你搞什么名堂? **3** (idm 习语) **cut a 'caper** jump about happily; act foolishly 雀跃; 愚蠢地行事.

ca·per[2] /ˈkeɪpə(r); ˋkepɚ/ *n* (**a**) prickly shrub 续随子(有刺灌木). (**b**) (usu *pl* 通常作复数) one of its buds pickled for use in sauces, etc 腌泡的续随子花蕾(用以制续随子酱等).

ca·per·cail·lie (also **ca·per·cail·zie**) /ˌkæpəˈkeɪlɪ; ˌkæpɚˋkelɪ/ *n* type of large grouse 松鸡.

ca·pil·lary /kəˈpɪlərɪ; *US* ˈkæpɪlerɪ; ˋkæpl̩ˌɛrɪ/ *n* any of the very narrow blood vessels connecting arteries and veins in the body 毛细管; 毛细血管.

□ **caˌpillary a'ttraction** force by which a liquid is drawn along a very narrow tube 毛细(管)吸引; 毛细吸力.

cap·ital[1] /ˈkæpɪtl; ˋkæpətl̩/ *n* **1** town or city that is the centre of government of a country, state or province 首都; 首府; 省会: *Cairo is the capital of Egypt.* 开罗是埃及的首都. ○ [attrib 作定语] *London, Paris and Rome are capital cities.* 伦敦、巴黎、罗马都是国都. **2** (also **capital letter**) letter of the form and size used to begin a name or a sentence 大写字母: *In this sentence, the word BIG is in capitals.* 本句中BIG一字用的是大写字母. ○ *Write your name in block capitals, please.* 姓名请用大写. **3** head or top part of a column 柱头; 柱顶. ⇨ illus at COLUMN 见COLUMN之插图.

▷ **cap·ital** *adj* [usu attrib 通常作定语] **1** involving punishment by death 死刑的: *a capital offence* 死罪 ○ *capital punishment*, ie the death penalty 死刑. **2** (of letters) having the form and size used to begin a name or a sentence (指字母)大写的: *London is spelt with a capital 'L'.* London一字中L是大写的. **3** very serious 极严重的: *a capital error* 大错. **4** (*dated* 旧 *Brit*) excellent 极好的: *What a capital idea!* 真是一个好主意!

cap·ital[2] /ˈkæpɪtl; ˋkæpətl̩/ *n* **1** [U] wealth or property that may be used to produce more wealth 资本; 资金. **2** [sing] sum of money used to start a business 本钱: *set up a business with a starting capital of £100 000* 先拿100 000英镑当本钱创业. **3** [U] accumulated material wealth owned by a person or a business 个人或企业积累的物质财富: [attrib 作定语] *capital assets* 资本资产. **4** [U] capitalists or their interests 资本家; 资方: *capital and labour* 资方与劳方. **5** (idm 习语) **make capital (out) of sth** use (a situation, etc) to one's own advantage 利用: *The Opposition parties made (political) capital out of the disagreements within the Cabinet.* 反对党利用内阁的分歧而捞取(政治)资本.

□ **capital ex'penditure** money spent by a business on buildings, equipment, etc 基本建设费用.

capital 'gain profits made from the sale of investments or property 资本收益. **capital 'gains tax** tax on such profits 资本收益税.

capital 'goods goods (eg ships, railways, machinery,

etc) used in producing other goods 资本货物(用以生产其他货物的货物，如船只、铁路、机器等). Cf 参看 CONSUMER GOODS (CONSUMER).

capital in'tensive (of industrial processes) needing the investment of very large sums of money (as contrasted with a very large number of workers) (指工业生产过程)资本密集的. Cf 参看 LABOUR INTENSIVE (LABOUR[1]).

capital 'levy general tax on private wealth or property 资产税. Cf 参看 INCOME TAX (INCOME).

capital 'sum single payment of money, eg to an insured person 最高金额(如付予投保人的赔偿金额).

capital 'transfer transfer of money or property from one person to another, eg by inheritance 资本转移(如继承财物).

capital 'transfer tax tax on such a transfer 资本转移税.

cap·it·al·ism /ˈkæpɪtəlɪzəm; ˋkæpətl̩ˌɪzəm/ *n* [U] economic system in which a country's trade and industry are controlled by private owners for profit, rather than by the State 资本主义.

▷ **cap·it·al·ist** *n* **1** person who owns or controls much capital[2](1); rich person 资本家; 富人. **2** person who supports capitalism 资本主义者. — *adj* based on or supporting capitalism 资本主义的: *a capitalist economy* 资本主义经济. **capitalistic** /ˌkæpɪtəˈlɪstɪk; ˌkæpɪtl̩ˋɪstɪk/ *adj*. Cf 参看 SOCIALISM.

cap·it·al·ize, -ise /ˈkæpɪtəlaɪz; ˋkæpətl̩ˌaɪz/ *v* [Tn] **1** write or print (sth) with capital[1](2) letters 用大写字母书写或印刷. **2** convert (sth) into, use as or provide with capital[2](1) 将(某事物)转作资本、用作资本或资本化. **3** (phr v) **capitalize on sth** use sth to one's own advantage; profit from sth 利用某事物; 从某事物中获利: *capitalize on the mistakes made by a rival firm* 从对方公司的错误中获益. ▷ **cap·it·al·iza·tion, -isation** /ˌkæpɪtəlaɪˈzeɪʃn; *US* -lɪˈzeɪʃn; ˌkæpətl̩əˋzeʃən/ *n* [U].

cap·ita·tion /ˌkæpɪˈteɪʃn; ˌkæpəˋteʃən/ *n* tax, fee or grant of an equal amount for each person 人头税; 按人收费; 按人计算的补助费: [attrib 作定语] *a capiˈtation allowance* 按人计算的津贴.

Cap·itol /ˈkæpɪtl; ˋkæpətl̩/ *n* **the Capitol** [sing] building in Washington in which the United States Congress meets 美国国会大厦.

ca·pit·ulate /kəˈpɪtʃʊleɪt; kəˋpɪtʃəˌlet/ *v* [I, Ipr] ~ **(to sb)** surrender (to sb), esp on agreed conditions (向某人)投降(尤指根据商定的条件).

▷ **ca·pit·ula·tion** /kəˌpɪtʃʊˈleɪʃn; kəˌpɪtʃəˋleʃən/ *n* [C, U] (act of) capitulating (尤指根据商定条件的)投降.

ca·pon /ˈkeɪpɒn, ˈkeɪpən; ˋkepɑn/ *n* domestic cock[1](1) castrated and fattened for eating (养肥以供食用的)阉鸡.

cap·pucci·no /kæpʊˈtʃiːnəʊ; ˌkæpəˋtʃino/ *n* (*pl* ~**s**) (*Italian* 意) espresso coffee with hot milk added 卡普契诺咖啡(蒸汽加压所煮的咖啡, 并加热奶).

ca·price /kəˈpriːs; kəˋpris/ *n* **1 (a)** [C] sudden change in attitude or behaviour with no obvious cause; whim 态度或行为无明显缘故的突然改变; 突如其来的念头. **(b)** [U] tendency to such changes 有上述突然改变的倾向. **2** [C] short lively piece of music in an irregular style 短小的随想曲.

ca·pri·cious /kəˈprɪʃəs; kəˋprɪʃəs/ *adj* characterized by sudden changes in attitude or behaviour; unpredictable; impulsive (态度或行为)反复无常的, 变幻莫测的, 任性的: *Romantic heroines are often capricious.* 浪漫的女主人公往往难以捉摸. ○ (*fig* 比喻) *a capricious climate*, ie one that is always changing 多变的气候. ▷ **ca·pri·ciously** *adv*. **ca·pri·cious·ness** *n* [U].

Cap·ri·corn /ˈkæprɪkɔːn; ˋkæprɪˌkɔrn/ *n* **1** the tenth sign of the zodiac, the Goat 摩羯宫(黄道第十宫); 山羊座. **2** [C] person born under the influence of this sign 属摩羯宫星座的人. ⇨Usage at ZODIAC 用法见 ZODIAC. ⇨ illus at ZODIAC 见 ZODIAC 之插图.

cap·sicum /ˈkæpsɪkəm; ˋkæpsɪkəm/ *n* **(a)** tropical plant with seed-pods containing hot-tasting seeds 番椒, 辣椒(植物). **(b)** one of these pods used as a vegetable 番椒, 辣椒(蔬菜). Cf 参看 PEPPER 2.

cap·size /kæpˈsaɪz; *US* ˈkæpsaɪz; ˋkæpˌsaɪz/ *v* [I, Tn] (cause a boat to) overturn or be overturned (使船)翻, 倾覆: *The boat capsized in heavy seas.* 船在大海中倾覆了.

cap·stan /ˈkæpstən; ˋkæpstən/ *n* thick revolving post or cylinder round which a rope or cable is wound, eg to raise a ship's anchor 绞盘; 起锚机.

cap·sule /ˈkæpsjuːl; *US* ˈkæpsl; ˋkæpsl̩/ *n* **1** seed-case of a plant that opens when the seeds are ripe 蒴; 荚. **2** small soluble case containing a dose of medicine and swallowed with it (装一剂药物的)胶囊. **3** detachable compartment for men or instruments in a spacecraft 航天舱; 太空舱.

Capt *abbr* 缩写 = Captain: *Capt (Terence) Jones* (特伦斯·)琼斯上尉.

cap·tain /ˈkæptɪn; ˋkæptɪn/ *n* **1** person in charge of a ship or civil aircraft 船长; 舰长; (民航机的)机长. **2 (a)** officer in the British Army between the ranks of lieutenant and major (英)陆军上尉. ⇨App 9 见附录 9. **(b)** officer in the British Navy between the ranks of commander and admiral (英)海军上校. ⇨App 9 见附录 9. **3** person given authority over a group or team; leader 队长; 组长: *He was (the) captain of the football team for five years.* 他当了五年的足球队长. **4** (idm 习语) **a captain of 'industry** person who manages a large industrial company 工业巨头.

▷ **cap·tain** *v* [Tn] be captain of (a football team, etc) 担任(足球队等的)队长: *Who is captaining the side today?* 今天这队的队长是谁?

cap·taincy /ˈkæptɪnsɪ; ˋkæptənsɪ/ *n* **(a)** [C, U] position of captain 船长、舰长、陆军上尉、海军上校或队长等的职位: *take over the captaincy* 接任船长一职 ○ *Captaincy suits him.* 他适合当舰长. **(b)** [C] period of being captain 船长、舰长、陆军上尉、海军上校或队长等的任期: *during her captaincy* 在她担任舰长期间. **(c)** [U] quality of a captain's actions 船长、舰长、陆军上尉、海军上校或队长等的能力: *showing fine captaincy* 表现出任职船长的才干.

cap·tion /ˈkæpʃn; ˋkæpʃən/ *n* **1** short title or heading of an article in a magazine, etc (杂志等文章中的)标题, 题目. **2** words printed with an illustration or a photograph in order to describe or explain it (附于插图、照片上的)说明文字. **3** words shown on a cinema or television screen, eg to establish the scene of a story (eg 'New York 1981') (电影片或电视上的)字幕(如'纽约 1981 年').

cap·tious /ˈkæpʃəs; ˋkæpʃəs/ *adj* (*fml* 文) fond of criticizing or raising objections about unimportant matters; quibbling 好吹毛求疵的; 好挑剔的. ▷ **cap·tiously** *adv*. **cap·tious·ness** *n* [U].

cap·tiv·ate /ˈkæptɪveɪt; ˋkæptəˌvet/ *v* [Tn] fascinate (sb); charm; enchant 迷住(某人); 迷惑: *He was captivated by her beauty.* 他被她的美色迷住了.

▷ **cap·tiv·at·ing** *adj* fascinating; charming 有迷惑力的; 使人神魂颠倒的: *a captivating woman* 迷人的女子 ○ *He found her captivating.* 他觉得她很迷人.

cap·tiva·tion /ˌkæptɪˈveɪʃn; ˌkæptəˋveʃən/ *n* [U].

cap·tive /ˈkæptɪv; ˋkæptɪv/ *adj* **1** [esp attrib 尤作定语] held as a prisoner; unable to escape 被俘虏的; 逃不掉的: *a captive bird* 被捕获的鸟. **2** (idm 习语) **hold/take sb 'captive/'prisoner** keep or take sb as a prisoner 囚禁或俘虏某人: *They were held captive by masked gunmen.* 他们被蒙面的持枪歹徒劫持了.

▷ **cap·tive** *n* captive person or animal 被捉住的人或动物: *Three of the captives tried to escape.* 捉住的有三个企图逃走.

cap·tiv·ity /kæpˈtɪvətɪ; kæpˋtɪvətɪ/ *n* [U] state of being captive 被俘; 被捕; 囚禁: *He was held in captivity for three years.* 他被囚禁三年. ○ *Wild animals don't breed well in captivity.* 圈着的野生动物繁殖不好.

□ **captive 'audience** audience with little or no freedom to go away and therefore easily persuaded to listen or watch 被动听众, 被动观众(无法轻易离开者, 故易受诱导): *Television advertisers can exploit a captive audience.* 电视广告商能利用被动观众.

captive bal'loon balloon held to the ground by a cable 系留气球(用绳索系在地面上的).

captor /ˈkæptə(r); ˋkæptɚ/ *n* person who captures a person or an animal 捕捉者; 捕获者: *The hostages were well treated by their captors.* 那些人质受到劫持者的善待.

cap·ture /ˈkæptʃə(r); ˋkæptʃɚ/ *v* [Tn] **1** take (sb/sth) as

C

a prisoner 俘获(某人[某物]): *capture an escaped convict* 捉拿逃犯 ○ (*fig* 比喻) *This advertisement will capture the attention of TV audiences.* 这广告将引起电视观众的注意. **2** take or win (sth) by force or skill 用武力或技巧夺取或赢得(某物): *capture a town* 占领城镇 ○ *capture one's opponent's queen*, ie in a game of chess 捉住对方的后(国际象棋中). **3** succeed in representing (sb/sth) in a picture, on film, etc 捕捉(画面或影片中的某人[某物]): *capture a baby's smile in a photograph* 拍摄到婴儿的微笑.
▷ **cap·ture** *n* **1** [U] capturing or being captured 捕捉或被捕捉: *the capture of a thief* 捕捉窃贼 ○ *He evaded capture for three days.* 他逃避追捕已三日. **2** [C] person or thing captured 被捕获的人或物; 俘虏; 战利品.

C

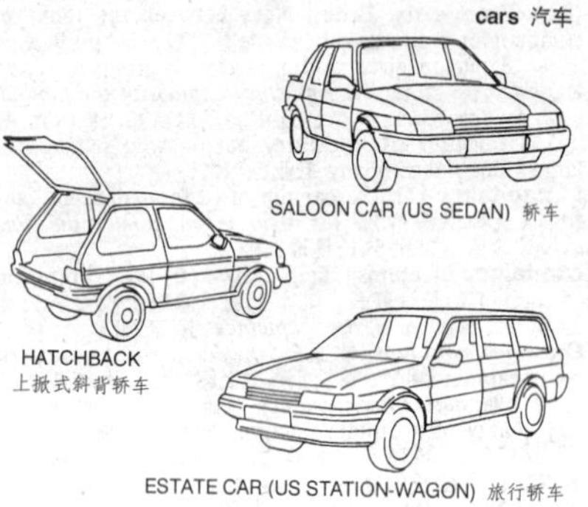

car /kɑː(r); kɑr/ *n* **1** (also **'motor car**, *esp US* **automobile**) motor vehicle with (usu four) wheels for carrying passengers 汽车: *buy a new car* 买新汽车 ○ *What kind of car do you have?* 你的汽车是什么样的? ○ *We're going (to London) by car.* 我们开车去(伦敦). ⇨illus at App 1 见附录1之插图, page xii. ⇨illus 见插图. **2** (in compound *ns* 用以构成复合名词) (**a**) railway carriage of a specified type (某类型的)火车车厢: *a dining-/sleeping-car*. (**b**) = CARRIAGE 2. (**c**) (*US*) any railway carriage or van 火车车厢: *a freight car.* **3** passenger compartment of an airship, a balloon, a cable railway or a lift (飞艇、气球、缆车或电梯的)载人舱室.
□ **'car-boot sale** (*esp Brit*) (*US* **garage sale**) outdoor sale at which people sell unwanted possessions, etc from the boots of their cars 汽车行李箱货物出售(将不想要的东西置于自己的汽车行李箱中出售).
'carfare *n* (*US*) money that one must pay to travel on a bus or streetcar (公共汽车或电车的)车费.
'car-ferry *n* sea or air ferry for carrying cars (eg across the English Channel) 载运汽车过海的渡轮或运输机(如渡英吉利海峡的); 汽车渡轮; 汽车运输机.
'car-park (*US* **parking-lot**) *n* (usu outdoor) area for parking cars (通常为露天的)汽车停车场: *a multi-storey car-park* 多层停车场.
'car-port *n* shelter for a car, consisting of a roof supported by posts (有棚架的)汽车间.
'carsick *adj* [usu pred 通常作表语] affected with nausea caused by the movement of a car 晕车: *He's feeling carsick.* 他觉得晕车. **'carsickness** *n* [U].

ca·rafe /kə'ræf; kə'ræf/ *n* **1** glass container in which wine or water are served at meals (餐桌上盛酒或水的)玻璃瓶. ⇨illus at BOTTLE 见 BOTTLE 之插图. **2** amount contained in this 一瓶的量: *I can't drink more than half a carafe.* 我顶多能喝半瓶.

cara·mel /'kærəmel; 'kærəml/ *n* **1** [U] burnt sugar used for colouring and flavouring food (食物着色或调味用的)焦糖. **2** [U, C] type of toffee tasting like this (含焦糖味的)太妃糖: *a piece of caramel* 一块焦糖味太妃糖. **3** [U] colour of caramel; light brown 焦糖色; 淡褐色.
▷ **cara·mel·ize, -ise** /'kærəməlaɪz; 'kærəmə,laɪz/ *v* [I, Tn] (cause sth to) turn into caramel (使某物)变成焦糖.

cara·pace /'kærəpeɪs; 'kærə,pes/ *n* shell on the back of a tortoise or crustacean (龟或其他甲壳类动物的)甲壳.

carat /'kærət; 'kærət/ *n* (*abbr* 缩写 **ct**) **1** unit of weight (200 milligrams) for precious stones 克拉(宝石重量单位, 等于200毫克). **2** (*US* **karat**) unit of measurement of the purity of gold (pure gold being 24 carats) 开(黄金纯度单位, 纯金为24开): *a 20-carat gold ring* 20开的金戒指 ○ *a ring of 20 carats* 20开的戒指.

cara·van /'kærəvæn; 'kærə,væn/ *n* **1** (*Brit*) (*US* **trailer**) large vehicle on wheels, equipped for living in and usu towed by a motor vehicle (可供居住的)拖车(通常由机动车拖行). **2** covered cart or wagon used for living in, and able to be pulled by a horse (供居住可用马拉的)篷车: *a gypsy caravan* 吉卜赛人的篷车. **3** group of people (eg merchants) travelling together across the desert (穿过沙漠地带的)旅行队(如商队).
▷ **cara·van** *v* (**-nn-**) [I] (usu 通常作 **go caravanning**) have a holiday in a caravan 乘拖车度假: *We're going caravanning in Spain this summer.* 我们今年夏天要乘拖车到西班牙度假.

ca·ra·van·serai /,kærə'vænsərɪ, -səraɪ; ,kærə'vænsərɪ, -sə,raɪ/ *n* (in some Eastern countries) inn with a large central courtyard where caravans (CARAVAN 3) can stay for the night (在东方某些国家中, 有大庭院可供沙漠旅行队过夜的)客店, 客栈.

ca·ra·way /'kærəweɪ; 'kærə,we/ *n* (**a**) [C] plant with spicy seeds that are used for flavouring bread, cakes, etc 葛缕子(植物, 籽味香, 用以为面包、糕饼等增味, 又名贳蒿). (**b**) [U] (also **'caraway seed**) these seeds used in cooking 葛缕子的籽(用于烹饪, 俗称贳蒿籽).

carb·ide /'kɑːbaɪd; 'kɑrbaɪd/ *n* compound of carbon, esp calcium carbide 碳化物; (尤指)碳化钙.

car·bine /'kɑːbaɪn; 'kɑrbaɪn/ *n* short light automatic rifle 卡宾枪.

car·bo·hyd·rate /,kɑːbəʊ'haɪdreɪt; ,kɑrbo'haɪdret/ *n* **1** [C, U] any of various types of organic compound, such as sugar and starch, containing carbon, hydrogen and oxygen 碳水化合物; 糖类. **2 carbohydrates** [pl] foods containing carbohydrate, considered to be fattening 淀粉质或糖类食物(可使身体发胖): *You eat too many carbohydrates!* 你吃淀粉质食物太多了!

car·bolic acid /kɑː,bɒlɪk 'æsɪd; kɑr'bɑlɪk 'æsɪd/ (also **phenol**) strong-smelling and powerful liquid used as an antiseptic and disinfectant 石碳酸, (苯)酚(味烈、药性强的防腐剂和消毒剂).

car·bon /'kɑːbən; 'kɑrbən/ *n* **1** [U] non-metallic chemical element that is present in all living matter and occurs in its pure form as diamond and graphite 碳. ⇨ App 10 见附录10. **2** [C] stick of carbon used in an electric arc lamp 炭精棒(用于电弧光灯). **3** [C] = CARBON PAPER. **4** [C] = CARBON COPY.
▷ **car·bon·ize, -ise** *v* [Tn] convert (sth) into carbon by burning 将(某物)烧成碳; 碳化. **car·bon·iza·tion, -isation** /,kɑːbənaɪ'zeɪʃn; *US* -nɪ'z-; ,kɑrbənɪ'zeʃən/ *n* [U].
□ **'carbon black** black powder made by partly burning oil, wood, etc, and used as a colouring or in the manufacture of rubber 碳黑(未完全燃烧的油、木材等的黑色粉末, 用于调色或橡胶生产).
,carbon 'copy 1 copy made with carbon paper 复写本; 副本: *make a carbon copy of a document* 用复写纸复写一文件. **2** (*fig* 比喻) exact copy or likeness 一模一样; 极相像: *She's a carbon copy of her sister.* 她跟她姐姐一模一样.
,carbon 'dating method of calculating the age of prehistoric objects by measuring the decay of radio-carbon in them 碳含量年代测定法.
,carbon di'oxide colourless odourless gas formed by the burning of carbon, or breathed out by animals from the lungs 二氧化碳.
,carbon mon'oxide poisonous gas formed when carbon burns incompletely, present eg in the exhaust fumes of petrol engines 一氧化碳.
'carbon paper (sheet of) thin paper coated with carbon or some other coloured substance and used between sheets of writing-paper for making copies 复写纸.

car·bon·ated /'kɑːbəneɪtɪd; 'kɑrbə,netɪd/ *adj* containing carbon dioxide; fizzy 含二氧化碳的; 发嘶嘶声的; 起泡的: *carbonated drinks* 含二氧化碳的饮料.

car·bonic acid /kɑːˌbɒnɪk ˈæsɪd; kɑrˋbɑnɪk ˋæsɪd/ weak acid made by dissolving carbon dioxide in water 碳酸.

car·bon·if·er·ous /ˌkɑːbəˈnɪfərəs; ˌkɑrbəˋnɪfərəs/ *adj* (*geology* 地质) **1** producing coal 产煤的: *carboniferous rocks* 产煤的岩层. **2 Carboniferous** of the geological period when coal deposits were formed 石炭纪的.

▷ **car·bon·if·er·ous** *n* the Carboniferous period 石炭纪.

Car·bor·un·dum /ˌkɑːbəˈrʌndəm; ˌkɑrbəˋrʌndəm/ *n* (*propr* 专利名) hard compound of carbon and silicon, used for polishing and grinding things 碳化硅; 金刚砂.

car·boy /ˈkɑːbɔɪ; ˋkɑrbɔɪ/ *n* large round glass or plastic bottle, usu enclosed in a protective framework, used for carrying dangerous liquids (大而圆的)玻璃瓶或塑料瓶(通常有护套, 用以运载危险液体).

car·buncle /ˈkɑːbʌŋkl; ˋkɑrbʌŋkl/ *n* **1** large inflamed swelling under the skin 痈. **2** bright-red gem with a rounded shape 红玉; 红宝石.

car·bur·et·tor /ˌkɑːbəˈretə (r); ˋkɑrbjəˌretɚ/ (*US* **car·bur·etor** /ˈkɑːrbəreɪtər; ˋkɑrbəˌretɚ/) *n* apparatus in a petrol engine for mixing fuel and air to make an explosive mixture 汽化器; 化油器. ⇨illus at App 1 见附录1之插图, page xii.

car·cass /ˈkɑːkəs; ˋkɑrkəs/ *n* **1** dead body of an animal, esp one prepared for cutting up as meat (动物的)尸体(尤指为切割供食用的): *vultures picking at a lion's carcass* 啄食狮子尸体的秃鹫. Cf 参看 CORPSE. **2** bones of a cooked bird 烹调过的禽鸟骨骼: *You might find a bit of meat left on the chicken carcass.* 鸡骨头上还可能有点儿肉呢. **3** (*joc or derog* 谑或贬) person's body (人的)身体: *Shift your carcass!* 别死呆在这儿, 躲开!

car·ci·no·gen /kɑːˈsɪnədʒen; kɑrˋsɪnədʒɛn/ *n* (*medical* 医) substance that produces cancer 致癌物.

▷ **car·ci·no·genic** /ˌkɑːsɪnəˈdʒenɪk; ˌkɑrsənəˋdʒɛnɪk/ *adj* (*medical* 医) producing cancer 致癌的.

car·cin·oma /ˌkɑːsɪˈnəʊmə; ˌkɑrsəˋnomə/ *n* (*pl* **~s** or **~ta** /-tə; -tə/) (*medical* 医) cancerous growth 癌.

card[1] /kɑːd; kɑrd/ *n* **1** [U] thick stiff paper or thin pasteboard 厚纸片; 薄纸板. **2** [C] piece of this for writing or printing on, used to identify a person or to record information or as proof of membership 卡片: *an identity card* 身分证 ○ *a record card* 记录卡 ○ *a membership card* 会员卡. **3** [C] piece of this with a picture on it, for sending greetings, messages, etc 贺卡; 慰问卡; 明信片: *a Christmas/birthday card* 圣诞[生日]卡 ○ *a get-well card*, ie one sent to sb who is unwell 康复祝卡 ○ *David sent us a card* (ie a postcard) *from Spain.* 大卫从西班牙给我们寄来一张明信片. **4** [C] = ˈPLAYING-CARD: *a pack of cards* 一副纸牌. **5 cards** [pl] games played with a set of playing-cards; card-playing 纸牌游戏: *win/lose at cards* 纸牌戏中赢[输] ○ *Let's play cards.* 咱们玩纸牌吧. **6** [C] programme of events at a race-meeting, etc (赛马、赛跑等比赛的)节目单, 项目单. **7** [C] (*dated infml* 旧, 口) odd or amusing person 怪人; 有趣的人: *Bertie's quite a card.* 伯蒂真是个怪人. **8** (idm 习语) **one's best/strongest ˈcard** one's strongest or most effective argument 某人的王牌、绝招或最强有力的论据. **(have) a card up one's sleeve** sth secret held in reserve until needed 锦囊妙计. **get one's ˈcards/give sb his ˈcards** (*infml* 口) be dismissed/dismiss sb from a job 开除; 解雇. **have the cards/odds stacked aˈgainst one** ⇨ STACK. **hold/keep one's cards ˌclose to one's ˈchest** be secretive about one's intentions 秘而不宣; 不露声色. **a house of cards** ⇨ HOUSE. **lay/put one's ˈcards on the table** be honest and open about one's resources and intentions 摊牌; 将实力与意图公开: *We can only reach agreement if we both put our cards on the table.* 我们双方只有摊开来说才能达成协议. **make a ˈcard** (in card-games) win a trick with a particular card (纸牌戏中)以一牌赢一墩. **on the cards** (*infml* 口) likely or possible 多半; 可能的: *An early general election is certainly on the cards.* 早日举行大选确有可能. **play one's ˈcards well, right, etc** act in the most effective way to achieve sth 做事精明; 处理得当: *You could end up running this company if you play your cards right.* 你要是处理得当, 到头来这个公司能归你掌管. **show one's hand/cards** ⇨ SHOW[2].

□ ˈ**card-carrying member** registered member of a political party, trade union, etc 正式的党员、工会会员等: *a card-carrying member of the Communist party* 共产党正式党员.

ˈ**card-game** *n* game using playing-cards 纸牌游戏: *Bridge, poker and whist are card-games.* 桥牌、扑克和惠斯特都是纸牌游戏.

ˈ**card index** = INDEX 1b.

ˈ**card-sharp** (also ˈ**card-sharper**) *n* person who earns a living by cheating at card-games 以纸牌骗赌为生的人.

ˈ**card-table** *n* (esp folding) table for playing cards on (尤指折叠的)纸牌桌.

ˈ**card vote** = BLOCK VOTE (BLOCK[1]).

card[2] /kɑːd; kɑrd/ *n* wire brush or toothed instrument for cleaning or combing wool (清理或梳理毛的)硬刷, 梳子.

▷ **card** *v* [Tn] clean or comb (wool) with this (用硬刷或梳子)刷, 梳(毛).

car·da·mom /ˈkɑːdəməm; ˋkɑrdəməm/ *n* **(a)** [C] E Indian plant 小豆蔻(东印度植物). **(b)** [U] its seeds used as a spice 小豆蔻的子(用以调味).

card·board /ˈkɑːdbɔːd; ˋkɑrdˌbɔrd/ *n* [U] **1** thick stiff type of paper or pasteboard used for making boxes, binding books, etc 硬纸板(用以制盒子、装订书籍等): [attrib 作定语] *a cardboard box* 纸箱; 纸盒. **2** [attrib 作定语] (*fig* 比喻) without real substance or worth 无实质的; 无价值的: *a cardboard figure, character, dictator* 有名无实的人物、角色、独裁者.

car·diac /ˈkɑːdɪæk; ˋkɑrdɪˌæk/ *adj* of or relating to the heart or heart disease 心脏的; 心脏病的: *cardiac muscles, disease, patients* 心肌、心脏病、心脏病患者 ○ *cardiac arrest*, ie temporary or permanent stopping of the heartbeat 心跳停止.

car·di·gan /ˈkɑːdɪgən; ˋkɑrdɪgən/ *n* knitted woollen jacket, usu with no collar and with buttons at the front 毛衣(通常指无领有扣前对襟的).

car·dinal[1] /ˈkɑːdɪnl; ˋkɑrdn̩əl/ *adj* [usu attrib 通常作定语] most important; chief; fundamental 最重要的; 主要的; 基本的: *cardinal sins, errors, virtues, etc* 大罪、大错、大德.

▷ **car·dinal** *n* (also ˌ**cardinal** ˈ**number**) whole number representing quantity, eg 1, 2, 3, etc 基数(如1、2、3等). Cf 参看 ORDINAL. ⇨App 4 见附录4.

□ ˌ**cardinal** ˈ**points** the four main points of the compass, ie North, South, East and West 基本方位(罗盘上的东南西北等四个主要方位).

car·dinal[2] /ˈkɑːdɪnl; ˋkɑrdn̩əl/ *adj, n* [U] (of a) deep red colour 深红色(的).

car·dinal[3] /ˈkɑːdɪnl; ˋkɑrdn̩əl/ *n* any of a group of senior Roman Catholic priests who elect the Pope 红衣主教; 枢机主教.

cardi(o)- *comb form* 构词成分 of the heart 心脏的: *cardiogram* ○ *cardiologist*.

car·di·ology /ˌkɑːdɪˈɒlədʒɪ; ˌkɑrdiˋɑlədʒɪ/ *n* [U] branch of medicine concerned with the heart and its diseases 心脏病学. ▷ **car·di·olo·gist** /-dʒɪst; -dʒɪst/ *n*.

care[1] /keə(r); kɛr/ *n* **1** [U] **~ (over sth/in doing sth)** **(a)** serious attention or thought 密切的注意; 审慎的思索: *She arranged the flowers with great care.* 她仔细地插花. ○ *You should take more care over your work.* 你对工作应该更认真些. **(b)** caution to avoid damage or loss 小心; 谨慎: *Care is needed when crossing the road.* 过马路时要小心. ○ *Fragile — handle with care*, eg as a warning on a container holding glass. 易碎——小心轻放(如容器内有玻璃的警告语). **2** [U] **~ (for sb)** sympathetic concern 关怀; 关心: *a mother's care for her children* 母亲对孩子的关怀 ○ *Old people need loving care and attention.* 老人需要爱护和照顾. **3** **(a)** [U] worry; anxiety; troubled state of mind 忧虑; 担心; 操心; 烦恼: *free from care* 无忧无虑. **(b)** [C esp *pl* 尤作复数] cause of or reason for worry 忧虑的起因或缘故: *weighed down by the cares of a demanding job* 被费力的工作压垮 ○ *not have a care in the world*, ie have no worries or responsibilities 无尘世之忧(无牵无挂). **4** (idm 习语) **care of sb** (*abbr* 缩写 **c/o**) (esp written on envelopes) at the address of sb (尤指书写于信封上的字样)由某人转交: *Write to him care of his solicitor.* 写给他的信件由律师转交. **have a ˈcare** (*dated* 旧) be more careful 更当心些. **in the care of sb** in sb's charge; under sb's supervision 由某人负责; 由某人照管: *in the care of a doctor* 由医生照料 ○ *They left the child in a friend's care.* 他们把孩子交给朋友照看. **take care (that.../to do sth)** be careful or cautious 当心; 小心: *Take care (that) you don't drink too much/not to drink too much.* 当心别喝多了. ○ *Good bye, and take care!* 再见, 多保重! **take care of oneself/sb/sth (a)** make sure that one/sb is safe and well; look after oneself/sb 照看; 照料; 照顾: *My sister is taking care of the children while we're away.* 我们不在的时候, 由我妹妹照看孩子. ○ *He's old enough to take care of himself.* 他大了, 能照顾自己了. **(b)** be responsible for sb/sth; deal with sb/sth 负责某人[某事]; 处理某人[某事]: *Mr Smith takes care of marketing and publicity.* 史密斯先生负责产品的销售与推广. ○ *Her secretary took care of all her appointments.* 她的秘书处理她的一切约会. ⇨ Usage at CARE[2] 用法见 CARE[2]. **take/put sb into/put sb in 'care** put (esp a child) in a home owned by a local authority(2) for special treatment 把(尤指儿童)交给地方当局的福利院照顾: *The social worker advised them to put their handicapped child into care.* 社会工作者建议他们将其残疾儿送到福利院去.

□ **'carefree** *adj* without responsibilities or worries; cheerful 无忧无虑的; 逍遥自在的; 快乐的: *young and carefree* 年幼而无忧的.

'careworn *adj* showing signs of much worry 忧心忡忡的; 操心的: *an old and careworn face* 苍老而忧伤的面孔.

care[2] /keə(r); kɛr/ *v* **1** [I, Ipr, Tw] **~ (about sth)** be worried, concerned or interested 忧虑; 关心; 惦念: *He failed the examination but he didn't seem to care.* 他考试不及格却似乎并不在乎. ○ *Don't you care about this country's future?* 难道你不为国家前途担忧吗? ○ *I don't think she cares (about) what happens to her children.* 我认为她并不关心她孩子的事. ○ *All she cares about is her social life.* 她关心的只是她的社交活动. ⇨Usage 见所附用法. **2** [Ipr, It] **~ for sth** (in negative or interrogative sentences, esp with *would* 用于否定句或疑问句, 尤与would连用) be willing or agree (to do sth); wish or like (to do sth) 愿意或同意(做某事); 希望或喜欢(做某事): *Would you care for a drink?* 你愿意喝点儿酒吗? ○ *Would you care to go for a walk?* 你愿意散散步吗? ⇨Usage at WANT[1] 用法见 WANT[1]. **3** (idm 习语) **for all one/sb cares** considering how little one/sb cares 自己[某人]漠不关心: *I might as well be dead for all he cares.* 我即使死了他也毫不关心. **not care 'less** (*infml* 口) be completely uninterested or unmoved by sth 对某事完全不感兴趣或无动于衷: *I couldn't care less who wins the match.* 我才不管这场比赛谁胜呢. **who 'cares?** (*infml* 口) nobody cares; I don't care 无人关心; 我不管: *'Who do you think will be the next Prime Minister?' 'Who cares?'* '你认为下届首相会是谁呢?' '谁管那个?' **4** (phr v) **care for sb (a)** like or love sb 喜欢或爱某人: *He cares for her deeply.* 他深深地爱着她. **(b)** be responsible for sb; look after sb; take care of sb 对某人负责; 照看某人; 照顾某人: *care for the sick* 照看病人 ○ *Who will care for him if his wife dies?* 假若他妻子死了, 谁照顾他? **care for sb/sth** (in negative or interrogative sentences 用于否定句或疑问句) have a taste or liking for sb/sth 对某人[某事物]爱好或喜爱: *I don't care much for opera.* 我不太喜欢歌剧. ○ *I like him but I don't care for her.* 我喜欢他, 却不太喜欢她.

▷ **car·ing** /'keərɪŋ; 'kɛrɪŋ/ *adj* [esp attrib 尤作定语] showing or feeling care[1](2) 表示或感到关怀或关心的: *caring parents* 有责任心的父母 ○ *Children need a caring environment.* 儿童需要一个受关怀的环境.

NOTE ON USAGE 用法: **1** Both **take care of** (somebody or something) and **care for** (someone) can mean 'look after' ☆ **take care of**(某人或某事物)和**care for**(某人)均可指'照看': *She takes great care of her children.* 她精心照看孩子. ○ *He's caring for his elderly parents.* 他正照顾着年迈的父母. **2 Care for** can also mean 'like' or 'love' ☆ **care for** 还可意为'喜欢'或'爱': *I'm fond of her but I don't care for her husband.* 我喜欢她, 但不喜欢她丈夫. **3 Care for** something and **care to do** something mean 'wish' or 'like' and are rather formal. ☆ **care for**某事物和**care to do**某事物意为'希望'或'喜欢', 均较庄重. They are mostly used with *would* in negative sentences and in questions 这两个词组在否定句和疑问句中多与would连用: *Would you care for a swim?* 你想去游泳吗? ○ *I wouldn't care to do her job.* 我不喜欢做她的工作. **4 Care (about)** (somebody or something) means 'be interested' or 'be concerned'. It is also mostly used in negative sentences and in questions ☆ **care (about)**(某人或某事物)意为'感兴趣'或'关心', 也多用于否定句和疑问句: *Don't you care about anybody?* 你难道谁也不关心吗? ○ *I don't care (about) what happens to him.* 我才不管他的事呢.

ca·reen /kə'ri:n; kə'rin/ *v* **1** [Tn] turn (a ship) on its side (esp for cleaning or repairing) 将(船)倾侧(尤指为清刷或修理). **2** [I] (of a ship) turn over or tilt (指船)倾侧, 倾斜. **3** [Ipr] (*US*) rush forward with a swaying or swerving motion 摇摇摆摆向前冲: *The driver lost control and the car careened down the hill.* 因司机失控, 那辆汽车就横冲直撞地冲下山去.

ca·reer /kə'rɪə(r); kə'rɪr/ *n* **1** [C] profession or occupation with opportunities for advancement or promotion 职业; 事业; 生涯: *a career in accountancy, journalism, politics, etc* 会计、新闻工作、政治等生涯 ○ *She chose an academic career.* 她选择了学术界职业. ○ [attrib 作定语] *a career diplomat*, ie a professional one 职业外交家. **2** [C] progress through life; development of a political party, etc 生命的历程; 政党等的发展: *look back on a successful career* 对成功经历的回顾. **3** [U] quick or violent forward movement 迅速的前进; 猛冲: *in full career*, ie at full speed 全速前进 ○ *stop sb in mid career*, ie as he is rushing along 在他飞奔时止住他.

▷ **ca·reer** *v* [Ipr, Ip] move about quickly and often dangerously 猛冲(常为危险地): *careering down the road on a bicycle* 骑着自行车沿路飞奔而去 ○ *The car careered off the road into a ditch.* 汽车冲出路面, 陷进沟里.

ca·reer·ist /kə'rɪərɪst; kə'rɪrɪst/ *n* (*often derog* 常作贬义) person who is keen to advance his or her career by any possible means 不择手段向上爬的人; 野心家.

□ **ca'reer girl** (also **ca'reer woman**) (*esp sexist or derog* 尤含性别偏见或贬义) woman who is more interested in a professional career than in eg getting married and having children (视事业重于结婚生子等的)职业妇女.

care·ful /'keəfl; 'kɛrfəl/ *adj* **1** [pred 作表语] **~ (about/of/with sth); ~ (about/in) doing sth** taking care; cautious 小心; 当心; 警惕: *Be careful not to/that you don't hurt her feelings.* 当心别伤了她的感情. ○ *Be careful with the glasses*, ie Don't break them. 小心玻璃杯. ○ *Be careful of the dog; it sometimes bites people.* 留心那条狗, 有时候咬人. ○ *Be careful (about/of) what you say to him.* 对他说话可得小心. ○ *Be careful (about/in) crossing the road.* 过马路要留神. ○ *He's very careful with his money*, ie He doesn't spend it on unimportant things. 他用钱很仔细. **2 (a)** giving serious attention and thought; painstaking 聚精会神的; 深思熟虑的; 审慎的; 苦心的: *a careful worker* 一丝不苟的工作者. **(b)** done with care 精心的: *a careful piece of work* 精细的作品 ○ *a careful examination of the facts* 认真的核实. ▷ **care·fully** /'keəfəlɪ; 'kɛrfəlɪ/ *adv*: *Please listen carefully.* 请注意听. ○ *I always drive more carefully at night.* 我夜晚开车总是更加小心. **care·ful·ness** *n* [U].

care·less /'keəlɪs; 'kɛrlɪs/ *adj* **1 ~ (about/of sth)** not taking care; inattentive; thoughtless 不小心的; 不注意的; 粗心的: *a careless driver, worker, etc* 粗心大意的司机、工作者等 ○ *careless about spelling, money, one's appearance* 对拼写、金钱、仪表粗心大意的. **2** resulting from lack of care 由粗心引起的: *a careless error, mistake, etc* 疏忽性的错误. ▷ **care·lessly** *adv*. **care·less·ness** *n* [U].

caress /kə'res; kə'rɛs/ *n* loving touch or stroke 爱抚; 抚摩.

▷ **caress** *v* [Tn] touch or stroke (sb/sth) lovingly 爱抚或抚摩(某人[某物]): *She caressed his hand.* 她抚摩他的手.

caret /'kærət; 'kærət/ *n* symbol (∧) used to show where sth is to be inserted in written or printed material 脱字号, 加字号(∧).

care·taker /'keəteɪkə(r); 'kɛr,tekɚ/ *n* (*Brit*) (*US*

janitor) person who is employed to look after a house, building, etc 看门人(受雇看管房屋、建筑物等的人): *the school caretaker* 学校的门卫.

▷ **care·taker** *adj* [attrib 作定语] holding power temporarily; interim 暂时代理的; 临时的: *a caretaker administration, government, prime minister* 代理行政、看守政府、代首相.

cargo /ˈkɑːɡəʊ; ˋkɑrgo/ *n* (*pl* **~es**; *US* **~s**) [C, U] (load of) goods carried in a ship or aircraft (用船或飞行器运载的)货物(量): [attrib 作定语] *a cargo ship* 货船.

NOTE ON USAGE 用法: **1** Compare **cargo**, **freight** and **goods** ☆ 试比较 **cargo**、**freight**、**goods** 这三个词. These words are used before the names of vehicles that transport things rather than passengers. They can also refer to the objects transported 这三个词均用于货运的(而非客运的)运载工具名称之前, 也可指所运载的货物: *A cargo plane/ship/vessel carries cargo.* 货运飞机[货轮/货船]是运载货物的. ○ *A goods/(US) freight train carries goods/freight.* 货运列车是运载货物的. ('货运'一词, 英式英语用 goods, 美式英语用 freight.) ○ *A passenger train sometimes also has goods wagons/(US) freight cars.* 客运列车有时也有货车车厢. ('货车车厢'英式英语为 goods wagon, 美式英语为 freight car.) **2 Cargo** [C] can also indicate a particular load that is being transported ☆ **cargo** 还可指所运载货物的量: *A cargo of steel was lost at sea.* 有一货轮的钢材在海上遗失了. **3 Freight** [U] also indicates the action of transporting ☆ **freight** 也可指运输工作: *We can send it by air/sea freight.* 我们可以空运[海运]. ○ *What is the freight charge?* 运费多少钱? In this sense **freight** can also be a verb ☆ **freight** 意为运输时, 也可作动词: *You can freight your belongings by air or sea.* 你可把东西经空运或海运运去.

ca·ri·bou /ˈkærɪbuː; ˋkærəˌbu/ *n* (*pl* unchanged or **~s** 复数或不变或作 **caribous**) N American reindeer (北美洲产的)驯鹿: *a herd of fifty caribou(s)* 五十只驯鹿.

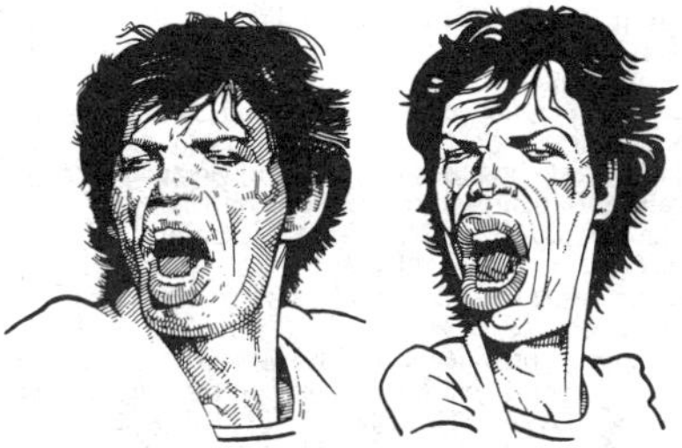

PORTRAIT 肖像 CARICATURE 漫画

ca·ri·ca·ture /ˈkærɪkətjʊə(r); ˋkærɪkəˌtjʊr/ *n* (**a**) [C] picture, description or imitation of sb/sth that exaggerates certain characteristics in order to amuse or ridicule 漫画; 夸张的描述或模仿: *draw a caricature of a politician* 画一政客的漫画 ○ *He does very funny caricatures of all his friends.* 他夸张地模仿了所有的朋友, 非常滑稽. ⇨ illus 见插图. (**b**) [U] art of doing this 漫画艺术; 滑稽或讽刺的模仿艺术.

▷ **ca·ri·ca·ture** *v* [Tn] make or give a caricature of (sb/sth) 用漫画表现或夸张描述、模仿(某人[某事物]). **ca·ri·ca·tur·ist** *n*.

car·ies /ˈkeəriːz; ˋkɛriz/ *n* [U] (*medical* 医) decay in bones or teeth 骨疡; 龋: *dental caries* 龋齿.

ca·ril·lon /kəˈrɪljən; *US* ˈkærəlɒn; ˋkærəˌlɑn/ *n* **1** set of bells sounded either from a keyboard or mechanically 编钟; 钟琴. **2** tune played on bells 钟乐曲.

ca·ri·ous /ˈkeərɪəs; ˋkɛrɪəs/ *adj* (*medical* 医) (esp of bones or teeth) decayed; affected with caries (尤指骨或齿)腐蚀的, 患骨疡的, 龋的.

Car·mel·ite /ˈkɑːməlaɪt; ˋkɑrmḷˌaɪt/ *n, adj* (friar or nun) belonging to a very strict religious order founded in 1155 加尔默罗会的(修士或修女).

car·mine /ˈkɑːmaɪn; ˋkɑrmaɪn/ *adj, n* [U] (of a) deep red colour 深红色(的); 洋红色(的).

carn·age /ˈkɑːnɪdʒ; ˋkɑrnɪdʒ/ *n* [U] killing of many people 大屠杀: *a scene of carnage*, eg a battlefield 大屠杀的场面(如战场).

car·nal /ˈkɑːnl; ˋkɑrnəl/ *adj* (*fml* 文) of the body; sexual or sensual 肉体的; 性的; 感官的: *carnal desires* 肉欲. ▷ **car·nally** /ˈkɑːnəlɪ; ˋkɑrnəlɪ/ *adv*.

car·na·tion /kɑːˈneɪʃn; kɑrˋneʃən/ *n* (**a**) garden plant with sweet-smelling white, pink or red flowers 麝香石竹; 康乃馨. (**b**) one of these flowers 康乃馨: *wear a carnation in one's buttonhole* 钮扣孔插着康乃馨. ⇨ illus at App 1 见附录 1 之插图, page ii.

car·ni·val /ˈkɑːnɪvl; ˋkɑrnəvḷ/ *n* (**a**) [C, U] (period of) public festivities and merry-making occurring at a regular time of year, eg in Roman Catholic countries during the week before Lent 狂欢节; 嘉年华会(天主教国家大斋期前一周内的狂欢): [attrib 作定语] *a carnival atmosphere* 狂欢节的气氛. (**b**) [C] festival of this kind, usu with a procession 狂欢节(通常有游行活动): *a street carnival* 街道上的狂欢节景象.

car·ni·vore /ˈkɑːnɪvɔː(r); ˋkɑrnəˌvɔr/ *n* flesh-eating animal 肉食动物. Cf 参看 HERBIVORE.

▷ **car·ni·vor·ous** /kɑːˈnɪvərəs; kɑrˋnɪvərəs/ *adj* flesh-eating 食肉的.

carol /ˈkærəl; ˋkærəl/ *n* joyful song, esp a Christmas hymn 欢乐之歌(尤指圣诞颂歌): *a Christmas carol* 圣诞颂歌 ○ *carol singers*, ie singers who visit people's houses at Christmas to sing carols and collect money, usu for charity 颂歌队(圣诞节挨户唱圣诞颂歌募捐的歌手, 通常为慈善募捐).

▷ **carol** *v* (**-ll-**; *US* **-l-**) [I] **1** sing joyfully 欢乐地唱. **2** (usu 通常作 **go carolling**) sing Christmas carols 去唱圣诞颂歌: *We often go carolling* (ie go from house to house, singing carols) *at Christmas.* 我们在圣诞节常去唱颂歌(挨门挨户唱颂歌). **ca·rol·ler** *n*.

ca·rotid /kəˈrɒtɪd; kəˋrɑtɪd/ *adj, n* (relating to) either of the two large blood-vessels (**carotid arteries**) in the neck, carrying blood to the head 颈动脉(的).

ca·rouse /kəˈraʊz; kəˋraʊz/ *v* [I] (*dated* 旧) drink and be merry with others (at a noisy meal, party, etc) (在热闹的宴会上)狂饮作乐.

▷ **ca·rou·sal** /kəˈraʊzl; kəˋraʊzḷ/ [C, U] (*dated* 旧) (noisy party with) drinking and merry-making 痛饮狂欢的(热闹的宴会).

ca·rou·sel (*US* **car·rou·sel**) /ˌkærəˈsel; ˌkærəˋsɛl/ *n* **1** (*US*) = ROUNDABOUT 1. **2** (esp at an airport) revolving apparatus or moving belt on which luggage is placed for collection by passengers (尤指机场的)旋转式行李传送带. **3** circular holder that feeds slides (SLIDE[1] 4a) into a projector (将幻灯片送入幻灯机内的)卡盘.

carp[1] /kɑːp; kɑrp/ *n* (*pl* unchanged 复数不变) type of large edible freshwater fish that lives in lakes and ponds 鲤鱼.

carp[2] /kɑːp; kɑrp/ *v* [I, Ipr] **~ (at/about sb/sth)** (*derog* 贬) complain continually about unimportant matters 挑剔; 吹毛求疵; 找茬儿: *have a carping tongue* 有一张刻薄嘴 ○ *carping criticism* 吹毛求疵的批评 ○ *She's always carping at her children.* 她老挑孩子的毛病.

carpal /ˈkɑːpl; ˋkɑrpḷ/ *adj* (*anatomy* 解) of the wrist 腕的.

▷ **carpal** *n* (*anatomy* 解) any of the bones in the wrist 腕骨. ⇨ illus at SKELETON 见 SKELETON 之插图.

car·pen·ter /ˈkɑːpəntə(r); ˋkɑrpəntɚ/ *n* person whose job is making or repairing wooden objects and structures 木匠. Cf 参看 JOINER.

▷ **car·pen·try** /-trɪ; -trɪ/ *n* [U] art or work of a carpenter 木工工艺; 木作: *learn carpentry* 学木工 ○ *a fine piece of carpentry* 精致的木工艺品.

car·pet /ˈkɑːpɪt; ˋkɑrpɪt/ *n* **1** (**a**) [U] thick woollen or synthetic fabric for covering floors 地毯. (**b**) [C] piece of this shaped to fit a particular room (适用于某房间的)全屋地毯: *lay a carpet*, ie fit it to a floor 铺地毯 ○ *We have fitted carpets* (ie carpets from wall to wall) *in our house.* 我们家已全铺了地毯(覆盖全部地板的地毯). ○ *We need a new bedroom carpet.* 我们需要一块卧室用的新地毯. Cf 参看 RED CARPET (RED[1]). **2** [C] thick layer of sth on the ground 地上的一厚层的东西: *a* *carpet of leaves, moss, snow, etc* 一厚层的叶子、苔、雪等. **3** (idm 习语) **on the 'carpet** (*infml* 口) summoned before sb in authority to be reprimanded 被叫去受训斥: *The boss had me on the carpet over my expenses claim.* 因为索取报销费的事, 老板把我叫去训了一顿. **pull the carpet/rug from under sb's feet** ⇨ PULL². **sweep sth under the carpet** ⇨ SWEEP¹.

▷ **car·pet** *v* **1** [Tn, Tn·pr] cover (sth) with or as if with a carpet 以地毯或好像以地毯覆盖(某物): *carpet the stairs* 在台阶上铺上地毯 ○ *a lawn carpeted with fallen leaves* 被落叶覆盖着的草坪. **2** [Tn esp passive 尤用于被动语态] (*infml* 口) reprimand (sb) 申斥, 责骂(某人): *be carpeted by one's boss* 遭老板申斥.

C

□ **'carpet-bag** *n* (formerly) travelling bag made of carpet (旧时)毯制旅行袋. **'carpet-bagger** *n* (*derog* 贬) political candidate, etc who hopes for success in an area where he is not known and is therefore resented (在某地区因无名声而受排斥却希望获胜的)政治上的候选人等.

'carpet-slippers *n* [pl] soft slippers with woollen or cloth uppers, worn indoors (室内穿用, 以毛绒或布作面的)软拖鞋.

'carpet-sweeper *n* device with revolving brushes for sweeping carpets (有旋转刷的)扫地毯器.

car·riage /ˈkærɪdʒ; ˋkærɪdʒ/ *n* **1** [C] (also **coach**) vehicle (usu with four wheels), pulled by a horse or horses, for carrying people (通常为四轮的载客的)马车. **2** [C] (*Brit* also **coach**) (*US* **car**) railway coach for carrying passengers (火车)客车厢: *a first-/second-class carriage* 头等[二等]车厢. **3** [U] (cost of) transporting goods from one place to another 货运(费): *carriage forward*, ie The cost of carriage is to be paid by the receiver. 运费由收货人支付. ○ *carriage free/paid*, ie The cost of carriage is paid by the sender. 运费免付[已付](已由发货人付讫). **4** [C] = GUN-CARRIAGE (GUN). **5** [C] moving part of a machine that supports or moves another part (机器的)移动托架: *a typewriter carriage* 打字机的滑动架. **6** [sing] (*dated* 旧) way in which sb holds and moves his head and body 仪态; 举止; 姿势: *have a very upright carriage* 挺着腰板.

□ **'carriageway** *n* part of a road on which vehicles travel 车道: *the northbound carriageway of a motorway* 高速公路的北行车道.

car·rier /ˈkærɪə(r); ˋkærɪɚ/ *n* **1** person or thing that carries sth 运送某物的人或物. **2** person or company that carries goods or people for payment 运货人; 货运公司; 客运公司: *Your carrier for this flight is British Airways.* 你的这一班机是英国航空公司的飞机. **3** (usu metal) framework fixed to a bicycle, etc for carrying luggage or a small child (自行车等的)行李架: *strap a parcel to the carrier* 把包裹捆到行李架上. **4** person or animal that can transmit a disease to others without suffering from it 带菌者(可传染疾病而本身不受感染的人或动物); 传染病的媒介: *Mosquitoes are carriers of malaria.* 蚊子是疟疾的传播媒介. Cf 参看 VECTOR 2. **5** = AIRCRAFT-CARRIER (AIRCRAFT). **6** = CARRIER BAG.

□ **'carrier bag** (*Brit*) paper or plastic bag for carrying shopping (装载所购商品的)纸袋或塑料袋.

'carrier pigeon pigeon trained to carry messages tied to its leg or neck 信鸽.

car·rion /ˈkærɪən; ˋkærɪən/ *n* [U] dead and decaying flesh 腐肉.

□ **'carrion crow** type of crow that eats carrion and small animals (一种吃腐肉及小动物的)乌鸦.

car·rot /ˈkærət; ˋkærət/ *n* **1** (**a**) [C] plant with a long pointed orange root 胡萝卜. (**b**) [C, U] this root eaten as a vegetable 胡萝卜(蔬菜): *boiled beef and carrots* 清炖牛肉胡萝卜 ○ *Have some more carrots.* 再吃点儿胡萝卜. ○ *grated carrot* 擦碎的胡萝卜. **2** [C] (*fig* 比喻) reward or advantage promised to sb to persuade him to do sth 说服某人做某事所许诺的报酬或利益: *hold out/offer a carrot to sb* 利诱某人. **3** (idm 习语) **the carrot and the stick** the hope of reward and the threat of punishment as a means of making sb try harder 胡萝卜加大棒; 软硬兼施; 威逼利诱: [attrib 作定语] *a carrot-and-stick approach* 胡萝卜加大棒的方法; 威逼利诱.

▷ **car·roty** *adj* (of hair) having an orange-red colour (指毛发)橘红色的.

car·rou·sel (*US*) = CAROUSEL.

carry /ˈkærɪ; ˋkærɪ/ *v* (*pt, pp* **carried**) **1** [Tn, Tn·pr, Tn·p] (**a**) support the weight of (sb/sth) and take (him/it) from place to place; take from one place to another 携带, 搬运, 传送, 运送(某人[某物]): *carry shopping, a suitcase, a rucksack, etc* 携带着购买的东西、手提箱、背包等 ○ *a train carrying commuters to and from work* 运送通勤者上下班的火车 ○ *The car had carried him 500 miles before it broke down.* 汽车载着他行驶了500英里以后抛锚了. ○ *She carried her baby in her arms.* 她怀抱着婴儿. ○ *He broke his leg during the match and had to be carried off.* 他在比赛中撞断了腿而被抬走. ○ *Seeds can be carried for long distances by the wind.* 种子能被风传送得很远. ○ *The injured were carried away on stretchers.* 用担架把受伤的人抬走了. (**b**) (of pipes, wires, etc) contain and direct the flow of (water, an electric current, etc); take; conduct (指管道、金属丝等)输送, 传导(水、电流等): *a pipeline carrying oil* 输油管 ○ *The veins carry blood to the heart.* 静脉把血液输送进心脏. ⇨Usage 见所附用法. **2** [Tn] have (sth) with one 持有; 带有: *Police in many countries carry guns.* 许多国家的警察都带枪. ○ *I never carry much money (with me).* 我(身上)从来不多带钱. ○ (*fig* 比喻) *He'll carry the memory of the experience (with him) for the rest of his life.* 他能把这一经历记一辈子. ⇨Usage at WEAR² 用法见 WEAR². **3** [Tn] (*dated or fml* 旧或文) (used esp in the continuous tenses 尤用于进行时态) be pregnant with (sb) 怀(胎): *She was carrying twins.* 她怀着双胞胎. **4** [Tn] (esp of sth that does not move) support the weight of (sth) (尤指不动的东西)支撑, 承载(某物): *These pillars carry the weight of the roof.* 这些柱子支撑着屋顶的重量. ○ *A road bridge has to carry a lot of traffic.* 高架路得承载很多车辆. ○ (*fig* 比喻) *He is carrying the department (on his shoulders)*, ie It is only functioning because of his efforts and abilities. 他主持着这个部门. **5** [Tn] (**a**) have (sth) as an attribute; possess 有(某特性); 具有: *His voice carries the ring of authority.* 他的声音中带有权威的口气. (**b**) have (sth) as a result; involve; entail 有(某种结果); 含有; 使承担: *Power carries great responsibilty.* 有权力就要承担重任. ○ *Crimes of violence carry heavy penalties.* 暴力罪行要承受严厉的惩罚. **6** [Tn, Tn·pr, Tn·p] take (sth) to a specified point or in a specified direction 使(某事物)延伸至某一点或向某一方向: *The war was carried into enemy territory.* 战争已伸展到敌方领土. ○ *His ability carried him to the top of his profession.* 他有才干能在本行业中首屈一指. ○ *He carries modesty to extremes*, ie is too modest. 他谦虚得过分. **7** [Tn] (in adding figures) transfer (a figure) to the next column (加法)进(位). **8** [Tn esp passive 尤用于被动语态] approve (sth) by a majority of votes (以多数票)通过(某事): *The bill/motion/resolution was carried by 340 votes to 210.* 这一提案[动议/决议]以340票对210票获得通过. **9** [Tn] win the support or sympathy of (sb) 赢得(某人)的支持或同情: *His moving speech was enough to carry the audience.* 他讲话感人足以赢得听众同情. **10** [Tn no passive 不用于被动语态] **~ oneself** hold or move one's head or body in a specified way 使头或身体呈现某种姿态: *She carries herself well.* 她体态优美. **11** (**a**) [In/pr] (of a missile, etc) cover a specified distance (指抛射物等)射至某距离: *The full-back's kick carried 50 metres into the crowd.* 后卫把球踢出50米远, 射入人群中. (**b**) [I] (of a sound, voice, etc) be audible at a distance (指声音等)达到可听见的某距离: *A public speaker needs a voice that carries (well).* 演说家要有(很远都能听到的)洪亮嗓音. **12** [Tn] (of a newspaper or broadcast) include (sth) in its content; contain (指报纸或广播)登载, 刊出, 播出(某事): *Today's papers carry full reports of the President's visit.* 今天报纸上登载了总统访问的详尽报道. **13** [Tn] (of a shop) have (sth) for sale; include in its regular stock (指商店)出售(某物); 有货: *I'm sorry, this shop doesn't carry cigarettes.* 对不起, 本店不卖香烟. **14** (idm 习语) **as fast as one's legs can carry one** ⇨ FAST¹. **carry all/everything be'fore one** be completely successful 完全成功; 大获全胜. **carry the can (for sth)** (*infml* 口) accept the responsibility or blame (for sth) (为某事)承担责任或承受责难. **carry coals to 'Newcastle** take goods to a place where they are already plentiful; supply sth unnecessarily 多此一举. **carry the day** ⇨ DAY. **carry/gain one's 'point** ⇨

POINT[1]. **carry/take sth too, etc far** ⇨ FAR[2]. **carry the war into the enemy's camp** attack (rather than being content to defend) 转(守)为攻; 反攻. **carry ˈweight** be influential or important 有影响; 有分量; 有力: *Her opinion carries (great) weight (with the chairman).* 她的意见(对主席)(很)有影响. **fetch and carry** ⇨ FETCH. **15** (phr v) **carry sb away** (usu passive 通常用于被动语态) cause sb to lose self-control or be very excited 使某人失去自制力或非常兴奋: *He tends to get carried away when watching wrestling on TV.* 他一看电视中的摔跤就很兴奋.

carry sb back (to sth) take sb back in memory 使某人回忆起: *The sound of seagulls carried her back to childhood holidays by the sea.* 她听到海鸥的叫声就回忆起童年时在海边度假的情景.

carry sth forward (in bookkeeping) transfer (the total of figures in a column or on a page) to a new column or page (簿记)将(一栏或一页的总数)转记于另一栏或另一页; 结转.

carry sth off win sth 赢得某物: *She carried off most of the prizes for swimming.* 她获得游泳项目的大多数奖. **carry it/sth off** handle a (difficult) situation successfully 成功地应付(困难)局面: *He carried the speech off well despite feeling very nervous.* 尽管他感到非常紧张, 但总算把演讲顺利地讲完了.

carry ˈon (*infml* 口) argue, quarrel or complain noisily; behave strangely 吵吵闹闹; 举动失常: *He does carry on, doesn't he?* 他真有点儿疯疯癫癫的, 是吧? **carry on (with sth/doing sth)**; **carry sth on** continue (doing sth) 继续(做某事): *Carry on (working/with your work) while I'm away.* 我不在的时候, 要继续做(工作[你的工作]). ○ *They decided to carry on* (eg continue their walk) *in spite of the weather.* 他们决定不管天气好坏都坚持着(如继续走). ○ *Carry on the good work!* 好好干下去! **carry on (with sb)** (*infml* 口) (used esp in the continuous tenses 尤用于进行时态) have an affair(5) with sb 与某人有暧昧关系: *She's carrying on with her boss.* 她和老板有暧昧关系. ○ *They've been carrying on for years.* 他们的暧昧关系已经有很多年了. **carry sth on (a)** take part in sth; conduct or hold sth 参加某事; 进行或举行某事: *carry on a conversation, discussion, dialogue, etc* 进行谈话、讨论、对话等. **(b)** conduct or transact sth 进行或经营某事物: *carry on a business* 经营事业.

carry sth out (a) do sth as required or specified; fulfil sth 实施; 执行; 实行; 落实; 贯彻; 完成; 实现: *carry out a promise, a threat, a plan, an order* 实践诺言、进行威胁、实施计划、执行命令. **(b)** perform or conduct (an experiment, etc) 进行(实验等): *carry out an enquiry, an investigation, a survey, etc* 进行查询、调查、勘查 ○ *Extensive tests have been carried out on the patient.* 对患者进行了多次试验.

carry sth over (a) postpone sth 将某事物延后. **(b)** = CARRY STH FORWARD.

carry sb through (sth) help sb to survive a difficult period 帮助某人渡过难关: *His determination carried him through (the ordeal).* 他靠坚定的信心渡过了难关. **carry sth through** complete sth successfully 成功地完成某事物: *It's a difficult job but she's the person to carry it through.* 这是件艰巨的工作, 但她是能胜任的.

▷ **carry** *n* **1** [U] **(a)** range of a gun (枪炮的)射程. **(b)** distance that a golf ball travels before hitting the ground (高尔夫球落地前的)飞行距离. **2** [sing] act of carrying sb/sth 携、带、持、抱、抬、扛、背或载某人[某物]: *Would you like me to give the baby a carry?* 你愿意让我抱抱婴儿吗?

□ **ˈcarry-all** *n* (*US*) = HOLDALL.

ˈcarry-cot *n* portable cot for a baby 手提式婴儿床.

carryings-ˈon *n* [pl] (*infml* 口) noisy or excited behaviour 喧闹的或激动的样子: *Did you hear the carryings-on next door last night?* 你听见没听见昨晚隔壁闹翻天了?

ˈcarry-on *n* (*infml* 口 *esp Brit*) [sing] fuss 大惊小怪; 忙乱: *I've never heard such a carry-on!* 我从来没听见过这样大惊小怪的事!

ˈcarry-out *n* (*Scot or US* 用于苏格兰或美国) = TAKE-AWAY (TAKE[1]).

NOTE ON USAGE 用法: **Carry**, **bear**, **cart**, **hump** and **lug** share the meaning of 'take (somebody or something) from one place to another'. ☆ **carry**、**bear**、**cart**、**hump**、**lug** 均意为'将(某人或某物)从一处移至另一处'. **Carry** is the most general term for the moving of loads of all weights. ☆ **carry** 一词最常用, 其所移动之物可轻可重. It can refer to passenger transport 这个词还可指客运: *She came in carrying an important-looking piece of paper.* 她进来时, 拿着一份看来很重要的文件. ○ *Could you carry this box to my car for me, please?* 请你把这个箱子给我搬到我的汽车那里可以吗? ○ *The plane was carrying 250 passengers when it crashed.* 飞机失事时载有250名乘客. When **bear** indicates movement it is formal ☆ **bear** 指移动时, 含义较庄重: *The ambassador arrived bearing gifts for the Queen.* 大使携礼物觐见女王. ○ *The hero was borne aloft on the shoulders of the crowd.* 这个英雄被人们高擎肩上. **Cart** means 'carry (away) (as if) in a cart' ☆ **cart** 意为'(好像)用大车运(走)': *We've asked the Council to come and cart away all this rubbish.* 我们已经要求市政局来把这些垃圾运走. Informally it suggests force or unwillingness 这个词在口语中含有强迫或不自愿的意思: *The police carted the protesters off to jail.* 警察把抗议者押送监狱. ○ *I've been carting these books around for him all over the place.* 我一直为他把书搬来搬去. **Hump** suggests that the load is heavy and difficult to move and is carried on one's back or shoulders ☆ **hump** 指以背或扛的方式移动笨重而难以移动之物: *We've spent all day humping furniture up and down stairs.* 我们花了一整天的时间楼上楼下地搬运家具. **Lug** indicates that what is carried is pulled or dragged behind unwillingly and/or with difficulty ☆ **lug** 指不自愿地、艰难地拉或拽: *Do I have to lug those suitcases all the way to the station?* 难道非要我把那些手提箱一直拉到车站去吗?

cart /kɑːt; kɑrt/ *n* **1 (a)** vehicle with two or four wheels used for carrying loads and usu pulled by a horse (通常为马拉的两轮或四轮的)大车: *a horse and cart* 一套马车. Cf 参看 WAGON 1. **(b)** (also **ˈhandcart**) light vehicle with wheels that is pulled or pushed by hand 手推车. **2** (idm 习语) **put the ˌcart before the ˈhorse** reverse the logical order of things, eg by saying that the result of sth is what caused it 本末倒置; 因果颠倒.

▷ **cart** *v* [Tn, Tn·pr, Tn·p] **1** carry (sth) in a cart 用大车拉(某物): *carting hay* 用大车拉干草 ○ *cart away the rubbish* 把垃圾拉走. **2** (*infml* 口) carry (sth) in the hands 拿; 提: *I've been carting these cases around all day.* 我整天都提着这些箱子. ⇨Usage at CARRY 用法见 CARRY.

carter *n* person whose job is driving carts or transporting goods 赶大车的人; 车把势.

□ **ˈcart-horse** *n* large strong horse used for heavy work (用以做重活的强壮的)大马.

ˈcart-load *n* amount that a cart holds 一辆大车所载的量.

ˈcart-track *n* rough track not suitable for motor vehicles (不适于机动车行驶的)大车道.

ˈcart-wheel *n* **1** wheel of a cart, with thick wooden spokes and a metal rim 马车轮. **2** sideways somersault 侧手翻: *do/turn cartwheels* 做[翻]侧手翻. — *v* [I] perform a cart-wheel 做侧手翻.

carte blanche /ˌkɑːt ˈblɒnʃ; ˈkɑrtˈblɑnʃ/ (*French* 法) complete freedom to act as one thinks best 全权处理: *give sb/have carte blanche* 授予某人[具有]全权.

car·tel /kɑːˈtel; ˈkɑrtl/ *n* [CGp] group of business firms which combine to control production and marketing, and to avoid competing with one another 卡特尔, 同业联盟(以控制产量、销售及防止相互竞争).

car·til·age /ˈkɑːtɪlɪdʒ; ˈkɑrtl̩ɪdʒ/ *n* **(a)** [U] tough white flexible tissue attached to the bones of animals; gristle 软骨: *I've damaged a cartilage in my knee.* 我伤了膝关节的软骨. **(b)** [C] structure made of this 软骨结构.

▷ **car·ti·la·gin·ous** /ˌkɑːtɪˈlædʒɪnəs; ˌkɑrtl̩ˈædʒənəs/ *adj* of or like cartilage 软骨的; 像软骨的.

car·to·grapher /kɑːˈtɒɡrəfə(r); kɑrˈtɑɡrəfɚ/ *n* person who draws maps and charts 制图者(绘制地图和图表者).

▷ **car·to·graphy** /kɑːˈtɒɡrəfɪ; kɑrˈtɑɡrəfɪ/ *n* [U] art of drawing maps and charts 制图学; 制图法. **car·to·graphic** /ˌkɑːtəˈɡræfɪk; ˌkɑrtəˈɡræfɪk/ *adj.*

C

car·ton /ˈkɑːtn; ˋkɑrtn̩/ *n* light cardboard or plastic box for holding goods 纸板箱; 纸板盒: *a carton of milk, cream, yoghurt, etc* 一纸盒奶、奶油、酸奶等 ○ *a carton of 200 cigarettes*, ie with 10 packets of 20 一条香烟(共10包, 每包20支). ⇨illus at BOX 见 BOX 之插图.

cartoon 漫画

car·toon /kɑːˈtuːn; kɑrˋtun/ *n* **1** (**a**) amusing drawing in a newspaper or magazine, esp one that comments satirically on current events (报刊上的)漫画; (尤指)时事讽刺画. ⇨illus 见插图. (**b**) sequence of these telling a story (报刊上的)连环漫画, 连环讽刺画. **2** (also **animated cartoon**) film made by photographing a series of gradually changing drawings, giving an illusion of movement 动画片; 卡通片: *a Walt Disney cartoon* 迪斯尼动画片. **3** drawing made by an artist as a preliminary sketch for a painting, tapestry, fresco, etc 草图; 底图.

▷ **car·toon·ist** *n* person who draws cartoons (CARTOON 1a) 漫画家.

cart·ridge /ˈkɑːtrɪdʒ; ˋkɑrtrɪdʒ/ *n* **1** (*US* **shell**) tube or case containing explosive (for blasting), or explosive with a bullet or shot (for firing from a gun) 子弹; 弹药筒; 弹壳. ⇨illus at GUN 见 GUN 之插图. Cf 参看 SHELL 3, SHOT[1] 4. **2** detachable end of a pick-up on a record player, holding the stylus (唱机的)唱头; (拾音器的)心座. **3** sealed case containing recording tape, photographic film or ink, that is put into a tape-deck, camera or pen 录音带盒; 胶卷盒; 钢笔囊.

□ ˈ**cartridge-belt** *n* belt with loops for holding cartridges (CARTRIDGE 1) 子弹带.

ˈ**cartridge-clip** *n* = CLIP[1] 2.

ˈ**cartridge paper** thick strong paper for drawing on 图画纸.

carve /kɑːv; kɑrv/ *v* **1** (**a**) [I, Ipr, Tn, Tn·pr] **~ (in sth); ~ sth (out of/from/of/in sth)** form (sth) by cutting away material from wood or stone 雕刻; 雕刻成(某物): *Michelangelo carved in marble.* 米开朗琪罗在大理石上雕刻. ○ *The statue was carved (out of stone).* 这座像是(用石头)雕刻的. (**b**) [Tn, Tn·pr] **~ sth (into sth)** cut or chip (solid material) in order to form sth 切, 削, 凿或刻(成某物): *carve wood* 削木头. **2** [Tn, Tn·pr] inscribe (sth) by cutting on a surface 刻记(某事物): *carve one's initials on a tree trunk* 在树干上刻自己名字的缩写字母. **3** [I, Tn, Dn·n, Dn·pr] **~ sth (for sb)** cut (cooked meat) into slices for eating 把(熟肉)切成片供食用: *Would you like to carve?* 你喜欢切片吃吗? ○ *carve a joint, turkey, leg of mutton, etc* 切肉、火鸡、羊腿等 ○ *Please carve me another slice.* 请再给我切一片. **4** (phr v) **carve sth out (for oneself)** build (one's career, reputation, etc) by hard work 靠勤奋创(业)或树(名声)等: *She carved out a name for herself as a reporter.* 她靠苦干而成了有名的记者. **carve sth up** (*infml* 口) divide sth into parts or slices 将某物分割成份或片; 瓜分: *The territory was carved up by the occupying powers.* 领土被侵占者瓜分.

▷ **carver** *n* **1** person who carves 雕刻者; 切肉的人. **2** = CARVING KNIFE.

carv·ing *n* carved object or design 雕刻品; 雕刻术.

□ ˈ**carving knife** knife used for carving meat 切肉刀. ⇨illus at KNIFE 见 KNIFE 之插图.

ca·ry·atid /ˌkærɪˈætɪd; ˌkærɪˋætɪd/ *n* (*architecture* 建) statue of a female figure used as a supporting pillar in a building 女像柱.

cas·cade /kæˈskeɪd; kæsˋked/ *n* **1** waterfall, esp one of a series forming a large waterfall 瀑布(尤指大瀑布的分支). **2** (*fig* 比喻) thing that falls or hangs in a way that suggests a waterfall 瀑布状下垂的东西: *a cascade of blonde hair* 金发垂髻.

▷ **cas·cade** *v* [I, Ipr, Ip] fall in or like a cascade 如瀑布落下; 如瀑布状下垂: *Water cascaded down the mountainside.* 水如瀑布般自山边下泻. ○ *Her golden hair cascaded down her back.* 她的金发像瀑布似的披在背后.

cas·cara /kæˈskɑːrə; kæsˋkɛrə/ *n* [U] type of laxative made from the bark of a N American tree 药鼠李皮(北美一种树皮制成的轻泻剂).

case[1] /keɪs; kes/ *n* **1** [C] instance or example of the occurrence of sth 事例; 实例; 情形: *The company only dismisses its employees in cases of gross misconduct.* 公司仅在雇员严重失职的情形下才予以解雇. ○ *It's a clear case of blackmail!* 这显然是敲诈! **2 the case** [sing] actual state of affairs; situation 实情; 情况: *Is it the case* (ie Is it true) *that the company's sales have dropped?* 公司销售额下降一事属实吗? ○ *If that is the case* (ie If the situation is as stated), *you will have to work much harder.* 果真如此(情况一如所述), 你就得更加努力了. **3** [C usu *sing* 通常作单数] circumstances or special conditions relating to a person or thing 与某人或某事物有关的环境或特殊情况: *In your case, we are prepared to be lenient.* 根据你的情况, 我们拟予从宽处理. ○ *I cannot make an exception in your case*, ie for you and not for others. 我不能为你破例. **4** [C] instance of a disease or an injury; person suffering from this 病例; 病症; 患者: *a case of typhoid* 伤寒患者 ○ *Cases of smallpox are becoming rare.* 天花病例日益罕见. **5** [C] person having medical, psychiatric, etc treatment 接受内科、精神科等治疗的病人: *This boy is a sad case. His parents are divorced and he himself is severely handicapped.* 这个男孩儿是个可怜的病儿, 父母离婚, 本人又严重残废. **6** [C] matter that is being officially investigated, esp by the police 被官方(尤指警方)调查的事情; 案件: *a murder case/a case of murder* 谋杀案. **7** [C] (**a**) question to be decided in a court of law; lawsuit 诉讼案: *The case will be heard in court next week.* 这一案件下星期审理. ○ *When does your case come before the court?* 你的案子什么时候开庭审讯? (**b**) (usu *sing* 通常作单数) set of facts or arguments supporting one side in a lawsuit, debate, etc 诉讼、辩论等的一方的辩护事实、理由、论点或论据: *the case for the defence/prosecution* 有利于辩方[控方]的案情陈述 ○ *the case for/against the abolition of the death penalty* 拥护[反对]废除死刑的理由 ○ *You have a very strong case.* 你的论据很有力. **8** [U, C] (*grammar*) (change in the) form of a noun, or pronoun, etc (esp in inflected languages) that shows its relationship to another word 格(尤指屈折语中, 表示名词或代词等与另一词的关系的形式及其变化): *the nominative case* 主格 ○ *the accusative case* 宾格 ○ *Latin nouns have case, number and gender.* 拉丁语名词有格、数和性. Cf 参看 DECLENSION. **9** [sing] (*infml* 口) eccentric person 怪人: *He really is a case!* 他真是个怪人! **10** (idm 习语) **a case in ˈpoint** example that is relevant to the matter being discussed 与所谈论的事有关的事例; 例证. **as the ˌcase may ˈbe** (used when describing two or more possible alternatives) as will be determined by the circumstances (用于两种或多种可能性)看情形, 根据具体情况: *There may be an announcement about this tomorrow — or not, as the case may be.* 这件事明天可能宣布 —— 也可能不宣布, 看情形吧. **in ˈany case** whatever happens or may have happened 无论如何; 总之. **(just) in case (...)** because of the possibility of sth happening 因为可能发生某事; 以防万一; 万一: *It may rain — you'd better take an umbrella (just) in case (it does).* 可能下雨 —— 你最好带把伞, 以防万一(下起来). **in case of sth** if sth happens 若发生某事; 假如: *In case of fire, ring the alarm bell.* 遇火警时立即按警铃. **in ˈno case** in no circumstances 在任何情形下决不; 无论如何都不. **in ˈthat case** if that happens or has happened; if that is the state of affairs 既然那样; 假若是那样的话: *You don't like your job? In that case why don't you leave?* 你不喜欢这份工作? 那你怎么不辞掉呢? **make out a case (for sth)** give arguments in favour of sth 提出对某事有利的论据: *The report makes out a strong case for increased spending on hospitals.* 这份报告提出了对增加

医疗开支的有力论据. **meet the case** ⇨ MEET[1]. **prove one's/the case/point** ⇨ PROVE.

□ ˈ**case-book** *n* written record kept by doctors, lawyers, etc of cases they have dealt with (医生、律师等保存的自己曾处理过的)病历、案例等记录.

ˈ**case grammar** (*linguistics* 语言) type of transformational grammar in which the case relationships are used to describe the deep structure of sentences 格的语法(转换语法的一种类型, 以格的关系来描述句子的深层结构).

ˌ**case** ˈ**history** record of a person's background, medical history, etc for use in professional treatment (eg by a doctor) 个案记录; 病历.

ˈ**case-law** *n* [U] law based on decisions made by judges in earlier cases 判例法(以过去的判例为根据的法律). Cf 参看 COMMON LAW (COMMON[1]), STATUTE LAW (STATUTE).

ˈ**case-load** *n* all those people for whom a doctor, social worker, etc is responsible (医生、社会工作者等所负责的)总人数, 工作量.

ˈ**case-study** *n* study of the development of a person or group of people over a period of time 个案研究(对一个人或一些人在一段时间的情况发展的研究).

ˈ**casework** *n* [U] social work involving the study of individuals or families with problems (对有问题的个人或家庭所做的)社会工作. ˈ**caseworker** *n*.

case[2] /keɪs; kes/ *n* **1** (**a**) (often in compounds 常用以构成复合词) any of various types of container or protective covering (各种类型的)容器、套、罩或包装: *a jewel case* ○ *a pencil case* ○ *a packing-case*, ie a large wooden box for packing goods in ○ *Exhibits in museums are often displayed in glass cases.* 博物馆中的展品常摆放在玻璃橱里. (**b**) this with its contents; amount that it contains (各种类型的)容器及其内容或容量: *a case* (ie 12 bottles) *of champagne* 一箱香槟酒(12瓶). ⇨illus at BOX 见BOX之插图. **2** suitcase 手提箱: *Could you carry my case for me?* 你给我提着手提箱可以吗?

▷ **case** *v* **1** [Tn] enclose (sth) in a case; encase 把(某物)装于容器中; 使装箱; 使装盒. **2** (idm 习语) **case the joint** (*sl* 俚) inspect a place carefully (esp before robbing it) 仔细探察一处所(尤指于抢劫前). **cas·ing** *n* [U, C] protective covering 包装; 套; 罩: *wrapped in rubber casing* 包在橡胶套中.

□ ˈ**case-hardened** *adj* made callous by experience 由于经历多而变得硬心肠或无感情的; 老于世故而冷酷无情的.

ca·sein /ˈkeɪsiːn; ˈkesɪn/ *n* [U] protein that is found in milk and that forms the basis of cheese 酪蛋白; 酪素.

case·ment /ˈkeɪsmənt; ˈkesmənt/ *n* (also **casement window**) window that opens on hinges like a door 门式窗. ⇨illus at App 1 见附录1之插图, page vi.

cash /kæʃ; kæʃ/ *n* **1** [U] (**a**) money in coins or notes 钱(硬币或纸币); 现款; 现金: *pay (in) cash* 付现金 ○ *I have no cash on me — may I pay by cheque?* 我没带现款——可以付支票吗? ○ *I never carry much cash with me.* 我从不多带现款. (**b**) (*infml* 口) money in any form; wealth (任何形式的)金钱; 财富: *I'm short of cash at the moment.* 我现在缺钱. **2** (idm 习语) **cash** ˈ**down** with immediate payment of cash 即付现款; 现款交易. **cash on de**ˈ**livery** system of paying for goods when they are delivered 货到付款.

▷ **cash** *v* **1** [Tn, Dn·n, Dn·pr] **~ sth (for sb)** exchange sth for cash 将某物兑换成现金: *cash a cheque (for sb)* (给某人)把支票兑现. **2** (phr v) **cash in (on sth)** take advantage of or profit from sth 从某事物中获得利益或利润: *The shops are cashing in on temporary shortages by raising prices.* 商店趁一时缺货而提高价格从中获利. **cash·able** *adj* that can be cashed 可兑现的; 可兑换现金的.

□ ˌ**cash and** ˈ**carry 1** system in which the buyer pays for goods in cash and takes them away himself 现款自运(顾客付现款自行将所购物品运走的制度). **2** shop operating this system 现款自运商店(实行上述制度的商店): *buy food in bulk at the local cash and carry* 在本地现款自运商店购买大批食物.

ˈ**cashcard** plastic card issued by a bank to its customers for use in a cash dispenser 自动提款卡.

ˈ**cash crop** crop grown for selling, rather than for use by the grower 商品作物(为出售而非自用的农作物). Cf 参看 SUBSISTENCE CROP (SUBSIST).

ˈ**cash desk** desk or counter where payment is made in a shop 付款柜台; 付款处.

ˈ**cash dispenser** machine (in or outside a bank) from which cash can be obtained when a personal coded card is inserted and a special code-number keyed 自动提款机.

ˈ**cash flow** movement of money into and out of a business as goods are bought and sold 现金周转: [attrib 作定语] *a healthy cash flow situation*, eg having enough money to make payments when required to do so 健康的现金周转状况.

ˈ**cashpoint** *n* = CASH DISPENSER.

ˈ**cash register** machine used in shops, etc that has a drawer for keeping money in, and displays and records the amount of each purchase 现金收入记录机.

C

cashew /ˈkæʃuː; ˈkæʃu/ *n* **1** tropical American tree (美洲热带的)槚如树, 腰果树. **2** (also ˈ**cashew nut**) its small edible kidney-shaped nut 腰果. ⇨illus at NUT 见NUT之插图.

cash·ier[1] /kæˈʃɪə(r); kæˈʃɪr/ *n* person whose job is to receive and pay out money in a bank, shop, hotel, etc 出纳员.

cash·ier[2] /kæˈʃɪə(r); kæˈʃɪr/ *v* [Tn] dismiss (an army officer) from service, esp with dishonour 革除(军官)职务.

cash·mere /ˌkæʃˈmɪə(r); ˈkæʃmɪr/ *n* [U] fine soft wool, esp that made from the hair of a type of Asian goat 开士米; 山羊绒: [attrib 作定语] *a* ˌ*cashmere* ˈ*sweater* 开士米毛衣.

ca·sino /kəˈsiːnəʊ; kəˈsino/ *n* (*pl* **~s**) public building or room for gambling and other amusements 赌场; 娱乐场.

cask /kɑːsk; *US* kæsk; kæsk/ *n* (**a**) barrel, esp for alcoholic drinks (尤指盛酒精饮料的)桶. (**b**) amount that it contains 一桶的量.

cas·ket /ˈkɑːskɪt; *US* ˈkæskɪt; ˈkæskɪt/ *n* **1** small (usu decorated) box for holding letters, jewels or other valuable things (收藏信件、珠宝或其他贵重物品的, 常为有装饰的)小箱. **2** (*US*) coffin 棺材.

cas·sava /kəˈsɑːvə; kəˈsɑvə/ *n* **1** [C] tropical plant with starchy roots 木薯. **2** [U] starch or flour obtained from these roots, used to make tapioca 木薯粉.

cas·ser·ole /ˈkæsərəʊl; ˈkæsəˌrol/ *n* (**a**) [C] covered heat-proof dish in which meat, etc is cooked and then served at table 焙盘(烹饪肉食等的带盖浅锅, 也可上桌); 沙锅. ⇨illus at PAN 见PAN之插图. (**b**) [C, U] food cooked in a casserole 用焙盘或沙锅烹饪的食物; 焙盘炖菜: *a/some chicken casserole* 一份[一些]沙锅鸡.

▷ **cas·ser·ole** *v* [Tn] cook (meat, etc) in a casserole 用焙盘或沙锅烹饪(肉食等).

cas·sette /kəˈset; kəˈsɛt/ *n* small sealed case containing a reel of film or magnetic tape (盛胶卷或磁带等的)封闭小盒: [attrib 作定语] *a cassette recorder*, ie a tape-recorder with which cassettes are used 盒式录音机.

cas·sock /ˈkæsək; ˈkæsək/ *n* long (usu black or red) garment worn by certain clergymen and members of a church choir 法衣(某些教士和教会唱诗班成员所穿的长袍, 通常为黑色或红色).

cast[1] /kɑːst; *US* kæst; kæst/ *v* (*pt, pp* **cast**) **1** [Tn, Tn·pr, Tn·p] throw (sth), esp deliberately or with force 扔; 投; 掷; 抛: *cast a stone* 扔石头 ○ *The angler cast his line (into the water).* 钓鱼的人把鱼线抛入水中. **2** [Tn] allow (sth) to fall or drop; shed 脱落; 掉: *Snakes cast their skins.* 蛇能蜕皮. ○ *The horse cast a shoe*, ie One of its shoes came off. 这匹马的一只蹄铁脱落了. **3** [Tn, Tn·pr] turn or send (sth) in a particular direction; direct 向某一方向转或送(某物): *He cast a furtive glance at her.* 他偷偷瞥了她一眼. ○ *The tree cast* (ie caused there to be) *a long shadow (on the grass).* 树(在草地上)投下长长的影子. ○ (*fig* 比喻) *The tragedy cast a shadow on/over their lives*, ie made them gloomy and depressed. 这一悲剧在他们的生命中投下了一片阴影(使他们愁闷、沮丧). ○ (*fig* 比喻) *His muddled evidence casts doubt on his reliability as a witness.* 他的证词糊里糊涂, 使人对他作为见证人的可靠性产生了怀疑. **4** (**a**) [Tn] shape (molten metal, etc) by pouring it into a mould 浇铸(熔化的金属等): *cast bronze* 浇铸青铜. (**b**) [Tn, Tn·pr] **~ sth (in sth)** make (an object) in this way 铸造(某物): *a statue cast in bronze* 青铜铸成的像 ○ (*fig* 比喻) *The* *novel is cast in the form of a diary.* 这部小说是以日记的形式写的. **5** (**a**) [I, Tn] choose actors to play parts in (a play, film, etc) 挑选演员扮演(影剧等中的)角色: *We're casting (the play) next week.* 我们下星期挑选(话剧)演员. (**b**) [Tn, Tn·pr] **~ sb (as sb)**; **~ sb (in sth)** give sb a part in a play, etc 选派某人扮演戏剧等中的角色: *He was cast as Othello/cast in the role of Othello.* 选派他扮演奥赛罗的角色. **6** (idm 习语) **cast 'anchor** lower an anchor 抛锚. **cast aspersions (on sb/sth)** make damaging or derogatory remarks (about sb/sth) 中伤或诽谤(某人[某事物]): *How dare you cast aspersions on my wife's character!* 你竟敢诽谤我妻子的人格! **cast one's bread upon the waters** (*fml or rhet* 文或修辞) do good deeds without expecting anything in return 做好事不图回报. **cast an eye/one's eye(s) over sb/sth** look or examine sb/sth quickly 很快地看或查某人[某事物]: *Would you cast your eye over these calculations to check that they are correct?* 你看一下这些计算数字, 检查是否正确, 好吗? **cast/shed/throw light on sth** ⇨ LIGHT[1]. **cast/draw lots** ⇨ LOT[3]. **cast one's mind back (to sth)** think about the past 回顾; 回想: *She cast her mind back to her wedding-day.* 她回顾结婚的那一天. **cast one's net wide** cover a wide field of supply, activity, inquiry, etc 撒开大网(广泛地供应、活动、查询等): *The company is casting its net wide in its search for a new sales director.* 公司撒开大网到处物色新的销售主任. **cast pearls before swine** (*saying* 谚) offer beautiful or valuable things to people who cannot appreciate them 明珠暗投. **cast a spell on sb/sth** put sb/sth under the influence of a magic spell 用符咒迷惑某人[某事物]. **cast a/one's 'vote** give a vote 投票. **the die is cast** ⇨ DIE[3]. **7** (phr v) **cast about/around for sth** try to find or think of sth hurriedly 匆忙寻找或考虑某事物: *He cast about desperately for something to say.* 他搜索枯肠找话说. **cast sb/sth aside** abandon sb/sth as useless or unwanted; discard sb/sth 抛弃; 排除; 消除; 废除: *She has cast her old friends aside.* 她把老朋友都撇在一边. ○ *He cast aside all his inhibitions.* 他抛弃了一切禁忌. **cast sb away** (usu passive 通常用于被动语态) leave sb somewhere as a result of a shipwreck 某人因沉船而流落某处: *be cast away on a desert island* (因沉船)被撇在荒岛上. **cast sb down** (usu passive 通常用于被动语态) cause sb to become depressed 使某人沮丧: *He is not easily cast down.* 很少见他情绪低落. Cf 参看 DOWNCAST. **cast (sth) off** (**a**) untie the ropes holding a boat in position; release (a boat) in this way 解缆; 解缆放(船). (**b**) (in knitting) remove (stitches) from the needles (指编织毛线等)收(针). **cast sb/sth off** abandon or reject sb/sth 抛弃或驳回某人[某事物]: *She's cast off three boy-friends in a month.* 她一个月里就甩了三个男朋友. **cast (sth) on** (in knitting) put (the first line of stiches) on a needle (指编织毛线等)起(针). **cast sb out** (*fml* 文) (esp passive 尤用于被动语态) drive sb away; expel 把某人赶走; 逐出. Cf 参看 OUTCAST.

▷ **cast·ing** *n* **1** [C] object made by casting (CAST[1] 4a) molten metal, etc 铸件. **2** [U] process of choosing actors for a play, film, etc 挑选演员(演话剧、电影等): *a strange bit of casting* 演员选得有些怪.

□ **'castaway** *n* person who has been shipwrecked and left in an isolated place 沉船遇难流落在与外界隔绝之地的人.

,casting 'vote vote given (eg by a chairman) to decide an issue when votes on each side are equal 决定票(当各方票数相等时, 由主席所作的决定性投票).

,cast 'iron hard alloy of iron made by casting in a mould 铸铁; 生铁. Cf 参看 WROUGHT IRON (WROUGHT).

,cast-'iron *adj* **1** made of cast iron 铸铁制的; 生铁造的. **2** (*fig* 比喻) very strong; that cannot be broken 强壮的; 打不破的: *He has a ,cast-iron consti'tution.* 他的身体是铁打的. ○ *They won't find her guilty. She's got a ,cast-iron de'fence.* 他们无法给她定罪. 她的答辩无懈可击.

'cast-off *adj* [attrib 作定语] (esp of clothes) no longer wanted; discarded (尤指衣物)不再要的, 被丢弃的: *cast-off shoes* 被丢弃的鞋 ○ *a cast-off lover* 被抛弃的情人. — *n* (usu *pl* 通常作复数) garment which the original owner will not wear again 原主人不再穿的衣物: *He wears his brother's cast-offs.* 他穿着他哥哥的旧衣服.

cast[2] /kɑːst; *US* kæst; kæst/ *n* **1** [C] act of throwing sth 扔; 投; 掷; 抛: *the cast of the dice* 掷色子 ○ *make a cast with a fishing-line/net* 抛鱼线[撒鱼网]. **2** [C] (**a**) object made by pouring or pressing soft material into a mould 铸件; 塑件. (**b**) mould used to make such an object 模子; 模型. (**c**) = PLASTER CAST (PLASTER). **3** [CGp] all the actors in a play, etc 戏剧等的全体演员: *a film with a distinguished cast*, ie with famous actors in it 名演员联合演出的电影 ○ *a cast of thousands*, eg for an epic film 成千上万的演出人员(如史诗影片的) ○ [attrib 作定语] *a 'cast list* 演出人员表. **4** [sing] type or kind (of sth) (某事物的)类型: *He has an unusual cast of mind.* 他的头脑不寻常. **5** [C] = WORM-CAST (WORM). **6** [C] (*dated* 旧) slight squint 轻度斜视眼: *She has a cast in one eye.* 她一只眼轻度斜视.

cas·ta·nets /ˌkæstəˈnets; ˌkæstəˈnɛts/ *n* [pl] pair of shell-shaped pieces of wood or ivory clicked together with the fingers, esp as a rhythmic accompaniment to a Spanish dance 响板(木头或象牙制成的一对贝壳形板, 用手指拍合作响, 尤作西班牙舞蹈的伴奏器).

caste /kɑːst; kæst/ *n* **1** [C] any of the hereditary Hindu social classes 印度的社会等级: *the lowest caste* 最低阶层 ○ [attrib 作定语] *the caste system* (印度的)社会等级制度. **2** [C] any exclusive social class 任何排他的社会阶层. **3** [U] social system based on rigid distinctions of birth, rank, wealth, etc 种姓(按照血统、阶级、财富等严格区分的社会制度). **4** (idm 习语) **lose caste** ⇨ LOSE.

cas·tel·lated /ˈkæstəleɪtɪd; ˈkæstəˌletɪd/ *adj* having turrets or battlements like a castle (似城堡的)有角楼或城垛的; 有雉堞的.

cas·tig·ate /ˈkæstɪgeɪt; ˈkæstəˌget/ *v* [Tn] (*fml* 文) scold, criticize or punish (sb) severely 严厉责骂、批评或惩罚(某人). ▷ **cas·tiga·tion** /ˌkæstɪˈgeɪʃn; ˌkæstəˈgeʃən/ *n* [C, U]

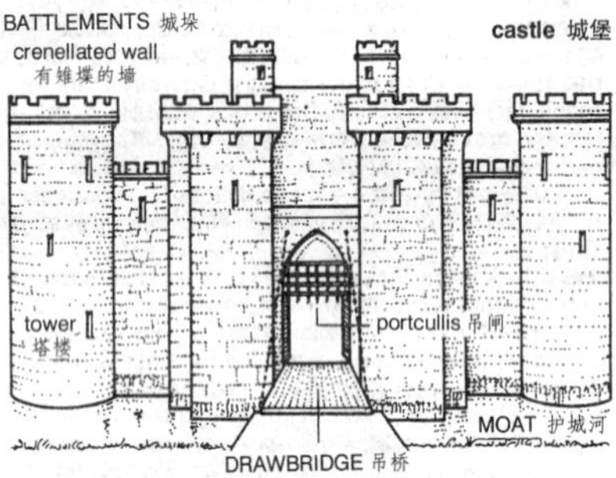

castle /ˈkɑːsl; *US* ˈkæsl; ˈkæsl/ *n* **1** large fortified building or group of buildings with thick walls, towers, battlements and sometimes a moat 城堡; 堡垒: *a medieval castle* 中世纪的城堡 ○ *Windsor Castle* 温莎宫. ⇨illus 见插图. **2** (also **rook**) (in chess) any of the four pieces placed in the corner squares of the board at the start of a game (国际象棋的)车. ⇨illus at CHESS 见CHESS之插图. **3** (idm 习语) **(build) castles in the 'air/in 'Spain** (have) plans or hopes that are unlikely to be realized; day-dreams 空中楼阁; 白日梦. **an Englishman's home is his castle** ⇨ ENGLISHMAN (ENGLISH).

▷ **castle** *v* [I] (as a single move in chess) move either castle to the square next to the king and the king to the square on the other side of that castle (国际象棋中的一步)用车护王.

castor (also **caster**) /ˈkɑːstə(r); *US* ˈkæs-; ˈkæstɚ/ *n* **1** any of the small swivelling wheels fixed to the bottom of a piece of furniture so that it can be moved easily (家具的)小脚轮. ⇨illus at App 1 见附录1之插图, page xvi. **2** small container with holes in the top for sprinkling sugar, etc 调味瓶(顶端有小孔, 用以撒糖等).

□ **,castor 'sugar** (also **,caster 'sugar**) white sugar in fine grains 细白砂糖.

castor oil /ˌkɑːstər ˈɔɪl; *US* ˈkæstər ɔɪl; ˈkæstɚ ˌɔɪl/ thick yellowish oil obtained from the seeds of a tropical plant and used as a laxative and a lubricant 蓖麻油.

cas·trate /kæ'streɪt; *US* 'kæstreɪt; 'kæstret/ *v* [Tn] remove the testicles of (a male animal or person); geld 割除(雄性动物或男子的)睾丸; 阉割; 去势: *A bullock is a castrated bull.* 阉牛是去势的公牛. ▷ **cas·tra·tion** /kæ'streɪʃn; kæs'treʃən/ *n* [U].

cas·ual /'kæʒʊəl; 'kæʒʊəl/ *adj* **1** [esp attrib 尤作定语] happening by chance 偶然的; 碰巧的: *a casual encounter, meeting, visit, etc* 邂逅、不期而遇、不意的拜访. **2** (**a**) [esp attrib 尤作定语] made or done without much care or thought; offhand 不经意的; 随便的; 马虎的; 临时的: *a casual remark* 漫不经心的话. (**b**) (*derog* 贬) showing little concern; nonchalant; irresponsible 漠不关心的; 无动于衷的; 不负责任的: *His attitude to his job is rather casual.* 他的工作态度不太认真. (**c**) [esp attrib 尤作定语] not methodical or thorough; not serious 无条理的; 不彻底的; 不认真的: *a casual inspection* 草率的检查 ○ *a casual glance at a book* 胡乱看一本书 ○ *a casual observer, reader, etc* 马虎的观察者、读者等. **3** (of clothes) for informal occasions; not formal (衣物)便服的, 非正式的: *casual wear* 便装. **4** [attrib 作定语] not permanent; irregular; part-time 非永久的; 不定期的; 部分时间的: *earn one's living by casual labour* 靠做短工为生 ○ *a casual labourer* 临时工 ○ *casual sex*, ie not involving a lasting relationship 萍水相逢的性行为(非持久的关系). **5** [attrib 作定语] slight; superficial 轻微的; 表面的; 肤浅的: *a casual acquaintance* 泛泛之交.

▷ **casu·ally** /'kæʒʊəlɪ; 'kæʒʊəlɪ/ *adv*: *meet sb casually* 巧遇某人 ○ *casually dressed* 穿得随便的 ○ *casually employed* 短期雇用的.

cas·ual·ness *n* [U].

cas·uals *n* [pl] informal clothes, esp men's slip-on shoes 便装(尤指男用无带、扣的鞋).

casu·alty /'kæʒʊəltɪ; 'kæʒʊəltɪ/ *n* **1** person who is killed or injured in war or in an accident (战争或事故中的)伤亡者: *Heavy casualties were reported* (ie It was reported that many people had been killed) *in the fighting.* 据报战斗中伤亡惨重(很多人被杀). ○ (*fig* 比喻) *Mr Jones was the first casualty of the firm's cut-backs*, ie the first to lose his job because of them. 琼斯先生在公司裁员中首当其冲(第一个被裁掉). ○ [attrib 作定语] *a casualty list* 伤亡名单. **2** thing that is lost, damaged or destroyed in an accident 事故中损失的物品: *The cottage was a casualty of the forest fire.* 那小屋被森林大火烧毁. **3** (also '**casualty ward**, '**casualty department**, *US* **emergency**) part of a hospital where people who have been hurt in accidents are taken for urgent treatment 急诊室.

ca·su·istry /'kæzjʊɪstrɪ; 'kæʒʊɪstrɪ/ *n* [U] (*fml usu derog* 文, 通常作贬义) resolving of moral problems, esp by the use of clever but false reasoning; sophistry 诡辩; 曲解; 诡辩术.

▷ **ca·su·ist** *n* (*fml usu derog* 文, 通常作贬义) person who is skilled in casuistry 诡辩家.

ca·su·istic /ˌkæzjʊ'ɪstɪk; ˌkæʒʊ'ɪstɪk/ (also **ca·su·ist·ical**) /-tɪkl; -tɪkl/ *adj*. **ca·su·ist·ic·ally** /-tɪklɪ; -tɪklɪ/ *adv*.

casus belli /ˌkɑːsʊs 'beliː, ˌkeɪsəs 'belaɪ; 'kesəs 'bɛlaɪ/ (*Latin* 拉) act or event which starts a war or is thought to justify starting a war 开战的理由、原因、借口、行动或事件.

cat[1] /kæt; kæt/ *n* **1** [C] small furry domesticated animal often kept as a pet or for catching mice 猫: *We've got three cats and a dog.* 我们有三只猫和一只狗. ○ [attrib 作定语] '*cat food* 猫食. ⇨illus at MOUSE 见 MOUSE 之插图. **2** [C] wild animal related to this 猫科动物: *big 'cats*, ie lions, tigers, leopards, etc 大的猫科动物(狮、虎、豹等) ○ [attrib 作定语] *the cat family* 猫科. ⇨illus 见插图. **3** [C] (*derog* 贬) malicious woman 狠毒的女人. **4 the cat** [sing] = CAT-O'-NINE-TAILS. **5** (idm 习语) **be the cat's 'whiskers/'pyjamas** (*infml* 口) be the best thing, person, idea, etc 了不起的东西、人、主意等: *He thinks he's the cat's whiskers*, ie has a high opinion of himself. 他自命不凡. **a cat-and-dog life** a life in which partners are frequently or constantly quarrelling (在一起居住者)经常吵架的生活. **a cat in hell's chance (of doing sth)** (*infml* 口) no chance at all 一点儿机会也没有. **curiosity killed the cat** ⇨ CURIOSITY. **let the 'cat out of the bag** reveal a secret carelessly or by mistake (无意中)泄露秘密; 露马脚: *I wanted mother's present to be a secret, but my sister let the cat out of the bag.* 给母亲的礼物我原想保密, 可是妹妹却露了马脚. **like a ˌcat on hot 'bricks** (*infml* 口) very nervous 非常紧张; 像热锅上的蚂蚁; 如坐针毡: *He was like a cat on hot bricks before his driving test.* 他面临驾驶考试, 紧张得像热锅上的蚂蚁. **no room to swing a cat** ⇨ ROOM. **play cat and mouse/play a cat-and-mouse game with sb** (*infml* 口) keep sb in a state of uncertain expectation, treating him alternately cruelly and kindly 对某人时好时坏、忽冷忽热. **put/set the 'cat among the pigeons** (*infml* 口) introduce sb/sth that is likely to cause trouble or disturbance 引来可能招惹是非或麻烦的人或事物: *The new security guard's a burglar — that'll set the cat among the pigeons!* 新来的守卫是小偷——这下子可要鸡犬不宁了. **rain cats and 'dogs** ⇨ RAIN[2]. **wait for the cat to jump/to see which way the cat jumps** ⇨ WAIT[1].

□ '**cat burglar** (*Brit*) burglar who enters houses by climbing up walls, drain-pipes, etc (沿墙壁或水管潜入屋内的)小偷, 飞贼.

ˌ**cat-o'-'nine-tails** *n* [sing] whip with nine knotted lashes, formerly used for flogging prisoners 九尾鞭(由九条带纥绌的鞭条做的鞭子, 旧时用以抽打囚犯).

ˌ**cat's-'cradle** *n* game in which string is looped round and between the fingers to form patterns 挑绷子, 翻绳儿(将细绳绕于手指上做成各种花样的游戏).

'**Cat's-eye** *n* (*propr* 专利名) any one of a line of reflecting studs marking the centre or edge of a road as a guide to traffic when it is dark 猫眼(安置在道路中央或边缘的小反光镜, 组成一线, 于黑暗中指示交通用的).

'**cat's-paw** *n* person who is used by sb else to do sth risky or unpleasant 被人利用做冒险或厌恶事情的人.

cat[2] /kæt; kæt/ *n* (*US infml* 口) = CATERPILLAR TRACTOR (CATERPILLAR).

CAT /ˌsiː eɪ 'tiː; ˌsi e 'ti *or, in informal use* 俗读作 kæt; kæt/ *abbr* 缩写 = (*Brit*) College of Advanced Technology 工学院.

cata·clysm /'kætəklɪzəm; 'kætəˌklɪzəm/ *n* sudden violent change or disaster, eg a flood, an earthquake, a revolution or a war 突发的剧烈变动或灾难(如洪水、地震、革命或战争). ▷ **cata·clys·mic** /ˌkætə'klɪzmɪk; ˌkætə'klɪzmɪk/ *adj*: *the cataclysmic events of 1939-45* 1939-1945 年间的战乱.

cata·combs /'kætəkuːmz; *US* -kəʊmz; 'kætəˌkomz/ *n* [pl] series of underground tunnels with openings along the sides for burying the dead (as in ancient Rome) 地下墓穴(如古罗马的).

cata·falque /'kætəfælk; 'kætəˌfælk/ *n* decorated platform on which the coffin of a distinguished person lies before or during a funeral 灵柩台.

cata·lepsy /ˈkætəlepsɪ; ˋkætəˌlɛpsɪ/ *n* [U] disease which causes a person to become temporarily unconscious and his body rigid 强直性昏厥; 僵住症.
▷ **cata·leptic** /ˌkætəˈleptɪk; ˌkætəˋlɛptɪk/ *adj* of or suffering from catalepsy 强直性昏厥的; 患僵住症的. — *n* person suffering from catalepsy 僵住症患者.

cata·logue (*US* also **cata·log**) /ˈkætəlɒg; *US* -lɔːg; ˋkætḷˌɔg/ *n* **1** (book or booklet containing a) complete list of items, usu in a special order and with a description of each 目录; 目录册: *a library catalogue* 图书目录 ○ *an exhibition catalogue* 展览目录. **2** (*fig* 比喻) series 系列: *a catalogue of disasters* 一连串的灾难.
▷ **cata·logue** *v* [Tn] list (sth) in a catalogue 将(某事物)编成目录, 列入目录.

C

cata·lysis /kəˈtæləsɪs; kəˋtæləsɪs/ *n* [U] process of speeding up a chemical reaction with a catalyst 催化作用; 触媒作用.
▷ **cata·lytic** /ˌkætəˈlɪtɪk; ˌkætḷˋɪtɪk/ *adj* of or causing catalysis 催化作用的; 起催化作用的.

cata·lyst /ˈkætəlɪst; ˋkætḷɪst/ *n* **1** substance that speeds up a chemical reaction without itself changing 催化剂; 触媒剂. **2** (*fig* 比喻) person or thing that causes a change 促使变化的人或事物: *The offer of a new job provided just the catalyst she needed.* 这份新工作正是她所需要转变的契机.

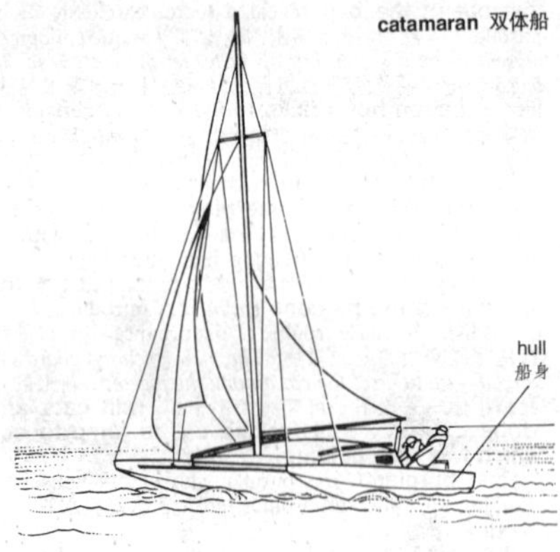

catamaran 双体船

cata·ma·ran /ˌkætəməˈræn; ˌkætəməˋræn/ *n* **1** sailing-boat with two parallel hulls 双体船. ⇨illus 见插图. **2** raft made of two boats or logs fastened side by side (两只船或木排组成的)筏子.

catapult 弹弓

cata·pult /ˈkætəpʌlt; ˋkætəˌpʌlt/ *n* **1** (*US* **slingshot**) Y-shaped stick with a piece of elastic attached to it, used esp by children for shooting stones 弹弓(尤指儿童玩的). ⇨illus 见插图. **2** (in ancient times) machine for throwing heavy stones in war (古时)石弩. **3** apparatus for launching gliders or for launching aircraft from the deck of a ship (使滑翔机或飞行器从轮船甲板上升空的)弹射器.
▷ **cata·pult** *v* **1** [Tn, Tn·pr] shoot or launch (sth) from a catapult 用弹弓、石弩或弹射器射出或弹射(某物). **2** [Ipr, Tn·pr] (cause sb/sth to) be thrown suddenly and with force (使某物)被猛力掷出: *In the crash the driver (was) catapulted through the windscreen.* 在事故中司机从挡风玻璃中(被)弹了出来.

cat·ar·act /ˈkætərækt; ˋkætəˌrækt/ *n* **1** large steep waterfall (大而陡的)瀑布. **2** (*medical* 医) (**a**) disease in which the lens of the eye becomes cloudy, causing partial or total blindness 白内障. (**b**) area clouded in this way 白内障的晶状体: *an operation to remove cataracts* 白内障(晶状体)摘除手术.

ca·tarrh /kəˈtɑː(r); kəˋtɑr/ *n* [U] (**a**) inflammation of the mucous membrane of the nose and throat, causing an increased flow of mucus 卡他; (鼻喉)黏膜炎. (**b**) mucus forming in this way (鼻喉)黏液: *I've a bad cold and I'm full of catarrh.* 我得了重感冒, 总流鼻涕.

cata·strophe /kəˈtæstrəfɪ; kəˋtæstrəfɪ/ *n* sudden great disaster or misfortune 突如其来的大灾难或大灾祸: *The earthquake was a terrible catastrophe.* 这次地震是可怕的灾难. ▷ **cata·strophic** /ˌkætəˈstrɒfɪk; ˌkætəˋstrɑfɪk/ *adj*: *a catastrophic failure* 灾难性的失败. **cata·stroph·ic·ally** *adv*.

cat·call /ˈkætkɔːl; ˋkætˌkɔl/ *n* shrill whistle expressing disapproval (表示反对的)嘘声: *The Minister's speech was greeted with jeers and catcalls.* 这位大臣的讲话遭到嘲笑, 嘘声四起.
▷ **cat·call** *v* [I] make catcalls 发出嘘声.

catch[1] /kætʃ; kætʃ/ *v* (*pt, pp* **caught** /kɔːt; kɔt/) **1** (**a**) [Tn] stop and hold (a moving object) esp in the hands 接住(运动的物体)(尤指用手): *I threw a ball to her and she caught it.* 我把球扔给她, 她接住了. ○ *Our dog likes catching biscuits in its mouth.* 我们的狗喜欢用嘴接饼干. (**b**) [Tn, Tn·p] **~ sb (out)** (in cricket) dismiss (a batsman) by catching the ball he has hit before it touches the ground (板球)在球触地之前接住球而迫使(击球员)出场; 接杀出局. **2** [Tn, Tn·pr] capture (sb/sth) after a chase, in a trap, etc; seize and hold 捉住; 抓住; 逮住; 捕获: *catch a thief* 捉贼 ○ *Cats catch mice.* 猫捉老鼠. ○ *How many fish did you catch?* 你捕到多少鱼? ○ *I caught him* (ie met him and stopped him) *just as he was leaving the building.* 他正要离开大楼的时候, 我把他截住了. ○ *catch sb by the arm, throat, scruff of the neck, etc* 抓住某人的胳臂、掐住某人的脖子等. **3** [Ipr, Cn·g] find or discover (sb doing sth); take by surprise 发现或发觉(某人正做某事); 突然抓住: *I caught her with her fingers in the biscuit tin.* 我看见她手指还在饼干盒里呢. ○ *I caught a boy stealing apples from the garden.* 我撞见一个男孩儿偷园里的苹果. ○ *You won't catch me working* (ie I would never work) *on a Sunday!* 你决见不到我在星期日工作! **4** [Tn] be in time for (and get on) (sth) 及时赶到; 赶上: *catch a bus, plane, train, etc* 赶上公共汽车、飞机、火车等 ○ *catch the post*, ie post letters before the box is emptied by the postman 赶上邮局的一班收信时刻(在邮递员将信箱里的信取走之前寄出). **5** [Tn] (*US infml* 口) see or hear (sth); attend 看或听(某事物); 参加: *Let's eat now and maybe we could catch a movie later.* 咱们现在就吃, 说不定吃完能赶场电影. **6** [I, Ipr, Tn, Tn·pr] **~ (sth) (in/on sth)** (cause sth to) become fixed, stuck or entangled in or on sth (使某物)固着、卡住、钩住、缠住、绊住、夹住或挂住某物: *The lock won't catch*, ie cannot be fastened. 这锁锁不上了. ○ *Her dress caught on a nail.* 她的衣服让钉子给钩住了. ○ *He caught his thumb in the door.* 他的拇指让门夹了. ○ *He caught his foot on a tree root and stumbled.* 他一只脚被树根绊住而跌倒了. **7** [Tn] become infected with (an illness) 感染上, 传染上(疾病): *catch (a) cold* 患感冒 ○ *catch 'flu, pneumonia, bronchitis, etc* 染上流感、肺炎、支气管炎等. **8** [Tn] hear (sth); understand 听见(某事物); 理解; 了解: *Sorry, I didn't quite catch what you said.* 对不起, 我没听清你的话. ○ *I don't catch your meaning.* 我不明白你的意思. **9** [Tn, Tn·pr, Dn·n] hit (sth) 击中(某物): *The stone caught him on the side of the head.* 那块石头击中他头部的侧面. ○ *She caught him a blow on the chin.* 她打了他下巴一拳. **10** [I] begin to burn 烧着; 着火: *These logs are wet: they won't catch.* 这些木头很湿, 点不着. **11** [Tn] reproduce (sth) accurately 精确地再现(某事物): *The artist has caught her smile perfectly.* 艺术家巧妙地捕捉住她的笑容. **12** (idm 习语) **be caught/taken short** ⇨ SHORT[2]. **catch sb ˈat it** = CATCH SB RED-HANDED. **catch sb's atˈtention/ˈeye** attract sb's attention 吸引某人的注意: *Try to catch the waiter's eye.* 招呼服务员. ○ *A newspaper headline caught his attention.* 报纸的大标题引起他的注意. **catch one's ˈbreath**

stop breathing for a moment (because of fear, shock, etc) (因恐惧、震惊等)一时停止呼吸, 屏息: *He caught his breath in surprise.* 他惊奇得屏住了呼吸. **catch one's death (of cold)** (*infml* 口) catch a severe cold 患重感冒: *Don't go out without a coat: you'll catch your death.* 别不穿外套出去, 会得重感冒的. **catch/take sb's fancy** ⇨ FANCY[1]. **catch 'fire** begin to burn, esp accidentally 烧着, 着火(尤指意外地): *She was standing too close to the fireplace and her dress caught fire.* 她站得离壁炉太近了, 衣服烧着了. **catch it** (*infml* 口) be punished or scolded 受罚; 挨骂: *If your father finds you here you'll really catch it!* 要是你父亲知道你在这里, 你非挨骂不可! **catch sb 'napping** find sb not paying attention 发现某人精神不集中: *Don't let the boss catch you napping!* 别让老板发现你走神儿! **catch sb on the wrong 'foot** catch sb when he is not ready or expecting sth 乘某人不备, 出其不意. **catch sb red-'handed** discover sb in the act of doing sth wrong or committing a crime 当场发现某人正做坏事或犯罪. **catch sight/a glimpse of sb/sth** see sb/sth for a moment 一眼瞥见某人[某事物]: *She caught sight of a car in the distance.* 她一眼瞥见远处的汽车. ○ *He caught a glimpse of her before she vanished into the crowd.* 他看见她一闪就在人群中消失了. **catch the 'sun** become sun-burned 晒焦; 晒黑: *Your back looks sore — you've really caught the sun today.* 你后背红了 —— 今天真晒坏了. **catch/take sb unawares** ⇨ UNAWARES (UNAWARE). **catch sb with his pants/trousers down** (*infml* 口) catch or trap sb when he is unprepared or not being watchful 乘某人措手不及; 乘其不备; 出其不意; 冷不防. **the early bird catches the worm** ⇨ EARLY. **set a sprat to catch a mackerel** ⇨ SPRAT. **set a thief to catch a thief** ⇨ THIEF. **13** (phr v) **catch at sth** = CLUTCH AT STH (CLUTCH). **ˌcatch 'on (to sth)** (*infml* 口) understand (sth) 理解, 了解, 懂(某事物): *He is very quick/slow to catch 'on.* 他理解得很快[很慢]. **ˌcatch 'on (with sb)** (*infml* 口) become popular or fashionable 受欢迎; 变得流行: *Mini-skirts first caught on in the 1960's.* 超短裙是在六十年代开始流行的. **ˌcatch sb 'out** show that sb is ignorant or doing sth wrong 显出某人无知或犯错误: *Ask me anything you like — you won't catch me out.* 你尽管问吧 —— 决问不倒我. **ˌcatch 'up (with sb)**; **ˌcatch sb 'up** reach (and sometimes overtake) sb who is ahead (eg in a race); reach the same stage as sb 赶上(有时超过)某人; 达到与某人相同的境界: *Go on in front. I'll soon catch you up/catch up (with you).* 你先走. 我很快就赶上你. ○ *After missing a term through illness he had to work hard to catch up (with the others).* 他因病一学期未上课, 得努力赶上(其他同学). **ˌcatch 'up on sth** (**a**) spend extra time doing sth, in order to compensate for having neglected it 用额外时间做某事(以弥补所耽误的时间): *I've got a lot of work to catch 'up on.* 我有很多工作得赶着做. (**b**) acquire information about sth belatedly 事后了解对某事物的情况: *Come over for a chat so we can catch up on each other's news.* 来聊聊天, 彼此好通通最近的消息. **be ˌcaught 'up in sth** be absorbed or involved in sth 被卷入或陷入某事物中: *She was caught up in the anti-nuclear movement.* 她投身于反核运动.

▷ **catcher** *n* (in baseball) fielder who stands behind the batter (棒球)接球手. ⇨illus at BASEBALL 见 BASEBALL 之插图.

catch·ing *adj* (of a disease) infectious (指疾病)传染性的.

catchy *adj* (**-ier, -iest**) (of a tune) pleasant and easy to remember (指曲调)悦耳易记的.

□ **'catch-all** *n* (*esp US*) **1** thing for holding many small objects 装零星物品的东西. **2** word, phrase, etc that covers a range of possibilities without describing any of them precisely 笼统的词语.

'catch crop crop grown between rows of other crops 间作.

catch[2] /kætʃ; kætʃ/ *n* **1** act of catching (esp a ball) 抓住(尤指球): *a difficult catch* 难接的球. **2** (amount of) sth caught 所捕获的某事物(的量): *a huge catch of fish* 捕获大量的鱼 ○ (*infml* 口) *He's a good catch*, ie worth getting as a husband. 他是个好对象(值得嫁给他). **3** device for fastening sth 固着某物的装置: *The catch on my handbag is broken.* 我的手提包的扣坏了. **4** hidden difficulty or disadvantage 潜在的困难或不利因素: *The house is very cheap. There must be a catch somewhere.* 这所房子非常便宜. 这里面一定有蹊跷. ○ [attrib 作定语] *a 'catch question*, ie one intended to trick sb 怪问题(使人上当的问题). **5** type of humorous song for three or more singers, each starting at a different time 轮唱曲. **6** (idm 习语) **catch-22** /ˌkætʃ twentɪˈtuː; ˌkætʃ ˌtwɛntɪˋtu/ (*sl* 俚) dilemma faced by sb who is bound to suffer, whichever course of action he takes 进退维谷: [attrib 作定语] *a catch-22 situation* 进退维谷的情况.

catch·ment area /ˈkætʃmənt eərɪə; ˋkætʃmənt ˌɛrɪə/ **1** (also **catchment basin**) area from which rainfall flows into a river, reservoir, etc 集水盆地(雨水由此处流入江河、水库等). **2** (also **catchment**) area from which people are sent to a particular school, hospital, etc 属区(人们由此处被送到某学校、医院等): *a school with a large catchment area* 有大范围招生区的学校.

catch·penny /ˈkætʃpenɪ; ˋkætʃˌpɛnɪ/ *adj* [attrib 作定语] designed to make money 专为赚钱的: *a catchpenny novel, title, device, trick* 专为赚钱的小说、头衔、装置、花招.

catch·phrase /ˈkætʃfreɪz; ˋkætʃˌfrez/ *n* well-known phrase first used by, and later associated with, an entertainer, political leader, etc 名言; 警语.

catch·word /ˈkætʃwɜːd; ˋkætʃˌwɝd/ *n* **1** word or phrase placed where it will attract attention, eg above a paragraph in a newspaper article 醒目的字或词语(如报章段落中的小标题). **2** first or last word of a page in a dictionary, printed above the columns (词典上的)眉题.

cat·ech·ism /ˈkætəkɪzəm; ˋkætəˌkɪzəm/ *n* (**a**) [U] summary of the principles of a religion in the form of questions and answers 教义问答. (**b**) [C] series of such questions, used for religious instruction 教义问答集.

cat·ech·ize, -ise /ˈkætəkaɪz; ˋkætəˌkaɪz/ *v* [Tn] teach (sb) (esp about religion) by means of questions and answers 用问答教学法教(某人)(尤指宗教内容).

cat·egor·ical /ˌkætəˈɡɒrɪkl; *US* -ɡɔːr-; ˌkætəˋɡɔrɪkl/ *adj* (of a statement) unconditional; absolute; explicit (指陈述)无条件的, 绝对的, 明确的: *a categorical denial, refusal, etc* 断然的否认、拒绝等. ▷ **cat·egor·ic·ally** /-klɪ; -klɪ/ *adv*.

cat·egory /ˈkætəɡərɪ; *US* -ɡɔːrɪ; ˋkætəˌɡorɪ/ *n* class or group of things in a complete system of grouping 种类; 类别; 范畴: *place things in categories* 分门别类.

▷ **cat·egor·ize, -ise** /ˈkætəɡəraɪz; ˋkætəɡəˌraɪz/ *v* [Tn] place (sth) in a category 将(某事物)分类.

ca·ter /ˈkeɪtə(r); ˋketɚ/ *v* **1** (**a**) [I, Ipr] **~ (for sth/sb)** provide food and services, esp at social functions 提供饮食及服务(尤指社交方面): *cater for a party, banquet, etc* 为聚会、宴会等备办食物 ○ *Fifty is a lot of people to cater for!* 承办五十人的饮食可够多的! (**b**) [Tn] (*esp US*) provide food and services for (a party, banquet, etc) 为(聚会、宴会等)提供饮食及服务. **2** [Ipr] (**a**) **~ for sb/sth** provide what is needed or desired by sb/sth 由某人[某事物]提供、迎合: *TV must cater for many different tastes.* 电视节目必须迎合各种人的爱好. (**b**) **~ to sth** try to satisfy a particular need or demand 满足某种需要或要求: *newspapers catering to people's love of scandal* 迎合人们爱看丑闻消息的报纸.

▷ **ca·terer** *n* **1** person whose job is providing food for large social events 承办酒席的人. **2** owner or manager of a hotel, restaurant, etc (旅馆、饭店等的)老板, 经理.

ca·ter·ing *n* [U] (trade of) providing food, etc for social events 承办酒席(的行业): *Who did the catering for your son's wedding?* 谁承办你儿子婚礼的酒席?

cat·er·pil·lar /ˈkætəpɪlə(r); ˋkætɚˌpɪlɚ/ *n* **1** larva of a butterfly or moth 毛虫, 蠋(蝶或蛾的幼虫). ⇨illus at BUTTERFLY 见 BUTTERFLY 之插图. **2** (**a**) (also **Caterpillar track**) (*propr* 专利名) endless belt passing round the wheels of a tractor or tank, enabling it to travel over rough ground 履带. (**b**) (also **Caterpillar tractor**, *abbr* 缩写 **cat**) tractor fitted with such a belt 履带拖拉机.

cat·er·waul /ˈkætəwɔːl; ˋkætɚˌwɔl/ *v* [I] make a cat's shrill howling cry 发出猫叫春的声音: *Do stop caterwauling, children!* 孩子们, 别像猫似的乱叫!

▷ **cat·er·waul** *n* [sing] shrill cry of or like a cat (像)猫叫春的声音.

cat·fish /ˈkætfɪʃ; ˋkætˌfɪʃ/ *n* (*pl* unchanged 复数不变) large (usu freshwater) fish with whisker-like feelers round its mouth 鲶鱼.

cat·gut /ˈkætgʌt; ˋkæt,gʌt/ *n* [U] thin strong cord made from the dried intestines of animals and used for the strings of violins, tennis rackets, etc（小提琴、网球拍等用的）肠线.

Cath *abbr* 缩写 = Catholic.

cath·ar·sis /kəˈθɑːsɪs; kəˈθɑrsɪs/ *n* (*pl* **-ses** /-siːz; -siz/) **1** [C, U] (instance of the) release of strong feelings through the effect of art, esp drama（通过艺术作用，尤指戏剧）强烈情感的发抒. **2** [U] (*medical* 医) emptying of the bowels 导泻; 通便.

▷ **cath·artic** /kəˈθɑːtɪk; kəˈθɑrtɪk/ *adj* causing catharsis; purgative 导泻的; 通便的. — *n* (*medical* 医) purgative drug 泻药.

ca·thed·ral /kəˈθiːdrəl; kəˈθidrəl/ *n* main church of a district under the care of a bishop 总教堂; 大教堂: [attrib 作定语] *a cathedral city* 有大教堂的城市.

Cath·er·ine wheel /ˈkæθrɪn wiːl; ˌkæθrɪn ˋhwil/ *n* type of firework that spins when lit 转轮烟火.

cath·eter /ˈkæθɪtə(r); ˋkæθətɚ/ *n* (*medical* 医) thin tube used to drain fluids from the body, esp one that is inserted into the bladder to extract urine 导管;（尤指）导尿管.

▷ **cath·et·er·ize, -ise** [Tn] insert a catheter into (sb/sth) 将导管插入（某人［某物］）.

cath·ode /ˈkæθəʊd; ˋkæθod/ *n* negative electrode, by which an electric current leaves a device such as a battery 阴极; 负极. Cf 参看 ANODE.

□ ˌ**cathode** ˈ**ray** beam of electrons from the cathode in a vacuum tube 阴极射线. ˌ**cathode** ˈ**ray tube** vacuum tube, eg the picture tube of a TV set, in which cathode rays produce a luminous image on a fluorescent screen 阴极射线管.

Cath·olic /ˈkæθəlɪk; ˋkæθəlɪk/ *adj* **1** = ROMAN CATHOLIC (ROMAN): *the Catholic Church* 天主教会 ○ *a Catholic priest, school* 天主教教士、学校. Cf 参看 PROTESTANT. **2** (also **catholic**) of or relating to all Christians or the whole Christian Church 天主教的; 与天主教有关的.

▷ **Cath·olic** *n* (*abbr* 缩写 **Cath**) member of the Roman Catholic Church 天主教徒: *Is she a Catholic or a Protestant?* 她是天主教徒还是新教徒?

Cath·oli·cism /kəˈθɒləsɪzəm; kəˋθɑlə,sɪzəm/ *n* [U] = ROMAN CATHOLICISM (ROMAN).

cath·olic /ˈkæθəlɪk; ˋkæθəlɪk/ *adj* including many or most things; general; universal 包罗万象的; 广泛的; 普遍的: *have catholic tastes, interests, views, etc* 广泛的爱好、兴趣、意见等.

▷ **cath·oli·city** /ˌkæθəˈlɪsətɪ; ˌkæθəˋlɪsətɪ/ *n* [U] universality or breadth (esp of interests) 普遍性, 广泛性（尤指兴趣）.

cat·kin /ˈkætkɪn; ˋkætkɪn/ *n* tuft of soft downy flowers hanging from the twigs of such trees as willows or birches 柔荑花序（垂于柳树或桦树枝头的软毛花穗）.

cat·mint /ˈkætmɪnt; ˋkæt,mɪnt/ (also **catnip**) *n* [U] aromatic plant with blue flowers whose smell is attractive to cats 猫薄荷; 樟脑草.

cat·nap /ˈkætnæp; ˋkætnæp/ *n* short sleep; doze 小睡; 瞌睡; 盹儿.

▷ **cat·nap** *v* (**-pp-**) [I] have a catnap 小睡片刻; 打瞌睡; 打盹儿.

cat·nip /ˈkætnɪp; ˋkætnɪp/ *n* [U] = CATMINT.

cat·suit /ˈkætsuːt; ˋkæt,sut/ *n* close-fitting garment that covers the body from the neck to the feet（从颈至足全身的）紧身衣.

cattle /ˈkætl; ˋkætl̩/ *n* [pl *v*] animals with horns and cloven hoofs such as cows, bulls and bullocks, bred for their milk or meat; oxen 牛（总称）: *a herd of cattle* 一群牛 ○ *twenty head of cattle*, eg twenty cows 二十头牛 ○ *The prisoners were herded like cattle.* 囚犯像牲口一样被赶到一起. ○ [attrib 作定语] ˈ*cattle breeding* 饲养牛 ○ ˈ*cattle sheds* 牛棚.

□ ˈ**cattle-cake** *n* [U] small blocks of concentrated food fed to cattle 牛饲料.

ˈ**cattle-grid** *n* (usu metal) grid covering a ditch in a road so that vehicles can pass but not cattle, sheep, etc 拦畜沟栅（通常为金属制的架子，置于路中的沟上，车辆可通过而牛羊等无法通过）.

catty /ˈkætɪ; ˋkætɪ/ *adj* (**-ier, -iest**) (also **cat·tish**) malicious; spiteful 恶毒的; 恶意的: *catty remarks* 恶毒的话. ▷ **cat·tily** *adv*. **cat·ti·ness** *n* [U].

cat·walk /ˈkætwɔːk; ˋkæt,wɔk/ *n* raised narrow footway along a bridge, over a theatre stage, etc（桥梁、舞台等的）狭窄的人行道.

Cau·ca·sian /kɔːˈkeɪzɪən, kɔːˈkeɪʒn; kɔˋkeʒən/ (also **Cau·ca·soid** /ˈkɔːkəzɔɪd; ˋkɔkə,sɔɪd/) *adj* of or relating to the 'white' or light-skinned racial division of mankind 白种人的; 高加索的; 高加索人的.

▷ **Cau·ca·sian** *n* Caucasian person 白种人; 高加索人.

cau·cus /ˈkɔːkəs; ˋkɔkəs/ *n* [CGp] (*sometimes derog* 有时作贬义) **1** (meeting of the) parliamentary members of a particular political party or any other legislature 政党或立法机关的议会成员（的会议）. **2** (*US*) (meeting of the) members or leaders of a particular political party to choose candidates, decide policy, etc 政党的决策干部（的会议）. **3** local organizing committee of a political party, which decides policy, etc 政党的地方决策委员会.

caught *pt, pp* of CATCH[1].

caul /kɔːl; kɔl/ *n* (*anatomy* 解) (**a**) membrane enclosing a foetus in the womb 胎膜. (**b**) part of this that is sometimes found on a child's head at birth（在幼儿出生时头部有时带有的）部分胎膜.

caul·dron (also **cal·dron**) /ˈkɔːldrən; ˋkɔldrən/ *n* large deep pot for boiling things in 大锅.

cau·li·flower /ˈkɒlɪflaʊə(r); *US* ˈkɔːlɪ-; ˋkɔlə,flaʊɚ/ *n* [C, U] type of cabbage with a large dense white head of flowers, eaten as a vegetable 花椰菜; 菜花: *Have some more cauliflower.* 再吃点菜花. ⇨illus at CABBAGE 见 CABBAGE 之插图.

□ **cauliflower** ˈ**cheese** (*Brit*) cauliflower cooked and served with a cheese sauce 奶酪菜花.

cauliflower ˈ**ear** (*Brit*) ear that has become swollen after repeated blows, eg in boxing 菜花耳（被反复殴打而肿胀的耳朵，如在拳击赛中的）.

caulk (also *esp US* **calk**) /kɔːk; kɔk/ *v* [Tn] (**a**) make (esp a boat) watertight by filling the seams or joints with waterproof material（用防水材料填充缝隙或连接处）使（尤指船）不漏水. (**b**) fill up (esp cracks in wood) with a sticky substance 用黏性物质填塞（尤指木缝）; 泥（缝）.

causal /ˈkɔːzl; ˋkɔzl̩/ *adj* **1** of or forming a cause; relating to cause and effect 原因的; 构成原因的; 因果关系的. **2** (*grammar*) expressing or indicating a cause 表示原因的: *'Because' is a causal conjunction.* because 一词是表示原因的连接词.

▷ **caus·al·ity** /kɔːˈzælətɪ; kɔˋzælətɪ/ (also **causation**) *n* [U] (**a**) relationship between cause and effect 因果关系. (**b**) principle that nothing can happen without a cause 因果性.

causa·tion /kɔːˈzeɪʃn; kɔˋzeʃən/ *n* [U] **1** the causing or producing of an effect 起因; 原因. **2** = CAUSALITY (CAUSAL).

caus·at·ive /ˈkɔːzətɪv; ˋkɔzətɪv/ *adj* **1** acting as a cause 成为原因的. **2** (*grammar*) (of words or forms of words) expressing a cause（指词或词形）使役的: *'Blacken' is a causative verb meaning 'cause to become black'.* blacken 是使役动词, 意思是'使变黑'.

cause /kɔːz; kɔz/ *n* **1** [C] that which produces an effect; thing, event, person, etc that makes sth happen 原因; 导致某事物发生的事物、人等: *What was the cause of the fire?* 火灾是怎样引起的? ○ *Smoking is one of the causes of heart disease.* 吸烟是引起心脏病的一种病因. ○ *Police are investigating the causes of the explosion.* 警方正在调查爆炸的原因. **2** [U] **~ (for sth)** reason 理由; 缘故: *There is no cause for anxiety.* 不必忧虑. ○ *You have no cause for complaint/no cause to complain.* 你没有理由抱怨. ○ *She is never absent from work without good cause.* 她决不无故缺勤. ⇨Usage at REASON[1] 用法见 REASON[1]. **3** [C] aim, principle or movement that is strongly defended or supported 极力维护或支持的目标、原则或运动; 事业: *a good cause*, ie one that deserves to be supported, eg a charity 高尚的目标（应为之尽力的目标, 如慈善事业）○ *He fought for the republican cause in the civil war.* 他在内战中为共和事业而战. ○ *Her life was devoted to the cause of justice.* 她为正义事业而献身. **4** [C] (*law* 律) question to be resolved in a court of law 诉讼的问题或事由: *pleading one's cause* 辩护; 分辩. **5** (idm 习语) **a lost cause** ⇨ LOSE[2]. **make common cause with sb** ⇨ COMMON[1]. **the root cause** ⇨ ROOT[1].

▷ **cause** *v* [Tn, Tnt, Dn·n, Dn·pr] **~ sth (for sb)** be the cause of (sth); make happen 造成(某事物); 使发生: *Smoking can cause lung cancer.* 吸烟可致肺癌. ○ *What caused the explosion?* 爆炸是怎样引起的? ○ *The cold weather caused the plants to die.* 天气寒冷冻死了植物. ○ *He caused his parents much unhappiness.* 他弄得父母很不愉快. ○ *She's always causing trouble for people.* 她总是给人添麻烦.

NOTE ON USAGE 用法: The verbs **cause**, **bring about** and **make** indicate how a certain result, situation or event happens ☆ **cause**、**bring about**、**make** 均表示某结果、某情况或某事情是怎样造成或发生的. These verbs are used in a variety of patterns. 这几个动词可用于多种句型. **Bring about** and **cause** can be used with a direct object indicating the result ☆ **bring about** 和 **cause** 可与表示结果的直接宾语连用. **Bring about** is more formal and refers to a less direct cause ☆ **bring about** 较文, 所表示的因果关系不那么直接: *Smoking can cause lung cancer.* 吸烟可致肺癌. ○ *The war brought about a reduction in the birth-rate.* 战争导致出生率下降. **Cause** can connect the result with the person, etc affected ☆ **cause** 可指所产生的结果与所涉及的人等有关: *My car has caused me a lot of trouble.* 我的汽车给我带来很多麻烦. ○ *His parents were caused a lot of worry by his laziness.* 他很懒惰, 使父母大伤脑筋. **Cause** and **make** can be used with (*to* +) an infinitive, but not in the passive ☆ **cause** 和 **make** 可与(to +)不定式连用, 但不可用于被动语态: *The pepper in the food caused me to/made me sneeze.* 这食物中的胡椒味儿呛得我直打喷嚏. When **make** means 'compel', it can be used in the passive (with *to* + infinitive) 当 **make** 意为'迫使'时, 可用于被动语态(与 to + 不定式连用): *They made him pay for the damage he had done/He was made to pay for the damage he had done.* 那些人叫他赔偿由他造成的损失[他被迫赔偿自己所造成的损失].

cause·way /ˈkɔːzweɪ; ˈkɔz,we/ *n* raised road or path, esp across low or wet ground 堤道, 砌道(尤指通过低洼或潮湿地带的).

caus·tic /ˈkɔːstɪk; ˈkɔstɪk/ *adj* **1** that can burn or destroy things by chemical action 腐蚀性的; 苛性的. **2** (*fig* 比喻) (of comments) sarcastic; cutting (指评论)讽刺的; 挖苦的: *caustic remarks* 刻薄话 ○ *a caustic wit* 言词尖刻的人.
▷ **caus·tic·ally** /-klɪ; -kl̩ɪ/ *adv* in a caustic(2) way 讽刺地; 挖苦地.
□ ˌ**caustic** ˈ**soda** = SODIUM HYDROXIDE (SODIUM).

caut·er·ize, -ise /ˈkɔːtəraɪz; ˈkɔtə,raɪz/ *v* [Tn] burn the surface of (body tissue) with a caustic substance or hot iron to destroy infection or stop bleeding (用腐蚀性物质或烙铁)烧灼(表皮组织)以消毒或止血: *cauterize a snake-bite* 烧灼蛇咬伤口.

cau·tion /ˈkɔːʃn; ˈkɔʃən/ *n* **1** [U] being careful to avoid danger or mistakes; prudence 小心; 谨慎; 慎重: *Proceed with caution.* 小心行事. ○ *You should exercise extreme caution when driving in fog.* 在雾中开车要极为小心. **2** [C] warning, esp one given to sb who has committed a minor crime, that further action will be taken if he commits it again 警告(尤指某人已犯轻罪, 下不为例): *let sb off with a caution* 给某人一个警告而放过他. **3** [sing] (*dated infml* 旧, 口) amusing or surprising person 使人发笑或惊奇的人. **4** (idm 习语) **throw, fling, etc caution to the winds** stop being cautious in one's actions or when deciding what to do 不顾一切; 鲁莽行事.
▷ **cau·tion** *v* **1** (**a**) [Tn, Dn·t] warn (sb) to be careful 提醒或警告(某人)要小心: *We were cautioned not to drive too fast.* 人家提醒我们车不要开得太快. (**b**) [Ipr, Tn·pr] **~ (sb) against sth** warn or advise (sb) against sth 警告或劝告(某人)防止某事物: *I would caution against undue optimism.* 我奉劝不要过于乐观. **2** [Tn] give a caution(2) to (sb) 对(某人)给予警告: *be cautioned by a judge* 受到法官的警告.
cau·tion·ary /ˈkɔːʃənərɪ; *US* ˈkɔːʃənerɪ; ˈkɔʃən,ɛrɪ/ *adj* giving advice or a warning 给予劝告或警告的: *a cautionary tale* 警世的故事.

cau·tious /ˈkɔːʃəs; ˈkɔʃəs/ *adj* **~ (about/of sb/sth)** showing or having caution(1); careful 小心的; 谨慎的; 细心的: *a cautious driver* 谨慎的司机 ○ *cautious of strangers* 提防陌生人 ○ *cautious about spending money* 用钱仔细. ▷ **cau·tiously** *adv*. **cau·tious·ness** *n* [U].

ca·val·cade /ˌkævlˈkeɪd; ˌkævl̩ˈked/ *n* procession of people on horseback, in cars, etc 骑马、乘车等的行列.

ca·va·lier /ˌkævəˈlɪə(r); ˌkævəˈlɪr/ *n* **1 Cavalier** supporter of Charles I in the English Civil War (英国内战中)拥护查理一世的人, 保皇党党员. Cf 参看 ROUNDHEAD (ROUND²). **2** (*joc* 谑) man escorting a woman (陪伴女子的)护花使者.
▷ **ca·va·lier** *adj* [esp attrib 尤作定语] offhand; discourteous 随便的; 不礼貌的: *display a cavalier attitude towards the feelings of others* 对别人的感情满不在乎 ○ *treat sb in a cavalier manner* 慢待某人.

C

cav·alry /ˈkævlrɪ; ˈkævl̩rɪ/ *n* [CGp] soldiers fighting on horseback (esp formerly) or in armoured vehicles 骑兵(尤指旧时的); 装甲兵: [attrib 作定语] *a cavalry officer/regiment* 装甲兵军官[团]. Cf 参看 INFANTRY.

cave /keɪv; kev/ *n* hollow place in the side of a cliff or hill, or underground 洞穴.
▷ **cave** *v* **1** [I] (usu 通常作 **go caving**) explore caves as a sport 洞穴探险运动: *He likes caving.* 他喜欢洞穴探险运动. **2** (phr v) **cave in** fall inwards; collapse 塌陷; 坍方; 坍塌: *The roof of the tunnel caved in (on the workmen).* 隧道顶坍塌(压住工人). ○ (*fig* 比喻) *All opposition to the scheme has caved in.* 所有反对这一计划的意见都否定了.
□ ˈ**cave-dweller** *n* = CAVEMAN.
ˈ**cave-in** *n* sudden collapse of a roof, etc (屋顶等)突然坍塌.
caveman /ˈkeɪvmæn; ˈkev,mæn/ *n* (*pl* **-men** /ˈkeɪvmen; ˈkev,mɛn/) **1** person living in caves, esp in prehistoric times 穴居人(尤指史前时代的). **2** (*infml* 口) man of crude or violent feelings and behaviour 野蛮人; 粗野的人.

cav·eat /ˈkævɪæt, *also* ˈkeɪvɪæt; ˈkævɪ,æt, ˈkevɪ,æt/ *n* **1** (*fml* 文) warning; proviso 警告; 限制性条款: *I recommend the deal, but with certain caveats.* 我介绍这笔交易, 但有几项要提请注意. **2** (*law* 律) procedure for requesting a court to suspend proceedings until the opposition has been heard 中止诉讼的申请.

cav·ern /ˈkævən; ˈkævɚn/ *n* cave, esp a large or dark one 洞穴(尤指大而黑的).
▷ **cav·ern·ous** *adj* like a cavern; large and deep 像大洞穴的; 大而深的: *cavernous depths* 像大洞穴般的深度 ○ *cavernous eyes* 深陷的眼睛.

cavi·are (also **cav·iar**) /ˈkævɪɑː(r); ˌkævɪˈɑr/ *n* [U] **1** pickled roe of sturgeon or other large fish, eaten as a delicacy 鱼子酱. **2** (idm 习语) **be** ˌ**caviare to the** ˈ**general** (*dated or joc* 旧或谑) be too refined or delicate to be appreciated by ordinary people 过于高雅而不为一般人所欣赏; 阳春白雪.

cavil /ˈkævl; ˈkævl̩/ *v* (**-ll-**; *US* **-l-**) [I, Ipr] **~ (at sth)** (*fml* 文) make unnecessary complaints (about sth) (对某事物)无端指摘, 挑剔, 吹毛求疵: *He cavilled at being asked to cook his own breakfast.* 他嗔怪让他自己做早饭.

cav·ity /ˈkævətɪ; ˈkævətɪ/ *n* empty space within sth solid, eg a hole in a tooth 腔, 洞(如牙齿中的洞).
□ ˌ**cavity** ˈ**wall** wall consisting of two separate walls with a space between, designed to give extra insulation 夹壁墙(两道墙中间有空隙, 用以增强绝缘性).

ca·vort /kəˈvɔːt; kəˈvɔrt/ *v* [I, Ip] **~ (about/around)** jump about excitedly 欢跃; 跳跃: *Stop cavorting around and sit still, just for five minutes!* 别欢蹦乱跳的, 坐好了, 就五分钟!

caw /kɔː; kɔ/ *n* harsh cry of a crow, rook or raven 乌鸦的叫声.
▷ **caw** *v* [I] make this cry (乌鸦)叫; 发出乌鸦的叫声; 呱呱地叫.

cay·enne /keɪˈen; keˈɛn/ *n* [U] (also ˌ**cayenne** ˈ**pepper**) type of hot red powdered pepper(1), used for seasoning foods 辣椒粉.

cay·man (also **cai·man**) /ˈkeɪmən; ˈkemən/ *n* type of S American reptile like an alligator (南美的)大鳄鱼.

CB /ˌsiː ˈbiː; ˌsi ˈbi/ *abbr* 缩写 = **1** citizens' band: *broadcast a message on CB radio* 在无线电民用频带中广播消息. **2** (*Brit*) Companion (of the Order) of the Bath 最低级巴思爵士.

CBC /ˌsi: bi: ˈsi:; ˌsi bi ˋsi/ *abbr* 缩写 = Canadian Broadcasting Corporation 加拿大广播公司: *a CBC news programme* 加拿大广播公司新闻节目 ○ *listen to (the) CBC* 收听加拿大广播公司的广播.

CBE /ˌsi: bi: ˈi:; ˌsi bi ˋi/ *abbr* 缩写 = (*Brit*) Commander (of the Order) of the British Empire 英帝国二等勋位爵士; 英帝国司令勋章: *be (made) a CBE* (成)为英帝国二等勋位爵士 ○ *John Adams CBE* 英帝国二等勋位爵士约翰·亚当斯. Cf 参看 DBE, KBE, MBE.

CBI /ˌsi: bi: ˈaɪ:; ˌsi bi ˋaɪ/ *abbr* 缩写 = Confederation of British Industry 英国工业联合会.

CBS /ˌsi: bi: ˈes; ˌsi bi ˋɛs/ *abbr* 缩写 = (*US*) Columbia Broadcasting System 哥伦比亚广播公司: *a CBS news broadcast* 哥伦比亚广播公司的新闻广播 ○ *listen to CBS* 收听哥伦比亚广播公司的广播.

C

cc /ˌsi: ˈsi:; ˌsi ˋsi/ *abbr* 缩写 = **1** (*commerce* 商) carbon copy (to) 副本(交): *to Luke Petersen, cc Janet Gold, Marion Ryde* 交卢克·彼得森, 副本交珍妮特·戈尔德、马里恩·赖德. **2** cubic centimetre(s) 立方厘米: *an 850cc engine* 850立方厘米的发动机.

Cdr (also **Cmdr**) *abbr* 缩写 = Commander: *Cdr (John) Stone* (约翰)斯通指挥官.

Cdre (also **Cmdre**) *abbr* 缩写 = Commodore: *Cdre (James) Wingfield* (詹姆斯)温菲尔德海军准将.

CDT /ˌsi: di: ˈti:; ˌsi di ˋti/ *abbr* 缩写 = (*US*) Central Daylight Time 中部夏令时间.

CE *abbr* 缩写 = Church of England 英国国教: *a CE junior school* 英国国教初级学校. Cf 参看 C OF E.

cease /si:s; sis/ *v* (*fml* 文) **1** [I, It, Tn, Tg] come or bring (sth) to an end; stop 停止; 中止: *Hostilities* (ie Fighting) *between the two sides ceased at midnight.* 双方在午夜停止敌对行动(战斗). ○ *The officer ordered his men to cease fire*, ie stop shooting. 长官命令士兵停火(停止射击). ○ *That department has ceased to exist.* 那部门已不复存在. ○ *The factory has ceased making bicycles.* 那工厂已停止生产自行车了. **2** (idm 习语) **wonders will never cease** ⇨ WONDER *n*.

▷ **cease** *n* (idm 习语) **without ˈcease** (*fml* 文) without stopping; continuously 不停地; 不断地.

cease·less *adj* not stopping; without end; continuous 不停的; 不绝的; 不断的: *His ceaseless chatter began to annoy me.* 他不停的唠叨使我厌烦起来. **cease·lessly** *adv*.

□ ˌ**cease-ˈfire** *n* **1** signal to stop firing guns in war 战争中的停火信号: *order a cease-fire* 命令停火. **2** temporary period of truce 休战: *negotiate a cease-fire* 谈判休战.

ce·dar /ˈsi:də(r); ˋsidɚ/ *n* (**a**) [C] tall evergreen coniferous tree 雪松. (**b**) (also **cedarwood** /ˈsi:dəwʊd; sidɚˌwʊd/) [U] its hard red sweet-smelling wood, used for making boxes, furniture, pencils, etc 雪松木材(用以制造箱子、家具、铅笔等): [attrib 作定语] *a ˌcedar ˈchest* 雪松木的箱子.

cede /si:d; sid/ *v* [Tn, Dn·pr] **~ sth (to sb)** give up one's rights to or possession of sth 割让, 让予, 放弃(某事物的权利或所有权): *cede territory to a neighbouring state* 把领土割让给邻国.

ce·dilla /sɪˈdɪlə; sɪˋdɪlə/ *n* mark put under the c (̧) in certain languages (eg French and Portuguese) to show that it is pronounced /s; s/, as in *façade* 下加符, 尾形符(某些语言中, 如法语和葡萄牙语, 字母c下面的一撇 ' ̧', 表示发/s; s/音, 如façade中的).

ceil·ing /ˈsi:lɪŋ; ˋsilɪŋ/ *n* **1** top inner surface of a room 天花板; 顶篷: *Mind you don't bump your head on the low ceiling.* 天花板很低, 留神别碰头. **2** cloud level 云幕高度. **3** maximum altitude at which a particular aircraft can normally fly 一航空器所能飞的最高限度; 升限; 上升限度: *an aircraft with a ceiling of 20 000 ft* 一架能飞20 000英尺高的飞机. **4** upper limit 上限: *The government has set a wages and prices ceiling of 10%.* 政府规定工资和物价提高的最高限度为10%. **5** (idm 习语) **hit the ceiling/roof** ⇨ HIT 1.

cel·an·dine /ˈseləndaɪn; ˋsɛlənˌdaɪn/ *n* small wild plant with yellow flowers 白屈菜.

ce·leb·rant /ˈselɪbrənt; ˋsɛləbrənt/ *n* priest leading a church service, esp the Eucharist (主持宗教仪式的)教士(尤指主持圣餐者).

cel·eb·rate /ˈselɪbreɪt; ˋsɛləˌbret/ *v* **1** (**a**) [Tn] mark (a happy or important day, event, etc) with festivities and rejoicing 庆祝; 祝贺: *celebrate Christmas, sb's birthday, a wedding anniversary, etc* 庆祝圣诞节、某人的生日、结婚纪念日等 ○ *celebrate a victory, success, etc* 庆祝胜利、成功等. (**b**) [I] enjoy oneself in some way on such an occasion (为庆祝)寻欢作乐: *It's my birthday — let's celebrate!* eg with alcoholic drink. 今天是我的生日——咱们庆祝一下吧! **2** [Tn] (of a priest) lead (a religious ceremony) (指神父)主持(宗教仪式): *celebrate Mass/the Eucharist* 主持弥撒[圣餐]. **3** [Tn] (*fml* 文) praise (sb/sth); honour 赞扬, 赞美(某人[某事物]); 称赞; 歌颂: *Odysseus's heroic exploits are celebrated in 'The Odyssey'.* 《奥德赛》史诗中歌颂了奥德修斯的丰功伟绩.

▷ **cel·eb·rated** *adj* **~ (for sth)** famous 著名的; 驰名的: *a celebrated actress, writer, pianist, etc* 著名的女演员、作家、钢琴家等 ○ *Burgundy is celebrated for its fine wines.* 勃艮第以盛产美酒而驰名.

cel·eb·ra·tion /ˌselɪˈbreɪʃn; ˌsɛləˋbreʃən/ *n* [C, U] (act or occasion of) celebrating 庆祝或祝贺(的活动或场合): *birthday celebrations* 生日庆祝会 ○ *a day of celebration* 庆祝日.

ce·leb·rity /sɪˈlebrətɪ; səˋlɛbrətɪ/ *n* **1** [C] famous person 名人; 闻人: *celebrities of stage and screen*, ie well-known actors and film stars 舞台和影视界名人(著名的演员和电影明星). **2** [U] being famous; fame 著名; 名望; 名声.

ce·ler·ity /sɪˈlerətɪ; səˋlɛrətɪ/ *n* [U] (*arch* 古) quickness 敏捷; 迅速.

cel·ery /ˈselərɪ; ˋsɛlərɪ/ *n* [U] garden plant with crisp stems that are used in salads or as a vegetable 芹菜: *a bunch/stick/head of celery* 一捆[根/棵]芹菜 ○ [attrib 作定语] *celery soup* 芹菜汤.

ce·les·tial /sɪˈlestɪəl; *US* -tʃl; səˋlɛstʃəl/ *adj* **1** [attrib 作定语] of the sky 天的; 天空的: *celestial bodies*, eg the sun and the stars 天体(如太阳和星球). **2** of heaven; divine 天上的; 神的; 天才的; 非凡的: (*fig* 比喻) *the celestial beauty of her voice* 她歌喉之美如闻天籁. Cf 参看 TERRESTRIAL.

cel·ib·ate /ˈselɪbət; ˋsɛləbɪt/ *adj* **1** remaining unmarried, esp for religious reasons 不结婚的(尤指为宗教原因). **2** not having sexual relations 没有性关系的.

▷ **cel·ib·acy** /ˈselɪbəsɪ; ˋsɛləbəsɪ/ *n* [U] (state of) living unmarried, esp for religious reasons 独身生活(的状况)(尤指为宗教原因): *Catholic priests take a vow of celibacy.* 天主教神父发誓不结婚. **cel·ib·ate** *n* unmarried person; person not having sexual relations 独身者; 没有性关系的人.

cell /sel; sɛl/ *n* **1** very small room, eg for a monk in a monastery or for one or more prisoners in a prison 小房间(如修道院里的密室或狱中的牢房). **2** compartment in a honeycomb (蜂房的)巢室. **3** device for producing an electric current by chemical action, eg the metal plates in acid inside a battery 电池. **4** microscopic unit of living matter, containing a nucleus 细胞: *Human tissue is made up of cells.* 人体的组织是由细胞构成的. ○ *cancer cells* 癌细胞. **5** small group of people forming a centre of (esp revolutionary) political activity (尤指革命的)政治活动小组: *a terrorist cell* 恐怖分子的小组.

cel·lar /ˈselə(r); ˋsɛlɚ/ *n* **1** underground room for storing things (贮藏东西用的)地下室, 地窖: *a coal cellar* 地下煤窖. **2** = WINE-CELLAR (WINE).

cello /ˈtʃeləʊ; ˋtʃɛlo/ *n* (*pl* **~s**) stringed musical instrument like a large violin, held between the knees by a seated player 大提琴. ⇨illus at App 1 见附录1之插图, page xi.

▷ **cell·ist** /ˈtʃelɪst; ˋtʃɛlɪst/ *n* person who plays the cello 大提琴演奏者.

Cel·lo·phane /ˈseləfeɪn; ˋsɛləˌfen/ *n* [U] (*propr* 专利名) thin transparent material made from viscose and used for wrapping things (包装用的)玻璃纸: [attrib 作定语] *cellophane wrapping* 玻璃纸包装.

cel·lu·lar /ˈseljʊlə(r); ˋsɛljəlɚ/ *adj* **1** of or consisting of cells (CELL 4) 细胞的; 由细胞组成的: *cellular tissue* 细胞组织. **2** (of textile materials) loosely woven (指纺织材料)松织的: *cellular blankets* 松织的毯子.

cel·lu·loid /ˈseljʊlɔɪd; ˋsɛljəˌlɔɪd/ *n* [U] **1** plastic made from cellulose nitrate and camphor, used for making many things, eg toys, toilet articles and (formerly) photographic film 赛璐珞. **2** (*dated* 旧) cinema films 电影片: [attrib 作定语] *the celluloid heroes of one's youth*

某人青年时代的电影明星.

cel·lu·lose /ˈseljʊləʊs; ˋsɛljəˌlos/ *n* [U] **1** organic substance that forms the main part of all plants and trees and is used in making plastics, paper, etc 纤维素(构成植物主要组成部分的有机化合物, 用以制造塑料、纸等). **2** any of various compounds of this used in making paint or lacquer 纤维素的衍生物(用以制造颜料或油漆).

Cel·sius /ˈselsɪəs; ˋsɛlsɪəs/ *adj* = CENTIGRADE: *Boiling point is 100° Celsius.* 沸点是100摄氏度.

Celt /kelt; *US* selt; sɛlt/ *n* (**a**) member of an ancient W European people some of whom settled in Britain before the coming of the Romans 凯尔特人(古代西欧人, 其中有些人在罗马人来到之前已定居于不列颠). (**b**) one of their descendants, esp in Ireland, Wales, Scotland, Cornwall or Brittany 凯尔特人(尤指爱尔兰、威尔士、苏格兰、康沃尔或布列塔尼的).
▷ **Celtic** *n*, *adj* (language) of the Celts 凯尔特人的(语言).

ce·ment /sɪˈment; səˋmɛnt/ *n* [U] **1** grey powder, made by burning lime and clay, that sets hard after mixing with water and is used in building to stick bricks together or for making very hard surfaces 水泥. **2** (**a**) any similar soft substance that sets firm and is used for sticking things together 任何类似水泥的软物质; 胶合剂; 接合剂. Cf 参看 ADHESIVE *n*, GLUE. (**b**) substance for filling holes in teeth (补牙用的)粘固粉.
▷ **ce·ment** *v* **1** [Tn] cover (sth) with cement(1) 用水泥铺(某物). **2** [Tn, Tn·p] **~ A and B (together)** join things together (as) with cement (如)用水泥粘合东西: *He cemented the bricks into place.* 他用水泥砌砖. **3** [Tn] (*fig* 比喻) establish (sth) firmly; strengthen 将(某事物)结合在一起; 加强; 巩固: *cement a friendship* 加强友谊.

cem·et·ery /ˈsemətrɪ; *US* ˈseməterɪ; ˋsɛməˌtɛrɪ/ *n* area of land, not a churchyard, used for burying the dead (非教堂的)墓地, 公墓.

ceno·taph /ˈsenətɑ:f; *US* -tæf; ˋsɛnəˌtæf/ *n* monument in memory of people buried elsewhere, esp soldiers killed in war (为葬于别处的死者, 尤指阵亡者, 所立的)纪念碑.

cen·ser /ˈsensə(r); ˋsɛnsɚ/ *n* container in which incense is burnt in churches (教堂中的)香炉.

cen·sor /ˈsensə(r); ˋsɛnsɚ/ *n* **1** person authorized to examine books, films, plays, letters, etc and remove parts which are considered indecent, offensive, politically unacceptable or (esp in war) a threat to security (书籍、电影、戏剧、信件等的)检查员: *the British Board of Film Censors* 英国影片审查委员会. **2** (in ancient Rome) official who prepared a register of all citizens and supervised public morals (古罗马负责登记全体市民并监督公众道德行为的)监察官.
▷ **cen·sor** *v* [Tn] examine or remove parts from (sth), as a censor (作为检查员)检查或删剪(某物): *the censored version of a film* 经过检查的电影版本.
cen·sor·ship *n* [U] act or policy of censoring books, etc 书籍等的检查或其政策: *Strict censorship is enforced in some countries.* 某些国家的书刊检查很严.

cen·sori·ous /senˈsɔ:rɪəs; sɛnˋsorɪəs/ *adj* tending to find faults in people or things; severely critical 爱挑剔的; 吹毛求疵的; 苛刻批评的. ▷ **cen·sori·ously** *adv*. **cen·sori·ous·ness** *n* [U].

cen·sure /ˈsenʃə(r); ˋsɛnʃɚ/ *v* [Tn, Tn·pr] **~ sb (for sth)** criticize sb severely; rebuke sb formally 严厉批评某人; 正式责备某人: *Two MPs were censured by the Speaker.* 有两个议员遭到议长的责备.
▷ **cen·sure** *n* [U] strong criticism or condemnation; reprimand 指责; 谴责; 斥责: *pass a vote of censure (on sb)* 通过(对某人的)不信任投票 ○ *lay oneself open to* (ie risk) *public censure* 给人以责难的口实.

cen·sus /ˈsensəs; ˋsɛnsəs/ *n* (*pl* **~es**) official counting of a country's population or of other classes of things, eg traffic, for statistical purposes 人口统计; 人口调查; 人口普查.

cent /sent; sɛnt/ *n* (**a**) one 100th part of a US dollar or of certain other metric units of currency 分(一美元或某些十进制货币单位的百分之一). (**b**) (*abbrs* 缩写 **c, ct**) coin of this value 分值的硬币. ⇨App 4 见附录4.

cent *abbr* 缩写 = century(1b): *in the 20th cent* 在20世纪. Cf 参看 C 2.

cen·taur /ˈsentɔ:(r); ˋsɛntɔr/ *n* (in Greek mythology) one of a tribe of creatures with a man's head, arms and upper body on a horse's body and legs (希腊神话中的)半人半马怪(上半身为人下半身为马).

cen·ten·ar·ian /ˌsentɪˈneərɪən; ˌsɛntəˋnɛrɪən/ *n*, *adj* (person who is) 100 years old or more 百岁或百岁以上的(人); 人瑞.

cen·ten·ary /senˈti:nərɪ; *US* ˈsentənerɪ; ˋsɛntəˌnɛrɪ/ (*US* also **centennial**) *n* 100th anniversary of sth 某事物的第100周年纪念: *The club will celebrate its centenary next year.* 该俱乐部明年要庆祝一百周年纪念 ○ [attrib 作定语] *centenary year* 一百周年纪念的一年 ○ *centenary celebrations* 一百周年纪念庆典.

cent·en·nial /senˈtenɪəl; sɛnˋtɛnɪəl/ *n* (*US*) = CENTENARY.
▷ **cent·en·nial** *adj* **1** occurring every 100 years 每100年的. **2** of a centenary 一百周年纪念的. **cent·en·nially** *adv*.

center /ˈsentə(r); ˋsɛntɚ/ (*US*) = CENTRE.

cent(i)- *comb form* 构词成分 (forming *ns* 用以构成名词) **1** hundred 一百: *centigrade* ○ *centipede*. **2** (in the metric system) one hundredth part of (十进制中的)百分之一: *centimetre*. ⇨App 11 见附录11.

cen·ti·grade /ˈsentɪgreɪd; ˋsɛntəˌgred/ (also **Celsius**) *adj* (*abbr* 缩写 **C**) of or using a temperature scale with the freezing-point of water at 0° and the boiling-point at 100° 摄氏温度计的: *a centigrade thermometer* 摄氏温度计 ○ *20°C means twenty degrees centigrade* 20°C的意思是二十摄氏度. Cf 参看 FAHRENHEIT. ⇨App 4, 5 见附录4、5.

cen·ti·gram (also **cen·ti·gramme**) /ˈsentɪgræm; ˋsɛntəˌgræm/ *n* one 100th part of a gram 厘克(百分之一克). ⇨App 5 见附录5.

cen·ti·litre (*US* **cen·ti·liter**) /ˈsentɪli:tə(r); ˋsɛntəˌlitɚ/ *n* (*abbr* 缩写 **cl**) one 100th part of a litre 厘升(百分之一升).

cent·ime /ˈsɒnti:m; ˋsɑntim/ *n* (**a**) one 100th part of a franc 生丁(百分之一法郎). (**b**) coin of this value 生丁值的硬币.

cen·ti·metre /ˈsentɪmi:tə(r); ˋsɛntəˌmitɚ/ *n* (*abbr* 缩写 **cm**) one 100th part of a metre 厘米(百分之一米). ⇨App 4, 5 见附录4、5.

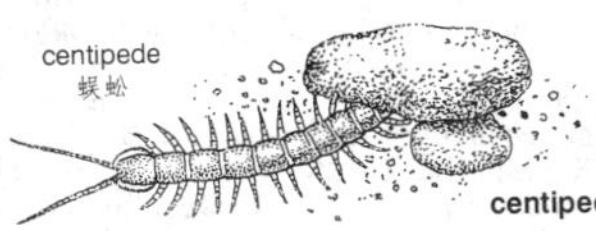

centipede 蜈蚣

cen·ti·pede /ˈsentɪpi:d; ˋsɛntəˌpid/ *n* small crawling insect-like creature with a long thin body, numerous joints and a pair of legs at each joint 蜈蚣; 马陆. ⇨illus 见插图.

CENTO (also **Cento**) /ˈsentəʊ; ˋsɛnto/ *abbr* 缩写 = Central Treaty Organization (a military and economic alliance of Britain, Iran, Pakistan and Turkey) 中央条约组织(英国、伊朗、巴基斯坦、土耳其的军事和经济联盟).

cent·ral /ˈsentrəl; ˋsɛntrəl/ *adj* **1** (**a**) of, at, near or forming the centre of sth 中心的; 中央的; 在中心的; 形成中心的: *We live in central London.* 我们住在伦敦中部. ○ *Our house is very central*, ie is in or close to the centre of the town. 我们的房子就在市中心. ○ *the central plains of N America* 北美洲的中部平原. (**b**) easily reached from surrounding areas; convenient 容易从四周到达的; 方便的: *a theatre with a very central location* 地处中心的剧场. **2** most important; main; principal 最重要的; 主要的; 首要的: *the central point of an argument* 争论的焦点 ○ *the central character in a novel* 小说的中心人物 ○ *Reducing inflation is central to* (ie a major part of) *the government's economic policy.* 缩减通货膨胀是政府经济政策的重点. **3** having overall power or control 有全部权力或控制力的: *central government*, ie the government of a whole country, as contrasted with local government 中央政府(区别于地方政府) ○ *the central committee*, eg of a political party

中央委员会(如一政党的).

▷ **cen·tral·ism** /ˈsentrəlɪzəm; ˈsɛntrəl,ɪzəm/ *n* [U] principle or system of centralizing 中央集权制; 集中制. **cen·tral·ist** *n, adj*. **cen·tral·ize, -ise** /ˈsentrəlaɪz; ˈsɛntrəl,aɪz/ *v* [I, Tn] (cause sth to) come under the control of one central authority (使某事物)归中央管; 实行中央集权制: *Is government becoming too centralized?* 政府的权力是否越来越过分集中了? **cen·tral·iza·tion, -isation** /ˌsentrəlaɪˈzeɪʃn; *US* -lɪˈz-; ˌsɛntrələˈzeʃən/ *n* [U]: *the centralization of power* 权力的集中.

cen·trally /ˈsentrəlɪ; ˈsɛntrəlɪ/ *adv*.

□ ˌ**central** ˈ**bank** national bank that does business with the Government and other banks, and issues currency 中央银行.

ˌ**central** ˈ**heating** system for heating a building from one source by circulating hot water or hot air in pipes or by linked radiators 中央暖气系统; 集中供热设备.

central ˈ**nervous system** part of the nervous system consisting of the brain and spinal cord 中枢神经系统.

ˌ**central** ˈ**processor** part of a computer that controls and co-ordinates the activities of other units and performs the actions specified in the program 中心处理机.

ˌ**central reser**ˈ**vation** grass or asphalt strip that separates the two sides of a motorway 中央分车带. ⇨ illus at App 1 见附录1之插图, page xiii.

ˌ**Central** ˈ**Standard Time** (*US*) (*abbr* 缩写 **CST**) standard time used in a zone that includes the central states of the US 中央标准时间.

centre (*US* **center**) /ˈsentə(r); ˈsɛntɚ/ *n* **1** [C] point that is equally distant from all sides of sth; middle point or part of sth 中心点; 中心; 中央: *the centre of a circle* 圆心 ○ *the centre of London* 伦敦市的中心 ○ *a town centre* 市中心. ⇨illus at CIRCLE 见 CIRCLE 之插图. **2** [C] point towards which people's interest is directed 使人感兴趣的集中点: *Children like to be the centre of attention.* 儿童喜欢引人注意. ○ *The Prime Minister is at the centre of a political row over leaked Cabinet documents.* 首相是内阁文件泄密政治纠纷的中心人物. **3** [C] place from which administration is organized 行政机构所在地; 中枢: *a centre of power* 权力的核心 ○ *London is a centre of government.* 伦敦是政府所在地. **4** [C] place (eg a town or group of buildings) where certain activities or facilities are concentrated 活动集中的地方(如城镇或一群建筑物): *a centre of industry, commerce, the steel trade, etc* 工业、商业、钢铁贸易等的中心 ○ *a shopping, sports, leisure, community centre* 购物、运动、娱乐、社区中心. **5** (esp **the centre**) [sing, Gp] moderate political position or party, ie one between the extremes of left and right 政治上的中间立场或中间党派: *This country lacks an effective party of the centre.* 这个国家缺少一个能起作用的中立党派. ○ *Are her views to the left or right of centre?* 她的观点是中间偏左还是偏右? ○ [attrib 作定语] *a centre party* 中立的党. **6** [C] (**a**) (in football, hockey, etc) centre-forward (足球、曲棍球等)中锋. (**b**) (in Rugby football) either of two players in the middle of the line of three-quarters (橄榄球)中后卫. **7** [C] (in football, hockey, etc) kick or hit from the side towards the middle of the pitch (足球、曲棍球等)从一边向球场中央之传球. **8** (idm 习语) **left, right and centre** ⇨ LEFT².

▷ **centre** *v* **1** [Tn] place (sth) in or at the centre 将(某物)放在中央. **2** [I, Tn] (in football, hockey, etc) kick or hit (the ball) from the side towards the middle of the pitch (足球、曲棍球等)将(球)传到球场的中央. ⇨illus at ASSOCIATION FOOTBALL 见 ASSOCIATION FOOTBALL 之插图. **3** (phr v) **centre (sth) on/upon/round sb/sth** have sb/sth as its centre or main concern or theme; be concentrated or concentrate on sb/sth 将某人[某事物]当作中心、重点或主题; 集中于某人[某事物]: *The social life of the village centres round the local sports club.* 村民的社交活动都集中在当地的体育俱乐部. ○ *Her research is centred on the social effects of unemployment.* 她的研究课题是失业对社会的影响. ○ *Public interest centres on the outcome of next week's by-election.* 公众的注意力集中在下周的补选结果上.

□ ˈ**centre-bit** *n* tool for boring holes in wood 三叉钻头; 中心钻.

ˈ**centreboard** *n* moveable board that can be raised or lowered through a slot in the keel of a sailing-boat to prevent drifting 中插板(船底中心防止船漂移的垂直升降板). ⇨illus at DINGHY 见 DINGHY 之插图.

ˈ**centre-fold** *n* large coloured picture folded to form the middle pages of a newspaper or magazine 中间摺页(报纸或杂志中间的大张彩色夹页).

ˌ**centre-**ˈ**forward** (also **centre**) *n* (in football, hockey, etc) player or position in the middle of the forward line (足球、曲棍球等)中锋或中锋的位置: *play (at) centre-forward* 担任中锋.

ˌ**centre-**ˈ**half** *n* (in football, hockey, etc) player or position in the middle of the half-back line (足球、曲棍球等)中前卫或中前卫的位置.

ˌ**centre of** ˈ**gravity** point around which the weight of an object is evenly distributed 重心.

ˈ**centre-piece** *n* (**a**) ornament for the centre of a table, etc (桌子等的)中心装饰. (**b**) most important item, eg in a display 最重要的项目(如展览中的).

ˌ**centre** ˈ**spread** two facing middle pages of a newspaper or magazine (报纸或杂志的)中间跨页.

cen·tri·fu·gal /senˈtrɪfjʊgl, *also* ˌsentrɪˈfju:gl; sɛnˈtrɪfjugl/ *adj* (**a**) moving away from the centre or axis 离心的. (**b**) of or using centrifugal force 离心力的; 用离心力的.

□ **cen**ˌ**trifugal** ˈ**force** force that appears to cause an object travelling round a centre to fly outwards and away from its circular path 离心力.

cent·ri·fuge /ˈsentrɪfju:dʒ; ˈsɛntrə,fjudʒ/ *n* rotating machine using centrifugal force to separate substances, eg milk and cream 离心机; 离心分离机.

cent·ri·petal /senˈtrɪpɪtl, *also* ˌsentrɪˈpi:tl; sɛnˈtrɪpətl/ *adj* moving towards the centre or axis 向心的; 向轴心的.

cent·rist /ˈsentrɪst; ˈsɛntrɪst/ *n* person who holds moderate political views (政治上的)中间派成员. ▷ **cent·rism** /-ɪzəm; -ɪzəm/ *n* [U].

cen·tur·ion /senˈtjʊərɪən; *US* -ˈtʊər-; sɛnˈturɪən/ *n* (in ancient Rome) officer commanding a unit of 100 soldiers (古罗马的)百人队队长.

cen·tury /ˈsentʃərɪ; ˈsɛntʃərɪ/ *n* **1** (**a**) period of 100 years 100年. (**b**) (*abbr* 缩写 **c, cent**) any of the periods of 100 years before or after the death of Jesus Christ 世纪(指耶稣基督去世以前或以后每100年的期间): *the 20th century*, ie AD 1900-1999 第20世纪(公元1900-1999年) ○ *at the turn of the century*, ie when one ends and the next begins 在两个世纪之交(在一个世纪结束, 下一个世纪开始时). **2** (in cricket) score of 100 runs by one batsman in an innings (板球)(击球员在一局所得的)百分: *make/score a century* 得百分 ○ *a double century*, ie 200 runs in an innings 双百分(一局得200分).

ce·ramic /sɪˈræmɪk; səˈræmɪk/ *adj* of or relating to pottery 陶器的; 与陶器有关的.

▷ **ce·ram·ics** *n* **1** [sing *v*] art of making and decorating pottery 陶器制法; 陶器工艺. **2** [pl] objects made of clay, porcelain, etc 陶器制品.

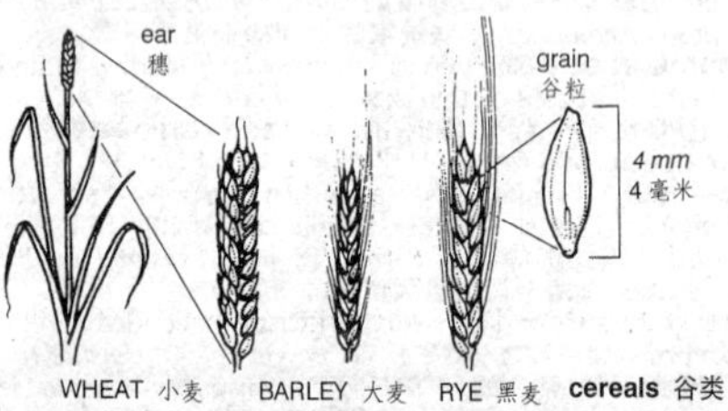

cereals 谷类

cer·eal /ˈsɪərɪəl; ˈsɪrɪəl/ *n* (**a**) [C] any of various types of grass producing edible grains, eg wheat, rye, oats, barley 谷类植物. ⇨illus 见插图. (**b**) [U] grain produced by such a grass 谷物: [attrib 作定语] *cereal products* 谷物产品. (**c**) [C, U] (any of various types of) food made from the grain of cereals 谷类食物; 麦片粥: ˈ*breakfast cereals* 早餐用的谷类食品 ○ *a bowl of cereal* 一碗麦片粥.

ce·re·bel·lum /ˌserɪˈbeləm; ˌsɛrəˈbɛləm/ *n* (*pl* **-la** /-lə; -lə/ or **-lums** /-ləmz; -ləmz/) (*anatomy* 解) part of the brain that controls voluntary muscle movements 小脑.

ce·reb·ral /ˈserɪbrəl; US səˈri:brəl; səˈribrəl/ *adj* **1** of the brain 脑的; 大脑的: *a cerebral haemorrhage* 脑溢血. **2** intellectual (rather than emotional) 理智的(非感情的): *His poetry is very cerebral.* 他的诗很有理性.

□ **cerebral ˈpalsy** disease in which a person's movements become jerky and uncontrolled because of brain damage before or at birth 脑性麻痹. Cf 参看 SPASTIC.

ce·reb·ra·tion /serɪˈbreɪʃn; ˌsɛrəˋbreʃən/ *n* [U] (*fml or rhet or joc* 文或修辞或谑) working of the brain; thinking 大脑活动; 思想; 思考.

ce·re·mo·nial /ˌserɪˈməʊnɪəl; ˌsɛrəˋmonɪəl/ *adj* of, used for or involving a ceremony; formal 礼仪的; 仪式的; 正式的: *ceremonial dress* 礼服 ○ *a ceremonial occasion* 正式场合.

▷ **ce·re·mo·nial** *n* [C, U] system of rules and procedures for ceremonies or formal occasions 礼仪; 仪式: *the ceremonials of religion* 宗教仪式 ○ *performed with due ceremonial* 按照适当礼仪进行.

ce·re·mo·ni·ally /-nɪəlɪ; -nɪəlɪ/ *adv*.

ce·re·mony /ˈserɪmənɪ; US -məʊnɪ; ˋsɛrəˌmonɪ/ *n* **1** [C] formal act or series of formal acts performed on a religious or public occasion 典礼; 仪式: *a marriage/wedding ceremony* 婚礼. **2** [U] formal display or behaviour; formality 礼节; 礼貌; 礼仪: *There's no need for ceremony between friends.* 朋友之间不必拘礼. ○ *The Queen was crowned with much ceremony.* 女王加冕礼仪很隆重. **3** (idm 习语) **stand on ˈceremony** behave formally 拘于礼节: *Please don't stand on ceremony* (ie Please be natural and relaxed) *with me*. 请勿拘礼.

▷ **ce·re·mo·ni·ous** /ˌserɪˈməʊnɪəs; ˌsɛrəˋmonɪəs/ *adj* (**a**) full of ceremony; very formal 仪式隆重的; 讲究礼仪的. (**b**) elaborately performed 郑重其事的; 礼节过分的: *He unveiled the picture with a ceremonious gesture.* 他郑重其事地为这幅画揭幕. **ce·re·mo·ni·ously** *adv*.

ce·rise /səˈri:z, səˈri:s; US -i:z; səˋriz/ *adj, n* [U] (of a) light clear red colour 鲜红色(的).

CERN (also **Cern**) /sɜ:n; sɝn/ *abbr* 缩写 = European Organization for Nuclear Research (French *Conseil Européen pour la Recherche Nucléaire*) 欧洲原子核研究组织(源自法文*Conseil Européen pour la Recherche Nucléaire*).

cert /sɜ:t; sɝt/ *n* (*Brit infml* 口) thing that is sure to happen, be successful, etc; certainty 必然发生的事情; 确实的事情: *Black Widow is a (dead) cert for* (ie is sure to win) *the next race*. '黑寡妇'马下一场比赛赢定了.

cert *abbr* 缩写 = certified.

cer·tain /ˈsɜ:tn; ˋsɝtn̩/ *adj* **1** [pred 作表语] **~ (that...)**; **~ (to do sth)** sure beyond doubt; that can be relied on 无疑; 确定: *It is certain that he will agree/He is certain to agree.* 肯定他会同意[他一定同意]. ○ *One thing is certain: I'm not coming here again.* 有一件事可以肯定, 我再也不来了. **2** [pred 作表语] **~ (that...)**; **~ (of/about sth)** positive in one's mind; completely sure 确信; 肯定: *I'm certain (that) she saw me.* 我肯定她看见我了. ○ *She saw me: I'm certain of that.* 她看见我了, 这一点我可以肯定. ○ *I'm not certain (of) what she wants.* 我不清楚她想要什么. **3** [attrib 作定语] sure to come, happen or be effective; assured 一定会来到、发生或生效的; 有把握的: *There is no certain cure for this disease.* 这种病没有特效药. ○ *They face certain death unless they can be rescued today.* 他们除非今天获救, 否则必死无疑. **4** [attrib 作定语] specific but not named or stated 某(不指明的或不说出的): *For certain reasons I will be unable to attend the meeting.* 因为某种原因, 我不能出席这次会议. ○ *The terrorists will only release their hostages on certain conditions.* 恐怖分子只有在某些条件下才释放人质. **5** [attrib 作定语] named but not known 说出姓名但不认识的: *A certain Mr Brown telephoned while you were out.* 你出去的时候, 有个叫布朗的先生来过电话. **6** [attrib 作定语] slight; some 稍微的; 一些的; 一点儿的: *There was a certain coldness in her attitude towards me.* 她对我的态度有点儿冷淡. ○ *I felt a certain reluctance to tell her the news.* 我不太愿意告诉她这个消息. **7** (idm 习语) **for ˈcertain** without doubt 无疑地; 确定地: *I couldn't say for certain when he'll arrive.* 我说不准他什么时候到. ○ *I don't yet know for certain.* 我知道得不确切. **make certain (that...)** inquire in order to be sure about sth 弄清楚; 弄明白; 弄确实: *I think there's a train at 8.20 but you ought to make certain.* 我想8点20分有一班火车, 不过你应该打听清楚. **make certain of sth/of doing sth** do sth in order to be sure of (doing) sth else 采取行动以便确有把握做其他事: *You'd better leave now if you want to make certain of getting there on time.* 你要想准时到达那里就最好马上走.

▷ **cer·tain** *pron* **~ of...** some particular members of (a group of people or things) (人或物中的)某些: *Certain of those present had had too much to drink.* 有些出席的人喝得太多了.

cer·tainly *adv* **1** without doubt; definitely 无疑地; 确定地: *He will certainly die if you don't call a doctor.* 你不请大夫来, 他就得死了. Cf 参看 SURELY. **2** (used in answer to questions 用于回答问题) of course 当然: *'May I borrow your pen for a moment?' 'Certainly.'* '我可以借用一下你的钢笔吗?' '当然可以.' ○ *'Do you consider yourself a rude person?' 'Certainly not!'* '你认为你是个粗鲁的人吗?''当然不是!'

cer·tainty /ˈsɜ:tntɪ; ˋsɝtn̩tɪ/ *n* **1** [C] thing that is certain 确定的事情: *England will lose the match — that's a certainty!* 这场比赛英格兰要输——这是肯定的! ○ *That horse is a certainty*, ie is certain to win. 那匹马赢定了(准赢). **2** [U] state of being certain 确知; 确信; 确实; 必然: *I can't say with any certainty where I shall be next week.* 我说不准我下星期在什么地方. ○ *We can have no certainty of success.* 我们没有成功的把握.

NOTE ON USAGE 用法: **Sure** and **certain** are often used in the same way ☆ **sure** 和 **certain** 的用法常常是相同的: *They're sure/certain to be late.* 他们一定迟到. ○ *I'm sure/certain (that) they'll be late.* 我肯定他们得迟到. ○ *One thing was sure/certain: they'd be late.* 有一件事是确定无疑的, 他们得迟到. ○ *They made sure/certain (that) they weren't late.* 他们有把握不迟到. With 'it' as an indefinite subject or object only **certain** can be used ☆ it 作不定主语或不定宾语时, 只可用 **certain** 与之连用: *It was certain/I thought it certain that they would be late.* 肯定[我肯定]他们要迟到. **Sure** can sound weaker than **certain**, especially in conversation ☆ **sure** 的语气听起来比 **certain** 弱些, 特别是在对话中: *I'm sure he'll manage it*, ie I think/hope he will. 我确信他能办到(即我认为[希望]他能办到).

Cert Ed /ˌsɜ:t ˈed; ˌsɝt ˋɛd/ *abbr* 缩写 = Certificate in Education 教育学证书: *have/be a Cert Ed* 有教育学证书 ○ *Jim Smith BA Cert Ed* 吉姆·史密斯文学士, 持有教育学证书.

cer·ti·fi·able /ˌsɜ:tɪˈfaɪəbl; ˋsɝtəˌfaɪəbl̩/ *adj* that can or should be certified, esp as insane 可证明的, 应证明的(尤指证明为精神病患者): *He's certifiable*, ie mad. 可证明他是精神病患者.

cer·ti·fic·ate /səˈtɪfɪkət; sɝˋtɪfəkɪt/ *n* official written or printed statement that may be used as proof or evidence of certain facts 证(明)书: *a ˈbirth/ˈmarriage/ˈdeath certificate* 出生[结婚/死亡]证书 ○ *an examination certificate*, ie proving that sb has passed an examination 及格证明书.

▷ **cer·ti·fic·ated** /-keɪtɪd; -ˌketɪd/ *adj* having been awarded a certificate; qualified 授予证明书的; 合格的.

cer·ti·fica·tion /ˌsɜ:tɪfɪˈkeɪʃn; ˌsɝtəfəˋkeʃən/ *n* [U] action of certifying or state of being certified 证明.

□ **Cerˌtificate of ˌSecondary Eduˈcation** (in Britain) former examination in a range of subjects taken by pupils aged 15 and over 中等教育证书(英国年满15岁的学生参加的各科考试). Cf 参看 GENERAL CERTIFICATE OF EDUCATION (GENERAL), GENERAL CERTIFICATE OF SECONDARY EDUCATION (GENERAL).

cer·tify /ˈsɜ:tɪfaɪ; ˋsɝtəˌfaɪ/ *v* (*pt, pp* **-fied**) **1** [Tn, Tf, Cn·a, Cn·n/a, Cn·t] **~ sb/sth as sth** formally declare (sth), esp in writing or on a printed document (尤指书面)证明(某事物): *a document certifying sb's birth* 证明某人出生的文件 ○ *He certified (that) it was his wife's handwriting.* 他证明那是他妻子的手迹. ○ *The accused has been certified (as) insane/certified to be insane.* 被告有书面证明为精神失常. **2** [Tn esp passive 尤用于被动语态] officially declare (sb) to be insane 正式证明(某人)精神失常: *He was certified and sent to a mental* *hospital.* 他经诊断为精神失常而送往精神病院.

□ ˌ**certified** ˈ**cheque** (*US*) cheque that is guaranteed by the bank 保付支票(由银行担保的支票).

cer·ti·tude /ˈsɜːtɪtjuːd; *US* -tuːd; ˋsɝtəˌtud/ *n* [U] (*fml* 文) feeling of certainty; lack of doubt 确信; 确定无疑.

cer·vix /ˈsɜːvɪks; ˋsɝvɪks/ *n* (*pl* **cer·vi·ces** /ˈsɜːvɪsiːz; ˋsɝvəˌsiz/ or **~es** /-vɪksɪz; -vɪksɪz/) (*anatomy* 解) narrow part of the womb where it joins the vagina 子宫颈. ⇨illus at FEMALE 见 FEMALE 之插图.

▷ **cer·vical** /sɜːˈvaɪkl; *US* ˈsɜːvɪkl; ˋsɝvɪkl/ *adj* [esp attrib 尤作定语] of or relating to the cervix 子宫颈的; 与子宫颈有关的: *cervical cancer* 子宫颈癌 ○ *a cervical smear*, ie one taken from the cervix to test for cancer 子宫颈涂片(取自子宫颈的涂片, 用以检验子宫颈癌).

Ce·sar·ian (also **Ce·sar·ean**) = CAESAREAN.

ces·sa·tion /seˈseɪʃn; sɛˋseʃən/ *n* [U, C] (*fml* 文) action or act of ceasing; pause 停止; 中止; 中断: *The bombardment continued without cessation.* 轰炸持续不断地进行着. ○ *a temporary cessation of hostilities* 暂时停战.

ces·sion /ˈseʃn; ˋsɛʃən/ *n* (*fml* 文) (**a**) [U] action of ceding sth, esp land or rights 让与或割让某事物(尤指土地或权利). (**b**) [C] thing that is ceded, esp land 被割让的事物(尤指土地).

cess·pit /ˈsespɪt; ˋsɛsˌpɪt/ (also **cess·pool** /ˈsespuːl; ˋsɛsˌpul/) *n* **1** covered pit where liquid waste or sewage is stored temporarily (有盖的)污水坑, 粪坑. **2** (*fig* 比喻) dirty or corrupt place 污秽的场所: *a cesspool of vice* 罪恶的渊薮.

CET /ˌsiː iː ˈtiː; ˌsi i ˋti/ *abbr* 缩写 = Central European Time 欧洲中部时间.

cf /ˌsiː ˈef; ˌsi ˋɛf/ *abbr* 缩写 = compare (Latin *confer*) 参看; 试比较(源自拉丁文 *confer*). Cf 参看 CP.

CFE /ˌsiː ef ˈiː; ˌsi ɛf ˋi/ *abbr* 缩写 = (*Brit*) College of Further Education 进修学院.

ch (also **chap**) *abbr* 缩写 = chapter(1): *the Gospel of St John ch 9 v 4* 《圣约翰福音》第 9 章第 4 节.

Chab·lis /ˈʃæbliː; ʃæˋbli/ *n* [U] dry white wine from E France 沙布利白葡萄酒(产自法国东部的无甜味白葡萄酒).

cha-cha /ˈtʃɑː tʃɑː; ˋtʃɑtʃɑ/ (also ˌ**cha-cha-**ˈ**cha**) *n* (**~s**) ballroom dance performed with small steps and swaying hip movements 恰恰舞(一种小步摆臀的交际舞): *dance/do the cha-cha* 跳恰恰舞.

chafe /tʃeɪf; tʃef/ *v* **1** [I, Ipr] **~ (at/under sth)** become irritated or impatient (because of sth) (因某事物)恼怒或不耐烦: *The passengers sat chafing at the long delay.* 乘客们因长时间的耽搁而坐得很不耐烦. ○ *chafe under an illness* 因病而烦躁. **2** [I, Tn] (cause sth to) become sore by rubbing (使某物)因摩擦而疼痛: *Her skin chafes easily.* 她的皮肤一擦就疼. ○ *His shirt collar chafed his neck.* 他的衬衫领口把脖子摩疼了. ○ *chafed hands* 摩疼的手. **3** [Tn] warm (sth) by rubbing, esp with the hands 摩擦(某物)而生热(尤指手): *chafe a baby's feet* 擦热婴儿的脚.

▷ **chafe** *n* sore place on the skin caused by rubbing (皮肤受摩擦的)疼处.

chaff[1] /tʃɑːf; *US* tʃæf; tʃæf/ *n* [U] **1** outer covering of corn, etc, separated from the grain by threshing or winnowing 谷物的皮壳. Cf 参看 HUSK. **2** hay or straw cut up as food for cattle (切碎作饲料用的)干草, 草料. **3** (idm 习语) **separate the wheat from the chaff** ⇨ SEPARATE[2].

chaff[2] /tʃɑːf; *US* tʃæf; tʃæf/ *v* [Tn, Tn·pr] **~ sb (about sth)** (*dated or fml* 旧或文) tease sb in a good-natured way (善意地)戏弄某人, 开某人的玩笑: *They chaffed him about his love-life.* 他们拿他的爱情生活开玩笑.

▷ **chaff** *n* [U] good-natured teasing or joking (善意的)戏弄或玩笑.

chaf·finch /ˈtʃæfɪntʃ; ˋtʃæˌfɪntʃ/ *n* common type of European finch 苍头燕雀. ⇨illus at App 1 见附录1之插图, page iv.

chafing-dish /ˈtʃeɪfɪŋ dɪʃ; ˋtʃefɪŋ dɪʃ/ *n* (*dated* 旧) pan with a heater underneath it for cooking food or keeping it warm at table (在餐桌上烹饪或使食物保温的)火锅.

chag·rin /ˈʃægrɪn; *US* ʃəˈgriːn; ʃəˋgrɪn/ *n* [U] feeling of disappointment or annoyance (at having failed, made a mistake, etc) (因失败、犯错等)失望, 灰心, 懊恼: *Much to his chagrin, he came last in the race.* 他因跑个倒数第一而垂头丧气.

▷ **chag·rin** *v* [Tn usu passive 通常用于被动语态] affect (sb) with chagrin 使(某人)懊恼, 悔恨: *be/feel chagrined at/by sth* 对[因]某事物而[感到]懊恼.

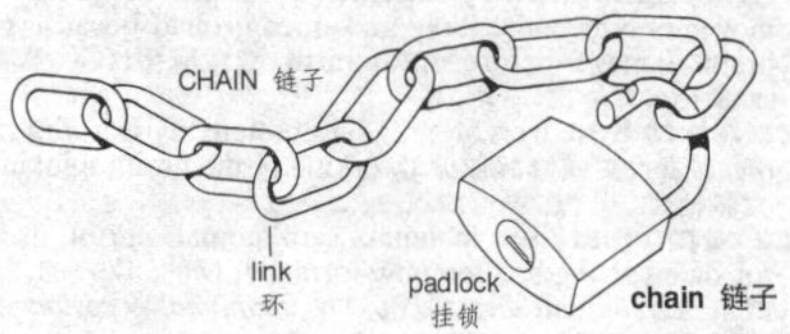

chain /tʃeɪn; tʃen/ *n* **1** (**a**) [C, U] (length of) connected metal links or rings, used for hauling or supporting weights or for fastening or restraining things 链子; 链条: *keep a dog on a chain* 用链子把狗拴住 ○ *pull the chain*, ie to flush the toilet 拉链子(冲抽水马桶) ○ *Remember to put the chain on the door when you lock it.* 锁门时别忘挂防盗链. ○ *a length of chain* 一截链条. (**b**) [C] length or loop of chain used for a specific purpose (有某种用途的)一截或一圈链条: *a bicycle chain*, ie for transmitting power from the pedals to the wheels 自行车链条 ○ *The mayor wore her chain of office round her neck.* 市长戴带着象征她官职的项链儿. ○ *She wore a locket hanging on a silver chain.* 她戴着银项链儿, 坠着个挂盒. ⇨illus at App 1 见附录1之插图, page xiii. ⇨illus 见插图. **2** [C usu *pl* 通常作复数] (*fig* 比喻) thing that confines or restrains 束缚或限制的事物: *the chains of poverty* 贫困的桎梏. **3** [C] series of connected things 一系列的事物: *a chain of mountains/a mountain chain* 连绵的山[山脉] ○ *a chain of circumstances, events, ideas* 一系列的情况、事件、意见. **4** [C] group of shops or hotels owned by the same company 同一公司所属的商店或旅店; 联号: *a chain of supermarkets/a supermarket chain* 超级市场联号. **5** [C] (formerly) unit of length (66 feet) for measuring land (旧时)测链(测量土地的长度单位, 等于66英尺). ⇨App 5 见附录5. **6** (idm 习语) **in chains** (**a**) (of a prisoner) bound with chains (指囚犯)用链锁住的. (**b**) not free; kept as a prisoner 不自由; 被囚禁.

▷ **chain** *v* [Tn esp passive 尤用于被动语态, Tn·pr, Tn·p] **~ sb/sth (to sb/sth)**; **~ sb/sth (up)** fasten or confine sb/sth with or as if with a chain 用链子或像用鏈子一樣拴住或束縛住某人[某事物]: *prisoners chained to a wall, each other* 用链子锁在墙上、互相锁住的囚犯 ○ *chain (up) a dog for the night* 晚上用链子把狗拴起来 ○ (*fig* 比喻) *Too many women feel chained to the kitchen sink*, ie feel that they spend all their time doing housework. 很多妇女觉得自己被拴在了厨房的洗涤槽上.

□ ˈ**chain-gang** *n* (*US*) group of prisoners chained together or forced to work in chains 用链子拴在一起的囚犯.

ˈ**chain-letter** *n* letter sent to several people each of whom is asked to make copies of it and send them to other people who will do the same 连锁信(寄给数人的信, 要求每个收信人复制数份再分寄给他人, 如此延续下去).

ˈ**chain-mail** *n* [U] armour made of metal rings linked together 锁子甲.

ˌ**chain re**ˈ**action** (**a**) chemical change forming products which themselves cause more changes so that new compounds are produced 连锁反应. (**b**) series of events each of which causes the next 连锁式反应的一系列事件: *The Government fear the strike may produce a chain reaction in other industries.* 政府害怕罢工可能在其他行业产生连锁反应.

ˈ**chain-saw** *n* saw with teeth set on an endless chain and driven by a motor 链锯.

ˈ**chain-smoke** *v* [I, Tn] smoke (cigarettes or cigars) continuously, esp by lighting each from the one just smoked 一枝接一枝不断地吸(香烟或雪茄). ˈ**chain-smoker** *n*.

ˈ**chain-stitch** *n* (**a**) [U] (in crochet or embroidery) type of sewing in which each stitch makes a loop through which the next stitch is taken (钩针或刺绣织品的)链状工艺. (**b**) [C] stitch made in this way 链状针脚.

ˈ**chain-store** *n* any of a series of similar shops owned by the same company 联号(同一公司所属的一系列类似商店之一).

chair /tʃeə(r); tʃɛr/ *n* **1** [C] moveable seat with a back and sometimes with arms, for one person to sit on 椅子: *a table and chairs* 桌子和椅子 ○ *Have/Take a chair*, ie Sit down. 入座[就座](坐下). ⇨illus at App 1 见附录1之插图, page xvi. **2 the chair** [sing] (position of the) person in charge of a meeting 主持会议的主席(的席位或职位): *She takes the chair in all our meetings.* 她担任我们一切会议的主席. ○ *Who is in the chair today?* 今天谁当主席? ○ *All remarks should be addressed to the chair.* 所有意见均应向主席提出. **3** [C] position of a university professor; professorship 大学教授的职位: *He holds the chair of philosophy at Oxford.* 他任牛津大学哲学教授. **4 the chair** [sing] (*US infml* 口) = THE ELECTRIC CHAIR (ELECTRIC).

▷ **chair** *v* **1** [Tn] act as chairman of (sth) 担任(某事务)的主席: *chair a meeting* 主持会议. **2** [Tn, Tn·pr] (*Brit*) carry (sb who has won sth) in a sitting position on the shoulders of a group 扛着(得胜者)(坐在人们的肩上): *The winning team chaired their captain off the field.* 获胜的队扛着队长走出场地.

□ ˈ**chair-lift** *n* series of chairs suspended from an endless cable for carrying people up and down a mountain, etc 架空吊椅(运送人上山下山等用的一系列循环吊椅).

ˈ**chairman** /-mən; -mən/ (*pl* **-men**, *fem* 阴性作 ˈ**chairwoman**) **1** person in charge of a meeting (主持会议的)主席: *'Madam Chairman, ladies and gentlemen,' began the speaker.* 发言人开始讲话: '主席、女士们、先生们'. **2** permanent president of a committee, board of directors of a company, etc (委员会、公司董事会等的)委员长, 董事长, 主席: *chairman of the board of governors (of a school)* (学校的)理事会会长 ○ *the chairman's report*, ie the annual report of a company, presented at its annual general meeting (公司在年会上作出的)年度报告.

ˈ**chairperson** *n* chairman or chairwoman (男或女)主席.

NOTE ON USAGE 用法: The affix **-man** is used in a lot of words (eg **chairman**) to indicate positions and occupations which today are filled by both women and men. ☆ **-man** 这一词缀用于很多词中(如 **chairman** 主席), 所指的职位和职务今日男女均可充任. To avoid sexual bias and unnecessary repetition (*chairman or chairwoman*) **-person** can be used 为免除性别偏颇和不必要的重复(chairman or chairwoman), 可用 **-person** 这一词缀: *chairperson, spokesperson, business person, etc* 主席、发言人、商人等. **Chair** is increasingly used to mean chairman or chairwoman ☆ **chair** 一词逐渐多用作主席, 男女均可: *She was the chair of the planning committee.* 她曾任计划委员会主席.

chaise longue /ˌʃeɪz ˈlɒŋ; *US* ˈlɔːŋ; ˈʃez ˈlɔŋg/ (*pl* **chaises longues** /ˌʃeɪz ˈlɒŋ; *US* ˈlɔːŋ; ˈʃez ˈlɔŋg/) (*French* 法) low chair with a long seat on which the person sitting can stretch out his legs 躺椅.

chalet 小木屋

cha·let /ˈʃæleɪ; ʃæˈle/ *n* **1** (esp in Switzerland) type of mountain hut or cottage built of wood and with an overhanging roof (尤指瑞士山区的)小木屋. ⇨illus 见插图. **2** house built in a similar style (类似这种形式的)房屋. **3** small hut in a holiday camp, etc (度假等用的)小屋.

chal·ice /ˈtʃælɪs; ˋtʃælɪs/ *n* large cup for holding wine, esp one from which consecrated wine is drunk at the Eucharist 大酒杯; (尤指)圣餐杯. ⇨illus at App 1 见附录1之插图, page viii.

chalk /tʃɔːk; tʃɔk/ *n* **1** [U] type of soft white rock used for burning to make lime 白垩: [attrib 作定语] *the chalk downs of southern England* 英格兰南部的白垩质高地. **2** (**a**) [U] this or a similar substance made into white or coloured sticks for writing or drawing on blackboards 制造白色或彩色粉笔的白垩或类似的物质: *a stick of chalk* 一枝粉笔 ○ *a picture drawn in chalk* 粉笔画 ○ *a teacher with chalk on his jacket* 外衣上有粉笔末的教师 ○ [attrib 作定语] *chalk dust* 粉笔末. (**b**) [C] one of these sticks 粉笔: *(a box of) coloured chalks* (一盒)彩色粉笔. **3** (idm 习语) **different as chalk and/from cheese** ⇨ DIFFERENT. **not by a long chalk/shot** ⇨ LONG[1].

▷ **chalk** *v* **1** [I, Tn] write, draw or mark (sth) with chalk 用粉笔写、画、涂(某物). **2** (phr v) **chalk sth out** draw (the outline of sth) with chalk 用粉笔画(某物的轮廓): *The boys chalked out goalposts on the playground wall.* 男孩子们在运动场的墙上用粉笔画上了球门柱. **chalk sth up** (*infml* 口) (**a**) write sth with chalk, esp on a blackboard (尤指在黑板上)用粉笔写: *chalk up one's score*, eg when playing darts 用粉笔写出自己得的分数(如玩投镖游戏时). (**b**) achieve or register (a success) 获得或取得(成功): *The team has chalked up its fifth win in a row.* 这队一连五次取得胜利. **chalk sth up (to sb/sth)** give credit (to sb or sb's account) for sth, esp drinks, etc bought in a pub (尤指在小酒店买饮品等)记(某人的帐): *Chalk this round up to me, please, barman.* 服务员, 请把这些人的费用记在我的帐上.

chalky *adj* (**-ier**, **-iest**) of or like chalk 白垩的; 似白垩的. **chalki·ness** *n* [U].

□ ˈ**chalkboard** *n* = BLACKBOARD (BLACK[1]).

chal·lenge[1] /ˈtʃælɪndʒ; ˋtʃælɪndʒ/ *n* **1 ~ (to sb) (to do sth)** invitation or call (to sb) to take part in a game, contest, fight etc to prove who is better, stronger, more able, etc 约请或要(某人)参加比赛、竞赛、战斗等以证明谁更好、更强、更能干等; 邀请比赛; 挑战: *issue/accept a challenge* 发出[接受]挑战. **2** order given by a sentry to stop and say who one is 哨兵发出的止步命令, 并问来者是谁: *The sentry gave the challenge, 'Who goes there?'* 哨兵查问: 谁在那儿? **3 ~ (to sth)** statement or action which questions or disputes (sth) 对(某事物)表示怀疑或争论的言论或行为异议; 质问; 怀疑: *a serious challenge to the Prime Minister's authority* 对首相的权威性郑重提出的异议. **4** difficult, demanding or stimulating task 艰巨的、高难度的或有激励性的任务: *She likes her job to be a challenge.* 她喜欢艰巨的工作. ○ *Reducing the gap between rich and poor is one of the main challenges facing the government.* 缩小贫富之间的差距是政府面临的主要难题之一. **5** formal objection, eg to a member of a jury 正式的反对(如反对陪审团的一个成员).

chal·lenge[2] /ˈtʃælɪndʒ; ˋtʃælɪndʒ/ *v* **1** [Tn, Tn·pr, Dn·t] **~ sb (to sth)** invite sb to do sth (esp to take part in a contest or to prove or justify sth) 要求某人做某事(尤指参加竞赛或证明某事正当): *challenge sb to a duel, a game of tennis* 要求某人参加决斗、网球赛 ○ *She challenged the newspaper to prove its story.* 她要求这家报纸证实报道的真实性. **2** [Tn] order (sb) to stop and say who he is 命令(某人)停步并说出是谁; 问口令: *The sentry challenged the stranger at the gates.* 哨兵查问在门口的陌生人. **3** [Tn] question the truth, rightness or validity of (sth); dispute 怀疑(某事)的真实性、正确性或有效性; 提出异议: *challenge sb's authority/right to do sth* 怀疑某人是否有权力[权利]做某事 ○ *challenge a claim, an assertion, a verdict* 对某要求、主张、判决质疑 ○ *This new discovery challenges traditional beliefs.* 这项新的发现对传统观念提出了异议. **4** [Tn] test the ability of (sb); stimulate 考验(某人)的能力; 激励; 鞭策: *The job doesn't really challenge him.* 这项工作不能真正考验

他. **5** [Tn] make a formal objection to (esp a member of a jury) 宣布反对(尤指陪审团某成员).

▷ **chal·len·ger** *n* person who challenges, esp in sport 提出竞争要求的人(尤指体育运动中); 挑战者.

chal·len·ging *adj* offering problems that test sb's ability; stimulating (为考验某人的能力)提出难题的; 激励的; 挑战的: *a challenging job, test, assignment, etc* 激励人的工作、考验、任务等.

cham·ber /ˈtʃeɪmbə(r); ˋtʃembɚ/ *n* **1** [C] (formerly) room, esp a bedroom (旧时)房间, (尤指)寝室. **2** **chambers** [pl] (**a**) judge's room for hearing cases that do not need to be taken into court 法官的办公室(用以审理不需要提出诉讼的案件). (**b**) (*Brit*) set of rooms in a larger building, esp the offices in the Inns of Court used by barristers for interviewing clients, etc 大建筑物中的成套房间; (尤指法律协会的)办公室(讼务律师用以接待委托人等的). **3** [C, CGp] (hall used by an) administrative or legislative assembly, eg one of the houses of a parliament 行政或立法机构(用的大厅)(如议会的会议厅): *The members left the council chamber.* 议员们离开了会议厅. ○ *the Upper/Lower Chamber*, eg (in Britain) the House of Lords/Commons 上[下]议院(如英国的上[下]议院). **4** [C] (**a**) enclosed space or cavity in the body of an animal, in a plant or in some kinds of machinery (动植物体内或某些机器中封闭的)洞穴, 腔, 室: *the chambers of the heart*, ie the auricle and the ventricle 心腔(心房与心室) ○ *a combustion chamber* 燃烧室. ⇨illus at PISTON 见 PISTON 之插图. (**b**) enclosed space under the ground 地下的封闭空间; 洞穴: *The cavers discovered a vast underground chamber.* 探穴人发现了一个地下大洞穴. **5** [C] part of a gun that holds the bullets 枪膛; 炮膛.

□ ˈ**chamber concert** concert of chamber music 室内乐音乐会.

ˈ**chambermaid** *n* woman whose job is cleaning and tidying bedrooms, usu in a hotel 以打扫和整理卧室为工作的妇女(通常指旅馆中的); 女服务员; 女侍.

ˈ**chamber music** music written for a small group of players (eg a string quartet) 为小乐队演奏谱写的乐曲(如弦乐四重奏); 室内乐.

ˌ**chamber of** ˈ**commerce** group of businessmen organized to promote local commercial interests 商会.

ˌ**chamber of** ˈ**horrors** place full of horrifying things, eg the room of criminals in Madame Tussaud's waxworks 充满恐怖事物的地方(如图索德夫人蜡像馆中的罪犯塑像室).

ˈ**chamber orchestra** small orchestra, esp one that performs baroque and early classical music 室内乐队(尤指表演巴罗克风格的作品和早期经典乐曲的小乐队).

ˈ**chamber-pot** *n* pottery vessel for urine, used in bedrooms 尿壶; 尿盆; 尿桶.

cham·ber·lain /ˈtʃeɪmbəlɪn; ˋtʃembɚlɪn/ *n* (formerly) official who managed the household of a monarch or nobleman (旧时)管理君主或贵族家务的人员; 管家.

cha·meleon /kəˈmiːlɪən; kəˋmilɪən/ *n* **1** any of various types of small lizard that can change colour according to its surroundings 避役(能变色的小蜥蜴); 变色龙. **2** (*fig* 比喻) person who changes his behaviour or opinions to suit the situation 改变行为或看法以适应情况的人.

cham·ois /ˈʃæmwɑː; *US* ˈʃæmɪ; ˋʃæmɪ/ *n* (*pl* unchanged 复数不变) type of small antelope living in the mountains of Europe and Asia (欧洲和亚洲山区的)小羚羊.

□ ˈ**chamois-leather** (also **shammy-leather** /ˈʃæmɪ leðə(r); ˋʃæmɪ ˋlɛðɚ/, ˈ**shammy**) *n* (**a**) [U] soft leather made from the skin of goats, sheep, deer, etc (由山羊、绵羊、鹿等的皮制成的)软皮革. (**b**) [C] piece of this 软皮革: *polish the car with a shammy* 用软皮擦汽车.

chamo·mile = CAMOMILE.

champ¹ /tʃæmp; tʃæmp/ *v* **1** [I, Tn] (esp of horses) chew (food) noisily (尤指马)大声嚼(食物). **2** [Ipr, Tn] **~ (at/on) sth** (of horses) bite at sth nervously or impatiently (指马)急躁地或不耐烦地咬某物: *horses champing at the bit* 咬着嚼子的马. **3** [I, Ipr, It] **~ (at sth)** (used esp in the continuous tenses 尤用于进行时态) be eager or impatient, esp to begin sth 急切或不耐烦(尤指开始做某事物): *He was champing with rage at the delay.* 他对这一延误着急上火. ○ *The boys were champing to start.* 男孩儿们恨不得马上就出发. **4** (idm 习语) ˌ**champ at the** ˈ**bit** (*infml* 口) be restlessly impatient to start doing sth 迫不及待要做某事.

champ² /tʃæmp; tʃæmp/ *n* (*infml* 口) = CHAMPION 2.

cham·pagne /ʃæmˈpeɪn; ʃæmˋpen/ *n* **1** [C, U] (any of various types of) sparkling white wine from E France 香槟酒: *a* ˌ*glass of cham*ˈ*pagne* 一杯香槟酒 ○ [attrib 作定语] ˌ*champagne* ˈ*cocktails* 香槟鸡尾酒. **2** [U] colour of this; pale straw colour 香槟酒的颜色; 淡草色; 淡黄色.

cham·pion /ˈtʃæmpɪən; ˋtʃæmpɪən/ *n* **1** person, team, animal or plant that has defeated or excelled all others in a competition 冠军; 优胜者: *a chess champion* 国际象棋冠军 ○ *The English football team were world champions in 1966.* 英格兰足球队是1966年的世界冠军. ○ *the heavyweight (boxing) champion of the world* 重量级(拳击)世界冠军 ○ [attrib 作定语] *a champion swimmer, horse, marrow* 优胜的游泳运动员、马、西葫芦. **2** person who fights, argues or speaks in support of another or of a cause(3) 支持他人或某一事业而进行战斗、辩护或解释说明的人; 斗士; 拥护者: *a champion of the poor/of women's rights* 穷苦人的[妇女权利的]卫士.

▷ **cham·pion** *v* [Tn] support the cause of (sb/sth); defend vigorously 支持(某人[某事物])的事业; 维护; 卫护: *champion the cause of gay rights* 维护同性恋权利.

cham·pi·on·ship *n* **1** [C often *pl* 常作复数] contest to decide who is the champion 锦标赛: *win the world championship* 赢得世界冠军 ○ *The European championships are being held in Rome.* 欧洲锦标赛正在罗马举行. ○ [attrib 作定语] *a championship medal* 冠军奖章. **2** [C] position of being a champion 冠军地位: *The championship is ours.* 冠军是我们的. ⇨Usage at SPORT 用法见 SPORT. **3** [U] vigorous support 有力的支持: *her championship of our cause* 她对我们事业的有力支持.

chance¹ /tʃɑːns; *US* tʃæns; tʃæns/ *n* **1** [U] way in which things happen without any cause that can be seen or understood; luck; fortune 无任何可见到的或可了解的原因而发生的情况; 机会; 运气: *Chance plays a big part in many board games.* 在许多棋类游戏中, 大多靠碰运气取胜. ○ *It was (pure) chance our meeting in Paris/that we met in Paris.* 我们在巴黎相遇(纯)属巧合. ○ *trust to chance* 凭机会; 碰运气 ○ *leave nothing to chance*, ie take great care in planning sth to reduce the chance of bad luck 不靠运气(极仔细地计划某事物以减少不利的可能性) ○ *a game of chance*, ie one decided by luck, not skill 靠碰运气的游戏 ○ [attrib 作定语] *a chance meeting, encounter, occurrence, happening, etc* 巧遇、偶然相遇、偶发事件、偶然发生的事. **2** **~ of (doing) sth/to do sth/that...** [C, U] possibility; likelihood 可能性: *Is there any chance of getting tickets for tonight's performance?* 有可能得到今晚演出的票吗? ○ *What are the chances of his coming?* 他来的可能性有多大? ○ *She has a good chance/no chance/not much chance/only a slim chance of winning.* 她大有希望[没有可能/没什么希望/只有些微的可能]获胜. ○ *What chance of success do we have?* 我们成功的把握有多大? ○ *There's a faint chance that you'll find him at home.* 在他家里找到他的可能性很小. **3** [C] **~ (of doing sth/to do sth)** occasion when success seems very probable; opportunity 很有可能成功的时机; 机会: *It was the chance she had been waiting for.* 这就是她一直等待的机会. ○ *You won't get another chance of going there.* 你没有再到那里去的机会了. ○ *Please give me a chance to explain.* 请给我个机会让我解释一下. ○ *You'd be a fool to ignore a chance like that.* 你放弃掉那样的机会可太蠢了. ○ *This is your big chance!* ie your best opportunity of success. 这是你的大好机会! ⇨Usage at OPPORTUNITY 用法见 OPPORTUNITY. **4** [C] risk; gamble 冒险; 赌博: *This road may not be the one we want — but that's a chance we're going to have to take.* 我们要走的并不是这条路——但我们还是要冒险试一试. **5** [C] unplanned event, esp a lucky one; accident 意外事件; (尤指)机会; 机遇: *By a happy chance a policeman was passing as I was attacked.* 在我受到攻击时, 幸好有个警察经过. **6** (idm 习语) **as** ˌ**chance would** ˈ**have it** by coincidence; as it happens 凑巧; 碰巧: *As chance would have it he was going to London as well and was able to give me a lift.* 赶巧他也去伦敦, 所以能载我一程. **by** ˈ**any chance** perhaps;

possibly 或许; 可能: *Would you by any chance have change for £5?* 你能找换5英镑的零钱吗? **by 'chance** by accident; accidentally; unintentionally 偶然地; 意外地; 非有意地: *I met her quite by chance.* 我遇见她完全是偶然的. **a cat in hell's chance** ⇨ CAT[1]. **'chance would be a fine thing** (*infml* 口) I would like to do sth but will never have an opportunity to do it 愿作某事但永远没有机会去作. **the chances are (that) ...** (*infml* 口) it is likely that... 很可能...: *The chances are that she'll be coming.* 很可能她要来. **an even chance** ⇨ EVEN[1]. **even chances/odds/money** ⇨ EVEN[1]. **a fighting chance** ⇨ FIGHT[1]. **give sb/sth half a 'chance** give sb/sth some opportunity of being or doing sth 给某人[某事物]一些机会去成为或去做某事物: *She's keen and I'm sure she'll succeed given half a chance.* 她聪明机智, 只要有点儿机会我肯定她会成功. **have an eye for/on/to the main chance** ⇨ EYE[1]. **no chance** (*infml* 口) there is no possibility of that 没有可能; 没有希望. **not have a chance/hope in hell** ⇨ HELL. **on the (off) chance (of doing sth/that...)** in the hope of sth happening, although it is unlikely 希望某事发生(虽然可能性不大); 抱(一线)希望: *I didn't think you'd be at home, but I just called on the 'off chance.* 我想你不会在家的, 只是抱着一线希望给你打个电话. **a sporting chance** ⇨ SPORTING. **stand a chance (of sth/of doing sth)** have a chance of (achieving) sth 有(完成)某事物的希望; 有达到某目的的机会: *He stands a (good/fair) chance of passing the examination.* 他考试及格(大[很])有希望. **take a 'chance (on sth)** attempt to do sth, in spite of the possibility of failure; take a risk 试图做成某事物(虽然有失败的可能性); 冒险; 碰运气. **take 'chances** behave riskily 冒险: *You should never take chances when driving a car.* 开车时决不应冒险. **take one's 'chance** profit as much as one can from one's opportunities 从自己的机遇中尽量取得利益.

chance[2] /tʃɑ:ns; *US* tʃæns; tʃæns/ *v* **1** (*fml* 文) happen by chance 偶然发生; 碰巧: *She chanced to be in/It chanced that she was in when he called.* 他打电话时碰巧她在家. ⇨Usage at APPEAR 用法见 APPEAR. **2** [Tn, Tg] (*infml* 口) risk (sth) 冒(某事的)险: *'Take an umbrella.' 'No — I'll chance it* (ie risk getting wet).' '带着雨伞吧.' '不带了 —— 豁出去了(可能被淋湿).' ○ *We'll have to chance meeting an enemy patrol.* 我们不得不冒着可能遇上敌人巡逻兵的危险. **3** (idm 习语) **ˌchance one's 'arm** (*infml* 口) take a risk, although it is likely that one will fail (尽管可能失败)仍冒险试一试. **4** (phr v) **chance on sb/sth** (*fml* 文) happen to meet sb or find sth 偶然遇见某人; 偶然发现某事物.

chan·cel /'tʃɑ:nsl; *US* 'tʃænsl; 'tʃænsl̩/ *n* part of a church near the altar, used by the priests and the choir 圣坛(教堂中靠近祭坛部分, 供牧师和唱诗班用). ⇨illus at App 1 见附录1之插图, page viii.

chan·cel·lery /'tʃɑ:nsələrı; *US* 'tʃæns-; 'tʃænsələrı/ *n* **1** [C] position, department or official residence of a chancellor 大臣的职位、部门或官邸. **2** [Gp] staff in a chancellor's department 大臣部门中的全体工作人员. **3** [C] office where business is done in an embassy or a consulate 大使馆或领事馆的办事处.

chan·cel·lor /'tʃɑ:nsələ(r); *US* 'tʃæns-; 'tʃænsələ˞/ *n* **1** head of government in Austria etc (奥地利等国的)总理, 首相. **2** (*Brit*) honorary head of some universities (某些大学的)名誉校长: *chancellor of London University* 伦敦大学的名誉校长. **3** State or law official of various kinds 政府的或司法的各类官员: *the Lord Chancellor*, ie the highest judge (and chairman of the House of Lords) 大法官(及上议院议长).

□ **ˌChancellor of the Ex'chequer** (*Brit*) cabinet minister responsible for finance 财政大臣.

chan·cery /'tʃɑ:nsərı; *US* 'tʃænsərı; 'tʃænsərı/ *n* **1** (*Brit*) Lord Chancellor's division of the High Court of Justice 高等法院的大法官法院. **2** (*US*) court that settles cases according to general principles of justice and fairness not covered by the law; court of equity 衡平法院(以正义公平即衡平为总原则, 审理不属普通法范围的案件的法院). **3** office where public records are kept 档案馆; 档案室. **4** (idm 习语) **ward in chancery** ⇨ WARD.

chancy /'tʃɑ:nsı; 'tʃænsı/ *adj* (**-ier**, **-iest**) risky; uncertain 冒险的; 不确定的: *a chancy business* 冒险的生意. ▷ **chan·cily** *adj*.

chan·de·lier /ˌʃændə'lıə(r); ˌʃændl̩'ır/ *n* ornamental hanging light with branches for several bulbs or candles 枝形吊灯(有分枝的装饰吊灯, 可装几盏灯或蜡烛).

chand·ler /'tʃɑ:ndlə(r); *US* 'tʃænd-; 'tʃændlə˞/ *n* (also **ship's chandler**) dealer in ropes, canvas and other supplies for ships 船用杂货商(经售绳索、帆布及其他船用物品的商人).

change[1] /tʃeındʒ; tʃendʒ/ *v* **1** [I, Tn] (cause sb/sth to) become different; alter (使某人[某事物])变; 改变: *You've changed a lot since I last saw you.* 自从我上次见到你以来, 你改变了很多. ○ *Our plans have changed.* 我们的计划已经改变了. ○ *change one's attitude, ideas, opinion, etc* 改变态度、主意、意见等 ○ *an event which changed the course of history* 改变历史进程的事件. ⇨ Usage 见所附用法. **2 (a)** [Ipr, Tn·pr] **~ (sb/sth) (from sth) to/into sth** (cause sb/sth to) pass from one form to another (使某人[某事物])改变形式: *Caterpillars change into butterflies or moths.* 毛虫能变成蝴蝶或蛾子. ○ *The witch changed the prince into a frog.* 巫婆把王子变成了青蛙. **(b)** [I, Ipr, Tn·pr] **~ (sb/sth) (from A) (to/into B)** (cause sb/sth to) pass from one stage to another (使某人[某事物])进入另一阶段: *The traffic lights have changed (from red to green).* 交通灯由红灯变绿灯了. ○ *Britain changed to a metric system of currency in 1970.* 1970年英国已改用公制货币. **3 (a)** [Tn, Tn·pr] **~ sb/sth (for sb/sth)** take or use another instead of sb/sth; replace sb/sth with another 替换或代替某人[某事物]: *change one's doctor* 另找一位医生看病 ○ *change one's job* 换一份工作 ○ *change one's address*, ie move to a new home 更改地址 ○ *change a light bulb* 换个灯泡 ○ *change gear*, ie engage a different gear in a car, etc in order to travel at a higher or lower speed 换挡(汽车等换另一排挡, 以加速或减速行车) ○ *I must change these trousers* (ie put on a clean pair) — *they've got oil on them.* 我必须换换裤子(换一条干净的)—— 上面弄上油了. ○ *I'm thinking of changing my car for a bigger one.* 我正在考虑换辆大汽车. **(b)** [Tn] move from one (thing, direction, etc) to another; switch 转换, 转变(事物、方向等): *change sides*, eg in a war, debate, etc 转变立场(如在战争、辩论中等) ○ *The ship changed course*, ie began to travel in a different direction. 轮船改变了航向. ○ *The wind has changed direction.* 风向变了. **(c)** [Tn, Tn·pr] **~ sth (with sb)** (used with a *pl* object 与复数宾语连用) (of two people) exchange (positions, places, etc) (指两人)交换(位置、地方等): *Can we change seats?/Can I change seats with you?* 咱们可以换换座位吗? [我可以和你换个座位吗?] **(d)** [I, Ipr, Tn] **~ (from sth to sth)** go from one (train, bus, etc) to another 换乘(火车、公共汽车等): *Change (trains) at Crewe for Stockport.* 在克鲁换(火)车到斯托克波特去. ○ *This is where we change from car to bus.* 这就是我们从小汽车换乘公共汽车的地方. ○ *All change!* ie This train stops here; everyone must leave it. 所有乘客全部换车! (本次列车已到终点站, 所有乘客均须下车.) **(e)** [Tn] put different clothes or covering on (sb/sth) 给(某人[某物])换上衣服或覆盖物: *change* (ie put a clean nappy on) *the baby* 给婴儿换尿布 ○ *change* (ie put clean sheets on) *the beds* 换床单. **4** [I, Ipr] **~ (out of sth) (into sth)** take off one's clothes and put others on 换衣服; 更衣: *go upstairs to change* 到楼上换衣服 ○ *change* (ie into more formal clothes) *for dinner* 换上宴会服 ○ *Go and change out of those damp clothes into something dry.* 去把湿衣服脱掉换上干的. **5** [Tn, Tn·pr] **~ sth (for/into sth)** give or receive (money) in exchange for the equivalent sum in coins or notes of smaller value or in a different currency 兑换(钱): *Can you change a five-pound note?* 你能换开五英镑的票子吗? ○ *I need to change my dollars into francs.* 我需要把美金换成法郎. **6** (idm 习语) **change 'hands** pass into another person's possession 归另一人所有; 转手: *The house has changed hands several times recently.* 这房子最近几经转手. **change/swap horses in midstream** ⇨ HORSE. **change one's/sb's 'mind** alter one's decision or opinion 改变决定或意见: *Nothing will make me change my mind.* 任何事情都不能使我改变主意. **change 'places (with sb)** (of two people, groups, etc) exchange positions, seats, etc (指两人、组等)交换地位、座位等: *Let me change places with*

C

you/Let's change places so you can be next to the window. 我和你换换地方吧[咱们换换地方吧, 这样你就能靠近窗户]. **change one's spots** (try to) be or do sth that is against one's nature (试图)违反本性或做违反本性的事; 改变本性. **change step** adjust one's step when marching so that one is marching in the correct rhythm 行军时调整步伐跟上节奏. ˌ**change the ˈsubject** start talking about sth different 开始谈其他的事; 改变话题. ˌ**change one's ˈtune** (*infml* 口) alter one's manner or attitude, eg becoming humble instead of insolent 改变举止或态度(如前倨后恭). **change one's ways** start to live one's life differently, esp in order to suit changed circumstances 开始过另一种生活(尤指为适应环境的改变). **chop and change** ⇨ CHOP[3]. **7** (phr v) **change back (into sb/sth)** return to one's earlier form, character, etc 回复到原来的样子、特性等: *Cats can never change back into kittens.* 老猫绝变不成小猫. **change back (into sth)** take off one's clothes and put on others that one was wearing earlier 换上原来穿的衣物: *Can I change back into my jeans now?* 现在我能换上原来穿的牛仔裤了吗? **change sth back (into sth)** give back (money) and receive the equivalent sum in the original currency 将(钱)换成原来的货币: *change back francs into dollars* 将法郎换成原来的美元. ˌ**change ˈdown** engage a lower gear when driving a car, etc (开汽车等时)换成低挡. ˌ**change ˈover (from sth) (to sth)** change from one system or position to another 改变制度或地位: *The country has changed over from military to democratic rule.* 这个国家已经由军事统治转变为民主领导. ˌ**change ˈup** engage a higher gear when driving a car, etc (开汽车等时)换成高挡.

▷ **change·able** /ˈtʃeɪndʒəbl; ˌtʃendʒəˈbl/ *adj* **1** tending to change; often changing 易变的; 常变的: *a changeable person, mood* 喜怒无常的人、情绪 ○ *changeable weather* 多变的天气. **2** that can be changed 能被改变的.

□ ˈ**change-over** *n* change from one system to another 制度的改变: *a peaceful change-over to civilian rule* 和平地转变为文官统治.

NOTE ON USAGE 用法: **Change** has a general use and indicates any act of making something different ☆ **change** 的词义很广, 表示使某事物改变的任何作用: *Most English women change their names when they marry.* 英国妇女大多因结婚而改姓. ○ *He changed the design of the house completely.* 他完全更改了房屋的设计. **Alter** indicates the making of a small difference in the appearance, character, use, etc of something ☆ **alter** 表示使某事物在外观、性质、用途等方面稍作改变: *I'll have to alter the diagram. I've made a mistake.* 我得修改图表. 我出了点儿错. **Modify** is more formal. ☆ **modify** 一词较文. When applied to objects, especially machines, it suggests a partial change in structure or function 用于物体时, 尤指用于机器时, 表示结构或功能的部分改变: *The car has been modified for racing.* 这辆汽车已改装为赛车. It can also indicate the softening of attitudes, opinions, etc 这个词还可表示态度、意见等的软化: *He'll have to modify his views if he wants to be elected.* 他要想当选就得把观点改得缓和些. **Vary** describes the changing of something or its parts, often temporarily and repeatedly ☆ **vary** 所指某事物或其部分的改变常为暂时的或反复的: *It's better to vary your diet rather than eat the same things all the time.* 你最好变换一下饮食, 不要总吃同样的东西. All these verbs (except **modify**) can also be used intransitively 所有这些动词(除 **modify** 外)还均可用作不及物动词: *Her expression changed when she heard the news.* 她听到这一消息时表情就变了. ○ *This place hasn't altered since I was a girl.* 从我幼时起, 这地方就没发生过变化. ○ *Political opinions vary according to wealth, age, etc.* 政治见解因财富、年龄等不同而有所区别.

change[2] /tʃeɪndʒ; tʃendʒ/ *n* **1** [C, U] **~ (in/to sth)** (act of) making or becoming different; alteration 变化(的行动); 改变; 变更; 变动: *a change in the weather* 天气的变化 ○ *There has been a change in the programme.* 节目有变动. ○ *The Government plans to make important changes to the tax system.* 政府计划对税收制度作重大改变. ○ *Doctors say there is no change in the patient's condition.* 医生说病人的情况没有变化. ○ *Are you for or against change?* 你赞同还是反对改动? **2** [C] **~ (of sth)** (**a**) act of changing one thing for another 从一事物改换成另一事物的行动: *a change of job* 换工作 ○ *Please note my change of address.* 请注意我改换了地址. ○ *The party needs a change of leader.* 这个党需要更换领袖. ○ *This is the third change of government the country has seen in two years.* 这次是国家两年来的第三次政府更替. (**b**) thing used in place of another or others 替代物: *Don't forget to take a change of* (ie a second set of) *clothes.* 不要忘记带着替换的衣服. **3** [C] **~ (from sth) (to sth)** (**a**) act of going from one train or bus to another 换车; 转车: *He had to make a quick change at Crewe.* 他得在克鲁迅速换车. (**b**) changed or different routine, occupation or surroundings 改换后的或另一路线、职业或环境: *a welcome change from town to country life* 从城市到乡村生活的喜人变化 ○ *She badly needs a change.* 她亟须改变一下. **4** [U] (**a**) coins or notes of lower values equivalent to a single coin or note of a higher value 辅币: *Can you give me/Have you got change for a five-pound note?* 你能否给我[你有没有]五英镑的辅币? (**b**) coins of low value 低值硬币: *I've no small change.* 我没有零钱. (**c**) money returned when the price of sth is less than the amount given in payment 找回的钱; 找给的钱: *Don't forget your change!* 不要忘了找你的钱! ○ *25p change* 找给25便士. **5** (idm 习语) **a change for the ˈbetter/ˈworse** improvement/worsening of sth that already exists or that has gone before 现有的或曾有过的某事物的改善[变坏]: *The situation is now so bad that any change is likely to be a change for the better.* 目前情况恶劣, 只要有变化就是向好处变. **a** ˌ**change of ˈair/ˈclimate** different conditions or surroundings 换换条件或环境: *A change of air* (eg a holiday away from home) *will do you good.* 换换环境(如离家度假)对你有好处. **a** ˌ**change of ˈheart** great change in one's attitude or feelings, esp towards greater friendliness or co-operation 态度或感情的巨大变化(尤指对增进友好或合作关系). **the** ˌ**change of ˈlife** (*euph* 婉) = MENOPAUSE. **for a ˈchange** to vary one's routine; for the sake of variety 为了改变常规; 为了有变化: *We usually go to France in the summer, but this year we're going to Spain for a change.* 我们夏天通常去法国, 但今年为了换个地方我们去西班牙. **get no change out of sb** (*infml* 口) receive no help, information, etc from sb 从某人处得不到帮助、信息等. **ring the changes** ⇨ RING[2].

▷ **change·less** *adj* never changing 从不改变的.

change·ling /ˈtʃeɪndʒlɪŋ; ˈtʃendʒlɪŋ/ *n* child or thing believed to have been secretly substituted for another (据信是被偷换了的)儿童, 东西.

chan·nel /ˈtʃænl; ˈtʃænl/ *n* **1** [C] (**a**) sunken bed of a river, stream or canal 河床. (**b**) passage along which a liquid may flow (液体的)通道. **2** [C] navigable part of a stretch of water, deeper than the parts on either side of it 航道: *The channel is marked by buoys.* 航道有浮标标明. **3** (**a**) [C] stretch of water joining two seas 海峡. (**b**) **the Channel** [sing] = THE ENGLISH CHANNEL (ENGLISH): [attrib 作定语] *The Channel crossing was very calm.* 这次横渡英吉利海峡风平浪静. **4** [C] (*fig* 比喻) any way by which news, information, etc may travel (新闻、信息等传递的)途径, 线路: *Your complaint must be made through the proper channels.* 你的意见必须通过正当途径投诉. ○ *He has secret channels of information.* 他有秘密的消息来源. **5** [C] (**a**) band of frequencies (FREQUENCY 2) used for broadcasting a particular set of radio or television programmes 频道. (**b**) particular television station 某电视台: *What's your favourite channel?* 你喜欢哪个电视台?

▷ **chan·nel** *v* (**-ll-**; *US* ALSO **-l-**) **1** [Tn] form a channel or channels in (sth) 在(某物)上形成槽或沟: *Deep grooves channelled the soft rock.* 在软岩石上形成许多深槽. **2** [Tn, Tn·pr] carry (sth) in a channel; direct 经水道运送(某物); 引导: *Water is channelled through a series of irrigation canals.* 把水引入一系列灌溉渠中. ○ (*fig* 比喻) *We must channel all our energies into the new scheme.* 我们必须把一切精力都用到新的计划上.

chant /tʃɑːnt; tʃænt/ *n* **1** simple tune to which psalms or canticles are fitted by singing several syllables or words to the same note 圣歌. **2** words sung or shouted rhythmically and repeatedly (有节奏地、反复地)唱的

或喊叫的词语: *The team's supporters sang a victory chant.* 拥护这个队的人有节奏地反复喊着胜利的口号.
▷ **chant** *v* [I, Tn] **1** sing or recite (a psalm, etc) as a chant (如圣歌般)歌唱或背诵(赞美诗等): *chant the liturgy* 在礼拜仪式上唱圣歌. **2** sing or shout (sth) rhythmically and repeatedly (有节奏地、反复地)唱或喊叫(某词语): *'We are the champions!' chanted the football fans.* 足球迷们有节奏地反复喊叫: '我们是冠军.'

chanty, chantey (*US*) = SHANTY.

chaos /ˈkeɪɒs; ˈkeɑs/ *n* [U] complete disorder or confusion 混乱; 紊乱: *The burglars left the house in (a state of) chaos.* 窃贼走后房屋中一片凌乱. ○ *The wintry weather has caused chaos on the roads.* 因风雪交加道路上混乱不堪.
▷ **cha·otic** /keɪˈɒtɪk; keˈɑtɪk/ *adj* in a state of chaos; completely disorganized 处于混乱状态的; 完全无秩序的: *With no one to keep order the situation in the classroom was chaotic.* 因无人维持秩序, 教室里一片混乱. **cha·ot·ic·ally** /keɪˈɒtɪklɪ; keˈɑtɪklɪ/ *adv*.

chap[1] /tʃæp; tʃæp/ *v* (**-pp-**) (**a**) [I] (of the skin) become cracked, rough or sore (指皮肤)皲裂, 变粗糙, 疼痛: *My skin soon chaps in cold weather.* 我的皮肤在寒冷天气很快就裂了. (**b**) [Tn esp passive 尤用于被动语态] cause (sth) to become cracked, rough or sore 使(某物)皲裂、变粗糙或疼痛: *chapped lips* 皲裂的嘴唇 ○ *hands and face chapped by the cold* 因寒冷而皲裂的手和脸.
▷ **chap** *n* sore crack in the skin (皮肤上疼痛的)皲裂处, 裂口.

chap[2] /tʃæp; tʃæp/ *n* (*infml* 口 *esp Brit*) man or boy; fellow 男子; 小伙子; 傢伙: *Be a good chap and open the door for me, would you?* 好兄弟, 给我开开门行吗?

chap *abbr* 缩写 = chapter(1).

chapel /ˈtʃæpl; ˈtʃæpl̩/ *n* **1** [C] small building or room used for Christian worship, eg in a school, prison, large private house, etc (基督徒礼拜用的)小教堂或房间(如学校、监狱、私人大宅等中的): *a college chapel* 学院小教堂 ○ *Chapel is* (ie Services in chapel are) *at 8 o'clock.* (小教堂的)礼拜在8点钟举行. **2** [C] separate part of a church or cathedral with its own altar, used for small services and private prayer 私人祈祷处(教堂或大教堂中有自己祭坛的独立部分, 用于小规模礼拜或私人祈祷): *a ˈLady chapel*, ie one dedicated to Mary, the mother of Jesus 圣母堂(供奉耶稣之母马利亚的礼拜堂). ⇨illus at App 1 见附录1之插图, page viii. **3** [C] (*Brit*) place used for Christian worship by Nonconformists (非英国国教徒礼拜基督的)教堂: *a Methodist ˈchapel* 卫理公会教堂 ○ *She goes to/attends chapel regularly.* 她经常去新教徒教堂作礼拜. ○ (*dated* 旧) *Are they church or chapel?* ie Do they belong to the Anglican Church or to a Nonconformist denomination? 他们是英国国教徒还是非国教徒? **4** [CGp] (members of a) branch of a trade union in a newspaper office or printing house 报社或印刷厂工会(会员): *The chapel voted against a strike.* 印刷工会投票反对罢工. **5** [C] (*esp US*) local branch of a club, society, etc 俱乐部、社团等的地方分部.

chap·eron /ˈʃæpərəʊn; ˈʃæpəˌron/ *n* (esp formerly) older person, usu a woman, who looks after a girl or a young unmarried woman on social occasions (尤指旧时)在社交场合照顾少女或未婚女子的年长者(通常为妇女); 年长女伴; 保护人.
▷ **chap·eron** *v* [Tn] act as a chaperon for (sb) 当(某人的)年长女伴.
chap·er·on·age *n* [U].

chap·lain /ˈtʃæplɪn; ˈtʃæplɪn/ *n* clergyman attached to the chapel of a school, prison, etc, or serving in the armed forces (学校、监狱、军队等的)教士: *an army chaplain* 随军教士. Cf 参看 PADRE.
▷ **chap·laincy** *n* position, period of office or house of a chaplain 随军教士的职位、任期或住所.

chap·let /ˈtʃæplɪt; ˈtʃæplɪt/ *n* **1** wreath of leaves, flowers, jewels, etc for the head 花冠(叶子、花、珠宝等做成的环, 用作头饰). **2** short string of beads for counting prayers (祈祷时计数用的)短串珠.

chap·ter /ˈtʃæptə(r); ˈtʃæptɚ/ *n* **1** [C] (*abbrs* 缩写 **ch, chap**) (usu numbered) division of a book (通常为编序的)(书中的)章, 篇, 回: *I've just finished Chapter 3.* 我刚看完第3章. **2** [C] period of time 时期: *the most glorious chapter in our country's history* 我国历史上最光辉的时期. **3** [Gp] (**a**) all the canons of a cathedral or the members of a monastery or convent 大教堂的全体教士或修道院或女修道院的全体成员. (**b**) [C] meeting of these 大教堂或修道院的会议. **4** (idm 习语) ˌ**chapter and ˈverse** exact reference to a passage or an authority; exact details of sth (某段或某权威论述的)准确出处; (某事物的)准确细节: *I can't quote chapter and verse but I can give you the main points the author was making.* 我无法引用确切的原文, 但是我可以告诉你作者所述的要点. **a** ˌ**chapter of ˈaccidents** series or sequence of unfortunate events 一系列的或一连串的不幸事件.

char[1] /tʃɑː(r); tʃɑr/ *v* (**-rr-**) (**a**) [I, Tn] (cause sth to) become black by burning; scorch (使某物)燃烧而变黑; 烧焦: *charred wood* 烧焦的木头. (**b**) [Tn] reduce (sth) to charcoal by burning 使(某物)燃烧成焦炭: *the charred remains of the bonfire* 营火的余烬.

char[2] /tʃɑːr; tʃɑr/ *n* (*Brit*) = CHARWOMAN.
▷ **char** *v* (**-rr-**) [I] work as a charwoman 做打杂女工.

char[3] /tʃɑː(r); tʃɑr/ *n* [U] (*dated Brit infml* 旧, 口) tea 茶: *a cup of char* 一杯茶.

cha·ra·banc /ˈʃærəbæŋ; ˈʃærəˌbæŋ/ *n* (*dated* 旧 *Brit*) early type of bus with bench seats facing forward, used esp for pleasure trips 大型游览车(旧式公共汽车, 有面向前的板凳, 尤用于游览).

char·ac·ter /ˈkærəktə(r); ˈkærɪktɚ/ *n* **1** [C] (**a**) mental or moral qualities that make a person, group, nation, etc different from others (个人、集体、民族等特有的)品质, 特性: *What does her handwriting tell you about her character?* 你从她的笔迹中看到她有什么个性? ○ *His character is very different from his wife's.* 他和他妻子的性格迥然不同. ○ *The British character is often said to be phlegmatic.* 英国人的性格常说成是冷漠的. (**b**) all those features that make a thing, a place, an event, etc what it is and different from others (事物、地方、事件等的)特点, 特征, 特性, 特色: *the character of the desert landscape* 沙漠景色的特点 ○ *The whole character of the village has changed since I was last here.* 自从我上次到这里以来, 这个村庄的特色完全改变了. ○ *The wedding took on the character of* (ie became like) *a farce when the vicar fell flat on his face.* 牧师摔了个大马趴, 婚礼变得像出笑剧. **2** [U] (**a**) striking individuality 显著的个性: *drab houses with no character* 没有特色的单调房屋. (**b**) moral strength 道德的力量; 品格; 品德: *a woman of character* 有道德的女子 ○ *It takes character to say a thing like that.* 说那样的话需要有骨气. ○ *Some people think military service is character-building.* 有些人认为服兵役能陶冶情操. **3** [C] (**a**) (*infml* 口) person, esp an odd or unpleasant one 人(尤指古怪或令人讨厌的人): *He looks a suspicious character.* 他像个可疑的人. (**b**) (*approv* 褒) person who is not ordinary or typical; person with individuality 与众不同的人; 有个性的人: *She's a real/quite a character!* 她真[很]有个性! **4** [C] person in a novel, play, etc (小说、戏剧等中的)人物: *the characters in the novels of Charles Dickens* 狄更斯小说中的人物. **5** [C] reputation, esp a good one 名声(尤指好名声); 声望: *damage sb's character* 损害某人的名声. **6** [C] letter, sign or mark used in a system of writing or printing (用于书写或印刷系统的)字母、符号或记号: *Chinese, Greek, Russian, etc characters* 汉字、希腊字母、俄文字母. **7** (idm 习语) **in/out of character** typical/not typical of a person's character(1a) 合乎[不合乎]某人的性格: *Her behaviour last night was quite out of character.* 她昨晚的举止与她的性格很不相符.
▷ **char·act·er·less** *adj* (*derog* 贬) without character (2a); uninteresting; ordinary 无特征的; 无趣的; 平庸的: *a characterless place* 无特色的地方.
□ ˈ**character actor**, ˈ**character actress** actor who specializes in playing odd or eccentric characters 性格演员.
ˈ**character reference** (*Brit*) written description of a person's qualities; testimonial (对人的品质的)书面描述, 证明书.

char·ac·ter·istic /ˌkærəktəˈrɪstɪk; ˌkærɪktəˈrɪstɪk/ *adj* ~ (**of sb/sth**) forming part of the character(1a) of a person or thing; typical 构成人或事物特征之一部分的; 典型性的: *He spoke with characteristic enthusiasm.* 他以特有的热情说话. ○ *Such bluntness is characteristic of* *him.* 他就是这么迟钝.

▷ **char·ac·ter·istic** *n* distinguishing feature 与众不同的特征: *What characteristics distinguish the Americans from the Canadians?* 美国人和加拿大人的特征有什么不同? ○ *Arrogance is one of his less attractive characteristics.* 骄傲自大是他的一个缺点.

char·ac·ter·ist·ic·ally *adv*: *Characteristically she took the joke very well.* 从她的性格来说, 她经得起那个玩笑.

char·ac·ter·ize, -ise /ˈkærəktəraɪz; ˋkærɪktə,raɪz/ *v* **1** [Cn·n/a] **~ sb/sth as sth** describe or portray the character of sb/sth as sth 将某人[某事物]的特点描述成或刻画成某事物: *The novelist characterizes his heroine as capricious and passionate.* 这位小说家把女主人公刻画成反复无常而又多情的人. **2** [Tn esp passive 尤用于被动语态] be typical of (sb/sth); be characteristic of 表现(某人[某事物])的典型; 以...为特征: *the rolling downs that characterize this part of England* 英格兰这一地区特有的开阔的丘陵地 ○ *The giraffe is characterized by its very long neck.* 长颈鹿以其长颈为特征.

▷ **char·ac·ter·iza·tion, -isation** /-raɪˈzeɪʃn; -raɪˋzeʃən/ *n* [U] action or process of characterizing (CHARACTERIZE 1), esp the portrayal of human character in novels, plays, etc 描述, 刻画, 塑造(尤指人物性格): *Jane Austen's skill at characterization* 简·奥斯汀刻画人物的技巧.

cha·rade /ʃəˈrɑːd; *US* ʃəˈreɪd; ʃəˋred/ *n* **1 charades** [sing *v*] game in which one team acts a series of little plays containing syllables of a word which the other team tries to guess 哑谜猜字游戏(一组进行若干短小的表演, 表示一字的各音节, 由另一组猜字). **2** [C] scene in a game of charades 这种游戏的表演. **3** [C] (*fig* 比喻) absurd and obvious pretence 荒唐可笑又显而易见的伪装.

char·coal /ˈtʃɑːkəʊl; ˋtʃɑr,kol/ *n* **1** [U] black substance made by burning wood slowly in an oven with a little air, used as a filtering material or as fuel or for drawing 木炭: *a stick/piece/lump of charcoal* 一根、一块木炭 ○ [attrib 作定语] *a charcoal sketch* 炭笔素描. **2** (also **charcoal ˈgrey**) [U] very dark grey colour 深灰色.

□ ˈ**charcoal-burner** *n* (formerly) person making charcoal (旧时)烧炭者.

chard /tʃɑːd; tʃɑrd/ *n* [U] (also **Swiss chard**) type of beet whose leaves are eaten as a vegetable 莙达菜(其叶可做蔬菜的一种甜菜).

charge[1] /tʃɑːdʒ; tʃɑrdʒ/ *n* **1** [C] claim that a person has done wrong, esp a formal claim that he has committed a crime; accusation 指责; 指控; (尤指)控告: *arrested on a charge of murder/a murder charge* 以谋杀罪被捕 ○ *I resent the charges of incompetence made against me.* 说我无能, 我感到很气愤. **2** [C] rushing violent attack (by soldiers, wild animals, footballers, etc) (士兵、野兽、足球队员等)猛攻: *lead a charge* 带头进攻. **3** [C] price asked for goods or services (货物或服务所需的)费用: *an admission/entry charge*, eg to visit a museum 入场[门]费(如参观博物馆) ○ *His charges are very reasonable.* 他要的价钱很公道. ○ *All goods are delivered free of charge.* 一切物品免费送货. ⇨Usage at PRICE 用法见PRICE. **4** (**a**) [U] responsible possession; care; custody 掌管; 照管; 监护: *leave a child in a friend's charge* 把孩子留给朋友照管 ○ *He assumed full charge of the firm in his father's absence.* 他在父亲不在时全权掌管公司. (**b**) [C] (*fml* 文) person or thing left in sb's care 留给某人照管的人或事物: *He became his uncle's charge after his parents died.* 他在父母去世后, 由叔父抚养. **5** [C] (*fml* 文) task; duty 任务; 责任. **6** [C] amount of explosive needed to fire a gun or cause an explosion (开枪放炮或产生爆炸所需的)炸药量. **7** [C] (**a**) amount of electricity put into a battery or contained in a substance 充电量; 电荷: *a positive/negative charge* 正[负]电荷. (**b**) energy stored chemically for conversion into electricity (以化学物质贮存的可转化为电的)能量. **8** [C] (*fml* 文) instructions; directions 指示; 命令: *the judge's charge to the jury*, ie his advice to them about their verdict 法官给陪审团的指示(引导他们作出裁断). **9** (idm 习语) **bring a charge (of sth) against sb** formally accuse sb (of a crime, etc) 正式控告某人(某罪行等). **a charge on sb/sth** person or thing that must be paid for as part of a particular area of expenditure 必须为某人或某事物支付的某项开支: *They are a charge on the rates.* 这是(征收)房地产税的金额. **face a charge/charges** ⇨ FACE[2]. **give sb in ˈcharge** (*esp Brit*) hand sb over to the police 把某人交给警方. **have charge of sth** have responsibility for sth 对某事物有责任. **in charge (of sb/sth)** in a position of control or command (over sb/sth) 处于控制或支配(某人[某事物])的地位: *Who's in charge here?* 这儿谁负责? ○ *He was left in charge of the shop while the manager was away.* 经理不在时, 他负责这个商店. **in/under sb's charge** in the care of sb 在某人照看下: *These patients are under the charge of Dr Wilson.* 这些病人由威尔逊医生治疗. **lay sth to sb's charge** (*fml* 文) accuse sb of sth 控告某人犯某罪. **prefer a charge/charges** ⇨ PREFER. **reverse the charges** ⇨ REVERSE[3]. **take charge (of sth)** take control of sth; become responsible for sth 控制或掌管某事物;承担某事物的责任: *The department was badly organized until she took charge (of it).* 这个部门在她负责以前组织工作做得很差.

□ ˈ**charge account** (*US*) = CREDIT ACCOUNT (CREDIT[1]).

ˈ**charge-sheet** *n* (*Brit*) record kept in a police station of charges (CHARGE[1] 1) made 保存在警察局的控告记录.

charge[2] /tʃɑːdʒ; tʃɑrdʒ/ *v* **1** (**a**) [Tn, Tn·pr] **~ sb (with sth)** accuse sb of sth, esp formally in a court of law 以某事指控某人; (尤指在法庭上)控告某人: *He was charged with murder.* 他被控犯谋杀罪. ○ *She charged me with neglecting my duty.* 她指控我玩忽职守. (**b**) [Tf] (*fml* 文) claim; assert 声称; 断言: *It is charged* (ie in a court of law) *that on 30 November, the accused....* 现指控被告于11月30日.... **2** (**a**) [I, Ipr, Tn] **~ ((at) sb/sth)** rush forward and attack (sb/sth) 进攻: *The troops charged (at) the enemy lines.* 部队进攻敌军防线. ○ *One of our strikers was violently charged by a defender*, ie in a game of football. 我方一前锋受到对方后卫的猛冲拦截(足球赛中). (**b**) [Ipr, Ip] **~ down, in, up, etc** rush in the specified direction 向某方向冲去: *The children charged down the stairs.* 孩子们冲下楼梯. **3** [I, Ipr, Tn, Tn·pr, Dn·n] **~ (sb/sth) for sth; ~ (sb) sth (for sth)** ask (an amount) as a price 要价: *How much do you charge for mending shoes?* 修鞋要多少钱? ○ *As long as you've paid in advance we won't charge you for delivery.* 只要你预先付款, 我们就不收你送货费. ○ *I'm not going there again — they charged (me) £1 for a cup of coffee!* 我再也不到那儿去了——一杯咖啡就要了(我)1英镑! **4** [Tn] (**a**) load (a gun) 为(枪炮)装弹药. (**b**) (*fml* 文) fill (a glass) 注满(杯子): *Please charge your glasses and drink a toast to the bride and groom!* 请各位将酒杯斟满, 向新娘、新郎祝酒! **5** (**a**) [Tn] put a charge[1](7a) into (sth) 给(某物)充电: *charge a battery* 给蓄电池充电. (**b**) [esp passive 尤用于被动语态: Tn, Tn·pr] **~ sth (with sth)** (*fig* 比喻) fill sth (with an emotion) 使某事物充满(情感): *a voice charged with tension* 充满紧张情绪的声音 ○ *The atmosphere was charged with excitement.* 气氛中充满了激情. **6** [Tn, Cn·t] (*fml* 文) give (sb) a responsibility; command; instruct 交给(某人)责任; 命令; 指示: *I charge you not to forget what I have said.* 你千万别忘记我的话. ○ *The judge charged the jury*, ie advised them about their verdict. 法官对陪审团作指示(引导他们作出裁断). **7** (phr v) **charge sth (up) to sb; charge sth up** record sth as a debt to be paid by sb 将某人的欠款记在帐上: *Please charge these goods (up) to my account.* 请把这些货物记在我的帐上. **charge sb/oneself with sth** (*fml* 文) give sb/oneself a duty or responsibility 使某人[自己]承担任务或责任: *She was charged with an important mission.* 她被委以重任.

charge·able /ˈtʃɑːdʒəbl; ˋtʃɑrdʒəbḷ/ *adj* **1** (**a**) able or liable to be charged (CHARGE[2] 1a) 可被指控的; 可能被控告的: *If you steal, you are chargeable with theft.* 如果偷窃就可能被控偷窃罪. (**b**) liable to result in a legal charge 可能导致控告后果的: *a chargeable offence* 可能导致遭控告的过失. **2 ~ to sb** (of a debt) to be paid by sb or put on sb's account (指债款)应由某人偿付的或记在某人帐上的: *Any expenses you may incur will be chargeable to the company.* 你的所有开销都可以由公司偿付.

chargé d'affaires /ˌʃɑːʒeɪ dæˈfeə(r); ʃɑrˋʒe dæˋfɛr/ *n* (*pl* **chargés d'affaires** /ˌʃɑːʒeɪ dæˈfeə(r); ʃɑrˋʒe dæˋfɛr/) **1** diplomat who takes the place of an ambassador or a minister when the ambassador or minister is absent 代

理大使(大使或公使不在时代替大使或公使的外交官). **2** diplomat below the rank of ambassador or minister who heads a diplomatic mission in a minor country 代办(低于大使或公使的外交官, 率领出使小国的使团).

char·ger /ˈtʃɑːdʒə(r); ˋtʃɑrdʒɚ/ *n* (*arch* 古) horse ridden by a soldier in battle; cavalry horse 军马; 战马.

cha·riot /ˈtʃærɪət; ˋtʃærɪət/ *n* horse-drawn open vehicle with two wheels, used in ancient times in battle and for racing 敞篷双轮马车(古代用于战争或竞赛).
▷ **cha·ri·ot·eer** /ˌtʃærɪəˈtɪə(r); ˌtʃærɪətˋɪr/ *n* person driving a chariot (敞篷马车的)驭者.

cha·risma /kəˈrɪzmə; kəˋrɪzmə/ *n* (*pl* **~s** or **~ta**) **1** [U] power to inspire devotion and enthusiasm 吸引人效忠的能力; 号召力: *a politician with charisma* 有一呼百应能力的政客. **2** [C] (*religion* 宗) power or talent given by God 神授的力量或才能.
▷ **cha·ris·matic** /ˌkærɪzˈmætɪk; ˌkærɪzˋmætɪk/ *adj* **1** having charisma 有号召力的; 有神授能力的: *a charismatic figure, leader, politician, etc* 有号召力的人物、领袖、政治家等. **2** (of a religious group) emphasizing the divine gifts, eg the power to heal the sick (指宗教组织)崇尚神赐天赋的(如治病的力量). **cha·rismat·ic·ally** /-klɪ; -klɪ/ *adv*.

char·it·able /ˈtʃærətəbl; ˋtʃærətəbl̩/ *adj* **~ (to/towards sb)** **1** generous in giving money, food, etc to poor people (给穷人钱、食物等)慷慨的, 慈善的. **2** of, for or connected with a charity(4) or charities 慈善组织的; 为慈善组织的; 关于慈善组织的: *a charitable institution, organization, body, etc* 慈善机构、组织、团体等 ○ *a charitable venture*, ie one to raise money for charity 慈善事业. **3** kind in one's attitude to others 宽厚的; 慈爱的: *That wasn't a very charitable remark.* 那话说得可不太厚道. ▷ **char·it·ably** /-blɪ; -blɪ/ *adv*.

char·ity /ˈtʃærətɪ; ˋtʃærətɪ/ *n* **1** [U] loving kindness towards others 慈善; 慈悲; 慈爱; 仁爱. **2** [U] tolerance in judging others; kindness; leniency 宽容; 宽厚; 仁慈; 宽大: *judge people with charity* 宽厚度人. **3** [U] (**a**) (generosity in) giving money, food, help, etc to the needy 施舍; 布施; 慷慨: *do sth out of charity* 出于慷慨助人而做某事物 ○ *raise money for charity* 为施舍助人而集资 ○ [attrib 作定语] *a charity ball, concert, jumble sale, etc* 慈善舞会、音乐会、义卖等. (**b**) help given in this way (慷慨施舍的)帮助: *live on/off charity* 靠赈济生活. **4** [C] society or organization for helping the needy 慈善团体: *Many charities sent money to help the victims of the famine.* 许多慈善团体捐款赈济饥民. **5** (idm 习语) **charity begins at ˈhome** (*saying* 谚) a person's first duty is to help and care for his own family 慈善先惠及家人(一个人的首要责任是帮助和照顾自己的家庭).

char·lady /ˈtʃɑːleɪdɪ; ˋtʃɑrˌledɪ/ *n* = CHARWOMAN.

char·latan /ˈʃɑːlətən; ˋʃɑrlətn̩/ *n* person who falsely claims to have special knowledge or skill, esp in medicine 冒充内行的人; (尤指)庸医; 江湖医生. ▷ **char·lat·an·ism** *n* [U].

Charles·ton /ˈtʃɑːlstən; ˋtʃɑrlztən/ *n* fast dance, popular in the 1920's, in which the knees are turned inwards and the legs kicked sideways 查尔斯顿舞(流行于20世纪20年代的快步舞, 舞时膝盖内屈, 腿向两侧踢).

char·lie /ˈtʃɑːlɪ; ˋtʃɑrlɪ/ *n* (*Brit infml* 口) foolish person 蠢人: *You must have felt a proper charlie!* 你一定觉得自己很蠢! ○ *He looks a real charlie in that hat.* 他戴那顶帽子看起来真像个傻瓜.

charm¹ /tʃɑːm; tʃɑrm/ *n* **1** (**a**) [U] power of pleasing, fascinating or attracting people; attractiveness 迷人或吸引人的力量; 魅力: *a woman of great charm* 极为迷人的女子 ○ *He has a lot of charm.* 他很有魅力. ○ *the charm of the countryside in spring* 郊外的春光明媚. (**b**) [C] pleasing or attractive feature or quality 吸引人的特点或性质; 妩媚: *a woman's charms*, ie her beauty or attractive manner 一女子的妩媚. **2** [C] (**a**) object worn because it is believed to protect the wearer and bring good luck 护身符. (**b**) small ornament worn on a chain or bracelet (装在链上或手镯上的)小饰物: [attrib 作定语] *a ˈcharm bracelet* 带有饰物的手镯. **3** [C] act or words believed to have magic power; magic spell 魔法; 咒符; 咒语. **4** (idm 习语) ˌ**work like a ˈcharm** (*infml* 口) be immediately and completely successful 迅速地而完全地获得成功: *Those new pills you gave me worked like a charm.* 你给我的那些新药丸真是药到病除.

charm² /tʃɑːm; tʃɑrm/ *v* [Tn] **1** please, fascinate or attract (sb); delight 取悦, 迷住或吸引(某人); 使欣喜: *He charms everyone he meets.* 他使他遇见的每一个人都感到愉快. ○ *He was charmed by her vivacity and high spirits.* 她的活泼与兴高采烈的情绪把他迷住了. **2** influence or protect (sb/sth) by or as if by magic (如有魔法般)影响或保护(某人[某事物]): *He has a charmed life*, ie has escaped many dangers, as if protected by magic. 他的生命似有神灵保护(多次脱险似有神助). **3** (phr v) **charm sth from/out of sb/sth** get sth from sb/sth by using charm 使用迷人手段从某人[某事物]处得到某事物: *She could charm the birds from the trees!* 她有沉鱼落雁的魅力!
▷ **charmer** *n* person who charms people of the opposite sex 对异性有吸引力的人.
charm·ing *adj* delightful 令人高兴的; 迷人的; 可爱的: *a charming man, village, song* 令人喜爱的男子、村庄、歌. **charm·ingly** *adv*.

charnel-house /ˈtʃɑːnl haʊs; ˋtʃɑrnl̩ ˌhaʊs/ *n* (formerly) place for keeping dead human bodies or bones (旧时)存放人的尸体或骸骨的地方.

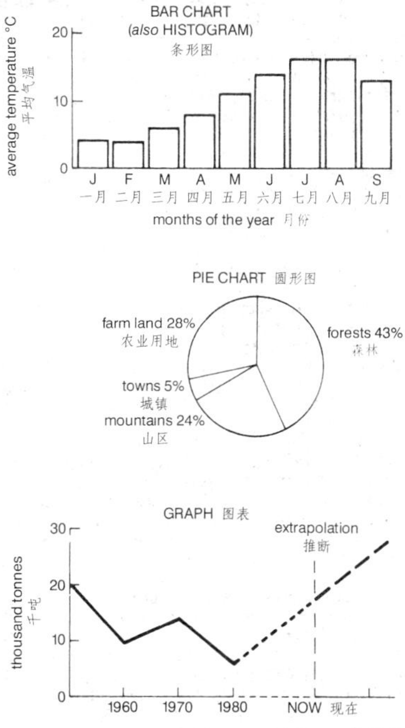

charts 图表

chart /tʃɑːt; tʃɑrt/ *n* **1** [C] (**a**) detailed map used to help navigation at sea, showing coasts, rocks, the depth of the sea, etc 航海图: *a naval chart* 海军航图. (**b**) similar map for navigation by air 航空地图. **2** [C] map, diagram, graph or table giving clear information, esp about sth that changes over a period of time 地图; 示意图; 曲线图或表: *a weather chart* 天气图 ○ *a temperature chart*, ie one showing changes in a person's temperature 体温图表 ○ *a sales chart*, ie one showing the level of a company's sales 销售图. ⇨illus 见插图. Cf 参看 MAP, PLAN 2. **3 the charts** [pl] weekly list of the best-selling pop music records (流行音乐唱片最畅销的)每周选录.
▷ **chart** *v* **1** [Tn] make a chart of (sth); map 绘制(某事物)的图表; 绘制…的地图. **2** [Tn] record or follow (sth) on or as if on a chart (犹如)在图表上记录或跟踪某事物: *Scientists are carefully charting the progress of the spacecraft.* 科学家密切跟踪航天器的运行.

C

char·ter /ˈtʃɑːtə(r); ˋtʃɑrtɚ/ *n* **1** (**a**) written statement by a ruler or a government granting certain rights and privileges to a town, company, university, etc 特许状(统治者或政府给予一城市、公司、大学等的某些权利或特权的证书): *privileges granted by royal charter* 皇家特许状所给予的特权. (**b**) written statement of the main functions and principles of an organization or institution; constitution (写明某组织或机构的主要职责与原则的)章程, 宪章. **2** hiring of a ship, an aircraft or a vehicle for a particular purpose or group of people (为某目的或某团体对船只、飞机或车辆的)包租: [attrib 作定语] *a ˈcharter plane* 包机.

▷ **char·ter** *v* [Tn] **1** grant a charter(2) to (sb/sth) 准予(某人[某事物])包租(船只、飞机或车辆). **2** hire (an aircraft, etc) for a particular purpose (为某目的)包租(飞机等): *a chartered plane* 包机.

char·tered /ˈtʃɑːtəd; ˋtʃɑrtɚd/ *adj* [attrib 作定语] qualified according to the rules of a professional association which has a royal charter (根据持有皇家特许状的专业协会的规章)合格的: *a chartered engineer, librarian, surveyor, etc* 特许工程师、图书馆馆长、检测官等. ˌ**chartered acˈcountant** (*Brit*) (*US* ˌ**certified** ˌ**public acˈcountant**) fully trained and qualified accountant 特许会计师.

□ ˈ**charter flight** flight by a chartered aircraft 包机航班.

ˈ**charter-party** *n* (*commerce* 商) agreement for the hire of a ship for a particular voyage or period of time 租船契约; 租船合同.

Chart·ism /ˈtʃɑːtɪzəm; ˋtʃɑrtɪzəm/ *n* [U] movement in Britain in the 1830's seeking electoral and social reform 宪章运动(英国19世纪30年代争取普选和社会改革的运动). ▷ **Chart·ist** /ˈtʃɑːtɪst; ˋtʃɑrtɪst/ *n*.

char·treuse /ʃɑːˈtrɜːz; *US* ʃɑːˈtruːz; ʃɑrˋtruz/ *n* [U] **1** green or yellow liqueur made with herbs 荨麻酒(加药草酿制, 呈绿色或黄色). **2** yellowish-green colour 黄绿色.

char·wo·man /ˈtʃɑːwʊmən; ˋtʃɑr,wʊmən/ (also **char-lady, char**) *n* woman employed to clean a house, an office building, etc 女清洁工

chary /ˈtʃeərɪ; ˋtʃɛrɪ/ *adj* (**-ier, -iest**) ~ **(of sth)** **1** cautious; wary 小心的; 谨慎的; 仔细的: *chary of lending money* 贷款谨慎的. **2** sparing 节省的; 舍不得的: *chary of giving praise*, ie seldom praising people 不轻易赞扬人的. ▷ **char·ily** *adv*.

Cha·ryb·dis /kəˈrɪbdɪs; kəˋrɪbdɪs/ *n* (idm 习语) **between Scylla and Charybdis** ⇨ SCYLLA.

chase[1] /tʃeɪs; tʃes/ *v* **1** [Ipr, Tn] ~ **(after) sb/sth** run after in order to capture or overtake sb/sth 追捕; 追逐; 追赶; 追击: *My dog likes chasing rabbits.* 我的狗喜欢追逐兔子. ○ *He chased (after) the burglar but couldn't catch him.* 他追赶窃贼却未捉住. **2** [Ipr, Tn] ~ **(after) sb** make sexual advances to sb in an unsubtle way 露骨地向某人求爱: *He's always chasing (after) women.* 他不断地追逐女人. **3** [Tn] (*infml* 口) try to win (sth) 试图赢获(某事物): *Liverpool are chasing their third league title in four years.* 利物浦队正全力以赴准备四年后第三次赢获联赛冠军. **4** (phr v) **chase about, around, etc** rush or hurry in the specified direction 向某方向急奔: *I've been chasing around town all morning looking for a present for her.* 为了送给她一件礼物, 我一上午都在全市奔走寻找. **chase sb/sth away, off, out, etc** force sb/sth to run away, etc; drive sb/sth away, etc 赶走; 驱逐: *chase the cat out of the kitchen* 把猫赶出厨房. **chase sb up** (*Brit infml* 口) contact sb and try to obtain esp money or information 向某人追讨或索要(尤指钱或信息): *chase up clients with outstanding debts* 向委托人追索未清还的债款. **chase sth up** (*Brit infml* 口) try to investigate sth or make sth happen more quickly 追查或催促某事物: *chase up a delayed order* 追查逾期的订货单.

chase[2] /tʃeɪs; tʃes/ *n* **1** act of chasing; pursuit 追捕; 追逐; 追赶; 追击; 追寻: *The criminal was caught after a car chase.* 开着汽车追来追去才把罪犯捉住. **2** (idm 习语) **give ˈchase** begin to run after sb/sth 开始追逐某人[某事物]: *After the robbery the police immediately gave chase.* 劫案发生后警方立即跟踪追击. ˌ**give up the ˈchase** stop chasing sb/sth 停止追赶某人[某物]. **a wild goose chase** ⇨ WILD.

chase[3] /tʃeɪs; tʃes/ *v* [Tn] cut patterns or designs on (metal); engrave or emboss 在(金属)上镂刻图案或花样; 雕刻; 刻浮雕: *chased silver* 雕花银器.

chaser /ˈtʃeɪsə(r); ˋtʃesɚ/ *n* **1** horse for steeplechasing (越野赛或障碍赛的)马. **2** (*infml* 口) drink taken after another of a different kind, eg a weaker alcoholic drink after a strong one (喝完一种饮料后再喝的另一种的)饮料(如烈酒之后的淡酒).

chasm /ˈkæzəm; ˋkæzəm/ *n* **1** deep opening in the ground; abyss; gorge (地上的)深坑; 深渊; 峡谷. **2** (*fig* 比喻) wide difference of feelings or interests between people, groups, etc (人、团体等的情感或利益的)巨大差距, 分歧: *the vast chasm separating rich and poor* 贫富的鸿沟.

chas·sis /ˈʃæsɪ; ˋʃæsɪ/ *n* (*pl* unchanged 复数不变 /ˈʃæsɪz; ˋʃæsɪz/) framework on which the body and working parts of a vehicle, radio or television are built (车辆的)底盘, 车架; (收音机或电视机的)底盘, 框架. ⇨illus at App 1 见附录1之插图, page xii.

chaste /tʃeɪst; tʃest/ *adj* **1** (*dated* 旧) not having had sexual intercourse; virgin 没有经过性交的; 童贞的. **2** not having sexual intercourse except with the person to whom one is married (性生活)忠于配偶的. **3** pure; virtuous 纯真的; 有道德的. **4** simple in style; not ornate (风格)简单的; 不修饰的. ▷ **chastely** *adv*.

chasten /ˈtʃeɪsn; ˋtʃesn/ *v* [Tn] **1** punish (sb) in order to correct or improve; discipline 惩罚(某人)(使之改正或改进); 惩戒. **2** subdue (sb); restrain 遏制(某人); 制止: *a chastening experience* 使人抑制的感受 ○ *He was chastened by his failure.* 他因失败而一蹶不振.

chas·tise /tʃæˈstaɪz; tʃæsˋtaɪz/ *v* [Tn] (*fml* 文) punish (sb) severely, esp by beating 严惩(某人)(尤指责打).

▷ **chas·tise·ment** /tʃæˈstaɪzmənt, *also* ˈtʃæstɪzmənt; tʃæsˋtaɪzmənt; ˋtʃæstɪzmənt/ *n* [C, U] (*fml* 文) severe punishment 严惩.

chast·ity /ˈtʃæstətɪ; ˋtʃæstətɪ/ *n* [U] (state of) being chaste (1, 2, 3) 童贞; 贞洁; 贞操; 纯洁; 正派: *vows of chastity*, eg those taken by a nun or a monk 贞操誓言(如修女或修道士所发的).

chas·uble /ˈtʃæzjʊbl; ˋtʃæzjʊbl/ *n* loose garment worn over all other vestments by a priest celebrating the Eucharist 十字褡(神父行圣餐礼时穿在最外层的宽松长袍).

chat /tʃæt; tʃæt/ *n* [C, U] friendly informal conversation 聊天; 闲谈: *I had a long chat with her (about her job).* (关于她的工作)我和她聊了很久. ○ *That's enough chat — get back to work.* 别再聊了——回去工作吧. ⇨Usage at TALK[1] 用法见TALK[1].

▷ **chat** *v* (**-tt-**) **1** [I, Ipr, Ip] ~ **(away)**; ~ **(to/with sb) (about sth)** have a chat 聊天; 闲谈: *They were chatting (away) in the corner.* 他们在角落里闲谈. ○ *What were you chatting to him about?* 你和他聊了些什么? **2** (phr v) **chat sb up** (*Brit infml* 口) talk to sb in a friendly or flirtatious manner in order to gain his or her confidence 和某人亲切地或轻佻地交谈(以获取信任): *Who was that pretty girl you were chatting up last night?* 昨晚你与之谈笑风生的那个漂亮姑娘是谁?

chatty *adj* (**-ier, -iest**) **1** fond of chatting 爱闲聊的; 爱聊天的. **2** resembling chat; informal 闲聊般的; 非正式的: *a chatty description* 随便的描述. **chat·tily** *adv*. **chat·ti·ness** *n* [U].

□ ˈ**chat show** television or radio programme in which (esp well-known) people are interviewed 电视或无线电采访节目(尤指对知名人士的).

chât·eau /ˈʃætəʊ; *US* ʃæˈtəʊ; ʃæˋto/ *n* (*pl* **~x** /-təʊz; -toz/) castle or large country house in France 法国的城堡或大别墅.

chat·tel /ˈtʃætl; ˋtʃætl/ *n* (idm 习语) **sb's goods and chattels** ⇨ GOODS.

chat·ter /ˈtʃætə(r); ˋtʃætɚ/ *v* **1** [I, Ipr, Ip] ~ **(away/on) (about sth)** talk quickly, continuously or foolishly about unimportant matters 唠叨; 喋喋不休: *Do stop chattering on about the weather when I'm trying to read.* 别再没完没了地唠叨天气了, 我要看书了. **2** [I, Ip] ~ **(away)** (of birds and monkeys) make short repeated high-pitched noises (指鸟和猴)短促连声尖叫, 啾啾叫, 吱吱叫: *sparrows chattering in the trees* 在树上啾啾叫的麻雀. **3** [I, Ip] ~ **(together)** (of the teeth) strike together with a clicking sound because of cold or fear

(指牙齿)打颤.

▷ **chat·ter** *n* [U] **1** continuous rapid talk 唠叨的话: *I've had enough of your constant chatter.* 我已经听够你那没完没了的唠叨话. **2** chattering sound 吱吱叫的声音: *the chatter of monkeys* 猴子的吱吱叫声.

□ **'chatterbox** *n* talkative person, esp a child 话多的人(尤指小孩).

chauf·feur /ˈʃəʊfə(r); *US* ʃəʊˈfɜːr; ʃoˈfɝ/ *n* person employed to drive a car, esp for sb rich or important 受雇开车的人; (尤指富人或要人的)司机.

▷ **chauf·feur** *v* [Tn] drive (sb) as a chauffeur 任司机为(某人)开车.

chau·vin·ism /ˈʃəʊvɪnɪzəm; ˈʃovɪnˌɪzəm/ *n* [U] **1** aggressive and irrational belief that one's own country is better than all others 沙文主义. **2** = MALE CHAUVINISM (MALE).

▷ **chau·vin·ist** /ˈʃəʊvɪnɪst; ˈʃovɪnɪst/ *n, adj* (person) displaying or feeling chauvinism 沙文主义的; 沙文主义者. **chau·vin·ist·ic** /ˌʃəʊvɪˈnɪstɪk; ˌʃovɪˈnɪstɪk/ *adj.* **chauvin·ist·ic·ally** /-klɪ; -klɪ/ *adv.*

ChB /ˌsiː eɪtʃ ˈbiː; ˌsi etʃ ˈbi/ *abbr* 缩写 = Bachelor of Surgery (Latin *Chirurgiae Baccalaureus*) 外科医学士(源自拉丁文 *Chirurgiae Baccalaureus*): *have/be a ChB* 有外科医学士学位[为外科医学士] ○ *Philip Watt MB, ChB* 菲利浦·瓦特内科医学士, 外科医学士.

cheap /tʃiːp; tʃip/ *adj* (**-er, -est**) **1** (**a**) low in price; costing little money 廉价的; 花钱少的; 便宜的: *cheap tickets, fares* 廉价票、便宜的交通费 ○ *the cheap seats in a theatre* 剧院的廉价座位 ○ *Cauliflowers are very cheap at the moment.* 菜花现在很便宜. (**b**) worth more than the cost; offering good value 合算的; 实惠的; 价钱好的: *£3 is very cheap for a hardback book.* 花3英镑买精装书很上算. **2** charging low prices 要价低的: *a cheap hairdresser, restaurant* 要价低的理发师、饭馆. **3** of poor quality; shoddy 品质低劣的; 质量差的: *cheap furniture, jewellery, shoes* 劣质家具、珠宝、鞋 ○ *a cheap and nasty bottle of wine* 一瓶质量低劣的、难喝的葡萄酒. **4** insincere; shallow(2) 不真诚的; 肤浅的: *cheap flattery* 虚伪的奉承. **5** (of people, words or actions) not worthy of respect; despicable; contemptible (指人、词语或行为)不值得尊敬的, 卑鄙的, 可耻的: *a cheap gibe, joke, remark, retort, etc* 低级的嘲弄、玩笑、言语、反驳等 ○ *That was a cheap trick to play on her.* 那样捉弄她是可耻的. ○ *He's just a cheap crook.* 他纯粹是个卑鄙的无赖. ○ *His treatment of her made her feel cheap.* 他那样对待她, 她觉得很丢脸. **6** (*esp US*) excessively careful with one's money; mean; stingy 对钱过分仔细的; 吝啬的; 小气的. **7** (idm 习语) **cheap/common as dirt** ⇨ DIRT. **cheap at the price** so well worth having that the price, however high it is, does not seem too much 无论价钱多么高都值得: *The holiday will be very expensive but if it helps to make you fit and healthy again it will be cheap at the price.* 度假要花很多钱, 但能助你恢复健康, 花钱再多也值得. ˌ**hold sth ˈcheap** (*fml* 文) consider sth to be of little value or importance 认为某事物无价值或不重要; 轻视. ˌ**make oneself ˈcheap** do sth which causes other people to respect one less 做出让人看不起的事. **on the ˈcheap** (*infml* 口) without paying the usual, or a fair, price 没有付通常的或公道的价钱; 便宜的: *buy, sell, get sth on the cheap* 便宜地买、卖、得到某事物.

▷ **cheap** *adv* (*infml* 口) **1** for a low price 廉价地: *get sth cheap* 廉价买到某物 ○ *sell sth off cheap* 廉价卖出某物. **2** (idm 习语) ˌ**go ˈcheap** (*infml* 口) be offered for sale at a low price 廉价卖: *The local shop has some radios going cheap.* 本地商店有些廉价的收音机.

cheaply *adv* **1** for a low price 廉价地: *buy, sell, get sth cheaply* 廉价买、卖、得到某事物. **2** in a cheap(1a) manner 廉价地; 便宜地: *The room was cheaply furnished.* 屋里配置了便宜的家具. **3** (idm 习语) **get off lightly/cheaply** ⇨ LIGHTLY (LIGHT[3]).

cheap·ness *n* [U].

cheapen /ˈtʃiːpən; ˈtʃipən/ *v* **1** [Tn] (cause sth to) become cheap or cheaper 减价: *cheapen the cost of sth* 降低某事物的价钱. **2** [Tn] make (oneself/sth) less worthy of respect; degrade 降低(自己[某事物])的身价; 贬低: *It's only cheapening yourself to behave like that.* 那样做只能使你自贬身价.

cheap·jack /ˈtʃiːpdʒæk; ˈtʃipˌdʒæk/ *n* person who sells inferior goods at low prices 廉价出售劣质品的人; 廉价品商贩.

▷ **cheap·jack** *adj* inferior; shoddy 劣质的; 低级的.

cheap·skate /ˈtʃiːpskeɪt; ˈtʃipˌsket/ *n* (*infml* 口 *esp US*) mean or stingy person; miser 吝啬的人; 小气的人; 财迷; 守财奴.

cheat /tʃiːt; tʃit/ *v* **1** [I, Ipr] **~ (at sth)** act dishonestly or unfairly in order to win an advantage or profit 欺骗: *accuse sb of cheating at cards* 指责某人玩纸牌时作弊. **2** [Tn] trick or deceive (sb/sth) 欺骗或瞒哄(某人[某事物]): *cheat the taxman*, ie avoid one's taxes 欺瞒税务局(逃税) ○ (*fig* 比喻) *cheat death*, ie come close to dying but stay alive by luck or cunning 死里逃生. **3** [Ipr, Tn] **~ (on) sb** (*esp US*) be unfaithful to one's wife, husband or lover 不忠实于妻子、丈夫或情人. **4** (phr v) **cheat sb (out) of sth** prevent sb from having sth, esp in an unfair or a dishonest way 防止某人得到某事物(尤指以不正当或不诚实的手段): *He was cheated (out) of his rightful inheritance.* 他依法应得的遗产被人骗走了.

▷ **cheat** *n* **1** person who cheats, esp in a game 骗子; (尤指游戏或比赛中的)作弊者. **2** dishonest trick 欺骗手段.

check[1] /tʃek; tʃɛk/ *v* **1** (**a**) [I, Ip, Tf no passive 不用于被动语态, Tw no passive 不用于被动语态] **~ (up)** make sure of sth by examining or investigating it (用检查或调查的方法)印证某事物: *I think I remembered to switch the oven off but you'd better check (up) (that I did).* 我好像记得把烤箱关了, 但你最好再查看一下(我是否关了). ○ *Could you go and check if the baby's asleep?* 你去看看孩子睡了没有好吗? (**b**) [Tn] examine (sth) in order to make sure that it is correct, safe, satisfactory or in good condition 检查; 检验; 核对; 核实: *check the oil*, ie make sure there is enough oil in a car engine 检查机油(确保汽车发动机中的油足够) ○ *check the tyres*, ie make sure there is enough air in a car's tyres 检查轮胎(确保汽车轮胎气足) ○ *check the items against the list*, ie to see that it tallies 照清单查点各项(看是否相符) ○ *He must check his work more carefully — it's full of mistakes.* 他检查工作时要再仔细一些——到处是错. **2** [Tn] (**a**) cause (sb/sth) to stop or go more slowly; slow down; control 使(某人[某事物])停止或缓慢进行; 减缓; 控制: *check the enemy's advance* 阻止敌军前进 ○ *check the flow of blood from a wound* 为伤口止血 ○ *The Government is determined to check the growth of public spending.* 政府立意控制公共开支的增长. (**b**) hold (sth) back; restrain (sth/oneself) 阻止住(某事物); 抑制(某事物); 克制(自己): *unable to check one's laughter, tears, anger* 控制不住笑声、眼泪、愤怒. **3** [I] stop suddenly 突然停止: *She went forward a few yards, checked and turned back.* 她向前走了几码, 突然停住脚步又返回来. **4** [I, Tn] (in chess) put (one's opponent) in a position in which he must move his king to prevent its capture (国际象棋中)将(对方的王). Cf 参看 CHECKMATE. **5** [Tn] (*US*) (**a**) leave (hats, coats, etc) to be stored for a short period 暂存(帽子、大衣等). (**b**) leave (luggage, etc) ready to be despatched 托运(行李等). **6** (phr v) **check in (at...)**; **check into...** register as a guest at a hotel or as a passenger at an airport, etc (为住旅馆或登机等)办理登记手续: *Passengers should check in for flight BA 125 to Berlin.* 去柏林的英航125航班旅客请办理登机手续. **check sth in** (**a**) leave or accept sth to be transported by train or by air 托运, 收运(经火车或飞机运送之物): *check in one's luggage* 托运行李. (**b**) (*esp US*) leave or accept sth for safe keeping in a cloakroom or left-luggage office (在衣帽间或行李寄存处)存取某物: *Is there a place we can check in our coats?* 有暂存大衣的地方吗? **check sth off** mark (items on a list) as correct or as having been dealt with (在清单的项目上)作记号表示正确或已处理; 核对. **check (up) on sb** investigate sb's behaviour, background, etc 调查某人的行为、背景等: *The police are checking up on him.* 警方正在调查他. **check (up) on sth** examine sth to discover if it is true, safe, correct, etc 检查某事物(是否真实、安全、正确等). **check out (of...)** pay one's bill and leave a hotel 办理旅馆付帐及退房手续. **check sth out** (*esp US*) = CHECK UP ON STH.

▷ **checker** *n* person who checks (esp stores, orders, etc) 审核员(尤指审核存货、定货单等者).

□ **ˈcheck-in** *n* **1** act of checking in at an airport 在机

场登记登机: [attrib 作定语] *the check-in desk* 办理登机手续的柜台 ○ *one's check-in time* 办理登机手续的时间. **2** place where one checks in at an airport before a flight (在机场的飞机起飞前的)登记处.

ˈ**checking account** (*US*) = CURRENT ACCOUNT (CURRENT[1]).

ˈ**checklist** *n* list of items to be marked as present or having been dealt with (对现有的或已处理的项目进行查点的)清单: *a checklist of things to take on holiday* 度假携带物品的清单.

ˈ**check-out** *n* **1** act of checking out (CHECK[1] 6) 办理旅馆付帐及退房手续. **2** place where customers pay for goods in a supermarket (超级市场中的)付款处.

ˈ**check-point** *n* place, eg on a frontier, where travellers are stopped and their vehicles and documents inspected 检查站(如于边境处的).

C

ˈ**checkroom** *n* (*US*) (**a**) cloakroom in a hotel, theatre, etc (旅馆、剧院等的)衣帽间. (**b**) left-luggage office 行李寄存处.

ˈ**check-up** *n* thorough examination, esp a medical one 全面检查; (尤指)体格检查: *go for/have a check-up* 去[作]体检.

check[2] /tʃek; tʃɛk/ *n* **1** [C] **~ (on sth)** (**a**) examination to make sure that sth is correct, safe, satisfactory or in good condition 检查(以确保某事物正确、安全、满意或处于良好状态): *Could you give the tyres a check, please?* 你能给检查一下轮胎吗? ○ *We conduct regular checks on the quality of our products.* 我们对产品做例行质量检查. (**b**) method of testing the accuracy or genuineness of sth 检验(以测试某事物准确度或真假). **2** [C] **~ (on sb)** investigation 调查: *The police made a check on all the victim's friends.* 警方对受害者所有的朋友进行了调查. **3** [C] (**a**) slowing down or stopping; pause 减慢; 停止; 暂停: *a check in the rate of production* 生产速度减慢. (**b**) **~ (on sth)** thing that restrains or stops sth 制止或停止某事物的事物: *The presence of the army should act as a check on civil unrest.* 有了军队应能制止民间的动乱. **4** [sing] (in chess) situation in which a player must move his king in order to prevent its capture by his opponent (国际象棋中)将军: *You're in check!* 将你一军! Cf 参看 CHECKMATE. **5** [C] (*US*) = CHEQUE. **6** [C] (*US*) = BILL[1]: *I'll ask the waiter for the check.* 我找服务员要帐单. **7** [C] (*US*) ticket or token used to identify and reclaim clothing or property left in a cloakroom or left-luggage office 存放证, 寄存牌(用以领取寄存物品的存根或收据). **8** [C] (*US*) = TICK[1]. **9** (idm 习语) **hold/keep sth in ˈcheck** prevent sth from advancing or increasing; control sth 抑止; 约束; 制止: *keep one's temper in check* 控制自己不发脾气 ○ *The epidemic was held in check by widespread vaccination.* 这种传染病靠广泛的预防注射已受到控制. **take a rain check** ⇨ RAIN[1].

▷ **check** *interj* (in chess) call made to one's opponent to show that his king is in check (国际象棋中)将, 将军(向对方的呼叫).

□ ˈ**checkbook** *n* (*US*) = CHEQUE-BOOK (CHEQUE).

check[3] /tʃek; tʃɛk/ *n* (**a**) [C] pattern of crossed lines (often in different colours) forming squares 方格图案: *Which do you want for your new dress, a stripe or a check?* 你要哪种料子来做新连衣裙, 条子的还是方格的? (**b**) [U] cloth with this pattern 方格布: [attrib 作定语] *a check skirt, jacket, table-cloth* 方格的裙子、短上衣、桌布.

▷ **checked** /tʃekt; tʃɛkt/ *adj* having a check pattern 方格图形的: *checked material* 方格形材料.

checker /ˈtʃekə(r); ˈtʃɛkɚ/ *v* (*US*) = CHEQUER.

checkers /ˈtʃekəz; ˈtʃɛkɚz/ *n* [sing *v*] (*US*) = DRAUGHTS.

□ ˈ**checkerboard** *n* (*US*) = DRAUGHTBOARD (DRAUGHT).

check·mate /ˈtʃekmeɪt; ˈtʃɛkˌmet/ (also **mate**) *n* [sing] **1** (in chess) situation in which one player cannot prevent the capture of his king and the other player is therefore the winner (国际象棋中)将死. Cf 参看 CHECK[2] 4. **2** total defeat 彻底失败.

▷ **check·mate** *v* [Tn] **1** (in chess) put (one's opponent) in a position in which he cannot prevent the capture of his king (国际象棋中)将死(对方). Cf 参看 CHECK[1] 4. **2** defeat (sb/sth) totally; frustrate 使(某人[某事物])彻底失败; 挫败. — *interj* (in chess) call made when checkmating one's opponent 将, 将军(国际象棋中将死对方时的呼叫).

Ched·dar /ˈtʃedə(r); ˈtʃɛdɚ/ *n* [U] type of firm yellowish cheese 切德干酪(一种淡黄色的硬奶酪).

cheek /tʃi:k; tʃik/ *n* **1** [C] either side of the face below the eye 面颊; 脸蛋儿: *healthy pink cheeks* 健康的红面颊 ○ *dancing cheek to cheek*, ie with the cheek of one partner touching that of the other 跳贴面舞(面颊接触舞伴面颊). ⇨illus at HEAD 见 HEAD 之插图. **2** [C] (*infml* 口) either of the buttocks 屁股(指半边). **3** [U, sing] impertinent talk or behaviour; impudence 无礼的、冒失的、不当的话或行为; 厚颜无耻: *That's enough of your cheek!* 不要恬不知耻! ○ *He had the cheek to ask me to do his work for him.* 他居然有脸叫我替他工作. ○ *What (a) cheek!* ie How very cheeky! 真没皮没脸! **4** (idm 习语) ˌ**cheek by ˈjowl (with sb/sth)** close together 紧紧靠着: *live/lie cheek by jowl* 亲密地生活[躺在一起]. ˌ**turn the other ˈcheek** accept violent attack without being violent oneself 受到猛烈攻击而不还手. **with tongue in cheek** ⇨ TONGUE.

▷ **cheek** *v* [Tn] speak cheekily to (sb) 对(某人)厚颜无耻地说.

-cheeked (forming compound *adjs* 用以构成复合形容词) having the specified type of cheeks 有某种面颊的: *a rosy-cheeked boy.*

cheeky *adj* (**-ier, -iest**) (of a person, his manner, etc) lacking respect, esp in a bold or cheerful way; impertinent; impudent (指人、言谈、举止等)厚脸皮的, 放肆的, 鲁莽的, 厚颜无耻的: *a cheeky boy, remark* 厚脸皮的男孩儿、言语. **cheek·ily** *adv*. **chee·ki·ness** *n* [U].

□ ˈ**cheek-bone** *n* bone below the eye 颧骨.

cheep /tʃi:p; tʃip/ *n* weak shrill cry of a young bird (雏鸟的)吱吱叫声.

▷ **cheep** *v* [I] make this cry 作吱吱叫.

cheer[1] /tʃɪə(r); tʃɪr/ *v* **1** [I, Tn] give shouts of joy, praise, support or encouragement to (sb) 向(某人)欢呼; 喝彩: *The crowd cheered loudly as the Queen appeared.* 女王出现时群众高声欢呼. ○ *The winning team were cheered by their supporters.* 获胜的队受到热情观众的喝彩. **2** [Tn] give comfort, hope, support or encouragement to (sb); gladden 给(某人)安慰、希望、支持或鼓励; 使欢喜: *He was greatly cheered by the news.* 他听到这个消息非常高兴. **3** (phr v) **cheer sb on** encourage sb to make greater efforts by cheering 鼓舞或鼓励某人更加努力: *The crowd cheered the runners on as they started the last lap.* 赛跑进入最后一圈时, 观众为运动员加油鼓劲. **cheer (sb) up** (cause sb to) become happier or more cheerful (使某人)更高兴或更快活: *Try and cheer up a bit; life isn't that bad!* 想办法高兴点儿, 生活并不是那么糟! ○ *You look as though you need cheering up*, ie to be cheered up. 看来你需要振作起来. ○ (*fig* 比喻) *Flowers always cheer a room up.* 房间里一有花就满室生辉.

▷ **cheer·ing** *adj* encouraging; gladdening 令人鼓舞的; 令人欢喜的: *cheering news* 令人振奋的消息. — *n* [U]: *The cheering could be heard half a mile away.* 半英里以外都可以听到欢呼声.

cheer[2] /tʃɪə(r); tʃɪr/ *n* **1** [C] shout of joy, praise, support or encouragement 欢呼声; 喝彩声: *the cheers of the crowd* 群众的欢呼声 ○ *Three cheers for* (ie Shout 'hurray' three times to show admiration for) *the bride and groom!* 向新娘、新郎三次欢呼! **2** [U] (*arch* 古) happiness and hopefulness 欢愉与乐观: *Christmas should be a time of great cheer.* 圣诞节应是欢乐的时刻.

□ ˈ**cheer-leader** *n* (*esp US*) person who leads the cheering by a crowd, esp at a sporting event 带领观众欢呼的人; (尤指体育比赛中的)啦啦队长.

cheer·ful /ˈtʃɪəfl; ˈtʃɪrfəl/ *adj* **1** (**a**) in good spirits; happy 兴高采烈的; 精神振奋的; 快乐的: *a cheerful smile, disposition* 欢快的微笑、性情 ○ *You're very cheerful today.* 你今天很快活. (**b**) causing happiness; pleasant 令人快活的; 令人高兴的: *The news isn't very cheerful, I'm afraid.* 我看这个消息不太乐观. **2** pleasantly bright 欢快明亮的: *cheerful colours* 悦目的色彩 ○ *a cheerful room* 使人感到愉快的房间. **3** not grudging; willing 愿意的: *a cheerful worker* 肯干的工人. ▷ **cheer·fully** /-fəlɪ; -fəlɪ/ *adv*: *accept sth, smile, whistle, work cheerfully* 欢快地接受某事物、微笑、吹口哨、工作. **cheer·ful·ness** *n* [U].

cheerio /ˌtʃɪərɪˈəʊ; ˈtʃɪrɪˌo/ *interj* (*Brit infml* 口) goodbye 再见.

cheer·less /ˈtʃɪəlɪs; ˋtʃɪrlɪs/ *adj* gloomy; dreary 阴暗的; 惨淡的: *a cold, cheerless day* 寒冷阴暗的一天 ○ *a damp, cheerless room* 潮湿阴暗的房间. ▷ **cheer·lessly** *adv.* **cheer·less·ness** *n* [U].

cheers /tʃɪəz; tʃɪrz/ *interj* (*infml* 口 *esp Brit*) **1** (used as a toast when drinking 用于祝酒) good health! 祝你健康 **2** goodbye; cheerio 再见: *Cheers! See you tomorrow night.* 再见! 明晚见. **3** thank you 谢谢.

cheery /ˈtʃɪərɪ; ˋtʃɪrɪ/ *adj* (**-ier, -iest**) lively and cheerful; genial 喜气洋洋的; 兴高采烈的; 亲切的: *a cheery smile, greeting, wave* 喜气洋洋的微笑、致意、招手. ▷ **cheer·ily** *adv.* **cheeri·ness** *n* [U].

cheese /tʃi:z; tʃiz/ *n* **1** (**a**) [U] food made from milk curds 干酪; 奶酪: *Cheddar cheese* 切德干酪 ○ *a lump/piece/slice of cheese* 一大块[块/片]干酪 ○ [attrib 作定语] *a cheese sandwich* 干酪三明治. (**b**) [C] particular type of this 某种干酪: *a selection of French cheeses* 精选法国干酪. (**c**) [C] shaped and wrapped portion or mass of this (制成一定形状及有包装的)干酪, 奶酪: *two cream cheeses* 两块乳脂干酪. **2** [U] type of thick jam 稠果酱: *lemon, damson cheese* 柠檬、洋李果酱. **3** (idm 习语) **a big cheese** ⇨ BIG. **different as chalk and/from cheese** ⇨ DIFFERENT.

▷ **cheese** *v* (phr v) **cheese sb off** (esp passive 尤用于被动语态) (*infml* 口) make sb annoyed, bored or frustrated 使某人烦恼、厌烦或灰心: *He's cheesed off with his job.* 他厌倦他的工作.

cheesy *adj* (**-ier, -iest**) like cheese in taste or smell (味道或气味)像干酪的.

□ ˈ**cheese-board** *n* board for cutting cheese on 干酪板(切干酪用的板).

ˈ**cheeseburger** *n* hamburger with a slice of cheese in it 干酪汉堡包.

ˈ**cheese-paring** *n* [U] (*derog* 贬) excessive carefulness in the spending of money; stinginess 花钱过分仔细; 吝啬. — *adj* (*derog* 贬) stingy; mean 吝啬的; 小气的.

cheese·cake /ˈtʃi:zkeɪk; ˋtʃiz,kek/ *n* **1** [C, U] type of tart made with cream cheese, eggs, sugar, etc on a base of pastry or crushed biscuits 奶酪饼(以油酥面或碎饼干作底, 上有乳脂奶酪、蛋、糖等制成的糕饼): *a cherry cheesecake* 樱桃奶酪饼 ○ *Have some more cheesecake.* 请再用一些奶酪饼. **2** [U] (*infml* 口) pictures of women with shapely bodies, esp as used in advertisements (身材匀称的)女子照片(尤指用于广告的).

cheese·cloth /ˈtʃi:zklɒθ; *US* -klɔ:θ; ˋtʃiz,klɔθ/ *n* [U] thin, loosely woven, cotton fabric 薄纱织物: [attrib 作定语] *a cheesecloth shirt* 薄纱衬衫.

chee·tah /ˈtʃi:tə; ˋtʃitə/ *n* African wild animal of the cat family with black spots and long legs, and able to run very fast 猎豹(产于非洲, 有黑色斑点, 腿长善跑).

chef /ʃef; ʃɛf/ *n* professional cook, esp the chief cook in a restaurant 厨师; (尤指饭店的)厨师长.

chef-d'oeuvre /ʃeɪ ˈdɜ:vrə; ʃe ˋdœvrə/ *n* (*pl* **chefsd'oeuvre** /ʃeɪ ˈdɜ:vrə; ʃe ˋdœvrə/) (*French* 法) masterpiece 杰作.

chem·ical /ˈkemɪkl; ˋkɛmɪkl/ *adj* **1** of or relating to chemistry 化学的; 关于化学的: *the chemical industry* 化学工业. **2** produced by or using chemistry or chemicals 用化学方法或化学品产生的或生产的: *a chemical experiment* 化学实验 ○ *a chemical reaction*, ie one causing changes in the structure of atoms or molecules 化学反应(造成原子或分子结构变化的反应).

▷ **chem·ical** *n* substance obtained by or used in a chemical process 在化学反应中得到的或使用的物质.

chem·ic·ally /-klɪ; -klɪ/ *adv.*

□ ˌ**chemical engiˈneering** engineering that deals with processes involving chemical changes and with the equipment needed for these 化学工程. ˌ**chemical engiˈneer** *n.*

ˌ**chemical ˈwarfare** use of poisonous gases and other harmful chemicals in war 化学战.

che·mise /ʃəˈmi:z; ʃəˋmiz/ *n* (**a**) loose-fitting undergarment hanging straight from the shoulders, formerly worn by women (直筒式的)宽松内衣(旧时女子穿的). (**b**) dress similar to this (直筒式的)宽松连衣裙.

chem·ist /ˈkemɪst; ˋkɛmɪst/ *n* **1** (*US* **druggist**) person who prepares and sells medicines, and usu also sells cosmetics, toiletries, etc; pharmacist 药剂师; 药商: *buy aspirin at the chemist's* (ie chemist's shop) *on the corner* 在大街拐角的药房买阿司匹林. Cf 参看 PHARMACIST. **2** expert in chemistry 化学专家; 化学家.

chem·istry /ˈkemɪstrɪ; ˋkɛmɪstrɪ/ *n* [U] **1** scientific study of the structure of substances, how they react when combined or in contact with one another, and how they behave under different conditions 化学: *Chemistry was her favourite subject at school.* 她上学时最喜欢化学. ○ [attrib 作定语] *a chemistry lesson* 化学课. **2** chemical structure, properties (PROPERTY 4) and reactions of a particular substance 某物质的化学组成、性质和反应: *the chemistry of copper* 铜的化学组成、性质和反应. **3** any mysterious or complex change or process 任何神秘的或复杂的变化或过程: *the strange chemistry that causes two people to fall in love* 使两人相爱的不可思议的过程.

chemo·ther·apy /ˌki:məʊˈθerəpɪ; ˌkimoˋθɛrəpɪ/ *n* [U] treatment of disease by drugs and other chemical substances 化学疗法.

che·nille /ʃəˈni:l; ʃəˈnil/ *n* [U] (**a**) thick velvety cord used for trimming furniture 雪尼尔线, 绳绒线(用以装饰家具的天鹅绒粗线). (**b**) fabric made of this 雪尼尔线的织物.

cheque (*US* **check**) /tʃek; tʃɛk/ *n* **1** (special printed form on which one writes an) order to a bank to pay a sum of money from one's account to another person 支票: *write (sb)/sign a cheque for £50* 给(某人)开[签]一张50英镑的支票 ○ *Are you paying in cash or by cheque?* 您付现款还是付支票? **2** (idm 习语) **a blank cheque** ⇨ BLANK.

□ ˈ**cheque-book** (*US* ˈ**checkbook**) *n* book of printed cheques 支票簿.

ˈ**cheque card** card issued by a bank to sb who has an account with it, guaranteeing payment of his cheques up to a specified amount 支票保付卡(银行发给存户的卡片, 保证支付其高达某预定限额的支票).

chequer (*US* **checker**) /ˈtʃekə(r); ˋtʃɛkɚ/ *n* pattern of squares, usu of alternate colours 方格图案(通常为交错颜色的). ⇨illus at PATTERN 见 PATTERN 之插图.

▷ **chequer** *v* [Tn esp passive 尤用于被动语态] mark (sth) with a pattern of squares or patches of different colours or shades 使(某物)呈现方格图案或不同颜色或不同深浅的方格: *a lawn chequered with sunlight and shade* 有阳光和阴影交错的草坪.

chequered (*US* **checkered**) *adj* [esp attrib 尤作定语] (*fig* 比喻) marked by periods of good and bad fortune 好运与恶运交替的: *a chequered career/history/past* 荣辱盛衰的事业[历史/过去].

cher·ish /ˈtʃerɪʃ; ˋtʃɛrɪʃ/ *v* [Tn] **1** protect or tend (sb/sth) lovingly; care for 爱护或珍爱(某人[某事物]); 关心. **2** be fond of (sb/sth); love 喜爱(某人[某事物]); 爱. **3** keep (a feeling or an idea) in one's mind or heart and think of it with pleasure 怀有(某种感情或想法); 怀念: *cherish the memory of one's dead mother* 怀念先母 ○ *cherish the hope of winning an Olympic medal* 盼望获奥林匹克奖牌 ○ *He cherishes the illusion that she's in love with him.* 他怀有一种幻想, 认为她已经爱上他了.

che·root /ʃəˈru:t; ʃəˋrut/ *n* cigar with both ends open (两端都开口的)雪茄烟.

cherry /ˈtʃerɪ; ˋtʃɛrɪ/ *n* **1** [C] small soft round fruit (red or black when ripe) containing a stone 樱桃. ⇨illus at FRUIT 见 FRUIT 之插图. **2** (**a**) (also ˈ**cherry-tree**) [C] tree on which this fruit grows 樱桃树: *a flowering cherry* 开花的樱桃树 ○ [attrib 作定语] *cherry blossom* 樱桃花. (**b**) [U] wood of this tree 樱桃木. **2** [U] (also ˌ**cherry ˈred**) bright red colour 樱桃色; 鲜红色: [attrib 作定语] *cherry lips* 樱唇. **3** (idm 习语) **have/get two bites at the cherry** ⇨ BITE[2].

cherub /ˈtʃerəb; ˋtʃɛrəb/ *n* **1** (*pl* **~im** /ˈtʃerəbɪm; ˋtʃɛrəbɪm/) (*Bible* 圣经) one of the second highest order of angels, usu represented in paintings as a plump child with wings 二级天使(通常绘作圆胖有翼的孩子). ⇨ illus at ANGEL 见 ANGEL 之插图. Cf 参看 SERAPH. **2** (*pl* **~s**) (**a**) (in art) angelic plump child with wings (艺术上的)天使般的圆胖而有翼的孩子. (**b**) sweet or innocent-looking child 可爱的或天真无邪的孩子.

▷ **cher·ubic** /tʃɪˈru:bɪk; tʃəˋrubɪk/ *adj* (esp of a child) with a plump and innocent face (尤指孩子)有着胖乎乎而天真无邪的面孔的.

cher·vil /ˈtʃɜ:vɪl; ˋtʃɝvɪl/ *n* [U] (**a**) type of garden herb 有喙欧芹. (**b**) its leaves used to flavour soups and salads 有喙欧芹叶(用作汤羹和色拉的调料).

C

chess /tʃes; tʃɛs/ *n* [U] game for two people, played on a board with pieces that are moved in an attempt to checkmate the opponent's king 国际象棋. ⇨illus 见插图.

□ ˈ**chessboard** *n* chequered board with 64 black and white squares on which chess and draughts are played (国际象棋的)棋盘.

chess-man /ˈtʃesmæn; ˋtʃɛs,mæn/ *n* (*pl* **-men** /-men; -,mɛn/) any of the pieces used in the game of chess (国际象棋的)棋子. ⇨illus 见插图.

chest /tʃest; tʃɛst/ *n* **1** large strong box for storing or shipping things in 大箱子: *a* ˈ*tea chest* 茶叶箱 ○ *a* ˈ*medicine chest* 药品箱 ○ *a* ˈ*tool chest* 工具箱. **2** upper front part of the body from the neck to the stomach 胸部: *a hairy chest* 多毛的胸部 ○ *What size are you round the chest?* 你的胸围是多少? ○ [attrib 作定语] ˈ*chest pains* 胸部疼痛 ○ *a* ˈ*chest cold*, ie one that affects the lungs 重感冒. ⇨illus at HUMAN 见 HUMAN 之插图. **3** (idm 习语) ˌ**get sth off one's** ˈ**chest** (*infml* 口) say sth that one has wanted to say for a long time 说出积存已久的话: *You're obviously worried about something; why not get it off your chest?* 你显然有心事, 何不一吐为快? **hold/keep one's cards close to one's chest** ⇨ CARD[1].

▷ **-chested** (forming compound *adjs* 用以构成复合形容词) having the specified type of chest 有某种胸部的: ˌ*broad-*ˈ*chested* ○ ˌ*bare-*ˈ*chested* ○ *She's* ˌ*flat-*ˈ*chested*, ie She has very small breasts. 她胸部扁平(乳房很小).

chesty *adj* (*Brit infml* 口) tending to suffer from or showing the symptoms of bronchial disease 易患支气管疾病的; 有支气管疾患症状的: *She often gets chesty in wet weather.* 在潮湿天气, 她经常犯支气管炎. ○ *a chesty cough* 患支气管炎引起的咳嗽. **chesti·ness** *n* [U].

□ ˌ**chest of** ˈ**drawers** (*US* also **bureau**) piece of furniture with drawers for storing clothes in (有抽屉的)衣橱. ⇨illus at App 1 见附录1之插图, page xvi.

ches·ter·field /ˈtʃestəfi:ld; ˋtʃɛstɚ,fild/ *n* sofa with a padded back, seat and ends (靠背、座位和两端都有垫料的)长沙发.

chest·nut /ˈtʃesnʌt; ˋtʃɛs,nʌt/ *n* **1** (**a**) (also ˈ**chestnut tree**) [C] any of various types of tree producing smooth reddish-brown nuts enclosed in prickly cases (those of some types being edible) 栗树. (**b**) [C] one of these nuts 栗子: *roast chestnuts* 炒栗子 ○ [attrib 作定语] *chestnut stuffing*, ie a mixture of chestnuts, herbs, etc used to stuff a chicken, turkey, etc 栗子馅(用以填充鸡、火鸡等). ⇨illus at NUT 见 NUT 之插图. (**c**) wood of the chestnut tree 栗木: [attrib 作定语] *a chestnut table* 栗木桌子. **2** [U] deep reddish-brown colour 栗色(深棕红色): [attrib 作定语] *chestnut hair* 栗色的头发 ○ *a chestnut mare* 栗色的雌马. **3** [C] horse of this colour 栗色马. **4** [C] (*infml* 口) old joke or story that is no longer amusing (因陈腐而无味的)笑话或故事: *an old chestnut* 老掉牙的笑话[故事].

chev·ron /ˈʃevrən; ˋʃɛvrən/ *n* bent line or stripe in the shape of a normal or upside-down V, worn by a policeman or soldier to show his rank (警察或士兵所佩带以示衔级的)V形或Λ形标志.

chew /tʃu:; tʃu/ *v* **1** [I, Tn, Tn·p] **~ sth (up)** work or grind (food) between the teeth 嚼碎或咀嚼(食物): *Chew your food well before you swallow it.* 食物要先嚼烂再下咽. **2** (idm 习语) **bite off more than one can chew** ⇨ BITE[1]. ˌ**chew the** ˈ**cud (of sth)** reflect upon sth already said or done; ponder sth 回味、体味、玩味某事物; 深思某事物. ˌ**chew the** ˈ**fat**/ˈ**rag** (*infml* 口) talk about sth, often in a grumbling or argumentative way 谈论某事物(常为以抱怨或争辩的方式); 发牢骚; 唠叨; 拌嘴. **3** (phr v) **chew sth over** (*infml* 口) think about sth slowly and carefully (从容审慎地)细想某事物: ˌ*chew over a* ˈ*problem* 仔细考虑一个问题 ○ *I'll give you till tomorrow to* ˌ*chew it* ˈ*over.* 我给你一天时间考虑考虑这问题.

▷ **chew** *n* **1** act of chewing 咀嚼. **2** thing that can be chewed, eg a sweet or a piece of tobacco 可以咀嚼的东西(如糖果或烟草).

□ ˈ**chewing-gum** (also **gum**) *n* [U] sticky substance flavoured and sweetened for prolonged chewing 口香糖.

Chi·anti /kɪˈæntɪ; kɪˋæntɪ/ *n* [C, U] (particular type of) dry red or white wine, from central Italy 基安蒂葡萄酒(意大利中部产的不甜的红的或白的葡萄酒).

chiaro·scuro /kɪ,ɑ:rəˈskʊərəʊ; kɪ,ɑrəˋskjʊro/ *n* [U] (*art* 美术) **1** treatment of the light and dark parts in a painting 明暗对照法(绘画中明暗部分的处理法). **2** use of contrast in literature, music, etc (文学、音乐等中使用的)对比法.

chic /ʃi:k; ʃik/ *adj* elegant and stylish 高雅的: *She always looks very chic.* 她的样子总是很高雅.

▷ **chic** *n* [U] stylishness and elegance 高雅: *She dresses with chic.* 她的穿着雅致.

chi·canery /ʃɪˈkeɪnərɪ; ʃɪˋkenərɪ/ *n* **1** [U] use of clever but misleading talk in order to trick sb, esp in legal matters; dishonest practice 耍花招哄骗别人(尤指于法律事务中); 不诚实的行为: *accuse a politician of chicanery* 谴责一政客的欺骗手段. **2** [C] trick or deception 哄骗; 欺骗.

chick /tʃɪk; tʃɪk/ *n* **1** young bird, esp a young chicken, just before or after hatching (即将孵出的或刚孵出的)雏鸟; (尤指)小鸡: *a hen with her chicks* 母鸡及其小鸡. **2** (*dated sexist* 旧, 性别偏见) young woman 黄毛丫头.

chicken /ˈtʃɪkɪn; ˋtʃɪkɪn/ *n* **1** [C] young bird, esp of the domestic fowl 雏鸟; (尤指)小鸡. ⇨illus at App 1 见附录1之插图, page v. **2** (**a**) [C] domestic fowl kept for its eggs or meat 鸡: *keep chickens* 养鸡. Cf 参看 COCK[1], HEN. (**b**) [U] its flesh eaten as food 鸡肉: *slices of roast chicken* 烧烤鸡肉片. **3** [C] (*sl* 俚) coward 胆小鬼; 懦夫. **4** [U] (*sl* 俚) children's game that tests sb's courage in the face of danger (儿童的)胆量比试游戏. **5** (idm 习语) **be** ˌ**no (spring)** ˈ**chicken** (*infml* 口) (esp of women) be no longer young (尤指女子)已不年轻. **count one's chickens** ⇨ COUNT[1].

▷ **chicken** *v* (phr v) **chicken out (of sth)** (*infml* 口) decide not to do sth because one is afraid 因害怕而决定不做某事: *He had an appointment to see the dentist but he chickened out (of it) at the last moment.* 他已预约治牙, 但到时候却不敢去了.

chicken *adj* [pred 作表语] (*sl* 俚) cowardly 胆小; 怯懦.

□ ˈ**chicken-feed** *n* [U] **1** food for poultry 家禽饲料. **2** (*fig infml* 比喻, 口) small amount, esp of money 少量(尤指钱): *Your salary is chicken-feed compared to what you could earn in America.* 你的薪水和美国的相比, 太少了.

ˌ**chicken-**ˈ**hearted** *adj* lacking courage; cowardly 缺乏勇气的; 胆小的.

ˈ**chicken-pox** *n* [U] disease, esp of children, with a mild fever and itchy red spots on the skin 水痘: *catch chicken-pox* 患水痘.

ˈ**chicken-run** *n* area surrounded by a fence where chickens are kept 鸡圈.

ˈ**chicken wire** type of thin wire netting 细铁丝网.

chick-pea /ˈtʃɪk pi:; ˋtʃɪk,pi/ *n* (**a**) Asian plant grown for its edible pea-like seeds 鹰嘴豆(亚洲产, 豆状籽可食). (**b**) one of these seeds 鹰嘴豆(豆粒).

chick·weed /ˈtʃɪkwi:d; ˋtʃɪk,wid/ *n* [U] common type of weed with small white flowers 繁缕(欧洲常见的小草, 开白花).

chicle /ˈtʃɪkl; ˋtʃɪkl/ *n* [U] milky juice of a tropical American tree, the main ingredient of chewing-gum 糖胶树胶(美洲热带树的乳汁, 制口香糖的主要原料).

chic·ory /ˈtʃɪkərɪ; ˋtʃɪkərɪ/ *n* [U] (**a**) (also **endive**) blue-flowered plant, the leaves of which are eaten raw in salads 菊苣(开蓝花, 叶可作色拉). (**b**) these leaves 菊苣叶. (**c**) root of this plant, roasted, ground and used with or instead of coffee 菊苣根(烤后磨碎与咖啡同用

或作其代用品).

chide /'tʃaɪd; tʃaɪd/ *v* (*pt* **chided** /'tʃaɪdɪd; 'tʃaɪdɪd/ or **chid** /tʃɪd; tʃɪd/, *pp* **chided**, **chid** or **chidden** /'tʃɪdn; 'tʃɪdn/) [Tn, Tn·pr] **~ sb (for sth)** (*dated or fml* 旧或文) rebuke; scold 指责; 责骂: *She chided him for his laziness.* 她责备他懒惰.

chief /tʃi:f; tʃif/ *n* **1** leader or ruler, esp of a tribe or clan 领袖; 统治者; (尤指)酋长, 族长. **2** person with the highest rank in an organization, a department, etc (组织、部门等的)最高级别的人, 首长, 领导人, 主任: *a chief of police* 警长.

▷ **chief** *adj* **1** [esp attrib 尤作定语] most important; main; principal 最重要的; 主要的; 首要的: *the chief rivers of India* 印度主要的河流 ○ *The chief thing to remember is...* 要记住的最重要的事是... ○ *Smoking is one of the chief causes of lung cancer.* 吸烟是导致肺癌的主要成因之一. **2** [attrib 作定语] having the highest rank or authority 最高级别的; 最高权威的: *the chief priest* 祭司长. **chiefly** *adv* (**a**) above all; principally 首先; 首要地: *The Government is chiefly concerned with controlling inflation.* 政府的当务之急是控制通货膨胀. (**b**) mostly; mainly 大部分; 主要地: *Air consists chiefly of nitrogen.* 空气主要由氮气组成.

□ **Chief 'Constable** (*Brit*) head of the police force in a particular area (一地区的)警察局长.

,Chief of 'Staff (in the armed forces) highest ranking member of the group of officers serving under and advising a commander (军队的)参谋长.

-in-'chief (forming compound *ns* 用以构成复合名词): *editor-in-chief*, ie chief editor ○ *commander-in-chief*.

chief·tain /'tʃi:ftən; 'tʃiftən/ *n* leader of a tribe or clan; chief (部落或氏族的)首领, 领袖; 酋长: *a Highland chieftain* 高地族长.

chif·fon /'ʃɪfɒn; *US* ʃɪ'fɒn; ʃɪ'fɑn/ *n* [U] thin, almost transparent fabric made of silk, nylon, etc 雪纺绸, 薄绸(丝、尼龙等制成的近乎透明的薄织物): [attrib 作定语] *a chiffon scarf* 丝头巾.

chi·gnon /'ʃi:njɒn; 'ʃinjɑn/ *n* woman's hair twisted into a coil or thick knot at the back of the head 发髻.

chi·hua·hua /tʃɪ'wɑ:wə; *US* tʃɪ'wɑ:wɑ:; tʃɪ'wɑwɑ/ *n* type of very small smooth-haired dog, originally from Mexico 奇瓦瓦狗(毛光滑的小狗, 产自墨西哥).

chil·blain /'tʃɪlbleɪn; 'tʃɪl,blen/ *n* (usu *pl* 通常作复数) painful swelling, esp on the hand or foot, caused by exposure to cold 冻疮.

child /tʃaɪld; tʃaɪld/ *n* (*pl* **children** /'tʃɪldrən; 'tʃɪldrən/) **1** (**a**) young human being below the age of puberty; boy or girl 儿童: *a child of six*, ie one who is six years old 六岁的儿童 ○ [attrib 作定语] *a child actor* 儿童演员. (**b**) son or daughter (of any age) (任何年龄的)儿子或女儿: *an only child*, ie one with no brothers or sisters 独生子女 ○ *She is married with three children.* 她已婚, 有三个孩子. ⇨App 8 见附录8. (**c**) unborn or newly born human being; baby 胎儿; 婴儿: *She is expecting* (ie is pregnant with) *her first child.* 她不久要生头胎. **2** (**a**) person who behaves like a child 行为像孩子的人: *You wouldn't think a man of forty could be such a child.* 想不到四十岁的人竟像个孩子. (**b**) inexperienced person 没有经验的人: *He's a child in financial matters.* 他在财务方面毫无经验. **3 ~ of sth** person or thing strongly influenced by a period, place or person 受某时期、地方或人强烈影响的人或事物; 产儿; 产物: *She's a real child of the (19)60's.* 她是真正的(二十世纪)六十年代的产儿. **4** (idm 习语) **be with child** (*arch* 古) be pregnant 怀孕. **the child is father of the man** (*saying* 谚) the experiences of childhood determine a person's character as an adult 童年的经历可决定成年后的性格. **'child's play** (*infml* 口) thing that is very easy to do 容易做的事: *It's not a difficult climb — it should be child's play for an experienced mountaineer.* 这次攀登并不难——对于有经验的登山运动员应是轻而易举的事. **an only child** ⇨ ONLY[1]. **spare the rod and spoil the child** ⇨ SPARE[2].

▷ **child·hood** /'tʃaɪldhʊd; 'tʃaɪld,hʊd/ *n* **1** [U, C] condition or period of being a child 童年; 幼年时代: *the joys of childhood* 童年的快乐 ○ *She had an unhappy childhood.* 她的童年很不幸. ○ [attrib 作定语] *childhood memories* 童年的回忆. **2** (idm 习语) **a/one's second 'childhood** (*often joc* 常作戏谑语) period in later life when one acts as one did as a child 行为像孩提时的晚年时期; 老小孩: *He's in his second childhood, playing with his grandson's toy trains.* 他返老还童, 玩儿他孙子的玩具火车.

child·less *adj* having no children 无子女的: *a childless couple/marriage* 无子女的夫妻[婚姻生活].

□ **'child-bearing** *n* [U] giving birth to children 生孩子: [attrib 作定语] *She's past child-bearing age.* 她已过生育年龄.

child 'benefit (*Brit*) payment made by the Government to parents of children up to a certain age 儿童补助金(政府发给儿童的父母, 到儿童某一年龄为止).

'childbirth *n* [U] process of giving birth to a child 分娩: *She died in childbirth.* 她分娩时死亡.

'childlike *adj* (*esp approv* 尤作褒义) like or characteristic of a child; innocent; not devious 孩子般的; 孩子气的; 天真的; 无邪的: *childlike enjoyment, trust, honesty, etc* 孩子般的欢乐、信任、诚实等. Cf 参看 CHILDISH.

'child-minder *n* (*esp Brit*) person who is paid to look after children, esp those of parents who are both at work 受雇照顾孩子的人(尤指因孩子父母都工作).

'child-proof *adj* (of equipment, appliances, etc) which cannot be operated, opened, damaged, etc by a young child (指设备、用具等)防儿童的(不能被幼儿开动、打开、损坏...的): *Most car doors are now fitted with child-proof locks.* 汽车门现在大都装有预防儿童开启的锁.

child·ish /'tʃaɪldɪʃ; 'tʃaɪldɪʃ/ (**a**) (characteristic) of a child 孩子(特有)的: *childish laughter* 孩子的笑声. (**b**) (*derog* 贬) (of an adult) (behaving) like a child; immature; silly (指成人)(举止)像孩子的, 幼稚的, 傻里傻气的: *Don't be so childish!* 不要这么孩子气! ○ *a childish attitude, fear, remark* 幼稚的态度、恐惧、言语. Cf 参看 CHILDLIKE (CHILD). ▷ **child·ishly** *adv*: *behave childishly* 表现得像孩子. **child·ish·ness** *n* [U].

chili (*US*) = CHILLI.

chill /tʃɪl; tʃɪl/ *n* **1** [sing] unpleasant coldness in the air, in the body, in water, etc 寒冷: *There's quite a chill in the air this morning.* 今晨空气很寒冷. **2** [C] illness caused by cold and damp, with shivering of the body; feverish cold 受寒; 着凉; 感冒发烧: *catch a chill* 着凉. **3** [sing] (*fig* 比喻) feeling of gloom or depression 冷淡; 寒心: *The bad news cast a chill over the gathering.* 这坏消息使参加聚会的人颇为扫兴.

▷ **chill** *v* **1** [Tn] make (sb/sth) cold 使(某人)感到冷; 使(某物)冷却: *The March wind chilled us.* 三月的风使我们感到十分寒冷. ○ (*fig* 比喻) *His sinister threat chilled* (ie frightened) *all who heard it.* 他这一凶恶的威胁使所有听到的人不寒而栗. **2** (**a**) [I, Tn] (cause food and drink to) become cool, eg in a refrigerator (指食物和饮料)变凉或冷却(如在冰箱中): *Let the pudding chill for an hour.* 把布丁冰镇一小时. ○ *This wine is best served chilled.* 这种葡萄酒最好冷饮. (**b**) [Tn] preserve (food) at a low temperature without freezing it 冷藏(在低温而未冰冻的情况下保存)(食物): *chilled beef* 冷藏的牛肉. **3** [Tn] lessen (sth); dampen 减少(某事物); 减轻: *The raw weather chilled our enthusiasm for a swim.* 天气阴冷, 我们游泳的兴致大减. **4** (idm 习语) **chill sb to the 'bone/'marrow** make sb very cold 使某人感到非常冷: *Come by the fire — you must be chilled to the marrow!* 到火旁边来吧——你一定冻坏了.

chill *adj* = CHILLY: *a chill wind* 寒风.

chil·ling /'tʃɪlɪŋ; 'tʃɪlɪŋ/ *adj* frightening 吓人的: *a chilling ghost story* 吓人的鬼故事.

chilly /'tʃɪlɪ; 'tʃɪlɪ/ *adj* (**-ier**, **-iest**) **1** rather cold; unpleasantly cold 寒冷的; 冷得难受的: *a chilly day, morning, room* 寒冷的天、早晨、房间 ○ *feel chilly* 感到寒冷. **2** (*fig* 比喻) unfriendly 冷淡的; 不友好的: *a chilly welcome, reception, stare* 冷淡的迎接、接待、注视 ○ *chilly politeness* 冷淡的客套. **chil·li·ness** *n* [U].

chilli (*US* **chili**) /'tʃɪlɪ; 'tʃɪlɪ/ *n* (*pl* **chillies**; *US* **chilies**) [C, U] small pod of a type of pepper plant, often dried or made into powder and used to give a hot taste to food 辣椒: *How much chilli did you put in the curry?* 你在咖喱食品中放了多少辣椒? ○ [attrib 作定语] *chilli peppers* 辣椒 ○ *'chilli powder* 辣椒粉.

□ **,chilli con 'carne** /kɒn 'kɑ:nɪ; kɑn 'kɑrnɪ/ stew of minced beef and kidney beans, flavoured with chillies or chilli powder 辣味牛肉末炖菜豆.

chime /tʃaɪm; tʃaɪm/ *n* **1** set of tuned bells 成套编钟; 排钟: *a chime of bells* 一套编钟. **2** series of notes sounded by such a set 编钟发出的声音: *ring the chimes* 敲编钟 ○ *the chime of church bells/of the clock* 教堂钟[时钟]的钟声.

▷ **chime** *v* **1** (**a**) [I] (of bells) sound a chime; ring (指钟)敲出乐声; 响: *cathedral bells chiming* 大教堂钟声在响. (**b**) [Tn] cause (bells) to ring 使(钟)响; 敲. **2** [I, Tn] (of bells or a clock) show (the time) by ringing (指钟或时钟)响声报(时): *The church clock chimed (at) midnight.* 教堂午夜钟响报时. **3** (phr v) **chime in (with sth)** (*infml* 口) interrupt a conversation 插话: *He kept chiming in with his own opinions.* 他不断插话发表意见. **chime (in) with sth** (*infml* 口) fit sth; suit sth 符合某事; 适合某事: *It's good that your plans chime (in) with ours.* 你们的计划和我们的相吻合, 真是好极了.

chi·mera (also **chi·maera**) /kaɪˈmɪərə; kaɪˈmɪrə/ *n* **1** imaginary monster made up of parts of several different animals (由几种动物的各部分构成的)假想的怪物. **2** (*fig* 比喻) wild or impossible idea 不可能实现的想法; 幻想; 妄想.

▷ **chi·mer·ical** /kaɪˈmerɪkl; kaɪˈmɛrɪkl/ *adj* unreal; fanciful 不真实的; 奇异的: *chimerical ideas, schemes, etc* 异想天开的主意、计划等.

chim·ney /ˈtʃɪmnɪ; ˈtʃɪmnɪ/ *n* **1** structure through which smoke or steam is carried away from a fire, furnace, etc and through the roof or wall of a building 烟囱: *a blocked chimney* 堵塞的烟囱 ○ *factory chimneys* 工厂的烟囱. ⇨illus at App 1 见附录1之插图, page vii. **2** glass tube that protects the flame of an oil-lamp from draughts (油灯的)玻璃灯罩. **3** (in mountaineering) narrow opening in a rock or cliff up which a person may climb (登山中)(岩石或峭壁中的)狭孔(可供人攀登的). ⇨illus at MOUNTAIN 见 MOUNTAIN 之插图.

□ ˈ**chimney-breast** *n* projecting part of the wall of a room which encloses the bottom of the chimney and the fireplace 壁炉腔.

ˈ**chimney-piece** *n* = MANTELPIECE.

ˈ**chimney-pot** *n* short metal or earthenware pipe fitted to the top of a chimney 烟囱管帽(装在烟囱顶上的短的金属管或陶管). ⇨illus at App 1 见附录1之插图, page vii.

ˈ**chimney-stack** *n* group of chimneys standing together, esp on a roof 烟囱体(立在一起的一组烟囱, 尤指屋顶上的).

ˈ**chimney-sweep** (also **sweep**) *n* person whose job is removing soot, etc from inside chimneys 烟囱清洁工.

chimp /tʃɪmp; tʃɪmp/ *n* (*infml* 口) chimpanzee 黑猩猩.

chim·pan·zee /ˌtʃɪmpənˈziː, ˌtʃɪmpænˈziː; ˌtʃɪmpænˈzi/ *n* type of small African ape 黑猩猩. ⇨illus at APE 见 APE 之插图.

chin /tʃɪn; tʃɪn/ *n* **1** part of the face below the mouth; front part of the lower jaw 颏; 下巴: *a double chin*, ie a fold of fat under the chin 双下巴. ⇨illus at HEAD 见 HEAD 之插图. **2** (idm 习语) **chuck sb under the chin** ⇨ CHUCK[1]. **keep one's ˈchin up** (*infml* 口) remain cheerful in difficult circumstances 在困难环境下仍然乐观; 毫不气馁.

▷ **chin·less** *adj* **1** having a small chin, regarded as a sign of a weak character 小下巴的(视为性格懦弱的标志). **2** (idm 习语) **a chinless ˈwonder** (*Brit infml* 口) (esp young upper-class) person with a weak character (尤指上层社会的青年)性格懦弱者.

□ ˈ**chin-strap** *n* strap on a helmet, etc, that fastens under the chin 下颏带(钢盔等上系在颏下的带子).

ˈ**chin-wag** *n* (*Brit infml* 口) chat 聊天; 闲谈: *have a chin-wag* 聊天.

China /ˈtʃaɪnə; ˈtʃaɪnə/ (also **People's Republic of China**) country in eastern Asia, the third-largest and most populous country in the world 中国; 中华人民共和国.

china /ˈtʃaɪnə; ˈtʃaɪnə/ *n* [U] **1** (**a**) fine baked and glazed white clay; porcelain 瓷; 瓷料; 瓷器: *made of china* 瓷制的 ○ [attrib 作定语] *a china vase* 瓷花瓶. (**b**) objects made of this, eg cups, saucers, plates 瓷制品(如杯、碟、盘): *household china* 家用瓷器. **2** (idm 习语) **a bull in a china shop** ⇨ BULL[1].

□**china ˈclay** = KAOLIN.

ˈ**china-cupboard** *n* cupboard in which china is kept or displayed 瓷器柜(放置或展示瓷器的柜).

ˈ**chinaware** *n* [U] = CHINA 1.

chine /tʃaɪn; tʃaɪn/ *n* (**a**) animal's backbone (动物的)脊骨, 脊柱, 脊椎. (**b**) joint of meat including part of this 脊肉(带部分脊骨的肉); 排骨肉.

Chinese /tʃaɪˈniːz; tʃaɪˈniz/ *adj* of China, its language or its people 中国的; 汉语的; 中文的; 中国人的.

▷ **Chinese** *n* **1** [C] native of China or person of Chinese descent 中国人; 华裔. **2** [U] language of China 汉语; 中文.

chink[1] /tʃɪŋk; tʃɪŋk/ *n* **1** narrow opening; crack; slit 缝隙; 裂口; 裂缝: *Sunlight entered the room through a chink in the curtains.* 阳光穿过窗帘的缝隙照射到室内. ○ *He peeped through a chink in the fence.* 他从围栏的缝隙窥视. **2** (idm 习语) **a chink in sb's ˈarmour** weak point or flaw in sb's argument, character, etc (论点、性格等的)弱点或缺陷.

chink[2] /tʃɪŋk; tʃɪŋk/ *n* **~ (of sth)** light ringing sound (as) of coins, glasses, etc striking together (硬币、玻璃杯等相互轻碰的)叮当声: *the chink of crockery* 陶器相碰发出的叮当声.

▷ **chink** *v* [I, Ip, Tn, Tn·p] **~ (A and B) (together)** (cause things to) make this sound (使)发叮当声: *We chinked glasses and drank each other's health.* 我们叮叮当当地碰杯为彼此的健康祝酒.

chintz /tʃɪnts; tʃɪnts/ *n* [U] type of (usu glazed) cotton cloth with a printed design, used for curtains, furniture covers, etc (通常擦光的)印花棉布(用作窗帘、家具罩布等).

chip[1] /tʃɪp; tʃɪp/ *n* **1** thin piece cut or broken off from wood, stone, china, glass, etc (木、石、瓷、玻璃等切割下或碰下的)薄片, 破片, 碎块, 碎屑: *a chip of wood* 木屑. **2** place from which such a piece has been broken (这种碎块所留下的)缺损处: *This mug has a chip in it.* 这个缸子上有个缺口. ⇨illus 见插图. **3** (*US* **French ˈfry**) (usu *pl* 通常作复数) thin strip of potato fried in deep fat 炸马铃薯条: *a plate of chips* 一盘炸土豆条 ○ *fish and ˈchips*, ie fish coated in batter, fried and served with chips 炸鱼和炸土豆条. ⇨illus at POTATO 见 POTATO 之插图. **4** (*US*) = CRISP *n*. **5** flat plastic counter[2](1) used to represent money, esp in gambling 筹码(用以代钱, 尤用于赌博). **6** = MICROCHIP. **7** (also ˈ**chip shot**) (esp in golf and football) shot or kick that travels steeply upwards and then lands within a short distance (尤指高尔夫球和足球)高球. **8** (idm 习语) **a ˌchip off the old ˈblock** (*infml* 口) person (esp a man or boy) who is like his father in character 性格像父亲的人(尤指男的). **have a ˈchip on one's shoulder** (*infml* 口) be bitter, resentful or defiant because one feels that one's past, background, physical appearance, etc, causes other people to be prejudiced against one 因感到自己的过去、背景、外貌等使别人产生偏见而怀恨、不满或对抗: *She's got a chip on her shoulder about not having gone to university.* 她因为没有进入大学而愤愤不平. **have had one's ˈchips** (*Brit sl* 俚) be dead, dying or defeated 已死、垂死或受挫. **when the chips are down** (*infml* 口) when a crisis point is reached 危急关头: *When the chips were down he found the courage to carry on.* 他在关键时刻勇于坚持到底.

□ ˈ**chipboard** *n* [U] building material made of compressed wood chips and resin 刨花板(用压缩木片和树脂制成的建筑材料).

chip[2] /tʃɪp; tʃɪp/ *v* **1** (**a**) [Tn] break or cut (sth) at the edge or surface (在边缘或表面)打破或切削(某物): *a badly chipped saucer* 边缘严重破损的碟子 ○ *chip a tooth* 锛了牙齿 ○ *He chipped one of my best glasses.* 他碰坏了我最好的玻璃杯. ⇨illus 见插图. (**b**) [I] (tend to) break at the edge or surface (易于)从边缘或表面破裂: *Be careful with these plates — they chip very easily.* 小心这些

盘子——边缘容易破损. ○ *The paint is chipping badly.* 油漆在严重剥落. **2** (**a**) [Tn·pr, Tn·p] **~ sth from/off sth; ~ sth off** break or cut (a small piece) from the edge or surface of sth 从某物的边缘或表面折下或切下(一小块): *A piece was chipped off the piano when we moved house.* 我们搬家时钢琴碰掉了一小块. ○ *We chipped the old plaster (away)* (ie removed it in small pieces) *from the wall.* 我们把旧墙皮从墙上铲掉. (**b**) [Ipr, Ip] **~ off (sth)** be broken off in small pieces 呈小块掉下; 剥落: *The paint has chipped off where the table touches the wall.* 桌子接触墙壁的地方漆皮已剥落. **3** [Tn] shape or carve (sth) by cutting the edge or surface (with an axe, chisel, etc) (用斧、凿等切削边缘或表面)雕刻(某物)或使(某物)成形; 砍成; 凿成. **4** [Tn esp passive 尤用于被动语态] make (potatoes) into chips (CHIP[1] 3) 将(土豆)切成小条: *chipped potatoes* 土豆条. **5** [I, Tn] (esp in golf and football, etc) strike or kick (the ball) so that it travels steeply upwards and then lands within a short distance (尤指高尔夫球或足球)打高或踢高(球). **6** (phr v) **chip away at sth** continuously break off small pieces from sth 从某物上不断除去小块: *chipping away at a block of marble with a chisel* 用凿子在大理石上不停地凿 ○ (*fig* 比喻) *He kept chipping away at the problem until he had solved it.* 他一直在琢磨这一问题, 直到把它解决为止. **chip in (with sth)** (*infml* 口) (**a**) join in or interrupt a conversation 参加谈话或插嘴: *She chipped in with some interesting remarks.* 她插进一些话, 说得很有趣. (**b**) contribute (money) 凑(钱); 捐(款): *If everyone chips 'in we'll be able to buy her a really nice leaving present.* 若每个人都凑些钱, 就能真正给她买件好的送别礼物.

▷ **chip·pings** *n* [pl] chips of stone, etc used for making a road surface (石头等的)碎块(用于铺路面); 碎石: *Danger! Loose chippings*, eg as a warning to motorists. 危险! 小心路面碎石(如用以警告开车的人).

chip·munk /ˈtʃɪpmʌŋk; ˋtʃɪpmʌŋk/ *n* small striped squirrel-like N American animal 花鼠(北美洲产, 有条纹, 似松鼠).

chi·po·lata /ˌtʃɪpəˈlɑːtə; ˌtʃɪpəˋlɑtə/ *n* (*esp Brit*) small sausage 小香肠.

Chip·pen·dale /ˈtʃɪpəndeɪl; ˋtʃɪpənˌdel/ *n* [U] elegant style of 18th-century English furniture 奇彭代尔式家具(18 世纪英国精美的家具): [attrib 作定语] *Chippendale chairs* 奇彭代尔式的椅子.

chi·ro·pod·ist /kɪˈrɒpədɪst; kaɪˋrɑpədɪst/ (*US* **podiatrist**) *n* person whose job is treating or preventing minor disorders of people's feet 足科治疗师.

▷ **chi·ro·pody** /kɪˈrɒpədɪ; kaɪˋrɑpədɪ/ (*US* **podiatry**) *n* [U] such treatment 足病治疗与预防术.

chiro·practor /ˈkaɪərəʊpræktə(r); ˋkaɪrəˌpræktɚ/ *n* person whose job is treating diseases by manipulating people's joints, esp those of the spine 按摩师.

▷ **chiro·practic** /ˌkaɪərəʊˈpræktɪk; ˌkaɪrəˋpræktɪk/ *n* [U] such treatment 按摩(尤指脊关节)疗法.

chirp /tʃɜːp; tʃɝp/ *n* short sharp sound made by a small bird or a cricket (小鸟或蟋蟀发出的)短而尖的叫声; 啁啾声; 唧唧声: *the chirp of a sparrow* 麻雀叽叽喳喳的叫声.

▷ **chirp** *v* [I, Ip] make this sound 作唧唧声: *birds chirping (away) merrily in the trees* 树林中快乐地叽叽喳喳叫(个不停)的小鸟.

chirpy /ˈtʃɜːpɪ; ˋtʃɝpɪ/ *adj* (**-ier, -iest**) (*Brit infml* 口) lively and cheerful 活泼的; 快活的: *You seem very chirpy today!* 今天你好像很快活似的! ▷ **chirp·ily** *adv*: *whistle chirpily* 快活地吹口哨. **chirpi·ness** *n* [U].

chir·rup /ˈtʃɪrəp; ˋtʃɪrəp/ *n* series of chirps 连续的唧唧声.

▷ **chir·rup** *v* (**-p-**) [I] make a chirrup; twitter 唧唧叫.

chisel 凿子

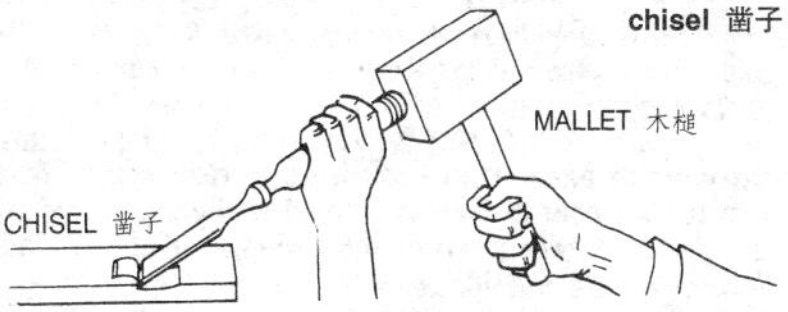

chisel /ˈtʃɪzl; ˋtʃɪzl̩/ *n* tool with a sharp cutting edge at the end, for shaping wood, stone or metal 凿子; 錾子. ⇨ illus 见插图.

▷ **chisel** *v* (**-ll-**; *US* also **-l-**) **1** [Tn, Tn·pr] (**a**) **~ sth (into sth)** cut or shape sth with a chisel 用凿子或錾子凿开或凿成某物: *The sculptor chiselled the lump of marble into a fine statue.* 雕刻家把大理石块凿成优美的雕像. ○ (*fig* 比喻) *a woman with (finely) chiselled features*, ie a sharply defined face 眉清目秀的女人. (**b**) **~ sth (out of sth)** form sth using a chisel 用凿子做成某物: *a temple chiselled out of solid rock* 在岩石中凿出的庙宇. **2** [Tn, Tn·pr] **~ sb (out of sth)** (*sl* 俚) cheat or swindle sb 欺骗或诈骗某人.

chis·el·ler *n* (*US* also **chis·eler**) person who chisels (CHISEL 2) people; swindler 骗子.

chit[1] /tʃɪt; tʃɪt/ *n* **1** young child 幼儿. **2** (*usu derog* 通常作贬义) small or thin young woman 瘦小的少女: *a mere chit of a girl* 只是个黄毛丫头.

chit[2] /tʃɪt; tʃɪt/ *n* **1** short written note or letter 便条; 短信. **2** note showing an amount of money owed, eg for drinks at a hotel 欠条, 记帐单(如用旅馆中的饮料): *Can I sign a chit for the drinks I've ordered?* 我要的饮料可以记帐吗?

chit-chat /ˈtʃɪt tʃæt; ˋtʃɪt ˌtʃæt/ *n* [U] (*infml* 口) chat; gossip 闲谈; 聊天.

chiv·alry /ˈʃɪvəlrɪ; ˋʃɪvl̩rɪ/ *n* [U] **1** (**a**) (in the Middle Ages) ideal qualities expected of a knight, such as courage, honour, courtesy and concern for the weak and helpless (中世纪的)骑士精神(如勇气、荣誉感、谦恭及扶助弱小等). (**b**) religious, moral and social system of the Middle Ages, based on these qualities 骑士制度: *the age of chivalry* 骑士制度时代. **2** courtesy and considerate behaviour, esp towards women 谦恭有礼及体贴殷勤(尤指对女子).

▷ **chiv·al·rous** /ˈʃɪvlrəs; ˋʃɪvl̩rəs/ *adj* **1** (in the Middle Ages) showing the qualities of a perfect knight (中世纪的)表现出完美的骑士精神的. **2** (of men) courteous and considerate towards women; gallant (指男子)对女子谦恭有礼及体贴殷勤的, 有骑士风度的: *a chivalrous old gentleman* 彬彬有礼的绅士. **chiv·al·rously** *adv*.

chive /tʃaɪv; tʃaɪv/ *n* [C] (**a**) small herb with purple flowers and slender onion-flavoured leaves 细香葱(开紫花, 叶狭长有洋葱味). (**b**) (usu *pl* 通常作复数) these leaves chopped and used to flavour or decorate salads, etc 细香葱叶(作色拉调料或装饰用切碎的).

chivvy (also **chivy**) /ˈtʃɪvɪ; ˋtʃɪvɪ/ *v* (*pt, pp* **chivvied, chivied**) [Tn, Tn·pr, Tn·p, Cn·t] **~ sb (into sth/along)** (*infml* 口) continuously urge sb to do sth, often in an annoying way 不断催促某人做某事(常使人烦恼): *His mother kept on chivvying him to get his hair cut.* 他母亲一直唠唠叨叨地催他去理发.

chlor·ide /ˈklɔːraɪd; ˋklɔraɪd/ *n* [U] compound of chlorine and one other element 氯化物: *sodium chloride* 氯化钠.

chlor·ine /ˈklɔːriːn; ˋklɔrin/ *n* [U] chemical element, a poisonous greenish-yellow gas with a pungent smell, used to sterilize water and in industry 氯. ⇨App 10 见附录10.

▷ **chlor·in·ate** /ˈklɔːrɪneɪt; ˋklɔrɪˌnet/ *v* [Tn] treat or sterilize (esp water) with chlorine 用氯处理或消毒(尤指水): *Is the swimming-pool chlorinated?* 游泳池的水用氯消毒了吗? **chlor·ina·tion** /ˌklɔːrɪˈneɪʃn; ˌklɔrɪˋneʃən/ *n* [U].

chlo·ro·form /ˈklɒrəfɔːm; *US* ˈklɔːr-; ˋklɔrəˌfɔrm/ *n* [U] colourless liquid, the vapour of which makes a person unconscious when it is breathed in 氯仿.

▷ **chlo·ro·form** *v* [Tn] make (sb) unconscious with this 用氯仿使(某人)失去知觉.

chloro·phyll /ˈklɒrəfɪl; *US* ˈklɔːr-; ˋklɔrəˌfɪl/ *n* [U] green substance in plants that absorbs energy from sunlight to help them grow 叶绿素. Cf 参看 PHOTOSYNTHESIS.

ChM /ˌsiː eɪtʃ ˈem; ˌsi etʃ ˋɛm/ *abbr* 缩写 = Master of Surgery (Latin *Chirurgiae Magister*) 外科硕士(源自拉丁文 *Chirurgiae Magister*): *have/be a ChM* 有外科硕士学位[为外科硕士] ○ *John Wall ChM* 约翰·沃尔外科硕士.

choc /tʃɒk; tʃɑk/ *n* (*Brit infml* 口) chocolate 巧克力: *a box of chocs* 一盒巧克力.

□ **'choc-ice** (also **'choc-bar**) *n* (*Brit*) small block of ice-cream thinly coated with chocolate 巧克力脆皮冰棍儿.

chock /tʃɒk; tʃɑk/ *n* block or wedge used to prevent a wheel, barrel, door, etc, from moving (用以防止轮子、桶、门等移动的)垫块.
▷ **chock** *v* [Tn] wedge (sth) with a chock or chocks 用垫块塞住(某物).
□ ˌ**chock-a-ˈblock** *adj* [pred 作表语] **~ (with sth/sb)** completely full; tightly packed 充满; 塞满: *The town centre was chock-a-block (with traffic).* 市中心(车辆)挤得水泄不通.
chock-ˈfull *adj* [pred 作表语] **~ (of sth/sb)** completely full 充满: *The dustbin is chock-full (of rubbish).* 垃圾箱塞满了(垃圾).

choc·olate /ˈtʃɒklət; ˈtʃɑkəlɪt/ *n* **1** [U] brown edible substance in the form of powder or a block, made from roasted and crushed cacao seeds 巧克力. **2** [U, C] sweet made of or coated with this 巧克力糖; 夹心巧克力糖: *a bar of (milk/plain) chocolate* 一条(牛奶的[纯的])巧克力糖 ○ *a box of chocolates* 一盒巧克力糖 ○ *Have another chocolate.* 再吃一块巧克力糖. **3** [U] drink made by mixing powdered chocolate with hot water or milk 巧克力粉与热水或奶混合制成的饮料: *a mug of hot chocolate* 一缸子热巧克力饮料. **4** [sing] colour of chocolate; dark brown 巧克力色; 深褐色.
▷ **choc·olate** *adj* **1** made or coated with chocolate 用巧克力制成的; 有巧克力糖衣的: *chocolate sauce* 巧克力汁 ○ *a chocolate biscuit* 巧克力饼干. **2** having the colour of chocolate; dark brown 巧克力色的; 深褐色的: *a chocolate carpet* 深褐色地毯.

choice /tʃɔɪs; tʃɔɪs/ *n* **1** [C] **~ (between A and B)** act of choosing between two or more possibilities 挑选; 选择: *make a choice* 做出选择 ○ *We are faced with a difficult choice.* 我们面临困难的抉择. ○ *What influenced you most in your choice of career?* 在你选择职业时, 对你影响最大的因素是什么? **2** [U] right or possibility of choosing 选择的权利或可能性: *He had no choice but to resign*, ie Resigning was the only thing he could do. 他除了辞职别无他途. ○ *If I had the choice, I would retire at thirty.* 假如我有选择的余地, 我三十岁就退休. **3** [C] one of two or more possibilities from which sb may choose; alternative 可供选择的可能性之一; 另一选择: *You have several choices open to you.* 有几种可能性供你选择. **4** [C] person or thing chosen 选中的人或物; 中选者: *She wouldn't be my choice as Prime Minister.* 她不是我看中做首相的人. ○ *I don't like his choice of* (ie the people he chooses as his) *friends.* 我不喜欢他找的那类朋友. **5** [U] variety from which to choose; range 供选择的种类; 范围: *There's not much choice in the shops.* 这些商店中没有多少可挑选的东西. **6** (idm 习语) **be spoilt for choice** ⇨ SPOIL. **for choice** preferably 宁可. **of one's choice** that one chooses 某人所选定的: *First prize in the competition will be a meal at the restaurant of your choice.* 获头奖者可自选饭店用一餐. **out of/from choice** willingly 愿意地: *do sth out of choice* 出于自愿做某事物. **you pays your money and you takes your choice** ⇨ PAY[2].
▷ **choice** *adj* (**-r, -st**) **1** [esp attrib 尤作定语] (esp of fruit and vegetables) of very good quality (尤指水果和蔬菜)优质的. **2** carefully chosen 精选的: *She summed up the situation in a few choice phrases.* 她言简意赅地总结了情况. ○ (*joc* 谑) *He used some pretty choice* (ie rude or offensive) *language!* 他使用粗鄙的语言!

choir /ˈkwaɪə(r); kwaɪr/ *n* **1** [CGp] organized group of singers, esp one that performs in church services 合唱队(尤指教堂作礼拜时合唱者的); 唱诗班: *She sings in the school choir.* 她在校唱诗班唱歌. **2** [C] part of a church where these singers sit 教堂中唱诗班坐的席位: [attrib 作定语] *choir stalls* 唱诗班席位. ⇨illus at App 1 见附录1之插图, page viii.
□ ˈ**choirboy** *n* boy who sings in a church choir 唱诗班的男童歌手.
ˈ**choirmaster** *n* person who trains and conducts a choir 唱诗班指挥.
ˈ**choir school** school attached to or associated with a cathedral or college 唱诗班学校(附属于大教堂或学院或与之有关的学校).

choke /tʃəʊk; tʃok/ *v* **1** [I, Ipr] **~ (on sth)** be unable to breathe because one's windpipe is blocked by sth 窒息: *She choked (to death) on a fish bone.* 鱼刺把她卡住而窒息(致死). **2** [Tn] cause (sb) to stop breathing by squeezing or blocking the windpipe; (of smoke, etc) make (sb) unable to breathe easily (掐住或阻塞气管)使(某人)停止呼吸; (指烟等)使(某人)难以呼吸; 呛: *choke the life out of sb* 扼死某人 ○ *The fumes almost choked me.* 烟雾几乎把我呛死. **3** [I, Ipr, Tn] **~ (with sth)** (cause sb to) become speechless (使某人)说不出话来: *She was choking with emotion.* 她激动得说不出话来. ○ *Anger choked his words.* 他气得说不出话来. **4** [Tn, Tn·pr esp passive 尤用于被动语态, Tn·p esp passive 尤用于被动语态] **~ sth (up) (with sth)** block or fill (a passage, space, etc); clog or smother sth 阻塞, 充满(通道、空间等); 填满某物; 窒息某物: *The drains are choked (up) with dead leaves.* 下水道被枯叶堵住. ○ *The garden is choked with weeds.* 花园杂草丛生. **5** (phr v) **choke sth back** restrain or suppress sth 克制、抑制、忍住或压制某事物: *choke back one's tears, anger, indignation* 忍住眼泪、愤怒、义愤. **choke sth down** swallow sth with difficulty 困难地咽下某物. **choke sb off** (*infml* 口) (**a**) interrupt sb rudely or abruptly 粗鲁地或突然阻止某人. (**b**) reprimand sb severely (for doing sth) 严厉申斥某人(之所为).
▷ **choke** *n* **1** act or sound of choking 窒息; 窒息时发出的声音. **2** (knob which operates the) valve controlling the flow of air into a petrol engine 阻风门(开关)(控制进入汽油机空气量的阀门): *Won't your car start? Try giving it a bit more choke*, ie letting more air into the engine by pulling out the choke. 你的汽车不能启动啦? 把阻风门开大一点儿(外拉阻风门钮让更多的空气进入发动机). ⇨illus at App 1 见附录1之插图, page xii.
choked *adj* [pred 作表语] **~ (about sth)** (*infml* 口) upset; angry 心烦; 愤怒: *He was pretty choked about being dropped from the team.* 他因为队里未选用他而耿耿于怀.

choker /ˈtʃəʊkə(r); ˈtʃokɚ/ *n* close-fitting necklace or band of material worn round the throat by women (女子紧围颈部的)项链或箍带: *a pearl choker* 短的珍珠项链.

chol·era /ˈkɒlərə; ˈkɑlərə/ *n* [U] infectious and often fatal disease causing severe diarrhoea and vomiting, common in hot countries 霍乱: *an outbreak of cholera* 霍乱突然蔓延 ○ [attrib 作定语] *a cholera epidemic* 霍乱流行.

chol·eric /ˈkɒlərɪk; ˈkɑlərɪk/ *adj* easily angered; bad-tempered 易怒的; 坏脾气的.

cho·les·terol /kəˈlestərɒl; kəˈlɛstəˌrol/ *n* [U] fatty substance found in animal fluids and tissue, thought to cause hardening of the arteries 胆固醇: [attrib 作定语] *A high cholesterol level in the blood can cause heart disease.* 血液中胆固醇含量高可导致心脏病.

choose /tʃu:z; tʃuz/ *v* (*pt* **chose** /tʃəʊz; tʃoz/, *pp* **chosen** /ˈtʃəʊzn; ˈtʃozn̩/) **1** [I, Ipr, Tn, Tn·pr, Cn·n/a, Cn·t] **~ (between A and/or B)**; **~ (A) (from B)**; **~ sb/sth as sth** pick out or select (sb/sth that one prefers or considers the best, most suitable, etc) from a number of alternatives 选择, 挑选, 选取(某人[某事物]): *choose carefully* 细心挑选 ○ *She had to choose between giving up her job or hiring a nanny.* 她得在放弃工作和雇用保姆两者间作一选择. ○ *We offer a wide range of holidays to choose from.* 我们提供各种旅游度假方式可供选择. ○ *choose a carpet, career, chairman* 挑选地毯、选择职业、选举主席 ○ *We have to choose a new manager from a short-list of five candidates.* 我们得从五位候选人中挑选新经理. ○ *The Americans chose Mr Clinton as president/to be president.* 美国人选举了克林顿先生任[当]总统. **2** (**a**) [Tw no passive 不用于被动语态, Tt] decide (to do one thing rather than another) 决定(做一事而不做另一事): *Have you chosen what you want for your birthday?* 你过生日要什么东西决定了吗? ○ *We chose to go by train.* 我们决定乘火车去. (**b**) [I, Tt] like; prefer 喜欢; 愿意: *You may do as you choose.* 你喜欢怎么做就怎么做. ○ *The author chooses to remain anonymous.* 作者愿不署名. **3** (idm 习语) **pick and choose** ⇨ PICK[3]. **there is nothing, not much, little, etc to choose between A and B** there is very little difference between two or more things or people 事物与事物或人与人之间无甚差别.

NOTE ON USAGE 用法: **Select** suggests a more

carefully considered decision than **choose** ☆ 用 **select** 表示所作出的决定比用 **choose** 考虑得更为周到: *Our shops select only the very best quality produce.* 我们商店都是精选的质量最高的产品. **Pick** is less formal than **select** ☆ **pick** 比 **select** 通俗: *Who are you going to pick for the team?* 你打算挑选谁参加这个队? **Choose** suggests a freely made decision and can refer to a decision between only two items. (We usually **select** or **pick** from a number greater than two) 用 **choose** 表示的是自由作出的决定, 可仅指两者之间. (不止两项时通常用 **select** 或 **pick**): *She chose the red sweater rather than the pink one.* 她选中那件红毛衣而不要那件粉红的. **Opt (for)** refers to the choice of courses of action rather than of items and suggests the weighing up of advantages and disadvantages ☆ **opt (for)** 所指的选择对象是行动而不是项目, 且有权衡利弊之意: *Most people opt for buying their own homes rather than renting them.* 大多数人愿意买房子而不愿意租房子.

choosy (also **choosey**) /ˈtʃuːzɪ; ˋtʃuzɪ/ *adj* (**-sier**, **-siest**) (*infml* 口) careful in choosing; fussy or hard to please 精心挑选的; 挑剔的; 难以取悦的: *She's very choosy about who she goes out with.* 她愿意和谁幽会不愿意和谁幽会是很挑剔的. ▷ **choosi·ness** *n* [U].

chop[1] /tʃɒp; tʃɑp/ *v* (**-pp-**) **1** [Tn, Tn·pr, Tn·p] **~ sth (up) (into sth)** cut sth into pieces with an axe, a knife, etc (用斧、刀等)将某物切碎, 劈开, 剁碎: *chopping wood in the garden* 在花园中劈木头 ○ *He chopped the logs (up) into firewood*, ie into sticks. 他把原木劈成了柴. ○ *Chop the meat into cubes before frying it.* 把肉切成方块再炸. ○ *finely chopped onions, carrots, parsley, etc* 剁碎的洋葱、胡萝卜、芫荽等. **2** [Tn] hit (sth) with a short downward stroke or blow 剁, 砍(某物). ⇨Usage at CUT[1] 用法见 CUT[1]. **3** [Tn esp passive 尤用于被动语态] (*Brit infml* 口) stop or greatly reduce (sth) 终止或削减(某事物): *Bus services in this area have been chopped.* 这一地区的公共汽车班次已大为削减. **4** (phr v) **chop at sth** aim blows at sth with an axe, a knife, etc (用斧、刀等)向某物砍或劈. **chop sth down** cause sth to fall down by cutting it at the base 砍倒(某物): *chop down a dead tree* 砍倒枯树. **chop sth off (sth)** remove sth (from sth) by cutting with an axe, etc (用斧等)砍掉某物: *He chopped a branch off the tree.* 他从树上砍下一根树枝. ○ (*infml* 口) *Charles I had his head chopped off.* 查里一世遭斩首. **chop a/one's way through sth** make a path through sth by chopping branches, etc (砍掉树枝等)开路穿过某处.

chop[2] /tʃɒp; tʃɑp/ *n* **1** [C] (**a**) cutting stroke, esp one made with an axe 砍, 劈(尤指用斧): *She cut down the sapling with one chop.* 她一斧子就把树苗砍倒了. (**b**) chopping blow, esp one made with the side of the hand 砍击(尤指用掌侧); 掌劈: *a karate chop* 空手道掌劈. **2** [C] thick slice of meat, usu including a rib 粗肉条(通常带肋骨); 排骨: *a pork/lamb/mutton chop* 猪[羔羊/羊]排骨. **3 the chop** [sing] (*sl* 俚 *esp Brit*) act of dismissing or killing sb; act of discontinuing sth 辞退某人; 杀掉某人; 中止某事物: *She got the chop after ten years with the company.* 她在公司工作十年后遭解雇. ○ *The public spending cuts will mean the chop for several hospitals.* 削减公费开支意味着要砍掉几所医院.

chop[3] /tʃɒp; tʃɑp/ *v* (**-pp-**) **1** (idm 习语) ˌ**chop and** ˈ**change** keep changing one's plans, opinions, etc 不断改变计划、意见等; 变化无常. **2** (phr v) **chop about/round** (of the wind) change direction suddenly (指风)突然改变方向. ⇨Usage at CUT[1] 用法见 CUT[1].

chop·per /ˈtʃɒpə(r); ˋtʃɑpɚ/ *n* **1** chopping tool, esp a short axe or a butcher's heavy knife with a large blade 砍割工具(尤指短斧或屠夫的宽刃重刀); 砍刀; 屠刀. **2** (*infml* 口) helicopter 直升飞机.

choppy /ˈtʃɒpɪ; ˋtʃɑpɪ/ *adj* (**-ier**, **-iest**) (of the sea) moving in short broken waves; slightly rough (指海洋)有浪花起伏的, 稍有波浪的. ▷ **choppi·ness** *n* [U].

chop·sticks /ˈtʃɒpstɪks; ˋtʃɑpˌstɪks/ *n* [pl] pair of thin sticks made of wood, ivory, etc, used in China, Japan, etc for lifting food to the mouth 筷子.

chop-suey /ˌtʃɒpˈsuːɪ; ˋtʃɑpˋsuɪ/ *n* [U] Chinese dish of small pieces of meat fried with rice and vegetables 炒饭.

choral /ˈkɔːrəl; ˋkɔrəl/ *adj* of, composed for or sung by a choir 唱诗班的; 为唱诗班创作的; 由唱诗班演唱的: *a choral society* 唱诗班合唱团 ○ *choral evensong* 合唱晚祷 ○ *Beethoven's choral symphony* 贝多芬的合唱交响曲.

chor·ale /kəˈrɑːl; koˋrɑl/ *n* **1** (music for a) hymn sung by a choir and congregation together, as part of a church service 众赞歌(曲调). **2** (*esp US*) group of singers; choir 合唱队; 唱诗班.

chord[1] /kɔːd; kɔrd/ *n* (in music) combination of notes usu sounded together in harmony (音乐的)和弦, 和音.

chord[2] /kɔːd; kɔrd/ *n* **1** (*mathematics* 数) straight line that joins two points on the circumference of a circle or the ends of an arc 弦(与圆的两点或弧的两端相交的直线). ⇨illus at CIRCLE 见 CIRCLE 之插图. **2** string of a harp, etc (竖琴等的)弦. **3** (idm 习语) **strike a chord** ⇨ STRIKE[2]. **touch the right chord** ⇨ TOUCH[2].

chore /tʃɔː(r); tʃɔr/ *n* **1** small routine task 日常的零星事务; 琐事: *do the chores*, eg the housework 干杂活儿(如家务活儿) ○ *household/domestic chores*, ie dusting, ironing, making the beds, etc 家务杂活儿(打扫、熨衣、铺床等). **2** unpleasant or tiring task 讨厌的或累人的工作: *She finds shopping a chore.* 她认为买东西是烦人的事.

cho·reo·graph /ˈkɒrɪəgrɑːf, *also* -græf; *US* ˈkɔːrɪəgræf; ˋkɔrɪəˌgræf/ *v* [Tn] design and arrange steps and dances for (a ballet, etc) 为(芭蕾舞等)设计舞步与编舞; 设计舞蹈动作.

cho·reo·graphy /ˌkɒrɪˈɒgrəfɪ; *US* ˌkɔːrɪ-; ˌkɔrɪˋɑgrəfɪ/ *n* [U] (art of designing and arranging) steps for ballet and dancing on stage (芭蕾舞和其他舞台舞的)舞步(的设计与编排艺术). ▷ **chor·eo·grapher** /ˌkɒrɪˈɒgrəfə(r); *US* ˌkɔːrɪ-; ˌkɔrɪˋɑgrəfɚ/ *n*. **cho·reo·graphic** /ˌkɒrɪəˈgræfɪk; *US* ˌkɔːrɪ-; ˌkɔrɪəˋgræfɪk/ *adj*.

chor·is·ter /ˈkɒrɪstə(r); *US* ˈkɔːr-; ˋkɔrɪstɚ/ *n* member of a choir, esp a choirboy 唱诗班歌手(尤指男童歌手).

chortle /ˈtʃɔːtl; ˋtʃɔrtl/ *n* loud chuckle of pleasure or amusement 大声的笑; 咯咯的笑.

▷ **chortle** *v* [I] utter a chortle 哈哈大笑; 咯咯笑: *chortle with delight at a joke* 让笑话逗得哈哈大笑.

NOTE ON USAGE 用法: **Chuckle** and **chortle** both indicate laughing with pleasure and satisfaction. ☆ **chuckle** 和 **chortle** 均指因高兴和满足而笑. **Chuckling** is usually quiet and may be a response to private thoughts or reading ☆ **chuckling** 通常是低声或无声的, 也可为独自思考和阅读的反应: *He chuckled to himself when he remembered the trick he'd played on them.* 他想起捉弄他们的事就忍俊不禁. **Chortling** is usually louder and more public ☆ **chortling** 通常声音较大, 而且多是当众的: *When I told them what had happened to me, they all chortled with mirth.* 我把我的事告诉他们以后, 他们咯咯地笑起来了.

chorus /ˈkɔːrəs; ˋkɔrəs/ *n* **1** [CGp] (usu large) group of singers; choir (通常为大型的)合唱团; 唱诗班: *the Bath Festival Chorus* 巴斯音乐节大合唱团. **2** [C] piece of music, usu part of a larger work, composed for such a group 合唱曲: *the Hallelujah Chorus* 哈利路亚合唱曲. **3** [C] part of a song that is sung after each verse, esp by a group of people (歌曲中的)合唱部分: *Bill sang the verses and everyone joined in the chorus.* 比尔先唱独唱部分, 然后大家一起合唱. **4** [C] thing said or shouted by many people together 齐声说或齐声喊的内容: *a chorus of boos, cheers, laughter, etc* 齐声喊呸、欢呼、大笑等 ○ *The proposal was greeted with a chorus of approval.* 大家对该建议异口同声表示赞成. **5** [CGp] group of performers who sing and dance in a musical comedy (歌舞喜剧中的)歌舞队: [attrib 作定语] *a chorus line* (歌舞喜剧中的)歌舞队唱词. **6** [CGp] (in ancient Greek drama) group of singers and dancers who comment on the events of the play (古希腊戏剧中)(为剧中事件作评注的)歌舞队. **7** [C] (esp in Elizabethan drama) actor who speaks the prologue and epilogue of a play (尤指伊丽莎白时代戏剧中)(宣读开场白和收场白的)男演员. **8** (idm 习语) **in chorus** all together; in unison 一起; 同时; 一齐; 一致: *act, speak, answer in chorus* 一致行动、异口同声地说、同时回答.

▷ **chorus** *v* [Tn] sing or say (sth) all together 同时唱或说(某事): *The crowd chorused their approval (of the decision).* 群众(对该决定)齐声表示赞成.

□ ˈ**chorus-girl** *n* girl or young woman who sings or dances in a chorus(5) (歌舞喜剧中的)歌舞队女演员.

chose, chosen *pt, pp* of CHOOSE.

chough /tʃʌf; tʃʌf/ *n* type of crow with red legs and a red beak 山鸦(红腿红嘴的鸦).

chow[1] /tʃaʊ; tʃaʊ/ *n* type of dog with a thick coat, originally from China (原产于中国的一种被毛厚的)狗.

chow[2] /tʃaʊ; tʃaʊ/ *n* [U] (*sl* 俚) food 食物.

chow·der /ˈtʃaʊdə(r); ˋtʃaʊdɚ/ *n* [U] (*US*) thick soup or stew made with vegetables and fish (用蔬菜与鱼烹调的)浓汤或杂烩: *clam chowder* 蛤肉杂烩汤.

chow mein /ˌtʃaʊ ˈmeɪn; ˋtʃaʊ ˋmen/ *n* [U] Chinese dish of fried noodles with shredded meat and vegetables 炒面.

C

Christ /kraɪst; kraɪst/ *n* (**a**) (also **Jesus, Jesus Christ** /ˌdʒiːzəs ˈkraɪst; ˌdʒizəs ˋkraɪst/) the founder of the Christian religion 基督. (**b**) image or picture of Christ 基督的图像.

▷ **Christ** *interj* (also **Jesus, Jesus Christ**) (⚠ *infml* 讳, 口) (expressing anger, annoyance, surprise, etc 表示愤怒、烦恼、惊讶等): *Christ! We're running out of petrol.* 天哪! 我们的汽油要用完了.

□ ˈ**Christlike** *adj* like Christ in character or action (性格或行为)像基督的: *showing Christlike humility* (表现出)像基督那样谦卑的.

chris·ten /ˈkrɪsn; ˋkrɪsn̩/ *v* **1** [Tn] receive (sb) into the Christian Church by sprinkling water on his head and giving him a name 为(某人)施洗礼(在头上洒水并为之命名以加入基督教). Cf 参看 BAPTIZE. **2** [esp passive 尤用于被动语态: Tn, Cn·n] (**a**) give a name to (sb) at such a ceremony (在洗礼仪式上)为(某人)命名: *The child was christened Mary.* 这孩子洗礼时命名为玛丽. (**b**) give a name to (esp a ship when it is launched) 为(尤指下水的轮船)命名. **3** [Tn] (*fig infml* 比喻, 口) use (sth) for the first time 第一次使用(某物): *Let's have a drink to christen our new sherry glasses.* 让我们为使用我们新的雪利酒杯喝点儿酒.

▷ **chris·ten·ing** /ˈkrɪsnɪŋ; ˋkrɪsn̩ɪŋ/ *n* ceremony in which sb is christened; baptism 洗礼(给某人施洗礼命名的仪式): [attrib 作定语] *a christening service* 洗礼仪式.

Chris·ten·dom /ˈkrɪsndəm; ˋkrɪsn̩dəm/ *n* [sing] (*fml* 文) (**a**) all Christian people throughout the world (全世界所有的)基督教徒. (**b**) (*dated* 旧) the Christian countries of the world (全世界的)基督教国家. ⇨ Usage at CHRISTIAN 用法见 CHRISTIAN.

Chris·tian /ˈkrɪstʃən; ˋkrɪstʃən/ *adj* **1** of or based on the teachings of Christ or the doctrines of Christianity 基督教导的; 根据基督教导的; 基督教义的; 根据基督教义的: *the Christian Church, faith, religion* 基督教教堂、基督教的信仰、基督教 ○ *a Christian upbringing* 基督教义的熏陶. **2** of or believing in the Christian religion 基督教的; 信仰基督教的: *a Christian country* 信仰基督教的国家. **3** of Christians 基督教徒的: *the Christian sector of the city* 城市的基督教徒区. **4** showing the qualities of a Christian; kind and humane 表现出基督徒的品质的; 仁慈与慈悲的: *That's not a very Christian way to behave.* 那可不太像基督徒的行为.

▷ **Chris·tian** *n* **1** person who believes in the Christian religion 信仰基督教的人; 基督徒. **2** (*infml* 口) person who has Christian qualities 有基督徒品质的人.

Chris·ti·an·ity /ˌkrɪstɪˈænətɪ; ˌkrɪstʃɪˋænətɪ/ *n* [U] **1** the religion based on the belief that Christ was the son of God, and on his teachings 基督教(基于相信基督是上帝之子并信仰其教导的宗教): *She was converted to Christianity.* 她已皈依基督教. **2** (**a**) being a Christian 基督徒身分: *He derives strength from his Christianity.* 他身为基督徒而从中获得力量. (**b**) Christian character or qualities 基督徒的特性或品质.

□ **the ˌChristian ˈEra** the period of history from the birth of Christ to the present day 基督纪元; 公元.

ˈ**Christian name** (*US* also ˈ**given name**) name given to sb when he is christened; first name 教名(洗礼时所取者); 名字. ⇨ Usage at NAME[1] 用法见 NAME[1].

ˌ**Christian ˈScience** religious system which claims that disease can be cured through Christian faith, without medical treatment 基督教科学派(主张靠基督教的信仰无须医药即可治愈疾病的教派). ˌ**Christian ˈScientist** person who believes in this system 基督教科学派信徒.

NOTE ON USAGE 用法: **Christianity, Islam** and **Judaism** are the names of religions or faiths followed by **Christians, Muslims** and **Jews** respectively. ☆ **Christianity**、**Islam**、**Judaism** 是分别由基督教徒、伊斯兰教徒、犹太教徒信奉的宗教或信仰. The word **Christendom**, which is now dated, refers to all Christian countries or all Christians in the world. ☆ **Christendom** 一词现已过时, 意为世界上所有的基督教国家或所有的基督教徒. Historically it has been used to mean the whole world from a European point of view 从欧洲人的观点来看, 这个词在历史上用以指全世界: *Rome was the greatest city in all Christendom.* 罗马是当时世界上最伟大的城市. **Jewry** is the collective name for all Jews ☆ **Jewry** 是全体犹太人的统称: *British Jewry* 英国的犹太人. **Muhammedanism** (now dated) is an alternative name for **Islam**, used particularly by non-Muslims ☆ **Muhammedanism** 一词(现已过时)是 **Islam** 的别称, 尤为非穆斯林所使用.

Christ·mas /ˈkrɪsməs; ˋkrɪsməs/ *n* **1** (also ˌ**Christmas ˈDay**) annual celebration by Christians of the birth of Christ (on 25 December) 圣诞节(12月25日): [attrib 作定语] *Christmas dinner, presents* 圣诞节晚餐、礼物. **2** (also ˈ**Christmas-time**, ˈ**Christmas-tide**) period of several days before and after Christmas Day 圣诞节节期(圣诞节前后的几天): *spend Christmas with one's family* 和全家一起过圣诞节 ○ [attrib 作定语] *the Christmas holidays* 圣诞节假期.

▷ **Christ·massy** /ˈkrɪsməsɪ; ˋkrɪsməsɪ/ *adj* (*infml* 口) typical of Christmas; looking festive 有圣诞节特点的; 像节日的.

□ ˈ**Christmas box** *n* (*Brit*) small gift, usu of money, given at Christmas, esp to sb (eg a postman or a milkman) who provides a service throughout the year 圣诞节的节礼(通常为赏钱, 尤指酬谢全年服务的人, 如邮递员或送牛奶的人).

ˈ**Christmas cake** rich fruit cake, usu covered with marzipan and icing and eaten at Christmas 圣诞节蛋糕(多水果的糕饼, 通常覆有杏仁蛋白糊、糖霜等, 于圣诞节食用).

ˈ**Christmas card** greetings card sent to friends at Christmas 圣诞卡.

ˌ**Christmas ˈcracker** = CRACKER 2B.

ˌ**Christmas ˈEve** (evening of the) day before Christmas Day, 24 December 圣诞节前夕, 圣诞夜(圣诞节的前一天, 12月24日或当晚).

ˌ**Christmas ˈpudding** rich steamed pudding made with dried fruit and eaten at Christmas 圣诞节布丁(干果制成的蒸糕, 于圣诞节食用).

ˈ**Christmas tree** evergreen or artificial tree decorated with lights, tinsel, etc at Christmas 圣诞树(圣诞节时摆设的常绿树或人造树, 装饰有灯、闪光的金属丝、片等).

chro·matic /krəʊˈmætɪk; kroˋmætɪk/ *adj* **1** (**a**) of colour 有颜色的. (**b**) in bright colours 颜色鲜艳的. **2** (*music* 音) having the notes of the chromatic scale 有半音阶的; 半音的.

□ **chroˌmatic ˈscale** (*music* 音) series of notes rising or falling in semitones 半音音阶.

chrome /krəʊm; krom/ *n* [U] **1** chromium (esp when used as a protective coating on other metals) 铬. **2** yellow colouring matter obtained from a compound of chromium and used in paints 铬黄.

□ ˌ**chrome ˈsteel** alloy of steel and chromium 铬钢.

chro·mium /ˈkrəʊmɪəm; ˋkromɪəm/ *n* [U] metallic chemical element used in making alloys (such as stainless steel) and as a shiny protective coating on other metals 铬: *chromium plating*, eg on a car bumper 镀铬(如在汽车保险杠上) ○ *chromium-plated* 镀铬的. ⇨ App 10 见附录 10.

chro·mo·some /ˈkrəʊməsəʊm; ˋkroməˌsom/ *n* (*biology* 生) any of the tiny threads or rods in animal and plant cells, carrying genes 染色体.

chronic /ˈkrɒnɪk; ˋkrɑnɪk/ *adj* **1** (esp of a disease) lasting for a long time; continually recurring (尤指疾病)长期的, 慢性的; 连续复发的: *chronic bronchitis, arthritis, etc* 慢性支气管炎、关节炎等 ○ *the country's chronic unemployment problem* 国家的长期失业问题. Cf 参看 ACUTE. **2** having had a disease or a habit for a long time 长期患病的; 长期有某种习惯的: *a chronic alcoholic, invalid, etc* 长期酗酒的、病弱的等. **3** (*Brit sl*

俚) very bad 极坏的: *The film was absolutely chronic.* 这个电影糟透了. ▷ **chron·ic·ally** /ˈkrɒnɪklɪ; ˋkrɑnɪklɪ/ *adv*: *the chronically ill* 患有慢性病的.

chron·icle /ˈkrɒnɪkl; ˋkrɑnɪkl/ *n* (often *pl* 常作复数) record of historical events in the order in which they happened 编年史: *He consulted the chronicles of the period.* 他参考了这一时期的编年史.

▷ **chron·icle** *v* [Tn] record (sth) in a chronicle 将(某事物)载入编年史: *chronicling the events of a war* 把战争中的重大事件载入编年史中. **chron·ic·ler** /ˈkrɒnɪklə(r); ˋkrɑnɪklɚ/ *n*.

chron(o)- *comb form* 构词成分 of or relating to time 时间的; 有关时间的: *chronology* ○ *chronometer*.

chro·no·lo·gical /ˌkrɒnəˈlɒdʒɪkl; ˌkrɑnəˋlɑdʒɪkl/ *adj* arranged in the order in which they occurred 按时间的前后顺序排列的: *a chronological list of Shakespeare's plays*, ie in the order in which they were written 莎士比亚戏剧的编年表. ▷ **chro·no·lo·gic·ally** /-klɪ; -klɪ/ *adv*.

chro·no·logy /krəˈnɒlədʒɪ; krəˋnɑlədʒɪ/ *n* **1** [U] science of fixing the dates of historical events 年代学. **2** [C] arrangement or list of events in the order in which they occurred 年表: *a chronology of Mozart's life* 莫札特生平年表.

chro·no·meter /krəˈnɒmɪtə(r); krəˋnɑmətɚ/ *n* instrument that keeps very accurate time, used esp for navigating at sea 极准确的记时仪器; (尤指用于航海的)精密记时计; 天文钟.

chrys·alis /ˈkrɪsəlɪs; ˋkrɪslɪs/ *n* (*pl* ~es) **1** form of an insect at the stage of its life when it changes from a grub to an adult insect, esp a butterfly or moth; pupa 蛹; (尤指)蝶蛹, 蛾蛹. ⇨illus at BUTTERFLY 见 BUTTERFLY 之插图. **2** hard case that encloses an insect during this stage 蛹壳.

chrys·an·themum /krɪˈsænθəməm; krɪsˋænθəməm/ *n* (**a**) garden plant with brightly coloured flowers 菊花. (**b**) one of these flowers 菊花(花朵). ⇨illus at App 1 见附录1之插图, page ii.

chub /tʃʌb; tʃʌb/ *n* (*pl* unchanged 复数不变) small freshwater fish with a thick body 查布鱼(一种小型体粗的淡水鱼).

chubby /ˈtʃʌbɪ; ˋtʃʌbɪ/ *adj* (**-ier, -iest**) round and plump; slightly fat 圆胖丰满的; 稍胖的: *chubby cheeks* 圆胖脸 ○ *a chubby child* 胖乎乎的孩子. ⇨Usage at FAT[1] 用法见 FAT[1]. ▷ **chub·bi·ness** *n* [U].

chuck[1] /tʃʌk; tʃʌk/ *v* **1** [Tn, Tn·pr, Tn·p, Dn·n] (*infml* 口) throw (sth) carelessly or casually (胡乱地或随便地)扔、抛(某物): *Chuck it in the bin!* 把它扔到垃圾桶里去! ○ *chuck old clothes away/out* 把旧衣服扔掉[出去] ○ *Chuck me (over) the newspaper if you've finished reading it.* 你看完了报就扔给我. **2** [Tn, Tn·p] **~ sb/sth (in/up)** (*infml* 口) give up sb/sth; abandon 抛弃某人[某事物]; 放弃: *She's just chucked her boy-friend*, ie ended her relationship with him. 她刚刚甩了男朋友. ○ *He chucked in his job last week.* 上星期他辞掉了工作. **3** (idm 习语) **chuck it** (*sl* 俚) stop doing sth immediately 立即停止做某事物: *I'm sick of your sarcastic remarks — just chuck it* (ie stop making them), *will you?* 我已经听腻了你的冷嘲热讽——别说了, 行吗? **chuck sb under the chin** touch or stroke sb lovingly or playfully under the chin 爱抚或抚弄某人的下巴. **4** (phr v) **chuck sb out (of sth)** (*infml* 口) force sb to leave (a place) 迫使某人离开(某地); 撵走: *They were chucked out of the pub for being too rowdy.* 他们因为太吵闹被撵出酒馆. ○ *He failed his exams and was chucked out of university.* 他考试不及格, 被大学开除.

▷ **chuck** *n* **1** playful touch or stroke under the chin 抚弄或抚摸下巴. **2** (idm 习语) **give sb/get the chuck** (*infml* 口) dismiss or reject sb/be dismissed or rejected 辞退或拒绝某人[被辞退或拒绝].

□ **chucker-out** /ˌtʃʌkər ˈaʊt; ˌtʃʌkɚˋaʊt/ *n* (*infml* 口) person whose job is to remove troublesome people from public-houses, meetings, etc (受雇从酒馆、会议等中撵走捣乱者的)保安人员.

chuck[2] /tʃʌk; tʃʌk/ *n* (**a**) part of a lathe that grips the object to be worked on 卡盘, 夹盘(车床上用以夹住工件的部分). (**b**) part of a drill that grips the bit 夹头(钻或钻床上用以夹住钻头的部分). ⇨illus at DRILL 见 DRILL 之插图.

chuck[3] /tʃʌk; tʃʌk/ *n* [U] (also ˈ**chuck steak**) cut[2](5) of beef taken from the neck to the ribs (牛的从颈到肋骨的)颈肉.

chuckle /ˈtʃʌkl; ˋtʃʌkl/ *v* [I, Ipr] laugh quietly or to oneself 轻声地笑; 暗自笑: *He chuckled (to himself) as he read the newpaper.* 他看报时暗暗(独自)发笑. ○ *What are you chuckling about?* 你独自笑什么? ⇨Usage at CHORTLE 用法见 CHORTLE.

▷ **chuckle** *n* quiet or partly suppressed laugh 轻声的笑; 忍俊不禁: *She gave a chuckle of delight.* 她高兴得笑出声来.

chuffed /tʃʌft; tʃʌft/ *adj* [pred 作表语] **~ (about/at sth)** (*Brit infml* 口) very pleased 愉快: *look/feel chuffed* 看起来[感到]很愉快 ○ *She was chuffed at/about getting a pay rise.* 她因获加薪而洋洋得意.

chug /tʃʌg; tʃʌg/ *v* (**-gg-**) **1** [I] make the short dull repeated sound of an engine running slowly (发动机缓慢运转时)发出(持续而单调的)短声; 发出突突声. **2** (phr v) **chug along, down, up, etc** move steadily in the specified direction while making this sound (发出突突声朝某方向)稳稳行进: *The boat chugged along the canal.* 小船稳稳地顺着运河突突地航行.

▷ **chug** *n* sound made by a chugging engine (发动机缓慢运转时发出的)突突声.

chum /tʃʌm; tʃʌm/ *n* (*infml* 口) close friend 好友: *an old school chum* 老同学.

▷ **chum** *v* (**-mm-**) (phr v) **chum up (with sb)** (*infml* 口) become very friendly (with sb) (与某人)成为好友.

chummy *adj* (*infml* 口) very friendly 非常友好的. **chum·mily** *adv*. **chum·mi·ness** *n* [U].

chump /tʃʌmp; tʃʌmp/ *n* **1** (*infml* 口) foolish person 傻瓜; 笨蛋: *Don't be such a chump!* 不要这么傻了! **2** short thick block of wood 短而厚的木块. **3** (*Brit* also ˌ**chump** ˈ**chop**) thick end of a loin of lamb or mutton 羊腰部的厚肉. **4** (idm 习语) **off one's** ˈ**chump** (*dated Brit sl* 旧, 俚) crazy 发疯; 发狂.

chunk /tʃʌŋk; tʃʌŋk/ *n* **1** thick solid piece cut or broken off sth (从某物上切下或折下的)大块: *a chunk of bread, meat, ice, wood, etc* 一大块面包、肉、冰、木头等. **2** (*infml* 口) fairly large amount (of sth) (某物)相当大的部分: *I've completed a fair chunk of my article.* 我已经把文章的一大部分写完了.

chunky /ˈtʃʌŋkɪ; ˋtʃʌŋkɪ/ *adj* (**-ier, -iest**) **1** having a short thick body; stocky 身体短粗的; 矮胖的; 敦实的: *a chunky footballer* 敦实的足球运动员. **2** containing chunks of fruit, etc 含有大块水果等的: *chunky marmalade* 橙块果酱. **3** (of clothes) made of thick bulky (usu woollen) material (指衣物)用厚而蓬松材料(通常为毛料)制的: *a chunky sweater* 厚毛衣. ▷ **chunk·ily** *adv*: *He's chunkily built.* 他长得很结实. **chun·ki·ness** *n* [U].

church /tʃɜːtʃ; tʃɝtʃ/ *n* **1** [C] building used for public Christian worship 教堂: *The procession moved into the church.* 人们陆续进入教堂. ○ [attrib 作定语] *a church steeple* 教堂的尖顶 ○ *a church service* 教堂的礼拜仪式. ⇨illus at App 1 见附录1之插图, page viii. **2** [U] service in such a building; public worship (教堂的)礼拜仪式; (会众的)礼拜: *Church begins/is at 9 o'clock.* 礼拜仪式9点开始. ○ *How often do you go to church?* 你隔多久去做一次礼拜? ○ *They're in/at church*, ie attending a service. 他们在做礼拜. ⇨Usage at SCHOOL[1] 用法见 SCHOOL[1]. **3 the Church** [sing] all Christians regarded as a group 全体基督教徒: *The Church has a duty to condemn violence.* 基督徒有责任谴责暴力. **4 Church** [C] particular group of Christians; denomination 基督教教派; 派别: *the Anglican Church* 英国国教; 圣公会 ○ *the Catholic Church* 天主教 ○ *the Free Churches* 自由教会. **5 the Church** [sing] (**a**) (esp the Christian) religion regarded as an established institution (尤指基督教的)教会, 宗教: *the conflict between (the) Church and (the) State* 政教冲突. (**b**) the ministers of the Christian religion; the clergy or clerical profession 基督教牧师; 教士; 神职: *go into/enter the Church*, ie become a Christian minister 开始担任神职(成为基督教牧师).

□ ˈ**churchgoer** *n* person who goes to church services regularly 按时去教堂做礼拜的人.

the ˌ**Church of** ˈ**England** the established Protestant Church in England; the Anglican Church 英国国教会; 圣公会.

C

church'warden *n* (in a Church of England parish) one of usu two elected officials responsible for church money and property (英国国教教区的)教会执事(通常为选出的两名执事之一, 负责教会财务和财产).

'churchyard *n* enclosed area of land round a church, often used for burials 教堂的庭院(常用作墓地).

churl /tʃɜ:l; tʃɝl/ *n* (*dated* 旧) bad-mannered or bad-tempered person 举止或脾气不佳的人; 粗暴的人. ▷ **churl·ish** *adj*: *It seems churlish to refuse such a generous offer.* 拒绝这样慷慨的建议未免有些失礼. **churl·ishly** *adv*. **churl·ish·ness** *n* [U].

churn /tʃɜ:n; tʃɝn/ *n* **1** machine in which milk or cream is beaten to make butter 搅乳器(用以搅拌牛奶或乳脂以制成黄油的机器). **2** (*Brit*) large (usu metal) container in which milk is carried from a farm 奶桶(通常为金属的).

▷ **churn** *v* **1** [Tn] (**a**) beat (milk or cream) to make butter 搅拌(牛奶或乳脂)以制黄油. (**b**) make (butter) in this way (用此种方法)制(黄油). **2** (**a**) [Tn, Tn·p] ~ **sth (up)** cause sth to move violently; stir or disturb sth 使某物猛动; 搅动; 扰乱某物: *motor boats churning (up) the peaceful waters of the bay* 激荡着海湾平静水面的汽艇 ○ *The earth had been churned up by the wheels of the tractor.* 拖拉机轮子把泥土掀了起来. ○ (*fig* 比喻) *The bitter argument left her feeling churned up* (ie agitated and upset) *inside.* 这场激烈的争论使她忐忑不安. (**b**) [I] (esp of liquids) move about violently (尤指液体)翻腾: *the churning waters of a whirlpool* 旋涡翻腾的水 ○ *His stomach churned with nausea.* 他的胃翻腾欲呕. **3** (phr v) **churn sth out** (*infml* 口) produce sth (usu of bad quality) in large amounts 大量生产某物(通常质量恶劣); 粗制滥造: *She churns out romantic novels.* 她写了很多浪漫小说, 质量很差.

chute /ʃu:t; ʃut/ *n* **1** sloping or vertical passage down which things can slide or be dropped (物件可以滑下或落下的)斜的或垂直的通道, 斜道, 滑道, 斜槽, 立槽: *a rubbish chute*, eg from the upper storeys of a high building 垃圾滑道(如高层建筑自上面各层通到下面的管道). **2** (*infml* 口) parachute 降落伞.

chut·ney /'tʃʌtnɪ; 'tʃʌtnɪ/ *n* [U] hot-tasting mixture of fruit, vinegar, sugar and spices, eaten with curries, cold meat, cheese, etc 酸辣酱(水果、醋、糖和香料的混合物, 与咖喱、冷肉、奶酪等一起食用): *green tomato chutney* 绿西红柿酸辣酱.

CI *abbr* 缩写 = (*Brit*) Channel Islands (Jersey, Guernsey, Alderney and Sark) 海峡群岛(泽西、根西、奥尔德尼、萨克等四岛): *St Peter Port, Guernsey, CI*, eg in an address 海峡群岛根西岛圣彼得港(如用于通讯处).

CIA /ˌsi: aɪ 'eɪ; ˌsi aɪ 'e/ *abbr* 缩写 = (*US*) Central Intelligence Agency 中央情报局: *working for the CIA* 为中央情报局工作. Cf 参看 FBI.

ci·cada /sɪ'kɑ:də; *US* sɪ'keɪdə; sɪ'kedə/ *n* insect like a grasshopper, common in hot countries, the male of which makes a shrill chirping noise 蝉.

ci·ca·trice /'sɪkətrɪs; 'sɪkətrɪs/ (also **ci·ca·trix** /'sɪkətrɪks; 'sɪkətrɪks/) *n* (*pl* **-trices** /sɪkə'traɪsi:z; sɪkə'traɪsiz/) scar left by a wound that has healed 疤; 伤痕; 疤痕.

CID /ˌsi: aɪ 'di:; ˌsi aɪ 'di/ *abbr* 缩写 = (*Brit*) Criminal Investigation Department 刑事调查局: *an inspector from the CID* 刑事调查局的调查员.

-cide *comb form* 构词成分 (forming *ns* 用以构成名词) **1** act of killing sb 杀(人): *genocide* ○ *patricide*. **2** person or thing that kills 可致死的人或物: *insecticide* ○ *fungicide*.

▷ **-cidal** *comb form* 构词成分 (forming *adjs* 用以构成形容词) of or related to killing 杀的; 有关杀的: *homicidal*.

cider /'saɪdə(r); 'saɪdɚ/ *n* **1** (also **cyder**) [U] drink made from fermented apple-juice 苹果酒: *dry/sweet cider* 不甜的[甜的]苹果酒 ○ [attrib 作定语] *cider apples* 制酒的苹果. Cf 参看 PERRY. **2** [U] (*US* also **sweet cider**) non-alcoholic drink made from apples 苹果汁. **3** [C] drink or glass of either of these 一些或一杯苹果酒或苹果汁: *Two ciders, please.* 请来两杯苹果酒.

□ **'cider-press** *n* machine for squeezing the juice from apples 苹果榨汁器.

cif /ˌsi: aɪ 'ef; ˌsi aɪ 'ɛf/ *abbr* 缩写 = (*commerce* 商) cost, insurance, freight (included in the price) 到岸价(包括成本、保险费、运费): *The invoice was for £35 cif.* 发票为到岸价35英镑.

ci·gar /sɪ'gɑ:(r); sɪ'gɑr/ *n* tight roll of tobacco leaves for smoking 雪茄烟: [attrib 作定语] *the smell of cigar smoke* 雪茄烟的气味.

ci·gar·ette (*US* also **ci·garet**) /ˌsɪgə'ret; *US* 'sɪgəret; 'sɪgəˌrɛt/ *n* roll of shredded tobacco enclosed in thin paper for smoking 纸烟; 香烟; 烟卷.

□ **ciga'rette-case** *n* small flat (usu metal) box for holding cigarettes 香烟盒(装香烟的小扁盒, 通常为金属的).

ciga'rette-holder *n* tube in one end of which a cigarette may be put for smoking 烟嘴.

ciga'rette-lighter (also **lighter**) *n* device that produces a small flame for lighting cigarettes and cigars 打火机.

ciga'rette-paper *n* [C, U] (piece of) thin paper in which tobacco is rolled to make cigarettes 卷烟纸.

C-in-C /ˌsi: ɪn 'si:; ˌsi ɪn 'si/ *abbr* 缩写 = Commander-in-Chief.

cinch /sɪntʃ; sɪntʃ/ *n* (*sl* 俚) **1** easy task 容易做的事情: *'How was the exam?' 'It was a cinch!'* '考试怎么样?' '很容易!' **2** sure or certain thing 必然发生的事: *He's a cinch to win the race.* 他肯定会赢得这次比赛. **3** (*US*) = GIRTH 2.

▷ **cinch** *v* [Tn] (*US*) fasten a girth(2) on (a horse) 给(马)系上肚带.

cin·der /'sɪndə(r); 'sɪndɚ/ *n* **1** [C] small piece of partly burnt coal, wood, etc that is no longer burning but may still be hot 煤渣, 炭渣, 炉渣等(不再燃烧但仍可能有余热). **2 cinders** [pl] ashes 灰. **3** (idm 习语) **burn, etc sth to a 'cinder** cook (food) until it is hard and black 将(食物)做煳: *The cakes were burnt to a cinder.* 饼烤煳了.

□ **'cinder-track** *n* running-track made with finely crushed cinders 灰渣跑道.

Cin·der·ella /ˌsɪndə'relə; ˌsɪndə'rɛlə/ *n* **1** girl or woman whose beauty or abilities have not been recognized 灰姑娘; (美貌或能力未被赏识的)女子. **2** person or thing that has been persistently neglected 长期被忽视的人或物; 被埋没的人: *This department has been the Cinderella of the company for far too long.* 这个部门在公司不受重视由来已久.

cine- *comb form* 构词成分 of the cinema 电影的: *cine-projector*.

cine-camera /'sɪnɪ kæmərə; 'sɪnɪ ˌkæmərə/ *n* camera used for taking moving pictures 电影摄影机.

cine-film /'sɪnɪ fɪlm; 'sɪnɪ ˌfɪlm/ *n* [C, U] film used for taking moving pictures 电影胶片.

cin·ema /'sɪnəmɑ:, 'sɪnəmə; 'sɪnəmə/ *n* **1** [C] (*US* **movie house, movie theatre**) building in which motion-picture films are shown 电影院: *go to the cinema*, ie to see a film 去看电影. **2** (also **the cinema**) [sing] (*esp Brit*) (*US* **the movies**) films as an art-form or an industry 电影艺术; 电影业: *She's interested in (the) cinema.* 她对电影艺术很感兴趣. ○ *He works in the cinema.* 他从事电影业.

▷ **cine·matic** /ˌsɪnə'mætɪk; ˌsɪnɪ'mætɪk/ *adj* of or relating to cinema 电影的; 有关电影的.

cine·ma·to·graphy /ˌsɪnəmə'tɒgrəfɪ; ˌsɪnəmə'tɑgrəfɪ/ *n* [U] art or science of making motion-picture films 摄制电影的艺术. **cine·ma·to·grapher** /ˌsɪnəmə'tɒgrəfə(r); ˌsɪnəmə'tɑgrəfɚ/ *n*. **cine·ma·to·graphic** /ˌsɪnəmætə'græfɪk; ˌsɪnəˌmætə'græfɪk/ *adj*.

cine-projector /'sɪnɪ prədʒektə(r); 'sɪnɪ prəˌdʒɛktɚ/ *n* machine for showing moving pictures on a screen 电影放映机.

cin·na·mon /'sɪnəmən; 'sɪnəmən/ *n* **1** (**a**) [U] spice made from the inner bark of a SE Asian tree 桂皮. (**b**) [C] this tree 肉桂; 桂. **2** [U] yellowish-brown colour 黄褐色.

ci·pher (also **cy·pher**) /'saɪfə(r); 'saɪfɚ/ *n* **1** (**a**) [C, U] (method of) secret writing in which a set of letters or symbols is used to represent others; code 密码编写(的方法); 密码: *a message in cipher* 密码信. (**b**) [C] message written in this way 用密码写的信息. (**c**) [C] key[1](5b) to a secret message 密码索引; 密码检索本. **2** [C] the symbol 0, representing nought or zero 0(代表无或零的符号); 零. **3** [C] any of the numbers from 1 to 9 从1至9的任何阿拉伯数字. **4** [C] (*fig derog* 比喻,

贬) person or thing of no importance 不重要的人或物: *a mere cipher* 无足轻重的人.

▷ **ci·pher** *v* [Tn] write (a message) in secret writing; encode 用密码书写(信息); 译成密码.

circa /ˈsɜ:kə; ˈsɝkə/ *prep* (*Latin* 拉) (*abbrs* 缩写 **c, ca**) (with dates) about (与日期连用)大约: *born circa 150 BC* 生于公元前约150年.

circle 圆

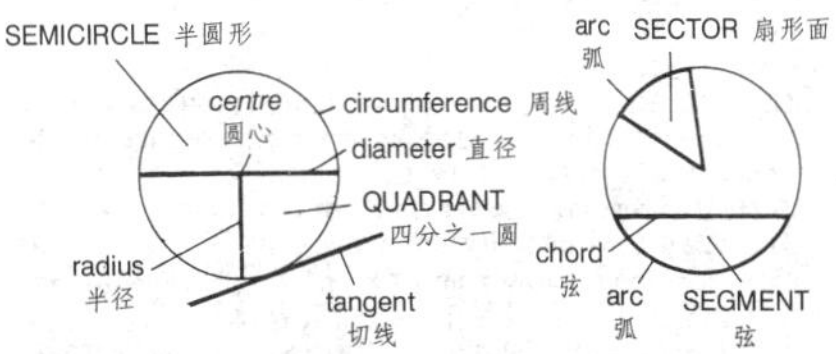

circle /ˈsɜ:kl; ˈsɝkl̩/ *n* **1** (round space enclosed by a) curved line every point on which is the same distance from the centre 圆周; 圆; 圆形空间: *Use your compasses to draw a circle.* 用圆规画圆. ⇨App 5 见附录5. ⇨illus 见插图. **2** thing shaped like this; ring 圆形物; 环; 圈: *a circle of trees, hills, spectators* 一圈树、小山、旁观者 ○ *standing in a circle* 站成一圈. **3** (*US* **balcony**) group of seats in curved and banked rows raised above the floor level of a theatre, cinema, concert-hall, etc 楼厅包厢(剧院、电影院、音乐厅等的半圆形楼座): *We've booked seats in the circle.* 我们预订了楼厅包厢的座位. ⇨illus at App 1 见附录1之插图, page ix. **4** group of people who are connected by having the same interests, profession, etc (有共同兴趣、职业等的人形成的)圈子, 阶层, 界: *be well known in business, political, theatrical, etc circles*, ie among people connected with business, politics, the theatre, etc 在商、政、戏剧等界中知名 ○ *move in fashionable circles* 进入上层社会 ○ *She has a large circle of friends.* 她交游很广. **5** (idm 习语) **come full circle** ⇨ FULL. **go round in ˈcircles** work busily at a task without making any progress 工作忙忙碌碌而无进展; 瞎忙. **square the circle** ⇨ SQUARE[3]. **a vicious circle** ⇨ VICIOUS.

▷ **circle** *v* **1** [I, Ipr, Ip] **~ (about/around/round) (over sb/sth)** move in a circle, esp in the air 转圈(尤指在空中); 盘旋; 环行: *vultures circling (round) over a dead animal* 在死的动物上空盘旋的秃鹫. **2** [Tn] (**a**) move in or form a circle round (sb/sth) 围绕(某人[某物])转圈; 盘旋; 环行: *The plane circled the airport before landing.* 飞机着陆前围绕机场盘旋. ○ *The moon circles the earth every 28 days.* 月亮每28天绕地球一圈. ○ *a town circled by hills* 群山环绕的城镇. (**b**) draw a circle round (sth) 围绕(某物)画圈: *spelling mistakes circled in red ink* 用红笔圈起的拼写错误.

circ·let /ˈsɜ:klɪt; ˈsɝklɪt/ *n* circular band, eg of precious metal, flowers, etc, worn round the head as an ornament 圆箍饰环(如贵金属、花等制的).

cir·cuit /ˈsɜ:kɪt; ˈsɝkɪt/ *n* **1** line, route or journey round a place 围绕一地方的线、路线或旅程; 周线; 圈: *The circuit of the city walls is three miles.* 环绕本市城墙的周长是三英里. ○ *The earth takes a year to make a circuit of* (ie go round) *the sun.* 地球绕太阳一周需要一年时间. ○ *She ran four circuits of the track.* 她在跑道上跑了四圈. **2** (**a**) complete path along which an electric current flows 电路: *There must be a break in the circuit.* 电路中一定有断路. (**b**) apparatus with a sequence of conductors, valves, etc, through which an electric current flows 电器装置: [attrib 作定语] *a circuit diagram*, ie one showing the connections in such an apparatus 电路图. **3** (**a**) regular journey made by a judge round a particular area to hear cases in court 巡回审判(法官定期巡回某地区): *go on circuit*, ie make this journey 进行巡回审判 ○ [attrib 作定语] *a circuit judge* 巡回法官. (**b**) area covered by such a journey 巡回审判地区. **4** (in sport) series of tournaments in which the same players regularly take part 联赛: *the American golf circuit* 美国高尔夫球联赛. **5** group of Methodist churches sharing the same preachers within a particular area (在某地区有同一批传教士的)卫理公会组织.

□ ˈ**circuit-breaker** *n* automatic device for interrupting an electric current 断路器(自动切断电路的装置).

ˈ**circuit training** method of training using a series of different athletic exercises 循环训练法(用一系列体育项目锻炼的方法).

cir·cu·it·ous /səˈkju:ɪtəs; sɝˈkjuɪtəs/ *adj* (*fml* 文) long and indirect; roundabout 迂回的; 绕行的: *a circuitous route* 迂回的路线. ▷ **cir·cu·it·ously** *adv*.

cir·cu·lar /ˈsɜ:kjʊlə(r); ˈsɝkjələ/ *adj* **1** shaped like a circle; round 圆形的; 环绕的. **2** moving round a circle 环程移动的; 循环的: *a circular tour*, ie one taking a route that brings travellers back to the starting-point 环程旅行. **3** (of reasoning) using the point it is trying to prove as evidence for its conclusion (指推理)循环论证的: *a circular argument* 循环论证. **4** [usu attrib 通常作定语] sent to a large number of people 送达很多人的; 传阅的: *a circular letter* 传阅的信件.

▷ **cir·cu·lar** *n* printed letter, notice or advertisement sent to a large number of people (送达很多人的)印刷信件、通知或宣传品; 传阅文件.

cir·cu·lar·ity /ˌsɜ:kjʊˈlærətɪ; ˌsɝkjəˈlærətɪ/ *n* [U].

cir·cu·lar·ize, -ise /ˈsɜ:kjʊləraɪz; ˈsɝkjələˌraɪz/ *v* [Tn] send a circular to (sb) 发通知给(某人).

□ ˌ**circular ˈsaw** *n* rotating metal disc with a serrated edge used for cutting wood, etc 圆锯.

cir·cu·late /ˈsɜ:kjʊleɪt; ˈsɝkjəˌlet/ *v* **1** (**a**) [I, Ipr, Tn, Tn·pr] (cause sth to) go round continuously (使某物)循环: *Blood circulates through the body.* 血液在体内循环. (**b**) [I] move about freely 流通: *open a window to allow the air to circulate* 开窗使空气流通. **2** [I, Ipr, Tn, Tn·pr] (cause sth to) pass from one place, person, etc to another (使某事物)流传, 传播: *The news of her death circulated* (ie spread) *quickly.* 她死去的消息迅速传开. ○ *The host and hostess circulated (among their guests).* 男女主人(在客人间)走来走去招待客人. ○ *circulate a letter* 传阅信件. **3** [Tn] inform (sb) by means of a circular 发通知告知(某人): *Have you been circulated with details of the conference?* 你收到会议详情的通知了吗?

cir·cu·la·tion /ˌsɜ:kjʊˈleɪʃn; ˌsɝkjəˈleʃən/ *n* **1** [C, U] movement of blood round the body from and back to the heart 血液循环: *have (a) good/bad circulation* 血液循环良好[不佳]. **2** [U] (**a**) passing of sth from one person or place to another; spread 流传; 传播: *the circulation of news, information, rumours, etc* 新闻、信息、谣言的传播. (**b**) state of circulating or being circulated 流通: *Police say a number of forged banknotes are in circulation.* 警方称市面上有一定数量的伪钞. ○ *Pound notes have been withdrawn from circulation.* 一英镑面值的钞票已停止流通. ○ (*fig* 比喻) *She's been ill but now she's back in circulation*, ie going out and meeting people again. 她一直生病, 但现在又重新参加活动了. **3** [C] number of copies of a newspaper, magazine, etc sold to the public 报纸、杂志等售出的份数; 发行额; 销售量: *a newspaper with a (daily) circulation of more than one million* (日)销售量超过一百万份的报纸 ○ [attrib 作定语] *circulation figures* 销售数字.

cir·cu·lat·ory /ˌsɜ:kjʊˈleɪtərɪ; *US* ˈsɜ:kjələtɔ:rɪ; ˈsɝkjələˌtɔrɪ/ *adj* of or relating to the circulation of blood 血液循环的; 有关血液循环的: *circulatory disorders* 血液循环失调.

cir·cum·cise /ˈsɜ:kəmsaɪz; ˈsɝkəmˌsaɪz/ *v* [Tn] (**a**) cut off the foreskin of (a male person) as a religious rite or for medical reasons 切除(某男子)的包皮. (**b**) cut off the clitoris of (a female person) 切除(某女子)的阴蒂.

▷ **cir·cum·cis·ion** /ˌsɜ:kəmˈsɪʒn; ˌsɝkəmˈsɪʒən/ *n* [C, U] (action or ceremony of) circumcising 割礼; 包皮环切术; 阴蒂切除术.

cir·cum·fer·ence /səˈkʌmfərəns; sɝˈkʌmfərəns/ *n* (**a**) line that marks out a circle or other curved figure[1](2b) 周线; 周缘; 圆周. ⇨App 5 见附录5. (**b**) distance round this 周长: *The circumference of the earth is almost 25 000 miles/The earth is almost 25 000 miles in circumference.* 地球的圆周长约为25 000英里. ⇨illus at CIRCLE 见CIRCLE之插图. Cf 参看 PERIMETER.

cir·cum·flex /ˈsɜ:kəmfleks; ˈsɝkəmˌflɛks/ *n* (also **circumflex accent**) mark put over a vowel in French and some other languages to show how it is pronounced, as in *rôle* or *fête* (标在法文或其他文字元音字母上)表示如何发音的符号(如在 rôle 或 fête 中的).

cir·cum·lo·cu·tion /ˌsɜːkəmləˈkjuːʃn; ˌsɝkəmloˈkjuʃən/ *n* [C, U] (instance of the) use of many words to say sth that could be said in a few words 累赘的说法; 迂回的说法. ▷ **cir·cum·lo·cu·tory** /ˌsɜːkəmˈlɒkjʊtərɪ; ˌsɝkəmˈlɑkjəˌtɔrɪ/ *adj*.

cir·cum·nav·ig·ate /ˌsɜːkəmˈnævɪgeɪt; ˌsɝkəmˈnævəˌget/ *v* [Tn] (*fml* 文) sail round (esp the world) 环绕(尤指地球)航行: *Magellan was the first person to circumnavigate the globe.* 麦哲伦是第一个环球航行的人. ▷ **cir·cum·nav·iga·tion** /ˌsɜːkəmˌnævɪˈgeɪʃn; ˌsɝkəmˌnævəˈgeʃən/ *n* [C, U].

C

cir·cum·scribe /ˈsɜːkəmskraɪb; ˌsɝkəmˈskraɪb/ *v* [Tn] **1** (*fml* 文) restrict (sth) within limits; confine 将(某事物)限制于一定范围内; 约束: *a life circumscribed by poverty* 受制于贫穷的一生. **2** draw a line round (a geometrical figure) so that it touches all the outside points 画(几何图形的)外接圆: *circumscribe a square* 画正方形的外接圆.

▷ **cir·cum·scrip·tion** /ˌsɜːkəmˈskrɪpʃn; ˌsɝkəmˈskrɪpʃən/ *n* [U] circumscribing or being circumscribed 限制; 受限制; 画外接圆.

cir·cum·spect /ˈsɜːkəmspekt; ˈsɝkəmˌspɛkt/ *adj* [usu pred 通常作表语] considering everything carefully before acting; cautious; wary 小心; 慎重; 细心.

▷ **cir·cum·spec·tion** /ˌsɜːkəmˈspekʃn; ˌsɝkəmˈspɛkʃən/ *n* [U] caution; prudence 小心; 谨慎: *proceeding with great circumspection* 小心谨慎地进行.

cir·cum·spectly *adv*.

cir·cum·stance /ˈsɜːkəmstəns; ˈsɝkəmˌstæns/ *n* **1** [C usu *pl* 通常作复数] condition or fact connected with an event or action 环境; 情形; 情况: *What were the circumstances of/surrounding her death?* ie Where, when and how did she die? 她是在什么情况下死的? (她是在何地、何时及如何死的?) ○ *She was found dead in suspicious circumstances,* ie She may have been murdered. 她死的情形可疑(她可能是被谋杀的). ○ *He was a victim of circumstance(s),* ie What happened to him was beyond his control. 他是客观环境的牺牲者(他所遇到的事是他无法控制的). ○ *Circumstances forced us to change our plans.* 客观情况迫使我们改变了计划. **2 circumstances** [pl] financial position 经济状况: *What are his circumstances?* 他的经济状况如何? ○ *in easy/poor circumstances,* ie having much/not enough money 处于富裕[贫穷]境况. **3** (idm 习语) **in/under the ˈcircumstances** this being the case; such being the state of affairs 在这种情况下; 情形既然如此: *Under the circumstances* (eg because the salary offered was too low) *he felt unable to accept the job.* 在这种情况下(如所提的薪金太低), 他觉得无法接受这项工作. ○ *She coped well in the circumstances,* eg even though she was feeling ill. 她在这种情况下仍处理得当(如虽然身体不适). **in/under no circumstances** in no case; never 在任何情况下决不; 无论如何不: *Under no circumstances should you lend him any money.* 你无论如何都不该把钱借给他. **in straitened circumstances** ⇨ STRAITENED. **pomp and circumstance** ⇨ POMP.

cir·cum·stan·tial /ˌsɜːkəmˈstænʃl; ˌsɝkəmˈstænʃəl/ *adj* **1** (of a description) giving full details (指描述)详细的. **2** (of evidence) consisting of details that strongly suggest sth but do not prove it (指证据)有充分细节却无法证实的: *You can't convict a man of a crime on circumstantial evidence alone.* 不能只靠旁证就判定一个人有罪. ▷ **cir·cum·stan·tially** /-nʃəlɪ; -nʃəlɪ/ *adv*.

cir·cum·vent /ˌsɜːkəmˈvent; ˌsɝkəmˈvɛnt/ *v* [Tn] (*fml* 文) find a way of overcoming or avoiding (sth) 设法克服或避免(某事物); 规避; 回避: *circumvent a law, rule, problem, difficulty* 规避一法规、规则、问题、困难. ▷ **cir·cum·ven·tion** /ˌsɜːkəmˈvenʃn; ˌsɝkəmˈvɛnʃən/ *n* [U].

cir·cus /ˈsɜːkəs; ˈsɝkəs/ *n* **1** (**a**) [CGp] travelling company of entertainers, including acrobats, riders, clowns and performing animals 马戏团. (**b**) **the circus** [sing] public performance given by such a company, usu in a large tent 马戏表演(通常在大帐篷中): *go to the circus* 看马戏表演. **2** [C] (*infml* 口) scene of lively action 热闹的场面. **3** [C] (*Brit*) (in place-names 用于地名) open space in a town where several streets meet (城市中数条街道相会聚的)广场: *Piccadilly Circus* 皮卡迪利广场. Cf 参看 ROUNDABOUT *n* 2. **4** [C] (in ancient Rome) round or oval arena for chariot racing and public games (古罗马)(圆形或椭圆形的)竞技场.

cir·rho·sis /sɪˈrəʊsɪs; sɪˈrosɪs/ *n* [U] chronic and often fatal disease of the liver, suffered esp by alcoholics 肝硬变; 肝硬化: *cirrhosis of the liver* 肝硬化.

cir·rus /ˈsɪrəs; ˈsɪrəs/ *n* (*pl* **cirri** /ˈsɪraɪ; ˈsɪraɪ/) [U] type of light wispy cloud, high in the sky 卷云: [attrib 作定语] *cirrus clouds* 卷云.

cissy = SISSY.

Cis·ter·cian /sɪˈstɜːʃn; sɪsˈtɝʃən/ *n, adj* (monk or nun) of a religious order founded as a stricter branch of the Benedictines 西多会的(修士或修女).

cis·tern /ˈsɪstən; ˈsɪstɚn/ *n* water tank, esp one connected to a lavatory or in the roof of a house with pipes to taps on lower storeys (抽水马桶的)水箱; (位于屋顶有水管通往低层的)贮水槽, 蓄水池.

cit·adel /ˈsɪtədəl; ˈsɪtədl/ *n* fortress on high ground overlooking and protecting a city (建于高处的)城堡, 堡垒.

cite /saɪt; saɪt/ *v* [Tn] **1** (**a**) speak or write (words taken from a passage, a book, an author, etc); quote 引用; 引述: *She cited (a verse from) (a poem by) Keats.* 她引述济慈(诗中的)词句. (**b**) mention (sth) as an example or to support an argument; refer to 引证(某事物)(为例或以支持一论点): *She cited the high unemployment figures as evidence of the failure of government policy.* 她引证庞大的失业数字以证明政府政策的失误. **2** (*US*) officially commend (esp a soldier) for bravery; mention 表扬(尤指士兵)勇敢; 嘉奖; 表彰: *He was cited in dispatches.* 他在战报中受到表扬. **3** (*law* 律) summon (sb) to appear in a court of law 召(某人)出庭; 传讯: *be cited in divorce proceedings* 因离婚案被传讯.

▷ **ci·ta·tion** /saɪˈteɪʃn; saɪˈteʃən/ *n* **1** (**a**) [U] action of citing sth 引用; 引述; 引证. (**b**) [C] passage cited; quotation 引文; 引语; 语录: *Some dictionary writers use citations to show what words mean.* 有些辞典的编纂者用引文作例证以解释词义. **2** [C] (*US*) (**a**) official commendation of a soldier for bravery (对某士兵的勇敢的)表扬, 表彰, 嘉奖. (**b**) written description of the reasons for this (说明某士兵勇敢的)嘉奖令.

cit·izen /ˈsɪtɪzn; ˈsɪtəzn̩/ *n* **1** person who has full rights as a member of a country, either by birth or by being granted such rights 公民: *an American citizen* 美国公民 ○ *She is German by birth but is now a French citizen.* 她在德国出生而现在是法国公民. **2** person who lives in a town or city 市民: *the citizens of Rome* 罗马市民. **3** (*esp US*) = CIVILIAN.

▷ **cit·izen·ship** *n* [U] (status of) being a citizen, esp of a particular country, with the rights and duties that involves 公民资格, 公民身分(尤指公民的权利和义务): *apply for/be granted British citizenship* 申请[被给予]英国国籍.

□ **ˌcitizen's aˈrrest** arrest(1) made by a member of the public (allowable in certain cases under common law) 公民采取的逮捕行动(根据英国法律中的普通法在某些情况下准许的).

ˌcitizens' ˈband range of radio frequencies used by members of the public for local communication 民用无线电波段.

NOTE ON USAGE 用法: **Citizen** and **subject** both indicate a person who has the rights given by a state to its members, eg the right to vote. ☆ **citizen** 和 **subject** 二词均指享有国家给予的权利(如选举权)的人. **Subject** is used when the state is ruled by a monarch. ☆ **subject** 用于君主制国家. **Citizen** is used in all types of state but especially republics ☆ **citizen** 用于任何类型的国家, 但尤用于共和国: *a British subject/citizen* 英国的臣民[公民] ○ *a French citizen* 法国的公民.

cit·ric acid /ˌsɪtrɪk ˈæsɪd; ˌsɪtrɪk ˈæsɪd/ (*chemistry* 化) acid present in the juice of oranges, lemons, limes, etc 柠檬酸.

cit·ron /ˈsɪtrən; ˈsɪtrən/ *n* **1** pale yellow fruit like a lemon but larger, less sour and with a thicker skin 枸橼; 香橼. **2** small Asian tree bearing this fruit 香橼树.

cit·rus /ˈsɪtrəs; ˋsɪtrəs/ *n* any of a group of related trees including the lemon, lime, orange and grapefruit 柑橘属果树: [attrib 作定语] *citrus fruit* 柑橘属水果.

▷ **cit·rous** *adj* of or relating to these trees or their fruit 柑橘(树)的; 有关柑橘(树)的.

city /ˈsɪtɪ; ˋsɪtɪ/ *n* **1** [C] large and important town 城市; 都市; 市: *Which is the world's largest city?* 世界上最大的城市是哪个? ○ [attrib 作定语] *the city ˈcentre*, ie the central area of a city 市中心. **2** [C] (**a**) (*Brit*) town with special rights given by royal charter and usu containing a cathedral 特许市(由皇家特许状赋予特权, 且通常有大教堂的城市): *the city of York* 约克特许市. (**b**) (*US*) town given special rights by State charter 特许市(由国家特许状赋予特权的城市). **3** [CGp] all the people living in a city, as a group 全市居民: *The city turned out to welcome back its victorious team.* 全市居民倾城而出迎接凯旋球队. **4 the City** [sing] the oldest part of London, now its commercial and financial centre 伦敦商业区(伦敦最古老的部分, 现为商业及金融中心): *She works in the City*, eg as a stockbroker. 她在伦敦商业区工作(如做证券经纪人). ○ *The City reacted sharply to the fall in oil prices.* 伦敦商业区对油价下跌反应强烈. **5** (idm 习语) **the freedom of the city** ⇨ FREEDOM.

□ ˈ**city desk 1** (*Brit*) department of a newspaper dealing with financial news (报纸的)财经新闻部. **2** (*US*) department of a newspaper dealing with local news (报纸的)本地新闻部.

ˌ**city ˈeditor 1** (*Brit*) (on a newspaper) journalist responsible for financial news (报纸的)负责财经新闻的编辑. **2** (*US*) (on a newspaper) journalist responsible for local news (报纸的)负责本地新闻的编辑.

ˌ**city-ˈstate** *n* (formerly) independent state consisting of a city and the surrounding area (eg Athens in ancient times) (旧时)城邦(由一城市和周围地区组成的独立国家, 如古代雅典).

civet /ˈsɪvɪt; ˋsɪvɪt/ *n* **1** (also ˈ**civet-cat**) [C] small spotted catlike animal living in central Africa and S Asia 灵猫(产于中非和南亚). **2** [U] strong-smelling substance obtained from its glands and used in making perfume 灵猫香(用做香料).

civic /ˈsɪvɪk; ˋsɪvɪk/ *adj* [usu attrib 通常作定语] **1** of a town or city; municipal 集镇的; 城市的; 市的: *a civic function*, eg the opening of a new hospital by the mayor of a town 城市的庆典(如市长为新医院剪彩). **2** of citizens or citizenship 公民的; 公民身分的; 市民的: *civic pride*, ie citizens' pride in their town 市民的自豪(市民对自己城市的自豪) ○ *civic duties, responsibilities etc* 公民的义务、责任.

▷ **civics** /ˈsɪvɪks; ˋsɪvɪks/ *n* [sing *v*] study of municipal government and the rights and responsibilities of citizens 公民学(研究市政和公民的权利与责任的学科).

□ ˌ**civic ˈcentre** (*Brit*) area in which the public buildings of a town (eg the town hall, library, etc) are grouped together 市中心(城市公共建筑, 如市政厅、图书馆等集中的地区).

civ·ies = CIVVIES.

civil /ˈsɪvl; ˋsɪvḷ/ *adj* **1** of or relating to the citizens of a country 公民的; 民间的; 国内的: *civil disorder*, eg rioting 民间的动乱 ○ *civil strife*, eg fighting between different political or religious groups within a country 内乱. **2** of or relating to ordinary citizens rather than the armed forces or the Church 普通公民的(非军队的或教会的); 文职的; 文官的: *civil government* 文官政府. **3** polite and helpful 礼貌的; 助人的; 文明的: *How very civil of you!* 你多么彬彬有礼呀! ○ *Keep a civil tongue in your head!* ie Don't speak rudely! 说话要文明有礼! **4** involving civil law rather than criminal law 民法的(非刑法的): *civil cases* 民事案件 ○ *a civil court* 民事诉讼法庭. Cf 参看 CRIMINAL 2 (CRIME).

▷ **ci·vil·ity** /sɪˈvɪlətɪ; səˋvɪlətɪ/ *n* [C, U] (*fml* 文) (act of) politeness 礼貌; 客气: *You should show more civility to your host.* 你是客人, 应该对主人有礼貌.

civ·illy /ˈsɪvəlɪ; ˋsɪvḷɪ/ *adv* politely 有礼貌地.

□ ˌ**civil deˈfence** organizing of civilians to protect people and property during air raids or other enemy attacks in wartime 民防.

ˌ**civil disoˈbedience** refusal to obey certain laws, pay taxes, etc, as a peaceful means of (esp political) protest (人民针对政府的)非暴力反抗: *a campaign of civil disobedience* 非暴力反抗运动.

ˌ**civil engiˈneering** design and building of roads, railways, bridges, canals, etc 土木工程. ˌ**civil engiˈneer** 土木工程师.

ˌ**civil ˈlaw** law dealing with the private rights of citizens, rather than with crime 民法.

ˌ**civil ˈliberty** individual's freedom of action, limited only by laws designed to protect the community 公民自由.

ˈ**civil list** (*Brit*) allowance of money made by Parliament for the household expenses of the Royal Family 王室年俸.

ˌ**civil ˈmarriage** marriage which does not involve a religious ceremony but is recognized by law 公证结婚(未经宗教仪式但为法律承认的婚姻).

ˌ**civil ˈrights** rights of each citizen to freedom and equality (eg in voting and employment) regardless of sex, race or religion 公民权. ˌ**civil ˈrights movement** organized movement aiming to establish full civil rights for a particular group of citizens, eg for Blacks in the USA 民权运动.

ˌ**civil ˈservant** person employed by the Civil Service (政府中的)公务员, 文职人员, 文官.

the ˌCivil ˈService (**a**) [sing] all government departments other than the armed forces (政府中的)文职部门, 行政机关: *She works in the Civil Service*, eg in the Home Office. 她在政府行政机关中工作(如在内政部). (**b**) [Gp] all the people employed in these (政府文职部门中的)全体公务员: *The Civil Service is/are threatening to strike.* 政府行政部门的全体公务员威胁要举行罢工.

ˌ**civil ˈwar** war between groups of citizens of the same country 内战: *the Spanish Civil War* 西班牙内战.

ci·vil·ian /sɪˈvɪlɪən; səˋvɪljən/ *n* person not serving in the armed forces or the police force 平民, 百姓(不在军队或警察部队中服役的人): *Two soldiers and one civilian were killed in the explosion.* 在爆炸中有两个士兵和一个平民被炸死. ○ [attrib 作定语] *He left the army and returned to civilian life.* 他退伍后恢复平民生活.

ci·vil·iza·tion, -isation /ˌsɪvəlaɪˈzeɪʃn; *US* -əlɪˈz-; ˌsɪvḷəˋzeʃən/ *n* **1** [U] becoming or making sb civilized 开化; 教化: *The civilization of mankind has taken thousands of years.* 人类经数千年才文明开化. **2** (**a**) [U] (esp advanced) state of human social development (尤指高级的)文明, 文明阶段. (**b**) [C] culture and way of life of a people, nation or period regarded as a stage in the development of organized society (一民族、国家或时期的)文化和生活方式: *the civilizations of ancient Egypt and Babylon* 古埃及和巴比伦文化. **3** [U] civilized conditions or society 文明的环境; 文明社会; 文明世界: *live far from civilization*, ie far from a large town or city 在远离文明世界的地方生活(远离大城市) ○ (*joc* 谑) *It's good to get back to civilization after living in a tent for two weeks!* 在帐篷里过了两个星期后, 又回到文明社会可真舒服!

civ·il·ize, -ise /ˈsɪvəlaɪz; ˋsɪvḷˌaɪz/ *v* [Tn] **1** cause (sb/sth) to improve from a primitive stage of human society to a more developed one 使(某人[某物])开化, 文明: *civilize a jungle tribe* 使丛林部族开化. **2** improve the behaviour or manners of (sb); refine 改善(某人)的举止行为; 教化: *His wife has had a civilizing influence on him.* 他妻子对改进他言谈举止有潜移默化的影响.

▷ **civ·il·ized, -ised** /ˈsɪvəlaɪzd; ˋsɪvḷˌaɪzd/ *adj* polite; refined 有礼貌的; 文雅的: *civilized society, behaviour* 有礼貌的社会、行为.

civ·vies (also **civ·ies**) /ˈsɪvɪz; ˋsɪvɪz/ *n* [pl] (*dated Brit sl* 旧, 俚) clothes worn by civilians, ie not military uniform 便服(平民穿的衣服, 即非军服).

Civvy Street /ˈsɪvɪ striːt; ˋsɪvɪ ˋstrit/ (*dated Brit sl* 旧, 俚) civilian life 平民生活.

cl *abbr* 缩写 = **1** (*pl* unchanged or **cls** 复数或不变或作 **cls**) centilitre: *75 cl* 75 厘升. **2** class: *two 2nd cl tickets* 两张二等票.

clack /klæk; klæk/ *n* short sharp sound (as) of hard objects being struck together (硬物相碰的)短促而尖锐的声响: *the clack of high heels on a stone floor* 高跟鞋在石地上的咔咔声 ○ *the clack of knitting needles, a typewriter* 织针、打字机的啪嗒声.

▷ **clack** *v* [I, Tn] (cause sth to) make this sound (使某

物)作咯哒声: (*fig* 比喻) *Pay no attention to clacking tongues*, ie to people gossiping. 不理会叽叽喳喳的饶舌.

clad /klæd; klæd/ *adj* **1** (used after an *adv*, with *in* and a noun, or in compounds 用于副词后, 与 in 及名词连用或用于复合词) (*dated or fml* 旧或文) dressed; clothed 穿衣的: *warmly, scantily clad* 穿着暖暖的、单薄的 ○ *motor-cyclists clad in leather/leather-clad motor-cyclists* 穿皮衣的摩托车手. **2** (in compounds 用以构成复合词) (*fml* 文) covered 覆盖的: *an ivy-clad tower* 爬满常春藤的塔 ○ *iron-clad battleships* 装甲战列舰.

clad·ding /ˈklædɪŋ; ˋklædɪŋ/ *n* [U] protective covering applied to the surface of a material or the outside walls of a building 覆面(施加于材料表面或建筑物外壁的保护层).

C

claim[1] /kleɪm; klem/ *v* **1** (**a**) [Tn] demand or request (sth) because it is or one believes it is one's right or one's property 要求或索要(某事物)(因是应得的权利或财物): *claim diplomatic immunity, the protection of the law, etc* 要求外交豁免、法律保护等 ○ *After the Duke's death, his eldest son claimed the title.* 公爵死后, 其长子要求继承爵位. ○ *She claims ownership* (ie says she is the rightful owner) *of the land.* 她对这块土地的产权提出要求(称她是合法所有人). ○ *claim an item of lost property* 认领丢失的财物 ○ (*fig* 比喻) *Gardening claims* (ie takes up) *much of my time in the summer.* 夏天, 园艺工作需要(占去)我大量时间. (**b**) [I, Ipr, Tn] **~ (for sth)** demand (money) under an insurance policy, as compensation, etc 凭保险单要求赔偿(款项); 索赔: *Have you claimed (the insurance) yet?* 你索取(保险金)了吗? ○ *You can always claim on the insurance.* 反正出了事可按保险索赔. ○ *claim for damages* 要求损害赔偿金. **2** [Tn, Tf, Tt] state or declare (sth) as a fact (without being able to prove it); assert 声称; 宣称; 断言: *claim knowledge* (ie to have knowledge) *of sth* 自称知道某事 ○ *After the battle both sides claimed victory.* 战斗结束后, 双方均宣称获胜. ○ *She claims (that) she is related to the Queen/claims to be related to the Queen.* 她声称和女王有亲属关系. **3** [Tn] (of things) need (sth); deserve (指事物)需要, 值得: *important matters claiming one's attention* 值得注意的重要事情. **4** [Tn] (of a disaster, an accident, etc) cause the loss or death of (sb) (指灾难、事故等)使(某人)失踪或死亡: *The earthquake claimed thousands of lives/victims.* 地震夺去数以千计的[人]罹难者的生命. **5** (phr v) **claim sth back** ask for sth to be returned 要回某物; 索回: *You can claim your money back if the goods are damaged.* 货物有损坏, 可以要求退钱.

claim[2] /kleɪm; klem/ *n* **1** [C] (**a**) **~ (for sth)** demand for a sum of money (as insurance, compensation, a wage increase, etc) 索款(作为保险金、赔偿、增薪等): *put in/make a claim for damages, a pay rise, etc* 提出损害赔偿、增薪等要求. (**b**) sum of money demanded 索要的金额: *That's a very large claim!* 索要的是一大笔钱! **2** [C, U] **~ (to sth)**; **~ (on sb/sth)** right to sth 对某事物的权利: *His claim to ownership is invalid.* 他的所有权是无效的. ○ *a claim to the throne* 对获得王位的权利 ○ *You have no claim on* (ie no right to ask for) *my sympathy.* 你没有要我同情的权利. ○ *His only claim to fame* (ie The only remarkable thing about him) *is that he once met Stalin.* 他唯一出风头的事是他与斯大林有一面之缘. **3** [C] statement of sth as a fact; assertion 称某事为事实的陈述; 声称; 断言: *Nobody believed his claim that he was innocent/to be innocent.* 他说他清白, 谁也不相信. **4** [C] thing claimed, esp a piece of land 索要之物(尤指土地). **5** (idm 习语) **lay claim to sth** (**a**) state that one has a right to sth 声称对某事物有权利: *lay claim to an inheritance, an estate, a property, etc* 声称对遗产、产业、财产等有权利. (**b**) (usu negative 通常作否定) state that one has knowledge, understanding, a skill, etc 自称有知识、智力、技能等: *I lay no claim to being an expert economist.* 我决不自命为经济学专家. **stake a/one's claim** ⇨ STAKE.

▷ **claim·ant** /ˈkleɪmənt; ˋklemənt/ *n* person who makes a claim[2](1a), esp in law 索偿者(尤指在法律上).

clair·voy·ance /kleəˈvɔɪəns; klɛrˋvɔɪəns/ *n* [U] supposed power of seeing in the mind either future events or things that exist or are happening out of sight (超人的)视力, 洞察力.

▷ **clair·voy·ant** /kleəˈvɔɪənt; klɛrˋvɔɪənt/ *n, adj* (person) having such power 有超人视力的(人); 有洞察力的(人).

clam /klæm; klæm/ *n* large shellfish with a hinged shell 蛤; 蛤蜊; 蚌.

▷ **clam** *v* (**-mm-**) **1** [I] (*US*) (usu 通常作 **go clamming**) dig for clams (on a beach) (在沙滩上)挖蛤. **2** (phr v) **clam up** (*infml* 口) become silent; refuse to speak 沉默不语; 拒不说话: *He always clammed up when we asked him about his family.* 我们一问到他的家庭时, 他总是闭口不言.

□ ˈ**clambake** *n* (*US*) picnic on the sea-shore at which clams and other seafood are cooked and eaten 烤蚌野餐(在海滨以蛤和其他海味为主的野餐).

clam·ber /ˈklæmbə(r); ˋklæmbɚ/ *v* [I, Ipr, Ip] climb, esp with difficulty or effort, using the hands and feet 攀爬, 攀登(尤指艰难地或费力地): *The children clambered over the rocks.* 孩子们吃力地爬过了岩石.

▷ **clam·ber** *n* (esp *sing* 尤作单数) difficult or awkward climb 困难的或麻烦的攀登.

clammy /ˈklæmɪ; ˋklæmɪ/ *adj* (**-ier, -iest**) unpleasantly moist and sticky; damp 又潮又黏的; 潮湿的: *clammy hands* 又湿又黏的手 ○ *a face clammy with sweat* 汗涔涔的脸 ○ *clammy* (ie close or humid) *weather* 潮湿的天气.

▷ **clam·mily** *adv.* **clam·mi·ness** *n* [U].

clam·our (*US* **clamor**) /ˈklæmə(r); ˋklæmɚ/ *n* [C, U] **1** loud confused noise, esp of shouting 喧哗声(尤指喊叫声); 喧闹; 吵闹. **2 ~ (for/against sth)** loud demand or protest 大声的要求或抗议: *a clamour for revenge* 复仇的喊声.

▷ **clam·our** (*US* **clamor**) *v* **1** [I] make a clamour(1) 喧哗; 吵闹. **2** [Ipr, It] **~ for/against sth** make a loud demand or protest 大声地要求或抗议: *The public are clamouring for a change of government.* 公众大声疾呼要求撤换政府. ○ *The baby clamoured to be fed.* 婴儿饿得大声哭叫.

clam·or·ous /ˈklæmərəs; ˋklæmərəs/ *adj* (*fml* 文) making loud demands or protests 大声要求的; 大声抗议的.

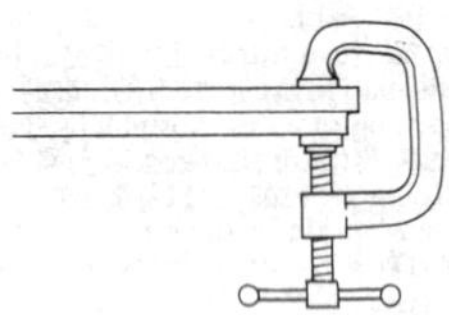

clamp /klæmp; klæmp/ *n* **1** (also **cramp**) device for holding things tightly together, usu by means of a screw 夹具; 夹钳. **2** piece of wood, metal, etc used for strengthening other materials or fastening things together 夹板; 压板. ⇨illus 见插图

▷ **clamp** *v* **1** [Tn] grip or hold (sth) (as if) with a clamp (像)用夹具夹住(某物): *He kept his pipe clamped between his teeth.* 他一直叼着烟斗. **2** [Tn, Tn·pr] **~ A and B (together)**; **~ A to B** fasten (one thing to another) with a clamp 用夹具将(一物与另一物)夹紧, 固定住: *clamp two boards together* 把两块板夹在一起. **3** (phr v) **clamp down on sb/sth** (*infml* 口) become stricter about sth; use one's authority against sb or to prevent or suppress sth 对某事更严格; 利用权势反对某人或防止或压制某事: *The Government intends to clamp down on soccer hooliganism.* 政府拟采取措施严禁在足球比赛中闹事.

□ ˈ**clamp-down** *n* sudden policy of increased strictness in preventing or suppressing sth (为防止或压制某事而突然采取的)严格的政策.

clan /klæn; klæn/ *n* [CGp] **1** group of families, esp in Scotland, descended from a common ancestor 宗族; 家族; (尤指苏格兰的)氏族: *the ˈCampbell clan/the clan ˈCampbell* 坎贝尔氏族. **2** (*infml* 口) large family forming a close group 大家族; 大家庭. **3** group of people closely connected by similar aims, interests, etc; coterie 集团; 帮会; 宗派.

▷ **clan·nish** *adj* (*often derog* 常作贬义) (of members of a group) associating closely with each other and

showing little interest in other people（指集团的成员）抱成一团的. **clan·nishly** *adv*. **clan·nish·ness** *n* [U].
□ **'clansman** /-mən; -mən/ *n* (*pl* **-men**) /-mən; -mən/ (*fem* 阴性作 **'clanswoman, -women**) member of a clan 宗族、家族、氏族或集团等的成员.

clan·des·tine /klæn'destɪn; klæn`dɛstɪn/ *adj* (*fml* 文) done secretly; kept secret; surreptitious 秘密的; 保密的; 暗中的: *a clan,destine 'marriage* 秘密结婚.

clang /klæŋ; klæŋ/ *n* loud ringing sound (as) of metal being struck（金属敲击的）铿锵声, 叮当声: *the clang of the school bell* 校铃的叮当声.
▷ **clang** *v* [I, Tn] (cause sth to) make this sound（使某物）发出哐啷声: *The prison gates clanged shut.* 监狱的大门哐啷一声关上了.

clanger /'klæŋə(r); `klæŋɚ/ *n* (*Brit infml* 口) **1** obvious and embarrassing mistake; gaffe（明显而使人难为情的）错误; 出丑. **2** (idm 习语) **drop a brick/clanger** ⇨ DROP[2].

clang·our (*US* **clangor**) /'klæŋə(r), 'klæŋgə(r); `klæŋɚ/ *n* [U] continued clanging noise; series of clangs 连续的铿锵声; 一连串的叮当声. ▷ **clan·gor·ous** /'klæŋərəs, 'klæŋgərəs; `klæŋərəs/ *adj*.

clank /klæŋk; klæŋk/ *n* dull metallic sound (as) of chains striking together（如铁链撞击在一起的）低沉的金属声, 叮当声.
▷ **clank** *v* [I, Tn] (cause sth to) make this sound（使某物）发出叮当声: *The chains clanked as the drawbridge opened.* 吊桥放下时, 铁链发出叮当声.

clap[1] /klæp; klæp/ *v* (**-pp-**) **1** (**a**) [Tn, Tn·p] **~ sth (together)** strike (the palms of one's hands) together 拍(手); 鼓(掌): *She clapped her hands in delight.* 她高兴地拍起手来. ○ *They clapped their hands in time to the music.* 他们随着音乐的节拍鼓起掌来. (**b**) [I, Tn] do this continually to show approval of (sb/sth); applaud 不断鼓掌以示赞许（某人[某事物]）; 鼓掌欢迎: *The audience clapped (her/her speech) enthusiastically.* 听众热情地（为她[为她的讲话]）鼓起掌来. **2** [Tn·pr] **~ sb on sth** strike or slap sb lightly with an open hand, usu in a friendly way（用手掌）轻轻拍打某人(通常为友好地): *clap sb on the back* 轻拍某人的背. **3** (idm 习语) **clap/lay/set eyes on sb/sth** ⇨ EYE[1]. **clap hold of sb/sth** (*infml* 口) seize sb/sth suddenly or with force 突然或用力抓住某人[某物]: *Here, clap hold of this!* 喂, 抓住这个! **clap sb in/into jail, prison, etc** (*infml* 口) put sb in prison quickly (often without a trial) 迅速将某人关进监狱(常未经审讯). **4** (phr v) **clap sth on (sth)** (*infml* 口) add sth to the price of sth, esp in an unwelcome way 涨价, 提价(尤指不得人心的): *The Government has clapped an extra ten pence on a packet of cigarettes.* 政府对每包香烟额外提价十便士. **(be) clapped out** (*Brit infml* 口) (of people or things) completely worn out or exhausted（指人）筋疲力尽; (指物)破烂不堪: *a clapped-out old bicycle* 破烂不堪的旧自行车.
▷ **clap** *n* **1** [sing] act or sound of clapping (CLAP[1] 1a) 鼓掌; 掌声: *Let's give her a big clap*, ie applaud her. 咱们给她用力鼓掌. **2** [C] **~ on sth** friendly slap 善意的拍打: *give sb a clap on the back* 在某人背上拍一下. **3** [C] sudden loud noise 突然的巨响: *a clap of thunder* 雷鸣.

clap[2] /klæp; klæp/ (also **the clap**) *n* [U] (*sl* 俚) venereal disease, esp gonorrhoea 花柳病; (尤指)淋病.

clap·board /'klæpbɔ:d; *US* 'klæbɔ:rd; `klæbɚd/ (*US*) = WEATHER-BOARD (WEATHER[1]).

clap·per /'klæpə(r); `klæpɚ/ *n* **1** piece of metal, etc fixed loosely inside a bell and making it sound by striking the side（钟铃的）击锤; 钟舌; 铃舌. ⇨illus at BELL 见 BELL 之插图. **2** (idm 习语) **like the 'clappers** (*Brit infml* 口) very fast or hard; vigorously 很快; 很用力; 强有力地: *go, run, work, etc like the clappers* 一个劲儿地走、跑、工作等.
□ **'clapper-board** *n* (in film-making) pair of hinged boards brought together sharply to help in synchronizing the sound and the picture at the start of filming（拍电影时用的）拍板, 场记板.

clap·trap /'klæptræp; `klæp,træp/ *n* [U] worthless, insincere or pretentious talk; nonsense 无价值的、不诚恳的或虚伪的话; 废话: *What a load of claptrap!* 废话真多!

claret /'klærət; `klærət/ *n* (**a**) [C, U] (any of various types of) dry red wine, esp from the Bordeaux area of France 干红葡萄酒(尤指法国波尔多地区产的): *I prefer Burgundy to claret.* 我喜欢勃艮第葡萄酒, 不喜欢波尔多产的葡萄酒. (**b**) [U] colour of this 深红色(此种酒的颜色). Cf 参看 BORDEAUX.
▷ **claret** *adj* dark red 深红色的.

cla·rify /'klærɪfaɪ; `klærə,faɪ/ *v* (*pt, pp* **-fied**) **1** [I, Tn] (cause sth to) become clear or easier to understand（使某事物）清楚易懂; 澄清: *clarify a remark, statement* 澄清一项意见、声明 ○ *I hope that what I say will clarify the situation.* 我希望我说的话能澄清这一情况. **2** [Tn] remove impurities from (fats), eg by heating 除去(油脂)中的杂质(如用加热法): *clarified butter* 已除去杂质的黄油.
▷ **cla·ri·fica·tion** /,klærɪfɪ'keɪʃn; ,klærəfə`keʃən/ *n* [U] clarifying or being clarified 澄清; 被澄清: *The whole issue needs clarification.* 整个问题都需要澄清.

cla·ri·net /,klærə'net; ,klærə`nɛt/ *n* musical instrument of the woodwind group with finger-holes and keys 单簧管; 竖笛. ⇨illus at App 1 见附录1之插图, page x.
▷ **cla·ri·net·tist** (also **cla·ri·net·ist**) *n* person who plays the clarinet 单簧管或竖笛吹奏者.

clar·ion /'klærɪən; `klærɪən/ *adj* [attrib 作定语] loud, clear and rousing 响亮、清澈而又有激励作用的: *a clarion call to action* 激励人行动起来的鲜明口号.

clar·ity /'klærətɪ; `klærətɪ/ *n* [U] clearness; lucidity 清楚; 明晰; 清澈: *clarity of expression, thinking, vision* 表达、思维、视觉清楚.

clash[1] /klæʃ; klæʃ/ *v* **1** [I, Ip, Tn, Tn·p] **~ (sth and sth) (together)** (cause things to) strike together with a loud, harsh noise（使）发出巨大刺耳的撞击声: *Their swords clashed.* 他们的剑互相撞击, 铿锵有声. ○ *She clashed the cymbals together.* 她敲铙钹. **2** [I, Ipr] (**a**) **~ (with sb)** come together and fight 冲突; 交战: *The two armies clashed.* 两军交战. ○ *Demonstrators clashed with police.* 示威者与警察发生冲突. (**b**) **~ (with sb) (on/over sth)** disagree seriously (about sth)（对某事）重大分歧: *The Government clashed with the Opposition/The Government and the Opposition clashed on the question of unemployment.* 政府与反对党在失业问题上有重大分歧. **3** [I, Ipr] **~ (with sth)** happen inconveniently at the same time (as sth else)（与另一事）时间上冲突: *It's a pity the two concerts clash; I wanted to go to both of them.* 真可惜两个音乐会时间上有冲突, 我本来想两个都去. ○ *Your party clashes with a wedding I'm going to.* 你们的聚会和我要去参加的婚礼时间上有冲突. **4** [I, Ipr] **~ (with sth)** (of colours, designs, etc) not match or harmonize（指颜色、花样等）不相配, 不和谐: *The (colour of the) wallpaper clashes with the (colour of the) carpet/The wallpaper and the carpet clash.* 壁纸(的颜色)和地毯(的颜色)不和谐.

clash[2] /klæʃ; klæʃ/ *n* **1** clashing noise 碰撞声; 撞击声: *a clash of cymbals, swords* 铙钹、剑的撞击声. **2** (**a**) **~ (with sb/sth); ~ (between A and B)** violent contact; fight 激烈的冲突; 打斗: *clashes between police and demonstrators* 警察与示威者间的冲突. (**b**) **~ (with sb/sth) (on/over sth); ~ (between sb and sb) (on/over sth)** serious disagreement; argument 重大的分歧; 争论: *a clash between the Prime Minister and the leader of the Opposition on defence spending* 首相与反对党领袖在国防开支上的争论. (**c**) serious difference; conflict 极大的区别; 冲突: *a clash of interests, personalities, cultures, opinions* 利益、个性、文化、意见的巨大的差别. **3 ~ (between A and B)** coinciding of events or dates 事情或日期的冲突: *a clash between two classes* 两堂课在时间上的冲突. **4** failure of colours, designs, etc to match or harmonize（颜色、花样等的）不相配或不和谐.

clasp[1] /klɑ:sp; *US* klæsp; klæsp/ *n* **1** device for fastening things (eg the ends of a belt or a necklace) together 钩子, 扣子, 扣环(如腰带或项链的两端): *The clasp of my brooch is broken.* 我胸针的钩子坏了. **2** (**a**) firm hold with the hand; grasp; grip 紧握; 抓; 攥: *He held her hand in a firm clasp.* 他紧紧握着她的手. (**b**) embrace 拥抱.
□ **'clasp-knife** *n* folding knife with a catch for holding the blade open 弹簧折刀.

clasp[2] /klɑ:sp; *US* klæsp; klæsp/ *v* **1** (**a**) [Tn, Tn·p] hold (sb/sth) tightly in the hand 握紧（某人[某物]）; 紧握; 攥: *She was clasping a knife.* 她攥着一把刀. ○ *They* *clasped hands* (ie held each other's hands) *briefly before saying goodbye.* 他们匆匆握手告别. ○ *His hands were clasped (together) in prayer.* 他祈祷时双手十指交叉(在一起)握着. (**b**) [Tn, Tn·pr] hold (sb) tightly with the arms; embrace 抱紧(某人); 拥抱: *He clasped her to his chest.* 他把她紧紧地抱在怀里. ○ *They stood clasped in each other's arms.* 他们站着相互拥抱. **2** [I, Tn, Tn·pr] be fastened or fasten (sth) with a clasp[1](1) 被扣紧; 被钩紧: *clasp a bracelet round one's wrist* 将手镯戴在手腕上.

class /klɑːs; *US* klæs; klæs/ *n* **1** (**a**) [CGp] group of people at the same social or economic level 阶级; 阶层; 社会等级: *the working/middle/upper class* 工人阶级[中产阶级/上层社会] ○ *the professional class(es)* 专业阶层. (**b**) [U] system that divides people into such groups 阶级制度: [attrib 作定语] *class differences, distinctions, divisions, etc* 阶级差别、界限、划分. **2** (**a**) [CGp] group of students taught together 班级: *We were in the same class at school.* 我们上学时在同一班. ○ *Form 4 is/are a difficult class to teach.* 四年级很难教. (**b**) [C] occasion when this group meets to be taught; lesson 上课; 课: *I have a maths class at 9 o'clock.* 我9点钟有数学课. (**c**) [CGp] (*US*) group of students who finish their studies at school or university in a particular year (毕业生的)同届: *the class of '82* 1982年届. **3** [C] set of people, animals or things grouped together, esp according to quality 级, 等, 等级, 种类(尤指按质量划分的): *As an actress Jane is not in the same class as* (ie is not as good as) *Susan.* 作为演员, 简不如苏珊. ○ [attrib 作定语] *a top-class athlete* 一流运动员. **4** [U] (*infml* 口) high quality; excellence; distinction 高质量; 优秀; 优异: *She's got (a lot of) class.* 她(实在)很有气质. ○ [attrib 作定语] *a class (tennis) player* 优秀(网球)运动员. **5** [C] (esp in compounds 尤用以构成复合词) one of several different levels of comfort, etc available to travellers in a train, plane, bus, etc (火车、飞机、公共汽车等的)等级: *first class* ○ *tourist class* ○ [attrib 作定语] *a second-class compartment*, eg on a train. **6** [C] (*Brit*) (esp in compounds 尤用以构成复合词) one of several grades of achievement in a university degree examination (大学学位考试成绩的)等级: *a first-/second-/third-class (honours) degree*. **7** [C] (*biology* 生) second highest group into which animals and plants are divided, below a phylum and including several orders (ORDER[1] 9) (动植物分类的)纲. Cf 参看 FAMILY 4, GENUS 1, SPECIES. 1. **8** (idm 习语) **in a class of one's/its 'own; in a class by one'self/it'self** better than everyone/anything else of his/its kind; unequalled 独一无二; 无以伦比: *Pele was in a class of his own as a footballer.* 贝利是举世无双的足球健将.

▷ **class** *v* [Tn, Cn·n/a] **~ sb/sth (as sth)** place sb/sth in a class(1b); classify sb/sth 将某人[某事物]归入某类; 把…分类: *Immigrant workers were classed as resident aliens.* 移民来的工人已归入外侨类.

class·less *adj* **1** not clearly belonging to any particular social class 不明显属于某一阶级或阶层的: *a classless accent* 无任何阶层特征的口音. **2** without social classes 无阶级的: *a classless society* 无阶级的社会.

classy /ˈklɑːsɪ; *US* ˈklæsɪ; ˈklæsɪ/ *adj* (**-ier**, **-iest**) (*infml* 口) of high quality; stylish; superior 高质量的; 时髦的; 优等的: *a classy hotel* 高级旅馆.

□ **'class-conscious** *adj* aware of belonging to a particular social class or of the differences between social classes 意识到属于某阶级的; 有阶级意识的. **'class-consciousness** *n* [U].

'class-feeling *n* [U] feelings of hostility between social classes 阶级意识(阶级间的敌意).

'class-list *n* (*Brit*) list showing the class of degree achieved by university students in their final examinations (大学生最后考试的)学位成绩名单.

'class-mate *n* person who was or is in the same class as oneself at school 同班同学: *We were class-mates at primary school.* 我们在小学是同班同学.

'class-room *n* room where a class of pupils or students is taught 教室.

the 'class struggle (also **the 'class war**) (esp in Marxist thought) the continuing fight for economic and political power between the capitalist ruling class and the working class (尤指马克思主义思想的)阶级斗争.

clas·sic[1] /ˈklæsɪk; ˋklæsɪk/ *adj* [esp attrib 尤作定语] **1** having a high quality that is recognized and unquestioned; of lasting value and importance 最优秀的; 第一流的; 经典的: *a classic novel, work of scholarship, game of football* 最佳的小说、学术著作、足球赛. **2** very typical 典型的: *a classic example* 典型的例子 ○ *classic symptoms of pneumonia* 肺炎的典型症状 ○ *a classic case of malnutrition* 营养不良的典型病例. **3** (**a**) simple, harmonious and restrained; classical(3) 典雅的; 古雅的. (**b**) (of clothes, designs, etc) having a simple traditional style that is not affected by changes in fashion (指衣服、设计等)传统式样的: *a classic dress* 传统的连衣裙. **4** famous through being long established (因为时已久)著名的; 传统的: *one of the classic events of the sporting calendar* 体育运动日程表中传统比赛项目之一.

clas·sic[2] /ˈklæsɪk; ˋklæsɪk/ *n* **1** [C] writer, artist or work of art recognized as being of high quality and lasting value 文豪; 大艺术家; 杰作; 名著; 经典著作: *This novel may well become a classic.* 这本小说很可能成为经典著作. ○ *She enjoys reading the classics*, ie the great works of literature. 她喜欢读经典著作. **2** [C] outstanding example of its kind 优秀的典范: *The (football) match was a classic.* 那场(足球)比赛堪称典范. **3 Classics** [sing *v*] (study of) ancient Greek and Roman language and literature 古代希腊与罗马的语言和文学(的研究): *She studied Classics at university.* 她在大学学习古希腊与古罗马的语言文学. **4** [C] garment that is classic[1](3b) in style 传统样式的服装.

clas·sical /ˈklæsɪkl; ˋklæsɪkl/ *adj* [esp attrib 尤作定语] **1** of, relating to or influenced by the art and literature of ancient Greece and Rome 古希腊与古罗马文学艺术的; 受古希腊与古罗马文学艺术影响的: *classical studies* 古希腊与古罗马文学艺术的研究 ○ *a classical scholar*, ie an expert in Latin and Greek 研究古希腊与古罗马文学艺术的学者(拉丁文与希腊文专家) ○ *a classical education*, ie one based on the study of Latin and Greek 以学习拉丁文与希腊文为基础的教育 ○ *classical architecture* 古希腊与古罗马式的建筑风格. **2** (**a**) (of music) serious and traditional in style (指音乐)古典的(风格严谨而传统的): *the classical music of India* 印度的古典音乐. Cf 参看 POP[3]. (**b**) (of music) (characteristic) of the period 1750-1800 (指音乐)表现1750-1800年时期(特征)的; 古典派的: *classical composers such as Mozart and Haydn* 古典派的作曲家如莫札特和海顿 ○ *the classical symphony* 古典派的交响乐. **3** simple, restrained and harmonious in style 风格朴实、严谨及和谐的: *a classical elegance* 典雅. ▷ **clas·sic·ally** /ˈklæsɪkəlɪ; ˋklæsɪklɪ/ *adv*.

clas·si·cism /ˈklæsɪsɪzəm; ˋklæsəˌsɪzəm/ *n* [U] **1** (following of the) style and principles of classical(1) art and literature (遵循)古典主义, 古典文学艺术的风格与原则. Cf 参看 IDEALISM 2, REALISM 2, ROMANTICISM (ROMANTIC). **2** simplicity and regularity of style or form (风格或形式的)朴素和正规.

▷ **clas·si·cist** /ˈklæsɪsɪst; ˋklæsəsɪst/ *n* **1** person who follows classicism in art or literature 古典主义者. **2** expert in or student of ancient Greek or Latin 古希腊文或拉丁文的专家或学者.

clas·si·fica·tion /ˌklæsɪfɪˈkeɪʃn; ˌklæsəfəˋkeʃən/ *n* **1** [U] classifying or being classified 分类; 分级. **2** [C] group or class into which sth is put (某事物所归入的)类别, 种类, 门类. **3** [U] (*biology* 生) placing of animals and plants into groups according to similarities of structure, origin, etc (动植物的)分类(法). **4** [C] (in libraries, etc) system of grouping books, magazines, etc according to their subject (图书馆等中的)编目.

clas·sify /ˈklæsɪfaɪ; ˋklæsəˌfaɪ/ *v* (*pt, pp* **-fied**) **1** (**a**) [Tn] arrange (sth) systematically in classes or groups 将(某事物)编排, 分类: *The books in the library are classified by/according to subject.* 图书馆的书是按照[根据]科目分类的. (**b**) [Tn, Cn·n/a] **~ sb/sth (as sth)** place sb/sth in a particular class(3) 将某人[某事物]归类: *Would you classify her novels as serious literature or as mere entertainment?* 你认为她的小说属于文学类呢, 还是属于通俗读物类? **2** [Tn] declare (information, documents, etc) to be officially secret and available only to certain people 将(资料、文件等)定为官方密件而仅供某些人使用.

▷ **clas·si·fi·able** /ˈklæsɪfaɪəbl; ˋklæsəˌfaɪəbl/ *adj* that can be classified 可分类的.

clas·si·fied *adj* [usu attrib 通常作定语] **1** arranged in groups 分类的: *a classified directory*, ie one in which the names of firms, etc are entered under labelled headings, eg builders, electricians, plumbers 分类电话簿. **2** declared officially secret (by a government) and available only to certain people (由政府)定为机密而仅供某些人使用的: *classified information, documents* 机密情报、文件.

□ **ˌclassified adˈvertisements** (also **ˌclassified ˈads** /ædz; ædz/, *esp US* **ˈwant ads**) small advertisements placed in a newspaper, etc by people wishing to buy or sell sth, employ sb, find a job, etc 分类广告.

clat·ter /ˈklætə(r); ˈklætɚ/ *n* [sing] continuous noise (as) of hard objects falling or knocking against each other (硬物落下或相撞时发出的)连续撞击声: *the clatter of cutlery, horse's hoofs, a typewriter* 刀叉、马蹄、打字机的咔嗒声.

▷ **clat·ter** *v* **1** [I, Ipr, Tn] (cause sth to) make a clatter (使某物)发出连续咔嗒声: *Don't clatter your knives and forks.* 不要将刀叉相碰出声. **2** (phr v) **clatter across, down, in, etc** move across, etc, making a clatter 发出连续咔嗒声地跨过等: *The children clattered* (ie ran noisily) *downstairs.* 孩子们噔噔地跑下楼. ○ *The cart clattered over the cobble-stones.* 马车咔嗒咔嗒响着经过大卵石路.

clause /klɔːz; klɔz/ *n* **1** (*grammar*) group of words that includes a subject[1](4a) and a verb, forming a sentence or part of a sentence 从句; 分句; 子句: *The sentence 'He often visits Spain because he likes the climate' consists of a main clause and a subordinate clause.* He often visits Spain because he likes the climate 一句中有一个主句和一个从句. **2** paragraph or section in a legal document (eg a will, contract or treaty) stating a particular obligation, condition, etc (在法律文件如遗嘱、合同或条约中, 陈述具体义务、条件等的)段落或章节; 条款: *There is a clause in the contract forbidding tenants to sublet.* 合同中列有条款, 禁止承租人转租.

claus·tro·pho·bia /ˌklɔːstrəˈfəʊbɪə; ˌklɔstrəˈfobɪə/ *n* [U] abnormal fear of being in an enclosed space 幽闭恐怖(症).

▷ **claus·tro·pho·bic** /ˌklɔːstrəˈfəʊbɪk; ˌklɔstrəˈfobɪk/ *adj* suffering from or causing claustrophobia 患幽闭恐怖(症)的; 诱发幽闭恐怖(症)的: *feel claustrophobic* 感到幽闭恐怖 ○ *a claustrophobic little room* 使人感到幽闭恐怖的房间.

clavi·chord /ˈklævɪkɔːd; ˈklævəˌkɔrd/ *n* early type of keyboard instrument with a very soft tone 击弦键琴(钢琴的前身).

clav·icle /ˈklævɪkl; ˈklævəkḷ/ *n* (*anatomy* 解) collar-bone 锁骨. ⇨illus at SKELETON 见 SKELETON 之插图.

claw /klɔː; klɔ/ *n* **1** (**a**) any of the pointed nails (NAIL[1]) on the feet of some mammals, birds and reptiles 爪(某些哺乳类、鸟类和爬行类动物的尖利脚趾甲): *Cats have sharp claws.* 猫有尖爪. (**b**) (esp in birds) foot with claws (尤指鸟类)带爪的脚: *The eagle held a mouse in its claws.* 鹰用爪抓住了老鼠. **2** pincers of a shellfish (甲壳类动物的)钳, 螯: *a lobster's claw* 龙虾的螯. ⇨ illus at SHELLFISH 见 SHELLFISH 之插图. **3** mechanical device like a claw, used for gripping and lifting things 爪形器具(用以抓住或提起物件). **4** (idm 习语) **get one's claws into sb** (*infml* 口) (esp of a woman) attach oneself to (a partner) in a determined way (尤指女子)依附于伴侣: *She's really got her claws into him!* 她完全依靠他了!

▷ **claw** *v* **1** [Ipr, Tn] **~ (at) sb/sth** (try to) scratch or tear sb/sth with a claw or claws or with one's finger-nails (试图)用爪或指甲抓或撕某人[某物]; 搔; 挠; 刮: *The cats clawed at each other.* 猫用爪子互相抓. ○ *The prisoner clawed at the cell door in desperation.* 囚犯绝望地乱抓牢房的门. ○ *His face was badly clawed.* 他的脸给抓坏了. **2** (idm 习语) **claw one's way across, up, through, etc** move across, etc by using the claws or the hands 用爪或手爬行过去等: *They slowly clawed their way up the cliff.* 他们缓慢地爬上峭壁. **3** (phr v) **claw sth back** (of a government) recover, esp by taxation, money paid as an allowance to people who are not thought to need financial help (指政府)(尤指用税收)收回认为不需资助者的补助金.

□ **ˈclaw-back** *n* act of clawing sth back 收回补助金.

ˈclaw-hammer *n* hammer with one end of its head bent and divided for pulling out nails 羊角榔头; 拔钉锤. ⇨illus at HAMMER 见 HAMMER 之插图.

clay /kleɪ; kle/ *n* **1** [U] stiff sticky earth that becomes hard when baked, used for making bricks and pottery 黏土: [attrib 作定语] *clay soil* 黏质土壤 ○ *clay tiles* 陶土瓦. **2** (idm 习语) **have feet of clay** ⇨ FOOT[1].

▷ **clayey** /kleɪɪ; ˈkle·ɪ/ *adj* like, containing or covered with clay 像黏土的; 含有黏土的; 粘着黏土的.

□ **clay ˈpigeon** breakable disc thrown in the air as a target for shooting at 泥鸽靶(掷到空中作射击靶子的易碎圆盘): [attrib 作定语] *clay ˈpigeon shooting* 泥鸽靶射击.

clay ˈpipe tobacco pipe made of clay pottery 陶制烟斗.

clay·more /ˈkleɪmɔː(r); ˈklemɔr/ *n* large two-edged sword, formerly used by Scottish Highlanders (旧时苏格兰高地人用的)双刃大刀.

clean[1] /kliːn; klin/ *adj* (**-er, -est**) **1** (**a**) free from dirt or impurities 清洁的; 干净的; 无杂质的: *clean hands* 干净的手 ○ *clean air*, ie free from smoke, etc 清洁的空气 ○ *a clean wound*, ie one that is not infected 未感染的伤口 ○ *wash, wipe, scrub, brush, etc sth clean* 把某物洗、擦、擦洗、刷…干净. (**b**) that has been washed since it was last worn or used 洗过的: *a clean dress, towel, knife* 洗过的连衣裙、手巾、小刀 ○ *He wears clean socks every day.* 他每天穿新洗的袜子. ○ *put clean sheets on a bed* 把洗过的床单铺在床上. (**c**) having clean habits; caring about cleanliness 爱干净的; 讲究清洁的: *Cats are clean animals.* 猫很爱干净. **2** not yet used; unmarked 尚未用过的; 未作过标记的: *a clean sheet of paper* 一张白纸. **3** (**a**) not obscene or indecent 不猥亵的; 不下流的: *Keep it clean!* ie Don't tell dirty jokes! 嘴干净点! (别开下流玩笑!) (**b**) (*dated* 旧) good; innocent 好的; 无辜的; 清白的: *lead a clean life* 过清白的生活. (**c**) showing or having no record of offences 无过失记录的: *a clean driving-licence*, ie one with no endorsements 无违章记录的驾驶执照 ○ *She has a clean record.* 她无违法记录. (**d**) keeping to the rules; not unfair 遵守规则的; 公平的; 正当的; 不违例的: *a hard-fought but clean match* 激烈而规矩的比赛 ○ *a clean tackle*, eg in a game of football 正当的抢截(如在足球赛中). **4** having a simple and pleasing shape; well-formed 外形简洁美观的; 形状好的: *a car with clean lines* 美观的汽车. **5** with a smooth edge or surface; regular; even 边或面光滑的; 规则的; 均匀的; 整齐的: *A sharp knife makes a clean cut.* 快刀切得整齐. ○ *a clean break*, eg the breaking of a bone in one place 整齐的断裂处(如骨折于一处). **6** (esp in sport) skilfully and accurately done (尤指体育运动)动作纯熟准确的, 干净利落的: *a clean hit, stroke, blow, etc* 干净利落的击中目标、一击、一拳等. **7** (*infml* 口) (of a nuclear weapon) producing little radioactivity (指核武器)几乎无放射性尘埃的. **8** (idm 习语) **(as) clean as a new ˈpin** (*infml* 口) very clean and tidy 非常整洁. **(as) clean as a ˈwhistle** (*infml* 口) (**a**) very clean 非常清洁. (**b**) skilfully; deftly 熟练地; 灵巧地: *The dog jumped through the hoop as clean as a whistle*, ie without touching it. 狗灵巧地跳过钻圈(没有触到圈). **a clean bill of ˈhealth** report showing that one's health is good, esp after illness 健康状况良好的报告(尤指病后): *The doctor gave him a clean bill of health.* 医生给他一份健康良好的报告. **a clean ˈsheet/ˈslate** record of work or behaviour that does not show any wrongdoing in the past 过去工作或操行中无过错的记录: *He came out of prison hoping to start (life) again with a clean sheet*, ie with his previous offences forgotten. 他出狱后希望重新做人. **(make) a clean sweep (of sth)** (**a**) the removing of things or people that are thought to be unnecessary 去掉认为不必要的事物或人; 清除; 撤换: *The new manager made a clean sweep of the department.* 新经理清除了部门中的冗员. (**b**) victory in all of a group of similar or related competitions, games, etc (在所有有关竞争、比赛等中)大获全胜: *The Russians made a clean sweep of (the medals in) the gymnastics events.* 俄罗斯运动员囊括体操项目奖牌. **keep one's nose clean** ⇨ NOSE[1]. **make a clean break (with sth)** change one's previous manner of living entirely 完全改变以前的生活方式: *He's made a*

C

clean break with the past. 他完全改变了过去的生活方式. **make a clean breast of sth** make a full confession of sth 完全承认某事物: *He made a clean breast of his crime to the police.* 他向警方如实招供. **show a clean pair of heels** ⇨ SHOW². **wipe the slate clean** ⇨ WIPE.

▷ **clean** *adv* **1** completely; entirely 彻底地; 完全地; 全部地: *The bullet went clean through his shoulder.* 子弹穿透他的肩膀. ○ *The thief got clean away.* 窃贼逃得无影无踪. ○ *I clean forgot about it.* 我把它忘得一干二净. ○ *The batsman was clean bowled,* ie without the ball hitting the bat or the pads first. 击球员被迫出局(球未先击中球板或护胫). **2** (idm 习语) **come clean (with sb) (about sth)** (*infml* 口) make a full and honest confession 全盘招供; 和盘托出: *I've got to come 'clean (with you) — I was the one who broke the window.* 我(向你)说实话——窗户是我打破的.

C

□ ˌ**clean-'cut** *adj* (**a**) clearly outlined 轮廓清楚的: *ˌclean-cut 'features* 轮廓清楚的脸型. (**b**) (*approv* 褒) looking neat and respectable 外貌整洁体面的: *a ˌclean-cut 'student* 整洁体面的学生.

ˌ**clean-'limbed** *adj* (*approv* 褒) (esp of young people) having well-formed and slender limbs (尤指年轻人)体形优美四肢修长的.

ˌ**clean-'shaven** *adj* (of men) not having a moustache or a beard (指男子)胡须刮得干净的.

clean² /kli:n; klin/ *v* **1** (**a**) [Tn] make (sth) clean or free of dirt, etc 使(某物)清洁或无灰尘等: *clean the windows, one's shoes, one's teeth* 擦窗户、擦鞋、刷牙 ○ *I must have this suit cleaned,* ie at the dry-cleaner's. 我得把这套衣服送去干洗. ○ *The cat sat cleaning itself.* 猫坐着舔干净自己的身体. (**b**) [I] become clean 变干净: *This floor cleans easily,* ie is easy to clean. 这地面容易擦洗干净. **2** (phr v) **clean sth down** clean sth thoroughly by wiping or brushing it 擦净或刷净某物: *clean down the walls* 擦净墙壁. **clean sth from/off sth** remove sth from sth by brushing, scraping, wiping, etc 从某物上将他物刷掉、刮掉、擦掉等: *She cleaned the dirt from her finger-nails.* 她从指甲里剔掉污垢. **clean sth out** clean the inside of sth thoroughly 彻底将某物内部弄得干干净净: *clean out the stables* 彻底清扫马厩. **clean sb out (of sth)** (*infml* 口) use up or take all sb's money; take or buy all sb's stock 将某人所有的钱用完或取走; 将某人所有的存货取走或买走: *I haven't a penny left; buying drinks for everyone has cleaned me out completely.* 我一个便士都没有了, 给大家买饮料把我的钱全花光了. ○ *The burglars cleaned her out of all her jewellery.* 窃贼把她所有的首饰都偷走了. **clean (oneself) up** (*infml* 口) wash oneself 把身体洗干净: *My hands are filthy; I'd better go and clean (myself) up.* 我的手脏了, 最好去洗洗. **clean (sth) up** (**a**) remove (dirt, rubbish, etc) from a place to clean it; make (a place) clean by removing dirt, etc 除去(污物、垃圾等)把一地方打扫干净; 除去污物等使(一地方)干净: *The workmen cleaned up (the mess) before they left.* 工人们清理(杂物)后就走了. ○ *clean up (a room) after a party* 聚会后(把房间)打扫干净. (**b**) (*infml* 口) make or win (a lot of money) 挣得或赢得(很多钱): *He cleaned up a small fortune.* 他发了一笔小财. **clean sth up** remove criminals, harmful influences, etc from sth 从某事物中清除罪犯、有害影响等: *The mayor is determined to clean up the city.* 市长决心清除市内的不良现象. ○ *a campaign to clean up* (ie reduce the amount of sex and violence shown on) *television* 清除电视中不良现象的运动(减少播放色情和暴力的节目).

□ **'cleaning woman** woman employed to clean offices, a private house, etc 女清洁工.

'clean-up *n* (**a**) removal of dirt, etc from a person or place 清洗; 打扫. (**b**) removal of criminals, etc 清除罪犯等.

cleaner /'kli:nə(r); 'klinɚ/ *n* **1** (esp in compounds 尤用以构成复合词) person or thing that cleans 做清扫工作的人或物: *an 'office cleaner* 办公室清洁工 ○ *a 'floor cleaner,* ie a substance that removes grease, stains, etc from floors 地板除垢剂(从地板上清除油渍、污点之物). **2 cleaners** [pl] place where clothes and fabrics are cleaned, esp with chemicals 洗衣店: *send a suit to the cleaners* 把一套衣服送到洗衣店去. **3** (idm 习语) **take sb to the 'cleaners** (*infml* 口) (**a**) rob or cheat sb of his money 抢或骗某人的钱. (**b**) criticize sb harshly 粗暴地批评某人.

cleanly¹ /'kli:nlı; 'klinlı/ *adv* easily; smoothly 容易地; 光洁地: *Blunt scissors don't cut cleanly.* 钝剪刀剪不齐. ○ *catch a ball cleanly,* ie without fumbling 利落地接住球.

cleanly² /'klenlı; 'klɛnlı/ *adj* (**-ier, -iest**) habitually clean; having clean habits 习惯上清洁的; 有清洁习惯的: *Cats are cleanly animals.* 猫很爱清洁.

▷ **clean·li·ness** *n* [U] being clean 清洁; 干净.

cleanse /'klenz; klɛnz/ *v* [Tn, Tn·pr] **~ sb/sth (of sth)** make thoroughly clean 使彻底清洁; 清洗: *a cleansing cream,* ie one that cleans the skin 洁肤膏(使皮肤清洁的乳剂) ○ (*fig fml* 比喻, 文) *She felt cleansed of her sins after confession.* 她忏悔之后觉得自己的罪洗清了.

▷ **cleanser** *n* substance that cleanses, eg a detergent or a lotion 清洁剂.

clear¹ /klıə(r); klır/ *adj* (**-er** /'klıərə(r); 'klırɚ/, **-est** /'klıərıst; 'klırıst/) **1** (**a**) easy to see through; transparent 清澈的; 透明的: *clear glass* 透明的玻璃 ○ *the clear water of a mountain lake* 山上清澈的湖水. (**b**) without cloud or mist 无云雾的; 晴朗的: *a clear sky, day* 晴朗的天空、一天 ○ *clear weather* 无云雾的天气. (**c**) without spots or blemishes 无污点或瑕疵的; 洁净的: *clear skin* 洁净的皮肤 ○ *a clear complexion* 洁净的面孔. **2** (**a**) easy to see or hear; distinct 易看清或听清的; 清晰的: *a clear photograph* 清晰的照片 ○ *a clear reflection in the water* 水中清晰的倒影 ○ *a clear voice, speaker, sound* 清晰的嗓音、扬声器、声音. (**b**) easy to understand 易懂的; 明白的: *a clear explanation, article, meaning* 易懂的解释、文章、意思 ○ *You'll do as you're told, is that clear?* 让你怎么做就怎么做, 明白吗? **3 ~ (about/on sth)** without doubt, confusion or difficulty; certain 无疑的; 不混淆的; 无困难的; 肯定的: *a clear thinker* 思维清楚的思考者 ○ *a clear understanding of the problems* 对问题透彻的了解 ○ *My memory is not clear on that point.* 那一点我记不清楚了. ○ *Are you quite clear about what the job involves?* 这一工作涉及哪些内容, 你都明白吗? **4 ~ (to sb)** evident; obvious; definite 明显的; 显然的; 明确的: *a clear case of cheating* 明显的欺骗 ○ *have a clear advantage/lead,* eg in a contest 明显的优势[领先](如在比赛中) ○ *It is quite clear that she is not coming.* 很清楚, 她不来了. **5 ~ (of sth)** (**a**) free from obstructions, obstacles, difficulties or dangers 无阻塞、障碍、困难或危险的: *a clear view* 一览无遗 ○ *Wait until the road is clear (of traffic) before crossing.* 等路上无车辆来往时, 再穿过马路. ○ *I want to keep next weekend clear so that I can do some gardening.* 我要留出下周末的时间作些园艺工作. (**b**) free from guilt 无罪的; 无辜的: *have a clear conscience* 问心无愧. (**c**) free from sth undesirable 无厌恶之物的: *clear of debt* 无债务的 ○ *You are now clear of all suspicion.* 你现在已经没有嫌疑了. **6** [pred 作表语] **~ (of sb/sth)** not touching sth; away from sth 不触及某事物; 与某事物有距离: *The plane climbed until it was clear of the clouds.* 飞机爬升穿出了云层. ○ *Park (your car) about nine inches clear of the kerb.* (把你的汽车)停放在离路边石九英寸的地方. **7** [attrib 作定语] complete 整整的; 十足的: *Allow three clear days for the letter to arrive.* 信要整整三天才能到达. ○ *The bill was passed by a clear* (ie fairly large) *majority.* 议案获绝对多数票通过. **8** [attrib 作定语] (of a sum of money) with nothing to be deducted; net (指一笔钱)不再扣除的, 纯的, 净的: *a clear profit* 净利. **9** (idm 习语) **(as) clear as a 'bell** clearly and easily heard 清楚而容易听到的. **(as) clear as 'day** easy to see or understand; obvious 显而易见的; 易懂的; 显然的. **(as) clear as 'mud** (*infml* 口) very unclear; not apparent or well explained 很不清楚的; 不明显的; 未解释清楚的. **the coast is clear** ⇨ COAST¹. **in the 'clear** (*infml* 口) no longer in danger or suspected of sth 不再有危险的; 不再因某事物受嫌疑: *She was very ill for a few days but doctors say she's now in the clear.* 她大病了几天, 但医生说她现在已无危险. **make oneself 'clear** express oneself clearly 把自己的意思表达清楚: *Do I make myself clear?* 我讲得清楚吗? **make sth 'clear/'plain (to sb)** make sth fully understood 使某事物被充分理解: *I made it clear to him that I rejected his proposal.* 我清楚地告诉他, 我拒绝了他的建议.

▷ **clearly** *adv* **1** in a clear manner; distinctly 清楚地;

明白地；明显地：*speak clearly* 清楚地说 ○ *It is too dark to see clearly.* 天太黑看不清楚. **2** obviously; undoubtedly 显然地；无疑地：*That clearly cannot be true.* 显然那不是真的.

clear·ness *n* [U] state of being clear; clarity 清楚；明白；清澈；透明：*the clearness of the atmosphere* 空气清新 ○ *clearness of vision* 视觉清楚.

□ ˌ**clear-ˈheaded** *adj* thinking or understanding clearly; sensible 头脑清楚的；明事理的. ˌ**clearˈheadedly** *adv.* ˌ**clear-ˈheadedness** *n* [U].

ˌ**clear-ˈsighted** *adj* seeing, understanding or thinking clearly; discerning 观察、理解或思维清楚的；有眼力的.

ˈ**clearway** *n* (*Brit*) road other than a motorway on which vehicles may not normally stop or park 畅通路（公路上的不准停车路段，与高速公路不同）.

clear[2] /klɪə(r); klɪr/ *adv* **1** clearly; distinctly 清楚地；明白地；明显地：*I can hear you loud and clear.* 你的声音很大，我听得很清楚. **2 ~ (of sth)** out of the way of sth; no longer near or touching sth 不阻碍某事物；不再接触或接近某事物：*Stand clear of the doors.* 别站在门口挡道. ○ *He managed to leap clear of* (ie out of) *the burning car.* 他设法从燃烧着的汽车中跳了出来. ○ *He jumped three inches clear of* (ie above) *the bar.* 他跳得比杆儿高出三英寸. **3** completely 彻底；完全：*The prisoner got clear away.* 该囚犯逃之夭夭了. **4** (idm 习语) **keep/stay/steer clear (of sb/sth)** avoid meeting sb or becoming involved with sth or going near a place or using sth 避免见到某人或涉及某事物或接近某处或使用某物：*Try to keep clear of trouble.* 尽量避免麻烦. ○ *I prefer to keep clear of town during the rush-hour.* 我不愿意在交通拥挤的时间去市区. ○ (*infml* 口) *His doctor advised him to steer clear of alcohol.* 医生建议他不要喝酒. **pull sb/sth clear** ⇨ PULL[2].

□ ˌ**clear-ˈcut** *adj* not vague; definite 不含混的；明确的：ˌ*clear-cut* ˈ*plans, proˈposals, diˈstinctions* 明确的计划、提议、区分.

clear[3] /klɪə(r); klɪr/ *v* **1 (a)** [I] become transparent 变得透明：*The muddy water slowly cleared.* 有泥的水慢慢地变清了. **(b)** [I] (of the sky or the weather) become free of cloud or rain（指天空或天气）变为无云或无雨；转晴：*The sky cleared after the storm.* 暴风雨过后，天空转晴了. **(c)** [I, Ip] **~ (away)** (of fog, smoke, etc) disappear（指雾、烟等）消散：*It was a fine day once the mist had cleared.* 雾消散后是个晴天. **2 (a)** [Tn, Tn·pr] **~ A (of B)/~ B (from A)** remove (sth that is unwanted or no longer needed) (from a place)（从某处）移走（不要的东西）：*clear the table,* eg take away dirty plates, etc after a meal 收拾桌子（饭后拿走脏盘子等）○ *clear one's throat,* ie remove phlegm from one's throat by coughing slightly 清清嗓子 ○ *clear the streets of snow/clear snow from the streets* 清除街道上的积雪 ○ *The land was cleared of trees.* 地上的树已清除. ○ (*fig* 比喻) *clear one's mind of doubt* 消除心中疑团. **(b)** [Tn] remove (data that is no longer required) from the memory of a computer or calculator（从电脑或计算器中）消除（数据）. **3** [Tn, Tn·pr] **~ sb (of sth)** show or declare sb to be innocent 表明或宣称某人无辜：*clear one's name* 表明自己名声清白 ○ *She was cleared of all charges.* 对她的一切控告均已撤消. **4** [Tn] get past or over (sth) without touching it 经过或越过（某物）（但不触及）：*The horse cleared the fence easily.* 那匹马轻易地越过了篱笆. ○ *The car only just cleared* (ie nearly hit) *the gatepost.* 汽车险些碰上门柱. ○ *The winner cleared six feet,* ie jumped six feet without touching the bar. 优胜者跳过六英尺. **5 (a)** [Tn, Tn·pr] get permission for or allow (a ship, plane or cargo) to leave or enter a place or be unloaded 准予（船、飞机或货物）通过：*clear goods through customs,* ie by paying the necessary duties 为货物报关（交税）○ *clear a plane for take-off* 准予飞机起飞. **(b)** [Tn] (of goods) pass through (sth) after satisfying official requirements（指货物）（符合官方规定）通过（某物）：*Our baggage has cleared customs.* 我们的行李已通过海关检查. **6** [Tn esp passive 尤用于被动语态] **(a)** officially approve (sb) before he is given special work or allowed to see or handle secret information 正式批准（某人）可做机密工作或接触机密资料：*She's been cleared by security.* 她经保安部门批准可做机密工作. **(b)** declare (sth) to be acceptable 决定（某事物）可接受：*clear an article for publication* 决定一篇文章可以发表. **7** [Tn] pass (a cheque) through a clearing-house (CLEAR[3])（经票据交换所）结算，清算（支票）. **8** [Tn] earn (money) as gain or profit 赚（钱）：*clear £1 000 on a deal* 一项交易赚1 000英镑 ○ *clear* (ie make enough money to cover) *one's expenses* 赚得足够开销的钱. **9** [Tn] repay (sth) fully 清偿（某事物）：*clear one's debts, a loan, etc* 还清自己的债务、贷款等. **10** [I, Tn] (in football, hockey, etc) kick or hit (the ball) away from the area near the goal（足球、曲棍球等中）踢或击（球）使之离开球门区. **11** (idm 习语) **clear the ˈair** lessen or remove fears, worries or suspicions by talking about them openly（公开倾诉以）减轻或消除恐惧、忧虑或疑虑：*A frank discussion can help to clear the air.* 坦率的谈论有助于消除疑虑. **clear the ˈdecks** (*infml* 口) prepare for a particular activity, event, etc by removing anything that is not essential to it（清除不必要的东西）准备某项行动、活动等. **12** (phr v) **clear (sth) away** remove (objects) in order to leave a clear space 移走（物件）以留出空间：*clear away the dishes* 收走碟子. **clear off** (*infml* 口) (esp imperative 尤用于祈使句) go or run away 走开；跑开：*You've no right to be here. Clear off!* 你无权在这儿. 走开！○ *He cleared off as soon as he saw the policeman coming.* 他一看到警察来了，就逃跑了. **clear sth off** complete the payment of sth 付清某物的款：*clear off a debt* 付清债务. **clear out (of...)** (*infml* 口) leave (a place) quickly 迅速离开（某地）：*He cleared out before the police arrived.* 警察尚未来到，他就急忙溜掉了. **clear sth out** make sth empty or tidy by removing what is inside it 清除某物内部将其腾空或使之整洁：*clear out the attic* 清理顶楼. **clear up (a)** (of the weather) become fine or bright（指天气）转晴：*I hope it clears up this afternoon.* 我希望今天下午天气转晴. **(b)** (of an illness, infection, etc) disappear as good health returns 痊愈：*Has your rash cleared up yet?* 你的皮疹好了吗？**clear (sth) up** make (sth) tidy 使（某物）整洁；清理：*Please clear up (the mess in here) before you go.* 你走以前请（把这里的杂乱东西）整理好. **clear sth up** remove doubt about sth; solve sth 清除对某事的疑虑；解决某事物：*clear up a mystery, difficulty, misunderstanding, etc* 清除疑团、解决困难、解除误会. **clear sb/sth with sb/sth** have sb/sth inspected or approved by sb in authority 使某人[某事物]经过某权威人士检验或批准：*You'll have to clear it with management.* 此事你必须得到管理部门准许.

□ ˈ**clearing bank** (*Brit*) any bank belonging to a clearing-house 票据交换银行.

ˈ**clearing-house** *n* office at which banks exchange cheques and then pay in cash the amount they still owe each other 票据交换所.

clear·ance /ˈklɪərəns; ˈklɪrəns/ *n* **1** [C, U] (act of) clearing, removing or tidying sth 清理、清除或整理某事物：ˈ*slum clearance,* ie knocking down of slum houses 清拆贫民窟（拆除贫民窟的房屋）○ [attrib 作定语] *a* ˈ*clearance sale,* ie one in which all unwanted stock in a shop is sold at reduced prices（商店）清货大贱卖. **2** [C] (in football, hockey, etc) act of kicking or striking the ball away from the goal（足球、曲棍球等）将球踢出或击出球门区的动作：*a fine clearance by the full-back* 后卫将球一脚踢出球门区. **3** [C, U] space left clear when one object moves past or under another 净空，余隙，量（一物从另一物旁边或下面经过时，两者间的空隙）：*a clearance of only two feet,* eg for a ship moving through a canal 仅两英尺的净空（如船通过运河时）○ *There is not much clearance for tall vehicles passing under this bridge.* 高大车辆在这桥下通过时没有多大余隙. **4 (a)** [C, U] (document giving) authorization or permission, eg for a ship or plane to leave a place or for goods to pass through customs(2) 许可（证）（如准予船只或飞机离开或货物通过海关的）：*get clearance for take-off* 得到起飞的许可. **(b)** [U] official permission for sb to work with secret information, etc 正式批准某人参与机密工作等的许可：*give sb security clearance* 保安部门给予某人的机密工作许可. **5** [C, U] clearing of cheques at a clearing-house (CLEAR[3])（票据交换所内的）支票交换，结算，清算.

clear·ing /ˈklɪərɪŋ; ˈklɪrɪŋ/ *n* open space from which trees have been cleared in a forest（森林中树木砍伐后的）空地.

cleat /kli:t; klit/ *n* **1** small wooden or metal bar fastened to sth, on which ropes may be fastened by winding (固定在某物上的)木棒或金属棒(用以缠绕绳索); 拴; 楔子. **2** (usu *pl* 通常作复数) strip of rubber, wood, etc fastened to the sole of a boot or shoe, or to a gangway, to prevent slipping 防滑条. **3** V-shaped wedge V形楔; 羊角.

cleav·age /'kli:vɪdʒ; `klivɪdʒ/ *n* **1** [C] (**a**) split or division 分裂; 分开: (*fig* 比喻) *a deep cleavage within the ruling party* 执政党内部严重的分裂. (**b**) line along which material such as rock or wood splits (岩石或木等材料的)裂纹. **2** [C, U] (*infml* 口) hollow between a woman's breasts that can be seen above the low neckline of a dress 乳沟(女子乳房间的凹处, 穿低领连衣裙时所见者): *That new gown shows a large amount of (her) cleavage!* 那件新的女长服袒露出(她)大部分乳沟!

C

cleave[1] /kli:v; kliv/ *v* (*pt* **cleaved** /kli:vd; klivd/, **clove** /kləʊv; klov/ or **cleft** /kleft; klɛft/, *pp* **cleaved**, **cloven** /'kləʊvn; `klovən/ or **cleft**) **1** [I] break or split, esp along a natural line 裂开, 分开(尤指沿天然纹理): *This wood cleaves easily.* 这种木材容易裂. **2** [Tn, Tn·pr, Cn·a] divide (sth) by chopping (with a heavy axe, etc); split (用大斧等)劈开(某物); 使分开: *cleave a block of wood in two* 把一块木头劈成两半 ○ *cleave a man's head open with a sword* 用剑劈开人头. **3** [Ipr, Tn, Tn·pr] ~ **through sth/~ sth (through sth)** make a way through (sth) (as if) by cutting (好像)开路般穿过(某物): *The ship's bows cleaved (through) the waves.* 轮船破浪前进. ○ *cleave a path through the jungle* 在丛林中开出一条路 ○ (*fig* 比喻) *cleaving one's way/a path through the crowd* 从拥挤的人群中穿过. **4** (idm 习语) **be (caught) in a cleft 'stick** be trapped in a situation where it is difficult to decide what to do 陷入进退两难的境地.

□ ˌ**cleft 'palate** deformed condition in which the roof of a person's mouth is split at birth 腭裂(出生时腭板裂开的畸形).

cleave[2] /kli:v; kliv/ *v* (*pt* **cleaved** /kli:vd; klivd/ or **clave** /kleɪv; klev/, *pp* **cleaved**) [Ipr] ~ **to sb/sth** (*arch* 古) remain attached or faithful to sb/sth 依恋或忠实于某人[某事物].

cleaver /'kli:və(r); `klivɚ/ *n* heavy knife with a broad blade used by a butcher for chopping meat (屠夫剁肉用的)宽刃大刀.

clef /klef; klɛf/ *n* (*music* 音) symbol at the beginning of a stave showing the pitch of the notes 谱号(谱表开始处的符号, 用以表示音符的音高: *treble/bass/alto clef* 高音[低音/中音]谱号. ⇨ illus at MUSIC 见 MUSIC 之插图.

cleft[1] /kleft; klɛft/ *n* crack or split occurring naturally (eg in the ground or in rock) (自然形成的)裂缝, 裂口(如地上或岩石中的).

cleft[2] *pt, pp* of CLEAVE[1].

cle·ma·tis /'klemətɪs, *also* klə'meɪtɪs; `klɛmətɪs/ *n* [U, C] climbing plant with white, purple or pink flowers 铁线莲(攀缘植物, 开白色、紫色或粉红色花).

clem·ent /'klemənt; `klɛmənt/ *adj* (*fml* 文) **1** (esp of weather) mild (尤指天气)温和的. **2** showing mercy 仁慈的.

▷ **clem·ency** /'klemənsɪ; `klɛmənsɪ/ *n* [U] (*fml* 文) **1** mildness (esp of weather) 温和(尤指天气). **2** mercy (esp when punishing sb) 仁慈(尤指惩罚某人时): *He appealed to the judge for clemency.* 他乞求法官开恩.

clem·en·tine /'kleməntі:n; `klɛmənˌtin/ *n* type of small orange 小柑橘.

clench /klentʃ; klɛntʃ/ *v* **1** [Tn] close (sth) tightly or press (two things) firmly together 紧闭(某物); 将(两物)紧压在一起: *clench one's fist/jaws/teeth* 攥紧拳头[咬紧牙关/咬牙] ○ *a clenched-fist salute* 握拳礼. **2** [Tn, Tn·pr] ~ **sb/sth (in/with sth)** grasp or hold sb/sth firmly 抓紧或握紧某人[某物]: *clench the railings (with both hands)* (双手)紧握栏杆 ○ *money clenched tightly in one's fist* 在拳头里攥着的钱.

clere·story /'klɪəstɔ:rɪ; `klɪrˌstorɪ/ *n* upper part of a wall in a large church, with a row of windows, above the roofs of the aisles 高侧墙(大教堂墙壁的上部, 高于侧廊的屋顶, 有一排高侧窗).

clergy /'klɜ:dʒɪ; `klɝdʒɪ/ *n* [pl *v*] people who have been ordained as priests or ministers of esp the Christian Church 神职人员; (尤指基督教的)教士或牧师: *All the local clergy attended the ceremony.* 当地所有的牧师出席了仪式. ○ *The new proposals affect both clergy and laity.* 新的建议与神职人员和俗人都有关系. Cf 参看 LAITY 1.

□ '**clergyman** /'klɜ:dʒɪmən; `klɝdʒɪmən/ *n* (*pl* **-men** /-mən; -mən/) priest or minister of the Christian Church, esp the Church of England (基督教的)教士或牧师(尤指英国国教会的).

cleric /'klerɪk; `klɛrɪk/ *n* (*dated* 旧) clergyman 教士; 牧师.

cler·ical /'klerɪkl; `klɛrɪkl̩/ *adj* **1** of, for or made by a clerk(1) or clerks 文书或办事员的: '*clerical work* 文书的工作 ○ *a* ˌ*clerical* '*error*, ie one made in copying or calculating sth 笔误(抄写或计算中的错误). **2** of or for the clergy 教士的; 牧师的; 神职人员的: *a* ˌ*clerical* '*collar*, ie one that fastens at the back, worn by clergymen 牧师领(牧师用的颈后系扣的领).

cleri·hew /'klerɪhju:; `klɛrɪhju/ *n* short comic poem, usu consisting of two rhyming couplets with lines of varying length 克莱里休诗体(通常含有两个押韵的幽默对句, 诗句长短不等).

clerk /klɑ:k; *US* klɜ:rk; klɝk/ *n* **1** person employed in an office, a shop, etc to keep records, accounts, etc 文书; 办事员; 事务员: *a* '*bank clerk* 银行办事员 ○ *a* '*filing clerk* 档案管理员. **2** official in charge of the records of a council, court, etc (议会、法院等的)书记员, 秘书: *the Town* '*Clerk* 市政府秘书 ○ *the Clerk to the* '*Council* 议会秘书 ○ *the Clerk of the* '*Court* 法院书记员 ○ *clerk of (the)* '*works*, ie person responsible for materials, etc for building work done by contract 工程管理员. **3** (*US*) (**a**) (also '**desk clerk**) assistant in a hotel 旅馆接待员. (**b**) assistant in a shop 店员. **4** (*arch* 古) clergyman 教士; 牧师.

▷ **clerk** /klɜ:rk; klɝk/ *v* [I] (*US*) work as a clerk(1), esp in a shop 做办事员; (尤指)做店员.

clever /'klevə(r); `klɛvɚ/ *adj* (**-er** /'klevərə(r); `klɛvərɚ/, **-est** /'klevərɪst; `klɛvərɪst/) **1** (**a**) quick at learning and understanding things; intelligent 敏于学习和理解的; 机灵的; 聪明的; 伶俐的: *clever at arithmetic* 擅长算术的 ○ *a clever student* 聪明的学生 ○ *Clever girl!* 伶俐的姑娘! (**b**) skilful; nimble 熟练的; 灵巧的: *be clever with money, a needle, one's hands* 擅长理财、针线活儿好、手巧 ○ *be clever at making excuses* 善于找借口 ○ *How clever of you to do that!* 你那样做真太聪明了! **2** (of things, ideas, actions, etc); showing intelligence or skill; ingenious (指事物、主意、举动等)表现出聪明或灵巧的; 精巧的: *a clever scheme* 精明的计划 ○ *a clever little gadget* 灵巧的小玩意儿. **3** (*infml derog* 口, 贬) quick-witted or smart, often in a cheeky way 机敏的, 精明的, 耍小聪明的(常指厚颜无耻的): *Are you trying to be clever?* 你想耍心眼儿吗? ○ *He was too clever for* (ie He outwitted) *us.* 他太精明了(我们斗不过). ▷ **cleverly** *adv*. **clever·ness** *n* [U].

□ '**clever-clever** *adj* [usu pred 通常作表语] (*infml derog* 口, 贬) trying to appear clever 卖弄小聪明.

'**clever Dick** (*infml derog* 口, 贬) person who thinks he is always right or knows everything 自以为一贯正确或无所不知的人: *She's such a clever Dick.* 她是个老正确.

clew /klu:; klu/ *n* **1** (*nautical* 海) metal loop attached to the lower corner of a sail 帆耳(连在帆下角的金属环). **2** loop holding the strings of a hammock 吊床上穿绳索的环.

▷ **clew** *v* [Tn, Tn·p] ~ **sth (up/down)** (*nautical* 海) raise or lower (a sail) 升或降(帆).

cli·ché /'kli:ʃeɪ; *US* kli:'ʃeɪ; kli'ʃe/ *n* (**a**) [C] phrase or idea which is used so often that it has become stale or meaningless 陈腐的词语或主意; 陈词滥调: *a cliché-ridden style* 堆砌陈腐词藻的风格. (**b**) [U] use of such phrases 使用陈词滥调: *Cliché is a feature of bad journalism.* 使用套语是拙劣的新闻体的特点.

click[1] /klɪk; klɪk/ *n* short sharp sound (like that of a key turning in a lock) 短而尖的声音(像用钥匙开锁的声音); 咔嗒声: *the click of a switch* 开关的咔嗒声 ○ *He saluted with a click of his heels.* 他立正敬礼, 鞋后跟发出咔嗒一声.

click[2] /klɪk; klɪk/ *v* **1** [I, Ipr, Tn] (cause sth to) make a slight sharp sound (as of a key turning in a lock) (使某物)发出轻微尖声(像钥匙在锁中转动的声音); (使某物)发咔嗒声: *The door clicked shut.* 门咔嗒一声关上了. ○ *The new part clicked into place.* 新零件咔嗒一声就装好了. ○ *a clicking noise* 咔嗒咔嗒的响声 ○ *click one's* *tongue/heels/fingers* 使舌头[鞋后跟/手指]发出咔嗒声. **2** [I, Ipr] ~ **(with sb)** (*Brit infml* 口) (**a**) become friendly at once 很快成为好朋友: *We met on holiday and just clicked immediately.* 我们在假日相识, 一见如故. (**b**) become popular (with sb) 为(某人)所喜爱: *The film has really clicked with young audiences.* 这部电影深受年轻观众的喜爱. **3** [I] (*infml* 口) suddenly become clear or understood 突然明白或理解: *I puzzled over it for hours before it finally clicked.* 我对这一问题茫然不解, 几小时后终于顿开茅塞.

cli·ent /ˈklaɪənt; ˋklaɪənt/ *n* **1** person who receives help or advice from a professional person (eg a lawyer, an accountant, a social worker, an architect, etc) (律师、会计师、社会工作者、建筑师等的)委托人, 当事人. **2** customer in a shop (商店的)顾客, 主顾.

cli·en·tele /ˌkli:ənˈtel; *US* ˌklaɪənˈtel; ˌklaɪənˋtɛl/ *n* [Gp, U] **1** customers or clients as a group 顾客, 委托人(总称): *an international clientele* 国际顾客. **2** patrons of a theatre, restaurant, etc (剧院、饭馆等的)顾客.

cliff /klɪf; klɪf/ *n* steep, usu high, face of rock, esp at the edge of the sea 峭壁, 悬崖(尤指在海边的). ⇨illus at COAST 见COAST之插图.

□ ˈ**cliff-hanger** *n* story or contest whose outcome is uncertain till the end (到终局时才见分晓的)故事或比赛. ˈ**cliff-hanging** *adj.*

cli·mac·teric /klaɪˈmæktərɪk; klaɪˋmæktərɪk/ *n* period of life when physical powers begin to decline, eg (for women) the menopause 更年期(如妇女绝经期).

cli·mac·tic /klaɪˈmæktɪk; klaɪˋmæktɪk/ *adj* forming a climax 形成高潮的.

cli·mate /ˈklaɪmɪt; ˋklaɪmɪt/ *n* **1** (**a**) regular pattern of weather conditions (temperature, rainfall, winds, etc) of a particular region 气候: *Britain has a temperate climate.* 英国气候温和. (**b**) area or region with certain weather conditions 有某种天气情况的地区: *She moved to a warmer climate.* 她迁往气候较温暖的地方. **2** general attitude or feeling; atmosphere 一般的态度或感觉; 风气; 思潮; 倾向: *a climate of suspicion* 怀疑的风气 ○ *the present political climate* 当前的政治气候 ○ *the current climate of opinion*, ie the general or fashionable attitude to an aspect of life, policy, etc 目前的舆论气氛(对生活、政策等方面). **3** (idm 习语) **a change of air/climate** ⇨ CHANGE².

▷ **cli·matic** /klaɪˈmætɪk; klaɪˋmætɪk/ *adj* of climate 气候的. **cli·matic·ally** /-klɪ; -klɪ/ *adv.*

cli·ma·to·logy /ˌklaɪməˈtɒlədʒɪ; ˌklaɪməˋtɑlədʒɪ/ *n* [U] science or study of climate 气候学.

cli·max /ˈklaɪmæks; ˋklaɪmæks/ *n* **1** (**a**) most interesting or significant event or point in time; culmination 顶点, 极点, 高潮(最有趣或最有意义的事件或时刻): *the climax of his political career* 在他政治生涯中的顶点 ○ *The climax of the celebration was a firework display.* 庆祝会的高潮是燃放烟火. (**b**) most intense part (esp of a play, piece of music, etc) 最紧张激烈的部分; (尤指戏剧, 乐曲等的)高潮: *The music approached a climax.* 乐曲接近高潮. ○ *His intervention brought their quarrel to a climax.* 他一干预使他们的口角达到最激烈程度. **2** peak of sexual pleasure; orgasm 性高潮.

▷ **cli·max** *v* **1** [I, Ipr, Tn, Tn·pr] ~ **(sth) (in/with sth)** bring (sth) to or come to a climax(1a) 使(某事物)达到顶点, 极点, 高潮: *Her career climaxed in the award of an Oscar.* 她荣获奥斯卡金像奖是她事业的顶峰. **2** [I] reach the peak of sexual pleasure 达到性高潮.

climb /klaɪm; klaɪm/ *v* **1** (**a**) [Tn] go up or over (sth) by effort, esp using one's hands and feet 攀登, 攀爬, 爬上, 爬过(某物): *climb a wall, a mountain, a tree, a rope, the stairs* 爬墙、山、树、绳、楼梯 ○ *The car slowly climbed the hill.* 汽车缓慢地爬上山坡. (**b**) [I, Ipr, Ip] go or come in the specified direction, esp upwards, by effort 攀爬: *climb up/down a ladder, along a ridge, into a car, out of bed, over a gate, through a hedge, etc* 爬上[下]梯子、爬越山岭、爬进汽车、爬下床、爬越大门、爬过篱笆 ○ *climb into/out of one's clothes*, ie get dressed/undressed 穿上[脱下]衣服 ○ *This is where we start climbing*, ie upwards. 这就是我们向上爬的地方. ○ *Monkeys can climb well.* 猴子善于攀爬. **2** [I] (**a**) go up mountains, etc as a sport 登山(运动): *He likes to go climbing at weekends.* 他喜欢在周末做登山运动. (**b**) (of aircraft, the sun, etc) go higher in the sky (指飞机、太阳等)上升: *The plane climbed to 20 000 feet.* 飞机上升到20 000英尺. (**c**) slope upwards 倾斜向上: *The road climbs steeply for several miles.* 这条路有几英里向上倾斜得很陡. (**d**) (of plants) grow up a wall or some other support by clinging or twining (指植物)缘墙或其他支撑物向上生长: *a climbing rose* 攀缘而上的玫瑰. **3** [I] rise in social rank, etc by one's own effort (靠自己努力)提高社会地位等. **4** [I] (of currency, temperature, etc) increase in value, etc (指货币)增值; (指温度等)上升: *The dollar has been climbing steadily all week.* 整个星期美元一直在稳步增值. **5** (idm 习语) **climb/jump on the bandwagon** ⇨ BANDWAGON (BAND). **6** (phr v) **climb down (over sth)** (*infml* 口) admit a mistake or withdraw from a position in an argument, etc (在辩论等中)认错, 让步: *As new facts became known, the Government was forced to climb down over its handling of the spy scandal.* 新的事实已众所周知, 政府被迫承认处理间谍丑事失当.

▷ **climb** *n* **1** act or instance of climbing 攀登: *an exhausting climb* 令人筋疲力尽的攀登 ○ *a rapid climb to stardom* 很快爬上明星地位. **2** place or distance (to be) climbed 要攀登到的地方或距离: *It's an hour's climb to the summit.* 到顶峰有一小时的攀登路程.

climber *n* **1** person who climbs (esp mountains) 攀登的人; (尤指)登山者. **2** (*infml* 口) person who tries to improve his status in society 尽力改善自己社会地位的人: *a social climber* 社会上向上爬的人. **3** climbing plant 攀缘植物. ⇨illus at App 1 见附录1之插图, page vii.

□ ˈ**climb-down** *n* act of admitting one was mistaken, etc 认错; 让步; 屈服.

ˈ**climbing-frame** *n* structure of joined bars, etc for children to climb (儿童玩的)攀爬架.

clime /klaɪm; klaɪm/ *n* (usu *pl* 通常作复数) (*arch or joc* 古或谑) country; climate(1b) 地区; 气候: *seeking summer climes* 去找有夏季的地方.

clinch /klɪntʃ; klɪntʃ/ *v* **1** [Tn] fix (a nail or rivet) firmly in place by hammering sideways the end that sticks out 敲弯(穿出的钉尖)使之牢固. **2** [Tn] (*infml* 口) confirm or settle (sth) finally 最终确定或解决(某事物): *clinch a deal/an argument/a bargain* 成交[解决争端/谈妥买卖]. **3** [I] (esp of boxers) hold each other tightly with the arms (尤指拳击手)互相扭抱: *The boxers clinched and the referee had to separate them.* 拳击手扭抱在一起, 裁判让他们分开. ○ (*infml* 口) *The scene ended as the lovers clinched.* 这一幕结束时, 情人相互拥抱在一起.

▷ **clinch** *n* (**a**) (in boxing) act or instance of clinching (CLINCH 3) (拳击中)扭抱: *get into a clinch* 扭抱在一起 ○ *break a clinch* 将扭抱的拳击手分开. (**b**) (*infml* 口) embrace 拥抱.

clincher *n* (*infml* 口) point or remark that settles an argument, etc 起决定性作用的论点或言语.

cline /klaɪn; klaɪn/ *n* (*biology* 生) graded sequence of differences; continuum 生态群; 群体连续体.

cling /klɪŋ; klɪŋ/ *v* (*pt, pp* **clung** /klʌŋ; klʌŋ/) **1** [Ipr, Ip] ~ **(on) to sb/sth; ~ on; ~ together** hold on tightly to sb/sth 紧抓住或抱住某人[某物]: *survivors clinging to a raft* 紧抓住木筏的生还者 ○ *They clung to each other/clung together as they said goodbye.* 他们告别时, 紧紧地拥抱在一起. ○ *Cling on tight!* 抓紧! **2** [Ipr] ~ **(on) to sth** be unwilling to abandon sth; refuse to give sth up 舍不得放弃某事物; 拒绝放弃某事物: *cling to a belief, an opinion, a theory, etc* 坚持一种信仰、意见、理论等 ○ *cling to one's possessions* 舍不得放弃财物 ○ *She clung to the hope that he was still alive.* 她始终抱着一个希望, 就是他仍活着. **3** [I, Ipr] ~ **(to sth)** become attached to sth; stick to sth 附着于某物: *The smell of smoke clings (to one's clothes) for a long time.* 烟味长久附着(在衣服上)不散. ○ *a dress that clings to* (ie fits closely so as to show the shape of) *the body* 紧贴身体(显出体形)的连衣裙. **4** [Ipr] ~ **to sb/sth** stay close to sb/sth 紧靠着某人[某物]: *The ship clung to the coastline.* 船紧靠着海岸线. ○ *Don't cling to the kerb when you're driving.* 不要紧贴路边开车. **5** [I, Ipr] ~ **(to sb)** (*esp derog* 尤作贬义) be emotionally dependent on sb; stay too close to sb 感情上依靠某人; 太接近某人; 依恋: *Small children cling to their mothers.* 小孩子都缠着母亲. **6** (idm 习语) **cling/stick to sb like a leech** ⇨ LEECH.

▷ **cling·ing** *adj* **1** (of clothes) sticking to the body and

C

showing its shape (指衣服)紧身显出体形的. **2** emotionally dependent 感情上依附他人的: *a clinging boyfriend* 缠绵不已的男朋友.

clingy *adj* (*infml* 口): *a shy, clingy child* 腼腆、依附他人的孩子.

□ ˈ**cling film** thin transparent plastic film used for wrapping food, etc 保鲜纸, 保鲜膜(用以包裹食品等的透明塑料薄膜). Cf 参看 SHRINK-WRAP (SHRINK).

clinic /ˈklɪnɪk; ˋklɪnɪk/ *n* **1** private or specialized hospital (私人的)诊所; 专科医院: *He is being treated at a private clinic.* 他正在私人诊所接受治疗. **2** place or session at which specialized medical treatment or advice is given to visiting patients (门诊治疗的)部、科、室或过程: *a dental, diabetic, fracture, etc clinic* 牙科、糖尿病科、骨科 ○ *She is attending the antenatal clinic.* 她正接受产前检查. **3** occasion in a hospital when students learn by watching how a specialist examines and treats his patients 临床见习.

C

clin·ical /ˈklɪnɪkl; ˋklɪnɪkl̩/ *adj* **1** [attrib 作定语] of or relating to the examination and treatment of patients and their illnesses 临床的; 有关临床的: *clinical medicine* 临床医学 ○ *clinical training*, ie the part of a doctor's training done in a hospital 临床实习. **2** coldly objective; unfeeling 冷静客观的; 无感情的: *He watched her suffering with clinical detachment.* 他冷静客观地看着她遭受的痛苦. **3** (of a room, building, etc) very plain; undecorated (指房间、建筑物等)非常朴素的; 不装饰的: *the clinical style of some modern architecture* 某些现代建筑的朴实风格. ▷ **clin·ic·ally** *adv*: *clinically dead*, ie judged to be dead from the condition of the body 临床死亡的(从身体的情况判断为死亡).

□ ˌ**clinical therˈmometer** instrument for measuring the temperature of the human body 体温计; 体温表.

clink[1] /klɪŋk; klɪŋk/ *n* sharp ringing sound (as) of small pieces of metal or glass knocking together (好像)(小块金属或玻璃相撞的)叮当声: *the clink of coins, keys, glasses* 硬币、钥匙、玻璃杯相碰的叮当声.

▷ **clink** *v* [I, Tn] (cause sth to) make this sound (使某物)发叮当声: *coins clinking in his pocket* 在他衣袋里叮当作响的硬币 ○ *They clinked glasses and drank each other's health.* 他们碰杯互祝健康.

clink[2] /klɪŋk; klɪŋk/ *n* [sing] (*sl* 俚) prison 监狱; 牢房: *be (put) in (the) clink* (送去)坐牢.

clinker /ˈklɪŋkə(r); ˋklɪŋkɚ/ *n* [U] rough stony material left in a furnace, etc after coal has burnt (熔炉等内的)熔渣, 渣块, 煤渣.

clinker-built /ˈklɪŋkə bɪlt; ˋklɪŋkɚˌbɪlt/ *adj* (of a boat) made with the outside planks or metal plates overlapping downwards (指船)瓦叠式外壳的, 鱼鳞式外壳的.

clip[1] /klɪp; klɪp/ *n* [C] **1** (esp in compounds 尤用以构成复合词) any of various wire or metal devices used for holding things together (金属制的)夹子; 别针; 曲别针: *a* ˈ*paper-clip* ○ *a* ˈ*hair-clip* ○ ˈ*bicycle-clips*. **2** (also ˈ**cartridge clip**) set of cartridges in a metal holder that is placed in a rifle, etc for firing 子弹夹. **3** piece of jewellery fastened to clothes by a clip 饰物别针(用别针别在衣服上的珠宝饰物): *a diamond* ˈ*clip* 钻石别针.

▷ **clip** *v* **(-pp-)** [Ipr, Ip, Tn·pr, Tn·p] **~ (sth) (on)to sth; ~ (sth) on; ~ (A and B) together** be fastened or fasten (sth) to sth else with a clip 用别针别在某物上; 用夹子夹在某物上: *Do you clip those ear-rings on/Do those ear-rings clip on?* 你的[这种]耳环是夹上去的吗? ○ *There was a cheque clipped to the back of the letter.* 在信背面夹着一张支票. ○ *clip documents together* 把文件夹在一起.

□ ˈ**clipboard** *n* portable board with a clip at the top for holding papers 带夹子的写字板.

ˈ**clip-on** *n* (usu *pl* 通常作复数), *adj* [attrib 作定语] (object) that is fastened to sth with a clip 夹式的(用夹子夹在某物上的)(物体): *Are your ear-rings clip-ons?* 你的耳环是夹式的吗? ○ *a clip-on bow-tie* 夹式蝶形领结.

clip[2] /klɪp; klɪp/ *v* **1** [Tn, Cn·a] cut (sth) with scissors or shears, esp in order to shorten it; trim (用剪刀)剪(某物); (尤指)剪短; 修剪: *clip a hedge, one's finger-nails* 修剪树篱、指甲 ○ *clip a sheep*, ie cut off its hair for wool 剪羊毛 ○ *The dog's fur was clipped short for the show.* 为参加狗展把狗的毛剪短了. **2** [Tn] make a hole in (a bus or train ticket) to show that it has been used (在公共汽车票或火车票上)剪孔; 剪(票). **3** [Tn] omit (parts of words) when speaking (说话时)省略(部分话); 删节: *a clipped accent* 缩略的语音 ○ *He clipped his words when speaking.* 他说话时把词语缩短了. **4** [Tn, Tn·pr] (*infml* 口) hit (sb/sth) sharply 猛击(某人[某物]): *clip sb's ear/clip sb on the ear* 打某人耳光. **5** (idm 习语) **clip sb's** ˈ**wings** prevent sb from being active or from doing what he is ambitious to do 阻止某人活动; 扼杀某人雄心: *Having a new baby to look after has clipped her wings a bit.* 她有个新生婴儿要照看, 活动难免受些限制. **6** (phr v) **clip sth out of sth** remove sth from sth else with scissors, etc 从某物上剪掉另一物: *clip an article out of the newspaper* 从报纸上剪下一篇文章.

▷ **clip** *n* **1** act of clipping 剪; 修剪. **2** amount of wool cut from a (flock of) sheep at one time 一次从(一群羊)身上剪下的羊毛量. **3** (*infml* 口) sharp blow 猛打: *She gave him a clip round the ear.* 她打了他一记耳光. **4** short extract from a film 电影的片段. **5** (idm 习语) **at a fair, good, etc** ˈ**clip** (*infml* 口) at a fast speed 快速地: *The old car was travelling at quite a clip.* 那辆旧汽车开得相当快.

clip·ping *n* **1** (usu *pl* 通常作复数) piece cut off 剪下的一块: *hair, nail, hedge clippings* 剪下的头发、指甲、篱笆. **2** (*esp US*) = CUTTING[1] 1.

□ ˈ**clip-joint** *n* (*sl* 俚) place of entertainment, esp a night-club, that overcharges its customers 向顾客索价过高的娱乐场所(尤指夜总会).

NOTE ON USAGE 用法: Compare **clip**, **pare**, **prune**, **trim** and **shave**. 试比较 **clip**、**pare**、**prune**、**trim**、**shave** 这几个词. These verbs refer to cutting off an unwanted part to make an object smaller, tidier, etc. 这些动词均指剪切掉不需要的部分使物体更小、更整齐些等. Note that with all except **pare** the direct object can be either **(a)** the main body that is made smaller, smoother, etc or **(b)** the part that is cut off. 注意除 **pare** 外, 其他各词的直接宾语可为 **(a)** 被剪小或剪整齐等的主体, 或为 **(b)** 所剪切掉的部分. **Shave** is generally used of hair on the body ☆ **shave** 一般用于身体上的毛发: **(a)** *Monks shave their heads.* 和尚都剃头. **(b)** *She shaved the hairs off her legs.* 她刮掉了腿上的寒毛. We **trim** something to make it tidy ☆ **trim** 某物是为使之整齐: **(a)** *trim one's beard, a hedge* 修剪胡须、树篱. **(b)** *She trimmed the loose threads from her skirt.* 她把裙子上的线头剪掉了. **Clip** can relate to cutting off an unwanted part or to removing a part in order to keep it ☆ **clip** 可指剪掉不需要的部分, 也可指剪下要保留的部分: **(a)** *Have you finished clipping the hedge?* 你把树篱剪完了吗? **(b)** *I want to clip that picture from the magazine.* 我要把杂志上的那张照片剪下来. We **prune** plants to make them grow stronger 我们修剪(**prune**)植物使之生长得更壮: **(a)** *The roses need pruning.* 玫瑰需要修剪了. **(b)** *I've pruned all the dead branches off the tree.* 我已经把树上的枯枝都剪掉了. **Pare** indicates removing the outer layer or edge of something ☆ **pare** 指除掉某物的外层或边缘: *She pared the apple with a sharp knife.* 她用快刀削苹果.

clip-clop /ˈklɪp klɒp; ˌklɪp ˋklɑp/ *n* sound (like that) of horses' hoofs on a hard surface (像)马蹄在硬路面上发出的声音; 嘚嘚声.

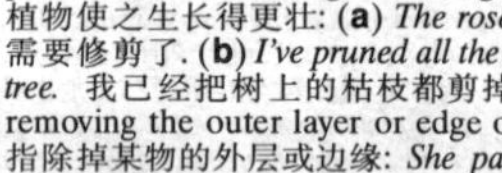

GARDENING SHEARS 修篱剪

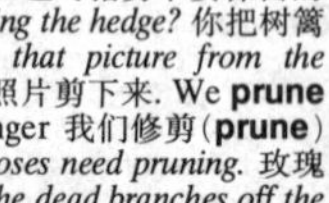

SECATEURS (*also* CLIPPERS) 修枝剪

NAIL CLIPPERS 指甲剪

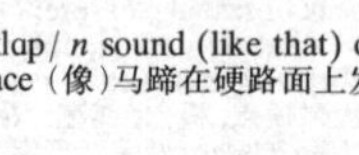

HAIRDRESSER'S CLIPPERS 推子

clip·per /ˈklɪpə(r); ˈklɪpɚ/ *n* **1 clippers** [pl] instrument for clipping nails, hair, hedges, etc 剪指甲、毛发、树篱等的工具; 剪刀; 指甲刀; 推子; 羊毛剪: *(a pair of) nail clippers* (一把)指甲剪. ⇨illus 见插图. **2** fast sailing-ship 快速帆船.

clique /kli:k; klik/ *n* [CGp] (*sometimes derog* 有时作贬义) small group of people, often with shared interests, who associate closely and exclude others from their group 小集团; 派系; 朋党: *The club is dominated by a small clique of intellectuals.* 这俱乐部被知识分子小集团把持着.

▷ **cliquy** (also **cliquey**, **cliquish**) *adj* (*derog* 贬) **(a)** (of people) tending to form a clique (指人)有结成小集团倾向的. **(b)** dominated by a clique or cliques 被小集团所把持的: *Our department is very cliquy.* 我们的部门由小集团把持着.

clit·oris /ˈklɪtərɪs; ˈklɪtərɪs/ *n* small part of the female genitals which becomes larger when the female is sexually excited 阴蒂; 阴核. ▷ **clit·oral** /ˈklɪtərəl; ˈklɪtərəl/ *adj*.

Cllr *abbr* 缩写 = (*Brit*) Councillor: *Cllr Michael Booth* 迈克尔·布思议员.

cloak 斗篷

cloak /kləʊk; klok/ *n* **1** [C] sleeveless outer garment hanging loosely from the shoulders, usu worn out of doors 斗篷; 披风. ⇨illus 见插图. **2** [sing] (*fig* 比喻) thing that hides or covers 隐藏或掩盖的事物: *They left under (the) cloak of darkness.* 他们在黑暗的遮掩下离开了. ○ *The spy's activities were concealed by the cloak of diplomacy.* 间谍的活动是在外交的掩护下暗中进行的.

▷ **cloak** *v* [Tn, Tn·pr] **~ sth (in sth)** (*usu fig* 通常作比喻) cover or hide (as if) with a cloak (好像)用斗篷掩盖或隐藏: *The negotiations were cloaked in secrecy.* 谈判是秘密进行的.

□ ˌ**cloak-and-ˈdagger** *adj* [attrib 作定语] (of a story, film, etc) involving intrigue and espionage (指故事、电影等)有阴谋和间谍活动内容的.

cloak·room /ˈkləʊkrʊm; ˈklok,rʊm/ *n* **1** room (usu in a public building) where coats, hats, etc may be left for a time 衣帽间(通常设于公共场所内). **2** (*Brit euph* 婉) lavatory 厕所: *the ladies' cloakroom* 女厕所.

clob·ber[1] /ˈklɒbə(r); ˈklɑbɚ/ *v* [Tn] (*infml* 口) **1** strike (sb) heavily and repeatedly 连续重击(某人): (*fig* 比喻) *The police intend to clobber drunk drivers*, ie punish them severely. 警方拟持续不断地严惩醉酒驾驶者. ○ *The new tax laws will clobber small businesses*, ie harm them financially. 新税法对小型企业, 将是一连串的打击. **2** defeat (sb/sth) completely 彻底挫败(某人[某事物]): *Our team got clobbered on Saturday.* 我们队星期六一败涂地. **3** criticize (sb/sth) severely 狠狠地批评(某人[某事物]).

clob·ber[2] /ˈklɒbə(r); ˈklɑbɚ/ *n* [U] (*Brit infml* 口) clothing or equipment (esp for a specific activity) 服装或设备(尤指为某特定活动的): *You should see the clobber he takes when he goes climbing!* 你真该看看他去登山时带的服装和设备!

cloche /klɒʃ; kloʃ/ *n* **1** portable glass or plastic cover used to protect outdoor plants (保护室外植物的)轻便玻璃罩, 塑料罩. **2** woman's close-fitting bell-shaped hat (紧套于头上的)钟形女帽.

clock[1] /klɒk; klɑk/ *n* **1** instrument for measuring and showing time (not carried or worn like a watch) 时钟. **2** (*infml* 口) instrument (eg a taxi meter or a milometer) for measuring and recording things other than time 计量和记录仪器(如计程车计费表或里程表): *a second-hand car with 20 000 miles on the clock* 里程表上显示已行驶20 000英里的二手车. **3** (idm 习语) **around/round the ˈclock** all day and all night 整天整夜; 夜以继日: *Surgeons are working round the clock to save his life.* 外科医生们正在日夜工作以抢救他的生命. ○ [attrib 作定语] *Doctors must provide a round-the-clock service.* 必须昼夜不停地有医生应诊. **beat the clock** ⇨ BEAT[1]. **put the ˈclock back** return to a past age or to old-fashioned ideas, laws, customs, etc 开倒车; 倒行逆施: *The new censorship law will put the clock back (by) 50 years.* 新的审查条例是开倒车, 要退回到50年前的水平. **put the clock/clocks forward/back** (in countries which have official summer time) change the time, usu by one hour, at the beginning/end of summer (夏时制)将时钟拨快[拨回](通常为一小时): *Remember to put your clocks back (one hour) tonight.* 记住今天晚上把钟拨回(一小时). **watch the clock** ⇨ WATCH[2]. ˌ**work against the ˈclock** work fast in order to finish a task before a certain time (为在某一时间完成任务)加快工作; 抢时间做.

▷ ˈ**clock·wise** *adv*, *adj* moving in a curve in the same direction as the hands of a clock 顺时针方向(的): *turn the key clockwise/in a clockwise direction* 顺时针方向转动钥匙. Cf 参看 ANTI-CLOCKWISE.

□ ˈ**clock-face** *n* part of a clock that shows the time, usu marked with numbers 钟面.

ˌ**clock ˈgolf** game in which players putt a golf-ball into a hole from points in a circle round it 钟面式高尔夫球戏.

ˈ**clock tower** tall structure, usu forming part of a building, with a clock at the top 钟楼.

ˈ**clock-watcher** *n* worker who is always checking the time to know when he may stop working 总看钟点等候下班的工作人员. ˈ**clock-watching** *n* [U].

clock[2] /klɒk; klɑk/ *v* **1** [Tn] record the time of (sth) with a stop-watch; time 用跑表记录(某事)的时间; 计时. **2** [Tn, Tn·p] **~ sth (up)** achieve or register (the stated time, distance or speed) 达到或记录(所说时间、距离或速度): *He clocked 9.6 seconds in the 100 metres.* 他用9.6秒跑完100米. ○ *My car has clocked up 50 000 miles.* 我的汽车已有50 000英里行车记录. **3** (idm 习语) ˈ**clock sb one** (*Brit infml* 口) hit sb, esp in the face 打某人(尤指打耳光): *If you do that again, I'll clock you one.* 你要再那么干, 我就打你耳光. **4** (phr v) **clock (sb) in/on**; **clock (sb) out/off**; *US* **punch (sb) in/out** record the time that one (or sb else) arrives at or leaves work, esp by means of an automatic device 记录上下班时间(尤指用自动设施): *Workers usually clock off at 5.30.* 工人们通常在5时30分下班. ○ *What is ˈclock-in/clocking-ˈin time at your office?* 你们办事处几点上班?

clock·work /ˈklɒkwɜːk; ˈklɑk,wɝk/ *n* [U] **1** mechanism with wheels and springs, like that of a clock (有似时钟的齿轮和发条的)机械: [attrib 作定语] *a clockwork toy*, ie one driven by clockwork 机械玩具 ○ *with clockwork* (ie absolute) *precision* 极精确 ○ *as regular as clockwork*, ie very punctual 总是非常准时. **2** (idm 习语) **like ˈclockwork** with perfect regularity and precision; smoothly 极有规律性和准确性地; 顺利地; 精确地: *The operation went like clockwork.* 手术进行得极为顺利.

clod /klɒd; klɑd/ *n* lump of earth or clay 土块; 泥块.

clod·hop·per /ˈklɒdhɒpə(r); klɑd,hɑpɚ/ *n* (*infml* 口) **1** (*derog* 贬) clumsy person 笨蛋. **2** (*usu pl* 通常作复数) (*joc* 谑) large heavy shoe 大而重的鞋.

clog[1] /klɒg; klɑg/ *n* shoe made entirely of wood or with a wooden sole 全木制的或有木底的鞋; 木屐.

□ ˈ**clog-dance** *n* dance performed by people wearing clogs 木屐舞.

clog[2] /klɒg; klɑg/ *v* (**-gg-**) [I, Ipr, Ip, Tn, Tn·pr, Tn·p] **~ (sth) (up) (with sth)** (cause sth to) become blocked with thick or sticky material (稠的或黏的材料)阻塞, 塞住: *The pipes are clogging up.* 管子渐渐被堵塞. ○ *a drain clogged up with dead leaves* 枯叶堵住的排水道 ○ *pores clogged with dirt* 被脏物堵塞的毛孔 ○ *That heavy oil will clog up the machinery*, ie prevent it from working properly. 这种重油会妨碍机器的运转. ○ (*fig* 比喻)

Don't clog (up) your memory with useless facts. 别满脑子装着那些没用的事.

clois·ter /ˈklɔɪstə(r); ˈklɔɪstɚ/ *n* **1** [C, often *pl* 常作复数] covered passage around an open court or quadrangle, with a wall on the outer side and columns or arches on the inner side, esp within a convent or college, or attached to a cathedral 回廊. **2** (**a**) [C] convent or monastery 修道院. (**b**) [sing] life in a convent or monastery 修道院的生活: *the calm of the cloister* 修道院的幽静.

▷ **clois·ter** *v* [Tn, Tn·p] **~ oneself/sb (away)** shut oneself/sb away (as if) in a cloister 使自己[某人]与世隔绝(像在修道院内): *He cloistered himself away with his books.* 他只顾埋头读书. **clois·tered** *adj* secluded; sheltered 隐居的; 隐匿的: *a cloistered life* 隐居的生活.

C

clone /kləʊn; klon/ *n* **1** (*biology* 生) (any of a) group of plants or organisms produced asexually from one ancestor 无性繁殖系(的个体). **2** (*computing* 计) computer designed to copy the functions of another (usu more expensive) model 仿制的计算机(通常指仿制较贵的): *an IBM clone* 仿IBM型号的计算机.

▷ **clone** *v* [I, Tn] (cause sth to) grow as a clone (使某物)无性繁殖.

close[1] /kləʊs; klos/ *adj* (**-r**, **-st**) **1** [pred 作表语] **~ (to sb/sth); ~ (together)** near in space or time (在空间或时间上)接近: *This station is our closest*, ie the nearest one to our home. 这个站离我们最近. ○ *The church is close to the school.* 教堂离学校很近. ○ *The two buildings are close together.* 这两座建筑物距离很近. ○ *The children are close to each other in age.* 孩子们彼此的年龄很接近. ○ *Their birthdays are very close together.* 他们的生日紧挨着. **2** (**a**) near in relationship 关系很近的: *a close relative* 近亲. (**b**) **~ (to sb)** intimate; dear 亲近的; 亲密的: *a close friend* 密友 ○ *She is very close to her father/She and her father are very close.* 她和父亲的关系很亲密. **3** to a high degree 高度的; 极度的: *in close proximity*, ie almost touching 极为接近 ○ *There's a close resemblance/similarity*, ie They are very alike. 有极为相像[相似]之处. **4** with little or no space between; dense; compact 中间无空隙的; 浓缩的; 挤紧的: *material with a close texture* 质地紧密的材料 ○ *The soldiers advanced in close formation.* 士兵排成密集队形前进. **5** (of a competition, game, etc) in which the competitors are almost equal (指竞赛、游戏等)参赛者几乎平手的, 势均力敌的, 棋逢对手的, 旗鼓相当的, 难分高下的: *a close contest, match, election, etc* 势均力敌的竞赛、比赛、选举等 ○ *a close finish* 几乎平手的结局 ○ *The game was closer than the score suggests.* 实际的比赛与所得的分数相比更难分高下. **6** [attrib 作定语] careful; thorough; detailed 仔细的; 彻底的; 详细的: *On closer examination the painting proved to be a fake.* 再经仔细观察, 证实那幅画是赝品. ○ *pay close attention to sth* 密切关注(某事物) ○ *close reasoning*, ie showing each step clearly 严谨的推理(把每一步骤都表示清楚) ○ *a close* (ie exact) *translation* 紧扣原文的翻译(准确的). **7** [attrib 作定语] strict; rigorous 严格的; 严厉的: *in close confinement* 被严密监禁 ○ *be (kept) under close arrest*, ie carefully guarded 被严密拘禁(戒备森严) ○ *keep sth a close secret* 对某事物严守秘密. **8** (**a**) (of the weather) humid; oppressive; heavy (指天气)潮湿的, 闷热的, 沉闷的: *It's very close and thundery today.* 今天天气阴沉有雷. (**b**) (of a room) without fresh air; stuffy (指房间)没有新鲜空气的, 不通气的: *a close atmosphere* 窒闷的空气 ○ *Open a window — it's very close in here.* 打开窗户吧——这里很闷气. **9** (*phonetics* 语音) (of vowels) pronounced with the tongue raised close to the roof of the mouth (指元音)闭塞音的(发音时将舌抬起接近上腭): *The English vowels /iː/ and /uː/ are close.* 英语元音中的/iː/和/uː/是闭元音. **10** [pred 作表语] secretive; reticent 遮遮掩掩; 沉默寡言: *be close about sth* 对某事物守口如瓶. **11** [pred 作表语] mean; stingy 吝啬; 小气: *He's very close with his money.* 他用钱很吝啬. **12** near to the surface; very short 离表面很近的; 很短的: *A new razor gives a close shave.* 新刀片刮得很干净. **13** (idm 习语) **at ˌclose ˈquarters** very near 非常近的: *fighting at close quarters* 近战. **a ˌclose ˈcall** (*infml* 口) almost an accident, a disaster or a failure 几乎造成事故、灾难或失败: *We didn't actually hit the other car, but it was a close call.* 我们倒并未撞上那辆汽车, 可险些出了事. **a ˌclose ˈshave** situation in which one only just manages to escape an accident, a disaster, etc 勉强脱离危险、灾难等; 死里逃生; 九死一生. **a close/near thing** ⇨ THING. **close to/near the bone** ⇨ BONE. **close/dear/near to sb's heart** ⇨ HEART. **close/near to home** ⇨ HOME[1]. **hold/keep one's cards close to one's chest** ⇨ CARD[1]. **keep a close ˈeye/ˈwatch on sb/sth** watch sb/sth carefully 密切注视某人[某事物]. **keep/lie ˈclose** stay hidden; not show oneself 躲藏; 不露面: *He decided to lie close for a while.* 他决定躲一躲.

▷ **closely** *adv* in a close manner 接近地; 紧密地; 严密地; 密切地: *listen closely*, ie carefully 仔细地听 ○ *follow an argument closely* 密切注意一议论的进行 ○ *a closely contested election* 旗鼓相当的竞选 ○ *She closely resembles her mother.* 她非常像她母亲. ○ *The two events are closely connected.* 这两件事有密切的联系.

close·ness *n* [U].

□ **ˈclose season** (also *esp US* **ˈclosed season**) time of the year when it is illegal to kill certain animals, birds and fish because they are breeding 禁猎期.

close[2] /kləʊs; klos/ *adv* **1** leaving little space between; in a close position 中间无空隙地; 位置接近地: *They live quite close.* 他们住得很近. ○ *hold sb close*, ie embrace sb tightly 紧紧地拥抱某人 ○ *follow close behind sb* 紧跟在某人背后 ○ *She stood close (up) against the wall.* 她紧靠着墙站着. **2** (idm 习语) **close ˈby (sb/sth)** at a short distance (from sb/sth) 离(某人[某事物])不远. **close on** almost; nearly 几乎; 差不多: *She is ˌclose on ˈsixty.* 她接近六十岁了. ○ *It's ˌclose on ˈmidnight.* 已近午夜了. **close up (to sb/sth)** very near in space to sb/sth 离(某人[某事物])很近: *She snuggled close up to him.* 她紧紧地挨着他. **run sb/sth ˈclose** be nearly as good, fast, successful, etc as sb/sth else 接近某人[某事物]那样好、快、成功等: *We run our competitors close for price and quality.* 在价格和质量上, 我们差不多都赶上我们的竞争对手了. **sail close/near to the wind** ⇨ SAIL.

□ **ˌclose-ˈcropped** (also **ˌclose-ˈcut**) *adj* (of hair, grass, etc) cut very short (指毛、发、草等)剪得很短的.

ˌclose-ˈfitting *adj* (of clothes) fitting close to the body (指衣物)紧身的.

ˌclose-ˈgrained (of wood) in which the lines formed by growth are close together (指木材)纹理细密的.

ˌclose-ˈhauled *adj* (*nautical* 海) (of a sailing-ship) with the sails set for sailing as nearly as possible in the direction from which the wind is blowing (指帆船)迎风航行的.

ˌclose-ˈknit *adj* (of a group of people) bound together by shared beliefs, interests, etc (指集体)(为共同的信念、利益等)结合在一起的: *the ˌclose-knit comˈmunity of a small village* 小村庄中关系密切的村民.

ˌclose-ˈrun *adj* [usu attrib 通常作定语] (of a race, competition, etc) won by a very small margin (指竞赛、竞争等)险胜: *The election was a ˌclose-run ˈthing.* 这次竞选仅获险胜.

ˌclose-ˈset *adj* situated very close together 位置靠近的: *ˌclose-set ˈeyes, ˈteeth* 相距很近的双眼、长得很密的牙齿.

ˈclose-up *n* [C, U] photograph or film taken very close to sb/sth and giving a detailed view of him/it (照片或电影的)特写; 特写镜头: *a close-up of a human eye* 人的一只眼睛的特写 ○ *a television scene filmed in close-up* 以特写镜头拍摄的电视画面.

close[3] /kləʊs; klos/ *n* **1** (esp in street names 尤用于街道名称) street closed off at one end; cul-de-sac 一头不通的街道; 死巷; 死胡同: *Brookside Close* 布鲁克赛德巷. **2** grounds and buildings surrounding and belonging to a cathedral, an abbey, etc (大教堂、寺院等的)周围的场地和建筑物.

close[4] /kləʊz; kloz/ *v* **1** [I, Tn] (cause sth to) move so as to cover an opening; shut (使某物)关, 闭: *The door closed quietly.* 门轻轻地关上了. ○ *This box/The lid of this box doesn't close properly*, ie The lid doesn't fit. 盒子[盒子的盖]盖不严. ○ *close a door, a window, the curtains, etc* 关门、关窗户、拉上帘子 ○ *If you close your eyes, you can't see anything.* 若闭上眼睛, 那就什么都看不见了. **2** [I, Tn, Tn·pr] **~ sth (to sb/sth)** be or declare sth to be not open 不开; 关闭某事物: *The shops close* (ie stop trading) *at 5.30.* 商店5时30分关闭(停止营业). ○

Wednesday is early-ˈclosing day, ie the day when the shops are not open in the afternoon. 星期三提早关门(该日商店下午不开门). ○ *The theatres have closed for the summer.* 戏院现已歇夏. ○ *The museum is closed (to visitors) on Sundays.* 星期日博物馆(对参观者)不开放. ○ *This road is closed to motor vehicles.* 这条路机动车不准通行. **3** [I, Ipr, Tn, Tn·pr] (cause sth to) come to an end (使某事物)终止: *The closing* (ie last) *day/date for applications is 1 May.* 申请的截止日[日期]是5月1日. ○ *The speaker closed (the meeting) with a word of thanks to the chairman.* 演讲者向主席道了谢,(会议)就结束了. ○ *As far as I am concerned the matter is closed,* ie it will not be discussed further. 对我来说,事情已了结. ○ *Steel shares closed at £15,* ie This was their value at the end of the day's business on the Stock Exchange. 钢铁股票收盘价为15英镑. ⇨Usage 见所附用法. **4** [I, Tn] (cause sth to) become smaller or narrower (使某物)变小或变窄: *The gap between the two runners is beginning to close,* ie One runner is catching the other up. 两个赛跑者的差距开始缩短. **5** (idm 习语) **a closed ˈbook (to sb)** subject about which one knows nothing 自己一无所知的科目: *Nuclear physics is a closed book to most of us.* 我们大多数人对原子核物理学一窍不通. **beˌhind closed ˈdoors** without the public being allowed to attend; in private 不准公众旁听的; 秘密的: *The meeting was held behind closed doors.* 会议秘密进行. **close a ˈdeal (with sb)** agree to the terms of a business agreement 同意交易协定的条款; 成交. **close one's ˈeyes to sth** ignore sth 不理会某事物; 视而不见; 熟视无睹: *The Government seems to be closing its eyes to the plight of the unemployed.* 政府似乎对失业者的困境熟视无睹. **close one's ˈmind to sth** be unwilling to think about sth seriously 不愿认真思考某事物; 拒不考虑某事物. **close (the/one's) ˈranks (a)** (of soldiers) come closer together in a line or lines (指士兵)排紧, 列队靠拢. **(b)** (of members of a group) forget disagreements and unite in order to protect or defend common interests (指团体中的成员)求同存异, 团结一致保卫或捍卫共同利益: *In times of crisis party members should close ranks.* 在紧要关头, 党员应该团结起来. **shut/close one's eyes to sth** ⇨ EYE[1]. **with one's eyes shut/closed** ⇨ EYE[1].

6 (phr v) **close around/round/over sb/sth** surround and enclose or grip sb/sth 围住并包围或钳制某人[某事物]: *His hand closed over the money.* 他手中紧握着钱. ○ *She felt his arms close tightly around her.* 她觉得他把她搂得很紧.

close ˈdown (of a radio or television station) stop broadcasting (指无线电台或电视台)停止广播: *It is midnight and we are now closing down.* 时间已到午夜, 本台现在停止广播. **close (sth) down** (cause sth to) stop functioning or operating; shut (sth) down permanently (使)停止运转或操作; 永久关闭; 倒闭: *Many businesses have closed down because of the recession.* 因经济衰退许多企业纷纷倒闭.

close ˈin (of days) gradually become shorter (指白天)渐渐变短: *The days are closing in now that autumn is here.* 秋天来到了, 白天渐渐短了. **close in (on sb/sth) (a)** come nearer and attack from several directions 从四面八方逼近并攻击: *The enemy is closing in (on us).* 敌人从四面八方(向我们)逼近. **(b)** surround or envelop sb/sth 围绕或笼罩某人[某事物]: *Darkness was gradually closing in.* 暮色渐渐降临.

close ˈup (of a wound) heal (指伤口)愈合: *The cut took a long time to close up.* 伤口经过很长时间才愈合. **close (sth) up (a)** come or bring (sth) closer together 使靠紧、靠近或靠拢: *The sergeant-major ordered the men to close up.* 军士长命令士兵靠拢. **(b)** shut (sth), esp temporarily (尤指暂时)关闭(某事物): *Sorry, madam, we're closing up for lunch.* 很抱歉, 小姐, 我们现在要关门吃午饭. ○ *He closes the shop up at 5.30.* 他在5点30分停止营业.

close with sb (a) accept an offer made by sb 接受或同意某人提出的条件. **(b)** (*dated* 旧) (of soldiers) come together and start fighting (指士兵)短兵相接: *close with the enemy* 与敌人短兵相接. **close with sth** accept (an offer) 接受或同意(提出的条件).

□ ˈ**close-down** *n* act of closing (sth) down 关闭(某物).

ˈ**closing price** (usu *pl* 通常作复数) price of a share at the end of a day's business on the Stock Exchange 收市价格(证券交易所中当日某股票收盘时的价格).

ˈ**closing-time** *n* time when a shop, public house, etc ends business for the day (商店、酒馆等的)停止营业时间.

NOTE ON USAGE 用法: Generally, **close** means the same as **shut** and is more formal ☆ **close** 通常与 **shut** 的意思相同, 但较庄重: *Shut/Close the door!* 把门关上! ○ *The box won't shut/close.* 这个盒子关不上. When referring to the opening hours of public places, both **shut** and **close** are used 指公众场所的开放或营业时间时, 用 **shut** 和 **close** 均可: *Shops/Offices shut/close at 5.30.* 商店[办事处]5点30分停止营业[办公]. Note **closed** in the following example 注意以下例句中要用 **closed**: *Museums are closed to the public on Mondays.* 博物馆每逢星期一闭馆. **Close** can mean 'terminate' and 'make smaller' ☆ **close** 可意为'终止'和'使更小': *The meeting was closed after the demonstrators interrupted it.* 会议遭示威者干扰而结束. ○ *Some politicians aim at closing the gap between rich and poor.* 有些政治家的奋斗目标在于缩小贫富的差距. It is also used of roads, railways, etc 这个词还可用于街道、公路、铁路等: *They've closed the road because of an accident.* 这条路因发生事故而被封闭. **Lock** means to close a door, box, suitcase, etc and fasten it with a lock and key. ☆ **lock** 意为把门、盒子、箱子等关上, 再用锁(和钥匙)锁上.

close[5] /kləʊz; kloz/ *n* [sing] **1** end of a period of time or an activity (一段时间或一活动的)终结, 结束, 末尾: *at the close of the day* 在黄昏时候 ○ *towards the close of the 17th century* 将近17世纪末叶 ○ *The day had reached its close.* 天已黑了. ○ *at close of play,* ie at the end of the day's play in a cricket match 当天在板球比赛结束的时候. **2** (idm 习语) **bring sth/come/draw to a ˈclose** end or conclude sth 结束某事物: *The ceremony was brought to a close by the singing of the national anthem.* 典礼在国歌的歌声中结束.

closed /kləʊzd; klozd/ *adj* **1 (a)** not communicating with or influenced by others; self-contained 不与他人来往的; 不受他人影响的; 有自治力的; 封闭的: *a closed society, economy* 闭关自守的社会、经济. **(b)** [esp attrib 尤作定语] limited to certain people; exclusive 只限于某些人的; 不随便吸收新成员的: *a closed membership* 限定的成员资格 ○ *a closed scholarship* 限于部分人的奖学金. **2** unwilling to accept new ideas 不愿接受新思想的: *He has a closed mind.* 他思想闭塞僵化.

□ ˌ**closed-ˌcircuit ˈtelevision** television system in which signals are transmitted by wires to a limited number of receivers 闭路电视.

ˈ**closed season** (*esp US*) = CLOSE SEASON (CLOSE[1]).

ˌ**closed ˈshop** factory, business, etc whose employees must be members of a specified trade union (只雇用工会会员的)工厂、企业等: [attrib 作定语] *a closed-shop agreement* 只雇用工会会员的劳资协议.

closet /ˈklɒzɪt; ˈklɑzɪt/ *n* **1** (*esp US*) cupboard or small room for storing things (储存物品的)柜橱或小房间. **2** (*arch* 古) small room for private meetings 私人的小议事室.

▷ **closet** *adj* [attrib 作定语] secret 秘密的: *I never knew he was a closet queen,* ie homosexual. 我从来不知道他暗地里搞同性恋. ○ *I suspect he's a closet fascist.* 我怀疑他是地下法西斯分子.

closet *v* [usu passive 通常用于被动语态: Tn, Tn·pr, Tn·p] **~ A and B (together); ~ A with B** shut sb away in a room for a private meeting 把某人关在房间里作私人会晤: *He was closeted with the manager/He and the manager were closeted together for three hours.* 他与经理在密室会谈[他们在密室里一起商谈了三个小时].

clos·ure /ˈkləʊʒə(r); ˈkloʒɚ/ *n* [C, U] **1** closing or being closed 关闭; 终止; 结束: *pit closures,* eg closing of coal-mines because they are uneconomic 矿山关闭(如因不经济而关闭煤矿) ○ *The threat of closure affected the workers' morale.* 工厂行将倒闭一事影响着工人的士气. **2** (*US* **cloture**) (in a parliament or other legislative body) method of ending a debate by taking a vote (国会或其他立法议会中的)借投票表决以终止辩论的方法: *move the closure* 提议以投票表决终止辩论 ○ *apply the* *closure to a debate* 以投票表决终止辩论. Cf 参看 GUILLOTINE 3.

clot /klɒt; klɑt/ *n* **1** half-solid lump formed from a liquid, eg from blood when it is exposed to the air (液体结成的)凝块(如血块): *blood clots* 血块. **2** (*Brit infml joc* 口, 谑) stupid person; fool 笨蛋; 傻瓜: *You silly clot!* 你这个大笨蛋!

▷ **clot** *v* (**-tt-**) [I, Tn] (cause sth to) form clots (使某物)凝固: *A haemophiliac's blood will not clot properly.* 血友病患者的血液凝固不良.

□ ˌ**clotted** ˈ**cream** (*Brit*) thick cream made by scalding milk 凝结的乳脂(将乳类加热煮沸而成).

cloth /klɒθ; *US* klɔːθ; klɔθ/ *n* (*pl* **~s** /klɒθs; *US* klɔːðz; klɔðz/) **1** [U] material made by weaving cotton, wool, silk, etc (棉、毛、丝等织的)料子, 布料, 毛料, 丝绸: *enough cloth to make a suit* 够做一身衣服的料子 ○ *good quality woollen cloth* 优质毛料 ○ [attrib 作定语] *a cloth binding* 布面装订. **2** [C] (esp in compounds 尤用以构成复合词) piece of cloth used for a special purpose 作某种用途的布块: *a* ˈ*dishcloth* ○ *a* ˈ*floorcloth* ○ *a* ˈ*table-cloth*. **3 the cloth** [sing] clothes worn by the clergy, seen as a symbol of their profession 教士服, 牧师服(被视为神职的标志): *the respect due to his cloth* 因他任神职而受到的尊敬 ○ *a man of the cloth*, ie a clergyman 一位神职人员(传教士). **4** (idm 习语) **cut one's coat according to one's cloth** ⇨ COAT.

clothe /kləʊð; kloð/ *v* (**a**) [usu passive 通常用于被动语态: Tn, Tn·pr] **~ sb/oneself (in sth)** put clothes on sb/oneself; dress 给某人[自己]穿上衣物; 穿(衣物): *clothed from head to foot in white* 从头到脚穿戴一身白的 ○ *warmly clothed* 穿得暖的. (**b**) [Tn] provide clothes for (sb) 供给(某人)衣物: *He can barely feed and clothe his family.* 他勉强能给予全家人温饱. (**c**) [Tn·pr] **~ sth in sth** cover sth as if with clothes (像穿衣物般)覆盖某物: *a landscape clothed in mist* 笼罩于雾中的风景.

clothes /kləʊðz; *US* kləʊz; kloz/ *n* [pl] (not used with numerals 不可与数字连用) covering for a person's body; garments 衣物; 衣服; 服装: *warm, fashionable, expensive, etc clothes* 温暖的、时髦的、昂贵的衣物 ○ *put on/take off one's clothes* 穿上[脱下]衣物.

□ ˈ**clothes-basket** *n* basket for clothes which need to be washed or have been washed 放置待洗的或洗净的衣物的篮子.

ˈ**clothes-brush** *n* brush for removing dust, mud, hair, etc from clothes 衣刷.

ˈ**clothes-hanger** *n* = HANGER 1.

ˈ**clothes-horse** *n* frame on which clothes are hung to air after they have been washed and dried 晒衣架.

ˈ**clothes-line** *n* rope stretched between posts on which washed clothes, etc are hung to dry 晾衣绳. ⇨illus at App 1 见附录1之插图, page vii.

ˈ**clothes moth** = MOTH 2.

ˈ**clothes-peg** (*Brit*) (*US* ˈ**clothes-pin**) *n* wooden or plastic clip for fastening clothes to a clothes-line (用于晾衣绳的)衣夹. ⇨illus at PEG 见 PEG 之插图.

cloth·ing /ˈkləʊðɪŋ; ˈkloðɪŋ/ *n* [U] **1** clothes 衣物; 服装: *articles/items of clothing* 衣物 ○ *waterproof clothing* 防水服; 雨衣. ⇨App 4 见附录4. **2** (idm 习语) **a wolf in sheep's clothing** ⇨ WOLF.

clo·ture /ˈkləʊtʃə(r); ˈklotʃɚ/ *n* (*US*) = CLOSURE.

cloud¹ /klaʊd; klaʊd/ *n* **1** [C, U] (separate mass of) visible water vapour floating in the sky 云: *black clouds appearing from the west* 西方出现的乌云 ○ *There wasn't a cloud in the sky.* 天空无云. ○ *The top of the mountain was covered in cloud.* 浮云遮盖着山顶. **2** [C] (**a**) mass of smoke, dust, sand, etc in the air (空中的烟、尘、沙等的)团. (**b**) mass of insects moving together in the sky (天空中昆虫的)群: *a cloud of locusts* 一群飞蝗. **3** [C] blurred patch in a liquid or on a transparent object (液体或透明物体中的)混浊斑. **4** [C] (*fig* 比喻) thing that causes unhappiness, uncertainty, etc 造成不愉快、不明朗等的事物: *A cloud of suspicion is hanging over him.* 有一团疑云笼罩着他. ○ *Her arrival cast a cloud (of gloom) over the party.* 她一来给聚会蒙上了一层阴影. **5** (idm 习语) **every cloud has a silver** ˈ**lining** (*saying* 谚) there is always a comforting or more hopeful side to a sad or difficult situation 乌云背后总有一线光芒(在逆境中总有值得宽慰的或有希望的一面). **have one's head in the clouds** ⇨ HEAD¹. **on cloud** ˈ**nine** (*infml* 口) extremely happy 极快乐: *He was on cloud nine after winning the competition.* 他在比赛获胜后欣喜若狂. **under a** ˈ**cloud** in disgrace or under suspicion 失体面; 受怀疑.

▷ **cloud·less** *adj* without clouds; clear 无云的; 晴朗的: *a cloudless sky* 晴朗的天空.

cloudy *adj* (**-ier**, **-iest**) **1** covered with clouds 多云的; 乌云密布的: *a cloudy sky* 多云的天空. **2** (esp of liquids) not clear or transparent (尤指液体)混浊的, 不透明的. **cloudi·ness** *n* [U].

□ ˈ**cloud-bank** *n* thick mass of low cloud 低垂浓密的云团.

ˈ**cloudburst** *n* sudden and violent rainstorm 骤雨; 暴雨.

ˌ**cloud** ˈ**chamber** (*physics* 物) device containing vapour in which the paths of charged particles, X-rays and gamma rays can be observed by the trail of tiny drops of condensed vapour they produce 云室(一种含饱和水蒸气的辐射探测器, 遇有粒子、X射线和伽马射线通过时, 可形成凝结的细小水滴的径迹).

cloud-ˈ**cuckoo-land** *n* ideal place or state of affairs that exists only in the mind of an impractical or unrealistic person (脱离现实的)理想境界.

cloud² /klaʊd; klaʊd/ *v* **1** [I, Tn] (cause sth to) become dull, unclear or indistinct (使某事物)变得阴沉暗淡不清楚、不明朗或不清晰: *Her eyes clouded with tears.* 她泪眼模糊. ○ *Tears clouded her eyes.* 眼泪使她的眼睛朦胧不清. ○ *Steam clouded the mirror*, ie covered it with condensation. 蒸气把镜子弄得模糊不清. ○ (*fig* 比喻) *Old age has clouded his judgement.* 他年事已高, 判断力减弱了. ○ *Don't cloud the issue*, ie Don't make it unnecessarily complicated. 不要把问题搞得复杂化. **2** [I, Ip] **~ (over)** (of sb's face) show sadness or worry (指某人的脸)显得阴沉或忧伤: *His face clouded (over) when he heard the news.* 他听到这一消息, 脸就沉了下来. **3** [Tn] spoil (sth); threaten 毁坏(某事物); 威胁: *cloud sb's enjoyment, happiness, etc* 冲淡了某人的兴致、欢乐等 ○ *I hope this disagreement won't cloud our friendship.* 我希望这一分歧不会影响我们的友谊. **4** (phr v) **cloud** ˈ**over** (of the sky) become covered with clouds (指天空)布满了云.

clout /klaʊt; klaʊt/ *n* (*infml* 口) **1** [C] heavy blow with the hand or a hard object (用手或硬物)猛击, 敲, 打: *get a clout across the back of the head* 脑后受到狠狠一击. **2** [U] power or influence 权力; 影响力: *This union hasn't much clout with the Government.* 这个组织对政府没有什么影响力.

▷ **clout** *v* [Tn] (*infml* 口) hit (sb/sth) heavily with the hand or a hard object (用手或硬物)猛击, 打(某人[某物]).

clove¹ *pt* of CLEAVE¹.

clove² /kləʊv; klov/ *n* dried unopened flower-bud of the tropical myrtle tree, used as a spice 丁香(一种热带树的干花苞, 用作香料或调味品).

clove³ /kləʊv; klov/ *n* one of the small separate sections of a compound bulb (复合鳞茎的)瓣: *a clove of garlic* 一瓣蒜. ⇨illus at ONION 见 ONION 之插图.

clove hitch /ˈkləʊv hɪtʃ; ˈklov ˌhɪtʃ/ knot used to fasten a rope round a pole, bar, etc 卷结(用绳绕过杆、柱等的一种结绳法).

cloven *pp* of CLEAVE¹.

clover /ˈkləʊvə(r); ˈklovɚ/ *n* **1** [U] small plant with (usu) three leaves on each stalk, and purple, pink or white flowers, grown as food for cattle, etc 车轴草(一种矮小植物, 可作牧草, 每一叶柄上通常有三片叶子, 花呈紫色、粉红色或白色): *(a)* ˌ*four-leaf/-leaved* ˈ*clover*, ie a rare type of clover with four leaves, thought to bring good luck to anyone who finds it 四叶车轴草(一种稀有的车轴草品种, 叶柄上有四片叶子, 认为可给发现它的人带来好运). **2** (idm 习语) **in clover** (*infml* 口) in comfort or luxury 安逸; 舒适; 富裕: *be/live in clover* 生活优裕.

□ ˈ**clover-leaf** *n* (*pl* **-leafs** or **-leaves** /liːvz; ˌlivz/) motorway intersection in a pattern resembling a four-leaf clover, allowing traffic to move in any of four directions 蝶式立体交叉桥(车辆可向任何方向行驶的高速公路立交桥).

clown /klaʊn; klaʊn/ *n* **1** comic entertainer (esp in a circus) who paints his face and dresses in a ridiculous way and performs funny or foolish tricks 滑稽演员；（尤指马戏团的）小丑. **2** person who is always behaving comically 举止一贯滑稽可笑的人.

▷ **clown** *v* [I, Ip] **~ (about/around)** (*usu derog* 通常作贬义) act in a foolish or comical way, like a clown 扮小丑: *Stop clowning around!* 不要再像小丑那样胡闹了!

clown·ish *adj* of or like a clown 丑角的; 像小丑的.

cloy /klɔɪ; klɔɪ/ *v* (*dated fml* 旧, 文) **1** [I] (of sth sweet or pleasurable) become unpleasant by being tasted or experienced too often（指甜食或美好的事物）因过多而生厌; 吃腻; 玩腻: *The pleasures of idleness soon cloy.* 无所事事的享乐很快就使人厌烦了. **2** [Tn esp passive 尤用于被动语态] sicken (sb) with too much sweetness or pleasure（因吃甜食过多或享乐过度）使（某人）生腻, 生厌: *cloyed with rich food* 吃腻美食.

▷ **cloy·ing** *adj* (of food, etc) sickeningly sweet（指食物等）甜得发腻的: (*fig* 比喻) *a cloying smile, manner* 嬉皮笑脸的微笑、态度.

cloze test /ˈkləʊz test; ˋkloz ˌtɛst/ comprehension test in which the person being tested tries to fill in words that have been left out of a text 填空测验（阅读理解力测验, 被测者须填出选文中删去的词语以测验理解力）.

club[1] /klʌb; klʌb/ *n* (esp in compounds 尤用以构成复合词) **1** (**a**) [C] group of people who meet together regularly to participate in a particular activity (esp a sport) or for relaxation（尤指体育等活动的）社团; 会社; 俱乐部: *a cricket, football, rugby, etc club* ○ *a working men's club* ○ *a youth club*. (**b**) [C] building or rooms used by a club（俱乐部所用的）建筑物或房屋: *have a drink at the golf club* ○ [attrib 作定语] *the club bar* 俱乐部酒吧间. **2** [CGp, C] (organization owning a) building where elected (usu male) members may stay temporarily, have meals, read the newspapers, etc（通常为男性会员的）社团建筑物, 会所: *The club has/have decided to increase subscriptions.* 会所决定增加报刊订阅份数. ○ *He's a member of several London clubs.* 他是伦敦几个会所的成员. **3** [C] commercial organization offering benefits to members who agree to make regular payments of money（为会员提供利益的）商业组织: *a book club*. **4** [C] = NIGHT-CLUB (NIGHT). **5** (idm 习语) **in the club** (*Brit sl* 俚) pregnant 怀孕. **join the club** ⇨ JOIN.

▷ **club** *v* (**-bb-**) (phr v) **club together (to do sth)** (of the members of a group) make contributions of money, etc so that the total can be used for a specific purpose（指某集体中的成员）（为某目的）凑钱, 分摊费用: *They clubbed together to buy the chairman a present.* 他们出份子给主席买礼物.

club·bable /ˈklʌbəbl; ˋklʌbəbl̩/ *adj* suitable to be a member of a club; sociable 有资格做俱乐部会员的; 善于交际的.

□ ˈ**club car** (*US*) first-class railway carriage offering comfortable seats and refreshments 有舒适座位及小吃的火车车厢.

ˈ**clubhouse** *n* building used by a sports club, esp a golf club 俱乐部会所.

ˌ**club** ˈ**sandwich** (*esp US*) sandwich consisting of three slices of bread or toast and two layers of meat, lettuce, tomato, etc 总会三明治（三片面包夹有两层肉、生菜、蕃茄等的三明治）.

club[2] /klʌb; klʌb/ *n* **1** heavy stick with one end thicker than the other, used as a weapon（一端粗一端细的沉重的）棍棒（可用作武器）. **2** stick with a specially shaped end for hitting the ball in golf and hockey 高尔夫球棒; 曲棍球棒. ⇨illus at GOLF 见 GOLF 之插图.

▷ **club** *v* (**-bb-**) [Tn] hit or beat (sb/sth) with a club or heavy object（用棍棒或重物）打、击（某人［某物］）: *The soldiers clubbed him (to death) with their rifles.* 士兵用枪托打（死了）他.

□ ˌ**club-**ˈ**foot** *n* (**a**) [C] foot that is deformed from birth（先天性的）畸形足. (**b**) [U] condition of having such a foot 生有畸形足. ˌ**club-**ˈ**footed** *adj*.

ˌ**club-**ˈ**root** *n* [U] disease affecting cabbages and similar plants, with swelling of the roots（甘蓝等植物的）根肿病.

club[3] /klʌb; klʌb/ *n* (**a**) **clubs** [sing or pl *v*] suit of playing-cards with a black three-leaf design on them（纸牌戏的）梅花: *Clubs is/are trumps.* 梅花是王牌. ○ *the ace of clubs* 梅花幺. (**b**) [C] playing-card of this suit 梅花牌: *play a club* 出梅花牌. ⇨illus at PLAYING-CARD 见 PLAYING-CARD 之插图.

cluck /klʌk; klʌk/ *n* noise that a hen makes, eg when calling her chicks（母鸡的）咯咯叫声（如呼唤小鸡时）.

▷ **cluck** *v* **1** [I] make a cluck 发出咯咯声. **2** [I, Tn] (of people) express (disapproval, etc) by making a similar noise（指人）发出表示不同意等的声音.

clue /klu:; klu/ *n* **1 ~ (to sth)** fact or piece of evidence that helps to solve a problem or reveal the truth in an investigation 线索; 端倪: *The only clue to the identity of the murderer was a half-smoked cigarette.* 鉴定谋杀者的唯一线索是一枝吸了一半的香烟. ○ *We have no clue as to where she went after she left home.* 我们对她离家后去往何处毫无线索. **2** word or words indicating the answer to be inserted in a crossword puzzle（纵横填字字谜中对应填词语的）提示词语. **3** (idm 习语) **not have a** ˈ**clue** (*infml* 口) (**a**) not know (anything about) sth; not know how to do sth 对某事物一无所知; 不知如何做某事物: *'When does the train leave?' 'I haven't a clue.'* '火车什么时候开?' '我完全不知道.' (**b**) (*derog* 贬) be stupid or incompetent 愚笨; 无能: *'Don't ask him to do it — he hasn't a clue.'* '不要叫他做——他没本事.'

▷ **clue** *v* (phr v) **clue sb up (about/on sth)** (*infml* 口) (usu passive 通常用于被动语态) make sb well-informed (about sth) 使某人熟知（某事物）: *She's really clued up on politics.* 她对政治非常博学多闻.

clue·less /klu:lɪs; ˋklulɪs/ *adj* (*infml derog* 口, 贬) stupid or incompetent 愚笨的; 无能的: *He's absolutely clueless.* 他毫无本事.

clump[1] /klʌmp; klʌmp/ *n* group or cluster (esp of trees, shrubs or plants)（尤指树木或花草的）丛: *a small clump of oak trees* 橡树丛.

▷ **clump** *v* [Tn, Tn·p esp passive 尤用于被动语态] **~ sth (together)** form a clump or arrange sth in a clump 形成一丛; 将某物聚集成堆: *The children's shoes were all clumped together in a corner.* 孩子们的鞋都堆在角落里.

clump[2] /klʌmp; klʌmp/ *v* [Ipr, Ip] **~ about, around, etc** walk in the specified direction putting the feet down heavily 以沉重的脚步向某方向行走: *clumping about (the room) in heavy boots* 穿着笨重的靴子（在屋里）走来走去.

▷ **clump** *n* [sing] sound of heavy footsteps 沉重的脚步声: *the clump of boots* 靴子的咯咯声.

clumsy /ˈklʌmzɪ; ˋklʌmzɪ/ *adj* (**-ier, -iest**) **1** awkward and ungraceful in movement or shape（行动或形状）笨拙而难看的: *You clumsy oaf — that's the second glass you've broken today!* 你这个笨傢伙——这是你今天打碎的第二个玻璃杯! **2** (of tools, furniture, etc) difficult to use or move; not well designed（指工具、家具等）难用的, 难移动的; 设计欠佳的: *a clumsy sideboard, pair of scissors* 不好用的碗柜、剪刀 ○ *It's not easy walking in these clumsy shoes.* 穿着这双笨重的鞋走路真难受. **3** done without tact or skill 无策略的; 无技巧的: *a clumsy apology, reply, speech, etc* 生硬的道歉、回答、讲话等 ○ *a clumsy forgery*, ie one that is easy to detect 粗劣的伪造品（容易识破的）. ▷ **clum·sily** *adv*. **clum·si·ness** *n* [U].

clung *pt, pp* of CLING.

clunk /klʌŋk; klʌŋk/ *n* dull sound (as) of heavy metal objects striking together（沉重的金属物件的）碰击声, 哐啷声.

▷ **clunk** *v* [I] make this sound 发出哐啷声.

clus·ter /ˈklʌstə(r); ˋklʌstɚ/ *n* **1** number of things of the same kind growing closely together（丛生的）簇, 丛, 团, 串: *a cluster of berries, flowers, curls* 一簇浆果、花、鬈发 ○ *ivy growing in thick clusters* 成丛生长的常春藤. **2** number of people, animals or things grouped closely together（任何的）群, 堆, 组, 团, 串: *a cluster of houses, spectators, bees, islands, diamonds, stars* 密密匝匝的房屋、观众、蜜蜂、岛屿、钻石、星星 ○ *a consonant cluster*, eg *str* in *strong* 辅音连缀（如 strong 中的 str）.

▷ **clus·ter** *v* (phr v) **cluster/be clustered (together) round sb/sth** form a cluster round sb/sth; surround sb/sth closely 聚集在某人［某物］的周围; 丛生; 群聚: *roses clustering round the window* 绕着窗户丛生的玫瑰花 ○ *The village clusters round the church.* 村子的房屋围绕在教堂的四周. ○ *Reporters (were) clustered round the Prime Minister.* 记者把首相团团围住.

C

clutch[1] /klʌtʃ; klʌtʃ/ *v* **1** (**a**) [Tn] seize (sb/sth) eagerly 急忙抓住(某人[某事物]): *He clutched the rope we threw to him.* 他急忙抓住我们扔给他的绳子. (**b**) [Tn, Tn·pr] hold (sb/sth) tightly in the hand(s) 紧紧地抱住、握住(某人[某物]): *clutch a baby in one's arms* 双臂抱住婴儿 ○ *Mary was clutching her doll to her chest.* 玛丽把洋娃娃抱在怀里. **2** (idm 习语) **clutch at a straw/straws** try to grasp a slight opportunity to escape, rescue sb, etc in desperate circumstances 临危极力抓住渺茫的机会逃脱、救人等. **3** (phr v) **clutch at sth** try to seize sth 试图抓住某事物: *He clutched at the branch but couldn't reach it.* 他想抓住树枝, 可是没够着.

▷ **clutch** *n* **1** (**a**) [C] act of clutching or seizing 抓; 握; 抱: *make a clutch at sth* 想抓取某事物. (**b**) [sing] act of holding sth in the fingers or the hands; grip 抓; 握; 捏; 攥. **2 clutches** [pl] power or control (used esp as in the expressions shown) 势力范围, 控制(尤用于以下示例): *be in sb's clutches* 在某人控制下 ○ *fall into the clutches of sb/sth* 落入某人[某事物]的势力范围 ○ *have sb in one's clutches* 把某人控制住 ○ *escape from sb's clutches* 摆脱某人的控制. **3** [C] (**a**) device that connects and disconnects working parts in a machine (esp the engine and gears in a motor vehicle) 接合器; (尤指)离合器: *let in/out the clutch*, ie when changing gear 接合[分离]离合器(换挡时) ○ *She released the clutch and the car began to move.* 她放开离合器, 汽车就动了. (**b**) pedal that operates this device 离合器踏板: *take one's foot off the clutch* 把脚从离合器踏板上抬起. ⇨illus at App 1 见附录1之插图, page xii.

clutch[2] /klʌtʃ; klʌtʃ/ *n* (**a**) set of eggs that a hen sits on and that hatch together 母鸡一次所孵的蛋; 一窝蛋. (**b**) group of young chickens that hatch from these eggs 一窝小鸡.

clut·ter /ˈklʌtə(r); ˋklʌtɚ/ *n* (*derog* 贬) (**a**) [U] (esp unnecessary or unwanted) things lying about untidily 凌乱的东西: *How can you work with so much clutter on your desk?* 书桌上有这么多乱七八糟的东西, 你怎么能工作呢? (**b**) [sing] untidy state 杂乱; 凌乱: *His room is always in a clutter.* 他的房间总是凌乱不堪.

▷ **clut·ter** *v* [esp passive 尤用于被动语态: Tn, Tn·p] **~ sth (up)** fill or cover sth in an untidy way 胡乱地填满、塞满或覆盖住某事物: *a room cluttered (up) with unnecessary furniture* 塞满不必要的家具的房间 ○ *Don't clutter up my desk — I've just tidied it.* 不要在我的书桌上乱放东西——我刚收拾好. ○ (*fig* 比喻) *His head is cluttered (up) with useless facts.* 他满脑子杂七杂八的闲事.

cm *abbr* 缩写 = (*pl* unchanged or **cms** 复数或不变或作 **cms**) centimetre: *600 cm × 140 cm*, ie as a measure of area 600厘米 × 140厘米.

Cmdr *abbr* 缩写 = CDR.

Cmdre *abbr* 缩写 = CDRE.

CND /ˌsiː en ˈdiː; ˌsi ɛn ˋdi/ *abbr* 缩写 = (*Brit*) Campaign for Nuclear Disarmament 核裁军运动.

co- *pref* 前缀 (used fairly widely with *adjs, advs, ns* and *vs* 可与许多形容词、副词、名词、动词结合) together; jointly 共同; 一起; 联合: *co-produced* ○ *co-operatively* ○ *co-driver* ○ *co-star.*

CO /ˌsiː ˈəʊ; ˌsi ˋo/ *abbr* 缩写 = Commanding Officer 指挥官.

Co *abbr* 缩写 = **1** (*esp commerce* 尤用于商业) company: *Pearce, Briggs & Co* 皮尔斯—布里格斯公司 ○ *the Stylewise Furniture Co* 斯泰尔怀斯家具公司 ○ (*infml* 口) *Were Jane and Mary and Co* /ˈmeərɪ ən kəʊ; ˋmɛrɪ ən ko/ *at the party?* 简和玛丽他们来参加聚会了吗? **2** county 郡: *Co Down, Northern Ireland* 北爱尔兰当郡.

c/o /ˌsiː ˈəʊ; ˌsi ˋo/ *abbr* 缩写 = (on letters, etc addressed to sb staying at sb else's house) care of (用于信件等)由…转交: *Mr Peter Brown c/o Mme Marie Duval....* 玛丽·杜瓦尔夫人转交彼得·布朗先生.

coach[1] /kəʊtʃ; kotʃ/ *n* **1** bus (usu with a single deck) for carrying passengers over long distances 长途公共汽车(通常指单层的): *travel by overnight coach to Scotland* 乘坐夜间长途汽车去苏格兰 ○ [attrib 作定语] *a coach station* 长途汽车站 ○ *a coach tour of Italy* 乘长途汽车游览意大利. **2** = CARRIAGE 2. **3** large four-wheeled carriage pulled by horses and used (esp formerly) for carrying passengers 四轮大马车(尤指旧时载客的): *a ˈstage-coach* 公共马车. **4** (idm 习语) **drive a coach and horses through sth** ⇨ DRIVE[1].

□ **coachman** /ˈkəʊtʃmən; ˋkotʃmən/ *n* (*pl* **-men** /-mən; -mən/) driver of a horse-drawn carriage 马车夫.

ˈ**coachwork** *n* [U] main outside structure of a road or railway vehicle (公路或铁路车辆的)车身外壳.

coach[2] /kəʊtʃ; kotʃ/ *n* **1** person who trains sportsmen, esp for contests (运动员的)教练: *a tennis, football, swimming, etc coach* 网球、足球、游泳等的教练. **2** teacher who gives private lessons to prepare students for examinations (私人的)辅导教师.

▷ **coach** *v* (**a**) [Tn, Tn·pr] **~ sb (for/in sth)** teach or train sb, esp for an examination or a sporting contest 辅导或训练某人(尤指为参加考试或比赛): *coach a swimmer for the Olympics* 训练准备参加奥林匹克运动会的游泳运动员 ○ *coach sb in maths* 辅导某人数学 ○ *She has talent but she will need coaching.* 她有天分, 但需要指导. (**b**) [I] work or act as a coach 辅导或训练的工作或活动: *She'll be coaching all summer.* 她整个夏天将要作辅导工作. ⇨Usage at TEACH 用法见 TEACH.

co·agu·late /kəʊˈægjʊleɪt; koˋægjə,let/ *v* [I, Tn] (cause sth to) change from a liquid to a thick and semi-solid state; clot (使液体)变为半固体状态; 凝固: *Blood coagulates in air.* 血液遇到空气就凝结. ○ *Air coagulates blood.* 空气能使血液凝结. ▷ **co·agu·la·tion** /kəʊˌægjʊˈleɪʃn; ko,ægjəˋleʃən/ *n* [U].

coal /kəʊl; kol/ *n* **1** (**a**) [U] black mineral found below the ground, used for burning to supply heat and to make coal gas and coal tar 煤: *put more coal on the fire* 往火里再加些煤 ○ [attrib 作定语] *a coal fire* 煤火 ○ *coal dust* 煤末. (**b**) [C] piece of this material, esp one that is burning (尤指燃烧着的)煤块: *A hot coal fell out of the fire and burnt the carpet.* 火炉里掉出一块炽热的煤把地毯烧了. **2** (idm 习语) **carry coals to Newcastle** ⇨ CARRY. **haul sb over the coals** ⇨ HAUL. **heap coals of fire on sb's head** ⇨ HEAP.

▷ **coal** *v* **1** [Tn] load a supply of coal into (a ship) 给(轮船)加煤, 上煤, 装煤. **2** [I] (of a ship) be loaded with a supply of coal (指轮船)被加煤, 上煤, 装煤.

□ ˌ**coal-ˈblack** *adj* very dark 极黑的: *ˌcoal-black ˈeyes* 乌黑的眼睛.

ˈ**coal-face** (also **face**) *n* part of a coal-seam from which coal is being cut 煤层中的采掘面: *work at the coal-face* 采煤工作.

ˈ**coalfield** *n* district in which coal is mined 采煤区.

ˈ**coal gas** [U] mixture of gases produced from coal, used for lighting and heating 煤气.

ˈ**coal-hole** *n* small cellar for storing coal 贮藏煤的地下室; 地下小煤库.

ˈ**coal-mine** (also **pit**) *n* place underground where coal is dug 煤矿. ˈ**coal-miner** *n* person whose job is digging coal in a coal-mine 煤矿工人.

ˈ**coal oil** *n* (*US*) = PARAFFIN.

ˈ**coal-scuttle** (also **scuttle**) *n* container for coal, usu kept by the fireside 煤斗, 煤桶(通常置于炉边的).

ˈ**coal-seam** *n* layer of coal under the ground 煤层.

ˌ**coal ˈtar** thick black sticky substance produced when gas is made from coal 煤焦油.

co·alesce /ˌkəʊəˈles; ˌkoəˋlɛs/ *v* [I] (*fml* 文) combine and form one group, substance, mass, etc 联合; 结合; 合并: *The views of party leaders coalesced to form a coherent policy.* 党的领导人的各种观点已统一为一致的政策. ▷ **co·ales·cence** /ˌkəʊəˈlesns; ˌkoəˋlɛsn̩s/ *n* [U].

co·ali·tion /ˌkəʊəˈlɪʃn; ˌkoəˋlɪʃən/ *n* **1** [U] action of uniting into one body or group 结合; 联合. **2** [CGp] temporary alliance between political parties, usu in order to form a government 政党间的暂时联合(通常为成立联合政府的): *form a coalition* 结成同盟 ○ *a left-wing coalition* 左翼联盟 ○ [attrib 作定语] *a coalition government* 联合政府.

coam·ing /ˈkəʊmɪŋ; ˋkomɪŋ/ *n* raised rim round a ship's hatches to keep water out 舱口栏板(船舱口周围防水流入的突起边缘).

coarse /kɔːs; kɔrs/ *adj* (**-r, -st**) **1** (**a**) consisting of large particles; not fine 有大颗粒的; 粗糙的; 粗的: *coarse sand, salt, etc* 粗沙、粗盐等. (**b**) rough or loose in texture (表面或质地)粗糙的, 稀松的: *bags made from coarse linen* 用粗亚麻制的口袋 ○ *a coarse complexion/skin* 粗糙的颜面[皮肤]. **2** (of food, wine, etc) of low quality; inferior (指食物、酒等)低劣的, 粗劣的. **3** (**a**)

not refined; vulgar 不高雅的; 粗俗的: *coarse manners, laughter, tastes, etc* 粗俗的举止、笑声、兴味等. (**b**) indecent or obscene 下流的; 猥亵的; 淫秽的: *coarse jokes, humour, language, etc* 粗鄙笑话、幽默、语言等.
▷ **coarsely** *adv*: *chop onions coarsely*, ie into large pieces 把洋葱剁成大块.
coar·sen /ˈkɔːsn; ˋkɔrsn̩/ *v* [I, Tn] (cause sth to) become coarse (使某物)变粗糙: *The sea air coarsened her skin.* 海上的空气使她的皮肤粗糙了.
coarse·ness *n* [U].
□ ˌ**coarse** ˈ**fish** freshwater fish other than salmon and trout (除鲑和鳟以外的)淡水鱼. ˌ**coarse** ˈ**fishing** trying to catch coarse fish as a sport 捕捉淡水鱼(作为娱乐活动).

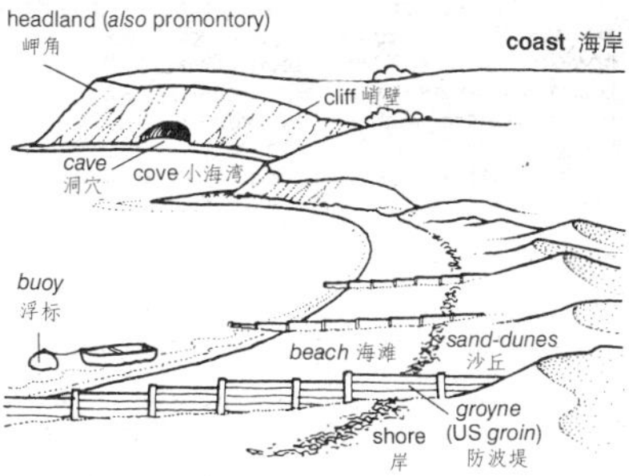

coast[1] /kəʊst; kost/ *n* **1** land bordering the sea 海岸: *The ship was wrecked on the Kent coast.* 该船在肯特海岸遇难. ○ *islands off the Scottish coast* 苏格兰沿海的岛屿 ○ *a village on the south coast*, eg of England 南海岸的村子(如英格兰南海岸) ○ *spend a day by the coast*, ie the seaside 在海滨度一日 ○ [attrib 作定语] *a coast road*, ie one that follows the line of the coast 沿海岸线的道路. ⇨illus 见插图. **2** (idm 习语) **the** ˌ**coast is** ˈ**clear** (*infml* 口) there is no danger of being seen or caught 没有被发现或被捉住的危险: *They waited until the coast was clear before loading the stolen goods into the van.* 他们待四下无人时就把赃物装进货车.
▷ **coastal** *adj* [usu attrib 通常作定语] of or near a coast 海岸的; 沿海的: *coastal waters* 近海水域 ○ *a coastal town, area, etc* 沿海的城镇、地区等. Cf 参看 INLAND 1.
□ ˈ**coastguard** *n* [C, CGp] (one of a) group of people employed to watch the coast and report passing ships, prevent smuggling, etc (受雇监视、报告过往船只、防止走私等的)海岸警卫队(员).
ˈ**coastline** *n* shape or outline of a coast 海岸的轮廓; 海岸线: *a rugged, rocky, indented, etc coastline* 崎岖的、多石的、弯弯曲曲的…海岸线.

NOTE ON USAGE 用法: **Coast** and **shore** both indicate land lying beside large areas of water. ☆ **coast** 和 **shore** 均指邻接大片水域的陆地. **Shore** suggests the limits of a lake or sea, or a narrow strip of land next to the water ☆ **shore** 指湖或海的边缘或水边的狭长的陆地: *They camped on the shore of Lake Bala.* 他们在巴拉湖畔宿营. ○ *The survivors swam to the shore.* 幸存者游上了岸. The land at the edge of a river or stream is a **bank.** 江河或溪流边上的陆地叫做 **bank.** ☆ **Coast** can refer to a wider area of land or a long stretch of land next to the sea or ocean ☆ **coast** 可指邻接海或洋的较宽阔的或狭长的地域: *We live at/on the coast.* 我们住在海滨. ○ *the Atlantic coast of South America* 南美洲的大西洋海岸. The **beach** is usually the sloping part of the **shore** often covered by the sea at high tide ☆ **beach** 通常指 **shore** 的倾斜部分, 往往在涨潮时被潮水漫过: *The beach was crowded with sunbathers.* 沙滩上挤满了作日光浴的人们. The **seaside** is a coastal area where people go on holiday ☆ **seaside** 是指人们前往度假的沿海地区: *Brighton is a famous seaside resort.* 布赖顿是著名的海滨胜地. ○ *We're spending August at the seaside.* 我们八月份要在海滨度过.

coast[2] /kəʊst; kost/ *v* **1** [I, Ipr, Ip] (**a**) move, esp downhill (in a car, on a bicycle, etc), without using power (不使用动力, 尤指向山下)移动, 滑行(乘汽车、骑自行车等): *coast down a hill* (ie in neutral gear) *to save petrol* 滑行下山以省汽油(如使用空挡) ○ *coasting along on a bicycle*, ie without pedalling 骑在自行车上滑行(不用脚蹬). (**b**) (*fig* 比喻) make progress without much effort 不很费力而取得进展: *The Socialists are coasting to victory* (ie winning easily) *in the election.* 社会党人在选举中会轻易获胜. **2** [I] sail (from port to port) along a coast 沿着海岸(从一港口到另一港口)航行.
coaster /ˈkəʊstə(r); ˋkostɚ/ *n* **1** (**a**) small mat put under a drinking-glass to protect a polished table, etc from drips 杯垫. (**b**) small tray for holding a decanter, wine bottle, etc (放饮料瓶、酒瓶等的)小托盘. **2** ship that sails from port to port along a coast (沿海岸各港口航行的)轮船.
coat /kəʊt; kot/ *n* **1** long outer garment with sleeves, usu fastened at the front with buttons 大衣: *a waterproof, fur, leather, etc coat* 防水的、皮毛的、皮革的等大衣. **2** woman's jacket worn with a skirt (与裙子配套穿的女用)短外套: *a tweed coat and skirt* 粗花呢的外套和裙子. **3** fur, hair or wool covering an animal's body (动物的)皮毛: *a dog with a smooth, shaggy, etc coat* 长有光滑毛的、粗毛的狗 ○ *animals in their winter coats*, ie grown long for extra warmth 长有冬季皮毛的动物(毛长而更保暖). **4** layer of paint or some other substance put on a surface at one time (涂颜料等的)一层: *give sth a second coat of paint* 在某物上涂上第二层颜料. **5** (idm 习语) ˌ**cut one's** ˈ**coat ac**ˌ**cording to one's** ˈ**cloth** (*saying* 谚) spend money or produce sth within the limits of what one can afford 量力而行; 量入为出: *We wanted to buy a bigger house than this but we had to cut our coat according to our cloth.* 我们原想买比这个大些的房子, 但是得量力而为呀. **turn one's coat** desert one side, party, etc and join another, esp because it is profitable or advantageous to do so 背弃自己的一方、党派等而加入另一方(尤指因有利可图或有好处); 变节; 背叛; 改变立场.
▷ **coat** *v* [Tn, Tn·pr] **~ sb/sth (in/with sth)** cover sb/sth with a layer of sth 为某人[某物]加上一层东西: *coat fish in batter* 把鱼蘸上一层面、蛋、奶调成的糊 ○ *biscuits coated with chocolate* 外层有巧克力的饼干 ○ *furniture coated with dust* 落上灰尘的家具 ○ *a coated tongue* 有苔的舌头. **coat·ing** *n* **1** [C] thin layer or covering 薄层; 外层: *a coating of wax, chocolate, paint* 一层蜡、巧克力、颜料. **2** [U] material for making coats (COAT 1, 2) (做大衣或女外套的)面料.
□ ˈ**coat-hanger** *n* = HANGER.

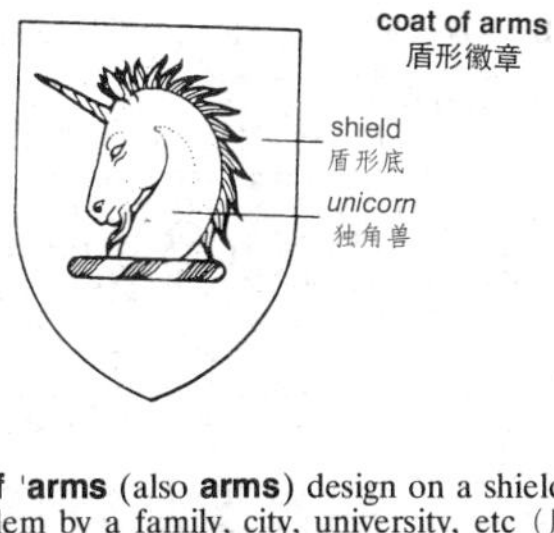

ˌ**coat of** ˈ**arms** (also **arms**) design on a shield used as an emblem by a family, city, university, etc (用作某家族、城市、大学等的标志的)盾形徽章. ⇨illus 见插图.
ˌ**coat of** ˈ**mail** piece of armour made of interlocking metal rings or plates and worn on the upper part of the body 铠甲; 锁子甲.
ˈ**coat-tails** *n* [pl] divided tapering part at the back of a tailcoat (TAIL) (燕尾服的)尾部.
coax /ˈkəʊks; koks/ *v* [Tn, Tn·pr, Cn·t] **1 ~ sb (into/out of (doing) sth)** persuade sb gently or gradually 劝诱或哄劝某人: *He coaxed her into letting him take her to the cinema.* 他哄得她同意带她去看电影. ○ *She coaxed*

him out of his bad temper. 她循循善诱地劝他改掉坏脾气. ○ *coax a child to take its medicine* 哄小孩儿吃药 ○ (*fig* 比喻) *coax a fire with* (ie make it burn by adding) *paraffin* 加上煤油把火点着. **2** (phr v) **coax sth out of/from sb** obtain sth from sb by gentle persuasion 用好言好语劝说某人以得到某事物: *I had to coax the information out of him.* 我得用好话套出他掌握的情况. ○ *She coaxed a smile from the baby.* 她哄得婴儿一笑.

▷ **coax·ing** *n* [U] attempts to persuade sb 试图劝诱某人: *It took a lot of coaxing before he agreed.* 劝说了很久他才同意. ○ (*fig* 比喻) *With a little coaxing* (ie After several attempts) *the engine started.* 发动机打了几次火才发动起来. **coax·ingly** *adv*: *speak coaxingly* 苦口婆心地说.

C

cob /kɒb; kɑb/ *n* **1** strong short-legged horse for riding (供乘骑用的)强壮而腿短的马. **2** male swan 雄天鹅. **3** (also ˈ**cob-nut**) large type of hazel-nut 欧洲榛子. **4** = CORN-COB (CORN[1]): *corn on the cob* 玉米棒子.

co·balt /ˈkəʊbɔːlt; ˈkobɔlt/ *n* [U] **1** chemical element, a hard silvery-white metal used in many alloys 钴. ⇨App 10 见附录10. **2** deep-blue colouring matter made from compounds of this, used to colour glass and pottery 钴类颜料(深蓝色, 用于玻璃及陶瓷着色): [attrib 作定语] *cobalt blue* 钴蓝.

cob·ber /ˈkɒbə(r); ˈkɑbɚ/ *n* (*Austral infml* 澳, 口) (esp used as a form of address between men 尤用作男子间的称呼) friend; mate 朋友; 同伴.

cobble[1] /ˈkɒbl; ˈkɑbl̩/ (also ˈ**cobble-stone**) *n* rounded stone formerly used for covering the surfaces of roads, etc (旧时用于铺路面等的)圆石, 鹅卵石: *The cart clattered over the cobble-stones.* 马车啊啊地驶过石子路.

▷ **cobble** *v* [Tn usu passive 通常用于被动语态] cover the surface of (a road) with cobbles 用圆石铺(路)面: *cobbled streets* 用圆石铺的街道.

cobble /ˈkɒbl; ˈkɑbl̩/ *v* **1** [Tn] repair (shoes) 修补(鞋). **2** [Tn, Tn·p] **~ sth (together)** put sth together or make sth hastily or clumsily 胡乱拼凑; 粗制滥造: *The student cobbled together an essay in half an hour.* 这个学生用半小时草草拼凑了一篇文章.

cob·bler /ˈkɒblə(r); ˈkɑblɚ/ *n* **1** (*becoming dated* 渐旧) person who repairs shoes 修鞋匠; 补鞋匠. **2** (*esp US*) fruit pie with a thick cake-like crust 脆皮水果馅饼. **3** (*esp US*) iced drink made with wine, lemon and sugar (用酒、柠檬和糖制成的)冷饮料.

cob·blers /ˈkɒbləz; ˈkɑblɚz/ *n* [sing *v*] (*Brit sl* 俚) nonsense; rubbish 胡说; 废话: *What a load of (old) cobblers!* 胡说八道!

COBOL (also **Cobol**) /ˈkəʊbɒl; ˈkoˌbɔl/ *abbr* 缩写 = (*computing* 计) common business-oriented language, a programming language designed for use in commerce 通用商业语言(为商业用途而设计的程序语言).

co·bra /ˈkəʊbrə; ˈkobrə/ *n* poisonous snake found in India and Africa 眼镜蛇. ⇨illus at SNAKE 见SNAKE之插图.

cob·web /ˈkɒbweb; ˈkɑbˌwɛb/ *n* **1** fine network of threads made by a spider 蜘蛛网. **2** single thread of this 蜘蛛丝. Cf 参看 WEB 1.

coca /ˈkəʊkə; ˈkokə/ *n* (**a**) [C] S American shrub 古柯(南美灌木). (**b**) [U] its dried leaves from which cocaine is obtained 古柯树的干叶(可提取可卡因).

Coca-Cola /ˌkəʊkə ˈkəʊlə; ˌkokəˈkolə/ (also *infml* 口语亦作 **Coke**) *n* (*propr* 专利名) (**a**) [U] popular non-alcoholic carbonated drink 可口可乐. (**b**) [C] bottle or glass of this 一瓶或一杯可口可乐.

co·caine /kəʊˈkeɪn; koˈken/ *n* [U] drug used as a local anaesthetic by doctors, and as a stimulant by drug addicts 可卡因; 古柯碱.

coc·cyx /ˈkɒksɪks; ˈkɑksɪks/ *n* (*pl* **~es** or **coccyges** /ˈkɒksɪdʒiːz; kɑkˈsədʒiz/) (*anatomy* 解) small bone at the bottom of the spine 尾骨. ⇨illus at SKELETON 见SKELETON之插图.

coch·in·eal /ˌkɒtʃɪˈniːl; ˌkɑtʃəˈnil/ *n* [U] bright red colouring-matter made from the dried bodies of certain tropical American insects 胭脂虫红(由南美热带胭脂虫干骸制成的鲜红色物质).

coch·lea /ˈkɒklɪə; ˈkɑklɪə/ *n* (*pl* **-leae** /-lɪiː; -lɪˌi/) (*anatomy* 解) spiral-shaped part of the inner ear 耳蜗. ⇨illus at EAR 见EAR之插图.

cock[1] /kɒk; kɑk/ *n* **1** (*US* **rooster**) [C] adult male bird of the domestic fowl 公鸡. ⇨illus at App 1 见附录1之插图, page v. Cf 参看 HEN. **2** (esp in compounds 尤用以构成复合词) male of any other bird, esp of a game bird 雄鸟(尤指猎禽): *a ˌcock ˈpheasant* 雄雉 ○ *a ˌcock ˈsparrow* 雄麻雀 ○ *a ˌcock ˈrobin* 雄鸲. **3** [sing] (*Brit sl* 俚) (used as a form of address between men 男子互称用语) friend; mate 朋友; 老兄; 老弟. **4** (idm 习语) **a ˌcock-and-ˈbull story** absurd and improbable story, esp one used as an excuse or explanation 无稽之谈(尤指用作借口或解释的): *He told us some cock-and-bull story about having lost all his money.* 他鬼话连篇, 告诉我们把钱都丢了. ˌ**cock of the ˈwalk** person who dominates others within a group 人群中支配他人的人; 头子; 头头. **live like fighting cocks** ⇨ LIVE[2].

□ **cock-a-doodle-doo** /ˌkɒk ə ˌduːdl ˈduː; ˈkɑk ə ˌdudl̩ ˈdu/ *n* (**a**) noise made by a cock[1](1) (公鸡叫的)喔喔声. (**b**) (used by and to children 儿语) cock 公鸡.

ˌ**cock-a-ˈhoop** *adj* [usu pred 通常作表语] very pleased, esp about being successful 得意扬扬(尤指由于成功): *She's cock-a-hoop about getting the job.* 她为得到这份工作而自鸣得意.

ˌ**cock-a-ˈleekie** /ˌkɒk ə ˈliːkɪ; ˌkɑk ə ˈlikɪ/ *n* [U] Scottish soup made of chicken boiled with vegetables. (苏格兰的)韭菜鸡汤.

ˈ**cock-crow** *n* [U] dawn 黎明: *wake at cock-crow* 黎明时醒来.

ˈ**cock-fight** *n* fight between (usu two) cocks fitted with sharp metal spurs on their feet, watched as a sport 斗鸡. ˈ**cock-fighting** *n* [U].

cock[2] /kɒk; kɑk/ *n* **1** [C] tap or valve controlling the flow of a liquid or gas in a pipe 龙头; 旋塞. **2** [C] hammer of a gun (枪的)击铁. **3** [C] (⚠ *sl* 讳, 俚) penis 鸡巴. **4** [U] (*sl* 俚) nonsense; rubbish 胡说; 废话: *a load of cock* 胡说八道. **5** (idm 习语) **at half/full ˈcock** (of a gun with a hammer that is raised before firing) half ready/ready to be fired (指枪击铁扳开)半开[全开]准备发射. **go off at ˌhalf ˈcock** (*infml* 口) start before preparations are complete, so that the effect or result is not satisfactory 仓促行事; 操之过急.

cock[3] /kɒk; kɑk/ *v* **1** [Tn, Tn·pr, Tn·p] **~ sth (up)** cause sth to be upright or erect; raise sth 使某物竖起; 使某物翘起; 举起某物: *The horse cocked (up) its ears when it heard the noise.* 那马听到声音就竖起了耳朵. ○ *The dog cocked its leg (against the lamppost)*, ie in order to urinate. 狗(对着灯柱)抬起一只腿(撒尿). **2** [Tn, Tn·pr] cause (sth) to tilt or slant 使(某物)倾斜; 歪斜: *She cocked her hat at a jaunty angle.* 她把帽子歪戴成俏皮的样子. ○ *The bird cocked its head to/on one side.* 鸟把头斜向[到]一侧. **3** [Tn] raise the cock[2](2) of (a gun) ready for firing 扳起(枪)的击铁准备射击. **4** (idm 习语) **cock a snook at sb/sth** (**a**) make a rude gesture at sb by putting one's thumb to one's nose 以拇指抵鼻对某人做不礼貌手势. (**b**) show cheeky contempt for or defiance of sb/sth 对某人[某事物]表示蔑视或不屑一顾: *cocking a snook at authority* 对权威的蔑视. **5** (phr v) **cock sth up** (*Brit infml* 口) spoil or ruin sth by incompetence; bungle sth 把某事物搞糟: *The travel agent completely cocked up the arrangements for our holiday.* 旅行社把我们假日的安排搞得一塌糊涂. ○ *Trust him to cock it/things up!* 保管他会把它[事情]搞糟!

□ ˌ**cocked ˈhat 1** hat with the brim turned up on three sides 三角帽(帽檐三面卷起的). **2** (idm 习语) **knock sb/sth into a cocked hat** ⇨ KNOCK[2].

ˈ**cock-up** *n* (*Brit infml* 口) act of bungling sth; mess 搞糟; 混乱: *She made a complete cock-up of the arrangements.* 她把计划安排全弄糟了. ○ *What a cock-up!* 一团糟!

cock[4] /kɒk; kɑk/ *n* small cone-shaped pile of straw or hay (小圆锥形的)稻草堆, 干草堆.

▷ **cock** *v* [Tn] pile (straw or hay) in cocks 将(稻草或干草)堆成锥形堆; 堆草堆.

cock·ade /kɒˈkeɪd; kɑkˈed/ *n* piece of ribbon tied in a knot and worn on a hat as a badge 帽子上作为徽章的带结.

cock·atoo /ˌkɒkəˈtuː; ˌkɑkəˈtu/ *n* (*pl* **~s**) type of parrot with a large crest 凤头鹦鹉; 葵花鹦鹉.

cock·chafer /ˈkɒktʃeɪfə(r); ˈkɑkˌtʃefɚ/ (also ˈ**may-bug**) *n* large beetle that flies at night with a loud whirring sound and feeds on leaves 金龟(甲虫).

cocker /ˈkɒkə(r); ˋkɑkɚ/ *n* (also ˌ**cocker ˈspaniel**) small spaniel with golden-brown fur (金褐色毛的)西班牙猎鸡狗. ⇨illus at App 1 见附录1之插图, page iii.

cock·erel /ˈkɒkərəl; ˋkɑkərəl/ *n* young cock[1](1) not more than one year old (未满一岁的)小公鸡.

cock-eyed /ˈkɒk aɪd; ˋkɑkˌaɪd/ *adj* (*infml* 口) **1** not straight or level; crooked 不正的; 不平的; 歪的: *That picture on the wall looks cock-eyed to me.* 我看墙上那幅画歪了. **2** having a squint; squinting 斜视的; 斜眼看的. **3** impractical; absurd 不现实的; 荒唐的: *a cock-eyed scheme* 荒唐的计划.

cockle /ˈkɒkl; ˋkɑkl̩/ *n* **1** (**a**) small edible shellfish 鸟蛤(可食的小蛤). (**b**) its shell 鸟蛤壳. **2** (also ˈ**cockle-shell**) small shallow boat 浅底小船. **3** (idm 习语) **warm the cockles** ⇨ WARM[2].

cock·ney /ˈkɒknɪ; ˋkɑknɪ/ *n* **1** [C] native of London, esp of the East End of the city 伦敦人(尤指东区人). **2** [U] dialect spoken by cockneys 伦敦人的方言; 伦敦土话.
▷ **cock·ney** *adj* [esp attrib 尤作定语] of cockneys or their dialect 伦敦人的; 伦敦土话的: *a cockney accent* 伦敦口音 ○ *cockney humour, slang, wit* 伦敦人的幽默、俚语、机智.

cock·pit /ˈkɒkpɪt; ˋkɑkˌpɪt/ *n* **1** compartment for the pilot and crew of an aircraft or a spaceship (飞行器中机组人员的)座舱, 驾驶舱. ⇨illus at AIRCRAFT 见 AIRCRAFT 之插图. **2** driver's seat in a racing car (赛车手的)驾驶座. **3** enclosed part of a small yacht containing the wheel (小游艇的)座舱. ⇨illus at YACHT 见 YACHT 之插图. **4** (**a**) (formerly) place used for cock-fights (旧时)斗鸡场. (**b**) place where many battles have been fought (进行过多次战役的)战场: *Belgium has been called the cockpit of Europe.* 比利时被称作欧洲的战场.

cock-roach /ˈkɒkrəʊtʃ; ˋkɑkˌrotʃ/ (also **roach**) *n* large dark-brown insect that infests kitchens and bathrooms 蟑螂.

cocks·comb /ˈkɒkskəʊm; ˋkɑksˌkom/ *n* red fleshy crest on the head of a cock[1](1) (公鸡的)鸡冠.

cock·sure /ˌkɒkˈʃɔ:(r); *US* ˌkɒkˈʃʊər; ˋkɑkˋʃʊr/ *adj* ~ **(about/of sth)** (*infml* 口) arrogantly or offensively confident 过于自信的: *He's so cocksure — I'd love to see him proved wrong.* 他过分自信——我倒想看看他栽跟头.

cock·tail /ˈkɒkteɪl; ˋkɑkˌtel/ *n* **1** [C] alcoholic drink consisting of a spirit or spirits mixed with fruit juice, etc 鸡尾酒: [attrib 作定语] *a cocktail party* 鸡尾酒会. **2** [C, U] dish of seafood or fruit (used esp in the expressions shown) 用海鲜或水果做的菜(尤用于下列示例): *(a) prawn cocktail*, ie a mixture of prawns and mayonnaise eaten as a first course 大虾冷盘(用作西餐第一道菜) ○ *(a) fruit cocktail*, ie a mixture of small pieces of fruit, usu eaten as a dessert 什锦水果丁(通常作西餐最后的甜食). **3** [C] (*infml* 口) any mixture of substances 任何混合物: *a lethal cocktail of drugs* 致命的混合药物.

cocky /ˈkɒkɪ; ˋkɑkɪ/ *adj* (**-ier, -iest**) (*infml* 口) conceited; arrogant 自高自大的; 趾高气扬的. ▷ **cock·ily** *adv*. **cocki·ness** *n* [U].

coco /ˈkəʊkəʊ; ˋkoko/ *n* (*pl* **~s**) = COCONUT PALM (COCONUT).

co·coa /ˈkəʊkəʊ; ˋkoko/ *n* (**a**) [U] dark brown powder made from crushed cacao seeds; powdered chocolate 可可粉; 巧克力粉. (**b**) [C, U] (cup of a) hot drink made from this with milk or water (一杯)可可与牛奶或水调成的热饮料: *a mug of cocoa* 一大杯可可.

co·co·nut /ˈkəʊkənʌt; ˋkokəˌnʌt/ *n* (**a**) [C] large hard-shelled seed of the coconut palm, with an edible white lining and filled with milky juice 椰子. (**b**) [U] the edible lining of this, often shredded and used to flavour cakes, biscuits, etc 椰子肉; 椰丝; 椰蓉: [attrib 作定语] *coconut icing* 椰霜.
□ ˌ**coconut ˈmatting** floor covering made from the tough fibre of the coconut's outer husk 用椰壳纤维做的垫子.
ˈ**coconut palm** (also **coco**, ˈ**coco-palm**) tropical tree on which coconuts grow 椰树.
ˈ**coconut shy** fairground stall where people try to knock coconuts off stands by throwing balls at them 在娱乐场上用球击椰子的游戏摊位.

co·coon /kəˈku:n; kəˋkun/ *n* **1** silky covering made by an insect larva to protect itself while it is a chrysalis 茧. **2** any soft protective covering 任何保护性软套: *wrapped in a cocoon of blankets* 裹在毯子里.
▷ **co·coon** *v* [esp passive 尤用于被动语态: Tn, Tn·pr] cover or wrap (sb/sth) in a cocoon 将(某人[某物])盖在或裹在保护层里: *cocooned in luxury* 在奢侈的环境中.

cod /kɒd; kɑd/ *n* (*pl* unchanged 复数不变) **1** (also ˈ**cod·fish**) [C] large sea fish 鳕. **2** [U] its flesh eaten as food (食用的)鳕鱼肉.
□ ˌ**cod-liver ˈoil** *n* [U] oil obtained from cod livers, rich in vitamins A and D and used as a medicine 鱼肝油.

COD /ˌsi: əʊ ˈdi:; ˋsɪ ˌo ˋdi/ **1** (*Brit*) cash on delivery 货到付款. **2** (*US*) collect (payment) on delivery 货到收(款).

coda /ˈkəʊdə; ˋkodə/ *n* (*music* 音) final passage of a piece of music (乐曲的)尾声.

coddle /ˈkɒdl; ˋkɑdl̩/ *v* [Tn] **1** treat (sb) with great care and tenderness 悉心照料(某人): *He'll need to be coddled after his illness.* 他病后需要悉心照料. **2** cook (eggs) in water just below boiling-point (在刚刚低于沸点的水中)煮(鸡蛋).

code /kəʊd; kod/ *n* **1** [C, U] (often in compounds 常用以构成复合词) (**a**) (system of) words, letters, symbols, etc that represent others, used for secret messages or for presenting or recording information briefly 密码; 暗号; 代码; 代号; 电码: *a letter in code* 密码信 ○ *break/crack* (ie decipher) *a code* 解译[破译]密码 ○ *a ˈpost-code/ˈpostal code*. (**b**) (system of) pre-arranged signals used to send messages by machine 用机器传送的信号(的系统): *ˌMorse ˈcode*. **2** [C] set of instructions for programming a computer 编码(计算机编制程序的成套指令). **3** [C] (**a**) set of laws or rules arranged in a system (系统编排的)法律, 规章, 章程, 法典: *the penal ˈcode* 刑法 ○ *the highway ˈcode* 公路法规. (**b**) set of moral principles accepted by society or a group of people 道德准则: *a code of beˈhaviour/ˈhonour* 行为[社交礼仪]准则 ○ *a code of ˈpractice*, ie a set of professional standards agreed on by members of a particular profession 行业规则.
▷ **code** *v* [Tn] put or write (sth) in code 将(某事物)编成或写成密码、代码或电码等: *coded messages* 用密码编写的信息.

cod·eine /ˈkəʊdi:n; ˋkodɪˌin/ *n* [U] drug made from opium, used to relieve pain or help people to sleep 可待因(由鸦片制成的药物, 用以镇痛或安眠).

co·dex /ˈkəʊdeks; ˋkodɛks/ *n* (*pl* **codices** /ˈkəʊdɪsɪ:z; ˋkodəˌsɪz/) handwritten book of ancient texts (古书的)手抄本.

codger /ˈkɒdʒə(r); ˋkɑdʒɚ/ *n* (*infml* 口) man, esp an old or peculiar one 男人(尤指老人或古怪的人): *He's a funny old codger.* 他这个人可真怪.

co·di·cil /ˈkəʊdɪsɪl; *US* ˈkɒdəsl; ˋkɑdəsl̩/ *n* (*law* 律) later addition to a will, esp one that changes part of it 遗嘱修改附录: *She added a codicil to her will just before she died.* 她临终前在遗嘱上加了附录.

co·dify /ˈkəʊdɪfaɪ; *US* ˈkɒdəfaɪ; ˋkɑdəˌfaɪ/ *v* (*pt, pp* **-fied**) [Tn] arrange (laws, rules, etc) systematically into a code(3a) 将(法律、规则等)编成法典.
▷ **co·di·fica·tion** /ˌkəʊdɪfɪˈkeɪʃn; *US* ˌkɒd-; ˌkɑdəfəˋkeʃən/ *n* [U].

cod·piece /ˈkɒdpi:s; ˋkɑdˌpis/ *n* (in 15th and 16th century dress) bag or flap covering the opening at the front of a man's breeches (15、16世纪服装)遮阴布(男子短马裤前面的遮袋或遮盖).

cods·wal·lop /ˈkɒdzˌwɒləp; ˋkɑdzˌwɑləp/ *n* [U] (*Brit infml* 口) nonsense; rubbish 胡说; 废话: *He's talking (a load of) codswallop.* 他(满口)胡说八道.

coed /ˌkəʊˈed; ˋkoˋɛd/ *n* (*infml* 口 *esp US*) female student at a coeducational school or college (男女合校的)女生.
▷ **coed** *adj* (*infml* 口) coeducational 男女合校的: *Is your school coed?* 你们学校是男女合校吗? ○ *a ˌcoed ˈschool* 男女合校的学校.

co·edu·ca·tion /ˌkəʊedʒʊˈkeɪʃn; ˌkoɛdʒəˋkeʃən/ *n* [U] education of girls and boys together 男女合校的教育.
▷ **co·edu·ca·tional** /-ˈkeɪʃənl; -ˋkeʃənl̩/ *adj*.

C

co·ef·fi·cient /ˌkəʊɪˈfɪʃnt; ˌkoəˈfɪʃənt/ *n* **1** (*mathematics* 数) quantity placed before and multiplying another quantity 系数: *In 3xy, 3 is the coefficient of xy.* 在3xy中，3是xy的系数. **2** (*physics* 物) measure of a particular property of a substance under specified conditions 系数: *the coefficient of friction* 摩擦系数.

co·erce /kəʊˈɜːs; koˈɝs/ *v* [Tn, Tn·pr] **~ sb (into sth/doing sth)** (*fml* 文) make sb do sth by using force or threats; compel sb to do sth 强制或胁迫某人做某事: *coerce sb into submission* 迫使某人屈服 ○ *They were coerced into signing the contract.* 他们被迫签了合同.

▷ **co·er·cion** /kəʊˈɜːʃn; *US* -ʒn; koˈɝʒən/ *n* [U] coercing or being coerced 强迫; 胁迫; 被迫: *He paid the money under coercion.* 他被迫付了钱.

co·er·cive /kəʊˈɜːsɪv; koˈɝsɪv/ *adj* using force or threats 强迫的; 胁迫的: *coercive methods, measures, tactics, etc* 强迫的方法、手段、策略等.

co·eval /ˌkəʊˈiːvl; koˈivl̩/ *adj* **~ (with sb/sth)** (*fml* 文) existing at the same time or having the same age as sb/sth else; contemporary 同年代的; 同时代的; 同年龄的; 同时期的.

▷ **co·eval** *n* (*fml* 文) coeval person or thing 同时代的人; 同年代的事物.

co·ex·ist /ˌkəʊɪgˈzɪst; ˌko·ɪgˈzɪst/ *v* [I, Ipr] **~ (with sb/sth)** (**a**) exist together at the same time or in the same place 同时或同地存在; 共处; 共存. (**b**) (of opposing countries or groups) exist together without fighting (指对立的国家或集团)和平共处.

▷ **co·ex·ist·ence** *n* [U] coexisting 共处; 共存: *peaceful coexistence*, ie tolerance of each other by countries, groups, etc with different political systems, beliefs, etc 和平共处.

C of E /ˌsiː əv ˈiː; ˌsi əv ˈi/ *abbr* 缩写 = Church of England: *Are you C of E?* 你是英国国教徒吗? Cf 参看 CE.

cof·fee /ˈkɒfɪ; *US* ˈkɔːfɪ; ˈkɔfɪ/ *n* **1** [U] (powder obtained by grinding the roasted) seeds of the coffee tree 咖啡豆; 咖啡粉: *half a pound of coffee* 半磅咖啡 ○ *instant coffee*, ie coffee powder that dissolves in boiling water 速溶咖啡 ○ [attrib 作定语] *a coffee cake*, ie one flavoured with coffee 咖啡蛋糕. **2** (**a**) [U] drink made by adding hot water to ground or powdered coffee 咖啡(热饮料): *a cup of coffee* 一杯咖啡 ○ *make some coffee* 煮咖啡. (**b**) [C] cup of this drink 一杯咖啡: *Two black/white coffees, please*, ie without/with milk. 请来两杯不加奶的[加奶的]咖啡. **3** [U] colour of coffee mixed with milk; light brown 咖啡色(咖啡加奶的颜色); 浅褐色: [attrib 作定语] *a coffee carpet* 咖啡色的地毯.

□ ˈ**coffee bar** (*Brit*) place serving coffee, non-alcoholic drinks and snacks 咖啡馆.

ˈ**coffee bean** seed of the coffee tree 咖啡豆.

ˈ**coffee grinder** (also ˈ**coffee-mill**) machine for grinding roasted coffee beans 咖啡磨.

ˈ**coffee-house** *n* (formerly) place serving coffee and other refreshments, esp one that was a fashionable meeting-place in 18th century London (旧时)咖啡馆(尤指18世纪伦敦上流社会的).

ˈ**coffee shop** (*US*) small restaurant serving coffee and simple meals (供应咖啡和便饭的)小饭馆.

ˈ**coffee-table** *n* small low table 咖啡桌. ⇨illus at App 1 见附录1之插图, page xvi. ˈ**coffee-table book** large expensive illustrated book, often placed where visitors may look at it 精装大开本画册(常放在客人能看到的地方).

ˈ**coffee tree** tropical shrub on which coffee beans grow 咖啡树.

cof·fer /ˈkɒfə(r); ˈkɔfɚ/ *n* **1** [C] large strong box for holding money or other valuables; chest 保险柜; 保险箱; 箱子. **2 coffers** [pl] (*fml* 文) store of money; treasury; funds 金库; 资金: *The nation's coffers are empty.* 国库空虚. **3** [C] (*architecture* 建) ornamental sunken panel in a ceiling, dome, etc 镶板; 藻井(天花板、圆屋顶等凹陷的装饰镶嵌板). **4** (also ˈ**coffer-dam**) [C] watertight structure built or placed round an area of water which can then be pumped dry to allow building work (eg on a bridge) to be done inside it 围堰; 沉箱.

cof·fin /ˈkɒfɪn; ˈkɔfɪn/ *n* **1** box in which a dead body is buried or cremated 棺材. **2** (idm 习语) **a nail in sb's/sth's coffin** ⇨ NAIL.

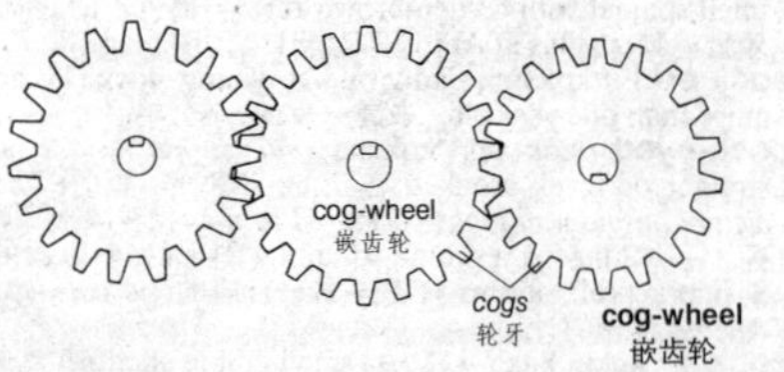

cog /kɒg; kɑg/ **1** each of a series of teeth on the edge of a wheel, that fit between those of a similar wheel, so that each wheel can cause the other one to move (齿轮的)轮牙; 轮齿. ⇨illus 见插图. **2** (idm 习语) **a cog in the maˈchine** (*infml* 口) person who plays a necessary but small part in a large organization or process 不重要的但不可少的人.

□ ˈ**cog-railway** *n* (*esp US*) = RACK-RAILWAY (RACK[1]).

ˈ**cog-wheel** *n* wheel with teeth round the edge 嵌齿轮. ⇨illus 见插图.

co·gent /ˈkəʊdʒənt; ˈkodʒənt/ *adj* (of arguments, reasons, etc) convincing; strong (指论据、道理等)令人信服的; 强有力的: *He produced cogent reasons for the change of policy.* 他对改变政策提出了充分的理由.

▷ **co·gency** /ˈkəʊdʒənsɪ; ˈkodʒənsɪ/ *n* [U] (of arguments, reasons, etc) quality of being convincing; strength (指论据、道理等的)说服力; 中肯.

co·gently *adv*: *Her case was cogently argued.* 她的案件辩驳得很有说服力.

co·git·ate /ˈkɒdʒɪteɪt; ˈkɑdʒəˌtet/ *v* [I, Ipr, Tn] **~ (about/on) sth** (*fml or joc* 文或谑) think deeply about sth 深思某事物; 仔细思考.

▷ **co·gita·tion** /ˌkɒdʒɪˈteɪʃn; ˌkɑdʒəˈteʃən/ *n* [C, U] (*fml* 文) (act of) thinking deeply 深思; 仔细思考: *After much cogitation I have decided to resign.* 我经过再三考虑后决定辞职.

cognac /ˈkɒnjæk; ˈkɑnjæk/ *n* (**a**) [U] (type of) fine brandy made in W France 科尼亚克白兰地酒(法国西部产的精美的白兰地酒). (**b**) [C] glass of this 一杯科尼亚克白兰地酒.

cog·nate /ˈkɒgneɪt; ˈkɑgnet/ *adj* **~ (with sth)** **1** (*linguistics* 语言) (of a word or language) having the same source or origin as another one (指词或语言)同源的: *The German word 'Haus' is cognate with the English word 'house'.* 德语的Haus一词和英语的house一词同源. ○ *German and Dutch are cognate languages.* 德语和荷兰语为同源语言. **2** having many things in common; related 有许多共同点的; 相关的: *Physics and astronomy are cognate sciences.* 物理学和天文学是相关联的科学.

▷ **cog·nate** *n* (*linguistics* 语言) word that is cognate with another 同源词: *'Haus' and 'house' are cognates.* Haus与house为同源词.

cog·ni·tion /kɒgˈnɪʃn; kɑgˈnɪʃən/ *n* [U] (*psychology* 心) action or process of acquiring knowledge, by reasoning or by intuition or through the senses 认知; 认识; 认识力.

▷ **cog·nit·ive** /ˈkɒgnɪtɪv; ˈkɑgnətɪv/ *adj* of or relating to cognition 认知的; 有关认识的: *a child's cognitive development* 儿童认识能力的发展.

cog·niz·ance /ˈkɒgnɪzəns; ˈkɑgnəzəns/ *n* [U] **1** (*fml* 文) knowledge; awareness 知觉; 获知; 认识: *have cognizance of sth* 认识到某事物. **2** (*esp law* 尤用于法律) scope or extent of sb's knowledge or concern 审理; 审理权; 审判权: *These matters fall within/go beyond the cognizance of this court.* 这些问题在本法庭审理范围之内[外]. **3** (idm 习语) **take cognizance of sth** (*esp law* 尤用于法律) take notice of sth; acknowledge sth officially 注意到某事物; 正式获知某事物; 受理: *take cognizance of new evidence* 注意到新的证据.

▷ **cog·niz·ant** *adj* [pred 作表语] **~ of sth** (*fml* 文) having knowledge of sth; aware of sth 知道某事物; 认识某事物.

co·gnos·cente /ˌkɒnjəˈʃentɪ; ˌkɑnjəˈʃente/ *n* (*pl* **cognoscenti**) (*Italian* 意) (usu *pl* 通常作复数) connoisseur 鉴赏家; 鉴别家; 内行; 行家: *a restaurant favoured by the cognoscenti* 美食家爱光顾的饭馆.

co·habit /kəʊˈhæbɪt; koˋhæbɪt/ *v* [I, Ipr] **~ (with sb)** (*fml* 文) (usu of an unmarried couple) live together (通常指未婚的双方)同居: *They were cohabiting for three years before their marriage.* 他们同居了三年才结婚. ▷ **co·hab·ita·tion** /ˌkəʊhæbɪˈteɪʃn; koˌhæbəˋteʃən/ *n* [U].

co·here /kəʊˈhɪə(r); koˋhɪr/ *v* [I] **1** stick together in a mass or group 黏合; 凝聚. Cf 参看 COHESION 1. **2** (of ideas, reasoning, etc) be connected logically; be consistent (指看法、推理等)逻辑上衔接, 前后一致, 连贯.

▷ **co·her·ent** /ˌkəʊˈhɪərənt; koˋhɪrənt/ *adj* (of ideas, thoughts, speech, reasoning, etc) connected logically or consistent; easy to understand; clear (指看法、思想、言语、推理等)有条理的, 前后一致的, 易懂的, 清楚的: *a coherent analysis, argument, description, etc* 前后一致的分析、论证、描述等 ○ *The Government lacks a coherent economic policy.* 政府的经济政策缺乏一致性. ○ *He's not very coherent on the telephone.* 他打电话时语无伦次. **co·her·ence** /-rəns; -rəns/ (also **co·her·ency**) *n* [U] being coherent 连贯性; 一致性. **co·her·ently** *adv*: *express one's ideas coherently* 条理清楚地表明意见. Cf 参看 INCOHERENT.

co·he·sion /kəʊˈhiːʒn; koˋhiʒən/ *n* [U] **1** tendency to stick together; unity 结合; 结合力; 团结: *the cohesion of the family unit* 家庭成员的团结 ○ *a lack of cohesion* 缺乏结合力. Cf 参看 COHERE 1. **2** (*physics* 物) force that causes molecules to stick together 内聚力; 凝聚力.

▷ **co·hes·ive** /kəʊˈhiːsɪv; koˋhisɪv/ *adj* (**a**) tending to stick together 黏合性的; 有结合力的: *a cohesive social unit* 紧密团结的社团. (**b**) producing cohesion 产生结合力的; 产生内聚力的: *cohesive forces* 内聚力. **co·hes·ively** *adv*. **co·hes·ive·ness** *n* [U].

co·hort /ˈkəʊhɔːt; ˋkohɔrt/ *n* [CGp] **1** (in the army of ancient Rome) each of the ten units forming a legion (古罗马军队的)步兵大队(军团的十分之一). **2** number of people banded together 一群人; 一帮人.

COI /ˌsiː əʊ ˈaɪ; ˌsi o ˋaɪ/ *abbr* 缩写 = (*Brit*) Central Office of Information 中央新闻署.

coif /kɔɪf; kɔɪf/ *n* (formerly) close-fitting cap covering the top, back and sides of the head (旧时)科伊夫帽(覆盖着头的顶部、后部及两侧的紧帽).

coif·feur /kwɑːˈfɜː(r); ˌkwɑˋfɝ/ (*fem* 阴性作 **coif·feuse** /kwɑːˈfɜːz; kwɑˋfɝz/) *n* (*French* 法) hairdresser 理发师.

coif·fure /kwɑːˈfjʊə(r); kwɑˋfjʊr/ *n* (*French* 法) way in which (esp a woman's) hair is arranged; hairstyle 发式(尤指女子的); 发型.

coil /kɔɪl; kɔɪl/ *v* [Ipr, Ip, Tn, Tn·pr, Tn·p] **~ (oneself/sth) round sth/up** wind or twist (oneself/sth) into a continuous circular or spiral shape 将(自己[某物])卷或盘成圈或螺旋形: *The snake coiled (itself) round the branch.* 蛇(把身体)盘绕在树枝上. ○ *coil (up) a length of rope, flex, wire, etc* 卷(起)一段绳子、花线、金属丝等.

▷ **coil** *n* **1** length of rope, etc wound into a series of loops 缠成许多圈的绳子等: *a coil of flex* 一盘花线. **2** single ring or loop of rope, etc (绳等的)环, 圈: *the thick coils of a python* 盘卷着的大蟒 ○ *a coil of hair* 发圈. **3** length of coated wire wound in a spiral to conduct an electric current 线圈. **4** = INTRA-UTERINE DEVICE (INTRA-UTERINE).

coin /kɔɪn; kɔɪn/ *n* **1** (**a**) [C] piece of metal used as money 硬币: *two gold coins* 两枚金币 ○ *a handful of coins* 一把硬币. (**b**) [U] money made of metal 硬币: *£5 in coin* 5英镑的硬币. **2** (idm 习语) **the other side of the coin** ⇨ SIDE[1]. **pay sb in his own/the same coin** ⇨ PAY[2].

▷ **coin** *v* **1** [Tn] (**a**) make (coins) by stamping metal (冲压金属)制造(硬币). (**b**) make (metal) into coins 将(金属)制成硬币. **2** [Tn] invent (a new word or phrase) 创造(新词语): *coin words for new products* 为新产品创造新词. **3** (idm 习语) **ˈcoin it/money** (*infml* 口) earn a lot of money easily or quickly 赚大钱; 发大财. **to coin a ˈphrase** (**a**) (used to introduce a new expression, or a well-known expression that one has changed slightly 采用一新词语或略改动一现成词语时, 可用此短语作引子). (**b**) (*ironic* 反语) (used to apologize for using a well-known expression rather than an original one 因无创意而使用一现成词语时, 用此短语自嘲).

coin·age /ˈkɔɪnɪdʒ; ˋkɔɪnɪdʒ/ *n* **1** [U] (**a**) making coins 造硬币. (**b**) coins made 所造的硬币. **2** [U] system of coins in use (现行的)硬币币制: *decimal coinage* 十进位硬币币制. **3** (**a**) [U] inventing of a new word or phrase 创造新词语. (**b**) [C] newly invented word or phrase 新创的词语: *I haven't heard that expression before — is it a recent coinage?* 我以前从未听到过这个词语 —— 是最近新造的吗?

co·in·cide /ˌkəʊɪnˈsaɪd; ˌko·ɪnˋsaɪd/ *v* [I, Ipr] **~ (with sth)** **1** (of events) occur at the same time or occupy the same period of time as sth else (指事情)同时发生: *Her arrival coincided with our departure.* 她来到时我们正好离开. ○ *Our holidays don't coincide.* 我们的假期不在同一时间. **2** (of two or more objects) occupy the same amount of space (指至少两个物体)占据同一空间. **3** be identical or very similar to sth else 与他事物相符或极相似: *Their stories coincided.* 他们的叙述一致. ○ *Her taste in music coincides with her husband's/Their tastes in music coincide.* 她在音乐方面的爱好与她丈夫一致[他们在音乐方面的爱好一致].

co·in·cid·ence /kəʊˈɪnsɪdəns; koˋɪnsədəns/ *n* **1** [C, U] (instance of the) occurrence of similar events or circumstances at the same time by chance 巧合(的事): *'I'm going to Paris next week.' 'What a coincidence! So am I.'* '我准备下周去巴黎.' '真巧! 我也去.' ○ *By a strange coincidence we happened to be travelling on the same train.* 巧得出奇, 我们正好坐同一列火车. ○ *The plot of the novel relies too much on coincidence to be realistic.* 这部小说的情节多靠巧合安排而无真实感. **2** [U] coinciding of events, tastes, stories, etc (事情、口味、故事等)相合, 符合, 一致.

co·in·cid·ent /kəʊˈɪnsɪdənt; koˋɪnsədənt/ *adj* (*fml* 文) happening at the same time by chance 巧合的.

▷ **co·in·cid·ental** /kəʊˌɪnsɪˈdentl; koˌɪnsəˋdɛntl̩/ *adj* [usu pred 通常作表语] resulting from coincidence 由巧合造成: *The similarity between these two essays is too great to be coincidental*, ie One must have been copied from the other. 这两篇文章雷同的地方很多, 并非巧合所致(一定是一篇抄袭另一篇). **co·in·cid·ent·ally** *adv*.

coir /ˈkɔɪə(r); ˋkɔɪr/ *n* [U] fibre from the outer husk of coconuts, used for making ropes, matting etc 椰子外壳纤维(用以编绳、席等).

co·itus /ˈkəʊɪtəs; ˋko·ɪtəs/ (also **co·ition** /kəʊˈɪʃn; koˋɪʃən/) *n* [U] (*medical or fml* 医或文) sexual intercourse 性交. ▷ **co·ital** /ˈkəʊɪtl; ˋkoətəl/ *adj*.

coke[1] /kəʊk; kok/ *n* [U] black substance remaining after coal gas and coal tar have been removed from coal, used as a fuel 焦炭; 焦煤: [attrib 作定语] *a coke furnace* 炼焦炉.

▷ **coke** *v* [Tn] convert (coal) into coke 将(煤)制成焦炭.

coke[2] (also **Coke**) /kəʊk; kok/ *n* [C, U] (*propr infml* 专利名, 口) = COCA-COLA.

coke[3] /kəʊk; kok/ *n* [U] (*sl* 俚) cocaine 可卡因.

col /kɒl; kɑl/ *n* pass in a mountain range 山口.

cola (also **kola**) /ˈkəʊlə; ˋkolə/ *n* **1** [C] W African tree 可乐果树(生长于西非洲). **2** [U] carbonated non-alcoholic drink flavoured with the seeds of this tree 可乐饮料.

□ **ˈcola-nut** (also **kola-nut**) *n* seed of the cola tree, used as a flavouring or chewed 可乐树的坚果(作调味或咀嚼用).

Col *abbr* 缩写 = Colonel: *Col (Terence) Lloyd* (特伦斯)劳埃德上校.

col *abbr* 缩写 = column(3).

col·an·der (also **cullender**) /ˈkʌləndə(r); ˋkʌləndɚ/ *n* metal or plastic bowl with many small holes in it, used to drain water from vegetables, etc, esp after cooking 滤盆; 滤锅; 漏勺.

cold[1] /kəʊld; kold/ *adj* (**-er, -est**) **1** of low temperature, esp when compared to the temperature of the human body 冷的; 寒冷的: *feel cold* 觉得冷 ○ *have cold hands, feet, ears, etc* 冰凉的手、脚、耳等 ○ *a cold bath, climate, day, house, room, wind, winter* 冷水浴、寒冷的气候、冷天、寒冷的房屋、冰凉的房间、冷风、寒冷的冬天 ○ *cold weather, water* 寒冷的天气、冷水 ○ *It/The weather is getting colder.* 天[天气]渐冷了. Cf 参看 HOT, WARM[1]. **2** (of food or drink) not heated; having cooled after being heated or cooked (指食物或饮料)未加热的; 已

冷却的: *Would you like tea or a cold drink?* 你喜欢要茶还是要冷饮? ○ *have cold meat and salad for supper* 晚饭吃凉肉和色拉 ○ *Don't let your dinner get cold*, ie Eat it while it is still warm. 不要让饭凉了(趁热吃). **3** (**a**) (of a person, his manner, etc) without friendliness, kindness or enthusiasm; without emotion (指人、态度等)不友好的; 不和气的; 不热情的; 冷淡的: *a cold look, stare, welcome, reception, etc* 冷淡的表情、目光、迎接、接待等 ○ *cold fury*, ie violent anger kept under control 强忍住的怒火. (**b**) sexually unresponsive; frigid 无性欲反应的; 性冷感的. **4** suggesting coldness; creating an impression of coldness 显示出寒冷的; 产生冷的印象的: *a cold grey colour* 冷灰色 ○ *cold skies* 令人有寒冷感觉的天空. **5** (in children's games) not close to finding a hidden object, the correct answer, etc (儿童游戏中)远离隐藏物的, 远未猜中的. **6** [pred 作表语] (*infml* 口) unconscious (used esp in the expression shown) 无知觉(尤用于下列示例): *knock sb (out) cold* 击昏某人. **7** [pred 作表语] dead 死. **8** (idm 习语) **blow hot and cold** ⇨ BLOW[1]. ˌ**cold** ˈ**comfort** thing that offers little or no consolation 不起(什么)安慰作用的事物: *After losing my job it was cold comfort to be told I'd won the office raffle.* 我失去工作以后, 听说我抽中了公司的奖券, 有同画饼. **a** ˌ**cold** ˈ**fish** (*derog* 贬) person who shows no emotion or is very aloof 无热情的人; 冷漠的人. ˌ**cold** ˈ**turkey** (*sl* 俚 *esp US*) (**a**) way of treating a drug addict by suddenly stopping all his doses of the drug instead of gradually reducing them 使有毒瘾者突然停用毒品而不是逐渐减少剂量的处理方法. (**b**) frank statement of the truth, often about sth unpleasant 直言不讳; 照实说: *talk cold turkey to/with sb* 对[与]某人直言不讳. **get/have cold** ˈ**feet** (*infml* 口) become/be afraid or reluctant to do sth (esp sth risky or dangerous) 临阵退缩或胆怯: *He got cold feet at the last minute.* 他事到临头却退缩了. **give sb/get the cold** ˈ**shoulder** treat sb/be treated in a deliberately unfriendly way 故意冷落某人. **in cold** ˈ**blood** without feeling pity or remorse; deliberately and callously 残忍地; 蓄意地; 冷酷地: *kill, murder, shoot, etc sb in cold blood* 残忍地将某人杀死、谋杀、射杀等. **leave sb cold** ⇨ LEAVE[1]. **make sb's blood run cold** ⇨ BLOOD[1]. **pour/throw cold** ˈ**water on sth** be discouraging or unenthusiastic about sth 对某事物泼冷水(泄气或不热心): *pour cold water on sb's plans, ideas, hopes, etc* 对某人的计划、主意、希望泼冷水.

▷ **coldly** *adv* in an unfriendly or unenthusiastic way 不友好地; 冷淡地: *stare coldly at sb* 冷冷地盯着某人.

cold·ness *n* [U] state of being cold 寒冷; 冷淡: *his coldness* (ie unfriendly manner) *towards her* 他对她的冷淡态度.

□ ˌ**cold-**ˈ**blooded** /-ˈblʌdɪd; -ˋblʌdɪd/ *adj* **1** (*biology* 生) having a blood temperature which varies with the temperature of the surroundings 冷血的(血液温度随环境温度的高低而改变的): *Reptiles are cold-blooded.* 爬行动物是冷血的. **2** (*derog* 贬) (of people or actions) without pity; cruel (指人或行动)无情的, 残酷的: *a cold-blooded murderer, murder* 残忍的谋杀者、谋杀.

ˈ**cold chisel** chisel used to cut cold metal 冷凿, 冷錾(凿冷金属的凿子或錾子).

ˈ**cold cream** ointment for cleansing and softening the skin 冷霜; 润肤膏.

ˈ**cold cuts** (*esp US*) cooked meat, sliced and served cold (冷吃的)肉片.

ˈ**cold frame** small glass-covered frame used to protect young plants 冷床, 阳畦(用以保护幼小植物的小玻璃罩).

ˌ**cold-**ˈ**hearted** /-ˈhɑ:tɪd; -ˋhɑrtɪd/ *adj* without sympathy or kindness; unkind 无同情心的; 无仁慈心的; 无情的.

ˌ**cold-**ˈ**shoulder** *v* [Tn] be deliberately unfriendly to (sb); snub 冷淡, 慢待(某人); 冷落.

ˈ**cold snap** sudden short period of cold weather (突然的短时间的)冷天气; 骤冷; 乍冷.

ˌ**cold** ˈ**storage** storing of things in a refrigerated place to preserve them 冷藏: (*fig* 比喻) *put a plan, an idea, etc into cold storage*, ie decide not to use it immediately but to reserve it for later 将计划、主意等搁置起来(决定暂时不用而保留备用).

ˌ**cold** ˈ**sweat** state in which sb sweats and feels cold at the same time, caused by fear or illness 冷汗: *be in a cold sweat (about sth)* (为某事物)出一身冷汗.

ˌ**cold** ˈ**war** state of hostility between nations involving the use of propaganda, threats and economic pressure but no actual fighting 冷战: [attrib 作定语] *cold-war attitudes, diplomacy, rhetoric* 冷战的态度、外交、辞令.

cold[2] /kəʊld; kold/ *n* **1** [U] lack of heat or warmth; low temperature (esp in the atmosphere) 冷; 寒冷: *shiver with cold* 冻得发抖 ○ *the heat of summer and the cold of winter* 夏暑冬寒 ○ *Don't stand outside in the cold.* 不要站在外面冻着. ○ *She doesn't seem to feel the cold.* 她似乎不觉得冷. **2** [C, U] infectious illness of the nose or throat or both, with catarrh, sneezing, coughing, etc 伤风; 感冒: *a bad, heavy, slight cold* 严重、重、轻感冒 ○ *have a cold in the head/on the chest* 患伤风头疼[伤风咳嗽] ○ *catch (a) cold* 患感冒. **3** (idm 习语) **(leave sb/be)** ˌ**out in the** ˈ**cold** excluded from a group or an activity; ignored 被排斥在某集体或某项活动之外的; 不被理睬的: *When the coalition was formed, the Republicans were left out in the cold.* 各党形成联盟时, 共和党人被排斥在外.

□ ˈ**cold sore** (*infml* 口) cluster of painful blisters near or in the mouth, caused by a virus 唇疱疹.

cole·slaw /ˈkəʊlslɔ:; ˋkol,slɔ/ *n* [U] finely shredded raw cabbage mixed with dressing(3) and eaten as a salad 凉拌洋白菜丝.

colic /ˈkɒlɪk; ˋkɑlɪk/ *n* [U] severe pain in the abdomen, suffered esp by babies 绞痛(尤指婴儿患的).

▷ **col·icky** *adj* of, like or suffering from colic (似)绞痛的; 患绞痛的.

col·itis /kəˈlaɪtɪs; kəˋlaɪtɪs/ *n* [U] (*medical* 医) inflammation of the lining of the colon[1] 结肠炎.

col·lab·or·ate /kəˈlæbəreɪt; kəˋlæbə,ret/ *v* [I, Ipr] **1 ~ (with sb) (on sth)** work together (with sb), esp to create or produce sth (与某人)合作; 协作(尤指创造或生产某事物): *She collaborated with her sister/She and her sister collaborated on a biography of their father.* 她和姐姐合作写父亲的传记. **2 ~ (with sb)** (*derog* 贬) help enemy forces occupying one's country 通敌; 勾结敌人: *He was suspected of collaborating (with the enemy).* 怀疑他(与敌人)勾结.

▷ **col·lab·ora·tion** /kə,læbəˈreɪʃn; kə,læbəˋreʃən/ *n* [U] **1 ~ (with sb) (on sth); ~ (between A and B)** collaborating (COLLABORATE 1) 合作; 协作: *She wrote the book in collaboration with her sister*, ie They wrote it together. 她和姐姐合作写成此书. **2 ~ (with sb)** helping enemy forces occupying one's country 通敌.

col·lab·or·ator /kəˈlæbəreɪtə(r); kəˋlæbə,retɚ/ person who collaborates 合作者; 协作者; 通敌者.

col·lage /ˈkɒlɑ:ʒ; *US* kəˈlɑ:ʒ; kəˋlɑʒ/ *n* [C, U] (picture made by) fixing pieces of paper, cloth, photographs, etc to a surface (用纸片、布片、照片等碎片)拼贴; 拼贴画.

col·lapse /kəˈlæps; kəˋlæps/ *v* **1** [I] (break into pieces and) fall down or in suddenly (破碎并)突然倒塌, 坍塌, 塌陷: *The whole building collapsed.* 整个建筑倒塌了. ○ *The roof collapsed under the weight of snow.* 雪把房顶压塌了. ○ *The wind caused the tent to collapse.* 风把帐篷吹塌了. **2** [I, Ipr] (of a person) fall down (and usu become unconscious) because of illness, tiredness, etc (指人)晕倒(因病、累等): *He collapsed in the street and died on the way to hospital.* 他在大街上晕倒, 在送往医院途中死去. ○ *collapse in a heap on the floor* 晕倒在地板上. **3** [I] (**a**) fail suddenly or completely; break down 突然或完全垮下; 失败; 衰退: *His health collapsed under the pressure of work.* 他的身体被工作压垮了. ○ *The enterprise collapsed through lack of support.* 该企业因无力支持而倒闭. ○ *Talks between management and unions have collapsed.* 资方和工会的谈判失败了. (**b**) be defeated or destroyed 被击败; 被摧毁: *All opposition to the scheme has collapsed.* 对这一计划的反对意见都已驳倒. **4** [I] (of prices, currencies, etc) suddenly decrease in value (指价格、货币等)突然降价; 暴跌: *Share prices collapsed after news of poor trading figures.* 交投数额不佳使股票价格暴跌. **5** [I, Tn] (cause sth to) fold into a compact shape (使某物)折叠或套缩: *a chair that collapses for easy storage* 为便于存放而折叠起来的椅子. **6** [I, Tn] (cause a lung or blood vessel to) become a flattened mass (指肺或血管)(使)萎陷: *a collapsed lung* 萎陷的肺.

▷ **col·lapse** *n* [sing] **1** sudden fall; collapsing 突然倒

下; 倒塌; 坍塌: *the collapse of the building, roof, bridge, etc* 建筑物、房顶、桥梁等的倒塌. **2** failure; breakdown 垮下; 失败; 崩溃: *the collapse of negotiations, sb's health, law and order* 谈判破裂、身体垮掉、法治败坏 ○ *The economy is in a state of (total) collapse.* 经济处于(完全)崩溃状态. **3** sudden decrease in value 暴跌: *the collapse of share prices, the dollar, the market* 股票价格、美元、市场价格暴跌.

col·laps·ible *adj* that can be folded into a compact shape 可折叠成紧凑形状的; 可套缩的: *a collapsible bicycle, boat, chair* 可折叠的自行车、小艇、椅子.

col·lar /ˈkɒlə(r); ˋkɑlɚ/ *n* **1** band, upright or folded over, round the neck of a shirt, coat, dress, etc 衣领: *turn one's collar up against the wind*, ie to keep one's neck warm 竖起领子挡风 ○ *grab sb by the collar* 抓住某人的领子 ○ [attrib 作定语] *What is your collar size?* 你的衣领尺寸是多少? ○ *a stiff collar*, ie a starched detachable one, worn with a shirt 硬领(浆过的可卸下的领子). ⇨illus at JACKET 见 JACKET 之插图. **2** band of leather, metal, etc put round an animal's (esp a dog's) neck 戴在动物(尤指狗)颈部的项圈: *Our dog has its name on its collar.* 我们的狗的项圈上有它的名字. **3** metal band or ring joining two pipes, rods or shafts, esp in a machine (连接两条管、杆或轴的)圈; 箍(尤指机器中的). **4** (idm 习语) **hot under the collar** ⇨ HOT.

▷ **col·lar** *v* [Tn] (**a**) seize (sb) by the collar; capture 揪住(某人)的领子; 捉住; 拉住: *The policeman collared the thief.* 警察把小偷捉住了. ○ (*infml* 口) *She collared me* (ie stopped me in order to talk to me) *as I was leaving the building.* 我正要离开大楼时, 她把我拉住了(和我谈话). (**b**) (*dated infml* 旧, 口) take (sth) without permission 未经允许拿走(某物); 窃取; 偷走: *Who's collared my pen?* 谁拿走我的钢笔了?

□ ˈ**collar-bone** *n* bone joining the breastbone and the shoulder-blade 锁骨. ⇨illus at SKELETON 见 SKELETON 之插图.

ˈ**collar-stud** *n* small piece of metal or plastic for fastening a detachable collar to a shirt (可将活领子扣在衬衫上的)领扣.

col·late /kəˈleɪt; kəˋlet/ *v* **1** [Tn, Tn·pr] **~ A and B/~ A with B** examine and compare (two books, manuscripts, etc) in order to find the differences between them 核对, 校对(书、底稿等): *collate a new edition with an earlier one* 将新版本与旧版本进行核对. **2** [Tn] collect together and arrange (information, pages of a book, etc) in the correct order 检点并整理(书页等).

▷ **col·la·tion** /kəˈleɪʃn; kəˋleʃən/ *n* [U] action of collating 核对; 整理.

col·lat·eral /kəˈlætərəl; kəˋlætərəl/ *adj* **1** side by side; parallel 并排的; 平行的; 并行的. **2** connected but less important; additional 有关的(但为次要的); 附属的; 附带的; 附加的: *collateral evidence* 旁证 ○ *a collateral aim* 附带的目的. **3** descended from the same ancestor, but by a different line 同一祖先而不同支的; 旁系的: *a collateral branch of the family* 这家族的旁支.

▷ **col·lat·eral** *n* [U] (also **colˌlateral seˈcurity**) property pledged as a guarantee for the repayment of a loan 抵押物; 担保品: *The bank will insist on collateral for a loan of that size.* 银行对这样的大笔贷款一定要有抵押物.

col·la·tion /kəˈleɪʃn; kəˋleʃən/ *n* (*fml* 文) light meal, esp at an unusual time 小吃: *a cold collation* 冷餐.

col·league /ˈkɒli:g; ˋkɑlig/ *n* person with whom one works, esp in a profession or business 同事; 同僚: *the Prime Minister's Cabinet colleagues* 首相的内阁同僚 ○ *David is a colleague of mine/David and I are colleagues.* 戴维是我的同事[戴维和我是同事].

col·lect[1] /kəˈlekt; kəˋlɛkt/ *v* **1** [Tn, Tn·p] **~ sth (up/together)** bring or gather sth together 收集; 搜集; 凑集: *collect (up) the empty glasses, dirty plates, waste paper* 收集空瓶、脏碟、废纸 ○ *collect together one's belongings* 收拾起自己的东西 ○ *the collected works of Dickens*, ie a series of books containing everything he wrote 狄更斯全集. **2** [I] come together; assemble or accumulate; gather 聚集; 召集; 积累; 集合; 齐集: *A crowd soon collected at the scene of the accident.* 群众迅速聚集在出事现场. ○ *Dust had collected on the window-sill.* 窗台上积了灰尘. **3** [I, Tn] obtain (money, contributions, etc) from a number of people or places 募捐; 募集; 征集: *He's collecting (money) for famine relief.* 他正在为赈济饥民募捐. ○ *The Inland Revenue is responsible for collecting income tax.* 税务局负责征收所得税. **4** [Tn] obtain specimens of (sth) as a hobby or for study 搜集(某物)的样品(作为爱好或为了研究); 采集标本: *collect stamps, old coins, matchboxes, first editions* 搜集邮票、硬币、火柴盒、初版物. **5** [Tn, Tn·pr] call for and take away (sb/sth); fetch 领走, 带走(某人); 拿走, 取走, 收走(某物): *The dustmen collect the rubbish once a week.* 垃圾工每周运走一次垃圾. ○ *collect a child from school* 从学校接回孩子 ○ *collect a suit from the cleaners* 从洗衣店取回衣服. **6** [Tn] regain or recover control of (oneself, one's thoughts, etc) 使(自己)镇定; 使(思想)集中: *collect oneself after a shock* 受惊之后镇定下来 ○ *collect one's thoughts before an interview* 面试之前先定定神儿. **7** (idm 习语) **collect/gather one's wits** ⇨ WIT.

▷ **col·lect** *adj, adv* (*US*) (of a telephone call) to be paid for by the receiver (指打电话)由受话人付钱(的): *a collect call* 受话人付款的电话 ○ *call sb collect*, ie transfer the charge 给某人打电话由受话人付款.

col·lected *adj* [pred 作表语] in control of oneself; calm (used esp in the expression shown) 镇定, 镇静, 冷静, 泰然自若(尤用于以下示例): *She always stays cool, calm and collected in a crisis.* 她在危难时总是很冷静、镇定如常、泰然自若. **col·lect·edly** *adv*.

col·lect[2] /ˈkɒlekt; ˋkɑlɛkt/ *n* (in the Anglican or the Roman Catholic Church) short prayer, usu to be read on a particular day (英国国教或天主教的)短祈祷文.

col·lec·tion /kəˈlekʃn; kəˋlɛkʃən/ *n* **1** [C, U] (act of) collecting (COLLECT[1] 5) sth 拿走、取走或收走某物: *There are two collections a day from this letter-box*, ie The postman empties it twice a day. 这个信筒每天收信两次(邮递员每天取走两次). ○ *The council is responsible for refuse collection.* 市政局负责清除垃圾废物. **2** [C] group of objects that have been collected (COLLECT[1] 4) systematically 一系列搜集物; 收藏品: *a fine collection of paintings*, eg in an art gallery 精美的绘画收藏品(如在美术馆中) ○ *a stamp, coin, record, etc collection* 邮票、硬币、唱片等的收藏品 ○ *a collection of poems*, ie a group of poems published in one volume 诗集. **3** [C] range of new clothes, etc offered for sale by a designer or manufacturer 时装展销: *You are invited to view our autumn collection.* 秋装展销, 敬请光临. **4** [C] (**a**) collecting (COLLECT[1] 3) of money during a church service or a meeting (在教堂礼拜或聚会期间的)募捐: *The collection will be taken (up)/made after the sermon.* 教堂讲道之后将进行募捐. ○ *a collection for famine relief* 赈济饥民的募捐. (**b**) sum of money collected in this way 募捐的钱: *a large collection* 大批捐款. **5** [C] heap or pile of objects; group of people 成堆物品; 人群: *a collection of junk, rubbish, etc* 一堆废旧物品、垃圾等 ○ *an odd collection of people* 一群稀奇古怪的人.

col·lect·ive /kəˈlektɪv; kəˋlɛktɪv/ *adj* of, by or relating to a group or society as a whole; joint; shared 集体的; 整个社会的; 共同的; 共有的: *collective action, effort, guilt, responsibility, wisdom* 集体的行动、努力、罪责、责任、智慧 ○ *collective leadership*, ie government by a group rather than an individual 集体领导. Cf 参看 INDIVIDUAL 2.

▷ **col·lect·ive** *n* **1** (**a**) [C] organization or enterprise (esp a farm) owned and controlled by the people who work in it 集体组织; 集体企业; (尤指)集体农场: *a workers' collective* 工人的集体组织. (**b**) [CGp] these people as a group 集体. **2** [C] = COLLECTIVE NOUN.

col·lect·ively *adv*.

col·lect·iv·ism /-ɪzəm; -ɪzəm/ *n* [U] theory advocating the ownership and control of land and the means of production by the whole community or by the State, for the benefit of everyone 集体主义. **col·lect·iv·ist** *n, adj*.

col·lect·iv·ize, -ise /kəˈlektɪvaɪz; kəˋlɛktɪˌvaɪz/ *v* [Tn] change (farms, industries, land, etc) from private ownership to ownership by the State 使(农场、工业、土地等)集体化, 国有化. **col·lect·iv·iza·tion, -isation** /kəˌlektɪvaɪˈzeɪʃn; *US* -vɪˈz-; kəˌlɛktəvəˋzeʃən/ *n* [U].

□ **colˌlective ˈbargaining** negotiation (about pay, working conditions, etc) between a trade union and an employer 劳资双方(关于工资、工作条件等)的集体谈判.

colˌlective ˈfarm (esp in Communist countries) farm

or group of farms owned by the State and run by the workers（尤指共产主义国家的）集体农场或农庄.

col,lective 'noun (*grammar*) noun that is singular in form but can refer to a number of people or things and agree with a plural verb 集合名词(形式上为单数而意为复数的名词, 要求与复数动词一致): *'Flock' and 'committee' are collective nouns.* flock和committee都是集合名词.

col,lective 'ownership ownership of land, the means of production, etc by all the members of a community for the benefit of everyone 集体所有制.

col·lector /kə'lektə(r); kə'lektɚ/ *n* (esp in compounds 尤用以构成复合词) person who collects (COLLECT[1] 4) things 收集人; 收藏家: *a 'stamp-collector* ○ *a 'tax-collector* ○ *a 'ticket- collector*, eg at a railway station.

□ **col'lector's item** (also **col'lector's piece**) thing worth putting in a collection because of its beauty, rarity, etc 值得收集的物品.

col·leen /'kɒli:n; 'kɑlin/ *n (Irish* 爱尔兰) young woman; girl 少女; 姑娘; 女孩儿.

col·lege /'kɒlɪdʒ; 'kɑlɪdʒ/ *n* **1** [C, U] institution for higher education or professional training 学院; 职业学校: *a college of further education*, ie providing educational and vocational courses for adults 进修学院 ○ *the Royal College of Art* 皇家艺术学院 ○ *a secretarial college* 秘书学校 ○ *Our daughter is going to college* (ie starting a course of study at a university or a college) *in the autumn.* 我们的女儿秋天就要上大学了. ○ *She's at* (ie studying at) *college.* 她在大学读书. ⇨Usage at SCHOOL[1] 用法见SCHOOL[1]. **2** (**a**) [C] (in Britain) any of a number of independent institutions within certain universities, each having its own teachers, students and buildings（英国）某些大学内独立的学院: *the Oxford and Cambridge colleges* 牛津和剑桥的学院 ○ *New College, Oxford* 牛津新学院. (**b**) (in the US) university, or part of one, offering undergraduate courses（美国）大学; （大学中的）学院. **3** [C, U] building or buildings of a college(2) 学院的建筑物: *Are you living in college?* 你住在学院里吗? ○ [attrib 作定语] *a college chapel* 学院附属教堂. **4** [CGp] staff and/or students of a college(1) 学院的职员或学生或全体师生员工. **5** [C] (*Brit*) (in names) school（用作名称）学校: *Eton College* 伊顿学院. **6** [C] organized group of professional people with particular aims, duties or privileges 有某种目的、责任或特权的专业人员的组织; 学会; 社团: *the Royal College of Surgeons* 皇家外科医生学会 ○ *the College of Cardinals*, ie the whole group of them, esp as advisers and electors of the Pope（天主教）枢机主教团; （尤指）红衣主教团.

col·legi·ate /kə'li:dʒɪət; kə'lidʒɪɪt/ *adj* [usu attrib 通常作定语] **1** of or relating to a college or its students 学院的; 学院学生的. **2** consisting of or having colleges 由学院组成的; 有学院的: *Oxford is a collegiate university.* 牛津是由学院组成的大学.

col·lide /kə'laɪd; kə'laɪd/ *v* [I, Ipr] **~ (with sb/sth) 1** (of moving objects or people) strike violently against sth or each other（指运动中的物体或人）猛撞某物或互撞: *As the bus turned the corner, it collided with a van.* 公共汽车转过拐角时与客货车相撞. ○ *The bus and the van collided.* 公共汽车与客货车相撞. ○ *The ships collided in the fog.* 轮船在雾中相撞. **2** (of people, aims, opinions, etc) be in disagreement or opposition; conflict（指人、目的、意见等）不一致或相反; 冲突: *The interests of the two countries collide.* 两国的利益发生冲突.

col·lie /'kɒlɪ; 'kɑlɪ/ *n* sheep-dog with shaggy hair and a long pointed muzzle 柯利牧羊狗(毛粗, 嘴长而尖). ⇨ illus at App 1 见附录1之插图, page iii.

col·lier /'kɒlɪə(r); 'kɑljɚ/ *n* (*esp Brit*) **1** coal-miner 煤矿工人. **2** ship that carries coal as its cargo 运煤船.

col·li·ery /'kɒlɪərɪ; 'kɑljərɪ/ *n* (*esp Brit*) coal-mine with its buildings 煤矿及其建筑物.

col·li·sion /kə'lɪʒn; kə'lɪʒən/ *n* [C, U] **~ (with sb/sth); ~ (between A and B) 1** (instance of) one object or person striking against another; (instance of) colliding; crash（物与物或人与人）相撞, 碰撞, 撞坏: *a (head-on) collision between two cars* 两车(迎头)相撞 ○ *The liner was in collision* (ie collided) *with an oil-tanker.* 客轮与油轮相撞. ○ *The two ships were in/came into collision.* 两艘轮船相撞. **2** strong disagreement; conflict or clash of opposing aims, ideas, opinions, etc 抵触; （相反的目的、看法、意见等的）冲突: *Her political activities brought her into collision with the law.* 她的政治活动触犯了法律.

□ **col'lision course** course or action that is certain to lead to a collision with sb/sth 必然与某人[某事物]相冲突的进程或行动: *The Government and the unions are on a collision course.* 政府和工会必将发生冲突.

col·loc·ate /'kɒləkeɪt; 'kɑlo,ket/ *v* [I, Ipr] **~ (with sth)** (*linguistics* 语言) (of words) be regularly used together in a language; combine（指词语）经常一起使用; 搭配; 配合: *'Weak' collocates with 'tea' but 'feeble' does not.* weak可与tea搭配, 而feeble则不可. ○ *'Weak' and 'tea' collocate.* weak可与tea相搭配.

▷ **col·loca·tion** /,kɒlə'keɪʃn; ,kɑlə'keʃən/ *n* **1** [U] collocating（词语的）搭配, 相配. **2** [C] regular combination of words 经常搭配着用的词语: *'Strong tea' and 'by accident' are English collocations.* strong tea与by accident是英语经常搭配的词组.

col·lo·quial /kə'ləʊkwɪəl; kə'lokwɪəl/ *adj* (of words, phrases, etc) belonging to or suitable for normal conversation but not formal speech or writing（指词语等）口语的, 口头的. Cf 参看 INFORMAL, SLANG.

▷ **col·lo·qui·al·ism** *n* colloquial word or phrase 口语的词语: *The phrase 'on the blink' in the sentence 'The radio's on the blink'* (ie not working properly) *is a colloquialism.* 在 The radio's on the blink(收音机坏了)一句中的 on the blink(坏了)这一词组是口语用语.

col·lo·qui·ally /-kwɪəlɪ; -kwɪəlɪ/ *adv*.

col·lo·quy /'kɒləkwɪ; 'kɑləkwɪ/ *n* [C, U] (*fml* 文) conversation 交谈; 会谈.

col·lude /kə'lu:d; kə'lud/ *v* [I, Ipr] **~ (with sb)** plot or conspire to deceive or cheat others 阴谋或密谋欺骗他人.

col·lu·sion /kə'lu:ʒn; kə'luʒən/ *n* [U] **~ (with sb); ~ (between sb and sb)** (*fml* 文) secret agreement or co-operation between two or more people with the aim of deceiving or cheating others 勾结; 串通共谋: *There was collusion between the two witnesses*, eg They gave the same false evidence to protect the defendant. 两个证人串通一气(如两人作同样伪证包庇被告). ○ *She acted in collusion with the other witness.* 她与另一证人串通一气.

▷ **col·lus·ive** /kə'lu:sɪv; kə'lusɪv/ *adj*.

col·ly·wobbles /'kɒlɪwɒblz; 'kɑlɪ,wɑblz/ *n* [pl] (*infml* 口) **1** pain or rumbling in the stomach 肚子痛或咕噜咕噜响. **2** feeling of fear or nervousness 害怕; 紧张不安: *have an attack of (the) collywobbles* 有害怕的感觉.

co·logne /kə'ləʊn; kə'lon/ *n* [U] = EAU-DE-COLOGNE.

co·lon[1] /'kəʊlən; 'kolən/ *n* lower part of the large intestine 结肠. ⇨illus at DIGESTIVE 见 DIGESTIVE 之插图.

co·lon[2] /'kəʊlən; 'kolən/ *n* punctuation mark (:) used in writing and printing to show that what follows is an example, list or summary of what precedes it, or a contrasting idea 冒号(:). ⇨App 3 见附录3. Cf 参看 SEMICOLON.

col·onel /'kɜ:nl; 'kɝnl/ *n* (**a**) army officer between the ranks of lieutenant-colonel and brigadier, commanding a regiment（陆军）上校. (**b**) officer of similar rank in the US air force（美国空军）上校. ⇨App 9 见附录9.

co·lo·nial /kə'ləʊnɪəl; kə'lonɪəl/ *adj* [esp attrib 尤作定语] **1** of, relating to or possessing a colony(1a) or colonies 殖民地的; 占有殖民地的: *France was once a colonial power.* 法国一度是占有殖民地的强国. ○ *Kenya was under (British) colonial rule for many years.* 肯尼亚曾多年受(英国)殖民统治. **2** (*esp US*) in a style of architecture typical of a colony, esp that used in the British colonies in N America in the 17th and 18th centuries 典型的殖民地建筑风格的(尤指于17和18世纪在北美的英国殖民地所采用的): *colonial residences in New England* 在新英格兰的有殖民地建筑风格的住宅 ○ *a colonial-style ranch* 殖民地建筑式的大牧场.

▷ **co·lo·nial** *n* person living in a colony who is not a member of the native population 住在殖民地而非土著的人.

co·lo·ni·al·ism *n* [U] policy of acquiring colonies and keeping them dependent 殖民主义; 殖民政策. **co·lo·ni·al·ist** *n* supporter of colonialism 殖民主义者.

col·on·ist /'kɒlənɪst; 'kɑlənɪst/ *n* person who settles in an area and colonizes it 移居并开拓殖民地的人; 殖民者.

col·on·ize, -ise /'kɒlənaɪz; 'kɑlə,naɪz/ *v* [Tn] establish a colony in (an area); establish (an area) as a colony 在(一地区)建立殖民地; 把(某地区)开拓为殖民地: *Britain colonized many parts of Africa.* 英国在非洲开拓了许多殖民地. ○ *Britain was colonized by the Romans.* 不列颠曾沦为罗马人的殖民地.

▷ **col·on·iza·tion, -isation** /ˌkɒlənaɪˈzeɪʃn; *US* -nɪˈz-; ˌkɑlənəˈzeʃən/ *n* [U] colonizing or being colonized 殖民地化; 被殖民地化: *the colonization of N America by the British and French.* 英国和法国对北美洲的殖民地化.

col·on·nade /ˌkɒləˈneɪd; ˌkɑləˈned/ *n* row of columns, usu with equal spaces between them and often supporting a roof, etc 列柱; 柱廊.

▷ **col·on·naded** /ˌkɒləˈneɪdɪd; ˌkɑləˈnedɪd/ *adj* having a colonnade 有柱廊的.

col·ony /ˈkɒlənɪ; ˈkɑlənɪ/ *n* **1** (**a**) [C] country or area settled or conquered by people from another country and controlled by that country 殖民地: *a former British colony*, eg Australia 前英国殖民地(如澳大利亚). Cf 参看 PROTECTORATE 1. (**b**) [CGp] group of people who settle in a colony 移居到殖民地的人群. **2** [CGp] (**a**) group of people from a foreign country living in a particular city or country 移民群体; 侨民群体: *the American colony in Paris* 巴黎的美国人区. (**b**) group of people with the same occupation, interest, etc living together in the same place 住在同一地方有相同职业、兴趣等的人群: *an artists' colony* 聚居的艺术家 ○ *a nudist colony* 裸体者群. **3** [CGp] (*biology* 生) group of animals or plants living or growing in the same place (生活或生长在同一地方的动物或植物的)群, 集群, 群体: *a colony of ants* 蚁群 ○ *a seal colony* 海豹群.

col·or (*US*) = COLOUR.

col·ora·tura /ˌkɒlərəˈtʊərə; ˌkɑlərəˈtʊrə/ *n* **1** [U] elaborate or ornamental passages in vocal music (声乐中的)花腔. **2** [C] (also **coloratura soprano**) female singer who specializes in singing such passages 花腔女高音歌手.

co·los·sal /kəˈlɒsl; kəˈlɑsl/ *adj* very large; immense; huge 巨大的; 广大的; 庞大的: *a colossal building, man, price, amount* 巨大的建筑物、巨人、高价、庞大数量.

co·los·sus /kəˈlɒsəs; kəˈlɑsəs/ *n* (*pl* **-lossi** /-ˈlɒsaɪ; -ˈlɑsaɪ/ or **~es** /-ˈlɒsəsɪz; -ˈlɑsəsɪz/) **1** statue much larger than life size (远超于实体的)塑像; 巨像. **2** person or thing of very great size, importance, ability, etc 非常巨大、重要、有能量等的人或事物: *Mozart is a colossus among composers.* 莫札特是作曲家中的巨匠.

col·our[1] (*US* **color**) /ˈkʌlə(r); ˈkʌlɚ/ *n* **1** (**a**) [U] visible quality that objects have, produced by rays of light of different wavelengths being reflected by them 颜色: *The garden was a mass of colour.* 花园中五彩缤纷. ○ *You need more colour in this room.* 你这房间的色调需要丰富些. (**b**) [C] particular type of this (某种)颜色: *Red, orange, green and purple are all colours.* 红、橙、绿、紫都是颜色. ○ *'What colour is the sky?' 'It's blue.'* '天空是什么颜色的?''是蓝的.' ○ *a sky the colour of lead*, ie a grey sky 像铅一样颜色的天空(灰色天空). **2** (**a**) [C, U] substance (eg paint or dye) used to give colour to sth 颜料(如油漆、染料): *paint in ˈwater-colour(s)* 水彩画 ○ *use plenty of bright colour in a painting* 画中使用了大量鲜艳的颜色. (**b**) [U] use of all colours, not only black and white 彩色: *Is the film in colour or black and white?* 这胶卷是彩色的还是黑白的? ○ [attrib 作定语] *colour photography, television, printing* 彩色摄影术、电视、印刷. **3** [U] redness of the face, usu regarded as a sign of good health (used esp as in the expressions shown) 脸色, 气色(尤用于以下示例): *He has very little colour*, ie is very pale. 他脸色不好(苍白). ○ *change colour*, ie become paler or redder than usual 变脸色(变得较平常苍白或红润) ○ *lose colour*, ie become paler 失去红润 ○ *She has a high colour*, ie a very red complexion. 她气色很好. ○ *The fresh air brought colour to her cheeks.* 因空气新鲜, 她双颊红润. **4** [U] colour of the skin as a racial characteristic 肤色(作为种族特征): *be discriminated against on account of one's colour/on grounds of colour* 因为肤色[由于肤色]的关系受到歧视 ○ [attrib 作定语] *colour prejudice* 不同肤色的种族偏见. **5 colours** [pl] coloured badge, ribbon, clothes, etc worn to show one is a member of a particular team, school, political party, etc or worn by a racehorse to show who owns it 彩色徽章、绶带、衣物等(用以表示为某队、校、政党等的成员由参赛的马披戴作其主人的标识). **6 colours** [pl] (*Brit*) award given to a regular or outstanding member of a sports team, esp in a school 颁给体育运动队, 尤指校队正式成员或杰出成员的奖: *get/win one's (football) colours* 得到[赢得](足球)奖. **7 colours** [pl] flag(s) of a ship or regiment 船旗; 团旗; 军旗: *salute the colours* 向军旗敬礼. **8** [U] (**a**) interesting detail or qualities; vividness 有趣的细节; 令人感兴趣的特性; 生动: *Her description of the area is full of colour.* 她对这地区的描述绘声绘色. (**b**) distinctive quality of sound in music; tone 音色; 音质; 音品; 格调: *orchestral colour* 管弦乐的音色 ○ *His playing lacks colour.* 他的演奏没有什么格调. **9** (idm 习语) **give/lend ˈcolour to sth** make sth seem true or probable 使某事物显得真实或可信: *The scars on his body lent colour to his claim that he had been tortured.* 他说他受过折磨拷打, 从他身上的伤疤看来倒也可信. **lose colour** ⇨ LOSE. **nail one's colours to the mast** ⇨ NAIL *v*. **off colour** (*infml* 口) unwell; ill 不舒服; 有病: *feel, look, seem a bit off colour* 感觉、看起来、似乎有点不舒服. **see the colour of sb's ˈmoney** make sure that sb has enough money to pay for sth 弄清某人的钱是否足以偿付某事物: *Don't let him have the car until you've seen the colour of his money.* 先弄清他确实有钱再把汽车给他. **trooping the colour** ⇨ TROOP. **one's true colours** ⇨ TRUE. **under false colours** ⇨ FALSE. **with flying colours** ⇨ FLYING.

▷ **col·our·ful** (*US* **col·or·ful**) /-fl; -fəl/ *adj* **1** full of colour; bright 鲜艳的; 鲜明的: *a colourful dress, scene* 艳丽的连衣裙、景色 ○ *colourful material* 颜色鲜明的材料. **2** interesting or exciting; vivid 有趣的; 激动人心的; 生动活泼的: *a colourful character, life, story, period of history* 活泼的性格、活跃的生活、生动的故事、丰富多彩的历史时期.

col·our·less (*US* **col·or·less**) *adj* **1** without colour; pale 无色的; 苍白的: *a colourless liquid*, eg water 无色的液体(如水) ○ *colourless cheeks* 苍白的面颊. **2** dull and uninteresting 呆板而无趣的: *a colourless character, existence, style* 呆板而无趣的性格、生活、格调.

□ **ˈcolour-bar** *n* (*US* **ˈcolor line**) legal or social discrimination between people of different races, esp between whites and non-whites 肤色障碍(法律上的或社会上的种族歧视, 尤指白种人与非白种人之间的).

ˈcolour-blind *adj* unable to see the difference between certain colours, esp red and green 色盲的. **ˈcolour-blindness** *n* [U].

ˈcolour code system of marking things (eg electrical wires, parts of a filing system, etc) with different colours to help people to distinguish between them 色标, 色码(用不同颜色对物件, 如电线、档案分目等作的标记). **ˈcolour-coded** *adj* marked in this way 用颜色标记的.

ˈcolour-fast *adj* (of a fabric) having a colour that will not change or fade when it is washed (指纤维织物)不褪色的.

ˈcolour scheme arrangement of colours, esp in the decoration and furnishing of a room 色彩调配(尤指室内装修): *I don't like the colour scheme in their sitting-room.* 我不喜欢他们起居室的色调.

col·our[2] (*US* **color**) /ˈkʌlə(r); ˈkʌlɚ/ *v* **1** [Tn, Cn·a] put colour on (sth), eg by painting, dyeing or staining 给(某物)着色(如以绘、漆、印、染等方式): *colour a picture* 给画片着色 ○ *colour a wall green* 把墙壁涂成绿色. **2** (**a**) [I] become coloured; change colour 变为有色; 改变颜色: *It is autumn and the leaves are beginning to colour*, ie turn brown. 秋天到了, 叶子开始变黄了. (**b**) [I, Ipr, Ip] **~ (up) (at sth)** become red in the face; blush 脸红: *She coloured (with embarrassment) at his remarks.* 她听到他的话(因受窘)而脸红了. **3** [Tn esp passive 尤用于被动语态] affect (sth), esp in a negative way; distort 影响(某事物)(尤指不良方面); 歪曲: *His attitude to sex is coloured by his strict upbringing.* 他所受到的严厉教养, 影响了他对两性的态度. ○ *Don't allow personal loyalty to colour your judgement.* 不要因讲义气而影响了你的判断. ○ *She gave a highly coloured* (ie exaggerated) *account of her travels.* 她把旅行的事大大地渲染(夸张)了一番. **4** (phr v) **colour sth in** fill (a particular area, shape, etc) with colour 给(某面积、图形等)着色: *The child coloured in all the shapes on the page with a crayon.* 那孩子用蜡笔把这页上所有的图形都涂上了颜色.

▷ **col·oured** (*US* **col·ored**) *adj* **1** (often in compounds 常用以构成复合词) having colour; having the specified colour 有色的; 有某种颜色的: *coloured chalks* 彩色粉笔 ○ *ˈcream-coloured* 奶油色的 ○ *ˈflesh-coloured* 肉色的. **2** (**a**) (*becoming dated* 渐旧) (of people) of a race that does not have a white skin (指人)有色人种的(非白皮肤种族的). (**b**) **Coloured** (in S Africa) of mixed race (在南非洲)混血种的人.

col·our·ing *n* **1** [U] action of putting colour on sth 给某物着色; 上色; 染色; 涂色: *Children enjoy colouring*, eg with crayons. 儿童都喜欢涂颜色(如用蜡笔). ○ [attrib 作定语] *a colouring book* (为练习涂色用的)空白画册. **2** [U] (**a**) way or style in which sth is coloured 着色法. (**b**) way in which an artist uses colour in paintings (艺术家在绘画中的)用色风格, 色调. **3** [U] colour of a person's skin; complexion 肤色; 面色: *She has (a) very fair colouring.* 她面色白皙. **4** [C, U] (type of) substance used to give a particular colour to sth, esp to food 着色剂(尤指用于食物的): *This yoghurt contains no artificial flavouring or colouring.* 这种酸乳酪不含人造香料或着色剂.

colt /kəʊlt; kolt/ *n* **1** young male horse up to the age of 4 or 5 (四五岁或以下的)小雄马. Cf 参看 FILLY, GELDING (GELD), STALLION. **2** young inexperienced person, esp a member of a junior sports team 没有经验的年轻人(尤指青年运动队队员): *He plays for the colts*, eg the junior team of a football club. 他是青年队队员(如足球俱乐部的青年队).

▷ **colt·ish** /ˈkəʊltɪʃ; ˈkoltɪʃ/ *adj* like a colt; frisky 像小马的; 活泼的.

col·ter (*US*) = COULTER.

col·um·bine /ˈkɒləmbaɪn; ˈkɑləm,baɪn/ *n* garden plant with flowers that have thin pointed petals 耧斗菜(园艺植物, 花瓣细而尖).

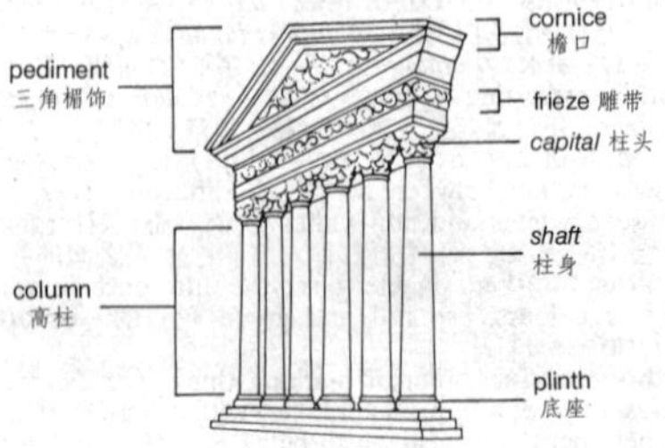

col·umn /ˈkɒləm; ˈkɑləm/ *n* **1** tall pillar, usu round and made of stone, either supporting part of the roof of a building or standing alone as a monument 高柱; (通常为)石制圆柱, 支柱, 纪念柱: *The temple is supported by massive columns.* 此庙由粗大的柱子支撑. ○ *Nelson's Column is a famous monument in London.* 纳尔逊纪念碑是伦敦著名的纪念碑. ⇨illus 见插图. **2** thing shaped like a column 圆柱形物: *a column of smoke*, ie smoke rising straight up 烟柱(直上的烟) ○ *the ˌspinal ˈcolumn*, ie the backbone 脊柱(脊骨) ○ *a column of mercury*, ie in a thermometer 水银柱(温度计中). **3** (*abbr* 缩写 **col**) one of two or more vertical sections of printed material on a page (印刷品每页上的)列, 栏: *Each page of this dictionary has two columns of text.* 本词典每页上有两列正文. **4** part of a newspaper regularly dealing with a particular subject or written by the same journalist (报纸的)专栏: *the ˈfashion, ˈmotoring, fiˈnancial, etc column* 时装、汽车、财经等专栏 ○ *the correspondence columns of 'The Times'* 《泰晤士报》上的通讯栏 ○ *I always read her column in the local paper.* 我经常在当地报纸上看她的专栏文章. **5** (**a**) long line of vehicles, ships, etc following one behind the other 长列(排成长行的车辆、船只等). (**b**) large group of soldiers, tanks, etc moving forward in short rows 纵队(短排前进的大队士兵、坦克车等). **6** series of numbers arranged one under the other 纵行数字: *add up a long column of figures* 把一串纵行数字相加.

▷ **col·um·nist** /ˈkɒləmnɪst; ˈkɑləmnɪst/ *n* journalist who regularly writes an article commenting on politics, current events, etc for a newspaper or magazine 专栏作家: *a political columnist* 政论专栏作家.

coma /ˈkəʊmə; ˈkomə/ *n* state of deep unconsciousness, usu lasting a long time and caused by severe injury or illness 昏迷(状态): *go into a coma* 进入昏迷状态 ○ *He was in a coma for several weeks.* 他昏迷了几个星期.

▷ **co·ma·tose** /ˈkəʊmətəʊs; ˈkomə,tos/ *adj* **1** in a coma; deeply unconscious 昏迷的; 不省人事的. **2** sleepy; drowsy; sluggish 想睡的; 困乏的; 怠惰的; 没精打采的: *feeling comatose after a large meal* 大吃一顿后感到困倦.

comb /kəʊm; kom/ *n* **1** [C] (**a**) piece of metal, plastic or bone with teeth, used for tidying and arranging the hair 梳子; 篦子. (**b**) small piece of plastic or bone with teeth, worn by women to hold the hair in place or as an ornament 发插(用以使头发固定或作头饰). **2** [C usu *sing* 通常作单数] act of combing the hair 梳理(毛发); 梳(头): *Your hair needs a (good) comb.* 你的头发需要(好好)梳一梳. **3** [C] thing shaped or used like a comb, esp a device for tidying and straightening wool, cotton, etc to prepare it for manufacture 梳状物; 精梳机. **4** [C, U] = HONEYCOMB. **5** [C] red fleshy growth on the head of a domestic fowl, esp a cock (家禽的)冠; (尤指)公鸡冠. ⇨illus at App 1 见附录1之插图, page v. **6** (idm 习语) **with a fine-tooth comb** ⇨ FINE[2].

▷ **comb** *v* **1** [Tn] pass a comb through (the hair) in order to tidy or arrange it 梳理(毛发); 梳(头): *Don't forget to comb your hair before you go out!* 不要忘记临出门梳梳头! **2** [Tn] prepare (wool, cotton, etc) for manufacture by tidying and straightening it with a comb (3) (用精梳机)精梳(毛、棉等). **3** [Ipr, Tn, Tn·pr] **~ (through) sth (for sb/sth)** search sth thoroughly 彻底搜寻某物: *He combed through the files searching for evidence of fraud.* 他详查档案, 寻找欺诈行为的证据. ○ *Police are combing the woods for the missing children.* 警察搜遍树林以寻找失踪的孩子. **4** (phr v) **comb sth out** remove knots, tangles, etc from or shape (the hair) with a comb 梳去(发结和乱处等); 梳整(发型). **comb sth out (of sth)** (**a**) remove (dirt, tangles, etc) from the hair with a comb 梳去毛发中(的脏物或结团处): *She combed the mud out of the dog's fur.* 她梳去狗的皮毛中的泥土. (**b**) remove (unwanted people or things) from a group 从群体中清除(不需要的人或物).

com·bat /ˈkɒmbæt; ˈkɑmbæt/ *n* [C, U] fight or fighting between two people, armies, etc (两人、两军等的)格斗, 搏斗, 战斗: *armed/unarmed combat*, ie with/without weapons 武装的[非武装的]斗争 ○ *The troops were exhausted after months of fierce combat.* 部队经过几个月的激战已筋疲力尽. ○ [attrib 作定语] *a combat jacket, mission, zone* (野战用夹克式)军上衣、战斗任务、战区.

▷ **com·bat** *v* [Ipr, Tn] **~ (against/with) sb/sth** (**a**) fight or struggle against sb/sth 与(某人[某事物])战斗, 斗争, 搏斗: *combat the enemy* 与敌人作战. (**b**) try to reduce, weaken or destroy sth 试图减少、减弱或消灭(某事物): *combating disease, inflation, terrorism* 与疾病、通货膨胀、恐怖主义作斗争.

com·bat·ant /ˈkɒmbətənt; ˈkɑmbətənt/ *n, adj* (person) involved in fighting in a war 参战者; 战士: *In modern wars, both combatants and non-combatants* (ie civilians) *are killed.* 在现代战争中, 战斗人员与非战斗人员(平民)都可能死亡.

com·bat·ive /ˈkɒmbətɪv; ˈkɑmbətɪv/ *adj* eager or ready to fight or argue 斗志旺盛的; 好斗的; 好争论的: *in a combative mood* 斗志昂扬. **com·bat·ively** *adv*.

com·bina·tion /ˌkɒmbɪˈneɪʃn; ˌkɑmbəˈneʃən/ *n* **1** [U] joining or mixing together of two or more things or people; state of being joined or mixed together (两个或两个以上事物或人)结合, 混合, 联合, 组合, 合并, 化合: *It is the combination of wit and political analysis that makes his articles so readable.* 他的生花妙笔与政治分析相得益彰, 使他的文章脍炙人口. ○ *The firm is working on a new product in combination with several overseas partners.* 公司正在联合几家海外合伙人制造新产品. **2** [C] number of things or people joined or mixed together; mixture; blend 结合到一起的事物或人; 混合物; 联合体: *Pink is a combination of red and white.* 粉红色是红色与白色的混合色. ○ *A combination of factors led to her decision to resign.* 综合各种因素之后她决定辞职. ○ *The architecture in the town centre is a successful combination of old and new.* 市中心的建筑风格是古今结合, 浑然一体. ○ *What an unusual combination of* *flavours!* 多么不寻常的混合风味! **3** [C] sequence of numbers or letters used to open a combination lock (用以开启暗码锁的)数字或字母组合. **4** [C] (*Brit*) motor-bike with a side-car attached to it 带挎斗的摩托车. **5 combinations** [pl] (formerly) one-piece undergarment covering the body and legs (旧时)衫裤相连的内衣.

□ **combi'nation lock** type of lock (eg on a safe) that can only be opened by turning a set of dials until they show a particular sequence of numbers or letters 暗码锁(如保险柜上的).

com·bine[1] /kəm'baɪn; kəm'baɪn/ *v* **1** [I, Ipr, Tn, Tn·pr] **~ (with sth)**; **~ A and B/A with B** (cause things to) join or mix together to form a whole (使物件)结合或混合形成一整体; 联合; 组合; 合并; 化合: *Hydrogen and oxygen combine/Hydrogen combines with oxygen to form water.* 氢与氧化合成水. ○ *Circumstances have combined to ruin our plans for a holiday.* 各种情况凑在一起破坏了我们的假日计划. ○ *Combine the eggs with a little flour and heat the mixture gently.* 把鸡蛋和少量面粉调匀, 用文火加热. ○ *a kitchen and dining-room combined*, ie one room used as both 厨房兼饭厅 ○ *Success was achieved by the combined efforts of the whole team.* 全队齐心协力取得了胜利. **2** [Tn, Tn·pr] **~ A and B/A with B** do (two or more things) at the same time or have (two or more different qualities) as a characteristic 同时做(不止一件事); 兼有(不止一种)特性: *combine business with pleasure* 寓工作于娱乐之中 ○ *He combines arrogance and incompetence in his dealings with the staff.* 他在与工作人员交往中既傲慢又无能.

□ **com'bining form** (*linguistics* 语言) form of a word which can combine with another word or another combining form to form a new word, eg *Anglo-*, *-philia* 构词成分(能与另一词或另一构词成分构成新词者, 如Anglo-、-philia). ⇨ Detailed Guide 1.4.

com·bine[2] /'kɒmbaɪn; 'kɑmbaɪn/ *n* **1** group of people or firms acting together in business 业务上合作的人们或企业; 联合企业. **2** (also ˌ**combine 'harvester**) agricultural machine that both reaps and threshes grain 联合收割机. Cf 参看 HARVESTER (HARVEST).

com·bust·ible /kəm'bʌstəbl; kəm'bʌstəbḷ/ *adj* **1** that can catch fire and burn easily 可燃的; 易燃的: *Petrol is (highly) combustible.* 汽油(极)易燃. **2** (*fig* 比喻) (of people) excitable (指人)易激动的: *a combustible temperament* 易冲动的脾气.

▷ **com·bust·ible** *n* (usu *pl* 通常作复数) combustible substance or material 易燃物; 可燃物.

com·bus·tion /kəm'bʌstʃən; kəm'bʌstʃən/ *n* [U] **1** process of burning 燃烧. **2** chemical process in which substances combine with oxygen in air, producing heat and light 燃烧过程.

□ **com·'bustion chamber** enclosed space in which 'combustion(2) takes place, eg the space above the piston in an internal-combustion engine 燃烧室.

come /kʌm; kʌm/ *v* (*pt* **came** /keɪm; kem/, *pp* **come**) **1** (**a**) [I, Ipr, Ip] **~ (to...) (from...)** move to, towards, into, etc a place where the speaker or writer is, or a place being referred to by him 来(指行动过程): *She came into the room and shut the door.* 她进到屋子里来, 然后关上了门. ○ *She came slowly down the stairs.* 她慢慢地走下楼来. ○ *He has come all the way from Leeds to look for a job.* 他从利兹远道而来寻找工作. ○ *Come and visit us again soon!* 希望你不久再来坐一坐! ○ *She comes to work by bus.* 她上班乘公共汽车来. ○ *Are you coming out for a walk?* 你要出来散散步吗? ○ *Our son is coming home for Christmas.* 我们的儿子准备回家来过圣诞节. ○ *Come here!* 到这儿来! ⇨Usage at AND 用法见AND. ⇨Usage at VISIT 用法见VISIT. (**b**) [I, Ipr] **~ (to...)** arrive at a place where the speaker or writer is or at a place being referred to by him 来(指到达): *They came to a river.* 他们来到河边. ○ *They came* (eg arrived at my house) *at 8 o'clock.* 他们8点钟来到(如到我家). ○ *What time will you be coming?* 你几点钟来? ○ *Have any letters come for me?* 有给我的来信吗? ○ *I've come to collect my book/come for my book.* 我来取我的书. ○ *Help has come at last.* 终于得到了帮助. ○ *There's a storm coming*, ie approaching. 暴风雨要来了. ○ *Spring came late this year.* 今年春天来得晚了. ○ *The time has come* (ie Now is the moment) *to act.* 该行动的时候到了. (**c**) [I, Ipr] **~ (to sth) (with sb)** move in order to be with sb at a particular place or be present at an event 来(相聚或出席): *I've only come for an hour.* 我来到这里仅仅一小时. ○ *Are you coming (to the cinema) with us tonight?* 今晚你来和我们一起(看电影)吗? ○ *'Would you like to come to dinner next Friday?' 'I'd love to.'* '下星期五来吃饭好吗?' '好哇.' ○ *Are you coming to my party?* 你来参加我的聚会吗? ○ *Who are you coming with?* 你和谁一起来? ○ *I'll be coming with Keith.* 我和基思一起来. (**d**) (used with the present participle 与现在分词连用) take part in the specified activity, esp a sport, usu with other people 来(参加某活动, 尤指体育运动, 通常和他人一起): *Why don't you come ice-skating (with us) tonight?* 今晚来(和我们一起)溜冰好吗? **2** [I] travel (a specified distance) 行进(某段距离): *We've come fifty miles since lunch.* 我们午饭后走了五十英里了. ○ (*fig* 比喻) *This company has come a long way* (ie made a lot of progress) *in the last five years.* 最近五年这个公司已经前进了一大步. **3** (used with a present participle to show that sb/sth moves in the way specified or that sb is doing sth while moving 与现在分词连用, 表示某人[某事物]按某方式行进或某人在行进中做某事): *He came hurrying* (ie hurried) *to see her as soon as he heard she was ill.* 他一听说她病了就立刻赶来看她. ○ *The children came running* (ie ran) *to meet us.* 孩子们跑着来迎接我们. ○ *She came sobbing* (ie was sobbing as she came) *into the room.* 她哭着进屋来了. ○ *Sunlight came streaming through the window.* 阳光从窗子射进来. **4** [La, Ipr] (not in the continuous tenses 不用于进行时态) occupy a particular position in space or time; occur 占据一定的空间或时间; 发生; 出现: *Easter comes early this year.* 今年复活节来得早. ○ *She came first* (ie received the highest mark) *in the examination.* 她在这次考试中得第一. ○ (*fig* 比喻) *His family comes first*, ie is the most important thing in his life. 他把家庭放在第一位. ○ *May comes between April and June.* 五月在四月与六月之间. ○ *'A' comes before 'B' in the alphabet.* 在字母表中A在B的前面. ○ *Her death came as a terrible shock (to us).* 她的死(使我们)极为震惊. ○ *Her resignation came as a surprise/It came as a surprise when she resigned.* 她辞职的事大家都感到惊讶. **5** [I] (not in the continuous tenses 不用于进行时态) (of goods, products, etc) be available (指货物、产品等)有(货), 买得到: *This dress comes in three sizes.* 这种衣服有三种尺码. ○ *Do these shoes come in black?* 这种鞋有黑色的吗? ○ *New cars don't come cheap*, ie They are expensive. 新汽车没有便宜的. **6** [La] become; prove to be 变成; 证实是: *My shoe laces have come undone.* 我的鞋带松开了. ○ *This envelope has come unstuck.* 这个信封开了. ○ *The handle has come loose.* 这个把柄松了. ○ *It comes cheaper if you buy things in bulk.* 成批买东西就便宜些. ○ *Everything will come right in the end.* 一切问题终会解决. **7** [It] reach a point at which one realizes, understands, believes, etc sth 达到(对某事物认识、理解、相信等的境界): *She had come to see the problem in a new light.* 她对这问题已有新的认识. ○ *In time he came to love her.* 他终于爱上了她. ○ *I have come to believe that the Government's economic policy is misguided.* 我认识到政府的经济政策已步入歧途. **8** [It] (used in questions after *how* to ask for an explanation or a reason for sth 用于疑问句中的how之后, 要求对某事物作出解释或说明理由): *How did he come to break his leg?* 他怎么把腿弄折了呢? ○ *How do you come to be so late?* 你怎么迟到这么长时间呢? Cf 参看 HOW COME (COME 13). **9** [Ln] **~ sth (with sb)** (*infml* 口) behave like or play the part of sth 举止像...; 扮演某事物的角色: *Don't come the bully with me!* 不要跟我无理取闹! ○ *She tried to come the innocent with me.* 她在我面前装出清白无辜的样子. **10** (*infml* 口) (used before an expression of time 用于表示时间的词语之前) when the specified time comes 当某时刻到来时: *We'll have been married for two years come Christmas.* 到圣诞节时我们就结婚两年了. ○ *Come* (ie By) *next week she'll have changed her mind.* 到下星期她就要改变主意了. **11** [I] (*infml* 口) have an orgasm 达到性高潮. **12** (used with *to* or *into* + *n* in many expressions to show that the state or condition indicated by the *n* has been reached 与to或into加名词连用可构成许多固定词组, 表示已达到该名词所示的状态, 如 *At last winter came* *to an end*, ie ended 冬天终于结束了; *The trees are coming into leaf*, ie starting to grow leaves 树木开始长出叶子; for similar expressions, see entries for *ns* 类似固定词组见有关名词词条, 如 **come to blows** ⇨ BLOW). **13** (idm 习语) **be as ˌclever, ˌstupid, etc as they ˈcome** (*infml* 口) be very clever, stupid, etc 非常聪明、愚蠢等. **come again?** (*infml* 口) (used to ask sb to repeat sth because one doesn't understand it or can hardly believe it 因未听懂或难以置信, 要求某人重复一遍时使用): *'She's an entomologist.' 'Come again?' 'An entomologist — she studies insects.'* '她是昆虫学家.' '请再说一遍.' '昆虫学家——她研究昆虫.' **ˌcome and ˈgo** exist or be present in a place for a short time and then stop or depart 时来时去; 时有时无; 时隐时现: *The pain in my leg comes and goes*, ie Sometimes my leg is painful and sometimes it is not. 我的腿有时疼有时不疼. ○ *Governments come and go* (ie One government is replaced by another) *but does anything really change?* 政府换来换去, 但有什么真正的改变呢? **come ˈeasily, ˈnaturally, etc to sb** (of an activity, skill, etc) be easy, natural, etc for sb to do (指活动、技能等)某人做起来容易、生来就会等: *Acting comes naturally to her.* 她生来就会表演. **ˌcome over ˈdizzy, ˈfaint, ˈgiddy, etc** (*infml* 口) suddenly feel dizzy, faint, giddy, etc 突然感到头晕目眩、要昏倒、发晕等: *I suddenly came over (all) funny/queer and had to lie down.* 我突然感到身体不舒服[眩晕], 只好躺下. **come to ˈnothing; not come to ˈanything** have no useful or successful result; be a complete failure 毫无结果; 完全失败: *All her plans have come to nothing.* 她所有的计划都落空了. ○ *How sad that his efforts should come to nothing.* 他的一切努力完全付诸东流, 多么可悲呀. **come to oneˈself** return to one's normal state 恢复自己的常态: *The shock made her hesitate for a moment but she quickly came to herself again.* 这一打击使她踌躇片刻, 但很快就又恢复正常了. **come to ˈthat; if it comes to ˈthat** (*infml* 口) (used to introduce sth that is connected with and in addition to sth just mentioned 用以引出与刚提到的事物有联系而作补充的事物): *He looks just like his dog — come to that, so does his wife!* 他看上去就像他的狗一样——说起像来, 连他妻子也像! **ˌcome what ˈmay** whatever happens; in spite of difficulties or problems that may arise 不论发生什么事情; 不管出现什么样的困难和问题: *He promised to support her come what may.* 他答应不论发生什么事都支持她. **how come (...)?** (*infml* 口) how does/did it happen (that...)?; what is the explanation (of sth)? 怎么发生的?; (某事物)怎样解释?: *If she spent five years in Paris, how come she can't speak a word of French?* 她假若在巴黎呆了五年, 怎么一句法语都不会说呢? ○ *You were an hour late this morning, how ˈcome?* 今天早晨你迟到了一小时, 怎么回事? **not ˈcome to much** not be, become or do anything of importance 不重要; 不足道; 无关紧要: *He'll never come to much* (ie have a successful career), *he's too lazy.* 他绝不会有什么作为, 因为他太懒. ○ *I don't think her idea of becoming a journalist ever came to much.* 我认为她当新闻记者的想法没什么名堂. **to ˈcome** (used after a *n* 用于名词之后) in the future 在将来: *In years to come...* 未来的岁月 ○ *for some time to come*, ie for a period of time in the future 在将来的一段时间里. **when it comes to sth/doing sth** when it is a case, matter or question of (doing) sth 当涉及(做)某事物的情况、事情或问题时: *I'm as good a cook as she is except when it comes to (making) pastry.* 我做饭做得和她一样好, 就是不会做油酥馅饼. (For other idioms containing **come**, see entries for *ns*, *adjs*, etc 与 **come** 搭配的其他习语见有关名词、形容词等的词条, 如 **come a cropper** ⇨ CROPPER; **come clean** ⇨ CLEAN.)

14 (phr v) **come aˈbout** (of a sailing-boat) change direction (指帆船)改变方向. **come about (that...)** happen 发生: *Can you tell me how the accident came aˈbout?* 你能告诉我事故是怎样发生的吗? ○ *How did it come about that he knew where we were?* 他是怎么知道我们在什么地方的呢?

come aˈcross (also **come ˈover**) (**a**) be understood or communicated 被理解; 被传达: *He spoke for a long time but his meaning did not really come across.* 他讲了很长时间, 但他的意思没有人真正理解. (**b**) make an impression of the specified type 使人产生某种印象: *She comes across well/badly in interviews.* 她在面试中给人留下很好的[很坏的]印象. ○ *He came across as sympathetic/a sympathetic person.* 他给人以有同情心的印象. **come across sb/sth** meet or find sb/sth by chance 偶然遇见或发现某人[某事物]; 碰见: *I ˌcame across an old ˈschool friend in Oxford Street this morning.* 今天早上我在牛津大街碰见一位老校友. ○ *She ˌcame across some old ˈphotographs in a drawer.* 她在抽屉里偶然发现一些旧照片. **come aˈcross (with sth)** (*dated infml* 旧, 口) give or hand over (money, information, etc) 给或交给(钱、资料等): *He owes me five pounds but I doubt if he'll ever come across (with it).* 他欠我五英镑, 我怀疑是否能还给我(这笔钱).

come after sb chase or pursue sb 追赶或追逐某人: *The farmer came after the intruders with a big stick.* 农夫拿着大棒追赶闯进来的人.

come aˈlong (**a**) arrive; appear 到达; 出现: *When the right opportunity comes along, she'll take it.* 待适当的机会来临, 她就能抓住. ○ *'Is she married?' 'No. She says she's waiting for the right man to come along.'* '她结婚了吗?' '没有. 她说她在等待着意中人的出现.' (**b**) = COME ON d. (**c**) = COME ON e.

come aˈpart break or fall into pieces 破裂; 摔碎: *The teapot just came apart in my hands.* 茶壶就在我手中裂开了.

come at sb attack sb 攻击某人: *She came ˌat me with a ˈrolling-pin.* 她用擀面杖向我打来. **come at sth** discover (facts, the truth, etc) 发现(事实、真相等): *The truth is often difficult to ˈcome at.* 事情真相往往难以发现.

come around (to sth) = COME ROUND (TO STH).

come aˈway (from sth) become detached (from sth) (与某物)脱离: *The plaster had started to come away from the wall.* 灰泥已经开始从墙上脱落. **come away with sth** leave a place with (a feeling, an impression, etc) (带着某种感觉、印象等)离开某地: *We came away with the distinct impression that all was not well with their marriage.* 我们离去时有一种清楚的印象: 他们的婚姻并非十分美满.

come ˈback (**a**) return 回来: *You came back* (ie came home) *very late last night.* 昨晚你回来得很晚. ○ *The colour is coming back to her cheeks.* 她的面颊上又泛出红晕. (**b**) become popular, successful or fashionable again 又成为流行的、成功的或时髦的: *Miniskirts are starting to come back.* 超短裙又开始流行了. (**c**) (of a rule, law or system) be restored or reintroduced (指规章、法律或制度)恢复, 规复: *Some people would like to see the death penalty come back.* 有些人希望恢复死刑. **come ˈback at sb** reply to sb forcefully or angrily (强有力地或气愤地)答复或反驳某人: *She came back at the speaker with some sharp questions.* 她用一些尖锐的问题反驳讲话人. **come ˈback (to sb)** return to the memory 恢复记忆; 回想起: *It's all coming back to me now*, ie I'm beginning to remember everything. 现在我全都想起来了. ○ *Your French will soon come back.* 你的法语很快就能重新运用自如. **come ˈback to sb (on sth)** reply to sb about sth after a period of time (经过一段时间后)(就某事物)答复某人: *Can I come back to you on that one* (ie on that subject) *later?* 我可以过一会儿再谈你那件事吗?

come before sb/sth (**a**) be presented to sb/sth for discussion, decision or judgement 被提交给某人[某事物]进行讨论、作出决定或判决: *The case ˌcomes before the ˈcourt next week.* 这件案子下星期提交法庭审理. (**b**) have greater importance than sb/sth else 比某人[某事物]更重要: *Fighting poverty and unemployment should come before all other political considerations.* 解决贫穷和失业问题比所有其他政治问题都更重要.

come between sb and sb interfere with or harm a relationship between two people 干预或损害两人之间的关系; 离间: *It's not a good idea to come between a man and his wife.* 最好不要介入人家夫妻间的事. ○ *I'd hate anything to come between us.* 我痛恨影响我们关系的一切事物. **come between sb and sth** prevent sb from doing or having sth 妨碍某人做某事物或得到某事物: *He never lets anything come between him and his evening pint of beer.* 什么事也不能妨碍他晚上喝啤酒.

ˈcome by sth (**a**) obtain sth, usu by effort 得到某事物(通常靠努力): *Jobs are hard to come by these days.* 近来

很难找到工作. ○ *I hope that money was honestly come by.* 我希望那笔钱来得正当. **(b)** receive sth by chance 偶然获得某事物: *How did you come by that scratch on your cheek?* 你脸上的抓伤是怎么来的?

come 'down (a) collapse 塌下; 坍塌: *The ceiling came down.* 天花板塌了. **(b)** (of rain, snow, etc) fall (指雨、雪等)落下: *The rain came down in torrents.* 下着倾盆大雨. **(c)** (of an aircraft) land or fall from the sky (指飞行器)着陆, 从空中掉下: *We were forced to come down in a field.* 我们被迫在田地里着陆. ○ *Two of our fighters came down inside enemy lines.* 我方有两架战斗机坠落在敌方. **(d)** (of prices, the temperature, etc) become lower; fall (指价格、温度等)降低; 下降: *The price of petrol is coming down/Petrol is coming down in price.* 汽油价格在下跌. **come 'down (from...)** (*Brit*) leave a university (esp Oxford or Cambridge) after finishing one's studies 大学毕业(尤指于牛津或剑桥): *When did you come down (from Oxford)?* 你什么时候(从牛津)大学毕业的? **come down (from...) (to...)** come from one place to another, esp from the North of England to London, or from a city or large town to a smaller place 从一处来到另一处(尤指从英格兰北部到伦敦或由城镇到较小的地方): *We hope to come down to London next week.* 我们希望下星期南下到伦敦. ○ *They've recently come down from London to live in the village.* 他们最近已经从伦敦搬到乡村来住. **come 'down on sb** (*infml* 口) **(a)** criticize sb severely; rebuke sb 申斥某人; 训斥某人: *Don't come down too hard on her.* 不要太严厉地申斥她. **(b)** punish sb 惩罚某人: *The courts are coming down heavily on young offenders.* 法庭从严惩处年轻罪犯. **come down on sb for sth** (*infml* 口) demand (payment or money) from sb 向某人索取(报酬或钱): *His creditors came down on him for prompt payment of his bills.* 债权人催他尽快付帐. **come down to sb** be passed from one generation to another 一代传一代: *stories that came down to us from our forefathers* 祖祖辈辈传下来的故事. **come down to sth/doing sth** (*infml* 口) be forced by poverty, etc to do sth that one would never do normally; be reduced to sth 因贫穷等被迫去做正常情况下决不做的事; 沦落为...: *He had come down to begging.* 他已沦为乞丐. **come down to sth (a)** reach as far down as (a specified point) 下垂到(某一点): *Her hair comes down to her waist.* 她的头发垂到腰部. **(b)** be able to be summarized as sth; be a question of sth 可归结为某事物; 是某事物的问题: *It comes down to two choices: you either improve your work, or you leave.* 归结起来有两条出路: 你或者改进工作, 或者辞职. ○ *The whole dispute comes down to a power struggle between management and trade unions.* 全部争论其实就是资方与工会间的权力斗争. **come down with sth** become ill with (an illness) 得某病; 因某病病倒: *I came down with flu and was unable to go to work.* 我得了流感, 不能去上班.

come 'forward present oneself 站出来; 自告奋勇; 挺身而出: *come forward with help, information, money* 自告奋勇提供帮助、信息、金钱 ○ *Police have asked witnesses of the accident to come forward.* 警方要求事故的目击者挺身而出予以协助.

come from... (not used in the continuous tenses 不用于进行时态) have as one's birthplace or place of residence 为自己的出生地; 为自己的居住地: *She comes from London.* 她是伦敦人. ○ *Where do you come from?* 你是什么地方的人? **come from.../sth** be a product of (a place or a thing) (某地或某事物)的产品: *Much of the butter eaten in England comes from New Zealand.* 在英国食用的黄油多产自新西兰. ○ *Milk comes from cows and goats.* 常见的奶是牛奶和羊奶. **come from sth** (also **come of sth**) be descended from sth 出身于: *She comes from a long line of actresses.* 她出身于演员世家. **come from doing sth** = COME OF STH/DOING STH.

come in (a) (of the tide) move towards the land; rise (指潮水)涌向陆地; 涨: *The tide was coming in fast.* 潮水涨得很快. **(b)** finish a race in a particular position 赛跑取得的名次: *Which horse came in first?* 哪匹马跑第一? **(c)** (of a batsman in cricket) come to the wicket at the start of one's innings (指板球戏中的击球手)(轮到击球开始时)来到三柱门前就位: *Who's coming in next?* 该谁到三柱门击球了? **(d)** become fashionable 时兴; 流行; 时髦: *Long hair for men came in in the sixties.* 男子留长发在六十年代流行. **(e)** become available (at a particular time of the year) (在一年的某一时间)有(货); 可以买到: *English strawberries usually come in in late June.* 英国草莓通常在六月下旬上市. **(f)** be elected 当选: *The socialists came in at the last election.* 社会党人在上次选举中当选. **(g)** be received as income 收入; 进项: *She has a thousand pounds a month coming in from her investments.* 她每月从投资中得到一千英镑收入. **(h)** have a part to play in sth 在某事物中起作用: *I understand the plan perfectly, but I can't see where I come in.* 我完全了解这项计划, 但不知道我能起什么作用? **(i)** (of news, a report, etc) be received by a television station, the offices of a newspaper, etc (指新闻、报道等)被电视台、报社等收到: *News is coming in of a serious train crash in Scotland.* 刚刚收到的消息说, 苏格兰发生火车撞车重大事故. **(j)** contribute to a discussion 参与讨论: *Would you like to come in at this point, Prime Minister?* 首相, 您愿意在此刻发表意见吗? **come in for sth** be the object of sth; attract sth; receive sth 是某事物的对象; 吸引某事物; 获得某事物: *The Government's economic policies have come in for much criticism in the newspapers.* 政府的经济政策遭到报章多方抨击. **come in on sth** have a part or share in sth; join sth (在某事物中)有一份; 参与某事物: *If you want to come in on the scheme, you must decide now.* 你要参与这项计划就必须现在决定. **come in with sb** (*infml* 口) join sb in a scheme, venture, etc (在一项计划、企业等中)联合某人; 合资经营.

come into sth inherit sth 继承某事物: *She came into a fortune when her uncle died.* 她叔叔死后她继承了财产.

'come of sth = COME FROM STH. **come of sth/doing sth** (also **come from doing sth**) be the result of sth 是某事物的结果: *He promised to help, but I don't think anything will come of it.* 他答应帮忙, 但我想不会有任何结果. ○ *This is what comes of being over-confident.* 这就是过于自信的结果. ○ *No harm can come of trying.* 不妨试一试.

come off (a) be able to be removed 能被去掉: *'Does this knob come off?' 'No, it's fixed on permanently.'* '这个把手能拆下来吗?' '不能, 那是固定的.' ○ *These stains won't come off, I'm afraid.* 我看, 这些污点去不掉. **(b)** (*infml* 口) take place; happen 举行; 发生: *When's the wedding coming off?* 婚礼什么时候举行? ○ *Did your proposed trip to Rome ever come off?* 你提出的到罗马旅行, 后来去了吗? **(c)** (*infml* 口) (of a plan, scheme, etc) be successful; have the intended effect or result (指计划、方案等)成功; 达到预期的效果或结果: *Her attempt to break the world record nearly came off.* 她想要打破世界纪录, 已接近成功. ○ *The film doesn't quite come off.* 这部电影不很成功. **(d)** (*infml* 口) (followed by an *adv* 后接副词) fare; get on 进展; 进行: *He always comes off badly in fights.* 他在拳击比赛中总是很糟糕. ○ *Who came off best in the debate?* 在辩论中谁最出色? **come off (sth) (a)** fall from sth 从某物上掉下: *come off one's bicycle, horse, etc* 从自行车、马等上跌下. **(b)** become detached or separated from sth 从某物上脱落或分离: *When I tried to lift the jug, the handle came off (in my hand).* 我刚一提这个罐, 把儿就掉了(握在我手中). ○ *Lipstick often comes off on wine glasses.* 口红常能印到酒杯上. ○ *A button has come off my coat.* 我的大衣掉了一颗扣子. **come 'off it** (*infml* 口) (used in the imperative to tell sb to stop saying things that one thinks or knows are untrue 用于祈使句, 要某人不再说不确之事): *Come off it! England don't have a chance of winning the match.* 别胡扯了! 英格兰没有希望赢得这场比赛. **come off sth** (of an amount of money) be removed from (a price) (指钱数)从(价钱)中减去: *I've heard that ten pence a gallon is coming off the price of petrol.* 我听说汽油价格每加仑要减十便士.

come on (a) (of an actor) walk onto the stage (指演员)出台, 登场, 上场. **(b)** (of a sportsman) join a team as a substitute during a match (指运动员)(在比赛中)上场做替补队员: *Robson came on in place of Wilkins ten minutes before the end of the game.* 比赛结束前十分钟罗布森上场替代威尔金斯. **(c)** (of a bowler in cricket) begin to bowl (指板球投球手)开始投球: *Botham came on to bowl after lunch.* 午饭后博瑟姆开始投球. **(d)** (also **come along**) make progress; grow; improve 取得

进步; 生长; 改善; 发展; 发育: *The garden is coming on nicely.* 这个花园里花草茂盛. ○ *Her baby is coming on well.* 她的婴儿发育良好. ○ *His French has come on a lot since he joined the conversation class.* 他自从参加了会话班, 法语取得了很大进步. (**e**) (also **come along**) (used in the imperative to encourage sb to do sth, esp to hurry, try harder or make an effort 用于祈使句以鼓励某人做某事, 尤指促其加速、努力或试一试): *Come on, we'll be late for the theatre.* 快点吧, 我们去戏院要迟到了. ○ *Come along now, someone must know the answer.* 试试吧, 一定有人能够回答. (**f**) begin 开始: *I think I have a cold coming 'on.* 我看我要感冒了. ○ *The rain came on/It ˌcame on to 'rain.* 下起雨来了. ○ *It's getting colder: winter is coming 'on.* 天渐冷了, 冬天来了. (**g**) (of a film, play, etc) be shown or performed (指电影、戏剧等)上演, 演出: *There's a new play coming on at the local theatre next week.* 下星期本地剧院有新戏上演. **come on/upon sb/sth** (*fml* 文) meet or find sb/sth by chance 偶然遇见或发现某人[某事物]: *I came upon a group of children playing in the street.* 我遇到一群孩子在街上玩耍.

come 'out (**a**) stop work; strike 停止工作; 罢工: *The miners have come out (on strike).* 矿工已罢工. (**b**) (of a young girl) be formally introduced to high society (指少女)初进社交界: *Fiona came out last season.* 菲奥纳上一季初次参加社交活动. ○ *a coming-out ball* 少女初进社交界舞会. (**c**) (of the sun, moon or stars) become visible; appear (指太阳、月亮或星星)露出, 出现: *The rain stopped and the sun came out.* 雨停了, 太阳出来了. (**d**) (of flowers, etc) begin to grow; appear; flower (指花朵等)开始长出, 吐艳, 开花: *The crocuses came out late this year because of the cold weather.* 因为天气寒冷, 今年藏红花开得晚. (**e**) be produced or published 出版或发表: *When is her new novel coming out?* 她的新小说何时问世? (**f**) (of news, the truth, etc) become known; be told or revealed (指消息、真相等)周知, 传出, 透露: *The full story came out at the trial.* 事件的始末在审判时才真相大白. ○ *It came out that he'd been telling a pack of lies.* 后来才知道他一直在说谎. (**g**) (of photographs) be developed (指照片)显影, 显出, 洗出: *Our holiday photos didn't come out*, eg because the film was faulty. 我们假日的照片冲洗不出来(如因胶卷有毛病). (**h**) be revealed or shown clearly 显示得或表示得很清楚: *The bride comes out well* (ie looks attractive) *in the photographs.* 像片上新娘照得很好. ○ *His arrogance comes out in every speech he makes.* 他每次讲话都显得很傲慢. ○ *Her best qualities come out in a crisis.* 在危急关头显露出了她的优秀品质. ○ *The meaning of the poem doesn't really come out in his interpretation.* 他并没有把这首诗的意义真正揭示出来. (**i**) (of words, a speech, etc) be spoken (指词语、言论等)说出, 讲出: *My statement didn't come out quite as* (ie appeared to have a different meaning from the one) *I had intended.* 我说出的话和我原先想要表达的意思不尽相同. (**j**) (of a sum, problem, etc) be solved (指算数题、问题等)解出, 解决: *I can't make this equation come out.* 我不会解这个方程式. (**k**) declare openly that one is a homosexual 公开表白是同性恋者: *She's been much happier since she came out.* 她公开了自己是同性恋者以后就快活多了. (**l**) have a specified position in a test, examination, etc (在测验、考试等中)得某名次: *She came out first in the examination.* 她考试得第一名. **come out (of sth)** (**a**) (of an object) be removed from a place where it is fixed (指物体)(从固着处)除掉: *The little girl's tooth came out when she bit into the apple.* 这小女孩在咬苹果时, 她的牙掉了. ○ *I can't get this screw to come out of the wall.* 我无法把这颗螺丝钉从墙上取出. (**b**) (of a mark, stain, etc) be removed from sth by washing, cleaning, etc (指标记、污点等)(用洗刷等方法)除掉: *These ink stains won't come out (of my dress).* (我的连衣裙上的)这些墨水点洗不掉. ○ *Will the colour come out* (ie fade or disappear) *if the material is washed?* 这料子洗时掉色吗? **come out against sth** say publicly that one is opposed to sth 公开说反对某事物: *In her speech, the Minister came out against any change to the existing law.* 这位部长在她的讲话中表示不同意对现行法律作任何更改. **come out at sth** amount to a particular cost or sum 合计成本、费用或总数: *The total cost comes out at £500.* 总计费用为500英镑. **come out in sth** become partially covered in (spots, pimples, etc) (局部)布满(斑点、粉刺、皮疹等): *Hot weather makes her come out in a rash.* 因天气炎热, 她起了皮疹. **come out with sth** say sth; utter sth 说某事物; 说出某事物: *He came out with a stream of abuse.* 他讲了一连串的污言秽语. ○ *She sometimes comes out with the most extraordinary remarks.* 她有时说出的话妙语如珠.

come over = COME ACROSS. **come over (to...)** = COME ROUND (TO...). **come over (to...) (from...)** move from one (usu distant) place to another 从一地(通常为远处)来到另一地: *Why don't you come over to England for a holiday?* 你怎么不到英国来度假呢? ○ *Her grandparents came over* (eg to America) *from Ireland during the famine.* 她的祖父母是在饥荒时期从爱尔兰来的(如到美国). **come 'over sb** (of a feeling) affect sb (指某种感觉)刺激或影响某人: *A fit of dizziness came over her.* 她感到一阵头晕目眩. ○ *I can't think what came over me*, ie I do not know what caused me to behave in that way. 我不知道我是怎么了(我不知道是什么原因使我有那种举动). **come over (to sth)** change from one side, opinion, etc to another 改变立场或意见等: *She will never come over to our side.* 她决不会站到我们这边来.

come 'round (**a**) come by a longer route than usual 绕道而来: *The road was blocked so we had to come round by the fields.* 道路堵塞了, 所以我们只好由田间绕道而来. (**b**) (of a regular event) arrive; recur (指有规律的事情)来到; 发生: *Christmas seems to come round quicker every year.* 圣诞节似乎一年比一年来得快. (**c**) (also **come 'to**) regain consciousness, esp after fainting 恢复知觉; 苏醒: *Pour some water on his face — he'll soon come round.* 往他脸上泼些水——他很快就能醒过来. ○ *Your husband hasn't yet come round after the anaesthetic.* 你丈夫麻醉后还没有苏醒. (**d**) (*infml* 口) become happy again after being in a bad mood (情绪不好之后)又愉快起来: *Don't scold the boy; he'll come round in time.* 不要责骂这孩子, 他过了那一阵就会好的. **come round (to...)** (also **come over (to...)**) visit sb or a place (usu within the same town, city, etc) 访问或参观(通常为同一城镇等的)某人或某地: *Why don't you come round (to my flat) this evening?* 今晚你来(我家), 好吗? ○ *Do come round and see us some time.* 务必抽空来坐坐. **come round (to sth)** (also **come around (to sth)**) be converted to sb else's opinion or view 转变成与别人一致的看法或观点: *She will never come round (to our way of thinking).* 她决不会改变态度(与我们的想法一致). **come round to sth/doing sth** (*infml* 口) do sth after a long delay (长时间拖延后)做某事: *It was several weeks before I eventually came round to answering her letter.* 过了几星期之后我才终于给她回信.

come 'through (of news, a message) arrive by telephone, radio, etc or through official channels (指新闻、信息)(由电话、无线电等或经官方渠道)传来: *A message is just coming through.* 有消息刚刚传来. ○ *Your posting has just come through: you're going to Hong Kong.* 你的调令刚到: 你要去香港了. **come through (sth)** recover from a serious illness or avoid serious injury; survive (sth) (重病后)康复; 避免受到严重伤害; (经某事物后)还活着: *He's very ill but doctors expect him to come 'through.* 他病得很重, 但医生预料他能康复. ○ *With such a weak heart she was lucky to come through (the operation).* 她心脏很弱, (手术后)能活下来就是万幸. ○ *She came through without even a scratch*, eg was not even slightly injured in the accident. 她安然脱险. ○ *He has come through two world wars.* 他身经两次世界大战, 劫后余生.

come 'to (**a**) = COME ROUND. (**b**) (of a boat) stop (指船)停下: *The police launch hailed to us to come to.* 警方汽艇招呼我们停下来. **'come to sb (that...)** (of an idea) occur to sb (指看法)被某人想出: *The idea came to him in his bath.* 他洗澡时想出了这个主意. ○ *It suddenly came to her that she had been wrong all along.* 她突然想到她一开始就错了. **ˌcome to 'sth** (**a**) amount to sth; be equal to sth 共计为某数; 等于某数: *The bill came to £30.* 帐款共计30英镑. ○ *I never expected those few items to come to so much.* 我绝想不到就那么几项合计起来竟要这么多钱. (**b**) (used esp with *this*, *that* or *what* as object 尤以 this、that 或 what 作宾

语时与之连用) reach a particular (usu bad) situation or state of affairs 达到某种(通常为坏的)情况或状态: *The doctors will operate if it proves necessary — but it may not come to that.* 医生认为必要时便动手术——但可能不致如此. ○ *'There's been another terrorist bomb attack.' 'Really? I don't know what the world is coming to.'* '又发生一次恐怖分子炸弹爆炸事件.' '真的吗? 不知道这个世界要变成什么样子了.' ○ *Things have come to such a state in the company that he's thinking of resigning.* 公司的事情已经到了这种地步, 因此他正在考虑辞职. ○ *Who'd have thought things would come to this* (ie become so bad or unpleasant)? 谁想到过事情会发展到这种地步(变得这么糟或不愉快)? **come to sb (from sb)** (of money, property, etc) be given or left to sb as an inheritance (指钱、财产等)作为遗产送给或留给某人: *The farm came to him on his father's death.* 他父亲死时把农场留给他了. ○ *He has a lot of money coming to him when his uncle dies.* 他的叔父死后他承受了一大笔钱.
come under sth (a) be included within a certain category 归入某类; 编入: *What heading does this come under?* 这个编在什么标题之下? (b) be the target of sth 是某事物的目标: *We came under heavy enemy fire.* 我们遭到敌人猛烈攻击.
come 'up (a) (of plants) appear above the soil (指植物)长出地面: *The snowdrops are just beginning to come up.* 雪花莲刚刚开始长出地面. (b) (of the sun) rise (指太阳)升起: *We watched the sun come up.* 我们观看日出. (c) (of soldiers, supplies, etc) be moved to the front line (指士兵、给养等)被送往前线. (d) occur; arise 发生; 出现: *We'll let you know if any vacancies come up.* 一有空缺我们就通知你. ○ *I'm afraid something urgent has come up; I won't be able to see you tonight.* 很抱歉, 有些急事; 今晚不能见你了. (e) be mentioned or discussed; arise 被提及; 被讨论; 出现: *The subject came up in conversation.* 这个问题是在谈话中提到的. ○ *The question is bound to come up at the meeting.* 会上必然要讨论这个问题. (f) be dealt with by a court 由法庭审理: *Her divorce case comes up next month.* 她的离婚案件下月审理. (g) (of a lottery ticket, number, etc) be drawn; win (指彩票、数字抽奖等)抽中, 中奖, 赢: *My number came up and I won £100.* 我的数字彩票中奖了, 我赢得100英镑. **come 'up (to...)** (*Brit*) begin one's studies at a university (esp at Oxford or Cambridge) 开始上大学(尤指牛津或剑桥): *She came up (to Oxford) in 1982.* 她1982年(到牛津)上大学. **come up (to...) (from...)** come to one place from another, esp from a smaller place to London or from the South to the North of England 从一地来到另一地(尤指由小地方到伦敦或由英格兰南部到北部); 上伦敦; 北上: *She often comes up to London* (eg from Oxford) *at weekends.* 她常在周末(如由牛津)上伦敦来. ○ *Why don't you come up to Scotland for a few days?* 你怎么不北上到苏格兰来住几天? **come up against sb/sth** be faced with or opposed by sb/sth 面对某人[某事物]; 被某人[某事物]反对: *We expect to come up against a lot of opposition to the scheme.* 我们预计这个计划要遭到很多人反对. **come up for sth** be considered as an applicant or a candidate for sth 作某事的申请人或候选人: *She comes up for re-election next year.* 在明年的重选中她参加竞选. **come up to sth** (a) reach up as far as (a specified point) 升到(某点): *The water came up to my neck.* 水升到我的颈部. (b) reach (an acceptable level or standard) 达到(认可的水平或标准): *His performance didn't really come up to his usual high standard.* 他没有真正表现出平日的高水平来. ○ *Their holiday in France didn't come up to expectations.* 他们在法国度假未尽如人意. **come 'up with sth** find or produce (an answer, a solution, etc) 找到或提出(答案、办法等): *She came up with a new idea for increasing sales.* 她想出了增加销售量的新主意.
come upon sb/sth = COME ON SB/STH.

▷ **come** *interj* (used to encourage sb to be sensible or reasonable, or to rebuke sb slightly 用以鼓励某人使之理智或合情合理或用以轻责某人): *Oh come (now), things aren't as bad as you say.* 嗳, 好了, 事情并不像你说的那样糟. ○ *Come, come, Miss Jones, be careful what you say.* 得啦, 得啦, 琼斯小姐, 说话要当心.

□ **'come-back** *n* **1** return to a former (successful) position 恢复到原先的(成功)地位: *an ageing pop star trying to make/stage a come-back* 年事已高的流行曲歌星, 打算重返歌坛. **2** (*infml* 口) reply or retort to a critical or hostile remark (对批评的或恶意的话的)回答或反驳. **3** way of obtaining compensation or redress 得到补偿或补救的方法: *If you're not insured and you get burgled, you have no come-back.* 没投保险而遭偷窃, 就得不到赔偿.

'come-down *n* (usu *sing* 通常作单数) (*infml* 口) loss of importance or social position 失去重要性或社会地位; 败落; 没落: *Having to work as a clerk is a bit of a come-down after running his own business.* 他原来经营自己的买卖, 现在不得已去当小职员, 可谓家道中落了.

,come-'hither *adj* [attrib 作定语] (*dated infml* 旧, 口) flirtatious; inviting 挑逗性的; 勾引人的; 诱人的: *a ,come-hither 'look, 'smile, etc* 挑逗性的一瞥、一笑等.

'come-on *n* (usu *sing* 通常作单数) (*infml* 口) gesture, remark, etc indicating that sb (esp a woman) is trying to attract sb sexually (某人, 尤指女人, 试图吸引异性的)姿势、言语等: *She gave him the come-on.* 她勾引他.

co·median /kəˈmiːdɪən; kəˋmidɪən/ *n* **1** (*fem* 阴性作 **co·medi·enne** /kə,miːdɪˈen; kə,midɪˋɛn/) (a) entertainer who tells jokes, performs sketches (SKETCH 3), etc to amuse an audience (说笑话、演滑稽剧等的)演员. (b) actor or actress who plays comic parts 喜剧演员. **2** person who is always behaving comically 滑稽的人.

com·edy /ˈkɒmədɪ; ˋkɑmədɪ/ *n* **1** (a) [C] light or amusing play or film, usu with a happy ending 喜剧. (b) [U] plays or films of this type 喜剧; 喜剧片: *I prefer comedy to tragedy.* 我喜欢喜剧, 不喜欢悲剧. Cf 参看 TRAGEDY. **2** [U] amusing aspect of sth; humour 某事物的有趣方面; 幽默: *He didn't appreciate the comedy of the situation.* 他没有意识到处境的有趣方面. ○ *the slapstick comedy of silent films* 无声电影的滑稽趣味.

□ **comedy of manners** comedy that presents a satirical portrayal of social life 风尚喜剧(讽刺社交生活的喜剧).

comely /ˈkʌmlɪ; ˋkʌmlɪ/ *adj* (**-lier**, **-liest**) (*dated or fml* 旧或文) (esp of a woman) good-looking; attractive (尤指女子)好看的, 标致的, 有吸引力的. ▷ **come·li·ness** *n* [U].

comer /ˈkʌmə(r); ˋkʌmɚ/ *n* **1** person who comes (used esp as in the expressions shown) 来者(尤用于下列示例): *The race is open to all comers*, ie Anyone may take part in it. 这项竞赛任何人都可参加. ○ *Late-comers will not be allowed in.* 迟到者不得入内. **2** (*infml* 口 *esp US*) person who is likely to be successful; promising person 可能成功的人; 有前途的人.

com·est·ibles /kəˈmestəblz; kəˋmɛstəbl̩z/ *n* [pl] (*fml* 文) things to eat 食物; 食品.

comet /ˈkɒmɪt; ˋkɑmɪt/ *n* object that moves round the sun and looks like a bright star with a long, less bright tail 彗星.

come-uppance /kʌmˈʌpəns; kʌmˋʌpəns/ *n* (*infml* 口) deserved punishment; retribution (used esp as in the expression shown) 应得的惩罚, 报应(尤用于下列示例): *get one's come-uppance* 遭报应.

com·fort /ˈkʌmfət; ˋkʌmfɚt/ *n* **1** [U] state of being free from suffering, pain or anxiety; state of physical or mental well-being 舒适; 身心健康: *live in comfort* 生活舒适 ○ *They did everything for our comfort.* 他们尽力使我们觉得舒适. **2** [U] help or kindness to sb who is suffering; consolation (对受苦者的)帮助或仁爱; 安慰: *a few words of comfort* 几句安慰的话 ○ *The news brought comfort to all of us.* 这消息给我们大家带来了安慰. **3** [sing] person or thing that brings relief or consolation 给予援助或安慰的人或事物: *Her children are a great comfort to her.* 她的孩子是她极大的安慰. ○ *It's a comfort to know that she is safe.* 知道她平安无事是令人宽慰的事. **4** [C esp *pl* 尤作复数] thing that creates physical ease or well-being 使身体舒适或健康的事物: *The hotel has all modern comforts/every modern comfort*, eg central heating, hot and cold water, etc. 这家旅馆设有各种现代化的舒适设施(如集中供暖、冷热水等). ○ *He likes his comforts.* 他喜欢自己舒适的生活条件. **5** (idm 习语) **cold comfort** ⇨ COLD[1].

▷ **com·fort** *v* [Tn] give comfort(2) to (sb) 安慰(某人): *comfort a dying man* 安慰垂死的人 ○ *The child ran to its mother to be comforted.* 孩子跑到母亲身边以求得到安慰.

com·fort·less *adj* without comforts (COMFORT 4) 无舒适生活设施的: *a comfortless room* 无舒适设施的房间.

□ ˈ**comfort station** (*US euph* 婉) public lavatory 公共厕所.

com·fort·able /ˈkʌmftəbl; *US* -fərt-; ˋkʌmfɚtəbl̩/ *adj* **1** allowing, producing or having pleasant bodily relaxation 舒适的; 安逸的; 使人舒服的: *a comfortable bed, position* 舒适的床、姿势 ○ *She made herself comfortable in a big chair.* 她舒舒服服地坐在大椅子上. ○ *The patient is comfortable* (ie is not in pain) *after his operation.* 病人手术后感觉良好. **2** having or ensuring freedom from anxiety 无忧无虑的: *a comfortable life, job* 无忧无虑的生活、工作. **3** [pred 作表语] (*infml* 口) quite wealthy 富足: *They may not be millionaires but they're certainly very comfortable.* 他们尽管不算百万富翁, 却也丰衣足食. **4** more than adequate; reasonably large 充裕的; 相当大的: *a comfortable income* 丰厚的收入 ○ *She won by a comfortable margin.* 她获胜成绩远远超过其他人.

C

▷ **com·fort·ably** /-təblɪ; -təblɪ/ *adv* **1** in a comfortable way 舒适地; 舒服地: *comfortably ensconced in a big armchair* 舒适地稳坐在单座沙发上. **2** by a clear margin 充裕地: *The favourite won the race comfortably.* 那个大热门以明显优势获胜. **3** (idm 习语) ˌ**comfortably** ˈ**off** having enough money to live in comfort 生活宽裕.

com·forter /ˈkʌmfətə(r); ˋkʌmfɚtɚ/ *n* **1** person who comforts 安慰者. **2** (*US*) quilt 被子. **3** (*Brit*) (*US* **pacifier**) = DUMMY. **4** (*dated* 旧 *Brit*) woollen scarf worn round the neck 毛围巾.

comfy /ˈkʌmfɪ; ˋkʌmfɪ/ *adj* (**-ier**, **-iest**) (*infml* 口) comfortable 舒适的; 舒服的.

comic /ˈkɒmɪk; ˋkɑmɪk/ *adj* **1** [usu attrib 通常作定语] causing people to laugh; funny 使人发笑的; 可笑的; 滑稽的: *a comic song, performance, etc* 滑稽的歌曲、表演等 ○ *His accident with the microphone brought some welcome comic relief to a very dull party.* 他撞上了话筒, 这给极沉闷的聚会带来了些欢乐. **2** [attrib 作定语] of, containing or using comedy 喜剧的; 有喜剧成分的; 运用喜剧的: *comic opera* 喜剧歌剧 ○ *a comic actor* 喜剧演员.

▷ **comic** *n* **1** comedian 喜剧演员: *a popular TV comic* 观众喜爱的电视喜剧演员. **2** (*US* ˈ**comic book**) children's magazine containing stories told mainly through pictures (儿童的)连环画册.

com·ical /ˈkɒmɪkl; ˋkɑmɪkl̩/ *adj* (odd and) amusing (古怪而)可笑的, 滑稽的: *He looked highly comical wearing that tiny hat.* 他戴着那顶小帽子, 看上去真滑稽. **com·ic·ally** /-klɪ; -klɪ/ *adv*: *clothes that were almost comically inappropriate* 因不合适而近乎滑稽的衣物.

□ **comic** ˈ**strip** (also ˈ**strip cartoon**) sequence of drawings telling a humorous or adventure story, printed in newspapers, etc (报纸上的)连环漫画.

com·ing /ˈkʌmɪŋ; ˋkʌmɪŋ/ *n* **1** arrival 抵达; 来到; 到达; 到来: *the coming of the space age* 太空时代的到来. **2** (idm 习语) ˌ**comings and** ˈ**goings** (*infml* 口) arrivals and departures 来来往往: *the constant comings and goings at a hotel* 旅馆中旅客不断的来来往往 ○ *With all the comings and goings* (eg of visitors) *I haven't been able to do any work at all.* 有这么多人来来往往(如来访者), 我根本不能工作.

comma /ˈkɒmə; ˋkɑmə/ *n* punctuation mark (,) to indicate a light pause or break between parts of a sentence 逗号(,). ⇨App 3 见附录 3.

com·mand[1] /kəˈmɑːnd; *US* -ˈmænd; kəˋmænd/ *v* **1** [I, Tn, Tf, Dn·t] (of sb in authority) tell (sb) that he must do sth; order (指有权者)叫(某人)必须做某事; 命令: *Do as I command (you).* 照我命令(你的)去做. ○ (*fml* 文) *The tribunal has commanded that all copies of the book (must) be destroyed.* 法庭命令(必须)将这本书的所有印本都销毁. ○ *The officer commanded his men to fire.* 军官命令士兵开火. ⇨Usage at ORDER[2] 用法见 ORDER[2]. **2** [I, Tn] have authority (over sb/sth); be in control (of) 有(支配某人[某事物])的权力; 控制: *Does seniority give one the right to command?* 难道年长资深就有权发号施令吗? ○ *The ship's captain commands all the officers and men.* 舰长统率舰上全体官兵. **3** [Tn no passive 不用于被动语态] be able to use (sth); have at one's disposal 能使用(某事物); 由某人随意支配; 掌握; 掌管: *command funds, skill, resources, etc* 掌握资金、技巧、资源等 ○ *She commands great wealth*, ie is very rich. 她很富有. ○ *A government minister commands the services of many officials.* 政府部长掌管许多官员的工作. ○ (*fig* 比喻) *The house commands a fine view*, ie A fine view can be seen from it. 从这所房子处可一览优美景色. **4** [Tn no passive 不用于被动语态] deserve and get (sth) 应得; 值得; 博得: *Great men command our respect.* 伟人受到我们尊敬. ○ *The plight of the famine victims commands everyone's sympathy.* 饥民的苦境值得大家同情. **5** [Tn no passive 不用于被动语态] (of a place, fort, etc) be positioned so as to control (sth) (指地方、堡垒等)因地利而能控制(某事物): *The castle commanded the entrance to the valley.* 该城堡控制着峡谷的入口.

▷ **com·mand·ing** *adj* **1** [attrib 作定语] having the authority to give formal orders 有权发出正式命令的; 指挥的: *one's commanding officer* 上级指挥官. **2** [usu attrib 通常作定语] in a position to control or dominate 处于控制或支配地位的: *The fort occupies a commanding position.* 这堡垒占据控制地位. ○ *One team has already built up a commanding lead.* 有一个队已经遥遥领先. **3** [usu attrib 通常作定语] seeming to have authority; impressive 像有权威的; 给人深刻印象的: *a commanding voice, tone, look, etc* 威严的声音、声调、神态等.

com·mand[2] /kəˈmɑːnd; *US* -ˈmænd; kəˋmænd/ *n* **1** [C] (**a**) order 命令: *Her commands were quickly obeyed.* 她的命令已迅速执行. ○ *Give your commands in a loud, confident voice.* 发命令声音要洪亮、坚定. (**b**) (*computing* 计) instruction to a computer (给计算机的)指令. **2** [U] (*esp military* 尤用于军事) control; authority (used esp with the *vs* and *preps* shown) 控制, 指挥(尤与下列动词和介词连用): *to have/take command of a regiment, etc* 负责[担任]团等部队的指挥 ○ *He should not be given command of troops.* 不应该把部队的指挥权交给他. ○ *Who is in command* (ie in charge) *here?* 这里由谁负责? ○ *General Smith is in command of the army.* 史密斯将军统率陆军. ○ *The army is under the command of General Smith.* 这支军队由史密斯将军指挥. ○ *He has twenty men under his command.* 他指挥着二十人. **3 Command** [C] part of an army, air force, etc organized and controlled separately (单独组织指挥的)陆军、空军等的一部分; 部队; 军区: *Western Command* 西部部队 ○ *Bomber Command* 轰炸机组的指挥部. **4** [U, sing] **~ (of sth)** ability to use or control sth; mastery 使用或控制某事物的能力; 掌握: *He has (a) good command of the French language*, ie can speak it well. 他精通法语. ○ *He has enormous funds at his command.* 他掌握着巨额资金. ○ *He has no command over himself*, ie cannot control his feelings, temper, etc. 他不能克制自己. **5** (idm 习语) **at /by sb's com**ˈ**mand** (*fml* 文) having been ordered by sb 奉某人之命的; 受某人指挥的: *I am here at the King's command.* 在下奉谕旨至此. **at the word of command** ⇨ WORD. **be at sb's com**ˈ**mand** be ready to obey sb 听候某人吩咐. **your wish is my command** ⇨ WISH.

□ **com**ˈ**mand module** part of a spacecraft carrying the crew and control equipment 指挥舱(飞行器中的).

comˌ**mand per**ˈ**formance** performance (of a play, film, etc) given at the request of a head of State (who usu attends) 奉国家元首之命的演出(戏剧、电影等); (通常为)御前演出.

comˈ**mand post** headquarters of a military unit (军事单位的)指挥所[部].

com·mand·ant /ˌkɒmənˈdænt; ˌkɑmənˋdænt/ *n* commanding officer, esp of a prisoner-of-war camp, military academy, etc 指挥官; 司令; (尤指)战俘营的首长, 军事院校的校长等.

com·man·deer /ˌkɒmənˈdɪə(r); ˌkɑmənˋdɪr/ *v* [Tn] take possession or control of (vehicles, buildings, etc) forcibly or for official (esp military) purposes 强取, 强占, 征用(车辆、建筑物等)(尤指作军用).

com·mander /kəˈmɑːndə(r); *US* -ˈmæn-; ˌkəˋmændɚ/ *n* **1** person who commands 指挥官; 司令; 队长: *the commander of the expedition* 探险队队长. **2** (*Brit*) (**a**) officer in the British Navy immediately below the rank of captain 海军中校. ⇨App 9 见附录 9. (**b**) officer of high rank in London's Metropolitan Police (伦敦警务处的)高级警官.

□ **com,mander-in-'chief** *n* (*pl* **commanders-in-chief**) commander of all the armed forces of a country 总司令.

com·mand·ment /kə'mɑːndmənt; *US* -'mænd-; kə'mændmənt/ *n* (**a**) (*fml* 文) command; order 戒律; 命令: *obeying God's commandments* 恪守上帝的戒律. (**b**) **Commandment** (in the Bible) any of the ten laws given by God to Moses (《圣经》中)上帝给摩西的十诫之一: *the Ten Commandments* 十诫.

com·mando /kə'mɑːndəʊ; *US* -'mæn-; kə'mændo/ *n* (*pl* **~s** or **~es**) (member of a) group of soldiers specially trained for carrying out quick raids in enemy areas 突击队(员).

com·mem·or·ate /kə'meməreɪt; kə'mɛmə,ret/ *v* [Tn] (**a**) keep (a great person, event, etc) in people's memories 纪念(伟人、大事件等): *We commemorate the founding of our nation with a public holiday.* 我们放假一日以庆祝国庆. (**b**) (of a statue, monument, etc) be a reminder of (sb/sth) (指雕像、纪念碑等)作为对(某人[某事物])的纪念: *This memorial commemorates those who died in the war.* 这座纪念碑是纪念战争中牺牲者的.

▷ **com·mem·ora·tion** /kə,memə'reɪʃn; kə,mɛmə'reʃən/ *n* [C, U] (act of or ceremony for) commemorating 纪念; 庆祝; 纪念仪式: *a statue in commemoration of a national hero* 纪念民族英雄的雕像.

com·mem·ora·tive /kə'memərətɪv; *US* -'memәreɪt-; kə'mɛmə,retɪv/ *adj* helping to commemorate (有助于)纪念的: *commemorative stamps, medals, etc* 纪念邮票、奖章等.

com·mence /kə'mens; kə'mɛns/ *v* [I, Tn, Tg] (*fml* 文) begin (sth); start 开始(某事物): *Shall we commence (the ceremony)?* 开始(举行仪式)好吗? ○ *After grace had been said, we commenced eating.* 我们做过感恩祷告后就开始吃饭.

▷ **com·mence·ment** *n* [U, C usu *sing* 通常作单数] **1** (*fml* 文) beginning 开始. **2** (*esp US*) ceremony at which academic degrees are officially given 学位颁授典礼.

com·mend /kə'mend; kə'mɛnd/ *v* **1** [Tn, Tn·pr] (**a**) **~ sb (on/for sth)**; **~ sb/sth (to sb)** speak favourably to or of sb/sth; praise sb/sth 表扬某人[某事物]; 称赞某人[某事物]: *Her teaching was highly commended.* 她的教学工作受到高度赞扬. ○ *I commended the chef on the excellent meal. I later wrote to commend him to his employer, the restaurant owner.* 我称赞厨师做的菜味道好. 随后我给雇用他的餐馆老板写了封信表扬他. (**b**) **~ sb/sth (to sb)** (*fml* 文) recommend sb/sth 推荐某人[某事物]: *That's excellent advice; I commend it to you*, ie suggest that you accept it. 那意见极好, 我把它推荐给你. **2** [Tn·pr] **~ oneself/itself to sb** (*fml* 文) be acceptable to sb; be liked by sb 为某人所接受; 被某人喜爱: *Will this government proposal commend itself to the public?* 政府的这项建议公众能欢迎吗? **3** [Tn·pr] **~ sth to sb** (*fml* 文) give sth to sb so that it will be kept safe; entrust sth to sb 将某物托付给某人保管; 将某事物委托给某人: *commend one's soul to God* 把自己的灵魂托付给上帝.

▷ **com·mend·able** /-əbl; -əbḷ/ *adj* deserving praise (even if perhaps not completely successful) 值得称赞的(即使并非完全成功). **com·mend·ably** /-əblɪ; -əblɪ/ *adv*.

com·menda·tion /,kɒmen'deɪʃn; ,kɑmən'deʃən/ *n* (**a**) [U] praise; approval 称赞; 赞成. (**b**) [C] **~ (for sth)** (award involving the) giving of special praise 表扬; 奖状; 奖励: *a commendation for bravery* 因勇敢而受奖 ○ *Her painting won a commendation from the teacher.* 她的画博得老师的赞扬.

com·men·sur·ate /kə'menʃərət; kə'mɛnʃərɪt/ *adj* **~(to/with sth)** (*fml* 文) in the right proportion (to sth); appropriate (与某事物)成比例的, 适当的, 相称的: *Her low salary is not commensurate with her abilities.* 她的薪水很低, 与她的能力不相称.

com·ment /'kɒment; 'kɑmɛnt/ *n* **1** [C, U] **~ (on sth)** written or spoken remark giving an opinion on, explaining or criticizing (an event, a person, a situation, etc) 意见; 解释; 评论; 批评: *Have you any comment(s) to make on the recent developments?* 你对最近的事态发展有什么评论吗? ○ *The scandal caused a lot of comment*, ie of talk, gossip, etc. 这件丑闻遭到很多议论. **2** (idm 习语) **,no 'comment** (said in reply to a question) I have nothing to say about that (回答问题时所说)无可奉告: *'Will you resign, Minister?' 'No comment!'* '部长, 你是要辞职吗?' '无可奉告.'

▷ **com·ment** *v* [I, Ipr, Tf] **~ (on sth)** make comments; give one's opinion 评论; 发表意见: *Asked about the date of the election, the Prime Minister commented that no decision had yet been made.* 首相对询问选举日期一事称尚未作出决定.

com·ment·ary /'kɒməntrɪ; *US* -terɪ; 'kɑmən,tɛrɪ/ *n* **1** [C, U] **~ (on/of sth)** spoken description of an event as it happens 实况报道; 现场解说: *a broadcast commentary of a football match* 足球赛实况的广播报道. **2** [C] **~ (on sth)** set of explanatory notes on a book, etc (对书等的)集注: *a Bible commentary* 《圣经》集注.

com·ment·ate /'kɒmenteɪt; 'kɑmən,tet/ *v* [I, Ipr] **~ (on sth)** (**a**) describe, esp on TV or radio, an event as it happens 实况报道(尤指电视或无线电广播): *commentate on an athletics meeting* 运动会实况报道. (**b**) (usu not in the continuous tenses 通常不用于进行时态) do this regularly, as a job 作(实况报道的)解说员.

▷ **com·ment·ator** /'kɒmenteɪtə(r); 'kɑmən,tetɚ/ *n* **~ (on sth)** **1** person who commentates (实况报道的)解说员. **2** person who comments 评论员: *an informed commentator on political events* 消息灵通的政治评论员. **3** writer of a commentary(2) 集注的作者.

com·merce /'kɒmɜːs; 'kɑmɝs/ *n* [U] trade (esp between countries); buying and selling of goods 商业; (尤指国际间的)贸易: *We must promote commerce with neighbouring countries.* 我们必须促进与邻国的贸易.

com·mer·cial /kə'mɜːʃl; kə'mɝʃəl/ *adj* **1** (**a**) of or for commerce 商业的; 贸易的: *commercial law, activity, art* 商业的法规、活动、技巧. (**b**) [usu attrib 通常作定语] of business practices and activities generally 商务的: *doing a commercial course at the local college* 在本地学院学商科. **2** (**a**) [attrib 作定语] from the point of view of profit 从营利角度出发的: *The play was a commercial success*, ie made money. 这出戏从营利角度看, 很成功(赚钱). (**b**) making or intended to make a profit 营利的; 以获利为目的的: *commercial theatre, music, etc* 以获利为目的的剧院、音乐等 ○ *Oil is present in commercial quantities*, ie There is enough to make extraction profitable. 石油的储量有商业开采价值. ○ *Her novels are well written and commercial as well.* 她的小说写得好, 销路也广. **3** (of TV or radio) financed by broadcast advertisements (指电视或无线电广播)靠广告收入的, 商业性的: *I work for a commercial radio station.* 我在商业广播电台工作.

▷ **com·mer·cial** *n* advertisement on TV or radio (电视或无线电中的)广告.

com·mer·cial·ism /kə'mɜːʃəlɪzəm; kə'mɝʃəl,ɪzəm/ *n* [U] (*often derog* 常作贬义) practices and attitudes concerned with the making of profit 商业主义; 营利主义: *excessive commercialism in the theatre* 该戏院过分追求利润的经营方式. **com·mer·cial·ize, -ise** /kə'mɜːʃəlaɪz; kə'mɝʃəl,aɪz/ *v* [Tn] (*often derog* 常作贬义) (try to) make money out of (sth) (试图)通过(某事物)赚钱; 商业化: *Sport has become much more commercialized in recent years.* 体育运动近几年更加商业化了. **com·mer·cially** /-ʃəlɪ; -ʃəlɪ/ *adv*: *Commercially, the play was a failure, though the critics loved it.* 从营利角度看这出戏失败了, 然而评论家却很赞赏.

□ **com,mercial 'traveller** person who travels over a large area visiting shops, etc with samples of goods, trying to obtain orders 旅行推销员.

com,mercial 'vehicle van, lorry, etc for transporting goods 商用机动车.

com·mis·er·ate /kə'mɪzəreɪt; kə'mɪzə,ret/ *v* [I, Ipr] **~ (with sb) (on/over sth)** (*fml* 文) feel, or say that one feels, sympathy 同情; 怜悯: *I commiserated with her on the loss of her job.* 她失去了工作, 我很同情她.

▷ **com·mis·era·tion** /kə,mɪzə'reɪʃn; kə,mɪzə'reʃən/ *n* [C usu *pl*, U 作可数名词时通常作复数, 亦作不可数名词] **~ (on/over sth)** (*fml or joc* 文或谑) (expression of) sympathy for sb (对某人表示的)同情(的言语): *I*

C

expressed my commiserations on his misfortune. 我对他的不幸表示同情. ○ *'I lost again.' 'Commiserations* (ie I am sorry)!' '我又赔钱了.' '真遗憾!'

com·mis·sar /ˈkɒmɪsɑː(r); ˌkɑməˈsɑr/ *n* **1** (formerly) head of a government department in the USSR (旧时)人民委员(苏联政府的部长). **2** (formerly) officer in the army of the USSR giving political instruction (旧时)政治委员(苏联军队中的).

com·mis·sion /kəˈmɪʃn; kəˈmɪʃən/ *n* **1** [C] **~ (to do sth)** action, task or piece of work given to sb to do (交付某人进行的)行动、任务或工作; 委托: *She has received many commissions to design public buildings.* 她接受多项委托, 设计公共建筑. **2** (often 常作 **Commission**) [C] **(a)** group of people authorized to carry out a task (受权执行任务的)委员会: *the Civil Service Commission*, ie the body that selects staff for the Civil Service 公务员叙用委员会(遴选公务员的机构). **(b) ~ (on sth)** group of people officially set up to make an inquiry and write a report 考查团; 调查团: *a Royal Commission on* (ie reporting on) *betting and gambling* 由英王委派的赌博调查团. **3** [U] **~ (of sth)** (*fml* 文) doing (sth wrong or illegal 做(坏事或不法的事)): *the commission of a crime* 犯罪 ○ *a sin of commission* (ie actually doing sth wrong) *rather than omission* 违法罪(主动做坏事)而不是疏忽罪. **4** [C, U] payment to sb for selling goods which increases with the quantity of goods sold 佣金; 回扣; 酬劳金: *You get (a) 10% commission on everything you sell.* 你可从售出的每种货物中得到10%佣金. ○ *earn £2000 (in) commission* 挣得2000英镑酬劳金 ○ *She is working for us on commission*, ie is not paid a salary. 她按挣回扣方式为我们工作(没有薪水). **5** [C] (document signed by the monarch appointing sb to the) rank of an officer in the armed services (帝王签署授予某人的)军官资格(的委任状): *He resigned his commission to take up a civilian job.* 他辞去军职而从事平民工作. **6** (idm 习语) **in/into comˈmission** (esp of a ship) in/into service (尤指船、舰)在使用中, 服现役: *Some wartime vessels are still in commission.* 有些战时的军舰仍在服役. **ˌout of comˈmission (a)** (esp of a ship) not in service (尤指船、舰)不在使用中; 退出现役: *With several of their planes temporarily out of commission, the airline is losing money.* 航空公司因有几架飞机暂时不能使用而正在赔钱. **(b)** (*fig* 比喻) not available; not working 不能得到; 不工作: *I got flu and was out of commission for a week.* 我得了流感,一星期没工作.

▷ **com·mis·sion** *v* **1 (a)** [Tn, Dn·t] give a commission (1) to (sb) 交付(某人)任务或工作; 委托: *commission an artist to paint a picture* 委托画家画一幅画. **(b)** [Tn] give sb the job of making (sth) 交付某人制作(某物)的工作: *He commissioned a statue of his wife.* 他请人制作他妻子的雕像. **2** [usu passive 通常用于被动语态: Tn, Cn·n, Cn·n/a] **~ sb as sth** appoint sb officially by means of a commission (5) 正式授予某人军官资格(的委任状): *She was commissioned (as a) lieutenant in the Women's Army Corps.* 她被委任为陆军妇女队的中尉. **3** [Tn] bring (machinery, equipment, etc) into operation 使(机器、设备等)开始使用: *The nuclear plant now being built is expected to be commissioned in five years' time.* 正在建造的核电站预计在五年后投产.

□ **comˌmissioned ˈofficer** officer in the armed forces who holds a commission (持有委任状的)军官.

com·mis·sion·aire /kəˌmɪʃəˈneə(r); kəˌmɪʃənˈɛr/ *n* (*esp Brit*) uniformed attendant at the entrance to a cinema, theatre, hotel, etc who opens the door for people, finds them taxis, etc. (穿制服的)看门人(在电影院、剧场、旅馆等的入口, 为人开门、叫计程车等).

com·mis·sioner /kəˈmɪʃənə(r); kəˈmɪʃənə/ *n* **1** (usu 通常作 **Commissioner**) member of a commission, esp one with particular duties 委员(尤指有某职责的); 长官: *the Commissioners of Inland Revenue*, ie those who are in charge of tax collection in Britain 税务局长(负责英国税务的) ○ *the Civil Service Commissioners*, ie those who conduct Civil Service examinations in Britain 公务员叙用委员会委员(负责英国文官考试的). **2** public official of high rank 高级公共事务官员: *The London police force is headed by a commissioner.* 伦敦警察由局长领导. ○ *In British India, district commissioners had judicial powers.* 在过去的英属印度, 地区长官有审判权.

□ **Comˌmissioner for ˈOaths** (*Brit*) solicitor with special authority, to whom people can swear oaths relating to legal documents 宣誓公证人(有权为他人的宣誓作证的律师).

com·mit /kəˈmɪt; kəˈmɪt/ *v* **(-tt-) 1** [Tn] do (sth illegal, wrong or foolish) 做(不合法的、错的或愚蠢的事); 犯: *commit murder, suicide, theft, a blunder, an unforgiveable error, etc* 犯凶杀、自杀、偷窃、大错、不可原谅的错误等. **2** [Tn·pr] **~ sb/sth to sth** give or transfer sb/sth to (a state or place) for safe keeping, treatment, etc 将某人[某事物]置于(某状态)或交与或转交(某处)保留、处理等: *commit a man to prison*, ie have him put in prison 把一男子送进监狱 ○ *commit a patient to a mental hospital* 把病人送进精神病院 ○ *commit sth to paper/to writing*, ie write sth down 把某事写下来 ○ *The body was committed to the flames*, ie was burnt. 遗体被火化. ○ *commit a list to memory*, ie memorize it 记住一份名单. **3** [Tn, Tn·pr, Cn·t] **~ sb/oneself (to sth/to doing sth)** make it impossible for sb/oneself not to do sth, or to do sth else, esp because of a promise; pledge sb/oneself 使某人[自己]不能不做某事或不做另事(尤指因有承诺); 向某人[自己]保证: *I can't come on Sunday: I'm already committed*, ie I've arranged to do sth else. 星期天我不能来, 我有事. ○ *commit oneself to a course of action* 决定采取一行动 ○ *Signing this form commits you to buying the goods.* 你签此表格后就一定要买这批货. ○ *The company has committed funds to an advertising campaign.* 公司已决定拨款作广告宣传. ○ *This regiment is already committed to* (ie It has been settled that it will fight on) *the eastern front.* 该团承担东线的战斗任务. ○ *He has committed himself to support his brother's children.* 他已答应抚养他弟弟的孩子. **4** [Tn, Tn·pr] **~ oneself (on sth)** give one's opinion openly so that it is difficult to change it 公开表明自己的意见(因而难以更改): *I asked her what she thought, but she refused to commit herself.* 我问她她是怎么想的, 但她拒不表示意见. Cf 参看 NON-COMMITTAL. **5** [Tn, Tn·pr] **~ sb (for sth)** send sb to a higher court to be tried 将(某人)送交高一级法院受审: *The magistrates committed him for trial at the Old Bailey.* 地方法官把他送往伦敦中央刑事法院受审.

▷ **com·mit·tal** /kəˈmɪtl; kəˈmɪtl/ *n* [U] action of committing (COMMIT 2), esp to prison 交与; 转交; (尤指)入狱, 交押, 收监: [attrib 作定语] *At the committal proceedings the police withdrew their case.* 警方在转交诉讼程序中撤销了案件.

com·mit·ted *adj* (*usu approv* 通常作褒义) devoted (to a cause, one's job, etc) (对事业、本职工作等)尽忠的, 坚定的: *a committed Christian, doctor, teacher, communist* 虔诚的基督徒、尽责的医生、严师、坚定的共产党员. Cf 参看 UNCOMMITTED.

com·mit·ment *n* **1** [U] **~ (to sth)** committing or being committed (COMMIT 2): *the commitment of a patient to a mental hospital* 把病人送进精神病院 ○ *the commitment of funds to medicine* 对医学方面的拨款. **2** [C] **~ (to sth/to do sth)** thing one has promised to do; pledge; undertaking 承诺; 允诺; 保证; 承担: *I'm overworked at the moment — I've taken on too many commitments.* 我目前劳累过度——应承的事情太多了. ○ *a commitment to pay £100 to charity* 承担捐赠慈善事业100英镑的义务. **3** [U] (*approv* 褒) state of being dedicated or devoted (to sth) 致力, 献身(于某事物): *We're looking for someone with a real sense of commitment to the job.* 我们在寻求对此工作真正能尽职尽责的人.

com·mit·tee /kəˈmɪtɪ; kəˈmɪtɪ/ *n* [CGp] group of people appointed (usu by a larger group) to deal with a particular matter (通常由较大团体所委派以处理某事务的)委员会: *be/sit on a committee* 任委员会委员 ○ *The committee has/have decided to dismiss him.* 委员会已决定辞退他. ○ *the transport committee* 运输委员会 ○ *This was discussed in committee*, ie by the committee. 这事已经委员会讨论. ○ [attrib 作定语] *a committee meeting, member, decision* 委员会的会议、成员、决定.

com·mode /kəˈməʊd; kəˈmod/ *n* **1** piece of bedroom furniture to hold a chamber-pot 便桶箱(放便桶的寝室家具). **2** chest of drawers (有抽屉的)柜橱.

com·modi·ous /kəˈməʊdɪəs; kəˈmodɪəs/ *adj* (*fml* 文) having a lot of space available for use; roomy 宽敞的: *a commodious house, cupboard, suitcase* 宽敞的房屋、橱

柜、手提箱.

com·mod·ity /kəˈmɒdətɪ; kəˈmɑdətɪ/ *n* **1** thing bought in a shop and put to use, esp in the home 商品;（尤指）日用品: *household commodities*, eg pots and pans, cleaning materials, etc 家庭日用品 ○ (*fig* 比喻) *I lead a very busy life, so spare time is a very precious commodity to me.* 我的生活非常忙, 空余时间对我来说是非常珍贵的. **2** (*finance* 财) article, product or material that is exchanged in (esp international) trade 商品; 货物;（尤指国际贸易中的）物品、产品或材料: *Trading in commodities was brisk.* 商品交易兴旺. ○ [attrib 作定语] *the commodity/commodities market* 商品市场.

com·mo·dore /ˈkɒmədɔ:(r); ˈkɑmə,dɔr/ *n* **1** officer in the British Navy between the ranks of captain and rear-admiral（英国海军的）准将. ⇨App 9 见附录 9. **2** president of a yacht club（游艇俱乐部的）主席. **3** senior captain of a shipping line（航运公司的）资深船长: *the commodore of the Cunard Line* 丘纳德航运公司的资深船长.

com·mon[1] /ˈkɒmən; ˈkɑmən/ *adj* **1** usual or familiar; happening or found often and in many places 普通的; 通常的; 常见的: *a common flower, sight, event* 普通的花、风景、事件 ○ *the common cold* 感冒 ○ *Is this word in common use?* ie Is it commonly used? 这个词常用吗? ○ *Robbery is not common in this area.* 这个地区劫案不常见. ○ *Pine trees are common throughout the world.* 松树在世界各处都很常见. Cf 参看 UNCOMMON. **2** [attrib 作定语] **~ (to sb/sth)** shared by, belonging to, done by or affecting two or more people, or most of a group or society 共有的; 共同做的; 共同受到的: *common property, ownership* 共有的财产、所有权 ○ *We share a common purpose.* 我们有共同的目标. ○ *He and I have a common interest: we both collect stamps.* 我和他有共同的爱好, 我们都集邮. ○ *He is French, she is German, but they have English as a common language*, ie they can both speak English. 他是法国人, 她是德国人, 但他们以英语作为共同的语言. ○ *measures taken for the common good*, ie for the benefit of everyone 为了共同的利益而采取的措施 ○ *A fruity quality is common to all wine made from this grape.* 用这种葡萄酿制的所有的葡萄酒有共同的醇味. **3** [attrib 作定语] without special rank or quality; ordinary 一般的, 平常的（没有特殊的级别或特性）: *He's not an officer, but a common soldier.* 他不是军官而是普通士兵. ○ *the common people*, ie the average citizens of a country 老百姓 ○ *common salt* 食盐. **4** (*infml derog* 口, 贬) (of people, their behaviour and belongings) (typical) of the lower classes of society, showing a lack of taste and refinement; vulgar（指人、其行为及所有物）（典型的）下层社会的, 低级趣味的, 庸俗的, 粗俗的: *common manners, accents, clothes* 粗鄙的举止、口音、衣物 ○ *She's so common, shouting like that so all the neighbours can hear!* 她非常粗俗, 大喊大叫, 周围的人都能听到! **5** (*mathematics* 数) belonging to two or more quantities 公共的: *a common denominator/factor/multiple* 公分母［公因子/公倍数］. **6** (idm 习语) **be common/public knowledge** ⇨ KNOWLEDGE. **(as) ˌcommon as ˈdirt/ˈmuck** (*infml derog* 口, 贬) (of people) very common[1](4)（指人）极庸俗的. **ˌcommon or ˈgarden** ordinary; not unusual 平常的; 普通的: *It isn't a rare bird, just a common or garden sparrow.* 那不是稀有的鸟, 只不过是普通的麻雀. **the ˌcommon ˈtouch** ability (esp of sb of high rank) to deal with and talk to ordinary people in a friendly way and without condescension 平易近人的美德（尤指居高位的）: *A politician needs the common touch.* 政治家需要有平易近人的美德. **ˌmake common ˈcause (with sb)** (*fml* 文) unite to pursue a shared objective 联合起来追求共同的目标: *The rebel factions made common cause (with each other) to overthrow the regime.* 各造反派（彼此）联合起来共同推翻政府.

▷ **com·monly** *adv* **1** usually; very often 通常地; 常常地: *That very commonly happens.* 那种事常常发生. ○ *Thomas, commonly known as Tom.* 托马斯, 通常称为汤姆. **2** (*infml derog* 口, 贬) in a common[1](4) manner 庸俗地.

□ **ˌcommon ˈdecency** polite behaviour to be expected from a reasonable person 普通礼貌: *You'd think he'd have the common decency to apologize for what he said.* 你还以为他懂礼貌, 会为他说的话道歉.

ˌcommon ˈground [U] shared opinions, interests, aims, etc 共同的意见、利益、目标等: *The two rival parties have no common ground between them.* 这两个敌对的党派之间没有共同点.

ˈcommon land [U] land that belongs to or may be used by the community, esp in a village 公地（为地区全体居民, 尤指村庄, 所有并使用的土地）. Cf 参看 COMMON[2].

ˌcommon ˈlaw [U] (in England) law developed from old customs and from decisions made by judges, ie not created by Parliament（英国的）普通法, 习惯法（由古老习俗或由法官判例演变而来的法律, 即非由国会制定者）. Cf 参看 CASE LAW (CASE[1]), STATUTE LAW (STATUTE).

ˌcommon-law ˈwife, ˌcommon-law husband person with whom a man or woman has lived for some time and who is recognized as a wife or husband under common law, without a formal marriage ceremony 按普通法结合的妻子、丈夫（未举行正式婚礼, 男女已同居一定时间, 为普通法认可者）.

the ˌCommon ˈMarket (also **the European Economic Community**) economic association, established in 1958, and now including Belgium, Britain, Denmark, France, Greece, Ireland, Italy, Luxembourg, the Netherlands, Portugal, Spain and Germany, whose members give each other mutual trading advantages 共同市场（又名欧洲经济共同体）.

ˌcommon ˈnoun (*grammar*) word that can refer to any member of a class of similar things (eg *book* or *knife*) 普通名词（可以指同类事物其中之一的词, 如 book、knife）.

ˈcommon-room *n* room for use of the teachers or students of a school, college, etc when they are not in class（教师或学生的）公共休息室.

ˌcommon ˈsense practical good sense gained from experience of life, not by special study 常识; 情理: [attrib 作定语] *I like her common-sense approach to everyday problems.* 我喜欢她在处理日常问题上通情达理的方法.

ˌcommon ˈtime (*music* 音) two or four beats (esp four crotchets) in a bar 普通拍子（每小节两拍或四拍, 尤指四个四分音符）.

com·mon[2] /ˈkɒmən; ˈkɑmən/ *n* **1** area of unfenced grassland which anyone may use, usu in or near a village 公地（无篱笆墙的公用草地, 通常在村内或村子附近）: *Saturday afternoon cricket on the village common.* 星期六下午在村子空地上举行的板球赛. Cf 参看 COMMON LAND (COMMON[1]). **2** (idm 习语) **have sth in common (with sb/sth)** share interests, characteristics, etc 有共同的利益、特点等: *Jane and I have nothing in common.* 简和我毫无共同之处. ○ *I have nothing in common with Jane.* 我和简毫无共同之处. **in common** for or by all of a group 共同(的); 共有(的); 共用(的): *land owned in common by the residents* 居民公有的土地. **in common with sb/sth** together with sb/sth; like sb/sth 与某人［某事物］一起; 像某人［某事物］一样: *In common with many others, she applied for a training place.* 她已和许多人一起申请参加训练.

com·moner /ˈkɒmənə(r); ˈkɑmənɚ/ *n* one of the common people, not a member of the nobility 平民（非贵族）. Cf 参看 ARISTOCRAT, NOBLEMAN (NOBLE).

com·mon·place /ˈkɒmənpleɪs; ˈkɑmən,ples/ *adj* (*often derog* 常作贬义) ordinary; not interesting 平常的; 平凡的; 寻常的; 不引起兴趣的: *He's not at all exciting, in fact he's really rather commonplace.* 他毫不出奇, 实际上平庸得很.

▷ **com·mon·place** *n* **1** remark, etc that is ordinary or unoriginal; truism（平淡的或无见地的）言语; 陈词滥调; 老生常谈: *a conversation full of mere commonplaces* 充满陈词滥调的谈话 ○ *He uttered a few commonplaces about peace and democracy.* 他泛泛地谈了几句关于和平与民主的话. **2** event, topic, etc that is ordinary or usual（普通的或寻常的）事情、主题等: *Air travel is a commonplace nowadays.* 现在坐飞机是平常事.

com·mons /ˈkɒmənz; ˈkɑmənz/ *n* [pl] **1 the commons** (*arch* 古) the common people 平民百姓. **2 the Commons** (*Brit*) **(a)** = THE HOUSE OF COMMONS (HOUSE). **(b)** the members of the House of Commons 下议院议员: *the Lords and the Commons* 上议院和下议院的议员. **3** (idm 习语) **short commons** ⇨ SHORT[1].

C

com·mon·wealth /ˈkɒmənwelθ; ˋkɑmən,wɛlθ/ *n* **1** [C] (**a**) independent State or community 独立的国家或团体、集体: *measures for the good of the commonwealth* 有利于集体的措施. (**b**) group of States that have chosen to be politically linked (政治上相结合的国家组成的)集团: *the Commonwealth of Australia* 澳大利亚联邦. **2 the Commonwealth** [sing] the association consisting of the UK and various independent States (previously subject to Britain) and dependencies 英联邦(由联合王国及原所辖的自治省和属地组成的联邦).

com·mo·tion /kəˈməʊʃn; kəˋmoʃən/ *n* [U, C] (instance of) noisy confusion or excitement 嘈杂混乱; 骚动不安; 骚扰; 暴乱: *The children are making a lot of commotion.* 孩子们闹作一团. ○ *Suddenly, there was a great commotion next door.* 突然隔壁发生了巨大的骚乱.

C

com·munal /ˈkɒmjʊnl, kəˈmju:nl; ˋkɑmjʊnl/ *adj* **1** (**a**) for the use of all; shared 全体共用的; 分享的: *communal land, facilities* 共用的土地、设施 ○ *The flat has four separate bedrooms and a communal kitchen.* 这个单元有四间卧室和一间共用的厨房. (**b**) of or for a community 集体的; 为集体的: *communal life, work* 集体的生活、工作. **2** between different groups in a community (集体中的)各个小群体之间的: *communal strife, disturbances, etc* 派别间的冲突、纷争等 ○ *communal riots between religious sects* 不同教派之间的暴力冲突. ▷ **com·mun·ally** *adv*.

com·mune[1] /kəˈmju:n; kəˋmjun/ *v* [I, Ipr, Ip] **~ (with sb/sth)**; **~ (together)** talk to sb intimately; feel close to sb/sth 与某人亲密地交谈; 与某人[某事物]亲近: *commune with one's friends* 和朋友亲密谈心 ○ *commune with God in prayer* 祈祷时与上帝作灵的沟通 ○ *walking in the woods, communing with nature* 在林中散步, 沉浸于大自然中 ○ *friends communing together* 在一起亲密交谈的朋友.

com·mune[2] /ˈkɒmju:n; ˋkɑmjun/ *n* [CGp] **1** group of people, not all of one family, living together and sharing property and responsibilities 共同生活、共享财产、分担责任而并非都是一家人的群体; 公社. **2** (in France, Belgium, Italy, Spain) smallest unit of local government, with a mayor and council (法国、比利时、意大利、西班牙的)最小的地方行政区(有市长和地方议会).

com·mun·ic·able /kəˈmju:nɪkəbl; kəˋmjunɪkəbḷ/ *adj* that can be communicated or transmitted 可传染的; 可传送的: *complex ideas not easily communicable to non-experts* 对非专业人员不易说清楚的复杂想法 ○ *a communicable disease* 传染病.

com·mun·ic·ant /kəˈmju:nɪkənt; kəˋmjunɪkənt/ *n* **1** person who receives Communion, esp regularly 领受圣餐者(尤指经常领受者). **2** (*fml* 文) person who gives information; informer 提供情况的人; 告发者; 检举人; 报信人.

com·mun·ic·ate /kəˈmju:nɪkeɪt; kəˋmjunə,ket/ *v* **1** [Tn, Tn·pr] **~ sth (to sb/sth)** (**a**) make sth known; convey sth 使某事物被人知晓; 传送某事物: *This poem communicates the author's despair.* 这首诗流露出作者的绝望心情. ○ *The officer communicated his orders to the men by radio.* 军官用无线电向士兵下达命令. (**b**) pass on sth; transmit sth 传递某事物; 传播: *communicate a disease* 传播疾病. **2** (**a**) [I, Ipr] **~ (with sb)** exchange information, news, ideas, etc 交流情况、交换消息、交流思想等: *The police communicate (with each other) by radio.* 警察通过无线电(互相)联络. (**b**) [I] convey one's ideas, feelings, etc clearly to others 将想法感情等清楚地传达给别人: *A politician must be able to communicate.* 政治家必须善于表达自己的观点. **3** [I, Ipr] **~ (with sth)** be connected 被联系; 被联接; 被沟通: *My garden communicates with the one next door by means of a gate.* 我的花园有道门与邻家的相通 ○ *communicating rooms*, ie rooms with a connecting door 通间(带通门的房间).

com·mun·ica·tion /kə,mju:nɪˈkeɪʃn; kə,mjunəˋkeʃən/ *n* **1** [U] act of communicating(1b, 2a, 2b) 传递; 传播; 交流; 交换; 传达; 表达; 传意; 通信; 通讯; 联络: *the communication of disease* 疾病的传染 ○ *Being deaf and dumb makes communication very difficult.* 又聋又哑很难与人交往. **2** [C] (*usu fml* 通常作文雅语) thing that is communicated; message (被传递的)事物; 信息; 消息: *to receive a secret communication* 得到一个秘密消息. **3** [U] (also **communications** [pl]) means of communicating, eg roads, railways, telephone and telegraph lines between places, or radio and TV 交流的方式方法或工具(如公路、铁路、电话及两地间的电报线路或无线电、电视等): *Telephone communications between the two cities have been restored.* 两城市间的电话联系已经恢复. ○ *The heavy snow has prevented all communication with the highlands.* 大雪阻断了与高地之间的一切联系. ○ [attrib 作定语] *a communication satellite, link, etc* 通讯卫星、通讯线路等 ○ *a world communications network* 环球通讯网. **4** (idm 习语) **be in communication with sb** exchange information regularly with sb, usu by letter or telephone 经常与某人互通情况(通常为通过书信或电话).

□ **communiˈcation cord** cord that passes along the length of a train inside the coaches, and that passengers can pull to stop the train in an emergency (火车车厢内供乘客紧急制动时拉的)警报索.

com·mun·ic·at·ive /kəˈmju:nɪkətɪv; *US* -keɪtɪv; kəˋmjunə,ketɪv/ *adj* ready and willing to talk and give information 愿意交谈并提供信息的: *I don't find Peter very communicative.* 我觉得彼得很不爱说话. Cf 参看 RESERVED.

com·mu·nion /kəˈmju:nɪən; kəˋmjunjən/ *n* **1 Communion** [U] (also **Holy Communion**) (in the Christian Church) celebration of the Lord's Supper (基督教教会的)圣餐仪式: *go to Communion*, ie attend church for this celebration 领圣餐(去教堂参加此仪式) ○ [attrib 作定语] *Communion wine* 圣餐酒. Cf 参看 EUCHARIST. **2** [C] group of people with the same religious beliefs 教会; 教派: *We belong to the same communion.* 我们属于同一教会. **3** [U] **~ (with sb/sth)** (*fml* 文) state of sharing or exchanging the same thoughts or feelings 思想感情相同或交融: *poets who are in communion with nature* 与大自然情感交融的诗人.

com·mu·ni·qué /kəˈmju:nɪkeɪ; *US* kə,mju:nəˈkeɪ; kə,mjunəˋke/ *n* official announcement, esp to the press 官方公报(尤指对新闻界发布的): *A government communiqué, issued this morning, states that...* 今晨发布的政府公报宣称....

com·mun·ism /ˈkɒmjʊnɪzəm; ˋkɑmjʊ,nɪzəm/ *n* [U] **1** social and economic system in which there is no private ownership and the means of production belong to all members of society 共产主义. **2 Communism** (**a**) political doctrine or movement that aims to establish such a society 共产主义学说; 共产主义运动. (**b**) system of government by a ruling Communist Party 共产主义制度.

▷ **com·mun·ist** /ˈkɒmjʊnɪst; ˋkɑmjʊnɪst/ *n* **1** supporter of communism 共产主义者. **2 Communist** member of a Communist party or movement 共产党员; 共产主义运动的成员. — *adj* characterized by, supporting or relating to communism 共产主义的: *have communist ideals* 有共产主义理想 ○ *a Communist country, government, party, etc* 共产主义的国家、政府、政党等. **com·mun·istic** /,kɒmjʊˈnɪstɪk; ,kɑmjʊˋnɪstɪk/ *adj*.

□ **the ˈCommunist Party 1** political party supporting Communism 共产党. **2** (in Communist countries) single official ruling party of the State (共产主义国家的)单一执政党.

com·mun·ity /kəˈmju:nətɪ; kəˋmjunətɪ/ *n* **1 the community** [sing] the people living in one place, district or country, considered as a whole 社区; 团体; 集体; 社会: *work for the good of the community* 为集体利益服务 ○ [attrib 作定语] *community service* 社会服务工作 **2** [CGp] group of people of the same religion, race, occupation, etc, or with shared interests 宗教信仰、种族、职业等方面相同的人构成的集体; 有共同利益的集体: *the British community in Paris* 在巴黎的英国侨民团体 ○ *a community of monks*, ie a group of the same order living together 僧侣团体. **3** [U] condition of sharing, having things in common, being alike in some way 共享, 共有; 共同; 相同: *community of interests* 利益的一致 ○ [attrib 作定语] *a community spirit*, ie a feeling of sharing the same attitudes, interests, etc 集体精神.

□ **comˈmunity centre** place where the people of a neighbourhood can meet for sporting activities, education classes, social occasions, etc 社区活动中心.

comˈmunity chest (*US*) fund for helping local people in financial need 社区福利基金.

comˈmunity home (*Brit*) centre where young

offenders are kept for training, before their release 失足青少年教养所.

com'munity singing organized singing in which all present may take part (在场的人都参加的)大合唱.

com·mut·ator /ˈkɒmjuːteɪtə(r); ˈkɑmjʊˌtetɚ/ *n* device for altering the direction of an electric current 整流器; 换向器.

com·mute /kəˈmjuːt; kəˈmjut/ *v* **1** [I, Ipr, Ip] travel regularly by bus, train or car between one's place of work (usu in a city) and one's home (usu at a distance) 通勤(乘汽车或火车经常往返于市区工作处与郊区住所之间): *She commutes from Oxford to London every day.* 她每天通勤于牛津和伦敦之间. ○ *She lives in Oxford and commutes (in).* 她住在牛津而通勤来往. **2** [Tn, Tn·pr] **~ sth (to sth)** replace (one punishment) by another that is less severe 减(刑): *commute a death sentence (to one of life imprisonment)* 将死刑减刑(改为无期徒刑) ○ *She was given a commuted sentence.* 她获减刑判决. **3** [Tn, Tn·pr] **~ sth (for/into sth)** change sth, esp one form of payment, for or into sth else 改变某事物(尤指付款方式): *commute one's pension* 改变退休金的付款方式 ○ *commute an annuity into a lump sum* 将年金改为一次性总付款.

▷ **com·mut·able** /kəˈmjuːtəbl; kəˈmjutəbḷ/ *adj* **~ (for/into sth)** that can be made, paid, etc in a different form 可用不同方式制造、偿付等的: *A pension is often commutable into a lump sum.* 养老金常可改为一次性总付款.

com·muta·tion /ˌkɒmjuːˈteɪʃn; ˌkɑmjʊˈteʃən/ *n* **1** [C, U] replacement of one punishment by another that is less severe 减刑: *He appealed for (a) commutation of the death sentence to life imprisonment.* 他已上诉请求将死刑减为无期徒刑. **2** (**a**) [U] replacing one method of payment by another, eg a lump sum instead of a pension 变换付款方法(如以一次性总付款代替年金). (**b**) [C] payment made in this way 以上述方式付的款.

commu'tation ticket (*US*) bus or train ticket valid for a fixed number of trips during a given period of time (公共汽车或火车的)长期车票. Cf 参看 SEASON TICKET (SEASON).

com·muter *n* person who commutes (COMMUTE 1) 通勤者: *The five o'clock train is always packed with commuters.* 五点钟那趟车总是挤满了通勤者. ○ [attrib 作定语] *the commuter belt*, ie the area around a large city, from which people commute to work 通勤者居住带(环绕在大城市周围的通勤者居住区).

com·pact[1] /kəmˈpækt; kəmˈpækt/ *adj* **1** (**a**) closely packed together 装填紧密的: *a compact mass of sand* 坚实的沙堆 ○ *Stamp the soil down so that it's compact.* 把泥土踩结实. (**b**) neatly fitted in a small space (在一个小空间里)整齐填满的: *a compact flat, car, kit* 小型的单元、汽车、箱子等 ○ *The computer looks compact and functional.* 这个计算机看起来小巧而实用. **2** (of literary style) condensed; concise (指文体)简洁的, 紧凑的.

▷ **com·pact** *v* [Tn usu passive 通常用于被动语态] press (sth) firmly together 将(某物)紧压在一起: *The compacted snow on the pavement turned to ice.* 人行道上被踩实的雪已变成了冰.

com·pact·ly *adv*.

com·pact·ness *n* [U].

□ **comˌpact 'disc** /*also* ˌkɒmpækt ˈdɪsk; ˌkɑmpækt ˈdɪsk/ small disc for reproducing recorded sound by laser action 激光唱片.

com·pact[2] /ˈkɒmpækt; ˈkɑmpækt/ *n* agreement or contract between two or more parties 协议; 条约; 契约; 合同: *The two states made a compact to co-operate against terrorism.* 两国签订了反恐怖主义合作协议.

com·pact[3] /ˈkɒmpækt; ˈkɑmpækt/ *n* **1** small flat portable case for face-powder, usu also containing a powder-puff and a mirror 小粉盒(通常带粉扑和镜子). **2** (*esp US*) small car 小型汽车.

com·pan·ion /kəmˈpænɪən; kəmˈpænjən/ *n* **1** (**a**) person or animal that goes with, or spends much time with, another (相伴的)人或动物; 同伴; 伙伴: *my companions on the journey* 我的旅伴 ○ *A dog is a faithful companion.* 狗是忠实的伙伴. ○ (*fig* 比喻) *Fear was the hostage's constant companion.* 恐惧的心情始终缠绕着人质. (**b**) person who shares in the work, pleasures, misfortunes, etc of another 与另一人共事、同甘共苦等的人: *companions in arms*, ie fellow soldiers 战友 ○ *companions in misfortune*, ie people suffering together 共患难的人. (**c**) person with similar tastes, interests, etc 有共同兴趣、爱好等的人: *She's an excellent companion.* 她是个好伴侣. ○ *They're 'drinking companions.* 他们是酒友. ○ *His brother is not much of a companion for him.* 他哥哥和他志趣不大相投. **2** person employed to live with another (esp sb old or ill) as a friend 受雇的陪伴人(如朋友般与雇主, 尤指老人或病人, 一起生活者): *to take a post as a ˌpaid com'panion* 受雇作陪伴人. **3** one of a matching pair or set of things (成双、成对或成套的)物品之一: [attrib 作定语] *The companion volume will soon be published.* 这卷书的姊妹篇即将问世. **4** (used in book titles 用于书的题目) handbook; reference book 手册; 参考书: *the ˌGardener's Com'panion* 《园艺指南》. **5 Companion** member of certain distinguished orders (ORDER[1] 10a) 有某等勋位的人: *Comˌpanion of 'Honour* 勋爵. **6** (idm 习语) **a boon companion** ⇨ BOON[2].

▷ **com·pan·ion·able** *adj* friendly; sociable 友好的; 好交际的.

com·pan·ion·ship *n* [U] relationship between friends or companions 友谊; 朋友或伴侣的关系: *the companionship of old friends* 老交情 ○ *She turned to me for companionship.* 她找上我, 要与我为伴.

companion-way /kəmˈpænɪən weɪ; kəmˈpænjən ˌwe/ (also **companion**) *n* staircase from a ship's deck to the saloon or cabins 舱梯(由甲板通往大厅或船舱的阶梯).

com·pany /ˈkʌmpənɪ; ˈkʌmpənɪ/ *n* **1** [U] being together with another or others 陪伴; 与他人在一起: *I enjoy his company*, ie I like being with him. 我喜欢和他在一起. ○ *be good, bad, etc company*, ie be pleasant, unpleasant, etc to be with 令人愉快、不快等的伙伴. **2** [U] group of people together; number of guests 一群人; 一伙; 客人; 来宾: *She told the assembled company what had happened.* 她把发生的事告诉了聚会的人. ○ *We're expecting company* (ie guests, visitors) *next week.* 我们下星期有客来访. **3** (often 常作 **Company**) [CGp] group of people united for business or commercial purposes 公司; 商行: *a manufacturing company* 制造公司. Cf 参看 FIRM 2. **4** [CGp] group of people working together 同事; 同仁: *a company of players*, ie a number of actors regularly performing together 演出团(常在一起演出的演员) ○ *a theatrical company* 剧团 ○ *the ship's company*, ie the crew 全体船员. **5** [CGp] subdivision of an infantry battalion, usu commanded by a captain or a major 连队(步兵的营以下的单位, 通常由上尉或少校指挥). **6** (idm 习语) **the 'company one keeps** the type of people with whom one spends one's time 经常与之为伍的人; 伙伴: (*saying* 谚) *You may know a man by the company he keeps*, ie judge his character by his friends. 观其友则知其人. **for company** as a companion 作伴; 一起: *I hate going out alone: I take my daughter for company.* 我不愿独自一人出门, 带女儿作个伴. **get into/keep bad 'company** associate with undesirable people 与坏人交往. **in company** in the presence of others 当着别人的面: *It's bad manners to whisper in company.* 当着别人窃窃私语是不礼貌的行为. **in company with sb** together with sb 和某人一起: *I, in company with many others, feel this decision was wrong.* 我, 还有许多人, 都觉得这个决定是错误的. **in good 'company** doing the same as other, better people do 与他人、比自己强的人做得一样: *'I'm late again!' 'Well, you're in good company. The boss isn't here yet.'* '我又迟到了!' '没关系, 有跟你做伴儿的. 老板还没来呢.' **keep sb company** remain with sb so that he is not alone 陪伴某人; 给某人做伴: *I'll stay here and keep you company.* 我留下陪你. **part company** ⇨ PART[2]. **present company excepted** ⇨ PRESENT[1]. **two's company (, three's a crowd)** (*saying* 谚) (used esp of people in love) it is better for two people to be alone with each other and without others present (尤指恋人)两人为伴(三人添乱).

com·par·able /ˈkɒmpərəbl; ˈkɑmpərəbl/ *adj* **~ (to/with sb/sth)** able or suitable to be compared 可比较的; 适合相比的: *The achievements of an athlete and a writer are not comparable.* 运动员的成就与作家的成就不能相提并论. ○ *His work is comparable with the very* best. 他的工作可与最优秀的相比.

com·par·at·ive /kəmˈpærətɪv; kəmˈpærətɪv/ *adj* **1** involving comparison or comparing 比较的; 相比的: *comparative linguistics, religion, etc* 比较语言学、宗教等 ○ *a comparative study of the social systems of two countries*, ie one that analyses the similarities and differences between them 两国社会制度的比较研究. **2** measured or judged by comparing; relative 经比较而衡量或判断的; 相对的; 比较而言的: *living in comparative comfort*, eg compared with others, or with one's own life at an earlier period 生活比较舒适(如与他人或与自己以前相比) ○ *In a poor country, owning a bicycle is a sign of comparative wealth.* 在贫穷的国家里, 有辆自行车就是比较富裕的象征. **3** (*grammar*) (of adjectives and adverbs) expressing a greater degree or 'more', eg *better, worse, slower, more difficult* (指形容词和副词)比较级的(如 better、worse、slower、more difficult). Cf 参看 SUPERLATIVE 2.

▷ **com·par·at·ive** *n* (*grammar*) form of adjectives and adverbs that expresses a greater degree (形容词和副词的)比较级形式: *'Better' is the comparative of 'good'.* better 是 good 的比较级.

com·par·at·ively *adv* as compared to sth or sb else 比较地: *comparatively wealthy, small, good, old* 比较富裕的、小的、好的、老的.

com·pare /kəmˈpeə(r); kəmˈpɛr/ *v* **1** [Tn, Tn·pr] **~ A and B; ~ A with/to B** examine people or things to see how they are alike and how they are different 比较: *Compare (the style of) the two poems.* 将这两首诗(的风格)加以比较. ○ *If you compare her work with his/If you compare their work, you'll find hers is much better.* 要是把他俩的工作比较一下, 就会发现她的好得多. Cf 参看 CF, CP *abbrs* 缩写. **2** [Tn·pr] **~ A to B** show the likeness between sb/sth and sb/sth else 显示某人[某事物]与他人[他事物]相同: *Poets have compared sleep to death.* 诗人把睡眠比作死亡. ○ *A beginner's painting can't be compared to that of an expert*, ie is very different in quality. 初学者的画不能与专家的相比(水平极不相同). **3** [Ipr] **~ with sb/sth** be compared with or be worthy to be compared with sb/sth 和某人[某事物]相比或值得相比: *This cannot compare with that*, ie No comparison is possible because they are so different. 这个无法与那个相比(因二者相去甚远, 不能相比). ○ *He cannot compare with* (ie is not nearly as great as) *Shakespeare as a writer of tragedies.* 在悲剧写作方面他根本不能与莎士比亚相比. **4** [Tn] (*grammar*) form the comparative and superlative degrees of (an adjective or adverb) 构成(形容词或副词的)比较级和最高级. **5** (idm 习语) **compare ˈnotes (with sb)** exchange ideas or opinions 交换意见、观点、看法: *We saw the play separately and compared notes afterwards.* 我们各自看了那出戏, 后来交换了意见.

▷ **com·pare** *n* (idm 习语) **beyond comˈpare** (*fml* 文) to such an extent that no comparison can be made with anything or anyone else 无可比拟; 举世无双; 绝伦; 绝顶: *She is lovely beyond compare.* 她真是可爱得无与伦比.

com·par·ison /kəmˈpærɪsn; kəmˈpærəsn̩/ *n* **1** [U] comparing 比较: *He showed us a good tyre for comparison (with the worn one).* 他给我们看一个好轮胎(与磨损的)作比较. **2** [C] **~ (of A and/to/with B); ~ (between A and B)** act of comparing 相比; 对比; 对照: *the comparison of the heart to/with a pump* 把心脏比作唧筒 ○ *It is often useful to make a comparison between two things.* 将两件事物相比较往往是有益的. **3** (idm 习语) **bear/stand comparison with sb/sth** be able to be compared favourably with sb/sth 比得上某人[某事物]; 不亚于某人[某事物]: *That's a good dictionary, but it doesn't bear comparison with this one.* 那是本好词典, 但比不上这本. **by/in comparison (with sb/sth)** when compared 相比之下; 比较起来: *The tallest buildings in London are small in comparison with those in New York.* 伦敦最高的建筑物与纽约的一比就矮了. **comparisons are odious** (*saying* 谚) people and things should be judged on their own merits and not measured against sb/sth else 人和事物应以本身的好坏来衡量, 不应以他人[他事物]作尺度; 人比人, 气死人. **there's no comˈparison** (used to emphasize the difference between two people or things being compared 用以强调相比较的两人之间或两事物之间的差别): *'Is he as good as her at chess?' 'There's no comparison'*, ie She is much better. '他下棋也像她下得一样好吗?' '根本不能比(她下得好得多).'

com·part·ment /kəmˈpɑːtmənt; kəmˈpɑrtmənt/ *n* any of the sections into which a larger area or enclosed space, esp a railway carriage, is divided 隔间(尤指火车车厢中的); 车室: *The first-class compartments are in front.* 头等车室在前面. ○ *a case with separate compartments for shoes, jewellery, etc* 分格存放鞋、珠宝等的箱子.

▷ **com·part·men·tal·ize, -ise** /-ˈmentəlaɪz; -ˈmɛntl̩ˌaɪz/ *v* [Tn, Tn·pr] **~ sth (into sth)** divide sth into compartments or categories 将某事物分成隔间或部分: *Life today is compartmentalized into work and leisure.* 现今生活分成工作和闲暇两部分.

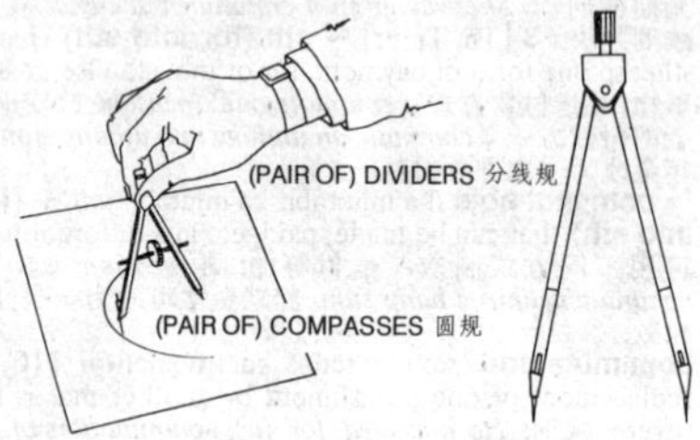

com·pass[1] /ˈkʌmpəs; ˈkʌmpəs/ *n* **1** [C] **(a)** (also **magnetic compass**) device for finding direction, with a needle that points to magnetic north 指南针; 罗盘; 罗经: *the points of the compass*, ie N, NE, E, SE, S, SW, W, NW, etc 罗经上的方位(北、东北、东、东南、南、西南、西、西北等). **(b)** similar device for determining direction (指示方向的)类似装置: *a radio compass* 无线电罗经. **2** [C] (also **compasses** [pl]) V-shaped instrument with two legs joined by a hinge, used for drawing circles, measuring distances on a map or chart, etc 圆规; 两脚规: *a pair of compasses* 一只圆规. ⇨illus 见插图. **3** [U] scope; range 界限; 范围: *beyond the compass of the human mind* 超出人类智力范围 ○ *the compass of a singer's voice*, ie the range from the lowest to the highest note that he or she can reach 歌手的音域.

com·pass[2] /ˈkʌmpəs; ˈkʌmpəs/ *v* [Tn] (*arch* 古) = ENCOMPASS 2.

com·pas·sion /kəmˈpæʃn; kəmˈpæʃən/ *n* [U] **~ (for sb)** pity for the sufferings of others, making one want to help them 同情; 怜悯: *be filled with compassion* 充满怜悯 ○ *a woman of great compassion* 富有同情心的女子 ○ *The plight of the refugees arouses our compassion.* 难民的困苦引起我们的同情. ○ *Out of* (ie Because of) *compassion for her terrible suffering they allowed her to stay.* 他们因为同情她的悲惨遭遇而准许她居留. ○ *They took compassion on her children and offered them a home.* 他们因可怜她的孩子而给他们提供了住处.

▷ **com·pas·sion·ate** /kəmˈpæʃənət; kəmˈpæʃənɪt/ *adj* showing or feeling compassion 表示怜悯的; 有同情心的. **com·pas·sion·ately** *adv*. **compassionate leave** (*Brit*) leave[2](1) granted (eg to a member of the armed forces) because of some special personal circumstance 特殊私事假(如准予军人的): *She was allowed compassionate leave from work to attend her father's funeral.* 她获准丧假为父亲送葬.

com·pat·ible /kəmˈpætəbl; kəmˈpætəbl̩/ *adj* **~ (with sb/sth)** **(a)** (of people, ideas, arguments, principles, etc) suited; that can exist together (指人、想法、论点、原则等)适合的; 适宜的; 能共存的; 符合的; 相容的: *The couple separated because they were not compatible.* 这对夫妻因不合而分居. ○ *driving a car at a speed compatible with safety*, ie at a safe speed 以符合安全要求的速度驾驶. **(b)** (of equipment) that can be used together (指设备)可协同使用的, 兼容的: *This printer is compatible with most microcomputers.* 这台打印机是与大多数微型电子计算机兼容的.

▷ **com·pat·ib·il·ity** /kəm,pætə'bɪlətɪ; kəm,pætə'bɪlətɪ/ *n* [U] **~ (with sb/sth); ~ (between A and B)** state of being compatible 适合; 共存; 符合; 相容.
com·pat·ibly /-əblɪ; -əblɪ/ *adv*.

com·pat·riot /kəm'pætrɪət; *US* -'peɪt-; kəm'petrɪət/ *n* person who was born in, or is a citizen of, the same country as another; fellow-countryman 同胞; 同国人.

com·peer /'kɒmpɪə(r); 'kɑmpɪr/ *n* (*fml* 文) person of equal status or ability (地位、能力)相等的人; 同辈人; 同代人: *be much respected by one's compeers* 备受同辈尊重.

com·pel /kəm'pel; kəm'pɛl/ *v* **(-ll-)** **1** [Cn·t] (*fml* 文) make (sb) do sth; force 使(某人)做某事; 强迫: *We cannot compel you to (do it), but we think you should.* 我们不能强迫你(去做), 但认为你应该做. ○ *I was compelled to* (ie I had to) *acknowledge the force of his argument.* 我不得不承认他的论据有力. Cf 参看 IMPEL. **2** [Tn no passive 不用于被动语态] (*fml* 文) (**a**) get (sth) by force or pressure; make necessary 强夺、强求(某物); 强迫; 使必须: *You can compel obedience, but not affection.* 可以逼人服从, 却无法逼人生爱. ○ *Circumstances have compelled a change of plan.* 因情况所迫, 计划已经改变. (**b**) (not in the continuous tenses 不用于进行时态) (*fig* 比喻) inspire (sth) irresistibly (不可抗拒地)激起, 激发(某事物): *His courage compels universal admiration.* 他的勇气不禁令人肃然起敬.
▷ **com·pel·ling** *adj* (**a**) extremely interesting and exciting, so that one has to pay attention 使人非注意不可的: *a compelling novel, account, story, etc* 引人入胜的小说、报道、故事等. (**b**) that one must accept or agree with 必须接受或同意的: *a compelling reason, argument, etc* 不得不同意的理由、论点. Cf 参看 COMPULSION.

com·pen·di·ous /kəm'pendɪəs; kəm'pɛndɪəs/ *adj* (*fml* 文) giving a lot of information briefly 扼要的; 简要的; 简明的; 精练的; 简练的: *a compendious writer, handbook, catalogue* 文笔简练的作家、简明手册、要目.

com·pen·dium /kəm'pendɪəm; kəm'pɛndɪəm/ *n* (*pl* **~s** or **-ia**) **~ (of sth)** **1** brief but full account; summary 简洁而全面的叙述; 摘要; 概要; 纲要: *This encyclopedia is truly a compendium of knowledge.* 这部百科全书真正是知识宝库. **2** (*Brit*) set of different board games sold in one box (装在一个盒子里出售的)各种棋类游戏用具.

com·pens·ate /'kɒmpenseɪt; 'kɑmpɛn,set/ *v* [Ipr, Tn, Tn·pr] **~ (sb) for sth** give (sb) sth good to balance or lessen the bad effect of damage, loss, injury, etc; recompense 补偿; 赔偿; 报偿; 报酬: *Nothing can compensate for the loss of one's health.* 失去健康是无法补偿的. ○ *The animal's good sense of smell compensates for its poor eyesight.* 这动物嗅觉灵敏弥补了视力之不足. ○ *She was compensated by the insurance company for her injuries.* 她受伤后获得保险公司的赔偿.
▷ **com·pens·at·ory** /,kɒmpen'seɪtərɪ; *US* kəm'pensə-tɔ:rɪ; kəm'pɛnsə,torɪ/ *adj* compensating 补偿的; 赔偿的; 报偿的; 报酬的: *compensatory payments* 赔款.

com·pensa·tion /,kɒmpen'seɪʃn; ,kɑmpɛn'seʃən/ *n* **~ (for sth)** (**a**) [U] compensating 补偿; 赔偿; 报偿: *Compensation of injured workers has cost the company a lot.* 公司花了一大笔钱赔偿受伤的工人. (**b**) [U, C] thing given to compensate 补偿或赔偿的物或款; 报酬: *receive £5000 in compensation/by way of compensation/as a compensation for injury* 因受伤获5000英镑赔偿 ○ *My job is hard, but it has its compensations*, ie pleasant aspects that make it seem less bad. 我的工作虽苦, 但也有所补偿(有好的方面因而不觉得太苦).

compère /'kɒmpeə(r); 'kɑmpɛr/ *n* (*Brit*) person who introduces the performers in a variety programme or game show, esp on radio or television (杂耍、游戏等表演的)主持人(尤指广播或电视中的).
▷ **compère** *v* [Tn] (*Brit*) act as a compere for (a show) 当(演出的)主持人.

com·pete /kəm'pi:t; kəm'pit/ *v* [I, Ipr, It] **~ (against/with sb) (in sth) (for sth)** try to win sth by defeating others who are trying to do the same 竞争; 对抗; 比赛: *Several companies are competing (against/with each other) for the contract/to gain the contract.* 几家公司正为争取一项合同而互相竞争. ○ *a horse that has competed in the Grand National four times* 参加过四次'英国大赛马'的马 ○ *We have limited funds and several competing claims, so it is hard to choose between them.* 我们的基金有限而争相申请的却有几处, 因此难于做出抉择.

com·pet·ence /'kɒmpɪtəns; 'kɑmpətəns/ *n* [U] **1 ~ (for/as/in sth); ~ (in doing sth/to do sth)** being competent; ability 胜任; 能力; 称职: *No one doubts her competence as a teacher.* 谁也不怀疑她能胜任教师工作. ○ *competence in solving problems* 解决问题的能力. **2 ~ (to do sth)** (of a court, a judge, etc) legal authority (指法院、法官等的)管辖权, 权限: *matters within/beyond the competence of the court*, ie ones that it can/cannot legally deal with 法院权限以内[以外]的事(法院依法能[不能]解决的事).

com·pet·ent /'kɒmpɪtənt; 'kɑmpətənt/ *adj* **1 ~ (as/at/in sth); ~ (to do sth)** (of people) having the necessary ability, authority, skill, knowledge, etc (指人)有能力、权力、技能、知识等的; 能胜任的; 能干的: *a highly competent driver* 技术高超的司机 ○ *competent at/in one's work* 能胜任工作的 ○ *He's not competent to look after young children.* 他没有看小孩的本事. **2** quite good, but not excellent 不错的(但并不出色): *a competent piece of work* 良好的作品 ○ *The novel may be a best seller, but it's no more than a competent piece of writing.* 这部小说就算能畅销, 也不过是平平之作. ▷ **com·pet·ently** *adv*

com·peti·tion /,kɒmpə'tɪʃn; ,kɑmpə'tɪʃən/ *n* **1** [C] event in which people compete; contest 比赛; 竞赛: *boxing, chess, beauty competitions* 拳击、棋类、选美竞赛 ○ *He came first in the poetry competition.* 他获诗歌比赛第一名. ⇨Usage at SPORT 用法见SPORT. **2** [U] **~ (between/with sb) (for sth)** competing; activity in which people compete 竞争; 角逐: *Competition between bidders for this valuable painting has been keen.* 拍卖时各出价人对这幅名画竞争很激烈. ○ *We're in competition with* (ie competing against) *several other companies for the contract.* 我们与另几家公司角逐争取这项合同. **3 the competition** [sing or pl *v*] those competing against sb 竞争者; 对手: *She had a chance to see the competition* (ie the other people who were trying to get the same job as she was) *before the interview.* 她在面试之前有机会见到了对手(与她竞争同一职位者).

com·pet·it·ive /kəm'petətɪv; kəm'pɛtətɪv/ *adj* **1** of or involving competition 比赛的; 竞争的: *competitive examinations for government posts* 公职遴选考试 ○ *competitive sports* 竞技性体育运动 ○ *the competitive spirit*, ie enjoying competition 竞争精神(乐于竞争). **2 ~ (with sb/sth)** able to do as well as or better than others 不逊于、不亚于、胜过或超过他人的: *Our firm is no longer competitive in world markets.* 我们公司在世界市场上已不占优势. ○ *a shop offering competitive prices*, ie as low as in any other shop 在价格上有竞争力的商店. **3** (of people) having a strong urge to win (指人)求胜心切的, 急于取胜的: *You have to be highly competitive to do well in sport nowadays.* 如今必须有高度的竞争意识才能在体育运动中取胜. ▷ **com·pet·it·ively** *adv*: *competitively priced goods* 在价格上有竞争力的货物.

com·pet·itor /kəm'petɪtə(r); kəm'pɛtətɚ/ *n* person who competes 竞争者; 比赛者; 对手; 敌手: *The firm has better products than its competitors*, ie than rival firms. 这公司的产品比其对手的好(比与其竞争的其他公司). Cf 参看 CONTESTANT (CONTEST).

com·pile /kəm'paɪl; kəm'paɪl/ *v* **1** [Tn, Tn·pr] (**a**) **~ sth (for/from sth)** collect (information) and arrange it in a book, list, report, etc 收集(资料)并编辑(成书、表、报告等): *compiling statistics for a report on traffic accidents* 为交通事故报告汇集统计数字. (**b**) **~ sth (from sth)** produce (a book, list, report, etc) in this way 编纂, 编辑, 编制, 编写(书、表、报告等): *The police have compiled a list of suspects.* 警方已编制了涉嫌者名单. ○ *a guidebook compiled from a variety of sources* 汇集多方资料编辑的旅行指南. **2** [Tn] (*computing* 计) turn instructions in a high-level language into (information in a form that a particular computer can understand and act on) 编译(将高级语言指令转换成代码, 使某计算机可识别并照其执行).
▷ **com·pila·tion** /,kɒmpɪ'leɪʃn; ,kɑmpɪ'leʃən/ *n* (**a**) [U] compiling 编辑; 编纂; 编制; 编写; 编译. (**b**) [C] thing that is compiled 编辑物: *Her latest album is a compilation of all her best singles.* 她最新的一套唱片是她的最佳单曲唱片的汇集.

com·piler /kɒmˈpaɪlə(r); kəmˈpaɪlɚ/ *n* **1** person who compiles 编辑者; 汇编者; 编纂者. **2** (*computing* 计) computer program that turns instructions in a high-level language into a form that the computer can understand and act on 将高级语言指令转换为计算机可识别并照其执行的编译程序.

com·pla·cency /kəmˈpleɪsnsɪ; kəmˈplesn̩sɪ/ (also **com·pla·cence** /-ˈpleɪsns; -ˈplesn̩s/) *n* **~ (about sb/ sth)** (*usu derog* 通常作贬义) calm feeling of satisfaction with oneself, one's work, etc 自满; 自得: *There's no room for complacency; we must continue to try to improve.* 我们不能自满, 必须继续努力改进.

C

com·pla·cent /kəmˈpleɪsnt; kəmˈplesn̩t/ *adj* **~ (about sb/sth)** (*usu derog* 通常作贬义) calmly satisfied with oneself, one's work, etc 自满的; 自鸣得意的: *a complacent smile, manner, tone of voice* 自满的微笑、姿态、声调 ○ *We must not be complacent about our achievements; there is still a lot to be done.* 我们绝不能满足于自己的成绩, 还有很多事情要做. ▷ **com·pla·cently** *adv*.

com·plain /kəmˈpleɪn; kəmˈplen/ *v* **1** [I, Ipr, Tf, Dpr·f] **~ (to sb) (about/at sth)** (*often derog* 常作贬义) say that one is dissatisfied, unhappy, etc 投诉; 抱怨; 诉苦; 发牢骚: *You're always complaining!* 你总是发牢骚! ○ (*infml* 口) *'What was the weather like on your holiday?' 'Oh, I can't complain'*, ie It was as good as could be expected. '你度假时天气怎么样?' '嗬, 没说的(要多好有多好).' ○ *She complained to me about his rudeness.* 她向我诉苦说他粗鲁. ○ *He complained (to the waiter) that his meal was cold.* 他(向服务员)抱怨说饭菜是凉的. **2** (phr v) **complain of sth** report (a pain, etc) 诉说(病痛等); 主诉: *The patient is complaining of acute earache.* 病人说耳部剧痛. ▷ **com·plain·ingly** *adv*: *'Why me?' he asked complainingly.* '为什么偏偏是我呢?' 他不满地问.

com·plain·ant /kəmˈpleɪnənt; kəmˈplenənt/ *n* (*law* 律) = PLAINTIFF.

com·plaint /kəmˈpleɪnt; kəmˈplent/ *n* **1** [U] complaining 抱怨; 埋怨; 不满: *The road-works caused much complaint among local residents.* 修路引起周围居民很多怨言. ○ *You have no cause/grounds for complaint.* 你没有理由抱怨. **2** [C] **~ (about/of sth); ~ (that...)** **(a)** reason for dissatisfaction 不满的原因: *I have a number of complaints about the hotel room you've given me.* 我对你给我的旅馆房间有几点不满意见. **(b)** statement of dissatisfaction 申诉; 投诉; 诉苦; 控诉; 控告: *She lodged a complaint about the noise.* 她就噪音问题提出投诉. ○ *submit a formal complaint* 提出正式控告 ○ *We've received a lot of complaints of bad workmanship.* 很多人向我们投诉产品工艺低劣. ○ *Management ignored our complaints that washing facilities were inadequate.* 我们投诉卫生设备不足, 管理部门不予理睬. ○ [attrib 作定语] *follow the complaints procedure* 按照投诉程序. **3** [C] (*sometimes euph* 有时作委婉语) illness; disease 疾病; 病: *a heart complaint* 心脏病 ○ *childhood complaints*, ie illnesses common among children 小儿常见病.

com·plais·ance /kəmˈpleɪzəns; kəmˈplezn̩s/ *n* [U] (*fml* 文) willingness to do what pleases others 讨好; 殷勤. ▷ **com·plais·ant** /-zənt; -zn̩t/ *adj* (*fml* 文) ready to please; obliging 讨好的; 殷勤的: *a complaisant husband* 殷勤的丈夫.

com·ple·ment /ˈkɒmplɪmənt; ˈkɑmpləmənt/ *n* **1 ~ (to sth)** thing that goes well or suitably with sth else, or makes it complete 相配合的事物; 补充物; 补足物: *Rice makes an excellent complement to a curry dish.* 有咖喱的菜配米饭最妙. **2** the complete number or quantity needed or allowed 需要的或允许的数额: *We've taken on our full complement of new trainees for this year.* 我们今年招收的新学员已经满额了. ○ *the ship's complement*, ie all the officers and other sailors 船上的编制名额(全体军官和水兵或高级船员和水手). **3** (*grammar*) word (s), esp adjectives and nouns, used after linking verbs such as *be* and *become*, and describing the subject of the verb 补语(尤指在连系动词如be、become等之后, 用以描述动词之主语的形容词或名词): *In the sentence 'I'm angry', 'angry' is the complement.* 在I'm angry一句中, angry是补语.

▷ **com·ple·ment** /ˈkɒmplɪmənt; ˈkɑmpləˌmɛnt/ *v* [Tn] combine well (and often contrastingly) with (sth) to form a whole 与(某事物)结合(相辅相成): *His business skill complements her flair for design.* 他的经营技巧和她的设计才能相辅相成. Cf 参看 COMPLIMENT.

com·ple·ment·ary /ˌkɒmplɪˈmentrɪ; ˌkɑmpləˈmɛntərɪ/ *adj* **~ (to sth)** combining well to form a balanced whole 紧密结合成相称的整体: *They have complementary personalities*, ie Each has qualities which the other lacks. 他们二人的性格可取长补短(各自有对方缺乏的性格). ○ *His personality is complementary to hers.* 他的个性与她的相反相成. ˌ**complementary ˈangle** either of two angles which together make 90° 余角(两角之和为90°这两个角就互为余角). ˌ**complementary ˈcolour** colour of light which when combined with a given colour makes white light (eg blue with yellow) 互补色(混合后产生白色光的两种色光, 如蓝和黄).

com·plete[1] /kəmˈpliːt; kəmˈplit/ *adj* **1** having all its parts; whole 完整的; 完全的; 全部的; 整个的: *a complete set, collection, etc* 完善的设备、全部收藏等 ○ *a complete edition of Shakespeare's works*, ie one that includes all of them 莎士比亚全集 ○ *a radio complete with a carrying case*, ie having it as an additional feature 带套的手提收音机. **2** [pred 作表语] finished; ended 完成; 结束: *When will the building work be complete?* 建筑工作何时完成? **3** [usu attrib 通常作定语] thorough; in every way; total 彻底的; 全面的; 完全的: *a complete stranger, idiot, nonentity* 素不相识的人、十足的白痴、完全的虚构 ○ *It was a complete surprise to me.* 这对我完全是件意外的事.

▷ **com·pletely** *adv* wholly; totally 完整地; 完全地; 圆满地: *completely innocent, happy, successful* 完全无辜、十分高兴、圆满成功.

com·plete·ness *n* [U].

com·plete[2] /kəmˈpliːt; kəmˈplit/ *v* [Tn] **1** **(a)** make (sth) whole or perfect 使(某事物)圆满、完善: *I only need one volume to complete my set of Dickens's novels.* 我那套狄更斯小说只差一卷就能配齐了. ○ *A few words of praise from her would have completed his happiness.* 她要是能夸他两句, 他也就心满意足了. **(b)** bring (sth) to an end; finish 使(某事物)结束; 完成: *When will the railway be completed?* 铁路何时竣工? **2** fill in (a form, etc) 填(表格等): *Complete your application in ink.* 用钢笔填申请表.

com·ple·tion /kəmˈpliːʃn; kəmˈpliʃən/ *n* [U] **1** **(a)** action of completing 完成(指动作): *Completion of the building work is taking longer than expected.* 建筑工程的竣工比预计的时间要长. **(b)** state of being complete 完成: *The film is nearing completion.* 电影制作即将完成. ○ [attrib 作定语] *its completion date* 完成的日期. **2** (*commerce* 商) formal completing of a contract of sale (销售契约手续的)正式完成: *You may move into the house on completion.* 办完房屋买卖契约手续后, 你就可以搬进去.

com·plex[1] /ˈkɒmpleks; *US* kəmˈpleks; kəmˈplɛks/ *adj* **(a)** made up of (usu several) closely connected parts 由密切联系的部分组成的; 联合的; 复合的: *a complex system, network, etc* 联合的体系、网等 ○ (*grammar*) *a complex sentence*, ie one containing subordinate clauses 主从复合句(含有从句的句子). **(b)** difficult to understand or explain because there are many different parts (因有很多部分)难于理解或解释的; 复杂的: *a complex argument, theory, subject, etc* 复杂的论证、理论、学科等. Cf 参看 COMPLICATED (COMPLICATE).

▷ **com·plex·ity** /kəmˈpleksətɪ; kəmˈplɛksətɪ/ *n* **(a)** [U] state of being complex 复杂性; 错综复杂的状态: *a problem of great complexity* 极复杂的问题. **(b)** [C] complex thing 复杂的事物: *the complexities of higher mathematics* 高等数学的难题.

com·plex[2] /ˈkɒmpleks; ˈkɑmplɛks/ *n* **1** group of connected or similar things 相联或相似的综合事物: *a big industrial complex*, ie a site with factories, etc 大型工业联合体(建有工厂等的场地) ○ *a sports/leisure complex*, ie a set of buildings or facilities for sports/ leisure 运动的[娱乐的]综合场所. **2** **(a)** (*psychology* 心) abnormal mental state resulting from past experience or suppressed desires 情结(由以往的经历或被压抑的欲望引起的精神失常状态): *a persecution complex* 受迫害情结 ○ *an inferiority complex* 自卑情结. **(b)** (*infml* 口) obsessive concern or fear 无法摆脱的忧虑或恐惧: *He has a complex about his weight/has a* *weight complex.* 他对自己的体重提心吊胆.

com·plex·ion /kəmˈplekʃn; kəmˋplɛkʃən/ *n* **1** natural colour and appearance of the skin of the face (天生的)面色, 脸色, 面貌: *a good, dark, fair, sallow, etc complexion* 脸色好、黑、白、黄等. **2** (usu *sing* 通常作单数) general character or aspect of sth 某事物总的特性或方面: *Her resignation puts a different complexion on things*, ie changes one's view of the affair. 她一辞职则情随事迁(使人改变了对事务的看法). ○ *a victory that changed the complexion of the war*, ie made the probable result different, gave hope of an early end, etc 扭转战局的胜利.

com·pli·ance /kəmˈplaɪəns; kəmˋplaɪəns/ *n* [U] ~ **(with sth)** **1** action in accordance with a request or command; obedience 服从; 听从; 遵从; 顺从: *Compliance (with the rules) is expected of all members.* 要求全体人员都遵守(制度). ○ *In compliance with your wishes* (ie As you have requested) *we have withdrawn our suggestion.* 遵照你的要求我们已将建议撤销. **2** (*usu derog* 通常作贬义) tendency to agree (too readily) to do what others want 百依百顺; 承颜候色. Cf 参看 COMPLY.

com·pli·ant /kəmˈplaɪənt; kəmˋplaɪənt/ *adj* ~ **(with sb/sth)** (*usu derog* 通常作贬义) (too) willing to comply (with other people, with rules, etc) (对于他人、规章等)(过于)顺从的, 百依百顺的, 惟命是听的: *The Government, compliant as ever, gave in to their demands.* 政府同往常一样唯唯诺诺, 对他们的要求作出让步.

com·plic·ate /ˈkɒmplɪkeɪt; ˋkɑmpləˏket/ *v* [Tn] make (sth) more difficult to do, understand or deal with 使(某事)复杂化: *Her refusal to help complicates matters.* 她不肯帮忙, 事情就更难办了.

▷ **com·plic·at·ed** *adj* **(a)** (*often derog* 常作贬义) made up of many interconnected parts 结构复杂的: *complicated wiring, machinery* 复杂的线路、机器 ○ *a complicated diagram* 复杂的图表. **(b)** difficult to understand or explain because there are many different parts (因复杂)难于理解或解释的: *a complicated situation, process, relationship, plot* 复杂的情况、过程、关系、情节 ○ *He's married to her, and she's in love with his brother-in-law, and...oh, it's too complicated to explain!* 他已经跟她结了婚, 可她又爱上他姐夫, 而且...哎, 太乱了, 说不清! Cf 参看 COMPLEX[1].

com·plica·tion /ˌkɒmplɪˈkeɪʃn; ˏkɑmpləˋkeʃən/ *n* **1** [U] state of being complex, intricate or difficult; involved condition 复杂、错综或困难的状态; 复杂的情况: *I have enough complication in my life without having to look after your sick pets!* 即使不给你照看那些生病的小宠物, 我生活里的麻烦事就已经够多了! **2** [C] thing that makes a situation more complex or difficult 使情况更加复杂或困难的事物: *A further complication was Fred's refusal to travel by air.* 更麻烦的是弗雷德不肯坐飞机. **3 complications** [pl] (*medical* 医) new illness, or new development of an illness, that makes treatment more difficult 并发症: *Complications set in, and the patient died.* 病人因出现并发症而死亡.

com·pli·city /kəmˈplɪsətɪ; kəmˋplɪsətɪ/ *n* [U] ~ **(in sth)** action of taking part with another person (in a crime or some other wrongdoing); shared responsibility 合谋; 串通: *He was suspected of complicity in her murder.* 他涉嫌合谋将她杀害.

com·pli·ment /ˈkɒmplɪmənt; ˋkɑmpləmənt/ *n* **1** [C] ~ **(on sth)** expression of praise, admiration, approval, etc 赞美、敬佩、赞成等的表示: *One likes to hear compliments on one's appearance.* 人人都爱听夸奖自己容貌的话. ○ *She paid me a very charming compliment on my paintings*, ie praised them. 她极为赞赏我的画. ○ (*fig* 比喻) *These beautiful flowers are a compliment to the gardener's skill*, ie show how skilful he is. 这些艳丽的花朵就是对园丁技艺的赞美. **2 compliments** [pl] (*fml* 文) greetings, usu as part of a message 致意, 问候, 祝贺(通常作为传达音讯的一部分): *My compliments to your wife*, ie Please give her a greeting from me. 向您的夫人致意(请转达我的问候). ○ *Compliments of the season*, eg said at Christmas or the New Year. 谨致节日的祝贺(如在圣诞节或新年时说的). ○ *The flowers are with the compliments of* (ie are a gift from) *the management.* 这鲜花是主管部门送的礼物. **3** (idm 习语) **a left-handed compliment** ⇨ LEFT-HANDED (LEFT[2]).

▷ **com·pli·ment** /ˈkɒmplɪment; ˋkɑmpləˏmɛnt/ *v* [Tn, Tn·pr] ~ **sb (on sth)** express praise or admiration of sb (对某人)表示赞美或敬佩: *I complimented her on her skilful performance.* 我钦佩她娴熟的技艺. Cf 参看 COMPLEMENT.

□ **ˈcompliment slip** small piece of paper, usu with the words 'with compliments' on it, sent with a free sample, gift, etc (附在样品、礼品上, 通常写有'敬赠'字样的)赠礼便条.

com·pli·ment·ary /ˌkɒmplɪˈmentrɪ; ˏkɑmpləˋmɛntərɪ/ *adj* **1** expressing admiration, praise, etc 表示崇敬、赞美、称赞、赞许等的: *a complimentary remark, review, pat on the back* 赞美的言辞、褒扬的评论、在背上拍一下的赞许表示 ○ *She was highly complimentary about my paintings.* 她对我的画给予了高度评价. **2** given free of charge by the producer or owner (生产者或所有者给的)赠品: *a complimentary seat, ticket, copy of a book* 优待席、赠券、赠书.

com·pline /ˈkɒmplɪn; ˋkɑmplɪn/ *n* [U] (in the Roman Catholic and High Anglican church) last service of the day (天主教和英国圣公会的)晚祷: *attend compline* 参加晚祷.

com·ply /kəmˈplaɪ; kəmˋplaɪ/ *v* (*pt, pp* **complied**) [I, Ipr] ~ **(with sth)** do as one is requested, commanded, etc; obey 按要求、命令去做; 依从; 顺从; 听从; 服从: *She was told to pay the fine, but refused to comply.* 通知她交纳罚款, 但她拒不服从. ○ *The rules must be complied with*, ie obeyed. 这些规章制度必须遵守. Cf 参看 COMPLIANCE.

com·pon·ent /kəmˈpəʊnənt; kəmˋponənt/ *n* any of the parts of which sth is made (某事物的)组成部分; 成分; 零部件: *the components of an engine, a camera, etc* 发动机、照相机等的部件 ○ *a factory supplying components for the car industry* 为汽车制造业提供零部件的工厂 ○ (*fig* 比喻) *Surprise is an essential component of my plan.* 我这项计划主要就是想使人惊喜一下.

▷ **com·pon·ent** *adj* [attrib 作定语] being one of the parts of a whole (整体中的)一部分的; 组成的: *analysing the component parts of a sentence* 分析句子的成分.

com·port /kəmˈpɔːt; kəmˋpɔrt/ *v* [Tn·pr] ~ **oneself with sth** (*fml* 文) conduct oneself in the specified way; behave (行为)表现: *comport oneself with dignity/in a dignified manner* 举止庄重.

▷ **com·port·ment** *n* [U] (*fml* 文) behaviour 举止; 行为; 表现.

com·pose /kəmˈpəʊz; kəmˋpoz/ *v* **1 (a)** [I, Tn] write (music, opera, etc) 写, 创作(乐曲、歌剧等): *She began to compose (songs) at an early age.* 她年轻时就已开始创作(歌曲). **(b)** [Tn] (*fml* 文) write (a poem, speech, etc) 写(诗、讲稿等): *I'm composing a formal reply to the letter.* 我正写一封郑重其事的回信. **2** [Tn no passive 不用于被动语态] (not in the continuous tenses 不用于进行时态) (*fml* 文) (of parts or elements of sth) form (a whole); constitute (指某事物的部分或成分)构成(整体); 组成: *the short scenes that compose the play* 组成该剧的各场. ⇨Usage at COMPRISE 用法见 COMPRISE. **3** [Tn no passive 不用于被动语态] bring (oneself/sth) under control; calm 使(自己[某事物])安定, 平静, 镇静, 冷静: *His mind was in such a whirl that he could hardly compose his thoughts.* 他心乱如麻难以镇定下来. ○ *Please compose yourself; there's no need to get excited!* 请镇静, 不必激动! Cf 参看 COMPOSURE. **4** [Tn] put (printing type) in order, to form words, paragraphs, pages, etc 将(铅字)排成词、段、页等. Cf 参看 COMPOSITOR.

▷ **com·posed** *adj* **1** [pred 作表语] ~ **of sth** made up or formed from sth (由某事物)组成或构成: *Water is composed of hydrogen and oxygen.* 水是由氢和氧化合而成的. ○ *The committee was composed mainly of teachers and parents.* 委员会主要由教师和学生家长组成. ⇨ Usage at COMPRISE 用法见 COMPRISE. **2** with one's feelings under control; calm 控制住感情的; 克制的; 镇静的; 平静的: *a composed person, manner, look* 镇静的人、态度、表情. **com·posedly** /kəmˈpəʊzɪdlɪ; kəmˋpozɪdlɪ/ *adv*: *She talked composedly to reporters about her terrible ordeal.* 她沉着地向记者谈了自己可怕的经历.

com·poser /kəmˈpəʊzə(r); kəmˋpozɚ/ *n* person who

composes (esp music) 创作者(尤指乐曲的).

com·pos·ite /ˈkɒmpəzɪt; kɑmˈpɑzɪt/ *n, adj* [attrib 作定语] (thing) made up of different parts or materials (由不同的成分或材料)组成的(事物); 混合的; 合成的; 混合物: *The play is a composite of reality and fiction.* 这出戏是现实与虚构的混合物. ○ *a composite substance* 混合物 ○ *a composite illustration,* ie one made by putting together two or more separate pictures 拼图.

com·posi·tion /ˌkɒmpəˈzɪʃn; ˌkɑmpəˈzɪʃən/ *n* **1** [C] thing composed, eg a piece of music, a poem or a book 作品(如乐曲、诗或书): *'Swan Lake' is one of Tchaikovsky's best-known compositions.*《天鹅湖》是柴可夫斯基最著名的作品之一. **2** [U] (**a**) action of composing sth, eg a piece of music or writing, type for printing, etc 创作: *He played a piano sonata of his own composition*, ie that he himself had composed. 他演奏了一首自己创作的钢琴奏鸣曲. (**b**) art of composing music 作曲艺术: *studying composition at music school* 在音乐学校学习作曲艺术. **3** [C] short piece of non-fictional writing done as a school or college exercise; essay 作文; 散文. **4** [U] the parts of which sth is made; make-up 成分; 组成部分: *the composition of the soil* 土壤的成分 ○ (*fig* 比喻) *He has a touch of madness in his composition*, ie He is a little mad. 他有点疯疯癫癫的. **5** [U] arrangement of elements in a painting, photograph, etc (绘画、摄影等的)构图: *Her drawing is competent, but her composition is poor.* 她的画有功力, 但布局欠佳. **6** [C, U] substance, esp an artificial one, composed of more than one material (尤指人工)合成的物质: *a composition used as flooring material* 合成的地板材料 ○ [attrib 作定语] *a composition floor* 合成地板.

com·pos·itor /kəmˈpɒzɪtə(r); kəmˈpɑzɪtɚ/ *n* skilled person who composes (COMPOSE 4) type for printing 排字工人.

com·pos men·tis /ˌkɒmpəs ˈmentɪs; ˈkɑmpəsˈmɛntɪs/ (also **compos**) *adj* [pred 作表语] (*Latin infml or joc* 拉, 口或谑) having control of one's mind; sane 能控制住神志; 心智健全: *He's not quite compos mentis*, ie He's a little mad. 他有点儿疯.

com·post /ˈkɒmpɒst; ˈkɑmpost/ *n* [U, C] mixture of decayed organic matter, manure, etc added to soil to improve the growth of plants 混合肥料; 堆肥.

▷ **com·post** *v* [Tn] (**a**) make (sth) into compost 将(某物)制成堆肥: *composting the kitchen waste* 用厨房里的垃圾制堆肥. (**b**) put compost on or in (sth) 给(某物)施堆肥: *compost the flower-beds* 给花坛施堆肥.

com·pos·ure /kəmˈpəʊʒə(r); kəmˈpoʒɚ/ *n* [U] state of being calm in mind or behaviour 心情、举止平静的状态; 镇静; 沉着: *keep/lose/regain one's composure* 保持[不再/恢复]平静 ○ *He showed great composure in a difficult situation.* 他在困难环境中表现得极沉着. Cf 参看 COMPOSE 3.

com·pound[1] /ˈkɒmpaʊnd; ˈkɑmpaʊnd/ *n* **1** (**a**) thing made up of two or more separate things combined together 复合物. (**b**) substance consisting of two or more elements chemically combined 化合物: *Common salt is a compound of sodium and chlorine.* 食盐是钠和氯的化合物. Cf 参看 ELEMENT 3, MIXTURE 3. **2** (*grammar*) noun, adjective, etc composed of two or more words or parts of words (written as one or more words, or joined by a hyphen) 复合词: *'Bus conductor', 'dark-haired' and 'policeman' are compounds.* bus conductor、dark-haired、policeman 都是复合词. ▷ **com·pound** *adj* [attrib 作定语]: *an insect's compound eye* 昆虫的复眼 ○ *compound nouns, adjectives, etc* 复合名词、复合形容词.

□ ˌ**compound ˈfracture** breaking of a bone in which part of the bone comes through the skin 有创骨折.

ˌ**compound ˈinterest** interest paid on both the original capital and the interest added to it 复利. Cf 参看 SIMPLE INTEREST (SIMPLE).

ˌ**compound ˈsentence** (*grammar*) sentence containing two or more co-ordinate clauses (linked by *and*, *but*, etc) 并列复合句.

com·pound[2] /kəmˈpaʊnd; kəmˈpaʊnd/ *v* **1** (**a**) [Tn] mix (sth) together 将(某物)混合, 搀合: *the vat in which the chemicals are compounded* 混合化学药品用的大桶. (**b**) [usu passive 通常用于被动语态: Tn, Tn·pr] **~ sth (of/from sth)** make sth by mixing (用混合方法)制造(某物): *a medicine compounded of* (ie made of) *herbs* 用草药混合制成的药 ○ (*fig* 比喻) *Her character was compounded in equal parts of meanness and generosity.* 她的为人慷慨吝啬参半. **2** [Tn] make (sth bad) worse by causing further harm (因进一步伤害)使(坏事)更坏: *Initial planning errors were compounded by carelessness in carrying the plan out.* 计划原来就有错误, 再加上执行中的粗心大意就更糟了. **3** [I, Ipr, Tn] **~ (with sb) (for sth)** (*commerce* 商) reach an agreement (about sth); settle (a debt, etc) (就某事)达成协议; 和解妥协; 了结(债务等): *He compounded with his creditors for a postponement of payment.* 他与债权人达成协议延期付款. **4** [Tn] (*law* 律) agree not to reveal (a crime), thus seeming not to disapprove of it 同意不揭发(罪行)(似并不反对该行为); 私了: *guilty of compounding a felony* 对重罪案件私了罪.

com·pound[3] /ˈkɒmpaʊnd; ˈkɑmpaʊnd/ *n* (**a**) area enclosed by buildings, esp in a military camp or a prison camp 有建筑物围绕的场地(尤指军营、监狱中的). (**b**) (in India, China, etc) area enclosed by a fence, etc, in which a house or factory stands (在印度、中国等)用围墙等圈起来的场地(内有房屋或工厂); 院子.

com·pre·hend /ˌkɒmprɪˈhend; ˌkɑmprɪˈhɛnd/ *v* **1** [Tn, Tf, Tw] understand (sth) fully 全面理解、了解、领会(某事物): *failing to comprehend the full seriousness of the situation* 未能充分理解形势的严重性 ○ *I cannot comprehend how you could have been so stupid.* 我真不明白你怎么那么蠢. **2** [Tn] (*fml* 文) include (sth) 包含、包括(某事物).

com·pre·hens·ible /ˌkɒmprɪˈhensəbl; ˌkɑmprɪˈhɛnsəbl/ *adj* **~ (to sb)** that can be understood fully 能充分理解的: *a book that is comprehensible only to specialists* 只有专家才看得懂的书.

▷ **com·pre·hens·ib·il·ity** /ˌkɒmprɪˌhensəˈbɪlətɪ; ˌkɑmprɪˌhɛnsəˈbɪlətɪ/ *n* [U].

com·pre·hen·sion /ˌkɒmprɪˈhenʃn; ˌkɑmprɪˈhɛnʃən/ *n* **1** [U] (power of) understanding 理解(力): *a problem above/beyond sb's comprehension*, ie one that he cannot understand 某人不能理解的问题. **2** [U, C] exercise aimed at improving or testing one's understanding of a language (written or spoken) 理解力练习(旨在提高或测验某人书面语或口语的理解能力): *a French comprehension* 法语理解力练习 ○ [attrib 作定语] *a compreˈhension test* 理解力测试.

com·pre·hens·ive /ˌkɒmprɪˈhensɪv; ˌkɑmprɪˈhɛnsɪv/ *adj* **1** that includes (nearly) everything (几乎)包罗万象的; 全面的: *a comprehensive description, account, report, etc* 全面的描述、叙述、报道等 ○ *She has a comprehensive grasp of the subject.* 她已全面掌握了这一学科. **2** (*Brit*) (of education) for pupils of all abilities in the same school (指教育)(具有不同能力的学生)同在一校的, 综合的.

▷ **com·pre·hens·ive** *n* (*Brit infml* 口) comprehensive school 综合学校.

com·pre·hens·ively *adv*: *Our football team was comprehensively* (ie thoroughly) *defeated.* 我们的足球队一败如水.

com·pre·hens·ive·ness *n* [U].

□ ˌ**comprehensive inˈsurance** insurance on motor vehicles that covers most risks, including fire, theft, damage and risks to the driver and others 综合保险(机动车辆的多种保险, 包括火险、盗窃险、毁坏险和司机及第三者事故保险等).

compreˈhensive school (*Brit*) large secondary school at which children of all abilities are taught 综合中学(招收具有不同能力的学生的大型中学).

com·press[1] /kəmˈpres; kəmˈprɛs/ *v* [Tn, Tn·pr] **~ sth (into sth) 1** press sth together; force sth into a small(er) space 压紧; 将某物压进(较)小的空间; 挤压; 压缩: *compressed air*, ie at higher than atmospheric pressure 压缩空气 ○ *compressing straw into blocks for burning* 将干草压成块供燃烧. **2** express (ideas, etc) in a shorter form; condense 使(意见等)简短, 精简, 浓缩: *compress an argument into just a few sentences* 将论点概括成几句话 ○ *The film compresses several years into half an hour.* 这电影将几年的事压缩于半小时内.

▷ **com·pres·sion** /kəmˈpreʃn; kəmˈprɛʃən/ *n* [U] **1** compressing or being compressed 压缩: *the compression* *of gas* 气体的压缩. **2** process of reducing the volume of the fuel mixture of an internal combustion engine, to increase its pressure before it is ignited (内燃机的)压缩冲程.

com·press·or /kəm'presə(r); kəm'prɛsɚ/ *n* (part of a) machine that compresses air or other gases 压缩机; 压气机.

com·press² /'kɒmpres; 'kɑmprɛs/ *n* pad or cloth pressed on to a part of the body to stop bleeding, reduce fever, etc (用以止血、退烧等的)敷布, 压布: *a cold/hot compress* 冷[热]敷布.

com·prise /kəm'praɪz; kəm'praɪz/ *v* [Tn] (not in the continuous tenses 不用于进行时态) (**a**) have as parts or members; be made up of 包括; 包含; 构成; 组成: *a committee comprising people of widely differing views* 由观点极不相同的成员组成的委员会. (**b**) be the parts or members of (sth); together form 为(某事物)的部分或成员; 组成; 包括: *Two small boys and a dog comprised the street entertainer's only audience.* 两个小男孩和一条狗成了街头艺人仅有的观众.

NOTE ON USAGE 用法: Note the use of **comprise.** 注意**comprise**一词的用法. It can mean **1 consist of** or **be composed of** ie be formed of 这个词可意为**1 consist of**或**be composed of**, 即由…形成、组成或构成: *The British Parliament comprises/consists of/is composed of the House of Commons and the House of Lords.* 英国国会是由下议院和上议院组成的. **2 compose** or **constitute,** ie form 亦可意为 **2 compose**或**constitute**, 即形成、组成或构成: *The House of Commons and the House of Lords comprise/compose/constitute the British Parliament.* 下议院和上议院组成了英国国会. This use of **comprise** is less common and careful speakers avoid **be comprised of** in sense 1. ☆ **comprise**一词的这一用法并不多见, 用词考究的人避免用**be comprised of**于上述第1义.

com·prom·ise /'kɒmprəmaɪz; 'kɑmprə,maɪz/ *n* (**a**) [U] giving up of certain demands by each side in a dispute, so that an agreement may be reached which satisfies both to some extent 妥协; 和解; 谅解; 折衷: *Most wage claims are settled by compromise.* 对提高工资的要求大多都能折衷解决. ○ [attrib 作定语] *work out a compromise agreement* 制定出折衷协议. (**b**) [C] **~ (between/on sth)** settlement reached in this way (以上述方法取得的)和解: *Can the two sides reach a compromise?* 双方能互让和解吗? ○ *The final proposals were a rather unsuccessful compromise between the need for profitability and the demands of local conservationists.* 最终的方案是受益者和地区自然资源保护者之间颇为勉强的相互妥协.

▷ **com·prom·ise** *v* **1** [I, Ipr] **~ (on sth)** settle a dispute, etc by making a compromise 以折衷方法解决争论、争端、分歧: *I wanted to go to Greece, and my wife wanted to go to Spain, so we compromised on* (ie agreed to go to) *Italy.* 我想去希腊, 可我妻子想去西班牙, 于是我们折衷了一下, 去意大利. **2** [Tn] bring (sth/sb/oneself) into danger or under suspicion by foolish behaviour (因行为愚蠢)使(某事物[某人/自己])陷入危险境地或受到怀疑: *He has irretrievably compromised himself by accepting money from them.* 他因收了他们的钱铸成大错害了自己. ○ *He was photographed in compromising situations* (ie ones that showed him behaving immorally) *with a call-girl.* 他和应召女郎在有伤风化的情况下让人拍了照片. **3** [Tn] modify (sth); weaken 修改, 更改(某事物); 减轻; 减弱; 缓和: *She refused to compromise her principles,* ie insisted on keeping to them. 她的原则寸步不让.

com·pul·sion /kəm'pʌlʃn; kəm'pʌlʃən/ *n* **~ (to do sth)** **1** [U] compelling or being compelled 强迫; 强制; 被迫: *I refuse to act under compulsion,* ie because I am forced to. 我决不能让人逼着做事. ○ *You need feel under no compulsion to accept,* ie do not have to accept. 你不必勉强接受. **2** [C] urge (esp to behave in an irrational way) that one cannot resist (不能克制的)欲望, 冲动, 要求(尤指不合情理的行为): *a compulsion to destroy things* 毁物欲.

com·puls·ive /kəm'pʌlsɪv; kəm'pʌlsɪv/ *adj* **1** extremely interesting; fascinating 极有趣的; 令人着迷的: *a compulsive novel about politics* 有关政治的有趣的小说. **2** (**a**) caused by an obsession 因着迷而引起的; 强迫性的; 强制性的; 上瘾的: *compulsive gambling, eating, etc* 上瘾的赌博、强迫性进食等. (**b**) (of people) forced to do sth by an obsession (指人)因着迷而被迫做的, 强迫性的: *a compulsive eater, TV viewer, gambler* 对食物、电视、赌博着迷的人 ○ *He's a compulsive liar,* ie He lies repeatedly. 他说谎成性. ▷ **com·puls·ively** *adv*: *a compulsively readable book* 引人入胜、非读不可的书.

com·puls·ory /kəm'pʌlsərɪ; kəm'pʌlsərɪ/ *adj* that must be done; required by the rules, etc; obligatory 必须做的; 按规定要做的; 有责任的; 有义务的: *Is military service compulsory in your country?* 你们国家实行义务兵役制吗? ○ *Is English a compulsory subject?* 英语是必修科目吗? ▷ **com·puls·or·ily** /kəm'pʌlsərəlɪ; kəm'pʌlsərəlɪ/ *adv*.

com·punc·tion /kəm'pʌŋkʃn; kəm'pʌŋkʃən/ *n* [U] **~ (about doing sth)** (*fml* 文) (usu in negative sentences 通常用于否定句) feeling of guilt or regret for one's action 内疚; 后悔; 懊悔: *She kept us waiting without the slightest compunction.* 她一直让我们等着却毫无歉意. ○ *If I could find the people responsible, I would have no compunction about telling the police.* 我要知道是谁干的就去报警而毫不后悔.

com·pu·ta·tion /,kɒmpju:'teɪʃn; ,kɑmpjə'teʃən/ *n* (**a**) [C, U] (*fml* 文) (act of) computing; calculation 计算; 估计: *A quick computation revealed that we would not make a profit.* 粗略计算后可以看出我们无利可图. ○ *Addition and division are forms of computation.* 加法和除法都是计算方法. ○ *It will cost £5 000 at the lowest computation.* 估计最少也值5 000英镑. (**b**) [U] use of a computer for calculation 计算机的使用.

▷ **com·pu·ta·tional** *adj* [usu attrib 通常作定语] using computers 使用计算机的: *computational linguistics* 计算机语言学.

com·pute /kəm'pju:t; kəm'pjut/ *v* [Tn, Tn·pr] **~ sth (at sth)** **1** calculate sth with a computer 用计算机计算: *Scientists have computed the probable course of the rocket.* 科学家用计算机计算了火箭可能运行的轨道. **2** (*fml* 文) calculate sth; work sth out 估计某事物; 将某事物算出: *He computed his losses at £5 000.* 他估计自己损失5 000英镑.

▷ **com·put·ing** *n* [U] operation of computers 计算机的运算: [attrib 作定语] *a computing course* 计算机运算课程.

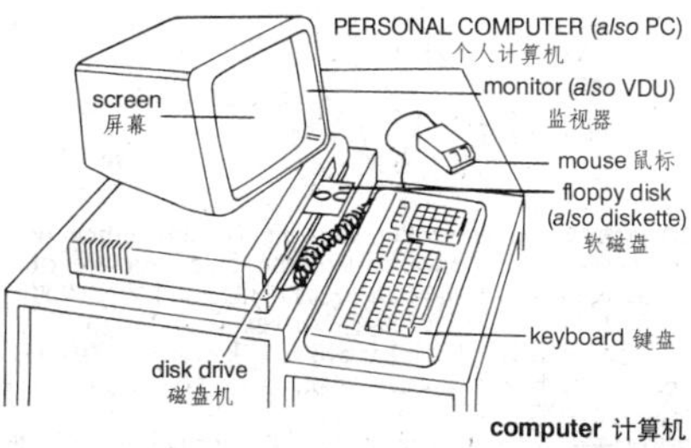

computer 计算机

com·puter /kəm'pju:tə(r); kəm'pjutɚ/ *n* electronic device for storing and analysing information fed into it, making calculations, or controlling machinery automatically 计算机; 电脑: *Is the information available on the computer?* 计算机中有这个资料吗? ○ *The accounts are processed by computer.* 这帐目是用计算机处理的. ○ *a digital computer* 数字计算机 ○ [attrib 作定语] *a computer programmer* 计算机程序设计员 ⇨illus 见插图.

▷ **com·pu·ter·ize, -ise** /-təraɪz; -tə,raɪz/ *v* [Tn] (**a**) provide a computer to do the work of or for (sth) 用计算机做(某事); 使计算机化: *The accounts section has been completely computerized.* 会计科已完全计算机化了. (**b**) store (information) in a computer 将(资料)存入计算机: *The firm has computerized its records.* 公司已将纪录存入计算机. **com·pu·ter·iza·tion, -isation** /kəm,pju:təraɪ'zeɪʃn; *US* -rɪ'z-; kəm,pjutərə'zeʃən/ *n* [U].

com·rade /ˈkɒmreɪd; *US* -ræd; ˋkɑmræd/ *n* **1** fellow member of a trade-union, or of a socialist or communist political party, etc (工会或社会主义、共产主义政党等的)会员，党员，同志: *We must fight for our rights, comrades!* 同志们，我们必须为自己的权利而斗争! **2** (*dated* 旧) trusted companion who shares one's activities (共同参与活动的)忠实伙伴: *We were comrades in the war.* 我们从前是战友. ○ [attrib 作定语] *an old comrades association*, ie of people who had been in the army, etc together 老兵协会. ▷ **com·radely** /ˈkɒmreɪdlɪ; ˋkɑmrædlɪ/ *adj*: *some comradely advice* 同志般的劝告. **com·rade·ship** /ˈkɒmreɪdʃɪp; ˋkɑmræd,ʃɪp/ *n* [U].

□ ˌ**comrade-in-ˈarms** *n* (*pl* ˌ**comrades-in-ˈarms**) fellow soldier 战友: (*fig* 比喻) *They'd long been comrades-in-arms in the Labour Party.* 他们长期以来在工党中就是战友.

con[1] /kɒn; kɑn/ *n* [sing] (*sl* 俚) instance of cheating sb; confidence trick 欺骗; 骗局: *This so-called bargain is just a con!* 这种所谓的大减价不过是个骗局! ○ [attrib 作定语] *a con trick* 欺骗的手段 ○ *He's a real con artist/merchant*, ie swindler. 他是个不折不扣的假艺术家[商人](骗子).

▷ **con** *v* (**-nn-**) [Tn, Tn·pr] **~ sb (into doing sth/out of sth)** (*infml* 口) swindle or persuade sb after gaining his trust 诈骗; 哄骗: *You can't con me — you're not really ill!* 你骗不了我 —— 你根本就没病! ○ *I was conned into buying a useless car.* 我受人骗买了辆不能用的汽车. ○ *She conned me out of £100.* 她骗走我100英镑.

□ **con man** /ˈkɒn mæn; ˋkɑn ,mæn/ (*pl* **con men** /ˈkɒn men; ˋkɑn mɛn/) (*infml* 口) *person who swindles others* into giving him money, etc 骗取他人钱财等的人; 骗子.

con[2] /kɒn; kɑn/ *n* (*sl* 俚) = CONVICT *n*.

con[3] /kɒn; kɑn/ *n* (idm 习语) **the pros and cons** ⇨ PRO[1].

con·cat·ena·tion /kənˌkætɪˈneɪʃn; kən,kætṇˋeʃən/ *n* **~ (of sth)** (*fml* 文) series of things or events linked together 一系列互相关联的事物: *an unfortunate concatenation of mishaps* 接连的不幸.

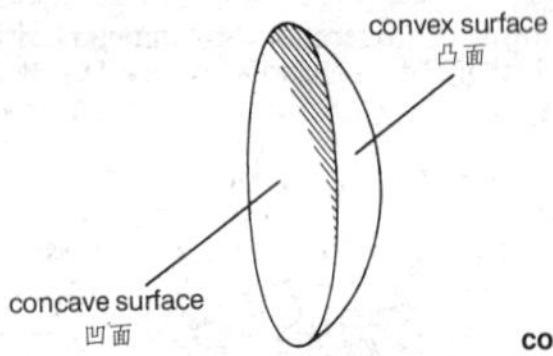

concave 凹的

con·cave /ˈkɒŋkeɪv; kɑnˋkev/ *adj* (of an outline or a surface) curved inwards like the inner surface of a sphere or ball (指轮廓或表面)凹的(如球体或球的内部). ⇨illus 见插图. Cf 参看 CONVEX.

▷ **con·cav·ity** /ˌkɒnˈkævətɪ; kɑnˋkævətɪ/ *n* (**a**) [U] quality of being concave 凹状; 凹形. (**b**) [C] concave surface 凹面.

con·ceal /kənˈsiːl; kənˋsil/ *v* [Tn, Tn·pr] **~ sth/sb (from sb/sth)** keep sth/sb from being seen or known about; hide sth/sb 隐藏、掩盖或隐瞒某事物[某人]: *a tape recorder concealed in a drawer* 藏在抽屉里的录音机 ○ *He tried to conceal his heavy drinking from his family.* 他极力对家人隐瞒自己酗酒的事. ○ *There's a concealed entrance just round the corner.* 拐角处有个隐蔽入口. ○ *He spoke with ill-concealed contempt for his audience.* 他讲话时流露出对听众的蔑视.

▷ **con·ceal·ment** *n* [U] acton of concealing or state of being concealed 隐藏; 掩盖; 隐瞒: *Stay in concealment until the danger has passed.* 藏着别动，等危险过后再出来.

con·cede /kənˈsiːd; kənˋsid/ *v* **1** [Tn, Tf, Dn·n, Dn·pr] **~ sth (to sb)** admit that sth is true, valid, proper, etc 承认某事属实、有效、合理等: *concede a point (to sb) in an argument* 在辩论中承认(某人的)某一点正确 ○ *concede defeat*, ie admit that one has lost 承认失败 ○ *I was forced to concede that she might be right.* 我不得不承认可能是她对. ○ *It's certainly big, I'll concede you that.* 那确实很大，在这一点上我向你认输. **2** [Tn, Dn·pr] **~ sth (to sb)** give sth away; allow (sb else) to have sth 将(某物)让出; 允许(他人)得到(某物): *We cannot concede any of our territory*, ie allow another country to have it. 我们寸土不让(不让他国得到). ○ *England conceded a goal (to their opponents) in the first minute.* 英格兰队在第一分钟就输(给对方)一分. **3** [I, Tn] admit that one has lost (a game, an election, etc) 承认自己输掉(一局、一次竞选等): *The chess-player conceded (the game) when he saw that his position was hopeless.* 棋手一看出自己陷入绝境，就承认(那局)输了. Cf 参看 CONCESSION 1.

con·ceit /kənˈsiːt; kənˋsit/ *n* **1** [U] excessive pride in oneself or in one's powers, abilities, etc 骄傲; 自负; 自高自大: *The conceit of the man — comparing his own work with Picasso's!* 这个自高自大的人 —— 竟把自己的作品跟毕加索的相比! **2** [C] (*fml* 文) cleverly-phrased witty expression (esp in a work of literature) 俏皮诙谐的词语(尤指于文学作品中); 字字珠玑.

▷ **con·ceited** *adj* full of conceit 极其自负的: *insufferably conceited* 难以容忍地自负. **con·ceit·edly** /-ɪdlɪ; -ɪdlɪ/ *adv*.

con·ceive /kənˈsiːv; kənˋsiv/ *v* **1** [I, Tn] become pregnant (with a child) 怀孕; 受孕: *She was told she couldn't conceive.* 她得知自己不能怀孕. ○ *The child was conceived on the night of their wedding.* 那孩子是在他们新婚之夜怀上的. **2** [Ipr, Tn, Tf, Tw, Cn·n/a] **~ of sth; ~ sth (as sth)** form (an idea, a plan, etc) in the mind; imagine sth 想出(主意、计划等); 构思; 想像某事物: *It was then that I conceived the notion of running away.* 就在那时我产生了逃跑的念头. ○ *I cannot conceive* (ie do not believe) *that he would wish to harm us.* 我不能想像(不相信)他会伤害我们. ○ *I cannot conceive why you allowed the child to go alone*, ie I think you were very foolish to allow it. 我真想不通你为什么让孩子一个人走(我认为你这样做很蠢). ○ *The ancients conceived (of) the world as (being) flat*, ie They thought it was flat. 古人认为地球是扁的.

▷ **con·ceiv·able** /-əbl; -əbḷ/ *adj* that can be conceived or believed; imaginable 可想到的; 可相信的; 可想像的: *It is hardly conceivable (to me) that she should do such a thing.* (我)简直难以想像她会干这种事. ○ *We tried it in every conceivable combination.* 我们把能想到的各种组合都试了一遍. **con·ceiv·ably** /-əblɪ; -əblɪ/ *adv*: *He couldn't conceivably have* (ie I don't believe he could have) *meant what he said.* 他的话想来不会是他的原意.

con·cen·trate /ˈkɒnsntreɪt; ˋkɑnsṇ,tret/ *v* **1** (**a**) [I, Ipr, Tn, Tn·pr] **~ (sth) (on sth/doing sth)** focus (one's attention, effort, etc) exclusively and intensely on sth, not thinking about other less important things 全神贯注，精神集中，专心致志(于某事物): *I can't concentrate (on my studies) with all that noise going on.* 吵闹声不绝于耳，我精神无法集中(于学习). ○ *We must concentrate our efforts on improving education.* 我们必须致力于改进教育工作. (**b**) [Ipr] **~ on sth** do one particular thing and no other 做某件事(而不做其他事): *Having failed my French exams, I decided to concentrate on science subjects.* 我因法语考试不及格而决心专攻理科. ○ *This firm concentrates on the European market.* 这公司把工作重点集中在欧洲市场. **2** [Ipr, Tn·pr] come or bring together at one place 集合; 集中: *Birds concentrate (in places) where food is abundant.* 鸟聚集在食物丰盛的地方. ○ *Troops are concentrating south of the river.* 军队正向河的南边集结. ○ *The Government's plan is to concentrate new industries in areas of high unemployment.* 政府的计划是将新的工业集中于高失业区. **3** [Tn] increase the strength of (a solution) by reducing its volume (eg by boiling it) 浓缩. **4** (idm 习语) ˌ**concentrate the/one's ˈmind** make sb consider sth urgently and seriously 使某人急切地、认真地考虑某事: *The threat of going bankrupt is very unpleasant but it certainly concentrates the mind.* 即将破产的威胁虽令人极烦恼，但确也能逼迫人开动脑筋.

▷ **con·cen·trate** *n* [C, U] substance or solution made by concentrating (CONCENTRATE 3) 经浓缩而制成的物质或溶液浓缩物; 浓缩液: *an orange concentrate which you dilute with water* 兑水饮用的浓缩橙汁.

con·cen·trated *adj* **1** intense 极度的; 紧张的; 加强的;

强烈的: *concentrated study, hate, effort* 紧张的学习、强烈的仇恨、专心致志的努力 ○ *concentrated fire*, ie the firing of guns all aimed at one point 集中的火力. **2** increased in strength or value by the evaporation of liquid 浓缩的: *a concentrated solution* 浓缩的溶液 ○ *concentrated food* 浓缩食品.

con·cen·tra·tion /ˌkɒnsnˈtreɪʃn; ˌkɑnsn̩ˈtreʃən/ *n* **1** [U] **~ (on sth)** (power of) concentrating (on sth) 集中(于某事物)(之力): *Stress and tiredness often result in a lack of concentration.* 紧张和疲劳常使人精神不集中. ○ *a book that requires great concentration* 需全神贯注才能看懂的书 ○ *I found it hard to keep my concentration with such a noise going on.* 吵闹声不绝于耳, 我很难保持精神集中. **2** [C] **~ (of sth)** grouping of people or things 人或事物的聚集、集中或集合: *concentrations of enemy troops, industrial buildings* 敌军、工业建筑物的集中.

□ **concenˈtration camp** (esp in Nazi Germany) prison consisting usu of a set of buildings inside a fence, where political prisoners, prisoners of war, etc were kept in very bad conditions (尤指纳粹德国的)集中营.

con·cent·ric /kənˈsentrɪk; kənˈsɛntrɪk/ *adj* **~ (with sth)** (of circles) having the same centre (指数个圆)有同一中心的: *concentric rings* 同心环. Cf 参看 ECCENTRIC 2.

con·cept /ˈkɒnsept; ˈkɑnsɛpt/ *n* **~ (of sth/that...)** idea underlying sth; general notion 观念; 概念: *the concept of freedom, meaning* 自由的、意义的概念 ○ *He can't grasp the basic concepts of mathematics.* 他掌握不了数学的基本概念. ○ *She seemed unfamiliar with the concept that everyone should have an equal opportunity.* 看来她不大熟悉机会均等这个概念.

▷ **con·cep·tual** /kənˈseptʃʊəl; kənˈsɛptʃʊəl/ *adj* of or based on concepts 观念的; 概念的; 观念上的; 概念上的.

con·cep·tion /kənˈsepʃn; kənˈsɛpʃən/ *n* **1** [U, C] conceiving (CONCEIVE 1) or being conceived 怀孕; 受孕: *the moment of conception* 受孕的一刻 ○ *an unplanned conception* 计划外怀孕. **2** (**a**) [U] thinking of (an idea or a plan) (主意或计划的)构思, 构想, 设想: *The plan, brilliant in its conception, failed because of inadequate preparation.* 那计划的构想倒是十分宏伟, 但终因准备不足而告吹. (**b**) [C] **~ (of sb/sth/that...)** idea, plan or intention 主意; 计划; 意图: *The new play is a brilliant conception.* 这出新剧真了不起. ○ *I have no conception of* (ie do not know) *what you mean.* 我完全不懂你的意思.

con·cern[1] /kənˈsɜːn; kənˈsɝn/ *v* **1** [Tn] (**a**) be the business of (sb); be important to; affect 是(某人)的事; 对...有重要性; 影响: *Don't interfere in what doesn't concern you.* 别管与自己无关的事. ○ *The loss was a tragedy for all concerned*, ie all those affected by it. 那损失对一切有关的人来说都是极为痛心的. ○ *Where the children are concerned...*, ie In matters where one must think of them... 关系到孩子们的问题... ○ *To whom it may concern...*, eg at the beginning of a public notice or a testimonial of sb's character, ability, etc 敬启者... (**b**) be about (sth); have as a subject 关于(某事物); 作为议题: *a report that concerns drug abuse* 关于滥用毒品的报告. **2** [Tn·pr] **~ oneself with/in/about sth** be busy with sth; interest oneself in sth 忙于(某事); 关心(某事): *There's no need to concern yourself with this matter; we're dealing with it.* 你不用管这事了, 我们正在处理. **3** [Tn] worry (sb); trouble; bother 使(某人)担忧; 使烦恼; 打扰: *Our losses are beginning to concern me.* 我们的损失使我担起心来. **4** (idm 习语) **as/so far as sb/sth is concerned** ⇨ FAR[2]. **be concerned in sth** have some connection with or responsibility for sth 与某事有牵连或对某事负有责任: *He was concerned in the crime.* 他与那起罪案有牵连. **be concerned to do sth** have it as one's business to do sth 把做某事视为自己的事. **be concerned with sth** be about sth 与某事物有关; 涉及某事物: *Her latest documentary is concerned with youth unemployment.* 她最近的一部纪录片是关于青年人失业问题的.

▷ **con·cerned** *adj* **~ (about/for sth/that...)** worried; troubled 担心的; 烦恼的; 忧虑的: *Concerned parents held a meeting.* 忧心忡忡的家长们开了一次会. ○ *We're all concerned for her safety.* 我们都为她的安全担忧. ○ *I'm concerned that they may have got lost.* 我担心他们可能迷路了. **con·cern·edly** /-ˈsɜːnɪdlɪ; -ˈsɝnɪdlɪ/ *adv*.

con·cern·ing *prep* about (sb/sth) 关于(某人[某事物]): *a letter concerning your complaint* 关于你投诉的信件.

con·cern[2] /kənˈsɜːn; kənˈsɝn/ *n* **1** (**a**) [U] **~ (for/about/over sth/sb); ~ (that...)** worry; anxiety 担心; 忧虑; 焦虑; 焦急: *There is no cause for concern.* 不必发愁. ○ *There is now considerable concern for their safety.* 现在对他们的安全相当担心. ○ *public concern about corruption* 公众对于腐败现象的忧虑 ○ *There is growing concern that they may have been killed.* 现在越来越担心他们可能已遭杀害. (**b**) [C] cause of anxiety 焦虑的原因: *Our main concern is that they are not receiving enough help.* 我们最忧虑的是他们一直没有得到足够的帮助. **2** [C] thing that is important or interesting to sb 对某人来说是重要的或感兴趣的事物: *What are your main concerns as a writer?* 你身为作家, 对什么最感兴趣? ○ *It's no concern of mine*, ie I am not involved in it or I have no responsibility for it. 这事与我无关. ○ *What concern is it of yours?* ie Why do you take an interest in it or interfere with it? 那与你有什么关系? **3** [C] company; business 企业; 公司; 商行: *a huge industrial concern* 巨大的工业企业 ○ *Our little corner shop is no longer a paying concern*, ie is no longer profitable. 我们这个街头小店已赚不到钱了. **4** [C] **~ (in sth)** share 股分: *He has a concern in* (ie is a part-owner of) *the business.* 他在企业中有股分(他是股东之一). **5** (idm 习语) **a going concern** ⇨ GOING.

con·cert /ˈkɒnsət; ˈkɑnsɝt/ *n* **1** musical entertainment given in public by one or more performers 音乐会: *an orchestral concert* 管弦乐音乐会 ○ *give a concert for charity* 举行慈善义演音乐会 ○ [attrib 作定语] *a concert pianist, hall, performance* 在音乐会上演奏的钢琴家、音乐厅、音乐会演出. Cf 参看 RECITAL. **2** (idm 习语) **at ˌconcert ˈpitch** in a state of full efficiency or readiness 处于效率极高或充分准备的状态. **in ˈconcert** giving a live public performance rather than a recorded one 现场演出的(并非事先录音的). **in concert (with sb/sth)** (*fml* 文) co-operating together 合作: *working in concert with his colleagues* 与他的同事合作.

□ **ˈconcert-goer** *n* person who attends concerts (esp of classical music) 出席音乐会(尤指古典音乐会)的人.

ˌconcert ˈgrand grand piano of the largest size, for concerts (音乐会用的)大钢琴.

ˌconcert-ˈmaster (*US*) = LEADER 2.

con·cer·ted /kənˈsɜːtɪd; kənˈsɝtɪd/ *adj* [usu attrib 通常作定语] arranged or done in co-operation 共同筹划的; 合作的: *a concerted effort, attack, campaign* 共同努力、联合攻击、协同作战 ○ *concerted action by several police forces* 警方数部门的联合行动.

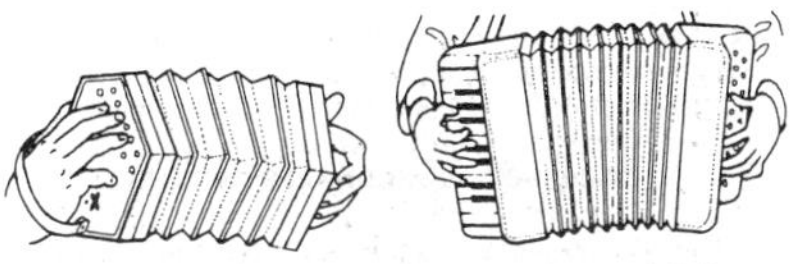

CONCERTINA 六角手风琴　　ACCORDION 手风琴

con·cer·tina /ˌkɒnsəˈtiːnə; ˌkɑnsɚˈtinə/ *n* musical instrument like a small accordion, consisting of a closed pleated tube, held in the hands and played by pressing the ends together to force air past reeds (REED 2) 六角手风琴. ⇨illus 见插图.

▷ **con·cer·tina** *v* (*pt, pp* **concertinaed**, *pres p* **concertinaing**) [I] fold up (as if) by being pressed together from each end (像)(从各端受挤压)折起: *The lorry had concertinaed after crashing into the tree.* 卡车撞到大树后折在一起.

con·certo /kənˈtʃeətəʊ, -ˈtʃɜːt-; kənˈtʃɛrto/ *n* (*pl* **~s**) musical composition for one or more solo instruments and an orchestra 协奏曲: *a ˈpiano concerto* 钢琴协奏曲 ○ *a concerto for two violins* 双小提琴协奏曲.

con·ces·sion /kənˈseʃn; kənˈsɛʃən/ *n* **1 ~ (to sb/sth)** (**a**) [U] conceding 承认; 让出; 允许: *There is a call for the concession of certain rights.* 要求承认某些权利. (**b**)

[C] thing granted or yielded, esp after discussion, an argument, etc 妥协，让步(尤指经协商或辩论等): *Employers made concessions to the workers in negotiations.* 资方在与工人谈判中作出了让步. ○ *As a concession to her inexperience they allowed her to have some help.* 他们体谅她缺乏经验，允许她获得些帮助. Cf 参看 CONCEDE. **2** [C] price reduction for certain categories of people (对某类人)减价: *special concessions on all bus fares for old people* 所有公共汽车票对老年人特价. **3** [C] ~ **(to do sth)** right given or sold to sb by the owner(s) of sth, allowing him to use or operate it 特许权(由某事物的所有者授予或售予某人的使用或经营之权利): *oil/mining concessions*, ie allowing oil or minerals to be extracted from the ground 石油[矿产]开采权 ○ *a concession to drill for oil* 石油钻探权.

▷ **con·ces·sion·ary** /kən'seʃənərɪ; US -nerɪ; kən'sɛʃə-n,ɛrɪ/ *adj* involving a concession(2) (对某类人)减价的: *concessionary rates/prices* (对某类人)减低的费用[价格].

con·ces·sion·aire /kən,seʃə'neə(r); kən,sɛʃən'ɛr/ *n* person who has been granted a concession(3), esp for the use of land or for trading 特许权获得者(尤指土地使用权或贸易权).

con·cess·ive /kən'sesɪv; kən'sɛsɪv/ *adj* (*grammar*) expressing concession(1) 表示承认、允许、妥协或让步的: *a concessive clause*, eg one introduced by *as*, *although* or *even if*, indicating a contrast with the main clause 让步从句(如由as、although或even if引导的表示与主句意思相反的从句).

conch /kɒntʃ; kɑntʃ/ *n* **(a)** shellfish with a large spiral shell 海螺(有大螺旋贝壳的贝类). **(b)** shell of this creature 海螺壳.

▷ **concho·logy** /kɒŋ'kɒlədʒɪ; kɑŋ'kɑlədʒɪ/ *n* [U] study of shells and shellfish 贝类学; 贝壳学.

con·ci·li·ate /kən'sɪlɪeɪt; kən'sɪlɪ,et/ *v* **1** [Tn] make (sb) less angry or more friendly (esp by being pleasant or making some concessions) 使(某人)息怒或友好(尤指经抚慰或让步); 安抚; 抚慰; 劝慰: *conciliate outraged customers* 劝慰盛怒的顾客. **2** [I, Ipr, Tn] ~ **(between sb and sb)** bring (people who are disagreeing) into agreement 使(有分歧的人)意见一致; 调解; 调停: *conciliate (between) the parties in a dispute* 调解双方(之间)的争端.

▷ **con·ci·li·ation** /kən,sɪlɪ'eɪʃn; kən,sɪlɪ'eʃən/ *n* [U] conciliating or being conciliated (受到)抚慰或调解: [attrib 作定语] *A conciliation service helps to settle disputes between employers and workers.* 调解机构协助解决劳资纠纷.

con·ci·li·at·ory /kən'sɪlɪətərɪ; US -tɔ:rɪ; kən'sɪlɪə,torɪ/ *adj* intended or likely to conciliate 意图或可能抚慰或调解的: *a conciliatory gesture, smile, remark* 愿和解的姿态、微笑、言语.

con·cise /kən'saɪs; kən'saɪs/ *adj* (of speech or writing) giving a lot of information in few words; brief (指语言或文字)用少数词语传达大量信息的; 简明的; 言简意赅的: *a concise summary, account, etc* 简明的摘要、报道等. ▷ **con·cisely** *adv*. **con·cise·ness**, **con·cis·ion** /kən'sɪʒn; kən'sɪʒən/ *ns* [U].

con·clave /'kɒŋkleɪv; 'kɑŋklev/ *n* private meeting (eg of cardinals to elect a Pope) 秘密会议(如红衣主教选举教皇者): *sit/meet in conclave*, ie hold a private meeting 参加[举行]秘密会议.

con·clude /kən'klu:d; kən'klud/ *v* **1** [I, Ipr, Tn, Tn·pr] ~ **(sth) (with sth)** (*usu fml* 通常作文雅语) come or bring (sth) to an end (使)(某事物)结束: *a few concluding remarks* 几句结束语 ○ *The meeting concluded at 8 o'clock.* 会议于8时结束. ○ *The story concludes with the hero's death.* 这故事随主人公死亡而告终. ○ *He concluded by saying that...* 他结束讲话时说... ○ *She concluded her talk with a funny story.* 她以一个有趣的故事结束谈话. **2** [Tn·pr, Tf] ~ **sth from sth** come to believe sth as a result of reasoning (经推理)相信某事物: *Those are the facts; what do you conclude from them?* 这些都是事实，你能从中得出什么结论? ○ *The jury concluded, from the evidence, that she was guilty.* 陪审团根据证据作出结论, 认定她有罪. **3** [Tn, Tn·pr] ~ **sth (with sb)** arrange and settle (a treaty, etc) formally and finally 达成; 决定; 缔结(条约等): *Britain concluded a trade agreement with China.* 英国和中国签署了贸易协定. ○ *Once the price had been agreed, a deal was quickly concluded.* 价格一经商定, 交易很快就达成了. **4** [Tf no passive 不用于被动语态, Tt] (*esp US*) decide, esp after discussion 决定(尤指经讨论或协商): *We concluded to go out/that we would go out.* 我们决定出去.

con·clu·sion /kən'klu:ʒn; kən'kluʒən/ *n* **1** [C usu *sing* 通常作单数] end 结束; 结尾: *at the conclusion of his speech* 他讲话的结尾 ○ *bring sth to a speedy conclusion* 将某事物迅速结束. **2** [C] ~ **(that...)** belief or opinion that is the result of reasoning (由推理而得出的)信念或意见, 结论: *I came to/reached the conclusion that he'd been lying.* 我看他是在说谎. ○ *What conclusions do you draw (from the evidence you've heard)?* 你从(你听到的证据)中得出什么结论? **3** [U] formal and final arranging or settling of sth 决定; 协定; 达成; 缔结: *Hostilities ended with the conclusion of a peace treaty.* 和平条约签定以后, 战事随之结束. **4** (idm 习语) **a foregone conclusion** ⇨ FOREGONE. **in conclusion** lastly 最后: *In conclusion I'd like to say that...* 最后, 我想说.... **jump to conclusions** ⇨ JUMP[2].

con·clus·ive /kən'klu:sɪv; kən'klusɪv/ *adj* (of facts, evidence, etc) convincing; ending doubt (指事实、证据等)令人信服的, 确凿的, 消除怀疑的: *Her fingerprints on the gun were conclusive proof of her guilt.* 她在枪上留下的指纹就是她犯罪的确凿证据. ▷ **con·clus·ively** *adv*.

con·coct /kən'kɒkt; kən'kɑkt/ *v* [Tn] (*often derog* 常作贬义) **1** make (sth) by mixing ingredients (esp ones that do not usu go together) 将(尤指通常不相配合的)成分混合成某物; 调制: *concoct a drink out of sherry and lemon juice* 用雪利酒和柠檬汁配制成的饮料. **2** (*derog* 贬) invent (a story, an excuse, etc) 编造, 捏造(谎言、借口等): *She'd concocted some unlikely tale about the train being cancelled.* 她胡编了一通瞎话, 说什么那班火车给取消了.

▷ **con·coc·tion** /kən'kɒkʃn; kən'kɑkʃən/ *n* **(a)** [U] concocting 调制; 编造; 捏造. **(b)** [C] thing that is concocted; (esp liquid) mixture 配制而成的物品; (尤指液体的)混合物: *Do you expect me to drink this vile concoction?* 你难道想让我喝这种乌七八糟的东西?

con·com·it·ant /kən'kɒmɪtənt; kən'kɑmətənt/ *adj* ~ **(with sth)** (*fml* 文) accompanying; happening together 伴随的; 同时发生或出现的: *concomitant circumstances, events, etc* 伴随的情况、事情等 ○ *travel and all its concomitant discomforts* 旅行及随之而来的不适.

▷ **con·com·it·ant** *n* ~ **(of sth)** (*fml* 文) thing that typically happens with sth else 伴随发生的事; 伴随物: *the infirmities that are the concomitants of old age* 年老而虚弱.

con·cord /'kɒŋkɔ:d; 'kɑŋkɔrd/ *n* [U] **1** (*fml* 文) harmony between people; lack of quarrelling and unfriendliness (人与人之间的)和谐, 一致, 和睦: *living in concord (with neighbouring states)* (与邻国)和睦相处. Cf 参看 DISCORD. **2** (*grammar*) agreement between words in gender, number, etc, eg between a verb and a plural noun as its subject (词与词之间在性、数等方面的)一致(如动词及其作主语的复数名词之间的).

con·cord·ance /kən'kɔ:dəns; kən'kɔrdṇs/ *n* alphabetical index of the words used by an author or in a book (作家所使用的或书籍中的)按字母顺序排列的索引: *a 'Bible concordance* 《圣经》词语索引 ○ *a concordance to Shakespeare* 莎士比亚词语索引.

con·cord·ant /kən'kɔ:dənt; kən'kɔrdṇt/ *adj* ~ **(with sth)** (*fml* 文) in agreement; appropriate 一致的; 协调的; 恰当的; 适合的: *practice concordant with our principles* 与我们的原则相符的做法.

con·cordat /kən'kɔ:dæt; kən'kɔrdæt/ *n* agreement, esp between a State and the Church on church affairs 协定; 协约; (尤指一政府与教会之间就宗教事务所订立的)政教协定.

con·course /'kɒŋkɔ:s; 'kɑnkɔrs/ *n* **1** open area forming part of a building or large complex, where people may walk about 宽敞的大厅; 广场: *The ticket office is at the rear of the station concourse*, ie its main hall. 售票处在车站大厅的后部. **2** (*fml* 文) gathering of people or things; crowd (人或事物的)聚集, 汇集; 群众: *a vast concourse of pilgrims* 大群的朝圣者.

con·crete[1] /'kɒŋkri:t; 'kɑnkrit/ *adj* **1** existing in material form; that can be touched, felt, etc 以物质形式存在的;

具体的; 实体的: *Physics deals with the forces acting on concrete objects.* 物理学研究作用于物体上的力. Cf 参看 ABSTRACT. **2** definite; positive 确实的; 明确的; 确定的: *concrete proposals, evidence, facts* 明确的建议、确实的证据; 确定的事实 ○ *The police have nothing concrete to go on.* 警方没有任何确实的东西作依据. ▷ **con·cretely** *adv*.

□ ˌ**concrete** ˈ**music** music composed of natural sounds that are recorded and then rearranged 具体音乐(将自然音响录制后重新改编而成者).

ˌ**concrete** ˈ**poetry** poetry that uses its visual appearance on the page to achieve its effect 具体诗歌(从版面上的视觉形象来达到效果的诗歌).

con·crete² /ˈkɒŋkriːt; ˋkɑnkrit/ *n* [U] building material made by mixing cement with sand, gravel, etc and water 混凝土: *a slab of concrete* 混凝土板 ○ *modern buildings made of concrete* 用混凝土建造的现代建筑物 ○ [attrib 作定语] *a concrete path, wall, etc* 混凝土的路、墙等.

▷ **con·crete** *v* [Tn, Tn·p] **~ sth (over)** cover sth with concrete 用混凝土覆盖; 铺设: *concrete a road (over)* 用混凝土铺路.

□ ˈ**concrete mixer** revolving container used to mix the ingredients of concrete 混凝土搅拌机.

con·cre·tion /kənˈkriːʃn; kənˋkriʃən/ *n* (*fml* 文) mass formed when sth soft or liquid becomes hard or solid 凝结; 凝固; 固结.

con·cu·bine /ˈkɒŋkjʊbaɪn; ˋkɑŋkjuˌbaɪn/ *n* (in countries where a man can legally have more than one wife) woman who lives with a man but is of lower status than a wife (一夫多妻制国家中的)妾, 姨太太, 小老婆: *The sultan's wives and concubines live in the harem.* 苏丹的妻妾住在后宫.

con·cu·pis·cence /kənˈkjuːpɪsns; kɑnˋkjupəsṇs/ *n* [U] (*fml often derog* 文, 常作贬义) strong sexual desire; lust 强烈的性欲; 淫欲; 色欲; 肉欲.

con·cur /kənˈkɜː(r); kənˋkɝ/ *v* (**-rr-**) (*fml* 文) **1** [I, Ipr] **~ (with sb/sth) (in sth)** agree; express agreement 同意; 表示意见一致: *She has expressed her opposition to the plan, and I fully concur (with her) (in this matter).* 她对计划表示反对, (在这一问题上)我完全同意(她的意见). **2** [I, It] (of events, etc) happen together; coincide (指事情等)同时发生: *Everything concurred to produce a successful result.* 所有的事都同时发生而产生了圆满的结果.

▷ **con·cur·rence** /kənˈkʌrəns; kənˋkɝəns/ *n* (*fml* 文) **1** [U, sing] agreement 同意; 一致: *With your concurrence* (ie If you agree), *I will confirm the arrangement.* 你若同意, 我就把这项安排定下来了. ○ *a concurrence* (ie similarity) *of ideas, views, etc* 意见、观点等一致. **2** [sing] occurrence at the same time 同时发生或出现: *an unfortunate concurrence of events* 事情不幸同时发生.

con·cur·rent /kənˈkʌrənt; kənˋkɝənt/ *adj* **~ (with sth)** existing, happening or done at the same time 同时存在的、发生的或完成的: *developments concurrent with this* 与此同时发生的事物. **con·cur·rently** *adv*: *He was given two prison sentences, to run concurrently.* 他两罪均判监禁, 同期执行.

con·cuss /kənˈkʌs; kənˋkʌs/ *v* [Tn esp passive 尤用于被动语态] injure (sb's brain) by a blow or by violent shaking 使(脑)震荡: *He was badly concussed in the collision.* 在猛烈碰撞时他的脑部受到严重损伤.

con·cus·sion /kənˈkʌʃn; kənˋkʌʃən/ *n* [C, U] (**a**) injury to the brain caused by a blow, violent shaking, etc, resulting in temporary unconsciousness 脑震荡: *The patient is suffering from severe concussion following a blow to the head.* 患者头部受击后患严重脑震荡. (**b**) violent shaking or shock (caused eg by a blow, an explosion, etc) 猛烈的摇动或震动(如因撞击、爆炸等所致): *a mighty tremor followed by minor concussions* 巨大的震动及随后的轻微震荡.

con·demn /kənˈdem; kənˋdɛm/ *v* **1** [Tn, Tn·pr, Cn·n/a] **~ sb/sth (for/as sth)** say that one disapproves of sb/sth 谴责; 责备; 指摘: *We all condemn cruelty to children.* 我们一致谴责虐待儿童的行为. ○ *The papers were quick to condemn him for his mistake.* 报纸及时地指摘他的错误. ○ *She is often condemned as uncaring.* 她常因不关心别人而受到责难. **2** [Tn, Cn·n/a] **~ sth (as sth)** say officially that (sth) is faulty or not fit for use 官方宣称(某事物)有缺陷或不宜使用: *The meat was condemned as unfit for human consumption.* 这种肉已宣布不适宜人们食用. ○ *a condemned building* 已公布为不宜使用的建筑物. **3** (**a**) [Tn, Tn·pr, Cn·t] **~ sb (to sth/to do sth)** (*law* 律) say what sb's punishment is to be; sentence sb (esp to death) 宣告某人要受的惩罚; 判某人刑(尤指死刑): *condemn sb to death/hard labour* 判处某人死刑[劳役] ○ *He was found guilty and condemned to be shot.* 他被判有罪, 处以枪决. (**b**) [Tn] make (sb) appear guilty 使(某人)显示出有罪: *His nervous looks condemned him.* 他神色紧张, 显出有罪的样子. **4** [esp passive 尤用于被动语态: Tn·pr, Cn·t] **~ sb to sth/to do sth** make sb take or accept sth unwelcome or unpleasant; doom sb 使某人接受不好的某事物; 使某人注定: *an unhappy worker, condemned to a job he hates* 闷闷不乐的工作者, 无奈何要做他厌恶的工作 ○ *As an old person, one is often condemned to live alone.* 老年人常出于无奈而独自生活.

▷ **con·dem·na·tion** /ˌkɒndemˈneɪʃn; ˌkɑndɛmˋneʃən/ *n* (**a**) [U] condemning or being condemned 谴责; 判罪; 注定. (**b**) [C] instance of this 谴责; 判罪; 注定: *many condemnations of her action* 对她行为的多方谴责.

□ **conˌdemned** ˈ**cell** cell where a person who has been sentenced to death is kept 死囚牢房.

con·densa·tion /ˌkɒndenˈseɪʃn; ˌkɑndɛnˋseʃən/ *n* **1** [U, C] condensing or being condensed 浓缩; 凝结; 简缩; 缩写: *the condensation of steam to water* 蒸气之凝结为水 ○ *The report is a brilliant condensation of several years' work.* 这报告是几年工作的精华. **2** [U] drops of liquid formed on a surface when vapour condenses (蒸气凝结在表面上的)液滴: *His shaving mirror was covered with condensation.* 他的剃须镜上有一层小水珠.

□ ˌ**condenˈsation trail** = VAPOUR TRAIL (VAPOUR).

con·dense /kənˈdens; kənˋdɛns/ *v* **1** [I, Ipr, Tn, Tn·pr] **~ (sth) (into/to sth)** (**a**) (cause sth to) become thicker or more concentrated (使某物)变稠或变浓; 浓缩: *Soup condenses when boiled*, ie by losing most of the water. 汤煮过后就浓了(失去大量的水分). ○ *condensed milk, soup, etc* 炼乳、浓缩汤等. (**b**) (cause sth to) change from gas or vapour to a liquid (使某物)由气体或蒸气变成液体; 凝结: *Steam condenses/is condensed into water when it touches a cold surface.* 蒸气接触冷的表面而凝结成水珠. ⇨Usage at WATER¹ 用法见 WATER¹. **2** [Tn, Tn·pr] **~ sth (into sth)** put sth into fewer words 简缩; 摘要; 简述: *condense a long report into a brief summary* 将长篇报告简缩为摘要.

con·denser /kənˈdensə(r); kənˋdɛnsɚ/ *n* **1** device for cooling vapour and condensing it to liquid 冷凝器. **2** device for receiving and storing an electric charge (esp in a car engine) 电容器. **3** mirror or lens that concentrates light, eg in a film projector 聚光镜; 聚光器.

con·des·cend /ˌkɒndɪˈsend; ˌkɑndɪˋsɛnd/ *v* **1** [It] (*often derog* 常作贬义) do sth that one regards as undignified or below one's level of importance 屈尊; 俯就: *She actually condescended to say hello to me in the street today.* 她今天在街上竟能屈尊跟我打招呼. ○ (*ironic* 反语) *Perhaps your father would condescend to help with the washing-up!* 令尊大人或可纡尊降贵帮助刷锅洗碗吧! **2** [I, Ipr] **~ (to sb)** (*derog* 贬) behave kindly or graciously, but in a way that shows one feels that one is better than other people (带有优越感地)故意表示和蔼可亲: *I do wish he wouldn't condescend to the junior staff in his department.* 我但愿他不要假惺惺地纡尊降贵接近部门里的低级员工.

▷ **con·des·cend·ing** *adj*: *a condescending person* 屈尊俯就的人 ○ *condescending behaviour* 屈尊的行为 ○ *She's so condescending!* 她隐藏优越感太惺惺作态! **con·des·cend·ingly** *adv*.

con·des·cen·sion /ˌkɒndɪˈsenʃn; ˌkɑndɪˋsɛnʃən/ *n* [U] condescending (behaviour) 屈尊; 俯就.

con·dign /kənˈdaɪn; kənˋdaɪn/ *adj* (*fml* 文) (of punishment, etc) severe and well deserved (指惩罚)严厉而适当的; 罪有应得的.

con·di·ment /ˈkɒndɪmənt; ˋkɑndəmənt/ *n* [C esp *pl*, U 作可数名词时尤作复数, 亦作不可数名词] seasoning (eg salt or pepper) used to give flavour and relish to food 调味品, 佐料(如盐或胡椒).

con·di·tion¹ /kənˈdɪʃn; kənˋdɪʃən/ *n* **1** [sing] particular state of existence 状态; 处境; 地位; 身分: *the human*

C

condition 人类的处境 ○ *the condition of slavery*, ie being a slave 奴隶的身分. **2** [sing, U] (**a**) present state of a thing 现状; 状况; 情况: *be in good, poor, excellent, etc condition* 处于好的、坏的、极佳的等状况 ○ *the rusty condition of the bicycle* 自行车生锈的状况 ○ *The ship is not in a condition/is in no condition* (ie is unfit) *to make a long voyage.* 此船的现状不适宜远航. (**b**) physical fitness; health 健康状况; 健康: *He's in excellent condition for a man of his age.* 他就其年龄而言, 身体极好. ○ *I've had no exercise for ages; I'm really out of condition*, ie unfit. 我已多时没运动了, 现在健康状况欠佳. ○ *She's in no condition* (ie is not well enough) *to travel.* 她的身体状况不宜旅行(不甚健康). **3** [C] (**a**) thing needed to make sth else possible; thing on which another thing depends 条件: *One of the conditions of the job is that you should be able to drive*, ie In order to get the job you must be able to drive. 做这项工作的其中一个条件是要会开车. ○ *He was allowed to go out, but his parents made it a condition that he should get home before midnight.* 他父母允许他出去, 但规定他要在午夜前回家. ○ *I'll let you borrow it on one condition: (that) you lend me your bicycle in return.* 我借给你也行, 但有个条件, 你得把你的自行车借给我. (**b**) thing required as part of an agreement, a contract, etc; stipulation 条款; 规定; 约定; 条件: *the terms and conditions of the lease* 契约的条款与条件. **4 conditions** [pl] circumstances 环境; 情况: *under existing conditions* 在现有的情况下 ○ *poor working conditions* 恶劣的工作环境 ○ *firemen having to operate in very difficult conditions* 须在极困难的情况下工作的消防队员. **5** [C] illness; ailment 疾病: *a heart, liver, brain, etc condition* 心脏、肝脏、脑等的疾病 ○ *What is the treatment for this condition?* 这种病用什么方法治疗? **6** [C] (*dated* 旧) position in society; rank 社会地位; 阶级; 等级: *people of every condition/of all conditions* 社会各阶层人士. **7** (idm 习语) **in mint condition** ⇨ MINT². **on condition (that)...** only if; provided (that) 在...条件下; 倘若...: *You can go out on condition that you wear an overcoat.* 你要穿上外衣才能出去. **on no condition** (*fml* 文) not at all 一点也不; 决不: *You must on no condition tell him what happened.* 你决不能把发生的事情告诉他.

con·di·tion² /ˌkən'dɪʃn; kən'dɪʃən/ *v* **1** [Tn] have an important effect on (sb/sth); determine 对(某人[某事物])有重要影响; 决定: *Environment conditions an animal's development.* 环境能影响动物的成长. **2** [Tn, Tn·pr, Cn·t] **~ sb/sth (to sth/to do sth)** accustom sb/sth; train sb/sth 使某人[某事物]习惯; 训练某人[某事物]: *We have all been conditioned by our upbringing.* 我们都习惯于所受的教养. ○ *It didn't take them long to become conditioned to the new environment.* 他们不久就适应了新环境. ○ *Animals can be conditioned to expect food at certain times.* 可以训练动物定时等待喂食. **3** [Tn] put (sth) into a proper or desired state for use 使(某事物)达到适当的或合要求的状况(以供使用): *leather conditioned by a special process* 经特殊加工的皮革 ○ *a lotion that conditions the skin*, ie keeps it healthy 护肤剂.

▷ **con·di·tioner** /kən'dɪʃənə(r); kən'dɪʃənɚ/ *n* [C, U] thing or substance that conditions, esp a liquid that keeps the hair healthy and shiny 调理的物品或物质; (尤指)护发剂, 护发素.

□ **conˌditioned 'reflex** response that a person or an animal is trained to make to a particular stimulus (even if it is not a normal or natural response) 条件反射.

con·di·tional /kən'dɪʃənl; kən'dɪʃənḷ/ *adj* (**a**) **~ (on/upon sth)** depending on sth 依赖某事物的; 含有条件的: *conditional approval, acceptance, etc* 含有条件的批准、接受等 ○ *Payment of the money is conditional upon delivery of the goods*, ie If the goods are not delivered, the money will not be paid. 货到方可付款(货不到则不付款). (**b**) (*esp grammar* 尤作语法用语) containing or implying a condition¹(3a) or qualification 有条件的; 受制约的: *a conditional clause*, ie one beginning with *if* or *unless* 条件从句(由if或unless起首的从句). ▷ **condi·tion·ally** /-ʃənəlɪ; -ʃənḷɪ/ *adv*.

con·dole /kən'dəʊl; kən'dol/ *v* [Ipr] **~ with sb (on sth)** (*fml* 文) express sympathy (for a misfortune, bereavement, etc) (对不幸、丧失亲人等)表示同情, 吊慰; 吊唁.

▷ **con·dol·ence** /kən'dəʊləns; kən'doləns/ *n* [U, C often *pl* 常作复数] (expression of) sympathy 同情; 吊慰; 吊唁: *a letter of condolence* 吊唁信 ○ *Please accept my condolences.* 谨致吊慰之意.

con·dom /'kɒndəm; 'kʌndəm/ (also *esp US* **prophylactic**) *n* contraceptive sheath worn on the penis during sexual intercourse (男用)避孕套, 保险套; 阴茎套.

con·do·min·ium /ˌkɒndə'mɪnɪəm; ˌkɑndə'mɪnɪəm/ *n* **1** country governed jointly by two or more other states (由另两国或多国)共管的国家. **2** (*US*) (apartment in a) block of apartments, each of which is owned by its occupier (产权为居住者自有的)公寓(的单元).

con·done /kən'dəʊn; kən'don/ *v* [Tn, Tg, Tsg] treat or regard (an offence) as if it were not serious or wrong; overlook; forgive 容忍(过失); 宽恕; 原谅: *condone violence, adultery, fraud, etc* 宽恕暴行、奸情、欺诈行为等 ○ *Not punishing them amounts to condoning their crime.* 不惩罚他们就等于纵容他们的罪行. ▷ **con·dona·tion** /ˌkɒndəʊ'neɪʃn; ˌkɑndo'neʃən/ *n* [U] (*fml* 文).

con·dor /'kɒndɔː(r); 'kɑndɚ/ *n* type of large vulture found mainly in S America 神鹰(主要产于南美).

con·duce /kən'djuːs; *US* -'duːs; kən'dus/ *v* [Ipr] **~ to/towards sth** (*fml* 文) help to bring sth about 有助于产生(某事物); 导致; 有益于: *A good diet conduces to good health.* 良好的饮食有益于健康.

▷ **con·du·cive** /kən'djuːsɪv; *US* -'duːs-; kən'dusɪv/ *adj* [pred 作表语] **~ to sth** allowing or helping sth to happen 容许或有助于某事物发生; 有益: *These noisy conditions aren't really conducive to concentrated work.* 这嘈杂的环境实在不利于专心工作.

con·duct¹ /'kɒndʌkt; 'kɑndʌkt/ *n* [U] **1** person's behaviour (esp its moral aspect) (人的)行为(尤指道德方面); 品德; 品行: *the rules of conduct* 行为准则 ○ *The prisoner was released early because of good conduct.* 这罪犯因表现良好提前获释. **2 ~ of sth** manner of directing or managing (a business, campaign, etc) (对业务、作战等的)指导、指挥、管理或经营(的方式): *There was growing criticism of the Government's conduct of the war.* 政府领导作战的方式受到越来越多的批评.

con·duct² /kən'dʌkt; kən'dʌkt/ *v* **1** [Tn·pr, Tn·p] lead or guide (sb/sth) 领导、指导、引导或带领(某人[某事物]): *I asked the attendant to conduct him to the door/conduct him out.* 我让服务员领他到门口[领他出去]. ○ *A guide conducted the visitors round the museum.* 导游带领游客参观博物馆. ○ *We were given a conducted* (ie guided) *tour of the cathedral.* 我们在有人引导下参观了大教堂. **2** (**a**) [Tn] direct (sth); control; manage 指挥(某事物); 控制; 操纵; 管理; 主持; 经营: *conduct business, a meeting, negotiations, etc* 经营生意、主持会议、主持谈判等 ○ *She was appointed to conduct the advertising campaign.* 她被委派主持宣传活动. (**b**) [I, Tn] direct the performance of (an orchestra, a choir, a piece of music, etc) 指挥(管弦乐队、合唱团、乐曲等)的演出: *a concert by the Philharmonic Orchestra, conducted by Sir Colin Davis* 由科林·戴维斯爵士指挥、爱乐交响乐团演出的音乐会. **3** [Tn·pr] **~ oneself well, badly, etc** (*fml* 文) behave in the specified way (行为)表现: *conduct oneself honourably, with dignity, like a gentleman* 行为光明磊落、端庄高尚、像正人君子 ○ *How did the prisoner conduct himself?* 那犯人表现如何? **4** [Tn] (of a substance) allow (heat, electric current, etc) to pass along or through it (指物质)传导(热、电流等): *Copper conducts electricity better than other materials do.* 铜的导电性能比其他材料好.

▷ **con·duc·tion** /kən'dʌkʃn; kən'dʌkʃən/ *n* [U] conducting of electric current along wires or of heat by contact (电流或热量的)传导; 导电; 导热.

con·duct·ive /kən'dʌktɪv; kən'dʌktɪv/ *adj* that can conduct heat, electricity, etc 导热的; 导电的; 能传导的.

con·duct·iv·ity /ˌkɒndʌk'tɪvətɪ; ˌkɑndʌk'tɪvətɪ/ *n* [U] property or power of conducting heat, electricity, etc 传导(热、电等的)性质或能力; 传导性; 传导力.

con·ductor /kən'dʌktə(r); kən'dʌktɚ/ *n* **1** person who directs the performance of an orchestra, a choir, etc (esp by standing in front of them and gesturing with his arms) (管弦乐队、合唱团等的)指挥. **2** (**a**) (*Brit*) person who collects fares on a bus (公共汽车上的)收票员. (**b**) (*US*) (*Brit* **guard**) person in charge of a train

(火车上的)乘务员，列车员(英式英语用**guard**)。**3** substance that conducts heat or electric current 导体(导热或导电的物质): *a 'lightning conductor* 避雷器 ○ *Wood is a poor conductor.* 木头是不良导体.

▷ **con·duc·tress** /kən'dʌktrɪs; kən'dʌktrɪs/ *n* (*Brit*) woman conductor on a bus (公共汽车上的)女收票员.

□ **con'ductor rail** rail (laid parallel to the tracks) from which a railway locomotive picks up electric current 导电轨, 接触轨(与路轨平行的轨道, 可供机车导入电流).

con·duit /'kɒndɪt; US 'kɒnduːɪt, -dwɪt; 'kɑndʊɪt/ *n* (**a**) large pipe through which liquids flow 大水管. (**b**) tube enclosing insulated electric wires 导线管.

cone /kəʊn; kon/ *n* **1** solid body that narrows to a point from a circular flat base (实心的)圆锥体. ⇨illus at CUBE 见CUBE之插图. **2** solid or hollow thing that has this shape, eg an edible container for ice-cream, a warning sign for road-works, etc (实心的或中空的)圆锥形物(如用以盛冰激凌的可食的锥形蛋卷、修路时放置的锥形警告路标等). ⇨illus at App 1 见附录1之插图, page xiii. **3** fruit of certain evergreen trees (fir, pine, cedar) made of overlapping woody scales 球果(某些常绿树, 如枞、松、雪松的果实). ⇨illus at App 1 见附录1之插图, page i.

▷ **cone** *v* (phr v) **cone sth off** mark or separate sth with cones 用锥形标志标明或隔开: *cone off a section of motorway during repairs* 用锥形标志隔开维修中的一段高速公路 ○ *cone off parking spaces that must not be used* 用锥形标志标明不准使用的停车位置.

co·ney = CONY.

con·fab /'kɒnfæb; 'kɑnfæb/ *n* (*dated infml* 旧, 口) private friendly conversation; chat 私下的亲切交谈; 闲谈; 闲聊; 聊天.

con·fec·tion /kən'fekʃn; kən'fɛkʃən/ *n* (*fml* 文) thing made with sweet ingredients 甜食.

▷ **con·fec·tioner** *n* person who (makes and) sells sweets, cakes, etc (制作和)销售糖果、糕点的人; 甜食师傅; 甜食商: *I bought it at the confectioner's (shop).* 那是我从糖果店买来的. **con·fec·tion·ery** /kən'fekʃənərɪ; US -ʃənerɪ; kən'fɛkʃən,ɛrɪ/ *n* (**a**) [U] sweets, chocolates, cakes, etc 糖果、巧克力、糕点等. (**b**) [C] confectioner's business or shop 糖果糕点业或商店.

con·fed·er·acy /kən'fedərəsɪ; kən'fɛdərəsɪ/ *n* **1** [C] alliance or league, esp of states 联盟或同盟(尤指国家的). **2 the (Southern) Confederacy** [sing] the Confederate States 美国南部邦联.

con·fed·er·ate[1] /kən'fedərət; kən'fɛdərɪt/ *adj* joined together by an agreement or a treaty 联盟的; 同盟的; 联邦的: *the Confederate States of America* 美国南部邦联.

▷ **con·fed·er·ate** *n* **1** person one works with (esp in sth illegal or secret); accomplice 同伙; 合谋者; 同党; 共犯: *his confederates in the crime* 他的共犯. **2 Confederate** supporter of the Confederate States 南部邦联的支持者.

□ **Confederate States** the eleven states that separated from the US in 1860-61 and caused the American Civil War 美国南部邦联(由1860-1861年脱离美利坚合众国的十一个州组成, 后导致美国南北战争).

con·fed·er·ate[2] /kən'fedəreɪt; kən'fɛdə,ret/ *v* [I, Ipr] ~ **(with sb/sth)** join together in a larger organization for mutual benefit (为共同利益而)联合; 结盟.

▷ **con·fed·era·tion** /kən,fedə'reɪʃn; kən,fɛdə'reʃən/ *n* (**a**) [U] confederating or being confederated 结盟. (**b**) [C] organization of smaller groups that have joined together for mutual benefit 同盟; 联盟; 邦联: *the Confederation of British Industry* 英国工业联合会.

con·fer /kən'fɜː(r); kən'fɝ/ *v* (**-rr-**) **1** [I, Ipr] ~ **(with sb) (on/about sth)** have discussions (esp in order to exchange opinions or get advice) 讨论; 探讨; 商谈; 商议; 协商; 请教: *She withdrew to confer with her advisers before announcing a decision.* 她先去请教顾问然后再来宣布决定. **2** [Tn, Tn·pr] ~ **sth (on sb)** give or grant (a degree or title) to sb 授予某人(学位或头衔): *The Queen conferred knighthoods on several distinguished men.* 女王将爵士头衔授予几位杰出人士. ○ (*fig* 比喻) *He behaves as if high rank automatically confers the right to be obeyed.* 他的表现好像是身居高位就自然有权使人俯首听命.

▷ **con·fer·ment** *n* [U, C] (*fml* 文) giving or granting (of degrees, honours, etc) (学位荣誉等的)授予.

con·fer·ence /'kɒnfərəns; 'kɑnfərəns/ *n* [C, U] (meeting for) discussion or exchange of views 讨论(会); 协商(会); 会议: *Many international conferences are held in Geneva.* 许多国际会议在日内瓦举行. ○ *The Director is in conference now.* 主任正在开会.

con·fess /kən'fes; kən'fɛs/ *v* **1** (**a**) [I, Ipr, Tn, Tf, Dn·pr] ~ **(to sth/doing sth)**; ~ **(sth) (to sb)** say or admit, often formally (that one has done wrong, committed a crime, etc) 承认(错误、罪行等); 供认; 坦白: *The prisoner refused to confess (his crime).* 该犯拒不招供(罪行). ○ *She finally confessed (to having stolen the money).* 她最后招认了(偷了那笔钱). ○ *He confessed that he had murdered her.* 他供认他杀害了她. (**b**) [Ipr, Tf, Cn·a, Cn·t] acknowledge, often reluctantly 承认(常为不情愿地): *She confessed to (having) a dread of spiders*, ie admitted that she was afraid of them. 她承认她害怕蜘蛛. ○ *I'm rather bored, I must confess.* 说老实话, 我真有点厌烦. ○ *He confessed himself (to be) totally ignorant of their plans.* 他承认自己对于他们的计划一无所知. **2** (**a**) [I, Ipr, Tn, Tn·pr, Tf, Dpr·f] ~ **(sth) (to sb)** (esp in the Roman Catholic Church) tell (one's sins) formally to a priest (尤指天主教)向神父忏悔, 告罪, 告解: *He confessed (to the priest) that he had sinned.* 他(向神父)忏悔他犯了罪. (**b**) [Tn] (of a priest) hear the sins of (sb) in this way (指神父)听取(某人)的忏悔: *The priest confessed the criminal.* 神父听取那罪犯的忏悔.

▷ **con·fess·edly** /-ɪdlɪ; -ɪdlɪ/ *adv* by sb's own admission 自己供认地.

con·fes·sion /kən'feʃn; kən'fɛʃən/ *n* **1** [C, U] statement of one's guilt; confessing 供认; 招供; 承认; 坦白; 交代: *to make a full confession of one's crimes* 对自己所犯罪行供认不讳. **2** [C, U] (in the Roman Catholic Church) formal admission of one's sins to a priest (指天主教)向神父忏悔; 告罪; 告解: *The priest will hear confessions in English and French.* 这位神父可听取用英语和法语的告解. ○ *I always go to confession on Fridays.* 我总是每星期五去作忏悔. **3** [C] declaration of one's religious beliefs, principles, etc (表明宗教信仰、准则等的)声明: *a confession of faith* 信仰声明.

con·fes·sional /kən'feʃənl; kən'fɛʃənəl/ *n* private, usu enclosed, place in a church where a priest sits to hear confessions (教堂中神父听取忏悔的)告解室: *the secrets of the confessional* 在告解室中吐露的隐情.

con·fessor /kən'fesə(r); kən'fɛsɚ/ *n* priest who hears confessions 听取忏悔的神父; 告解神父.

con·fetti /kən'fetɪ; kən'fɛtɪ/ *n* [sing *v*] small pieces of coloured paper thrown over the bride and bridegroom at a wedding (婚礼时投撒在新娘和新郎身上的)五彩纸屑.

con·fid·ant /,kɒnfɪ'dænt; ,kɑnfə'dænt/ *n* trusted person to whom one speaks about one's private affairs or secrets (可以向之披露私事或内心秘密的)知己, 密友.

con·fide /kən'faɪd; kən'faɪd/ *v* **1** (**a**) [Tf, Dn·pr, Dpr·f] ~ **sth to sb** tell (a secret) to sb 向某人吐露(秘密): *She confided her troubles to a friend.* 她向朋友倾吐了内心的烦恼. ○ *He confided (to me) that he had applied for another job.* 他(向我)吐露说他已申请了另一份工作. (**b**) [Tn·pr] ~ **sb/sth to sb/sth** (*fml* 文) give sb/sth to sb to be looked after; entrust 委托某人照料某人[某事物]; 托付: *Can I confide my children to your care?* 托你照顾一下我的孩子好吗? **2** (phr v) **confide in sb** trust sb enough to tell a secret to him 充分信赖某人(可告知秘密者): *There's no one here I can confide in.* 这里没有一个我可以信赖的人.

▷ **con·fid·ing** *adj* [usu attrib 通常作定语] trusting; not suspicious 易信任人的; 深信不疑的: *She was a practised swindler and took advantage of the old man's confiding nature.* 她是一个行骗的老手, 利用了那个老人生性轻信以售其奸. **con·fid·ingly** *adv*.

con·fid·ence /'kɒnfɪdəns; 'kɑnfədəns/ *n* **1** [U] (**a**) ~ **(in sb/sth)** firm trust (in sb, in sb's ability, or in what is said, reported, etc) 坚定的信赖: *to have/lose confidence in sb* 对某人抱有[失去]信心 ○ *I have little confidence in him.* 我对他没有什么信心. ○ *Don't put too much confidence in what the papers say.* 不要过分相信报纸上的话. ○ *There is a lack of confidence in the Government*, ie People do not believe that its policies are wise. 人民

C

对政府缺乏信心. (**b**) feeling of certainty; trust in one's own ability 把握; 自信心: *He answered the questions with confidence.* 他很有把握地回答了那个问题. ○ *You are too shy: you should have more confidence (in yourself).* 你太缩手缩脚了, 应该增强(自)信心. **2** [C] secret which is told to sb 知心话; 私房话: *The two girls sat in a corner exchanging confidences.* 那两个女孩子坐在角落里说着悄悄话. **3** (idm 习语) **in (strict) confidence** as a secret 当作秘密: *I'm telling you this in (strict) confidence — so don't breathe a word of it.* 我现在告诉你这件事是个(绝对的)秘密——千万不可外传. **take sb into one's confidence** tell sb one's secrets, etc 向某人吐露内心的秘密等.

C

□ **'confidence trick** act of swindling sb by first gaining his trust 骗局(从赢得信任人手使某人受骗). **'confidence trickster** (also *infml* 口语亦作 **'con man**) person who swindles people in this way (以此术行骗的)骗子.

con·fid·ent /ˈkɒnfɪdənt; ˋkɑnfədənt/ *adj* **~ (of sth/that ...)** feeling or showing trust in oneself or one's ability 自信的; 有信心的; 有把握的: *a confident smile, manner, speech* 显示信心的微笑、态度、讲话等 ○ *feel confident of succeeding/that one will succeed* 有信心能成功 ○ *He is confident of victory.* 他对胜利充满信心. ▷ **con·fid·ently** *adv*.

con·fid·en·tial /ˌkɒnfɪˈdenʃl; ˌkɑnfəˋdɛnʃəl/ *adj* **1** to be kept secret; not to be made known to others 恪守秘密的; 机密的: *confidential information, files, letters* 机密情报、文件、信件. **2** [attrib 作定语] trusted with secrets 获得信任参与机密的: *a confidential secretary* 机要秘书. **3** trusting 表示信任的: *speaking in a confidential tone* 用表示信任的口吻说话. ▷ **con·fid·en·ti·al·ity** /ˌkɒnfɪˌdenʃɪˈæləti; ˌkɑnfɪˌdɛnʃɪˋælɪtɪ/ *n* [U]. **con·fid·en·tially** /-ʃəli; -ʃəlɪ/ *adv*: *He told me confidentially that he's thinking of resigning next year.* 他私下告诉我他打算明年辞职.

con·fig·ura·tion /kənˌfɪgəˈreɪʃn; *US* -ˌfɪgjʊˈreɪʃn; kənˌfɪgjəˋreʃən/ *n* arrangement of the parts of sth; shape or outline 某物的构造、结构、布局; 形状; 外观: *the configuration of the earth's surface, the vocal tract, the solar system* 地球表面的形状; 发音系统的构造; 太阳系的分布.

con·fig·ure /kənˈfɪgə(r); *US* kənˈfɪgjər; kənˋfɪgjɚ/ *v* [Tn] (*esp computing* 尤作计算机术语) arrange (sth) for a particular purpose, usu so that it is compatible with other equipment 装配, 配置(某物)(通常为与其他装置兼容).

con·fine /kənˈfaɪn; kənˋfaɪn/ *v* **1** [Tn, Tn·pr] **~ sb/sth (in/to sth)** keep (a person or an animal) in a restricted space 限制在某空间以内: *Is it cruel to confine a bird in a cage?* 把鸟关在笼子里残忍不残忍? ○ *After her operation, she was confined to bed for a week.* 她手术之后已卧床一星期了. ○ *I should hate to be confined in an office all day.* 我讨厌整天关在办公室里. **2** [Tn·pr] **~ sb/sth to sth** restrict or keep sb/sth within certain limits 将某人[某事物]限制在一定范围以内: *I wish the speaker would confine himself to the subject.* 我希望演讲者不要离题. ○ *Confine your criticism to matters you understand.* 发表评论时不要超出自己所了解的事情的范围.

▷ **con·fined** *adj* (of space) limited; restricted (指空间)有限的, 受限制的: *It is hard to work efficiently in such a confined space.* 在这样狭小的空间里工作很难提高效率.

con·fine·ment *n* **1** [U] being confined; imprisonment 限制; 监禁: *to be placed in confinement*, ie in a prison, mental hospital, etc 被监禁, 禁闭(坐牢、被关进精神病院里等) ○ *The prisoner was sentenced to three months' solitary confinement*, ie kept apart from other prisoners. 那犯人被判处单独监禁三个月(与其他犯人隔离). **2** (**a**) [U] time during which a baby is being born 分娩期: *Her confinement was approaching.* 她的分娩期临近了. (**b**) [C] instance of this; birth 分娩; 生育: *The doctor has been called to a home confinement*, ie a birth taking place at the mother's home rather than in hospital. 那医生被请到产妇家里接生.

con·fines /ˈkɒnfaɪnz; ˋkɑnfaɪnz/ *n* [pl] (*fml* 文) limits; borders; boundaries 界限; 边界; 范围: *beyond the confines of human knowledge* 超出人类知识的范围 ○ *within the confines of family life* 在家庭生活的范围内.

con·firm /kənˈfɜːm; kənˋfɝm/ *v* **1** [Tn, Tf] provide evidence for the truth or correctness of (a report, an opinion, etc); establish the truth of 证实, 证明(报告、意见等)的正确性; 确认: *The rumours of an attack were later confirmed.* 发动攻击的谣传后来得到了证实. ○ *The announcement confirmed my suspicions.* 这项通告证明了我的猜疑属实. ○ *Please write to confirm your reservation*, ie send a letter to support a booking made by telephone. 请来信确认一下您所预订的项目(来信确认在电话中预订的项目). ○ *When asked, she confirmed that she was going to retire.* 有人问她时, 她肯定了她将要退休. **2** [Tn, Tn·pr, Cn·n/a] **~sth; ~ sb (as/in sth)** ratify (a treaty, appointment, etc); make definite or establish more firmly (power, a position, etc) 批准(条约、任命等); 肯定, 巩固或加强(权力、地位等): *The new minister will be confirmed in office by the Queen.* 新的部长将由女王批准任职. ○ *After a six-month probationary period, she was confirmed in her post.* 经过六个月的试用期之后, 她获准正式任该职. ○ *The incident confirmed him in* (ie established more firmly) *his dislike of dogs.* 出了这件事之后他就更加不喜欢狗了. **3** [Tn] admit (sb) to full membership of the Christian Church (教会)给(某人)施坚信礼(使之成为正式教徒): *She was baptized when she was a month old and confirmed when she was thirteen.* 她出生一个月时受洗礼, 十三岁时行坚信礼.

▷ **con·firmed** *adj* [attrib 作定语] settled in a particular habit or state 习惯的; 根深蒂固的: *a confirmed bachelor*, ie a single man who is unlikely to marry 抱独身主义的男子 ○ *a confirmed drunkard, gambler, etc* 饮酒、赌博等成癖的人.

con·firma·tion /ˌkɒnfəˈmeɪʃn; ˌkɑnfɚˋmeʃən/ *n* [U, C] confirming or being confirmed 证实; 证明; 批准; 肯定; 巩固; 加强; 坚信礼: *We are waiting for confirmation of our onward reservations*, ie waiting to be told that our further travel bookings are still valid. 我们在等候通知预定的下一步行程是否落实. ○ *The bishop conducted a number of confirmations at the service.* 主教在仪式上为许多人施行了坚信礼.

con·fis·cate /ˈkɒnfɪskeɪt; ˋkɑnfɪsˌket/ *v* [Tn] take possession of (sb's property) by authority, without payment or compensation 没收(某人的财产); 充公: *The headmaster confiscated Tommy's pea-shooter.* 校长没收了汤米的射豆枪. ○ *If you are caught smuggling goods into the country, they will probably be confiscated.* 假若查出你向该国走私货物, 你的货物准得没收. ▷ **con·fis·ca·tion** /ˌkɒnfɪˈskeɪʃn; ˌkɑnfɪsˋkeʃən/ *n* [C, U].

con·flag·ra·tion /ˌkɒnfləˈgreɪʃn; ˌkɑnfləˋgreʃən/ *n* (*fml* 文) great and destructive fire 大火; 大火灾.

con·flate /kənˈfleɪt; kənˋflet/ *v* [Tn usu passive 通常用于被动语态] combine (two sets of information, texts, etc) into one 将(两种资料、文本等)合而为一; 混合: *The results of the two experiments were conflated.* 这两项实验的结果合并在一起了. ○ *Can these two definitions be conflated, or must they be kept separate?* 这两个定义可以合成一个呢, 还是必须分开? ▷ **con·fla·tion** /kənˈfleɪʃn; kənˋfleʃən/ *n* [U, C].

con·flict /ˈkɒnflɪkt; ˋkɑnflɪkt/ *n* [C, U] **1** (**a**) struggle; fight 斗争; 战斗: *soldiers involved in armed conflict* 遭遇武装冲突的士兵. (**b**) (*fig* 比喻) serious disagreement; argument; controversy 冲突; 争执; 争论; 论战: *a long and bitter conflict between employers and workers* 劳资双方旷日持久的激烈争执. **2** (of opinions, desires, etc) opposition; difference; clash (意见、欲望等)不合, 分歧, 抵触: *the conflict between one's duty and one's desires* 责任与欲望之间的矛盾 ○ *a conflict of interests*, ie between the achievement of one aim and that of another 利害冲突 ○ *Your statement is in conflict with the rest of the evidence.* 你的陈述同其余证据有矛盾.

▷ **con·flict** /kənˈflɪkt; kənˋflɪkt/ *v* [I, Ipr] **~ (with sth)** be in opposition or disagreement; be incompatible; clash 不合; 不一致; 冲突; 抵触: *A and B conflict/A conflicts with B.* A和B相冲突. ○ The statements of the two witnesses *conflict.* 两个证人的证词不一致. ○ *Their account of events conflicts with ours.* 他们对事件的说法与我们的说法截然不同.

con·flu·ence /ˈkɒnfluəns; ˋkɑnfluəns/ *n* **1** place where two rivers flow together and become one (两河)汇流点,

汇合处: *the confluence of the Blue Nile and the White Nile* 青尼罗河与白尼罗河的交汇处. **2** (*fml* 文) coming together, esp of large numbers of people 汇合, 汇集(尤指大群的人).

▷ **con·flu·ent** /ˈkɒnfluənt; ˋkɑnfluənt/ *adj* (*fml* 文) flowing or coming together; uniting 汇流的; 汇合的; 联合的.

con·form /kənˈfɔːm; kənˋfɔrm/ *v* **1** [I, Ipr] **~ (to sth)** keep to or comply with (generally accepted rules, standards, etc) 符合或遵守(公认的规则、准则等): *her refusal to conform (to the normal social conventions)* 她的拒绝遵从(正常的社会习俗) ○ *The building does not conform to safety regulations.* 这座建筑物不符合安全条例. **2** [Ipr] **~ with/to sth** agree or be consistent with sth 与某事物相符合或相一致: *His ideas do not conform with mine.* 他的想法跟我的不一致.

▷ **con·form·ist** /kənˈfɔːmɪst; kənˋfɔrmɪst/ *n* person who conforms to accepted behaviour, the established religion, etc 循规蹈矩的人; 墨守成规的人: *She's too much of a conformist to wear silly clothes.* 她很古板, 不穿那些奇装异服.

con·form·ity /kənˈfɔːmətɪ; kənˋfɔrmətɪ/ *n* **1** [U] **~ (to/with sth)** (*fml* 文) (behaviour, etc) conforming to established rules, customs, etc 符合, 依照(法规、习俗等)(的行为等). **2** (idm 习语) **in conformity with sth** (*fml* 文) in accordance with sth; obeying sth 与某事物相一致; 顺从某事物: *act in conformity with the rules, law, etc* 依照规定、法律等行事 ○ *in conformity with your request, instructions, wishes, etc* 遵照你的要求、指示、愿望等.

con·forma·tion /ˌkɒnfɔːˈmeɪʃn; ˌkɑnfɔrˋmeʃən/ *n* [U, C] (*fml* 文) way in which sth is formed; structure 构造; 结构.

con·found /kənˈfaʊnd; kɑnˋfaʊnd/ *v* **1** [Tn] (*dated or fml* 旧或文) puzzle and surprise (sb); perplex 使(某人)困惑和惊奇; 使迷惑: *His behaviour amazed and confounded her.* 他的所作所为让她感到既惊愕又困惑. ○ *I was confounded to hear that*... 我听到...感到大惑不解. **2** [Tn, Tn·pr] **~ sth (with sth)** (*dated* 旧) confuse (ideas, etc) 使(思想等)混乱. **3** [Tn] (*dated or fml* 旧或文) (**a**) defeat (sb) 击败(某人): *confound an enemy, a rival, a critic, etc* 击败敌人、对手、批评者等. (**b**) prevent (sth); thwart 防碍, 挫败(某事物): *confound a plan, an attempt, etc* 挫败计划、企图等. **4** [Tn] (*infml* 口) (used as an *interj* to express anger 用作叹词表示愤怒): Confound it! 真讨厌! ○ Confound you! 去你的!

▷ **con·foun·ded** *adj* [attrib 作定语] (*infml* 口) (used to emphasize one's annoyance 用以强调厌烦之意): *You're a confounded nuisance!* 你真讨厌死了! **confoun·dedly** *adv* (*infml* 口) very 非常: *It's confoundedly hot.* 极热的.

con·front /kənˈfrʌnt; kənˋfrʌnt/ *v* **1** [Tn·pr] **~ sb with sb/sth** make sb face or consider sb/sth unpleasant, difficult, etc 使某人面对或正视令人不快、令人头疼等的人[事物]: *They confronted the prisoner with his accusers.* 他们让犯人与原告对质. ○ *When confronted with the evidence of her guilt, she confessed.* 她面对罪证供认不讳. **2** [Tn] (**a**) (of a difficulty, etc) face (sb) threateningly; oppose (指困难等)临到(某人)头上; 面临: *the problems confronting us* 摆在我们面前的问题 ○ *Confronted by an angry crowd the police retreated.* 警察面对愤怒的人群只好后撤了. (**b**) face (sth) defiantly 对抗或面对(某事物): *A soldier often has to confront danger.* 士兵常常要身临险境.

▷ **con·fronta·tion** /ˌkɒnfrʌnˈteɪʃn; ˌkɑnfrʌnˋteʃən/ *n* [C, U] (instance of) angry opposition 对抗; 对抗的事物: *a confrontation between the Government and the unions* 政府与工会之间的对抗.

Con·fu·cian /kənˈfjuːʃn; kənˋfjuʃən/ *adj*, *n* (follower) of Confucius /kənˈfjuːʃəs; kənˋfjuʃəs/, the Chinese philosopher and teacher (551-479 BC) 孔子的; 崇奉孔子的; 儒家的; 孔子的信徒.

con·fuse /kənˈfjuːz; kənˋfjuz/ *v* **1** [Tn usu passive 通常用于被动语态] make (sb) unable to think clearly; puzzle; bewilder 把(某人)弄糊涂; 使迷惑; 使为难: *They confused me by asking so many questions.* 他们提了一大堆问题, 把我都弄糊涂了. **2** [Tn] put (sth) into disorder; upset 把(某事物)搞乱; 打乱: *Her unexpected arrival confused all our plans.* 她突然来到把我们所有的计划全打乱了. **3** [Tn, Tn·pr] **~ A and/with B** mistake one person or thing for another 把此人或此物误当作彼人或彼物; 混淆: *I always confuse the sisters: they look so alike.* 我总是分不出这对姐妹, 她们看上去简直一模一样. ○ *Don't confuse Austria and/with Australia.* 不要把奥地利跟澳大利亚弄混淆了. ○ *This construction should not be confused with the regular passive.* 这种句法结构不可与按规则变化的被动语态相混淆. **4** [Tn] make (sth) unclear; muddle 使(某事物)模糊不清; 使含糊: *a confused argument* 自相矛盾的论点 ○ *Don't confuse the issue*, eg by introducing irrelevant topics. 不要把问题搅乱(如提出无关的话题).

▷ **con·fused** *adj* **1** unable to think clearly; bewildered 糊涂的; 迷乱的: *All your changes of plan have made me totally confused.* 你把计划改来改去, 我都糊涂了. ○ *The old lady easily gets confused.* 这个老太婆容易迷糊. **2** mixed up; not clear 混杂的; 不清楚的: *a confused account of what happened* 对发生的事杂乱无章的叙述. **con·fus·edly** /-ɪdlɪ; -ɪdlɪ/ *adv*.

con·fus·ing *adj* difficult to understand; puzzling 莫名其妙的; 难以理解的: *a most confusing speech* 完全莫名其妙的讲话 ○ *The instructions on the box are very confusing.* 盒子上的使用说明含混不清. **con·fus·ingly** *adv*.

con·fu·sion /kənˈfjuːʒn; kənˋfjuʒən/ *n* [U] **1** bewilderment or embarrassment 迷乱; 惶惑: *gazing in confusion at the strange sight* 惶惑地凝视着这种奇怪的景象. **2** disorder 混乱; 杂乱: *Her unexpected arrival threw us into total confusion.* 她来得很突然, 使我们完全不知所措. **3** mistaking of one person or thing for another 混淆; 混同: *There has been some confusion of names.* 有些名字弄混了. **4** state of uncertainty 不确定状态: *There is some confusion about what the right procedure should be.* 对应该采取怎样的步骤这一点还不太明确.

con·fute /kənˈfjuːt; kənˋfjut/ *v* [Tn] (*fml* 文) prove (a person or an argument) to be wrong 证明(某人或某论点)有误; 驳倒. ▷ **con·fu·ta·tion** /ˌkɒnfjuːˈteɪʃn; ˌkɑnfjuˋteʃən/ *n* [U, C].

conga /ˈkɒŋgə; ˋkɑŋgə/ *n* (music for a) lively dance in which the dancers follow a leader linked together in a long winding line 康茄舞; 康茄舞乐曲.

con·geal /kənˈdʒiːl; kənˋdʒil/ *v* [I, Tn] (of a liquid) (cause to) become thick or solid, esp by cooling (指液体)(使)变浓或凝结(尤指遇冷冻结): *The blood had congealed round the cut on her knee.* 血液在她的膝盖伤口周围凝固了. ○ *Use hot water to rinse the congealed fat off the dinner plates.* 用热水把菜盘上凝结的油渍冲洗掉.

con·gen·ial /kənˈdʒiːnɪəl; kənˋdʒinjəl/ *adj* **1** (of people) pleasing because of similarities in temperament, interests, etc (指人)(因性情、志趣等相近)彼此合得来的, 意气相投的: *a congenial companion* 情投意合的伴侣. **2 ~ (to sb)** agreeable or pleasant because suited to one's nature or tastes 适合于自己的天性或癖好的: *a congenial climate, environment, hobby* 适意的气候、环境、消遣 ○ *I find this aspect of my job particularly congenial.* 我觉得我的工作的这一方面特别适合于我.

▷ **con·geni·al·ity** /kənˌdʒiːnɪˈælətɪ; kənˌdʒinɪˋælətɪ/ *n* [U]. **con·geni·ally** /-ɪəlɪ; -jəlɪ/ *adv*.

con·gen·ital /kənˈdʒenɪtl; kənˋdʒɛnətl̩/ *adj* **1** (of diseases, etc) present from or before birth (指疾病等)天生的, 先天的: *congenital defects, blindness, etc* 先天性缺陷、失明等. **2** [attrib 作定语] (of people) born with a certain illness or condition (指人)生来有某种疾病或状况的: *a congenital idiot, syphilitic, etc* 先天性白痴、梅毒患者等.

con·ger /ˈkɒŋgə(r); ˋkɑŋgɚ/ *n* (also ˌ**conger ˈeel**) large type of sea eel 康吉鳗(一种大海鳗).

con·gested /kənˈdʒestɪd; kənˋdʒɛstɪd/ *adj* **1 ~ (with sth)** too full; overcrowded 拥挤不堪的; 充塞的: *streets congested with traffic* 交通拥塞的街道. **2** (**a**) (of parts of the body, eg the lungs) abnormally full of blood (指身体的部分, 如肺部)充血的. (**b**) (of the nose) blocked with mucus (指鼻子)因鼻涕多而不通的: *He had a cold and was very congested.* 他患了感冒, 鼻子不通.

con·ges·tion /kənˈdʒestʃən; kənˋdʒɛstʃən/ *n* [U] state of being congested 拥挤; 充塞; 充血; 鼻腔阻塞: *traffic* *congestion* 交通拥塞 ○ *congestion of the lungs* 肺充血.

con·glom·er·ate /kən'glɒmərət; kən`glɑmərɪt/ *n* **1** materials gathered together into a rounded mass (聚集成团的)聚合物. **2** rock made of small stones held together by cement, dried clay, etc (由小石块用水泥、泥等黏结而成的)岩块. **3** (*commerce* 商) large corporation formed by merging several different firms (通过合并若干企业而组建的)大公司, 企业集团: *a mining, chemical, etc conglomerate* 矿业、化工等企业集团.

▷ **con·glom·era·tion** /kənˌglɒmə'reɪʃn; kənˌglɑmə're-ʃən/ *n* **1** [C] (*infml* 口) assortment of different things gathered together or found in the same place 聚集物; 收集物: *a conglomeration of rusty old machinery* 一堆生锈的旧机器. **2** [U] process of becoming, or state of being, a conglomerate 聚集过程; 组建成企业集团的过程; 聚集状态.

C

con·gratu·late /kən'grætʃʊleɪt; kən`grætʃəˌlet/ *v* [Tn, Tn·pr] **1 ~ sb (on sth)** tell sb that one is pleased about his good fortune or achievements 祝贺; 庆贺; 道喜: *congratulate sb on his marriage, new job, good exam results, etc* 祝贺某人结婚、找到新工作、考试成绩优良等. **2 ~ oneself (on/upon (doing) sth)** consider oneself fortunate or successful; be proud (of sth) 认为自己幸运或成功; (为某事物而)自鸣得意: *You can congratulate yourself on having done a good job.* 你的工作做得很出色, 你应该感到自豪.

▷ **con·gratu·lat·ory** /kən'grætʃʊlətərɪ; *US* -tɔ:rɪ; kən-`grætʃələˌtorɪ/ *adj* [usu attrib 通常作定语] intended to congratulate 祝贺的: *congratulatory words, letters, telegrams, etc* 贺词、贺信、贺电.

con·gratu·la·tion /kənˌgrætʃʊ'leɪʃn; kənˌgrætʃə`leʃən/ *n* **1** [U] congratulating or being congratulated 祝贺或受到祝贺: *a speech of congratulation for the winner* 对获胜者的贺词. **2 congratulations** [pl] **(a)** words of congratulation 贺词: *offer sb one's congratulations on his success* 祝贺某人成功. **(b)** (used as an *interj* 用作叹词): *You've passed your driving test? Congratulations!* 你驾驶测验合格了? 向你道喜! ○ *Congratulations on winning the prize!* 祝贺你获奖!

con·greg·ate /'kɒŋgrɪgeɪt; `kɑŋgrɪˌget/ *v* [I] come together in a crowd 集合; 聚集: *A crowd quickly congregated (round the speaker).* 大群的人迅速地(在演说者周围)聚集起来.

con·grega·tion /ˌkɒŋgrɪ'geɪʃn; ˌkɑŋgrɪ`geʃən/ *n* [CGp] **1** group of people gathered together for religious worship (usu excluding the priest and choir) (参加宗教礼拜式的)会众(通常不包括牧师和唱诗班). **2** group of people who regularly attend a particular church, etc 教堂会众(定期参加某教会活动等的人群).

▷ **con·grega·tional** *adj* [usu attrib 通常作定语] **1** of a congregation 会众的. **2 Congregational** of a union of Christian churches in which individual congregations are responsible for their own affairs 公理会的.

con·gress /'kɒŋgres; *US* -grəs; `kɑŋgrəs/ *n* [CGp] **1** formal meeting or series of meetings for discussion between representatives 代表大会: *a medical, international, etc congress* 医学、国际等会议 ○ *the Church Congress* 教会代表大会. **2 Congress** law-making body, eg of the USA 国会(立法机关, 如美国国会). Cf 参看 SENATE 1.

▷ **con·gres·sional** *adj* /kən'greʃənl; kən`greʃənl/ of a congress or Congress 代表大会的; 国会的; 最高立法机关的: *a congressional investigation, committee* 代表大会的审查、委员会等.

□ '**Con·gress·man** /-mən; -mən/ *n* (*pl* **-men** /-mən; -mən), '**Con·gress·woman** *n* (*pl* **-women**) member of the US Congress 美国国会议员.

con·gru·ent /'kɒŋgrʊənt; `kɑŋgrʊənt/ *adj* **1** (*geometry* 几) having the same size and shape 全等的: *congruent triangles* 全等三角形. **2** (also **congruous**) **~ (with sth)** (*fml* 文) suitable; fitting 适合的; 适当的; 相称的: *measures congruent with the seriousness of the situation* 针对情况的严重性而采取的措施.

con·gru·ous /'kɒŋgrʊəs; `kɑŋgrʊəs/ *adj* **~ (with sth)** (*fml* 文) = CONGRUENT 2. ▷ **con·gru·ity** /kɒŋ'gru:ətɪ; kən`gruətɪ/ *n* [U].

conic /'kɒnɪk; `kɑnɪk/ *adj* (*geometry* 几) of a cone 圆锥的: *conic sections*, ie the shapes formed when a cone is intersected by a plane 圆锥截面.

▷ **con·ical** /'kɒnɪkl; `kɑnɪkl/ *adj* cone-shaped 圆锥形的: *a conical hat, shell, hill* 锥形的帽子、贝壳、小山.

con·ifer /'kɒnɪfə(r), *also* 'kəʊn-; `kɑnəfɚ; `kon-/ *n* type of tree (eg pine, fir) that bears cones (CONE 3) 针叶树(如松树、枞树、结球果).

▷ **con·ifer·ous** /kə'nɪfərəs; *US* kəʊ'n-; ko`nɪfərəs/ *adj* (of trees) bearing cones (指树)结球果的, 针叶树的.

con·jec·ture /kən'dʒektʃə(r); kən`dʒɛktʃɚ/ *v* [I, Ipr, Tn, Tf] **~ (about sth)** (*fml* 文) form (and express) an opinion not based on firm evidence; guess 推测; 猜测: *It was just as I had conjectured.* 这正如我所猜测的. ○ *Don't conjecture about the outcome.* 不要对结果妄加猜测. ○ *What made you conjecture that?* 是什么促使你推测出这样的结论?

▷ **con·jec·ture** *n* **1** [C] guess 猜测; 推测: *I was right in my conjectures.* 我所猜测的都应验了. **2** [U] guessing 猜测; 推测: *What the real cause was is open to conjecture.* 真正的原因是什么尽可任凭猜测. ○ *Your theory is pure conjecture.* 你的理论纯粹是主观臆测. **con·jec·tural** /kən'dʒektʃərəl; kən`dʒɛktʃərəl/ *adj* based on conjecture 推测的; 猜测的.

con·join /kən'dʒɔɪn; kən`dʒɔɪn/ *v* [I, Tn] (*fml* 文) (cause people or things to) join together; unite (使)结合; 联合.

▷ **con·joint** /kən'dʒɔɪnt, 'kɒndʒɔɪnt; kən`dʒɔɪnt/ *adj* (*fml* 文) united; associated 结合的; 联合的. **con·jointly** *adv*.

con·jugal /'kɒndʒʊgl; `kɑndʒʊgl/ *adj* (*fml* 文) of marriage or the relationship between a husband and a wife 婚姻的; 夫妻之间的: *conjugal life, bliss, rights* 婚姻的生活、美满、权利. ▷ **con·jug·ally** /-gəlɪ; -glɪ/ *adv*.

con·jug·ate /'kɒndʒʊgeɪt; `kɑndʒʊˌget/ *v* (*grammar*) **1** [Tn] give the different forms of (a verb), as they vary according to number, tense, etc 列举(动词)的变化形式(单复数、时态等). **2** [I] (of a verb) have different forms showing number, tense, etc (指动词)有数、时态等词形变化: *How does this verb conjugate?* 这个动词有哪些变化形式?

▷ **con·juga·tion** /ˌkɒndʒʊ'geɪʃn; ˌkɑndʒə`geʃən/ *n* **1** [C, U] (method of) conjugating 动词的词形变化(法): *a verb with an irregular conjugation* 不规则的动词. **2** [C] class of verbs that conjugate in the same way 词形变化相似的一类动词: *Latin verbs of the second conjugation* 属于第二种变化法的拉丁语动词.

con·junc·tion /kən'dʒʌŋkʃn; kən`dʒʌŋkʃən/ *n* **1** [C] (*grammar*) word that joins words, phrases or sentences, eg *and, but, or* 连词(用以连接词、词组或句子的词, 如and、but、or). **2** (*fml* 文) **(a)** [C] combination (of events, etc) (事件等的)结合, 同时发生: *an unusual conjunction of circumstances* 各种情况偶然的巧合. **(b)** [U] joining or being joined together; blend 结合; 连在一起; 混和: *the conjunction of workmanship and artistry in making jewellery* 在珠宝饰物的制造中手工与艺术的结合. **3** (idm 习语) **in conjunction with sb/sth** together with sb/sth 与某人[某事物]一道: *We are working in conjunction with the police.* 我们与警方配合进行工作.

con·junct·ive /kən'dʒʌŋktɪv; kən`dʒʌŋktɪv/ *adj* (*esp grammar* 尤作语法用语) that joins or connects 连接的; 联结的: *a conjunctive adverb* 连接副词.

▷ **con·junct·ive** *n* conjuction(1) 连词.

con·junc·tiv·itis /kənˌdʒʌŋktɪ'vaɪtɪs; kənˌdʒʌŋktə`vaɪtɪs/ *n* [U] inflammation of the thin transparent membrane which covers the eyeball 结膜炎.

con·junc·ture /kən'dʒʌŋktʃə(r); kən`dʒʌŋktʃɚ/ *n* (*fml* 文) combination (of events or circumstances); conjunction(2a) (事件或情况的)结合; 同时发生.

con·jure[1] /'kʌndʒə(r); `kʌndʒɚ/ *v* **1** [I] do clever tricks which seem magical, esp with quick movements of the hands 变戏法; 变魔术(尤指手法敏捷的): *learn how to conjure* 学变戏法. **2** (idm 习语) **a name to conjure with** ⇨ NAME. **3** (phr v) **conjure sth up (a)** make sth appear as a picture in the mind 使某事物浮现于脑际: *a tune which conjures up pleasant memories* 唤起美好回忆的曲调. **(b)** ask (a spirit) to appear (esp by using a magic ceremony) 祈求(鬼魂)显灵(尤指使用巫术的): *conjure up the spirits of the dead* 念咒召死者的魂灵. **conjure sth up; conjure sth (up) from/out of**

sth make sth appear suddenly or unexpectedly, as if by magic (如变戏法般)使某事物突然地或意外地出现: *I had lost my pen, but she conjured up another one for me from somewhere.* 我把钢笔弄丢了，可是她像变戏法似的不知从什么地方又给我弄来一枝. ○ *conjuring a delicious meal out of a few unpromising ingredients* 用一些毫不出奇的材料做出了一顿美餐.

▷ **con·jurer** (also **con·juror**) /ˈkʌndʒərə(r); ˋkʌndʒərɚ/ *n* person who performs conjuring tricks 变戏法的人; 魔术师. Cf 参看 MAGICIAN (MAGIC).

con·jur·ing /ˈkʌndʒərɪŋ; ˋkʌndʒərɪŋ/ *n* [U] performing of clever tricks which seem magical, esp involving quick movements of the hands 变戏法; 变魔术: [attrib 作定语] *a ˈconjuring trick* 戏法; 魔术; 把戏.

con·jure[2] /kənˈdʒʊə(r); kənˋdʒʊr/ *v* [Tn, Dn·t] (*fml* 文) appeal solemnly to (sb) 祈求, 恳求(某人): *Be on your guard, I conjure you.* 千万要警惕呀, 我恳求你. ○ *I conjure you most earnestly to reconsider your position.* 我最诚恳地请求你重新考虑一下你的立场. ▷ **con·jura·tion** /ˌkɒndʒʊˈreɪʃn; ˌkɑndʒʊˋreʃən/ *n* [U].

conk[1] /kɒŋk; kɑŋk/ *n* (*Brit sl* 俚) nose 鼻子.

conk[2] /kɒŋk; kɑŋk/ *v* (phr v) **conk out** (*infml* 口) **(a)** (of a machine) stop working (指机器)停止运转, 失灵: *The car conked out at the crossroads.* 汽车在十字路口抛锚了. **(b)** (of people) become exhausted and stop; fall asleep, faint or die (指人)筋疲力尽而停止, 入睡, 昏迷, 死去: *Grandad usually conks out* (ie sleeps) *for an hour or so after lunch.* 爷爷吃过午饭往往要睡一个小时左右.

conker /ˈkɒŋkə(r); ˋkɑŋkɚ/ *n* (*infml* 口 *esp Brit*) horse-chestnut 七叶树果. ⇨illus at App 1 见附录1之插图, page i.

con man ⇨ CON.

con·nect /kəˈnekt; kəˋnɛkt/ *v* **1** [I, Ipr, Ip, Tn, Tn·pr, Tn·p] **~ (sth) (up) (to/with sth)** come or bring together or into contact; join 连接; 联结; 结合: *The wires connect (up) under the floor.* 电线是在地板下接通的. ○ *Where does the cooker connect with the gas-pipe?* 煤气炉在什么地方与煤气管道衔接? ○ *The two towns are connected by a railway.* 这两个市镇通火车. ○ *A railway connects Oxford and/with Reading.* 牛津与雷丁之间有铁路相连. ○ *Connect the fridge (up) to the electricity supply.* 接通冰箱的电源. ○ *The thigh bone is connected to the hip bone.* 股骨连着髋骨. ○ *The two rooms have a connecting door*, ie so that you can go straight from one room into the other. 这两个房间有门相通. ○ an ill-connected narrative 缺乏连贯性的叙述. **2 (a)** [Tn, Tn·pr usu passive 通常用于被动语态] **~ sb (with sb/sth)** associate sb (with sb/sth); relate sb (to sb/sth) 使某人(与某人[某事物])有联系; 使有关系: *a man connected with known criminals* 与人所共知的罪犯有关系的人 ○ *The two men are connected by marriage.* 这两个男子是姻亲. ○ *She is connected with a noble family.* 她是某名门望族的亲戚. **(b)** [Tn, Tn·pr] **~ sb/sth (with sb/sth)** think of (different things or people) as being related to each other 用想像把(不同事物或人)联系起来; 联想: *I was surprised to hear them mentioned together: I've never connected them before.* 听到有人把他们俩扯在一起, 我感到很惊奇, 我以前从未想到过他们之间有什么关系. ○ *People connect Vienna with waltzes and coffee-houses.* 人们一提到维也纳就会联想到华尔兹圆舞曲和咖啡馆. **3** [I, Ipr] **~ (with sth)** (of a train, plane, etc) be timed to arrive so that passengers can transfer from or to another train, plane, etc (指火车、飞机等)安排好到达时间以便使中转的旅客换乘另一火车、飞机等; 实行联运: *These two planes connect.* 这两架班机在时间上互相衔接. ○ *The 9:00 am train from London connects with the 12:05 pm from Crewe.* 上午9时自伦敦开出的列车可接上下午12时05分自克鲁开出的列车. ○ *There's a connecting flight at midday.* 中午有一次联运航班. **4** [Tn, Tn·pr] **~ sb (with sb)** (of a telephonist) put sb into contact by telephone (话务员)给某人接通电话: *Hold on, I'll just connect you (with Miss Jones).* 请等一下, 我这就给您接通(琼斯小姐的电话). **5** [I, Ipr] **~ (with sb/sth)** (*infml* 口) (of a blow, etc) strike or touch (指打击等)击中或碰到: *a wild swing which failed to connect (with his chin)* 抡臂猛击, 却未击中(他的下巴). Cf 参看 WELL-CONNECTED (WELL[3]).

□ **conˈnecting rod** rod linking the piston and the crankshaft in an engine 活塞杆.

con·nec·tion (*Brit* also **con·nex·ion**) /kəˈnekʃn; kəˋnɛkʃən/ *n* **1 (a)** [U] connecting or being connected 连接; 联结: *How long will the connection of the telephone take?* ie How long will it take to install a telephone and connect it to the exchange? 安装电话机与总机接通要多长时间? **(b)** [C] **~ between sth and sth; ~ with/to sth** point where two things are connected; thing that connects 连接点; 连接物: *There's a faulty connection in the fuse-box.* 保险丝盒里接错了线. ○ *What is the connection between the two ideas*, ie How are they linked? 这两个概念之间有什么联系? ○ *Is there a connection between smoking and lung cancer?* 吸烟跟肺癌是否有关? ○ *His dismissal has no connection with* (ie is not due to) *the quality of his work.* 他被解雇一事与他的工作好坏无关. **2** [C] train, plane, etc timed to leave a station, airport, etc soon after the arrival of another, enabling passengers to change from one to the other (供中转旅客及时换乘的)联运交通工具(如火车、飞机等): *The train was late and I missed my connection.* 列车误点了, 我没能赶上联运. **3** [C usu *pl* 通常作复数] person whom one knows socially or through business, esp one who has influence or high rank 熟人, 生意上的关系户(尤指有权有势的): *I heard about it through one of my business connections.* 我通过一个生意上的关系户知道了这件事. **4 connections** [pl] relatives 亲属; 亲戚: *She is British but also has German connections.* 她是英国人, 但也有一些德国亲戚. **5** (idm 习语) **in connection with sb/sth** with reference to sb/sth 与某人[某事物]有关: *I am writing to you in connection with your job application.* 此信是有关你求职一事的. **in this/that connection** (*fml* 文) with reference to this/that 关于这[那]一点.

con·nect·ive /kəˈnektɪv; kəˋnɛktɪv/ *adj* that connects things 连接的; 起连接作用的: *connective tissue* 结缔组织.

▷ **con·nect·ive** *n* thing that connects, esp a linking word 连接物; (尤指)联结词.

conning-tower /ˈkɒnɪŋ taʊə(r); ˋkɑnɪŋ ˌtaʊɚ/ *n* raised structure on a submarine containing the periscope (潜水艇上带有潜望镜的)瞭望塔.

con·nive /kəˈnaɪv; kəˋnaɪv/ *v* [Ipr] **~ at sth** (*derog* 贬) disregard or seem to allow (a wrong action) 对错误行为视若无睹; 默许; 纵容: *Not to protest is to connive at the destruction of the environment.* 对于破坏环境的行为不加反对就等于纵容.

▷ **con·niv·ance** /kəˈnaɪvəns; kəˋnaɪvəns/ *n* [U] **~ (at/in sth)** conniving (at a wrong action) 默许, 纵容(错误的行为): *a crime carried out with the connivance of/in connivance with the police* 在警方的纵容下所犯的罪行.

con·niv·ing *adj* acting slyly and unpleasantly so as to harm others 搞阴谋的; 暗算他人的: *You conniving bastard!* 你这个阴险的傢伙!

con·nois·seur /ˌkɒnəˈsɜː(r); ˌkɑnəˋsɝ/ *n* person with good judgement on matters in which appreciation of fineness or beauty is needed, esp the fine arts (尤指艺术品的)鉴赏家, 鉴定家, 行家: *a connoisseur of painting, antiques, wine* 绘画、古瓷、古董、葡萄酒鉴定家.

con·note /kəˈnəʊt; kəˋnot/ *v* [Tn, Tf] (of words) suggest (sth) in addition to the main meaning (指词语)含有某种附加意义: *a term connoting disapproval/that one disapproves of sth* 暗含不赞成[不赞成某事物]的词语.

▷ **con·no·ta·tion** /ˌkɒnəˈteɪʃn; ˌkɑnəˋteʃən/ *n* idea which a word makes one think of in addition to the main meaning 隐含意义; 言外之意: *The word 'hack' means 'journalist' but has derogatory connotations.* hack 一词意为'新闻记者', 但含贬义.

con·nu·bial /kəˈnjuːbɪəl; *US* -ˈnuː-; kəˋnubɪəl/ *adj* (*fml or joc* 文或谑) of marriage; of husband and wife 婚姻的; 夫妻的: *connubial life, bliss, etc* 夫妻生活、和睦等.

con·quer /ˈkɒŋkə(r); ˋkɑŋkɚ/ *v* [Tn] **1 (a)** take possession of (sth) by force 以武力占领, 征服(某事物): *The Normans conquered England in 1066.* 诺曼人于1066年征服了英国. **(b)** (*fig* 比喻) gain the admiration, love, etc of (sb/sth) 赢得(某人[某事物])的赞誉、爱慕等: *He set out to conquer the literary world of London.* 他决心赢得伦敦文学界的赞誉. ○ *She has conquered the hearts of many men*, ie they have fallen in love with her. 她已使许多男子倾心. **2 (a)** defeat (an enemy, a rival, etc) 击败

C

(敌人、对手等): *England conquered their main rivals in the first round of the competition.* 英格兰队在第一轮比赛中就击败了主要对手. **(b)** (*fig* 比喻) overcome (an obstacle, emotion, etc) 克服(障碍、情绪等): *The mountain was not conquered* (ie successfully climbed) *until 1953.* 1953年以前, 从未有人能攀登到这座山的山顶. ○ *Smallpox has finally been conquered.* 天花终于遏制住了. ○ *You must conquer your fear of driving.* 你必须克服驾驶车辆的恐惧心理.

▷ **con·queror** /ˈkɒŋkərə(r); ˋkɑŋkərɚ/ *n* person who conquers 征服者: *William the Conqueror*, ie King William I of England. 征服者威廉(英国国王威廉一世).

con·quest /ˈkɒŋkwest; ˋkɑŋkwɛst/ *n* **1** [U] conquering (eg of a country and its people); defeat 征服(如某国家及其人民); 击败: *the Norman Conquest*, ie of England by the Normans in 1066 诺曼人的征服(即1066年诺曼人征服英国) ○ *the conquest of cancer* 战胜癌症. **2** [C] **(a)** thing got by conquering 掠取物; 战利品: *the Roman conquests in Africa* 罗马人在非洲的征服所得. **(b)** person whose admiration or (esp) love has been gained 仰慕者; 崇拜者; (尤指)爱情的俘虏: *He is one of her many conquests.* 她倾倒众生, 他是其中之一. ○ *You've made quite a conquest there*, ie He or she likes you! 你很招人喜爱!

con·quis·ta·dor /kɒnˈkwɪstədɔː(r); kɑnˋkwɪstə,dɔr/ *n* (*pl* **~s** or **~es**) one of the Spanish conquerors of Mexico and Peru in the 16th century (16世纪征服墨西哥和秘鲁的)西班牙征服者.

Cons *abbr* 缩写 = (*Brit politics* 政) Conservative: *James Crofton (Cons)* 詹姆斯·克洛夫顿(保守党人).

con·san·guin·ity /ˌkɒnsæŋˈgwɪnətɪ; ˌkɑnsæŋˋgwɪnətɪ/ *n* [U] (*fml* 文) relationship by being descended from the same family 血亲; 血缘; 血族: *close ties of consanguinity* 很近的血亲关系.

con·science /ˈkɒnʃəns; ˋkɑnʃəns/ *n* [C, U] **1** person's awareness of right and wrong with regard to his own thoughts and actions 良心; 是非感: *have a clear/guilty conscience*, ie feel one has done right/wrong 问心无[有]愧 ○ *After she had committed the crime, her conscience was troubled*, ie she felt very guilty. 她犯罪后, 良心上感到很不安. ○ *She cheerfully cheats and lies; she's got no conscience at all.* 她以撒谎和骗人为乐, 完全没有良心. ○ *I must go. It's a matter of conscience*, ie I think it would be morally wrong not to go. 我必须去, 这是有关良心的事(不去对不起自己的良心). ○ *prisoners of conscience*, ie people imprisoned because they believe it is wrong to support a political system, etc 政治犯(认为拥护某政治制度等是错误的因而被关押者). **2** (idm 习语) **ease sb's conscience/mind** ⇨ EASE[2]. **have sth on one's conscience** feel troubled about sth one has done or failed to do 因做了某事或未能做某事而内疚: *He has several murders on his conscience.* 他因为谋害了几个人而受到良心的谴责. **in all conscience** by any reasonable standard 当然; 的确; 凭良心: *You cannot in all conscience regard that as fair pay.* 你在良心上总不能认为那样的报酬算是合理的吧. **on one's ˈconscience** making one feel one has done wrong, or left sth undone 使人觉得自己做错了事或该做某事而未做: *It's still on my conscience that I didn't warn her in time.* 我未能及时提醒她, 这事至今使我耿耿于怀. **search one's heart/conscience** ⇨ SEARCH.

□ **ˈconscience money** money paid to make one feel less guilty, esp when one should have paid it before 为求心安而付出的钱(尤指早就应付的钱).

ˈconscience-stricken /-strɪkən; -ˌstrɪkən/ filled with remorse 于心不安的; 受良心责备的.

con·scien·tious /ˌkɒnʃɪˈenʃəs; ˌkɑnʃɪˋɛnʃəs/ *adj* **1** (of people or conduct) careful to do what one ought to do, and do it as well as one can (指人或行为)认真的, 尽责的: *a conscientious worker, pupil, attitude* 勤勤恳恳的工作人员、学生、态度. **2** (of actions) done with great care and attention (指行动)小心谨慎的: *This essay is a most conscientious piece of work.* 这篇论文是精雕细刻的工作. ▷ **con·scien·tiously** *adv*. **con·scien·tious·ness** *n* [U].

□ **ˌconscientious obˈjector** person who refuses to serve in the armed forces because he thinks it is morally wrong (因觉不合道义)拒服兵役者. Cf 参看 PACIFIST (PACIFISM).

con·scious /ˈkɒnʃəs; ˋkɑnʃəs/ *adj* **1** knowing what is going on around one because one is able to use bodily senses and mental powers; awake 感觉到的; 意识到的; 清醒的: *He was in a coma for days, but now he's (fully) conscious again.* 他昏迷了几天, 但现在又(完全)清醒了. ○ *She spoke to us in her conscious moments.* 她神志清醒时跟我们说过话. **2 ~ of sth/that...** aware; noticing 知道的; 察觉的; 注意到的: *be conscious of being watched/that one is being watched* 察觉有人在监视自己 ○ *Are you conscious (of) how people will regard such behaviour?* 你知道人们对这种行为是怎样看待的吗? **3** (of actions, feelings, etc) realized by oneself; intentional (指行为、感情等)自觉的; 蓄意的: *One's conscious motives are often different from one's subconscious ones.* 一个人有明显动机的举动跟下意识的举动往往截然不同. ○ *I had to make a conscious effort not to be rude to him.* 我得刻意约束自己不要对他粗鲁. **4** being particularly aware of and interested in the thing mentioned 对所提到的事物具有深刻认识和浓厚兴趣的: *trying to make the workers more politically conscious* 努力提高工人的政治觉悟 ○ *Teenagers are very ˈfashion-conscious.* 青少年很讲究时髦. ▷ **consciously** *adv*.

con·scious·ness /ˈkɒnʃəsnɪs; ˋkɑnʃəsnɪs/ *n* [U] **1 (a)** state of being conscious(1) 知觉; 清醒状态: *The blow caused him to lose consciousness.* 那一击打得他失去了知觉. ○ *recover/regain consciousness after an accident* 事故之后恢复知觉. **(b) ~ (of sth/that...)** state of being aware; awareness 明了; 觉悟: *my consciousness of her needs* 我对她的需求的了解 ○ *class consciousness*, ie awareness of the struggle between social classes and strong attachment to one's own class 阶级觉悟. **2** all the ideas, thoughts, feelings, etc of a person or people 意识: *attitudes that are deeply ingrained in the English consciousness* 深深扎根于英国人意识中的看法.

con·script /kənˈskrɪpt; kənˋskrɪpt/ *v* [Tn, Tn·pr] **~ sb (into sth)** force sb by law to serve in the armed forces 征召某人服兵役: *conscripted into the army* 被征入伍 ○ (*fig* 比喻) *I got conscripted into the team when their top player was injured.* 他们的尖子队员受了伤, 就把我召去了. Cf 参看 DRAFT.

▷ **con·script** /ˈkɒnskrɪpt; ˋkɑnskrɪpt/ *n* person who has been conscripted 被征入伍者; 应征人员: [attrib 作定语] *conscript soldiers* 应征士兵 ○ *a conscript army* 应征部队. Cf 参看 VOLUNTEER 2.

con·scrip·tion /kənˈskrɪpʃn; kənˋskrɪpʃən/ *n* [U] conscripting of people into the armed forces 征兵; 招兵.

con·sec·rate /ˈkɒnsɪkreɪt; ˋkɑnsɪˌkret/ *v* **1** [Tn, Cn·n] bring (sth) into religious use or (sb) into a religious office by a special ceremony 把(某事物)奉献(作宗教用途); 行仪式使(某人)就任圣职: *The new church was consecrated by the Bishop of Chester.* 在切斯特的主教主持下举行了新教堂的奉献礼. ○ *He was consecrated Archbishop last year.* 他于去年就任大主教之圣职. **2** [Tn·pr] **~ sth/sb to sth** reserve sth/sb for or devote sth/sb to a special (esp religious) purpose 将某物[某人]留给或献给某事物[某人]作某种(尤指宗教的)用途: *consecrate one's life to the service of God, to the relief of suffering* 献身于为神服务[解除世人苦难]的事业. Cf 参看 DEDICATE 3.

▷ **con·sec·ra·tion** /ˌkɒnsɪˈkreɪʃn; ˌkɑnsɪˋkreʃən/ *n* [C, U] (instance of) consecrating or being consecrated 献祭; 献身; 授圣职的仪式: *the consecration of a bishop*, ie the ceremony at which a priest is made a bishop 主教授职礼(由神父升为主教的仪式).

con·sec·ut·ive /kənˈsekjʊtɪv; kənˋsɛkjətɪv/ *adj* coming one after the other without interruption; following continuously 顺序来的; 连续不断的: *on three consecutive days, Monday, Tuesday and Wednesday* 星期一、星期二、星期三连续三天. ▷ **con·sec·ut·ively** *adv*.

con·sensus /kənˈsensəs; kənˋsɛnsəs/ *n* [C, U] **~ (on sth/that...)** agreement in opinion; collective opinion 意见一致; 共同看法: *The two parties have reached a consensus.* 这两个政党达成了一致意见. ○ *There is broad consensus (of opinion) in the country on this issue.* 对这一问题举国上下(舆论)普遍一致. ○ [attrib 作定语] *consensus politics*, ie the practice of proposing policies which will be given support by (nearly) all parties 以协商为基础的政治.

con·sent /kən'sent; kən'sɛnt/ *v* [I, Ipr, It] **~ (to sth)** give agreement or permission 同意; 允许: *She made the proposal, and I readily consented (to it).* 她提出了这个建议, 我欣然同意. ○ *She won't consent to him staying out late/to his staying out late.* 她不允许他呆在外面太晚. ○ *They finally consented* (ie agreed) *to go with us.* 他们终于同意了和我们一块走. ○ *sex between consenting adults*, ie who both agree to it 成年人之间两相情愿的性行为.
▷ **con·sent** *n* [U] **1 ~ (to sth)** agreement; permission 同意; 允许: *Her parents refused their consent to the marriage.* 她的父母不答应这门婚事. ○ *He gave his consent for the project to get under way.* 他同意将这个计划付诸实施. ○ *She was chosen as leader by common consent*, ie Everyone agreed to the choice. 她是经一致同意而当选为领导人的. ○ *Silence implies consent*, ie One is assumed to agree if one remains silent. 沉默意味着同意. **2** (idm 习语) **with one consent** (*arch* 古) unanimously 一致同意地.

con·sequence /'kɒnsɪkwəns; *US* -kwens; 'kɑnsə,kwɛns/ *n* **1** [C usu *pl* 通常作复数] thing that is a result or an effect of sth else 结果; 后果; 影响: *Her investment had disastrous consequences: she lost everything she owned.* 她的投资结果很惨, 血本无归. ○ *be ready to take/suffer/bear the consequences of one's actions*, ie accept the bad things which happen as a result 准备承担自己行动的后果 ○ *recent developments which could have far-reaching consequences for the country's economy* 最近的事态变化, 能够对国家的经济产生深远影响. **2** [U] (*fml* 文) importance 重要性: *It is of no consequence.* 这无关紧要. ○ *He may be a man of consequence* (ie an important man or man of high rank) *in his own country, but he's nobody here.* 他在自己的国家中尽管举足轻重, 但在此地却毫不显眼. **3** (idm 习语) **in consequence (of sth)** (*infml* 口) as a result (of sth) 由于(某事物)的缘故; 因而: *She was found guilty, and lost her job in consequence (of it).* 她被判有罪, 因而失去了工作.

con·sequent /'kɒnsɪkwənt; 'kɑnsə,kwɛnt/ *adj* **~ (on/upon sth)** (*fml* 文) following sth as a result or an effect 由某事物引起的; 随之发生的: *his resignation and the consequent public uproar* 他的辞职以及由此而引起的公众的哗然 ○ *the rise in prices consequent upon the failure of the crops* 由于农作物歉收而引起的物价上涨.
▷ **con·sequently** *adv* as a result; therefore 所以; 因而: *My car broke down and consequently I was late.* 我的汽车坏了, 所以我迟到了.

con·sequen·tial /,kɒnsɪ'kwenʃl; ,kɑnsə'kwɛnʃəl/ *adj* (*fml* 文) **1** following as a result or an effect (esp indirect) 随之发生的(尤指间接发生的); 余波所及的: *She was injured and suffered a consequential loss of earnings.* 她受了伤因而收入受损. **2** (**a**) of far-reaching importance 有深远重要性的. (**b**) (*derog* 贬) (of a person) self-important; pompous (指人)自高自大的, 自负的. ▷ **con·sequen·tial·ly** /-ʃəlɪ; -ʃəlɪ/ *adv*.

con·ser·vancy /kən'sɜ:vənsɪ; kən'sɝvənsɪ/ *n* (*Brit*) **1** (often 常作 **Conservancy**) [CGp] group of officials controlling a port, a river, an area of land, etc (港口、河道、地区等的)管理机构: *the Thames Conservancy* 泰晤士河管理委员会 ○ *the Nature Conservancy* 自然资源管理委员会. **2** [U] official conservation (of forests, etc) 政府(对森林等)的保护.

con·ser·va·tion /,kɒnsə'veɪʃn; ,kɑnsɚ'veʃən/ *n* [U] **1** prevention of loss, waste, damage, destruction, etc 保存; 保护; 避免损失、浪费、破坏、损坏等: *the conservation of forests, water resources, old buildings, etc* 对森林、水源、古老建筑等的保护 ○ *wildlife conservation* 对野生动物的保护 ○ (*physics* 物) *the conservation of energy*, ie the principle that the total quantity of energy in the universe never varies 能量守恒. **2** preservation of the natural environment 对自然环境的保护: *She is interested in conservation.* 她对保护环境这个问题十分关心.
▷ **con·ser·va·tion·ist** /-ʃənɪst; -ʃənɪst/ *n* person who is interested in conservation(2) 关心环保问题的人; 自然环境保护论者.
□ **conser'vation area** (*Brit*) area protected by law from changes that would damage its natural or architectural character 保护区(受法律保护维持其原有的自然风貌或建筑特色的地区.

con·ser·vat·ism /kən'sɜ:vətɪzəm; kən'sɝvə,tɪzəm/ *n* [U] **1** tendency to resist great or sudden change (esp in politics) 抗拒巨变或突变(尤指政治方面)的倾向; 保守性: *people's innate conservatism* 人们固有的保守性. **2** (usu 通常作 **Conservatism**) the principles of the Conservative Party in British politics 保守主义(英国政界保守党的基本信条).

con·ser·vat·ive /kən'sɜ:vətɪv; kən'sɝvətɪv/ *adj* **1** opposed to great or sudden change 反对做大的或突然的改变的; 保守的; 守旧的: *Old people are usually more conservative than young people.* 老年人通常比年轻人保守. **2** (usu 通常作 **Conservative**) of the British Conservative Party 英国保守党的: *Conservative principles, candidates, voters.* 英国保守党的政策、候选人、投票者. **3** cautious; moderate; avoiding extremes 谨慎的; 稳健的; 避免过激的: *There must have been a thousand people there, at a conservative estimate*, ie a low one. 按照保守的估计, 那里一定有一千人. ○ *She is conservative in the way she dresses.* 她在衣着上很保守.
▷ **con·ser·vat·ive** *n* **1** conservative person 思想保守者; 因循守旧者. **2** (usu 通常作 **Conservative**) member of the British Conservative Party 英国保守党党员.
con·ser·vat·ive·ly *adv*.
□ **the Con'servative Party** one of the main British political parties, which supports capitalism and opposes socialism 保守党(英国主要政党之一, 该党拥护资本主义而反对社会主义). Cf 参看 THE LABOUR PARTY (LABOUR[1]), THE LIBERAL DEMOCRATS (LIBERAL).

con·ser·va·toire /kən'sɜ:vətwɑ:(r); kən,sɝvə'twɑr/ (also **conservatory**) *n* school of music, drama, etc, esp in Europe (音乐、戏剧等)专科学校(尤指欧洲大陆的).

con·ser·vat·ory /kən'sɜ:vətrɪ; *US* -tɔ:rɪ; kən'sɝvə,tɔrɪ/ *n* **1** room with glass walls and roof used to protect plants from cold, built against an outside wall of a house, and with a door into the house 温室. ⇨illus at App 1 见附录1之插图, page vii. **2** = CONSERVATOIRE.

con·serve /kən'sɜ:v; kən'sɝv/ *v* [Tn] prevent (sth) from being changed, lost or destroyed 使(某事物)不变质、不受损失或不被损坏; 保护; 保藏; 保存: *conserve one's strength, health, resources, etc* 保住体力、健康、资源等 ○ *new laws to conserve wildlife in the area* 保护该地区野生动物的新法令. Cf 参看 PRESERVE.
▷ **con·serve** /'kɒnsɜ:v; 'kɑnsɝv/ *n* [C usu *pl*, U 作可数名词时通常作复数, 亦作不可数名词] jam, typically with quite large pieces of fruit in it 果酱(尤为带成块水果的); 蜜饯; 果脯. Cf 参看 PRESERVE *n*.

con·sider /kən'sɪdə(r); kən'sɪdɚ/ *v* **1** [Tn, Tn·pr, Tw, Tg] **~ sb/sth (for/as sth)** think about sb/sth, esp in order to make a decision; contemplate sb/sth 考虑某人[某事物](尤指以做决定为目的者); 细想: *We have considered your application carefully, but cannot offer you the job.* 我们已经仔细地考虑了你的申请, 认为不能聘请你做这份工作. ○ *consider sb for a job/as a candidate* 考虑让某人做某工作[作候选人] ○ *Have you considered how to get there?* 你是否考虑过如何到达那里? ○ *We are considering going to Canada*, ie we may go there. 我们正考虑到加拿大去. **2** [Tf, Cn·a, Cn·n, Cn·n/a, Cn·t] **~ sb/sth as sth** be of the opinion; regard sb/sth as sth 认为; 视某人[某事物]为: *We consider that you are not to blame.* 我们认为不该责怪你. ○ *We consider this (to be) very important.* 我们认为这非常重要. ○ *Do you consider it wise to interfere?* 你认为应该干预吗? ○ *He will be considered a weak leader.* 他会被认为是个软弱无能的领导人. ○ *a painting previously considered as worthless, but which now turns out to be very valuable* 一幅先前认为毫无价值的画, 现在却变成了珍品 ○ *He's generally considered to have the finest tenor voice in the country.* 现在公认他是该国最佳的男高音歌手. ○ (*fml* 文) *He's very well considered* (ie people have a high opinion of him) *within the company.* 他在公司中受到很高的评价. ○ *Consider yourself* (ie You are) *under arrest.* 你已被逮捕. **3** [Tn] take (sth) into account; make allowances for 考虑到(某事物); 体谅: *We must consider the feelings of other people.* 我们必须顾及他人的感情. ○ *In judging him you should consider his youth.* 在对他进行评审时, 你应该考虑到他还年轻. **4** [Tn] (*fml* 文) look at (sb/sth) carefully 细看(某人[某事物]): *He stood considering the painting for some minutes.* 他站在那幅画前凝视了几分钟. **5** (idm 习语) **all**

things considered ⇨ THING. ˌone's conˌsidered oˈpinion one's opinion arrived at after some thought 经仔细考虑后得出的意见: *It's my considered opinion that you should resign.* 我仔细考虑后认为你应该辞职.

con·sid·er·able /kənˈsɪdərəbl; kənˋsɪdərəbl/ *adj* great in amount or size 相当多的; 相当大的: *a considerable quantity, sum, distance, etc* 相当大的数量、数目、距离等 ○ *bought at considerable expense* 花很多钱买到的.

▷ **con·sid·er·ably** /-əblɪ; -əblɪ/ *adv* much; a great deal 非常; 很; 相当地: *It's considerably colder this morning.* 今早冷得多.

con·sid·er·ate /kənˈsɪdərət; kənˋsɪdərɪt/ *adj* **~ (towards sb); ~ (of sb) (to do sth)** careful not to hurt or inconvenience others; thoughtful 为他人着想的; 考虑周到的: *a considerate person, act, attitude* 体贴别人的人、行为、态度等 ○ *considerate towards her employees* 能体谅她那些雇员 ○ *It was considerate of you not to play the piano while I was asleep.* 在我睡觉时你不弹钢琴, 真是体贴入微. ▷ **con·sid·er·ately** *adv.* **consid·er·ate·ness** *n* [U].

con·sid·era·tion /kənˌsɪdəˈreɪʃn; kənˌsɪdəˋreʃən/ *n* **1** [U] action of considering (CONSIDER 1) or thinking about sth 考虑: *Please give the matter your careful consideration.* 此事请你仔细考虑. ○ *The proposals are still under consideration,* ie being considered. 那些提议仍在审议中. **2** [U] **~ (for sb/sth)** quality of being sensitive or thoughtful towards others, their feelings, etc (对他人、他人的情绪等的)顾及, 体贴: *He has never shown much consideration for his wife's needs.* 他从来不大考虑妻子的需要. ○ *Out of consideration for the bereaved family's feelings the papers did not print the story.* 由于考虑到那个家庭失去亲人的痛苦, 报纸没有刊登那件事. **3** [C] thing that must be thought about or taken into account; reason 要考虑的事; 考虑到的事; 原因; 因素: *Time is an important consideration in this case.* 在这种情况下, 时间是一个要考虑的重要因素. ○ *Several considerations have influenced my decision.* 有好几个因素影响了我的决定. **4** [C] (*fml* 文) reward; payment 报酬; 酬金: *I will do it for you for a small consideration (of £50).* 我愿替你做这件事, 只消给我一点小小的报酬(50英镑). **5** (idm 习语) **in consideration of sth** (*fml* 文) in return for sth; on account of sth 作为对...的回报; 考虑到: *a small payment in consideration of sb's services* 答谢某人服务的微薄酬金. **leave sth out of account/consideration** ⇨ LEAVE[1]. **take sth into consideration** take account of sth; make allowances for sth 考虑某事物; 体谅某事物: *I always take fuel consumption into consideration when buying a car.* 我买汽车时总要把燃油消耗量考虑在内.

con·sider·ing /kənˈsɪdərɪŋ; kənˋsɪdərɪŋ/ *prep, conj* in view of (the fact that); taking into consideration 考虑到; 就...而言: *She's very active, considering her age.* 就她的年龄来说, 她是够活跃的. ○ *Considering he's only just started, he knows quite a lot about it.* 考虑到他只是刚刚开始, 他对此的了解已经不少了. ○ *You've done very well, considering,* eg in view of the adverse circumstances. 考虑到不利的条件因素, 你已经做得够好的了.

con·sign /kənˈsaɪn; kənˋsaɪn/ *v* **1** [Tn·pr] (*fml* 文) **(a) ~ sb/sth to sb/sth** hand over sb/sth to sb/sth; give sb/sth up to sb/sth 把某人[某事物]移交给某人[某事物]; 交付: *consign a child to/into its uncle's care* 把小孩交给他叔叔照料 ○ *consign one's soul to God* 把灵魂托付给上帝 ○ (*fig* 比喻) *The body was consigned to the flames,* ie burned. 尸体被送去焚化(火葬). **(b) ~ sth to sth** put (sth unwanted) away 把(不要之物)移走: *an old chair that had been consigned to the attic* 搬到了阁楼上的旧椅子. **2** [Tn, Tn·pr] **~ sth (to sb)** send (goods, etc) for delivery (esp to a buyer) 发运, 托运(货物等)给对方(尤指买主): *The goods have been consigned (to you) by rail.* 货物已交由铁路发运(给贵方).

▷ **con·signee** /ˌkɒnsaɪˈniː; ˌkɑnsaɪˋni/ *n* person to whom sth is consigned (CONSIGN 2) 收货人; 收件人.

con·signer, con·signor /-nə(r); -nɚ/ *ns* person who consigns goods 发货人; 寄件人; 托运人.

con·sign·ment *n* **1** [U] consigning 移交; 交付; 移走; 发运; 托运. **2** [C] goods consigned 所运送之物: *a consignment of wheat bound for Europe* 发往欧洲的小麦. **3** (idm 习语) **on consignment** with payment to be made after the goods have been sold by the receiver 以寄售方式(货物售出后始行付款): *take/send/ship/supply goods on consignment* 以寄售方式接受[送交/装运]货物.

□ **conˈsignment note** note sent with a consignment of goods, giving details of the goods 发货单; 货运清单.

con·sist /kənˈsɪst; kənˋsɪst/ *v* (not in the continuous tenses 不用于进行时态) (phr v) **consist of sth (a)** be composed or made up of sth 由某事物组成或构成: *The committee consists of ten members.* 委员会由十人组成. ○ *a mixture consisting of flour and water* 面粉和水的混合物. ⇨Usage at COMPRISE 用法见 COMPRISE. **(b) consist in sth** (*fml* 文) have sth as its chief or only element or feature 以某事物为其主要的或唯一的因素或特点; 存在于某事物之中: *The beauty of the plan consists in its simplicity.* 这计划的好处就在于简单易行.

con·sist·ence /kənˈsɪstəns; kənˋsɪstəns/ *n* [U] = CONSISTENCY 1.

con·sist·ency /kənˈsɪstənsɪ; kənˋsɪstənsɪ/ *n* **1** (also **consistence**) [U] (*approv* 褒) quality of being consistent(1) 一贯性; 一致性: *His views lack consistency: one day he's a conservative, the next he's a liberal.* 他的观点缺乏一贯性: 时而保守, 时而开明. **2** [C, U] degree of thickness, firmness or solidity, esp of thick liquids, or of sth made by mixing with a liquid 强度; 硬度; (尤指)浓度: *Mix flour and liquid to the right consistency.* 把面粉和液体混合到适当的浓度. ○ *mixtures of various consistencies* 各种不同浓度的混合物 ○ *It should have the consistency of thick soup.* 这应该有浓汤那样的浓度.

con·sist·ent /kənˈsɪstənt; kənˋsɪstənt/ *adj* **1** (*approv* 褒) (of a person, his behaviour, his views, etc) always keeping to the same pattern or style; unchanging (指人、人的行为、观点等)一贯的, 前后一致的: *You're not very consistent: first you condemn me, then you praise me.* 你前后矛盾, 开头责备我, 接着又夸奖我. **2** [pred 作表语] **~ (with sth)** in agreement 一致; 相符: *What you say now is not consistent with what you said last week.* 你现在说的话与你上星期说过的话不相符. ○ *The pattern of injuries is consistent with* (ie could have been caused by) *an attack with a knife.* 这些伤口与刀伤的情形正相符合(可能因刀伤所致). ○ *I left as early as was consistent with politeness.* 我在不失礼的情况下, 提前离去了. ▷ **con·sist·ent·ly** *adv.*

con·sola·tion /ˌkɒnsəˈleɪʃn; ˌkɑnsəˋleʃən/ *n* **1** [U] consoling or being consoled 安慰; 慰问; 慰藉: *a few words of consolation* 几句安慰的话 ○ *Money is no consolation when you don't like your work,* ie does not make up for not liking it. 要是不喜欢所做的工作, 给的钱多也没用. **2** [C] person or thing that consoles 带来安慰的人或事物: *Your company has been a great consolation to me.* 有你为伴我感到极大的安慰. ○ *At least you weren't hurt — that's one consolation,* ie one good aspect of an otherwise bad situation. 至少你没有受到伤害——这是不幸中的幸事.

□ **consoˈlation prize** prize given to sb who has just missed winning or has come last 安慰奖(授予未能获胜或名列末位者以资鼓励的奖赏): (*fig* 比喻) *She missed out on the top job, but as a consolation prize was made deputy chairman.* 她失去了就任最高职位的机会, 但还算是中了安慰奖, 她被任命为副董事长.

con·sol·at·ory /kənˈsɒlətərɪ; *US* -tɔːrɪ; kənˋsɑləˌtorɪ/ *adj* tending or intended to console; comforting 安慰的; 慰问的: *a consolatory letter, remark, etc* 慰问信、安慰话等.

con·sole[1] /kənˈsəʊl; kənˋsol/ *v* [Tn, Tn·pr] **~ sb (for/on sth)** give comfort or sympathy to (sb who is unhappy, disappointed, etc) 安慰, 慰问(某人): *Nothing could console him when his pet dog died.* 他的爱犬死后, 什么事情也不能使他宽慰. ○ *console sb for/on a loss* 安慰受到损失的人 ○ *He consoled himself with the thought that it might have been worse.* 他聊以自慰的是幸亏事情没有更糟.

▷ **con·sol·able** *adj* able to be consoled 可安慰的; 可告慰的.

con·sole[2] /ˈkɒnsəʊl; ˋkɑnsol/ *n* **1** panel for the controls of electronic or mechanical equipment (电子或机械装置的)控制板, 操纵板, 仪表盘, 操纵台. **2** radio or TV cabinet designed to stand on the floor (落地式的收音机或电视机的)机壳. **3** frame containing the keyboard and other controls of an organ 风琴的操作台(包括键盘及其他操作件). **4** bracket to support a shelf (搁板的)

支架.

con·sol·id·ate /kənˈsɒlɪdeɪt; kənˋsɑləˏdet/ *v* **1** [I, Tn] (cause sth to) become more solid, secure, or strong 使某事物巩固; 加固; 加强: *The time has come for the firm to consolidate after several years of rapid expansion.* 公司经过几年的迅速发展之后, 该整顿一下了. ○ *With his new play he has consolidated his position as the country's leading dramatist.* 他有了新创作的剧本, 巩固了他在国内的杰出剧作家的地位. **2** [I, Ipr, Tn, Tn·pr] **~ (sth) (into sth)** (*commerce* 商) (cause things to) unite or combine (into one) (使事物)联合或合并: *All the debts have been consolidated.* 所有债务均已合并. ○ *The two companies consolidated for greater efficiency.* 这两家公司已合并以提高效率.

▷ **con·sol·ida·tion** /kənˌsɒlɪˈdeɪʃn; kənˏsɑləˋdeʃən/ *n* [U] consolidating or being consolidated 巩固; 联合: *the consolidation of the party's position at the top of the opinion polls* 在民意测验中该党名列第一的地位得以巩固.

□ **conˌsolidated anˈnuities** consols (英国政府发行的)统一公债.

the Conˌsolidated ˈFund (in Britain) government fund into which money obtained by taxation is paid, used esp to pay interest on the national debt (英国)统一基金(政府所设基金, 由税收拨给款项, 主要用以支付公债利息).

con·sols /ˈkɒnsɒlz; ˋkɑnsɑlz/ *n* [pl] type of British government stock(5b) that pays a low rate of interest (英国政府发行的低利息的)统一公债.

con·sommé /kənˈsɒmeɪ; *US* ˌkɒnsəˈmeɪ; ˏkɑnsəˋme/ *n* [U] clear meat soup 清炖肉汤.

con·son·ance /ˈkɒnsənəns; ˋkɑnsənəns/ *n* [U] (*fml* 文) **1** harmony 协调. **2** (*fig* 比喻) **~ (with sth)** agreement 一致: *actions which were not in consonance with his words* 与他的言论不一致的行为.

con·son·ant[1] /ˈkɒnsənənt; ˋkɑnsənənt/ *n* (*phonetics* 语音) (**a**) speech sound produced by completely or partially obstructing the air being breathed out through the mouth 辅音. (**b**) letter of the alphabet or phonetic symbol for such a sound: *b, c, d, f,* etc 辅音字母, (音标中的)辅音符号(如b, c, d, f等). Cf 参看 VOWEL.

con·son·ant[2] /ˈkɒnsənənt; ˋkɑnsənənt/ *adj* **~ with sth** (*fml* 文) in agreement; suitable; ˈconsistent(2) 一致的; 适合的; 符合的: *behaving with a dignity consonant with his rank* 举止带有与其地位相称的尊贵气派.

con·sort[1] /ˈkɒnsɔːt; ˋkɑnsɔrt/ *n* husband or wife, esp of a ruler 配偶(尤指君主的夫或妻): *the prince consort,* ie the reigning queen's husband 王夫(在位女王的丈夫).

con·sort[2] /kənˈsɔːt; kənˋsɔrt/ *v* (*fml* 文) **1** [Ipr, Ip] **~ with sb/together** (*esp derog* 尤作贬义) spend time with sb/together; associate with sb 与某人交往; 结交: *He'd been consorting with known criminals.* 他一直与那些臭名昭著的罪犯有交往. **2** [Ipr] **~ with sth** go well with sth; be in harmony with sth 与某事物相符; 与某事物协调: *dubious practices which consort ill with* (ie contradict) *his public statements on morality* 与其满口仁义道德大相径庭而令人生疑的行为.

con·sor·tium /kənˈsɔːtɪəm; *US* -ˈsɔːrʃɪəm; kənˋsɔrʃɪəm/ *n* (*pl* **-tia** /-tɪə; *US* -ʃɪə; -ʃɪə/) temporary association of a number of countries, companies, banks, etc for a common purpose (若干国家、公司、银行等为一共同目的而临时组合的)协会, 协营, 联营, 集团: *A consortium of construction companies will build the power-station.* 由建筑公司组成的集团将建造该发电站.

con·spectus /kənˈspektəs; kənˋspɛktəs/ *n* (*pl* **~es**) (*fml* 文) general view or survey of a subject, etc (某科目等的)概览, 概要, 大纲.

con·spicu·ous /kənˈspɪkjʊəs; kənˋspɪkjʊəs/ *adj* **1 ~ (for sth)** easily seen; noticeable; remarkable 显而易见的; 明显的; 惹人注目的: *If you're walking along a badly-lit road at night you should wear conspicuous clothes.* 晚上在照明很差的路上行走, 应该穿显眼的衣物. ○ (*ironic* 反语) *She wasn't exactly conspicuous for her helpfulness,* ie wasn't helpful. 她并不那么乐于助人. ○ *make oneself conspicuous,* ie attract attention by unusual behaviour, wearing unusual clothes, etc 出风头(借与众不同的举动、衣着等以惹人注目). **2** (idm 习语) **conˌspicuous by one's ˈabsence** noticeably absent when one ought to be present (本该到场)因未到场而引人注意: *When it came to cleaning up afterwards, the boys were conspicuous by their absence.* 后来轮到做卫生时, 这些男孩却不在场, 引起了大家的注意. ▷ **con·spicu·ous·ly** *adv*: *conspicuously absent* 因缺席而引人注意. **con·spicu·ous·ness** *n* [U].

con·spir·acy /kənˈspɪrəsɪ; kənˋspɪrəsɪ/ *n* **~ (to sth/to do sth) 1** [U] act of conspiring, esp joint planning of a crime 阴谋活动(尤指共谋犯罪): *accused of conspiracy to murder* 被控参与谋杀罪. **2** [C] plan made by conspiring 阴谋; 共谋: *a conspiracy to overthrow the Government* 颠覆政府的阴谋 ○ *a conspiracy of silence,* ie an agreement not to talk publicly about sth which should not remain secret 保持缄默的密约(对本不该保密的事不公开谈论的约定). Cf 参看 PLOT[2] 2.

con·spire /kənˈspaɪə(r); kənˋspaɪr/ *v* **1** [I, Ipr, Ip, It] **~ (with sb) (against sb); ~ (together) (against sb)** make secret plans (with others), esp to do wrong (与他人)密谋(尤指干坏事): *conspire with others against one's leader* 与他人共谋反对上司 ○ *They conspired to overthrow the Government.* 他们共同密谋颠覆政府. **2** [Ipr, It] **~ against sb/sth** (of events) seem to act together; combine disadvantageously for sb/sth (指事情)似乎同时发生对某人[某事物]不利: *circumstances conspiring against our success* 阻碍我们成功的各种情况凑在一起 ○ *events that conspired to bring about his downfall* 导致他垮台的种种事件同时发生.

▷ **con·spir·ator** /kənˈspɪrətə(r); kənˋspɪrətɚ/ *n* person who conspires 搞阴谋的人; 阴谋家.

con·spir·at·or·ial /kənˌspɪrəˈtɔːrɪəl; kənˏspɪrəˋtɔrɪəl/ *adj* of or like conspirators or conspiracy (似)阴谋家的; 阴谋的; (似)搞阴谋的: *She handed the note to me with a conspiratorial air.* 她鬼鬼祟祟地把字条交给了我.

con·stable /ˈkʌnstəbl; *US* ˈkɒn-; ˋkɑnstəbḷ/ *n* = POLICE CONSTABLE (POLICE): [attrib 作定语] *Constable Johnson* 约翰逊警察.

▷ **con·stab·ul·ary** /kənˈstæbjʊlərɪ; *US* -lerɪ; kənˋstæbjəˏlɛrɪ/ *n* [Gp] police force of a particular area, town, etc (某地区、城镇等的)警察部队: *the Royal Ulster Constabulary* 皇家北爱尔兰警察队.

con·stancy /ˈkɒnstənsɪ; ˋkɑnstənsɪ/ *n* [U] (*approv* 褒) **1** quality of being firm and unchanging 坚定性; 持久性: *constancy of purpose* 目标的坚定性. **2** faithfulness 忠诚: *a husband's constancy* 丈夫的忠贞不渝.

con·stant /ˈkɒnstənt; ˋkɑnstənt/ *adj* **1** [usu attrib 通常作定语] going on all the time; happening again and again 经常的; 不断发生的: *constant chattering, complaints, interruptions* 没完没了的饶舌、抱怨、打搅 ○ *This entrance is in constant use; do not block it.* 这个入口经常使用, 不要挡住. **2** unchanging; fixed 不变的; 恒定的; 稳定的: *a constant speed, value, etc* 恒定速度、恒值等 ○ *Pressure in the container remains constant.* 容器中的压力保持恒定不变. **3** [usu attrib 通常作定语] (*approv* 褒) firm; faithful 坚定的; 忠实的: *a constant friend, companion, supporter, etc* 忠实的朋友、伴侣、支持者等.

▷ **con·stant** *n* (*mathematics or physics* 数或物) number or quantity that does not vary 常数; 常量; 恒量. Cf 参看 VARIABLE *n*.

con·stantly *adv* continuously; frequently 不断地; 经常地: *He's constantly disturbing me.* 他老是打扰我. ○ *She worries constantly.* 她经常苦恼.

con·stel·la·tion /ˌkɒnstəˈleɪʃn; ˏkɑnstəˋleʃən/ *n* **1** named group of stars (eg *the Great Bear*) 星座(经命名的星群, 如大熊星座). **2** (*fig* 比喻) group of associated or similar people or things 相关的或相似的人群或事物: *a constellation of Hollywood talent* 好莱坞的一群才俊.

con·sterna·tion /ˌkɒnstəˈneɪʃn; ˏkɑnstɚˋneʃən/ *n* [U] surprise and anxiety; great dismay 惊恐; 惊愕; 惊慌: *filled with consternation* 惊恐万状 ○ *To her consternation, he asked her to make a speech.* 她感到惊慌的是他要求她发言.

con·stip·at·ed /ˈkɒnstɪpeɪtɪd; ˋkɑnstəˏpetɪd/ *adj* unable to empty the bowels 便秘的: *If you're constipated you should eat more roughage.* 假若便秘就应该多吃粗糙食物.

▷ **con·stipa·tion** /ˌkɒnstɪˈpeɪʃn; ˏkɑnstəˋpeʃən/ *n* [U] state of being constipated 便秘.

con·stitu·ency /kənˈstɪtjʊənsɪ; kənˋstɪtʃʊənsɪ/ *n* [CGp] (**a**) (body of voters living in a) district having its own elected representative in parliament 选区; 选区的选民. (**b**) group of people with the same interests that one can turn to for support (一批有共同利益的)支持者, 拥护者, 追随者: *Mr Jones has a natural constituency among steel workers.* 琼斯先生在钢铁工人中自有一批人拥护.

con·stitu·ent /kən'stɪtjʊənt; kən'stɪtʃʊənt/ *adj* [attrib 作定语] forming or helping to make a whole 组成的; 构成的: *Analyse the sentence into its constituent parts.* 把这句子的各个成分加以分析.

▷ **con·stitu·ent** *n* **1** member of a constituency 选区的选民. **2** component part 成分: *the constituents of the mixture* 混合物的成分.

□ **con,stituent as'sembly** one which has the power to make or alter a political constitution 立宪议会(负责制定或修改宪法的权力机构).

C

con·sti·tute /'kɒnstɪtju:t; 'kɑnstə,tut/ *v* **1** [Tn] (not in the continuous tenses 不用于进行时态) (*fml* 文) make up or form (a whole); be the components of 组成, 构成(某整体); 为...之成分: *Twelve months constitute a year.* 十二个月为一年. ○ *The committee is constituted of members of all three parties.* 委员会由所有三个政党的成员组成. ○ (*fig* 比喻) *He is so constituted* (ie His nature is such) *that he can accept criticism without resentment.* 他豁达大度, 能接受批评而不怀恨在心. ⇨ Usage at COMPRISE 用法见 COMPRISE. **2** [Ln] (not in the continuous tenses 不用于进行时态) be 是: *My decision does not constitute* (ie should not be regarded as) *a precedent.* 我的决定下不为例. ○ *The defeat constitutes a major set-back for our diplomacy.* 这次失败是我们外交上的重大挫折. **3** [Tn] give formal authority to (a group of people); establish 正式授权给(某团体); 建立: *The committee had been improperly constituted, and therefore had no legal power.* 该委员会的建立不合规定, 因而没有合法的权力. **4** [Cn·n] (*fml* 文) give (sb) formal authority to hold (a position, etc); appoint 任命(某人)担任(某职位等); 委派: *He seemed to have constituted himself our representative.* 他俨然自封为我们的代表.

con·sti·tu·tion /,kɒnstɪ'tju:ʃn; *US* -'tu:ʃn; ,kɑnstə'tuʃən/ *n* **1** [C] (system of) laws and principles according to which a state is governed 宪法(的体制): *Britain has an unwritten constitution, and the United States has a written constitution.* 英国有不成文的宪法, 美国有成文的宪法. **2** (**a**) [U] (*fml* 文) action or manner of constituting (CONSTITUTE 1, 3, 4) 组织、建立、任命、授权的举动或方式: *the constitution of an advisory group* 咨询小组的组成. (**b**) [C] (*fml* 文) general structure of a thing 事物的一般结构: *the constitution of the solar spectrum* 太阳光谱的构成. **3** [C] condition of a person's body with regard to health, strength, etc 人的健康、体力等状况; 体质; 体格: *a robust/weak constitution* 强壮的[虚弱的]体质 ○ *Only people with a strong constitution should go climbing.* 只有身体强健的人才可以去登山.

con·sti·tu·tional /,kɒnstɪ'tju:ʃənl; *US* -'tu:-; ,kɑnstə'tu-ʃənl/ *adj* **1** of a constitution(1) 宪法的; 符合宪法的; 立宪的: *constitutional government, reform, etc* 立宪政体、宪法的修改 ○ *a constitutional ruler*, ie one controlled or limited by a constitution 立宪君主(受宪法控制或限制的君主) ○ *They claimed that the new law was not constitutional*, ie not allowed by the constitution. 他们声称这项新法律不符合宪法. **2** of a person's constitution (3) 体质的; 体格的: *constitutional weakness, robustness, etc* 体质的虚弱、强健等.

▷ **con·sti·tu·tional** *n* (*dated or joc* 旧或谑) short walk taken to improve or maintain one's health 保健散步: *go for/take a constitutional* 进行健身散步.

con·sti·tu·tion·al·ism /-ʃənəlɪzəm; -ʃənlɪzəm/ *n* [U] (belief in) constitutional government or constitutional principles 立宪、政体; 立宪主义; 拥护宪政; 拥护立宪主义.

con·sti·tu·tion·ally /-ʃənəlɪ; -ʃənlɪ/ *adj*.

con·stitu·tive /'kɒnstɪtju:tɪv, kən'stɪtjʊtɪv; *US also* -'stɪtʃʊ-; 'kɑnstə,tjutɪv, -stɪtʃʊ-/ *adj* (*fml* 文) having the power to take action, make appointments, etc 有权采取行动、任命等的: *a constitutive committee* 有采取行动及任命权的委员会.

con·strain /kən'streɪn; kən'stren/ *v* [Tn, Cn·t] (*fml* 文) make (sb) do sth by strong (moral) persuasion or by force 力劝, 强迫(某人)做某事: *As an artist he didn't consider himself constrained* (ie restricted) *by the same rules of social conduct as other people.* 他认为自己是艺术家, 不必像一般人那样要受社会行为准则的束缚. ○ *I feel constrained to write* (ie I feel I must write) *and complain in the strongest possible terms.* 我深感责无旁贷, 必须笔诛墨伐.

▷ **con·strained** *adj* (of voice, manner, etc) forced; uneasy; unnatural (指声音、态度等)勉强的, 受拘束的, 不自然的. **con·strain·edly** /-ɪdlɪ; -ɪdlɪ/ *adv*.

con·straint /kən'streɪnt; kən'strent/ *n* **1** [U] constraining or being constrained 约束; 强制: *act under constraint*, ie because one is forced to do so 受逼迫而行动. **2** [C] **~ (on sth)** thing that limits or restricts 限制性或约束性的事物: *There are no constraints on your choice of subject for the essay*, ie You can choose whatever subject you like. 文章内容不拘, 你可任选. **3** [U] (*fml* 文) strained manner; unwillingness to be friendly; uneasiness 不自然的态度; 假情假意; 拘束感: *I was aware of a certain constraint on their part when they were in my presence.* 我觉察到我在时他们有些拘束.

con·strict /kən'strɪkt; kən'strɪkt/ *v* [Tn] make (sth) tight, smaller or narrower 使(某事物)缩紧, 缩小或缩窄: *a tight collar that constricts the neck* 紧卡脖子的衣领 ○ *administering a drug that constricts the blood vessels* 施用收缩血管的药 ○ (*fig* 比喻) *Our way of life is rather constricted* (ie We cannot do so many things) *now that our income is so reduced.* 由于我们的收入减少了这么多, 我们的生活方式受到一定限制.

▷ **con·stric·tion** /kən'strɪkʃn; kən'strɪkʃən/ *n* **1** [U] constricting 紧缩; 收缩. **2** [C] (**a**) feeling of tightness 紧缩或压迫的感觉: *a constriction in the chest* 胸部的压迫感. (**b**) thing that constricts 紧缩的事物: *the constrictions of life on a low income* 低收入的节衣缩食.

con·struct /kən'strʌkt; kən'strʌkt/ *v* [Tn] **1** build (sth); put or fit together; form 建筑, 建造(某物); 构成; 形成: *construct a factory, an aircraft, a model, a sentence, a theory* 建工厂; 造飞机; 制作模型; 造句; 建立理论 ○ *a hut constructed (out) of branches* 用树枝搭成的棚屋 ○ *a well-constructed novel* 结构完善的小说. **2** (*geometry* 几) draw (a line, figure, etc) in accordance with certain rules (按照某种规则)画(线), 作(图).

▷ **con·structor** *n* person who constructs things 建筑者; 建造者: *oil-rig constructors* 采油设备承造商.

con·struc·tion /kən'strʌkʃn; kən'strʌkʃən/ *n* **1** [U] action or manner of constructing; being constructed 建筑, 建造的活动或方式; 施工; 建设: *the construction of new roads* 新道路的施工 ○ *The new railway is still under construction*, ie being constructed. 新铁路尚在敷设中. ○ *The wall is of very solid construction*, ie is solidly constructed. 这堵墙构筑得非常坚固. ○ [attrib 作定语] *the construction industry*, ie the building of roads, bridges, buildings, etc 建筑业. **2** [C] thing constructed; structure; building 建造物; 构造物; 建筑物: *a complex construction of wood and glass* 木和玻璃综合结构的建筑物 ○ *The shelter is a brick construction.* 掩护所是用砖构筑的. **3** [C] way in which words are put together to form a phrase, clause or sentence 造句法: *This dictionary gives the meanings of words and also illustrates the constructions they can be used in.* 本词典提供词义解释, 并举例说明遣词造句的方法. **4** [C] (*fml* 文) sense in which words, statements, etc are to be understood; meaning (对词语、言辞等所作的)解释, 意义, 意思: *What construction do you put on his actions?* ie How do you understand their purpose? 你对他的行为作何解释? ○ *The sentence does not bear such a construction*, ie cannot be understood in that way. 这句话并不含有那样的意思. Cf 参看 CONSTRUE 1.

con·struct·ive /kən'strʌktɪv; kən'strʌktɪv/ *adj* having a useful purpose, helpful 建设性的; 有助益的: *constructive criticism, proposals, remarks, etc* 建设性的批评、提议、评论等. ▷ **con·struct·ive·ly** *adv*.

con·strue /kən'stru:; kən'stru/ *v* **1** [Tn, Tw, Cn·n/a] **~ sth (as sth)** (*fml* 文) explain the meaning of (words, sentences, actions, etc); interpret sth 解释(词语、句子、行为等)的意义; 理解: *How do you construe what he did?* 你对他之所为作何解释? ○ *Her remarks were wrongly construed*, ie were misunderstood. 她的话被误解了. ○ *I construed his statement as a refusal.* 据我看他的说法就是拒绝. Cf 参看 CONSTRUCTION 4. **2** (**a**) [Tn] (*grammar*) analyse the syntax of (a sentence) 对(句子)

作句法分析. (**b**) [I, Tn] (*dated* 旧) translate (a piece of text, esp from Latin or Greek) 翻译(文章的片断, 尤指原文为拉丁文或希腊文).

con·sul /ˈkɒnsl; ˋkɑnsl/ *n* **1** official appointed by a state to live in a foreign city in order to help people from his own country who are travelling or living there, and protect their interests 领事: *the British Consul in Marseilles* 英国驻马赛领事. Cf 参看 HIGH COMMISSIONER (HIGH[1]). **2** either of the two magistrates who ruled in ancient Rome before it became an Empire (古罗马成为帝国之前的)两执政官之一. **3** any one of the three chief magistrates of the French Republic (1799-1804) (1799-1804 年法兰西共和国的)三个主要执政官之一.

▷ **con·su·lar** /ˈkɒnsjʊlə(r); *US* -səl-; ˋkɑnslɚ/ *adj* of a consul 领事的; 执政官的.

con·sul·ship /-ʃɪp; -ˏʃɪp/ *n* **1** position of a consul 领事或执政官的职位: *appointed to the consulship* 被任命为领事或执政官. **2** period of time during which a consul holds his position 领事或执政官的任期.

con·sul·ate /ˈkɒnsjʊlət; *US* -səl-; ˋkɑnslɪt/ *n* **1** offices of a consul(1) 领事馆: *the British consulate in Marseilles* 英国驻马赛领事馆. Cf 参看 EMBASSY 1, HIGH COMMISSION (HIGH[1]). **2 the Consulate** period of consular government in France 法国的执政府统治时期.

con·sult /kənˈsʌlt; kənˋsʌlt/ *v* **1** [Tn, Tn·pr] **~ sb/sth (about sth)** go to (a person, book, etc) for information, advice, etc (为获取资料、得到指点等)请教(别人), 查阅(书)等: *consult one's lawyer, a map, a dictionary* 请教律师、查看地图、查阅词典 ○ *a consulting engineer*, ie one who has specialized knowledge and gives advice 顾问工程师 ○ *I consulted a doctor about my pains.* 我找过医生诊治病痛. **2** [Ipr] **~ with sb** discuss matters with sb; confer with sb 与某人商量(事情); 与某人磋商: *consult with one's partners* 与合伙人商量.

□ **conˈsulting room** room where a doctor talks to and examines patients 诊察室.

con·sult·ant /kənˈsʌltənt; kənˋsʌltənt/ *n* **1 ~ (on sth)** person who gives expert advice (in business, law, etc) (商业、法律等方面的)顾问: *a firm of management consultants* 管理咨询公司 ○ *the president's consultant on economic affairs* 总统的经济事务顾问. **2 ~ (in sth)** (in Britain) hospital doctor of senior rank (英国)顾问医师, 会诊医师: *a consultant in obstetrics* 产科顾问医师 ○ [attrib 作定语] *a consultant surgeon* 外科顾问医师. Cf 参看 REGISTRAR 2.

con·sul·ta·tion /ˌkɒnslˈteɪʃn; ˌkɑnslˋteʃən/ *n* **1** [U] consulting or being consulted 请教; 咨询; 磋商: *acting in consultation with the director*, ie with his advice and agreement 在征询过主任的意见并得其同意后行事 ○ *consultation of a dictionary* 查词典. **2** [C] (**a**) meeting for discussion 讨论会: *top-level consultations between the US and Russian delegations* 美俄代表团之间最高级别的磋商. (**b**) meeting to discuss, or seek advice about, a sick person 会诊.

con·sult·at·ive /kənˈsʌltətɪv; kənˋsʌltətɪv/ *adj* of or for consulting; advisory 咨询的; 供咨询的; 顾问的: *a consultative committee, document, etc* 咨询委员会、文件等.

con·sume /kənˈsjuːm; *US* -ˈsuːm; kənˋsum/ *v* [Tn] **1** (**a**) use (sth) up 用尽, 消耗, 花费(某事物): *consume resources, time, stores, etc* 耗尽资源、时间、存物等 ○ *The car consumes a lot of fuel.* 这辆汽车很费汽油. ○ (*rhet* 修辞) *He soon consumed his fortune*, ie spent the money wastefully. 他很快就把财产挥霍殆尽. (**b**) destroy (sb/sth) by fire, decay, etc (因火烧、衰败等)毁掉(某人[某物]): *The fire quickly consumed the wooden hut.* 火焰很快地吞噬了那所小木屋. ○ (*fig* 比喻) *be consumed* (ie filled) *with envy, hatred, greed, etc* 心中充满了忌妒、仇恨、贪欲等. **2** (*fml* 文) eat or drink (sth) 吃或喝(某物).

▷ **con·sum·ing** *adj* [attrib 作定语] that obsesses or dominates sb 使人着迷的; 支配人的: *Building model trains is his consuming passion.* 制作模型火车是他废寝忘食的爱好.

con·sumer /kənˈsjuːmə(r); *US* -suː-; kənˋsumɚ/ *n* person who buys goods or uses services 消费者; 顾客; 用户: *Consumers are encouraged to complain about faulty goods.* 要鼓励消费者对劣质商品投诉. ○ *electricity consumers* 电力的用户 ○ [attrib 作定语] *consumer rights, protection, etc* 消费者的权利、保障等. Cf 参看 PRODUCER.

▷ **con·sumer·ism** /-ɪzəm; -ɪzəm/ *n* [U] (campaigning for the) protection of consumers' interests 消费者利益的保护(运动).

□ **conˌsumer ˈdurables** = DURABLES (DURABLE).

conˈsumer goods goods bought and used by individual customers, eg food, clothing, domestic appliances 消费品. Cf 参看 CAPITAL GOODS (CAPITAL[2]).

con·sum·mate[1] /kənˈsʌmət; kənˋsʌmɪt/ *adj* [attrib 作定语] (*fml* 文) highly skilled; perfect 技艺高超的; 尽善尽美的: *a consummate artist, performance, piece of work* 高超的艺术家、演出、作品 ○ *She dealt with the problem with consummate skill.* 她以巧妙的手腕处理了这个问题. ○ (*derog* 贬) *a consummate liar* 瞎话大王.

con·sum·mate[2] /ˈkɒnsəmeɪt; ˋkɑnsəˌmet/ *v* [Tn] (*fml* 文) **1** make (sth) complete or perfect 使(某事物)完整或圆满: *This award consummates my life's work.* 这个奖是我一生努力的圆满结果. **2** make (a marriage) legally complete by having sexual intercourse 完(婚)(行房).

▷ **con·sum·ma·tion** /ˌkɒnsəˈmeɪʃn; ˌkɑnsəˋmeʃən/ *n* [C, U] action or point of completing, making perfect, or fulfilling 完成; 臻于圆满; 实现: *the consummation of one's life's work, one's ambitions, a marriage* 毕生努力的圆满成功、夙愿的得偿、完婚.

con·sump·tion /kənˈsʌmpʃn; kənˋsʌmpʃən/ *n* [U] **1** (**a**) using up of food, energy, resources, etc (食物、能量、资源等的)消耗: *The meat was declared unfit for human consumption.* 这种肉已宣布不适宜人们食用. ○ *conspicuous consumption which is an affront to people on low incomes* 使低收入者感到自惭形秽的那种铺张. (**b**) quantity used 消耗量: *We have measured the car's fuel consumption.* 我们测量了这辆汽车的汽油消耗量. **2** (*dated* 旧) tuberculosis of the lungs 肺痨; 肺结核.

con·sump·tive /kənˈsʌmptɪv; kənˋsʌmptɪv/ *adj* (*dated* 旧) suffering or tending to suffer from consumption(2) (可能)患肺痨的.

▷ **con·sump·tive** *n* consumptive person 肺痨患者.

cont *abbr* 缩写 = **1** contents. **2** (also **contd**) continued: *cont on p 74* 下接第 74 页.

con·tact /ˈkɒntækt; ˋkɑntækt/ *n* **1** [U] **~ (with sb/sth)** (**a**) state of touching (used esp with the *vs* shown) 接触(尤与下列示例中动词连用): *The two substances are now in contact (with each other), and a chemical reaction is occurring.* 现在这两种物质(互相)接触产生了化学反应. ○ *His hand came into contact with* (ie touched) *a hot surface.* 他的手触到热物体的表面. ○ *The label sticks on contact*, ie when it touches a surface. 这标签一接触即可贴上. ○ (*fig* 比喻) *The troops came into contact with* (ie met) *the enemy.* 部队已与敌人交锋(遭遇). ○ (*fig* 比喻) *Pupils must be brought into contact with* (ie exposed to) *new ideas.* 应该引导学生接触新思想. (**b**) communication 通讯; 联系; 交往: *in constant radio/telephone contact (with sb)* (与某人)经常保持无线电[电话]联系 ○ *Beyond a certain distance we are out of contact with our headquarters.* 我们跟总部超过一定距离通讯就会中断. ○ *She's lost contact with her son*, ie no longer hears from him, knows where he is, etc. 她跟儿子失去了联系. ○ *two people avoiding eye contact*, ie avoiding looking directly at each other 避免目光接触的两人. **2** [C] instance of meeting or communicating 接触; 会晤; 通讯; 联系; 交往: *extensive contacts with firms abroad* 与国外公司的广泛的联系. **3** [C] person one has met or will meet, esp one who can be helpful 已接触或将接触的人(尤指于己有利的人): *I have a useful contact in New York.* 我在纽约有个有用的人可以联系. **4** [C] (**a**) electrical connection 电流的接触; 电的接通: *A poor contact causes power to fail occasionally.* 接触不良有时会造成断电. (**b**) device that makes an electrical connection 接触器; 电气接头; 触头: *The switches close the contacts and complete the circuit.* 这些开关可使接触器接通电流形成回路. **5** [C] (*medical* 医) person who may be infectious because he has recently been near to sb who has a contagious disease (因接触传染病人)可能受到传染者. **6** (idm 习语) **make contact (with sb/sth)** succeed in speaking to or meeting sb/sth 与某人[某事物]交谈、会晤或取得联系: *They made contact with headquarters by radio.* 他们用无线电跟总部联络上

了. ○ *I finally made contact with her in Paris.* 我终于在巴黎同她取得了联系. **make/break 'contact** complete/interrupt an electric circuit 接通[切断]电流.

▷ **con·tact** /kən'tækt, 'kɒntækt; 'kɑntækt/ *v* [Tn] reach (sb/sth) by telephone, radio, letter, etc; communicate with (用电话、无线电、书信等与某人[某事物])联系; 与...来往: *Where can I contact you tomorrow?* 明天我在哪里能跟你联系?

□ **contact lens** /ˌkɒntækt 'lenz; 'kɑntækt ˌlɛnz/ lens made of thin plastic placed on the surface of the eye to improve vision 接触眼镜; 隐形眼镜片.

'contact print photographic print made by placing a negative directly onto the printing paper and exposing it to light 接触印相照片(将底片直接置于印相纸上进行曝光而成).

C

con·ta·gion /kən'teɪdʒən; kən'tedʒən/ *n* **1** [U] spreading of disease by being close to or touching other people (接)触(传)染. **2** [C] disease that can be spread by contact接触传染病: *Fear spread through the crowd like a contagion*, ie quickly and harmfully. 人们心中的恐惧就像瘟疫似的蔓延开来. Cf 参看 INFECTION.

con·ta·gious /kən'teɪdʒəs; kən'tedʒəs/ *adj* **1 (a)** (of a disease) spreading by contact (指疾病)(接)触(传)染的: *Scarlet fever is highly contagious.* 猩红热传染性很强. **(b)** (of a person) having a disease that can be spread to others by contact (指人)患传染病的, 带触染原的. **2** (*fig* 比喻) spreading easily from one person to another 容易感染他人的; 感染性的: *contagious laughter, enthusiasm, etc* 容易感染别人的笑声、热情等 ○ *Yawning is contagious.* 打呵欠是有感染性的. ▷ **con·ta·giously** *adv*. Cf 参看 INFECTIOUS.

con·tain /kən'teɪn; kən'ten/ *v* [Tn] (not in the continuous tenses 不用于进行时态) **1 (a)** have or hold (sth) within itself 包含; 含有: *The atlas contains forty maps.* 这地图集共有四十幅地图. ○ *Whisky contains a large percentage of alcohol.* 威士忌所含酒精的百分比很高. ○ *What does that box contain?* 那个盒子里装的是什么? ○ *Her statement contained several inaccuracies.* 她的言词有几处不确切. **(b)** be capable of holding (sth) 可容纳(某事物): *This barrel contains 50 litres.* 这个桶容量为50升. **2 (a)** keep (sth/oneself) under control; keep within limits; hold back 控制(某事物[自己]); 抑制; 克制: *I was so furious I couldn't contain myself*, ie had to express my feelings. 我气极了, 无法克制自己. ○ *Please contain your enthusiasm for a moment.* 请你暂且控制住感情. ○ *She could hardly contain her excitement.* 她抑制不住内心的激动. **(b)** prevent (sth) from spreading harmfully or becoming more serious 阻止(某事物)的蔓延或恶化: *Has the revolt been contained?* 叛乱是否已受到遏止? **3** (*geometry* 几) form the boundary of (sth) 作(某事物)的边: *the angle contained by two sides of a triangle* 三角形两边的夹角. **4** (*mathematics* 数) be capable of being divided by (a number) exactly 可被(某数)除尽; (某数)可整除: *12 contains 2, 3, 4 and 6* 12可被2、3、4、6除尽.

▷ **con·tain·ment** *n* [U] keeping sth within limits, so that it cannot spread harmfully 阻止; 遏制: *Until we'd built up sufficient forces to drive the invaders back, we pursued a policy of containment.* 我们对入侵之敌采取牵制的方针, 以备组织好兵力将之击退.

con·tainer /kən'teɪnə(r); kən'tenɚ/ *n* **1** box, bottle, etc in which sth is kept, transported, etc 容器(如箱、瓶等): *The radioactive material is stored in a special radiation-proof container.* 放射性材料贮存在防辐射的特殊容器内. **2** large metal box of standard size for transporting goods by road, rail, sea or air 货柜; 集装箱: [attrib 作定语] *a 'container train/ship/lorry*, ie one designed to transport such containers 载货柜的列车[货船/卡车] ○ *'container traffic, depots, etc* 货柜运输、货运站等.

▷ **con·tain·er·ize, -ise** /kən'teɪnəraɪz; kən'tenəˌraɪz/ *v* [Tn] **1** pack (goods) into a container(1, 2) 将(货物)装入容器或货柜(集装箱). **2** convert (a dock, ship, etc) so that it can use containers (CONTAINER 2) 使(码头、船舶等)货柜化(集装箱化). **con·tain·er·iza·tion, -isation** /kənˌteɪnəraɪ'zeɪʃn; *US* -rɪ'z-; kənˌtenərə'zeʃən/ *n* [U].

con·tam·in·ate /kən'tæmɪneɪt; kən'tæməˌnet/ *v* [Tn, Tn·pr] **~ sth/sb (with sth)** make sth/sb impure by adding dangerous or disease-carrying substances 使某事物[某人]受污染: *contaminated clothing*, eg by radioactive material 受污染的衣物(如受放射性物质污染) ○ *a river contaminated by chemicals* 受到化学物质污染的河流 ○ *Flies contaminate food.* 苍蝇可污染食物. ○ (*fig* 比喻) *They are contaminating the minds of our young people with these subversive ideas.* 他们这些颠覆作乱的思想是对我们年轻人的精神污染.

▷ **con·tam·in·ant** /kən'tæmɪnənt; kən'tæmənənt/ *n* (*fml* 文) substance that contaminates things 污染物; 污染物质.

con·tam·ina·tion /kənˌtæmɪ'neɪʃn; kənˌtæmə'neʃən/ *n* [U] contaminating or being contaminated 污染: *contamination of the water supply* 给水系统的污染.

contd *abbr* 缩写 = CONT 2.

con·tem·plate /'kɒntempleɪt; 'kɑntəmˌplet/ *v* **1 (a)** [Tn, Tw] look at or consider (sth) thoughtfully 凝视, 打量, 思忖, 沉思(某事物): *She stood contemplating the painting.* 她站着审视那幅图画. ○ *He contemplated what the future would be like without the children.* 他思忖着要是没有这些孩子, 将来又如何. **(b)** [I, Tn, Tw] meditate (upon sth), esp as a religious practice 冥思(某事物)(尤指一种宗教仪式): *a few quiet minutes in the middle of the day to sit and contemplate* 中午时分静坐冥思的几分钟 ○ *contemplating the death of Our Lord* 默祷上主之死难. **2** [Tn, Tg, Tsg] consider the possibility of (sth) 考虑(某事物)的可能性; 盘算; 预料: *She is contemplating a visit to* (ie may visit) *London.* 她正打算去伦敦观光. ○ *I'm not contemplating retiring* (ie I do not intend to retire) *yet.* 我尚未考虑退休问题. ○ *We don't contemplate him opposing our plan*, ie do not expect that he will oppose it. 我们预料他不会反对我们的计划.

▷ **con·tem·pla·tion** /ˌkɒntem'pleɪʃn; ˌkɑntəm'pleʃən/ *n* **1 (a)** [U] action of looking at sth/sb thoughtfully 凝视; 注视: *He returned to his contemplation of the fire.* 他重又凝视着那炉火. **(b)** [U, C] deep thought; meditation 沉思; 冥思: *He sat there deep in contemplation.* 他坐在那里沉思着. ○ *I'm sorry to interrupt your contemplations, but...* 很抱歉打断了您的沉思, 可是.... **2** [U] consideration; intention 考虑; 意图: *the Government's contemplation of new measures* 政府采取新措施的意图.

con·tem·plat·ive /kən'templətɪv, 'kɒntempleɪtɪv; 'kɑntəmˌpletɪv/ *adj* **1** fond of contemplation; thoughtful 好沉思的; 深思熟虑的: *a contemplative person, manner, look* 深思熟虑的人、态度、表情. **2** engaging in religious meditation 进行默观的: *a contemplative order of nuns* 注重默观的修女团. **con·tem·plat·ively** *adv*.

con·tem·por·an·eous /kənˌtempə'reɪnɪəs; kənˌtɛmpə'renɪəs/ *adj* **~ (with sb/sth)** (*fml* 文) existing or happening at the same time 同时存在或发生的; 同时期的; 同时代的: *contemporaneous events, developments, etc* 同时期的事件、发展等. ▷ **con·tem·por·an·eously** *adv*.

con·tem·por·ary /kən'temprərɪ; *US* -pərerɪ; kən'tɛmpəˌrɛrɪ/ *adj* **1 ~ (with sb/sth)** of the time or period being referred to; belonging to the same time 属于该时代或该时期的; 属于同一时代的: *Many contemporary writers condemned the emperor's actions.* 当时的许多作家都谴责该皇帝的行径. ○ *a contemporary record of events*, ie one made by people living at that time 同时代的大事记 ○ *Dickens was contemporary with Thackeray.* 狄更斯与萨克莱属于同一时代. **2** of the present time; modern 当代的; 现代的: *contemporary events, fashions* 当代事件、款式 ○ *furniture of contemporary style* 现代风格的家具. ⇨Usage at NEW 用法见 NEW.

▷ **con·tem·por·ary** *n* person who lives or lived at the same time as another 同期的人; 同辈: *She and I were contemporaries at college.* 她和我在学院里是同学.

con·tempt /kən'tempt; kən'tɛmpt/ *n* [U] **1 (a) ~ (for sb/sth)** feeling that sb/sth is completely worthless and cannot be respected 轻视; 蔑视: *I feel nothing but contempt for people who treat children so cruelly.* 我鄙视如此虐待孩子的人. ○ *I shall treat that suggestion with the contempt it deserves.* 我对那项建议理所当然嗤之以鼻. **(b)** (*fml* 文) state of being regarded as worthless and shameful 微不足道; 耻辱: *behaviour which is generally held in contempt*, ie despised 被人看不起的行为. **2 ~ of/for sth** disregard (of rules, danger, etc) 藐视, 不顾(规则、危险等): *She rushed forward in complete contempt of danger.* 她完全不顾危险往前冲去. ○

remarks which betray a staggering contempt for the truth, ie are completely untrue 全然不顾事情真相的言论. **3** (idm 习语) **beneath con'tempt** completely unworthy of respect 不齿: *Such conduct is beneath contempt.* 这种举动为人所不齿. **familiarity breeds contempt** ⇨ FAMILIARITY.

▷ **con·tempt·ible** /kən'temptəbl; kən'tɛmptəbl/ *adj* deserving contempt; despicable 不齿于人的; 可鄙的: *contemptible cowardice* 可鄙的胆怯.

con·temp·tu·ous /kən'temptʃuəs; kən'tɛmptʃuəs/ *adj* **~ (of sth/sb)** feeling or showing contempt 鄙视的; 表示轻蔑的: *a contemptuous person, attitude, remark* 傲慢的人、态度、言语等 ○ *He threw it away with a contemptuous gesture.* 他带着不屑一顾的样子把它扔了. ○ *be contemptuous of public opinion* 蔑视舆论. **con·temp·tu·ously** *adv*.

□ **con,tempt of 'court** (also **contempt**) disobedience to an order made by a court of law; disrespect for a court or judge 蔑视法庭(不服从法庭或法官的命令): *She was jailed for contempt (of court).* 她因藐视(法庭)罪被监禁.

con·tend /kən'tend; kən'tɛnd/ *v* **1** [Ipr] **~ with/against sb/sth; ~ for sth** struggle in order to overcome a rival, competitor or difficulty (与对手)竞争; (与他人)争夺; (与困难)拼搏: *Several teams are contending for* (ie trying to win) *the prize.* 有几个队在争夺锦标. ○ *She's had a lot of problems to contend with.* 她有许多问题要解决. ○ *the captains of the contending* (ie rival) *teams* 参与争夺的各个队的队长. **2** [Tf no passive 不用于被动语态] put forward (sth) as one's opinion; argue; assert 主张(某事物); 争辩; 认为: *I would contend that unemployment is our most serious social evil.* 我认为失业是我们社会最为严重的弊病.

▷ **con·tender** *n* person who tries to win sth in competition with others 竞争者; 争夺者; 对手: *the two contenders for the heavyweight title* 重量级冠军的两名争夺者.

con·tent[1] /kən'tent; kən'tɛnt/ *adj* [pred 作表语] **~ (with sth); ~ to do sth** satisfied with what one has; not wanting more; happy 知足; 满足; 满意; 愉快: *Are you content with your present salary?* 你对你现在的薪水满意吗? ○ *Now that she has apologized, I am content.* 既然她已经道了歉, 我也就满意了. ○ *He is content to stay in his present job.* 他对现在的工作心满意足. ○ *He is content to remain where he is now.* 他安于现状. Cf 参看 CONTENTED.

▷ **con·tent** *n* **1** [U] state of being content 满足; 满意: *the quiet content of a well-fed child* 孩子喂饱后不哭不闹的满足状. **2** (idm 习语) **to one's heart's content** ⇨ HEART.

con·tent *v* [Tn·pr] **~ oneself with sth** accept sth, even though one would have liked more or better 满足或满意于某事物(虽然可能有更高的要求): *As there's no cream, we'll have to content ourselves with black coffee.* 既然没有奶油, 我们只好喝清咖啡算了.

con·tented *adj* showing or feeling content; satisfied 表示或感到满意或满足的; 心满意足的: *a contented person, cat, smile, etc* 心满意足的人、猫、微笑等. **con·tent·edly** *adv*.

con·tent·ment *n* [U] state of being content 满足; 满意: *with a smile of contentment* 带着心满意足的微笑.

con·tent[2] /'kɒntent; 'kantɛnt/ *n* **1 contents** [pl] that which is contained in sth 所容纳之物; 所含之物; 内容: *the contents of a room, box, bottle, pocket* 屋、盒、瓶、衣袋里的东西 ○ *The drawer had been emptied of its contents.* 抽屉已经腾空了. ○ *She hadn't read the letter and so was unaware of its contents.* 她没有看那封信, 所以不知道信的内容. ○ *At the front of the book is a table of contents, giving details of what is in the book.* 书的前部有目录, 详列了书中的内容. **2** [sing] that which is written or spoken about in a book, an article, a programme, a speech, etc (书、文章、节目、演说等的)内容: *The content of your essay is excellent, but it's not very well expressed.* 你那篇文章的内容好极了, 但是表达方式不太好. **3** [sing] (preceded by a *n* 用于名词之后) amount of sth contained in sth else 容量; 含量: *the silver content of a coin* 硬币中银的含量 ○ *food with a high fat content* 脂肪含量高的食物.

con·ten·tion /kən'tenʃn; kən'tɛnʃən/ *n* **1** [U] **~ (for sth/to do sth)** contending (CONTEND 1); competition 争夺; 竞争: *two teams in contention for the title/to win the title*, ie competing for it 争夺冠军的两个队. **2** [U] contending (CONTEND 2); angry disagreement 争辩; 争论; 争吵: *This is not a time for contention.* 这不是争论的时候. **3** [C] **~ (that...)** assertion made in an argument (辩论时提出的)论点: *It is my contention that...* 我的论点是.... **4** (idm 习语) **a bone of contention** ⇨ BONE.

con·ten·tious /kən'tenʃəs; kən'tɛnʃəs/ *adj* **1** liking to argue; quarrelsome 爱争论的; 好争吵的. **2** likely to cause disagreement 可能引起争议的: *a contentious book, law, speech* 有争议的书、法律、讲话 ○ *a contentious clause in a treaty* 条约中可能有异议的条款.

con·test /kən'test; kən'tɛst/ *v* [Tn] **1** claim that (sth) is wrong or not proper; dispute 对(某事物)予以驳斥; 争论: *contest a statement, point, etc* 对某说法、论点等加以驳斥 ○ *contest a will*, ie try to show it was not properly made in law 对遗嘱提出质疑. **2** (take part in and) try to win (sth) (参与并)争取赢得(某事物): *As a protest, the party has decided not to contest this election.* 该党已决定不参加此次选举, 以示抗议. ○ *contest a seat in Parliament* 争夺国会席位 ○ *a hotly contested game*, ie one in which the participants play very hard and the result is close 激烈角逐的一局.

▷ **con·test** /'kɒntest; 'kantɛst/ *n* **1** event in which people compete against each other for a prize; competition 比赛; 竞赛: *a boxing, archery, dancing, beauty, etc contest* 拳击、射箭、舞蹈、选美等比赛 ○ (*fig* 比喻) *The election was so one-sided that it was really no contest*, ie only one side was likely to win. 选举呈现一边倒的局面, 实际上毫无竞争可言. ⇨Usage at SPORT 用法见 SPORT. **2 ~ (for sth)** struggle to gain control 争取获得控制权: *a contest for the top job in the union* 为争取协会的最高职位而进行的角逐.

con·test·ant /kən'testənt; kən'tɛstənt/ *n* **~ (for sth)** person who is in a contest; competitor 竞争者; 比赛者.

con·text /'kɒntekst; 'kantɛkst/ *n* [C, U] **1** words that come before and after a word, phrase, statement, etc, helping to show what its meaning is (某词、词组、语句等的)上下文: *Can't you guess the meaning of the word from the context?* 你能联系上下文猜出这个词的意思吗? ○ *Don't quote my words out of context*, eg so as to mislead people about what I mean. 对我的话不要断章取义. **2** circumstances in which sth happens or in which sth is to be considered (某事物产生的或应考虑到的)环境, 背景: *In the context of the present economic crisis it seems unwise to lower taxes.* 鉴于当前的经济危机, 降低税率似乎不妥. ○ *You have to see these changes in context: they're part of a larger plan.* 看待这些改革必须要纵观全局, 这些改革是大局中的局部.

▷ **con·tex·tual** /kən'tekstʃuəl; kən'tɛkstʃuəl/ *adj* of or according to context 上下文的; 根据上下文的; 有来龙去脉的: *Contextual clues can help one to find the meaning.* 上下文所提供的线索有助于了解其意义.

con·tigu·ous /kən'tɪgjuəs; kən'tɪgjuəs/ *adj* **~ (to/with sth)** (*fml* 文) touching; neighbouring; near 挨着的; 相邻的; 邻近的: *the northern province and contiguous areas* 北方省份及邻近区域 ○ *The garden is contiguous to the field.* 这个花园紧挨着农田.

▷ **con·ti·gu·ity** /ˌkɒntɪ'gju:ətɪ; ˌkantɪ'gjuətɪ/ *n* [U] (*fml* 文) being contiguous 接触; 相邻; 邻近.

con·tin·ence /'kɒntɪnəns; 'kantənəns/ *n* [U] **1** (*fml* 文) control of one's feelings, esp in sexual matters (感情的)节制; (尤指)节制性欲. **2** (*medical* 医) ability to control one's bladder and bowels 大小便的自控能力.

con·tin·ent[1] /'kɒntɪnənt; 'kantənənt/ *n* **1** each of the main land masses of the Earth (Europe, Asia, Africa, etc) (地球上的)大洲之一(欧洲、亚洲、非洲等); 洲; 大陆. **2 the Continent** [sing] (*Brit*) the mainland of Europe 欧洲大陆: *holidaying on the Continent* 在欧洲大陆度假.

▷ **con·tin·ental** /ˌkɒntɪ'nentl; ˌkantə'nɛntl/ *adj* **1** belonging to or typical of a continent 大陆的; 大陆性的: *a ˌcontinental 'climate* 大陆性气候. **2** (also **Continental**) (*Brit*) of the mainland of Europe 欧洲大陆的: *ˌcontinental 'wars, al'liances, etc* 欧洲大陆的战争、联盟等 ○ *a continental holiday* 在欧洲大陆的假日.

con·tin·ental *n* (*Brit often derog* 常作贬义) inhabitant

of the mainland of Europe (欧洲)大陆人.

□ ˌ**continental** ˈ**breakfast** light breakfast typically consisting only of coffee and rolls with jam 欧洲大陆式早餐(仅有咖啡和果酱面包). Cf 参看 ENGLISH BREAKFAST (ENGLISH). ˌ**continental** ˈ**drift** the slow movement of the continents towards and away from each other during the history of the Earth 大陆漂移(地球史上各大陆之间产生相对位移的缓慢运动).

con·tin·ent² /ˈkɒntɪnənt; ˋkɑntənənt/ *adj* **1** (*fml* 文) having control of one's feelings and (esp sexual) desires 有节制的; 节制欲望的(尤指性欲). **2** (*medical* 医) able to control one's bladder and bowels 大小便控制力正常的.

C

con·tin·gency /kənˈtɪndʒənsɪ; kənˋtɪndʒənsɪ/ *n* event that may or may not occur; event that happens by chance 可能发生也可能不发生的事件; 偶发事件: *Be prepared for all possible contingencies*, ie for whatever may happen. 要准备应付一切可能发生的事件. ○ [attrib 作定语] *contingency plans/arrangements* 应变计划[安排].

con·tin·gent¹ /kənˈtɪndʒənt; kənˋtɪndʒənt/ *adj* (*fml* 文) **1 ~ on/upon sth** dependent on sth that may or may not happen 依可能发生也可能不发生的情况而定: *Our success is contingent upon your continued help.* 我们的成功全靠你的不断帮助. **2** uncertain; accidental 不能确定的; 偶然的: *a contingent advantage, effect, etc* 意外的好处、结果等.

con·tin·gent² /kənˈtɪndʒənt; kənˋtɪndʒənt/ *n* [CGp] **1** number of troops supplied to form part of a larger force 分遣队; 小分队: *a small British contingent in the UN peace-keeping force* 联合国维持和平部队的英国小分队. **2** group of people sharing particular characteristics (eg place of origin) attending a gathering 参加某集会的一批具有某共同点(如所属地区)的人; 代表团: *A large contingent from Japan was present at the conference.* 来自日本的一个大代表团出席了会议. ○ *There were the usual protests from the anti-abortion contingent.* 反对堕胎的人照例提出了抗议.

con·tinual /kənˈtɪnjʊəl; kənˋtɪnjʊəl/ *adj* (*esp derog* 尤作贬义) going on all the time without stopping, or repeatedly 继续不断的; 一再重复的: *continual rain, talking, interruptions* 不停的雨、谈话、打扰 ○ *How do we prevent these continual breakdowns?* 我们如何防止这些一再出现的故障?

▷ **con·tinu·ally** /-jʊəlɪ; -jʊəlɪ/ *adv* without stopping; repeatedly 不停地; 一再地: *They're continually arguing.* 他们争吵不休. ○ *I continually have to remind him of his responsibilities.* 我得一再提醒他记住他的责任.

NOTE ON USAGE 用法: Compare **continual** and **continuous.** 试比较 **continual** 和 **continuous**. **Continual** usually describes an action which is repeated again and again ☆ **continual** 一般指多次重复的动作: *Please stop your continual questions.* 请不要再接二连三地提问了. ○ *He was continually late for work.* 他上班总是迟到. **Continuous** indicates that the action or object carries on without stopping or interruption ☆ **continuous** 表示动作或物体继续不停地或不间断地进行下去: *They chattered continuously for an hour.* 他们唠唠叨叨足有一个小时. ○ *a continuous flow of traffic* 接连不断的来往车辆.

con·tinu·ance /kənˈtɪnjʊəns; kənˋtɪnjʊəns/ *n* [sing] (*fml* 文) continuing existence; remaining; staying 继续的存在; 持续; 停留: *Can we hope for a continuance of this fine weather?* 我们能够指望这样的好天气再持续一段时间吗? ○ *We can no longer support the President's continuance in office.* 我们不能再支持总统连任.

con·tinua·tion /kənˌtɪnjʊˈeɪʃn; kənˌtɪnjʊˋeʃən/ *n* **1** [U, sing] **(a)** carrying sth on beyond a certain point without stopping; prolongation 继续; 延续; 持续: *He argued for a continuation of the search.* 他主张继续进行搜查. **(b)** starting again after a stop; resumption (停止后的)再开始; (中断后的)再继续: *Continuation of play after the tea interval was ruled out by rain.* 原定茶点小憩后继续进行的比赛因下雨而取消了. **2** [C] thing that continues or extends sth else (某事物的)延续或延长部分: *This road is a continuation of the motorway.* 这条公路是高速公路的延伸. **3** [C] (*US law* 律) temporary stopping of a trial; adjournment (法庭的)休庭, 休会.

con·tinue /kənˈtɪnju:; kənˋtɪnjʊ/ *v* **1** [I, Ipr, Ip, Tn, Tn·pr, Tn·p] (cause sth to) go or move further (使某事物)继续, 延续: *How far does the road continue?* 这条路有多长? ○ *The desert continued as far as the eye could see.* 沙漠一直伸展到视线的尽头. ○ *We continued up the mountain on horseback.* 我们骑着马继续上山. ○ *They continued down until they came to some pockets of natural gas.* 他们继续往下钻, 终于找到了一些天然气的气井. ○ *It's been decided to continue the motorway (to the coast)*, ie build more of it until it reaches the coast. 已决定将高速公路延长(至海滨). **2** [La, I, Ipr, Tn, Tt, Tg] **~ (with sth)** (cause sth to) go on existing or happening; not stop (使某事物)继续存在或不断发生; 不停: *Circumstances continue (to be) favourable.* 情况仍然是有利的. ○ *Wet weather may continue for a few more days.* 多雨的天气可能还要持续好几天. ○ *We will continue (with) the payments for another year.* 我们这样的报酬还要再维持一年. ○ *In spite of my efforts to pacify it the baby continued to cry/continued crying.* 尽管我已尽力哄这婴儿, 可是他还是哭个不停. ○ *How can you continue to work/continue working with all that noise going on?* 你在那不停的噪声中怎么能工作得下去呀? **3** [Ipr] stay; remain 留在原处; 继续保持: *He is to continue as manager.* 他要继续当经理. ○ *continue at school, in one's job, etc* 继续求学、任职等. **4 (a)** [I, Tn, Tt, Tg] start again after stopping; resume (停止后)再开始; (中断后)再继续: *The story continues/is continued in the next issue of the magazine.* 这个故事在该杂志的下一期里继续刊载. ○ *We continued to rehearse/continued rehearsing the chorus after the break.* 休息之后我们继续排练合唱节目. **(b)** [I, Tn] speak or say (sth) again after stopping (停顿后)继续说: *Please continue; I didn't mean to interrupt.* 请往下说, 我不是有意打断你的话的. ○ *'And what's more,' he continued, 'they wouldn't even let me in!'* '这还不算,' 他接着说: '他们甚至不让我进去!'

▷ **con·tinued** *adj* [attrib 作定语] going on without stopping 继续不停的: *continued opposition, resistance, etc* 持续的反对、抵抗等.

con·tinu·ity /ˌkɒntɪˈnju:ətɪ; *US* -ˈnu:-; ˌkɑntəˋnuətɪ/ *n* [U] **1** state of being continuous 继续; 连续: *We must ensure continuity of fuel supplies.* 我们应该确保燃料供给不中断. **2** logical connection between parts of a sequence 连续性; 持续性: *This article lacks continuity; the writer keeps jumping from one subject to another.* 这篇文章缺乏连贯性, 作者一味东拉西扯, 格局无章. **3** (*cinema or TV* 影或视) correct sequence of action in a film, etc (电影等各场景的)串联, 衔接: *Continuity is ensured by using the same props in successive scenes.* 在连续的场景中使用同样的道具以确保前后衔接. ○ [attrib 作定语] *a contiˈnuity girl*, ie one who makes sure the correct sequence is kept 女场记员(负责各场的顺序衔接正确无误者). **4** (*broadcasting* 播) connecting comments, announcements, etc made between broadcasts (广播节目之间主持人的)串联词、说明词等: [attrib 作定语] *a continuity announcer* 插白广播员.

con·tinu·ous /kənˈtɪnjʊəs; kənˋtɪnjʊəs/ *adj* going on without stopping or being interrupted 继续不停的; 不间断的: *Is this a continuous flight, or do we stop off anywhere?* 我们是不着陆的连续飞行呢, 还是要在中途的什么地方停一停? ○ *Our political institutions are in continuous evolution.* 我们的政治制度正在不断发展中. ○ *A continuous belt feeds components into the machine.* 无极带把零件送入机器里. ○ *continuous assessment*, ie evaluation of a student's progress throughout a course of study (instead of by examination alone) 连续性评定(对学生在整个学习过程中所取得的进步的评价, 用以代替单独的考试). ⇨Usage at CONTINUAL 用法见 CONTINUAL. ▷ **con·tinu·ously** *adv.*

□ **conˈtinuous tense** (also **progressive tense**) (*grammar*) phrase consisting of part of *be* and a verb ending in *-ing* which expresses an action that continues over a period of time, as in 'I am/was writing', 'They are/were singing' 进行时态(由 be 的一种形式和以 -ing 结尾的动词构成的词组, 表示持续一段时间的动作, 如: 'I am/was writing', 'They are/were singing').

con·tinuum /kənˈtɪnjʊəm; kənˋtɪnjʊəm/ *n* (*pl* **~s** or **-ua** /-jʊə; -jʊə/) graded sequence of things of a similar kind, so that the ones next to each other are almost identical, but the ones at either end are quite distinct; cline 连续统一体.

con·tort /kənˈtɔːt; kənˋtɔrt/ *v* [I, Ipr, Tn] **~ (sth) (with sth)** (cause sth to) twist out of its natural shape (使某物)扭曲, 走样: *Her face contorted/was contorted with pain.* 她的脸因疼痛而走了样. ○ *contorted branches, limbs, etc* 弯弯曲曲的枝桠、主枝等 ○ (*fig* 比喻) *a contorted* (ie too complicated) *explanation, excuse, etc* 拐弯抹角的解释、辩解等.

contortionist 柔软杂技表演者

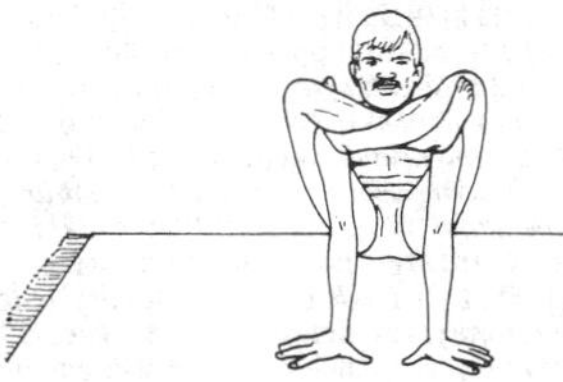

▷ **con·tor·tion** /kənˈtɔːʃn; kənˋtɔrʃən/ (**a**) [U] contorting or being contorted (esp of the face or body) 扭曲, 扭歪, 走样(尤指脸部或躯体). (**b**) [C] instance or result of this 扭曲; 扭歪; 走样: *the contortions of a yoga expert* 瑜伽高手的柔软动作. **con·tor·tion·ist** /-ʃənɪst; -ʃənɪst/ *n* person who is skilled in contorting his body 柔软杂技表演者.

con·tour /ˈkɒntʊə(r); ˋkantʊr/ *n* **1** outward curve of sth/sb (eg a coast, mountain range, body) thought of as defining its shape 轮廓, 外形(如海岸、山脉、身体的轮廓线): *the smooth contours of a sculpture* 雕塑物的平滑的轮廓线. **2** (also **ˈcontour line**) line on a map joining points that are the same height above sea level 等高线. ⇨illus at MAP 见MAP之插图.

▷ **con·tour** *v* [Tn] **1** mark (a map) with contour lines 在(地图)上标出等高线. **2** build (a road) so that it follows the contours of a hill (顺着山的起伏)修筑(道路).

□ **ˈcontour map** map with contour lines representing fixed intervals on the ground, eg of 25 metres 等高线地图.

contra- *comb form* 构词成分 against 反对; 相反: *contraflow*.

contra- *pref* 前缀 **1** (with *vs* and *ns* 用于动词和名词之前) opposite to; against 与...相反; 反对: *contra-distinction* ○ *contra-indication* ○ *ˈcontraflow*. **2** (with *ns* 用于名词之前) (*music* 音) having a pitch an octave below 声音低八度的: *contra-bassoon*.

con·tra·band /ˈkɒntrəbænd; ˋkantrəˌbænd/ *n* [U] goods brought into or taken out of a country illegally (非法带入或带出国境的)违禁品; 走私货: [attrib 作定语] *contraband goods* 违禁货物.

con·tra·cep·tion /ˌkɒntrəˈsepʃn; ˌkantrəˋsɛpʃən/ *n* [U] preventing of conception(1) 避孕; 节育.

▷ **con·tra·cept·ive** /ˌkɒntrəˈseptɪv; ˌkantrəˋsɛptɪv/ *n* device or drug for preventing conception 避孕器; 避孕剂. — *adj* preventing conception 避孕的; 避孕用的: *a contraceptive pill, device, drug, etc* 避孕丸、避孕器、避孕剂.

con·tract[1] /ˈkɒntrækt; ˋkantrækt/ *n* **1 ~ (with sb) (for sth/to do sth)** legally binding agreement, usu in writing 合同; 契约: *You shouldn't enter into/make a contract until you have studied its provisions carefully.* 你应该先仔细研究合同的条款, 然后再签订. ○ *We have a contract with the Government for the supply of vehicles/to supply vehicles.* 我们在提供车辆方面与政府订有合约. ○ *When the legal formalities have been settled, the buyer and seller of a house can exchange contracts,* ie to complete their agreement legally. 房子的买方和卖方办妥法律手续即可交换契约. ○ *He has agreed salary terms and is ready to sign a new contract,* ie of employment. 他同意了薪金条件, 准备签新合同. ○ *I'm not a permanent employee; I'm working here on a fixed-term contract.* 我并不是永久雇员, 而是根据定期合同在此工作的. ○ [attrib 作定语] *the contract price, date, etc,* ie the price, date, etc agreed to 合同价格、日期等 ○ *a contract worker,* ie employed on a contract 合同工. **2** (idm 习语) **be under contract (to sb)** have made a contract to work (for sb) 立约(为某人)工作: *a pop group that is under contract to one of the big record companies* 与一家大唱片公司签有合约的流行音乐乐队. **put sth out to ˈcontract** invite people to make a contract to do work, supply (goods, etc) 请人承包工作、供货等事: *We haven't the resources to do the work ourselves, so we'll put it out to contract.* 我们自己无法做这项工作, 所以要承包出去.

▷ **con·trac·tual** /kənˈtræktʃʊəl; kənˋtræktʃʊəl/ *adj* of or contained in a contract 合同的; 契约性的: *contractual liability, obligations, etc* 合同责任、义务等.

□ **ˌcontract ˈbridge** type of bridge[2] in which a player can gain points only with tricks which he had undertaken to win before the game started 定约桥牌.

con·tract[2] /kənˈtrækt; kənˋtrækt/ *v* **1** (**a**) [Ipr, It] **~ with sb for sth** make (a legal agreement) with sb for a purpose 与某人签订(合同或契约): *contract with a firm for the supply of fuel,* ie agree to buy fuel from it 与一家公司就供应燃料一事签订合同 ○ *Having contracted (with them) to do the repairs, we cannot withdraw now.* 我们(与他们)订有维修合约, 现在不能撤消. (**b**) [Tn, Tn·pr] **~ sth (with sb)** (*fml* 文) enter into or undertake sth formally 正式缔结或确定(某事物): *She had contracted a most unsuitable marriage.* 她订下的婚约极不匹配. ○ *contract an alliance with a neighbouring state* 与邻国缔结同盟. **2** [Tn] (**a**) catch or develop (an illness) 感染(疾病): *contract measles, a cold, etc* 患麻疹、感冒等. (**b**) (*fml* 文) acquire (sth) 招致(某事物): *contract debts, bad habits* 负债、染上恶习. **3** (phr v) **contract ˈout (of sth)** (*Brit*) withdraw from, or not enter into, an agreement which applies to a large group 退出或不参加某合约: *You can contract out (of the pension scheme) if you wish.* 你愿意的话, 可以退出(这个养老金计划). **contract sth out (to sb)** arrange for (work) to be done by another firm rather than one's own 把工作包出去(让别人做).

▷ **con·tractor** *n* person or firm that does jobs (esp construction) under contract 订约者; (尤指建筑工程的)承包人, 承包商: *a building contractor* 承建商 ○ *a firm of defence contractors,* ie who make weapons, etc 军火承包商 ○ *Who were the contractors on the new motorway?* ie Who built it? 谁是这条新高速公路的承包人?

con·tract[3] /kənˈtrækt; kənˋtrækt/ *v* [I, Ipr, Tn, Tn·pr] **~ (sth) (to sth) 1** make or become smaller or shorter (使)缩小, 缩短, 缩约: *Metals contract as they get cooler.* 金属遇冷则收缩. ○ *'I will' can be contracted to 'I'll'.* I will可缩写为I'll. ○ (*fig* 比喻) *Our business has contracted a lot recently.* 我们的生意近来大为减少了. **2** (cause sth to) become tighter or narrower; constrict (使某物)紧缩或收缩; 缩: *contract a muscle* 收缩肌肉 ○ *The tunnel contracts to a narrow passageway as you go deeper.* 再往里走, 坑道缩小成了一条窄窄的通道. Cf 参看 EXPAND.

▷ **con·tract·ible** *adj* that can be contracted 可收缩的; 有收缩性的.

con·tract·ile /kənˈtræktaɪl; *US* -tl; kənˋtræktl/ *adj* (*fml* 文) that can contract or be contracted 可收缩的; 有收缩力的; 有收缩性的: *contractile tissue* 可缩组织.

con·trac·tion /kənˈtrækʃn; kənˋtrækʃən/ *n* **1** [U] contracting or being contracted 缩小; 缩短; 紧缩; 收缩: *the contraction of a muscle* 肌肉的收缩. **2** [C] (*medical* 医) tightening of the womb that occurs at intervals in the hours preceding childbirth (分娩时阵发性的)子宫收缩. **3** [C] shortened form at a word 词的缩约形式; 缩约词: *'Can't' is a contraction of 'cannot'.* can't是cannot的缩约形式.

con·tra·dict /ˌkɒntrəˈdɪkt; ˌkantrəˋdɪkt/ *v* **1** [I, Tn] say sth that conflicts with (sth said or written) by (sb), suggesting that the person is mistaken or not telling the truth 反驳(某人)的(言论或文字); 批驳; 驳斥: *That is true, and don't you dare contradict (me).* 这是事实, 你还敢(跟我)犟嘴. ○ *The speaker had got confused, and started contradicting himself.* 演讲者弄糊涂了, 说话自相矛盾起来. **2** [Tn] (of facts, evidence, etc) be contrary to (sth); conflict with (指事实、证据等)与(某事物)相反, 或相矛盾: *The two statements contradict each other.*

两种说法互相抵触. ○ *The report contradicts what we heard yesterday.* 这个报告与我们昨天听到的有矛盾.

▷ **con·tra·dic·tion** /ˌkɒntrəˈdɪkʃn; ˌkɑntrəˈdɪkʃən/ *n* **1** (**a**) [U] contradicting 反驳; 矛盾; 对立: *She will permit no contradiction.* 她决不允许有异议. (**b**) [C] instance of this 矛盾: *That's a flat contradiction of what you said before.* 这可和你以前说的恰恰相反. **2 ~ (between sth and sth)** (**a**) [U] absence of agreement (between statements, facts, etc) (两种说法、事实等之间的)不一致, 矛盾, 对立: *I find no contradiction between his publicly expressed opinions and his private actions.* 我觉得他的公开言论与私下行为并无二致. ○ *His private actions are in direct contradiction to/with* (ie directly contradict) *his publicly expressed opinions.* 他私下的行为跟公开的言论完全是两码事. (**b**) [C] instance of this 不一致; 矛盾; 对立: *It's a contradiction to love animals and yet wear furs.* 又爱护动物又穿毛皮服装, 是自相矛盾的. **3** (idm 习语) **a ˌcontradiction in ˈterms** statement containing two words which contradict each other's meaning 语词矛盾: *'A generous miser' is a contradiction in terms.* '慷慨的吝啬鬼'在用词上自相矛盾.

con·tra·dict·ory /ˌkɒntrəˈdɪktərɪ; ˌkɑntrəˈdɪktərɪ/ *adj* contradicting 互相矛盾的; 互相对立的: *contradictory statements, reports, etc* 互相矛盾的说法、报告等.

con·tra·dis·tinc·tion /ˌkɒntrədɪˈstɪŋkʃn; ˌkɑntrədɪˈstɪŋkʃən/ *n* (idm 习语) **in contradistinction to sth/sb** (*fml* 文) by contrast with sth/sb; as opposed to sth/sb 以别于某事物[某人]; 与某事物[某人]相反: *I refer specifically to permanent residents, in contradistinction to temporary visitors.* 我是专指永久居民而言, 以别于临时访客.

con·tra·flow /ˈkɒntrəfləʊ; ˈkɑntrəˌflo/ *n* [U, C] transferring of traffic from its usual half of the road to the other half, so that it shares the lane with traffic coming in the other direction 逆道行驶(车辆在迎面来车一边的道路上逆行): [attrib 作定语] *While repairs are being carried out on this part of the motorway, a contraflow system is in operation.* 高速公路的这一部分正进行维修, 现实行逆道行驶. ⇨ illus at App 1 见附录1之插图, page xiii.

contra-indication /ˌkɒntrəɪndɪˈkeɪʃn; ˌkɑntrəˌɪndəˈkeʃən/ *n* (*medical* 医) sign that a particular drug may be harmful 禁忌症; 禁忌征象: *The contra-indications listed for the pills meant that she could not take them.* 这种药丸所列的禁忌症表明, 她不能服用.

con·tralto /kənˈtræltəʊ; kənˈtrælto/ (also **alto**) *n* (*pl* **~s**) **1** lowest female voice 女低音: *She sings contralto.* 她唱女低音. **2** woman with, or musical part to be sung by, such a voice 女低音歌手; 乐曲的女低音部分: *A gifted young contralto.* 有天赋的年轻女低音歌手.

con·trap·tion /kənˈtræpʃn; kənˈtræpʃən/ *n* (*infml* 口) apparatus or device, esp a strange or complicated one 器械或装置(尤指新奇或复杂的玩意儿): *a peculiar contraption for removing pips from oranges* 可以除去柑橘的子的稀奇玩意儿.

con·tra·puntal /ˌkɒntrəˈpʌntl; ˌkɑntrəˈpʌntl/ *adj* (*music* 音) of or in counterpoint 对位法的; 复调音乐的.

con·trari·wise /ˈkɒntrərɪwaɪz; *US* -trerɪ-; ˈkɑntrerɪˌwaɪz/ *adv* **1** on the contrary; on the other hand 相反; 在另一方面: *He always gives permission; she, contrariwise, always refuses it.* 他总是予以应允; 她则相反, 总是拒绝. ○ *'Don't you find him very rude?' 'Contrariwise! I think he's most polite.'* '你是否觉得他很粗野?' '恰恰相反! 我认为他非常有礼貌.' **2** in the opposite way 以相反的方式: *I work from left to right, he works contrariwise.* 我从左边干到右边, 他从右边干到左边. **3** /kənˈtreərɪwaɪz; kənˈtrerɪwaɪz/ perversely; in a way that shows opposition 一意孤行地; 表示相反地; 作对地: *They know they're not allowed to park there, but, contrariwise, they always do.* 他们明知不准在那里停车, 却偏偏总要把车停在那里.

con·trary[1] /ˈkɒntrərɪ; *US* -trerɪ; ˈkɑntrerɪ/ *adj* [usu attrib 通常作定语] opposite in nature, tendency or direction (在性质、倾向或方向等上)相反的, 相违的: *contrary beliefs* 截然相反的信仰 ○ *traffic moving in contrary directions* 来来往往的车辆 ○ *'Hot' and 'cold' are contrary terms.* '热'和'冷'是一对反义词. ○ *The ship was delayed by contrary winds*, ie blowing against the direction of travel. 航船因遇逆风而延误了.

▷ **con·trar·ily** /-rɪlɪ; *US* -rəlɪ; -rəlɪ/ *adv* in a contrary manner 相反地; 反而.

□ **contrary to** *prep* in opposition to (sth); against 违反(某事物); 对抗: *be contrary to the law, rules, etc* 违反法律、规则等 ○ *The results were contrary to expectation.* 结果与预期的相反. ○ *Contrary to the doctor's orders, he had gone back to work.* 他不听医生的吩咐, 又回去工作了.

con·trary[2] /ˈkɒntrərɪ; *US* -trerɪ; ˈkɑntrerɪ/ *n* **1 the contrary** [sing] the opposite 反面; 对立面: *The contrary of 'wet' is 'dry'.* '湿'的对立面是'干'. ○ *I've never opposed it. The contrary is true: I've always supported it.* 我从未反对过它. 恰恰相反: 我一贯支持它. **2** (idm 习语) **by contraries** in an opposite way to what is expected 与预期的相反: *Many events in our lives go by contraries.* 我们的生活中有不少事与愿违的情况. **on the ˈcontrary** the opposite is true; not at all 与此相反; 正相反: *It doesn't seem ugly to me; on the contrary, I think it's rather beautiful.* 我觉得它并不丑, 恰恰相反, 它挺美. **to the ˈcontrary** indicating or proving the opposite 与此相反(的): *I will come on Monday unless you write to the contrary*, ie telling me not to come. 我将于星期一前来, 除非你写信叫我别来. ○ *I will continue to believe it until I get proof to the contrary*, ie that it is not true. 我仍然相信这一点, 除非能证明它与此相反.

con·trary[3] /kənˈtreərɪ; kənˈtrerɪ/ *adj* obstinately refusing to help or obey 好与人作对的; 执拗的: *He's an awkward, contrary child.* 他是个又麻烦又不听话的孩子.

▷ **con·trar·ily** *adv.* **con·trari·ness** *n* [U].

con·trast[1] /kənˈtrɑːst; *US* -ˈtræst; kənˈtræst/ *v* **1** [Tn, Tn·pr] **~ A and/with B** compare (two people or things) so that differences are made clear 对比(以显出两人或事物的差异): *It is interesting to contrast the two writers.* 将这两位作家加以比较是很有意思的. ○ *contrast his work and/with hers* 把他的作品与她的作品加以比较. **2** [I, Ipr] **~ (with sb/sth)** show a difference when compared (通过对比)显出差异; 形成对照: *Her actions contrasted sharply with her promises.* 她的行动与她的诺言有天壤之别. ○ *Her actions and her promises contrasted sharply*, ie She did not do as she had promised. 她的行动与她的诺言相去甚远.

con·trast[2] /ˈkɒntrɑːst; *US* -træst; ˈkɑntræst/ *n* **~ (to/with sb/sth); ~ (between A and B) 1** [U] action of contrasting 对比; 相比: *Careful contrast of the two plans shows up some key differences.* 把这两个计划仔细地加以对比就可以看出一些关键性的差异. ○ *His white hair was in sharp contrast to* (ie was very noticeably different from) *his dark skin.* 他的白头发与黑皮肤形成了鲜明的对比. ○ *She had almost failed the exam, but her sister, by contrast, had done very well.* 她考试差点不及格, 而她的妹妹相比之下考得很好. ○ *In contrast with their system, ours seems very old-fashioned.* 我们的制度与他们的相比, 显得过于守旧了. **2** [C, U] difference clearly seen when unlike things are compared or put together; thing showing such a difference 明显的差异; 对照: *The white walls make a contrast with the black carpet.* 白色的墙壁与黑色的地毯形成了鲜明的对照. ○ *There is a remarkable contrast between the two brothers.* 他们兄弟俩截然不同. ○ *The work you did today is quite a contrast to* (eg noticeably better/worse than) *what you did last week.* 你今天干的活儿跟你上周干的判然不同(如明显地要好[不如]). ○ *The contrast of light and shade is important in photography.* 在摄影艺术中明暗的反差是很重要的.

con·tra·vene /ˌkɒntrəˈviːn; ˌkɑntrəˈvin/ *v* [Tn] **1** act or be contrary to (a law, etc); break 违犯(法律等); 违反: *You are contravening the regulations.* 你违反了规定. ○ *Her actions contravene the rules.* 她的所作所为违反了规定. **2** (of things) conflict with (sth); not agree with (指事物)与(某事物)相抵触; 不合于...: *This evidence contravenes our theory.* 这个证据跟我们的理论不相符.

▷ **con·tra·ven·tion** /ˌkɒntrəˈvenʃn; ˌkɑntrəˈvɛnʃən/ *n* [C, U] (act of) contravening (a law, etc) (对法律等的)违犯, 违反: *a blatant contravention of the treaty* 公然违背条约的行为 ○ *acting in direct contravention of* (ie against) *my wishes* 跟我的愿望完全背道而驰.

con·tre·temps /ˈkɒntrətɒm; ˈkɑntrəˌtɑ̃/ *n* (*pl* unchanged 复数不变) (*French fml or joc* 法, 文或谑) unfortunate event; mishap; set-back 不幸事件; 灾祸; 挫折.

con·trib·ute /kən'trɪbju:t; kən'trɪbjut/ *v* **1** [I, Ipr, Tn, Tn·pr, Tw] **~ (sth) (to/towards sth)** give one's share of (money, help, advice, etc) to help a joint cause 出(钱、力、主意等); 捐助; 捐赠; 贡献: *contribute (ten pounds) to a charity collection* 捐献(十镑)给慈善事业 ○ *contribute aid for refugees* 向难民提供援助 ○ *Everyone should contribute what he or she can afford.* 人人都应该尽自己的能力作贡献. ○ *The chairman encourages everyone to contribute to* (ie take part in) *the discussion.* 主席鼓励大家参与讨论. **2** [Ipr] **~ to sth** increase sth; add to sth 增加某事物; 添加到某事物中: *Her work has contributed enormously to our understanding of this difficult subject.* 她的著作极有助于我们对这个困难问题的了解. **3** [Ipr] **~ to sth** help to cause sth 促成某事物: *Does smoking contribute to lung cancer?* 吸烟会导致肺癌吗? **4** [Ipr, Tn·pr] **~ (sth) to sth** write (articles, etc) for a publication 撰稿; 投(稿): *She has contributed (several poems) to literary magazines.* 她给文学刊物投了(几首诗)稿.

▷ **con·trib·utor** *n* person who contributes (money to a fund, articles to a magazine, etc) 捐款人; 捐助者; 投稿者.

con·tri·bu·tion /ˌkɒntrɪ'bju:ʃn; ˌkɑntrə'bjuʃən/ *n* **~ (to/towards sth)** (**a**) [U] action of contributing 捐款; 捐助; 贡献; 促成; 投稿: *the contribution of money to charity* 慈善捐款. (**b**) [C] thing contributed 捐赠物; 稿件: *a small contribution* (ie of money) *to the collection* 少量捐款 ○ *The editor is short of contributions* (ie articles) *for the May issue.* 编辑缺少五月号刊物用的稿件. ○ (*fig* 比喻) *The signing of such a treaty would be a major contribution towards* (ie would help greatly to bring about) *world peace.* 签订这样一项条约, 是对世界和平的重大贡献.

con·trib·ut·ory /kən'trɪbjʊtərɪ; *US* -tɔ:rɪ; kən'trɪbjəˌtɔrɪ/ *adj* [usu attrib 通常作定语] **1** helping to cause sth 促成某事物的; 有助于某事物的: *a contributory factor, cause, etc* 起促成作用的因素、原因等 ○ *contributory negligence*, eg that helped to cause an accident 共同过失(受伤一方因本身疏忽造成的事故). **2** paid for by contributions 由捐助支付的: *a conˌtributory 'pension scheme*, ie paid for by both employers and employees 共集年金制(由雇主和职工共同出资).

con·trite /'kɒntraɪt; 'kɑntraɪt/ *adj* filled with or showing deep regret for having done wrong; repentant 痛悔前非的; 悔恨不已的: *a contrite apology, manner* 深表懊悔的致歉、样子 ○ *She was contrite the morning after her angry outburst.* 她发了一顿脾气之后一早上追悔莫及. ▷ **con·tritely** *adv*.

con·tri·tion /kən'trɪʃn; kən'trɪʃən/ *n* [U] deep regret for having doing wrong; repentance 悔恨; 痛悔; 忏悔.

con·triv·ance /kən'traɪvəns; kən'traɪvəns/ *n* **1** [C] **~ (for doing sth/to do sth)** (**a**) device or tool, esp one made by an individual for a particular purpose 机械装置或用具(尤指为某用途而特制之物): *a contrivance for cutting curved shapes* 可作曲线切削的用具 ○ *He erected some contrivance for storing rain-water.* 他装设了一种贮存雨水的器具. (**b**) complicated or deceitful plan 计谋; 骗术: *an ingenious contrivance to get her to sign the document without reading it* 为使她不经过目就签署文件的妙计. **2** [U] capacity to do or accomplish sth 能力: *Some things are beyond human contrivance.* 有些事情人们是无能为力的. **3** [U] action of contriving 发明; 设计: *the contrivance of an effective method* 一种实用方法的产生.

con·trive /kən'traɪv; kən'traɪv/ *v* (*fml* 文) **1** [Tn] plan (sth) cleverly or deceitfully; invent; design 谋划或策划(某事); 发明; 设计: *contrive a device, an experiment, a means of escape* 设计一个装置; 筹划一项实验; 策划逃跑 ○ *contrive a way of avoiding paying tax* 设法逃税 ○ *Their sudden outburst was obviously genuine; it couldn't have been contrived.* 他们突如其来的发作显然是真的, 这是装不出来的. **2** [Tt] manage (to do sth) in spite of difficulties 想尽办法做某事物: *contrive to live on a small income* 靠菲薄的收入精打细算过日子 ○ (*ironic* 反语) *He contrived to make matters worse*, ie unintentionally made them worse by what he did. 他弄巧成拙.

▷ **con·trived** *adj* (*derog* 贬) **1** planned in advance rather than being spontaneous or genuine 人为的; 策划的; 非自发的; 虚假的: *a contrived incident intended to mislead the newspapers* 企图蒙蔽报界的人为事件. **2** obviously invented; not lifelike 杜撰的; 缺乏真实性的: *a novel with a very contrived plot* 情节十分虚假的小说.

con·trol[1] /kən'trəʊl; kən'trol/ *n* **1** [U] **~ (of/over sb/sth)** power or authority to direct, order or limit (指挥、命令或限制的)能力, 权力; 控制; 支配; 管理: *children who lack parental control*, ie are not kept in order by their parents 缺乏父母管教的孩子 ○ *He has no control over his emotions.* 他控制不住自己的感情. ○ *In the latest elections our party has got/gained control (of the council).* 在这次选举中, 本党获得了(对议会的)控制权. ○ *She managed to keep control of her car on the ice.* 她在冰上开车时, 尽力控制住了汽车. ○ *A military government took control (of the country).* 军政府接管了(国家). ○ *The city is in/under the control of enemy forces.* 该城现处于敌军的控制之下. ○ *The pilot lost control of the plane.* 飞行员失去了对飞机的控制. ○ *He got so angry he lost control (of himself)*, ie started to behave wildly. 他气得无法自制. ○ *Due to circumstances beyond/outside our control, we cannot land here.* 由于出现了我们无法控制的情况, 我们不能在此着陆. **2** [U] management; guidance; restriction 管制; 指导; 限制: *control of traffic/traffic control* 交通管制 ○ *control of foreign exchange* 外汇管理 ○ *She argued for import control*, ie the restricting of imports. 她主张实行进口限制. ○ [attrib 作定语] *arms-control talks* 军备控制谈判. **3** [C] **~ (on sth)** means of limiting or regulating 限制或管理的手段: *government controls on trade and industry* 政府对工商业的管理措施 ○ *The arms trade should be subject to rigorous controls.* 对军火贸易应该严加限制. **4** [C] standard of comparison for checking the results of an experiment (实验的)对照标准: *One group was treated with the new drug, and a second group was treated with the old one as a control.* 对一组使用新药, 对另一组则使用旧药以资对照. ○ [attrib 作定语] *a con'trol group* 作为对照的一组. **5** [C usu *pl* 通常作复数] switches, levers, etc by which a machine is operated or regulated (机器的)操纵装置(如开关、操纵杆等): *the controls of an aircraft*, ie for direction, height, etc 飞行器的操纵装置 ○ *The pilot is at the controls.* 飞行员在掌握操纵仪. ○ *the volume control of a radio*, ie the one which regulates loudness 收音机的音量调节器 ○ *a studio with an array of electronic controls* 有一系列电子控制装置的播音室 ○ [attrib 作定语] *a control panel, board, lever, etc* 操纵盘、板、杆等. **6** [sing] place from which orders are issued or at which checks are made 指挥部; 检查站: *Mission control ordered the spacecraft to return to earth.* 指挥部命令宇宙飞船返回地球. ○ *Our papers are checked as we go through passport control at the airport.* 我们通过机场查验护照的关卡时, 查验了我们的证件. **7** (idm 习语) **be in control (of sth)** direct, manage or rule (sth) 指挥、管理或支配(某事物): *She may be old, but she's still in control (of all that is happening).* 她尽管人已老了, 然而仍由她掌管(一切事情). ○ *Who's in control of the project?* 谁是这个项目的负责人? ○ *Enemy forces are in control of the city.* 敌军控制着这座城市. **be/get out of con'trol** be/become no longer manageable 失去控制: *The children are out of control.* 管不住这些孩子了. ○ *Inflation has got out of control.* 通货膨胀已失去控制. **bring/get sth/be under con'trol** subdue or master sth/be subdued or mastered 抑制; 控制: *You must get your spending under control.* 你必须节制开支. ○ *The fire has been brought under control.* 火势已受到控制. ○ *Don't worry; everything's under control*, ie all difficulties are being dealt with. 别担心, 一切都在控制之下.

□ **con'trol tower** building at an airport from which the taking off and landing of aircraft is controlled (机场的)指挥塔, 指挥调度台; 塔台.

con·trol[2] /kən'trəʊl; kən'trol/ *v* (**-ll-**) [Tn] **1** have power or authority over (sb/sth) 控制, 操纵, 管理, 支配(某人[某事物]): *a dictator who controlled the country for over 50 years* 统治该国达50多年之久的独裁者 ○ *Can't you control that child* (ie make it behave properly)? 你管不了那个孩子吗? ○ *an aircraft which is hard to control at high speeds* 高速飞行难以控制的飞机 ○ *I was so furious I couldn't control myself, and I hit him.* 我气得不得了, 就打了他. **2** regulate (sth) 管理(某事物): *control traffic, immigration, supplies, prices* 管理交通、移民事务、物资供应、物价 ○ *This knob controls the radio's* *volume.* 这个旋钮可调节收音机的音量. ○ *government efforts to control inflation,* ie stop it getting worse 政府控制通货膨胀的努力. **3** check (sth); verify 检查(某事物); 检验: *regular inspections to control product quality* 对产品质量的常规检查.

▷ **con·trol·lable** *adj* that can be controlled 可控制的; 可操纵的; 可管理的; 可支配的: *Drugs can make violent patients controllable.* 麻醉药可使狂躁病人安静下来.

con·trol·ler *n* person who controls or directs sth, esp a department or division of a large organization (尤指大机构中部门的)负责人: *the controller of BBC Radio* 英国广播公司广播电台负责人 ○ *an air-traffic controller* 航空调度员.

C

□ **con,trolling 'interest** (*finance* 财) possession of enough stock(5b) of a company to control decision-making 控股权益: *have a controlling interest in a company* 在某公司中有控股权益.

con·tro·ver·sial /ˌkɒntrəˈvɜːʃl; ˌkɑntrəˈvɝʃəl/ *adj* causing or likely to cause controversy 引起或可能引起争论的: *a controversial person, decision, organization, book* 有争议的人物、决定、组织、书.

▷ **con·tro·ver·sial·ist** /-ʃəlɪst; -ʃəlɪst/ *n* (*fml* 文) person who is good at or fond of controversy 善辩者; 好辩者.

con·tro·ver·sially /-ʃəlɪ; -ʃəlɪ/ *adv.*

con·tro·versy /ˈkɒntrəvɜːsɪ, kənˈtrɒvəsɪ; ˈkɑntrəˌvɝsɪ/ *n* [U, C] **~ (about/over sth)** public discussion or argument, often rather angry, about sth which many people disagree with 公开辩论; 论战: *The appointment of the new director aroused a lot of controversy,* ie Many people publicly disagreed with it. 新负责人的任命引起了激烈的争论. ○ *a bitter controversy about/over the siting of the new airport* 对新机场选址问题的剧烈争论.

con·tro·vert /ˌkɒntrəˈvɜːt; ˈkɑntrəˌvɝt/ *v* [Tn] (*fml* 文) deny the truth of (sth); argue about 否定(某事物); 争论; 反驳: *a fact that cannot be controverted* 无可置辩的事实.

con·tu·ma·cious /ˌkɒntjuːˈmeɪʃəs; *US* -tuː-; ˌkɑntuˈmeʃəs/ *adj* (*fml* 文) obstinate and disobedient 固执的; 桀骜不驯的; 顽抗的. ▷ **con·tu·ma·ciously** *adv.*

con·tu·macy /ˈkɒntjʊməsɪ; *US* kənˈtuːməsɪ; ˈkɑntuməsɪ/ *n* (*fml* 文) (**a**) [U] obstinate resistance or disobedience 顽抗; 抗命. (**b**) [C] instance of this 顽抗.

con·tumely /ˈkɒntjuːmlɪ; *US* kənˈtuːməlɪ; kənˈtuməlɪ/ *n* (*fml* 文) (**a**) [U] insulting language or treatment 无礼的言辞或行为. (**b**) [C] instance of this; humiliating insult 侮慢无礼.

con·tuse /kənˈtjuːz; *US* -ˈtuːz; kənˈtuz/ *v* [Tn esp passive 尤用于被动语态] (*medical* 医) injure (a part of the body) without breaking the skin; bruise 挫伤(身体某部); 使产生青肿.

▷ **con·tu·sion** /kənˈtjuːʒn; *US* -ˈtuː-; kənˈtjuʒən/ *n* (*medical* 医) bruise 挫伤; 青肿.

con·un·drum /kəˈnʌndrəm; kəˈnʌndrəm/ *n* **1** question, usu with a pun in its answer, that is asked for fun; riddle 问题(答案通常为双关语的); 谜语. **2** puzzling problem 伤脑筋的问题: *an issue that is a real conundrum for the experts* 使专家们大伤脑筋的问题.

con·ur·ba·tion /ˌkɒnɜːˈbeɪʃn; ˌkɑnɝˈbeʃən/ *n* large urban area formed by the expansion and joining together of several smaller towns 集合城市(由几个小城镇扩展连合而构成大的城市区域).

con·valesce /ˌkɒnvəˈles; ˌkɑnvəˈlɛs/ *v* [I] regain one's health and strength after an illness 恢复健康和体力; 康复: *She went to the seaside to convalesce after her stay in hospital.* 她经过住院治疗后, 前往海滨养病.

▷ **con·val·es·cence** /ˌkɒnvəˈlesns; ˌkɑnvəˈlɛsn̩s/ *n* [sing, U] (period of) gradual recovery of health and strength 康复(期). **con·val·es·cent** /ˌkɒnvəˈlesnt; ˌkɑnvəˈlɛsn̩t/ *n, adj* (person who is) recovering from illness 康复中的(病人): *a convalescent home,* ie a type of hospital where people convalesce 疗养所.

con·vec·tion /kənˈvekʃn; kənˈvɛkʃən/ *n* [U] transmission of heat from one part of a liquid or gas to another by the movement of heated substances (热的)对流.

con·vector /kənˈvektə(r); kənˈvɛktɚ/ *n* (also **con,vector 'heater**) room heater that warms air by passing it over hot surfaces and then circulates it 对流加热器.

con·vene /kənˈviːn; kənˈvin/ *v* **1** [Tn] summon (people) to come together; arrange (a meeting, etc) 召集(人们); 召开(会议等): *convene the members, a committee, etc* 召集成员、委员会会议等. **2** [I] come together (for a meeting, etc) 集合(开会等): *The tribunal will convene tomorrow.* 法庭将于明日开庭.

▷ **con·vener** (also **con·venor**) *n* (**a**) person who convenes meetings (会议)召集人. (**b**) (*Brit*) senior trade union official in a factory or some other place of work 工会领导人: *the works convenor* 该厂的工会领导人.

con·veni·ence /kənˈviːnɪəns; kənˈvinjəns/ *n* **1** [U] quality of being convenient or suitable; freedom from trouble or difficulty 方便; 便利; 适宜; 省事: *a library planned for the users' convenience* 旨在方便读者的图书馆 ○ *I keep my reference books near my desk for convenience.* 我把参考书放在书桌旁用着方便. ○ *It was a marriage of convenience,* ie They married for material advantage, not for love. 那是一门贪图财利的亲事. **2** [C] (**a**) arrangement, appliance or device that is useful, helpful or suitable 有用、有益或适宜的安排、用具或设施: *It was a great convenience to have the doctor living near us.* 有医生住在我们附近真是太方便了. ○ *The house has all the modern conveniences,* eg central heating, hot water supply, etc. 这所房屋有各种现代化的设施(如集中供暖、热水供应等设备). (**b**) (*Brit euph* 婉) lavatory for the use of the general public (公共)厕所: *There is a public convenience on the corner of the street.* 在街道的拐角处有公共厕所. **3** (idm 习语) **at one's con'venience** when and where it suits one 在方便的时候及在适宜的地方: *With a caravan, you can stop at your own convenience; you're not dependent on hotels.* 开着一辆大篷车, 可以随意停下来, 不用住旅馆. **at your earliest con'venience** ⇨ EARLY. **a flag of convenience** ⇨ FLAG[1].

□ **con'venience food** food (eg in a tin, packet, etc) that needs very litttle preparation after being bought 方便食品.

con·veni·ent /kənˈviːnɪənt; kənˈvinjənt/ *adj* **~ (for sb/sth) 1** fitting in well with people's needs or plans; giving no trouble or difficulty; suitable 适合需要的; 方便的; 省心的; 省事的; 合适的: *I can't see him now; it's not convenient.* 我现在不便见他. ○ *Will it be convenient for you to start work tomorrow?* 你明天开始工作方便吗? ○ *We must arrange a convenient time and place for the meeting.* 我们必须安排一个合适的时间和地点开会. ○ *A bicycle's often far more convenient than a car in busy cities.* 在热闹的都市里骑自行车往往比坐汽车方便得多. **2** situated nearby; easily accessible 近便的; 容易到达的: (*infml* 口) *a house that is convenient for* (ie is near) *the shops* 靠近店铺的房屋 ○ *It's useful to have a convenient supermarket.* 附近有家超级市场实在方便.

▷ **con·veni·ently** *adv* in a convenient manner 方便地: *My house is conveniently near a bus-stop.* 我家离公共汽车站不远, 非常方便.

con·vent /ˈkɒnvənt; *US* -vent; ˈkɑnvɛnt/ *n* building(s) in which a community of nuns lives 女修道院: *enter a convent,* ie become a nun 当修女 ○ [attrib 作定语] *a convent school,* ie one run by nuns 修女会开办的学校. Cf 参看 MONASTERY, NUNNERY (NUN).

con·ven·tion /kənˈvenʃn; kənˈvɛnʃən/ *n* **1** [C] conference of members of a profession, political party, etc (某一职业、政党等之人士召开的)大会: *a teachers', dentists', etc convention* 教师的、牙科医生的会议 ○ *hold a convention* 召开大会 ○ *the US Democratic Party Convention,* ie to elect a candidate for President 美国民主党代表大会(会上选出总统候选人). **2** (**a**) [U] general, usu unspoken, agreement about how people should act or behave in certain circumstances (某种情况下的)习俗, 惯例: *Convention dictates that a minister should resign in such a situation.* 依照常规大臣在这种情况下应该辞职. ○ *By convention the deputy leader is always a woman.* 按照惯例这一领导人的副职总是由女子担任. ○ *defy convention by wearing outrageous clothes* 穿着奇装异服以对抗习俗 ○ *a slave to convention,* ie sb who always follows accepted ways of doing things 传统的奴隶(墨守成规的人). (**b**) [C] customary practice 惯常作法; 惯例: *the conventions which govern stock-market dealing* 证券交易所遵循的惯例. **3** [C] agreement between states, rulers, etc that is less formal than a treaty (国家、首脑等之间的)协议, 协定: *the Geneva Convention*, ie about the treatment of prisoners of war, etc (关于战俘待遇等问题的)日内瓦协定.

con·ven·tional /kən'venʃənl; kən'vɛnʃənḷ/ *adj* **1** (**a**) (*often derog* 常作贬义) based on convention(2a) 依照惯例的; 约定俗成的; 因循守旧的: *conventional clothes, behaviour* 老一套的衣物、行为 ○ *She's so conventional in her views.* 她的观点太保守. ○ *He made a few conventional remarks about the weather.* 他说了几句关于天气的客套话. ○ *The conventional wisdom is that high wage rises increase inflation*, ie That is the generally accepted view. 人们普遍认同的看法是工资增长过快会加剧通货膨胀. (**b**) following what is traditional or customary 依照传统的; 符合习俗的: *a conventional design, method* 传统的式样、方法. **2** (esp of weapons) not nuclear (尤指武器)常规的, 非核的: *conventional missiles, warfare, etc* 常规的导弹、战争等 ○ *a conventional power station*, ie fuelled by oil or coal, rather than being powered by a nuclear reactor 使用普通燃料的发电厂(以石油或煤为燃料而非使用核动力的).

▷ **con·ven·tion·al·ity** /kən,venʃən'ælətɪ; kən,vɛnʃən-'ælətɪ/ *n* (**a**) [U] conventional quality or character 传统性; 因循性: *the timid conventionality of his designs* 他在设计中对传统的亦步亦趋. (**b**) [C] conventional remark, attitude, etc 因循守旧的言语、态度等.

con·ven·tion·al·ize, -ise /kən'venʃənəlaɪz; kən'vɛnʃənḷ,aɪz/ *v* [Tn] make (sb/sth) conventional 使(某人[某事物])符合惯例.

con·ven·tion·ally /-ʃənəlɪ; -ʃənḷɪ/ *adv*: *conventionally dressed, designed, etc* 传统穿戴的、式样的等.

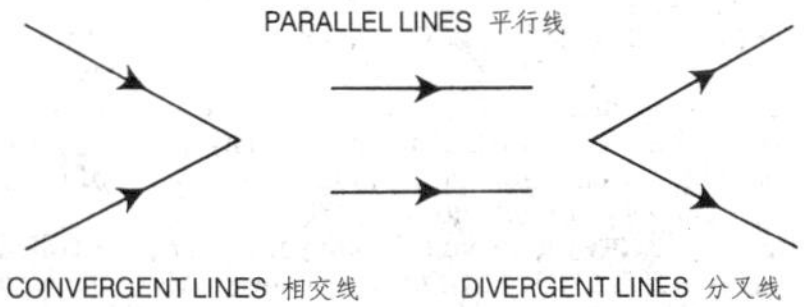

con·verge /kən'vɜːdʒ; kən'vɝdʒ/ *v* **1** [I, Ipr] **~ (on sb/sth); ~ (at sth)** (of lines, moving objects, etc) (come towards each other and) meet at a point (指线条、运动的物体等)会于一点, 向一点会合; 聚集: *armies converging on the capital city* 向首都集结的各路军队 ○ *Parallel lines converge at infinity.* 平行线永不相交. ○ *Enthusiasts from around the world converge on* (ie come to) *Le Mans for the annual car race.* 热心的观众从世界各地涌到勒芒市观看一年一度的汽车比赛. **2** [I] (*fig* 比喻) (tend to) become similar or identical (趋于)相似或相同: *Our previously opposed views are beginning to converge.* 我们原来相互对立的观点开始趋于一致. ○ *Capitalism and socialism will not eventually converge.* 资本主义和社会主义最终不会合而为一. ▷ **con·ver·gence** /kən'vɜːdʒəns; kən'vɝdʒəns/ *n* [U]. **con·ver·gent** /kən'vɜːdʒənt; kən'vɝdʒənt/ *adj*: *convergent lines, opinions* 相交的线条; 趋于一致的意见. ⇨illus 见插图. Cf 参看 DIVERGE.

con·vers·ant /kən'vɜːsnt; kən'vɝsnt/ *adj* [pred 作表语] **~ with sth** (*fml* 文) having knowledge of sth; familiar with sth (对某事物)精通, 熟悉: *thoroughly conversant with all the rules* 对所有的规则了如指掌.

con·ver·sa·tion /,kɒnvə'seɪʃn; ,kɑnvɚ'seʃən/ *n* **~ (with sb) (about sth)** (**a**) [C] informal talk 交谈; 谈话; 谈天: *having a quiet conversation with a friend* 跟朋友静静地谈天 ○ *She tended to monopolize the conversation.* 她说个没完, 使别人插不上嘴. (**b**) [U] informal talking 交谈; 谈话; 谈天: *He was deep in conversation with his accountant.* 他与会计深入交谈. ○ *It can be very difficult, making conversation at a party*, ie trying to think of things to say. 在聚会时有时很难找话题跟人应酬. ⇨ Usage at TALK[1] 用法见 TALK[1].

▷ **con·ver·sa·tional** /-ʃənl; -ʃənḷ/ *adj* (**a**) [attrib 作定语] of talking 谈话的: *her limited conversational powers* 她那有限的口才. (**b**) appropriate to conversation; colloquial 适用于会话的; 口语的: *a conversational tone, manner, etc* 会话语调、方式等.

con·ver·sa·tion·al·ist /-ʃənəlɪst; -ʃənḷɪst/ *n* talker 交谈者: *a fluent conversationalist* 健谈的人.

con·verse[1] /kən'vɜːs; kən'vɝs/ *v* [I, Ipr, Ip] **~ (with sb) (about sth); ~ (together)** (*fml* 文) talk 交谈: *She sat conversing with the President.* 她坐着与总统交谈.

con·verse[2] /'kɒnvɜːs; 'kɑnvɝs/ **the converse** *n* [sing] **1** the opposite 相反的事物: *He says she is satisfied, but I believe the converse to be true: she is very dissatisfied.* 他说她已心满意足了, 不过我认为实际情况相反: 她很不满意. **2** (in logic) statement made by reversing two elements of another statement (逻辑学)反题(将一语句中的两个成分颠倒后所成的语句): *'He is happy but not rich' is the converse of 'He is rich but not happy'.* '他乐而不富'是'他富而不乐'的反题.

▷ **con·verse** *adj* [usu attrib 通常作定语] opposite to sth 与(某事物)相反的; 逆的: *They hold converse opinions.* 他们持相反意见. **con·versely** *adv*: *You can add the fluid to the powder or, conversely, the powder to the fluid.* 可以将液体加到粉末里, 或者相反, 将粉末加到液体里.

con·ver·sion /kən'vɜːʃn; *US* kən'vɜːrʒn; kən'vɝʒən/ *n* **~ (from sth) (into/to sth)** **1** [U] converting or being converted 转变; 变换: *the conversion of a barn into a house, of pounds into dollars* 仓房之改建为寓所、英镑之兑换成美元 ○ *Conversion to gas central heating will save you a lot of money.* 改用煤气集中供暖将节省大笔开支. ○ [attrib 作定语] *a metric conversion table*, ie showing how to change metric amounts into or out of another system, by calculation 公制换算表. **2** [C] instance of this 转变: *a building firm which specializes in house conversions*, eg converting large houses into several flats 专营改建房屋的建筑公司(如将大房屋改建为几个单元者) ○ *He kicked a penalty goal and two conversions*, ie in Rugby football. 他一次罚球得分, 两次触地后射门得分(在橄榄球赛中). ○ *He used to support monetarist economics, but he underwent quite a conversion* (ie changed his opinion) *when he saw how it increased unemployment.* 他一向赞同货币经济理论, 然而当他看到这种理论加重了失业现象之后, 他彻底改变了看法.

con·vert[1] /kən'vɜːt; kən'vɝt/ *v* **1** (**a**) [I, Ipr, Tn, Tn·pr] **~ (sth) (from sth) (into/to sth)** change (sth) from one form or use to another 改变(某事物)的形式或用途: *Britain converted to a decimal currency system in 1971.* 英国于1971年改用十进制货币体系. ○ *a ferry that was converted to carry troops during the war* 战争期间改作运兵船的渡轮 ○ *a converted flat*, ie made by dividing up a large house 改建而成的一套房间(将大的房屋分隔而成者) ○ *convert rags into paper, a house into flats, pounds into francs* 用碎布屑造纸、把一所房屋改建成几个单元、把英镑兑换成法郎 ○ *The room was converted from a kitchen to a lavatory.* 这房间由厨房改成了厕所. (**b**) [Ipr] **~ into/to sth** be able to be changed from one form or use to another 可改变形式或用途: *a sofa that converts (in)to a bed* 可改为床铺的沙发. **2** [I, Ipr, Tn, Tn·pr] **~ (sb) (from sth) (to sth)** change one's beliefs, esp one's religion; persuade sb to change his beliefs (使)改变信仰(尤指宗教信仰): *He's converted to Catholicism.* 他已皈依天主教. ○ *convert sb from atheism to Christianity* 使某人放弃无神论, 改信基督教. **3** [Tn] (in Rugby football) gain extra points after scoring (a try) by kicking a goal (在橄榄球赛中)(触地得分后再射)踢中球门获得附加分. **4** (idm 习语) **preach to the converted** ⇨ PREACH.

▷ **con·verter, con·vertor** *ns* **1** (*physics* 物) (**a**) device for converting alternating current to direct current or vice versa 变流器, 逆变器. (**b**) device that changes the wavelength of a radio signal 变频器. **2** vessel for refining molten metal 转炉(冶炼金属的容器).

con·vert[2] /'kɒnvɜːt; 'kɑnvɝt/ *n* **~ (to sth)** person converted to a different belief, esp a different religion 改变信仰(尤指宗教信仰)的人; 皈依者: *a convert to socialism* 改而信奉社会主义的人 ○ *Already the new newspaper is winning/gaining converts*, ie people who used to read other newspapers. 这家新报纸已经逐渐把其他报纸的读者争取过来.

con·vert·ible /kən'vɜːtəbl; kən'vɝtəbḷ/ *adj* **~ (into/to sth)** that can be converted 可改变的; 可转换的; 可兑换的: *a sofa that is convertible (into a bed)* 可改(为床铺)的沙发 ○ *convertible currencies*, ie that can be exchanged

for those of other countries 可兑换的货币.
▷ **con·vert·ib·il·ity** /kən,vɜ:tə'bɪlətɪ; kən,vɝtə'bɪlətɪ/ *n* [U]. **con·vert·ible** *n* car with a roof that can be folded down or removed 折篷汽车.

con·vex /'kɒnveks; 'kɑnvɛks/ *adj* with a curved surface like the outside of a ball 凸圆的; 凸面的: *a convex lens, mirror, etc* 凸透镜; 凸面镜等. ⇨illus at CONCAVE 见CONCAVE之插图. Cf 参看 CONCAVE.
▷ **con·vex·ity** /kɒn'veksətɪ; kən'vɛksətɪ/ *n* [U] state of being convex 凸; 凸状.

con·vey /kən'veɪ; kən've/ *v* **1** [Tn, Tn·pr] **~ sb/sth (from...) (to...)** (*fml* 文) take sb/sth; carry sb/sth; transmit sb/sth 运载; 运送某人[某物]: *Pipes convey hot water from the boiler to the radiators.* 通过管道把热水从锅炉输送到散热器里. ○ *This train conveys both passengers and goods.* 这列火车既载人又载货. ○ *a message conveyed by radio* 由无线电传递的讯息. **2** [Tn, Tf, Tw, Dn·pr, Dpr·f, Dpr·w] **~ sth (to sb)** make (ideas, feelings, etc) known to another person 表达或传达(思想、感情等): *a poem that perfectly conveys (to the reader) the poet's feelings/what the poet feels* (向读者)充分地表达出诗人思想感情的诗篇 ○ *Words cannot convey how delighted I was.* 言辞无法表达我内心的喜悦. ○ *Please convey my good wishes to your mother.* 请向您母亲转达我的祝愿. ○ *Blenkinsop? No, the name doesn't convey anything to me*, ie I do not know or recognize it. Blenkinsop? 我不知道这个名字. **3** [Tn·pr] **~ sth (to sb)** (*law* 律) transfer full legal rights to the ownership of (land, property, etc) to sb 转让(土地、财产等).
▷ **con·veyor**, **con·veyer** *ns* person or thing that conveys 运送者; 传送者; 传达者; 转让者; 运输设备; 传送装置: *one of the largest conveyors of passenger traffic* 最大的客运工具之一. **con'veyor belt** (also **conveyor**) continuous belt or band that moves on rollers and is used for transporting loads (eg products in a factory, luggage at an airport) 传送带.

con·vey·ance /kən'veɪəns; kən'veəns/ *n* **1** [U] (*fml* 文) conveying 运送; 传送; 传达; 转让: *the conveyance of goods by rail* 铁路货运. **2** [C] (*fml* 文) thing that conveys; vehicle 运输设备; 运载工具; 车辆: *old-fashioned conveyances* 老式运载工具 ○ *a public conveyance* 公共运输设备. **3** (*law* 律) **(a)** [U] conveying property 转让财产: *an expert in conveyance* 承办产权转让事务的专家. **(b)** [C] document that conveys property 产权转让证书: *draw up a conveyance* 拟就产权转让证书.
▷ **con·vey·an·cer** *n* person who prepares conveyances (CONVEYANCE 3b) 备办产权转让证书的人员.
con·vey·an·cing *n* [U] conveying of property 财产的转让.

con·vict /kən'vɪkt; kən'vɪkt/ *v* [Tn, Tn·pr] **~ sb (of sth)** (of a jury or judge) declare in a lawcourt that sb is guilty (of a crime) (指陪审团或法官)宣判某人有(...)罪: *She has twice been convicted (of fraud).* 她已有两次被判(诈骗)罪. ○ *a convicted murderer* 已定罪的谋杀犯.
▷ **con·vict** /'kɒnvɪkt; 'kɑnvɪkt/ (also *infml* 口语亦作 **con**) *n* person who has been convicted of crime and is being punished, esp by imprisonment 已决犯; (已定罪并服刑的, 尤指监禁的)囚犯: *an escaped convict* 逃犯.

con·vic·tion /kən'vɪkʃn; kən'vɪkʃən/ *n* **1 ~ (for sth)** **(a)** [U] the convicting of a person for a crime 定罪; 科刑: *an offence which carries, on conviction, a sentence of not more than five years' imprisonment* 定罪后可判处五年以下监禁的罪行. **(b)** [C] instance of this 定罪: *She has six convictions for theft.* 她有六次因盗窃而被判刑. **2** [U, C] **~ (that...)** firm opinion or belief 坚定的看法或信仰: *It's my conviction* (ie I firmly believe) *that complacency is at the root of our troubles.* 我深信自满情绪是我们各种问题的根源. ○ *Do you always act in accordance with your convictions?* 你是否一贯地本着你的信念行事? **3** [U] believable quality 可信性: *She'd made such promises before, and they lacked conviction/didn't carry much conviction.* 她以前也作过这样的许诺, 但都不足信. **4** (idm 习语) **be open to conviction** ⇨ OPEN[1]. **have/lack the courage of one's convictions** ⇨ COURAGE.

con·vince /kən'vɪns; kən'vɪns/ *v* **1** [Tn, Tn·pr, Dn·f] **~ sb (of sth)** make sb feel certain; cause sb to realize 使某人确信; 使某人明白: *How can I convince you (of her honesty)?* 我怎样才能使你相信(她很诚实)呢? ○ *What she said convinced me that I was mistaken.* 她的一番话使我认识到我错了. ○ *I was convinced* (ie sure) *I saw you there, but it must have been someone else.* 我原来真以为看见你在那里, 一定是看错了人. **2** [Cn·t] (*esp US*) persuade 说服: *What convinced you to vote for them?* 究竟是什么使得你愿意投他们的票?
▷ **con·vinced** *adj* [attrib 作定语] firm in one's belief 坚信不移的; 有坚定信仰的: *a convinced Christian* 虔诚的基督徒.

con·vin·cible /kən'vɪnsəbl; kən'vɪnsəbḷ/ *adj* willing to be convinced 可被说服的; 可喻之以理的.

con·vin·cing *adj* that convinces 令人信服的: *a convincing speech, argument, liar* 有说服力的讲话、言之成理的论据、很能蛊惑人的瞎话大王等. **con·vin·cingly** *adv*: *a convincingly argued statement* 雄辩的陈辞.

con·viv·ial /kən'vɪvɪəl; kən'vɪvɪəl/ *adj* (*esp fml* 尤作文雅语) **1** cheerful and sociable; fond of being with others 愉快而随和的; 好交际的: *convivial companions* 喜欢交际的朋友. **2** full of shared pleasure and friendliness 联欢的; 联谊的: *a convivial evening, atmosphere* 欢乐的夜晚、气氛.
▷ **con·vi·vi·al·ity** /kən,vɪvɪ'ælətɪ; kən,vɪvɪ'ælətɪ/ *n* [U] **1** cheerfulness; sociability 欢乐; 交游. **2** shared pleasure, esp with drinking and eating 联欢(尤指饮宴作乐).
con·viv·ially /-ɪəlɪ; -ɪəlɪ/ *adv*.

con·voca·tion /,kɒnvə'keɪʃn; ,kɑnvə'keʃən/ *n* **1** [CGp] formal assembly, esp the legislative body of the Church of England or of the graduates of some universities (正式的)集会(尤指英国国教会制定规章的机构的会议或某些大学的毕业生评议会): *Convocation has/have ruled that...* 会议规定如下.... **2** [U] (*fml* 文) convoking; calling together 召集.

con·voke /kən'vəʊk; kən'vok/ *v* [Tn] (*fml* 文) call together or summon (a meeting, etc) 召集, 召开(会议等): *convoke Parliament* 召开国会.

con·vo·luted /'kɒnvəlu:tɪd; 'kɑnvə,lutɪd/ *adj* **1** coiled; twisted 盘绕的; 卷曲的: *the convoluted folds of the brain* 盘绕成团的脑回. **2** (*fig* 比喻) complicated and difficult to follow 复杂的; 费解的: *a convoluted argument, explanation, etc* 玄之又玄的论点、解释等.

con·vo·lu·tion /,kɒnvə'lu:ʃn; ,kɑnvə'luʃən/ *n* (usu *pl* 通常作复数) coil; twist 盘绕; 拳曲: *ornate carving with lots of curves and convolutions* 有很多曲线和回旋的雕饰 ○ (*fig* 比喻) *the bizarre convolutions of the plot* 情节的离奇曲折.

con·vol·vu·lus /kən'vɒlvjʊləs; kən'vɑlvjələs/ *n* (*pl* **~es**) [C, U] type of twining plant with trumpet-shaped flowers 旋花植物(开喇叭状的花).

con·voy[1] /'kɒnvɔɪ; 'kɑnvɔɪ/ *n* **1 (a)** group of vehicles or ships travelling together 车队; 船队: *a large convoy of coal lorries* 由运煤卡车组成的庞大车队. **(b)** group of vehicles or ships being escorted for protection while travelling 被护送的车队或船队: *The convoy was attacked by submarines.* 被护送的船队受到了潜水艇的攻击. **2** (idm 习语) **in 'convoy** (of travelling vehicles) as a group; together (指行进中的交通工具)组成一队; 结队: *The supply ships travelled in convoy.* 补给船结队航行. **under 'convoy** escorted by a protecting force 在护卫下: *The missiles were moved under convoy.* 导弹在护卫之下转移.

con·voy[2] /'kɒnvɔɪ; 'kɑnvɔɪ/ *v* [Tn·pr, Tn·p] (esp of a warship) travel with (other ships) in a group to protect them; escort 尤指战舰为(其他船只)护航: *The troop ships were convoyed across the Atlantic.* 运兵船被护送渡过大西洋. ○ (*fig* 比喻) *parents taking it in turns to convoy children to and from school while the attacker was on the losse* 在该暴徒仍逍遥法外期间, 轮流护送孩子往返学校的家长.

con·vulse /kən'vʌls; kən'vʌls/ *v* [Tn usu passive 通常用于被动语态] cause (sb/sth) to make sudden violent uncontrollable movements 使(某人[某事物])剧烈震动: *convulsed with laughter, anger, toothache* 笑得前仰后合、气得暴跳如雷、牙齿疼得使脸抽搐变形 ○ *a country convulsed by earthquakes* 遭受震灾的国家 ○ (*fig* 比喻) *Riots convulsed the cities*, ie caused violent disturbance. 动乱震撼着这些城市.

con·vul·sion /kənˈvʌlʃn; kənˈvʌlʃən/ *n* **1** (usu *pl* 通常作复数) sudden violent uncontrollable body movement, caused by contraction of muscles 痉挛; 抽搐: *The child reacted to the drug by going into convulsions.* 这孩子全身痉挛, 对药物有反应. **2** violent disturbance 大乱; 乱子: *The leader's assassination led to political convulsions*, eg an attempt at revolution. 领导人遇刺引起了政治动乱. **3 convulsions** [pl] uncontrollable laughter 捧腹大笑: *The story was so funny it had us in convulsions.* 这故事滑稽极了, 使我们笑得不亦乐乎.

con·vuls·ive /kənˈvʌlsɪv; kənˈvʌlsɪv/ *adj* **1** having, producing or consisting of convulsions (产生)痉挛的; 抽搐的: *a convulsive movement, spasm, etc* 抽搐的动作、发作等. **2** violently disturbing 大乱的: *convulsive upheavals, such as urban riots* 大动荡, 如城市动乱. ▷ **con·vuls·ively** *adv*.

cony (also **coney**) /ˈkəʊnɪ; ˈkonɪ/ *n* (*pl* **conies**) **1** [U] fur of the rabbit used to make coats, etc (做大衣等用的)兔毛皮. **2** [C] (*arch* 古) rabbit 兔子.

coo[1] /ku:; ku/ *v* (*pt, pp* **cooed** /ku:d; kud/, *pres p* **cooing**) **1** [I] (of a dove or pigeon) make its characteristic soft cry (指鸽子)发咕咕声. **2** (*infml* 口) (**a**) [I] make a soft murmuring sound like that of a dove 发类似鸽叫的细语声: *a baby cooing* 婴儿的细语. (**b**) [Tn] say (sth) in a soft murmur 柔声地说: *'It will be all right,' she cooed soothingly.* '就会好起来的,'她轻柔地安慰说. **3** (idm 习语) **bill and coo** ⇨ BILL[2].

▷ **coo** *n* (*pl* **coos**) soft murmuring sound (like that) of a dove 鸽子的咕咕声; 喁喁细语声.

coo[2] /ku:; ku/ *interj* (*Brit infml* 口) (used to express surprise 用以表示惊讶).

cook /kʊk; kuk/ *v* **1** (**a**) [I, Ipr, Tn, Dn·n, Dn·pr] **~ sth (for sb)** prepare (food) by heating, eg boiling, baking, roasting, frying 烹调(如煮、焙、烤、炸); 做饭菜: *Where did you learn to cook?* 你在哪里学的烹饪? ○ *These potatoes aren't (properly) cooked!* 这些马铃薯还没熟(透)! ○ *a cooked breakfast* 做好了的早餐 ○ *He cooked me my dinner.* 他给我做了饭. ○ *I like to cook (Chinese dishes) for my family.* 我喜欢给家里人做(中国菜)饭. (**b**) [I] be prepared in this way 煮, 焙, 烤, 炸; 烹调: *The vegetables are cooking.* 蔬菜正在做着. ○ *The meat cooks slowly.* 肉熟得慢. ○ *These apples cook well*, ie taste good when cooked. 这种苹果宜于熟吃. ⇨Usage 见所附用法. **2** [Tn] (*infml derog* 口, 贬) alter (sth) secretly or dishonestly so as to deceive; falsify 窜改(某物); 捏造: *He was sent to prison for cooking the books*, ie dishonestly changing the financial records, esp for personal profit. 他因窜改帐目而入狱. ○ *cook the accounts, statistics, figures* 窜改帐目、统计资料、数字. **3** [I] (used in the continuous tenses 用于进行时态) (*infml* 口) be planned; happen as a result of plotting 在筹划中; (经过策划而)发生: *What's cooking?* 发生了什么事? ○ *Everybody is being secretive: there's something cooking.* 每个人都鬼鬼祟祟, 一定出了什么事情. **4** (idm 习语) ˌ**cook the** ˈ**books** (*infml* 口) falsify facts or figures in order to make one's financial position seem better than it really is 伪造帐目; 做假帐. **cook sb's** ˈ**goose** (*infml* 口) ensure that sb fails 使某人彻底失败: *When the police found his fingerprints he knew his goose was cooked*, ie knew that he would be caught. 警方发现了他的指纹, 他意识到自己已经完了. **5** (phr v) **cook sth up** (*infml* 口) invent sth, esp in order to deceive 编造某事物(尤指行骗): *cook up an excuse, a story, a bizarre theory, etc* 编造借口、故事、怪论等.

▷ **cook** *n* **1** person who cooks food 厨师; 厨子; 炊事员: *employed as a cook in a hotel* 受雇为旅馆厨师 ○ *I'm not much of a cook*, ie I don't cook well. 我做不好饭菜. ○ *Were you the cook?* ie Did you cook this food? 是你做饭吗? Cf 参看 CHEF. **2** (idm 习语) ˌ**too many** ˌ**cooks** ˌ**spoil the** ˈ**broth** (*saying* 谚) if too many people are involved in sth, it will not be done properly 厨子多了做坏了汤(人多反倒误事): *I know they only meant to help, but it was a case of too many 'cooks, I'm afraid.* 我知道他们一心想帮忙, 可惜人多反而坏了事.

cook·ing *n* [U] process of preparing food by heating 烹调过程; 烹饪方法: *She does all the cooking.* 烹饪的事都由她做. ○ *Chinese 'cooking* 中国式烹饪 ○ [attrib 作定语] *'cooking apples, sherry, etc*, ie apples, sherry, etc suitable for cooking rather than eating raw or drinking 烹饪用的苹果、雪利酒等.

□ ˈ**cookbook** *n* = COOKERY BOOK (COOKERY).

ˈ**cookhouse** *n* detached or outdoor kitchen, eg in a camp 独立的或露天的厨房(如野营时搭盖的厨房).

NOTE ON USAGE 用法: When cooking we generally use **1** boiling water (in a saucepan) or **2** boiling fat/oil (in a frying-pan) or **3** dry heat (in an oven or under a grill). 使用 cook 一词时, 一般是指用(1)沸水(置于深锅中)或(2)热的动[植]物油(置于煎锅中)或(3)直接加热(置于烤炉中或烤架上). **1** We **boil** vegetables, eggs, rice, etc by covering them with water and heating it. 将蔬菜、鸡蛋、大米等浸于水中煮叫 **boil**. ☆ We **steam** fish, puddings, etc by placing the food above boiling water. 将鱼、布丁等置于沸水上蒸叫 **steam**. ☆ **2** Meat, fish, vegetables, etc can be **fried** in shallow oil or fat. 将肉、鱼、蔬菜等放在少许植物油或动物油里煎叫 **fry**. ☆ Chips, chicken pieces, etc can be completely covered by oil and **deep-fried.** 将土豆条、鸡块等完全浸入油中炸叫 **deep-fry**. ☆ We **sauté** vegetables very quickly in a small amount of oil. 用少量油将蔬菜很快一炒叫 **sauté**. ☆ **3** We **roast** large pieces of meat, potatoes, etc and we **bake** bread, cakes, etc in the oven. 在烤箱里烘烤大块的肉、土豆等叫 **roast**, 烘烤面包、糕饼等叫 **bake**. ☆ Small or flat pieces of meat, fish, etc are **grilled** (*US* **broiled**) by being placed under direct heat. 将小块的或切成片的肉、鱼等置于发热器下面烘烤叫 **grill**(美式英语叫 **broil**). ☆ **Boil, fry, roast** and **bake** can be used in two types of sentence ☆ **boil**、**fry**、**roast**、**bake** 可用于以下两种句型: *We boil potatoes* and *The potatoes are boiling.* **Steam, sauté** and **grill** are generally only used in the first pattern. ☆ **steam**、**sauté**、**grill** 一般只用于以上第一种句型. With **boil** we often use the container to refer to its contents 用 **boil** 时常以容器借代其所盛之物: *The kettle's boiling.* 壶开了.

cooker /ˈkʊkə(r); ˈkukɚ/ *n* **1** kitchen appliance for cooking, consisting of an oven with a hob on top and often also a grill 炉具(包括炉子、炉子上的搁架, 常带有烤架): *a 'gas cooker* 煤气炉 ○ *an e'lectric cooker* 电炉. Cf 参看 STOVE 1. **2** type of fruit, esp an apple, grown for cooking 烹饪用的水果(尤指苹果): *These apples are good cookers.* 这些苹果宜于烹饪. Cf 参看 EATING APPLE (EAT).

cook·ery /ˈkʊkərɪ; ˈkukərɪ/ *n* [U] art and practice of cooking 烹调技术; 烹饪方法: [attrib 作定语] *a cookery course, school, etc* 烹饪课程、学校等.

□ ˈ**cookery book** (also ˈ**cookbook**) book giving recipes and instructions on cooking 烹饪书; 食谱.

cookie (also **cooky**) /ˈkʊkɪ; ˈkukɪ/ (*pl* **-kies**) *n* (*US*) **1** biscuit 饼干. **2** (*infml* 口) person 人; 家伙: *He's a tough cookie.* 他是个硬汉子. **3** (idm 习语) **that's the way the cookie crumbles** ⇨ WAY[1].

cool[1] /ku:l; kul/ *adj* (**-er, -est**) **1** (**a**) fairly cold; not hot or warm 凉的; 不热的: *a cool breeze, day, surface* 凉爽的微风、一天、表面 ○ *cool autumn weather* 秋凉天气 ○ *Let's sit in the shade and keep cool.* 咱们坐在阴凉处乘乘凉吧. ○ *The coffee's not cool enough to drink.* 咖啡还不够凉, 不能喝. (**b**) giving a (usu pleasant) feeling of being not too warm 凉快的; 凉爽的: *a cool room, dress, etc* 凉爽的房间、连衣裙等 ○ *a cool cotton shirt* 凉快的棉布衬衫. (**c**) (of colours) suggesting coolness (指颜色)给人以凉爽感觉的, 冷色的: *a room painted in cool greens and blues* 涂上能给人以凉爽感觉的绿色和蓝色的房间. **2** calm; unexcited 冷静的; 镇定的: *Keep cool!* 保持冷静! ○ *She always remains cool, calm and collected in a crisis.* 她在危难中总能保持冷静、平静和镇静. ○ *He has a cool head*, ie doesn't get agitated. 他头脑冷静(不易冲动). **3 ~ (about sth); ~ (towards sb)** not showing interest, enthusiasm or friendliness 冷淡的; 冷漠的; 冷冰冰的: *She was decidedly cool about the proposal.* 她对这个提议漠然置之. ○ *They gave the Prime Minister a cool reception.* 他们很冷淡地接待了这位首相. **4** calmly bold or impudent 满不在乎的; 厚颜无耻的: *You should have seen the cool way she took my radio without even asking.* 你没瞧见她那满不在乎的样子, 连问也不问就把我的收音机拿走了. **5** [attrib 作定语] (*infml* 口) (said esp of sums of money, distances, etc, emphasizing their largeness 附加于钱、距离等数目之

前以强调其数目之大): *The car cost a cool twenty thousand.* 这辆汽车足足两万元. **6** (*dated sl* 旧, 俚 *esp US*) pleasant; fine 令人愉快的; 棒的: *Her guy's real cool.* 她的男朋友真帅. **7** (idm 习语) **(as) ˌcool as a ˈcucumber** very calm and controlled, esp in difficult circumstances (尤指在困难情况下)从容不迫的; 泰然自若的. **a cool ˈcustomer** (*infml* 口) calmly bold or impudent person 行若无事的人; 无耻之徒: *She just took out her purse and paid a thousand in cash: what a cool customer!* 她从容地掏出钱夹付了一千镑现金, 多么豪爽! **play it ˈcool** (*infml* 口) deal calmly with a situation; not get excited 泰然处之.

▷ **cool** *n* **1 the cool** [sing] cool air or place; coolness 凉爽的空气或地方; 凉快: *step out of the sun into the cool* 到阴凉处去躲避烈日 ○ *the pleasant cool of the evening* 傍晚时的凉爽宜人. **2** (idm 习语) **keep/lose one's cool** (*infml* 口) remain calm/get excited, angry, etc 保持冷静[情不自禁、怒不可遏]等.

coolly /ˈku:llɪ; ˈkullɪ/ *adv* in a cool[1](3) way 冷淡地; 冷漠地; 冷冰冰地: *He received my suggestion coolly*, ie unenthusiastically. 他对待我的建议十分冷淡.

cool·ness *n* [U] quality of being cool[1](3) 冷淡; 冷漠; 冷冰冰: *I noticed a certain coolness* (ie lack of friendliness) *between them.* 我察觉到他们彼此有些冷淡.

□ ˌ**cool-ˈheaded** *adj* calm; not flustered or excitable 头脑冷静的; 不慌不忙的.

cool[2] /ku:l; kul/ *v* **1** [I, Ip, Tn, Tn·p] **~ (sth/sb) (down/off)** become or make cool or cooler (使)变凉: *The hot metal contracts as it cools (down).* 热的金属一冷(下来)就收缩. ○ *Let the hot pie cool (off) before serving.* 热馅饼凉了再吃. ○ *A cooling drink is welcome on a hot day.* 在热天清凉饮料很受欢迎. ○ (*fig* 比喻) *Her unresponsiveness failed to cool his ardour.* 她对他无动于衷, 这并未能冷却他的感情. **2** (idm 习语) **ˈcool it** (*sl* 俚) calm down 冷静下来: *Cool it! Don't get so excited!* 静一静吧! 别那么激动! ˌ**cool one's ˈheels** be kept waiting 等下去: *Let him cool his heels for a while: that'll teach him to be impolite.* 让他等一会儿吧, 好教训教训他别那么没礼貌. **3** (phr v) **cool (sb) down/off** (cause sb to) become calm, less excited or less enthusiastic (使某人)冷静、镇静或降低热情: *She's very angry; don't speak to her until she's cooled down a bit.* 她气极了, 等她消消气再跟她说话. ○ *A day in jail cooled him off.* 一天的铁窗生活使他冷静了下来.

□ ˌ**cooling-ˈoff period** (in industrial disputes) compulsory delay before a strike, to allow a compromise to be reached (劳资纠纷中的)冷却期.

ˈ**cooling tower** large container used in industry to cool water before it is re-used 冷却塔.

cool·ant /ˈku:lənt; ˈkulənt/ *n* [C, U] (type of) fluid used for cooling (eg in nuclear reactors) 冷却剂.

cooler /ˈku:lə(r); ˈkulɚ/ *n* **1** [C] container in which things are cooled 冷却器: *a wine cooler* 冰酒器. **2 the cooler** [sing] (*sl* 俚) prison 牢房: *two years in the cooler* 两年监禁.

coolie /ˈku:lɪ; ˈkulɪ/ *n* (*dated* ⚠ *derog* 旧, 讳, 贬) unskilled Asian labourer (亚洲的)苦力.

coon /ku:n; kun/ *n* **1** (*infml* 口 *esp US*) raccoon 浣熊: [attrib 作定语] *a coon-skin cap* 浣熊皮的帽子. **2** (⚠ *sl derog* 讳, 俚, 贬) black person 黑人.

coop /ku:p; kup/ *n* cage for poultry (家禽的)笼子.

▷ **coop** *v* (phr v) **coop sb/sth up (in sth)** (usu passive 通常用于被动语态) restrict the freedom of sb/sth by keeping him/it inside; confine sb/sth 将某人[某物]关入(...内)以限制其自由; 拘禁某人[某物]: *I've been cooped up indoors all day.* 我在屋里关了一整天.

co-op /ˈkəʊ ɒp; ˈko ˌɑp/ *n* (*infml* 口) **1** [C] co-operative 合作社: *a wine produced by the local growers' co-op* 本地种植者合作社所生产的葡萄酒. **2 the Co-op** [sing] (in Britain) (shop or supermarket belonging to a) large retail chain founded originally to provide low-priced goods and share out its profits amongst purchasers (英国的)消费合作社(大型廉价零售网, 可使顾客分享其利润); 隶属于消费合作社的商店或超级市场: *He does all his shopping at the Co-op.* 他无论什么东西都在消费合作社购买.

cooper /ˈku:pə(r); ˈkupɚ/ *n* maker of barrels 桶匠.

co-operate /kəʊˈɒpəreɪt; koˈɑpəˌret/ *v* **1** [I, Ipr] **~ (with sb) (in doing/to do sth); ~ (with sb) (on sth)** work or act together with another or others (与他人)合作, 协作: *co-operate with one's friends in raising/to raise money* 与朋友合作集资 ○ *The two schools are co-operating on the project.* 这两所学校在这一项目上进行协作. **2** [I] be helpful and do as one is asked 配合; 协助: *'If you co-operate we'll let you go,' said the policeman.* '你只要协助我们, 就放你走,'警察说道. ▷ **co-operator** *n*.

co-operation /kəʊˌɒpəˈreɪʃn; koˌɑpəˈreʃən/ *n* [U] **1 ~ (with sb) (in doing sth/on sth); ~ (between A and B) (in doing sth/on sth)** acting or working together for a common purpose 合作; 协作: *a report produced by the Government in co-operation with the chemical industry* 政府在化工部门的配合下所提出的一份报告 ○ *co-operation between the police and the public in catching the criminal* 在追捕罪犯过程中警方与公众之间的相互配合. **2** willingness to be helpful and do as one is asked 乐于协助或配合的态度: *Please clear the gangways, ladies and gentlemen. Thank you for your co-operation.* 女士们、先生们: 请别堵住通道. 谢谢诸位大力协助.

co-operative /kəʊˈɒpərətɪv; koˈɑpərətɪv/ *adj* **1** [usu attrib 通常作定语] marked by co-operation; joint 合作性质的; 联营的: *a co-operative venture, attempt, etc* 合作的企业、尝试等. **2** willing to be helpful 愿意协助的: *The school was very co-operative when we made a film there.* 我们到该校拍摄影片时, 获校方大力协助. **3** [usu attrib 通常作定语] (*commerce* 商) owned and run by those participating, with profits shared by them 共同掌握所有权和管理权并分享其利的; 合作的: *a co-operative farm* 合作农场 ○ *The co-operative movement started in Britain in the 19th century; co-operative societies set up shops to sell low-priced goods to poor people.* 19世纪英国开始了合作社运动, 许多合作机构开办商店向贫民出售廉价物品.

▷ **co-operative** *n* co-operative(3) business or other organization 合作企业或其他组织: *agricultural co-operatives in India and China* 印度和中国的农业合作社 ○ *The bicycle factory is now a workers' co-operative.* 这家自行车制造厂现在是工人的集体企业. ○ *a housing co-operative*, ie in which a house or group of houses is jointly owned by those who live there 住宅业主团体(其住宅之所有权属于全体住户).

co-operatively *adv*.

co-opt /kəʊˈɒpt; koˈɑpt/ *v* [Tn, Tn·pr] **~ sb (onto sth)** (of the members of a committee) vote for the appointment of sb as an extra member of the committee (指委员会的成员)增选某人为新委员: *co-opt a new member onto the committee* 增补一名新委员.

co-ordinate[1] /kəʊˈɔ:dɪnət; koˈɔrdn̩ɪt/ *n* **1** (often 常作 **coordinate**) either of two numbers or letters used to fix the position of a point on a graph or map 坐标: *the x and y coordinates on a graph* 图表上的x和y坐标 ○ *coordinates of latitude and longitude* 经纬度 ○ [attrib 作定语] *co-ordinate geometry*, ie geometry using co-ordinates 解析几何. ⇨illus at MAP 见MAP之插图. **2 co-ordinates** [pl] matched items of women's clothing (女子的)配套衣物.

□ **co-ordinate ˈclause** (*grammar*) one of two or more clauses in a sentence that are equal in importance, have similar patterns and are often joined by *and*, *or*, *but*, etc 并列分句(一个句子中所含有的至少两个地位相等、结构相似的分句之一, 常以and、or、but等词相连接). Cf 参看 SUBORDINATE CLAUSE (SUBORDINATE).

co-ordinate[2] /kəʊˈɔ:dɪneɪt; koˈɔrdn̩ˌet/ *v* [Tn, Tn·pr] **~ sth (with sth)** cause (different parts, limbs, etc) to function together efficiently 使(各部分、肢体等)协调, 协同动作: *co-ordinate one's movements when swimming* 游泳时协调动作 ○ *We must co-ordinate our efforts* (ie work together) *to help the flood victims.* 我们应该同心协力以援助遭水灾的灾民. ○ *The plan was not* (ie Its parts were not) *very well co-ordinated.* 这计划的各部分配合得不够好.

▷ **co-ordination** /ˌkəʊˌɔ:dɪˈneɪʃn; koˌɔrdn̩ˈeʃən/ *n* [U] **1 ~ (with sb/sth)** action of co-ordinating 协调; 协同动作: *the co-ordination of the work of several people* 几个人的协作 ○ *the perfect co-ordination of hand and eye* 手和眼完美的协调动作 ○ *a pamphlet produced by the*

Government in co-ordination with (ie working together with) *the Sports Council* 政府在体育协会的配合下发行的小册子. **2** ability to control one's movements properly 协调自己动作的能力: *have good/poor co-ordination* 善于[不善于]协调自己的动作 ○ *You need excellent co-ordination for ball games.* 做球类运动, 要善于协调自己的动作.

co-ordinator *n* person who co-ordinates 协调人: *The campaign needs an effective co-ordinator.* 这个运动需要一个有能力的协调人.

coot /ku:t; kut/ *n* **1** type of water-bird with a white spot on the forehead 蹼鸡, 白骨顶(额上有白斑的一种水鸟). ⇨illus at App 1 见附录1之插图, page v. **2** (idm 习语) **bald as a coot** ⇨ BALD.

cop[1] /kɒp; kap/ *n* (*sl* 俚) policeman (男)警察.

cop[2] /kɒp; kap/ *v* **(-pp-)** (*sl* 俚) **1** [Tn] receive (sth); suffer 获得(某事物); 遭受: *He copped a nasty whack on the head.* 他头上受一重击. ○ *The heavy rain missed the north of the country altogether, and the south copped the lot.* 该国南部大雨滂沱而北部却滴雨未落. **2** (**a**) [Tn, Tng] discover (sb) in the act of doing sth wrong; catch 发现(某人)在干坏事; 抓住: *If I cop you cheating again you'll be in trouble.* 我要再发现你骗人, 决不轻饶. (**b**) [Tn, Tn·pr] **~ sb (for sth)** arrest sb 逮捕某人: *He was copped for speeding.* 他因超速行车被捕. **3** (idm 习语) **cop hold of sth** take hold of sth; grasp sth 握住某物; 抓住某物: *Here, cop hold of the screwdriver while I try the hammer.* 喂, 握住这把改锥, 我用锄头试试. ˈ**cop it** be punished 受罚: *When he finds out who broke his radio, you'll really cop it!* 要是他知道了是谁把他的收音机弄坏了, 准够你受的! **4** (phr v) **cop ˈout (of sth)** (*derog* 贬) fail to do what one ought to do, esp through fear 退避, 回避, 逃避(尤指因恐惧): *He was boasting about how brave he was at the start, but copped out (of it) at the finish.* 他起初夸耀自己勇敢, 到头来却打了退堂鼓.

▷ **cop** *n* (idm 习语) **a fair cop** ⇨ FAIR[1]. **not much ˈcop** (*sl* 俚) not very good 不太好: *He's not much cop as a boxer.* 他是个蹩脚的拳击手.

□ ˈ**cop-out** *n* (*sl derog* 俚, 贬) act of or excuse for copping out 逃避的行为或借口: *The TV debate was a cop-out: it didn't tackle any of the real issues.* 电视辩论不过是虚晃一枪, 并未解决任何实际问题.

co·part·ner /ˌkəʊˈpɑ:tnə(r); koˈpɑrtnɚ/ *n* partner or associate in a business (企业的)合伙人.

▷ **co·part·ner·ship** *n* **1** [U] system of having copartners in business (企业的)合伙. **2** [C] pair or group of copartners 一对或一群合伙者.

cope[1] /kəʊp; kop/ *v* [I, Ipr] **~ (with sb/sth)** manage successfully; be able to deal with sth difficult 对付; (善于)处理(棘手之事): *cope with problems, difficulties, misfortune, etc* 对付问题、困难、灾祸等 ○ *Her husband's left her and the kids are running wild, so it's not surprising that she can't cope.* 她丈夫离开了她, 孩子们又不听管教, 难怪她束手无策. ○ *There was too much work for our computer to cope with.* 我们的计算机要干的工作太多, 简直应接不暇.

cope[2] /kəʊp; kop/ *n* long loose cloak worn by priests on some special occasions (教士在某些场合穿的)斗篷式长袍.

co·peck (also **ko·peck**) /ˈkəʊpek, ˈkɒpek; ˈkopɛk/ *n* unit of currency in the former Soviet Union; 100th part of a rouble 戈比(前苏联货币单位, 为一卢布的百分之一).

Co·per·nican /kəˈpɜ:nɪkən; koˈpɝnɪkən/ *adj* of Copernicus /kəˈpɜ:nɪkəs; koˈpɝnɪkəs/ (1473-1543), a Polish astronomer, who was the first to propose the theory that the planets move around the sun 哥白尼的(哥白尼, 1473-1543 年, 波兰天文学家, 日心说的创始人): *the Copernican system* 哥白尼体系.

co-pilot /ˌkəʊ ˈpaɪlət; ˈkoˌpaɪlət/ *n* assistant pilot in an aircraft (飞行器的)副驾驶员.

coping /ˈkəʊpɪŋ; ˈkopɪŋ/ *n* (*architecture* 建) top row of bricks or masonry, usu sloping, on a wall (墙上端的)压顶, 盖顶.

□ ˈ**coping-stone** *n* (*esp Brit*) stone used in a coping 压顶石: (*fig fml* 比喻, 文) *The final scene is the coping-stone of the play,* ie, the climax, which completes it appropriately. 这个剧的最后一场是压轴戏.

co·pi·ous /ˈkəʊpɪəs; ˈkopɪəs/ *adj* **1** plentiful; abundant 丰富的; 大量的: *copious flowers, tears, words* 许多花、眼泪、话 ○ *She supports her theory with copious evidence.* 她以大量的例证来充实自己的理论. ○ *I took copious notes.* 我作了详细的笔记. **2** (of a writer) writing or having written much; prolific (指作家)多产的: *a copious writer of detective stories* 写侦探小说的多产作家. ▷ **co·pi·ously** *adv*.

cop·per[1] /ˈkɒpə(r); ˈkapɚ/ *n* **1** [U] chemical element, a common reddish-brown metal 铜; 紫铜; 红铜: *the mining of copper in central Africa* 中部非洲的铜矿开采业 ○ *Is the pipe copper or lead?* 这管子是铜的呢还是铅的? ○ [attrib 作定语] *a copper pipe, wire, alloy, etc* 铜管、丝、合金等 ○ *her copper-coloured hair* 她那红棕色的头发. ⇨App 10 见附录10. **2** [C] (*esp Brit*) coin made of copper or a copper alloy 铜币: *It only costs a few coppers,* ie is cheap. 这只值几个铜板(很便宜). **3** [C] (*esp Brit*) large metal vessel, esp one in which clothes were formerly washed by boiling 大锅(尤指旧时用以煮洗衣物的). Cf 参看 BOILER 3.

□ ˌ**copper ˈbeech** type of beech tree with copper-coloured leaves 紫叶山毛榉.

ˌ**copper-ˈbottomed** *adj* (*esp Brit*) safe in every way; certain not to fail 绝对安全的; 万无一失的: *a copper-bottomed guarantee, assurance, deal, etc* 可靠的保证、绝对的把握、毫无风险的交易.

ˈ**copperhead** *n* poisonous snake found in the US 铜头蛇(一种毒蛇, 产于美国).

ˌ**copperˈplate** *n* polished copper plate on which designs, etc are engraved 铜凹版(镌刻有图案等的抛光铜板). ˌ**copperplate ˈwriting, handwriting** (also **copperplate**) neat old-fashioned formal handwriting with looped sloping letters that are joined to each other 铜版体(一种老式手写体, 笔画匀称、倾斜、互相连接).

cop·per[2] /ˈkɒpə(r); ˈkapɚ/ *n* (*infml* 口) policeman (男)警察.

cop·pice /ˈkɒpɪs; ˈkapɪs/ *n* = COPSE.

copra /ˈkɒprə; ˈkaprə/ *n* [U] dried coconut, from which oil is extracted to make soap, etc 干椰子仁(可榨油以制肥皂等).

copse /kɒps; kaps/ (also **coppice**) *n* small area of woodland with thick undergrowth and trees 矮林; 萌生林.

Copt /kɒpt; kapt/ *n* **1** member of the Coptic Church 科普特教徒. **2** Egyptian who is descended from the ancient Egyptians 科普特人(古埃及人后裔的埃及人).

▷ **Coptic** /ˈkɒptɪk; ˈkaptɪk/ *adj* of the Copts 科普特教徒的; 科普特人的: *Coptic language, traditions* 科普特语、传统. — *n* [U] language used in the Coptic Church (科普特教会使用的)科普特语.

□ **the ˌCoptic ˈChurch** the ancient Christian Church of Egypt, now with members in Egypt and Ethiopia 科普特教会(古代埃及建立的基督教会, 现今在埃及和埃塞俄比亚均有教徒).

cop·ula /ˈkɒpjʊlə; ˈkapjələ/ *n* (*grammar*) type of verb that connects a subject with its complement 系词(即连系动词, 用以连结主语及其补语): *In 'George became ill', the verb 'became' is a copula.* 在 George became ill 一句中, became 是系词.

cop·ulate /ˈkɒpjʊleɪt; ˈkapjəˌlet/ *v* [I, Ipr] **~ (with sb/sth)** (*fml* 文) (esp of animals) have sexual intercourse (尤指动物)交配, 交尾: *The male bird performs a sort of mating dance before copulating with the female.* 这种雄鸟在与雌鸟交尾以前要跳一种交欢舞.

▷ **cop·ula·tion** /ˌkɒpjʊˈleɪʃn; ˌkapjəˈleʃən/ *n* [U] act of copulating 交配; 交尾.

copu·lat·ive /ˈkɒpjʊlətɪv; *US* -leɪtɪv; ˈkapjəˌletɪv/ *adj* (*fml* 文) having a connecting function 有连系作用的. — *n* (*grammar*) word that connects (and implies that meanings are added together 系词; 连系词; 连词; 连接词): *'And' is a copulative.* and 是连词.

copy[1] /ˈkɒpɪ; ˈkapɪ/ *n* **1** [C] thing made to look like another, esp a reproduction of a letter, picture, etc 复制品(尤指信件的复写件、图片的复印件等): *Is this the original drawing or is it a copy?* 这是原画还是模本? ○ *a perfect copy* 以假乱真的仿造物 ○ *Make three carbon copies of the letter.* 把这信复制三份. ○ *Photocopies cost 6p per copy.* 影印文件每份收费6便士. **2** [C] individual example of a book, newspaper, record, etc of which many have been made (书、报纸、唱片等物品的)一本,

一份, 一张, 一件: *If you can't afford a new copy of the book, perhaps you can find a second-hand one.* 这书要是你买不起新的, 你或许能找到一本旧的. ○ *You receive the top copy of the receipt, and we keep the carbon.* 你把这收据上面的原件收下, 我们保留下面的复写件. **3** [U] material that is to be printed 原稿: *The journalist has handed in her copy.* 这个女记者交了稿. ○ *The government crisis will make good copy*, ie will make an interesting or exciting newspaper story. 政府的危机将成为新闻报道的好题材. ○ *We can give you the text on computer disk, or as hard copy*, ie as writing or printing on paper. 我们可以给你一份计算机磁盘的文本, 也可以给你一份硬拷贝(手抄本或打印本).

C

□ ˈ**copy-cat** *n* (*infml derog* 口, 贬) person who always imitates others 一味模仿他人者.

ˈ**copy desk** (*US*) desk in a newspaper office where copy[1](3) is edited and prepared for printing (报社的)编辑办公桌.

ˈ**copy-typist** *n* typist who types out written material (书面材料的)打字员.

ˈ**copy-writer** *n* person who writes advertising or publicity copy[1](3) 广告或宣传文字的撰稿人.

copy[2] /ˈkɒpɪ; ˋkɑpɪ/ *v* (*pt, pp* **copied**) **1** (**a**) [Tn, Tn·pr, Tn·p] **~ sth (down/out) (from sth) (in/into sth)** make a written copy(1) of sth 抄写; 复写某物: *copy out a letter*, ie write it out again completely 缮写出信函的复本 ○ *The teacher wrote the sums on the board, and the children copied them down in their exercise books.* 老师把算术题写在黑板上, 学生再抄写在自己的练习本上. ○ *copy notes (from a book, etc) into a notebook* 把(书等的)要点抄录在笔记本上. (**b**) [Tn, Tn·pr] make a copy (1) of (sth) 复制; 复印: *copy documents on a photocopier* 用复印机复印文件. **2** [Tn] (try to) do the same as (sb else); imitate 仿效, 追随(他人); 模仿: *She's a good writer: try to copy her style.* 她是出色的作家, 你不妨学学她的写作风格. ○ *Don't always copy what the others do; use your own ideas.* 不要老是蹈袭他人, 你应该有主见. **3** [I, Ipr] **~ (from sb)** cheat by writing or doing the same thing as sb else 抄袭; 做假: *She was punished for copying during the examination.* 她因考试抄袭作弊而受到处罚.

▷ **copier** *n* machine that makes copies of documents on paper, esp by photographing them 复印机.

copy·ist *n* **1** person who makes copies of eg old documents 缮写员(如古旧文件的抄写人员). **2** imitator 模仿者: *This painting is by a copyist.* 这幅画出自临模家之手.

copy-book /ˈkɒpɪbʊk; ˋkɑpɪ,bʊk/ *n* **1** exercise book containing models of handwriting for learners to imitate (有书写范例的)习字簿. **2** [attrib 作定语] perfect; textbook 十全十美的; 堪称典范的: *It was a copy-book operation by the police; all the criminals were arrested and all the stolen property quickly recovered.* 警方这一行动十分漂亮, 将罪犯一网打尽, 迅速起获所有赃物. **3** [attrib 作定语] (*dated* 旧) unoriginal; commonplace 陈腐的; 平淡无奇的: *copy-book maxims, sentiments, etc* 陈腐的格言、观点等. **4** (idm 习语) **blot one's copy-book** ⇨ BLOT[2].

copy·right /ˈkɒpɪraɪt; ˋkɑpɪ,raɪt/ *n* [U, C] **~ (on sth)** exclusive legal right, held for a certain number of years, to print, publish, sell, broadcast, perform, film or record an original work or any part of it 版权: *Copyright expires 50 years after the death of the author.* 版权在作者死后50年即行终止. ○ *The poem is still under copyright, so you have to pay to quote it.* 该诗仍然享有版权, 因此你必须支付引用费. ○ *sued for breach of copyright/for infringing copyright* 因侵犯版权被控告 ○ *Who owns the copyright on this song?* 谁享有这首歌的版权?

▷ **copy·right** *v* [Tn] obtain copyright for (a book, etc) 获得(书等)的版权.

copy·right *adj* protected by copyright 受版权保护的: *This material is copyright.* 本资料享有版权.

coquetry /ˈkɒkɪtrɪ; ˋkokɪtrɪ/ *n* (*fml* 文) (**a**) [U] flirting 调情; 卖俏. (**b**) [C] instance of this; flirtatious act 调情; 卖弄风情.

coquette /kɒˈket; koˋkɛt/ *n* (*fml often derog* 文, 常作贬义) girl or woman who flirts 卖弄风情的女子.

▷ **coquet·tish** /kɒˈketɪʃ; koˋkɛtɪʃ/ *adj* of or like a coquette 卖弄风情的; 卖俏似的: *a coquettish smile, manner* 卖弄风情的微笑、样子. **coquet·tishly** *adv*.

cor·acle /ˈkɒrəkl; ˋkɑrəkl/ *n* small light boat made of wickerwork and covered with watertight materials, used by fishermen on Welsh and Irish rivers and lakes (威尔士及爱尔兰渔民用的)轻便小船(用枝条编成, 覆以防水材料).

coral /ˈkɒrəl; *US* ˈkɔːrəl; ˋkɔrəl/ *n* **1** [U] red, pink or white hard substance formed on the sea bed from the skeletons of tiny animals known as polyps 珊瑚: *a necklace made of coral* 珊瑚项链. **2** [C] coral-producing animal; polyp 珊瑚虫; 水螅.

▷ **coral** *adj* like coral in colour; pink or red 珊瑚色的; 粉的或红的: *coral lipstick* 粉红色的口红.

□ ˌ**coral** ˈ**island** island formed by the growth of coral 珊瑚岛.

ˌ**coral** ˈ**reef** reef formed by the growth of coral 珊瑚礁.

cor ang·lais /ˌkɔːr ˈɒŋgleɪ; *US*- ɔːŋˈgleɪ; ˌkɔr ɔŋˋgle/ (*pl* **cors anglais**) (*music* 音) woodwind instrument similar to the oboe, but larger and playing lower notes 英国管(一种类似双簧管而形状较大、音调较低的木管乐器).

cor·bel /ˈkɔːbl; ˋkɔrbḷ/ *n* (*architecture* 建) stone or timber projection from a wall to support sth (eg an arch) 梁托; 翅托; 托臂.

cord /kɔːd; kɔrd/ *n* **1** [C, U] (piece of) long thin flexible material made of twisted strands, thicker than string and thinner than rope (细)绳: *parcels tied with cord* 用绳子捆扎的包裹. **2** [C] part of the body like a cord in being long, thin and flexible 身体上细长柔韧有如绳子的部分: *the spinal cord* 脊髓 ○ *the vocal cords* 声带. **3** [C, U] (*esp US*) = FLEX. **4** (*infml* 口) (**a**) [U] corduroy 灯芯绒: [attrib 作定语] *cord trousers, skirts, etc* 灯芯绒的裤子、裙子等. (**b**) **cords** [pl] corduroy trousers 灯芯绒裤子: *a man wearing blue cords* 穿蓝色灯芯绒裤的男子.

cord·age /ˈkɔːdɪdʒ; ˋkɔrdɪdʒ/ *n* [U] cords, ropes, etc, esp the rigging of a ship 绳索(尤指船缆).

cor·dial[1] /ˈkɔːdɪəl; *US* ˈkɔːrdʒəl; ˋkɔrdʒəl/ *adj* **1** sincere and friendly 诚恳的; 热诚的; 亲切的; 友好的: *a cordial smile, welcome, handshake, etc* 热诚的微笑、欢迎、握手等. **2** [usu attrib 通常作定语] (of dislike) strongly felt (指厌恶)深深感到的: *cordial hatred, detestation, loathing* 无比的憎恨、憎恶、厌恶.

▷ **cor·di·al·ity** /ˌkɔːdɪˈælətɪ; *US* ˌkɔːrdʒɪ-; ˌkɔrdʒɪˋælətɪ/ *n* **1** [U] quality of being cordial[1](1) 诚恳; 热诚. **2** **cordialities** [pl] (*fml* 文) expressions of cordial[1](1) feeling 热情友好的表示: *After the cordialities, we sat down to talk.* 我们热情友好地相互致意, 然后坐下来进行会谈. **cor·di·ally** /-dɪəlɪ; *US* -dʒəlɪ; -dʒəlɪ/ *adv*.

cor·dial[2] /ˈkɔːdɪəl; *US* ˈkɔːrdʒəl; ˋkɔrdʒəl/ *n* [U, C] (*Brit*) sweetened non-alcoholic drink typically made from fruit juice (不含酒精的)甜饮料(多由果汁制成): *lime juice cordial* 酸橙汁饮料.

cord·ite /ˈkɔːdaɪt; ˋkɔrdaɪt/ *n* [U] smokeless explosive substance used in bullets, shells, bombs, etc 柯达炸药; (柯达)无烟火药.

cor·don /ˈkɔːdn; ˋkɔrdṇ/ *n* **1** line or ring of policemen, soldiers, etc, esp one which guards sth or prevents people entering or leaving an area (由警察、士兵等组成的)警戒线, 防卫圈: *Demonstrators tried to break through the police cordon.* 示威群众企图突破警察的封锁线. **2** ornamental ribbon or braid of an order[1](10a), usu worn across the shoulder (代表勋位的)饰带或穗带(通常斜挂在肩上); 绶带. **3** fruit-tree with all its side branches cut off so that it grows as a single stem, usu against a wall or along wires (剪去一切枝桠的)单干果树(通常倚墙或沿金属线生长).

▷ **cor·don** *v* (phr v) **cordon sth off** separate or enclose sth by means of a cordon(1) 以警戒线分隔或包围: *Police cordoned off the area until the bomb was defused.* 警方封锁了这个区域直至拆除炸弹的引信为止.

cor·don bleu /ˌkɔːdɒn ˈblɜː; kɔrˋdɔ̃ˋblœ/ *adj* [usu attrib 通常作定语] (*French* 法) (of a cook, dish, etc) of the highest standard of skill in cooking, esp classical French cooking (指厨师、菜肴等)第一流手艺的(尤指法国传统烹饪): *cordon bleu cuisine* 第一流名厨所治佳肴.

cor·du·roy /ˈkɔːdərɔɪ; ˋkɔrdə,rɔɪ/ *n* **1** [U] strong cotton cloth covered with parallel soft raised ridges made up of short tufts 灯芯绒: [attrib 作定语] *a corduroy jacket* 灯芯绒夹克. **2** **corduroys** [pl] trousers made of this

cloth 灯芯绒裤子: *a pair of corduroys* 一条灯芯绒裤子.
□ ˌ**corduroy ˈroad** (*esp US*) road made of tree trunks laid side-by-side across swampy land (将树干并排横铺于湿软之地面而成的)木排路.

core /kɔː(r); kɔr/ *n* **1** (usu hard) centre of such fruits as the apple and pear, containing the seeds 果心(如苹果核、梨核). **2** (**a**) central part of a magnet or an induction coil 磁铁心; 线圈心. (**b**) (*geology* 地质) central part of the planet earth 地核: *The earth has a core and a mantle around it.* 地球的中心是地核, 地核的周围是地幔. (**c**) (*physics* 物) central part of a nuclear reactor, where the fuel rods are kept and the nuclear reaction takes place (核反应堆中的)活性区, 反应堆心. (**d**) (*computing* 计) very small magnetizable metal ring used formerly in a computer's memory for storing one bit³ of data (存储器的)磁心. (**e**) inner strand of an electric cable (电缆的)芯线. **3** most important part of sth 核心: *Let's get to the core of the argument.* 咱们进入实质性的辩论吧. ○ *This concept is at the very core of her theory.* 这个概念是她的理论的核心. ○ [attrib 作定语] *English is a subject on the core curriculum*, ie one which all the students have to do. 英语是一门基础课程. **4** (idm 习语) **to the ˈcore** right to the centre 达到中心: *rotten to the core*, ie completely bad 烂透了的 ○ *He is English to the core*, ie completely English in manner, speech, dress, etc. 他是地地道道的英国人. ○ *Her refusal shocked us to the core*, ie utterly. 她拒绝后我们大吃一惊.
▷ **core** *v* [Tn] take out the core of (sth) 去掉(某物)的中心部分: *core an apple* 挖去苹果的果心.

CORE (also **Core**) /kɔː(r); kɔr/ *abbr* 缩写 = (*US*) Congress of Racial Equality 争取种族平等大会.

co-religionist /ˌkəʊrɪˈlɪdʒənɪst; ˌko·rɪˈlɪdʒənɪst/ *n* (*fml* 文) person who belongs to the same religion as sb else 信奉同一宗教的人.

co-respondent /ˌkəʊ rɪˈspɒndənt; ˌko·rɪˈspɑndənt/ *n* (*law* 律) (formerly) person accused of committing adultery with the respondent in a divorce case (旧时离婚诉讼中被控通奸的)共同被告: *cite* (ie name) *sb as co-respondent* 指某人为共同被告.

corgi /ˈkɔːgɪ; ˈkɔrgɪ/ *n* breed of small Welsh dog 柯吉犬(一种小狗, 产于威尔士).

co·ri·an·der /ˌkɒrɪˈændə(r); *US* ˌkɔːr-; ˌkɔrɪˈændɚ/ *n* [U] plant whose leaves and dried seeds are used in cooking, to give a special taste 芫荽; 香菜.

Co·rin·thian /kəˈrɪnθɪən; kəˈrɪnθɪən/ *adj* **1** of Corinth /ˈkɒrɪnθ; ˈkɔrɪnθ/ in (ancient) Greece (古)希腊科林斯的. **2** (*architecture* 建) of the most highly decorated of the five classical orders (ORDER¹ 13) of Greek architecture, incorporating carvings of leaves 科林斯式的(希腊建筑五种古典柱式中最华丽者, 其特征为饰有叶形的雕花): *a Corinthian column* 科林斯圆柱. Cf 参看 DORIC, IONIC.
▷ **Co·rin·thian** *n* native of Corinth 科林斯人.

cork /kɔːk; kɔrk/ *n* **1** [U] light springy buoyant substance that is the thick bark of a type of oak tree growing around the Mediterranean 栓皮; 软木: *Cork is often used for insulation.* 栓皮经常用作绝缘材料. ○ [attrib 作定语] *cork tiles, table mats, etc* 软木砖、桌垫等. **2** [C] bottle-stopper made of this 软木瓶塞: *draw/pull out the cork* 拔出软木塞. ⇨illus at BOTTLE 见 BOTTLE 之插图.
▷ **cork** *v* **1** [Tn, Tn·p] **~ sth (up)** close or seal (a bottle, barrel, etc) with a cork or sth similar 用软木塞等物封堵(瓶、桶等): *cork a bottle* 塞住瓶子. **2** (phr v) **cork sth up** (*infml* 口) not express (feelings, etc) 抑制(感情等): *Don't cork it all up: if you feel angry, show it.* 别什么都闷在心里, 你有气就发泄出来.
corked *adj* (of wine) made bad by a decayed cork (指酒)有腐坏的软木塞异味的.
□ ˈ**corkscrew** *n* device for pulling corks from bottles 瓶塞钻(拔软木瓶塞用的).

cork·age /ˈkɔːkɪdʒ; ˈkɔrkɪdʒ/ *n* [U] charge made by a restaurant for opening wine a customer has bought elsewhere 开瓶费(饭店对顾客自备的酒收取的).

corm /kɔːm; kɔrm/ *n* (*botany* 植) underground reproductive part of certain plants (eg crocus and gladiolus), similar in appearance to a bulb(1), from which the new stalk grows each year 球茎. ⇨illus at App 1 见附录 1 之插图, page ii.

cor·mor·ant /ˈkɔːmərənt; ˈkɔrmərənt/ *n* large, long-necked, dark-coloured bird which lives near sea coasts and eats fish 鸬鹚. ⇨illus at App 1 见附录 1 之插图, page v.

corn 玉蜀黍

corn¹ /kɔːn; kɔrn/ *n* **1** [U] (**a**) (*esp Brit*) (seed of) any of various grain plants, chiefly wheat, oats, rye and maize; such plants while growing 谷物: *grinding corn to make flour* 把谷物磨成粉 ○ *a field of corn* 一片庄稼 ○ *a ˈcorn-field* 庄稼地 ○ *a sheaf of corn* 一捆谷物. (**b**) (*esp US*) maize 玉蜀黍; 玉米. ⇨illus 见插图. **2** [U] (*infml derog* 口, 贬) music, verse, drama, etc that is banal, sentimental or hackneyed 平庸、感伤或陈腐的音乐、诗歌、戏剧等: *a romantic ballad that is pure corn* 极为感伤的浪漫小曲.
▷ **corny** /ˈkɔːnɪ; ˈkɔrnɪ/ *adj* (**-ier**, **-iest**) (*infml derog* 口, 贬) (**a**) too often heard or repeated; hackneyed 老生常谈的; 陈腐的: *a corny joke* 老掉牙的笑话. (**b**) banal; sentimental 平庸乏味的; 多愁善感的: *a corny song* 伤感的歌曲.
□ ˈ**corn-cob** *n* hard cylindrical part at the top of a maize stalk, on which the grains grow 玉米穗轴. ⇨illus 见插图.
ˈ**corn-exchange** *n* place where corn is bought and sold 谷物市场.
ˈ**cornflakes** *n* [pl] breakfast cereal made of maize that has been crushed and heated to make it crisp 玉米片(一种早餐食品).
ˈ**cornflour** (*US* ˈ**cornstarch**) *n* [U] finely ground flour made esp from maize or rice 谷物磨成的粉; (尤指)玉米面, 米粉.
ˈ**cornflower** *n* any of various plants growing wild in corn-fields, esp a blue-flowered kind that is also grown in gardens 矢车菊.
the ˈCorn Laws (*history* 史) set of British laws, repealed in 1846, which restricted import of corn to keep prices high 谷物法(英国法令, 旨在限制谷物进口以维持高价, 于 1846 年废除).
ˌ**corn on the ˈcob** maize cooked with all the grains still attached to the stalk (熟的)玉米棒子.
ˈ**corn pone** (*US* also **pone**) /pəʊn; pon/ baked or fried maize bread (烤的或煎的)玉米面包.
ˈ**cornstarch** *n* [U] (*US*) = CORNFLOUR.

corn² /kɔːn; kɔrn/ *n* **1** small, often painful, area of hardened skin on the foot, esp on the toe 鸡眼. **2** (idm 习语) **tread on sb's corns/toes** ⇨TREAD.

cor·nea /ˈkɔːnɪə; ˈkɔrnɪə/ *n* (*anatomy* 解) transparent outer covering of the eye, which protects the pupil and iris 角膜. ⇨illus at EYE 见 EYE 之插图.
▷ **cor·neal** /ˈkɔːnɪəl; ˈkɔrnɪəl/ *adj* of the cornea 角膜的: *a corneal graft* 角膜移植片.

corned /kɔːnd; kɔrnd/ *adj* (of meat) preserved in salt (指肉)腌制的: *corned beef/pork* 咸的牛肉[猪肉].

cor·ne·lian /kɔːˈniːlɪən; kɔrˈniljən/ *n* semi-precious stone of a reddish, reddish-brown or white colour 光玉髓(次等宝石, 呈红色、红褐色或白色).

cor·ner¹ /ˈkɔːnə(r); ˈkɔrnɚ/ *n* **1** place where two lines, sides, edges or surfaces meet; angle enclosed by two walls, sides, etc that meet 角儿; 角落: *A square has four corners; a cube has eight.* 正方形有四个角儿; 立方体有八个角儿. ○ *standing at a street corner* 站在街角儿上 ○ *the shop on/at the corner* 位于街角儿的商店 ○ *In the corner of the room stood a big old chair.* 屋角儿放着一把旧的大椅子. ○ *The address is in the top right-hand corner* *of the letter.* 地址在这封信的右上角儿. ○ *When I turned the corner (of the street) he had disappeared.* 我拐过街角儿时他已经不见了. ○ *He hit his knee on the corner of the table.* 他的膝盖撞在桌子角儿上了. ○ [attrib 作定语] *the corner shop*, ie on the corner of two streets 街角儿处的商店. **2** (**a**) hidden, secret or remote place 隐蔽的、秘密的或偏僻的处所: *money hidden in odd corners* 藏在秘密地方的钱. (**b**) region; part; area 区域; 部分; 地区: *She lives in a quiet corner of Yorkshire.* 她住在约克郡的一个僻静的地区. **3** difficult or awkward situation 困境; 窘况: *Having lied that I still had the money, I was in rather a corner when they asked me to hand it over.* 因我谎称钱仍在我处, 所以他们要我交出时, 我很尴尬. ○ *She'll need luck to get out of a tight corner like that.* 她要靠运气才能摆脱那样的困境. ○ *The interviewer had driven her into a corner.* 面试主持人把她追问得很窘. **4** (usu *sing* 通常作单数) **~ (in sth)** (*commerce* 商) complete ownership or control of supplies of sth, enabling one to decide its price 囤积; 垄断: *a company with a corner in tin ore, wheat, etc* 垄断锡矿石、小麦等市场的一家公司. **5** (also ˈ**corner-kick**) (in soccer) kick from the corner of the field, given to a team when an opposing player kicks the ball over his own goal-line (英式足球)角球. **6** (in boxing and wrestling 拳击或摔跤运动中) (**a**) any of the four corners of the ring (拳击场及摔跤场的)场角: *In the blue corner, Buster Smith.* 蓝方, 巴斯特·史密斯. (**b**) [CGp] group of people (eg trainers) who help a fighter during intervals in the match (比赛休息时向场上队员提供帮助的)辅助人员(如教练员): *His corner advised him to retire.* 教练员建议他退场. ⇨illus at BOXING 见 BOXING 之插图. **7** (idm 习语) **cut** ˈ**corners** (**a**) drive round corners in a wide curve rather than at a sharp angle (驾驶时)拐小弯而不拐大弯. (**b**) do sth in the easiest and quickest way, often by ignoring rules, being careless, etc (做事)走捷径, 图省事(常为忽视规则、粗心大意等): *We've had to cut a few corners to get your visa ready in time.* 我们得简化手续才能将你的签证及时办妥. **cut (off) a** ˈ**corner** (*esp Brit*) go across the corner of sth, not properly around it 不绕角儿走而取捷径斜穿: *The lawn is damaged here because people cut (off) the corner.* 由于人们不绕角儿走而抄近道, 这里的草坪已踩坏了. **the four corners of the earth** the most distance parts of the the earth 世界各个角落; 天涯海角: *Former students of this school are now working in the four corners of the earth.* 该校的校友现在世界各地工作. **out of the corner of one's eye** by looking sharply sideways 瞟; 睨视: *I caught sight of her out of the corner of my eye.* 我用眼一瞟, 看见了她. **(just) round the** ˈ**corner** very near 很近: *Her house is (just) round the corner.* 她家离此不远. ○ *Good times are just round the corner*, ie will soon happen. 好日子近在眼前. **turn the** ˈ**corner** pass a critical point in an illness, a period of difficulty, etc and begin to improve (疾病、困难时期等)渡过危险期, 渡过难关.

▷ **-**ˈ**cornered** (in compound *adjs* 用以构成复合形容词) **1** with the specified number of corners 有某数量边角的: *a* ˌ*three-cornered* ˈ*hat*. **2** with the specified number of participants 有某数量参与者的: *The election was a three-cornered fight between Conservatives, Labour and SLD.* 这次选举是保守党、工党以及社会民主党三方的较量.

□ ˈ**corner-stone** *n* **1** stone that forms the base of a corner of a building, often laid in position at a ceremony 奠基石. **2** (*fig* 比喻) thing on which sth is built; foundation 基础: *Hard work was the corner-stone of his success.* 努力奋斗是他成功的基础.

cor·ner[2] /ˈkɔ:nə(r); ˋkɔrnɚ/ *v* **1** [Tn] (**a**) get (a person or an animal) into a position from which it is hard to escape 使(某人或某动物)走投无路: *The escaped prisoner was cornered at last.* 那逃犯最后走投无路了. ○ *The runaway horse was cornered in a field.* 那匹跑掉的马在田地里被圈住了. (**b**) put (sb) into a difficult situation 使(某人)陷于困境: *The interviewer cornered the politician with a particularly tricky question.* 采访者用一个极其巧妙的问题难住了那个政客. **2** [I] (of a vehicle or driver) turn a corner (指车或司机)转弯: *The car corners well*, ie remains steady on curves. 这车转弯转得很平稳. ○ *Don't corner so fast!* 转弯别转得太快! **3** [Tn] (*commerce* 商) gain monopoly control of (sth) 垄断(某事物): *corner the market in silver* 垄断白银市场.

cor·net /ˈkɔ:nɪt; ˋkɔrnɪt/ *n* **1** brass instrument, like a trumpet but smaller, typically played in brass bands 短号. **2** (*Brit*) cone-shaped container for ice-cream, made of thin crisp biscuit (盛冰激凌的)圆锥形蛋卷.

cor·nice /ˈkɔ:nɪs; ˋkɔrnɪs/ *n* (*architecture* 建) **1** ornamental moulding, eg in plaster, round the walls of a room, just below the ceiling 檐口(墙顶上带装饰的突出体, 如用灰泥制的). ⇨illus at COLUMN 见 COLUMN 之插图. **2** horizontal strip of carved wood or stone along the top of an outside wall (沿外墙的雕木或石刻的)飞檐. **3** overhanging mass of snow or rock on the side of a mountain 雪檐(冻结在悬崖边缘的悬垂的冰雪块; (向外突出的)悬崖.

Corn·ish /ˈkɔ:nɪʃ; ˋkɔrnɪʃ/ *adj* of Cornwall (英国)康沃尔郡的.

□ ˌ**Cornish** ˈ**pasty** small pie consisting of pastry filled with meat and vegetables 康沃尔馅饼(以肉和菜为馅做成的小点心).

cor·nu·co·pia /ˌkɔ:njuˈkəupɪə; ˌkɔrnəˋkopɪə/ *n* **1** (also **horn of** ˈ**plenty**) ornamental animal's horn shown in art as overflowing with flowers, fruit and corn, symbolizing abundance 丰饶角(艺术作品中象征丰饶的羊角, 角内呈现满溢的鲜花、水果及谷物). **2** (*fml fig* 文, 比喻) abundant source 富饶之源; 宝藏: *The book is a cornucopia of information.* 书是知识的宝库.

co·rolla /kəˈrɒlə; kəˋrɑlə/ *n* (*botany* 植) ring of petals forming the cup of a flower 花冠.

co·rol·lary /kəˈrɒlərɪ; *US* ˈkɒrəlerɪ; ˋkɔrəˌlɛrɪ/ *n* **~ (of/to sth)** (*fml* 文) natural consequence or result; thing that logically must be so, once sth else has been established 自然的结果; 推断: *Neither of them knew about it, and the corollary of that is that someone else revealed the secret.* 他们两人并不知道这回事, 因此一定是另外有人泄露了秘密.

co·rona /kəˈrəunə; kəˋronə/ *n* (*pl* **~s** /-nəz; -nəz/ **~e** /-ni:; -ni/) (also **aureola**, **aureole, halo**) (*astronomy* 天) ring of light seen round the sun or moon, eg during an eclipse 日冕; 日华; 月华.

cor·on·ary /ˈkɒrənrɪ; *US* ˈkɔ:rənerɪ; ˋkɔrəˌnɛrɪ/ *adj* (*anatomy* 解) of the arteries supplying blood to the heart 冠状动脉的: *coronary arteries* 冠状动脉.

□ ˌ**coronary throm**ˈ**bosis** (also *infml* 口语亦作 **coronary**) blocking of a coronary artery by a clot of blood, damaging the heart and possibly causing death; heart attack 冠状动脉血栓; 心脏病发作.

cor·ona·tion /ˌkɒrəˈneɪʃn; *US* ˌkɔ:r-; ˌkɔrəˋneʃən/ *n* ceremony of crowning a king, a queen or some other sovereign ruler 加冕礼: *the coronation of Elizabeth II* 伊丽莎白二世的加冕礼 ○ [attrib 作定语] *the coronation day, robes, coach* 加冕日、袍、马车等.

cor·oner /ˈkɒrənə(r); *US* ˈkɔ:r-; ˋkɔrənɚ/ *n* official who investigates any violent or suspicious death 验尸官; 死因裁判官.

□ ˌ**coroner's** ˈ**inquest** proceedings held by a coroner, at which evidence about a death is presented and a jury gives a verdict on its cause 验尸.

cor·onet /ˈkɒrənet; *US* ˈkɔ:r-; ˋkɔrənɪt/ *n* **1** small crown worn by a peer or peeress (贵族戴的)小冠冕. **2** garland of flowers worn on the head (带在头上的)花环.

Corp *abbr* 缩写 = **1** (also **Cpl**) Corporal: *Corp (Simon) Grey* (西蒙·)格雷下士. **2** (*US*) corporation: *West Coast Motor Corp* 西海岸汽车公司.

cor·poral[1] /ˈkɔ:pərəl; ˋkɔrpərəl/ *adj* (*fml* 文) of the human body 人体的.

□ ˌ**corporal** ˈ**punishment** physical punishment, eg by whipping, beating 体罚(如鞭打).

cor·poral[2] /ˈkɔ:pərəl; ˋkɔrpərəl/ *n* non-commissioned officer below the rank of sergeant in an army or air force (陆军或空军的)下士. ⇨App 9 见附录 9.

cor·por·ate /ˈkɔ:pərət; ˋkɔrpərɪt/ *adj* **1** of or shared by all the members of a group; collective 团体的; 共同的: *corporate responsibility, action, etc* 共同的责任、行动等. **2** of or belonging to a corporation(2a, b) 法人团体的; 公司的: *corporate planning policy, etc* 公司的计划、方针等 ○ *Corporate executives usually have high salaries.* 公司里的管理人员一般享有高薪. **3** united in a single group 结成一个团体的: *a corporate body* 团体.

cor·pora·tion /ˌkɔːpəˈreɪʃn; ˌkɔrpəˈreʃən/ *n* **1** [CGp] (*esp Brit*) group of people elected to govern a town; council 市政当局: *the Lord Mayor and Corporation of the City of London* 伦敦市长及市政当局 ○ *the municipal corporation* 市行政机关 ○ [attrib 作定语] *corporation services, transport, refuse collection, etc* 市政机关管理的部门、运输、垃圾收集服务等. **2** [CGp] (*abbr* 缩写 **corp**) (**a**) group of people authorized to act as an individual, eg for business purposes 法人团体(如贸易公司): *Broadcasting authorities are often public corporations.* 广播事业管理机构一般为公营公司. (**b**) (*esp US*) business company 公司: *large multinational corporations* 大跨国公司. **3** [C] (*joc* 谑 *esp Brit*) large fat stomach 大肚皮.

□ ˌ**corpoˈration tax** tax paid by business companies on profits 公司税.

cor·por·eal /kɔːˈpɔːrɪəl; kɔrˈpɔrɪəl/ *adj* (*fml* 文) **1** of or for the body; bodily 肉体的; 身体的; 身体所需的: *corporeal needs*, eg food and drink 维持生命的必需品; 身体的需要(如食物和饮料). **2** material, rather than spiritual 物质的(与精神的相对): *He is very religious; corporeal world has little interest for him.* 他虔信宗教,对物质上的享受不感兴趣.

corps /kɔː(r); kɔr/ *n* (*pl* unchanged 复数不变 /kɔːz; kɔrz/) [CGp] **1** (**a**) military force made up of two or more divisions 兵团, 军(军事单位, 由两个或两个以上师的兵力组成): *the 6th Army Corps* 陆军第6兵团. (**b**) one of the technical branches of an army (陆军的)特种部队: *the ˌRoyal ˌArmy ˈMedical Corps* 英国皇家陆军医疗队. **2** group of people involved in a particular activity 从事某活动的集体: *the Diploˈmatic Corps*, ie all the ambassadors, attachés, etc of foreign states in a particular country 外交使节团 ○ *the ˈpress corps*, ie journalists 记者团.

□ **corps de ballet** /ˌkɔː də ˈbæleɪ; ˌkɔr də bæˈle/ (*French* 法) dancers in a ballet company who dance together as a group 芭蕾舞团.

corpse /kɔːps; kɔrps/ *n* dead body (esp of a human being) 尸体(尤指人的). Cf 参看 CARCASS.

cor·pulent /ˈkɔːpjʊlənt; ˈkɔrpjələnt/ *adj* (*fml esp euph* 文, 尤作委婉语) (of a person or his body) fat (指人或人的身体)肥胖的. ▷ **cor·pu·lence** /ˈkɔːpjʊləns; ˈkɔrpjələns/ *n* [U].

cor·pus /ˈkɔːpəs; ˈkɔrpəs/ *n* (*pl* **corpora** /ˈkɔːpərə; ˈkɔrpərə/) collection of written (or sometimes spoken) texts (书面的, 有时为口语的)资料, 文集, 汇编: *analyse a corpus of spoken dialect* 分析口语方言的汇集资料 ○ *the entire corpus of Milton's works* 米尔顿作品的全集.

cor·puscle /ˈkɔːpʌsl; ˈkɔrpʌsl/ *n* (*anatomy* 解) any of the red or white cells in the blood (红或白)血球.

cor·ral /kəˈrɑːl; *US* -ˈræl; kəˈræl/ *n* (*esp US*) **1** enclosure for horses, cattle, etc on a ranch or farm (牧场或农场上关马、牛等的)畜栏. **2** defensive circle of wagons, etc; laager (形成防御圈的)车阵.

▷ **cor·ral** *v* (**-ll-**) **1** [Tn] drive (cattle, etc) into or shut up in a corral 把(牛等)赶入或关进畜栏. **2** [Tn] form (wagons, etc) into a corral 把(车辆等)布成车阵.

cor·rect[1] /kəˈrekt; kəˈrɛkt/ *adj* **1** true; right; accurate 正确的; 对的; 准确的: *the correct answer* 正确的答案 ○ *Do you have the correct time?* 你的表准吗? ○ *The description is correct in every detail.* 每个细节的叙述都很准确. ○ *Would I be correct in thinking that you are Jenkins?* ie Are you Jenkins? 我想你就是詹金斯吧? ○ *'Are you Jenkins?' 'That's correct.'* '你是詹金斯吗?' '是的.' **2** (of behaviour, manners, dress, etc) in accordance with accepted standards or convention; proper (指行为、礼貌、衣着等)符合公认标准的, 得体的: *Such casual dress would not be correct for a formal occasion.* 这样的便服不宜在正式的场合穿. ○ *a very correct young lady* 举止很得体的年轻女士. ▷ **cor·rectly** *adv*: *answer correctly* 正确地回答 ○ *behave very correctly* 举止十分得体. **cor·rect·ness** *n* [U].

cor·rect[2] /kəˈrekt; kəˈrɛkt/ *v* [Tn] **1** (**a**) make (sth) right or accurate; remove the mistakes from 改正(某事物); 修改; 纠正: *correct spelling, mistakes, misconceptions* 改正拼写错误、谬误、错误的观念 ○ *I corrected my watch by the time signal.* 我按照报时信号对的表. ○ *Please correct my pronunciation if I go wrong.* 假若我的发音不准就请你纠正. ○ *Spectacles correct faulty eyesight.* 眼镜可以矫正视力缺陷. ○ *'It was in April — no, May,' he said, correcting himself.* '那是在四月份 —— 不, 在五月份,' 他改口说. (**b**) (of a teacher, etc) mark the errors in (sth) (指教师等)批改(某项作业的)错处: *correct an essay, a test, etc* 批改作文、测验题等. **2** point out the mistakes or faults of (sb) 指出(某人)的错误或过失: *'Correct me if I'm wrong, but isn't that a llama?' 'No, it's not.' 'I stand corrected'*, ie You have pointed out my mistake. '那是美洲驼吗? 要是我说错了, 就请指出来.' '那不是.' '多谢您指正.' **3** adjust (sth) so as to make it accurate 校正(某事物): *Turn the wheel to the right to correct the steering.* 把方向盘往右边转转, 好修正驾驶上的偏差. ○ *Add salt to correct the seasoning.* 加点盐把味道调好.

cor·rec·tion /kəˈrekʃn; kəˈrɛkʃən/ *n* **1** [U] correcting 改正; 修改; 批改; 校正: *the correction of exam papers* 试卷的批改. **2** [C] right mark, etc put in place of sth wrong 错误之处的批改记号: *a written exercise with corrections in red ink* 用红笔批改过的书面作业. **3** [U] (*fml* 文) punishment 惩治: *the correction of young delinquents* 失足少年的改造 ○ (*arch* 古) *a house of correction*, ie prison 感化院(监狱).

cor·rect·ive /kəˈrektɪv; kəˈrɛktɪv/ *adj* having the effect of correcting sth 有改正作用的; 矫正的: *corrective training*, eg for young offenders 管教(如对失足少年) ○ *corrective surgery for a deformed leg* 医治腿部畸形的矫正外科.

▷ **cor·rect·ive** *n* ~ **(to sth)** thing that produces an opposing view which is more accurate, fairer, etc 纠正错误看法之物: *These artefacts are correctives to the usual view of these people as completely uncivilized.* 通常认为这些人完全没有开化, 这些工艺品改变了人们的这种看法.

cor·rel·ate /ˈkɒrəleɪt; *US* ˈkɔːr-; ˈkɔrəˌlet/ *v* [I, Ipr, Tn, Tn·pr] ~ **(with sth)**; ~ **A and/with B** have a mutual relation or connection, esp of affecting or depending on each other; (try to) show such a relation or connection between sth and sth else 相关或相互关联; (尤指)相互影响或相互依存; (试图)显示某事物与他事物的上述关系或联系: *The results of this experiment do not correlate with the results of earlier ones.* 这次试验的结果与以往试验的结果毫不相干. ○ *Researchers cannot correlate the two sets of figures.* 研究者们看不出这两组数字有什么联系. ○ *We can often correlate age with frequency of illness.* 年龄的大小往往与发病率有关.

▷ **cor·rela·tion** /ˌkɒrəˈleɪʃn; *US* ˌkɔːr-; ˌkɔrəˈleʃən/ *n* [sing, U] ~ **(with sth)**; ~ **(between A and B)** mutual relationship 相互的关系: *the correlation between sb's height and weight* 身高与体重之间的关系.

cor·rel·at·ive /kɒˈrelətɪv; kəˈrɛlətɪv/ *adj* having or showing a relation to sth else 相关的; 显示相互关系的: *'Either' and 'or' are correlative conjunctions.* either 和 or 是关联连词.

cor·res·pond /ˌkɒrɪˈspɒnd; *US* ˌkɔːr-; ˌkɔrəˈspɑnd/ *v* [I, Ipr] **1** ~ **(with sth)** be in agreement; not contradict sth or each other 相一致; 相符合: *Your account of events corresponds with hers.* 你说的情况跟她说的相符. ○ *Your account and hers correspond.* 你的说法跟她的说法一致. ○ *The written record of our conversation doesn't correspond with* (ie is different from) *what was actually said.* 对我们交谈所作的文字记录与我们的原话不符. ○ *Does the name on the envelope correspond with the name on the letter inside?* 信封上的名字与里面信上的名字是否相同? **2** ~ **(to sth)** be equivalent or similar 相当的; 相似的: *The American Congress corresponds to the British Parliament.* 美国的国会相当于英国的议会. **3** ~ **(with sb)** exchange letters 通信: *We've corresponded (with each other)* (ie written to each other) *for years but I've never actually met him.* 我们已(互相)通信多年了, 可是我从未见过他本人.

▷ **cor·res·pond·ing** *adj* that corresponds 相符的; 相当的; 通信的: *Imports in the first three months have increased by 10 per cent compared with the corresponding period last year.* 第一季度的进口额与去年同期相比增长了百分之十. **cor·res·pond·ingly** *adv*: *The new exam is longer and correspondingly more difficult to pass.* 新的考试需时较长, 因而相应地较难及格.

cor·res·pond·ence /ˌkɒrɪˈspɒndəns; *US* ˌkɔːr-; ˌkɔrəˈspɑndəns/ *n* **1** [C, U] ~ **(with sth/between sth and**

C

sth) agreement; similarity 一致; 相似: *a close/not much correspondence between the two accounts* 两种叙述接近[不太]一致. **2** [U] **~ (with sb)** letter-writing; letters 通信; 信件: *She has a lot of correspondence to deal with.* 她有大批信件需要处理. ○ *I refused to enter into any correspondence* (ie exchange letters) *with him about it.* 我决不就这一问题与他通信. ○ *Is commercial correspondence taught at the school?* 学校里是否教授商业函件?

□ **corre'spondence course** course of study using books, exercises, etc sent by post 函授课程.

cor·res·pond·ent /ˌkɒrɪ'spɒndənt; US ˌkɔ:r-; ˌkɔrə'spɑndənt/ *n* **1** person who contributes news or comments regularly to a newspaper, radio station, etc, esp from abroad (报刊、广播电台等的)通讯员, 记者(尤指派驻国外的): *our Hong Kong, Middle East, etc correspondent* 我们派驻香港、中东的通讯员 ○ *a foreign, war, cricket correspondent,* ie sb gathering news in a foreign country, in a war, about cricket 国外、战地、板球比赛通讯记者. **2** person who writes letters to another 通信者: *He's a good/poor correspondent,* ie writes regularly/seldom. 他是个勤于[懒于]写信的人.

cor·ridor /'kɒrɪdɔ:(r); US 'kɔ:r-; 'kɔrədɚ/ *n* **1** long narrow passage, from which doors open into rooms or compartments 过道; 走廊. **2** long narrow strip of land belonging to one country that passes through the land of another country 一国领土穿越他国境内的狭长地带. **3** (idm 习语) **the corridors of 'power** the higher levels of the Government and administration, where important decisions are made 权力走廊(政府及行政部门进行重要决策的较高阶层): *an issue much discussed in the corridors of power* 在领导核心中进行了充分讨论的问题.

□ **'corridor train** train with coaches which have compartments opening into a corridor 包厢列车.

cor·ri·gendum /ˌkɒrɪ'dʒendəm; US ˌkɔ:r-; ˌkɔrɪ'dʒɛndəm/ *n* (*pl* **-da** /-də; -də/) corrected error, esp one of a list printed at the beginning of a book 已改正的错误; (尤指书前的)勘误表. Cf 参看 ERRATUM.

cor·rob·or·ate /kə'rɒbəreɪt; kə'rɑbəˌret/ *v* [Tn] confirm or give support to (a statement, belief, theory, etc) 证实, 支持(某种说法、信仰、理论等): *Experiments have corroborated her predictions.* 实验证实了她的预言.

▷ **cor·rob·ora·tion** /kəˌrɒbə'reɪʃn; kəˌrɑbə'reʃən/ *n* [U] confirmation or support by further evidence, esp from a different source; additional evidence 进一步的证实(尤指另有来源的); 进一步的证据: *His possession of the gun is corroboration of his guilt.* 他藏有枪是他犯罪的又一证据. ○ *In corroboration of his story* (ie to give support to it) *he produced a signed statement from his employer.* 为了进一步证明他所说的是事实, 他出示了一份雇主签了字的文件.

cor·rob·or·at·ive /kə'rɒbərətɪv; US -reɪtɪv; kə'rɑbəˌretɪv/ *adj* tending to corroborate 确证(性)的: *corroborative reports, evidence, etc* 可以进一步说明问题的报告、证据等.

cor·rode /kə'rəʊd; kə'rod/ *v* [I, Ip, Tn, Tn·p] **~ (sth) (away)** be destroyed or destroy (sth) slowly, esp by chemical action 腐蚀, 侵蚀(某物)(尤指化学作用): *The metal has corroded (away) because of rust.* 该金属已锈蚀. ○ *Acid has corroded the iron (away).* 酸把铁腐蚀了. ○ (*fig* 比喻) *a bitter envy that had corroded their friendship* 使他们的友谊遭到损害的强烈的忌妒.

▷ **cor·ro·sion** /kə'rəʊʒn; kə'roʒən/ *n* [U] corroding or being corroded; corroded area or part 腐蚀; 受腐蚀的部位: *Clean off any corrosion before applying the paint.* 先除去所有的锈迹再上油漆.

cor·ros·ive /kə'rəʊsɪv; kə'rosɪv/ *n, adj* (substance) that corrodes 腐蚀性的(物质): *Rust and acids are corrosive.* 锈及酸类都是腐蚀性物质.

cor·rug·ate /'kɒrəgeɪt; US 'kɔ:r-; 'kɔrəˌget/ *v* [I, Tn usu passive 通常用于被动语态] be shaped or shape (sth) into folds, wrinkles or furrows (使某物)起皱褶, 起皱纹, 起波纹: *His brow corrugated with the effort of thinking.* 他皱着眉头用心地思考. ○ *muddy roads corrugated* (ie rutted and furrowed) *by cart-wheels* 被大车压出了一道道辙印的泥泞的道路.

▷ **cor·rug·ated** /'kɒrəgeɪtɪd; 'kɔrəˌgetɪd/ *adj* folded, wrinkled or furrowed 起皱褶的; 起皱纹的; 起波纹的:

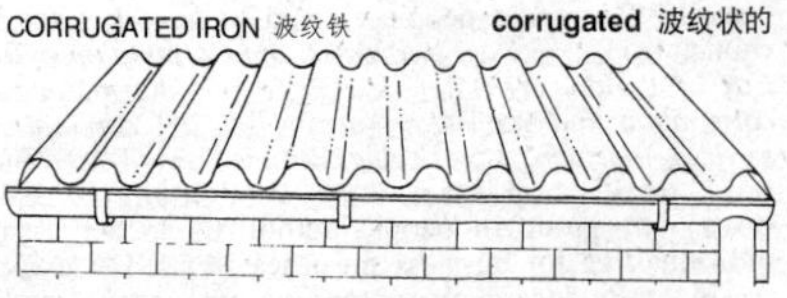

corrugated cardboard, ie used for packing fragile goods 瓦楞纸板 ○ *a corrugated roof,* ie made of corrugated iron 瓦楞铁的屋顶. ⇨illus 见插图.

cor·ruga·tion /ˌkɒrə'geɪʃn; US ˌkɔ:r-; ˌkɔrə'geʃən/ *n* fold; wrinkle 皱褶; 皱纹.

□ ˌ**corrugated 'iron** sheet iron pressed into curving folds, used for roofs, fences, etc 波纹铁; 瓦楞铁.

cor·rupt¹ /kə'rʌpt; kə'rʌpt/ *adj* **1** (**a**) immoral, esp sexually 不道德的; 堕落的; (尤指)有伤风化的: *corrupt morals, behaviour, etc* 腐败的风气、行为等 ○ *a thoroughly corrupt novel which young people should not be allowed to read* 应该不准年轻人阅读的极其伤风败俗的小说. (**b**) dishonest, esp through accepting bribes 不诚实的; 营私舞弊的; (尤指)贪污受贿的: *corrupt officials who won't issue permits unless you bribe them* 不行贿就不给办理许可证的贪官污吏 ○ *corrupt practices,* eg the offering and accepting of bribes 舞弊行为(如行贿受贿). **2** (of languages, texts, etc) containing errors or changes (指语言、文本等)有错误的, 有改动的: *a corrupt manuscript* 有错误的文稿. **3** (*arch* 古) impure 不纯的: *corrupt air/blood* 不洁的空气[血液]. ▷ **cor·ruptly** *adv.* **cor·rupt·ness** *n* [U].

cor·rupt² /kə'rʌpt; kə'rʌpt/ *v* [I, Tn] make (sb/sth) corrupt 使(某人或某事物)堕落, 腐化; 贿赂(某人或某事物): *young people whose morals have been corrupted* 道德败坏的年轻人 ○ *corrupt an official,* ie gain his favour by offering bribes 贿赂官员 ○ *Pornography is defined by its 'tendency to deprave or corrupt'.* 是不是色情作品, 要看它有没有'诱人堕落或伤风败俗的倾向'.

▷ **cor·rupt·ible** *adj* that can be corrupted 容易被腐蚀的; 可贿买的: *corruptible young people, government officials, etc* 易被腐蚀的年轻人、政府官员等.

cor·rupt·ib·il·ity /kəˌrʌptə'bɪlətɪ; kəˌrʌptə'bɪlətɪ/ *n* [U].

cor·rup·tion /kə'rʌpʃn; kə'rʌpʃən/ *n* [U] **1** corrupting or being corrupted 堕落; 腐化; 腐败; 败坏; 贿赂: *officials who are open to corruption,* ie can be bribed 可以买通的官员 ○ *claiming that sex and violence on TV led to the corruption of young people* 断言电视中所宣扬的色情和暴力会诱使年轻人堕落. **2** (*fml* 文) decay 腐烂: *the corruption of the body after death* 尸体的腐烂.

cors·age /kɔ:'sɑ:ʒ; kɔr'sɑʒ/ *n* small bouquet of flowers worn on the upper part of a woman's dress (女服上身佩带的)小花束.

cor·sair /'kɔ:seə(r); 'kɔrsɛr/ *n* (*history* 史) pirate or pirate ship attacking ships of European countries, esp off the coast of N Africa 海盗(船)(尤指活动于北非沿岸以欧洲国家之船只为攻击目标的).

corse·let (also **cors·let**) /'kɔ:slɪt; 'kɔrslɪt/ *n* suit of armour, esp one covering the back, chest and stomach only 护身铠甲(尤指专门用以防护背部、胸部及腹部的).

cor·set /'kɔ:sɪt; 'kɔrsɪt/ *n* close-fitting undergarment worn to shape the body, or support it in case of injury (为衬托身体曲线而穿的)紧身内衣; (为支撑受到损伤的身体而穿的)紧身胸衣.

cor·tege (also **cor·tège**) /kɔ:'teɪʒ; kɔr'tɛʒ/ *n* [CGp] (*French* 法) solemn procession, esp for a funeral 庄严肃穆的队伍(尤指送葬行列).

cor·tex /'kɔ:teks; 'kɔrtɛks/ *n* (*pl* **cortices** /'kɔ:tɪsi:z; 'kɔrtɪˌsiz/) **1** (*medical* 医) outer layer of the brain or other organ (脑或其他器官的)皮层, 皮: *the cerebral cortex* 大脑皮层 ○ *the renal cortex,* ie the outer layer of the kidney 肾皮层(肾的表层). **2** outer layer of a plant, eg the bark of a tree 植物的表层(如树皮).

▷ **cor·tical** /'kɔ:tɪkl; 'kɔrtɪkḷ/ *adj* of the cortex 皮层的; 表层的.

cor·tis·one /'kɔ:tɪzəʊn; 'kɔrtɪˌson/ *n* [U] (*propr* 专利名) hormone from the adrenal gland, often made synthetically, used medically in the treatment of arthritis and some allergies 可的松.

co·run·dum /kəˈrʌndəm; kəˋrʌndəm/ *n* [U] hard crystallized mineral used chiefly in abrasives, or in powder form for polishing 刚玉; 刚石; 金刚砂.

co·rus·cate /ˈkɒrəskeɪt; *US* ˈkɔːr-; ˋkɔrəs,ket/ *v* [I] (*fml* 文) flash; sparkle 闪耀; 闪烁: (*fig* 比喻) *coruscating wit/humour* 焕发的才智[绝妙的幽默]. ▷ **co·rus·ca·tion** /ˌkɒrəˈskeɪʃn; *US* ˌkɔːr-; ˌkɔrəsˋkeʃən/ *n* [C, U].

cor·vette /kɔːˈvet; kɔrˋvɛt/ *n* **1** small fast warship designed for escorting merchant ships (为商船护航的)轻型护卫舰. **2** (formerly) warship with sails and a single row of guns (旧时)木帆炮舰(设有单排炮位).

cos[1] /kɒs; kɑs/ *n* [C, U] (also ˌ**cos** ˈ**lettuce**) (type of) long-leaved lettuce (一种)长叶莴苣.

cos[2] (also **'cos**) /kəz; kəz/ *conj* (*infml* 口) (esp in spoken English) because 因为.

cos /kɒs; kɑs/ *abbr* 缩写 = (*mathematics* 数) cosine. Cf 参看 SIN *abbr* 缩写.

co·sec /ˈkəʊsek; ˋkosɪk/ *abbr* 缩写 = cosecant.

co·sec·ant /ˌkəʊˈsiːkənt; koˋsikənt/ *n* (*abbr* 缩写 **cosec**) (*mathematics* 数) in a right-angled triangle, the ratio of the length of the hypotenuse to that of the opposite side 余割.

co·set /ˈkəʊset; ˋkosɛt/ *n* (*mathematics* 数) set that can be added to an existing set to produce a more inclusive larger set 傍系; 陪集.

cosh /kɒʃ; kɑʃ/ *n* (*esp Brit*) length of lead pipe, rubber tubing filled with metal, etc, used for hitting people 短棍, 铅管, 内充金属的橡皮管等(用以打人).

▷ **cosh** *v* [Tn] (*esp Brit*) hit (sb) with a cosh 用短棍打(某人): *The train robbers coshed the guard.* 抢劫列车的匪徒用短棍袭击列车长.

co-signatory /ˌkəʊˈsɪgnətərɪ; *US* -tɔːrɪ; koˋsɪgnə,torɪ/ *n* **~ (of/to sth)** person, state, etc signing jointly with others 连署者(人、国家等): *The US and the former Soviet Union were co-signatories of/to the treaty.* 美国和前苏联都是条约的签署国.

co·sine /ˈkəʊsaɪn; ˋkosaɪn/ *n* (*abbr* 缩写 **cos**) (*mathematics* 数) in a right-angled triangle, the ratio of the length of a side adjacent to one of the acute angles to the length of the hypotenuse 余弦. Cf 参看 SINE, TANGENT 2.

cos·metic /kɒzˈmetɪk; kɑzˋmɛtɪk/ *n* (usu *pl* 通常作复数) substance for putting on the body, esp the face, to make it beautiful 化妆品(尤指用于面部的): *Lipstick and hair conditioner are cosmetics.* 口红和护发素都是化妆品.

▷ **cos·metic** *adj* **1** used as a cosmetic 化妆用的; 美容的: *cosmetic preparations* 梳妆打扮. **2** (*usu derog* 通常作贬义) intended to improve only the appearance of sth 装点门面的: *The reforms he claims to have made are in fact merely cosmetic.* 他自称已经实行的改革实际上只不过是摆摆样子罢了. **cos·met·ic·ally** /-klɪ; -klɪ/ *adv*.

cos·met·ician /ˌkɒzməˈtɪʃn; ˌkɑzməˋtɪʃən/ *n* person who sells cosmetics or advises on their use 化妆品经销商; 美容师.

□ **cos**ˌ**metic** ˈ**surgery** surgery performed to restore or improve one's outward appearance (rather than restore health) 整容外科.

cos·mic /ˈkɒzmɪk; ˋkɑzmɪk/ *adj* [usu attrib 通常作定语] of the whole universe or cosmos 宇宙的: *Physics is governed by cosmic laws.* 物理学受宇宙法则的制约. ○ (*fig* 比喻) *a disaster of cosmic proportions*, ie very great 天大的灾难.

□ ˌ**cosmic** ˈ**dust** fine particles of matter that gather into clouds in outer space 宇宙尘.

ˌ**cosmic** ˈ**rays** radiation that reaches the earth from outer space 宇宙射线.

cos·mog·ony /kɒzˈmɒgənɪ; kɑzˋmɑgənɪ/ (also **cosmology**) *n* theory of the origin and development of the universe 天体演化学.

cos·mo·logy /kɒzˈmɒlədʒɪ; kɑzˋmɑlədʒɪ/ *n* **1** [U] scientific study of the universe and its origin and development 宇宙学. **2** [C] = COSMOGONY. ▷ **cos·mo·lo·gist** /-ˈmɒlədʒɪst; -ˋmɑlədʒɪst/ *n*.

cos·mo·naut /ˈkɒzmənɔːt; ˋkɑzmə,nɔt/ *n* Russian astronaut (俄罗斯的)宇航员, 太空人.

cos·mo·pol·itan /ˌkɒzməˈpɒlɪtən; ˌkɑzməˋpɑlətn/ *adj* **1** (**a**) containing people from all over the world 世界性的; 有各国人的: *a cosmopolitan city, club etc* 国际的都市、俱乐部等 ○ *the cosmopolitan gatherings at the United Nations Assembly* 联合国大会的各种世界性集会. (**b**) (*botany or zoology* 植或动) occurring in most parts of the world 遍布世界各地的: *a cosmopolitan plant* 遍生于世界各地的植物. **2** (*approv* 褒) (free from national prejudice because of) having wide experience of the world 无民族偏见的; 四海一家的: *a cosmopolitan person, outlook etc* 四海为家的人、观念等.

▷ **cos·mo·pol·itan** *n* cosmopolitan(2) person 四海为家者; 世界主义者.

cos·mos /ˈkɒzmɒs; ˋkɑzməs/ **the cosmos** *n* [sing] the universe, ie all space, seen as a well-ordered system 宇宙.

cos·set /ˈkɒsɪt; ˋkɑsɪt/ *v* [Tn] (*derog* 贬) protect (sb/sth) too carefully; pamper 宠爱, 溺爱, 纵容(某人[某事物]): *industry cosseted by tariffs on foreign imports* 由于向外国货征收进口税而得天独厚的产业.

cost[1] /kɒst; *US* kɔːst; kɔst/ *v* (*pt, pp* **cost**) (with the *n* phrase indicating price, etc often preceded by an indirect object 在表示代价等的名词词组前常加间接宾语) **1** [In/pr] (not usu in the continuous tenses 通常不用于进行时态) be obtainable at the price of; require the payment of 价钱为; 需花费: *These chairs cost £40 each.* 这些椅子每把价钱为40英镑. ○ *How much/What does it cost?* 这东西值多少钱? ○ *It costs too much.* 这东西价钱太贵. ○ *The meal cost us £30.* 这顿饭花了我们30英镑. ○ *It costs (them) £1 000 a year to run a car.* 使用一辆汽车每年(他们)要花1 000英镑. **2** [In/pr] (*fig* 比喻) (not usu in the continuous tenses 通常不用于进行时态) (**a**) result in the loss of (sth) 使付出(代价); 使丧失(某事物): *Dangerous driving could cost you your life.* 开车不注意安全有生命危险. ○ *The scandal cost her her career*, ie resulted in her having to resign, being dismissed, etc. 这件丑事毁了她的前程. (**b**) require a certain effort or sacrifice 需做出某种努力或牺牲: *Her irresponsible behaviour cost her father many sleepless nights.* 她那不负责任的行为使她父亲许多夜不得安眠. ○ *Compiling a dictionary costs much time and patience.* 编纂词典要用很多的时间, 要有极大的耐心. **3** [Tn] (*pt, pp* **~ed**) (*commerce* 商) estimate the price to be charged for (an article or a service), based on the expense of producing or performing it 估价; 定价; 估计成本; 按成本作价: *Has this project been costed?* 这项工程估价了吗? **4** [Tn] (*infml* 口) be expensive for (sb) 对(某人)来说代价高昂: *You can have the de luxe model if you like, but it'll cost you.* 你愿意的话, 可以买高级的, 不过得花很多钱. **5** (idm 习语) **charge/cost/pay sb the earth** ⇨ EARTH. **cost sb** ˈ**dear** cause sb to suffer loss or injury 使某人付出沉重的代价: *That mistake cost him dear: he lost the game because of it.* 那个差错使他付出了沉重的代价: 他因而输了这一局. **6** (phr v) **cost sth out** estimate the cost of sth 估算某事物的成本或价钱: *I thought I could afford it, then I costed it out properly and found it was too expensive.* 我以为能负担得起那费用, 后来认真估算了一下才知道过于昂贵.

▷ **cost·ing** *n* [C, U] (*commerce* 商) estimation or fixing of prices or costs 估价; 定价; 成本计算; 作价: *When we had done the costings on the project, it was clear it would not be economical to go ahead with it.* 我们计算了成本, 清楚表明这项工程不合算. ○ [attrib 作定语] *the costing department, clerk etc* 成本会计部门、会计等.

cost[2] /kɒst; *US* kɔːst; kɔst/ *n* **1** [U, C] price (to be) paid for a thing 价钱; 价格; 费用: *the high cost of car repairs* 昂贵的汽车修理费 ○ *the costs involved in starting a business* 开创一企业所需要的资金 ○ *She built the house without regard to cost*, ie not caring if it would be expensive. 她盖这所房子根本不在乎花多少钱. ○ *the cost of living/living costs*, ie the general level of prices 生活费用 ○ *the cost-of-living index* 生活费用指数. ⇨ Usage at PRICE 用法见 PRICE. **2** [U, sing] that which is used, needed or given to obtain sth; effort, loss or sacrifice (为得到某事物而付的)代价; 努力; 损失; 牺牲: *the cost in time and labour* 时间和精力方面的消耗 ○ *The battle was won at (a) great cost in human lives.* 牺牲了许多人的生命才换来了这次战役的胜利. **3 costs** [pl] (*law* 律) expense of having sth settled in a law-court 诉讼费用: *pay a £50 fine and £25 costs* 缴纳50英镑罚金和25英镑诉讼费. **4** (idm 习语) **at** ˈ**all costs** as the

C

supremely important consideration 不惜任何代价: *We must at all costs prevent them from finding out about the plan.* 我们无论如何不能让他们探知这个计划. **at 'cost** at cost price 按成本价格: *goods sold at cost* 按成本价格出售的货物. **at the cost of sth** involving the loss or sacrifice of sth 以牺牲某事物为代价: *She saved him from drowning, but only at the cost of her own life.* 他遇溺时她把他救了, 但却牺牲了自己的生命. **count the cost** ⇨ COUNT[1]. **to one's 'cost** to one's loss or disadvantage 付了代价; 吃了苦头: *Wasp stings are serious, as I know to my cost*, ie as I know because I have suffered from them. 让黄蜂蜇了可不好受, 我吃过这苦头.

C

□ **'cost accountant, cost clerk** person who keeps a record of the expenses in a business, etc 成本会计.

ˌcost 'benefit (*economics* 经) the relation of the cost of sth to the benefit it gives 成本效益: [attrib 作定语] *cost-benefit analysis* 成本效益分析.

ˌcost-ef'fective *adj* giving enough profit, benefit, etc compared to money spent 成本效益好的; 合算的: *It isn't cost-effective to build cars in such small quantities.* 这么小批量地制造汽车不划算. **ˌcost-ef'fectiveness** *n* [U].

'cost price (*commerce* 商) cost of producing sth or the price at which it may be bought wholesale 成本价格. Cf 参看 SELLING PRICE (SELL).

co-star /'kəʊ stɑ:(r); 'koˋstɑr/ *v* **(-rr-)** (*cinema or TV* 影或视) **1** [Tn no passive 不用于被动语态] (of a film, etc) have (a star(4)) with status equal to that of another or others (指电影等)由(某明星)与其他明星联合主演: *The film co-starred Robert Redford (and Paul Newman).* 这部影片由罗伯特·雷德福(和保罗·纽曼)联合主演. **2** [I, Ipr] **~ (with sb)** appear as a star with sb (与某人)联合主演, 合演: *Laurence Olivier is in the film, and Maggie Smith co-stars (with him).* 劳伦斯·奥利维尔演这部影片, 玛吉·史密斯(与他)联合演出.

▷ **co-star** /'kəʊstɑ:(r); 'kostɑr/ *n* person who co-stars 联合主演者; 合演的明星: *His co-star in the film was Maggie Smith.* 他在这部影片中的搭档是玛吉·史密斯.

cost·er·mon·ger /'kɒstəmʌŋgə(r); 'kɑstɚˌmʌŋgɚ/ *n* (*dated* 旧 *Brit*) person who sells fruit, vegetables, etc from a barrow in the street (推小车沿街叫卖水果、蔬菜等的)小贩.

costly /'kɒstlı; *US* 'kɔ:st-; 'kɔstlı/ *adj* **(-ier, -iest)** costing much; expensive 费钱的; 昂贵的: *It would be too costly to repair the car.* 修理这辆汽车要花很多钱. ○ *a costly mistake*, ie one involving great loss 造成重大损失的错误. ▷ **cost·li·ness** *n* [U].

cos·tume /'kɒstju:m; *US* -tu:m; 'kɑstum/ *n* **1** [C, U] garment or style of dress, esp of a particular period or group or for a particular activity 服装, 服装式样(尤指用于某时期、某团体或某活动的): *People wore historical costumes for the parade.* 人们穿着古装参加游行. ○ *The actor came on in full costume*, ie wearing all his stage clothes. 那个男演员身穿全套戏装登场. ○ *Scotsmen in Highland costume*, ie wearing kilts, etc 身穿高地服装的苏格兰男子 ○ *skiing costume* 滑雪服 ○ [attrib 作定语] *a 'costume piece/play/drama*, ie one in which the actors wear historical costume 古装剧. **2** [C] (*dated* 旧) woman's suit (ie a skirt and short coat of the same material) 女套装(面料相同的裙子和西服短上衣).

▷ **cos·tu·mier** /kɒ'stju:mıə(r); *US* -'stu:-; kɑs'tumıɚ/ *n* person who makes, deals in, or hires out costumes, esp for theatrical performances 服装制作人经销商或出租商(尤指戏装): *a theatrical costumier* 舞台服装制作人.

□ **'costume jewellery** jewellery made with artificial gems 人造珠宝饰物.

cosy (*US* **cozy**) /'kəʊzı; 'kozı/ *adj* **(-ier, -iest)** (*approv* 褒) **1** (warm and) comfortable (暖和而)舒适的: *a cosy room, chair, feeling* 舒适的房间、椅子、感觉 ○ *a nice cosy little house* 美妙舒适的房子 ○ *I felt all cosy tucked up in bed.* 我钻进被窝里, 暖暖和和舒服极了. ○ (*fig derog* 比喻, 贬) *He's had it too cosy in that job; we ought to keep a stricter check on him.* 他那工作太轻松了, 我们应当经常对他进行严格的检查. **2** intimate and friendly 亲切友好的: *a cosy chat by the fireside* 在炉边的亲切闲谈.

▷ **co·sily** *adv*: *sitting cosily in my armchair* 舒舒服服地坐在单座沙发上.

co·si·ness *n* [U]. **cosy** *n* cover to keep a teapot or boiled egg hot (茶壶、煮熟的蛋的)保温罩.

cot /kɒt; kɑt/ *n* **1** (*Brit*) (*US* **crib**) bed for a young child, usu with sides to prevent the child falling out 幼儿床(通常设有栏杆). ⇨illus at App 1 见附录1之插图, page xvi. **2** (*US*) simple narrow bed, eg a camp-bed, or a bunk bed on a ship 简易床(如行军床或船上的铺位).

□ **'cot-death** *n* [C, U] sudden unexplained death of a sleeping baby 婴儿猝死.

co·tan·gent /kəʊ'tændʒənt; ko'tændʒənt/ *n* (*abbr* 缩写 **cot**) (*mathematics* 数) tangent of the complement of a given angle 余切.

cote /kəʊt; kot/ *n* (in compounds 用以构成复合词) shed, shelter or enclosure for domestic animals or birds (家畜或家禽的)棚, 圈, 栏: *a 'dove-cote* ○ *a 'sheep-cote.*

co-tenant /ˌkəʊ 'tenənt; ko'tɛnənt/ *n* joint tenant 共同承租人; 合租人; 共同佃户.

co·terie /'kəʊtərı; 'kotərı/ *n* [CGp] (*often derog* 常作贬义) small group of people with shared activities, interests, tastes, etc, esp one that tends to be exclusive (由有共同的活动、兴趣、爱好等人组成的)小圈子, (尤指排外的)小集团: *a literary coterie* 一帮文人.

co·term·in·ous /ˌkəʊ'tɜ:mınəs; ko'tɝmənəs/ *adj* [usu pred 通常作表语] **~ (with sth)** (*fml* 文) having a shared boundary 有共同边界; 毗邻.

cot·tage /'kɒtıdʒ; 'kɑtıdʒ/ *n* small simple house, esp in the country 简陋的小屋; (尤指)村舍: *farm labourers' cottages* 农场雇工的小屋.

▷ **cot·tager** /'kɒtıdʒə(r); 'kɑtıdʒɚ/ *n* person who lives in a cottage 住农舍者; 村民.

□ **ˌcottage 'cheese** type of soft white cheese made from skimmed milk 农家乳酪(一种脱脂的白色软干酪).

ˌcottage 'hospital (*Brit*) small hospital in the country 乡间诊疗所.

ˌcottage 'industry business that can be carried on at home, esp skilled manual work such as knitting, pottery, some kinds of weaving, etc 家庭手工业(如针织、制陶、某些编织等).

ˌcottage 'loaf (*Brit*) loaf consisting of a large round mass of bread with a smaller one on top 农家面包(大小两个圆面包相叠的).

ˌcottage 'pie = SHEPHERD'S PIE (SHEPHERD).

cotter-pin /'kɒtə pın; 'kɑtɚˌpın/ *n* (*engineering* 工) pin used to hold parts of machinery in place 开尾销; 扁销.

cot·ton[1] /'kɒtn; 'kɑtn̩/ *n* [U] **1** **(a)** soft white fibrous substance round the seeds of a tropical plant, used for making thread, cloth, etc 棉花: *bales of cotton* 大包小包的棉花. **(b)** this plant when growing 棉树; 棉株: [attrib 作定语] *working in the cotton fields* 在棉田里干活. **2** **(a)** thread spun from cotton yarn 棉线: *a needle and cotton* 针和线. **(b)** cloth made from this 棉布: [attrib 作定语] *a cotton dress* 棉布连衣裙.

□ **ˌcotton 'candy** (*US*) = CANDY-FLOSS (CANDY).

ˌcotton seed 'oil oil obtained from cotton seed 棉籽油.

'cottontail *n* type of small N American rabbit 棉尾兔(产于北美洲的小兔).

ˌcotton 'wool soft fluffy absorbent material, originally made from raw cotton, used for bandaging, cleaning, padding, etc 脱脂棉: (*fig* 比喻) *You shouldn't wrap your children in cotton wool*, ie protect them too much from the world. 你不该对孩子娇生惯养.

cot·ton[2] /kɒtn; kɑtn̩/ *v* (phr v) **cotton on (to sth)** (*Brit infml* 口) come to understand or realize sth 明白; 认识到: *At last she's cottoned on to what they mean.* 最后她终于明白了他们的意思. **cotton to sb** (*US infml* 口) take a liking to sb 对某人产生好感.

coty·le·don /ˌkɒtı'li:dn; ˌkɑtl̩'idn̩/ *n* (*botany* 植) first leaf growing from a seed 子叶.

couch[1] /kaʊtʃ; kaʊtʃ/ *n* long bedlike seat for sitting or lying on; sofa (坐卧两用的)长沙发: *on the psychiatrist's couch* 在精神病医生的诊察台上.

couch[2] /kaʊtʃ; kaʊtʃ/ *v* **1** [Tn·pr usu passive 通常用于被动语态] **~ sth (in sth)** (*fml* 文) express (a thought, an idea, etc) (in words) (用词语)表达(思想、概念等): *His letter was couched in conciliatory terms.* 他那封信里使用了表示和解的言辞. ○ *a carefully couched reply* 措辞

谨慎的答复. **2** [I] (*arch* 古) (of animals) lie flat, either in hiding or ready to jump forward (指动物)蹲伏, 趴下(或为躲藏或准备跃起).

couch·ant /ˈkaʊtʃənt; ˋkaʊtʃənt/ *adj* (usu directly after a *n* 通常直接用于名词之后) (*heraldry* 纹) (of an animal on a coat of arms) lying with the body resting on the legs and the head raised (指纹章上的动物)昂首蹲伏的: *a lion couchant* 昂首蹲伏的狮子像. Cf 参看 RAMPANT 3.

couch·ette /kuːˈʃet; kuˋʃɛt/ *n* (*French* 法) bed in a railway carriage which can be folded down to make the back of a seat during the day (列车的)坐卧两用铺位(可折叠成靠背椅).

couch-grass /ˈkaʊtʃ grɑːs, ˈkuːtʃ-; *US* -ˈgræs; ˋkaʊtʃ græs/ (also **couch**) *n* [U] type of grass with long creeping roots 匍匐冰草; 茅草.

cou·gar /ˈkuːgə(r); ˋkugɚ/ *n* (*esp US*) = PUMA.

cough /kɒf; *US* kɔːf; kɔf/ *v* **1** [I] send out air from the lungs violently and noisily, esp to clear one's throat or when one has a cold, etc 咳嗽: *She was coughing (away) all night.* 她咳了一整夜. ○ (*fig* 比喻) *The engine coughed and spluttered into life*, ie started noisily. 这发动机起动时喀喀作响. **2** [Tn, Tn·p] **~ sth (up)** get sth out of the throat or lungs by coughing 咳出某物: *He'd been coughing up blood.* 他那时一直在咳血. **3** (phr v) **cough (sth) up** (*Brit infml* 口) say or produce sth reluctantly 勉强说出某话; 不情愿地提供某物: *He owes us money, but he won't cough (it) up.* 他欠我们钱, 却不愿还帐. ○ *Come on, cough up: who did it?* 好了, 说出来, 是谁干的?

▷ **cough** *n* **1** [C] act or sound of coughing 咳嗽; 咳嗽声: *She gave a quiet cough to attract my attention.* 她轻轻地咳了一声好引起我注意. **2** [sing] illness, infection, etc that causes a person to cough often 咳嗽: *have a bad cough* 咳嗽得很厉害 ○ [attrib 作定语] ˈ*cough medicine, mixture, etc*, ie taken to relieve a cough 止咳的药、合剂等.

could[1] /kəd; kəd; *strong form* 强读式 kʊd; kud/ *modal v* (*neg* 否定式 **could not**, *contracted form* 缩约式 **couldn't** /ˈkʊdnt; ˋkudn̩t/) **1** (indicating permission 表示允准): *Could I use your phone?* 让我用一下你的电话好吗? ○ *Could I borrow your bicycle?* 我可以借一下你的自行车吗? ○ *Could I come round next week?* 我下星期来拜访好吗? ⇨Usage 1 at MAY[1] 见MAY[1]所附用法第1项. **2** (indicating requests 表示请求): *Could you baby-sit for us on Friday?* 星期五你替我们照看小孩行吗? ○ *Could you type one more letter before you go?* 你临走以前再打一封信行吗? ○ *Do you think I could have a cigarette?* 我可以吸支香烟吗? **3** (indicating result 表示结果): *I'm so unhappy I could weep.* 我难过得要哭. ○ *What's for dinner? I could eat a horse.* 吃什么饭? 我饿得要命. **4** (indicating possibility 表示可能性): *You could be right, I suppose.* 我想可能是你对. ○ *My wife's in hospital — our baby could arrive at any time.* 我妻子住进了医院——我们的小宝宝随时都可能出生. ○ *Don't worry — they could have just forgotten to phone.* 别担心——他们很可能只是忘了打电话. ○ *Somebody must have opened the cage — the lion couldn't have escaped on its own.* 一定是有人打开了笼子——因为狮子是不可能自己跑出来的. ○ *You could at least have sent a card*, ie It was possible but you didn't do it. 你本来至少可以寄张明信片来吧. ⇨Usage 2 at MAY[1] 见MAY[1]所附用法第2项. **5** (indicating suggestions 表示建议): *We could write a letter to the headmaster.* 我们不妨给校长写封信. ○ *You could always try his home number.* 实在不行的话, 你还可以试一试他家的电话号码. ⇨Usage 3 at SHALL 见SHALL所附用法第3项.

could[2] *pt* of CAN[2].

coul·ter (*US* **col·ter**) /ˈkəʊltə(r); ˋkoltɚ/ *n* metal blade fixed vertically in front of a ploughshare, to cut the soil before it is lifted and turned by the share 犁刀.

coun·cil /ˈkaʊnsl; ˋkaʊnsl̩/ *n* [CGp] **1** group of people elected to manage affairs in a city, county, etc 会议; 政务会; 议会: *a city/county council* 市[郡]议会 ○ *The local council is/are in charge of repairing roads.* 地方议会负责维修道路. ○ [attrib 作定语] *council services, elections* 议会的部门、选举. **2** group of people appointed or elected to give advice, make rules, manage affairs, etc (顾问、立法、管理等)委员会: *A council of elders governs the tribe.* 有个叫长老会的组织治理这个部落. ○ *In Britain, the Design Council gives awards for good industrial design.* 在英国, 设计委员会给优秀的工业产品设计颁奖. ○ *a council of war*, ie a meeting of leaders, military commanders, etc to discuss tactics 军事会议.

□ ˈ**council-chamber** *n* large room in which a council meets 会议室.

ˈ**council estate** (*Brit*) housing estate (HOUSING 1) built by a city, county, etc 市、郡等的统建住房.

ˈ**council flat**, ˈ**council house** (*Brit*) flat/house built or provided by a city, county, etc 市、郡等统建或提供的公寓[房屋].

coun·cil·lor (*US* also **coun·cilor**) /ˈkaʊnsələ(r); ˋkaunslɚ/ *n* member of a council (市、郡等的)政务会委员; 议员: *Councillor Jones* 琼斯议员.

coun·sel[1] /ˈkaʊnsl; ˋkaunsl̩/ *n* **1** [U] (*fml* 文) advice; suggestions 劝告; 建议: *Listen to the counsel of your elders.* 听从长辈的劝告吧. ○ *wise counsel* 高明的建议. **2** [C] (*pl* unchanged 复数不变) barrister conducting a law case 讼务律师: *counsel for the defence/prosecution* 被告[原告]的律师 ○ *The court heard counsel for both sides.* 法庭听取了双方律师的陈述. Cf 参看 KING'S COUNSEL (KING). **3** (idm 习语) **a counsel of perˈfection** advice that is very good but is difficult or impossible to follow 难以照办的好建议. **hold/take counsel with sb** (*fml* 文) consult sb 与某人商量. **keep one's own ˈcounsel** keep one's opinions, plans, etc secret 将自己的意见、计划等保密. **take ˈcounsel together** (*fml* 文) consult each other 共同商量.

coun·sel[2] /ˈkaʊnsl; ˋkaunsl̩/ *v* (**-ll-**; *US also* **-l-**) **1** [Tn] give professional advice to (sb with a problem) 向(某人)提供专业建议: *a psychiatrist who counsels alcoholics* 对酗酒者提出辅导的精神病科医生. **2** [Tn] give (the stated advice) 提出(劝告): *I would counsel caution in such a case.* 我奉劝在此情况下务必小心. **3** [Dn·t] (*fml* 文) advise 劝告; 建议: *He counselled them to give up the plan.* 他建议他们放弃这项计划.

▷ **coun·sel·ling** /-səlɪŋ; -slɪŋ/ *n* [U] advice, esp from a professional person (尤指行家的)意见: *psychiatric/financial counselling* 精神辅导[财务咨询] ○ [attrib 作定语] *a student counselling service* 辅导学生的工作.

coun·sel·lor (*US* also **coun·selor**) /ˈkaʊnsələ(r); ˋkaunslɚ/ *n* **1** adviser 顾问: *a wise counsellor in time of need* 困难时的好参谋 ○ *a marriage guidance counsellor* 婚姻问题顾问. **2** (*US or Irish* 用于美国或爱尔兰) lawyer 律师.

count[1] /kaʊnt; kaunt/ *v* **1** [I, Ipr] **~ (from sth) (to sth)** say or name numbers in order 数; 计数: *He can't count yet.* 他还不会数数. ○ *count from 1 to 20* 从1数到20 ○ *I can count (up) to 100.* 我能数到100. **2** [Tn, Tn·p] **~ sth (up)** calculate the total of sth 算某物的总数: *Don't forget to count your change.* 别忘了数一数你的零钱. ○ *Have the votes been counted up yet?* 选票算好了没有? **3** [Tn] include (sb/sth) in a calculation 把(某人[某物])计算在内: *fifty people, not counting the children* 五十人, 儿童除外. **4** (**a**) [I, Ipr] **~ (for sth)** be of value or importance 有价值; 有重要性: *Her opinion counts because of her experience.* 因为她有经验, 所以她的意见很重要. ○ *Knowledge without common sense counts for little.* 光有学问而无常识, 则这种学问无甚价值. ○ *We've only a few bullets left, so make each one count*, ie use it effectively. 我们只剩几颗子弹了, 因此要弹不虚发. (**b**) [I, Ipr] **~ (as sth)** be accepted or valid 认可; 有效: *You didn't shut your eyes before you made the wish, so it doesn't count!* 你祈求实现愿望时没闭上眼睛, 所以不算数! ○ *A few lines of rhyming doggerel don't count as poetry.* 几行押韵的蹩脚诗算不上是诗. **5** [Cn·a, Cn·n, Cn·n/a] **~ sb/sth (as) sb/sth** consider sb/sth to be sb/sth 认为(某事物或某人)…: *I count myself lucky to have a job.* 我有工作实在很幸运. ○ *I count him a good judge of character.* 我认为他很会判断别人品性的好坏. ○ *We count her as one of our oldest friends.* 我们把她看作交情最久的一个朋友. **6** (idm 习语) **count one's ˈblessings** be grateful for what one has 知足: *Don't complain! Count your blessings!* 别怨天尤人了! 你应该知足! **count one's ˈchickens (before they are ˈhatched)** be too confident that sth will be successful 小鸡还没孵出, 先计算鸡数; 打如意算盘. **count the**

C

cost (of sth) suffer the consequences of a careless or foolish action 因粗心或做了蠢事而吃苦头; 自作自受: *The town is now counting the cost of its failure to provide adequate flood protection.* 该镇未采取适当的防洪措施, 现在吃到了苦头. **7** (phr v) **count against sb; count sth against sb** be considered/consider sth to be to the disadvantage of sb 认为(某事物)对某人不利: *Your criminal record could count against you in finding a job.* 你有前科对你找工作很不利. ○ *He is young and inexperienced, but please do not count that against him.* 他年轻又无经验, 但请不要因此而小看他. **count among sb/sth; count sb/sth among sb/sth** be regarded/ regard sb/sth as one of the stated group 视某人[某事物]为某集体的一员: *She counts among the most gifted of the current generation of composers.* 她算是当代最有才华的一位作曲家. ○ *I no longer count him among my friends.* 我不再把他当作朋友. **count down** signal the approach of a moment (eg for launching a space vehicle) by counting seconds backwards, eg 10, 9, 8, 7... 倒数计秒(如10、9、8、7...). **count sb/sth in** include sb/sth 把某人[某事物]算在内: *See how many plates we have, but don't count in the cracked ones.* 看看我们有多少个盘子, 但不要算有裂纹的. ○ *If you're all going to the party, you can count me in,* ie I will come with you. 要是你们全都去参加聚会, 就可以把我也算上. **count on sb/sth** rely on sb/sth with confidence 依靠、依赖、信赖或指望某人[某事物]: *count on sb's help/on sb to help* 依靠某人的帮助 ○ *Don't count on a salary increase this year,* ie You may not get one. 别指望今年会加薪. **count sb/sth out** (**a**) count (things) one by one, esp slowly (慢慢地)逐个数东西: *The old lady counted out thirty pence and gave it to the shop assistant.* 老太婆一个个地数出三十便士给了售货员. (**b**) count up to ten over (a boxer who has been knocked down), signifying his defeat 对被击倒的拳击者数到十后判其失败: *The referee counted him out in the first round.* 裁判判定他在第一回合被击败. (**c**) (*infml* 口) not include sb/sth 不包括某人[某事物]: *If it's going to be a rowdy party, you can count me out,* ie I shall certainly not attend. 要是弄成了吵吵闹闹的聚会, 我可不参加. **count towards sth** be included as a qualification for sth (按照获得某事物的条件)被包括在内: *These payments will count towards your pension.* 你付的这些款项将来算在你的养老金里. **count up to sth** reach the specified total; add up to sth 达到某总数; 共计: *These small contributions soon count up to a sizeable amount.* 这些捐款很快就集少成多, 总数相当可观.

▷ **count·able** *adj* that can be counted 可数的. **'countable noun** = COUNT NOUN (COUNT[2]).

□ **'counting-house** *n* (*dated* 旧) building or room where accounts are kept, eg in a bank 会计室; 帐房.

'countdown *n* ~ **(to sth)** (**a**) [C] counting seconds backwards to zero before firing a rocket, etc 倒数秒. (**b**) [sing] (*fig* 比喻) period immediately before sth important happens 大事临近的时期: *the countdown to the local election* 地方选举日益临近的时候.

count[2] /kaʊnt; kaunt/ *n* **1** [C] action of counting; number reached by counting 计数; 数出的数: *a second count of the votes in an election* 选举中的第二次点票 ○ *I want you to start on a count of 5,* ie after I have counted up to 5. 我要你在我数到5时开始. ○ *By my count* (ie As I have counted them) *that's five cakes you've had already.* 我数着你已经吃了五块蛋糕. **2** [C usu *sing* 通常作单数] total number of things found in a sample tested 样品中被检验物的含量: *a high pollen count* 花粉含量高. **3** (usu 通常作 **the count**) [sing] (in boxing) act of counting sb out (COUNT[1] 7) (拳击比赛中对被击倒的某人)数十(而判其失败): (*fig* 比喻) *Little Jimmy was really out for the count* (ie completely exhausted) *after that long tiring day.* 小吉米劳累了一天已经筋疲力尽了. **4** [C] (**a**) (*law* 律) any of a group of offences of which a person is accused (被控的)事项, 罪状: *two counts of forgery and one of fraud* 两项伪造罪和一项诈骗罪 ○ *She was found guilty on all counts.* 她被判各项罪名成立. (**b**) any of a set of points made in a discussion or an argument (讨论或争论的)事项, 问题: *I disagree with you on both counts.* 我对你的两个论点均未敢苟同. **5** (idm 习语) **keep/lose 'count (of sth)** know/not know how many there are of sth 知[不知]其数: *So many arrived at once that I lost count (of them).* 同时来了这么多, 我数不清了.

□ **'count noun** (also **'countable noun**) (*grammar*) noun that can be used in the plural and with such words as *many* and *few* 可数名词: *Count nouns are marked* [C] *in this dictionary.* 在本词典中, 可数名词均以[C]为标记.

count[3] /kaʊnt; kaunt/ *n* title of a nobleman in France, Italy, etc, equal in rank to a British earl (法、意等国家的)伯爵(相当于英国的earl). Cf 参看 COUNTESS.

coun·ten·ance[1] /ˈkaʊntənəns; ˋkauntənəns/ *n* (*fml* 文) **1** [C] (expression on sb's) face 面孔; 面容; 面部表情: *a woman with a fierce countenance/of fierce countenance* 面目凶恶的女子. **2** [U] support; approval 支持; 赞成; 批准: *I would not give/lend countenance to such a plan.* 我不赞同这样的计划. **3** (idm 习语) **keep one's 'countenance** (*fml* 文) maintain one's composure, esp by not laughing 保持沉稳(尤指忍住不笑). **put/stare sb out of 'countenance** (*dated* 旧) make sb feel embarrassed or at fault by staring at him 盯得某人发慌或不知所措.

coun·ten·ance[2] /ˈkaʊntənəns; ˋkauntənəns/ *v* [Tn, Tg, Tsg] (*fml* 文) support or approve (sth) 支持, 赞成, 批准(某事物): *countenance a fraud* 怂恿诈骗 ○ *How could you countenance such behaviour?* 你怎么能纵容这种行为? ○ *They would never countenance lying.* 他们对说谎的行为决不姑息.

coun·ter[1] /ˈkaʊntə(r); ˋkauntɚ/ *n* **1** long narrow flat surface over which goods are sold or served or business done in a shop, bank, etc (商店、银行等的)柜台. **2** (idm 习语) **over the 'counter** (of medicines) without a prescription(1a) (指药品)无处方: *These tablets are available over the counter.* 这些药片无需处方可直接购买. **under the 'counter** (of goods bought or sold in shops) secretly (指商店买卖货物)暗中交易, 走后门: *In Britain pornography was once sold under the counter.* 在英国, 色情书画曾一度在暗地里出售.

coun·ter[2] /ˈkaʊntə(r); ˋkauntɚ/ *n* **1** small disc used for playing or scoring in certain board games 筹码. **2** (used in compounds 用以构成复合词) device for counting repeated mechanical actions 计数器: *an engine's rev-counter* 发动机转速计. **3** thing that can be exchanged for sth else 可与他物交换之物: *Our missiles will be a useful bargaining counter in our negotiations with the Russians,* ie may be given up in exchange for concessions. 在我们与俄国人的谈判中, 我们的导弹是讨价还价的有利资本.

coun·ter[3] /ˈkaʊntə(r); ˋkauntɚ/ *adv* ~ **to sth** in the opposite direction to sth; in opposition to sth; contrary to sth 与某事物的方向相反; 相反地: *act counter to sb's wishes* 违背某人的意愿 ○ *Economic trends are running counter to the forecasts.* 经济发展趋势与预测的结果截然相反.

coun·ter[4] /ˈkaʊntə(r); ˋkauntɚ/ *v* [Ipr, Tn, Tn·pr, Tf] ~ **with sth; ~ sb/sth (with sth)** respond to (sb/sth) with an opposing view, a return attack, etc 反对, 反击(某人[某事物]): *The champion countered with his right,* ie responded to a blow with a right-handed punch. 这位卫冕者挥起右拳还击. ○ *They countered our proposal with one of their own.* 他们针对我们的建议提出了一项相反的建议. ○ *The minister countered his critics with a strong speech defending his policies.* 这位部长慷慨陈词为其政策辩护, 反驳批评他的人. ○ *I pointed out the shortcomings of the scheme, but he countered that the plans were not yet finished.* 我指出那方案的缺点, 但他申辩说各项计划尚未完成.

counter- *comb form* 构词成分 (forming *ns, vs, adjs* and *advs* 用以构成名词、动词、形容词以及副词) **1** opposite in direction or effect 方向或作用相反: *counter-attraction* ○ *counter-productive.* **2** made in response to, or so as to defeat 回击: *counter-attack* ○ *counter-espionage.* **3** corresponding 对应的; 对等的: *counterpart.* ⇨Usage at ANTI- 用法见 ANTI-.

coun·ter·act /ˌkaʊntəˈrækt; ˌkauntɚˋækt/ *v* [Tn] act against and reduce the force or effect of (sth) 对抗; 抵消: *counteract (the effects of) a poison, sb's bad influence, etc* 消解毒性(的作用)、清除某人的不良影响 ○ *We must counteract extremism in the party.* 我们应该抵制党内的极端主义.

▷ **coun·ter·ac·tion** /ˌkaʊntəˈrækʃn; ˌkaʊntɚˈækʃən/ *n* [U] counteracting 对抗; 抵消; 中和.

counter-attack /ˈkaʊntər ətæk; ˈkaʊntərəˌtæk/ *n* attack made in response to an enemy's attack 反攻; 反击.

▷ **counter-attack** *v* [I, Tn] make a counter-attack on (sb/sth) 反击(某人[某事物]).

counter-attraction /ˌkaʊntər əˈtrækʃn; ˌkaʊntərəˈtrækʃən/ *n* **~ (to sth)** rival attraction 反引力; 对抗物: *There are so many counter-attractions these days that the live theatre is losing its audiences.* 当今其他方面的吸引力太强, 所以戏剧舞台的观众越来越少.

coun·ter·bal·ance /ˈkaʊntəbæləns; ˈkaʊntɚˌbæləns/ (also **counterpoise**) *n* **~ (to sth)** weight or force that balances another 平衡重; 平衡块; 平衡锤; 平衡力.

▷ **coun·ter·bal·ance** /ˌkaʊntəˈbæləns; ˌkaʊntɚˈbæləns/ *v* [Tn] act as a counterbalance to (sb/sth) 对(某人[某事物])起平衡作用: *His level-headedness counterbalances her impetuousness.* 他头脑冷静, 这可抵消一些她的急躁情绪.

coun·ter·blast /ˈkaʊntəblɑːst; *US* -blæst; ˈkaʊntɚˌblæst/ *n* **~ (to sth)** powerful reply 有力的反驳: *Her article was a counterblast to her critics.* 她的文章有力地回击了那些批评者.

coun·ter·claim /ˈkaʊntəkleɪm; ˈkaʊntɚˌklem/ *n* claim made in opposition to another claim 反要求; 反诉: *Amongst all the claims and counterclaims it was hard to say who was telling the truth.* 所有这些要求和反要求, 很难说谁说的是实话.

counter-clockwise /ˌkaʊntə ˈklɒkwaɪz; ˌkaʊntɚˈklɑkˌwaɪz/ *adv* (*US*) = ANTI-CLOCKWISE.

counter-espionage /ˌkaʊntər ˈespɪənɑːʒ; ˌkaʊntɚˈɛspɪənɪdʒ/ *n* [U] action taken against an enemy's spying 反间谍行动.

coun·ter·feit /ˈkaʊntəfɪt; ˈkaʊntɚfɪt/ *n, adj* (thing) made or done so that it is very similar to another thing, in order to deceive; fake 伪造的; 假冒的; 伪造物; 赝品: *counterfeit money, jewels, etc* 假钱币、珠宝等 ○ *This ten-dollar bill is a counterfeit.* 这张十元钞票是伪钞. Cf 参看 FORGERY (FORGE²).

▷ **coun·ter·feit** *v* [Tn] copy or imitate (coins, handwriting, etc) in order to deceive 伪造, 仿造(钱币等); 模仿(笔迹等): *a gang of criminals counterfeiting ten-pound notes* 伪造十镑假钞票的犯罪集团. Cf 参看 FORGE² 2. **coun·ter·feiter** *n* person who counterfeits money, etc (钱币等的)伪造者, 仿制者. Cf 参看 FORGER (FORGE²).

coun·ter·foil /ˈkaʊntəfɔɪl; ˈkaʊntɚˌfɔɪl/ *n* part of a cheque, ticket, etc which can be detached and kept as a record; stub (支票、票据等的)存根.

counter-insurgency /ˌkaʊntər ɪnˈsɜːdʒənsɪ; ˌkaʊntɚ ɪnˈsɝdʒənsɪ/ *n* [U] measures taken to prevent enemy troops from entering one's territory, esp in small groups 反敌军侵入(尤指小股渗入)本国领土的措施; 反渗入对策.

counter-intelligence /ˌkaʊntər ɪnˈtelɪdʒəns; ˌkaʊntɚ ɪnˈtɛlədʒəns/ *n* [U] measures taken to stop an enemy country from finding out one's secrets, to give them false information, etc 反情报措施.

counter-intuitive /ˌkaʊntər ɪnˈtjuːɪtɪv; ˌkaʊntɚ ɪnˈtjuɪtɪv/ *adj* contrary to what one would naturally expect 与情理中的预料相反的; 反直觉的: *His solution to the problem is counter-intuitive.* 他解决这问题的方法是出人意表的.

counter-irritant /ˌkaʊntər ˈɪrɪtənt; ˌkaʊntɚˈɪrətənt/ *n* (*medical* 医) substance put on the skin to make it sore, and thus to relieve greater pain deeper in the body, eg rheumatism 抗刺激剂.

coun·ter·mand /ˌkaʊntəˈmɑːnd; *US* -ˈmænd; ˌkaʊntɚˈmænd/ *v* [Tn] cancel (a command or an order already given), esp by giving a new and opposite one 撤销, 撤回(成命或订单)(尤指代之以新的、内容相反的).

coun·ter·meas·ure /ˌkaʊntəmeʒə(r); ˈkaʊntɚˌmɛʒɚ/ *n* (often *pl* 常作复数) course of action taken to remove, prevent, or protect against sth undesirable or dangerous 对策: *countermeasures against a threatened strike* 为防止一触即发的罢工而采取的对策.

counter-offer /ˈkaʊntərɒfə(r); ˈkaʊntɚˌɑfɚ/ *n* offer made in response to, and esp to defeat, an offer made by sb else 反提议; 还价: *The first company made a very attractive counter-offer and won the order.* 第一家公司的还盘很有吸引力, 从而赢得了订单.

coun·ter·pane /ˈkaʊntəpeɪn; ˈkaʊntɚˌpen/ *n* (*dated* 旧) covering for a bed; bedspread 床罩; 床单.

coun·ter·part /ˈkaʊntəpɑːt; ˈkaʊntɚˌpɑrt/ *n* person or thing that corresponds to or has the same function as sb or sth else 相对应或具有相同功能的人或物: *The sales director phoned her counterpart in the other firm*, ie the other firm's sales director. 销售部的女经理给另一家公司的销售部经理打了电话.

coun·ter·plot /ˈkaʊntəplɒt; ˈkaʊntɚˌplɑt/ *n* plot made to defeat another plot 反计; 对抗策略.

▷ **coun·ter·plot** *v* (**-tt-**) [I, Ipr] **~ (against sb/sth)** make a counterplot 施反计; 将计就计.

coun·ter·point /ˈkaʊntəpɔɪnt; ˈkaʊntɚˌpɔɪnt/ *n* (*music* 音) **1** [C] melody added as an accompaniment to another 对位旋律: (*fig* 比喻) *The dark curtains make an interesting counterpoint to* (ie contrast with) *the lighter walls.* 深色的窗帘与浅色的墙壁形成有趣的对比. **2** [U] art or practice of combining melodies according to fixed rules 对位; 对位法.

coun·ter·poise /ˈkaʊntəpɔɪz; ˈkaʊntɚˌpɔɪz/ *n* (*fml* 文) **1** [C] = COUNTERBALANCE. **2** [U] state of being in balance; equilibrium 平衡; 均衡: *The two nations' nuclear forces are in perfect counterpoise*, ie are equal. 这两国的核力量完全均衡.

counter-productive /ˌkaʊntə prəˈdʌktɪv; ˌkaʊntɚ prəˈdʌktɪv/ *adj* having the opposite effect to that intended 产生相反效果的; 适得其反的; 事与愿违的: *It's counter-productive to be too tough: it just makes the staff resentful.* 过于严厉则适得其反, 使全体工作人员愤愤不平. ▷ **counter-productively** *adv*. **counterproductiveness** *n* [U].

counter-revolution /ˌkaʊntə ˌrevəˈluːʃn; ˌkaʊntɚˌrɛvəˈluʃən/ *n* [C, U] revolution that overthrows the political regime introduced by a previous revolution; activity intended to bring this about 反革命; 反革命活动; 反动: *stage a counter-revolution* 进行反革命活动 ○ *the forces of counter-revolution* 反动势力.

▷ **counter-revolutionary** /-ˈluːʃənərɪ; *US* -nerɪ; -ˈluʃənˌɛrɪ/ *adj* of a counter-revolution 反革命的: *counter-revolutionary movements, ideas, etc* 反革命运动、思想等. — *n* person who opposes or tries to overthrow a revolution 反革命分子; 反动分子.

coun·ter·sign¹ /ˈkaʊntəsaɪn; ˈkaʊntɚˌsaɪn/ *v* [Tn] sign (a document, etc already signed by another person 副署; 会签): *a cheque countersigned on the back* 背书支票.

coun·ter·sign² /ˈkaʊntəsaɪn; ˈkaʊntɚˌsaɪn/ *n* secret word which must be spoken to a guard, etc before one is allowed to pass; password 回令(回应警卫人员等的暗语以便通行): *give the countersign* 应答回令.

coun·ter·sink /ˈkaʊntəsɪŋk; ˈkaʊntɚˌsɪŋk/ *v* (*pt* **-sank** /-sæŋk; -ˌsæŋk/, *pp* **-sunk** /-sʌŋk; -ˌsʌŋk/) [Tn usu passive 通常用于被动语态] **1** enlarge the top of (a hole) so that the head of a screw or bolt fits into it level with or below the surrounding surface 钻埋头孔. **2** insert (a screw or bolt) into such an enlarged hole 将(螺钉或螺栓)旋入埋头孔中.

counter-tenor /ˌkaʊntəˈtenə(r); ˌkaʊntɚˈtɛnɚ/ *n* (*music* 音) (man with a) voice higher than tenor; male alto 男高音(歌手).

coun·ter·vail·ing /ˈkaʊntəveɪlɪŋ; ˈkaʊntɚˌvelɪŋ/ *adj* [attrib 作定语] (*fml* 文) compensating 补偿; 弥补; 抵销: *all the disadvantages without any of the countervailing advantages* 没有任何好处作为补偿的一切不利情况.

count·ess /ˈkaʊntɪs; ˈkaʊntɪs/ *n* **1** wife or widow of a count or earl 伯爵夫人; 伯爵遗孀. **2** woman with the rank of a count or earl 女伯爵.

count·less /ˈkaʊntlɪs; ˈkaʊntlɪs/ *adj* [esp attrib 尤作定语] numerous; too many to be counted 无数的; 多得数不清的: *I've told her countless times.* 我告诉她无数次了.

coun·tri·fied /ˈkʌntrɪfaɪd; ˈkʌntrɪˌfaɪd/ *adj* **1** having typical features of the countryside (eg open fields, trees, etc); rural 有乡村特色的(如旷野、树林等); 乡村的: *quite a countrified area* 乡野气息十足的地区. **2** (*derog* 贬) having the unsophisticated ways, views, etc of country people; rustic 具有乡下人土里土气方式、见解等的; 粗俗的.

coun·try /ˈkʌntrɪ; ˈkʌntrɪ/ *n* **1 (a)** [C] area of land that forms a politically independent unit; nation; state 国; 国家: *European countries* 欧洲各国 ○ *There will be rain in all parts of the country.* 全国各地将有雨. (**b**) **the country** [sing] the people of a country(1a); the nation as a whole 全国人民; 全民: *The whole country resisted the invaders.* 全民抗击侵略者. ⇨Usage 见所附用法. **2 the country** [sing] land away from towns and cities, typically with fields, woods, etc and used for agriculture 乡下; 乡村; 田野: *live in the country* 住在乡下 ○ *a day in the country* 乡间一日 ○ *We travelled across country,* ie across fields, etc or not by a main road. 我们走在田野上. ○ [attrib 作定语] *country roads, life, areas* 乡村的道路、生活、地区. **3** [U] (often with a preceding *adj* 常用于形容词之后) area of land (esp with regard to its physical or geographical features) 地区, 区域(尤指带有某种地形或地势的): *rough, marshy, etc country* 崎岖不平的、多沼泽的 ... 地区 ○ *We passed through miles of wooded country.* 我们经过了大片的森林地带. ○ *This is unknown country to me,* ie I have not been here before, or (*fig* 比喻) This is an unfamiliar topic to me. 我以前没到过这里(或作: 我对这问题一窍不通). **4** [U] (*esp US*) country-and-western music 乡村与西部音乐: [attrib 作定语] *a country singer* 乡村音乐的歌手 ○ *country music* 乡村音乐的乐曲. **5** (idm 习语) **a country ˈcousin** (*infml esp derog* 口, 尤作贬义) person who is not used to town life and ways 乡下人; 乡巴佬. **go to the ˈcountry** (*Brit*) dissolve Parliament and hold a general election 解散议会举行大选.

□ ˌ**country-and-ˈwestern** *n* [U] (*abbr* 缩写 **C and W**) type of music that derives from the folk music of the southern and western US 乡村与西部音乐(源于美国南部及西部地区的一种民间音乐): [attrib 作定语] *a country-and-western singer* 乡村与西部音乐的歌手.

ˈ**country club** club in the country where members take part in outdoor sports, etc 乡村俱乐部(会员可在其中做户外运动等).

ˌ**country ˈdance** (*esp Brit*) traditional dance in which couples are arranged in two long lines or face inward from four sides 土风舞.

ˌ**country-ˈhouse** *n* large house in the country surrounded by an estate, typically owned by a rich person 乡间宅第(富人的大宅, 周围为其产业).

ˌ**country ˈseat** = SEAT[1] 8.

NOTE ON USAGE 用法: **Country** is the most usual and neutral word for a geographical area identified by a name, such as France or China ☆ **country** 是最普通的中性词, 指可借 France 或 China 这样的名称加以识别的地理区域: *We passed through four countries on our way to Greece.* 我们在前往希腊的途中经过了四个国家. The word **state** emphasizes the political organization of the area under an independent government, and it can refer to the government itself ☆ **state** 这个词侧重指某一有独立性的政府所治理的地区的政权机构, 亦可指政府本身: *the member states of the EEC* 欧洲经济共同体成员国 ○ *a one-party state* 一党政权 ○ *The State provides free education and health care.* 政府实行免费教育和公费医疗制度. A **state** may also be a constituent part of the larger unit ☆ **state** 亦可能指较大单位的组成部分: *There are 13 states in Malaysia.* 马来西亚有十三个州. **Nation** also indicates a political unit and is more formal than **state** ☆ **nation** 亦指政治单位, 较 **state** 更为庄重: *the United Nations* 联合国 ○ *the Association of South-East Asian Nations* 东南亚国家联盟. In addition, it can suggest a community of people who share a history and language but may not have their own country or state 此外, 这个词还可指某些群体, 虽然有共同的历史和语言, 却可能没有自己的国家或政权: *The Jewish nation is scattered around the world.* 犹太民族散居于世界各地. **Land** is more formal or poetic ☆ **land** 较为庄重, 多见于诗中: *Exiles long to return to their native land.* 流亡者们渴望回到自己的祖国.

coun·try·man /ˈkʌntrɪmən; ˋkʌntrɪmən/ *n* (*pl* -men /-mən; -mən/, *fem* 阴性作 **coun·try·wo·man** /ˈkʌntrɪwʊmən; ˋkʌntrɪˌwʊmən/, *pl* **-women**) **1** person living in or born in the same country(1a) as sb else 同国人; 同胞: *a hero much loved by his countrymen* 深受同胞爱戴的英雄. **2** person living in or born in the country(2) 乡下人.

coun·try·side /ˈkʌntrɪsaɪd; ˋkʌntrɪˌsaɪd/ *n* (usu 通常作 **the countryside**) [sing] fields, wooded areas, etc outside towns and cities 郊外; 乡村; 野外: *The English countryside looks at its best in spring.* 英国的乡村在春天景色最美. ○ *the preservation of the countryside* 郊野地区的保护.

county /ˈkaʊntɪ; ˋkaʊntɪ/ *n* **1** administrative division of Britain, the largest unit of local government 郡(英国最大的地方行政区): *the county of Kent* 肯特郡 ○ [attrib 作定语] *a county boundary, councillor* 郡的边界线、郡政务委员会委员 ○ *county cricket* 郡际板球赛. Cf 参看 PROVINCE 1, STATE[1] 3. **2** (in US and other countries) subdivision of a state (美国及其他国家的)县(州以下的行政区).

▷ **county** *adj* (*Brit infml sometimes derog* 口, 有时作贬义) having the life-style and habits of English upper-class landowners (eg fond of foxhunting) 有英国大地主生活方式和习惯的(如爱好猎狐); 有郡中豪绅习气的: *She's awfully county.* 她十足地主派头. ○ *He belongs to the county set,* ie people having this life-style. 他属于郡中豪绅阶层.

□ ˌ**county ˈcouncil** body elected to govern a county 郡政务委员会; 郡议会.

ˌ**county ˈcourt** (in England) local lawcourt where non-criminal cases are dealt with (英国的)郡法院(负责审理民事案件). Cf 参看 CROWN COURT (CROWN[1]).

ˌ**county ˈtown** (*esp Brit*), ˌ**county ˈseat** (*esp US*) main town of a county, the centre of its administration 郡首府; 县城.

coup /kuː; ku/ *n* (*pl* **~s** /kuːz; kuz/) **1** surprising and successful action 意外而成功的行动: *She pulled off a great coup in getting the president to agree to an interview.* 她竟然办到了让总统同意接受采访. **2** (also *French* 法语借词 **coup d'état** /kuː deɪˈtɑː; ˋkudeˋta/, *pl* **coups d'état** /kuː deɪˈtɑː; ˋkudeˋta/) sudden unconstitutional, often violent, change of government 政变: *The army staged a coup (d'état).* 军方发动了一场政变. ○ *a bloodless coup* 不流血的政变.

□ **coup de grâce** /ˌkuː də ˈgrɑːs; *US* ˈgræs; kudəˋgrɑːs/ (*pl* **coups de grâce** /ˌkuː də ˈgrɑːs; *US* -ˈgræs; kudəˋgrɑːs/) blow that kills a person or an animal, esp for reasons of mercy 致命的一击(尤指为解除垂死时痛苦者): (*fig* 比喻) *Poor exam results dealt the coup de grâce to* (ie ended) *his hopes of staying on at university.* 他考试成绩不好, 继续念大学的希望一下子破灭了.

coupé /ˈkuːpeɪ; kuˋpe/ *n* **1** (*US* **coupe** /kuːp; kup/) two-door car with a sloping back (斜背双门的)汽车. **2** closed horse-drawn carriage with an inside seat for two people and an outside seat for the driver 双座轿式马车(内有两人座位, 外有驭者席).

couple[1] /ˈkʌpl; ˋkʌpḷ/ *n* **1** two people or things that are seen together or associated, esp a man and woman together 一对, 一双(尤指男女): *married couples* 对对夫妻 ○ *courting couples* 对对情侣 ○ *Several couples were on the dance floor.* 有几对舞伴在跳舞. ○ *I won't have any more whiskies; I've had a couple already.* 我不能再喝威士忌了, 我已经喝了几杯了. **2** (idm 习语) **a couple of people/things** (**a**) two people/things 两人; 两件事物: *I saw a couple of men get out.* 我看见有两个人出去了. ○ *I'll stay for a couple more hours.* 我再多待两个小时. (**b**) a small number of people/things 几个人; 几件事物: *She jogs a couple of miles every morning.* 她每天早上要慢跑几英里. **in two/a couple of shakes** ⇨ SHAKE[2].

couple[2] /ˈkʌpl; ˋkʌpḷ/ *v* **1** [Tn, Tn·pr, Tn·p] **~ A on (to B); ~ A and B (together)** fasten or join (two things, esp two railway carriages) together 连接或连结(两物, 尤指两节列车车厢): *The dining-car was coupled on (to the last coach).* 餐车已挂(在末节车厢)上. **2** [Tn·pr] **~ sb/sth with sb/sth** link or associate sb/sth with sb/sth 将某人[某事物]与某人[某事物]联系在一起: *The name of Mozart is coupled with the city of Salzburg.* 莫扎特的名字是与萨尔茨堡城联系在一起的. ○ *The bad light, coupled with* (ie together with) *the wet ground, made play very difficult.* 光线不足兼之地面潮湿, 比赛难以进行. **3** [I] (*arch or rhet* 古或修辞) (of two people) have sexual intercourse (指两人)性交, 云雨.

▷ **coup·ling** /ˈkʌplɪŋ; ˋkʌplɪŋ/ *n* **1** (**a**) [U] act of joining 连结. (**b**) [C, U] (*arch or rhet* 古或修辞) (act of) sexual intercourse 性交; 云雨. **2** [C] link connecting two parts, esp two railway carriages or other vehicles 连接器;(尤指列车等的)车钩, 挂钩.

coup·let /ˈkʌplɪt; ˋkʌplɪt/ *n* two successive lines of verse of equal length 相连的两行长度相同的诗句; 对句: *a rhyming couplet* 押韵的对句.

cou·pon /ˈku:pɒn; ˋkupɑn/ *n* **1** small, usu detachable, piece of paper that gives the holder the right to do or receive sth (eg goods in exchange) 证明持有人有做某事或获得某物之权利的票据(通常可撕下): *petrol coupons* 汽油配给券 ○ *10p off if you use this coupon* 凭此券可优惠10便士. **2** printed form, often cut out from a newspaper, etc, used to enter a competition, order goods, etc (通常剪自报刊等的)参赛表, 订货单等: *fill in a football coupon*, ie for a football pool competition 填写足球比赛的彩票(赌足球比赛的输赢).

cour·age /ˈkʌrɪdʒ; ˋkɝɪdʒ/ *n* **1** [U] ability to control fear when facing danger, pain, etc; bravery 勇气; 胆量: *He showed great courage in battle.* 他在战斗中表现得十分勇敢. ○ *She didn't have the courage to refuse.* 她没有勇气拒绝. ○ *I plucked up/summoned up my courage* (ie controlled my fear) *and asked her to marry me.* 我鼓起勇气向她求婚. **2** (idm 习语) **Dutch courage** ⇨ DUTCH. **have/lack the courage of one's conˈvictions** be/not be brave enough to do what one feels to be right 有[没有]勇气做自己认为对的事. **lose courage** ⇨ LOSE. **pluck up courage** ⇨ PLUCK. **screw up one's courage** ⇨ SCREW. **take one's ˌcourage in both ˈhands** make oneself do sth which one is afraid of 鼓起勇气做事.

▷ **cour·age·ous** /kəˈreɪdʒəs; kəˋredʒəs/ *adj* brave; fearless 勇敢的; 无畏的: *It was courageous of her to oppose her boss.* 她真有胆量, 竟敢对抗上司. **cour·age·ously** *adv*.

cour·gette /kɔ:ˈʒet; kʊrˋʒɛt/ *n* (*Brit*) (*US* **zucchini**) small green marrow(2) eaten as a vegetable 小胡瓜. ⇨ illus at MARROW 见MARROW之插图.

cour·ier /ˈkʊrɪə(r); ˋkʊrɪɚ/ *n* **1** person employed to guide and assist a group of tourists 旅游团的服务员; 导游. **2** messenger carrying news or important papers (传递消息或重要文件的)信使, 通讯员.

course[1] /kɔ:s; kors/ *n* **1** [sing] forward movement in time (时间的)进程, 过程: *In the course of* (ie During) *my long life I've known many changes.* 我在漫长的一生中饱经沧桑. ○ *the course of history* 历史的进程 ○ *I didn't sleep once during the entire course of the journey.* 我在整个旅程中没有睡过一次觉. **2** [C] **(a)** direction or route followed by a ship or an aircraft or by a river, boundary line, etc (船只或飞行器的)航向, 航线; (河流、界线等的)走向, 所经之路: *The plane was on/off course*, ie following/not following the right course. 飞机航向正确[偏离航向]. ○ *The course of the ship was due north.* 这条船的航行方向是正北. ○ *The captain set a course for* (ie towards) *New York.* 船长定好航向驶向纽约. ○ *the course of the River Thames* 泰晤士河的河道 ○ (*arch* 古) *the stars in their courses*, ie the way they appear to move 在轨道中运行的星球 ○ (*fig* 比喻) *The course of the argument suddenly changed*, ie It turned to a different subject. 辩论的方向突然变了(转到了别的论题上). **(b)** way of acting or proceeding 行动的途径; 做法: *What courses are open to us?* 我们可以采取什么办法? ○ *The Government's present course will only lead to disaster.* 政府的现行方针后患无穷. ○ *The wisest course would be to ignore it.* 上上策是不予理睬. **3** [C] **(a)** ~ **(in/on sth)** (*education* 教) series of lessons, lectures, etc (成系列的)课题、讲座等: *a French, a chemistry, an art course* 法语的、化学的、艺术的课程 ○ *an elementary course in maths* 初级数学课程 ○ *taking a refresher course to improve my driving* 参加补习训练以提高自己的驾驶技术. **(b)** ~ **(of sth)** (*medical* 医) series (of treatments, pills, etc) (治病、服药等)疗程: *prescribe a course of injections, X-ray treatment, etc* 开一个注射X射线等疗程的处方. **4** [C] **(a)** area for playing golf (高尔夫球)球场: *a ˈgolf-course* 高尔夫球场. ⇨illus at GOLF 见GOLF之插图. **(b)** stretch of land or water for races 跑道; 赛船水道: *a ˈrace-course*, ie for horse-races 赛马跑道 ○ *a five-mile rowing course* 五英里长赛艇水道. **5** [C] any of the separate parts of a meal, eg soup, dessert 一道菜(如汤、点心): *a five-course dinner* 有五道菜的正餐 ○ *The main course was a vegetable stew.* 主菜是炖蔬菜. **6** [C] continuous layer of brick, rock, etc in a wall (砌成墙壁的砖、石等的)层: *a damp(-proof) course* 防潮层. **7** (idm 习语) **a course of action** activity planned to achieve sth; procedure followed to get sth done 行动步骤; 办事程序: *What is the best course of action we can take?* 我们采取什么办法最好? **be par for the course** ⇨ PAR[1]. **in course of sth** undergoing the specified process 在...的过程中: *a house in course of construction*, ie being built 建造中的房屋. **in the course of sth** during sth 在...期间: *in the course of our conversation*, ie while we were talking 在我们谈话时. **in (the) course of ˈtime** when (enough) time has passed; eventually 总有一天; 最终: *Be patient: you will be promoted in the course of time.* 别着急, 你总有一天会获得提升的. **in due course** ⇨ DUE[1]. **in the ordinary, normal, etc course of events, things, etc** as things usually happen; normally 在一般情况下; 通常: *In the ordinary course of events, I visit her once a week.* 在一般情况下, 我每周去看她一次. **a matter of course** ⇨ MATTER[1]. **a middle course** ⇨ MIDDLE. **of course** naturally; certainly 自然; 当然: *'Do you study hard?' 'Of course I do.'* '你很用功吗?''当然用功.' ○ *'Did she take it?' 'Of course not.'* '她拿走了吗?''当然没拿.' ○ *That was 40 years ago, but of course you wouldn't remember it.* 那是40年以前的事, 你自然想不起来了. **run/take its ˈcourse** develop as is usual; proceed to the usual end 听其自然发展; 按常规进行: *We can't cure the disease; it must run its course.* 我们治不了这种疾病, 只好听其自然. ○ *The decision cannot be reversed; the law must take its course*, ie the punishment must be carried out. 判决是不能更改的, 有法必依. **stay the course** ⇨ STAY.

course[2] /kɔ:s; kors/ *v* [Ipr, Ip] (*esp rhet* 尤作修辞) (esp of liquids) move or flow freely (尤指液体)流动: *The blood coursed through his veins.* 血在他的血管中流动. ○ *Tears coursed down her cheeks.* 眼泪沿着她的面颊流下来.

▷ **cours·ing** /ˈkɔ:sɪŋ; ˋkorsɪŋ/ *n* [U] sport of hunting hares with dogs which follow them using sight rather than scent (凭猎犬视觉而不凭嗅觉追捕野兔的)狩猎运动.

court[1] /kɔ:t; kort/ *n* **1** **(a)** [C, U] place where trials or other law cases are held 法庭; 法院: *a ˈcourt-room* 法庭 ○ *a ˈmagistrate's court* 地方法院 ○ *a crown ˈcourt* (英格兰及威尔士的)地方刑事法院 ○ *a court of assize, a court of quarter-sessions*, ie courts in England and Wales before 1971 巡回法庭、季审法院(1971年以前英格兰及威尔士的法院) ○ *a (military or naval) court of inquiry*, ie one that deals with cases of indiscipline, etc (陆军或海军的)调查法庭(负责审理违纪等案件) ○ *The prisoner was brought to court for trial.* 囚犯被提到法庭受审. ○ *She had to appear in court to give evidence.* 她须出庭作证. ○ [attrib 作定语] *a court usher, reporter* 法院传达员、书记员 ○ *The case was settled out of court*, ie was settled without the need for it to be tried in court. 此案已在庭外和解. ○ *an out-of-court settlement* 庭外和解. **(b) the court** [sing] people present in a court-room, esp those who administer justice 出庭人员; (尤指)审判人员: *The court rose* (ie stood up) *as the judge entered.* 法官出庭时全体到庭人员起立. ○ *Please tell the court all you know.* 请把你所知道的一切告诉本庭审判人员. Cf 参看 LAWCOURT (LAW). **2** (often 常作 **Court**) **(a)** [C, U] official residence of a sovereign 宫廷; 朝廷: *the Court of St James*, ie the court of the British sovereign 英国宫廷 ○ *She had been received at all the courts of Europe.* 她曾获欧洲各君主召见. ○ *be presented at court*, ie make one's first official appearance at the sovereign's court 初次觐见君主 ○ [attrib 作定语] *the court jester* 宫廷中的小丑. **(b) the court** [sing] (institution consisting of the) sovereign and all his or her advisers, officials, family, etc 宫廷; 朝廷: *The court moves to the country in the summer.* 夏天王室上下都移居到乡下去. **3** [C] (*sport* 体) indoor or outdoor space marked out for tennis or similar ball games (网球等的室内或室外)球场: *a ˈtennis/ˈsquash court* 网球[壁球]场 ○ *Do you prefer grass or hard courts?* 你喜欢草地球场还是硬地球场? ○ *Players must behave well on court.* 比赛者应该遵守场上规则. ⇨illus at TENNIS 见TENNIS之插图. **4** (also **ˈcourtyard**) [C] unroofed space partially or completely enclosed by walls or buildings, eg in a castle or an old inn; the buildings around such a space 庭院, 院子, 天井(如城堡或古时客栈中的); 庭院周围的建筑物. **5** (idm 习语) **the ball is in sb's/one's court** ⇨ BALL[1]. **go to court (over sth)** apply to have a case heard and decided by a court of law 起诉; 打官司. **hold 'court** entertain visitors, admirers, etc 接待来访者、敬慕者等: *The film star held court in the hotel lobby.* 这位电影明星在旅馆的大厅里接见了影迷. **laugh sb/sth out of court** ⇨ LAUGH. **pay court to sb** ⇨ PAY[2]. **put sth out of 'court** make sth not worthy of consideration 使某事物不被重视: *The sheer cost of the scheme puts it right out of court.* 这一方案所需费用庞大, 不值得考虑. **take sb to 'court** make a charge against sb, to be settled in court; prosecute sb 起诉某人; 控告某人: *I took her to court for repayment of the debt.* 我为索取债务而起诉她.

C

□ **'court-card** *n* (also **face-card**) playing-card that is a king, queen or jack 头像牌(纸牌中的K、Q或J).

'court-house *n* (**a**) building containing courts of law 法院(指建筑物). (**b**) (*US*) administrative offices of a county 县政府.

,court of 'law = LAWCOURT (LAW).

,court 'order legal order made by a judge in court, telling sb to do or not do sth 法院指令.

court[2] /kɔːt; kɔrt/ *v* **1 (a)** [Tn] (*dated* 旧) (of a man) try to win the affections of (a woman), with a view to marriage (指男子)向(女子)献殷勤; 向(女子)求爱或求婚: *He had been courting Jane for six months.* 他追求简已有六个月之久. (**b**) [I] (*esp dated* 尤作旧) spend time together, with a view to marriage 谈情说爱; 谈恋爱: *The two have been courting for a year.* 两人恋爱已有一年之久. ○ *There were several courting couples in the park.* 公园里有几对谈情说爱的男女. **2** [Tn] (**a**) try to gain the favour of (a rich or influential person) 讨好(有钱或有势的人): *He has been courting the director, hoping to get the leading role in the play.* 他一直在讨好导演, 想在剧中扮演主角. (**b**) (*often derog* 常作贬义) try to win or obtain (sth) 设法赢得或获得(某事物): *court sb's approval, support, favour, etc* 取悦于某人以获其同意、支持、好感等 ○ *court applause* 博取掌声. **3** [Tn no passive 不用于被动语态] do sth that might lead to (sth unpleasant); risk 招致; 招惹; 导致; 冒…之险: *court failure, defeat, death, etc* 导致挫折、失败、死亡等 ○ *To go on such an expedition without enough supplies would be to court disaster.* 没有足够的补给就进行这种远征是会闯祸的.

cour·te·ous /ˈkɜːtɪəs; ˈkɝtɪəs/ *adj* having or showing good manners; polite 彬彬有礼的; 客气的. ▷ **cour·te·ously** *adv*.

cour·tesan /ˌkɔːtɪˈzæn; *US* ˈkɔːtɪzn; ˈkortəzn̩/ *n* (formerly) prostitute with wealthy or aristocratic clients (旧时)(伺候富豪或贵族的)高等娼妓.

cour·tesy /ˈkɜːtəsɪ; ˈkɝtəsɪ/ *n* **1** [U] courteous behaviour; good manners 礼貌; 客气: *They didn't even have the courtesy to apologize.* 他们也不道个歉, 真没有礼貌. ○ *It would only have been common courtesy to say thank you.* 说声谢谢不过是普通的礼貌. **2** [C] courteous remark or act 客气话; 礼貌的举止: *Do me the courtesy of listening* (ie Please listen) *to what I have to say.* 请听我说几句话. **3** (idm 习语) **(by) courtesy of sb** by the permission, kindness or favour of sb 承蒙某人允许; 蒙某人的好意: *This programme comes by courtesy of* (ie is sponsored or paid for by) *a local company.* 本节目由本地的一家公司提供(赞助或出资).

□ **'courtesy title** (*Brit*) title conventionally given to sb (eg the son or daughter of a lord) but with no legal validity 礼貌性的尊称(无法律效力的习惯称谓, 如对勋爵子女的尊称).

court·ier /ˈkɔːtɪə(r); ˈkortɪɚ/ *n* companion or assistant of a sovereign at court 侍臣; 廷臣: *the King and his courtiers* 国王及其朝臣.

courtly /ˈkɔːtlɪ; ˈkortlɪ/ *adj* (**-ier, -iest**) polite and dignified 谦和而有威严的: *the old gentleman's courtly manners* 这位老先生谦和而有威严的样子. ▷ **court·li·ness** *n* [U].

court mar·tial /ˌkɔːtˈmɑːʃl; ˈkortˈmarʃəl/ *n* (*pl* **courts martial**) court for trying offences against military law; trial by such a court 军事法庭; 军法审判: *He faced a court martial for disobeying orders.* 他因不服从命令受到军法审判.

▷ **court-martial** *v* (**-ll-**; *US* **-l-**) [Tn, Tn·pr] **~ sb (for sth)** try sb in such a court 以军法审判某人: *be court-martialled for neglect of duty* 因玩忽职守受到军法审判.

court·ship /ˈkɔːt-ʃɪp; ˈkortʃɪp/ *n* **1** [U] courting (COURT[2] 1). **2** [C] period during which this lasts 求爱期; 追求期: *They married after a brief courtship.* 他们恋爱不久就结婚了.

court·yard /ˈkɔːtjɑːd; ˈkort,jard/ *n* = COURT[1] 4.

cousin /ˈkʌzn; ˈkʌzn̩/ *n* **1** (also **first cousin**) child of one's uncle or aunt 堂[表]兄弟姐妹: *She is my cousin.* 她是我的表姐. ○ *We are cousins*, ie children of each other's aunts/uncles. 我们是表亲. Cf 参看 SECOND COUSIN (SECOND[1]). ⇨ App 8 见附录8. **2** (idm 习语) **a country cousin** ⇨ COUNTRY.

▷ **cous·inly** *adj* of or suitable for cousins 堂[表]兄弟姐妹的; 合于堂[表]亲戚关系的: *cousinly affection* 堂[表]兄弟姐妹之间的亲情.

cou·ture /kuːˈtʊə(r); kuˈtʊr/ *n* [U] (*French* 法) = HAUTE COUTURE: [attrib 作定语] *couture clothes/dresses* 女式时装.

▷ **cou·tur·ier** /kuːˈtʊərɪeɪ; kuˈtʊrɪɚ/ *n* person who designs and makes high-fashion clothes for women 女式时装设计师或裁缝.

cove[1] /kəʊv; kov/ *n* small bay[2] 小海湾; 小湾. ⇨illus at COAST 见COAST之插图.

cove[2] /kəʊv; kov/ *n* (*dated Brit infml* 旧, 口) man 男子: *What a strange cove he is!* 他这人真怪!

coven /ˈkʌvn; ˈkʌvən/ *n* meeting or group of witches 巫婆的聚会; 女巫团.

cov·en·ant /ˈkʌvənənt; ˈkʌvənənt/ *n* **1** (*law* 律) formal agreement that is legally binding (有法律约束力的)协议, 盟约, 公约. **2** formal promise to pay money regularly to a charity, trust(5), etc (向慈善事业、信托基金会等定期捐款的)契约.

▷ **cov·en·ant** *v* [Ipr, Tn, Tn·pr, Tf, Tt] **~ for sth; ~ sth (to/with sb)** promise or agree to (sth) under the terms of a covenant 立约承诺或同意(某事物): *I've covenanted (for) £100/covenanted (with them) to pay/that I'll pay £100 a year.* 我立约承诺每年捐款100英镑.

Cov·en·try /ˈkɒvəntrɪ; ˈkʌvəntrɪ/ *n* (idm 习语) **send sb to Coventry** ⇨SEND.

cover[1] /ˈkʌvə(r); ˈkʌvɚ/ *v* **1 (a)** [Tn, Tn·pr, Tn·p] **~ sth (up/over) (with sth)** place sth over or in front of sth; hide or protect sth in this way 覆盖或遮掩某物; (以覆盖或遮掩方式)隐藏或保护某物: *Cover the table with a cloth.* 在桌子上铺上台布. ○ *He covered (up) the body with a sheet.* 他用单子盖住那具尸体. ○ *She covered her knees (up) with a blanket.* 她把毯子盖在膝盖上. ○ *The hole was covered (over) with canvas.* 这个洞被帆布遮盖住了. ○ *He covered the cushion with new material.* 他给靠垫蒙上了新的料子. ○ *He laughed to cover* (ie hide) *his nervousness.* 他哈哈大笑以遮掩紧张的心情. ○ *She covered her face with her hands.* 她双手掩面. (**b**) [Tn] lie or extend over the surface of (sth) 平铺或展开在(某物)之表面; 盖住: *Snow covered the ground.* 积雪覆盖了大地. ○ *Flood water covered the fields by the river.* 洪水淹没了河边的田地. ○ *Rubble covered the pavement.* 人行道上铺了碎石块. **2** [Tn·pr] **~ sb/sth in/with sth** sprinkle, splash or scatter a layer of liquid, dust, etc on sb/sth 在某人[某物]上洒上、溅上或撒上一层液体、尘土等: *I was covered in/with mud by a passing car.* 一辆过路的汽车溅了我一身泥. ○ *The wind blew from the desert and covered everything with sand.* 沙漠那边吹来的风把所有的东西都蒙上了一层沙子. **3** [Tn] include (sth); deal with 包括(某事物); 涉及; 处理; 适用于: *research that covers a wide field* 涉及范围很广的研究工作 ○ *Her lectures covered the subject thoroughly.* 她的演讲对这个问题阐述得很透彻. ○ *Is that word covered in the dictionary?* 这部词典里有那个单词吗? ○ *Do the rules cover* (ie Can they be made to apply to) *a case like this?* 这些规则是否适用于这样的情况? ○ *the salesman covering the northern part of the country*, ie selling to people in that region 负责在该国北部地区促销的推销员. **4** [Tn] (of money) be enough for (sth) (指钱)够(某事物)之用: *£10 will cover our petrol for the journey.* 10英镑就足够支付我们旅行的汽油费. ○ *The firm barely covers (its) costs; it hasn't made a profit for years.* 该公司几乎入不敷出, 已经多年没有盈利了. **5** [Tn] travel (a certain distance) 走(一段路程): *By sunset we had covered thirty miles.* 到日落的时候, 我们已走了三十英里. **6** [Tn] (of a journalist) report on (a major event such as a trial, an election, a riot, etc) (指新闻记者)报道(审判、选举、动乱之类的大事): *cover the Labour Party's annual conference* 报道工党年会新闻. **7** [I, Ipr] **~ (for sb)** do sb's work, duties, etc during his absence 代替某人工作、履行职责等: *I'll cover for Jane while she's on holiday.* 简休假时我替补她工作. **8** [Tn, Tn·pr] **~ sb/sth (against/for sth)** insure sb/sth against loss, etc 给某人[某事物]保险: *Are you fully covered against/for fire and theft?* 你是否保了足够的火险和盗窃险? **9** [Tn] (**a**) protect (sb) by shooting at a potential attacker (以火力)掩护(某人): *Cover me while I move forward.* 我前进时, 你掩护我. ○ *The artillery gave us covering fire*, ie shot to protect us. 炮火掩护着我们. (**b**) (of guns, fortresses, etc) be in a position to shoot at and therefore control (an area, a road, etc); dominate (指枪炮、堡垒等)射程达到, 掩护, 控制(某区域、道路等); 支配: *Our guns covered every approach to the town.* 我们的炮火控制了通往市区的各条道路. (**c**) keep aiming a gun at sb (so that he cannot shoot or escape) (用枪炮)瞄准某人(使其不能还击或逃跑): *Cover her while I phone the police.* 你用枪看住她, 我给警方打电话. ○ *Keep them covered!* 把枪口对准他们! **10** [Tn] (of a male animal, esp a horse) copulate with (a female) (指雄性动物与(雌性动物)交配(尤指马). **11** (idm 习语) **cover/hide a multitude of sins** ⇨ MULTITUDE. **cover one's tracks** leave no evidence of where one has been or what one has been doing 掩盖行踪或所做的事的痕迹. **cover oneself with glory** (*rhet* 修辞) acquire fame and honour 获得名声及荣誉: *The regiment covered itself with glory in the invasion battle.* 该团在反侵略的战斗中赫赫有名. **12** (phr v) **cover sth in** put a protective covering over (an open space) 给露天场所加顶: *We're having the yard/passage/terrace covered in.* 我们给院子[过道/阳台]加了顶子. **cover (oneself) up** (**a**) dress warmly 穿暖和: *Do cover (yourself) up: it's freezing outside.* 衣服穿暖一点: 外面冷极了. (**b**) put on (extra) clothes, esp to avoid embarrassment (多)穿衣物, (尤指以免尴尬). **cover (sth) up** (*derog* 贬) make efforts to conceal a mistake, sth illegal, etc 掩盖错误、非法的事物等: *The government is trying to cover up the scandal.* 政府企图遮掩这件丑事. **cover up for sb** conceal sb's mistakes, crimes, etc in order to protect him 为某人掩饰错误或隐瞒罪行等.

▷ **cov·ered** *adj* **1 ~ in/with sth** [pred 作表语] having a great number or amount of sth 大量: *trees covered in/with blossom/fruit* 开满鲜花[结满果实]的树 ○ (*fig* 比喻) *I was covered in/with confusion*, ie very confused and embarrassed. 我深感不安. **2** having a cover, esp a roof 有遮盖物的; (尤指)有顶的: *a covered way* 有顶篷的通道.

cov·er·ing /ˈkʌvərɪŋ; ˋkʌvərɪŋ/ *n* thing that covers 掩蔽物; 遮盖物: *a light covering of snow on the ground* 地上一层薄薄的雪.

□ ˌ**covered ˈwagon** (*US*) large wagon with an arched canvas roof, used by pioneers for travel westward across the prairies (美国拓荒者的)大篷车.

ˌ**covering ˈletter** letter sent with a document, or with goods, etc, typically explaining the contents (随公文、货物等发出的通常用以说明其内容的)附信.

ˈ**cover-up** *n* (*derog* 贬) act of concealing a mistake, sth illegal, etc 文过饰非; 护短: *She said nothing was stolen, but that's just a cover-up.* 她说什么东西也没被偷, 那不过是掩饰罢了.

cover^2 /ˈkʌvə(r); ˋkʌvɚ/ *n* **1** [C] (**a**) thing that covers 掩蔽物; 覆盖物; 罩子; 套子: *a plastic cover for a typewriter* 打字机的塑料外罩 ○ *Some chairs are fitted with loose covers.* 有些椅子配有椅套. (**b**) top; lid 顶子; 盖子: *the cover of a saucepan* 长柄锅的锅盖. **2** [U] place or area giving shelter or protection 隐蔽处; 避难所; 庇护所: *There was nowhere we could take cover* (ie go for protection) *from the storm.* 我们没有地方躲避这场风暴. ○ *The land was flat and treeless and gave no cover to the troops.* 该处地势平坦又没有树木, 部队无处隐蔽. ○ *The bicycles are kept under cover*, eg in a shelter, shed, etc. 自行车存放在棚子下面. **3** [C] either or both of the thick protective outer pages of a book, magazine, etc, esp the front cover (书刊等的)封面: *a book with a leather cover* 一本有皮面的书 ○ *The magazine had a picture of a horse on the cover*, ie the front cover. 这本杂志封面上画着一匹马. ○ *read a book from cover to cover*, ie from beginning to end 从头到尾读完一本书. **4 the covers** [pl] bedclothes 毯子; 被子: *push back the covers and get out of bed* 掀开被子起床. **5** [C usu *sing* 通常作单数] (**a**) **~ (for sth)** means of concealing sth illegal, secret, etc 隐瞒非法事物、秘密等的手段: *His business was a cover for drug dealing.* 他的商行是进行毒品交易的幌子. (**b**) false identity 虚假的身分; 伪装: *The spy's cover was that she was a consultant engineer.* 那女间谍伪装成顾问工程师. ○ *The agent's cover had been broken/blown* (ie revealed), *and he had to leave the country.* 那特务暴露了身分, 只好离开该国. **6** [U] protection from attack 防护; 掩护: *Artillery gave cover* (ie fired at the enemy to stop them firing back) *while the infantry advanced.* 炮火掩护步兵前进. ○ *For this operation we need plenty of air cover*, ie protection by military aircraft. 为进行这次军事行动, 我们需要充足的空中掩护. **7** [U] **~ (for sb)** performance of another person's work, duties, etc during his absence 代替他人工作、履行职责等; 替补; 代劳: *This doctor provides emergency cover (for sick colleagues).* 这位医生代(患病的同事)急诊值班. **8** [U] **~ (against sth)** insurance (against loss, injury, etc) 保险(以防损失、伤亡等): *a policy that gives cover against fire* 投保火险的保险单. **9** [C] envelope or wrapper 封套; 封皮: *a first-day cover*, ie an envelope with a newly issued stamp on it 首日封(贴有新发行的邮票的信封) ○ *under plain cover*, ie in an envelope or a parcel that does not show the sender, contents, etc 在未写明寄件人、内容等的信封或包裹内 ○ (*commerce* 商) *under separate cover*, ie in a separate parcel or envelope 在另一包裹或另函内. **10** [U] woods or undergrowth that can conceal animals, etc 动物等隐身的树林或矮树丛: *cover for game birds* 猎禽的藏身处 ○ *The fox broke* (ie left) *cover and ran across the field.* 狐狸离开了它所隐身的树林, 窜过了农田. Cf 参看 COVERT^2. **11** [C] place laid at table for a meal (餐桌上布置的)席位: *Covers were laid for six.* 布置了六个席位. **12** (**a**) **the covers** [pl] (in cricket) area to the right of and in front of the batsman (板球)外场防守区(击球员右方及前方的区域): *fielding in the covers* 在外场防守区进行防守. (**b**) [C] player who fields in the covers 外场防守员: *The ball went past cover.* 球越过了外场防守员. **13** (idm 习语) **under cover of sth** (**a**) concealed by sth 在某事物掩护下: *We travelled under cover of darkness.* 我们在夜幕掩护下行进. (**b**) with pretence of sth 以某事物为借口; 借某事物之名: *under cover of friendship* 借友谊之名 ○ *crimes committed under cover of patriotism* 打着爱国的旗号犯下的罪行.

□ ˈ**cover charge** (in a restaurant) charge to be paid in addition to the cost of food and drink (餐馆中饮食费用以外的)服务费, 附加费.

ˈ**cover girl** girl whose photograph appears on the cover of a magazine (刊物上的)封面女郎.

ˈ**cover note** (*Brit*) document from an insurance company showing that one is insured, issued to cover the period before a policy is officially in force (保险公司于保单正式生效以前提供临时保险的)临时保单.

cov·er·age /ˈkʌvərɪdʒ; ˋkʌvərɪdʒ/ *n* [U] **1** reporting of events, etc 新闻报道: *TV coverage of the election campaign* 有关竞选活动的电视报道 ○ *There's little coverage of foreign news in the newspaper.* 报纸上几乎没有国外新闻的报道. **2** extent to which sth is covered 覆盖范围; 覆盖程度: *a thicker paint which gives good coverage* 严严实实的一层厚漆 ○ *a dictionary with poor coverage of American words* 所收美式词语不多的词典.

cov·er·alls /ˈkʌvərɔːlz; ˋkʌvəˌrɔlz/ *n* [pl] (*US*) = OVERALLS (OVERALL^2 2).

cov·er·let /ˈkʌvəlɪt; ˋkʌvɚlɪt/ *n* bedspread 床罩.

cov·ert^1 /ˈkʌvət; *US* ˈkəʊvɜːrt; ˋkovɚt/ *adj* concealed; not open; secret 隐蔽的; 不公开的; 秘密的: *covert glances, threats, payments* 偷偷的一瞥、暗中的威胁、秘密的付款 ○ *the covert activities of a spy* 间谍的秘密活动. ▷ **cov·ertly** *adv*. Cf 参看 OVERT.

cov·ert^2 /ˈkʌvə(r); ˋkʌvɚt/ *n* area of thick low bushes, trees, etc in which animals, esp hunted animals, hide 动物(尤指猎物)藏身的矮树丛、树林等. Cf 参看 COVER^2

C

10.

covet /ˈkʌvɪt; ˋkʌvɪt/ *v* [Tn] (*usu derog* 通常作贬义) want very much to possess (esp sth that belongs to sb else) 贪求(尤指别人的东西); 觊觎: *covet sb's position, status, possessions, rewards* 觊觎某人的职位、地位、财产、报酬 ○ *this year's winner of the coveted Nobel Prize*, ie which everyone would like to win 许多人梦寐以求的诺贝尔奖之本年度获得者.

▷ **cov·et·ous** *adj* **~ (of sth)** (*derog* 贬) having or showing a strong desire to possess (esp sth that belongs to sb else) 贪求(尤指别人的东西)的: *covetous of his high salary* 觊觎他的高薪的 ○ *a covetous look, glance, etc* 贪婪的眼色、一瞥等. **cov·et·ously** *adv*. **cov·et·ous·ness** *n* [U].

covey /ˈkʌvɪ; ˋkʌvɪ/ *n* (*pl* **~s**) [CGp] small flock of partridges 一小群鹧鸪.

cow suckling its calf
给小牛喂奶的母牛

cow[1] /kaʊ; kaʊ/ *n* **1** fully-grown female of any animal of the ox family, esp the domestic kind kept by farmers to produce milk and beef 母牛(尤指奶牛和菜牛): *milking the cows* 给奶牛挤奶 ○ *a herd of cows* 一群母牛. ⇨illus 见插图. Cf 参看 BULL[1] 1, CALF, HEIFER. **2** female elephant, rhinoceros, whale, etc 雌性的象、犀牛、鲸等. Cf 参看 BULL[1] 2. **3** (⚠ *derog sl* 讳, 贬, 俚) woman 女子: *You stupid cow!* 你这蠢女人! **4** (idm 习语) **a sacred cow** ⇨ SACRED. **till the ˈcows come home** (*infml* 口) for a very long time; for ever 长时间; 永远: *You can talk till the cows come home: you'll never make me change my mind.* 你就是说出大天来, 也休想改变我的主意.

□ **ˈcowbell** *n* bell hung round a cow's neck so that the cow can be found by the sound of its ringing 牛颈铃.

ˈcowcatcher *n* (*US*) metal frame fixed to the front of a railway engine to push obstacles off the track (机车的)排障器.

ˈcowgirl *n* girl or woman who looks after cows 牧牛女; 饲牛女工.

ˈcowhand *n* person who looks after cows 牧牛人; 饲牛工.

ˈcowherd *n* (*dated* 旧) person who looks after grazing cows 放牛人; 牧牛工.

ˈcowhide *n* **1** [U, C] leather made from the skin of a cow 牛皮; 牛革. **2** [C] strip of this leather used as whip 牛皮鞭.

ˈcowman /-mən; -mən/ *n* (*pl* **-men**) man who looks after cows 牧牛人; 牧牛工.

ˈcow-pat *n* flat round mass of cow-dung on the ground (一团)牛屎.

ˈcowshed *n* farm building where cows are kept when not outside, or where they are milked 牛棚; 牛舍.

cow[2] /kaʊ; kaʊ/ *v* [esp passive 尤用于被动语态: Tn, Tn·pr] **~ sb (into sth/into doing sth)** make sb do as one wants by frightening him; intimidate sb 胁迫某人(做某事); 恐吓某人: *The men were cowed into total submission.* 这些人被吓得服服帖帖. ○ *a cowed* (ie frightened and submissive) *look* 畏惧而顺从的样子.

cow·ard /ˈkaʊəd; ˋkaʊɚd/ *n* (*derog* 贬) person who lacks courage; person who runs away from danger 胆小鬼; 懦夫: *You miserable coward!* 你这可怜的胆小鬼! ○ *I'm a terrible coward when it comes to dealing with sick people*, ie It scares me and I avoid it. 我一和病人打交道就提心吊胆.

▷ **cow·ard·ice** /ˈkaʊədɪs; ˋkaʊɚdɪs/ *n* [U] (*derog* 贬) feelings or behaviour of a coward; fearfulness 胆小; 怯懦: *a battle lost owing to the troops' cowardice* 由于部队畏缩不前而招致的战斗失利 ○ *abject cowardice* 可鄙的怯懦行为.

cow·ardly *adj* (*derog* 贬) lacking courage; of or like a coward 胆小的; 怯懦的; (似)胆小鬼的: *cowardly lies, behaviour, actions* 怯懦的谎言、行为、举动 ○ *It was cowardly of you not to admit your mistake.* 你不承认错误就不是好样儿的.

cow·boy /ˈkaʊbɔɪ; ˋkaʊˌbɔɪ/ *n* **1** man, usu on horseback, who looks after grazing cattle in the western parts of the US (美国西部的)牛仔, 牧童: [attrib 作定语] *a cowboy movie*, ie one featuring adventures in the American West 牛仔影片. **2** (*Brit infml derog* 口, 贬) tradesman or businessman whose work, business practices, etc are incompetent or dishonest 无能的或不老实的商人或经营者: *The house has all these defects because it was built by cowboys.* 这所房屋有这么多毛病, 其原因就在于承建者都是滑头. ○ [attrib 作定语] *cowboy builders, stockbrokers, etc* 不老实的建筑商、证券经纪人等.

cower /ˈkaʊə(r); ˋkaʊɚ/ *v* [I, Ipr, Ip] crouch down or move backwards in fear or distress (因畏惧或痛苦)蜷缩, 退缩: *He cowered away/back as she raised her hand to hit him.* 她扬手打他, 他立即退缩开[向后退缩]. ○ *The dog cowered (down) under the table.* 那只狗吓得蜷伏在桌子底下.

cowl /kaʊl; kaʊl/ *n* **1** large hood on a monk's gown (修士道袍上的)大兜帽. **2** cap for a chimney, ventilating pipe, etc, usu of metal and often revolving with the wind, which is designed to improve the flow of air or smoke 通风帽; 烟囱罩(可随风旋转以利通风或排烟). ⇨illus at App 1 见附录1之插图, page vii.

▷ **cowl·ing** *n* removable metal covering for an engine, esp on an aircraft (发动机上可拆卸的)金属罩(尤指飞行器上的). ⇨illus at AIRCRAFT 见 AIRCRAFT 之插图.

cow·lick /ˈkaʊlɪk; ˋkaʊˌlɪk/ *n* (*infml* 口) tuft of hair just above the forehead that will not lie flat (额前翘起的)一绺头发.

cow·pox /ˈkaʊpɒks; ˋkaʊˌpɑks/ *n* [U] mild contagious disease of cattle caused by a virus (which is also used in making smallpox vaccine) 牛痘.

cow·rie /ˈkaʊrɪ; ˋkaʊrɪ/ *n* small shell formerly used as money in parts of Africa and Asia 宝贝(旧时在非洲及亚洲的部分地区用作钱币的小贝壳).

cow·slip /ˈkaʊslɪp; ˋkaʊˌslɪp/ *n* small plant with yellow flowers, growing wild in temperate countries 黄花九轮草(生长于温带国家).

cox /kɒks; kɑks/ *n* person who steers a rowing-boat, esp in races 划艇(尤指赛艇)的舵手.

▷ **cox** *v* [I, Tn] act as cox of (a rowing-boat) 当(划艇)的舵手: *He coxed the Oxford boat.* 他担任牛津大学赛船的掌舵人.

cox·comb /ˈkɒkskəʊm; ˋkɑksˌkom/ *n* (*arch* 古) foolish conceited man, esp one who pays too much attention to his clothes 自命不凡的蠢傢伙(尤指过分注意衣着者).

cox·swain /ˈkɒksn; ˋkɑksn̩/ *n* **1** man in charge of a ship's rowing-boat and its crew 船上管理划艇及其船员的人. **2** (*fml* 文) cox 小艇的掌舵人.

Coy /kɔɪ; kɔɪ/ *abbr* 缩写 = (army) company.

coy /kɔɪ; kɔɪ/ *adj* (**-er, -est**) (*usu derog* 通常作贬义) **1** pretending to be shy or modest 假装害羞的; 忸怩作态的; 故作谦虚的: *She gave a coy smile when he paid her a compliment.* 他恭维她时, 她忸怩作态地笑了一笑. **2** reluctant to give information, answer questions, etc; secretive 不肯明说的; 不肯作答的; 含糊其词的: *He was a bit coy when asked about the source of his income.* 问起他收入的来源, 他就有些吞吞吐吐. ▷ **coyly** *adv*. **coy·ness** *n* [U].

coy·ote /kɔɪˈəʊtɪ; *US* kaɪəʊt; ˋkaɪot/ *n* small wolf of the plains of western N America 郊狼(北美洲西部原野上的小狼).

coypu /ˈkɔɪpu:; ˋkɔɪpu/ *n* beaver-like water-rodent from S America, bred for its fur 河狸鼠(状若海狸, 产于南美洲, 人工饲养以取其毛皮).

cozy (*US*) = COSY.

CP /ˌsi: ˈpi:; ˌsi ˋpi/ *abbr* 缩写 = Communist Party: *join the CP* 加入共产党.

cp *abbr* 缩写 = compare. Cf 参看 CF.

Cpl *abbr* 缩写 = CORP 1.

cps /ˌsi: pi: ˈes; ˌsi pi ˋɛs/ *abbr* 缩写 = (also **c/s**) (*physics* 物) cycles per second 每秒周数; 周/秒.

crab[1] /kræb; kræb/ *n* **1** (**a**) [C] ten-legged shellfish 蟹. ⇨illus at SHELLFISH 见 SHELLFISH 之插图. (**b**) [U] its flesh as food 蟹肉: *dressed crab*, ie prepared for eating

加作料的蟹肉. **2 the Crab** [sing] the fourth sign of the zodiac; Cancer 巨蟹宫(黄道第四宫); 巨蟹星座. **3** [C] (*infml* 口) = CRAB-LOUSE. **4** (idm 习语) **catch a crab** ⇨ CATCH[1].

▷ **crab·wise** /ˈkræbwaɪz; ˋkræb,waɪz/ *adv* sideways, often in a stiff or ungainly way (常为僵硬或笨拙的方式)横向地, 蟹行般地: *shuffle crabwise across the floor* 拖着脚在室内横着走过去.

□ **ˈcrab-louse** *n* parasitic insect found in the hairy parts of the body 阴虱.

crab[2] /kræb; kræb/ *v* (**-bb-**) [I, Ipr] **~ (about sth)** (*infml derog* 口, 贬) complain; grumble; criticize 抱怨; 挑剔; 批评: *The boss is always crabbing about my work.* 老板对我的工作总是横挑鼻子竖挑眼.

crab-apple /ˈkræbæpl; ˋkræb,æpl/ (also **crab**) *n* **1** wild apple-tree 花红树; 沙果树; 海棠树. **2** its hard sour fruit 花红; 沙果; 海棠.

crabbed /ˈkræbɪd *or, rarely,* 罕读作 ˈkræbd; ˋkræbɪd/ *adj* **1** (of handwriting) small and difficult to read (指字迹)细小难辨的. **2** = CRABBY.

crabby /ˈkræbɪ; ˋkræbɪ/ *adj* (**-ier, -iest**) (*infml* 口) bad-tempered; irritable 脾气乖戾的; 易怒的.

crack[1] /kræk; kræk/ *n* **1 ~ (in sth)** **(a)** line along which sth has broken, but not into separate parts 裂缝; 裂纹: *a cup with bad cracks in it* 有很多裂纹的杯子 ○ *Don't go skating today — there are dangerous cracks in the ice.* 今天别去溜冰了 —— 冰上有裂缝很危险. ○ (*fig* 比喻) *The cracks* (ie defects) *in the Government's economic policy are beginning to show.* 政府经济政策上的失误已渐渐明显. ⇨illus at CHIP 见CHIP之插图. **(b)** narrow opening 缝隙: *She looked through a crack in the curtains.* 她透过帘子的缝隙观望. ○ *Open the door a crack*, ie Open it very slightly. 把门打开一条缝(打开一点点). **2** sudden sharp noise 爆裂声; 噼啪声: *the crack of a pistol shot* 噼噼啪啪的手枪声 ○ *a crack of thunder* 一声霹雳. **3 ~ (on sth)** sharp blow, usu one that can be heard 重击(通常为可听到响声的): *give sb/get a crack on the head* 吧的一声打在某人的头上[头上挨了一下子]. **4 ~ (about sth)** (*infml* 口) clever and amusing remark, often critical; joke 俏皮话(常为挖苦人的); 笑话: *She made a crack about his fatness.* 她取笑他肥胖. **5 ~ at sth/doing sth** (*infml* 口) attempt at sth 试做某事物: *Have another crack at solving this puzzle.* 再试一试把这个难题解决了吧. **6** (idm 习语) **the crack of ˈdawn** (*infml* 口) very early in the morning 黎明; 破晓: *get up at the crack of dawn* 黎明即起. **the crack of ˈdoom** the end of the world 世界末日: (*fig* 比喻) *To get a bus here you have to wait till the crack of doom*, ie an extremely long time. 在这儿真要等到世界末日(很久很久以后)才能有公共汽车. **a fair crack of the whip** ⇨ FAIR[1]. **paper over the cracks** ⇨ PAPER.

▷ **crack** *adj* [attrib 作定语] very clever or expert; excellent 精明能干的; 技艺高超的; 优秀的: *a crack regiment* 劲旅 ○ *He's a crack shot*, ie expert at shooting. 他是神枪手.

□ **ˈcrack-brained** *adj* (*infml* 口) crazy; foolish 疯狂的; 愚蠢的: *a crack-brained idea, scheme, etc* 愚蠢的念头、计谋等.

crack[2] /kræk; kræk/ *v* **1** [I, Tn] (cause to) develop a crack[1](1a) or cracks (使)开裂, 破裂, 爆裂: *The ice cracked as I stepped onto it.* 我一踩冰就裂了. ○ *You can crack this toughened glass, but you can't break it.* 这种韧化玻璃只裂不碎. ○ *She has cracked a bone in her arm.* 她手臂有一处骨裂. ○ *a cracked mug* 有裂纹的缸子. **2** [Tn, Cn·a] break (sth) open or into pieces 砸开或砸碎(某物): *crack a nut* 把坚果砸碎 ○ *crack a safe*, ie open it to steal from it 砸开保险箱 ○ *crack a casing open* 噼里啪啦打开包装. **3** [Tn, Tn·pr] **sth (on/against sth)** hit sth sharply 猛击某物: *I cracked my head on the low door-frame.* 我的头撞在低矮的门框上了. **4** [I, Tn no passive 不用于被动语态] (cause sth to) make a sharp sound (使某物)发出爆裂声; (使某物)噼啪作响: *crack a whip, one's knuckles* 抽鞭子、屈指节噼啪作响 ○ *The hunter's rifle cracked and the deer fell dead.* 猎人的枪一响, 鹿即倒地而死. **5** [I, Tn] (cause sb to) cease to resist; (cause sth to) fail (使某人)屈服; (使某事物)垮台: *The suspect cracked under questioning.* 嫌疑分子在审问之下招供了. ○ *They finally cracked the defence and scored a goal.* 他们终于突破了防守, 射进一球. **6** [Tn] (*infml* 口) solve (a problem, etc) 解决(问题等): *The calculation was difficult, but we finally cracked it.* 计算起来很费劲, 然而我们终于解决了. ○ *crack a code*, ie decipher it 破译密码. **7** [I] (of the voice) change in depth, loudness, etc suddenly and uncontrollably (指嗓音)突然而失控地改变音色、音量等: *In a voice cracking with emotion, he announced the death of his father.* 他悲恸失声地宣布了父亲去世的消息. ○ *A boy's voice cracks* (ie becomes deeper) *at puberty.* 男孩在青春期嗓音改变(声音变粗). **8** [Tn] (*infml* 口) open (a bottle, esp of alcoholic drink) and drink its contents 开(瓶, 尤指酒瓶)饮用. **9** [Tn] (*infml* 口) tell (a joke) 说(笑话). **10** [Tn] (*chemistry* 化) break down (heavy oils) by heat and pressure to produce lighter oils 使裂化(利用高温高压从质量较重的石油里制取轻油). **11** (idm 习语) **cracked ˈup to be sth** (usu negative 通常作否定) (*infml* 口) reputed to be sth 号称: *He's not such a good writer as he's cracked up to be.* 他并不像人们所吹捧的那样是什么杰出的作家. **get ˈcracking** (*infml* 口) begin, esp energetically 开始; (尤指)大干起来: *There's a lot to be done, so let's get cracking.* 工作很多, 咱们开始干吧. **12** (phr v) **crack down (on sb/sth)** impose more severe treatment or restrictions on sb/sth (对某人[某事物])严加处置或限制: *Police are cracking down on drug dealers.* 警方现对贩毒分子严惩不贷. **crack up** (*infml* 口) lose one's physical or mental health (身体)垮掉; (精神)崩溃: *You'll crack up if you go on working so hard.* 你继续这样拼命干下去, 身体会吃不消的.

▷ **cracked** /krækt; krækt/ *adj* [usu pred 通常作表语] (*infml* 口) mad; crazy 疯狂; 狂热.

crack·ing /ˈkrækɪŋ; ˋkrækɪŋ/ *adj* [usu attrib 通常作定语] (*Brit infml* 口) excellent 精彩的; 棒的: *That was a cracking shot he played.* 他这一下打得妙极了.

□ **ˈcrack-down** *n* **~ (on sb/sth)** severe measures to restrict or discourage undesirable or criminal people or actions 制裁; 取缔: *a crack-down on tax evasion* 对逃税行为的严厉打击.

ˈcrack-up *n* (*infml* 口) loss of physical or mental health (身体的)衰退; (精神的)崩溃: *a crack-up due to overwork* 因操劳过度而招致的身体的衰退.

cracker /ˈkrækə(r); ˋkrækɚ/ *n* **1** thin flaky dry biscuit, typically eaten with cheese 薄脆饼干(多与干酪一起食用). **2** **(a)** small firework that explodes with a sharp sound 爆竹; 鞭炮. **(b)** (also **Christmas cracker**) party toy consisting of a cardboard tube wrapped in paper that makes a sharp explosive sound as its ends are pulled apart, with a small gift, paper hat, etc inside 彩包爆竹(一种宴会时的娱乐用品, 为一硬的纸筒, 内装小件礼品、纸帽等, 用纸包裹好, 两端一拉即噼啪作响): *a box of crackers* 一盒彩包爆竹. **3** (*Brit infml approv* 口, 褒) attractive girl or woman 迷人的姑娘; 有魅力的女子: *What a little cracker she is!* 她真是小美人! **4 crackers** [pl] = NUTCRACKERS (NUT).

crack·ers /ˈkrækəz; ˋkrækɚz/ *adj* [pred 作表语] (*Brit infml* 口) mad; crazy 疯狂; 狂热: *That noise is driving me crackers/making me go crackers.* 那噪声吵得我简直要发狂. ○ *You must be crackers!* 你一定是疯了!

crackle /ˈkrækl; ˋkrækl/ *v* [I] make small cracking sounds, as when dry sticks burn 发轻微的爆裂声(如干柴燃烧时的响声); 发噼啪声: *a crackling camp-fire* 噼啪作响的营火 ○ *The twigs crackled as we trod on them.* 我们践踏树枝时, 树枝噼啪作响. ○ (*fig* 比喻) *The atmosphere crackled with tension as the two boxers stepped into the ring.* 这两名拳手一登场, 气氛顿时紧张起来.

▷ **crackle** *n* [U] series of small cracking sounds 一连串轻微的爆裂声; 噼里啪拉的响声: *the distant crackle of machine-gun fire* 远处机枪的格格声 ○ *Can you get rid of the crackle on my radio?* 你能把我那收音机的杂音除掉吗?

crack·ling /ˈkræklɪŋ; ˋkræklɪŋ/ *n* [U] **1** small cracking sounds 轻微爆裂声; 噼啪声. **2** crisp skin on roast pork (烤猪肉的)脆皮.

□ **ˈcrackle-ware** *n* [U] china, etc covered with a network of what appear to be tiny cracks 有细碎纹饰的陶瓷器.

crack·pot /ˈkrækpɒt; ˋkræk,pɑt/ *n* (*infml* 口) eccentric person with strange or impractical ideas (想法怪异或不

切实际的)怪人, 狂人: [attrib 作定语] *crackpot ideas, schemes, etc* 异想天开的念头、计划等.

cracks·man /ˈkræksmən; ˋkræksmən/ *n* (*pl* **-men**) (*dated* 旧) burglar 窃贼.

-cracy *comb form* 构词成分 (forming *ns* 用以构成名词) government or rule of 统治: *democracy* ○ *technocracy* ○ *bureaucracy*. Cf 参看 -CRAT.

cradle /ˈkreɪdl; ˋkredl̩/ *n* **1** small bed for a baby, usu shaped like a box with curved parts underneath so that it can move from side to side 摇篮: *The mother rocked the baby to sleep in its cradle.* 母亲摇动摇篮使婴儿入睡. ⇨illus at App 1 见附录1之插图, page xvi. **2 ~ of sth** (usu *sing* 通常作单数) (*fig* 比喻) place where sth begins 发源地; 策源地; 发祥地: *Greece, the cradle of Western culture.* 希腊, 西方文化的发源地. **3** (**a**) framework that looks like or is used like a cradle, eg the structure on which a ship rests while it is being repaired or built 形状或用途近似摇篮的框架(如修造船舶时用以支承的托架). (**b**) platform that can be moved up and down an outside wall by means of ropes and pulleys, used by window-cleaners, painters, etc (擦窗工人、油漆工人等使用的依靠绳索及滑轮可沿外墙上下移动的)吊架, 吊篮. **4** part of a telephone on which the receiver rests (电话机的)听筒架, 叉簧. **5** (idm 习语) **from the ˌcradle to the ˈgrave** from birth to death 从生到死; 一生.

▷ **cradle** *v* [Tn, Tn·pr] **~ sb/sth (in sth)** place or hold sb/sth (as if) in a cradle 将某人[某物](如同)置于摇篮中: *cradle a child in one's arms,* ie hold it gently, esp rocking it from side to side 把孩子抱在怀里轻轻摇晃.

craft /krɑ:ft; *US* kræft; kræft/ *n* **1** [C] occupation, esp one that needs skill in the use of the hands; such a skill or technique 行业; (尤指)手工业; 手艺; 工艺: *the potter's craft* 陶器业 ○ *teach arts and crafts in a school* 在学校里教工艺美术 ○ *He's a master of the actor's craft.* 他演技精湛. **2** (*pl* unchanged 复数不变) [C] (**a**) boat; ship 船舶: *Hundreds of small craft accompany the liner into harbour.* 数百只小艇随同这艘班轮驶入港湾. Cf 参看 VESSEL 1. (**b**) aircraft; spacecraft 飞行器; 宇宙飞船: *The astronauts piloted their craft down to the lunar surface.* 宇航员驾驶宇宙飞船在月球表面降落. **3** [U] (*fml derog* 文, 贬) skill in deceiving; cunning 骗术; 狡诈: *achieving by craft and guile what he could not manage by honest means* 玩弄诡计和手腕以实现其用正当手段无法实现的企图.

▷ **craft** *v* [Tn usu passive 通常用于被动语态] make (sth) skilfully, esp by hand 精工制作(某物)(尤指用手工): *a beautiful hand-crafted silver goblet* 美观的手工精制的高脚银杯.

-craft (forming compound *ns* 用以构成复合名词): *handicraft* ○ *needlecraft* ○ *stagecraft*.

crafty *adj* (**-ier**, **-iest**) (*usu derog* 通常作贬义) clever in using indirect or deceitful methods to get what one wants; cunning 诡计多端的; 狡猾的: *a crafty politician* 老奸巨猾的政客 ○ *He's a crafty old fox.* 他是一只狡猾的老狐狸. **craft·ily** *adv*. **crafti·ness** *n* [U].

crafts·man /ˈkrɑ:ftsmən; *US* ˈkræfts-; ˋkræftsmən/ *n* (*pl* **-men**) **1** skilled workman, esp one who makes things by hand 匠人; 能工巧匠(尤指手艺人). **2** person who attends carefully to the details of a creative task 对创作刻意求工的人: *In symphonic writing he is the master craftsman.* 他在交响乐曲的创作上堪称技艺大师.

▷ **crafts·man·ship** *n* [U] **1** skilled workmanship 技艺; 手艺. **2** careful attention to details, etc 精工细作; 刻意求工.

crag /kræg; kræg/ *n* high, steep or rugged mass of rock 悬崖; 峭壁; 绝壁; 巉岩.

▷ **craggy** *adj* (**-ier**, **-iest**) **1** having many crags 多峭壁的; 多巉岩的. **2** (*usu approv* 通常作褒义) (of the face) having strong-looking prominent features (cheek-bones, nose, etc) and deep lines (指面部)五官轮廓分明的: *his handsome craggy features* 他那五官轮廓分明的英俊相貌.

cram /kræm; kræm/ *v* **1** (**a**) [Tn·pr, Tn·p] **~ sth (into sth/in)** push or force too much of sth into sth 将某物塞进某物中; 尽力塞入: *cram food into one's mouth, papers into a drawer* 把食物塞到嘴里、文件塞进抽屉里 ○ *The room's full; we can't cram any more people in.* 屋里满满的, 再也挤不进去人了. (**b**) [usu passive 通常用于被动语态: Tn, Tn·pr] **~ sth (with sth)** make sth (too) full 塞满某物; 将某物塞得满满的: *cram one's mouth with food* 往嘴里塞满食物 ○ *an essay crammed with quotations* 引语连篇的文章 ○ *The restaurant was crammed (with people).* 餐厅里挤满了(人). **2 ~ (for sth)** (**a**) [I, Ipr] (*infml* 口) learn a lot of facts in a short time, esp for an examination 突击式学习(尤指为应考): *cram for a chemistry test* 为应付化学考试而临时抱佛脚. (**b**) [Tn] teach (sb) in this way 以注入方式教(某人): *cram pupils* 以填鸭方式教学生.

▷ **cram·mer** *n* (*dated infml* 旧, 口) special school where students are crammed (CRAM 2b) (搞注入式教学的)专门学校或补习班.

□ ˌ**cram-ˈfull** *adj* [usu pred 通常作表语] (*infml* 口) very full 很满: *cram-full of people* 人挤得很满.

cramp[1] /kræmp; kræmp/ *n* **1** [U] sudden and painful tightening of the muscles, usu caused by cold or too much exercise, making movement difficult 痉挛; 抽筋: *The swimmer got cramp in his legs and had to be helped out of the water.* 游泳者两腿抽筋, 不得不由他人救助出水. ○ *writer's cramp*, ie in the muscles of the hand 书写痉挛. **2 cramps** [pl] (*esp US*) severe pain in the stomach 绞痛.

cramp[2] /kræmp; kræmp/ *v* **1** [Tn esp passive 尤用于被动语态] give insufficient space or scope to (sb/sth); hinder or prevent the movement or development of (sb/sth) 限制在狭小的范围内; 阻碍或妨碍(某人[某事物])的活动或发展: *All these difficulties cramped his progress.* 所有这些困难阻碍了他的进步. ○ *I feel cramped by the limitations of my job.* 我觉得受工作束缚, 没有什么奔头儿. **2** (idm 习语) **be cramped for ˈroom/ˈspace** be without enough room, etc 缺乏足够的空间等的: *We're a bit cramped for space in this attic.* 在这间阁楼里我们有点活动不开. **cramp sb's ˈstyle** (*infml* 口) prevent sb from doing sth freely, or as well as he can 使某人不能放开手脚; 使某人不能施展其才能: *It cramps my style to have you watching over me all the time.* 你老是盯着我使我放不开手脚.

▷ **cramped** *adj* **1** (of handwriting) with small letters close together, and therefore difficult to read (指字迹)又小又密而难以辨认的, 密密麻麻的. **2** (of space) narrow and restricted (指空间)狭小的, 受限制的: *Our accommodation is rather cramped.* 我们住的地方很挤.

cramp[3] /kræmp; kræmp/ *n* **1** (also ˈ**cramp-iron**) metal bar with bent ends, used in building for holding together timbers or blocks of stone 两爪钉; 扣钉; 爬钉; 弯头钢筋. **2** = CLAMP 1.

▷ **cramp** *v* [Tn] fasten (sth) with a cramp 用两爪钉钩紧(某物): *cramp a beam, wall, etc* 用两爪钉把梁、墙等接连在一起.

cram·pon /ˈkræmpɒn; ˋkræmpɑn/ *n* (usu *pl* 通常作复数) metal plate with spikes, worn on shoes for walking or climbing on ice and snow (在冰雪上行走及爬坡时安装在鞋底的)带铁钉鞋底.

cran·berry /ˈkrænbərɪ; *US* -berɪ; ˋkrænˌbɛrɪ/ *n* small red slightly sour berry of a small bush, used for making jelly and sauce 越橘.

crane[1] /kreɪn; kren/ *n* **1** large bird with long legs, neck and beak 鹤. **2** machine or vehicle with a long movable arm from which heavy weights can be hung in order to lift or move them 吊车; 起重机. ⇨illus at OIL 见OIL之插图.

crane[2] /kreɪn; kren/ *v* [I, Ipr, Tn, Tn·pr] stretch (one's neck) 伸长(脖子): *crane (forward) in order to get a better view* (向前)伸着脖子好看得清楚一些 ○ *crane one's neck to see sth* 伸长脖子观看某物.

crane-fly /ˈkreɪn flaɪ; ˋkren flaɪ/ (also *infml* 口语亦作 **daddy-ˈlong-legs**) *n* type of fly with very long legs 大蚊(一种足部很长的飞虫).

cra·nium /ˈkreɪnɪəm; ˋkrenɪəm/ *n* (*pl* **~s** or **crania** /ˈkreɪnɪə; ˋkrenɪə/) (*anatomy* 解) bony part of the head enclosing the brain; skull 头盖骨; 颅骨.

▷ **cra·nial** /ˈkreɪnɪəl; ˋkrenɪəl/ *adj* (*anatomy* 解) of the skull 头盖骨的; 颅骨的.

crank[1] /kræŋk; kræŋk/ *n* L-shaped bar and handle for converting to-and-fro movement to circular movement (用以将往复运动变换为圆周运动的)曲柄, 曲轴: *The pedals of a cycle are attached to a crank.* 自行车的踏板与曲柄相连. ⇨illus at App 1 见附录1之插图, page xiii.

▷ **crank** *v* [Tn, Tn·p] ~ **sth (up)** cause sth to turn by means of a crank 用曲柄转动某物: *crank (up) an engine*, ie start it with a crank 用曲柄启动发动机.

□ ˈ**crankshaft** *n* shaft that turns or is turned by a crank 曲柄轴.

crank[2] /kræŋk; kræŋk/ *n* (*derog* 贬) person with strange fixed ideas, esp on a particular subject; eccentric person 有古怪成见的人(尤指在某问题上); 有怪癖的人: *a health-food crank*, ie one who insists on eating unusual food for health reasons 对保健食品有偏好怪癖的人.

▷ **cranky** *adj* (**-ier**, **-iest**) (*infml derog* 口, 贬) **1** strange; eccentric 古怪的; 怪僻的: *a cranky person, idea* 古怪的人、念头. **2** (of machines, etc) unreliable; shaky; unsteady (指机器等)靠不住的; 摇晃的; 不稳的: *a rattling, cranky old engine* 格格作响的、摇晃不稳的旧发动机. **3** (*US*) bad-tempered 脾气坏的.

cranny /ˈkrænɪ; ˋkrænɪ/ *n* **1** small cavity or opening, eg in a wall 小洞, 小窟窿(如墙壁上的). **2** (idm 习语) **every nook and cranny** ⇨ NOOK.

▷ **cran·nied** *adj* full of crannies 满是窟窿的.

crap /kræp; kræp/ *v* (**-pp-**) [I] (⚠ *sl* 讳, 俚) defecate 拉屎: *a dog crapping on the lawn* 在草坪上拉屎的狗.

▷ **crap** *n* (⚠ *sl* 讳, 俚) **1** [U] excrement 屎. **2** [sing] act of defecating 拉屎: *have a crap* 拉屎. **3** [U] nonsense; rubbish 胡扯; 废话: *You do talk a load of crap!* 你净胡说八道!

crappy *adj* (*sl* 俚) bad; worthless; unpleasant 糟糕的; 毫无价值的; 令人生厌的: *a crappy book, party, programme* 没有意思的书、聚会、节目.

crape /kreɪp; krep/ *n* [U] black silk or cotton material with a wrinkled surface, formerly worn as a sign of mourning (旧时为表示哀悼而披戴的)黑色绉绸或绉布. Cf 参看 CREPE.

craps /kræps; kræps/ *n* [sing *v*] (also ˈ**crap-shooting** [U]) (*US*) gambling game played with two dice 掷双色子的赌博戏: *shoot craps*, ie play this game 掷双色子赌博.

▷ **crap** *adj* [attrib 作定语] of or for craps 掷双色子赌博的: *a crap game* 掷双色子的赌博.

crapu·lent /ˈkræpjʊlənt; ˋkræpjulənt/ *adj* (*fml* 文) feeling unwell as a result of eating or drinking too much 因饮食过量而感到不适的. ▷ **crapu·lence** /-ləns; -ləns/ *n* [U].

crash[1] /kræʃ; kræʃ/ *n* **1** (**a**) (usu *sing* 通常作单数) (loud noise made by a) violent fall, blow or breakage 坠落(声); 撞击(声); 破裂(声): *the crash of dishes being dropped* 摔碎盘碟的声音 ○ *The tree fell with a great crash.* 那棵树哗啦一声倒了. ○ *His words were drowned in a crash of thunder.* 他的话为一阵雷声所淹没. (**b**) accident involving a vehicle in a collision or some other impact 撞车; (车辆等)碰撞: *a crash in which two cars collided* 两辆汽车相撞的事故 ○ *a* ˈ*car crash*/*an* ˈ*air crash* 汽车撞车事故[飞机坠毁]. **2** collapse, esp of a business or stock-market 崩溃; 垮台; (尤指)倒闭; (证券市场)暴跌: *The great financial crash in 1929 ruined international trade.* 1929年的经济大萧条摧毁了国际贸易.

▷ **crash** *adj* [attrib 作定语] done intensively to achieve quick results 突击式的; 速成的: *a crash course in computer programming* 计算机程序设计速成课程 ○ *a crash diet* 速效饮食.

crash *adv* with a crash 哗啦一声地: *The vase fell crash on to the tiles.* 花瓶哗啦一声掉在瓷砖上.

□ ˈ**crash barrier** fence, rail, etc to restrain crowds, divide vehicles travelling in opposite directions on a motorway, etc (限制人群通行的)隔离栅; (高速公路等的双程行车道之间的)防撞护栏. ⇨illus at App 1 见附录1之插图, page xiii.

ˈ**crash-dive** *n* sudden dive made by a submarine or an aircraft, eg to avoid being attacked (潜艇或飞机为免受攻击而实行的)紧急下潜或下降. — *v* [I] dive in this way (潜艇)紧急下潜; (飞机)紧急下降.

ˈ**crash helmet** hat made of very strong material (eg metal), worn by motor-cyclists, racing drivers, etc to protect the head (摩托车手、赛车驾驶员等戴的)防撞头盔.

ˌ**crash-**ˈ**land** *v* [I, Tn] land (an aircraft) or be landed roughly in an emergency, usu with resulting damage (使飞行器)强行着陆. ˌ**crash-**ˈ**landing** *n* landing of this kind 强行着陆: *make a crash-landing* 实行强行着陆.

crash[2] /kræʃ; kræʃ/ *v* **1** (**a**) [Ipr, Ip, Tn·pr, Tn·p] fall or strike (sth) suddenly and noisily 突然倒下, 撞击(某物)发出声响: *The rocks crashed (down) onto the car.* 岩石轰隆一声砸在汽车上. ○ *The tree crashed through the window.* 树哗啦一声倒入窗内. ○ *The dishes crashed to the floor.* 碗碟哗啦一声掉在地板上. ○ *She crashed the plates (down) on the table.* 她哗啦一声把那些盘子摔到桌上. (**b**) [I, Ipr, Tn, Tn·pr] ~ **(sth) (into sth)** (cause sth to) have a collision (使某物)猛撞: *The plane crashed (into the mountain).* 飞机撞毁(在山上)了. ○ *He crashed his car (into a wall).* 他把汽车撞(到墙上)了. ○ *a crashed car, plane* 撞毁的汽车、坠毁的飞机. (**c**) [Ipr, Ip, Tn·pr, Tn·p] (cause sth to) move noisily or violently (使某物)轰然或猛然冲, 闯: *an enraged elephant crashing about in the undergrowth* 被激怒了的大象, 在矮树丛中东奔西窜 ○ *He crashed the trolley through the doors.* 他推着小脚轮车乒乒乓乓地过了几道门. **2** [I] make a loud noise 发出巨响: *The thunder crashed.* 雷声隆隆. **3** [I] (of a business company, government, etc) fail suddenly; collapse (指企业、政府等)突然倒台, 崩溃: *The company crashed with debts of £2 million.* 那家公司因负债2百万英镑而告破产. **4** [Tn] (*infml* 口) = GATECRASH (GATE). **5** [Ipr, Ip] ~ **(out)** (*sl* 俚 *esp US*) sleep in an improvised bed, esp when very tired 在临时床铺上睡觉(尤指困极时): *Mind if I crash (out) on your floor tonight?* 今晚我在你家打地铺行吗? **6** (idm 习语) **a crashing** ˈ**bore** very boring person 讨厌鬼.

crass /kræs; kræs/ *adj* (**-er**, **-est**) (*fml derog* 文, 贬) **1** [attrib 作定语] complete; very great; utter 完全的; 十足的; 彻头彻尾的: *crass stupidity, ignorance, etc* 极度的愚钝、无知等. **2** very stupid; insensitive 愚不可及的; 感觉迟钝的: *Don't talk to him: he's so crass.* 别跟他费口舌了, 他太笨了. ▷ **crassly** *adv.* **crass·ness** *n* [U].

-crat *comb form* 构词成分 (forming *ns* 用以构成名词) member or supporter of a type of government or rule 某政体或统治形式的成员或拥护者: *democrat* ○ *technocrat* ○ *bureaucrat.* ▷ **-cratic** (forming *adjs* 用以构成形容词): *aristocratic.*

crate /kreɪt; kret/ *n* **1** (**a**) large wooden container for transporting goods (运货用的)大木箱, 板条箱: *a crate of car components* 一箱汽车零部件. (**b**) container made of metal, plastic, etc divided into compartments for transporting or storing bottles 周转箱(运送或存放瓶子的分格容器): *a crate of milk* 一箱牛奶. ⇨illus at BOX 见 BOX 之插图. **2** (**a**) (*sl joc* 俚, 谑) worn-out car 破旧的汽车. (**b**) (*dated air force sl* 旧, 空军, 俚) aircraft 飞机.

▷ **crate** *v* [Tn, Tn·p] ~ **sth (up)** put sth in a crate 将某物装入大木箱或板条箱中: *crating (up) a machine* 把机器装入大木箱中.

crater /ˈkreɪtə(r); ˋkretɚ/ *n* **1** hole in the top of a volcano 火山口. ⇨illus at VOLCANO 见 VOLCANO 之插图. **2** hole in the ground made by the explosion of a bomb or shell, or by a meteorite landing, etc 弹坑或陨石坑等.

□ ˈ**crater** ˈ**lake** lake in the crater of an extinct volcano 火山口湖.

cra·vat /krəˈvæt; krəˋvæt/ *n* short strip of decorative material worn by men round the neck, folded inside the collar of a shirt 男用围巾(系于衬衫衣领内).

crave /kreɪv; krev/ *v* **1** [Ipr, Tn] ~ **(for) sth** have a strong desire for sth 渴望; 渴求某事物: *I was craving for a drink.* 我非常想喝一点. ○ *giving her the admiration she craves* 给予她渴望得到的赞赏. **2** [Tn] (*arch* 古) ask for (sth) earnestly; beg for 恳求(某事物); 祈求: *crave sb's mercy/forgiveness/indulgence* 恳求某人宽恕[原谅/赦免].

▷ **crav·ing** *n* ~**(for sth)** strong desire 强烈的愿望: *a craving for food* 想吃东西的强烈愿望.

craven /ˈkreɪvn; ˋkrevən/ *adj* (*fml derog* 文, 贬) cowardly 怯懦的; 胆小的: *craven behaviour, submission, etc* 怯懦的行为、顺服的举动 ○ *a craven deserter* 胆怯的逃兵.

craw·fish /ˈkrɔ:fɪʃ; ˋkrɔˌfɪʃ/ *n* (*pl* unchanged 复数不变) = CRAYFISH.

crawl /krɔ:l; krɔl/ *v* **1** [I, Ipr, Ip] (**a**) move slowly, with the body on or close to the ground, or on hands and knees 爬; 爬行; 匍匐行进: *a snake crawling along (the ground)* 在(地上)爬行的蛇 ○ *A baby crawls (around) before it can walk.* 婴儿先能(到处)爬, 然后才会走. ○

The wounded man crawled to the phone. 那伤者爬到电话跟前. (**b**) (of traffic, vehicles, etc) move very slowly (指来往行人、车辆等)缓慢地行进, 徐缓而行: *The traffic crawled over the bridge in the rush-hour.* 在高峰时刻桥上的车辆行驶缓慢. **2** [Ipr] **~ with sth** (esp in the continuous tenses 尤用于进行时态) be covered with, or full of, things that crawl 爬满; 满是爬行之物: *The ground was crawling with ants.* 地上满是蚂蚁. ○ (*fig* 比喻) *The area was crawling with* (ie was full of) *police.* 这个地区布满了警察. **3** [I, Ipr] **~ (to sb)** (*infml derog* 口, 贬) try to gain sb's favour by praising him, doing what will please him, etc 拍马屁: *She's always crawling (to the boss).* 她老是拍(上司的)马屁. **4** (idm 习语) **make one's/sb's flesh crawl/creep** ⇨ FLESH.

C

▷ **crawl** *n* **1** (**a**) [sing] (*derog* 贬) very slow pace 极慢的速度: *traffic moving at a crawl* 缓慢蠕动的来往车辆. (**b**) [C] crawling movement 爬动: *the baby's laborious crawl* 婴儿费劲的爬动. **2** (often 常作 **the crawl**) [sing] fast swimming stroke using overarm movements of each arm in turn, accompanied by rapid kicks with the feet 爬泳; 自由泳: *Can you do the crawl?* 你会自由泳吗?

crawler *n* **1** [C] (*infml derog* 口, 贬) person who crawls (CRAWL 3) 奴颜婢膝的人; 马屁精. **2 crawlers** [pl] overalls made for a baby to crawl about in (婴儿穿的)连衫罩裤.

cray·fish /ˈkreɪfɪʃ; ˋkreˌfɪʃ/ (also **crawfish**) *n* (*pl* unchanged 复数不变) freshwater shellfish like a small lobster (淡水的)螯虾, 小龙虾.

crayon /ˈkreɪən; ˋkreən/ *n* pencil or stick of soft coloured chalk, wax or charcoal, used for drawing (绘画用的)铅笔, 彩色粉笔, 蜡笔, 炭笔: [attrib 作定语] *a crayon drawing* 彩色蜡笔画.

▷ **crayon** *v* [I, Tn] draw (sth) with crayons 用彩色粉笔、蜡笔或炭笔绘画.

craze /kreɪz; krez/ *n* (**a**) **~ (for sth)** enthusiastic, usu brief, interest in sth 对某事物的狂热(通常为时短暂): *a craze for collecting beer-mats* 对搜集啤酒杯垫子的浓厚兴趣 ○ *the current punk-hairstyle craze* 时下对鲜艳彩色发式的狂热. (**b**) object of such an interest 狂热的对象: *Skateboards are the latest craze.* 滑板运动是目前最时兴的玩意儿.

crazed /kreɪzd; krezd/ (also **half-crazed**) *adj* **~ (with sth)** wildly excited; insane 狂热的; 疯狂的: *a crazed look, expression, etc* 狂热的样子、表情等 ○ *She was crazed with grief.* 她悲痛欲绝. ○ *drug-crazed fanatics* 嗜毒如命的瘾君子.

crazy /ˈkreɪzɪ; ˋkrezɪ/ *adj* (**-ier, -iest**) **1** (*infml* 口) (**a**) insane 疯狂的; 精神失常的: *He's crazy; he ought to be locked up.* 他疯了, 应该把他关起来. ○ *That noise is driving me crazy/making me go crazy*, ie annoying me very much. 那噪声吵得我要发狂. (**b**) very foolish; not sensible 荒唐的; 糊涂的: *a crazy person, idea, suggestion* 荒唐的人、念头、建议等 ○ *You must be crazy to go walking in such awful weather.* 你一定头脑发昏了, 这么恶劣的天气还去散步. ○ *She's crazy to lend him the money.* 她把钱借给他, 真糊涂. **2** [pred 作表语] **~ (about sth/sb)** (*infml* 口) wildly excited; enthusiastic 狂热; 热衷: *The kids went crazy when the film star appeared.* 那位影星一出场, 孩子们欣喜若狂. ○ *I'm crazy about steam-engines.* 我对蒸汽机着了迷. ○ *She's crazy about him*, ie loves him a lot. 她为他而神魂颠倒. **3** [attrib 作定语] (of pavements, quilts, etc) made up of irregularly shaped pieces fitted together (指人行道、被褥等)由不规则的碎块拼成的: *crazy paving* 碎纹石路. **4** (idm 习语) **like ˈcrazy** (used as an *adv* 用如副词) (*infml* 口) very intensely; very much 极度; 非常: *work, talk, etc like crazy* 拼命干、讲等 ○ *run like crazy*, ie very fast 拼命跑. ▷ **cra·zily** *adv*. **cra·zi·ness** *n* [U].

creak /kri:k; krik/ *v* [I] make a harsh sound like that of an unoiled door-hinge, or badly-fitting floor-boards when trodden on (作)嘎吱声(如缺油的门铰链或松动的地板踩上去时所发出的刺耳声音): *The wooden cart creaked as it moved along.* 这辆板车走动时嘎吱嘎吱地响. ○ *the creaking joints of an old man* 老头儿咯吧作响的关节.

▷ **creak** *n* such a sound 嘎吱声. **creaky** *adj* (**-ier, -iest**) that creaks 嘎吱作响的: *a creaky floor-board* 嘎吱作响的地板 ○ (*fig* 比喻) *The Government's policy is looking rather creaky*, ie as if about to fail. 政府的政策看来行不通了. **creak·ily** *adv*.

cream[1] /kri:m; krim/ *n* **1** [U] thick yellowish-white liquid that is the fatty part of milk 奶油; 乳脂: *peaches and cream* 奶油桃子 ○ *put cream in one's coffee* 在咖啡里加奶油 ○ *whipped cream* 搅打过的奶油 ○ [attrib 作定语] *cream buns, cake, etc*, ie containing cream 奶油面包、蛋糕等. **2** [C, U] type of food containing or similar to cream 含奶油食品; 奶油状食品: *ice-cream* 冰激凌 ○ *chocolate creams*, ie soft chocolate sweets 巧克力奶糖. **3** [U] smooth paste or thick liquid used as a cosmetic, in medicine, for polishing, etc 乳霜; 乳膏: *ˈface-cream* ○ *ˈcold-cream* ○ *antiseptic cream*. **4 the cream** (also **the crème de la crème**) [sing] **~ (of sth)** the best part of sth 精华; 精髓: *the cream of the crop* 最好的一部分庄稼 ○ *The cream of this year's graduates will get high-paid jobs.* 本届毕业的高材生将获得高薪职位.

▷ **cream** *adj* yellowish-white 淡黄色的; 乳白色的: *a cream dress, jacket, etc* 米色的衣服、夹克等 ○ *cream paper* 淡黄色的纸.

cream·ery /ˈkri:mərɪ; ˋkrimərɪ/ *n* **1** place where milk, cream, butter, etc are sold 乳制品商店. **2** place where butter and cheese are made 乳品厂.

creamy *adj* (**-ier, -iest**) looking and feeling like cream; containing much cream 奶油状的; 奶油般的; 含有大量奶油的: *creamy soup, yoghurt, etc* 奶油汤、酸奶.

□ **ˌcream ˈcheese** soft white cheese containing a lot of cream 奶油干酪.

ˌcream of ˈtartar purified form of tartaric acid, used for making baking powder 酒石; 酒石酸氢钾.

ˈcream ˈtea (Brit) meal consisting of tea with scones, jam and whipped cream (英国)奶油茶点.

cream[2] /kri:m; krim/ *v* [Tn] **1** mash (cooked vegetables, esp potatoes) with added milk or butter until they are soft and smooth 将(熟的蔬菜, 尤指土豆)制成糊状并加入牛奶或黄油. **2** mix (sth) together into a soft smooth paste 将某物搅和成糊状混合物: *cream butter and sugar* 将黄油和糖搅成糊状. **3** (phr v) **cream sb/sth off** take away (the best people or things) 带走(最拔尖的人或物): *The most able pupils are creamed off and put into special classes.* 最有才华的学生被挑选出来编入特别班. ○ *Our best scientists are being creamed off by other countries.* 我们最优秀的科学家被其他国家吸引而外流.

crease /kri:s; kris/ *n* **1** line made on cloth, paper, etc by crushing, folding or pressing 折线; 折缝; 折痕; 皱纹: *iron a crease into one's trousers* 用熨斗在裤子上烫一道折线 ○ *crease-resistant cloth*, ie that does not easily get creases in it 防皱布. **2** wrinkle in the skin, esp on the face 皮肤上(尤指面部)的皱纹: *creases round an old man's eyes* 老人眼边的皱纹. **3** (in cricket) white line made at each end of the pitch to mark the positions of the bowler and batsman (板球)标示投球手和击球手位置的白线. ⇨illus at CRICKET 见 CRICKET 之插图.

▷ **crease** *v* **1** [I, Tn] (cause sth to) get creases; make a crease or creases in (sth) (使某物)起皱; 弄皱(某物): *material that creases easily* 容易起皱的布料 ○ *Pack the clothes carefully so that you don't crease them.* 把衣服细心装好, 免得弄皱了. **2** [Tn, Tn·p] **~ sb (up)** (*Brit infml* 口) amuse sb greatly 使某人乐不可支: *Her jokes really creased me (up).* 她的笑话真笑得我直不起腰来.

cre·ate /kri:ˈeɪt; krɪˋet/ *v* **1** [Tn] cause (sth) to exist; make (sth new or original) 创造; 创建; 创作: *God created the world.* 上帝创造世界. ○ *A novelist creates characters and a plot.* 小说家塑造人物并设计作品的情节. ○ *create a role*, ie (of an actor) be the first to play it 创演角色(指演员为某一角色的最初扮演者) ○ *create more jobs* 提供更多的就业机会. **2** [Tn] have (sth) as a result; produce 引起; 产生: *His shabby appearance creates a bad impression.* 他那寒酸的样子给人留下不好的印象. ○ *The outrageous book created a sensation.* 那部耸人听闻的书曾轰动一时. ○ *create a fuss*, ie express anger, annoyance, etc 发脾气. **3** [Tn, Cn·n esp passive 尤用于被动语态] give (sb) a certain rank 任命; 册封: *create eight new peers* 新封了八个贵族 ○ *He was created Baron of Banthorp.* 他被封为班绍普男爵. **4** [I] (*Brit infml* 口) be angry, cause trouble, etc 生气; 惹事: *She really created because she wasn't served first.* 她的确生气了, 因为没有首先为她服务.

cre·ation /kri:ˈeɪʃn; krɪˋeʃən/ *n* **1** (**a**) [U] action of creating 创造；产生：*the creation of the world in seven days* 七天的创世过程 ○ *the creation of a good impression* 良好印象的产生 ○ *Economic conditions may be responsible for the creation of social unrest.* 经济状况不佳可能是造成社会动乱的根源. (**b**) (usu 通常作 **the Creation**) [sing] making of the world, esp by God as told in the Bible 创造世界(尤指《圣经》中所说的上帝创造世界). **2** (often 常作 **Creation**) [U] all created things 所有的创造物；天地万物：*all of God's creation* 神所创造的一切 ○ *the biggest liar in Creation*, ie a very great liar 瞎话大王. **3** [C] (**a**) thing made, esp by means of skill or intelligence 创造物；(尤指凭借技艺和才智的)作品：*the creations of poets and artists* 诗人和艺术家的作品 ○ *The chef had produced one of his most spectacular creations, a whole roasted swan.* 这位厨师做出了他最拿手的好菜——一整只烤天鹅. (**b**) new type of garment or hat (服装或帽子的)新式样：*the latest creations from London's fashion houses* 伦敦时装商店的最新款式服装.

cre·at·ive /kriːˈeɪtɪv; krɪˋetɪv/ *adj* **1** [attrib 作定语] of or involving creation 创造的；创造性的；创作的：*The writer described the creative process.* 这位作家叙述了创作的过程. ○ *He teaches creative writing*, ie teaches people to write fiction, plays, etc. 他教写作. **2** able to create 有创造力的：*She's very creative; she writes and paints.* 她很有创作能力，既从事写作又从事绘画. ▷ **cre·at·ively** *adv*. **cre·at·ive·ness** *n* [U]. **cre·at·iv·ity** /ˌkriːeɪˈtɪvətɪ; ˌkrieˋtɪvətɪ/ *n* [U].

cre·ator /kriːˈeɪtə(r); krɪˋetɚ/ *n* **1** [C] person who creates 创造者；创作者：*Shakespeare, the creator of Hamlet* 莎士比亚——哈姆雷特的塑造者. **2 the Creator** [sing] God 上帝；造物主.

crea·ture /ˈkriːtʃə(r); ˋkritʃɚ/ *n* **1** living being, esp an animal 生物；(尤指)动物：*dumb creatures*, ie animals 不会说话的动物 ○ *Your dog's a ferocious creature!* 你的狗真凶！○ *creatures from Mars* 来自火星的生物. **2** (with a preceding *adj* 用于形容词之后) person 人：*What a lovely creature!* ie a beautiful woman. 多么美丽的女人哪！○ *a poor creature*, ie a pitiable person 可怜的人. **3** (idm 习语) **sb's creature/the creature of sb** (*fml derog* 文，贬) person who is totally dependent on sb else, and does whatever he wants 受人支配者；(他人的)驯服工具；奴才；走狗：*The king would appoint one of his creatures to the post.* 国王要派他的一名奴仆去任这差事. **a creature of ˈhabit** person whose daily life tends to be governed by habit 习惯的奴隶(日常生活受制于习惯的人).

□ ˌ**creature ˈcomforts** things needed for bodily comfort, eg food, drink, warmth, etc 物质享受所需之事物(如饮食、保暖等).

crèche /kreɪʃ, kreʃ; kreʃ/ *n* **1** (*Brit*) nursery where babies are looked after while their mothers work 托儿所. **2** (*US*) = CRIB.

cre·dence /ˈkriːdns; ˋkridn̩s/ *n* (idm 习语) **attach/give credence to sth** (*fml* 文) believe (gossip, reports, etc) 相信(流言蜚语、传言等)：*I attach little credence to what she says.* 我对她的话姑妄听之. **lend credence to sth/gain credence** (*fml* 文) make sth/become more believable 使某事物[变得]更为可信.

cre·den·tials /krɪˈdenʃlz; krɪˋdɛnʃəlz/ *n* [pl] **1 ~ (for/as sth); ~ (to do sth)** qualities, achievements, etc that make one suitable; qualifications (学历、资历等的)资格：*She has the perfect credentials for the job.* 她做这工作完全够格. **2** documents showing that a person is what he claims to be, is trustworthy, etc (某人合乎条件、可以信任等的)证明书，证件：*I examined his credentials.* 我查验了他的证件.

cred·ible /ˈkredəbl; ˋkrɛdəbl/ *adj* that can be believed; believable 可信的；可靠的：*a credible witness, statement, report* 可信的证人、陈词、报道 ○ *It seems barely credible*, ie seems almost impossible to believe. 这似乎难以置信. ○ *Is there a credible alternative to the nuclear deterrent?* 是否有可以取代核威慑力量的可靠办法？

▷ **cred·ib·il·ity** /ˌkredəˈbɪlətɪ; ˌkrɛdəˋbɪlətɪ/ *n* [U] **1** quality of being believable 可信性；可靠性. **2** quality of being generally accepted and trusted 信用；信誉：*After the recent scandal the Government has lost all credibility.* 经过最近这次丑闻之后，政府完全失去了人们的信任.

cred·ibly /-əblɪ; -əblɪ/ *adv*: *I am credibly informed that…*, ie I have been told by sb who can be believed. 我从可靠的方面获悉….

□ ˌ**crediˈbility gap** difference between what sb says and what is generally thought to be true 信用差距(某人所说的话与公众认为的真相之间的差距)：*the growing credibility gap that crippled Nixon's presidency* 危及尼克松的总统地位的不断扩大的信用差距.

credit[1] /ˈkredɪt; ˋkrɛdɪt/ *n* **1** (**a**) [U] permission to delay payment for goods and services until after they have been received; system of paying in this way 赊购；赊购制度：*refuse/grant sb credit* 拒绝[允许]某人赊购物品 ○ *No credit is given at this shop*, ie Payment must be in cash. 本店概不赊欠. ○ *I bought it on credit*, ie did not have to pay for it until some time after I got it. 我以赊购方式买下了它. ○ *High interest rates make credit expensive.* 由于利率很高，赊购并不划算. ○ *give sb six months' interest-free credit*, ie allow sb to pay within six months, without adding an extra charge for interest 给予某人六个月的无息赊欠期 ○ [attrib 作定语] *a credit period, agreement, limit* 赊欠期限、协议、限额. (**b**) [U] sum of money in sb's bank account (某人银行帐户中的)存款数额：*How much do I have to my credit?* ie How much money is in my account? 我帐上有多少存款？○ *Your account is in credit*, ie There is money in it. 你的帐上有余额. ○ [attrib 作定语] *I have a credit balance of £250.* 我帐上有250英镑的存款余额. (**c**) [C] sum of money lent by a bank, etc; loan (银行等的)借款；贷款：*The bank refused further credits to the company.* 银行拒绝再向这家公司提供贷款. (**d**) [C] (in bookkeeping) (written record of a) payment received (簿记中的)付方，贷方：*Is this item a debit or a credit?* 这笔帐属于借方还是属于贷方？Cf 参看 DEBIT. **2** [U] **~ (for sth)** praise; approval; recognition (used esp with the *vs* shown) 称赞；赏识；表扬(尤与以下示例中的动词连用)：*He got all the credit for the discovery.* 这一发现全都归功于他了. ○ *I can't take any credit; the others did all the work.* 我不能接受任何荣誉，所有的工作都是别人做的. ○ *She was given the credit for what I had done.* 事情是我做的，她却受到称赞. ○ *At least give him credit for trying*, ie praise him, even though he did not succeed. 至少也应该肯定他敢于尝试(虽未取得成功也该给予表扬). ○ *Give credit where it's due.* 该表扬就给予表扬. ○ *There was little credit for those who had worked hardest.* 几乎没表扬那些工作最努力的人. ○ *His courage has brought great credit to/reflects credit on* (ie gives a good reputation to) *his regiment.* 他很勇敢使他所在的团大为增光. **3** [U] belief; trust; confidence 相信；信任；信赖：*The rumour is gaining credit*, ie More and more people believe it. 相信那谣言的人越来越多了. ○ *Recent developments lend credit to* (ie strengthen belief in) *previous reports.* 最近的事态发展说明先前的报道是可靠的. **4 credits** [pl] (also **credit titles**) list of actors, director, cameramen, etc who worked on a film, TV programme, etc, shown at the beginning or end 片头字幕，片尾字幕(在电影、电视节目等的片头或片尾所显示的演员、导演、摄制人员等的名单). **5** [C] (*US education* 教) entry on a record showing that a student has completed a course 学分：*gain credits in Math and English* 取得数学课和英语课的学分. **6** [sing] addition to the reputation or good name of sb/sth 为某人[某事物]增光：*This brilliant pupil is a credit to his teachers.* 这名优秀生为老师增了光. **7** (idm 习语) **be to sb's credit; do sb credit; do credit to sb/sth** make sb worthy of praise 使某人值得赞扬：*Jack, to his credit, refused to get involved.* 杰克好就好在拒不参与. ○ *It is greatly to your credit that you gave back the money you found; your honesty does you credit.* 你拾金不昧是非常难能可贵的；你很诚实，应该受表扬. ○ *His improved performance does credit to his trainer.* 他的表演有进步，这应该归功于他的教练. ○ *It does her credit that she managed not to get angry.* 她沉住气没发脾气，这是值得称赞的. **have sth to one's credit** have achieved sth 完成某事物：*He is only thirty, and already he has four films to his credit*, ie he has made four films. 他才三十岁，却已拍过四部影片了.

□ ˈ**credit account** (*US* **charge account**) account with a shop, store, etc that allows one to pay for goods at fixed intervals (eg monthly) rather than immediately 赊销帐项(商店等为顾客定期，如按月，付款赊购物品

C

的帐项).
ˈ**credit card** card that allows its holder to buy goods and services on credit 信用卡.
ˈ**credit note** (*commerce* 商) note given to a customer who has returned goods to the seller, allowing him to have other goods with a value equal to those returned 信用票据, 贷方单据(退货顾客用以换取等值的其他货物的凭证).
ˈ**credit rating** assessment of how reliable sb is in paying for goods bought on credit (对某人以记帐方式购物的付款情况作出的)信誉评估, 信用等级.
ˈ**credit-side** *n* right-hand side of an account, on which payments received are recorded 付方; 贷方: (*fig* 比喻) *We've lost some experienced players, but on the credit-side* (ie at least there is this favourable aspect) *there are some useful young ones coming into the team.* 我们少了一些有经验的运动员, 然而事情也有好的一面, 有些年轻的生力军加入了本队.
ˈ**credit squeeze** government policy of controlling inflation by making it difficult to borrow money, eg by raising interest rates 信用紧缩(政府为控制通货膨胀而采取的措施, 如借提高利率以增加借款之困难).
ˈ**credit transfer** transfer of money direct from one bank account to another, without using a cheque 银行转帐.
ˈ**credit-worthy** *adj* (of people, business firms, etc) accepted as safe to give credit to, because reliable in making repayment (指人、工商企业等)信用可靠的, 有资格接受贷款的. ˈ**credit-worthiness** *n* [U].

credit[2] /ˈkredɪt; ˋkrɛdɪt/ *v* **1** [Tn·pr] **~ sb/sth with sth; ~ sth to sb/sth** (**a**) believe that sb/sth has sth; attribute sth to sb/sth 认为某人[某事物]有某事物; 把某事物归功于某人[某事物]: *Until now I've always credited you with more sense.* 在这以前, 我一直都认为你不至如此糊涂. ○ *The relics are credited with miraculous powers.* 这些早期遗物被认为具有神奇的力量. ○ *Miraculous powers are credited to the relics.* 人们认为这些早期遗物具有神奇的力量. (**b**) record an amount as being paid into sb's bank account 把金额记入某人银行帐户的贷方: *credit a customer with £8* 把8英镑记入客户贷方 ○ *credit £8 to a customer/an account* 在客户[帐户]的贷方记入8英镑. **2** [Tn] (used mainly in questions and negative sentences 主要用于疑问句及否定句) believe (sth) 相信(某事物): *Would you credit it?* ie It is incredible. 你相信吗? ○ *I can barely credit what she said.* 我简直不能相信她的话.

cred·it·able /ˈkredɪtəbl; ˋkrɛdɪtəbl̩/ *adj* **~ (to sb)** deserving praise (although perhaps not outstandingly good); bringing credit[1](2) 值得赞扬的(虽然可能并非特别好); 带来荣誉的: *a creditable attempt, performance, etc* 值得赞扬的努力、表现等 ○ *creditable work, progress, etc* 应予肯定的工作、进步等 ○ *conduct that is very creditable to him* 给他带来极好声誉的行为. ▷ **cred·it·ably** /ˈkredɪtəblɪ; ˋkrɛdɪtəblɪ/ *adv*: *She performed very creditably in the exam.* 她考得好极了.

cred·itor /ˈkredɪtə(r); ˋkrɛdɪtɚ/ *n* person to whom money is owed 债主; 债权人: *His creditors are demanding to be paid.* 他的那些债主正在讨债.

credo /ˈkriːdəʊ, ˈkreɪdəʊ; ˋkrido, ˋkredo/ *n* (*pl* **~s**) creed 信条: *her extremist political credo* 她那极端主义的政治信条.

cre·du·lity /krɪˈdjuːlətɪ; *US* -ˈduː-; krəˋdulətɪ/ *n* [U] too great a readiness to believe things 轻信: *a statement which stretches/strains one's credulity to the limit,* ie is almost impossible to believe 简直难以置信的陈述.

credu·lous /ˈkredjʊləs; *US* -dʒə-; ˋkrɛdʒələs/ *adj* too ready to believe things 轻信的: *credulous people who believe what the advertisements say* 轻信广告的人. ▷ **credu·lously** *adv*.

creed /kriːd; krid/ *n* **1** [C] system of beliefs or opinions, esp religious beliefs 信条, 教义(尤指宗教信仰): *people of all colours and creeds,* ie of all sorts 各种肤色和各种宗教信仰的人 ○ *What is your political creed?* 你的政治信仰如何? **2 the Creed** [sing] short summary of Christian belief, esp as said or sung as part of a church service 使徒信条.

creek /kriːk; *US also* krɪk; krik/ *n* **1** (*Brit*) narrow stretch of water flowing inland from a coast; inlet 小海湾; 小港湾. **2** (*US*) small river; stream 小河; 溪流. **3** (idm 习语) **up the ˈcreek** (*infml* 口) in difficulties 处于困境: *I'm really up the creek without my car.* 我没有了汽车实在不方便.

creel /kriːl; kril/ *n* angler's wicker basket for holding the fish he catches (钓鱼者用的)鱼篓.

creep /kriːp; krip/ *v* (*pt, pp* **crept**) **1** [Ipr, Ip] move slowly, quietly or stealthily, esp crouching low 慢慢地、悄悄地或偷偷地移动(尤指弯着腰走): *The cat crept silently towards the bird.* 那只猫一声不响地接近那只鸟. ○ *She crept up to him from behind.* 她从后面蹑手蹑脚地走近他. ○ *The thief crept along the corridor.* 那个贼偷偷摸摸地穿过走廊. ○ (*fig* 比喻) *A feeling of drowsiness crept over him.* 他不禁感到昏昏欲睡. ○ (*fig* 比喻) *Old age creeps up on you* (ie approaches you stealthily) *before you realize it.* 人不知不觉地就变老了. ⇨Usage at PROWL 用法见PROWL. **2** [I, Ipr, Ip] (of plants) grow along the ground, up walls, etc (指植物)蔓生, 匍匐, 攀附: *Ivy had crept up the castle walls.* 常春藤爬上了城堡的围墙. ○ *a creeping vine* 蔓生的葡萄树. **3** (idm 习语) **make one's/sb's flesh crawl/creep** ⇨ FLESH.
▷ **creep** *n* **1** (*infml derog* 口, 贬) person who tries to win sb's favour by always agreeing with him, doing things for him, etc 溜须拍马的人. **2** (idm 习语) **give sb the ˈcreeps** (*infml* 口) (**a**) (of fear or horror) cause an unpleasant sensation in the skin, as if things are creeping over it (指恐惧或憎恶)毛骨悚然, 汗毛直竖, 起鸡皮疙瘩. (**b**) make sb feel extreme dislike; repel sb 使某人厌恶或反感: *I don't like him: he gives me the creeps.* 我不喜欢他, 他这人很讨厌.
creep·ing *adj* [attrib 作定语] (of sth bad) gradual (指坏事)逐渐发展的, 日趋严重的: *The disease results in creeping paralysis.* 这种病可发展成脊髓痨. ○ *creeping inflation in the housing market* 房产价格的不断上涨.

creeper /ˈkriːpə(r); ˋkripɚ/ *n* plant that grows along the ground, up walls, etc, often winding itself round other plants 匍匐植物; 攀援植物.

creepy /ˈkriːpɪ; ˋkripɪ/ *adj* (**-ier**, **-iest**) (*infml* 口) **1** causing or having an unpleasant feeling of fear or horror 令人毛骨悚然的; 不寒而栗的: *a creepy ghost story* 令人毛骨悚然的鬼故事 ○ *a sight that makes you feel creepy* 使人不寒而栗的情景. **2** disturbingly strange 怪异的; 离奇的: *That was a really creepy coincidence.* 那样的巧合实在太离奇了.

creepy-crawly /ˌkriːpɪˈkrɔːlɪ; ˌkripɪˋkrɔlɪ/ *n* (*infml esp joc* 口, 尤作戏谑语) insect, spider, etc thought of as unpleasant or frightening (使人厌恶或使人害怕的)昆虫、蜘蛛等.

cre·mate /krɪˈmeɪt; ˋkrimet/ *v* [Tn] burn (a dead body) to ashes, esp ceremonially at a funeral 火化(尸体); (尤指)火葬: *He wants to be cremated, not buried.* 他要火葬, 不要土葬.
▷ **cre·ma·tion** /krɪˈmeɪʃn; krɪˋmeʃən/ *n* [C, U] (act of) cremating 火化; 火葬.
crem·at·or·ium /ˌkreməˈtɔːrɪəm; ˌkrɛməˋtɔrɪəm/ *n* (*pl* **~s** or **-oria** /-ɔːrɪə; -ɔrɪə/) (also *esp US* **crem·at·ory**) /ˈkremətərɪ; *US* -tɔːrɪ; ˋkriməˌtorɪ/ building in which bodies are cremated 火葬场.

crème de la crème /ˌkrem də lɑː ˈkrem; ˌkrɛmdəla-ˋkrɛm/ *n* **the crème de la crème** (*French* 法) = CREAM 4.

crème de menthe /ˌkrem də ˈmɒnθ; krɛmdəˋmɛnθ/ *n* [U, C] (*French* 法) sweet thick green liqueur flavoured with peppermint 薄荷甜酒.

cren·el·lated (*US* **-el·ated**) /ˈkrenəleɪtɪd; ˋkrɛnl̩ˌetɪd/ *adj* having battlements 有雉堞的: *a crenellated castle/wall* 有雉堞的城堡[墙]. ⇨illus at CASTLE 见CASTLE之插图.

cre·ole /ˈkriːəʊl; ˋkriol/ *n* **1** [C, U] language formed by a blending of two other languages, and used as the main language in the community in which it is spoken 混合语(由不同语言混合而成, 用作某群体的主要语言). Cf 参看 PIDGIN. **2** (usu 通常作 **Creole**) [C] (**a**) descendant (either direct or of mixed European and African descent) of the original European settlers in the West Indies or Spanish America (西印度群岛的或通用西班牙语的美洲国家的)克里奥尔人(欧洲初期移民的后裔, 或这些移民与非洲人的混血后代). (**b**) descendant of the original French or Spanish settlers in the southern states of the USA (美国南方各州的)克里奥尔人(法国

或西班牙初期移民的后裔): [attrib 作定语] *Creole cuisine* 克里奥尔式烹饪.

creo·sote /ˈkrɪəsəʊt; ˋkriə,sot/ *n* [U] thick brown oily liquid obtained from coal tar, used to preserve wood 杂酚油, 木馏油(木材防腐剂).

▷ **creo·sote** *v* [Tn] paint (sth) with creosote 用杂酚油涂(某物).

crepe (also ˌ**crêpe**) /ˈkreɪp; krep/ *n* **1** [U] light thin fabric with a wrinkled surface 绉绸; 绉布; 绉织品. Cf 参看 CRAPE. **2** (also ˌ**crepe ˈrubber**) [U] tough rubber produced in sheets with a wrinkled surface, used for the soles of shoes 绉胶: *crepe-soled shoes* 绉胶底的鞋.

□ ˌ**crepe ˈpaper** thin paper with a wavy or wrinkled surface 绉纹纸.

crep·it·ate /ˈkrepɪteɪt; ˋkrɛpə,tet/ *v* [I] (*fml or medical* 文或医) make sharp crackling or grating sounds 发爆裂声; 发磨擦声.

▷ **crep·ita·tion** /ˌkrepɪˈteɪʃn; ˌkrɛpəˋteʃən/ *n* [U, C] (*fml or medical* 文或医) crepitating (sound) 爆裂声; 磨擦声: *the telltale crepitation of a broken bone* 显示骨折的爆裂声.

crept *pt, pp* of CREEP.

cre·pus·cu·lar /krɪˈpʌskjʊlə(r); krɪˋpʌskjələ˞/ *adj* (*fml* 文) **1** of or like twilight; dim 黎明或黄昏(般)的; 朦胧的; 昏暗的: *crepuscular shadows* 阴影. **2** (of animals) active at twilight or dawn (指动物)在黎明或黄昏时分活动的: *Bats are crepuscular creatures.* 蝙蝠是在黎明或黄昏时分活动的动物.

cres·cendo /krɪˈʃendəʊ; krəˋʃɛndo/ *adj, adv* (*music* 音) of or with increasing loudness (指音乐)渐强的: *a crescendo passage* 渐强的乐节.

▷ **cres·cendo** *n* (*pl* **~s**) **1** (*music* 音) gradual increase in loudness (音量的)渐强. **2** (*fig* 比喻) climax; high point 高潮; 顶点: *The advertising campaign reached a crescendo at Christmas.* 在圣诞节期间, 广告战已达到高潮. Cf 参看 DIMINUENDO.

crescent 新月形状

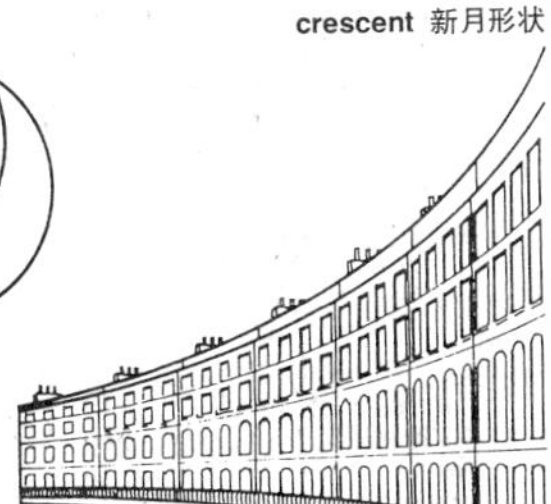

cres·cent /ˈkresnt; ˋkrɛsn̩t/ *n* **1** [C] (**a**) (thing with a) narrow curved shape that tapers to a point at each end, like the new moon 新月形(物); 月牙形(物). (**b**) (street consisting of a) semicircular row of houses or other buildings 半圆形的一排房屋或其他建筑物; 半圆形的街区 ⇨illus 见插图. **2 the Crescent** [sing] (*fig* 比喻) the faith and religion of Islam 伊斯兰教: *the Cross* (ie Christianity) *and the Crescent* 基督教和伊斯兰教.

cress /kres; krɛs/ *n* [U] any of various small plants with hot-tasting leaves used in salads and sandwiches 水芹(叶味辛辣, 用于色拉和三明治).

crest /krest; krɛst/ *n* **1** tuft of feathers on a bird's head 羽冠. **2** (**a**) top of a slope or hill 坡顶; 山顶. (**b**) white top of a large wave 浪尖; 波峰. ⇨illus at SURFING 见SURFING之插图. **3** design above the shield on a coat of arms, often represented on a seal or on notepaper (盾形纹章上方的)饰章(常用于印信或信笺): *the family crest*, ie one above the family's coat of arms 家族饰章(标记于家族的盾形纹章上方的). **4** (**a**) decorative tuft or plume formerly worn on top of a soldier's helmet (旧时军人头盔顶上的)羽饰. (**b**) (*fig rhet* 比喻, 修辞) helmet 头盔. **5** (idm 习语) **on the crest of a ˈwave** at the point of greatest success, happiness, etc 在最成功、最得意的时候: *After its election victory, the party was on the crest of a wave.* 该党在选举获胜后如日中天.

▷ **crest** *v* **1** [Tn] reach the crest of (a hill, etc) 达到(山等)的顶端: *As we crested the hill, we saw the castle.* 我们登上山顶, 看见了城堡. **2** [I] (of a wave) form into a crest (指波浪)形成浪尖.

crested *adj* [attrib 作定语] **1** having a crest(3) 有饰章的: *crested notepaper* 有饰章的信笺. **2** (used in names of birds 用在鸟类名称中) having a crest(1) 有羽冠的: *the great crested grebe* 有羽冠的大鸊鷉.

crest·fal·len /ˈkrestfɔːlən; ˋkrɛst,fɔlən/ *adj* sad because of unexpected failure, disappointment, etc 垂头丧气的; 心灰意懒的.

cre·ta·ceous /krɪˈteɪʃəs; krɪˋteʃəs/ *adj* (*geology* 地质) **1** of or like chalk 白垩质的; 似白垩的: *cretaceous rock* 白垩质的岩石. **2 Cretaceous** of the geological period when chalk-rocks were formed 白垩纪: *Cretaceous fossils* 白垩纪的化石.

C

cretin /ˈkretɪn; *US* ˈkriːtn; ˋkritɪn/ *n* **1** (*medical* 医) person who is deformed and of very low intelligence because of a disease of the thyroid gland 呆小病(克汀病)患者. **2** (⚠ *offensive* 讳, 蔑) very stupid person 笨蛋; 白痴: *Why did you do that, you cretin?* 你为什么做那事, 你这个笨蛋? ▷ **cret·in·ous** /ˈkretɪnəs; *US* ˈkriːt-; ˋkritɪnəs/ *adj*.

cre·tonne /ˈkretɒn; krɪˋtɑn/ *n* [U] thick cotton cloth with printed designs, used for curtains, furniture covers, etc 印花厚棉布(作窗帘、家具套等).

cre·vasse /krɪˈvæs; krəˋvæs/ *n* deep open crack in the ice of a glacier (冰川的)裂口, 裂隙.

crev·ice /ˈkrevɪs; ˋkrɛvɪs/ *n* narrow opening or crack in a rock, wall, etc (岩石、墙壁等的)裂缝, 缺口.

crew[1] /kruː; kru/ *n* [CGp] **1** (**a**) people working on a ship, an aircraft, an oil-rig, etc (轮船、飞行器、钻井平台等上的)工作人员. (**b**) these people, except the officers (上述的)工作人员(不包括高级职员): *the officers and crew of the SS London* 伦敦号轮船的全体工作人员. (**c**) rowing team 划艇队: *the Cambridge crew* 剑桥大学赛艇队. **2** group of people working together; gang 一道工作的班子; 队; 组: *a track-repair crew* 轨道维修组 ○ *a camera crew* 电影(或电视)摄制组. **3** (*usu derog* 通常作贬义) group of people (人的)一伙, 一帮: *The people she'd invited were a pretty motley crew.* 她请的人相当杂.

▷ **crew** *v* [I, Ipr, Tn] **~ (for sb/on sth)** act as (a member of) the crew on (sth) 充当(某集体)的工作人员: *Will you crew for me on my yacht?* 你愿意在我的快艇上当水手吗? ○ *Men are needed to crew the lifeboat.* 需要有人来做救生艇的船员.

□ ˈ**crew cut** very short hair-style for men 平头.

ˈ**crew neck** type of round close-fitting collar, esp on a pullover 圆式紧衣领(尤指套头毛衣的). ⇨illus at NECK 见NECK之插图.

crew[2] *pt* of CROW[2].

crib[1] /krɪb; krɪb/ *n* **1** [C] wooden framework for holding animal food; manger 饲料槽. **2** [C] (*esp US*) = COT 1. **3** (*US* **crèche**) [C] model, eg in a church at Christmas, representing Christ's birth in Bethlehem 马厩图(如基督教会圣诞节所陈列的马厩模型, 展示基督在伯利恒诞生之情景). **4** [U] = CRIBBAGE.

▷ **crib** *v* (**-bb-**) [Tn, Tn·p] **~ sb (up)** (*arch* 古) confine sb in a small space 将某人关在狭小的空间内.

crib[2] /krɪb; krɪb/ *n* **1** thing copied dishonestly from the work of another, eg in an examination 抄袭他人之物(如考试中): *This answer must be a crib: it's exactly the same as Jones's.* 这个答案可能是抄袭来的, 跟琼斯的答案一模一样. **2** thing used as an aid to understanding, eg an exact translation of a foreign text one is studying 有助于理解之物(如学外语者用的对照译文).

▷ **crib** *v* (**-bb-**) [I, Ipr, Tn, Tn·pr] **~ (sth) (from/off sb)** copy (another student's written work) dishonestly 抄袭(另一学生的作业等): *In the exam, I cribbed (an answer) from the girl next to me.* 考试时我抄袭了挨着我坐的一个女生的答案.

crib·bage /ˈkrɪbɪdʒ; ˋkrɪbɪdʒ/ (also **crib**) *n* [U] card-game for two, three or four players, in which the score is kept by putting small pegs in holes in a board 一种两人、三人或四人玩的纸牌游戏(用木钉插在有孔的木板上记分).

□ ˈ**cribbage board** board for keeping the score in

cribbage 玩上述纸牌戏时用来插木钉的记分板.

crick /krɪk; krɪk/ *n* [sing] painful stiffness, esp in the neck 痛性强直(尤指颈肌): *to have/get a crick in one's neck/back* 患颈部[背部]肌肉痛性强直.

▷ **crick** *v* [Tn] get a crick in (sth) 引起(身体某处)肌肉强直: *to crick one's neck/back* 引起颈部[背部]肌肉强直.

cricket[1] /ˈkrɪkɪt; ˋkrɪkɪt/ *n* small brown jumping insect that makes a shrill sound by rubbing its front wings together 蟋蟀: *the chirping of crickets* 蟋蟀的唧唧叫声.

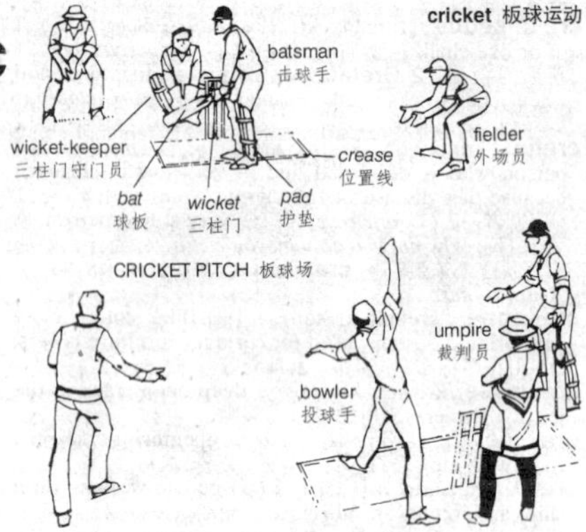

cricket[2] /ˈkrɪkɪt; ˋkrɪkɪt/ *n* **1** [U] game played on grass by two teams of 11 players each, in which a ball is bowled at stumps and a batsman tries to hit it with a bat, and the score is made in runs 板球运动: [attrib 作定语] *a cricket match, ball, team etc* 板球比赛、板球运动用的球、板球队等. ⇨illus 见插图. ⇨App 4 见附录4. **2** (idm 习语) **not ˈcricket** (*dated Brit sl* 旧, 俚) unfair; not honourable 不公正; 不光明磊落: *You can't do it without telling him; it just isn't cricket.* 你不能不告诉他一声就做那件事, 这不够光明磊落.

▷ **crick·eter** *n* cricket player 板球运动员.

cried *pt, pp* of CRY[1].

crier /ˈkraɪə(r); ˋkraɪɚ/ *n* = TOWN CRIER (TOWN).

cries /kraɪz; kraɪz/ **1** *3rd pers sing pres t* of CRY[1]. **2** *pl* of CRY[2].

cri·key /ˈkraɪkɪ; ˋkraɪkɪ/ *interj* (*Brit infml* 口) (used to express surprise, fear, etc 用以表示惊讶、恐惧等): *Crikey! What a big dog!* 嗳呀! 好大的狗哇!

crime /kraɪm; kraɪm/ *n* **1** (**a**) [C] offence for which one may be punished by law 罪; 罪行: *commit a serious crime* 犯重罪 ○ *a minor crime like shoplifting* 入店行窃之类的小罪 ○ *convicted of crimes against humanity* 被判犯有违反人性的罪行. (**b**) [U] such offences; law-breaking 犯罪活动; 不法行为: *an increase in crime* 犯罪活动的增加 ○ *The police prevent and detect crime.* 警察的职责是防止和侦查犯罪活动. ○ *He took to a life of crime*, ie became a criminal. 他已沦为罪犯. ○ [attrib 作定语] *crime prevention, rates* 防止犯罪的措施、犯罪率 ○ *crime fiction, writers, novels, etc*, ie dealing with crime, its detection, etc 描写犯罪活动的小说、作家、长篇小说等. **2** (usu 通常作 **a crime**) [sing] foolish or immoral act 愚蠢的行为; 缺德行为: *It's a crime to waste money like that.* 那样浪费金钱是一种罪过. ○ *It's a crime the way he bullies his children.* 像他那样欺负自己的孩子真缺德.

▷ **crim·inal** /ˈkrɪmɪnl; ˋkrɪmənḷ/ *adj* **1** [usu attrib 通常作定语] of or being crime 刑事的; 犯罪的: *criminal offences, damage, negligence, etc* 刑事犯罪、损害罪、过失罪等. **2** [attrib 作定语] concerned with crime 关于犯罪的: *criminal law* 刑法 ○ *a criminal lawyer* 刑事辩护律师. Cf 参看 CIVIL 4. **3** disgraceful; immoral 可耻的; 不道德的: *a criminal waste of public money* 浪费公款的可耻行为 ○ *It's criminal the way she lies and cheats to get what she wants.* 她用说谎和欺诈的手段来满足自己的欲望, 真可耻. — *n* person who commits a crime or crimes 犯人; 罪犯. **crim·in·ally** /-nəlɪ; -nḷɪ/ *adv*: *criminally insane* 疯狂地进行犯罪活动的.

crim·ino·logy /ˌkrɪmɪˈnɒlədʒɪ; ˌkrɪməˋnɑlədʒɪ/ *n* [U] scientific study of crime 犯罪学. ▷ **crim·ino·lo·gist** /-dʒɪst; -dʒɪst/ *n*.

crimp /krɪmp; krɪmp/ *v* [Tn] (**a**) press (cloth, paper, etc) into small folds or ridges 把(布、纸等)压出小的褶痕或皱纹. (**b**) make (hair) wavy by pressing with a hot iron 把(毛发)烫成拳曲状; 烫发.

crim·plene /ˈkrɪmpli:n; ˋkrɪmplin/ *n* [U] (*propr* 专利名) cloth that does not crease easily, often used for dresses, shirts, etc 克林普纶(一种不易起皱的布料).

crim·son /ˈkrɪmzn; ˋkrɪmzn̩/ *adj, n* [U] (of a) deep red 深红色(的); 绯红(的).

▷ **crim·son** *v* [I, Tn] (*fml* 文) (cause sb/sth to) become crimson (使某人[某事物])呈现红色; 变成深红色: *crimson* (ie blush) *with embarrassment* 因难为情而脸红.

□ ˌ**crimson ˈlake** = LAKE[2].

cringe /krɪndʒ; krɪndʒ/ *v* **1** [I, Ipr] **~ (at/from sth)** move back or lower one's body in fear; cower (因恐惧而)退缩, 蜷缩; 畏缩: *a child cringing in terror* 吓得直退缩的孩子 ○ *The dog cringed at the sight of the whip.* 那只狗见到鞭子就退缩了. ○ (*fig* 比喻) *I cringe with embarrassment* (ie feel very embarrassed) *when I reread those first stories I wrote.* 我重读了我初期编写的故事, 感到十分难为情. **2** [I, Ipr] **~ (to/before sb)** (*derog* 贬) behave too humbly towards sb who is more powerful 卑躬屈膝: *She's always cringing to the boss.* 她在上司面前总是卑躬屈膝.

crinkle /ˈkrɪŋkl; ˋkrɪŋkḷ/ *n* wrinkle or thin crease, esp in material such as tin foil or paper, or in skin 褶痕, 皱纹(尤指锡箔或纸等材料上或皮肤上的).

▷ **crinkle** *v* [I, Ip, Tn, Tn·p] **~ (sth) (up)** (cause sth to) have crinkles; produce crinkles in (sth) (使某物)起皱; 使(某物)出现皱纹: *crinkle the tin foil (up) by squeezing it* 把锡箔压出皱纹 ○ *the dead plant's crinkled leaves* 死亡植物的皱叶.

crinkly /ˈkrɪŋklɪ; ˋkrɪŋklɪ/ *adj* (**-ier, -iest**) (**a**) having crinkles 有皱纹的. (**b**) (of hair) having tight curls (指毛发)拳曲得很厉害的.

crin·ol·ine /ˈkrɪnəlɪn; ˋkrɪnḷɪn/ *n* light framework covered with fabric, formerly worn under a long skirt to make it stand out 裙撑(为表面包上织物的轻质支架, 旧时女子用以撑起长裙).

cripes /kraɪps; kraɪps/ *interj* (*dated sl* 旧, 俚) (used to express astonishment, etc 用以表示惊讶等): *Cripes! It just disappeared!* 啊呀! 那东西不见了!

cripple /ˈkrɪpl; ˋkrɪpḷ/ *n* person who is unable to walk or move properly because of disease or injury to the spine or legs 瘸子; 伤残人.

▷ **cripple** *v* [Tn usu passive 通常用于被动语态] **1** make (sb) a cripple 使(某人)成为瘸子; 使(某人)残废: *crippled by polio* 因患小儿麻痹症而致残 ○ *crippled with rheumatism* 因患风湿病而瘸腿 ○ *their crippled daughter* 他们那伤残的女儿. **2** (*fig* 比喻) damage or weaken (sth) seriously 严重损坏或削弱(某事物): *a ship crippled by a storm* 在暴风雨中受到严重损坏的船只 ○ *The business has been crippled by losses.* 这家企业因亏损而陷入困境. ○ *The country has crippling* (ie extremely large) *debts.* 这个国家债务极重.

cri·sis /ˈkraɪsɪs; ˋkraɪsɪs/ *n* (*pl* **crises** /ˈkraɪsi:z; ˋkraɪsiz/) [C, U] time of great difficulty or danger; decisive moment in illness, life, history, etc 危机; (疾病、生命、历史等的)决定性时刻: *a financial, political, domestic, etc crisis* 财政、政治、国内等危机 ○ *come to/reach a crisis* 陷入危机 ○ *In times of crisis it's good to have a friend to turn to.* 危难时好在有朋友可以投奔. ○ *a government in crisis*, ie going through a difficult period 危机中的政府 ○ *The fever passed its crisis*, ie its most dangerous point. 发烧已过了危险期. ○ [attrib 作定语] *The Government is holding crisis talks with the unions.* 政府正与工会组织举行解决危机的会谈.

crisp /krɪsp; krɪsp/ *adj* (**-er, -est**) (*usu approv* 通常作褒义) **1** (**a**) (esp of food) hard, dry and easily broken (尤指食品)脆的: *a crisp biscuit* 脆饼干 ○ *crisp pastry, toast, etc* 酥脆的糕饼、再烤的面包片等 ○ *The snow was crisp underfoot.* 雪踩上去是脆的. (**b**) (esp of fruit or vegetables) firm and fresh (尤指水果、蔬菜)脆生而新鲜的: *a crisp apple, lettuce, etc* 脆生而新鲜的苹果、生菜等. (**c**) (esp of paper) slightly stiff (尤指纸张)挺括的: *a crisp new £5 note* 一张挺括的5英镑新钞票. **2** (of the air or the weather) dry and cold (指空气、天气)干冷的: *a crisp winter morning* 冬天的一个干冷的早晨 ○ *the crisp air of an autumn day* 秋日的凉爽空气. **3** (of curls in hair) tight (指毛发的拳曲状)紧的. **4** (of sb's manner, way of speaking, etc) brisk, precise and decisive (指态度、说话方式等)干脆的, 斩钉截铁的: *a crisp order* 果断坚决的命令 ○ *crisp speech* 干净利落的讲话 ○ *a crisp and clear answer* 干脆明确的回答.

▷ **crisp** *n* **1** (also **po,tato 'crisp**, *US* **potato chip**, **chip**) thin slice of potato, fried and dried, often flavoured and sold in packets 油炸土豆片(常以小包装出售). ⇨illus at POTATO 见 POTATO之插图. **2** (idm 习语) **burn sth to a crisp** ⇨ BURN. **crisp** *v* [Tn, Tn·p] **~ sth (up)** make sth crisp 使某物变脆: *crisp the bread up in the oven* 把面包放在烤箱里烤脆.

crisply *adv* in a crisp(4) manner 干脆地; 斩钉截铁地.

crisp·ness *n* [U].

crispy *adj* (**-ier**, **-iest**) (*infml* 口) = CRISP *adj* 1a, b: *crispy bacon* 发脆的腌猪肉.

criss-cross /ˈkrɪskrɒs; *US* -krɔːs; ˋkrɪs,krɔs/ *adj* [attrib 作定语], *adv* with lines crossing each other 十字形的; 纵横交错地: *a criss-cross pattern, design, etc* 十字形图案、花样等 ○ *electricity cables erected criss-cross over the countryside* 纵横交错地架设在乡村地区的电缆.

▷ **criss-cross** *v* **1** [I, Tn] form a criss-cross pattern (on sth) (在某物上)构成十字图案: *Railway lines criss-cross in a dense network.* 铁路线纵横交错密如蛛网. ○ *Rivers criss-cross the landscape.* 河流纵横交错点缀着此处风景. **2** [Tn, Tn·pr usu passive 通常用于被动语态] **~ sth (with sth)** mark sth with lines that cross 在某物上作十字形标记: *a sheet criss-crossed with pencil marks* 用铅笔画有十字记号的一张纸.

cri·terion /kraɪˈtɪərɪən; kraɪˋtɪrɪən/ *n* (*pl* **-ria** /-rɪə; -rɪə/) standard by which sth is judged (评判的)标准, 尺度: *Success in making money is not always a good criterion of success in life.* 能挣钱并不一定是衡量人生幸福的可靠标准. ○ *What are the criteria for deciding* (ie How do we decide) *who gets the prize?* 评定获奖者以什么作标准?

critic /ˈkrɪtɪk; ˋkrɪtɪk/ *n* **1** person who expresses a low opinion of sb/sth, points out faults in sb/sth, etc 批评者: *I am my own severest critic.* 我是个严于律己者. ○ *She confounded her critics by breaking the record*, ie They said she would not be able to do so, but she did. 她打破了纪录, 这把批评她的人弄得狼狈不堪. **2** person who evaluates and describes the quality of sth, esp works of art, literature, music, etc 评论员, 评论家(尤指对艺术、文学、音乐等作品): *a music, theatre, literary, etc critic* 音乐、戏剧、文学等评论员 ○ *a play praised by the critics* 评论家交口称誉的剧本.

crit·ical /ˈkrɪtɪkl; ˋkrɪtɪkl/ *adj* **1 ~ (of sb/sth)** looking for faults; pointing out faults 找出毛病的; 指出缺点的; 批评的; 非难的: *a critical remark, report, etc* 批评性的议论、报道等 ○ *The inquiry was critical of her work.* 该项调查对她的工作提出了批评. ○ (*derog* 贬) *Why are you always so critical?* 你怎么老是这样吹毛求疵? ○ (*approv* 褒) *Try to develop a more critical attitude, instead of accepting everything at face value.* 要学会对一切事物一丝不苟, 而不要注重表面现象. **2** [attrib 作定语] of the art of making judgements on literature, art, etc (文学、艺术等)评论手法的: *In the current critical climate her work is not popular.* 在当前的评论风气的影响下, 她的作品不怎么受欢迎. ○ *The film has received critical acclaim*, ie praise from the critics. 影片得到了评论界的赞誉. **3** of or at a crisis; decisive; crucial 危机中的; 危急时刻的; 决定性的; 关键的: *We are at a critical time in our history.* 我们正处于历史的紧要关头. ○ *The patient's condition is critical*, ie He is very ill and may die. 病人情况危殆. ○ *Her help was critical* (ie of great importance) *during the emergency.* 在紧急的情况下她的援助至为重要. **4** (idm 习语) **go 'critical** (of a nuclear reactor) reach a state where a nuclear reaction sustains itself (指核反应堆)达到临界状态. ▷ **crit·ic·ally** /-ɪklɪ; -ɪklɪ/ *adv*: *speak critically of sb* 非议某人 ○ *He is critically ill.* 他病得很重.

□ **,critical 'path analysis** the study of a set of operations (eg in building a ship) to decide the quickest and most efficient order in which to do them 关键途径分析法(分析整体工作以制定出最快、最有效的程序). **,critical 'temperature** temperature below which a gas cannot be liquefied 临界温度.

cri·ti·cism /ˈkrɪtɪsɪzəm; ˋkrɪtə,sɪzəm/ *n* **1** (**a**) [U] looking for faults; pointing out faults 批评; 非难: *a scheme that is open to criticism* 有待批评的方案 ○ *He hates/can't take criticism*, ie being criticized. 他不喜欢[不能接受]别人的批评. (**b**) [C] remark that points out a fault or faults 批评意见: *I have two criticisms of your plan.* 我对你的计划有两条批评意见. **2** (**a**) [U] art of making judgements on literature, art, etc 文学、艺术等的评论: *literary criticism* 文学批评. (**b**) [C] such a judgement 评论文章.

cri·ti·cize, -ise /ˈkrɪtɪsaɪz; ˋkrɪtə,saɪz/ *v* **1** [I, Tn, Tn·pr, Tsg] **~ sb/sth (for sth)** point out the faults of sb/sth 批评某人[某事物]; 挑剔; 非难: *Stop criticizing (my work)!* 别再挑剔(我那作品)了! ○ *He was criticized by the committee for failing to report the accident.* 他由于未对事故进行汇报而受到委员会的批评. ○ *He criticized my taking risks.* 他批评了我的冒险举动. **2** [Tn] form and express a judgement on (a work of art, literature, etc) 评论(艺术、文学等作品): *teaching students how to criticize poetry* 向学生讲授评论诗歌的方法.

cri·tique /krɪˈtiːk; krɪˋtik/ *n* critical analysis 批评性的分析; 评论; 评论文章: *The book presents a critique of the Government's policies.* 该书对政府的政策作出了批评性的分析.

croak /krəʊk; krok/ *n* deep hoarse sound, like that made by a frog 深沉而嘶哑的声音; (蛙的)呱呱叫声.

▷ **croak** *v* **1** [I] (of a frog, etc) utter a croak or croaks (指蛙等)发深沉而嘶哑的声音, 呱呱叫. **2** [I, Tn, Tn·p] **~ sth (out)** (of a person) speak or say sth with a deep hoarse voice (指人)用低沉而嘶哑的声音说话: *She could only croak because of her heavy cold.* 她因患重感冒只能用沙哑的声音说话. ○ *He croaked (out) a few words.* 他低沉而沙哑地说出一些话来. **3** [I] (*sl* 俚) die 死亡.

cro·chet /ˈkrəʊʃeɪ; *US* krəʊˈʃeɪ; kroˋʃe/ *n* [U] (**a**) method of making fabric by looping thread into a pattern of connected stitches, using a hooked needle (called a **crochet-hook**) 钩针编织. (**b**) fabric made in this way 钩针编织品.

▷ **cro·chet** *v* (*pt, pp* **~ed** /-ʃeɪd; -ˋʃed/) [I, Tn] make (sth, eg a shawl) in this way 用钩针编织(某物, 如围巾): *a crocheted skirt* 钩针编织的裙子.

crock[1] /krɒk; krɑk/ *n* (*dated* 旧) **1** [C] large earthenware pot or jar, eg for containing water 瓦罐, 坛子(如盛水用的). **2 crocks** [pl] = CROCKERY. **3** [C usu *pl* 通常作复数] broken piece of earthenware 陶器碎片.

crock[2] /krɒk; krɑk/ *n* (*Brit infml* 口) **1** old useless vehicle 破旧无用的车辆. **2** old or worn-out person or animal 老年或体衰的人或动物: *What does a young girl like you want with an old crock like me?* 像你这样一个年轻的姑娘要我这样一个老朽做什么呢?

▷ **crocked** /krɒkt; krɑkt/ *adj* (*Brit infml* 口) injured or broken 受伤的; 损坏的: *My arm's crocked.* 我的手臂受伤了.

crock·ery /ˈkrɒkərɪ; ˋkrɑkərɪ/ *n* [U] (also **crocks** [*pl*]) cups, plates, dishes, etc made of baked clay 陶器, 瓦器(如杯、盘、碟等用黏土烧制的器皿).

cro·co·dile /ˈkrɒkədaɪl; ˋkrɑkə,daɪl/ *n* **1** large river reptile with a hard skin, a long body and tail, and very big tapering jaws, that lives in hot parts of the world 鳄鱼. Cf 参看 ALLIGATOR. **2** (*Brit infml* 口) long line of schoolchildren walking in pairs 两人一排成纵列行进的学童. **3** (idm 习语) **'crocodile tears** insincere sorrow 鳄鱼的眼泪(假悲伤): *She shed crocodile tears* (ie pretended to be sorry) *when she dismissed him from his job.* 她把他解雇时, 流出了鳄鱼的眼泪(假装难过).

cro·cus /ˈkrəʊkəs; ˋkrokəs/ *n* (*pl* **~es** /-sɪz; sɪz/) small plant that produces yellow, purple or white flowers early in spring 番红花(一种小植物, 花黄色、紫色或白色, 初春时开放). ⇨illus at App 1 见附录1之插图, page ii.

Croe·sus /ˈkriːsəs; ˋkrisəs/ *n* wealthy king in Asia Minor in the 6th century BC 克罗伊斯(公元前6世纪小亚细亚一富有的国王: (*saying* 谚) *as rich as Croesus*, ie very rich 像克罗伊斯那样富有(非常富有).

croft /krɒft; *US* krɔ:ft; krɔft/ *n* (*Brit*) **1** small farm, esp in Scotland 小农场(尤指苏格兰的). **2** (*arch* 古) small enclosed field 圈起来的小块土地.
▷ **crofter** *n* person who rents or owns a small farm, esp in Scotland 小农场的佃农或主人(尤指苏格兰的).

crois·sant /ˈkrwʌsɒŋ; krwɑˈsɑn/ *n* (*French* 法) crescent-shaped bun made of light flaky pastry, eaten esp at breakfast 新月形面包(一种松软的酥皮点心, 尤于早餐中食用). ⇨illus at BREAD 见 BREAD 之插图.

crom·lech /ˈkrɒmlek; ˈkrɑmlɛk/ (also **dolmen**) *n* prehistoric circle of large tall stones 史前时期由很高的巨石排成的圆圈.

crone /krəʊn; kron/ *n* (*usu derog* 通常作贬义) ugly withered old woman 干瘪丑陋的老太婆.

C

crony /ˈkrəʊnɪ; ˈkronɪ/ *n* (*derog* 贬) close friend or companion 密友; 亲密的伙伴: *He spends every evening drinking in the pub with his cronies.* 他每天晚上都跟知心朋友到酒馆喝酒.

crook /krʊk; krʊk/ *n* **1** (*infml* 口) person who is habitually dishonest 一贯耍花招的人; 行骗或行窃的老手: *The crooks got away with* (ie The criminals stole) *most of the money.* 那坏蛋把那笔钱的大部分都偷走了. ○ *That used-car salesman is a real crook.* 那个卖旧汽车的商人是个地地道道的骗子. **2** bend or curve, eg in a river or path 弯曲; 弯子; (河流、道路等的)弯曲处: *carry sth in the crook of one's arm*, ie on one's arm, at the inside of the bent elbow 臂弯里挎着某物. **3** (**a**) long stick with a rounded hook at one end, as used in former times by shepherds for catching sheep 一端有弯钩的长棍杖(如旧时牧羊人捕羊所用的). (**b**) long staff similar to this, carried ceremonially by a bishop; crosier 主教举行仪式时手持的权杖(形如牧羊人之手杖). **4** (idm 习语) **by hook or by crook** ⇨ HOOK[1].
▷ **crook** *v* [Tn] bend (esp one's finger or arm) 使(尤指手指或手臂)弯曲: *She crooked her little finger as she drank her tea.* 她喝茶时弯起小指头. **crook** *adj* [usu pred 通常作表语] (*Austral infml* 澳, 口) ill 有病: *I'm feeling a bit crook.* 我感到有点不适.
□ ˈ**crook-back** *n, adj* (*arch* 古) hunch-back(ed) 驼背(的). ˈ**crook-backed** *adj*.

crooked /ˈkrʊkɪd; ˈkrʊkɪd/ *adj* (**-er, -est**) **1** not straight or level; twisted, bent or curved 歪的; 扭曲的; 弯曲的: *a crooked lane, branch, table* 弯曲的小巷、树枝; 歪斜的桌子 ○ *a crooked smile*, ie in which the mouth slopes down at one side 歪斜着嘴的一笑 ○ *You've got your hat on crooked.* 你把帽子戴歪了. **2** (*infml* 口) (of people or actions) dishonest; illegal (指人或行为)不老实的, 不正当的: *a crooked businessman, deal* 奸商、非法经营. ▷ **crook·edly** *adv*. **crook·ed·ness** *n* [U].

croon /kru:n; krun/ *v* [I, Ipr, Tn, Tn·pr] **~ (sth) (to sb)** hum, sing or say (sth) softly and gently 柔情地轻哼、轻唱或低声述说(某事物): *croon soothingly (to a child)* (给孩子)低声唱歌 ○ *croon a sentimental tune* 轻哼感伤的曲调 ○ *croon a baby to sleep* 低声哼唱哄婴儿睡觉 ○ *'What a beautiful little baby,' she crooned.* '多么逗人爱的小宝贝儿啊,'她柔声细语地说.
▷ **crooner** *n* singer of the 1930's or 1940's who sang sentimental songs (二十世纪三十或四十年代演唱感伤歌曲的)歌手.

crop /krɒp; krɑp/ *n* **1** (**a**) [C] amount of grain, hay, fruit, etc grown in one year or season (谷物、干草、水果等一年或一季的)收成, 产量: *the potato crop* 马铃薯的产量 ○ *a good crop of rice* 稻谷的丰收 ○ *a bumper* (ie very large) *crop* 特大的丰收 ○ [attrib 作表语] *a crop failure* 歉收. (**b**) **crops** [pl] agricultural plants in the fields 农作物; 庄稼: *treat the crops with fertilizer* 给农作物施肥. **2** [sing] **~ of sth** group of people or quantity of things appearing or produced at the same time (同时出现或产生的)一群(人), 一批(事物): *this year's crop of students* 本届大学生 ○ *The programme brought quite a crop of complaints from viewers.* 该节目招致观众诸多不满. **3** [C] very short hair-cut 极短的发式; 平头. **4** [C] bag-like part of a bird's throat where food is prepared for digestion before passing into the stomach 嗉子; 嗉囊. **5** [C] (also ˈ**hunting-crop**) whip with a short loop instead of a lash, used by riders 猎鞭(骑手用的, 端部有小圈). **6** (idm 习语) **neck and crop** ⇨ NECK.
▷ **crop** *v* (**-pp-**) **1** [Tn, Cn·a] (**a**) cut short (sb's hair or an animal's ears, tail, etc) 剪短(某人的头发、动物的耳朵或尾巴等): *with hair cropped (short)* 头发剪得很短. (**b**) (of animals) bite the tops off and eat (grass, plants, etc) (指动物)啃吃(青草、其他植物等): *Sheep had cropped the grass (short).* 羊把草啃(短)了. **2** [I] (of plants, fields, etc) bear a crop (指植物、田地等)收获: *The beans cropped well this year.* 今年豆子丰收. **3** (phr v) **crop up** appear or happen, esp unexpectedly 出现或发生(尤指意外地): *All sorts of difficulties cropped up.* 各种各样的困难意想不到地出现了. ○ *The subject cropped up as we talked.* 我们交谈时无意中涉及到了这个问题.
□ ˈ**crop-dusting**, ˈ**crop-spraying** *ns* [U] dusting/spraying of crops with fertilizer or insecticide, eg from low-flying aircraft 作物喷粉(如自低飞的飞机中喷撒肥料或杀虫剂).

crop·per /ˈkrɒpə(r); ˈkrɑpɚ/ *n* **1** (following *adjs* 用于形容词之后) plant that produces a crop of the specified kind 作物: *a good, bad, heavy, light, etc cropper* 高产的、低产的、产量高的、产量低的...作物. **2** (idm 习语) **come a ˈcropper** (*infml* 口) (**a**) fall over 摔倒. (**b**) fail 失败.

cro·quet /ˈkrəʊkeɪ; *US* krəʊˈkeɪ; kroˈke/ *n* [U] game played on a lawn, using wooden mallets to knock wooden balls through hoops 槌球游戏(在草坪上进行, 以木槌击木球钻小圈).

cro·quette /krəʊˈket; kroˈkɛt/ *n* ball of mashed potato, fish, etc coated with bread-crumbs and cooked in fat 炸丸子(用土豆泥、碎鱼肉等裹以面包屑炸成的).

crore /krɔ:(r); kror/ *n* (*Indian* 印度) ten million 十兆; 一千万: *a crore of rupees* 一千万卢比.

cro·sier (also **cro·zier**) /ˈkrəʊzɪə(r); *US* ˈkrəʊʒər; ˈkroʒɚ/ *n* bishop's long ceremonial staff, usu shaped like a shepherd's crook (主教的)权杖.

cross 十字

SWASTIKA 卐字 MALTESE CROSS 马耳他十字 LATIN CROSS 拉丁式十字架

cross[1] /krɒs; *US* krɔ:s; krɔs/ *n* **1** [C] (**a**) mark made by drawing one line across another, eg x or + 十字形或叉形记号(如×或+): *The place is marked on the map with a cross.* 那个地方在地图上以十字形记号标出. ○ *make one's cross*, ie put a cross on a document instead of one's signature, eg if one cannot write 画十字, 画押(在文件上画个十字代替签名, 如文盲之所为). (**b**) line or stroke forming part of a letter, eg the horizontal stroke on a 't' (字母中的)一横(如 t 中的横线). **2** (**a**) **the Cross** [sing] the frame made of a long vertical piece of wood with a shorter horizontal piece joined to it near the top, on which Christ was crucified (基督被钉死在上面的)十字架. (**b**) [C] thing representing this, as a Christian emblem (作为基督徒标记的)十字架模型: *She wore a small silver cross on a chain round her neck.* 她脖子上戴着项链, 上面挂着个银的小十字架. ⇨illus at App 1 见附录1之插图, page viii. (**c**) [C] thing, esp a monument, in the form of a cross, eg a stone one in a village market-place 十字形物品(尤指纪念物, 如乡村市集上的十字形纪念石碑). (**d**) [C usu *sing* 通常作单数] cross-shaped sign made with the right hand as a Christian religious act 画十字的动作(用右手比划, 为基督徒的宗教行为): *The priest made a cross over her head.* 牧师在她头上画了一个十字. (**e**) **the Cross** [sing] (*fig* 比喻) the Christian religion 基督教: *the Cross and the Crescent*, ie Christianity and Islam 基督教与伊斯兰教. **3** (usu 通常作 **Cross**) [C] small cross-shaped piece of metal awarded as a medal for courage, etc (为表彰英勇行为等而授予的)十字勋章: *the Victoria Cross* 维多利亚十字勋章 ○ *the Distinguished Service Cross* 优异服务十字勋章. **4** [C usu *sing* 通常作单数] **~ (between A and B)** (**a**) animal or plant that is the offspring of different breeds or varieties (动物或植物的)杂交品种, 混合种: *A mule is a cross between a horse and an ass.* 骡是马和驴交配而生的杂种. (**b**) (*fig* 比喻) mixture of two different things (两种不同物的)混合物: *a play that is a cross between farce and tragedy* 把闹剧和悲剧结合成

一体的戏. **5** [C] source of sorrow, worry, etc; problem 悲哀、苦恼等的根源; 问题: *We all have our crosses to bear.* 每个人都有苦难需要承受. **6** (idm 习语) **cut sth on the 'cross** cut cloth, etc diagonally 把布等对角剪开.

cross[2] /krɒs; *US* krɔːs; krɔs/ *v* **1** [I, Ipr, Ip, Tn] **~ (over) (from sth/to sth)** go across; pass or extend from one side to the other side of (sth) 横穿: *The river is too deep; we can't cross (over).* 河太深, 我们过不去. ○ *cross from Dover to Calais* 从多佛横渡到加来 ○ *cross a road, a river, a bridge, a desert, the sea, the mountains* 过马路、过河、过桥、穿过沙漠、越过大海、翻过高山 ○ *Electricity cables cross the valley.* 电缆跨过山谷. **2** (**a**) [I] pass across each other 交叉: *The roads cross just outside the village.* 那两条路就在村外交叉. ○ (*fig* 比喻) *Our paths crossed* (ie We met by chance) *several times.* 我们碰上好几次了. (**b**) [I, Tn no passive 不用于被动语态] (of people travelling, letters in the post) meet and pass (each other) (指行人)对面而过; (指邮寄中的信件)互相错过: *We crossed each other on the way.* 我们在途中对脸而过. ○ *Our letters crossed in the post.* 我们的信在邮寄途中错过去了. **3** [Tn] put or place (sth) across or over sth else of the same type 使(某物)交叉: *cross one's legs*, ie place one leg over the other, esp at the thighs 盘腿 ○ *cross one's arms on one's chest* 交叉两臂于胸前 ○ *a flag with a design of two crossed keys* 有两把钥匙相交叉图案的旗帜 ○ *a crossed line*, ie interruption of a telephone call because of a wrong connection 交扰线路(电话因岔线而产生的干扰). **4** [Tn] draw a line across (sth) 画横线于(某物): *cross the t's* 写t上的一横 ○ *cross a cheque*, ie draw two lines across it so that it can only be paid through a bank 在支票上画两条平行线(则该支票只能经由银行兑现) ○ *a crossed cheque*, ie a cheque marked in this way 画线支票. **5** [Tn no passive 不用于被动语态] **~ oneself** make the sign of the cross[1](2a) on one's chest 用手在胸前画十字: *He 'crossed himself as he passed the church.* 他经过教堂时用手在胸前画十字. **6** [Tn] obstruct, oppose or contradict (sb, his plans or wishes); thwart 阻挠, 反对, 违背(某人、其计划或意愿); 使受挫: *She doesn't like to be crossed.* 她不喜欢有人跟她作对. ○ *He crosses me in everything.* 他处处与我作对. ○ *to be crossed in love*, ie fail to win the love of sb one loves 在恋爱上受到挫折. **7** [Tn, Tn·pr] **~ sth (with sth)** cause (two different types of animal or plant) to produce offspring 使(不同种的动物或植物)杂交: *to cross a horse with an ass* 使马与驴杂交 ○ *Varieties of roses can be crossed to vary their colour.* 不同品种的玫瑰可以杂交以改变其颜色. **8** (idm 习语) **ˌcross one's ˌbridges when one 'comes to them** not worry about a problem before it actually arrives 问题来了再解决不迟(勿为尚未发生的事情烦恼): *We'll cross that bridge when we come to it.* 船到桥头自然直, 等出了问题我们再解决不迟. **cross my 'heart (and hope to die)** (*infml saying* 口, 谚) (used to emphasize the honesty or sincerity of what one says or promises 用以强调所说属实): *I saw him do it: cross my heart.* 我看见他干的, 我可以发誓. **cross one's 'fingers** hope that one's plans will be successful 祈求成功: *I'm crossing my fingers that my proposal will be accepted.* 但愿我的建议能被采纳. ○ *Keep your fingers crossed!* 祈求好运吧! **cross one's 'mind** (of thoughts, etc) come into one's mind (指想法等)出现, 掠过: *It never crossed my mind that she might lose*, ie I confidently expected her to win. 我从未想到她会失败. **ˌcross sb's ˌpalm with 'silver** give sb (esp a fortune-teller) a coin 给某人(尤指算命者)钱. **ˌcross sb's 'path** meet sb, usu by chance 与某人相遇(通常指不期而遇): *I hope I never cross her path again.* 但愿我永远不再遇见她. **ˌcross the 'Rubicon** take an action or start a process which is important and which cannot be reversed 断然采取有进无退的重大行动; 破釜沉舟. **cross 'swords (with sb)** fight or argue (with sb) (与某人)交锋, 争论: *The chairman and I have crossed swords before over this issue.* 我和主席以前曾经对这问题进行过辩论. **dot one's i's and cross one's t's** ⇨ DOT. **get, have, etc one's lines crossed** ⇨ LINE[1]. **get one's wires crossed** ⇨ WIRE. **9** (phr v) **cross sth off (sth); cross sth out/through** remove sth by drawing a line through it 画掉某物: *We can cross his name off (the list), as he's not coming.* 他既然不来了, 我们可以把他的名字(从名单中)划掉. ○ *Two words have been crossed out.* 有两个词删掉了.

cross[3] /krɒs; *US* krɔːs; krɔs/ *adj* (**-er, -est**) **1 ~ (with sb) (about sth)** (*infml* 口) rather angry 生气的; 恼怒的: *I was cross with him for being late.* 他迟到了, 我很生气. ○ *What are you so cross about?* 你为什么发那么大的火啊? ○ *She gave me a cross look.* 她瞪了我一眼. **2** [attrib 作定语] (of winds) contrary; opposed (指风)逆的, 反向的: *Strong cross breezes make it difficult for boats to leave harbour.* 逆风很强刮得船难以离港. Cf 参看 CROSS-WIND. ▷ **cross·ly** *adv*. **cross·ness** *n* [U].

cross- *comb form* 构词成分 (forming *ns, vs, adjs* and *advs* 用以构成名词、动词、形容词、副词) movement or action from one thing to another or across 自一事物到另一事物的运动或动作; 横跨; 穿越: *cross-current* ○ *cross-fertilize* ○ *cross-cultural* ○ *cross-country* ○ *cross-Channel ferries*.

cross·bar /ˈkrɒsbɑː(r); *US* ˈkrɔːs-; ˈkrɔsˌbɑr/ *n* horizontal bar, eg one joining the two upright posts of a football goal, or the front and rear ends of a bicycle frame 横杠; (足球门上的)横木; (自行车架上的)横梁. ⇨ illus at App 1 见附录1之插图, page xiii.

cross·beam /ˈkrɒsbiːm; *US* ˈkrɔːs-; ˈkrɔsˌbim/ *n* horizontal beam between two supporting parts of a structure; girder 横梁; 大梁.

cross-benches /ˈkrɒsbentʃɪz; *US* ˈkrɔːs-; ˈkrɔsˌbɛntʃɪz/ *n* [pl] seats in the British parliament occupied by those members who do not regularly support a particular political party 中立议员席(英国议会中不固定追随任何政党的议员席位).
▷ **cross-bencher** *n* member of parliament who usu sits on these seats 中立议员.

cross-bones /ˈkrɒsbəʊnz; *US* ˈkrɔːs-; ˈkrɔsˌbonz/ *n* [pl] ⇨ SKULL AND CROSS-BONES (SKULL).

cross·bow /ˈkrɒsbəʊ; *US* ˈkrɔːs-; ˈkrɔsˌbo/ *n* small powerful bow mounted horizontally on a grooved support where the arrow is held and then released by pulling a trigger 十字弓, 弩(一种小型的强弓). Cf 参看 LONGBOW (LONG[1]).

cross-bred /ˈkrɒsbred; *US* ˈkrɔːs-; ˈkrɔsˌbrɛd/ *adj* produced by different species or varieties breeding together 杂种的; 杂交的: *a cross-bred sheep, dog, etc* 杂种的羊、狗等.

cross-breed /ˈkrɒsbriːd; *US* ˈkrɔːs-; ˈkrɔsˌbrid/ *n* animal, plant, etc produced by the breeding of different species or varieties (动植物等的)杂交品种.
▷ **cross-breed** *v* [I, Tn] breed (sth) in this way 杂交繁育(某物).

cross-check /ˌkrɒs ˈtʃek; *US* ˌkrɔːs; ˌkrɔsˈtʃɛk/ *v* [I, Tn, Tn·pr] **~ sth (against sth)** make sure that information, a calculation, etc is correct by consulting a different source, using a different method, etc (从不同方面、以不同方法等)核实(情报), 核对(计算结果等): *Cross-check your answer by using a calculator.* 用计算器核对一下你的答案.
▷ **ˈcross-check** *n* check made in this way 查证; 复核.

cross-country /ˌkrɒs ˈkʌntrɪ; *US* ˌkrɔːs; ˈkrɔsˈkʌntrɪ/ *adj* [usu attrib 通常作定语], *adv* across fields, etc rather than on main roads 越野(的): *a ˌcross-country 'run, 'race, etc* 越野跑步、赛跑等 ○ *travel cross-country* 越野.
▷ **cross-country** *n* cross-country race 越野赛跑: *enter for the mile and the cross-country* 报名参加一英里和越野两项赛跑.

cross-current /ˈkrɒs kʌrənt; *US* krɔːs; ˈkrɔsˌkɝənt/ *n* **1** current that crosses another 交叉水流. **2** (*fig* 比喻) body of beliefs, views, etc contrary to those of the majority 与多数人相反的信仰、观点等: *a cross-current of opinion against the prevailing view* 反潮流的观点.

cross-cut /ˈkrɒskʌt; *US* ˈkrɔːs-; ˈkrɔsˌkʌt/ *adj* [usu attrib 通常作定语] (of a saw, etc) with teeth designed for cutting across the grain of wood (指锯等)有为横割木纹而设计的锯齿的: *a cross-cut saw/blade* 横截锯[刀刃].

cross-examine /ˌkrɒs ɪɡˈzæmɪn; *US* ˌkrɔːs; ˈkrɔsɪɡ-ˈzæmɪn/ *v* [Tn] **1** (*esp law* 尤用于法律) question (sb) carefully to test the correctness of answers given to previous questions 严诘, 盘问(某人): *The prosecution lawyer cross-examined the defence witness.* 控方律师诘问被告一方的证人. **2** question (sb) aggressively or in great detail 追问, 详询(某人): *Whenever he comes in late his wife cross-examines him about where he's spent the evening.* 每逢他晚归, 妻子总要追问他晚上到哪里去了. Cf 参看 EXAMINE 3.

▷ **cross-examiner** *n.*

cross-examination /ˌkrɒs ɪɡˌzæmɪˈneɪʃn; *US* ˌkrɔːs; ˋkrɔsɪɡˌzæməˈneʃən/ *n* [U, C] (instance of) cross-examining 严诘; 盘问; 追问; 详询: *He broke down under cross-examination* (ie while being cross-examined) *and admitted the truth.* 他经不起严密的诘问而供认了事实.

cross-eyed /ˈkrɒsaɪd; *US* ˈkrɔːs-; ˋkrɔsˈaɪd/ *adj* with one or both eyes turned inwards towards the nose 内斜视的; 斗鸡眼的.

cross-fertilize, -ise /ˌkrɒs ˈfɜːtəlaɪz; *US* ˌkrɔːs; ˋkrɔsˈfɝtḷˌaɪz/ *v* [Tn] **1** (*botany* 植) fertilize (a plant) by using pollen from a different type of plant 以异种花粉使(植物)受精; 使异花受精. **2** (*fig* 比喻) stimulate (sb/sth) usefully or positively with ideas from a different field, etc (从不同方面以有益的或积极的思想)影响(某人[某事物]): *Literary studies have been cross-fertilized by new ideas in linguistics.* 文学研究从语言学方面的新见解中受益良多. ▷ **cross-fertilization, -isation** /ˌkrɒs ˌfɜːtəlaɪˈzeɪʃn; *US* ˌkrɔːs ˌfɜːrtlɪˈzeɪʃn; ˋkrɔsˌfɝtḷəˋzeʃən/ *n* [U, C].

cross-fire /ˈkrɒsfaɪə(r); *US* ˈkrɔːs-; ˋkrɔsˌfaɪr/ *n* [U] **1** (*military* 军) firing of guns from two or more points so that the bullets, shells, etc cross each other 交叉火力. **2** (*fig* 比喻) situation in which two people or groups are arguing, competing, etc and another is unwillingly involved 被波及的状况: *When two industrial giants clash, small companies can get caught in the cross-fire,* ie harmed incidentally. 两大企业争斗之下, 小公司遭受池鱼之殃.

cross-grained /ˌkrɒs ˈɡreɪnd; *US* ˌkrɔːs; ˋkrɔsˈɡrend/ *adj* **1** (of wood) with the grain running diagonally or across rather than in a straight line (指木材)斜纹的, 纹理交织的. **2** difficult to please or get on with 难讨好的; 难相处的.

cross-hatch /ˈkrɒs hætʃ; *US* ˌkrɔːs; ˋkrɔsˌhætʃ/ *v* [Tn] mark or shade (sth) with sets of crossing parallel lines 用平行线相交的网线给(某物)加上标记或阴影: *cross-hatch an area on a map* 在地图上用网线标出某一区域.

▷ **cross-hatching** *n* [U] pattern of such lines 网线图型; 网线法.

cross·ing /ˈkrɒsɪŋ; *US* ˈkrɔːs-; ˋkrɔsɪŋ/ *n* **1** journey across a sea, wide river, etc (经大海、大河等的)横越, 横渡: *a rough crossing from Dover to Calais* 从多佛港到加来港之艰险的横渡. **2** place where two roads, two railways, or a road and a railway, cross 十字路口; (铁路的)交叉道口; (公路与铁路的)平交道口. Cf 参看 LEVEL CROSSING (LEVEL[1]). **3** (**a**) place, esp on a street, where pedestrians can cross safely 人行横道. Cf 参看 PEDESTRIAN CROSSING (PEDESTRIAN), PELICAN CROSSING (PELICAN), ZEBRA CROSSING (ZEBRA). (**b**) place where one crosses from one country to another (由一国至另一国的)过境处: *arrested by guards at the border crossing* 在越境地点被卫兵逮捕.

cross-legged /ˌkrɒs ˈleɡd; *US* ˌkrɔːs; ˋkrɔsˈlɛɡɪd, -ˈlɛɡd/ *adv* with one leg over the other, esp at the ankles 盘着腿: *sitting cross-legged on the floor* 盘着腿席地而坐. ⇨ illus 见插图.

cross-patch /ˈkrɒspætʃ; *US* ˈkrɔːs-; ˋkrɔsˌpætʃ/ *n* (*dated infml* 旧, 口) bad-tempered person 脾气很坏的人.

cross-piece /ˈkrɒs piːs; *US* ˈkrɔːs; ˋkrɔsˌpis/ *n* piece (of a structure, tool, etc) lying or fixed across another piece (指一结构、用具等上的)横档, 横杆.

cross-ply /ˈkrɒsplaɪ; *US* ˈkrɔːs-; ˋkrɔsˌplaɪ/ *adj* (of tyres) having layers of fabric with cords lying crosswise (指轮胎)有交叉帘布层的. Cf 参看 RADIAL.

cross-purposes /ˌkrɒs ˈpɜːpəsɪz; *US* ˌkrɔːs; ˋkrɔsˈpɝpəsɪz/ *n*(idm 习语) **at cross-ˈpurposes** (of people or groups) misunderstanding what the other side is talking about or concerned with (指人或团体)相互误解: *We're at cross-purposes: I'm talking about astronomy, you're talking about astrology.* 我们彼此误解了: 我谈的是天文学, 你谈的是占星术.

cross-question /ˌkrɒs ˈkwestʃən; *US* ˌkrɔːs; ˋkrɔsˈkwɛstʃən/ *v* [Tn] question (sb) thoroughly and often aggressively; cross-examine(2) 追问, 诘问(某人).

cross-reference /ˌkrɒs ˈrefrəns; *US* ˌkrɔːs; ˋkrɔsˈrɛfərəns/ *n* **~ (to sth)** note directing a reader to another part of a book, file, etc for further information 互见; 相互参照的诠释: *follow up all the cross-references* 参阅所有标明相互参照的注释.

▷ **cross-reference** *v* [Tn usu passive 通常用于被动语态] pvovide (a book, etc) with cross-references 给(书等)编制相互参照注释.

cross·roads /ˈkrɒsrəʊdz; *US* ˈkrɔːs-; ˋkrɔsˌrodz/ *n* **1** [sing *v*] place where two roads meet and cross 十字路口: *We came to a crossroads.* 我们来到了十字路口. **2** (idm 习语) **at a/the ˈcrossroads** at a decisive point in one's life, career, etc (人生、经历等)处于关键时期, 面临重大抉择: *Our business is at the crossroads: if this deal succeeds, our future is assured; if not, we shall be bankrupt.* 我们的商号正处在紧要关头: 倘若此番交易成功, 前途自无问题, 否则就要破产.

cross-section /ˌkrɒs ˈsekʃn; *US* ˌkrɔːs; ˋkrɔsˈsɛkʃən/ *n* **1** (picture of the) surface formed by cutting through sth, esp at right angles 截面(图); 断面(图); 剖面(图): *examining a cross-section of the kidney under the microscope* 在显微镜下检查肾的切面 ○ *The girder is square in cross-section.* 这个大梁的截面是方形的. **2** typical or representative sample 典型; 样品: *a cross-section of the electors, population, etc* 选民、全体居民等中的一群具有代表性的人物 ○ *a broad cross-section of opinion* 具有广泛代表性的看法.

cross-stitch /ˈkrɒs stɪtʃ; *US* ˈkrɔːs; ˋkrɔsˌstɪtʃ/ *n* **1** [C] stitch formed by two stitches crossing each other 十字形针法. **2** [U] needlework in which this stitch is used 采用十字形针法的刺绣.

cross-talk /ˈkrɒs tɔːk; *US* ˈkrɔːs; ˋkrɔsˌtɔk/ *n* [U] (*Brit*) rapid dialogue, eg between two comedians 机敏的对白(如两个滑稽演员之间的对话).

cross-town /ˈkrɒstaʊn; *US* ˈkrɔːs-; ˋkrɔsˌtaʊn/ *adj* [attrib 作定语] (*US*) going across a town (rather than in and out of the centre) 穿过城镇的: *a cross-town bus* 穿越市区的公共汽车.

cross-trees /ˈkrɒstriːz; *US* ˈkrɔːs-; ˋkrɔsˌtriz/ *n* [pl] (*nautical* 海) two horizontal pieces of wood fastened to a lower mast to support the mast above and to support ropes, etc 桅顶横杆.

cross·walk /ˈkrɒswɔːk; *US* ˈkrɔːs-; ˋkrɔsˌwɔk/ *n* (*US*) = PEDESTRIAN CROSSING (PEDESTRIAN).

cross-wind /ˈkrɒswɪnd; *US* ˈkrɔːs-; ˋkrɔsˌwɪnd/ *n* wind blowing across the direction in which cars, aircraft, etc are travelling 侧风: *Strong cross-winds blew the aircraft off course.* 强劲的侧风把飞机吹得偏离了航线.

cross·wise /ˈkrɒswaɪz; *US* ˈkrɔːs-; ˋkrɔsˌwaɪz/ *adj* [attrib 作定语], *adv* **1** across, esp diagonally 贯穿的; (尤指)斜穿的: *a yellow flag with a red band going crosswise from top left to bottom right* 有一道红色的条纹从左上方斜穿到右下方的黄旗. **2** in the form of a cross 贯穿地; 斜穿地.

cross·word /ˈkrɒswɜːd; *US* ˈkrɔːs-; ˋkrɔsˌwɝd/ *n* (also **ˈcrossword puzzle**) puzzle in which words indicated by numbered clues have to be inserted vertically (clues *down*) and horizontally (clues *across*) in spaces on a chequered square 纵横字谜. ⇨ illus 见插图.

crotch /krɒtʃ; kratʃ/ (also **crutch**) *n* place where a person's legs, or trouser legs, join at the top (人体的)胯部; 裤裆.

crossword 纵横字迷

crot·chet /ˈkrɒtʃɪt; ˋkrɑtʃɪt/ *n* (*US* ˈ**quarter note**) (*music* 音) note equal to half a minim 四分音符. ⇨illus at MUSIC 见 MUSIC 之插图.

crot·chety /ˈkrɒtʃɪtɪ; ˋkrɑtʃɪtɪ/ *adj* (*infml* 口) bad-tempered 脾气坏的.

crouch /kraʊtʃ; kraʊtʃ/ *v* [I, Ip] lower the body by bending the knees, eg in fear or to hide 蹲; 蹲伏: *The cat crouched, ready to leap.* 那只猫弓着身子, 准备扑过去. ○ *I crouched behind the sofa.* 我蹲在沙发后面.
▷ **crouch** *n* [sing] crouching position 蹲着的姿势: *drop down into a crouch* 蹲下. ⇨illus at KNEEL 见 KNEEL 之插图.

croup[1] /kru:p; krup/ *n* [U] disease of children, in which there is coughing and difficulty in breathing 格鲁布, 哮吼(儿科疾病).

croup[2] /kru:p; krup/ *n* rump or buttocks of certain animals, esp the horse (某些动物, 尤指马的)臀部. ⇨ illus at HORSE 见 HORSE 之插图.

crou·pier /ˈkru:pɪə; *US* -pɪər; ˋkrupɪɚ/ *n* person in charge of a gambling table, who deals out the cards, throws the dice, etc and pays out money to the winner(s) 赌台上的主持人(负责发牌、掷色子等, 并付赢者钱).

crou·ton /ˈkru:tɒn; kruˋtɑn/ *n* (*French* 法) cube of toasted or fried bread, usu served with soup 烤的或炸的面包丁(通常放在汤里).

crow[1] /krəʊ; kro/ *n* **1** any of various types of large black bird with a harsh cry 乌鸦. ⇨illus at App 1 见附录1之插图, page iv. **2** (idm 习语) **as the** ˈ**crow flies** in a straight line 成直线. **stone the crows** ⇨ STONE.
□ ˈ**crow's-feet** *n* [pl] wrinkles in the skin around the outer corner of the eye 眼角皱纹.
ˈ**crow's-nest** *n* platform fixed to the top of a ship's mast from which sb can see clearly a long way in all directions 桅顶瞭望台.

crow[2] /krəʊ; kro/ *v* (*pt* **crowed** or, in archaic use, 古语拼作 **crew** /kru: ; kru /, *pp* **crowed**) **1** [I] (of a cock) make a loud shrill cry, esp at dawn (指公鸡)喔喔叫(尤指黎明时). **2** [I] (of a baby) make sounds showing pleasure (指婴儿)欢叫. **3** [I, Ipr] **~ (over sb/sth)** (*derog* 贬) express gleeful triumph (about one's success, etc) (因成功等而)得意洋洋, 自鸣得意: *She won the competition and won't stop crowing (over her rivals/her rivals' failure).* 她在比赛中获得了胜利, (在对手[对手的失败]面前)简直得意忘形.
▷ **crow** *n* [sing] crowing sound (公鸡的)喔喔叫声; (婴儿的)欢叫声.

crow·bar /ˈkrəʊbɑ:(r); ˋkro,bɑr/ *n* straight iron bar, usu with a hooked end, used as a lever to open crates, move heavy objects, etc 撬棍; 铁撬.

crowd[1] /kraʊd; kraʊd/ *n* **1** [CGp] (**a**) large number of people gathered together in the open 人群: *A crowd had already collected outside the embassy gates.* 使馆大门外已经聚集了一群人. ○ *He pushed his way through the crowd.* 他在人群中往前挤. ○ *Police had to break up the crowd.* 警察不得不驱散人群. ○ [attrib 作定语] *crowd control* 人群控制. (**b**) mass of spectators; audience 观众; 听众: *The match attracted a large crowd.* 那项比赛吸引了大批观众. ○ *The crowd cheered the winning hit.* 观众为那致胜的一击喝彩. **2 the crowd** [sing] (*derog* 贬) people in general 人们: *move with the crowd*, ie do as everybody else does 随大溜. **3** [CGp] (*infml* 口) group; company 一伙人; 一帮人: *I don't associate with that crowd.* 我不跟那伙人打交道. **4** (idm 习语) **crowds/a (whole) crowd (of)** very many (people) 许许多多(人): *There were crowds of people waiting to get in.* 有许许多多的人在等着进去. ○ *A whole crowd of us arrived at the party uninvited.* 我们这一大批不速之客来到了聚会场所. **follow the crowd** ⇨ FOLLOW.
□ ˈ**crowd-puller** *n* (*infml* 口) person or thing that attracts a large audience 吸引大批观众(或听众)的人或事物.

crowd[2] /kraʊd; kraʊd/ *v* **1** [Ipr, Ip] **~ around/round (sb)** gather closely around (sb) 聚集在(某人)周围: *People crowded round to get a better view.* 人们争相围观. ○ *Pupils crowded round (their teacher) to ask questions.* 小学生围着(老师)提问题. **2** [Tn] fill (a space) so that there is little room to move 充塞(某空间): *Tourists crowded the pavement.* 游客把人行道挤得水泄不通. ○ *crowd a restaurant, theatre, beach, etc* 挤满餐厅、剧院、海滨等. **3** [Tn] (*infml* 口) put pressure on (sb); harass 给(某人)施加压力; 逼迫: *Don't crowd me: give me time to think!* 不要逼我: 给我时间让我想想! **4** (idm 习语) **crowd on** ˈ**sail** (*nautical* 海) raise many sails in order to increase speed 扬起许多风帆(以增加速度). **5** (phr v) **crowd in on sb** (of thoughts, etc) come into the mind in large numbers (指想法等)大量涌现: *Memories crowded in on me.* 往事一齐涌上我心头. **crowd into sth; crowd in** move in large numbers into a small space 大批涌入(某狭小空间内): *Supporters crowded through the gates into the stadium.* 来捧场的人挤过大门, 涌入运动场. ○ *We'd all crowded into Harriet's small sitting-room.* 我们大家涌进了哈丽特那狭小的客厅. ○ (*fig* 比喻) *Disturbing thoughts crowded into my mind.* 我心乱如麻. **crowd sb/sth into sth; crowd sb/sth in** put many people or things into a small space or period of time; cram (sb/sth) into sth 使很多人或物挤进狭小空间或在短时期涌现出来; 勉强塞入: *They crowd people into the buses.* 他们让许多人挤进公共汽车里. ○ *Guests were crowded into the few remaining rooms.* 把客人都挤在剩余的几个房间里了. ○ *She crowds too much detail into her paintings.* 她的画过于繁杂. **crowd sb/sth out (of sth)** (**a**) keep sb/sth out of a space by filling it oneself 挤占某空间使某人[某物]无法进入: *The restaurant's regular customers are being crowded out by tourists.* 这家餐馆的老主顾被游客挤得不得其门而入. (**b**) prevent sb/sth from operating successfully 排挤某人[某事物]: *Small shops are being crowded out by the big supermarkets.* 小商店受到大型超级市场不断排挤.
▷ **crowded** *adj* **1** having (too) many people 人(太)多的; 拥挤的: *crowded buses, roads, hotels* 拥挤的公共汽车、繁忙的道路、住满人的旅馆. **2** (*fig* 比喻) **~ (with sth)** full (of sth) (被某事物)占满的: *days crowded with activity* 忙得不可开交的日子 ○ *We had a very crowded schedule on the trip.* 我们的旅行日程排得满满的.

crown[1] /kraʊn; kraʊn/ *n* **1** (**a**) [C] ornamental head-dress made of gold, jewels, etc worn by a king or queen on official occasions 王冠; 皇冠. (**b**) (**the Crown** or **the crown**) [sing] the State as represented by a king or queen as its head 王国: *land owned by the Crown* 王国的土地 ○ *a minister of the Crown* 王国的大臣 ○ *Who appears for the Crown* (ie Who is prosecuting the accused person on behalf of the State) *in this case?* 谁在该案中代表王国政府出庭? ○ [attrib 作定语] *Crown land, property, etc* 王国政府的土地、财产等 ○ *a crown witness*, ie for the prosecution in a criminal case 刑事案件中提起公诉一方的证人. (**c**) **the crown** [sing] the office or power of a king or queen 王位; 王权: *She refused the crown*, ie refused to become queen. 她拒不接受王位. ○ *relinquish the crown*, ie abdicate 放弃王位. **2** [C] circle or wreath of flowers, leaves, etc worn on the head, esp as a sign of victory, or as a reward 花冠(用花、叶等做的环状物, 戴在头上, 尤指象征胜利或作为奖赏者): *Christ's crown of thorns* 基督的荆冠 ○ (*fig* 比喻) *two boxers fighting it out for the world heavyweight crown*, ie championship 争夺世界重量级冠军宝座的两名拳击手. **3** (usu 通常作 **the crown**) [sing] (**a**) top of the head or of a hat 头顶; 帽顶. (**b**) top part of anything 物之顶部: *the crown of a hill, tree* 山顶; 树颠 ○ *the crown* (ie the highest part of the curved surface) *of a road* 弯曲路面的最高部分 ○ *A motor cycle overtook us on the crown* (ie the middle or most curved part) *of the bend.* 有一辆摩托车在拐弯处超过了我们. **4** [C] (**a**) part of the tooth that is visible outside the gum 齿冠. (**b**) artificial replacement for this 假齿冠. **5** [C] crown-

C

shaped emblem or ornament, eg a crest or badge 王冠或花冠状的标记或饰物(如纹章或徽章): *A major has a crown on the shoulder of his uniform.* 一名少校在制服的肩部有个王冠形的纹章. **6** [C] former British coin worth 5 shillings (25p) 5先令(25便士)的英国旧币.

□ ˌ**crown** ˈ**colony** colony ruled directly by the British government (英国政府)直辖殖民地.

ˌ**crown** ˈ**court** (in England and Wales) local court in which serious criminal cases are tried (英格兰及威尔士的)地方刑事法院. Cf 参看 COUNTY COURT (COUNTY).

ˌ**crown** ˈ**jewels** crown and other regalia worn or carried by a king or queen on formal occasions (君主于正式场合穿戴的或携带的)王冠及其他象征王权之物, 御宝.

C

ˌ**crown** ˈ**prince** prince who will become the next king 王储; 皇太子.

ˌ**crown prin**ˈ**cess** wife of a crown prince 储妃.

crown² /kraʊn; kraun/ *v* **1** [Tn, Cn·n] put a crown on the head of (a new king or queen) as a sign of royal power 为(新立为王者)加冕: *She was crowned (queen) in 1952.* 她于1952年继(王)位. ○ *the crowned heads* (ie kings and queens) *of Europe* 欧洲各国的君主. **2** [Tn, Tn·pr usu passive 通常用于被动语态] **~ sth (with sth)** (**a**) (*rhet* 修辞) form or cover the top of sth 形成或覆盖某物之顶部: *The hill is crowned with a wood.* 山顶上长满了树. ○ *Beautiful fair hair crowns her head.* 她长着一头浅色的秀发. (**b**) complete or conclude sth in a worthy or perfect way 圆满完成或结束某事物: *The award of this prize crowned his career.* 他荣获此奖, 这是他事业的顶峰. ○ *efforts that were finally crowned with success* 最终必将成功之努力. **3** [Tn] (*infml* 口) hit (sb) on the head 打击(某人)头部: *Shut up or I'll crown you.* 住口, 要不我就砸烂你的脑袋. **4** [Tn] (also **cap**) put an artificial top on (a tooth) 为(牙齿)镶上假齿冠. Cf 参看 CROWN¹ 4. **5** (idm 习语) **to crown it** ˈ**all** as the final event in a series of fortunate or unfortunate events 更使人高兴的是; 更糟的是: *It was cold, raining, and, to crown it all, we had to walk home.* 天气寒冷, 又下着雨, 而最倒霉的是, 我们得走着回家.

▷ **crown·ing** *adj* [attrib 作定语] making perfect or complete 获得圆满成功的; 达到顶点的: *The performance provided the crowning touch to the evening's entertainments.* 该项演出使晚会锦上添花. ○ *the crowning success of her career* 她一生成就的顶峰 ○ *Her crowning glory is her hair.* 她最引以为荣的是她的头发. ○ *The crowning* (ie most extreme) *irony was that I didn't even like her.* 最使人啼笑皆非的是我根本就不喜欢她.

cro·zier = CROSIER.

cru·cial /ˈkru:ʃl; ˈkruʃəl/ *adj* **~ (to/for sth)** very important; decisive 至关重要的; 决定性的: *a crucial decision, issue, factor* 关键性的决定、问题、因素 ○ *at the crucial moment* 在紧要关头 ○ *Getting this contract is crucial to the future of our company.* 签订此项合同对本公司的前途至关重要. ▷ **cru·cially** /-ʃəlɪ; -ʃəlɪ/ *adv*.

cru·cible /ˈkru:sɪbl; ˈkrusəbl/ *n* **1** pot in which metals are melted 坩埚. **2** (*fig rhet* 比喻, 修辞) severe test or trial 严峻的考验: *The alliance had been forged in the crucible of war.* 这个联盟经受了战争的严峻考验.

cru·ci·fix /ˈkru:sɪfɪks; ˈkrusəˌfɪks/ *n* model of the Cross with the figure of Jesus on it 有耶稣像的十字架.

cru·ci·fix·ion /ˌkru:sɪˈfɪkʃn; ˌkrusəˈfɪkʃən/ *n* [C, U] (instance of) crucifying or being crucified 钉死在十字架上: *the Crucifixion,* ie of Jesus 耶稣受难像

cru·ci·form /ˈkru:sɪfɔ:m; ˈkrusəˌfɔrm/ *adj* cross-shaped 十字形的.

cru·cify /ˈkru:sɪfaɪ; ˈkrusəˌfaɪ/ *v* (*pt, pp* **-fied**) [Tn] **1** kill (sb) by nailing or tying him to a cross¹(2a) 把(某人)钉死在十字架上. **2** (*fig infml* 比喻, 口) deal with (sb) very severely 折磨, 虐待(某人): *The minister was crucified* (ie very severely criticized) *in the press for his handling of the affair.* 部长对此事的处理手法受到新闻界的严厉抨击.

crud /krʌd; krʌd/ *n* (*infml* 口 *esp US*) **1** [U] slimy or sticky substance; sth dirty or unwanted 黏糊糊的脏东西; 污垢; 渣滓: *all the crud in the bottom of the saucepan* 锅底部的积垢. **2** [C] (*offensive* 蔑) unpleasant person 讨厌的人.

▷ **cruddy** *adj* (*infml* 口 *esp US*) unpleasant 讨厌的.

crude /kru:d; krud/ *adj* (**-r**, **-st**) **1** [usu attrib 通常作定语] in the natural state; unrefined 天然的; 未提炼的: *crude oil, sugar, ore, etc* 原油、粗糖、原矿. **2** (**a**) not well finished; not completely worked out; rough 粗陋的; 未完成的; 粗糙的: *a crude sketch, method, approximation* 粗略的草图、方法、估计 ○ *His paintings are rather crude,* ie not skilfully done. 他画的画还不够成熟. ○ *I made my own crude garden furniture.* 我给我那园子做了一套简陋的家具. (**b**) not showing taste or refinement; coarse 粗俗的; 粗鲁的: *crude manners* 粗鲁的举止 ○ *He made some crude* (ie sexually offensive) *jokes.* 他说了一些粗俗的(淫秽的)笑话.

▷ **crudely** *adv*: *crudely assembled* 粗略地汇集起来的 ○ *express oneself crudely* 粗略地说说自己的看法.

cru·dity /ˈkru:dɪtɪ; ˈkrudətɪ/ *n* [U] **1** state or quality of being crude (2a) 粗陋; 粗糙; 欠成熟: *the crudity of his drawing* 他画的画不够成熟. **2** crude(2b) behaviour, remarks, etc 粗俗或粗鲁的行为、词语等: *I'd never met such crudity before.* 我从未见过这样粗鲁的行径.

cruel /krʊəl; ˈkruəl/ *adj* (**-ller**, **-llest**) **1** (*derog* 贬) **~ (to sb/sth)** (of people) making others suffer, esp intentionally (指人)残暴的, 残忍的, 残酷的: *a cruel boss, master, dictator, etc* 残暴的老板、主人、独裁者等 ○ *people oppressed by a cruel tyranny* 受残酷暴政压制的人们 ○ *Don't be cruel to animals.* 不要虐待动物. **2** causing pain or suffering 使人痛苦的; 让人受难的: *a cruel blow, punishment, disease* 叫人吃不消的打击、惩罚、疾病 ○ *cruel* (ie bad) *luck* 恶运 ○ *War is cruel.* 战争是残酷无情的. ▷ **cruelly** /ˈkrʊəlɪ; ˈkruəlɪ/ *adv*: *I was cruelly deceived.* 我被骗得很惨.

cruelty /ˈkrʊəltɪ; ˈkruəltɪ/ *n* **1** [U] **~ (to sb/sth)** readiness to cause pain or suffering to others; cruel actions 残暴; 残忍; 残酷: *his cruelty to his children* 他对自己孩子的虐待 ○ *He saw a lot of cruelty in the prison camp.* 他在集中营里看到许多惨不忍睹的事. **2** [C usu *pl* 通常作复数] cruel act 残暴的举动: *the tyrant's infamous cruelties* 该暴君可耻的凶残行径.

cruet /ˈkru:ɪt; ˈkruɪt/ *n* **1** small glass bottle containing oil or vinegar for use at meals (餐桌上的)调味品瓶. **2** (also ˈ**cruet-stand**) stand for holding cruets and containers for salt, pepper, mustard, etc 调味品瓶架.

cruise /kru:z; kruz/ *v* **1** [I, Ipr, Ip] sail about, either for pleasure or, in wartime, looking for enemy ships (航船)巡游, 巡航: *a destroyer cruising about (in) the Baltic Sea* 在波罗的海游弋的驱逐舰. **2** (**a**) [I, Ipr, Ip] (of a motor vehicle or an aircraft) travel at a moderate speed, using fuel efficiently (指机动车辆或飞行器)(以节省燃料的)中等速度行进: *cruising at 10 000 ft/350 miles per hour* 以每小时10 000英尺[350英里]的中速航行 ○ *a cruising speed of 50 miles per hour* 每小时50英里的中等速度. (**b**) [I, Ipr, Ip] drive a vehicle at a moderate speed 以中等速度行驶: *Taxis cruised about, hoping to pick up late fares.* 计程车以中等速度转来转去, 希望能招揽到晚归的乘客. **3** [I] (*sl* 俚) (esp of a homosexual) go about in public places looking for someone to have sex with (尤指同性恋者)在公共场所寻找性伴侣.

▷ **cruise** *n* pleasure voyage 海上航游; 乘船游览: *go on/for a cruise* 作一次海上航游 ○ *a round-the-world cruise* 乘船周游世界.

cruiser /ˈkruˈzə(r); ˈkruzə/ *n* **1** large warship 巡洋舰. **2** (also ˈ**cabin-cruiser**) motor boat with sleeping accommodation, etc, used for pleasure trips 机动游艇(有住宿设备等).

□ ˈ**cruise missile** missile, usu with a nuclear warhead, that flies at low altitude and is guided by its own computer 巡航导弹.

crumb /krʌm; krʌm/ *n* **1** [C] very small piece, esp of bread, cake or biscuit, which has fallen off a larger piece 碎屑(尤指面包、糕饼或饼干的): *sweep the crumbs off the table* 把桌上的食品屑扫掉. **2** [U] soft inner part of a loaf of bread 面包心. **3** [C] small piece or amount 少许; 一点儿: *a few crumbs of information* 点滴消息 ○ *I failed my exam, and my only crumb of comfort* (ie the only thing that consoles me) *is that I can take it again.* 我没考及格, 唯一可宽慰的是还能补考. **4** [C] (*infml* 口 *esp US*) contemptible person 可鄙的傢伙: *You little crumb!* 你这无耻小人!

crumble /ˈkrʌmbl; ˈkrʌmbl/ *v* **1** [I, Ipr, Ip, Tn, Tn·pr, Tn·p] **~ (sth) (into/to sth)**; **~ (sth) (up)** (cause sth to) be broken or rubbed into very small pieces (将某物)

弄碎; 碎成细屑: *crumble one's bread*, ie break it into crumbs 把面包弄碎 ○ *The bricks slowly crumbled in the long frost.* 砖块在长期寒冷的情况下慢慢地碎裂了. ○ *crumbling walls*, ie that are breaking apart 破裂的墙壁. **2** [I, Ipr] **~ (into/to sth)** (*fig* 比喻) gradually deteriorate or come to an end 渐渐垮掉; 走向末路: *The great empire began to crumble.* 这个大帝国开始衰落了. ○ *hopes that crumbled to dust* 破灭的希望 ○ *Their marriage is crumbling.* 他们的婚姻开始出现裂痕. **3** (idm 习语) **that's the way the cookie crumbles** ⇨ WAY[1].

▷ **crumble** *n* [U, C] pudding of stewed fruit with a crumbly topping of pastry, breadcrumbs, etc 酥皮水果点心: *apple, rhubarb, etc crumble* 苹果、大黄等点心.

crum·bly /ˈkrʌmblɪ; ˋkrʌmblɪ/ *adj* (**-ier, -iest**) that crumbles easily 易碎的: *crumbly bread, soil, etc* 易碎的面包、土壤等.

crumbs /krʌmz; krʌmz/ *interj* (*Brit infml* 口) (used to express surprise, apprehension, etc 用以表示惊骇、忧虑等).

crummy /ˈkrʌmɪ; ˋkrʌmɪ/ *adj* (**-ier, -iest**) (*infml* 口) bad; worthless; unpleasant 糟糕的; 毫无价值的; 令人厌恶的: *a crummy little street in the worst part of town* 城中最差之地段的一条邋遢的小街.

crum·pet /ˈkrʌmpɪt; ˋkrʌmpɪt/ *n* **1** [C] (in Britain) flat round unsweetened cake, usu toasted and eaten hot with butter (英国)烤面饼(通常涂上黄油热吃). **2** [U] (*Brit sl sexist* 俚, 性别偏见) women, regarded simply as sexually desirable objects (视为性对象的)女子: *There's not much crumpet around at this party.* 在这次聚会中看不到多少性感的女子. **3** (idm 习语) **a bit of crumpet/fluff/skirt/stuff** ⇨ BIT[1].

crumple /ˈkrʌmpl; ˋkrʌmpl/ *v* **1** [I, Ipr, Ip, Tn, Tn·pr, Tn·p] **~ (sth) (into sth); ~ (sth) (up)** (cause sth to) be pressed or crushed into folds or creases (将某物)压皱: *material that crumples easily* 容易起皱的衣料 ○ *a crumpled (up) suit* 皱皱巴巴的一套西装 ○ *The front of the car crumpled on impact.* 汽车的前部被撞瘪了. ○ *He crumpled the paper (up) into a ball.* 他把那张纸揉成一团. ○ (*fig* 比喻) *The child's face crumpled up and he began to cry.* 孩子脸一皱哭了起来. **2** [I, Ip] **~ (up)** (*fig* 比喻) come suddenly to an end; collapse 垮掉; 崩溃: *Her resistance to the proposal has crumpled.* 她对这个建议的抵触情绪化为乌有了.

crunch /krʌntʃ; krʌntʃ/ (also **scrunch**) *v* **1** [Tn, Tn·p] **~ sth (up)** crush sth noisily with the teeth when eating 嘎吱嘎吱地咬或嚼某物: *crunch peanuts, biscuits, etc* 嚼花生、饼干等 ○ *The dog was crunching a bone.* 那只狗在啃一块骨头. **2** [I, Tn] (cause sth to) make a harsh grating noise (使某物)发出刺耳的碎裂声: *The frozen snow crunched under our feet.* 冻结的雪在我们的脚下嘎吱作响. ○ *The wheels crunched the gravel.* 车轮碾在碎石上嘎吱嘎吱地响.

▷ **crunch** *n* **1** (also **scrunch**) (usu *sing* 通常作单数) noise made by crunching; act of crunching 碎裂声; 使发出碎裂声的动作: *There was a crunch as he bit the apple.* 在他咬苹果时, 发出嘎扎一响. **2** (idm 习语) **if/when it comes to the ˈcrunch; if/when the ˈcrunch comes** if/when the decisive moment comes 当关键时刻到来时: *He always says he'll help, but when it comes to the crunch, he does nothing.* 他口口声声说他一定帮忙, 然而事到临头他什么也不帮.

crunchy *adj* (**-ier, -iest**) (*often approv* 常作褒义) firm and crisp, and making a sharp sound when broken or crushed 硬而脆的; 碎裂时声音尖利的: *crunchy biscuits, snow* 松脆的饼干; 沙沙作响的积雪.

crup·per /ˈkrʌpə(r); ˋkrʌpɚ/ *n* **1** leather strap fixed to a saddle or harness and looped under a horse's tail 后鞧(拴在马鞍或挽具上兜过马尾的皮带). **2** rear part of a horse, above the back legs (马的)臀部.

cru·sade /kruːˈseɪd; kruˋsed/ *n* **1** any one of the military expeditions by the European Christian countries to recover the Holy Land from the Muslims in the Middle Ages 十字军(远征). **2 ~ (for/against sth); ~ (to do sth)** any struggle or campaign for sth believed to be good, or against sth believed to be bad (为争取好的或反对坏的事物的)斗争或运动: *a crusade against corruption* 反腐化运动.

▷ **cru·sade** *v* [I, Ipr] **~ (for/against sth)** take part in a crusade 参加十字军; 参与某种正义行动: *crusading for fairer treatment of minorities* 参与争取少数民族平等权利的运动. **cru·sader** *n* person taking part in a crusade 十字军战士; 某种正义行动的参与者.

crush[1] /krʌʃ; krʌʃ/ *v* **1** [Tn, Tn·pr] press or squeeze (sth/sb) hard so that there is breakage or injury 压(或挤)坏, 压(或挤)伤(某物[某人]): *Don't crush the box; it has flowers in it.* 别把盒子压破了, 里面有花. ○ *Wine is made by crushing grapes.* 葡萄酒是压榨葡萄制成的. ○ *Several people were crushed to death by the falling rocks.* 有几个人被落下来的岩石压死了. **2** [Tn, Tn·p] **~ sth (up)** break sth hard into small pieces or into powder by pressing 捣(或碾)碎某物; 把某物捣(或碾)成粉末: *Huge hammers crush (up) the rocks.* 用大锤把岩石砸成了碎块. **3** [I, Tn] (cause sth to) become full of creases or irregular folds (使某物)显得皱皱巴巴的: *The clothes were badly crushed in the suitcase.* 衣服压在箱子里皱得不像样子了. ○ *Some synthetic materials do not crush easily.* 有些化纤衣料不易起皱. **4** [Tn] defeat (sb/sth) completely; subdue 消灭, 击溃, 镇压(某人[某事物]); 制服: *The rebellion was crushed by government forces.* 政府军已把叛乱镇压下去. ○ *Her refusal crushed all our hopes.* 她一拒绝, 我们的希望就全都破灭了. ○ *He felt completely crushed* (ie humiliated) *by her last remark.* 他听到她最后的一番话感到深受凌辱. **5** (phr v) **crush (sb/sth) into, past, through, etc sth** (cause sb/sth to) move into or through a narrow space by pressing or pushing (使某人[某物])挤入或挤过: *A large crowd crushed past (the barrier).* 大群的人挤过了(障碍物). ○ *You can't crush twenty people into such a tiny room.* 不能让二十个人挤进这样一个狭小的房间里. ○ *The postman tried to crush the packet through the letter-box.* 邮递员使劲把邮件塞进信箱里. **crush sth out (of sth)** remove sth by pressing or squeezing 挤出或榨出某物: *crush the juice out of oranges* 榨橙子汁 ○ (*fig* 比喻) *With his hands round her throat he crushed the life out of her.* 他双手扼住她的喉咙把她掐死了.

▷ **crush·ing** *adj* [usu attrib 通常作定语] **1** overwhelming 压倒的: *a crushing defeat, blow, etc* 惨重的失败、打击等. **2** intended to subdue or humiliate 企图制服或羞辱对方的: *a crushing look, remark, etc* 让人受不了的脸色、话语等. **crush·ingly** *adv*.

crush[2] /krʌʃ; krʌʃ/ *n* **1** [sing] crowd of people pressed close together 拥挤的人群: *a big crush in the theatre bar* 剧院小卖部里拥挤不堪的人群 ○ *I couldn't get through the crush.* 我无法从人群中挤过去. **2** [C] **~ (on sb)** (*infml* 口) strong but typically brief liking (for sb); infatuation (对某人的)强烈而短暂的喜爱, 迷恋: *Schoolchildren often have/get crushes on teachers.* 小学生往往很钦佩老师. **3** [U] (*Brit*) drink made from fruit juice 果汁饮料: *lemon crush* 柠檬饮料.

□ **ˈcrush barrier** fence put up to control crowds 防挤栏杆.

crust /krʌst; krʌst/ *n* **1** (**a**) [C, U] hard outer surface of a loaf of bread; pastry covering of a pie, tart, etc 面包皮; 糕饼等的酥皮: *a white loaf with a crisp brown crust* 有焦皮的白面包 ○ *Cut the crusts off when you make sandwiches.* 做三明治时要把焦皮切掉. ⇨illus at BREAD 见 BREAD 之插图. (**b**) [C] (*esp rhet* 尤作修辞) slice of bread, esp a thin dry one 面包片(尤指薄而干的): (*fig* 比喻) *He'd share his last crust with you*, ie is very unselfish. 他就是剩下最后一片面包也会与你分享. **2** [C, U] hard surface 硬的表面: *a thin crust of ice, frozen snow, etc* 薄薄的一层冰、冻结的雪等 ○ *the Earth's crust*, ie the part nearest its surface 地壳. **3** [C, U] hard deposit on the inside of a bottle of wine, esp old port (葡萄酒的)沉淀物. **4** (idm 习语) **the upper crust** ⇨ UPPER.

▷ **crust** *v* (phr v) **crust over** become covered with a crust 表层变硬: *The surface of the liquid gradually crusted over.* 液体表面渐渐地结了一层皮. **crusted** *adj* **1** [usu pred 通常作表语] **~ (with sth)** having a hardened covering; encrusted 有硬壳; 结壳: *walls crusted with dirt* 积满污垢的墙. **2** [usu attrib 通常作定语] (of port) blended from different vintages and matured in bottles (指红葡萄酒)由不同年份的葡萄酒混合装瓶使之醇和.

crus·ta·cean /krʌˈsteɪʃn; krʌsˋteʃən/ *n* any of various types of animal (eg crabs, lobsters, shrimps) that have a hard outer shell and live mostly in water; shellfish 甲壳纲动物(如蟹、虾); 贝类.

crusty /ˈkrʌstɪ; ˋkrʌstɪ/ *adj* (**-ier, -iest**) **1** having or resembling a crisp crust 有(或似)脆皮的: *crusty French bread* 有脆皮的法式面包 ○ *a crusty pizza base* 形成脆的硬皮的意大利烤饼的底部. **2** (*infml* 口) (esp of older people or their behaviour) easily angered; short-tempered (尤指上年纪的人或其行为)动辄发火的, 急性子的: *a crusty old soldier* 脾气暴躁的老兵.

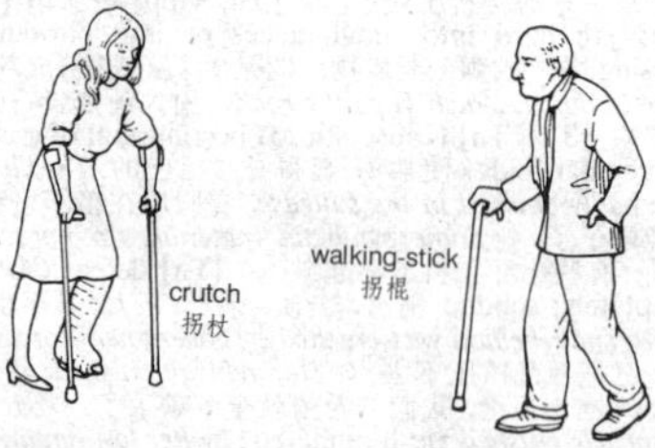

crutch /krʌtʃ; krʌtʃ/ *n* **1** support in the form of a pole, placed under the armpit to help a lame person to walk (病人用的)拐杖: *a pair of crutches* 一副拐杖 ○ *go about on crutches* 撑着一副拐杖走来走去. ⇨illus 见插图. **2** (*fig* 比喻) person or thing that provides help or support 提供帮助或支持的人或事物: *He uses his wife as a kind of crutch because of his lack of confidence.* 他缺乏自信心, 总把妻子当作主心骨. **3** = CROTCH.

crux /krʌks; krʌks/ *n* [sing] most vital or difficult part of a matter, an issue, etc 事情、问题等最重要或最棘手的部分: *Now we come to the crux of the problem.* 现在我们来谈问题的症结所在.

cry[1] /kraɪ; kraɪ/ *v* (*pt, pp* **cried**) **1** [I, Ipr, Tn no passive 不用于被动语态] **~ (for/over sth/sb)**; **~ (with sth)** weep; shed (tears) 哭; 流(泪): *He cried because he had hurt his knee.* 他摔伤膝盖哭了起来. ○ *cry for joy*, ie because one is happy 喜极而泣 ○ *The child was crying for* (ie because he wanted) *his mother.* 那孩子哭着要妈妈. ○ *cry with pain, hunger, etc* 痛、饿…得哭起来 ○ *How many tears have I cried over* (ie because of) *you?* 我为你流了多少眼泪呀! ⇨Usage 见所附用法. **2** (**a**) [I, Ip] **~ (out)** (of people, animals, birds) make loud wordless sounds expressing fear, pain, etc (指人、野兽、禽鸟)大叫(表示恐惧、疼痛等): *The monkeys cry (out) shrilly when they see danger.* 猴子遇到危险时尖声大叫. ○ *She cried (out) in pain when her tooth was pulled out.* 她拔牙时痛得叫了起来. ⇨Usage at SHOUT 用法见SHOUT. (**b**) [Ipr, Ip, Tn no passive 不用于被动语态] **~ (out) (for sth)** call out loudly in words; exclaim 喊; 喊叫; 呼喊: *He cried (out) for mercy.* 他大声求饶. ○ *'Help, help!' he cried.* '救命啊, 救命啊!' 他喊道. ○ (*rhet* 修辞) *But what about the workers, I hear you cry*, ie say. 然而工人们又如何呢, 你说说看. **3** [Tn] (*dated* 旧) announce (goods, etc) for sale by calling out 叫卖(商品等): *cry one's wares* 叫卖货物. **4** (idm 习语) **cry one's ˈeyes/ˈheart out** weep bitterly 痛哭. **cry over spilt ˈmilk** express regret for sth that has happened and cannot be remedied 为已经发生而无法补救的事懊悔: *You've broken it now; it's no use crying over spilt milk!* 你现在既已把它损坏了, 后悔是没有用的! **cry/sob oneself to sleep** ⇨ SLEEP[1]. **cry ˈwolf** say there is danger when there is none 喊狼来了; 发假警报. **for ˌcrying out ˈloud** (used to express protest 用以表示抗议): *For crying out loud! Why did you do that?* 我的天哪! 你为什么要干那种事? **laugh till/until one cries** ⇨ LAUGH. **5** (phr v) **cry sth down** say that sth is not very good, important, etc 贬低某事物: *Don't cry down her real achievements.* 不要贬低她真正的成就. **cry off** withdraw from sth one has promised to do 取消自己的诺言; 打退堂鼓: *I said I would go, but had to cry off at the last moment.* 我是说过要去的, 但事到临头却不得不改变了主意. **cry out for sth** demand sth; require sth 要求某事物; 需要某事物: *People are crying out for free elections.* 人民要求自由选举. ○ *This system is crying out for reform*, ie urgently needs to be reformed. 这种制度亟需改革.

NOTE ON USAGE 用法: Compare **cry, sob, weep, wail** and **whimper.** 试比较**cry**、**sob**、**weep**、**wail**、**whimper**这五个词. They all indicate people expressing emotions, often with tears. 这些词均指强烈感情的表现, 常伴有眼泪. **Cry** has the widest use and may be the result of unhappiness, joy, etc or, especially with babies, of physical discomfort ☆ **cry** 使用最广, 可为出于难过、喜悦等或因身体不适(尤指小儿): *The little boy was crying because he was lost.* 那小孩因迷路而哭. ○ *Babies cry when they are hungry.* 婴儿肚子饿了就哭. **Weep** is more formal than cry and can suggest stronger emotions ☆ **weep** 比cry文雅, 可表示更为强烈的感情: *The hostages wept for joy on their release.* 人质获释时喜极而泣. **Sob** indicates crying with irregular and noisy breathing ☆ **sob** 意为啜泣. It is usually associated with misery 通常与伤心事有关: *He sobbed for hours when his cat died.* 他的猫死了, 他抽抽搭搭地哭了半天. Children **whimper** with fear or in complaint 儿童因害怕或抱怨而哭用**whimper**. ☆ **Wail** indicates long noisy crying in grief or complaint ☆ **wail** 意为痛哭或嚎啕大哭(因悲痛或哀怨): *The mourners were wailing loudly.* 送葬的人都嚎啕大哭. Note that all these verbs can be used instead of 'say' to indicate a way of speaking 注意以上各词均可代替'say'使用, 表示这种说话的方式: *'I've lost my daddy,' the little boy cried/sobbed/wept/whimpered/wailed.* '我找不到爸爸了,' 小孩哭着[抽抽搭搭地/哭哭啼啼地/呜呜咽咽地/痛哭流涕地]说.

cry[2] /kraɪ; kraɪ/ *n* **1** [C] (**a**) loud wordless sound expressing grief, pain, joy, etc 大叫声(表示悲伤、疼痛、喜悦): *a cry of terror* 惊恐的叫声 ○ *the cry of an animal in pain* 动物的疼叫声. (**b**) loud utterance of words; call; shout 叫喊; 呼喊; 呼叫: *angry cries from the mob* 闹事的人群愤怒的叫喊. (**c**) (usu *sing* 通常作单数) characteristic call of an animal or a bird 动物的嚎叫; 鸟鸣: *the cry of the rook* 秃鼻乌鸦的鸣叫. **2** [sing] act or period of weeping 哭的动作或期间: *Have a good long cry: it will do you good.* 痛痛快快地哭一场吧, 哭出来就好受了. **3** [C] (*dated* 旧) words shouted to give information 大声传叫的话语: *the cry of the night-watchman* 守夜人的大声传叫 ○ *the old street cries of London, eg 'Fresh herrings!'* 伦敦街上熟悉的叫卖声, 如'鲜鲱鱼!' **4** [C] (esp in compounds 尤用以构成复合词) slogan or phrase, used for a principle or cause 口号; 标语: *a 'battle-cry* ○ *a 'war-cry* ○ *'Lower taxes' was their cry* (ie their public demand). 他们的口号是'减税'. **5** (idm 习语) **a far cry from sth/from doing sth** ⇨ FAR[1]. **hue and cry** ⇨ HUE[2]. **in full cry** ⇨ FULL.

□ **'cry-baby** *n* (*infml derog* 口, 贬) person who weeps too often or without good reason 动不动就哭的人: *He's a dreadful cry-baby.* 他简直一碰就哭.

cry·ing /ˈkraɪɪŋ; ˋkraɪɪŋ/ *adj* [attrib 作定语] **1** (esp of sth bad, wrong, etc) extremely bad and shocking (尤指坏事)极糟糕的, 令人震惊的: *It's a crying shame, the way they treat their children.* 他们对待子女的做法真是太不像话了. **2** great and urgent (used esp in the expression shown) 重要而紧急的(尤用于以下示例): *a crying need* 迫切的需要.

cryo·genics /ˌkraɪəˈdʒenɪks; ˌkraɪəˋdʒɛnɪks/ *n* [sing *v*] scientific study or use of very low temperatures 低温学. ▷ **cryo·genic** *adj*.

crypt /krɪpt; krɪpt/ *n* room beneath the floor of a church (教堂的)地下室.

cryptic /ˈkrɪptɪk; ˋkrɪptɪk/ *adj* with a meaning that is hidden or not easily understood; mysterious 含有隐义的; 晦涩难懂的; 神秘的: *a cryptic remark, message, smile, etc* 令人困惑的言语、信息、微笑等. ▷ **crypt·ic·ally** /-klɪ; -klɪ/ *adv*: *'Yes and no,' she replied cryptically.* '又是又不是,' 她神乎其神地回答说.

crypt(o)- *comb form* 构词成分 (forming *ns* 用以构成名词) hidden; secret 隐藏的; 秘密的: *cryptogram* ○ *a ˌcrypto-'fascist*, ie a person who has fascist sympathies but keeps them secret.

cryp·to·gam /ˈkrɪptəgæm; ˋkrɪptəˌgæm/ *n* any flowerless plant, such as a fern, moss or fungus 隐花植物(无花植物, 如蕨类、苔藓类或菌类).

cryp·to·gram /ˈkrɪptəgræm; ˋkrɪptəˌgræm/ *n* message

written in code 密码材料; 密码文件.

crys·tal /ˈkrɪstl; ˋkrɪstl̩/ *n* **1** (**a**) [U] transparent colourless mineral, such as quartz 无色透明的矿物(如石英); 水晶. (**b**) [C] piece of this, esp when used as an ornament 水晶石; (尤指)水晶饰品: *a necklace of crystals* 水晶珠项链 ○ [attrib 作定语] *a crystal bracelet, watch, etc* 水晶镯子、石英表. **2** [U] high-quality glassware, made into bowls, vases, glasses, etc 晶质玻璃制品(如碗、瓶、杯等): *The dining-table shone with silver and crystal.* 餐桌上摆的银制餐具和晶质玻璃器皿闪闪发光. ○ [attrib 作定语] *a crystal vase, chandelier, etc* 晶质玻璃花瓶、吊灯等. **3** [C] (*chemistry* 化) regular many-sided shape which the molecules of a substance form when it is solid 结晶(体): *sugar and salt crystals* 糖和盐的结晶体 ○ *snow and ice crystals* 雪和冰的结晶体. **4** [C] (*US*) glass or plastic cover of the face of a watch 表蒙子.

□ ˌ**crystal** ˈ**ball** clear glass sphere in which future events can supposedly be seen 水晶球(据说可用以窥见未来情况的透明玻璃球).

ˌ**crystal** ˈ**clear 1** (of glass, water, etc) entirely clear (指玻璃、水等)完全透明的. **2** (*fig* 比喻) very easy to understand; completely understood 浅近易懂的; 明明白白的: *She made her meaning crystal clear.* 她把她的意思解释得清清楚楚.

ˈ**crystal-gazing** *n* [U] **1** looking into a crystal ball 水晶球占卜术. **2** (*fig* 比喻) attempting to foretell future events 预测未来.

ˈ**crystal set** early type of radio set 晶体检波接收机, 矿石收音机(早期的收音机).

crys·tal·line /ˈkrɪstəlaɪn; ˋkrɪstl̩ˌaɪn/ *adj* **1** made of or resembling crystals 水晶制的; 水晶般的: *crystalline structure, minerals, etc* 晶体的结构、矿物等. **2** (*fml* 文) very clear; transparent 清澈明净的; 透明的: *water of crystalline purity* 清澈纯净的水.

crys·tal·lize, -ise /ˈkrɪstəlaɪz; ˋkrɪstl̩ˌaɪz/ *v* **1** [I, Tn] (cause sth to) form into crystals (使某物)结晶. **2** [I, Ipr, Tn, Tn·pr] **~ (sth) (into sth)** (*fig* 比喻) (of ideas, plans, etc) become clear and definite; cause (ideas, plans, etc) to become clear and definite (指思想、计划等)变得清晰而明确; 使(思想、计划等)具体化: *His vague ideas crystallized into a definite plan.* 他那些模糊的想法变成了一个明确的计划. ○ *Reading your book helped crystallize my views.* 我阅读你的著作有助于澄清我的思想.

▷ **crys·tal·liza·tion, -isation** /ˌkrɪstəlaɪˈzeɪʃn; *US* -lɪˈz-; ˋkrɪstl̩əˋzeʃən/ *n* [U].

crys·tal·lized, -ised *adj* (esp of fruit) preserved in sugar and covered with sugar-crystals (尤指水果)蜜饯的, 有糖霜的: *a box of crystallized oranges* 一盒蜜饯橙饼.

c/s *abbr* 缩写 = CPS.

CSE /ˌsi: es ˈi:; ˌsi ɛs ˋi/ *abbr* 缩写 = (*Brit*) Certificate of Secondary Education 中学文凭: *have 4 CSEs* 中学文凭考试有4科合格 ○ *take CSE in 6 subjects* 中学文凭考试中报考6门科目. Cf 参看 GCE, GCSE.

CSM /ˌsi: es ˈem; ˌsi ɛs ˋɛm/ *abbr* 缩写 = (*Brit*) Company Sergeant-Major 连的军士长.

CST /ˌsi: es ˈti:; ˌsi ɛs ˋti/ *abbr* 缩写 = (*US*) Central Standard Time 中部标准时间.

ct *abbr* 缩写 = (*pl* **cts**) **1** carat: *an 18 ct gold ring* 一只18克拉的金戒指. **2** cent: *50 cts* 50分钱.

cu *abbr* 缩写 = cubic: *a volume of 2 cu m*, ie 2 cubic metres 2立方米体积.

cub /kʌb; kʌb/ *n* **1** [C] young fox, bear, lion, tiger, etc (狐、熊、狮、虎等的)幼兽. **2** (**a**) **the Cubs** [pl] junior branch of the Scout Association 幼童军: *to join the Cubs* 加入幼童军. (**b**) **Cub** [C] (also ˈ**Cub Scout**) member of this 幼童军成员. **3** (*dated* 旧) rude young man 毛头小伙子: *You cheeky young cub!* 你这莽撞的毛头小伙子!

□ ˈ**cub reporter** young and inexperienced newspaper reporter 年轻缺少经验的记者.

cubby-hole /ˈkʌbɪ həʊl; ˋkʌbɪˌhol/ *n* small enclosed space or room 围起来的小天地; 小房间: *My office is a cubby-hole in the basement.* 我的办公室是在地下室的一个小房间.

cube /kju:b; kjub/ *n* **1** (**a**) (*geometry* 几) solid body with six equal square sides 立方体; 立方形. ⇨illus 见插图. (**b**) six-sided piece of sth, esp food 立方形的东西(尤指食物): *an ice cube* 冰块儿 ○ *Cut the meat into cubes.* 把肉切成一块一块的. **2** (*mathematics* 数) result of multiplying a number by itself twice 立方(三次幂): *The cube of 5 (5^3) is 125 ($5 \times 5 \times 5 = 125$).* 5的立方($5^3$)是125($5\times5\times5=125$). ⇨App 5 见附录5.

▷ **cube** *v* **1** [Tn usu passive 通常用于被动语态] (*mathematics* 数) multiply (a number) by itself twice 使(某数)自乘两次; 求(某数)立方: *10 cubed is 1 000.* 10的立方为1 000. **2** [Tn] cut (food) into cubes 把(食物)切成块状.

□ ˌ**cube** ˈ**root** number which, when cubed, produces the stated number 立方根: *The cube root of 64 ($\sqrt[3]{64}$) is 4 ($4 \times 4 \times 4 = 64$).* 64的立方根($\sqrt[3]{64}$)是4($4\times4\times4=64$).

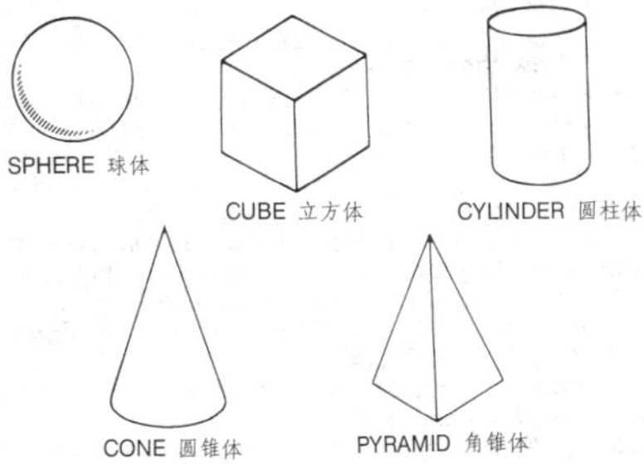

cube and other three-dimensional shapes
立方体及其他形状的立体

cu·bic /ˈkju:bɪk; ˋkjubɪk/ *adj* **1** [attrib 作定语] (**a**) having the volume of a cube with sides of the specified length 具有立方体积的; 立方的: *a cubic metre of coal* 一立方米的煤 ○ *a car with a 2 000 cc capacity*, ie 2 000 cubic centimetres 汽缸容量为2 000立方厘米的汽车. (**b**) measured or expressed in cubic units 用立方单位度量或表示的: *cubic content* 容量; 容积. **2** (having the shape) of a cube 立方形的: *a cubic figure* 立方形.

cu·bical /ˈkju:bɪkl; ˋkjubɪkl̩/ *adj* = CUBIC 2.

cu·bicle /ˈkju:bɪkl; ˋkjubɪkl̩/ *n* small compartment made by separating off part of a larger room, eg for dressing, undressing or sleeping in (大房间中隔出的)小室.

cu·bism /ˈkju:bɪzəm; ˋkjubɪzəm/ *n* [U] modern style of art in which objects are represented as if they are made up of geometrical shapes 立体主义; 立体派.

▷ **cu·bist** /ˈkju:bɪst; ˋkjubɪst/ *adj* (in the style) of cubism 立体主义的; 立体主义风格的. — *n* cubist artist 立体派艺术家.

cuck·old /ˈkʌkəʊld; ˋkʌkl̩d/ *n* (*arch usu derog* 古, 通常作贬义) man whose wife has committed adultery 妻子与人通奸的人.

▷ **cuck·old** *v* [Tn] (*arch* 古) (**a**) (of a man) make (another man) a cuckold by having sex with his wife (指男子)(与某人妻子通奸)使(某人)当乌龟. (**b**) (of a woman) make (her husband) a cuckold by having sex with another man (指女子)(与人通奸)使(丈夫)当乌龟.

cuckoo[1] /ˈkʊku:; ˋkʊku/ *n* migratory bird with a call that sounds like its name, that leaves its eggs in the nests of other birds 杜鹃; 布谷; 子规; 杜宇.

□ ˈ**cuckoo clock** clock which strikes the hours with sounds like a cuckoo's call 布谷鸟自鸣钟(报时似布谷鸟的叫声).

cuckoo[2] /ˈkʊku:; ˋkʊku/ *adj* [usu pred 通常作表语] (*infml* 口) foolish; mad 愚蠢; 疯狂: *He has gone absolutely cuckoo.* 他简直疯了.

cu·cum·ber /ˈkju:kʌmbə(r); ˋkjukʌmbɚ/ *n* **1** (**a**) [C, U] long green-skinned fleshy vegetable used raw in sandwiches and salads, or pickled 黄瓜: *a huge cucumber* 一条大黄瓜 ○ *Have some cucumber.* 吃点黄瓜吧. ○ [attrib 作定语] *cucumber salad, sandwiches, etc* 有黄瓜的色拉、三明治等. ⇨illus at SALAD 见SALAD之插图. (**b**) [C] plant that produces this 黄瓜藤. **2** (idm 习语) **cool as a cucumber** ⇨ COOL[1].

cud /kʌd; kʌd/ *n* **1** [U] food that cattle, etc bring back from the stomach into the mouth to chew again 反刍的食物(牛等自胃部返回口中再次咀嚼的食物). **2** (idm 习语) **chew the cud** ⇨ CHEW.

cuddle /ˈkʌdl; ˋkʌdḷ/ *v* **1** [I, Tn] hold (sb, sth, each other) close and lovingly in one's arms 搂抱(某人、某物); (互相)拥抱: *The lovers kissed and cuddled on the sofa.* 那对恋人在沙发上又是接吻又是搂抱. ○ *The child cuddled her doll (to her chest).* 那孩子(怀里)抱着玩具娃娃. **2** (phr v) **cuddle up (to/against sb/sth)**; **cuddle up (together)** lie close and comfortably; nestle 挨在一起舒适地躺着; 偎依: *She cuddled up to her mother.* 她偎依着母亲. ○ *They cuddled up (together) under the blanket.* 他们盖着毯子(在一起)搂着.

▷ **cuddle** *n* [sing] act of cuddling; hug 搂抱; 拥抱: *have a cuddle together* 搂抱在一起.

cuddle·some /-səm; -səm/, **cud·dly** /ˈkʌdlɪ; ˋkʌdlɪ/ (**-ier, -iest**) *adjs* (*infml* 口) pleasant to cuddle 不由得想搂抱的; 可爱的: *a cuddly teddy bear* 可爱的玩具熊.

cud·gel /ˈkʌdʒl; ˋkʌdʒəl/ *n* **1** short thick stick or club 粗而短的棍棒. **2** (idm 习语) **take up the cudgels for/on behalf of sb/sth** (start to) defend or support sb/sth strongly (奋起)保卫或支持某人[某事物]. ▷ **cud·gel** *v* (**-ll**; *US* also **-l-**) **1** [Tn] hit (sb) with a cudgel 用粗而短的棍棒打(某人). **2** (idm 习语) **cudgel one's ˈbrains** think very hard 冥思苦索; 绞尽脑汁: *Hard as I cudgelled my brains, I couldn't remember her name.* 尽管我苦思苦想, 还是想不起她的名字.

cue[1] /kjuː; kju/ *n* **1 ~ (for sth/to do sth)** thing said or done to signal sb's turn to say or do sth, esp in a theatrical or other performance 提示, 暗示(尤指戏剧等演出中对某人起暗示作用的道白或动作): *Actors have to learn their cues* (ie the last words of the speeches just before their own speeches) *as well as their own lines.* 演员不仅要记住台词, 还要记住其他演员的暗示. ○ *When I nod my head, that's your cue to interrupt the meeting.* 我一点头, 就是暗示你把会议中断. ○ (*fig* 比喻) *And they all lived happily ever afterwards — which sounds like the cue* (ie an appropriate moment) *for a song.* 从此以后他们全都过上了幸福的生活——这句话听起来像是舞台提示, 说完就开始唱歌. **2** example of how to behave, what to do, etc (行为、行动等的)榜样: *take one's cue from sb*, ie be guided by the way sb does sth 照某人的样子去做 ○ *Follow her cue, and one day you'll be a great scholar.* 你以她为榜样, 总有一天会成为博学之士. **3** (idm 习语) **(right) on cue** at exactly the appropriate or expected moment 就在这时候: *He said she would be back very soon and, right on cue, she walked in.* 他说她很快就回来, 说着说着, 她走进来了.

▷ **cue** *v* (*pres p* **cueing**) [Tn, Tn·p] **~ sb (in)** give a cue to sb (to do sth) 提示, 暗示某人(做某事): *I'll cue you in* (ie give you a signal to start) *by nodding my head.* 我一点头, 你就开始.

cue[2] /kjuː; kju/ *n* long tapering leather-tipped stick used for striking the ball in snooker, billiards, etc (打台球用的)球杆. ⇨illus at SNOOKER 见 SNOOKER 之插图.

cuff[1] /kʌf; kʌf/ *n* **1** [C] end of a coat or shirt sleeve at the wrist 袖口: *frayed cuffs* 磨破的袖口. ⇨illus at JACKET 见 JACKET 之插图. **2** (*US*) = TURN-UP (TURN[1]). **3 cuffs** [pl] (*sl* 俚) handcuffs 手铐. **4** (idm 习语) ˌ**off the ˈcuff** without previous thought or preparation 未经思考; 未经准备: *make a remark off the cuff* 即席发言 ○ [attrib 作定语] *an ˌoff-the-cuff ˈjoke, ˈremark, etc* 随口而出的笑话、言语等.

□ ˈ**cuff-link** *n* (usu *pl* 通常作复数) one of a pair of fasteners for shirt cuffs (衬衫的)袖扣: *a pair of cuff-links* 一对袖扣.

cuff[2] /kʌf; kʌf/ *v* [Tn] give (sb) a light blow with the open hand, esp on the head 用掌轻拍(某人)(尤指头部). ▷ **cuff** *n* such a blow (用掌的)轻拍.

cuir·ass /kwɪˈræs; kwɪˋræs/ *n* piece of armour protecting the upper body, consisting of a breastplate and back-plate fastened together (由胸甲和背甲两部分合成的)上半身铠甲.

cuis·ine /kwɪˈziːn; kwɪˋzin/ *n* [U] (*French* 法) (style of) cooking 烹饪(风味): *French, Italian, etc cuisine* 法国、意大利菜 ○ *a restaurant where the cuisine is excellent* 饭菜精美的餐馆.

cul-de-sac /ˈkʌl də sæk; ˋkʌldəˋsæk/ *n* (*pl* **cul-de-sacs**) (*French* 法) street open at one end only; blind alley 一端不通的街道; 死胡同.

cu·lin·ary /ˈkʌlɪnərɪ; *US* -nerɪ; ˋkjuləˌnɛrɪ/ *adj* of or for cooking 烹饪的; 烹饪用的: *culinary skill, implements* 烹饪技术、用具 ○ *a culinary triumph*, ie a very well cooked dish or meal 精心烹调的美味.

cull /kʌl; kʌl/ *v* **1** [Tn] **(a)** kill (a certain number of usu weaker animals) in a herd, in order to reduce its size 杀掉(一定数量的通常为体弱的动物)以减少兽群总数; 剔除: *Deer are culled by hunters.* 猎人把鹿杀掉了一批. **(b)** reduce (the herd) in this way 用有选择地杀掉一部分的方法减少(牧群的数量): *The herd must be culled.* 必须有选择地杀掉部分牧畜. **2** [Tn, Tn·pr] **~ sth (from sth)** select or obtain sth from various different sources 从各个不同的方面挑选出或获得某事物: *information culled from various reference books* 从各种参考书中摘出的资料.

▷ **cull** *n* **1** [C] act of culling 剔除; 挑选: *an annual seal cull* 一年一度对体弱海豹的杀戮. **2** [sing] animal(s) culled 剔出来杀掉的动物: *sell the cull as meat* 出售被剔出来杀掉的动物以供食用.

cul·len·der = COLANDER.

cul·min·ate /ˈkʌlmɪneɪt; ˋkʌlməˌnet/ *v* [Ipr] **~ in sth** (*fml* 文) have the specified final conclusion or result 终于获得某种结局或结果: *a long struggle that culminated in success* 终于取得胜利的长期斗争 ○ *Her career culminated in her appointment as director.* 她一生事业的顶峰是当上了董事. ○ *a series of border clashes which culminated in full-scale war* 导致全面战争的一连串的边界冲突事件.

▷ **cul·mina·tion** /ˌkʌlmɪˈneɪʃn; ˌkʌlməˋneʃən/ *n* [sing] eventual conclusion or result 结局; 结果: *the successful culmination of a long campaign* 一场持久战的胜利结束.

cu·lottes /kjuːˈlɒts; kjuˋlɑts/ *n* [pl] women's wide shorts that look like a skirt (女用的)裙裤: *a pair of culottes* 一条裙裤.

culp·able /ˈkʌlpəbl; ˋkʌlpəbḷ/ *adj* **~ (for sth)** deserving blame; blameworthy 应受责备的; 难辞其咎的: *I cannot be held culpable (for their mistakes).* 不能(把他们的错误)归咎于我. ○ (*law* 律) *culpable negligence*, ie failure to do what one should do 应受惩罚的玩忽行为. ▷ **culp·ab·il·ity** /ˌkʌlpəˈbɪlətɪ; ˌkʌlpəˋbɪlətɪ/ *n* [U]. **culp·ably** /ˈkʌlpəblɪ; ˋkʌlpəblɪ/ *adv*.

cul·prit /ˈkʌlprɪt; ˋkʌlprɪt/ *n* person who has done sth wrong; offender 犯过者; 犯罪者: *Someone broke a cup: who was the culprit?* 有人把杯子打碎了, 是谁干的? ○ *Police are searching for the culprits.* 警方正在搜捕罪犯.

cult /kʌlt; kʌlt/ *n* **1** system of religious worship, esp one that is expressed in rituals 宗教的膜拜; (尤指)膜拜仪式: *the mysterious nature-worship cults of these ancient peoples* 这些先民向大自然的神秘膜拜仪式. **2 ~ (of sb/sth)** (*often derog* 常作贬义) devotion to or admiration of sb/sth 狂热的献身或崇拜: *the cult of physical fitness* 对身体健美的狂热追求 ○ *a personality cult*, ie admiration of a person rather than of what he does or the office he holds 个人崇拜. **3** popular fashion or craze 时尚; 一时的狂热: *the current pop music cult* 流行音乐的热潮 ○ [attrib 作定语] *a ˈcult word*, ie one used because it is fashionable among members of a particular (usu small) group 时髦用词 ○ *an artist with a cult following*, ie who is admired by such a group 有狂热追随者的艺术家.

cul·tiv·able /ˈkʌltɪvəbl; ˋkʌltəvəbḷ/ *adj* that can be cultivated 可耕的; 可种植的; 可培养的: *cultivable soil, land, etc* 可耕的土壤、土地等.

cul·tiv·ate /ˈkʌltɪveɪt; ˋkʌltəˌvet/ *v* [Tn] **1 (a)** prepare and use (land, soil, etc) for growing crops 耕(地等); 耕作. **(b)** grow (crops) 种植(庄稼). **2 (a)** make (the mind, feelings, etc) more educated and refined 陶冶(思想、感情等): *reading the best authors in an attempt to cultivate her mind* 她为陶冶情操而阅读最优秀作家的作品. **(b)** (*sometimes derog* 有时作贬义) (try to) acquire or develop (a relationship, an attitude, etc) (力求)建立或发展(某种关系)、采取(某种态度): *cultivating the friendship of influential people* 巴结有权势的人 ○ *cultivate an air of indifference* 采取无动于衷的态度. **(c)** (*sometimes derog* 有时作贬义) (try to) win the friendship or support of (sb) (力求)获得(某人)的友谊或支持: *You must cultivate people who can help you in*

business. 你得结交在业务上对你有用的人.
▷ **cul·ti·vated** *adj* (of people, manners, etc) having or showing good taste and refinement (指人、态度等)趣味高雅的, 有修养的.

cul·ti·va·tion /ˌkʌltɪˈveɪʃn; ˌkʌltəˈveʃən/ *n* [U] cultivating (CULTIVATE 1) or being cultivated 耕作; 耕种: *the cultivation of the soil* 耕作 ○ *land that is under cultivation*, ie is being cultivated 耕种的土地 ○ *bring land into cultivation* 开垦荒地.

cul·tiv·ator /ˈkʌltɪveɪtə(r); ˈkʌltəˌvetɚ/ *n* **1** machine for breaking up soil, destroying weeds, etc 耕耘机. **2** person who cultivates (CULTIVATE 1) 耕种者.

cul·tural /ˈkʌltʃərəl; ˈkʌltʃərəl/ *adj* of or involving culture 文化的; 与文化有关的: *cultural differences, activities, etc* 文化的差异、活动等 ○ *cultural studies*, eg of art, literature, etc 人文学科(如艺术、文学等) ○ *a cultural desert*, ie a place with few cultural activities 文化沙漠.
▷ **cul·tur·ally** /-rəlɪ; -rəlɪ/ *adv*.

cul·ture /ˈkʌltʃə(r); ˈkʌltʃɚ/ *n* **1** [U] (**a**) refined understanding and appreciation of art, literature, etc 文化(对于文艺等的深刻的了解和鉴赏): *a society without much culture* 文化不发达的社会 ○ *She is a woman of considerable culture.* 她是个文化修养很高的女子. ○ *Universities should be centres of culture.* 大学应该是文化的中心. (**b**) (*often derog* 常作贬义) art, literature, etc collectively 文化(文学、艺术等的总称): *tourists coming to Venice in search of culture* 前来威尼斯附庸风雅的游客. **2** [U] state of intellectual development of a society 文化(一个社会智力发展的状况): *twentieth-century mass culture* 二十世纪的大众文化 ○ *a period of high/low culture* 文化高[低]的时期. **3** [U, C] particular form of intellectual expression, eg in art and literature 文化(智力表现的形式, 如体现于文艺方面): *We owe much to Greek culture.* 我们得益于希腊文化之处甚多. ○ *She has studied the cultures of Oriental countries.* 她研究过东方各国的文化. **4** [U, C] customs, arts, social institutions, etc of a particular group or people 文化(某群体或民族的风俗、人文现象、社会惯例等): *the culture of the Eskimos* 爱斯基摩人的文化 ○ *working-class culture* 工人阶级的文化. **5** [U] development through training, exercise, treatment, etc 锻炼; 训练; 修养: *physical culture*, ie developing one's muscles and fitness by doing exercises 体育 ○ *The culture of the mind is vital.* 修心养性是极其重要的. **6** [U] growing of plants or rearing of certain types of animal (eg bees, silkworms, etc) to obtain a crop or improve the species (植物的)栽培; (动物, 如蜂、蚕等, 良种的)培育: *bulb culture*, ie the growing of flowers from bulbs 鳞茎植物的栽培. **7** [C] (*biology* 生) group of bacteria grown for medical or scientific study 培养的细菌: *a culture of cholera germs* 培养出的霍乱菌.
▷ **cul·tured** *adj* (of people) appreciating art, literature, etc; refined; cultivated (指人)懂文学、艺术等的, 有教养的, 文雅的.
□ ˈ**cultured pearl** pearl formed by an oyster into which a piece of grit has been placed 养殖珍珠.
ˈ**culture shock** confusion and disorientation caused by contact with a civilization other than one's own 文化冲击.
ˈ**culture vulture** (*infml, joc or derog* 口, 谑或贬) person eager to acquire culture 贪求文化的人.

cul·vert /ˈkʌlvət; ˈkʌlvɚt/ *n* drain that crosses beneath a road, railway, etc; underground channel for electrical cables (公路、铁路等的)涵洞; 地下电缆道.

cum /kʌm; kʌm/ *prep* (used to link two ns 用以联结两个名词) also used as; as well as 兼作; 和: *a bedroom-cum-sitting-room* 卧室、客厅两用房间 ○ *a barman-cum-waiter* 酒吧(男)服务员兼招待员.

cum·ber·some /ˈkʌmbəsəm; ˈkʌmbɚsəm/ *adj* **1** heavy and difficult to carry, wear, etc (对于携带、穿戴等)笨重的: *a cumbersome parcel, overcoat* 沉重的包裹、大衣. **2** slow and inefficient 迟缓而缺乏效率的: *the university's cumbersome administrative procedures* 这所大学拖拖拉拉的行政工作.

cumin /ˈkʌmɪn; ˈkʌmɪn/ *n* [U] (plant with) pleasant-smelling seeds used for flavouring 欧莳萝; 小茴香; 欧莳萝子; 小茴香子(气味芳香, 用作调味品).

cum·mer·bund /ˈkʌməbʌnd; ˈkʌmɚˌbʌnd/ *n* sash worn around the waist, esp under a dinner-jacket 腰带(尤指男子穿晚礼服时用的).

cu·mu·lat·ive /ˈkjuːmjʊlətɪv; *US* -leɪtɪv; ˈkjumjəˌletɪv/ *adj* gradually increasing in amount, force, etc by one addition after another (数量、力量等)渐增的, 累积的: *the cumulative effect of several illnesses* 几种疾病日积月累造成的影响. ▷ **cu·mu·lat·ively** *adv*.

cu·mulus /ˈkjuːmjʊləs; ˈkjumjələs/ *n* (*pl* **-li** /-laɪ; -ˌlaɪ/) [U, C] cloud formed of rounded masses heaped on a flat base 积云.

cu·nei·form /ˈkjuːnɪfɔːm; *US* kjuːˈnɪəfɔːrm; kjuˈnɪəˌfɔrm/ *adj* wedge-shaped 楔形的: *cuneiform characters*, ie as used in old Persian or Assyrian writing 楔形文字(如古代波斯文或亚述文所用的).

cun·ni·lin·gus /ˌkʌnɪˈlɪŋgəs; ˌkʌnəˈlɪŋgəs/ *n* [U] stimulation of a woman's outer sexual organs with the mouth or tongue 舐阴(用口或舌刺激女性外生殖器之性行为): *perform cunnilingus on sb* 对某人作舐阴举动.

cun·ning /ˈkʌnɪŋ; ˈkʌnɪŋ/ *adj* **1** (**a**) clever at deceiving people 善于骗人的: *a cunning liar, spy, cheat, etc* 诡计多端的说谎者、间谍、骗子等 ○ *He's a cunning old fox.* 他是诡计多端的老狐狸. (**b**) showing this kind of cleverness 狡猾的; 诡诈的: *a cunning smile, trick, plot, etc* 狡猾的微笑、行骗手段、计谋等. **2** ingenious 灵巧的; 巧妙的: *a cunning device for cracking nuts* 打开坚果用的巧妙器械. **3** (*US*) attractive; cute 有吸引力的; 可爱的: *a cunning baby, kitten, etc* 逗人爱的婴儿、小猫等.
▷ **cun·ning** *n* [U] cunning behaviour or quality 欺诈行为; 狡猾: *When he couldn't get what he wanted openly and honestly, he resorted to low cunning.* 他用光明正大的方法得不到的东西, 就采取卑鄙的欺诈手段.
cun·ningly *adv*: *cunningly concealed* 狡猾地加以掩盖的.

cunt /kʌnt; kʌnt/ *n* (⚠ *offensive* 讳, 蔑) **1** (*sl* 俚) (**a**) vagina 屄; 阴道. (**b**) outer female sexual organs 女性外生殖器. **2** (*derog sl* 贬, 俚) unpleasant person 讨厌的人: *You stupid cunt!* 你这笨蛋!

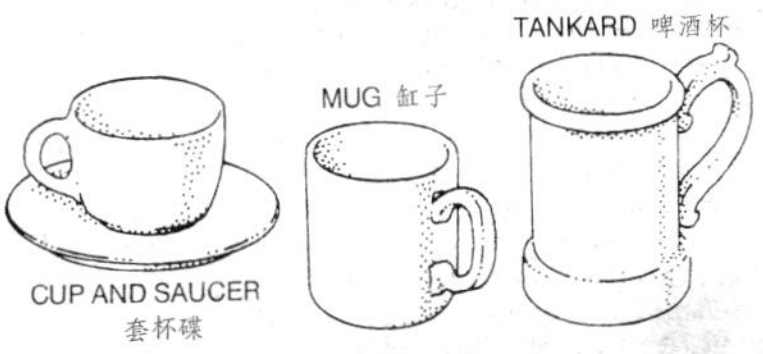

cup[1] /kʌp; kʌp/ *n* **1** [C] small bowl-shaped container, usu with a handle, for drinking tea, coffee, etc from; its contents; the amount it will hold 杯子; 杯中之物; 一杯之量: *a ˈteacup* 茶杯 ○ *a ˌcup and ˈsaucer* 一套杯碟 ○ *a ˌcup of ˈcoffee* 一杯咖啡 ○ *a paper cup* 纸杯 ○ *She drank a whole cup of milk.* 她喝了满满一杯牛奶. ○ *Use two cups of flour for the cake*, ie as a measure in cooking. 用两杯面粉做蛋糕(用作烹饪的量器). ○ (*fig rhet* 比喻, 修辞) *My cup (of joy) is full/overflowing*, ie I am extremely happy. 我快乐极了. ⇨illus 见插图. **2** [C] (**a**) vessel, usu of gold or silver, awarded as a prize in a competition 奖杯: *teams competing for the World Cup*, eg in football 争夺世界杯的球队(如足球赛中) ○ *He's won several cups for shooting.* 他曾多次荣获射击比赛的奖杯. (**b**) such a competition 优胜杯赛; 锦标赛: *We got knocked out of the Cup in the first round.* 我们在锦标赛的第一轮比赛中就被淘汰了. **3** [C] = CHALICE. **4** [C] thing shaped like a deep narrow bowl 杯形物: *an ˈegg-cup* 蛋杯 ○ *the cup in which an acorn grows* 长橡果的壳斗 ○ *the cups of a bra* 胸罩的罩杯 ○ *She wears a ˈD cup*, ie size of bra. 她戴罩杯尺寸为D的胸罩. **5** [U] drink made from wine, cider, etc with other flavourings added (由葡萄酒、苹果酒等加其他调料制成的)混合饮料: *ˈclaret-cup* 红葡萄酒混合饮料 ○ *ˈcider-cup* 苹果酒混合饮料. **6** (idm 习语) **(not) sb's cup of ˈtea** (*infml* 口) (not) what sb likes, is interested in, etc (非)某人所喜爱、所关注等的: *Skiing isn't really my cup of tea.* 滑雪不算是我的嗜好. **in one's ˈcups** (*dated fml* 旧, 文) drunk 喝醉的. **there's many a slip 'twixt cup and lip** ⇨ SLIP[1].

▷ **cup·ful** /ˈkʌpfʊl; ˋkʌp,fʊl/ *n* amount that a cup will hold 一杯的容量.

□ ˌ**cup ˈfinal** (usu 通常作 **Cup Final**) final match to decide the winner of a knock-out competition, esp in football 优胜杯决赛(尤指足球).

ˈ**cup-tie** *n* match between teams competing for a cup, esp in football 优胜杯淘汰赛(尤指足球).

cup[2] /kʌp; kʌp/ *v* **(-pp-)** **1** [Tn] form (esp one's hands) into the shape of a cup 做成杯状(尤指用手窝成): *She cupped her hands round her mouth and shouted.* 她窝起两只手掌围着嘴喊. **2** [Tn, Tn·pr] **~ sth (in/with sth)** hold sth as if in cup 把某物放入杯状物中: *cup one's chin in one's hands* 窝起两只手掌托住下巴.

C

cup·board /ˈkʌbəd; ˋkʌbɚd/ *n* **1** set of shelves with a door or doors in front, either built into the wall of a room or as a separate piece of furniture, used for storing food, clothes, dishes, etc (放食物、衣物、碗碟等的)柜橱: *a* ˌ*kitchen* ˈ*cupboard* 厨房用的橱柜 ○ *an* ˈ*airing cupboard*, ie for airing clothes 烘柜(用以烘干衣物) ○ (*fig* 比喻) *They ask for more funds, but the cupboard is bare*, ie there is no money to give them. 他们要求提供更多的资金, 然而我们已囊空如洗. ○ [attrib 作定语] *not enough cupboard space* 橱柜里放不下. ⇨ illus at App 1 见附录1之插图, page xvi. **2** (idm 习语) ˈ**cupboard love** affection that is shown, esp by a child, in order to gain sth by it (为获得某事物)讨人喜欢(尤指小孩): *It's only cupboard love; he wants some sweets!* 别看他那么讨人喜欢, 他要吃糖! **a skeleton in the cupboard** ⇨ SKELETON.

Cu·pid /ˈkju:pɪd; ˋkjupɪd/ *n* **1** the Roman god of love 丘比特(罗马神话中的爱神). **2 cupid** [C] (picture or statue of a) beautiful boy with wings and a bow and arrow, representing love (生有双翼, 手持弓矢, 视为爱的化身的)美男孩(的画像或塑像); 丘比特像.

cu·pid·ity /kju:ˈpɪdətɪ; kjuˋpɪdətɪ/ *n* [U] (*fml* 文) greed, esp for money or possessions 贪婪; (尤指)贪财物.

cu·pola /ˈkju:pələ; ˋkjupələ/ *n* (**a**) small dome forming (part of) a roof 圆屋顶. (**b**) ceiling of this 穹顶天花板.

cuppa /ˈkʌpə; ˋkʌpə/ *n* (*Brit infml* 口) cup of tea 一杯茶: *Shall we have a cuppa?* 咱们喝杯茶好吗?

cupro-nickel /ˌkju:prəʊˈnɪkl; ˌkjuproˋnɪkḷ/ *n* [U] alloy of copper and nickel used for making coins 铜镍合金(用以制造硬币).

cur /kɜ:(r); kɝ/ *n* (*dated* 旧) **1** vicious or bad-tempered dog, esp a mongrel 恶犬(尤指杂种狗). **2** (*fig* 比喻) cowardly or worthless man 胆小鬼; 不中用的傢伙: *You treacherous cur!* 你这个背信弃义的傢伙!

cur·able /ˈkjʊərəbl; ˋkjʊrəbḷ/ *adj* that can be cured 可治愈的: *Some types of cancer are curable.* 有些癌症是可以治愈的. ▷ **cur·ab·il·ity** /ˌkjʊərəˈbɪlətɪ; ˌkjʊrəˋbɪlətɪ/ *n* [U].

cura·çao (also **cura·çoa**) /ˌkjʊərəˈsəʊ; *US* -ˈsaʊ; ˌkjʊrəˋsaʊ/ *n* [U] liqueur flavoured with the peel of bitter oranges 库拉索酒(一种用苦橙皮调味的甜酒).

cur·acy /ˈkjʊərəsɪ; ˋkjʊrəsɪ/ *n* curate's job or position; holding of such a job or position 助理牧师的职务或职位; 助理牧师的身分: *a curacy at a church in Oxford* 牛津一座教堂中的助理牧师职位 ○ *during his curacy* 在他担任助理牧师期间.

cur·ate /ˈkjʊərət; ˋkjʊrɪt/ *n* **1** (in the Church of England) clergyman who helps a parish priest (英国国教会的)助理牧师. Cf 参看 VICAR. **2** (idm 习语) **a curate's** ˈ**egg** (*Brit usu derog* 通常作贬义) thing with both good and bad aspects 瑕瑜互见之物.

cur·at·ive /ˈkjʊərətɪv; ˋkjʊrətɪv/ *adj* helping to, able to or intended to cure illness, etc 有助于治疗的; 有疗效的; 以治病等为目的的: *the curative properties of a herb* 药草的治疗性能.

cur·ator /kjʊəˈreɪtə(r); *US also* ˈkjʊərətər; kjuˋretɚ/ *n* person in charge of a museum, an art gallery, etc (博物馆、美术馆等的)馆长.

curb /kɜ:b; kɝb/ *n* **1 ~ (on sth)** thing that restrains or controls 起约束或控制作用的事物: *put/keep a curb on one's anger, feelings, etc* 抑制怒火、感情等 ○ *government curbs on spending* 政府对开支的限制. **2** strap or chain passing under a horse's jaw, used to restrain the horse 马勒, 马嚼子(横放在马嘴里的皮带或铁链, 用以驾御马匹). **3** (*esp US*) = KERB.

▷ **curb** *v* [Tn] **1** prevent (sth) from getting out of control; restrain 防止(某事物)失控; 约束: *curb one's anger, feelings, etc* 抑制怒火、感情等 ○ *curb spending, waste, etc* 限制开支、浪费等. **2** control (a horse) by means of a curb 勒住(马).

curd /kɜ:d; kɝd/ *n* **1** (usu 通常作 **curds** [pl]) thick soft substance formed when milk turns sour, used to make cheese 凝乳(牛奶发酵而形成的稠而软的物质, 可制奶酪): ˌ*curds and* ˈ*whey* 凝乳和乳清 ○ [attrib 作定语] *curd* ˈ*cheese* 凝乳制的干酪. **2** [U] (in compounds 用以构成复合词) substance made to look like curds 做成凝乳状的物质: ˌ*lemon-*ˈ*curd*, ie made from eggs, butter and sugar, flavoured with lemon, and used like jam ○ *soya-*ˈ*bean curd*.

curdle /ˈkɜ:dl; ˋkɝdḷ/ *v* [I, Tn] (cause sth to) form into curds (使某物)结成凝乳: *The milk has curdled*, ie become sour. 牛奶凝结了(变酸了). ○ *Lemon juice curdles milk.* 柠檬汁可使牛奶结成凝乳. ○ (*fig* 比喻) *a scream which was enough to curdle one's blood/make one's blood curdle*, ie fill one with horror 让人心惊胆战的尖叫声.

cure[1] /kjʊə(r); kjʊr/ *v* **1** (**a**) [Tn, Tn·pr] **~ sb (of sth)** make sb healthy again 治愈某人: *The doctors cured her of cancer.* 医生治好了她的癌症. (**b**) [Tn] provide a successful remedy for (an illness, etc) 治好(疾病等): *This illness cannot be cured easily.* 这种病不好治. **2** (**a**) [Tn] (*fig* 比喻) find a solution to (sth); put an end to 解决(某事物); 了结: *Ministers hoped that import controls might cure the economy's serious inflation.* 部长们希望实行进口控制或可抑止经济上严重的通货膨胀. (**b**) [Tn·pr] **~ sb of sth** (*fig* 比喻) stop sb from behaving unpleasantly, harmfully, etc 矫正某人的不良行为: *That nasty shock cured him of his inquisitiveness for ever.* 那一沉重教训根除了他凡事爱打听的毛病. **3** [Tn] treat (meat, fish, tobacco, etc) by salting it, smoking it, drying it, etc in order to keep it in good condition (用腌、熏、烤等方法)加工处理(肉、鱼、烟草等): *well-cured bacon* 精制的熏猪肉. **4** (idm 习语) **kill or cure** ⇨ KILL.

cure[2] /kjʊə(r); kjʊr/ *n* **1** [C] act of curing or process of being cured 治疗; 治愈: *The doctor cannot guarantee a cure.* 医生不能保证治愈. ○ *Her cure took six weeks.* 她的病用了六个星期才治好. ○ *effect/work a cure* 治愈[治疗]. **2** [C, U] **~ (for sth)** substance or treatment that cures; remedy 药物; 疗法: *Is there a certain cure for cancer yet?* 癌症迄今有无有效的治疗方法? ○ *a disease with no known cure* 迄今仍然无法可治的疾病 ○ *He has tried all sorts of cures, but without success.* 他已试用过各种各样的疗法, 但仍不见效. ○ (*fig* 比喻) *What is the cure for the plight of the homeless?* 帮助无家可归者摆脱困境有何措施? **3** [C, U] (*fml* 文) duties of a priest 牧师的职务: *the cure of souls*, ie looking after people's spiritual welfare 拯救灵魂的工作 ○ *obtain/resign a cure*, ie a position as a priest 就任[辞去]牧师职务. **4** (idm 习语) **prevention is better than cure** ⇨ PREVENTION.

cur·few /ˈkɜ:fju:; ˋkɝfju/ *n* signal or time after which people must stay indoors until the next day 宵禁: *an 11 o'clock curfew* 从11点钟起宵禁 ○ *impose a curfew*, eg under martial law 实行宵禁(如根据戒严法) ○ *lift/end a curfew* 解除宵禁 ○ *Don't go out after curfew.* 宵禁时不要外出.

curio /ˈkjʊərɪəʊ; ˋkjʊrɪ,o/ *n* (*pl* **~s**) small object that is quite rare or unusual 小件的珍奇物品: *his valuable collection of curios* 他搜集的贵重珍品.

curi·os·ity /ˌkjʊərɪˈɒsətɪ; ˌkjʊrɪˋɑsətɪ/ *n* **1** [U] **~ (about sth/to do sth)** being curious(1a); inquisitiveness 好奇心; 爱打听的癖性: *curiosity about distant lands* 对于遥远国家的好奇心 ○ *her burning curiosity to know what's going on* 她想知道发生了何事的强烈欲望 ○ *He gave in to curiosity and opened the letter addressed to his sister.* 他抑制不住好奇心, 拆开了别人写给他妹妹的信. **2** [C] strange or unusual thing or person; strange or rare object 稀奇或罕见的事物或人; 奇物; 珍品: *She is so eccentric that she is regarded as a bit of a curiosity.* 她非常古怪, 算是个奇人. **3** (idm 习语) **curiosity killed the** ˈ**cat** (*saying* 谚) (said to sb to stop him being too inquisitive 谓某人不可过于好奇的用语).

curi·ous /ˈkjʊərɪəs; ˋkjʊrɪəs/ *adj* **1 ~ (about sth/to do sth)** (**a**) (*approv* 褒) eager to know or learn 富于好奇心的; 有求知欲的; 感兴趣的: *curious about the origin of mankind/the structure of atoms* 对人类的起源[原子的结

构]有兴趣的 ○ *I'm curious to know what she said.* 我真想知道她说了什么. ○ *He is a curious boy who is always asking questions.* 他是个有求知欲的孩子, 老是问这问那. (**b**) (*derog* 贬) having or showing too much interest in the affairs of others 对别人的事情过分感兴趣的; 爱管闲事的: *curious neighbours* 爱打听别人闲事的邻居 ○ *She's always so curious about my work.* 她总爱打听我的工作. ○ *Hide it where curious eyes won't see it.* 把它藏在好事者看不见的地方. ○ *Don't be so curious!* 别这么好奇! **2** strange; unusual 奇特的; 不寻常的: *She looks rather curious with green hair.* 她头发是绿的, 样子有点古怪. ○ *What a curious thing to say.* 说的多么离奇. ○ *Isn't he a curious-looking little man?* 他长得怎么那么怪呀? ○ *It's curious that he didn't tell you.* 他没有告诉你, 实在反常. ▷ **curi·ously** *adv*: *She was there all day but, curiously, I didn't see her.* 她一整天都在那里, 然而奇怪的是, 我却没有看见她.

curl[1] /kɜːl; kɝl/ *n* **1** [C] thing, esp a small bunch of hair, that curves round and round like a spiral or the thread of a screw 卷状物; 螺旋状物; (尤指)一绺鬈发: *curls (of hair) falling over her shoulder* 垂在她肩上的鬈发 ○ *hair falling in curls over her shoulders* 呈卷状垂于她两肩的头发 ○ *the little boy's golden curls*, ie curly hair 这小男孩的金色鬈发 ○ *a curl of smoke rising from a cigarette* 从香烟上面缭绕升起的一缕烟 ○ *'Of course not,' he said, with a curl of his lip*, ie expressing scorn. '当然不是,' 他嘴一撇(表示鄙夷)地说. **2** [U] plant disease in which the leaves curl up (植物的)卷叶病.

▷ **curly** *adj* (**-ier**, **-iest**) curling; full of curls 拳曲的; 曲曲弯弯的: *curly hair* 鬈发 ○ *a curly pattern* 线条曲曲弯弯的图样 ○ *a ˌcurly-headed ˈgirl* 有一头鬈发的姑娘. ⇨illus at HAIR 见 HAIR 之插图.

curl[2] /kɜːl; kɝl/ *v* **1** [I, Ip, Tn, Tn·p] **~ (sth) (up)** (**a**) (cause sth to) form into a curl or curls; coil (使某物)弯曲; 盘绕: *She has curled (up) her hair.* 她已经卷过头发. ○ *Does her hair curl naturally?* 她的头发是生来就鬈的吗? (**b**) (cause sth to) form into a curved shape, esp so that the edges are rolled up (使某物)呈拳曲状(尤指边缘): *The frost made the leaves curl (up).* 叶子受霜冻而卷了起来. ○ *The heat curled the paper (up).* 纸张受热而打卷儿. **2** [Ipr, Ip] move in a spiral; coil 旋绕; 盘绕: *The smoke curled upwards.* 烟气袅袅上升. ○ *The plant's tendrils curled up the stick.* 植物的卷须盘绕在枯枝上. **3** (idm 习语) **curl one's lip** put on a sneering expression 撇嘴(表示轻蔑). **make sb's hair curl** ⇨ HAIR. **4** (phr v) **curl up** (**a**) lie or sit with curved back and one's legs drawn up close to the body (躺或坐)蜷作一团: *curl up with a book* 弯着身子看书 ○ *The dog curled up in front of the fire.* 那只狗蜷伏在火炉前面. (**b**) bend at the waist 弯腰: *A blow to the stomach made him curl up.* 他腹部受到一击而直不起腰来. **curl (sb) up** (*infml* 口) (**a**) (cause sb to) feel very embarrassed (使某人)感到非常难堪: *My father's bad jokes always make me curl up.* 父亲那些要不得的玩笑总是让我很难为情. (**b**) (cause sb to) laugh heartily (使某人)开怀大笑: *I just curled up when I saw her dressed as a clown.* 我见她打扮得像个小丑, 把我笑得直不起腰来.

▷ **ˈcurler** *n* small cylinder around which wet or warm hair is wound to curl it 卷发夹.

□ **ˈcurling-tongs**, **ˈcurling-irons** *ns* [pl] metal device for curling hair using heat (烫鬈发用的)卷发钳.

cur·lew /ˈkɜːljuː; ˋkɝlju/ *n* water bird with a long thin beak that curves downwards 杓鹬(一种滨鸟, 喙长而下弯). ⇨illus at App 1 见附录1之插图, page v.

curl·ing /ˈkɜːlɪŋ; ˋkɝlɪŋ/ *n* [U] game played on ice, esp in Scotland, with heavy flat round stones which are slid along the ice towards a mark 冰上溜石游戏(将圆底石片滑向一目标, 尤风行于苏格兰).

cur·mud·geon /kɜːˈmʌdʒən; kɚˋmʌdʒən/ *n* (*dated* 旧) bad-tempered person 脾气不好的人. ▷ **cur·mud·geonly** *adj*: *a curmudgeonly person, act* 暴戾的人、行为.

cur·rant /ˈkʌrənt; ˋkɝənt/ *n* **1** small sweet dried seedless grape used in cookery 无子葡萄干: [attrib 作定语] *a currant bun* 葡萄干小圆面包. **2** (usu in compounds 通常用以构成复合词) (cultivated bush with) small black, red or white fruit growing in clusters 茶藨子; 醋栗; 醋栗树: *blackcurrants* ○ *redcurrants*.

cur·rency /ˈkʌrənsɪ; ˋkɝənsɪ/ *n* **1** [C, U] money system in use in a country 通货; 货币: *gold/paper currency* 金[纸]币 ○ *trading in foreign currencies* 以外汇为支付手段的贸易 ○ *decimal currency* 十进制货币 ○ *a strong currency* 强通货 ○ [attrib 作定语] *a currency crisis, deal, etc* 货币的危机、交易等. **2** [U] (state of being in) common or general use (used esp with the *vs* shown) 流通, 通用, 流行(尤与以下动词连用): *ideas which had enjoyed a brief currency* (ie were briefly popular) *during the eighteenth century* 在十八世纪风行一时的观点 ○ *The rumour soon gained currency*, ie became widespread. 谣言很快传开了. ○ *Newspaper stories gave currency to this scandal*, ie spread it. 报刊所作的报道使这丑闻广为传布.

cur·rent[1] /ˈkʌrənt; ˋkɝənt/ *adj* **1** [usu attrib 通常作定语] of the present time; happening now 现在的; 现行的; 当前发生的: *current issues, problems, prices* 目前的议题、问题、价格 ○ *the current issue of a magazine* 最新一期的杂志 ○ *the current year*, ie this year 今年 ○ *current events in India* 印度的要闻 ○ *her current boy-friend* 她现在的男朋友. **2** in common or general use; generally accepted 通用的; 通行的; 被普遍接受的: *current opinions, beliefs, etc* 普遍的看法、信仰等 ○ *words that are no longer current* 已不通用的词 ○ *a rumour that is current* (ie widely known) *in the city* 在城里广为传播的谣言. ⇨Usage at NEW 用法见 NEW.

▷ **cur·rently** *adv* at the present time 当前; 时下: *our director, who is currently in London* 本公司的董事, 现在伦敦.

□ **ˌcurrent acˈcount** (*esp Brit*) (*US* **checking account**) bank account from which money can be drawn without previous notice 活期存款帐户. Cf 参看 DEPOSIT ACCOUNT (DEPOSIT[2]), SAVINGS ACCOUNT (SAVING).

ˌcurrent afˈfairs events of political importance happening in the world at the present time 时事.

ˌcurrent ˈassets (*commerce* 商) assets which change in the course of business (eg money owed) 流动资产. Cf 参看 FIXED ASSETS (FIX[1]).

cur·rent[2] /ˈkʌrənt; ˋkɝənt/ *n* **1** [C] movement of water, air, etc flowing in a certain direction through slower-moving or still water, air, etc (水、气等的)流, 流动: *The swimmer was swept away by the current.* 那个游泳的人被激流卷走了. ○ *She had to swim against the current.* 她必须逆着水流往上游. ○ *Currents of warm air keep the hang-gliders aloft.* 悬挂式滑翔机借着暖气流在高空飞行. **2** [U, sing] flow of electricity through sth or along a wire or cable 电流: *a 15-amp current* 强度为15安培的电流 ○ *Turn on the current.* 接通电源. ○ *A sudden surge in the current made the lights fuse.* 电压突然增加烧断了保险丝而使电灯熄灭. Cf 参看 ALTERNATING CURRENT (ALTERNATE[2]), DIRECT CURRENT (DIRECT[1]). **3** [C] course or movement (of events, opinions, etc); trend (事件、见解等的)趋向, 趋势, 倾向: *Nothing disturbs the peaceful current of life in the village.* 没有任何事干扰村里一向平静的生活. ○ *We must try to counteract the present current of anti-government feeling.* 我们应该努力消除目前的这股反政府情绪.

cur·ric·ulum /kəˈrɪkjʊləm; kəˋrɪkjələm/ *n* (*pl* **~s** or **-la** /-lə; -lə/) subjects included in a course of study or taught at a particular school, college, etc (全部的)课程: *Is German on your school's curriculum?* 你们学校有德语课吗? Cf 参看 SYLLABUS.

□ **curriculum vitae** /kəˌrɪkjʊləm ˈviːtaɪ; kəˌrɪkjələm ˋvitaɪ/ (abbr 缩写 **cv**) (*US* also **résumé**) brief account of sb's previous career, usu sumitted with an application for a job (个人的)简历, 履历.

curry[1] /ˈkʌrɪ; ˋkɝɪ/ *n* [C, U] dish of meat, fish, vegetables, etc cooked with certain hot-tasting spices, usu served with rice 用咖喱烹调的菜: *a chicken, beef, etc curry* 一道咖喱鸡、牛肉等 ○ *eat too much curry* 吃过多用咖喱烹调的菜.

▷ **curried** *adj* [usu attrib 通常作定语] cooked with certain hot-tasting spices 用咖喱烹调的: *curried chicken, beef, etc* 咖喱鸡、牛肉等.

□ **ˌcurry powder** mixture of turmeric, cumin and other spices ground to a powder and used to make curry 咖喱粉.

curry[2] /ˈkʌrɪ; ˋkɝɪ/ *v* (*pt, pp* **curried**) **1** [Tn] rub down and clean (a horse) with a curry-comb (用马梳)梳刷, 梳洗(马). **2** (idm 习语) **curry favour (with sb)**

(*derog* 贬) try to gain sb's favour by flattery, etc 拍某人马屁.

□ 'curry-comb *n* pad with rubber or plastic teeth for rubbing down a horse 马梳.

curse[1] /kɜ:s; kɝs/ *n* **1** [C] impolite or obscene word or words used to express violent anger 咒骂语: *angrily muttering curses* 愤怒地低声咒骂. **2** [sing] word or words spoken with the aim of punishing, injuring or destroying sb/sth 咒; 咒语: *The witch put a curse on him*, ie used a curse against him. 女巫念咒诅咒他. ○ *be under a curse*, ie suffer as a result of a curse 遭受诅咒 ○ *lift a curse*, ie cancel it 解除咒语. **3** [C] cause of evil, harm, destruction, etc 祸根; 祸由: *the curse of inflation* 通货膨胀的祸害 ○ *Gambling is often a curse.* 赌博往往是个祸根. ○ *His wealth proved a curse to him.* 他的财富到头来害了他. **4 the curse** [sing] (*dated infml* 旧, 口) menstruation 月经; 行经: *I've got the curse today.* 我今天来月经了.

C

curse[2] /kɜ:s; kɝs/ *v* **1** (**a**) [I, Ipr, Tn] ~ **(at sb/sth)** utter curses (CURSE[1] 2) (against sb/sth) 诅咒(某人[某事物]): *to curse and swear* 咒骂 ○ *He cursed (at) his bad luck.* 他诅咒自己运气不好. ○ *I cursed her for spoiling my plans.* 我诅咒她坏了我的事. (**b**) [Tn] use a curse (CURSE[1] 2) against (sb/sth) 念咒语诅咒(某人[某事物]): *The witch-doctor has cursed our cattle.* 巫医念了咒语想叫我家的牛遭殃. **2** (phr v) **be cursed with sth** be afflicted with sth, esp habitually; have the stated bad thing 受某事物之害(尤指经常); 为某事物所苦: *be cursed with bad health, a violent temper, bad luck, etc* 因身体有病、脾气暴躁、命运不好等而吃苦头.

▷ **cursed** /'kɜ:sɪd; 'kɝsɪd/ *adj* [attrib 作定语] (used to show annoyance 用以表示恼怒) hateful; unpleasant 可恨的; 讨厌的: *This work is a cursed nuisance.* 这种工作讨厌死了. **curs·edly** *adv.*

curs·ive /'kɜ:sɪv; 'kɝsɪv/ *adj* (of handwriting) with letters rounded and joined together (指书法)草书的, 草体的.

cursor /'kɜ:sə(r); 'kɝsɚ/ *n* (*computing* 计) movable dot on a VDU screen that indicates a particular position 光标.

curs·ory /'kɜ:sərɪ; 'kɝsərɪ/ *adj* (*often derog* 常作贬义) done quickly and not thoroughly; (too) hurried 粗略的; 草率的; 仓促的: *a cursory glance, look, inspection, etc* 匆匆的一瞥、粗略的一看、草草的检查等 ○ *He put aside the papers after a cursory study.* 他把文件稍一过目就放到一边了. ▷ **curs·or·ily** /'kɜ:sərəlɪ; 'kɝsərəlɪ/ *adv.*

curt /kɜ:t; kɝt/ *adj* (*derog* 贬) (of a speaker, his manner, what he says) rudely brief; abrupt (指说话者、态度、话语)简单粗暴的, 唐突无礼的: *a curt answer, rebuke, etc* 唐突无礼的回答、责难等 ○ *He's rather curt when he's angry.* 他生气时不免有些失礼. ○ *I was a little curt with him*, ie spoke sharply to him. 我有点冒犯了他(言语尖刻). ▷ **curtly** *adv.* **curt·ness** *n* [U].

cur·tail /kɜ:'teɪl; kɝ'tel/ *v* [Tn] make (sth) shorter or less; reduce 缩短, 减少(某事物); 削减: *curtail a speech, one's holidays* 缩短讲话、假期 ○ *We must try to curtail our spending.* 我们必须尽力缩减开支. ○ *Illness has curtailed her sporting activities.* 她因病而减少了体育活动.

▷ **cur·tail·ment** *n* [C, U] (act of) curtailing 缩短; 减少; 削减.

cur·tain /'kɜ:tn; 'kɝtn̩/ *n* **1** [C] (**a**) (*US* **drape**) piece of material hung to cover a window, and usu movable sideways 窗帘: *draw the curtains*, ie pull them across the window(s) 把窗帘拉上 ○ *lace curtains* 花边窗帘. (**b**) similar piece of material hung up as a screen 作屏幕用的帘子: *Pull the curtains round the patient's bed.* 把病床周围的床帷拉上. ○ *a shower curtain* 浴帘. **2** [sing] (**a**) screen of heavy material that can be raised or lowered at the front of a stage (舞台的)幕: *The curtain rises/goes up*, ie The play/act begins. 幕启(演出开始). ○ *The curtain falls/comes down*, ie The play/act ends. 幕落(演出结束). ○ (*fig* 比喻) *The curtain has fallen on her long and distinguished career*, ie Her career has ended. 她那漫长而成就斐然的生涯已告结束. ⇨illus at App 1 见附录1之插图, page ix. (**b**) (*fig* 比喻) raising or lowering of such a curtain 开幕或闭幕: *Tonight's curtain is at 7. 30*, ie the play begins at 7. 30. 今晚的演出七点半开始. ○ *After the final curtain* (ie After the play had ended) *we went backstage.* 演出结束后我们到后台去了. **3** [C esp *sing* 尤作单数] (*fig* 比喻) thing that screens, covers, protects, etc 掩蔽物; 覆盖物; 防护物: *a curtain of fog, mist, etc* 一层雾幕、薄雾等 ○ *A curtain of rain swept over the valley.* 瓢泼大雨冲刷着这个谷地. ○ *the curtain of secrecy that hides the Government's intentions* 掩盖政府意图的烟幕. **4 curtains** [pl] **~s (for sb/sth)** (*infml* 口) hopeless situation; the end 绝望的处境; 完蛋: *When I saw he had a gun, I knew it was curtains for me.* 我一见到他拿着枪, 就知道这下子我算完了. **5** (idm 习语) **ring up/down the curtain** ⇨ RING[2].

▷ **cur·tain** *v* **1** [Tn] provide (a window, an alcove, etc) with a curtain or curtains 给(窗户、凹室等)装上帘子: *curtained windows* 挂窗帘的窗户 ○ *enough material to curtain all the rooms* 够给所有的房间装上窗帘的布料. **2** (phr v) **curtain sth off** separate or divide sth with a curtain or curtains 把某物用帘幕隔开: *curtain off part of a room* 把房间的一部分用布幔分隔开.

□ 'curtain-call *n* actor's appearance in front of the curtain at the end of a play to receive applause 谢幕: *The performers took* (ie made) *their curtain-call.* 演出人员出场谢幕.

ˌcurtain-raiser *n* ~ **(to sth)** (**a**) short piece performed before the main play 序幕(正剧演出前的短剧). (**b**) thing that precedes a similar but larger or more important event 序幕, 前奏(重大事件的开端): *border incidents that were curtain-raisers to a full-scale war* 引发一场全面战争的边境事件.

curt·sey (also **curtsy**) /'kɜ:tsɪ; 'kɝtsɪ/ *n* bend of the knees with one foot in front of the other, performed by women as a sign of respect, eg to a monarch (女子行的)屈膝礼: *make/drop/bob a curtsey (to sb)* (向某人)行屈膝礼.

▷ **curt·sey** (also **curtsy**) *v* (*pt, pp* **curtseyed, curtsied**) [I, Ipr] **~ (to sb)** make a curtsey 行屈膝礼: *curtsey to the Queen* 向女王行屈膝礼.

cur·va·ceous /kɜ:'veɪʃəs; kɝ'veʃəs/ *adj* (*esp sexist* 尤含性别偏见) (of a woman) having an attractively rounded figure (指女子)标致丰腴的.

cur·va·ture /'kɜ:vətʃə(r); *US* -tʃʊər; 'kɝvəˌtʃʊr/ *n* [U] curved form; curving 弯曲形状; 弯曲: *the curvature of the earth's surface* 地球表面的曲度 ○ *to suffer from curvature of the spine* 患脊柱弯曲症.

curve /kɜ:v; kɝv/ *n* **1** line of which no part is straight and which changes direction without angles 曲线; 弧线: *a curve on a graph* 图表上的曲线. **2** thing shaped like this 曲线状物; 弯曲物: *a curve in the road* 道路的弯曲处 ○ *a pattern full of curves and angles* 满是曲线和尖角的图案 ○ *her attractive curves*, ie pleasantly rounded figure 她那富于曲线美的身段.

▷ **curve** *v* **1** [I, Tn] (cause sth to) form a curve (使某物)成曲线形: *The road curved suddenly to the left.* 那条路突然向左转弯. ○ *a knife with a curved blade* 刀身弯曲的小刀. **2** [Ipr, Ip] move in a curve 沿曲线移动: *The spear curved through the air.* 标枪在空中沿曲线运动.

curvy *adj* (**-ier, -iest**) (*infml* 口) **1** curving; curved 弯曲的; 弧状的: *curvy lines* 曲线. **2** curvaceous 有曲线美的.

cush·ion /'kʊʃn; 'kʊʃən/ *n* **1** small bag filled with soft material, feathers, etc, used to make a seat more comfortable, to kneel on, etc (坐、跪等时用的)软垫, 靠垫, 垫子. **2** mass of sth soft 柔软如垫之物: *a cushion of moss on the rock* 岩石上的一层青苔 ○ *A hovercraft rides on a cushion of air.* 气垫船悬浮在气垫上行驶. ○ *a 'pin-cushion* 针插 ○ (*fig* 比喻) *The three goals we scored in the first half give us a useful cushion* (ie protect us) *against defeat.* 我们在上半场比赛中射进的三个球可以使我们稳操胜券. **3** soft bouncy lining of the inside edges of a snooker or billiard table, from which balls rebound (台球台内侧边缘的)弹性衬里. ⇨illus at SNOOKER 见SNOOKER之插图.

▷ **cush·ion** *v* **1** [Tn] soften (sth) by absorbing the effect of impact 对(某事物)起缓冲作用: *Powerful shock absorbers cushion our landing.* 有效的减震装置缓解了我们着陆时的冲撞力. **2** [Tn, Tn·pr] **~ sb/sth (against/from sth)** (*fig* 比喻) protect sb/sth (from sth harmful), sometimes excessively 保护某人[某事物](有时过分): *a child who has been cushioned from unpleasant experiences* 备受关怀而生活得无忧无虑的孩

子 ○ *Wage increases have cushioned us from the effects of higher prices.* 工资提高后减轻了物价上涨对我们的影响.

cushy /ˈkʊʃɪ; ˋkʊʃɪ/ *adj* (**-ier, -iest**) (*infml often derog* 口, 常作贬义) **1** (esp of a job) not requiring much effort (尤指工作)轻松的, 不费劲的: *Her job's so cushy: she does next to nothing and earns a fortune.* 她的工作真轻松: 几乎无所事事却能挣大钱. ○ *It's a cushy life for the rich.* 有钱人日子过得很舒服. **2** (idm 习语) **a cushy ˈnumber** (*infml* 口) job or situation in life that is pleasant, easy and undemanding 愉快、轻松又不费心劳神的工作或生活状况: *He's got himself a very cushy little number.* 他弄到了一份美差.

cusp /kʌsp; kʌsp/ *n* pointed end where two curves meet (两弧线相交所形成的)尖端: *the cusp of a crescent/a leaf* 月牙[叶子]的尖端.

cuss /kʌs; kʌs/ *n* (*infml* 口) **1** curse 诅咒. **2** (preceded by an *adj* 用于形容词之后) person 人; 傢伙: *He's an awkward/queer old cuss.* 他是个笨手笨脚的[古里古怪的]傢伙. **3** (idm 习语) **not give a ˈcuss/ˈdamn (about sb/sth)** be completely unworried 一点不在乎.

cus·sed /ˈkʌsɪd; ˋkʌsɪd/ *adj* (*infml derog* 口, 贬) (of people) unwilling to agree or co-operate; obstinate; contrary (3)(指人)执拗的, 固执的, 好作对的: *She's so cussed she always does the opposite of what you ask.* 她这人真是牛脾气, 总是与你的要求背道而驰. ▷ **cus·sedly** *adv*. **cus·sed·ness** *n* [U] (*fig* 比喻): *It rained, with the usual cussedness of the English weather.* 天不作美, 英国的天气往往专门与人作对.

cus·tard /ˈkʌstəd; ˋkʌstɚd/ *n* [U] sweet sauce, typically yellow, eaten with fruit, pastry, etc as a dessert, and made from flavoured cornflour mixed with sugar and milk 蛋奶沙司(一种甜食, 与水果、糕饼等一同食用): *apple pie and custard* 苹果馅饼加蛋奶沙司.

□ **custard ˈpie** flat round mass of soft wet or foamy matter, like a pie, which performers throw at each other in slapstick comedy 蛋奶糕饼(松软或黏稠的圆饼, 在闹剧中演员常用以掷打对方).

cus·to·dial /kʌˈstəʊdɪəl; kʌsˋtodɪəl/ *adj* (*law* 律) involving imprisonment 监禁的; 拘留的: *a custodial sentence* 予以监禁的判决.

cus·to·dian /kʌˈstəʊdɪən; kʌsˋtodɪən/ *n* person who takes care of or looks after sth 看管人; 监护人: *a self-appointed custodian of public morals* 自封的公共道德的卫道士.

cus·tody /ˈkʌstədɪ; ˋkʌstədɪ/ *n* [U] **1** (right or duty of) taking care of sb/sth 监管、监护(的权利或责任): *leave one's valuables in safe custody*, eg in a bank 将贵重物品妥善保管(如于银行中) ○ *When his parents died, he was placed in the custody of his aunt.* 他的父母去世以后, 他就交由姑妈照管. ○ *The court gave the mother custody of the child*, eg after a divorce. 法庭把孩子判给母亲照管(如在离婚以后). ○ *parents involved in a battle over custody*, ie disputing who should have the right to look after the children 为孩子的监护权而争得不可开交的父母. **2** imprisonment while awaiting trial 拘留; 羁押: *The magistrate remanded him in custody for two weeks.* 法官命令把他拘留两星期. ○ *be held in custody* 被拘留 ○ *take sb into custody*, ie arrest him 将某人拘捕.

cus·tom[1] /ˈkʌstəm; ˋkʌstəm/ *n* **1** (**a**) [C, U] usual, generally accepted and long-established way of behaving or doing things 习俗; 风俗: *It is difficult to get used to another country's customs.* 要适应另一国家的风俗习惯是很困难的. ○ *the customs of the Eskimos* 爱斯基摩人的风俗 ○ *a slave to custom*, ie sb who does what most people do and have always done 习俗的奴隶 ○ *procedures laid down by ancient custom* 依照古老的习俗制定的程序. (**b**) [C] thing that sb habitually does; practice 个人的习惯: *It is my custom to rise early.* 早起是我的习惯. **2** [U] regular purchases from a tradesman, shop, etc 经常向某商人、商店等购物: *We would like to have your custom*, ie would like you to buy our goods. 我们欢迎您经常惠顾. ○ *We've lost a lot of custom since our prices went up*, ie Fewer goods have been bought from us. 自从提价以后, 我们失去了许多顾客的生意. ○ *I shall withdraw my custom* (ie stop buying goods) *from that shop.* 我不再去那家商店买东西了.

cus·tom[2] /ˈkʌstəm; ˋkʌstəm/ *adj* [attrib 作定语] made as the buyer specifies, rather than as a standard model 定做的: *a custom car* 定制的汽车.

▷ **cus·tom·ize, -ise** *v* [Tn] make or alter (esp a car) according to the buyer's or owner's wishes 按顾主或物主的意思制造或改制(尤指汽车).

□ ˌ**custom-ˈbuilt** (also ˌ**custom-ˈmade**) *adj* built or made as the buyer specifies 按顾主的具体要求建造或制造的; 定做的: *a* ˌ*custom-built* ˈ*car* 按买主的要求制造的汽车 ○ ˈ*custom-made* ˈ*clothes,* ˈ*shoes, etc* 定做的衣物、鞋等.

cus·tom·ary /ˈkʌstəmərɪ; *US* -merɪ; ˋkʌstəmˌɛrɪ/ *adj* according to custom; usual 合乎习俗的; 依照习俗的; 习惯上的: *Is it customary to tip waiters in your country?* 在贵国依照惯例是否应该付给服务员小费? ○ *She gave the customary speech of thanks to the chairman.* 她照例向主席致感谢辞. ▷ **cus·tom·ar·ily** /ˈkʌstəmərəlɪ; *US* ˌkʌstəˈmerəlɪ; ˋkʌstəmˌɛrəlɪ/ *adv*.

cus·tomer /ˈkʌstəmə(r); ˋkʌstəmɚ/ *n* **1** person who buys sth from a tradesman, shop, etc 顾客; 主顾: *one of the shop's best customers* 该店最好的顾客之一. **2** (*infml* 口) (preceded by an *adj* 用于形容词之后) person 人; 傢伙: *a queer, awkward, rum, tough, etc customer* 古怪的、难对付的、不好惹的、倔头倔脑的...傢伙 ○ *an ugly customer* 面目可憎的傢伙 ○ *a cool customer*, eg one who remains calm in a crisis 冷汉子(如临危镇静的人).

cus·toms /ˈkʌstəmz; ˋkʌstəmz/ *n* [pl] **1** taxes payable to the Government on goods imported from other countries; import duties 进口税; 关税: *pay customs on sth* 为某物缴纳进口税. **2** (also **the Customs**) government department that collects these taxes 海关: *The Customs have found heroin hidden in freight.* 海关查出了隐藏在货物中的海洛因. ○ *How long does it take to get through customs?* ie have one's baggage examined by customs officers at a port, airport, etc 海关检查要用多少时间? ○ [attrib 作定语] *a customs officer, search, check* 海关官员、检查、查验 ○ *customs duty, formalities, etc* 海关税、手续等. Cf 参看 EXCISE[1].

□ ˈ**customs house** office, esp at a port, where customs duties are collected (尤指港口的)海关.

ˈ**customs union** agreement between states on what customs duties are to be paid on each other's goods 关税联盟(国与国之间就双方货物的征税问题缔结的协定).

cut[1] /kʌt; kʌt/ *v* (**-tt-**; *pt, pp* **cut**) **1** [Ipr, Tn] make an opening, slit or wound in (sth) with a sharp-edged tool, (eg a knife or a pair of scissors) 切; 割; 剪; 砍: *You need a powerful saw to cut through metal.* 切割金属需用强劲的锯. ○ *He cut himself/his face shaving.* 他刮胡须时割破了脸. ○ *She cut her finger on a piece of broken glass.* 她被一块碎玻璃划伤了手指. ○ *cut sb's throat*, ie kill sb with a deep wound in the throat 割断某人咽喉. **2** (**a**) [Tn, Tn·pr, Dn·n, Dn·pr] **~ sth (from sth); ~ sth (for sb)** remove sth (from sth larger) using a knife, etc (用刀等自较大物体上)切下、割下、剪下或砍下某物: *cut some flowers* 剪下一些花朵 ○ *How many slices of bread shall I cut* (ie from the loaf)? 我该切多少片面包? ○ *She cut a slice of beef from the joint.* 她从大块的牛肉上切下一片来. ○ *Please cut me a piece of cake/cut a piece of cake for me.* 请给我切块蛋糕. ○ *Cut yourself some pineapple.* 你自己切点菠萝吃吧. ○ *Cut some pineapple for your sister.* 给你姐姐切几片菠萝吧. (**b**) [Tn, Tn·pr, Tn·p] **~ sth (in/into sth)** divide sth (into smaller pieces) with a knife, etc (用刀等)把某物切割成小块: *Will you cut the cake?* 请你切蛋糕好吗? ○ *If you cut the bread* (ie into slices) *we'll make some toast.* 你要是把面包切成片, 我们就烤点儿面包片. ○ *She cut the meat into cubes.* 她把肉切成小块儿. ○ *cut apples into halves, thirds, quarters, etc* 把苹果切成两半、三瓣、四瓣等 ○ *The bus was cut in half/in two by the train.* 公共汽车被火车撞成两截. (**c**) [Tn] separate (sth) into two pieces; divide (把某物)一分为二; 分割: *cut a rope, cable, thread, etc* 割断绳子、缆索、线等 ○ *Don't cut the string, untie the knots.* 别剪断绳子, 把结解开. ○ *The Minister cut the tape to open a new section of the motorway.* 部长为一段新高速公路的竣工剪彩. (**d**) [Tn, Cn·a] shorten (sth) by cutting; trim 剪短(某物); 修剪: *cut one's hair, one's nails, a hedge* 剪头发、指甲、树篱 ○ *cut* (ie mow) *the grass* 刈草 ○ *He has had his hair cut (short).* 他理发了. (**e**) [Tn, Tn·pr] make or form (sth) by removing material with a cutting tool 切成, 剪成, 挖成, 刻成(某物): *cut a diamond* 雕琢

C

钻石 ○ *The climbers cut steps in the ice.* 登山者在冰上凿出踏脚处. ○ *cut a hole in a piece of paper* 在纸上挖个洞 ○ *cut one's initials on a tree* 在树上刻自己姓名的首字母. ⇨Usage 见所附用法. **3** [I] (**a**) be capable of being cut 可被切、剪等: *Sandstone cuts easily.* 砂岩容易切割. (**b**) be capable of cutting 可用以切、剪等: *This knife won't cut.* 这把刀不快. **4** [Tn] cause physical or mental pain to (sb) 使(某人)感到疼痛或痛苦: *His cruel remarks cut her deeply.* 他那些无情的话伤透了她的心. **5** [Tn] harvest (a crop) 收割(庄稼): *The wheat has been cut.* 小麦已经收割. **6** [Tn] (of a line) cross (another line) (指直线)(与另一直线)相交: *Let the point where AB cuts CD be called E.* 设AB线与CD线的相交点为E. ○ *The line cuts the circle at two points.* 一直线与圆相交于两点. **7** [I, Tn] lift and turn up part of (a pack of playing-cards) in order to decide who is to deal, play first, etc 切牌(从一副纸牌中拿起一部分翻转过来以决定由谁发牌、谁先出牌等): *Let's cut for dealer.* 咱们切牌决定由谁发牌吧. ○ *cut the cards/pack* 切牌. **8** (**a**) [Tn, Tn·pr] reduce (sth) by removing a part of it 削减(某事物): *cut prices, taxes, spending, production* 削价、减税、紧缩开支、减少产量 ○ *His salary has been cut (by ten per cent).* 他的薪水减少了(百分之十). ○ *The new bus service cuts the travelling time by half.* 新的公共汽车交通服务使运行时间减少了一半. ○ *Could you cut your essay from 10 000 to 5 000 words?* 请把你的那篇文章从10 000字删减到5 000字行吗? (**b**) [Tn, Tn·pr] **~ sth (from sth)** remove sth (from sth); leave out or omit sth 删除, 删节(某物): *Two scenes were cut by the censor.* 有两个镜头被审查员剪掉了. (**c**) [Tn] (*infml* 口) stop (sth) 停止(某事): *Cut the chatter and get on with your work!* 别唠唠叨叨了, 继续工作吧! **9** (**a**) [Tn] prepare (a film or tape) by removing or rearranging parts of it; edit 剪辑(影片或磁带); 编辑. (**b**) [I] (usu imperative 通常用于祈使句) stop filming or recording 停止拍片或录音、录像: *The director shouted 'Cut!'* 导演喊了一声'停!' (**c**) [Ipr] **~ (from sth) to sth** (in films, radio or television) move quickly from one scene to another (电影、电视)转换画面; (无线电)瞬间转换: *The scene cuts from the shop to the street.* 镜头从商店转换到街道. **10** [Tn] switch off (a light, car engine, etc) 关上(电灯、汽车发动机等). **11** [Tn] (*infml* 口) stay away from (sth) deliberately; not attend 不出席; 不到场: *cut a class, lecture, tutorial, etc* 旷课、不听讲座、不上辅导课. **12** [Tn] (*infml* 口) refuse to recognize (sb) 不认, 不理睬(某人): *She cut me (dead) in the street the other day.* 几天前她在街上竟把我视若路人. **13** [I, Tn] (in cricket) hit (the ball) in the direction one is facing with the bat held horizontally (板球)切击(横握球板向正面方向击球): *He cut the ball to the boundary.* 他把球切击到边线. **14** [Tn] have (a new tooth) beginning to appear through the gum 开始长(新牙). **15** [Tn, Tn·pr] **~ sth (with sth)** (*esp US*) make sth less pure; dilute or weaken sth 往某物中掺入杂质; 将某物冲淡或稀释: *cut whisky with water* 往威士忌酒里掺些水. **16** [Tn] record music on (a gramophone record) 灌制(唱片): *The Beatles cut their first disc in 1962.* 披头士乐队于1962年灌了第一张唱片. **17** (idm 习语) **cut and ˈrun** (*sl* 俚) make a quick or sudden escape 急忙逃走. (For other idioms containing **cut**, see entries for the *ns, adjs*, etc 与**cut**搭配的其他习语见有关名词、形容语等的词条, 如**cut corners** ⇨ CORNER; **cut it/things fine** ⇨ FINE[3].) **18** (phr v) **cut across sth** not correspond to (the usual divisions between groups) 与(通常的分类)不符: *Opinion on this issue cuts across traditional political boundaries.* 人们对这问题的看法, 超越了他们沿袭至今的政治界线. **cut across, along, through, etc (sth)** go across, etc (sth), esp in order to shorten one's route 穿过(某地)(尤指抄近路): *I usually cut across/through the park on my way home.* 我在回家途中通常抄近路穿过公园.

cut at sb/sth try to sever, open or wound sb/sth with a knife, etc 试图用刀等截断、破开或伤害某人[某事物]: *His attacker cut at him with a razor.* 袭击者用剃刀去割他. ○ *She cut at the rope in an attempt to free herself.* 她割绳索以求脱身.

cut sth away (from sth) remove sth (from sth) by cutting (自某物上)切除, 剪去, 破掉某物: *They cut away all the dead branches from the tree.* 他们把树上的枯枝通通砍掉了.

cut sth back shorten (a bush, shrub, etc) by cutting off shoots and branches close to the stem; prune sth 修剪(矮树、灌木等); 给某树剪枝: *cut back a rose bush* 给玫瑰树剪枝. **cut sth back; cut back (on sth)** reduce sth considerably 大量削减某事物: *If we don't sell more goods, we'll have to cut back (on) production.* 我们若不能增加货物的销售量, 就必须大幅度降低产量. Cf 参看 CUT-BACK.

cut sb ˈdown (*fml* 文) (**a**) kill or injure sb by striking him with a sword or some other sharp weapon (用刀剑等锐利武器)杀死或杀伤某人. (**b**) (usu passive 通常用于被动语态) kill sb 杀死某人; 夺去某人生命: *He was cut down by pneumonia at an early age.* 他年纪轻轻的就被肺炎夺去了生命. **cut sth down** (**a**) cause sth to fall down by cutting it at the base (自基础部分)砍倒: *cut down a tree* 砍倒一棵树. (**b**) reduce the length of sth; shorten sth 缩短某物; 删减某物: *cut down a pair of trousers* 把裤子改短 ○ *Your article's too long — please cut it down to 1 000 words.* 你的文章太长 —— 请把它删减到1 000字. **cut sth down; cut down (on sth)** reduce the amount or quantity of sth; consume, use or buy less (of sth) 减少某事物的数额或数量; 减少消耗, 少用或少买(某物): *cut down one's expenses* 减少开支 ○ *The doctor told him to cut down his consumption of fat.* 医生建议他减少脂肪的摄取量. ○ *I won't have a cigarette, thanks — I'm trying to cut down (on them)*, ie smoke fewer. 谢谢, 我不抽烟 —— 我正在尽量少抽. **cut sb down (to sth)** persuade sb to reduce a price 说服某人降低价格: *He was asking £400 for the car, but we cut him down to £350.* 这辆汽车他要价400英镑, 但是我们把价杀到350英镑.

cut sb/sth from sth remove sb/sth from a larger object by cutting 将某人[某物]从一较大物体中分出: *cut a branch from a tree* 砍下树枝 ○ *The injured driver was cut from the wreckage of his car.* 把汽车残骸破开才救出了受伤的司机.

cut ˈin (on sb/sth) (of a vehicle or driver) move suddenly in front of another vehicle, leaving little space between the two vehicles (指车辆或司机)超车抢道: *The lorry overtook me and then cut in (on me).* 那辆卡车超越我的车后, 突然插入我前方的位置. **cut in (on sb/sth); cut into sth** interrupt sb/sth 打断、打搅某人[某事物]: *She kept cutting in on/cutting into our conversation.* 我们谈话时她老是插嘴. **cut sb in (on sth)** (*infml* 口) give sb a share of the profit (in a business or an activity) 让某人分享利润: *cut sb in on a deal* 让某人入伙做生意.

cut sb ˈoff (**a**) (often passive 常用于被动语态) interrupt sb speaking on the telephone by breaking the connection 切断电话线路使某人通话中断: *We were cut off in the middle of our conversation.* 我们正交谈时, 线路被切断了. ○ *'Operator, I've just been cut off.'* '话务员, 线路断了.' (**b**) leave sb nothing in one's will; disinherit sb 剥夺某人的继承权: *He cut his son off without a penny.* 他完全剥夺了儿子的继承权. (**c**) (usu passive 通常用于被动语态) cause sb to die sooner than is normal 夭折: *a young man cut off in his prime* 英年早逝的年轻人. **cut sb/sth off** (often passive 常用于被动语态) stop the supply of sth to sb 停止向某人供应某物: *If you don't pay your gas bill soon you may be cut off.* 你若不立即付清煤气费, 就要停止向你供气. ○ *Our water supply has been cut off.* 我们断水了. ○ *Her father cut off* (ie stopped paying) *her allowance.* 她父亲不再给她零用钱了. **cut sth off** block or obstruct sth 阻碍或阻断某事物: *cut off the enemy's retreat* 切断敌人的退路 ○ *cut off an escape route* 堵住逃跑的道路 ○ *The fence cuts off our view of the sea.* 篱笆挡住了我们观望大海的视线. **cut sth off (sth)** remove sth (from sth larger) by cutting 切下; 割下; 剪下; 砍下: *Mind you don't cut your fingers off!* 小心别切断了手指头! ○ *King Charles I had his head cut off.* 英王查理一世遭斩首. ○ *He cut off a metre of cloth from the roll.* 他从那卷布上剪下一米. ○ *The winner cut ten seconds off* (eg ran the distance ten seconds quicker than) *the world record.* 获胜者比世界记录快十秒. **cut sb/sth off (from sb/sth)** (often passive 常用于被动语态) prevent sb/sth from leaving or reaching a place or communicating with people outside a place 切断某人[某事物]的去路或来路; 使某人[某事物]与外界隔绝:

an army cut off from its base 与基地失去联络的军队 ○ *The children were cut off* (eg stranded on a rock) *by the incoming tide.* 涨潮把孩子们困住了(如困在岩石上). ○ *The village was cut off (from the outside world) by heavy snow for a month.* 村庄被大雪封住(而不能与外界联系)达一个月. ○ *She feels very cut off* (ie isolated) *living in the country.* 她生活在乡间感到很闭塞.

cut sth open open sth by cutting 切开或破开某物: *She fell and cut her head open*, ie suffered a deep wound to the head. 她摔倒了, 撞破了脑袋.

cut 'out stop functioning 不再起作用: *One of the aircraft's engines cut out.* 飞机的一个发动机失灵了. **cut sth out** (**a**) make sth by cutting 切成、剪成、砍出或开辟出某事物: *cut out a path through the jungle* 在丛林中开辟出一条小路 ○ (*fig* 比喻) *He's cut out a niche* (ie found a suitable job) *for himself in politics.* 他已跻身于政界. (**b**) cut the shapes of different parts of (a garment) from a piece of material 裁剪(衣服): *cut out a dress* 裁剪一件连衣裙. (**c**) (*infml* 口) (esp imperative 尤用于祈使句) stop doing or saying (sth annoying) 不再做(恼人的事); 不再说(恼人的话): *I'm sick of you two squabbling — just cut it out!* 你们两个吵来吵去真烦人 —— 快打住吧! (**d**) (*infml* 口) leave sth out; omit sth 去掉或省略某事物: *You can cut out the unimportant details.* 你可以删掉不重要的细节. (**e**) (*infml* 口) stop doing, using or consuming sth 停止做某事; 停止使用或消耗某物: *cut out sweets in order to lose weight* 为了减轻体重而戒食糖果. **cut sth out (of sth)** (**a**) remove sth (from sth larger) by cutting 切去, 剪下或砍掉某物: *cut an article out of the newspaper* 把报上的一篇文章剪下来. **be cut out for sth**; **be cut out to be sth** (*infml* 口) have the qualities and abilities needed for sth; (of two people) be well matched 有(做)某事所需要的素质和才能; (指两人)相当, 相配: *He's not cut out for teaching/to be a teacher.* 他不是当教师的材料. ○ *Sally and Michael seem to be cut out for each other.* 萨莉和迈克尔看起来很相配.

cut sth through sth make a path or passage through sth by cutting 开出一条路: *The prisoners cut their way through the barbed wire and escaped.* 囚犯们从铁丝网中开出一条路逃跑了.

cut sb up (**a**) (*infml* 口) injure sb with cuts and bruises 割伤, 挫伤某人: *He was badly cut up in the fight.* 他在斗殴中被打得遍体鳞伤. (**b**) destroy sb 毁掉某人: *cut up the enemy's forces* 摧毁敌军. (**c**) (*infml* 口) (usu passive 通常用于被动语态) cause sb to be emotionally upset 使某人伤心: *He was badly cut up by the death of his son.* 他因儿子死了极为悲伤. **cut sth up** divide sth into small pieces with a knife, etc 用刀等把某物分成小块; 切碎; 剪碎: *cut up vegetables* 把蔬菜切碎.

□ **'cutaway** *n* drawing or model of a house, machine, etc with the front part absent to show what is inside (房屋、机器等的)剖面图, 剖面模型: [attrib 作定语] *a cutaway model/diagram* 剖面模型[图].

'cut-back *n* reduction 减少: *cut-backs in public spending* 削减公共费用.

,cut 'glass glass with patterns cut in it 雕花玻璃: [attrib 作定语] *a ,cut-glass 'vase* 雕花玻璃的花瓶.

'cut-off *n* **1** point at which sth is ended; limit 截止点; 界限: [attrib 作定语] *reach the cut-off point* 达到截止点. **2** device for stopping a flow of water, electricity, etc (水流、电流等的)截断装置, 断流器.

'cut-out *n* **1** shape (to be) cut out of paper or cardboard 用纸或硬纸板剪的图形: *a cardboard cut-out* 硬纸板剪的图样. **2** device that switches off or breaks an electric circuit 断流器, 保险装置(用以切断电路).

,cut-'price (*US* **,cut-'rate**) *adj* [esp attrib 尤作定语] (**a**) sold at a reduced price 减价出售的: *,cut-price 'goods* 削价商品 ○ *I bought it cut-price.* 我买的是廉价货. (**b**) selling goods at reduced prices 卖削价商品的: *a ,cut-price 'store* 卖削价商品的商店.

NOTE ON USAGE 用法: Compare **cut, saw, chop, hack, slash** and **tear.** 试比较**cut**、**saw**、**chop**、**hack**、**slash**、**tear**这几个词. Notice that they are used with a variety of prepositions and particles. 注意这些词总是与各类介词及小品词连用. **Cut** has the widest use and indicates making an opening in something or removing a part of something with a (usually) sharp instrument or object ☆ **cut**使用最广, 意为用(通常指)利器破开某物或除去某物之一部分: *She cut her finger on some broken glass.* 她被碎玻璃划破了手指. ○ *He cut the advertisement out of the newspaper.* 他把那广告从报纸上剪了下来. We **saw** wood by cutting it with a saw and **chop** it by cutting it with an axe 用锯锯木头为**saw**, 用斧子劈木头为**chop**: *We can saw off any dead branches and chop them for firewood.* 我们可以把枯枝锯掉劈成柴. **Hack** suggests hitting something with violent cutting blows, usually in order to destroy or remove it completely ☆ **hack**指劈或砍某物, 通常旨在将其彻底毁坏或清除: *The explorers hacked (away) at the undergrowth to make a path.* 勘探人员披荆斩棘开辟道路. ○ *Developers have destroyed the landscape by hacking down all the trees.* 土地开发商把树都砍掉了, 破坏了风景. **Slash** indicates damaging or injuring somebody or something with long swinging cuts of a knife or sword ☆ **slash**指挥动刀剑猛砍或猛劈某人或某物: *The football hooligans had slashed some of the seats in the train.* 足球迷中的流氓用刀砍坏了列车上的一些座位. We **tear** things by pulling them apart with our hands 用手把东西扯破为**tear**: *Can I tear this article out of the newspaper?* 我可以把这篇文章从报纸上撕下来吗? ○ *She tore up his letter in anger.* 她愤怒地撕毁了他的信.

cut[2] /kʌt; kʌt/ *n* **1** wound or opening made with a knife, pair of scissors, etc (刀、剪刀等留下的)伤口, 破口: *a deep cut in the leg* 腿上很深的伤口 ○ *cuts on the face* 脸上的伤口 ○ *make a cut in sth* 在某物上划一刀 ○ *a cut in the edge of the cloth* 在布的边沿上剪的一道口子. **2** (**a**) act of cutting 切; 割; 剪; 砍: *Your hair could do with a cut*, ie is too long. 你该理发了. (**b**) stroke made with a knife, sword, whip, etc (刀、剑、鞭子等的)抡, 挥, 削, 砍, 击, 抽: *a cut across the hand* 手上挨的一鞭子. **3** ~ **(in sth)** reduction in size, length, amount, etc (体积、长度、数量等的)减小, 减短, 减少: *a cut in expenditure, prices, production* 费用、价格、产量的降低 ○ *He had to take a cut in (his) salary.* 他不得不接受减薪. ○ *tax cuts* 减税 ○ *a power cut*, ie temporary reduction or stoppage of an electric current 电力不足(电力暂时性的减弱或断电). **4** ~ **(in sth)** act of removing part of a play, film, book, etc (戏剧、影片、书等的)删节, 删剪: *There are several cuts in the film*, ie parts that have been cut out by the censor. 影片中有几处给剪掉了. ○ *Where can we make a cut in this long article?* 这篇长文在什么地方可以删掉一些? **5** piece of meat cut from the carcass of an animal (从屠宰后动物躯体上)切下的肉块: *a lean cut of pork* 一块瘦猪肉 ○ *a cut off the joint*, ie a slice from a cooked joint of meat 从一大块熟肉上切下的一片. **6** style in which a garment is made by cutting (服装剪裁的)式样, 款式: *I don't like the cut of his new suit.* 我不喜欢他那套新衣服的式样. **7** (in cricket) stroke played in the direction one is facing with the bat held horizontally (板球中的)切球: *a cut to the boundary* 切至边线的一击. **8** remark, etc that hurts sb's feelings 伤人感情的言语等: *What she said was a cut at* (ie was directed at) *me.* 她的话是冲着我来的. **9** (*infml* 口) share of the profits from sth (从利润中分得的)份额: *Your cut will be £200.* 你的一份是200英镑. **10** (idm 习语) **a cut above sb/sth** (*infml* 口) rather better than sb/sth 略优于某人[某事物]: *Her work is a cut above that of the others.* 她干的工作比别人要好些. ○ *She's a cut above the rest (of her colleagues).* 她比其他(共事的)人略胜一筹. **cut and 'thrust (of sth)** lively argument; attack and counter-attack 激烈的争论; 交锋: *the cut and thrust of parliamentary debate* 议会辩论中的唇枪舌剑. **the cut of sb's 'jib** (*dated* 旧) person's appearance, manner or style 人的外貌、姿态或风度: *I must say I didn't like the cut of his jib.* 说实在的, 我不喜欢他那个样子. **a short cut** ⇨ SHORT[1].

cute /kju:t; kjut/ *adj* (**-r**, **-st**) (*sometimes derog* 有时作贬义) **1** attractive; pretty and charming 有吸引力的; 漂亮的; 逗人喜爱的: *Isn't she a cute baby?* 她是多么逗人喜爱的婴儿啊! ○ *unbearably cute paintings of little furry animals* 那些画着毛绒绒的小动物的图画, 艳丽得俗不可耐. **2** (*infml* 口 *esp US*) sharp-witted; clever 机灵的; 聪明的: *It was cute of you to spot that.* 你能把那个挑出来真是精得很. ○ *I have had enough of your cute remarks.* 你那些高论我已经听腻了. ○ *Don't be so cute!* 别那么

鬼! ▷ **cutely** *adv*. **cute·ness** *n* [U].

cut·icle /ˈkjuːtɪkl; ˋkjutɪkl/ *n* skin at the base of a finger-nail or toe-nail (手指甲或脚趾甲根部的)外皮. ⇨illus at HAND 见 HAND 之插图.

cut·lass /ˈkʌtləs; ˋkʌtləs/ *n* short sword with a slightly curved blade, used formerly by sailors (刀身略弯的)短刀(旧时水手用的). ⇨illus at SWORD 见 SWORD 之插图.

cut·ler /ˈkʌtlə(r); ˋkʌtlɚ/ *n* person who makes, sells or repairs knives and other cutting tools (制造或修理刀具的)刀匠, 卖刀人, 刀剪商.

▷ **cut·lery** /ˈkʌtlərɪ; ˋkʌtlərɪ/ *n* [U] knives, forks and spoons used for eating and serving food (刀、叉、匙等)餐具: [attrib 作定语] *a cutlery box, set, etc* 餐具盒、一套餐具.

C

cut·let /ˈkʌtlɪt; ˋkʌtlɪt/ *n* **1** thick slice of meat or fish typically cooked by frying or grilling 厚肉片, 厚鱼片(尤指经过煎炸或炙烤的): *a lamb, veal, salmon, etc cutlet* 羊肉、牛肉、鲑鱼...片. **2** minced meat or other food shaped to look like a cutlet (肉末或其他食物做成像肉片的)薄饼: *a nut cutlet* 坚果饼.

cut·purse /ˈkʌtpɜːs; ˋkʌt,pɝs/ *n* (*arch* 古) pickpocket 扒手.

cut·ter /ˈkʌtə(r); ˋkʌtɚ/ *n* **1 (a)** person or thing that cuts 切割者; 切削工人; 裁剪者; 切割工具; 裁剪工具: *a tailor's* ˈ*cutter*, ie who cuts out cloth 成衣店的剪裁师 ○ *a ci*ˈ*gar cutter*, ie a small tool for cutting the end off cigars 雪茄切头器(用以切开雪茄烟前端者). **(b) cutters** [pl] (esp in compounds 尤用以构成复合词) cutting tool 切割工具: ˈ*wire-cutters* ○ ˈ*bolt-cutters*. **2 (a)** sailing-boat with one mast 独桅帆船. **(b)** ship's boat, used for trips between ship and shore (附属于大船, 用以穿行于大船和海岸之间的)小艇.

cut·throat /ˈkʌtθrəʊt; ˋkʌt,θrot/ *adj* [usu attrib 通常作定语] ruthless; intense 凶残的; 极度的; 剧烈的: *cutthroat competition, business practices* 你死我活的竞争、残酷无情的商业手段.

□ ˌ**cutthroat** ˈ**razor** razor consisting of a long blade attached to a handle (有手柄而刀身长的)剃刀, 刮脸刀.

cut·ting[1] /ˈkʌtɪŋ; ˋkʌtɪŋ/ *n* **1** (*US* **clipping**) article, story, etc cut from a newspaper, etc and kept for reference 剪报; 剪辑资料. **2** piece cut off a plant to be used to grow a new plant 插枝, 插条(从植物上截取供扦插的枝条): *chrysanthemum cuttings* 菊花插枝 ○ *take a cutting (from a rose)* (从玫瑰树上)剪枝以供扦插. **3** (also **cut**) unroofed passage dug through high ground for a road, railway or canal (在高地上挖的)路基或河床.

□ ˈ**cutting-room** *n* room where film is edited (影片的)剪辑室.

cut·ting[2] /ˈkʌtɪŋ; ˋkʌtɪŋ/ *adj* **1** [attrib 作定语] (of wind) sharply and unpleasantly cold (指风)严寒的, 刺骨的. **2** hurtful; sarcastic 刺人的; 挖苦人的: *cutting remarks, criticism, etc* 尖酸刻薄的言语、批评等.

▷ **cut·tingly** *adv* in a cutting[2](2) way 刺人地; 挖苦地: ... *she said cuttingly* ... 她冷言冷语地说.

cuttle·fish /ˈkʌtlfɪʃ; ˋkʌtl̩,fɪʃ/ *n* sea animal with ten arms (tentacles), which sends out black fluid when threatened 乌贼; 墨鱼.

cut·worm /ˈkʌtwɜːm; ˋkʌt,wɝm/ *n* any of various types of caterpillar that eat the stems of young plants near the ground 切根虫, 地老虎(夜蛾的幼虫).

cv /ˌsiː ˈviː; ˌsi ˋvi/ *abbr* 缩写 = record of a person's education and employment (Latin *curriculum vitae*) 履历(源自拉丁文 *curriculum vitae*).

cwm /kuːm, kʊm; kum/ *n* rounded valley or hollow on a mountain 圆形的山谷或山上的大圆坑.

cwt *abbr* 缩写 = (*pl* **cwts**) hundredweight (Latin *centum* + English *weight*) 英担(源自拉丁文 *centum* + 英文 *weight*): *a ½ cwt sack of potatoes* 一袋半英担装的土豆.

-cy (also **-acy**) *suff* 后缀 **1** (with *adjs* and *ns* forming *ns* 与形容词和名词结合构成名词) state or quality of 状态; 性质: *accuracy* ○ *supremacy* ○ *infancy*. **2** (with *ns* forming *ns* 与名词结合构成名词) status or position of 地位; 职位: *baronetcy* ○ *chaplaincy*.

cy·an·ide /ˈsaɪənaɪd; ˋsaɪə,naɪd/ *n* [U] highly poisonous chemical compound 氰化物.

cy·ber·net·ics /ˌsaɪbəˈnetɪks; ˌsaɪbɚˋnɛtɪks/ *n* [sing *v*] science of communication and control, esp concerned with comparing human and animal brains with machines and electronic devices 控制论(对信息传递和控制的研究, 尤涉及人及动物大脑与机器及电子装置的差异).

▷ **cy·ber·netic** *adj*.

cyc·la·mate /ˈsaɪkləmeɪt, ˈsɪk-; ˋsaɪklə,met/ *n* chemical compound used as an artificial sweetener 环己氨基磺酸盐(一种化合物, 用作人工增甜剂).

cyc·la·men /ˈsɪkləmən; ˋsɪkləmən/ *n* any of several types of plant with pink, purple or white flowers that have backward-turning petals 仙客来(植物名, 花呈粉红色、紫色或白色, 花瓣向后翻).

cycle /ˈsaɪkl; ˋsaɪkl/ *n* **1** series of events that are regularly repeated in the same order 循环; 周期: *the cycle of the seasons* 四季的循环 ○ *the cycle of economic booms and slumps* 经济繁荣和经济萧条的周期变化. **2** complete set or series, eg of songs or poems 整套, 整个系列(如组歌或组诗): *a Schubert song cycle* 舒伯特的组歌. **3** (*infml* 口) bicycle, motor cycle, etc 自行车、摩托车等: [attrib 作定语] *a cycle shop, race* 自行车商店、比赛. Cf 参看 BIKE.

▷ **cycle** *v* [I, Ipr, Ip] ride a bicycle 骑自行车: *go cycling* 去骑自行车 ○ *He cycles to work every day.* 他每天骑自行车上班. ○ *She cycled along (the street).* 她(沿着街道)骑着自行车.

cyc·lic /ˈsaɪklɪk; ˋsaɪklɪk/ (also **cyc·lical** /ˈsaɪklɪkl; ˋsaɪklɪkl̩/) *adj* recurring in cycles; regularly repeated 循环的; 有规律地重复的: *the cyclical nature of economic activity* 经济活动的周期性质. ▷ **cyc·lic·ally** *adv*.

cyc·list /ˈsaɪklɪst; ˋsaɪklɪst/ *n* person who rides a bicycle 骑自行车的人.

cyc·lone /ˈsaɪkləʊn; ˋsaɪklon/ *n* **1** system of winds turning round a calm area of low pressure 气旋. **2** violent destructive wind-storm 暴风. Cf 参看 HURRICANE, TYPHOON.

▷ **cyc·lonic** /saɪˈklɒnɪk; saɪˋklɑnɪk/ *adj* of or like a cyclone (似)气旋的; (似)暴风的.

Cyc·lo·pean /saɪˈkləʊpɪən; ˌsaɪkləˋpiən/ *adj* **1** of or like a Cyclops (/ˈsaɪklɒps; ˋsaɪklɑps/), a one-eyed giant in Greek myth (希腊神话独眼巨人)库克罗普斯的; (似)独眼巨人的. **2** (*rhet* 修辞) huge; immense 巨大的; 庞大的.

cyc·lo·style /ˈsaɪkləstaɪl; ˋsaɪklə,staɪl/ *n* machine for printing copies from a stencil, used esp before the introduction of photocopiers 油印机.

▷ **cyc·lo·style** *v* [Tn] produce (copies) with this 油印(材料): *some cyclostyled copies of his speech* 他的讲话的几分油印材料.

cy·clo·tron /ˈsaɪklətrɒn; ˋsaɪklə,trɑn/ *n* device for making atomic particles move at a very high speed, used for experiments in nuclear research 回旋加速器.

cyder = CIDER.

cyg·net /ˈsɪgnɪt; ˋsɪgnɪt/ *n* young swan 幼天鹅.

cy·lin·der /ˈsɪlɪndə(r); ˋsɪlɪndɚ/ *n* **1 (a)** (*geometry* 几) solid or hollow curved body with circular ends and straight sides 圆柱, (圆)柱体(实心或空心); 柱面. ⇨illus at CUBE 见 CUBE 之插图. **(b)** thing shaped like this 圆柱状物: *The string is wound round a cardboard cylinder.* 线缠绕在纸筒上. ○ *the cylinder of a revolver*, ie the part in which the cartridges are placed 左轮手枪的旋转弹膛. **2** cylinder-shaped hollow part inside which the piston moves in an engine (发动机的)汽缸: *a six-cylinder engine/car* 六缸发动机[六缸发动机汽车]. ⇨illus at PISTON 见 PISTON 之插图. **3** (idm 习语) **working/firing on all** ˈ**cylinders** (*infml* 口) (operating) with full power or effort 开足马力; 竭尽全力: *The office is working on all cylinders to get the job finished.* 办公室人员正在竭尽全力争取把这工作干完.

▷ **cy·lin·drical** /sɪˈlɪndrɪkl; sɪˋlɪndrɪkl̩/ *adj* cylinder-shaped 圆柱形的; 圆筒状的.

□ ˈ**cylinder block** part of an engine that contains the cylinders (CYLINDER 2) 汽缸体; 汽缸组.

ˈ**cylinder head** removable part that fits onto the top of a cylinder block 汽缸盖.

cym·bal /ˈsɪmbl; ˋsɪmbl̩/ *n* (usu *pl* 通常作复数) one of a pair of round brass plates struck together or hit with a stick to produce a clanging sound 钹. ⇨illus at App 1 见附录1之插图, page xi.

cynic /ˈsɪnɪk; ˋsɪnɪk/ *n* **1** person who believes that people do not do things for good, sincere or noble reasons, but only for their own advantage 愤世嫉俗者. **2 Cynic** member of a school of ancient Greek philosophy that despised ease and comfort (古希腊哲学)犬儒学派的成员.

▷ **cyn·ical** /ˈsɪnɪkl; ˋsɪnɪkəl/ *adj* **1** of or like a cynic 愤世嫉俗的: *a cynical remark, attitude, smile* 愤世嫉俗的话语、态度、微笑 ○ *They've grown rather cynical about democracy*, ie no longer believe that it is an honest system. 他们逐渐感到所谓民主制度也不过尔尔. **2** contemptuously selfish and concerned only with one's own interests 自私得为人所不齿的; 心中只有自己的: *a cynical disregard for others' safety* 只顾自己不顾他人安危的可耻行为 ○ *The footballer brought down his opponent with a cynical foul.* 那个足球队员恶意犯规把对方绊倒了. **cyn·ic·ally** /-klɪ; -klɪ/ *adv*.

cyn·icism /ˈsɪnɪsɪzəm; ˋsɪnəsɪzəm/ *n* [U] cynical attitude 愤世嫉俗的态度.

cy·nos·ure /ˈsɪnəzjʊə(r); *US* ˈsaɪnəʃʊər; ˋsaɪnə,ʃʊr/ *n* (*fml* 文) person or thing that attracts everybody's attention or admiration; centre of attraction 众人所瞩目的或所倾慕的人或事物; 注意力所集中的地方: *She was the cynosure of all eyes*, ie Everyone looked at her. 她是众目所瞩的人.

cy·pher = CIPHER.

cy·press /ˈsaɪprəs; ˋsaɪprəs/ *n* type of tall thin cone-bearing evergreen tree with dark leaves and hard wood 柏树. ⇨ illus at App 1 见附录1之插图, page i.

Cyr·il·lic /sɪˈrɪlɪk; sɪˋrɪlɪk/ *adj* of the alphabet used for Slavonic languages such as Russian and Bulgarian 西里尔字母(斯拉夫语言中, 如俄语和保加利亚语所用的字母): *a Cyrillic letter, text, etc* 西里尔字母、文献等. Cf 参看 THE ROMAN ALPHABET (ROMAN).

cyst /sɪst; sɪst/ *n* hollow organ, bladder, etc in the body, containing liquid matter 胞囊; 胞; 囊: *an ovarian cyst* 卵巢囊肿.

cyst·itis /sɪˈstaɪtɪs; sɪsˋtaɪtɪs/ *n* [U] (*medical* 医) inflammation of the bladder 膀胱炎.

czar, czar·ina = TSAR, TSARINA.

Czech /tʃek; tʃɛk/ *n* **1** [C] (**a**) native of the Czech Republic, formerly Bohemia 捷克人; 波希米亚人. (**b**) = CZECHO-SLOVAK. **2** [U] (formerly 旧时) language of Czechoslovakia 捷克斯洛伐克语.

▷ **Czech** *adj* **1** of the Czech Republic or Bohemia 捷克的; 波希米亚的. **2** = CZECHOSLOVAK.

Czecho·slo·vak /ˌtʃekəˈsləʊvæk; ˌtʃɛkəˋslovæk/ (also **Czecho·slo·va·kian** /ˌtʃekəsləˈvækɪən; ˌtʃɛkəsloˋvækɪən/) *n, adj* (formerly 旧时) (native) of Czechoslovakia 捷克斯洛伐克的; 捷克斯洛伐克人.

C

D d

D, d /di:; di/ *n* (*pl* **D's, d's** /di:z; diz/) **1** the fourth letter of the English alphabet 英语字母表的第四个字母: *'David' begins and ends with a 'D'/D.* David一字的开头和结尾都是D. **2 D** (*music* 音) the second note in the scale of C major C大调音阶中的第二音或音符. **3 D** academic mark indicating a low standard of work 学业成绩为低等的评价符号.

D *abbr* 缩写 = (*US politics* 政) Democrat; Democratic. Cf 参看 R 3.

D (also **d**) *symb* 符号 Roman numeral for 500 罗马数字的500. Cf 参看 D-DAY.

d *abbr* 缩写 = **1** (in former British currency 英国旧币) penny; pennies or pence (Latin *denarius*; *denarii*) 便士(源自拉丁文*denarius*; *denarii*): *a 2d stamp* 一张2便士的邮票 ○ *6d each* 每个6便士. Cf 参看 P 2. **2** died: *Emily Jane Clifton d 1865* 埃米莉·简·克利夫顿, 1865年卒. Cf 参看 B.

D

-d ⇨ -ED.

DA *abbr* 缩写 = **1** deposit account. **2** (*US*) District Attorney.

dab[1] /dæb; dæb/ *v* (**-bb-**) **1** [Tn] press (sth) lightly and gently 轻触, 轻压(某物): *She dabbed her eyes (with a tissue).* 她(用纸巾)轻轻地按了按眼睛. **2** [Ipr] **~ at sth** lightly touch sth by pressing but not rubbing 轻触某物(但不揉擦): *She dabbed at the cut with cotton wool.* 她用药棉轻轻地按了按伤口. **3** (phr v) **dab sth on/off (sth)** apply/remove (sth) with light quick strokes 轻而快地搽、涂[去掉](某物): *dab paint on a picture* 在画上轻轻点上颜色 ○ *dab off the excess water* 轻轻地按, 吸掉多余的水.

▷ **dab** *n* **1** [C] (**a**) small quantity (of paint, etc) put on a surface (涂上的)少量(颜色等). (**b**) act of lightly touching or pressing sth without rubbing 轻触或轻压某物(但不揉擦): *One dab with blotting-paper and the ink was dry.* 用吸墨纸轻轻按了一下, 墨水就干了. **2 dabs** [pl] (*Brit sl* 俚) fingerprints 指纹印.

dab[2] /dæb; dæb/ *n* type of flat-fish 黄盖鲽(鱼).

dab[3] /dæb; dæb/ *n* (idm 习语) **(be) a dab (hand) (at sth)** (*Brit infml* 口) very skilled 能手; 熟手: *a dab hand at golf, at rolling cigarettes* 高尔夫球、卷香烟的能手.

dabble /ˈdæbl; ˋdæbl̩/ *v* **1** [Tn, Tn·pr] **~ sth (in sth)** splash (hands, feet, etc) around in water (用手脚等)溅水, 戏水: *She dabbled her fingers in the fountain.* 她用手指在喷泉中玩水. **2** [I, Ipr] **~ (in/at sth)** take part without serious intentions 涉猎; 涉足: *He just dabbles in politics.* 他仅浅涉政治而已. ▷ **dab·bler** /ˈdæblə(r); ˋdæblɚ/ *n*: *He's not a dedicated musician, just a dabbler.* 他并不是专门的音乐家, 只不过是个业余爱好者.

dab·chick /ˈdæbtʃɪk; ˋdæbtʃɪk/ *n* small water-bird of the grebe family (䴙䴘科的)小水鸟.

dace /deɪs; des/ *n* (*pl* unchanged 复数不变) small freshwater fish 鲦鱼(一种小淡水鱼).

da·cha /ˈdætʃə; ˋdɑtʃə/ *n* country house or villa in Russia (俄国的)乡间邸宅或别墅.

dachs·hund /ˈdækshʊnd; ˋdɑks,hʊnd/ *n* type of small dog with a long body and short legs 猎獾狗(一种身长腿短的狗). ⇨illus at App 1 见附录1之插图, page iii.

Dacron /ˈdækrɒn, ˈdeɪkrɒn; dæk,rɑn, ˋde,krɑn/ *n* [U] (*US propr* 专利名) = TERYLENE.

dac·tyl /ˈdæktɪl; ˋdæktɪl/ *n* metrical foot consisting of one stressed syllable followed by two unstressed syllables, as in the line "ˈunder the/ ˈblossom that/ˈhangs on the/ˈbough" 扬抑抑格(即一重音节后接两个轻音的音步, 如 ˈunder the/ˈblossom that/ˈhangs on the/ˈbough). ▷ **dac·tylic** /dækˈtɪlɪk; dækˋtɪlɪk/ *adj*: *a dactylic line/verse* 扬抑抑格的诗句[诗].

dad /dæd; dæd/ *n* (*infml* 口) father 爸爸; 爹爹.

daddy /ˈdædɪ; ˋdædɪ/ *n* (used esp by and to children 尤作儿语) father 爸爸; 爹爹.

□ ˌ**daddy-ˈlong-legs** *n* (*infml* 口) = CRANE-FLY.

dado /ˈdeɪdəʊ; ˋdedo/ *n* (*pl* **~s**; *US* **~es**) lower part of the wall of a room, when it is different from the upper part in colour or material 护壁板; 墙裙.

dae·mon /ˈdi:mən; ˋdimən/ *n* **1** (esp in Greek mythology) supernatural being that is half god, half man (尤指希腊神话中的)半人半神的精灵. **2** spirit that inspires sb to action or creativity 守护神.

daf·fo·dil /ˈdæfədɪl; ˋdæfəˌdɪl/ *n* yellow flower with a tall stem and long narrow leaves that grows from a bulb 水仙花. ⇨illus at App 1 见附录1之插图, page ii.

daft /dɑ:ft; *US* dæft; dæft/ *adj* (**-er, -est**) (*infml* 口) foolish; silly 傻的; 愚蠢的: *Don't be so daft!* 别那么傻了! ○ *He's gone a bit daft (in the head),* ie He has become slightly insane. 他(头脑)有些发痴. ▷ **daft·ness** *n* [U].

dag·ger /ˈdægə(r); ˋdægɚ/ *n* **1** short pointed two-edged knife used as a weapon 短剑; 匕首. ⇨illus at KNIFE 见KNIFE之插图. **2** printer's mark (†) used to refer the reader to a footnote, etc 剑号(即†, 用以指示读者参看脚注的印刷符号). **3** (idm 习语) **at daggers drawn (with sb)** very hostile (towards sb) (对某人)剑拔弩张: *She's at daggers drawn with her colleagues.* 她与同事们水火不相容. ○ *He and his partner are at daggers drawn.* 他和伙伴势不两立. **look daggers at sb** look very angrily at sb 对某人怒目而视: *He looked daggers at me when I told him he was lazy.* 我说他懒惰, 他就狠狠地瞪了我一眼. Cf 参看 CLOAK-AND-DAGGER (CLOAK).

dago /ˈdeɪgəʊ; ˋdego/ *n* (*pl* **~s**) (⚠ *sl offensive* 讳, 俚, 蔑) dark-skinned foreigner, esp an Italian, a Spaniard or a Portuguese 肤色深的外国人(尤指意大利人、西班牙人或葡萄牙人).

da·guerre·otype /dəˈgerətaɪp; dəˋgɛrəˌtaɪp/ *n* early type of photograph using a chemically treated plate (早期的)银板照相.

dah·lia /ˈdeɪlɪə; *US* ˈdælɪə; ˋdæljə/ *n* garden plant with brightly coloured flowers 大丽花.

Dáil Éire·ann /ˌdɔɪl ˈeərən; ˋdɔɪl ˋɛrən/ (also **the Dáil**) the legislative assembly of the Republic of Ireland 爱尔兰共和国的众议院.

daily /ˈdeɪlɪ; ˋdelɪ/ *adj* [attrib 作定语], *adv* **1** done, produced or happening every day 每日(的): *a daily routine, visit, newspaper* 日常工作、日访、日报 ○ *The machines are inspected daily.* 机器每日均经检查. **2** (idm 习语) **one's daily bread** (**a**) one's daily food 每日的粮食. (**b**) (*infml* 口) one's livelihood 生计: *That's how I earn my daily bread.* 我是这样维持生活的. **one's daily dozen** (*infml* 口) a few routine exercises performed each day in order to keep oneself fit 每日体操.

▷ **daily** *n* **1** newspaper published every weekday 日报. **2** (also **daily help**) (*Brit infml* 口) = HELP[2] 3.

dainty /ˈdeɪntɪ; ˋdentɪ/ *adj* (**-ier, -iest**) **1** (of things) small and pretty (指物)小巧的, 精致的: *dainty porcelain, lace, etc* 小巧精致的瓷器、花边等. **2** (**a**) (of people) neat and delicate(2) in build or movement (指人)(体形或举止)娇美的, 秀丽的, 优美的: *a dainty child* 娇小玲珑的孩子. (**b**) (of people) having refined taste[1](5) and manners; fastidious, esp about food (指人)讲究的, (尤指对食物)挑剔的: *a dainty eater* 饮食讲究的人. **3** having a pleasant taste; delicious 可口的; 美味的: *a dainty morsel* 美味的少量食物.

▷ **dain·tily** *adv* in a dainty way 优美地; 精致地; 娇美地; 讲究地: *a daintily dressed doll* 服饰精美的娃娃. **dain·ti·ness** *n* [U].

dainty (usu *pl* 通常作复数) *n* small tasty piece of food, esp a small cake 量少而味美的食物; (尤指)小点心.

dai·quiri /ˈdækərɪ, ˈdaɪ-; ˋdaɪkərɪ/ *n* (*esp US*) iced drink made with rum, lime juice and sugar 代基里酒(以朗姆酒、酸橙汁加糖调制的冷饮).

dairy /ˈdeərɪ; ˋdɛrɪ/ *n* **1** place where milk is kept and milk products are made 牛奶场; 奶品场: [attrib 作定语] *dairy cream* 奶品场制的乳脂. **2** shop where milk, butter, eggs, etc are sold (出售牛奶、黄油、鸡蛋等的)乳品店.

□ ˈ**dairy cattle** cows kept to produce milk, not meat 乳牛.
ˈ**dairy farm** farm that produces mainly milk and butter 奶场.
ˈ**dairymaid** *n* woman who works in a dairy(1) 奶场女工.
ˈ**dairyman** /-mən; -mən/ *n* (*pl* **-men**) (**a**) dealer in milk, etc 奶品商. (**b**) man who works in a dairy(1) 奶场男工.
ˈ**dairy produce** food made from milk, eg butter, cheese, yoghurt 乳制品(如黄油、干酪、酸乳酪).

dais /ˈdeɪɪs; ˋde·ɪs/ *n* (*pl* **-es** /-sɪz; -sɪz/) raised platform, esp at one end of a room, for a speaker, etc 讲台.

daisy /ˈdeɪzɪ; ˋdezɪ/ *n* **1** (**a**) small white flower with a yellow centre, usually growing wild 雏菊(花). ⇨illus at App 1 见附录1之插图, page ii. (**b**) any of many different types of plant with similar flowers, ie with petals that radiate from the centre like the spokes of a wheel 雏菊(植物). **2** (idm 习语) **fresh as a daisy** ⇨ FRESH. **push up daisies** ⇨ PUSH[2].
□ ˈ**daisy wheel** small wheel used in a printer or an electric typewriter, with characters arranged around the circumference 菊花轮(印字机或电动打字机上的印字轮). Cf 参看 GOLF BALL (GOLF).

dale /deɪl; del/ *n* **1** valley, esp in Northern England (尤指英格兰北部的)山谷: *the Yorkshire Dales* 约克郡山谷. **2** (idm 习语) **up hill and down dale** ⇨ HILL.

dal·li·ance /ˈdælɪəns; ˋdælɪəns/ *n* [U] (*fml* 文) frivolous behaviour, esp flirtation 轻浮的举动; (尤指)调情: *to spend time in idle dalliance* 浪荡地消磨时间.

dally /ˈdælɪ; ˋdælɪ/ *v* (*pt, pp* **dallied**) **1** [I, Ipr] **~ (over sth)** waste time 浪费时间: *Come on. Don't dally!* 好了, 别浪费时间了! ○ *She dallies over her work and rarely finishes it.* 她工作吊儿郎当, 很少能把工作做完. **2** (phr v) **dally with sb/sth** treat sb/sth frivolously 戏弄、玩弄某人[某事物]: *She merely dallied with him/his affections*, ie flirted with him without really caring for him. 她只是玩弄他[他的感情]. **dally with sth** think about (an idea, etc) but not seriously (不认真地)考虑(意见等): *dally with a proposal* 马马虎虎考虑一项提议.

Dal·ma·tian /dælˈmeɪʃn; dælˋmeʃən/ *n* large short-haired dog, white with dark spots 达尔马提亚狗(一种短毛大狗, 毛色白, 带有黑色斑点). ⇨illus at App 1 见附录1之插图, page iii.

dam[1] /dæm; dæm/ *n* **1** barrier (made of concrete, earth, etc) built across a river to hold back the water and form a reservoir, prevent flooding, etc 水坝; 水堤; 水闸. **2** reservoir formed by such a barrier 水坝围成的水库.
▷ **dam** *v* **1** [Tn, Tn·p] **~ sth (up)** build a dam across (a river, valley, etc) 建水坝于(河、谷等). **2** (phr v) **dam sth up** (*fig* 比喻) hold back (emotions, etc) 抑制(情感等): *to dam up one's feelings* 抑制住自己的感情.

dam[2] /dæm; dæm/ *n* mother of a four-footed animal 母兽.

dam·age /ˈdæmɪdʒ; ˋdæmɪdʒ/ *n* **1** [U] **~ (to sth)** loss of value, attractiveness or usefulness caused by an event, accident, etc 损失; 损害; 损毁: *The accident did a lot of damage to the car.* 这一事故把汽车损坏得很厉害. ○ *storm damage to crops* 暴风雨对农作物的损害 ○ *damage to her reputation* 对她名誉的损害. **2 damages** [pl] money paid or claimed as compensation for damage (1), loss or injury 损害赔偿金: *The court awarded £5 000 (in) damages to the injured man.* 法院判给伤者5 000英镑损害赔偿费. **3** (idm 习语) **what's the ˈdamage?** (*Brit infml* 口) what does/did sth cost? 某物要多少钱?: *'I need a new coat.' 'Oh yes? What's the damage?'* '我需要件新外衣了.' '是吗? 要花多少钱?'
▷ **dam·age** *v* [Tn] cause damage to (sth) 损害; 损坏; 损毁; 损伤: *damage a fence, a car, furniture, etc* 损坏栅栏、汽车、家具等 ○ *damage sb's career* 损害某人的事业 ○ *damage relations between two countries* 损害两国的关系.
dam·aging *adj* **~ (to sth)** having a bad effect 有害的: *Smoking can be damaging to your health.* 吸烟对身体有害. ○ *to make damaging allegations* 提出诋毁性的责难.

dam·ask /ˈdæməsk; ˋdæməsk/ *n* [U] **1** silk or linen material, with designs made visible by the reflection of light 缎子; 花缎; 锦缎; 织花麻布: [attrib 作定语] *a damask table-cloth* 织花桌布. **2** steel with a pattern of wavy lines or with inlaid gold or silver 大马士革钢(带有波纹图案或镶有金银).
□ ˌ**damask** ˈ**rose** bright pink, sweet-scented type of rose 粉红色玫瑰.

dame /deɪm; dem/ *n* **1** (*US sl* 俚) woman 妇女: *Gee! What a dame!* 嘿! 多标致的女人! **2 Dame** (*Brit*) (title of a) woman, who has been awarded an order[1](10a) of knighthood (获有爵位的)夫人(的头衔). **3** (also **pantomime dame**) elderly female comic character in pantomime, usu played by a man (童话剧中常由男性扮演的滑稽的)老太婆.

damn[1] /dæm; dæm/ *v* **1** [Tn] (of God) condemn (sb) to suffer in hell (指上帝)罚(某人)入地狱受罪. **2** [Tn] criticize (sth) severely 严厉地批评(某事物): *The play was damned by the reviewers.* 这出戏被评论家批评得一无是处. **3** [Tn] (also *euph* 委婉语作 **darn**) (*infml* 口) (esp as an *interj*, used to express annoyance, anger, etc 尤用作感叹词, 表示厌烦、愤怒等): *Damn! I've lost my pen.* 倒霉! 我钢笔丢了. ○ *Damn this useless typewriter!* 这个破打字机真该死! **4** (idm 习语) **as near as damn it/dammit** ⇨ NEAR[2]. **damn the consequences, expense, etc** never mind the difficulties 不顾一切: *Let's enjoy ourselves and damn the consequences.* 咱们不管三七二十一, 且玩个儿痛快. **(I'm) damned if ...** (*infml* 口) I certainly do, will, etc not ...; I absolutely refuse to ... 我决不...; 我绝对不...: *I'm damned if I'm going to let her get away with that!* 我决不能就这样放过她! ○ *Damned if I know!* ie I certainly don't know. 我根本就不知道! **damn sb/sth with faint ˈpraise** imply criticism by not praising enough 名褒实贬. **I'll be damned!** (*infml* 口) (used as an expression of surprise 用以表示惊奇): *Well I'll be damned: she won after all!* 好傢伙, 她居然胜了! **publish and be damned** ⇨ PUBLISH.
▷ **damn·ing** *adj* very unfavourable 非常不利的: *damning criticism, evidence* 致命的批评、证据 ○ *a damning remark, etc* 极为不利的言语等 ○ *She said some pretty damning things about him.* 她说了他一些坏话.

damn[2] /dæm; dæm/ *n* (idm 习语) **not be worth a damn, etc** ⇨ WORTH. **not care/give a ˈdamn (about sb/sth)** (*infml* 口) not care at all 毫不在乎: *I don't give a damn what you say, I'm going.* 不管你怎么说, 我走定了.
▷ **damn** *adj* [attrib 作定语] (*infml* 口) (expressing disapproval, anger, impatience, etc 表示不满、愤怒、不耐烦等): *Where's that damn book?* 那本该死的书在哪里? ○ *My damn car has broken down!* 我的混账汽车坏了!
damn *adv* (*infml* 口) **1** (**a**) (expressing disapproval, anger, etc 表示不满、愤怒等) very 非常: *Don't be so damn silly!* 别那么傻了! ○ *You know damn well what I mean!* 你清清楚楚明白我的意思! (**b**) (expressing approval, etc 表示同意等) very 非常: *damn good, clever, etc* 非常好、聪明等 ○ *We got out of there pretty damn fast.* 我们很快就离开了那个地方. **2** (idm 习语) **damn ˈall** (*infml* 口) nothing at all 完全没有: *I earned damn all last week.* 我上星期分文没挣. ○ [attrib 作定语] *It's damn all use you telling me that now!* 你现在才告诉我, 管什么用!

dam·nable /ˈdæmnəbl; ˋdæmnəbl̩/ *adj* (**a**) deserving disapproval; wicked; disgraceful 可恶的; 恶劣的; 不名誉的: *damnable behaviour, crimes, etc* 恶劣的行为、罪行等. (**b**) (*dated infml* 旧, 口) very bad 极坏的: *damnable weather* 糟糕的天气. ▷ **dam·nably** /ˈdæmnəblɪ; ˋdæmnəblɪ/ *adv*.

dam·na·tion /dæmˈneɪʃn; dæmˋneʃən/ *n* [U] **1** state of being damned 遭天罚: *to suffer eternal damnation* 受到永远的惩罚. **2** (*dated* 旧) (used as an *interj* to express annoyance, anger, etc 用作感叹词, 表示厌烦、愤怒等): *Damnation! I've lost my umbrella.* 糟糕! 我把雨伞丢了.

damned /dæmd; dæmd/ *adj, adv* = DAMN *adj*, DAMN *adv* 1.
▷ **the damned** *n* [pl *v*] people who suffer in hell 在地狱中受罪的人: *the torments of the damned* 地狱中的人受的折磨.
damned·est /ˈdæmdɪst; ˋdæmdɪst/ (idm 习语) **do/try one's ˈdamnedest** do/try one's best 尽自己最大的努力: *She did her damnedest to get it done on time.* 她竭尽全力按时完成了.

damp[1] /dæmp; dæmp/ *adj* (**-er, -est**) **1** not completely dry; slightly wet 不完全干燥的; 潮湿的: *damp clothes* 潮湿的衣服 ○ *a damp surface* 潮湿的表面 ○ *Don't sleep between damp sheets.* 睡觉时不要用潮湿的被褥. **2** (idm 习语) **a damp 'squib** (*infml* 口) event, etc that is much less impressive than expected 未达预期效果的事等: *The party was a bit of a damp squib.* 这次聚会有些扫兴.
▷ **damp** *n* [U] **1** state of being damp 潮湿: *Air the clothes to get the damp out.* 晾晾衣服以驱潮气. ○ *Don't stay outside in the damp*, ie in the damp atmosphere. 外面潮湿, 不要待在外面. **2** = FIRE-DAMP (FIRE[1]).
damply *adv.*
damp·ness *n* [U].
□ **'damp-proof course** (also **'damp course**) layer of material near the bottom of a wall to stop damp rising from the ground 防湿层(在墙基处阻止湿气由地面上升的一层建筑材料).

damp[2] /dæmp; dæmp/ *v* **1** [Tn] = DAMPEN 1. **2** [Tn, Tn·p] **~ sth (down)** (**a**) reduce (noise, etc) 减低(声音等): *Soft material damps down vibrations.* 柔软的材料可防震. (**b**) make (sth) less strong; restrain 使(某物)减弱; 抑制: *damp (down) sb's spirits, energy, ardour, etc* 打击某人的情绪、干劲、热情等. **3** (phr v) **damp sth down** cause sth to burn more slowly (by adding ash, etc or reducing the flow of air) 使某物燃烧缓慢(加入灰等或减弱气流): *We damped the fire down before we went to bed.* 我们临睡觉前封好了火.

dampen /ˈdæmpən; ˋdæmpən/ *v* **1** [Tn] make (sth) damp 使(某物)潮湿: *I always dampen shirts before ironing them.* 我总是把衬衫先弄潮湿再熨. **2** [Tn, Tn·p] **~ sth (down)** make (sth) less strong; restrain 使(某事物)减弱; 抑制: *dampen (down) sb's spirits, enthusiasm, etc* 打击某人的情绪、热情等.

damper /ˈdæmpə(r); ˋdæmpɚ/ *n* **1** movable metal plate that controls the flow of air into a fire in a stove, furnace, etc 气门; 气闸. **2** small pad that is pressed against a piano-string to stop it vibrating 制音器(终止钢琴弦震动的小毡块). **3** (idm 习语) **put a damper on sth** (*infml* 口) cause (an event, atmosphere, etc) to be less cheerful, excited, etc 使(事情、气氛等)受到抑制, 减弱: *Their argument put a bit of a damper on the party.* 他们的争论使聚会颇为扫兴.

dam·sel /ˈdæmzl; ˋdæmzl/ *n* **1** (*arch* 古) girl; young unmarried woman 姑娘; 闺女; 未婚少女. **2** (idm 习语) **a damsel in distress** (*joc* 谑) woman who needs help 需要帮助的女子: *Most men will help a damsel in distress.* 男人多愿帮助有困难的女子.

dam·son /ˈdæmzn; ˋdæmzn̩/ *n* **1** (**a**) type of fruit tree that produces a small dark-purple plum 西洋李子树. (**b**) its fruit 西洋李子: [attrib 作定语] *damson jam/jelly* 西洋李子酱[冻]. **2** dark-purple colour 深紫色: [attrib 作定语] *a damson dress* 深紫色连衣裙.

dance[1] /dɑːns; *US* dæns; dæns/ *n* **1** (**a**) [C] (series of) movements and steps in time to music 跳舞; 舞蹈; 舞步: [attrib 作定语] *to learn new dance steps* 学新舞步. (**b**) [C] type of dance (某种)舞: *The rumba is a Latin-American dance.* 伦巴舞是拉丁美洲的舞蹈. (**c**) [C] one round or turn of a dance (一个舞曲或乐曲的)舞: *May I have the next dance?* 下一个舞可否请你和我一起跳? (**d**) [C] music for a dance 舞曲: *a gipsy dance played on the violin* 小提琴奏的吉卜赛舞曲. (**e**) (also **the dance**) [U] dancing as an art form 舞蹈艺术: *She has written a book on (the) dance.* 她写了一本关于舞蹈的书. **2** [C] social gathering at which people dance 舞会: *to hold a dance in the village hall* 在村庄会堂举行舞会. **3** (idm 习语) **lead sb a dance** ⇨ LEAD[3]. **a song and dance** ⇨ SONG.
□ **'dance-band** *n* band that plays music for dancing 为跳舞伴奏的乐团.
'dance-hall *n* hall for public dances, which one pays to enter (交费入场的)舞厅, 舞场. Cf 参看 BALLROOM (BALL[2]).

dance[2] /dɑːns; *US* dæns; dæns/ *v* **1** (**a**) [I, Ipr, Ip] move rhythmically in a series of steps, alone, with a partner or in a group, usu in time to music 跳舞: *We danced to the disco music.* 我们跟着迪斯科乐曲跳舞. ○ *Would you like to dance?* 请你跟我跳个舞好吗? ○ *I danced with her all night.* 我整晚都跟她共舞. (**b**) [Tn] perform (a certain kind of dance, ballet, etc) 跳(某种舞): *to dance a waltz, the cha-cha, etc* 跳华尔兹舞、恰恰舞等. **2** [I, Ipr, Ip] move in a lively way, usu up and down (尤指上下)跳跃, 雀跃: *leaves dancing in the wind* 随风飘舞的树叶 ○ *a boat dancing on the waves* 随波漂荡的小船 ○ *to dance for joy/with rage* 高兴得[气得]直跳. **3** [Tn·pr, Tn·p] cause (sb) to dance 使(某人)跳跃: *She danced the little child round the room.* 她逗得小孩满屋蹦蹦跳跳. ○ *He danced the baby* (ie bounced it up and down) *on his knee.* 他把婴儿放在膝上颠着玩. **4** (idm 习语) **dance attendance (up)on sb** (*fml* 文) follow sb about, attending to his wishes 侍候某人, 听其差遣: *She loves to have servants dance attendance (up)on her.* 她喜欢仆人前呼后拥地侍候她. **dance to sb's tune** do as sb demands 听某人指挥.
▷ **dan·cer** (**a**) person who dances 跳舞的人: *He's a good dancer.* 他跳舞跳得好. (**b**) person who dances for payment 舞蹈演员: *She's a (tap-/ballet) dancer.* 她是(踢跶舞[芭蕾舞])舞蹈演员.
dan·cing *n* [U] moving rhythmically in time to music 跳舞: *'tap-dancing* 跳踢跶舞 ○ *'reggae dancing* 跳雷盖舞.
'dancing-girl *n* woman who dances professionally, often in a group 女舞蹈演员; 跳舞女郎. **'dancing shoes** light shoes worn for dancing 舞鞋.

dan·delion /ˈdændɪlaɪən; ˋdændɪˌlaɪən/ *n* small wild plant with a bright yellow flower and leaves with notched edges 蒲公英. ⇨ illus at App 1 见附录1之插图, page ii.

dan·der /ˈdændə(r); ˋdændɚ/ *n* (idm 习语) **get sb's/one's 'dander up** (*infml* 口) make sb/become angry 使某人发怒: *It really got my dander up when she began accusing me of dishonesty.* 她指责我不诚实, 可真把我惹火了.

dandle /ˈdændl; ˋdændl̩/ *v* [Tn] move (esp a child) up and down on one's knee(s) or in one's arms (在膝上或怀里)颠动(孩子等): *He dandled the baby to make it stop crying.* 他颠动着婴儿, 哄他不再哭.

dan·druff /ˈdændrʌf; ˋdændrəf/ *n* [U] small flakes of dead skin from the scalp, usu seen in the hair; scurf 头皮屑: *This shampoo will cure your dandruff.* 这种洗发水可除掉头皮屑.

dandy[1] /ˈdændɪ; ˋdændɪ/ *n* man who cares too much about the smartness of his clothes and his appearance 过分注意衣着和外表的男人; 花花公子.
▷ **dan·di·fied** /ˈdændɪfaɪd; ˋdændɪˌfaɪd/ *adj* like or typical of a dandy 像花花公子的: *dandified clothes* 像花花公子穿的衣服.

dandy[2] /ˈdændɪ; ˋdændɪ/ *adj* (**-ier, -iest**) (*infml* 口 *esp US*) very good; excellent 极好的; 优秀的: *all fine and dandy* 非常好 ○ *That's just dandy!* 那太好了!

Dane /deɪn; den/ *n* native of Denmark 丹麦人.

dan·ger /ˈdeɪndʒə(r); ˋdendʒɚ/ *n* **1** [U] **~ (of sth)** chance of suffering damage, loss, injury, etc; risk 危险; 风险: *There's a lot of danger in rock climbing.* 攀登岩壁非常危险. ○ *Danger — thin ice!* 危险——薄冰! ○ *In war, a soldier's life is full of danger.* 在战争中, 士兵的生命充满了危险. ○ *Is there any danger of fire?* 有遭火灾的危险吗? ○ *She was very ill, but is now out of danger*, ie not likely to die. 她病重, 但现已脱险. ○ *Ships out in this storm are in great danger*, ie very liable to suffer damage, etc. 轮船在这种风暴中出航要冒极大风险. ○ *His life was in danger.* 他有生命危险. **2** [C] **~ (to sb/sth)** person or thing that may cause damage, injury, pain, etc; hazard 可能造成损伤、疼痛等的人或物; 危害: *be afraid of hidden dangers* 害怕潜伏的危险 ○ *Smoking is a danger to health.* 吸烟危害健康. ○ *That woman is a danger to society.* 那个女人是社会上的危险人物. **3** (idm 习语) **on the 'danger list** (*infml* 口) very ill and near to death 病危; 病入膏肓: *She was on the danger list, but is much better now.* 她曾一度病危, 现在好多了.
□ **'danger money** extra pay for dangerous work 危险工作津贴.

dan·ger·ous /ˈdeɪndʒərəs; ˋdendʒərəs/ *adj* **~ (for sb/sth)** likely to cause danger or be a danger 有危险的; 危险的: *a dangerous bridge, journey* 危险的桥梁、旅程 ○ *The river is dangerous for swimmers.* 在这条河里游泳有危险. ○ *This machine is dangerous: the wiring is faulty.* 这个机器有危险: 电线有毛病.
▷ **dan·ger·ously** *adv*: *driving dangerously* 危险驾驶 ○ *dangerously ill*, ie so ill that one might die 病危.

dangle /ˈdæŋgl; ˋdæŋgl/ *v* **1** (**a**) [I] hang or swing loosely 悬吊着或摆动不定: *a bunch of keys dangling at the end of a chain* 在链子一端悬吊着的一串钥匙. (**b**) [Tn] hold (sth) so that it swings loosely 拿着(某物)使其摆动: *He dangled his watch in front of the baby.* 他在婴儿面前摇晃着表. **2** (phr v) **dangle sth before/in front of sb** offer sth temptingly to sb 以某事物招引某人: *The prospect of promotion was dangled before him.* 晋升的希望在吸引着他.

Dan·ish /ˈdeɪnɪʃ; ˋdenɪʃ/ *n, adj* (language) of Denmark and the Danes 丹麦的; 丹麦人的; 丹麦语(的).
□ ˌ**Danish** ˈ**blue** type of soft white cheese with blue veins 丹麦蓝奶酪(有蓝色纹的白色软奶酪).
ˌ**Danish** ˈ**pastry** pastry cake containing apple, almond paste, etc, with icing, nuts, etc on top 丹麦糕饼(以苹果、杏仁糊等为馅, 上面覆有糖霜、坚果仁等).

dank /dæŋk; dæŋk/ *adj* (**-er, -est**) unpleasantly damp and cold 阴湿的; 阴冷的: *a dank cellar, cave, etc* 阴湿的地窖、洞穴等. ▷ **dank·ness** *n* [U].

dap·per /ˈdæpə(r); ˋdæpɚ/ *adj* (*approv* 褒) (usu of a small person) neat and smart in appearance; nimble in movement (通常指矮小的人)整洁漂亮的, 动作敏捷的: *What a dapper little man!* 好一个短小精悍的人!

dapple /ˈdæpl; ˋdæpl/ *v* [Tn] mark (sth) with (often rounded) patches of different colour or shades of colour 使(某物)有斑点(常为圆形): *The sun shining through the leaves dappled the ground.* 阳光穿过树叶照射在地上, 现出一块块亮斑.
▷ **dappled** *adj* having (often rounded) patches of different colour or shades of colour 有(常为圆形)斑点的: *a dappled deer/horse* 有斑点的鹿[马] ○ *dappled shade*, eg when the sun shines through leaves 斑斑的阴影(如阳光穿过树叶所形成的).
□ ˌ**dapple-**ˈ**grey** *n, adj* (horse that is) grey with darker patches 灰色而有深色斑点的(马).

Darby and Joan /ˌdɑːbɪ ən ˈdʒəʊn; ˋdɑrbɪ ən ˋdʒon/ old and loving married couple 恩爱的老年夫妇.
□ ˌ**Darby and** ˈ**Joan club** (*Brit*) social club for old (esp married) people 老年人(尤指老年夫妇)俱乐部.

dare[1] /deə(r); dɛr/ *modal v* (*neg* 否定式 **dare not**, *contracted form* 缩约式 **daren't** /deənt; dɛrnt/; *rare or fml pt* 罕用或文学语言用过去式 **dared** /deəd; dɛrd/, *neg* 否定式 **dared not**) **1** (used esp in negative sentences and questions, after *if/whether*, or with *hardly, never, no one, nobody* 尤用于否定句及疑问句中, 在if/whether之后, 或与hardly、never、no one、nobody连用) have sufficient courage or impudence (to do sth) 敢; 敢于; 竟敢; 胆敢: *I daren't ask her for a rise.* 我不敢要求她加薪. ○ *What's the matter — daren't you read what it says?* 怎么了 —— 你难道不敢把上面写的念出来吗? ○ *I wonder whether he dare stand up in public.* 我不知道他敢不敢站在大庭广众面前. ○ *They hardly dared breathe as somebody walked past the door!* 有人在门前走过, 他们几乎不敢呼吸了! ○ *If you ever dare call me that name again, you'll be sorry.* 你胆敢再那样叫我, 你就后悔莫及了. ○ *Nobody dared lift their eyes from the ground.* 没有人敢把视线离开地面. **2** (idm 习语) **how** ˈ**dare you, he, she, etc** (used to express indignation at the actions of others 用以表示对他人举动的愤慨): *How dare you suggest that I copied your notes!* 你竟敢认为我抄了你的笔记! ○ *How dare he take my bicycle without even asking!* 他怎么连问都不问就敢把我的自行车骑走了! **I dare say** I accept (sth) as a true or possible fact 我相信; 可能: *I* ˌ*dare say you* ˈ*are British but you still need a passport to prove it.* 我相信你是英国人, 但仍需有护照加以证明. ○ *'I would imagine he's forgotten.' '*ˌ*dare* ˈ*say!'* '我猜想他忘记了.' '很可能!'

dare[2] /deə(r); dɛr/ *v* **1** [Tt] have sufficient courage 敢; 敢于; 竟敢; 胆敢: *I don't know how she dares wear that dress.* 我不知道她怎么敢穿那件连衣裙. ○ *I've never dared go back to look.* 我再也不敢回去看一眼了. ○ *Privatize the national parks? They'd never dare, would they?* 把国家公园私营化? 他们绝对不敢, 对吗? ○ *How did you dare to tell her?* 你怎么竟敢告诉她了? ○ *Don't (you) dare leave the room!* (你)敢离开这间屋子! **2** [Tn, Dn·t] suggest to (sb) that he tries to do sth beyond his courage or ability; challenge 激(某人)做某事; 挑战: *Throw it at him! I dare you!* 向他投掷! 我谅你也不敢! ○ *I dare you to tell your mother!* 我谅你不敢告诉你母亲! ○ *Somebody dared me to jump off the bridge into the river.* 有人激我敢不敢从桥上跳进河里. **3** [Tn no passive 不用于被动语态] (*fml* 文) take the risk of having to face (sth) 冒着(某事物)的风险: *He dared his grandfather's displeasure when he left the family business.* 他不顾祖父的不悦, 放下了家族的生意.
▷ **dare** *n* (usu *sing* 通常作单数) **1** challenge to do sth dangerous or difficult 做危险的或困难的事的胆量; 挑战: *'Why did you climb onto the roof?' 'It was a dare.'* '你为什么爬到屋顶上去了?' '试试胆量.' **2** (idm 习语) **for a** ˈ**dare** because one has received a challenge 因受到激将: *He only entered the competition for a dare.* 他只是因为受人激将才参加竞赛.
□ **daredevil** /ˈdeədevl; ˋdɛrˌdɛvl/ *n* person who is foolishly bold or reckless 蛮勇的人; 冒失鬼: *He's a daredevil on the racing-track.* 他在跑道上十分胆大鲁莽. ○ [attrib 作定语] *a* ˌ*daredevil* ˈ*pilot* 蛮干的飞行员 ○ *Don't try any of those daredevil stunts.* 不要要那些天不怕地不怕的绝招.

dar·ing /ˈdeərɪŋ; ˋdɛrɪŋ/ *n* [U] adventurous courage; boldness 冒险精神; 勇气; 胆量: *the daring of the mountain climber* 爬山者的冒险精神 ○ *an ambitious plan of great daring*, ie that is bold and new 大胆创新的计划.
▷ **dar·ing** *adj* **1** courageous 勇敢的; 英勇的: *a daring person, exploit, attack* 勇敢的人、英雄的业绩、勇猛的进击. **2** bold in a new or unusual way (出奇地)大胆的: *a daring plan, innovation, etc* 别出心裁的大胆计划、革新等 ○ *a daring new art form* 别具一格的创新艺术形式 ○ *She said some daring* (ie bold and possibly shocking) *things.* 她说了一些泼天大胆的话. **dar·ingly** *adv.*

dark[1] /dɑːk; dɑrk/ *n* **1 the dark** [sing] absence of light 黑暗; 无光: *All the lights went out and we were left in the dark.* 所有的灯都熄了, 周围一片黑暗. ○ *Are you afraid of the dark?* 你怕黑吗? **2** (idm 习语) **before/after dark** before/after the sun goes down 在天黑以前[以后]: *Try to get home before dark.* 尽量在天黑以前回家. ○ *I'm afraid to go out after dark in the city.* 在城里, 我害怕天黑后出门. **(be/keep sb) in the** ˈ**dark (about sth)** in a state of ignorance 无知; 不知: *I was in the dark about it until she told me.* 这件事在她告诉我之前, 我毫不知情. ○ *We were kept completely in the dark about his plan to sell the company.* 对他计划将公司出售一事, 我们一直蒙在鼓里. **a leap/shot in the** ˈ**dark** action, answer, etc that is risked in the hope that it is correct 盲目冒险的干、回答等: *It's hard to know exactly what to do — we'll just have to take a shot in the dark.* 很难说怎么办才对 —— 我们只好瞎碰. **whistle in the dark** ⇨ WHISTLE.

dark[2] /dɑːk; dɑrk/ *adj* (**-er, -est**) **1** with no or very little light 黑暗的: *a dark room, street, corner, etc* 黑暗的房间、街道、角落等 ○ *It's awfully dark in here: put the light on.* 这里太黑了, 开灯吧. ○ *It's too dark to play outside.* 外面黑得玩儿不了. **2** (**a**) (of a colour) not reflecting much light; closer in shade(6) to black than to white 暗色的; 深色的: *dark green, red, grey, etc* 深绿色、深红色、深灰色 ○ *a dark dress, suit, etc* 深色的连衣裙、西装等 ○ *dark-brown eyes* 深棕色的眼睛. (**b**) having brown(ish) or black skin or hair 有棕色或黑色皮肤或毛发的: *a dark youth, complexion* 皮肤黝黑的青年[棕黑的肤色] ○ *I have one fair and one dark child.* 我有两个孩子, 一个头发是金色的, 一个是黑色的. **3** (*fig* 比喻) (**a**) hidden; mysterious 隐藏的; 神秘的: *a dark secret/mystery* 无人知道的秘密[神秘事情]. (**b**) difficult to understand; obscure 难理解的; 意义不明的: *Your meaning is too dark for me.* 你的意思我很难理解. **4** (*fig* 比喻) gloomy; sad 悲观的; 忧郁的; 忧愁的: *dark predictions about the future* 对前途悲观的预测 ○ *You always look on the dark side of things*, ie are always pessimistic. 你总是着眼于事物的黑暗面(总是悲观). **5** evil 邪恶的; 恶毒的: *dark powers/influence* 罪恶的权力[影响]. **6** (idm 习语) **a dark** ˈ**horse** person who hides special personal qualities or abilities 黑马(有本事而深藏不露的人): *He's a bit of a dark horse: he was earning a fortune, but nobody knew.* 他可算是藏龙卧虎: 赚大钱, 可谁也不知道. **keep it/sth dark (from sb)** keep sth secret 保密: *I'm getting married again, but keep it dark, will you?* 我要再婚了, 可要保密呀, 行吗?
▷ **darkly** *adv* (*fig* 比喻) **1** mysteriously 神秘地: *She*

D

hinted ˈ*darkly at strange events.* 她神秘地暗示着事非寻常. **2** gloomily 悲观地; 忧郁地: *He spoke darkly of possible future disaster.* 他悲观地说将来可能大难临头.

dark·ness *n* [U] state of being dark 黑暗: *The room was in complete darkness.* 室内一片漆黑.

□ **the ˈDark Ages** period of (European) history between the end of the Roman Empire and the tenth century AD 黑暗时代(从罗马帝国灭亡至公元第十世纪的欧洲历史时期).

the ˌDark ˈContinent (name given to) Africa before it was fully explored 黑暗大陆(非洲未完全开发时之称).

ˌdark ˈglasses spectacles with tinted lenses 墨镜.

ˈdark-room *n* room which can be made dark, used for processing photographs (冲洗相片用的)暗室, 暗房.

darken /ˈdɑːkən; ˋdɑrkən/ *v* [I, Tn] **1** (cause sth to) become dark (使某物)变黑暗: *We darkened the room to show the film.* 我们把房间弄暗以放影片. ○ *The sky darkened as the storm approached.* 风雨欲来, 天色黑暗. **2** (idm 习语) **darken sb's ˈdoor** (*joc or rhet* 谑或修辞) come as an unwanted or reluctant visitor to sb's house 不受欢迎的人到访: *Go! And never darken my door again!* 走吧! 下次不要再到我家来了!

darky (also **darkie**) /ˈdɑːkɪ; ˋdɑrkɪ/ *n* (⚠ *infml offensive* 讳, 口, 蔑) black or coloured person 黑鬼(黑人或有色人).

dar·ling /ˈdɑːlɪŋ; ˋdɑrlɪŋ/ *n* (**a**) person or thing much liked or loved 心爱的人: *She's a little darling!* 她是小宝贝! ○ *He's the darling* (ie favourite subject) *of the media just now.* 他是当前传播媒介中最红的人(最受欢迎的人). (**b**) (as a form of address 作为称呼): *My darling! How sweet of you to come!* 亲爱的! 你来到这里多让人高兴啊!

▷ **dar·ling** *adj* [attrib 作定语] **1** dearly loved 心爱的; 可爱的. **2** (*infml* 口) charming; pleasing 迷人的; 使人愉快的: *What a darling little room!* 多么讨人喜欢的小屋子!

darn[1] /dɑːn; dɑrn/ *v* [I, Tn] mend (a garment) by passing a thread through the material in two directions 织补(衣物): *My socks have been darned again and again.* 我的袜子已经补了又补. ○ *I must darn the hole in my pocket.* 我得把口袋补一补.

▷ **darn** *n* place mended by darning 织补之处.

darn·ing *n* [U] task of darning; things needing to be darned 织补的工作; 需织补的东西: *I hate darning.* 我讨厌织补活儿. ○ *We sat doing the darning.* 我们坐着织补.

ˈdarning-needle *n* large sewing needle used for darning 织补用的大针.

darn[2] /dɑːn; dɑrn/ *v* [Tn] (*infml euph* 口, 婉) = DAMN[1] 3: *Well, I'll be darned!* 啊呀, 好家伙! ○ *Darn it! She beat me again!* 倒霉! 她又比我强了! ○ *Darn those blasted kids!* 这些缺德孩子真该死!

▷ **darn** (also **darned**) *adj* (*infml euph* 口, 婉) (used to express annoyance, impatience, etc 用以表示烦恼、不耐烦等): *That darn(ed) cat has eaten my supper!* 这个死猫把我的晚饭吃掉了! — *adv* (*infml euph approv or derog* 口, 婉, 褒或贬) extremely; very 极端; 非常: *a darn(ed) good try* 好好试一下 ○ *What a darn(ed) stupid thing to say!* 这话说得多么愚蠢!

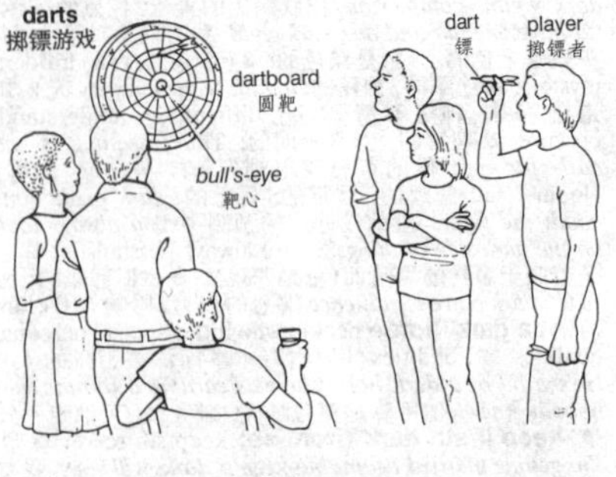

dart[1] /dɑːt; dɑrt/ *n* **1** [C] small pointed missile (often with feathers to aid flight) used as a weapon or in the game of darts 镖; 飞镖. **2** [sing] sudden fast movement 猛冲; 突进: *She made a dart for the exit.* 她冲向出口. **3** [C] (in dressmaking) stitched tapering fold (制衣)捏褶. **4 darts** [sing *v*] game in which darts are thrown at a target marked with numbers for scoring 掷镖游戏: *Darts is often played in English pubs.* 英国酒馆里常有掷镖游戏. ⇨illus 见插图.

□ **ˈdartboard** *n* circular board used as the target in the game of darts 掷镖游戏用的圆靶.

dart[2] /dɑːt; dɑrt/ *v* [Ipr, Ip, Tn·pr, Tn·p] (cause sth to) move suddenly and quickly in the specified direction (使某物)猛冲, 突进: *The mouse darted away when I approached.* 我走近时, 老鼠就飞快逃跑了. ○ *Swallows are darting through the air.* 燕子在空中掠过. ○ *She darted into the doorway to hide.* 她冲到门口躲藏起来. ○ *The snake darted out its tongue.* 蛇飞快地吐着芯子. ○ *She darted an angry look* (ie suddenly glanced angrily) *at him.* 她狠狠地瞥了他一眼. ⇨Usage at WHIZ 用法见WHIZ.

dash[1] /dæʃ; dæʃ/ *n* **1** [sing] **~ (for sth)** sudden forward movement 突进; 猛冲: *to make a dash for freedom, shelter* 为获自由、遮掩处而急奔 ○ *We jumped into the car and made a dash for the ferry.* 我们跳上汽车, 冲向码头. ○ *Mother said lunch was ready and there was a mad dash for the table.* 母亲说午饭做好了, 大家一下子都向饭桌奔去. **2** [C usu *sing* 通常作单数] (*esp US*) short race; sprint 短跑; 短距离赛跑: *the 100-metres dash* 100米赛跑. **3** [C esp *sing* 尤作单数] **a ~ (of sth)** small amount of sth added or mixed 少量搀和物或混合物: *a dash of salt* 少许盐 ○ *red with a dash of blue* 略为发蓝的红色 ○ *The flag adds a dash of colour to the grey building.* 那面旗子装点着灰秃秃的大楼. **4** [sing] **~ (of sth)** (sound of) liquid striking or being thrown against sth 冲击或溅洒液体(的声音): *the dash of waves on the rocks* 波浪拍打岩石的声音 ○ *A dash of water in his face will revive him.* 向他脸上泼水能使他苏醒. **5** [C] horizontal stroke (—) used in writing, printing and Morse code 破折号(——). ⇨App 3 见附录3. **6** [U] ability to act vigorously; energy 活力; 冲劲儿; 精力; 干劲: *an officer famous for his skill and dash* 以干练和干劲闻名的官员. **7** [C] (*infml* 口) = DASHBOARD. **8** (idm 习语) **cut a ˈdash** be exciting and stylish (in appearance or behaviour) (外表或举止)神气, 有气派, 帅: *He really cuts a dash in his smart new uniform.* 他穿着漂亮的新制服真是神气十足. **make a bolt/dash/run for it** ⇨ BOLT[2].

□ **ˈdashboard** (also **facia, fascia**) *n* board or panel below the windscreen of a motor vehicle, carrying various instruments and controls (机动车辆的)仪表板. ⇨illus at App 1 见附录1之插图, page xii.

dash[2] /dæʃ; dæʃ/ *v* **1** [I, Ipr, Ip] move suddenly and quickly; rush 猛冲; 突进: *I must dash* (ie leave quickly), *I'm late.* 我得赶紧走了, 已经晚了. ○ *He dashed off with the money.* 他带着钱跑了. ○ *She dashed into the shop.* 她冲进商店里. ○ *An ambulance dashed to the scene of the accident.* 救护车风驰电掣赶往事故现场. **2** [Ipr, Tn·pr, Tn·p] (cause sth to) strike forcefully (使某物)猛撞, 撞击, 碰撞: *Waves dashed against the harbour wall.* 波浪撞击着港口的墙基. ○ *He dashed the glass to the ground.* 他把玻璃杯狠狠摔在地上. ○ *The boat was dashed against the rocks.* 小船猛撞在礁石上. ○ *A passing car dashed mud all over us.* 一辆汽车飞驰而过, 溅了我们满身泥. **3** (idm 习语) **dash (it)!** (*infml euph* 口, 婉) (used as a milder way of saying *damn* 用如damn一词, 语气稍轻): *Dash it! I've broken my pen.* 糟了! 我把钢笔弄断了. **4 dash/shatter sb's hopes** ⇨ HOPE. **5** (phr v) **dash sth off** write or draw sth quickly 匆匆地写或画某事物: *She dashed off a letter to her mother.* 她给母亲匆匆写了一封信.

▷ **dash·ing** *adj* (**a**) lively and exciting 精神振奋的; 精神抖擞的: *a dashing rider, officer, etc* 雄赳赳的骑马人、官员等. (**b**) (of clothes) smart and interesting (指衣服)漂亮而有趣的, 帅: *a dashing uniform, hat, etc* 很帅的制服、帽子等. **dash·ingly** *adv*.

data /ˈdeɪtə, *also* ˈdɑːtə; *US* ˈdætə; ˋdætə/ *n* (**a**) [U or pl] facts or information used in deciding or discussing sth 资料: *Very little data is available.* 现有的资料十分不足. ○ *The data is/are still being analysed.* 资料仍在分析中. (**b**) [usu sing *v* 通常与单数动词连用] (*computing* 计)

information prepared for or stored by a computer 数据: [attrib 作定语] *data analysis, capture, retrieval* 数据分析、捕捉、检索 ○ *data protection*, ie legal restrictions on access to data stored in a computer 数据保护.

□ ˈ**data bank** centre with a comprehensive file of computer data 数据库.

ˈ**database** *n* large store of computerized data, esp lists or abstracts of reports, etc 数据单元.

ˌ**data-ˈprocessing** *n* [U] performing of computer operations on data to analyze it, solve problems, etc 数据处理.

ˌ**data ˈcapture** process of collecting data for use in a computer 数据捕捉; 数据收集.

NOTE ON USAGE 用法: There are a lot of nouns in English of Latin or Greek origin. 英语名词中有很多来自拉丁语或希腊语. They often end in **-us, -a, -um, -on,** etc. 这些词多以 **-us**、**-a**、**-um**、**-on** 等结尾. The plural forms of these nouns can cause difficulty. 这些名词的复数形式可能会造成困难. **1** Some, especially scientific terms, have kept their original singular and plural forms 有些词, 特别是科学术语, 仍保留着原来的单复数形式: *bacillus, bacilli* ○ *larva, larvae* ○ *criterion, criteria.* **2** Many, especially those in general use, now only have a regular English plural form 其中很多词, 特别是常用词, 现在只有合乎英语规则的复数形式: *arena, arenas* ○ *circus, circuses* ○ *electron, electrons.* **3** Some have alternative plural forms, which are both acceptable. 有些词, 有两种复数形式, 均可使用. The Latin form is more formal 拉丁语式的复数形式较庄重: *focus, focuses/foci* ○ *formula, formulas/formulae* ○ *spectrum, spectrums/spectra.* **4** There is uncertainty with some nouns as to whether they are singular or plural 有些名词到底是单数还是复数, 难以确定: *This data is correct* and *These data are correct* are both acceptable. 数据正确(英文句中用is或are均可). Paraphernalia (a Greek plural) is used as a singular noun ☆ paraphernalia(希腊语复数)一字用作单数名词: *All my fishing paraphernalia is in the car.* 我的鱼具都在汽车里. Media (*sing* medium) is sometimes incorrectly used as a singular noun ☆ media(单数为medium)一字有时误用作单数名词: *The media are* (NOT *is*) *often accused of being biased.* 传播媒介常遭指责, 认为有偏见(英文句中不可用is).

date[1] /deɪt; det/ *n* **1** [C] (**a**) specific numbered day of the month, or specific year, usu given to show when sth happened or is to happen 日期; 日子; 年份: *Today's date is the 23rd of June.* 今天是6月23日. ○ *'What's the date?' 'The 10th.'* '日期是几号?' '10号.' ○ *Has the date of the meeting been fixed?* 开会的日期决定了吗? ○ *'When was the date of the Battle of Waterloo?' 'June 1815.'* '滑铁卢战役是在何时?' '1815年6月.' (**b**) indication written, printed or stamped (on a letter, coin, etc) of the time when it was written, made, etc (信件、硬币等)注明的日期: *There's no date on this cheque.* 这张支票上没有日期. ○ *The manuscript bears the date 10 April 1937.* 手稿上注着1937年4月10日. ⇨App 4 见附录4. **2** [U] period of time in history, eg one to which antiquities belong (古物等所属的)时代, 年代: *This vase is of an earlier date* (ie is older) *than that one.* 这个花瓶的年代比那个的早. **3** [C] (*infml* 口) (**a**) appointment to meet sb at a particular time (约好时间的)会晤: *We made a date to go to the opera.* 我们约好去看歌剧. (**b**) meeting with a person of the opposite sex (和异性的)约会: *I have a date (with my girl-friend) tonight.* 我今晚(和女朋友)有个约会. (**c**) (*esp US*) person with whom one has a date[1](3b) (异性的)约会对象: *My date is meeting me at seven.* 我的对象七点钟跟我见面. **4** (idm 习语) **(be/go) ˌout of ˈdate** (**a**) no longer fashionable 不再流行的; 过时的: *Will denim jeans ever go out of date?* 粗布牛仔裤会过时吗? ○ [attrib 作定语] *ˌout-of-date ˈclothes, iˈdeas, ˈslang* 过时的衣服、陈旧的思想、已废的俚语. (**b**) no longer valid 过期的; 失效的: *My passport is out of date.* 我的护照已经过期了. **to date** so far; up to now 迄今; 至今; 到目前为止: *To date, we have not received any replies.* 我们至今还未接到答复. ○ *This is the biggest donation we've had to date.* 这是到目前为止我们所收到的最大一项捐赠. **(be/bring sb/sth) ˌup to ˈdate** (**a**) modern; fashionable 现代的; 时新的: *She wears clothes that are right up to date.* 她穿着最时新的衣服. (**b**) according to what is now known or required 据目前所知或所要求的: *The list is up to date now that we've added the new members' names.* 我们把新成员的名字已经加进去了, 这份名单是最全的了. ○ [attrib 作定语] *ˌup-to-date ˈstyles, ˈmethods, ˈbooks* 最新的式样、方法、书籍.

▷ **date·less** *adj* never becoming unfashionable or dated 历久弥新的; 永不过时的.

□ ˈ**date-line** *n* (**a**) (also **international date-line**) imaginary line running from north to south 180° from Greenwich, east and west of which the date differs by one day (国际)日界线(距格林威治180°自北向南的一条假想线, 此线以东及以西的地区日期相差一日). (**b**) line in a newspaper above an article, etc, that shows the time and place of writing 日期行(报章中一篇文字上方注明撰写时间和地点的一行文字).

ˈ**date-stamp** *n* adjustable rubber stamp for printing the date on documents, etc 日期戳子.

date[2] /deɪt; det/ *v* **1** [Tn] write a date[1](1a) on (sth) 在(某物)上写上日期: *Don't forget to date your cheque.* 不要忘记在支票上写上日期. ○ *His last letter was dated 24 May.* 他最后一封信的日期是5月24日. **2** [Tn] determine the age of (sth) 鉴定(某物)的年代: *the method of dating rocks, fossils, tools, paintings* 鉴定岩石、化石、工具、绘画的年代的方法. **3** [I, Tn] seem or make (sb/sth) seem old-fashioned 显得过时; 使(某人[某物])显得过时: *Young people's clothes date quickly nowadays.* 现在年轻人的衣服转眼就过时. ○ *Your taste in pop music really dates you.* 你所喜爱的流行音乐真使你显得脱离了时代. **4** [Ipr] **~ back to/from...** have existed since 自某时代存在至今: *This castle dates from the 14th century*, ie was built then. 这座城堡建于14世纪. ○ *Our partnership dates back to* (ie We have been partners since) *1960.* 我们从1960年就合伙了. **5** [I, Tn] (*infml* 口 *esp US*) go on a date[1](3b) with (sb), once or regularly (与异性)约会: *They've been dating for a long time.* 他们一直频频约会. ○ *I only dated her once.* 我和她只约会过一次.

▷ **dat·able** *adj.*

dated *adj* old-fashioned; no longer in use 旧式的; 不时兴的; 过时的: *His clothes look so dated.* 他的衣服早就过时了. ○ *She uses rather dated words and phrases.* 她使用的词语未免太陈旧了.

date[3] /deɪt; det/ *n* **1** brown sweet edible fruit of a palm tree common in N Africa and S W Asia 枣. **2** (usu 通常作 ˈ**date-palm**) this tree 枣树.

dat·ive /ˈdeɪtɪv; ˈdetɪv/ *n* (*grammar*) special form of a noun, a pronoun or an adjective used (in some inflected languages) to indicate or describe esp the person who receives sth or benefits from an action 与格(某些屈折语中的名词、代词或形容词的一种形式, 用以表示所指的人物接受某事物或从一行动中获益).

▷ **dat·ive** *adj* of or in the dative 与格的.

daub /dɔːb; dɔb/ *v* **1** [Tn, Tn·pr, Tn·p] **~ A on (B); ~ B (with A)** put (a soft substance) on (a surface) in a rough or careless way (胡乱)涂抹: *He daubed some red paint on (the canvas).* 他(在油画布上)涂上了一些红颜色. ○ *She daubed her face with thick make-up.* 她面部化妆很浓. ○ *trousers daubed* (ie made dirty) *with mud* 沾上泥的裤子. **2** [I, Tn] (*infml* 口) paint (pictures) without skill or artistry 胡乱地画.

▷ **daub** *n* **1** [C, U] (covering of) soft sticky material, eg clay, for walls (一层)涂料. **2** [C] badly painted picture 拙劣的画.

dauber *n* (*derog* 贬) unskilful painter 拙劣的画匠.

daugh·ter /ˈdɔːtə(r); ˈdɔtɚ/ *n* one's female child 女儿. ⇨App 8 见附录8.

□ **daughter-in-law** /ˈdɔːtər ɪn lɔː; ˈdɔtərɪnˌlɔ/ *n* (*pl* **~s-in-law** /ˈdɔːtəz ɪn lɔ; ˈdɔtɚzɪnˌlɔ/) wife of one's son 儿媳妇. ⇨App 8 见附录8.

daunt /dɔːnt; dɔnt/ *v* **1** [Tn usu passive 通常用于被动语态] discourage (sb); frighten 使(某人)气馁; 威吓: *I was rather daunted by the thought of addressing such an audience.* 我一想到要对这样的听众讲话, 就有些胆小. **2** (idm 习语) **nothing ˈdaunted** (*fml or joc* 文或谑) not at all discouraged 毫无惧色; 毫不气馁: *Their guide deserted them, but, nothing daunted, they pressed on into* *the jungle.* 向导离他们而去，但是他们毫不气馁，仍向森林进发.

▷ **daunt·ing** *adj* discouraging; frightening 使人气馁的; 吓人的: *The prospect of meeting the President is quite daunting.* 一想到要会见总统就足以令人心悸.

daunt·less /ˈdɔ:ntlɪs; ˈdɔntlɪs/ *adj* not easily discouraged or frightened 勇敢的; 无畏的: *dauntless bravery* 英勇绝伦. **daunt·lessly** *adv*.

dau·phin /ˈdɔ:fɪn; ˈdɔfɪn/ *n* (formerly) title of the King of France's eldest son (旧时)法国皇太子的称号.

dav·en·port /ˈdævnpɔ:t; ˈdævən,pɔrt/ *n* **1** (*Brit*) writing desk with drawers and a hinged top 翻板写字台(带有抽屉, 桌面有合叶可翻开). **2** (*US*) large sofa for two or three people, esp one that can be converted into a bed 长沙发(可坐两三人); (尤指)沙发床.

davit /ˈdævɪt; ˈdævɪt/ *n* small crane[1](2) on a ship, usu one of a pair, used for supporting, lowering and raising a ship's boat (轮船上的)吊艇柱, 吊艇架.

D

Davy Jones's locker (*infml often joc* 口, 常作戏谑语) the bottom of the sea 海底: *Their ship was sent to Davy Jones's locker*, ie was sunk. 他们的轮船去见龙王爷了(沉没了).

dawdle /ˈdɔ:dl; ˈdɔdl/ *v* (**a**) [I] be slow; waste time 缓慢; 浪费时间: *Stop dawdling and hurry up: we're late.* 别磨磨蹭蹭了, 快点儿吧: 咱们晚了. ○ *She doesn't get her work done because she's always dawdling.* 她没做完, 总是磨洋工. (**b**) (phr v) **dawdle sth away** waste (time) 浪费(时间): *He dawdles the hours away watching television.* 他把时间都荒废在看电视上了. ▷ **dawd·ler** /ˈdɔ:dlə(r); ˈdɔdlɚ/ *n*.

dawn[1] /dɔ:n; dɔn/ *n* [U, C] **1** time of day when light first appears; daybreak 黎明; 破晓; 拂晓: *We must start at dawn.* 我们必须天一亮就启程. ○ *He works from dawn till dusk.* 他从天亮工作到天黑. ○ *It's almost dawn.* 天差不多要亮了. **2** (*fig* 比喻) beginning; first signs of sth 开始; 开端; 发端: *the dawn of hope, love, intelligence, civilization* 希望、爱情、智力、文明的开端 ○ *the dawn of a new age* 新时代的曙光. **3** (idm 习语) **the crack of dawn** ⇨ CRACK[1].

□ ˌ**dawn** ˈ**chorus** sound of birds singing in the early morning 清晨的鸟啼声.

dawn[2] /dɔ:n; dɔn/ *v* **1** [I] (often with *it* as subject 常用it作主语) begin to grow light 破晓: *It was dawning as we left.* 我们离开时天开始亮了. ○ *When day dawned, we could see the damage the storm had caused.* 天亮时, 我们可以看到风暴造成的灾害. **2** [I, Ipr] **~ (on sb)** gradually become clear to sb's mind; become evident (to sb) (某人)逐渐明白: *It finally dawned (on me) that he had been lying.* 最后(我)才明白他一直在撒谎. ○ *The truth began to dawn on him.* 他开始弄明白真相.

day /deɪ; de/ *n* **1** (**a**) [U] time between sunrise and sunset 白天; 日间: *He has been working all day.* 他整天都在工作. ○ *When I woke up, it was already day.* 我醒来时已是白天. (**b**) [C] period of 24 hours 一天; 一昼夜: *There are seven days in a week.* 一周有七天. ○ *I saw Tom three days ago.* 我三天前见过汤姆. ○ *I shall see Mary in a few days' time*, ie a few days from now. 我几天后就能见到玛丽. ○ *'What day of the week is it?' 'It's Monday.'* '今天星期几?' '今天星期一.' ⇨App 5 见附录5. (**c**) [C] hours of the day when one works 一天工作的时间; 工作日: *I've done a good day's work.* 我已做完足足一天的工作. ○ *Have you had a hard day at the office?* 你今天在办公室是否忙得不可开交? ○ *Her working day is seven hours.* 她一天工作七小时. ○ *The employees are demanding a six-hour day and a five-day week.* 雇员要求每日工作六小时, 每周工作五天. **2 days** [pl] specified time; period 某段时间; 时期; 时代: *in his younger days* 在他的年轻时代 ○ *I was much happier in those days*, ie at that time. 我在那时期快乐得多. ○ *in the days of Queen Victoria* 在维多利亚女王时代 ○ *in days of old/in the old days*, ie in former times 昔日. **3** (idm 习语) **all in a day's** ˈ**work** part of the normal routine 每日常规的一部分; 日常工作: *Injecting animals is all in a day's work for a vet.* 给动物注射是兽医的日常工作. **at the end of the day** ⇨ END[1]. **break of day** ⇨ BREAK[2]. **by day/night** during daylight hours/after dark 白天; 日间 *[夜间; 天黑后]*: *The fugitives travelled by night and rested by day.* 逃亡者夜行而昼伏. **call it a day** ⇨ CALL[2]. **carry/win the** ˈ**day** (*infml* 口) be successful against sb/sth 成功; 获胜: *Despite strong opposition, the ruling party carried the day.* 执政党尽管遭到强烈反对, 还是获胜了. **clear as day** ⇨ CLEAR[1]. **day after** ˈ**day** for many days; continuously 日复一日; 多日; 连续地: *Day after day she waited in vain for him to telephone her.* 日复一日, 她徒劳地等待他的电话. **the day after to**ˈ**morrow** 后天: *If today is Wednesday, the day after tomorrow will be Friday.* 今天要是星期三, 后天就是星期五. **the day before** ˈ**yesterday** 前天: *If today is Wednesday, the day before yesterday was Monday.* 今天要是星期三, 前天就是星期一. **day by** ˈ**day** as time goes by 一天一天地; 逐日: *Day by day she learnt more about her job.* 她日益了解自己的工作了. **day** ˈ**in, day** ˈ**out** every day without exception 一天接一天地; 日复一日; 每天: *Day in, day out, no matter what the weather is like, she walks ten miles.* 她不管天气如何, 每天总是不间断地步行十英里. **a day of** ˈ**reckoning** (*fml* 文) time when wrongdoers will be punished 做坏事的人得到惩罚的日子: *You're enjoying yourself now, but a day of reckoning will come.* 别看你现在逍遥, 将来会遭报应的. **sb's/sth's days are** ˈ**numbered** sb/sth is soon going to die, fail, lose favour, etc 某人*[某事物]*即将死亡、失败、失宠等; 活不久; 寿命长不了: *He has a serious illness, and his days are numbered.* 他患重病, 不久人世了. ○ *This factory is no longer profitable, so its days are numbered*, ie it will soon close. 这家工厂赚不到钱了, 很快就要倒闭. **early days** ⇨ EARLY. **end one's days/life** ⇨ END[2]. **every dog has his/its day** ⇨ DOG[1]. **fall on evil days** ⇨ EVIL. **from day to** ˈ**day**; **from** ˌ**one day to the** ˈ**next** within a short period of time 在短时间内: *Things change from day to day.* 事情一天一变. ○ *You don't know what his mood will be from one day to the next.* 真说不上他的情绪今天怎样明天又怎样. **the good/bad old days** ⇨ OLD. **happy as the day is long** ⇨ HAPPY. **have had one's** ˈ**day** be no longer successful, prosperous, powerful, etc 不再顺利、兴旺、强大等: *He was a great singer once but now he's had his day.* 他曾是个红歌星, 但现在风华已去. ○ *Colonialism has had its day*, ie is over. 殖民主义已日薄西山. **have seen/known better days** ⇨ BETTER[1]. **high days and holidays** ⇨ HIGH[1]. **if he's, she's, etc a** ˈ**day** (in speaking of sb's age) at least (论某人年龄)至少: *He's eighty if he's a day!* 他至少八十岁了! **in all one's born days** ⇨ BORN. **in** ˈ**this day and age** nowadays 现时代; 当今. **in one's** ˈ**day** in one's lifetime; in a period of success, prosperity, power, etc 一生; 成功、兴盛、强大等的时期; 鼎盛时期: *In his day, he was a very influential politician.* 他在走红时是非常有影响力的政治家. ○ *She was a great beauty in her day*, ie when she was young. 她年轻时是个绝代美人. **it's not sb's** ˈ**day** (*infml* 口) sb is especially unlucky 某人特别不幸运; 倒霉: *My car broke down, then I locked myself out: it's just not my day!* 我的汽车坏了, 又把自己锁在外边, 真倒霉透了! **make sb's** ˈ**day** (*infml* 口) make sb very happy 使某人非常高兴: *If she wins, it'll make her day.* 她要是赢了, 她就太高兴了. **late in the day** ⇨ LATE[2]. **the livelong day/night** ⇨ LIVELONG. **night and day** ⇨ NIGHT. **a** ˌ**nine days'** ˈ**wonder** person or thing that attracts attention for a short time but is soon forgotten 昙花一现的人或事物: *As a pop star she was a nine days' wonder: she only made one successful record.* 她是个昙花一现的歌星, 只录制过一张受欢迎的唱片. ˈ**one day** at a particular time in the future 将来某一天; 有朝一日: *One day I'll get my revenge.* 有朝一日我要报仇. **one fine day** ⇨ FINE[2]. ˈ**one of these (fine) days** soon 不久: *One of these days he'll realize what a fool he's been.* 不久他就会明白他一直是多么愚蠢. **one of those** ˈ**days** an especially unpleasant or unlucky day 特别不愉快或不幸的日子: *I've had one of those days: my train was late, and I lost my wallet.* 这一天我真不幸: 火车晚点, 我又丢了钱包. **the order of the day** ⇨ ORDER[1]. **the other** ˈ**day** recently 最近: *I saw her (only) the other day.* 我(就)在最近见过她. **pass the time of day** ⇨ PASS[2]. **peep of day** ⇨ PEEP[1]. **the present day** ⇨ PRESENT[1]. **a red-letter day** ⇨ RED[1]. **Rome was not built in a day** ⇨ BUILD. **salad days** ⇨ SALAD. **save, etc sth for a rainy day** ⇨ RAINY. ˈ**some day** at some time in the future 他日; 将来有一天: *Some day I'll come back and marry her.* 总有一天我要回来娶她. ˈ**that'll be the day** (*ironic* 反语)

that's very unlikely 不太可能: *'He says he'll do the washing-up.' 'That'll be the day!'* '他说他要洗碗.' '没那么回事!' **'these days** nowadays 如今; 当今. **,this day 'fortnight** a fortnight from today 两星期后的今天. **,this day 'week** a week from today 一星期后的今天. **'those were the days** that was a happier, better, etc time 那是过去的幸福、美好等的日子: *Do you remember when we first got married? Those were the days!* 你还记得我们刚结婚那时吗? 那时多幸福! **to the 'day** exactly 一天都不差; 正好: *It's three years to the day since we met.* 我们整整三年没见面了. **to this 'day** even now 至今: *To this day, I still don't know why she did it.* 至今我仍不明白她为什么干那件事. **turn night into day** ⇨ NIGHT.

□ **'day-book** (*commerce* 商) *n* book for recording sales as they take place, before transferring them later to a ledger (转入总帐之前的)日记帐, 流水帐.

'day-boy, 'day-girl *ns* pupil who attends a boarding-school daily but sleeps at home (寄宿学校中的)走读生.

'daybreak *n* dawn 破晓; 黎明: *We will leave at daybreak.* 我们在黎明时动身.

,day 'care care for small children away from home, during the day 日托: *Day care is provided by the company she works for.* 她工作的那家公司有日托. ○ [attrib 作定语] *a 'day-care centre* 日托托儿所.

'day-dream *n* idle and pleasant thoughts that distract one's attention from the present 白日梦: *She stared out of the window, lost in day-dreams.* 她凝视窗外, 陷入白日梦中. — *v* [I, Ipr] **~ (about sth)** enjoy such thoughts 想入非非; 空想; 幻想: *He sat in the classroom, day-dreaming (about the holidays).* 他坐在教室里幻想着(度假).

'day-long *adj* [attrib 作定语], *adv* (lasting) for the whole day 整天(的); 终日(的).

'day nursery place where small children are looked after while their parents are at work 日托托儿所.

,day 'off day on which one does not have to work 休息日: *I work from Tuesday to Saturday, and Sunday and Monday are my days off.* 我从星期二到星期六工作, 星期日和星期一休息.

,day re'lease system of allowing employees days off work for education 脱产进修; 给假若干天调训制.

,day-re'turn *n* return ticket (often at a reduced price) for passengers travelling both ways on the same day 当日往返票(票价常较低).

'day-room *n* room (in a hospital, hostel, etc) where residents can sit, relax, watch TV, etc during the day 医院、招待所等里面供住客白天休息看电视等的房间.

'day-school *n* school attended daily by pupils living at home 日校; 走读学校. Cf 参看 BOARDING-SCHOOL (BOARD[2]).

'day shift (group of workers who work for a) fixed period during the day 日班(工人). Cf 参看 NIGHT SHIFT (NIGHT).

'daytime *n* [U] time between sunrise and sunset 白天; 日间: *You hardly ever see owls in the daytime.* 白天几乎看不到猫头鹰.

,day-to-'day *adj* [attrib 作定语] **(a)** planning for only one day at a time 逐日的(每次只作一天的计划的): *I have organized the cleaning on a ,day-to-'day basis, until the usual cleaner returns.* 我已安排了清洁工回来前的逐日清洁工作. **(b)** involving daily routine 每日常规工作的: *She has been looking after the ,day-to-day admini'stration.* 她一直在照管日常的行政工作.

day·light /'deɪlaɪt; 'de,laɪt/ *n* **1** [U] light during daytime 日光; 白昼: *The colours look different when viewed in daylight.* 在日光下看, 颜色显得不同. ○ *I haven't seen your garden in daylight before.* 我以前还没有在白天看过你的花园呢. ○ *before daylight*, ie before dawn 天亮前; 黎明前. **2** (idm 习语) **broad daylight** ⇨ BROAD[1]. **,daylight 'robbery** (*infml* 口) charging too much 要价过高: *Three pounds for two sandwiches? It's daylight robbery!* 两个三明治要三镑? 简直是敲竹杠! **see 'daylight** understand sth that was previously puzzling 理解了曾感到困惑的事: *I struggled with the problem for hours before I saw daylight.* 这个问题我费了几小时才弄明白.

□ **,daylight 'saving** [U] way of making darkness fall later during summer by making clocks show a later time on a date in spring 日光节约; 夏令时. **,daylight 'saving time** (*US* also **'daylight time**) period when this is in effect 实行夏令时的期间. Cf 参看 SUMMER TIME (SUMMER).

day·lights /'deɪlaɪts; 'de,laɪts/ *n* [pl] (idm 习语) **beat/knock the (living) daylights out of sb** (*infml* 口) beat sb very severely 狠打某人: *If I catch you stealing again, I'll beat the daylights out of you!* 假如再让我逮着你偷东西, 看我怎么揍你! **frighten/scare the (living) daylights out of sb** (*infml* 口) frighten sb very much 使某人非常惊恐.

daze /deɪz; dez/ *v* [Tn usu passive 通常用于被动语态] **(a)** make (sb) confused and unable to react properly 使(某人)迷乱而不能做出正确反应; 使茫然: *dazed with drugs* 在麻醉剂影响下神志不清 ○ *The blow on the head dazed him for a moment.* 他头上受了一击后就昏眩了片刻. **(b)** surprise and bewilder (sb) 使(某人)惊奇与迷惑: *I was dazed by her sudden offer.* 她突然提出此事, 我感到惊奇而不知所措.

▷ **daze** *n* (idm 习语) **in a daze** in a confused state 处于茫然状态: *I've been in a complete daze since hearing the sad news.* 我听到那坏消息, 一直全然不知所措.

dazed /deɪzd; dezd/ *adj*: *a dazed look, manner, etc* 茫然的神态、举止等.

dazzle /'dæzl; 'dæzl/ *v* [Tn usu passive 通常用于被动语态] **(a)** blind (sb) briefly with too much light, brilliance, etc (因强光、闪烁等)使(某人)目眩, 眼花缭乱: *I was dazzled by his headlights.* 他的车头灯照得我目眩. **(b)** (*fig* 比喻) impress (sb) greatly through splendour, ability, etc 使(某人)赞许, 称奇: *He was dazzled by her beauty and wit.* 她聪明貌美使他为之神魂颠倒.

▷ **dazzle** *n* [U] splendour; brilliance 壮丽; 光辉: *all the dazzle of the circus* 马戏团所见之光怪陆离.

daz·zling *adj*: *a dazzling display of sporting skill* 运动技巧的精湛表演.

dB *abbr* 缩写 = decibel(s).

DBE /,di: bi: 'i:; ,di bi i/ *abbr* 缩写 = (*Brit*) Dame Commander (of the Order) of the British Empire 英帝国高级女勋爵士; 英帝国爵级司令勋衔: *be made a DBE* 获封英帝国高级女勋爵士 ○ *Dame Susan Peters DBE* 苏珊·彼得斯英帝国高级女勋爵士. Cf 参看 CBE, KBE, MBE.

DC /,di: 'si:; ,di 'si/ *abbr* 缩写 = **1** (*music* 音) repeat from the beginning (Italian *da capo*) 从头再奏(源自意大利文*da capo*). **2** District of Columbia 哥伦比亚特区: *Washington, DC* 美国首都华盛顿. **3** (also **dc**) direct current (DIRECT[1]). Cf 参看 AC.

DD /,di: 'di:; ,di 'di/ *abbr* 缩写 = Doctor of Divinity 神学博士: *have/be a DD* 有神学博士学位[为神学博士] ○ *Colin Green DD* 科林·格林神学博士.

D-day /'di: deɪ; 'di,de/ *n* **1** day (6 June 1944) on which the Allied forces landed in N France during the Second World War 第二次世界大战盟军在法国北部的登陆日(1944年6月6日). **2** date on which something important is due to happen 重大事件将要发生的日期: *As D-day approached we still weren't ready to move house.* 日子快到了, 我们还没准备好搬家.

DDT /,di: di: 'ti:; ,di di 'ti/ *abbr* 缩写 = dichlorodiphenyl-trichloroethane (a colourless chemical that kills insects and is also harmful to animals) 滴滴涕; 二氯二苯基三氯乙烷.

de- *pref* 前缀 (with *vs* and related *adjs, advs* and *ns* 与动词、形容词、副词、名词结合) **1** opposite or negative of ...的反义或否定: *defrost* ○ *decentralization.* **2** removal of 除掉...: *defuse* ○ *derailment.*

dea·con /'di:kən; 'dikən/ *n* **1** (in Christian churches with ordained priests, eg the Church of England) minister ranking below a priest (有委任牧师的基督教会, 如英国国教圣公会中的)会吏. **2** (in nonconformist churches) lay person who deals with church business affairs (在英国不从国教派教会中的)执事, 助祭.

▷ **dea·con·ess** /,di:kə'nes, *also* 'di:kənɪs; 'dikənɪs/ *n* woman with duties similar to those of a deacon 任上项两义职责的女子; 女会吏; 女执事; 女助祭.

dead /ded; dɛd/ *adj* **1** **(a)** no longer alive 死的: *a dead person, animal* 死的人、动物 ○ *dead flowers, cells* 凋谢的花、死的细胞 ○ *The tiger fell dead.* 老虎倒地死去.

(**b**) never having been alive; inanimate 无生命的; 无生气的: *dead matter*, eg rock 无生命的物质(如岩石). **2** (**a**) without movement or activity 无活动的: *The town is dead now the mine has closed.* 因矿井已关闭, 镇上一片死气沉沉. ○ *in the dead hours of the night*, ie when everything is quiet 在夜深人静时. (**b**) (*infml* 口) without interest and liveliness; dull 无趣的; 无生气的; 呆滞的: *What a dead place this is!* 这地方多没意思! ○ *The acting was rather dead.* 表演十分乏味. **3** no longer used, effective, valid, etc 不再使用的、已无作用的、已失效的等: *This debate is now dead.* 辩论现已过去. ○ *My love for him is dead.* 我不再爱他了. ○ *a dead language*, eg Latin 死的语言(如拉丁语). **4** (**a**) numb from cold, anaesthetic, etc 冻僵的; 麻木的: *My dead fingers could not untie the knot.* 我的手指麻木了, 解不开结. (**b**) [pred 作表语] **~ to sth** not feeling (pity, guilt, etc) 无动于衷; 无感觉: *He was dead to all feelings of shame.* 他恬不知耻. **5** [attrib 作定语] complete; absolute 全然地; 完全地: *dead calm, silence, etc* 死一般的平静、沉寂等 ○ *come to a dead stop*, ie stop suddenly 猛然停住 ○ *dead centre*, ie exact centre 正中心 ○ *a dead shot*, ie a person who shoots very accurately 神枪手 ○ *a dead sleep*, ie a very deep sleep 熟睡 ○ *He's a dead cert/certainty for* (ie He will certainly win) *the 100 metres.* 他稳拿百米第一. **6** that does, can or will no longer function 不(能)再起作用的: *a dead match*, ie one that has been struck 已擦过的火柴 ○ *a dead battery*, ie one without power 没电的电池 ○ *The telephone went dead*, ie produced no more sounds. 电话没声了. **7** [usu attrib 通常作定语] (**a**) (of sounds) not resonant; dull (指声音)无共鸣的, 沉闷的: *It fell with a dead thud.* 它砰的一声倒了下来. (**b**) (of colours) not brilliant (指颜色)不鲜艳的: *The walls were a dead brown colour.* 墙是暗褐色的. **8** (*sport* 体) (**a**) (of a ball) outside the playing area (指球)界外的, 死的. (**b**) (of the ground) tending to make balls rolling on it stop quickly (指场地)(对球的滚动)阻力大的: *Rain had made the pitch rather dead.* 场地因雨而阻力增大. **9** (idm 习语) **be a dead ringer for sb** (*sl* 俚) be very like sb in appearance 外貌上很像某人: *She's a dead ringer for a girl I used to know.* 她酷似以前我认识的一个女孩. **be the dead spit of sb** (*infml* 口) look exactly like sb else 极像某人. **cut sb dead** pretend not to have seen sb; refuse to greet sb 装着没看见某人; 拒不向某人打招呼. **(as) ˌdead as a/the ˈdodo** (*infml* 口) no longer effective, valid, interesting, etc 已无作用的、已失效的、不再吸引人注意的等: *This organization is as dead as a dodo.* 这个组织已不复存在. **(as) ˌdead as a ˈdoornail/as ˈmutton** (*infml* 口) quite dead 完全死了的: *It lay there with its eyes closed, dead as a doornail.* 它躺在那里眼睛闭着, 确实死了. **a dead ˈduck** (*infml* 口) scheme, etc which has been abandoned, or will fail 被放弃的或将失败的计划等: *The plan is a dead duck: there's no money.* 计划告吹了: 没有钱. **a dead ˈend** (**a**) = CUL-DE-SAC. (**b**) point at which one can make no further progress in work, an enquiry, etc 工作、查询等不能再进展的阶段: *be at/come to a dead end* 陷入僵局 ○ *With the failure of the experiment, we had reached a dead end.* 试验失败了, 我们一筹莫展. ○ [attrib 作定语] *a ˌdead-end ˈjob/caˈreer*, ie one that offers no prospect of promotion 无晋升希望的工作[职业]. **the dead hand of sth** oppressive influence of sth 某事物的恶劣影响; 流毒: *The dead hand of bureaucracy is slowing our progress.* 官僚主义的流毒拖慢了我们的进步. **a dead ˈletter** (**a**) rule or law that is generally ignored 被普遍忽视的规章或法律. (**b**) outdated custom, issue or topic 过时的习俗、论点或话题: *Many people say that détente is now a dead letter.* 很多人说缓和国际紧张局势的论调已是明日黄花. (**c**) letter kept by the post office because they cannot find either the person to whom it was sent or the person who sent it 死信(无法投递的信件). **a dead ˈloss** (*sl* 俚) person or thing of no help or use to anyone 对谁都无用的人或物: *This pen is a dead loss: it just won't write properly.* 这枝笔没用了: 书写很不流畅. **ˌdead men ˌtell no ˈtales** (*saying* 谚) if a person is killed he cannot cause difficulties by revealing sth that one does not wish to be known 死人不会泄密. **ˌdead men's ˈshoes** job that one takes over from sb who has left unexpectedly or died 从突然离开或去世的某人手中接过来的工作: *She got early promotion by stepping into dead men's shoes.* 她因补缺而得以提早晋升. **ˌdead to the ˈworld** fast asleep 熟睡. **ˌdead ˈwood** useless or unneeded people, material, papers, etc 无用的或不需要的人、材料、文件等: *There is too much dead wood among the teaching staff.* 教师中尸位素餐者众. ○ *The new manager wants to cut out the dead wood and streamline production.* 新经理想精简机构以提高生产效率. **drop dead** ⇨ DROP². **flog a dead horse** ⇨ FLOG. **in a dead ˈfaint** completely unconscious 完全失去知觉. **over my dead ˈbody** (used to express one's strong opposition to sth 用以表示对某事物的强烈反对): *They'll demolish this house over my dead body.* 我死也不让他们拆这所房子. ○ *'I'm going out.' 'Over my dead body!'* '我要出去.' '除非我死了!' **the quick and the dead** ⇨ QUICK. **wake the dead** ⇨ WAKE¹. **wouldn't be seen ˈdead in, at, with, etc sth/doing sth** (*infml* 口) would refuse to be in, at, with, etc sth 绝不涉于某事物: *That dress is so ugly I wouldn't be seen dead in it.* 那件连衣裙真难看, 我宁死也不穿. ○ *She wouldn't be seen dead jogging; she hates exercise.* 她就是不愿跑步; 她讨厌运动.

▷ **dead** *adv* **1** completely; absolutely; thoroughly 完全地; 绝对地; 彻底地: *dead tired/drunk* 极度疲倦[酩酊大醉] ○ *dead sure/certain* 绝对肯定[无疑] ○ *dead level/straight* 非常平[直] ○ *You're dead right!* 你完全正确! ○ *dead slow*, ie as slowly as possible 极慢 ○ *dead ahead*, ie directly ahead 正前方 ○ *be dead against* (ie absolutely opposed to) *sth* 坚决反对某事物. **2** (idm 习语) **ˌdead ˈbeat** (*infml* 口) very tired; exhausted 精疲力竭; 筋疲力尽. **(be) ˌdead ˈset against sb/sth** (be) strongly opposed to sb/sth 强烈反对某人[某事物]. **(be) dead set on sth** (be) determined to do sth 决心做某事物: *He's dead set on getting a new job.* 他打定主意要找个新工作. **stop dead** ⇨ STOP¹.

dead *n* **1 the dead** [pl *v*] those who have died 已死的人: *We carried the dead and (the) wounded off the battlefield.* 我们把伤亡者抬出了战场. **2** (idm 习语) **in the/at ˌdead of ˈnight** in the quietest part of the night 在夜阑人静时: *We escaped at dead of night, when the guards were asleep.* 我们在夜静卫兵熟睡时逃跑了. **in the ˌdead of ˈwinter** in the coldest part of winter 在隆冬.

□ **ˈdead-beat** *n* (*infml* 口) person who has no job and no money and has lost the will to live an active life 失业而穷途潦倒的人.

ˌdead ˈheat result in a race when two competitors finish at exactly the same time 两个竞赛者同时到达终点的比赛成绩.

ˌdead man's ˈhandle handle on an electric train that cuts off the power if it is released (电动机车中自动切断电源的)安全手柄.

ˌdead-ˈpan *adj* expressionless 无表情的: *a ˌdead-pan ˈface/ˈlook* 无表情的脸[目光] ○ *ˌdead-pan ˈhumour*, ie when the speaker pretends to be very serious 无表情的幽默(说话人故作严肃认真).

ˌdead ˈreckoning calculation of one's position by log²(1) or compass (when visibility is bad) (当能见度很低时)靠测程仪或罗盘定位的测定法.

ˌdead ˈweight heavy lifeless mass 重物: *The drunken man was a dead weight in my arms.* 这个醉汉在我怀里死沉.

deaden /ˈdedn; ˋdɛdn̩/ *v* **1** [Tn] lessen the force or intensity of (sth) 减低(某物)的力量或强度: *drugs to deaden the pain* 镇痛药 ○ *My thick clothing deadened the blow.* 我的厚衣减轻了打击的力量. ○ *Your constant criticism has deadened their enthusiasm.* 你接二连三地批评降低了他们的热情. **2** [Tn·pr] **~ sb to sth** make sb insensitive to sth 使某人对某事的感觉迟钝: *Unhappiness had deadened her to the lives of others.* 她遭遇不幸, 因而对别人的生活也无动于衷.

dead·line /ˈdedlaɪn; ˋdɛdˌlaɪn/ *n* point in time by which sth must be done 截止时间(必须完成某事物的期限): *meet, miss a deadline* 如期、超过期限 ○ *I have a March deadline for the novel*, ie It must be finished by March. 我那本小说必须在三月完成.

dead·lock /ˈdedlɒk; ˋdɛdˌlɑk/ *n* [C, U] complete failure to reach agreement or to settle a quarrel or grievance 僵局: *The negotiations have reached deadlock.* 谈判陷入僵局. ○ *We can only make minor concessions, but it might* *break the deadlock*, ie allow a compromise. 我们只能做些较小的让步,但这就可能打破僵局.

deadly /ˈdedlɪ; ˋdɛdlɪ/ *adj* (**-ier, -iest**) **1** causing, or likely to cause, death (可能)致命的: *deadly poison* 剧毒 ○ *deadly weapons* 致命的武器. **2** (*fig* 比喻) extremely effective, so that no defence is possible 极有效的(因而无法防御): *His aim is deadly*, ie so accurate that he can kill easily. 他弹无虚发. ○ *She uses wit with deadly effect.* 她聪明机智,使人难以招架. **3** [attrib 作定语] filled with hate 充满仇恨的: *They are deadly enemies.* 他们是死敌. **4** [attrib 作定语] like that of death 如死一样的: *deadly paleness, coldness, silence* 死一样的苍白、冰冷、沉寂. **5** [attrib 作定语] extreme 极端的; 非常的: *deadly seriousness* 极其严肃 ○ *I'm in deadly earnest.* 我是非常认真的. **6** (*infml* 口) very boring 令人生厌的: *The concert was absolutely deadly.* 那音乐会十分枯燥. **7** (idm 习语) **the (seven) deadly ˈsins** serious sins that result in damnation 受上帝惩罚的(七)大重罪.

▷ **deadly** *adv* (**a**) as if dead 死一样地: *deadly pale/cold* 死一样地苍白[冰冷]. (**b**) (*infml* 口) extremely 极端地; 非常地: *deadly serious, boring, dull, etc* 非常严肃、无聊、乏味等.

dead·li·ness *n* [U].

□ ˌ**deadly** ˈ**nightshade** poisonous plant with red flowers and black berries 颠茄.

deaf /def; dɛf/ *adj* (**-er, -est**) **1** unable to hear at all or to hear well 聋的: *go deaf* 变聋 ○ *be deaf in one ear* 一只耳聋 ○ *He's getting deafer in his old age.* 他年纪大了耳朵越来越聋. **2** [pred 作表语] **~ to sth** unwilling to listen to sth 对某事听不进: *be deaf to all advice, requests, entreaties, etc* 对一切劝告、要求、恳求等充耳不闻. **3** (idm 习语) **(as)** ˌ**deaf as a** ˈ**post**/ˈ**doorpost** (*infml* 口) very deaf 非常聋的. **fall on deaf** ˈ**ears** be ignored or unnoticed by others 被别人忽视; 不受注意: *All her appeals for help fell on deaf ears.* 她屡屡求助均无人理会. **turn a deaf** ˈ**ear (to sb/sth)** refuse to listen (to sb/sth) 不肯听取(某人的话[某事物]); 对...充耳不闻: *She turned a deaf ear to our warnings and got lost.* 她对我们的警告充耳不闻,结果迷失了方向.

▷ **deaf** *n* **the deaf** [pl *v*] deaf people 耳聋的人: *television subtitles for the deaf* 为聋人做的电视对白字幕.

deaf·ness *n* [U].

□ ˈ**deaf-aid** *n* small (usu electronic) device that helps a person to hear; hearing-aid 助听器.

ˌ**deaf-and-**ˈ**dumb** unable to hear or speak 聋哑的; 不能听或说的: [attrib 作定语] *a* ˌ*deaf-and-dumb* ˈ*child* 聋哑儿 ○ *the* ˌ*deaf-and-dumb* ˈ*alphabet*, ie in which signs made with the hands are used for letters or words 聋哑人用的字母(以手势表示字母或词语者); 聋哑人手语.

ˌ**deaf** ˈ**mute** person who is deaf and dumb 聋哑人.

deafen /ˈdefn; ˋdɛfən/ *v* [Tn] (**a**) make (sb) feel deaf or unable to hear sounds around him by making a very loud noise 使(某人)感到震耳欲聋: *We're being deafened by next door's stereo.* 隔壁的立体声音响要把我们耳朵震聋. (**b**) make (sb) deaf 使(某人)耳聋: *The head injury deafened her for life.* 她头部受伤以致终身耳聋.

▷ **deafen·ing** *adj* very loud 震耳欲聋的: *deafening thunder* 震耳欲聋的雷声 ○ *Please turn the radio down — the noise is deafening.* 请把收音机的声音开小一点——声音大得震耳欲聋. **deafen·ingly** *adv*: *deafeningly loud* 声大得震耳欲聋.

deal[1] /diːl; dil/ *n* [U] (*esp Brit*) (planks of) fir or pine wood 冷杉木或松木(的板): *made of white deal* 白松木制的 ○ [attrib 作定语] *a deal table, floor, etc* 杉木桌、地板等.

deal[2] /diːl; dil/ *n* (idm 习语) **a good/great deal (of sth)** much; a lot 很多; 大量: *spend a good deal of money* 花很多的钱 ○ *take a great deal of trouble* 费很大的事 ○ *be a great deal better* 好多了 ○ *see sb a great deal*, ie often 常见某人.

deal[3] /diːl; dil/ *v* (*pt, pp* **dealt** /delt; dɛlt/) **1** [I, Ipr, Tn, Tn·p, Dn·n, Dn·pr] **~ sth (out)**; **~ sth (to sb)** distribute (cards) in a game (纸牌戏中)发(牌): *Whose turn is it to deal (the cards)?* 该谁发(牌)了? ○ *She dealt me four cards.* 她发给我四张牌. **2** (idm 习语) **deal sb/sth a** ˈ**blow**; **deal a blow to sb/sth** (*fml* 文) (**a**) hit sb/sth 打击某人[某事物]: *She dealt him a tremendous blow with the poker.* 她用拨火棒重重地打了他一下. (**b**) cause sb a setback, shock, etc 使某人受到挫折、震惊等: *Her death dealt us a terrible blow.* 她一死对我们打击很大. **deal well, badly, etc by/with sb** (*dated or fml* 旧或文) treat sb well, etc 对某人好、坏等: *He has always dealt well by me.* 他一贯对我很好. ○ *You've been badly dealt with.* 你一直受到虐待. **wheel and deal** ⇨ WHEEL. **3** (phr v) **deal in sth** (**a**) sell sth; trade in sth 卖某物; 经营某物: *My bank deals in stocks and shares now.* 我们银行现在经营债券与股票. ○ *We deal in hardware but not software.* 我们只经营硬件而不经营软件. (**b**) (*derog* 贬) concern oneself with sth; indulge in sth 忙于某事物; 沉溺于某事物: *deal in gossip and slander*, ie make a habit of gossiping about and slandering people 惯于搬弄是非和诽谤别人. **deal sb in** give cards to (a new player in a game) (纸牌戏中)发牌(给新参加者). **deal sth out** give sth out to a number of people; distribute sth 将某物分发给一些人; 分发某物: *The profits will be dealt out among the investors.* 红利将分发给投资者. ○ *The judge dealt out harsh sentences to the rioters.* 法官对暴乱者处以严刑. **deal with sb** tackle the problem or task set by sb; behave towards sb 处理某人所提出的问题或任务; 对待、对付某人: *How would you deal with an armed burglar?* 你怎样对付闯进来的持有武器的强盗? ○ *They try to deal politely with angry customers.* 他们尽量对发怒的顾客彬彬有礼. **deal with sb/sth** have social, business, etc relations with sb 与某人有社交、商业等关系: *I hate dealing with large impersonal companies.* 我讨厌与那些没有人情味的大公司打交道. ○ *We don't deal with* (ie negotiate with) *terrorists.* 我们不与恐怖分子打交道. **deal with sth** (**a**) attend to (a problem, task, etc); manage sth 处理(问题、任务等); 料理某事: *You dealt with an awkward situation very tactfully.* 你很巧妙地处理了一个困难的局面. ○ *Haven't you dealt with* (ie replied to) *that letter yet?* 那封信你答复了吗? (**b**) take or have sth as a subject; discuss sth 以某事物作为内容; 讨论某事物: *The next chapter deals with verbs.* 下一章讨论动词. ○ *I'll deal with decimals in the next lesson.* 下一堂课我要讲小数.

deal[4] /diːl; dil/ *n* **1** agreement, esp in business, on certain terms for buying or doing sth 协议; (尤指)交易: *to make/conclude/close/finalize a deal (with sb)* (与某人)达成一笔交易 ○ *We did a deal with the management on overtime.* 在加班问题上我们与管理部门达成一项协议. ○ *They both wanted to use the car, so they did a deal*, ie reached a compromise. 他们双方都想用这辆汽车, 因而达成了折衷的协议. ○ *It's a deal!* ie I agree to your terms. 我同意你的条件. ○ *The deal fell through*, ie No agreement was reached. 交易告吹. **2** (in games) distribution of playing-cards (纸牌戏中)发牌: *After the deal, play begins.* 发完牌之后, 纸牌游戏即开始. ○ *It's your deal*, ie your turn to deal the cards. 该你发牌了. **3** (idm 习语) **big deal!** ⇨ BIG. **a fair/square** ˈ**deal** fair treatment in a bargain 公平交易: *We offer you a fair deal on furniture*, ie We sell it at fair prices. 我们卖家具价钱公道. **make the best of a bad deal** ⇨ BEST[3]. **a new deal** ⇨ NEW. **a raw/rough** ˈ**deal** (*infml* 口) unfair treatment 不公平的待遇: *If she lost her job for being late once, she got a pretty raw deal.* 她若只因迟到一次就失去了工作, 这样对她未免太不公平了.

dealer /ˈdiːlə(r); ˋdilɚ/ *n* **1** person who distributes playing-cards 发牌者. **2 ~ (in sth)** trader 商人: *a used-car dealer* 旧车商 ○ *a furniture dealer* 家具商 ○ *a dealer in* (ie sb who buys and sells) *stolen goods* 买卖赃物的商人.

NOTE ON USAGE 用法: **Dealers, traders** and **merchants** are all people who earn money from selling goods. ☆ **dealers**、**traders**、**merchants** 都是以出售货物赚钱的人. **1** A **trader** works informally and casually selling household goods, etc, especially in a market ☆ **trader** 的工作是非正式的及临时性的, 出售的是日用百货等, 尤指在市场中出售者: *a market/street trader* 市场[走街]商人. A **trader** can also be a company buying and selling internationally ☆ **trader** 还可指从事国际贸易的公司: *The company is an international trader in grain.* 这家公司是国际粮食贸易公司. **2** A **merchant** sells particular (often imported) goods in large quantities ☆ **merchant** 是指大批量出售某种(常为进口的)货物的商人: *He's a coal, wine,*

D

timber, tea, etc merchant. 他是经营煤、酒、木材、茶等的商人. **3** A **dealer** sells especially individual objects and has a specialized knowledge of these ☆ **dealer** 是指专门出售某类物品, 并对之有专业知识的商人: *She's an antique, a used-car, etc dealer.* 她是经营古董、旧车等的商人. **Dealer** is also used of someone who buys and sells illegally ☆ **dealer** 还可指做非法买卖者: *He's a dealer in drugs/stolen goods.* 他是个毒品贩子[贼赃贩子].

deal·ing /ˈdi:lɪŋ; ˋdilɪŋ/ *n* **1** [U] way of behaving, esp in business 作风; (尤指)经营作风: *Our company is proud of its reputation for fair dealing.* 我们公司以享有经营作风正派的美誉而感到自豪. **2** (idm 习语) **have dealings (with sb)** have relations (with sb), esp in business (与某人)有关系(尤指在商业上): *I'll have no further dealings with him.* 我再不和他打交道了. ○ *We've had no previous dealings with this company.* 我们以前和这家公司没有商业往来.

dealt *pt, pp* of DEAL[3].

D

dean /di:n; din/ *n* **1** clergyman who is head of a cathedral chapter 教长(大教堂教士中职位最高者); 主任牧师. **2** (also ˌ**rural** ˈ**dean**) (*esp Brit*) clergyman who is responsible for a number of parishes (乡区的)主任牧师(主管若干牧区). **3** (**a**) (in some universities) person who is responsible for discipline (在某些大学中的)学监. (**b**) head of a university department of studies (大学的)系主任: *dean of the faculty of law* 法律系系主任. **4** (*US*) = DOYEN.

▷ **dean·ery** /ˈdi:nərɪ; ˋdinərɪ/ *n* (**a**) office or house of a dean(1,2) 教长、主任牧师或乡区牧师的办公室或住宅. (**b**) group of parishes under a rural dean 乡区主任牧师管辖下的若干牧区.

dear /dɪə(r); dɪr/ *adj* (**-er, -est**) **1 ~ (to sb)** loved (by sb); greatly valued 亲爱的; 极为珍贵的: *my dear wife* 我亲爱的妻子 ○ *his dearest possessions, friends* 他最宝贵的所有物、朋友 ○ *My daughter is very dear to me.* 我的女儿是我的宝贝. ○ *He lost everything that was dear to him.* 他失去了自己珍爱的一切东西. **2** (used attributively with *little* and *old* to show fondness 作定语与 little 及 old 连用表示亲昵之意): *What a dear little child!* 多么可爱的孩子! ○ *Dear old Paul!* 亲爱的保罗! **3** (used attributively as a form of address in letters, and politely or ironically in speech 冠于信函中的称谓及用于言语, 以示礼貌或讽刺): *Dear Sir/Madam* 敬启者 ○ *Dear Mr Bond* 邦德先生台鉴 ○ *My dear fellow, surely you don't mean that!* 亲爱的朋友, 那决不是你的本意吧! **4** [usu pred 通常作表语] (*Brit*) expensive 昂贵: *Clothes are getting dearer.* 衣服越来越贵了. ○ *dear money*, ie money on which a high rate of interest must be paid 须付高利的钱 ○ *That shop is too dear for me*, ie Its prices are too high. 对我来说, 这家商店的价格太高了. **5** (idm 习语) **close/dear/near to sb's heart** ⇨ HEART. **for dear life** vigorously or desperately (as if trying to save oneself from death) 拼命地: *run, swim, pull, shout, argue for dear life* 拼命地跑、游、拉、喊、争论. **hold sb/sth** ˈ**dear** (*rhet* 修辞) cherish sb/sth; value sb/sth highly 喜爱某人[某事物]; 高度重视某人[某事物]: *I said farewell to those I hold dear.* 我向我所喜爱的人们道别. ○ *the ideals we hold dear* 我们极为珍惜的理想. **one's nearest and dearest** ⇨ NEAR[1].

▷ **dear** *adv* **1** at a high cost 高价地; 昂贵地: *If you want to make money, buy cheap and sell dear.* 要想赚钱就得贱买贵卖. **2** (idm 习语) **cost sb dear** ⇨ COST[1].

dear *n* **1** lovable person 可爱的人: *Isn't that baby a dear?* 多可爱的婴儿啊! ○ *Thank you, you are a dear.* 谢谢你, 你真是好人. ○ *Be a dear and* (ie Please) *give me that book.* 做做好事, 把那本书给我吧. **2** (used to address sb one knows very well 用以称呼极熟悉的人): *Yes, dear, I'll write to mother.* 是的, 亲爱的, 我要给妈妈写信. ○ *Come here, my dear.* 上这儿来, 亲爱的.

dear *interj* (used in expressions of surprise, impatience, dismay, etc 用以表示惊奇、不耐烦、惊恐等): *Oh dear! I think I've lost it!* 糟糕! 我可能把它给丢了! ○ *Dear me! What a mess!* 天哪! 乱成什么样子了!

dear·est /ˈdɪərɪst; ˋdɪrɪst/ *n* (used to address sb one likes very much 用以称呼非常喜爱的人): *Come, (my) dearest, let's go home.* 好啦, 亲爱的, 咱们回家吧.

dearly *adv* **1** very much 非常地: *He loves his mother dearly.* 他极爱他的母亲. ○ *She would dearly like to get that job.* 她非常想得到那份工作. **2** (*fig rhet* 比喻, 修辞) with great loss, damage, etc (损失、损坏等)极大地: *She paid dearly for her mistake*, ie It caused her many problems. 她为自己的错误付出极大代价. ○ *Victory was dearly bought*, eg because many soldiers died. 胜利来之不易(如因牺牲了很多士兵). **3** (idm 习语) **sell one's life dearly** ⇨ SELL.

dear·ness *n* [U].

dearth /dɜ:θ; dɝθ/ *n* [sing] **~ (of sth)** shortage; scarcity 缺乏; 稀少: *There seems to be a dearth of good young players at the moment.* 目前似乎好的年轻选手太少了.

deary (also **dearie**) /ˈdɪərɪ; ˋdɪrɪ/ *n* (*infml* 口) (used by an older person to a much younger one 长者对年幼者用) dear(1); darling 亲爱的; 宝贝儿.

death /deθ; dɛθ/ *n* **1** [C] dying or being killed 死; 死亡: *Her death was a shock to him.* 她的死对他是个打击. ○ *There have been more deaths from drowning.* 溺水死亡人数有所增加. ○ *A bad driver was responsible for their deaths.* 他们的死是个技术不佳的司机造成的. **2** [U] end of life; state of being dead 生命的终止; 死亡的状态: *Food poisoning can cause death.* 食物中毒可导致死亡. ○ *burn, starve, stab, etc sb to death*, ie until he is dead 把某人烧死、饿死、刺死等 ○ *You're drinking yourself to death.* 你这样喝酒, 非喝死不可. ○ (*usu joc* 通常作戏谑语) *Don't work yourself to death*, ie Don't work too hard. 别把自己累死. ○ *One mistake could mean death for him*, ie could result in his being killed. 一个错误足可置他于死地. ○ *sentenced to death*, ie to be executed 被判死刑 ○ *eyes closed in death* 死后闭合的双眼 ○ *united in death*, eg of a husband and a wife in the same grave 死后合葬(如夫妇同葬一墓). **3** (also **Death**) [U] power that destroys life, pictured as a person 死神: *Death is often shown in pictures as a human skeleton.* 死神常被画成骷髅. **4** [U] **~ of sth** ending or destruction of sth 终止; 毁灭: *the death of one's plans, hopes, etc* 计划的破产、希望的破灭 ○ *the death of capitalism* 资本主义的灭亡. **5** (idm 习语) **(be) at death's** ˈ**door** (*often ironic* 常作反语) so ill that one may die 病得要死: *Stop groaning! You're not at death's door!* 别哼哼了! 你还不至于死呢! **(be) at the point of death** ⇨ POINT[1]. **be the death of sb** (**a**) be the cause of sb's death 成为某人致死的原因: *That motorbike will be the death of you.* 那辆摩托车就会要了你的命. (**b**) (*often joc* 常作戏谑语) cause sb great worry 引起某人极大忧虑: *Those kids will be the death of me, coming home so late every night.* 那些孩子真把我气死了, 每天这么晚才回家. **be** ˌ**in at the** ˈ**death** be present when sth fails, comes to an end, etc 目睹某事物失败、终结等: *The TV cameras were in at the death and filmed the arrest.* 进行逮捕时正好有电视摄像机录下了这场面. **bore sb to death/tears** ⇨ BORE[2]. **catch one's death** ⇨ CATCH[1]. **dice with death** ⇨ DICE. **die the death** ⇨ DIE[2]. ˌ**do sth to** ˈ**death** perform (a play, a piece of music, etc) so often that people become tired of seeing or hearing it (剧本、乐曲等)频频演出而令人感到厌倦不愿再看或再听: *That idea's been done to death.* 那主意听得腻死人了. **a fate worse than death** ⇨ FATE. **flog sth to death** ⇨ FLOG. **frighten/scare sb to death/out of his wits** ⇨ FRIGHTEN. **the kiss of death** ⇨ KISS. **like grim death** ⇨ GRIM. **a matter of life and death** ⇨ MATTER[1]. **put sb to death** execute sb; kill sb 处死某人; 杀死某人: *The prisoner was put to death (by firing squad) at dawn.* 那囚犯在黎明时被(行刑队)处决. **sick to death of sb/sth** ⇨ SICK. **sudden death** ⇨ SUDDEN. **tickled pink/to death** ⇨ TICKLE. **to the death** until sb is dead 直至某人死亡: *a fight to the death* 拼到死的搏斗.

□ ˈ**deathbed** *n* bed in which a person is dying or dies 临终时卧的床: *He forgave her on his deathbed*, ie as he lay dying. 他在临终时原谅了她. ○ [attrib 作定语] *a deathbed confession* 临终的忏悔.

ˈ**death-blow** *n* (**a**) blow that kills 致命的打击. (**b**) event, act, etc that destroys or puts an end to sth 使某事物毁灭、终结的事件、行动等: *Losing the contract was a death-blow to the company.* 失去这一份合同的生意使公司受到致命的打击.

ˈ**death certificate** official form that states the cause and time of sb's death 死亡证明书.

ˈ**death duty** (*Brit*) (formerly) tax paid on property

after the owner's death, now called *capital transfer tax* (旧时)遗产税(现称资产转让税).

ˈ**death-mask** *n* cast²(2a) taken from the face of a person who has just died 从刚死的人面部制取的模型.

ˈ**death penalty** punishment of being executed for a crime 死刑.

ˈ**death rate** yearly number of deaths per 1 000 people in a group 死亡率(每年每1 000人中的死亡人数).

ˈ**death-rattle** *n* rattling sound in the throat of a dying person 临终前喉头发出的呼噜声.

ˌ**death ˈrow** (also **death house**) (*US*) group of prison cells for those condemned to death 死囚的牢房.

ˈ**death's head** human skull as an emblem of death 象征死亡的骷髅头.

ˈ**death-toll** *n* number of people killed (eg in a war or an earthquake) 死亡名单(如在战争或地震中).

ˈ**death-trap** *n* (**a**) place where many people have died in accidents 死亡陷阱(造成许多人在事故中死亡的地方): *That sharp bend is a death-trap for motorists.* 那个急转弯是开汽车的人的死亡陷阱. (**b**) place where many people could die (eg in a fire) 可使许多人死亡的地方(如火场): *The cars blocking the exits could turn this place into a death-trap.* 那些汽车堵住出口能把这地方变成遭难场所.

ˈ**death-warrant** *n* **1** (**a**) written order that sb should be executed 死刑执行令. (**b**) act, decision, etc that causes the end of sth 使某事物终止的行动、决定等: *The tax is a death-warrant for small businesses.* 交税是小企业的致命负担. **2** (idm 习语) **sign sb's/one's own death-warrant** ⇨ SIGN².

ˌ**death-watch** ˈ**beetle** small beetle whose larva bores into wood with a ticking sound 红毛窃蠹(一种小甲虫).

ˈ**death-wish** *n* (often subconscious) desire for one's own or sb else's death (常为潜意识的)希望自己或他人死亡的想法.

death·less /ˈdeθlɪs; ˋdɛθlɪs/ *adj* (*fml* 文) never to be forgotten; immortal 永恒的; 永生的; 不朽的: *deathless fame, glory, etc* 不朽的声誉、荣誉等 ○ (*ironic* 反语) *The letter was written in his usual deathless* (ie bad, unmemorable) *prose.* 他这封信是用其万世不变的笔调写成的.

death·like /ˈdeθlaɪk; ˋdɛθˌlaɪk/ *adj* like that of death 像死一样的: *a deathlike silence/paleness* 死寂[死样的苍白].

deathly /ˈdeθlɪ; ˋdɛθlɪ/ *adj* (**-lier**, **-liest**) like or suggesting death 死一般的; 有死亡含义的: *a deathly stillness/hush/silence/pallor* 死一般的平静[寂静/苍白]. ▷ **deathly** *adv*: *deathly pale/cold* 死人一样地苍白[冰凉].

deb /deb; dɛb/ *n* (*infml* 口) = DEBUTANTE.

dé·bâcle /deɪˈbɑːkl; deˋbɑkḷ/ *n* (**a**) sudden and complete failure; fiasco 突然的大失败; 惨败: *His first performance was a débâcle: the audience booed him off the stage.* 他的首场演出一败涂地, 观众发出嘘声把他轰下了台. (**b**) retreat by beaten troops who run away scared and in disorder 败军在慌乱中的溃逃: *Many men were shot or captured in the débâcle.* 败军在溃逃时有很多人被击毙或俘虏.

debar /dɪˈbɑː(r); dɪˋbɑr/ *v* (**-rr-**) [esp passive 尤用于被动语态: Tn, Tn·pr] **~ sb (from sth)** (**a**) shut sb out (of a place) 将某人排斥在(某地之)外: *People in jeans were debarred (from the club).* 穿牛仔裤的人均未准进入(俱乐部). (**b**) prevent sb (from exercising a right, etc) 阻止某人(行使某项权利等): *Convicted criminals are debarred from voting in elections.* 已判刑的罪犯均被褫夺选举投票权.

de·bark /dɪˈbɑːk; dɪˋbɑrk/ *v* [I, Ipr, Tn, Tn·pr] **~ (sb/sth) (from sth)** = DISEMBARK. ▷ **de·barka·tion** /ˌdiːbɑːˈkeɪʃn; ˌdibarˋkeʃən/ *n* [U] = DISEMBARKATION.

de·base /dɪˈbeɪs; dɪˋbes/ *v* [Tn] **1** lower the quality, status or value of (sth) 降低(某物的)质量、地位或价值: *Sport is being debased by commercialism.* 体育运动的价值受商业化影响而逐渐下降. ○ *You debase yourself by telling such lies.* 你说这些谎话就降低了身分. **2** lower the value of (coins) by using less valuable metal in them 降低(硬币的)价值(减少含贵金属的成色). ▷ **de·base·ment** *n* [U].

de·bat·able /dɪˈbeɪtəbl; dɪˋbetəbḷ/ *adj* not certain; open to question; arguable 不肯定的; 有待解决的; 可争议的: *It's debatable whether or not the reforms have improved conditions.* 改革是否改善了现状, 这问题仍有争议. ○ *a debatable point, claim, etc* 有争论的观点、要求等. ▷ **de·bat·ably** /-blɪ; -blɪ/ *adv*.

de·bate /dɪˈbeɪt; dɪˋbet/ *n* [C, U] (**a**) formal argument or discussion of a question, eg at a public meeting or in Parliament, with two or more opposing speakers, and often ending in a vote (正式的)辩论, 讨论(如在公众集会或议会中, 常以表决结束): *After a long debate, the House of Commons approved the bill.* 经过长时间的辩论, 下议院通过了议案. ○ *to open the debate*, ie be the first to speak 开始辩论(第一个发言) ○ *the motion under debate*, ie being discussed 在辩论中的动议. (**b**) argument or discussion in general (一般性的)辩论, 讨论: *After much debate, we decided to move to Oxford.* 我们经充分讨论决定迁往牛津. ○ *We had long debates at college about politics.* 我们上大学时曾长时间地辩论政治问题. ○ *Her resignation caused much public debate.* 她辞职一事引起群众议论纷纷.

▷ **de·bate** *v* **1** [I, Ipr, Tn, Tw, Tg] **~ (about sth)** have a debate(2) about (sth); discuss (sth) 对(某事)进行辩论; 讨论(某事): *What are they debating (about)?* 他们在辩论什么? ○ *We're just debating what to do next.* 我们正讨论下一步该做什么事. ○ *They debated closing the factory.* 他们争论是否关闭工厂. **2** [Tn, Tw, Tg] think (sth) over in order to decide 考虑(某事物)以决定: *I debated it for a while, then decided not to go.* 我反复考虑后决定不去. ○ *I'm debating where to go on holiday.* 我在琢磨到何处度假. ○ *He debated buying a new car, but didn't in the end.* 他思量很久是否买辆新汽车, 但最后还是没买. **de·bater** *n* person who debates (DEBATE 1) 辩论的人.

de·bauch /dɪˈbɔːtʃ; dɪˋbɔtʃ/ *v* [Tn] make (sb) act immorally by using bad influence 诱使(某人)做不道德的事: *He debauched* (ie seduced) *many innocent girls.* 他诱使许多清白的女子堕落了.

▷ **de·bauch** *n* occasion of excessive drinking or immoral behaviour, usu involving several people 狂饮或放荡的场合(通常有数人参加): *go on a drunken debauch* 进行狂饮作乐.

de·bauched *adj* immoral, esp sexually 不道德的; (尤指)淫荡的: *to live a debauched life* 过着淫逸生活.

de·bauch·ee /ˌdebɔːˈtʃiː; ˌdɛbɔˋtʃi/ *n* debauched person 道德败坏的人.

de·bauch·ery /dɪˈbɔːtʃərɪ; dɪˋbɔtʃərɪ/ *n* (**a**) [U] immoral behaviour, esp in sexual matters 道德败坏; (尤指)淫荡: *a life of debauchery* 放荡淫逸的生活. (**b**) [C] example or period of this 放荡; 淫逸: *His debaucheries ruined his health.* 他生活放荡因而身体亏损.

de·ben·ture /dɪˈbentʃə(r); dɪˋbɛntʃɚ/ *n* certificate given by a business corporation, etc as a receipt for money lent at a fixed rate of interest until the loan is repaid 债券: [attrib 作定语] *debenture shares* 债券股.

de·bil·it·ate /dɪˈbɪlɪteɪt; dɪˋbɪləˌtet/ *v* [Tn] make (a person or his body) very weak 使(人或人的身体)非常虚弱: *a debilitating illness, climate* 使人虚弱的疾病、气候 ○ *She has been debilitated by dysentery.* 她让痢疾搞得身体非常虚弱. ○ (*fig* 比喻) *Huge debts are debilitating their economy.* 沉重的债务大大削弱了他们的经济.

de·bil·ity /dɪˈbɪlətɪ; dɪˋbɪlətɪ/ *n* [U] physical weakness 身体的虚弱: *After her operation she suffered from general debility.* 她在手术后感到全身虚弱.

debit /ˈdebɪt; ˋdɛbɪt/ *n* (**a**) (in bookkeeping) written note in an account of a sum owed or paid out (簿记中的)收方, 借方. (**b**) sum withdrawn from an account 从帐户中提取的款项: *My bank account shows two debits of £5 each.* 我的银行帐户借方记入了两笔5英镑的款项. Cf 参看 CREDIT, DIRECT DEBIT (DIRECT¹).

▷ **debit** *v* [Tn, Tn·pr] **~ sth (against/to sb/sth); ~sb/sth (with sth)** record (a sum of money) owed or withdrawn (by sb) 将(款额)记入(某人帐户的)收方, 借方: *Debit £5 against my account.* 在我的帐户借方记入5英镑. ○ *Debit £50 to me.* 把50英镑记入我的帐户借方. ○ *She/Her account was debited with £50.* 在她的帐户借方记入了50英镑.

□ ˈ**debit side** left-hand side of an account, on which debits are entered 收方, 借方(簿记帐户的左方, 记载借贷的款项).

de·bon·air /ˌdebəˈneə(r); ˌdɛbəˋnɛr/ *adj* (usu of men)

cheerful and self-assured (通常指男人)愉快而自信的: *He strolled about, looking very debonair in his elegant new suit.* 他穿了一身讲究的新衣服逛来逛去，显得颇为惬意.

de·bouch /dɪˈbaʊtʃ; dɪˋbuʃ/ *v* [I, Ipr] **~ (into sth)** (**a**) (*military* 军) (of troops) come out into open ground (指部队)进入开阔地: *The army debouched from the mountains into a wide plain.* 军队从山里开出，进入宽阔平原. (**b**) (of a river, road, etc) merge into a larger body or area (指河流、道路等)进入一较大区域: *The stream debouches into the estuary.* 这条河流入河口湾.

de·brief /di:ˈbri:f; diˋbrif/ *v* [Tn, Tn·pr] (*esp military* 尤用于军事) question (a soldier, an astronaut, a diplomat, etc) esp about a mission that he has just completed 询问(士兵、宇航员、外交人员等)执行任务的情况: *a debriefing session* 情况查询会 ○ *While being debriefed the defector named two double agents.* 在询问过程中叛变者供出了两名双重间谍. ○ *Pilots were debriefed on the bombing raid.* 驾驶员汇报了空袭情况. Cf 参看 BRIEF[2].

D

deb·ris /ˈdeɪbri:; *US* dəˈbri:; dəˋbri/ *n* [U] scattered fragments; wreckage 散落的碎片; 残骸: *After the crash, debris from the plane was scattered over a large area.* 飞机坠毁后，残骸散落在一大片土地上. ○ *searching among the debris after the explosion* 爆炸后在瓦砾中进行的搜寻.

debt /det; dɛt/ *n* **1** (**a**) [C] sum of money owed to sb that has not yet been paid 债务; 欠款: *If I pay all my debts I'll have no money left.* 我若还清所有欠债就分文不剩了. (**b**) [U] owing money, esp when one cannot pay 欠债(尤指无法偿还的): *We were poor, but we avoided debt.* 我们穷是穷，但还不至于背债. **2** [C usu *sing* 通常作单数] (*fig* 比喻) obligation to sb for their help, kindness, etc 人情债: *I'm happy to acknowledge my debt to my teachers.* 我能有机会向老师们表示感谢，我觉得十分高兴. ○ *owe sb a debt of gratitude* 欠某人恩情. **3** (idm 习语) **be ˌin/ˌout of ˈdebt** owe/not owe a lot of money 欠[不欠]债. **be in sb's ˈdebt** (*fml* 文) feel grateful to sb for his help, kindness, etc 欠某人之情: *You saved my life: I am forever in your debt.* 你救了我的命: 我永远感恩不尽. **ˌget/ˌrun into ˈdebt** reach a stage where one owes a lot of money 负债. **ˌget out of ˈdebt** reach a stage where one no longer owes money 还清欠款. **a ˌdebt of ˈhonour** debt that one feels morally obliged to pay even though one is not required by law to do so 信誉债(无法律约束力而道义上有责任偿还者).

▷ **debtor** /ˈdetə(r); ˋdɛtɚ/ *n* person who owes money to sb 债务人: *receive payment from one's debtors* 从债务人处收到付款.

de·bug /ˌdi:ˈbʌg; diˋbʌg/ *v* (**-gg-**) [Tn] (*infml* 口) **1** find and remove defects in (a computer program, machine, etc) 检测并排除(计算机程序、机器等)中的故障. **2** find and remove hidden microphones from (a room, house, etc) 从(房屋等)中找出并除掉窃听器: *The place has been completely debugged.* 这地方的窃听器已彻底清除.

de·bunk /ˌdi:ˈbʌŋk; diˋbʌŋk/ *v* [Tn] show that the reputation of (a person, an idea, an institution, etc) is undeserved or exaggerated 揭穿(某人、某思想、某机构等)名不副实: *debunk fashionable opinions* 指出流行一时的说法的不是.

dé·but (also **debut**) /ˈdeɪbju:; *US* dɪˈbju:; dɪˋbju/ *n* first appearance in public as a performer (on stage, etc) 演员首次(登台等)演出: *He marked his début by beating the champion.* 他初次上阵即击败了冠军而一鸣惊人. ○ *She's making her New York début at Carnegie Hall.* 她在卡内基音乐堂举行她在纽约的首次演出.

dé·but·ante /ˈdebju:tɑ:nt; ˌdɛbjʊˋtɑnt/ (also *infml* 口语亦作 **deb**) *n* young woman making her first appearance in fashionable society 初次在上流社会的社交场合露面的少女.

deca- *comb form* 构词成分 ten 十: *decathlon.* ⇨App 11 见附录11.

Dec *abbr* 缩写 = December: *5 Dec 1909* 1909年12月5日.

dec (also **decd**) *abbr* 缩写 = deceased: *Simon Day dec* 西蒙·戴(已故).

dec·ade /ˈdekeɪd; ˋdɛked/ *n* period of ten years 十年: *the first decade of the 20th century,* ie 1900-1909 20世纪最初的十年(1900-1909).

dec·ad·ence /ˈdekədəns; ˋdɛkədəns/ *n* [U] (**a**) (falling to a) lower level (in morals, art, literature, etc) esp after a period at a high level (道德伦理、艺术、文学等的)衰落，堕落(尤指经过一鼎盛时期后): *the decadence of late Victorian art* 维多利亚晚期文艺的衰落. (**b**) attitude or behaviour that shows this 表现出此种衰落的态度或行为: *the decadence of the rich Western countries* 富裕的西方国家中的颓废行为. ▷ **dec·ad·ent** /ˈdekədənt; ˋdɛkədənt/ *adj*: *a decadent society, style* 堕落的社会、作风 ○ *decadent behaviour* 颓废的行为.

de·caf·fein·ated /ˌdi:ˈkæfɪneɪtɪd; diˋkæfə,netɪd/ *adj* with most or all of the caffeine removed (大部或全部)除去咖啡因的: *decaffeinated coffee* 除去咖啡因的咖啡.

Deca·logue /ˈdekəlɒg; *US* -lɔ:g; ˋdɛkə,lɔg/ *n* **the Decalogue** (in the Bible) the Ten Commandments given to Moses by God (《圣经》中的)十诫.

de·camp /dɪˈkæmp; dɪˋkæmp/ *v* **1** [I, Ipr] **~ (with sth)** go away suddenly and often secretly (taking sth with one) (突然而常为秘密地)(携某物)逃走: *She has decamped with all our money.* 她携带我们所有的钱潜逃了. **2** [I] leave a camp or a place where one has camped 撤营; 离开宿营地: *The soldiers decamped at dawn.* 士兵在黎明时撤离了营地.

de·cant /dɪˈkænt; dɪˋkænt/ *v* [Tn, Tn·pr] **~ sth (into sth)** pour (wine, etc) from a bottle into another container, esp slowly so that the sediment is left behind 将(酒等)自瓶中倒入另一容器(尤指慢倒以留下沉淀).

▷ **de·canter** *n* (usu decorative) glass bottle with a stopper into which wine, etc may be decanted before serving (通常为有装饰的)带瓶塞的玻璃瓶(用以盛除去沉淀的酒等). ⇨illus at BOTTLE 见 BOTTLE 之插图.

de·cap·it·ate /dɪˈkæpɪteɪt; dɪˋkæpə,tet/ *v* [Tn] cut the head off (esp a person or an animal) 杀头(可指人或动物). ▷ **de·cap·ita·tion** /dɪˌkæpɪˈteɪʃn; dɪ,kæpəˋteʃən/ *n* [U, C].

de·car·bon·ize, -ise /ˌdi:ˈkɑ:bənaɪz; diˋkɑrbən,aɪz/ (also *infml* 口语亦作 **de·coke**) *v* [Tn] remove carbon from (esp the cylinders of an internal combustion engine) 除去(尤指内燃机汽缸)中的碳.

dec·ath·lon /dɪˈkæθlɒn; dɪˋkæθlɑn/ *n* athletic contest in which each participant must take part in all of ten events 十项全能运动.

▷ **dec·ath·lete** /dɪˈkæθli:t; dɪˋkæθ,lit/ *n* athlete who competes in a decathlon 完成十项全能运动的运动员.

de·cay /dɪˈkeɪ; dɪˋke/ *v* **1** [I, Tn] (cause sth to) become bad; rot; decompose (使某物)变坏，腐烂，变质: *decaying teeth, vegetables* 龋齿、腐烂的蔬菜 ○ *Sugar decays your teeth.* 糖能腐蚀牙齿. **2** [I] lose power, vigour, influence, etc 失去权力、活力、影响等: *a decaying culture, society, regime, etc* 衰退的文化、社会、政权等 ○ *Our powers decay* (ie We become less strong, alert, etc) *in old age.* 我们的体力、精力在老年时就衰退.

▷ **de·cay** *n* [U] (state reached by the process of) decaying 腐败、衰退的状态: *ˈtooth decay* 蛀牙 ○ *The empire is in decay.* 帝国在衰亡. ○ *The feudal system slowly fell into decay,* ie stopped working. 封建制度在缓慢地衰亡.

de·cease /dɪˈsi:s; dɪˋsis/ *n* [U] (*law or fml* 律或文) death (of a person) (人的)死亡.

▷ **de·ceased** *adj* dead 死的: *a deceased father, uncle, spouse, etc* 已故的父亲、叔父、配偶等 ○ *Both her parents are deceased.* 她的双亲均已辞世.

the de·ceased *n* (*pl* unchanged 复数不变) (*law or fml* 律或文) person who has died, esp recently 已死的人(尤指死去不久者).

de·ceit /dɪˈsi:t; dɪˋsit/ *n* **1** [U] deliberately leading sb to believe or accept sth that is false, usu so as to get sth for oneself; deceiving 欺骗; 欺诈: *practice deceit on sb* 对某人进行欺骗 ○ *She won her promotion by deceit.* 她用欺骗手段得以晋升. **2** [C] dishonest act or statement 不诚实的行为或言语: *She got them to hand over all their money by a wicked deceit.* 她用卑鄙的手段使他们把所有的钱移交给她.

▷ **de·ceit·ful** /dɪˈsi:tfl; dɪˋsitfəl/ *adj* **1** often deceiving people; dishonest 惯于欺骗的; 不诚实的: *You've been going there without telling me, you deceitful child!* 你一直在瞒着我到那地方去，你这不诚实的孩子! **2** intended to mislead 有意误导的: *deceitful words, behaviour* 使人

受骗的话、行为. **de·ceit·fully** /-fʊlɪ; -fəlɪ/ *adv*. **de·ceit·ful·ness** *n* [U].

de·ceive /dɪˈsi:v; dɪˋsiv/ *v* [Tn, Tn·pr] **1 ~ sb/oneself (into doing sth)** make sb believe sth that is not true (so as to make him do sth); deliberately mislead sb 欺骗某人(去做某事); 使自己信以为真(去做某事); 故意使(某人)误解: *You can't pass exams without working, so don't deceive yourself (into thinking you can).* 不努力是考不及格的, 因此不要欺骗自己(以为可以及格). ○ *We were deceived into believing that he could help us.* 我们受骗了, 还以为他能帮助我们. ○ *His friendly manner did not deceive us for long.* 他那热情的样子并没把我们欺骗多久. **2 ~ sb (with sb)** be sexually unfaithful to (one's spouse, etc) (指性行为)对(配偶等)不忠: *He's been deceiving his wife with another woman for months.* 他几个月来一直瞒着妻子与另一女人来往.
▷ **de·ceiver** /-və(r); -vɚ/ *n* person who deceives 骗子.

de·cel·er·ate /ˌdi:ˈseləreɪt; diˋsɛləˌret/ *v* [I, Tn] (cause sth to) slow down (使某物)减速. Cf 参看 ACCELERATE.
▷ **de·cel·era·tion** /ˌdi:seləˈreɪʃn; diˌsɛləˋreʃən/ *n* [U] (**a**) slowing down or being caused to slow down 减速. (**b**) rate of decrease of speed per unit of time 单位时间内的减速率.

De·cem·ber /dɪˈsembə(r); dɪˋsɛmbɚ/ *n* [U, C] (*abbr* 缩写 **Dec**) the twelfth month of the year, next after November 十二月.
For the uses of *December* see the examples at *April*. 关于December的用法见April词条中的示例.

de·cency /ˈdi:snsɪ; ˋdisṇsɪ/ *n* **1** [U] quality of being or appearing as respectable people would wish 正派; 端庄; 高雅; 体面: *an offence against decency*, eg appearing naked in public 有伤风化之举(如当众裸体) ○ *Have the decency to* (ie Be polite and) *apologize for what you did!* 讲点礼貌, 为你所做的事道歉! **2 the decencies** [pl] standards of respectable behaviour in society 社会上高尚文雅行为的标准: *We must observe the decencies and attend the funeral.* 我们要遵照礼仪参加葬礼.

de·cent /ˈdi:snt; ˋdisṇt/ *adj* **1** (**a**) proper; acceptable 适当的; 可接受的: *We must provide decent housing for the poor.* 我们必须为穷苦人提供适当的住房. ○ *The hospital has no decent equipment.* 这家医院没有像样的设备. ○ *He's done the decent thing and resigned.* 他做了件体面的事, 辞职了. (**b**) not likely to shock or embarrass others; modest 不致使别人吃惊或难堪的; 适度的; 得体的: *That dress isn't decent.* 那件连衣裙不够体面. ○ (*infml* 口) *Are you decent?* ie Are you properly dressed? 你的穿戴得体吗? ○ *Never tell stories that are not decent*, ie that are obscene. 切勿讲不雅的故事. Cf 参看 INDECENT. **2** satisfactory; quite good 令人满意的; 相当好的: *earn a decent wage, living, etc* 赚可观的工资、生活费等 ○ *That was quite a decent lunch.* 那顿午餐相当不错. ○ *They're a decent firm to work for*, ie They treat their employees well. 在那家公司工作挺不错. ○ *He's a thoroughly decent* (ie honourable) *man.* 他是个极为正直的人.
▷ **de·cently** *adv* in a decent(1, 2) manner 合适地; 适度地; 体面地: *decently dressed* 衣着体面的 ○ *behave decently* 规规矩矩地行事.

de·cen·tral·ize, -ise /ˌdi:ˈsentrəlaɪz; diˋsɛntrəlˌaɪz/ *v* [I, Tn] **1** transfer (power, authority, etc) from central government to regional government 权力下放; 将(权力、权限等)自中央政府转到地方政府: *If we decentralize, the provinces will have more autonomy.* 我们把权力下放, 各省就有更多的自主权. **2** distribute (industry, workers, population, etc) over a wider area away from the centre 将(工业、工人、人口等)自集中点分散到较大的区域内. ▷ **de·cen·tral·iza·tion, -isa·tion** /ˌdi:sentrəlaɪˈzeɪʃn; *US* -lɪˈz-; ˌdisɛntrələˋzeʃən/ *n* [U].

de·cep·tion /dɪˈsepʃn; dɪˋsɛpʃən/ *n* **1** [U] deceiving or being deceived 欺骗: *obtain sth by deception* 用欺骗手段获得某事物 ○ *practise deception on the public* 欺骗公众. **2** [C] trick intended to deceive 骗术; 诡计: *It was an innocent deception, meant as a joke.* 那是无伤大雅的鬼把戏, 开个玩笑而已.

de·cept·ive /dɪˈseptɪv; dɪˋsɛptɪv/ *adj* likely to deceive; misleading 可能欺骗的; 导致误解的: *Appearances are often deceptive*, ie Things are not always what they seem to be. 外表往往是靠不住的. ○ *Her simple style is deceptive: what she has to say is very profound.* 别以为她的工作方法简单, 她说出话来是很有分量的. ▷ **de·cept·ively** *adv*: *The tank is deceptively small: it actually holds quite a lot.* 这容器看上去很小, 实际上可以装很多东西.

deci- *comb form* 构词成分 (in the metric system) one tenth part of (公制的)十分之一: *decilitre* ○ *decimetre.* ⇨App 11 见附录11.

deci·bel /ˈdesɪbel; ˋdɛsəˌbɛl/ *n* unit for measuring the relative loudness of sounds, or for measuring power levels in electrical communications 分贝.

de·cide /dɪˈsaɪd; dɪˋsaɪd/ *v* **1** [I, Ipr, Tn, Tn·pr] settle (a dispute, an issue or a case); give a judgement on (sth) 解决(争端、问题或案件); 对(某事物)作出判断: *The judge will decide (the case) tomorrow.* 法官明天判决此案. ○ *It's difficult to decide between the two.* 很难在这两者之间决定取舍. ○ *The judge decided for/against the plaintiff.* 法官判决原告胜诉[败诉]. ○ *Her argument decided the issue in his favour.* 她的论据促成问题的解决对他有利. **2** (**a**) [I, Ipr, Tn, Tf, Tw, Tt] **~ (on/against sth/sb)** consider and come to a conclusion; make up one's mind; resolve 考虑后作出决定; 下决心; 决定: *With so many choices, it's hard to decide (what to buy).* 有这么多可选择的, 真难决定(买什么). ○ *After seeing all the candidates we've decided on* (ie chosen) *this one.* 我们见了所有的候选人, 决定选这位. ○ *decide against changing one's job* 决定不改变工作 ○ *I never thought she'd decide that!* 我从来没想到她会决定此事! ○ *It has been decided that the book should be revised.* 已经决定这本书要重新修订. ○ *She decided not to go alone.* 她决定不单独去. (**b**) [Ipr, Tn, Tw] (of events, actions, etc) have an important, definite effect on (sth) (指事件、行动等)对某事物有重要的、肯定的效果: *I wanted to be a painter, but circumstances decided otherwise*, ie forced me to be something else. 我本想当画家, 可是环境对我另作安排. ○ *A chance meeting decided my career.* 偶然的会面决定了我的事业. ○ *This last game will decide who is to be champion.* 最后一局将决定谁是冠军. **3** [Tn, Tn·pr, Tnt] cause (sb) to reach a decision 使(某人)作出决定: *What finally decided you against it?* 是什么事情使你最后决定不做此事? ○ *That decided me to leave my job.* 那件事使我决定离职.
▷ **de·cided** *adj* **1** [attrib 作定语] clear; definite 清楚的; 明确的; 肯定的: *There is a decided difference between the two sisters.* 这对姐妹之间有明显不同之处. ○ *a person of decided views* 有明确看法的人. **2 ~ (about sth)** determined 坚决的; 坚定的: *a decided effort to improve sales* 提高销售量的坚决努力 ○ *He won't go: he's quite decided about it.* 他绝不去: 他对此事很坚定. **de·cidedly** *adv* definitely; undoubtedly 肯定地; 无疑地: *I feel decidedly unwell this morning.* 我今天上午确实感到不舒服.
de·cider *n* game, race, etc to settle a contest between competitors who have previously finished equal 在成平局的竞赛者之间决定胜负的一局、比赛等.

de·cidu·ous /dɪˈsɪdjʊəs, dɪˈsɪdʒʊəs; dɪˋsɪdʒʊəs/ *adj* (of a tree) that loses its leaves annually, usu in autumn (指树木)每年(通常在秋季)落叶的: *deciduous forests* 落叶林. Cf 参看 EVERGREEN. ⇨illus at App 1 见附录1之插图, page i.

deci·litre /ˈdesɪli:tə(r); ˋdɛsəˌlitɚ/ *n* unit of capacity in the metric system, equal to one tenth of a litre 分升(十分之一升).

decimal /ˈdesɪml; ˋdɛsəmḷ/ *adj* based on or reckoned in tens or tenths 十进位的: *decimal coinage/currency* 十进币制.
▷ ˌ**decimal** *n* (also ˌ**decimal** ˈ**fraction**) fraction expressed in tenths, hundredths, etc (以十分之一、百分之一等表示的)小数: *The decimal 0.61 stands for 61 hundredths.* 小数0.61代表百分之六十一. ⇨App 4 见附录4.
decim·al·ize, -ise /-məlaɪz; -məˌlaɪz/ *v* **1** [Tn] express a number as a decimal fraction 以小数表示一数字: *$1\frac{1}{2}$ decimalized is 1.5.* $1\frac{1}{2}$以小数表示为1.5. **2** [I, Tn] change (currency) to a decimal system 将(货币)改为十进制: *The country decided to decimalize (its coinage).* 这个国家决定将货币改为十进制. **decim·al·iza·tion, -isa·tion** /ˌdesɪməlaɪˈzeɪʃn; *US* -lɪˈz-; ˌdɛsəməlɪˋzeʃən/ *n* [U].

□ ˌ**decimal** ˈ**point** dot or point placed after the unit figure in the writing of decimals, eg in 15.61 小数点(如15.61中的小数点).

ˈ**decimal system** system of numbers, measures or currency based on the number ten 十进制.

decim·ate /ˈdesɪmeɪt; ˋdɛsəˌmet/ *v* [Tn] (**a**) kill or destroy a large part of (sth) 杀死或毁坏(某物)之大部: *Disease has decimated the population.* 疾病使大部分人死亡. (**b**) (*infml* 口) reduce (sth) considerably 相当程度地减少、降低(某事物): *Student numbers have been decimated by cuts in grants.* 助学金削减后, 学生人数大大减少. ▷ **decima·tion** /desɪˈmeɪʃn; ˌdɛsəˈmeʃən/ *n* [U].

deci·metre /ˈdesɪmiːtə(r); ˋdɛsəˌmitɚ/ *n* unit of length in the metric system, equal to one tenth of a metre 分米(一米的十分之一).

de·cipher /dɪˈsaɪfə(r); dɪˋsaɪfɚ/ *v* [Tn, Tw] succeed in understanding (a coded message, bad handwriting, etc) 破译(密码); 辨认(潦草字迹): *I can't decipher what is inscribed on the pillar.* 我认不出刻在柱子上的是什么. ○ (*infml* 口) *Can you decipher her scrawl?* 你能辨认出她乱写的是什么吗?

▷ **de·cipher·able** /dɪˈsaɪfrəbl; dɪˋsaɪfrəbl/ *adj* that can be deciphered 可译解的; 可破译的; 可辨认得出的.

de·cision /dɪˈsɪʒn; dɪˋsɪʒən/ *n* **1 ~ (on/against sth); ~ (to do sth)** (**a**) [U] deciding; making up one's mind 决定; 决心: *It's a matter for personal decision,* ie Everybody must decide for themselves. 这是须由个人作决定的问题. (**b**) [C] conclusion reached; judgement 得到的结论; 判断: *arrive at/come to/make/reach a decision* 作出决定 ○ *his decision against going on holiday* 他不休假的决定 ○ *We took the difficult decision to leave.* 我们好不容易才作出离开的决定. ○ *Her decision to retire surprised us all.* 她决定退休, 我们大为惊讶. ○ *give a decision on an issue* 就某问题作出决定 ○ *The judge's decision was to award damages to the defendant.* 法官判决赔偿被告损失. ○ *Discussion should be part of the decision-making process.* 进行讨论该是作决定的过程. **2** [U] ability to decide quickly 迅速决定的能力: *Anyone who lacks decision* (ie who hesitates, can't decide questions) *shouldn't be a leader.* 不果断的人不应做领导.

de·cisive /dɪˈsaɪsɪv; dɪˋsaɪsɪv/ *adj* **1** having a particular, important or conclusive effect 有特殊、重要或决定性效果的: *a decisive victory, battle, moment* 决定性的胜利、战役、时刻 ○ *The injury to their key player could be a decisive factor in the game.* 他们主力队员受伤可能是这场比赛决定胜负的因素. **2** having or showing the ability to decide quickly 果断的; 决断的: *a decisive person, answer, manner* 果断的人、回答、方式 ○ *Be decisive — tell them exactly what you think should be done!* 果断些——确切地告诉他们你认为应该怎么做!

▷ **de·cisively** *adv*: *act, answer decisively* 果断地行动、回答. **de·cisive·ness** *n* [U].

deck[1] /dek; dɛk/ *n* **1** (**a**) any of the floors of a ship in or above the hull 甲板: *My cabin is on E deck.* 我的舱位在E层甲板. ○ *below deck(s),* ie in(to) the space under the main deck 在主甲板之下. ⇨illus at YACHT 见 YACHT 之插图. (**b**) any similar area, eg the floor of a bus 任何类似甲板的地方(如公共汽车的层面): *the top deck of a double-decker bus* 双层公共汽车的顶层. **2** (*esp US*) pack of playing-cards 一副纸牌. **3** (**a**) platform on which the turntable and pick-up arm of a record-player rest 电唱机的转盘及拾音器臂的支托面. (**b**) device for holding and playing magnetic tape, discs, etc in sound-recording equipment or a computer 录音设备或计算机中放磁带或磁盘的装置. **4** (idm 习语) **clear the decks** ⇨ CLEAR[3]. **hit the deck** ⇨ HIT[1]. **on deck** (**a**) on the main deck of a ship 在船的主甲板上. (**b**) (*esp US*) ready for action, duty, etc 准备行动、执行任务等.

▷ **deck** *v* [Tn] (*US infml* 口) knock (sb) to the ground 将(某人)打倒在地: *He decked him with his first punch.* 他第一拳就把他打倒在地.

-decker (forming compound *ns* and *adjs* 用以构成复合名词及形容词) having a specified number of decks or layers 有某数目的甲板或层面的: *a* ˌ*double-/*ˌ*single-decker* ˈ*bus* ○ *a* ˌ*triple-decker* ˈ*sandwich,* ie one with three layers of bread.

□ ˈ**deck-chair** *n* portable folding chair with a (usu) canvas seat on a wood or metal frame, used out of doors, eg in parks and on the beach (户外用的)折叠帆布躺椅. ⇨illus at App 1 见附录1之插图, page vii.

ˈ**deck-hand** *n* member of a ship's crew who works on deck 在甲板上工作的海员.

deck[2] /dek; dɛk/ *v* [esp passive 尤用于被动语态: Tn, Tn·pr, Tn·p] **~ sb/sth (out) (in/with sth)** decorate sb/sth 装饰某人[某物]: *streets decked with flags* 挂着旗子的街道 ○ *She was decked out in her finest clothes.* 她穿着她最好的衣服.

de·claim /dɪˈkleɪm; dɪˋklem/ *v* **1** [I, Tn] speak (sth) as if addressing an audience (像演讲般)说(话): *A preacher stood declaiming in the town centre.* 传教士站在市镇中心慷慨陈词. ○ *He declaims his poetry,* ie recites it formally and with great feeling. 他朗诵自己的诗歌. **2** [Ipr] **~ against sb/sth** attack sb/sth in words 抨击某人[某事物]: *She wrote a book declaiming against our corrupt society.* 她写了一本书抨击我们这腐败的社会.

de·clama·tion /ˌdekləˈmeɪʃn; ˌdɛkləˋmeʃən/ *n* (**a**) [U] declaiming 朗诵: *the declamation of poetry* 诗歌朗诵. (**b**) [C] formal speech, esp one made with great feeling 正式演说; (尤指)慷慨陈词.

▷ **de·clam·at·ory** /dɪˈklæmətərɪ; *US* -tɔːrɪ; dɪˋklæməˌtɔrɪ/ *adj* formal and rhetorical; (spoken) with great feeling 正式的及遣词讲究的; (说话)慷慨激昂的: *her high-flown declamatory style* 她的夸张而雄辩的风格.

de·clara·tion /ˌdekləˈreɪʃn; ˌdɛkləˋreʃən/ *n* **1** (**a**) [U] declaring; formally announcing 宣言; 宣布; 正式声明: *He was in favour of the declaration of a truce.* 他赞成宣布停战. (**b**) [C] formal announcement 宣言; 公告: *a declaration of war* 宣战 ○ *the Declaration of Human Rights,* ie by the United Nations, stating an individual's basic rights 人权宣言. **2** [C] written notification 书面通知: *a declaration of income,* ie made to the tax authorities 收益申报(向税务部门所做的) ○ *a customs declaration,* ie a form giving details of the contents of a parcel, consignment, etc on which duty may be payable 报关单(详列包裹、托运品中应纳税项目的申报表).

de·clare /dɪˈkleə(r); dɪˋklɛr/ *v* **1** (**a**) [Tn, Tf, Tw, Cn·a, Cn·n, Cn·t, Dpr·f, Dpr·w] formally announce (sth); make known clearly 正式宣布(某事); 表明: *'I'm not coming with you — and that's final!' declared Mary.* '我不跟你去——这是最后决定!'玛丽郑重地说. ○ *declare that the war is over* 宣布战争结束 ○ *They then declared (to us all) what had been decided.* 他们然后(对我们全体)宣布所作出的决定. ○ *They declared him (to be) the winner.* 他们宣布他为得胜者. ○ *I declare the meeting closed.* 我宣布会议结束. (**b**) [Tf, Cn·a, Cn·t] say (sth) solemnly 郑重地说(某事): *He declared that he was innocent.* 他郑重声明他是清白的. ○ *She was declared (to be) guilty.* 已宣判她有罪. **2** [Ipr] **~ for/against sth/sb** say that one is/is not in favour of sth/sb 表示赞成[不赞成]某事物[某人]: *The commission declared against the proposed scheme.* 委员会反对所提的计划. **3** [Tn] tell the tax authorities about (one's income), or customs officers about (dutiable goods brought into a country) 向税务部门申报(自己的收益)或向海关官员申报(应纳税的物品): *You must declare all you have earned in the last year.* 你必须申报去年的总收入. ○ *Have you anything to declare?* 你有什么要申报纳税的吗? **4** [I, Cn·a] (in cricket) choose to end one's team's innings before all ten wickets have fallen (板球)(在十个击球员并未全部出局时)宣布本队不再继续击球: *The captain declared (the innings closed) at a score of 395 for 5 wickets.* 队长在五人出局得395分时宣布不再继续击球. **5** (idm 习语) **declare an/one's** ˈ**interest** reveal to others any facts that might be thought to influence one's opinions or actions on a particular issue 申报利益. **declare trumps** (in card-games) say which suit will be trumps (纸牌戏中)宣布哪一花色牌为王牌. **declare** ˈ**war (on/against sb)** announce that one is at war (with sb) (向某人)宣战: *War has been declared.* 已经宣战了.

▷ **de·clared** *adj* [attrib 作定语] that sb has openly admitted to be such 公开宣称的: *He's a declared atheist.* 他自称是无神论者. ○ *Her declared ambition is to become a politician.* 她公开声称她的抱负是要当政治家.

de·clas·sify /ˌdiːˈklæsɪfaɪ; diˋklæsəˌfaɪ/ *v* (*pt, pp* **-fied**) [Tn] declare (information) to be no longer secret 宣布(资料)不再保密: *Plans for nuclear plants have been declassified.* 建造核装备的计划已不再保密. ▷ **de·clas·si·fica·tion** /ˌdiːˌklæsɪfɪˈkeɪʃn; diˌklæsəfəˋkeʃən/ *n* [U].

de·clen·sion /dɪˈklenʃn; dɪˋklɛnʃən/ *n* (*grammar*) (**a**) [U] varying the endings of nouns and pronouns according to their function in a sentence (名词和代词在句中的)词尾变化. Cf 参看 CASE[1] 8. (**b**) [C] class of words with the same range of endings for the different cases (CASE[1] 8) 在各格中词尾同形的一类词: *In Latin, the nominative case of first declension nouns ends in 'a'.* 在拉丁文中, 属于第一类词形变化的名词的主格以 a 结尾.

de·clina·tion /ˌdeklɪˈneɪʃn; ˌdɛkləˋneʃən/ *n* [U, C] (*physics* 物) deviation of the needle of a compass, east or west from true north (罗盘指针的)偏差(如正北偏东或偏西); 磁偏角.

de·cline[1] /dɪˈklaɪn; dɪˋklaɪn/ *v* **1** [I, Tn, Tt] say 'no' to (sth); refuse (sth offered), usu politely 拒绝(接受某物); (通常指)谢绝: *I invited her to join us, but she declined.* 我邀请她和我们在一起, 可是她婉言谢绝了. ○ *decline an invitation to dinner* 谢绝宴请 ○ *He declined to discuss his plans.* 他拒绝讨论他的计划. **2** [I] become smaller, weaker, fewer, etc; diminish 变小; 变弱; 变少: *Her influence declined after she lost the election.* 她落选后其影响力大为降低. ○ *a declining birth-rate* 逐渐下降的出生率 ○ *declining sales* 销售量下降 ○ *He spent his declining years* (ie those at the end of his life) *in the country.* 他在乡村度过晚年. **3** (*grammar*) (**a**) [Tn] vary the endings of (nouns and pronouns) according to their function in a sentence 改变(名词和代词)的词尾(根据其在句中的作用). (**b**) [I] (of nouns and pronouns) vary in this way (指名词和代词)按此方式变化.

de·cline[2] /dɪˈklaɪn; dɪˋklaɪn/ *n* **1 ~ (in sth)** gradual and continuous loss of strength, power, numbers, etc; declining (力量、权力、数量等的)消减: *the decline of the Roman Empire* 罗马帝国的衰亡 ○ *a decline in population, prices, popularity* 人口、价格、声望的降低. **2** (idm 习语) **fall/go into a deˈcline** lose strength, influence, etc 失去力量、影响等: *After his wife's death, he fell into a decline.* 他在妻子死后一蹶不振. ○ *The company has gone into a decline because of falling demand.* 由于市场需求下降, 这家公司的生意每况愈下. **on the deˈcline** becoming weaker, fewer, etc 在消减; 在衰退: *She is on the decline, and may die soon.* 她身体越来越弱, 恐不久于人世. ○ *The number of robberies in the area is on the decline.* 这地区的劫案在减少.

de·cliv·ity /dɪˈklɪvətɪ; dɪˋklɪvətɪ/ *n* (*fml* 文) downward slope 下斜. Cf 参看 ACCLIVITY.

de·clutch /ˌdiːˈklʌtʃ; diˋklʌtʃ/ *v* [I] disconnect the clutch (of a motor vehicle) before changing gear 分离(机动车辆的)离合器(以便换挡).

de·code /ˌdiːˈkəʊd; diˋkod/ *v* [Tn] (**a**) find the meaning of (sth written in code) 译(码); 解(码). (**b**) analyse and interpret (an electronic signal) 分析及译解电子信号. Cf 参看 ENCODE.

▷ **de·coder** *n* (**a**) person or device that changes a code into understandable language 译码员; 译码器. (**b**) device that decodes an electronic signal 译解电子信号的机器.

de·coke /ˌdiːˈkəʊk; diˋkok/ *v* [Tn] (*infml* 口) = DECARBONIZE.

dé·col·leté /deɪˈkɒlteɪ; *US* -kɒlˈteɪ; ˌdekalˋte/ *adj* (*French* 法) (**a**) (of a dress, etc) with a low neckline (指连衣裙等)低领的, 袒胸露肩的. (**b**) [pred 作表语] (of a woman) wearing a dress, etc with a low neckline (指妇女)穿低领衣, 穿袒胸露肩衣: *She was daringly décolleté.* 她大胆地穿着袒胸露肩的衣服.

▷ **dé·col·let·age** /ˌdeɪkɒlˈtɑːʒ; ˌdekalˋtaʒ/ *n* [U] (*French* 法) low neckline (on a dress, etc) 袒胸露肩衣的低领.

de·col·on·ize, -ise /ˌdiːˈkɒlənaɪz; diˋkaləˌnaɪz/ *v* [I, Tn] give independent status to (a colony) 给(殖民地)独立地位; 使非殖民化. ▷ **de·col·on·iza·tion, -isa·tion** /ˌdiːˌkɒlənaɪˈzeɪʃn; *US* -nɪˈz-; ˌdiˌkalənəˋzeʃən/ *n* [U].

de·com·pose /ˌdiːkəmˈpəʊz; ˌdikəmˋpoz/ *v* **1** [I, Tn] (cause sth to) become bad or rotten; decay (使某物)变坏, 腐烂: *a decomposing corpse* 腐尸. **2** [Tn] separate (a substance, light, etc) into its parts 分解(某物质、光线等): *A prism decomposes light.* 棱镜可以分解光线. ▷ **de·com·posi·tion** /ˌdiːkɒmpəˈzɪʃn; ˌdikampəˋzɪʃən/ *n* [U].

de·com·press /ˌdiːkəmˈpres; ˌdikəmˋprɛs/ *v* [Tn] (**a**) gradually release the air pressure on (esp a deep-sea diver returning to the surface) 给(尤指重返水面的深海潜水者)逐渐减压. (**b**) reduce compression in (a chamber, vessel, etc) 减低(气室、容器等)内的压力. ▷ **de·com·pres·sion** /ˌdiːkəmˈpreʃn; ˌdikəmˋprɛʃən/ *n* [U]: [attrib 作定语] *a decompression chamber*, ie one in which divers may return to normal pressure 减压室(潜水者于其中可恢复到正常压力).

de·con·gest·ant /ˌdiːkənˈdʒestənt; ˌdikənˋdʒɛstənt/ *n* [C, U] (*medicine* 药) substance that relieves congestion, esp in the nose 消除(尤指鼻中)充血的药物. ▷ **de·con·gest·ant** *adj*: *decongestant tablets* 减轻充血的药片.

de·con·tam·in·ate /ˌdiːkənˈtæmɪneɪt; ˌdikənˋtæməˌnet/ *v* [Tn] remove (esp radioactive) contamination from (a building, clothes, an area, etc) (自建筑物、衣物、地区等)排除(尤指放射性的)污染. ▷ **de·con·tam·ina·tion** /ˌdiːkənˌtæmɪˈneɪʃn; ˌdikənˌtæməˋneʃən/ *n* [U].

de·con·trol /ˌdiːkənˈtrəʊl; ˌdikənˋtrol/ *v* (**-ll-**) [Tn] remove controls (such as those imposed by a government during a war or an emergency) from (trade in certain goods) 解除对(某些货物交易)的控制或管制.

dé·cor /ˈdeɪkɔː(r); *US* deɪˈkɔːr; deˋkɔr/ *n* [U, sing] furnishing and decoration of a room, stage, etc (房间、舞台等的)布置, 装饰: *a stylish, modern décor* 有风格的、现代的装饰 ○ *Who designed the décor?* 这装潢是谁设计的?

dec·or·ate /ˈdekəreɪt; ˋdɛkəˌret/ *v* **1** [Tn, Tn·pr] **~ sth (with sth)** make sth (more) beautiful by adding ornaments to it 装饰某事物: *Bright posters decorate the streets.* 鲜艳的广告招贴画点缀着街道. ○ *The building was decorated with flags.* 这座建筑物有旗子作装饰. ○ *decorate a Christmas tree with coloured lights* 用彩色灯装饰圣诞树. **2** [I, Tn] put paint, plaster, wallpaper, etc on (a room, house, etc) 在(房屋等)上添加漆、泥灰、壁纸等: *We're decorating (the kitchen) again this summer.* 今年夏天我们又要修饰厨房. **3** [Tn, Tn·pr] **~ sb (for sth)** give a medal or some other award to sb 授予某人奖章或其他奖状: *Several soldiers were decorated for bravery.* 有几名士兵因英勇而获奖章.

▷ **dec·or·ator** *n* person whose job is painting and wallpapering rooms, houses, etc (给房屋等)粉刷和糊壁纸的人: *Arthur Jones, painter and decorator* 油漆粉刷修饰工阿瑟·琼斯.

dec·ora·tion /ˌdekəˈreɪʃn; ˌdɛkəˋreʃən/ *n* **1** [U] decorating or being decorated 装饰; 装潢: *When will they finish the decoration of the bathroom?* 他们什么时候才把盥洗室装饰好? **2** [U, C] thing used for decorating 装饰品: *the carved decoration around the doorway* 门口周围的雕刻装饰 ○ *Christmas decorations* 圣诞节装饰品. **3** [C] medal, ribbon, etc given and worn as an honour or award 奖章; 绶带.

dec·or·at·ive /ˈdekərətɪv; *US* ˈdekəreɪtɪv; ˋdɛkəˌretɪv/ *adj* that makes sth look (more) beautiful 装饰的; 作装饰用的: *decorative icing on the cake* 糕点上的装饰性糖霜 ○ *The coloured lights are very decorative.* 有这些彩灯大为生色.

dec·or·ous /ˈdekərəs; ˋdɛkərəs/ *adj* dignified and socially acceptable 端庄得体的: *decorous behaviour, speech* 高雅的举止、言谈. ▷ **dec·or·ously** *adv*.

de·corum /dɪˈkɔːrəm; dɪˋkɔrəm/ *n* [U] dignified and socially acceptable behaviour 端庄得体: *In the presence of elderly visitors our son was a model of decorum.* 我们的儿子在来访的长辈面前彬彬有礼.

de·coy /ˈdiːkɔɪ; ˋdikɔɪ/ *n* (**a**) (real or imitation) bird or animal used to attract others so that they can be shot or trapped (用于诱捕鸟兽的)动物(或仿制物). (**b**) (*fig* 比喻) person or thing used to lure sb into a position of danger 用于引诱某人落入圈套的人或物.

▷ **de·coy** /dɪˈkɔɪ; dɪˋkɔɪ/ *v* [Tn, Tn·pr] trick (a person or an animal) into a place of danger by using a decoy 用诱饵诱骗(某人或动物)落入圈套: *He was decoyed by a*

D

false message (into entering enemy territory). 他被假情报诱骗(进入敌区)。

de·crease /dɪ'kri:s; dɪ'kris/ *v* [I, Tn] (cause sth to) become smaller or fewer; diminish (使某物)变小或变少; 减少: *Student numbers have decreased by 500.* 学生人数减少了500名. ○ *Interest in the sport is decreasing.* 人们对此项运动的兴趣已逐渐淡薄.

▷ **de·crease** /'di:kri:s; 'dikris/ *n* **1 ~ (in sth)** (**a**) [U] decreasing; reduction 减少; 降低: *some decrease in the crime rate* 犯罪率的少许降低. (**b**) [C] amount by which sth decreases 减少的量: *a decrease of 3% in the rate of inflation* 通货膨胀率降低3% ○ *There has been a decrease in imports.* 进口货物有所减少. **2** (idm 习语) **on the 'decrease** decreasing 在减少: *Is crime on the decrease?* 犯罪案件是否在减少?

de·cree /dɪ'kri:; dɪ'kri/ *n* **1** order given by a ruler or an authority and having the force of a law 命令; 法令: *issue a decree* 颁布法令 ○ *rule by decree,* ie without seeking people's consent 以法令统治(不征求人民的同意). **2** judgement or decision of certain law-courts (法院的)判决, 裁定.

D

▷ **de·cree** *v* (*pt, pp* **decreed**) [Tn, Tf, Tw] order (sth) (as if) by decree 发布(命令); 颁布(法令): *The governor decreed a day of mourning.* 地方长官发布哀悼一日的命令. ○ (*fig* 比喻) *Fate decreed that they would not meet again.* 他们受命运的安排再也不能相会.

□ **de,cree 'absolute** order of a lawcourt by which two people are finally divorced 法院作出的离婚判决.

de,cree 'nisi /'naɪsɪ, 'naɪsaɪ; 'naɪsaɪ/ order of a lawcourt that two people will be divorced after a fixed period, unless good reasons are given why they should not (除非有正当理由, 否则在指定日期后即行生效的)离婚判决令.

NOTE ON USAGE 用法: When talking about giving orders, **decree** and **dictate** can be used of individuals in positions of authority. 谈到发命令, **decree** 和 **dictate** 均可指下达者为掌权的个人. **Decree** usually suggests the public announcement of a decision made by a ruler or government without consulting others ☆ **decree** 通常指统治者或政府不与别人商议而公开宣布的决定: *The dictator decreed that his birthday would be a public holiday.* 该独裁者发布命令, 将其生日定为公众假期. **Dictate** indicates people using their power over others ☆ **dictate** 用以指人用权力支配他人: *Her skills were in such demand that she could dictate her own salary.* 她因其技术奇货可居, 故可以主宰自己的薪金待遇. **Ordain** and **prescribe** suggest a more impersonal authority such as the law. ☆ **ordain** 和 **prescribe** 多用以指如法律等非个人的权力. **Ordain** is formal and can be used of God ☆ **ordain** 含庄重色彩, 可用以指上帝: *Is it ordained in heaven that women should work in the home?* 女人就该在家里干活儿, 这是上天的旨意吗? **Prescribe** is used of the law ☆ **prescribe** 用于法律方面: *Regulations prescribe certain standards for building materials.* 有规章规定建筑材料的某些标准.

de·crepit /dɪ'krepɪt; dɪ'krɛpɪt/ *adj* made weak by age or hard use 衰老的; 老朽的; 破旧的: *a decrepit person, horse, bicycle* 苍老的人、衰老的马、破旧的自行车.

▷ **de·crep·it·ude** /dɪ'krepɪtju:d; *US* -tu:d; dɪ'krɛpɪtud/ *n* [U] state of being decrepit 衰老; 老朽; 破旧.

de·cry /dɪ'kraɪ; dɪ'kraɪ/ *v* (*pt, pp* **decried**) [Tn, Cn·n/a] **~ sb/sth (as sth)** speak critically of sb/sth to make him/it seem less valuable, useful, etc; disparage sb/sth 诋毁某人[某事物]以贬低其价值: *He decried her efforts (as a waste of time).* 他贬低她所作的努力(认为是浪费时间).

ded·ic·ate /'dedɪkeɪt; 'dɛdə,ket/ *v* **1** [Tn·pr] **~ oneself/sth to sth** give or devote (oneself, time, effort, etc) to (a noble cause or purpose) 将(自己、时间、精力等)奉献给(崇高的事业或目的): *She dedicated her life to helping the poor.* 她毕生致力于帮助穷人. ○ *dedicate oneself to one's work* 献身于自己的工作. **2** [Tn·pr] **~ sth to sb** address (one's book, a piece of one's music, etc) to sb as a way of showing respect, by putting his name at the beginning 在(自己所著之书、音乐作品等)的前部题献词: *She dedicated her first book to her husband.* 她把自己的第一本书献给了丈夫. **3** [Tn, Tn·pr] **~ sth (to sb/sth)** devote (a church, etc) with solemn ceremonies (to God, to a saint or to sacred use) 以庄严的仪式将(教堂等)奉献(给上帝、圣徒等): *The chapel was dedicated in 1880.* 这座小教堂于1880年举行献堂礼. Cf 参看 CONSECRATE.

▷ **ded·ic·ated** *adj* **1** devoted to sth; committed 献身于某事物的; 专心致志的: *a dedicated worker, priest, teacher, etc* 有献身精神的工作者、牧师、教师等. **2** [esp attrib 尤作定语] (esp of computer equipment) designed for one particular purpose only (尤指计算机设备)为某特殊目的而设计的, 专用的: *a dedicated word processor* 专门的文字处理机.

ded·ica·tion /,dedɪ'keɪʃn; ,dɛdə'keʃən/ *n* **~ (to sth) 1** [U] devotion to a cause or an aim 对某事业或目的的忠诚; 奉献: *I admire the priest's dedication.* 我钦佩这位牧师的奉献精神. **2** (**a**) [U] action of dedicating a book, piece of music, etc to sb 题献词. (**b**) [C] words used in doing this 献词. **3** [U] dedicating (of a church, etc) (教堂的)献堂礼; 启用典礼.

de·duce /dɪ'dju:s; dɪ'djus/ *v* [Tn, Tn·pr, Tf, Tw] **~ sth (from sth)** arrive at (facts, a theory, etc) by reasoning; infer sth 用推理的方法获致(实情、理论等); 演绎; 推断: *If a = b and b = c, we can deduce that a = c.* 设a = b, b = c, 可以推断a = c. ○ *Detectives deduced from the clues who had committed the crime.* 侦探根据所掌握的线索推断出作案的人.

▷ **de·du·cible** /dɪ'dju:səbl; *US* dɪ'du:səbl; dɪ'dusəbl/ *adj* that may be deduced 可以推断的; 可以演绎的.

de·duct /dɪ'dʌkt; dɪ'dʌkt/ *v* [Tn, Tn·pr] **~ sth (from sth)** take away (an amount or a part) 减去; 扣除: *Tax is deducted from your salary.* 税款从薪金中扣除. Cf 参看 SUBTRACT.

▷ **de·duct·ible** /dɪ'dʌktəbl; dɪ'dʌktəbl/ *adj* that may be deducted from one's taxable earnings (从应纳税的收入中)可扣除的: *Money spent on business expenses is deductible.* 业务方面的开支是可扣除税款的.

de·duc·tion /dɪ'dʌkʃn; dɪ'dʌkʃən/ *n* **~ (from sth) 1** (**a**) [U] reasoning from general principles to a particular case; deducing 推演; 推理; 演绎: *a philosopher skilled in deduction* 擅长推理的哲学家. (**b**) [C] conclusion reached by reasoning (推理所得出的)结论: *It's an obvious deduction that she is guilty.* 推断出的明显结论是她有罪. Cf 参看 INDUCTION 3. **2** (**a**) [U] deducting 扣除; 减除: *the deduction of tax from earnings* 从收入中扣除税金. (**b**) [C] amount deducted 扣除的量: *deductions from pay for insurance and pension* 自工资中扣出作保险金和退休金的数额.

▷ **de·duct·ive** /dɪ'dʌktɪv; dɪ'dʌktɪv/ *adj* of, using or reasoning by deduction(1a) 推理的; 运用推理的; 以演绎去推断的. **de·duct·ively** *adv*.

deed /di:d; did/ *n* **1** (*fml* 文) act; thing done 行动; 所做之事: *be rewarded for one's good deeds* 因做好事而受到奖赏 ○ *deeds of heroism* 英雄事迹 ○ *Deeds are better than words when people need help.* 在需要帮助时, 行动胜于语言. ⇨Usage at ACT[1] 用法见 ACT[1]. **2** (often *pl* 常作复数) (*law* 律) signed agreement, esp about the ownership of property or legal rights 契约, 证书(尤指有关房地产或合法权利者).

□ **'deed-box** *n* strong box for keeping deeds and other documents 契据文件保险箱.

,deed of 'covenant signed promise to pay a regular amount of money annually to a person, society, etc enabling the receiver to reclaim in addition the tax paid on the amount by the giver 付款契据(承诺每年付予某人、某社团一定金额的契约, 受款人可据此兼获付款人为此款所付之税额).

'deed poll legal deed made by one person only, esp to change his name 单边契据(尤指改名者).

deem /di:m; dim/ *v* [Tf, Tnt esp passive 尤用于被动语态, Cn·a esp passive 尤用于被动语态, Cn·n] (*fml* 文) consider; regard 认为; 视为: *He deemed that it was his duty to help.* 他认为他有责任加以援助. ○ *She was deemed (to be) the winner.* 人们认为是她获胜. ○ *It is deemed advisable.* 这认为是可取的. ○ *I deem it a great honour to be invited to address you.* 要我向诸位讲几句话, 我觉得非常荣幸.

deep[1] /di:p; dip/ *adj* (**-er, -est**) **1** (**a**) extending a long way from top to bottom 深的(从顶端延伸到底部): *a deep well, river, trench, box* 深的井、河、沟、箱子. Cf 参

看 SHALLOW. (**b**) extending a long way from the surface or edge 深的(从表面或边缘延伸): *a deep wound, cleft, border, shelf* 深进去的伤口、裂缝、边缘、搁板 ○ *a big, deep-chested wrestler* 身材魁梧、胸部很厚的摔跤者. (**c**) (after *ns*, with words specifying how far 用于名词后, 与说明多远的词连用) extending down, back or in 深的(向下、向后、向里延伸): *water six feet deep* 六英尺深的水 ○ *a plot of land 100 feet deep*, ie going back this distance from a road, fence, etc 深远达100英尺的土地 ○ *People stood twenty deep* (ie in lines of twenty people one behind the other) *to see her go past.* 人们一层层站成二十排以观看她经过的情形. **2** (**a**) [attrib 作定语] taking in or giving out a lot of air 深的(吸进或呼出大量空气): *a deep sigh/breath* 深深的叹息[呼吸]. (**b**) going a long way down or through sth 深的(沿某物向下或穿过某物): *a deep thrust/dive* 深刺[深潜]. **3** (of sounds) low in pitch; not shrill (指声音)低沉的, 不尖锐的: *a deep voice, note, rumbling, etc* 低沉的嗓音、音调、隆隆声等. **4** (of sleep) from which one is not easily awakened (指睡眠)不易醒的, 酣睡的. **5** (of colours) strong; vivid (指颜色)浓重的, 鲜明的, 鲜艳的: *a deep red* 深红色. **6** [pred 作表语] **~ in sth** (**a**) far down in sth 在某物深远处: *with his hands deep in his pockets* 双手深插在衣袋里 ○ *rocks deep in the earth* 地下深处的岩石. (**b**) absorbed in sth; concentrating on sth 专心于或集中于某事物: *deep in thought, study, a book* 沉思、专心于学习、全神贯注于书中. (**c**) very involved in sth; overwhelmed by sth 深陷于某事物; 被某事物的负担压倒: *deep in debt, difficulties* 深陷于债务、困难之中. **7** [usu attrib 通常作定语] (*fig* 比喻) (**a**) difficult to understand or find out 难以理解的; 难以发现的: *a deep mystery, secret, etc* 难以理解的奥妙、难以发现的秘密. (**b**) learned; profound 博学的; 渊博的; 造诣深的: *a deep thinker* 知识渊博的思想家 ○ *a person with deep insight* 具有远见卓识的人 ○ *a deep discussion* 深入的讨论. (**c**) concealing one's real feelings, motives, etc; devious 隐藏自己真正感情、动机等的; 狡猾的; 不诚实的: *He's a deep one.* 他是个城府很深的人. **8** (**a**) (of emotions) strongly felt; intense (指情感)可强烈感觉到的, 强烈的, 剧烈的: *deep outrage, shame, sympathy, etc* 强烈的愤怒、羞辱、同情心等. (**b**) extreme 极度的: *in deep disgrace, trouble* 在极度的耻辱、苦恼中. **9** (idm 习语) **beauty is only skin deep** ⇨ BEAUTY. **between the devil and the deep blue sea** ⇨ DEVIL[1]. **go off the ˈdeep end** (*infml* 口) become extremely angry or emotional 变得极度愤怒或激动: *When I said I'd broken it, she really went off the deep end.* 我说我把它给弄坏了, 她可真气极了. **in deep ˈwater(s)** in trouble or difficulty 处于麻烦或困难之中: *Having lost her passport, she is now in deep water.* 她丢了护照身陷困厄. **of the blackest/deepest dye** ⇨ DYE[2]. **throw sb in at the deep end** (*infml* 口) introduce sb to the most difficult part of an activity, esp one for which he is not prepared 使某人做最困难的事(尤指其无准备的).

▷ **-deep** (forming compound *adjs* 用以构成复合形容词) as far as a specified point 远至某一点: *They stood knee-deep in the snow.* 他们站在没膝深的雪里. ○ *The grass was ankle-deep.* 草深至脚踝处.

deepen /ˈdi:pən; ˋdipən/ *v* [I, Tn] (cause sth to) become deep or deeper 变深; 使(某物)更深; 加深: *The water deepened after the dam was built.* 堤坝建成后水已加深. ○ *The mystery deepens*, ie becomes harder to understand. 这奥秘更难理解了. ○ *deepen a channel* 加深航道 ○ *the deepening colours of the evening sky* 逐渐昏暗的暮色.

deeply *adv* **1** a long way down or through sth 深深地: *The dog bit deeply into his arm.* 狗咬了他的胳臂, 咬得很深. **2** greatly; intensely 极大地; 强烈地: *deeply interested, indebted, impressed* 极感兴趣的、极为感激的、印象极深的 ○ *She felt her mother's death deeply.* 她对母亲的死深感悲痛.

deep·ness *n* [U].

□ ˈ**deep-sea**, ˈ**deep-water** *adjs* [attrib 作定语] of or in the deeper parts of the sea, away from the coast (远离海岸)在海水较深部分的: ˌ*deep-sea* ˈ*fishing* 深海捕鱼 ○ *a* ˌ*deep-sea* ˈ*diver* 深海潜水者.

the ˌ**deep** ˈ**South** southern states of the USA, esp Georgia, Alabama, Mississippi, Louisiana and South Carolina 美国南部诸州.

ˌ**deep** ˈ**space** far distant regions beyond the earth's atmosphere or the solar system 深空(地球大气层外或太阳系外遥远的空间).

deep[2] /di:p; dip/ *adv* (**-er**, **-est**) **1** far down or in 深深地: *We had to dig deeper to find water.* 我们必须再挖深些才能找到水. ○ *They dived deep into the ocean.* 他们深深地潜入海中. ○ *The gold lies deep in the earth.* 黄金埋藏于地下深处. ○ *He went on studying deep into the night.* 他继续学习至深夜. **2** (idm 习语) **deep ˈdown** (*infml* 口) in reality; in spite of appearances 实际上; 在心底: *She seems indifferent, but deep down she's very pleased.* 她貌似无动于衷, 其实心里非常高兴. **go ˈdeep** (of attitudes, beliefs, etc) be strongly and naturally held or felt (指态度、信仰等)强烈, 坚定: *Her faith goes very deep.* 她的信念很坚定. ○ *Your maternal instincts go deeper than you think.* 你的母性本能远比你想像的强. **still waters run deep** ⇨ STILL[1].

□ ˌ**deep-ˈfreeze** *v* (*pt* ˌ**deep-ˈfroze**, *pp* ˌ**deep-ˈfrozen**) [Tn] freeze (food) quickly in order to preserve it for long periods 迅速冷冻(食物)(以便保存): ˌ*deep-frozen* ˈ*fish* 速冻鱼. — *n* = FREEZER 1.

ˌ**deep-ˈfry** *v* (*pt, pp* ˌ**deep-ˈfried**) [Tn] fry (food) in hot fat that completely covers it 油炸(食物). ⇨Usage at COOK 用法见 COOK.

ˌ**deep-ˈlaid** *adj* [usu attrib 通常作定语] (of schemes, etc) secretly and carefully planned (指计划、阴谋等)秘密而仔细策划的.

ˌ**deep-ˈmined** *adj* (of coal) taken from far down in the earth (指煤)从地下深处开采的. Cf 参看 OPEN-CAST (OPEN[1]).

ˌ**deep-ˈrooted**, ˌ**deep-ˈseated** *adjs* profound; not easily removed 深深的; 不易移动的: ˌ*deep-rooted dis*ˈ*like,* ˈ*prejudice, su*ˈ*spicion, etc* 难以消除的憎恶、偏见、怀疑等 ○ *The causes of the trouble are deep-seated.* 这一问题的产生由来已久.

deep[3] /di:p; dip/ *n* **the deep** [sing] (*dated or fml* 旧或文) the sea 海洋.

deer 鹿

deer /dɪə(r); dɪr/ *n* (*pl* unchanged 复数不变) any of several types of graceful, quick-running, ruminant animal, the male of which has antlers 鹿. ⇨illus 见插图.

□ ˈ**deerskin** *n* [U] (leather made of) deer's skin 鹿皮; 鹿皮革: [attrib 作定语] ˌ*deerskin* ˈ*sandals* 鹿皮凉鞋.

deer·stalker /ˈdɪəstɔ:kə(r); ˋdɪrˌstɔkɚ/ *n* cloth cap with two peaks, one in front and the other behind, and flaps for covering the ears 猎鹿帽(有前后两个遮檐, 帽边可遮耳). ⇨illus at HAT 见 HAT 之插图.

de-escalate /ˌdi: ˈeskəleɪt; diˋɛskəˌlet/ *v* [Tn] reduce the level or intensity of (a war, the arms race, etc) 使(战争、军备竞赛等)降级. ▷ **de-escalation** /di: ˌeskəˈleɪʃn; diˌɛskəˋleʃən/ *n* [U].

de·face /dɪˈfeɪs; dɪˋfes/ *v* [Tn] spoil the appearance or legibility of (sth) by marking or damaging the surface 损坏(某物)的外观或清晰度: *Don't deface library books.* 不要污损图书馆的书籍. ○ *The wall has been defaced with slogans.* 那堵墙因贴有标语而面目全非.

▷ **de·face·ment** *n* [U] defacing or being defaced 损坏外表.

de facto /ˌdeɪ ˈfæktəʊ; deˋfækto/ (*Latin* 拉) existing in actual fact, whether rightly or not 实际上存在的(不论合法与否): *a de facto ruler, government, right* 实际上存在的统治者、政府、权利 ○ *Though his kingship was challenged, he continued to rule de facto.* 虽然他做国王的身分为人诟病, 但他仍大权在握. Cf 参看 DE JURE.

de·fame /dɪˈfeɪm; dɪˋfem/ *v* [Tn] attack the good reputation of (sb); say bad things about (sb) 破坏(某人)的声誉; 说(某人)的坏话; 诽谤; 中伤: *The article is an attempt to defame an honest man.* 这篇文章旨在诋毁一个正直的人.

▷ **de·fama·tion** /ˌdefəˈmeɪʃn; ˌdɛfəˋmeʃən/ *n* [U] defaming or being defamed 诽谤; 中伤: *defamation of character* 对品性的中伤.

de·fam·at·ory /dɪˈfæmətrɪ; *US* -tɔːrɪ; dɪˋfæməˌtɔrɪ/ *adj* intended to defame 诽谤的; 中伤的: *a defamatory statement, book, etc* 诽谤他人的言语、书等.

de·fault[1] /dɪˈfɔːlt; dɪˋfɔlt/ *n* **1** [U] (*esp law* 尤用于法律) failure to do sth, esp to pay a debt or appear in court 不做某事; (尤指)不还债, 不出庭. **2** (idm 习语) **by deˈfault** because the other party, team, etc does not appear 因对方、他队等未出场: *win a case/a game by default* 因对方未出席[未出场]而赢得诉讼[比赛]. **in default of sth/sb** (*fml* 文) because or in case sth/sb is absent 因某物[某人]未在场; 在无某物[某人]时: *He was acquitted in default of strong evidence of his guilt.* 因无确凿证据而判他无罪. ○ *The committee will not meet in default of a chairman.* 没有主席委员会就不开会.

D

de·fault[2] /dɪˈfɔːlt; dɪˋfɔlt/ *v* (**a**) [I] fail to do what one is supposed to do (eg to appear in a lawcourt) 未做应做的事(如出庭); 不履行; 不到场; 不出庭: *A party to the contract defaulted.* 订契约的一方未到场. (**b**) [I, Ipr] ~ **(on sth)** fail to pay (a debt, etc) 未付(债等): *default on hire purchase payments* 未付应分期付的款.

▷ **de·faulter** *n* **1** person who defaults 不履行职责者; 未到场者; 不出庭者; 未付款者. **2** soldier guilty of a military offence 触犯军纪的士兵.

de·feat /dɪˈfiːt; dɪˋfit/ *v* **1** [Tn, Tn·pr] win a victory over (sb); overcome 战胜(某人); 击败: *The enemy was defeated in a decisive battle.* 敌人在一场决定性的战斗中被击败. ○ *He has been soundly defeated at chess.* 他在国际象棋比赛中一败涂地. **2** [Tn] (*infml* 口) be puzzling for (sb); baffle 使(某人)困惑; 难住: *I've tried to solve the problem, but it defeats me!* 这个问题我想解决, 但把我难倒了! ○ *Why you stay indoors on a beautiful day like this defeats me!* 天气这样好你却呆在屋里, 真叫人莫名其妙! **3** [Tn] (**a**) stop (hopes, aims, etc) from becoming reality; thwart 使(希望、目的等)不能实现; 阻挠; 挫败: *By not working hard enough you defeat your own purpose.* 你因不太努力, 所以达不到自己的目的. (**b**) prevent (an attempt, a proposal, etc) from succeeding 阻挠(一企图、提案等): *We've defeated moves to build another office block.* 我们已否决另建一座办公楼的动议.

▷ **de·feat** *n* (**a**) [U] defeating or being defeated 击败; 失败: *suffer defeat* 遭到失败 ○ *I never consider the possibility of defeat.* 我从未考虑有失败的可能性. (**b**) [C] instance of this 失败: *six wins and two defeats for the team* 该队之六胜二负.

de·feat·ism /-ɪzəm; -ɪzəm/ *n* [U] attitude or behaviour that shows one expects not to succeed 失败主义: *Not bothering to vote is a sure sign of defeatism.* 连投票都不投, 纯粹是失败主义. **de·feat·ist** /-ɪst; -ɪst/ *n* person who shows defeatism 失败主义者. — *adj*: *I don't approve of your defeatist attitude.* 我不赞成你这种失败主义的态度.

de·fec·ate /ˈdefəkeɪt; ˋdɛfəˌket/ *v* [I] (*fml* 文) push out waste from the body through the anus 排粪; 大便; 出恭.

▷ **de·feca·tion** /ˌdefəˈkeɪʃn; ˌdɛfəˋkeʃən/ *n* [U].

de·fect[1] /ˈdiːfekt, *also* dɪˈfekt; ˋdifɛkt, dɪˋfɛkt/ *n* fault or lack that spoils a person or thing 缺点; 不足之处; 毛病; 瑕疵: *a defect of character* 性格上的缺陷 ○ *mechanical defects in a car* 汽车的机械缺陷 ○ *defects in the education system* 教育制度的不足之处. ⇨Usage at MISTAKE[1] 用法见 MISTAKE[1].

de·fect[2] /dɪˈfekt; dɪˋfɛkt/ *v* [I, Ipr] ~ **(from sth) (to sth)** leave a party, cause, country, etc, and go to another 背叛; 叛变; 叛党; 脱党; 叛国; 投敌; 变节: *She defected from the Liberals and joined the Socialists.* 她脱离自由党, 加入了社会党. ○ *One of our spies has defected to the enemy.* 我们的一名特工已叛变投敌. ▷ **de·fector** *n*: *a high-ranking defector seeking political asylum* 寻求政治庇护的任高职的背叛者.

de·fec·tion /dɪˈfekʃn; dɪˋfɛkʃən/ *n* ~ **(from sth) 1** (**a**) [U] deserting a party, cause, religion, etc (对党派、事业、宗教等的)背叛, 叛变, 变节. (**b**) [C] instance of this 背叛; 叛变; 叛党; 脱党; 叛教; 变节: *Discontent in the party will lead to further defections.* 党内的不满情绪将导致更多的党员脱党. **2** (**a**) [U] leaving one's country permanently, usu because one disagrees with its political system 去国(通常因不赞同其政治制度). (**b**) [C] instance of this 去国: *defections from a racist system* 脱离有种族歧视制度的祖国.

de·fect·ive /dɪˈfektɪv; dɪˋfɛktɪv/ *adj* ~ **(in sth)** having a defect or defects; imperfect or incomplete 有缺点的; 不完美的; 不完全的: *a defective machine, method, theory* 有缺陷的机器、方法、理论 ○ *defective in workmanship, character* 技艺不高的、性格上有缺陷的 ○ *Her hearing was found to be slightly defective.* 她的听力稍弱. ○ *a defective verb*, ie one without the full range of endings that other verbs have, eg *must* 不完全变化动词(不似其他的有全部词尾变化的动词). ▷ **de·fect·ively** *adv*. **de·fect·ive·ness** *n* [U].

de·fence (*US* **de·fense**) /dɪˈfens; dɪˋfɛns/ *n* **1** [U] ~ **(against sth)** (**a**) defending from attack; fighting against attack 防御; 防护; 保卫: *They planned the defence of the town.* 他们订出了该城的防御计划. ○ *to fight in defence of one's country* 为保卫祖国而战 ○ *weapons of offence and defence* 进攻的和防御的武器. (**b**) [C] weapon, barrier, etc used for defending or protecting 用于保卫或保护的武器、屏障等: *The high wall was built as a defence against intruders.* 修建这堵高墙作为屏障以防外人闯入. ○ *The country's defences are weak.* 该国的防御能力薄弱. ○ *coastal defences*, ie against attack from the sea 海岸防御工事 ○ *Antibodies are the body's defences against infection.* 抗体是身体抵御感染的武器. (**c**) [U] military measures for protecting a country 国防方面的军事措施: *A lot of money is spent on defence.* 国防方面的开支很大. **2** (**a**) [C, U] ~ **(against sth)** (esp legal) argument used to answer an accusation or support an idea (尤指法律上)答辩, 辩护: *counsel for the defence* 辩护律师 ○ *The lawyer produced a clever defence of his client.* 律师机智地为委托人辩护. ○ *The book is a brilliant defence of* (ie argues in favour of) *our policies.* 这本书出色地捍卫了我们的政策. ○ *She spoke in defence of her religious beliefs.* 她为其宗教信仰辩护. (**b**) **the defence** [Gp] lawyer(s) acting for an accused person 辩护律师: *The defence argue/argues that the evidence is weak.* 辩护律师提出理由认为证据不充分. Cf 参看 PROSECUTION 2. **3** (*sport* 体) (**a**) [U] protection of a goal or part of the playing area from opponents' attacks 防守: *She plays in defence.* 她打后卫. (**b**) (usu 通常作 **the defence**) [Gp] members of a team involved in this 防守队员; 后卫: *He has been brought in to strengthen the defence.* 已请他来加强后卫力量. Cf 参看 OFFENSE. (**c**) [C] sporting contest in which a champion is challenged 冠军卫冕的比赛: *his third successful defence of the title* 他第三次卫冕成功.

▷ **de·fence·less** *adj* having no defence; unable to defend oneself 没有防卫的; 不能保护自己的: *a defenceless child, animal, city* 没有自卫能力的孩子、动物、城市. **de·fence·lessly** *adv*. **de·fence·less·ness** *n* [U].

de·fend /dɪˈfend; dɪˋfɛnd/ *v* **1** [Tn, Tn·pr] ~ **sb/sth (from/against sb/sth)** (**a**) protect sb/sth from harm; guard sb/sth 保护某人[某物]免受伤害; 保卫某人[某事物]: *When the dog attacked me, I defended myself with a stick.* 那狗扑向我时, 我用棍子自卫. ○ *defend sb from attack, an attacker, injury* 保护某人免受攻击、免遭袭击者攻打、以免受伤 ○ *defend one's country against enemies* 卫国抗敌. (**b**) act, speak or write in support of sb/sth 为支持某人[某事]而行动、说话或写文章: *defend one's actions, cause, ideas, leader* 为自己的行为、事业、想法、领导辩护 ○ *The newspaper defended her against the accusations.* 报纸为她辩护, 驳斥对她的指责. ○ *defend a lawsuit*, ie fight against it in court 对诉讼案进行辩护 ○ *You'll need stronger evidence to defend your claim to the inheritance.* 你需要更强有力的证据才能为你的遗产继承权进行辩护. **2** (**a**) [I, Tn, Tn·pr] (*sport* 体) protect (the goal, etc) from one's opponents 防守(球门等); 防卫: *Some players are better at defending.* 有些运动员较擅长打防卫. ○ *They had three players defending the goal (against attack).* 他们有三个队员防守球门. (**b**) [Tn] (of a sports champion) take part in a contest to keep (one's position) (指运动冠军)参加卫冕

的比赛: *She's running to defend her 400 metres title.* 她为蝉联400米冠军而参赛. ▷ **de·fender** *n*: *He had to beat several defenders to score.* 他要冲破几名后卫的拦截才能得分.

de·fend·ant /dɪˈfendənt; dɪˋfɛndənt/ *n* person accused or sued in a legal case 被告; 被告人. Cf 参看 PLAINTIFF.

de·fens·ible /dɪˈfensəbl; dɪˋfɛnsəbl/ *adj* that can be defended 可保卫的; 可防御的; 可辩护的: *a defensible castle, position, theory* 能防御的城堡、可防守的阵地、站得住脚的理论.

de·fens·ive /dɪˈfensɪv; dɪˋfɛnsɪv/ *adj* **1** used for or intended for defending 防御用的; 防御性的: *defensive warfare, measures* 防御战、防御措施 ○ *a defensive weapon system to destroy missiles approaching the country* 摧毁射向该国的导弹的防御武器系统. **2 ~ (about sb/sth)** showing anxiety to avoid criticism or attack; hiding faults 防备批评或攻击的; 隐藏缺点的: *When asked to explain her behaviour, she gave a very defensive answer.* 有人问她为什么要这样做, 她则极力为自己辩解. ○ *She's very defensive about her part in the affair.* 她极力掩盖她在此事中充当的角色. Cf 参看 OFFENSIVE 3.

▷ **de·fens·ive** *n* (idm 习语) **on the defensive** expecting to be attacked or criticized 进行防御; 采取守势: *The team was thrown on(to) the defensive as their opponents rallied.* 该队在对手重整旗鼓后, 被迫采取守势. ○ *Talk about boy-friends always puts her on the defensive.* 一谈到男朋友, 她总是戒心十足.

de·fens·ively *adv*.

de·fens·ive·ness *n* [U].

de·fer[1] /dɪˈfɜ:(r); dɪˋfɝ/ *v* **(-rr-)** [Tn, Tn·pr, Tg] **~ sth (to sth)** delay sth until a later time; postpone sth 使(某事)延期; 推迟: *deferred payment*, ie made in instalments after purchase 分期付款 ○ *defer one's departure to a later date* 推迟行期 ○ *defer making a decision* 暂缓决定. ▷ **de·fer·ment**, **de·fer·ral** /dɪˈfɜ:rəl; dɪˋfɝəl/ *ns* [U, C].

□ **deˌferred ˈshares** shares (SHARE[1] 3) on which dividends are paid only after they have been paid on all other shares 延期付息股份.

de·fer[2] /dɪˈfɜ:(r); dɪˋfɝ/ *v* **(-rr-)** [Ipr] **~ to sb/sth** give way to sb or sb's wishes, judgement, etc, usu out of respect 服从某人的意愿、判断等; (通常为)遵从: *On technical matters, I defer to the experts.* 在技术问题上, 我遵从专家的意见. ○ *I defer to your greater experience in such things.* 在这些问题上, 我尊重你丰富的经验.

de·fer·ence /ˈdefərəns; ˋdɛfərəns/ *n* [U] **1** giving way to the views, wishes, etc of others, usu out of respect; respect 遵从; 服从; 顺从; 尊敬; 尊重; 敬重: *treat one's elders with due deference* 以应有的尊敬对待较自己年长的人 ○ *show deference to a judge* 表示对裁判的尊重. **2** (idm 习语) **in deference to sb/sth** out of respect for sb/sth 出于对某人[某事物]的尊重: *In deference to our host I decided not to challenge his controversial remarks.* 我出于对主人的尊敬, 不对他那易引起争论的话表示异议.

▷ **de·fer·en·tial** /ˌdefəˈrenʃl; ˌdɛfəˋrɛnʃəl/ *adj* showing deference 顺从的; 恭顺的. **de·fer·en·tially** /-ʃəlɪ; -ʃəlɪ/ *adv*.

de·fi·ance /dɪˈfaɪəns; dɪˋfaɪəns/ *n* **1** [U] open disobedience or resistance; refusal to give way to authority or opposition; defying 违抗; 反抗; 藐视; 蔑视: *The protesters showed their defiance of the official ban on demonstrations.* 抗议者藐视官方的示威禁令. **2** (idm 习语) **glare defiance at sb/sth** ⇨ GLARE[2]. **in defiance of sb/sth** in spite of sb/sth; ignoring sb/sth 不顾某人[某事物]; 无视某人[某事物]: *act in defiance of orders* 违抗命令的行动 ○ *She wanted him to stay, but he left in defiance of her wishes.* 她要他留下来, 但他并不理会, 还是走了.

de·fi·ant /dɪˈfaɪənt; dɪˋfaɪənt/ *adj* showing defiance; openly opposing or resisting sb/sth 违抗的; 反抗的; 藐视的; 蔑视的: *a defiant manner, look, speech* 蔑视的态度、神色、话语. ▷ **de·fi·antly** *adv*.

de·fi·ciency /dɪˈfɪʃnsɪ; dɪˋfɪʃənsɪ/ *n* **~ (in/of sth)** **1** (**a**) [U] state of lacking sth essential 缺乏; 缺少: *Deficiency in vitamins/Vitamin deficiency can lead to illness.* 身体缺乏维生素就会生病. (**b**) [C] instance of this; shortage 缺乏; 匮乏; 短缺: *suffering from a deficiency of iron* 患缺铁质症状 ○ *deficiency diseases*, ie those caused by a deficiency of eg vitamins in diet 营养缺乏病. **2** [C] lack of a necessary quality; fault 缺点; 缺陷; 毛病: *She can't hide her deficiencies as a writer.* 她无法掩盖她身为作家的不足之处.

de·fi·cient /dɪˈfɪʃnt; dɪˋfɪʃənt/ *adj* (**a**) [usu pred 通常作表语] **~ in sth** lacking in sth 缺乏; 缺少: *be deficient in skill, experience, knowledge, etc* 缺乏技巧、经验、知识等 ○ *a diet deficient in iron* 缺铁质的日常饮食. (**b**) (*fml* 文) incomplete; inadequate 不完全的; 不完美的; 不适当的; 不充足的: *deficient funds, supplies* 不充足的资金、供应 ○ *Our knowledge of the matter is deficient.* 我们对此事了解不足.

de·fi·cit /ˈdefɪsɪt; ˋdɛfəsɪt/ *n* (**a**) amount by which sth, esp a sum of money, is too small 不足额(尤指款项): *We raised £100, and we need £250: that's a deficit of £150.* 我们筹措了100英镑而我们需要250英镑, 还缺150英镑. (**b**) excess of debts over income; amount of this excess 亏空额; 赤字: *Tax was low and state spending was high, resulting in a budget deficit.* 税率低而政府支出大, 结果出现预算赤字. Cf 参看 SURPLUS.

de·fied *pt, pp* of DEFY.

de·file[1] /dɪˈfaɪl; dɪˋfaɪl/ *v* [Tn] (*fml or rhet* 文或修辞) **1** make (sth) dirty or impure 使(某物)肮脏或不纯: *rivers defiled by pollution* 受污染的河流 ○ (*fig* 比喻) *a noble cause defiled by the greed of its supporters* 被拥护者的贪婪所玷污的高尚事业. **2** make (sth) unfit for holy ceremonies; desecrate 亵渎(神明): *The altar had been defiled by vandals.* 圣坛遭到破坏公物的人故意损坏.

▷ **de·file·ment** *n* [U] defiling or being defiled 污损; 弄脏; 亵渎.

de·file[2] /ˈdi:faɪl; ˋdifaɪl/ *n* narrow pass through mountains 山中的狭道.

▷ **de·file** *v* [I] (of troops) march in single file or a narrow column (指部队)成单行或纵队行进.

de·fine /dɪˈfaɪn; dɪˋfaɪn/ *v* **1** [Tn, Cn·n/a] **~ sth (as sth)** state precisely the meaning of (eg words) 给(词语等)下定义. **2** [Tn, Tw] state (sth) clearly; explain (sth) 阐明(某事); 解释(某事): *The powers of a judge are defined by law.* 法官的权力是由法律规定的. ○ *It's hard to define exactly what has changed.* 很难解释清楚到底发生了什么变化. **3** [Tn] show (a line, shape, feature, etc) clearly; outline 清楚地显示出(线条、形状、特征等); 画出...的轮廓: *When boundaries between countries are not clearly defined, there is usually trouble.* 国与国的边界未明确划定则通常会发生纠纷. ○ *The mountain was sharply defined against the eastern sky.* 那座山在东方天空的衬托下显得轮廓分明. ○ *a well-defined profile* 轮廓清晰的侧面像.

▷ **de·fin·able** /-əbl; -əbl/ *adj* that can be defined 可下定义的; 可以解释的; 能显示形状、特征等的.

def·in·ite /ˈdefɪnət; ˋdɛfənɪt/ *adj* (**a**) clear; not doubtful 清楚的; 明确的; 确切的: *a definite decision, opinion, result, change* 明确的决定、意见、结果、变化 ○ *I have no definite plans for tomorrow.* 我明天没有确切的计划. ○ *I want a definite answer, 'yes' or 'no'.* 我要一个明确的答复, '是'还是'不是'. (**b**) [pred 作表语] **~ (about sth/that...)** sure; certain 肯定; 有把握: *He seemed definite about what had happened.* 他好像对所发生的事情很清楚. ○ *It's now definite that the plane crashed.* 现已肯定那架飞机已坠毁.

▷ **def·in·itely** /ˈdefɪnətlɪ; ˋdɛfənɪtlɪ/ *adv* **1** in a definite manner 明确地; 清楚地: *She states her views very definitely.* 她非常明确地阐述自己的观点. **2** certainly; undoubtedly 肯定地; 确实地: *That is definitely correct.* 那肯定正确. ○ *Definitely not*, ie No. 肯定不. **3** (*infml* 口) (in answer to questions) yes; certainly (用于回答问题)是的, 当然: *'Are you coming?' 'Definitely!'* '你来吗?' '一定来!'

□ **ˌdefinite ˈarticle** the word 'the' 定冠词'the'. Cf 参看 INDEFINITE ARTICLE (INDEFINITE).

def·ini·tion /ˌdefɪˈnɪʃn; ˌdɛfəˋnɪʃən/ *n* **1** (**a**) [U] stating the exact meaning (of words, etc) (词语等的)释义: *Dictionary writers must be skilled in the art of definition.* 词书编纂者必须精于给词语下定义的技巧. (**b**) [C] statement that gives the exact meaning (of words, etc) (词语等的)定义: *Definitions should not be more difficult to understand than the words they define.* 词语的定义不应比所解释的词语更难理解. **2** [U] (**a**) clearness of outline; making or being distinct in outline (轮廓的)清晰(度); 鲜明(度): *The photograph has poor definition.*

D

这张照片轮廓很不清楚. ○ *They concentrated on better definition of the optical image.* 他们致力于提高该光学影像的鲜明度. (**b**) power of a lens (in a camera or telescope) to show clear outlines (照相机或望远镜中)透镜的分解力, 解像力. **3** (**a**) [U] clear statement; outlining 清楚的说明; 划出的轮廓: *My duties require clearer definition.* 我的职责需要更清楚的说明. (**b**) [C] instance of this; outline 清楚的说明; 轮廓: *The book attempts a definition of his role in world politics.* 该书要阐明的是他在世界政局中的作用.

de·fin·it·ive /dɪˈfɪnətɪv; dɪˈfɪnətɪv/ *adj* clear and having final authority; that cannot or need not be changed 明确的; 有权威的; 不能或不必改变的; 决定性的: *a definitive answer, solution, verdict, etc* 明确的答复、确切的解决方法、陪审团的最终裁决 ○ *Her book is the definitive work on Milton.* 她的书是论述米尔顿的权威著作. ○ *a definitive edition*, eg one revised by the author himself 选定版(如作者亲自修订的版本). ▷ **de·fin·it·ively** *adv*.

D

de·flate *v* **1** /dɪˈfleɪt; dɪˈflet/ [Tn] (**a**) let air or gas out of (a balloon, tyre, etc); let down 放出(气球、轮胎等)的气. (**b**) (*fig* 比喻) make (sb, esp sb proud or too confident) feel or appear embarrassed or discouraged 使(某人, 尤指骄傲的或自负的人)尴尬, 泄气: *I felt quite deflated by your nasty remark.* 你那些难听的话使我觉得无地自容. ○ *Nothing could deflate his ego/pomposity*, ie make him less self-assured or pompous. 任何事都不能削弱他的自信心[气焰]. **2** /ˌdiːˈfleɪt; diˈflet/ [I, Tn] reduce the amount of money in circulation in (an economy), in order to lower prices or keep them steady 紧缩(通货): *The Government decided to deflate.* 政府决定紧缩通货. Cf 参看 INFLATE, REFLATE.

▷ **de·fla·tion** /-eɪʃn; -eʃən/ *n* [U] action of deflating (DEFLATE 2) or state of being deflated 泄气.

de·fla·tion·ary /ˌdiːˈfleɪʃnərɪ; *US* -nerɪ; diˈfleʃən,ɛrɪ/ *adj* causing or intended to cause monetary deflation 通货紧缩的: *a deflationary policy, measure, etc* 紧缩通货的方针、措施等.

de·flect /dɪˈflekt; dɪˈflɛkt/ *v* **1** [I, Ipr, Tn, Tn·pr] **~ (sth) (from sth)** (cause sth to) turn from its direction of movement (使某物)运动转向: *The missile deflected from its trajectory.* 导弹已偏离轨道. ○ *The ball hit one of the defenders and was deflected into the net.* 球射中一名后卫后反弹进网. ○ *The bullet hit a wall and was deflected from its course.* 子弹击中墙壁而改变了方向. **2** [Tn, Tn·pr] **~ sb (from sth)** (*fig* 比喻) turn sb away from his intended course of action 使某人改变原来的计划: *not easily deflected from one's purpose/aim* 不容易改变自己的意图[目的].

▷ **de·flec·tion** /dɪˈflekʃn; dɪˈflɛkʃən/ *n* **1** (**a**) [U] deflecting (DEFLECT 1) or being deflected 转向. (**b**) [C] instance or amount of this 转向; 偏斜度: *The smallest deflection of the missile could bring disaster.* 导弹有极微小的偏斜也可能酿出大祸. **2** [C, U] (amount of the) movement of a pointer or needle on a measuring device from its zero position 偏差(度).

de·flower /ˌdiːˈflaʊə(r); diˈflaʊɚ/ *v* [Tn] (*arch or euph* 古或婉) deprive (a woman) of her virginity, usu by sexual intercourse 使(女子)失去童贞.

de·fo·li·ate /ˌdiːˈfəʊlɪeɪt; diˈfolɪ,et/ *v* [Tn] destroy the leaves of (trees or plants) 毁掉(树木或花草)的叶: *forests defoliated by chemicals in the air* 被空气中的化学物质毁掉树叶的林木.

▷ **de·fo·li·ant** /ˌdiːˈfəʊlɪənt; diˈfolɪənt/ *n* chemical used on trees and plants to destroy the leaves 脱叶剂.

de·fo·li·ation /ˌdiːfəʊlɪˈeɪʃn; di,folɪˈeʃən/ *n* [U].

de·for·est /ˌdiːˈfɒrɪst; *US* -ˈfɔːr-; diˈfɔrɪst/ (also **disafforest**) *v* [Tn] remove forests from (a place) 除掉(某地)的森林. ▷ **de·for·esta·tion** /diːˌfɒrɪˈsteɪʃn; *US* -ˌfɔːr-; di,fɔrəsˈteʃən/ *n* [U].

de·form /dɪˈfɔːm; dɪˈfɔrm/ *v* [Tn] spoil the shape or appearance of (sth) 毁坏(某物的)形状或外观; 使(某物)变形或成畸形: *deform a structure, limb, spine* 使一结构、肢体、脊柱变形.

▷ **de·forma·tion** /ˌdiːfɔːˈmeɪʃn; ,difɔrˈmeʃən/ *n* (**a**) [U] process of deforming 变形; 畸形. (**b**) [C] result of this 变形的结果: *a deformation of the spine* 脊柱的畸变.

de·formed *adj* (of the body, or part of it) badly or unnaturally shaped (指身体或身体之局部)严重变形的, 畸形的: *She has a deformed foot and can't walk very easily.* 她有一只脚畸形, 行动不方便.

de·form·ity /dɪˈfɔːmətɪ; dɪˈfɔrmətɪ/ *n* (**a**) [U] being deformed 变形; 畸形. (**b**) [C] deformed part, esp of the body 变形的部分(尤指身体的): *deformities caused by poor diet* 饮食不良造成的畸形 ○ *He was born with a slight deformity of the foot which made him limp.* 他的脚稍有先天畸形, 走起路来一瘸一拐的.

de·fraud /dɪˈfrɔːd; dɪˈfrɔd/ *v* [Tn, Tn·pr] **~ sb (of sth)** get sth from sb by deception; cheat sb 从某人处骗取某物; 欺骗某人: *She was defrauded of her money by a dishonest accountant.* 她的钱被一个奸诈的会计骗去了.

de·fray /dɪˈfreɪ; dɪˈfre/ *v* [Tn] (*fml* 文) provide money for (sth); pay for (sth) 为(某事物)付款; 支付: *defray expenses, costs, etc* 支付开销、费用等 ○ *My father has to defray my education.* 我父亲得支付我的教育费用. ▷ **de·frayal** /dɪˈfreɪəl; dɪˈfreəl/ *n* [U].

de·frock /ˌdiːˈfrɒk; diˈfrɑk/ *v* [Tn] = UNFROCK.

de·frost /ˌdiːˈfrɒst; *US* ˌdiːˈfrɔːst; diˈfrɔst/ *v* **1** [Tn] remove ice or frost from (sth) 除去(某物)的冰或霜: *defrost the fridge, the car windscreen* 给冰箱、汽车挡风玻璃除霜. **2** [I, Tn] (cause sth to) become unfrozen (使某物)解冻: *A frozen chicken should be allowed to defrost completely before cooking.* 冻鸡应彻底解冻后再烹调. ⇨Usage at WATER[1] 用法见WATER[1]. Cf 参看 UNFREEZE 1.

deft /deft; dɛft/ *adj* **~ (at sth/doing sth)** skilful and quick, esp with the hands 熟练的, 灵巧的, 敏捷的(尤指用手): *With deft fingers she untangled the wire.* 她用灵巧的手指解开了金属线. ○ *She is deft at dealing with reporters.* 她善于与记者周旋. ▷ **deftly** *adv*. **deft·ness** *n* [U].

de·funct /dɪˈfʌŋkt; dɪˈfʌŋkt/ *adj* (*fml or joc* 文或谑) (**a**) (of people) dead (指人)死的. (**b**) (of practices, laws, etc) no longer in use (指做法、法律等)不再使用的, 过时的. (**c**) no longer effective or treated with respect 失效的; 不再受尊重的: *a defunct organization* 瘫痪的组织.

de·fuse /ˌdiːˈfjuːz; diˈfjuz/ *v* [Tn] **1** remove or make useless the device that sets off (a bomb, etc) 拆除(炸弹等)的引信. **2** (*fig* 比喻) reduce the dangerous tension in (a difficult situation) 缓和(困难局面)的紧张状态: *defuse tension, anger, a crisis* 减弱紧张气氛、平息怒火、缓和危急局面.

defy /dɪˈfaɪ; dɪˈfaɪ/ *v* (*pt, pp* **de·fied**) **1** [Tn] (**a**) disobey or refuse to respect (sb, an authority, etc) 违抗, 反抗, 藐视, 蔑视(某人、权威等): *They defied their parents and got married.* 他们违抗父母的意愿而结婚了. ○ *defy the Government, the law, etc* 蔑视政府、法律等. (**b**) refuse to give in to (sb/sth); resist boldly 拒绝向(某人[某事物])让步; 勇敢地抵抗: *The army defied the enemy's forces.* 这支军队英勇抗敌. **2** [Tn] be so difficult as to make (sth) impossible (因有困难)使(某事)不可能, 办不到: *The door defied all attempts to open it.* 这门用什么办法也打不开. ○ *The problem defied solution*, ie could not be solved. 此问题无法解决. **3** [Dn·t] challenge (sb) to do sth one believes he cannot or will not do 激(某人)做其不能或不愿做的事: *I defy you to prove I have cheated.* 我谅你无法证实我欺骗了人.

deg *abbr* 缩写 = (also *symb* 符号为 °) degree (of temperature) (温)度: *42 degs/42° Fahrenheit* 42华氏度.

de·gen·er·ate /dɪˈdʒenəreɪt; dɪˈdʒɛnə,ret/ *v* [I, Ipr] **~ (from sth) (into sth)** pass into a worse physical, mental or moral state than one which is considered normal or desirable (体力或精神)衰退; 堕落; 恶化: *His health is degenerating rapidly.* 他的健康状况迅速恶化. ○ *Her commitment to a great cause degenerated from a crusade into an obsession.* 她致力于一伟大事业, 但其崇高的奋斗精神已变质成为偏执的狂热.

▷ **de·gen·er·ate** /dɪˈdʒenərət; dɪˈdʒɛnərət/ *adj* having lost the physical, mental or moral qualities that are considered normal or desirable 衰弱的; 颓废的; 堕落的: *a degenerate art, society, age* 堕落的艺术、社会、时代. **de·gen·er·acy** /dɪˈdʒenərəsɪ; dɪˈdʒɛnərəsɪ/ *n* [U] (**a**) state of being degenerate 堕落; 恶化; 退化. (**b**) process of becoming degenerate 堕落、恶化、退化的过程.

de·gen·er·ate /dɪˈdʒenərət; dɪˈdʒɛnərət/ *n* degenerate

person or animal 堕落的人; 退化的动物: *This degenerate seduced my daughter!* 这个道德败坏的人勾引我的女儿!

de·gen·era·tion /dɪˌdʒenəˈreɪʃn; dɪˌdʒɛnəˈreʃən/ *n* [U] (**a**) process of degenerating 堕落、恶化、退化的过程: *Ageing is accompanied by a slow degeneration of his mental faculties.* 他随着年纪增长, 智力逐渐衰退. (**b**) state of being degenerate 堕落; 恶化; 退化.

de·grade /dɪˈgreɪd; dɪˋgred/ *v* **1** [Tn] cause (sb) to be less moral and less deserving of respect 贬低(某人); 降低(某人)的身分; 使(某人)丢脸: *degrade oneself by cheating and telling lies* 因欺骗和说谎而降低自己的身分 ○ *I felt degraded by having to ask for money.* 我出于无奈向别人要钱而自觉有失尊严. **2** [I, Ipr, Tn, Tn·pr] (*chemistry or biology* 化或生) (cause sth to) become less complex in structure (使某物)降解, 分解, 退化: *degrade molecules into atoms* 将分子降解为原子.

▷ **de·grada·tion** /ˌdegrəˈdeɪʃn; ˌdɛgrəˋdeʃən/ *n* [U] degrading or being degraded 堕落; 降解; 递降分解; 退化: *living in utter degradation*, eg extreme poverty 生活十分潦倒 ○ *Being sent to prison was the final degradation.* 堕落到最后的地步就是被关进监狱.

de·gree /dɪˈgriː; dɪˋgri/ *n* **1** [C] unit of measurement for angles 度, 度数(角的量度单位): *an angle of ninety degrees (90°)*, ie a right angle 90度角(直角) ○ *one degree of latitude*, ie about 69 miles 纬度的1度(约69英里). ⇨App 5 见附录5. **2** [C] (*abbr* 缩写 **deg**) unit of measurement for temperature 度, 度数(温度的量度单位): *Water freezes at 32 degrees Fahrenheit (32° F) or zero/nought degrees Celsius (0° C).* 水结成冰的温度是32华氏度(32°F)或零摄氏度(0°C). ⇨App 5 见附录5. **3** [C, U] step or stage in a scale or series 程度; 等级: *She shows a high degree of skill in her work.* 她在工作中表现出高度的技巧. ○ *He was not in the slightest degree interested*, ie was completely uninterested. 他丝毫不感兴趣. ○ *To what degree* (ie To what extent, How much) *was he involved in the crimes?* 他在多大程度上参与了这些犯罪活动? ○ *She has also been affected, but to a lesser degree.* 她也受到波及, 但程度较轻. ○ *I agree with you to some/a certain degree.* 我在某种程度上同意你的意见. **4** [U] (*arch* 古) position in society 在社会上的地位: *people of high/low degree* 高[低]阶层的人. **5** [C] academic title; rank or grade given by a university or college to sb who has passed an examination, written a thesis, etc 学位: *take* (ie be awarded) *a degree in law/a law degree* 获得法律学位 ○ *the degree of Master of Arts (MA)* 文学硕士学位. **6** [C] (esp in compounds with *first*, *second*, etc 尤用于有 first、second 等的复合词中) step in a scale of seriousness 严重的程度: *murder in the ˌfirst deˈgree*, ie (in US), of the most serious kind ○ [attrib 作定语] *ˌfirst-degree ˈmurder* ○ *ˌthird-degree* (ie very serious) *ˈburns*. **7** [C] (*grammar*) each of the three forms of comparison of an adjective or adverb 形容词或副词比较等级的三种形式之一: *degrees of comparison* 比较的等级 ○ *'Good', 'better' and 'best' are the positive, comparative and superlative degrees of 'good'.* good、better、best 是 good 的原级、比较级、最高级. **8** (idm 习语) **by deˈgrees** gradually 逐渐地: *By degrees their friendship grew into love.* 他们的友谊渐渐发展成爱情. **to a deˈgree** (*infml* 口) very 非常; 很: *The film was boring to a degree.* 这部影片非常枯燥. **to the nth degree** ⇨ NTH.

de·hu·man·ize, -ise /ˌdiːˈhjuːmənaɪz; diˋhjuməˌnaɪz/ *v* [Tn] take human qualities away from (sb) 使(某人)失去人性: *Torture always dehumanizes both the torturer and his victim.* 严刑拷打往往使施刑者和受刑者都丧失人性. ▷ **de·hu·man·iza·tion, -isation** /diːˌhjuːmənaɪˈzeɪʃn; *US* -nɪˈz-; diˌhjumənəˋzeʃən/ *n* [U].

de·hyd·rate /ˌdiːˈhaɪdreɪt; diˋhaɪdret/ *v* **1** [Tn esp passive 尤用于被动语态] remove water or moisture from (esp food, to preserve it) 从(尤指食物)中去掉水分或潮气(以便保存); 脱水: *dehydrated vegetables, eggs, milk*, eg in powdered form 脱水蔬菜、蛋、牛奶(如呈粉末状). **2** [I] (of the body, tissues, etc) lose water or moisture (指身体、组织等)脱水, 失水: *Her body had dehydrated dangerously with the heat.* 她因受酷热身体脱水, 情况危殆.

▷ **de·hyd·ra·tion** /ˌdiːhaɪˈdreɪʃn; ˌdihaɪˋdreʃən/ *n* [U] (**a**) loss of water or moisture 失水; 脱水: *dying of dehydration* 因脱水而奄奄一息. (**b**) state of being dehydrated 脱水状态.

de-ice /ˌdiː ˈaɪs; diˋaɪs/ *v* [Tn] remove ice from or prevent ice forming on (sth) 除去(某物)上的冰; 防止(某物)的表面结冰: *de-ice a windscreen* 除去挡风玻璃上的冰.

▷ **de-icer** *n* [C, U] substance put on a surface, esp by spraying, to remove ice or stop it forming 除冰剂(尤指喷剂).

deify /ˈdiːɪfaɪ; ˋdiəˌfaɪ/ *v* (*pt, pp* **-fied**) [Tn] make a god of (sb/sth); worship as a god 将(某人[某事物])奉若神明; 神化: *Primitive peoples deified the sun.* 原始民族将太阳奉作神.

▷ **dei·fica·tion** /ˌdiːɪfɪˈkeɪʃn; ˌdiəfəˋkeʃən/ *n* [U] deifying or being deified 神化: *the deification of a Roman emperor* 对罗马皇帝的神化.

deign /deɪn; den/ *v* [Tt] (*sometimes derog or ironic* 有时作贬义或作反语) be kind or gracious enough (to do sth); condescend 屈尊, 俯就(做某事): *He walked past me without even deigning to look at me.* 他从我身旁走过, 竟没有屈尊看我一眼.

de·ism /ˈdiːɪzəm; ˋdiɪzəm/ *n* [U] belief in the existence of God that is based more on natural laws of the world than on divine revelation 自然神论(一种对神的信仰, 其理论基础是大自然的规律而不是神的启示). Cf 参看 THEISM.

▷ **de·ist** /ˈdiːɪst; ˋdiɪst/ *n* person who holds such a belief 自然神论者.

de·ity /ˈdiːɪtɪ; ˋdiətɪ/ *n* **1** (**a**) [C] god or goddess 神; 女神: *Roman deities* 罗马诸神. (**b**) **the Deity** [sing] God 上帝. **2** [U] divine quality or nature; state of being a god or goddess 神性; 神的身分.

déjà vu /ˌdeɪʒɑː ˈvjuː; deʒɑˋvju/ (*French* 法) [U] **1** feeling that one remembers an event or scene that one has not experienced or seen before 似曾经历, 似曾相见(认为自己曾经历过或见过某事物的幻觉): *I had an odd sense of déjà vu just as you said that.* 你刚才提到的事, 我有一种似曾经历过的奇怪幻觉. **2** (*infml* 口) feeling that one has experienced sth too often 对某事经历过多的感觉: *There was an awful feeling of déjà vu at the annual office party.* 对一年一度的同事聚会, 总有一种年年如是的厌倦感.

de·jected /dɪˈdʒektɪd; dɪˋdʒɛktɪd/ *adj* depressed; sad 沮丧的; 垂头丧气的; 情绪低落的; 郁郁不乐的: *dejected-looking campers in the rain* 在雨中神情沮丧的露营者 ○ *Repeated failure had left them feeling very dejected.* 他们三番五次失败后情绪非常低落. ▷ **de·ject·edly** *adv*.

de·jec·tion /dɪˈdʒekʃn; dɪˋdʒɛkʃən/ *n* [U] sad or dejected state; depression 忧郁; 沮丧; 情绪低落: *The loser sat slumped in dejection.* 失败者垂头丧气地坐着, 全身瘫软.

de jure /ˌdeɪ ˈdʒʊərɪ; deˋdʒʊrɪ/ (*Latin* 拉) by right; according to law 根据权利; 根据法律; 法律上: *the de jure king* 合法的国王 ○ *be king de jure* 依法获得王位. Cf 参看 DE FACTO.

dekko /ˈdekəʊ; ˋdɛko/ *n* (idm 习语) **have a dekko (at sth)** (*dated Brit sl* 旧, 俚) have a look 看一眼; 瞧; 瞥: *Have a dekko at this wheel: the tyre's flat.* 瞧瞧这个轮子, 轮胎瘪了.

de·lay /dɪˈleɪ; dɪˋle/ *v* **1** [I, In/pr, Tn] (cause sb to) be slow or late 使(某人)慢或迟到; 耽搁; 延误: *Don't delay! Book your holiday today!* 别拖延! 今天就定下你休假的日子! ○ *She delayed (for) two hours and missed the train.* 她耽搁两个小时, 把火车误了. ○ *I was delayed by the traffic.* 因交通阻塞, 我迟到了. **2** [Tn, Tg] put (sth) off until later; postpone 推迟(某事); 延期: *We must delay our journey until the weather improves.* 我们必须把旅行推迟, 等天气好转再说. ○ *Why have they delayed opening the school?* 他们为什么延期开学?

▷ **de·lay** *n* **1** [U] delaying or being delayed 耽搁; 延误; 推迟; 延期: *We must leave without delay.* 我们必须立即离开. **2** [C] amount of time for which sb/sth is delayed 被耽搁或推迟的时间: *There was a delay (of two hours) before the plane took off.* 飞机起飞推迟了(两个小时).

□ **deˌlayed-ˈaction** *adj* [usu attrib 通常作定语] operating after an interval of time 在隔一段时间后进行的: *a deˌlayed-action ˈfuse, ˈbomb, ˈcamera* 延时熔断器、

定时炸弹、自拍照相机.

de·lect·able /dɪˈlektəbl; dɪˈlɛktəbl/ *adj* (*fml* 文) (esp of food) delightful; pleasant (尤指食物)令人喜爱的, 合意的, 美味的: *a delectable meal* 美餐 ○ (*fig* 比喻) *What a delectable little girl!* 多么可爱的小姑娘! ▷ **de·lect·ably** /-əblɪ; -əblɪ/ *adv*.

de·lecta·tion /ˌdiːlekˈteɪʃn; ˌdilɛkˈteʃən/ *n* [U] (*fml or joc* 文或谑) enjoyment; entertainment 欢娱; 享乐: *And now for your further delectation, we present a selection of popular melodies.* 为使你们更加愉快, 我们奉献给你们一组精选的流行歌曲.

del·eg·ate[1] /ˈdeləgət; ˈdɛləgɪt/ *n* person chosen or elected by others to express their views (eg at a meeting or conference) 代表(如出席会议者).

del·eg·ate[2] /ˈdelɪgeɪt; ˈdɛləˌget/ *v* **1** [Tn, Tn·pr, Tnt] **~ sb (to sth)** **(a)** choose or send sb as a representative 挑选或委派某人作代表: *delegate sb to a conference/to attend a conference* 选派某人作代表出席会议. **(b)** choose sb to carry out (duties, a task, etc) 挑选或委派某人执行(职责、任务等): *The new manager was delegated to reorganize the department.* 派这位新经理重新组织该部门. **2** [I, Tn, Tn·pr] **~ (sth) (to sb)** entrust (duties, rights, etc) to sb in a lower position or grade 将(职责、权利等)委托给下级; 授权给: *A boss must know how to delegate (work).* 当老板的要知人善任. ○ *The job had to be delegated to an assistant.* 这项工作得交给助手去做.

del·ega·tion /ˌdelɪˈgeɪʃn; ˌdɛləˈgeʃən/ *n* **1** [U] delegating or being delegated 代表; 委托. **2** [CGp] group of delegates 代表团: *She refused to meet the union delegation.* 她拒绝接见工会代表团.

de·lete /dɪˈliːt; dɪˈlit/ *v* [Tn, Tn·pr] **~ sth (from sth)** cross out or deliberately omit (sth written or printed) 删除或删略(文字): *The editor deleted the last paragraph (from the article).* 编辑删除了(文章的)最后一段.

▷ **de·le·tion** /dɪˈliːʃn; dɪˈliʃən/ *n* **(a)** [U] deleting or being deleted 删除. **(b)** [C] word, passage, etc that has been deleted 删除的词、段落等.

de·le·teri·ous /ˌdelɪˈtɪərɪəs; ˌdɛləˈtɪrɪəs/ *adj* **~ (to sb/sth)** (*fml* 文) harmful 有害的: *have a deleterious effect on a child's development* 对孩子的发育有不良影响. ▷ **de·le·teri·ously** *adv*.

delft /delft; dɛlft/ (also **delft·ware** /ˈdelftweə(r); ˈdɛlft-ˌwɛr/) *n* [U] type of glazed earthenware, usu with blue decoration 代尔夫特陶器(通常有蓝色图案).

deli /ˈdelɪ; ˈdɛlɪ/ *n* (*infml* 口) delicatessen shop 熟食店.

de·lib·er·ate[1] /dɪˈlɪbərət; dɪˈlɪbərɪt/ *adj* **1** done on purpose; intentional 故意的; 有意的; 蓄意的: *a deliberate insult, lie, act* 蓄意的侮辱、存心编造的谎言、故意的行为. **2** unhurried; careful 不慌不忙的; 小心翼翼的; 审慎的: *She has a slow, deliberate way of talking.* 她谈话的方式缓慢而审慎. ○ *making very deliberate gestures for emphasis* 做出非常沉稳的手势以示强调. ▷ **de·lib·er·ately** *adv*: *a deliberately calm tone of voice* 从容不迫的平静声调 ○ *She said it deliberately to provoke me.* 她故意说这件事向我挑衅.

de·lib·er·ate[2] /dɪˈlɪbəreɪt; dɪˈlɪbəˌret/ *v* [I, Ipr, Tw] **~ (about/on sth)** (*fml* 文) think or talk carefully 仔细考虑或谈论: *We had no time to deliberate (on the problem).* 我们没有时间仔细思考(这个问题). ○ *deliberate what action to take* 仔细考虑要采取的行动 ○ *deliberate whether to leave or not* 认真琢磨是否离开.

de·lib·era·tion /dɪˌlɪbəˈreɪʃn; dɪˌlɪbəˈreʃən/ *n* **1** [U, C] careful consideration or discussion 仔细的考虑或商议; 审议: *After long deliberation, they decided not to buy.* 他们商量了很长时间后, 决定不买了. ○ *What was the result of your deliberation(s)?* 你仔细考虑后结果如何? **2** [U] slowness of movement; carefulness 缓慢; 从容; 审慎: *speak, take aim, walk with great deliberation* 从容不迫地说、瞄准、散步.

del·ic·acy /ˈdelɪkəsɪ; ˈdɛləkəsɪ/ *n* **1** [U] softness or tenderness when touched 柔软; 细嫩: *the delicacy of the fabric, a child's skin* 纤维的柔软、小孩皮肤的娇嫩. **2** [U] delicate structure; fineness 精致; 优雅: *the delicacy of her features* 她那清秀的容貌. **3** **(a)** [U] skill or careful treatment 精巧; 小心的处理: *the delicacy of her playing, workmanship, carving* 她演奏、手艺、雕刻的精巧. **(b)** [U] tact and restraint in human relations; sensitivity (人际关系中的)技巧和谨慎; 敏感: *She spoke with delicacy of our recent loss.* 她机敏婉转地谈到我们最近的损失. ○ *Don't forget the delicacy of our position*, ie Remember the need for tact, etc. 不要忘记我们的处境, 需谨慎从事. **4** [U] (of colours, food, smells) pleasantness that does not strongly affect the senses (指颜色、食物、气味)柔和, 精美, 清香: *a shade, wine, scent of great delicacy* 精美的灯罩、醇香的葡萄酒、芬芳的气味. **5** [C] type of food thought to be delicious, esp in a particular place 珍馐, 佳肴(尤指有某处风味的): *The local people regard these crabs as a great delicacy.* 当地人认为这些螃蟹是珍馐美味.

del·ic·ate /ˈdelɪkət; ˈdɛləkət/ *adj* **1** soft or tender when touched; made of sth fine or thin 柔软的; 柔和的; 娇嫩的: *as delicate as silk* 柔软如丝绸 ○ *a baby's delicate skin* 婴儿娇嫩的皮肤. **2** very carefully made or formed; fine; exquisite 精致的; 优美的; 精巧的: *a delicate mechanism, structure, etc* 精巧的机械装置、结构等 ○ *the delicate beauty of a snowflake* 雪花的精美. **3** **(a)** easily injured or damaged; fragile 容易受伤或受损的; 易碎的; 脆弱的: *delicate china* 易碎的瓷器 ○ *a delicate plant* 娇弱的植物. **(b)** becoming ill easily; not strong 容易生病的; 不强壮的: *a delicate child, constitution* 瘦弱的孩子、身躯 ○ *She has been in delicate health for some time.* 她身体欠佳已有些时日了. **4** **(a)** showing or needing much skill or careful treatment 精致的; 需技巧的; 精心处理的: *the delicate craftsmanship of a fine watch* 制造好表的精湛技艺 ○ *a delicate surgical operation*, eg on sb's eyes 精细的外科手术(如眼科手术) ○ *her delicate playing of the sonata* 她演奏奏鸣曲的娴熟技巧. **(b)** showing or needing tact and good judgement in human relations; sensitive (在人际关系中)有技巧的, 得当的, 得体的, 微妙的: *I admired your delicate handling of the situation.* 我很钦佩你这样巧妙地处理了这种局面. ○ *We're conducting very delicate negotiations.* 我们正在进行十分审慎的谈判. **5** (of the senses or of instruments) able to detect or show very small changes or differences; sensitive (指感官、仪器)精密的, 灵敏的: *a delicate sense of smell/touch* 灵敏的嗅觉[触觉] ○ *Only a very delicate thermometer can measure such tiny changes in temperature.* 只有非常灵敏的温度计才能测出这样微小的温度变化. **6** **(a)** (of colours) not intense; soft (指颜色)柔和的, 淡的, 浅的: *a delicate shade of pink* 淡粉红色. **(b)** (of food or its taste) pleasing and not strongly flavoured (指食物或味道)美味的, 清淡可口的: *the gentle, delicate flavour of salmon* 鲑鱼清淡可口的味道 ○ *Veal is too delicate for a spicy sauce.* 小牛肉清淡可口不宜多加调料. **(c)** (of smell) pleasing and not strong (指气味)柔和的, 淡的: *a delicate perfume, fragrance, aroma, etc* 淡雅的香水、芳香、香气等. ▷ **del·ic·ately** *adv*: *delicately carved statues* 雕刻精致的塑像 ○ *a delicately phrased compliment* 措词高雅的赞词.

de·li·ca·tes·sen /ˌdelɪkəˈtesn; ˌdɛləkəˈtɛsn̩/ *n* **(a)** [C] shop selling prepared foods, often unusual or imported, ready for serving (esp cooked meat, smoked fish, cheeses, etc) 熟食店(尤指供应熟肉、熏鱼、干酪等的). **(b)** [U] such food 熟食.

de·li·cious /dɪˈlɪʃəs; dɪˈlɪʃəs/ *adj* giving pleasure, esp to the senses of taste and smell 美味的; 可口的; 芳香的: *a delicious meal, cake, flavour* 可口的饭、糕点、味道 ○ *It smells delicious!* 闻起来多香啊! ○ (*fig* 比喻) *What a delicious joke!* 多有趣的笑话! ▷ **de·li·ciously** *adv*: *a deliciously creamy soup* 可口的奶油汤.

de·light[1] /dɪˈlaɪt; dɪˈlaɪt/ *n* **1** [U] great pleasure; joy 高兴; 快乐; 愉快: *give delight to sb* 使某人快乐 ○ *To our great delight, the day turned out fine.* 我们感到高兴的是天气转晴了. **2** [C] cause or source of pleasure 使人高兴的原因: *Her singing is a delight.* 她的歌声使人快乐. ○ *the delights of living in the country* 在乡村生活的乐趣. **3** (idm 习语) **take delight in sth/doing sth** find pleasure in sth/doing sth (esp sth cruel or wrong) 以某事物[做某事]为乐(尤指残忍的事或坏事): *He takes great delight in proving others wrong.* 他的极大乐趣是证实别人错了.

▷ **de·light·ful** /-fl; -fəl/ *adj* **~ (to sb)** giving delight 使人快乐的; 令人愉快的: *a delightful holiday, melody, conversation* 令人愉快的假日、曲调、谈话 ○ *No news could be more delightful to me.* 这消息最令我高兴. **de·light·fully** /-fəlɪ; -fəlɪ/ *adv*.

de·light[2] /dɪˈlaɪt; dɪˋlaɪt/ *v* **1** [Tn] give great pleasure to (sb); please greatly 给(某人)乐趣; 使愉快: *Her singing delighted everyone.* 她的歌声使大家很愉快. **2** [Ipr no passive 不用于被动语态, It] **~ in sth/doing sth** take great (and often cruel) pleasure in sth; enjoy sth 以某事物为乐(常为残忍的事); 喜好某事物: *He delights in teasing his younger sister.* 他以戏弄他妹妹为乐. ○ (*fml* 文) *She delights to be surrounded by admirers.* 她喜欢身边簇拥着爱慕她的人.

▷ **de·lighted** *adj* **~ (at sth/to do sth/that...)** very pleased; showing delight 非常高兴的; 显示愉快的: *a delighted smile, look, child* 愉快的微笑、样子、小孩 ○ *I'm delighted at your success/to hear of your success/that you succeeded.* 我对你的成功[听到你成功的消息/对你已获成功]感到很高兴. ○ *'Will you come to the party?' 'I'd be delighted (to)!'* '你来参加聚会吗?' '很愿意来!'

de·limit /diːˈlɪmɪt; dɪˋlɪmɪt/ *v* [Tn] fix the limits or boundaries of (sth) 确定(某事物)的范围或界线: *The first chapter delimits her area of research.* 第一章阐明了她的研究领域. ▷ **de·lim·ita·tion** /diːˌlɪmɪˈteɪʃn; dɪˌlɪməˋteʃən/ *n* [C, U].

de·lin·eate /dɪˈlɪnieɪt; dɪˋlɪnɪˌet/ *v* [Tn] (*fml* 文) show (sth) by drawing or describing; portray 画出或描述出(某事物); 描绘; 描写: *delineate sb's features, character* 描绘某人的面貌、性格 ○ *delineate one's plans* 描述某人的计划. ▷ **de·lin·eation** /dɪˌlɪnɪˈeɪʃn; dɪˌlɪnɪˋeʃən/ *n* [C, U].

de·lin·quency /dɪˈlɪŋkwənsɪ; dɪˋlɪŋkwənsɪ/ *n* (**a**) [U, C] minor crime such as vandalism, esp when committed by young people 不严重的罪(如破坏公物, 尤指青少年所为者): *juvenile delinquency* 少年犯罪. (**b**) [U] failure to perform one's duty 失职: *The captain's delinquency led to the loss of the ship.* 船长失职而损失了一艘轮船.

de·lin·quent /dɪˈlɪŋkwənt; dɪˋlɪŋkwənt/ *n, adj* (person) doing wrong or failing to perform a duty 做错事的或失职的(人): *a juvenile delinquent* 少年违法者 ○ *delinquent behaviour* 失职行为 ○ *a delinquent soldier* 犯过的士兵.

de·li·ques·cent /ˌdelɪˈkwesnt; ˌdɛləˋkwɛsn̩t/ *adj* (*chemistry* 化) becoming liquid by absorbing moisture from the air 潮解的.

de·li·ri·ous /dɪˈlɪrɪəs; dɪˋlɪrɪəs/ *adj* **1** (**a**) suffering from delirium 神志昏乱的; 谵妄的: *He's so delirious he doesn't know where he is.* 他精神错乱, 竟不知自己身在何处. (**b**) showing the effects of delirium 显示精神错乱的: *a delirious condition, reply* 狂乱的状态、回答. **2** (*fig* 比喻) very excited and happy 非常激动的; 特别愉快的: *The children were delirious (with joy) as they opened the parcels.* 孩子们打开包裹时欣喜若狂. ▷ **de·li·ri·ously** *adv*: *raving deliriously* 疯狂地吼叫 ○ *deliriously happy* 狂喜.

de·li·rium /dɪˈlɪrɪəm; dɪˋlɪrɪəm/ *n* [U] **1** mental disturbance caused by (esp feverish) illness, resulting in restlessness and often wild talk 精神错乱, 说胡话(尤指因发烧等引起者): *exhausted by the fever and delirium* 因发烧说胡话而疲惫不堪. **2** (*fig* 比喻) excited happiness 狂喜.

□ **deˌlirium ˈtremens** /-ˈtriːmenz; -ˋtrimənz/ (*abbr* 缩写 **DT(s)**) delirium caused by extreme alcoholism 震颤性谵妄(由过度嗜酒引起).

de·liver /dɪˈlɪvə(r); dɪˋlɪvɚ/ *v* **1** [I, Ipr, Tn, Tn·pr] **~ (sth) (to sb/sth)** take (letters, parcels, goods, etc) to the places or people they are addressed to 递送, 传送(信件、包裹、货物等): *We deliver (your order) to your door!* 我们送货上门! ○ *A courier delivered the parcels (to our office).* 送急件的人将包裹送来(送到我们办公室)了. ○ *Did you deliver my message to my father?* 你把我的信息传给我父亲了吗? **2** (**a**) [Tn·pr only passive 只用于被动语态] **be ~ed of sb** (*fml* 文) give birth to (a child) 生(小孩儿): *She was delivered of a healthy boy.* 她生了一个健康的男孩儿. (**b**) [Tn] help a mother to give birth to (a child) 协助产妇分娩; 助产; 接生: *Her baby was delivered by her own doctor.* 她的婴儿是由她自己的医生给接生的. (**c**) [Tn·pr] **~ oneself of sth** (*fml* 文) state sth 发言; 发表: *deliver oneself of an opinion, a judgement, etc* 发表意见、看法等. **3** [Tn, Tn·pr, Tn·p] **~ sth (up/over) (to sb)** (*fml* 文) give sth up; hand sth over; surrender sth 放弃某事物; 交出某物: *deliver (up) a fortress to the enemy* 弃守要塞任敌人占据 ○ *deliver over one's property to one's children* 把财产交给子女. **4** [Tn, Tn·pr] give (a lecture, sermon, speech, etc) 授(课); 讲(道); 讲(话): *She delivered a talk on philosophy to the society.* 她给学会作了一次有关哲学的讲话. **5** [Tn, Tn·pr] **~ sb (from sth)** (*arch* 古) rescue sb (from sth); save sb; free sb 拯救某人; 解救某人; 释放某人: *May God deliver us from evil.* 愿上帝拯救我们脱离罪恶. **6** (**a**) [Tn] throw or launch (sth) in flight; release 投掷, 发射(某物); 放出: *In cricket, the ball is delivered overarm.* 打板球时, 要举臂过肩掷球. ○ *The missile is delivered from underground.* 这种导弹由地下发射. (**b**) [Tn, Tn·pr] give (a blow) 给予(打击): *deliver a blow to the jaw* 给颔部一击 ○ (*fig* 比喻) *The teacher delivered a sharp rebuke to the class.* 教师尖刻地申斥了全班学生. **7** (*infml* 口) (**a**) [I, Ipr] **~ (on sth)** give what is expected or promised 不负所望; 履行诺言: *They promise to finish the job in June, but can they deliver (on that)?* 他们答应六月份完成这项工作, 但他们能说到做到吗? (**b**) [Tn] achieve (a level of performance) 达到(某一能力、性能等的水平): *The new model delivers speed and fuel economy.* 这种新型设计能提高速度、节约燃料. ○ *If you can't deliver improved sales figures, you're fired!* 你要是不能提高销售额, 就把你解雇! **8** (idm 习语) **come up with/deliver the goods** ⇨ GOODS.

▷ **de·liv·erer** *n* **1** person who delivers (DELIVER 1, 2, 3, 4) 递送者; 助产者; 述说者; 放弃者; 交付者; 授课者; 讲道者; 演讲者. **2** rescuer; saviour 拯救者; 救星.

de·liv·er·ance /dɪˈlɪvərəns; dɪˋlɪvərəns/ *n* [U] **~ (from sth)** being freed or rescued 被释放; 被拯救: *They prayed for an early deliverance from captivity.* 他们为早日获释而祈祷.

de·liv·ery /dɪˈlɪvərɪ; dɪˋlɪvərɪ/ *n* **1** (**a**) [U] delivering (of letters, goods, etc) 递送, 投递, 交付(信件、货物等): *Your order is ready for delivery.* 你订购的货物可随时交付. ○ *Please pay on* (ie at the time of) *delivery.* 请于交货时付款. (**b**) [C] goods, mail, etc delivered (递送或交付的)货物、邮件等: *We had a big delivery of coal today.* 今天我们收到大批订购的煤. (**c**) [C] instance of delivering (parcels, goods, etc) (包裹、货物等的)递送, 交付: *We have two postal deliveries each day.* 我们每天收到两次信. **2** [C, U] process of birth 分娩: *an easy/difficult delivery* 顺[难]产 ○ *the first stage of delivery* 第一产程. **3** [sing] manner of speaking (in lectures, etc) (在讲课等中的)讲话方式, 风度, 态度: *Her poor delivery spoilt an otherwise good speech.* 她的演讲在各方面都很好, 却因表达技巧差而功亏一篑. **4** (**a**) [U] throwing or launching in flight (of a ball, missile, etc) (球的)投掷; (导弹的)发射. (**b**) [C] ball thrown (esp one bowled in cricket or thrown in baseball) 投掷的球(尤指板球或棒球): *a fast, hostile delivery* 快速投球、投出刁球. **5** (idm 习语) **cash on delivery** ⇨ CASH. **take delivery (of sth)** receive sth 收到某物: *When can you take delivery of the car?* 你什么时候才能收到那辆汽车?

□ **deˈlivery note** (*esp Brit*) note, usu in duplicate, sent with goods and signed by the person receiving them 送货单(通常有副本, 与货物一起送出, 由收货人签收).

deˈlivery van (*US* **deˈlivery truck**) van used for delivering goods 厢式送货车.

dell /del; dɛl/ *n* small valley, usu with trees on its sides 小山谷(通常两边有树).

de·louse /ˌdiːˈlaʊs; diˋlaʊs/ *v* [Tn] remove the lice from (sb/sth) 消灭(某人[某物])的虱子.

Del·phic /ˈdelfɪk; ˋdɛlfɪk/ *adj* **1** of the ancient Greek oracle at Delphi 特尔斐之古希腊神谕的. **2** mysterious or unclear because more than one meaning is possible 深奥难解的; 含义不明的; 意义模棱两可的: *a Delphic utterance* 语意含混不清的话.

del·phi·nium /delˈfɪnɪəm; dɛlˋfɪnɪəm/ *n* garden plant with tall spikes of (usu blue) flowers 飞燕草(园艺植物, 开穗状花, 通常为蓝色).

delta /ˈdeltə; ˋdɛltə/ *n* **1** the fourth letter of the Greek alphabet (Δ, δ) 希腊字母表的第四个字母(Δ, δ). **2** triangular area of alluvial land at a river's mouth, enclosed or crossed by branches of the river (河口的)三角洲: *the Nile Delta* 尼罗河三角洲.

□ ˌ**delta wing ˈaircraft** aircraft with swept-back wings that give it a triangular appearance 三角翼飞机.

de·lude /dɪˈluːd; dɪˋlud/ *v* [Tn, Tn·pr] **~ sb (with sth/into doing sth)** deliberately mislead sb; deceive sb 诳

惑某人; 欺骗某人; 哄骗某人: *a poor deluded fool* 受骗的可怜傻瓜 ○ *delude sb with empty promises* 以虚假的诺言哄骗某人 ○ *delude oneself with false hopes* 以虚幻的希望欺骗自己 ○ *delude sb/oneself into believing that...* 欺骗某人[自己]误以为....

de·luge /ˈdelju:dʒ; ˋdɛljudʒ/ *n* **1** (**a**) great flood or rush of water 洪水; 大水流: *When the snow melts, the mountain stream becomes a deluge.* 雪融化时, 山间溪流变成山洪暴发. (**b**) heavy fall of rain 大暴雨; 倾盆大雨: *I got caught in the deluge on the way home.* 我在回家的路上遇到倾盆大雨. **2** (*fig* 比喻) great quantity of sth that comes all at once 同时涌来的大量事物: *a deluge of work, words, letters* 涌来的大量工作、滔滔不绝的话、纷至沓来的信件.

▷ **de·luge** *v* [esp passive 尤用于被动语态: Tn, Tn·pr] **1 ~ sth (with sth)** flood sth (with sth) (以某物)淹没某物: *The town was deluged with thick slimy mud.* 该城到处都是又厚又黏的泥. **2 ~ sb/sth (with sth)** (*fig* 比喻) send or give sb/sth a very large quantity of sth (事物)涌现: *I was deluged with phone calls.* 我的电话应接不暇. ○ *We advertised the job and were deluged with applications.* 我们登出了这项工作的广告, 收到的申请书不计其数.

D

de·lu·sion /dɪˈlu:ʒn; dɪˋluʒən/ *n* **1** [U] deluding or being deluded 诳惑; 欺骗: *His arguments sound convincing but they're based on delusion.* 他的论据听起来似乎有理, 但根本上是欺骗性的. **2** [C] false opinion or belief, esp one that may be a symptom of madness 幻想, 妄想, 错觉(尤指可能因精神错乱所致): *be under a delusion/under the delusion that...* 有...的错觉 ○ *suffer from delusions* 患妄想症 ○ *Your hopes of promotion are a mere delusion.* 你提升的希望只不过是一种幻想. **3** (idm 习语) **delusions of ˈgrandeur** false belief in one's own importance 妄自尊大: *She wants to travel first-class: she must have delusions of grandeur.* 她想坐头等舱旅行, 她一定自以为很了不起.

de·lus·ive /dɪˈlu:sɪv; dɪˋlusɪv/ *adj* not real; misleading 不真实的; 诳惑的; 骗人的; 使人产生错觉的: *a delusive belief, impression, etc* 虚妄的信念、使人产生错觉的印象. ▷ **de·lus·ively** *adv*.

de luxe /dəˈlʌks, *also* -ˈlʊks; dɪˋlʌks, -ˋlʊks/ *adj* [esp attrib 尤作定语] of a very high quality, high standard of comfort, etc 高质量的; 豪华的: *a de luxe hotel, car, bed* 舒适的旅馆、汽车、床 ○ *the de luxe edition of a book*, eg with a special leather binding 书的精装本.

delve /delv; dɛlv/ *v* **1** [Ipr] **~ in/into sth** (**a**) search or rummage in sth 在某物中搜寻或翻查: *She delved in her bag and pulled out a pen.* 她在提包里翻找, 拿出一枝钢笔. ○ *delve into a drawer, box, pocket, etc for sth* 在抽屉、盒子、衣袋等里寻找某物. (**b**) try to find information about sth; study sth 探索; 钻研: *a writer delving in medieval French literature* 研究中世纪法国文学的作家 ○ *She delved into the origins of the custom.* 她探究这种习俗的起源. **2** [I] (*arch* 古) dig 挖掘.

Dem *abbr* 缩写 = (*US*) Democrat; Democratic. Cf 参看 Rep 2.

de·mag·net·ize, -ise /ˌdi:ˈmægnɪtaɪz; diˋmægnəˌtaɪz/ *v* [Tn] remove the magnetic properties of (sth) 除去(某物)的磁性. ▷ **de·mag·net·iza·tion, -isation** /ˌdi:mægnɪtaɪˈzeɪʃn; ˌdimægnətəˋzeʃən/ *n*.

dem·agogue /ˈdeməgɒg; ˋdɛməˌgɑg/ *n* political leader who tries to win people's support by using emotional and often unreasonable arguments 蛊惑民心的政客.

▷ **dem·agogic** /ˌdeməˈgɒgɪk; ˌdɛməˋgɑgɪk/ *adj* of or like a demagogue (似)蛊惑民心的政客的; 蛊惑民心的; 煽动性的.

dem·agogy /ˈdeməgɒgɪ; ˋdɛməˌgɑgɪ/ *n* [U] principles and methods of a demagogue 蛊惑民心的策略和手段.

de·mand[1] /dɪˈmɑ:nd; *US* dɪˈmænd; dɪˋmænd/ *n* **1** [C] **~ (for sb to do sth); ~ (for sth/that...)** command, or sth which is given as if it was a command 要求; 请求: *receive a tax demand* 接到纳税通知 ○ *It is impossible to satisfy all your demands.* 满足你所有的要求是不可能的. ○ *The workers' demands for higher pay were refused by the employers.* 工人要求提高工资遭到雇主拒绝. ○ *There have been fresh demands for the Prime Minister to resign.* 人们最近不断要求首相辞职. ○ *demands for reform/that there should be reform* 改革要求. **2** [U] **~ (for sth/sb)** desire of customers for goods or services which they wish to buy or use (顾客的)需求, 需要: *We blame poor overseas demand for the car's failure.* 我们将汽车滞销归咎于海外需求量太低. ○ *Demand for skilled workers is high; but there is no demand for unskilled ones.* 非常需要熟练工人, 但却不需要生手. ○ *Demand for fish this month exceeds supply.* 本月份鱼供不应求. **3** [C] (also **deˈmand note**) note that requires sb to pay money owed, eg income tax 缴款通知. **4** (idm 习语) **in deˈmand** much wanted; popular 非常需要的; 受欢迎的: *Good secretaries are always in demand.* 好的秘书总是很多人都需要的. ○ *She is in great demand as a singer.* 她是个十分受欢迎的歌手. **make demands of/on sb** oblige sb to use a lot of skill, strength, etc 需要某人用高度技巧、很大力气等: *This new aircraft makes tremendous demands of the pilot.* 这种新飞机需要飞行员有极高的技巧. **on deˈmand** whenever asked for 一经要求: *a cheque payable on demand* 即时兑现的支票 ○ *She's in favour of abortion on demand.* 对于人工流产, 她赞成有求必应.

□ **deˈmand bill**, **deˈmand loan** (*esp US*) bill/loan that must be paid when payment is demanded 即付汇票[活期贷款]. Cf 参看 SUPPLY AND DEMAND (SUPPLY).

de·mand[2] /dɪˈmɑ:nd; *US* dɪˈmænd; dɪˋmænd/ *v* **1** [Tn, Tf, Tt] ask for (sth) as if one is commanding, or as if one has a right to do so 要求, 请求(某事物): *demand an apology (from sb)* 要求(某人)道歉 ○ *The workers are demanding better pay.* 工人要求提高工资. ○ *She demanded (to know) my business.* 她过问我的事情. ○ *He demands that he be told/demands to be told everything.* 他要求将一切都告诉他. **2** [Tn] require (sth); need 需求(某事物); 需要: *This sort of work demands great patience.* 这种工作需要极大耐性. ○ *Does the letter demand an immediate answer?* ie Must it be answered at once? 这封信需要立即答复吗?

de·mand·ing /dɪˈmɑ:ndɪŋ; *US* dɪˈmændɪŋ; dɪˋmændɪŋ/ *adj* (**a**) (of a task, etc) needing much patience, skill, effort, etc (指任务等)需要很大耐性、技巧、努力等的: *a demanding job, schedule, etc* 需要高度技巧的工作、需努力才能实现的计划. (**b**) (of a person) making others work hard, meet high standards, etc (指人)对他人要求高的, 苛求的: *a demanding boss, father, etc* 苛求的老板、父亲等 ○ *Children are so demanding: they need constant attention.* 孩子们总有所求, 需要时刻照顾他们.

de·marc·ate /ˈdi:mɑ:keɪt; dɪˋmɑrket/ *v* [Tn] mark or fix the limits of (sth) 标出或确定(某事物)的界线: *The playing area is demarcated by a white line.* 运动场地以白线为界.

de·marca·tion /ˌdi:mɑ:ˈkeɪʃn; ˌdimɑrˋkeʃən/ *n* [U, C] (marking of a) limit or boundary, esp between types of work considered by trade unions to belong to workers in different trades 划界线; 界线; (尤指工会认为属于不同行业间的)工种界线: *a line of demarcation* 分界线 ○ [attrib 作定语] *demarcation disputes in industry* 工业上工种界线的纠纷.

dé·marche /ˈdeɪmɑ:ʃ; deˋmɑrʃ/ *n* (*French* 法) political step or proceeding 政治上的步骤或手段.

de·mean /dɪˈmi:n; dɪˋmin/ *v* [Tn, Tnt] **~ oneself** lower oneself in dignity; deprive oneself of others' respect 降低自己的身分; 失去别人的尊重; 贬低自己: *Don't demean yourself by telling such obvious lies.* 你不要用这种明显的谎言自贬人格. ○ *I wouldn't demean myself to ask for favours from them.* 我不会降低身分向他们求情.

▷ **de·mean·ing** *adj* lowering (sb's) dignity; degrading 降低身分的; 卑微的; 堕落的: *He found it very demeaning to have to work for his former employee.* 他觉得要为他以前的雇员工作很失身分.

de·mean·our (*US* **-nor**) /dɪˈmi:nə(r); dɪˋminɚ/ *n* [U] (*fml* 文) way of behaving; conduct 行为; 举止: *I dislike his arrogant demeanour.* 我讨厌他那傲慢的行为.

de·men·ted /dɪˈmentɪd; dɪˋmɛntɪd/ *adj* (**a**) mad 疯狂的: *a poor, demented creature* 可怜的疯子. (**b**) (*fig infml* 比喻, 口) agitated because of worry, anger, etc (因忧虑、愤怒等)焦躁不安的: *When her child was two hours late, she became quite demented.* 她孩子晚了两个小时, 她心急如焚. ▷ **de·ment·edly** *adv*.

de·men·tia /dɪˈmenʃə; dɪˋmɛnʃə/ *n* [U] (*medical* 医) madness with loss of powers of thinking due to brain disease or injury 痴呆.

□ **dementia praecox** /dɪˌmenʃə ˈpri:kɒks; dɪˌmɛnʃə

ˋpri,kɑks/ (*fml* 文) schizophrenia 早发性痴呆症; 精神分裂症.

dem·er·ara /ˌdeməˈreərə; ˌdɛməˈrɛrə/ *n* [U] (also ˌ**demerara** ˈ**sugar**) light-brown raw cane sugar 浅褐色蔗糖.

de·merit /diːˈmerɪt; diˋmɛrɪt/ *n* (*fml* 文) fault; defect 缺点; 不足; 欠缺: *consider the merits and demerits of a system* 考虑一个制度的长处和短处.

de·mesne /dɪˈmeɪn; dɪˋmen/ *n* (*law* 律) (**a**) [U] possession and use of land as one's own property 土地的领有和使用(作为私产): *land held in demesne* 领有的地产. (**b**) [C] estate with land held in this way, ie without tenants living on it 领有供自用的地产(即无佃户租用).

demi- *pref* 前缀 (with *ns* 与名词结合) half; partly 半; 部分: *demigod*.

demi·god /ˈdemɪgɒd; ˋdɛmə,gɑd/ *n* (in classical mythology) being who is partly divine and partly human, esp the offspring of a god or goddess and a human (古典神话中)半神半人(尤指神与人所生的后代).

demi·john /ˈdemɪdʒɒn; ˋdɛmə,dʒɑn/ *n* large bottle with a narrow neck, often in a wickerwork case 细颈大瓶(常置于柳条套中).

de·mil·it·ar·ize, -ise /ˌdiːˈmɪlɪtəraɪz; diˋmɪlətə,raɪz/ *v* [Tn] remove military forces or installations from (an area) as a result of a treaty or an agreement 从(一地区)撤军或拆除军事设施: *a demilitarized zone* 非军事区. ▷ **de·mil·it·ar·iza·tion, -isation** /ˌdiːˌmɪlɪtəraɪˈzeɪʃn; *US* -rɪˈz-; di,mɪlətərɪˋzeʃən/ *n* [U, Gp].

demi-monde /ˈdemɪmɒnd; ˋdɛmɪ,mɑnd/ *n* [Gp] (*French* 法) **1** group of people whose actions are thought to be not entirely legal, respectable, etc 不正派的一群人: *the demi-monde of gambling clubs and sleazy bars* 赌场和低级酒吧里不正派的人. **2** (formerly) women thought to be not entirely respectable and for this reason not acceptable to society (旧时)因不正派而为社会嫌弃的女子.

de·mise /dɪˈmaɪz; dɪˋmaɪz/ *n* [sing] **1** (*fml* 文) death 死; 死亡. **2** (*fig* 比喻) end or failure (of an enterprise, etc) 停业; 倒闭: *This loss led to the demise of the business.* 这一损失导致了公司的倒闭.

de·mist /ˌdiːˈmɪst; diˋmɪst/ *v* [Tn] remove the mist from (eg the windscreen of a car) 除去(如汽车挡风玻璃)上面的雾水.

▷ **de·mister** (*US* **de·froster**) *n* device that warms (esp the windscreen of a vehicle) to stop mist forming 除雾器(尤指车辆挡风玻璃的).

dem(o)- *comb form* 构词成分 of people or population 人的; 人口的: *demagogue* ○ *democracy* ○ *demographic*.

demo /ˈdeməʊ; ˋdɛmo/ *n* (*pl* **~s**) (*infml* 口 *esp Brit*) = demonstration(3).

de·mob /ˌdiːˈmɒb; diˋmɑb/ *v* (**-bb-**) [Tn] (*Brit infml* 口) = demobilize (sb).

▷ **de·mob** *n* [U] (*Brit infml* 口) = demobilization.

de·mo·bil·ize, -ise /diːˈməʊbəlaɪz; diˋmobə,laɪz/ *v* [Tn] release (sb) from military service 使(某人)复员, 退伍; 遣散(军队). ▷ **de·mo·bil·iza·tion, -isation** /ˌdiːˌməʊbəlaɪˈzeɪʃn; *US* -lɪˈz-; ˌdimobəlɪˋzeʃən/ *n* [U].

demo·cracy /dɪˈmɒkrəsɪ; dəˋmɑkrəsɪ/ *n* **1** (**a**) [U] system of government by the whole people of a country, esp through representatives whom they elect 民主; 民主政治; 民主政体; 民主制度: *parliamentary democracy* 议会民主政体. (**b**) [C] country having such a system 民主国家: *the Western democracies* 西方的民主国家. **2** [C, U] (country with a) government that allows freedom of speech, religion and political opinion, that upholds the rule of law and majority rule and that respects the rights of minorities 民主政府; 有民主政府的国家: *the principles of democracy* 民主政府的原则. **3** (**a**) [U] treatment of each other by citizens as equals, without social class divisions 民主精神; 民主作风: *Is there more democracy in Australia than in Britain?* 澳大利亚比英国更民主吗? (**b**) [C] society where such conditions exist 民主社会. **4** [U] control of an organization by its members, who take part in the making of decisions (一组织由其成员的)民主管理: *industrial democracy* 企业的民主管理.

demo·crat /ˈdeməkræt; ˋdɛmə,kræt/ *n* **1** person who believes in or supports democracy 民主主义者. **2 Democrat** (*abbr* 缩写 **D**) member or supporter of the Democratic Party of the US 美国民主党的党员或拥护者. Cf 参看 REPUBLICAN 2.

demo·cratic /ˌdeməˈkrætɪk; ˌdɛməˋkrætɪk/ *adj* **1** based on the principles of democracy (1a) 民主的; 民主政治的; 民主政体的: *democratic rights, elections* 民主的权利、选举 ○ *democratic government, rule, etc* 民主的政府、统治等. **2** of or supporting democracy(3); paying no or little attention to class divisions based on birth or wealth 民主作风的; 平等的: *a democratic society, outlook* 民主的社会、观点. **3** of or supporting control of an organization by its members 民主管理的: *democratic involvement, participation, etc* 参与民主管理、参加民主管理. ▷ **demo·crat·ic·ally** /-klɪ; -klɪ/ *adv*: *democratically elected, decided, etc* 民主选举的、民主决定的.

□ **Demoˈcratic Party** one of the two main political parties in the US 民主党(美国两大主要政党之一). Cf 参看 REPUBLICAN PARTY (REPUBLICAN).

demo·crat·ize, -ise /dɪˈmɒkrətaɪz; dəˋmɑkrə,taɪz/ *v* [Tn] make (sth) democratic 使(某事)民主化: *democratize the administration of an organization* 使一组织的管理民主化. ▷ **demo·crat·iza·tion, -isation** /dɪˌmɒkrətaɪˈzeɪʃn; dɪ,mɑkrətəˋzeʃən/ *n* [U].

demo·graphy /dɪˈmɒgrəfɪ; dɪˋmɑgrəfɪ/ *n* [U] study of statistics of births, deaths, diseases, etc in order to show the state of a community 人口统计学; 人口学.

▷ **demo·grapher** /dɪˈmɒgrəfə(r); dɪˋmɑgrəfɚ/ *n* expert in such studies 人口统计学家; 人口学家.

demo·graphic /ˌdeməˈgræfɪk; ˌdɛməˋgræfɪk/ *adj*.

de·mol·ish /dɪˈmɒlɪʃ; dɪˋmɑlɪʃ/ *v* [Tn] **1** (**a**) pull or knock down (a building, etc) 拆毁, 拆除(建筑物等): *They've demolished the slum district.* 贫民区已拆除. (**b**) (*fig* 比喻) destroy (a theory, etc) 推翻, 驳倒(理论等): *Her article brilliantly demolishes his argument.* 她的文章精辟地批驳了他的论点. **2** (*fig joc* 比喻, 谑) eat (sth) greedily 贪婪地吃(某物): *She demolished two whole pies.* 她贪婪地吃下两个馅饼. ▷ **de·moli·tion** /ˌdeməˈlɪʃn; ˌdɛməˋlɪʃən/ *n* [U, C]: *the demolition of the houses* 房屋的拆除 ○ [attrib 作定语] *demolition contractors* 做拆除工作的承包者.

de·mon /ˈdiːmən; ˋdimən/ *n* **1** wicked or cruel spirit 恶魔; 魔鬼: *medieval carvings of demons* 中世纪的魔鬼雕像. **2** (*infml* 口) (**a**) person thought to be wicked, mischievous, etc 恶人; 恶棍; 调皮鬼: *Your son's a little demon.* 你儿子是个小调皮鬼. (**b**) **~ (for sth)** energetic person 精力充沛的人: *She's a demon for work*, ie works very hard. 她工作起来精力充沛. ○ [attrib 作定语] *a demon worker* 精力过人的工作者. (**c**) fierce or aggressive player 勇猛的运动员; 攻击型的运动员: [attrib 作定语] *a demon bowler* 勇猛的投球手. **3** (idm 习语) **the demon ˈdrink** (*joc* 谑) alcoholic drink, esp when it is the cause of wild noisy behaviour 含酒精的饮料(尤指饮后使人撒酒疯者): *He's very violent: it's the demon drink, you know.* 他大撒酒疯, 你要知道就是因为喝了那种酒. ▷ **de·monic** /diːˈmɒnɪk; diˋmɑnɪk/ *adj*: *demonic energy* 过人的精力.

de·mon·et·ize, -ise /ˌdiːˈmʌnɪtaɪz; diˋmʌnə,taɪz/ *v* stop (a metal) being used as currency 使(某金属)不再用作货币. ▷ **de·mon·et·iza·tion, -isa·tion** /diːˌmʌnɪtaɪˈzeɪʃn; *US* -tɪˈz-; di,mʌnətɪˋzeʃən/ *n* [U].

de·mo·niac /dɪˈməʊnɪæk; dɪˋmonɪ,æk/ (also **de·moni·acal** /ˌdiːməˈnaɪəkl; ˌdiməˋnaɪəkl/) *adj* (**a**) very evil; devilish 邪恶的; 凶恶的; 恶魔般的: *demoniac tortures, plans* 酷刑、邪恶的计划. (**b**) frenzied; fiercely energetic 疯狂的; 精力极充沛的: *demoniac energy, fury, etc* 逾常的精力、狂怒等.

dem·on·strable /ˈdemənstrəbl; *US* dɪˈmɒnstrəbl; ˋdɪmɑnstrəbl/ *adj* that can be shown or proved 可表明的; 可证实的: *a demonstrable lie, inaccuracy, etc* 明显的谎言、误差等. ▷ **dem·on·strab·il·ity** /ˌdemənstrəˈbɪlətɪ; ˌdɛmənstrəˋbɪlətɪ/ *n* [U]. **de·mon·strably** /-blɪ; -blɪ/ *adv*.

dem·on·strate /ˈdemənstreɪt; ˋdɛmən,stret/ *v* **1** (**a**) [Tn, Tn·pr, Tf, Tw] **~ sth (to sb)** show sth clearly by giving proof or evidence 证明; 论证: *demonstrate the truth of a statement (to sb)* (向某人)证明一说法的真实性 ○ *How do you demonstrate that the pressure remains constant?* 你怎样证明压力一直不变? ○ *Can you* *demonstrate what you mean by that?* 你那样做能说明你的意思吗? **(b)** [Tn, Tf, Tw] be an example of (sth); show 是(某事物)的实例; 表明; 表示: *The election demonstrates democracy in action.* 这次选举是以实际行动体现了民主. ○ *His sudden departure demonstrates that he's unreliable/how unreliable he is.* 他突然离去表明他不可靠[他多么不可靠]. **2** [Tn, Tn·pr, Tw] **~ sth (to sb)** show and explain how sth works or a way of doing sth 示范并解释某物如何操作或使用: *An assistant demonstrated the washing machine (to customers).* 店员(向顾客)示范如何使用洗衣机. ○ *She demonstrated how best to defend oneself.* 她示范最有效的自卫方法. **3** [I, Ipr] **~ (against/in favour of sb/sth)** take part in a public rally, etc, usu as a protest or to show support 示威; 进行示威集会或游行: *Thousands demonstrated against the price increases.* 数以千计的人举行示威, 抗议物价上涨. **4** [Tn] express (sth) by one's actions 用行动表达(某事): *Workers have already demonstrated their opposition to the plans.* 工人们已经表明反对这些方案. ○ *demonstrate strong feelings* 显示出强烈的感情.

D

de·mon·stra·tion /ˌdemənˈstreɪʃn; ˌdɛmənˈstreʃən/ *n* **1** [C, U] (instance of) showing sth by giving proof or evidence 证明; 论证: *convinced by (a) scientific demonstration* 以科学的论证使人信服 ○ *a demonstration of a law of physics* 证明一物理定律. **2** [C, U] (instance of) showing and explaining how sth works (对某物如何操作的)示范, 解释: *a demonstration of the computer's functions* 计算机功能的示范表演. ⇨Usage 见所附用法. **3** [C] **~ (against/in favour of sb/sth)** public, often organized, rally or march protesting against or supporting sb/sth (抗议或拥护某人[某事], 常为有组织的)集会或游行: *a mass demonstration in support of the régime* 拥护该政权的群众集会. **4** [C] outward sign; example 表现; 表示; 实例: *a demonstration of affection*, eg embracing sb 爱的表示(如拥抱某人) ○ *a clear demonstration of their intentions* 他们明显表示意图.

NOTE ON USAGE 用法: **1** A **demonstration** and a **display** do not require a specific or permanent site. ☆ **demonstration** 和 **display** 不必有特定的或永久的地点. At a **demonstration** one sees how something works or is done 在 **demonstration** 中可以看到某事物的操作情形: *a cookery demonstration* 烹饪表演 ○ *a demonstration of a new car* 新汽车的使用示范. **2** A **display** is often for public entertainment ☆ **display** 常用于公共娱乐方面: *a flying, fireworks, fashion, etc display* 飞行、烟火、时装等表演. **3** A **trade exhibition/show/fair** is held in an **exhibition hall** or **centre** where commercial or industrial goods are advertised ☆ **trade exhibition / show / fair** 是在 **exhibition hall** 或 **centre** 中举办的, 用以宣传工商业产品: *a book fair* 书展 ○ *the World Trade Fair* 世界贸易博览会 ○ *the Motor Show* 机动车辆展览 ○ *the Great Exhibition* 大型展览会. **4** A **show** can also be of domestic animals or plants, often in competition for prizes. ☆ **show** 还可作豢养的动物展览或栽培的花草展览, 常为有奖竞赛. Paintings, drawings, etc are displayed in an **exhibition** 绘画等则在 **exhibition** 中展出: *the Chelsea Flower Show* 切尔西花展 ○ *a horse show* 马展 ○ *an art exhibition* 美术展览会. **5** A **fair** or **funfair** is also a collection of entertainments (roundabouts, stalls, etc) travelling from town to town. ☆ **fair** 或 **funfair** 也可作巡回的娱乐集会(有旋转木马、游戏摊位等).

de·mon·strat·ive /dɪˈmɒnstrətɪv; dɪˈmɑnstrətɪv/ *adj* **1** **(a)** (of people) showing the feelings readily (指人)易流露感情的, 喜怒形于色的: *Some people are more demonstrative than others.* 有些人较爱流露感情. **(b)** expressing feelings, esp affection, openly 公开表露感情的(尤指爱慕之情): *He's very demonstrative: he kissed me on both cheeks.* 他热情奔放, 吻了我的双颊. **2** (*grammar*) (of a determiner or pronoun) indicating the person or thing referred to (指限定词或代词)指示的: *In 'This is my bike', 'this' is a demonstrative pronoun.* 在 This is my bike 一句中, this 是指示代词. ▷ **de·mon·strat·ively** *adv.* **de·mon·strat·ive·ness** *n* [U]: *embarrassed by demonstrativeness* 受公开表露的爱慕之情所窘.

dem·on·strator /ˈdemənstreɪtə(r); ˈdɛmənˌstretɚ/ *n* **1** person who teaches or explains by demonstrating (DEMONSTRATE 2) 示范助教: *The demonstrators set up apparatus for the experiment.* 示范助教安排好了实验装置. **2** person who demonstrates (DEMONSTRATE 3) 示威者; 游行者; 集会者: *The noisy demonstrators were dispersed by the police.* 喧嚷的示威者遭警察驱散.

de·mor·al·ize, -ise /dɪˈmɒrəlaɪz; *US* -ˈmɔːr-; dɪˈmɔrəlˌaɪz/ *v* [Tn] weaken the courage or self-confidence of (sb); dishearten 削弱(某人)的勇气或自信心; 使泄气; 使士气低落: *The troops were thoroughly demoralized by this set-back.* 这一挫败使部队士气丧失殆尽. ○ *feel very demoralized* 觉得十分沮丧 ○ *The news is very demoralizing.* 这消息很使人泄气. Cf 参看 DISPIRIT. ▷ **de·mor·al·iza·tion, -isa·tion** /dɪˌmɒrəlaɪˈzeɪʃn; *US* -ˌmɔːrələˈz-; dɪˌmɔrələˈzeʃən/ *n* [U].

de·mote /ˌdiːˈməʊt; dɪˈmot/ *v* [Tn, Tn·pr] **~ sb (from sth) (to sth)** reduce sb to a lower rank or grade 将某人降级或降职: *He was demoted from sergeant to corporal.* 他由中士降到下士. Cf 参看 PROMOTE. ▷ **de·mo·tion** /ˌdiːˈməʊʃn; dɪˈmoʃən/ *n* [C, U].

dem·otic /dɪˈmɒtɪk; dɪˈmɑtɪk/ *adj* of or used by ordinary people 民众的; 通俗的: *demotic Greek*, ie the informal, esp spoken, form of modern Greek 现代希腊语的通俗形式(尤指口语).

de·mur /dɪˈmɜː(r); dɪˈmɝ/ *v* (**-rr-**) [I, Ipr] **~ (at sth)** (*fml* 文) express a doubt (about sth) or an objection (to sth) (对某事物)表示怀疑或反对: *I suggested putting the matter to a vote, but the chairman demurred.* 我建议对此事投票表决, 但主席表示反对.

▷ **de·mur** *n* (idm 习语) **without deˈmur** without objecting or hesitating 无异议地; 不犹豫地.

de·mure /dɪˈmjʊə(r); dɪˈmjʊr/ *adj* **(a)** (pretending to be) quiet, serious and modest (故作)娴静的, 严肃的, 谦虚的: *a very demure young lady* 假装矜持的少女. **(b)** suggesting that one is demure 显示娴静的、严肃的、谦虚的: *a demure smile, reply, etc* 娴静的微笑、谦逊的回答. ▷ **de·murely** *adv.* **de·mure·ness** *n* [U].

de·mys·tify /ˌdiːˈmɪstɪfaɪ; diˈmɪstəˌfaɪ/ *v* (*pt, pp* **-fied**) [Tn] make (sth) less mysterious; make clear 使(某事物)非神秘化; 弄清楚: *We are trying to demystify the workings of government.* 我们要尽量使政府工作公开化. ▷ **de·mys·ti·fica·tion** /ˌdiːˌmɪstɪfɪˈkeɪʃn; ˌdimɪstəfəˈkeʃən/ *n* [U] action of making sth less mysterious 非神秘化: *The demystification of the Resurrection upsets many Christians.* 把耶稣的复活作非神秘化解释使许多基督徒不快.

den /den; dɛn/ *n* **1** animal's hidden home, eg a cave 兽穴; 窝(如山洞): *a bear's/lion's den* 熊的[狮子的]洞穴. **2** (*derog* 贬) secret meeting-place 秘密相聚之处: *an ˈopium den* 鸦片烟窟 ○ *a den of thieves* 贼窝. **3** (*infml* 口) room in a home where a person can work or study without being disturbed (家中的)私室, 书斋: *retire to one's den* 回到自己的私室. **4** (idm 习语) **beard the lion in his den** ⇨ BEARD[2]. **a den of iˈniquity/ˈvice** (*often joc* 常作戏谑语) a place where evil or immoral activities go on 进行罪恶活动的地方: *He thought of New York as a den of iniquity.* 他认为纽约是个藏污纳垢之处.

de·na·tion·al·ize, -ise /ˌdiːˈnæʃənəlaɪz; diˈnæʃənlˌaɪz/ *v* [Tn] put (a nationalized industry) back into private ownership, usu by selling shares in it; privatize 将(国营工业)恢复为私营; 使非国有化; 使私有化. Cf 参看 NATIONALIZE 1. ▷ **de·na·tional·iza·tion, -isa·tion** /ˌdiːˌnæʃənəlaɪˈzeɪʃn; *US* -lɪˈz-; diˌnæʃənəlɪˈzeʃən/ *n* [U].

de·na·tured /ˌdiːˈneɪtʃəd; diˈnetʃɚd/ *adj* [esp attrib 尤作定语] **(a)** made unfit for eating and drinking (but possibly still usable for other purposes) 不适于食用或饮用的; 变性的: *denatured alcohol* 变性酒精. **(b)** having lost its natural qualities 已失去天然特性的: *denatured rubber*, ie no longer elastic 失去弹性的橡胶.

deni·able /dɪˈnaɪəbl; dɪˈnaɪəbl̩/ *adj* that can be denied 可否认的; 可否定的; 可拒绝的: *I suppose these changes are deniable?* ie We might convince others they are not true. 我想这些更动可以驳回吧?

de·nial /dɪˈnaɪəl; dɪˈnaɪəl/ *n* **1** [C] **~ (of sth/that...)** statement that sth is not true 否认: *the prisoner's repeated denials of the charges against him* 囚犯对被控罪名再三否认 ○ *an official denial that there would be an* *election in May* 官方对五月份要进行选举一事加以否认. **2** [C, U] **(a)** **~ of sth** refusal to grant (justice, rights, etc) (对公正处理、权利等的)拒绝, 拒不给予: *condemn the denial of basic human freedoms* 谴责剥夺基本的自由权. **(b)** **~ (of sth)** refusal (of a request, etc) (对要求等的)拒绝: *the denial of his request for leave* 对他请假予以拒绝.

den·ier /ˈdenɪə(r); ˋdɛnɪr/ *n* unit for measuring fineness of rayon, nylon and silk yarns 旦尼尔, 旦(人造丝、尼龙、丝、纱线的纤度单位): [attrib 作定语] *30 denier stockings* 30旦的长袜.

den·ig·rate /ˈdenɪɡreɪt; ˋdɛnəˌɡret/ *v* [Tn] claim (unfairly) that (sb/sth) is inferior, worthless, etc; belittle 诋毁; 贬低; 诬蔑: *denigrate sb's character, achievements, etc* 诋毁某人的人格、成就等. ▷ **den·ig·ra·tion** /ˌdenɪˈɡreɪʃn; ˌdɛnəˋɡreʃən/ *n* [U].

denim /ˈdenɪm; ˋdɛnəm/ *n* **1** [U] hard-wearing twilled cotton cloth (used for jeans, overalls, etc) 斜纹粗棉布(用于制牛仔裤、工作服、罩衫等). **2** **denims** [pl] (*infml* 口) jeans made from this 斜纹粗棉布制的牛仔裤.

den·izen /ˈdenɪzn; ˋdɛnəzn̩/ *n* (*fml or joc* 文或谑) person or type of animal or plant living or growing permanently in a place 长久生长于某地的人或动植物: *polar bears, denizens of the frozen north* 北极熊, 北极冰天雪地的老住户 ○ *Blenkinsop, a respected denizen of our school*, ie a teacher who has been there for a long time. 布伦金索普, 我校长期备受尊敬的教师.

de·nom·ina·tion /dɪˌnɒmɪˈneɪʃn; dɪˌnɑməˋneʃən/ *n* **1** (*fml* 文) name, esp of a general class or type; classification 名称(尤指种类名称); 分类: *agreed denominations for various species of fish* 各种鱼的公认的分类. **2** religious group or sect 宗教派别: *The Protestant denominations include the Methodists, the Presbyterians and the Baptists.* 新教派别包括卫理公会派、长老会派、浸礼派. **3** class or unit of measurement or money 度量衡或货币的单位: *The US coin of the lowest denomination is the cent.* 美国硬币的最小单位是美分. ○ *We can reduce fractions to the same denomination* 分数可以化为同分母, 如 $\frac{1}{2}$, $\frac{5}{8}$ = $\frac{8}{16}$, $\frac{10}{16}$.

▷ **de·nom·ina·tional** /-ˈneɪʃənl; -ˋneʃənl̩/ *adj* of denominations (DENOMINATION 2) 宗教派别的: *denominational schools* 各教派的学校.

de·nom·in·ator /dɪˈnɒmɪneɪtə(r); dɪˋnɑməˌnetɚ/ *n* (*mathematics* 数) number below the line in a fraction, showing how many parts the whole is divided into, eg 4 in $\frac{3}{4}$ 分母(如 $\frac{3}{4}$ 中的 4). Cf 参看 NUMERATOR.

de·note /dɪˈnəʊt; dɪˋnot/ *v* **(a)** [Tn] be the name, sign or symbol of (sth); refer to 作为(某事物)的名称、符号或象征; 指的是: *What does the term 'organic' denote?* organic一词指的是什么? ○ *In algebra, the sign x usually denotes an unknown quantity.* 在代数中, x 符号通常代表一未知的量. **(b)** [Tn, Tf] indicate (sth) 表示(某事物): *The mark ⋏ denotes an omission.* 增补号(⋏)表示有脱漏. ○ *This mark denotes that a word has been deleted.* 这个符号表示有个词已删掉.

denoue·ment /ˌdeɪˈnuːmɒŋ; *US* ˌdeɪnuːˈmɔːŋ; ˌdenuˋmɑ̃/ *n* last part, esp of a novel, play, etc, in which everything is settled or made clear 最后部分; (尤指小说、戏剧等的)结局: *In a surprising denouement, she becomes a nun.* 结局出人意表, 她当修女了.

de·nounce /dɪˈnaʊns; dɪˋnaʊns/ *v* **1** **(a)** [Tn, Tn·pr, Cn·a] **~ sb (to sb) (as sth)** give information (to the authorities) against sb (向当局)告发某人: *An informer denounced him to the police (as a terrorist).* 检举人已向警方告发他(是恐怖分子). **(b)** [Tn, Cn·a] **~ sb/sth (as sth)** say that sb/sth is wrong, unlawful, etc 谴责; 指责; 斥责: *She strongly denounced the Government's hypocrisy.* 她强烈谴责政府虚伪. ○ *Union officials denounced the action as a breach of the agreement.* 工会负责人谴责这一行动破坏了协议. **2** [Tn] announce one's withdrawal from (a treaty, etc) 宣布退出(条约等).

dense /dens; dɛns/ *adj* **(-r, -st)** **1** **(a)** very heavy in relation to each unit of volume 密度大的: *a dense substance, rock, star* 密度大的物质、岩石、星星. **(b)** (of liquids or vapour) not easily seen through (指液体、水气或烟雾)不易看透的, 浓的: *dense fog/smoke* 大雾[浓烟]. **2** (of people and things) crowded together in great numbers (指人和物)稠密的, 密集的: *a dense crowd, forest* 密集的人群、茂密的森林. **3** (*infml* 口) stupid 愚蠢的: *How can you be so dense?* 你怎么能如此愚蠢?

▷ **densely** *adv*: *a densely populated country* 人口稠密的国家 ○ *densely wooded*, ie covered with trees growing close together 森林茂密的. **dense·ness** *n* [U].

dens·ity /ˈdensətɪ; ˋdɛnsətɪ/ *n* **1** [U] quality of being dense(1b, 2) 浓度; 密度: *the density of a forest, the fog, etc* 森林的密度、雾的浓度. **2** [C, U] (*physics* 物) relation of mass to volume 密度(质量与体积的关系).

dent /dent; dɛnt/ *n* **1** (also **dint**) hollow place in a hard even surface made by a blow or pressure 凹陷; 凹部; 凹痕: *a dent in the boot of my car* 我的汽车行李箱上的凹痕. **2** (idm 习语) **(make) a dent in sth** (*infml* 口) (cause) a reduction in sth 减少; 削减; 削弱: *a dent in one's pride* 自尊心的挫伤 ○ *The repairs made a dent in our funds*, ie cost us a lot. 这次修理用去了我们很多钱.

▷ **dent** *v* **(a)** [Tn] make a dent or dents in (sth) 在(某物)上造成凹痕: *The back of the car was badly dented in a collision.* 这辆汽车后部在碰撞中造成很大的凹陷. **(b)** [I] get a dent or dents 出现凹痕: *a metal that dents easily* 容易出现凹痕的金属.

dental /ˈdentl; ˋdɛntl̩/ *adj* **1** of or for the teeth 牙齿的; 牙科的: *dental care, treatment, etc* 牙齿的保护、治疗等. **2** (*phonetics* 语音) pronounced with the tip of the tongue near or touching the upper front teeth 齿音的: *dental sounds* 齿音, 如 /θ/、/ð/.

□ **ˈdental floss** soft thread used for cleaning the gaps between the teeth 洁牙线(用以使牙缝清洁的软线).

ˌdental hyˈgienist /ˈdentl haɪˈdʒiːnɪst; ˌdɛntl̩ haɪˋdʒinɪst/ person who works, usu for a dentist, cleaning and polishing people's teeth 牙科保健员.

ˈdental plate = PLATE[1] 9.

ˈdental surgeon dentist 牙科医师.

den·ti·frice /ˈdentɪfrɪs; ˋdɛntəˌfrɪs/ *n* [U] (*fml* 文) powder or paste used for cleaning the teeth 牙粉; 牙膏.

dent·ist /ˈdentɪst; ˋdɛntɪst/ *n* person whose work is filling, cleaning and taking out teeth, and fitting artificial teeth 牙科医生.

▷ **den·tistry** /ˈdentɪstrɪ; ˋdɛntɪstrɪ/ *n* [U] work of a dentist 牙科学; 牙医术.

den·ture /ˈdentʃə(r); ˋdɛntʃɚ/ *n* (usu *pl* 通常作复数) = PLATE[1] 9: *a set of dentures* 一副假牙.

de·nude /dɪˈnjuːd; *US* -ˈnuːd; dɪˋnud/ *v* [esp passive 尤用于被动语态: Tn, Tn·pr] **~ sth (of sth)** make sth bare; take the covering off sth 使某物裸露; 去掉遮掩; 剥光: *trees denuded of leaves* 叶子落尽的秃树 ○ *hillsides denuded of trees* 无树的秃山坡. ▷ **de·nuda·tion** /ˌdiːnjuːˈdeɪʃn; *US* -nuː-; ˌdinuˋdeʃən/ *n* [U].

de·nun·ci·ation /dɪˌnʌnsɪˈeɪʃn; dɪˌnʌnsɪˋeʃən/ *n* [C, U] (act of) denouncing 谴责; 斥责: *her fierce denunciation(s) of her enemies* 她对仇敌的强烈谴责.

deny /dɪˈnaɪ; dɪˋnaɪ/ *v* (*pt, pp* **de·nied**) **1** [Tn, Tf, Tnt, Tg] say that (sth) is not true 否认, 否定(某事): *deny a statement, a claim, an accusation, a charge, etc* 否认一个说法、否定某人声称的事、否认一项指责、否认一项指控 ○ *deny that sth is true* 否定某事属实 ○ (*fml* 文) *She denied this to be the case.* 她不承认情况是这样. ○ *He denied knowing anything about it.* 他否认知道此事. ○ *He denied that he was involved.* 他否认与己有关. ○ *There is no denying the fact that...*, ie Everyone must admit that... 无可否认.... Cf 参看 AFFIRM. **2** [Dn·n, Dn·pr] **~ sth (to sb)** refuse to give sb, or prevent sb from having, (sth asked for or wanted) 拒不给予某人(所求或所需之物); 阻止某人获得(所求或所需之物): *He gave to his friends what he denied to his family.* 他宁可赠予朋友也不给家里人. ○ *She was angry at being denied the opportunity to see me.* 因不准她见我, 她非常生气. ○ *He denies himself nothing.* 他对自己极为放纵. **3** [Tn] say that one knows nothing about (sth); refuse to acknowledge; disown 声称对(某事)毫无所知; 拒绝承认; 否认与己有关: *He denied any knowledge of their plans*, ie claimed to know nothing about them. 他声称对他们的计划一无所知. ○ (*fml* 文) *He denied the signature*, ie said that it was not his. 他拒不承认这是他的签字.

de·odor·ant /diːˈəʊdərənt; diˋodərənt/ *n* [U, C] substance that removes or disguises (esp bodily) odours 除臭剂, 防臭剂(尤指除体臭者).

de·odor·ize, -ise /diːˈəʊdəraɪz; diˋodə,raɪz/ *v* [Tn] remove (esp bad) smells from (sb/sth) 除去(某人[某物])的臭味.

dep *abbr* 缩写 = **1** depart(s); departed; departing; departure: *dep Paris 23.05 hrs* 23时05分自巴黎开出. Cf 参看 ARR 2. **2** deputy.

de·part /dɪˈpɑːt; dɪˋpɑrt/ *v* (*fml* 文) **1** [I, Ipr] **~ (for...) (from...)** go away; leave 走开; 离开: *We departed for London at 10 am.* 我们上午10点动身去伦敦. ○ *The 10.15 to Leeds departs from platform 4.* 10点15分开往利兹的火车在第4站台上车. **2** (idm 习语) **depart (from) this ˈlife** (*arch or rhet* 古或修辞) die 去世; 亡故. **3** (phr v) **depart from sth** behave in a way that differs from (what is usual or expected) 背离; 违反: *depart from routine, standard practice, old customs, etc* 违反常规、惯例、旧风俗等 ○ *depart from the truth*, ie not be truthful 背离事实.

de·par·ted /dɪˈpɑːtɪd; dɪˋpɑrtɪd/ *adj* [esp attrib 尤作定语] **1** (*fml or euph* 文或婉) dead 死去的; 故去的: *our departed heroes*, eg soldiers who died in battle 我们那些与世长辞的英雄(如阵亡的士兵) ○ *your dear departed brother* 你挚爱的已故兄长. **2** (*fml* 文) past; bygone 过去的; 以往的: *thinking of departed glories* 怀念过去的光荣.

▷ **the departed** *n* (*pl* unchanged 复数不变) person who has died 死去的人: *pray for the soul(s) of the departed* 为死者的灵魂祈祷.

D

de·part·ment /dɪˈpɑːtmənt; dɪˋpɑrtmənt/ *n* **1** (*abbr* 缩写 **Dept**) each of several divisions of a government, business, shop, university, etc (政府、企业、商店、大学等的)部, 司, 局, 处, 科, 部门, 系: *the Department of the Environment* 环境部 ○ *the Education Department* 教育部 ○ *the export sales department* 出口销售部 ○ *the men's clothing department* 男装部. **2** area of activity or knowledge 活动范围; 知识领域: *Don't ask me about our finances: that's my wife's department.* 我们家的经济情况你别问我, 那是我妻子的事. **3** administrative district, eg in France 行政区, 省(如法国的).

▷ **de·part·mental** /ˌdiːpɑːtˈmentl; ˌdipɑrtˋmɛntl/ *adj* of a department, rather than the whole organization 部门的(非整个组织的): *a departmental manager, meeting* 部门的经理、会议.

□ **deˈpartment store** large shop where many kinds of goods are sold in different departments 百货公司.

de·par·ture /dɪˈpɑːtʃə(r); dɪˋpɑrtʃɚ/ *n* **1** (**a**) [U] **~ (from...)** departing; going away 离开; 离去: *His departure was quite unexpected.* 他这一走很出人意料. ○ [attrib 作定语] *the departure lounge*, ie in an airport 候机室. (**b**) [C] instance of this 离开; 离去: *notices showing arrivals and departures of trains* 列车到达和开出时刻的公告. **2** (**a**) [C, U] **~ from sth** action different from (what is usual or expected) 背离; 违反: *a departure from old customs, the standard procedure, etc* 同旧习俗、标准程序等相违. (**b**) [C] course of action; venture 行动; 大胆行事: *Working on a farm is a new departure for him.* 对他来说, 在农场工作是一种新的尝试. **3** (idm 习语) **a point of departure** ⇨ POINT[1].

de·pend /dɪˈpend; dɪˋpɛnd/ *v* **1** (idm 习语) **that deˈpends; it (all) deˈpends** (used alone, or at the beginning of a sentence 单独使用, 或用于句首) the result will be decided by sth mentioned or implied 那得看情况: *'Can I come?' 'That depends: there might not be room in the car.'* '我能来吗?' '那要看情况, 汽车里可能没有空座了.' ○ *It depends how you tackle the problem.* 那取决于你如何解决这个问题. **2** (phr v) **depend on/upon sb/sth** (**a**) be sure, or confidently expect, that sth will happen 确信; 坚信; 信赖: *I'm depending on you coming.* 我肯定你会来的. ○ *You can never depend on his arriving on time.* 决不可指望他能准时到达. ○ (*ironic* 反语) *You can depend on her to be* (ie She always is) *late.* 可以担保她必定迟到. ○ *Depend on it* (ie You can be sure): *we won't give up.* 可以打包票, 我们决不会放弃. (**b**) (be able to) believe that sb/sth will be reliable (能)相信某人[某事物]可靠: *You can't depend on the train arriving on time.* 千万不要认为这列火车能正点到达. ○ *She's a woman who can be depended on.* 她是个可以信赖的人. **depend on sb/sth (for sth)** (usu not in the continuous tenses 通常不用于进行时态) (**a**) need sb/sth for a particular purpose (因某目的)需要某人[某事物]: *I haven't got a car, so I have to depend on the buses.* 我没有汽车, 所以我得乘公共汽车. ○ *We depend on the radio for news.* 我们靠收音机听新闻. (**b**) get money or other help from sb/sth 从某人[某事物]处得到钱或其他帮助: *This area depends on the mining industry.* 这个地区以采矿业为经济基础. ○ *Children depend on their parents for food and clothing.* 儿童靠父母供给衣食. **depend on sth** be decided by sth; follow from sth 视某事物而定; 取决于某事物: *A lot will depend on how she responds to the challenge.* 在很大程度上将取决于她对这一难题的反应. ○ *How much is produced depends on how hard we work.* 产量的大小在于我们努力的程度.

▷ **de·pend·able** *adj* that may be depended on 可信赖的; 可靠的: *a dependable friend, car, service* 可靠的朋友、汽车、服务. **de·pend·ab·il·ity** /dɪˌpendəˈbɪlətɪ; dɪˌpɛndəˋbɪlətɪ/ *n* [U]. **de·pend·ably** /-əblɪ; -əblɪ/ *adv*.

de·pend·ant (also *esp US* **-ent**) /dɪˈpendənt; dɪˋpɛndənt/ *n* person who depends on others for a home, food, etc 依赖他人生活者; 受扶养者.

de·pend·ence /dɪˈpendəns; dɪˋpɛndəns/ *n* [U] **~ on/upon sb/sth** **1** trust in sb/sth; reliance on sb/sth 信赖; 信任: *my complete dependence on her skill and experience* 我对她的技巧和经验的完全信赖. **2** (**a**) state of having to be supported by others 依赖: *Find a job and end your dependence on your parents.* 找个工作, 别再依赖你父母了. (**b**) state of being affected by or needing sb/sth 依靠; 指望: *the dependence of the crops on the weather* 收成靠天 ○ *medical treatment for drug/alcohol dependence* 戒除毒瘾[酒瘾]的治疗.

de·pend·ency /dɪˈpendənsɪ; dɪˋpɛndənsɪ/ *n* country governed or controlled by another 附属国; 附属地: *The Hawaiian Islands are no longer a dependency of the USA.* 夏威夷群岛已不再是美国的属地.

de·pend·ent /dɪˈpendənt; dɪˋpɛndənt/ *adj* **1 ~ (on/upon sb/sth)** needing support from sb 需要某人支持的; 依靠的; 依赖的: *a woman with several dependent children* 带着几个无法自理的孩子的女人 ○ *be dependent on one's parents, a grant* 依靠父母[补助]. **2** [pred 作表语] **~ on/upon sth** affected or decided by sth 取决于某事物: *Success is dependent on how hard you work.* 成败取决于努力的程度. **3** [pred 作表语] **~ on/upon sth** needing sth physically 肉体上需要某物: *be dependent on drugs/alcohol* 有毒瘾[酒瘾]. ▷ **de·pend·ent** *n* (*esp US*) = DEPENDANT.

□ **deˌpendent ˈclause** = SUBORDINATE CLAUSE (SUBORDINATE).

de·pict /dɪˈpɪkt; dɪˋpɪkt/ *v* [Tn, Cn·n/a, Cn·g] (**a**) show (sb/sth) as a picture; portray 描绘(某人[某事物]); 描画: *a picture depicting him as a clown* 把他画成小丑的画 ○ *The drawing depicts her sitting on a sofa.* 这幅画画的是她坐在沙发上的姿势. (**b**) describe (sth) in words 描述, 描写(某事物): *Her novel depicts life in modern London (as an ordeal).* 她的小说描写的是伦敦现代的生活(苦不堪言). ▷ **de·pic·tion** /dɪˈpɪkʃn; dɪˋpɪkʃən/ *n* [U, C].

de·pil·at·ory /dɪˈpɪlətrɪ; *US* -tɔːrɪ; dɪˋpɪlə,torɪ/ *n, adj* (liquid, cream, etc) used for removing excess hair 用以脱毛的(液、膏、霜、油等); 脱毛的; 脱毛剂.

de·plane /ˌdiːˈpleɪn; diˋplen/ *v* [I, Tn] (cause sb to) leave an aircraft (使某人)下飞机: *The troops (were) deplaned an hour later.* 部队一个小时后下了飞机.

de·plete /dɪˈpliːt; dɪˋplit/ *v* [Tn, Tn·pr] reduce greatly the quantity, size, power or value of (sth) 大量削减(某物)的数量、能力或价值; 消耗: *Our stock of food is greatly depleted.* 我们的食物储备已消耗殆尽. ○ *This expense has depleted our funds.* 这笔花费已使我们的资金所剩无几. ○ *a lake depleted of fish*, ie with many of the fish gone 几乎无鱼的湖.

▷ **de·ple·tion** /dɪˈpliːʃn; dɪˋpliʃən/ *n* [U] depleting or being depleted 削减; 消耗.

de·plore /dɪˈplɔː(r); dɪˋplɔr/ *v* [Tn] (**a**) be shocked or offended by (sth); condemn 被(某事物)震惊或触犯; 谴责: *She deplored his scandalous actions.* 她谴责他那令人愤慨的行为. (**b**) feel sorrow or regret about (sth) 对(某事物)感到悲伤或悔恨.

▷ **de·plor·able** /dɪˈplɔːrəbl; dɪˋplɔrəbl/ *adj* that is, or should be, condemned (应)受谴责的: *a deplorable attitude, speech* 应受谴责的态度、讲话 ○ *The acting was deplorable!* 这种演技糟透了! **de·plor·ably** /-əblɪ; -əblɪ/ *adv*.

de·ploy /dɪˈplɔɪ; dɪˋplɔɪ/ *v* **(a)** [I, Tn] (cause troops, etc to) move into the correct position for battle (使部队等)进入战斗位置; 调度, 部署(军队等): *The infantry began to deploy at dawn.* 步兵黎明时开始进入战斗位置. ○ *Artillery was deployed in the west.* 炮兵部署在西边. **(b)** [Tn] use (sth) effectively 有效地使用(某物): *deploy one's arguments, resources, etc* 有效地利用论据、资源等. ▷ **de·ploy·ment** *n* [U].

de·pon·ent /dɪˈpəʊnənt; dɪˋponənt/ *n* (*law* 律) person who makes a written statement for use in a lawcourt (给法庭提供书面证词的)证人.

de·popu·late /ˌdiːˈpɒpjʊleɪt; diˋpɑpjəˌlet/ *v* [Tn] reduce the number of people living in (a city, state, etc) 减少(某城市、州等)的人口: *a country depopulated by war, famine, disease, etc* 因战争、饥荒、疾病等而人口下降的国家. ▷ **de·popu·la·tion** /ˌdiːpɒpjʊˈleɪʃn; ˌdipɑpjəˋleʃən/ *n* [U].

de·port /dɪˈpɔːt; dɪˋpɔrt/ *v* [Tn, Tn·pr] **~ sb (from ...)** legally force (a foreigner, criminal, etc) to leave a country 将(外国人、罪犯等)驱逐出境: *He was convicted of drug offences and deported.* 他被判犯有毒品罪而遭驱逐出境.
▷ **de·porta·tion** /ˌdiːpɔːˈteɪʃn; ˌdipɔrˋteʃən/ *n* [C, U] (instance of) deporting or being deported 驱逐出境: *Years ago convicted criminals in England could face deportation to Australia.* 很多年以前, 英国已定罪的犯人可能被驱逐到澳大利亚.
de·portee /ˌdiːpɔːˈtiː; ˌdipɔrˋti/ *n* person who is or has been deported 被驱逐出境的人.

de·port·ment /dɪˈpɔːtmənt; dɪˋpɔrtmənt/ *n* [U] (*fml* 文) **(a)** (*Brit*) way of standing and walking; bearing 举止; 风度; 仪态: *Young ladies used to have lessons in deportment.* 少女以前要上仪态课. **(b)** (*US*) behaviour 行为; 举止.

de·pose /dɪˈpəʊz; dɪˋpoz/ *v* **1** [Tn] remove (esp a ruler such as a king) from power 罢免, 革除, 废黜(尤指统治者, 如国王). **2** [Ipr, Tf] **~ to doing sth** (*law* 律) give (usu written) evidence, esp on oath in a lawcourt (通常以书面)证明, 作证(尤指在法庭宣誓): *depose to having seen sth* 宣誓证明曾目睹某事物 ○ *depose that one saw sth* 宣誓证明亲眼见到某事物. Cf 参看 DEPOSITION.

de·posit[1] /dɪˈpɒzɪt; dɪˋpɑzɪt/ *v* [Tn, Tn·pr] **1 (a)** put (money) into a bank, esp to earn interest, etc 将(钱)存入银行: *The cheque was only deposited yesterday, so it hasn't been cleared yet.* 这张支票昨天才存入银行, 所以尚未兑现. **(b) ~ sth (with sb)** give (sth valuable or important) to sb to be kept in a safe place 将(有价值的或重要之物)交与某人保管: *deposit papers with one's lawyer* 将文件交与律师保管. **2 (a)** pay (sth) as part of a larger sum, the rest of which is to be paid later 付(定金): *I had to deposit 10% of the price of the house.* 我必须先付房价的10%作定钱. **(b)** pay (a sum) as a guarantee in case one damages or loses sth one is renting 付(押金): *You must deposit £500 as well as the first month's rent.* 你必须付500英镑押金及第一个月的租赁费. **3 ~ sth (on sth)** (*fml* 文) **(a)** lay or put sth down 放下某物: *He deposited the books on the desk.* 他把书放在办公桌上了. ○ *Some insects deposit their eggs on the ground.* 有些昆虫把卵产在地上. **(b)** (esp of liquids or a river) cause (mud, silt, etc) to settle (尤指液体、河流)使(淤泥等)沉积: *The Nile floods the fields and deposits mud on them.* 尼罗河泛滥, 在田野上淤积一层泥.

de·posit[2] /dɪˈpɒzɪt; dɪˋpɑzɪt/ *n* **1** [C] sum paid into an account, eg at a bank 存款: *a £10 deposit* 10英镑的存款 ○ *She made two deposits of £500 last month.* 她上月存了两笔500英镑的款. **2** [C] **~ (on sth) (a)** payment of a part of a larger sum, the rest of which is to be paid later 定金; 定钱: *The shop promised to keep the goods for me if I paid a deposit.* 商店答应, 倘若我付定金就给我保留这批货. **(b)** sum that sb pays in advance, in case he damages or loses sth he is renting 押金; 保证金: *I had to pay a £500 deposit to the landlord before I could move into the house.* 我得付给房东500英镑押金才能搬进房里去. **3** [C, U] **(a)** layer of matter laid down by a liquid, river, etc (液体、河流等的)沉积物: *A thick deposit of mud lay on the fields when the flood went down.* 洪水退后, 田野上留下一层厚泥. **(b)** layer of matter (often deep in the earth) that has accumulated naturally (常为在地层深处的)沉积物, 矿床: *Valuable deposits of oil have been found by drilling.* 通过钻探发现很有开采价值的油层. **4** (idm 习语) **on deˈposit** in a deposit account 在定期存款帐户中: *have £2 000 on deposit* 有2 000英镑定期存款.
□ **deˈposit account** type of account, usu at a bank, in which money earns interest but cannot be taken out unless the bank is warned in advance 定期存款帐户. Cf 参看 CURRENT ACCOUNT (CURRENT[1]), SAVINGS ACCOUNT (SAVING).

de·pos·ition /ˌdepəˈzɪʃn; ˌdɛpəˋzɪʃən/ *n* **1** [U] removing (a ruler such as a king) from power; dethronement (对国王等统治者的)废黜, 罢免. **2** [U, C] (*law* 律) (action of making a) statement on oath 宣誓作证; (经宣誓的)证词: *The accused has made a deposition.* 被告已宣誓作证. Cf 参看 DEPOSE.

de·pos·itor /dɪˈpɒzɪtə(r); dɪˋpɑzɪtɚ/ *n* person who deposits (eg money in a bank) 存放者(如在银行存钱); 存户; 储户.

de·pos·itory /dɪˈpɒzɪtərɪ; dɪˋpɑzəˌtorɪ/ *n* place where things, eg furniture, are stored; storehouse 储藏室; 仓库.

de·pot /ˈdepəʊ; ˋdɛpo/ *n* **(1) (a)** storehouse, esp for military supplies; warehouse 仓库; (尤指)军需库; 栈房. **(b)** place where vehicles, eg buses, are kept 车库(如公共汽车的). **(2)** (*US*) railway or bus station 火车站; 公共汽车站.

de·prave /dɪˈpreɪv; dɪˋprev/ *v* [Tn esp passive 尤用于被动语态] (*fml* 文) make (sb) morally bad; corrupt 使(某人)道德败坏; 使堕落; 使腐化: *a man depraved by bad company* 被坏朋友带坏的人.
▷ **de·prava·tion** /ˌdeprəˈveɪʃn; ˌdɛprəˋveʃən/ *n* [U].
de·praved /dɪˈpreɪvd; dɪˋprevd/ *adj* morally bad; corrupt 道德败坏的; 堕落的; 腐化的: *depraved thoughts, morals, companions* 堕落的思想、道德、伙伴 ○ *He was totally depraved.* 他彻底堕落了.

de·pravity /dɪˈprævətɪ; dɪˋprævətɪ/ *n* **1** [U] state of being depraved; corruption 堕落; 腐化: *a life of depravity* 腐化的生活 ○ *sunk in depravity* 堕落. **2** [C] depraved act 堕落的行为: *the depravities of a corrupt ruler* 腐败的统治者的堕落行为.

de·prec·ate /ˈdeprəkeɪt; ˋdɛprəˌket/ *v* (*fml* 文) **(a)** [Tn, Tw, Tg, Tsg] feel and express disapproval of (sth) 对(某事物)表示不赞成; 反对: *Hasty action is to be deprecated.* 切不可草率行事. ○ *He deprecates (her) changing the party's policy.* 他不赞成(她)改变党的方针. **(b)** [Tn, Tw] feel embarrassed or displeased by (sb's flattery, etc) 因(某人的奉承等)觉得难为情或不自在: *deprecate sb's compliments, condescending charm* 对某人的奉承话、屈尊俯就的态度觉得不自在.
▷ **de·prec·at·ing** *adj*: *a deprecating smile* 不以为然的微笑. **de·prec·at·ingly** adv. **de·prec·at·ory** /ˌdeprɪˈkeɪtərɪ; *US* -tɔːrɪ; ˋdɛprəkəˌtorɪ/ *adj*: *a deprecatory remark, view, etc* 表示不悦的言语、观点等.

de·pre·ci·ate /dɪˈpriːʃɪeɪt; dɪˋpriʃɪˌet/ *v* **1** [I] become less valuable 贬值: *Shares in the company have depreciated.* 该公司的股票已经贬值. **2** [Tn] state that (sth) is not valuable, important, etc; disparage 贬低; 轻视: *Don't depreciate my efforts to help/what I have done.* 不要轻视我为帮忙所付出的努力[我已做的事]. ▷ **de·pre·ci·ation** /dɪˌpriːʃɪˈeɪʃn; dɪˌpriʃɪˋeʃən/ *n* [C, U]: *suffer a sharp depreciation* 遭受巨大贬值损失. **de·pre·ci·at·ory** /dɪˈpriːʃətərɪ; *US* -tɔːrɪ; dɪˋpriʃəˌtorɪ/ *adj*: *depreciatory remarks about a great achievement* 对一巨大成就的轻蔑言论.

de·preda·tion /ˌdeprəˈdeɪʃn; ˌdɛprɪˋdeʃən/ *n* [pl] (*fml* 文) damage caused by an attack, accident, etc (由攻击、事故等造成的)损坏, 破坏: *The town survived the depredations of marauding gangs.* 这个城镇经受住了打家劫舍的匪徒造成的破坏. ○ *the depredations of the storm* 暴风雨的蹂躏.

de·press /dɪˈpres; dɪˋprɛs/ *v* [Tn] **1** make (sb) sad and without enthusiasm 使(某人)忧愁, 消沉, 沮丧: *Wet weather always depresses me.* 我在阴雨天总是心灰意懒. **2** press, push or pull (sth) down 将(某物)压下, 推下, 拉下: *depress a lever, a piano key, a button, etc* 压杠杆、按钢琴键、按钮. **3** make (esp trade) less active 使(尤指贸易)不活跃, 不景气, 萧条: *depress a market* 使市场萧条 ○ *depress sales* 使销售额下降 ○ *A rise in oil prices*

D

depresses the car market. 油价上涨导致汽车市场不景气.
▷ **de·press·ant** /-ənt; -nt/ *n, adj* (substance) that reduces mental or physical activity 抑制(脑力或体力活动)的(药物): *a depressant drug* 抑制药.

de·pressed *adj* sad and without enthusiasm 忧愁的; 消沉的; 沮丧的: *depressed about the election results* 因选举结果而垂头丧气.

de·press·ing *adj* making one feel depressed 令人忧愁的; 使人沮丧的: *a depressing sight, prospect, film* 令人沮丧的景象、前景、影片. **de·press·ingly** *adv*: *The crime rate is depressingly high.* 犯罪率太高, 令人忧心忡忡.

□ ˌ**depressed ˈarea** part of a country where there is little economic activity (resulting in poverty and unemployment) (一国的)经济萧条地区.

de·pres·sion /dɪˈpreʃn; dɪˈprɛʃən/ *n* **1** [U] being depressed; low spirits 忧愁; 沮丧; 消沉: *He committed suicide during a fit of depression.* 他一时想不开, 自杀了. **2** [C] hollow sunken place in the surface of sth, esp the ground; dip 凹陷处; (尤指)洼地, 坑: *depressions on the face of the moon* 月球表面的凹陷处 ○ *The soldiers hid from the enemy in a slight depression.* 士兵们隐藏在低洼处, 躲过了敌人. **3** [C] period when there is little economic activity, and usu poverty and unemployment 经济萧条期. **4** [C] **(a)** (winds caused by a) lowering of atmospheric pressure 气压降低(形成的气流). **(b)** area where this happens 低气压区: *a depression over Iceland* 冰岛上空的低气压区. Cf 参看 ANTICYCLONE.

de·press·ive /dɪˈpresɪv; dɪˈprɛsɪv/ *adj* **1** tending to depress; of depression 忧愁的; 压抑的; 沮丧的; 抑郁的: *a depressive drug, illness* 易产生抑郁的药物、疾病. **2** intended to reduce trading activity 为减少贸易活动的: *a depressive financial policy* 为抑制贸易活动而采取的金融方针.

▷ **de·press·ive** *n* person who often suffers from depression(1) 经常忧愁、沮丧、消沉的人.

de·pres·sur·ize, -ise /ˌdiːˈpreʃəraɪz; diˈprɛʃəˌraɪz/ *v* [Tn] reduce the pressure of air or gas in (a vessel, cabin, etc) 减低, 降低(容器、舱室等)的气压. ▷ **de·pres·sur·iza·tion, -isation** *n* [U].

de·prive /dɪˈpraɪv; dɪˈpraɪv/ *v* [Tn·pr] **~ sb/sth of sth** take sth away from sb/sth; prevent sb/sth from enjoying or using sth 剥夺某人[某事物]的某事物; 阻止某人[某事物]享有或使用某事物: *deprived of one's civil rights* 剥夺某人的公民权 ○ *trees that deprive a house of light* 遮住房中光线的树 ○ (*joc* 谑) *Are you depriving us of your company* (ie leaving us)? 你要舍我们而去吗?

▷ **de·priva·tion** /ˌdeprɪˈveɪʃn; ˌdɛprɪˈveʃən/ *n* **1** [U] **(a)** depriving or being deprived 剥夺: *suffer deprivation of one's rights as a citizen* 公民权遭到剥夺. **(b)** state of not having the normal benefits of adequate food, etc; poverty 贫乏; 穷困: *widespread deprivation caused by unemployment* 由失业造成的普遍贫困现象. **2** [C] thing of which one is deprived 被剥夺的事物; 丧失的事物: *Missing the holiday was a great deprivation.* 错过假日是极大的损失.

de·prived *adj* without the normal benefits of adequate food, housing, health care, etc 贫困的; 穷苦的: *a deprived childhood, background, area* 贫苦的童年、出身、地区 ○ *The poorest and most deprived people will receive special government help.* 最穷的、生活条件最差的人可得到政府的特别援助.

Dept *abbr* 缩写 = Department(1): *Linguistics Dept*, eg of a university 语言学系(如大学的).

depth /depθ; dɛpθ/ *n* **1** [C, U] **(a)** distance from the top down 深, 深度(从上至下的距离): *the depth of the well, mine, box, trunk* 井、矿井、盒、行李箱的深度 ○ *Water was found at a depth of 30 ft.* 在30英尺深处找到了水. ○ *At what depth does the wreck lie?* 沉船位置的深度是多少? ⇨illus at DIMENSION 见DIMENSION之插图. **(b)** distance from the front to the back 宽, 宽度(从前至后的距离): *shelves with a depth of 8 ins* 8英寸宽的搁板. **(c)** distance from the surface inwards 深, 深度(从表面向内部的距离): *the depth of a wound, crack, etc* 伤口、裂缝等的深度. **2** [C, U] **(a)** (of colours, darkness, etc) intensity (指颜色、黑暗等)浓度, 强度. **(b)** (of sounds) lowness in pitch (指声音)低沉. **3** [U] **(a)** (of feelings, etc) sincerity; intensity (指感情等)诚挚, 真诚, 强烈: *the depth of her love* 她爱情的真挚. **(b)** ability to understand or explain difficult ideas 领悟或解释深奥意念的能力: *a writer of great depth and wisdom* 极具领悟力和智慧的作家. **(c)** having or showing this ability 上述能力的体现: *a novel that lacks depth* 缺乏深度的小说. **4** (idm 习语) ˌ**in ˈdepth** thoroughly 完全地; 彻底地; 深入地: *to study a subject in depth* 深入研究一科目 ○ [attrib 作定语] *an* ˌ*in-depth* ˈ*study* 深入的研究. **in the ~(s) of sth** when or where sth is deepest, most severe, etc 在最深处; 在最严峻的时刻: *in the depth of winter* 在隆冬 ○ *in the depths of despair* 在绝望的深渊 ○ *in the depth of the country*, ie a long way from a town 在偏远的乡村. **(be/get) out of one's depth (a)** (be/go) in water too deep to stand in 在深得不能站立的水中: *If you can't swim, don't get out of your depth.* 不会游泳就不要到水深没顶的地方去. **(b)** (be/become) unable to understand a subject or topic 不能理解: *When they start talking about economics, I'm out of my depth.* 他们一谈起经济学, 我就一窍不通了. **plumb the depths of sth** ⇨ PLUMB.

□ ˈ**depth charge** bomb used against submarines that explodes under water 深水炸弹. Cf 参看 MINE² 2.

de·pu·ta·tion /ˌdepjʊˈteɪʃn; ˌdɛpjəˈteʃən/ *n* [CGp] group of people given the right to act or speak for others 代表团.

de·pute /dɪˈpjuːt; dɪˈpjut/ *v* (*fml* 文) **1** [Dn·pr] **~ sth to sb** give (one's work, authority, etc) to sb else 将(工作、职权等)交予某人: *He deputed the running of the department to an assistant.* 他把部门的管理工作委托给助手了. **2** [Dn·t] give (sb else) authority to act or speak on one's behalf 给予(某人)代表行事或发言之权: *They were deputed to put our views to the assembly.* 他们代表我们向议会表达我们的观点.

depu·tize, -ise /ˈdepjʊtaɪz; ˈdɛpjəˌtaɪz/ *v* [I, Ipr] **~ (for sb)** act or speak on sb's behalf 代表某人行事或说话: *Dr Mitchell's ill so I'm deputizing (for her).* 米切尔博士病了, 所以我做代理(她的)工作.

dep·uty /ˈdepjʊtɪ; ˈdɛpjətɪ/ *n* **1** person who is given work, authority, etc (eg during sb's absence) 代理人; 代表: *I'm acting as deputy till the headmaster returns.* 我在校长回来前代行他的职务. **2** person who is immediately below the head of a business, school, etc (企业、学校等领导人的)副手: *the Director General and his deputy* 董事长及其副手 ○ [attrib 作定语] *the deputy headmistress* 女副校长. **3** (in some countries, eg France) member of a legislative assembly (某些国家中, 如法国的)议员.

de·rail /dɪˈreɪl; dɪˈrel/ *v* [Tn] cause (a train, etc) to go off the rails 使(火车等)脱轨: *The engine was derailed by a tree lying across the line.* 有一棵树横在铁轨上, 造成机车出轨. ▷ **de·rail·ment** *n*.

de·ranged /dɪˈreɪndʒd; dɪˈrendʒd/ *adj* unable to act and think normally, esp because of mental illness; seriously disturbed 精神错乱的; (尤指)有精神病的; 精神失常的: *She's completely deranged.* 她完全精神错乱了. ○ *a deranged attacker, mind, laugh* 疯狂的攻击者、失常的心态、狂笑. **de·range·ment** *n* [U].

derby¹ /ˈdɑːbɪ; *US* ˈdɜːrbɪ; ˈdɝbɪ/ *n* **1 the Derby** [sing] annual horse race at Epsom, England 德比马赛(英国埃普瑟姆一年一度的马赛). **2** [C] (*US*) any of several annual horse races (每年举行的任何的)马赛. **3** [C] any important sporting contest (任何重要的)运动比赛: *a local derby*, ie between local teams 本地的运动比赛.

□ ˈ**Derby Day** day when the Derby is run (in June) (英国埃普瑟姆一年一度的)马赛日(在六月份).

derby² /ˈdɜːrbɪ; ˈdɝbɪ/ *n* (*US*) = BOWLER².

de·regu·late /ˌdiːˈregjʊleɪt; diˈrɛgjəˌlet/ *v* [Tn] remove the regulations from (sth) 撤销对(某事物)的规定、管制: *deregulate the price of oil* 撤销对石油价格的管制. ▷ **de·regu·la·tion** *n* [U].

der·el·ict /ˈderəlɪkt; ˈdɛrəˌlɪkt/ *adj* deserted and allowed to fall into ruins; dilapidated 弃置的; 破旧的; 坍塌的: *a derelict house* 弃置的房屋 ○ *derelict areas* 离弃的地区.

▷ **der·el·ic·tion** /ˌderəˈlɪkʃn; ˌdɛrəˈlɪkʃən/ *n* **1** [U] being derelict 遗弃; 弃置: *a house in a state of dereliction* 弃置的房屋. **2** (idm 习语) ˌ**dereliction of ˈduty** (*fml* 文) (deliberate) failure to do what one ought to do 失职: *be guilty of a serious dereliction of duty* 犯严重失职罪.

de·res·trict /ˌdiːrɪˈstrɪkt; ˌdirɪˈstrɪkt/ *v* [Tn] remove a restriction, esp a speed limit, from (sth) 取消对(某事

物)的限制(尤指车速): *derestrict a road* 取消对一公路的速度限制.

de·ride /dɪˈraɪd; dɪˋraɪd/ *v* [Tn, Cn·n/a] **~ sb/sth (as sth)** treat sb/sth as funny and not worthy of serious attention; mock sb/sth 嘲笑; 嘲弄: *They derided his efforts (as childish).* 他们嘲笑他的做法(很幼稚).

de rigueur /də rɪˈgɜ:(r); dərɪˋgɝ/ (*French* 法) required by etiquette or custom 按照礼仪或风俗所要求的: *Evening dress is de rigueur at the Casino.* 在赌博娱乐场要穿晚礼服.

de·ri·sion /dɪˈrɪʒn; dɪˋrɪʒən/ *n* [U] ridicule or mockery 嘲笑; 嘲弄; 笑柄: *be an object of general derision*, ie be derided by everybody 是大家嘲弄的对象 ○ *Her naive attitude provoked their derision.* 她那天真的态度受到他们嘲笑.

de·ris·ive /dɪˈraɪsɪv; dɪˋraɪsɪv/ *adj* showing ridicule or mockery 嘲笑的; 嘲弄的: *derisive laughter, booing, etc* 嘲弄的笑声、嘘声等. ▷ **de·ris·ively** *adv*.

de·ris·ory /dɪˈraɪsərɪ; dɪˋraɪsərɪ/ *adj* **1** so small or unimportant that it is not worth considering seriously 不值一哂的: *a derisory offer*, eg £100 for a car that is worth £1 000 低得可笑的出价(如对价值1 000英镑的汽车, 出价100英镑). **2** = DERISIVE.

de·riva·tion /ˌderɪˈveɪʃn; ˌdɛrəˋveʃən/ *n* **1** [U] development or origin (esp of words) 发展; 起源; (尤指词语的)派生: *the derivation of words from Latin* 词语自拉丁文的派生 ○ *a word of French derivation* 由法语派生的词. **2** [C] **(a)** first form and meaning of a word 词源. **(b)** later change of form and meaning 派生的词形和词义: *give the derivations of words* 指出词语的派生词形和词义.

de·riv·at·ive /dɪˈrɪvətɪv; dəˋrɪvətɪv/ *adj* (*usu derog* 通常作贬义) derived from sth else; not original 由他事物演变的; 非独创的: *a derivative design, style, etc* 蹈袭前人的设计、式样等.

▷ **de·riv·at·ive** *n* derived word or thing 派生词; 衍生物: *'Assertion' is a derivative of 'assert'.* assertion是assert的派生词.

de·rive /dɪˈraɪv; dəˋraɪv/ *v* **1** [Tn·pr] **~ sth from sth** (*fml* 文) obtain sth from sth; get sth from sth 得到; 获取: *derive great pleasure from one's studies* 从学习中获得极大乐趣 ○ *She derived no benefit from the course of drugs.* 她用药经此疗程后并无好转. **2** **(a)** [Ipr] **~ from sth** have sth as a starting-point, source or origin; originate from sth 源自; 源于: *Thousands of English words derive from Latin.* 英语中有成千上万的词源自拉丁文. **(b)** [Tn·pr] **~ sth from sth** trace sth from (a source) 对某事物追本穷源: *We can derive the word 'derelict' from the Latin 'derelictus'.* derelict这一词的起源可以追溯到拉丁文的derelictus.

derm(a)- *comb form* 构词成分 of skin 皮肤的: *dermatology* ○ *dermatitis*.

der·ma·titis /ˌdɜ:məˈtaɪtɪs; ˌdɝməˋtaɪtɪs/ *n* [U] (*medical* 医) inflammation of the skin 皮炎.

der·ma·to·logy /ˌdɜ:məˈtɒlədʒɪ; ˌdɝməˋtɑlədʒɪ/ *n* [U] medical study of the skin and its diseases, etc 皮肤学; 皮肤病学.

▷ **der·ma·to·logist** /ˌdɜ:məˈtɒlədʒɪst; ˌdɝməˋtɑlədʒɪst/ *n* expert in dermatology 皮肤学专家; 皮肤病专家.

dermis /ˈdɜ:mɪs; ˋdɝmɪs/ *n* (*anatomy* 解) layer of skin below the epidermis 真皮(表皮下面的皮层).

der·og·ate /ˈderəgeɪt; ˋdɛrəˌget/ *v* [Ipr] **~ from sth** (*fml* 文) cause sth to seem inferior; detract from sth 贬低; 减损; 毁损: *remarks derogating from her merits, qualities, virtues, etc* 贬低她的优点、品质、美德等的言语.

de·rog·at·ory /dɪˈrɒgətrɪ; *US* -tɔ:rɪ; dɪˋrɑgəˌtɔrɪ/ *adj* (*abbr* **derog** in this dictionary 本词典缩写作 **derog**) showing a hostile or critical attitude (to sb's reputation, etc); insulting 贬低的; 毁损的; 贬抑的; 侮辱的: *The word 'pig' is a derogatory term for policeman.* pig是个侮辱警察的词. ○ *remarks that were highly derogatory* 极伤人的言语.

der·rick /ˈderɪk; ˋdɛrɪk/ *n* **1** large crane for moving or lifting heavy weights, esp on a ship 转臂起重机; (尤指轮船上的)桅杆起重机. **2** framework over an oil well or borehole, to hold the drilling machinery, etc 井架; 钻塔. Cf 参看 OIL RIG (OIL).

derring-do /ˌderɪŋˈdu:; ˋdɛrɪŋˋdu/ *n* [U] (*arch or joc* 古或谑) heroic deeds 英勇事迹: *stirring tales of derring-do* 讲述英勇事迹的激动人心的故事.

derv /dɜ:v; dɝv/ *n* [U] (*Brit*) fuel oil for diesel engines (from *d*iesel-*e*ngined *r*oad *v*ehicle) 柴油机燃油(由diesel-engined road vehicle 四词的首字母组成).

der·vish /ˈdɜ:vɪʃ; ˋdɝvɪʃ/ *n* member of a Muslim religious order (伊斯兰教的)托钵僧: *dancing dervishes*, ie those who take part in whirling dances 跳旋转舞蹈的托钵僧.

DES /ˌdi: i: ˈes; ˌdi i ˋɛs/ *abbr* 缩写 = (*Brit*) Department of Education and Science 教育暨科学部: *DES grants* 教育暨科学部拨款.

de·sal·in·ate /ˌdi:ˈsælɪneɪt; diˋsæləˌnet/ *v* [Tn] remove salt from (esp sea-water) 从(尤指海水)中除去盐分; 使脱盐. ▷ **de·sal·ina·tion** /ˌdi:ˌsælɪˈneɪʃn; ˌdisæləˋneʃən/ *n* [U].

de·scale /ˌdi:ˈskeɪl; diˋskel/ *v* [Tn] remove scale[1](3) from (eg the inside of boilers and kettles) 从(如锅炉和水壶的内壁)上除去水碱, 水锈.

des·cant /ˈdeskænt; ˋdɛskænt/ *n* (*music* 音) treble accompaniment (often improvised) which is sung or played to a melody 高音部伴奏或伴唱(常为即兴的).

▷ **des·cant** /dɪˈskænt; dɪˋskænt/ [Ipr] **~ on/upon sth** **1** (*music* 音) sing or play a descant on sth 为某乐曲作高音伴奏或伴唱. **2** (*fml* 文) talk for a long time about sth; comment on sth 长时间谈论某事; 评论某物: *descant endlessly on the Government's failings* 无尽无休地谈论政府的过失.

D

des·cend /dɪˈsend; dɪˋsɛnd/ *v* **1** (*fml* 文) **(a)** [I, Tn] come or go down (sth) 下来; 下去; 下降: *The balloon descended gradually as the air came out.* 气球空气外逸而缓缓下降. ○ *She descended the stairs.* 她走下楼梯. **(b)** [I] (of a hill, etc) lead downwards; slope (指山等)下倾, 下斜: *We turned the corner and saw that the road descended steeply.* 我们转过弯, 看到路陡然下倾. **2** [Ipr] **~ from sb** (of properties, qualities, rights) pass from father to son; be inherited by sb from sb (指财产、气质、权利)由父传子, 从某人处继承, 传下, 遗传: *The title descends to me from my father.* 这个头衔是由我父亲传给我的. **3** [I] (*fml* 文) (of night, darkness) fall (指夜、黑暗)降临: *Night descends quickly in the tropics.* 热带地区黑夜来得很快. **4** (idm 习语) **be descended from sb** have sb as an ancestor 为某人的后裔: *She claims to be descended from royalty.* 她声称她是皇室后裔. **5** (phr v) **descend on/upon sb/sth** **(a)** attack sb/sth suddenly 袭击某人[某物]: *The police descended on their hide-out.* 警察突袭了他们的藏身处. **(b)** visit sb/sth unexpectedly or inconveniently 出乎意料地或不合时宜地去见某人[来到某处]: *My sister's family is descending on us this weekend.* 想不到我姐姐一家本周末要到我们这里来. **descend to sth** (no passive 不用于被动语态) do or say sth that is mean and unworthy of one; stoop to sth 做或说卑鄙无耻的事; 降低身分或人格做某事: *descend to fraud, abuse, bad language* 堕落到去欺诈、辱骂、使用下流语言.

▷ **des·cend·ant** /-ənt; -ənt/ *n* person descended from another 后代; 后裔: *the descendants of Queen Victoria* 维多利亚女王的后裔. Cf 参看 ANCESTOR 1.

des·cent /dɪˈsent; dɪˋsɛnt/ *n* **1** **(a)** [C usu *sing* 通常作单数] coming or going down 下来; 下去: *The plane began its descent into Paris.* 飞机到巴黎开始降落. **(b)** [C] slope 斜坡: *Here there is a gradual descent to the sea.* 这里有个通向海的缓坡. **2** [U] origins; ancestry 出身; 血统; 祖先; 祖籍: *of French descent*, ie having French ancestors 祖籍法国 ○ *He traces his descent from the Stuart kings.* 他的祖先可追溯至斯图亚特国王. **3** [C] **~ (on/upon sb/sth)** (*fig* 比喻) **(a)** attack 攻击; 袭击: *the invaders' descent on the town* 入侵者对该城的攻击. **(b)** unexpected or inconvenient visit 出乎意料的或不合时宜的到访: *a sudden descent by tax officials* 税务官员之突然到来. **4** [sing] change to behaviour that is low and unworthy 堕落: *a sharp descent to violent abuse* 突然粗俗得破口大骂.

de·scribe /dɪˈskraɪb; dɪˋskraɪb/ *v* **1** [Tn, Tw, Cn·n/a, Dn·pr, Dpr·w] **~ sb/sth (to/for sb)**; **~ sb/sth as sth** say what sb/sth is like; depict sth in words 描述某人[某事物]; 叙述某事物; 形容: *Words cannot describe the beauty of the scene.* 那景色之美难以言传. ○ *Describe (to me) how you were received.* (跟我)说说接待你的情况. ○

She described it as red with pink frills. 她将之描述为红色的带有粉红色饰边. **2** [Cn·n/a] **~ sb/sth as sth** state sb/sth to be sth; call 叫做; 称做: *I hesitate to describe him as really clever.* 我很难说他真聪明. ○ *He describes himself as a doctor.* 他自称是医生. **3** [Tn] (**a**) draw (esp a geometrical figure) 画(尤指几何图形): *describe a circle with a pair of compasses* 用圆规画圆. (**b**) move along (a line, curve, etc) 沿(直线、曲线等)移动: *A bullet describes a curved path in the air.* 子弹在空中作曲线运动.

de·scrip·tion /dɪˈskrɪpʃn; dɪˋskrɪpʃən/ *n* **1** (**a**) [U] saying in words what sb/sth is like 对某人[某事物]的描述、叙述、形容: *He's not very good at description.* 他不大擅长描写叙述. ○ *The scenery was beautiful beyond description.* 那风景美丽得难以形容. (**b**) [C] picture in words 描绘: *Can you give me a description of the thief?* 你能给我形容一下那个窃贼的模样吗? **2** (preceded by *of* and an *adj* or *some, every, etc* 用于of和形容词或some、every等之后) (*infml* 口) type; sort 类型; 种类: *boats of every description* 各种类型的船 ○ *a house of some description* 某种类型的房子 ○ *wearing a dress of no particular description*, ie a very ordinary dress 穿着很普通的连衣裙 ○ *medals, coins and things of that description* 那一类的纪念章、硬币、东西. **3** (idm 习语) **answer to a description** ⇨ ANSWER². **beggar description** ⇨ BEGGAR.

D

de·script·ive /dɪˈskrɪptɪv; dɪˋskrɪptɪv/ *adj* **1** (**a**) giving a picture in words 描述的; 描写的: *a descriptive passage in a novel* 小说中的一段描写. (**b**) describing sth with skill 精于描述的: *a very descriptive account of a journey* 对旅程十分生动的叙述 ○ *The report was so descriptive, I felt as if I were there.* 这报道写得活色生香, 我也宛如身临其境. **2** (*grammar*) describing how language is actually used, without giving rules for how it ought to be used 描写语言的(描述语言的使用实况而不规定使用规则的).
▷ **de·script·ively** *adv*. **de·script·ive·ness** *n* [U].

des·cry /dɪˈskraɪ; dɪˋskraɪ/ *v* (*pt, pp* **descried**) [Tn] (*fml* 文) see (sth) esp a long way away; catch sight of 看见(某物)(尤指从远处); 望见: *I descry a sail on the horizon.* 我看见在天水交接处的轮船.

de·sec·rate /ˈdesɪkreɪt; ˋdɛsɪˌkret/ *n* [Tn] treat (a sacred thing or place) in an unworthy or evil way 亵渎(圣物或圣地): *desecrate a grave, chapel, monument, etc* 亵渎坟墓、小教堂、纪念碑等.
▷ **de·sec·ra·tion** /ˌdesɪˈkreɪʃn; ˌdɛsɪˋkreʃən/ *n* [U] desecrating or being desecrated 亵渎.

de·seg·reg·ate /ˌdiːˈsegrɪgeɪt; diˋsɛgrɪget/ *v* [Tn] end racial segregation in (sth) 废除(某事物)的种族隔离: *desegregate schools, buses* 废除学校里、公共汽车里的种族隔离. ▷ **de·seg·rega·tion** /ˌdiːˌsegrɪˈgeɪʃn; diˌsɛgrɪˋgeʃən/ *n* [U].

de·se·lect /ˌdiːsɪˈlekt; ˌdisəˋlɛkt/ *v* [Tn] (*Brit*) (of a local constituency party) reject (the existing Member of Parliament) as a candidate at a forthcoming election (指地方选区政党)否决(现任议员)作下届候选人. ▷ **de·se·lec·tion** *n* [U].

de·sens·it·ize, -ise /ˌdiːˈsensɪtaɪz; diˋsɛnsəˌtaɪz/ *v* [Tn] make (a patient, nerve, etc) insensitive or less sensitive to light, pain, etc 使(病人、神经等)对光、疼痛等无感觉或不敏感; 使脱敏: *desensitize an area of skin* 使一块皮肤脱敏 ○ (*fig* 比喻) *people who are morally desensitized* 道德观念不强的人. ▷ **de·sens·it·iza·tion, -isa·tion** /ˌdiːˌsensɪtaɪˈzeɪʃn; *US* -təˈz-; ˌdisɛnsətəˋzeʃən/ *n* [U].

de·sert¹ /dɪˈzɜːt; dɪˋzɝt/ *v* **1** [Tn] (**a**) go away from (a place) without intending ever to return 离弃(一地方); 放弃; 遗弃: *desert a house, city, etc* 离弃一所房屋、一座城市等 ○ *The village had been hurriedly deserted, perhaps because terrorists were in the area.* 全村人都匆匆逃走了, 或许因为该地区有恐怖分子. (**b**) leave (sb) without help or support; abandon 离弃(某人); 抛弃: *He deserted his wife and children and went abroad.* 他抛弃了妻子儿女, 出国去了. ○ *He has become so rude that his friends are deserting him.* 他变得十分粗野, 朋友们都不和他来往了. **2** [I, Ipr, Tn] leave (esp service in the armed forces, or a ship) without authority or permission; run away 擅自离开(尤指军中或船上的职守); 逃跑; 潜逃: *A soldier who deserts (his post) in time of war is punished severely.* 战争期间开小差的士兵要受到严惩. ○ *desert from the army* 开小差. **3** [Tn] fail (sb) when needed 在关键时使(某人)失望: *His courage/presence of mind deserted him.* 他丧失了勇气[再不能镇定自若].
▷ **de·serted** *adj* (**a**) with no one present 无人的: *a deserted street, area, etc* 空无一人的街道、地区等 ○ *The office was quite deserted.* 这个办公室里没有人. (**b**) abandoned 被离弃的; 被遗弃的; 被抛弃的: *a deserted hut, house, etc* 被离弃的小屋、房子等 ○ *a deserted wife*, ie one whose husband has left her 遭遗弃的妻子.
de·serter *n* person who deserts (desert¹ 2) 擅离职守者; 开小差者; 潜逃者.
de·ser·tion /dɪˈzɜːʃn; dɪˋzɝʃən/ *n* [C, U] (instance of) deserting or being deserted 离弃; 遗弃; 抛弃; 开小差: *Is desertion grounds for divorce?* 被配偶遗弃是离婚的理由吗? ○ *Desertion from the army is punishable by death.* 开小差可处死刑.

des·ert² /ˈdezət; ˋdɛzɚt/ *n* [C, U] (large area of) barren land, with very little water and vegetation, often sand-covered 沙漠; 荒漠; 荒原: *Vast areas of land have become desert.* 广大的地区均已变成沙漠. ○ *the Sahara Desert* 撒哈拉大沙漠 ○ [attrib 作定语] *desert wastes, sands, etc* 不毛的荒地、沙漠等.
□ ˌ**desert ˈisland** uninhabited island (esp in the tropics) 无人居住的岛(尤指热带地区的).

de·serts /dɪˈzɜːts; dɪˋzɝts/ *n* [pl] what one deserves 应得到的事物: *be rewarded/punished according to one's deserts* 受到应得的奖赏[惩罚] ○ *get/meet with one's just deserts* 得到应得的奖赏或惩罚.

de·serve /dɪˈzɜːv; dɪˋzɝv/ *v* (not used in the continuous tenses 不用于进行时态) **1** [Tn, Tt] be sth or have done sth for which one should receive (a reward, special treatment, etc); be entitled to; merit 应受(奖赏、特殊待遇等); 应得; 值得: *The article deserves careful study.* 这篇文章值得仔细研究. ○ *She deserves a reward for her efforts.* 她积极努力, 应得到奖赏. ○ *He richly deserved all that happened to him.* 他得到这一切确是受之无愧. ○ *They deserve to be sent to prison.* 他们应该入狱. ○ *much deserved praise* 受之无愧的赞扬. **2** (idm 习语) **deserve well/ill of sb** (*fml* 文) be worthy of good/bad treatment by sb 应该受到某人好的[坏的]待遇: *She deserves well of her employers.* 她应当受到雇主善待. **one good turn deserves another** ⇨ TURN².
▷ **de·serv·edly** /dɪˈzɜːvɪdlɪ; dɪˋzɝvɪdlɪ/ *adv* according to what is deserved; justly; rightly 应得地; 理所当然地; 恰如其分地: *She was deservedly praised.* 她受到了应得的表扬.

de·ser·ving /dɪˈzɜːvɪŋ; dɪˋzɝvɪŋ/ *adj* **~ (of sth)** worthy of help, praise, a reward, etc (帮助、赞扬、奖励等)应得的, 值得的: *give money to a deserving cause* 把钱捐给值得赞助的事业 ○ *be deserving of sympathy* 值得同情的 ○ *a very deserving case*, eg sb who used to be generous and now needs help 很值得帮助的人.

dés·ha·billé /ˌdeɪzæˈbiːeɪ; ˌdɛzəˋbil/ *n* [U] (*French* 法) state of being only partly dressed 衣着仅部分遮体: *appear in déshabillé* 出现时衣着随便.

de·sic·cant /ˈdesɪkənt; ˋdɛsəkənt/ *n* substance that absorbs moisture, and is often used to keep food in good condition 干燥剂.

de·sic·cate /ˈdesɪkeɪt; ˋdɛsəˌket/ *v* [Tn] remove all the moisture from (esp solid food) to preserve it 除去(尤指食物的)水分; 使脱水: *desiccated fruit/coconut* 水果[椰子]干.

de·sid·er·atum /dɪˌzɪdəˈrɑːtəm; dɪˌsɪdəˋretəm/ *n* (*pl* **-rata** /-ˈrɑːtə; -ˋrɑtə/) (*fml* 文) thing that is lacking and needed 需要的东西: *The report on the hospital mentions such desiderata as a supply of clean laundry.* 报告中提到该医院需要干净的洗换物品.

de·sign /dɪˈzaɪn; dɪˋzaɪn/ *n* **1** (**a**) [C] **~ (for sth)** drawing or outline from which sth may be made 图样; 设计图: *designs for a dress, a garden, an aircraft* 连衣裙、花园、飞机的设计图. (**b**) [U] art of making such drawings, etc 设计术; 制图术: *study textile design* 学习纺织品设计术 ○ *industrial design* 工业设计. **2** [U] general arrangement or planning (of a building, book, machine, picture, etc) (建筑物、书、机器、画等的)设计, 布局: *The building seats 2 000 people, but is of poor design.* 这座建筑物可容纳2 000人, 但设计很差. ○ *A machine of faulty design will not sell well.* 设计不良的机器销路不会好. **3** [C] arrangement of lines, shapes or figures as decoration on a carpet, vase, etc; pattern (地毯、花瓶等上的)装饰图案; 图案: *a bowl with a flower design* 有花卉图案的碗. **4** [U, C] purpose; intention 目的; 打算; 意向: *We don't know if it was done by accident or by design*, ie deliberately. 我们不知道那是偶然的还是故意的. ○ *His evil designs were frustrated.* 他的罪恶企图未能得逞. **5** (idm 习语) **have designs on sb/sth** intend to harm sb/sth or take sb/sth for oneself 企图伤害某人[某事物]; 企图将某人[某事物]据为己有: *She has designs on his money.* 她觊觎他的钱财. ○ *He has designs on her*, eg wants to seduce her. 他对她存心不良(如想诱奸她).

▷ **de·sign** *v* **1** (**a**) [I, Tn, Dn·n, Dn·pr] **~ sth (for sb/sth)** decide how sth will look, work, etc, esp by making plans, drawings or models of it 设计; 制图: *Do the Italians really design better than we do?* 意大利人真比我们会设计吗? ○ *design a car, a dress, a tool, an office* 设计汽车、连衣裙、工具、办公室 ○ *They've designed us a superb studio.* 他们给我们设计了一个极好的工作室. ○ *We design kitchens for today's cooks.* 我们为当今一代的厨师设计厨房. (**b**) [Tn, Tn·pr] think of and plan (a system, procedure, etc); devise 想出, 计划(一系统、步骤等); 谋划: *Can anyone design a better timetable?* 有人能定出更好的时间表吗? ○ *We shall have to design a new curriculum for the third year.* 我们得设计出三年级的新课程. **2** (idm 习语) **be designed for sb/sth**; **be designed as sth**; **be designed to do sth** be made or planned for a particular purpose or use 为某目的或用途而制造或计划: *The gloves were designed for extremely cold climates.* 这些手套是为严寒地区制造的. ○ *This course is designed as an introduction to the subject.* 这门课程是作为该科目的入门课而开设的. ○ *The route was designed to relieve traffic congestion.* 这条路是为缓解交通拥挤而开辟的. **de·sign·edly** /-ɪdlɪ; -ɪdlɪ/ *adv* intentionally; on purpose 有意地; 蓄意地; 故意地. **de·sign·ing** *n* [U] art of making designs (for machinery, dresses, etc) (机械、服装等的)设计术.

des·ig·nate[1] /ˈdezɪgneɪt, -nət; ˋdɛzɪg,net, -nət/ *adj* (following *ns* 用于名词之后) appointed to a job (but not yet having officially started it) 已受委任(而尚未上任)的: *the editor, director, archbishop, etc designate* 已受委任的编辑、董事、大主教等.

des·ig·nate[2] /ˈdezɪgneɪt; ˋdɛzɪg,net/ *v* **1** [Tn] mark or point out (sth) clearly 清楚地标出或指出(某事物): *designate the boundaries of sth* 标出某事物的分界线. **2** [esp passive 尤用于被动语态: Cn·n, Cn·n/a] **~ sb/sth (as) sth** (*fml* 文) (**a**) choose sb/sth for a special purpose 为某目的选择某人[某事物]: *The town has been designated (as) a development area.* 该城已被定为开发区. (**b**) give a particular name, title or position to sb 给某人某名称、称号、职务或地位: *She was designated (as) sportswoman of the year.* 她被命名为本年度的体坛明星. ○ *The chairman has designated Christina as his successor.* 主席已指定克里斯蒂娜作他的继任人.

des·ig·na·tion /ˌdezɪgˈneɪʃn; ˌdɛzɪgˋneʃən/ *n* (*fml* 文) **1** [U] **~ (as sth)** appointing of sb to an office 任命; 委派. **2** [C] name, title or description 名称; 称号; 称呼: *His official designation is Financial Controller.* 他的职称是财务总监.

de·signer /dɪˈzaɪnə(r); dɪˋzaɪnɚ/ *n* person whose job is designing (eg machinery, furniture, fashionable clothes) 设计者(如机器、家具、时装的设计人): *an industrial designer* 工业设计师 ○ *dressed by a leading New York designer* 穿着纽约主要设计师设计的服装 ○ [attrib 作定语] *designer jeans* 标有设计师姓名的牛仔裤 ○ (*joc* 谑) *designer stubble*, ie an unshaven look deliberately cultivated for effect (讲派头而不刮脸的)胡子拉碴.

de·sign·ing /dɪˈzaɪnɪŋ; dɪˋzaɪnɪŋ/ *adj* [usu attrib 通常作定语] (*derog* 贬) wanting to carry out one's own secret plans; cunning 别有用心的; 狡猾的: *Designing colleagues stopped them from promoting me.* 有些别有用心的同事阻止他们提拔我.

de·sir·able /dɪˈzaɪərəbl; dɪˋzaɪrəbl̩/ *adj* **1 ~ (that...)** worth having; to be wished for 值得有的; 想望的; 称心的; 合意的: *a desirable residence, solution* 称心的住所、解决方法 ○ *It is most desirable that they should both come.* 他们两人都来, 这最好不过了. **2** (of a person) arousing sexual desire (指人)引起性欲的, 性感的: *a very desirable woman* 非常性感的女子.

▷ **de·sir·ab·il·ity** /dɪˌzaɪərəˈbɪlətɪ; dɪˌzaɪrəˋbɪlətɪ/ *n* [U]. **de·sir·ably** /-rəblɪ; -rəblɪ/ *adv*.

de·sire[1] /dɪˈzaɪə(r); dɪˋzaɪr/ *n* **1** (**a**) [U] **~ (for sth/to do sth)** strong sexual longing 性欲; 情欲; 肉欲: *my desire for her/to make love with her* 我对她的强烈的情欲[与她做爱的强烈欲望]. (**b**) [C] instance of this 性欲; 情欲; 肉欲: *passionate, intense, strong, etc desires* 热切的、极大的、强烈的...性欲 ○ *satisfy one's desires* 满足性欲. **2** (**a**) [U] **~ (for sth/to do sth)** longing; craving 渴望; 欲望; 渴求; 热望: *They had little desire for wealth/to get rich.* 他们对财富[致富]无大欲望. ○ *his country's desire for friendly relations/to establish friendly relations* 他们国家对友好关系[建立友好关系]的热望. (**b**) [C] instance of this; wish 渴望; 欲望; 渴求; 热望: *enough to satisfy all your desires* 完全能满足你所有的愿望. **3** [C] person or thing that is wished for 想望的人或物: *She is my heart's desire.* 她是我心上人.

de·sire[2] /dɪˈzaɪə(r); dɪˋzaɪr/ *v* **1** (**a**) [Tn, Tf, Tt, Tnt] (*fml* 文) wish for (sth); want 希望得到(某事物); 想要: *We all desire happiness and health.* 我们都希望幸福和健康. ○ *Our holiday was all that could be desired*, ie was entirely satisfactory. 我们的假日称心如意. ○ *She desires you to come/that you come at once.* 她希望你立即来. ○ *I have long desired to meet them.* 我一直渴望见到他们. (**b**) [Tn] be sexually attracted to (sb) 被(某异性)吸引: *She desires his young, strong body.* 他年轻强壮的身体使她春心荡漾. **2** (idm 习语) **leave a lot, etc to be desired** ⇨ LEAVE[1].

de·sir·ous /dɪˈzaɪərəs; dɪˋzaɪrəs/ *adj* [pred 作表语] **~ of sth/doing sth**; **~ that...** (*fml or rhet* 文或修辞) having a wish for (sth); wanting 希望; 渴望: *desirous of peace* 渴望和平 ○ *desirous of restoring relations between our two countries* 渴望恢复我们两国之间的关系 ○ *desirous that these initiatives should lead to further exchanges* 希望这些主动的行动能促进交流.

de·sist /dɪˈzɪst; dɪˋzɪst/ *v* [I, Ipr] **~ (from sth/doing sth)** (*fml* 文) stop sth/doing sth; cease 停止某事物[不再做某事物]; 停止; 结束: *I wish he'd desist from entertaining his friends at all hours of the day and night.* 但愿他别再昼夜不分地招待他的朋友.

desk /desk; dɛsk/ *n* **1** piece of furniture with a flat or sloping top, often with drawers, at which one can read, write or do business 书桌; 办公桌: *an office desk* 办公桌 ○ *children seated at their desks* 坐在各自书桌前的儿童 ○ [attrib 作定语] *a desk job* 办公室的工作. ⇨illus at App 1 见附录1之插图, page xvi. **2** table or counter in a public building behind which a receptionist, cashier, etc works (接待员、出纳员等的)桌子, 柜台: *an enquiry/information desk* 问询处[问讯处] ○ *leave a message at the desk of the hotel* 在旅馆的服务处留言. **3** office, eg in a newspaper or ministry, that handles a particular matter 办事处(如报社或政府部门的); 部; 司; 组: *Jefferies is running the sports desk.* 杰弗里斯负责体育新闻组.

□ ˈ**desk clerk** (*US*) = CLERK 3.

ˈ**desk-top** /-tɒp; -,tɑp/ *n* top of a desk 桌面: [attrib 作定语] *a desk-top computer*, ie one that fits on a desk 台式计算机 ○ [attrib 作定语] *desk-top publishing*, ie using a microcomputer and (esp a laser) printer to produce high-quality printed material 桌面出版(使用微型计算机和印字机, 尤指激光印字机印刷的).

des·ol·ate /ˈdesələt; ˋdɛsl̩ɪt/ *adj* **1** (of a place) deserted and miserable (指地方)无人烟的, 荒凉的, 荒芜的: *a desolate industrial landscape* 工业废墟 ○ *a desolate, windswept moorland area* 荒凉的、受强风吹袭的高沼地区. **2** miserable and without friends; lonely and sad 凄凉而无友的; 孤凄的: *a desolate person, life, existence* 孤独而凄凉的人、生活、生活情况 ○ *We all felt absolutely desolate when she left.* 她走后, 我们都觉得万分孤寂.

▷ **des·ol·ate** /ˈdesəleɪt; ˋdɛsl̩,et/ *v* [Tn esp passive 尤用于被动语态] **1** leave (a place) ruined and deserted 使(某处)沦为废墟; 使荒凉: *a city desolated by civil strife* 遭内乱破坏的城市. **2** make (sb) sad and hopeless 使(某人)悲伤绝望: *a family desolated by the loss of a child* 因失去孩子而悲痛欲绝的一家人. **des·ol·ately** *adv*. **des·ola·tion** /ˌdesəˈleɪʃn; ˌdɛsəˋleʃən/ *n* [U]

D

1 desolating or being desolated (DESOLATE *v* 1) 遗弃; 荒凉; 破坏: *the desolation caused by war* 战争造成的满目疮痍. **2** misery; loneliness 凄凉; 孤寂: *her utter desolation when she heard the bad news* 她听到那坏消息时极度悲伤.

des·pair /dɪˈspeə(r); dɪˈspɛr/ *n* **1** [U] state of having lost all hope 失去一切希望; 绝望: *Your stupidity will drive me to* (ie make me feel) *despair.* 你愚蠢得使我寒心. ○ *He gave up the struggle in despair.* 他绝望地放弃了斗争. ○ *She was overcome by despair.* 她已完全绝望. ○ *his despair of ever seeing his family again* 他再也见不到他家里人的绝望心情. **2** (idm 习语) **be the despair of sb** make sb give up hope 使某人放弃希望: *Your son is the despair of all his teachers*, ie They no longer expect to be able to teach him anything. 你的儿子在所有教师的心目中已毫无希望了.

▷ **des·pair** *v* [I, Ipr] **~ (of sb/sth)** (*fml* 文) have lost all hope (esp that sb/sth will improve) 失去全部希望; 绝望: *We've despair of him; he can't keep a job for more than six months.* 我们对他已经绝望了, 他做什么工作都不能超过半年.

des·pair·ing /dɪˈspeərɪŋ; dɪˈspɛrɪŋ/ *adj* showing despair 表现绝望的; 绝望的: *a despairing look/gesture* 绝望的神色[姿态]. **des·pair·ingly** *adv*: *look despairingly at the judge* 绝望地看着法官.

des·patch /dɪˈspætʃ; dɪˈspætʃ/ *n, v* = DISPATCH.

des·per·ado /ˌdespəˈrɑːdəʊ; ˌdɛspəˈrɑdo/ *n* (*pl* **~es**; *US* also **~s**) (*dated* 旧) man who commits dangerous, esp criminal, acts without worrying about himself or other people 亡命之徒; 暴徒: *the desperadoes who robbed the mail-train* 抢劫邮车的亡命徒.

des·per·ate /ˈdespərət; ˈdɛspərɪt/ *adj* **1** feeling or showing great despair and ready to do anything regardless of danger 感到绝望而不惜冒险的; 拼命的; 不顾一切的: *The prisoners grew more desperate.* 囚徒们在绝望中更加不顾死活了. ○ *She wrote me a desperate letter.* 她给我写了一封信表示因绝望而不惜孤注一掷. **2** [attrib 作定语] violent and sometimes against the law 凶暴的; 犯法的: *a desperate criminal, act, robbery* 无法无天的罪犯、行为、抢劫. **3** [usu pred 通常作表语] **~ (for sth/to do sth)** in great need (of sth/to do sth) 极需要(某事物[做某事]): *They're desperate for money.* 他们极需钱. ○ (*infml* 口) *Have you got some water? I'm desperate (for a drink).* 你有水吗? 我很想喝(一点). ○ *I'm desperate to see her.* 我很想见到她. **4** extremely serious or dangerous 极严重的; 极危险的: *a desperate situation, shortage, illness* 危局、奇缺、重病 ○ *The state of the country is desperate.* 该国局势危殆. **5** [usu attrib 通常作定语] giving little hope of success; tried when all else has failed 成功希望渺茫的; 孤注一掷的: *a desperate remedy, measure, etc* 成功希望渺茫的补救方法、孤注一掷的措施.

▷ **des·per·ately** *adv*.

des·pera·tion /ˌdespəˈreɪʃn; ˌdɛspəˈreʃən/ *n* [U] state of being desperate(1) 拼命; 不顾一切; 不顾死活: *driven to desperation* 被逼得铤而走险 ○ *In desperation I pleaded with the attackers.* 我不顾一切向攻击者哀求.

de·spic·able /dɪˈspɪkəbl, ˈdespɪkəbl; dɪˈspɪkəbḷ, ˈdɛspɪkəbḷ/ *adj* **~ (of sb) (to do sth)** deserving to be despised; contemptible 可鄙的; 卑鄙的: *a despicable action, gesture* 可鄙的行动、姿势 ○ *a despicable rogue* 卑鄙的无赖. ▷ **de·spic·ably** /-əblɪ; -əblɪ/ *adv*: *behave despicably* 举动卑鄙.

des·pise /dɪˈspaɪz; dɪˈspaɪz/ *v* [Tn, Tn·pr] **~ sb/sth (for sth)** feel contempt for sb/sth; consider sb/sth as worthless 鄙视、藐视、看不起某人[某事物]: *despise his hypocrisy, meanness, conceit, etc* 鄙视他的虚伪、吝啬、自负等 ○ *Strike-breakers are often despised by their workmates.* 破坏罢工的人常为同事所不齿.

des·pite /dɪˈspaɪt; dɪˈspaɪt/ *prep* without being affected by (the factors mentioned) 尽管; 不管; 不顾: *They had a wonderful holiday, despite the bad weather.* 尽管天气不好, 他们的假日还是过得极为愉快. ○ *Despite wanting to see him again, she refused to reply to his letters.* 她尽管很想再见到他, 但却不愿给他回信. ○ *Despite what others say, I think he's a very nice chap.* 不管别人怎么说, 我仍认为他这个人很好. Cf 参看 IN SPITE OF (SPITE).

de·spoil /dɪˈspɔɪl; dɪˈspɔɪl/ *v* [Tn, Tn·pr] **~sth (of sth)** (*fml* 文) rob (a place) of sth valuable; plunder sth 从(某处)抢劫有价值之物; 掠夺某物: *Museums have despoiled India of many priceless treasures.* 博物馆里有许多从印度掠夺来的无价之宝.

des·pond·ent /dɪˈspɒndənt; dɪˈspɑndənt/ *adj* **~ (about sth)** having or showing loss of hope; wretched 失望的; 沮丧的; 消沉的; 苦恼的: *a despondent loser, mood, look* 沮丧的失败者、情绪、神情 ○ *Don't be so despondent.* 不要这样泄气.

▷ **des·pond·ency** /dɪˈspɒndənsɪ; dɪˈspɑndənsɪ/ *n* [U] loss of hope; misery 泄气; 沮丧; 失望; 苦恼: *her despondency about having no job* 她因失业而意志消沉.

des·pond·ently *adv*.

des·pot /ˈdespɒt; ˈdɛspət/ *n* ruler with unlimited powers, esp a cruel and oppressive one; tyrant 有至高无上权力的统治者; (尤指)暴君: *an enlightened despot* 开明的专制君主.

▷ **des·potic** /dɪˈspɒtɪk; dɪˈspɑtɪk/ *adj* of or like a despot 专制暴君的; 似暴君的; 专横的: *a despotic headmaster* 专横的校长. **des·pot·ic·ally** /-klɪ; -klɪ/ *adv*.

des·pot·ism /ˈdespətɪzəm; ˈdɛspəˌtɪzəm/ *n* [U] rule of a despot; tyranny 专制君主的统治; 暴政.

des·sert /dɪˈzɜːt; dɪˈzɝt/ (also **sweet**) *n* **(a)** [C] any sweet dish, (eg pie, tart, ice-cream) eaten at the end of a meal (饭后的)甜食(如馅饼、果馅饼、冰激凌): *a pineapple dessert* 菠萝甜食. Cf 参看 AFTERS, PUDDING 1. **(b)** [U] course in which this dish is served (用作最后一道菜的)甜食: *Shall we move on to dessert?* 咱们上甜食好吗? ○ [attrib 作定语] *a dessert apple, wine, etc*, ie served with or for dessert 作为甜食的苹果、餐末甜酒.

□ **deˈssert-spoon** *n* **(a)** medium-sized spoon 点心匙; 中型匙. ⇨illus at SPOON 见 SPOON 之插图. **(b)** (also **deˈssert-spoonful**) /-fʊl; -ˌfʊl/ amount held by this 一点心匙的量.

des·tina·tion /ˌdestɪˈneɪʃn; ˌdɛstəˈneʃən/ *n* place to which sb/sth is going or being sent 目的地: *Tokyo was our final destination.* 东京是我们的最终目的地. ○ *arrive at/reach one's destination* 到达目的地.

des·tined /ˈdestɪnd; ˈdɛstɪnd/ *adj* [pred 作表语] (*fml* 文) **1 ~ for sth/to do sth; be ~ that...** having a future which has been decided or planned beforehand 命中注定; 注定; 预定: *Coming from a theatrical family, I was destined for a career on the stage*, ie I was expected to be an actor. 我生于戏剧工作者之家, 注定了我的舞台生涯. ○ *They were destined never to meet again*, ie Fate had decided they should not meet again. 他们命中注定再也无缘相遇了. ○ *It was destined that they would marry.* 他们结婚是缘分. **2 ~ for...** on the way to (a place) 去, 到, 往, 赴(某处): *a letter, a traveller, an aircraft destined for London* 往伦敦的信、游客、飞机.

des·tiny /ˈdestɪnɪ; ˈdɛstənɪ/ *n* **1** [U] power believed to control events 命运: *Destiny drew us together.* 命运把我们连在一起了. **2** [C] that which happens to sb/sth (thought to be decided beforehand by fate) 定数; 天命: *It was his destiny to die in a foreign country.* 他注定要客死异国. ○ *events which shaped his destiny* 决定他命运的事件.

des·ti·tute /ˈdestɪtjuːt; *US* -tuːt; ˈdɛstəˌtut/ *adj* **1** without money, food, etc and other things necessary for life; impoverished 穷困的; 贫穷的; 穷苦的: *When he died, his family was left destitute.* 他死后家人衣食无着. **2** [pred 作表语] **~ of sth** (*fml* 文) lacking sth 缺少某事物: *officials who are destitute of ordinary human feelings* 毫无感情的官员.

▷ **des·ti·tu·tion** /ˌdestɪˈtjuːʃn; *US* -ˈtuːʃn; ˌdɛstəˈtuʃən/ *n* [U] being destitute 匮乏; 穷困: *live in complete destitution* 生活一贫如洗.

des·troy /dɪˈstrɔɪ; dɪˈstrɔɪ/ *v* **1** [Tn] damage (sth) so badly that it no longer exists, works, etc; wreck 摧毁, 毁坏(某物): *a house destroyed by bombs, fire, explosion* 被炸弹、大火、爆炸毁掉的房子 ○ *Vandals destroyed the bus.* 恣意破坏公物的人毁坏了这辆公共汽车. ○ *They've destroyed all the evidence.* 他们销毁了一切证据. ○ (*fig* 比喻) *destroy sb's hopes, career, reputation* 毁掉某人的希望、事业、名誉. **2** [Tn esp passive 尤用于被动语态] kill (a dog, horse, etc) deliberately, usu because it is sick or unwanted 杀死(狗、马等)(通常因其生病或不能保留); 人道毁灭: *The injured dog had to be destroyed.* 这只受伤的狗要予以人道毁灭.

▷ **des·troyer** *n* **1** (*fml* 文) person or thing that

destroys 破坏者: *Death, the destroyer* 死神, 生灵之毁灭者. **2** small fast warship for protecting larger warships or convoys of merchant ships 驱逐舰.

de·struct·ible /dɪˈstrʌktəbl; dɪˈstrʌktəbḷ/ *adj* that can be destroyed 可破坏的; 可摧毁的; 可毁灭的. ▷ **de·struct·ib·il·ity** /dɪˌstrʌktəˈbɪlətɪ; dɪˌstrʌktəˈbɪlətɪ/ *n* [U].

de·struc·tion /dɪˈstrʌkʃn; dɪˈstrʌkʃən/ *n* [U] (**a**) destroying or being destroyed 破坏; 摧毁; 毁灭: *the total destruction of a town by an earthquake* 地震对一小镇之彻底毁坏. (**b**) person or thing that destroys or ruins 破坏者; 毁灭者: *Gambling was his destruction.* 赌博把他毁了.

de·struct·ive /dɪˈstrʌktɪv; dɪˈstrʌktɪv/ *adj* (**a**) causing destruction or serious damage 造成毁灭或严重破坏的; 毁灭性的: *the destructive force of the storm* 暴风雨的破坏力. (**b**) wanting or tending to destroy 想要破坏的; 会造成破坏的: *destructive urges* 想搞破坏的欲望 ○ *Are all small children so destructive?* 是不是儿童都很喜欢破坏? ○ *destructive criticism*, ie making no positive suggestions for improvement 破坏性的批评. ▷ **de·struct·ive·ly** *adv*. **de·struct·ive·ness** *n* [U].

de·suet·ude /dɪˈsjuːɪtjuːd; *US* -tuːd; ˈdɛswɪˌtud/ *n* (idm 习语) **fall into deˈsuetude** (*fml* 文) cease being used 已不用; 废止: *customs, fashions, words that have fallen into desuetude* 已经废弃的风俗、式样、词语.

des·ul·tory /ˈdesəltrɪ; *US* -tɔːrɪ; ˈdɛsəlˌtorɪ/ *adj* going from one thing to another, without a definite plan or purpose; unmethodical 不连贯的; 漫无计划或目的的; 无条理的: *desultory reading, work* 漫无目的的阅读、漫无计划的工作 ○ *desultory attempts to help* 毫无计划的随意帮助. ▷ **des·ul·tor·ily** *adv*. **des·ul·tori·ness** *n* [U].

Det *abbr* 缩写 = Detective.

de·tach /dɪˈtætʃ; dɪˈtætʃ/ *v* **1** [Tn, Tn·pr] **~ sth (from sth)** unfasten sth from sth; disconnect sth 将某物拆下; 拆开某物; 分开某物: *detach a link from a chain* 从链子上拆下一个链环 ○ *a coach detached from a train* 从火车上脱离的一节车厢. Cf 参看 ATTACH 1. **2** [Tn, Tn·pr] **~ sb/sth (from sth)** (*military* 军) send (a group of soldiers, ships, etc) away from the main force, esp to do special duties 派遣, 分遣(兵员、船舰等)(尤指执行特殊任务): *A number of men were detached to guard the right flank.* 派遣了一些士兵守卫右翼.

▷ **de·tached** *adj* **1** (**a**) not influenced by others; impartial 不受他人影响的; 不偏不倚的; 公正的: *a detached mind, assessment, judgement, etc* 不偏不倚的见解、评价、判断等 ○ *take a detached view of sth* 对某事物采取公正的观点. (**b**) not feeling emotional or involved 不动感情的; 冷静的; 客观的; 超然的: *her detached response to the crisis* 她对这危机的客观的反应. **2** (of a house) not joined to another on either side (指房子)两边不与其他房子相连的, 独立的. ⇨illus at App 1 见附录1之插图, page vii.

de·tach·able /-əbl; -əbḷ/ *adj* that can be detached 可拆开的; 可分离的; 可分遣的: *a detachable lining in a coat* 大衣的活衬里.

de·tach·ment /dɪˈtætʃmənt; dɪˈtætʃmənt/ *n* **1** [U] detaching or being detached 派遣; 分遣: *the detachment of units from the main force* 从主力部队派遣的小分队. **2** [U] (**a**) state of being not influenced by others 不受他人影响; 独立; 客观: *show detachment in one's judgements* 表现出独立的见解. (**b**) lack of emotion; indifference 冷静; 超然: *He answered with an air of detachment.* 他以超然的神态回答. **3** [C] group of soldiers, ships, etc sent away from a larger group, esp to do special duties 分遣队; 支队; 特遣舰队: *a detachment of signallers* 通讯兵支队.

de·tail[1] /ˈdiːteɪl; *US* dɪˈteɪl; dɪˈtel/ *n* **1** [C] small, particular fact or item 细目; 细节; 详情: *Please give me all the details.* 请告诉我全部详情. ○ *I checked every detail of her research.* 我核对了她的学术研究的各个细节. ○ *The details of the costume were totally authentic.* 这件古装的每个小地方都完全真实. ○ *Spare me the details!* ie Don't provide any. 别给我讲细枝末节了! **2** [U] (**a**) small, particular aspects of sth 细微的方面: *A good organizer pays attention to detail.* 善于组织者考虑问题无微不至. ○ *a novelist with an eye for detail*, eg who includes many small, realistic facts 刻划入微的小说家. (**b**) smaller or less important parts of a picture, pattern, etc (绘画、图案等的)较小的或次要的部分: *The overall composition of the picture is good but some of the detail is distracting.* 这幅画的构图不错, 但有些细微处稍嫌喧宾夺主. **3** [C] (*military* 军) group of soldiers given special duties 特遣队; 小分队: *the cookhouse detail* 营地炊事班. **4** (idm 习语) **go into ˈdetail(s)** speak or write about all aspects of sth 详细叙述: *He refused to go into details about his plans.* 他不肯详述他计划的细节. **in ˈdetail** discussing all facts or items fully 详细地: *to explain/describe sth in detail* 详细解释[叙述]某事物.

de·tail[2] /ˈdiːteɪl; *US* dɪˈteɪl; dɪˈtel/ *v* **1** [Tn, Dn·pr] **~ sth (to/for sb)** list sth fully, item by item; describe sth fully (to/for sb) 逐项列出; (向[为]某人)详述某事物: *The computer's features are detailed in our brochure.* 该计算机的特点在我们的小册子中有详细介绍. ○ *an inventory detailing all the goods in a shop* 逐项列出的商店货物清单 ○ *I detailed our plans to her.* 我向她详细讲述了我们的计划. **2** [Tn, Tn·pr, Dn·t] **~ sb (for sth)** choose or appoint sb for special duties 选出或指派某人执行特殊任务: *detail soldiers for guard duty/to guard a bridge* 派士兵值勤[守桥].

▷ **de·tailed** *adj* having many details or paying great attention to details; thorough 详细的; 极注意细节的; 详尽的; 完全的: *a detailed description, account, analysis, etc* 详尽的叙述、报道、分析等.

de·tain /dɪˈteɪn; dɪˈten/ *v* [Tn] **1** prevent (sb) from leaving or doing sth; delay 阻止(某人)离开或做某事; 耽搁; 延误: *She was detained in the office by unexpected callers.* 有些临时访客把她耽搁在办公室里了. ○ *This question need not detain us long*, ie can be settled quickly. 这个问题不必耽搁我们很长时间. **2** keep (sb) in custody; lock up 拘留(某人); 扣押: *The police detained him for questioning.* 警方对他进行拘留审问.

▷ **de·tainee** /ˌdiːteɪˈniː; diˌteˈni/ *n* person who is detained (by police, etc, eg sb suspected of a violent crime, terrorism, etc) 被拘留者.

de·tect /dɪˈtekt; dɪˈtɛkt/ *v* [Tn] (**a**) discover or recognize that (sth) is present 发现、察觉或查出(某事物): *The dentist could detect no decay in her teeth.* 牙医检查了她的牙, 未见有龋齿. ○ *instruments that can detect minute amounts of radiation* 能检测极微量辐射的仪器 ○ *Do I detect a note of irony in your voice?* 听起来你是在说反话吧? (**b**) investigate and solve (crime, etc) 侦察, 侦查(罪案等): *This police officer's job is to detect fraud.* 这位警官负责侦查欺诈案.

▷ **de·tector** *n* device for detecting changes in pressure or temperature, metals, explosives, etc 探测器.

de·tec·tion /dɪˈtekʃn; dɪˈtɛkʃən/ *n* [U] detecting; discovering 发现; 察觉; 侦查; 探测: *the detection of radioactivity* 对放射性的探测 ○ *the detection of crime* 对罪行的侦查 ○ *try to escape detection by disguising oneself* 乔装打扮以躲过侦察者的耳目.

de·tect·ive /dɪˈtektɪv; dɪˈtɛktɪv/ *n* person, esp a police officer, whose job it is to investigate and solve crimes 侦探: *employ a private detective* 雇用一名私人侦探.

□ **deˈtective story, deˈtective novel** story in which the main interest is a puzzling crime and the process of solving it 侦探小说.

dé·tente /ˌdeɪˈtɑːnt; deˈtɑnt/ *n* [U] (*French* 法) lessening of dangerous tension, esp between countries (紧张关系的)缓和(尤指国与国间的).

de·ten·tion /dɪˈtenʃn; dɪˈtɛnʃən/ *n* [U] (**a**) detaining or being detained, esp in prison 阻止; 滞留; 拘留; (尤指)监禁: *detention without trial* 未经审判的关押. (**b**) punishment of being kept at school after it has closed 课后留校的惩罚: *be given two hours' detention* 被罚留校两小时.

□ **deˈtention centre** place where young offenders are kept in detention for a short time 青少年管教所.

de·ter /dɪˈtɜː(r); dɪˈtɝ/ *v* (**-rr-**) [Tn, Tn·pr] **~ sb (from doing sth)** make sb decide not to do sth 使某人决定不做某事物: *Failure did not deter him (from making another attempt).* 他并未因失败而畏缩不前. ○ *I was deterred from emigrating by the thought of leaving my family.* 我舍不得离开家, 所以决定不移居国外了.

de·ter·gent /dɪˈtɜːdʒənt; dɪˈtɝdʒənt/ *n* [U, C], *adj* (substance) that removes dirt, eg from the surface of clothes or dishes 洗涤剂; 去污剂; 洗涤的; 去污的: *Most* *synthetic detergents are in the form of powder or liquid.* 大多数合成洗涤剂呈粉状或液态.

de·teri·or·ate /dɪˈtɪərɪəreɪt; dɪˈtɪrɪə,ret/ *v* [I, Ipr] **~ (into sth)** become worse in quality or condition 变坏; 变质; 恶化: *Leather can deteriorate in damp conditions.* 皮革受潮可变质. ○ *The discussion deteriorated into a bitter quarrel.* 这场讨论演变成了激烈的争吵. ▷ **de·teri·ora·tion** /dɪˌtɪərɪəˈreɪʃn; dɪ,tɪrɪəˈreʃən/ *n* [U]: *a deterioration in superpower relations* 超级大国之间关系的恶化.

de·ter·min·ant /dɪˈtɜːmɪnənt; dɪˈtɝmənənt/ *n, adj* (*fml* 文) (thing) that determines or decides how or if sth happens 决定因素; 决定性的: *The main determinant of economic success is our ability to control inflation.* 经济方面的成就主要取决于我们控制通货膨胀的能力.

de·ter·min·ate /dɪˈtɜːmɪnət; dɪˈtɝmənɪt/ *adj* (*fml* 文) limited in range or scope; definite 限定的; 确定的.

de·ter·mina·tion /dɪˌtɜːmɪˈneɪʃn; dɪ,tɝməˈneʃən/ *n* [U] **1 ~ (to do sth)** quality of being firmly committed to doing sth; resoluteness 决心; 坚定性: *a leader with courage and determination* 果敢的领导者 ○ *with an air of determination*, ie showing this quality 带着一副坚定的神态 ○ *her dogged determination to learn English* 她学英语的那种坚定不移的决心. **2** precise fixing (of sth); deciding (对某事物的)确定; 决定: *the determination of future policy* 未来政策的确定. **3** finding out (of an amount, a quality, etc); calculation (数量、质量等的)测定; 计算: *the determination of a ship's position/the exact composition of a substance* 船的方位[某种物质的准确成分]的测定.

de·ter·min·at·ive /dɪˈtɜːmɪnətɪv; *US* -neɪtɪv; dɪˈtɝmə-,netɪv/ *adj* (*fml* 文) having the power to determine or limit sth (对某事物)有决定力的, 有限制力的: *a determinative factor in his psychological development* 在他心理发展过程中的决定因素.

▷ **de·ter·min·at·ive** *n* thing having the power to determine or limit sth 决定因素.

de·ter·mine /dɪˈtɜːmɪn; dɪˈtɝmɪn/ *v* **1** [Tn, Tw] (*fml* 文) fix (sth) precisely; decide 确定(某事物); 决定: *determine a date for a meeting* 确定会议日期 ○ *His future has not been determined, but he may study medicine.* 他将来何去何从尚未决定, 但有可能学医. ○ *She will determine how it is to be done.* 她会决定这件事的做法. **2** [Tn, Tw] (*fml* 文) find out (sth that is not known); calculate 测定, 找出(某未知事物); 算出: *determine the meaning of a word/what a word means* 确定某词的含义 ○ *determine exactly what happened* 查出究竟发生了什么事 ○ *determine the speed of light, how high a mountain is* 测定光速、山有多高. **3** [Ipr, Tf, Tw, Tt] **~ on/upon sth** decide firmly that sth will be done; make up one's mind about sth; resolve 决定做某事; 对某事下定决心; 决心: *We determined on an early start/(that) we'd make an early start.* 我们决定早些出发. ○ *determine on proving/to prove sb's innocence* 决心要证实某人无辜 ○ *They have determined where the new school will be built.* 他们已决定在何处建校. ○ *He determined to learn Greek.* 他决定学希腊语. **4** [Tn·pr] **~ sb against sth** (*fml* 文) make sb decide not to do sth 使某人决定不做某事: *That determined her against leaving home.* 那件事使她决定不离开家了. **5** [Tn] decisively influence (sth); fix 对(某事物)产生决定性的影响; 决定: *Do heredity and environment determine one's character?* 遗传与环境可以决定一个人的性格吗? ○ *The exam results could determine your career.* 考试成绩可能会决定你的前途.

▷ **de·ter·mined** /dɪˈtɜːmɪnd; dɪˈtɝmɪnd/ *adj* **~ (to do sth)** with one's mind firmly made up; resolute 有决心的; 意志坚定的; 坚决的: *a determined fighter, look, attitude* 坚定的战士、神情、态度 ○ *I'm determined to succeed.* 我决心要努力获得成功.

de·ter·miner /dɪˈtɜːmɪnə(r); dɪˈtɝmɪnɚ/ *n* (*grammar*) word, eg *the, some, my*, that comes before a noun to show how the noun is being used 限定词(置于名词前, 对该名词起限定作用的词, 如 the、some、my).

de·ter·min·ism /dɪˈtɜːmɪnɪzəm; dɪˈtɝmən,ɪzəm/ *n* [U] (*philosophy* 哲) belief that one is not free to choose the sort of person one wants to be, or how one behaves, because these things are decided by one's background, surroundings, etc 决定论(认为个人并无选择个性或行为的自由, 因为这一切都由其背景、环境等所决定).

de·ter·rent /dɪˈterənt; *US* -ˈtɜː-; dɪˈtɝənt/ *n, adj* (thing) that deters or is meant to deter 起制止作用的(事物); 遏止的(因素); 威慑的(力量): *His punishment will be a deterrent to others.* 惩罚他以儆效尤. ○ *deterrent weapons, measures* 具威慑性的武器、遏制性的手段.

▷ **de·ter·rence** /dɪˈterəns; *US* -ˈtɜː-; dɪˈtɝəns/ *n* [U] action of deterring 阻止; 遏止; 威慑: *nuclear deterrence*, ie (a policy of) having nuclear weapons in order to make an enemy too frightened to attack 核威慑.

de·test /dɪˈtest; dɪˈtest/ *v* [Tn, Tg, Tsg] dislike (sb/sth) very much; hate 憎恶, 憎恨(某人[某事物]); 厌恶; 讨厌: *detest dogs* 讨厌狗 ○ *detest having to get up early* 很不喜欢早起身 ○ *I detest people complaining.* 我讨厌人发牢骚.

▷ **de·test·able** /-əbl; -əbḷ/ *adj* that one hates; hateful 令人憎恨的; 可憎的; 可恶的; 讨厌的: *a detestable habit* 可恶的习惯. **de·test·ably** /-əblɪ; -əblɪ/ *adv*.

de·testa·tion /ˌdiːteˈsteɪʃn; ,dɪtɛsˈteʃən/ *n* [U] strong dislike; hatred 强烈的厌恶; 憎恶.

de·throne /ˌdiːˈθrəʊn; diˈθron/ *v* [Tn] **(a)** remove (a ruler) from the throne; depose 废黜(君主). **(b)** (*fig* 比喻) remove (sb) from a position of authority or influence 使(某人)失去权势; 撵下台; 挤走: *a government adviser dethroned by a younger expert* 被较年轻的专家挤走的政府顾问. ▷ **de·throne·ment** *n* [C, U].

det·on·ate /ˈdetəneɪt; ˈdɛtə,net/ *v* [I, Tn] (cause sth to) explode; (be) set off (使某物)爆炸; 引爆; 起爆: *The bomb failed to detonate.* 炸弹没爆炸. ○ *an explosive charge detonated by remote control* 遥控起爆的炸药.

▷ **det·ona·tion** /ˌdetəˈneɪʃn; ,dɛtəˈneʃən/ *n* [C, U] explosion 爆炸; 起爆.

det·on·ator /ˈdetəneɪtə(r); ˈdɛtə,netɚ/ *n* part of a bomb, etc that explodes first, setting off the full explosion 起爆管; 雷管; 信管.

de·tour /ˈdiːtʊə(r); *US* dɪˈtʊər; dɪˈtʊr/ *n* (*esp US*) route that avoids a blocked road, etc; deviation (绕开受阻道路等的)绕行路线, 迂回路线: *We had to make a detour round the floods.* 我们为避开洪水得绕道而行. Cf 参看 DIVERSION.

▷ **de·tour** *v* [I, Tn] avoid (sth) by making a detour 绕道以避开(某物); 绕过(某物): *We had to detour a road-block.* 我们得绕过路障.

de·tox·ify /ˌdiːˈtɒksɪfaɪ; diˈtɑksə,faɪ/ *v* (*pt, pp* **-fied**) [Tn] remove poison or harmful substances from (sb/sth) 清除(某人[某物])的毒素或有害物质; 为(某人[某物])解毒: *detoxify the bloodstream* 清除血液中的毒素.

▷ **de·toxi·fica·tion** /ˌdiːˌtɒksɪfɪˈkeɪʃn; di,tɑksəfəˈkeʃən/ *n* [U] action of removing poison or harmful substances, eg addictive drugs 解毒; (对如毒品等有害物质的)清除: [attrib 作定语] *a detoxification centre*, ie where drug addicts or alcoholics are treated 戒毒(或戒酒)中心.

de·tract /dɪˈtrækt; dɪˈtrækt/ *v* [Ipr] **~ from sth** make sth seem less valuable or important 减损某事物的价值或重要性; 贬低: *detract from the merit, value, worth, excellence, etc of sth* 有损于某事物的好处、重要性、价值、优点等 ○ *criticism that detracts from her achievements* 贬低她成就的批评 ○ *This unpleasant incident detracted from our enjoyment of the evening.* 这件不愉快的事情使我们当晚兴致大减.

▷ **de·trac·tion** /dɪˈtrækʃn; dɪˈtrækʃən/ *n* [U] unfair criticism of sb/sth; belittling 不恰当的批评; 贬低; 贬抑.

de·tractor *n* person who criticizes sb/sth unfairly 诋毁者; 贬低者: *The scheme is better than its detractors suggest.* 这计划比贬低它的人所说的要好.

de·train /ˌdiːˈtreɪn; diˈtren/ *v* [I, Tn] (*fml* 文) leave or cause (sb) to leave a railway train 下火车; 使(某人)下火车: *The troops detrained near the battle zone.* 部队在战区附近下了火车.

de·trib·al·ize, -ise /ˌdiːˈtraɪbəlaɪz; diˈtraɪbə,laɪz/ *v* [Tn] cause (sb) to abandon tribal customs; end tribal organization in (a society) 使(某人)摒弃部落习俗; 解散(某社会)中的部落组织: *detribalized Indians in South America* 解散南美洲印第安人的部落. ▷ **de·trib·al·iza·tion, -isa·tion** /ˌdiːˌtraɪbəlaɪˈzeɪʃn; *US* -lɪˈz-; di,traɪbəlɪˈzeʃən/ [U].

det·ri·ment /ˈdetrɪmənt; ˈdɛtrəmənt/ *n* (idm 习语) **to the detriment of sb/sth; without detriment to sb/sth** harming/not harming sb/sth 对某人[某事物]有害

[无害]; 有损于[无损于]某人[某事物]: *He works long hours, to the detriment of his health.* 他长时间地工作, 有损健康. ○ *This tax cannot be introduced without detriment to the economy.* 这一税制一旦施行, 必然会危害国民经济.

▷ **det·ri·mental** /ˌdetrɪˈmentl; ˌdɛtrəˋmɛntl/ *adj* **~ (to sb/sth)** harmful 有害的; 不利的: *The measures had a detrimental effect.* 这些措施已产生不良影响. ○ *activities detrimental to our interests* 损及我们利益的活动. **det·ri·ment·ally** /-təlɪ; -tl̩ɪ/ *adv*: *detrimentally affected* 受到不良影响.

de·tritus /dɪˈtraɪtəs; dɪˋtraɪtəs/ *n* [U] matter such as sand, silt or gravel produced by the wearing away of rocks, etc (岩石等风化而形成的)泥沙, 碎石, 岩屑; 风化物.

de trop /dəˈtrəʊ; dəˋtro/ *adj* [pred 作表语] (*French* 法) not wanted; unwelcome 不需要; 无用; 不受欢迎: *Their intimate conversation made me feel de trop.* 他们亲切交谈, 使我感到自己是个多余的人.

deuce[1] /dju:s; *US* du:s; dus/ *n* **1** two on playing-cards or dice (shown as pips and/or numbers) (纸牌或色子上的)两点(以点和[或]数字表示). **2** (in tennis) score of 40-all, after which either side must gain two successive points to win the game (网球赛中)40 平(其后一方须连胜两球方为胜).

deuce[2] /dju:s; *US* du:s; dus/ *n* (*dated infml euph* 旧, 口, 婉) **1 the deuce** [sing] (used as an expression of annoyance 用以表示烦恼、厌恶等): *The deuce! I've lost my keys!* 真倒霉, 钥匙丢了! ○ *Who/What/Where the deuce is that?* 到底是哪个傢伙[是什么鬼名堂/在什么鬼地方]? ○ *What the deuce is going on?* 讨厌, 到底是怎么回事? **2** (idm 习语) **the deuce of a sth** a very bad case of sth 非常糟糕; 十分严重: *I've got the deuce of a headache.* 我头痛极了.

▷ **deuced** /dju:st, ˈdju:sɪd; *US* du:st; dust/ *adj* (used as an expression of annoyance 用以表示烦恼、厌恶等): *Where's that deuced boy?* 那坏小子上哪儿去了? — *adv* very 很; 非常: *What deuced bad luck!* 倒霉死了! **deucedly** /ˈdju:sɪdlɪ; *US* ˈdu:-; ˋdusɪdlɪ/ *adv* very 很; 非常.

Deutsch·mark /ˈdɔɪtʃmɑ:k; ˋdɔɪtʃ,mɑrk/ *n* (*abbr* 缩写 **DM**) unit of money in the Federal Republic of Germany 马克(德国货币单位).

de·value /ˌdi:ˈvælju:; diˋvælju/ *v* [Tn] (**a**) reduce the value of (a currency) in relation to other currencies or gold 使(某种货币)贬值: *devalue the dollar, pound, mark, etc* 使美元、英镑、马克等贬值. (**b**) reduce the value or worth of (sth) 降低(某事物)的价值; 贬低(某事物)的重要性: *criticism that devalues our work* 贬低我们工作成绩的批评.

▷ **de·valu·ation** /ˌdi:væljʊˈeɪʃn; ˌdivæljuˋeʃən/ *n* [C, U] (instance of) reducing a currency to a lower fixed value 货币贬值: *There's been a further devaluation of the dollar.* 美元继续贬值.

dev·ast·ate /ˈdevəsteɪt; ˋdɛvəs,tet/ *v* [Tn] (**a**) completely destroy (sth); ruin 彻底毁坏(某事物); 毁灭; 摧毁: *a house devastated by a bomb* 被炸弹炸毁的房子 ○ *War devastated the country.* 战争摧毁了这个国家. (**b**) (*infml* 口) shock (sb); overwhelm 令(某人)震惊; 使(某人)难以承受: *She was devastated by his death.* 她因他去世而悲痛欲绝. ○ *I was devastated by the news of the crash.* 我获悉失事的消息感到十分震惊.

▷ **dev·ast·at·ing** /ˈdevəsteɪtɪŋ; ˋdɛvəs,tetɪŋ/ *adj* **1** very destructive 破坏力极强的; 毁灭性的: *a devastating war, famine, storm, etc* 毁灭性的战争、饥荒、风暴等. **2** causing severe shock 令人十分震惊的; 具有强大冲击力的: *devastating criticism, news* 猛烈的抨击、惊人的消息. **3** (*fig infml* 比喻, 口) striking; impressive 突出的; 醒目的; 令人钦佩的: *devastating wit* 非凡的机智 ○ *She looked devastating*, ie very beautiful. 她貌美绝伦. **dev·ast·at·ingly** *adv*.

dev·asta·tion /ˌdevəˈsteɪʃn; ˌdɛvəsˋteʃən/ *n* [U] devastating or being devastated 毁灭: *complete, utter devastation* 完全的、彻底的毁灭.

de·velop /dɪˈveləp; dɪˋvɛləp/ *v* **1** [I, Ipr, Tn, Tn·pr] **~ (sb/sth) (from sth) (into sth)** (cause sb/sth to) grow gradually; become or make more mature, advanced or organized (使某人[某事物])发展, 发育, 成长, 发达: *The child is developing well.* 这孩子发育良好. ○ *The plot for the novel gradually developed in my mind.* 我逐步构想出小说的情节. ○ *The argument developed into a bitter quarrel.* 这场辩论逐渐变成了激烈的争吵. ○ *We've developed the project from an original idea by Stephen.* 我们根据斯蒂芬的设想制定了这个计划. ○ *The place has developed from a fishing port into a thriving tourist centre.* 这地方由原来的渔港发展成一个繁荣的旅游胜地. **2** [I, Tn] (cause sth to) become noticeable, visible or active (使某事物)出现, 明显化, 显露, 变得活跃: *Symptoms of malaria developed*, ie appeared. 疟疾的症状出现了. ○ *The car has developed signs of rust*, ie is becoming rusty. 这辆汽车出现了锈迹. **3** (*photography* 摄) (**a**) [Tn] treat (an exposed film) with chemicals so that the picture can be seen 冲洗(已曝光的底片); 使(已曝光的底片)显影: *take a film to be developed* 将胶卷送去冲洗. (**b**) [I] (of the image on an exposed film or plate) become visible (指底片上的图像)显影. **4** [Tn] use (land) for the building of houses, etc and so increase its value 在(土地)上建筑房屋等; 开发(土地): *The site is being developed by a London property company.* 这块地正在由伦敦的一家地产公司开发利用.

▷ **de·veloped** *adj* **1** advanced; mature 先进的; 发达的; 成熟的: *a highly developed system of agriculture* 十分发达的农业体系 ○ *She is well developed for her age.* 她比她的实际年龄看来早熟. **2** (*economics* 经) (of a country, an area, etc) with a highly organized economy (指国家、地区等)经济发达的: *one of the less developed countries* 发达程度较低的国家之一.

de·vel·oper *n* **1** (*photography* 摄) substance used to develop films 显影剂. **2** person or company that develops land 土地开发者; 土地开发公司.

de·vel·op·ing *adj* trying to become economically advanced 经济发展中的: *a developing country* 发展中的国家 ○ *the developing world* 发展中的世界.

de·vel·op·ment /dɪˈveləpmənt; dɪˋvɛləpmənt/ *n* **1** [U] developing or being developed (DEVELOP 1, 2, 3, 4) 发展; 发达; 发育; 成长; 出现; 显影; 开发: *the healthy development of children* 儿童的健康成长 ○ *encourage the development of small businesses* 鼓励小公司的发展 ○ *land that is ready for development*, ie ready to be built on 可以开发的土地(可在上面营建). **2** [C] (**a**) new stage or event 新的阶段; 新事态: *the latest development in the continuing crisis* 这段持续危机的最新情况 ○ *We must await further developments.* 我们必须等待事态的进一步发展. (**b**) new product or invention 新产品; 新发明: *Our electrically-powered car is an exciting new development.* 我们的电动汽车是一项令人鼓舞的新发明. **3** [C] piece of land with new buildings on it 新近建造了房屋的一块土地; 新开发地: *a commercial development on the outskirts of the town* 在城郊的新商业区.

□ **deˈvelopment area** (*Brit*) poor area where new industries are encouraged in order to create jobs 待开发区(鼓励发展新工业以提供就业机会的贫穷地区).

de·vi·ant /ˈdi:vɪənt; ˋdivɪənt/ *n, adj* (*often derog* 常作贬义) (person who is) different in moral or social standards from what is considered normal 偏离正常的道德或社会标准的(人); 离经叛道的(人): *a sexual deviant who assaults children* 蹂躏儿童的性变态者 ○ *deviant behaviour* 不轨的行为.

▷ **de·vi·ance** /-vɪəns; -vɪəns/, **de·vi·ancy** *ns* [U] deviant tendencies or behaviour 反常的倾向或行为.

de·vi·ate /ˈdi:vɪeɪt; ˋdivɪ,et/ *v* [Ipr] **~ from sth** stop following (a course, standard, etc) 偏离(路线、标准等); 背离: *The plane deviated from its usual route.* 飞机偏离了正常的航线. ○ *I will never deviate from what I believe to be right.* 我绝不背离我自信正确的道路. ○ *deviate from one's plan, the norm, the accepted procedure, etc* 偏离自己的计划、标准、一般的程序等.

de·vi·ation /ˌdi:vɪˈeɪʃn; ˌdivɪˋeʃən/ *n* **~ (from sth)** **1** (**a**) [U] not following the normal or expected course, plan, etc; deviating 偏离正常的或原定的路线、计划等; 偏向; 偏差: *There was little deviation from his usual routine.* 他没有什么反常的举动. ○ *sexual deviation* 性变态行为. (**b**) [C] instance of this 偏差; 逸出常轨: *a deviation from the rules* 违背规则. **2** [U] (*politics* 政) moving away from the beliefs held by the group to which one belongs 背离自己所属集团的信条; 背盟: *Party ideologists accused her of deviation.* 党内理论家谴

D

责她背离了党的信条. **3** [C] difference between a numerical value and a norm or average 偏差; 离差: *a compass deviation of 5°*, ie from true north 罗盘自差5度(相对于正北而言).

▷ **de·vi·ation·ism** /-ʃənɪzəm; -ʃənɪzm/ *n* [U] practice of political deviation 政治上的离经叛道. **de·vi·ation·ist** /-ʃənɪst; -ʃənɪst/ *n*.

de·vice /dɪˈvaɪs; dɪˋvaɪs/ *n* **1** thing made or adapted for a special purpose (为某种用途而制作或改装的)装置, 器具: *a device for measuring pressure* 测压装置 ○ *a labour-saving device* 节省劳力的装置 ○ *an explosive device* 爆破装置 ○ *a nuclear device*, eg a nuclear bomb or missile 核子装置(如核弹或核导弹). ⇨Usage at MACHINE 用法见MACHINE. **2** (*literature* 文学) metaphor, combination of words, etc used by a writer to produce an effect on the reader (作者用以感染读者的)手法, 技巧(如隐喻、词语搭配等): *a stylistic device* 文体表现手法. **3** scheme; trick 策略; 计策; 诡计; 计谋: *Her illness is merely a device to avoid seeing him.* 她所谓生病只不过是避免见他的花招而已. **4** symbol or figure used as a sign by a noble family, eg on a crest or shield (贵族用作家族标志的)图案(如用于饰章或盾形徽的): *a heraldic device* 纹章图案. **5** (idm 习语) **leave sb to his own devices** ⇨ LEAVE[1].

D

devil[1] /ˈdevl; ˋdɛvl/ *n* **1** (**a**) **the Devil** supreme evil being; Satan 魔鬼; 撒旦: *The Devil tempted Adam and Eve.* 魔鬼诱惑了亚当和夏娃. (**b**) wicked spirit 魔鬼; 鬼怪: *He believes in devils and witches.* 他相信魔鬼、巫婆这类事. **2** (*infml* 口) (**a**) wicked or mischievous person 恶人; 坏蛋; 调皮鬼; 淘气鬼: *My niece is a little devil.* 我的侄女是个调皮鬼. ○ *He's a devil with* (ie flirts with) *the ladies.* 他是个玩弄女性的傢伙. (**b**) (used for emphasis 用以加强语气) person 人; 傢伙: *The poor/lucky devil!* 多可怜[幸运]的傢伙! ○ *Which silly devil left the fire on all day?* 是哪个笨蛋没将炉火熄掉, 烧了这一整天? **3** (idm 习语) **be a ˈdevil** (*infml joc* 口, 谑) used to encourage sb to do sth he is hesitating to do 用以在某人迟疑时鼓励他去做某事: *Go on, be a devil — tell me what they said.* 来, 怕什么——尽管告诉我他们说了些什么. **better the devil you know** ⇨ BETTER[2]. **between the ˌdevil and the ˌdeep (blue) ˈsea** in a situation where there are two equally unacceptable alternatives 进退维谷; 左右为难. **the devil** (used for emphasis in questions 在疑问句中用以加强语气): *What/Who/Why/Where the devil is that?* 到底是什么鬼名堂[是哪个傢伙/是为什么/是在什么鬼地方]? **the (very) ˈdevil** (sth) difficult or unpleasant 困难的或令人不愉快的(事物): *This job is the very devil.* 这工作十分棘手. ○ *These pans are the (very) devil to clean.* 这些锅太难洗干净了. **the ˈdevil you will/won't, she can/can't, etc** (*infml* 口) (used to emphasize a statement of refusal, an expression of surprise, etc 用作强调表示拒绝、惊讶等的语句): *'I'm going to a party.' 'The devil you are!'*, ie I forbid it. '我要去参加一个聚会.' '你敢!' (我不准). **the ˌdevil looks ˌafter his ˈown** (*saying* 谚) success comes to those who deserve it least 魔鬼保佑恶人(最不配成功者却能获得成功); 小人行大运. **the devil makes work for idle hands** (*saying* 谚) when people do not have enough work to do, they get into or make trouble 闲则生非. **a devil of a sth/sb** (*dated infml* 旧, 口) (used for emphasis 用以加强语气) very remarkable, difficult, awkward, etc thing or person 非常突出、麻烦、糟糕等的事或人: *a devil of a pretty woman* 漂亮得不得了的女人. **devil's ˈadvocate** person who speaks against sb or sth simply to encourage discussion 故意提出异议以激发辩论的人; 故意唱反调的人: *I don't really believe in capital punishment, I'm just playing the devil's advocate.* 我并非真正主张应该有死刑, 只是故意唱唱反调罢了. **the devil's own luck** very good luck 极佳的运气; 鸿运. **the devil take the ˈhindmost** everybody should look after himself and not care about others 魔鬼专抓落后的(人人应自保, 不可顾他人); 要鬼捉不到, 抢在人前逃: *In this business you have to be tough, and the devil take the hindmost.* 干这一行必须心狠, 谁顾别人谁吃亏. **give the devil his ˈdue** be just, even to those who do not deserve it 不管人好人坏, 都要公平对待; 平心而论. **go to the ˈdevil!** (*dated* 旧) damn you! 去你的! 见鬼去吧! **have a/the devil of a job doing sth** (*infml* 口) find sth very difficult 觉得某事十分困难: *I'm having a devil of a job fixing my car.* 我修我这辆汽车可费劲了. **like the ˈdevil** (*infml* 口) very hard, intensively, etc 很卖力地、强烈地等; 拼命地: *run, work like the devil* 拼命跑、干. **needs must when the devil drives** ⇨ NEEDS (NEED). **play the devil with sth** (*infml* 口) harm or make sth worse 伤害; 使某事物恶化: *Cold weather plays the devil with my rheumatism.* 天一冷, 我的风湿病就犯了. **speak/talk of the ˈdevil** (*saying infml* 谚, 口) (said when sb one has been talking about appears 用于说到某人, 某人就到的场合). **there'll be the ˈdevil to pay** (*infml* 口) there will be trouble as the result of sth 那就麻烦了; 那就糟糕了; 那就要倒霉了: *There'll be the devil to pay if you scratch my car!* 你要是划坏了我的汽车你就有麻烦了! **the world, the flesh and the devil** ⇨ WORLD.

□ **ˌdevil-may-ˈcare** *adj* [esp attrib 尤作定语] reckless 肆无忌惮的; 不顾一切的.

devil[2] /ˈdevl; ˋdɛvl/ *v* (**-ll-**; *US* **-l-**) **1** [Tn] grill (sth) with mustard, curry, etc 加芥末、咖喱等烧烤(某物): *devilled kidneys/ham/turkey* 加辛辣调味品的烤腰子[火腿/火鸡]. **2** [I, Ipr] **~ (for sb)** (*Brit*) work as an assistant to (a barrister) 给(律师)做助手.

dev·il·ish /ˈdevəlɪʃ; ˋdɛvəlɪʃ/ *adj* wicked; cruel 邪恶的; 恶毒的; 残忍的: *a devilish plan* 毒计 ○ *devilish cunning* 奸诈.

▷ **dev·il·ish** *adv* (*dated infml* 旧, 口) very 很; 非常: *devilish hot* 热得要命.

de·vil·ishly *adv*: *devilishly cruel, cunning, etc* 穷凶极恶、极为狡诈.

de·vil·ish·ness *n* [U].

dev·il·ment /ˈdevlmənt; ˋdɛvlmənt/ (also **dev·ilry** /ˈdevlrɪ; ˋdɛvlrɪ/) *n* **1** [U] high spirits; mischief 高昂的情绪; 恶作剧; 玩笑: *She played a trick on him out of sheer devilment.* 她捉弄他完全是为了寻开心. **2** [C] mischievous act 恶作剧; 开玩笑: *She's up to some devilry or other.* 她正要搞个恶作剧什么的.

de·vi·ous /ˈdiːvɪəs; ˋdivɪəs/ *adj* **1** cunning; dishonest 刁滑的; 不诚实的: *a devious lawyer, scheme, trick* 刁滑的律师、阴谋、诡计 ○ *get rich by devious means* 以不正当的手段致富. **2** (of a route, path, etc) winding; not straight (指道路等)弯曲的, 蜿蜒的, 不直的: *The coach followed a rather devious course to its destination.* 长途汽车要绕很多弯路才到达目的地. ▷ **de·vi·ously** *adv*. **de·vi·ous·ness** *n* [U].

de·vise /dɪˈvaɪz; dɪˋvaɪz/ *v* [Tn] think out (a plan, system, tool, etc); invent 想出, 设计(计划、制度、工具等); 发明: *devise a scheme for redeveloping the city centre* 制定市中心重建计划 ○ *devise a new type of transistor* 发明一种新晶体管.

de·vi·tal·ize, -ise /ˌdiːˈvaɪtəlaɪz; diˋvaɪtlˌaɪz/ *v* [Tn] take strength and vigour away from (sb/sth) 使(某人[某事物])失去活力; 消耗(某人[某事物])的力量: *a nation devitalized by a sustained war effort* 因持续的战事而大伤元气的国家. ▷ **de·vi·tal·iza·tion, -isa·tion** /ˌdiːˌvaɪtəlaɪˈzeɪʃn; *US* -lɪˈz-; diˌvaɪtlɪˈzeʃən/ *n* [U].

de·void /dɪˈvɔɪd; dɪˋvɔɪd/ *adj* [pred 作表语] **~ of sth** without sth; completely lacking in sth 没有或毫无某事物: *a criminal utterly devoid of conscience* 天良丧尽的罪犯.

de·volu·tion /ˌdiːvəˈluːʃn; *US* ˌdev-; ˌdɛvəˋluʃən/ *n* [U] transfer of power or authority, esp from central government to regional authorities (尤指中央政府向地方政府)移交权力, 下放权力, 分权.

de·volve /dɪˈvɒlv; dɪˋvɑlv/ *v* (*fml* 文) **1** [Ipr] **~ on/upon sb** (of work, duties) be transferred or passed to sb (指工作、职务)移交给某人: *When the President is ill, his duties devolve upon the Vice-President.* 总统生病时, 其职务交由副总统代理. **2** [Tn, Tn·pr] **~ sth (to/upon sb)** transfer (work, duties, etc) to sb 将(工作、职务等)转交给某人: *More power is to be devolved to regional government.* 要将更多的权力交给地方政府.

de·vote /dɪˈvəʊt; dɪˋvot/ *v* [Tn·pr] **~ oneself/sth to sb/sth** give (one's time, energy, etc) to sb/sth; dedicate 为某人[某事物]付出(时间、精力等); 向某人[某事物]奉献(时间、精力等); 献身于某事物: *devote oneself to a noble cause* 献身于一项崇高的事业 ○ *devote all one's efforts to one's task* 全力以赴地工作.

▷ **de·voted** *adj* **~ (to sb/sth)** very loving or loyal 热爱的; 非常忠实的; 全心全意的: *a devoted son, friend,* supporter, etc 孝子、忠实的朋友、不遗余力的支持者 ○ *She is devoted to her children.* 她深爱她的孩子. **de·vot·edly** *adv*.

de·votee /ˌdevəˈtiː; ˌdɛvəˋti/ *n* (**a**) person who is devoted to sth; enthusiast 致力于、献身于某事物的人; 热心者; 某事物的迷恋者: *a devotee of sport, music, crime fiction, etc* 热衷于体育运动、音乐、侦探小说等的人. (**b**) zealous supporter (of a sect, etc) (某一宗派等的)热情拥护者.

de·vo·tion /dɪˈvəʊʃn; dɪˋvoʃən/ *n* **1** [U] **~ (to sb/sth)** (**a**) deep strong love 深爱; 挚爱: *a mother's devotion to her children* 母亲对子女深深的疼爱. (**b**) giving of oneself (to a person, cause, etc); loyalty 献身; 忠心: *devotion to duty* 忠于职守 ○ *a teacher's devotion to her task* 教师全心全意投入其工作的态度 ○ *our devotion to our leader* 我们对领袖的忠诚. **2** (**a**) [U] religious zeal; devoutness 宗教热情; 虔诚: *a life of great devotion* 信仰诚笃的一生. (**b**) [C] prayer or religious practice 祈祷; 灵修; 宗教仪式: *a traditional devotion like the Way of the Cross* 有如天主教'拜苦路'的传统宗教仪式 ○ *a priest at his devotions*, ie praying 正在祈祷的教士.

▷ **de·vo·tional** /-ʃənl; -ʃənl̩/ *adj* of or used in religious worship 崇拜的; 灵修的; 祈祷的: *devotional literature* 灵修书刊.

de·vour /dɪˈvaʊə(r); dɪˋvaʊr/ *v* **1** [Tn] (**a**) eat (sth) hungrily or greedily 贪婪地吃(某物); 吞食(某物): *devour the food ravenously* 狼吞虎咽地吃东西. (**b**) (*fig* 比喻) look at (sb/sth) avidly 贪婪地、全神贯注地看(某人[某事物]): *She devoured the new detective story.* 她如饥似渴地读那本新侦探小说. ○ *He devoured her with his eyes*, ie looked at her lustfully. 他用色迷迷的目光盯着她. (**c**) (*fig* 比喻) destroy (sth) 毁灭, 吞噬(某事物): *Fire devoured a huge area of forest.* 大火吞噬了大片森林. **2** (idm 习语) **be devoured by sth** be filled with (curiosity, anxiety, etc) 心中充满了(好奇、忧虑等).

de·vout /dɪˈvaʊt; dɪˋvaʊt/ *adj* **1** sincerely religious; pious 虔信宗教的; 虔诚的: *a devout Muslim, prayer* 虔诚的穆斯林、祈祷. **2** sincere; deeply felt 诚挚的; 真诚的; 衷心的; 发自内心的: *a devout hope, wish, etc* 衷心的希望、祝愿等. ▷ **de·voutly** *adv*: *It is devoutly to be wished*, ie something I hope very much will happen. 这是我衷心希望的. **de·vout·ness** *n* [U].

dew /djuː; *US* duː; du/ *n* [U] tiny drops of moisture condensed on cool surfaces from water vapour in the air, esp at night 露水: *The grass was wet with dew.* 草被露水沾湿了.

▷ **dewy** *adj* wet with dew 为露水所湿的; 带露水的. ˌ**dewy-ˈeyed** *adj* naïve and trusting 单纯天真、易轻信人的: *You can't be too dewy-eyed if you want to succeed.* 要成功就不能太天真.

□ ˈ**dewdrop** *n* drop of dew 露珠.

dew·lap /ˈdjuːlæp; *US* ˈduː-; ˋduˌlæp/ *n* fold of loose skin hanging down from the throat of an animal such as a cow or an ox (牛等)自喉部垂下的松皮; 喉垂.

dex·ter·ity /dekˈsterətɪ; dɛkˋstɛrətɪ/ *n* [U] skill, esp in using one's hands 技巧, 灵巧(尤指用手的); 灵活的手法: *A juggler needs great dexterity.* 玩杂耍的人要有非常灵巧的手. ○ (*fig* 比喻) *The negotiations will call for considerable dexterity.* 进行这些谈判需要相当圆滑的手腕.

dex·ter·ous (also **dex·trous**) /ˈdekstrəs; ˋdɛkstrəs/ *adj* (**a**) skilful with one's hands 善于用手的; 手巧的: *She's very dexterous with the knitting needles.* 她擅长用织针. (**b**) skilfully performed 表现灵巧的: *a dextrous movement* 灵巧的动作. ▷ **dex·ter·ously** (also **dex·trously**) *adv*.

dex·trose /ˈdekstrəʊs, -əʊz; ˋdɛkstros, -oz/ *n* [U] form of glucose 右旋糖(葡萄糖的一种).

DG /ˌdiː ˈdʒiː; ˌdi ˋdʒi/ *abbr* 缩写 = **1** (on coins) by the grace of God (Latin *Dei Gratia*) (硬币上的字样)蒙上帝之恩, 蒙主恩宠(源自拉丁文 *Dei Gratia*). **2** thanks be to God (Latin *Deo Gratias*) 感谢上帝(源自拉丁文 *Deo Gratias*). **3** director-general.

dhoti /ˈdəʊtɪ; ˋdotɪ/ *n* loincloth worn by male Hindus (印度男子用的)缠腰布.

dhow /daʊ; daʊ/ *n* ship with one mast used along the coasts of Arab countries (阿拉伯国家沿海使用的)单桅帆船.

DHSS /ˌdiː eɪtʃ es ˈes; ˌdi etʃ ɛs ˋɛs/ *abbr* 缩写 = (*Brit*) Department of Health and Social Security 卫生和社会保险部.

di- *pref* 前缀 **1** (with *ns* 后与名词结合) two; double 二; 双; 二重; 二倍: *dicotyledon*. **2** (*chemistry* 化) (with *ns* in names of chemical compounds 后与名词结合构成化合物名称) containing two atoms or groups of the specified type 含有两个原子的; 含有两组某一类型物质的: *dioxide* ○ *dichromate*. Cf 参看 BI-, TRI-.

dia·betes /ˌdaɪəˈbiːtiːz; ˌdaɪəˋbitiz/ *n* [U] disease of the pancreas which prevents sugar and starch being properly absorbed 糖尿病.

dia·betic /ˌdaɪəˈbetɪk; ˌdaɪəˋbɛtɪk/ *adj* of diabetes 糖尿病的.

▷ **dia·betic** *n* person suffering from diabetes 糖尿病患者.

dia·bolic /ˌdaɪəˈbɒlɪk; ˌdaɪəˋbɑlɪk/ *adj* (**a**) of or like a devil 魔鬼的; 魔鬼似的. (**b**) clever and evil; wicked 奸邪的; 阴毒的; 毒辣的: *diabolic plan, trick, etc* 阴毒的计划、诡计等.

▷ **dia·bol·ical** /-lɪkl; -lɪkl̩/ *adj* **1** = DIABOLIC. **2** (*Brit infml* 口) very bad 很坏的; 很差的; 糟糕的: *The film was diabolical.* 这部电影糟透了. ○ *a diabolical liberty*, ie an act that one resents very much 极放肆的举动. **dia·bol·ic·ally** /-klɪ; -klɪ/ *adv*.

dia·critic /ˌdaɪəˈkrɪtɪk; ˌdaɪəˋkrɪtɪk/ *n* (also **dia·crit·ical** /-kl; -kl̩/) *adj* [attrib 作定语] mark (eg an accent, a diaeresis or a cedilla) placed above or below a written or printed letter to indicate different sounds (标于书面字母上方或下方以表示其不同发音的)变音符号(如重音符、分音符或下加符).

▷ **dia·critic** of diacritic mark 变音符号的.

dia·dem /ˈdaɪədem; ˋdaɪəˌdɛm/ *n* crown worn as a sign of royal power 王冠, 冕(王权的象征).

di·aer·esis (also **di·er·esis**) /daɪˈerəsɪs; daɪˋɛrəsɪs/ *n* (*pl* **-eses** /-əsiːz; -əˌsiz/) mark (eg as in *naïve*) placed over a vowel to show that it is sounded separately from the vowel before it 分音符(标于元音之上以示其与前一元音分别发音, 如 naïve 中的¨). Cf 参看 UMLAUT.

dia·gnose /ˈdaɪəgnəʊz; *US* ˌdaɪəgˈnəʊs; ˌdaɪəgˋnos/ *v* [Tn, Cn·n/a] **~ sth (as sth)** find out the nature of (esp an illness) by observing its symptoms 判断; (尤指)诊断(疾病): *The doctor diagnosed measles.* 医生诊断出麻疹. ○ *diagnosed the tumour as benign* 诊断该肿瘤为良性的 ○ (*fig* 比喻) *The book diagnoses our present economic ills*, ie shows what is wrong with the economy. 该书针砭我们经济中现存的弊病.

dia·gnosis /ˌdaɪəgˈnəʊsɪs; ˌdaɪəgˋnosɪs/ *n* (*pl* **-noses** /-ˈnəʊsiːz; -ˋnosiz/) (**a**) [U] diagnosing 诊断; 确定毛病; 判断问题: *make one's diagnosis* 进行诊断 ○ *a doctor skilled in diagnosis* 诊断准确的医生 ○ *accurate diagnosis of an electrical fault* 电气故障的准确判定. Cf 参看 PROGNOSIS. (**b**) [C] (statement of the) result of diagnosing 诊断结果; 诊断书.

dia·gnostic /ˌdaɪəgˈnɒstɪk; ˌdaɪəgˋnɑstɪk/ *adj* [usu attrib 通常作定语] of diagnosis 诊断的; 判断的: *diagnostic skill, training, etc* 诊断的技术、训练等 ○ *symptoms that were of little diagnostic value*, ie that did not indicate the patient's disease 对诊断是何疾病无甚参考价值的症状(即该症状显示不出是何疾病).

di·ag·onal /daɪˈægənl; daɪˋægənl̩/ *adj* (**a**) crossing a straight-sided figure, eg a rectangle, from corner to corner (长方形等直边图形的)对角的, 对角线的. ⇨ illus at VERTICAL 见 VERTICAL 之插图. (**b**) slanting; oblique 倾斜的; 斜线的: *diagonal stripes* 斜纹. (**c**) crossed by slanting lines 有斜线的; 斜纹的.

▷ **di·ag·onal** *n* straight line crossing a straight-sided figure from corner to corner; slanting line 对角线; 斜线. **di·ag·on·ally** /-nəlɪ; -nl̩ɪ/ *adv*.

dia·gram /ˈdaɪəgræm; ˋdaɪəˌgræm/ *n* drawing or plan that uses simple lines rather than realistic details to explain or illustrate a machine, structure, process, etc 图解; 图表; 示意图: *a diagram of a gear-box, a rail network* 齿轮箱、铁路网的图解. ▷ **dia·gram·matic** /ˌdaɪəgrəˈmætɪk; ˌdaɪəgrəˋmætɪk/ *adj*: *a diagrammatic map* 图解地图. **dia·gram·mat·ic·ally** /-klɪ; -klɪ/ *adv*.

dial /ˈdaɪəl; ˋdaɪəl/ *n* **1** face of a clock or watch 钟面; 表面. **2** similar face or flat plate with a scale and a pointer for measuring weight, volume, pressure, the amount of gas used, etc 仪表盘; 标度盘; 刻度盘: *the dial of an* *electricity meter* 电表盘. **3** plate or disc, etc on a radio or television set showing the wavelengths or channels (收音机)调谐指示板; (电视机)频道显示盘. **4 (a)** disc on a telephone that is turned when making a call (电话)拨号盘. **(b)** set of keys on a telephone that are pressed when making a call (按键式电话的)按键盘.

▷ **dial** *v* (**-ll-**; *US* **-l-**) [I, Tn] use a telephone dial to call (a number or telephone service) 打电话; 拨(电话号码): *dial 01-230-1212* 拨 01-230-1212 ○ *dial the operator* 打给接线员. **'dialling code** numbers for an area or a country that are dialled before the number of the person one wants to speak to 电话区域号码: *The dialling code for the London area is 01.* 伦敦地区的电话区号是01. **'dialling tone** sound heard on the telephone showing that one can begin to dial the number wanted (电话内传出表示可拨号的)拨号音. ⇨App 4 见附录4.

dia·lect /ˈdaɪəlekt; ˋdaɪəˌlɛkt/ *n* [C, U] form of a language (grammar, vocabulary and pronunciation) used in a part of a country or by a class of people 方言; 土语; 地方话: *the Yorkshire dialect* 约克郡方言 ○ *a play written in dialect* 用方言写的剧本 ○ [attrib 作定语] *dialect words, pronunciations, etc* 方言词、方音. Cf 参看 ACCENT 3, BROGUE. ▷ **dia·lectal** /ˌdaɪəˈlektl; ˌdaɪəˋlɛktḷ/ *adj*: *dialectal differences between two areas* 两个地区方言的差别.

D

dia·lec·tic /ˌdaɪəˈlektɪk; ˌdaɪəˋlɛktɪk/ *n* [U] (also **dia·lec·tics** [sing *v*]) (*philosophy* 哲) **1** art of discovering and testing truths by discussion and logical argument 逻辑论证法(通过讨论与逻辑推理揭示并检验真理的方法). **2** criticism that deals with metaphysical contradictions and how to solve them 辩证法(研究抽象矛盾及其解决方法的学说).

▷ **dia·lect·ical** /-kl; -kḷ/ *adj* of or relating to dialectic 逻辑论证的; 有关逻辑论证的; 辩证的; 有关辩证法的: *dialectical method* 逻辑论证的方法. **dia,lectical ma'terialism** Marxist theory that political and historical events are due to the conflict of social forces caused by man's material needs 辩证唯物主义. **dia·lect·ic·ally** /-klɪ; -klɪ/ *adv*.

dia·lec·ti·cian /ˌdaɪəlekˈtɪʃn; ˌdaɪəlɛkˋtɪʃən/ *n* person who is skilled in dialectic 擅长逻辑论证者; 辩证学家.

dia·logue (*US* also **dia·log**) /ˈdaɪəlɒg; *US* -lɔːg; ˋdaɪəˌlɔg/ *n* **1 (a)** [U, C] (writing in the form of a) conversation or talk 对话; 用对话体写的文字: *Most plays are written in dialogue.* 大多数戏剧都是用对话体写的. ○ *a novel with long descriptions and little dialogue* 描述多而对话少的小说. **(b)** [C] conversation, esp in literature, plays and films (尤指文学、戏剧、电影中的)对话, 对白: *a long dialogue in the opening scene* 开场的大段对白. **2** [C, U] discussion between people with different opinions 意见分歧者之间的讨论; 意见交换; 磋商: *a useful dialogue on common problems* 就共同问题进行的有益的磋商 ○ *More dialogue between world leaders is needed.* 世界各国领导人之间需要多交换意见.

dia·lysis /ˌdaɪˈælɪsɪs; daɪˋæləsɪs/ *n* (*pl* **-lyses** /-lɪsiːz; -ləˌsiz/) [U, C] (*medical* 医) process of purifying blood by passing it through a membrane, used esp for treating patients with damaged kidneys 透析, 渗析(通过薄膜过滤来净化血液的方法, 尤用于治疗肾脏损伤的病人): *renal dialysis* 肾透析 ○ [attrib 作定语] *a dialysis machine* 透析机.

di·amanté /daɪəˈmæntɪ, dɪəˈmɒnteɪ; ˌdaɪəmɑnˋte/ *adj* decorated with powdered crystal or some other sparkling substance 饰以水晶粉或其他闪光物的: *diamanté ear-rings* 珠光耳环.

dia·meter /daɪˈæmɪtə(r); daɪˋæmətɚ/ *n* (length of a) straight line connecting the centre of a circle or sphere, or of the base of a cylinder, to two points on its sides 直径: *the diameter of a tree-trunk* 树干的直径 ○ *a lens that magnifies 20 diameters*, ie makes an object look 20 times longer, wider, etc than it is 放大20倍的透镜. ⇨App 5 见附录5. ⇨illus at CIRCLE 见 CIRCLE 之插图.

▷ **dia·met·rical** /ˌdaɪəˈmetrɪkl; ˌdaɪəˋmɛtrɪkḷ/ *adj* of or along a diameter 直径的; 沿直径的.

dia·met·ric·ally /ˌdaɪəˈmetrɪklɪ; ˌdaɪəˋmɛtrɪklɪ/ *adv* completely; entirely 完全地; 全然地: *diametrically opposed/opposite* 完全相反的.

dia·mond /ˈdaɪəmənd; ˋdaɪəmənd/ *n* **1 (a)** [U, C] transparent precious stone of pure carbon in crystallized form, the hardest substance known 金刚石; 金刚钻; 钻石: *a ring with a diamond in it* 钻石戒指 ○ [attrib 作定语] *a diamond ring, necklace, etc* 钻石戒指、项链等. **(b)** [C] piece of this (often artificially made) used in industry, esp for cutting glass or as a stylus for playing records (常为人造的)工业用金刚石; (尤指)金刚石玻璃刀, 宝石唱针. **2** [C] figure with four equal sides and with angles that are not right angles 菱形. **3 (a)** **diamonds** [sing or pl *v*] suit of playing-cards marked with red diamond shapes 红方块花色的纸牌: *the five of diamonds* 方块五 ○ *Diamonds is/are trumps.* 方块为王牌. **(b)** [C] playing-card of this suit 方块牌: *play a diamond* 出一张方块. ⇨illus at PLAYING-CARD 见 PLAYING-CARD 之插图. **4** [C] (in baseball) space inside the lines connecting the bases (棒球)内野(四垒连线内的场地). **5** (idm 习语) **a rough diamond** ⇨ ROUGH[1].

□ **,diamond 'jubilee** (celebration of a) 60th anniversary 60周年(纪念). Cf 参看 GOLDEN JUBILEE (GOLDEN), SILVER JUBILEE (SILVER).

,diamond 'wedding 60th anniversary of a wedding 钻石婚(结婚60周年纪念). Cf 参看 GOLDEN WEDDING (GOLDEN), SILVER WEDDING (SILVER).

di·aper /ˈdaɪəpə(r); *US also* ˈdaɪpər; ˋdaɪəpɚ, ˋdaɪpɚ/ *n* **1** [U] linen or cotton fabric with a pattern of small diamonds on it 有菱形花格的麻或棉织物. **2** [C] (*US*) = NAPPY.

dia·phan·ous /daɪˈæfənəs; daɪˋæfənəs/ *adj* (of fabric) light, very fine and almost transparent (指织物)又轻又薄而半透明的: *a diaphanous veil* 半透明的面纱 ○ *a dress of diaphanous silk* 薄如蝉翼的绸服.

dia·phragm /ˈdaɪəfræm; ˋdaɪəˌfræm/ *n* **1** wall of muscle, between the chest and the abdomen, that helps to control breathing 膈; 膈膜; 横膈膜. ⇨illus at RESPIRE 见 RESPIRE 之插图. **2** arrangement of thin plates in a camera that control how much light is let in through the lens 光圈; 光孔; 光阑. **3** vibrating disc or cone producing sound-waves, eg in telephone receivers, loudspeakers, etc 振动膜(如电话听筒及扬声器等中的). **4** (also **Dutch 'cap, cap**) thin plastic or rubber membrane that is fitted over the neck of the womb before intercourse to prevent conception 子宫帽(避孕用具).

dia·rrhoea (*US* **dia·rrhea**) /ˌdaɪəˈrɪə; ˌdaɪəˋriə/ *n* [U] condition that causes waste matter to be emptied from the bowels frequently and in a watery form 腹泻: *have a bad attack of diarrhoea* 患了严重的腹泻.

di·ary /ˈdaɪərɪ; ˋdaɪərɪ/ *n* (book used for a) daily record of events, thoughts, appointments, etc 日记; 日志; 日记簿: *keep* (ie write regularly in) *a diary* 记日记.

▷ **di·ar·ist** /ˈdaɪərɪst; ˋdaɪərɪst/ *n* person who writes a diary, esp one that is later published 写日记的人, 日记作者(尤指内容供日后发表者).

Dia·spora /daɪˈæspərə; daɪˋæspərə/ *n* **the Diaspora** [sing] **(a)** settling of the Jews among various non-Jewish communities after they had been exiled in 538 BC 犹太人于公元前538年被逐出故土后散居各地. **(b)** places where they settled 犹太人散居的各个地方: *People from every country of the Diaspora now live in Israel.* 当年流落他乡的犹太人现在生活在以色列.

dia·stase /ˈdaɪəsteɪs; ˋdaɪəˌstes/ *n* [U] enzyme that converts starch to sugar, important in digestion 淀粉酶; 糖化酶.

di·atom /ˈdaɪətəm; *US* -tɒm; ˋdaɪəˌtɑm/ *n* any of various types of microscopic one-cell plants living in water and forming fossil deposits 硅藻.

dia·tonic /ˌdaɪəˈtɒnɪk; ˌdaɪəˋtɑnɪk/ *adj* (*music* 音) using the notes of the major or minor scale[2](6) only, not of the chromatic scale 用自然音阶的.

dia·tribe /ˈdaɪətraɪb; ˋdaɪəˌtraɪb/ *n* **~ (against sb/sth)** lengthy and bitter attack in words 长篇抨击; 长时间的谩骂: *a diatribe against the police state* 对警察国家的连声怒骂.

dibble /ˈdɪbl; ˋdɪbḷ/ (also **dib·ber** /ˈdɪbə(r); ˋdɪbɚ/) *n* short wooden tool with a pointed end, used for making holes in the ground for seeds or young plants 点播器; 挖穴器.

▷ **dibble** *v* (phr v) **dibble sth in** put (plants, etc) in the ground using a dibble 用点播器栽种(植物等); 点播.

dice 色子

dice /daɪs; daɪs/ *n* (*pl* unchanged 复数不变) **1** (**a**) [C] small cube of wood, bone, plastic, etc that has a different number of spots on each side, from one to six, used in games of chance 色子; 骰子: *a pair of dice* 一对色子 ○ *shake/roll/throw the dice* 摇[滚/掷]色子. ⇨illus 见插图. (**b**) [U] game played with this 掷色子游戏: *play dice* 玩掷色子游戏. **2** (idm 习语) **load the dice** ⇨ LOAD². **no 'dice** (*sl* 俚 *esp US*) no agreement (to sth requested) 不同意(某要求); 拒绝; 不行: *'Shall we change the plan?' 'No dice, we'll stick with the original one.'* '我们变动一下计划好吗?' '不行, 我们要按原计划行事.'

▷ **dice** *v* **1** [I] gamble using dice 用色子赌博. **2** [Tn, Tn·p] cut (meat, vegetables, etc) into small cubes 将(肉、蔬菜等)切成小方块, 切成丁: *Dice the beetroot (up) neatly.* 将甜菜根切成整齐的小方块. **3** (idm 习语) **dice with death** (*infml* 口) risk one's life 冒生命危险; 玩儿命.

dicey /ˈdaɪsɪ; ˋdaɪsɪ/ *adj* (**dicier**, **diciest**) (*infml* 口) risky; dangerous 冒险的; 危险的: *The fog made driving a bit dicey.* 在这大雾中开车有些危险.

di·cho·tomy /daɪˈkɒtəmɪ; daɪˋkɑtəmɪ/ *n* **~ (between A and B)** (*fml* 文) separation into or between two groups or things that are opposed, entirely different, etc 一分为二; 二分; 二分法: *the dichotomy between peace and war* 和平与战争之一分为二 ○ *They set up a false dichotomy between working and raising a family*, ie wrongly claim that one cannot do both. 他们错误地把工作与养育儿女两者对立起来.

dick /dɪk; dɪk/ *n* **1** (⚠ *infml* 讳, 口) penis 屌, 鸡巴(阴茎). **2** (*dated infml* 旧, 口 *esp US*) detective 侦探: *The thief was caught by the hotel dick.* 那个贼被旅店的巡察职员抓住了.

dick·ens /ˈdɪkɪnz; ˋdɪkɪnz/ *n* **the dickens** (*infml euph* 口, 婉) (used to give emphasis, esp in questions) the Devil (用以加强语气, 尤于疑问句中)相当于 the Devil: *Who/What/Where the dickens is that?* 到底是谁[是什么/在哪儿]? ○ *We had the dickens of a job finding the place.* 我们费了九牛二虎之力才找到这地方.

Dick·ens·ian /dɪˈkenzɪən; dɪˋkɛnzɪən/ *adj* of or like the novels of Dickens, which often describe eccentric characters and bad social conditions 狄更斯笔下的; 像狄更斯小说的: *a Dickensian slum* (似)狄更斯笔下的贫民窟.

dicker /ˈdɪkə(r); ˋdɪkɚ/ *v* [I, Ipr] **~ (with sb) (for sth)** argue (with the seller) about the price of sth; haggle (与卖主)讲价钱; 讨价还价: *She dickered (with the shopkeeper) for the best fruit.* 她要买店里最好的水果而(跟店主)讨价还价.

dicky¹ (also **dickey**) /ˈdɪkɪ; ˋdɪkɪ/ *n* (*infml* 口) **1** (also **'dicky-seat**) (*Brit dated* 旧) small extra folding seat at the back of some old-fashioned two-seater cars (旧式两座位汽车后部的)折叠加座. **2** (*dated* 旧) false shirt-front 衬衫的假襟.

□ **'dicky-bird** *n* **1** (used by or to young children 儿语) bird 鸟儿. **2** (idm 习语) **not say a dicky-bird** ⇨ SAY.

dicky² /ˈdɪkɪ; ˋdɪkɪ/ *adj* (**-ier**, **-iest**) (*dated Brit infml* 旧, 口) not healthy or strong 不健康的; 虚弱的; 不结实的; 脆弱的: *That ladder looks a bit dicky.* 那梯子看起来不太结实. ○ *have a dicky heart* 虚弱的心脏.

di·co·ty·le·don /ˌdaɪkɒtəˈliːdən; ˌdaɪkɑtlˋidn̩/ *n* flowering plant that has two leaves growing from the seed at the embryo stage 双子叶植物.

Dic·ta·phone /ˈdɪktəfəʊn; ˋdɪktəˌfon/ *n* (*propr* 专利名) machine that records speech, esp dictated letters, and plays it back so that a secretary can type it out (录下口授信函等然后播放以供秘书打出的)录音机; 口授录音机.

dic·tate /dɪkˈteɪt; *US* ˈdɪkteɪt; ˋdɪktet/ *v* **1** [I, Ipr, Tn, Tn·pr] **~ (sth) (to sb)** say or read aloud (words to be typed, written down or recorded on tape) 口授; 读出(文字, 作听写或录音): *dictate a letter to one's secretary* 向秘书口授信稿 ○ *The teacher dictated a passage to the class.* 教师读出一段文章让全班听写. **2** [Tn, Tn·pr] **~ sth (to sb)** state or order sth with the force of authority 强行规定; 指令; 指定: *dictate terms to a defeated enemy* 向战败的敌人指定条件. **3** (phr v) **dictate to sb** (esp passive 尤用于被动语态) give orders to sb, esp in an officious way 指使某人; (尤指)向某人发号施令: *I refuse to be dictated to by you.* 我不愿被你呼来唤去的. ○ *You can't dictate to people how they should live.* 不能强行规定人们应该怎样生活. ⇨ Usage at DECREE 用法见 DECREE.

▷ **dic·tate** *n* /ˈdɪkteɪt; ˋdɪktet/ (usu *pl* 通常作复数) command (esp one that reason, conscience, etc prompts one to obey) (尤指在理智、良心等驱使下必须执行的)命令, 指令: *Follow the dictates of common sense*, ie Do what common sense tells you to do. 按常识行事.

dic·ta·tion /dɪkˈteɪʃn; dɪkˋteʃən/ *n* **1** [U] action of giving or taking sth dictated 口授; 听写; 命令: *shorthand dictation* 速记. **2** [C] passage, etc that is dictated 用作口授、听写的文字: *three English dictations* 三段英语听写文字.

dic·tator /dɪkˈteɪtə(r); *US* ˈdɪkteɪtər; ˋdɪktetɚ/ *n* **1** ruler who has total power over his country, esp one who has obtained it by force and uses it in a cruel way 独裁者. **2** (*fig infml* 比喻, 口) person who insists that people do what he wants 霸道的人; 爱发号施令者: *Our boss is a bit of a dictator.* 我们的老板有点霸道.

▷ **dic·tat·or·ial** /ˌdɪktəˈtɔːrɪəl; ˌdɪktəˋtɔrɪəl/ *adj* (**a**) of or like a dictator 独裁者的; 似独裁者的; 独裁的: *dictatorial government, powers, etc* 独裁政治、权力等. (**b**) fond of giving orders; domineering 爱发号施令的; 霸道的; 专横的; 盛气凌人的: *a dictatorial teacher, manner, tone* 专横的教师、态度、语气. **dic·tat·ori·ally** /-əlɪ; -əlɪ/ *adv*.

dic·tator·ship *n* **1** [C, U] (country with) government by a dictator 独裁政治; 专政; 专制; 独裁国家; 专制国家. **2** [C] rank or office of a dictator 独裁者的地位或职位.

dic·tion /ˈdɪkʃn; ˋdɪkʃən/ *n* [U] (**a**) style or manner of speaking or (sometimes) writing 说话(有时亦指写作)的方式; 语言风格: *Clarity of diction is vital for a public speaker.* 发音清晰对演说家至关重要. (**b**) choice and use of words 词语的选择; 遣词用字; 措辞.

dic·tion·ary /ˈdɪkʃənrɪ; *US* -nerɪ; ˋdɪkʃəˌnɛrɪ/ *n* (**a**) book that lists and explains the words of a language, or gives translations of them into one or more other languages, and is usu arranged in alphabetical order 字典; 词典: *an English dictionary* 英语词典. (**b**) similar book that explains the terms of a particular subject 专业词典: *a dictionary of architecture* 建筑学词典.

dictum /ˈdɪktəm; ˋdɪktəm/ *n* (*pl* **~s** or **-ta** /-tə; -tə/) (**a**) saying; maxim 名言; 格言: *the well-known dictum 'Knowledge is power'* 著名的格言'知识就是力量'. (**b**) formal expression of opinion 正式发表的权威性意见.

did *pt* of DO.

di·dactic /dɪˈdæktɪk, daɪ-; daɪˋdæktɪk/ *adj* (*fml* 文) **1** intended to teach 教导的; 教诲性的; 说教的: *didactic poetry, methods* 教诲诗、教导方法. **2** (*usu derog* 通常作贬义) that seems to treat the listener, reader, etc like a child in school 对待听者、读者等有如小学生似的; 教书式的: *I don't like her didactic way of explaining everything.* 我不喜欢她那种像教小孩子一样解释一切的方法. ▷ **di·dact·ic·ally** /-klɪ; -klɪ/ *adv*.

diddle /ˈdɪdl; ˋdɪdl̩/ *v* [Tn, Tn·pr] **~ sb (out of sth)** (*infml* 口) cheat sb, esp in small matters 欺骗某人; (尤指在小事上)哄骗: *I've been diddled! Half of these tomatoes are bad!* 我上当了! 这些番茄一半是坏的! ○ *They've diddled me out of the rent!* 他们骗去了我的租金!

didn't ⇨ DO.

die¹ /daɪ; daɪ/ *n* block of hard metal with a design, etc cut into it, used for shaping coins, printing-type, medals, etc or for stamping paper, leather, etc so that designs stand out from the surface 金属模; 硬模; 印模; 钢印.

□ **'die-cast** *adj* made by casting metal in a mould 用印

D

模铸造的: *die-cast toys*, eg small models of cars 用印模铸造的玩具(如小汽车模型).

die[2] /daɪ; daɪ/ *v* (*pt, pp* **died**, *pres p* **dying**) **1** (**a**) [I, Ipr] stop living; come to the end of one's life 死; 死亡; 死去: *Flowers soon die without water.* 花如果没有水很快就会枯死. ○ *die of an illness, hunger, grief* 因疾病、饥饿、悲伤而死 ○ *die from a wound* 受伤不治而死 ○ *die by violence* 横死 ○ *die by one's own hand*, ie commit suicide 自尽 ○ *die for one's country* 为国捐躯 ○ *die through neglect* 因疏忽而送命 ○ *die in battle* 阵亡 ○ *one's dying wish/words/breath*, ie uttered just before death 临终愿望[遗言/最后一口气] ○ *I'll love you to my dying day*, ie until I die. 我爱你至死不渝. (**b**) [La, Ln] be (sth) when one dies 死时处于(某种状态); 死时具备(某种身分): *die happy, poor, young, etc* 在幸福中、穷困中、年轻时...死亡 ○ *die a beggar, martyr, etc* 在乞讨生活中死去、殉道. (**c**) [Tn] have (a particular kind of death) 以(某死亡方式)而终: *die a lingering, natural, violent, etc death* 弥留许久后死去、寿终正寝、横死. **2** [I] (*fig* 比喻) cease to exist; disappear 不复存在; 消失; 消亡: *love that will never die* 永不止息的爱 ○ *dying traditions, customs, etc* 行将消失的传统、习俗等 ○ *His secret died with him*, ie He died without telling it to anyone. 他的秘密随他一同入土了. ○ *The flame died*, ie went out. 火熄了. **3** (idm 习语) **be dying for sth/to do sth** have a strong desire for sth 极想; 渴望: *I'm dying for something to eat.* 我极想吃点东西. ○ *She's dying to know where you've been.* 她极想知道你到哪儿去了. **die the 'death** (*joc* 谑) end suddenly and completely 突然中止; 戛然而止: *After getting bad reviews the play quickly died the death.* 这出戏遭到恶评后, 很快就寿终正寝了. **die 'hard** only be changed, disappear, etc with great difficulty 很难改变、消失等; 顽固; 死硬: *Old habits die hard.* 积习难移. **die in one's 'bed** die of old age or illness 老死; 病故. **die in 'harness** die while still working 在工作期间死去; 死于岗位. **die laughing** (*infml* 口) laugh a lot 笑死了: *It was so funny, I nearly died laughing.* 太好玩了, 我差点笑死了. **die/fall/drop like flies** ⇨ FLY[1]. **die with one's 'boots on/in one's 'boots** die while still vigorous and active 暴毙. **one's last/dying breath** ⇨ BREATH. **never say die** ⇨ SAY. **4** (phr v) **die away** become so faint or weak that it is no longer noticeable 减弱(以至察觉不到); 淡化: *The noise of the car died away in the distance.* 汽车的声音消失在远方. ○ *The breeze has died away.* 微风渐渐止住了. **die down** gradually become less strong, loud, noticeable, etc 逐渐减弱、降低、察觉不到等: *flames, storms, pain dying down* 火焰越来越小、风暴渐渐减弱、疼痛逐渐消失 ○ *These rumours will soon die down.* 这些谣言不久就会逐渐消失. **die off** die one by one 一一死去; 先后死去: *The members of the family had all died off.* 这家人一个个都死了. **die out** (**a**) (of a family, species, etc) no longer have any members left alive (指家族、物种等)死光, 灭绝, 绝迹: *The moth's habitat is being destroyed and it has nearly died out.* 这种蛾子因栖息地正受到破坏, 几乎绝种了. (**b**) (of a custom, practice, etc) no longer be common (指习俗、做法等)消失, 过时: *The old traditions are dying out.* 旧传统正在消失.

□ **'die-hard** *n* person who is stubborn, esp in resisting change 顽固分子, 死硬分子(尤指反对变革者): *A few die-hards are trying to stop the reforms.* 一小撮死硬派企图中止改革. ○ [attrib 作定语] *a die-hard conservative, campaigner, sceptic* 死硬的保守分子、搞运动的人、怀疑论者.

die[3] /daɪ; daɪ/ *n* **1** (*dated* 旧) = DICE. **2** (idm 习语) **the die is cast** (*saying* 谚) a decision has been made and cannot be changed 事已决定, 不可更改; 木已成舟. **straight as an arrow/a die** = STRAIGHT[1].

di·er·esis (*US*) = DIAERESIS.

diesel /'diːzl; 'dizl/ *n* **1** [C] (also **'diesel engine**) oil-burning engine (used eg for buses and locomotives) in which fuel is ignited by sudden compression 柴油机: [attrib 作定语] *a diesel lorry, train, etc* 柴油机运货卡车、火车等. **2** [U] (also **'diesel fuel, 'diesel oil**) heavy fuel oil used in diesel engines 柴油. **3** [C] locomotive, motor vehicle or ship that uses diesel fuel 柴油机机车、机动车或船.

□ **ˌdiesel-'electric** *adj* driven by electric current from a generator driven by a diesel engine 用柴油发电机驱动的: *a diesel-electric train* 柴油电力驱动的火车.

diet[1] /'daɪət; 'daɪət/ *n* **1** [C] sort of food that is usually eaten (by a person, community, etc) (某人、共同生活的人等)通常吃的食物; 日常食物: *the Japanese diet of rice, vegetables and fish* 米、蔬菜、鱼等日本人常吃的食物 ○ *Too rich a diet* (ie Too much rich food) *is not good for you.* 吃太多油腻的食物对你身体不好. ○ *illnesses caused by poor diet* 饮食欠佳导致的疾病. **2** [C] limited variety or amount of food that a person is allowed to eat, eg for medical reasons or in order to lose weight 限定的食物种类或数量, 规定食谱(如为治疗疾病或减轻体重的): *a salt-free diet* 无盐食谱 ○ [attrib 作定语] *diet aids* 食疗. **3** [sing] **~ of sth** (*fig* 比喻) so much of sth that it becomes boring or unpleasant 多得令人生厌的事物: *the constant diet of soap operas on TV* 多得使人腻烦的电视连续剧. **4** (idm 习语) **(be/go/put sb) on a diet** allowed to eat only some foods or a little food, because of illness or to lose weight 用规定食谱, 控制饮食, 节食(因病或为减轻体重): *The doctor says I've got to go on a diet.* 医生说我得节食.

▷ **diet** *v* [I] (be allowed to) eat only some foods or a little food, esp to lose weight 只(准)吃某类食物或少量食物; (尤指为减轻体重)节食: *You ought to diet and take more exercise.* 你应该节食并多做运动.

di·et·ary /'daɪətərɪ; *US* -erɪ; 'daɪəˌtɛrɪ/ *adj*: *dietary habits* 饮食习惯 ○ *dietary rules*, eg forbidding certain foods 饮食规定(如禁食某些食物).

di·et·etic /ˌdaɪə'tetɪk; ˌdaɪə'tɛtɪk/ *adj* of diet and nutrition 饮食的; 特定饮食的; 营养的.

di·et·et·ics *n* [sing *v*] science of diet and nutrition 饮食学; 营养学.

di·eti·cian (also **di·eti·tian**) /ˌdaɪə'tɪʃn; ˌdaɪə'tɪʃən/ *n* expert in dietetics 饮食学家; 营养学家.

diet[2] /'daɪət; 'daɪət/ *n* **1** (esp formerly) series of meetings to discuss national, international or church affairs (尤指旧时)讨论国内、国际或宗教事务的一系列会议, 大会. **2** law-making assembly in certain countries, eg Japan (日本等国的)国会, 议会.

dif·fer /'dɪfə(r); 'dɪfɚ/ *v* [I, Ipr] **1 ~ (from sb/sth)** not be the same (as sb/sth); be unlike (与某人[某事物])不同, 不一样, 有区别; 不像; 相异: *The brothers differ widely in their tastes.* 他们弟兄的爱好大相径庭. ○ *Tastes differ*, ie Different people like different things. 人各有所好. ○ *have differing tastes, views, etc* 有不同的爱好、观点等 ○ *In this respect, French differs from English/French and English differ.* 在这方面, 法语不同于英语[法语与英语有区别]. **2 ~ (with/from sb) (about/on sth)** disagree; not share the same opinion 不同意; 持异议: *I'm sorry to differ with you on that.* 对不起, 在那一点上我与你看法不同. ○ *We differ on many things.* 我们在很多事情上意见都不一致. **3** (idm 习语) **agree to differ** ⇨ AGREE. **I beg to differ** ⇨ BEG.

dif·fer·ence /'dɪfrəns; 'dɪfrəns/ *n* **1** [C] **~ (between A and B); ~ (in/of sth)** state or way in which two people or things are not the same, or in which sb/sth has changed 差别; 差异; 不同之处; 变化; 变化之处: *the marked differences between the two children* 两个孩子之间的显著差别 ○ *Did you notice a difference (in her)?* 你注意到(她)有什么变化吗? ○ *It's easy to tell the difference* (ie distinguish) *between butter and margarine.* 区别黄油和人造黄油是很容易的. ○ *a difference of approach* 方法的不同. **2** [C, U] **~ (in sth) (between A and B)** amount or degree in which two things are not the same or sth has changed 差距; 差额; 变化程度: *There's an age difference of six years between them*, ie One of them is six years older than the other. 他们俩相差六岁. ○ *I'll lend you 90% of the money and you'll have to find the difference*, ie the other 10%. 我借给你这笔钱的90%, 其余的(10%)你自己解决. ○ *We measured the difference(s) in temperature.* 我们测量了温度的变化. ○ *There's not much difference in price between the two computers.* 这两种计算机价格没多大差别. **3** [C] **~ (between A and B) (over sth)** disagreement, often involving a quarrel 意见不合, 争执(常引起争吵者): *Settle your differences and be friends again.* 你们消除分歧, 言归于好罢. ○ *We had a difference of opinion* (ie argued) *over who had won.* 我们在究竟是谁获胜的问题上发生了争执. **4** (idm 习语) **as near as makes no difference** ⇨ NEAR[2]. **for all the 'difference it/sth**

makes considering how little difference it/sth makes 鉴于那事物[某事物]作用甚微; 尽管有所差别. **make a, no, some, etc difference (to sb/sth)** (**a**) have an, no, some, etc effect (on sb/sth) (对某人[某事物])有、没有、有些...作用或影响: *The rain didn't make much difference (to the game).* 这场雨(对比赛)没多大影响. ○ *The sea air has made a difference to* (ie improved) *her health.* 海上的空气改善了她的健康状况. ○ *A hot bath makes all the difference* (ie makes you feel better) *in the morning.* 上午洗个热水澡能让人精神振奋. (**b**) be important, unimportant, etc (to sb/sth); matter (对某人[某事物])重要、不重要等; 要紧、不要紧等: *It makes no difference (to me) what you say: I'm not going.* 不管你怎么说(对我来说)都无所谓, 反正我不去. ○ *It won't make much difference whether you go today or tomorrow.* 你今天去也好, 明天去也好, 关系不大. ○ *Does that make any difference?* ie Is it important, need we consider it? 那要紧吗? ○ *Yes, it makes all the difference*, ie is very important. 是的, 非常重要. **make a difference between** treat differently 区别对待; 不同样对待: *She makes no difference between her two sons.* 她对两个儿子一视同仁. **sink one's differences** ⇨ SINK[1]. **split the difference** ⇨ SPLIT. **with a ˈdifference** (following *ns* 用于名词之后) special; unusual 特别的; 与众不同的: *She's an opera singer with a difference: she can act well!* 她这个歌剧演唱家与众不同, 因为她还擅长表演!

dif·fer·ent /ˈdɪfrənt; ˋdɪfrənt/ *adj* **1** ~ **(from/to sb/sth)**; *esp US* ~ **(than sb/sth)** not the same (as sb/sth) 不同的; 不一样的; 有区别的: *the same product with a different name* 名称不同的同一种产品 ○ *The room looks different with the furniture gone.* 家具搬走之后, 这房间变了样了. ○ *Their tastes are different from/to mine.* 他们的爱好与我的不同. ○ *She is wearing a different dress every time I see her.* 我每次见到她时, 她穿的衣服都不重样. **2** separate; distinct 分别的; 彼此分开的; 各不相同的: *I called on three different occasions, but he was out.* 我打了三次电话, 他都不在. ○ *They are sold in different colours*, ie a variety of colours. 这批货有多种颜色供选购. **3** (idm 习语) **(as) ˌdifferent as ˌchalk and/from ˈcheese** completely different 天差地远; 迥然不同. **a (very) different kettle of fish** (*infml* 口) a completely different person or thing from the one previously mentioned 与所提及的人或事物完全不同者; 另一码事. **know different** ⇨ KNOW. **sing a different song/tune** ⇨ SING. ▷ **dif·fer·ently** *adv*.

NOTE ON USAGE 用法: British and US English differ as regards the prepositions used after **different.** 接在 **different** 后面的介词, 在英式英语和美式英语中有所不同. **1** Before a noun or adverbial phrase, both **from** and **to** are acceptable in British English. 若用在名词或状语短语前, 英式英语使用 **from** 和 **to** 均可. Some speakers prefer **from**. 有的人喜欢用 **from**. **Different than** is not usual ☆ **different than** 则不常用: *He's very different from/to his brother.* 他跟他哥哥很不同. ○ *This visit is very different from/to last time.* 这次的访问与上次大不一样. In US English **than** is commonly used (not **to**) 在美式英语中, **than** 使用得较普遍(**to** 则不常见): *Your trains are different from/than ours.* 你们的火车跟我们的不一样. ○ *You look different than before.* 你看上去跟从前不同了. **2** In both varieties, but especially in US English, **than** is an alternative to **from** before a clause 在以上两种英语中, 尤其是美式英语, 从句前既可用 **from** 亦可用 **than**: *His appearance was very different from what I'd expected/His appearance was very different than I'd expected.* 他的容貌与我想像的相去甚远.

dif·fer·en·tial /ˌdɪfəˈrenʃl; ˏdɪfəˋrɛnʃəl/ *adj* [attrib 作定语] of, showing or depending on a difference 不同的; 有分别的; 基于差别的; 区别性的: *differential treatment of applicants for jobs*, eg varying according to their education, etc 对求职者区别对待(如根据学历等) ○ *Non-EEC countries pay a higher differential tariff.* 欧洲经济共同体以外的国家须付高于成员国的差别关税.

▷ **dif·fer·en·tial** *n* **1** (also ˌ**differential** ˈ**wage**) (*esp Brit*) difference in rates of pay for different types of work or workers (不同工种或工人的)工资级差: *a dispute about the differential between men and women workers* 有关男女工不同酬的争议. **2** (also ˌ**differential** ˈ**gear**) gear enabling a vehicle's back wheels to turn at different speeds when going round corners (车辆转弯时使两后轮以不同速度转动的)差速器. ⇨ illus at App 1 见附录1之插图, page xii.

□ ˌ**differential** ˈ**calculus** (*mathematics* 数) branch of calculus concerned with calculating rates of change, maximum and minimum values, etc 微分(学). Cf 参看 INTEGRAL CALCULUS (INTEGRAL).

dif·fer·en·ti·ate /ˌdɪfəˈrenʃɪeɪt; ˏdɪfəˋrɛnʃɪˏet/ *v* **1** (**a**) [Ipr, Tn, Tn·pr] ~ **between A and B**; ~ **A (from B)** see or show (two things) to be different; show sth to be different (from sth else) 看出或指出(两者)不同; 辨别; 区别; 区分: *Can you differentiate between the two varieties?* 你能辨别这两个品种吗? ○ *Can you differentiate one variety from the other?* 你能将这两个品种区别开来吗? ○ *One character is not clearly differentiated from another.* 人物之间的区别没有明显刻划出来. (**b**) [Tn, Tn·pr] ~ **sth (from sth)** be a mark of difference between (people or things); distinguish 构成(人或事物)间的差别; 使(人或事物)有差别: *The male's orange beak differentiates it from the female.* 那种鸟雄鸟的喙呈橙色, 与雌鸟不同. **2** [Ipr] ~ **between A and B** treat (people or things) in a different way, esp unfairly; discriminate 区别对待(人或事物)(尤指不公平地): *It is wrong to differentiate between people according to their family background.* 根据出身不同而区别待人是不对的. ▷ **dif·fer·en·ti·ation** /ˌdɪfərenʃɪˈeɪʃn; ˏdɪfəˏrɛnʃɪˋeʃən/ *n* [U].

dif·fi·cult /ˈdɪfɪkəlt; ˋdɪfəkəlt/ *adj* **1** ~ **(to do sth)** (of tasks) requiring effort or skill; not easy (指任务)需要精力或技术的; 困难的; 不易的: *a difficult problem, language, translation* 难题、难学的语言、难做的翻译 ○ *She finds it difficult to stop smoking.* 她觉得戒烟很不容易. ○ *This mountain is difficult to climb/It is difficult to climb this mountain.* 这座山很难爬[爬这座山可不容易]. ○ *Their refusal puts us in a difficult position.* 他们拒绝后, 我们便陷入了困境. ○ *They made it difficult for me to see her.* 他们从中作梗, 让我不易见到她. ○ *13 is a difficult age*, ie Children have problems then. 13岁是个出麻烦的年龄. **2** (of people) not easy to please or satisfy; unwilling to co-operate (指人)不易取悦的, 不易满足的, 不易相处的, 不愿合作的, 执拗的: *a difficult child, customer, boss, etc* 难哄的小孩、难对付的顾客、难讨好的上司 ○ *Don't be difficult: just lend us the money.* 别难为人了, 还是把钱借给我们罢. **3** (idm 习语) **easy/difficult of approach** ⇨ APPROACH.

dif·fi·culty /ˈdɪfɪkəltɪ; ˋdɪfəˏkəltɪ/ *n* **1** [U] ~ **(in sth/in doing sth)** state or quality of being difficult; trouble or effort that sth involves 困难; 艰难; 困难性; 难度: *the sheer difficulty of the task* 这项任务的高难度 ○ *Bad planning will lead to difficulty later.* 计划不善会给今后带来困难. ○ *do sth with/without difficulty* 费劲地[不费劲地]做某事 ○ *She got the door open, but only with some difficulty.* 她倒是把门打开了, 但却花了些力气. ○ *I had the greatest difficulty in persuading her.* 我为了说服她, 费了好大的劲. ○ *We had no difficulty (in) finding the house.* 我们毫不费劲地找到了那所房子. **2** [C usu *pl* 通常作复数] difficult thing to do, understand or deal with 难做、难懂、难应付的事; 难事; 难点; 难题: *the difficulties of English syntax* 英语句法的难点 ○ *be working under some difficulty*, ie in difficult circumstances 在艰苦的条件下工作 ○ *She met with many difficulties when travelling.* 她在旅行时遇到了许多伤脑筋的事. ○ *financial difficulties*, ie problems about money 财务困难 ○ *We got into difficulty/difficulties with the rent*, ie found it hard to pay. 我们付不出租钱了. ○ *I want to marry her, but my parents are making/creating difficulties*, ie making things hard for us. 我想娶她, 但我父母从中阻挠.

dif·fid·ent /ˈdɪfɪdənt; ˋdɪfədənt/ *adj* ~ **(about sth)** not having or showing much belief in one's own abilities; lacking self-confidence 对自己的能力缺乏信心的; 露出怯态的; 缺乏自信的: *an able but diffident young student* 能干但缺乏自信的青年学生 ○ *Don't be so diffident about your talents.* 别对自己的才能如此缺乏信心. ▷ **dif·fid·ence** /-dəns; -dəns/ *n* [U]. **dif·fid·ently** *adv*.

dif·fract /dɪˈfrækt; dɪˋfrækt/ *v* [Tn] break up (a beam of light) into a series of dark and light bands or into the coloured bands of the spectrum 使(一束光)衍射(即将

D

一束光分解为一系列明暗有别的光带或有色的光谱谱带，旧作绕射）. ▷ **dif·frac·tion** /dɪˈfrækʃn; dɪˈfrækʃən/ *n* [U].

dif·fuse[1] /dɪˈfju:z; dɪˈfjuz/ *v* **1** [Tn] spread (sth) all around; send out in all directions 散布；传播: *diffuse a scent, an odour, light, heat, learning, knowledge* 散发香气、散发气味、传送光、传导热、传授学问、传播知识 ○ *He diffuses enthusiasm all around him.* 他热情奔放. ○ *posters diffusing party propaganda* 政党的宣传海报 ○ *diffused lighting*, ie not coming directly from one source 漫射光照明(非直接来自单一的光源). **2** [I, Tn] (cause gases or liquids to) mix slowly 使(气体或液体)慢慢混合，扩散: *A drop of milk diffused in the water, and it became cloudy.* 一滴奶在水中扩散开来，使水变得混浊不清了.

▷ **dif·fusion** /dɪˈfju:ʒn; dɪˈfjuʒən/ *n* [U] diffusing or being diffused 散布；传播；弥漫；扩散: *the diffusion of knowledge through books and lectures* 通过书本和授课进行的知识传播 ○ *the diffusion of gases and liquids* 气体和液体的扩散.

dif·fuse[2] /dɪˈfju:s; dɪˈfjus/ *adj* **1** spread out; not concentrated 散开的；不集中的；漫射的；扩散的: *diffuse light* 漫射光. **2** using too many words; not concise 堆砌词藻的；不简洁的；冗赘的: *a diffuse writer, style* 行文冗赘的作者、冗赘的文体. ▷ **dif·fusely** *adv*. **dif·fuse·ness** *n* [U].

dig[1] /dɪg; dɪg/ *v* (**-gg-**; *pt, pp* **dug** /dʌg; dʌg/) **1** (**a**) [I, Ipr, Ip, Tn, Tn·pr, Tn·p] use one's hands, a spade, a machine, etc to break up and move (earth, etc); advance by doing this 挖，掘(泥土等): *I spent the morning digging.* 我整个上午都在不停地挖. ○ *They are digging through the hill to make a tunnel.* 他们正在凿山建一条隧道. ○ *dig down into the soil* 往土里深挖 ○ *It is difficult to dig the ground when it is frozen.* 地面冻住了就不易挖掘. ○ *dig the soil away from the bottom of the wall* 将墙根的泥挖出来. (**b**) [Tn] make (a hole, etc) by doing this 挖出(洞等)；凿出；打(洞): *dig a pit, tunnel, shaft, etc* 挖坑、隧道、升降井等. (**c**) [Ipr] **~ for sth** search for (gold, etc) by doing this 采掘探寻(黄金等)；探矿: *We are digging for mineral deposits.* 我们正在掘地探矿. **2** (*dated infml* 旧，口) (**a**) [Tn] enjoy (sth); appreciate 喜欢(某事物)；欣赏: *I don't dig modern jazz.* 我不喜欢现代爵士乐. (**b**) [I, Tn] understand (sth) 明白(某事物)；懂: *I don't dig that crazy stuff.* 我不懂那种没意思的玩意儿. ○ *You dig?* 你懂了吗? **3** (idm 习语) ˌ**dig one's** ˈ**heels**/ˈ**toes in** be stubborn; refuse to give in 固执己见；寸步不让. **dig sb in the ribs** nudge or prod sb hard in the side 用肘碰或戳某人的肋部. **dig one's own grave** do sth which causes one's own downfall 自掘坟墓；自取灭亡. **4** (phr v) **dig in**; **dig into sth** (*infml* 口) (begin to) eat hungrily or enthusiastically (开始)贪婪地吃，津津有味地吃: *The food's ready, so dig in!* 吃的弄好了，放量吃罢! **dig sth in**; **dig sth into sth** (**a**) mix sth with soil by digging 在翻地时将某物混入土壤中: *The manure should be well dug in.* 在翻地时应把肥料均匀地混入土壤中. (**b**) push or thrust sth into sth 推入；插入；戳进；刺入: *dig a fork into a pie* 用餐叉叉馅饼 ○ *The rider dug his spurs into the horse's flank.* 骑马者用靴刺戳了戳马的侧腹. ○ *The dog dug its teeth in.* 那只狗一口咬下去. **dig oneself in** (**a**) (*military* 军) (of soldiers) protect oneself by digging a trench, etc (指士兵)挖壕沟等以掩蔽自己，挖掩体. (**b**) (*infml* 口) establish oneself securely (in a place, job, etc) (在职位、工作等方面)使自己站稳脚跟，巩固自己的地位: *He has dug himself in well at the college now.* 如今他在学院已站住脚了. **dig sb/sth out (of sth)** (**a**) get sb/sth out by digging 挖出某人[某物]: *They dug the potatoes out (of the ground).* 他们(从地里)挖出了马铃薯. ○ *He was buried by an avalanche and had to be dug out.* 他遇雪崩被埋住了，得把他挖出来. (**b**) get sth by searching or study 搜出或钻研出某事物；探索；查明: *dig information out of books and reports* 从书和报告中查找资料 ○ *dig out the truth* 探明实情. (**c**) (*infml* 口) take out (sth not easy to get at) 取出(不易找到的东西)；翻出: *dig out an old photo from the drawer* 从抽屉中翻出一张旧照片. **dig sth over** prepare (ground) thoroughly by digging 翻挖(土地)；刨地: *dig the garden over* 给花园翻地. **dig sth up** (**a**) break up (soil, etc) by digging 挖掘(泥土等)；垦地: *dig up land for a new garden* 为建一座新花园而垦地. (**b**) remove (sth) from the ground by digging 从地里挖出(某物): *We dug up the tree by its roots.* 我们将树连根挖起. (**c**) reveal and remove from the ground by digging (sth that has been buried or hidden) 从地里挖掘出(掩埋或藏起的东西)；掘到: *An old Greek statue was dug up here last month.* 上个月在这儿挖出了一尊古希腊雕像. (**d**) (*fig* 比喻) discover (information, etc); reveal sth 找出(情报等)；透露某事: *Newspapers love to dig up scandal.* 报纸就是爱把丑事儿揭出来.

dig[2] /dɪg; dɪg/ *n* **1** (**a**) poke; prod 戳；刺；捣: *give sb a dig in the ribs* 戳某人的肋部. (**b**) **~ (at sb)** (*fig* 比喻) remark that is meant to irritate or upset sb 故意让某人生气的言语；恼人的话；挖苦: *She makes mean little digs at him.* 她冲他说一些刻薄的挖苦话. **2** (**a**) act of digging 挖；掘；翻挖；刺；戳: *I gave the vegetable plot a quick dig.* 我把菜地很快翻了一遍. (**b**) site being explored by archaeologists 考古发掘地.

di·gest[1] /ˈdaɪdʒest; ˈdaɪdʒɛst/ *n* short condensed account; summary 摘要；概要: *a digest of the week's news* 一周新闻摘要.

di·gest[2] /dɪˈdʒest, daɪ-; dəˈdʒɛst, daɪ-/ *v* **1** (**a**) [Tn] change (food) in the stomach and bowels so that it can be used by the body 消化(食物): *Fish is easy to digest when you're ill.* 生病时吃鱼容易消化. (**b**) [I] (of food) be changed in this way (指食物)被消化: *It takes hours for a meal to digest.* 一顿饭要几小时才能消化掉. **2** [Tn] take (information) in mentally; fully understand 吸收(信息)；完全理解；彻底领会: *Have you digested the report yet?* 这个报告你吃透了吗?

▷ **di·gest·ible** /dɪˈdʒestəbl, daɪ-; dəˈdʒɛstəbl, daɪ-/ *adj* that can be digested 可消化的；可吸收的. **di·gest·ib·il·ity** /dɪˌdʒestəˈbɪlətɪ, daɪ-; dəˌdʒɛstəˈbɪlətɪ, daɪ-/ *n* [U].

di·ges·tion /dɪˈdʒestʃən, daɪ-; dəˈdʒɛstʃən, daɪ-/ *n* (**a**) [U] digesting 消化；吸收；领悟: *foods which aid digestion* 助消化的食物. (**b**) [C usu *sing* 通常作单数] power of digesting food 消化能力；消化力: *have a good/poor digestion* 消化力强[弱].

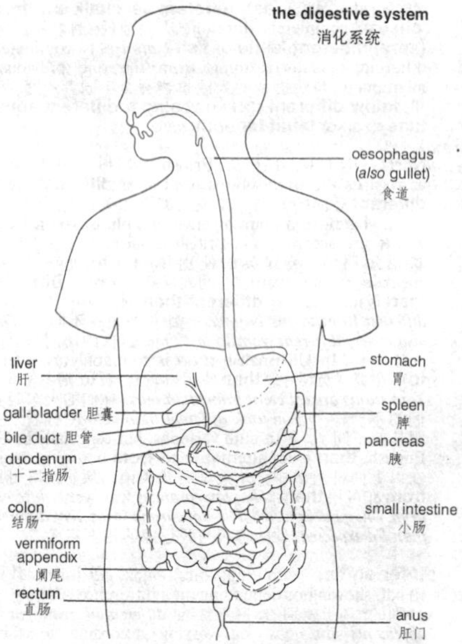

di·gest·ive /dɪˈdʒestɪv, daɪ-; dəˈdʒɛstɪv, daɪ-/ *adj* [usu attrib 通常作定语] of digestion (of food) 消化(食物)的: *the digestive process, juices* 消化过程、消化液 ○ *suffer from digestive trouble* 患消化系统的疾病.

□ **diˌgestive ˈbiscuit** (also **digestive**) (*Brit*) round, not very sweet, biscuit made from wholemeal flour 消化饼干.

di'gestive system organs of the body that digest food 消化系统. ⇨illus 见插图.

dig·ger /ˈdɪɡə(r); ˋdɪɡɚ/ *n* **1** person who digs 挖掘者; 采掘者. **2** mechanical excavator 挖掘机; 挖掘器. **3** (*sl* 俚) Australian or New Zealander, esp a soldier 澳大利亚人, 新西兰人(尤指士兵).

dig·ging /ˈdɪɡɪŋ; ˋdɪɡɪŋ/ *n* **1** [U] action of digging 挖掘; 采掘. **2 diggings** [pl] place where people dig for tin, gold, etc (开采锡、黄金等的)矿场, 矿区.

di·git /ˈdɪdʒɪt; ˋdɪdʒɪt/ *n* **1** (*mathematics* 数) any of the ten Arabic numerals 0 to 9 (阿拉伯数字中)0到9的任何一个数字: *The number 57306 contains five digits.* 57306是个五位数. **2** (*anatomy* 解) finger or toe 手指; 脚趾.

▷ **di·gital** /ˈdɪdʒɪtl; ˋdɪdʒɪtl/ *adj* **1** showing amounts by means of numbers 数字的; 数字显示的. **2** of fingers or toes 手指的; 脚趾的. ˌ**digital** ˈ**clock**, ˌ**digital** ˈ**watch** clock/watch that shows the time by digits rather than hands 数字式时钟[手表]. ˌ**digital comˈputer** device that makes calculations, etc with data represented as a series of digits 数字计算机. Cf 参看 ANALOGUE COMPUTER (ANALOGUE). ˌ**digital reˈcording** [C, U] (recording made by a) process of converting sound into a series of electrical pulses (representing binary digits) 数字录声(把声频信号变换成与二元数字相应的一串脉冲的过程及以此方式进行的录声).

dig·nify /ˈdɪɡnɪfaɪ; ˋdɪɡnəˌfaɪ/ *v* (*pt, pp* **-fied**) (*fml* 文) **1** [Tn] make (sth) seem worthy or impressive; give dignity to 使(某事物)显得有尊严、崇高; 给(某事物)增光: *a ceremony dignified by the presence of the ambassador* 因大使光临而生辉的典礼. **2** [Tn, Tn·pr] **~ sb/sth (with sth)** give an important-sounding name to sb/sth 用尊贵的名字称呼某人[某事物]; 美其名曰: *dignify a small collection of books with the name of library* 藏书不多, 却美其名曰图书馆 ○ *I wouldn't dignify this trash by calling it a novel.* 这部劣等作品我是不会美称为小说的.

▷ **dig·ni·fied** *adj* having or showing dignity 有尊严的; 高贵的; 显得高尚的; 高雅的; 庄严的: *a dignified person, walk, bow* 高贵的人、庄重的步态、高雅的鞠躬礼.

dig·nit·ary /ˈdɪɡnɪtərɪ; *US* -terɪ; ˋdɪɡnəˌtɛrɪ/ *n* (*fml* 文) person with a high rank or position 显要人物; 权贵: *civic dignitaries*, eg the mayor and councillors 市政要人(如市长和议员).

dig·nity /ˈdɪɡnətɪ; ˋdɪɡnətɪ/ *n* **1** [U] quality that earns or deserves respect; true worth 高尚的品质; 可贵的品质; 真正的价值; 尊严; 尊贵: *the dignity of labour* 劳动的尊严 ○ *Only a truly free person has human dignity.* 只有真正自由的人才具有人的尊严. **2** [U] calm or serious manner or style 庄严的举止; 端庄的仪态: *She kept her dignity despite the booing.* 尽管嘘声四起, 她依旧泰然自若. **3** [C] (*fml* 文) high or honourable rank, post or title 高位或显要职衔: *The Queen conferred the dignity of a peerage on him.* 女王封他为贵族. **4** (idm 习语) **beˌneath one's ˈdignity** (*often ironic* 常作反语) below one's social, moral, etc standards 有失身分、尊严、体面等: *Some husbands still think it beneath their dignity to do the shopping.* 有些做丈夫的至今仍然认为让他们去买东西是件丢面子的事. ˌ**stand on one's ˈdignity** insist on behaving or being treated in a special way because one thinks oneself important (因自爱)保持尊严; (因自命不凡)摆架子: *She doesn't stand on her dignity and treat the rest of us as servants.* 她没有端着架子把我们当作仆人对待.

di·graph /ˈdaɪɡrɑːf; *US* -ɡræf; ˋdaɪɡræf/ *n* two letters that represent a single sound (eg *sh* /ʃ; ʃ/, *ea* /iː; i/ in *sheaf*) 二合字母(代表一个单音的两个字母, 如sheaf中sh代表/ʃ; ʃ/, ea代表/iː; i/).

di·gress /daɪˈɡres; daɪˋɡrɛs/ *v* [I, Ipr] **~ (from sth)** turn or wander (from the main topic) in speech or writing 说话或写作时偏离(主题); 离题: *Don't digress (from the subject) when lecturing.* 讲课时不要岔开(主题).

▷ **di·gres·sion** /daɪˈɡreʃn; daɪˋɡrɛʃən/ *n* (**a**) [U] digressing 离题. (**b**) [C] passage, etc in which one digresses 题外话; 枝节内容: *If you'll allow a slight digression,...* 请允许我说几句题外话....

digs /dɪɡz; dɪɡz/ *n* [pl] (*Brit infml* 口) room(s) rented in sb else's house; lodgings 在他人房屋里租用的房间; 寄宿房间; 寄宿处: *the high cost of living in digs* 寄宿的高费用 ○ *take digs in London* 在伦敦寄宿.

dike (also **dyke**) /daɪk; daɪk/ *n* **1** ditch (for allowing water to flow away from land) 排水沟. **2** long wall of earth, etc (to keep back water and prevent flooding) (拦水防洪的)土堤, 堤坝. **3** (⚠ *sl* 讳, 俚) lesbian, esp a masculine one 同性恋女子(尤指男性化者).

▷ **dike** *v* [I, Tn] make or provide (sth) with a dike(1, 2) 建排水沟; 筑堤.

dik·tat /ˈdɪktæt; dɪkˋtɑt/ *n* [C, U] (*derog* 贬) order, esp an unreasonable one, that must be obeyed 命令, 指令, 勒令(尤指不合理而又必须服从的): *refuse to accept the foreign diktat* 拒绝接受这道外国的苛刻命令.

di·lap·id·ated /dɪˈlæpɪdeɪtɪd; dəˋlæpəˌdetɪd/ *adj* (of furniture, buildings, etc) falling to pieces; in a bad state of repair (指家具、建筑物等)残破的, 破烂的, 失修的: *a dilapidated chair, bed, etc* 破椅子、床等 ○ *a dilapidated-looking car* 破破烂烂的汽车. ▷ **di·lap·ida·tion** /dɪˌlæpɪˈdeɪʃn; dəˌlæpəˋdeʃən/ *n* [U]: *in a dreadful state of dilapidation* 处于破败不堪的状态.

di·late /daɪˈleɪt; daɪˋlet/ *v* **1** [I, Tn] (cause sth to) become wider, larger or further open (使某物)扩大, 膨胀, 张大: *The pupils of your eyes dilate when you enter a dark room.* 进入黑暗的房间时, 瞳孔就扩大. ○ *The horse dilated its nostrils.* 那匹马张大了鼻孔. **2** (phr v) **dilate on sth** (*fml* 文) speak or write about sth for a long time 详述某事; 铺叙某事: *a chapter in which she dilates on the benefits of vegetarianism* 她详述素食好处的一章.

▷ **di·la·tion** /daɪˈleɪʃn; daɪˋleʃən/ *n* [U] dilating or being dilated 扩大; 膨胀; 张大; 详述.

dil·at·ory /ˈdɪlətərɪ; *US* -tɔːrɪ; ˋdɪləˌtɔrɪ/ *adj* (*fml* 文) (**a**) **~ (in doing sth)** slow in acting 行动缓慢的; 迟缓的: *The Government has been dilatory in condemning the outrage.* 政府迟迟才谴责是次暴行. (**b**) causing delay 拖拉的; 拖延的: *dilatory behaviour, actions, etc* 拖拉的行为、行动等. ▷ **dil·at·or·ily** *adv*. **dil·at·ori·ness** *n* [U].

di·lemma /dɪˈlemə, daɪ-; dəˋlɛmə, daɪ-/ *n* **1** situation in which one has to choose between two undesirable things or courses of action 进退两难的窘境; 进退维谷的困境: *be in/place sb in a dilemma* 陷入[置某人于]进退两难之境. **2** (idm 习语) **on the horns of a dilemma** ⇨ HORN.

di·let·tante /ˌdɪlɪˈtæntɪ; ˌdɪləˋtæntɪ/ *n* (*pl* **~s** or **-ti** /-tiː; -ti/) (*often derog* 常作贬义) person who studies or does sth, but without serious interest or understanding 浮泛的涉猎者; 浅尝辄止者: *a musical dilettante* 粗通音乐的人. ▷ **di·let·tant·ish** /-ˈtæntɪʃ; -ˋtæntɪʃ/ *adj*: *a dilettantish follower of the arts* 蜻蜓点水般学艺术的人.

di·li·gence /ˈdɪlɪdʒəns; ˋdɪlədʒəns/ *n* [U] **~ (in sth/in doing sth)** steady effort; careful hard work 不懈的努力; 勤勉; 勤奋; 认真刻苦: *She shows great diligence in her school work.* 她做作业非常用功. ○ *He pursues his aims with diligence.* 他努力追求自己的奋斗目标.

di·li·gent /ˈdɪlɪdʒənt; ˋdɪlədʒənt/ *adj* **~ (in sth/in doing sth)** showing care and effort (in what one does); hard-working 认真刻苦的; 勤勉的; 勤奋的; 用功的: *a diligent worker, pupil, etc* 勤奋的工作者、学生等 ○ *They're very diligent in keeping records.* 他们做记录十分认真. ▷ **dili·gently** *adv*.

dill /dɪl; dɪl/ *n* [U] herb with scented leaves and seeds used for flavouring pickles 莳萝; 小茴香.

dilly /ˈdɪlɪ; ˋdɪlɪ/ *n* (*US infml* 口) person or thing considered excellent or remarkable 杰出人物; 突出人物; 突出事物; 显眼的事物: *She had a dilly of a bruise on her arm.* 她手臂上有一块显眼的伤痕.

dilly-dally /ˈdɪlɪ dælɪ; ˋdɪlɪˌdælɪ/ (*pt, pp* **-dallied**) *v* [I] (*infml* 口) waste time; dawdle 浪费时间; 磨蹭; 闲混: *Don't dilly-dally! Make up your mind!* 别磨蹭了! 拿定主意吧!

di·lute /daɪˈljuːt; *US* -ˈluːt; daɪˋlut/ *v* [Tn, Tn·pr] **~ sth (with sth)** **1** make (a liquid or colour) thinner or weaker (by adding water or another liquid) 使(液体)变稀; 使(颜色)变淡; 稀释; 冲淡; 搀水: *dilute wine with water* 搀水把酒冲淡. **2** (*fig* 比喻) make (sth) weaker in force, effect, etc 削弱(某事物)的力量、效果等; 使减色; 降低: *diluting standards in our schools* 降低我们各校的水平.

▷ **di·lute** *adj* (of acids, etc) weakened by diluting (指酸液等)稀释的, 冲淡了的, 搀水的: *dilute sulphuric acid*

稀硫酸.

di·lu·tion /daɪˈljuːʃn; *US* -ˈluː-; daɪˈluʃən/ *n* (**a**) [U] diluting or being diluted 稀释; 冲淡. (**b**) [C] thing that is diluted 被稀释[冲淡]之物.

dim /dɪm; dɪm/ *adj* (**-mmer, -mmest**) **1** (**a**) where or which one cannot see well; not bright 光线暗淡的; 看不清的; 不光亮的; 昏暗的; 阴暗的: *a dim corridor with no windows* 没有窗户的昏暗走廊 ○ *the dim outline of buildings on a dark night* 黑夜里建筑物朦胧的轮廓 ○ *reading by dim candle-light* 就着微弱的烛光读书. (**b**) not clearly remembered; faint 记不清的; 记忆模糊的: *a dim memory/recollection* 淡淡的记忆[回忆]. **2** (*infml* 口) (of people) lacking intelligence (指人)愚笨的. **3** (of the eyes, eyesight) not able to see well (指眼睛)看不清东西的; (视力)差的, 模糊的: *His sight is getting dim.* 他的视力越来越差了. ○ *eyes dim with tears* 迷离的泪眼. **4** (idm 习语) **dim and distant** (*joc* 谑) long past 很久以前: *Once, in the dim and distant past, I was a student here.* 我早八辈子的时候在这儿读过书.

▷ **dim** *v* (**-mm-**) [I, Tn] (cause sth to) become dim 变暗淡或模糊; 使(某事物)暗淡或模糊: *The stage lights (were) dimmed, and the play's first act was over.* 舞台灯光暗了下去, 这出戏的第一幕结束了. ○ *Old age hasn't dimmed her memory.* 她虽然年事已高, 但记忆并未模糊.

dimly *adv* in a dim manner 暗淡地; 模糊地; 朦胧地; 迟钝地: *a dimly-lit room* 灯光微弱的房间 ○ *I can dimly* (ie only just) *remember my fourth birthday.* 我隐约记得自己过四岁生日时的情景. ○ *react rather dimly to a question* 回答问题时相当迟钝.

dim·ness *n* [U].

□ ˈ**dim-wit** *n* (*infml* 口) stupid person 笨蛋; 傻子. ˌ**dim-ˈwitted** *adj* (*infml* 口) stupid 愚笨的.

dime /daɪm; daɪm/ *n* **1** coin of the US and Canada worth ten cents 美国、加拿大的10分铸币. ⇨App 4 见附录4. **2** (idm 习语) **a ˌdime a ˈdozen** (*infml* 口) nearly worthless or very common 几乎一文不值的; 极便宜的; 很普通的: *Novels like this one are a dime a dozen: write something original!* 这样的小说多得很, 还是写些新鲜的东西罢!

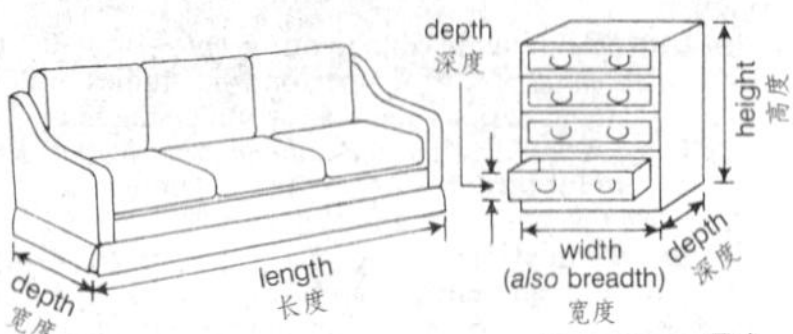

dimensions 量度

di·men·sion /dɪˈmenʃn, daɪ-; dəˈmɛnʃən, daɪ-/ *n* **1** [C, U] measurement of any sort (breadth, length, thickness, height, etc) (空间的)任何一种量度(宽度、长度、厚度、高度等): *What are the dimensions of the room?* 这房间的面积是多少? ⇨App 4 见附录4. ⇨ illus 见插图. **2** **dimensions** [pl] size; extent 大小; 体积; 程度; 范围: *a creature of huge dimensions* 体形庞大的动物 ○ (*fig* 比喻) *I did not realized the dimensions of the problem.* 我未曾意识到问题的严重程度. **3** [C] (*fig* 比喻) aspect 方面; 侧面: *There is a dimension to the problem that we have not discussed.* 这问题还有一方面我们没讨论过.

▷ **-di·men·sional** /-ʃənəl; -ʃənl̩/ (forming compound *adjs* 用以构成复合形容词) having the specified number of dimensions …维的; …方面的: *A square is two-dimensional and a cube is three-dimensional.* 正方形是二维的(平面的), 而正六面体则是三维的(立体的).

NOTE ON USAGE 用法: **1** It is sometimes difficult to decide whether **length** (*adj* **long**), **width** (*adj* **wide**) or **depth** (*adj* **deep**) is the correct term for a particular measurement. 对于物体某一边的量度, 在 **length** (adj **long**)、**width** (adj **wide**) 或 **depth** (adj **deep**) 中选用哪个才对, 有时颇难确定. The measurements of a room or of a rectangular area or object are the **length** (measured along the longer sides) and the **width** (measured along the shorter sides) 量度房间或长方形的面积或物体, 用 **length** (长度, 沿较长的边量得)和 **width** (宽度, 沿较短的边量得)表示: *The garage is 6 metres long and 3 metres wide.* 汽车房长6米, 宽3米. When describing a piece of furniture that has a front and a back, both **length** and **width** can be used for the longer sides and **depth** is used for the measurement from front to back. 在形容一件有前后之分的家具时, **length** 和 **width** 均可用以指较长的边, 而 **depth** (深度)则指从前面到后面的尺寸. **Length** is generally used when the measurement of the front is much greater than that of the depth. 若前面的长短远远超过深度, 一般用 **length**. ☆ **Width** is used when the measurements of the front and of the depth are similar. 若前面的长短与深度相似, 则用 **width**. (See illustration 见插图.) **2** Compare **wide** and **broad**. 试比较 **wide** 和 **broad**. **Wide** is the more general word but **broad** is used of parts of the body ☆ **wide** 适用范围较广, **broad** 则特指身体的部位: *a broad nose* 大鼻子 ○ *broad shoulders* 宽阔的双肩. Otherwise it is more formal than **wide** and is often used, especially in literary language, to describe features of the landscape 在其他情况下, **broad** 比 **wide** 更文雅, 尤其在文学语言中常用以描绘景色: *a broad river* 宽阔的河 ○ *a broad expanse of unspoilt country* 一片广袤的、自然美未受破坏的郊野.

di·min·ish /dɪˈmɪnɪʃ; dəˈmɪnɪʃ/ *v* [I, Tn] **1** (cause sth to) become smaller or less; decrease 变小; 变少; 使(某事物)变小; 使(某事物)变少; 缩小; 减少; 降低: *His strength has diminished over the years.* 经过这许多年月, 他的体力不如从前了. ○ *Nothing could diminish her enthusiasm for the project.* 什么也不能影响她对这项计划的热忱. ○ *diminishing hopes, supplies, funds* 逐渐渺茫的希望、渐渐用完的物资、渐渐枯竭的资金. **2** (*fig* 比喻) make (sb/sth) seem less important than it really is; devalue 减低(某人[某事物]的重要性; 贬低: *The opposition are trying to diminish our achievements.* 反对党企图贬低我们的成就. **3** (*music* 音) decrease (an interval) by a semitone 将(音程)减半音: *a diminished seventh* 减七度.

□ **diˌminished responsiˈbility** (*law* 律) state of mind in which an accused person cannot be held fully responsible for a crime 减轻的刑事责任(被告因精神失常不能对其罪行完全负责).

di·minu·endo /dɪˌmɪnjʊˈendəʊ; dəˌmɪnjʊˈɛndo/ *adj, adv* (*music* 音) of or with a gradual decrease in loudness 渐弱(的); 音量逐渐减轻(的): *a diminuendo passage* 渐弱的乐节. ▷ **di·minu·endo** *n* (*pl* **~s**) (*music* 音) gradual decrease in loudness 渐弱.

di·mi·nu·tion /ˌdɪmɪˈnjuːʃn; *US* -ˈnuːʃn; ˌdɪməˈnuʃən/ *n* (**a**) [U] diminishing or being diminished; reduction 变小; 变少; 缩小; 减少; 缩减: *the diminution of one's resources* 资源的减少. (**b**) [C] amount of this; reduction 缩小量; 减少量: *hoping for a small diminution in taxes* 希望税捐略微减少.

di·min·ut·ive /dɪˈmɪnjʊtɪv; dəˈmɪnjətɪv/ *adj* **1** unusually or remarkably small 小得出奇的; 特小的: *her diminutive figure* 她那小小的身材. **2** (*grammar*) (of a suffix) indicating smallness (指后缀)表示小的.

▷ **di·min·ut·ive** *n* word formed by the use of a suffix of this kind, eg *eaglet* (= a young eagle), *kitchenette* (= a small kitchen) 由这类后缀构成的词(如 eaglet 小雕, kitchenette 小厨房).

dim·ity /ˈdɪmɪtɪ; ˈdɪmətɪ/ *n* [U] type of cotton cloth woven with raised strips or designs, used for bed covers, curtains, etc 凸纹棉布, 提花布(用作床罩、帷幕等).

dim·mer /ˈdɪmə(r); ˈdɪmɚ/ *n* (also ˈ**dimmer switch**) device with which one can vary the brightness of an electric light 调光器; 变光器.

dimple /ˈdɪmpl; ˈdɪmpl̩/ *n* (**a**) small natural hollow in the chin or cheek (either permanent, or which appears eg when a person smiles) (下巴或脸颊上自然的)小窝, 酒窝, 靥. (**b**) slight hollow on a surface (esp of glass or water) 浅凹(尤指玻璃表面的小坑或水面的波纹).

▷ **dimple** *v* [I, Tn] (cause sth to) form dimples (使某物)出现酒窝, 形成浅坑, 起波纹: *Her cheeks dimpled as she smiled.* 她一笑, 脸上露出了酒窝. ○ *The surface of the water was dimpled by the breeze.* 轻风拂动水面, 荡起了涟漪.

din /dɪn; dɪn/ *n* [U, sing] continuing loud confused noise

持续的嘈杂声；不停的喧闹：*They made so much din that I couldn't hear you.* 他们太吵了，我听不见你说的话. ○ *Don't make such a din!* 别吵啦！○ *make/kick up a din* 大闹一场.

▷ **din** *v* **(-nn-)** **1** (idm 习语) **din in sb's ears** sound or echo in one's ears 在耳中轰鸣；在耳中回响；聒耳：*They drove away from the city centre, the roar of the traffic still dinning in their ears.* 他们驶出了市中心，但车来人往的喧嚣声仍在耳中回响. **2** (phr v) **din sth into sb** tell sb sth again and again in a forceful way 向某人再三强调某事；就某事反复叮嘱某人：*I dinned it into him that he had to manage things differently.* 我三番五次告诉他得改一改处理事情的方法了.

DIN *abbr* 缩写 = (of a scale of film speeds) German Industry Standard (German *Deutsche Industrie-Norm*) (指胶卷感光度)德国工业标准(源自德文*Deutsche Industrie-Norm*). Cf 参看 ASA 2, ISO.

dine /daɪn; daɪn/ *v* **1** [I, Ipr] **~ (on sth)** (*fml* 文) eat dinner 进餐；用饭：*We dined on smoked salmon.* 我们晚餐吃的是熏鲑鱼. **2** [Tn] (*fml* 文) give a dinner for (sb) 设宴款待(某人)；宴请(某人)；请(某人)吃饭：*We're dining the ambassador this week.* 我们本星期宴请大使. **3** (idm 习语) **wine and dine** ⇨ WINE *v*. **4** (phr v) **dine out** dine away from one's home (eg at a restaurant or in the home of friends) 在外吃饭，出去吃(如在饭馆或朋友家)；下馆子.

□ 'dining-car *n* railway carriage in which meals are served 餐车.

'dining-room *n* room in which meals are eaten 饭厅；餐室；餐厅.

'dining-table *n* table used for eating on 餐桌；饭桌. ⇨ illus at App 1 见附录1之插图, page xvi.

diner /ˈdaɪnə(r); ˈdaɪnɚ/ *n* **1** person eating dinner 吃饭的人；就餐者；餐馆顾客. **2** dining-car on a train 餐车. **3** (*US*) small restaurant, usu beside a highway 小饭馆(通常位于公路边者).

din·ette /daɪˈnet; daɪˈnɛt/ *n* (*esp US*) small room or part of a room, esp a kitchen, used for eating 小饭厅；厨房或其他房间内辟作吃饭用的一部分地方.

ding-dong /ˌdɪŋˈdɒŋ; ˈdɪŋˌdɑŋ/ *n* **1** sound of bells striking again and again 钟、铃声；叮当声音. **2** (*infml* 口) heated argument 激烈的争论；争吵：*I had a bit of a ding-dong with him about his mistakes.* 就他的错误我跟他吵了两句. ○ [attrib 作定语] *a ˌding-dong ˈstruggle, ˈbattle, etc* 激烈的斗争、战斗等.

▷ **ding-dong** *adv* with the sound of bells striking again and again (钟、铃)叮当作响地，发出当当声地；叮叮当当声地：*a clock striking ding-dong* 当当报时的钟.

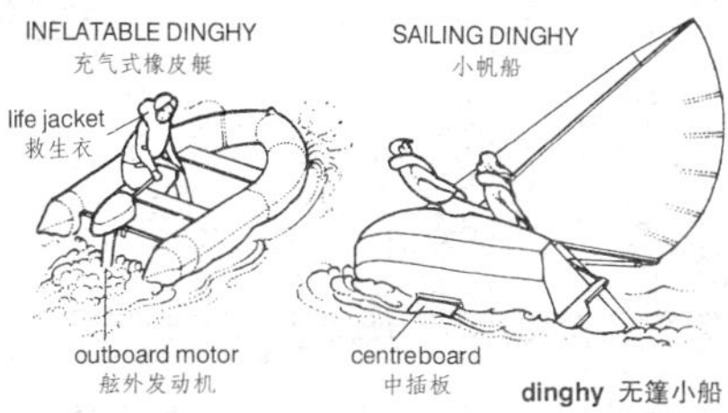

dinghy 无篷小船

dinghy /ˈdɪŋɡɪ; ˈdɪŋɡɪ/ *n* **(a)** any of various types of small open boat 无篷小船；小艇：*a sailing dinghy* 小帆船. **(b)** inflatable rubber boat (used esp for rescuing passengers from ships and aircraft) 充气式橡皮艇；橡皮救生艇. ⇨illus 见插图. Cf 参看 YACHT.

dingle /ˈdɪŋɡl; ˈdɪŋɡl/ *n* deep hollow in the landscape, usu with trees 深谷(通常有树木).

dingo /ˈdɪŋɡəʊ; ˈdɪŋɡo/ *n* (*pl* **~es**) wild Australian dog 澳洲野犬.

dingy /ˈdɪndʒɪ; ˈdɪndʒɪ/ *adj* **(-ier, -iest)** dirty-looking; not cheerful or bright; drab 肮脏的；邋遢的；无生气的；无光泽的；暗淡的；昏黑的；死气沉沉的：*a dingy room in a cheap hotel* 低级旅馆中又黑又脏的房间 ○ *a dingy manufacturing town* 污浊的工业小镇. ▷ **din·gily** *adv*. **din·gi·ness** *n* [U].

dining ⇨ DINE.

dinky /ˈdɪŋkɪ; ˈdɪŋkɪ/ *adj* **(-ier, -iest)** (*infml* 口) **(a)** (*Brit*) small and attractively neat 小巧的；精致的：*What a dinky little hat!* 多漂亮的小帽子！○ *a dinky red car* 精致的红色小汽车. **(b)** (*US*) small and insignificant 不起眼的；无足轻重的.

din·ner /ˈdɪnə(r); ˈdɪnɚ/ *n* **1** [C, U] main meal of the day, whether eaten at midday or in the evening 正餐(一日间的主餐，中午或晚上吃均可)：*It's time for dinner.* 该吃饭了. ○ *Have you had dinner yet?* 你吃过饭了吗？○ (*US*) *Did you eat dinner yet?* 你吃过饭了吗？○ *She didn't eat much dinner.* 她这顿饭没吃多少. ○ *I never eat a big dinner.* 我向来饭量不大. ○ *They're at* (ie eating) *dinner.* 他们正在用餐. ○ *four dinners at £10 per person* 四客饭，每客10英镑 ○ *Shall we ask him to dinner?* 我们请她吃饭好吗？⇨Usage 见所附用法. **2** [C] **(a)** (usu large) formal social gathering at which this meal is eaten (通常指大型的)宴会：*A dinner was given for the ambassador.* 宴请大使. **(b)** (also **'dinner-party**) private social gathering where this meal is eaten 宴会：*give a dinner for friends* 设宴招待朋友. **3** (idm 习语) **a dog's breakfast/dinner** ⇨ DOG[1].

□ **'dinner-jacket** *n* (*Brit*) (*US* **tuxedo**) jacket, usu black, worn with a bow-tie and (usu) matching trousers at formal occasions in the evening (男用)晚礼服.

'dinner service, **'dinner set** set of plates, dishes, etc for dinner 成套餐具.

NOTE ON USAGE 用法：The use of the terms **lunch, dinner, supper** and **tea** varies between social classes in Britain and to some extent between regions. 在英国，因社会阶层不同，**lunch**、**dinner**、**supper**、**tea** 这四个词的用法也不尽相同，而且在一定程度上亦有地区性差别. If the midday meal is called **lunch,** the evening meal is **dinner** or **supper.** 若午餐称作 **lunch**，则晚餐即为 **dinner** 或 **supper**. ☆ In this case **tea** consists of a drink and cake or biscuits in the afternoon. 在这种情况下，**tea** 则指下午的茶点，包括饮料和糕点、饼干之类. If the midday meal is called **dinner** then the evening meal is **tea** or **supper.** 若午餐称作 **dinner**，则晚餐即是 **tea** 或 **supper**. ☆ In this case **supper** may be a light snack before bedtime. 这时，**supper** 可能指临睡前吃的夜宵. At school, children have **school dinner/lunch** at midday or they may take a **packed/sandwich lunch** with them. 在校学生中午吃的要么是 **school dinner / lunch** (学校午餐)，要么是自己带去的 **packed / sandwich lunch** (盒装[三明治]午餐).

dinosaur 恐龙

di·no·saur /ˈdaɪnəsɔː(r); ˈdaɪnəˌsɔr/ *n* large extinct reptile 恐龙.

dint /dɪnt; dɪnt/ *n* **1** = DENT. **2** (idm 习语) **by dint of sth** by means of sth 凭借某事物的力量；通过某事物的作用：*He succeeded by dint of hard work.* 他通过辛勤努力获得成功.

dio·cese /ˈdaɪəsɪs; ˈdaɪəˌsis/ *n* district for which a bishop is responsible 主教管区；(某主教的)教区.

▷ **di·ocesan** /daɪˈɒsɪsn; daɪˈɑsəsn̩/ *adj* of a diocese 主教管区的；教区的.

di·ox·ide /daɪˈɒksaɪd; daɪˈɑksaɪd/ *n* [U] (*chemistry* 化) oxide formed by combining two atoms of oxygen and one atom of another element 二氧化物：*carbon dioxide* 二氧化碳.

dip[1] /dɪp; dɪp/ *v* **(-pp-)** **1** [Tn, Tn·pr, Tn·p] **~ sth (into sth); ~ sth (in)** put or lower sth into a liquid 将某物放入或伸入液体中；浸；泡；蘸：*Dip your pen (into the ink).*

将钢笔(在墨水中)蘸一蘸. ○ *Dip your fingers in to see how hot the water is.* 把手指伸进水里看有多热. ○ *dip sheep*, ie immerse them in a liquid that disinfects them or kills vermin 给羊洗药浴 ○ *dip candles*, ie make them by dipping a wick into melted fat 浸制蜡烛 ○ *to dip a garment*, ie put it in a liquid dye to change its colour 浸染衣服. **2** [I, Ipr, Ip] go below a surface or level 下降到某一平面以下; 下跌到某一高度[水平]以下: *The birds rose and dipped in flight.* 鸟儿在飞行中时高时低. ○ *The sun dipped (down) below the horizon.* 太阳落到地平线下了. **3** [I, Tn, Tn·pr] (cause sth to) go down and then up again (使某物)向下再向上; (使某物)下降后再上升: *The branches dipped in the wind.* 树枝在风中上下颤动着. ○ *dip the headlights of a car*, ie lower their beams (so as not to dazzle the driver of another car) 将汽车前灯的远光调为近光(改用低位光束, 以免使另一辆车上的驾驶者眼花) ○ *Dip your head under the low arch.* 在低矮的门拱下要低头. **4** [I, Ip] slope downward 向下倾斜: *The land dips (down) gently to the south.* 这块地微微向南倾. **5** (phr v) **dip into sth** (**a**) take money from (eg one's savings) 从(如自己的储蓄)中取出钱: *dip into one's purse*, ie spend money 掏腰包(花钱). (**b**) make a brief study of (a book, an author, etc) 翻阅, 浏览(书、某作者的作品等): *I've only had time to dip into the report.* 这份报告我只来得及浏览了一遍.

□ ˈ**dip-stick** *n* rod for dipping into a tank or some other container to measure the depth of the liquid in it (esp oil in the sump of an engine) 浸量尺; (尤指测量发动机润滑油的)量油尺. ⇨illus at App 1 见附录1之插图, page xii.

ˈ**dip-switch** *n* (*Brit*) switch for dipping a motor vehicle's headlights 调节汽车前灯远近光的开关; 汽车大灯调光开关.

dip[2] /dɪp; dɪp/ *n* **1** [C] act of dipping (DIP[1]) 浸; 蘸. **2** [C] (*infml* 口) quick swim or bathe 为时不长的游泳或(在河海中)洗澡: *have/take/go for a dip* 去水里泡一泡. **3** [U] cleansing liquid for dipping sheep (给羊药浴用的)清洗液, 药浴液. **4** [U, C] any of several types of thick sauce into which biscuits or pieces of vegetable are dipped before being eaten (用来蘸着吃饼干或小片蔬菜的)调味酱: *cheese dip* 奶酪酱. **5** [C] downward slope 斜坡: *a dip in the road* 路上的斜坡 ○ *a dip among the hills* 山中的斜坡.

Dip *abbr* 缩写 = Diploma.

Dip Ed /ˌdɪp ˈed; ˌdɪp ˋɛd/ *abbr* 缩写 = Diploma in Education 教育学文凭: *have/be a Dip Ed* 持有[已获]教育学文凭 ○ *Mary Hall BA Dip Ed* 玛丽·霍尔, 文学士、教育学文凭持有者.

diph·theria /dɪfˈθɪərɪə; dɪfˋθɪrɪə/ *n* [U] serious contagious disease of the throat causing difficulty in breathing 白喉.

diph·thong /ˈdɪfθɒŋ; *US* -θɔːŋ; ˋdɪfθɔŋ/ *n* union of two vowel sounds or vowel letters, eg the sounds /aɪ; aɪ/ in *pipe* /paɪp; paɪp/, the letters *ou* in *doubt* 二合元音, 复合元音, 双元音(如 pipe / paɪp; paɪp / 中的/aɪ; aɪ/ 音); 复合元音字母(如 doubt 中的 ou). Cf 参看 MONOPHTHONG.

dip·loma /dɪˈpləʊmə; dɪˋplomə/ *n* (*abbr* 缩写 **Dip**) certificate awarded for passing an examination, completing a course of study, etc 毕业证书; 毕业文凭: *a diploma in architecture* 建筑学文凭.

dip·lo·macy /dɪˈpləʊməsɪ; dɪˋploməsɪ/ *n* [U] **1** management of relations between countries by each country's representatives abroad; skill in this 外交; 外交手段; 外交手腕; 外交术: *International problems must be solved by diplomacy, not war.* 国际问题应通过外交途径来解决, 不应诉诸战争. **2** art of or skill in dealing with people; tact 处理人际关系的方法、技巧; 交际手腕; 处世之道.

dip·lo·mat /ˈdɪpləmæt; ˋdɪpləˌmæt/ *n* **1** person in the diplomatic service, eg an ambassador 外交官(如大使); 外交家. **2** person clever at dealing with people; tactful person 通权达变的人; 有交际手腕的人; 机智练达的人.

dip·lo·matic /ˌdɪpləˈmætɪk; ˌdɪpləˋmætɪk/ *adj* **1** of diplomacy(1) 外交的: *settle disputes by diplomatic means* 通过外交手段解决纷争. **2** tactful; having or showing diplomacy(2) 圆通的; 灵活变通的; 有手腕的; 策略的: *a diplomatic answer, move, etc* 很策略的回答、一步等 ○ *be diplomatic in dealing with people* 与人打交道老练得体. ▷ **dip·lo·mat·ic·ally** /-klɪ; -klɪ/ *adv*.

□ ˌ**diplomatic** ˈ**bag** any container for official letters, goods, etc sent to or from an embassy 外交邮袋; 外交信袋.

diploˈmatic corps all the ambassadors and embassy staff in a country 外交使节团.

diploˌmatic imˈmunity privilege granted to diplomatic staff working abroad, by which they may not be arrested, taxed, etc 外交豁免权; 外交特权.

diploˈmatic service all the officials who conduct a country's diplomacy 外交部门.

dip·lo·mat·ist /dɪˈpləʊmətɪst; dɪˈplomətɪst/ *n* (*fml* 文) = DIPLOMAT.

dip·per /ˈdɪpə(r); ˈdɪpɚ/ *n* **1** cup-shaped container with a long handle, for ladling out liquids 长柄勺. **2** type of diving bird 河乌(一种潜水鸟). Cf 参看 PLOUGH 2.

dip·so·ma·nia /ˌdɪpsəˈmeɪnɪə; ˌdɪpsəˋmenɪə/ *n* [U] extreme dependence on alcoholic drink 嗜酒狂; 间发性酒狂.

▷ **dip·so·ma·niac** /ˌdɪpsəˈmeɪnɪæk; ˌdɪpsəˈmenɪˌæk/ *n*, *adj* (person) suffering from dipsomania 间发性酒狂患者; 嗜酒狂的.

dip·tych /ˈdɪptɪk; ˋdɪptɪk/ *n* painting or carving, esp on an altar, on two hinged panels that can be closed like a book 折合式双连画, 折合式双连雕刻品(尤指置于圣坛上者).

dire /ˈdaɪə(r); daɪr/ *adj* **1** (*fml* 文) dreadful; terrible 可怕的; 极糟的: *a dire situation, crisis, etc* 可怕的处境、严重的危难 ○ *The firm is in dire straits* (ie in a very difficult situation) *and may go bankrupt.* 这商行已陷入岌岌可危的境地, 可能要破产了. ○ (*joc* 谑) *The film we saw was absolutely dire!* 我们看的那部电影差劲透了! **2** (*infml* 口) extreme 极端的: *We're in dire need of your help.* 我们太需要你的帮助了.

dir·ect[1] /dɪˈrekt, daɪ-; dəˋrɛkt, daɪ-/ *adj* **1** [esp attrib 尤作定语] (going) straight; not curved or crooked; not turned aside 直的; 笔直的; 径直的: *follow a direct course, route, etc* 沿笔直的航线、路线等行进 ○ *a direct flight*, ie without stopping or changing planes 直飞航班 ○ *a direct train*, ie that goes to a passenger's destination without stopping beforehand 直达列车 ○ *a direct hit/shot*, ie not turned aside by hitting sth else first 直接命中 ○ *the direct rays of the sun*, ie not reflected from or screened by sth 直射的阳光. **2** (**a**) with nothing or no one in between; immediate 直接的; 当中没有其他事物的; 不经其他人的; 亲自的; 最接近的: *a direct result, link, connection* 直接的结果、关系、联系 ○ *I'm in direct contact with the hijackers.* 我与劫机者保持着直接的联系. (**b**) (of descent in a family) passing through sb's children, grandchildren, etc, rather than through his brothers, sisters, cousins, etc (指家族血统)直系的: *She descends in a direct line from the country's first President.* 她是这个国家的首任总统的直系后裔. **3** straightforward; frank 率直的; 坦率的; 坦白的; 直言的: *a direct person, manner, answer* 直性子的人、坦率的态度、直截了当的回答 ○ *She has a direct way of speaking.* 她说话直爽. ○ *He is very direct, so you always know what his real views are.* 他为人很直率, 所以总能知道他的真实想法. **4** [attrib 作定语] exact; complete 恰好的; 完全的: *the direct opposite* 截然相反的事物 ○ *Your reply today is in direct contradiction to what you said last week.* 你今天的答复跟你上星期说的恰好相反. Cf 参看 INDIRECT.

▷ **dir·ect** *adv* **1** without interrupting a journey; using a straight route 中途不停地; 径直地; 笔直地: *The train goes there direct.* 这趟列车直达那里. **2** with no one in between; personally 亲自地; 直接地: *I prefer to deal with him direct.* 还是我直接跟他打交道为好.

dir·ect·ness [U] *n*.

□ **diˌrect ˈaccess** (*computing* 计) = RANDOM ACCESS (RANDOM).

diˌrect ˈaction use of strikes, violence, etc instead of negotiation to achieve one's demands 直接行动(用罢工、暴力等方式而不经协商来达到目的).

diˌrect ˈcurrent (*abbr* 缩写 **DC**) electric current flowing in one direction 直流电. Cf 参看 ALTERNATING CURRENT (ALTERNATE[2]).

diˌrect ˈdebit order to a bank that allows sb else to withdraw agreed amounts of money from one's account on agreed dates, esp to pay bills 直接借记. Cf 参看

STANDING ORDER (STANDING).

di,rect 'object (*grammar*) noun, noun phrase or noun clause which is directly affected by the action of a verb 直接宾语. Cf 参看 OBJECT[1] 5.

di,rect 'speech (use of a) speaker's actual words 说话者的原话; 原话的直接引用; 直接引语.

di'rect tax tax that one pays direct to the Government (eg income tax) rather than eg sales tax which is paid to the seller before being passed on 直接税.

dir·ect[2] /dɪ'rekt, daɪ-; də'rɛkt, daɪ-/ *v* **1** [Tn, Tn·pr] **~ sb (to...)** tell or show sb how to get somewhere 给某人指路: *Can you direct me (to the station)?* 你告诉我(到车站)怎么走好吗? **2 (a)** [Tn, Tn·pr] **~ sth (to...)** (*fml* 文) address (a letter, parcel, etc) 在(信件、包裹等)上写姓名地址: *Shall I direct the letter to his business address or to his home address?* 我该把这封信寄到他的办公地点还是寄到他家里呢? **(b)** [Tn·pr] **~ sth to/at sb** (*fml* 文) intend that a particular person or group should notice (what one says or does) 让某人或某类人注意(自己所说的话或所做的事): *Let me direct these remarks to the younger students.* 这些话还是让我来对低年级的学生说罢. ○ *advertising directed mainly at young consumers* 主要针对年轻消费者的广告. **3 (a)** [Tn] manage (sth/sb); control 管理(某事物[某人]); 监督; 指导: *She directed the planning of the festival.* 她统管节日活动的筹划. ○ *direct a group of workers* 指挥一群工作人员. **(b)** [I, Tn] be in charge of (actors, a film, a play, etc) 担任导演; 指导(演员)的演出; 为(电影、戏剧等)作导演: *I'd rather act than direct.* 我愿意当演员, 不愿意当导演. ○ *Who directed the play?* 这出戏是谁导演的? **4** [Tn·pr] **~ sth to/towards...; ~ sth at sth** (*fml* 文) turn or aim sth in a particular direction 使某事物转向或对准某一方向: *The guide directed our attention to the other picture.* 讲解员要我们注意另一幅画. ○ *We directed our steps towards home.* 我们朝家走去. ○ *direct a blow at sb's head* 向某人的头部打去 ○ *Our efforts should be directed towards greater efficiency.* 我们应该努力提高效率. **5** [Tf, Dn·t] (*fml* 文) order; command 指示; 命令: *The owners directed that the factory be closed.* 厂主下令关厂. ○ *The officer directed them to advance.* 指挥官命令他们前进. ⇨Usage at ORDER[2] 用法见 ORDER[2].

dir·ec·tion /dɪ'rekʃn, daɪ-; də'rɛkʃən, daɪ-/ *n* **1 (a)** [C] course taken by a moving person or thing; way that a person or thing looks or faces 方向: *Tom went off in one direction and Harry in another.* 汤姆朝一个方向走, 哈里则朝另一个方向走. ○ *The aircraft was flying in a northerly direction.* 飞机正在向北飞去. ○ *The signpost points in a westerly direction.* 路标指向西. ○ *When the police arrived, the crowd scattered in all directions.* 警察一到, 人群就向四面八方散开了. **(b)** [C] (*fig* 比喻) way in which sb/sth develops or is developed 趋向; 趋势; 动向: *new directions in current research* 当前研究的新动向 ○ *That is the present direction of government thinking.* 这就是如今政府考虑问题的取向. ○ *We're making changes in various directions*, ie of various types. 我们正在多方面进行改革. **2** [C usu *pl* 通常作复数] information or instructions about what to do, where to go, how to do sth, etc 指南; 指示; 说明书; 用法说明; 操作说明: *Simple directions for assembling the model are printed on the box.* 盒上印有装配模型的简要说明. ○ *I gave him full directions to enable him to find the house.* 我向他作了详细说明, 好让他能找到那房子. **3 directions** [pl] address on a letter, parcel, etc (信件、包裹等上的)姓名地址: *The parcel was returned to the sender because the directions were incorrect.* 包裹因姓名地址有误而退给了寄件人. **4** [U] management; supervision; guidance 管理; 监督; 指导; 指点: *He did the work under my direction.* 他在我的指导下做这件事. ○ *She was entrusted with the direction of the project.* 她受委托负责这项计划. ○ *He feels the need for firm direction*, ie wants sb to guide and advise him. 他感到需要有人好好地指点自己.

▷ **dir·ec·tional** /-ʃənl; -ʃənl/ *adj* of direction in space 方向的; 定向的: *a directional aerial*, ie one that transmits or receives radio signals in one direction only 定向天线.

□ **di'rection-finder** *n* radio device that shows the direction from which radio signals are coming 无线电测向仪.

dir·ect·ive /dɪ'rektɪv, daɪ-; də'rɛktɪv, daɪ-/ *n* official instruction 正式的指示; 官方的指示; 指令: *a directive from headquarters calling for increased output* 总部要求提高产量的指示.

dir·ectly /dɪ'rektlɪ, daɪ-; də'rɛktlɪ, daɪ-/ *adv* **1** in a direct line or manner; straight 径直地; 直接地; 坦率地; 直爽地: *He looked directly at us.* 他正视着我们. ○ *directly in front of me* 在我的正前方 ○ *She's directly responsible to the Minister.* 她直接受部长领导. ○ *She speaks very directly to people.* 她对人说话非常直率. ○ *directly opposite* 正好相反. **2 (a)** at once; immediately 立即; 马上: *Come in directly.* 立刻进来吧. **(b)** in a short time 不久; 很快地: *I'll be there directly.* 我很快就到.

▷ **dir·ectly** *conj* as soon as 一俟; 一...就...: *I went home directly I had finished work.* 我一干完活就回家了.

dir·ector /dɪ'rektə(r), daɪ-; də'rɛktɚ, daɪ-/ *n* **1 (a)** person who manages, esp as a member of a board[1](7), the affairs of a business company 主管; (尤指)董事. **(b)** person who is in charge of an institution, a college, etc (事业机构、学院等的)负责人; 署长; 厅长; 局长; 处长; 院长; 校长; 所长; 主任: *the orchestra's musical director* 乐团的音乐总监. **2** person in charge of a film, play, etc who supervises and instructs the actors, camera crew and other staff 导演. Cf 参看 PRODUCER 2.

▷ **dir·ector·ship** *n* **(a)** position of a director 主管(如董事、局长、主任等)职位; 导演的职位. **(b)** time during which a director holds his position 主管任期; 担任导演的期间.

□ **di,rector-'general** *n* main administrator of a large organization (大机构的)主要管理者; 总裁; 总监; 总干事.

dir·ect·or·ate /dɪ'rektərət, daɪ-; də'rɛktərɪt, daɪ-/ *n* **1** position or office of a director 主管(如董事、局长、主任等)职位或职务; 导演的职位或职务. **2** board of directors 董事会; 理事会.

dir·ect·ory /dɪ'rektərɪ, daɪ-; də'rɛktərɪ, daɪ-/ *n* (book with a) list of telephone subscribers, business firms, etc of an area, or members of a profession, etc, usu arranged alphabetically 电话簿; 商行名录; 人名地址录.

dirge /dɜ:dʒ; dɝdʒ/ *n* **(a)** song sung at a burial or for a dead person 挽歌. **(b)** (*infml derog* 口, 贬) mournful song 忧伤的歌; 哀歌.

di·ri·gible /'dɪrɪdʒəbl; 'dɪrədʒəbḷ/ *n* old-fashioned air balloon 旧式充气飞艇.

dirk /dɜ:k; dɝk/ *n* (*Scot* 苏格兰) type of dagger 一种短剑.

dirndl /'dɜ:ndl; 'dɝndḷ/ *n* dress with a full wide skirt and a close-fitting bodice 紧身连衣裙.

dirt /dɜ:t; dɝt/ *n* [U] **1** matter that is not clean (eg dust, soil, mud), esp when it is where it is not wanted (eg on the skin, on clothes, in buildings) 污垢; 灰尘; 尘垢; 脏土; 污泥: *His clothes were covered with dirt.* 他的衣服蒙上了灰尘. ○ *How can I get the dirt off the walls?* 我怎样才能把墙上的污垢去掉呢? **2** loose earth or soil 松土; 散土: *a pile of dirt beside a newly-dug trench* 在新挖的沟渠旁的一堆土. **3** (*infml* 口) obscene thought or talk 下流想法; 下流话: *Be quiet! We don't want to hear that kind of dirt!* 别说了! 我们不想听那种下流话! **4** (*infml* 口) excrement 排泄物; 粪便; 屎: *a pile of dog dirt on the road* 路上的一堆狗屎. **5** (*infml* 口) malicious gossip 恶意中伤的闲话: *He likes to hear all the dirt about his colleagues.* 他就爱听有关同事的流言蜚语. **6** (idm 习语) **(as) cheap/common as 'dirt** (*infml derog* 口, 贬) vulgar; low-class 低贱的; 下贱的: *Don't invite her! She's as common as dirt.* 别请她来! 她是个贱货. **dish the dirt** ⇨ DISH[2]. **fling/throw dirt at sb** say slanderous things about sb 说某人坏话; 给某人脸上抹黑. **treat sb like dirt/a dog** ⇨ TREAT.

□ **,dirt 'cheap** (*infml* 口) very cheap(ly) 非常便宜(的).

'dirt farmer (*US*) farmer who does all his own work, without hired help 自耕农.

,dirt 'road (*US*) unpaved country road, made of earth or gravel that has been pressed down 泥路; 土路; 石子路.

'dirt-track *n* track made of cinders, etc (eg for motor-cycle races) 用煤渣等铺的跑道(如用于摩托车比赛的).

dirty[1] /'dɜ:tɪ; 'dɝtɪ/ *adj* (**-ier**, **-iest**) **1 (a)** not clean; covered with dirt 肮脏的; 龌龊的; 污秽的; 有尘垢的: *dirty hands, clothes, floors* 脏的手、衣服、地板.

D

(**b**) causing one to be dirty 将人弄脏的: *a dirty job* 肮脏的工作 ○ *dirty work* 脏活. **2** (of the weather) rough; stormy (指天气)恶劣的, 糟糕的; 风雨交加的: *I'm glad I don't have to go out on such a dirty night.* 我庆幸自己不必在天气这样恶劣的夜晚外出. **3** [attrib 作定语] (of colours) not bright or clear (指颜色)不鲜艳的, 暗淡的: *a dirty brown sofa* 暗褐色的沙发. **4** obscene 下流的; 黄色的: *dirty book, joke, etc* 下流的书、笑话等 ○ *You've got a dirty mind*, ie You have impure thoughts. 你满脑子下流事. **5** [usu attrib 通常作定语] (*infml* 口) unfair; underhand 不公正的; 卑劣的; 不光明正大的; 阴险的: *That's a dirty lie!* 胡说八道! ○ *You dirty rat! How could you do a thing like that?* 你这个不要脸的东西, 这种事你都做得出? ○ *That was a mean and dirty thing to do!* 做出那种事真够卑鄙无耻的! **6** (idm 习语) **a dirty old man** (*infml* 口) older man who takes an unhealthy interest in sex, or in young girls as sexually attractive 老色鬼; 老淫棍. **a dirty weekend** (*esp joc* 尤作戏谑语) weekend spent intimately (and often illicitly) with a sexual partner 风流的周末(与性伴侣厮混). **(be) a dirty 'word** thing or idea that is disliked or not respected 不喜欢的或不正经的事物或想法: *My children think that work is a dirty word!* 我的孩子都觉得工作顶讨厌! **(do sb's) 'dirty work** (do) the tasks that sb else does not like or cannot face (做)他人不想做或难以应付的工作: *I had to tell them they'd lost their jobs: I always have to do the boss's dirty work (for him).* 我得对他们说他们被开除了, 我总得替老板(出面)做这种倒霉事儿. **do the dirty on sb** cheat or betray sb 欺骗某人; 出卖某人; 要弄某人; 对某人玩花招. **give sb/get a dirty 'look** look at sb disapprovingly or in disgust 厌恶地看着某人[遭人白眼]. **wash one's dirty linen in public** ⇨ WASH[2].

D

▷ **dirt·ily** *adv*.

dirty *adv* **1** (*infml* 口) very 很; 非常: *He was carrying a dirty great box.* 他提着一只大得不得了的箱子. **2** (idm 习语) **talk dirty** ⇨ TALK.

dirty[2] /ˈdɜːtɪ; ˋdɝtɪ/ *v* (*pt, pp* **dirt·ied**) [I, Tn] become or make (sth) dirty 变脏; 使(某物)变脏; 弄脏(某物): *White gloves dirty easily.* 白手套很容易脏. ○ *Don't dirty your new dress.* 别把你的新衣服弄脏了.

dis- *pref* 前缀 (with *adjs, advs, ns* and *vs* 后与形容词、副词、名词、动词结合) negative, reverse or opposite of 表示否定、相反或相对: *dishonest* ○ *disagreeably* ○ *disagreement* ○ *disengage.* ⇨Usage at UN- 用法见 UN-.

dis·ab·il·ity /ˌdɪsəˈbɪlətɪ; ˌdɪsəˋbɪlətɪ/ *n* **1** [U] state of being disabled; incapacity 无能力; 丧失能力; 伤残: *Physical disability causes mental anguish.* 生理伤残会引起心理苦闷. **2** [C] thing that disables; lack of sth necessary 导致丧失能力的事物; 残疾; 缺乏必需的条件: *She swims well despite her disabilities.* 她虽然身有残疾, 却是个游泳好手. ○ *Her lack of experience is a severe disability.* 她缺乏经验, 这是个很不利的条件. ○ [attrib 作定语] *a disability pension* 伤残补助费; 伤残抚恤金.

dis·able /dɪsˈeɪbl; dɪsˋebl̩/ *v* [Tn] make (sb) unable to do sth, esp by making a limb or limbs useless 使(某人)丧失能力; 使(某人)残废(尤指肢体): *a soldier disabled by leg wounds* 腿部受伤致残的士兵.

▷ **dis·abled** *adj* unable to use a limb or limbs 丧失使用肢体能力的; 肢体有残疾的: *a disabled child in a wheelchair* 坐轮椅的残疾儿童. **the disabled** *n* [pl *v*] people who are disabled 残疾人; 伤残人: *walking aids for the disabled* 帮助残疾人行走的器具.

dis·able·ment *n* [U].

dis·ab·use /ˌdɪsəˈbjuːz; ˌdɪsəˋbjuz/ *v* [Tn·pr] **~ sb of sth** (*fml* 文) free sb of (false ideas) 去掉某人的(错误想法); 纠正; 矫正: *disabuse sb of mistaken notions, false assumptions, etc* 使某人去掉错误的观点、错误的设想等.

dis·ad·vant·age /ˌdɪsədˈvɑːntɪdʒ; *US* -ˈvæn-; ˌdɪsədˋvæntɪdʒ/ *n* **1** unfavourable condition; thing that tends to prevent sb succeeding, making progress, etc 不利条件; 阻碍成功、进步等的事物; 不便之处: *The other candidate's main disadvantage is her age.* 另一候选人的主要不利条件是她的年龄问题. ○ *The lack of decent public transport is a great disadvantage.* 没有适当的公共交通工具是很不方便的. **2** (idm 习语) **put sb/be at a disadvantage** put sb/be in an unfavourable position 置某人于[处于]不利境地: *His inability to speak French puts him at a disadvantage.* 他不会说法语, 这使他很吃亏. **to sb's disadvantage** (*fml* 文) damaging sb or his reputation; causing some loss to sb 对某人不利; 有损声誉; 使某人吃亏: *rumours to his disadvantage*, eg that discredit him 对他不利的谣言(如有损其名誉者) ○ *It would be to your disadvantage to invest in the project*, ie You might lose money. 你在这项工程上投资, 可能要吃亏.

▷ **dis·ad·vant·aged** *adj* socially or economically deprived 社会地位低下的; 卑贱的; 贫困的; 贫贱的: *More state help is needed for the disadvantaged sections of the community.* 国家需要向社区的贫困阶层提供更多救济. **the disadvantaged** *n* [pl *v*] people who are disadvantaged 社会底层的人: *appeals on behalf of the disadvantaged* 为社会底层的人所作的呼吁.

dis·ad·vant·age·ous /ˌdɪsædvɑːnˈteɪdʒəs; *US* -væn-; dɪsˌædvænˋtedʒəs/ *adj* **~ (to sb)** causing a disadvantage 不利的; 引起不方便的: *in a disadvantageous position* 处于不利的境地. **dis·ad·van·tage·ously** *adv*.

dis·af·fec·ted /ˌdɪsəˈfektɪd; ˌdɪsəˋfɛktɪd/ *adj* discontented; disloyal 不满的; 不忠的: *Disaffected members have left to form a new party.* 那些不忠分子脱党另组了一个新党.

▷ **dis·af·fec·tion** /ˌdɪsəˈfekʃn; ˌdɪsəˋfɛkʃən/ *n* [U] discontent that often leads to disloyalty (常为导致不忠的)不满, 离心离德.

dis·af·for·est /ˌdɪsəˈfɒrɪst; *US* -ˈfɔːr-; ˌdɪsəˋfɔrɪst/ *v* [Tn] = DEFOREST.

dis·ag·ree /ˌdɪsəˈgriː; ˌdɪsəˋgri/ *v* (*pt, pp* **-reed**) **1** [I, Ipr] (**a**) **~ (with sb/sth) (about/on sth)** have a different opinion (from sb); not agree 持(与某人)不同的观点; (与某人)有分歧; 不同意: *Even friends sometimes disagree.* 即便是朋友也有时意见不一. ○ *disagree with sb/what sb says/sb's decision* 不同意某人的观点[某人的话/某人的决定] ○ *We disagreed on future plans.* 我们对未来的计划产生了分歧. (**b**) **~ (with sth)** not match; be different 不符; 不一致; 不同: *The reports from Rome disagree with those from Milan.* 罗马的报道与米兰的不符. Cf 参看 AGREE. **2** (phr v) **disagree with sb** (of food, climate) have a bad effect on sb; cause sb to feel unwell (指食物、气候)对某人有不良影响, 有害于某人, 使某人不舒服: *I feel sick: that fish disagreed with me.* 我感到恶心, 那条鱼吃得我不舒服.

dis·ag·ree·able /ˌdɪsəˈgriːəbl; ˌdɪsəˋgriəbl/ *adj* unpleasant 令人不快的; 讨厌的; 不合意的; 别扭的: *a disagreeable person, mood, experience* 令人不愉快的人、情绪、经历. ▷ **dis·ag·ree·able·ness** *n* [U]. **dis·ag·ree·ably** /-əblɪ; -əblɪ/ *adv*.

dis·ag·ree·ment /ˌdɪsəˈgriːmənt; ˌdɪsəˋgrimənt/ *n* **1** [U] **~ (about/on sth)** disagreeing; lack of agreement 分歧; 不一致; 意见不合: *total disagreement on how to proceed* 对于如何继续进行, 意见完全不同. **2** [C] instance of this; difference of opinion 分歧; 意见不合: *disagreements between colleagues* 同事间的意见分歧.

dis·al·low /ˌdɪsəˈlaʊ; ˌdɪsəˋlaʊ/ *v* [Tn] refuse to accept (sth) as valid 不承认(某事物)有效; 不接受; 不准; 驳回: *disallow a claim, goal* 不接受要求、进球无效.

dis·ap·pear /ˌdɪsəˈpɪə(r); ˌdɪsəˋpɪr/ *v* **1** [I] (**a**) no longer be visible; vanish 消失; 失踪: *The plane disappeared behind a cloud.* 飞机飞入云中不见了. ○ *The rash soon disappeared.* 疹子很快就消了. (**b**) stop existing 不复存在: *His anger soon disappeared.* 他的怒气一会儿就消了. ○ *The problem won't just disappear.* 这问题不会就这样不了了之的. (**c**) be lost, esp without explanation 遗失(尤指无法解释的): *My passport has disappeared: it was in my pocket a moment ago.* 我的护照丢了, 刚才还在口袋里呢. ○ (*euph* 婉) *Things tend to disappear when he's around*, ie He steals them. 只要有他在, 东西就爱丢. **2** (idm 习语) **do a disappearing act** disappear, esp when needed or being looked for 失去踪影(尤指被需要或寻找时): *It's typical of Bob to do a disappearing act just when there's work to be done!* 一有事情要做, 鲍勃就没人影儿了, 他就是这样!

▷ **dis·ap·pear·ance** /-ˈpɪərəns; -ˋpɪrəns/ *n* (**a**) [U] act or fact of disappearing 消失; 失踪; 丢失: *At first nobody noticed the child's disappearance.* 起初谁都没有注意到小孩不见了. (**b**) [C] instance of sb disappearing, eg because he has been murdered or kidnapped 失踪(如被谋杀或绑架); 失踪案: *Most disappearances are the result* *of the terrorist activity.* 大多数的失踪案都是恐怖分子造成的.

dis·ap·point /ˌdɪsəˈpɔɪnt; ˌdɪsəˋpɔɪnt/ *v* [Tn] **1** fail to be or do sth as good, interesting etc as was hoped for or desired or expected by (sb) 使(某人)失望: *The tenor disappointed us by singing flat.* 那位男高音歌手调门儿唱得很低, 十分扫兴. ○ *I can't disappoint my public by retiring.* 我可不能退休, 否则大家会失望的. ○ *Don't disappoint me by being late again.* 别再迟到了, 不要叫我失望. ○ *I've often been disappointed in love*, ie not been loved in return by sb I have loved. 我经常情场失意. **2** prevent (hope, plan, etc) from becoming reality 使(希望、计划等)不能实现: *disappoint sb's expectations, sb's calculations, etc* 使某人的希望破灭、使某人的如意算盘落空.

▷ **dis·ap·pointed** *adj* **~ (about/at sth); ~ (in/with sb/sth); ~ (to do sth/that...)** sad or dissatisfied because sb has failed, some desired event has not happened, etc 失望的; 失意的; 受挫的: *be disappointed about/at sb's failure* 对某人的失败感到失望 ○ *I was disappointed with his performance.* 他的表现令我失望. ○ *I'm disappointed in you: I expected you to win.* 你让我失望了, 我本来指望你能赢的. ○ *He was disappointed to hear they were not coming.* 他听说他们不来了, 感到很扫兴. ○ *I was disappointed not to be chosen.* 我没被挑中, 感到很沮丧. **dis·ap·point·edly** *adv*.

dis·ap·point·ing *adj* causing sb to be disappointed 令人失望的; 扫兴的: *a disappointing novel* 令人失望的小说 ○ *The weather this summer has been disappointing.* 今年夏天的天气一直使人不痛快. **dis·ap·point·ingly** *adv*: *Disappointingly, he had nothing new to show us.* 他没什么新鲜东西给我们看, 使人感到失望.

dis·ap·point·ment /ˌdɪsəˈpɔɪntmənt; ˌdɪsəˋpɔɪntmənt/ *n* **1** [U] being disappointed 失望; 沮丧: *To our great disappointment, it rained on the day of the picnic.* 使我们大失所望的是野餐那天下起雨来了. **2** [C] **~ (to sb)** person or thing that disappoints 令人失望的人或事物: *Not getting the job was a terrible disappointment.* 得不到那份工作, 叫人失望极了. ○ *His children are a disappointment to him.* 他的孩子让他感到失望.

dis·ap·proba·tion /ˌdɪsˌæprəˈbeɪʃn; ˌdɪsæprəˋbeʃən/ *n* (*fml* 文) [U] disapproval 反对; 非难; 不准.

dis·ap·prove /ˌdɪsəˈpruːv; ˌdɪsəˋpruv/ *v* [I, Ipr] **~ (of sb/sth)** consider (sb/sth) to be bad, immoral, foolish, etc 认为(某人[某事物])不好、不道德、不明智等; 不赞成; 反对: *She wants to be an actress, but her parents disapprove (of her intentions).* 她想当演员, 但她父母不赞成(她的想法).

▷ **dis·ap·proval** /-ˈpruːvl; -ˋpruvḷ/ *n* [U] not approving (of sb/sth) 不赞同; 反对: *her disapproval of my methods* 她对我所用的方式的反对 ○ *He shook his head in disapproval*, ie to show that he disapproved. 他摇了摇头表示反对.

dis·ap·prov·ing *adj* showing disapproval 表示反对的: *a disapproving look, frown, etc* 不以为然的样子、皱起眉头表示不赞成. **dis·ap·prov·ingly** *adv*: *When I suggested a drink, she coughed disapprovingly.* 我提议喝一杯时, 她咳了一下表示反对.

dis·arm /dɪsˈɑːm; dɪsˋɑrm/ *v* **1** [Tn] take weapons away from (sb) 缴(某人)的械; 解除(某人)的武装: *Five hundred rebels were captured and disarmed.* 五百名造反者被俘获并缴了械. **2** [I] (of nations) reduce the size of or abolish one's armed forces; give up one's weapons (指国家)裁减军备, 裁军, 解除武装: *The superpowers are unlikely to disarm completely.* 超级大国不太可能彻底裁军. **3** [Tn] make (sb) less suspicious, angry, hostile, etc 消除(某人)的疑虑、怒气、敌意等: *By frankly admitting he wasn't a brilliant player, he disarmed us all.* 他坦率地承认自己并非高手, 让我们都放下心来. ○ *I felt angry, but her smile disarmed me.* 我动气了, 但她一笑, 又将我的气儿给消了.

▷ **dis·arma·ment** /dɪsˈɑːməmənt; dɪsˋɑrməmənt/ *n* [U] disarming or being disarmed (DISARM 2) 解除武装; 裁军: *nuclear disarmament*, ie giving up nuclear weapons 核武器的裁减 ○ [attrib 作定语] *a disarmament conference* 裁军会议.

dis·arm·ing *adj* that disarms (DISARM 3) 消解他人的疑虑、怒气、敌意等的: *her disarming smile, frankness, charm, etc* 她那能化敌为友的微笑、坦率、魅力等.

dis·arm·ingly *adv*: *disarmingly frank, honest, etc* 坦率、诚实…得让人放心.

dis·ar·range /ˌdɪsəˈreɪndʒ; ˌdɪsəˋrendʒ/ *v* [Tn] (*fml* 文) (**a**) make (sth) disorderly or untidy 使(某物)不整齐; 弄乱(某物): *disarrange sb's papers, hair* 弄乱某人的文件、头发. (**b**) upset (sth); disturb 打乱(某事); 扰乱: *Her sudden departure has disarranged my plans.* 她突然离去, 打乱了我的计划. ▷ **dis·ar·range·ment** *n* [U].

dis·ar·ray /ˌdɪsəˈreɪ; ˌdɪsəˋre/ *n* [U] state in which people or things are no longer properly organized 混乱; 紊乱: *The troops fled in disarray.* 部队仓皇逃散. ○ *Changing offices has left my papers in complete disarray.* 办公室搬迁, 使我的文件全部乱了套了.

dis·as·so·ci·ate = DISSOCIATE.

dis·as·ter /dɪˈzɑːstə(r); *US* -ˈzæs-; dɪzˋæstɚ/ *n* **1** [C] (**a**) event that causes great harm or damage, eg a fire, a serious defeat, the loss of a large sum of money 灾难; 灾祸; 灾害: *Thousands died in the disaster.* 数千人死于这场灾祸. ○ *Losing your job needn't be such a disaster.* 你不必把丢了工作看成是大难临头. ○ *a natural disaster*, ie an accident, such as an earthquake or a flood, that is not caused by human beings 自然灾害. (**b**) (*infml* 口) person or thing that is a complete failure 彻底失败的人或事物: *As a teacher, he's a disaster.* 他是个很糟糕的教师. ○ *The play's first night was a disaster.* 这出戏头一晚就演砸了. **2** [U] failure 失败: *His career is a story of utter disaster.* 他在事业上一事无成.

▷ **dis·ast·rous** /dɪˈzɑːstrəs; *US* -zˈæs-; dɪzˋæstrəs/ *adj* being or causing a disaster 灾难性的; 造成灾害的; 失败的: *disastrous floods* 灾难性的洪水 ○ *a defeat that was disastrous to the country* 给国家带来灾难的一场败仗 ○ *Buying this house was a disastrous step: it's going to have a main road built behind it.* 买下这所房子是一大失策, 因为房后就要建一条公路了. **dis·ast·rously** *adv*.

□ **diˈsaster area** area affected by a disaster, eg an earthquake, floods, etc 灾区: *declare a place a disaster area* 宣布某地为灾区.

dis·avow /ˌdɪsəˈvaʊ; ˌdɪsəˋvaʊ/ *v* [Tn] (*fml* 文) say one does not know of, is not responsible for, or does not approve of (sth) 否认, 不承认, 不赞成(某事): *She disavows any part* (ie says she was not involved) *in the plot.* 她否认参与了这一密谋. ▷ **dis·avowal** /-ˈvaʊəl; -ˋvaʊəl/ *n* [C, U].

dis·band /dɪsˈbænd; dɪsˋbænd/ *v* [I, Tn] (cause sth to) stop operating as an organization; break up (使组织、机构等)解散, 散伙, 解体: *The regiment disbanded when the war was over.* 战争结束后, 这个团就解散了. ○ *disband a club, society, etc* 解散俱乐部、社团等. ▷ **dis·band·ment** *n* [U].

dis·be·lieve /ˌdɪsbɪˈliːv; ˌdɪsbəˋliv/ *v* **1** [Tn] refuse to believe (sb/sth) 不相信(某人[某事物]): *I disbelieve every word you say.* 你说的我一句都不信. ○ *You have no reason to disbelieve their account of what happened.* 你不应该不信他们对事情经过的叙述. **2** [Ipr] **~ in sb/sth** not accept the existence of (sth) 不相信(某事物)的存在: *disbelieve in ghosts* 不相信有鬼.

▷ **dis·be·lief** /ˌdɪsbɪˈliːf; ˌdɪsbəˋlif/ *n* [U] lack of belief; failure to believe 不相信; 怀疑: *He listened in disbelief to this extraordinary story.* 他满腹疑惑地听着这个离奇的故事. Cf 参看 UNBELIEF.

dis·burse /dɪsˈbɜːs; dɪsˋbɝs/ *v* [Tn] (*fml* 文) pay out (money) 支付(钱): *funds disbursed for travelling expenses* 用于支付旅行费用的款子.

▷ **dis·burse·ment** *n* (*fml* 文) (**a**) [U] paying out money 支付; 支出. (**b**) [C] sum of money paid out 付出款; 支出额.

disc (also *esp US* **disk**) /dɪsk; dɪsk/ *n* **1** flat thin round plate, eg a coin 扁平的圆盘状物(如硬币) **2** small flat object of any shape 小的扁平物体: *He wears an identity disc round his neck.* 他脖子上挂着身分牌儿. **3** round surface that appears to be flat 似扁平的圆面: *the moon's disc* 月轮. **4** = RECORD[1] 3: *recordings on disc and cassette* 唱片和盒式磁带上的录音. **5** (*anatomy* 解) layer of cartilage between the bones of the spine 椎骨间的软骨层; 椎间盘: *a slipped disc*, ie one that is slightly dislocated 突出的椎间盘(即轻微错位).

□ ˈ**disc brake** brake which consists of a flat plate pressed against a rotating plate at the centre of a (car) wheel 盘式制动器. Cf 参看 DRUM BRAKE (DRUM[1]).

ˈ**disc harrow** harrow with discs instead of teeth 圆盘耙(与钉耙相对).

ˈ**disc jockey** (*abbr* 缩写 **DJ**) person who plays and comments on recorded popular music, esp on radio or TV 流行音乐节目主持人(尤指在广播或电视上).

dis·card /dɪˈskɑ:d; dɪsˋkɑrd/ *v* [Tn] (**a**) throw (sth) out or away 扔掉, 丢弃(某物): *old, discarded clothes* 扔掉的旧衣服. (**b**) stop using, wearing, etc (sth that is no longer useful) 不再使用, 不再穿戴(已没用的物品): *discard one's winter clothes in spring* 春天里换下冬装 ○ (*fig* 比喻) *discard outdated beliefs* 抛弃过时的信仰. (**c**) give up (unwanted playing-cards) 打出(无用的牌); 出(牌): *She discarded a four, and picked up a king.* 她打出一张四点的牌, 抓起一张K.

▷ **dis·card** /ˈdɪskɑ:d; ˋdɪskɑrd/ *n* card or cards discarded in a card-game; discarded thing (在牌戏中)打出的牌; 废弃的东西.

dis·cern /dɪˈsɜ:n; dɪˋsɝn/ *v* [Tn] see (sth) clearly (with the senses or the mind), esp with an effort 看出, 识别, 辨认(某事物)(尤指需费力): *In the gloom I could only just discern the outline of a building.* 在黑暗中我只能依稀分辨出一座建筑物的轮廓来. ○ *One can faintly discern the flavour of lemon.* 可以隐约觉得有一点柠檬味. ○ *discern sb's true intentions* 弄清某人的真实意图.

▷ **dis·cern·ible** *adj* that can just be discerned 依稀可辨的.

dis·cern·ing *adj* (*approv* 褒) showing careful judgement 识别力强的; 有洞察力的: *She is a very discerning art critic.* 她是位眼光敏锐的艺术评论家.

dis·cern·ment *n* [U] ability to judge well; insight 识别能力; 洞察力.

dis·charge[1] /dɪsˈtʃɑ:dʒ; dɪsˋtʃɑrdʒ/ *v* **1** [Tn] unload (a ship); unload (cargo) from a ship 从(船)上卸货; 将(货物)从船上卸下; 卸船. **2** [I, Tn] give or send out (liquid, gas, electric current, etc) 放出(液体、气体、电流等); 排放: *The Nile discharges* (ie flows) *into the Mediterranean.* 尼罗河流入地中海. ○ *The sewers discharge (their contents) into the sea.* 下水管道将污物排入大海. ○ *Lightning is caused by clouds discharging electricity.* 闪电是由云层放电产生的. ○ *The wound is discharging (pus).* 伤口正在流脓. **3** [Tn] (**a**) fire (a gun etc) 开(枪炮等): *The rifle was discharged accidently.* 步枪走火了. (**b**) launch (eg a flying weapon) 射出(如飞行武器): *arrows discharged at the enemy* 射向敌人的箭. **4** [Tn] give official permission for (sb) to leave, eg after he has carried out a duty 准许(某人)离开; 放行; 遣散; 释放: *discharge a soldier, patient, etc* 批准士兵退伍、准许病人出院 ○ *The accused man was found not guilty and discharged.* 被告男子被判无罪而获释. ○ *The members of the jury were discharged.* 陪审员都解散了. ○ *a discharged bankrupt*, ie sb who has been bankrupt, has done what the court requires, and has no further obligation to the court 解除债务的破产者(已执行法庭规定而无其他义务的破产者). **5** [Tn] (*fml* 文) (**a**) pay (a debt) 清偿(债务). (**b**) perform (a duty) 执行(任务); 尽(职): *She undertook to discharge all the responsibilities of a Minister.* 她承担了做部长的所有责任.

dis·charge[2] /ˈdɪstʃɑ:dʒ; ˋdɪstʃɑrdʒ/ *n* **1** [U] discharging or being discharged 卸货; 排放; 开火; 发射; 准许离开; 获准离开; 偿还; 行使: *the discharge of cargo* 卸货 ○ *the discharge of water from the reservoir* 水库的放水 ○ *the accidental discharge of a rifle* 步枪的走火 ○ *After his discharge from the army, he went to Canada.* 他退役后到加拿大去了. ○ *money accepted in full discharge of a debt* 所收到的全部债款 ○ *the conscientious discharge of one's duties* 尽忠职守. **2** [U, C] that which is discharged (DISCHARGE[1] 2) 排放出的物体: *The wound hasn't healed — there's still some/a discharge,* ie it is still producing pus. 伤口没好, 还有些分泌物.

dis·ciple /dɪˈsaɪpl; dɪˋsaɪpl/ *n* follower of a religious, political, artistic, etc leader or teacher (宗教、政治、艺术等领袖人物或导师的)追随者, 门徒, 信徒.

dis·cip·lin·ar·ian /ˌdɪsəplɪˈneərɪən; ˌdɪsəplɪnˋɛrɪən/ *n* person who believes in strict discipline 严格执行纪律者; 严守纪律者: *a good/strict/poor disciplinarian* 能[严格/不能]执行纪律者 ○ *He's no disciplinarian*, ie He does not or cannot maintain discipline. 他不能维持纪律.

dis·cip·line[1] /ˈdɪsɪplɪn; ˋdɪsəplɪn/ *n* **1** (**a**) [U] training, esp of the mind and character, aimed at producing self-control, obedience, etc 训练, 锻炼, 磨练(尤指在智力和品德方面): *school discipline* 学校的训练 ○ *Strict discipline is imposed on army recruits.* 新兵受到严格的训练. ○ *monastic discipline* 僧侣的修行. (**b**) [U] result of such training; ordered behaviour, eg of schoolchildren, soldiers 纪律; 风纪: *The soldiers showed perfect discipline under fire.* 士兵在枪林弹雨中严守军纪. ○ *The children are happy at the school, but they lack discipline.* 孩子们在学校里很快活, 但很散漫. **2** [C] (**a**) method by which training may be given 训练方式: *Yoga is a good discipline for learning to relax.* 要学会身心松弛, 瑜珈功是一种有效的锻炼方法. (**b**) set rules for conduct 行为准则. **3** [U] punishment 处罚; 处分: *the teacher's cruel discipline* 该教师施予的残酷处罚. **4** [C] branch of knowledge; subject of instruction 学科; 教学科目: *scientific disciplines* 科学科目.

▷ **dis·cip·lin·ary** /ˈdɪsɪplɪnərɪ; *US* -nerɪ; ˋdɪsəplɪnˌɛrɪ/ *adj* concerning discipline 有关训练的; 有关纪律的; 有关惩处的; 有关学科的: *disciplinary measures, problems, etc* 纪律上的措施、问题等 ○ *a disciplinary hearing*, eg of a soldier accused of an offence 惩戒审讯(如审问违纪士兵者).

dis·cip·line[2] /ˈdɪsɪplɪn; ˋdɪsəˌplɪn/ *v* **1** [Tn, Cn·t] train (sb/sth) to be obedient, self-controlled, skilful, etc 训练, 训导, 管教(某人[某物]): *a well/badly disciplined orchestra, football team, etc* 训练有素的[缺乏训练的]管弦乐队、足球队等 ○ *Parents have to discipline their children.* 做父母的须管教子女. ○ *You must discipline yourself to finish your work on time.* 你必须严格要求自己按时完成任务. **2** [Tn] punish (sb) 处罚, 处分(某人): *The teacher disciplined the class by giving them extra homework.* 那教师布置额外的家庭作业来处罚学生.

dis·claim /dɪsˈkleɪm; dɪsˋklem/ *v* [Tn, Tg] say that one does not have (sth); renounce 声称没有(某事物); 否认; 放弃: *The gang disclaimed all responsibility for the explosion*, ie said they did not cause it. 这个匪帮声称与这次爆炸事件毫无关系. ○ *She disclaimed ownership of the vehicle.* 她放弃了这辆车的所有权.

▷ **dis·claimer** *n* statement that disclaims 否认某事物的声明; 放弃某事物的声明: *to issue/send a disclaimer* 发表声明加以否认.

dis·close /dɪsˈkləʊz; dɪsˋkloz/ *v* (*fml* 文) (**a**) [Tn, Dn·pr] **~ sth (to sb)** allow sth to be seen 使某物显露: *He opened the box, disclosing the contents (to the audience).* 他打开盒子, 露出里面的东西(给观众看). (**b**) [Tn, Tf, Tw, Dn·pr, Dpr·f, Dpr·w] **~sth (to sb)** make sth known 公开某事; 透露某事: *refuse to disclose one's name and address* 拒绝透露自己的姓名地址 ○ *The Government disclosed that another diplomat has been arrested for spying.* 政府透露, 又有一名外交官因间谍罪被捕. ○ *She wouldn't disclose her friend's whereabouts to the police.* 她不愿把她朋友的下落告诉警方.

▷ **dis·clos·ure** /dɪsˈkləʊʒə(r); dɪsˋkloʒɚ/ *n* (**a**) [U] making sth known 公开; 透露: *the magazine's disclosure of defence secrets* 该杂志对防务内幕的透露. (**b**) [C] thing, esp a secret, that is made known 被公开的事情; (尤指)被透露的秘闻: *startling disclosures of police brutality* 揭发警察暴行的惊人消息.

disco /ˈdɪskəʊ; ˋdɪsko/ *n* (*pl* **~s**) (also **discotheque** /ˈdɪskətek; ˋdɪskəˌtɛk/) **1** club, party, etc, usu with flashing lights, where people dance to recorded pop music 迪斯科舞厅; 迪斯科舞会: *Is there a good disco round here?* 附近有像样的迪斯科舞厅吗? **2** equipment that produces the sound and lighting effects of a disco (迪斯科舞厅的)音响及灯光效果设备: *We're hiring a disco for the party.* 我们为这次聚会租用一套迪斯科舞厅用的设备.

□ ˈ**disco dancing** modern popular dancing with no fixed steps, with or without a partner 迪斯科舞.

ˈ**disco music** type of music played in discos 迪斯科音乐.

dis·colour (*US* **dis·color**) /dɪsˈkʌlə(r); dɪsˋkʌlɚ/ *v* **1** [Tn] change or spoil the colour of (sth) 使(某物)变色; 使(某物)退色: *Smoking discolours the teeth.* 吸烟会使牙齿变色. **2** [I] (of colour) change or be spoilt (指颜色)变化, 变色, 退色.

▷ **dis·col·ora·tion** /ˌdɪskʌləˈreɪʃn; ˌdɪskʌləˋreʃən/ *n* (**a**) [U] process of discolouring 变色; 退色: *some discoloration of the paintwork* 漆皮儿的少许退色. (**b**)

[C] discoloured spot; stain 变色点; 退色点; 污点.

dis·comfit /dɪsˈkʌmfɪt; dɪsˋkʌmfɪt/ *v* [Tn] (*fml* 文) confuse or embarrass (sb) 使(某人)困惑、尴尬或狼狈: *be discomfited by rude questions* 因他人提出的问题粗鄙而感到尴尬. ▷ **dis·com·fit·ure** /dɪsˈkʌmfɪtʃə(r); dɪsˋkʌmfɪtʃɚ/ *n* [U]: *a look, air, expression, etc of discomfiture* 狼狈的神色、样子、表情等.

dis·com·fort /dɪsˈkʌmfət; dɪsˋkʌmfɚt/ *n* **1** (**a**) [U] lack of comfort; slight pain 不舒服; 不适; 轻微的病痛: *He still suffers considerable discomfort from his injury.* 他因那次受伤至今仍颇感不适. (**b**) [C] thing that causes this 使人不舒服或不适的事情: *the discomforts of travel* 旅行的诸多不便. **2** [U] mental unease; embarrassment 不安; 不痛快.

dis·com·mode /ˌdɪskəˈməʊd; ˌdɪskəˋmod/ *v* [Tn] (*fml* 文) cause (sb) inconvenience 使(某人)不便; 给(某人)添麻烦; 打搅(某人).

dis·com·pose /ˌdɪskəmˈpəʊz; ˌdɪskəmˋpoz/ *v* [Tn] (*fml* 文) make (sb) feel uneasy or uncomfortable 使(某人)感到不安或不舒服. ▷ **dis·com·pos·ure** /ˌdɪskəmˈpəʊʒə(r); ˌdɪskəmˋpoʒɚ/ *n* [U].

dis·con·cert /ˌdɪskənˈsɜːt; ˌdɪskənˋsɝt/ *v* [Tn usu passive 通常用于被动语态] cause (sb) to feel confused, upset or embarrassed 使(某人)感到困惑、不安或尴尬: *He was disconcerted to find the other guests formally dressed.* 他看到其他客人都穿得正正经经的, 觉得很尴尬. ▷ **dis·con·certed** *adj*: *a disconcerted look, glance, tone of voice, etc* 不安的神情、一瞥、语调等. **dis·con·cert·ing** *adj*: *a disconcerting reply, stare, silence, manner, etc* 令人难堪的回答、注视、沉默、举止等. **dis·con·cert·ingly** *adv*.

dis·con·nect /ˌdɪskəˈnekt; ˌdɪskəˋnɛkt/ *v* [Tn, Tn·pr] ~ **A (from B)** detach sth (from sth); undo a connection 使某物(与某物)分离; 割断, 切断(联系); 使不连接: *If you don't pay your bills they'll disconnect your electricity/gas.* 若不付费用, 就要停止供应电力[煤气]. ○ *disconnect a TV (from the power supply)*, ie unplug it 切断电视机的电源 ○ *Operator, I/we have been disconnected*, ie I have lost contact with the person I was telephoning. 话务员, 我[我们]的线断了(我跟对方的通话中断了).

▷ **dis·con·nec·ted** *adj* (of speech or writing) lacking in order; incoherent (指言语或文字)无条理的, 不连贯的: *the disconnected ramblings of an old man* 老人东拉西扯的唠叨. **dis·con·nec·tedly** *adv*.

dis·con·nec·tion *n* [U].

dis·con·sol·ate /dɪsˈkɒnsələt; dɪsˋkɑnslɪt/ *adj* unhappy, esp at the loss of sb/sth; refusing to be comforted 不快乐的, 忧郁的(尤指因失去某人[某事物]); 拒绝接受安慰的: *The death of her father left Mary disconsolate.* 玛丽因父亲去世而伤心难过. ▷ **dis·con·sol·ately** *adv*.

dis·con·tent /ˌdɪskənˈtent; ˌdɪskənˋtɛnt/ (also **dis·con·tent·ment** /ˌdɪskənˈtentmənt; ˌdɪskənˋtɛntmənt/) *n* [U] ~ **(with sth)** lack of satisfaction 不满; 不满足; 不满意: *The strikes were a sign of discontent (with poor pay).* 那些罢工事件是(对低薪)不满的一种表示.

▷ **dis·con·tented** *adj* dissatisifed 不满的; 不满足的; 不满意的: *discontented with one's job* 对自己的职业不满意. **dis·con·tent·edly** *adv*.

dis·con·tinue /ˌdɪskənˈtɪnjuː; ˌdɪskənˋtɪnjʊ/ *v* [I, Tn, Tg] (cause sth to) come to an end; stop (doing sth) 终止, 中断(某事); 中止(进行某事): *I'll have to discontinue these weekly visits.* 我每周一次的访问得停止了. ○ *The local rail service (was) discontinued in 1958.* 当地的铁路运输在1958年中断了.

▷ **dis·con·tinu·ation** /ˌdɪskəntɪnjʊˈeɪʃn; ˌdɪskənˌtɪnjʊˋeʃən/ (also **dis·con·tinu·ance** /ˌdɪskənˈtɪnjʊəns; ˌdɪskənˋtɪnjʊəns/) *n* [U] ending the availability, production, etc of sth 终止某事物的供应、生产等: *the discontinuation of our loss-making products* 我们的亏本产品的停产.

dis·con·tinu·ous /ˌdɪskənˈtɪnjʊəs; ˌdɪskənˋtɪnjʊəs/ *adj* not continuous; intermittent. **dis·con·tinu·ously** *adv*.

dis·cord /ˈdɪskɔːd; ˋdɪskɔrd/ *n* (*fml* 文) **1** (**a**) [U] disagreement; quarrelling 不和; 纷争: *A note of discord crept into their relationship.* 他们的关系出现了裂痕. (**b**) [C] instance of this 不和; 争吵. **2** (*music* 音) (**a**) [U] lack of harmony between notes sounded together 不谐和. (**b**) [C] instance of this; unpleasant sound 不谐和的音调; 刺耳的音调. Cf 参看 CONCORD. **3** (idm 习语) **an/the apple of discord** ⇨ APPLE.

▷ **dis·cord·ance** /dɪˈskɔːdəns; dɪsˋkɔrdn̩s/ *n* [U].

dis·cord·ant /dɪˈskɔːdənt; dɪsˋkɔrdn̩t/ *adj* **1** [usu attrib 通常作定语] not in agreement; conflicting 不一致的; 相互冲突的: *discordant views, interests, etc* 不一致的观点、利益等. **2** (of sounds) harsh (指声音)刺耳的. **dis·cord·antly** *adv*.

dis·co·theque = DISCO.

dis·count[1] /ˈdɪskaʊnt; ˋdɪskaʊnt/ *n* [U, C] **1** amount of money taken off the cost of sth 从某物的价格中扣去的数目; 折扣: *We give (a) 10% discount for cash*, ie for immediate payment. 现金付款, 我们予以九折优待. **2** (*commerce* 商) amount deducted for paying a bill of exchange 折息贴现. Cf 参看 REBATE. **3** (idm 习语) **at a discount** (**a**) at a reduced price 打折扣; 减价. (**b**) (*fig* 比喻) not highly valued; unfashionable 不受重视的; 不时兴的: *Concern for others seems to be at (something of) a discount today.* 如今好像不兴关心别人了.

□ ˈ**discount house** **1** (*Brit commerce* 商) establishment which deals in discounts (DISCOUNT[1] 2) 贴现公司; 贴现银行. **2** (*US*) = DISCOUNT SHOP.

ˈ**discount shop** (also ˈ**discount store**, ˈ**discount warehouse**) shop which regularly sells goods at less than the usual price 廉价商店.

dis·count[2] /dɪsˈkaʊnt; *US* ˈdɪskaʊnt; ˋdɪskaʊnt/ *v* [Tn] **1** regard (sth) as unimportant or untrue; ignore (sb/sth) 不重视, 不相信, 不理会(某人[某事物]): *You can discount what Jack said: he's a dreadful liar.* 杰克说的话你不必当真, 他可是个说谎大王. **2** (*commerce* 商) buy or sell (a bill of exchange) for less than it will be worth when due 将(票据)贴现.

dis·coun·ten·ance /dɪsˈkaʊntɪnəns; dɪsˋkaʊntənəns/ *v* [Tn] (*fml* 文) disapprove of (sb); discourage 不赞成(某人)的言行; 不支持.

dis·cour·age /dɪˈskʌrɪdʒ; dɪsˋkɝɪdʒ/ *v* **1** [Tn, Tn·pr] ~ **sb (from doing sth)** take away sb's confidence or hope of doing sth 使某人丧失(做某事的)信心; 使某人泄气: *Don't discourage her; she's doing her best.* 别泄她的气, 她正尽力做呢. **2** (**a**) [Tn] try to stop (sth) 设法阻止(某事物): *Parents should discourage smoking.* 做父母的应该设法阻止子女吸烟. (**b**) [Tn·pr] ~ **sb from doing sth** persuade sb not to do sth 劝某人不要做某事: *Parents should discourage their children from smoking.* 做父母的应该劝子女不要吸烟.

▷ **dis·cour·aged** *adj*.

dis·cour·age·ment *n* (**a**) [U] action of discouraging; state of feeling discouraged 劝阻; 泄气. (**b**) [C] thing that discourages 使人泄气的事物; 挫折: *Despite all these discouragements, she refused to give up.* 她尽管遇到许多挫折, 却仍然不气馁.

dis·cour·aging *adj*: *a discouraging result, reply* 使人泄气的结果、回答. **dis·cour·agingly** *adv*.

dis·course /ˈdɪskɔːs; ˋdɪskɔrs/ *n* **1** [C] (*fml* 文) lengthy and serious treatment of a subject in speech or writing 论文; 演讲. **2** [U] (*linguistics* 语言) continuous piece of spoken or written language (口头或书面的连贯的)语段, 话语: *analyse the structure of discourse* 分析语段结构 ○ [attrib 作定语] *discourse analysis* 话语分析.

▷ **dis·course** /dɪˈskɔːs; dɪˋskɔrs/ *v* [Ipr] ~ **on/upon sth** (*fml* 文) talk, preach or lecture about sth (usu at length) (通常长篇大论地)论说、宣扬或讲授某事物: *The speaker discoursed knowledgeably on a variety of subjects.* 演讲者头头是道地论述了一系列问题.

dis·cour·teous /dɪsˈkɜːtɪəs; dɪsˋkɝtɪəs/ *adj* (*fml* 文) bad-mannered; impolite 不讲礼貌的; 无礼的; 粗鲁的: *It was discourteous of you to arrive late.* 你迟到了, 真没礼貌.

▷ **dis·cour·teously** *adv*.

dis·cour·tesy /dɪsˈkɜːtəsɪ; dɪsˋkɝtəsɪ/ *n* [U, C] (*fml* 文) impoliteness; rude act or comment 无礼; 失礼; 失礼的举动; 粗鲁的评论: *I must apologize for my discourtesy in arriving late.* 我要为迟到失礼而道歉.

dis·cover /dɪsˈkʌvə(r); dɪˋskʌvɚ/ *v* **1** [Tn, Tf, Tw] find or learn about (a place, fact, etc for the first time) 发现(某地、某事等): *Columbus discovered America.* 哥伦布发现了美洲. ○ *I've discovered a super restaurant near here!* 我在附近找到一家一流的餐馆! ○ *I never discovered how to start the engine.* 我怎么也学不会发动

D

引擎. Cf 参看 INVENT[1]. **2** [Tn, Tng] find (sb/sth) unexpectedly (出乎意料地)发现、碰见或撞见(某人[某事物]): *I discovered him kissing my wife.* 我撞见他在吻我的妻子. **3** [Tn, Tf, Tw, Tnt esp passive 尤用于被动语态] come to know or realize (sth) 了解到, 认识到, 发觉(某事物): *Did you ever discover who did it?* 你到底发现是谁干的了吗? ○ *We discovered that our luggage had been stolen.* 我们发觉行李被偷了. ○ *He was later discovered to have been a spy.* 后来发现他原来是间谍. ▷ **dis·cov·erer** *n*.

dis·cov·ery /dɪˈskʌvərɪ; dɪˈskʌvərɪ/ *n* **1** (**a**) [U] discovering or being discovered 发现; 发觉: *a voyage of discovery* 探索未知世界的航行 ○ *the discovery of Australia* 澳洲的发现 ○ *the discovery by Franklin that lightning is electricity* 富兰克林对闪电即是电这一发现. (**b**) [C] act of discovering 发现; 发觉: *Scientists have made many important discoveries.* 科学家作出了许多重大发现. ○ *He buried the treasure to prevent its discovery.* 他将财宝埋了起来以免被人发现. **2** [C] thing discovered 被发现的事物: *Like many discoveries, atomic power can be used for good or evil.* 正如人类发现的许多事物一样, 原子能既可用来为善, 也可用以作恶.

dis·credit[1] /dɪsˈkredɪt; dɪsˈkrɛdɪt/ *v* [Tn] **1** damage the good reputation of (sb/sth) 损害, 破坏, 败坏(某人[某事物])的名声: *The Government was discredited by the scandal.* 政府因这桩丑闻而名声败坏. **2** cause (sb/sth) to be disbelieved 使(某人[某事物])不可信, 受怀疑: *His theories were discredited by scientists.* 他的理论科学家很怀疑. **3** refuse to believe (sb/sth) 不相信(某人[某事物]): *There is no reason to discredit what she says.* 没理由不信她说的话.

dis·credit[2] /dɪsˈkredɪt; dɪsˈkrɛdɪt/ *n* **1** [U] loss of reputation or respect; dishonour 名誉的丧失; 名声的败坏; 丢脸: *Violent fans bring discredit on their teams.* 粗野的球迷给他们的球队丢脸. ○ *The police, to their discredit, arrived too late.* 警察来得太晚了, 真丢人. **2** [sing] **~ to sb/sth** person or thing that causes loss of respect to sb/sth 败坏名声的原因、人或事: *He is a discredit to his family.* 他是他们家的耻辱. **3** [U] disbelief; doubt 不信; 怀疑: *The findings of the report threw discredit on the protesters' claims.* 报告中展示的调查结果使抗议者的要求遭到了怀疑.

▷ **dis·cred·it·able** /-əbl; -əbḷ/ *adj* causing a loss of reputation; dishonourable 败坏名声的; 不名誉的; 丢脸的: *discreditable conduct, methods, tactics, etc* 不名誉的行为、方法、伎俩等. **dis·cred·it·ably** /-əblɪ; -əblɪ/ *adv*.

dis·creet /dɪˈskri:t; dɪˈskrit/ *adj* careful or showing good judgement in what one says or does; not too obvious 言谈举止谨慎的; 言行审慎的; 不显眼的: *We must be extremely discreet; my husband suspects something.* 我们必须极为小心才是, 我丈夫已起疑了. ○ *I should make a few discreet enquires about the firm before you sign anything.* 我应该先审慎打探一下这家公司的底细, 然后您再签字. ○ (*fig* 比喻) *a discreet perfume*, ie one that is not too obvious 香气清淡的香水. ▷ **dis·creetly** *adv*.

dis·crep·ancy /dɪˈskrepənsɪ; dɪˈskrɛpənsɪ/ *n* **~ (between A and B)** [C, U] difference; failure to agree 差异; 不符; 不一致: *There is (a) considerable discrepancy/There were many discrepancies between the two versions of the affair.* 这件事的两种说法有很大出入. ▷ **dis·crep·ant** *adj*.

dis·crete /dɪˈskri:t; dɪˈskrit/ *adj* separate; distinct 分离的; 截然分开的: *discrete particles* 独立的粒子 ○ *a series of discrete events* 一系列互不相关的事件. ▷ **dis·cretely** *adv*. **dis·crete·ness** *n* [U].

dis·cre·tion /dɪˈskreʃn; dɪˈskrɛʃən/ *n* [U] **1** quality of being discreet; good judgement 谨慎; 慎重; 审慎; 明智: *to act with discretion* 谨慎行事 ○ *This is a secret, but I know I can count on your discretion*, ie be sure you won't tell anyone. 这可是个秘密, 不过我知道你嘴稳(肯定不会告诉别人). **2** freedom to decide for oneself what should be done 自行决断的自由: *Don't keep asking me what to do; use your own discretion.* 不要老是问我该做什么事, 你自行决定吧. **3** (idm 习语) **the age/years of diˈscretion** maturity; age when one is considered able to judge and decide for oneself 成年; 解事年龄; 责任年龄. **at sb's discretion** on the basis of sb's judgement 依据某人的见解: *A supplementary grant may be awarded at the discretion of the committee.* 委员会可能酌情追加一笔补助金. **diˌscretion is the ˌbetter part of ˈvalour** (*saying usu joc* 谚, 通常作戏谑语) there is no point in taking unnecessary risks 不知进退非真勇(不必作无谓的冒险).

▷ **dis·cre·tion·ary** /dɪˈskreʃənərɪ; *US* dɪˈskreʃənerɪ; dɪˈskrɛʃənˌɛrɪ/ *adj* [esp attrib 尤作定语] used, adopted, etc when considered necessary 根据需要而使用的、采取的等; 便宜施行的: *discretionary powers, measures, etc* 可便宜施行的权力、机动措施. ○ *discretionary payments to old people* 酌情发放给老年人的补助金.

dis·crim·in·ate /dɪˈskrɪmɪneɪt; dɪˈskrɪməˌnet/ *v* **1** [I, Ipr, Tn·pr] **~ (between A and B); ~ A from B** see or make a difference (between two things) 分别, 辨别, 区分(两事物): *discriminate between two cases/one case from another* 区分两件事[将一件事与另一件事区分开] ○ *The law discriminates between accidental and intentional killing.* 意外杀人和故意杀人在法律上是有区别的. **2** [Ipr] **~ against sb/in favour of sb** treat (one person or group) worse/better than others 歧视[偏袒](某人或某些人): *Society still discriminates against women/in favour of men.* 社会上仍然歧视女性[厚待男性].

▷ **dis·crim·in·at·ing** *adj* **1** showing good judgement and perception 判断力强的; 鉴别力强的; 知觉敏锐的: *discriminating taste, judgement, etc* 敏锐的鉴赏力、判断力等 ○ *a discriminating connoisseur, collector, customer, etc* 鉴赏力强的鉴赏家、收藏家、顾客等 ○ *She has an artist's discriminating eye.* 她具有艺术家特有的敏锐眼光. **2** = DISCRIMINATORY.

dis·crim·in·at·ory /dɪˈskrɪmɪnətərɪ; *US* dɪˈskrɪmɪnətɔ:rɪ; dɪˈskrɪmənəˈtorɪ/ *adj* discriminating against sb/sth (对待某人[某事物])不公平的, 歧视的: *discriminatory measures, policies, actions, tariffs* 不公平的措施、厚此薄彼的政策、歧视性的行为、差别关税.

dis·crim·ina·tion /dɪˌskrɪmɪˈneɪʃn; dɪˌskrɪməˈneʃən/ *n* [U] **1** good judgement and perception 辨别力; 识别力: *show discrimination in one's choice of friends, clothes, hobbies, etc* 在选择交友对象、服装、消遣形式等方面有鉴别力. **2 ~ (against/in favour of sb)** treating a person or group differently (usu worse) than others 歧视[偏袒](某人): *racial, sexual, religious, political, etc discrimination* 种族、性别、宗教、政治…歧视 ○ *This is a clear case of discrimination (against foreign imports)*. 这显然是(对进口货的)排斥.

dis·curs·ive /dɪˈskɜ:sɪv; dɪˈskɝsɪv/ *adj* (of the way a person speaks or writes) wandering from one point to another (指口头或书面的表达方式)东拉西扯的, 不着边际的: *a rather discursive account of the events* 对那些事件东拉西扯的描述. ▷ **dis·curs·ively** *adv*. **dis·curs·ive·ness** *n* [U].

discus 铁饼

dis·cus /ˈdɪskəs; ˈdɪskəs/ *n* (**a**) [C] heavy disc thrown in athletic contests 铁饼. (**b**) **the discus** [sing] discus-throwing event 铁饼项目; 铁饼比赛: *I see Britain did well in the discus.* 我看英国队在铁饼项目中表现不错. ⇨illus 见插图.

dis·cuss /dɪˈskʌs; dɪˈskʌs/ *v* [Tn, Tn·pr, Tw, Tg, Tsg] **~ sth (with sb)** talk or write about sth 谈论、讨论、议论、商量或论述某事物: *Jack was still discussing the game (with his friends) when I got there.* 我到那儿的时候, 杰克还在(跟朋友们)谈论那场比赛呢. ○ *We discussed when to go/when we should go.* 我们商量了什么时候动身. ○ *They discussed selling the house.* 他们商量过卖房子的事儿. ○ *We're here to discuss Ann's joining the club.* 我们这次碰头是为了谈谈安入会的事儿. ○ *Her latest book discusses the problems of the disabled.* 她

的新书论述残疾人的问题.

▷ **dis·cus·sion** /dɪˈskʌʃn; dɪˋskʌʃən/ *n* **1** [C, U] (instance of) discussing sth 谈论; 讨论; 议论; 商量; 论述: *After much discussion/several lengthy discussions they decided to accept our offer.* 经过反复讨论[多次长时间的讨论], 他们决定接受我们开的价. ⇨Usage at TALK[1] 用法见TALK[1]. **2** (idm 习语) **under discussion** being talked about 正在讨论中: *The plans have been under discussion for a year now, but no decision has been reached.* 那些计划讨论了一年了, 还是没有结果. ○ *the matter under discussion* 正在讨论中的那件事.

dis·dain /dɪsˈdeɪn; dɪsˋden/ *n* [U] feeling that sb/sth is not good enough to deserve one's respect; contempt 鄙视; 轻视; 蔑视: *a look/tone/expression of disdain* 鄙夷的神态[语气/表情] ○ *treating other people's ideas with disdain* 藐视别人的意见.

▷ **dis·dain** *v* **1** [Tn] treat (sth/sb) with disdain; despise 鄙视(某事物[某人]); 轻视; 蔑视: *disdain an invitation, an offer of help, a peace initiative* 不屑接受邀请、鄙视他人的援助、对和平建议不屑理会. **2** [Tg, Tt] (*fml* 文) refuse (doing/to do sth) because of one's disdain 不屑于(做某事): *He disdains going to the cinema/to sit with people like us.* 他不屑于去看电影[与我们这等人同席而坐].

dis·dain·ful /-fl; -fəl/ *adj* **~ (of sb/sth)** showing disdain 鄙视的; 轻蔑的; 藐视的: *a disdainful reply* 轻蔑的回答 ○ *He's disdainful of anyone from America.* 美洲来的人他都瞧不起. **dis·dain·fully** /-fəlɪ; -fəlɪ/ *adv.*

dis·ease /dɪˈziːz; dɪˋziz/ *n* [C, U] (case of) illness of the body, of the mind or of plants, caused by infection or internal disorder 疾病; 病患; (植物的)病害: *a serious, infectious, incurable disease* 重病、传染性疾病、不治之症 ○ *a disease of the nervous system* 神经系统的疾病 ○ *prevent/spread disease* 预防[传播]疾病.

▷ **dis·eased** *adj* suffering from a disease 患病的; 遭受病害的: *diseased kidneys, leaves* 患病的肾脏、有病害的叶子 ○ (*fig* 比喻) *a diseased society, mentality, imagination* 病态的社会、病态的心理、不健康的想像.

dis·em·bark /ˌdɪsɪmˈbɑːk; ˌdɪsɪmˋbɑrk/ (also **debark**) *v* (**a**) [I, Ipr] **~ (from sth)** (of people) leave a ship or an aircraft (指人)离船或下飞机等: *disembark from a ferry* 离渡船上岸. (**b**) [Tn, Tn·pr] **~ sb/sth (from sth)** cause (people or goods) to leave a ship or an aircraft 使(人)离船或下飞机等; 从船上或飞机上卸下(货物): *disembark passengers from the plane* 让乘客下飞机. ▷ **dis·em·barka·tion** /ˌdɪsembɑːˈkeɪʃn; ˌdɪsɛmbɑrˋkeʃən/ (also **debarkation**) *n* [U]: *After disembarkation, we went through passport control.* 我们下了飞机, 接受护照检查.

dis·em·bod·ied /ˌdɪsɪmˈbɒdɪd; ˌdɪsɪmˋbɑdɪd/ *adj* [usu attrib 通常作定语] **1** (of a soul or spirit) separated from the body (指灵魂或魂魄)从躯体中脱离出来的, 出窍的, 游荡的. **2** (*fig* 比喻) (of sounds) lacking any obvious source; eerie (指声音)没有明确来源的, 怪异的: *disembodied voices, screams, groans, etc* 神秘可怖的人声、尖叫、呻吟等.

dis·em·bowel /ˌdɪsɪmˈbaʊəl; ˌdɪsɪmˋbaʊəl/ *v* (**-ll-**; *US* also **-l-**) [Tn] remove the bowels of (sb), usu as part of an execution 取出(某人)的肠子(通常作为死刑的一部分).

dis·en·chant /ˌdɪsɪnˈtʃɑːnt; *US* ˌdɪsɪnˈtʃænt; ˌdɪsɪnˋtʃænt/ *v* [Tn] cause (sb) to lose his good opinion of sb/sth; disillusion 使(某人)对某人[某事物]不再着迷, 不抱幻想: *Her arrogance has disenchanted many of her former admirers.* 她为人高傲, 追求过她的许多人都已不再迷恋她了. ▷ **dis·en·chanted** *adj* **~ (with sb/sth)**: *His disenchanted supporters abandoned him.* 那些拥护他的人对他失去了幻想, 纷纷离他而去了. ○ *I'm becoming increasingly disenchanted with London.* 我对伦敦渐渐不那么眷恋了. **dis·en·chant·ment** *n* [U].

dis·en·cum·ber /ˌdɪsɪnˈkʌmbə(r); ˌdɪsɪnˋkʌmbɚ/ *v* [Tn, Tn·pr] **~ sb/sth (of sth)** (*fml* 文) free sb/sth from (a burden, an obstruction, etc) 使某人[某事物]解除(负担), 消除(障碍): *disencumber oneself of financial responsibilities, social commitments* 摆脱经济负担、社会义务.

dis·en·fran·chise /ˌdɪsɪnˈfræntʃaɪz; ˌdɪsɪnˋfræntʃaɪz/ *v* [Tn] = DISFRANCHISE.

dis·en·gage /ˌdɪsɪnˈɡeɪdʒ; ˌdɪsɪnˋɡedʒ/ *v* **1** [Tn, Tn·pr] **~ sth/sb (from sth/sb)** (*fml* 文) free or disconnect sth/sb from sth/sb that holds it/him firmly 放开; 挣脱开; 摆脱开: *Disengage the clutch* (ie from the gear mechanism) *before changing gear.* 先松开离合器再换挡. ○ (*joc* 谑) *He managed to disengage himself from Martha's embrace.* 他使劲儿挣脱了玛莎的拥抱. **2** [I, Ipr, Tn, Tn·pr] **~ (sb/sth) (from sth)** (*military* 军) (cause sb/sth to) stop fighting and withdraw (使某人[某物])脱离接触, 中止战斗: *The fighter planes quickly disengaged (from the combat).* 歼击机很快(从战斗中)撤出了. ○ *We must disengage our troops (from the conflict).* 我们必须把部队(从战斗中)撤出.

▷ **dis·en·gaged** *adj* [usu pred 通常作表语] (*fml* 文) (of a person) free from social or professional obligations (指人)没有社会或职业负担, 无牵无挂.

dis·en·gage·ment *n* [U].

dis·en·tangle /ˌdɪsɪnˈtæŋɡl; ˌdɪsɪnˋtæŋɡḷ/ *v* **1** [Tn] make (rope, hair, etc) straight and free of knots 将(绳索、毛发等)理直并解开其结子, 理顺. **2** [Tn, Tn·pr] **~ sth/sb (from sth)** free sth/sb from sth that hooks into it/him 使某事物[某人]摆脱开钩绊之物: *He tried to disentangle himself (from the bushes into which he had fallen).* 他竭力(从他跌入的灌木丛中)挣脱出来. ○ (*fig* 比喻) *I wish I could disentangle myself from Jill,* ie from my relationship with her. 我希望能摆脱跟吉尔的关系. ○ *disentangle the truth from a mass of lies* 把真话和一大堆谎言区分开. ▷ **dis·en·tangle·ment** *n* [U].

dis·equi·lib·rium /ˌdɪsiːkwɪˈlɪbrɪəm, *also* -ekw-; dɪsˌikwəˋlɪbrɪəm, -ɛkw-/ *n* [U] (*fml usu fig* 文, 通常作比喻) loss or lack of balance 失衡; 不平衡; 失调: *a disequilibrium in the military forces of the two countries* 两国之间军事力量的不平衡.

dis·es·tab·lish /ˌdɪsɪˈstæblɪʃ; ˌdɪsəˋstæblɪʃ/ *v* [Tn] end the official status of (a national Church) 废除(国教)的法定地位: *those who want to disestablish the Church of England* 主张废除英国国教的人. ▷ **dis·es·tab·lish·ment** *n* [U].

dis·fa·vour (*US* **dis·fa·vor**) /ˌdɪsˈfeɪvə(r); dɪsˋfevɚ/ *n* [U] dislike; disapproval (used esp as in the expressions shown) 不喜欢, 不赞成, 反感(尤用于以下示例): *regard sb/sth with disfavour* 不喜欢某人[某事物] ○ *incur sb's disfavour* 引起某人的反感 ○ *be in/fall into disfavour* 受冷遇[失宠].

dis·fig·ure /dɪsˈfɪɡə(r); *US* dɪsˈfɪɡjər; dɪsˋfɪɡjɚ/ *v* [Tn] spoil the appearance of (sb/sth) 毁损(某人[某物])的外观, 外貌; 毁容: *The accident disfigured him for life.* 那次事故使他破相, 终生无法恢复. ○ *a landscape disfigured by a power station* 被发电厂破坏了的风景. ▷ **dis·fig·ure·ment** *n* [U, C]: *the planners responsible for the disfigurement of the countryside* 使乡村景色遭到破坏的规划者.

dis·fran·chise /dɪsˈfræntʃaɪz; dɪsˋfræntʃaɪz/ (also **dis·en·fran·chise** /ˌdɪsɪnˈfræntʃaɪz; ˌdɪsɪnˋfræntʃaɪz/) *v* [Tn] take away the right to vote for a parliamentary representative from (a person or place) 剥夺(某人)选举议员的权利; 剥夺(某地)选派议员的权利. ▷ **dis·fran·chise·ment** /dɪsˈfræntʃɪzmənt; dɪsˋfræntʃɪzmənt/ (also **dis·en·fran·chise·ment** /ˌdɪsɪnˈf-; ˌdɪsɪnˋf-/) *n* [U].

dis·gorge /dɪsˈɡɔːdʒ; dɪsˋɡɔrdʒ/ *v* **1** [Tn, Tn·pr] **~ sth (from sth)** throw out (food, etc) from the stomach or throat; vomit sth 呕出, 吐出(食物等); 呕吐: *She was trying hard to disgorge a fish bone.* 她拼命想把鱼刺吐出来. **2** (**a**) [Ipr, Tn·pr] **~ (itself) into sth** (of a river) let (its waters) flow out, esp into the sea or another river (指江河)流出(尤指注入大海或汇入另一条河流): *The Avon disgorges (itself) into the Severn.* 埃文河流入塞文河. (**b**) [Ipr, Tn, Tn·pr] **~ from sth/into sth; ~ sth into sth; ~ sth (from sth) (into sth)** (*fig* 比喻) (let sth) pour out in a great mass (使某物)大量流出, 涌出: *Crowds disgorged from the theatre into the dark street.* 人流从戏院涌出, 进入了黑洞洞的街道. ○ *The holed tanker was disgorging oil.* 撞了个窟窿的油船正在喷油. **3** [I, Tn] (*infml joc* 口, 谑) unwillingly hand (sth) over or back 不情愿地将(某物)交出或交还; 吐出: *You owe me £5: come on, disgorge!* 你欠我5英镑, 快, 吐出来!

dis·grace[1] /dɪsˈɡreɪs; dɪsˋɡres/ *n* **1** [U] state in which others think that one has behaved badly and no longer deserves respect 出丑; 丢脸: *bring disgrace on oneself, one's family, etc* 给自己、家庭等丢脸 ○ *There is no disgrace in being poor.* 贫穷并不丢脸. **2** [sing] **~ (to**

D

sb/sth) thing or person that is so bad that one feels or should feel ashamed 令人感到羞耻的事物或人; 耻辱: *Your homework is a disgrace: rewrite it!* 你做的功课真丢人, 重做吧! ○ *These slums are a disgrace to the city.* 这些贫民窟是这座城市的耻辱. **3** (idm 习语) **(be) in disgrace (with sb)** (be) regarded with deep disfavour 很不讨人喜欢; 令人不喜爱: *He's in disgrace (with his father) because he told a lie.* 他撒了个谎, 惹得父亲很不痛快.

▷ **dis·grace·ful** /-fl; -fəl/ *adj* causing disgrace; very bad 可耻的; 丢脸的; 极坏的: *disgraceful manners, behaviour, etc* 丢人的举止、行为等 ○ *This cheating is disgraceful.* 这样骗人, 真不要脸. ○ *The bus is late again — it's absolutely disgraceful!* 这趟公共汽车又来迟了, 简直太不像话了! **dis·grace·fully** /-fəlɪ; -fəlɪ/ *adv*.

dis·grace² /dɪsˈgreɪs; dɪsˋgres/ *v* [Tn] **1** bring disgrace on (sb/sth); be a disgrace to 给(某人[某事物])丢脸; 给...带来耻辱: *Your behaviour disgraces us all.* 你的行为使我们大家丢脸. ○ *He got drunk and disgraced himself at the wedding.* 他在婚礼上喝多了, 出了洋相. **2** cause (sb) to lose a position of power, honour or favour 使(某人)失去权位、荣誉或不受喜爱: *After the defeat two generals were publicly disgraced.* 那两位将军吃了败仗之后, 在公众心目中威望扫地.

D

dis·gruntled /dɪsˈgrʌntld; dɪsˋgrʌntḷd/ *adj* **~ (at/about sth); ~ (with sb)** resentful because sth has happened to displease one 不高兴的; 不满的: *a disgruntled look, frown, scowl, etc* 不悦的样子、因不满而皱眉、怒容 ○ *She's still disgruntled about missing the party.* 她因错过了这一聚会而仍耿耿于怀.

dis·guise¹ /dɪsˈgaɪz; dɪsˋgaɪz/ *v* **1** [Tn, Tn·pr, Cn·n/a] **~ sb/sth (with sth); ~ sb/sth (as sb/sth)** make sb/sth look or sound different from normal; give sb/sth a false appearance (用伪装)使某人[某物]的外观或声音异常; 假装; 假扮; 装扮: *disguise one's voice* 不使用自己真实的声音 ○ *I disguised the spots on my face with make-up.* 我用化妆品盖住脸上的斑点. ○ *The raiders disguised themselves as security guards.* 袭击者都装扮成了保安人员. **2** [Tn] hide or cover up (eg one's real feelings or intentions) 隐藏, 遮掩(如真实的感情或用意): *I couldn't disguise my anger.* 我怒形于色. ○ *There's no disguising the fact* (ie It is clear) *that he's a liar.* 他爱撒谎, 这可是掩盖不了的.

dis·guise² /dɪsˈgaɪz; dɪsˋgaɪz/ *n* **1** [C, U] thing worn or used for disguising (供穿戴或使用的)伪装品: *put on (a) disguise* 伪装起来 ○ *wear a beard as a disguise* 戴上假须. **2** [U] disguised condition; disguising 伪装: *a master of disguise* 伪装的能手. **3** (idm 习语) **a blessing in disguise** ⇨ BLESSING. **in disguise** disguised 伪装的; 假装的; 假扮的: *I didn't recognize him: he was in disguise.* 我没认出他来, 他化了装了.

dis·gust¹ /dɪsˈgʌst; dɪsˋgʌst/ *n* [U] **~ (at sth)/(for/with sb)** strong dislike for sth/sb that one feels is not right or good 反感; 厌恶; 嫌恶: *his disgust at the sight of the rotting food* 他看到腐败的食物而感到恶心 ○ *The execution of political opponents aroused widespread disgust (with the regime).* 处决了政敌引起(对这个政权的)普遍反感. ○ *She turned away in disgust.* 她厌恶地把脸转开.

dis·gust² /dɪsˈgʌst; dɪsˋgʌst/ *v* [Tn] cause disgust in (sb) 使(某人)反感, 厌恶, 嫌恶: *The use of torture must disgust any civilized person.* 施用酷刑必为文明社会的人所不齿.

▷ **dis·gusted** *adj* **~ (at/by/with sb/sth)**: *We were (absolutely) disgusted at the size of the bill.* 我们看到帐单上的数额, 极为气愤.

dis·gust·edly /dɪsˈgʌstɪdlɪ; dɪsˋgʌstɪdlɪ/ *adv* with disgust 反感地; 厌恶地; 嫌恶地: *look disgustedly at sb* 厌恶地看着某人.

dis·gust·ing *adj* causing disgust 使人反感的; 使人厌恶的; 讨厌的: *disgusting personal habits* 令人厌恶的个人习惯 ○ *disgusting language* 不堪入耳的话.

dis·gust·ingly *adv* **(a)** in a disgusting way 使人反感地; 使人厌恶地. **(b)** (*joc* 谑) extremely 极端地: *be disgustingly fit, well-read, successful* 身体极棒、学富五车、极为成功.

dish¹ /dɪʃ; dɪʃ/ *n* **1 (a)** [C] container for holding or serving food (usu shallow and flat-bottomed) 盘; 碟: *a glass, an earthenware, a ceramic, a metal, etc dish* 玻璃的、陶的、瓷的、金属的...盘子 ⇨ illus at PLATE 见 PLATE 之插图. **(b)** [C] food, etc served in the container 一盘食物; 一碟食物; 一道菜; 菜肴: *a big dish of curry* 一大盘用咖喱作调味的菜. **(c) the dishes** [pl] plates, bowls, cups, etc used for a meal; crockery 餐具: *wash, do, dry, put away, etc the dishes* 洗、刷洗、弄干、放好...餐具. **2** [C] particular type of food prepared for a meal 具某种风味的饭菜: *a restaurant specializing in Indonesian dishes* 印度尼西亚风味的餐馆. **3** [C] object shaped like a dish or bowl, esp the large concave reflector of a radio telescope 盘状物; 盆状物; 凹形物; (尤指射电望远镜中巨大的)抛物面状天线. **4** [C esp *sing* 尤作单数] (*infml* 口) physically attractive person 外貌有吸引力的人; 漂亮的人: *Mary's new boy-friend's quite a dish, isn't he?* 玛丽新交的男朋友挺帅的, 是不是?

▷ **dish·ful** /ˈdɪʃfʊl; ˋdɪʃ,fʊl/ *n* about as much as a dish will hold 一盘的量; 一碟的量.

dishy /ˈdɪʃɪ; ˋdɪʃɪ/ *adj* (**-ier, -iest**) (*infml* 口) (of a person) physically attractive (指人)漂亮, 潇洒, 帅.

□ **ˈdishcloth** *n* cloth for washing dishes, etc (洗碗碟等用的)抹布.

ˈdishwasher *n* machine or person that washes dishes 刷洗碗碟的机器或人; 洗碟机; 洗碗机; 洗碗者.

ˈdish-water *n* [U] water used for washing dishes 洗碗碟的水: (*joc* 谑) *Her coffee tastes like dish-water,* ie It is weak and unpleasant. 她的咖啡喝起来像刷锅水.

dish² /dɪʃ; dɪʃ/ *v* **1** [Tn] (*Brit infml* 口) ruin (sb's hopes or chances); prevent (sb) from succeeding 使(某人的希望)破灭; 破坏(某人的机会); 使(某人)不能成功: *The scandal dished his hopes of being elected.* 这丑闻使他当选的希望破灭了. ○ *dish one's opponents* 击败对手. **2** (idm 习语) **dish it ˈout** (*infml* 口) attack sb fiercely with words or blows 大骂或猛揍某人: *Don't get into a fight with him: he can really dish it out.* 别跟他动手, 他揍起人来可凶了. **dish the ˈdirt** (*sl* 俚) gossip in an unkind way; say scandalous things about sb 说坏话; 揭某人的短儿: *journalists who dish the dirt about television stars* 揭电视明星疮疤的记者们. **3** (phr v) **dish sth out** give away a lot of sth 大量给予或分发: *There were students dishing out leaflets to passers-by.* 有学生向路人散发传单. ○ *dish out compliments, insults, abuse, etc* 大加赞扬、大肆侮辱、滔滔不绝地咒骂. **dish sth up (a)** put (food) on plates; serve sth 将(食物)盛在盘里; 上(菜). **(b)** (*derog* 贬) present or offer sth 提出或提供某事物: *They're dishing up the usual arguments in a new form.* 他们将老调子改头换面, 又端出来了.

dis·har·mony /dɪsˈhɑːmənɪ; dɪsˋhɑrmənɪ/ *n* [U] lack of harmony between people; disagreement 人与人之间的不和睦; 不协调; 不一致: *He noted the disharmony between husband and wife.* 他觉察出这对夫妇不太和睦.

▷ **dis·har·moni·ous** /ˌdɪshɑːˈməʊnɪəs; ˌdɪshɑrˋmonɪəs/ *adj*: *a disharmonious relationship* 不和谐的关系.

dis·hear·ten /dɪsˈhɑːtn; dɪsˋhɑrtn̩/ *v* [Tn] cause (sb) to lose hope or confidence 使(某人)失去希望或信心; 使(某人)灰心: *Don't let this set-back dishearten you.* 不要因这一挫折而气馁. ▷ **dis·hear·tening** /-ˈhɑːtnɪŋ; -ˋhɑrtnɪŋ/ *adj*: *disheartening news* 使人泄气的消息 ○ *a disheartening lack of interest* 使人失望的淡漠. **dis·hear·ten·ingly** *adv*.

dish·ev·elled (*US* **dis·hev·eled**) /dɪˈʃevld; dɪˋʃɛvḷd/ *adj* (of hair or clothes) untidy; ruffled (指毛发或衣服)不整齐的, 凌乱的.

dis·hon·est /dɪsˈɒnɪst; dɪsˋɑnɪst/ *adj* **1** (of a person) not honest (指人)不老实的, 不诚实的: *a dishonest trader, partner, etc* 奸商、耍滑头的合伙人. **2** [attrib 作定语] **(a)** intended to deceive or cheat 骗人的; 欺骗性的: *dishonest behaviour, goings-on, competition* 欺骗的行为、骗人的勾当、做了手脚的比赛. **(b)** (of money) not honestly obtained (指金钱)来路不正的: *dishonest earnings, gains, etc* 以不正当的方式获得的钱、利益等. ▷ **dis·hon·estly** *adv*. **dis·hon·esty** *n* [U].

dis·hon·our (*US* **dis·honor**) /dɪsˈɒnə(r); dɪsˋɑnɚ/ *n* [U, sing] (*fml or rhet* 文或修辞) loss of honour or respect 不名誉; 耻辱; 丢脸: *bring dishonour on one's family, country, regiment, etc* 使自己的家庭、国家、所在团等蒙羞.

▷ **dis·hon·our** *v* [Tn] (*fml* 文) **1** bring dishonour on (sb/sth) 使(某人[某事物])蒙羞; 败坏(某人[某事

物]）的名誉: *a cowardly act that dishonours his memory* 使他一想起便羞愧不已的怯懦之举. **2** (of a bank) refuse to cash (a cheque, etc) (指银行)拒绝兑现(支票等). Cf 参看 BOUNCE.

dis·hon·our·able /-nərəbl; -nɚəbl/ *adj* not honourable 不名誉的; 可耻的: *a dishonourable record, reputation, discharge from the army* 不光彩的履历、坏名声、被开除出军队这一不名誉事. **dis·hon·our·ably** /-nərəblɪ; -nɚəblɪ/ *adv*.

dis·il·lu·sion /ˌdɪsɪˈluːʒn; ˌdɪsɪˋluʒən/ *v* [Tn] destroy the pleasant but mistaken beliefs or ideals of (sb) 使(某人)醒悟, 理想或幻想破灭: *She still believes in Santa Claus and it would be cruel to disillusion her.* 她仍然相信有圣诞老人, 要是使她这一幻想破灭就于心不忍了.

▷ **dis·il·lu·sioned** *adj* **~ (with sb/sth)** disappointed in sb/sth that one had admired or believed in (对某人[某事物])大失所望, 幻想破灭: *Disillusioned voters want an alternative to the two main parties.* 失望的选民需要一个党派以取代这两个大党. ○ *She's disillusioned with life in general.* 她对生活各方面均不抱幻想了.

dis·il·lu·sion·ment (also **dis·il·lu·sion**) *n* [U] state of being disillusioned 幻灭; 醒悟: *the growing disillusionment with the Government's policies* 对政府政策产生越来越强烈的失望.

dis·in·cent·ive /ˌdɪsɪnˈsentɪv; ˌdɪsɪnˋsɛntɪv/ *n* **~ (to sth)** thing that discourages an action or effort 阻碍行动或发展的事物; 遏制因素: *Fixed wages and lack of promotion act as a disincentive to employees.* 工资固定又无晋升机会遏制了雇员的积极性.

dis·in·clina·tion /ˌdɪsɪnklɪˈneɪʃn; ˌdɪsɪnkləˋneʃən/ *n* [sing] **~ (for sth/to do sth)** (*fml* 文) unwillingness; reluctance 不情愿; 勉强: *a disinclination for work, exercise, politics* 不愿工作、锻炼、关心政治 ○ *his disinclination to tackle the causes of the problem* 他对问题的起因无心过问的态度.

dis·in·clined /ˌdɪsɪnˈklaɪnd; ˌdɪsɪnˋklaɪnd/ *adj* [pred 作表语] **~ (for sth/to do sth)** unwilling; reluctant 不情愿; 勉强: *feel disinclined for study, argument, discussion, etc* 不愿意学习、争辩、讨论等 ○ *She was disinclined to believe him.* 她对他的话半信半疑.

dis·in·fect /ˌdɪsɪnˈfekt; ˌdɪsɪnˋfɛkt/ *v* [Tn] clean (sth) by destroying germs that cause disease 为(某物)杀菌或消毒: *disinfect a wound, a surgical instrument, a hospital ward* 为伤口、外科手术器械、医院病房消毒.

▷ **dis·in·fect·ant** /ˌdɪsɪnˈfektənt; ˌdɪsɪnˋfɛktənt/ *n* [U, C] substance that disinfects 杀菌剂; 消毒剂: [attrib 作定语] *disinfectant liquid, cream, soap, etc* 消毒用的溶液、乳膏、肥皂等.

dis·in·fec·tion /ˌdɪsɪnˈfekʃn; ˌdɪsɪnˋfɛkʃən/ *n* [U].

dis·in·fest /ˌdɪsɪnˈfest; ˌdɪsɪnˋfɛst/ *v* [Tn] remove vermin or insects from (sb/sth) 为(某人[某物])消灭寄生虫、害虫、害鸟或害兽. ▷ **dis·in·festa·tion** /ˌdɪsɪnfeˈsteɪʃn; dɪsˌɪnfɛsˋteʃən/ *n* [U].

dis·in·forma·tion /dɪsˌɪnfəˈmeɪʃn; ˌdɪsɪnfɚˋmeʃən/ *n* [U] deliberately false information, esp given out by governments or intelligence services (故意透露的)假情报(尤指政府或情报部门). Cf 参看 MISINFORMATION (MISINFORM).

dis·in·genu·ous /ˌdɪsɪnˈdʒenjʊəs; ˌdɪsɪnˋdʒɛnjʊəs/ *adj* (*fml* 文) insincere, esp in pretending that one knows less about sth than one really does 不真诚的; (尤指)装作不知道的: *It would be disingenuous to claim that we hadn't suspected them.* 要是说我们当时还没有怀疑他们, 那就是言不由衷了. ▷ **dis·in·genu·ously** *adv*. **dis·in·genu·ous·ness** *n* [U].

dis·in·herit /ˌdɪsɪnˈherɪt; ˌdɪsɪnˋhɛrɪt/ *v* [Tn] prevent (sb) from inheriting one's property (by making a new will naming another person as heir) (重立遗嘱, 另定继承人以)阻止(某人)继承自己的财产; 取消或剥夺(某人)的继承权: *disinherit one's eldest son* 取消自己的长子的继承权. ▷ **dis·in·her·it·ance** /ˌdɪsɪnˈherɪtəns; ˌdɪsɪnˋhɛrətəns/ *n* [U].

dis·in·teg·rate /dɪsˈɪntɪgreɪt; dɪsˋɪntəˌgret/ *v* [I, Tn] **(a)** (cause sth to) break into small parts or pieces (使某物)碎裂, 崩裂: *The plane flew into a mountain and disintegrated on impact.* 飞机冲向一座山, 撞得粉碎. **(b)** (*fig* 比喻) (cause sth to) become less strong or united (使某物)衰微, 瓦解, 分崩离析: *The family is starting to disintegrate.* 这个家庭要破裂了. ▷ **dis·in·teg·ra·tion** /dɪsˌɪntɪˈgreɪʃn; dɪsˌɪntəˋgreʃən/ *n* [U]: *the gradual disintegration of traditional values* 传统价值观念的逐渐淡薄.

dis·in·ter /ˌdɪsɪnˈtɜː(r); ˌdɪsɪnˋtɝ/ *v* **(-rr-)** [Tn] (*fml* 文) dig up (sth buried) 挖出(被埋的某物): *The court granted him permission to disinter the body.* 法院批准他掘出尸体. ○ (*fig* 比喻) *disinter an old scandal* 将从前的一桩丑事儿抖出来. ▷ **dis·in·ter·ment** *n* [U, C].

dis·in·ter·es·ted /dɪsˈɪntrəstɪd; dɪsˋɪntrɪstɪd/ *adj* not influenced by personal feelings or interests; unbiased 无个人利害关系的; 公正无私的; 不偏不倚的: *a disinterested act of kindness* 没有私心杂念的好心的行为 ○ *My advice is quite disinterested.* 我的建议是正直无偏的. ⇨Usage at INTEREST[2] 用法见 INTEREST[2]. ▷ **dis·in·ter·es·tedly** *adv*. **dis·in·ter·es·ted·ness** *n* [U].

dis·in·vest /ˌdɪsɪnˈvest; ˌdɪsɪnˋvɛst/ *v* [I, Ipr] (*finance* 财) reduce or dispose of one's investment (in a place, company, etc) 缩减、收回或转让(在某地、某公司等的)投资.

dis·jointed /dɪsˈdʒɔɪntɪd; dɪsˋdʒɔɪntɪd/ *adj* (of talk, writing, etc) in which it is difficult to understand how the ideas, events, etc follow each other and develop (指说话、文章等)内容不连贯的, 支离破碎的: *The film was so disjointed that I couldn't tell you what the story was about.* 那部电影的情节支离破碎, 我简直说不出个所以然来. ▷ **dis·joint·edly** *adv*.

dis·junct·ive /dɪsˈdʒʌŋktɪv; dɪsˋdʒʌŋktɪv/ *adj* (*grammar*) (of a conjunction) showing opposition or contrast between two ideas (eg *either ... or*) (指连词)转折的, 反意的(如 either ... or).

disk /dɪsk; dɪsk/ *n* **1** (*esp US*) = DISC. **2** (*computing* 计) circular plate, coated with magnetic material, on which data can be recorded in a form that can be used by a computer 磁盘. Cf 参看 FLOPPY DISK (FLOP), HARD DISK (HARD[1]).

▷ **disk·ette** /dɪsˈket; dɪˋskɛt/ *n* = FLOPPY DISK (FLOP).

□ **ˈdisk drive** device which transfers data from a disk to the memory of a computer, or from the memory to the disk 磁盘驱动器; 磁盘机. ⇨illus at COMPUTER 见 COMPUTER 之插图.

dis·like /dɪsˈlaɪk; dɪsˋlaɪk/ *v* [Tn, Tg, Tsg] not like (sb/sth) 不喜欢, 讨厌(某人[某事物]): *My mother dislikes seeing you with me/dislikes our being together.* 我母亲不喜欢看到你和我在一起. ○ *I like cats but dislike dogs.* 我喜欢猫, 不喜欢狗. ○ *I dislike it when you whistle.* 我不爱听你吹口哨. ○ *If you go on like that you'll get yourself disliked*, ie become unpopular. 你再这样下去, 别人就不喜欢你了.

▷ **dis·like** *n* **1 (a)** [U] **~ (of sb/sth)** feeling of not liking 不喜欢; 反感: *a strong dislike of modern poetry* 对现代诗的强烈反感. **(b)** [C usu *pl* 通常作复数] thing that one dislikes 不喜欢的事物: *have one's pet dislikes* 有自己特别不喜欢的东西. **2** (idm 习语) **likes and dislikes** ⇨ LIKE[2]. **take a dislike to sb/sth** start disliking sb/sth 开始不喜欢某人[某事物]: *I don't know why, but I took a strong dislike to him as soon as I saw him.* 也不知为什么, 我一见他就十分讨厌他.

dis·lo·cate /ˈdɪsləkeɪt; *US* ˈdɪsləʊkeɪt; ˋdɪsloˌket/ *v* [Tn] **1** put (a bone) out of its proper position in a joint 使(骨头)脱位: *dislocate one's ankle, wrist, etc* 使脚踝、手腕等脱臼 ○ *a dislocated shoulder* 脱了臼的肩膀. **2** stop (a system, plan, etc) from working as it should; disrupt 扰乱(制度、计划等): *Flights have been dislocated by the fog.* 大雾将飞机的班次搅乱了. ▷ **dis·loca·tion** /ˌdɪsləˈkeɪʃn; *US* ˌdɪsləʊˈkeɪʃn; ˌdɪsloˋkeʃən/ *n* [C, U]: *treated her for a dislocation and muscle strain* 为她治疗脱臼和肌肉扭伤 ○ *The strike will cause some dislocation of rail traffic.* 这次罢工会给铁路交通造成一定的混乱.

dis·lodge /dɪsˈlɒdʒ; dɪsˋlɑdʒ/ *v* [Tn, Tn·pr] **~ sb/sth (from sth)** move or force sb/sth from a previously fixed position 将某人[某物]逐出或移开; 移去; 取出: *The wind dislodged some tiles (from the roof).* 风把瓦(从屋顶上)刮了下来. ○ *There's something between my teeth and I can't dislodge it.* 我牙缝里塞了点东西, 就是弄不出来. ○ (*fig* 比喻) *She became champion in 1982 and no one has been able to dislodge her.* 她于1982年获得冠军, 至今还没有人能把她从宝座上拉下来. ▷ **dis·lodge·ment** *n* [U].

dis·loyal /dɪsˈlɔɪəl; dɪsˋlɔɪəl/ *adj* **~ (to sb/sth)** not loyal; unfaithful 不忠实的; 不忠诚的: *be disloyal to a*

D

cause, one's country, one's associates 对事业不忠、对国家不忠、对同事不守信义. ▷ **dis·loy·ally** /-ˈlɔɪəlɪ; -ˋlɔɪəlɪ/ *adv*. **dis·loy·alty** /-ˈlɔɪəltɪ; -ˋlɔɪəltɪ/ *n* [U, C].

dis·mal /ˈdɪzməl; ˋdɪzml̩/ *adj* **1** causing or showing sadness; gloomy; miserable (使人)悲伤的; 凄凉的; 阴沉的; 悲惨的: *dismal weather, countryside* 阴沉沉的天气、乡村 ○ *The news was as dismal as ever.* 这消息还是叫人提不起劲来. ○ *a dismal manner, tone of voice, look, etc* 郁郁寡欢的样子、悲戚的语调、凄楚的神情等. **2** (*infml* 口) less good than expected; poor 差劲的; 不怎么样的: *a dismal performance in the elections* 在选举中差劲的表现. ▷ **dis·mally** /-məlɪ; -mlɪ/ *adv*.

dis·mantle /dɪsˈmæntl; dɪsˋmæntl/ *v* [Tn] **1** take (sth) to pieces 将(某物)拆开; 拆除(某物): *dismantle a faulty motor, machine, etc (for repairs)* 把有毛病的发动机、机器等拆开(以便修理) ○ *dismantle an exhibition, a theatrical set, etc* 把所有展品、戏剧布景等拆除 ○ (*fig* 比喻) *We should dismantle our inefficient tax system.* 我们这个效益很差的税收制度应该废除. **2** remove fittings and furnishings from (a building or ship) 拆除(建筑物或船只)的装备.

D

dis·may /dɪsˈmeɪ; dɪsˋme/ *n* [U] feeling of shock and discouragement 惊愕; 气馁; 灰心: *be filled/struck with dismay (at the news, etc)* (得到这消息等)极为震惊 ○ *He learned to his dismay that he had lost his job.* 他得知自己失去了工作, 十分伤心. ○ *We watched in blank dismay as she packed her bags.* 我们瞧着她打行李, 感到无可奈何.

▷ **dis·may** *v* [Tn usu passive 通常用于被动语态] fill (sb) with dismay 使(某人)惊愕或气馁: *We were all dismayed at his refusal to co-operate.* 他不肯合作使我们感到非常失望.

dis·mem·ber /dɪsˈmembə(r); dɪsˋmɛmbɚ/ *v* [Tn] **1** cut or tear off the limbs of (a person or an animal) 切断或分裂(人或动物)的肢体; 肢解: *The victim's dismembered body was found in a trunk.* 在一只大箱子里发现了受害者遭肢解的躯体. **2** divide (a country, etc) into parts; partition 瓜分(国家等); 分割. ▷ **dis·mem·ber·ment** *n* [U].

dis·miss /dɪsˈmɪs; dɪsˋmɪs/ *v* **1** [Tn, Tn·pr] **~ sb (from sth)** remove sb (esp an employee) from a position 免除某人(尤指雇员)的职务; 开除; 解雇: *workers who have been unfairly dismissed* 被无理解雇的工人. **2** [Tn, Tn·pr] **~ sb (from sth)** send sb away; allow sb to leave 把某人打发走; 让某人离开: *dismiss soldiers, a class* 遣散士兵、下课 ○ (*fml* 文) *The duchess dismissed the servant (from her presence).* 公爵夫人让那个仆人退下. **3** (**a**) [Tn, Tn·pr] **~ sb/sth (from sth)** put (thoughts, feelings, etc) out of one's mind 屏除(思想、感情等): *He tried without success to dismiss her/her memory from his thoughts.* 他尽量不去想她, 然而无济于事. (**b**) [Tn, Cn·n/a] **~ sb/sth (as sth)** consider sb/sth not worth thinking or talking about 对某人[某事物]不予理会或不屑一提: *She was dismissed as a dreamer.* 人们认为她是个空想家而不予理睬. ○ *dismiss a suggestion, an objection, an idea, etc* 不理会一建议、异议、主意等. **4** [Tn] (*law* 律) reject (a case, an appeal, etc) 驳回(诉案、上诉等). **5** [Tn] (in cricket) end the innings of (the other team or one of its batsmen) (板球赛中)迫使(对方球队或击球手)出局, 退场.

▷ **dis·missal** /dɪsˈmɪsl; dɪsˋmɪsl/ *n* (**a**) [U] action of dismissing 开除; 撤职; 解雇; 调离; 遣散; 屏除; 不予理会; 驳回; 退场: *a strike caused by the dismissal of two workers* 因解雇两名工人而引起的罢工事件 ○ *his rash dismissal of the offer* 他对该提议轻率的拒绝. (**b**) [C] event of being dismissed 被解雇、被撤职等的事件: *The dismissals led to a strike.* 雇主解雇工人导致了罢工事件.

dis·miss·ive *adj* **~ (of sb/sth)** dismissing in a rude, brief and casual way (以粗暴、轻率及漫不经心的态度)打发走或表示拒绝: *a dismissive gesture, tone of voice, shrug of the shoulders* 表示轻蔑的手势、语调、一耸肩 ○ *Reviewers were dismissive, and the play closed within a week.* 由于评论界持否定态度, 该剧上演不到一周便停止了. ○ *Don't be so dismissive of her talent.* 可别小看了她的才能. **dis·miss·ively** *adv*.

dis·mount /ˌdɪsˈmaʊnt; dɪsˋmaʊnt/ *v* **1** [I, Ipr] **~ (from sth)** get off (a motor cycle, bicycle, horse, etc) 下(摩托车、自行车、马等). Cf 参看 ALIGHT[2] 1. **2** [Tn] cause (sb) to fall, esp from a horse, etc 使(某人)掉下; (尤指)坠马等.

dis·obedi·ent /ˌdɪsəˈbiːdɪənt; ˌdɪsəˋbidɪənt/ *adj* not obedient 不顺从的; 不服从的: *a disobedient child* 不听话的孩子 ○ *I was very disobedient towards my father.* 我根本不听我父亲的话.

▷ **dis·obedi·ence** /-ɪəns; -ɪəns/ *n* [U] failure or refusal to obey 不顺从; 不服从: *an act of disobedience* 违抗行为 ○ *He was punished for his disobedience.* 他因不顺从而受到惩罚.

dis·obedi·ently *adv*.

dis·obey /ˌdɪsəˈbeɪ; ˌdɪsəˋbe/ *v* [I, Tn] not obey (a person, law, etc) 不服从, 违抗(某人、法律等).

dis·ob·lige /ˌdɪsəˈblaɪdʒ; ˌdɪsəˋblaɪdʒ/ *v* [Tn] (*fml* 文) refuse to help or co-operate with (sb) 不肯帮助(某人); 拒不与(某人)合作. ▷ **dis·ob·li·ging** *adj*: *a disobliging manner, person, response* 不愿合作的态度、人、反应 ○ *Sorry to be so disobliging, but I have no money to lend you.* 很抱歉, 爱莫能助, 我没有钱借给你. **dis·ob·li·gingly** *adv*.

dis·order /dɪsˈɔːdə(r); dɪsˋɔrdɚ/ *n* **1** [U] confused or untidy state; lack of order 混乱; 凌乱; 无秩序: *with one's papers, thoughts, financial affairs in (complete) disorder* 证件、思绪、财务(完全)乱七八糟地 ○ *Everyone began shouting at once and the meeting broke up in disorder.* 大家一下子全都喊叫起来, 会议秩序大乱而被迫中断. **2** (**a**) [U] disturbance of public order 骚乱: *The capital is calm, but continuing disorder has been reported elsewhere.* 首都一片平静, 然而据报道在别的地方仍有持续的骚乱. (**b**) [C] riot 动乱; 暴乱: *The announcement led to violent civil disorders.* 这项宣布引起了剧烈的内乱. **3** [C, U] disturbance of the normal working of the body or mind (身体或精神)不适, 疾病: *He's suffering from severe mental disorder.* 他患有严重的精神病. ○ *a disorder of the bowels* 闹肚子.

▷ **dis·order** *v* [Tn] disturb the order of (sth) 弄乱(某物): *disorder sb's papers, files, etc* 把某人的证件、档案等弄乱. **dis·or·dered** *adj* [usu attrib 通常作定语] suffering from lack of order or control 错乱的; 失调的: *a disordered imagination, flow of words* 精神错乱、语无伦次 ○ *He led a disordered life and died in poverty.* 他生活毫无规律, 于贫困中死去.

dis·or·derly *adj* [usu attrib 通常作定语] **1** untidy 凌乱的; 无秩序的: *a disorderly heap of clothes* 乱七八糟的一堆衣服. **2** (of people or behaviour) showing a lack of self-control; disturbing public order (指人或行为)不能律己的, 妨碍治安的: *a disorderly mob, demonstration, meeting, etc* 扰乱社会秩序的暴民、示威活动、集会等 ○ (*law* 律) *a disorderly house*, ie where prostitution or illegal gambling is carried on 妓院(或非法赌场). **3** (idm 习语) **drunk and disorderly** ⇨ DRUNK.

dis·or·der·li·ness *n* [U].

dis·or·gan·ize, -ise /dɪsˈɔːgənaɪz; dɪsˋɔrgəˌnaɪz/ *v* [Tn] spoil the organized way (sb/sth) is supposed to work 打乱(某人[某事物])的步骤或安排: *disorganize a schedule, plan, etc* 打乱程序、计划等.

▷ **dis·or·gan·iza·tion, -isation** /dɪsˌɔːgənaɪˈzeɪʃn; *US* -nɪˈz-; dɪsˌɔrgənəˋzeʃən/ *n* [U].

dis·or·gan·ized, -ised *adj* badly organized or planned 组织不善的; 计划不周的: *She's so disorganized she never gets anything done.* 她太缺乏条理了, 什么事也做不成. ○ *a disorganized lesson, holiday, household* 凌乱无序的课、计划不周的假期、杂乱无章的家务.

dis·ori·ent·ate /dɪsˈɔːrɪənteɪt; dɪsˋɔrɪɛnˌtet/ (also *esp US* **dis·ori·ent** /dɪsˈɔːrɪənt; dɪsˋɔrɪˌɛnt/) *v* [Tn esp passive 尤用于被动语态] **1** cause (sb) to lose all sense of direction 使(某人)迷失方向: *We were quite disorientated by the maze of streets.* 街道曲曲弯弯的, 把我们弄得迷失了方向. **2** confuse (sb) 使(某人)神志迷乱: *I felt completely disorientated with the jet lag.* 我乘长途飞机后因生理节奏失调而感到昏昏沉沉的. ▷ **dis·ori·enta·tion** /dɪsˌɔːrɪənˈteɪʃn; dɪsˌɔrɪənˋteʃən/ *n* [U].

dis·own /dɪsˈəʊn; dɪsˋon/ *v* [Tn] refuse to be connected with (sb/sth), esp because one is shocked by some action 与(某人[某事物])断绝关系, 脱离关系: *If you behave like that in front of my friends again, I'll disown you!* 你要是当着我朋友的面再那样做, 我就和你一刀两断!

dis·par·age /dɪˈspærɪdʒ; dɪˋspærɪdʒ/ *v* [Tn] suggest, esp unfairly, that (sb/sth) is of little value or importance 贬低, 轻视(某人[某事物])(尤指欠公允): *disparage sb's work, talents, achievements, character, etc* 贬低某人的作

品、才能、成就、品性等. ▷ **dis·par·age·ment** *n* [U]. **dis·par·aging** *adj*: *disparaging remarks, comments, etc* 贬低性的言语、评论等. **dis·par·agingly** *adv*: *speak disparagingly of sb/sb's efforts* 诋毁某人[某人的成就].

dis·par·ate /ˈdɪspərət; ˋdɪspərɪt/ *adj* (*fml* 文) so different in kind or degree that they cannot be compared 迥然不同的; 无法比较的: *The five experiments gave quite disparate results.* 这五次试验所获得的结果迥然不同. ▷ **dis·par·ately** *adv*.

dis·par·ity /dɪˈspærəti; dɪsˋpærətɪ/ *n* (*fml* 文) [U, C] difference or inequality 不同; 不等: *disparity in age, rank, income, status, etc* 年龄、级别、收入、地位等方面的差距 ○ *Comparison of the two accounts revealed numerous disparities.* 把两本帐一比较, 发现有许多出入.

dis·pas·sion·ate /dɪˈspæʃənət; dɪsˋpæʃənɪt/ *adj* (*approv* 褒) not influenced by emotion; impartial 不动感情的; 冷静的; 公平的: *a dispassionate view, observer, judgement* 客观公正的见解、观察家、评判. ▷ **dis·pas·sion·ately** *adv*: *She listened dispassionately but with great interest to both arguments.* 她平心静气地听着, 然而对双方的理由都极为注意.

dis·patch[1] (also **des·patch**) /dɪˈspætʃ; dɪˋspætʃ/ *v* **1** [Tn, Tn·pr] **~ sb/sth (to...)** send sb/sth off to a destination or for a special purpose 派遣(某人); 发送(某事物): *dispatch a letter, telegram, message, etc* 发信、电报、消息等 ○ *American warships have been dispatched to the area.* 美国军舰已派往该地区. **2** [Tn] finish (a job, meal, etc) quickly 迅速做完(工作); 匆匆吃完(饭): *The chairman dispatched the meeting in 20 minutes.* 主席仅用20分钟就结束了会议. **3** [Tn] give the death-blow to (sb/sth); kill 给予(某人[某物])致命的一击; 杀死: *A vet dispatched the injured horse.* 兽医把那匹受伤的马杀死了.

dis·patch[2] (also **des·patch**) /dɪˈspætʃ; dɪˋspætʃ/ *n* **1** (*fml* 文) [U] dispatching; being dispatched (被)派遣; 发送: *We welcome the dispatch of the peace-keeping force.* 我们对派出维持和平部队此举表示欢迎. **2** [C] **(a)** official message or report sent quickly (公事的)急件. **(b)** report sent to a newspaper or news agency (发给报刊或通讯社的)新闻报道; 电讯. **3** (idm 习语) **mentioned in dispatches** ⇨ MENTION. **with diˈspatch** (*dated* 旧) quickly and effectively 迅速而有效地: *act with dispatch* 行动利索.

□ **diˈspatch-box** *n* **(a)** container for carrying official documents (传送文件用的)公文箱. **(b) the Diˈspatch Box** box in the British Parliament next to which Ministers stand when speaking 英国议会中置于大臣站立发言处的箱子.

diˈspatch-rider *n* (usu military) messenger who travels by motor cycle (通常指军队中)骑摩托车的通讯员.

dis·pel /dɪˈspel; dɪˋspɛl/ *v* **(-ll-)** [Tn] drive (sth) away; cause to vanish 驱走(某事物); 使消失: *dispel sb's doubts/fears/worries* 消除某人的疑虑[恐惧/烦恼] ○ *The company is trying to dispel rumours about a take-over.* 公司力图澄清有关控制权转移的流言.

dis·pens·able /dɪˈspensəbl; dɪˋspɛnsəbl̩/ *adj* [usu pred 通常作表语] not necessary or essential 不必要; 不重要: *A garage is useful but dispensable.* 汽车房虽然有用, 但不必要.

dis·pens·ary /dɪˈspensəri; dɪˋspɛnsərɪ/ *n* **(a)** place in a hospital, school, etc where medicines are given out (医院、学校等的)药房. **(b)** place where patients are treated; clinic 医务室; 诊所.

dis·pensa·tion /ˌdɪspenˈseɪʃn; ˌdɪspənˋseʃən/ *n* **1** [U] (*fml* 文) action of dispensing or distributing 分配; 分发. **2** [U, C] (*fml* 文) apparent arrangement of events by Providence 神的安排; 天命; 天道. **3** [C, U] (*religion* 宗) (in the Roman Catholic Church) permission to break the normal rules of the church (天主教)特准(容许违反教会的常规), 豁免: *She needs a special dispensation to marry her cousin.* 她需要得到特准才能嫁给她的表亲. **4** [C] (*religion* 宗) religious system prevalent at a certain period 某一时代的宗教制度: *the Christian, Mosaic dispensation* 基督教的教规、摩西的律法.

dis·pense /dɪˈspens; dɪˋspɛns/ *v* **1** [Tn, Tn·pr] **~ sth (to sb)** **(a)** give sth out; distribute sth 施予某物; 分配某物: *On Saturday morning my father solemnly dispensed pocket money to each of the children.* 星期六上午我父亲郑重其事地给每个孩子发零花钱. ○ *a machine dispensing paper towels* 供应纸巾的机器. **(b)** (*law* 律) administer (justice) in court 执行(法律). **2** [Tn] prepare and give out (medicine, esp that prescribed by a doctor) 配(药)和发(药)(尤指按医生处方): (*Brit*) *a dispensing chemist* 药剂师 ○ *dispense a prescription*, ie medicine that has been prescribed 按处方配药. **3** (phr v) **dispense with sb/sth** manage without sb/sth; get rid of sb/sth 用不着某人[某事物]; 摆脱某人[某事物]: *He is not yet well enough to dispense with the pills.* 他尚未痊愈, 仍需吃药. ○ *Let's dispense with formalities!* 咱们不必拘礼了. ○ *Formalities were dispensed with*, ie People could speak frankly or naturally. 免除了客套. ○ *Automation has largely dispensed with the need for manual checking*, ie made it unnecessary. 实行了自动化就在很大程度上不需要人工检验了.

▷ **dis·penser** *n* **1** device from which towels, liquid soap, paper cups, etc may be obtained 自动售货机(出售毛巾、液体皂、纸杯等): *a cash dispenser* 自动提款机. **2** person who dispenses medicine 配药者; 药剂师.

dis·perse /dɪˈspɜːs; dɪˋspɝs/ *v* [I, Ipr, Tn, Tn·pr] (cause sb/sth to) go in different directions; scatter; break up (使某人[某物])散开; 消散; 驱散: *The crowd dispersed (in all directions).* 人群散开了. ○ *The wind dispersed the clouds.* 风把云吹散了.

▷ **dis·persal** /dɪˈspɜːsl; dɪˋspɝsl̩/ *n* [U] action or process of dispersing 分散; 消散: *They called for the peaceful dispersal of the demonstrators.* 他们要求示威者和平解散.

dis·per·sion /dɪˈspɜːʃn; *US* dɪˈspɜːrʒn; dɪˋspɝʒən/ *n* **(a)** [U] dispersal, esp of light 分散; 消散; (尤指光的)色散. **(b) the Dispersion** [sing] = THE DIASPORA.

dis·pirit /dɪˈspɪrɪt; dɪˋspɪrɪt/ *v* [Tn] discourage (sb); depress 使(某人)气馁; 使沮丧: *She refused to be dispirited by her long illness.* 她并未因长期患病而萎靡不振. Cf 参看 DEMORALIZE. ▷ **dis·pir·ited** *adj* [usu attrib 通常作定语]: *a dispirited air, look, expression, etc* 心灰意懒的样子、神色、表情等. **dis·pir·itedly** *adv*. **dis·pir·it·ing** *adj*: *Our lack of progress is very dispiriting.* 我们毫无进展真使人气馁.

dis·place /dɪsˈpleɪs; dɪsˋples/ *v* [Tn] **1** move (sb/sth) from the usual or correct place 使(某人[某物])离开原位. **2** (*fml* 文) take the place of (sb/sth) 取代, 替代, 置换(某人[某物]): *Moderates have displaced the extremists on the committee.* 在委员会中, 稳健派人士取代了激进派人士. ○ *Weeds tend to displace other plants.* 杂草越来越多, 有取代其他植物之势.

□ ˌ**displaced ˈperson** (*dated* 旧) refugee 难民; 流亡者.

dis·place·ment /dɪsˈpleɪsmənt; dɪsˋplesmənt/ *n* **1** [U] displacing or being displaced 移位; 取代. **2** [C] (*nautical* 海) weight of water displaced by a ship floating in it, used as a measure of the ship's size 排水量: *a ship with a displacement of 10 000 tons* 排水量为10 000吨的船只.

dis·play[1] /dɪˈspleɪ; dɪˋsple/ *v* [Tn, Tn·pr] **~ sth (to sb)** **1** put sth on show 展示、表露或陈列某事物: *display a notice, goods for sale, one's anger, one's wealth* 张贴布告、陈列商品、表现自己的愤怒、炫耀自己的财富 ○ *It's the first time the painting has been displayed to the public.* 这是该画首次公开展出. **2** show signs of having (a quality or an emotion, etc) 显示, 显露(某特性或情绪等): *display one's ignorance, arrogance, fear, etc* 显示出愚昧无知、狂妄自大、胆小怕事等 ○ *Her writing displays natural talent.* 她写的作品显示出她天赋极高.

dis·play[2] /dɪˈspleɪ; dɪˋsple/ *n* **1 (a)** act of displaying 展示; 表露; 陈列; 显示; 显露: *put on a firework display* 施放烟火 ○ *a display of karate, military might, courage, strength* 空手道的表演、军事威力的炫耀、勇气的表现、力量的显示 ○ *an appalling display of incompetence, prejudice, greed* 极其无能、偏颇、贪婪的表现. **(b)** goods, works of art, etc being displayed 陈列的货物、艺术品等: *The displays in Harrods are one of the sights in London.* 哈罗德百货公司的陈列品是伦敦一景. ⇨ Usage at DEMONSTRATION 用法见DEMONSTRATION. **2** (*computing* 计) words, pictures, etc shown on a visual display unit 荧屏上显示的词语、画面等. **3** (idm 习语) **on display** being displayed 被展示; 被陈列: *A* *collection of photographs was on display in the hall.* 大厅里展出了一辑照片. ○ *put sth on display*, ie display it 展出某物.

dis·please /dɪsˈpli:z; dɪsˈpliz/ *v* [Tn] make (sb) feel upset or angry; annoy 惹恼, 触怒(某人); 使生气: *He'd do anything rather than displease his parents.* 他无论如何也不会惹父母生气. ○ *Her insolence greatly displeased the judge.* 她傲慢无礼, 大大地触怒了法官. ▷ **dis·pleased** *adj* **~ (with sb/sth)**: *He was rather displeased with his friends (for not having phoned to say they were coming).* 他对朋友的做法有些不快(因为他们没有打电话告知要来). ○ *Many voters are displeased with the government's policies.* 许多选民不满政府的政策. **dis·pleas·ing** *adj* **~ (to sb/sth)**: *Modern music can at first seem displeasing to the ear.* 现代音乐乍听起来可能让人很不舒服. ○ *a displeasing habit (of talking too much)* 令人厌烦的(唠叨)习惯. **dis·pleas·ingly** *adv.*

dis·pleas·ure /dɪsˈpleʒə(r); dɪsˈplɛʒɚ/ *n* [U] displeased feeling; dissatisfaction 不悦; 不满: *His rash outburst incurred the displeasure of the judge.* 他勃然大怒使法官不悦. ○ *express one's displeasure at sth* 对某事物表示不满.

dis·port /dɪˈspɔ:t; dɪˈspɔrt/ *v* [Tn] **~ oneself** (*fml or joc* 文或谑) amuse oneself energetically 欢娱; 取乐: *children disporting themselves like puppies on the beach* 像一群小狗似的在海滩上嬉戏的儿童.

dis·pos·able /dɪˈspəʊzəbl; dɪˈspozəbl/ *adj* [esp attrib 尤作定语] **1** made to be thrown away after use 用完即可丢弃的; 一次性的: *disposable razors, nappies, syringes, plates* 一次性的剃刀、尿片、注射器、盘子. **2** (*finance* 财) available for use 可动用的: *disposable assets, capital, resources, etc* 可支配的资产、资本、资源等 ○ *disposable income*, ie that one can spend oneself after paying one's income tax, social security contributions, etc 可支配收入(缴纳所得税、社会福利金等之后自己可以动用的部分).

dis·posal /dɪˈspəʊzl; dɪˈspozl̩/ *n* **1** [U] action of getting rid of sth 清除; 处理; 处置: *The safe disposal of nuclear waste is a major problem.* 安全处置核废料是个大问题. ○ *a bomb disposal squad* 炸弹处理小组. **2** (idm 习语) **at one's/sb's disposal** available for one/sb to use as one wishes 供任意使用; 可自行支配: *Students have a well-stocked library at their disposal.* 学生有个藏书丰富的图书馆, 非常方便. ○ *The firm put a secretary at my disposal.* 公司给我配备了一名秘书.

dis·pose /dɪˈspəʊz; dɪˈspoz/ *v* **1** [Tn] (*fml* 文) place (sb/sth) in a suitable way; arrange 安排, 编排(某人[某事物]); 布置: *troops disposed in battle formation* 编成战斗队形的军队 ○ *dispose the chairs/singers in a semi-circle* 把椅子[唱歌的人]排成半圆形. **2** [Cn·t] (*fml* 文) make (sb) willing or ready to do sth 使(某人)愿意做某事物: *His criminal record does not dispose me to trust him.* 他有前科, 我不能轻易相信他. **3** (phr v) **dispose of sb/sth** (**a**) get rid of sb/sth that one does not want or cannot keep 去除、处理、舍弃某人[某物]: *a better way of disposing of household waste* 清除家中垃圾的好办法 ○ *He was forced to dispose of* (ie sell) *his art treasures.* 他被迫处理(卖)掉了自己的艺术珍藏. ○ *All the furniture has been disposed of.* 所有的家具都已处理掉了. (**b**) deal or finish with sb/sth that presents a problem 应付、解决、了结某人[某事物]: *She disposed of the champion in straight sets.* 她一盘未输战胜了冠军. ○ *The president ruthlessly disposed of his rivals*, eg dismissed them, had them killed. 这位总统无情地除掉了政敌(如将他们撤职或杀害). ○ *Their objections were easily disposed of*, ie successfully argued against. 他们的反对言论很容易就被驳倒了. (**c**) (no passive 不用于被动语态) (*fml* 文) have sb/sth available for use 随时可使用或支配某人[某事物]: *dispose of considerable wealth, power, influence, etc* 随时可支配可观的财富、行使很大的权力、施加很大的影响.

dis·posed /dɪˈspəʊzd; dɪˈspozd/ *adj* [pred 作表语] **1 ~ (to do sth)** wanting or prepared to do sth 想(做某事); 准备(做某事): *I'm not disposed to meet them at the moment.* 我不打算在此刻会见他们. ○ *You're most welcome to join us if you feel so disposed.* 你若有意参加, 我们无任欢迎. **2** (following an *adv* 用于副词之后) **~ towards sb/sth** inclined to think that sb/sth is/is not good or worthwhile 认为某人[某事物]好[不好]或有价值[无价值]: *well/ill disposed towards sb/sth* 对某人[某事物]有好感[无好感] ○ *She's favourably disposed towards new ideas.* 她对新思想持赞同的态度.

dis·posi·tion /ˌdɪspəˈzɪʃn; ˌdɪspəˈzɪʃən/ *n* [sing] **1** person's natural qualities of mind and character 性情; 性格: *a calm, irritable, cheerful, boastful, etc disposition* 沉静、易怒、开朗、自负等的性格. **2 ~ to sth/to do sth** (*fml* 文) inclination; tendency 意向; 倾向: *a disposition to jealousy/to be jealous* 爱忌妒 ○ *There was a general disposition to ignore the problem.* 人们一般都忽视了这个问题. **3** arrangement; placing 安排; 布置: *A defector revealed the disposition of the enemy fleet.* 有一名叛变者透露了敌方舰队的部署.

dis·pos·sess /ˌdɪspəˈzes; ˌdɪspəˈzɛs/ *v* [Tn, Tn·pr] **~ sb (of sth)** take away property, land, a house, etc from sb 夺走(某人的财产、土地、房屋等): *The nobles were dispossessed (of their estates) after the revolution.* 革命后剥夺了贵族们的地产.

▷ **the dis·pos·ses·sed** *n* [pl *v*] people who have been dispossessed 被剥夺权利者.

dis·pos·ses·sion /ˌdɪspəˈzeʃn; ˌdɪspəˈzɛʃən/ *n* [U].

dis·proof /dɪsˈpru:f; dɪsˈpruf/ *n* (*fml* 文) (**a**) [U] disproving 反证明. (**b**) [C] thing that disproves 反证物.

dis·pro·por·tion /ˌdɪsprəˈpɔ:ʃn; ˌdɪsprəˈpɔrʃən/ *n* [C, U] **~ (between sth and sth)** (instance of) being out of proportion 不均衡; 不相称; 不成比例: *disproportion in age, size, weight, importance* 年龄上的不相称、尺寸上的不匀称、重量上的不均衡、重要性上的不相等 ○ *the disproportion between her salary and her responsibilities* 她薪金与职责的不相称.

▷ **dis·pro·por·tion·ate** /ˌdɪsprəˈpɔ:ʃənət; ˌdɪsprəˈpɔrʃənɪt/ *adj* relatively too large or small, etc; out of proportion 过大或过小的; 不成比例的: *You spend a disproportionate amount of your time on sport.* 你在运动方面花费的时间过多. **dis·pro·por·tion·ately** *adv*: *Babies often seem to have disproportionately large heads.* 婴儿往往显得头部过大.

dis·prove /ˌdɪsˈpru:v; dɪsˈpruv/ *v* [Tn] show that (sth) is wrong or false 证明(某事物)有误或有假: *The allegations have been completely disproved.* 这些指控证明完全是无中生有.

dis·put·able /dɪˈspju:təbl; dɪˈspjutəbl/ *adj* that may be questioned or argued about 成问题的; 有争议的: *He made some very disputable claims about his record.* 他声称创造了新纪录, 那可大有争议. ▷ **dis·put·ably** /-əblɪ; -əblɪ/ *adv.*

dis·put·ant /dɪˈspju:tənt, *also* ˈdɪspjʊtənt; ˈdɪspjʊtənt/ *n* (*law or fml* 律或文) person who disputes 争论者; 辩论者.

dis·pu·ta·tion /ˌdɪspju:ˈteɪʃn; ˌdɪspjʊˈteʃən/ *n* (*fml* 文) **1** [C, U] (instance of) disputing; controversy 争论; 辩论. **2** [C] (*arch* 古) formal academic debate 学术讨论.

dis·pu·ta·tious /ˌdɪspju:ˈteɪʃəs; ˌdɪspjʊˈteʃəs/ *adj* (*fml* 文) fond of arguing; inclined to argue 爱争论的; 好辩的. ▷ **dis·pu·ta·tiously** *adv.*

dis·pute[1] /dɪˈspju:t; dɪˈspjut/ *n* **1** [U] argument; debate 争论; 辩论: *There has been much dispute over the question of legalized abortion.* 堕胎合法化问题引起了许多争论. ○ *It is a matter of dispute (whether they did the right thing).* (他们做得对还是不对,)这是有争议之处. ○ *Their conclusions are open to dispute.* 他们的结论可供商榷. **2** [C] quarrel; controversy 争吵; 争论; 辩论: *religious, political, industrial, etc disputes* 宗教上的争论、政治上的辩论、劳资纠纷 ○ *a border dispute that could easily become a war* 容易引发战争的边界争端. **3** (idm 习语) **beyond/past diˈspute** certain 无可争辩的; 确定无疑的: *Her courage is beyond all dispute.* 她的勇气是无可置疑的. **in diˈspute** that can be or is being argued about 可以争论; 在争议中: *The exact cause of the accident is still in dispute.* 事故的真正起因仍有争议. ○ *Your sincerity is not in dispute.* 你的诚恳是无可置辩的. **in dispute (with sb)** involved in a (usu industrial) dispute 涉及(通常为劳资关系上的)纠纷: *We're in dispute (with the management) about overtime rates.* 我们正(与资方)交涉加班费问题. **without diˈspute** certainly 毫无疑义; 无争论余地: *He is without dispute the better player.* 他无疑是较优秀的选手.

dis·pute[2] /dɪˈspju:t; dɪˈspjut/ *v* **1** [I, Ipr] **~ (with sb)** argue; debate 争论; 辩论: *Some people love to dispute* *(with everyone).* 有些人好(与人)争论. **2** **(a)** [Tn, Tw] argue about (sth) 争论(某事物): *They disputed at great length what they should do.* 他们对应该做什么这一问题进行了长时间的争论. **(b)** [Tn] question the truth or validity of (sth) 对(某事物)的真实性或有效性提出质询: *dispute a statement, claim, decision, etc* 对某项陈述、要求、决定等提出质疑 ○ *The election result was disputed.* 有人对选举的结果提出了异议. **3** [Tn] try to stop sb winning (sth) from one; fight for (sth) 捍卫(某事物); 争夺(某物): *Our soldiers disputed every inch of ground.* 我方战士寸土必争.

dis·qual·ify /dɪsˈkwɒlɪfaɪ; dɪsˈkwɑləˌfaɪ/ *v* (*pt, pp* **-fied**) [Tn, Tn·pr] **~ sb (from sth/doing sth)** prevent sb from doing sth, usu because he has broken a rule or is not able enough 制止某人做某事(通常因其违反规则或能力不够): *Her criminal record disqualifies her from serving on a jury.* 她有犯罪前科所以不能当陪审员. ○ *She was disqualified in the first round.* 她在第一局里就被淘汰了. ○ *The team has been disqualified from the competition.* 该队已被取消参赛资格. ▷ **dis·quali·fica·tion** /dɪsˌkwɒlɪfɪˈkeɪʃn; ˌdɪskwɑləfəˈkeʃən/ *n* [C, U]: *(a) disqualification for driving while drunk* 因酒后驾驶而被吊销执照.

dis·quiet /dɪsˈkwaɪət; dɪsˋkwaɪət/ *n* [U] anxiety 忧虑; 不安: *The strength of the dollar is causing considerable disquiet on the Stock Exchange.* 美元表现坚挺在证券交易所中引起很大的不安.

▷ **dis·quiet** *v* [Tn usu passive 通常用于被动语态] make (sb) anxious; worry 使(某人)忧虑不安; 使着急; 使担心: *be greatly disquieted by the fall in public support* 因公众支持率的下降而大为不安. **dis·quiet·ing** *adj* causing disquiet 令人不安的; 令人忧虑的: *disquieting news* 令人不安的消息. **dis·quiet·ingly** *adv*: *a disquietingly large number of accidents* 事故之多令人忧虑.

dis·quisi·tion /ˌdɪskwɪˈzɪʃn; ˌdɪskwəˈzɪʃən/ *n* **~ (on sth)** long elaborate spoken or written report or account (悉心作出的)长篇演讲或论文.

dis·reg·ard /ˌdɪsrɪˈgɑːd; ˌdɪsrɪˋgɑrd/ *v* [Tn] pay no attention to (eg a warning, an objection); treat (sth) as of no importance; ignore 不理会(如警告、反对意见); 不重视(某事物); 忽视: *He completely disregarded my point of view.* 他完全不理会我的观点. ○ *You can't just disregard the security problem!* 你可不能忽视安全问题!

▷ **dis·reg·ard** *n* [U sing] **~ (for/of sb/sth)** lack of attention or care 未加注意或留心; 忽视; 漠视: *She shows a total disregard for other people and their feelings.* 她显然丝毫也不顾及别人以及别人的感情. ○ *fire-fighters working with a complete disregard of their own safety* 奋不顾身的消防队员.

dis·repair /ˌdɪsrɪˈpeə(r); ˌdɪsrɪˋpɛr/ *n* [U] bad condition caused by lack of repairs 失修; 破损: *be in/fall into (a state of) disrepair* 需要修理.

dis·rep·ut·able /dɪsˈrepjʊtəbl; dɪsˋrɛpjətəbl/ *adj* **(a)** having a bad reputation 名声不好的; 不光彩的: *Soho is one of London's more disreputable areas.* 索霍区是伦敦名声较差的街区. **(b)** not respectable or looking respectable 不体面的; 不雅观的: *a disreputable suit, manner, appearance* 有失体面的服装、举止、外表 ○ *I've been accused of using disreputable methods to get what I want.* 我被指控采取不正当的手段以谋取私利. ▷ **dis·rep·ut·ably** /-əblɪ; -əblɪ/ *adv*.

dis·rep·ute /ˌdɪsrɪˈpjuːt; ˌdɪsrɪˋpjut/ *n* [U] state of having a bad reputation 名声不好; 不光彩: *The use of drugs is bringing the sport into disrepute.* 因有人服食禁药, 这项运动蒙受了耻辱. ○ *Since the scandal, the school has rather fallen into disrepute.* 自从发生了这件丑闻, 该校名声大为下降.

dis·re·spect /ˌdɪsrɪˈspekt; ˌdɪsrɪˋspɛkt/ *n* [U] **~ (to/towards sb/sth)** lack of respect; rudeness 不尊敬; 无礼: *He meant no disrespect by that remark*, ie did not mean to be rude. 他的话并无不敬之意. ○ *No disrespect (to you), but I think you are wrong.* 我(对你)没有别的意思, 只不过认为你错了.

▷ **dis·res·pect·ful** /-fl; -fəl/ *adj* **~ (to/towards sb/sth)** showing disrespect 无礼的; 不尊敬的: *We often criticize the Government, but we're never disrespectful towards the Royal Family.* 我们经常抨击政府, 但对皇室从无不敬之意. **dis·res·pect·fully** /-fəlɪ; -fəlɪ/ *adv*.

dis·robe /dɪsˈrəʊb; dɪsˋrob/ *v* [I] **(a)** (*fml or joc* 文或谑) undress 脱衣服. **(b)** take official or ceremonial robes off 脱去制服或礼服: *The Queen disrobed after the ceremony.* 女王在仪式过后脱去了王袍.

dis·rupt /dɪsˈrʌpt; dɪsˋrʌpt/ *v* [Tn] cause disorder in (sth) 将(某事物)弄乱; 扰乱(某事物): *Demonstrators succeeded in disrupting the meeting.* 示威者扰乱了会议. ○ *Fog disrupted traffic.* 大雾使交通陷于混乱.

▷ **dis·rup·tion** /dɪsˈrʌpʃn; dɪsˋrʌpʃən/ *n* [C, U]: *violent disruption caused by rioters* 暴徒们造成的大动乱 ○ *disruptions of our production schedule* 我们的生产计划之被打乱.

dis·rupt·ive /dɪsˈrʌptɪv; dɪsˋrʌptɪv/ *adj* causing disruption 制造混乱的: *A few disruptive students can easily ruin a class.* 只要有几个爱捣乱的学生, 就能把全班搅乱. **dis·rupt·ively** *adv*: *act, behave, etc disruptively* 存心捣乱.

dis·sat·is·fac·tion /ˌdɪˌsætɪsˈfækʃn; ˌdɪssætɪsˋfækʃən/ *n* [U] **~ (with sb/sth); ~ (at doing sth)** lack of satisfaction 不满意; 不满足: *Letters from viewers express their dissatisfaction with current programmes.* 电视观众来信表示对当前节目不满. ○ *MPs voice public dissatisfaction at having to pay higher taxes.* 下议院议员道出了公众对增加税收的不满.

dis·sat·is·fied /dɪˈsætɪsfaɪd; dɪsˋsætɪsˌfaɪd/ *adj* **~ (with sb/sth); ~ (at doing sth)** not satisfied; discontented 不满意的; 不满足的: *a dissatisfied customer* 感到不满意的顾客 ○ *I'm thoroughly dissatisfied with your work.* 我完全不满意你的工作. ○ *She's very dissatisfied at not getting a bonus.* 她因未能获得奖金而深为不满.

dis·sect /dɪˈsekt; dɪˋsɛkt/ *v* [Tn] **1** cut up (a dead body, a plant, etc) in order to study its structure 解剖(动植物等). **2** (*fig* 比喻) examine (a theory, an event, etc) in great detail 剖析(理论、事件等): *Commentators are still dissecting the election results.* 评论家仍在剖析此次选举的结果. ○ *The film has been minutely dissected by the critics.* 影评家对这部影片作了详细的分析.

▷ **dis·sec·tion** /dɪˈsekʃn; dɪˋsɛkʃən/ *n* [C, U] (instance of) dissecting or being dissected 解剖; 剖析: *Her first dissection made her change her mind about becoming a doctor.* 她进行了首次解剖后就改变了要当医生的想法.

dis·semble /dɪˈsembl; dɪˋsɛmbl/ *v* [I, Tn] (*fml* 文) hide or disguise (one's true thoughts and feelings); dissimulate 掩盖(真实的思想感情); 假装: *dissemble one's intentions, meaning, motives, etc* 掩盖自己的意图、意思、动机等.

▷ **dis·sem·bler** /dɪˈsemblə(r); dɪˋsɛmblɚ/ *n* (*fml* 文) person who dissembles 隐藏自己真实思想感情的人.

dis·sem·in·ate /dɪˈsemɪneɪt; dɪˋsɛməˌnet/ *v* [Tn] spread (ideas, beliefs, etc) widely 散布, 广为传播(思想、信仰等): *They use the press to disseminate right-wing views.* 他们利用报刊来传播右翼观点. ▷ **dis·sem·ina·tion** /dɪˌsemɪˈneɪʃn; dɪˌsɛməˋneʃən/ *n* [U].

dis·sen·sion /dɪˈsenʃn; dɪˋsɛnʃən/ *n* [U, C] angry disagreement 争执: *deal with dissension in the party* 处理党内斗争 ○ *Father's will caused much dissension among his children.* 父亲的遗嘱引起了子女之间的纷争.

dis·sent[1] /dɪˈsent; dɪˋsɛnt/ *n* [U] holding opinions which differ from common or officially held ones 持有异议(不同于普通的或官方的见解): *their public dissent from official party policy* 他们对党的官方政策公然表示异议的观点 ○ *In those days, religious dissent was not tolerated.* 那年头不容许对宗教信仰持异议.

dis·sent[2] /dɪˈsent; dɪˋsɛnt/ *v* [I, Ipr] **~ (from sth)** (*fml* 文) have or express opinions which are opposed to official views, religious teaching, etc 持异议(与官方观点、宗教教义等相反的见解); 不同意; 反对: *I wish to dissent (from the motion).* 我不同意(该动议). ○ *Those who dissented from Anglican teachings could be heavily fined.* 反对英国国教教义的人在过去可判巨额罚款.

▷ **dis·senter** *n* **(a)** person who dissents 持异议者; 不同意者; 反对者. **(b) Dissenter** Protestant who refuses to accept the doctrines of the Church of England (不赞成英国国教教义的)新教徒: *Presbyterians and other Dissenters* 长老会教友及其他新教徒.

dis·sent·ing *adj* [attrib 作定语]: *a dissenting voice, opinion, vote, etc* 反对的呼声、异议、反对票 ○ *a dissenting minister*, ie in a church that refuses to accept Anglican doctrine 不赞成英国国教教义的牧师. Cf 参看

D

NONCONFORMIST.

dis·ser·ta·tion /ˌdɪsəˈteɪʃn; ˌdɪsɚˈteʃən/ *n* [C] **~ (on sth)** long essay on a particular subject, esp one written for a doctorate or similar degree; thesis 专题论文; (尤指)博士学位之类的论文: *a dissertation on Arabic dialects* 论述阿拉伯语方言的论文.

dis·ser·vice /dɪsˈsɜːvɪs; dɪsˈsɝvɪs/ *n* **~ (to sb/sth)** [C, U] harmful or unhelpful action 损害; 危害; 伤害: *She did her cause (a) great disservice by concealing the truth.* 她隐瞒了真相, 这对她所参与的事业极为不利.

dis·sid·ent /ˈdɪsɪdənt; ˈdɪsədənt/ *n* person who strongly disagrees with or opposes official views and policies 持不同政见者: *left-wing dissidents* 左翼持不同政见者 ○ [attrib 作定语] *dissident groups, writings, opinions* 持不同政见者的组织、著作、观点. ▷ **dis·sid·ence** /ˈdɪsɪdəns; ˈdɪsədəns/ *n* [U].

dis·sim·ilar /dɪˈsɪmɪlə(r); dɪˈsɪmələ/ *adj* **~ (from/to sb/sth)** not the same; unlike 不相同的; 不相似的: *These wines are not dissimilar*, ie quite similar. 这些酒都差不多. ○ *Her latest book is quite dissimilar from her previous one.* 她新近写的这本书跟她以前写的截然不同. ▷ **dis·sim·il·arity** /ˌdɪsɪmɪˈlærətɪ; dɪˌsɪməˈlærətɪ/ *n* [C, U]: *They correct any dissimilarity between batches of work.* 他们改正各批活儿不统一之处. **dis·sim·ilarly** *adv*.

dis·simu·late /dɪˈsɪmjʊleɪt; dɪˈsɪmjəˌlet/ *v* [I, Tn] (*fml* 文) hide or disguise (one's thoughts and feelings); dissemble 隐藏, 掩盖(思想感情); 假装. ▷ **dis·simu·la·tion** /dɪˌsɪmjʊˈleɪʃn; dɪˌsɪmjəˈleʃən/ *n* [U, C].

dis·sip·ate /ˈdɪsɪpeɪt; ˈdɪsəˌpet/ *v* **1** [I, Tn] (cause sth to) scatter or vanish (使某事物)消散, 消失: *The mist quickly dissipated as the sun rose.* 太阳升起时雾很快就消散了. ○ *Her son's letter dissipated all her fears and anxiety.* 她儿子的来信消除了她一切恐惧和焦虑. **2** [Tn] waste (time, money, etc) foolishly 浪费(时间、金钱等): *dissipate one's efforts, energies, fortune* 浪费自己的精力、体力、财产.

▷ **dis·sip·ated** *adj* (*derog* 贬) given to foolish and harmful pleasures 放荡的; 浪荡的: *lead a thoroughly dissipated life* 过极为放荡的生活.

dis·sipa·tion /ˌdɪsɪˈpeɪʃn; ˌdɪsəˈpeʃən/ *n* [U] **1** dissipating or being dissipated 驱散; 消散; 浪费. **2** dissipated living 放荡的生活: *Years of dissipation had ruined his health.* 多年的放荡生活毁掉了他的健康.

dis·so·ci·ate /dɪˈsəʊʃɪeɪt; dɪˈsoʃɪˌet/ (also **dis·as·so·ci·ate**, /ˌdɪsəˈsəʊʃɪeɪt; ˌdɪsəˈsoʃɪˌət/) *v* [Tn·pr] **1 ~ sb/sth from sth** separate (people or things) in one's thoughts or feelings (在思想或感情方面)将(人或事物)分开: *dissociate two ideas/one idea from another* 把两个概念[一个概念与另一个概念]分开 ○ *You cannot dissociate the Government's actions from the policies which underlie them.* 不能把政府的措施同作为其根据的政策割裂开. **2 ~ oneself from sb/sth** say that one does not agree with or support sb/sth 声言不赞成或不支持某人[某事物]: *I wish to dissociate myself from those views.* 我想表明我本人是不赞成那些观点的. ▷ **dis·so·ci·ation** /dɪˌsəʊsɪˈeɪʃn; dɪˌsosɪˈeʃən/ (also **dis·as·so·ci·ation**) *n* [U].

dis·sol·uble /dɪˈsɒljʊbl; dɪˈsɑljəbl/ *adj* that can be dissolved 可溶解的: (*fig* 比喻) *Is a marriage dissoluble?* ie Can it be ended? 婚约能解除吗? ▷ **dis·sol·ub·il·ity** /dɪˌsɒljʊˈbɪlətɪ; dɪˌsɑljəˈbɪlətɪ/ *n* [U].

dis·sol·ute /ˈdɪsəluːt; ˈdɪsəˌlut/ *adj* immoral; dissipated 道德沦丧的; 放荡的: *lead a dissolute life* 过放荡的生活 ○ *a dissolute and worthless character* 行为放荡一无是处的人. ▷ **dis·sol·utely** *adv*. **dis·sol·ute·ness** *n* [U].

dis·solu·tion /ˌdɪsəˈluːʃn; ˌdɪsəˈluʃən/ *n* [C, U] **~ (of sth)** breaking up (of sth); dissolving 破裂; 瓦解; 解体; 分解; 溶解: *the dissolution of a marriage, a business partnership, the Roman Empire* 婚姻关系的解除、商业合伙关系的终止、罗马帝国的解体 ○ *the dissolution of Parliament*, ie the ending of the current session by the monarch before a general election 议会的解散(普选前君主解散本届议会).

dis·solve /dɪˈzɒlv; dɪˈzɑlv/ *v* **1 (a)** [Tn] (of a liquid) make (a solid) become liquid (指液体)使(固体)溶解: *Water dissolves salt.* 水能溶解盐. **(b)** [I, Ipr] **~ (in sth)** (of a solid) become part of a liquid (指固体)溶解: *Salt dissolves in water.* 盐在水中溶解. **(c)** [Tn, Tn·pr] **~ sth (in sth)** cause (a solid) to dissolve 使(固体)溶解: *Dissolve the salt in water.* 使盐在水中溶解. **2** [Tn, Tn·p] **~ sth (away)** remove or destroy (sth solid, esp dirt) 除去, 消除(某固体物质, 尤指脏物): *The cream dissolves facial hair.* 这种化妆品能清除脸上的汗毛. ○ *a powder that dissolves stains away* 消除色斑的粉剂. **3** [I, Ipr] **~ (in sth)** disappear; fade away 消失; 消散: *All his hopes dissolved at the terrible news.* 那个极坏的消息使他的一切希望都破灭了. ○ *The view dissolved in mist.* 那景色在雾中消失了. **4** [I, Tn] (cause sth to) come to an end (使某事物)终止, 结束, 解除, 解散: *Parliament dissolves tomorrow.* 议会定于明日解散. ○ *dissolve a business partnership, marriage, society, etc* 结束商业合伙关系、解除婚姻关系、解散会社. **5** [Ipr] **~ in sth** give way to emotion 情不自禁: *dissolve in tears/laughter/giggles* 不禁潸然泪下[哈哈大笑/咯咯地笑].

dis·son·ance /ˈdɪsənəns; ˈdɪsənəns/ *n* **1** [U] discord 不和谐; 不一致. **2** [C] (*music* 音) combination of notes that is discordant 不协和音.

dis·son·ant /ˈdɪsənənt; ˈdɪsənənt/ *adj* not harmonious; discordant 不和谐的; 不一致的. ▷ **dis·son·antly** *adv*.

dis·suade /dɪˈsweɪd; dɪˈswed/ *v* [Tn, Tn·pr] **~ sb (from sth/doing sth)** (try to) stop sb by advice or persuasion (企图)劝阻某人: *The police managed to dissuade him from jumping off the building.* 警方已设法劝他不要从大楼上跳下来.

▷ **dis·sua·sion** /dɪˈsweɪʒn; dɪˈsweʒən/ *n* [U].

dis·suas·ive /dɪˈsweɪsɪv; dɪˈswesɪv/ *adj* dissuading 劝阻的.

dis·taff /ˈdɪstɑːf; *US* ˈdɪstæf; ˈdɪstæf/ *n* **1** stick holding wool, flax, etc for spinning by hand (手工的)纺纱杆. **2** (idm 习语) **on the distaff side** on the mother's side of the family 母系的.

dis·tance[1] /ˈdɪstəns; ˈdɪstəns/ *n* **1** [C, U] (amount of) space between two points or places 距离; 间距: *A good cyclist can cover distances of over a hundred miles a day.* 自行车骑得好的人一天可以行驶一百多英里. ○ *It's a great/some/no distance from here*, ie very/fairly/not far away. 离此处很[相当/不]远. ○ *a short, long, great, etc distance* 短的、长的、很大的…距离 ○ *In the USA distance is measured in miles, not kilometres.* 在美国, 测量距离用英里, 不用公里. ○ *The beach is within walking distance of my house*, ie near enough to be reached easily on foot. 海滩离我家不远, 走几步就到了. ○ (*fig* 比喻) *at a distance of fifty years* 时隔五十年. ⇨App 4 见附录4. **2** [C, U] distant place or point 远处; 远方: *At a distance of six miles you can't see much.* 距离六英里以外的东西很难看清. ○ *He won't hit the target at that distance.* 他打不中那样远的目标的. **3** [U] being separated in space or by time (空间或时间的)相距: *Distance is no problem with modern telecommunications.* 在电信发达的今天, 相距遥远已不再是什么问题了. **4** [U] coldness or remoteness in personal relationships (人际关系的)冷淡, 疏远: *Is his distance a result of snobbery or shyness?* 他态度冷淡是因为他势利眼呢, 还是因为他腼腆? **5** (idm 习语) **go the ˈdistance** (esp in sports) continue to run, fight, etc until the end of a contest (尤指运动)继续跑完全程、赛足全局等: *Nobody thought he'd last 15 rounds, but he went the full distance.* 没有人认为他会坚持15个回合, 然而他终于打满了全局. ○ *You need perseverance to win in politics and I doubt if he can go the distance.* 在政治上, 需要矢志不移才能取胜, 我怀疑他能否坚持到底. **in the ˈdistance** far away 在远处; 在远方. **keep one's ˈdistance (from sb/sth) (a)** not get too close (to sb/sth) (与某人[某事物])保持一定距离: *I would keep my distance from that dog, if I were you!* 我要是你, 就离那条狗远一点! **(b)** not become friendly or familiar (with a person, cause, etc) (对人、事业等)冷淡, 疏远: *He was asked many times to join the party, but he always kept his distance.* 人家好几次要他参加那个政党, 但他的反应总是很冷淡. **keep sb at a ˈdistance** refuse to let sb become familiar or friendly 与某人保持一定距离; 不愿与某人亲近. Cf 参看 THE NEAR DISTANCE (NEAR[1]), THE MIDDLE DISTANCE (MIDDLE).

dis·tance[2] /ˈdɪstəns; ˈdɪstəns/ *v* **1** [Tn, Tn·pr] **~ sb (from sb/sth)** make sb less friendly or warm towards sb/sth 使某人与某人[某事物]保持距离、关系疏远或冷淡: *That stupid quarrel has distanced us.* 那一场无谓

的争吵使我们的关系疏远了. ○ *Voters have been distanced from the party by adverse publicity.* 选民受到反面宣传的影响, 对这个政党冷淡了. **2** [Tn·pr] **~ oneself from sb/sth** not approve of or become involved with sb/sth 与某人[某事物]保持距离; 对某人[某事物]持不赞同或不介入的态度: *She needs to distance herself from some of her more extreme supporters.* 她必须与拥护她的那些比较偏激的人保持一定的距离.

dis·tant /ˈdɪstənt; ˋdɪstənt/ *adj* **1** (sometimes used with measurements 有时与测量单位连用) far away in space or time (空间或时间)远隔的, 遥远的: *a distant land, cry, flash of light* 遥远的地方、远处的叫声、远处的闪光 ○ *the distant horizon, past* 遥远的天际、过去 ○ *The airport is about ten miles distant from the city.* 机场距离城市大约十英里远. **2 (a)** [attrib 作定语] (of people) not closely related (指人)远亲的: *She is a distant cousin of mine.* 她是我的远房表妹. **(b)** (of a connection, similarity, etc) not very strong or clear (指联结、相似性等)不太强的, 不明显的: *There is a distant connection between the two theories.* 这两种学说之间没有什么关联. **3** not very friendly; reserved 不太友好的; 不太热情的; 冷漠的: *a distant nod, attitude, greeting, manner* 不太热情的点头、态度、招呼、举止. **4** (idm 习语) **dim and distant** ⇨ DIM. ▷ **dis·tantly** *adv*: *We're distantly related.* 我们是远亲. ○ *His style distantly resembles that of Wilde.* 他的文风与王尔德略微有些相似. ○ *She smiled distantly at us.* 她朝我们淡然地微笑.

dis·taste /dɪsˈteɪst; dɪsˋtest/ *n* [U sing] **~ (for sb/sth)** dislike; aversion 不喜欢; 厌恶: *turn away in distaste* 厌恶地走开 ○ *a distaste for violent sports* 不喜欢剧烈的运动.

▷ **dis·taste·ful** /dɪsˈteɪstfl; dɪsˋtestfəl/ *adj* **~ (to sb)** unpleasant; disagreeable 使人不愉快的; 不合意的; 讨厌的: *distasteful behaviour* 讨厌的行为 ○ *a distasteful incident* 使人不愉快的事儿 ○ *Even the thought of her was distasteful to him.* 他即使一想起她来, 都感到恶心. **dis·taste·fully** /-fəlɪ; -fəlɪ/ *adv*. **dis·taste·ful·ness** /dɪsˈteɪstfəlnɪs; dɪsˋtestfəlnɪs/ *n* [U].

dis·tem·per[1] /dɪˈstempə(r); dɪsˋtɛmpɚ/ *n* [U] (*Brit*) (old method of painting with) colouring matter mixed with water and brushed on walls, etc 刷墙水粉; 用刷墙水粉涂刷的一种旧方法.

▷ **dis·tem·per** *v* [Tn, Cn·a] paint (sth) with distemper 用刷墙水粉涂刷(某物): *distemper the walls green* 用刷墙水粉把墙壁刷成绿色.

dis·tem·per[2] /dɪˈstempə(r); dɪsˋtɛmpɚ/ *n* [U] disease of dogs and some other animals, with coughing and weakness 温热(狗和其他动物的疾病).

dis·tend /dɪˈstend; dɪˋstɛnd/ *v* [I, Tn] (*fml* 文) (cause sth to) swell by means of pressure from inside (使某物)膨胀: *a distended intestine, stomach, vein, etc* 膨胀的肠、胃、静脉等.

▷ **dis·ten·sion** (*US* **dis·ten·tion**) /dɪˈstenʃn; dɪˋstɛnʃən/ *n* [U] swelling or being swollen 膨胀; 胀大.

dis·til (*US* **dis·till**) /dɪˈstɪl; dɪˋstɪl/ *v* **(-ll-)** **1** [Tn, Tn·pr] **~ sth (from sth)** **(a)** turn (a liquid) to vapour by heating, then collect the drops of liquid that condense from the vapour when cooled 蒸馏: *distil fresh water from sea-water* 用蒸馏法从海水中制取淡水. **(b)** make (spirits or essences) in this way 用蒸馏法制(酒或香精): *The Scots have distilled whisky for centuries.* 苏格兰人用蒸馏法制威士忌酒已有数百年历史. **2** [Tn, Tn·pr] **~ sth (from sth)** draw or derive sth (from sth) 吸取或提取某事物: *useful advice distilled from a lifetime's experience* 从一生的经历中得出的有益的教训. **3** (phr v) **distil sth off/out** purify (a liquid) by turning it to vapour, etc 用蒸馏法对(液体)提纯: *Sea-water can be made drinkable by distilling out the salt.* 可以用蒸馏法除去海水中的盐分以制取饮用水.

▷ **dis·til·la·tion** /ˌdɪstɪˈleɪʃn; ˌdɪstəˋleʃən/ *n* **1** [C, U] (substance made by) distilling 蒸馏; 馏出液; 馏出物. **2** [C, U] reduction; essence 摘要; 精华: *This book offers a distillation of Wittgenstein's thought in a mere fifty pages.* 这本书在不过五十页的篇幅里向人们提供了维特根斯坦思想的精髓.

dis·til·ler /dɪˈstɪlə(r); dɪˋstɪlɚ/ *n* person or company that distils (esp whisky, etc) 采用蒸馏法(尤指制威士忌酒等)的业者或公司; 酿酒者; 酿酒厂

▷ **dis·til·lery** /dɪˈstɪlərɪ; dɪˋstɪlərɪ/ *n* place where gin, whisky, etc are distilled (制造杜松子酒、威士忌酒等的)蒸馏所, 制酒厂. Cf 参看 BREWERY (BREW).

dis·tinct /dɪˈstɪŋkt; dɪˋstɪŋkt/ *adj* **1** easily heard, seen, felt or understood; definite 清楚的; 清晰的; 明显的; 明白的; 明确的: *The footprints are quite distinct; they must be fresh.* 足迹清晰易辨, 一定是不久前留下来的. ○ *I had the distinct impression that I was being watched.* 我很明显地感觉到有人在监视我. ○ *There was a distinct sense of embarrassment in the air.* 周围的气氛中有一种明显的侷促不安的感觉. **2 ~ (from sth)** different in kind; separate 种类不同的; 分开的: *Although they look similar, these plants are actually quite distinct.* 尽管这些植物看起来很相似, 实际上却属于完全不同的种类. ○ *Mozart's style is quite distinct from Haydn's.* 莫扎特在风格上与海顿截然不同. ○ *Astronomy, as distinct from astrology, is an exact science.* 天文学是一门严谨的科学, 与占星术完全不同.

▷ **dis·tinctly** *adv* in a distinct manner; clearly 清楚地; 明显地: *But I distinctly remember you promising to phone me!* 可我记得清清楚楚你是答应了要给我打电话!

dis·tinct·ness *n* [U].

dis·tinc·tion /dɪˈstɪŋkʃn; dɪˋstɪŋkʃən/ *n* **1** [C, U] **~ (between A and B)** difference or contrast between one person or thing and another 差别; 对比: *He drew a quite artificial distinction between men and women readers.* 他把男读者和女读者硬是人为地区分开来. ○ *I don't understand your distinction: surely all painting is art?* 我不明白你为什么要有所区分, 所有的绘画不都是艺术吗? **2** (*fml* 文) **(a)** [U] separation of things or people into different groups according to quality, grade, etc (事物或人按其质量、品质、等级等的)区分: *without distinction* (ie regardless) *of rank* 不分级别. **(b)** [C] detail that separates in this way (按此方式划分的)类别, 等级: *distinctions of birth and wealth* 按出身和财富划分的类别. **3** [C] mark of honour; title, decoration, etc 荣誉的标志; 荣衔、勋章等: *an academic distinction*, eg a doctor's degree 学术上的荣衔(如博士学位) ○ *win a distinction for bravery* 因表现英勇而获得勋章. **4** [U] quality of being excellent or distinguished 优秀; 卓越: *a writer, novel, work of distinction* 优秀的作家、小说、作品 ○ *She had the distinction of being the first woman to swim the Channel.* 她卓尔不群, 因为她是第一个横渡英吉利海峡的女子.

dis·tinct·ive /dɪˈstɪŋktɪv; dɪˋstɪŋktɪv/ *adj* **~ (of sth)** that distinguishes sth by making it different from others 特别的; 有特色的: *a distinctive appearance, style, smell* 特殊的外表、风格、气味 ○ *Long complex sentences are distinctive of Henry James's later style.* 亨利·詹姆斯晚期作品的风格特色是擅长使用长复合句. ▷ **dis·tinct·ively** *adv*: *distinctively coloured* 有特殊色彩的. **dis·tinct·ive·ness** *n* [U].

D

dis·tin·guish /dɪˈstɪŋgwɪʃ; dɪˋstɪŋgwɪʃ/ *v* **1** [Ipr, Tn·pr] **~ (between) A and B; ~ A from B** recognize the difference between (people or things) 区别, 辨别(人或事物): *People who cannot distinguish between colours are said to be colour-blind.* 不能辨别颜色的人称为色盲. ○ *The twins are so alike that no one can distinguish one from the other.* 这对孪生儿长得很像, 无人能分辨出谁是谁. **2** [Tn, Tn·pr] **~ A (from B)** **(a)** show the difference between (one person or thing and another) 显示(两者)之间的差别: *The male is distinguished (from the female) by its red beak.* 由喙部为红色这一特点可以辨认出其为雄性(以区别于雌性). **(b)** be a characteristic mark or property of sb/sth; make sb/sth different 为某人[某事物]之特征或特性; 使某人[某事物]有所不同: *Speech distinguishes human beings from the animals.* 使用言语是人类有别于动物的特征. **3** [Tn] manage to see, hear, etc (sth) 看清、听清...(某事物): *distinguish distant objects, a shape in the mist, a whispered conversation* 辨别出远处的物体、雾中的朦胧形象、窃窃私语声. **4** [Tn] **~ oneself** deserve to be noticed by doing sth very well (因善于做某事)受人注目, 出名: *She distinguished herself by her coolness and bravery.* 她因头脑冷静、敢作敢为而为人称道.

▷ **dis·tin·guish·able** /dɪˈstɪŋgwɪʃəbl; dɪˋstɪŋgwɪʃəbl/ *adj* [usu pred 通常作表语] **~ (from sb/sth)**: *The coast was barely distinguishable in the mist.* 在雾中很难看清海岸. ○ *Vipers are distinguishable from other snakes by their markings.* 根据蛇身上的斑纹就能把蝰蛇同其他蛇类区别开来.

dis·tin·guished *adj* **1** dignified in appearance or manner (外表或举止上)有尊严的, 高贵的: *I think grey hair makes you look rather distinguished.* 我觉得你灰白的头发使你看上去很有尊严. **2** showing remarkable qualities 卓越的; 杰出的: *a distinguished career* 非凡的事业 ○ *She is a distinguished novelist and philosopher.* 她是一个杰出的小说家和哲学家.

dis·tort /dɪˈstɔːt; dɪsˋtɔrt/ *v* [Tn] **1** pull or twist (sth) out of its usual shape 使(某物)变形; 扭曲, 弄歪(某物): *a heap of distorted metal* 一堆变了形的金属东西 ○ *a face distorted by pain* 因疼痛而扭曲的脸. **2** make (sth) look or sound unnatural 使(某物)失真: *a distorting mirror*, ie one which makes people look long and thin, short and fat, etc 哈哈镜 ○ *The announcement was so distorted that I couldn't understand what was said.* 通告播出的声音严重失真, 我听不懂说的是什么. **3** give a false account of (sth); misrepresent 歪曲(某事物); 曲解: *distort sb's words, motives, point of view, etc* 歪曲某人的言语、动机、观点等 ○ *The Government were accused of having systematically distorted the protesters' case.* 政府有计划地歪曲抗议者的观点而受到非难.

D

▷ **dis·tor·tion** /dɪˈstɔːʃn; dɪsˋtɔrʃən/ *n* [C, U] (instance of) distorting or being distorted 变形; 扭曲; 歪曲; 曲解: *a distortion of the facts* 对事实的歪曲.

dis·tract /dɪˈstrækt; dɪˋstrækt/ *v* [Tn, Tn·pr] **~ sb (from sth)** stop sb concentrating on sth 使某人分心; 分散或扰乱某人的注意力: *Children are so easily distracted.* 儿童的注意力很不容易集中. ○ *Don't distract my attention — I'm trying to study!* 别分散我的注意力——我正要学习呢! ○ *The film managed to distract me from these problems for a while.* 这部影片分散了我的注意力, 让我暂时忘记了这些难题.

▷ **dis·tracted** *adj* **~ (with/by sth)** unable to concentrate properly, esp because of one's strong feelings 精神不能集中的(尤指因激动): *distracted with joy, fear, sorrow, anxiety, etc* 因高兴、恐惧、悲伤、忧虑等而精神不能集中. **dis·tract·edly** *adv*: *He paced up and down distractedly.* 他心烦意乱地踱来踱去.

dis·tract·ing *adj*: *a very distracting noise* 很分散注意力的嘈杂声. **dis·tract·ingly** *adv*.

dis·trac·tion /dɪˈstrækʃn; dɪˋstrækʃən/ *n* **1** [U] distracting or being distracted 注意力分散; 精神不集中. **2** [C] noise, sight, etc that distracts the attention and prevents concentration 使人分心的事物(如噪声、景象等): *He found the noise of the photographers a distraction.* 他觉得摄影师们的嘈杂声分散了他的注意力. **3** [C] thing or event that amuses or entertains 娱乐; 消遣: *TV can be a welcome distraction after a hard day's work.* 辛苦一天之后, 看看电视有时算是很美的消遣. **4** [U] state of mental distress (精神上的)痛苦; 心烦意乱. **5** (idm 习语) **to diˈstraction** almost to a state of madness 几乎到了疯狂的地步: *He loves her to distraction.* 他爱她爱得发狂. ○ *You'll drive me to distraction with your silly questions!* 你的那些傻问题简直要我的命!

dis·train /dɪˈstreɪn; dɪˋstren/ *v* [I, Ipr] **~ (upon sb/sth)** (*law* 律) seize a person's property or belongings to force him to pay what he owes (esp rent) 扣押某人之财物(以迫使其偿付债款, 尤指租金).

▷ **dis·traint** *n* [U] act or process of distraining 扣押财物.

dis·trait /dɪˈstreɪ; dɪˋstre/ *adj* absent-minded; not paying attention 心不在焉的; 不注意的.

dis·traught /dɪˈstrɔːt; dɪˋstrɔt/ *adj* very troubled in mind with grief or worry 心烦意乱的; 忧心如焚的.

dis·tress[1] /dɪˈstres; dɪˋstrɛs/ *n* **1** (**a**) [U, sing] (cause of) great pain, sorrow, suffering, etc 极大的痛苦、悲伤、苦难等(的缘由): *Towards the end of the marathon several runners showed signs of distress.* 马拉松赛接近终点时, 有些参赛者显出极难受的样子. ○ *Her death was a great distress to all the family.* 她去世后全家人极为悲痛. (**b**) [U] (suffering caused by) lack of money, food, etc 贫困; 困苦: *The Government acted quickly to relieve the widespread distress caused by the earthquake.* 地震造成广泛地区的灾难, 政府迅速采取行动赈济灾民. **2** [U] state of being in danger or difficulty and requiring help 危难; 困境: *a ship in diˈstress* 遇险的船 ○ [attrib 作定语] *a diˈstress signal/call/flag* 呼救信号[求救呼叫/遇难信号旗]. **3** (idm 习语) **a damsel in distress** ⇨ DAMSEL.

▷ **dis·tress·ful** /dɪˈstresfl; dɪˋstrɛsfəl/ *adj* = DISTRESSING. **dis·tress·fully** *adv*.

dis·tress[2] /dɪˈstres; dɪˋstrɛs/ *v* [Tn usu passive 通常用于被动语态] cause distress to (sb/sth) 给(某人[某事物])带来痛苦、悲伤、苦难、贫困、困苦、危难等: *I was most distressed to hear the sad news of your father's death.* 我听到你父亲去世的噩耗, 十分难过. ○ *Please don't distress yourself,* ie don't worry. 请你不要忧愁了.

▷ **dis·tress·ing** (also **dis·tress·ful**) *adj* causing distress 使人痛苦的; 令人苦恼的: *distressing news* 使人难过的消息 ○ *a distressing sight* 令人伤感的情景. **dis·tress·ingly** (also **dis·tress·fully**) *adv*.

dis·trib·ute /dɪˈstrɪbjuːt; dɪˋstrɪbjʊt/ *v* [Tn, Tn·pr] **1 ~ sth (to/among sb/sth)** separate sth into parts and give a share to each person or thing 分发、分配某事物: *In a co-operative profits are distributed among the work-force.* 在合作社中, 利润是在全体劳动者中进行分配的. ○ *The demonstrators distributed leaflets to passers-by.* 示威者向行人分发传单. **2** spread (sth); scatter; place at different parts 使(某物)散开; 散布; 分散放置: *Baggage loaded onto an aircraft must be evenly distributed.* 飞机载运的行李应均匀放置在各个部位.

▷ **dis·tri·bu·tion** /ˌdɪstrɪˈbjuːʃn; ˌdɪstrəˈbjuʃən/ *n* [C, U] **1** (instance of) giving or being given to each of several people, etc 分发; 分配; 分送: *the distribution of catalogues, forms, prizes, etc* 目录、表格、奖品等的分发. **2** (instance of the) positioning or allocation of items, features, etc within an area 分布: *the distribution of schools in this district* 这个区里的学校分布情况 ○ *Pines have a very wide distribution.* 松树的分布很广.

dis·trib·utor /dɪˈstrɪbjʊtə(r); dɪˋstrɪbjətɚ/ *n* **1** person or thing that distributes, esp an agent who supplies goods to shops in a certain area 分发者; 分配者; (尤指)批发商. **2** device that passes electric current to the sparking-plugs in an engine 配电器; 配电盘.

dis·tribu·tive /dɪˈstrɪbjʊtɪv; dɪˋstrɪbjətɪv/ *adj* [usu attrib 通常作定语] **1** concerned with distribution(2) 关于分布的: *the distributive trades*, eg transport, retailing, etc 经销业(如运送、零售等). **2** (*grammar*) referring to each individual member of a class 分布的; 个别的: *'Each', 'every', 'either' and 'neither' are distributive pronouns.* each、every、either、neither都是分布代词. ▷ **dis·tribu·tively** *adv*.

dis·trict /ˈdɪstrɪkt; ˋdɪstrɪkt/ *n* **1** part of a country or town having a particular quality 地区; 区域: *mountainous, agricultural, outlying, poor, gloomy districts* 山区、农业区域、边远地区、贫穷地区、黑暗地区 ○ *the ˈLake District* (英格兰西北部的)湖区. **2** area of a country or town treated as an administrative unit 行政区: *a ˈpostal district* 邮政区 ○ *rural and urban districts*, ie units of local government 乡区和市区(地方行政单位) ○ [attrib 作定语] *district ˈcouncils* 区议会.

□ **ˌdistrict atˈtorney** (*US*) (*abbr* 缩写 **DA**) public prosecutor representing a State or the Federal government in a judicial district (代表州政府或联邦政府在管区内执法的)地方检察官.

ˌdistrict ˈnurse (*Brit dated* 旧) nurse visiting patients in their homes 区域护士(在区域内登门服务者).

dis·trust /dɪsˈtrʌst; dɪsˋtrʌst/ *n* [U, sing] lack of trust; suspicion 不信任; 怀疑: *Negotiations between unions and management are made more difficult by mutual distrust.* 工会和资方之间的谈判由于互不信任而愈加困难. ○ *He has a distrust of strangers.* 他不信任陌生人.

▷ **dis·trust** *v* [Tn] have no confidence or belief in (sb/sth) 不信任(某人[某事物]): *He's so suspicious he would distrust his own mother.* 他这人疑心太重, 连自己的母亲也不相信.

dis·trust·ful /-fʊl; -fəl/ *adj* having or showing distrust; suspicious 不信任的; 猜疑的. **dis·trust·fully** /-fəlɪ; -fəlɪ/ *adv*.

dis·turb /dɪˈstɜːb; dɪˋstɝb/ *v* [Tn] **1** move (sth) from a settled or usual position or state 搅乱, 弄乱(某事物): *Don't disturb the papers on my desk.* 别把我写字台上的文件弄乱了. **2** break the rest, concentration or calm of (sb/sth) 打扰, 干扰, 骚扰(某人[某事物]): *She opened the door quietly so as not to disturb the sleeping child.* 她轻轻地开门, 以免惊扰了睡着的孩子. ○ *Exam in Progress — Do Not Disturb* 正在考试——请勿打扰 ○ *No sound disturbed the silence of the evening.* 入夜时分, 万籁俱寂. **3** cause (sb) to worry 使(某人)烦恼或不安:

disturbing developments, reports, symptoms 使人感到不安的事态发展、报道、症状. **4** (idm 习语) **disturb the ˈpeace** (*law* 律) break the law by making too much noise, quarrelling or fighting publicly, etc 扰乱治安.
▷ **dis·turbed** *adj* (*psychology* 心) over-reacting to stress 困扰: *He is emotionally disturbed.* 他情绪困扰.

dis·turb·ance /dɪˈstɜːbəns; dɪsˋtɝbəns/ *n* **1** (**a**) [U] disturbing or being disturbed 搅乱; 弄乱; 打扰; 干扰; 骚扰; 烦扰. (**b**) [sing] person or thing that disturbs 进行骚扰的人或事物: *The teacher told him to leave as he was a disturbance to the other students.* 因为他干扰了其他学生, 所以老师叫他出去. **2** [C] instance of social unrest; riot 社会动乱; 骚乱: *violent disturbances in inner-city areas* 发生在市中心区的激烈骚乱. **3** [U] (*psychology* 心) over-reaction to stress 对压力的过度反应; 困扰: *suffer an emotional disturbance* 情绪受到困扰.

dis·union /dɪsˈjuːnɪən; dɪsˋjunjən/ *n* [U] (*fml* 文) **1** separating or being separated 分离; 分裂. **2** disagreement 分歧; 不和.

dis·unite /ˌdɪsjuːˈnaɪt; ˌdɪsjuˋnaɪt/ *v* [I, Tn] (cause sb/sth to) become separate (使某人[某事物])分离, 分裂.

dis·unity /dɪsˈjuːnətɪ; dɪsˋjunɪtɪ/ *n* [U] lack of unity; disagreement 不统一; 不一致; 不和: *There should be no disunity within our party.* 我们党内不应该存有分歧.

dis·use /dɪsˈjuːs; dɪsˋjus/ *n* [U] state of not being used 不用; 废弃: *rusty from disuse* 因弃置不用而生锈 ○ *words that have fallen into disuse* 废弃不用的词语.
▷ **dis·used** /dɪsˈjuːzd; dɪsˋjuzd/ *adj* no longer used 不再使用的: *a disused railway line* 停止运营的铁路线.

disyl·lable /dɪˈsɪləbl, daɪˈsɪləbl; dɪˋsɪləbl̩, daɪˋsɪləbl̩/ (*US* **dis·syl·lable** /ˌdɪs-; ˌdɪs-/) *n* disyllabic word or metrical foot 双音节词; 双音节韵步. Cf 参看 MONOSYLLABLE.
▷ **disyl·labic** /ˌdɪsɪˈlæbɪk, ˌdaɪsɪˈlæbɪk; ˌdɪsɪˋlæbɪk, ˌdaɪsəˋlæbɪk/ (*US* **dis·syl·labic** /ˌdɪs-; ˌdɪs-/) *adj* consisting of two syllables 双音节的.

ditch /dɪtʃ; dɪtʃ/ *n* **1** narrow channel dug at the edge of a field, road, etc, esp to hold or carry off water (田边、路边等挖掘的)沟(尤指用以蓄水或排水者). **2** (idm 习语) **dull as ditch-water** ⇨ DULL. **the last ditch** ⇨ LAST[1].
▷ **ditch** *v* **1** [I, Tn] land (an aircraft) in the sea in an emergency 使(飞行器)在海上紧急降落; 迫降: *A sudden engine failure forced the pilot to ditch (in the Irish Sea).* 由于发动机突然出现故障, 飞行员不得不(在爱尔兰海上)紧急降落. **2** [Tn] (*infml* 口) abandon (sb/sth); get rid of 抛弃(某人[某事物]); 摆脱: *I hear she's ditched her boy-friend*, ie stopped seeing him. 听说她把男朋友给甩了. ○ *When the road became impassable, we had to ditch the car and walk.* 道路无法通行时, 我们只好弃车步行. **3** [I] make or repair ditches 挖沟; 修沟: *hedging and ditching* 筑篱和挖沟.

dither /ˈdɪðə(r); ˋdɪðɚ/ *v* [I, Ipr] ~ **(about sth)** hesitate about what to do; be unable to decide 踌躇; 犹豫不决: *Stop dithering about which film you want to see or you'll miss them both!* 到底看哪一部影片, 别再犹豫了, 不然的话, 两部影片你都要耽误了!
▷ **dither** *n* **1** [sing] state of dithering 犹豫: *in a dither* 在犹豫中. **2** (idm 习语) **all of a ˈdither** (*infml* 口) very confused and unable to decide 心慌意乱的; 茫然无措的. **have the ˈdithers** (*infml* 口) hesitate anxiously 张皇失措.

ditto /ˈdɪtəʊ; ˋdɪto/ *n* (*abbr* 缩写 **do**) (used in lists to avoid repetition 用在表格中以避免重复) the same thing again 同上; 同前: *1 doz bottles white wine £2.25 a bottle; ditto red £3.* 一打白葡萄酒, 每瓶2.25英镑; 同上数量的红葡萄酒, 每瓶3英镑.
□ **ˈditto marks** marks (") representing *ditto* used in lists, tables, bills, etc (")表示'同上'或'同前'的符号(用于表格、目录、清单等中).

ditty /ˈdɪtɪ; ˋdɪtɪ/ *n* (*often joc* 常作戏谑语) short simple song 小曲; 小调.

di·ur·etic /ˌdaɪjʊˈretɪk; ˌdaɪjuˋrɛtɪk/ *n, adj* (*medical* 医) (substance) causing an increase in the flow of urine 利尿剂; 利尿的: *Coffee is a diuretic.* 咖啡是一种利尿剂. ○ *a diuretic drug* 利尿药.

di·urnal /daɪˈɜːnl; daɪˋɝnl̩/ *adj* **1** (*biology* 生) of the daytime; not nocturnal 白天的; 白昼的: *Unlike most other bats, this species is diurnal.* 这种蝙蝠与大多数蝙蝠不同, 是在日间活动的. **2** (*astronomy* 天) occupying one day 周日的: *the diurnal movement of the planets* 行星的周日运行. ▷ **di·urn·ally** *adv*.

Div *abbr* 缩写 = division(3b): *Manchester United, League Div 1* 曼彻斯特联队, 足球联赛甲组.

di·van /dɪˈvæn; *US* ˈdaɪvæn; ˋdaɪvæn/ *n* **1** long low couch without a back or arms (无靠背无扶手的)长沙发. **2** (also **diˌvan ˈbed**) low bed resembling this (像上述沙发的)矮床.

dive[1] /daɪv; daɪv/ *v* (*pt, pp* **dived**; *US* also *pt* **dove** /dəʊv; dov/) **1** [I, Ipr, Ip] ~ **(from/off sth) (into sth)**; ~ **(off/in)** go head first into water (头先入水)跳水: *He dived from the bridge to rescue the drowning child.* 他从桥上跳入水中去抢救那溺水儿童. **2** [I, Ipr, Ip] ~ **(down) (for sth)** (of a submarine, diver, etc) go under water or to a deeper level under water (指潜水艇、潜水员等)潜水: *The whale dived as the harpoon struck it.* 鲸鱼被鱼叉射中后潜入水中. ○ *dive for pearls* 潜水采珠. **3** [I, Ipr, Ip] (of an aircraft) go steeply downwards (指飞行器)急剧俯冲. **4** [Ipr] ~ **into, under, etc sth** move quickly in a specified direction 向某方向冲去或奔去: *dive under the bed* 很快钻到床底下 ○ *When the rain started, we dived into a cafe.* 雨下了起来, 我们立即跑进了一家小餐馆. **5** (phr v) **dive for sth** move quickly towards or in search of sth 扑向某物; 急忙搜寻某物: *dive for the phone, the gun, etc* 急忙过去拿听筒、枪等 ○ *We dived for cover when the storm started.* 暴风雨来临时, 我们急忙寻找躲避的地方. **dive into sth/in** (*fml* 文) (**a**) move one's hand quickly into sth 迅速将手伸入某物中: *dive into one's pocket, briefcase, etc* 立即把手伸进衣袋、公事包等. (**b**) involve oneself completely in sth 一心投入某事物: *dive into a new project* 潜心钻研一个新项目.
▷ **diver** *n* person who dives, esp one who works under water using a diving-suit 潜水者; (尤指)潜水员.
□ **ˈdive-bomb** *v* [I, Tn] (of an aeroplane, a pilot, etc) drop bombs on (sth) after having dived steeply downwards (指飞机、飞行员等)俯冲轰炸. **ˈdive-bomber** *n* aircraft designed to do this 俯冲轰炸机.
ˈdiving-bell *n* bell-shaped device supplied with air in which people can work under water 潜水钟.
ˈdiving-board *n* board for diving from (跳水用的)跳板.
ˈdiving-suit *n* watertight suit worn by divers with a helmet into which air can be pumped 潜水衣.

dive[2] /daɪv; daɪv/ *n* **1** act of diving 跳水或潜水的动作; 俯冲: *The goalkeeper made a spectacular dive to save the goal.* 守门员做了一个精彩的鱼跃动作救回一球. **2** (*infml* 口) disreputable bar, gambling club, etc 低级酒馆、赌场等: *a low dive* 下等酒吧.

di·verge /daɪˈvɜːdʒ; daɪˋvɝdʒ/ *v* **1** [I, Ipr] ~ **(from sth)** (**a**) (of lines, roads, etc) separate and go in different directions, becoming further apart (指线条、道路等)分叉, 岔开: *The M6 diverges from the M1 just north of Rugby.* 6号高速公路与1号高速公路在拉格比市以北处岔开. ○ (*fig* 比喻) *Until their paths diverged Lennon and McCartney wrote many hits together.* 伦农和麦卡特尼在分道扬镳之前一同写过许多成功之作. ⇨illus at CONVERGE 见CONVERGE之插图. (**b**) (*fml* 文) (of opinions, etc) differ (指意见等)分歧: *Our views diverged so greatly that it was impossible to agree.* 我们的观点存在着严重的分歧, 绝无调和余地. **2** [Ipr] ~ **from sth** turn away from (a plan, standard, etc) 偏离(计划、标准等): *diverge from the truth, norm, usual procedure* 不符合事实、规范、一般程序. Cf 参看 CONVERGE. ▷ **di·ver·gence** /daɪˈvɜːdʒəns; daɪˋvɝdʒəns/ (also **di·ver·gency** /-dʒənsɪ; -dʒənsɪ/) *n* [C, U]. **di·ver·gent** /-dʒənt; -dʒənt/ *adj*: *divergent paths, opinions* 岔路、歧见.

divers /ˈdaɪvəz; ˋdaɪvɚz/ *adj* (*arch* 古) various; several 各种各样的; 好几个的.

di·verse /daɪˈvɜːs; daɪˋvɝs/ *adj* of different kinds; varied 多种多样的; 不同的: *people from diverse cultures* 不同文化背景的人 ○ *Her interests are very diverse.* 她的兴趣非常广泛.

di·ver·sify /daɪˈvɜːsɪfaɪ; daɪˋvɝsəˌfaɪ/ *v* (*pt, pp* **-fied**) **1** [Tn] give variety to (sth); vary 使(某事物)多样化; 使不同: *diversify one's skills, interests, etc* 培养自己多方面的技能、兴趣等 ○ *We must try to diversify the syllabus to*

D

attract more students. 我们应该使教学大纲内容多样化，可以多吸引学生. **2** [I, Ipr] **~ (into sth)** (*commerce* 商) (esp of a business) vary the range of products, investments, etc in order to reduce risk or expand operations (尤指企业)从事多种经营，多元化: *The choice facing the company is simple: diversify or go bankrupt.* 摆在公司面前的道路不难选择：要么进行多种经营，要么破产. ○ *Some publishers are now diversifying into software.* 有些出版社目前正兼营软件. ▷ **di·ver·si·fica·tion** /daɪˌvɜːsɪfɪˈkeɪʃn; daɪˌvɝsəfəˈkeʃən/ *n* [U, C].

di·ver·sion /daɪˈvɜːʃn; *US* daɪˈvɜːrʒn; daɪˈvɝʒən/ *n* **1** (**a**) [U] action of turning sth aside or changing its direction 偏离；转向: *the diversion of a stream, one's thoughts* 河流的改道、思想的转变 ○ *the diversion of flights because of fog* 由于有雾而造成的班机航向偏离. (**b**) [C] instance of this 偏离；转向. **2** [C] (*esp Brit*) (*US* **detour**) alternative route for use by traffic when the usual road is temporarily closed (道路禁止通行时的)临时绕行路: *Sorry I'm late — there was a diversion.* 对不起，我迟到了——因为改道的缘故. **3** [C] entertaining activity, esp one that turns the attention from work, study, etc 消遣，娱乐(尤指使注意力从工作、学习等中转移开者): *the diversions of city life* 城市生活中的各种消遣 ○ *It's difficult to concentrate when there are so many diversions.* 娱乐活动多了就很难集中精神. **4** [C] thing designed to draw attention away from sth one does not want to be noticed 用以转移视线的事物；为转移注意力而制造的假象: *One of the gang created a diversion in the street while the others robbed the bank.* 一名匪徒在街上制造事端引人注目，其余匪徒则抢劫银行. ▷ **di·ver·sion·ary** /daɪˈvɜːʃənərɪ; *US* daɪˈvɜːrʒənerɪ; daɪˈvɝʒənˌɛrɪ/ *adj*: *diversionary action, tactics, raids, etc* 牵制性的行动、战术、突袭等.

di·vers·ity /daɪˈvɜːsətɪ; daɪˈvɝsətɪ/ *n* [U, sing] state of being varied; variety 多种多样；多样性: *a wide diversity of opinion* 看法上的众说纷纭.

di·vert /daɪˈvɜːt; daɪˈvɝt/ *v* **1** [Tn, Tn·pr] **~ sb/sth (from sth) (to sth)** turn sb/sth from one course to another 转移某人的注意力；使某事物转向: *divert traffic (from one road to another)* 使车辆绕道行驶 ○ *divert a ship (from its course)* 使船只转变航向 ○ *divert sb's attention, thoughts, energies, etc* 将某人的注意力、思想、精力等转移到别处. **2** [Tn] entertain or amuse (sb) 使(某人)得到消遣或娱乐: *Children are easily diverted.* 孩子们有娱乐就很高兴.

▷ **di·vert·ing** *adj* entertaining 可资消遣的；娱乐的；有趣的. **di·vert·ingly** *adv*.

di·vest /daɪˈvest; daɪˈvɛst/ *v* [Tn·pr] (*fml* 文) **1 ~ sb of sth** take off (sb's clothes) 脱去(某人的衣服): *divest a queen of her robes* 为女王脱去王袍. **2 ~ sb of sth** take away (sb's power, rights, responsibility, etc) 解除(某人的权力、权利、责任等): *The disgraced official was divested of all authority.* 该失势官员失去了一切权力. **3 ~ oneself of sth** rid oneself of (a feeling, an idea, etc) 使自己摆脱(某种感情、思想等): *He could not divest himself of the suspicion that his wife was being unfaithful.* 他无法消除自己的疑心，总觉得妻子不忠.

di·vide[1] /dɪˈvaɪd; dəˈvaɪd/ *v* **1** [I, Ipr, Ip, Tn, Tn·pr, Tn·p] **~ (sth) (up) (into sth)** (cause sth to) split or break into parts; separate (使某物)分割开；分开；分隔: *The train divides at York.* 这列火车在约克市调动车厢分途行驶. ○ *divide a large house (up) into flats* 把一所大房子分隔成若干套间 ○ *divide a novel (up) into chapters* 把一部小说划分为若干章节 ○ *divide the class (up) into small groups* 把那个班分成几个小组. **2** [Tn, Tn·pr, Tn·p] **~ sth (out/up) (between/among sb)** break sth into parts and give a share to each of a number of individuals 分或分配某事物: *divide out/up the money, food, reward* 分钱、食物、赏金 ○ *We divided the work between us.* 我们分担这工作. **3** [Tn, Tn·pr] **~ sth (between A and B)** split sth up, esp one's time, and use parts of it for different activities, etc; apportion sth 将某事物分割开；(尤指)分配时间；分派某事物: *He divides his energies between politics and business.* 他把一部分精力用来搞政治，一部分用来搞业务. **4** [Tn·pr] **~ A from B** separate or be the boundary between (two people or things) 将(两者)分隔开；在(两者)之间划分界线: *The English Channel divides England from France.* 英吉利海峡把英法两国分隔开来. **5** [Tn] cause (two or more people) to disagree 使(人)产生分歧: *This issue has divided the Government.* 这一问题在政府中引起意见分歧. ○ *The Government is divided (on this issue).* 政府(在这一问题上)意见不统一. **6** (**a**) [Tn·pr] **~ sth by sth** find out how many times one number is contained in another 某数除以某数: *30 divided by 6 is 5.* 30除以6等于5. (**b**) **~ into sth** be able to be multiplied to give another number (用某数)除某数: *5 divides into 30 6 times.* 用5除30等于6. **7** [I, Tn] (*esp Brit*) (cause Parliament to) vote, by separating into groups for and against a motion (使议会)分组表决: *After a long debate the House divided*, ie voted on the question. 议院经过长时间辩论之后，进行了分组表决. ○ *divide the House*, ie ask for a vote to be taken 要求议院付诸表决.

▷ **di·vider** *n* thing that divides sth 分隔物: *a 'room divider*, ie a screen, etc that divides a room into two parts 分隔房间的隔板.

di·vide[2] /dɪˈvaɪd; dəˈvaɪd/ *n* (*esp US*) line of high land separating two river systems; watershed 分水岭；分水线: *the Continental/Great Di'vide*, ie the watershed formed by the Rocky Mountains 大陆分水岭(落基山脉所形成的分水线).

di·vi·dend /ˈdɪvɪdend; ˈdɪvəˌdɛnd/ *n* **1** (*commerce* 商) share of profits paid to share-holders in a company, or to winners in a football pool (付给股票持有者的)股息，红利；(付给足球赛打赌赢家的)彩金: *declare a dividend*, ie state what proportion of profits are to be divided among share-holders 宣布发放股息 ○ *an annual dividend of 8%* 年度股息8%. **2** (*mathematics* 数) number that is to be divided by another 被除数. Cf 参看 DIVISOR. **3** (idm 习语) **pay dividends** ⇨ PAY[2].

di·viders /dɪˈvaɪdəz; dəˈvaɪdɚz/ *n* [pl] instrument used for measuring lines, angles, etc 分线规；两脚规: *a pair of dividers* 一副分线规. ⇨illus at COMPASS 见COMPASS之插图.

div·ina·tion /ˌdɪvɪˈneɪʃn; ˌdɪvəˈneʃən/ *n* [U] foretelling the future by supernatural means 占卜；(以超自然的方法)预测.

di·vine[1] /dɪˈvaɪn; dəˈvaɪn/ *adj* **1** [usu attrib 通常作定语] of, from or like God or a god 上帝或神的；上帝或神赐予的；如同神灵的: *Di,vine 'Service*, ie the public worship of God (公众对上帝的)礼拜. **2** (*infml* 口) wonderful, lovely, etc 极好的、可爱的等: *You look simply divine, darling!* 你简直动人极了，亲爱的! ▷ **di·vinely** *adv*: *You dance divinely.* 你跳舞跳得棒极了.

di·vine[2] /dɪˈvaɪn; dəˈvaɪn/ *v* [Tn, Tf] **1** (*fml* 文) sense (sth) by intuition; guess (凭直觉)意识到(某事物)；猜测: *divine sb's thoughts, sb's intentions, the truth* 领悟某人的思想、察觉某人的意图、猜出事情的真相. **2** reveal (sth hidden, esp the future) by magical means 占卜(某未知事物，尤指未来)；卜测；预卜: *Astrologers claim to be able to divine what the stars hold in store for us.* 占星家声称能预知祸福.

▷ **di·viner** (also **'water-diviner**) *n* person who divines, esp one who searches for underground water using a divining-rod 占卜者；(尤指)用占卜杖探寻地下水源的人.

□ **di'vining-rod** *n* Y-shaped stick used by a water-diviner (卜测水源者用的)占卜杖(呈Y形).

di·vin·ity /dɪˈvɪnətɪ; dəˈvɪnətɪ/ *n* **1** [U] quality of being divine[1](1) 神性: *the divinity of Christ* 基督的神性. **2** [C] god or goddess 神；女神: *the Roman, Greek, Egyptian divinities* 罗马、希腊、埃及诸神. **3** [U] theology 神学: *a doctor of divinity* 神学博士.

di·vis·ible /dɪˈvɪzəbl; dəˈvɪzəbl/ *adj* [usu pred 通常作表语] **~(by sth)** (*mathematics* 数) that can be divided, usu with no remainder 可除；(通常指)可除尽: *8 is divisible by 2 and 4, but not by 3.* 8可被2和4除尽，但不能被3除尽.

di·vi·sion /dɪˈvɪʒn; dəˈvɪʒən/ *n* **1** [U] (**a**) dividing or being divided 分；分割；划分: *the division of wealth* 财产的分配. (**b**) dividing one number by another 除；除法: *Are you any good at division?* 你的除法好吗? **2** [sing] (often preceded by an *adj* 常用于形容词之后) result of dividing 分的结果: *a fair/unfair division of money* 金钱的公平[不公平]分配. **3** [C] (**a**) any of the parts into which sth is divided 分出来的一部分. (**b**) (*abbr* 缩写

Div) major unit or section of an organization (组织或机构的)单位, 部门(如处、科、组、军队的师等): *the 'sales division of our company* 本公司的销售部 ○ *Our team plays in the first di'vision (of the football league).* 本队在(足球联赛)甲组参赛. ○ *the 'parachute division* 空降师. **4** [C] dividing line 分界线: *A hedge forms the division between her land and mine.* 有一道树篱在她的土地和我的土地之间形成了分界线. **5** [C, U] (instance of) disagreement or difference in thought, way of life, etc (思想、生活方式等的)歧异, 差别, 分化现象: *the deep/widening divisions in society today* 当今社会中巨大的[日益加大的]差距. **6** [C] (*esp Brit*) (in Parliament) act of voting (议会中的)分组表决: *The Bill was read without a division.* 该法案未经分组表决即进行宣读. ○ *The opposition threatened to force a division on the motion.* 反对派威胁要强行将该动议分组表决.

▷ **di·vi·sional** /dɪˈvɪʒənl; dəˈvɪʒənl/ *adj* [attrib 作定语] of a division(3) 分出的; 分支的; 师的: *di,visional com'mander, head'quarters, etc* 师长、师指挥部.

□ **di'vision-bell** *n* (*Brit*) bell rung to warn Members of Parliament not present in the House that there is to be a division(6) (英国议院通知场外议员的)分组表决铃.

di'vision lobby (also **lobby**) (*Brit*) (in Parliament) one of two corridors where Members of Parliament go to vote (议院中的)两个分组投票厅之一.

di'vision sign *n* sign (÷) placed between two numbers, showing that the first is to be divided by the second 除号(÷).

di·vis·ive /dɪˈvaɪsɪv; dəˈvaɪsɪv/ *adj* causing disagreement or disunity among people 造成不和的; 导致分裂的: *a divisive influence, policy, effect* 导致分裂的势力、政策、作用. ▷ **di·vis·ively** *adv.* **di·vis·ive·ness** *n* [U].

di·visor /dɪˈvaɪzə(r); dəˈvaɪzɚ/ *n* (*mathematics* 数) number by which another number is divided 除数. Cf 参看 DIVIDEND.

di·vorce[1] /dɪˈvɔːs; dəˈvɔrs/ *n* **1** [C, U] **~ (from sb)** (instance of the) legal ending of a marriage 离婚; 离异: *ask/sue for a divorce* 申请离婚 ○ *get/obtain a divorce* 获准离婚 ○ *grounds* (ie legal reasons) *for divorce* 离婚的理由(法律根据) ○ *Divorce is on the increase.* 离婚案不断增多. ○ [attrib 作定语] *start di'vorce proceedings* 提出离婚诉讼. **2** [C] (*fig* 比喻) ending of a connection; separation 断绝关系; 分离: *the divorce between religion and science* 宗教与科学分道扬镳.

di·vorce[2] /dɪˈvɔːs; dəˈvɔrs/ *v* **1** [Tn] legally end one's marriage to (sb) 与(某人)离婚: *They're divorcing each other/getting divorced.* 他们离婚了. **2** [Tn·pr esp passive 尤用于被动语态] **~ sb/sth from sth** (*fig* 比喻) separate sb/sth from sth, esp in a false way 使某人[某事物]与他事物分开(尤指错误地): *You can't divorce science from ethical questions.* 不能把科学与伦理问题截然分开. ○ *a politician totally divorced from* (ie unable to understand or deal with) *the real needs of the country* 与国家的实际需要完全脱节(对之不了解或束手无策)的政治家.

▷ **di·vor·cee** /dɪˌvɔːˈsiː; dəˌvɔrˈsi/ *n* divorced person 离了婚的人.

divot /ˈdɪvət; ˈdɪvət/ *n* piece of turf cut out by a golf club when making a stroke (高尔夫球棒击球时削起的一小块)草皮.

di·vulge /daɪˈvʌldʒ; dəˈvʌldʒ/ *v* [Tn, Tn·pr, Tw] **~ sth (to sb)** make known (sth secret) 泄露(秘密): *divulge a confidential report, sb's identity, one's age* 泄露机密、某人的身分、自己的年龄 ○ *I cannot divulge how much it cost.* 我不能把价钱泄露出来. ▷ **di·vul·gence** /daɪˈvʌldʒəns; dəˈvʌldʒəns/ *n* [U].

divvy /ˈdɪvɪ; ˈdɪvɪ/ *n* (*dated Brit infml* 旧, 口) dividend(1), esp one paid by a co-operative society (旧时)股息, 红利.

▷ **divvy** *v* (*pt, pp* **div·vied**) (phr v) **divvy sth up** (*infml* 口) share sth out; distribute 分某物; 分发: *They divvied up the winnings between them.* 他们瓜分了赢得的钱.

Dixie /ˈdɪksɪ; ˈdɪksɪ/ *n* (*US infml* 口) southern states of the US, esp those that formed the Confederacy in 1860-61 美国南部各州(尤指1860–1861年间组成邦联者).

□ **'Dixieland** /-lænd; -ˌlænd/ *n* **1** (*US*) = Dixie. **2** (also **dixieland**) [U] style of jazz with a strong two-beat rhythm, originating in New Orleans 迪克西兰爵士乐(每节两拍, 节奏感强, 源出新奥尔良): *Do you like Dixieland?* 你喜欢迪克西兰爵士乐吗? ○ [attrib 作定语] *a dixieland band* 演奏迪克西兰爵士乐的乐队.

DIY /ˌdiː aɪ ˈwaɪ; ˌdi aɪ ˈwaɪ/ *abbr* 缩写 = (*Brit infml* 口) do it yourself : *a DIY kit* 供购买者自行装配的成套零件 ○ *DIY enthusiasts* 喜欢自己动手干的人.

dizzy /ˈdɪzɪ; ˈdɪzɪ/ *adj* (**-ier**, **-iest**) **1** (of a person) feeling as if everything is spinning around; unable to balance; confused (指人)头晕的, 眩晕的, 失去平衡的, 昏乱的: *After another glass of whisky I began to feel dizzy.* 我又喝了一杯威士忌酒之后, 就觉得头晕目眩. **2** of or causing this feeling 使人眩晕的; 使人迷乱的: *a dizzy spell* 一阵头晕 ○ *a dizzy height, speed* 使人眩晕的高度、速度.

▷ **diz·zily** *adv.*

diz·zi·ness *n* [U].

dizzy *v* (*pt, pp* **diz·zied**) [Tn] make (sb) dizzy 使(某人)眩晕.

DJ /ˌdiː ˈdʒeɪ; ˌdi ˈdʒe/ *abbr* 缩写 = (*infml* 口) **1** (*Brit*) dinner-jacket. **2** disc jockey: *He's a radio DJ.* 他是电台的流行音乐节目主持人.

dl *abbr* 缩写 = (*pl* unchanged or **dls** 复数或不变或作 **dls**) decilitre: *10 dl* 10分升.

DLitt /ˌdiː ˈlɪt; ˌdi ˈlɪt/ (also **Litt D**) *abbr* 缩写 = Doctor of Letters 文学博士: *have/be a DLitt in English* 有英国文学博士学位[为英国文学博士] ○ *Jane Pearce DLitt* 简·皮尔斯文学博士.

DM (also **D-mark**) *abbr* 缩写 = unit of money in Germany (German *Deutsche Mark*) 马克(源自德文 *Deutsche Mark*): *DM 650* 650马克.

dm *abbr* 缩写 = (*pl* unchanged or **dms** 复数或不变或作 **dms**) decimetre: *15 dm* 15分米.

DMus /ˌdiːˈmʌs; ˌdiˈmʌs/ *abbr* 缩写 = Doctor of Music 音乐博士: *have/be a DMus* 有音乐博士学位[为音乐博士] ○ *Simon Potter DMus* 西蒙·波特音乐博士.

DNA /ˌdiː en ˈeɪ; ˌdi ɛn ˈe/ *abbr* 缩写 = (*chemistry* 化) deoxyribonucleic acid (the basic constituent of the gene) 脱氧核糖核酸(基因的基本成分).

do[1] /duː; du/ *aux v* (*neg* 否定式 **do not**, *contracted form* 缩约式 **don't** /dəʊnt; dont/; *3rd pers sing pres t* **does** /dəz; dəz; *strong form* 强读式 dʌz; dʌz/, *neg* 否定式 **does not**, *contracted form* 缩约式 **doesn't** /ˈdʌznt; ˈdʌznt/; *pt* **did** /dɪd; dɪd/, *neg* 否定式 **did not**, *contracted form* 缩约式 **didn't** /ˈdɪdnt; ˈdɪdnt/; *pp* **done** /dʌn; dʌn/) **1** (**a**) (used in front of a full *v* to form negative sentences and questions 用于实动词之前以构成否定句及疑问句): *I don't like fish.* 我不喜欢鱼. ○ *They didn't go to Paris.* 他们没去巴黎. ○ *Don't forget to write.* 别忘了写信. ○ *Does she speak French?* 她会说法语吗? ○ *Do you believe him?* 你相信他吗? ○ *Did they take you home?* 是他们把你送到家的吗? (**b**) (used to make tag questions 用以构成附加问句): *You live in London, don't you?* 你住在伦敦, 是吗? ○ *He married his boss's daughter, didn't he?* 他娶了老板的女儿, 是吗? ○ *She doesn't work here, does she?* 她不在此地工作, 是吗? **2** (used when no other *aux v* is present to emphasize that a verb is positive 用于句中无其他助动词时, 以加强动词的肯定语气): *He 'does look tired.* 他确实显得很疲倦. ○ *She 'did write to say thank you.* 她的确写信向你道谢了. ○ *Do shut up!* 住口! ○ *Do say you'll stay for supper!* 务必吃完晚饭再走! **3** (used to reverse the order of the subject and *v* when an *adv* or adverbial phrase is moved to the front 当副词或副词词组移置到句首时, 用以改变主语和动词的语序): *Not only does she speak Spanish, (but) she also knows how to type.* 她不但会说西班牙语, 还会打字呢. ○ (*fml* 文) *So much did they eat that they could not move for the next hour.* 他们吃得太多了, 一个小时都动弹不得. ○ (*fml* 文) Rarely did she request help but this was *a matter of urgency.* 她很少求助于人, 这事却是十分紧急. **4** (used to avoid repetition of a full *v* 用以代替实动词, 避免重复): *He drives faster than he did a year ago.* 他开车比一年以前快了. ○ *She works harder than he does.* 她工作比他努力. ○ *'Who won?' 'I did.'* '谁赢了?' '我赢了.'

do[2] /duː; du/ *v* (*3rd pers sing pres t* **does** /dʌz; dʌz/, *pt* **did** /dɪd; dɪd/, *pp* **done** /dʌn; dʌn/)

▸ CARRYING OUT AN ACTIVITY 进行一项活动 **1** [Tn] (used esp with *what, anything, nothing* and

D

something, to refer to actions which are unspecified or not yet known about 尤与what、anything、nothing、something连用, 指未指定的或未知的行为或动作): *'What are you doing this evening?' 'I'm going to the cinema.'* '今晚你打算做什么?''我打算去看电影.' ○ *'Are you doing anything tomorrow evening?'* '明晚你有事吗?' ○ *We will do what we can to help you.* 我们愿意尽力帮助你. ○ *The company ought to do something about the poor service.* 公司应该对服务质量不佳一事采取些措施. ○ *What does she want to do* (ie What career does she want) *when she leaves school?* 她中学毕业以后想做什么? ○ *There's nothing to do in this place*, ie no means of passing one's leisure time enjoyably. 这个地方没有好玩儿的(无法消磨空闲时间). ○ *He does nothing but complain/All he does is complain.* 他只会发牢骚. ○ *'It's so unfair that she's lost her job.' 'I know, but there's nothing we can do about it* (ie We can't change the situation.)' '她丢了工作, 真使人为她抱不平.''我知道, 但我们又有什么办法呢.' ○ *'What can I do for you?' 'I'd like a pound of apples, please.'* '您想买些什么呢?''请给我来一磅苹果.' **2** [I] act; behave 做; 行动; 表现: *Do as you wish/please.* 你愿意怎么干就怎么干吧. ○ *Do as I do.* 照我做的去做吧. ○ *Why can't you do as you're told* (ie be obedient) ? 你怎么不听话呀? **3** [Tn] work at, or carry out, (an activity or a task) 做; 进行(某项活动或工作): *do a university degree* 攻读大学学位 ○ *do research into French history* 研究法国历史 ○ *He still has to do his military service.* 他仍须服兵役. ○ *I have a number of important things to do today.* 今天我有许多重要事情要做. ○ *She does aerobics once a week.* 她每周进行一次健美操. **4** [Tn] (used esp with *the* + *n* or *my, his,* etc + *n* to refer to everyday tasks such as cleaning, washing, arranging, mending, etc 尤与 the + 名词或 my、his 等 + 名词连用, 指日常事务, 如打扫卫生、洗洗刷刷、整理家务、修修补补等): *do* (ie brush) *one's teeth* 刷牙 ○ *do* (ie wash up) *the dishes* 洗碗碟 ○ *do* (ie polish) *the silver* 擦光银器 ○ *do the flowers*, ie arrange them in vases 插花 ○ *I like the way you've done* (ie styled) *your hair.* 我喜欢你梳的发式. ○ *We'll have to get someone to do* (ie mend) *the roof.* 我们得找人来修理房顶. **5** [Tn] (used with *the, my, some, much,* etc + the *-ing* form of a *v* to refer to a wide range of actions 与 the、my、some、much 等 + 动词的 the -ing 形式连用, 指各种各样的行为或动作): *do the ironing, cooking, washing, etc* 熨烫衣服、烹调食物、洗洗刷刷 ○ *We usually do our shopping at the weekend.* 我们通常利用周末采购物品. ○ *You do the painting and I'll do the papering.* 你上油漆, 我贴壁纸. ○ *She did a lot of acting* (ie acted in a lot of plays) *when she was at university.* 她上大学时演过许多剧. ○ *He does some writing* (eg writes poems, novels, essays, etc) *in his spare time.* 他在业余时间写一些东西(如写诗、小说、散文等).

▸ STUDYING OR SOLVING 学习或解决问题 **6** [Tn] learn or study (sth) 学习或研究(某事物): *Do you do science at school?* 你在学校里学自然科学吗? ○ *do accountancy, engineering, law, etc*, eg as a professional training 学会计、工程、法律等 ○ *She did economics at Sheffield University.* 她曾在谢菲尔德大学攻读经济学. ○ *Have you done any* (ie studied any works by) *Shakespeare?* 你研究过莎士比亚的作品吗? **7** [Tn] find the answer to (sth); solve 解答(某事物); 解决: *I can't do this sum.* 我不会做这道算术题. ○ *I could never do simultaneous equations.* 我从来不会算联立方程式. ○ *Can you do crosswords?* 你会填纵横字谜吗?

▸ MAKING OR PRODUCING 做出或制作 **8** [Tn, Dn·n, Dn·pr] **~ sth (for sb)** produce sth; make sth 做出某事物; 制作某事物: *do a drawing, painting, sketch, etc* 作图样、绘画、素描 ○ *She did five copies of the agenda.* 她将议程表复制了五份. ○ *Does this pub do* (ie provide) *lunches?* 这家酒馆供应午餐吗? ○ *Who's doing* (ie organizing and preparing) *the food at the wedding reception?* 谁包办婚宴的酒席? ○ *I'll do a translation for you/do you a translation.* 我来为你翻译. **9** [Tn] deal with or attend to (sb/sth) 处理, 照料(某人的事[某事物]): *The barber said he'd do me* (ie cut my hair) *next.* 理发师说下一个给我理. **10** [Tn] put on or produce (a play, an opera, etc) 演出或编排(戏剧、歌剧等): *The Dramatic Society are doing 'Hamlet next year.* 戏剧社准备明年演出《哈姆雷特》. **11** [Tn] play the part of (sb); imitate (sb) 扮演(某人)的角色; 模仿(某人): *I thought he did Hamlet superbly.* 我觉得他扮演哈姆雷特一角很出色. ○ *She does Mrs. Thatcher rather well.* 她学撒切尔夫人的样子倒挺像哩. **12** [I, Tn, Tg] (used in the perfect tense or the passive 用于完成时态或被动语态) finish (sth); complete 结束(某事物); 完成: (*infml* 口) *Have you done* (ie finished what you were doing) ? 你做完了吗? ○ *I've done talking — it's time to act.* 我话已说完——该采取行动了. ○ *The work won't take too long to do.* 这工作不需要很长时间就能完成. ○ *Did you get your article done in time?* 你的论文按时写完了吗?

▸ COMPLETING AN ACTIVITY OR A JOURNEY 完成一项活动或走完一段路程 **13** [Tn] (**a**) travel over (a distance) 走完(一段路程): *How many miles did you do during your tour?* 你旅行了多少英里? ○ *My car does 40 miles to the gallon*, ie uses one gallon of petrol to travel 40 miles. 我的汽车每耗一加仑油可行驶40英里. (**b**) complete (a journey) 完成(旅行): *We did the journey (from London to Oxford) in an hour.* 我们用一小时走完了(从伦敦到牛津的)旅程. (**c**) travel at or reach (a speed) 以(某一速度)行进; 达到(某一速度): *The car was doing 90 miles an hour.* 汽车以每小时90英里的速度行驶. **14** [Tn] (*infml* 口) visit (a place) as a sightseer; see the sights of 游览(某地); 观光: *We did Tokyo in three days.* 我们在东京游览了三天. **15** [Tn] spend (a period of time) 度过(一段时间): *She did a year at university, but decided to give up the course.* 她在大学里读过一年书, 但后来决定放弃学业. ○ (*infml* 口) *He did six months (in prison) for burglary.* 他因盗窃罪(在监狱)服刑六个月.

▸ OTHER MEANINGS 其他意义 **16** [I, Ipr, Tn] **~ (for sb/sth); ~ (as sth)** be sufficient or satisfactory for (sb/sth) 足够或能满足(某人/某事物的需要): *'Can you lend me some money?' 'Certainly — will £10 do?'* '你能借给我一点钱吗?''当然可以——10英镑够了吗?' ○ *Will next Friday do for our meeting?* 我们的会议下星期五开行吗? ○ *These shoes won't do* (ie are not strong enough) *for climbing.* 这些鞋不适合于登山(不够结实). ○ *This log will do fine as a table for our picnic.* 这块大圆木很可以用做我们野餐的餐桌. ○ *This room will do (me) nicely, thank you*, ie It has all the comforts I need. 这个房间很适合我的需要, 谢谢你. **17** [I] (used with *advs,* or in questions after *how* 与副词连用, 或在疑问句中用于 how 之后) progress; perform 进展; 表现: *She's doing very well at school*, ie Her work is good. 她在学校里功课很好. ○ *How is the business doing?* 生意如何? ○ *Both mother and baby are doing well*, ie after the birth of the baby. 母子均平安. ○ *Everything in the garden is doing* (ie growing) *splendidly.* 花园里的一切植物都长得好极了. ○ *She did well out of* (ie profited from) *the deal.* 她在这笔交易中赚了许多钱. **18** [Tn] cook (sth) 烹制(某物): *Shall I do the casserole in the oven?* 我用烤箱做焙盘炖菜好吗? ○ *How would you like your steak done?* 你要的牛排要几成熟? **19** (**a**) [Tn esp passive 尤用于被动语态] (*infml* 口) cheat or swindle (sb) 欺骗或诈骗(某人): *This table isn't a genuine antique; I'm afraid you've been done!* ie you have paid a lot of money for an object of little value. 这张桌子并不是真正的古物, 看来你上当了. (**b**) [Tn] (*sl* 俚) rob or burgle (sth) 抢劫, 盗窃(某物): *The gang did a warehouse and a supermarket.* 那帮匪徒抢劫了一个仓库和一家超级市场. **20** (*sl* 俚) (**a**) [Tn] hurt or hit (sb) 伤害, 打击(某人): *Say that again and I'll do you!* 你要再说一次我就揍你! (**b**) [esp passive 尤用于被动语态: Tn, Tn·pr] **~ sb (for sth)** arrest or convict sb (for a crime) 逮捕某人; 宣判某人有罪: *He got done for speeding.* 他因超速行车而被抓住. **21** (idm 习语) **ˌdo as you would be ˈdone by** (*saying* 谚) one should treat others as one would like to be treated 你希望别人怎样待你, 你就应该怎样待别人; 己所不欲, 勿施于人. **be/have to do with sb/sth** be connected with or related to sb/sth 与某人[某事物]有联系或有关系: *'What do you want to see me about?' 'It's to do with that letter you sent me.'* '你想见我有什么事吗?''这事跟你写给我的那封信有关.' **have (got) something, nothing, a lot, etc to do with sb/sth** be connected or concerned to a specified extent with sb/sth 与某人[某事物]在所述程度上有联系或有关系: *Her job has something to do with computers.* 她的工作与计算机有些关系. ○ *Hard work has a lot to do with* (ie has contributed greatly towards) *her success.* 她获得的成功是和她的努力分不开的. ○ *'How much do you earn?' 'What's it got to do with you?'* '你挣多少钱?''这跟你有什么关系?' ○ *We don't have very much to do with our neighbours*, ie don't meet them socially. 我们与邻居没什么往来. **ˌhow do you ˈdo?** (used as a formal greeting when one meets sb for the first time 用作初次见面时的正式问候语). **it/that will never/won't ˈdo** (used to indicate that a state of affairs is unsatisfactory and should be changed or improved 用以表示情况或事情不能令人满意应加以改变或改善): *This is the third time you've been late for work this week; it simply won't do, I'm afraid.* 这是你在本周里第三次上班迟到了, 这可不行啊. **ˌnothing ˈdoing** (*sl* 俚) (used to refuse a request 用以拒绝一项请求): *'Could you lend me £10?' 'Nothing doing!'* '你借给我10英镑行吗?''不行!' **that ˈdoes it** (*infml* 口) (used to show that one will not tolerate sth any longer 用以表示不能再容忍某事物): *That does it! I've had enough of your sarcasm. I'm leaving.* 够了! 你那些挖苦人的话我已经受不了啦. 我走! **that's ˈdone it** (*infml* 口) (used to express dismay, anger, etc that a misfortune, an accident or a mistake has spoiled or ruined sth 当某种灾祸、事故或差错弄糟或毁坏某事物时, 用以表示惊慌、气愤等): *That's done it. We've run out of petrol. We'll never be in time for the train now.* 糟了. 我们的汽油用完了. 怎么也赶不上火车了. **that will ˈdo** (used esp to order sb to stop doing or saying sth 尤用以制止某人做或说某事物): *That'll do, you two; you're getting far too noisy.* 行啦, 你们两个人简直吵死了. (For other idioms containing **do**, see entries for *ns*, *adjs*, etc 与**do**搭配的其他习语见有关名词、形容词等的词条, 如 **do a bunk** ⇨ BUNK[2]; **easier said than done** ⇨ EASY.) **22** (phr v) **do away with sth** (*infml* 口) get rid of sth; abolish sth 摆脱某事物; 废除某事物: *She thinks it's time we did away with the monarchy.* 她认为该是废除君主制的时候了. ○ *The death penalty has been done away with in many European countries.* 许多欧洲国家已废除了死刑. **do away with oneself/sb** (*infml* 口) kill oneself/sb 自杀[杀死某人]: *She tried to do away with herself.* 她企图自杀.

do sb/sth down (*infml* 口) speak of sb/sth in a critical or an unfavourable way; criticize or disparage sb/sth 说某人[某事物]坏话; 指责或诋毁某人[某事物]: *He's always doing his friends down.* 他老是说朋友的坏话. ○ *It has become fashionable to do down traditional moral values.* 诋毁传统道德的价值已成为一种时髦事.

do for sb (*infml* 口) do housework for sb 替某人做家务: *Old Mrs Green has done for us for over 20 years.* 格林老太太替我们料理家务已有20多年了. ○ *They can't afford a home help, so they have to do for themselves.* 他们请不起女佣人, 所以只好自己做家务活. **do for sb/sth** (usu passive 通常用于被动语态) (*infml* 口) ruin, destroy or kill sb/sth 毁灭、破坏或杀死某人[某事物]: *Unless the Government provides more cash, the steel industry is done for.* 除非政府提供更多的资金, 否则钢铁工业准给毁了. **do for sth** (*infml* 口) (used in questions with *how* and *what* 用于疑问句中, 与how和what连用) manage to obtain 设法获得: *How/What did you do for coal during the miners' strike?* 矿工罢工期间你是怎样搞到煤的? **do sth for sb/sth** (*infml* 口) improve the appearance of sb/sth 使某人[某事物]改观: *That new hairstyle really does something/a lot for her.* 那种新的发式的确使她好看一些[好看多了].

do sb ˈin (*infml* 口) (**a**) kill sb 杀死某人: *She was so depressed she felt like doing herself in.* 她心灰意冷想要自杀. (**b**) = DO SB OVER. (**c**) (usu passive 通常用于被动语态) exhaust sb 使某人筋疲力尽: *Come in and sit down – you look done in.* 进来坐坐吧 —— 你看来累坏了. **do sth in** (*infml* 口) injure (a part of the body) 伤害到(身体某部): *He did his back in lifting heavy furniture.* 他在抬沉重的家具时扭伤了腰.

do sth out (*infml* 口) clean or tidy (a room, cupboard, etc) by removing unwanted things from it 清扫或清理(房间、柜橱等): *Your desk drawer needs doing out.* 你那书桌的抽屉需要清理. **do sb out of sth** (*infml* 口) prevent sb from having sth, esp in an unfair or a dishonest way 使某人得不到某事物(尤指以不光明正大的方式): *She was done out of her promotion.* 她受人算计而未获提升. **do sb ˈover** (*infml* 口) attack and beat sb severely 猛击某人; 痛打某人: *He was done over by a gang of thugs after a football match.* 他在足球比赛结束以后受到一帮暴徒的殴打. **do sth over** clean or redecorate the surfaces of sth 清理或重新装饰某物的表面: *The paintwork is beginning to flake; it'll need doing over/to be done over soon.* 油漆已成片脱落, 需要赶快重新上漆.

do sth to sb (*infml* 口) have an effect on sb; excite or stir sb 影响到某人; 刺激或煽动某人: *Her voice really does something to me.* 她的声音确实对我有一定影响. ○ *What have you done to your sister? She's very upset.* 你对你妹妹怎么了? 她难过极了. **do sth to sth** (esp in questions with *what* 尤用于疑问句中, 与what连用) cause sth to happen to sth 使对某事物产生影响: *What have you done to the television? It's not working properly.* 这电视机你是怎么弄的? 都不能正常收看了. ○ *What on earth have you done to your hair?* eg Why have you had it cut in that way? 你怎么把头发弄成这个样子?

do up be fastened; fasten 固定住; 扣上; 绑紧: *This skirt does up at the back.* 这条裙子是在后面系扣的. **do oneself ˈup** (*infml* 口) make oneself more attractive by putting on make-up, different clothes, etc 藉梳妆打扮、着奇装异服等使自己格外引人注目. **do sth up** (**a**) fasten (a coat, skirt, etc) with buttons, a zip, etc (用扣子、拉链等)固着(外套、裙子等): *He never bothers to do his jacket up.* 他总是不愿意系外衣的钮扣. ○ *She asked me to do up her dress for her at the back.* 她要我给她把衣服从后面系上. (**b**) make sth into a parcel or bundle; wrap or tie sth up 把某物打成包裹或捆扎在一起; 包住或捆扎某物: *She was carrying a parcel of books done up in brown paper.* 她提着一个棕色的纸包, 里面是书. (**c**) repair, redecorate or modernize (a house, room, etc) 修理、重新装饰或以现代化设备装修(房子、房间等): *If we decide to buy the cottage we'll have to do it up.* 我们若决定购买这座别墅, 就得重新进行装修. ○ *We're having the kitchen done up.* 我们正用现代化设备装修厨房.

do with sth (**a**) (used with *can* and *could* to express a need or desire for sth 与can和could连用, 表示需要或希望得到某事物): *You look as if you could do with* (ie as if you need) *a good night's sleep.* 你看来似乎需要好好睡上一夜. ○ *I could do with a stiff drink!* 我想要一杯烈酒. (**b**) (used in the negative with *can* and *could* 用于否定句中, 与can和could配合使用) tolerate sth 忍受某事物: *I can't do with his insolence.* 我忍受不了他那傲慢无礼的态度. ○ *If there's one thing I can't do with, it's untidiness.* 假若说有什么东西我无法忍受的话, 那就是不整洁. **do sth with sb/sth** (used in questions with *what* 用于疑问句中, 与what配合使用): *What have you done with* (ie Where have you put) *my umbrella?* 你把我的伞放在哪儿去了? ○ *Tell me what you did with yourselves* (ie how you passed the time) *on Sunday.* 告诉我你们怎样度过星期天的. ○ *What are we going to do with* (ie How are we going to use) *the food left over from the party?* 我们宴会上剩下的食物怎么办呢? ○ *She doesn't know what to do with herself.* 她不知道怎么办才好.

do without (sb/sth) (used esp with *can* and *could* 尤与can和could连用) manage without sb/sth 不用或没有某人[某事物]也行: *He can't do without (the services of) a secretary.* 他不能没有秘书(的协助). ○ *If we can't afford a car, we'll just have to do without (one).* 我们要是买不起汽车, 也就只好不用(汽车)了. ○ *I could have done without being* (ie I wish I hadn't been) *woken up at 3 o'clock in the morning.* 其实用不着在清晨3点钟就把我叫醒吧.

□ **ˌdo-ˈgooder** *n* (*infml often derog* 口, 常作贬义) person who performs or tries to perform good deeds, esp in an unrealistic, interfering or fussy way (力图)做好事的人(尤指方式不切实际、多管闲事或帮倒忙).

ˌdo it yourˈself (*abbr* 缩写 **DIY**) activity of constructing, repairing or decorating things oneself (rather than employing professional workers to do it) 自己动手干(建造、修理或装饰, 而不雇用专人): *She's very keen on do it yourself.* 她很喜欢自己干维修活儿. ○

[attrib 作定语] *a do-it-yourself shop* 出售成套零件供顾客自行装配的商店.

do³ /du:; du/ *n* (*pl* **dos** or **do's** /du:z; duz/) **1** (*Brit infml* 口) party 聚会: *I hear the Newtons are having a big do tonight.* 听说牛顿家里今晚举行盛大的宴会. **2** (*Brit sl* 俚) dishonest trick; swindle 花招; 骗局: *If you ask me, the whole thing's a do.* 依我说, 这事完全是个骗局. **3** (idm 习语) **do's and don'ts** /ˌdu:zənˈdəʊnts; ˌduzənˈdonts/ rules 规则; 准则: *If you want to lose weight, here are some do's and don'ts.* 想要减轻体重, 这是一些注意事项. **fair do/dos/do's** ⇨ FAIR¹.

do⁴ = DOH.

do *abbr* 缩写 = (also *symb* 符号为 ") ditto.

doc /dɒk; dɑk/ *n* (*infml* 口) (used as a term of address) doctor (用作称呼语)医生.

do·cile /ˈdəʊsaɪl; *US* ˈdɒsl; ˈdɑsl/ *adj* (of a person or an animal) easy to control (指人或动物)容易控制的, 驯服的: *a docile child, dog, personality* 温顺的孩子、狗、个性. ▷ **do·cilely** /-saɪllɪ; *US* -səlɪ; -slɪ/ *adv*. **do·cil·ity** /dəʊˈsɪlətɪ; doˈsɪlətɪ/ *n* [U].

D

dock¹ /dɒk; dɑk/ *n* **1** [C] part of a port, etc where ships go for loading, unloading or repair, esp one fitted with gates to control the water level 码头; 船埠; (尤指)船坞: *go into/be in dock* 进入[在]船坞 ○ [attrib 作定语] *dock workers* 码头工人. **2 docks** [pl] grouping of docks with the wharves, sheds, etc round them (设有码头、货棚等的)港区: *work at the docks* 在港区工作. **3** [C] (*esp US*) ship's berth; wharf 泊位; 码头.

▷ **docker** *n* person who loads and unloads ships 码头工人.

□ ˈ**dockland** /-lænd; -ˌlænd/ *n* [U, C] district near a dockyard (邻近船厂的)厂区.

ˈ**dockyard** *n* area with docks and equipment for building and repairing ships 造船厂; 修船厂.

dock² /dɒk; dɑk/ *v* **1** (**a**) [I] (of a ship) come into dock (指船)进港, 进入船坞. (**b**) [Tn] bring (a ship) into dock 领(船)入港. **2** (**a**) [I] (of spacecraft) join together (指宇宙飞船)对接: *docking manoeuvres/procedures* 对接操作[过程]. (**b**) [Tn] join (two or more spacecraft) together in space 使(宇宙飞船)在宇宙空间对接.

dock³ /dɒk; dɑk/ *n* **1** part of a criminal court where the accused sits during his trial (刑事法庭的)被告席: *The judge looked over to the prisoner in the dock.* 法官打量了被告席上的犯人. **2** (idm 习语) **put sb/be in the dock** accuse sb/be accused of doing sth wrong 指控某人[受到指控]: *This recent tragedy has put the manufacturers of the drug squarely in the dock.* 新近发生的这一悲惨事件使药品厂商受到指控.

dock⁴ /dɒk; dɑk/ *v* **1** [Tn] cut short (an animal's tail) 剪短(动物的尾巴). **2** [Tn, Tn·pr, Dn·n] **~ sth (from/off sth)** take away (part of sb's wages, rations, etc) 扣除(某人的部分工资、配给品等): *They've docked my salary.* 他们扣掉了我的一部分工资. ○ *dock 15% from/off sb's earnings* 从某人的收入中扣除15% ○ *They've docked me £20.* 他们扣了我20英镑.

dock⁵ /dɒk; dɑk/ *n* [U, C] common weed with large leaves 酸模(一种阔叶野草).

docket /ˈdɒkɪt; ˈdɑkɪt/ *n* **1** (*commerce* 商) document or label listing goods delivered, jobs done, contents of a package, etc 单据, 标签(送货单、完工报表、包裹单等). **2** (*US law* 律) list of cases awaiting trial 备审案件目录表; 诉讼摘录.

▷ **docket** *v* [Tn] (**a**) write (sth) on a docket 将(某事物)列入一览表. (**b**) label (sth) with a docket 给(某物)附上内容标签.

doc·tor /ˈdɒktə(r); ˈdɑktɚ/ *n* (*abbr* 缩写 **Dr**) **1** person who has been trained in medical science 医生; 大夫: *You'd better see a doctor about that cut.* 你最好去找医生看看你那伤口. ○ *Doctor Thompson* 汤普森医生. **2** person who has received the highest university degree 博士: *Doctor of Philosophy, Science, Letters, Law, etc* 哲学、理学、文学、法学等博士.

▷ **doc·tor** *v* [Tn] **1** (*infml* 口) give medical treatment for (sth) or to (sb) 医治(某病); 为(某人)治病: *doctor a cold, a child* 医治感冒、给小孩治病. **2** neuter (a cat, dog, etc) 阉割(猫、狗等). **3** (*infml* 口) add sth harmful to (food or drink) 将有害物质搀入(食物或饮料)中: *They doctored her fruit juice with vodka and she got very drunk.* 他们在她喝的果汁里搀入了伏特加酒致使她酩酊大醉. **4** (*infml* 口) change (sth) in order to deceive 窜改, 伪造(某事物): *doctor the evidence, the accounts, a report* 伪造证据、窜改帐目、作假报告.

doc·toral /ˈdɒktərəl; ˈdɑktərəl/ *adj* [attrib 作定语] of or relating to a doctorate 博士的; 博士学位的: *a doctoral thesis* 博士论文.

doc·tor·ate /ˈdɒktərət; ˈdɑktərɪt/ *n* highest university degree 博士学位: *She's studying for her doctorate.* 她正在攻读博士学位.

doc·trin·aire /ˌdɒktrɪˈneə(r); ˌdɑktrɪˈnɛr/ *adj* (*derog* 贬) rigidly applying a theory with no concern for practical problems 空谈理论的; 教条主义的: *doctrinaire attitudes, beliefs, criticisms* 教条主义的态度、信条、批评.

doc·trine /ˈdɒktrɪn; ˈdɑktrɪn/ *n* [C, U] (any of a) set of beliefs held by a church, political party, group of scientists, etc 教义; 主义; 学说; 信条: *Catholic doctrines* 天主教教义 ○ *Marxist doctrine* 马克思的学说 ○ *This is a matter of doctrine*, ie must be accepted as true. 这是个基本信条(必须承认其为真理). ▷ **doc·trinal** /dɒkˈtraɪnl; *US* ˈdɒktrɪnl; ˈdɑktrɪnl/ *adj* [attrib 作定语]: *doctrinal controversy* 有关教义的论争 ○ (*derog* 贬) *a rigidly doctrinal approach, response, upbringing* 教条式的方法、反应、教养.

docu·ment /ˈdɒkjʊmənt; ˈdɑkjəmənt/ *n* paper, form, book, etc giving information about sth, evidence or proof of sth 文件; 公文; 文献: *The spy stole secret government documents.* 间谍窃去了政府的秘密文件. ○ *study all the documents in a case*, ie one being heard in court 研究案件的全部证件 ○ *legal documents*, eg deeds of property, wills, etc 法律文件(如财产的契约、遗嘱等).

▷ **docu·ment** /ˈdɒkjʊment; ˈdɑkjəˌmɛnt/ *v* [Tn] prove or support (sth) with documents 用文件证实或证明(某事): *Can you document these claims?* 你能为这些要求提供证件吗? ○ *a badly-/well-documented report*, ie (not) supporting its statements by referring to evidence 证据不足[充足]的报告.

docu·menta·tion /ˌdɒkjʊmenˈteɪʃn; ˌdɑkjəmɛnˈteʃən/ *n* [U] **1** documenting or being documented 文件或证据的提供或备办. **2** documents provided as evidence or proof of sth 证件: *We haven't enough documentation to process your claim.* 我们还没有足够的证明文件来审理你的要求.

docu·ment·ary /ˌdɒkjʊˈmentrɪ; ˌdɑkjəˈmɛntərɪ/ *adj* [attrib 作定语] **1** consisting of documents 文件的; 文献的: *documentary evidence, proof, sources* 书面证据、证件、文件来源. **2** giving a factual report of some subject or activity, esp by using pictures, recordings, etc of people involved 记实的, 记录的(尤指提供图片、录音等材料): *a documentary account of the Vietnam war* 关于越南战争的记实报道 ○ *documentary films showing the lives of working people* 反映劳动人民生活的纪录片.

▷ **docu·ment·ary** /ˌdɒkjʊˈmentrɪ; ˌdɑkjəˈmɛntərɪ/ *n* documentary film, or radio or TV programme 纪录片; 记实的广播或电视节目: *a documentary on/about drug abuse* 关于滥用毒品的纪录片.

dod·der /ˈdɒdə(r); ˈdɑdɚ/ *v* [I, Ipr, Ip] (*infml* 口) move or act in a shaky unsteady way, because of old age or weakness (因年老或体弱)步履不稳, 摇摇晃晃: *He doddered down the street.* 他踉踉跄跄沿街走去. ○ *dodder along, about, around, etc* 颤颤悠悠地四处走动.

▷ **dod·derer** /ˈdɒdərə(r); ˈdɑdərɚ/ *n* **1** (*infml* 口) person who dodders 蹒跚而行的人. **2** (*derog* 贬) old person 老人.

dod·der·ing /ˈdɒdərɪŋ; ˈdɑdərɪŋ/ (also **dod·dery** /ˈdɒdərɪ; ˈdɑdərɪ/) *adjs* weak and uncertain in movement 行动无力而不稳的.

doddle /ˌdɒdl; ˈdɑdl/ *n* [sing] (*infml* 口) task or activity that is easily performed 轻而易举的任务或活动: *That hill's an absolute doddle (to climb).* (爬)上那座山岗毫不费力. ○ *It's no doddle being a teacher, you know.* 你知道, 当老师决非易事.

dodge¹ /dɒdʒ; dɑdʒ/ *v* **1** [I, Ipr, Ip, Tn] move quickly and suddenly to one side in order to avoid (sb/sth) 闪开; 躲开; 躲避: *He dodged to left and right as the gunman opened fire.* 持枪歹徒开火时他东躲西闪. ○ *She dodged round the corner.* 她在角落处躲躲闪闪. ○ (*fig* 比喻) *I'll leave early so as to dodge the rush-hour.* 我要早早动身以

避过交通拥挤时间. **2** [Tn, Tg] (*infml* 口) avoid doing (sth) by cleverness or trickery 施计避免做(某事物): *dodge military service* 逃避兵役 ○ *dodge awkward questions* 回避令人尴尬的问题 ○ *He always manages to dodge doing the housework.* 他总是千方百计避免做家务.

▷ **dodger** *n* (*infml* 口) person who avoids doing sth 逃避者; 回避者; 躲避者: *Make sure she pays her share — she's a bit of a dodger.* 她自己的一份一定要她付清——她可是有点能赖就赖.

dodge[2] /dɒdʒ; dɑdʒ/ *n* **1** (usu *sing* 通常作单数) quick movement to avoid sb/sth 躲闪; 闪避; 躲避: *make a sudden dodge to the right* 突然向右一闪. **2** (*infml* 口) clever trick; way of avoiding sth 妙计; 避免某事物的方法: *a tax dodge* 偷税的伎俩 ○ *She's up to all the dodges*, ie knows and uses them all. 她总是有躲避的方法.

dodgems /ˈdɒdʒəmz; ˈdɑdʒəmz/ *n* [pl] (also ˈ**dodgem cars**) (*Brit*) (at fun fairs) small electric cars whose drivers try to bump other cars while dodging those that try to bump them 碰碰车: *have a go on the dodgems* 去玩碰碰车.

dodgy /ˈdɒdʒɪ; ˈdɑdʒɪ/ *adj* (**-ier**, **-iest**) (*infml* 口 *esp Brit*) **1** (of a person) likely to be dishonest; cunning (指人)诡诈的, 狡猾的: *He's a dodgy bloke — I wouldn't trust him an inch.* 他是个诡计多端的傢伙——我一点都不相信他. **2** difficult or dangerous 困难的; 危险的: *Cycle across America? Sounds a bit dodgy to me.* 骑自行车横越美国? 听起来有些冒险.

dodo /ˈdəʊdəʊ; ˈdodo/ *n* (*pl* **~s** or **~es**) **1** large bird, now extinct, that was unable to fly and that lived on Mauritius 渡渡鸟(巨鸟, 不能飞行, 原产毛里求斯, 已绝种). **2** (idm 习语) **dead as a/the dodo** ⇨ DEAD.

doe /dəʊ; do/ *n* female deer, reindeer, rabbit or hare 雌鹿; 雌兔. ⇨illus at DEER 见 DEER 之插图. Cf 参看 FAWN[1], HIND[2], STAG 1.

DOE /ˌdiː əʊ ˈiː; ˌdi o ˈi/ *abbr* 缩写 = (*Brit*) Department of the Environment 环境事务部.

doer /ˈduːə(r); ˈduɚ/ *n* (*approv* 褒) person who does things rather than thinking or talking about them 实干家; 身体力行者: *We need more doers and fewer organizers.* 我们需要的是实干的人多些, 组织的人少些.

does ⇨ DO.

doff /dɒf; *US* dɔːf; dɔf/ *v* [Tn] (*fml* 文) take off (one's hat) 脱(帽). Cf 参看 DON[2].

dog[1] /dɒg; *US* dɔːg; dɔg/ *n* **1** [C] (**a**) common domestic animal kept by human beings for work, hunting, etc or as a pet 狗; 犬. ⇨illus at App 1 见附录1之插图, page iii. (**b**) male of this animal, or of the wolf or fox 公狗; 公狼; 公狐. Cf 参看 BITCH 1. (**c**) **the dogs** [pl] (*infml* 口) (betting on the result of) greyhound racing 赛狗(的赌博): *I won £10 on the dogs.* 我赛狗赢了10英镑. **2** [C] (**a**) (preceded by an *adj* 前用形容词修饰) (*dated infml* 旧, 口) fellow 人; 傢伙: *a sly, lucky, gay dog* 狡猾之徒、幸运儿、快乐的傢伙 ○ *You dirty* (ie dishonourable) *dog!* 你这个无耻的小人! (**b**) (*dated* 旧) wicked or worthless man 邪恶的人; 卑鄙之徒: *He's a vile dog!* 他是个无耻之徒! **3** [C] mechanical device for gripping things 卡具, 夹具(卡、夹等机械装置). **4** [C] = ANDIRON. **5** (idm 习语) **(a case of)** ˌ**dog eat** ˈ**dog** ruthless competition 残酷无情的竞争; 自相残杀. **a** ˌ**dog in the** ˈ**manger** person who stops others enjoying sth he cannot use or does not want 狗占马槽; 占着茅坑不拉屎的人: [attrib 作定语] *a* ˌ*dog-in-the-manger* ˈ*attitude* 占着茅坑不拉屎的态度. **a dog's** ˈ**breakfast**/ˈ**dinner** (*infml* 口) muddle or mess 乱糟糟; 一团糟: *He's made a real dog's breakfast of these accounts.* 他把这些帐目搞得一团糟. **dressed like a dog's dinner** ⇨ DRESS[2]. **every dog has his/its** ˈ**day** (*saying* 谚) everyone enjoys good luck or success sooner or later 凡人皆有得意时. **give a dog a bad** ˈ**name (and** ˈ**hang him)** (*saying* 谚) once a person has lost his reputation, it is difficult for him to regain it because others continue to condemn or suspect him 一朝坏名声, 十年洗不清; 名誉一毁, 万难挽回. **go to the** ˈ**dogs** (*infml* 口) (of an organization, institution, etc) change so that it is no longer as efficient, productive, etc as before (指组织、机构等)一蹶不振, 不复往日之盛, 大不如前: *This firm's gone to the dogs since you took over!* 这公司自你接手已大不如前! **a/the hair of the dog** ⇨ HAIR. **help a lame dog over a stile** ⇨ HELP[1]. **lead a dog's life**; **lead sb a dog's life** ⇨ LEAD[3]. **let sleeping dogs lie** ⇨ SLEEP[2]. **love me, love my dog** ⇨ LOVE[2]. **not have a** ˈ**dog's chance** have no chance at all 毫无机会; 绝无可能: *He hasn't a dog's chance of passing the exam.* 他这次考试毫无及格的可能. **put on the dog** (*US sl* 俚) show off 炫耀; 摆阔. **rain cats and dogs** ⇨ RAIN[2]. **the tail wagging the dog** ⇨ TAIL. **teach an old dog new tricks** ⇨ TEACH. **top dog** ⇨ TOP[1]. **treat sb like dirt/a dog** ⇨ TREAT.

▷ **dog·gie** (also **doggy**) /ˈdɒgɪ; *US* ˈdɔːgɪ; ˈdɔgɪ/ *n* (*infml* 口) (used by and to children 儿语) dog 小狗; 狗儿.

□ ˈ**dog-biscuit** *n* small hard biscuit fed to dogs (喂狗的)小块硬饼干.

ˈ**dogcart** *n* light two-wheeled horse-drawn vehicle 双轮轻便马车.

ˈ**dog-collar** *n* **1** collar for a dog 狗项圈. **2** (*infml* 口) stiff white collar worn by a clergyman (牧师穿的)白色硬领; 牧师领.

dog-eared 页角折卷的

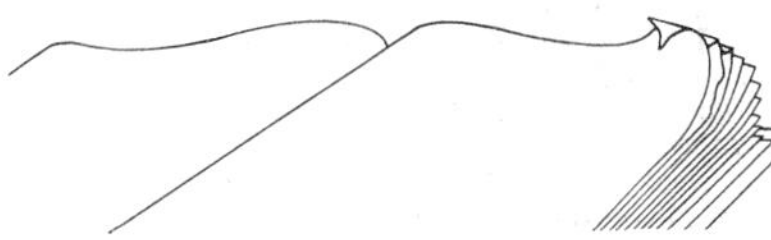

ˈ**dog-eared** *adj* (of a book) having the corners of many pages turned down through use (指书)翻旧而页角折卷的. ⇨illus 见插图.

ˈ**dogfight** *n* **1** close combat between fighter aircraft 战斗机近距离空战. **2** rough uncontrolled fight 混战.

ˈ**doghouse** *n* **1** (*US*) kennel 狗窝; 犬舍. **2** (idm 习语) **in the doghouse** in disgrace; out of favour 丢脸的; 不光彩的; 失宠的; 受冷落的.

ˈ**dog-like** *adj* [usu attrib 通常作定语] of or like a dog 狗的; 像狗的: *dog-like devotion, fidelity, etc* 像狗一般的忠心、忠实等.

ˈ**dog-leg** *n* sharp bend, esp on a golf-course 急转弯(尤指高尔夫球场的).

ˈ**dog-paddle** (also ˈ**doggie-paddle**) *n* [U] simple swimming stroke, with short quick movements of the arms and legs (游泳动作的)狗刨式. — *v* [I] swim in this way 用狗刨式游泳.

the ˈ**dog-star** *n* the star Sirius 天狼星(大犬座).

ˈ**dog-tired** *adj* [usu pred 通常作表语] very tired 极疲倦.

ˈ**dog-tooth** *n* (*architecture* 建) small pyramid-shaped ornament carved into stonework 犬牙饰.

ˈ**dog-trot** *n* gentle easy trot (从容的)小跑.

dog[2] /dɒg; *US* dɔːg; dɔg/ *v* (**-gg-**) [Tn] follow (sb) closely and persistently 紧随, 紧跟, 尾随(某人): *dog sb's footsteps* 跟踪某人 ○ (*fig* 比喻) *Her career was dogged by misfortune.* 她一生屡遭不幸.

dog days /ˈdɒgdeɪz; *US* ˈdɔːg; ˈdɔg ˌdez/ hottest period of the year (July and August) 一年中天气最热的时期(七月和八月); 三伏天.

doge /dəʊdʒ; dodʒ/ *n* (formerly) chief magistrate in the republics of Venice and Genoa (旧时)(威尼斯和热那亚两共和国的)总督.

dog·fish /ˈdɒgfɪʃ; *US* ˈdɔːg-; ˈdɔg ˌfɪʃ/ *n* (*pl* unchanged 复数不变) type of small shark 狗鲨.

dog·ged /ˈdɒgɪd; *US* ˈdɔːgɪd; ˈdɔgɪd/ *adj* [usu attrib 通常作定语] (*approv* 褒) determined; not giving up easily 顽强的; 不屈不挠的: *a dogged defence of the city* 对城市的顽强防守 ○ *Although he's less talented, he won by sheer dogged persistence.* 他虽然天赋不高, 但全凭坚韧的毅力赢得了胜利. ▷ **dog·gedly** *adv*. **dog·ged·ness** *n* [U].

dog·gerel /ˈdɒgərəl; *US* ˈdɔːgərəl; ˈdɔgərəl/ *n* [U] verse that (intentionally or not) produces a clumsy and ridiculous effect 歪诗; 蹩脚诗.

doggo /ˈdɒgəʊ; *US* ˈdɔːg-; ˈdɔgo/ *adv* (idm 习语) **lie doggo** ⇨ LIE.

dog·gone /ˈdɒgɒn; *US* ˈdɔːgɔːn; ˈdɔgˌgɔn/ *v* [Tn] (*US* *infml* 口) (used to express annoyance or surprise 用以表示恼怒或惊讶): *Doggone it!* 去它的! ○ *Well I'll be doggoned!* 嘿, 好家伙!

▷ **dog·gone** (also **dog·goned**) *adj* [attrib 作定语], *adv* (used to express annoyance or surprise 用以表示恼怒或惊讶): *I got another doggone traffic ticket.* 又给了我一张该死的交通违章罚款通知单. ○ *Don't drive so doggoned fast!* 别他妈开得这么快呀!

do·gie /ˈdəʊgɪ; ˋdogɪ/ *n* (*US*) motherless calf, esp on the range (失去母牛的)牛犊(尤指牧场中者).

dogma /ˈdɒgmə; *US* ˈdɔ:gmə; ˋdɔgmə/ *n* [C, U] belief or set of beliefs put forward by some authority, esp a Church, to be accepted as a matter of faith 教义; 教理; 教条; 信条: (*fig derog* 比喻, 贬) *political, social, economic, etc dogma*, ie ideas that are not expected to be questioned 政治的、社会的、经济的...信条.

dog·matic /dɒgˈmætɪk; *US* dɔ:gˈmætɪk; dɔgˋmætɪk/ *adj* **1** of or based on dogma 教义的; 教理的; 以教义为基础的: *dogmatic theology* 教义神学. **2** (*derog* 贬) that claims or suggests that sth is true without taking account of evidence or other opinions 武断的; 自以为是的: *a dogmatic attitude, approach, view, etc* 武断的态度、方法、看法等 ○ *You can't be dogmatic in matters of taste.* 对于个人爱好的事, 何必这样自以为是. ▷ **dog·mat·ic·ally** /-klɪ; -klɪ/ *adv*: *state sth dogmatically* 武断地主张某事物.

D

dog·mat·ism /ˈdɒgmətɪzəm; *US* ˈdɔ:gmətɪzəm; ˋdɔgmə,tɪzəm/ *n* [U] (*derog* 贬) (quality of) being dogmatic 教条主义; 武断: *the dogmatism of some music critics, popular preachers, etc* 某些音乐评论家、民众传道者等的教条主义观点.

▷ **dog·mat·ist** /-mətɪst; -mətɪst/ *n* (*derog* 贬) dogmatic person 教条主义者; 武断的人.

dog·mat·ize, -ise /ˈdɒgmətaɪz; *US* ˈdɔ:gmətaɪz; ˋdɔgmə,taɪz/ *v* [I, Ipr] **~ (about sth)** (*derog* 贬) make dogmatic statements 教条地或武断地表达: *You can't dogmatize about people's needs.* 对人民之所需不能武断.

dog·rose /ˈdɒgrəʊz; *US* ˈdɔ:g-; ˋdɔg,roz/ *n* wild rose, growing in hedges, etc 犬蔷薇(生长在树篱间的野蔷薇).

dogs·body /ˈdɒgzbɒdɪ; *US* ˈdɔ:g-; ˋdɔgz,bɑdɪ/ *n* (*Brit*) person who does boring or unpleasant jobs for others 勤杂工.

dog-watch /ˈdɒgwɒtʃ; *US* ˈdɔ:g-; ˋdɔg,wɑtʃ/ *n* (on ships) either of the two-hour watches (WATCH[1] 1a), 4 pm to 6 pm or 6 pm to 8 pm (船上)两小时值班(下午4至6时或6至8时).

dog·wood /ˈdɒgwʊd; *US* ˈdɔ:g-; ˋdɔg,wʊd/ *n* [U, C] wild flowering shrub 狗木(野生多花灌木).

doh (also **do**) /dəʊ; do/ *n* (*music* 音) (in tonic sol-fa) the first and eighth notes of any major scale (首调唱法的)任何大音阶第一音和第八音.

doily (also **doy·ley**, **doyly**) /ˈdɔɪlɪ; ˋdɔɪlɪ/ *n* small ornamental mat of lace, paper, etc placed under a dish or under a cake, etc on a plate (精细织品或纸品的)装饰性小垫(置于盘、碟下或衬在盘中糕点下者).

do·ings /ˈdu:ɪŋz; ˋduɪŋz/ *n* (*infml* 口) **1** [pl] things done or being done; activities 已做或正在做的事; 活动: *I've been hearing a lot about your doings.* 我常听到很多关于你做的事情. **2** [C] (*pl* unchanged 复数不变) (*Brit*) thing(s) needed 需要的东西: *Where's the doings for mending punctures?* 补车胎的傢伙(工具)在什么地方?

dol *abbr* 缩写 = (also *symb* 符号为 $) dollar(s) 元; 美元.

dol·drums /ˈdɒldrəmz; ˋdɑldrəmz/ *n* **1 the doldrums** [pl] parts of the ocean near the equator where there is little or no wind 赤道附近无风的海域; 赤道无风带. **2** (idm 习语) **in the ˈdoldrums** (**a**) feeling depressed; in low spirits 精神不振; 意志消沉; 无精打采: *He's been in the doldrums ever since she left him.* 自从她离开他以来, 他一直很消沉. (**b**) not active or making progress 不活跃; 无进展: *Despite these measures, the economy remains in the doldrums.* 尽管采取了这些措施, 经济状况仍然毫无起色.

dole[1] /dəʊl; dol/ *v* (phr v) **dole sth out** distribute (esp food, money, etc) in small amounts 少量发放(尤指食物、金钱等): *allowances grudgingly doled out to the elderly* 勉强发给老年人的少量津贴.

dole[2] /dəʊl; dol/ *n* **the dole** [sing] (*Brit infml* 口) weekly payment made by the state to unemployed people (政府每周发放的)失业救济金: *be/go on the dole*, ie register for/receive such payments 登记领取[领取]失业救济金.

dole·ful /ˈdəʊlfl; ˋdolfəl/ *adj* sad; mournful 悲伤的; 令人沮丧的: *a doleful face, manner, expression, etc* 愁眉苦脸、垂头丧气的样子、忧郁的表情. ▷ **dole·fully** /-fəlɪ; -fəlɪ/ *adv*. **dole·ful·ness** *n* [U].

doll[1] /dɒl; *US* dɔ:l; dɔl/ *n* **1** model of a baby or an adult, usu for a child to play with 玩偶; 玩具娃娃. **2** (*dated sl* 旧, 俚 *esp US*) attractive woman 漂亮女子: *She's quite a doll!* 她真是个美人!

□ ˈ**doll's house** **1** toy house used for playing with dolls (用以玩儿玩偶的)玩具小屋. **2** (*fig* 比喻) very small house 极小的房屋: *How do they all cram into that doll's house?* 那小小的房子怎么挤得下他们大家呢?

doll[2] /dɒl; *US* dɔ:l; dɔl/ *v* (*infml* 口) (phr v) **doll sb/oneself up** dress sb/oneself in a smart or showy way 把某人[自己]打扮得漂漂亮亮或花枝招展: *I'm going to get dolled up for the party.* 我马上好好打扮一下去参加聚会.

dol·lar /ˈdɒlə(r); ˋdɑlɚ/ *n* **1** [C] (*symb* 符号为 $) unit of money in the US, Canada, Australia, etc 元(美国、加拿大、澳大利亚等国的货币单位): *Oil from these fields is priced in dollars.* 这些油田产的油以美元定价. **2** [C] banknote or coin worth one dollar 一元的纸币或硬币: *Have you got any dollars?* 你带着钱呢吗? ⇨App 4 见附录4. **3 the dollar** [sing] (*finance* 财) value of the US dollar on international money markets 国际金融市场的美元价格: *The dollar closed two cents down.* 收市时一美元下降了二美分. **4** (idm 习语) **bet one's bottom dollar** ⇨ BET. **(feel, look, etc) like a million dollars** (*infml* 口) very fit, healthy, beautiful, etc 身体很好; 非常健康; 十分漂亮. **a/the sixty-four thousand dollar ˈquestion** important question that is very difficult to answer 很难回答的重大问题: *Will we all survive until the year 2 000? That's the sixty-four thousand dollar question.* 我们大家是否都能活到公元2 000年? 这个问题很难回答.

dol·lop /ˈdɒləp; ˋdɑləp/ *n* (*infml* 口) shapeless lump of sth soft, esp food (软而不成形的)一团, 一块(尤指食物): *a dollop of cream, jam, mashed potato, etc* 一团奶油、果酱、土豆泥等.

dolly /ˈdɒlɪ; *US* ˈdɔ:lɪ; ˋdɔlɪ/ *n* **1** (child's word for a) doll (儿语)洋娃娃. **2** (*cinema* 影) movable support for a cine or television camera 摄影机移动车.

□ ˈ**dolly-bird** (also **dolly**) *n* (*dated Brit infml sexist* 旧, 口, 性别偏见) pretty, fashionably dressed girl who is not thought of as very intelligent 漂亮、时髦却不大聪明的姑娘.

dol·men /ˈdɒlmen; ˋdɑlmɛn/ *n* = CROMLECH.

dol·or·ous /ˈdɒlərəs; *US* ˈdəʊlərəs; ˋdolərəs/ *adj* [usu attrib 通常作定语] (*fml* 文) sorrowful 哀伤的; 悲痛的.

dol·our (*US* **dolor**) /ˈdɒlə(r); *US* ˈdəʊlər; ˋdolɚ/ *n* [U, C] (*arch* 古) grief or sorrow 哀伤; 悲痛.

dolphin 海豚

dol·phin /ˈdɒlfɪn; ˋdɑlfɪn/ *n* mammal that looks like a large fish and lives in the sea 海豚. Cf 参看 PORPOISE.

dolt /dəʊlt; dolt/ *n* (*derog* 贬) stupid person 蠢人; 笨蛋; 傻瓜.

▷ **dolt·ish** *adj* stupid 愚蠢的; 愚笨的.

-dom *suff* 后缀 **1** (with *vs* and *adjs* forming *ns* 与动词和形容词结合构成名词) condition or state of ...的状况或地位: *boredom* ○ *freedom*. **2** (with *ns* 与名词结合) (**a**) rank or domain of ...的职位、级别、地位或领域: *dukedom* ○ *kingdom*. (**b**) group of ...的群体: *officialdom*.

do·main /dəʊˈmeɪn; doˋmen/ *n* **1** lands owned or ruled by a nobleman, government, etc (贵族、政府等的)领

地，领土: *trespass on the King's domain* 私闯国王领地 ○ (*fig* 比喻) *The kitchen is my wife's domain; she doesn't like me going into it.* 厨房是我妻子的领地，她不愿意让我进去. **2** field of thought, knowledge or activity (思想、知识或活动的)领域，范围，范畴: *(in) the domain of political science* (在)政治学领域(内) ○ *Military history is really outside my domain.* 我对军事史实在一窍不通.

dome /dəʊm; dom/ *n* **1** rounded roof with a circular base 穹顶; 圆屋顶: *the dome of St Paul's cathedral* 圣保罗大教堂的穹顶. **2** thing shaped like this 圆顶形物; 穹形物: *the dome of a hill, the night sky, a bald head* 山包、黑夜的天穹、光秃的头顶.
▷ **domed** *adj* [usu attrib 通常作定语] having or shaped like a dome 有穹顶的; 圆顶形的: *a domed forehead* 隆起的前额.

Domes·day Book /ˈdu:mzdeɪ bʊk; ˈdumzdeˌbʊk/ **the Domesday Book** record of the ownership, value etc of lands in England, made in 1086 by order of William the Conqueror 地籍簿(1086 年英王威廉一世钦定的地产清册).

do·mestic /dəˈmestɪk; dəˈmɛstɪk/ *adj* [usu attrib 通常作定语] **1** of the home, household or family 家庭的; 家务的: *domestic water, gas, etc supplies* 家庭用水、用气等的供应 ○ *a domestic help*, ie a servant, esp a cleaner 佣人(尤指清洁工) ○ *domestic bliss, unrest, upheavals, etc* 家庭的欢乐、不宁、剧变等 ○ *She's very domestic*, ie prefers home life to going out, or is good at and likes cooking, housework, etc. 她非常喜欢家庭生活(深居简出或善于烹饪、做家务等). **2** of or inside a particular country, not foreign or international 本国的; 国内的: *domestic trade, exports, production, etc* 国内贸易、本产出口、本地产品 ○ *domestic flights*, ie to and from places within a country 国内班机. **3** (of animals) kept on farms or as pets; not wild (指动物)驯养的，作宠物饲养的，非野生的.
▷ **do·mestic** *n* household servant, esp a cleaner 仆人，佣人(尤指清洁工).
do·mest·ic·ally /-klɪ; -klɪ/ *adv*.
□ **doˌmestic ˈscience** = HOME ECONOMICS (HOME).

do·mest·ic·ate /dəˈmestɪkeɪt; dəˈmɛstəˌket/ *v* [Tn esp passive 尤用于被动语态] **1** make (sb) used to or fond of housework and home life 使(某人)习惯于或喜爱家务和家庭生活: *He's become a lot more domesticated since his marriage.* 他婚后已非常恋家了. **2** tame (an animal) 驯养(动物). ▷ **do·mest·ica·tion** /dəˌmestɪˈkeɪʃn; dəˌmɛstəˈkeʃən/ *n* [U].

do·mest·icity /ˌdəʊmeˈstɪsətɪ, ˌdɒm-; ˌdomɛsˈtɪsətɪ, ˌdɑm-/ *n* [U] home or family life 家庭生活: *a scene of cosy domesticity* 闲适的家庭生活景象.

domi·cile /ˈdɒmɪsaɪl; ˈdɑməsl̩/ *n* (*fml or law* 文或律) a person's place of residence, esp as officially established for purposes of taxation, etc 住处，住所(尤指正式住址，据此履行纳税等法律义务者).
▷ **domi·ciled** *adj* [pred 作表语] having one's domicile in a place 有固定住所: *be domiciled in Britain, London, etc* 在英国、伦敦等有固定住所.

domi·cili·ary /ˌdɒmɪˈsɪlɪərɪ; *US* ˌdɒmɪˈsɪlɪerɪ; ˌdɑməˈsɪlɪˌɛrɪ/ *adj* [pred 作表语] (*fml* 文) of, to or at sb's home 住所的; 向住处; 在家中: *a domiciliary visit*, eg by a doctor or priest 家访(如医生、牧师等所进行的).

dom·in·ant[1] /ˈdɒmɪnənt; ˈdɑmənənt/ *adj* **1 ~ (in sth)** most important or prominent; dominating 最重要的; 最突出的; 占支配地位的: *She's the dominant child in the group.* 她是这一群孩子中的孩子头. ○ *the dominant flavour in a dish* 一份菜肴的主要香味 ○ *The castle stands in a dominant position above the town.* 古堡耸立在市镇中一个高处. **2** (*biology* 生) (of an inherited characteristic) appearing in offspring even when a genetically opposing characteristic is also inherited (指遗传特征)显性的，优势的. Cf 参看 RECESSIVE. ▷ **dom·in·ance** /-nəns; -nəns/ *n* [U]: *the absolute dominance of the governing party* 执政党的绝对优势.

dom·in·ant[2] /ˈdɒmɪnənt; ˈdɑmənənt/ *n* **1** (*music* 音) fifth note of a scale; chord or key based on this 音阶的第五音; 属音和弦; 属音. **2** (*biology* 生) dominant gene 显性基因.

dom·in·ate /ˈdɒmɪneɪt; ˈdɑməˌnet/ *v* **1** [I, Tn] (**a**) have control of or a very strong influence on (people, events, etc) 支配，统治，控制，影响(人、事等): *He has authority, but he doesn't try to dominate (others).* 他有权威，但并不想控制别人. ○ *She dominated the meeting by sheer force of character.* 她单凭个人气势就镇住了会场. (**b**) be the most obvious or important person or thing in (sth) 在(某事物)中处于优势或占上风; 占最重要地位: *Price tends to dominate all other considerations.* 首先考虑的往往是价格问题. ○ *My weekend was dominated by housework.* 我的周末全用在做家务上了. **2** [Tn] (of a high place) overlook (sth) (指高处)高于(某物): *The Acropolis dominates the city of Athens.* 雅典的卫城高耸于雅典全城之上. ▷ **dom·ina·tion** /ˌdɒmɪˈneɪʃn; ˌdɑməˈneʃən/ *n* [U]: *His defeat ended American domination of the sport.* 他的失利结束了美国在该项运动中称霸的地位. ○ *under foreign domination* 在外国统治下.

dom·in·eer /ˌdɒmɪˈnɪə(r); ˌdɑməˈnɪr/ *v* [I, Ipr] **~ (over sb)** (*derog* 贬) try to make sb do exactly what one wants by ordering him about, regardless of what he wants to do 对某人发号施令; 专横跋扈: *He domineered, and the rest of us hated it.* 他行事专横，我们大家都讨厌他这种作风.
▷ **dom·in·eer·ing** /ˌdɒmɪˈnɪərɪŋ; ˌdɑməˈnɪrɪŋ/ *adj* wanting to control others; overbearing 专横的; 跋扈的: *a domineering husband, manner, personality* 专横的丈夫、作风、个性. **dom·in·eer·ingly** *adv*.

Do·min·ican /dəˈmɪnɪkən; dəˈmɪnɪkən/ *adj* of the religious Order of Preachers founded by St Dominic, also called the Black Friars 多明我会的(多明我会为圣多明我创建的布道兄弟会，俗称黑衣兄弟会).
▷ **Do·min·ican** *n* priest, brother or nun in this order 多明我会神甫、修士或修女.

do·min·ion /dəˈmɪnɪən; dəˈmɪnjən/ *n* **1** [U] **~ (over sb/sth)** (*fml* 文) authority to rule; effective control 统治; 管辖: *under foreign dominion* 在外国统治下 ○ *have/be given dominion over peoples, lives, etc* 具有[被授予]统治各民族、生杀予夺等的权力. **2** [C] area controlled by one government or ruler 领土; 版图: *the vast dominions of the Chinese Empire* 中华帝国广阔的版图. **3** (often 常作 **Dominion**) [C] (formerly) any of the self-governing territories of the British Commonwealth (旧时)英联邦的自治领之一.

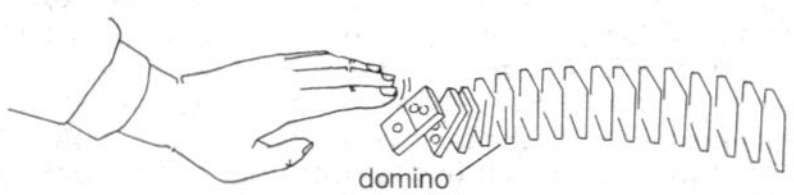

dom·ino /ˈdɒmɪnəʊ; ˈdɑməˌno/ *n* (*pl* **~es**) (**a**) [C] small flat oblong block marked on one side with two groups of dots, used in the game of dominoes 多米诺骨牌. (**b**) **dominoes** [sing *v*] game played with a set of 28 dominoes 28张一套的多米诺骨牌戏.
□ **ˈdomino effect** effect of one (esp political) event in one place making similar events happen one after the other elsewhere 多米诺效应(尤指政治方面): *Employers fear a domino effect if the strike is successful*, ie that there will be many other strikes as a result. 雇主们担心一旦罢工胜利就会引起多米诺效应. ⇨illus 见插图.

don[1] /dɒn; dɑn/ *n* **1** (*Brit*) teacher at a university, esp at an Oxford or a Cambridge college 大学教师(尤指在牛津大学或剑桥大学任教者). **2** title used before a man's Christian name in Spanish-speaking countries 先生(西班牙语国家对男子的尊称，用于教名前): *Don Felipe* 唐·菲力浦.
▷ **don·nish** /ˈdɒnɪʃ; ˈdɑnɪʃ/ *adj* (*esp Brit*) like (that of) a university don, who is usu considered to be clever, but unrealistic, forgetful, etc 像大学教师似的，学究式的(通常指聪明而不现实、健忘等): *a donnish remark, manner, sense of humour* 学究式的言语、仪态、幽默感.

don[2] /dɒn; dɑn/ *v* (**-nn-**) [Tn] (*fml* 文) put on (clothes, etc) 穿上，披上，戴上(衣物等): (*fig* 比喻) *He quickly donned a welcoming smile as his guests arrived.* 客人一到，他立刻笑脸相迎. Cf 参看 DOFF.

do·nate /dəʊˈneɪt; *US* ˈdəʊneɪt; ˈdonet/ *v* [Tn, Dn·pr] **~ sth (to sb/sth)** give (money, goods, etc), esp to a

charity; contribute sth 捐赠, 赠送(财物等)(尤指对慈善事业): *donate large sums to relief organizations* 向救济组织捐赠巨款.
▷ **do·na·tion** /dəʊˈneɪʃn; doˈneʃən/ *n* (**a**) [C] thing donated 捐赠物: *a donation to/for Amnesty International* 给大赦国际的捐款. (**b**) [U] donating or b ing donated 捐赠; 赠送.

done[1] *pp* of DO.

done[2] /dʌn; dʌn/ *adj* [pred 作表语] **1** (of food) cooked enough (指食物)煮熟: *The joint isn't quite done yet.* 这一大块肉煮得不太熟. **2** (*infml* 口) socially acceptable 社会上认可: *Smoking between courses simply isn't done.* 吃饭时在两道菜之间吸烟是不得体的. **3** (idm 习语) **be the done thing** be conventional or acceptable behaviour 符合传统的或可以容许的行为: *For most people it is still the done thing to get married.* 对于大多数人来说, 结婚仍然是天经地义的事. **be/have done with sb/sth** no longer work at sth or be involved with sb/sth 不再做某事物; 与某人[某事物]再无关系: *Let's spend another half an hour painting and then have done with it.* 我们再画半个小时把它画完吧. **over and done with** completely finished 完结; 了结; 结束: *Their relationship is over and done with.* 他们的关系完全断绝了. **what is done cannot be undone** (*saying* 谚) something that has already been done cannot be changed 已成定局, 无法改变; 木已成舟.
▷ **done** *interj* (used to show that one accepts an offer 用以表示接受一建议): *'I'll give you £500 for the car.' 'Done!'* '这辆汽车, 我给你500英镑.' '说定了!'

D

don·jon /ˈdɒndʒən; ˈdɑndʒən/ *n* large, strongly fortified central tower of a medieval castle 中世纪城堡中巨大而坚固的主塔.

Don Juan /ˌdɒn ˈdʒu:ən; dɑnˈdʒuən/ *n* (*infml* 口) man who has great sexual success with women 唐璜; 甚得女子欢心的男子: *Despite his looks he's said to be something of a Don Juan.* 尽管他其貌不扬, 但据说是个很得女人欢心的风流荡子.

don·key /ˈdɒŋkɪ; ˈdɑŋkɪ/ *n* (*pl* **~s**) **1** animal of the horse family, with short legs and long ears 驴. **2** stupid or stubborn person 愚蠢或固执的人: *He's an absolute donkey.* 他是个十足的蠢驴. **3** (idm 习语) **ˈdonkey's years** (*Brit infml* 口) a very long time 很长的时间; 很久; 猴年马月: *It's donkey's years since we've seen each other.* 我们有年头儿没见面了. ○ *The new motorway won't be ready for donkey's years.* 要修好新高速公路, 那得等到猴年马月了. **talk the hind legs off a donkey** ⇨ TALK[2].
□ **ˈdonkey engine** small extra engine, esp on a ship's deck 小型辅助发动机(尤指置于甲板上者).
ˈdonkey jacket workman's thick weatherproof jacket (工人穿的厚而短的)风雨衣.
ˈdonkey-work *n* [U] hard dull part of a job; drudgery 乏味而苦的工作; 苦活儿: *Typical — we do the donkey-work and he takes the credit!* 重活我们干, 功劳归他得——一向如此!

donor /ˈdəʊnə(r); ˈdonɚ/ *n* **1** person who gives or donates sth 捐赠者; 赠送者. **2** (*medical* 医) person who provides blood for transfusion, organs for transplantation, etc 献血者; 捐献器官者: *a blood donor* 献血者 ○ *The heart transplant will take place as soon as a suitable donor can be found.* 一旦找到适宜捐献心脏的人, 即可进行移植手术. ○ [attrib 作定语] *donor organs* 捐献的器官.

Don Quix·ote /ˌdɒn ˈkwɪksət; ˌdɑn ˈkwɪksət/ *n* person with high but completely unrealistic ideals; impractical dreamer 唐吉诃德(完全不切实际的理想主义者); 梦想者. Cf 参看 QUIXOTIC.

don't ⇨ DO.

doodle /ˈdu:dl; ˈdudḷ/ *v* [I, Ipr] make meaningless drawings, scribbles etc, while one is or should be thinking about sth else (当精神不集中于某事时)胡写, 乱画: *Stop doodling on my notebook!* 别在我的笔记本上乱画! ▷ **doodle** *n*: *a page covered in doodles* 胡写乱画的一页.

doom[1] /du:m; dum/ *n* [U] **1** (*rhet* 修辞) death or ruin; any terrible and inevitable fate 死亡; 毁灭; 劫数; 厄运: *meet/go to one's doom* 死亡 ○ *send a man to his doom* 使某人陷入绝境. **2** = DOOMSDAY. **3** (idm 习语) **the crack of doom** ⇨ CRACK[1]. **a prophet of doom** ⇨ PROPHET.

doom[2] /du:m; dum/ *v* [esp passive 尤用于被动语态: Tn, Tn·pr, Cn·t] **~ sb (to sth)** condemn sb (to death, destruction, failure, etc) 注定某人(死亡、毁灭、失败等): *The plan was doomed from the start.* 那计划从一开始就注定要失败. ○ *Are whales doomed to extinction?* 鲸鱼是否注定要绝种? ○ *We loathe each other, yet we seem doomed constantly to meet.* 我们相互厌恶, 但似乎偏偏冤家常碰头.

dooms·day /ˈdu:mzdeɪ; ˈdumzˌde/ *n* [U] **1** day of the Last Judgement; the end of the world 最后审判日; 世界末日. Cf 参看 DOMESDAY BOOK. **2** (idm 习语) **till ˈdoomsday** for ever; a long time 永远; 很长时间: *This work will take me till doomsday.* 这工作要花我一辈子的时间.

door /dɔ:(r); dɔr/ *n* **1** (**a**) movable barrier that closes the entrance to a building, room, cupboard, car, etc 门: *hinged/sliding/revolving doors* 有铰链的门[拉门/旋转门] ○ *hammer on the door* 砰砰地敲门 ○ *open, shut, close, lock, bolt the door* 开、关、闭、锁、栓门 ○ *the front/back door*, ie main door at the front/back of a house 前[后]门 ○ *a four-door saloon car* 四门轿车. ⇨ illus at App 1 见附录1之插图, pages vi, xii. (**b**) = DOORWAY. **2** (idm 习语) **at death's door** ⇨ DEATH. **behind closed doors** ⇨ CLOSE[4]. **by/through the back door** ⇨ BACK[2]. **darken sb's door** ⇨ DARKEN. **(from) ˌdoor to ˈdoor** (from) house to house 从一家门口到另一家门口: *The journey takes about an hour, door to door.* 从这家到那家的路程要用一小时. ○ *He went from door to door, selling encyclopaedias.* 他逐门逐户去推销百科全书. ○ [attrib 作定语] *a ˌdoor-to-door ˈsalesman* 挨户推销的售货员. **the door to sth** the means of getting or reaching sth 获得或达到某事物的门路或手段: *Our courses are the door to success in English.* 我们的课程是学习英语的成功之路. **a foot in the door** ⇨ FOOT[1]. **keep the wolf from the door** ⇨ WOLF. **lay sth at sb's ˈdoor** say that sb is responsible for sth that has gone wrong 归咎于某人: *The blame for the disaster has been laid firmly at the company's door.* 这场大祸罪责全在公司. **leave the door open** ⇨ LEAVE[1]. **lie at sb's door** ⇨ LIE[2]. **lock, etc the stable door after the horse has bolted** ⇨ STABLE[2]. **next ˈdoor (to sb/sth)** in the next building, room, etc 邻居; 隔壁; 邻室: *go next door to borrow some milk* 到邻居家借点牛奶 ○ *They live next door to the library.* 他们住在图书馆隔壁. **next door to** nearly; almost 几乎; 近乎; 差不多: *I'm afraid it's next door to impossible that we'll be there on time.* 看来我们几乎不可能按时到达那里了. **(be) on the ˈdoor** (*infml* 口) (at a public meeting, concert, etc) (stand) at the door, eg to collect tickets, give directions, etc (为公众集会、音乐会等)把门(如收票、指引方向等). **out of ˈdoors** in the open air 在户外; 在露天: *eat, sleep, walk, etc out of doors* 在户外吃、睡、散步等. **show sb the door; show sb to the door** ⇨ SHOW[2]. **shut/slam the door in sb's face** refuse to talk to or have any dealing with sb 拒绝与某人谈话; 拒绝与某人打交道. **shut the door on sth** ⇨ SHUT. **two, three, etc doors aˈlong/aˈway/ˈdown** in the next house but one, two, etc 在第二、第三…家: *Our other branch is just a few doors down the road.* 沿这条路再走几家就是我们的另一个分店.
□ **ˈdoorbell** *n* bell inside a building that can be rung by visitors outside 门铃. ⇨illus at App 1 见附录1之插图, page vi.
ˈdoor-frame *n* frame into which a door fits 门框.
ˈdoor-handle *n* handle that opens and closes a door (by releasing a latch) 门把儿; 门拉手. ⇨illus at App 1 见附录1之插图, page xii.
ˈdoor-keeper *n* = DOORMAN.
ˈdoorknob *n* round knob turned to open a door 球形门拉手.
ˈdoor-knocker *n* = KNOCKER.
ˈdoorman /-mən; -mən/ *n* (*pl* **-men** /-mən; -mən/) (*US*) = PORTER[2]: *Leave a message with the doorman.* 给看门人留个话.
ˈdoormat *n* **1** mat placed near a door, for wiping dirt from one's shoes (置于门前的)蹭鞋垫. **2** (*fig infml* 比喻, 口) person who allows others to treat him without respect 逆来顺受的人: *Stand up for yourself a bit —*

don't be such a doormat! 长点骨气吧——别老这么忍着任人践踏!

ˈ**doornail** *n* (idm 习语) **dead as a doornail** ⇨ DEAD.

ˈ**door-plate** *n* metal plate on a door showing the name of the person living or working in the room or building 门牌; 户名牌.

ˈ**doorpost** *n* (idm 习语) **deaf as a post/doorpost** ⇨ DEAF.

ˈ**doorstep** *n* **1** step leading up to (usu) an outside door 门阶: *empty milk bottles on the doorstep* 放在门阶上的空牛奶瓶. ⇨illus at App 1 见附录1之插图, page vi. **2** (idm 习语) **on one's ˈdoorstep** very near 很近: *In our holiday villas you'll have both the beach and the mountains on your doorstep.* 我们的度假别墅离海滩和山都很近.

ˈ**doorstop** *n* device to prevent a door from closing or from hitting a wall, etc when it is opened 制门器(防止门关闭的装置); 门碰头(防止门碰墙的装置).

ˈ**doorway** *n* opening, filled by a door, into a building, room, car, etc 门口: *in the doorway* 在门口.

dope /dəʊp; dop/ *n* **1** [U] (*sl* 俚) (**a**) harmful drug (eg hashish); narcotic 毒品(如大麻); 麻醉剂: [attrib 作定语] *a dope-addict* 吸毒成瘾者. (**b**) medicine, esp a sedative drug 药; (尤指)镇静剂. **2** [C] (*infml* 口) stupid person 笨蛋; 蠢货: *You've got the picture upside-down, you dope!* 你把画挂倒了, 你这笨蛋! **3** [U] **~ (on sb/sth)** (*sl* 俚) facts not generally known that are provided by a well-informed person 内幕消息; 消息灵通者透露的消息: *I want the dope on his criminal connections.* 我想知道他私通的内情. **4** [U] thick liquid used as a lubricant, varnish, etc (润滑油、涂料等)黏稠液体.

▷ **dope** *v* [Tn] (**a**) give a narcotic or stimulant drug to (esp a race-horse, an athlete, etc) 给(尤指参赛的马、运动员等)使用麻醉品或兴奋剂. (**b**) add a drug to (food, drink, etc) 在(食物、饮料等中)加麻醉剂.

dopey (also **dopy**) /ˈdəʊpɪ; ˈdopɪ/ *adj* (**-ier, -iest**) **1** (*infml* 口) dazed or sleepy, as if drugged 昏沉欲睡的; 似受到麻醉的: *I'm feeling really dopey this morning.* 今天上午我一直昏昏沉沉的. **2** (*sl* 俚) stupid 愚蠢的; 迟钝的.

Doric /ˈdɒrɪk; *US* ˈdɔːr-; ˈdɔrɪk/ *adj* (*architecture* 建) of the oldest and simplest of the five orders of classical Greek architecture 多利斯式的(古希腊建筑五种柱式中最古老、最简单者). Cf 参看 CORINTHIAN 2, IONIC.

dorm /dɔːm; dɔrm/ *n* (*infml* 口) dormitory 宿舍.

dor·mant /ˈdɔːmənt; ˈdɔrmənt/ *adj* temporarily inactive 暂时不活动的; 休眠的; 蛰伏的: *a dormant volcano*, ie neither extinct nor erupting 休眠火山 ○ *Many plants lie dormant throughout the winter*, ie alive but not growing. 许多植物冬天呈休眠状态. ○ *As soon as they met again his dormant love for her was rekindled.* 他们一见面, 他对她的旧情如干柴烈火般又重新燃起.

dormer /ˈdɔːmə(r); ˈdɔrmɚ/ (also ˌ**dormer-ˈwindow**) *n* upright window built in a sloping roof (建于斜屋顶上的)天窗, 老虎窗. ⇨illus at App 1 见附录1之插图, page vii.

dorm·it·ory /ˈdɔːmɪtrɪ; *US* -tɔːrɪ; ˈdɔrməˌtorɪ/ *n* **1** sleeping-room with a number of beds, esp in a school or some other institution 宿舍. **2** (*US*) building at a college, university, etc containing students' rooms for living and sleeping (大学等的)学生宿舍.

□ ˈ**dormitory town** (*Brit*) town from which people travel to work elsewhere 郊外住宅区.

dor·mouse /ˈdɔːmaʊs; ˈdɔrˌmaʊs/ *n* (*pl* **dor·mice** /ˈdɔːmaɪs; ˈdɔrˌmaɪs/) small animal like a mouse with a furry tail 榛睡鼠.

dor·sal /ˈdɔːsl; ˈdɔrsḷ/ *adj* [attrib 作定语] (*anatomy* 解) of or on the back of an animal or a plant (动植物的)背部的, 背侧的, 背上的: *the dorsal fin*, eg of a shark 背鳍(如鲨鱼的). ⇨illus at FISH 见 FISH 之插图. Cf 参看 VENTRAL.

dory[1] /ˈdɔːrɪ; ˈdɔrɪ/ *n* (*US*) light flat-bottomed rowing boat used by fishermen off the Atlantic coast of the US (美国东海岸渔民用的)轻型平底划艇.

dory[2] *n* [C, U] (also ˌ**John ˈDory**) type of edible seafish 海鲂.

dos·age /ˈdəʊsɪdʒ; ˈdosɪdʒ/ *n* (usu *sing* 通常作单数) amount of medicine to be taken at a time or over a period (药物一次或一阶段的)剂量: *Do not exceed the recommended dosage.* 不要超过规定的剂量.

do's and don'ts ⇨ DO[3] 3.

dose /dəʊs; dos/ *n* **1** amount of medicine to be taken at one time 一次剂量; 一剂; 一服: *give/administer the correct dose* 给规定的剂量. **2** amount of radiation received by sb/sth at one time (某人[某物]接受放射线的)一次剂量: *a lethal dose of radiation* 致死的辐射量. **3** (*fig infml* 比喻, 口) (**a**) any experience of sth unpleasant 不愉快的经历: *a dose of 'flu, boring conversation, bad weather* 一次流感、令人厌倦的谈话、恶劣的天气 ○ *I can only stand her in small doses*, ie for a short time. 我对她只能忍让片刻. (**b**) any experience of sth enjoyable 愉快的经历: *What you need is a good dose of laughter.* 你需要的是大笑一场. **4** (*sl* 俚) venereal infection 性病; 花柳病: *give sb/catch a dose* 把花柳病传染给某人[染上花柳病]. **5** (idm 习语) **like a dose of ˈsalts** (*sl* 俚) very fast 很快; 一下子: *He gets through his pay like a dose of salts, and by Monday he's broke.* 一发工资, 他就很快花个精光, 到了星期一便身无分文了.

▷ **dose** *v* [Tn, Tn·pr] **~ sb/oneself (with sth)** give sb/oneself a dose (of sth) 给某人[自己]一定剂量的药: *heavily dosed with pain-killing drugs* 大剂量地使用了止痛药.

doss /dɒs; dɑs/ *v* (phr v) **doss down** (*Brit sl* 俚) lie down to sleep, esp when one has not got a proper bed 凑合躺下睡觉, 将就过夜(尤指无适当的床): *We dossed down on Tony's floor after the party.* 聚会过后, 我们就躺在汤尼家的地板上睡了.

▷ **dosser** *n* (*Brit sl* 俚) person without a home who sleeps in the streets or in cheap lodgings; vagrant 露宿街头者; 常居于廉价客栈者; 流浪者.

□ ˈ**doss-house** *n* (*Brit sl* 俚) cheap lodging-house, esp one used by vagrants 廉价客栈(尤指供流浪者投宿者).

dos·sier /ˈdɒsɪeɪ; *US also* ˈdɔːsɪə(r); ˈdɑsɪˌe, ˈdɑsɪɚ/ *n* set of documents containing information about a person, an event, etc; file (有关人、事等的)材料, 卷宗, 档案.

dot /dɒt; dɑt/ *n* **1** small round mark 小圆点: *Join the dots up to complete the drawing.* 顺点连线把图画好. **2** such a mark used as a symbol in writing (eg above the letters i and j), mathematics (eg the decimal point), music, representing a short sound in Morse code, etc 字母上的点(如i和j上的); 小数点; 音乐符号上的点; 摩尔斯电码代表短音的点. ⇨App 3 见附录3. **3** anything resembling a dot; a small quantity 点状物; 少量, 微量, 一点儿: *The island was just a dot on the horizon.* 该岛只是天水交接处的一个黑点. ○ *I like just a dot of milk in my tea.* 我喜欢在茶里稍掺一点牛奶. **4** (idm 习语) **on the ˈdot** (*infml* 口) exactly on time, or at the time specified 准时地; 在指定的时刻: *He's very punctual — always arrives on the dot.* 他很守时——总是按时到. ○ *leave at 5 o'clock on the dot/on the dot of 5 o'clock* 准于五点整离开. **the year dot** ⇨ YEAR.

▷ **dot** *v* (**-tt-**) **1** [Tn] mark (sth) with a dot 以小圆点标出(某物). **2** [esp passive 尤用于被动语态: Tn·pr, Tn·p] place (things or people) here and there; scatter 将(物或人)分布各处; 分散: *The sky was dotted with stars.* 天空繁星密布. ○ *We've dotted a few chairs about.* 我们在周围放了几把椅子. **3** [Tn, Tn·pr, Dn·n](*infml* 口) hit (sb) 打, 击(某人): *He dotted me in the eye.* 他击中了我的眼睛. ○ *Shut up or I'll dot you one!* 闭嘴, 要不我就揍你! **4** (idm 习语) **dot one's/the ˌi's and cross one's/the ˈt's** complete the final details of a task 一丝不苟地完成任务.

□ ˌ**dot ˈmatrix** (*computing* 计) grid of dots used to form letters, numbers, etc in printing 点阵(印刷中用以组成字母、数字等的矩阵): [attrib 作定语] *a ˌdot matrix ˈprinter* 点阵打印机.

dotted ˈline **1** line of dots showing where sth is to be written on a document, form, etc 点线; 虚线. **2** (idm 习语) **sign on the dotted line** ⇨ SIGN[2].

dot·age /ˈdəʊtɪdʒ; ˈdotɪdʒ/ *n* (idm 习语) **in one's dotage** confused in one's mind because of old age 年老昏聩.

dote /dəʊt; dot/ *v* [Ipr] **~ on sb/sth** show (too) much fondness for sb/sth 热爱、溺爱或宠爱某人[某事物]: *She dotes on her grandchildren.* 她十分钟爱孙儿女. ○ *I just dote on hot buttered scones!* 我就是喜欢吃涂黄油的热司康饼!

▷ **dot·ing** *adj* [attrib 作定语] very or excessively loving and devoted 溺爱的; 偏爱的; 宠爱的: *a doting husband, son, parent, etc* 宠爱妻子的丈夫、非常孝顺的儿子、溺爱子女的家长. **dot·ingly** *adv*.

dottle /ˈdɒtl; ˈdɑtl̩/ *n* [U] partly burnt tobacco left in a pipe after smoking (烟斗中吸剩的)残烟丝.

dotty /ˈdɒtɪ; ˈdɑtɪ/ *adj* (**-ier, -iest**) (*infml* 口 *esp Brit*) **1** foolish; silly; eccentric 傻的; 蠢的; 古怪的: *She was getting a bit dotty and could never be left alone.* 她越来越见傻, 决不可无人照看. ○ *Not another of your dotty ideas for making money!* 你不要再出那些赚钱的馊主意了! **2** [pred 作表语] **~ about sb/sth** very fond of or enthusiastic about sb/sth 非常喜爱某人[某事物]; 对某人[某事物]极感兴趣: *She's dotty about this latest boyfriend.* 她非常喜欢这个新交的男朋友. ▷ **dot·ti·ness** *n* [U].

D

double[1] /ˈdʌbl; ˈdʌbl̩/ *adj* [usu attrib 通常作定语] **1** twice as much or as many (as usual) 加倍的; 两倍的: *a double helping* 一客双份的食物 ○ *two double whiskies* 两杯双份的威士忌酒 ○ *the new bleach with double strength for killing germs* 杀菌力特强的新型漂白剂. **2** having or made of two things or parts that are equal or similar 由两个相等或相似部分组成的; 双的: *Look, double yellow lines — you mustn't park here.* 喂, 这是双黄线——不能在这儿停车. ○ *'I didn't do nothing' is a double negative*, ie two negatives where only one is needed. I didn't do nothing 是双重的否定(只需一个否定词即可). ○ *a double-page advertisement* 一则占左右两页的广告 ○ *'Otter' is spelt with a double t.* otter 一字中有两个 t. **3** made for two people or things 供两人或两物用的; 双人的: *a double room, garage, etc* 双人房间、供停放两辆车的车房 ○ *a double wedding*, ie of two couples 两对新婚夫妇的婚礼. **4** combining two things or qualities 两种事物结合在一起的: *a double meaning, purpose, aim, etc* 双重意义、目的、目标等 ○ *the double advantage of being easy and cheap* 既方便又便宜的双重优点 ○ *She leads a double life*, ie Her life has two different (perhaps sharply contrasting) aspects, eg being a police officer and a drug dealer. 她过着双重生活(如又是警察又是毒品贩子). **5** (of flowers) having more than the usual number of petals (指花)重瓣的. **6** (idm 习语) **in double ˈharness** with a partner, or with a husband or wife 两人一起; 夫妻一起: *The brothers work in double harness.* 哥儿俩一起工作.

□ ˌ**double ˈagent** person who spies for two rival countries at the same time 双重间谍.

ˌ**double-ˈbass** (also **bass**) *n* largest and lowest-pitched instrument of the violin family 低音提琴. ⇨illus at App 1 见附录1之插图, page xi.

ˌ**double ˈbed** bed made for two people 双人床.

ˌ**double-ˈbedded** *adj* [usu attrib 通常作定语] (of a hotel room) having a double bed (or two single ones) (指旅馆房间)有双人床的, 有两张单人床的.

ˌ**double ˈbill** two films, plays, etc presented to an audience one after the other 双场(两场电影、戏剧等同场先后演出).

ˌ**double ˈbind** dilemma 进退两难.

ˌ**double ˈbluff** clever deception, eg telling an enemy the truth while knowing that he will assume you are lying 双重诈术(如告诉敌手实情而料其会以真为假).

ˌ**double ˈchin** fold of fat below the chin 双下巴.

ˌ**double ˈcream** (*Brit*) thick cream that contains a lot of milk fat 高脂奶油.

ˌ**double ˈdate** (*esp US infml* 口) date involving two (separate) couples 两对男女在一起的约会.

ˌ**double-ˈdealer** *n* (*derog* 贬) person who says one thing and means another; deceiver 口是心非的人; 两面派. ˌ**double-ˈdealing** *n* [U].

ˌ**double-ˈdecker** *n* **1** (*esp Brit*) bus with two floors 双层公共汽车. **2** (*esp US*) sandwich with two layers of filling 双层夹心三明治.

ˌ**double ˈDutch** (*Brit infml* 口) incomprehensible talk; written gibberish 莫名其妙的话; 晦涩的文字: *This article's so full of jargon it's just double Dutch to me.* 这文章满篇术语, 对我直如天书.

double entendre /ˌdu:bl ɑ:nˈtɑ:ndrə; ˌdubl̩ ɑnˈtɑndrə/ (*French* 法) word or phrase that can be understood in two ways, one of which contains a sexual allusion 双关语(其一有性的含意).

ˌ**double ˈentry** (*commerce* 商) system of bookkeeping in which each transaction is entered as a debit in one account and a credit in another 复式簿记.

ˌ**double ˈfigures** number that is 10 or over and 99 or less 两位数: *The inflation rate is into double figures*, ie above 10%. 通货膨胀率已进入两位数(10%以上).

ˌ**double ˈfirst** (graduate who gains a) first-class degree in two subjects at the same time or in successive years 双优荣誉学位(毕业生)(在两门学科中皆获优秀成绩者).

ˌ**double pneuˈmonia** pneumonia affecting both lungs 双肺肺炎.

ˌ**double ˈstandard** set of (usu moral) principles that discriminates against one of two groups, individuals, etc 双重标准(通常指道德方面): *He's got a double standard: it's all right for him to have affairs but not for her.* 他采取双重标准: 自己可以有外遇, 女方却不行.

ˌ**double ˈtake** delayed reaction to a situation, remark, etc, esp for comic effect (对情况、言语等)反应迟钝(尤指为产生滑稽效果者): *He did a double take when I said I was getting married.* 我告诉他我要结婚了, 他半天才恍然大悟.

ˈ**double-talk** *n* [U] way of talking that really means something very different from what it appears to mean, or nothing at all 指东说西或言之无物的话: *He gave us no real reasons, just the usual politician's double-talk.* 他没告诉我们真正理由, 只说了些政客常说的空话. — *v* [I, Tn·pr]: *double-talk one's way out of trouble* 说含糊其词的话以摆脱困境.

ˈ**double-think** *n* [U] (*derog* 贬) accepting or advocating contradictory ideas, principles, etc 思想矛盾(接受或提倡两种相矛盾的观念、原则等).

ˌ**double ˈtime** twice the usual wage, paid for working on a public holiday, etc (付给假日加班者的)双倍工资.

ˌ**double transitive ˈverb** (*linguistics* 语言) verb that takes an indirect object as well as a direct object, eg *offer* in *He offered me a job* 双及物动词(即要求直接宾语和间接宾语的动词, 如 He offered me a job 中的 offer).

double[2] /ˈdʌbl; ˈdʌbl̩/ *det* twice as much or as many (as usual, than sb/sth, etc) 两倍; 双倍: *His income is double hers.* 他的收入是她的两倍. ○ *He earns double what she does.* 他挣的比她挣的多一倍. ○ *We need double the amount we have.* 我们需要比现有的多一倍.

double[3] /ˈdʌbl; ˈdʌbl̩/ *adv* in twos or in two parts 成双; 成对; 成两部分: *When I saw her and her twin sister I thought I was seeing double.* 我看见她们孪生姐妹时还以为我把一个人看成俩了. ○ *sleep double*, ie two in a bed (for warmth, convenience, etc) 两人合睡一床(为取暖、方便等) ○ *fold a blanket double* 把毯子对折起来.

□ ˌ**double-ˈbarrelled** *adj* **1** (of a gun) having two barrels (指枪炮)双管的, 双筒的. **2** (*Brit*) (of a surname) having two parts, usu joined by a hyphen (as in *Day-Lewis*) (指姓)由两部分组成的(其间通常用连字符连结, 如 Day-Lewis).

ˌ**double-ˈbook** *v* [I, Tn] reserve (a particular hotel room, flight, ticket, etc) for more than one person at a time 为不止一人预订或保留(同一旅馆房间、飞机座位、票等): *They'd double-booked our seats and we had to wait for the next plane.* 他们把我们预订的座位又预订给他人了, 我们只好等下一班机了. ○ *They've double-booked me* (ie my seat, etc) *again!* 他们把我预订的(座位等)又重复预订给别人了! ˌ**double-ˈbooking** *n* [U, C].

ˌ**double-ˈbreasted** *adj* (of a coat or jacket) made to overlap across the chest (指大衣或夹克)有双排钮扣的.

ˌ**double-ˈcheck** *v* [I, Tn] check (sth) twice or with great care 复查; 仔细检查: *double-check figures, arrangements* 复核数字、审核计划. ˌ**double-ˈcheck** *n*: *do a double-check on sth* 复查某事.

ˌ**double-ˈcross** *v* [Tn] (*derog* 贬) cheat or betray (sb) after getting him to trust one (获取信任后)欺骗, 背叛, 出卖(某人). — *n*: *a double-cross that cost six lives* 损失了六条性命的叛卖行为.

ˌ**double-ˈdyed** *adj* [attrib 作定语] (*dated* 旧) very evil 邪恶的: *a ˌdouble-dyed ˈrogue, ˈscoundrel, etc* 罪恶多端的无赖、坏蛋等.

ˌ**double-ˈedged** *adj* **1** (of a knife, etc) having two edges (指刀等)双刃的. **2** (*fig* 比喻) (of a remark) having two possible meanings; ambiguous (指言语)模棱两可的, 含糊其辞的: *a ˌdouble-edged ˈargument, ˈcompliment, reˈply, etc* 语意含混的论据、恭维话、答复等.

ˌ**double-ˈfaced** *adj* insincere 伪善的.

ˌ**double-ˈglaze** *v* [Tn] fit two layers of glass to (the windows of a room, etc) to reduce heat loss, noise, etc 安两层玻璃于(窗户等): *The house is double-glazed back and front.* 这房子前后窗都是双层的. ˌ**double-ˈglazing** *n* [U]: *have double-glazing installed* 装有双层玻璃.

ˌ**double-ˈjointed** *adj* [usu pred 通常作表语] having very flexible joints that allow the fingers, arms or legs to bend backwards as well as forwards (手指、臂或腿)有双关节(可前后活动).

ˌ**double-ˈpark** *v* [I, Tn esp passive 尤用于被动语态] park (a car, etc) beside one already parked in a street 将(汽车等)并排停放于街道上另一汽车旁边: *Hurry up! I'm double-parked and the warden's coming.* 快点! 我这是并排停车, 检查员来啦.

ˌ**double-ˈquick** *adj, adv* (*infml* 口) very quick(ly) 快速(的); 急速(的).

ˌ**double-ˈstop** *v* [I, Tn] (*music* 音) play (two stopped notes) at the same time on a violin, etc (拉小提琴等时)奏双音.

double[4] /ˈdʌbl; ˋdʌbḷ/ *n* **1** [U] twice the (usual) number or amount 两倍; 加倍: *He's paid double for the same job.* 他做同样的工作, 而报酬比别人多一倍. **2** [C] **(a)** person or thing that looks very like another 酷似的人或物: *She's the double of her mother at the same age.* 她和她母亲年轻时十分相似. **(b)** (in a film) actor who replaces a star in the dangerous scenes (电影中的)特技替身演员. **3** [C] glass of spirits containing twice the usual amount 一杯双份的烈酒: *Two Scotches, please — and make those doubles, will you?* 请来两杯苏格兰威士忌——都要双份的, 好吗? **4** [C] bet on two horses in different races where any winnings from the first are staked again on the second 复式押注(下注于不同场次的两匹马, 第一场若赢即转押于第二场). **5 doubles** [pl] game (esp of tennis) in which one pair plays another 双打(尤指网球): *mixed doubles*, ie where each pair consists of a man and a woman 混合双打. **6 the double** [sing] (*sport* 体) two prizes won in similar competitions (在同类比赛中)两次获奖: *She's going for the double this year, the Olympics and the World Championship.* 今年她要争取奥林匹克赛和世界杯冠军赛的双料冠军. **7** [C] (in bridge) act of doubling (桥牌戏中)叫加倍. **8** [C] (in the game of darts) hit on the outer ring of the board, scoring double (投镖戏中)投中外环, 得分加倍. **9** (idm 习语) **at the ˈdouble** (*US* **on the ˈdouble**) (*infml* 口) quickly; hurrying 很快地; 赶紧地: *The boss wants you — you'd better get upstairs at the double.* 老板叫你——你最好赶紧上楼去. ˌ**double or ˈquits** paying twice what one owes or nothing at all, the decision being made by chance (eg throwing dice) 要么加倍赔钱, 要么欠款一笔勾销(如以掷色子决定).

double[5] /ˈdʌbl; ˋdʌbḷ/ *v* **1** [I, Tn] (cause sth to) become twice as much or as many (使某物)加倍: *The price of houses has virtually doubled over the past few years.* 房价这几年来简直涨了一倍. ○ *If you double all the quantities in the recipe it'll be enough for eight people.* 把菜谱上的各种用料都增加一倍, 就够八人吃了. **2** [Tn, Tn·p] **~ sth (up/over/across/back)** bend or fold sth in two 将某物对折: *double a blanket (over) for extra warmth* 为了暖和一些把毯子对折起来. **3** [Tn] (*nautical* 海) sail round (a cape, headland, promontory, etc) 绕(岬角、岛屿等)航行. **4** [Ipr] **~ as sth** **(a)** have a secondary function or use as sth 兼用作某物: *When we have guests, the sofa doubles as an extra bed.* 我们有客人时沙发可兼作临时的床用. **(b)** (of an actor) play (a second part) as well as another (指演员)兼任, 兼演: *His main part is the ghost, but he doubles as Fortinbras.* 他主要演剧中的鬼魂一角, 但也兼演福廷布拉斯. **5** [Tn] (*music* 音) play or sing the same music as (another instrument or voice) 兼奏(另一乐器); 兼唱(另一声部): *In this passage the violins double the sopranos.* 小提琴在本乐节兼作高音乐器演奏. **6** [I] (bridge) bid to cause the points lost or won by one's opponents to be twice as much as they would otherwise have been (桥牌)叫加倍. **7** (phr v) **double back** turn back in the opposite direction, esp unexpectedly 原路折回(尤指始料未及者): *The road ahead was flooded so we had to double back.* 前面的路已遭水淹, 我们只好原路折回. **double (sb) up** (cause sb to) bend the body (使某人)躬身, 弯腰: *be doubled up with laughter, pain, anger, etc* 笑、痛、气…得直不起腰. **double up (on sth/with sb)** (*infml* 口) share sth with another or others 共用: *We've only one room left: you'll have to double up with Peter.* 我们只余一个房间, 你只好和彼得合住一处了.

doub·let /ˈdʌblɪt; ˋdʌblɪt/ *n* **1** (formerly) short close-fitting jacket worn by men, with or without sleeves (旧时)男用紧身上衣或背心. **2** either of a pair of similar things, esp one of two words with the same origin but a different form or meaning, eg *hospital/hostel* 一对类似的东西中的一个; (尤指同源异形或异义的)双式词, 如 hospital/hostel.

doubly /ˈdʌblɪ; ˋdʌblɪ/ *adv* (used before *adjs* 用于形容词之前) **1** to twice the extent or amount 加倍地: *Make doubly sure that all the doors are locked*, ie check twice. 再查看一下是否所有的门都锁好了. **2** in two ways 两方面地; 双重地: *She is doubly gifted: as a writer and as an artist.* 她又是作家又是艺术家, 有双重天赋.

D

doubt[1] /daʊt; daʊt/ *n* **1** [U, C] **~ (about/as to sth); ~ (as to) whether...** (feeling of) uncertainty or disbelief 怀疑; 不确定; 不信任: *There's some doubt about his suitability for the job.* 他是否适合该工作有些疑问. ○ *There is (no) room for doubt.* (没)有怀疑的余地. ○ *I have grave doubts about her honesty.* 我很怀疑她是否诚实. ○ *The latest scientific discoveries cast doubt on earlier theories.* 科学上的最新发现使我们对以前的学说产生怀疑. ○ *She had her doubts (as to) whether he would come.* 她无法确定他是否来. ○ *Although a very religious man, he is still troubled by occasional doubts.* 他虽然笃信宗教, 但有时仍感到迷惘. **2** [U] **~ about sth/that...** (used after negatives to emphasize conviction 用于否定词后以强调深信不疑) reason for not believing sth 不相信: *There's not much doubt about it*, ie It is almost certain. 那件事情没有什么可疑之处. ○ *I have no doubt that you will succeed.* 我肯定你能成功. **3** (idm 习语) **beyond a/any ˈdoubt; beyond all (possible) ˈdoubt** certainly 无疑地: *She was beyond all doubt the finest ballerina of her day.* 她无疑是她那个时代最优秀的芭蕾舞演员. **give sb the benefit of the ˈdoubt** ⇨ BENEFIT. **in ˈdoubt** uncertain; undecided 不肯定的; 不确定的: *Their acceptance of the contract is still in doubt.* 他们是否接受那合同还说不准. ○ *If in doubt, don't*, ie Don't act unless you're certain. 没有把握就不要做. ˌ**no ˈdoubt** very probably 无疑地; 很可能: *No doubt he means to help, but in fact he just gets in the way.* 他确实是想帮忙, 然而事实上却只是帮倒忙. **without (a) ˈdoubt** certainly 无疑地; 确实地: *He is without doubt the cleverest student I've ever taught.* 他确实是我所教过的学生中最聪明的.

doubt[2] /daʊt; daʊt/ *v* [I, Tn, Tf] feel uncertain (about sth); question the truth of (sth) (对某事物)无把握, 有怀疑: *It is human to doubt.* 怀疑是人的天性. ○ *Do you doubt my word* (ie think I am not telling the truth)? 你怀疑我的话吗? ○ *I don't doubt that he'll come*, ie I'm sure he will. 我确信他会来. ○ *I doubt whether he'll come.* 我不敢肯定他来不来. ○ *I doubt if that was what he wanted.* 不知道那是不是他想要的. ▷ **doubter** *n*.

□ ˌ**doubting ˈThomas** person who refuses to believe sth until he has clear proof 有真凭实据才相信某事物的人: *She's a bit of a doubting Thomas — she won't believe you're back till she sees you.* 她是个眼见为实的人——除非她亲眼看见你, 否则绝不会相信你已经回来.

doubt·ful /ˈdaʊtfl; ˋdaʊtfəl/ *adj* **1** [usu pred 通常作表语] **~ (about sth/doing sth)** (of a person) feeling doubt; unsure (指人)感到怀疑, 不能确定: *feel doubtful about (the wisdom of) going/about whether to go or not* 拿不定主意去不去(不知道应否去). **2** causing doubt; uncertain 令人生疑的; 不肯定的: *The weather looks rather doubtful*, ie unsettled. 天气看来靠不住(可能会变天). ○ *a doubtful* (ie unreliable) *ally* 不可靠的盟友 ○ *It's a doubtful blessing*, ie It may or may not be one. 这是不是福不好说. **3** unlikely; improbable 未必的; 不大可能的: *It is extremely doubtful that anyone survived the explosion.* 在那场爆炸中很难有幸存者. **4** [attrib 作定

语] possibly dishonest, disreputable, etc; causing suspicion; questionable (诚实、名声等)不大好的, 可疑的, 有问题的: *a rather doubtful character, neighbourhood, past* 很可疑的人物、邻居、过去. ▷ **doubt·fully** /-fəlɪ; -fəlɪ/ *adv*.

doubt·less /ˈdaʊtlɪs; ˋdaʊtlɪs/ *adv* almost certainly; very probably 大概; 很可能: *Doubtless he'll be bringing his guitar, as usual.* 他很可能跟平常一样会带吉他来.

douche /duːʃ; duʃ/ *n* (device for directing a) stream of water into or onto a part of the body, esp the vagina, to clean it or for medical purposes (对身体部位, 尤指对阴道的)冲洗液, 灌洗液, 冲洗器, 灌洗器.

▷ **douche** *v* [I, Tn] treat (sth) with a douche 冲洗或灌洗(某部位).

dough /dəʊ; do/ *n* [U] **1** thick mixture of flour, water, etc ready to be baked into bread, pastry, etc (做面包、糕点等的)生面团. **2** (*sl* 俚) money 钱.

▷ **doughy** *adj* of or like dough; soft, pale and flabby (似)面团的; 柔软、苍白而松弛的: *a doughy complexion* 苍白的肤色.

□ ˈ**doughnut** *n* small cake, usu in the shape of a ring or a ball, made from sweetened dough cooked in fat 炸圈饼. ⇨illus at BREAD 见 BREAD 之插图.

doughty /ˈdaʊtɪ; ˋdaʊtɪ/ *adj* [usu attrib 通常作定语] (*arch or rhet* 古或修辞) brave and strong 勇敢而顽强的: *a doughty warrior* 勇猛的战士.

dour /dʊə(r); dur/ *adj* stern; severe; gloomy-looking; joyless 严厉的; 严格的; 脸色阴沉的; 闷闷不乐的: *dour looks* 抑郁的表情 ○ *a dour silence* 阴森森的寂静. ▷ **dourly** *adv*.

douse (also **dowse**) /daʊs; daus/ *v* **1** [Tn, Tn·pr] **~ sb/sth (in/with sth)** put sb/sth into (water); throw (water) over sb/sth 将某人[某物]放入(水中); 在某人[某物]上泼(水): *douse the flames/a fire* 浇灭火焰[炉火] ○ *As a joke, they doused him with a bucket of water.* 他们开玩笑, 把一桶水泼到他身上了. **2** [Tn] put out or turn off (a light) 熄, 灭, 关(灯).

dove[1] /dʌv; dʌv/ *n* **1** type of bird with short legs, a small head and a thick body, that makes a cooing sound and is often used as a symbol of peace 鸽子(常用作和平的象征). **2** (*fig* 比喻) person, esp a politician, who favours peace and negotiation rather than war or confrontation 温和派人物; (尤指)鸽派政治家. Cf 参看 HAWK[1] 2.

□ **dovecote** /ˈdʌvkɒt, *also* ˈdʌvkəʊt; ˋdʌv,kɑt ˋdʌv,kot/ *n* **1** building providing shelter and often nesting-boxes for pigeons and doves 鸽舍; 鸽房. **2** (idm 习语) **flutter the dovecotes** ⇨ FLUTTER.

dove[2] (*US*) *pt* of DIVE[1].

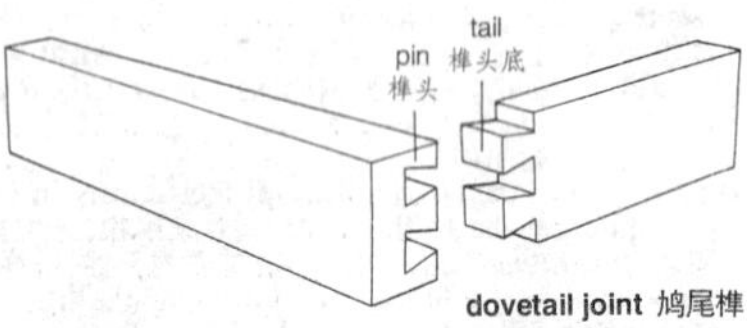

dovetail joint 鸠尾榫

dove·tail /ˈdʌvteɪl; ˋdʌv,tel/ *n* joint for fixing two pieces of wood together, with one piece cut in the shape of a wedge fitting into a groove of the same shape in the other 鸠尾榫; 楔形榫. ⇨illus 见插图.

▷ **dove·tail** *v* **1** [Tn] join (two pieces of wood) in this way 以鸠尾榫接合(两块木头). **2** [I, Ipr, Tn, Tn·pr] **~ (sth) (with sth)** (*fig* 比喻) fit together; combine neatly 吻合; 密合: *My plans dovetailed nicely with hers.* 我的计划和她的计划非常吻合.

dow·ager /ˈdaʊədʒə(r); ˋdaʊədʒɚ/ *n* **1** woman who holds a title or property because of her dead husband's position 因亡夫之地位而持有称号或财产的寡妇: [attrib 作定语] *the dowager duchess* 公爵遗孀. **2** (*infml* 口) dignified, usu wealthy, elderly woman 年长的贵妇人.

dowdy /ˈdaʊdɪ; ˋdaʊdɪ/ *adj* (**-ier, -iest**) (*derog* 贬) **1** (of clothes, etc) dull; unfashionable; drab (指衣物等)单调的, 过时的. **2** (of a person) dressed in dowdy clothes (指人)穿着单调的或过时的. ▷ **dow·dily** *adv*. **dow·di·ness** *n* [U].

dowel /ˈdaʊəl; ˋdaʊəl/ *n* wooden or metal pin with no head for holding two pieces of wood, metal, stone, etc together 暗榫; 暗钉; 合缝钉.

down[1] /daʊn; daʊn/ *adv part* (For special uses with many *vs*, see the *v* entries. 与动词搭配的特殊用法见有关动词词条.) **1** (**a**) from a higher to a lower level 从高到低; 向下: *pull down a blind* 拉下窗帘 ○ *fall, climb, jump, etc down* 跌下、爬下、跳下 ○ *The sun went down below the horizon.* 太阳落山, 消失于地平线下. ○ *The ice-cream slipped down easily — it was cold and delicious.* 冰激凌到嘴就化 —— 咽下去又凉快又可口. (**b**) (moving) from an upright position to a horizontal one 从竖着的位置(移动到)横着的位置; 倒下: *knock sb down* 把某人打倒 ○ *go and lie down* 去躺下. (**c**) with the body positioned at a lower level 使躯体处于较低位置: *sit, kneel, crouch, etc down* 坐下、跪下、蹲下 ○ *He bent down to pick up his gloves.* 他弯身拾起他的手套. Cf 参看 UP 1a. **2** (indicating place or state 指地点或状态): *Mary is not down yet*, ie She is in bed or still in an upstairs room. 玛丽还没下来呢(未下床或未下楼). ○ *The level of unemployment is down.* 失业率在下降. ○ *We're two goals down already*, ie The other team has scored two goals and we have scored none. 我们已落后两分. Cf 参看 UP 2. **3** (**a**) away from an important place, esp a large city 离开重要的地方(尤指大城市): *move down from London to the country* 离开伦敦搬到乡下. (**b**) (*Brit*) away from a university, esp Oxford or Cambridge 离开大学(尤指牛津或剑桥): *going down at the end of the year* 年底将大学毕业. (**c**) to or in the south of the country 向南方; 在南方: *living down south* 住在南方. Cf 参看 UP 4. **4** (indicating a decrease in volume, activity or quality 表示量或活动的减少或质量的下降): *boil the liquid down* 把液体煮得蒸发掉一些 ○ *calm/quieten/settle down* 宁静[安静/安顿]下来 ○ *The fire burnt down.* 火势渐渐减弱. ○ *The noise was dying down.* 噪声渐渐减低. ○ *The wine was watered down for the children.* 用水把葡萄酒冲淡给孩子喝. ○ *The heels of these shoes are quite worn down.* 鞋后跟磨损得很厉害. **5** (**a**) (written) on paper 在纸上(写): *write it down* 写下来 ○ *copy/note/put/take sth down* 抄下[摘记下/写下/记下]某事物. (**b**) added to a list 加入清单中: *Have you got me down for the team?* 你把我加进球队名单里了吗? **6 ~ (to sb/sth)** (indicating the upper (and lower) limits in a range 表示上(或下)限): *Everyone played well, from the captain down.* 上自队长下至每个队员都表现得很好. ○ *Nobody was free from suspicion, from the head girl down to the youngest pupil.* 上自首席女学长下至年龄最小的学生, 没有一个不受到怀疑的. **7** (**a**) (with a specified amount of money) spent or lost 花掉或失去(某钱数): *After paying all the bills, I found myself £5 down.* 付清所有帐单后, 我知道共花了5英镑. (**b**) as a deposit 作为定金: *Pay me £50 down and the rest at the end of the month.* 先付给我50英镑定金, 余款要月底付清. ○ [attrib 作定语] *Pay me £50 as a down payment.* 先付给我50英镑定钱. **8** (used in measuring one's progress through a series of individual people, things, etc 用以计算进度(如处理人、事物等的数量)): *That's 10 down, another 5 candidates to see yet.* 已经面试了10人, 还有5人要见. **9** (idm 习语) **be down on sb** (*infml* 口) feel, show or express disapproval or hostility towards sb 对某人感到、表示或表达出不满或有敌意: *She's terribly down on people who don't do things her way.* 她对不按她的要求做事的人十分不满. **be down to sb** be dependent on sb 依赖、依靠或依仗某人: *It's down to you now to look after the family business.* 现在得靠你照管家族生意了. **be down to sth** have only a little (money) left 只剩一点儿(钱): *be down to one's last penny, pound, etc* 只剩下最后一便士、一镑等 ○ *I'm afraid I can't buy you a drink — I'm down to my last 50p.* 很抱歉, 我不能请你喝什么了 —— 我只剩下50便士了. **be/go down with sth** have or catch an illness 有病; 得病: *Peter can't play tomorrow, he's (gone) down with flu.* 彼得明天不能参赛了, 他得了流感. ˌ**down and** ˈ**out** having no home, money, etc; destitute 无家、无钱等; 穷困潦倒: *He looked completely down and out.* 他看上去已穷困潦倒. ○ [attrib 作定语] *ˌdown-and-out ˌhomeless ˈpeople* 穷困潦倒、无家可归的人. **down below** in or to the basement of a building or to the hold of a ship, etc 在底下, 到底下(地下室、船舱等). ˌ**down** ˈ**stage (of sb/sth)** at or to the part of the stage nearest the audience 在(或向)舞台前

部: *move down stage (of the other actors)* 向舞台前方移动(到其他演员的前面). **down through sth** throughout (a considerable period of time) 经过(相当长的一段时间): *Down through the years this town has seen many changes.* 经过这些年, 这城市有了许多变化. **down 'under** (*infml* 口) in Australia 在澳大利亚: *Down under they speak their own kind of English.* 在澳大利亚, 人们说的是当地的英语. **down with sb/sth** (used to express a wish that a person, a group or an institution should be banned or abolished 用以表示打倒或取消某人、某团体或某机构): *Down with the government!* 打倒政府! ○ *Down with school uniforms!* 取消穿校服的规定!

□ **'down-and-out** *n* destitute person 穷困潦倒的人.

ˌdown-to-'earth *adj* practical; sensible 脚踏实地的; 现实的; 实际的: *He needs to marry a down-to-earth person who will organize his life for him.* 他需要娶个讲求实际的人做妻子好为他安排生活.

down[2] /daʊn; daʊn/ *prep* **1** from a high or higher point on (sth) to a lower one 从高处向下: *The stone rolled down the hill.* 石头滚下山. ○ *Tears ran down her face.* 眼泪从她脸上流下. ○ *Her hair hung down her back to her waist.* 她的长发披在后背直垂到腰间. **2** at or to a lower part of (sth) 在或向低处: *There's a bridge a mile down the river from here.* 从这里沿河往下一英里处有一座桥. **3** (of flat surfaces or areas) along; towards the direction in which one is facing (指平面或区域)沿着, 顺着(面对的方向): *He lives just down the street.* 他就住在街的那头. ○ *Go down the road till you reach the traffic lights.* 沿路前行直至有交通灯处. **4** (of periods of time) throughout (指时间段落)贯穿, 遍及: *an exhibition of costumes down the ages*, ie from all periods of history 历代服装展览.

down[3] /daʊn; daʊn/ *v* [Tn] **1** knock (sb) to the ground 将(某人)打倒在地上. **2** (*infml* 口) finish (a drink) quickly 很快喝下(饮料): *We downed our beer and left.* 我们一口气把啤酒喝光就走了. **3** (idm 习语) **ˌdown 'tools** (*Brit*) **(a)** (of workers) stop working, usu abruptly (指工人)停止工作(通常为突然地): *As soon as the clock strikes five, they down tools and off they go.* 钟一敲五点, 他们就撂下工作走人. **(b)** refuse to continue working, as in a strike 拒绝继续工作(如在罢工中).

down[4] /daʊn; daʊn/ *n* (idm 习语) **have a down on sb/sth** (*infml* 口) disapprove of or feel hostile towards sb/sth 讨厌或敌视某人[某事物]: *She's got a 'down on me; I don't know why.* 她很讨厌我, 我不知道为什么. **ups and downs** ⇨ UP *n*.

down[5] /daʊn; daʊn/ *n* [U] **1** very fine soft feathers 绒羽; 羽绒: *pillows filled with down* 羽绒枕头. **2** fine soft hair 绒毛; 汗毛; 软毛; 毫毛; 茸毛: *The first down was beginning to appear on the young boy's face.* 那小男孩的脸上渐渐长出了汗毛.

down·beat /ˈdaʊnbiːt; ˈdaʊnˌbit/ *n* (*music* 音) first beat of a bar (when the conductor's hand moves downwards) 下拍(乐队指挥向下的手势). Cf 参看 UPBEAT.

▷ **down·beat** *adj* (*infml* 口) **1** gloomy; pessimistic 忧郁的; 悲观的. **2** relaxed; not showing strong feelings 松弛的; 不强烈的.

down·cast /ˈdaʊnkɑːst; *US* ˈdaʊnkæst; ˈdaʊnˌkæst/ *adj* **1** (of eyes) looking downwards (指眼睛)目光向下的. **2** (of a person, an expression, etc) depressed; sad (指人、表情等)沮丧的, 悲哀的: *He seemed very downcast at the news.* 那消息似乎使他非常难过.

down draught (*US* **down draft**) /ˈdaʊn drɑːft; *US* dræft; ˈdaʊn ˌdræft/ downward current of air, esp one that moves down a chimney into a room 向下的气流(尤指从烟囱倒灌入室者).

downer /ˈdaʊnə(r); ˈdaʊnɚ/ *n* (*sl* 俚) **1** drug having a depressant effect, esp a barbiturate 抑制药, 镇静药(尤指巴比妥类). Cf 参看 UPPER *n* 2. **2** depressing experience, person, etc 令人沮丧的经历、人等: *What a downer that guy is!* 那家伙多让人泄气呀!

down·fall /ˈdaʊnfɔːl; ˈdaʊnˌfɔl/ *n* [sing] **1** fall from a position of prosperity or power 衰落; 败落; 垮台: *Greed led to his downfall.* 他贪得无厌而导致身败名裂. **2** thing that causes this 衰落、败落、垮台等的原因: *His vanity was his downfall.* 他因虚荣心太重而垮台.

down·grade /ˈdaʊngreɪd; ˈdaʊnˌgred/ *v* [Tn, Tn·pr] ~ **sb/sth (from sth) (to sth)** reduce sb/sth to a lower grade, rank or level of importance 使某人[某事物]降级、降职或降低重要性: *She's been downgraded (from principal) to deputy.* 她已(从校长)降为副校长. Cf 参看 UPGRADE.

down-hearted /ˌdaʊnˈhɑːtɪd; ˈdaʊnˈhɑrtɪd/ *adj* in low spirits; depressed 情绪低落的; 消沉的: *Don't be too down-hearted; things will get better.* 别那么垂头丧气, 事情会好起来的.

down·hill /ˌdaʊnˈhɪl; ˈdaʊnˌhɪl/ *adv* **1** towards the bottom of a hill; in a downward direction 向山下; 向下. **2** (idm 习语) **ˌgo down'hill** get worse (in health, fortune, social status, etc); deteriorate (健康状况、运气、社会地位等)走下坡路, 每况愈下; 恶化: *This part of the town used to be fashionable, but it's starting to go downhill.* 该市这一地区一度很繁华, 如今已江河日下.

▷ **down·hill** *adj* **1** [attrib 作定语] going or sloping towards the bottom of a hill 下山的; 下坡的; 向山下倾斜的: *a ˌdownhill 'race* 下山比赛. **2** (*infml* 口) easy compared to what came before (与前相较)容易的: *The difficult part is learning the new computer codes — after that it's all downhill.* 困难的部分是学会计算机的新编码——其余就轻而易举了.

Down·ing Street /ˈdaʊnɪŋ striːt; ˈdaʊnɪŋˌstrit/ **(a)** London street where the British Prime Minister's official residence is 唐宁街(伦敦街道名, 英国首相官邸所在地). **(b)** (*fig* 比喻) the Prime Minister or the British Government 英国首相; 英国政府: *Downing Street has so far refused to comment on these reports.* 英国政府对这些报道迄今不予置评.

down·load /ˌdaʊnˈləʊd; ˌdaʊnˈlod/ *v* [Tn, Tn·pr] (*computing* 计) transfer (a program, data, etc) from a large computer system to a smaller one 将(程序, 资料等)从大计算机系统输入小计算机系统.

down-market /ˌdaʊn ˈmɑːkɪt; ˈdaʊn ˌmɑrkɪt/ *adj* (of products, services, etc) designed to appeal to or satisfy people in the lower social classes (指产品、服务等)面向社会低层的, 低档的. Cf 参看 UP-MARKET.

down·pour /ˈdaʊnpɔː(r); ˈdaʊnˌpɔr/ *n* (usu *sing* 通常作单数) heavy, usu sudden, fall of rain 倾盆大雨: *be caught in a downpour* 遇上瓢泼大雨.

down·right /ˈdaʊnraɪt; ˈdaʊnˌraɪt/ *adj* [attrib 作定语] **1** (of sth undesirable) thorough; complete (指不喜欢的事物)彻底的, 十足的, 完全的: *a downright lie* 彻头彻尾的谎言 ○ *downright stupidity* 愚不可及. **2** frank; straightforward 坦白的; 直率的.

▷ **down·right** *adv* thoroughly 彻底地: *He wasn't just inconsiderate, he was downright rude.* 他岂止不体谅人, 简直是十分粗暴.

downs /daʊnz; daʊnz/ *n* [pl] **the downs** area of open rolling land, esp the chalk hills of S England 开阔的丘陵地(尤指英格兰南部的石灰岩丘陵): *the North, South, Sussex, etc Downs* 北部的、南部的、苏塞克斯的…丘陵地.

Down's syn·drome /ˈdaʊnz sɪndrəʊm; ˈdaʊnz ˌsɪndrom/ (also **mongolism**) abnormal condition in which a person is born with a broad flattened skull, slanting eyes and mental deficiency 唐氏综合征(一种头颅宽扁、眼斜的先天白痴).

down·stairs /ˌdaʊnˈsteəz; ˈdaʊnˈstɛrz/ *adv* **1** down the stairs 顺楼梯而下: *He fell downstairs and broke his wrist.* 他从楼梯跌下, 摔伤了手腕. **2** on or to a lower floor 在楼下; 往楼下: *They're waiting for us downstairs.* 他们在楼下等我们. Cf 参看 UPSTAIRS.

▷ **down·stairs** *adj* [attrib 作定语]: *the downstairs toilet* 楼下的厕所 **down·stairs** *n* [sing *v*] lower floor of a building, esp the ground floor 楼下(尤指一楼): *The whole downstairs needs repainting.* 楼下全层需要重新粉刷.

down·stream /ˌdaʊnˈstriːm; ˈdaʊnˈstrim/ *adv* in the direction in which a river flows 顺流而下; 朝下游方向: *drift, float, etc downstream* 顺流漂浮. Cf 参看 UPSTREAM.

down·town /ˌdaʊnˈtaʊn; ˈdaʊnˈtaʊn/ *adv* (*esp US*) to or in the centre of a city, esp the main business and commercial district 朝着或位于城市的中心区(尤指闹市及商业区): *go, move, live downtown* 前往、搬往、住在闹市 ○ [attrib 作定语] *downtown Manhattan* 曼哈顿商业区. Cf 参看 UPTOWN.

down·trodden /ˈdaʊntrɒdn; ˈdaʊnˈtrɑdn̩/ *adj* kept down and badly treated; oppressed 受蹂躏的; 受践踏的; 受压迫的: *downtrodden workers* 受压迫的工人.

down·ward /ˈdaʊnwəd; ˈdaʊnwɚd/ *adj* [usu attrib 通常

作定语] moving, leading or pointing to what is lower or less important 向下的; 下降的; 降低的: *a downward movement, slope* 下行、下坡 ○ *a downward trend in prices* 价格下降的趋势 ○ (*fig* 比喻) *on the downward path*, ie getting worse 走下坡路(日益恶化).

▷ **down·wards** (also **down·ward**) *adv* towards what is lower 向下地: *She laid the picture face downward on the table.* 她把那幅画正面朝下放在桌上. ○ *The garden sloped gently downwards towards the river.* 花园呈缓坡向河边倾斜. ⇨Usage at FORWARD[2] 用法见 FORWARD[2].

downy /ˈdaʊnɪ; ˋdaʊnɪ/ *adj* like or covered with down[5] 像绒毛的; 有羽绒的; 有软毛的.

dowry /ˈdaʊərɪ; ˋdaurɪ/ *n* [C, U] property or money brought by a bride to her husband 嫁妆; 嫁奁; 妆奁.

dowse[1] = DOUSE.

dowse[2] /daʊz; daus/ *v* [I, Ipr] **~ (for sth)** look for underground water or minerals by using a Y-shaped stick or rod that dips or shakes when it comes near water, etc 用占卜杖探水或探矿.

▷ **dowser** *n* person who does this; diviner 用占卜杖探水或探矿者.

D

doxo·logy /dɒkˈsɒlədʒɪ; dɑksˋɑlədʒɪ/ *n* hymn or other prayer praising God, esp one sung during a church service 三一颂; 赞美歌.

doyen /ˈdɔɪən; ˋdɔɪən/ (*US* usu 美式英语通常作 **dean** /di:n; din/) (*fem* 阴性作 **doy·enne** /dɔɪˈen; dɔɪˋɛn/) *n* senior member of a group, profession, etc (团体、职业等的)资深者, 老前辈, 元老: *She founded the club and is now our doyenne.* 她创建了这个俱乐部, 现在是我们的元老. ○ *the doyen of the French Department* 法语系的老前辈.

doy·ley, doyly = DOILY.

doz *abbr* 缩写 = dozen: *3 doz eggs* 3打鸡蛋.

doze /dəʊz; doz/ *v* [I, Ip] **1** sleep lightly 小睡; (打)瞌睡; 打盹儿. **2** (phr v) **doze off** fall into a light sleep 打(起)瞌睡(来); 打(起)盹儿(来): *I dozed off during the film.* 我看电影时打起盹儿来了.

▷ **doze** *n* (usu *sing* 通常作单数) short light sleep 小睡; 瞌睡; 盹儿: *I had a quick doze on the train.* 我在火车上打了一会儿瞌睡.

dozen /ˈdʌzn; ˋdʌzn̩/ *n* (*pl* **~s** or unchanged when counting sth 作量词时复数不变) (*abbr* 缩写 **doz**) **1** set of twelve (一)打(十二个): *Eggs are sold by the dozen.* 鸡蛋按打卖. ○ *They're 70p a dozen.* 这卖70便士一打. ○ *Pack them in dozens.* 按打装袋吧. ○ [attrib 作定语] *Half a dozen* (ie 6) *eggs, please.* 我要半打鸡蛋. ○ *We need three dozen boxes.* 我们需要三打盒子. ⇨App 4 见附录 4. **2** (idm 习语) **a baker's dozen** ⇨ BAKER. **one's daily dozen** ⇨ DAILY. **a dime a dozen** ⇨ DIME. **dozens of** (*infml* 口) lots of 许多: *She's got dozens of boy-friends.* 她的男朋友多极了. **talk, etc, nineteen to the ˈdozen** talk, etc continually 不停地谈、说等: *They were chatting away nineteen to the dozen.* 他们聊个没完. **(it is) ˌsix of ˈone and ˌhalf a dozen of the ˈother** there is very little difference between the one and the other 两者几无区别; 半斤八两: *I can't tell whether he or she is to blame — it's six of one and half a dozen of the other.* 我说不好他们俩谁是谁非——一个半斤, 一个八两.

dozy /ˈdəʊzɪ; ˋdozɪ/ *adj* (**-ier, -iest**) **1** sleepy 困倦的; 昏昏欲睡的: *I'm feeling a bit dozy this afternoon.* 今天下午我觉得有点困. **2** (*Brit infml* 口) stupid 愚蠢的: *Come on, you dozy lot — use your heads!* 快点, 你们这群笨蛋——开动脑筋嘛!

DPhil /ˌdi: ˈfɪl; ˌdi ˋfɪl/ *abbr* 缩写 = Doctor of Philosophy (哲学)博士: *have/be a DPhil in History* 有历史学博士学位[为历史学博士] ○ *Hugh Benson DPhil* 豪·本森哲学博士. Cf 参看 PhD.

DPP /ˌdi: pi: ˈpi:; ˌdi pi ˋpi/ *abbr* 缩写 = (*Brit*) Director of Public Prosecutions 检察官.

Dr *abbr* 缩写 = **1** (academic or medical) Doctor 博士; 医生: *Dr (James) Walker* (詹姆斯·)沃克医生(或博士). **2** (in street names) Drive (作街道名的)路, 大道: *21 Elm Dr* 埃尔姆大街21号.

dr *abbr* 缩写 = **1** drachma(s): *dr 500* 500德拉克马. **2** dram(s).

drab /dræb; dræb/ *adj* dull; uninteresting 单调的; 乏味的: *a drab evening, existence, personality* 单调乏味的夜晚、生活、个性 ○ *dressed in drab colours* 衣着色彩灰暗.

▷ **drably** *adv*. **drab·ness** *n* [U].

drachma /ˈdrækmə; ˋdrækmə/ *n* (*pl* **-mas** or **-mae** /-mi:; -mi/) unit of money in Greece 德拉克马(希腊货币单位).

Dra·con·ian /drəˈkəʊnɪən; dreˋkonɪən/ *adj* (*fml* 文) very harsh 严厉的; 严酷的: *Draconian measures, laws, policies, etc* 严厉的措施、法律、政策等.

draft[1] /drɑ:ft; *US* dræft; dræft/ *n* **1** [C] rough preliminary written version of sth 草稿; 草案: *This is only the draft of my speech, but what do you think of it?* 这仅仅是我演讲的草稿, 你认为怎样? ○ [attrib 作定语] *a draft amendment, copy, version* 修正草案、草稿、初稿. **2** (*finance* 财) (**a**) [C] written order to a bank to pay money to sb 汇票: *a draft on an American bank* 向一家美国银行提款的汇票. (**b**) [U] payment of money by means of such an order 汇票的支付. **3** [CGp] group of people chosen from a larger group for a special purpose 特遣队; 特别小组: *We're sending a fresh draft of nurses to the worst hit area.* 我们新派遣一组护理人员开赴受灾最重的地区. **4 the draft** [sing] (*US*) = CALL-UP (CALL[2]). **5** [C] (*US*) = DRAUGHT.

□ ˈ**draft-card** *n* (*US*) card summoning a man to serve in the armed forces 征兵卡.

ˈ**draft-dodger** *n* (*US*) man illegally evading the draft[1](4) 逃避兵役者.

draft[2] /drɑ:ft; *US* dræft; dræft/ *v* **1** [Tn] make a preliminary version of (a document) 草拟, 起草(文件): *draft a contract, parliamentary bill, treaty, etc* 起草一份合同、议会法案、条约等 ○ *I'm still drafting the first chapter.* 我还在草拟第一章. ○ *a badly drafted will* 草拟不当的遗嘱. **2** [Tn, Tn·pr, Tn·p] choose (people) and send them somewhere for a special task 选派; 抽调: *Extra police are being drafted in to control the crowds.* 现正额外抽调警察去控制人群. **3** [Tn, Tn·pr] **~ sb (into sth)** (*US*) conscript sb 征募; 征召: *be drafted into the Army, Navy, etc* 被征召加入陆军、海军等.

▷ **draftee** /ˌdrɑ:fˈti:; *US* ˌdræfˈti:; dræfˋti/ *n* (*US*) conscript 应征入伍者.

drafts·man /ˈdrɑ:ftsmən; *US* ˈdræfts-; ˋdræftsmən/ *n* (*pl* **-men**) **1** person responsible for the careful and exact wording of a legal document or parliamentary bill (法律文件或议会法案的)起草人. **2** (*US*) = DRAUGHTSMAN.

drafty (*US*) = DRAUGHTY.

drag[1] /dræg; dræg/ *n* **1** [C] thing made to be dragged, eg a drag-net, or heavy harrow (pulled over the ground to break up the soil) 供拖、拉之物(如拖网或重耙犁). **2** [U] resistance of the air to the movement of an aircraft (飞行器的)空气阻力. Cf 参看 LIFT *n* 4. **3** [sing] (*sl* 俚) boring person or thing 累赘的或使人生厌的人或事物: *Walking's a drag — let's take the car.* 走路太费事——我们坐汽车吧. **4** [U] (*sl* 俚) woman's clothes worn by a man 男子穿的女子服装: *in drag* (男子)穿着女服 ○ [attrib 作定语] *a drag artiste* 着女服的男艺人. **5** [C] (*sl* 俚) draw on a cigarette, etc 吸, 抽(香烟等). **6** [sing] **~ on sb/sth** (*infml* 口) person or thing that makes progress difficult 累赘的人或事物; 障碍: *She loves her family, but they're a drag on her career.* 她热爱自己的家庭, 但家庭却是她事业的累赘.

▷ **drag·ster** /ˈdrægstə(r); ˋdrægstɚ/ *n* car with a specially adapted motor for drag racing (改装成的)高速赛车.

□ ˈ**drag-hunt** *n* hunt in which dogs follow the trail of a strong-smelling object dragged over the ground 追猎(猎犬循地上臭迹追踪).

ˈ**drag-net** *n* (**a**) net pulled along the bottom of a river, etc, esp when searching for sth 拖网. (**b**) (*fig* 比喻) system of checks, raids, etc by the police for catching criminals 法网; 罗网; 兜捕.

ˈ**drag race** contest of acceleration between cars starting from a standstill 汽车加速赛. ˈ**drag racing**.

drag[2] /dræg; dræg/ *v* (**-gg-**) **1** [Tn, Tn·pr, Tn·p] pull (sb/sth) along with effort and difficulty 拖, 拉, 扯, 拽(某人[某物]): *The cat was dragging its broken leg.* 那只猫拖着断腿吃力地走. ○ *We dragged the fallen tree clear of the road.* 我们把倒下的树从路上拖走. ○ *drag oneself along, home* 拖着疲乏的身子前行、回家. ⇨illus at PULL 见 PULL 之插图. ⇨Usage at PULL[2] 用法见 PULL[2]. **2** [Ipr, Ip] move slowly and with effort 缓慢而吃力地行进: *She always drags behind.* 她总是在后面吃力地跟着.

3 [Tn·pr, Tn·p] (*fig* 比喻) persuade (sb) to come or go somewhere unwillingly 劝说(某人)勉为其难地来或去某处: *I could hardly drag the children away (from the party).* 我好不容易才把孩子们(从聚会中)劝走. ○ *She dragged herself out of bed, still half asleep.* 她挣扎着起了床, 犹自睡眼惺松. **4** [I, Ipr, Ip, Tn, Tn·pr] (cause sth to) trail on the ground (使某物)在地上拖拉: *Your coat's dragging in the mud.* 你的大衣拖到泥上了. ○ *The ship dragged her anchor during the storm,* ie The anchor did not stay in its place on the sea bottom. 船在暴风雨中拖动了锚链. **5** [I, Ip] **~ (on)** (of sth boring or irritating) go on too long (指乏味或恼人的事物)进行过久: *The film dragged terribly.* 电影演得拖拖拉拉. ○ *How much longer is this going to drag on?* 这事还要拖多久? **6** [Tn] search (the bottom of a river, lake, etc) with nets, hooks, etc 拖着网、钩等(沿河底、湖底等)搜索, 寻觅, 打捞: *They dragged the canal for the missing child.* 他们用拖网沿运河打捞失踪孩子的尸体. **7** (idm 习语) **drag one's 'feet/'heels** be deliberately slow or ineffective 故意拖沓或怠工: *I want to sell the house, but my husband is dragging his feet,* ie will not make a decision. 我想卖掉房子, 但我丈夫迟迟不作决定. **drag sb/sb's name through the mire/mud** bring disgrace to sb by behaving very badly 使某人蒙羞、丢丑. **8** (phr v) **drag sb down** make sb feel weak or depressed 使某人感到委顿或沮丧: *Hot weather always drags me down.* 天气一热我就浑身不适. **drag sb down (to sth)** (*infml* 口) bring sb to a lower social level, standard of behaviour, etc 使某人社会地位、行为标准等下降: *I'm afraid the children will all be dragged down to his level.* 我看他的孩子也要跟他学坏了. **drag sth in/into sth** introduce (a subject which has nothing to do with what is being talked about) into the conversation 在谈话中扯进不相关的事: *Must you drag politics into everything?* 你非得事事都把政治扯进来吗? **drag sb into doing sth** make sb take part in an activity against his will 硬拉某人参加某活动: *She had to be dragged into seeing the dentist.* 要她去牙科医生那里看病非得生拉硬拽不可. **drag sth out** make sth longer than necessary 使某事物不必要地拖延: *Let's not drag out this discussion, we've got to reach a decision.* 这场讨论别拖下去了, 我们得作个决定了. **drag sth out (of sb)** make sb reveal or give (information, etc) unwillingly 迫使某人透露或交代(情况等): *drag a confession, fact, concession, etc out of sb* 逼某人招供、说出事实、作出让步等. **drag sb up** (*Brit*) raise (a child) badly and without proper care 将(孩子)胡乱带大. **drag sth up** introduce unnecessarily into a conversation (a fact, story, etc that is considered unpleasant) 在谈话中扯进(不愉快的事情等): *She dragged up that incident just to embarrass me.* 她又扯起那件事故意想使我难堪.

drag·gled /ˈdræɡəld; ˋdræɡld/ *adj* = BEDRAGGLED.

drago·man /ˈdræɡəmən; ˋdræɡəmən/ *n* (*pl* **~s**) (esp formerly in some Middle Eastern countries) guide and interpreter (尤指旧时在某些中东国家的)导游和译员.

dragon 龙

dragon /ˈdræɡən; ˋdræɡən/ *n* **1** imaginary animal with wings and claws, able to breathe out fire 龙. ⇨illus 见插图. **2** (*fig derog* 比喻, 贬) fierce person, esp a woman 凶恶的人; (尤指)悍妇: *The woman in charge of the accounts department is an absolute dragon!* 会计科那个女科长是个十足的母夜叉!

dragon-fly /ˈdræɡənflaɪ; ˋdræɡən,flaɪ/ *n* insect with a long thin body and two pairs of wings 蜻蜓.

dra·goon /drəˈɡu:n; drəˋɡun/ *n* heavily-armed cavalryman 重骑兵.

▷ **dra·goon** *v* (phr v) **dragoon sb into doing sth** force sb to do sth; bully sb into doing sth 迫使或威胁某人做某事: *We were dragooned into going to the opera.* 我们迫不得已去看了那场歌剧.

drain[1] /dreɪn; dren/ *n* **1** pipe or channel that carries away sewage or other unwanted liquid 下水管; 下水道; 阴沟: *We had to call a plumber to unblock the drains.* 我们得叫管工来通一通下水道. ⇨illus at App 1 见附录1之插图, page vi. **2** (*US*) = PLUG-HOLE. **3** (idm 习语) **(go) down the 'drain** (*infml* 口) be wasted or spoilt 被浪费; 白费: *A single mistake and all that time and money would go down the drain.* 只要发生一个错误, 全部的时间和金钱就将尽付东流. **a drain on sb/sth** anything that continuously uses up sb's strength, time, money, etc 消耗精力、时间、金钱等的事物: *Military spending is a huge drain on the country's resources.* 军费开支是国家资源的一大消耗. **laugh like a drain** ⇨ LAUGH.

□ **'drain-pipe** *n* pipe used in a system of drains 排水管. ⇨illus at App 1 见附录1之插图, page vi. **ˌdrain-pipe 'trousers** (*infml dated* 口, 旧) tight-fitting trousers with straight narrow legs 瘦腿紧身裤.

drain[2] /dreɪn; dren/ *v* **1** [I, Ipr, Ip, Tn, Tn·pr, Tn·p] **~ (sth) (from sth); ~ (sth) (away/off)** (cause liquid to) flow away (使液体)流走: *All the blood drained from his face,* eg on hearing bad news. 他面无人色(如听到坏消息). ○ *The bath-water slowly drained away.* 浴池的水慢慢排走. ○ *The mechanic drained all the oil from the engine.* 机械工将发动机中的油全部放走. **2** [Tn, Cn·a] empty (a glass, etc) 喝光, 喝干(杯...中的饮料): *drain one's glass dry* 把杯中饮料喝光. **3** [I, Tn] (cause sth to) become dry as liquid flows away (使某物)流干, 滴干: *Leave the dishes to drain.* 让碟子控干. ○ *drain swamps/marshes* 排干沼泽地的水 ○ *Land must be well drained for some crops.* 某些作物要求土地有良好的排水性能. **4** [Tn, Tn·pr] **~ sb/sth (of sth)** (*fig* 比喻) make sb/sth weaker, poorer, etc by gradually using up his/its strength, money, etc 消耗或耗尽某人[某物]的精力、金钱等: *feel drained of energy* 觉得精疲力竭 ○ *a country drained of its manpower* 耗尽人力的国家. **5** (idm 习语) **drink/drain sth to the dregs** ⇨ DREGS. **6** (phr v) **drain away** (*fig* 比喻) gradually disappear or fade 逐渐消失或消退: *Her life was slowly draining away,* ie She was dying. 她的生命力在慢慢枯竭(她快死了).

□ **'draining-board** (*US* **'drainboard**) *n* sloping surface beside a sink, on which washed dishes, etc are put to drain (装在洗涤池边的)滴水板.

drain·age /ˈdreɪnɪdʒ; ˋdrenɪdʒ/ *n* [U] **1** draining or being drained 排水; 放水. **2** system of drains 排水系统. **3** what is drained off; sewage 排出的污水; 下水道的污物.

□ **'drainage-basin** *n* area from which water is drained away by a river (河流的)流域.

drake /dreɪk; drek/ *n* **1** male duck 雄鸭; 公鸭. Cf 参看 DUCK[1] 1. **2** (idm 习语) **play ducks and drakes with sb** ⇨ DUCKS AND DRAKES (DUCK[1]).

dram /dræm; dræm/ *n* **1** (*abbr* 缩写 **dr**) unit of weight, one-eighth of an ounce (apothecaries' weight) or one-sixteenth of an ounce (avoirdupois weight) 打兰(重量单位, 为药衡的 $\frac{1}{8}$ 盎司或常衡的 $\frac{1}{16}$ 盎司). **2** (*esp Scot* 尤用于苏格兰) small amount of alcoholic drink, esp whisky 少量的酒(尤指威士忌): *He's fond of his dram.* 他喜欢喝一点酒.

drama /ˈdrɑ:mə; ˋdrɑmə/ *n* **1 (a)** [C] play for the theatre, radio or TV 戏; 剧; 戏剧. **(b)** [U] plays as a branch of literature and as a performing art 戏剧文学; 戏剧艺术: *a masterpiece of Elizabethan drama* 伊丽莎白时代的戏剧杰作 ○ (*dated or fml* 旧或文) *lovers of the drama* 戏剧爱好者 ○ [attrib 作定语] *a drama critic, school, student* 戏剧评论家、学校、学者. **2** [C] series of exciting events 一连串紧张刺激的事件: *a real-life hospital drama* 医院中活生生的激动场面. **3** [U, C] excitement 激情: *Her life was full of drama.* 她的生活充满激动人心的事情. **4** (idm 习语) **make a drama out of sth** exaggerate a small problem or trivial incident 小题大做; 夸大其词: *He makes a drama out of a simple visit to the dentist.* 他把看牙这样一件小事弄得小题大做.

dra·matic /drəˈmætɪk; drəˋmætɪk/ *adj* **1** [attrib 作定语]

D

of drama 戏剧的: *a dramatic society* 戏剧协会 ○ *The play is a dramatic representation of a real event.* 这出话剧改编自真人真事. **2** exciting or impressive 戏剧性的; 激动人心的; 给人深刻印象的: *dramatic changes, developments, news* 激动人心的变化、发展、消息 ○ *Her opening words were dramatic.* 她的开场白十分动听.
▷ **dra·mat·ic·ally** /-klɪ; -klɪ/ *adv*: *Her attitude changed dramatically.* 她的态度突然大大改变.

dra·matics *n* [usu sing *v* 通常与单数动词连用] **1** study or practice of acting and producing plays 戏剧表演和创作的研究或实践: *amateur dramatics* 业余戏剧活动. **2** (*derog* 贬) exaggerated or over-emotional behaviour 夸张的或过分激动的行为: *I've had enough of your dramatics.* 我看够你装腔作势的表现了.
□ **dra,matic 'irony** effect produced in a drama, etc when the audience understands the implications of words or actions better than the characters do themselves 戏剧性讽示(一种戏剧效果, 观众领会到剧中人言行的含义而剧中人本身却未领会到).

D

dra·matis per·sonae /ˌdræmətɪs pɜːˈsəʊnaɪ; ˈdræmətɪs pɚˈsoni/ (*fml* 文) (list of the) characters in a play 剧中人物(表).

dram·at·ist /ˈdræmətɪst; ˈdræmətɪst/ *n* writer of plays 剧作家; 编剧.

dram·at·ize, -ise /ˈdræmətaɪz; ˈdræməˌtaɪz/ *v* **1** [Tn] make (eg a novel or an event) into a play 将(小说或事件)改编成剧本: *a dramatized documentary*, ie a play based on a report of real events 基于真实事件报道而改编成的戏剧. **2** [I, Tn] make (an incident, etc) seem more dramatic than it really is 使(事情)戏剧化; 夸张: *Don't believe everything she tells you; she tends to dramatize.* 她的话不可尽信; 她往往言过其实. ○ *The affair was dramatized by the press.* 新闻界把事情夸大了.
▷ **dram·at·iza·tion, -isation** /ˌdræmətaɪˈzeɪʃn, -tɪˈz-; ˌdræmətaɪˈzeʃən, -təˈz-/ *n* [U, C]: *a TV dramatization of the trial.* 据审判纪实改编成的电视剧.

drank *pt* of DRINK[3].

drape /dreɪp; drep/ *v* **1 (a)** [Tn·pr] **~ sth round/over sth** hang (cloth, curtains, a cloak, etc) loosely on sth 将(衣物、帘、幕、斗篷等)悬挂, 披: *a fur coat draped round her shoulders* 披在她肩上的皮大衣 ○ *Dust-sheets were draped over the furniture.* 家具上盖着防尘布. **(b)** [Tn, Tn·pr] **~ sb/sth (in/with sth)** cover or decorate sb/sth (with cloth, etc) (用布等)遮盖或装饰某人[某事物]: *Dracula appeared, draped in a huge cloak.* 吸血鬼披着一件大斗篷走了出来. ○ *walls draped with tapestries* 饰有挂毯的墙壁. **2** [Tn·pr] **~ sth round/over sth** allow sth to rest loosely on sth 将某物随便围在或放在另一物上: *She draped her arms around his neck.* 她伸开双臂轻轻地搂着他的脖子.
▷ **drape** *n* **1** [sing] way in which a curtain, dress, etc hangs (帘、幕、衣、裙等)悬挂状. **2** [C] (*US*) = CURTAIN.

draper /ˈdreɪpə(r); ˈdrepɚ/ *n* (*Brit*) shopkeeper who sells cloth and clothing 布商; 服装商.

drapery /ˈdreɪpərɪ; ˈdrepərɪ/ *n* **1** [U] (*Brit*) (*US* **dry goods**) draper's trade or goods 布料及服装业或所经售的货物: [attrib 作定语] *the drapery department* 布料及服装部. **2** [C, U] cloth, etc hanging in loose folds 打褶悬挂的布等.

dras·tic /ˈdræstɪk; ˈdræstɪk/ *adj* [usu attrib 通常作定语] **1** having a strong or violent effect 激烈的; 猛烈的; 烈性的: *Drastic measures will have to be taken to restore order.* 为恢复秩序必须采取严厉措施. **2** very serious 极严重的: *a drastic shortage of food* 食物的严重匮乏. ▷ **dras·tic·ally** /-klɪ; -klɪ/ *adv*.

drat /dræt; dræt/ *interj* (*infml* 口) (used to express one's annoyance with sb/sth 用以表示讨厌某人[某事物]): *Drat that child!* 讨厌的孩子! ▷ **drat·ted** *adj* [attrib 作定语] (*infml* 口): *This dratted pen won't work.* 这枝讨厌的钢笔写不出字来.

draught /drɑːft; dræft/ (*US* **draft** /dræft; dræft/) *n* **1** [C] current of air in a room or some other enclosed space 通风; 气流: *Can you close the door? There's an awful draught in here.* 你把门关上好吗? 这里过堂风太大. ○ *As the train began to move a pleasant draught cooled us all down.* 火车一开, 一阵凉风吹来, 我们顿感凉爽. **2** [U, sing] (*nautical* 海) depth of water needed to float a ship (船的)吃水深度: *vessels of shallow draught* 吃水浅的船只. **3** [C] one continuous process of swallowing liquid; the amount swallowed 一饮; 一口之量: *take a deep/long draught of beer* 喝一大口啤酒 ○ *He emptied his glass at one draught.* 他将杯中物一饮而尽. ○ (*fig* 比喻) *He took a deep draught of air into his lungs.* 他深深地吸了一口气. **4 draughts** (*Brit*) (*US* **checkers**) [sing *v*] table game for two players using 24 round pieces on a chequered board 国际跳棋(两人对下, 用24个圆形棋子在方格棋盘上进行). **5** (idm 习语) **on 'draught** drawn from a container, esp of beer from a barrel 从容器中汲取(尤指桶装的啤酒): *winter ale on draught* 桶装冬麦芽酒.
▷ **draught** *adj* [attrib 作定语] served on draught (自桶中汲取)散装的: *draught bitter, cider, lager, etc* 散装苦啤酒、苹果酒、贮藏啤酒等.
□ **'draught-board** (*Brit*) (*US* **'checkerboard**) *n* board (identical to a chessboard) used for playing draughts 国际跳棋棋盘.
'draughthorse *n* horse used for pulling loads 役马; 挽马. Cf 参看 PACK-ANIMAL (PACK[1]).

draughts·man /ˈdrɑːftsmən; ˈdræftsmən/ (*US* **drafts·man** /ˈdræfts-; ˈdræfts-/) *n* (*pl* **-men** /-mən; -mən/) **1** person whose job is to make plans and sketches of machinery, buildings, etc 起草人; 制图员. **2** person who can draw well 善画者; 美术家: *I'm no draughtsman, I'm afraid*, ie no good at drawing. 我根本不擅长画画. **3** (*Brit*) (*US* **checker**) piece used in the game of draughts 国际跳棋棋子.

draughty /ˈdrɑːftɪ; ˈdræftɪ/ (*US* **drafty** /ˈdræftɪ; ˈdræftɪ/) *adj* (**-ier, -iest**) with draughts of air blowing through 通风的; 有过堂风的; 有穿堂风的: *It's terribly draughty in here.* 这儿穿堂风大极了. ▷ **draugh·ti·ness** *n* [U].

draw[1] /drɔː; drɔ/ *n* **1 (a)** (usu *sing* 通常作单数) **~ (for sth)** act of picking at random tickets in a lottery, matches in a tournament, etc 抽奖; 抽签; 抓阄儿: *The draw for the raffle takes place on Saturday.* 抽彩仪式星期六举行. ○ *the draw for the second round of the European Cup* 为欧洲杯足球赛第二轮抽签. **(b)** lottery in which the winner is chosen this way 抽奖; 抽彩. Cf 参看 RAFFLE. **2** result of a game in which neither player or side wins 平局; 不分胜负: *The match ended in a draw 2-2.* 比赛以2比2打成平局结束. **3** (usu *sing* 通常作单数) person or thing that attracts people 有吸引力的人或事物: *A live band is always a good draw at a party.* 现场演奏的乐队在聚会上总是很吸引人的. **4** act of drawing at a cigarette, pipe, etc 吸烟; 抽烟斗. **5** (idm 习语) **the luck of the draw** ⇨ LUCK. **(be) quick/slow on the 'draw (a)** quick/slow at pulling out one's gun, etc 掏出枪等敏捷[迟缓]. **(b)** (*infml* 口) quick/slow to understand 领悟敏捷[迟钝]: *He's a nice lad, but a bit slow on the draw.* 他是个挺不错的小伙子, 就是头脑欠灵活.

draw[2] /drɔː; drɔ/ *v* (*pt* **drew** /druː; dru/, *pp* **drawn** /drɔːn; drɔn/) **1** [I, Tn] make (pictures or a picture of sth) with a pencil, etc 用铅笔等画(画): *You draw beautifully.* 你画得很好看. ○ *She drew a house.* 她画了一所房子. ○ *draw a diagram, plan, flow chart, etc* 画一示意图、平面图、流程图等 ○ (*fig* 比喻) *The report drew a grim picture of inefficiency and corruption.* 该报告描绘出一幅缺乏效率和贪污腐化的可怕情景. **2** [Ipr, Ip] move in the specified direction 向某方向移动: *The train drew in/into the station.* 火车进站. ○ *The car drew slowly away from the kerb.* 汽车慢慢驶离路边. ○ *One horse drew further and further ahead.* 有一匹马在前面, 把后面的落得越来越远了. ○ *A pilot boat drew alongside*, ie next to a ship. 一条领港船驶近船边. ○ (*fig* 比喻) *Christmas is drawing near.* 圣诞节日渐临近. ○ *His life was drawing peacefully to its close.* 他的生命正平静地走向结束. **3 (a)** [Tn·pr, Tn·p] pull or guide (sb/sth) into a new position 拉, 拖, 引导(某人[某物])到一新位置: *She drew a cover over the typewriter.* 她拿过罩子将打字机套上. ○ *I drew my chair up (to the table).* 我把椅子拉近(桌子). ○ *She drew me onto the balcony.* 她把我拉到阳台. ○ *I tried to draw him aside*, ie where I could talk to him privately. 我想把他拉到一边(以便私下和他谈谈). **(b)** [Tn, Tn·pr, Tn·p] (of horses, etc) pull or drag (eg a carriage, a plough) (指马匹等)拉, 拖(如车、犁等): *The Queen's coach was drawn by six horses.* 女王的御辇是由六匹马拉的. ⇨Usage at PULL[2] 用法见 PULL[2]. **(c)** [Tn] open or close (curtains, etc) 拉开, 拉上(帘、幕等). **4 (a)** [Tn·pr, Tn·p] **~ sth out of/from sth; ~ sth out** pull sth smoothly out of its present position 抽出、拔出或拉出某物: *draw a file from a drawer* 从抽屉里取出一份卷宗 ○ *I drew the record out of its sleeve.* 我从唱片套中抽出唱片. ○ *Can you draw the cork out?* 你能把瓶塞拔出来吗? **(b)** [Tn, Tn·pr] **~ sth (from sth)** take out (a gun, knife, etc) from its holder, esp in order to attack sb (从枪套、刀鞘等中)拔出(尤指旨在攻击): *She drew a revolver on me.* 她拔出手枪对准我. ○ *He came towards me with a drawn sword.* 他利剑出鞘, 冲我而来. **5** [Tn, Tn·pr] **~ sth (from sth)** gain or derive sth from study, experience, etc (used esp with the *ns* shown) 获取, 汲取(知识、经验等)(尤与下列名词连用): *What conclusions did you draw (from your study)?* 你(从研究中)得出什么结论? ○ *draw a moral from a story* 从故事中汲取教训 ○ *We can draw some lessons for the future (from this accident).* (从这起事故中)我们可以为今后汲取教训. **6** [Tn, Tn·pr] **~ sb (about/on sth)** make sb say more (about sth) 使某人说出(某事): *She wouldn't be drawn about her private life.* 关于她的私生活你就别想让她吐露半点. ○ *I wanted to hear about possible changes, but I couldn't draw them (on that).* 我很想听听可能会发生什么变动, 但是(关于这一点)不管怎么打听, 他们就是不说. **7 (a)** [Tn·pr, Tn·p] make (eg a liquid or gas) go in a particular direction by pumping, sucking, etc 将(如液体或气体)抽到, 吸往, 压至: *The engine draws water along the pipe.* 发动机将水沿管道抽来. ○ *The diaphragm draws air into the lungs.* 横膈膜向下运动让空气进入肺部. **(b)** [I] (of a chimney or fireplace) allow enough air to pass through a fire to make it burn properly (指烟囱或壁炉)通风(使火旺): *The flue should draw better once it's been swept.* 烟道一经清扫, 通风情况应好些. **(c)** [Ipr] **~ at/on sth** breathe in smoke from (a cigarette, etc) 吸, 抽(香烟等): *He drew thoughtfully on his pipe.* 他抽着烟斗, 若有所思. **8 (a)** [Tn, Tn·pr, Tn·p] **~ sth (from sth)** take sth from a larger supply 从某物中抽取或汲取: *draw water (from a well)* (从井中)汲水 ○ *He drew off a pint of beer from the barrel.* 他从酒桶里抽出一品脱啤酒. **(b)** [Tn·pr] **~ sth from sb/sth** obtain (sth one needs) from sb/sth 从某人[某物]取得(所需之物): *draw support, comfort, strength, etc from one's family* 从家庭获得支持、安慰、力量等 ○ *She drew inspiration from her childhood experiences.* 她从童年的经历中吸取了灵感. ○ *We draw our readers from all classes of society.* 我们吸引了来自社会各阶层的读者. **(c)** [Tn, Tn·pr] **~ sth (from sth)** take (money) from a bank account (从银行中)取, 提(款): *Can I draw £50 from my account?* 我可以从我的帐户上提取50英镑吗? **(d)** [Tn] receive (wages, etc) 收取, 领取(工资等): *It's good to be drawing a monthly salary again.* 现在可真好, 又可以领月薪了. **9** [Tn, Tn·pr] **(a) ~ sb (to sth)** attract or interest sb 吸引某人; 使某人感兴趣: *The film is drawing large audiences.* 这部影片很卖座. ○ *Her screams drew passers-by to the scene.* 她的叫喊声把过路人都吸引到现场. ○ *I felt drawn to this mysterious stranger.* 这个神秘的陌生人引起我的注意. ○ *What drew you to* (ie made you study) *medicine?* 是什么原因使你学医的? ○ *The course draws students from all over the country.* 这一课程吸引着全国各地的学生. **(b) ~ sth (from sb)** produce (a reaction or response) 产生(反应或回应): *draw tears, applause, laughter, etc* 使人落泪、博得掌声、引人捧腹 ○ *The idea has drawn much criticism from both sides.* 那主意招致双方的大量批评. ○ *The competition has drawn a large postbag.* 这场竞赛吸引人们寄来大量信件. **10** [Tn, Tn·pr] (*finance* 财) write out (a cheque, etc) 开出, 签发(支票等): *The bill was drawn on an American bank.* 所开票据是经由一家美国银行支付的. **11** [Ipr, Tn, Tn·pr] **~ for sth; ~ sth (from sth)** get or take sth by chance 抽签; 抓阄: *Before playing cards we drew for partners*, ie decided who would partner whom by drawing cards. 我们玩牌前用抓牌方式决定游戏伙伴. ○ *draw the winner/the winning ticket (in a raffle, etc)* (在抽彩等活动中)抽签决定中奖者 ○ *draw cards from a pack* 从一叠牌中抽牌 ○ *draw lots, names from a hat, etc* 抽签、从帽子里抓名字阄等 ○ *Italy have been drawn to play Spain in the World Cup.* 在世界杯足球赛中意大利队抓到阄儿定与西班牙队比赛. **12** [I, Tn] finish (a game, etc) without either side winning (比赛等)打成平局, 不分胜负: *The two teams drew.* 两队打平. ○ *draw three-all/for first place* 结局三平[都得第一] ○ *The match was drawn.* 比赛不分胜负. **13** [I] (of tea) infuse; brew (指茶)沏, 泡: *Let the tea draw (for three minutes).* 让茶叶泡开(到三分钟). **14** [Tn] (*nautical* 海) (of a ship) require (a certain depth of water) in which to float (船)吃水: *a ship drawing 20 feet* 吃水20英尺的船. **15** [Tn] (*dated* 旧) pull out (a tooth) 拔(牙). **16** [Tn] remove the inner organs of (a chicken, etc) 除去, 取出(鸡等的)内脏. **17** [Tn] pull back the string of (a bow) before firing an arrow 拉, 开(弓). **18** [Tn] mould a thin string of (metal, plastic, etc) by passing it through a small hole 将(金属、塑料等)拉成或拔成细丝. **19** (idm 习语) **at daggers drawn** ⇨ DAGGER. **cast/draw lots** ⇨ LOT[3]. **bring sth/come/draw to a close** ⇨CLOSE[5]. **draw an aˈnalogy, a comˈparison, a ˈparallel, etc between sth and sth** show how one thing is like or contrasts with another 作类比; 作对照. **draw (sb's) attention to sth** point sth out (to sb) 令(某人)注意某事物: *She drew my attention to an error in the report.* 她要我注意报告中的一处错误. ○ *I'm embarrassed about my mistake; please don't draw attention to it*, eg by mentioning it to others. 我出了这种错误很不好意思, 请不要和别人提起. **draw a ˈbead (on sb/sth)** (*infml* 口) aim carefully at sb/sth with a gun, etc 用枪等瞄准(某人[某物]). **draw a ˈblank** get no response or result 无回音; 无结果; 落空: *I tried looking him up in the directory but I drew a blank*, ie his name was not there. 我在电话簿上找他的名字, 但未找到. **draw ˈblood (a)** cause sb to bleed 使某人流血. **(b)** (*fig* 比喻) hurt sb's feelings 伤某人感情: *His wounding remarks clearly drew blood.* 他那尖酸刻薄的话显然很伤人. **draw ˈbreath (a)** pause to breathe deeply after an effort 喘; 歇口气. **(b)** live 活着: *as kind a man as ever drew breath* 世上一大好人 ○ *You won't want for a friend as long as I draw breath.* 只要我活着, 就永远是你的朋友. **draw a distinction between sth and sth** show how two things differ 指出两事物间的不同; 将两事物加以区分. **draw sb's ˈfire** make sb direct his anger, criticism, etc at oneself, so that others do not have to face it 吸引对方火力; 为别人打掩护. **draw one's first/last ˈbreath** be born/die 出生[死亡]. **draw in one's ˈhorns** become defensive or cautious, esp about one's finances 采取守势; 谨慎; (尤指)减缩开支: *You'll have to draw your horns in*, ie spend less money. 你得紧缩开支了. **draw the line at sth/doing sth** refuse to do or to tolerate sth 拒绝做某事物; 拒不容忍某事物: *I don't mind helping, but I draw the line at doing everything myself.* 我可以帮忙, 不过什么事都让我干, 那就不行了. ○ *A line has to be drawn somewhere — I can't go on lending you money.* 事情总得有个分寸 —— 我不能继续借给你钱了. **draw ˈstumps** (in cricket) mark the end of play (by removing the stumps) (板球戏中)结束比赛(撤走三柱门门柱). **draw sb's/sth's ˈteeth/ˈfangs** make sb/sth harmless 使某人[某事物]不能为害; 使无能为力: *Critics fear the bill will have its teeth drawn before it becomes law.* 评论家担心法案获通过时已锋芒尽失. **draw ˈtrumps** (in various card-games) play the trump suit until one's opponents have none left (在各种牌戏中)吊王牌. **draw oneself up to one's full ˈheight** stand as tall and straight as possible (esp as a sign of determination) 把身体挺得笔直(尤指表示下决心): *'Never!' she replied, drawing herself up to her full height.* '绝不!'她昂首挺胸站着, 十分坚决地回答. **draw a veil over sth** tactfully not say anything about sth 避而不谈某事: *I propose to draw a veil over the appalling events that followed.* 我建议不要谈及后来发生的那些骇人听闻的事. **20** (phr v) **draw back (from sth/doing sth)** not take action, esp because one feels unsure or nervous 撤回, 取消(尤因无把握或不安): *draw back from a declaration of/from declaring war* 取消宣战决定. **draw in** (of the hours of daylight) get shorter before winter (指白天的时间)渐短: *The days are drawing in.* 白天越来越短了. **draw sb into sth/doing sth; draw sb in** make sb take part in sth, esp against his will 使某人参加某事物(尤指勉强他人): *I found myself being drawn into another dreary argument.* 我发现竟然身不由己又参与了一次无聊的争论. ○ *We organize various social activities, but not all the members want to be drawn in.* 我们组织了各式各样的社

D

交活动，但并非所有会员都愿意参加. **draw on** (of a time or season) approach (指时间或季节)临近，接近: *Night was drawing on.* 夜渐深. **draw on/upon sth** use sth 使用; 利用; 运用: *We drew on her experience throughout the project.* 我们这一项目自始至终都借重她的经验. ○ *I shall have to draw on my savings.* 我只好动用我的储蓄. **draw sb on** attract or entice sb 吸引或引诱某人: *They drew investors on with visions of instant wealth.* 他们吸引了大批投资者，使他们以为可以立刻发财致富. **draw out** (of the hours of daylight) become longer in spring (指白天的时间)渐长. **draw sb out (about sth)** encourage sb to talk, etc 鼓励某人说话等: *He's very shy and needs to be drawn out.* 他很腼腆，需要鼓励才肯说话. ○ *I drew the old man out about his war experiences.* 我设法让那老人讲述了他的战争经历. **draw sth out** make (an event, etc) longer than usual 将(事情等)拖长: *She drew the interview out to over an hour.* 她把会见拖长，超过了一小时. ○ *a long-drawn-out discussion* 拖得很久的讨论. **draw up** (of a vehicle) come to a stop (指车辆等)停下来: *The taxi drew up outside the house.* 计程车停在房子外面. **draw sb up** (usu passive 通常用于被动语态) arrange (esp troops) in a special order 使(尤指部队)排好队形: *troops drawn up in ranks* 整好队形的部队. **draw sth up** write out (eg a contract, a list) 草拟或写出(如合同，名单).

□ ˈ**drawstring** *n* string that can be pulled so as to close a bag, purse, garment, etc (口袋、钱包、衣服等的)束带，拉绳.

draw·back /ˈdrɔːbæk; ˋdrɔ,bæk/ *n* **~ (of/to doing sth)** disadvantage; problem 不利条件; 缺点; 障碍: *The great drawback to living on a main road is the constant noise.* 住在通衢大道上的最大缺点就是噪声不断.

draw·bridge /ˈdrɔːbrɪdʒ; ˋdrɔ,brɪdʒ/ *n* bridge (esp formerly across the moat of a castle) that can be pulled up to stop people crossing 吊桥(尤指旧时跨越城堡护壕的): *lower/raise the drawbridge* 放下[拉起]吊桥. ⇨ illus at CASTLE 见CASTLE之插图.

drawer /drɔː(r); drɔr/ *n* **1** box-like container, with one or more handles but no lid, that slides in and out of a piece of furniture, etc 抽屉: *the middle drawer of my desk* 我的写字台中间的抽屉 ○ *clear out one's drawers* 清理抽屉. ⇨ illus at App 1 见附录1之插图, page xvi. **2** /ˈdrɔːə(r); ˋdrɔɚ/ **(a)** (*finance* 财) person who draws a cheque, etc (支票，票据等的)开票人，出票人. **(b)** person who draws pictures 制图者; 绘图员; 画者: *I'm not a very good drawer.* 我不擅长绘图.

drawers /drɔːz; drɔrz/ *n* [pl] (*dated* 旧) knickers or underpants 内裤: *a pair of drawers* 一条内裤.

draw·ing /ˈdrɔːɪŋ; ˋdrɔ·ɪŋ/ *n* **1** [U] art of representing objects by lines, with a pencil, chalk, etc 绘画(艺术); 制图(技巧): *classes in figure drawing* 人物素描课. **2** [C] picture made in this way 图画; 图样: *a collection of Italian drawings* 意大利素描集.

□ ˈ**drawing-board** *n* **1** flat board to which paper is fixed while a drawing is made 制图板; 绘图板. **2** (idm 习语) **(go) back to the drawing-board** prepare a new plan for sth because an earlier one has failed (失败后)重新做: *They've rejected our proposal, so it's back to the drawing-board, I'm afraid.* 他们已经拒绝了我们的建议，看来我们得从头来了.

ˈ**drawing-pin** (*US* ˈ**thumb-tack**) *n* flat-headed pin for fastening paper, etc to a board, wall, etc 图钉.

drawing-room /ˈdrɔːɪŋ rʊm, -ruːm; ˋdrɔ·ɪŋ,rʊm, -rum/ *n* room, esp in a large private house, in which people relax and guests are received and entertained 客厅(尤指私人大宅中的). Cf 参看 LIVING ROOM.

drawl /drɔːl; drɔl/ *v* [I, Tn, Tn·p] speak or say (sth) in a slow lazy manner, with drawn-out vowels 拖长腔调慢吞吞地说(话): *drawl (out) one's words* 拉长调说话.

▷ **drawl** *n* [sing] drawling manner of speaking 拖长腔调慢吞吞的说话方式: *a broad Texan drawl* 得克萨斯州人字字拉长调的说话方式.

drawn[1] /drɔːn; drɔn/ *adj* (of a person or his face) looking very tired or worried (指人或人脸)疲惫的，憔悴的，愁眉苦脸的: *She looked pale and drawn after weeks of sleepless nights.* 她经历了数周不眠之夜，看上去脸色苍白，形容憔悴.

drawn[2] *pp* of DRAW[2].

dray /dreɪ; dre/ *n* low flat cart for carrying heavy loads, esp barrels from a brewery 板车，大车(尤指装运酿造厂的大木桶者).

□ ˈ**dray-horse** *n* horse used for pulling a dray 拉板车的马.

dread /dred; drɛd/ *n* **1** [U, C] great fear; terror 恐惧; 畏惧: *He has always stood in dread of his father.* 他一见到他父亲就害怕. ○ *She has a dread of hospitals.* 她害怕医院. **2** [C] thing that is greatly feared 令人惧怕的事物: *Poverty is many people's constant dread.* 人常怕受穷.

▷ **dread** *v* [Tn, Tf, Tt, Tg, Tsg] fear (sth) greatly 惧怕，害怕，畏惧(某事): *dread illness/being ill* 害怕生病 ○ *I dread that I may never see you again.* 我很怕再也见不到你了. ○ *We all dread to think what will happen if the factory closes.* 假如工厂关闭可怎么办，我们想及此事都不寒而栗. ○ *The moment I had been dreading had arrived.* 使我一直忐忑不安的时刻已经来到. **dreaded** *adj* greatly feared 非常可怕的: *the dreaded scourge of smallpox* 可怕的天花祸害.

dread·ful /ˈdredfl; ˋdrɛdfəl/ *adj* **1** [esp attrib 尤作定语] causing great fear or suffering; shocking 产生极大恐惧或痛苦的; 使人震惊的: *a dreadful accident, disease, nightmare* 可怕的事故、疾病、恶梦 ○ *He has to live with the dreadful knowledge that he caused their deaths.* 他知道是自己使他们丧命而终生痛苦. **2** (*infml* 口) bad, boring or annoying 糟糕的; 讨厌的; 烦人的: *What dreadful weather!* 天气糟透了! ○ *a dreadful film, man, meal, country* 糟糕的影片、人、饭菜、国家 ○ *The noise was dreadful.* 噪声真讨厌. **3** [attrib 作定语] (*infml* 口) (used intensively 用以加强语气): *I'm afraid it's all a dreadful mistake.* 看来全都大错特错了.

▷ **dread·fully** /-fəlɪ; -fəlɪ/ *adv* **1** in a serious or shocking manner 严重地; 厉害地; 骇人地: *dreadfully injured* 严重受伤. **2** (*infml* 口) badly 糟糕: *This article is dreadfully written.* 这篇文章写得糟极了. **3** (*infml* 口) very 非常; 极其: *I'm afraid it's dreadfully late.* 我看已经太迟了.

dread·ful·ness *n* [U].

dread·locks /ˈdredlɒks; ˋdrɛd,lɑks/ *n* [pl] hair worn in long curled strands, esp by Rastafarians 拉斯塔法里式发绺(尤指非洲拉斯塔法里人所蓄满头又长又细的发辫). ⇨ illus at PLAIT 见 PLAIT 之插图.

dread·nought /ˈdrednɔːt; ˋdrɛd,nɔt/ *n* early 20th century battleship 无畏战舰(20世纪初的一种战舰).

dream[1] /driːm; drim/ *n* **1** [C] sequence of scenes and feelings occurring in the mind during sleep 梦: *I have a recurrent dream that I've turned into an elephant.* 我屡次梦见自己变成了大象. ○ *Good night — sweet dreams!* 晚安——祝你做好梦! **2** [sing] state of mind in which things happening around one seem unreal 如于梦中的心态: *be/live/go around in a (complete) dream* (全然)处于[生活在]梦幻中. **3** [C] ambition or ideal, esp when it is unrealistic 抱负; 理想; (尤指)梦想: *My son's dream is to be an astronaut.* 我儿子的理想是当宇航员. ○ *the car, holiday, home of your dreams* 你梦寐以求的汽车、假日、家园 ○ *If I win the tournament, it will be a dream come true*, ie something I wanted very much, but did not expect to happen. 我要是能赢得锦标赛，我的梦想就实现了. **4** [sing] (*infml* 口) beautiful or wonderful person or thing 美丽或美好的人或事物: *Her new dress is an absolute dream.* 她的新连衣裙漂亮极了. ○ [attrib 作定语] *a dream house, kitchen* 理想的房屋、厨房. **5** (idm 习语) **a bad ˈdream** situation that is so unpleasant one cannot believe it is real 噩梦般的处境: *You can't be leaving me — this is a bad dream!* 你千万不可离开我——这太可怕了! **beyond one's wildest dreams** ⇨ WILD. **go, etc like a ˈdream** (*infml* 口) work very well 极好用; 性能极佳: *My new car goes like a dream.* 我的新汽车开起来得心应手.

▷ **dream·less** *adj* [usu attrib 通常作定语] (of sleep) without dreams; deep and sound (指睡眠)无梦的，酣畅的.

□ ˈ**dream-land** /-lænd; -,lænd/ *n* [U] (*derog* 贬) pleasant but unrealistic situation imagined by sb 空想; 幻想: *You must be in dream-land if you think he'll pay that much!* 要是以为他会给那么多报酬，不啻是痴人说梦!

ˈ**dreamlike** *adj* like a dream 如梦的; 梦幻般的.

ˈ**dream world** state where sb imagines everything is the way he would like it to be 万事如意的理想境界; 理想世

界.

dream[2] /dri:m; drim/ *v* (*pt, pp* **dreamed** /dri:md; drimd/ or **dreamt** /dremt; drɛmt/) ➪Usage 见所附用法. **1** (**a**) [I] have a dream while asleep 做梦: *She claims she never dreams.* 她说她从来不做梦. (**b**) [Ipr, Tn, Tf] **~ (of sth/doing sth); ~ about sth/doing sth** experience sth in a dream 梦见某事物: *I dreamt about flying last night.* 昨夜我梦见我在飞翔. ○ *Was it real or did I dream it?* 是真的还是我当时在做梦? ○ *I dreamt (that) I could fly.* 我梦见我能飞翔. **2** [I, Ipr, Tn, Tf] **~ (of/about doing sth)** imagine sth 想像、幻想或梦想某事物: *I never promised to lend you my car: you must be dreaming!* 我从未答应过把汽车借给你: 你是在做梦吧! ○ *He dreams of one day becoming a famous violinist.* 他梦想有朝一日成为著名的小提琴家. ○ *Who'd have dreamt it? They're getting married!* 谁能想像得到? 他们竟然要结婚了! ○ *I never dreamt (that) I'd see you again.* 我绝没想到还能看见你. **3** (idm 习语) **not dream of sth/doing sth** not do sth under any circumstances 无论如何也不做某事物: *I should never have dreamt of saying such a thing.* 我无论如何也不会说出这样的话来. ○ *I'd never dream of allowing my child to do that.* 我决不允许我的孩子做那种事. **4** (phr v) **dream sth away** spend (time) idly 虚度(光阴): *She dreamt her life away, never really achieving anything.* 她虚度一生, 一事无成. **dream on** (*infml ironic* 口, 反语) continue to hope for sth that will not happen 痴心妄想: *So you want a rise? Dream on!* 那么说你想加薪? 做梦去吧! **dream sth up** (*infml* 口) think of (esp sth imaginative or foolish) 想入非非: *Trust you to dream up a crazy scheme like this!* 亏你想得出这种异想天开的计划!

▷ **dreamer** *n* **1** person who is dreaming 做梦的人. **2** (*usu derog* 通常作贬义) (**a**) person with (seemingly) impractical ideas, plans, etc 梦想家; 空想家: *People who said we would go to the moon used to be called dreamers.* 从前把那些说我们要登上月球的人都称之为空想家. (**b**) person who does not concentrate on what happens around him, but daydreams instead 做白日梦者: *Don't rely on his memory — he's a bit of a dreamer.* 不要相信他的记忆力 —— 他有点神不守舍的.

NOTE ON USAGE 用法: Several verbs have alternative regular and irregular past tense and past participle forms 有些动词兼有规则和不规则的过去式和过去分词的形式: **dream, dreamed/dreamt**; **spoil, spoiled/spoilt**. In British English the irregular form **(dreamt, spoilt,** etc) is preferred. 在英式英语中多用不规则的形式(**dreamt**、**spoilt** 等). The regular past tense is more often used when it describes an action that lasts some time 描述动作延续一段时间时, 多用规则的过去式: *He learnt his lesson.* 他得到了教训. ○ *She learned a lot about life from her mother.* 她从母亲那里学到不少做人的道理. ○ *He leant against the post and it broke.* 他往杆子上一倚, 杆子就断了. ○ *He leaned out of the window watching the parade.* 他从窗口探出身看游行. In US English there is a preference for the regular past tense and past participle forms (**dreamed, spoiled,** etc). 在美式英语中多用规则的过去式和过去分词的形式(**dreamed**、**spoiled** 等). In both British and US English the irregular form of the past participle is found in adjectival uses 在英式英语和美式英语中, 过去分词的不规则形式作形容词用: *a spoilt child* 宠坏了的孩子 ○ *spilt milk* 泼洒了的牛奶 ○ *a misspelt word* 拼错的字.

dreamy /ˈdri:mɪ; ˋdrimɪ/ *adj* (**-ier, -iest**) **1** (of a person) with thoughts far away from his present surroundings, work, etc (指人)心不在焉的. **2** vague or unclear 模糊的; 不清楚的: *a dreamy recollection of what happened* 对已发生的事情模糊的回忆. **3** (*infml* 口) pleasantly gentle and relaxing 轻柔的; 轻松恬静的: *dreamy music* 梦幻般柔曼的音乐. **4** (*infml* 口) wonderful 绝妙的; 极好的: *What a dreamy little house!* 多么小巧玲珑的房子啊! ▷ **dream·ily** /-ɪlɪ; -ɪlɪ/ *adv*. **dreami·ness** *n* [U].

dreary /ˈdrɪərɪ; ˋdrɪrɪ/ (also *arch* 古语作 **drear** /drɪə(r); drɪr/) *adj* (**-ier, -iest**) **1** that makes one sad or depressed; dismal; gloomy 使人闷闷不乐或沮丧的; 阴沉的; 忧郁的: *a dreary winter day* 沉闷的冬日. **2** (*infml* 口) boring; dull 令人厌烦的; 单调的; 枯燥的: *dreary people leading dreary lives* 过着无聊生活的无聊的人. ▷ **drear·ily** /ˈdrɪərəlɪ; ˋdrɪrəlɪ/ *adv*. **dreari·ness** *n* [U].

dredge[1] /dredʒ; drɛdʒ/ (also **dredger**) *n* machine for scooping or sucking mud, etc from the bottom of a river, canal, etc 挖泥机(从河底挖或吸泥等的机器).

▷ **dredge** *v* **1** [Tn] deepen or clear (a river, etc) with a dredge (用挖泥机)疏浚(河道等): *They have to dredge the canal so that ships can use it.* 他们须疏浚运河河道轮船方可通航. **2** [I, Ipr, Tn, Tn·pr, Tn·p] **~ sth (up) (from sth)** bring sth up using a dredge (用挖泥机)挖出或吸出某物: *dredge for oysters* 采捞牡蛎 ○ *We're dredging (up) mud (from the river bed).* 我们正在(从河床)挖淤泥. **3** (phr v) **dredge sth up** (*usu derog* 通常作贬义) mention sth that has been forgotten, esp sth that is unpleasant or embarrassing 重提旧事(尤指不愉快或令人难堪者): *dredge up details of that episode in Cairo* 重提已被遗忘的开罗事件中的许多细节. **dredger** (also **dredge**) *n* boat or machine used for dredging 挖泥船; 挖泥机.

dredge[2] /dredʒ; drɛdʒ/ *v* [Tn, Tn·pr] **~ A (with B); ~ B over/on A** sprinkle (food) with (flour, sugar, etc) (在食物上)撒(面粉、糖等): *dredge a cake with icing sugar* 把糖霜撒在蛋糕上 ○ *dredge icing sugar over a cake* 在蛋糕上撒糖霜.

▷ **dredger** *n* container with holes in the lid, used for dredging food 撒粉器(盖上有小孔, 用以向食物撒粉者).

dregs /dregz; drɛgz/ *n* [pl] **1** solid particles that sink to the bottom of certain liquids, esp wine and beer 沉淀物(尤指葡萄酒和啤酒中者). **2** (*fig* 比喻) worst and most useless part (of sth) 残渣; 渣滓: *the dregs of society* 社会的渣滓. **3** (idm 习语) **drink/drain sth to the ˈdregs** drink all of sth 喝干; 喝光.

drench /drentʃ; drɛntʃ/ *v* [esp passive 尤用于被动语态: Tn, Tn·pr, Tn·p] **1** make (sb/sth) completely wet 使(某人[某物])湿透: *We were caught in the storm and got drenched (through/to the skin).* 我们遇上大雨, 全都浇透了. ○ *be drenched with rain* 被雨浇透. **2 ~ sb/sth (in/with sth)** apply (a liquid) freely to sb/sth 在某人[某物]上大量使用(某液体): *drench oneself in perfume* 全身喷满香水 ○ *The poster wouldn't stick even though I drenched it with glue.* 我涂了大量胶水, 可那张海报就是贴不住.

▷ **drench·ing** *n* thorough wetting 湿透.

dress[1] /dres; drɛs/ *n* **1** [C] garment for a woman or girl, consisting of a bodice and skirt in one piece; frock 连衣裙; (上下连身的)女装: *She makes all her own dresses.* 她的连衣裙都是自己做的. **2** [U] clothes, esp outer garments, for either men or women 衣服(男女均可); (尤指)外衣: *casual/formal dress* 便服[礼服] ○ *evening dress* 晚礼服.

□ **ˈdress-circle** *n* (*Brit*) (*US* **first balcony**) first gallery in a theatre (where evening dress was formerly required) 戏院中楼厅的前排座位(从前要求坐该处的观众穿晚礼服). Cf 参看 MEZZANINE.

ˈdressmaker *n* person (esp a woman) who makes women's clothes (专做女服的)裁缝, (尤指)女裁缝. **ˈdressmaking** *n* [U].

ˈdress rehearsal **1** final rehearsal of a play, with the costumes, lighting, etc as they would be in a real performance 彩排. **2** (*fig* 比喻) practice 排演; 演习: *The earlier revolts had just been dress rehearsals for full-scale revolution.* 那些初期的反叛活动只不过是大规模革命行动的演习.

ˈdress-shirt *n* shirt, sometimes with a frilly front, worn with a dinner jacket 礼服衬衫(有时前襟有褶边装饰).

ˌdress ˈuniform elegant military dress worn by officers on ceremonial occasions 军礼服.

dress[2] /dres; drɛs/ *v* **1** [I, Tn] put clothes on (sb/oneself) 穿衣: *He takes ages to dress.* 他穿衣要用很长时间. ○ *Hurry up and get dressed!* 快点穿上衣服! ○ *Is she old enough to dress herself yet?* 她会自己穿衣服了吗? ○ *He was dressed as a woman*, ie wearing a woman's clothes. 他男扮女装. ○ *a woman dressed in green* 穿着绿衣服的女子. **2** [I, Ipr] put on evening dress 穿晚礼服: *Do I need to dress for the theatre?* 我去剧院需要穿晚礼服吗? **3** [I, Tn] provide (sb/oneself) with clothes 为(某人[自己])提供衣服: *dress well, badly, fashionably, gaudily, etc* 穿得好、不好、时髦、俗气等 ○ *She can*

D

hardly dress her children on the allowance he gives her. 他给她的那点钱连给孩子买衣服都不够. ○ *The princess is dressed by a rising young designer.* 公主的衣服是一位初露头角的年轻设计师设计的. **4** [Tn] decorate (sth) 装饰(某物): *dress a shop window*, ie arrange a display of goods in it 布置橱窗 ○ *dress a street with flags* 用旗子装饰街道 ○ *dress a Christmas tree with lights* 用彩灯装饰圣诞树. **5** [Tn] clean and bandage (a wound, etc) 清洗并包扎(伤口等). **6** [Tn] finish or treat the surface of (sth) 加工、处理或修整(某物的)表面: *dress leather, stone, etc* 鞣皮、琢石等. **7** [Tn] prepare (food) for cooking or eating 为烹调或食用准备(食物): *dress a chicken*, ie clean it ready for cooking 把鸡清洗好(待烹) ○ *dress a salad*, ie add a dressing to it before serving 给色拉加调味品. **8** [Tn] brush (a horse's coat); groom 梳刷(马的毛); 梳理. **9** [I, Tn] draw up (troops) in line 整队: *dress the ranks* 整队. **10** (idm 习语) **(be) dressed in sth** wearing sth 穿某物: *The bride was dressed in white.* 新娘穿一身白色的礼服. **(be) dressed like a dog's dinner** (*infml* 口) dressed very smartly or showily 穿着十分时髦或显眼. **(be) dressed (up) to 'kill** (*infml* 口) be dressed so as to attract attention and admiration, esp from the opposite sex 穿着引人注目(尤指吸引异性). **(be) dressed up to the nines** very elaborately dressed 穿着讲究. **mutton dressed as lamb** ⇨ MUTTON. **11** (phr v) **dress sb down** scold sb; tell sb off 训斥, 斥退(某人). **dress up** wear one's best clothes 穿上盛装: *Don't bother to dress up — come as you are.* 用不着穿讲究衣服——就穿平常的衣服来吧. **dress (sb) up (in sth/as sb/sth)** put on fancy dress, etc 化装打扮: *Children love dressing up.* 孩子们都喜欢化装打扮. ○ *dress (up) as a fairy, bandit, pirate, etc* 打扮成仙女、匪徒、海盗等 ○ *They were dressed up in Victorian clothes.* 他们化装成维多利亚时代的人. **dress sth up** (*fig* 比喻) make sth seem better or different by careful presentation 修饰; 掩饰: *The facts are quite clear; it's no use trying to dress them up.* 事实很清楚, 想掩饰是没有用的. ○ *rumours dressed up as hard news* 以假乱真的谣言.

□ **ˌdressing 'down** *n* severe scolding 痛骂; 厉斥: *give sb/get a (good) dressing down* 给某人[挨](好)一顿骂.

dress·age /ˈdresɑːʒ; drɛˈsɑʒ/ *n* [U] (**a**) training a horse to perform various movements that show its obedience to its rider 花式骑术训练. (**b**) display of such actions in a competition (马术比赛中)花式骑术表演.

dresser[1] /ˈdresə(r); ˈdrɛsɚ/ *n* **1** (used with an *adj* 与形容词连用) person who dresses in a specified way 以某种方式穿着的人: *a smart, scruffy, snappy, etc dresser* 衣着时髦者、邋遢者、漂亮者等. **2** (in a theatre) person who helps actors put on their costumes (在剧院中)服装师. **3** (*medical* 医) person who helps a surgeon during an operation 外科医生助手.

dresser[2] /ˈdresə(r); ˈdrɛsɚ/ *n* **1** (*esp Brit*) piece of kitchen furniture with shelves for dishes and cupboards below 碗柜; 碗橱. ⇨illus at App 1 见附录1之插图, page xvi. **2** (*US*) chest of drawers with a mirror on top 梳妆台.

dress·ing /ˈdresɪŋ; ˈdrɛsɪŋ/ *n* **1** [U] action of putting on clothes, bandaging wounds, etc 穿衣; 包扎伤口: *Dressing always takes her such a long time.* 她穿衣服总是要那么长时间. **2** [C, U] bandage, ointment, etc for treating a wound 敷料(处理伤口用的纱布、油膏等): *apply, change a dressing* 施、换敷料. **3** [C, U] sauce for food, esp a mixture of oil and vinegar for salads (食物)调料(尤指拌制色拉的油和醋的混合物): *salad dressing* 色拉调料. **4** [U] (*US*) = STUFFING.

□ **'dressing-gown** *n* (*US* usu 美式英语通常作 **bathrobe, robe**) loose gown worn indoors, usu before dressing 晨衣(通常为梳妆前在室内穿着的长而宽松的罩衫).

'dressing-room *n* room for changing one's clothes, esp one where an actor puts on his costume 更衣室; (尤指演员的)化妆室. ⇨illus at App 1 见附录1之插图, page ix.

'dressing-table *n* piece of bedroom furniture with a mirror and drawers, used esp by women when they dress, make up, etc 梳妆台. ⇨illus at App 1 见附录1之插图, page xvi.

dressy /ˈdresɪ; ˈdrɛsɪ/ *adj* (**-ier, -iest**) (*infml* 口) **1** (of a person) (fond of) wearing stylish or showy clothes (指人)穿着入时的, 爱穿花哨服装的: *They're a very dressy couple.* 他们俩是讲究穿着的一对儿. **2** (of clothes) elegant or elaborate, to be worn on special occasions (指衣物)漂亮的, 讲究的, 特殊场合穿的: *You can't wear that to the reception — it's not dressy enough.* 你不能穿那种衣服出席招待会——不太庄重.

drew *pt* of DRAW[2].

dribble /ˈdrɪbl; ˈdrɪbḷ/ *v* **1** [I, Ipr] allow saliva to run from the mouth 流口水; 流口涎: *The baby's just dribbled down my tie.* 孩子刚才淌口水弄湿了我的领带. **2** [I, Ipr, Ip, Tn, Tn·pr] (cause a liquid to) fall in drops or a thin stream (使液体)滴下或作细流: *water dribbling out (of a tap)* (从水龙头)滴下来的水 ○ *Dribble the oil into the beaten egg yolks.* 往打匀的蛋黄里一滴滴加油. **3** [I, Ipr, Tn, Tn·pr] (in football, hockey, etc) move (the ball) forward with repeated slight touches (足球、曲棍球等中)运球, 带球: *He dribbled (the ball) past the goalie to score.* 他带球越过守门员射门得分.

▷ **dribble** *n* (usu *sing* 通常作单数) **1** trickle 涓滴; 细滴: *a thin dribble of oil* 细线般滴下的油. **2** act of dribbling a ball 运球; 带球. **3** very small amount of a liquid 少量(液体): *There's only a dribble of coffee left, I'm afraid.* 看来只剩下一点点咖啡了.

drib·let /ˈdrɪblɪt; ˈdrɪblɪt/ *n* small amount 少量; 点滴; 零星: *in driblets*, ie a little at a time 一点点地.

dribs /drɪbz; ˈdrɪbz/ *n* [pl] (idm 习语) **in ˌdribs and 'drabs** (*infml* 口) in small amounts 少量; 一点点; 零零星星: *She paid me in dribs and drabs, not all at once.* 她零零星星地付给我钱, 而不是一次付清.

dried *pt, pp* of DRY[2].

drier[1] *compar of* DRY[1].

drier[2] *n* ⇨ DRY[2].

drift[1] /drɪft; drɪft/ *n* **1** [U] drifting movement 漂; 漂动; 漂流; 漂移: *the drift of the tide, current, wind, etc* 潮汐、水流、风等的缓缓流动. **2** [C] (*fig* 比喻) continuous uncontrolled movement or tendency towards sth bad (朝坏的方面发展的)倾向, 动向, 趋势: *a slow drift into debt, war, crisis, etc* 逐步走上借贷的道路、逐渐演变为战争、渐渐陷入危机. **3** [U] practice of being inactive and waiting for things to happen 不采取行动以等待事情发展的做法: *Is the Government's policy one of drift?* 政府采取的是否放任自流的政策? **4** [sing] (of speech, writing, etc) general meaning or sense; gist (指讲话、写作等)主旨, 大意, 含意: *My German isn't very good, but I got the general drift of what she said.* 我的德语不太好, 但她说的话我大致是明白的. **5** [C] mass of sth, esp snow or sand, piled up by the wind (风吹成的)堆积物, (尤指)雪堆, 沙堆: *deep snow-drifts* (风吹成的)厚厚的积雪. **6** [U] deposits of earth, gravel, rock, etc left behind by a glacier 冰碛. **7** [U] = DRIFTAGE.

▷ **drift·age** /-ɪdʒ; -ɪdʒ/ *n* [U] deviation by a ship from a set course, due to currents, winds, etc (船航行时受水流、风等影响对航线的)偏移, 偏差.

drift[2] /drɪft; drɪft/ *v* **1** [I, Ipr, Ip] be carried along gently by a current of air or water 飘移; 漂流: *We switched off the motor and started to drift (along).* 我们关闭发动机开始滑行. ○ *The boat drifted down the river.* 船顺河漂流而下. **2** [I, Ipr, Ip] (of snow, sand, etc) be piled into drifts by the wind (指雪、沙等)受风吹积: *Some roads are closed owing to drifting.* 有些道路因积雪而封闭. **3** [Tn, Tn·pr, Tn·p] cause (sth) to drift 使(某物)漂流, 飘动: *The logs are drifted downstream to the mill.* 那些原木沿河顺水漂到工厂. ○ *The wind drifted the snow into a high bank, blocking the road.* 风把雪吹积成长埂, 堵塞了道路. **4** [I, Ipr, Ip] (of people) move casually or aimlessly (指人)漫无目标地移动, 漂泊, 流浪: *The crowds drifted away from the stadium.* 人群慢慢从体育场散去. ○ *She finally drifted in two hours after everyone else.* 在大家到齐之后两小时, 她终于姗姗来到. ○ (*fig* 比喻) *He doesn't want a career, he's just drifting.* 他并不想要个固定职业, 只是碰到什么事做什么事. ○ *I didn't mean to be a teacher — I sort of drifted into it.* 我本来没想当教师——可谓无意间当上的. ○ *They used to be friends, but now they've drifted apart.* 他们原是朋友, 现在已经疏远了.

▷ **drifter** *n* **1** (*usu derog* 通常作贬义) aimless or rootless person 漂泊者; 流浪汉: *He's just a drifter — he can't settle down anywhere.* 他不过是个流浪汉——哪儿也呆不住. **2** boat used for fishing with a drift-net 飘网

渔船; 流网渔船.

□ ˈ**drift-ice** *n* [U] masses of broken ice floating in the sea, a river, etc 流冰.

ˈ**drift-net** *n* large net into which fish move with the tide 流网; 飘网.

ˈ**drift-wood** *n* [U] wood floating on the sea or washed ashore by it 浮木, 漂木(在海上漂流或被海水冲上岸的木头).

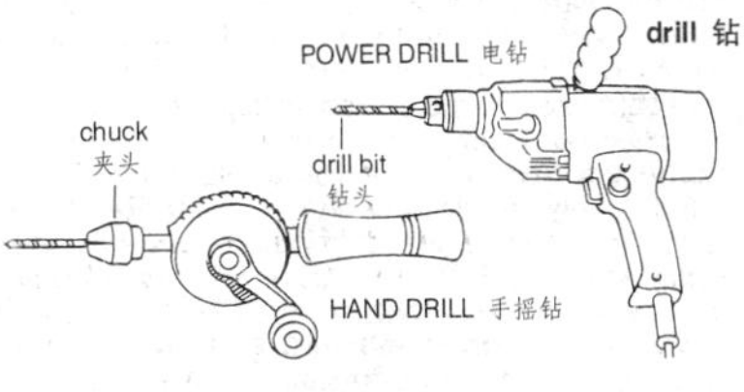

drill[1] /drɪl; drɪl/ *n* tool or machine with a detachable pointed end for making holes 钻; 钻床; 钻机: *a dentist's drill* 牙钻 ○ *a pneumatic drill* 风钻. Cf 参看 BIT[2] 2.

▷ **drill** *v* [I, Ipr, Tn, Tn·pr] make (a hole, etc) in some substance, esp with a drill 钻(孔), 打眼(尤指用钻机): *drill for oil* 钻井探油 ○ *They're drilling a new tunnel under the Thames.* 在泰晤士河河床下钻凿一条新隧道.

drill[2] /drɪl; drɪl/ *n* **1** [U] training in military exercises 军事训练; 操练: *New recruits have three hours of drill a day.* 新兵一天有三小时的操练. **2** (**a**) [U] thorough training by practical and usu repetitive exercises 练习: *regular drill to establish good habits* 有规则的训练以养成好习惯. (**b**) [C] such an exercise 训练; 练习: *pronunciˈation drills* 发音练习. **3** (**a**) [U] procedures to be followed in an emergency (紧急情况下的)步骤, 方法, 措施: *ˈlifeboat drill* 救生艇上的应急措施. (**b**) [C] practice session to test people's knowledge of this 演习: *There'll be a ˈfire-drill this morning.* 今天上午有消防演习. **4 the drill** [sing] (*Brit infml* 口) correct procedure for doing sth 做某事的正确方法; 程序; 步骤; 常规: *What's the drill for claiming expenses?* 费用报销的手续是怎样的? ○ *learn, know, teach sb the drill* 学习、了解、传授某人做某事的正确方法.

▷ **drill** *v* [I, Tn] be trained or train (sb) by means of drills 训练(某人); 操练; 演习: *The well-drilled crew managed to rescue most of the passengers.* 训练有素的机组人员设法营救出了大部分乘客.

drill[3] /drɪl; drɪl/ *n* **1** furrow 犁; 条播. **2** machine for making furrows, sowing seeds in them and covering the seeds 条播机. **3** row of seeds sown in this way 条播的一排种子.

▷ **drill** *v* [Tn] sow (seeds) in furrows 条播(种子).

drill[4] /drɪl; drɪl/ *n* [U] strong heavy linen or cotton cloth (粗斜纹的)麻布或棉布.

drill[5] /drɪl; drɪl/ *n* type of large African monkey 黑脸山魈(非洲产).

drily = DRYLY (DRY[1]).

drink[1] /drɪŋk; drɪŋk/ *n* **1** (**a**) [U, C] liquid for drinking 饮料: *food and drink* 食物与饮料 ○ *fizzy drinks* 发嘶嘶声起泡的饮料. (**b**) [C] amount of liquid drunk or served 一杯或一份饮料: *a drink of water* 一杯水. **2** (**a**) [U] alcoholic liquor 酒: *Isn't there any drink in the house?* 家里有酒吗? (**b**) [C] amount of this drunk or served 一杯或一份酒: *How about a quick drink?* 我们赶快喝杯酒好吗? ○ *Drinks are on me*, ie I will pay for them. 酒钱由我付. ○ *He's had one drink too many*, ie He is slightly drunk. 他有点醉了. **3** [U] habit of drinking too much alcohol 酗酒; 纵酒: *Drink is a growing problem among the young.* 年轻人的酗酒问题越来越严重. ○ *take to drink because of domestic problems* 受家庭问题困扰而耽于饮酒. **4 the drink** [sing] (*sl* 俚) the sea 海: *We crash-landed in the drink.* 我们在海上紧急降落. **5** (idm 习语) **be the ˌworse for ˈdrink** be very drunk 酩酊大醉. **the demon drink** ⇨ DEMON. **drive sb to drink** ⇨ DRIVE[1]. **meat and drink to sb** ⇨ MEAT.

drink[2] /drɪŋk; drɪŋk/ *v* (*pt* **drank** /dræŋk; dræŋk/, *pp* **drunk** /drʌŋk; drʌŋk/) **1** [I, Tn] take (liquid) into the mouth and swallow 喝; 饮: *Some horses were drinking at a trough.* 有些马在水槽边饮水. ○ *He drank a pint of milk in one go.* 他一口气喝了一品脱牛奶. **2** [Tn, Tn·p] **~ sth (in/up)** (of plants, the soil, etc) take in or absorb (usu water) (指植物、土壤等)吸收, 吸入(通常为水分). **3** [I] take alcohol 喝酒: *He never drinks.* 他滴酒不沾. ○ *They drink too much.* 他们喝酒喝得太多了. ○ *Don't drink and drive!* 切勿酒后开车! **4** [Tn·pr, Cn·a] bring (oneself) to a specified state by taking alcohol 使(自己)喝酒喝到某种程度: *You're drinking yourself to death.* 你这样喝酒要喝掉命的. ○ (*infml* 口) *They drank themselves stupid.* 他们喝得晕头转向. **5** (idm 习语) **drink sb's ˈhealth/drink a health to sb** (*fml* 文) express one's respect or good wishes for sb, by drinking a toast 向某人祝酒. **drink like a ˈfish** (*infml* 口) habitually drink large quantities of alcohol (习惯性地)豪饮. **drink/drain sth to the dregs** ⇨ DREGS. **drink sb under the ˈtable** (*infml* 口) drink more alcohol than sb else without becoming as drunk 灌醉某人(自己喝得更多但不醉). **you can take, etc a horse to water, but you can't make him drink** ⇨ HORSE. **6** (phr v) **drink sth down/up** drink the whole or the rest of sth, esp quickly 喝光, 喝干(尤指很快饮尽): *I know the medicine tastes nasty, but drink it down.* 我知道药味很苦, 不过还是一口灌下去吧. ○ (*Brit*) *drinking-ˈup time*, ie time allowed for finishing drinks before a public house closes (酒馆关门前允许顾客把酒喝完的)延长时间. **drink sth in** watch or listen to sth with great pleasure or interest 看得或听得出神: *They stood drinking in the beauty of the landscape.* 他们站在那儿尽情欣赏美景. **drink (sth) to sb/sth** express good wishes to sb/sth by drinking (a toast) 向某人[为某事]祝酒: *drink to sb's health, happiness, prosperity, etc* 为某人健康、幸福、成功等干杯 ○ *Let's drink to the success of your plans.* 让我们为你的计划成功干杯. ○ *I'll drink to that!* ie I agree. 我完全赞成!

▷ **drink·able** *adj* suitable or safe for drinking 可饮用的; 适合饮用的: *Is this water drinkable?* 这水可以喝吗? ○ (*fig* 比喻) *a drinkable* (ie pleasant but not particularly good) *wine* 尚可一喝的酒(不错但并非特好).

drinker *n* person who drinks (usu too much) alcohol 饮酒者; (通常指)酒徒: *a terrible/heavy/hardened/serious drinker* 酗酒者[豪饮者/酒鬼/酒徒].

drink·ing *n* [U]: *Drinking is known to be harmful.* 饮酒有害. ○ [attrib 作定语] *a ˈdrinking-bout* 一阵狂饮.

□ ˈ**drinking-fountain** *n* device supplying drinking-water in a public place (设于公共场所的)喷泉式饮水器.

ˈ**drinking-song** *n* song, usu about the pleasures of drinking, to be sung at drinkers' parties (酒会上的)饮酒歌.

ˈ**drinking-water** *n* [U] water safe for drinking 饮用水.

drip[1] /drɪp; drɪp/ *v* (**-pp-**) **1** (**a**) [Ipr, Ip] fall in drops 滴下: *Rain was dripping (down) from the trees.* 雨水从树上滴下. (**b**) [I, Tn, Tn·pr] let (liquid) fall in drops 让(液体)滴下: *Is that roof still dripping?* 那个屋顶还漏雨吗? ○ *a dripping tap* 滴水的龙头 ○ *He was dripping blood (onto the floor).* 他的血正在滴(到地板上). **2** (idm 习语) **be dripping with sth** be full of or covered with sth 充满; 布满: *His letter was dripping with flattery.* 他的信中充满阿谀之词. ○ *dripping with jewels* 浑身珠光宝气. **dripping/wringing wet** ⇨ WET.

□ ˌ**drip-ˈdry** *adj* (of a garment) able to dry quickly when hung up to drip (指衣服)能很快滴干的: *a ˌdrip-dry ˈshirt, ˈfabric* 能很快滴干的衬衫、织物.

NOTE ON USAGE 用法: **Drip, leak, ooze, run, seep** indicate the way in which a liquid escapes from a container or tap. ☆ **drip**、**leak**、**ooze**、**run**、**seep** 都表示液体从容器或活门流出的方式. Most (not **seep**) also indicate the way in which a container or tap allows a liquid to escape. 除 **seep** 外, 皆可指容器或活门使液体流出的方式. **1 Drip** = (allow sth to) fall in regular drops ☆ **drip** = (使某物)有规律地滴落: *Water is dripping from the pipe.* 水从管中滴落. *The pipe is dripping (water).* 管子在滴(水)呢. **2 Leak** = (allow sth to) get out (through a hole in sth) ☆ **leak** = (使某物从孔中)漏出: *Wine is leaking from the barrel.* 酒自桶中渗漏出来. *The barrel is leaking (wine).* 酒桶漏(酒). **3 Ooze** = (allow sth to) move slowly (out of sth) because thick ☆

ooze = (使某物)慢慢流出(因很稠): *Blood is oozing from the wound.* 血从伤口慢慢流出. *The wound is oozing (blood).* 伤口在出血. **4 Run** = (allow sth to) flow continuously (from sth) ☆ **run** = (使某物)连续不断流出: *Water is running from the tap.* 水从龙头中流出. *The tap is running.* 龙头在流水. **5 Seep** = move slowly (through a small opening in sth) ☆ **seep** = (从细孔中)慢慢流出: *Oil is seeping from the engine.* 油从发动机中渗出.

drip[2] /drɪp; drɪp/ *n* **1 (a)** [sing] series of drops of falling liquid (连续落下的)液滴: *the steady drip of water from a leaky tap* 从漏水的龙头中不断滴下的水滴. **(b)** [C] any one of these drops 一滴: *The roof is leaking — fetch a bucket to catch the drips.* 屋顶漏水——拿桶来接(水滴). **2** [C] (*medical* 医) device that lets (liquid food, medicine, etc) directly into a patient's vein 滴注器: *put sb on a drip*, ie fit such a device to a patient 给某人输液. **3** [C] (*sl* 俚) weak or boring person 软弱的或讨厌的人: *Don't be such a drip! Come and join in the fun.* 别呆在那里了! 过来一起玩儿吧.

D

drip·ping /ˈdrɪpɪŋ; ˋdrɪpɪŋ/ *n* [U] fat melted out of roast meat (烤肉上滴下的)油滴.

□ **ˈdripping-pan** *n* pan in which dripping collects during roasting (烤肉时用以承接的)接油盘.

drive[1] /draɪv; draɪv/ *v* (*pt* **drove** /drəʊv; drov/, *pp* **driven** /ˈdrɪvn; ˋdrɪvən/) **1 (a)** [I, Tn] (be able to) operate (a vehicle or locomotive) and direct its course (能)驾驶(车); 开(火车): *Can you drive?* 你会开车吗? ○ *He drives a taxi*, ie That is his job. 他开计程车. ○ *I drive* (ie own) *a Rolls-Royce.* 我开的是劳斯莱斯汽车. **(b)** [I, Ipr, Ip] come or go somewhere in a car, van, etc 开车来或去某处: *Did you drive* (ie come by car)*?* 你是开车来的吗? ○ *I drive to work.* 我开车上班. ○ *Don't stop — drive on!* 不要停——往前开! ⇨Usage at TRAVEL 用法见TRAVEL. **(c)** [Tn, Tn·pr, Tn·p] take (sb) somewhere in a car, taxi, etc 用汽车、计程车等送(某人)至某处: *Could you drive me to the station?* 你可以开车送我到车站去吗? **2** [Tn, Tn·pr, Tn·p] cause (animals or people) to move in some direction by shouts, blows, threats, etc 驱赶(动物或人): *some cattle being driven by a man on a horse* 骑马人驱赶着的一群牛 ○ *drive sheep into a field* 把羊赶到地里 ○ *They drove the enemy back*, ie forced them to retreat. 他们把敌人击退. ○ (*fig* 比喻) *I was driven out of the club.* 我被驱逐出俱乐部. **3** [Tn, Tn·pr, Tn·p] (of wind or water) carry (sth) along (指风或水)卷, 刮, 冲, 冲(某物): *Huge waves drove the yacht onto the rocks.* 巨浪把游艇卷到岩石上. ○ *dead leaves driven along by the wind* 风刮起的枯叶. **4** [I, Ipr] move rapidly or violently 急速地或猛烈地运动: *driving rain, hail, snow, etc* 如注的大雨、猛烈的冰雹、纷飞的大雪 ○ *The waves drove against the shore.* 波浪冲击着岸边. **5** [Tn·pr] **(a)** force (sth) to go in a specified direction or into a specified position 迫使(某物)移动或进入某位置; 打; 敲; 击; 戳; 拧: *drive a nail into wood, a stake into the ground, etc* 把钉子钉入木中、把桩打进地里 ○ (*fig* 比喻) *drive a proposal through Parliament* 迫使议会通过一项建议. **(b)** construct (sth) with difficulty (吃力地)建造(某物): *drive a new motorway across a mountain range.* 奋力修筑穿越山地的高速公路. ○ *They drove a tunnel through the rock.* 他们凿通一条穿过岩石的隧道. **6 (a)** [Tn, Tn·p] force (sb) to act 迫使(某人)行动: *A man driven by jealousy is capable of anything.* 嫉妒心可使人什么都做得出来. ○ *The urge to survive drove them on.* 求生的欲望驱使他们继续努力. **(b)** [Tn·pr, Cn·a, Cn·t] cause or compel (sb) to be in a specified state or do a specified thing 使或逼(某人)处于某种状态或做某事: *drive sb crazy/to insanity/out of his mind* 将某人逼疯[使某人精神失常/使某人丧失理智] ○ *Hunger drove her to steal.* 饥饿逼得她行窃. **(c)** [Tn] make (sb) work very hard, esp too hard 使(某人)努力(尤指过分): *Unless he stops driving himself like this he'll have a breakdown.* 他要是总这样拼命干下去是吃不消的. ○ *He drives the team relentlessly.* 他无情地鞭策全队苦练. **7** [I, Ipr, Tn, Tn·pr] (*sport* 体) hit and send (a ball, etc) forward with force, esp in tennis, golf or cricket 猛击, 猛抽(尤指网球、高尔夫球或板球): *drive (the ball) into the rough* (将球)击入深草区 ○ *He drove beautifully*, ie played this stroke well. 他这一球击得很漂亮. **8** [Tn esp passive 尤用于被动语态] (of electricity or some other power) keep (machinery) going (指电力或其他动力)驱动, 推动: *a steam-driven engine* 蒸汽机. **9** (idm 习语) **be driving at** (always with *what* as the object 必须以what 作宾语) be trying to do or say 意在; 意指; 打算: *What are you driving at?* 你是什么意思呢? ○ *I wish I knew what they were really driving at.* 我希望我能知道他们真实的意图. **drive a coach and horses through sth** disregard (eg a law or rule) in an obvious and a serious way without being punished, usu because of a loophole 钻(法律或规章的)空子. **drive a hard ˈbargain** insist on the best possible price, arrangements, etc when negotiating with sb 极力讨价还价. **drive sth home (to sb)** make sb realize sth, esp by saying it often, loudly, angrily, etc 使某人充分认识或理解某事物(尤指经常地、大声地、愤怒地说): *drive one's point home* 阐明自己的观点 ○ *I drove home to him that he must be here by ten.* 我跟他说得清清楚楚: 他必须十点钟以前到这里. **drive sth into sb's ˈhead** make sb remember sth, esp with difficulty (尤指费力地)使某人记住某事. **drive sb to ˈdrink** (*esp joc* 尤作戏谑语) make sb so worried, frustrated, etc that he starts drinking too much alcohol 使得某人借酒浇愁: *Working here is enough to drive anyone to drink.* 在这里干活足可以逼得人以喝酒解烦. **drive a wedge between A and B** make (friends, colleagues, etc) quarrel or start disliking each other 挑拨(朋友、同事等)不和或互相厌恶; 造成分裂. **let drive (at sb)** hit or aim blows at sb 打击某人; 朝某人打去. **needs must when the devil drives** ⇨ NEEDS. **pure as the driven snow** ⇨ PURE. **10** (phr v) **drive sb back on sth** force sb to use (resources, methods, etc) he would prefer to avoid using 迫使某人使用他本不愿用的(资源、方法等). **drive off (a)** (of a driver, car, etc) leave (指驾驶人、汽车等)开走, 离开. **(b)** (in golf) hit the ball to begin a game (高尔夫球戏中)发球. **drive sb off** take sb away in a car, etc 用汽车等把某人送走. **drive sb/sth off** defeat or chase away (an enemy or an attack) 击败, 击退(敌人或攻势).

□ **ˈdrive-in** *n* (*US*) place, esp a cinema or restaurant, where one is entertained, served, etc without leaving one's car 免下车的影院、餐厅等(顾客可安坐汽车中得到娱乐、饮食服务等): [attrib 作定语] *a drive-in bank* 免下车的银行.

ˈdriving-belt *n* belt that is turned by an engine, etc and that then makes machinery turn 传动皮带.

ˈdriving-licence *n* (*US* **driver's license**) licence to drive a motor vehicle 驾驶执照.

ˈdriving school school for teaching people to drive motor vehicles 机动车驾驶学校.

ˈdriving-test *n* test that must be passed to obtain a driving-licence 驾驶员为取得驾驶执照的考试.

ˈdriving-wheel *n* wheel that communicates power to other parts of a machine, or to which power is applied 驱动轮; 主动轮.

drive[2] /draɪv; draɪv/ *n* **1** [C] journey in a car, van, etc 乘汽车等之行: *Let's go for a drive in the country.* 我们开车到郊野去兜兜风吧. ○ *He took her out for a drive.* 他开车带她出去兜风. ○ *a forty minute, an hour's, a fifteen mile, etc drive* 四十分钟、一小时、十五英里等的驾驶路程. **2** [C] (*US* usu 美式英语通常作 **ˈdrive·way**) private road, etc by which vehicles can approach a house from the road or street (通往住宅的)私人车道. ⇨illus at App 1 见附录1之插图, page vii. **3** [C] (*sport* 体) stroke made by driving in tennis, golf, cricket, etc (网球、高尔夫球、板球等的)猛击, 猛抽. **4** [U] energy; ability to get things done 干劲; 能力; 魄力: *Our sales people need determination and drive.* 我们的推销人员需要有决心和干劲. **5** [C, U] (*psychology* 心) desire to attain a goal or satisfy a need 欲望; 内驱力: *(a) strong sexual drive* 强烈的性欲. **6** [C] **(a)** organized effort or campaign to achieve sth (为达到某目的而展开的)运动, 攻势: *a ˈsales, a reˈcruiting, an ˈexport, etc drive* 推销、征兵、出口等运动. **(b)** series of military attacks 一系列的军事攻击. **7** [C] (*Brit*) social gathering to play card-games 玩纸牌的聚会: *a ˈbridge/ˈwhist drive* 玩桥牌[惠斯特牌]的聚会. **8** [C, U] (apparatus for the) transmission of power to machinery 传动或驱动(装置): *electric, belt, fluid, etc drive* 电力、皮带、液压等传动 ○ *front-/rear-/*

four-wheel 'drive, ie where the engine makes the front, rear, or all four wheels turn 前轮[后轮/四轮]驱动 ○ *a car with left-hand drive*, ie with the steering wheel and other controls on the left 方向盘在左边的汽车 ○ [attrib 作定语] *the 'drive shaft* 驱动轴; 主动轴.

drivel /ˈdrɪvl; ˋdrɪvl/ *n* [U] silly nonsense 傻话; 胡言: *Don't talk drivel!* 别胡说八道!

▷ **drivel** *v* (-ll-; *US* -l-) [I, Ipr, Ip] **~ (on) (about sth)** talk or write drivel 说或写无聊的内容; 胡说; 胡写: *He was drivelling on about the meaning of life.* 他喋喋不休地胡诌什么人生的意义.

driven *pp* of DRIVE[1].

driver /ˈdraɪvə(r); ˋdraɪvɚ/ *n* **1** person who drives a vehicle 司机; 驾驶员; 马车夫: *a bus-, lorry-, taxi-driver* 公共汽车、卡车、计程车司机 ○ *a learner driver*, ie sb who has not yet passed a driving-test 实习司机. **2** (golf) club with a wooden head used for driving the ball from the tee (高尔夫球)球棒. **3** person who drives animals 驱赶动物者. **4** (idm 习语) **a back-seat driver** ⇨ BACK-SEAT (BACK[2]). **(be) in the 'driver's seat** in control 处于控制地位.

□ **'driver's license** (*US*) = DRIVING-LICENCE (DRIVE[1]).

drizzle /ˈdrɪzl; ˋdrɪzl/ *v* [I] rain in many fine drops 下蒙蒙细雨; 下毛毛雨: *It had been drizzling all day.* 下了一整天毛毛雨.

▷ **drizzle** *n* [U] fine misty rain 蒙蒙细雨; 毛毛雨.

drizzly /ˈdrɪzlɪ; ˋdrɪzlɪ/ *adj*: *a cold drizzly day* 下着蒙蒙细雨的寒冷的一天.

drogue /drəʊg; drog/ *n* funnel-shaped piece of material used as a wind-sock, sea anchor, target, etc (用作风向袋、海锚、靶子等的)锥形物.

□ **'drogue-parachute** *n* small parachute used to pull a larger one from its pack (用以将大降落伞由伞包中拖出的)小降落伞.

droll /drəʊl; drol/ *adj* amusing in an odd or a quaint way 离奇古怪的; 逗人乐的; 滑稽的: *a droll story* 离奇有趣的故事 ○ (*ironic* 反语) *So he thinks I'm going to apologize? How very droll!* 他还以为我要去道歉? 真滑稽!

▷ **droll·ery** /-ərɪ; -ərɪ/ *n* [C, U] (remark, etc showing) quaint humour 稀奇古怪的幽默(言语等).

drom·ed·ary /ˈdrɒmədərɪ; *US* -ədeɪɪ; ˋdrɑmə,dɛrɪ/ *n* animal of the camel family with only one hump 单峰骆驼. ⇨illus at CAMEL 见 CAMEL 之插图.

drone[1] /drəʊn; dron/ *n* **1** male honey-bee 雄蜂. Cf 参看 WORKER 3. **2** (*Brit derog* 贬) person who does no useful work and lives on others 不务正业而依赖他人为生者.

drone[2] /drəʊn; dron/ *v* **1** [I, Ip] make a low humming sound 发出嗡嗡声: *An aircraft droned overhead.* 飞机在上空发出嗡嗡声. **2** [I, Ip, Tn, Tn·p] talk, sing or say (sth) in a flat monotonous tone of voice (以低沉、单调的声调)谈, 唱, 说(某事): *The chairman droned on for hours.* 主席一直以沉闷的语调讲了几小时. ○ *drone (out) a hymn* 以低沉单调的声音唱赞美诗.

▷ **drone** *n* (usu *sing* 通常作单数) **1** low humming sound 嗡嗡声: *the drone of bees* 蜜蜂发出的嗡嗡声 ○ *the drone of a distant aircraft* 远处飞机发出的嗡嗡声. **2** monotonous talk 沉闷单调的谈话: *a steady drone from the lecturer* 讲演者枯燥的长篇言论. **3** (*music* 音) sustained bass note or chord, eg in bagpipe music 持续的低音或和音(如风笛乐曲中的).

drool /dru:l; drul/ *v* **1** [I] let saliva flow from the mouth; dribble 流口水; 流涎. **2** [I, Ipr] **~ (over sb/sth)** (*derog* 贬) show in a ridiculous way how much one enjoys or admires sb/sth 对某人[某事物]流露出痴迷的神情: *drooling over a photo of a pop star* 痴痴地望着流行曲歌星的照片.

droop /dru:p; drup/ *v* [I, Ipr, Ip] bend or hang downwards through tiredness or weakness (因疲倦或衰弱)弯曲或下垂; 发蔫: *flowers drooping for lack of water* 因缺水而发蔫的花 ○ *Her head drooped sadly.* 她悲伤地低着头. ○ (*fig* 比喻) *His spirits drooped at the news*, ie He became sad. 那消息使他情绪低落. ▷ **droopy** *adj* (**-ier, -iest**).

drop[1] /drɒp; drɑp/ *n* **1** [C] small rounded or pear-shaped mass of liquid (液体的)珠, 滴: *'rain-drops, 'tear-drops, etc* 雨滴、泪珠 ○ *drops of rain, dew, sweat, condensation, etc* 雨滴、露珠、汗珠、冷凝水珠 ○ *Pour the oil in drops into the mixture.* 将油滴入混合物. **2 drops** [pl] liquid medicine poured a drop at a time into the ears, eyes or nose 滴剂: *comfort drops*, eg used to make contact lenses easier to wear 润滑剂(如用以使隐形镜片容易配戴的). **3** [C esp *sing* 尤作单数] small quantity of liquid 少量的液体; 点滴: *I like my tea with just a drop of milk.* 我喜欢茶里加一点点牛奶. ○ (*fig* 比喻) *He's had a drop too much*, ie He is drunk. 他喝醉了. **4** [C] thing shaped like a drop, esp a sweet or a hanging ornament 滴状物; (尤指)糖果, 坠子饰物. **5** [sing] steep or vertical distance 倾斜的或垂直的距离: *There was a sheer drop of five hundred feet to the rocks below.* 至暗礁的垂直距离有五百英尺. **6** [sing] (*fig* 比喻) decrease 下降: *a drop in prices, temperatures, etc* 物价、温度等下降 ○ *a big drop in the number of people out of work* 失业人数大幅下降. **7** [C] act of dropping; thing that drops or is dropped 空投; 空投物: *Drops of supplies are being made to villages still cut off by the snow.* 目前正向大雪隔绝的村庄空投生活用品. **8** (idm 习语) **at the ,drop of a 'hat** without delay, hesitation or good reason 不拖延地; 不迟疑地; 无缘无故地: *You can't expect me to move my home at the drop of a hat.* 你别指望我说搬家就搬家. **(only) a ,drop in the 'bucket/ 'ocean** a quantity too small to make any improvement 沧海一粟; 杯水车薪: *Aid to the Third World is at present little more than a drop in the ocean.* 目前对第三世界的援助不过是杯水车薪.

▷ **drop·let** /ˈdrɒplɪt; ˋdrɑplɪt/ *n* small drop 小滴.

□ **'drop-goal** *n* (in Rugby football) goal scored with a drop-kick (橄榄球)以反弹踢法射中球门.

'drop-hammer, **'drop-forge**, **'drop-press** *ns* machine for shaping or stamping metal, using the force of a dropped weight 模锻压力机; 落锤.

'drop-kick *n* (in Rugby football) kick made as the ball bounces after being dropped to the ground (橄榄球)落地踢, 反弹踢. — *v* [I, Tn].

drop[2] /drɒp; drɑp/ *v* (**-pp-**) **1** [I, Ipr, Tn, Tn·pr] fall or allow (sth) to fall (by accident) 降落; 使(某物)(意外地)落下: *The bottle dropped and broke.* 瓶子掉下来摔碎了. ○ *The climber slipped and dropped to his death.* 攀登者一失足摔死了. ○ *Don't drop that or it'll break!* 别弄掉了, 不然会摔破的. **2** [I, Ipr, Ip, Tn, Tn·pr, Tn·p] fall or cause (sth) to fall (on purpose) 降落; (故意地)使(某物)落下: *She dropped to safety from the burning building.* 她从失火的建筑物上坠落到安全的地方. ○ *Medical supplies are being dropped to the stricken area.* 目前正将医药用品空投到灾区. ○ *Drop the hammer down to me.* 把锤子扔给我. **3** [I, Ipr] (of people and animals) collapse from exhaustion (指人和动物)(因筋疲力尽)倒下: *I feel ready to drop*, ie very tired. 我要累倒了. ○ (*fig* 比喻) *She expects everyone to work till they drop*, ie very hard. 她恨不得把个个人都累趴下为止. **4** [I, Ipr, Tn, Tn·pr] (cause sth to) become weaker, lower or less (使某事物)变弱、降低或减少: *The wind, temperature, water level, etc has dropped considerably.* 风势已减弱了、温度已下降了、水平面已降低了很多. ○ *His voice dropped to a whisper.* 他的声音已降低成轻声细语了. ○ *The cost of living seems set to drop for the third month in succession.* 生活费用持续下降, 眼看就快三个月了. **5** [I, Ipr, Ip] form a steep or vertical descent 形成险峻的或陡峭的斜坡: *The cliff drops sharply (away) (to the sea).* 悬崖呈陡坡状(伸入大海). **6** [Tn, Tn·pr, Tn·p] **~ sb/sth (off)** allow sb to get out of a car, etc; deliver sth on the way to somewhere else 让某人下汽车...; 中途顺便将某物送交某处: *Could you drop me (off) near the post office?* 你可以让我在邮局附近下车吗? **7** (*infml* 口) [Dn·n] send (a letter, etc) to sb 将(信件等)寄给某人: *drop sb a postcard* 给某人寄明信片. **8** [Tn, Tn·pr] **~ sb/sth (from sth)** omit sb/sth (by accident or on purpose) (偶然或有意地)略去某人[某事物]: *She's been dropped from the team because of injury.* 她因受伤而离队. ○ *Many dated expressions are being dropped from the new dictionary.* 这本新词典中删去了很多过时的词语. **9** [Tn] **(a)** stop seeing (sb) 不再与(某人)来往: *She's dropped most of her old friends — or they've dropped her!* 她已经与多数老朋友不再来往了——或者说他们不再与她来往了! **(b)** give up (a habit, custom, etc) 抛弃(习惯、风俗等). **(c)** stop doing or discussing (sth) 不再做(某事); 不再讨论(某事): *Drop everything and come here!* 把一切工作都放下, 到这里来! ○ *Let's* *drop the formalities: call me Mike.* 不要拘礼：叫我迈克吧。○ *Look, can we just drop the subject?* 我说，我们能不能别再谈这件事了？ **10** [Tn] (*infml* 口) lose (money), esp by gambling, etc 损失(金钱)(尤指因赌博等所致)：*I hear they've dropped over ten thousand on the deal.* 我听说他们那笔交易损失了一万多块钱. **11** [I, Tn] (*sl* 俚) take (illegal drugs) orally 口服(毒品). **12** (idm 习语) **die/drop/fall like flies** ⇨ FLY[1]. ˌ**drop one's ˈaitches** omit the 'h' sound from places in words where it is pronounced by educated speakers (often thought a sign of lower-class social origins) 略去单词中的h音(常视为出身低下的标志). **drop a ˈbrick/ˈclanger** (*infml* 口) say or do sth that is insulting or embarrassing without realizing that it is (无意中)说出或做出伤人的或令人发窘的事. **drop ˈdead** (**a**) (*infml* 口) die suddenly and unexpectedly 猝死；暴死. (**b**) (*sl* 俚) (used to tell sb forcefully and rudely to stop bothering one, interfering, etc 用以叫某人不要再打扰、干涉等，语气强硬而粗鲁). **drop a ˈhint (to sb)/drop (sb) a hint** make a suggestion indirectly or tactfully 间接地或策略地提出建议；暗示. **drop/dump sth in sb's lap** ⇨ LAP[1]. **drop sb a line** write a (usu short) letter to sb 给某人写信(通常指短信)：*Drop me a line to say when you're coming.* 给我写封短信告诉我你来的时间. **drop ˈnames** (*infml* 口) mention famous or powerful people one is supposed to know, so as to impress others 提及名人或有权势的人，让人以为自己认识这些人而对自己另眼相看. **drop a ˈstitch** (in knitting) let a stitch slip off the needle (编织)漏一针，脱一针，掉一针. **one's jaw drops** ⇨ JAW. **let sb/sth ˈdrop** do or say nothing more about sb/sth 不再提某人；不再做或不再提某事：*I suggest we let the matter drop.* 我建议咱们别再提这事了. **the penny drops** ⇨ PENNY. **13** (phr v) **drop back; drop behind (sb)** move or fall into position behind sb else 落后；落伍：*The two lovers dropped back so as to be alone.* 那对情人落在后面，为的是两人好单独在一起. ○ (*fig* 比喻) *Britain is increasingly dropping behind her competitors in this field.* 英国在这一领域日渐落后于竞争对手. **drop by/in/over/round; drop in on sb; drop into sth** pay a casual visit (to a person or place) 偶然访问(某人或某地)；顺便访问：*Drop round some time.* 有空就顺便来坐坐. ○ *I thought I'd drop in on you while I was passing.* 我曾想路过时就来看看你. ○ *Sorry we're late — we dropped into a pub on the way.* 对不起，我们迟到了——我们中途到酒馆去了. ⇨Usage at VISIT 用法见VISIT. **drop off** (*infml* 口) (**a**) fall into a light sleep; doze 打盹儿；打瞌睡：*I dropped off and missed the end of the film.* 我打了个盹儿，把影片的结尾给错过了. (**b**) become fewer or less 减少：*Traffic has dropped off since the by-pass opened.* 自从辅助道路通车后，这条路上来往车辆已经减少了. **drop out (of sth)** (**a**) withdraw (from an activity, a contest, etc) (从活动、竞赛等中)退出：*Since his defeat he's dropped out of politics.* 他失败后就不再从事政治活动了. (**b**) leave school, university, etc without finishing one's courses 中途退学；辍学：*She got a scholarship to Cambridge but dropped out a year later.* 她得到了剑桥大学的奖学金，但一年以后就退学了. (**c**) withdraw from conventional society 脱离传统社会.

▷ **drop·per** *n* instrument consisting of a short glass tube with a rubber bulb at one end for measuring out drops of medicine or other liquids 滴管.

drop·pings *n* [pl] excrement of animals or birds (鸟兽的)排泄物.

□ ˈ**drop-out** *n* person who withdraws from conventional society 脱离传统社会的人.

dropsy /ˈdrɒpsɪ; ˈdrɑpsɪ/ *n* [U] disease in which watery fluid collects in the body 水肿；浮肿. ▷ **drop·sical** /ˈdrɒpsɪkl; ˈdrɑpsɪkl/ *adj*.

dross /drɒs; *US* drɔːs; drɔs/ *n* [U] (**a**) scum of waste matter on melted metals 浮渣(浮在熔化的金属上的废物). (**b**) (*fig* 比喻) least valuable, attractive, etc part of sth 无价值、无吸引力之处：*The best players go off to the big clubs, leaving us the dross.* 最好的队员都投奔大俱乐部去了，就只给我们剩下些不中用的人.

drought /draʊt; draʊt/ *n* [C, U] (period of) continuous dry weather, esp when there is not enough water for people's needs 干旱(时期)：*areas of Africa affected by drought* 遭受旱灾的非洲地区.

drove[1] *pt* of DRIVE[1].

drove[2] /drəʊv; drov/ *n* **1** herd of cattle, flock of sheep, etc being made to move from one place to another (被驱赶从一地到另一地的)牛群、羊群等. **2** (usu *pl* 通常作复数) (*fig* 比喻) moving crowd of people or large number of things 移动的人群或大批的东西：*droves of sightseers* 一群群的游客 ○ *Letters of protest arrived in droves.* 抗议信大批涌来.

▷ **drover** *n* person who moves cattle, sheep, etc to market or to new pastures 将牛羊等驱赶到市场或牧场的人；驱赶牲畜者.

drown /draʊn; draʊn/ *v* **1** (**a**) [I, Ipr] die in water (or other liquid) because one is unable to breathe 淹死；溺死：*a drowning man* 快要淹死的人. (**b**) [Tn, Tn·pr] kill (a person or animal) in this way 溺死(人或动物)：*drown a kitten* 溺死小猫. **2** [Tn, Tn·pr] **~ sth (in sth)** flood or drench sth 淹没或浸透某物：*a drowned valley* 淹没的山谷 ○ *He drowned his meal in gravy.* 他把饭菜泡在肉汁里. **3** [Tn, Tn·p] **~ sb/sth (out)** (of a sound) be louder than (another sound) and prevent it being heard (指一声音)淹没(另一声音)：*She turned up the radio to drown (out) the noise of the traffic.* 她放大收音机的音量以压过来往车辆的嘈杂声. **4** (idm 习语) **drown one's ˈsorrows (in drink)** (*esp joc* 尤作戏谑语) get drunk in order to forget one's troubles 借酒浇愁. **(look) like a drowned ˈrat** soaking wet and miserable 湿得像落汤鸡.

drowse /draʊz; draʊz/ *v* **1** [I] be half asleep 假寐；半醒半睡；打瞌睡. **2** (phr v) **drowse sth away** spend (time) half asleep 半醒半睡地度过(时间)：*drowse away a hot afternoon* 打着瞌睡度过炎热的下午.

▷ **drowse** *n* [sing] state of being drowsy 假寐；瞌睡：*in a drowse* 在打瞌睡.

drowsy /ˈdraʊzɪ; ˈdraʊzɪ/ *adj* (**-ier, -iest**) **1** half asleep; feeling sleepy 半醒半睡的；昏昏欲睡的；困：*I'd just woken up and was still drowsy.* 我刚醒，还觉得困. ○ *This drug can make you drowsy.* 这种药会使你昏昏欲睡. **2** making one feel sleepy 使人发困的；使人昏昏欲睡的：*drowsy summer weather* 使人困倦的夏季天气. ▷ **drows·ily** /-əlɪ; -ɪlɪ/ *adv*: *murmur sth drowsily* 半醒半睡地低声述说某事. **drow·si·ness** *n* [U].

drub·bing /ˈdrʌbɪŋ; ˈdrʌbɪŋ/ *n* (idm 习语) **give sb/get a good ˈdrubbing** (**a**) beat sb/be beaten soundly 痛打某人[遭到痛打]. (**b**) (*fig* 比喻) defeat sb/be defeated thoroughly 彻底打败某人[遭到惨败].

drudge /drʌdʒ; drʌdʒ/ *n* person who has to do long hard boring jobs 长时间做繁重、乏味工作的人.

▷ **drudge** *v* [I, Ipr, Ip] **~ (away) (at sth)** do jobs of that kind 长时间做繁重、乏味的工作.

drudgery /-ərɪ; -ərɪ/ *n* [U] hard boring work 繁重、乏味的工作：*the endless drudgery of housework* 无尽无休的、单调乏味的家务 ○ *soulless drudgery* 无聊的繁重工作.

drug /drʌg; drʌg/ *n* **1** substance used as or in a medicine 药物；药剂；药材：*a pain-killing drug* 止痛药 ○ *The doctor has put me on drugs*, ie prescribed them for me. 医生给我开了药. **2** substance that affects the nervous system, esp one that is habit-forming, eg cocaine or heroin 影响神经系统的(尤指成瘾性的)物质(如古柯碱或海洛因)；麻醉药；毒品：*take/use/be on drugs* 吸毒 ○ *peddle/push drugs* 贩毒. **3** (idm 习语) **a drug on the ˈmarket** thing that cannot be sold because no one wants it 滞销品；滞销货.

▷ **drug** *v* (**-gg-**) [Tn] **1** add a drug(2) to (food or drink) (在食物或饮料中)投放麻醉药，下麻醉药. **2** give a drug(1, 2) to (sb), esp to make him unconscious 给某人使用麻醉药：*in a drugged stupor* 被药麻醉而不省人事.

□ ˈ**drug addict** person who cannot stop taking harmful drugs (DRUG 2) 有毒瘾者；吸毒者. ˈ**drug addiction**. ˈ**drug dealer**, ˈ**drug pusher** person who sells drugs (DRUG 2) illegally 贩毒者；毒品贩子.

drug·get /ˈdrʌgɪt; ˈdrʌgɪt/ *n* [C, U] (floor-covering made of) coarse woven fabric 粗线织物(制的地毯).

drug·gist /ˈdrʌgɪst; ˈdrʌgɪst/ *n* (*esp US*) = CHEMIST[1].

drug·store /ˈdrʌgstɔː(r); ˈdrʌgˌstɔr/ *n* (*US*) chemist's shop which also sells many kinds of goods and often serves light meals (兼营杂货及便餐的)药房，杂货店.

Druid /ˈdruːɪd; ˈdruɪd/ *n* priest of an ancient Celtic

religion 德鲁伊特(古代克尔特人中的祭司).

drum[1] /drʌm; drʌm/ *n* **1** (*music* 音) instrument consisting of a hollow round frame with plastic or skin stretched tightly across the open end(s) which is struck with sticks or the hands 鼓: *play the drum(s) in a band* 在乐队中打鼓. ⇨illus at App 1 见附录1之插图, page xi. **2** thing shaped like this instrument, eg a barrel for oil, a hollow cylinder on which wire is wound, or the container for clothes in a washing-machine or clothes drier 鼓状物(如桶、筒). ⇨illus at BARREL 见 BARREL 之插图. **3** = EAR-DRUM (EAR). **4** (idm 习语) **beat the drum** ⇨ BEAT[1].

□ ˈ**drumbeat** *n* (sound of a) stroke on a drum 鼓的一击(声).

ˈ**drum brake** brake in which curved pads press against the inner cylindrical part of a vehicle's wheel 鼓式制动器. Cf 参看 DISC BRAKE (DISC).

ˈ**drumhead** part of the drum that is hit 鼓面. ˌ**drumhead court-ˈmartial** trial held during a military operation 战地军法审判.

ˈ**drum-kit** *n* set of drums used in a band, etc 乐队等使用的成套的鼓.

ˌ**drum ˈmajor** **1** sergeant who leads a military band when it plays on parade (军乐队在行进中演奏的)指挥. **2** (*US*) male leader of a marching band (行进乐队的)男领队. ˌ**drum majoˈrette** /meɪdʒəˈret; ˌmedʒəˈrɛt/ (*esp US*) girl wearing a fancy costume who leads a marching band (乐队行进中着鲜艳服装的)女领队.

ˈ**drumstick** *n* **1** stick for playing a drum 鼓槌. ⇨illus at App 1 见附录1之插图, page xi. **2** lower part of the leg of a cooked chicken, turkey, etc (熟的)鸡、火鸡等的腿(状似鼓槌部分).

drum[2] /drʌm; drʌm/ *v* **(-mm-)** **1** [I] play a drum or drums 打鼓; 敲鼓; 击鼓. **2** [Ipr, Tn, Tn·pr] **~ (sth) on sth** make a drum-like sound on sth; tap or beat (sth) continuously (在某物上敲打)发出似鼓之声; 不停敲打(某物): *drum on the table with one's fingers* 用手指在桌上敲出鼓点声 ○ *drum one's feet on the floor* 跺脚. **3** (phr v) **drum sth into sb/into sb's head** make sb remember sth by repeating it often 经常重复某事使某人记住: *Our teacher used to drum our multiplication tables into us.* 我们老师过去老是让我们反复背诵乘法表. **drum sb out (of sth)** force sb to leave a group, an organization, etc, often in disgrace 迫使某人脱离(团体、组织等)(常为不名誉地): *drummed out of the club, the regiment* 被逐出俱乐部、团体. **drum sth up** try hard to get (support, customers, etc) 大力争取(支持、顾客等): *He's going round firms drumming up interest in the project.* 他到各公司游说以引起大家对该项目的兴趣.

▷ **drum·mer** *n* **1** person who plays a drum or drums 鼓手. **2** (*esp US infml* 口) commercial traveller 旅行推销员.

drum·ming *n* [U, sing] continuous rhythmical sound 连续的有节奏的声音: *the steady drumming of the rain on the tin roofs* 雨点打在铁皮屋顶上发出持续而有节奏的声音.

drunk /drʌŋk; drʌŋk/ *adj* **1** [usu pred 通常作表语] excited or confused by alcoholic drink 醉: *be blind/dead* (ie completely) *drunk* 烂醉 ○ *They've put vodka in her fruit juice to get her drunk.* 他们把伏特加酒倒入她的果汁中, 把她灌醉. ○ *get drunk on cider* 喝苹果酒而醉倒. **2** [pred 作表语] **~ with sth** behaving in a strange, often unpleasant, way (because of the excitement of sth) 陶醉; 飘飘然; 忘乎所以: *drunk with power, success, etc* 为权势、成功等而飘飘然. **3** (idm 习语) ˌ**drunk and ˈdisorderly** (*law* 律); ˌ**drunk and inˈcapable** behaving in an unpleasant, uncontrolled way while drunk 酒后失仪; 耍酒疯. **(as)** ˌ**drunk as a ˈlord** very drunk 酩酊大醉.

▷ **drunk** *n* person who is drunk 醉酒者; 醉鬼.

drunk·ard /-əd; -ərd/ *n* (*fml* 文) person who often gets drunk; alcoholic 酒鬼; 酒徒.

□ **drunˈkometer** *n* (*US*) = BREATHALYSER.

drunken /ˈdrʌŋkən; ˈdrʌŋkən/ *adj* [attrib 作定语] **1** drunk 醉的: *a drunken reveller* 喝醉的狂欢者. **2** who gets drunk regularly 常醉的: *her drunken boss, husband, etc* 她那经常醉醺醺的老板、丈夫等. **3** caused by or showing the effects of drink 因饮酒而引起的; 显出酒力的: *a drunken argument, fury, stupor, sleep* 酒后的争吵、狂暴、昏迷、沉睡 ○ *drunken laughter, voices, singing* 酒后的大笑、胡言乱语、歌声. ▷ **drunk·enly** *adv*: *stagger about drunkenly* 醉酒后步履蹒跚. **drunk·en·ness** *n* [U].

drupe /druːp; drup/ *n* (*botany* 植) fruit with juicy flesh surrounding a hard stone with a seed, eg an olive or a peach 核果(如橄榄、桃子).

dry[1] /draɪ; draɪ/ *adj* **(drier, driest)** **1** not (or no longer) wet, damp or sticky; without moisture 干的; 干燥的: *Is the washing dry yet?* 洗的衣服干了吗? ○ *Don't use this door until the paint is dry.* 油漆未干, 别走这个门. ○ *This pastry is too dry — add some water.* 做点心的面太干——加点儿水吧. **2** with little rainfall 少雨的; 干旱的: *a dry spell, climate, country* 干旱期、干燥的气候、干旱的国家 ○ *I hope it stays dry for our picnic.* 我盼着别下雨, 我们好去野餐. **3** not supplying liquid 不提供液体的; 干涸的: *The wells ran dry.* 井都干了. ○ *The cows are dry*, ie not producing milk. 那些母牛不产奶. **4** without liquid 无液体的: *a dry cough*, ie without phlegm 干咳(无痰) ○ *My throat feels dry.* 我嗓子发干. ○ *a dry shampoo*, ie in powder form 干洗发剂(粉状). **5** (of a country or region) where it is illegal to buy or sell alcoholic drink (指某国家或地区)禁酒的: *Some parts of Wales are dry on Sundays.* 威尔士的一些地区星期日禁酒. **6** (*infml* 口) (making one) thirsty (令人)口渴的: *I'm a bit dry.* 我有点儿渴. ○ *dry work* 令人口渴的工作. **7** [attrib 作定语] without butter 无黄油的: *dry bread, toast, etc* 无黄油的面包、烤面包片等. **8** (of wines, etc) not sweet or fruity (指酒等)干的(无甜味的或无水果味的): *a crisp dry white wine* 清新可口的干白葡萄酒 ○ *a dry sherry* 干雪利酒. **9** plain; without anything pleasant or interesting 平淡的; 枯燥的; 无趣味的; 干巴巴的: *They offered no apology, just a dry explanation for the delay.* 他们没有为延误道歉, 只做了个干巴巴的解释. **10** (of humour) pretending to be serious (指幽默)装成正经的: *a dry wit* 假装正经的诙谐. **11** unemotional; cold 不动感情的; 冷淡的: *a dry manner, greeting, tone of voice* 冷淡的态度、招呼、声调. **12** dull; boring 枯燥的; 乏味的: *Government reports tend to make rather dry reading.* 政府的报告往往读来枯燥无味. **13** (idm 习语) **boil dry** ⇨ BOIL[2]. **(as)** ˌ**dry as a ˈbone** completely dry 完全干燥的. **(as)** ˌ**dry as ˈdust** very boring 非常乏味的. **high and dry** ⇨ HIGH. **home and dry** ⇨ HOME[3]. **keep one's powder dry** ⇨ POWDER. **milk/suck sb/sth dry** obtain from sb all the money, help, information, etc he has to give 竭力从某人处获取其所有的金钱、帮助、消息等; 榨取. **not a dry eye in the house** (*joc* 谑) everybody in the audience was crying or deeply affected 观众都在哭或深受感动. ▷ **dryly** (also **drily**) /ˈdraɪlɪ; ˈdraɪlɪ/ *adv*: *'They're not likely to give you money,' he remarked dryly.* '他们不大可能给你钱,'他冷淡地说. **dry·ness** *n* [U].

□ ˌ**dry ˈbattery** electric battery with two or more dry cells 干电池组.

ˌ**dry ˈcell** cell in which the chemicals are in a firm paste which does not spill 干电池.

ˌ**dry-ˈclean** *v* [Tn] clean (clothes, etc) without water, using a solvent which evaporates quickly 干洗(衣服等). ˌ**dry-ˈcleaner** *n*: *The blankets are at the dry-cleaner's.* 毛毯都在干洗店里. ˌ**dry-ˈcleaning** *n* [U].

ˌ**dry ˈdock** dock from which water may be pumped out for work on a ship's bottom 干船坞: *a ship in dry dock for repairs* 在干船坞里待修的船.

ˌ**dry ˈgoods** **1** grain, fruit, etc 干(谷类、水果等)货物. **2** (*esp US*) clothing, textiles, etc (as opposed to groceries) 服装、纺织品等(与食品杂货相对).

ˌ**dry ˈice** solid carbon dioxide (used for refrigerating, theatrical effects, etc) 干冰(固态的二氧化碳, 用于冷却、舞台效果等).

ˌ**dry ˈland** land as distinct from sea, etc 陆地(区别于海洋等): *I'm no sailor and I couldn't wait to reach dry land.* 我晕船, 恨不得立刻上岸.

ˌ**dry ˈmeasure** measure of capacity for dry goods 干量(对干货物的计量单位).

ˈ**dry-nurse** *n* nurse who does not suckle the baby she is caring for (不喂奶的)保姆.

ˌ**dry ˈrot** **1** decay of wood, causing it to turn to powder (木材的)干腐(使其成为粉末). **2** fungi that cause this

D

使木材干腐的真菌. **3** (*fig* 比喻) force that gradually spoils eg an organization or moral standards but which is not easily noticed at first (初时不易发现的)逐渐腐蚀(组织、道德标准等)的力量.

ˌ**dry** ˈ**run** (*infml* 口) rehearsal or practice, eg for a ceremony or procedure 演习, 排练(如为典礼或礼仪): *Let's do/have a dry run.* 我们来排练一下.

ˈ**dry-shod** *adj, adv* without getting one's feet or shoes wet 未弄湿脚或鞋(的): *go ashore dry-shod* 上岸而未湿鞋.

ˈ**drystone** *adj* (of a stone wall) built without mortar (指石墙)无浆砌成的.

ˌ**dry-**ˈ**walling** *n* [U] building of drystone walls 无浆墙筑成的建筑物.

dry[2] /draɪ; draɪ/ *v* (*pt, pp* **dried**) **1** [I, Ip, Tn, Tn·p] (cause sb/sth to) become dry (使某人[某物])变干: *Leave the dishes to dry (off).* 把盘子放着晾干. ○ *Dry your hands on this towel.* 用这条毛巾把手擦干. **2** [I] (*infml* 口) (of an actor) forget one's lines (指演员)忘记台词. **3** (phr v) **dry (sb) out** (*infml* 口) treat (sb) or be treated for alcoholism (为某人)戒酒. **dry (sth) out** (cause sth soaked in water, etc to) become completely dry (使浸水等之物)完全变干, 干透: *Your clothes will take ages to dry out.* 你的衣服要很长时间才能干透. **dry up** (**a**) (of rivers, wells, etc) become completely dry (指河流、井等)干涸. (**b**) (*fig* 比喻) (of any source or supply) no longer be available (指资源或供应)耗尽, 枯竭: *If foreign aid dries up the situation will be desperate.* 倘若外援枯竭, 形势将极为严重. (**c**) (*infml* 口) stop talking 停止谈话; 住口; 住嘴: *Dry up and listen to me.* 住嘴, 听我说. (**d**) be unable to continue talking, esp because one has forgotten what one was going to say 不能继续谈下去(尤指忘记要说的话); 忘词儿. **dry (sth) up** dry (dishes, cutlery, etc) with a towel after washing them 用毛巾擦干(洗过的盘子、餐具等).

▷ **drier** (also **dryer**) /ˈdraɪə(r); ˋdraɪɚ/ *n* **1** (esp in compounds 尤用以构成复合词) machine that dries 脱水机: *a* ˈ*clothes drier* ○ *a* ˈ*hair-drier* ○ *a* ˈ*tumble-drier*. **2** substance mixed with paint or varnish to make it dry more quickly 干燥剂.

DSc /ˌdiː es ˈsiː; ˌdi ɛs ˋsi/ *abbr* 缩写 = Doctor of Science: *have/be a DSc in Physics* 有物理学博士学位[为物理学博士] ○ *Philip Jones DSc* 菲利普·琼斯理学博士.

DSO /ˌdiː es ˈəʊ; ˌdi ɛs ˋo/ *abbr* 缩写 = (*Brit*) (Companion of the) Distinguished Service Order 特殊功劳勋章(的勋位): *be awarded the DSO for bravery* 因勇敢荣获特殊功劳勋章.

DT /ˌdiː ˈtiː; ˌdi ˋti/ (also **DTs** /ˌdiː ˈtiːz; ˌdi ˋtiz/) *abbr* 缩写 = (*infml* 口) trembling delirium (Latin *delirium tremens*) 震颤性谵妄(源自拉丁文 *delirium tremens*): *have (an attack of) the DTs* 患震颤性谵妄.

dual /ˈdjuːəl; *US* ˈduːəl; ˋduəl/ *adj* [attrib 作定语] having two parts or aspects; double 两部分的; 二体的; 二重的; 双的: *his dual role as composer and conductor* 他兼作曲家及指挥的双重身分 ○ *She has dual nationality*, ie is a citizen of two different countries. 她兼有双重国籍. ▷ **du·al·ity** /djuːˈælətɪ; *US* duː-; duˋælətɪ/ [U] *n*.

□ ˌ**dual** ˈ**carriageway** (*Brit*) (*US* **divided highway**) road with a central strip dividing streams of traffic moving in opposite directions 双线车道.

ˌ**dual-con**ˈ**trol** *adj* (having) two linked sets of controls, allowing operation by either of two people 双重控制的, 复式操纵的(两人中任何一人皆可操纵): [attrib 作定语] *a* ˌ*dual-control* ˈ*car*, ie one used for driving lessons, in which the instructor can operate the clutch and brakes 双控汽车(用以教授驾驶技术, 教师在车上可操纵离合器和刹车).

ˌ**dual-**ˈ**purpose** *adj* serving two purposes 双重目的的; 两用的.

dub /dʌb; dʌb/ *v* (**-bb-**) **1** [Cn·n] make (a man) a knight by touching him on the shoulder with a sword 以剑触(某人)肩以封之为爵士. **2** [Cn·n] give (sb) a nickname 给(某人)起绰号; 起外号: *The papers dubbed them 'The Fab Four'.* 报刊给他们起了个绰号叫'四绝'. **3** [Tn, Tn·pr] **~ sth (into sth)** create, add to or replace the soundtrack of (a film), esp in a different language 为(影片)配音(尤指用不同的语言): *a dubbed version* 配音片 ○ *a German film dubbed into English* 用英语配音的德国影片.

dub·bin /ˈdʌbɪn; ˋdʌbɪn/ *n* [U] thick grease for making leather soft and waterproof (皮革用)软化防水油.

▷ **dub·bin** *v* [Tn] treat (esp boots) with dubbin 用软化防水油涂擦(尤指皮靴).

du·bi·ety /djuːˈbaɪətɪ; *US* duː-; duˋbaɪətɪ/ *n* (*fml* 文) **1** [U] feeling of doubt 怀疑; 疑惑. **2** [C] matter on which one is uncertain 不肯定的事.

du·bi·ous /ˈdjuːbɪəs; *US* ˈduː-; ˋdubɪəs/ *adj* **1** [esp pred 尤作表语] **~ (about sth/doing sth)** not certain and slightly suspicious about sth; doubtful 半信半疑; 可疑: *I remain dubious about her motives.* 我对她的动机仍存疑念. **2** (*derog* 贬) possibly or probably dishonest, disreputable or risky 不大可靠的; 名声不大好的; 冒风险的: *a rather dubious character* 名声不太好的人 ○ *a dubious business venture* 冒险的商业投机 ○ *His background is a trifle dubious, to say the least.* 起码可以说, 他的背景不大可靠. **3** uncertain in result; in doubt 结果未定的; 不能确定的: *The results of this policy will remain dubious for some time.* 这项政策的效果短期内难以确定. **4** (*esp ironic* 尤作反语) of which the value is doubtful; questionable 价值可疑的; 有问题的; 有争议的: *a dubious compliment*, ie a disguised insult 明褒实贬的恭维 ○ *She had the dubious honour of being the last woman to be hanged in England.* 她是英国最后一个受绞刑的女子, 这也算是有此殊荣吧. ▷ **du·bi·ously** *adv*. **du·bi·ous·ness** *n* [U].

du·cal /ˈdjuːkl; *US* ˈduːkl; ˋdukḷ/ *adj* [usu attrib 通常作定语] of or like a duke 公爵的; 似公爵的.

duch·ess /ˈdʌtʃɪs; ˋdʌtʃɪs/ *n* (in titles 称谓中作 **Duchess**) **1** wife or widow of a duke 公爵夫人; 公爵遗孀. **2** woman who holds ducal rank in her own right 女公爵.

duchy /ˈdʌtʃɪ; ˋdʌtʃɪ/ (also **dukedom** /ˈdjuːkdəm; *US* ˈduːk-; ˋdukdəm/) *n* territory of a duke or duchess 公爵的领地.

duck[1] /dʌk; dʌk/ *n* (*pl* unchanged or **~s** 复数或不变或作 **ducks**) **1** (**a**) [C] any of various types of common water-bird, domestic and wild 鸭; 野鸭: *ducks waddling about the yard* 在院子里一摇一摆走着的鸭子. ⇨illus at App 1 见附录1之插图, page v. (**b**) [C] female of this 雌鸭. Cf 参看 DRAKE. (**c**) [U] its flesh as food (食用的)鸭肉: *roast duck* 烤鸭. **2** [C usu *sing* 通常作单数] (also **ducky, ducks**) (*Brit infml* 口) (as a form of address) dear (作称呼)亲爱的, 宝贝儿. **3** [C] (in cricket) batsman's score of nought (板球)零分: *make a/be out for a duck* 得零分而出局 ○ *break one's duck*, ie score one's first run 首次得分. **4** (idm 习语) **a dead duck** ⇨ DEAD. **a lame duck** ⇨ LAME. **(take to sth) like a** ˌ**duck to** ˈ**water** without hesitation, fear or difficulty; naturally 像鸭子下水般; 不犹豫地; 不惧怕地; 无困难地; 自然地: *She's taken to teaching like a duck to water.* 她教起书来就像鸭子下水般轻而易举. **water off a duck's back** ⇨ WATER. **a sitting duck** ⇨ SIT.

▷ **duck·ling** /-lɪŋ; -lɪŋ/ *n* **1** (**a**) [C] young duck 雏鸭; 小鸭. (**b**) [U] its flesh as food (食用的)小鸭肉. **2** (idm 习语) **an ugly duckling** ⇨ UGLY.

□ ˈ**duck-boards** *n* [pl] boards used to spread one's weight when moving over muddy ground, a weak roof, etc (铺于泥泞地面、不牢的屋顶...上的)木板(用以分散人体重量).

ˌ**ducks and** ˈ**drakes** **1** children's game in which flat stones are bounced across the surface of the water 打水漂游戏. **2** (idm 习语) **play ducks and** ˈ**drakes with sth** spend (esp one's money) in a careless wasteful way 浪费; (尤指)挥霍.

ˈ**duckweed** *n* [U] plant that forms on the surface of ponds, etc 浮萍(生在池塘等表面的植物).

duck[2] /dʌk; dʌk/ *v* **1** [I, Ipr, Ip, Tn, Tn·pr, Tn·p] move (esp one's head) down quickly, to avoid being seen or hit 迅速低下(尤指头)(以免被看见或被打中): *I saw the gun and ducked under the window.* 我见到枪就迅速俯在窗下. ○ *Duck your head down!* 低下头! **2** [Tn, Tn·pr] push (sb) under water for a short time 使(某人)浸入水中片刻: *Her sisters ducked her in the river.* 她的姐妹把她按到河里. **3** [Ipr, Tn] (*infml* 口) **~ (out of) sth** avoid or dodge (a duty, responsibility etc) 躲避, 推脱, 推委(任务、责任等): *It's his turn to wash up but he'll try and duck out of it.* 轮到他刷锅洗碗, 他却想法儿逃避.

▷ **duck·ing** *n* thorough soaking 浸透: *give sb a ducking*, ie push him into or under the water 使某人全身湿透(将其推入水中).

duck[3] /dʌk; dʌk/ *n* **1** [U] strong linen or cotton cloth 坚固的麻布或棉布. **2 ducks** [pl] trousers made of this 这种布制成的裤子.

duct /dʌkt; dʌkt/ *n* **1** tube or channel carrying liquid, gas, electric or telephone wires, etc; (esp in an air-conditioning system) tube through which air passes (液体、气体、电线或电话线等通过的)管道, 槽; (尤指空调系统中的)输气管: *One of the air-ducts has become blocked.* 有一条输气管堵塞了. **2** tube in the body or in plants through which fluid, etc passes 人体中或植物中液体等经过的管: *ˈtear-ducts* 泪管.

□ ˌ**ductless ˈgland** gland from which hormones, etc pass directly into the bloodstream, not through a duct 无管腺; 内分泌腺.

duct·ile /ˈdʌktaɪl; US -tl; ˋdʌktḷ/ *adj* **1** (of metals) that can be pressed, beaten or pulled into fine strands without being heated (指金属)(不经加热)可锻的, 可延展的, 可拉成细丝的, 有韧性的. **2** (*fig fml* 比喻, 文) (of a person) easily led or influenced (指人)顺从的, 易受影响的. ▷ **duct·il·ity** /dʌkˈtɪlətɪ; dʌkˋtɪlətɪ/ *n* [U].

dud /dʌd; dʌd/ *n* (*infml* 口) thing or person that fails to work properly 无用的物或人; 废物: *Two of the fireworks in the box were duds.* 盒子里的烟火有两个是坏的. ○ *The new manager is a complete dud.* 新经理完全是个废物. ○ *This battery is a dud.* 这电池是废的.

▷ **dud** *adj* defective; worthless 有缺点的; 不完善的; 无价值的; 无用的 ○ *a dud cheque*, ie one that is forged or not backed by cash 无用的支票(假支票或空头支票).

dude /dju:d; US du:d; dud/ *n* (*US*) **1** city person, esp sb spending a holiday on a ranch 城里人(尤指在农场度假者): [attrib 作定语] *a dude ranch*, ie one used as a holiday centre 度假农场. **2** dandy 纨袴子弟; 花花公子. **3** (*sl* 俚) man 男人: *Who's that dude over there?* 那边的那个男的是谁?

dudgeon /ˈdʌdʒən; ˋdʌdʒən/ *n* (idm 习语) **in ˌhigh ˈdudgeon** angry, offended or resentful 恼怒; 愤怒; 忿恨: *He stormed out of the meeting in high dudgeon.* 他盛怒之下冲出会场.

duds /dʌdz; dʌdz/ *n* [pl] (*sl* 俚) clothes 衣服.

due[1] /dju:; US du:; du/ *adj* **1** [pred 作表语] **(a) ~ (to sb)** owed as a debt or an obligation 应支付; 应给予; 欠下: *Have they been paid the money due to them?* 他们是否已得到了应得的钱? ○ *I'm still due fifteen days' holiday.* 我还应有十五天假期. **(b) ~ for sth** owed sth; deserving sth 应有; 应得到: *She's due for promotion soon.* 她不久就要晋升了. **2** [pred 作表语] requiring immediate payment 须立即支付; 到期: *fall/become due* 到期 ○ *My rent isn't due till Wednesday.* 我的租金星期三才到期. **3** [pred 作表语] **~ (to do sth)** scheduled; arranged; expected 预定; 约定; 预期: *His book is due to be published in October.* 他的书预定十月份出版. ○ *The train is due (in)* (ie scheduled to arrive) *in five minutes.* 火车预定在5分钟后到达. **4** [attrib 作定语] suitable; right; proper 适当的; 正当的; 适宜的: *after due consideration* 经适当考虑之后 ○ *With all due respect, I disagree completely.* 不揣冒昧, 实不敢苟同. **5 ~ to sth/sb** caused by sb/sth; because of sb/sth 由某人[某事物]引起的; 由于某人[某事物]: *The team's success was largely due to her efforts.* 该队的成功在很大程度上是由于她的努力. **6** (idm 习语) **in ˌdue ˈcourse** at the appropriate time; eventually 在适当时机; 最终: *Your request will be dealt with in due course.* 你的要求将在适当时机予以处理.

NOTE ON USAGE 用法: **1** Some speakers are careful to use **due to** only after the verb *be* 有些说英语的人用 **due to** 一词很谨慎, 仅将之用于动词be后: *His lateness was due to the very heavy traffic on the motorway.* 他迟到是因高速公路上车辆过多所致. But it is also generally considered acceptable today as a synonym for **owing to**, which is used differently 但目前普遍认为可将 **due to** 看作是 **owing to** 的同义词, 而 **owing to** 的用法与之有别: *He was late owing to/due to the very heavy traffic.* 他迟到是因为交通拥挤. ○ *Due to/Owing to the heavy traffic, he was late.* 因交通拥挤, 他迟到了. **2 Due to** can be used immediately after a noun ☆ **due to** 可直接用于名词之后: *Accidents due to driving at high speed were very common that weekend.* 在那个周末因高速驾驶造成的交通事故很多.

due[2] /dju:; US du:; du/ *n* **1** [sing] thing that should be given to sb by right 某人理应得到的东西: *He received a large reward, which was no more than his due*, ie at least what he deserved. 他得到了巨大的酬劳, 这至少是他应得的. **2 dues** [pl] charges or fees, eg for membership of a club 应交纳的费用(如俱乐部的会费): *I haven't paid my dues yet.* 我还没交会费. **3** (idm 习语) **give sb his ˈdue** (*fml* 文) be fair to sb 公平对待某人: *She's a slow worker but, to give her her due, she does try very hard.* 她工作很慢, 但平心而论, 她确实非常努力. **give the devil his due** ⇨ DEVIL[1].

due[3] /dju:; US du:; du/ *adv* (of points of the compass) exactly (指罗盘的方位)正向: *sail due east* 向正东方航行 ○ *walk three miles due north* 向正北走三英里.

duel /ˈdju:əl; US ˈdu:əl; ˋduəl/ *n* **1** (formerly) formal fight between two men, using swords or pistols, esp to settle a point of honour (旧时)两男子的决斗(用剑或手枪, 尤指关系到名誉问题): *challenge sb to a duel* 向某人挑战进行决斗. **2** (*fig* 比喻) contest or struggle between two people, groups, etc (双方的)竞争, 斗争: *engage in a duel of words/wits* 双方斗嘴[斗智].

▷ **duel** *v* **(-ll-;** *US* also **-l-)** [I, Ipr] **~ (with sb)** fight a duel 决斗: *duelling pistols*, ie pistols used in a duel 用于决斗的手枪. **du·el·list** /ˈdju:əlɪst; ˋdjuəlɪst/ (*US* **du·el·ist** /ˈdu:əlɪst; ˋduəlɪst/) *n* person fighting a duel 决斗者.

du·enna /dju:ˈenə; *US* du:ˈenə; duˋɛnə/ *n* (esp in Spain and Portugal) elderly woman acting as governess and chaperon to the daughters of a family (尤指在西班牙和葡萄牙)(家庭里女孩子的)保姆, 陪媪.

duet /dju:ˈet; *US* du:ˈet; duˋɛt/ (also **duo**) *n* piece of music for two players or singers 二重奏曲; 二重唱曲: *a duet for violin and piano* 小提琴和钢琴的二重奏曲 ○ *We sang a duet.* 我们唱了一曲二重唱.

duff /dʌf; dʌf/ *adj* (*Brit sl* 俚) worthless or useless 无价值的; 无用的.

▷ **duff** *v* (*Brit sl* 俚) **1** [Tn] mishit (sth), esp in golf; bungle 未击中(某物)(尤指高尔夫球); 弄糟(某事): *He duffed his drive off the first tee.* 他开球第一杆就未击中. **2** (phr v) **duff sb up** punch or kick sb severely 狠打或狠踢某人.

duffer /ˈdʌfə(r); ˋdʌfɚ/ *n* (*dated infml* 旧, 口) stupid or incompetent person 笨蛋; 无能的人: *I was always a bit of a duffer at maths.* 我在数学方面总是有点笨.

duffle (also **duf·fel**) /ˈdʌfl; ˋdʌfḷ/ *n* [U] heavy woollen cloth with a soft surface 表面起绒的厚呢料.

□ ˈ**duffle bag** long tube-shaped canvas bag closed by a draw-string (抽口的长筒状)帆布包, 行李袋.

ˈ**duffle-coat** *n* coat made of duffle, usu with a hood, fastened with toggles 厚呢料制的外衣(通常有兜帽, 以套索扣紧).

dug[1] *pt, pp* of DIG[1].

dug[2] /dʌg; dʌg/ *n* udder; teat (牛羊等的)乳房, 乳头.

dug-out /ˈdʌg aʊt; ˋdʌgˌaʊt/ *n* **1** (also ˌ**dug-out caˈnoe**) canoe made by hollowing out a tree trunk 独木舟. **2** rough covered shelter, usu for soldiers, made by digging in the earth 掩蔽部, 防空洞(通常为士兵用的).

duke /dju:k; *US* du:k; duk/ *n* (in titles 称谓中作 **Duke**) (*fem* 阴性作 **duchess** /ˈdʌtʃɪs; ˋdʌtʃɪs/) **1** (title of a) nobleman of the highest rank 公爵(的称号): *the Duke and Duchess of Gloucester* 格洛斯特公爵及公爵夫人. **2** (in some parts of Europe, esp formerly) male ruler of a small independent state (欧洲某些地区, 尤指旧时)(独立的小国或公国的)君主.

▷ **duke·dom** *n* **1** position or rank of a duke 公爵的爵位; 君主的地位. **2** = DUCHY.

dul·cet /ˈdʌlsɪt; ˋdʌlsɪt/ *adj* [attrib 作定语] (*fml or joc* 文或谑) sounding sweet; pleasing to the ear 动听的; 悦耳的: (*ironic* 反语) *I thought I recognized your dulcet tones*, ie the sound of your voice. 我想我听出了你那美妙的嗓音.

dul·ci·mer /ˈdʌlsɪmə(r); ˋdʌlsəmɚ/ *n* musical instrument played by striking metal strings with two hammers 扬琴; 洋琴.

dull /dʌl; dʌl/ *adj* **(-er, -est) 1** not bright or clear 不鲜

明的; 不清楚的: *a dull colour, glow, thud* 暗淡的颜色、昏暗的光、沉闷的响声 ○ *dull* (ie cloudy) *weather* 阴沉的天气 ○ *dull of hearing*, ie slightly deaf 听力不佳. **2** slow in understanding; stupid 迟钝的; 呆笨的: *a dull pupil, class, mind* 迟钝的学生、一班学生、头脑. **3** lacking interest or excitement; boring; monotonous 枯燥无味的; 令人厌烦的; 单调的: *The conference was deadly dull.* 会议开得死气沉沉的. **4** not sharp 不锋利的; 钝的: *a dull knife* 钝刀. **5** (of pain) not felt sharply (指疼痛)感觉不明显的, 隐约感觉到的: *a dull ache* 隐约的疼痛. **6** (of trade) not busy; slow (指生意)萧条的, 清淡的: *There's always a dull period after the January sales.* 在一月份大减价之后市面总要有一段清淡时期. **7** (idm 习语) **(as) ˌdull as ˈditch-water** (*infml* 口) very boring 极沉闷乏味的.

▷ **dull** *v* [I, Tn] (cause sth to) become dull (使某事物)变钝, 变迟钝: *Watching television dulls one's wits.* 看电视能使人头脑迟钝. ○ *She took drugs to dull the pain.* 她吃了药以减轻疼痛. ○ (*fig* 比喻) *Time had dulled the edge of his grief.* 岁月流逝冲淡了他的忧伤.

D

dull·ness *n* [U].

dully *adj.*

dull·ard /ˈdʌləd; ˋdʌlɚd/ *n* person who thinks slowly; stupid person 头脑迟钝的人; 笨人.

duly /ˈdjuːlɪ; *US* ˈduːlɪ; ˋdulɪ/ *adv* **1** in a due, correct or proper manner (方式)正当地, 正确地, 适当地: *The president was duly elected.* 总统已正式选出. **2** at the due and proper time; punctually 按时地; 适时地; 准时地: *I duly knocked on his door at three o'clock.* 我准时在三点钟敲了他的门.

dumb /dʌm; dʌm/ *adj* (**-er, -est**) **1** unable to speak 哑的: *She's been dumb from birth.* 她生来即哑. ○ *our dumb friends*, ie animals 我们的不能言语的朋友(即动物) ○ (*fig* 比喻) *be struck dumb* (ie left speechless) *with horror, fear, amazement, etc* 因恐怖、恐惧、惊愕等而说不出话来. **2** [usu pred 通常作表语] temporarily silent; refusing to speak 暂时沉默; 拒绝说话: *They begged him to explain, but he remained dumb.* 他们请求他解释, 但他保持沉默不语. **3** (*infml* 口) stupid 愚蠢的: *That was a pretty dumb thing to do.* 那件事干得可真蠢. ○ *If the police question you, act dumb*, ie pretend you don't know anything. 警方要是盘问你, 就装作什么也不知道.

▷ **dumbly** *adv*. **dumb·ness** *n* [U].

□ ˈ**dumb show** communication using gestures but no words; mime 手语; 哑语; 哑剧.

ˌ**dumb ˈwaiter** (**a**) (*US* **lazy Susan**) stand with shelves for holding food ready to be served 食品台; 食品架. (**b**) small lift for carrying food, etc from one floor to another, esp in a restaurant 小型升降机(尤指饭店中传送食物者).

dumb-bell /ˈdʌmbel; ˋdʌmˌbɛl/ *n* **1** short bar with a weight at each end, used for exercising the muscles, esp those of the arms and shoulders 哑铃. **2** (*US infml* 口) stupid person 笨蛋; 蠢货.

dumb·found (also **dum·found**) /dʌmˈfaʊnd; dʌmˋfaʊnd/ *v* [Tn esp passive 尤用于被动语态] make (sb) speechless with surprise; astonish 使(某人)受惊而说不出话; 使(某人)惊讶: *We were completely dumbfounded by her rudeness.* 她粗鲁无礼, 把我们吓呆了.

dum·dum /ˈdʌmdʌm; ˋdʌmdʌm/ *n* (also **dumdum bullet**) soft-nosed bullet that expands on impact, causing a gaping wound 达姆弹.

dummy /ˈdʌmɪ; ˋdʌmɪ/ *n* **1** [C] model of the human figure, used for displaying or fitting clothes, etc (用于展示或试穿服装等的)人体模型: *a tailor's dummy* 服装店的人体模型. **2** [C] thing that appears to be real but is only an imitation 仿制品: *The bottles of whisky on display are all dummies.* 陈列的威士忌酒都是假的. **3** [C] (*esp Brit*) (*US* **comforter**, **pacifier**) rubber teat, not attached to a bottle, for a baby to suck (不装在瓶子上的)橡皮奶头. **4** [sing] (**a**) (in card-games, esp bridge) player whose cards are placed facing upwards on the table and played by his partner (纸牌游戏, 尤指桥牌)明手, 梦家(将牌摊出者). (**b**) these cards 明手、梦家摊出之牌: *She played a jack from dummy.* 她从明手摊出的牌中打出一张J. **5** [C] (*US infml* 口) stupid person 笨蛋; 蠢货.

□ ˌ**dummy ˈrun** trial or practice attack, performance, etc 攻击、表演等的试验或演习.

dump /dʌmp; dʌmp/ *v* [Tn, Tn·pr] **1** put (sth unwanted) in a place and leave as rubbish 丢弃(不需要的某物); 倾倒(垃圾): *Some people just dump their rubbish in the river.* 有些人径直往河里倒垃圾. ○ *Sealed containers of nuclear waste have been dumped in the sea.* 盛有核废料的密封容器被丢在海里. **2** put (sth) down carelessly, heavily or in a mass 将(某物)粗心地或猛力地放下或放成一堆: *dump a load of gravel, a pile of newspapers, a bundle of dirty clothes* 倾倒一车碎石、扔下一堆报纸、放下一包脏衣服 ○ *Just dump everything over there — I'll sort it out later.* 先把东西都堆在那边——我等会儿再整理. **3** (*infml often derog* 口, 常作贬义) leave or abandon (sb) 丢下或抛弃(某人): *She dumped the kids at her mother's and went to the theatre.* 她把孩子放在娘家就看戏去了. ○ *He's dumped his wife and gone off with one of his students.* 他丢下妻子, 跟自己的一个学生跑了. **4** (*derog commerce* 贬, 商) sell abroad at a very low price (goods that are not wanted in the home market) 向国外廉价倾销(国内市场不需要的货物). **5** (*computing* 计) transfer (data, etc) from one part of a system to another or from one storage system to another 转储(数据等). **6** (idm 习语) **drop/dump sth in sb's lap** ⇨ LAP[1].

▷ **dump** *n* **1** place where rubbish may be unloaded and left; rubbish-heap 垃圾场; 垃圾堆. Cf 参看 TIP[2] *n*. **2** temporary store of military supplies 军需品的临时存放处: *an ammuˈnition dump* 军火临时存放处. **3** (*infml derog* 口, 贬) dirty or unattractive place 肮脏的或讨厌的地方: *How can you live in this dump?* 你怎么住在这个破地方?

dumper *n* (also ˈ**dumper truck**, *US* ˈ**dumptruck**) small vehicle, used on building sites, etc, with a container that can be tilted to dump its contents (建筑工地上使用的, 有翻斗的)小型自卸载重车.

dump·ling /ˈdʌmplɪŋ; ˋdʌmplɪŋ/ *n* **1** small ball of dough steamed or boiled, eg in a stew 蒸的或煮的小面团; 汤团; 团子. **2** baked pudding made of dough filled with fruit (将水果放在面团中烘制而成的)水果布丁: *an apple dumpling* 苹果布丁. **3** (*infml* 口) short plump person 矮胖的人; 胖墩子.

dumps /dʌmps; dʌmps/ *n* [pl] (idm 习语) **(down) in the dumps** (*infml* 口) depressed; feeling gloomy 沮丧的; 抑郁的.

dumpy /ˈdʌmpɪ; ˋdʌmpɪ/ *adj* (**-ier**, **-iest**) (esp of a person) short and fat (尤指人)矮胖的. ▷ **dum·pi·ness** *n* [U].

dun[1] /dʌn; dʌn/ *adj, n* (of a) dull greyish-brown colour 暗褐色的; 暗褐色.

dun[2] /dʌn; dʌn/ *v* (**-nn-**) [Tn] persistently demand payment of a debt from (sb) (不断地向某人)讨债; 催讨债款.

dunce /dʌns; dʌns/ *n* person, esp a pupil, who is stupid or slow to learn (在学习上)愚笨的或迟钝的人(尤指学生).

□ ˈ**dunce's cap** pointed paper hat formerly given to dull pupils to wear in class as a punishment (旧时劣等生在课堂上戴的)圆锥形纸帽(以示惩罚).

dun·der·head /ˈdʌndəhed; ˋdʌndɚˌhɛd/ *n* (*derog* 贬) stupid person 笨人; 蠢材.

dune /djuːn; *US* duːn; dun/ (also ˈ**sand-dune**) *n* mound of loose dry sand formed by the wind (由于风吹而形成的)沙丘.

dung /dʌŋ; dʌŋ/ *n* [U] animal excrement, esp when used as manure 动物的粪便; (尤指)粪肥.

□ ˈ**dunghill** *n* heap of dung in a farmyard 粪堆.

dun·gar·ees /ˌdʌŋgəˈriːz; ˌdʌŋgəˋriz/ *n* [pl] overalls or trousers made of coarse cotton cloth (粗棉布制的)长工作服, 工装裤: *a pair of dungarees* 一条工装裤.

dun·geon /ˈdʌndʒən; ˋdʌndʒən/ *n* underground prison cell, esp in a castle 地牢(尤指城堡中者).

dunk /dʌŋk; dʌŋk/ *v* [Tn, Tn·pr] **~ sth/sb (in/into sth)** **1** dip (food) in liquid before eating 将(食物)浸入液体(再吃): *dunk a biscuit in one's coffee* 将饼干泡入咖啡. **2** submerge (sb/sth) briefly in water 将(某人[某物])在水中浸一下, 蘸一下: *They dunked her in the swimming-pool as a joke.* 他们跟她开玩笑, 把她往游泳池里浸了一下.

duo /ˈdjuːəʊ; *US* ˈduːəʊ; ˋduo/ *n* (*pl* **~s**) **1** pair of performers 成对的表演者: *a comedy duo* 一对喜剧演

员. **2** = DUET.

duo·decimal /ˌdjuːəʊˈdesɪml; *US* ˌduːəˈdesəml; ˌduəˈdɛsəml/ *adj* based on twelve or twelfths; proceeding by twelves 十二的; 十二分算的; 十二进制的: *a duodecimal system* 十二进制.

duo·denum /ˌdjuːəˈdiːnəm; *US* ˌduːəˈdiːnəm; ˌduəˈdinəm/ *n* (*anatomy* 解) first part of the small intestine, immediately below the stomach 十二指肠. ⇨illus at DIGESTIVE 见DIGESTIVE之插图. ▷ **duo·denal** /ˌdjuːəˈdiːnl; *US* ˌduːəˈdiːnl; ˌduəˈdinl/ *adj* [usu attrib 通常作定语]: *a duodenal ulcer* 十二指肠溃疡.

duo·logue /ˈdjuːəlɒg; *US* ˈduːəlɔːg; ˈduəˌlɔg/ *n* conversation between two people (二人的)对话.

dupe /djuːp; *US* duːp; dup/ *v* [Tn, Tn·pr] **~ sb (into doing sth)** deceive or trick sb (into doing sth) 欺骗或哄骗某人(做某事).
▷ **dupe** *n* person who is duped; fool 受骗的人; 傻子: *I won't be his dupe any longer.* 我再也不受他的骗了.

duple time /ˌdjuːpl ˈtaɪm; *US* duːpl; ˈdupl ˌtaɪm/ (*music* 音) rhythm with two beats in a bar 二拍子.

du·plex /ˈdjuːpleks; *US* ˈduːpleks; ˈduplɛks/ *adj* having two parts 有两部分的.
▷ **du·plex** *n* (*US*) **1** (**a**) building divided into two dwellings 毗联式建筑(分隔成两个住宅者). (**b**) either of these dwellings 毗联式建筑两个住宅中的一个. **2** (also **duplex apartment**) apartment on two floors 占两层楼的公寓套房.

du·plic·ate[1] /ˈdjuːplɪkət; *US* ˈduːpləkət; ˈdupləkɪt/ *adj* [attrib 作定语] **1** exactly like something else; identical (与另一物)完全一样的; 完全相同的: *a duplicate set of keys* (与另一套)完全相同的一套钥匙. **2** having two identical parts; twofold; double 两部分完全相同的; 双重的; 二倍的: *a duplicate receipt, form, etc* 双联式收据、表格等.
▷ **du·plic·ate** *n* **1** one of two or more things that are exactly alike; copy 相似物; 复制品: *Is this a duplicate or the original?* 这是复制件还是原件? **2** (idm 习语) **in duplicate** (of documents, etc) as two identical copies (指文件等)一式两份: *complete a form, prepare a contract, etc in duplicate* 填写表格、准备合同等一式两份.

du·plic·ate[2] /ˈdjuːplɪkeɪt; *US* ˈduːpləkeɪt; ˈdupləˌket/ *v* **1** [Tn esp passive 尤用于被动语态] make an exact copy of (sth) 复制(某物). **2** [Tn] do (sth) again, esp unnecessarily; repeat 再一次做(某事)(尤指无必要地); 重复: *This research merely duplicates work already done elsewhere.* 这项研究仅仅是重复别人已经做过的工作.
▷**du·plica·tion** /ˌdjuːplɪˈkeɪʃn; *US* ˌduːpləˈkeɪʃn; ˌdupləˈkeʃən/ *n* [U] duplicating or being duplicated 复制; 重复: *We must avoid wasteful duplication of effort.* 我们必须避免无谓的重复劳动.
du·plic·ator *n* machine for making copies of written or typed material 复印机.

du·pli·city /djuːˈplɪsətɪ; *US* duːˈplɪsətɪ; duˈplɪsətɪ/ *n* [U] (*fml* 文) deliberate deception 欺骗.

dur·able /ˈdjʊərəbl; *US* ˈdʊərəbl; ˈdurəbl/ *adj* lasting for a long time 持久的; 耐久的: *a durable peace, friendship, settlement* 持久的和平、永恒的友谊、永久的解决 ○ *trousers made of durable material* 耐穿的料子制成的裤子 ○ *This varnish provides a durable finish.* 这种清漆可作耐久的罩面漆.
▷ **dur·ab·il·ity** /ˌdjʊərəˈbɪlətɪ; *US* ˌdʊrəˈbɪlətɪ; ˌdurəˈbɪlətɪ/ *n* [U].
dur·ables *n* [pl] (also **conˌsumer ˈdurables**) goods expected to last for a long time after they have been bought, eg vacuum cleaners 耐用品(如吸尘器).

dura·tion /djʊˈreɪʃn; *US* dʊˈreɪʃn; duˈreʃən/ *n* [U] **1** time during which sth lasts or continues 持续时间; 期间: *of short, long, three years', etc duration* 短的、长的、持续三年的一段时间 ○ *for the duration of this government* 本届政府执政期间. **2** (idm 习语) **for the duration** (*infml* 口) (**a**) until the end of the war 在战争期间. (**b**) (*fig* 比喻) for a very long time 很长的时间: *Well, I'm stuck here for the duration,* eg for the whole term. 哎, 这段时间(如整个学期)我只得呆在这里了.

dur·ess /djʊˈres; *US* dʊˈres; duˈrɛs/ *n* [U] threats or force used to make sb do sth; (usu illegal) compulsion 威胁; 逼迫; (通常指非法的)强迫行动: *sign a confession under duress* 受威逼在供状上签字.

dur·ing /ˈdjʊərɪŋ; *US* ˈdʊr-; ˈdurɪŋ/ *prep* **1** throughout (a period of time taken by an action or event) 在...期间: *There are extra trains to the seaside during the summer.* 通往海滨的火车在夏季有加车. ○ *During his lifetime his work was never published.* 他的作品在他的有生之年从未出版过. ○ *He stopped for applause three times during his speech.* 他在讲话过程中曾停下三次等待掌声落下. **2** within (a specified period of time) 在(某段时间)内: *They only met twice during the whole time they were neighbours.* 他们在毗邻而居期间只见过两次面. ○ *There will be two intervals during the performance.* 演出期间将有两次休息. **3** at a particular time while (sth) progresses 在(某事)进行过程中的某一时间: *The phone rang during the meal.* 吃饭时电话铃响了. ○ *There was a bomb scare during the procession.* 在列队行进时因怀疑有炸弹而引起恐慌. ○ *Her husband was taken to hospital during the night.* 她丈夫在夜间被送进医院.

dusk /dʌsk; dʌsk/ *n* [U] time after twilight and before night 黄昏; 傍晚: *The street lights come on at dusk and go off at dawn.* 路灯在黄昏时开, 拂晓时关.

dusky /ˈdʌskɪ; ˈdʌskɪ/ *adj* (**-ier, -iest**) **1** shadowy; dim 昏暗的; 黑暗的; 暗淡的; 朦胧的: *the dusky light inside the cave* 山洞内昏暗的光线. **2** (**a**) dark-coloured 颜色深的; 颜色暗的: *dusky blue, red, etc* 深蓝、深红. (**b**) (*often offensive* 常作轻蔑语) dark-skinned 皮肤黑的; 肤色深的: *a dusky maiden* 皮肤黑的少女 ○ *dusky tribes* 肤色深的种族. ▷ **duski·ness** *n* [U].

D

dust[1] /dʌst; dʌst/ *n* [U] **1** fine dry powder consisting of particles of earth, dirt, etc 灰尘; 尘土; 尘埃: *a speck of dust* 一点灰尘 ○ *The old furniture was covered in dust.* 旧家具上有尘土. ○ *clouds of dust blowing in the wind* 风吹起的尘雾 ○ *gold, chalk, etc dust,* ie fine particles of gold, chalk, etc 金粉、粉笔灰 ○ [attrib 作定语] *A dust-cloud* (ie A whirlwind carrying clouds of dust) *swept across the plain.* 旋风卷着漫天尘土横扫平原. **2** (*rhet* 修辞) remains of a dead person 遗骸. **3** (idm 习语) **bite the dust** ⇨ BITE[1]. **dry as dust** ⇨ DRY[1]. **kick up/raise a ˈdust** (*infml* 口) make a fuss 引起骚乱. **shake the dust off one's feet** ⇨ SHAKE[1]. **throw dust in sb's eyes** prevent sb from seeing the truth by misleading him 蒙蔽某人, 使其不明真相. **when the dust has settled** when the present uncertainty, unpleasantness, etc is over 烟消云散; 疑云散尽; 愁云散尽.
□ **ˈdustbin** *n* (*Brit*) (*US* **garbage can, trash-can**) container for (esp household) rubbish (尤指家庭的)垃圾桶.
ˈdust bowl area that has lost its vegetation through drought, over-cultivation, etc (因旱灾、耕地使用过度等)失去植被的地区.
ˈdust-cart *n* (*Brit*) (*US* **garbage truck**) vehicle for collecting rubbish from dustbins 垃圾车.
ˈdust-cover *n* **1** cover used for protecting a computer, gramophone turntable, etc from dust (计算机、留声机转盘等的)防尘罩. **2** = DUST-JACKET. **3** = DUST-SHEET.
ˈdust-jacket *n* removable paper cover to protect the binding of a book 护封.
ˈdustman /-mən; -mən/ *n* (*pl* **-men** /-mən; -mən/) (*Brit*) (*US* **garbage man**) man employed by a local authority to empty dustbins and remove rubbish 清除垃圾的工人.
ˈdustpan *n* pan into which dust is brushed from the floor 簸箕.
ˈdust-sheet *n* sheet used for covering furniture that is not in use, to protect it from dust 家具罩单.
ˈdust-up *n* [sing] (*infml* 口) noisy quarrel or fight 争吵; 吵闹; 打架.

dust[2] /dʌst; dʌst/ *v* **1** (**a**) [Tn] remove dust from (sth) by wiping, brushing or flicking 将尘土从(某物)上抹去、刷去或拂去: *dust the furniture, books, living-room* 拭去家具上的、书上的、客厅里的灰尘. (**b**) [Tn·p] **~ sb down/off** remove dust from sb by brushing or flicking 将尘土从某人身上刷去或拂去: *Dust yourself down — you're covered in chalk.* 把你自己身上掸掸——上面都是粉笔末. **2** (phr v) **dust sth off** begin to practise sth, esp a skill or a language that one knows but has not used for some time 开始复习某事(尤指一段时间内搁置不用的技艺或语言): *I'll have to dust off my French if we're going to move to Paris.* 我们要是搬到巴黎去, 我就得把法语重新拾起来. **dust sth onto, over, etc sth**

sprinkle (sth powdery) over sth 将(粉状物)撒在某物表面: *dust sugar onto a cake* 将糖粉撒在蛋糕上. **dust sth with sth** sprinkle sth with (sth powdery) 以(粉状物)撒在某物上: *dust a cake with icing sugar* 将糖霜撒在蛋糕上.

▷ **duster** *n* cloth for dusting furniture, etc 布; 抹布.

dusty /ˈdʌstɪ; ˋdʌstɪ/ *adj* (**-ier, -iest**) **1** (**a**) full of dust; covered with dust 满是灰尘的; 落满灰尘的: *This room's rather dusty, I'm afraid.* 我看, 这间屋子的尘土未免太多了. (**b**) like dust 灰尘般的; 粉末状的. **2** (idm 习语) **a dusty answer** curt rejection of a request; unfriendly refusal (对要求的)轻率的回绝; 淡然的拒绝. **not so dusty** (*dated Brit infml* 旧, 口) fairly good 还好; 还不坏: *'How are you feeling?' 'Oh, not so dusty, thanks!'* '你身体怎样?' '啊, 还不错, 多谢!' ▷ **dusti·ness** *n* [U].

Dutch /dʌtʃ; dʌtʃ/ *adj* **1** of the Netherlands (Holland), its people or their language 荷兰的; 荷兰人的; 荷兰语的. **2** (idm 习语) **Dutch courage** (*infml joc* 口, 谑) courage that comes from drinking alcohol 酒后之勇. **a Dutch treat** a meal, an entertainment, etc at which each person pays for himself 各自付费的聚餐、娱乐等. **go Dutch (with sb)** share expenses 均摊费用. **talk (to sb) like a Dutch uncle** ⇨ TALK[2].

▷ **Dutch** *n* **1 the Dutch** [pl *v*] the people of the Netherlands 荷兰人. **2** [U] the language of the Dutch 荷兰语. Cf 参看 DOUBLE DUTCH (DOUBLE[1]).

□ ˌ**Dutch ˈauction** sale in which the price is gradually reduced until a buyer is found 降价式拍卖(逐渐降价直至有人购买为止).

ˌ**Dutch ˈbarn** farm building consisting of a roof supported on poles, without walls, used as a shelter for hay, etc (放干草等的)棚子.

ˌ**Dutch ˈcap** = DIAPHRAGM 4.

ˌ**Dutch ˈelm disease** disease that kills elm trees, caused by a fungus 荷兰榆树病.

ˈ**Dutchman** /-mən; -mən/ *n* (*pl* **-men**) **1** native of the Netherlands 荷兰人. **2** (idm 习语) **I'm a Dutchman!** (used to express incredulity 用以表示难以置信): *If he's only twenty-five, I'm a Dutchman!* 要说他只有二十五岁, 我才不信呢!

ˌ**Dutch ˈoven** covered container used for cooking meat, etc slowly 荷兰炖锅.

du·teous /ˈdjuːtɪəs; *US* ˈduː-; ˋdutɪəs/ *adj* (*fml* 文) = DUTIFUL.

du·ti·able /ˈdjuːtɪəbl; *US* ˈduː-; ˋdutɪəbḷ/ *adj* on which customs or other duties (DUTY 3) must be paid 应纳税的: *dutiable goods* 应纳税的货物.

du·ti·ful /ˈdjuːtɪfl; *US* ˈduː-; ˋdutɪfəl/ (also **duteous**) *adj* (*fml* 文) showing respect and obedience; fulfilling all one's obligations 恭敬顺从的; 尽职的: *a dutiful son, subject, servant, etc* 恭顺的儿子、顺从的国民、尽职的仆人. ▷ **du·ti·fully** /-fəlɪ; -fəlɪ/ *adv*: *He dutifully followed his commander's instructions.* 他恭顺地服从长官的命令. ○ *to serve one's country dutifully* 克尽厥职为国效力.

duty /ˈdjuːtɪ; *US* ˈduːtɪ; ˋdutɪ/ *n* **1** [C, U] moral or legal obligation (道德上的或法律上的)责任, 义务: *It's your duty to go.* 你得去, 那是你的责任. ○ *do one's duty* 尽职 ○ *It's not something I enjoy. I do it purely out of a sense of duty.* 那并不是我喜欢做的事, 我纯粹是出于责任感才做的. ○ *I'll have to go, I'm afraid — duty calls.* 看来我得走了——公务在身. **2** [C, U] task or action that sb must perform (某人必须执行的)任务或行动: *What are the duties of a traffic warden?* 街道停车管理员的职责是什么? ○ *I'm doing night duty this week.* 这个星期我上夜班. **3** [C, U] **~ (on sth)** tax charged on certain goods, esp on imports (某些货物, 尤指进口货物交纳的)税; 关税: *customs/excise duties* 关税[消费税]. Cf 参看 TARIFF 2. **4** (idm 习语) **one's bounden duty** ⇨ BOUNDEN. **dereliction of duty** ⇨ DERELICTION (DERELICT). **do duty for sth** serve as or act as a substitute for sth else 充作或当作另一事物的代替品: *An old wooden box did duty for a table.* 把旧木箱当作桌子. **in the line of duty** ⇨ LINE[1]. **on/off duty** (of nurses, police officers, etc) engaged/not engaged in one's regular work 值[不值]班; 上[不上]班: *I arrive at the hospital at eight o'clock, but I don't go on duty until nine.* 我八点钟就到医院了, 但是九点钟我才去值班. ○ [attrib 作定语] *off-duty activities, hours* 业余活动、时间.

□ ˌ**duty-ˈbound** *adj* [pred 作表语] obliged by duty 义不容辞: *I'm duty-bound to help him.* 就我来说, 帮助他是责无旁贷的.

ˌ**duty-ˈfree** *adj, adv* (of goods) that can be imported without payment of customs duties (指货物)免关税(的): *You're allowed 1½ litres of spirits duty-free.* 你可免税带进1½升烈性酒. ○ *There's a good duty-free shop* (ie one selling such goods) *on the ferry.* 渡船上有个挺不错的免税商店. ○ *buy cigarettes duty-free* 买免税香烟.

du·vet /ˈduːveɪ; duˋve/ *n* quilt filled with soft feathers, etc, used on a bed instead of a top sheet and blankets 羽绒被. Cf 参看 EIDERDOWN.

DV /ˌdiː ˈviː; ˌdi ˋvi/ *abbr* 缩写 = God being willing (Latin *Deo volente*) 如蒙上帝恩准, 如情况许可(源自拉丁文 *Deo volente*): *He should be back by Friday, DV*, ie if nothing prevents him. 他若一切顺利, 星期五就应该回来了.

dwarf /dwɔːf; dwɔrf/ *n* (*pl* **~s**) **1** person, animal or plant that is much smaller than the normal size 矮子; 侏儒; 矮小的动物或植物: [attrib 作定语] *a dwarf conifer* 矮小的针叶树. **2** (in fairy stories) creature like a very small man with magic powers (神话中的)有魔法的小矮人.

▷ **dwarf** *v* [Tn] **1** make (sb/sth) seem small by contrast or distance 使(某人[某物])相比之下显得小: *Our little dinghy was dwarfed by the big yacht.* 我们的小船跟大游艇一比显得很小. **2** prevent the full growth of (sth); stunt 阻碍(某物)充分生长发育; 阻碍生长.

dwell /dwel; dwɛl/ *v* (*pt, pp* **dwelt** /dwelt; dwɛlt/) **1** [Ipr] **~ in, at, etc . . .** (*arch or rhet* 古或修辞) live as an inhabitant of or reside at (a place) 住; 居住. **2** (phr v) **dwell on/upon sth** think, speak or write at length about sth 细想某事; 详述某事: *Let's not dwell on your past mistakes.* 我们不要再细说你过去的错误了.

▷ **dweller** *n* (esp in compound *ns* 尤用以构成复合名词) person or animal living in the place specified 住在某处的人或动物: ˈ*town-dwellers* ○ ˈ*flat-dwellers* ○ ˈ*cave-dwellers*.

dwell·ing *n* (*fml* 文) place of residence; house, flat, etc 住处; 住宅; 公寓: (*fml or joc* 文或谑) *my humble dwelling* 寒舍. ˈ**dwelling-house** *n* (*esp law* 尤用于法律) house used as a residence, not as a place of work 住宅.

dwindle /ˈdwɪndl; ˋdwɪndḷ/ *v* [I, Ipr, Ip] **~ (away) (to nothing)** become gradually less or smaller 逐渐变少或变小; 减少; 缩小: *dwindling hopes, popularity, profits* 逐渐消失的希望、日益低落的声望、日渐减少的利润 ○ *Their savings have dwindled (away) to nothing.* 他们的存款已减少到分文不剩了.

dye[1] /daɪ; daɪ/ *v* (*3rd pers sing pres t* **dyes**, *pt, pp* **dyed**, *pres p* **dyeing**) (**a**) [Tn, Cn·a] colour (sth), esp by dipping in a liquid 染(某物)(尤指浸渍法): *dye one's hair* 染发 ○ *dye a white dress blue* 将白色的连衣裙染成蓝色. (**b**) [I] be able to be dyed 能染上颜色: *a fabric that dyes well* 易染色的织物. ▷ **dyer** *n*.

□ ˌ**dyed-in-the-ˈwool** *adj* [usu attrib 通常作定语] (*usu derog* 通常作贬义) totally fixed in one's ideas, beliefs, etc (思想、信仰等)根深蒂固的, 顽固不化的: *a dyed-in-the-wool racist* 死心塌地的种族主义者.

dye[2] /daɪ; daɪ/ *n* [C, U] **1** substance used for dyeing 染料: *vegetable dyes* 植物染料 ○ *I bought some blue dye yesterday.* 我昨天买了些蓝颜料. **2** colour given by dyeing. 染料染上的颜色. **3** (idm 习语) **of the blackest/deepest dye** (*dated* 旧) of the worst kind 最坏的: *a villain, scoundrel, traitor, etc of the deepest dye* 罪大恶极的恶棍、流氓、叛徒等.

dy·ing ⇨ DIE.

dyke = DIKE.

dy·namic /daɪˈnæmɪk; daɪˋnæmɪk/ *adj* **1** of power or forces that produce movement 动力的. Cf 参看 STATIC 2. **2** (of a person) energetic and forceful (指人)精力充沛的, 有力的: *a dynamic personality* 精力充沛的人.

▷ **dy·namic** *n* [sing] force that produces change, action, or effects 产生变化、行动或影响的力量: *the inner dynamic of a historical period, social movement, work of art* 某一历史时期的、社会运动的、艺术品的内在力量.

dy·nam·ic·ally *adv*.

dy·namics /daɪˈnæmɪks; daɪˋnæmɪks/ *n* **1** [sing *v*]

branch of physics dealing with movement and force 动力学; 力学. **2** [pl] (*music* 音) amount of or variation in loudness 力度; 力度变化.

dy·nam·ism /ˈdaɪnəmɪzəm; ˋdaɪnə,mɪzəm/ *n* [U] **1** (in a person) quality of being dynamic (人的)精力, 活力, 干劲. **2** (*philosophy* 哲) theory that phenomena are the result of natural forces acting on each other 物力论(认为一切现象都是自然力相互作用的结果之理论).

dy·nam·ite /ˈdaɪnəmaɪt; ˋdaɪnə,maɪt/ *n* [U] **1** powerful explosive used in mining, etc 达纳炸药; 黄色炸药. **2** (*fig* 比喻) (**a**) thing likely to cause violent reactions 能引起强烈反应的事物: *The abortion issue is political dynamite.* 堕胎问题在政治上是个爆炸性的问题. (**b**) (*infml approv* 口, 褒) strikingly impressive person or thing 了不起的人或事物: *Their new album is sheer dynamite.* 他们这套新唱片一下子轰动起来.
▷ **dy·nam·ite** *v* [Tn] blow (sb/sth) up with dynamite 炸毁(某人[某物]).

dy·namo /ˈdaɪnəməʊ; ˋdaɪnə,mo/ *n* (*pl* **~s**) **1** device for converting steam-power, water-power, etc into electricity; generator 发电机. ⇨ illus at App 1 见附录1之插图, pages xii, xiii. **2** (*fig infml* 比喻, 口) intensely energetic person 精力充沛的人: *a human dynamo* 干劲十足的人.

dyn·asty /ˈdɪnəstɪ; *US* ˈdaɪ-; ˋdaɪnəstɪ/ *n* **1** series of rulers all belonging to the same family 朝代; 王朝: *the Tudor dynasty* 都铎王朝. **2** period during which a particular dynasty rules 某一王朝统治的时期; 朝; 代: *during the Ming dynasty* 在明朝. ▷ **dyn·astic** /dɪˈnæstɪk; *US* daɪ-; daɪˋnæstɪk/ *adj* [usu attrib 通常作定语]: *dynastic succession* 改朝换代.

dys·en·tery /ˈdɪsəntrɪ; *US* -terɪ; ˋdɪsn̩,tɛrɪ/ *n* [U] inflammation of the bowels, causing severe diarrhoea, usu with a discharge of mucus and blood 痢疾.

dys·lexia /dɪsˈleksɪə; dɪsˋlɛksɪə/ *n* [U] (*medical* 医) (also **word-blindness**) abnormal difficulty in reading and spelling, caused by a brain condition 诵读困难.
▷ **dys·lexic** /dɪsˈleksɪk; dɪsˋlɛksɪk/ *n*, *adj* (person) suffering from dyslexia 患诵读困难症的(人).

dys·pep·sia /dɪsˈpepsɪə; *US* dɪsˈpepʃə; dɪˋspɛpʃə/ *n* [U] (*fml* 文) indigestion 消化不良.
▷ **dys·peptic** /dɪsˈpeptɪk; dɪˋspɛptɪk/ *adj*, *n* (typical of a) person suffering from dyspepsia or the irritability that it causes 消化不良的; 消化不良患者; (因消化不良引起的)烦躁(的), 易怒(的).

dys·trophy /ˈdɪstrəfɪ; ˋdɪstrəfɪ/ *n* [U] (*medical* 医) inherited condition that causes a progressive weakening of the body tissues, esp the muscles 营养障碍; 营养不良: *muscular dystrophy* 因营养障碍造成的肌肉萎缩.

E e

E, e /i:; i/ *n* (*pl* **E's, e's** /i:z; iz/) **1** the fifth letter of the English alphabet 英语字母表的第五个字母: *'Eric' begins with an 'E'/E.* Eric一字以E字母开始. **2 E** (*music* 音) the third note in the scale of C major C大调音阶中的第三音或音符.

□ '**E number** code number, beginning with the letter E, used for indicating the additives in food and drink E数(以E字母开头的代号, 用以表明食品或饮料中的添加剂).

E *abbr* 缩写 = **1** (esp on electric plugs) earth (connection) (尤指标于电器插头上的)地线(接线). **2** east(ern): *E Asia* 东亚 ○ *London E10 6RL*, ie as a postal code 伦敦E10 6RL(邮政编码).

ea *abbr* 缩写 = each: *oranges 10p ea* 橙子10便士一个.

each /i:tʃ; itʃ/ *indef det* (used with *sing* [C] *ns* and *sing vs* 与单数可数名词和单数动词连用) (of two or more) every (person, thing, group, etc) considered individually 每一, 各个: *on each side of the road* 在路的每一边 ○ *a ring on each finger* 每个手指上一个指环 ○ *Each day passed without any news.* 每天都没有任何消息.

▷ **each** *indef pron* every individual member (of a group) 每个: *each of the boys, books, buildings* 每个男孩、每本书、每座建筑物 ○ *Each of them phoned to thank me.* 他们每个人都打电话来向我道谢. ○ *Each of us has a company car.* 我们每人都有一辆公司的汽车. (Cf 参看 *We each have a company car.*) ○ *I'll see each of you separately.* 我要分别地见你们每一个人. (Cf 参看 *I'll see you each separately.*) ○ *He gave us £5 each.* 他给我们每人5英镑.

each *indef adv* every one separately 每一个地; 各个地: *The cakes are 20p each.* 糕饼每块20便士.

each other 互相

□ **each** '**other** (used only as the object of a *v* or *prep* 仅用作动词或介词的宾语) the other one, reciprocally 互相; 彼此: *Paul and Linda helped each other*, ie Paul helped Linda and Linda helped Paul. 保罗和琳达互相帮助. ○ *We write to each other regularly.* 我们彼此经常通信. Cf 参看 ONE ANOTHER (ONE[3]).

NOTE ON USAGE 用法: **Each** and **every** are generally used as determiners before singular countable nouns. ☆ **each** 和 **every** 一般都作限定词, 用于单数可数名词之前. **Each** is used when the items in a group (of two or more) are considered individually ☆ **each** 用以指一个群体(至少两个)中个别的个体: *Each child learns at his or her own pace.* 每个儿童均按自己的进度学习. **Every** indicates that all the items in a group (of three or more) are being regarded as members of that group. ☆ **every** 指一个群体(至少三个)中侧重于全体的所有个体, 而不在个别的个体. It can be modified by some adverbs 这个词可以受某些副词修饰: *Every/Nearly every child in the school passed the swimming test.* 这所学校的每一个[几乎每一个]儿童游泳都及格了. **Each (one) of** and **every one of** come before plural nouns or pronouns, but the verb is still singular ☆ **each (one) of** 和 **every one of** 用于复数名词或代词之前, 然而动词仍用单数: *Each of the houses is slightly different.* 每所房子都稍有区别. ○ *I bought a dozen eggs and every one of them was bad.* 我买了一打鸡蛋, 每个都是坏的. ○ *She gave each (one) of her grandchildren 50p.* 她给每个孙儿50便士. **Each** can function as a pronoun on its own ☆ **each** 本身可作代词: *I asked all the children and each told a different story.* 我问过所有的孩子, 每个人的说法都不一样. It can also follow a plural subject or an indirect object with a plural verb 这个词还可以用于复数的主语之后或复数动词的间接宾语之后: *We each have a different point of view.* 我们每个人都有不同的观点.

eager /'i:gə(r); 'igɚ/ *adj* **1 ~ (for sth/to do sth)** full of interest or desire; keen 热切的; 渴望的; 热心的: *eager for success* 渴望成功 ○ *eager to please* 极想讨好(别人). **2** (idm 习语) **an eager 'beaver** (*sometimes derog* 有时作贬义) keen, hard-working and enthusiastic person 积极、努力又热心的人. ▷ **eagerly** *adv.* **eager·ness** *n* [U].

eagle /'i:gl; 'igl/ *n* **1** large strong bird of prey of the falcon family with very good eyesight 雕; 鹰. **2** (in golf) score of two strokes less than average (高尔夫球)比标准杆少两杆的分数. Cf 参看 BIRDIE 2, PAR[1] 3.

▷ **eag·let** /'i:glɪt; 'iglɪt/ *n* young eagle 小雕; 小鹰.

□ ˌ**eagle** '**eye** (usu *sing* 通常作单数) **1** very good eyesight 极好的视力. **2** keen watchfulness 敏锐的目光: *The teacher's eagle eye was always on us*, ie She noticed everything. 教师的锐利目光总是盯着我们(一举一动她都能注意到). ˌ**eagle-'eyed** *adj*.

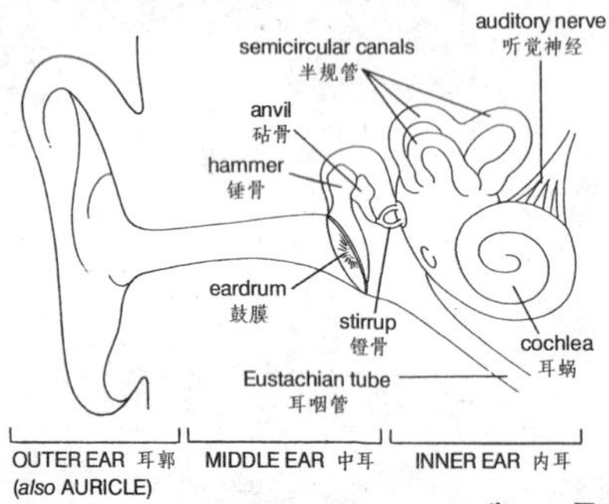

the ear 耳

ear[1] /ɪə(r); ɪr/ *n* **1** [C] organ of hearing; its outer part 耳, 耳朵; 外耳: *The doctor looked into my ears.* 医生检查我的耳朵. ○ *Rabbits have large ears.* 兔子的耳朵很长. ○ [attrib 作定语] *She's got an 'ear infection.* 她耳朵感染了. ⇨illus 见插图. **2** [sing] **an ~ (for sth)** sense of hearing; ability to discriminate sounds, esp in music and language 听觉; (尤指音乐和语言中的)辨音力, 听力: *She has a good ear for languages.* 她学语言的听力很好. **3** (idm 习语) **(be) all 'ears** (*infml* 口) listening attentively 倾听: *Tell me your news; I'm all ears.* 把你的新鲜事告诉我, 我洗耳恭听. **box sb's ears** ⇨ BOX[2]. **sth comes to/reaches sb's 'ears** sb finds out about sth, eg news or gossip 某事物(如消息或闲话)传到某人耳朵里: *If this news ever reaches her ears, she'll be furious.* 这个消息万一传到她的耳朵里, 她一定得大发雷霆. **din in one's ears** ⇨ DIN *v*. **sb's 'ears are burning** sb suspects that he is being talked about, esp in an unkind way 某人耳朵发烧(怀疑遭人议论, 尤指说坏话): *All this gossip about Sarah — her ears must be burning!* 都在说萨拉的闲话——她耳朵一定发烧了! **easy on the ear/eye** ⇨ EASY[1]. **fall on deaf ears** ⇨ DEAF. **feel one's ears burning** ⇨ FEEL[1]. **give sb/get a thick ear** ⇨ THICK. **go in (at) 'one ear and out (at) the 'other** be heard but either ignored or quickly forgotten 一耳进一耳出; 左耳进右耳出; 当作耳边风: *You've forgotten to buy the eggs! It* (ie What I tell you) *goes in one ear and out the other.* 你忘记买鸡蛋了! 把我跟你说的话当成耳旁风了. **have, get, win, etc sb's 'ear** have or get sb's favourable attention 获得某人的好感; 受到某人的重视. **have/keep an/one's ear to the 'ground** be aware of all that is happening and being said 注意周围的动静: *Peter'll know; he always keeps an ear to the ground.* 彼得会知道的, 他耳听八方. **have a word in sb's ear** ⇨ WORD. **keep one's ears/eyes open** ⇨ OPEN[1]. **lend an ear** ⇨ LEND. **make a pig's ear of sth** ⇨ PIG. **meet the ear/eye** ⇨ MEET[1]. **music to one's ears** ⇨ MUSIC. **not believe one's ears/eyes** ⇨ BELIEVE. **(be) out on one's 'ear** suddenly expelled, dismissed, etc 突遭驱逐、开除、解雇等. **play (sth) by 'ear** play (music) by remembering how it sounds, ie without seeing a printed form 凭记忆演奏(乐曲)(即不看乐谱). **play it by 'ear** (*infml* 口) act without preparation according to the demands of a situation; improvise 事前无准备而根据情况采取行动; 临时现做: *I've had no time to prepare for this meeting, so I'll have to play it by ear.* 我没有时间准备这次会议, 所以只好有什么谈什么. **prick up one's ears** ⇨ PRICK[2]. **shut one's ears to sth/sb** ⇨ SHUT. **smile, etc from ear to 'ear** smile, etc broadly, showing that one is very pleased or happy 眉开眼笑. **turn a deaf ear** ⇨ DEAF. **(be) up to one's ears/eyes in sth** very busy with or overwhelmed by sth 忙得不可开交; 深陷于某事物中: *I'm up to my ears in work at the moment.* 我现在工作忙极了. **walls have ears** ⇨ WALL. **with a flea in one's ear** ⇨ FLEA. **wet behind the ears** ⇨ WET. **with half an 'ear** not very attentively 不很注意地: *I was only listening to the radio with half an ear, while preparing some food.* 我正在做吃的, 没太留心听收音机.

▷ **-eared** /ɪəd; ɪrd/ (usu in compound *adjs* 通常用以构成复合形容词) having ears of a specified kind 有某种耳朵的: *the ˌlong-eared 'owl.*

ear·ful /ˈɪəfʊl; ˋɪrfʊl/ *n* [sing] (*infml* 口) (idm 习语) **give sb/get an 'earful** give or receive a long angry or abusive speech 说或听一番气愤的或辱骂的话: *If he bothers you again I'll give him an earful.* 如果他再来烦你, 我就训他一顿.

□ **'earache** *n* [U, sing] pain in the ear-drum 耳痛.

'ear-drop *n* (usu *pl* 通常作复数) liquid medication dropped into the ears 滴耳药水.

'ear-drum (also **drum**) *n* thin membrane in the inner part of the ear which vibrates when sound waves strike it 鼓膜. ⇨illus 见插图.

'ear-muff *n* (usu *pl* 通常作复数) either of a pair of ear-coverings connected by a band across the top of the head, and worn to protect the ears, esp from the cold (尤指防寒用的)耳罩: *a pair of green ear-muffs* 一副绿色的耳罩.

'earphone *n* (usu *pl* 通常作复数) (**a**) either of two receivers attached to each other so that they fit over the ears, used for listening to records, the radio, etc 耳机. (**b**) similar device with only one receiver that fits inside one ear 单耳机.

'ear-plug *n* (usu *pl* 通常作复数) either of two pieces of soft material put into the ears to keep out air, water or noise (防止空气、水或声音进入耳内的)耳塞.

'ear-ring *n* (often *pl* 常作复数) piece of jewellery worn in or on the ear lobe 耳环; 耳饰.

'earshot *n* [U] (idm 习语) **(be) out of/within 'earshot** where one cannot/can be heard 在听力范围之外[之内].

'ear-splitting *adj* very loud; shrill 极响的; 震耳的; 刺耳的: *an ear-splitting crash* 震耳欲聋的碰撞.

'ear-trumpet *n* trumpet-shaped tube formerly used by partially deaf people to magnify sound (旧时的)喇叭形助听器.

ear[2] /ɪə(r); ɪr/ *n* seed-bearing part of a cereal, eg wheat, barley, etc (麦子的)穗. ⇨illus at CEREAL 见CEREAL之插图.

earl /ɜːl; ɝl/ *n* (*fem* 阴性作 **countess**) (title of a) British nobleman ranking between a marquis and a viscount 伯爵(的衔头).

▷ **earl·dom** *n* rank of an earl 伯爵的爵位.

early /ˈɜːlɪ; ˋɝlɪ/ (**-ier, -iest**) *adj, adv* **1** near to the beginning of a period of time 早; 初; 初期: *the early morning* 清早 ○ *in early spring* 早春 ○ *in his early twenties*, ie aged between 20 and 23 or 24 (他)二十岁出头 ○ *early works (of a composer, poet, writer, etc)*, ie those written at the beginning of a career (作曲家、诗人、作家等的)早期作品 ○ *Two players were injured early in the season.* 有两名选手在该季开始不久就受了伤. Cf 参看 LATE[1] 2, LATE[2] 2. **2** before the usual or expected time 提前; 提早: *early peaches*, ie peaches that ripen early in the season 早熟的桃子 ○ *an early breakfast*, eg at 5 am 很早的早餐(如于早晨5时者) ○ *I got up early today.* 我今天起得很早. ○ *The bus arrived five minutes early.* 公共汽车早到了五分钟. Cf 参看 LATE[1] 1, LATE[2] 1. **3** (idm 习语) **at your earliest con'venience** (*fml esp commerce* 文, 尤用于商业) as soon as possible 尽早: *Please deliver the goods at your earliest convenience.* 请尽早送货. **bright and 'early** ⇨ BRIGHT. **an 'early bird** (*joc* 谑) person who arrives, gets up, etc early 早到、早起等的人: *You're an early bird this morning!* 你今天起得真早啊! **the ˌearly bird catches the 'worm** (*saying* 谚) the person who arrives, gets up, etc first will be successful 早起的鸟才能捉到虫; 捷足先登. **early 'days (yet)** (*esp Brit*) too soon to be sure how a situation, etc will develop 过早; 尚早: *I'm not sure if our book will be a success — it's early days yet.* 我们这本书是否受欢迎, 我没有把握——现在言之过早. **the early 'hours** very early in the morning, ie not long after midnight 深夜: *They were dancing till the early hours.* 他们跳舞跳到深夜. **an early/a late night** ⇨ NIGHT. **early 'on** soon after the start of a past event 在初期; 开始后不久: *I knew early on (in the film) that I wasn't going to enjoy it.* 电影一开演我就知道不会喜欢这部电影. **an early/late riser** ⇨ RISER (RISE[1]). **ˌearly to 'bed and ˌearly to 'rise (makes a man healthy, wealthy and wise)** (*saying* 谚) living sensibly and without excesses (will bring a person good health, money and wisdom) 睡得早, 起得早, (富足、聪明、身体好). **keep early 'hours** rise early or go to bed early 早起; 早睡. ▷ **earli·ness** *n* [U].

□ **early 'closing** (*Brit*) shutting of shops, etc on a particular afternoon every week (每周某一日下午商店等)停止营业: *It's early closing (day) today.* 今天照例下午停止营业.

early 'warning early indication (eg by radar) of the approach of enemy aircraft, missiles, etc 预先警报(敌人飞机、导弹等逼近的预先显示, 如由雷达显示): [attrib 作定语] *early 'warning system* 预先警报系统.

ear·mark /ˈɪəmɑːk; ˋɪrˌmɑrk/ *v* [Tn, Tn·pr] **~ sb/sth (for sth/sb)** assign or set aside sb/sth (to or for a special purpose) (为某目的)指定或安排某人[某事物]: *earmark a sum of money for research* 拨出一笔款项作研究经费 ○ *I've earmarked Peter for the job.* 我已派彼得做这事.

earn /ɜːn; ɝn/ *v* **1** [Tn] (**a**) get (money) by working 赚; 挣: *He earns £10 000 a year.* 他一年赚10 000英镑. ○ *She earned her living by singing in a nightclub.* 她靠在夜总会唱歌谋生. ○ *earned/unearned income* 劳动收入[非劳动收入]. (**b**) get (money) as a return on a loan or investment (贷款或投资)获得(利钱): *Money earns more in a high interest account.* 钱放在高利息的帐户里获利多. **2** [Tn, Dn·n] gain (sth deserved) in return for one's achievements, behaviour, etc (因自己的成就、行为等)得到(应得的事物); 博得; 使得: *You've certainly earned your retirement.* 你确已理当退休了. ○ *a well-earned rest* 应得的休息 ○ *His honesty earned him great respect.* 他因诚实而博得人们的尊敬. ○ *His bad manners earned him a sharp rebuke.* 他因为没有礼貌而受到责备. **3** (idm 习语) **earn/turn an honest penny** ⇨ HONEST. **ˌearn one's 'keep** work hard enough to cover the costs of one's food, accommodation, etc 挣钱维持生活.

▷ **earn·ings** *n* [pl] money earned 赚的钱; 生的利: *I've*

spent all my earnings. 我把赚的钱都花光了. ˌ**earnings-reˈlated** *adj* (of payments, etc) linked to and changing with one's earnings (指付款等)随个人收入而改变的: *an ˌearnings-related ˈpension scheme* 随个人收入而改变的退休金计划.

earn·est[1] /ˈɜːnɪst; ˋɝnɪst/ *adj* (too) serious; determined; not light-hearted (太)认真的; 坚决的; 不掉以轻心的: *a terribly earnest young man* 认真得不得了的年轻人.

▷ **earn·est** *n* (idm 习语) **in (dead/deadly/real) ˈearnest (a)** with determination and energy 有决心和精力: *It's beginning to snow in earnest*, ie heavily. 雪真的下起来了(下大了). **(b)** serious(ly); not joking(ly) 认真(地); 并非开玩笑(地): *When she threatened to report us, she was in dead earnest.* 她威胁说要告发我们, 她可是郑重其事说的.

earn·estly *adv*: *I earnestly beg you to reconsider your decision.* 我诚恳地请求你把你的决定再重新考虑一下.

earn·est·ness *n* [U].

earn·est[2] /ˈɜːnɪst; ˋɝnɪst/ *n* [sing] **1** sum of money paid as an instalment or a deposit to show that full payment will be made later 定金; 保证金. **2** thing meant as a sign or promise of what will follow 预示; 承诺; 保证: *As an earnest of my good intentions I will work overtime this week.* 我愿本周加班工作以示诚意.

E

earth /ɜːθ; ɝθ/ *n* **1** (usu 通常作 **the earth**) [sing] this world; the planet on which we live 世界; 地球: *The moon goes round the earth.* 月球环绕地球运转. ○ *I must be the happiest woman on earth!* 我一定是世界上最幸福的女人了. **2** [sing] land; the surface of the world as opposed to the sky or sea 大地; 陆地; 地面: *After a week at sea, it was good to feel the earth under our feet again.* 出海一周后, 又重新回到陆地上而感到愉快. ○ *The balloon burst and fell to earth.* 气球破裂而落到地上. **3** [U] soil 泥土: *a clod/lump of earth* 土块 ○ *fill a hole with earth* 用泥土填洞 ○ *cover the roots of a plant with earth* 用泥土把植物的根埋起来. ⇨Usage 见所附用法. **4** [C] hole of a wild animal, esp a fox or badger (野兽的, 尤指狐狸或獾的)洞穴; 兽穴. **5** [C usu *sing* 通常作单数] (*esp Brit*) (*US* **ground**) (wire that provides a) connection with the ground completing an electrical circuit 接地; 地线. **6** [C] (*chemistry* 化) any of several metallic oxides 几种金属氧化物之一: *an alkaline earth* 碱土金属氧化物 ○ *rare earths* 稀土金属元素. **7** (idm 习语) **charge, cost, pay, etc (sb) the ˈearth** (*infml* 口) charge, etc a lot of money 要付…很多钱: *I'd love that bike, but it costs the earth.* 我很喜欢那辆自行车, 可是贵得不得了. **come back/down to ˈearth (with a bang/bump)** (*infml* 口) stop day-dreaming; return to reality 不再做白日梦; 回到现实中来: *When his money ran out, he came down to earth (with a bump).* 他把钱用光时, 才(赫然)如梦初醒. **the ends of the earth** ⇨ END[1]. **the four corners of the earth** ⇨ CORNER. **go/run to earth/ground** hide oneself away to avoid being captured, etc 躲藏起来以免被捉住等. **how, why, where, who, etc on ˈearth/in the ˈworld** (*infml* 口) (used for emphasis 用以加强语气) how, etc ever 到底怎样…: *What on earth are you doing?* 你到底在干什么呢? ○ *How on earth did she manage that?* 她究竟怎么办到的呢? **(be, feel, look, etc) like nothing on ˈearth** (*infml* 口) very bad, unwell, peculiar, etc 糟糕、难受、特别极了等: *He looks like nothing on earth in those weird clothes.* 他穿着奇装异服难看极了. **move heaven and earth** ⇨ MOVE[2]. **promise the earth/moon** ⇨ PROMISE[2]. **run sb/sth to ˈearth** find sb/sth by searching hard 尽力追查某人[某事物]: *The police eventually ran him to earth in Paris.* 警察穷追不舍, 终于在巴黎找到了他. **the salt of the earth** ⇨ SALT. **wipe sth off the face of the earth/off the map** ⇨ WIPE.

▷ **earth** *v* **1** [Tn esp passive 尤用于被动语态] (*esp Brit*) connect (an electrical appliance, etc) with the ground 将(电器等)接地: *Is this plug earthed?* 这个插头接地了吗? **2** (phr v) **earth sth up** cover (the roots of a plant, etc) with earth 用土掩盖(植物等的根): *He earthed up the celery.* 他给芹菜培上了土.

earthy *adj* (**-ier, -iest**) **1** of or like earth or soil 泥土的; 像泥土的; 土壤的; 像土壤的: *an earthy smell* 泥土的气味. **2** (*fig* 比喻) (of people, jokes, etc) coarse; not refined or sensitive (指人、笑话等)粗俗的; 不文雅的; 土里土气的: *an earthy sense of humour* 粗俗的幽默感.

earthi·ness *n* [U].

□ ˈ**earth science** any of various sciences, such as geology or geography, concerned with the earth or part of it 地球科学(如地质学、地理学等).

ˈ**earthwork** *n* (formerly) large man-made bank of earth used as a fortification (旧时)土垒(用泥土筑成的大型防御工事): *the remains of ancient earthworks* 古代土垒的残骸.

ˈ**earthworm** *n* common type of worm that lives in the soil 蚯蚓(通称曲蟮). ⇨illus at WORM 见 WORM 之插图.

NOTE ON USAGE 用法: Compare **earth, ground, floor** and **soil.** 将 **earth**、**ground**、**floor**、**soil** 这几个词作一比较. **The earth** (also **Earth**) is the name of the planet where we live and **earth** can also refer to the solid land in contrast to the sky above ☆ **the earth**(亦大写作 **Earth**)是我们赖以生存的地球的名称, **earth** 还可指大地, 是相对于天空而言: *The parachutist floated gently down to earth.* 跳伞者轻飘飘地降落到地上. **Ground** indicates an area or distance on the earth's surface ☆ **ground** 指地面上的区域或距离: *The expedition covered a lot of ground.* 探险队到过很多地方. In addition, **the ground** is the solid surface under our feet when we are in the open air 此外, 当人们在露天活动时, **the ground** 可用以指地面: *You shouldn't sit on the ground when it's wet.* 地面潮湿时就不应该坐在地上. **The floor** is the solid surface under our feet inside a building ☆ **the floor** 指建筑物内的地面: *He left his clothes lying all over the floor.* 他把衣服扔得满地都是. **Ground, earth** and especially **soil** refer to the natural material in which trees and plants grow. ☆ **ground**、**earth**、特别是 **soil**, 均指土壤. **Ground** is an area of soil and earth ☆ **ground** 指土壤和土地的一个区域: *stony ground* 多石的地面 ○ *black earth* 黑土地 ○ *sandy soil* 沙土地.

earthen /ˈɜːθn; ˋɝθən/ *adj* [usu attrib 通常作定语] **1** made of earth 泥土做的: *earthen floors* (建筑物内的)泥土地面. **2** made of baked clay 用烧过的黏土做的; 陶制的: *earthen pots* 陶壶.

□ ˈ**earthenware** *n* [U] pottery made of baked clay 陶器: [attrib 作定语] *an earthenware bowl* 陶碗.

earthly /ˈɜːθlɪ; ˋɝθlɪ/ *adj* **1** of this world; not spiritual 现世的; 尘世的: *earthly joys, possessions* 尘世的享乐、财产. **2** (*infml* 口) (usu with a negative 通常与否定式连用) possible; conceivable 可能的; 可想像的: *You've no earthly hope of winning.* 你根本没有获胜的希望. **3** (idm 习语) **no earthly use** (*infml* 口) totally useless 完全无用的. **not have an ˈearthly** (*Brit infml* 口) not have the slightest chance or hope or idea 没有丝毫机会或希望或概念: *'Why isn't it working?' 'I haven't an earthly* (ie I don't know at all.)' '这怎么不灵呢?' '我一点儿都不知道.'

earth·quake /ˈɜːθkweɪk; ˋɝθˌkwek/ (also **quake**) *n* sudden violent movement of the earth's surface 地震.

ear·wig /ˈɪəwɪg; ˋɪrˌwɪg/ *n* small harmless insect with pincers at the rear end of its body 蠼螋(一种有尾铗的无害小昆虫).

ease[1] /iːz; iz/ *n* [U] **1** freedom from work, discomfort, pain or anxiety 安逸; 舒适; 无痛苦; 无忧虑: *a life of ease* 安逸舒适的生活 ○ *ease of mind* 心情舒畅 ○ *The injection brought him immediate ease.* 他经注射后疼痛顿消. Cf 参看 EASY[1] 2. **2** (idm 习语) **(stand) at ˈease** (as a military command 用作军事口令) (stand) with feet apart and hands behind the back 稍息. Cf 参看 ATTENTION 4. **(be/feel) at (one's) ˈease** (be/feel) comfortable and unworried; (be/feel) completely relaxed (感到)舒适而无忧虑; (感到)完全松弛: *I never feel at ease in his company.* 我跟他在一起总是感到很不自在. ○ *Finish the work at your ease*, ie in your own time. 你可以从容地把这项工作做完(在你方便时). **ill at ease** ⇨ ILL[1]. **put/set sb at (his, her, etc) ˈease** make sb feel comfortable, free from embarrassment, etc 使某人感到舒适、不拘束等: *He had been dreading their meeting but her warm welcome soon put him at his ease.* 他对彼此相见一直忐忑不安, 可是她热情相迎使他很快就无拘无束了. **put/set sb's mind at ease/rest** ⇨ MIND[1]. ˌ**take one's ˈease** stop working or worrying; relax 不再工作或忧虑; 休息; 轻松; 放心: *She sat down* and took her ease by the fire. 她坐在火旁休息一下. **with ˈease** without difficulty 容易地; 无困难地: *He passed the test with ease.* 他轻而易举地考及格了.

ease[2] /iːz; iz/ *v* **1** (**a**) [Tn] relieve (the body or mind) from pain, anxiety, discomfort, etc 减轻或消除(身体或精神上的)痛苦、忧虑、不适等: *The aspirins eased my headache.* 阿司匹林使我头疼减轻. ○ *Talking eased his anxiety.* 那一番谈话打消了他的顾虑. (**b**) [Tn·pr] **~ sb of sth** free sb from suffering, etc 消除某人的痛苦等: *Walking helped to ease him of his pain.* 他散了散步减轻了一些痛苦. **2** [I, Ip] (**a**) become less painful, severe, etc 减轻痛苦、严重程度等: *The pain eased.* 疼痛减轻了. (**b**) become less unpleasant or difficult 减轻不愉快的或困难的程度: *The situation has eased (off).* 情况已经缓和了. **3** [Tn] make (sth) looser or less tight; slacken 使(某物)放松; 松开: *The coat needs to be eased under the armpits.* 这件上衣的袖需放一放. **4** (idm 习语) **ease sb's ˈconscience/ˈmind** free sb from guilt, worry, etc 消除某人的内疚、忧虑等: *It would ease my mind to know where he was.* 要知道他在哪儿我就放心了. **5** (phr v) **ease (sb/sth) across, along, away, etc** (cause sb/sth to) move across, etc slowly and carefully (使)缓慢而小心地移动过去等: *He eased himself along the ledge to reach the terrified boy.* 他小心翼翼地沿着突出的檐向那惊惶失措的男孩靠近. ○ *She eased her injured foot into her shoe.* 她小心翼翼地把受伤的脚伸进鞋里. **ˌease ˈdown** reduce speed 减低速度: *Ease down: there's a sharp bend ahead.* 慢一点儿, 前面有个急转弯. **ˌease ˈoff/ˈup** become less severe, oppressive or urgent 减轻; 减缓; 缓和: *The tension between us has eased off a little.* 我们之间的紧张状况已经缓和一些. ○ *The flow of traffic eased off.* 交通已经通畅. ○ *I'm very busy just now; wait until things have eased up a little.* 我现在非常忙, 等事情缓一缓再说. **ease up on sb/sth** be more moderate with sb/sth 对某人[某事物]更适度、更有节制: *I should ease up on the cigarettes if I were you.* 我要是你, 我就再少抽些烟了.

easel /ˈiːzl; ˋizl/ *n* wooden frame for holding a blackboard or a picture (while it is being painted) 黑板架; 画架.

east /iːst; ist/ *n* [sing] (*abbr* 缩写 **E**) **1 the east** point of the horizon where the sun rises; one of the four main points of the compass 东; 东方: *The wind is blowing from the east.* 风从东方来. ○ *He lives to the east of* (ie further east than) *Exeter.* 他住在埃克塞特的东边. Cf 参看 NORTH, SOUTH, WEST. **2 the East** (**a**) countries of Asia, esp China and Japan 东方国家(亚洲的国家, 尤指中国和日本): *philosophies of the East* 东方国家的哲学 ○ *Yoga originated in the East.* 瑜伽起源于东方国家. (**b**) any part of the world to the east of Europe 欧洲以东的任何地区: *the Middle East* 中东 ○ *the Near East* 近东 ○ *the Far East* 远东. **3 the East** (*US*) eastern side of the USA 美国的东部地区: *I was born in the East, but now live in Los Angeles.* 我出生于东部, 但现在住在洛杉矶.

▷ **east** *adj* [attrib 作定语] **1** in or towards the east 在东方的; 向东方的: *He lives on the east coast.* 他住在东部海岸地区. **2** (of winds) from the east (指风)从东方来的: *an east wind* 东风. Cf 参看 EASTERLY.

east *adv* towards the east 向东方地: *My window faces east.* 我的窗户朝东. ○ *We are travelling east.* 我们向东方旅行. ○ *a town east of the Danube* 多瑙河以东的一个城镇.

east·ward /ˈiːstwəd; ˋistwɚd/ *adj* towards the east 向东的; 向东方的: *in an eastward direction* 在向东的方向.

east·ward, east·wards *adv*: *to travel eastwards* 向东方旅行. ⇨Usage at FORWARD[2] 用法见 FORWARD[2].

□ **eastbound** /ˈiːstbaʊnd; ˋistˌbaund/ *adj* travelling towards the east 向东方旅行的: *Is this the eastbound train?* 这是东行列车吗? ○ *the eastbound section of the motorway* 高速公路的东行段.

the ˌEast ˈEnd (*Brit*) thickly populated, mainly working-class part of East London 东区(伦敦东部的工人居住区, 人口稠密). Cf 参看 THE WEST END (WEST).

ˌEast-ˈEnder *n* person living in the East End 在伦敦东区居住的人.

Easter /ˈiːstə(r); ˋistɚ/ *n* annual Christian festival, that occurs on a Sunday in March or April, and celebrates the resurrection of Christ after the crucifixion; period about this time 复活节(基督徒一年一度的节日, 于3月或4月的一个星期日, 纪念耶稣在十字架上受刑死后复活); 复活节期间: [attrib 作定语] *ˌEaster ˈDay* 复活节日 ○ *ˌEaster ˈSunday* 复活节星期日 ○ *ˈEaster week*, ie the week beginning on Easter Sunday 复活节周(自复活节星期日起的一周) ○ *the Easter holidays* 复活节假期.

□ **ˈEaster egg** egg made of chocolate or a hen's egg with a painted or dyed shell, eaten at Easter 复活节彩蛋.

east·erly /ˈiːstəlɪ; ˋistɚlɪ/ *adj* [usu attrib 通常作定语], *adv* **1** in or towards the east 在东面(的); 向东面(的): *in an easterly direction* 朝东的方向. **2** (of winds) blowing from the east (指风)从东方吹来(的): *an easterly wind* 东风.

▷ **east·erly** *n* wind blowing from the east 东风: *strong easterlies at sea* 海上的强劲东风.

east·ern /ˈiːstən; ˋistɚn/ (also **Eastern**) *adj* [attrib 作定语] of, from or living in the east part of the world or of a specified region 东方的; 东部的; 来自东方的; 来自东部的; 居于东方的; 居于东部的: *Eastern customs, religions, etc* 东方的习俗、宗教等 ○ *the eastern seaboard of the USA* 美国东部沿海地区.

▷ **east·ern·most** /ˈiːstənməʊst; ˋistɚnˌmost/ *adj* situated farthest east 位于最东的; 位于极东的: *the easternmost city in Europe* 欧洲最东的城市.

□ **the ˌEastern ˈBloc** (formerly) communist countries of Eastern Europe considered as a group (旧时)东方集团(东欧共产主义国家, 视为一整体).

easy[1] /ˈiːzɪ; ˋizɪ/ *adj* (**-ier, -iest**) **1** not difficult; done or obtained without great effort 容易的; 不难的; 不费力的: *an easy exam* 容易的考试 ○ *It is an easy place to reach.* 那是个容易到达的地方. ○ *The place is easy to reach.* 那地方容易到达. **2** free from pain, discomfort, anxiety, trouble, etc 不再痛苦的; 舒适的; 安心的; 安逸的: *lead an easy life* 过安逸舒适的生活 ○ *My mind is easier now.* 现在我安心多了. Cf 参看 EASE[1] 1. **3** [attrib 作定语] not stiff or embarrassed 不生硬的; 不死板的; 不拘束的: *have easy manners* 举止从容. **4** [attrib 作定语] readily exploited, cheated, etc 易上当、受骗等的: *an easy victim* 容易吃亏的人 ○ *an easy prey* 容易受害的人. **5** (idm 习语) **as ˌeasy as ˈanything/as ˈpie/as ABˈC/as falling off a ˈlog/as ˈwinking** (*infml* 口) very easy or easily 极容易. **easy game** person or thing that can easily be attacked, exploited or made a victim 容易受攻击的人或事物; 容易吃亏、上当、受害的人. **easy/difficult of approach** ⇨ APPROACH *n*. **ˌeasy ˈmoney** money obtained either dishonestly or for little work 横财; 不义之财; 来得容易的钱. **ˌeasy on the ˈear/ˈeye** (*infml* 口) pleasant to listen to or look at 好听的; 好看的: *This music's easy on the ear late at night.* 这音乐夜晚听起来很好听. **an easy/a soft touch** ⇨ TOUCH[2]. **free and easy** ⇨ FREE[1]. **have an easy time (of it)** experience no difficulty in doing sth 在做某事物中无困难. **on easy ˈterms** (*commerce* 商) (of a loan) with a low rate of interest, or (of a purchase) allowing the buyer to pay gradually over a long period (指贷款)低息的; (指购物)分期付款的. **I'm ˈeasy** (*infml* 口 *esp Brit*) (replying when a choice has been offered) I have no preference (当被请求选择时, 回答)我无所谓(都一样). **take the easy way out** escape from a difficult or an awkward situation by the least demanding (and possibly not the most honourable) course of action 以最省事的做法(可能并非最得体者)回避困难的或尴尬的处境. **a woman of easy virtue** ⇨ WOMAN.

▷ **eas·ily** /ˈiːzəlɪ; ˋizlɪ/ *adv* **1** without difficulty 容易地; 无困难地: *I can easily finish it tonight.* 我今晚轻而易举就可把它做完. **2** without doubt 无疑地: *It's easily the best film I've seen this year.* 这无疑是我今年所看过的最好的电影. **3** possibly 可能地: *That could easily be the answer we're looking for.* 那可能就是我们正在寻找的办法.

easi·ness *n* [U].

□ **ˌeasy ˈchair** large comfortable armchair 安乐椅.

ˌeasyˈgoing *adj* (of people) relaxed in manner; placid and tolerant (指人)随便的; 温和宽容的: *My mother doesn't mind who comes to stay, she's very easygoing.* 我母亲不在乎有什么人来住, 她非常随和.

easy[2] /ˈiːzɪ; ˋizɪ/ *adv* (**-ier, -iest**) **1** (as a command 用作命令语) move sth gently and slowly 小心而缓慢地移动某事物: *Easy with that chair — one of its legs is loose.* 搬那把椅子要小心——有一条腿松了. **2** (idm 习语)

ˌ**easier** ˌ**said than** ˈ**done** more difficult to do than to talk about 说比做容易: *'Why don't you get yourself a job?' 'That's easier said than done.'* '你怎么不找个工作呢?' '说起来容易, 找起来难哪.' ˌ**easy** ˈ**come,** ˌ**easy** ˈ**go** (*saying* 谚) sth, esp money, obtained without difficulty is quickly lost or spent 来得容易, 去得快(尤指钱财): *I often win money at cards but never save a penny — 'easy come, easy go' is my motto.* 我玩纸牌经常赢, 可一分钱也存不住——我的俗话是'来得容易, 去得快'. ˈ**easy**/ˈ**gently** ˌ**does it** (*infml* 口) this job, etc should be done slowly and carefully 要慢些、小心些做这事等: *Take your time; easy does it.* 别着急, 慢慢来. ˌ**go** ˈ**easy** (*infml* 口) work less hard 省点劲儿; 别那么卖力: *You should go easy, you're getting tired.* 你要省点劲儿, 会累坏的. **go easy on/with sb/sth** (*infml* 口) be careful, gentle or moderate with sb/sth 对某人[某事物]谨慎、从容或有节制: *Go easy on the milk; we all want some.* 牛奶要匀着享用, 我们都想要一些. ○ *You should go easy on* (ie be less strict with) *that boy; he's only young.* 你应该对那个孩子宽容些, 他还小呢. ˌ**stand** ˈ**easy** (as a military command 用作军事口令) stand with more freedom of movement than when at ease (EASE[1] 2) 稍息(比at ease更随便些). **take it/things** ˈ**easy** relax; not work too hard or do too much 放松; 不过分努力; 不做过多: *I like to take things easy when I'm on holiday.* 我在假日愿意轻松一些.

E

eat /iːt; it/ *v* (*pt* **ate** /et; *US* eɪt; et/, *pp* **eaten** /ˈiːtn; ˈitn̩/) **1** [I, Ip, Tn, Tn·p] **~ (up)/~ sth (up)** take (solid food or soup) into the mouth and swallow it for nourishment 吃; 喝(汤): *He was too ill to eat.* 他病重得不能吃东西了. ○ *eat up* (ie finish eating) *now* 现在吃完 ○ *Eat (up) your dinner.* 你把饭吃(完)了. ○ *Lions eat meat*, ie Meat is their diet. 狮子吃肉. **2** [I] have a meal 吃饭: *Where shall we eat tonight?* 咱们今天晚上在哪儿吃饭? **3** (idm 习语) **dog eat dog** ⇨ DOG[1]. ˌ**eat sb a**ˈ**live**/ˌ**eat sb for** ˈ**breakfast** (*infml* 口) be able to dominate or exploit sb 能支配或剥削某人; 摆布; 宰割: *She'll eat him for breakfast.* 她将来能降住他. **eat one's** ˈ**heart out (for sb/sth)** endure envy, longing, frustration, etc in silence 默默地强忍妒忌、渴求、挫折等: *Since he left, she's been sitting at home eating her heart out.* 他走了以后, 她一直坐在家里, 心如刀割. ˌ**eat humble** ˈ**pie** be very apologetic 赔罪; 赔礼; 道歉: *When he realized his mistake, he had to eat humble pie.* 他认识到了自己的错误, 只好赔礼道歉. ˌ**eat like a** ˈ**horse** (*infml* 口) eat a lot 吃得很多. **eat out of sb's** ˈ**hand** be submissive and compliant towards sb 听命于某人: *She soon had the class eating out of her hand.* 她不久就把全班管得服服帖帖了. **eat sb out of** ˌ**house and** ˈ**home** (*infml often joc* 口, 常作戏谑语) (of people) eat a lot of food which sb else has paid for (指人)把某人吃穷: *I hope your brother won't stay much longer, he's eating us out of house and home!* 我希望你弟弟可别住太久了, 他要把咱们给吃穷了! **eat oneself** ˈ**sick (on sth)** (*infml* 口) eat so much (of sth) that one feels or is sick 吃(某物)太多而不适或生病: *The children would eat themselves sick on chocolate if I let them.* 我要是让孩子由着性儿吃巧克力, 他们会吃出病来. ˌ**eat one's** ˈ**words** admit that what one said was wrong 承认自己说错话. **have one's cake and eat it** ⇨ CAKE. **I'll** ˌ**eat my** ˈ**hat** (*infml* 口) (expression used by sb who believes that sth is so unlikely to happen that even to suggest it is absurd 某人认为发生某事物的可能性迹近荒谬时的用语): *Rob's always late — if he gets here on time I'll eat my hat.* 罗布总迟到——他要准时到这儿, 我把脑袋给你. **the proof of the pudding is in the eating** ⇨ PROOF[1]. **4** (phr v) **eat sth away/eat away at sth** erode 腐蚀; 侵蚀: *The river is eating away at the bank.* 河水侵蚀着两岸. **eat into sth** (**a**) consume sth; destroy; dissolve; corrode 消耗某事物; 毁坏; 分解; 腐蚀: *Acids eat into metal.* 酸能腐蚀金属. (**b**) (*fig* 比喻) consume a part of sth 消耗某事物的一部分: *Paying for that new carpet has eaten into my savings.* 付新地毯的款用去了我的一部分储蓄. **eat out** have a meal in a restaurant, etc rather than at home 在饭馆等处吃饭(不在家中吃): *I'm too tired to cook tonight; shall we eat out?* 我今晚累得不想做饭了, 咱们下饭馆好吗? **eat sb up** (*fig* 比喻) (usu passive 通常用于被动语态) consume; obsess; worry 操心; 烦扰; 担忧: *be eaten up with curiosity, anger, envy, etc* 受好奇心、愤怒、妒忌等煎熬 ○ *Jealousy was eating him up.* 嫉妒心在折磨着他.

▷ **eat·able** *adj* fit to be eaten; good to eat 可吃的; 好吃的: *Our school meals are hardly eatable.* 我们学校的饭菜简直没法吃. Cf 参看 EDIBLE. — *n* (usu *pl* 通常作复数); (*infml* 口) food 食物: *Have you brought the eatables?* 你带吃的来了吗?

eater *n* **1** person who eats (in a particular way) (以某种方式)吃东西的人: *He's a big, greedy, etc eater*, ie He eats a lot, eats greedily, etc. 他很能吃、很贪嘴等. **2** = EATING APPLE.

eats *n* [pl] (*infml* 口) food ready to be eaten 现成的食物: *There were plenty of eats, but not enough to drink.* 有很多吃的, 可是没什么喝的.

□ ˈ**eating apple** type of apple that is suitable for eating uncooked 适宜生吃的苹果(不用于烹饪者). Cf 参看 COOKER 2.

ˈ**eating-house** (also ˈ**eating-place**) *n* restaurant 饭馆; 饭店; 食堂.

eau-de-Cologne /ˌəʊ də kəˈləʊn; ˌodəkəˈlon/ *n* (also **co·logne**) [U] perfume made originally at Cologne 科隆香水.

eaves /iːvz; ivz/ *n* [pl] overhanging lower edges of a roof 屋檐: *birds nesting under the eaves* 在屋檐下筑巢的鸟. ⇨illus at App 1 见附录1之插图, page vii.

eaves·drop /ˈiːvzdrɒp; ˈivzˌdrɑp/ *v* [I, Ipr] (**-pp-**) **~ (on sb/sth)** listen secretly to a private conversation 偷听(私人谈话): *eavesdropping on the discussion, her parents* 偷听讨论、偷听她父母谈话. ▷ **eaves·drop·per** *n*.

ebb /eb; ɛb/ *v* [I, Ip] **~ (away)** **1** (of the tide) go out; recede (指潮水)退落; 退潮; 落潮. Cf 参看 FLOW 5. **2** (*fig* 比喻) grow less; become slowly weak or faint 减少; 衰落; 衰退: *Daylight was ebbing away.* 白昼在逐渐消失. ○ *Our enthusiasm soon began to ebb.* 我们的热情不久就凉下来了.

▷ **ebb** *n* [sing] **1** (usu 通常作 **the ebb**) (of a tide) the flowing out (指潮水)退落; 退潮; 落潮: *The tide is on the ebb*, ie is going out. 正在退潮. Cf 参看 FLOOD[2] 3. **2** (idm 习语) **at a low ebb** ⇨ LOW[1]. **the ebb and flow (of sth)** (of noise, fashions, etc) regular increase and decrease in intensity; constant fluctuation (指声音、流行式样等)消长, 兴衰; 不断长落, 起伏: *the ebb and flow of conversation* 谈话声此起彼伏. **on the** ˈ**ebb** diminishing; declining 正在减弱; 正在衰退; 正在衰落: *My luck is on the ebb.* 我的运气每况愈下.

□ ˌ**ebb** ˈ**tide** /ˌeb ˈtaɪd; ˈɛb ˌtaɪd/ = EBB *n* 1.

eb·ony /ˈebənɪ; ˈɛbənɪ/ *n* [U] hard black wood of a tropical tree 乌木; 黑檀.

▷ **eb·ony** *adj* **1** made of ebony 乌木做的: *the ebony keys on a piano* 钢琴上的乌木琴键. **2** black 黑色的: *ebony skin* 黝黑的皮肤.

ebul·li·ent /ɪˈbʌlɪənt, *also* ɪˈbʊlɪənt; ɪˈbʌljənt/ *adj* full of energy and excitement; exuberant 精力充沛的; 洋溢的; 奔放的.

▷ **ebul·li·ence** /-əns; -əns/ *n* [U] state of being ebullient; exuberance 精力充沛; 洋溢; 奔放: *She burst into the room with her usual ebullience, and immediately started talking to everyone.* 她像往常一样兴高采烈地冲进了房间, 立刻跟大家攀谈起来.

ebul·li·ently *adv*.

EC /iːˈsiː; ˌiˈsi/ *abbr* 缩写 = East Central 东部中央: *London EC1 4PW*, ie as a postal code 伦敦EC1 4PW(邮政编码).

ec·cent·ric /ɪkˈsentrɪk; ɪkˈsɛntrɪk/ *adj* **1** (of people, behaviour) unusual; peculiar; not conventional or normal (指人、举止)异常的; 古怪的; 不合常规的; 不正常的: *his eccentric habits* 他那古怪的习惯 ○ *an eccentric old lady* 一位古怪的老太太. **2** (**a**) (of circles) not having the same centre (指圆形)没有共同圆心的. Cf 参看 CONCENTRIC. (**b**) (of orbits) not circular (指轨道)不正圆的. (**c**) (of planets, etc) moving in an eccentric orbit (指行星等)在不正圆的轨道上运行的.

▷ **ec·cent·ric** *n* **1** eccentric person 古怪的人: *The club seemed to be full of eccentrics.* 这个俱乐部里好像都是怪人. **2** mechanical device consisting of a disc at the end of a shaft for changing circular movement into backward-and-forward movement 偏心器; 偏心轮.

ec·cent·ric·ally /-klɪ; -klɪ/ *adv*.

ec·cent·ri·city /ˌeksenˈtrɪsətɪ; ˌɛksɛnˈtrɪsətɪ/ *n* **1** [U] quality of being eccentric; strangeness of behaviour, etc 古怪; 怪异; 怪僻等: *eccentricity of style, clothing, manners, ideas* 古怪的样式、服装、举止、想法. **2** [C] instance of this; strange or unusual act or habit 古怪; 怪异; 怪僻: *One of his eccentricities is sleeping under the bed instead of on it.* 他的怪僻之一是睡觉睡在床底下而不睡在床上.

ec·cle·si·astic /ɪˌkliːzɪˈæstɪk; ɪˌklizɪˈæstɪk/ *n* clergyman (in the Christian Church) (基督教会的)传教士, 牧师.
▷ **ec·cle·si·ast·ical** /-kl; -kḷ/ *adj* [usu attrib 通常作定语] (**a**) of clergymen 传教士的; 牧师的. (**b**) of the Christian Church 基督教会的. **ec·cle·si·ast·ic·ally** /-klɪ; -klɪ/ *adv*.

ECG /ˌiː siː ˈdʒiː; ˌi si ˈdʒi/ *abbr* 缩写 = (*medical* 医) electrocardiogram: *have an ECG test* 作心电图检查.

ech·elon /ˈeʃəlɒn; ˈɛʃəˌlɑn/ *n* **1** level of authority or responsibility; rank in an organization 职权的等级; 级别: *the upper echelons of the Civil Service* 政府部门的高层. **2** step-like formation of troops, aircraft, ships, etc 梯形编队: *aircraft flying in echelon*, ie in a line stretching backwards to the left or right 成梯队飞行的飞机.

echo[1] /ˈekəʊ; ˈɛko/ *n* (*pl* **~es**) **1** (**a**) reflection and repetition of a sound, eg from a wall or inside an enclosed space 回声; 回音: *This cave has a good echo.* 这个洞的回声很大. (**b**) sound repeated in this way 反复的回声: *If you shout loudly, you'll hear the echo.* 如果大声喊, 就能听到回声. **2** (*fig* 比喻) person or thing that imitates another 模仿的人或事物: *He has no original opinions; he's just his father's echo.* 他没有主见, 只是随声附和他父亲的意见. ○ *There are many echoes of Shakespeare in his work.* 他的作品中有很多处模仿莎士比亚. **3** (idm 习语) **to the ˈecho** (*dated* 旧) long and loudly 长时间而大声地: *Her performance was cheered to the echo.* 她的表演获得长时间的喝彩.
□ **ˈecho-sounder** *n* instrument used for determining the depth of sth underneath a ship by measuring the time taken for sound waves to be echoed back from it 回声探测器.

echo[2] /ˈekəʊ; ˈɛko/ *v* **1** (**a**) [Tn, Tn·p] **~ sth (back)** (of places) send back (an echo) (指地方)传回(回声): *The valley echoed (back) his song.* 山谷中传回他唱歌的回声. (**b**) [Tn] (*fig* 比喻) (of people, places, etc) repeat (sth); imitate; recall (指人、地方等)重复(某事物); 模仿; 回忆: *They echoed their leader's every word.* 他们重复领袖的每一句话. **2** [I, Ipr] **~ (to/with sth)** (of places) repeat a sound (指地方)产生回声, 发出回声: *The hills echoed to the sound of their laughter.* 他们的笑声在山中产生回声. **3** [I, Ipr, Ip] (of sounds) be repeated as an echo (指声音)回响, 引起回声: *His footsteps echoed (in the empty hall).* 他的脚步声(在空荡荡的大堂里)产生了回声. ○ *Their shouts echoed through the forest.* 他们的叫喊声在林中回荡.

éclair /ɪˈkleə(r), eɪˈkleə(r); ɪˈklɛr, eˈklɛr/ *n* (also ˌ**chocolate éˈclair**) small finger-shaped pastry cake, filled with cream and iced with chocolate 巧克力棒糕(一种奶油馅巧克力糖衣的手指形小点心).

éclat /ˈeɪklɑː; *US* eɪˈklɑː; eˈklɑ/ *n* [U] **1** brilliance; conspicuous success 辉煌的成就; 显赫的功绩: *to perform with éclat* 大为成功地表演. **2** praise; applause 喝彩; 鼓掌: *Her latest novel was received with great éclat.* 她最新的小说备受赞赏.

ec·lectic /ɪˈklektɪk; ɪkˈlɛktɪk/ *adj* (*fml* 文) (of people, beliefs, etc) not restricted to one source of ideas, etc, but choosing from or using a wide range (指人、信仰等)不局限于一种思想的, 兼收并蓄的, 折衷的: *He has an eclectic taste in music.* 他爱好各种音乐.
▷ **ec·lectic** *n* person who works, thinks, etc in an eclectic way (工作、思想等)兼容并包的人.
ec·lect·ic·ally /-tɪklɪ; -tɪklɪ/ *adv*.
ec·lect·icism /ɪˈklektɪsɪzəm; ɪkˈlɛktɪˌsɪzəm/ *n* [U].

ec·lipse /ɪˈklɪps; ɪˈklɪps/ *n* [C] **1** blocking of the light of the sun (when the moon is between it and the earth) or of the moon (when the earth's shadow falls on it) 日食; 月食: *a total/partial eclipse of the sun* 日全[偏]食. **2** [C, U] (*fig* 比喻) loss of brilliance, fame, power, etc 光辉、声誉、权势等的丧失: *After suffering an eclipse, she is now famous again.* 她沉默一时期以后, 现在又名声大噪了. ○ *The writer's name remained in eclipse for many years after his death.* 这位作者死后很多年, 名字一直湮没无闻.
▷ **ec·lipse** *v* [Tn] **1** (of the moon, the sun, a planet, etc) cause an eclipse of (sth); cut off the light from (指月、日、行星等)形成(某种)食; 使...的光消失: *The sun is partly eclipsed (by the moon).* 太阳(被月球)遮住一部分(日偏食). **2** (*fig* 比喻) make (sb/sth) appear dull by comparison; outshine 使(某人[某事物])相形见绌; 使黯然失色: *He is eclipsed by his wife, who is much cleverer and more amusing than he is.* 他妻子比他聪明而有风趣, 显得他黯然失色.

eco- *comb form* 构词成分 (usu forming *ns* 通常用以构成名词) ecological or of ecology 生态的; 生态学的: *ecosystem* ○ *ecotype*.

eco·logy /iːˈkɒlədʒɪ; iˈkɑlədʒɪ/ *n* [U] (scientific study of) the relation of plants and living creatures to each other and to their surroundings 生态; 生态学: *Chemicals in the factory's sewage system have changed the ecology of the whole area.* 这座工厂排出的化学物质改变了整个地区的生态.
▷ **eco·lo·gical** /ˌiːkəˈlɒdʒɪkl; ˌikəˈlɑdʒɪkḷ/ *adj* of ecology 生态的; 生态学的: *the dangerous ecological effects of industry*, eg the pollution of the atmosphere, of rivers, etc 工业对生态的危害(如空气、河流等的污染等). **eco·lo·gic·ally** /-klɪ; -klɪ/ *adv*.
eco·lo·gist /iːˈkɒlədʒɪst; iˈkɑlədʒɪst/ *n* student of or expert in ecology 生态学研究者; 生态学家.

Econ *abbr* 缩写 = Economics: *James Rigg MSc* (ie Master of Science)*(Econ)* 詹姆斯·里格, 理学硕士(经济学).

eco·nomic /ˌiːkəˈnɒmɪk, ˌekəˈnɒmɪk; ˌikəˈnɑmɪk, ˌɛkəˈnɑmɪk/ *adj* **1** [attrib 作定语] of economics(1), or of an economy 经济学的; 经济的: *the government's economic policy* 政府的经济政策 ○ *economic development* 经济发展 ○ *economic sanctions*, ie punishment of another country by reducing or stopping trade with it 经济制裁. **2** [attrib 作定语] connected with trade and industry 与贸易和工业有关的: *economic geography*, ie studied mainly in connection with industry 经济地理. **3** designed to give a profit 为获取利润的; 有利可图的: *an economic rent*, ie one that brings the owner at least as much money as he has spent on the house 有利可图的租金(给业主带来至少相当其花费于该房产的钱者) ○ *It is not always economic for buses to run on Sundays.* 公共汽车星期日行驶不一定准能赚钱.

eco·nom·ical /ˌiːkəˈnɒmɪkl, ˌekəˈnɒmɪkl; ˌikəˈnɑmɪkḷ, ˌɛkəˈnɑmɪkḷ/ *adj* careful in the spending of money, time, etc and in the use of resources; not wasteful 经济的; 节俭的; 省时间的; 节约的: *an economical car to run*, eg one with low petrol consumption 节油汽车 ○ *She is economical with/in her use of salt when cooking.* 她烹饪时用盐很省. ○ *an economical style of writing*, ie one that does not waste words 简练的写作风格(不多费笔墨者).
▷ **eco·nom·ic·ally** /-klɪ; -klɪ/ *adv*: *His scheme is not economically sound.* 他的计划在经济上欠妥.

eco·nom·ics /ˌiːkəˈnɒmɪks, ˌekəˈnɒmɪks; ˌikəˈnɑmɪks, ˌɛkəˈnɑmɪks/ *n* [sing *v*] **1** science or principles of the production, distribution and consumption of goods esp with reference to cost 经济学; 经济原则: *the economics of publishing* 出版的经济原则. **2** condition of a country as regards its wealth 国家的经济状况: *third world economics* 第三世界的经济状况.

eco·nom·ist /ɪˈkɒnəmɪst; ɪˈkɑnəmɪst/ *n* student of or expert in economics 经济学研究者; 经济学家.

eco·nom·ize, -ise /ɪˈkɒnəmaɪz; ɪˈkɑnəˌmaɪz/ *v* [I, Ipr] **~ (on sth)** save (money, time, resources, etc); spend less than before; be economical 节省(金钱、时间、资源等); 紧缩开支; 节俭; 节约: *Our electricity bills are higher than we can afford — we must start to economize.* 我们的电费已经高得付不起了——得节省些了. ○ *economize on petrol* 节省汽油.

eco·nomy /ɪˈkɒnəmɪ; ɪˈkɑnəmɪ/ *n* **1** [C, U] (instance of) avoidance of waste (of money, strength, time, resources, etc) (金钱、力气、时间、资源等的)节省, 节约: *practise economy* 实行节约 ○ *It's an economy to buy good shoes; they cost more, but they last much longer than cheap ones.* 购买质量高的鞋很经济; 虽花钱多, 但比廉价鞋耐穿得多. ○ [attrib 作定语] *We're having an economy drive* (ie making a special effort to avoid waste or misuse of resources, etc) *at school.* 我们学校正开展节约运动(尽

E

量避免浪费或滥用资源). ○ *an economy pack*, ie a large amount of a product offered for sale at a reduced price 经济装(减价发售的大包装货品) ○ *economy class*, ie the cheapest class of (air) travel 经济舱(最低廉的客机舱位). **2** [U] control and management of money, resources, etc of a community, society, household, etc 理财: *political economy* 政治经济学 ○ *domestic economy* 国内经济. **3** [C] (often 常作 **the economy**) operation and management of a country's money supply, trade and industry; economic system (国家的)经济管理; 经济制度: *The state of the economy is very worrying.* 目前的经济状况令人十分担忧. ○ *The economies of Japan and China* 日本和中国的经济制度.

eco·sys·tem /ˈiːkəʊsɪstəm; ˋiko,sɪstəm/ *n* ecological unit consisting of a group of plants and living creatures interacting with each other and with their surroundings 生态系统.

ec·stasy /ˈekstəsɪ; ˋɛkstəsɪ/ *n* [U, C] (feeling or state of) great joy or happiness 狂喜: *in an ecstasy of delight* 欣喜若狂 ○ *religious ecstasy* 宗教的极乐境界 ○ *be in/go into/be thrown into ecstasy/ecstasies (over sth)* (对某事物)心醉神迷.

▷ **ec·static** /ɪkˈstætɪk; ɪkˋstætɪk/ *adj* causing or showing ecstasy 使人狂喜的; 欣喜若狂的: *He was ecstatic at the news of his daughter's birth.* 他获悉女儿出生不禁欣喜若狂. **ec·stat·ic·ally** /-klɪ; -klɪ/ *adv*.

E

ECT /ˌiː siː ˈtiː; ˌi si ˋti/ *abbr* 缩写 = (*medical* 医) electroconvulsive therapy (used eg on psychiatric patients) 电惊厥疗法, 电痉挛疗法(如施用于精神病人者).

-ectomy *comb form* 构词成分 (forming *ns* 用以构成名词) indicating removal by surgical operation (指通过外科手术)切除, 截除: *tonsillectomy* ○ *appendectomy*.

ec·to·plasm /ˈektəplæzəm; ˋɛktə,plæzəm/ *n* [U] substance that is thought by some to flow from a spiritualistic medium during a trance 灵媒体外质(据信为灵媒体在恍惚状态中发出的物质).

ECU *abbr* 缩写 = European Currency Unit (of the Common Market) (欧洲共同市场的)欧洲通货单位.

ecu·men·ical (also **oecu·men·ical**) /ˌiːkjuːˈmenɪkl, ˌekjuː-; ˌɛkjuˋmɛnɪkḷ/ *adj* **1** of or representing the whole Christian world or universal Church 全基督教的; 普世教会的; 大公的: *an Ecumenical Council*, eg of all the Roman Catholic Church as summoned by the Pope 大公会议(如由教皇召集的全体罗马天主教会议). **2** seeking the unity of the various Christian churches throughout the world 促进全世界基督教会联合的: *the ecumenical movement* 普世教会运动.

▷ **ecu·men·ic·al·ism** /-kəlɪzəm; -kə,lɪzəm/ (also **ecu·men·ism** /ɪˈkjuːmənɪzəm; ˋɛkjumə,nɪzəm/) *n* [U] belief in, or efforts towards, universal Christian unity 普世教会主义; 普世教会运动.

ecu·men·ic·ally /-klɪ; -klɪ/ *adv*.

ec·zema /ˈeksɪmə; *US* ɪgˈziːmə; ɪgˋzimə/ *n* [U] skin disease causing redness, severe itching and scaling of the skin 湿疹.

ed *abbr* 缩写 = **1** edited (by); edition; editor. **2** educated: *Peter Jeffries, b 1932, ed Tonbridge Sch* 彼得·杰弗里斯, 生于1932年, 曾就读于汤布里奇学校.

-ed (also **-d**) *suff* 后缀 (with *ns* forming *adjs* 与名词结合构成形容词) having (the characteristics of); affected with 有(某种特征)的; 受…影响的: *talented* ○ *bigoted* ○ *diseased* ○ *quick-witted* .

Edam /ˈiːdæm; *US also* ˈiːdəm; ˋidæm, ˋidəm/ *n* [U, C] hard round Dutch cheese, usu yellow with a red rind 埃丹干酪(荷兰圆形硬干酪, 通常为黄色, 包有红色外皮).

eddy /ˈedɪ; ˋɛdɪ/ *n* circular or spiral movement of water, air, fog, dust, etc (水、空气、雾、尘埃等的)旋涡; 涡流: *Eddies of mist rose from the valley.* 山谷中薄雾袅袅. ○ *Eddies of dust swirled in the road.* 路上尘埃滚滚.

▷ **eddy** *v* (*pt, pp* **eddied**) [I, Ip] move in or like an eddy; whirl 呈旋涡状运动; 旋转: (*fig* 比喻) *groups of tourists eddying continually about the main square of the city* 在该城主要广场上川流不息的成群旅客.

edel·weiss /ˈeɪdlvaɪs; ˋedḷ,vaɪs/ *n* (*pl* unchanged 复数不变) small Alpine plant with white flowers 火绒草(生长于阿尔卑斯高山地带, 开白花).

Eden /ˈiːdn; ˋidṇ/ *n* (also **the ˌgarden of ˈEden**) (*Bible* 圣经) beautiful garden where Adam and Eve lived in great happiness before they disobeyed God 伊甸园(亚当与夏娃背叛上帝前所居住的美丽乐园): (*fig* 比喻) *Life is no garden of Eden* (ie is unpleasant) *at the moment.* 现时的生活并非世外桃源.

edge[1] /edʒ; ɛdʒ/ *n* **1** sharp cutting part of a blade, knife, sword, or some other tool or weapon (刀片、刀、剑或其他工具或武器的)锋利部分; 刀口; 锋: *a knife with a sharp edge* 锋利的刀 ○ *put an edge on an axe*, ie sharpen it 给斧子开刃(磨快). **2** (line marking the) outside limit or boundary of a solid (flat) object, surface or area (扁的固体、物体表面或一范围的)外围界线, 边缘: *the edge of a coin, plate, record* 硬币、盘、唱片的边 ○ *He fell off the edge of the cliff.* 他从悬崖边上摔了下来. ○ *Don't put that glass on the edge of the table; it might fall off.* 不要把那杯子放在桌边, 可能掉下来. ○ *the water's edge* 水边 ○ *He lives at the edge of the forest.* 他住在森林边上. **3** (idm 习语) **give sb/get the (rough) edge of one's/sb's tongue** (*infml* 口) speak to sb/be spoken to by sb angrily, rudely, critically, etc 痛骂某人[被某人责骂]: *Her pupils often got the rough edge of her tongue when they disobeyed her.* 学生不听她的话时, 常遭到她粗暴的申斥. **have, etc an ˈedge to one's voice** have or show a degree of anger, nervousness, annoyance, etc in the way in which one speaks 言语中流露出愤怒、不安、厌烦等情绪: *She was trying to remain calm, but there was a distinct edge to her voice.* 她竭力想保持冷静, 但她的声音中却显然带着怒气. **have, etc an/the edge on/over sb/sth** (*infml* 口) have, etc a slight advantage over sb/sth 略胜过某人[某事物]: *The young tennis player definitely had the edge on his older opponent.* 这个年轻的网球运动员显然比那个年纪大的对手略胜一筹. **(be) on ˈedge** (be) nervous, excited or irritable 紧张不安的; 兴奋的; 易怒的; 烦躁的: *She was a bit on edge till she heard he was safe.* 她听到他安然无恙才放下心来. **on a razor's edge** ⇨ RAZOR. **set one's teeth on edge** ⇨ TOOTH. **take the edge off sth** reduce, dull or soften sth 减少、减轻或软化某物: *I need a sandwich to take the edge off my appetite.* 我需要一份三明治以解腹中之饥. ○ *His brother's failure took the edge off his own success.* 他哥哥的失败冲淡了他自己成功的喜悦.

▷ **-edged** /edʒd; ˋɛdʒd/ (forming compound *adjs* 用以构成复合形容词) having an edge or edges of a specified type 有某类刀口、边缘等的: *a ˌblunt-edged ˈknife* ○ *a ˌtwo-edged reˈmark*.

edge[2] /edʒ; ɛdʒ/ *v* **1** [Tn, Tn·pr usu passive 通常用于被动语态] **~ sth (with sth)** supply sth with a border 给(某物)加上边: *The handkerchief is edged with white lace.* 这块手帕镶着白色花边. ○ *a road edged with grass* 边沿长满青草的路. **2** (phr v) **edge (sth/one's way) across, along, away, back, etc** move slowly and carefully across, etc 缓慢而小心地横过等: *The climber edged carefully along the narrow rock ledge.* 爬山者沿着狭窄的岩架缓缓攀爬. ○ *I edged (my chair) towards the door.* 我慢慢向门口挪(椅子). ○ *The policeman slowly edged his way forward.* 警察慢慢地向前移动. **edge sb/sth out (of sth)** cause sb/sth gradually to lose a position or power 使某人[某物]逐渐丧失地位、力量或权力: *He was edged out of his job by his ambitious assistant.* 他那野心勃勃的助手逐渐谋取了他的职位. ○ *Their new product has edged all its competitors out of the market.* 他们的新产品已把所有的竞争者都挤出市场.

edge·ways /ˈedʒweɪz; ˋɛdʒ,wez/ (also **edge·wise** /ˈedʒwaɪz; ˋɛdʒ,waɪz/) *adv* **1** with the edge outwards or forwards; sideways 边缘向外或向前; 侧着; 斜着: *If you turn it edgeways you'll get the desk through the door.* 你把书桌斜过来就能通过这道门. **2** (idm 习语) **(not) get a word in edgeways** ⇨ WORD.

edging /ˈedʒɪŋ; ˋɛdʒɪŋ/ *n* [U, C] thing that forms the border or edge of sth 边缘; 边饰: *a/some lace edging on a dress* 连衣裙上的花边边饰.

□ **ˈedging-shears** *n* tool for trimming grass on the edges of a lawn 修剪草坪边缘的工具; 修边剪刀.

edgy /ˈedʒɪ; ˋɛdʒɪ/ *adj* (*infml* 口) nervous; easily upset or annoyed 紧张的; 易怒的; 暴躁的: *She's been very edgy recently, waiting for the examination results.* 她最近一直心绪不宁, 等待着考试的结果. ○ *She's always been an edgy type of person.* 她一向就是那种情绪紧张的人. ▷ **edgily** *adv*. **edgi·ness** *n* [U].

ed·ible /ˈedɪbl; ˋɛdəbḷ/ *adj* fit to be eaten 适宜食用的;

可以吃的: *This food is scarcely edible.* 这种食物算不上能吃. ○ *edible* (ie not poisonous) *wild berries* 可食用的野莓(无毒的). Cf 参看 EATABLE (EAT).

edict /ˈiːdɪkt; ˋidɪkt/ *n* order or proclamation issued by an authority 法令; 敕令; 公告: *by edict of the king* 根据国王的敕令 ○ *obey the edicts of parliament* 服从议会通过的法令.

edi·fica·tion /ˌedɪfɪˈkeɪʃn; ˌɛdəfəˋkeʃən/ *n* [U] (*fml or joc* 文或谑) improvement of mind or character 开导; 启发; 陶冶; 熏陶: *I am telling you this simply for your edification.* 我只是为了开导你才告诉你这件事的.

edi·fice /ˈedɪfɪs; ˋɛdəfɪs/ *n* (*fml or joc* 文或谑) large or imposing building 高大的或宏伟的建筑物: *the ruined edifice on the hill* 山上毁坏了的大厦 ○ (*fig* 比喻) *He had high ideals in his youth but gradually the whole edifice crumbled.* 他年轻时曾有过崇高的理想, 但渐渐地他的全部希望都破灭了.

edify /ˈedɪfaɪ; ˋɛdəˌfaɪ/ *v* (*pt, pp* **-fied**) [Tn] (*fml or joc* 文或谑) improve the mind or character of (sb) 开导或启发(某人).

▷ **edi·fy·ing** *adj* morally or intellectually improving (在道德或智力方面)开导的, 启发的: *edifying books* 陶冶情操的书籍 ○ *Travel is an edifying experience, especially for young people.* 旅游可以使人增广见闻, 年轻人更应该多参加旅游活动.

edit /ˈedɪt; ˋɛdɪt/ *v* [Tn] **1** prepare (a piece of writing, often another person's) for publication, eg in a book, newspaper, or magazine 编辑: *edit a Shakespeare play for use in schools* 编辑一部莎士比亚剧本供学校使用 ○ *edit a book of poetry* 编辑一本诗集. **2** be responsible for planning, directing and publishing (a newspaper, magazine, etc) 主编(报纸、杂志等). **3** prepare (a film, tape recording, radio or television programme, book, etc) by putting together collected parts in a suitable sequence 剪辑(电影、录音磁带、无线电或电视节目、书等). **4** arrange (data) for processing by a computer (用计算机)编辑(数据). **5** (phr v) **edit sth out (of sth)** remove (unwanted words, phrases, etc from a book, script, etc) in the process of editing 在编辑过程中删除(书、手稿等中的不必要的词语等): *They must have edited bits of the interview out.* 他们一定是把这次采访的一部分删掉了.

edi·tion /ɪˈdɪʃn; ɪˋdɪʃən/ *n* **1** (**a**) form in which a book is published 版本: *a paperback, hard-cover, de luxe, etc edition* 平装本, 硬皮本, 精装本等. (**b**) form in which a radio or television programme is broadcast 无线电或电视节目的广播形式. **2** total number of copies of a book, newspaper, etc issued at one time (书报等)一次发行的总数: *a first edition* 初版 ○ *a revised edition* 修订版 ○ *in its sixth edition* 出至第六版 ○ *the morning/evening/lunch-time edition of a newspaper* 报纸的早晨版[晚间版/中午版]. Cf 参看 IMPRESSION 6, REPRINT *n*.

ed·itor /ˈedɪtə(r); ˋɛdɪtɚ/ *n* person who edits (esp a book, newspaper, magazine, radio or television programme) or who is in charge of part of a newspaper 编辑; 编者: *the ˈsports, fiˈnancial, ˈfashion editor* 体育、金融、时装栏编辑. ▷ **ed·it·or·ship** *n* [U].

ed·it·or·ial /ˌedɪˈtɔːrɪəl; ˌɛdəˋtɔrɪəl/ *adj* [usu attrib 通常作定语] of an editor 编辑的: *the editorial office* 编辑部 ○ *editorial work* 编辑工作.

▷ **ed·it·or·ial** *n* special article in a newspaper, etc, giving an opinion on some topical issue (usu written by the editor) 社论; 社评.

EDP /ˌiː diː ˈpiː; ˌi di ˋpi/ *abbr* 缩写 = electronic data processing 电子数据处理.

EDT /ˌiː diː ˈtiː; ˌi di ˋti/ *abbr* 缩写 = (*US*) Eastern Daylight Time 东部夏令时间. Cf 参看 EST 1.

edu·cate /ˈedʒʊkeɪt; ˋɛdʒʊˌket/ *v* [Tn, Tn·pr, Cn·t] **~ sb (in sth)** train the mind and character of sb; teach sb; provide sb with an education 训练某人的思想和性格; 教某人; 教育某人: *The public should be educated in how to use energy more effectively.* 公众应受到合理地利用能源的教育. ○ *Parents should educate their children to behave well.* 父母应当教育子女守规矩. ○ *Where were you educated?* ie Which school(s), etc did you go to? 你在哪(些)所学校学习过? ⇨Usage at TEACH 用法见 TEACH.

▷ **edu·cated** /ˈedʒʊkeɪtɪd; ˋɛdʒʊˌketɪd/ *adj* **1** having been educated 受过教育的; 受过训练的: *a highly educated woman* 有高度教养的妇女 ○ *self-educated* 自修的 ○ *educated tastes in art* 在艺术方面有修养的鉴赏力. **2** (idm 习语) **an ˌeducated ˈguess** guess based on experience (and therefore probably correct) 根据经验做出的猜测(因此可能是正确的).

edu·cator *n* person who educates (esp professionally) 教育工作者; 教育家; 训练者.

edu·ca·tion /ˌedʒʊˈkeɪʃn; ˌɛdʒʊˋkeʃən/ *n* [U] **1** (system of) training and instruction (esp of children and young people in schools, colleges, etc) designed to give knowledge and develop skills 教育; 教育体制: *A child receives its early education at home.* 幼儿在家接受早期教育. ○ *primary/secondary/tertiary/adult education* 初等[中等/高等/成人]教育 ○ *No country can afford to neglect the education of its young people.* 任何国家都不能疏忽对年轻人的教育. **2** knowledge, abilities and the development of character and mental powers that result from such training (接受教育而获得的)知识, 能力, 修养, 智力: *intellectual, moral, physical, etc education* 智育、德育、体育等. **3** field of study dealing with how to teach 教育学: *a college of education* 教育学院 ○ *a lecturer in education* 教育学讲师.

▷ **edu·ca·tional** /-ʃənl; -ʃənḷ/ *adj* of, about or providing education 教育的; 与教育有关的; 有教育意义的: *an educational magazine* 教育杂志 ○ *I found the experience most educational.* 我认为这一经历极有教益. **edu·ca·tion·ally** /-ʃənəlɪ; -ʃənḷɪ/ *adv*.

edu·ca·tion·ist /ˌedʒʊˈkeɪʃənɪst; ˌɛdʒʊˋkeʃənɪst/ (also **edu·ca·tion·al·ist** /ˌedʒʊˈkeɪʃənəlɪst; ˌɛdʒʊˋkeʃənḷɪst/) *n* specialist in education 教育家.

-ee *suff* 后缀 **1** (with *vs* forming *ns* 与动词结合构成名词) person affected by 受动者: *employee* ○ *payee*. Cf 参看 -ER, -OR. **2** (with *adjs*, *vs* and *ns* forming *ns* 与形容词、动词、名词结合构成名词) person described as or concerned with 形容为…的人; 与…有关的人: *absentee* ○ *refugee*.

EEC /ˌiː iː ˈsiː; ˌi i ˋsi/ *abbr* 缩写 = European Economic Community (the Common Market) 欧洲经济共同体(共同市场): *join the EEC* 加入欧洲经济共同体 ○ *EEC members* 欧洲经济共同体成员.

EEG /ˌiː iː ˈdʒiː; ˌi i ˋdʒi/ *abbr* 缩写 = (*medical* 医) electroen-cephalogram: *give sb an EEG* 给某人做脑电图.

eel /iːl; il/ *n* long snake-like fish that is difficult to catch hold of 鳗; 鳗鲡; 白鳝: *jellied eels*, ie cooked and eaten cold in a savoury jelly 鳗鱼冻.

-eer *suff* 后缀 **1** (with *ns* forming *ns* 与名词结合构成名词) person concerned with 与…有关的人: *auctioneer* ○ *mountaineer*. **2** (with *ns* forming *vs* 与名词结合构成动词) (*often derog* 常作贬义) be concerned with 与…有关: *electioneer* ○ *profiteer*.

eerie (also **eery**) /ˈɪərɪ; ˋɪrɪ/ *adj* (**-ier**, **-iest**) causing a feeling of mystery and fear 引起神秘和恐怖感觉的; 可怕的; 怪异的: *an eerie scream* 恐怖的尖叫 ○ *an eerie silence* 可怕的沉寂. ▷ **eer·ily** /ˈɪərəlɪ; ˋɪrɪlɪ/ *adv*. **eeri·ness** /ˈɪərɪnɪs; ˋɪrɪnɪs/ *n* [U].

eff /ef; ɛf/ *v* (⚠ *euph* 讳, 婉) (phr v) **eff off** go away; fuck off 走开; 滚开: *I told him to eff off.* 我叫他滚蛋. ▷ **eff·ing** *adj*: *It's an effing nuisance.* 真是混账事.

ef·face /ɪˈfeɪs; ɪˋfes/ *v* [Tn] (*fml* 文) **1** rub or wipe (sth) out; cause to fade 擦去, 抹掉(某事物); 使淡薄; 使逐渐消失: *Time and weather had long ago effaced the inscription on the monument.* 岁月和风雨早已磨掉纪念碑上的铭文. ○ *Time alone will efface those unpleasant memories.* 只有时间才能使人淡忘那些不快的记忆. **2 ~ oneself** keep in the background in order to escape being noticed; make oneself appear unimportant 使自己不被人注意; 使自己显得无足轻重. ▷ **ef·face·ment** *n* [U].

ef·fect /ɪˈfekt; ɪˋfɛkt/ *n* **1** [C, U] **~ (on sb/sth)** change produced by an action or cause; result or outcome 效应; 结果; 后果: *the effects of heat on metal* 热对金属产生的效应 ○ *Did the medicine have any effect/a good effect?* 这药有什么疗效[疗效好]吗? ○ *The film had quite an effect on her.* 这影片对她影响极大. ○ *I tried to persuade him, but with little or no effect.* 我尽力劝他, 他根本不听. **2** [C, U] impression produced on the mind of the spectator, listener, reader, etc (esp in plays, films, broadcasts, paintings, etc) (观众、听众、读者等)头脑

E

中所产生的印象(尤指在戏剧、电影、广播、绘画等方面): *The general effect of the painting is overwhelming.* 这幅画给人总的印象是很有气势. ○ *The stage lighting gives the effect of a moonlit scene.* 舞台灯光产生月夜景色的效果. ○ *She only dresses like that for the effect it creates/for effect.* 她仅仅为了装样子才那样打扮. ○ *The science fiction film had some marvellous special effects.* 这部科幻电影有些特殊效果美妙绝伦. **3 effects** [pl] (*fml or law* 文或律) personal property; possessions 个人财产; 财物: *personal effects* 个人财产 ○ *household effects* 家庭财物. **4** (idm 习语) **bring/put sth into ef'fect** cause sth to come into use 使某物开始使用: *The new system will soon be put into effect.* 新系统即将启用. **come into ef'fect** (esp of laws, rules, etc) reach the stage of being in use (尤指法律、规则等)实行, 实施: *The new seat-belt regulations came into effect last week.* 新的安全带规则上周开始实施. **give effect to sth** (*fml* 文) cause sth to become active or produce a result 使某事物实行起来; 使生效: *The new ruling gives effect to the recommendations of the special committee.* 这一新裁定使特别委员会的推荐生效. **in ef'fect** (**a**) for practical purposes; in fact 实际上; 事实上: *The two systems are, in effect, identical.* 这两种制度实际上一模一样. (**b**) (of a rule, law, etc) in use (指规则、法律等)有效: *Some ancient laws are still in effect.* 有些古时的法律现在仍然有效. **of/to no ef'fect** not having the result intended or hoped for 没有预期的或希望的结果; 无效: *My warning was of no effect.* 我的警告无济于事. ○ *We warned them, but to no effect.* 我们警告过他们, 但完全没用. **strain after effects/an effect** ⇨ STRAIN[1]. **take ef'fect** (**a**) produce the result intended or required 产生预期的或要求的结果; 生效: *The aspirins soon took effect.* 服下的阿司匹林药片很快见效了. (**b**) come into force or use; become active 实施; 实行; 起作用: *The new law takes effect from tomorrow.* 新法令明日起实行. **to good, etc ef'fect** producing a good, etc result or impression 产生好的等结果或印象: *The room shows off her paintings to good effect.* 这个房间把她绘画的优点充分显示出来. **to this/that ef'fect** with this/that meaning or information 有这样[那样]的意思或内容: *He told me to get out, or words to that effect.* 他说了一句叫我走开之类的话. **to the effect that...** with the meaning, or giving the information, that... 大意为...: *He left a note to the effect that he would not be returning.* 他留下一张字条, 大意是说他不回来了.

▷ **ef·fect** *v* [Tn] (*fml* 文) bring (sth) about; cause to occur 使(某事物)产生; 使发生; 引起: *effect a cure, a change, a sale* 产生疗效、引起变化、实行大减价. ⇨ Usage at AFFECT[1] 用法见 AFFECT[1].

ef·fect·ive /ɪ'fektɪv; ɪ'fɛktɪv/ *adj* **1** (**a**) having an effect; producing the intended result 有效的; 产生预期结果的: *effective measures to reduce unemployment* 减少失业的有效措施 ○ *The law is no longer effective.* 该法令已失效. (**b**) making a striking impression 产生深刻印象的: *a very effective colour scheme* 非常醒目的色调 ○ *an effective speech* 精彩的演说. **2** [attrib 作定语] (**a**) actual or existing 实际的; 实在的; 现有的: *the effective membership of a society* 现有的全体会员. (**b**) fit for service or work 适于承担任务或工作的: *the effective strength of the army* 军队的战斗力.

▷ **ef·fect·ively** *adv* **1** in an effective way 有效地. **2** for practical purposes; in effect 事实上; 实际上: *This means that effectively we have no chance of finishing on time.* 这意味着我们实际上没有可能准时完成.

ef·fect·ive·ness *n* [U].

ef·fec·tual /ɪ'fektʃʊəl; ɪ'fɛktʃʊəl/ *adj* (*fml* 文) (not used of people) producing the intended result (不用于指人)产生预期结果的, 有效的: *take effectual action, measures, steps, etc* 采取有效行动、措施、步骤等. ▷ **ef·fec·tu·ally** /-əlɪ; -əlɪ/ *adv*.

ef·fem·in·ate /ɪ'femɪnət; ɪ'fɛmənɪt/ *adj* (*derog* 贬) (of a man or his behaviour) like a woman; unmanly (指男人或其行为)像女人的; 没男子气的: *an effeminate manner, voice, walk* 像女人的举止、声音、走路姿态. ▷ **ef·fem·in·acy** /ɪ'femɪnəsɪ; ɪ'fɛmənəsɪ/ *n* [U]. **ef·fem·in·ately** /-lɪ; -lɪ/ *adv*.

ef·fer·vesce /ˌefə'ves; ˌɛfɚ'vɛs/ *v* **1** [I] (of a liquid) release bubbles of gas; fizz (指液体)释放出气泡, 嘶嘶起泡. **2** [I, Ipr] **~ (with sth)** (*fml* 文) (of people) be happy, lively and excited (指人)愉快、活跃而兴奋. ▷ **ef·fer·ves·cence** /ˌefə'vesns; ˌɛfɚ'vɛsn̩s/ *n* [U]. **ef·fer·ves·cent** /-snt; -sn̩t/ *adj*.

ef·fete /ɪ'fi:t; ɪ'fit/ *adj* (**a**) weak, having lost power 衰弱的; 丧失权力的: *an effete civilization, empire, government, etc* 衰落的文明、没落的帝国、软弱的政府. (**b**) lacking vitality and strength; feeble 缺乏活力和力量的; 虚弱的: *an effete young man* 无精打采的年轻人. ▷ **ef·fete·ness** *n* [U].

ef·fi·ca·cious /ˌefɪ'keɪʃəs; ˌɛfə'keʃəs/ *adj* (*fml* 文) (not of people) producing the desired result; effective (不用以指人)有效的: *an efficacious treatment, medicine, etc* 有效的治疗、药品等.

▷ **ef·fi·ca·ciously** *adv*.

ef·fi·cacy /'efɪkəsɪ; 'ɛfəkəsɪ/ *n* [U] state or quality of being efficacious 有效性; 效能; 功效: *test the efficacy of a new drug* 测试新药的效能.

ef·fi·ci·ent /ɪ'fɪʃnt; ɪ'fɪʃənt/ *adj* **1** (of people) able to work well; capable (指人)能胜任的; 有能力的: *an efficient secretary, teacher, administrator, etc* 能干的秘书、教师、行政人员等 ○ *He's efficient at his job.* 他胜任工作. **2** (esp of tools, machines, systems, etc) producing a satisfactory result without wasting time or energy (尤指工具, 机器, 系统等)有效力的: *an efficient new filing system* 有效的新归档系统.

▷ **ef·fi·ci·ency** /ɪ'fɪʃnsɪ; ɪ'fɪʃənsɪ/ *n* [U] state or quality of being efficient 能力; 效力; 效能.

ef·fi·ci·ently /-lɪ; -lɪ/ *adv*: *get industry running more efficiently* 使工业经营管理效率更高.

ef·figy /'efɪdʒɪ; 'ɛfədʒɪ/ *n* **1** [C] carved figure or model representing a person or animal (人或动物的)雕像, 肖像, 模拟像: *stone effigies of Buddha* 石雕佛像 ○ *On 5 November British children burn effigies of Guy Fawkes.* 每逢11月5日英国儿童都焚烧盖伊·福克斯的模拟像. **2** (idm 习语) **in effigy** as a model 作为模拟像: *burn sb in effigy*, ie make a model of sb and burn it as a sign of hatred, etc 烧某人的模拟像(泄愤等).

ef·flor·es·cence /ˌeflɔ:'resns; ˌɛflɔ'rɛsn̩s/ *n* [U] (*fml esp fig* 文, 尤作比喻) action or time of bursting into flower 开花; 花期: *a period of great efflorescence in the arts* 艺术的全盛时期. ▷ **ef·flor·es·cent** /-snt; -sn̩t/ *adj*.

ef·flu·ent /'efluənt; 'ɛfluənt/ *n* **1** [U, C] (discharge of) liquid waste matter, sewage, etc, eg from a factory into a river 废液、污水等(的排放)(如从工厂排到河流): *The effluent from the factory makes the river unsafe for swimming.* 工厂放出的废水把这条河弄得不能游泳了. **2** [C] stream flowing from a larger stream or from a lake (从河或湖中流出的)支流, 小水流.

ef·fort /'efət; 'ɛfɚt/ *n* **1** [U] use of (much) strength and energy (to do sth) (做某事物使用的)力量和精力: *a waste of time and effort* 时间和精力的浪费 ○ *They lifted the heavy rock without effort.* 他们没费劲就把那块沉重的石头抬起来了. ○ *He must put more effort into his work.* 他必须更加努力工作. **2** [C] **~ (to do sth)** energetic attempt; struggle 努力; 奋斗: *His efforts were much appreciated.* 大家都夸他很努力. ○ *It was a real effort to stay awake through the film.* 真要强打着精神才能看完整部电影. ○ *I will make every effort* (ie do all I can) *to arrive on time.* 我将尽一切努力准时到达. **3** [C] result of an attempt 努力的结果: *That's a good effort*, ie That has been well done. 这事干得不错.

▷ **ef·fort·less** *adj* needing no or little effort 不需努力的; 不费力的: *She plays with seemingly effortless skill.* 她演奏得似乎毫不费力. **ef·fort·lessly** *adv*. **ef·fort·less·ness** *n* [U].

ef·front·ery /ɪ'frʌntərɪ; ɪ'frʌntərɪ/ *n* (**a**) [U] boldness or rudeness without shame; impertinence 厚颜无耻; 傲慢; 鲁莽; 无礼: *He had the effrontery to say I was lying.* 他竟敢说我撒谎. (**b**) [C esp *pl* 尤作复数] (*fml* 文) instance of this 厚颜无耻的行为; 傲慢鲁莽的举止: *Everyone is tired of their blatant effronteries.* 大家都厌恶他们粗俗.

ef·fu·sion /ɪ'fju:ʒn; ɪ'fjuʒən/ *n* **1** (*fml* 文) (**a**) [U] pouring out, esp of liquid 倾出; 流出: *an effusion of blood* 流血. (**b**) [C] quantity poured out 流出的量. **2** [C] (*usu derog* 通常作贬义) (esp unrestrained) pouring out of thoughts and feelings in words (尤指无约束的)思想和感情的流露; 抒发感情: *poetical effusions* 诗情奔放 ○ *effusions in love letters* 情书中的绵绵情意.

ef·fus·ive /ɪ'fju:sɪv; ɪ'fjusɪv/ *adj* (*often derog* 常作贬义)

E

showing (too much) feeling; too emotional (过分)流露感情的; 太动感情的: *Her effusive thanks embarrassed everybody.* 她道谢时非常激动, 弄得大家不好意思. ▷ **ef·fus·ively** *adv*. **ef·fus·ive·ness** *n* [U].

EFL /ˌiː ef ˈel; ˌi ɛf ˋɛl/ *abbr* 缩写 = (teaching, learning or studying) English as a Foreign Language 作为外语的英语(教学或研究). Cf 参看 ESL.

EFTA (also **Efta**) /ˈeftə; ˋɛftə/ *abbr* 缩写 = European Free Trade Association 欧洲自由贸易联盟: *In 1972 Britain left EFTA and joined the EEC.* 1972年英国脱离欧洲自由贸易联盟, 加入了欧洲经济共同体.

eg /ˌiː ˈdʒiː; ˋi ˋdʒi/ *abbr* 缩写 = for example; for instance (Latin *exempli gratia*) 例如(源自拉丁文 *exempli gratia*): *popular pets, eg dogs, cats, rabbits, etc* 大家喜爱的宠物, 如狗、猫、兔等. ⇨Usage at VIZ 用法见 VIZ.

egal·it·ar·ian /ɪˌgælɪˈteərɪən; ɪ,gæləˋtɛrɪən/ *n, adj* (person) showing or holding a belief in equal rights, benefits and opportunities for everybody 平等主义的; 平等主义者: *an egalitarian attitude to voting* 对投票持平等主义的态度. ▷ **egal·it·ar·ian·ism** /-ɪzəm; -ɪzəm/ *n* [U]

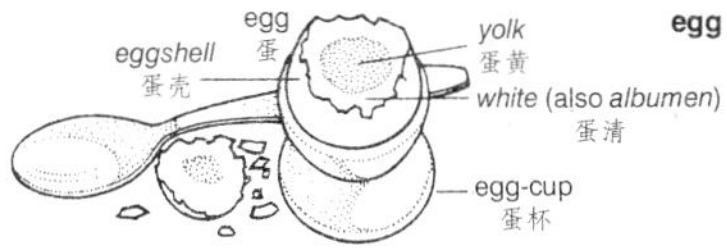

egg 蛋

egg[1] /eg; ɛg/ *n* **1** [C] in female mammals the cell from which the young is formed; ovum 卵; 卵子; 卵细胞: *The male sperm fertilizes the female egg.* 雄性的精子使雌性的卵子受精. **2** (**a**) [C] oval object from which young are hatched, laid by birds, reptiles, insects, etc and usu covered by a thin hard shell (鸟类、爬行动物、昆虫等产的)卵, 蛋: *The hen laid a large brown egg.* 这只母鸡下了一个大红皮蛋. ○ *The blackbird's nest contained four eggs.* 黑鹂巢里有四个蛋. ○ *ants' eggs* 蚂蚁卵. ⇨illus 见插图. (**b**) [U, C] (contents of) this, esp from a hen, used as food (用作食物的)蛋; (尤指)鸡蛋: *You've got some egg* (ie a bit of cooked egg) *on your shirt.* 你衬衫上沾了些鸡蛋. ○ *Do you want a boiled egg for breakfast?* 你早饭要吃煮鸡蛋吗? ○ *ducks' eggs* 鸭蛋. **3** (idm 习语) **a bad ˈegg/ˈlot** (*dated infml* 旧, 口) person considered to be dishonest and unreliable 不忠诚和不可信任的人; 坏蛋; 坏人. **a curate's egg** ⇨ CURATE. **get, have, be left with, etc ˈegg on/all over one's face** (*infml* 口) appear foolish 显得愚蠢: *He was left with egg all over his face when his forecast was proved wrong.* 他的预言证实是错的, 他显得很尴尬. **kill the goose that lays the golden egg** ⇨ KILL. **make an omelette without breaking eggs** ⇨ OMELETTE. **ˌput all one's ˌeggs in/into one ˈbasket** risk everything one has on the success of one plan, eg by putting all one's money into one business 孤注一掷(如将所有的钱投入一项生意上). **teach one's grandmother to suck eggs** ⇨ TEACH.

□ **ˈegg-beater** *n* = EGG-WHISK.

ˈegg-cup *n* small cup for holding a boiled egg 蛋杯(盛煮鸡蛋的小杯). ⇨illus 见插图.

ˈegghead *n* (*infml derog* 口, 贬) very intellectual person 很有学问的人: *The eggheads at the university know nothing about business.* 大学的饱学之士对做生意一窍不通.

ˈegg-plant *n* [C, U] (*esp US*) = AUBERGINE.

ˈeggshell *n* hard thin outer part of an egg 蛋壳. **eggshell ˈchina** very fine thin type of china 非常薄的细瓷器. **eggshell ˈpaint** type of paint that is neither glossy nor matt 蛋壳漆(一种光泽既不亮又不暗的漆).

ˈegg-timer *n* device for measuring time when boiling eggs 煮蛋计时器.

ˈegg-whisk (also **ˈegg-beater**) *n* device for beating eggs 打蛋器.

egg[2] /eg; ɛg/ *v* (phr v) **egg sb on (to do sth)** urge or strongly encourage sb to do sth 怂恿或鼓励某人做某事: *I didn't want to do it but Peter kept egging me ˈon.* 我本不想做那件事, 但彼得一直怂恿我.

eg·lan·tine /ˈeglәntaɪn; ˋɛglən,taɪn/ (also **sweet-briar**) *n* [U] type of wild rose 多花蔷薇; 野蔷薇.

ego /ˈegəʊ; *US* ˈiːgəʊ; ˋigo/ *n* **1** (*psychology* 心) individual's perception or experience of himself, esp in relation to other people or to the outside world; part of the mind that can think, feel and act 自我. Cf 参看 ID, SUPER-EGO. **2** (*infml* 口) self-esteem 自尊; 自负: *Losing the match made quite a dent in his ego.* 比赛失败对他的自尊心打击极大.

□ **ˈego-trip** *n* (*sl* 俚) self-centred activity 以自我为中心的活动: (*derog* 贬) *Her life is just one big ego-trip.* 她一生都是以自我为中心.

ego·cent·ric /ˌegəʊˈsentrɪk; *US* ˌiːg-; ˌigoˋsɛntrɪk/ *adj* considering only oneself; self-centred 只考虑自己的; 以自我为中心的. ▷ **ego·cent·ri·city** /-senˈtrɪsətɪ; -sɛnˋtrɪsətɪ/ *n* [U].

ego·ism /ˈegəʊɪzəm; *US* ˈiːg-; ˋigo,ɪzəm/ *n* [U] **1** (*usu derog* 通常作贬义) state of mind in which one is always thinking about oneself and what is best for oneself 总考虑个人和个人利益; 自私自利. **2** (*philosophy* 哲) theory that our actions are always caused by a wish to benefit ourselves 利己主义; 自我主义. Cf 参看 ALTRUISM.

▷ **ego·ist** /-ɪst; -ɪst/ *n* person who believes in or shows egoism 自私自利的人; 利己主义者; 自我主义者. **ego·istic** /ˌegəʊˈɪstɪk; *US* ˌiːg-; ˌigoˋɪstɪk/, **ego·ist·ical** /-kl; -kəl/ *adjs* of an egoist 自私自利的; 利己主义者的; 自我主义者的: *an egoistic act* 自私自利的行为. **ego·ist·ic·ally** /-klɪ; -klɪ/ *adv*.

egot·ism /ˈegəʊtɪzəm; *US* ˈiːg-; ˋigə,tɪzəm/ *n* [U] (*usu derog* 通常作贬义) practice of talking too often or too much about oneself; selfishness 自我中心; 自私自利.

▷ **egot·ist** /-tɪst; -tɪst/ *n* person who practises or shows egotism; selfish person 自我中心者; 自私自利者. **egot·istic** /ˌegəˈtɪstɪk; *US* ˌiːg-; ˌigəˋtɪstɪk/, **egot·ist·ical** /-kl; -kl/ *adjs* of egotism; of or like an egotist 利己主义的; 利己主义者的; 似自私自利者的. **egot·ist·ic·ally** /-klɪ; -klɪ/ *adv*.

egre·gious /ɪˈgriːdʒɪəs; ɪˋgridʒɪəs/ *adj* [usu attrib 通常作定语] (*fml* 文) (usu of sb/sth bad 通常指坏人[坏事物]) exceptional; outstanding 异乎寻常的; 突出的; 显著的: *egregious incompetence, cowardice, etc* 极其无能、胆怯...的表现 ○ *an egregious fool* 大傻瓜. ▷ **egre·giously** *adv*.

egress /ˈiːgres; ˋigrɛs/ *n* **1** [U] (*law* 律) (right of) going out 外出; 外出权. **2** [C] (*dated fml* 旧, 文) way out; exit 出路; 出口. Cf 参看 INGRESS.

eg·ret /ˈiːgrɪt; ˋigrɪt/ *n* type of heron with beautiful long white tail-feathers 白鹭.

eh /eɪ; e/ *interj* (*infml* 口) (used to express surprise or doubt, to invite agreement, or to ask for sth to be repeated 用以表示惊奇或怀疑、征求同意或请求重复某事): *'That was a good film, eh?'* '那是一部好影片, 对吗?' ○ *'I want to go home!' 'Eh?' 'I said I want to go home!'* '我想回家!' '嗯?' '我说我想回家!'

ei·der·down /ˈaɪdədaʊn; ˋaɪdɚ,daʊn/ *n* quilt for a bed filled with soft feathers or other soft material 用羽绒或其他轻软物填充的被褥. Cf 参看 DUVET.

eight /eɪt; et/ *pron, det* 8; one more than seven 8, 八(个). ⇨App 4 见附录4.

▷ **eight** *n* **1** the number 8 ☆ 8;八. **2** crew of eight people in a rowing boat 划艇的八人一组的船员: *Is the Oxford eight winning?* 牛津的划艇队能赢吗? **3** (idm 习语) **have had ˌone over the ˈeight** (*infml* 口) be slightly drunk 微醉.

eight- (in compounds 用以构成复合词) having eight of the thing specified 有八个...的.

eighth /eɪtθ; etθ/ *pron, det* 8th; next after seventh 第8, 第八(个). — *n* one of eight equal parts of sth 八分之一.

□ **eightsome** /ˈeɪtsəm; ˋetsəm/ *n* **1** group of eight people 八人一组. **2** game played by eight people 八人玩的游戏. **3** (also **ˌeightsome ˈreel**) lively Scottish dance for eight dancers 八人跳的轻快的苏格兰舞.

For the uses of *eight* and *eighth* see the examples at *five* and *fifth*. 关于 eight 和 eighth 的用法见 five 和 fifth 词条中的示例.

eight·een /ˌeɪˈtiːn; eˋtin/ *pron, det* 18; one more than seventeen 18, 十八(个). ⇨App 4 见附录4.

▷ **eight·een** *n* the number 18 ☆ 18;十八.

eight·eenth /ˌeɪˈtiːnθ; eˋtinθ/ *pron, det* 18th; next after seventeenth 第18, 第十八(个). — *n* one of eighteen equal parts of sth 十八分之一.

For the uses of *eighteen* and *eighteenth* see the examples at *five* and *fifth*. 关于eighteen和eighteenth的用法见five和fifth词条中的示例.

eighty /ˈeɪtɪ; ˋetɪ/ *pron, det* 80; one more than seventy-nine 80, 八十(个). ⇨App 4 见附录4.

▷ **eigh·ti·eth** /ˈeɪtɪəθ; ˋetɪɪθ/ *pron, det* 80th; next after seventy-ninth 第80, 第八十(个). — *n* one of eighty equal parts of sth 八十分之一.

eighty *n* **1** [C] the number 80 ☆ 80;八十. **2 the eighties** [pl] numbers, years or temperature from 80 to 89 从80到89的数目、年数或温度. **3** (idm 习语) **in one's eighties** between the ages of 80 and 90 在80岁到90岁之间.

For the uses of *eighty* and *eightieth* see the examples at *fifty*, *five* and *fifth*. 关于eighty和eightieth的用法见fifty、five和fifth词条中的示例.

ei·stedd·fod /ˌaɪˈsteðvɒd; aɪˋstɛðvɑd/ *n* annual gathering in Wales where poets and musicians compete 在威尔士举行的诗人与音乐家的比赛年会.

either /ˈaɪðə(r), ˈiːðə(r); ˋiðɚ/ *indef det, indef pron* one or the other of two (两者中的)一个. **(a)** (*det*): *You can park on either side of the street.* 在街道的哪边停车都可以. ○ *Keep either one of the forms.* 两张表格保留哪张都行. ○ *There's a staircase at either end* (ie both ends) *of the corridor.* 走廊两端都有楼梯. **(b)** (*pron*) (used with a *sing v* 与单数动词连用): *I've bought two cakes — you can have either.* 我买了两块蛋糕——你要哪块都行. ○ *Take one of the books on the table — either of them will do.* 从桌上拿一本书——两本中哪本都可以.

▷ **either** *indef adv* **1** (used after two negative *vs* 用于两个否定式之后): *I don't like the red shirt and I don't like the green one either*, ie I dislike both the red shirt and the green one. 我不喜欢这件红衬衫, 也不喜欢这件绿衬衫. ○ *Mary won't go and Peter won't go either.* 玛丽不去, 彼得也不去. (Cf 参看 *...and neither will Peter.*) ○ *He can't hear and he can hardly speak either.* 他既听不见也几乎不能说话. ⇨Usage at ALSO 用法见ALSO. **2** (used to emphasize a negative phrase 用于强调含否定意义的短语): *I know a good Italian restaurant. It's not far from here, either.* 我知道一家很好的意大利餐馆, 离这儿并不远. **3 either ... or ...** (used to show a choice of two alternatives 用于表示在两个可能性中任择其一): *either French or Spanish* 或法国的或西班牙的 ○ *I left it either on the table or in the drawer.* 我不是把它放在桌子上了, 就是放在抽屉里了. ○ *You can either write or phone to request a copy.* 既可以写信也可以打电话索取一本.

ejacu·late /ɪˈdʒækjʊleɪt; ɪˋdʒækjəˌlet/ *v* **1** [I] eject or rapidly discharge fluid, esp semen, from the body (从体内)射出或迅速排出液体; (尤指)射精. **2** [I, Tn] (*fml* 文) say (sth) suddenly and briefly; exclaim 突然而简短地说(某事); 呼喊.

▷ **ejacu·la·tion** /ɪˌdʒækjʊˈleɪʃn; ɪˌdʒækjəˋleʃən/ *n* **1** [C, U] sudden discharge or ejection of fluid, esp semen, from the body 从体内突然排出或射出液体; (尤指)射精. **2** [C] (*fml* 文) thing said suddenly and briefly; exclamation 突然说出的简短的话; 呼喊: *an ejaculation of surprise* 突然的惊叫.

eject /ɪˈdʒekt; ɪˋdʒɛkt/ *v* **1** [Tn, Tn·pr] **~ sb/sth (from sth)** (*fml* 文) force sb/sth out; expel sb/sth 强迫某人[某物]出去; 驱逐; 逐出某人[某物]: *The noisy youths were ejected from the cinema.* 吵闹的青年人都已从影院驱逐出去. ○ *Cartridges are ejected from the gun after firing.* 开枪后子弹壳从枪膛弹出. **2** [Tn] send (sth) out, usu violently or suddenly 喷出(某物): *lava ejected from a volcano* 从火山喷出的熔岩. **3** [I, Ipr] **~ (from sth)** be thrown quickly from an aircraft in an emergency, so that one can descend by parachute 在紧急情况下将人从飞行器中弹出(以便用降落伞降落): *As the plane fell rapidly towards the ground, the pilot had to eject.* 在飞机迅速落向地面时, 驾驶员只得弹射出来.

▷ **ejec·tion** /ɪˈdʒekʃn; ɪˋdʒɛkʃən/ *n* [U].

ejector /ɪˈdʒektə(r); ɪˋdʒɛktɚ/ *n* device for ejecting people or things 弹射器(弹射人或物的装置). **ejector seat** (*US* also **ejection seat**) seat in an aircraft that allows the pilot to eject(3) (飞行器上的)弹射座椅.

eke /iːk; ik/ *v* (phr v) **eke sth out (a)** make a small supply of sth last longer by adding sth else to it or by using it sparingly 使小量物品用的时间长(靠节省用量或以他物弥补): *They eked out their coal by collecting firewood.* 他们拣拾木柴以补充煤的不足. **(b)** manage to make (a living) laboriously by doing this 竭力维持(生活): *eking out a meagre existence* 勉强维持贫困的生活.

elab·or·ate /ɪˈlæbərət; ɪˋlæbərɪt/ *adj* very detailed and complicated; carefully prepared and finished 详尽而复杂的; 精心制作的: *elaborate plans* 详尽的计划 ○ *an elaborate hairstyle* 复杂的发型 ○ *an elaborate five-course meal* 有五道菜的一顿盛馔.

▷ **elab·or·ate** /ɪˈlæbəreɪt; ɪˋlæbəˌret/ **1** *v* [Tn] (*fml* 文) work (sth) out in detail 详细制定(某事物): *Please elaborate your plan.* 请做出详细的计划. **2** [I, Ipr] **~ (on sth)** describe or explain sth in detail 详尽解释或说明某事; 阐述: *You understand the situation; I needn't elaborate any further.* 你了解形势, 我无须赘述.

elab·ora·tion /ɪˌlæbəˈreɪʃn; ɪˌlæbəˋreʃən/ *n* **1** [U] working sth out, or discussing sth, in detail 详细制定, 详尽讨论某事物: *the further elaboration of a theory* 对一理论的深入探讨. **2** [C] additional, usu unnecessary, detail 附加细节(通常为不必要的): *The elaborations of the plot made it a difficult book to read.* 这本书因内容节外生枝而很难懂.

elab·or·ately *adv*: *an elaborately decorated room* 精心布置的房间.

elab·or·ate·ness *n* [U] state of being elaborate 详尽; 复杂; 精心制作.

élan /eɪˈlɑːn; eˋlɑ̃/ *n* [U] (*French* 法) vivacity; impetuousity; enthusiasm 活力; 冲动; 热情: *performing with great élan* 演出声情并茂.

eland /ˈiːlənd; ˋilənd/ *n* large African antelope 大角斑羚(非洲大羚羊).

elapse /ɪˈlæps; ɪˋlæps/ *v* [I] (*fml* 文) (of time) pass (指时间)过去, 消逝: *Three years have elapsed since we last met.* 我们上次相见至今已过了三年.

elastic /ɪˈlæstɪk; ɪˋlæstɪk/ *adj* **1** returning to its normal or previous size or shape after being pulled or pressed 有弹性的; 弹力的: *a bra with elastic straps* 有松紧带的乳罩 ○ *Rubber is elastic.* 橡皮有弹性. **2** (*fig* 比喻) not fixed or unalterable; adaptable; flexible 非固定的或不可改变的; 适应性强的; 灵活的: *Our plans are fairly elastic.* 我们的计划相当灵活.

▷ **elastic** *n* [U] **1** elastic cord or material, usu made with rubber thread 松紧带: *The elastic in my pants has gone*, ie has broken or perished. 我裤子的松紧带坏了(断了或老化了). ○ [attrib 作定语] *an elastic bandage* 弹性绷带. **2** (*US*) = RUBBER BAND (RUBBER).

elast·ic·ate /ɪˈlæstɪkeɪt; ɪˋlæstəˌket/ *v* [Tn usu passive 通常用于被动语态] insert elastic into (a fabric or garment) 将松紧带插入(织物或衣服): *a dress with an elasticated top* 上部有松紧带的连衣裙 ○ *an elasticated belt* 有松紧带的腰带.

elasti·city /ˌelæˈstɪsətɪ; *US* ɪˌlæ-; ɪˌlæsˋtɪsətɪ/ *n* [U] quality of being elastic 弹性; 弹力; 灵活性; 适应性.

□ **eˌlastic ˈband** (*US*) = RUBBER BAND (RUBBER).

Elastoplast /ɪˈlæstəplɑːst, -plæst; ɪˋlæstəˌplæst/ *n* [U] (*Brit propr* 专利名) adhesive dressing for cuts, etc 弹性绷带.

elated /ɪˈleɪtɪd; ɪˋletɪd/ *adj* **~ (at/by sth)** in high spirits; very happy or proud 情绪高昂的; 兴高采烈的; 非常愉快或自豪的: *an elated smile* 沾沾自喜的微笑 ○ *She was elated at/by the news.* 她听到这个消息喜出望外.

▷ **elatedly** /ɪˈleɪtɪdlɪ; ɪˋletɪdlɪ/ *adv*.

ela·tion /ɪˈleɪʃn; ɪˋleʃən/ *n* [U] high spirits; joy 兴高采烈; 欢欣鼓舞: *She was filled with elation when her daughter was born.* 她女儿出生时她十分欢喜.

el·bow /ˈelbəʊ; ˋɛlˌbo/ *n* **1** (outer part of the) joint where the arm bends 肘; 肘部: *He sat with his elbows on the table.* 他双肘支在桌上坐着. ⇨illus at HUMAN 见HUMAN之插图. **2** part of the sleeve of a coat, jacket, etc which covers this (衣服的)肘部: *a jacket patched at the elbows* 肘部打补丁的夹克. **3** sharp bend in a pipe, chimney, etc that is shaped like an elbow (形状似肘的)管子, 烟囱等的弯处; 弯管; 弯头. **4** (idm 习语) **at one's ˈelbow** very near; within reach 非常近; 可够得着. **give sb/get the ˈelbow** (*infml* 口) (cause sb to) be dismissed or rejected (使某人)被排斥或被拒绝: *She gave me the elbow when she started going out with Roger.*

她开始与罗杰外出约会，就把我撇开了. **more power to sb's elbow** ⇨ POWER. **not know one's arse from one's elbow** ⇨ KNOW. **out at (the) 'elbows** (**a**) (of a garment) old and full of holes (指衣服)捉襟见肘的. (**b**) (of a person) in old shabby clothes; badly dressed (指人)穿破旧衣服的, 衣衫褴褛的.

▷ **el·bow** *v* (phr v) **elbow sb out of the 'way/a'side** push sb to one side with the elbows 用肘将某人推到一边: *He elbowed me out of the way.* 他用肘部把我挤到一边. **elbow one's way into, through, etc (sth)** force (one's way) in a specified direction by using one's elbows 用肘朝某一方向强行开路: *He elbowed his way through the crowd.* 他用肘开路, 从人群中挤出. ○ *She elbowed her way forward.* 她用肘开路向前走.

□ **'elbow-grease** *n* [U] (*infml* 口) hard manual work, esp vigorous polishing or cleaning 费劲的体力活儿; (尤指)擦拭: *If you used a bit of elbow-grease you could get those boots clean.* 只要稍用些力就能把那双靴子擦干净.

'elbow-room *n* [U] space in which one can move freely 可以自由活动的空间: *I need (some) more elbow-room.* 我需要大一些的活动空间.

elder[1] /'eldə(r); 'ɛldɚ/ *adj* **1** (**a**) [attrib 作定语] (of people; esp two closely related members of a family) older; senior (指人, 尤指家庭中两个关系密切的成员)年长的, 年龄较大的: *my elder brother* 我的哥哥 ○ *her elder daughter*, ie the first-born of her two daughters 她的大女儿. (**b**) **the elder** (used without an immediately following *n* to refer to an earlier or later *n* 后面不紧接名词, 用以指前面或后面的名词) the older person, etc (of two) (两人中)年长者: *He is the elder of my two brothers.* 他是我两兄弟中年岁较大的. ○ *There go my two sons. Can you guess which is the elder?* 那是我的两个儿子. 你能猜出哪个大吗? **2 the elder** (*fml* 文) (used before or after sb's name to distinguish him from another person with the same name 用于某人名字之前或之后, 以区别与之同名者): *Pitt the elder* 大皮特 ○ *the elder Pitt* 大皮特. Cf 参看 YOUNG 3.

▷ **elder** *n* **1 my, etc elder** [sing] person older than me, etc 比我等年长的人: *He is her elder by several years.* 他比她大几岁. **2 elders** [pl] people of greater age and authority 年迈而有权威的人: *the village elders*, ie the old and respected people of the village 村中德高望重的前辈 ○ *Traditions were passed on by the elders of the tribe.* 部族的传统由长者承袭相传. **3** [C] official in a Presbyterian church (长老会中的)长老. **4** (idm 习语) **one's (elders and) betters** ⇨ BETTER[3] 2.

□ **,elder 'statesman** old and respected politician; person, usu retired, whose advice is still valued because of his long experience 政界元老(年迈而受尊重的政治家); 老顾问(因经验丰富而其意见仍受重视的人, 通常指退休者).

NOTE ON USAGE 用法: The usual comparative and superlative forms of **old** are **older** and **oldest** ☆ **old** 通常的比较级和最高级形式是**older**和**oldest**: *My brother is older than me.* 我哥哥比我年龄大. ○ *The cathedral is the oldest building in the city.* 这座大教堂是城里最古老的建筑. When comparing the ages of people, especially of members of a family, **elder** and **eldest** are often used, as adjectives and pronouns. 在比较人的年龄时, 特别是对于家庭成员, 经常使用**elder**和**eldest**, 用作形容词和代词. They cannot be used with *than* and as adjectives they can only be used before the noun 这两个词不可与than连用; 作形容词时, 只能用于名词前: *My elder sister lives in Canada.* 我姐姐住在加拿大. ○ *He was the elder of her two sons.* 他是她两个儿子中的长子. ○ *I'm the eldest in the family.* 我是全家年纪最大的.

el·der[2] /'eldə(r); 'ɛldɚ/ *n* any of several types of small tree with scented white flowers and red or black berries 接骨木.

□ **elderberry** /'eldəbrɪ; *US* 'eldərˌberɪ; 'ɛldɚˌbɛrɪ/ *n* fruit of an elder 接骨木浆果. **,elderberry 'wine** wine made from these berries 接骨木浆果酒.

eld·erly /'eldəlɪ; 'ɛldɚlɪ/ *adj* (*often euph* 常作委婉语) (of people) rather old; past middle age (指人)相当老的, 过了中年的, 上了年纪的: *He's very active for an elderly man.* 按老年人来说, 他非常活跃. ⇨Usage at OLD 用法见 OLD.

eld·est /'eldɪst; 'ɛldɪst/ *adj* [attrib 作定语], *n* (of people, esp of three or more closely related members of a family) first-born; oldest (指人, 尤指家中同辈的至少三个成员中的)第一个出生的, 年长的: *Jill is my eldest daughter.* 吉尔是我的长女. ○ *Jill is the eldest of my three children.* 吉尔是我三个孩子中年龄最大的. ○ *Jill is the eldest of three*, ie the oldest child in a family with three children. 吉尔是一家三个孩子中最大的. ○ *Jill is my eldest.* 吉尔是我的大孩子. ⇨Usage at ELDER[1] 用法见 ELDER[1].

el·dor·ado /ˌeldə'rɑːdəʊ; ˌɛldə'rɑdo/ *n* (*pl* **~s**) imaginary land or city rich in precious metals 想像中的黄金国或黄金市.

elect /ɪ'lekt; ɪ'lɛkt/ *v* **1** [Tn, Tn·pr, Cn·n, Cn·t] **~ sb (to sth)** choose sb by vote 选举某人: *They elected a new president.* 他们选举出一位新总统. ○ *She was elected to parliament last year.* 她去年被选进议会. ○ *We elected James (to be) chairman.* 我们选出詹姆斯当主席. **2** [Tt] (*fml* 文) choose or decide (to do sth) 选择或决定(做某事): *She elected to become a lawyer.* 她决定当律师.

▷ **elect** *adj* (after the *n*) chosen for a position but not yet occupying it (在名词后)当选而尚未就职的: *the president elect* 候任总统.

the elect *n* [pl *v*] (*fml* 文) people specially selected as the best 特别精选出来的人.

elec·tion /ɪ'lekʃn; ɪ'lɛkʃən/ *n* [U, C] (instance of) choosing or selection by vote (of candidates for a position, esp a political office) 选举(尤指从政): *In America, presidential elections are held every four years.* 美国总统选举每四年举行一次. ○ *He's standing for election.* 他是候选人. ○ [attrib 作定语] *the election results* 选举结果.

▷ **elec·tion·eer·ing** /ɪˌlekʃə'nɪərɪŋ; ɪˌlɛkʃən'ɪrɪŋ/ *n* [U] activity of trying to influence voters in an election by canvassing, making speeches, etc 竞选活动.

elect·ive /ɪ'lektɪv; ɪ'lɛktɪv/ *adj* **1** [usu attrib 通常作定语] having the power to elect 有选举权的: *an elective assembly* 有选举权的大会. **2** chosen or filled by election 选任的; 由选举产生的: *an elective office* 选任的职位. **3** (esp of an American university course, etc) not compulsory; optional (尤指美国大学课程等)非强迫的, 任选的, 选修的: *elective subjects* 选修科目. **4** not urgently necessary 非急需的: *elective surgery* 非急需施行的手术.

▷ **elect·ive** *n* (*esp US*) optional course or subject studied at school or college 学校的选修课或选修科目: *She is taking French as an elective next year.* 她明年选修法语.

elector /ɪ'lektə(r); ɪ'lɛktɚ/ *n* person who has the right to vote in an election 有选举权的人; 选民: *Many electors didn't vote today because of the bad weather.* 由于天气恶劣, 许多选民今天没有投票.

▷ **elect·oral** /ɪ'lektərəl; ɪ'lɛktərəl/ *adj* [attrib 作定语] of elections or electors 选举的; 选民的: *the electoral register/roll*, ie list of the electors in an area 选民登记册 ○ *In the USA the Electoral College elects the president.* 美国总统由总统选举团选举产生.

elect·or·ate /ɪ'lektərət; ɪ'lɛktərɪt/ *n* [CGp] all the qualified electors considered as a group 全体选民: *The electorate is/are disillusioned.* 全体选民大失所望.

elec·tric /ɪ'lektrɪk; ɪ'lɛktrɪk/ *adj* **1** [attrib 作定语] (**a**) producing electricity 发电的: *an electric generator* 发电机. (**b**) produced by electricity 由电产生的: *an electric current* 电流. ⇨App 11 见附录11. (**c**) used in the conveying of electricity 用于导电的: *an electric plug, socket, flex, etc* 电源插头、插座、皮线等. (**d**) using electrical power 使用电力的: *an electric cooker, iron, light, etc* 电炉、电熨斗、电灯等. **2** (*fig* 比喻) causing sudden excitement, esp in a group of people 使人(尤指人群)突然兴奋的: *an electric atmosphere* 令人激动的气氛 ○ *The news had an electric effect.* 这消息顿时使群情激昂.

□ **eˌlectric 'blanket** blanket that is warmed electrically 电热毯.

the eˌlectric 'chair (in the US) chair in which criminals are executed by electrocution (美国)电椅(以电刑处死罪犯的椅子).

eˌlectric 'eye (*infml* 口) = PHOTOELECTRIC CELL

(PHOTOELECTRIC).

e,lectric 'field (*physics* 物) area near an electric charge, in which a force is exerted on another charged particle 电场.

e,lectric 'razor = SHAVER (SHAVE).

e,lectric 'shock (also **shock**) effect of a sudden discharge of electricity through the body 触电; 电休克; 电震; 电击: *I got an electric shock from that faulty light switch.* 那个有毛病的电灯开关把我电了一下.

e,lectric 'storm violent atmospheric disturbance that produces electricity 电暴.

elec·trical /ɪ'lektrɪkl; ɪ'lɛktrɪkl/ *adj* of or concerned with electricity 电的; 与电有关的: *electrical engineering* 电机工程 ○ *This machine has an electrical fault.* 这台机器有电器故障. ▷ **elec·tric·ally** /-klɪ; -klɪ/ *adv*: *an electrically powered drill* 电钻.

elec·tri·cian /ɪ,lek'trɪʃn; ɪ,lɛk'trɪʃən/ *n* person whose job is to install, operate, repair, etc electrical equipment 电工: *Our washing machine has broken; I'll ring the electrician.* 我们的洗衣机坏了, 我得给电工打电话. ○ *We need an electrician to mend the iron.* 我们要请电工修理熨斗.

elec·tri·city /ɪ,lek'trɪsətɪ; ɪ,lɛk'trɪsətɪ/ *n* [U] **1** form of energy occurring in certain particles (electrons and protons) and hence in larger bodies, since they contain these 电. **2** supply of such energy in the form of electric current for lighting, heating, driving machines, etc 电流: *Don't leave the lights on — it wastes electricity.* 走时要随手关灯——以免浪费电. ○ *When did the village first get electricity?* 这个村何时通的电? **3** branch of science concerned with the study of this form of energy 电学.

elec·trify /ɪ'lektrɪfaɪ; ɪ'lɛktrə,faɪ/ *v* (*pt, pp* **-fied**) [Tn] **1** charge (sth) with electricity 给(某物)充电. **2** convert (a railway, etc) to the use of electric power 使(铁路等)改用电力; 使电气化. **3** (*fig* 比喻) stimulate (sb) as if by electricity; excite suddenly; startle 犹如以电刺激(某人); 使突然兴奋; 使吃惊: *the athlete's electrifying burst of speed* 运动员惊人的爆发速度.

▷ **elec·tri·fica·tion** /ɪ,lektrɪfɪ'keɪʃn; ɪ,lɛktrəfə'keʃən/ *n* [U] conversion to electricity 电气化: *the electrification of the railways*, ie from steam to electricity 铁路的电气化.

electr(o)- *comb form* 构词成分 of electricity 电的: *electrocardiogram* ○ *electrolysis*.

elec·tro·car·dio·gram /ɪ,lektrəʊ'kɑ:dɪəʊgræm; ɪ'lɛktro'kɑrdɪə,græm/ *n* (*abbr* 缩写 **ECG**) (*medical* 医) record of sb's heartbeat traced by an electrocardiograph, used in the diagnosis of heart disease 心电图.

elec·tro·car·dio·graph /,ɪlektrəʊ'kɑ:dɪəʊgrɑ:f; *US* -græf; ɪ'lɛktro'kɑrdɪə,græf/ *n* (*medical* 医) instrument that detects and records the electric activity in the muscles of the heart 心电图仪.

elec·tro·chem·istry /ɪ,lektrəʊ'kemɪstrɪ; ɪ,lɛktro'kɛmɪstrɪ/ *n* [U] application of electricity to chemical processes 电化学.

elec·tro·cute /ɪ'lektrəkju:t; ɪ'lɛktrə,kjut/ *v* [Tn usu passive 通常用于被动语态] kill (a person or an animal) by means of an electric current 电死(人或动物); 以电刑处死. ▷ **elec·tro·cu·tion** /ɪ,lektrə'kju:ʃn; ɪ,lɛktrə'kjuʃən/ *n* [U].

elec·trode /ɪ'lektrəʊd; ɪ'lɛktrod/ *n* (often *pl* 常作复数) either of two solid conductors by which an electric current enters or leaves a battery, etc; terminal 电极. Cf 参看 ANODE, CATHODE.

elec·tro·en·ceph·alo·graph /ɪ,lektrəʊen'sefələ,grɑ:f; *US* -græf; ɪ,lɛktroɛn'sɛfələ,græf/ *n* instrument for detecting and recording the electric current produced by the activity of the brain 脑电图仪.

▷ **elec·tro·en·ceph·alo·gram** /ɪ,lektrəʊen'sefələgræm; ɪ,lɛktroɛn'sɛfələ,græm/ *n* (*abbr* 缩写 **EEG**) pattern traced by an electroencephalograph 脑电图.

elec·tro·lysis /,ɪlek'trɒləsɪs; ɪ,lɛk'trɑləsɪs/ *n* [U] **1** separation of a substance into its chemical parts by an electric current 电解. **2** destruction of hair roots, tumours, etc by an electric current (for cosmetic or surgical reasons) 用电针除去发根、肿瘤等.

elec·tro·lyte /ɪ'lektrəlaɪt; ɪ'lɛktrə,laɪt/ *n* [C, U] (substance that can dissolve to produce a) solution able to conduct electric current, esp in an electric cell or battery 电解液; 电解质.

elec·tro·mag·net /ɪ,lektrəʊ'mægnɪt; ɪ,lɛktro'mægnɪt/ *n* (*physics* 物) piece of soft metal that becomes magnetic when an electric current is passed through the coil surrounding it 电磁铁; 电磁体.

▷ **elec·tro·mag·netic** /ɪ,lektrəʊmæg'netɪk; ɪ'lɛktromæg'nɛtɪk/ *adj* (*physics* 物) having both electrical and magnetic properties 电磁的: *electromagnetic waves*, eg X-rays, radio-waves, light waves 电磁波(如X射线、无线电波、光波). **elec·tro·mag·net·ism** *n* [U].

elec·tron /ɪ'lektrɒn; ɪ'lɛktrɑn/ *n* [C] (*physics* 物) minute particle of matter with a negative electric charge, found in all atoms 电子. Cf 参看 NEUTRON, POSITRON, PROTON.

▷ **elec·tronic** /,ɪlek'trɒnɪk; ɪ,lɛk'trɑnɪk/ *adj* [attrib 作定语] **1** (**a**) produced or operated by a flow of electrons 电子的: *an electronic calculator* 电子计算器. (**b**) concerned with electronic apparatus (eg computers) 与电子装置有关的(如计算机): *This dictionary is available in electronic form.* 这部词典有电子版本. ○ *electronic music*, ie produced by manipulating natural or artificial sounds with electronic equipment 电子音乐. **2** of or concerned with electrons or electronics 电子的; 电子学的; 关于电子的; 关于电子学的: *an electronic engineer* 电子工程师. **elec·tron·ic·ally** /-klɪ; -klɪ/ *adv*: *process data electronically*, ie using a computer 用电子计算机处理数据. ,**electronic 'mail** (also **email, e-mail**) sending text, diagrams, etc by means of computers linked to a telecommunication network 电子邮递(用计算机网络发送电文、图像等). ,**electronic 'mailbox** device for receiving and storing electronic mail 接受、储存电子邮递的装置.

elec·tron·ics *n* [sing *v*] **1** branch of science and technology that deals with the behaviour of electrons 电子学. **2** application of this, esp in developing equipment 电子学的应用: *He's an expert in electronics.* 他是电子应用专家. ○ [attrib 作定语] *the electronics industry* 电子工业.

□ **e,lectron 'microscope** very powerful microscope that uses beams of electrons instead of light rays 电子显微镜.

elec·tro·plate /ɪ'lektrəpleɪt; ɪ'lɛktrə,plet/ *v* [Tn usu passive 通常用于被动语态] cover (sth) with a thin layer of metal, usu silver, by electrolysis 电镀: *electroplated spoons* 电镀的勺.

el·eg·ant /'elɪgənt; 'ɛləgənt/ *adj* tasteful and stylish in appearance or manner (相貌或仪态)优雅的, 文雅的, 高雅的: *an elegant woman, coat, style of writing* 文雅的女人、高雅的外衣、优美的写作风格 ○ *elegant manners* 优雅的仪态. ▷ **el·eg·ance** /'elɪgəns; 'ɛləgəns/ *n* [U]. **el·eg·antly** *adv*: *He always dresses elegantly.* 他总是穿得很讲究.

ele·giac /,elɪ'dʒaɪək; ,ɛlə'dʒaɪək/ *adj* **1** (of poetic metre) suitable for elegies (指诗歌韵律)适于挽歌的: *elegiac couplets* 挽歌对句. **2** (*fml* 文) mournful; expressing sorrow 哀悼的; 表示悲伤的: *Her poetry has an elegiac quality.* 她的诗有伤感的情调.

elegy /'elədʒɪ; 'ɛlədʒɪ/ *n* poem or song expressing sorrow, esp for the dead; lament 挽歌; 哀歌; 挽诗.

ele·ment /'elɪmənt; 'ɛləmənt/ *n* **1** [C] **~ (in/of sth)** necessary or characteristic part of sth 要素; 特色: *Justice is an important element of good government.* 公正是仁政的要素. ○ *What a sensational story! It has all the elements of a soap opera.* 多么耸人听闻的事! 具备连续剧的一切要素. **2** [C usu *sing* 通常作单数] **~ of sth** small amount of sth; suggestion or trace of sth 某事物的少量; 某事物的启示或痕迹: *There's an element of truth in his story.* 他说的有些道理. ○ *There's always an element of danger in mountain climbing.* 登山总是有些危险的. **3** [C] (*chemistry* 化) any of about 100 substances which cannot be split by ordinary chemical methods into simpler substances 元素: *Water is composed of the elements hydrogen and oxygen.* 水是由氢元素和氧元素组成的. Cf 参看 COMPOUND[1] 1, MIXTURE 3. **4** [C] (according to ancient and medieval philosophers) any of the four substances, earth, air, fire and water, from which the universe was believed to be composed 要素(据古代和中世纪哲学家的观点, 认为构成宇宙的土、空气、火、水四种物质其中之一). **5 the elements** [pl] (*fml* 文) forces of nature, the weather, etc (esp bad weather) 自然力, 天气等(尤指坏天气): *exposed to (the* *fury of) the elements* 经受风吹雨打. **6** [C usu *sing* 通常作单数] natural or suitable environment or habitat 自然的或合适的环境或栖息地: *Water is a fish's natural element.* 水是鱼的自然栖息地. **7 elements** [pl] basic principles of a subject being studied; parts that must be learnt first (学科的)基本原则; 原理; 基础: *You must understand the elements of mathematics before we can proceed further.* 你必须先弄懂数学基础知识, 我们才能进一步学习. **8** [C] part of an electric kettle, etc that gives out heat 电阻丝(电壶等供热的部分): *This heater needs a new element.* 这个加热器需要一组新电阻丝. **9** (idm 习语) **in/out of one's ˈelement** in/not in one's accustomed or preferred surroundings; doing/not doing what one is good at and enjoys 在[不在]某人习惯或喜欢的环境中; 做[不做]某人擅长和喜欢的事: *I'm out of my element in political discussions.* 我不喜欢参加政治讨论. ○ *The children are really in their element playing on the beach.* 孩子们在沙滩上嬉戏真是乐得其所.

▷ **ele·mental** /ˌelɪˈmentl; ˌɛləˈmɛntl/ *adj* [esp attrib 尤作定语] **1** (*fml* 文) powerful; uncontrolled; like the forces of nature 强劲的; 失去控制的; 似自然力的: *the elemental fury of the storm* 暴风雨的肆虐. **2** basic 基本的: *an elemental truth* 基本事实.

ele·ment·ary /ˌelɪˈmentrɪ; ˌɛləˈmɛntərɪ/ *adj* **1** [attrib 作定语] **(a)** of or in the beginning stages (of a course of study) (一门课程的)入门阶段的, 初级的: *an elementary class* 初级班. **(b)** dealing with the simplest facts (of a subject); basic (一科目)基础的, 基本的: *elementary mathematics* 基础数学. **2** easy to solve or answer 容易解决的; 容易回答的: *The questions were so elementary that he easily passed the test.* 问题很好答, 他轻而易举就及格了.

□ ˌ**elementary** ˈ**particle** (*physics* 物) any of the subatomic particles thought not to consist of smaller particles 基本粒子.

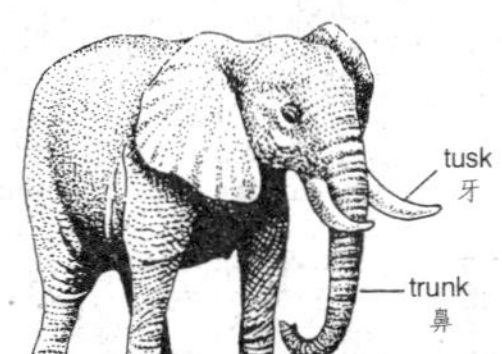

elephant 象

ele·phant /ˈelɪfənt; ˋɛləfənt/ *n* (*pl* unchanged or **~s** 复数或不变或作 **elephants**) **1** largest four-footed animal now living, with two curved ivory tusks, thick skin, and a long trunk 象: *a herd of elephant* 象群. ⇨illus 见插图. **2** (idm 习语) ˌ**elephants** ˌ**never** ˈ**forget** (*saying* 谚) elephants are noted for their good memories 象不忘事(象以记忆力良好著称). **a white elephant** ⇨ WHITE.

▷ **ele·phant·ine** /ˌelɪˈfæntaɪn; *US* -tiːn; ˌɛləˈfæntin/ *adj* (*derog or joc* 贬或谑) large and awkward like an elephant 似象一样大而笨拙的: *Their daughter is quite plump but their son is positively elephantine.* 他们的女儿很胖; 可是儿子呢, 简直像大象.

ele·phanti·asis /ˌelɪfənˈtaɪəsɪs; ˌɛləfənˋtaɪəsɪs/ *n* [U] disease, esp of tropical countries, in which limbs become abnormally enlarged and the skin thickens 象皮病(尤见于热带国家, 患者四肢异常肿大, 皮肤增厚).

el·ev·ate /ˈelɪveɪt; ˋɛləˌvet/ *v* [Tn, Tn·pr] **~ sb/sth (to sth)** (*fml* 文) **1** lift sb/sth up; raise sb/sth to a higher place or rank 将某人[某物]举起; 将某人[某物]提到更高的地位: *He's been elevated to the peerage*, ie made a peer. 他已升为贵族. **2** (*fig* 比喻) make (the mind, morals, etc) better or more educated 使(思想、道德等)更好; 使更有修养: *The teacher hoped to elevate the minds of her young pupils by reading them religious stories.* 教师希望给小学生读宗教故事来提高他们的修养.

▷ **el·ev·ated** *adj* (*fml* 文) fine or noble 好的; 高尚的: *elevated language, sentiments, thoughts* 高尚的语言、情操、思想.

el·ev·at·ing *adj* (*fml or joc* 文或谑) improving the mind or morals; uplifting 提高思想或道德的; 引人向上的: *an elevating book, sermon* 提高修养的书、布道 ○ *The experience wasn't terribly elevating.* 这种事不太有教益吧.

□ ˌ**elevated** ˈ**railway** (*US* **elevated railroad**) (*esp US*) railway built on piers (usu above the streets, etc of a town) 高架铁路.

el·eva·tion /ˌelɪˈveɪʃn; ˌɛləˋveʃən/ *n* **1** [C, U] (*fml* 文) elevating or being elevated 提高; 被提高: *elevation to the peerage* 升为贵族. **2** [U] (*fml* 文) nobility or dignity 高尚; 高贵; 尊贵: *elevation of language, style, thought* 语言、风格、思想的高尚. **3** [C] **(a)** height (of a place), esp above sea-level (某地方的)高度(尤指海拔): *The city is at an elevation of 2 000 metres.* 这座城市海拔2 000米. **(b)** (*fml* 文) hill or high place 小山; 高地: *a small elevation of the ground* 地面上的小隆起处. **4** [C] (architect's plan or drawing of) one side of a building (drawn to scale) (按比例绘制的)建筑物的正视图; 立视图: *the front/rear/side elevation of a house* 一座房子的正面[后面/侧面]立视图. **5** [C] angle that the direction of sth (esp a gun or planet) makes with the horizontal (尤指炮或行星的)仰角: *The gun has an elevation of 45 degrees.* 这门炮的仰角为45度.

el·ev·ator /ˈelɪveɪtə(r); ˋɛləˌvetɚ/ *n* **1** (*US*) = LIFT. **2** one of two movable parts in the tail of an aircraft that are used to make it climb or dive (飞行器的)升降舵. **3** tall storehouse for grain 高大的谷物仓库. **4** machine like a continuous belt with buckets at intervals, used for raising grain, goods, etc 斗式皮带输送机(用于向高处输送粮食、货物等).

E

el·even /ɪˈlevn; ɪˋlɛvən/ *pron, det* 11; one more than ten 11, 十一(个). ⇨App 4 见附录4.

▷ **el·even** *n* **1** the number 11 ☆ 11;十一. **2** team of eleven players for football, hockey or cricket 十一个人组成的足球、曲棍球、板球队.

eleven- (in compounds 用以构成复合词) having eleven of the thing specified 有十一个...的: *an eleven-mile walk.*

el·ev·enth /ɪˈlevnθ; ɪˋlɛvənθ/ *pron, det* 11th; next after tenth 第11, 第十一(个). — *n* one of eleven equal parts of sth 十一分之一.

□ eˌ**leven-**ˈ**plus** *n* [sing] (*Brit*) (esp formerly) examination taken at the age of eleven, to decide which type of secondary school a child should go to (尤指旧时)十一岁少年中学入学试(以决定升入中等学校的种类).

For the uses of *eleven* and *eleventh* see the examples at *five* and *fifth*. 关于 eleven 和 eleventh 的用法见 five 和 fifth 词条中的示例.

el·ev·enses /ɪˈlevnzɪz; ɪˋlɛvənzɪz/ *n* [usu sing *v* 通常与单数动词连用] (*Brit infml* 口) snack and/or drink taken at about eleven o'clock in the morning 午前茶点(上午十一时左右吃的点心和[或]喝的饮料).

elf /elf; ɛlf/ *n* (*pl* **elves** /elvz; ɛlvz/) type of small fairy; mischievous little creature 小精灵、小妖精、小淘气.

▷ **elfin** /ˈelfɪn; ˋɛlfɪn/ *adj* of or like an elf 小精灵的; 似小妖精的: *elfin music* 小精灵的乐曲 ○ *She has elfin features.* 她貌似小精灵.

elf·ish /ˈelfɪʃ; ˋɛlfɪʃ/ (also **elv·ish**) *adj* mischievous 调皮的; 顽皮的: *an elfish smile* 调皮的微笑.

eli·cit /ɪˈlɪsɪt; ɪˋlɪsɪt/ *v* [Tn, Tn·pr] **~ sth (from sb)** (*fml* 文) draw (facts, a response, etc) from sb, sometimes with difficulty 从某人处诱出, 探出(事实、反应等): *elicit a reply* 诱出答案 ○ *At last we've elicited the truth from him.* 我们终于从他那里探得真相.

elide /ɪˈlaɪd; ɪˋlaɪd/ *v* [Tn] leave out the sound of (part of a word) when pronouncing it 读音时省略(词的部分)读音: *The 't' in 'postman' may be elided.* postman 中的 t 可以省略不读. Cf 参看 ELISION.

eli·gible /ˈelɪdʒəbl; ˋɛlɪdʒəbḷ/ *adj* **~ (for sth/to do sth)** suitable or fit to be chosen; having the right or proper qualifications 适宜被选中的; 有恰当资格的; 合格的: *eligible for a pension, a job, an award* 有资格领取养老金、得到工作、获得奖品 ○ *eligible for promotion, membership* 适宜提升、得到会员身分 ○ *eligible to join a club* 有资格加入俱乐部 ○ *an eligible young man*, eg one who would be a satisfactory choice as a husband 合意的

年轻人(如可做佳婿者).

▷ **eli·gib·il·ity** /ˌelɪdʒəˈbɪlətɪ; ˌɛlɪdʒəˈbɪlətɪ/ *n* [U] state of being eligible 适宜入选; 有资格; 合格: *Her qualifications and experience confirm her eligibility for the job.* 她的资历和经验决定她适宜做这项工作.

elim·in·ate /ɪˈlɪmɪneɪt; ɪˋlɪməˌnet/ *v* **1** [Tn, Tn·pr] **~ sb/sth (from sth)** remove (esp sb/sth that is not wanted or needed) 消除, 清除, 排除(尤指不必要或不需要的某人[某物]): *eliminate mistakes from one's writing* 消除文字中的错误 ○ *The police have eliminated two suspects (from their enquiry).* 警方(从调查中)已排除了两名受嫌疑的人. ○ *eliminate waste matter from the body* 从体内排出废物. **2** [Tn] (*infml* 口) kill (sb) ruthlessly 干掉(某人): *The dictator had eliminated all his political opponents.* 独裁者已将所有政敌干掉. **3** [esp passive 尤用于被动语态: Tn, Tn·pr] **~ sb (from sth)** exclude sb from further stages in a competition, through defeat, etc 淘汰某人: *He was eliminated (from the contest) in the fourth round.* 他在第四轮(从比赛中)被淘汰. ▷ **elim·ina·tion** /ɪˌlɪmɪˈneɪʃn; ɪˌlɪməˋneʃən/ *n* [U].

eli·sion /ɪˈlɪʒn; ɪˋlɪʒən/ *n* (**a**) [U] leaving out of the sound of part of a word in pronunciation, as in *we'll, don't* and *let's* 读音时省略一字的部分读音(如we'll、don't、let's). (**b**) [C] instance of this 省略部分读音. Cf 参看 ELIDE.

E

élite /eɪˈliːt; ɪˋlit/ *n* [CGp] (*often derog* 常作贬义) social group considered to be the best or most important because of their power, talent, wealth, etc (由于有权力、才能、财富等)被视为最好的或最重要的社会集团; 精英; 尖子: *the ruling, scientific élite* 掌权的、科学方面的精英 ○ [attrib 作定语] *an élite force, regiment* 精锐部队、团.

▷ **élit·ism** /eɪˈliːtɪzəm; eˋlitɪzəm/ *n* [U] (*often derog* 常作贬义) (belief in a) system, leadership, etc that aims at developing an élite 旨在培养精英的体制、领导等(的主张); 精英主义: *Many people believe that private education encourages élitism.* 许多人认为私人办学可助长精英主义.

élit·ist /-tɪst; -tɪst/ *n* (*often derog* 常作贬义) person who believes in élitism 精英主义者. — *adj* of the élite or élitism 精英的; 主张培养精英的: *an élitist attitude to life* 卓尔不群的生活态度.

elixir /ɪˈlɪksə(r); ɪˋlɪksɚ/ *n* [U, C] **1** imaginary substance with which medieval scientists hoped to change metals into gold or make people live for ever (中世纪科学家希望得到的)炼金药, 长生不老药: *the elixir of life* 长生不老药. **2** imaginary cure for all ills (想像中的)灵丹妙药, 万灵药.

Eliza·bethan /ɪˌlɪzəˈbiːθn; ɪˌlɪzəˋbiθən/ *adj* [usu attrib 通常作定语] of the time of Queen Elizabeth I of England (1558-1603) 英国女王伊丽莎白一世时代的(1558–1603): *Elizabethan drama* 英国女王伊丽莎白一世时代的戏剧 ○ *The Elizabethan age was a time of exploration and discovery.* 英国女王伊丽莎白一世时代是探索和发现的时代.

▷ **Eliza·bethan** *n* person who lived during the reign of Queen Elizabeth I 伊丽莎白女王一世时代的人: *Shakespeare was an Elizabethan.* 莎士比亚是伊丽莎白女王一世时代的人.

elk /elk; ɛlk/ *n* (*pl* unchanged or **~s** 复数或不变或作 **elks**) (*Brit*) (*US* **moose**) [C] one of the largest types of living deer, found in N Europe, N Asia, and N America 犴, 驼鹿, 赤鹿(产于北欧、亚洲北部和北美洲).

el·lipse /ɪˈlɪps; ɪˋlɪps/ *n* regular oval 椭圆.

▷ **el·liptic** /ɪˈlɪptɪk; ɪˋlɪptɪk/, **el·lipt·ical** /ɪˈlɪptɪkl; ɪˋlɪptɪkḷ/ *adjs* shaped like an ellipse 似椭圆的.

el·lip·sis /ɪˈlɪpsɪs; ɪˋlɪpsɪs/ *n* (*pl* **-pses** /-psiːz; -psiz/) [C, U] (*grammar*) (instance of) leaving out a word or words from (the grammatical structure of) a sentence when the meaning can be understood without it/them 省略(指语法结构中的词语省略而不影响原意者): *The sentence 'He is dead and I alive' contains an ellipsis, ie of the word 'am'.* 在 He is dead and I alive一句中有一处省略, 即 am 这个词. ⇨App 3 见附录 3.

▷ **el·lipt·ical** /ɪˈlɪptɪkl; ɪˋlɪptɪkl/ *adj* containing ellipsis 省略的: *an elliptical style of writing,* ie one that implies more than is actually said (意在言外的)省略的文风. **el·lipt·ic·ally** /-klɪ; -klɪ/ *adj.*

elm /elm; ɛlm/ *n* [C] (also ˈ**elm tree**) **1** tall deciduous tree with broad rough-edged leaves 榆树: [attrib 作定语] *an elm forest* 榆树林. **2** [U] its hard heavy wood 榆木: *This bench is made of elm.* 这条长凳是榆木制的.

elocu·tion /ˌeləˈkjuːʃn; ˌɛləˋkjuʃən/ *n* [U] art or style of speaking clearly and effectively, esp in public 演说的艺术或风格: [attrib 作定语] *elocution lessons* 演说艺术课.

▷ **elocu·tion·ary** /-ənərɪ; *US* -ənerɪ; -ənˌɛrɪ/ *adj* of elocution 演讲艺术的.

elocu·tion·ist /-ʃənɪst; -ʃənɪst/ *n* person who teaches or is an expert in elocution 演说术教师; 演讲艺术家.

elong·ate /ˈiːlɒŋgeɪt; *US* ɪˈlɔːŋ-; ɪˋlɔŋget/ *v* [Tn] make (sth) longer 使(某物)更长; 伸长; 拉长.

▷ **elong·ated** /ˈiːlɒŋgeɪtɪd; *US* ɪˈlɔːŋ-; ɪˋlɔŋgetɪd/ *adj* (made) long and thin; stretched out (被拉得)细长的; 伸长的: *elongated figures in a painting* 画中的细长的人.

elonga·tion /ˌiːlɒŋˈgeɪʃn; *US* -lɔːŋ-; ˌilɔŋˋgeʃən/ *n* (**a**) [U] making or becoming longer 拉长; 伸长; 延长. (**b**) [C] thing that has been made longer (esp a line in a drawing, etc) 被拉长之物(尤指绘图中的线等).

elope /ɪˈləʊp; ɪˋlop/ *v* [I, Ipr] **~ (with sb)** run away with a lover, esp to get married 私奔: *The young couple eloped because their parents wouldn't let them marry.* 这对年轻人因父母不让他们结婚而私奔了. ○ *He eloped with one of his students.* 他和他的学生私奔了.

▷ **elope·ment** *n* [C, U].

elo·quence /ˈeləkwəns; ˋɛləkwəns/ *n* [U] (skilful use of) expressive language, esp to impress or persuade an audience 口才; 雄辩: *The crowd were swayed by his eloquence.* 他能言善辩打动了群众.

▷ **elo·quent** /-ənt; -ənt/ *adj* (*fml* 文) having or showing eloquence 有口才的; 雄辩的: *an eloquent speaker, speech* 雄辩的演讲者、讲话. **elo·quently** *adv.*

else /els; ɛls/ *adv* **1** (with indefinite, interrogative or negative *prons* and *advs* 与不定代词、疑问代词或否定代词或副词连用) in addition to or apart from (that already mentioned) 除(已提到的)以外; 另外; 其他: *Did you see anybody else,* ie any other person(s)? 你见到其他人了吗? ○ *Have you anything else to do?* 你还有别的事做吗? ○ *Ask somebody else to help you.* 请别人帮帮你吧. ○ *That must be somebody else's* (ie some other person's) *coat; it isn't mine.* 那一定是别人的外衣, 不是我的. ○ *Nothing else* (ie I want nothing more), *thank you.* 不要别的了, 谢谢你. ○ *We went to the cinema and nowhere else,* ie to no other place. 我们去电影院了, 没到其他地方去. ○ *I've tried to phone her six times today; what else can I do?* 我今天已给她打了六次电话, 都没接通, 我还能做什么呢? ○ *Who else was at the party?* 聚会上还有谁? ○ *How else* (ie In what other way) *would you do it?* 你做这件事还有别的办法吗? ○ *We have a bit of bread and little/not much else,* ie not much more. 我们有一点面包, 没有什么别的了. **2** (idm 习语) **or else** (**a**) otherwise; if not 否则; 要不然: *Run or else you'll be late.* 快跑, 不然你要迟到了. ○ *He must be joking or else he's mad.* 他准是开玩笑, 要不就是疯了. (**b**) (*infml* 口) (used to express a threat or warning 用以表示威胁或警告): *Give me the money or else!* 把钱给我, 不然的话, 哼!

else·where /ˌelsˈweə(r); *US* -ˈhweər; ˋɛlsˌhwɛr/ *adv* in, at or to some other place 在别处; 到别处: *Our favourite restaurant was full, so we had to go elsewhere.* 我们喜欢的饭馆已客满, 所以我们只得到别处去.

ELT /ˌiː el ˈtiː; ˌi ɛl ˋti/ *abbr* 缩写 = (principles and practice of) English Language Teaching (to non-native speakers) (对英语并非母语的人的)英语教学(的原则和方法).

elu·cid·ate /ɪˈluːsɪdeɪt; ɪˋlusəˌdet/ *v* [I, Tn] (*fml* 文) make (sth) clear; explain 使(某事物)清楚; 解释; 阐明: *You have not understood; allow me to elucidate.* 你没理解, 让我解释一下. ○ *elucidate a problem, mystery* 阐明一问题、弄清一奥秘 ○ *The notes helped to elucidate the most difficult parts of the text.* 这些注释有助于弄清文中最难懂的部分. ▷ **elu·cida·tion** /ɪˌluːsɪˈdeɪʃn; ɪˌlusəˋdeʃən/ *n* [U] (*fml* 文): *This requires elucidation.* 此事需要解释清楚.

elude /ɪˈluːd; ɪˋlud/ *v* [Tn] **1** escape (sb/sth), esp by a trick or cleverness; avoid 躲避(某人[某事物])(尤指用计谋或智慧); 逃避: *elude one's enemies* 避开敌人 ○ *He eluded capture for weeks by hiding underground.* 他为免被捕躲藏了几个星期. **2** escape the memory or understanding of (sb) (某人)不记得, 不理解: *I recognize her face, but her name eludes me*, ie I can't remember it. 我认得她的脸, 但想不起她的名字了.

elu·sive /ɪˈlu:sɪv; ɪˈlusɪv/ *adj* **(a)** tending to escape or disappear; difficult to capture 逃避的; 躲避的; 难以捕捉的: *a most elusive criminal* 极难逮捕的罪犯. **(b)** difficult to remember or understand 难以记忆的; 难以理解的; 难以捉摸的: *an elusive perfume* 难以捉摸的香味 ○ *an elusive word* 难记的词.

elver /ˈelvə(r); ˈɛlvɚ/ *n* young eel 幼鳗.

elves *pl* of ELF.

Elys·ium /ɪˈlɪzɪəm; ɪˈlɪzɪəm/ *n* **(a)** (in Greek myths) home of the blessed after death (希腊神话中的)天堂. **(b)** place or state of perfect happiness 极乐世界; 乐土. ▷ **Elys·ian** /ɪˈlɪzɪən; ɪˈlɪʒɪən/ *adj*: *the Elysian fields* 福地.

'em /əm; əm/ *pron* (*infml* 口) = THEM: *Don't let 'em get away!* 别让他们跑掉!

em- ⇨ EN-.

ema·ci·ated /ɪˈmeɪʃɪeɪtɪd; ɪˈmeʃɪˌetɪd/ *adj* made thin and weak 瘦弱的; 憔悴的: *very emaciated after a long illness* 久病之后非常憔悴 ○ *an emaciated child* 瘦弱的孩子. ⇨ Usage at THIN 用法见 THIN. ▷ **ema·ci·ation** /ɪˌmeɪsɪˈeɪʃn; ɪˌmesɪˈeʃən/ *n* [U].

email (also **e-mail**) /ˈi:meɪl; ˈiˌmel/ *n* [U] = ELECTRONIC MAIL (ELECTRON).

em·an·ate /ˈeməneɪt; ˈɛməˌnet/ *v* [Ipr] **~ from sth/sb** (*fml or joc* 文或谑) come or flow from sth/sb 来自某物[某人]; 从某物[某人]处流出, 飘出: *The idea originally emanated from his brother.* 这个主意最初是他哥哥出的. ○ *Delicious smells were emanating from the kitchen.* 香味从厨房飘了出来. ▷ **em·ana·tion** /ˌeməˈneɪʃn; ˌɛməˈneʃən/ *n* [C, U]: *The place gave off a strong emanation of evil.* 这地方是罪恶的渊薮.

eman·cip·ate /ɪˈmænsɪpeɪt; ɪˈmænsəˌpet/ *v* [Tn, Tn·pr] **~ sb (from sth)** set sb free, esp from political, legal or social restrictions 解放某人(尤指摆脱政治、法律或社会的束缚): *emancipate slaves* 解放奴隶 ○ *Women are still struggling to be fully emancipated*, ie to be given the same rights, opportunities, etc as men. 妇女仍在为彻底解放而奋斗(以获得与男子同等的权利、机会等).

▷ **eman·cipa·tion** /ɪˌmænsɪˈpeɪʃn; ɪˌmænsəˈpeʃən/ *n* [U] **(a)** action of emancipating 解放: *the emancipation of women* 妇女的解放. **(b)** state of being emancipated 获得解放.

emas·cu·late /ɪˈmæskjʊleɪt; ɪˈmæskjəˌlet/ *v* [Tn] (*fml* 文) **1** remove the sexual organs of (a male animal); castrate 使(某雄性动物)去势; 阉割. **2** deprive (sb/sth) of force or strength; weaken 使(某人[某事物])失去力量; 削弱: *an emasculated law* 被削弱了的法律. ▷ **emas·cu·la·tion** /ɪˌmæskjʊˈleɪʃn; ɪˌmæskjəˈleʃən/ *n*.

em·balm /ɪmˈbɑ:m; *US also* -bɑ:lm; ɪmˈbɑm, ɪmˈbɑlm/ *v* [Tn] **1** preserve (a dead body) from decay by using spices or chemicals (用香料或药物)保存(尸体): *The Egyptians used to embalm the bodies of their dead kings and queens.* 埃及人以前用药物保存国王和王后的尸体. **2** make (sth) fragrant 使(某物)充满香气. ▷ **em·balmer** /ɪmˈbɑ:mə(r); ɪmˈbɑmɚ/ *n*. **em·balm·ment** /ɪmˈbɑ:mmənt; *US also* -bɑ:lm-; ɪmˈbɑmmənt, -bɑlm-/ *n* [U].

em·bank·ment /ɪmˈbæŋkmənt; ɪmˈbæŋkmənt/ *n* wall or ridge of earth, stone, etc made to keep water back or to carry a railway or road over low ground 防水堤; 堤岸; (铁路或公路的)路堤: *the Thames Embankment* 泰晤士河河堤.

em·bargo /ɪmˈbɑ:gəʊ; ɪmˈbɑrgo/ *n* (*pl* **~es** /-gəʊz; -goz/) [C, U] **~ (on sth)** official order that forbids sth, esp trade, the movement of ships, etc 禁令; 禁止贸易令; 禁止船舶行驶令; 封港令等: *a gold embargo*, ie one that restricts or forbids the buying or selling of gold 限制或禁止黄金买卖令 ○ *an embargo on trade with other islands* 禁止与其他岛屿贸易令 ○ *lift/raise/remove an embargo on sth*, ie start trading in sth again 取消对某物的交易禁令(重新开放对某物的贸易) ○ *place sth under (an) embargo*, ie do no trade in sth 禁止对某物进行贸易.

▷ **em·bargo** *v* (*pt, pp* **~ed** /-gəʊd; -god/) [Tn] **1** put an embargo on (sth) 禁止(船只)出入港口; 禁运(某物). **2** seize (ships, goods, etc) for use by the State 征用(船只、货物等).

em·bark /ɪmˈbɑ:k; ɪmˈbɑrk/ *v* **1** [I, Ipr, Tn] **~ (for...)** (cause sb/sth to) go or be taken on board a ship or an aircraft (使某人[某物])乘船; 上船; 登机: *Passengers with cars must embark first.* 带汽车的乘客必须先上船. ○ *We embarked for Calais at midday.* 我们中午乘船去加来. ○ *The ship embarked passengers and cargo at an Italian port.* 这艘船在意大利一个港口载客装货. **2** (phr v) **embark on sth** start or engage in (esp sth new or difficult) 开始或从事(尤指新的或难的事): *embark on a long journey* 开始漫长的旅行 ○ *He embarked on a new career.* 他开始从事一新事业.

▷ **em·barka·tion** /ˌembɑ:ˈkeɪʃn; ˌɛmbɑrˈkeʃən/ *n* [C, U] action or process of embarking 乘船; 装载; 开始; 从事: *the port of embarkation* 登船装货港.

em·bar·rass /ɪmˈbærəs; ɪmˈbærəs/ *v* [Tn esp passive 尤用于被动语态] **(a)** cause (sb) to feel self-conscious, awkward or ashamed 使(某人)觉得不自然、忸怩、尴尬或害羞: *I was embarrassed by his comments about my clothes.* 他评论我的衣服使我很尴尬. ○ *Are you trying to embarrass me?* 你是想让我难堪吗? **(b)** cause mental discomfort or anxiety to (sb) 使(某人)不安或焦虑: *embarrassed by lack of money* 因缺钱而苦恼 ○ *financially embarrassed* 拮据.

▷ **em·bar·rass·ing** *adj*: *an embarrassing incident, question, mistake* 令人困窘的事、问题、错误. **em·bar·rass·ingly** *adv*.

em·bar·rass·ment *n* **1** **(a)** [U] embarrassing or being embarrassed 窘; 倔促不安; 焦急; 忧患: *He suffered much embarrassment in his youth.* 他年轻时饱经忧患. **(b)** [C] person or thing that embarrasses 令人困窘、不安、焦虑的人或事物: *He's an embarrassment to his family.* 他是家中叫人为难的人. ○ *financial embarrassments* 财务困难. **2** (idm 习语) **an embarrassment of 'riches** too many good things to do, choose from, etc 好东西太多而难以处理、难以选择等.

em·bassy /ˈembəsɪ; ˈɛmbəsɪ/ *n* **1** (official residence of an) ambassador and his staff 大使及其官员; 大使馆全体成员; 大使馆: *the American embassy in London* 美国驻伦敦大使馆 ○ *He is with* (ie working at) *the French embassy.* 他在法国大使馆工作. ○ [attrib 作定语] *embassy officials* 大使馆官员. Cf 参看 CONSULATE 1, HIGH COMMISSION (HIGH[1]). **2** (*dated* 旧) deputation sent to a foreign government 派往外国政府的代表团: *send sb/go/come on an embassy (to sb)* 派遣某人去[来]任赴外国政府代表团的成员(去某人处).

em·battled /ɪmˈbætld; ɛmˈbætld/ *adj* **1** **(a)** (of an army, etc) drawn up and prepared for battle (指军队等)严阵以待的; 做好战斗准备的: *embattled troops* 严阵以待的部队. **(b)** in a condition of defence; fortified against attack 处于防御状态的; 设防以抵御攻击的: *the embattled city* 设防的城市. **2** (of a tower or building) having battlements (指城楼或建筑物)有雉堞的.

em·bed /ɪmˈbed; ɪmˈbɛd/ *v* **(-dd-)** [usu passive 通常用于被动语态: Tn, Tn·pr] **~ sth (in sth)** fix sth deeply and firmly (in a surrounding mass) 将某物深而牢地固定于(周围的物体中): *stones embedded in rock* 嵌在岩石中的石块 ○ *The arrow embedded itself in the wall.* 箭牢牢地扎进墙里. ○ (*fig* 比喻) *The idea became embedded in his mind.* 这想法在他头脑中根深蒂固.

em·bel·lish /ɪmˈbelɪʃ; ɪmˈbɛlɪʃ/ *v* [Tn, Tn·pr] **~ sth (with sth)** **1** make sth beautiful by adding ornaments, etc 美化、装饰或修饰某物: *a dress embellished with lace and ribbons* 有花边和饰带的连衣裙. **2** improve (a story, statement, etc) by adding often untrue details, eg to make it more interesting or amusing 渲染; 添枝加叶(如使之更有趣、更可笑): *He often embellishes the tales of his travels.* 他常给他的旅游趣闻添枝加叶.

▷ **em·bel·lish·ment** *n* **(a)** [U] embellishing or being embellished 装饰; 渲染; 润色: *the embellishment of a book, a building, a speech* 对书的修饰、建筑物的装饰、言语的润色. **(b)** [C] thing that embellishes; artistic addition 装饰之物; 艺术性的增添物: *a 16th-century church with 18th-century embellishments* 有18世纪艺术装饰的16世纪的教堂.

em·ber /ˈembə(r); ˈɛmbɚ/ *n* (usu *pl* 通常作复数) small piece of burning or glowing wood or coal in a dying fire 余烬: *Only the embers of the bonfire remained.* 那篝火只有余烬尚存. ○ (*fig* 比喻) *the dying embers of a former passion* 昔日激情的将熄的余烬.

E

em·bezzle /ɪmˈbezl; ɪmˋbɛzl̩/ *v* [Tn] use (money placed in one's care) in a wrong way to benefit oneself 盗用, 挪用(款项): *embezzle the pension fund* 挪用抚恤金 ○ *The treasurer embezzled £2 000 of the club's money.* 司库盗用了俱乐部2 000英镑.

▷ **em·bez·zle·ment** *n* [C, U] (instance of) embezzling 盗用; 挪用: *petty embezzlements* 少量的盗用公款 ○ *He was found guilty of embezzlement.* 他被判盗用公款罪.

em·bezz·ler /ɪmˈbezlə(r); ɪmˋbɛzlɚ/ *n* person who embezzles 盗用者; 挪用公款者.

em·bit·ter /ɪmˈbɪtə(r); ɪmˋbɪtɚ/ *v* [Tn usu passive 通常用于被动语态] fill (sb/sth) with bitter feelings 使(某人)苦恼; 使(某事物)令人苦恼: *embittered by repeated failures* 因屡次失败而苦恼. ▷ **em·bit·ter·ment** *n* [U] (*fml* 文).

em·bla·zon /ɪmˈbleɪzən; ɪmˋblezn̩/ (also **bla·zon**) *v* [Tn] decorate (sth) with heraldic or other devices 以纹章或其他方式装饰(某物): *a shield emblazoned with dragons* 饰有龙纹的盾牌. ▷ **em·bla·zon·ment** *n* [U].

em·blem /ˈembləm; ˋɛmbləm/ *n* object that represents sth; symbol 象征; 标志; 标记: *The dove is an emblem of peace.* 鸽子是和平的象征. ○ *The ring was important to her as an emblem of their love.* 这枚戒指是他们爱情的象征, 对她至为重要. ○ *The thistle is the emblem of Scotland.* 蓟是苏格兰的标志.

▷ **em·blem·atic** /ˌembləˈmætɪk; ˌɛmbləˋmætɪk/ *adj* [usu pred 通常作表语] **~ (of sth)** (*fml* 文) serving as an emblem; symbolic 用作象征; 作为标志.

E

em·body /ɪmˈbɒdɪ; ɪmˋbɑdɪ/ *v* (*pt, pp* **-died**) [Tn, Tn·pr] **~ sth (in sth)** (*fml* 文) **1** express or give visible form to (ideas, feelings, etc) 体现(想法、感情等); 使(想法、感情等)具体化: *To me he embodies all the best qualities of a teacher.* 在我看来, 他本身体现了教师应有的一切优秀品质. **2** include or contain sth 包括或含有某物: *The latest computer model embodies many new features.* 最新型的计算机具备许多新功能.

▷ **em·bodi·ment** /ɪmˈbɒdɪmənt; ɪmˋbɑdɪmənt/ *n* person or thing that embodies sth or is embodied 体现某事物的人或物; 体现; 化身: *She's the embodiment of kindness.* 她是慈祥的化身.

em·bolden /ɪmˈbəʊldən; ɪmˋboldn̩/ *v* [esp passive 尤用于被动语态: Tn, Cn·t] (*dated or fml* 旧或文) give courage or confidence to (sb) 给(某人)勇气或信心; 给(某人)壮胆; 鼓励: *emboldened by drink* 饮酒后壮了胆的 ○ *His success emboldened him to expand his business.* 他有了成就因而激发他进一步扩展业务.

em·bol·ism /ˈembəlɪzəm; ˋɛmbəˌlɪzəm/ *n* (*medical* 医) blockage of an artery or a vein caused by a clot of blood, an air-bubble, etc 栓塞.

em·boss /ɪmˈbɒs; *US* -ˈbɔːs; ɪmˋbɔs/ *v* [esp passive 尤用于被动语态: Tn, Tn·pr] **~ A with B/~ B on A** decorate (the surface of sth) with a raised design; create (a raised design) on the surface of sth 在(某物的表面)装饰隆起的图案; 在某物表面制出(隆起的图案): *an address embossed on notepaper* 凸印在信纸上的地址 ○ *embossed stationery* 有压印浮雕花的信笺 ○ *a leather briefcase embossed with one's initials* 饰有浮凸的姓名首字母的皮公事包.

em·brace /ɪmˈbreɪs; ɪmˋbres/ *v* **1** [I, Tn] take (a person, etc) into one's arms as a sign of affection 拥抱(某人): *They embraced (each other) warmly.* 他们(相互)热情拥抱. ○ *She embraced her son before leaving.* 她在离开前拥抱着儿子. **2** [Tn] (*fml* 文) accept or take (an idea, etc) willingly 欣然接受或采取(某意见等): *embrace Christianity* 信奉基督教 ○ *embrace an offer, opportunity* 欣然接受提议、把握机会. **3** [Tn] (of things) include (指物)包括, 包含: *The term 'mankind' embraces men, women and children.* '人类'一词包括男人、女人和儿童.

▷ **em·brace** *n* act of embracing 拥抱; 接受; 包括; 包含: *He held her in a warm embrace.* 他热情地拥抱她. ○ *She tried to avoid his embraces.* 她极力不让他拥抱她.

em·bras·ure /ɪmˈbreɪʒə(r); ɛmˋbreʒɚ/ *n* [C] (**a**) opening for a door or window, wider on the inside than the outside, in an interior wall, esp of an old castle 斜面墙(内宽外窄的门窗的开口)(尤指古城堡的). (**b**) similar opening in a castle, fort, etc for shooting through (城堡、要塞等的)炮眼, 枪眼, 射击孔.

em·broca·tion /ˌembrəˈkeɪʃn; ˌɛmbroˋkeʃən/ *n* [U] liquid for rubbing on the body to ease muscular aches, stiffness, etc; liniment (缓解肌肉疼痛、僵硬等的)搽剂; 涂抹油: *A bit of embrocation will soothe your bruised knee.* 用一点搽剂可使你那青肿的膝部消肿.

em·broider /ɪmˈbrɔɪdə(r); ɪmˋbrɔɪdɚ/ *v* **1** [I, Tn, Tn·pr] **~ A (on B)/~ B (with A)** decorate (cloth) with needlework (在布上)刺绣: *She embroiders very well.* 她很会刺绣. ○ *She embroidered flowers on the cushion (in gold thread).* 她(用金线)在垫子上绣花. ○ *She embroidered the cushion with flowers.* 她把垫子绣上了花. **2** [Tn] (*fig* 比喻) add untrue details to (a story, etc) to make it more interesting (给故事等)添枝加叶: *embroider the truth, the tale, the facts, etc* 对真相、故事、事实等添油加醋地渲染.

▷ **em·broid·ery** /-dərɪ; -dərɪ/ *n* [U] **1** decoration with needlework 刺绣: *a beautiful piece of embroidery* 一件美丽的刺绣制品 ○ *He's good at embroidery.* 他擅长刺绣. **2** (*fig* 比喻) untrue details added for effect (为增强效果而加的)虚构细节: *A little embroidery made the story quite entertaining.* 增加了一点虚构细节使得故事相当有趣.

em·broil /ɪmˈbrɔɪl; ɛmˋbrɔɪl/ *v* [esp passive 尤用于被动语态: Tn, Tn·pr] **~ sb/oneself (in sth)** get sb/oneself involved (in a quarrel or difficult situation) 使某人[自己]卷入(争吵或困境中): *I don't want to become embroiled in their arguments.* 我不想卷入他们的争论中. ○ *They are embroiled in a war against their will.* 他们违背自己的意愿卷入一场战争之中.

em·bryo /ˈembrɪəʊ; ˋɛmbrɪˌo/ *n* (*pl* **~s** /-əʊz; -oz/) **1** (**a**) young animal or plant in the early stages of its development before birth (or before coming out of its egg or seed) 胚; 胚胎; 萌芽时期: *an aborted embryo* 流产的胚胎. Cf 参看 FOETUS. (**b**) (*fig* 比喻) plan, scheme, etc in its very early stages 初步的计划、方案等: *an embryo of an idea* 一个想法的雏形 ○ [attrib 作定语] *The project is still at the embryo stage.* 这个计划仍在酝酿阶段. **2** (idm 习语) **in embryo** existing but undeveloped 已存在但尚未发展的: *My plans are still very much in embryo.* 我的计划在很大程度上仍在酝酿中.

▷ **em·bry·ology** /ˌembrɪˈɒlədʒɪ; ˌɛmbrɪˋɑlədʒɪ/ *n* [U] scientific study of the formation and development of embryos 胚胎学. **em·bry·olo·gist** *n* /ˌembrɪˈɒlədʒɪst; ˌɛmbrɪˋɑlədʒɪst/ expert in this 胚胎学家.

em·bry·onic /ˌembrɪˈɒnɪk; ˌɛmbrɪˋɑnɪk/ *adj* [usu attrib 通常作定语] in an early stage of development 在发育的最初阶段的; 胚胎的: *an embryonic foetus* 刚刚发育的胎儿 ○ (*fig* 比喻) *The scheme is still in its embryonic stage.* 此方案仍在酝酿阶段.

em·cee /ˌemˈsiː; ˌɛmˋsi/ *n* (*infml* 口) master of ceremonies; compère 司仪; (节目的)主持人: *Who was (the) emcee of the show last night?* 谁是昨晚节目的主持人? Cf 参看 MC 1.

▷ **em·cee** *v* (*pt, pp* **emceed**) [I, Tn] act as master of ceremonies for (an event) 做司仪; 做(节目)主持人; 主持(节目): *Who's emceeing (the show) tonight?* 今晚谁主持(演出)?

emend /ɪˈmend; ɪˋmɛnd/ *v* [Tn] remove errors from (eg a text before printing) 校改; 校正; 校订; 修正(如文稿): *emend a passage in a book* 校正书中的一段.

▷ **emenda·tion** /ˌiːmenˈdeɪʃn; ˌimɛnˋdeʃən/ *n* (**a**) [U] action of emending (对文稿等的)修正; 校改; 校正; 校订. (**b**) [C] thing that is emended (对文稿等)修正、校改、校正或校订的内容: *minor emendations to the official statement* 对正式声明的些微修正.

em·er·ald /ˈemərəld; ˋɛmərəld/ *n* bright green precious stone 祖母绿; 纯绿柱石; 绿宝石; 翡翠: *two diamonds and an emerald* 两枚钻石和一枚绿宝石 ○ [attrib 作定语] *an emerald ring* 翡翠戒指.

▷ **em·er·ald** *adj, n* [U] (also **emerald ˈgreen**) (of a) bright green colour 绿宝石色(的); 翡翠绿(色): *an emerald hat* 翠绿色的帽子.

emerge /ɪˈmɜːdʒ; ɪˋmɝdʒ/ *v* [I, Ipr] **~ (from sth)** **1** (**a**) come out or up (from water, etc) (从水中等)出来, 现出, 露出: *The swimmer emerged from the lake.* 游泳者从湖中出来. ○ *The moon emerged from behind the clouds.* 月亮从云层后露出. (**b**) come into view or prominence 显现; 显露: *He emerged as leader at the age of thirty.* 他三十岁时初露锋芒担任了领袖. **2** (of facts, ideas, etc) become known (指事实、意见等)暴露, 知悉: *No new evidence emerged during the enquiry.* 在调查过程中未发现新证据.

▷ **emer·gence** /-dʒəns; -dʒəns/ *n* [U] action of emerging 出来; 现出; 出现; 显现; 暴露: *her emergence as a well-known artist* 她脱颖而出成为著名艺术家.

emer·gent /-dʒənt; -dʒənt/ *adj* [usu attrib 通常作定语] in the process of emerging 在出现过程中的: *the emergent countries of Africa*, ie those becoming politically independent and modernized, etc 非洲的新兴国家(那些政治上逐步独立和现代化等的国家).

emer·gency /ɪˈmɜːdʒənsɪ; ɪˋmɝdʒənsɪ/ *n* **1** [C, U] sudden serious event or situation requiring immediate action 紧急事件; 紧急情况: *You should only use this door in an emergency.* 在紧急情况下才能使用这扇门. ○ *The government has declared a state of emergency*, eg because of war, a natural disaster, etc. 政府已宣布进入紧急状态. ○ [attrib 作定语] *the emergency exit* 紧急出口. **2** [U] (*US*) = CASUALTY 3: [attrib 作定语] *the emergency ward* 急诊病室.

emer·itus /ɪˈmerɪtəs; ɪˋmɛrətəs/ *adj* (often placed after the *n*, and having a capital in titles 常置于名词后, 作头衔用时大写) (of a university teacher, esp a professor) retired, but keeping his title as an honour (指大学教师, 尤指教授)退休而保留头衔的: *the emeritus professor of biology* 生物学荣誉退休教授 ○ *a professor emeritus* 荣誉退休教授 ○ *Emeritus Professor Johnson* 约翰逊荣誉退休教授.

em·ery /ˈemərɪ; ˋɛmərɪ/ *n* [U] hard metallic substance used (esp in powdered form) for polishing, smoothing and grinding 金刚砂; 刚玉粉.

□ ˈ**emery-board** *n* small strip of wood or cardboard covered in emery, used for filing the finger-nails 指甲砂锉.

ˈ**emery-paper** *n* paper coated with emery, used for smoothing rough surfaces 砂纸.

em·etic /ɪˈmetɪk; ɪˋmɛtɪk/ *n, adj* (medicine) causing vomiting 催吐的; 催吐剂: *He was given an emetic (medicine) after eating poisonous berries.* 他吃了有毒的浆果, 已给了他催吐剂.

emig·rate /ˈemɪgreɪt; ˋɛmə͵gret/ *v* [I, Ipr] **~ (from ...) (to ...)** leave one's own country to go and live in another 移居外国: *emigrate from Britain to Australia to find work* 从英国移居到澳大利亚寻找工作. Cf 参看 IMMIGRATE.

▷ **emig·rant** /ˈemɪgrənt; ˋɛməgrənt/ *n* person who emigrates 移居外国者; 移民: *emigrants to Canada* 移居加拿大的人 ○ [attrib 作定语] *emigrant labourers* 移民他国的劳工.

emig·ra·tion /͵emɪˈgreɪʃn; ͵ɛməˋgreʃən/ *n* [U, C]: *the mass emigration of refugees in wartime* 战时大规模的逃难移民 ○ [attrib 作定语] *emigration officials* 管理移民的官员.

émi·gré /ˈemɪgreɪ; *US* ͵emɪˈgreɪ; ˋɛmə͵gre/ *n* (*French* 法) person who has left his own country, usu for political reasons 移居外国的人, 逃亡者, 流亡者(通常指因政治原因): *He was one of the émigrés who left France after the French Revolution.* 他是法国革命后离开法国的流亡者.

em·in·ence /ˈemɪnəns; ˋɛmənəns/ *n* **1** [U] state of being famous or distinguished 卓越; 著名: *reach eminence as a doctor* 成为名医 ○ *rise to eminence in one's profession* 在职业上出人头地. **2** [C] (*dated or fml* 旧或文) piece of rising ground; hill 高地; 山丘. **3 Eminence** [C] title used of or to a cardinal 阁下(对红衣主教的尊称): *His/Your Eminence* 主教阁下 ○ *Their/Your Eminences* 列位主教阁下.

em·in·ent /ˈemɪnənt; ˋɛmənənt/ *adj* **1** (of a person) famous and distinguished (指人)著名的, 杰出的, 卓越的: *an eminent architect* 杰出的建筑师 ○ *He is eminent both as a sculptor and as a portrait painter.* 他既是著名的雕刻家又是杰出的肖像画家. **2** [usu attrib 通常作定语] (of qualities) remarkable; outstanding (指品质、特性)明显的; 显著的; 突出的: *a man of eminent goodness* 品德优良的人.

▷ **em·in·ently** *adv* obviously; outstandingly 明显地; 显著地; 突出地: *She seems eminently suitable for the job.* 她看来极适合做这项工作.

emir /eˈmɪə(r); əˋmɪr/ (also **amir**) *n* title of various Muslim rulers 埃米尔(对穆斯林统治者的尊称).

▷ **emir·ate** /eˈmɪəreɪt; əˋmɪrɪt/ *n* position, reign or lands of an emir 埃米尔的地位、统治或领地: *the United Arab Emirates* 阿拉伯联合酋长国.

emis·sary /ˈemɪsərɪ; ˋɛmə͵sɛrɪ/ *n* person sent to deliver a message (often an unpleasant or a secret one) or to conduct negotiations (常为传送棘手信息的)使者, 密使, 谈判者.

emis·sion /ɪˈmɪʃn; ɪˋmɪʃən/ *n* **1** [U] (*fml* 文) sending out or giving off (of light, heat, fumes, matter, fluid from the body, etc) (光、热、烟、气、分泌物、体液等的)散发, 发射, 发出: *the emission of light from the sun* 阳光的照射. **2** [C] thing that is sent out or given off; discharge 散发之物、发出之物; 流出物; 排泄物: *a nocturnal emission*, ie the discharge of semen during sleep 夜间遗精.

emit /ɪˈmɪt; ɪˋmɪt/ *v* (**-tt-**) [Tn] give or send (sth) out; discharge 发射, 放射, 发出(某物); 排出; 排泄: *A volcano emits smoke, lava and ashes.* 火山喷射出烟、熔岩和灰烬. ○ *She emitted a cry of pain.* 她发出痛苦的呼叫. ○ *The cheese was emitting a strong smell.* 干酪散发出强烈的气味.

emol·li·ent /ɪˈmɒlɪənt; ɪˋmalɪənt/ *n, adj* (substance) that soothes and softens the skin 润肤的; 润肤剂: *Use an emollient for dry skin.* 干燥的皮肤要使用润肤剂. ○ *an emollient cream* 润肤霜.

emolu·ment /ɪˈmɒljʊmənt; ɪˋmaljəmənt/ *n* (usu *pl* 通常作复数) (*fml or rhet* 文或修辞) profit made from being employed; fee or salary 报酬; 酬金; 工资; 薪水: *Her emoluments as a teacher amounted to £8 500 a year.* 她任教年薪 8 500 英镑. ○ *He was paid a modest emolument.* 他获酬甚微.

emo·tion /ɪˈməʊʃn; ɪˋmoʃən/ *n* **1** [C] strong feeling of any kind 激情; 情感; 情绪: *Love, joy, hate, fear and jealousy are all emotions.* 爱情、喜悦、憎恨、恐惧、嫉妒都是强烈的感情. ○ *The speaker appealed to our emotions rather than to our minds.* 演讲者激发了我们的情感而不是启发我们的思考. **2** [U] excitement or disturbance of the mind or (more usu) the feelings 激动; 感动: *overcome by/with emotion* 为情感所动 ○ *He spoke of his dead wife with deep emotion.* 他提到亡妻感慨万分. ○ *She answered in a voice filled with emotion.* 她以激动的声音回答.

▷ **emo·tional** /-ʃənl; -ʃənḷ/ *adj* **1** [attrib 作定语] of the emotions 情感的: *emotional problems* 情感问题. **2** causing or showing emotions 引起情感的; 表示情感的: *an emotional response* 富于情感的反应 ○ *emotional music, language* 抒情的乐曲、语言. **3** having emotions that are easily excited 易激动的; 易动感情的: *an emotional man, actor, character, nature* 易动感情的男子、演员、性格、天性 ○ *She is embarrassingly emotional in public.* 她在大庭广众前常激动得让人难为情.

emo·tion·ally /-ʃənəlɪ; -ʃənḷɪ/ *adv*: *emotionally disturbed* 情绪波动.

emo·tion·less *adj* without emotion 没有情感的; 冷漠的.

emo·tive /ɪˈməʊtɪv; ɪˋmotɪv/ *adj* (of words, etc) tending to affect the emotions (指词等)激发情感的: *an emotive speech* 激动人心的讲话 ○ *Capital punishment is an emotive issue.* 应否有死刑是个容易引起感情用事的问题.

em·panel (also **im·panel**) /ɪmˈpænl; ɪmˋpænḷ/ *v* (**-ll-**; *US also* **-l-**) [Tn] (*fml* 文) list or select (sb) to serve on a jury 将(某人)列入陪审员名单; 选(某人)为陪审员.

em·pathy /ˈempəθɪ; ˋɛmpəθɪ/ *n* [U] **1** ability to imagine and share another person's feelings, experience, etc 感情移入, 同感(对他人的感情、经历等的想像力和感受力): *There is a strange empathy between the old lady and her grandson.* 老妇人和她孙子间有种莫名其妙的心灵相通的感觉. **2** ability to identify oneself mentally with eg a work of art that one is looking at, and so to understand its meaning 神入(全神贯注于某事物如一艺术品, 以理解其真谛的能力).

em·peror /ˈempərə(r); ˋɛmpərɚ/ *n* (*fem* 阴性作 **empress** /ˈemprɪs; ˋɛmprɪs/) ruler of an empire 皇帝: *the Roman emperors* 罗马皇帝 ○ *The Emperor Napoleon* 拿破仑皇帝.

em·phasis /ˈemfəsɪs; ˋɛmfəsɪs/ *n* (*pl* **-ases** /-əsiːz; -əsiz/) [C, U] **1** force or stress given to a word or words when spoken, to make the meaning clear or to show importance 加强语气; 强调: *give special emphasis to a phrase* 对一词组加强语气. **2 ~ (on sth)** (placing of) special meaning, value or importance (on sth) (付予某事物)特殊的意义、价值或重要性: *Some schools put/lay/place great emphasis on language study.* 有些学校极注重语言学习. ○ *The emphasis here is on hard work, not enjoyment.* 这里至关重要的是努力工作, 而不是享乐.

▷ **em·phas·ize, -ise** /ˈemfəsaɪz; ˋɛmfə,saɪz/ *v* [Tn, Tf] put emphasis on (sth); give emphasis to (sth); stress 强调; 着重; 加强(某词语)的语气; 重读: *Which word should I emphasize?* 我应该重读哪个词? ○ *He emphasized the importance of careful driving/that careful driving was important.* 他强调小心驾驶的重要性[小心驾驶很重要].

em·phatic /ɪmˈfætɪk; ɪmˋfætɪk/ *adj* **1** having, showing or using emphasis 加强语气的; 强调的; 重视的; 重点的; 着重的; 重读的: *an emphatic denial* 断然的否认 ○ *He was most emphatic that I should go.* 他极力强调我应该去. **2** definite and clear 肯定的; 明确的; 显著的: *an emphatic victory* 有目共睹的胜利. **em·phat·ic·ally** /-klɪ; -klɪ/ *adv*.

em·phys·ema /ˌemfɪˈsiːmə; ˌɛmfɪˋsimə/ *n* [U] (*medical* 医) disease that affects the lungs and makes breathing difficult 气肿; 肺气肿.

E

em·pire /ˈempaɪə(r); ˋɛmpaɪr/ *n* **1** [C] group of countries or states under a single ruler or ruling power 帝国: *the Roman Empire* 罗马帝国. **2** [U] (*fml* 文) supreme political power 帝权; 绝对支配权: *the responsibilities of empire* 有绝对支配权的统治. **3** [C] (*fig* 比喻) large commercial organization controlled by one person or group (由一人或一集团控制的)大企业组织: *a publishing empire* 大出版企业.

□ ˈ**empire-building** *n* [U] (*often derog* 常作贬义) process of deliberately acquiring extra territory, authority, etc 扩张领土、权力等.

em·pir·ical /ɪmˈpɪrɪkl; ɛmˋpɪrɪkl̩/ *adj* (of knowledge) based on observation or experiment, not on theory (指知识)以观察或实验为根据的(非理论的). Cf 参看 TRANSCENDENTAL.

▷ **em·pir·ic·ally** /-klɪ; -klɪ/ *adv*.

em·piri·cism /ɪmˈpɪrɪsɪzəm; ɛmˋpɪrə,sɪzəm/ *n* [U] use of empirical methods 观察或实验方法的运用; 经验主义.

em·piri·cist /-sɪst; -sɪst/ *n* person who works in an empirical way 以观察或实验方法工作的人; 经验主义者.

em·place·ment /ɪmˈpleɪsmənt; ɪmˋplesmənt/ *n* prepared position or platform for a heavy gun or guns 炮位; 炮台.

em·ploy /ɪmˈplɔɪ; ɪmˋplɔɪ/ *v* [Tn, Tn·pr, Cn·n/a, Cn·t] **1 ~ sb (in/on sth); ~ sb (as sth)** give work to sb, usu for payment 雇用某人: *She hasn't been employed* (ie has not had a job) *for six months now.* 她现在已半年没有工作了. ○ *They've just employed five new waiters.* 他们刚刚雇用了五个新服务员. ○ *He's employed on the oil rigs.* 他受雇在油井钻塔工作. ○ *She's employed as a taxi driver.* 她受雇任计程车司机. ○ *They employed him to look after the baby.* 他们聘请他照料婴儿. **2 ~ sb/sth (in/on sth); ~ sth (as sth)** (*fml* 文) make use of sb/sth; occupy (time, attention, etc) 使用某人[某事物]; 利用(时间、注意力等): *You could employ your spare time better.* 你可以把闲暇时间利用得好些. ○ *He was busily employed in cleaning his shoes.* 他忙着擦鞋. ○ *He employed his knife as a lever.* 他把刀子当杠杆用. ○ *The police employed force to open the door.* 警方强行把门打开了.

▷ **em·ploy** *n* [U] (*fml* 文) service or employment 服务; 工作; 职业; 雇用; 受雇: *I left their employ after an argument.* 我与他们争吵之后就辞掉了工作. ○ *How long has she been in your employ* (ie employed by you)? 你雇用她多长时间了?

em·ploy·able /-əbl; -əbl̩/ *adj* [usu pred 通常作表语] that can be employed 可雇用; 可使用.

em·ployee /ˌemplɔɪˈiː, *also* ɪmˈplɔiː; ˌɛmplɔɪˋi, ɪmˋplɔɪ·i/ *n* person who works for sb or for a company in return for wages 受雇者; 雇工; 雇员: *The manager sacked three employees.* 经理开除了三名雇员.

em·ployer *n* person or company that employs others 雇用者; 雇主: *They're not good employers*, ie They treat their workers badly. 他们不是好雇主.

em·ploy·ment /ɪmˈplɔɪmənt; ɪmˋplɔɪmənt/ *n* [U] **1** (**a**) act of employing 雇用; 使用: *The expansion of the factory will mean the employment of sixty extra workers.* 工厂的扩展意味着将增雇六十名工人. (**b**) state of being employed 受雇用; 被使用: *be in/out of regular full-time employment* 有[没有]固定的全日工作. **2** occupation (esp regular paid work) 职业: *give employment to sb* 雇用某人 ○ *find employment* 找工作 ○ [attrib 作定语] *government employment office* 政府就业事务处. ⇨ Usage at TRADE[1] 用法见 TRADE[1].

□ **emˈployment agency** private business that helps people to find work and employers to find workers 职业介绍所.

em·por·ium /ɪmˈpɔːrɪəm; ɛmˋpɔrɪəm/ *n* (*pl* **-riums** or **-ria** /-rɪə; -rɪə/) (*joc or fml* 谑或文) (**a**) centre of trade; market 贸易中心; 市场. (**b**) (*esp US*) large shop 大商店.

em·power /ɪmˈpaʊə(r); ɪmˋpaʊɚ/ *v* [Cn·t esp passive 尤用于被动语态] (*fml* 文) give lawful power or authority (to sb) to act 授权(给某人)采取行动: *The new laws empower the police to stop anybody in the street.* 新法令授予警方可在街上截停任何人的权力. ○ *The lawyer was empowered to pay all her bills.* 已授权给律师偿付她的一切帐项.

emp·ress /ˈemprɪs; ˋɛmprɪs/ *n* (**a**) female ruler of an empire 女皇. (**b**) wife or widow of an emperor 皇后.

empty[1] /ˈemptɪ; ˋɛmptɪ/ *adj* **1** (**a**) having nothing inside 空的: *an empty box* 空盒子 ○ *an empty lorry*, ie one without a load 空卡车 ○ *Your glass is empty.* 你的杯子空了. (**b**) with nobody in it 空无一人的: *an empty house, room, chair, bus* 空着的房子、房间、椅子、公共汽车 ○ *empty streets* 空无一人的街道 ○ *The cinema was half empty.* 电影院空着一半. **2** (**a**) [pred 作表语] **~ of sth** without or lacking in (a quality) 没有或缺乏(某种性质): (*fml* 文) *words empty of meaning* 无意义的话. (**b**) without sense or purpose 没有感知的; 没有意义的; 没有目的的: *empty threats, words, promises, dreams* 虚张声势的恐吓、空话、空洞的许诺、虚幻的梦想 ○ *My life feels empty now the children have left home.* 因为孩子们已离开了家, 我感到生活很空虚. **3** (*infml* 口) hungry 饥饿的: *I feel jolly empty!* 我饿极了! **4** (idm 习语) **on an empty ˈstomach** having eaten nothing 空腹: *It's not good to drink on an empty stomach.* 空着肚子喝酒不好.

▷ **emp·ties** *n* [pl] (*infml* 口) empty bottles, boxes, crates, etc 空瓶子、空盒子、空木箱等: *Put your empties on the doorstep for the milkman.* 把空奶瓶放到门阶上, 等送奶人来取.

empti·ness /ˈemptɪnɪs; ˋɛmptɪnɪs/ *n* [U].

□ ˌ**empty-ˈhanded** *adj* [pred 作表语] bringing back or taking away nothing 空手: *They always arrive at parties empty-handed.* 他们总是空着手参加聚会. ○ *return empty-handed from an unsuccessful shopping trip* 这趟购物之行什么也没买成, 空手而归.

ˌ**empty-ˈheaded** *adj* (of people) foolish and without common sense (指人)愚蠢的, 无头脑的: *an ˌempty-headed young ˈidiot* 没头脑的小笨蛋.

NOTE ON USAGE 用法: **Empty** and **full** have wide uses. ☆ **empty** 和 **full** 的使用范围很广. Any container or building can be **full** (of things or people) or **empty** 任何容器或建筑物都可为 **full** (有物或人)或 **empty**: *The theatre was almost empty last night.* 剧院昨晚几乎是空的. ○ *This bottle was full yesterday and now it's empty.* 这个瓶子昨天是满的, 现在已经空了. **Vacant** and **occupied** relate to the long-term use of a building, etc ☆ **vacant** 和 **occupied** 指对建筑物等的长期使用: *There are some vacant offices on the third floor.* 四楼有几间空着的办公室. ○ *All the flats are occupied now.* 所有的单元现在都已住满. They can also refer to the short-term use of a room, etc. 这两个词也可指短期使用房间等: *The lavatory is vacant.* 厕所现在无人使用. ○ *All the seats are occupied.* 所有的座位都坐满了.

empty[2] /ˈemptɪ; ˋɛmptɪ/ *v* (*pt, pp* **emptied**) **1** (**a**) [Tn, Tn·pr, Tn·p] **~ sth (out) (onto/into sth); ~ sth (of sth)** make sth empty 将某物弄空: *empty one's glass into the sink* 把杯里的东西倒进洗涤槽里. ○ *empty (out) a* *drawer* 把抽屉腾空 ○ *He emptied his pockets of their contents.* 他把衣袋里的东西全都掏出来了. ○ *This dreadful film soon emptied the cinema of people.* 这部电影很没意思, 电影院里的人很快就都走光了. (**b**) [I, Ipr] **~ (of sb/sth)** become empty 变空: *The streets soon emptied (of people) when the rain started.* 下起雨来了, 街道很快便空无一人了. ○ *The cistern empties in five minutes.* 贮水池五分钟就流干. **2** (**a**) [Tn, Tn·pr, Tn·p] **~ sth (out) (into/onto sth)** remove (the contents of sth) and put them somewhere else 将某物中的东西取出置于他处: *Have you emptied (out) the rubbish?* 你倒垃圾了吗? ○ *She emptied the milk into the pan.* 她把牛奶倒进锅里. ○ *We emptied the waste paper onto the floor.* 我们把废纸倒在地板上. (**b**) [I, Ipr] **~ (from/out of sth) (into/onto sth)** flow or pour out 流出; 倒出: *The water slowly emptied (from the cistern).* 水(从贮水池)缓缓流出. ○ *The Rhone empties into the Mediterranean.* 罗讷河流入地中海. ○ *The rubbish from the cart emptied onto the street.* 垃圾从大车上倾倒到街上.

emu /ˈiːmjuː; ˋimju/ *n* large Australian bird that runs quickly but cannot fly 鸸鹋(产于澳洲的大型鸟, 善跑而不能飞翔).

emu·late /ˈemjʊleɪt; ˋɛmjəˌlet/ *v* [Tn, Tn·pr] **~ sb (at sth)** (*fml* 文) try to do as well as or better than sb 赶超某人; 与某人竞争: *emulate her sister's sporting achievements* 赶超她姐姐的运动成绩 ○ *emulate her elder sister at the piano* 在钢琴演奏上与她姐姐竞争.

▷ **emu·la·tion** /ˌemjʊˈleɪʃn; ˌɛmjəˋleʃən/ *n* [U] (*fml* 文) action or state of emulating 赶超; 竞赛; 竞争: *She worked hard in emulation of her elder sister.* 她努力赶超姐姐.

emul·sify /ɪˈmʌlsɪfaɪ; ɪˋmʌlsəˌfaɪ/ *v* (*pt, pp* **-fied**) [I, Tn] become an emulsion or make an emulsion of (sth) 乳化; 使(某物)乳化: *The sauce has emulsified.* 调味汁已经乳化了. ○ *emulsify the oil* 使油乳化.

emul·sion /ɪˈmʌlʃn; ɪˋmʌlʃən/ *n* [C, U] **1** creamy liquid in which particles of oil or fat are evenly distributed 乳状液. **2** medicine or paint in this form 乳剂; 乳漆: [attrib 作定语] *emulsion paint*, ie paint that has a matt rather than a glossy finish when dry 乳状漆(干后无光泽的漆). **3** light-sensitive substance on the surface of photographic film 感光乳剂.

en- (also **em-**) *pref* 前缀 **1** (with *ns* or *vs* forming *vs* 与名词或动词结合构成动词) put into or on 放进; 放上: *encase* ○ *endanger* ○ *empanel*. **2** (with *adjs* or *ns* forming *vs* 与形容词或名词结合构成动词) make into; cause to be 变成; 变得; 使成为: *enlarge* ○ *enrich* ○ *empower*.

-en *suff* 后缀 **1** (with *ns* forming *adjs* 与名词结合构成形容词) made of 由…制成: *golden* ○ *wooden*. **2** (with *adjs* forming *vs* 与形容词结合构成动词) make or become 使; 变得: *blacken* ○ *sadden*.

en·able /ɪˈneɪbl; ɪnˋebl̩/ *v* **1** [Cn·t] make (sb) able to do sth by giving him the necessary authority or means 使(某人)能够做某事物: *This pass enables me to travel half-price on trains.* 我用这张通行证坐火车半价. ○ *A rabbit's large ears enable it to hear the slightest sound.* 兔子耳朵大能听到极微小的声音. **2** [Tn] make (sth) possible 使(某事)成为可能: *The conference will enable greater international co-operation.* 这次会议能进一步促进国际间的合作.

en·act /ɪˈnækt; ɪnˋækt/ *v* **1** [Tn esp passive 尤用于被动语态] (*fml* 文) perform (a part, play, etc) on, or as if on, the stage of a theatre 演出(戏剧等); 展现: *a one-act drama enacted by children* 儿童演出的独幕剧 ○ *A strange ritual was enacted before our eyes.* 在我们眼前展现出一种奇特的仪式. **2** [Tn esp passive 尤用于被动语态, Tf] (*fml or law* 文或律) make or pass (a decree) 制定或通过(法令): *enacted by Parliament* 由议会制定的 ○ *Be it further enacted that*... 再进一步规定....

▷ **en·act·ment** *n* **1** [U] (*fml or law* 文或律) enacting 演出; 展现; 制定; 规定; 通过: *the enactment of the drama* 该剧的演出 ○ *the enactment of the new bill* 新法案的制定. **2** [C] law 法律; 法令; 法规: *The enactment states that*... 法律规定....

en·amel /ɪˈnæml; ɪˋnæml̩/ *n* [U] **1** glass-like substance used for coating metal, pottery, etc for decoration or as protection 搪瓷; 珐琅; 瓷釉: *Some of the enamel on this pan is chipped off.* 这平底锅上的搪瓷有些已脱落. ○ [attrib 作定语] *enamel ware*, ie manufactured goods such as pots, pans, etc with hard enamel surfaces 搪瓷器皿 ○ *enamel paint*, ie paint that dries to make a hard glossy surface 瓷漆. **2** hard outer covering of teeth (牙齿的)珐琅质. ⇨illus at TOOTH 见 TOOTH 之插图.

▷ **en·amel** *v* (**-ll-**; *US also* **-l-**) [Tn] cover or decorate (sth) with enamel 给(某物)涂上瓷釉: *enamelled jewellery* 带瓷釉的首饰.

en·am·oured (*US* **en·am·ored**) /ɪˈnæməd; ɪnˋæmɚd/ *adj* [pred 作表语] **~ of/with sth** (*fml or joc* 文或谑) fond of or delighted by sth 喜欢某事物; 倾心于某事物: *enamoured of the sound of one's own voice* 陶醉于自己的嗓音 ○ *I'm not too enamoured with the idea of spending a whole day with him.* 我可不太喜欢一整天都跟他在一起.

en bloc /ˌɒn ˈblɒk; ɑnˋblɑk/ (*French* 法) all together; all at the same time 一起; 同时: *They left the meeting en bloc.* 他们一起离开了会场.

en·camp /ɪnˈkæmp; ɪnˋkæmp/ *v* [I, Tn esp passive 尤用于被动语态] settle in camp 扎营; 野营; 露营: *The soldiers are encamped in the forest.* 士兵在森林里安营. ○ (*fig* 比喻) *The strikers have been encamping outside the factory for weeks.* 罢工者数周来都在工厂外宿营.

▷ **en·camp·ment** *n* place where troops, etc are encamped 部队等的营地.

en·cap·sul·ate /ɪnˈkæpsjʊleɪt; ɪnˋkæpsəˌlet/ *v* [Tn, Tn·pr] **~ sth (in sth)** (*fml* 文) **1** enclose sth (as if) in a capsule (似)用胶囊包某物: *This story encapsulates scenes from his childhood.* 这个故事讲的是他童年的事. **2** express sth briefly; summarize sth 简述某事; 总结某事: *The chairman's short statement encapsulates the views of the committee.* 主席的简短陈辞概括了委员会的观点.

en·case /ɪnˈkeɪs; ɪnˋkes/ *v* [esp passive 尤用于被动语态: Tn, Tn·pr] **~ sth (in sth)** (*fml* 文) surround or cover sth (as) with a case (似)将某物置于箱、盒、套等之中: *His broken leg was encased in plaster.* 他折的腿打上了石膏.

-ence ⇨ -ANCE.

en·ceph·al·itis /ˌenkefəˈlaɪtɪs; ˌɛnsɛfəˋlaɪtɪs/ *n* [U] inflammation of the brain 脑炎.

en·chant /ɪnˈtʃɑːnt; *US* -ˈtʃænt; ɪnˋtʃænt/ *v* [Tn] fill (sb) with great delight 使(某人)极喜悦; 使(某人)陶醉: *enchanted by/with the singing of the children* 被孩子们的歌声迷住.

▷ **en·chanted** /-ɪd; -ɪd/ *adj* placed under a magic spell 中魔法的: *an enchanted garden*, eg in a fairy story 施过魔法的花园(如于童话故事中).

en·chanter *n* person who enchants 迷人的人; 施魔法的人.

en·chant·ing *adj* delightful 令人喜悦的; 迷人的; 可爱的: *What an enchanting little girl!* 多么可爱的小姑娘!

en·chant·ingly *adv*.

en·chant·ment *n* **1** [U] being enchanted 心醉; 销魂; 着迷. **2** [C] thing that enchants 令人心醉、销魂或着迷之物. **3** [U] delight 乐趣: *Dancing has lost all its enchantment for her.* 她已完全失去跳舞的乐趣.

en·chant·ress *n* /-trɪs; -trɪs/ woman who enchants or is enchanting 迷人的女子; 施魔法的女子: *seduced by an enchantress* 受一迷人女子的诱惑.

en·circle /ɪnˈsɜːkl; ɪnˋsɝkl̩/ *v* [Tn esp passive 尤用于被动语态] form a circle round; surround 环绕; 围绕; 包围: *a lake encircled by trees* 树木环绕着的湖 ○ *enemy troops encircling the town* 包围该城的敌军. ▷ **en·cir·cle·ment** *n* [U].

encl *abbr* 缩写 = (*commerce* 商) enclosed; enclosure (used eg at the end of a letter sent with one).

en·clave /ˈenkleɪv; ˋɛnklev/ *n* small territory of one state surrounded by that of another 飞地(被他国领土包围的一块领土): *British enclaves in Africa* 非洲的英国飞地 ○ (*fig* 比喻) *Switzerland was an enclave of peace in war-torn Europe.* 在饱经战争磨难的欧洲, 瑞士是和平的世外桃源.

en·close /ɪnˈkləʊz; ɪnˋkloz/ *v* [Tn, Tn·pr] **~ sth (with sth)** **1** (also **in·close**) put a wall, fence, etc round sth 用墙、篱笆等围住某物: *enclose a garden with a wall* 在花园周围筑起墙 ○ *an enclosed order of monks*, ie one that lives in isolation from the outside world 隐修士团. **2** put sth in an envelope, letter, parcel, etc 将某物放入封套、信件、包裹等中: *I'll enclose your letter with mine.* 我把你的信装在我的信里. ○ *A cheque for ten pounds is* *enclosed.* 附上一张十英镑的支票. ○ (*fml or commerce* 文或商) *Enclosed, please find*..., ie You will find, enclosed with this... 兹附上....

en·clos·ure /ɪnˈkləʊʒə(r); ɪnˋkloʒɚ/ *n* **1** (**a**) [U] enclosing of land 圈地: *opposed to the enclosure of common land* 反对把公地圈为私有. (**b**) [C] (also **in·clos·ure**) piece of land that is enclosed 被圈起的土地: *She keeps a horse in that enclosure.* 她在那个围栏里养了一匹马. ○ *the members' enclosure*, eg at a racecourse 会员座区(如赛马场上的). **2** [C] thing that is enclosed (esp with a letter) 附件(尤指信内的): *several enclosures in the envelope* 装在信封内的几分附件.

en·code /ɪnˈkəʊd; ɪnˋkod/ *v* [Tn esp passive 尤用于被动语态] (**a**) put (a message, etc) into code 将(信息等)译成代码. (**b**) (*computing* 计) put (data) into a coded form for processing by a computer 编码. Cf 参看 DECODE.

en·co·mium /enˈkəʊmɪəm; ɛnˋkomɪəm/ *n* (*pl* **-miums** or **-mia** /-mɪə; -mɪə/) (*fml* 文) very high praise in speech or writing 极高的赞颂; 推崇; 赞词; 颂词.

en·com·pass /ɪnˈkʌmpəs; ɪnˋkʌmpəs/ *v* [Tn] (*fml* 文) **1** include or comprise sth 包含或包括某事物: *The general arts course at the university encompasses a wide range of subjects.* 大学文科包括的科目范围很广. **2** (also **com·pass**) (*dated* 旧) surround 包围; 环绕: *a lake encompassed by mountains* 群山环抱的湖.

en·core /ˈɒŋkɔː(r); ˋɑŋkɔr/ *interj* (called out by an audience) Again! Repeat! (听众或观众喊出的)再来一个! 再来一次!

▷ **en·core** *n* (call for a) repetition (of a song, etc) or a further performance by the same person or people 再演(唱等)(的呼喊): *The violinist got an enthusiastic encore.* 听众热情要求小提琴手再演奏一曲. ○ *The group gave three encores.* 演出小组应听众之请又演出了三个节目.

en·coun·ter /ɪnˈkaʊntə(r); ɪnˋkaʊntɚ/ *v* [Tn] (*fml* 文) **1** meet or find oneself faced by (sth/sb unpleasant, dangerous, difficult, etc) 遇到或发现自己面临(令人不快的、危险的、困难的...某事[某人]): *I encountered many difficulties when I first started this job.* 我开始做这项工作时, 遇到许多困难. ○ *We encountered four enemy aircraft.* 我们遇到四架敌机. **2** meet (a friend, etc) unexpectedly 邂逅(友人等).

▷ **en·coun·ter** *n* ~ **(with sb/sth)** sudden or unexpected (esp hostile) meeting 突然的或意外的(尤指敌对的)相遇: *an encounter with an enemy* 与敌人的遭遇 ○ *I had a brief encounter with an angry client.* 我与一个生气的顾客一时发生了冲突.

en·cour·age /ɪnˈkʌrɪdʒ; ɪnˋkʌrɪdʒ/ *v* **1** [Tn, Tn·pr, Dn·t] **~ sb (in sth)** give support, confidence or hope to sb 鼓励或支持某人: *Don't encourage bad habits in a child.* 不要助长孩子的坏习惯. ○ *He felt encouraged by the progress he'd made.* 他取得了成绩而欢欣鼓舞. ○ *Her parents encouraged her in her studies.* 她的父母鼓励她好好学习. ○ *encourage sb to lose weight* 鼓励某人减轻体重. **2** [Tn] help (sth) to develop; stimulate 帮助(某事物)发展; 激励; 促进: *encourage exports* 促进出口.

▷ **en·cour·age·ment** *n* **~ (to sb) (to do sth)** (**a**) [U] action of encouraging 鼓励; 支持; 激励; 促进: *shouts of encouragement* 鼓劲的呼声. (**b**) [C] thing that encourages 鼓励、支持或促进的事物: *The teacher's words were a great encouragement to him.* 教师的话对他是极大的鼓舞.

en·cour·aging *adj*: *encouraging words, news, signs* 令人鼓舞的话、消息、迹象 ○ *This year's sales figures are very encouraging.* 今年的销售额很令人鼓舞. **en·cour·agingly** *adv*.

en·croach /ɪnˈkrəʊtʃ; ɪnˋkrotʃ/ *v* [I, Ipr] **~ (on/upon sth)** (*fml* 文) go beyond what is right or natural or desirable; intrude 超出正当的、自然的或适当的程度; 侵入; 侵害: *encroach on sb's property* 侵占某人的财产 ○ *encroach on the liberty of the individual* 侵犯个人自由 ○ *The sea is gradually encroaching (on the land)*, ie washing the land away. 海水渐渐侵蚀了陆地.

▷ **en·croach·ment** *n* **~ (on/upon sth)** (*fml* 文) (**a**) [U] action of encroaching 侵入; 侵害; 侵占: *I resent the encroachment on my time.* 我讨厌别人侵占我的时间. (**b**) [C] thing gained by encroaching 侵占或侵害之物: *encroachments made by the sea upon the land* 海水对陆地的侵蚀之处.

en·crust /ɪnˈkrʌst; ɪnˋkrʌst/ *v* **1** [usu passive 通常用于被动语态: Tn, Tn·pr] **~ sth (with sth)** cover (a surface) with a crust or thin hard coating, sometimes for decoration 在(表面)覆以薄而硬的壳或外层(有时作为装饰): *a gold vase encrusted with diamonds* 镶嵌钻石的金花瓶 ○ *an encrusted wound* 结痂的伤口. **2** [I] form into a crust 形成壳或硬皮: *Salt from the sea had encrusted on the dry sand.* 海水中的盐分在干燥的沙子上结成硬皮.

en·cum·ber /ɪnˈkʌmbə(r); ɪnˋkʌmbɚ/ *v* [usu passive 通常用于被动语态: Tn, Tn·pr] **~ sb/sth (with sth)** **1** prevent sb/sth from moving or acting freely and easily 阻碍或妨碍某人[某物]自由活动: *Travelling is difficult when you're encumbered with two small children and a heavy suitcase.* 旅行时带着两个孩子和一个沉重的手提箱, 真是寸步难移. ○ *encumbered with debts* 为债务所累. **2** (*derog* 贬) crowd sth; fill sth up 堆满某物; 充填某物: *a room encumbered with old and useless furniture* 堆满无用的旧家具的房间.

▷ **en·cum·brance** /ɪnˈkʌmbrəns; ɪnˋkʌmbrəns/ *n* [C] person or thing that encumbers 防碍者; 障碍物; 累赘; 负担.

en·cyc·lical /ɪnˈsɪklɪkl; ɛnˋsɪklɪkl/ *n* letter written by the Pope for wide circulation 教皇通谕.

en·cyc·lo·pe·dia (also **-pae·dia**) /ɪnˌsaɪkləˈpiːdɪə; ɪnˌsaɪkləˋpidɪə/ *n* book or set of books giving information about every branch of knowledge, or about one particular subject, with articles in alphabetical order 百科全书: *an encyclopedia of music* 音乐百科全书 ○ *a children's encyclopaedia* 儿童百科全书.

▷ **en·cyc·lo·pedic** (also **-paedic**) /ɪnˌsaɪkləˈpiːdɪk; ɪnˌsaɪkləˋpidɪk/ *adj* dealing with or having knowledge of a wide variety of subjects; comprehensive 百科全书的; 包含各种学科的; 学识渊博的; 广博的: *enˌcyclopedic ˈknowledge* 渊博的知识.

end[1] /end; ɛnd/ *n* **1** farthest or last part or point (of the length of sth); extreme limit 末端; 尽头; 极限: *the end of a road, stick, line* 路的终点、棍的顶端、线的末端 ○ *the house at the end of the street* 在街道尽头的房屋 ○ *join the end of the queue* 站在一排人的最后 ○ *the end of the tunnel* 隧道的终点 ○ *the west/east end* (ie the parts in the west/east) *of a town* 城镇的西[东]区 ○ *We've travelled from one end of Britain to the other.* 我们已从英国的这一头旅行到另一头. ○ [attrib 作定语] *the end house* 最末尾的房子 ○ *the end carriage*, ie in a train 末节车厢. **2** final part of sth; finish; conclusion 某事物的最后部分; 结束; 结论; 终结; 终止: *at the end of the day, month, year, century, etc* 在一日、月、年、世纪等之终结时 ○ *the end of a story* 故事的结尾 ○ *He said he'd love her till the end of time*, ie for ever. 他说天长地久永远爱她. ○ *the end of an era* 一个时代的终结. **3** small piece left over after sth has been used 某物使用后剩下的小块: *a cigarette end* 香烟头 ○ *candle ends* 蜡烛头. **4** (*often euph* 常作委婉语) death 死亡: *He's nearing his end*, ie is dying. 他已气息奄奄. ○ *She came to an untimely end*, ie died young. 她死的时候很年青. **5** aim or purpose 目的; 目标: *gain/win/achieve one's ends* 达到目的 ○ *with this end in view/to this end* 以此为目标[为达此目的]. **6** half of a sports pitch, etc defended or occupied by one team or player (球类比赛场地中的)半场: *At half-time the teams changed ends.* 比赛进行一半时, 双方交换了场地. **7** part or share (esp of a business, etc) with which a person is concerned 与某人有关的(尤指企业等的)部门或部分: *We need someone to handle the marketing end of the business.* 我们需要有人管理本公司的销售部. ○ *Are there any problems at your end?* 你那部门有问题吗? **8** (idm 习语) **at a loose end** ⇨ LOOSE[1]. **(be) at an end** finished 结束; 终结: *The war was at an end.* 战争结束了. **at the ˌend of one's ˈtether** having no power, patience, endurance, etc left 已无力量、耐性、耐力等: *I've been looking after four young children all day and I really am at the end of my tether!* 我整天都在照料四个小孩, 确实已筋疲力尽了! **(be) at the end of sth** finishing sth; having no more of sth 完成某事物; 已无某事物: *at the end of his patience* 他已再无耐性. **at the ˌend of the ˈday** when everything is taken into consideration 把一切都考虑进去: *At the end of the day the new manager is no better* *than the previous one.* 从各个方面来看，这位新经理并不比前任强. **at one's wits' end** ⇨ WIT. **be at/on the receiving end** ⇨ RECEIVE. **be the end** (*infml* 口) be the limit of what one can tolerate; be very bad, annoying, etc 可忍受的极限；非常糟、令人恼怒等: *This is the end — I'm never coming to this hotel again.* 可受够了——我再也不到这家旅馆来了. ○ *They really are the end!* 他们真令人恼火! **the beginning of the end** ⇨ BEGINNING (BEGIN). **bring sth/come/draw to an end** (cause sth to) finish, usu after lasting some time (使某事物)结束，终止(通常为已持续一段时间的): *The battle finally brought the war to an end.* 这一仗使这场战争终告结束. ○ *At last the meeting came to an end.* 会议终于结束了. **burn the candle at both ends** ⇨ BURN². **the business end** ⇨ BUSINESS. **come to a bad/sticky 'end** be led by one's actions to ruin, disgrace, punishment, an unpleasant death, etc 遭到报应；恶有恶报: *He'll come to a bad end one of these days.* 他总有一天会遭到恶报的. ○ *I like films where the villain comes to a sticky end!* 我喜欢恶有恶报的影片! **a dead end** ⇨ DEAD. **an ˌend in it'self** thing that is considered important in its own right, though possibly originally having another purpose 本身即很重要的事物(可能起初并不为主): *For the old lady buying the daily newspaper soon became an end in itself, since she really just wanted to chat with the shopkeeper.* 那老太太每天去买报纸，不多时便觉乐在其中，因为她主要是想和店主聊天. **the ˌend ˌjustifies the 'means** (*saying* 谚) even wrong or unfair methods may be allowed if the result or purpose of the action is good 只要目的正当，可以不择手段. **(reach) the ˌend of the 'line/'road** (reach) the point at which one does not wish, or cannot bear, to continue in the same way (达到)不希望的或不能容忍的地步: *It's sad that they got divorced but they had reached the end of the line together.* 他们离婚令人难过，但双方已达到无法容忍的地步了. **(not) the ˌend of the 'world** (not) completely disastrous for sb 对某人(不)是天大的灾难: *You must realize that failing one exam is not the end of the world.* 你要明白，一次不及格不是大不了的事. **(go to) the ˌends of the 'earth** (go to) the most remote parts of the world (去)天涯海角: (*fig* 比喻) *I'd go to the ends of the earth to see her again.* 哪怕走遍天涯海角，我也要再次见到她. **ˌend 'on** with the ends meeting 两端相遇: *The two ships collided end on,* ie The front (or back) of one struck the front (or back) of the other. 那两条船两端相撞了. **ˌend to 'end** in a line, with the ends touching 首尾相接成一行: *arrange the tables end to end* 将桌子连接排成一行. **get hold of the wrong end of the stick** ⇨ WRONG. **go off the deep end** ⇨ DEEP¹. **in the 'end** at last; finally 终于；最后: *He tried many different jobs; in the end he became a postman.* 他做过多种工作，最后当了邮递员. **keep one's 'end up** (*Brit infml* 口) continue to be cheerful and play one's part despite difficulties (不顾困难)仍乐观而尽本分，不泄气. **light at the end of the tunnel** ⇨ LIGHT¹. **make an end of sth** (*fml* 文) finish sth 结束某事物. **make (both) ends meet** earn enough money to live without getting into debt; balance one's income and expenditure 使收支相抵: *Being out of work and having two young children, they found it impossible to make ends meet.* 他们失了业，还要养活两个小孩，无法维持起码的生活. **make one's hair stand on end** ⇨ HAIR. **a means to an end** ⇨ MEANS¹. **no end of sth** (*infml* 口) very many or much; very great 无数的；大量的；巨大的: *I've had no end of problems recently.* 近来我的问题没完没了. ○ *We had no end of trouble getting them to agree.* 我们为让他们同意着实费尽了口舌. **not/never hear the end of sth** ⇨ HEAR. **odds and ends** ⇨ ODDS. **on 'end (a)** upright 直立；竖着: *He placed the box on (its) end and sat on it.* 他把箱子竖起来，坐在上面. **(b)** continuously 连续地: *They argued for two hours on end.* 他们连续争论了两小时. **put an 'end to one's life/oneself** kill oneself 自杀. **put an end/a stop to sth** stop sth from happening any more; abolish sth 终止或废止某事物: *The government is determined to put an end to terrorism.* 政府决心遏止恐怖主义活动. **the thin end of the wedge** ⇨ THIN. **throw sb in at the deep end** ⇨ DEEP¹. **to the bitter end** ⇨ BITTER. **without 'end** never reaching an end or finishing 无尽的；无穷的: *troubles without end* 无穷无尽的烦恼 ○ *world without end* 广袤无际的天地.

□ **'endpapers** *n* [pl] (usu blank) pages pasted to the inside covers of a book 环衬(书籍封面及封底内侧所贴的衬页，通常为空白页).

'end-product *n* final product of a manufacturing process 最终产品.

end² /end; ɛnd/ *v* **1** [I, Ipr, Tn, Tn·pr] (cause sth to) come to an end (使某事物)结束，终止: *The road ends here,* ie goes no further. 这条路到此为止. ○ *How does this story end?* 这故事的结局如何? ○ *They decided to end their relationship.* 他们决定结束彼此的关系. ○ *They ended the play with a song.* 他们以一首歌曲结束了这出剧. **2** (idm 习语) **the be-all and end-all** ⇨ BE¹. **ˌend it 'all; ˌend one's 'life** commit suicide 自杀: *He was so miserable that he seriously thought about ending it all.* 他难受得甚至认真考虑过要自杀. **ˌend one's 'days/'life (in sth)** spend the last part of one's life (in a particular state or place) (处于某状况下或在某处)度过余生: *The great singer ended his days in poverty.* 那位大歌唱家在贫困中度过残生. **3** (phr v) **end in sth (a)** have sth as its tip or ending 以某事物作为末端或结尾: *The word ends in -ous.* 此词以 -ous 结尾. **(b)** have sth as a result or conclusion 以某事物作为结果或结论: *Their long struggle ended in failure.* 他们长期斗争终告失败. ○ *The argument ended in tears.* 争吵到最后声泪俱下. ○ *The debate ended in uproar.* 那场争辩以大吵大闹收场. **end sth off (with sth/by doing sth)** finish sth (in a suitable or successful way) (妥当地或顺利地)结束某事物: *We ended off the meal with coffee and brandy.* 我们这顿饭最后喝的是咖啡和白兰地. ○ *He ended off his speech by telling a very funny joke.* 他最后讲了一个非常滑稽的笑话结束了讲话. **end up** reach or come to a certain place, state or action, esp by a lengthy route or process 到达或来到某处，达到某状态或采取某行动(尤指经一长路程或过程): *If you continue to steal you'll end up in prison.* 你要是继续行窃终归得进监狱. ○ *After much discussion about holidays abroad we ended up in Cornwall.* 我们反复商量到国外度假的事，最后决定去康沃尔. ○ *At first he refused to accept any responsibility but he ended up apologizing.* 最初他拒不承认有任何责任，到头来还是道了歉. ○ *If he carries on driving like that, he'll end up dead.* 他照这样开车，早晚得死于非命.

▷ **end·ing** *n* end, esp of a story, film, play or word 结尾，结局(尤指故事、电影、戏剧或词语): *a story with a happy ending* 结局圆满的故事.

en·dan·ger /ɪnˈdeɪndʒə(r); ɪnˈdendʒɚ/ *v* [Tn] cause danger to (sb/sth); put in danger 危及，危害(某人[某事物]); 使遭到危险: *Smoking endangers your health.* 吸烟危害健康. ○ *The giant panda is an endangered species,* ie is in danger of becoming extinct. 大熊猫是面临绝种危险的动物.

en·dear /ɪnˈdɪə(r); ɪnˈdɪr/ *v* [Tn·pr] **~ sb/oneself to sb** (*fml* 文) make sb/oneself loved or liked by sb 使某人[自己]受某人喜爱: *Her kindness to my children greatly endeared her to me.* 她对我的孩子很好，所以我十分喜爱她. ○ *He managed to endear himself to everybody.* 他有办法让大家都喜欢他.

▷ **en·dear·ing** *adj* causing or resulting in affection 使人喜爱的；讨人喜欢的: *an endearing remark, smile, habit* 讨人喜欢的话、微笑、习惯. **en·dear·ingly** *adv*.

en·dear·ment *n* [C, U] word or expression of affection 爱慕的词语；亲爱的表示: *He whispered endearments in her ear.* 他在她耳边说着悄悄话. ○ *'Darling' is a term of endearment.* '亲爱的'是亲昵语.

en·deav·our (*US* **-vor**) /ɪnˈdevə(r); ɪnˈdɛvɚ/ *n* (*fml* 文) attempt or effort 努力；尽力: *Please make every endeavour to arrive punctually.* 请尽量准时到达.

▷ **en·deav·our** *v* [It] (*fml* 文) try 努力；尽力；力图: *They endeavoured to make her happy but in vain.* 他们尽量使她快乐，却徒劳无功.

en·demic /enˈdemɪk; ɛnˈdɛmɪk/ *n, adj* [often pred 常作表语] (disease) that is regularly found in a particular country or area, or among a particular group of people 某国家、地区或某部分人中常见的(疾病)；地方性的(病): *Malaria is endemic in/to many hot countries.* 疟疾是热带许多国家的地方病. ○ (*fig* 比喻) *the violence endemic in the city* 该城中肆虐的暴力行为. Cf 参看 EPIDEMIC, PANDEMIC.

E

en·dive /ˈendɪv; *US* -daɪv; ˋɛndaɪv/ *n* [C, U] **1** (*US* also **escarole**) type of plant with curly leaves used as salad 苣荬菜(用作凉菜). **2** (*US*) = CHICORY.

end·less /ˈendlɪs; ˋɛndlɪs/ *adj* **1** (seemingly) without end (似乎)无止境的; 无穷尽的: *endless patience* 无限的耐心 ○ *an endless choice of things to do* 可做之事数之不尽 ○ *The hours of waiting seemed endless.* 等候了很多小时, 似乎无尽无休. **2** (of a belt, chain, cable, etc) with the ends joined; continuous (指带、链、缆等)两端相连的, 循环不断的: *wheels in a machine driven by an endless belt* 用无极带传动的机器轮子. ▷ **end·lessly** *adv*.

en·dorse /ɪnˈdɔ:s; ɪnˋdɔrs/ *v* [Tn] **1** write one's name on the back of (esp a cheque) 在(尤指支票)的背面签字; 背书. **2** (**a**) write comments, etc in or on the back of (a document) 在(文件)的背面写评论; 批注(公文). (**b**) (*Brit*) record details of a motoring offence in (a driving licence) 在(驾驶执照上)记录违章事项: *He's had his licence endorsed for dangerous driving.* 他的驾驶执照上载有危险驾驶记录. **3** give one's (official) approval or support to (a claim, statement, etc) (正式)赞同或支持(某要求、言论等): *I am afraid I can't endorse your opinion of the government's record.* 很抱歉, 你对政府功过的看法本人不敢苟同. **4** say in an advertisement that one uses and approves of (a product) 在广告上说本人使用并赞许(某产品): *Well-known sportsmen can earn large sums of money from manufacturers by endorsing clothes and equipment.* 著名运动员在广告中替厂家宣传运动服装和器械, 可获得巨额报酬.

▷ **en·dorse·ment** *n* (**a**) [U] act of endorsing 背书; 批注; (在执照上的)违章记录; 赞同; 支持: *the endorsement of a cheque* 支票的背书 ○ *official endorsement of the scheme* 对该计划的正式认可. (**b**) [C] instance of this; statement that endorses 背书; 批注; (在执照上的)违章记录; 赞同; 支持: *Her son has had two endorsements for speeding.* 她儿子的驾驶执照上有两次超速记录.

E

en·dow /ɪnˈdaʊ; ɪnˋdaʊ/ *v* **1** [Tn, Tn·pr] **~ sb/sth (with sth)** give money, property, etc to provide a regular income for (eg a school, a college) (经常性)资助, 捐助(如学校等): *endow a bed in a hospital* 资助医院的一个床位(即经常资助一名住院病人的全部医疗费用). **2** [Tn·pr usu passive 通常用于被动语态] **~ sb with sth** provide sb naturally with (any good quality or ability) 使某人天生具有(任何好的品质或能力): *She's endowed with intelligence as well as beauty.* 她生来聪明貌美.

▷ **en·dow·ment** *n* **1** [U] action of endowing (经常的)资助, 捐助: *the endowment of many schools by rich former pupils* 许多学校经常得到富裕校友的资助. **2** [C usu *pl* 通常作复数] money, property, etc given to provide an income 捐助的财物等: *The Oxford and Cambridge colleges have numerous endowments.* 牛津和剑桥大学有数不清的捐助财物. **3** [C usu *pl* 通常作复数] natural talent, quality or ability 天赋; 天资; 才能: *Not everyone is born with such endowments as you.* 并非所有的人生来都像你这样有天赋. **enˈdowment policy** form of life insurance where a certain sum is paid on a specified date to the insured person or is paid to that person's dependents if he dies before that date 养老保险.

en·due /ɪnˈdju:; *US* -ˈdu:; ɪnˋdu/ *v* [Tn·pr usu passive 通常用于被动语态] **~ sb with sth** (*fml* 文) provide or supply sb with a good quality, ability etc 给予或赋予某人好的品质、能力等: *endued with gentleness* 天赋的温顺.

en·dur·ance /ɪnˈdjʊərəns; *US* -ˈdʊə-; ɪnˋdurəns/ *n* [U] state or power of enduring 忍耐力: *He showed remarkable endurance throughout his illness.* 他生病的整个阶段都表现出非凡的忍耐力. ○ *His treatment of her was beyond endurance*, ie impossible to endure any longer. 他这样对待她是无法忍受的. ○ [attrib 作定语] *The soldiers eventually completed the endurance tests*, ie tests of how long they could endure harsh conditions. 士兵们终于完成了耐力测验. ○ (*fig* 比喻) *Jane's party was more of an endurance test than anything else.* 参加简举办的聚会完全是考验耐性.

en·dure /ɪnˈdjʊə(r); *US* -ˈdʊər; ɪnˋdur/ *v* **1** [I, Tn] suffer or undergo (sth painful or uncomfortable) patiently 忍受; 忍耐: *endure toothache* 忍受牙痛 ○ *He endured three years in prison for his religious beliefs.* 他因其宗教信仰而忍受系狱三年之苦. **2** [Tn, Tt, Tg] (esp in negative sentences 尤用于否定句) bear; tolerate 忍受; 容忍: *I can't endure that woman.* 我对那个女人忍无可忍. ○ *I can't endure to see/seeing children suffer.* 看着儿童受苦, 我可受不了. **3** [I] continue in existence; last 持续; 持久: *fame that will endure for ever* 将永世长存的声望 ○ *as long as life endures* 只要生命犹存 ○ *These traditions have endured throughout the ages.* 这些传统世代相传至今.

▷ **en·dur·able** /-rəbl; -rəbl/ *adj* that can be endured; bearable 可忍耐的; 可忍受的; 可容忍的: *He found the boredom scarcely endurable.* 他觉得这种厌烦难以忍受.

en·dur·ing *adj* continuing in existence; lasting 持续的; 持久的: *enduring memories* 永存的记忆 ○ *an enduring peace* 持久的和平 ○ *Her influence was the most enduring of all.* 她的影响是最持久的. **en·dur·ingly** *adv*.

end·ways /ˈendweɪz; ˋɛnd,wez/ (also **end·wise** /ˈendwaɪz; ˋɛnd,waɪz/) *adv* **1** with the end facing forwards 末端向前: *The bed was pushed endways into the bedroom.* 这张床已尾端朝前推入了卧室. **2** end to end 两端相接地: *The child put the toy cars together endways.* 孩子将玩具汽车两端相连摆在一起.

en·ema /ˈenɪmə; ˋɛnəmə/ *n* **1** injection of liquid into the rectum by means of a syringe (eg to clean out the bowels before an operation) 灌肠(如手术前): *give a patient an enema* 给病人灌肠. **2** liquid used for this 灌肠剂.

en·emy /ˈenəmɪ; ˋɛnəmɪ/ *n* **1** [C] person who strongly dislikes or wants to injure or attack sb/sth 敌人; 仇人; 仇敌: *Jane and Sarah used to be friends but now they are bitter enemies*, ie of each other. 简和萨拉以前是朋友而现在是死对头. ○ *His arrogance made him many enemies*, ie made many people hate him. 他妄自尊大, 树敌很多. **2** (**a**) **the enemy** [Gp] (armed) forces of a nation, side, etc with which one's country, side, etc is at war 敌军: *an encounter with the enemy* 与敌军的遭遇战 ○ *The enemy was/were forced to retreat.* 敌军被迫撤退了. ○ [attrib 作定语] *enemy forces, aircraft, ships, etc* 敌军、敌机、敌舰等 ○ *enemy propaganda* 敌方的宣传. (**b**) [C] member of such a hostile force 敌兵. **3** [C] anything that harms or weakens 危害或削弱之物: *Poverty and ignorance are the enemies of progress.* 贫穷和愚昧是进步的敌人. **4** (idm 习语) **one's own worst enemy** ⇨ WORST. **carry the war into the enemy's camp** ⇨ CARRY.

en·ergy /ˈenədʒɪ; ˋɛnədʒɪ/ *n* **1** [U] ability to act or work with strength and eagerness 精力; 干劲: *She's full of energy.* 她精力充沛. ○ *His work seemed to lack energy.* 他工作似乎缺乏干劲. ○ *It's a waste of time and energy.* 那简直是浪费时间和精力. **2 energies** [pl] person's powers available for working or other activities 精力; 活力: *I must concentrate my energies on decorating today.* 我今天必须集中精力搞装饰. ○ *apply/devote all one's energies to a task* 全力以赴. **3** [U] (*physics* 物) ability of matter or radiation to do work because of its motion or its mass or its electric charge, etc 能; 能量: *nuclear energy* 核能 ○ *electrical energy* 电能 ○ *kinetic energy* 动能. **4** [U] fuel and other resources used for operating machinery, etc 能源: *It is important to conserve energy.* 节省能源十分重要. ○ [attrib 作定语] *an energy crisis*, eg when sources of energy are scarce or unavailable 能源危机.

▷ **en·er·getic** /ˌenəˈdʒetɪk; ˌɛnəˋdʒɛtɪk/ full of or done with energy(1) 精力充沛的; 充满活力的: *an energetic child* 精力旺盛的孩子 ○ *take some energetic exercise* 做些剧烈的锻炼. **en·er·get·ic·ally** /-klɪ; -klɪ/ *adv*.

en·er·gize, -ise /ˈenədʒaɪz; ˋɛnə,dʒaɪz/ *v* [Tn] (**a**) give energy to (sb/sth) 给与(某人[某物])精力, 能量. (**b**) cause electricity to flow to (a device) 使电流入(一装置).

en·er·vate /ˈenəveɪt; ˋɛnə,vet/ *v* [Tn] cause (sb) to lose strength or energy 使(某人)失去力量或精力; 使衰弱: *an enervating climate* 使人无精打采的气候 ○ *a long, enervating illness* 长期而使人衰弱的病.

en famille /ˌɒn fæˈmi:; ˌanfæˋmi/ (*French* 法) at home; among one's family 在家; 与家人一起: *I always enjoy winter evenings spent en famille.* 我一向喜欢与家人共度冬宵.

en·fant ter·rible /ˌɒnfɒn teˈri:bl; ˌanfanteˋribl/ (*pl*

enfants terribles /ˌɒnfɒn teˈri:bl; ˌanfɑntɛˋribḷ/ (*French often joc* 法, 常作戏谑语) (esp young) person whose behaviour, ideas, etc annoy, shock or embarrass those with more conventional opinions (行为、想法等)使常人不悦、震惊或受窘的人(尤指年轻人): *Her advanced ideas have made her the enfant terrible of the art world.* 她一味标新立异, 在艺术界堪称一怪.

en·feeble /ɪnˈfi:bl; ɪnˋfibḷ/ *v* [Tn esp passive 尤用于被动语态] (*fml* 文) make weak or feeble 使衰弱; 使无力: *enfeebled by a long illness* 因长期患病而虚弱无力.

en·fold /ɪnˈfəʊld; ɪnˋfold/ *v* [Tn, Tn·pr] **~ sb/sth (in/with sth)** (*fml* 文) enclose sb/sth, esp in one's arms; clasp or embrace sb/sth 围住、圈起某人[某物]; 抱紧、拥抱某人[某物]: *He enfolded the child in an affectionate embrace.* 他疼爱那孩子而紧紧搂在怀里.

en·force /ɪnˈfɔ:s; ɪnˋfɔrs/ *v* **1** [Tn, Tn·pr] **~ sth (on sb)** force people to obey (a law, etc); make sth effective 强迫人服从(法律等); 使某事物生效; 实施; 执行: *The police are there to enforce the law.* 有警方管执法. **2** [Tn] make (sth) happen or bring (sth) about by force 迫使(某事)发生: *enforced silence, discipline, idleness* 被迫的沉默、强迫执行的纪律、被迫的无事可做. **3** [Tn] give greater force or strength to (an argument, a belief, etc) 加强(某论点、信念等): *Have you any statistics that would enforce your argument?* 你有没有支持自己论点的统计数字?

▷ **en·force·able** /-əbl; -əbḷ/ *adj* that can be enforced 可强迫的; 可实施的; 可强制执行的; 可加强的: *Such a strict law is not easily enforceable.* 这样严竣的法令不易实施.

en·force·ment *n* [U] enforcing or being enforced 强制; 实施; 执行; 加强: *strict enforcement of a new law* 新法令的强制执行.

en·franch·ise /ɪnˈfræntʃaɪz; ɪnˋfræntʃaɪz/ *v* [Tn esp passive 尤用于被动语态] (*fml* 文) **1** give (sb) political rights, esp the right to vote at parliamentary elections 给予(某人)政治权利(尤指议会选举权): *In Britain women were enfranchised in 1918.* 1918 年英国妇女获得议会选举权. **2** set free (slaves) 解放(奴隶). ▷ **en·franch·ise·ment** /ɪnˈfræntʃɪzmənt; ɪnˋfræntʃɪzmənt/ *n* [U].

Eng *abbr* 缩写 = **1** engineer(ing): *Tim Dale BSc (Eng)* 蒂姆·戴尔理科学士(工程学). **2** England; English.

en·gage /ɪnˈgeɪdʒ; ɪnˋgedʒ/ *v* **1** [Tn, Cn·n/a] **~ sb (as sth)** (*fml* 文) arrange to employ sb; hire sb 聘用某人; 雇用某人: *engage a new secretary* 聘用一新秘书 ○ *He's been engaged to decorate the house.* 他受雇装饰这所房子. ○ *She was engaged as an interpreter.* 她应聘当译员. **2** [Tn] (*fml* 文) occupy or attract (sb's thoughts, time, etc) 占用(某人的时间); 吸引(某人的注意力等): *Nothing engages his attention for long.* 什么事都无法使他长时间精神集中. ○ *The woman's plight engaged our sympathy.* 那女人的困难处境引起我们的同情. **3** [I, Tn] (*fml* 文) begin fighting with (sb) 与(某人)交战: *Our orders are to engage (the enemy) immediately.* 我们的命令是立即(与敌军)开战. ○ *The two armies were fiercely engaged for several hours.* 两军激战达数小时. **4** (**a**) [I, Ipr] **~ (with sth)** (of parts of a machine, etc) lock or fit together (指机器零件等)啮合, 衔接: *The two cog-wheels engaged and the machine started.* 那两个齿轮一啮合, 机器就启动了. ○ *One cog-wheel engages with another.* 一齿轮与另一齿轮啮合. (**b**) [Tn] cause (parts of a machine, etc) to lock together or fit into each other 使(机器零件等)啮合, 衔接: *engage the clutch/first gear*, eg in a car, when driving 使离合器啮合[挂一挡](如开车时). **5** [Tt] (*dated fml* 旧, 文) bind oneself by a promise; guarantee 允诺; 答应; 保证: *a lawyer engaged to undertake the sale of the house immediately* 受聘将房子立即出售的律师. **6** (phr v) **engage (sb) in sth** (cause sb to) take part in or be occupied in sth (使某人)参加某事或从事某事: *I have no time to engage in gossip.* 我无暇闲聊. ○ *be engaged in politics, business* 从政、做生意 ○ *I engaged him in conversation.* 我让他加入谈话.

▷ **en·gaged** *adj* [usu pred 通常作表语] **1** (of a person) busy; occupied (指人)忙着, 时间占用着: *I can't come to dinner on Tuesday; I'm otherwise engaged*, ie I've already arranged to do something else. 我星期二不能来参加宴会, 我有别的事. **2** (*Brit*) (*US* **busy**) (of a telephone line) in use (指电话线)使用着, 占线: *Sorry! That number's engaged.* 对不起! 这个号码现在占线. ○ [attrib 作定语] *the engaged tone/signal*, ie sound that tells the caller that the telephone line is engaged 占线声[占线信号]. **3 ~ (to sb)** (of a person or two people) having agreed to marry (指一人或两人)已订婚: *She's engaged to Peter.* 她与彼得订了婚. ○ *They're engaged (to be married)*, ie to each other. 他们俩订婚了. ○ *We've just got engaged.* 我们刚刚订婚. ○ [attrib 作定语] *an engaged couple*. 已订婚的双方. **4** (**a**) (esp of a toilet) occupied; already in use (尤指厕所)占用着, 使用着. (**b**) (of seats, tables, etc) reserved for later use (指座位、桌子等)预订.

en·ga·ging *adj* likely to attract or occupy the attention; charming 吸引注意力的; 迷人的: *an engaging smile, manner, person* 迷人的微笑、姿态、人. **en·ga·gingly** *adv*.

en·gage·ment /ɪnˈgeɪdʒmənt; ɪnˋgedʒmənt/ *n* **1** [C] agreement to marry 订婚: *Their engagement was announced in the local paper.* 他们订婚的消息已登在当地报纸上. **2** [C] arrangement to go somewhere, meet sb or do sth at a fixed time; appointment 约会: *I have several engagements for next week.* 我下周有几个约会. ○ *The orchestra has several concert engagements.* 这管弦乐队已安排好几场音乐会. **3** [C] (*fml* 文) formal promise or guarantee, esp in writing 正式的承诺或保证(尤指书面形式): *He doesn't have enough money to meet all his engagements*, ie to make the payments he has promised to make. 他无钱偿付承诺的一切债务. **4** [C] (*fml* 文) battle 战斗; 交战: *The general tried to avoid an engagement with the enemy.* 那位将军竭力避免与敌军交战. **5** [U] arrangement to employ; action of engaging 聘用的事宜; 雇用的行动: *the engagement of three new assistants* 聘用三名新助手的事. **6** [U] action or result of engaging (parts of a machine, etc) (机器零件等)啮合的动作或结果: *after engagement of the clutch* 离合器啮合后.

□ **enˈgagement ring** ring (usu containing precious stones) that a man gives to a woman when they agree to marry 订婚戒指(通常有宝石).

en·gen·der /ɪnˈdʒendə(r); ɪnˋdʒɛndɚ/ *v* [Tn] (*fml* 文) be the cause of (a situation or condition) 产生(某形势或状况); 造成; 引起: *Some people believe poverty engenders crime.* 有人认为贫困生罪恶.

en·gine /ˈendʒɪn; ˋɛndʒən/ *n* **1** machine with moving parts that converts energy such as heat, electricity, etc into motion 发动机; 引擎: *This car has a new engine.* 这辆汽车的发动机是新的. ○ *a steam/diesel/petrol engine* 蒸汽[柴油/汽油]发动机. **2** (also **lo·co·mot·ive**) machine that pulls or pushes a railway train 机车; 火车头: *I prefer to sit* (ie in a railway carriage) *facing the engine.* 我喜欢面朝机车坐(在火车车厢里). **3** (*arch* 古) machine or instrument 机器; 工具: *engines of war*, eg cannons 战争工具(如大炮) ○ *siege engines* 攻城器械.

□ **ˈengine-driver** *n* (*Brit*) (*US* **en·gin·eer**) person who drives a railway engine 火车司机.

en·gin·eer /ˌendʒɪˈnɪə(r); ˌɛndʒəˋnɪr/ *n* **1** person who designs, builds or maintains engines, machines, bridges, railways, mines, etc 工程师; 建筑师; 机械师: *a civil/mining/electrical/mechanical engineer* 土木[采矿/电气/机械]工程师. **2** skilled person who controls an engine or engines, esp on a ship or aircraft 操纵发动机的技师(尤指轮船或飞机上的): *the chief engineer on a cruise liner* 游轮的轮机长. **3** (*US*) = ENGINE-DRIVER (ENGINE). **4** soldier trained to design and build military works 工兵: *He's in the Royal Engineers*, ie a branch of the British Army. 他在皇家工兵部队服役(英国陆军的兵种).

▷ **en·gin·eer** *v* [Tn] **1** (*infml derog* 口, 贬) arrange or cause (sth), esp by cunning or secret means 安排或策动(某事物)(尤指用狡猾或秘密手段); 策划: *His enemies engineered his downfall.* 他的仇敌图谋把他搞垮. ○ *engineer a plot, scheme, revolt, etc* 策划阴谋、诡计、反叛等. **2** build or control (sth) as an engineer 建造或操纵(某事物).

en·gin·eer·ing /ˌendʒɪˈnɪərɪŋ; ˌɛndʒəˋnɪrɪŋ/ *n* [U] (**a**) practical application of scientific knowledge in the design, construction and control of machines, public services such as roads, bridges, etc, electrical apparatus, chemicals, etc 工程: *civil/electrical/chemical/mechanical* *engineering* 土木[电气/化学/机械]工程 ○ *The new bridge is a triumph of engineering.* 这座新桥是建筑工程的硕果. (**b**) work, science or profession of an engineer 工程; 工程学; 工程师行业: *She's studying engineering at university.* 她正在大学学习工程学. ○ [attrib 作定语] *an engineering degree* 工程学学位.

Eng·lish /ˈɪŋglɪʃ; ˋɪŋglɪʃ/ *n* **1** [U] the language of England, used in Britain, most countries in the British Commonwealth, the USA and some other countries 英语; 英文: *He speaks excellent English.* 他英语说得好极了. ○ *I must work to improve my English.* 我必须努力提高英语水平. **2 the English** [pl *v*] the people of England (sometimes wrongly used to mean the British, ie to include the Scots, the Welsh and the Irish) 英格兰人(有时误用以指英国人, 即除英格兰人外还包括苏格兰人、威尔士人、爱尔兰人). **3** (idm 习语) **in plain English** ⇨ PLAIN. **the King's/Queen's ˈEnglish** good, correct standard English 纯正标准的英语: *She speaks a dialect, not the Queen's English.* 她说一口方言, 不是标准英语.

▷ **Eng·lish** *adj* **1** of England or its people 英格兰的; 英格兰人的; 英国的; 英国人的: *the English countryside* 英国乡村 ○ *English characteristics* 英国人的特性 ○ *He is very English in his attitudes.* 他的态度英国味十足. **2** [attrib 作定语] of, written in, or spoken in the English language 英语的; 用英语写的; 用英语说的: *He's studying English literature.* 他在研究英国文学.

□ ˌ**English ˈbreakfast** breakfast usu consisting of cereals, cooked bacon and eggs, toast and marmalade, and tea or coffee 英国式早餐(通常包括麦片类、熏猪肉片、鸡蛋、烤面包片、果酱及茶或咖啡). Cf 参看 CONTINENTAL BREAKFAST (CONTINENT[1]).

the English ˈChannel (also **the Channel**) the area of the sea between England and France 英吉利海峡.

Englishman /-mən; -mən/ (*pl* **-men**), **Englishwoman** (*pl* **-women**) *ns* **1** person born in England or one whose parents are English or one who has become an English citizen 英格兰人; 英国人. **2** (idm 习语) **an ˌEnglishman's ˌhome is his ˈcastle** (*saying* 谚) an English person's home is a place where he may be private and safe and do as he wishes 英国人的家就是城堡(为私人随心所欲的安全天地).

en·grave /ɪnˈgreɪv; ɪnˋgrev/ *v* **1** [Tn, Tn·pr] **~ B on A/~ A (with B)** cut or carve (words, designs, etc) on (a hard surface) 在(硬物)上雕刻(字、画等): *His initials were engraved on the cigarette case.* 他姓名的首字母刻在香烟盒上. ○ *The cigarette case was engraved with his initials.* 这香烟盒上刻着他姓名的首字母. ○ *engraving a design on a metal plate*, eg for printing 在金属板上雕一图案(如用以印刷). **2** [Tn·pr esp passive 尤用于被动语态] **~ sth on sth** (*fig* 比喻) impress sth deeply on (the memory or mind) 将某事物深深留在(记忆或头脑中); 牢记; 铭记: *Memories of that terrible day are forever engraved on my mind.* 那可怕的一天永远留在我的记忆中.

▷ **en·graver** *n* person who engraves designs, etc on stone, metal, etc 雕刻师; 刻板工人.

en·grav·ing /ɪnˈgreɪvɪŋ; ɪnˋgrevɪŋ/ *n* **1** [U] art of cutting or carving designs on metal, stone, etc 雕刻术; 刻板术. **2** [C] picture printed from an engraved metal plate 版画: *I bought an old engraving of the High Street.* 我买了一张'大街'的旧版画.

en·gross /ɪnˈgrəʊs; ɪnˋgros/ *v* [Tn] **1** (usu passive 通常用于被动语态) occupy all the time or attention of (sb) 占去某人的全部时间或注意力; 使全神贯注: *be engrossed in one's work* 全神贯注于工作 ○ *an engrossing story* 引人入胜的故事. **2** (*law* 律) write (eg a legal document) in large letters or in formal legal style 以大字体或以正式法律文体写(如法律文件).

en·gulf /ɪnˈgʌlf; ɪnˋgʌlf/ *v* [Tn esp passive 尤用于被动语态] (*fml* 文) (of the sea, flames, etc) surround (sth) or cause (sth) to disappear; envelop (指海洋、火焰等)包围(某物)或使(某物)消失; 包住; 吞没: *a boat engulfed in/by the waves* 被浪涛吞没的小船 ○ (*fig* 比喻) *engulfed in silence, misery* 陷入寂静、痛苦之中.

en·hance /ɪnˈhɑːns; *US* -ˈhæns; ɪnˋhæns/ *v* [Tn] increase (the good qualities of sb/sth); make (sb/sth) look better 增强(某人[某事物]的优点); 使(某人[某事物])看起来更好; 提高; 美化: *enhance the status, reputation, position, etc of sb* 提高某人的身分、声望、地位 ○ *Those clothes do nothing to enhance her appearance.* 她穿那些衣服也并没显得更漂亮.

▷ **en·hance·ment** *n* (**a**) [U] action of enhancing 增强; 提高; 美化. (**b**) [C] thing that enhances 用以增强、提高或美化之物.

en·igma /ɪˈnɪgmə; ɪˋnɪgmə/ *n* question, person, thing, circumstance, etc that is difficult to understand; mystery 难于理解的问题、人、物、情况等; 奥秘: *I've known him for many years, but he remains something of an enigma to me.* 我与他相识多年, 他仍然难以捉摸.

▷ **en·ig·matic** /ˌenɪgˈmætɪk; ˌɛnɪgˋmætɪk/ *adj* difficult to understand; mysterious 难以理解的; 神秘的: *an enigmatic character, smile, statement* 莫名其妙的性格、微笑、说法. **en·ig·mat·ic·ally** /-klɪ; -klɪ/ *adv*.

en·join /ɪnˈdʒɔɪn; ɪnˋdʒɔɪn/ *v* [Tn, Tn·pr, Tf, Dn·t] **~ sth (on sb)** (*fml or law* 文或律) impose (an action or prohibition) on sb; order 将(一行动或禁令)强施于某人; 命令: *He enjoined obedience on his followers.* 他强迫随从服从. ○ *The leader enjoined that the rules should be obeyed.* 那位领导人命令必须遵守这些规则.

en·joy /ɪnˈdʒɔɪ; ɪnˋdʒɔɪ/ *v* **1** [Tn, Tg] get pleasure from 从…获得乐趣: *I enjoyed that meal.* 我很喜欢那顿饭. ○ *She enjoys playing tennis.* 她喜好打网球. **2** [Tn] have (sth) as an advantage or a benefit 享有(某事物): *enjoy good health, a high standard of living, great prosperity, etc* 享有健康、高生活水平、巨大成功等之福 ○ *Men and women should enjoy equal rights.* 男女应当享有平等权利. **3** (idm 习语) **enˈjoy oneself** experience pleasure; be happy 感到快乐; 过得愉快: *He enjoyed himself at the party.* 他在聚会上非常愉快. ○ *The children enjoyed themselves playing in the water.* 孩子们在水中玩得很高兴. ○ *I hope you enjoy yourself this evening.* 我希望你今晚过得愉快.

▷ **en·joy·able** /-əbl; -əbḷ/ *adj* giving joy; pleasant 使人愉快的; 令人快乐的: *an enjoyable weekend* 愉快的周末 ○ *The film was quite enjoyable.* 这部电影很有趣. **en·joy·ably** /-əblɪ; -əblɪ/ *adv*.

en·joy·ment /ɪnˈdʒɔɪmənt; ɪnˋdʒɔɪmənt/ *n* **1** [U] pleasure; satisfaction 愉快; 欢乐; 乐趣; 满意: *He spoiled my enjoyment of the film by talking all the time.* 他一直说话, 影响了我看电影的兴致. ○ *live only for enjoyment* 只为享乐活着. **2** [C] (*fml* 文) thing that gives pleasure or joy 令人愉快的事物; 乐事: *Gardening is one of her chief enjoyments.* 园艺工作是她的主要乐趣之一. **3** [U] (*fml* 文) possession and use 享有; 使用: *the enjoyment of equal rights* 享有平等权利.

en·kindle /ɪnˈkɪndl; ɛnˋkɪndḷ/ *v* [Tn] (*dated or fml* 旧或文) (**a**) cause (flames, passion, etc) to flare up 使(火焰、激情等)燃起. (**b**) inflame (sb) with passion, etc; arouse 使(某人)激动等; 引起; 唤起; 激起.

en·large /ɪnˈlɑːdʒ; ɪnˋlɑrdʒ/ *v* **1** (**a**) [I, Tn] (cause sth to) become larger (使某物)变大; 扩大; 增大: *I want to enlarge the lawn.* 我想把草坪扩大. (**b**) [Tn] reproduce (esp a photograph) on a larger scale 放大(尤指照片): *The police had the photograph of the missing girl enlarged.* 警方把失踪姑娘的照片放大了. **2** [Ipr] **~ on sth** say or write more about sth; add detail to sth 详述或详写某事; 增加某事的细节: *Can you enlarge on what has already been said?* 你能把所说的事再详尽地说说吗?

▷ **en·large·ment** *n* **1** [U] action of enlarging or being enlarged 扩大; 放大: *He's working on the enlargement of the business.* 他正在努力扩展业务. **2** [C] thing that has been enlarged, esp a photograph 已扩大或放大之物(尤指照片): *enlargements of the wedding photographs* 婚礼照片的放大照片. Cf 参看 REDUCTION.

en·lar·ger *n* apparatus for making photographic enlargements (照片)放大机.

en·lighten /ɪnˈlaɪtn; ɪnˋlaɪtṇ/ *v* [Tn, Tn·pr] **~ sb (as to sth)** give more knowledge or information to sb; free sb from false beliefs or ignorance 启发、启迪、教导或开导某人: *Can you enlighten me as to* (ie help me to understand better) *the new procedure?* 你能给我讲讲这新程序吗?

▷ **en·light·ened** *adj* [esp attrib 尤作定语] free from prejudice, ignorance, superstition, etc 摆脱偏见、无知、迷信等的; 开明的; 有知识的: *in these enlightened days* 在这开明的时代 ○ *enlightened opinions, attitudes, ideas, etc* 有见识的意见、开明的态度、进步的想法 ○ *an* *enlightened approach to teaching* 启发式教学法.

en·light·en·ment *n* [U] (*fml* 文) **1** act of enlightening or state of being enlightened 启发; 开导; 开明; 文明: *The teacher's attempts at enlightenment failed; I remained as confused as before.* 老师虽尽力开导却劳而无功, 我仍像以前一样糊涂. ○ *In an age of enlightenment such cruelty is unforgivable.* 在文明时代, 这么残忍是不能宽恕的. **2 the Enlightenment** period in the 18th century in Europe when some thinkers and writers believed that reason and science, not religion, would advance human progress (18世纪欧洲的)启蒙运动.

en·list /ɪn'lɪst; ɪn'lɪst/ *v* [I, Ipr, Tn, Tn·pr, Cn·n/a] **~ (sb) (in/for sth); ~ (sb) (as sth) 1** enter or cause (sb) to enter the armed forces 参军; 从军; 使(某人)入伍: *Have you enlisted yet?* 你参军了吗? ○ *He enlisted as a soldier in the army as soon as he was old enough.* 他年龄一到就入伍当兵了. ○ *They enlisted four hundred recruits for the navy.* 他们为海军征募了四百名新兵. **2 (a)** [Tn, Tn·pr] **~ sb/sth (in/for sth)** obtain (help, support, etc) 得到(帮助、支持等): *I've enlisted the co-operation of most of my neighbours in my campaign.* 我在这一活动中得到邻里多数人的支持. ○ *Can I enlist your help in raising the money?* 你能在我的筹款中赞助一些钱吗? **(b)** [Tn, Cn·t] get the support or help of (sb) 获得(某人)的支持或帮助: *We've enlisted a few volunteers to help clean the hall.* 我们已经找到几个人自愿协助打扫大厅. ○ *Sarah has been enlisted to organize the party.* 萨拉已应邀组织这一聚会.

▷ **en·list·ment** *n* **1** [U] enlisting or being enlisted 应征入伍; 征募; 获得; 取得. **2** [C] instance of this 应征入伍; 征募; 获得; 取得.

□ **enlisted man** (*esp US*) soldier, sailor or airman below a non-commissioned officer in rank 士兵.

en·liven /ɪn'laɪvn; ɪn'laɪvən/ *v* [Tn] make (sb/sth) more lively or cheerful 使(某人[某事物])更活跃或更愉快: *How can we enliven this party?* 我们怎样使这聚会热闹些呢?

en masse /ˌɒn 'mæs; ɑn'mæs/ (*French* 法) in a mass or crowd; all together 成群; 全体; 一齐; 一起: *Individually the children are delightful; en masse they can be unbearable.* 孩子们单独时还讨人喜欢, 一多了就受不了了. ○ *The Joneses are coming for lunch en masse — all twelve of them!* 琼斯一大家子人都来吃午饭——一共十二口人!

en·mesh /ɪn'meʃ; ɛn'mɛʃ/ *v* [Tn usu passive 通常用于被动语态, Tn·pr] **~ sb/sth (in sth)** (*usu fig* 通常作比喻) entangle (as) in a net 使(似)陷入网中: *He was enmeshed in a web of deceit and lies.* 他陷入坑绷拐骗的圈套.

en·mity /'enmətɪ; 'ɛnmətɪ/ *n* [U, C] condition or feeling of being an enemy; hostility 敌意; 仇恨; 不和; 作对: *I don't understand his enmity towards his parents.* 我不理解他为什么怨恨自己的父母. ○ *Personal enmities must be forgotten at a time of national crisis.* 民族危机当头, 必须捐弃个人恩怨.

en·noble /ɪ'nəʊbl; ɪ'nobl/ *v* [Tn] (*fml* 文) **1** make (sb) a member of the nobility 使(某人)成为贵族. **2** (*fig* 比喻) make (sb) dignified or more honourable 使(某人)高贵或崇高: *In a strange way she seemed ennobled by the grief she had experienced.* 她因历经艰辛而似乎出奇地备受敬重. ▷ **en·no·ble·ment** *n* [U].

en·nui /ɒ'nwi:; 'ɑnwi/ *n* [U] weariness of mind caused by lack of anything interesting or exciting to do; feeling of boredom 倦怠; 无聊: *Since losing his job, he has often experienced a profound sense of ennui.* 他自从失业以来, 常觉百无聊赖.

enorm·ity /ɪ'nɔ:mətɪ; ɪ'nɔrmətɪ/ *n* **1** [U] great wickedness 极恶; 凶恶: *The enormity of the crime has shocked even experienced policemen.* 这件罪行极端凶残, 连经历丰富的警察都感震惊. **2** [C, usu *pl* 通常作复数] (*fml* 文) serious crime 严重罪行: *Such enormities would not be tolerated today.* 这种严重罪行今日是不能容忍的. **3** [U] (*infml* 口) immense size; enormousness 巨大; 极大: *the enormity of the task of feeding all the famine victims* 为全部饥民提供粮食的巨大任务.

enorm·ous /ɪ'nɔ:məs; ɪ'nɔrməs/ *adj* very large; immense 巨大的; 极大的: *an enormous amount of money* 巨款 ○ *an enormous house* 巨大的房子.

▷ **enorm·ously** *adv* to a very great extent 在极大程度上: *enormously rich* 极富有 ○ *My tastes have changed enormously over the years.* 几年来我的爱好有了很大改变. ○ *I'm enormously grateful for your help.* 我非常感谢你的帮助.

enorm·ous·ness *n* [U].

enough[1] /ɪ'nʌf; ɪ'nʌf/ *indef det* (used in front of a plural *n* or a [U] *n* 用于复数名词或不可数名词前) **~ sth (for sb/sth); ~ sth (for sb) to do sth** as many or as much of sth as necessary; sufficient 足够的; 充足的: *Have you made enough copies?* 你复制的份数够吗? ○ *Have we got enough sandwiches for lunch?* 我们午饭的三明治够吃吗? ○ *Surely 15 minutes is enough time for you to have a coffee.* 你喝杯咖啡15分钟当然足够了. ○ *I've got enough money to pay for a taxi.* 我的钱够付计程车费的. ○ *There isn't enough space for my address.* 我写地址的地方不够. ○ (*dated* 旧) *There's food enough on the table.* 桌上的食物足够吃. ○ *We have time enough to get to the airport.* 我们来得及赶到机场.

▷ **enough** *indef pron* **1** as many or as much as necessary 充分; 足够: *Six bottles of wine will be enough.* 六瓶葡萄酒就够了. ○ *Is £100 enough for all your expenses?* 100英镑够你的全部开销吗? ○ *I hope enough of you are prepared to help with the show.* 我希望你们中能有足够的人手准备协助这场演出. ○ *They were able to save enough of their furniture to fill a room.* 他们能省出的家具足够装满一间屋子. **2** (idm 习语) **eˌnough is eˈnough** (*saying* 谚) it is unnecessary and possibly harmful to say or do more 适可而止. **have had eˈnough (of sth/sb)** be unable or unwilling to tolerate sth/sb any more 不能或不愿再容忍某事物[某人]: *After three years without promotion he decided he'd had enough and resigned.* 他三年未获提升, 认为已受够了, 便辞了职. ○ *I've had enough of her continual chatter.* 我已厌烦了她喋喋不休的闲谈. ○ *I'm surprised you haven't had enough of him yet — I found him very boring.* 你对他还没有受够, 我很惊讶——我觉得他很烦人.

enough[2] /ɪ'nʌf; ɪ'nʌf/ *adv* (used after *vs*, *adjs* and *advs* 用于动词、形容词和副词之后) **1 ~ (for sb/sth); ~ (to do sth/for doing sth)** to a satisfactory degree; sufficiently 达到满意的程度; 足够地; 充足地: *You don't practise enough at the piano.* 你钢琴弹奏练习得不够. ○ *Is the river deep enough for swimming/to swim in?* 在这条河里游泳水够深吗? ○ *At 14 you aren't old enough to buy alcohol.* 你才14岁, 不到买酒的年龄. ○ *She isn't good enough for* (ie to pass) *the exam.* 她功课不够好, 考不及格. ○ *I wish you'd write clearly enough for us to read it.* 但愿你能写得清楚点, 我们好能看明白. **2** (used to suggest that sth only deserves slight praise 用于表示某事物只值得略加赞扬) to a significant extent; fairly 达到一定的程度; 相当: *She plays well enough for a beginner.* 对于初学者说来, 她弹奏得已相当不错了. **3** (idm 习语) **curiously, oddly, strangely, etc enough** it is very curious, etc that... 稀奇的是...: *Strangely enough, I said the same thing to my wife only yesterday.* 说也奇怪, 我就在昨天也同妻子谈到这件事. **fair enough** ⇨ FAIR[2]. **sure enough** ⇨ SURE.

en pass·ant /ˌɒn 'pæsɒn; ˌɑnpɑ'sɑn/ (*French* 法) in passing; by the way 顺便: *He mentioned en passant that he was going away.* 他顺便提到他要离开的事.

en·quire, en·quiry = INQUIRE, INQUIRY.

en·rage /ɪn'reɪdʒ; ɪn'redʒ/ *v* [Tn esp passive 尤用于被动语态] make (sb) very angry 使(某人)非常愤怒; 激怒; 触怒: *enraged at/by sb's stupidity* 因某人的愚蠢而愤怒 ○ *His arrogance enraged her.* 他很傲慢, 她为此十分恼怒.

en·rap·ture /ɪn'ræptʃə(r); ɪn'ræptʃɚ/ *v* [Tn esp passive 尤用于被动语态] (*fml* 文) fill (sb) with great delight or joy 使(某人)非常喜悦或快乐: *We were enraptured by the view of the mountains.* 我们看到山峦景色, 心花怒放.

en·rich /ɪn'rɪtʃ; ɪn'rɪtʃ/ *v* [Tn, Tn·pr] **~ sb/sth (with sth) 1** make sb/sth rich or richer 使某人[某事物]富裕或更富裕: *a nation enriched by the profits from tourism* 因旅游业的赢利而富裕起来的国家. **2** improve the quality, flavour, etc of sth 改善某事物的质量、味道等: *soil enriched with fertilizer* 因施肥而肥沃的土壤 ○ *Reading enriches the mind.* 读书可以充实头脑. ▷ **en·rich·ment** *n* [U].

en·rol (also *esp US* **en·roll**) /ɪn'rəʊl; ɪn'rol/ *v* **(-ll-)** [I, Ipr, Tn, Tn·pr, Cn·n/a] **~ (sb) (in/as sth)** become or

E

make (sb) a member (of sth) 成为或使(某人)成为(某组织的)成员; 登记; 注册: *enrol in evening classes* 注册上晚间课程班 ○ *enrol new students* 招收新生 ○ *We enrolled him as a member of the society.* 我们吸收他为会员.

▷ **en·rol·ment** (also *esp US* **en·roll·ment**) *n* (**a**) [U] enrolling or being enrolled 登记; 注册; 人伍; 入会; 入学: *the enrolment of five new members* 五名新成员的注册. (**b**) [C] number of people enrolled 注册; 入会; 入学等的人数: *This school has an enrolment of 800 pupils.* 这所学校有800名学生注册.

en route /ˌɒn ˈruːt; ɑnˋrut/ **~ (from...) (to...); ~ (for...)** (*French* 法) on the way 在路上; 在中途: *We stopped at Paris en route from Rome to London.* 我们从罗马去伦敦的途中曾在巴黎停留. ○ *They passed through Paris en route for Rome.* 他们途经巴黎前往罗马.

Ens *abbr* 缩写 = Ensign: *Ens (Peter) Dwyer* 海军少尉(彼得)德怀尔.

en·sconce /ɪnˈskɒns; ɛnˋskɑns/ *v* [Tn·pr esp passive 尤用于被动语态] **~ oneself/sb in sth** (*fml or joc* 文或谑) establish or settle oneself in a safe, secret, comfortable, etc place 使自己定居或安顿在安全、秘密、舒适等的地方: *happily ensconced by the fire with a good book* 舒适地坐在火炉旁, 读着一本好书 ○ *We have ensconced ourselves in the most beautiful villa in the South of France.* 我们在法国南部最美丽的别墅里安顿下来.

en·semble /ɒnˈsɒmbl; ɑnˋsɑmbl/ *n* **1** thing viewed as a whole; general effect 整体; 总效果: *The arrangement of the furniture formed a pleasing ensemble.* 这些家具摆放得悦目而和谐. **2** complete matching set of (esp women's) clothes designed to be worn together 全套服装(尤指女装): *A pair of white shoes completed the striking ensemble.* 一双白鞋配这套醒目的服装已完美无缺了. **3** (**a**) passage of music in which all the performers play or sing together 合奏; 合唱. (**b**) group of musicians (smaller than an orchestra) who play together regularly 合奏组(比管弦乐队小): *a woodwind ensemble* 木管乐器合奏组.

en·shrine /ɪnˈʃraɪn; ɪnˋʃraɪn/ *v* (*fml* 文) (**a**) [Tn, Tn·pr] **~ sth (in sth)** place or keep sth (in, or as if in, a shrine or holy place) 放置或保存某物(于神龛或圣地): *relics enshrined in a casket* 在小箱中保存的遗物 ○ *memories enshrined in the heart* 珍藏于心中的记忆. (**b**) [Tn] serve as a shrine for (sth) 作为神龛以保存(某物): *The constitution enshrines the basic rights of all citizens.* 宪法中神圣地记载着全体公民的基本权利.

en·shroud /ɪnˈʃraʊd; ɪnˋʃraʊd/ *v* [Tn usu passive 通常用于被动语态] (*fml* 文) cover completely; hide from view 掩盖; 遮蔽; 隐蔽: *hills enshrouded in mist* 薄雾笼罩的群山 ○ *His background is enshrouded in mystery.* 他的来历背后有一层神秘的色彩.

en·sign /ˈensən; ˋɛnsn̩/ *n* **1** (**a**) (esp naval) flag or banner (尤指海军的)旗, 旗帜. (**b**) (*Brit*) special form of the national flag flown by ships (船上挂的特种的)国旗: *the red/white/blue ensign* 英国商船旗[英国皇家海军旗/英国海军预备舰队旗]. **2** (*US*) officer of the lowest rank in the navy 海军少尉. ⇨App 9 见附录9. **3** /ˈensaɪn; ˋɛnsaɪn/ (*Brit*) (formerly) infantry officer who carried the regimental flag (旧时)(陆军团的)掌旗官.

en·slave /ɪnˈsleɪv; ɪnˋslev/ *v* [Tn] (*often fig* 常作比喻) make a slave of (sb) 使某人成为奴隶: *Her beauty enslaved many young men.* 她的美貌倾倒了很多青年男子. ▷ **en·slave·ment** *n* [U].

en·snare /ɪnˈsneə(r); ɛnˋsnɛr/ *v* [Tn esp passive 尤用于被动语态, Tn·pr] **~ sb/sth (in sth)** (*often fig* 常作比喻) catch sb/sth in, or as if in, a trap or snare 用陷阱或圈套捕捉某人[某物]: *ensnared by love* 陷入情网 ○ *ensnare a rich husband* 千方百计嫁予富翁.

en·sue /ɪnˈsjuː; *US* -ˈsuː; ɛnˋsu/ *v* [I, Ipr] **~ (from sth)** happen afterwards or as a result; follow 继而发生; 因而产生; 接着: *Bitter arguments ensued from this misunderstanding.* 这一误会引发了激烈的争论. ○ *in the ensuing* (ie following) *debate* 在随后的辩论中.

en suite /ˌɒn ˈswiːt; ɑnˋswit/ (*French* 法) (of rooms, etc) forming a single unit (指房间等)构成独立单元: *Each bedroom in the hotel has a bathroom en suite.* 该旅馆每间卧室都有一洗澡间自成一套.

en·sure (*US* **in·sure**) /ɪnˈʃɔː(r); *US* ɪnˈʃʊər; ɪnˋʃʊr/ *v* **1** [Tn, Tf] make sure; guarantee 确保; 保证; 担保: *The book ensured his success.* 那本书确定了他的成就. ○ *Please ensure that all the lights are switched off at night.* 夜间请务必将所有的灯关掉. **2** [Dn·n] make (sb) certain to get (sth); assure 使(某人)一定得到(某事物); 保证得到: *These pills should ensure you a good night's sleep.* 服下这些药丸可保你睡一宿好觉.

ENT /ˌiː en ˈtiː; ˌi ɛn ˋti/ *abbr* 缩写 = (*medical* 医) ear, nose and throat 耳鼻喉: *an ENT specialist* 耳鼻喉专家.

-ent ⇨ -ANT.

en·tail /ɪnˈteɪl; ɪnˋtel/ *v* **1** [Tn] make (sth) necessary; involve 使(某事物)必要; 牵涉: *This job entails a lot of hard work.* 这项工作需要十分努力. ○ *That will entail an early start tomorrow morning.* 那就需要明晨很早动身. **2** [esp passive 尤用于被动语态: Tn, Tn·pr] **~ sth (on sb)** (*law* 律) leave (land) to a line of heirs in such a way that none of them can give it away or sell it 限定(地产)继承人: *The house and estate are entailed on the eldest daughter.* 这所房子和地产限定由长女继承. ○ *He would have sold the property long ago had it not been entailed.* 这些财产若非限定继承的话, 他早就卖掉了.

▷ **en·tail** *n* (*law* 律) (**a**) [U] practice of entailing (ENTAIL 2) land (地产的)限定继承. (**b**) [C] entailed property 限定继承的财产.

en·tangle /ɪnˈtæŋgl; ɪnˋtæŋgl/ *v* [Tn esp passive 尤用于被动语态, Tn·pr] **~ sb/sth/oneself (in/among/with sth)** **1** cause sb/sth/oneself to become twisted, tangled or caught (in sth) 使某人[某物/自己]缠绕, 纠缠于(某物中): *The bird got entangled in the wire netting.* 鸟被金属网缠住. ○ *a fishing line entangled among the weeds* 与杂草缠在一起的钓鱼线 ○ *Her long hair entangled itself in the rose bush.* 她的长发让玫瑰丛给钩住了. **2** (*fig* 比喻) involve sb/oneself (in difficulties or complicated circumstances) 使某人[自己]陷入(困难或复杂的环境中): *become entangled in money problems* 陷入金钱问题之中.

▷ **en·tan·gle·ment** *n* **1** [U] entangling or being entangled 缠住; 纠缠. **2** [C] (often *pl* 常作复数) situation that entangles 引起纠缠的情况; 纠纷: *entanglements with the police* 与警方的纠缠 ○ *emotional entanglements* 感情纠葛. **3 entanglements** [pl] (*military* 军) barrier of stakes and barbed wire to impede an enemy's advance (阻止敌人前进的)铁丝网.

en·tente /ɒnˈtɒnt; ɑnˋtɑnt/ *n* (**a**) [C, U] friendly understanding, esp between countries 相互谅解(尤指两国间). (**b**) [CGp] group of two or more countries having such an understanding between them 相互谅解的国家.

□ ˌ**entente cordiˈale** /ˌkɔːdɪˈɑːl; kɔrˋdjɑl/ entente between two governments, esp between those of Britain and France 两政府间的相互谅解(尤指英国与法国间).

en·ter /ˈentə(r); ˋɛntɚ/ *v* **1** (**a**) [I, Tn] come or go in or into (sth) 进来; 进去; 进入(某物)中: *Don't enter without knocking.* 进屋前先敲门. ○ *enter a room* 进屋 ○ *The train entered the tunnel.* 火车进了隧道. ○ *Where did the bullet enter the body?* 子弹是从身体的什么地方射入的? (**b**) [I] come or go onto a stage 登台; 上场: *Enter Hamlet/Hamlet enters,* eg stage directions in a printed play 哈姆雷特上场(如剧本的舞台说明). **2** [Tn no passive 不用于被动语态] become a member of (sth); gain admission to (sth) 成为(某组织)的成员; 得到进入(某组织)的允许: *enter a school, college, university, etc* 考上学校、学院、大学等 ○ *enter the Army/Navy/Air Force* 参加陆军[海军/空军] ○ *enter a profession* 从事一职业 ○ *enter the Church,* ie become a priest 成为牧师. **3** [Tn, Tn·pr, Tn·p] **~ sth (up) (in sth)** record (names, details, etc) in a book, computer, etc: register sth (在册子等上)记录名字、细节等; 登记某事物: *I haven't entered your name and occupation yet.* 我尚未记下你的名字和职业. ○ *All expenditure must be entered (up) in the account book.* 一切开支必须人帐. **4** (Tn) declare that one will take part in (a competition, etc) 报名参加(比赛等): *enter a race, an examination* 报名参加赛跑、考试. **5** [Tn] (*fml* 文) present (sth) for consideration 提出(某事物)供考虑: *enter a plea of not guilty* 提出无罪抗辩 ○ *enter a protest* 提出抗议. **6** (idm 习语) **enter the lists (against sb)** challenge sb or accept a challenge from sb to a contest 要求与某人比赛; 答应与某人比赛.

7 (phr v) **enter into sth** (**a**) begin to deal with sth 开始处理某事物: *Let's not enter into details at this stage.* 咱们不要在现阶段着手处理具体问题. (**b**) be able to understand and appreciate sth 能懂得并欣赏某事物; 领略; 体会: *enter into the spirit of an occasion*, ie begin to enjoy and feel part of it 领略个中乐趣. (**c**) (not passive 不用于被动语态) form part of sth 形成某事物的一部分: *This possibility never entered into our calculations.* 我们从未考虑过有这种可能性. **enter into sth (with sb)** begin sth; open sth 开始某事: *enter into negotiations with a business firm* 开始与一公司协商 ○ (*fml* 文) *I dared not enter into conversation with him.* 我未敢与他交谈. **enter on/upon sth** (*fml* 文) (**a**) make a start on sth; begin sth 着手做某事物; 开始某事: *enter upon a new career* 开始一新事业 ○ *The President has just entered upon another term of office.* 总统刚刚开始另一任期. (**b**) (*law* 律) take possession of sth; begin to enjoy sth 获得某物; 开始享有某物: *He entered on his inheritance when he was 21.* 他21岁时继承了财产. **enter (sb) for sth** give the name of (oneself or sb else) for a competition, race, etc 报名参加竞赛等: *I've entered for the high jump.* 我已报名参加跳高比赛. ○ *The teacher entered him for the examination.* 老师替他报名参加考试. ○ *enter a horse for a race* 给马报名参加赛跑.

en·teric /en'terɪk; ɛn'tɛrɪk/ *adj* [usu attrib 通常作定语] of the intestines 肠的: *enteric fever*, ie typhoid 肠热病(伤寒).

▷ **en·ter·itis** /ˌentə'raɪtɪs; ˌɛntə'raɪtɪs/ *n* [U] inflammation of the intestines 肠炎: *suffering from enteritis* 患肠炎.

en·ter·prise /'entəpraɪz; 'ɛntɚˌpraɪz/ *n* **1** [C] project or undertaking, esp one that is difficult or needs courage 事业, 计划(尤指困难的或需要勇气的): *his latest business enterprise* 他最新的企业规划 ○ *The music festival is a new enterprise which we hope will become an annual event.* 音乐会演是一项新生事物, 我们希望它能成为一年一度的盛会. Cf 参看 VENTURE 1. **2** [U] courage and willingness to be involved in such projects 事业心; 进取心; 勇气; 胆量: *a woman of great enterprise* 事业心极强的女子 ○ *He got the job because he showed the spirit of enterprise.* 他因为表现出进取精神, 所以得到了这份工作. **3** (**a**) [U] participation in projects; business activity 参与计划; 企业活动; 经营: *Conservative governments in Britain favour private enterprise rather than nationalization.* 英国的保守党政府赞成私人经营而反对国有化. (**b**) [C] business company or firm 事业单位; 企业单位; 公司; 商号; 商行: *one of the most successful enterprises of its kind* 同类企业中业绩极突出者.

▷ **en·ter·pris·ing** *adj* having or showing enterprise(2) 有事业心的; 表现出进取心的; 有胆量的: *an enterprising young man* 有进取心的年轻男子 ○ *She may not have been the cleverest candidate but she was certainly the most enterprising.* 她就算不是最聪明的候选人, 也肯定是最有事业心的. **en·ter·pris·ingly** *adv*.

en·ter·tain /ˌentə'teɪn; ˌɛntɚ'ten/ *v* **1** [I, Tn, Tn·pr] **~ sb (to sth)** receive sb as a guest; provide food and drink for sb, esp in one's home 宴客; 招待, 款待某人(尤指在自己家中): *I don't entertain very often.* 我不常在家请客. ○ *They do a lot of entertaining*, ie often give dinner parties, etc. 他们时常设宴待客. ○ *Bob and Liz entertained us to dinner last night.* 昨晚鲍勃和利兹设宴招待了我们. **2** [Tn, Tn·pr] **~ sb (with sth)** amuse sb 使某人快乐: *Could you entertain the children for an hour, while I make supper?* 我做晚饭时, 你能哄孩子们玩一个小时吗? ○ *He entertained us for hours with his stories and jokes.* 他给我们讲故事、说笑话, 让我们高兴了好几小时. **3** [Tn] (*fml* 文) (not in the continuous tenses 不用于进行时态) (**a**) be ready and willing to consider (sth) 愿意考虑(某事物): *He refused to entertain our proposal.* 他拒不考虑我们的提议. (**b**) hold (sth) in the mind or feelings 心里或感情上怀有(某事物): *entertain ideas, doubts, etc* 有想法、怀疑等.

▷ **en·ter·tainer** *n* person who entertains (ENTERTAIN 2), esp professionally (娱乐节目的)表演者; (尤指)艺人: *He's a popular television entertainer.* 他是大众喜爱的电视演员.

en·ter·tain·ing *adj* amusing and pleasing 使人愉快的; 有趣的: *a very entertaining film* 一部很有趣的电影 ○ *a most entertaining guest* 很有风趣的客人. **en·ter·tain·ingly** *adv*.

en·ter·tain·ment *n* **1** [U] entertaining or being entertained 宴客; 招待; 款待; 娱乐: *the entertainment of a group of foreign visitors* 宴请一批外宾 ○ *He fell in the water, much to the entertainment of the children.* 他掉进水里, 逗得孩子们乐不可支. ○ *a place of entertainment* 娱乐场所. **2** [C] thing that entertains; public performance (at a theatre, cinema, circus, etc) 娱乐; (在剧场、电影院、马戏团等的)演出: *The local entertainments are listed in the newspaper.* 报纸上登有本地的娱乐活动.

en·thral (also *esp US* **en·thrall**) /ɪn'θrɔːl; ɪn'θrɔl/ *v* (**-ll-**) [Tn esp passive 尤用于被动语态] capture the whole attention of (sb) as if by magic; please greatly; captivate (似以魔力)迷住(某人); 使极愉快; 迷住: *enthralled by her beauty* 被她的美色迷住. ▷ **en·thral·ling** *adj*: *an enthralling performance* 动人的演出. **en·thral·ment** (also *esp US* **en·thrall·ment**) *n* [U].

en·throne /ɪn'θrəʊn; ɪn'θron/ *v* [Tn esp passive 尤用于被动语态] (*fml* 文) place (a king, queen or bishop) on a throne, esp with ceremony; exalt 使(国王、女王或主教)登基, 就任(尤指举行仪式); 提升; 提拔: *The queen was enthroned in an ancient abbey.* 女王在一所古老的大教堂里举行登基仪式. ▷ **en·throne·ment** *n* [U, C].

en·thuse /ɪn'θjuːz; *US* -θuːz; ɪn'θuz/ *v* [I, Ipr] **~ (about/over sth/sb)** show great admiration or interest for 对…极为喜爱或极热心: *He hasn't stopped enthusing about his holiday since he returned.* 他度假归来, 对假日情趣仍津津乐道. ○ *They all enthused over the new baby.* 他们都极喜爱这个新生儿.

en·thu·si·asm /ɪn'θjuːzɪæzəm; *US* -'θuː-; ɪn'θuzɪˌæzəm/ *n* **~ (for/about sth)** **1** [U] strong feeling of admiration or interest; great eagerness 热爱; 热心; 热情: *The proposal aroused little enthusiasm in the group.* 该建议在这些人中未引起多大兴趣. ○ *feel no enthusiasm for/about an idea* 对某主意不感兴趣 ○ *an outburst of enthusiasm* 热情奔放 ○ *His enthusiasm made everyone else interested.* 他的热心激发了大家的兴致. **2** [C] object of this feeling 热中的事物: *One of my great enthusiasms is music.* 我的一大爱好就是音乐. ○ *Gardening is his latest enthusiasm.* 他近来爱好上园艺了.

▷ **en·thu·si·ast** /-'θjuːzɪæst; *US* -'θuː-; -'θuzɪˌæst/ *n* **~ (for/about sth)** person filled with enthusiasm 热情的人; 热心者; 热中者: *a sports enthusiast* 爱好运动的人 ○ *an enthusiast for/about all kinds of pop music* 酷爱各种流行音乐的人.

en·thu·si·astic /ɪnˌθjuːzɪ'æstɪk; *US* -θuː-; ɪnˌθuzɪ'æstɪk/ *adj* **~ (about/over sth/sb)** full of enthusiasm 热情的; 热心的: *He doesn't know much about the subject, but he's very enthusiastic.* 他对这事所知不多, 但却极感兴趣. ○ *She's very enthusiastic about singing.* 她非常喜欢唱歌. **en·thu·si·ast·ic·ally** /-klɪ; -klɪ/ *adv*: *She greeted him enthusiastically with a kiss.* 她热情地跟他打招呼并吻了他一下.

en·tice /ɪn'taɪs; ɪn'taɪs/ *v* [Tn, Tn·pr, Tn·p, Cn·t] **~ sb (away) (from sth); ~ sb (into sth/doing sth)** try to tempt or persuade sb, usu by offering sth pleasant or a reward 诱惑; 诱使; 怂恿: *Advertisements are designed to entice people into spending money/to spend money.* 广告宣传的目的是诱使人花钱. ○ *He enticed the young girl away from home.* 他把那小女孩诱惑得离开了家.

▷ **en·tice·ment** *n* **1** [U] enticing or being enticed 诱惑; 怂恿: *the enticement of a child into a car* 把一小孩哄进汽车里. **2** [C] thing that entices 诱惑物: *There were so many enticements offered that I could not refuse the job.* 这项工作有那么多优惠待遇, 使我难以拒绝.

en·ti·cing *adj* attractive or tempting 有吸引力的; 迷人的; 诱人的: *quite an enticing offer* 很诱人的条件 ○ *An enticing smell came from the bakery.* 从面包房里飘出了诱人的香味. **en·ti·cingly** *adv*.

en·tire /ɪn'taɪə(r); ɪn'taɪr/ *adj* [attrib 作定语] with no part left out; whole; complete 全部的; 整个的; 完全的: *The entire village was destroyed.* 整个村子被毁. ○ *I've wasted an entire day on this.* 我为此事浪费了一整天的时间. ○ *We are in entire agreement with you.* 我们完全同意你的意见.

▷ **en·tirely** *adv* completely 完全地: *entirely unnecessary* 完全不必要 ○ *Although they are twins, they look entirely different.* 他们虽是孪生, 但是相貌却完全不同. ○ *I'm not entirely happy with that idea.* 我对那个主意并不十分满意.

en·tir·ety /ɪn'taɪərətɪ; ɪn'taɪrtɪ/ *n* [U] state of being entire; completeness 整体; 全面: *We must examine the problem in its entirety*, ie as a whole, not in parts only. 我们要全面地研究这个问题.

en·title /ɪn'taɪtl; ɪn'taɪtl/ *v* **1** [Cn·n usu passive 通常用于被动语态] give a title to (a book, play, etc) 给(书、剧本等)取名; 定名: *He entitled the book 'Savage Love'.* 他给这本书取名为《野性的爱》. ○ *She read a poem entitled 'The Apple Tree'.* 她读了一首题为《苹果树》的诗. **2** [Tn·pr esp passive 尤用于被动语态, Tnt] **~ sb to sth** give sb a right to have or do sth 给予某人获得某事物或做某事的权利; 使某人有资格获得某事物或做某事: *You are not entitled to unemployment benefit if you have never worked.* 从未参加过工作, 就没有资格领取失业救济金. ○ *After a hard day's work she felt entitled to a rest.* 她劳累了一天, 觉得理应休息一下了. ○ *This ticket doesn't entitle you to travel first class.* 你这张票不能坐头等位.

▷ **en·title·ment** *n* **1** [U] entitling (ENTITLE 2) or being entitled 授权; 有资格: *We have no record of your entitlement to free travel.* 我们没有让你免费旅行的凭据. **2** [C] thing to which one is entitled 有权得到的东西: *Have you all taken your full holiday entitlements?* 你们大家是不是把应有的假期都用了呢?

en·tity /'entətɪ; 'ɛntətɪ/ *n* **1** [C] thing with distinct and real existence 实体: *a separate political entity* 独立的政治实体. **2** [U] (*fml* 文) thing's existence (contrasted with its qualities, relations with other things, etc) 事物的存在(区别于其属性、与其他事物的关系等).

E

en·tomb /ɪn'tu:m; ɪn'tum/ *v* [Tn usu passive 通常用于被动语态] (*fml* 文) (**a**) place (a person or an animal) in, or as if in, a tomb 将(人或动物)(似)置于墓中; 埋葬: *Many people were entombed in the rubble of the bombed buildings.* 很多人被埋在炸毁的建筑物的瓦砾里. (**b**) serve as a tomb for (a person or an animal) 用作(人或动物)的坟墓.

en·to·mo·logy /ˌentə'mɒlədʒɪ; ˌɛntə'mɑlədʒɪ/ *n* [U] scientific study of insects 昆虫学: *His hobby is entomology.* 他爱好昆虫学.

▷ **en·to·mo·lo·gical** /ˌentəmə'lɒdʒɪkl; ˌɛntəmə'lɑdʒɪkl/ *adj*.

en·to·mo·lo·gist /-dʒɪst; -dʒɪst/ *n* student of or expert in entomology 昆虫学研究者; 昆虫学家.

en·tour·age /ˌɒntʊ'rɑ:ʒ; ˌɑntu'rɑʒ/ *n* [CGp] all those who accompany and attend an important person 随从; 随行人员: *the President and his entourage* 总统及其随从 ○ (*fig* 比喻) *She always has an entourage of admiring young men.* 她周围总是簇拥着追求她的年轻人.

en·trails /'entreɪlz; 'ɛntrəlz/ *n* [pl] internal organs of a person or animal, esp the intestines 内脏; (尤指)肠: *The dish was made from the entrails of a sheep.* 这盘菜是羊杂碎.

en·trance[1] /'entrəns; 'ɛntrəns/ *n* **1** [C] **~ (to sth)** opening, gate, door, passage, etc by which one enters sth 入口; 门; 通道等: *Where's the entrance to the cave?* 这个洞穴的入口在哪里? ○ *There is a front and a back entrance to the house.* 这所房子有一个前门和一个后门. ○ *I'll meet you at the entrance to the theatre.* 我在剧院门口和你见面. **2** [U, C] **~ (into/onto sth)** coming or going in; entering 进来; 进去; 进入: *the Prime Minister's entrance into office* 首相就职 ○ *The hero makes his entrance (on stage) in Act 2.* 男主角在第二幕出场. ○ *An actor must learn his entrances and exits*, ie when to enter and leave the stage. 演员一定要懂得何时出场和退场. **3** [U] **~ (to sth)** right of entering; admission 进入的权利; 准予进入: *They were refused entrance to the club.* 他们被拒于俱乐部门外. ○ [attrib 作定语] *a university entrance examination* 大学入学考试 ○ *an entrance fee*, ie money paid so that one may enter an exhibition, etc or join a club, society, etc 入场费; 入会费.

en·trance[2] /ɪn'trɑ:ns; *US* -'træns; ɪn'træns/ *v* [usu passive 通常用于被动语态: Tn, Tn·pr] **~ sb (by/with sth)** fill sb with great emotion and delight as if by magic 使某人(着魔般)狂喜, 着迷: *entranced at the beautiful sight* 被美丽的景色迷住了 ○ *They were completely entranced by/with the music.* 他们完全陶醉在音乐中. ○ *We sat entranced by her beauty.* 我们坐在那里看着她的美貌出神.

ent·rant /'entrənt; 'ɛntrənt/ *n* **1 ~ (for sth)** person or animal that enters, esp for a race, a competition or an examination 参加者(尤指比赛、竞赛或考试): *There are fifty entrants for the dog show.* 有五十条狗参加狗展. ○ *university entrants* 大学入学试的考生. **2 ~ (to sth)** person who enters a profession 加入某行业的人: *an entrant to the diplomatic service* 初入外交界做事的人 ○ *women entrants to the police force* 新加入警察部队的妇女.

en·trap /ɪn'træp; ɪn'træp/ *v* (**-pp-**) [esp passive 尤用于被动语态: Tn, Tn·pr] (*fml* 文) **1 ~ sb/sth (by/in sth)** catch sb/sth (as) in a trap 使某人[某物]陷入圈套; 诱捕. **2 ~ sb (into doing sth)** trick or deceive sb 要弄或欺骗某人: *He felt he had been entrapped into marrying her.* 他觉得和她结婚是上了当.

en·treat /ɪn'tri:t; ɪn'trit/ *v* [Tn, Tn·pr, Dn·t] **~ (sth of) sb** (*fml* 文) ask sb (for sth) earnestly and feelingly; beg (为某事)恳求某人; 请求; 乞求: *Please don't go, I entreat you.* 我求求您, 请不要走. ○ *May I entreat a favour of you?* 您能帮帮忙吗? ○ *I entreat you to show mercy.* 我求您发发慈悲. ⇨Usage at ASK 用法见 ASK. ▷ **en·treat·ingly** *adv*.

en·treaty /ɪn'tri:tɪ; ɪn'tritɪ/ *n* [C, U] earnest request or requesting 恳求; 请求; 要求: *deaf to all entreaties* 对一切请求置若罔闻 ○ *with a look of entreaty* 恳求的神态.

en·trée /'ɒntreɪ; 'ɑntre/ *n* (*fml* 文) **1** [U, C] **~ (into sth)** right or privilege of admission or entry 获准进入的权利或特权: *Her wealth and reputation gave her (an) entrée into upper-class circles.* 她的财富和声望使她得以进入上层社会. **2** [C] dish served between the fish and meat courses at a formal dinner 在正式宴席上, 在鱼和肉两道主菜之间所上的菜: *What did you have as an entrée?* 在鱼和肉两道主菜之间, 你吃的是什么菜? ○ [attrib 作定语] *an entrée dish* 在鱼和肉两道主菜之间的一道菜.

en·trench (also **in·trench**) /ɪn'trentʃ; ɪn'trɛntʃ/ *v* [Tn usu passive 通常用于被动语态] **1** surround or protect (sb/sth) with a trench or trenches 用壕沟围绕或保护(某人[某物]): *The enemy were strongly entrenched on the other side of the river.* 敌军在河的对岸用坚固的壕沟防守. **2** (*fig sometimes derog* 比喻, 有时作贬义) establish (sth/sb) very firmly 牢固地确立(某人[某事物]): *entrenched ideas*, ie ones that are firmly fixed in the mind 根深蒂固的想法 ○ *entrenched rights*, ie those that are guaranteed by legislation 固有的权利 ○ *She is entrenched in her right-wing views.* 她的右翼观点根深蒂固.

▷ **en·trench·ment** *n* **1** [C] system of trenches made for defence 堑壕. **2** [U] action of entrenching or being entrenched 掘壕沟; 用壕沟防护.

en·tre·pôt /'ɒntrəpəʊ; 'ɑntrəˌpo/ *n* (**a**) warehouse where goods being sent from one place to another may be stored temporarily 货仓. (**b**) trading centre or port for the import, export, collection and distribution of goods (进出口)货物集散地, 贸易中心, 转口港.

en·tre·pren·eur /ˌɒntrəprə'nɜ:(r); ˌɑntrəprə'nɝ/ *n* **1** person who starts or organizes a commercial enterprise, esp one involving financial risk 企业家(尤指涉及财务风险的): *He would not have succeeded in such a risky business if he had not been such a clever entrepreneur.* 假若他不是那么精明强干的企业家, 就不会在这样冒险的事业中取得成功. **2** person who works under contract as an intermediary in the business affairs of others 承包人. ▷ **en·tre·pren·eur·ial** /-'nɜ:rɪəl; -'nɝɪəl/ *adj*: *entrepreneurial flair, skills, etc* 具有创业的才能、技巧等.

en·trust /ɪn'trʌst; ɪn'trʌst/ *v* [Tn·pr] **~ A to B /~ B with A** trust sb to take charge of sth/sb 委托某人负责某事物[照看某人]: *entrust an assistant with a task/entrust the task to an assistant* 把一项工作交给助手 ○ *Can I entrust you with the secret plans?* 我能把这些秘密计划委托给你吗? ○ *He's entrusted his children to me/to my care for the day.* 他托我照看一天孩子.

entry /'entrɪ; 'ɛntrɪ/ *n* **1** [C] **~ (into sth)** act of coming or going in 进入: *The children were surprised by the sudden entry of their teacher.* 老师突然进来把孩子们吓了一跳. ○ *the entry of the USA into world politics* 美国对世界政治的参与 ○ *The thieves had forced an entry into the building.* 窃贼闯进了楼内. **2** [U] **~ (to sth)** right of entering 进入权: *We can't go along that road because the sign says 'No Entry'.* 我们不能走那条路, 因为牌子上

写着'禁止入内'. ○ *He finally gained entry to the hotel by giving some money to the doorman.* 他给了门卫一些钱, 终于得以进入旅馆. ○ [attrib 作定语] *an entry visa*, ie a stamp or signature on a passport allowing sb to enter a particular country 入境签证. **3** [C] **(a)** (place of) entrance, esp a passage or small entrance hall 入口(处)(尤指过道、小门厅): *You can leave your umbrella in the entry.* 雨伞可放于入口处. ○ *the entry to a block of flats* 公寓大楼的入口处. **(b)** narrow passage between buildings 建筑物之间的甬道. **4 (a)** [C] **~ (in sth)** item written in a list, a diary, an account book, etc (写进清单、日记、帐本等的)项目: *There's no entry in his diary for that day.* 他的日记上没有那一天的记录. ○ *I'll have to check the entries in the ledger.* 我得核对一下总帐的项目. ○ *entries in a dictionary* 词典的条目. **(b)** [U] recording of such an item (这种项目的)记载, 记录, 登记: *The entry of all expenditure is necessary.* 有必要把一切开支入帐. **5 ~ (for sth) (a)** [C] person or thing that is entered for a competition 参加比赛的人或物: *fifty entries for the 800 metres* 有五十人参加800米赛跑 ○ *a last-minute entry for the pony race* 最后关头才参赛的马 ○ *This painting is my entry for the art competition.* 这幅画是我参加艺术比赛的作品. **(b)** [sing] list or total number of persons, etc entered for a competition (参加比赛的)名单、总人数等: *There's a large entry for the flower show this year.* 今年的花展有大量花卉参展.

Entry·phone /ˈentrɪfəʊn; ˋɛntrɪfon/ *n* (*propr* 专利名) type of telephone placed on the wall by the entrance to a building, esp a block of flats, to enable visitors to speak to individual occupants before being allowed to enter 对讲机(安装在公寓等建筑物入口处墙上的一种电话, 可使来访者与住户通话后获准入内).

en·twine /ɪnˈtwaɪn; ɪnˋtwaɪn/ *v* [Tn, Tn·pr] **~ sth (with/round sth) (a)** make sth by twisting one thing around another 编制(将一物缠绕在另一物上制成某物): *entwine a garland of flowers* 编制花冠. **(b)** wind one thing with or round another 缠绕; 挽; 搂: *They walked along with (their) arms entwined.* 他们挽着胳膊走去.

enu·mer·ate /ɪˈnju:məreɪt; *US* ɪˈnu:-; ɪˋnumə,ret/ *v* [Tn] name (things on a list) one by one; count 列出(清单上的事物); 数: *She enumerated the items we had to buy — sugar, tea, soap, etc.* 她列出了我们要购买的东西——糖、茶叶、肥皂等. ▷ **enu·mera·tion** /ɪˌnju:məˈreɪʃn; *US* ɪˌnu:-; ɪ,numəˋreʃən/ *n* [U, C].

enun·ci·ate /ɪˈnʌnsɪeɪt; ɪˋnʌnsɪ,et/ *v* **1** [I, Tn] say or pronounce (words or sounds) clearly (清晰地)念(字), 发(音): *That actor enunciates very well.* 那演员发音很清晰. ○ *She enunciated each word slowly for her students.* 她把每个字都给学生慢慢念清楚. **2** [Tn] express (a theory, etc) clearly or distinctly 阐明(理论等): *He is always willing to enunciate his opinions on the subject of politics.* 他总是愿意对政治问题发表意见. ▷ **enun·ci·ation** /ɪˌnʌnsɪˈeɪʃn; ɪ,nʌnsɪˋeʃən/ *n* [C, U].

en·velop /ɪnˈveləp; ɪnˋvɛləp/ *v* [Tn, Tn·pr] **~ sth/sb (in sth)** wrap sth/sb up; cover or surround sth/sb completely (in sth) 包住某事物[某人]; 将某事物[某人]覆盖, 包围(于某事物中): *mountains enveloped in cloud* 隐没在云中的群山 ○ *a baby enveloped in a blanket* 裹在毛毯中的婴儿 ○ *The coat was far too big — it completely enveloped him.* 大衣太大——把他整个儿包起来了. ○ (*fig* 比喻) *envelop a subject in mystery* 把某一问题弄得神秘莫测. ▷ **en·velop·ment** *n* [U].

en·vel·ope /ˈenvələʊp, *also* ˈɒn-; ˋɛnvə,lop, ˋɑnvə,lop/ *n* wrapper or covering, esp one made of paper for a letter 封套; 封皮; (尤指)信封: *writing paper and envelopes* 信纸和信封 ○ *an airmail envelope* 航空信封.

en·venom /ɪnˈvenəm; ɪnˋvɛnəm/ *v* [Tn esp passive 尤用于被动语态] (*fml* 文) **1** put poison on or in (eg a weapon) 置毒药于(如武器)上: *an envenomed dagger* 涂有毒药的匕首. **2** (*fig* 比喻) fill (sth/sb) with bitter hatred 使(某事物[某人])充满怨恨: *arguments envenomed with spite* 怀有恶意的争辩.

en·vi·able /ˈenvɪəbl; ˋɛnvɪəbl/ *adj* (of people or things) causing envy; desirable enough to cause envy (指人或物)引起忌妒的; 值得羡慕的: *an enviable achievement* 值得羡慕的成就 ○ *an enviable examination result* 值得羡慕的考试成绩 ○ *an enviable woman*, eg one whose life is happy and successful 令人羡慕的女人(如其生活幸福成功者). ▷ **en·vi·ably** /-blɪ; -blɪ/ *adv*: *enviably rich* 富得令人羡慕.

en·vi·ous /ˈenvɪəs; ˋɛnvɪəs/ *adj* **~ (of sb/sth)** full of envy; feeling, showing or expressing envy 满怀忌妒的; 表现出或表示忌妒或羡慕的: *I'm so envious of you getting an extra day's holiday.* 我真羡慕你得到一天额外的假期. ○ *She cast envious glances at her sister's dress.* 她以羡慕的目光看着姐姐的连衣裙. ○ *He was envious of his brother's success.* 他忌妒他哥哥的成功. ▷ **en·vi·ously** *adv*.

en·vir·on·ment /ɪnˈvaɪərənmənt; ɪnˋvaɪrənmənt/ *n* **1** [C, U] conditions, circumstances, etc affecting people's lives (影响人们生活的)情况、环境等: *An unhappy home environment can affect a child's behaviour.* 不愉快的家庭环境能影响儿童的行为. ○ *A noisy smoke-filled room is not the best environment to work in.* 房间里乌烟瘴气于工作十分不利. **2 the environment** [sing] natural conditions, eg land, air and water, in which we live (我们生活的)自然环境(如土地、空气、水): *Many people are concerned about the pollution of the environment.* 许多人都关心环境污染问题. ○ *measures to protect the environment*, ie prevent spoiling it further 保护环境的措施(防止进一步污染) ○ *the Department of the Environment*, ie the British Government department responsible for land planning, transport, preservation of public amenities, pollution control, protection of the coast and countryside, etc 环境事务部(英国政府部门, 负责土地规划、运输、保护公共设施、控制污染、保护海岸和乡村等).

▷ **en·vir·on·mental** /ɪnˌvaɪərənˈmentl; ɪn,vaɪrənˋmɛntl/ *adj* **1** of or caused by a person's environment 个人环境的; 由个人环境产生的: *disturbing environmental influences* 令人不安的环境影响. **2** of the environment 环境的: *environmental science* 环境科学. **en·vir·on·ment·al·ist** /ɪnˌvaɪərənˈmentəlɪst; ɪn,vaɪrənˋmɛntəlɪst/ *n* person who is concerned about and wants to improve or protect the environment 环境保护论者: [attrib 作定语] *an environmentalist protest* 环境保护论者的抗议. **en·vir·on·ment·ally** /-təlɪ; -tlɪ/ *adv*: *Building a new factory there would be environmentally disastrous.* 在那里建新工厂将严重损害环境.

en·vir·ons /ɪnˈvaɪərənz; ɪnˋvaɪrənz/ *n* [pl] (*fml* 文) districts surrounding a town, etc 郊区; 近郊等: *Berlin and its environs* 柏林及其郊区.

en·vis·age /ɪnˈvɪzɪdʒ; ɪnˋvɪzɪdʒ/ *v* [Tn, Tf, Tw, Tg, Tsg] picture (an event, action, etc) in the mind as a future possibility; imagine 展望; 想像: *Nobody can envisage the consequences of total nuclear war.* 没有人能想像出全面核子战争的后果. ○ *I can't envisage the plan('s) working.* 我无法设想计划能否行得通.

en·voy /ˈenvɔɪ; ˋɛnvɔɪ/ *n* **1** messenger or representative, esp one sent to deal with a foreign government 使者; 代表; (尤指)外交官: *the Archbishop of Canterbury's envoy* 坎特伯雷大主教的使者. **2** diplomatic agent next in rank below an ambassador 公使.

envy[1] /ˈenvɪ; ˋɛnvɪ/ *n* [U] **1 ~ (of sb); ~ (at/of sth)** feeling of discontent caused by sb else's good fortune or success, esp when one wishes this for oneself 忌妒; 羡慕: *He couldn't conceal his envy of me/envy at my success.* 他遮掩不住对我的忌妒[对我的成就的忌妒]. ○ *His new car excited their envy.* 他们很羡慕他的新汽车. ○ *They only say such unkind things about you out of envy*, ie because they are full of envy. 他们纯粹出于忌妒才说你这些坏话. **2** (idm 习语) **the envy of sb** thing that causes sb to feel envy 令人忌妒或羡慕的事物: *Her many talents were the envy of all her friends.* 她多才多艺, 所有的朋友都很羡慕她. ○ *He's the envy of the whole street.* 整条街的人都很羡慕他. Cf 参看 JEALOUSY.

envy[2] /ˈenvɪ; ˋɛnvɪ/ *v* (*pt, pp* **envied**) [Tn, Dn·n] feel envy of (sb) or at (sth) 忌妒或羡慕(某人[某事物]): *I envy you.* 我羡慕你. ○ *I have always envied your good luck.* 我一直羡慕你运气好. ○ *I don't envy him his money problems*, ie I'm happy I don't have them. 我庆幸自己没有他那些金钱的麻烦.

en·zyme /ˈenzaɪm; ˋɛnzaɪm/ *n* (*chemistry* 化) **1** organic chemical substance that is formed in living cells and assists chemical changes (eg in digestion) without being changed itself 酶; 酵素. **2** similar substance produced artificially for use in detergents, etc 人造酶(用于清洁剂等): *Washing powders containing enzymes are said to*

E

remove stains more efficiently. 据说含有人造酶的洗衣粉去污力强.

eon = AEON.

EP /ˌiː ˈpiː; ˌi ˈpi/ *abbr* 缩写 = extended-play (record) 慢速唱片; 密纹唱片: *a collection of EPs* 一批慢速唱片. Cf 参看 SINGLE *n* 5, LP.

epaul·ette (also *esp US* **epaulet**) /ˈepəlet; ˋɛpəˌlɛt/ *n* shoulder ornament on a naval or military officer's uniform (海军或陆军军官制服上的)肩章.

épée /ˈeɪpeɪ; eˋpe/ *n* thin sharp-pointed sword used (with the end blunted) in fencing (FENCE[2]) 重剑(钝化的击剑用剑). Cf 参看 FOIL[3], SABRE 2.

eph·em·era /ɪˈfemərə; əˋfɛmərə/ *n* [pl] things that are used, enjoyed, etc for only a short time and then forgotten 只可短期使用、享受等的事物.

eph·em·eral /ɪˈfemərəl; əˋfɛmərəl/ *adj* living, lasting, etc for a very short time (生存、持续等)短暂的: *ephemeral pleasures* 短暂的欢乐 ○ *Slang words are often ephemeral.* 俚语往往只流行于一时.

epic /ˈepɪk; ˋɛpɪk/ *n* **1** (**a**) long poem about the deeds of one or more great heroes, or a nation's past history 叙事诗; 史诗: *Homer's Iliad is a famous epic.* 荷马的《伊利亚特》是著名的史诗. (**b**) long film, story, etc dealing with heroic deeds and exciting adventures 叙述英雄事迹和历险的电影、故事等: *yet another epic about the Roman empire* 另一部关于罗马帝国的电影. **2** (*infml or joc* 口或谑) subject fit to be regarded as heroic 惊人之举: *Mending the car became something of an epic.* 修理汽车竟然也算是了不起的事.

▷ **epic** *adj* [usu attrib 通常作定语] of or like an epic; heroic; grand 史诗般的; 英勇的; 宏伟的: *an epic encounter, struggle, achievement* 可歌可泣的遭遇战、英勇的斗争、伟大的成就.

epi·centre (*US* **epi·center**) /ˈepɪsentə(r); ˋɛpɪˌsɛntɚ/ *n* (**a**) point at which an earthquake reaches the earth's surface 震中; 震央. (**b**) (*fig* 比喻) central point of a difficult situation 困难所在: *the epicentre of the riot* 暴乱的中心.

epi·cure /ˈepɪkjʊə(r); ˋɛpɪˌkjʊr/ *n* person who takes a special interest in and gets great pleasure from food and drink 美食家: *This cookery book has been written by a real epicure.* 这本食谱是由一位真正的美食家写的.

epi·cur·ean /ˌepɪkjʊˈriːən; ˌɛpɪkjʊˋriən/ *n, adj* (person who is) fond of pleasure and luxury 爱享乐的; 享乐主义者: *In his youth he was an extravagant epicurean.* 他年轻时是个花花公子. ○ *an epicurean feast* 丰盛的宴席.

epi·demic /ˌepɪˈdemɪk; ˌɛpəˋdɛmɪk/ *n, adj* (disease) spreading quickly among many people in the same place for a time 流行性的; 流行病: *an influenza epidemic* 流行性感冒 ○ (*fig* 比喻) *an epidemic of crime in our major cities* 在我们的大城市中罪案频仍 ○ *Football hooliganism is now reaching epidemic proportions.* 足球比赛中恣意闹事现已达愈演愈烈的地步. Cf 参看 ENDEMIC, PANDEMIC.

epi·dermis /ˌepɪˈdɜːmɪs; ˌɛpəˋdɝmɪs/ *n* [U, C] (*anatomy* 解) outer layer of the skin 表皮: *a damaged epidermis* 受损伤的表皮.

epi·dural /ˌepɪˈdjʊərəl; ˌɛpəˋdjʊrəl/ *adj* (*medical* 医) (of an anaesthetic) injected round the nerves in the spine and having the effect of anaesthetizing the lower part of the body (指麻醉剂)硬膜外的.

▷ **epi·dural** *n* epidural injection 硬膜外注射: *Epidurals are now often used during childbirth.* 现在分娩时常用硬膜外注射.

epi·glot·tis /ˌepɪˈglɒtɪs; ˌɛpəˋglɑtɪs/ *n* (*anatomy* 解) thin flap of tissue at the back of the tongue that covers the windpipe during swallowing to prevent food or drink from entering the lungs 会厌. ▷ **epi·glot·tal** /-ˈglɒtl; -ˋglɑtḷ/ *adj*.

epi·gram /ˈepɪgræm; ˋɛpəˌgræm/ *n* short poem or saying expressing an idea in a clever and amusing way 诙谐短诗; 警句: *The playwright Oscar Wilde was noted for his epigrams.* 剧作家奥斯卡·王尔德以他的诙谐短诗著称.

▷ **epi·gram·matic** /ˌepɪgrəˈmætɪk; ˌɛpəgrəˋmætɪk/ *adj* expressing things, or expressed, in a short and witty way 精警的: *an epigrammatic style* 善用警句的风格.

epi·lepsy /ˈepɪlepsɪ; ˋɛpəˌlɛpsɪ/ *n* [U] disease of the nervous system that causes a person to fall unconscious (often with violent uncontrolled movements of the body) 癫痫症; 羊痫风; 羊角风: *various forms of epilepsy* 各类的癫痫.

▷ **epi·leptic** /ˌepɪˈleptɪk; ˌɛpəˋlɛptɪk/ *adj* of epilepsy 癫痫的: *an epileptic fit* 癫痫发作. — *n* person who suffers from epilepsy 癫痫症患者: *She's been an epileptic from birth.* 她是先天性癫痫患者.

epi·logue /ˈepɪlɒg; ˋɛpəˌlɔg/ (*US* **epi·log** /-lɔːg; -lɒg/) *n* (**a**) part or section added at the end of a book, play, film, programme, etc, as a comment on the main action (书、剧本、电影、节目等的)结尾部分, 后记; 跋. (**b**) short speech or poem spoken by one of the characters at the end of a play (戏剧演出结束时由一个角色念的)收场白, 收场诗: *Fortinbras speaks the epilogue in Shakespeare's 'Hamlet'.* 在莎士比亚的《哈姆雷特》中, 由福丁布拉斯念收场白. Cf 参看 PROLOGUE.

Epi·phany /ɪˈpɪfənɪ; ɪˋpɪfənɪ/ *n* Christian festival held on 6 January, in memory of the coming of the Magi to the baby Jesus at Bethlehem 显现节, 主显节(每年1月6日纪念耶稣显灵的节日).

epis·copal /ɪˈpɪskəpl; ɪˋpɪskəpḷ/ *adj* (*fml* 文) of or governed by a bishop or bishops 主教的; 主教管辖的: *the Episcopal Church*, ie (esp) the Anglican Church in the US and Scotland (尤指美国和苏格兰的)圣公会. Cf 参看 PRESBYTERIAN.

▷ **epis·co·pa·lian** /ɪˌpɪskəˈpeɪlɪən; ɪˌpɪskəˋpelɪən/ *n, adj* (member) of an episcopal church 圣公会的; 圣公会教徒: *Are you a Roman Catholic or an Episcopalian?* 你是罗马天主教徒还是圣公会教徒?

epi·sio·tomy /əˌpiːzɪˈɒtəmɪ; əˌpizɪˋɑtəmɪ/ *n* (*medical* 医) cut made at the opening of the vagina during childbirth to aid the delivery of the baby 外阴切开术.

epis·ode /ˈepɪsəʊd; ˋɛpəˌsod/ *n* [C] **1** (description of an) event occurring as part of a long series of events as in a novel, one's life, etc (小说或人生等的)片段, 插曲: *That's an episode in my life I'd rather forget!* 那是我一生中但愿忘却的经历! ○ *One of the funniest episodes in the book occurs in Chapter 6.* 书中最有趣的部分是在第6章. **2** part of a TV or radio serial broadcast at one time (电视或无线电广播的)一集: *the final episode* 大结局 ○ *Listen to the next exciting episode tomorrow night.* 请于明晚收听精彩的下一集.

▷ **epis·odic** /ˌepɪˈsɒdɪk; ˌɛpəˋsɑdɪk/ *adj* (**a**) occurring irregularly; sporadic 偶然发生的; 分散性的: *episodic fits of depression* 阵发性抑郁症. (**b**) (of a story, novel, etc) containing or consisting of a series of events (指故事、小说等)由一系列片段组成的: *an episodic style* 描述一系列片段故事的写作风格.

epistle /ɪˈpɪsl; ɪˋpɪsḷ/ *n* **1** (*usu joc* 通常作戏谑语) letter 书信: *Her mother sends her a long epistle every week.* 她母亲每周给她写一封长信. **2 Epistle** (*Bible* 圣经) any of the letters included in the New Testament, written by the Apostles 《新约全书》中的使徒书信: *the Epistle of St Paul to the Romans* 《保罗达罗马人书》.

▷ **epis·tol·ary** /ɪˈpɪstələrɪ; *US* -lerɪ; ɪˋpɪstəˌlɛrɪ/ *adj* (*fml* 文) of, carried on by, or written in the form of letters 书信的; 用书信进行的; 书信体的: *an epistolary friendship* 书来信往的友谊 ○ *an epistolary novel* 书信体小说.

epi·taph /ˈepɪtɑːf; *US* -tæf; ˋɛpəˌtæf/ *n* words written or said about a dead person, esp words inscribed on a tombstone 悼文; 祭文; 悼词; (尤指)墓志铭.

epi·thet /ˈepɪθet; ˋɛpəˌθɛt/ *n* adjective or descriptive phrase that refers to the character or most important quality of sb/sth eg Alfred *the Great*, Attila *the Hun* (表示某人[某事物]性格或最主要特性的)修饰词或描述性短语(如阿尔弗烈德大王, 匈奴王阿提拉).

epi·tome /ɪˈpɪtəmɪ; ɪˋpɪtəmɪ/ *n* **1** thing that shows on a small scale all the characteristics of sth much larger 梗概; 缩影: *The divisions we see in this school are the epitome of those occurring throughout the whole country.* 我们在这所学校中看到的各个部门是全国各校的缩影. **2** person or thing that is a perfect example of a quality, type, etc 典型的人或事物: *the absolute epitome of a school teacher* 中小学教师的典范 ○ *She's the epitome of kindness.* 她是仁慈的化身. **3** (*dated* 旧) short summary of a book, speech, etc (书、演讲等的)摘要.

▷ **epi·tom·ize, -ise** /ɪˈpɪtəmaɪz; ɪˋpɪtəˌmaɪz/ *v* [Tn] be an epitome of (sth) 成为(某事物)的缩影: *He epitomizes everything I dislike.* 我讨厌的一切都在他身上体现出来

了. ○ *She epitomizes the loving mother.* 她是典型的慈母.

EPNS /ˌi: pi: en ˈes; ˌi pi ɛn ˋɛs/ *abbr* 缩写 = (on cutlery, tableware, etc) electroplated nickel silver (餐具等上的字样)电镀镍银.

epoch /ˈi:pɒk; *US* ˈepək; ˋɛpək/ *n* (beginning of a) period of time in history, life, the history of the earth, etc, esp one marked by notable events or characteristics 纪元; 时代; 时期: *Einstein's theory marked a new epoch in mathematics.* 爱因斯坦理论开创了数学的新纪元.

□ ˈ**epoch-making** *adj* (*fml or joc* 文或谑) important and remarkable enough to change the course of history and begin a new epoch 开新纪元的; 划时代的: *the epoch-making discovery of America* 发现美洲的划时代的创举 ○ *I told him his idea was not exactly epoch-making.* 我告诉他说他的思想算不上是划时代的.

Ep·som salts /ˌepsəm ˈsɔ:lts; ˋɛpsəm ˋsɔlts/ magnesium sulphate, a bitter white powder used medically to empty the bowels 泻盐.

equ·able /ˈekwəbl; ˋɛkwəbl/ *adj* **1** free from extremes of heat or cold; moderate 冷热适中的; 温和的: *an equable climate* 温和的气候. **2** (of a person) not easily upset or annoyed; even-tempered (指人)不易恼怒的, 性情温和的: *an equable temperament* 温和的性情 ○ *It's lucky that his parents are so equable.* 值得庆幸的是他双亲性情非常温和. ▷ **equ·ably** /ˈekwəblɪ; ˋɛkwəblɪ/ *adv*.

equal /ˈi:kwəl; ˋikwəl/ *adj* **1** the same in size, amount, value, number, degree, status, etc (大小、数量、价值、程度、状况等)相同的, 相等的, 同样的: *They are of equal height.* 他们一般高. ○ *Divide the cake into equal parts.* 把蛋糕分成等份. ○ *Equal amounts of flour and sugar should be added to the mixture.* 应在混合物中加入等量的面粉和糖. ○ *He speaks Arabic and English with equal ease.* 他说阿拉伯语和英语都一样自如. ○ *Women are demanding equal pay for equal work*, ie equal to that of men. 妇女要求同工同酬(与男人一样). ○ *In intelligence, the children are about equal.* 这些儿童在智力上大致相同. **2** [pred 作表语] **~ to sth/doing sth** having the strength, courage, ability, etc for sth 对某事物有力量、勇气、能力等; 能胜任: *She feels equal to the task.* 她认为能胜任该项工作. ○ *He's equal to* (ie able to deal with) *the occasion.* 他能应付这一局面. ○ *He doesn't seem equal to meeting our demands.* 他似乎不太合乎我们的要求. **3** (idm 习语) **on equal terms (with sb)** (meeting or speaking) as equals, with no difference in status or rank 平等相处; 地位相等: *Now that she has been promoted she is on equal terms with her ex-boss.* 她既然已升级, 就和原先的上司平起平坐了. **other things being equal** ⇨ THING.

▷ **equal** *n* person or thing equal to oneself in some way 和自己相当的人或事物: *He's my equal in strength.* 他和我力气一样大. ○ *She's the equal of her brother as far as intelligence is concerned.* 论智力, 她和她哥哥不相上下. ○ *We consider ourselves equals.* 我们彼此不分上下.

equal *v* (**-ll-**) (*US* **-l-**) [Tn, Tn·pr] **~ sb/sth (in sth)** be equal to sb/sth 与某人[某事物]相同或相等: *equalling the Olympic record* 平奥运会纪录 ○ *He is equalled by no one in kindness.* 没有人比他更善良.

equal·ity /ɪˈkwɒlətɪ; ɪˋkwɑlətɪ/ *n* [U] state of being equal 平等: *Women are still struggling for true equality with men.* 妇女仍在争取与男人真正平等. ○ *equality of opportunity*, ie having an equal chance of being considered for jobs, promotion, etc 机会均等(在求职、提升等方面有同等的机会).

equal·ize, -ise /ˈi:kwəlaɪz; ˋikwəlˌaɪz/ *v* [I, Tn] (cause sth to) become equal (in size, amount, etc) (使某事物)(在大小、数量等上)相等: *Germany were winning the match until just before the end when the other team equalized*, ie scored another goal to make the scores equal. 德国队眼看要赢得这场比赛, 而恰在终场前对方把比分扳平. **equal·iza·tion, -isation** /ˌi:kwəlaɪˈzeɪʃn; *US* -lɪˈz-; ˌikwələˋzeʃən/ *n* [U].

equally /ˈi:kwəlɪ; ˋikwəlɪ/ *adv* **1** in an equal manner or to an equal degree 相等地; 同等地: *They are equally clever.* 他们一样聪明. **2** in equal parts 均等: *They share the housework equally between them.* 他们平等分担家务. **3** also; similarly; in addition 也; 同样; 此外: *We must try to think about what is best for him; equally we must consider what he wants to do.* 我们要为他着想, 同时也要想到他愿意干什么.

equan·im·ity /ˌekwəˈnɪmətɪ; ˌikwəˋnɪmətɪ/ *n* [U] calmness of mind or temper 心情平静; 情绪镇定: *She maintained her equanimity throughout her long ordeal.* 她在长期的苦难中心情一直都很平静. ○ *Nothing disturbs his equanimity.* 没有任何事能扰乱他平静的心绪.

equate /ɪˈkweɪt; ɪˋkwet/ *v* [Tn, Tn·pr] **~ sth (to/with sth)** consider sth as equal or equivalent (to sth else) 认为某事物(与另一事物)相等或相仿: *You can't equate the education system of Britain to that of Germany.* 不能把英国教育制度与德国教育制度等同起来. ○ *He equates poverty with misery.* 他认为贫穷就是不幸.

equa·tion /ɪˈkweɪʒn; ɪˋkweʒən/ *n* **1** [C] (*mathematics* 数) statement that two expressions (connected by the sign =) are equal, eg *2x + 5 = 11* 等式(如 2x + 5 = 11). **2** [U] action of making equal or regarding as equal 等同; 相等: *The equation of wealth with happiness can be dangerous.* 把财富与幸福等同起来有时候很危险.

equator /ɪˈkweɪtə(r); ɪˋkwetɚ/ *n* imaginary line (or one drawn on a map, etc) around the earth at an equal distance from the North and South Poles 赤道: *It is very hot near the equator.* 赤道附近非常热. ⇨illus at GLOBE 见 GLOBE 之插图.

▷ **equat·or·ial** /ˌekwəˈtɔ:rɪəl; ˌɛkwəˋtorɪəl/ *adj* of or near the equator 赤道的; 赤道附近的: *an equatorial climate* 赤道的气候 ○ *equatorial jungles* 赤道附近的丛林.

equerry /ɪˈkwerɪ, *also* ˈekwərɪ; ɪˋkwɛrɪ, ˋɛkwərɪ/ *n* (in Britain) officer attending the king, the queen or a member of the royal family (英国的)王室侍从: *He is equerry to the Prince of Wales.* 他是威尔士亲王的侍从.

eques·trian /ɪˈkwestrɪən; ɪˋkwɛstrɪən/ *adj* [usu attrib 通常作定语] of horse-riding 骑马的: *equestrian skill* 骑术 ○ *an equestrian statue*, ie of a person on a horse 骑士塑像 ○ *equestrian events at the Olympic Games* 奥林匹克运动会的骑术比赛.

▷ **eques·trian** *n* person who is skilled at horse-riding 骑师.

equi- *comb form* 构词成分 equal; equally 同等的; 同等地: *equipoise* ○ *equidistant*.

equi·dist·ant /ˌi:kwɪˈdɪstənt; ˌikwəˋdɪstənt/ *adj* [pred 作表语] **~ (from sth)** (*fml* 文) at an equal distance (from two or more places, etc) 等距离: *Our house is equidistant from the two pubs in the village.* 我们的房子离村中两家酒馆距离相等.

equi·lat·eral /ˌi:kwɪˈlætərəl; ˌikwəˋlætərəl/ *adj* (*geometry* 几) having all sides equal 等边的: *an equilateral triangle* 等边三角形.

equi·lib·rium /ˌi:kwɪˈlɪbrɪəm, *also* ˌek-; ˌikwəˋlɪbrɪəm, ɛk-/ *n* [U] **1** state of being balanced 平衡; 均势: *This pair of scales is not in equilibrium.* 这个天平不平衡. ○ *He can't maintain enough equilibrium to ride a bike.* 他骑自行车不能保持平衡. **2** (*fig* 比喻) balanced state of mind, feelings, etc (心情、感情等)平静: *She lost her usual equilibrium and shouted at him angrily.* 她一反常态, 向他愤怒地叫喊.

equine /ˈekwaɪn; ˋikwaɪn/ *adj* of or like a horse or horses 马的; 似马的: *the equine species* 马类 ○ (*fig* 比喻) *He has a long equine face.* 他的脸像马脸那么长.

equi·nox /ˈi:kwɪnɒks, *also* ˈek-; ˋikwəˌnɑks, ɛk-/ *n* either of the two times in the year (around 21 March and 22 September) when the sun crosses the equator and day and night are of equal length 春分; 秋分: *spring/vernal equinox* 春分 ○ *autumnal equinox* 秋分. Cf 参看 SOLSTICE.

▷ **equi·noc·tial** /ˌi:kwɪˈnɒkʃl, *also* ˌek-; ˌikwəˋnɑkʃəl, ɛk-/ *adj* [usu attrib 通常作定语] of, at or near the equinox 春分或秋分时的; 在春分或秋分前后的: *equinoctial gales/tides* 春分或秋分时的暴风雨[潮汐].

equip /ɪˈkwɪp; ɪˋkwɪp/ *v* (**-pp-**) [Tn, Tn·pr] **~ sb/sth (with sth)** supply sb/sth (with what is needed, for a particular purpose) 配备; 装备: *They equipped themselves for the expedition.* 他们为远征治装. ○ *Please equip yourself with a sharp pencil and a rubber for the exam.* 请准备一枝尖的铅笔和一块橡皮参加考试. ○ *The soldiers were well equipped with weapons and ammunition.* 士兵们装备好了武器和弹药. ○ *A good education should equip you for life.* 有良好的教育能受用终生.

▷ **equip·ment** *n* [U] **1** things needed for a particular purpose 设备; 装备: *office equipment*, eg typewriters, photocopiers, stationery, etc 办公室的设备(如打字机、影印机、文具等) ○ *sports equipment* 运动器材 ○ *a factory with modern equipment* 有现代化设备的工厂. **2** action of equipping 装备; 配备: *The equipment of the photographic studio was expensive.* 装备摄影室的开支很大.

equi·poise /ˈekwɪpɔɪz; ˋɛkwə,pɔɪz/ *n* (*fml* 文) **1** [U] balanced state, esp of the mind; equilibrium 平衡状态; (尤指)心态平衡; 心情平静. **2** [C] thing that counterbalances 平衡物.

equit·able /ˈekwɪtəbl; ˋɛkwɪtəbḷ/ *adj* (*fml* 文) fair and just; reasonable 公正的; 合理的: *the most equitable solution to the dispute* 对该纠纷最公正的解决 ○ *Each person must have an equitable share.* 每人应得合理的一份. ▷ **equit·ably** /-blɪ; -blɪ/ *adv*.

equity /ˈekwətɪ; ˋɛkwətɪ/ *n* **1** [U] fairness; right judgement 公平; 公正的裁判: *The equity of the referee's decision was accepted by everyone.* 大家都同意裁判员的公正裁判. **2** [U] (*law* 律 *esp Brit*) principles of justice used to correct laws when these would seem unfair in special circumstances 衡平法. **3 equities** [pl] ordinary stocks and shares that carry no fixed interest (利息不定的)普通股.

E

equi·val·ent /ɪˈkwɪvələnt; ɪˋkwɪvələnt/ *adj* **~ (to sth)** equal in value, amount, meaning, importance, etc (价值、数量、意义、重要性等)相同的: *What is £5 equivalent to in French francs?* 5英镑相当于多少法国法郎? ○ *250 grams or an equivalent amount in ounces* 250克或与之相当的盎司.

▷ **equi·val·ence** /-ləns; -ləns/ *n* **1** [U] state or quality of being equivalent 均等; 等量. **2** [C] thing that is equivalent 相等物.

equi·val·ent *n* thing, amount or word that is equivalent 相等的事物或数量; 对应词: *the metric equivalent of two miles* 两英里的公制等距 ○ *Is there a French word that is the exact equivalent of the English word 'home'?* 法语中有没有和英语home完全一样的对应词?

equi·vocal /ɪˈkwɪvəkl; ɪˋkwɪvəkḷ/ *adj* **1** having a double or doubtful meaning; ambiguous 模棱两可的; 意义不明的: *The politician gave an equivocal answer.* 那政客的答复模棱两可. **2** (of behaviour, circumstances, etc) questionable; suspicious (指行为、情况等)不可靠的, 可疑的.

▷ **equi·voc·ate** /ɪˈkwɪvəkeɪt; ɪˋkwɪvə,ket/ *v* [I] speak in an ambiguous way to hide the truth or mislead people 说模棱两可的话; 支吾; 蒙混: *Don't equivocate with me — I want a straight answer to a straight question!* 别跟我绕弯子——我问的问题直截了当, 回答也要直截了当!

equi·voca·tion /ɪ,kwɪvəˈkeɪʃn; ɪ,kwɪvəˋkeʃən/ *n* **1** [U] use of equivocal statements to mislead people 用模棱两可的话迷惑人; 含糊其词. **2** [C] equivocal expression 暧昧语.

ER *abbr* 缩写 = (eg on post-boxes) Queen Elizabeth (Latin *Elizabetha Regina*) (如邮政信箱上的字样)伊丽莎白女王(源自拉丁文*Elizabetha Regina*). Cf 参看 GR.

-er *suff* 后缀 **1** (with *vs* forming *ns* 接在动词后构成名词) person or thing that does 施动的人或事物: *lover* ○ *computer*. Cf 参看 -EE, -OR. **2** (with *ns* forming *ns* 接在名词后构成名词) (**a**) person concerned with 与...有关的人: *astronomer* ○ *philosopher*. (**b**) person belonging to 属于...的人: *New Yorker* ○ *villager* ○ *sixth-former*. (**c**) thing that has 有...的东西: *three-wheeler* ○ *double-decker*.

era /ˈɪərə; ˋɪrə/ *n* [C] **1** period in history starting from a particular time or event 纪元; 年代; 时代: *the Elizabethan era* 伊丽莎白时代. **2** period in history marked by an important event or development (以重大事件或重要发展为标志的)历史时期, 时代: *the era of the miniskirt* 超短裙时代 ○ *We are living in the computer era.* 我们正生活在计算机时代.

erad·ic·ate /ɪˈrædɪkeɪt; ɪˋrædɪ,ket/ *v* [Tn] destroy (sth) completely; put an end to (sth) 根除, 消灭(某事物); 结束(某事物): *Smallpox has almost been eradicated.* 天花几乎已消灭. ○ *attempts to eradicate crime* 力图根除罪恶的行动.

▷ **erad·ica·tion** /ɪ,rædɪˈkeɪʃn; ɪ,rædɪˋkeʃən/ *n* [U].

erad·ic·ator /ɪˈrædɪkeɪtə(r); ɪˋrædɪ,ketɚ/ *n* [C, U] person or thing that eradicates, esp a chemical substance that removes ink marks 根除者; 消除物(尤指去墨水迹的化学物质): *a bottle of ink eradicator* 一瓶消字灵.

erase /ɪˈreɪz; *US* ɪˈreɪs; ɪˋres/ *v* **1** [Tn, Tn·pr] **~ sth (from sth)** rub or scrape sth out; remove all traces of sth 擦掉或刮掉某物; 消除某事物的痕迹: *erase pencil marks* 擦去铅笔的笔迹 ○ (*fig* 比喻) *She couldn't erase the incident from her memory.* 她难以忘却那次事故. **2** [Tn] remove a recording from (magnetic tape) 从(磁带)上抹去录音或录像.

▷ **eraser** /ɪˈreɪzə(r); *US* -sər; ɪˋresɚ/ *n* (*US*; *Brit fml* 文) (*Brit* also **rubber**) thing that erases, esp a piece of rubber, etc for removing pencil marks 清除用具(尤指擦去铅笔笔迹的橡皮等). **eraser head** device on a cassette or video player for erasing material recorded on magnetic tape (录音机或录像机上的)消磁器.

eras·ure /ɪˈreɪʒə(r); ɪˋreʒɚ/ *n* (*fml* 文) **1** [U] action of erasing 擦掉; 刮掉; 消除. **2** [C] (**a**) word, etc that has been erased 删掉的词等. (**b**) place or mark where sth has been erased 涂擦的痕迹: *erasures in a letter* 信中的涂擦痕迹.

ere /eə(r); ɛr/ *conj, prep* (*arch or rhet* 古或修辞) before 在...以前: *ere break of day* 破晓前 ○ *ere long*, ie soon 不久.

erect[1] /ɪˈrekt; ɪˋrɛkt/ *adj* **1** standing on end; upright; vertical 直立的; 竖直的; 垂直的: *stand erect* 笔直地站着 ○ *hold a banner erect* 将旗子举直. **2** (of a part of the body, esp the penis) swollen and stiff from sexual excitement (指身体的某部, 尤指阴茎)因性刺激而勃起的. ▷ **erect·ness** *n* [U].

erect[2] /ɪˈrekt; ɪˋrɛkt/ *v* [Tn] (*fml* 文) **1** build; set up; establish 建造; 设立; 创立: *erect a monument* 竖立纪念碑 ○ *A statue was erected to* (ie to honour the memory of) *Queen Victoria.* 为纪念维多利亚女王建起了一座雕像. **2** set upright; put up 竖起; 搭起: *erect a tent, a flagstaff* 搭起帐篷、竖起旗杆.

▷ **erec·tion** /ɪˈrekʃn; ɪˋrɛkʃən/ *n* **1** [U] (*fml* 文) action of erecting; state of being erected 建造; 设立; 创立: *The erection of the building took several months.* 建造这座建筑物花了好几个月的时间. **2** [C] (*fml sometimes derog* 文, 有时作贬义) thing that has been erected; building or structure 竖立物; 建筑物: *She calls the new opera house 'that hideous erection'.* 她把新歌剧院称作'那讨厌的庞然大物'. **3** [C] hardening and swelling (esp of the penis) in sexual excitement (性兴奋时, 尤指阴茎之)勃起: *get/have an erection* 产生勃起.

erec·tile /ɪˈrektaɪl; *US* -tl; ɪˋrɛktḷ/ *adj* (*anatomy* 解) (of parts of the body, esp the penis) that can become swollen and stiff from sexual excitement (指身体的某部, 尤指阴茎)能勃起的: *erectile tissue* 勃起组织.

erg /ɜːg; ɝg/ *n* unit of energy in the metric system 尔格(能量的公制单位).

ergo /ˈɜːgəʊ; ˋɝgo/ *adv* (*usu joc* 通常作戏谑语) therefore 所以; 因此.

er·go·nom·ics /,ɜːgəˈnɒmɪks; ,ɝgəˋnɑmɪks/ *n* [sing *v*] study of work and working conditions in order to improve people's efficiency 工效学; 工作环境改造学.

er·mine /ˈɜːmɪn; ˋɝmɪn/ *n* **1** [C] (*pl* unchanged or **~s** 复数或不变或作 **ermines**) small animal of the weasel family whose fur is brown in summer and white in winter 貂; 扫雪鼬. Cf 参看 FERRET, STOAT, WEASEL. **2** [U] its white winter fur, esp as used to trim the robes of judges, etc 白色貂皮(尤用于制法官等的长袍的饰边): *a gown trimmed with ermine* 饰以貂皮的长袍 ○ [attrib 作定语] *ermine robes* 白色貂皮袍.

erode /ɪˈrəʊd; ɪˋrod/ *v* [Tn esp passive 尤用于被动语态] (of acids, rain, wind, etc) destroy or wear (sth) away gradually (指酸、雨、风等)侵蚀, 腐蚀(某物): *Metals are eroded by acids.* 金属能被酸腐蚀. ○ *The sea has eroded the cliff face over the years.* 海水经年累月冲刷着峭壁的表面. ○ (*fig* 比喻) *The rights of the individual are being steadily eroded.* 个人的权利正逐渐受到侵犯.

▷ **ero·sion** /ɪˈrəʊʒn; ɪˋroʒən/ *n* [U] process of eroding or being eroded 侵蚀; 腐蚀: *the erosion of the coastline by the sea* 海水对海岸的冲刷 ○ *attempts to reduce soil erosion* 减少土壤侵蚀的做法 ○ (*fig* 比喻) *the steady erosion of the President's credibility* 总统的威信日渐丧失.

ero·sive /ɪˈrəʊsɪv; ɪˋrosɪv/ *adj*.

ero·gen·ous /ɪˈrɒdʒənəs; ɪˋrɑdʒənəs/ *adj* (of areas of

the body) particularly sensitive to sexual stimulation (指身体的某部)性欲发生的: e,rogenous 'zones 性欲发生区.

erotic /ɪˈrɒtɪk; ɪˈrɑtɪk/ *adj* of or arousing sexual desire 性欲的; 色情的; 引起性欲的: *erotic art, verse, photography, etc* 色情艺术、诗歌、摄影等 ○ *an erotic painting* 色情画 ○ *the erotic urge* 性冲动.
▷ **erot·ica** /ɪˈrɒtɪkə; ɪˈrɑtɪkə/ *n* [pl] books, pictures, etc intended to arouse sexual desire 色情书、画等: *a collection of erotica* 春宫录.
erot·ic·ally /-klɪ; -klɪ/ *adv*.
eroti·cism /ɪˈrɒtɪsɪzəm; ɪˈrɑtə,sɪzəm/ *n* [U] (quality of stimulating) sexual desire 性欲; 色情性: *the film's blatant eroticism* 影片露骨的色情性.

err /ɜ:(r); *US* eər; ɝ/ *v* (*fml* 文) **1** [I] (**a**) make mistakes; be wrong 犯错误; 出错. (**b**) do wrong; sin 做错事; 犯罪. **2** (idm 习语) **err on the side of sth** show too much of a (usu good) quality 过分表现某品质(通常指好的): *It's better to err on the side of tolerance* (ie be too tolerant rather than too severe) *when dealing with young offenders.* 对待失足的青少年宁可失之过宽(宁过宽而勿过严). **to ,err is 'human (to for,give di'vine)** (*saying* 谚) it is human nature to sin and make mistakes (and therefore one should be as forgiving as possible) 人孰无过(宽恕为上).

er·rand /ˈerənd; ˈɛrənd/ *n* **1** short journey to take a message, get or deliver goods, etc 短程差使(送信、取货或送货等): *He was tired of running errands for his sister.* 他已厌烦给姐姐当跑腿了. **2** object or purpose of such a journey 差事: *I've come on a special errand.* 我是专程来办一件差事的. **3** (idm 习语) **an errand of 'mercy** journey to bring help to sb who is in distress 帮助受困者之行; 雪中送炭. **a fool's errand** ⇨ FOOL[1].

er·rant /ˈerənt; ˈɛrənt/ *adj* (*arch or joc* 古或谑) **1** [attrib 作定语] doing wrong; misbehaving 犯错的; 行为不当的: *an ,errant* (ie unfaithful) *'husband/'wife* 不安分的丈夫[妻子]. **2** wandering in search of adventure (esp in the expression shown) 为冒险而周游的(尤用于以下示例): *a ,knight 'errant* 游侠.

er·ratic /ɪˈrætɪk; əˈrætɪk/ *adj* (*usu derog* 通常作贬义) irregular or uneven in movement, quality or behaviour; unreliable (动作、品质或行为)不规则的, 无常的, 不可靠的: *Deliveries of goods are erratic.* 不按规定送货. ○ *The singer gave an erratic performance.* 演唱者未唱出水平. ○ *This clock is rather erratic.* 这个钟不太准. ▷ **er·rat·ic·ally** /-klɪ; -klɪ/ *adv*: *Being out of practice the team played very erratically.* 这队因缺乏练习而表现失常.

er·ratum /eˈrɑ:təm; ɛˈrɑtəm/ *n* (*pl* **errata** /-tə; -tə/) (*fml* 文) error in printing or writing 印刷或书写的错误: *a list of errata* 勘误表 ○ *an erratum slip*, ie a piece of paper inserted into a book after printing, listing errors, misprints, etc 勘误附页.

er·ro·ne·ous /ɪˈrəʊnɪəs; ɪˈronɪəs/ *adj* (*fml* 文) incorrect; mistaken 不正确的; 错误的: *erroneous ideas, conclusions, statements, etc* 错误的观念、结论、说法等.
▷ **er·ro·ne·ously** *adv*: *a poem erroneously attributed to Shakespeare* 被误认为是莎士比亚写的诗.

error /ˈerə(r); ˈɛrɚ/ *n* **1** [C] thing done wrongly; mistake 错误; 差错: *spelling errors* 拼法错误 ○ *a computer error* 计算机错误 ○ *printer's errors*, ie misprints 印刷错误. **2** [U] state of being wrong in belief or behaviour 想法或行为的错误: *The letter was sent to you in error*, ie by mistake. 此信误送给你了. ○ *The accident was the result of human error.* 这事故是人为的错误造成的. **3** [C] (in calculations, etc) amount of inaccuracy (计算等的)误差: *an error of 2 per cent* 百分之二的误差. ⇨Usage at MISTAKE[1] 用法见MISTAKE[1]. **4** (idm 习语) **an ,error of 'judgement** a mistake in one's assessment of a situation, etc (对情况等的)判断错误. **the ,error of one's 'ways** aspects of one's way of life that are wrong and should be changed 生活中应改正的过失: *Jones used to be a thief, but now he's seen the error of his ways and is trying to rebuild his life.* 琼斯过去是小偷, 但是现已知过能改重新做人. **trial and error** ⇨ TRIAL.

er·satz /ˈeəzæts, ˈɜ:sɑ:ts; ɛrˈzɑts/ *adj* (*often derog* 常作贬义) imitation or substitute, usu inferior to the original 仿制的, 代用的(通常次于原物): *ersatz coffee, whisky, silk* 代用咖啡、仿制威士忌、人造丝.

eru·dite /ˈeru:daɪt; ˈɛrʊ,daɪt/ *adj* (*fml* 文) having or showing great learning; scholarly 博学的; 有学问的: *an erudite lecture* 博大精深的讲座.
▷ **eru·ditely** *adv*.
eru·di·tion /,eru:ˈdɪʃn; ,ɛrʊˈdɪʃən/ *n* [U] learning 学问: *display one's erudition* 炫耀自己的学识 ○ *a man of immense erudition* 饱学之士.

erupt /ɪˈrʌpt; ɪˈrʌpt/ *v* **1** [I] (of a volcano) suddenly throw out lava, etc (指火山)爆发: *It's many years since Mount Vesuvius last erupted.* 维苏威火山上一次爆发至今已有很多年了. **2** [I, Ipr] (*fig* 比喻) break out suddenly and violently 突然发生: *Violence has erupted on the streets.* 大街上突然发生了暴乱. ○ *The demonstration erupted into violence.* 示威游行中突然出现了武斗. ○ (*infml* 口) *When I saw the size of the bill I simply erupted*, ie became furiously angry. 我看到巨额帐单时简直火冒三丈. **3** [I] (of spots, etc) appear on the skin (指斑点等)在皮肤上出现: *A rash has erupted all over my back.* 我的背上出满了疹子.
▷ **erup·tion** /ɪˈrʌpʃn; ɪˈrʌpʃən/ *n* [C, U] **1** outbreak of a volcano 火山爆发. **2** (*fig* 比喻) outbreak of war, disease, etc (战争等)爆发; (疾病等)发作: *the eruption of hostilities* 战事爆发. **3** sudden appearance of spots, etc on the skin (斑疹等)突然在皮肤上出现; 出疹.

-ery (also **-ry**) *suff* 后缀 **1** (with *vs* and *ns* forming *ns* 与动词和名词结合构成名词) (**a**) place where ... 的地方: *bakery* ○ *brewery*. (**b**) art or practice of ... 的艺术或技术: *cookery* ○ *pottery*. **2** (with *ns* and *adjs* forming usu uncountable *ns* 与名词和形容词结合构成(通常为不可数)名词) (**a**) state or character of ... 的状态或性质: *snobbery* ○ *bravery* ○ *rivalry*. (**b**) group or collection of ... 的聚集: *machinery* ○ *greenery* ○ *gadgetry*.

ery·sip·elas /,erɪˈsɪpɪləs; ,ɛrəˈsɪpḷəs/ *n* [U] (*medical* 医) disease that causes fever and deep red inflammation of the skin 丹毒.

ESA /,i: es ˈeɪ; ,i ɛs ˈe/ *abbr* 缩写 = European Space Agency 欧洲航天局.

es·cal·ate /ˈeskəleɪt; ˈɛskə,let/ *v* [I, Tn] (cause sth to) increase or develop by successive stages; become or make (sth) more intense (使某事物)逐步增长或发展; (使某事物)更紧张: *the steadily escalating level of unemployment* 失业率日益上升 ○ *House prices have escalated rapidly.* 房价已急速上涨. ○ *The Government is deliberately escalating the war for political reasons.* 政府出于政治目的蓄意使战争逐步升级. ▷ **es·cala·tion** /,eskəˈleɪʃn; ,ɛskəˈleʃən/ *n*: *an escalation in food prices* 食物价格急剧上涨 ○ *try to prevent an escalation of the war* 竭力防止战争升级.

es·cal·ator /ˈeskəleɪtə(r); ˈɛskə,letɚ/ *n* moving staircase carrying people up or down between floors or different levels (in a shop, underground railway, etc) 自动扶梯.

es·cal·ope /eˈskælɒp; ɛˈskæləp/ *n* slice of boneless meat, usu coated in egg and breadcrumbs and fried 无骨肉片(通常裹以鸡蛋和面包屑油炸): *escalopes of veal* 小牛肉片.

es·cap·ade /,eskəˈpeɪd, ˈeskəpeɪd; ,ɛskəˈped, ˈɛskə,ped/ *n* daring, mischievous or adventurous act; prank 大胆的、顽皮的或冒险的行为; 恶作剧: *a foolish, childish, boyish, etc escapade* 愚蠢的、幼稚的、男孩子的恶作剧.

es·cape[1] /ɪˈskeɪp; ɪˈskep/ *v* **1** [I, Ipr] **~ (from sb/sth)** get free; get away (from imprisonment or control) (从监禁、管制中)逃脱, 逃走: *Two prisoners have escaped.* 有两个囚犯越狱了. ○ *A lion has escaped from its cage.* 有一头狮子从笼中逃走了. ○ *She longed to escape from her mother's domination.* 她渴望摆脱母亲的操纵. ○ (*fig* 比喻) *When life became too difficult, he escaped into a dream world of his own.* 生活太困难时, 他就躲进了自己梦幻世界之中. **2** [I, Ipr] **~ (from sth)** (of gases, liquids, etc) find a way out (of a container, etc); leak; seep out (指气体、液体等)漏出, 泄漏, 渗出: *There's gas escaping somewhere — can you smell it?* 有什么地方漏煤气了——你闻到了吗? ○ *Make a hole to let the water escape.* 弄个洞让水排出. ○ *heat escaping through a window* 从窗户散发出的热气. **3** [I, Tn no passive 不用于被动语态, Tg] keep free or safe from (sth unpleasant); avoid 避免或躲避(不愉快的事物); 免除: *Where can we go to escape the crowds?* 我们到哪里才能躲开这些人群? ○ *escape punishment/being punished* 避免惩罚[受罚] ○ *You can't escape the fact that...* 你不

E

能逃避这样的事实 .... **4** [Tn no passive 不用于被动语态] be forgotten or unnoticed by (sb/sth) 被遗忘; 未被注意: *Her name escapes me*, ie I can't remember it. 我想不起她的名字了. ○ *The fault escaped observation* (ie was not spotted) *for months.* 这故障数月来未引起注意. ○ *Nothing escapes you/your attention*, ie You notice everything. 什么也瞒不了你. **5** (idm 习语) **escape (sb's) 'notice** be missed or not noticed (by sb) 疏忽; 没注意到: *It won't have escaped your notice that I've been unusually busy recently.* 你一定注意到了我最近一直忙得不得了.

es·cape[2] /ɪ'skeɪp; ɪ'skep/ *n* **1** [C, U] **~ (from sth)** (act or action of) escaping; instance of having escaped 逃走; 逃脱: *Escape from Dartmoor prison is difficult.* 从达特穆尔监狱逃走非常困难. ○ *There have been few successful escapes from this prison.* 没有什么人能从这座监狱逃走. ○ *When the guard's back was turned, she made her escape.* 看守人一转过身去, 她就逃走了. **2** [C] means of escaping 逃走或逃生的手段: *The fire-escape is at the back of the building.* 太平门在建筑物的后面. ○ [attrib 作定语] *The police have just found the escape vehicle.* 警方刚找到逃走者使用的车辆. ○ *He showed us our escape route on the map.* 他在地图上指出我们逃走的路线. ○ *escape-pipe/-valve*, ie to release excess steam or water when the pressure is too great 排出管「阀」(压力过高时可释放出过剩的蒸汽或水). **3** [sing] (thing that provides a) temporary distraction from reality or dull routine 暂时逃避现实(的消遣事物): *He listens to music as an escape from the pressures of work.* 他听音乐以缓解一下工作的压力. **4** [C] leak 漏出: *an escape of gas* 漏出煤气. **5** (idm 习语) **make ˌgood one's e'scape** manage to escape completely and satisfactorily 设法逃脱.

□ **e'scape clause** (also **'get-out clause**) part of a contract that releases a person, etc from obligations under certain conditions (契约的)例外条款.

e'scape-hatch *n* emergency exit from a ship, an aircraft, etc (船只、飞行器等的)紧急出口.

e'scape velocity speed at which a spacecraft, etc must travel in order to leave the gravitational field of a planet, etc 逃逸速度(宇宙飞船等克服星球引力的速度).

es·capee /ɪˌskeɪ'piː; ˌɪske'pi/ *n* person who has escaped (esp from prison) 逃脱者; (尤指)越狱者.

es·cape·ment /ɪ'skeɪpmənt; ɪ'skepmənt/ *n* part of a clock or watch that regulates the movement (钟表的)擒纵器.

es·cap·ism /ɪ'skeɪpɪzəm; ɪ'skepɪzəm/ *n* [U] (*often derog* 常作贬义) (habit of) trying to forget unpleasant realities by means of entertainment, fantasy, etc 逃避现实(的习气): *Drug-taking is a form of escapism for some people.* 对有些人来说, 吸毒是一种逃避现实的手段.

▷ **es·cap·ist** /-pɪst; -pɪst/ *n* person whose behaviour is characterized by escapism 逃避现实的人: [attrib 作定语] *escapist literature*, eg romantic fiction 逃避现实的文学(如浪漫小说).

es·capo·logy /ˌeskə'pɒlədʒɪ; ˌɛskə'pɑlədʒɪ/ *n* [U] practice or technique of escaping from confinement (esp chains, bags, etc) as a form of entertainment 脱身术(表演)(尤指从铁链、口袋等中挣脱).

▷ **es·capo·lo·gist** /-lədʒɪst; -lədʒɪst/ *n* entertainer who specializes in this 脱身术表演者.

es·ca·role /'eskərəʊl; 'ɛskəˌrol/ *n* [C, U] = ENDIVE 1.

es·carp·ment /ɪ'skɑːpmənt; ɛ'skɑrpmənt/ *n* long steep slope or cliff separating two areas at different levels, usu a plateau and a low-lying plain (通常为处于高低两平原之间的)长而陡的坡或悬崖.

eschato·logy /ˌeskə'tɒlədʒɪ; ˌɛskə'tɑlədʒɪ/ *n* [U] (*religion* 宗) branch of theology concerned with the end of the world and God's judgement of mankind after death 末世论(神学的一个范畴, 研究世界的终局和人死后上帝的审判).

es·chew /ɪs'tʃuː; ɛs'tʃu/ *v* [Tn] (*fml* 文) keep away from (sth); abstain from; avoid 避开(某事物); 戒除; 回避: *eschew political discussion* 回避政治讨论.

es·cort[1] /'eskɔːt; 'ɛskɔrt/ *n* **1** [CGp] person or group of people, ships, vehicles, etc accompanying sb/sth to give protection or as an honour; person, etc accompanying valuable goods to guard them 进行护送的人、船、车辆等: *The government provided an armed escort for the visiting head of State.* 政府为到访的元首派出了武装卫队. ○ *The Queen's yacht had an escort of ten destroyers.* 有十艘驱逐舰为女王的游艇护航. ○ *The gold bullion was transported under police escort.* 金锭在警方的护送下运走了. ○ [attrib 作定语] *soldiers on escort duty* 执行护送任务的士兵. **2** [C] (*dated or fml* 旧或文) person, esp a man and usu not a regular companion, who accompanies a member of the opposite sex on a particular social occasion (在社交场合)陪伴异性的人(尤指男人而通常并非经常作伴者).

es·cort[2] /ɪ'skɔːt; ɪ'skɔrt/ *v* [Tn, Tn·pr, Tn·p] **~ sb (to sth)** accompany sb as an escort 护送某人: *a princess escorted by soldiers* 由士兵护送公主 ○ *May I escort you to the ball?* 我可以陪你去参加舞会吗? ○ *Her brother's friend escorted her home.* 她哥哥的朋友护送她回家.

es·crit·oire /ˌeskrɪ'twɑː(r); ˌɛskrɪ'twɑr/ *n* writing-desk with drawers for paper, envelopes, etc 写字台.

es·cut·cheon /ɪ'skʌtʃən; ɪ'skʌtʃən/ *n* **1** shield displaying a coat of arms 饰有纹章的盾. **2** (idm 习语) **a blot on sb's/the escutcheon** ⇨ BLOT[1].

-ese *suff* 后缀 **1** (with proper *ns* forming *adjs* and *ns* 与专有名词结合构成形容词和名词) (inhabitant or language) of ...的; ...的人; ...的语言: *(the) Milanese* ○ *(the) Japanese.* **2** (with *ns* forming *ns* 与名词结合构成名词) (*esp derog* 尤作贬义) in the literary style of ...的文体; ...的风格: *journalese* ○ *officialese.*

Es·kimo /'eskɪməʊ; 'ɛskəˌmo/ (*pl* unchanged or **~s** 复数或不变或作 **Eskimos** /-məʊz; -moz/) (also **In·nuit**, **In·uit**) *n* **1** [C] member of a people living in the Arctic regions of N America and E Siberia 爱斯基摩人: [attrib 作定语] *Eskimo art* 爱斯基摩艺术. **2** [U] language of this people 爱斯基摩语.

ESL /ˌiː es 'el; ˌi ɛs 'ɛl/ *abbr* 缩写 = (teaching, learning or studying) English as a Second Language 作为第二语言的英语(教学或研究). Cf 参看 EFL.

ESN /ˌiː es 'en; ˌi ɛs 'ɛn/ *abbr* 缩写 = educationally subnormal (because mentally handicapped) (因智力低下)教育逊常的.

eso·phagus (*US*) = OESOPHAGUS.

eso·teric /ˌesəʊ'terɪk, ˌiːsəʊ-; ˌɛsə'tɛrɪk/ *adj* (*fml* 文) likely to be understood by only those with a special knowledge or interest; mysterious; obscure 只有内行才懂的; 神秘的; 难懂的: *esoteric poetry, imagery, language, etc* 难懂的诗、意象、语言等.

ESP /ˌiː es 'piː; ˌi ɛs 'pi/ *abbr* 缩写 = **1** (teaching, learning or studying) English for Special/Specific (eg scientific, technical, etc) Purposes 专业英语(教学或研究). **2** extra-sensory perception 超感知觉.

esp *abbr* 缩写 = especially.

es·pa·drille /'espədrɪl; 'ɛspəˌdrɪl/ *n* light canvas shoe with a plaited rope sole (鞋底为绳索编结的)帆布便鞋.

es·pal·ier /ɪ'spælɪeɪ; *US* ɪ'spæljər; ɪ'spæljɚ/ *n* (tree or shrub whose branches are trained on a) wooden or wire frame in a garden 树棚; (树架上)枝杈盘绕的树.

es·pe·cial /ɪ'speʃl; ə'spɛʃəl/ *adj* (**a**) exceptional; outstanding; special 特别的; 突出的; 特殊的: *a matter of especial interest* 特别有趣的事. (**b**) belonging mainly to one person or thing; particular 特有的; 独有的: *for your especial benefit* 为了你特有的利益.

▷ **es·pe·cially** /ɪ'speʃəlɪ; ə'spɛʃlɪ/ *adv* in particular; specially 尤其; 特别: *This is especially for you.* 这是特别为你准备的. ○ *I love the country, especially in spring.* 我喜爱乡村, 尤其是在春天.

Es·per·anto /ˌespə'ræntəʊ; ˌɛspə'rænto/ *n* [U] artificial language designed for use by all nations 世界语.

es·pi·on·age /'espɪənɑːʒ; 'ɛspɪənɑʒ/ *n* [U] practice of spying or using spies to obtain secret information 间谍活动: *found guilty of espionage* 犯有间谍活动罪 ○ *engage in espionage* 从事间谍活动 ○ *industrial espionage*, ie spying on the secret plans of rival companies 工业情报刺探活动.

es·plan·ade /ˌesplə'neɪd; ˌɛsplə'ned/ *n* level area of open ground where people may walk, ride or drive for pleasure, esp by the sea (可供散步、骑马、开车游玩的)广场; (尤指)海滨广场.

es·pouse /ɪ'spaʊz; ɪ'spaʊz/ *v* [Tn] (*fml* 文) give one's support to (a cause, theory, etc) 支持, 拥护(某主张、理论等): *espousing feminism* 拥护女权主义.

▷ **es·pousal** /ɪˈspaʊzl; ɪˈspaʊzl/ *n* [U] (*fml* 文) ~ **of sth** espousing of (a cause, etc) 支持; 拥护: *his recent espousal of communism* 他最近对共产主义的拥护.

es·presso /eˈspresəʊ; ɛsˋprɛso/ *n* (*pl* ~**s**) [C, U] (cup of) coffee made by forcing boiling water under pressure through ground coffee (一杯)蒸馏咖啡: *'Two espressos, please.'* '请来两杯蒸馏咖啡.'

es·prit /eˈspriː; ɛˋspri/ *n* [U] (*French* 法) lively wit 机智. □ **esprit de corps** /eˌspriː də ˈkɔː(r); ɛˋspridəˋkɔr/ (*French* 法) loyalty and devotion uniting the members of a group 团结精神.

espy /ɪˈspaɪ; əˋspaɪ/ *v* (*pt, pp* **espied**) [Tn] (*dated or joc* 旧或谑) catch sight of (sb/sth) 看到(某人[某事物]): *Was it you I espied jogging in the park this morning?* 我今天早上看到在公园里有个人慢跑, 是你吗?

Esq *abbr* 缩写 = (*fml* 文 *esp Brit*) Esquire: *Edgar Broughton, Esq*, eg on a letter addressed to him 如用作书信中的称谓.

-esque *suff* 后缀 (used with *ns* to form *adjs* 与名词结合构成形容词) in the style or manner of ...的风格; ...的方式: *statuesque* ○ *Kiplingesque*.

Es·quire /ɪˈskwaɪə(r); *US* ˈes-; ˋɛs,kwaɪr/ *n* (*Brit fml* 文) (*abbr* 缩写 **Esq**) polite title added after a man's surname (instead of *Mr* before it), esp in addressing letters (用作男子的尊称, 加在姓后, 尤用于书信中, Mr 则用于姓前): *He wrote 'Peter Mitchell, Esq' on the envelope.* 他在信封上写了 Peter Mitchell, Esq.

-ess *suff* 后缀 (with *ns* forming *ns* 与名词结合构成名词) female 女的; 雌性的; 母的; 牝: *lioness* ○ *actress*.

NOTE ON USAGE 用法: The 'feminine' suffixes **-ess** and **-ette**, in such words as *poetess* and *usherette*, are frequently avoided today, because it is unnecessary to make a distinction between men and women doing the same job. ☆ **-ess** 和 **-ette** 这两个后缀表示'女的'之意(如 poetess 和 usherette), 现在已尽量避免使用, 因无必要将做同一工作的人区分男女. The same word can often be used to apply to both sexes 同一词往往用于男女均可: *author*, *host*, *manager*, *usher*. The use of an alternative word is sometimes possible; for example, instead of *headmaster* or *headmistress* we can use *headteacher*. 有时可用其他词替换, 如用 headteacher 而不用 headmaster 或 headmistress.

es·say[1] /ˈeseɪ; ˋɛse/ *n* piece of writing, usu short and in prose, on any one subject 文章; (尤指)短文, 小品文, 散文: *We had to write three essays in the history exam.* 我们考历史要写三篇短文.
▷ **es·say·ist** /-ɪst; -ɪst/ *n* writer of essays, esp for publication (文章的)作者: *Bacon was a famous essayist.* 培根是著名的散文家.

es·say[2] /eˈseɪ; ɛˋse/ *v* [Tn] (*dated fml* 旧, 文) try (sth); attempt 尝试(某事物); 企图: *essay a task* 试做一工作.
▷ **es·say** /ˈeseɪ; ɛˋse/ *n* (*dated fml* 旧, 文) ~ **(at/in sth)** attempt 试图.

es·sence /ˈesns; ˋɛsn̩s/ *n* **1** [U] that which makes a thing what it is; most important or indispensable quality of sth 本质; 精髓; 要素: *The essence of his argument is that capitalism cannot succeed.* 他的论点的核心是资本主义不能成功. ○ *She was the essence of kindness.* 她本性善良. **2** [C, U] extract of a plant, drug, etc, containing all its important qualities in concentrated form (植物、药物等的)精华, 精髓: *vanilla essence* 香草精 ○ *meat essences* 肉汁. **3** (idm 习语) **in ˈessence** fundamentally; essentially 大体上; 本质上: *The two arguments are in essence the same.* 这两个论点大致相同. **of the ˈessence** very important; indispensable 非常重要的; 不可缺少的: *Speed is of the essence in dealing with an emergency.* 在处理紧急事件时, 速度是非常重要的.

es·sen·tial /ɪˈsenʃl; əˋsɛnʃəl/ *adj* **1** [esp pred 尤作表语] ~ **(to/for sth)** necessary; indispensable; most important 必要; 不可缺少; 最重要: *Is money essential to happiness?* 金钱对于幸福是必不可少的吗? ○ *It's essential that you attend all the meetings.* 你务必要参加所有的会议. ○ *'Secretary wanted: previous experience essential.'* '招聘秘书: 须有经验.' **2** [attrib 作定语] relating to sb's/sth's basic nature; fundamental 本质的; 基本的: *His essential decency makes it impossible to dislike him.* 他十分正派, 使人不能不喜欢他. ○ *What is the essential theme of the play?* 这剧本的主题是什么?
▷ **es·sen·tial** *n* (usu *pl* 通常作复数) fundamentally necessary element or thing 要素; 要点: *A knowledge of French is an absolute essential.* 会些法语是非常必要的. ○ *the essentials of English grammar* 英语语法纲要 ○ *We only had time to pack a few essentials.* 我们只来得及装上几件必需品.
es·sen·tially /ɪˈsenʃəlɪ; əˋsɛnʃəlɪ/ *adv* in his/its true nature; basically 本质上; 基本上: *He's essentially a very generous man.* 他本质上是个十分慷慨的人.
□ **essential ˈoil** oil extracted from a plant and used in making perfume, flavourings, etc 香精油; 香料油.

EST /ˌiː es ˈtiː; ˌi ɛs ˋti/ *abbr* 缩写 = **1** (*US*) Eastern Standard Time 东部夏令时间. Cf 参看 EDT. **2** (*medical* 医) electro-shock treatment (used esp on psychiatric patients) 电休克疗法(尤用于精神病患者).

est (also **estd**) *abbr* 缩写 = **1** established: *Hyde, Jekyll and Co, est 1902* 海德杰基尔公司成立于1902年. **2** estimate(d).

es·tab·lish /ɪˈstæblɪʃ; əˋstæblɪʃ/ *v* **1** [Tn] set (sth) up on a firm or permanent basis 建立, 设立(某事物): *This business was established in 1860.* 这家公司成立于1860年. ○ *establish a close relationship with sb* 与某人建立起密切的关系. **2** [Tn only passive 只用于被动语态, Tn·pr only passive 只用于被动语态, Cn·n/a] ~ **sb/oneself (in sth) (as sth)** place sb/oneself in a position, office, etc, usu on a permanent basis 使某人[自己]任职; 安置; 安顿: *We are now comfortably established in our new house.* 我们现已在新居舒适地安顿下来了. ○ *He established himself as governor of the province.* 他当上了省长. ○ *She's now firmly established (in business) as an art dealer.* 她已稳固地奠定了艺术品商的地位. **3** [Tn, Tf, Tw] show (sth) to be true; prove 确定(某事物); 证实: *We've established his innocence/(the fact) that he's innocent.* 我们已证实他无罪. ○ *The police can't establish where he was at the time.* 警方无法确定当时他在哪里. **4** [Tn, Cn·n/a] cause people to accept (a belief, custom, claim, etc) 使人接受(信仰、风俗、要求等): *Established practices are difficult to change.* 积习难改. ○ *His second novel established his fame as a writer.* 他的第二部小说确立了他作家之名.
▷ **es·tab·lished** *adj* [attrib 作定语] (of a Church or religion) made official for a country (指教会或信仰)成为国教的: *Anglicanism is the established religion in England.* 英国圣公会是英国国教.

es·tab·lish·ment /ɪˈstæblɪʃmənt; əˋstæblɪʃmənt/ *n* **1** [U] action of creating or setting up 设立; 建立: *the establishment of a new college* 新学院的成立. **2** [C] (*fml or joc* 文或谑) (premises of a) business organization or large institution 商业机构或大型机关(的房屋建筑): *an educational establishment*, eg a school 教育机构(如学校) ○ *What made you come and work in this establishment?* 你到这个机构来工作的原因是什么? **3** [sing] group of people employed in an organization, a household, etc 一机构的雇员、家庭成员等: *We have a large establishment*, ie many staff. 我们员工编制很大(有许多职工). **4 the Establishment** [sing] *n* (*esp Brit often derog* 常作贬义) group of powerful people who influence or control policies, ideas, taste, etc and usually support what has been traditionally accepted 当权派(通常为守旧派): *the musical, intellectual, artistic, etc Establishment* 音乐界的、知识界的、艺术界等的当权派 ○ [attrib 作定语] *an Establishment figure* 一位当权派.

es·tate /ɪˈsteɪt; əˋstet/ *n* **1** [C] area of land, esp in the country, with one owner 地产; (尤指)庄园: *He owns a large estate in Scotland.* 他在苏格兰有大量地产. **2** [C] (*esp Brit*) large area of land developed for a specific purpose, eg for houses or factories 作某种用途的地区(如兴建房屋或工厂): *a housing/a trading/an industrial estate* 住宅区[商业区/工业区]. **3** [U, C] (*law* 律) all the money and property that a person owns, esp that which is left at death 个人财产; (尤指)遗产: *Her estate was divided between her four children.* 她的遗产分给了她的四个子女. **4** [C] (*dated fml* 旧, 文) political or social group or class 政治的或社会的集团或等级: *the three Estates of the Realm*, ie (in Britain) the bishops, the lords and the common people (欧洲封建时代的)三个等级(在英国为僧侣、贵族和平民). **5** [sing] (*dated fml* 旧, 文) condition; stage in life 状况; 生活阶段: *the*

E

holy estate of matrimony 已婚状况.

□ **es'tate agent** (*US* **realtor, real estate agent**) person whose job is to buy and sell houses for others 房地产经纪人.

es'tate car (also **shooting-brake**, *US* **station wagon**) car with a large area for luggage behind the rear folding seats and a door or doors at the back for easy loading 客货两用轿车; 旅行轿车. ⇨illus at CAR 见 CAR 之插图.

estd *abbr* 缩写 = EST.

es·teem /ɪ'sti:m; ə'stim/ *v* (*fml* 文) (not used in the continuous tenses 不用于进行时态) **1** [Tn] have a high opinion of (sb/sth); respect greatly 尊重, 尊敬(某人[某事物]): *I esteem his work highly.* 我非常尊重他的工作. **2** [Cn·n] consider; regard 考虑; 认为: *I esteem it a privilege to address such a distinguished audience.* 我认为能向各位贵宾演讲十分荣幸.

▷ **es·teem** *n* high regard; favourable opinion 尊重; 看重: *Since he behaved so badly he's gone down in my esteem*, ie I do not esteem him so highly. 他表现非常恶劣, 使我对他的看法一落千丈. ○ *She is held in great/high/low esteem by those who know her well.* 熟悉她的人都极为[甚为/不太]尊重她.

es·thete, es·thetic (*US*) = AESTHETE, AESTHETIC (AESTHETE).

es·tim·able /'estɪməbl; 'ɛstəməbl/ *adj* (*dated or fml* 旧或文) worthy of great respect 值得尊敬的.

es·tim·ate[1] /'estɪmət; 'ɛstəmɪt/ *n* **1** judgement or calculation of the approximate size, cost, value, etc of sth 估计; 估价: *I can give you a rough estimate of the number of bricks you will need.* 我可大略估算一下你需要多少砖. ○ *This is an outside estimate of the price*, ie an estimate of the highest probable price. 这是最高的估价. **2** statement of the price a builder, etc will probably charge for doing specified work (营造商等对承建工程的)报价: *We got estimates from three different contractors before accepting the lowest.* 我们得到三个承包商的报价后, 接受了价钱最低的. Cf 参看 QUOTATION 4. **3** judgement of the character or qualities of sb/sth (对某人[事物]性格或质量的)判断: *I don't know her well enough to form an estimate of her abilities.* 我对她不太了解, 无法对她的能力作出判断.

es·tim·ate[2] /'estɪmeɪt; 'ɛstə,met/ *v* **1** [Tn, Tn·pr, Tnt, Tf, Tw] **~ sth (at sth)** form an approximate idea of sth; calculate roughly the cost, size, value, etc of sth 估计: *We estimated his income at/to be about £8 000 a year.* 我们估计他一年的收入大约 8 000 英镑. ○ *She estimated that the work would take three months.* 她估计这项工作需要三个月. ○ *Can you estimate its length/how long it is?* 你能估计其长度[它有多长]吗? **2** [Ipr] **~ for sth** calculate the probable price of (a specified job) 估算(某项工作)的费用: *We asked our builder to estimate for the repair of the ceiling.* 我们要求营造商估算一下修理天花板的费用. Cf 参看 QUOTE 3.

es·tim·ation /,estɪ'meɪʃn; ,ɛstə'meʃən/ *n* **1** [U] judgement; opinion; regard 判断; 意见; 认为: *In my estimation, he's the more suitable candidate.* 我认为他是更合适的人选. **2** (idm 习语) **go up/down in sb's estimation** be regarded more/less highly by sb 增加[降低]对某人的尊敬: *She's certainly gone up in my estimation since she told the boss what she thought of him.* 她对老板讲了自己对他的看法后, 我就更加尊敬她了.

es·trange /ɪ'streɪndʒ; ɪ'strendʒ/ *v* [esp passive 尤用于被动语态: Tn, Tn·pr] **~ sb (from sb)** cause (sb formerly loving or friendly) to become unfriendly to sb 使(某人)疏远某人; 离间: *He's estranged from his wife*, ie no longer living with her. 他和妻子分居了. ○ *They are estranged.* 他们疏远了.

▷ **es·trange·ment** *n* **1** [U] state of being estranged 疏远. **2** [C] instance of this 疏远: *cause an estrangement between two old friends* 导致两个老朋友彼此疏远.

es·tu·ary /'estʃʊərɪ; *US* -ʊerɪ; 'ɛstʃʊ,ɛrɪ/ *n* [C] wide river mouth into which the tide flows 河口湾: *the Thames estuary* 泰晤士河河口.

ETA (also **eta**) /,i: ti: 'eɪ; ,i ti 'e/ *abbr* 缩写 = estimated time of arrival (when travelling) (旅行时)估计的到达时间: *leave London 10. 05, eta Paris 12. 30.* 10 时 05 分离开伦敦, 估计 12 时 30 分到达巴黎. Cf 参看 ETD.

et al /,et 'æl; ,ɛt 'æl/ *abbr* 缩写 = (*infml* 口) and other people or things (Latin *et alii/alia*) 以及其他人或事物(源自拉丁文 *et alii/alia*): *The concert included works by Mozart et al.* 音乐会上演奏莫扎特等人的作品.

et cet·era /ɪt 'setərə, et-; ɪt 'sɛtərə, ɛt-/ (*usu abbr* 通常缩写作 **etc**) and other similar things; and the rest; and so on 以及诸如此类的事物; 及其他等等; 等等.

et·cet·eras /ɪt'setərəz, et-; ɪt'sɛtərəz, ɛt-/ *n* [pl] (*infml* 口) the usual extra things 额外事物; 零星杂项: *It's not just the food for the guests I have to think about — there are all the etceteras as well.* 我要考虑的不仅仅是客人的食物——还有其他各种东西.

etch /etʃ; ɛtʃ/ *v* (**a**) [Tn, Tn·pr] **~ sth (on/onto sth)** use a needle and acid to make (a picture, etc) on a metal plate from which copies may be printed 用针和酸类在金属板上蚀刻(图画等): (*fig* 比喻) *The incident remained etched on her memory for years.* 那次事件多年来一直铭刻在她的记忆中. (**b**) [I] make pictures, etc in this way 蚀刻: *She enjoys etching.* 她喜爱作蚀刻画.

▷ **etcher** *n* person who etches 蚀刻师.

etch·ing *n* **1** [U] art of making etched prints 蚀刻术. **2** [C] copy printed from an etched plate 蚀刻板画: *Hanging on the wall was a fine etching of the church.* 挂在墙上的是一幅精致的教堂蚀刻板画.

ETD /,i: ti: 'di:; ,i ti 'di/ *abbr* 缩写 = estimated time of departure (when travelling) (旅行时)估计的离开时间: *arrive Paris 12.30, etd (for) Lyons 14.00* 12 时 30 分到达巴黎, 估计 14 时整启程前往里昂. Cf 参看 ETA.

eternal /ɪ'tɜ:nl; ɪ'tɝnl/ *adj* **1** without beginning or end; lasting or existing for ever 永久的; 永恒的; 不朽的: *the Eternal God* 上帝 ○ *eternal life*, ie life after death of the body 永生 ○ *eternal love* 永恒的爱. **2** [attrib 作定语] (*infml* 口) seeming never to stop; (too) frequent 似乎不停的; (过于)频繁的: *Stop this eternal chatter!* 不要啰嗦个不停! ○ *I am tired of your eternal arguments.* 我讨厌你那没完没了的争论. **3** (idm 习语) **the eternal 'triangle** situation in which two people are both in love with the same person of the opposite sex 三角恋爱. **the eternal 'verities** fundamental moral principles; laws of God 基本的道德准则; 永恒的真理.

▷ **etern·ally** /ɪ'tɜ:nəlɪ; ɪ'tɝnlɪ/ *adv* **1** throughout all time; for ever 永远地; 永久地. **2** (*infml* 口) (**a**) always 永远: *I'll be eternally grateful to you.* 我永远感激你. (**b**) (too) frequently (过于)频繁: *He's eternally telephoning me early in the morning.* 他总是大清早给我打电话.

□ **the Eternal 'City** Rome 不朽之城(即罗马).

etern·ity /ɪ'tɜ:nətɪ; ɪ'tɝnətɪ/ *n* **1** [U] (*fml* 文) time without end; state or time of life after death 永恒; 来世; 永生. **2 an eternity** [sing] (*infml* 口) a very long time that seems endless 漫长的时间: *It seemed an eternity before the police arrived.* 似乎等到猴年马月警察才来.

□ **e'ternity ring** finger-ring with gems set all round it symbolizing eternity 四周镶有宝石象征永恒的戒指: *He gave her an eternity ring when their son was born.* 他们的儿子出世后他送给她一枚表示永恒的戒指.

ether /'i:θə(r); 'iθɚ/ *n* [U] **1** colourless liquid made from alcohol, used in industry as a solvent to dissolve fats, etc and (esp formerly) medically as an anaesthetic 醚; 乙醚. **2** (also **aether**) (**a**) (*arch or joc* 古或谑) the upper air 上空: *Today's news goes into the ether and is soon forgotten.* 今天的新闻广播听后不久即置于脑后了. (**b**) type of substance formerly believed to fill all space through which light waves were thought to travel 以太.

eth·er·eal (also **aeth·er·ial**) /ɪ'θɪərɪəl; ɪ'θɪrɪəl/ *adj* **1** of unearthly delicacy and lightness; seeming too spiritual or fairy-like for this world 轻巧的; 超凡的: *ethereal music, beauty* 轻柔的音乐、超凡的美. **2** (*arch* 古) of the pure upper air above the clouds 苍天的.

ethic /'eθɪk; 'ɛθɪk/ *n* **1** system of moral principles; rules of conduct 道德标准; 行为准则: *the Puritan ethic* 清教徒的伦理观 ○ *the Christian ethic* 基督徒的伦理观. **2** **eth·ics** *n* (**a**) [sing *v*] science that deals with morals 伦理学: *Ethics is a branch of philosophy.* 伦理学是哲学的分科. (**b**) [pl] moral correctness 道德规范: *The ethics of his decision are doubtful.* 他的这一决定是否合乎道德规范值得怀疑. ○ *Medical ethics* (ie those observed by the medical profession) *forbid a doctor to have a love affair with a patient.* 行医道德有规定, 禁止医生与病人谈恋爱.

▷ **eth·ical** /-kl; -kl/ *adj* **1** of morals or moral questions

道德的; 道德上的问题的: *largely an ethical problem* 主要是道德问题 ○ *an ethical basis for education* 教育的道德基础. **2** morally correct 合乎道德的: *His behaviour has not been strictly ethical.* 他的行为不太道德. **eth·ic·ally** /-klɪ; -klɪ/ *adv*.

eth·nic /ˈeθnɪk; ˋɛθnɪk/ *adj* **1** of a national, racial or tribal group that has a common cultural tradition 民族的; 种族的; 部落的: *ethnic minorities, groups, communities, etc* 少数民族的; 族群的; 种族社区的等. **2** (typical) of a particular cultural group 某文化群体的(典型的): *ethnic clothes, food, music* 民族的服装、食物、音乐 ○ *an ethnic restaurant* 具有民族风味的饭店. ▷ **eth·nic·ally** /-klɪ; -klɪ/ *adv*.

eth·no·graphy /eθˈnɒgrəfɪ; ɛθˋnɑgrəfɪ/ *n* [U] scientific description of the different human races 人种志.

▷ **eth·no·grapher** /eθˈnɒgrəfə(r); ɛθˋnɑgrəfɚ/ *n* student of or expert in ethnography 人种志研究者; 人种志专家.

eth·no·graphic /ˌeθnəˈgræfɪk; ˌɛθnəˋgræfɪk/ *adj*.

eth·no·logy /eθˈnɒlədʒɪ; ɛθˋnɑlədʒɪ/ *n* [U] science of the different human races, their characteristics, relations to one another, etc 民族学. Cf 参看 ANTHROPOLOGY, SOCIOLOGY.

▷ **eth·no·lo·gical** /ˌeθnəˈlɒdʒɪkl; ˌɛθnəˋlɑdʒɪkl/ *adj* of ethnology 民族学的.

eth·no·lo·gist /eθˈnɒlədʒɪst; ɛθˋnɑlədʒɪst/ *n* student of or expert in ethnology 民族学研究者; 民族学家.

ethos /ˈi:θɒs; ˋiθɑs/ *n* (*fml* 文) characteristic spirit, moral values, ideas or beliefs of a group, community or culture (集体、社团、文化的)气质、道德观、思想或信仰: *the revolutionary ethos* 革命精神 ○ *His book captures exactly the ethos of Elizabethan England.* 他的书准确地描绘了英国伊丽莎白时代的风土人情.

ethyl al·co·hol /ˌeθɪl ˈælkəhɒl *or, rarely* 罕读作 ˌi:θaɪl-; ˌɛθəl ˋælkəˌhɔl/ base of alcoholic drinks, also used as a fuel or solvent 乙醇.

eti·ol·ate /ˈi:tɪəʊleɪt; ˋitɪəˌlet/ *v* [Tn] **1** (*botany* 植) make (a plant) pale through lack of light 使(植物)因缺乏日光而变白: *an etiolated seedling* 发黄的幼苗. **2** (*fml* 文) cause (sb) to become pale and weak 使(某人)苍白衰弱: *an etiolated adolescent* 面黄肌瘦的少年 ○ (*fig* 比喻) *an etiolated society* 颓废的社会. ▷ **eti·ola·tion** /ˌi:tɪəʊˈleɪʃn; ˌitɪəˋleʃən/ *n* [U].

eti·ology (*US*) = AETIOLOGY.

eti·quette /ˈetɪket, -kət; ˋɛtɪˌkɛt, -kət/ *n* [U] formal rules of correct and polite behaviour in society or among members of a profession 礼节; 礼仪: *Etiquette was considered very important in Victorian England.* 英国在维多利亚时代非常注重礼仪. ○ *medical, legal etiquette* 医务界的、法律界的成规.

et seq /ˌet ˈsek; ˌɛt ˋsɛk/ *abbr* 缩写 = (*pl* **et seqq**) and the following (page(s), item(s), etc) (Latin *et sequens/sequentia*) 以及下列(各页、各项等)(源自拉丁文 *et sequens/sequentia*): *for further information see pp 9 et seq* 详情见第 9 页起之各页.

-ette *suff* 后缀 (with *ns* forming *ns* 与名词结合构成名词) **1** small 小的: *cigarette* ○ *kitchenette*. **2** imitation 仿制: *flannelette* ○ *leatherette*. **3** female 女性: *usherette*. ⇨ Usage at -ESS 用法见 -ESS.

ety·mo·logy /ˌetɪˈmɒlədʒɪ; ˌɛtəˋmɑlədʒɪ/ *n* **1** [U] study of the origin and history of words and their meanings 词源学. **2** [C] account of the origin and history of a particular word 词源: *This dictionary does not give etymologies.* 这部词典不介绍词源.

▷ **ety·mo·lo·gical** /ˌetɪməˈlɒdʒɪkl; ˌɛtəməˋlɑdʒɪkl/ *adj* of etymology 词源学的; 词源的.

ety·mo·lo·gist /ˌetɪˈmɒlədʒɪst; ˌɛtəˋmɑlədʒɪst/ *n* student of or expert in etymology 词源学研究者; 词源学家.

eu·ca·lyptus /ˌju:kəˈlɪptəs; ˌjukəˋlɪptəs/ *n* (*pl* **~es** or **-lypti** /-ˈlɪptaɪ; -ˋlɪptaɪ/) **1** (also **euca'lyptus tree**) any of several types of tall evergreen trees (including the Australian gum-tree), from which oil, timber and gum are obtained 桉树属. **2** (also **euca'lyptus oil**) [U] oil obtained from its leaves, used as a treatment for colds 桉树油(用以治疗感冒).

eu·char·ist /ˈju:kərɪst; ˋjukərɪst/ *n* **the Eucharist** [sing] (the bread and wine taken at) the Christian ceremony based on Christ's last supper 圣餐; 圣体; (圣餐中用的)饼和葡萄酒. Cf 参看 COMMUNION.

eu·gen·ics /ju:ˈdʒenɪks; juˋdʒɛnɪks/ *n* [sing *v*] science of the production of healthy intelligent children with the aim of improving the human genetic stock[1](6) 优生学; 人种改良学.

eu·lo·gize, -ise /ˈju:lədʒaɪz; ˋjuləˌdʒaɪz/ *v* [I, Tn] (*fml or joc* 文或谑) praise (sb/sth) highly in speech or writing 称赞, 颂扬(某人[某事物]): *eulogizing over the vintage wine* 称誉佳酿.

▷ **eu·lo·gist** /ˈju:lədʒɪst; ˋjulədʒɪst/ *n* person who does this 颂扬者; 作颂词者.

eu·lo·gistic /ˌju:ləˈdʒɪstɪk; ˌjuləˋdʒɪstɪk/ *adj* (of a speech or piece of writing) full of high praise (指言语或文字)颂扬的: *eulogistic articles about his latest book* 对他的新书的赞扬文章.

eu·logy /ˈju:lədʒɪ; ˋjulədʒɪ/ *n* [C, U] (*esp fml* 尤作文雅语) (speech or piece of writing containing) high praise of a person or thing 颂词; 颂文: *a poem of eulogy to the princess* 献给公主的颂诗 ○ *Her latest film has brought eulogies from the critics.* 她最近的这部电影获得影评界的好评.

eu·nuch /ˈju:nək; ˋjunək/ *n* castrated man, esp one formerly employed in the women's quarters of some oriental courts 阉人; (尤指)宦官, 太监.

eu·phem·ism /ˈju:fəmɪzəm; ˋjufəˌmɪzəm/ *n* [C, U] (example of the) use of pleasant, mild or indirect words or phrases in place of more accurate or direct ones 委婉说法; 委婉话: *'Pass away' is a euphemism for 'die'.* '去世'是'死'的委婉说法. ○ *'Pass water' is a euphemism for 'urinate'.* '小便'是'排尿'的委婉语.

▷ **eu·phem·istic** /ˌju:fəˈmɪstɪk; ˌjufəˋmɪstɪk/ *adj* (of speech or writing) consisting of or containing euphemisms (指言语或文字)委婉的: *euphemistic language, expressions, terms, words, etc* 委婉的语言、用语、词语、言语等. **eu·phem·istic·ally** /-klɪ; -klɪ/ *adv*.

eu·pho·nium /ju:ˈfəʊnɪəm; juˋfonɪəm/ *n* large brass musical wind instrument, a type of tuba 次中音大号.

eu·phony /ˈju:fənɪ; ˋjufənɪ/ *n* (*fml* 文) (**a**) [U] pleasantness of sound, esp in words 声音(尤指语音)的和谐. (**b**) [C, U] pleasing sound 悦耳的声音: *the euphony of a speaker's voice* 演讲者的声音悦耳.

▷ **eu·phon·ious** /ju:ˈfəʊnɪəs; juˋfonɪəs/ *adj* of a pleasing sound 悦耳的: *euphonious musical notes* 悦耳的音调.

eu·phoria /ju:ˈfɔ:rɪə; juˋfɔrɪə/ *n* [U] intense feeling of happiness and pleasant excitement 愉快和兴奋的感觉: *She was still in a state of euphoria hours after her victory.* 她获胜后几小时仍喜气洋洋. ▷ **eu·phoric** /ju:ˈfɒrɪk; *US* -ˈfɔ:r-; juˋfɔrɪk/ *adj*: *euphoric shouts of victory* 胜利的欢呼声.

Eur·asia /jʊəˈreɪʒə; juˋreʒə/ *n* Europe and Asia 欧亚大陆.

▷ **Eur·asian** /jʊəˈreɪʒn; juˋreʒən/ *n, adj* (person) of mixed European and Asian parentage; of Europe and Asia 欧亚混血的(人); 欧亚大陆的.

eur·eka /jʊəˈri:kə; juˋrikə/ *interj* (*joc* 谑) I have found it! 我找到了! (a cry of triumph at making a discovery 有所发现时得意的呼声): *Eureka — a job at last!* 我找到了——终于找到工作了!

eu·rhyth·mics (also **eu·ryth-**) /ju:ˈrɪðmɪks; juˋrɪðmɪks/ *n* [sing *v*] (**a**) system of exercising the body through movement to music 韵律体操. (**b**) dancing in this style 韵律舞蹈.

Eur(o)- *comb form* 构词成分 European; of Europe 欧洲的: *Eurasian* ○ *Euro-Communist*.

Euro·cheque /ˈjʊərəʊtʃek; ˋjuroˌtʃɛk/ *n* (cheque issued under an) arrangement between European banks allowing customers in one country to cash cheques, etc in another 欧洲通用支票.

Euro·crat /ˈjʊərəkræt; ˋjurəˌkræt/ *n* person, esp one in a senior position, who works in the administration of the European Economic Community 欧洲经济共同体的官员(尤指高级官员): *the Brussels Eurocrats* 布鲁塞尔的欧洲经济共同体官员.

Euro·dol·lar /ˈjʊərəʊdɒlə(r); ˋjuroˌdɑlɚ/ *n* US dollar put into European banks to act as an international currency and help the financing of trade and commerce 欧洲美元(存入欧洲银行的美元).

Euro·pean /ˌjʊərəˈpɪən; ˌjurəˋpiən/ **1** *n, adj* (native) of Europe 欧洲的(土著): ˌ*European* ˈ*languages* 欧洲的语

言. **2** *adj* happening in or extending over Europe 在欧洲发生或传播的: *an author with European recognition* 名闻欧洲的作家.

□ **the European Economic Community** (*abbr* 缩写 **EEC**) = COMMON MARKET (COMMON[1]).

Eus·ta·chian tube /juːˌsteɪʃn ˈtjuːb; *US* -ˈtuːb; juˈsteʃən ˈtub/ (*anatomy* 解) narrow passage extending from the middle ear to the throat 耳咽管; 欧氏管: *The child has earache caused by blocked Eustachian tubes.* 这孩子因耳咽管堵塞而引起耳痛. ⇨illus at EAR 见EAR之插图.

eu·tha·nasia /ˌjuːθəˈneɪzɪə; *US* -ˈneɪʒə; ˌjuθəˈneʒə/ *n* [U] (bringing about of a) gentle and painless death for a person suffering from a painful incurable disease, extreme old age, etc 安乐死(术); 安死术: *It is against the law for doctors to practise euthanasia*, ie to kill patients to prevent suffering. 医生施行安死术是违法的.

evacu·ate /ɪˈvækjueɪt; ɪˈvækjuˌet/ *v* **1** [Tn, Tn·pr] **~ sb (from...) (to...)** remove sb from a place of danger to a safer place, esp in time of war 将某人移往较安全处(尤指战时); 疏散: *The children were evacuated to the country when the city was being bombed.* 城市遭到轰炸时, 儿童都疏散到乡下去了. **2** [Tn] (*esp military* 尤用于军事) leave or withdraw from (a place) esp because of danger 撤离(某处)(尤指因危险): *The soldiers evacuated the area as the enemy advanced.* 敌军推进时, 士兵都撤出了那地区. ○ *The region near the erupting volcano was evacuated rapidly.* 火山爆发处附近已迅速撤空. **3** [Tn, Tn·pr] (*fml* 文) **~ sth (of sth)** empty (esp the bowels) of their contents 排空(尤指肠).

▷ **evacu·ation** /ɪˌvækjuˈeɪʃn; ɪˌvækjuˈeʃən/ *n* **1** [U] act of evacuating or state of being evacuated 疏散; 撤离; 排空: *the evacuation of thousands of people after a flood* 洪水过后成千上万人离乡背井 ○ *the evacuation of a town* 城市的撤空. **2** [C] instance of this 疏散; 撤离; 排空.

evacuee /ɪˌvækjuˈiː; ɪˈvækjuˌi/ *n* person who is evacuated (EVACUATE 1) 被疏散者: *evacuees from the battle area* 来自战区的逃难者.

evade /ɪˈveɪd; ɪˈved/ *v* [Tn] **1** get or keep out of the way of (sb/sth) 躲开, 避开(某人[某事物]): *evade the police, an attack, an enemy* 躲避警察、袭击、敌人. **2** find a way of not doing (sth, esp sth that legally or morally ought to be done); avoid 逃避(尤指法律或道德上的责任): *evade military service* 逃避兵役 ○ *evade capture by the police* 躲避警方的追捕. **3** avoid answering (a question) fully or honestly 回避如实的答复(问题): *The policeman evaded all the difficult questions.* 那警察回避了所有难以答复的问题.

evalu·ate /ɪˈvæljueɪt; ɪˈvæljuˌet/ *v* [Tn] find out or form an idea of the amount or value of (sb/sth); assess 评价, 估计, 评估(某人[某事物]): (*fml* 文) *evaluate her chances of success* 估计她成功的机会 ○ *I can't evaluate his ability without seeing his work.* 我没有看到他的工作情况, 无法评论他的能力. ▷ **evalu·ation** /ɪˌvæljuˈeɪʃn; ɪˌvæljuˈeʃən/ *n* [C, U].

evan·es·cent /ˌiːvəˈnesnt; *US* ˌev-; ˌɛvəˈnɛsn̩t/ *adj* (*fml* 文) quickly fading; soon disappearing from memory 迅速消失的; 不久便淡忘的: *as evanescent as snowflakes on a river* 如雪花落入河中, 瞬即消失 ○ *a pop singer's evanescent fame* 流行歌曲演唱者一瞬即逝的声誉. ▷ **evan·es·cence** /-sns; -sn̩s/ *n* [U].

evan·gel·ical /ˌiːvænˈdʒelɪkl; ˌivænˈdʒɛlɪkl/ *adj* **1** of or according to the teachings of the Christian Gospel, or the Christian religion 福音的; 根据福音的. **2** of a Protestant group which believes that the soul can be saved only by faith in Christ 福音派新教会的.

▷ **evan·gel·ical** *n* member of this group 福音派新教信徒.

evan·gel·ic·al·ism /-əlɪzəm; -əlɪzəm/ *n* [U] evangelical (2) beliefs and teachings 福音派新教会的信仰与教义.

evan·gel·ist /ɪˈvændʒəlɪst; ɪˈvændʒəlɪst/ *n* **1** any one of the four writers (Matthew, Mark, Luke, John) of the Gospels in the Bible 四福音书作者(马太、马可、路加、约翰). **2** preacher of the Gospel, esp one who travels around holding evangelical(2) religious meetings 福音传道者; (尤指)布道家: *converted to Christianity by a fervent American evangelist* 受虔诚的美国布道家感化而皈依基督教 ▷ **evan·gel·ism** *n* [U]. **evan·gel·istic** /ɪˌvændʒəˈlɪstɪk; ɪˌvændʒəˈlɪstɪk/ *adj*.

evan·gel·ize, -ise /ɪˈvændʒəlaɪz; ɪˈvændʒəˌlaɪz/ *v* [I, Tn] (**a**) (*fml* 文) preach or spread the Christian gospel to (sb) with the aim of converting 宣讲福音使(某人)皈依基督教. (**b**) try to win support from (sb) for a cause 争取(某人)支持某事: *Health food supporters are always evangelizing.* 喜爱保健食品的人总爱劝别人都吃保健食品.

evap·or·ate /ɪˈvæpəreɪt; ɪˈvæpəˌret/ *v* **1** [I, Tn] (cause sth to) change into vapour and disappear (使某物)蒸发掉: *The water soon evaporated in the sunshine.* 水在阳光下不久就蒸发了. ○ *Heat evaporates water into steam.* 水受热变成水蒸气. ⇨Usage at WATER[1] 用法见 WATER[1]. **2** [I] (*fig* 比喻) be lost or cease to exist 消失; 不复存在: *His hopes evaporated*, ie he no longer felt any hope. 他的希望破灭了. ▷ **evap·ora·tion** /ɪˌvæpəˈreɪʃn; ɪˌvæpəˈreʃən/ *n* [U].

□ **eˌvaporated ˈmilk** thick unsweetened milk, usu bought in tins, which has had some of the liquid removed by evaporation 淡炼乳(通常为罐装): *The pudding was made with evaporated milk.* 这布丁是用淡炼乳做的.

eva·sion /ɪˈveɪʒn; ɪˈveʒən/ *n* **1** [C, U] keeping out of the way of sb; avoidance 躲避某人; 规避; 逃避: *the burglar's evasion of the police* 窃贼躲避警察 ○ *evasion of responsibility* 逃避责任 ○ *He's been accused of tax evasion.* 他被控逃税. **2** [C] statement, excuse, etc made to avoid fully answering a question (避免如实回答问题的)遁辞, 借口, 推托: *His answers to my questions were nothing but clever evasions.* 他回答我的问题时顾左右而言他.

evas·ive /ɪˈveɪsɪv; ɪˈvesɪv/ *adj* **1** (**a**) having the aim or intention of avoiding capture, of not giving a direct answer, etc 躲避的; 逃避的; 推诿的: *evasive tactics* 规避战术 ○ *Her manner was always very evasive; she would never look straight at me.* 她的样子总是躲躲闪闪的, 从来不正眼看我. (**b**) not direct or straightforward 不直接的; 不坦率的; 转弯抹角的: *an evasive answer to a question* 对问题躲躲闪闪的答复. **2** (idm 习语) **take evasive action** (esp of a plane, ship, etc in war) do sth in order to avoid danger, etc (尤指在战争中飞机、军舰等的)规避动作(以避免危险): *The pilot took evasive action to avoid a collision with the enemy aircraft.* 驾驶员采取规避动作以免与敌机相撞. ○ (*joc* 谑) *Stephen didn't want to see his sister, so he quickly took evasive action and hid under the bed.* 斯蒂芬不愿见他的姐姐, 便立即采取规避动作, 藏到床底下去了. ▷ **evas·ively** *adv*. **evas·ive·ness** *n* [U]: *Politicians are often accused of evasiveness.* 政客常因左右言他而受人指责.

Eve /iːv; iv/ *n* (in the Bible story of the Creation) the first woman on earth, created by God 夏娃(《圣经》故事《创世记》中上帝造的第一个女人): *Adam and Eve* 亚当和夏娃.

eve /iːv; iv/ *n* **1** day or evening before a religious festival or holiday (宗教节日或假日的)前日, 前夕: *Christmas Eve*, ie 24 Dec 圣诞节前夕(12月24日) ○ *New Year's Eve*, ie 31 Dec 除夕(12月31日). **2** time just before an important event 重大事件即将发生的时刻; 前夕: *the eve of the election* 选举前夕 ○ *on the eve of the race* 比赛前夕. **3** (*arch* 古) evening 傍晚: *a perfect summer eve* 美丽的夏日黄昏.

even[1] /ˈiːvn; ˈivən/ *adj* **1** level; smooth; flat 平的; 平滑的; 平坦的: *the most even part of the golf course* 高尔夫球场最平坦的地方 ○ *A billiard-table must be perfectly even.* 台球桌必须十分平. **2** unchanging in quality; regular; steady 均匀的; 有规律的; 稳定的: *This wine cellar stays at an even temperature all year round.* 这个酒窖常年保持恒温. ○ *an even colour* 均匀的颜色 ○ *even breathing* 均匀的呼吸 ○ *The child's pulse is now even.* 孩子的脉搏现在稳定了. **3** (**a**) (of amounts, distances, values) equal (指数量、距离、价值等)相等的: *Our scores are now even.* 我们的分数现在相等了. ○ *The two horses were even in the race.* 那两匹马比赛成绩相当. (**b**) (of two people or things) equally balanced or matched (指两个人或物)均衡的; 不相上下的: *I'd say the two players are pretty even.* 我认为这两个选手不相上下. ○ *an even game* 平局. **4** (of numbers) divisible by two with no remainder (指数目)偶数的: *4, 6, 8, 10, etc are even numbers.* 4、6、8、10 等是偶数. Cf 参看 ODD.

5 (of temperament, etc) not easily upset; calm（指性情等）稳定的, 温和的: *of an even disposition* 性情平和的 ○ *She has a very even temper.* 她的性情非常温和. ○ *an even-tempered baby* 温顺的婴儿. **6** (idm 习语) **an even 'chance (of doing sth)** an equally balanced probability (of sth happening or not)（某事发生与否的）可能性相等: *I'd say he has an even chance of winning the match.* 我认为她赢这场比赛有一半的机会. **be/get even (with sb)** have/get one's revenge on sb 向（某人）报复: *Bill swore he'd get even with his brother, who'd played a dirty trick on him.* 比尔上了哥哥的当, 发誓要报复. **break 'even** make neither a loss nor a profit 不赔不赚: *It will be a year before the firm makes a profit but at least it's breaking even.* 这家公司一年以后才能赢利, 现在至少已不赔不赚了. **even 'chances/'odds/'money** (also **evens**) **(a)** (in betting) equal probability of a horse, etc winning or losing（下赌注时）（赛马等）输赢的可能性相等: *It's even money whether the new horse comes first or last.* 这匹新马跑得最快或最慢的可能性是相同的. **(b)** equal probability of sth happening or not happening 某事发生与否的可能性相等: *It's even odds/The odds are even that he'll be late.* 他有一半的可能性要迟到. **honours are even** ⇨ HONOUR[1]. **on an even 'keel (a)** (of a ship) without movement to one side or the other（指船）不倾斜, 平稳. **(b)** (*fig* 比喻) maintaining steady undisturbed progress (in life)（生活）稳定的: *It took him a long time to get back on an even keel after his wife died.* 他妻子死后很久他情绪才稳定下来. **7** (phr v) **even out** become level or regular 变得平坦或稳定: *The path ran steeply up the hill and then evened out.* 这条路很陡, 到山上就平坦了. ○ *House prices keep rising and falling but they will eventually even out.* 房价有涨有落, 但终会稳定的. **even sth out** spread sth evenly over a period of time or among a number of people 将某事物平均分散到某段时间或分配给每个人: *Payments can be evened out on a monthly basis over the year.* 全部款项可以在一年中按月平均交纳. ○ *The manager tried to even out the distribution of work among his employees.* 经理把工作尽量平均分配给雇员. **even (sth) up** (cause sth to) become even or equal（使某事物）平均或相等: *That will even things up a bit*, ie make them more equal. 那样就平均一些了.

▷ **evenly** *adv* in an even manner 平坦地; 均匀地; 稳定地; 相等地: *evenly balanced/matched* 全部平衡的［相称的］○ *evenly divided/distributed* 平均分开的［分配的］.

even·ness /ˈiːvənnɪs; ˋivənnɪs/ *n* [U].

□ **ˌeven-ˈhanded** *adj* fair and impartial 公平的; 不偏不倚的: *ˌeven-handed ˈjustice* 公平的审判.

even[2] /ˈiːvn; ˋivən/ *adv* **1** (used to emphasize sth unexpected or surprising in what one is saying, or to invite a comparison with what might have happened, etc 用以加强出乎意料的语气或进而比较可能发生的事) 甚至; 连; 都; 即使: *He never even 'opened the letter*, ie so he certainly didn't read it. 他甚至都没把信打开. ○ *He didn't answer even 'my letter*, ie so he certainly didn't answer any others. 他连我的信都不回. ○ *It was cold there even in Ju'ly*, ie so it must have been very cold in winter. 那里即使七月份都很冷. ○ *Even a child can understand the book*, ie so adults certainly can. 甚至连孩子都看得懂这本书. **2** (used to emphasize a comparative 用以加强比较级的语气) still; yet 甚至; 还: *You know even less about it than I do.* 你对此事知道得比我还少. ○ *Sally drives fast, but Olive drives even faster.* 萨莉开车开得很快, 奥利夫开得更快. ○ *She's even more intelligent than her sister.* 她甚至比姐姐还聪明. **3** (used to add force to a more exact or precise version of a word, phrase, etc 用以强调某词语的更精确的说法) 甚至可以说; 其实: *It's an unattractive building, even ugly/ugly even.* 这座建筑物很不起眼, 甚至可以说很难看. **4** (idm 习语) **even a worm will turn** ⇨ WORM. **even as** (*fml* 文) (used as a compound *conj* 用作复合连词) just at the same time when (sb does sth, sth else happens) 正当; 恰恰: *Even as he shouted the warning the car skidded.* 就在他高喊注意的时候, 汽车滑动了. **even if/though** (used as *conjs* 用作连词) in spite of the fact or belief that; no matter whether 即使; 纵然; 尽管: *Even if I have to walk all the way I'll get there.* 即使我得一路走着去, 我也要走到那里. ○ *I like her even though she can be annoying.* 尽管她有时很恼人, 但我还是喜欢她. **ˌeven ˈnow/ˈthen (a)** in addition to previously; in spite of what has/had happened, etc 即使到这时: *I've shown him the photographs but even now he won't believe me.* 虽然我已给他看了照片, 他还是不相信我. ○ *Even then he would not admit his mistake.* 即使在这种情况下, 他还不承认错误. **(b)** (*fml* 文) (with continuous tenses only, often between the *aux* and the main *v* 仅用于进行时态, 常置于助动词与主要动词之间) at this or that precise moment 恰恰在这时: *The troops are even now preparing to march into the city.* 部队恰恰在这时准备开进城去. **ˌeven ˈso** (used as a *conj* 用作连词) in spite of that; nevertheless 尽管如此; 然而; 不过: *There are many spelling mistakes; even so it's quite a good essay.* 这篇文章有许多拼写错误, 然而仍不失之为好文章.

even·ing /ˈiːvnɪŋ; ˋivnɪŋ/ *n* **1** [C, U] part of the day between about 6p.m. and bedtime 晚上; 晚间: *I'll come round tomorrow evening.* 我明天晚上来. ○ *We were at home yesterday evening.* 我们昨天晚上在家. ○ *One warm summer evening.../On a warm summer evening...* 在夏天一个温暖的夜晚... ○ *In the evening I usually read.* 晚上我常常看书. ○ *Let's meet on Sunday evening.* 咱们星期日晚上见吧. ○ [attrib 作定语] *the evening show* 晚上的节目. **2** [C] outing or party of a specified type, happening in the evening 晚间的外出活动; 晚会: *A theatre evening* (ie an evening at the theatre) *has been arranged.* 已安排好一个戏剧晚会. ○ *musical evenings*, ie evenings especially for listening to or playing music 音乐晚会. **3** (*fig fml* 比喻, 文) the last part (esp of one's life) 最后部分; (尤指)晚年, 暮年: *in the evening of his life* 在他的晚年. ⇨Usage at MORNING 用法见 MORNING.

□ **'evening dress 1** [U] clothes worn for formal occasions in the evening 晚礼服: *Everyone was in evening dress.* 大家都穿着晚礼服. **2** [C] a woman's (long) formal dress 女装晚礼服: *All the evening dresses were beautiful.* 所有的女装晚礼服都很漂亮.

evening 'paper newspaper published after midday 晚报: *the local evening paper* 地方的晚报.

evening prayer = EVENSONG.

evening 'primrose plant with pale yellow flowers that open in the evenings 月见草: *Oil of evening primrose is used as a herbal medicine.* 月见草油可用作草药.

the evening 'star planet (Venus or Mercury) seen in the Western sky after sunset 昏星(即金星或水星).

even·song /ˈiːvnsɒŋ; ˋivənˌsɔŋ/ (also **ˌevening ˈprayer**) *n* service of evening prayer in the Church of England（英国国教的）晚祷: *We attended evensong as well as morning service.* 我们参加了晚祷和晨祷.

event /ɪˈvent; ɪˋvɛnt/ *n* **1** thing that happens, esp sth important; incident 事情; (尤指)大事, 事件: *one of the chief events of 1964* 1964年的主要大事之一 ○ *the chain* (ie sequence) *of events that led to the Prime Minister's resignation* 导致首相辞职的一连串事件 ○ *It was quite an event when a woman first became prime minister.* 首次由女人任首相倒是件大事. ⇨Usage at OCCURRENCE 用法见 OCCURRENCE. **2** any of the races, competitions, etc in a sports programme（体育运动的）比赛项目: *Which events have you entered for?* 你参加了哪几项比赛? ○ *The 800m is the fourth event of the afternoon.* 800米赛是下午的第四项比赛. **3** (idm 习语) **at 'all events/in 'any event** whatever happens; in any case 不管发生什么事; 在任何情况下; 无论如何: *In any event, the worst that she can do is say 'no'.* 不管怎样, 她大不了就是说个'不'字. **be wise after the event** ⇨ WISE. **in 'either event** whichever (of two things) happens（两件事情中）无论发生哪件事: *In either event, I'll be there to support you.* 无论这样或那样, 我都支持你. **a happy event** ⇨ HAPPY. **in 'that event** if that happens 如果那种情况发生; 如果是那样的话: *You could be right, and in that event they'll have to pay you back.* 可能是你对, 那样的话, 他们就得把钱还你. **in the e'vent** as it in fact happened; as it turned out 结果; 到头来: *I was worried about the hotel bill, but in the event I had enough money to pay.* 我一直担心旅馆的费用, 结果我的钱足够. **in the event of sth** (*fml* 文) if sth happens 万一; 倘若: *in the event of an accident* 万一发生事故 ○ *In the event of his death Sheila will inherit the money.* 一旦他故去, 希拉就会继承这笔钱. **a/the turn of events** ⇨ TURN[2].

▷ **event·ful** /-fl; -fəl/ *adj* full of memorable or notable events 有许多大事的: *He's had an eventful life.* 他一生

中有很多大事. ○ *an eventful year* 有许多大事的一年.

even·tide /ˈiːvntaɪd; ˋivən,taɪd/ *n* (*arch* 古) evening 晚上; 晚间.

□ **eventide home** home for elderly people 老年人之家.

event·ing /ɪˈventɪŋ; ɪˋvɛntɪŋ/ *n* [U] (*esp Brit*) sport of taking part in horse-riding competitions, esp three-day events involving cross-country riding, jumping and dressage 马术比赛运动(尤指历时三日的项目, 包括越野、跳越障碍、花式训马).

even·tual /ɪˈventʃʊəl; ɪˋvɛntʃʊəl/ *adj* [attrib 作定语] happening at last as a result; ultimate 最后的; 最终的: *his foolish behaviour and eventual failure* 他的愚蠢行为和最后的失败.

▷ **even·tu·ality** /ɪˌventʃʊˈælətɪ; ɪ,vɛntʃʊˋælətɪ/ *n* [C] (*fml* 文) possible event or result 可能发生的事情; 可能出现的结果: *We must consider every eventuality.* 我们什么事情都要考虑到.

even·tu·ally /-tʃʊəlɪ; -tʃʊəlɪ/ *adv* in the end; at last 最后; 终于: *He fell ill and eventually died.* 他患病而终于不治. ○ *Eventually he tired of trying so hard.* 他最后厌倦了这种艰苦的尝试.

ever /ˈevə(r); ˋɛvɚ/ *adv* **1** (usu in negative sentences and questions, or sentences expressing doubt or condition; usu placed before the *v* 通常用于否定句和疑问句, 或用于含有表示怀疑或条件成分的句中, 通常置于动词之前) at any time 在任何时候; 从来: *Nothing ever happens in this village.* 这个村里从未发生过任何事. ○ *Do you ever wish you were rich?* 你曾希望过自己很富吗? ○ *She seldom, if ever, goes to the cinema.* 她难得看电影. ○ *If you ever visit London, you must come and stay with us.* 你要是到伦敦来, 一定要到我们这里住住. **2** (with the perfect tenses in questions 用于疑问句中的完成时态) at any time up to the present 曾; 曾经: *'Have you ever flown a helicopter?' 'No, never.'* '你坐过直升飞机吗?' '没有, 从未坐过.' ○ *'Have you ever seen an elephant?' 'Yes I have.'* '你见过大象吗?' '见过.' ○ *I wondered if he'd ever stopped to think how I felt.* 我不知道他是否曾考虑过我的感受. (*Ever* is rarely used in the answer: say either 'Yes I have' or 'No, never', etc. ever很少作回答用语, 回答时用 'Yes, I have.' 或 'No, never.' 等) **3** (with comparatives after *than* or with superlatives 与比较级的词连用, 置于 than之后; 或与最高级的词连用) at any time (before/up till now) 在任何时候(之前[直至现在]): *It's raining harder than ever.* 雨下得更大了. ○ *This is the best work you've ever done.* 这是你所做的最好的工作. ○ *He hated her more than ever, when he got that letter.* 他接到那封信后, 越发憎恨她了. **4 ever-** (in compounds 用以构成复合词) always, continuously 总是; 不停地: *the ever-growing problem* ○ *the ever-increasing cost of food.* **5** (*infml dated* 口, 旧) (after **as**...**as**, as an intensifier 用于 **as ... as** 之后以加强语气): *Work as hard as ever you can!* 尽你最大努力工作! **6** (used after *when, where,* etc 用于when、where等之后): *When/Where/How ever did you lose it?* 你究竟在什么时候[什么地方/怎么]把它弄丢的? ○ *What ever do you mean?* 你到底是什么意思? **7** (idm 习语) **(as) bad, good, etc as ˈever; (as) badly, well, etc as ˈever** bad, badly, etc to the same degree as before (usu surprisingly so) 和以前一样坏、好...(通常含惊讶之意): *Despite the good weather forecast, the next morning was as wet as ever.* 尽管预报称天气很好, 但次日上午仍阴雨绵绵. ○ *He broke his arm last year but he plays the piano as skilfully as ever.* 他去年胳膊折了, 但现在弹起钢琴来仍像以前那样自如. **did you ever (...)!** (*infml* 口) (used as part of a rhetorical question or used alone to express surprise, indignation, disbelief, etc 用于反问句或单独使用, 表示惊讶、愤怒、怀疑等): *Did you ever hear such nonsense!* 你听过这种胡言乱语吗! ○ *It cost 50p to go to the toilet; well, did you ˈever!* 去一趟厕所要50便士; 哼, 真是闻所未闻! **ever and anon** (*dated or fml* 旧或文) several times, at regular intervals 几次; 一阵一阵地. **ever more** (*fml* 文) increasingly; more and more 越发地; 越来越: *She became ever more nervous as the interview continued.* 她在面试过程中越来越紧张. **ever since (...)** continuously since (a specified time) 自从: *ever since I was at school* 自从我上学以来. **ever so/ever such (a)** (*infml* 口 *esp Brit*) very; to a very great degree 非常; 在极大程度上: *He's ever so rich.* 他很富. ○ *ever such a handsome man* 非常漂亮的男子. **for ever and ˈever** (*rhet or joc* 修辞或谑): *Once he gets a drink in his hand he's here for ever and ever.* 他手里一有了酒就永远也动不了地方了. **if ˌever there ˈwas one** of that there is no doubt; that is certainly true 无可置疑; 确实: *That was a fine meal if ever there was one!* 那确实是一顿丰盛的饭! **yours ˈever/ever ˈyours** (*infml* 口) (sometimes used at the end of a letter, before the signature 有时用于书信结尾处的签字前).

ever·green /ˈevəgriːn; ˋɛvɚ,grin/ *n, adj* (tree, shrub) having green leaves throughout the year 常绿的(树): *The pine, cedar and spruce are evergreens.* 松树、雪松、云杉都是常绿的树. Cf 参看 DECIDUOUS. ⇨illus at App 1 见附录1之插图, page i.

ever·last·ing /ˌevəˈlɑːstɪŋ; *US* -ˈlæst-; ,ɛvɚˋlæstɪŋ/ *adj* **1** going on or lasting for ever 永久的; 永恒的: *everlasting fame, glory* 永久的声誉、光荣 ○ *everlasting life* 永生. **2** lasting a long time 持久的: *everlasting flowers*, ie flowers keeping shape and colour when dried 干后形状和颜色不变的花. **3** (*derog* 贬) repeated too often; lasting too long 多次重复的; 持续过长的: *I'm tired of his everlasting complaints.* 我厌倦了他没完没了的抱怨. **4 the Everlasting** God 上帝.

▷ **ever·last·ingly** *adv* (*infml* 口) in an everlasting(3) manner 多次重复地; 持续过长地: *everlastingly complaining* 喋喋不休地抱怨.

ever·more /ˌevəˈmɔː(r); ,ɛvɚˋmɔr/ *adv* for ever; always 永久; 永远: *for evermore* 永远地.

every /ˈevrɪ; ˋɛvrɪ/ *indef det* **1** (**a**) (used with *sing* [C] *ns* to refer to groups of three or more which are seen as wholes 与单数可数名词连用, 指至少三个, 视为一整体) each individual 每个; 所有的; 一切的: *Every child in the class passed the examination.* 班上所有的学生考试都及格了. ○ *I've got every record she has ever made.* 我已得到她灌的所有的唱片. ○ *I couldn't hear every word of his speech.* 他讲的话并非每句我都能听见. ○ *He examined every item in the set carefully.* 他仔细检查了这一套中的各项. (**b**) (used with *sing* [C] *ns* to emphasize the separate units 与单数可数名词连用, 侧重指各单项) each individual 每个; 每一; 各个: *He enjoyed every minute of his holiday.* 假日的每一分钟他都过得很愉快. ○ *I have had to work for every single penny I earned.* 我挣的每一便士都是辛苦工作得来的. ○ *They were watching her every movement.* 他们注视着她的每一个动作. ○ *Every time he phones I always seem to be in the bath.* 他每次来电话时, 我好像总是正在洗澡. ⇨Usage at EACH 用法见EACH. **2** (used with abstract *ns* 与抽象名词连用) all possible 所有可能的: *We have every reason to think he may still be alive.* 我们有充分理由认为他可能还活着. ○ *You have every chance of success.* 你完全有可能成功. **3** (used to indicate regular occurrence at specified intervals) each 每隔; 每逢; 每: *The buses go every 10 minutes.* 公共汽车每隔10分钟一辆. **4** (idm 习语) **every other** (**a**) all the other (people or things) 所有其他的(人或事物): *Every other girl except me is wearing jeans.* 除了我以外, 其他姑娘都穿着牛仔裤. (**b**) alternate 隔, 间(如隔周、间日等): *They visit us every other week.* 他们隔周到我们这儿来.

□ **everybody** /ˈevrɪbɒdɪ; ˋɛvrɪ,bɑdɪ/ (also **everyone** /ˈevrɪwʌn; ˋɛvrɪ,wʌn/) *indef pron* every person; all people 每个人; 人人; 所有的人: *The police questioned everybody in the room.* 警察询问了室内所有的人. ○ *It's impossible to remember everybody's name.* 把每个人的名字都记住是不可能的. ⇨Usage at SOMEBODY 用法见SOMEBODY.

everyday /ˈevrɪdeɪ; ˋɛvrɪˋde/ *adj* [attrib 作定语] used or happening daily; familiar 每天使用的; 每天发生的; 熟悉的; 日常的; 平常的: *an everyday occurrence* 日常之事 ○ *a compact dictionary for everyday use* 日常使用的袖珍词典.

everyplace /ˈevrɪpleɪs; ˋɛvrɪ,ples/ *indef adv* (*US infml* 口) = EVERYWHERE.

everything /ˈevrɪθɪŋ; ˋɛvrɪ,θɪŋ/ *indef pron* **1** all things 一切事物: *Everything was destroyed.* 一切都毁灭了. ○ *I'll tell you everything I know.* 我要把我知道的一切都告诉你. **2** the most important thing 最重要的事物: *Money isn't everything.* 金钱并不是最重要的.

everywhere /ˈevrɪweə(r); *US* -hweə(r); ˋɛvrɪ,hwɛr/ *indef adv* in or to every place 各处; 到处: *I've looked everywhere.* 我各处都看过了.

evict /ɪˈvɪkt; ɪˋvɪkt/ *v* [esp passive 尤用于被动语态: Tn, Tn·pr] **~ sb (from sth)** remove (a tenant) from a house or land, esp with the support of the law 将(房客或佃户)逐出(尤指依法): *They were evicted from their flat for not paying the rent.* 他们因不付房租而被赶出公寓.

▷ **evic·tion** /ɪˈvɪkʃn; ɪˋvɪkʃən/ *n* **~ (from sth)** **1** [U] evicting or being evicted (对房客或佃户的)驱逐: *He's had nowhere to live since his eviction.* 他自从被驱逐出住所以来, 就一直无处栖身. ○ [attrib 作定语] *an eviction order*, ie an order to leave given by the courts (对房客或佃户的)驱逐令. **2** [C] instance of this (对房客或佃户的)驱逐事件: *There have been four evictions from this street recently.* 最近这条街上已有四宗驱逐房客事件.

evid·ence /ˈevɪdəns; ˋɛvədəns/ *n* **1** [U] **~ (to do sth/that...)** (*esp law* 尤用于法律) information that gives a reason for believing sth or proves sth 根据; 证据; 证词: *There wasn't enough evidence to prove him guilty.* 没有充分的证据证明他有罪. ○ *Have you any evidence to support this statement?* 你这种说法有根据吗? ○ *His statement to the police was used in evidence against him.* 他对警方说的话已用作指证他的证据. ○ *A scientist must produce evidence in support of a theory.* 科学家必须提出证据以支持其理论. ○ *not a bit/piece/scrap/shred of evidence* 没有一点[一项/丝毫/点滴]证据. **2** [U, C] indication or trace 迹象; 痕迹: *The room bore evidence* (ie showed signs) *of a struggle.* 这房间里有搏斗过的痕迹. ○ *evidences of glacial action on the rocks* 岩石上的冰河留下的痕迹. **3** (idm 习语) **(be) in evidence** clearly or easily seen 显而易见的; 清楚的; 明显的: *He's the sort of man who likes to be very much in evidence at important meetings*, ie who likes to be seen and noticed. 他是非常喜欢在重大会议上出风头的那种人. **on the evidence of sth** using sth as evidence 用某事物作为证据: *On the evidence of their recent matches it's unlikely the Spanish team will win the cup.* 从西班牙队最近的比赛情况来看, 他们难以在这一锦标赛中夺标. **turn King's/Queen's ˈevidence** (*Brit*) (*US* **turn State's ˈevidence**) (of a criminal) give evidence in court against one's partners in order to receive a less severe sentence oneself (指罪犯)作污点证人(告发同犯的). **weigh the evidence** ⇨ WEIGH.

▷ **evid·ence** *v* [Tn] (*fml* 文) prove (sth) by evidence; be evidence of 证明(某事物): *His answer evidenced a guilty conscience.* 他的回答证明他良心有愧.

evid·ent /ˈevɪdənt; ˋɛvədənt/ *adj* **~ (to sb) (that...)** obvious (to the eye or mind); clear 明显的; 明白的; 清楚的: *It must be evident to all of you that he has made a mistake.* 你们一定很清楚, 他犯了错误. ○ *He looked at his children with evident pride.* 他看着自己的孩子, 充满自豪.

▷ **evid·ently** *adv* obviously; it appears that 明显地; 显然: *Evidently he has decided to leave.* 显然他已决定要离开.

evid·en·tial /ˌevɪˈdenʃl; ˌɛvəˋdɛnʃəl/ *adj* (*fml* 文) of, based on, or providing evidence 证据的; 凭证据的; 提供证据的: *evidential proof* 用作证据的证明.

evil /ˈiːvl; ˋivḷ/ *adj* **1** morally bad; wicked 道德败坏的; 邪恶的: *evil thoughts* 邪念 ○ *an evil man* 恶棍. **2** very unpleasant or harmful 令人不快的; 坏的; 有害的: *an evil smell* 难闻的气味 ○ *an evil temper* 坏脾气 ○ *evil weather* 恶劣的天气. **3** (idm 习语) **the evil ˈday, ˈhour, etc** time when sth unpleasant that one would like to avoid (but cannot) will happen 该着倒霉的日子、时刻等: *I know I need to go to the dentist but I've been putting off the evil day as long as possible.* 我明知得去看牙, 却尽可能把这倒霉日子往后拖. **(give sb) the evil ˈeye** supposed power to harm people by a look or glance 恶毒的目光. **the ˈEvil One** (*dated* 旧) the Devil 魔鬼; 恶魔. **an evil ˈtongue** tendency to say malicious things about people 说人坏话的恶习: *She has an evil tongue.* 她爱说别人坏话. **one's good/evil genius** ⇨ GENIUS. **fall on evil days** (*fml* 文) suffer hardship or misfortune 遭受苦难或不幸.

▷ **evil** *n* (*fml* 文) **1** [U] wrongdoing or wickedness 罪恶; 邪恶; 恶行: *the spirit of evil in man* 人类的邪恶灵魂 ○ *return good for evil* 以德报怨 ○ *speak no evil* 不说坏话 ○ *You cannot pretend there's no evil in the world.* 不要以为世界上没有罪恶. **2** [C] evil thing; disaster 邪恶之事; 灾难: *War, famine, and flood are terrible evils.* 战争、饥荒、洪水都是可怕的灾难. ○ *the evils of drink* 饮酒的害处. **3** (idm 习语) **the lesser of two evils** ⇨ LESSER. **a necessary evil** ⇨ NECESSARY.

evilly /ˈiːvəlɪ; ˋivḷɪ/ *adv* in an evil manner 邪恶地; 坏; 有害地: *He eyed her evilly.* 他狠狠地看着她.

□ ˈ**evildoer** *n* [C] (*fml* 文) person who does evil 作恶的人; 坏人: *thieves, murderers and other evildoers* 盗贼、谋杀者和其他犯罪分子.

ˌ**evil-ˈminded** *adj* having evil thoughts and desires 有邪念的; 恶毒的; 狠毒的: *a wicked, ˌevil-minded old ˈman* 邪恶的、狠毒的老头.

evince /ɪˈvɪns; ɪˋvɪns/ *v* [Tn] (*fml* 文) show clearly that one has (a feeling, quality, etc); exhibit 表现出(感情、特性等); 表明; 显示: *a child who evinces great intelligence* 表现出有极高智力的儿童 ○ *evincing powers of recovery* 显示出复原的生理机能.

evis·cer·ate /ɪˈvɪsəreɪt; ɪˋvɪsəˌret/ *v* [Tn] (*fml* 文) remove the internal organs of (a body); disembowel 切除内脏; 切除器官内容物.

evoc·at·ive /ɪˈvɒkətɪv; ɪˋvɑkətɪv/ *adj* **~ (of sth)** that evokes or is able to evoke memories, feelings, etc (of sth) 引起回忆的; 唤起感情的: *That smell is evocative of school.* 这种气味使人回想起学校来. ○ *evocative words* 引起回忆或感情的话.

evoke /ɪˈvəʊk; ɪˋvok/ *v* [Tn] **1** bring to mind (a feeling, memory, etc); summon up 引起或唤起(感情、记忆等): *The music evoked memories of her youth.* 这乐曲勾起她对青年时期的回忆. **2** (*fml* 文) produce or cause (a response, reaction, etc) 产生或引起(回应、反应等): *evoke admiration, surprise, interest, sympathy, etc* 产生羡慕之情、惊讶、兴趣、同情心等 ○ *Her speech evoked great anger.* 她的讲话引起极大愤慨. ▷ **evoca·tion** /ˌiːvəʊˈkeɪʃn; ˌivoˋkeʃən/ *n* [C, U] (*fml* 文).

evolu·tion /ˌiːvəˈluːʃn; *US* ˌev-; ˌɛvəˋluʃən/ *n* **1** [U] (*biology* 生) (theory of the) gradual development of the characteristics of plants and animals over many generations, esp the development of more complicated forms from earlier, simpler forms 进化; 进化论: *Darwin's theory of evolution* 达尔文的进化论. **2** [U] process of gradually developing; evolving 演化; 演进; 演变; 发展; 开展; 发育: *the evolution of farming methods* 耕种方法的演进 ○ *In politics Britain has preferred evolution to revolution*, ie gradual development to sudden violent change. 在政治上, 英国喜欢渐进而不喜欢革命. **3** [C] (*fml* 文) (of troops, warships, dancers, etc) movement according to plan (部队、军舰、跳舞者等)按照计划的行动或动作.

▷ **evolu·tion·ary** /ˌiːvəˈluːʃənrɪ; *US* ˌevəˈluːʃənerɪ; ˌɛvəˋluʃənˌɛrɪ/ *adj* (*fml* 文) of or resulting from (the theory of) evolution; developing 进化的; 由进化产生的; 进化论的; 发展的: *evolutionary processes* 进化过程.

evolve /ɪˈvɒlv; ɪˋvɑlv/ *v* **1** [I, Tn] (*fml* 文) (cause to) develop naturally and (usu) gradually (使)逐渐形成: *The American constitution was planned; the British constitution evolved.* 美国宪法是精心制定的, 英国宪法是约定俗成的. ○ *He has evolved a new theory after many years of research.* 他经过多年的研究, 逐渐总结出了新的理论. **2** [I] (*biology* 生) (of plants, animals, etc) gradually develop from a simple form to a more complex one (指植物、动物等)进化: *Many Victorians were shocked by the notion that Man had evolved from lower forms of life.* 在维多利亚时代, 许多人对于人是由低级生物进化而来的见解大为震惊.

ewe /juː; ju/ *n* female sheep 母羊; 雌羊; 牝羊. ⇨illus at SHEEP 见 SHEEP 之插图. Cf 参看 LAMB 1, RAM 1, TUP.

ewer /ˈjuːə(r); ˋjuɚ/ *n* large wide-mouthed jug for holding water, esp as formerly used with a basin in a bedroom without a piped water supply 大口水罐(尤指旧时无自来水时, 在卧室里与面盆共用者).

ex[1] /eks; ɛks/ *n* (*infml* 口) (*pl* **~es, ~'s**) former wife or husband; former boyfriend or girlfriend 前妻或前夫; 以前的男朋友或女朋友: *My ex shares custody of the children.* 我原先的配偶分担照顾孩子的责任. ○ *He is one of her many exes.* 他是她以前众多的男友之一.

ex[2] /eks; ɛks/ *prep* **1** (*commerce* 商) (of goods etc) as sold from (a ship, factory, etc) excluding cost of delivery to the buyer (指货物等)从(船上、工厂等处)交货(不包括运给买主的费用): *ex warehouse price* 仓库交货价.

E

2 excluding (sth); not included 除(某事物)外; 不包括; 不; 无; 未: *ex dividend*, ie not including a dividend that is about to be paid 除去红利 ○ *an ex-directory number* 未列入电话簿的电话号码.

ex- *pref* 前缀 (used widely with *ns* 可与许多名词结合) former 以前的: *ex-wife* ○ *ex-President* ○ *ex-convict*.

ex·acer·bate /ɪgˈzæsəbeɪt; ɪgˈzæsɚ,bet/ *v* [Tn] (*fml* 文) make (pain, disease, a situation) worse; aggravate 使(疼痛、疾病、情形)恶化; 加剧: *Scratching exacerbates a skin rash.* 皮疹搔后会恶化. ○ *Her mother's interference exacerbated the difficulties in their marriage.* 她母亲从中干预使他们的婚姻雪上加霜. ▷ **ex·acer·ba·tion** /ɪg,zæsəˈbeɪʃn; ɪg,zæsɚˈbeʃən/ *n* [U].

ex·act[1] /ɪgˈzækt; ɪgˈzækt/ *adj* **1** correct in every detail; precise 正确的; 准确的; 精确的: *What were his exact words?* 他的原话是怎么说的? ○ *I don't know the exact size of the room.* 我不知道这个房间的确切面积. ○ *He's in his mid-fifties; well, fifty-six to be exact* (ie more accurately). 他五十多岁; 嗯, 确切地说是五十六岁. **2** capable of being precise and accurate 严谨的; 精密的: *an exact scholar* 治学严谨的学者 ○ *She's a very exact person.* 她是个一丝不苟的人. ○ *the exact sciences*, ie those in which absolute precision is possible, eg mathematics 精密科学(如数学).

▷ **ex·ac·ti·tude** /ɪgˈzæktɪtju:d; *US* -tu:d; ɪgˈzæktə,tud/ *n* [U] (*fml* 文) over-correctness 极端的正确性或精确性: *He spoke with pompous exactitude.* 他以自视绝对正确的口吻说话.

E

ex·actly *adv* **1** quite; just 正; 恰恰: *That's exactly what I expected.* 那正是我想望的. ○ *You've arrived at exactly the right moment.* 你到得正是时候. **2** in precise detail; correctly 精确地; 正确地: *Your answer is exactly right.* 你回答得完全正确. ○ *Where exactly were you in France?* 你当时在法国的什么地方? **3** (as a reply or confirmation 用作答语或表示赞同用语) just so; you are quite right 确实如此; 完全正确: *'So she wants to sell the house and move to London.' 'Exactly.'* '那么说, 她是想把房子卖掉, 搬到伦敦去.' '对.' **4** (idm 习语) **not exactly** (*infml ironic* 口, 反语) by no means 决不; 一点也不: *He wasn't exactly pleased to see us; in fact he refused to open the door.* 他根本不愿见我们, 其实他连门都不开.

ex·act·ness *n* [U].

ex·act[2] /ɪgˈzækt; ɪgˈzækt/ *v* **1** [Tn, Tn·pr] **~ sth (from sb)** (**a**) demand and enforce the payment of sth 强索费用: *exact payment (from a client)* 逼迫(委托人)付款 ○ *The kidnappers exacted a ransom of £10 000 from the family.* 绑架者向这家人家勒索10 000英镑的赎金. (**b**) insist on and obtain sth 坚持要得到某事物: *exact obedience from one's staff* 坚持要全体工作人员服从. **2** [Tn] (of work, circumstances, etc) make (sth) necessary; require (指工作、环境等)使(某事物)不可或缺; 要求; 需要: (*fml* 文) *Her work exacts great care and attention to detail.* 她的工作需要极为细心, 一丝不苟.

▷ **ex·act·ing** *adj* making great demands; requiring great effort 苛求的; 严格的; 需极努力的: *an exacting teacher* 严师 ○ *an exacting piece of work* 费力的工作.

ex·ac·tion /ɪgˈzækʃn; ɪgˈzækʃən/ *n* (*fml* 文) **1** (**a**) [U] action of exacting money, etc (对金钱等的)强索, 强求: *the exaction of income tax* 强征所得税. (**b**) [C] something that is exacted, esp a tax that is considered to be too high 强索之物; (尤指)苛税: *unreasonable exactions* 不合理的苛捐杂税. **2** [C] great demand (on one's time, strength, etc) (对某人时间、精力等的)极大需求: *the exactions of a senior post in government* 在政府中任高职要日理万机.

ex·ag·ger·ate /ɪgˈzædʒəreɪt; ɪgˈzædʒə,ret/ *v* [I, Tn] make (sth) seem larger, better, worse, etc than it really is; stretch (a description) beyond the truth 夸张; 夸大; 言过其实: *He always exaggerates to make his stories more amusing.* 他总爱添枝加叶, 把故事讲得更有趣. ○ *You are exaggerating the difficulties.* 你把困难夸大了. ○ *That dress exaggerates her height.* 她穿那件连衣裙显得高了.

▷ **ex·ag·ger·ated** *adj* (**a**) made to seem larger, better, worse, etc than it really is 夸张的; 夸大的; 言过其实的: *a highly exaggerated version of the incident* 对那件小事极为夸张的说法 ○ *He has an exaggerated sense of his own importance.* 他自视过高. (**b**) produced, stated, etc in a false or an unnatural way; distorted 虚假的; 不自然的; 歪曲的: *an exaggerated laugh* 矫揉造作的笑声 ○ *a clown's exaggerated make-up* 对丑角过火的化装 ○ *with exaggerated politeness* 虚情假意的礼貌. **ex·ag·ger·atedly** *adv*.

ex·ag·gera·tion /ɪg,zædʒəˈreɪʃn; ɪg,zædʒəˈreʃən/ *n* **1** [U] action of exaggerating 夸张; 夸大; 言过其实. **2** [C] exaggerated description, statement, etc 夸张的描述、说法等: *a story full of exaggerations* 通篇夸夸其谈的故事.

ex·alt /ɪgˈzɔ:lt; ɪgˈzɔlt/ *v* [Tn] (*fml* 文) **1** make (sb) higher in rank or greater in power 提升, 提拔(某人). **2** praise (sb) highly 高度赞扬(某人). ▷ **ex·alted** *adj* (*fml or joc* 文或谑): *a person of exalted rank* 地位高的人 ○ *from his exalted position in the firm* 从他在公司的高职位上.

ex·al·ta·tion /ˌegzɔ:lˈteɪʃn; ,ɛgzɔlˈteʃən/ *n* [U] state of spiritual delight; elation 兴奋; 得意洋洋; 兴高采烈.

exam /ɪgˈzæm; ɪgˈzæm/ *n* (*infml* 口) examination(2) 考试: *school exams* 学校的考试.

ex·am·ina·tion /ɪg,zæmɪˈneɪʃn; ɪg,zæməˈneʃən/ *n* **1** [U] action of examining; being examined 检查; 调查; 被检查: *Careful examination of the ruins revealed new evidence.* 仔细检查了废墟后发现了新的证据. ○ *On* (ie As a result of) *further examination it was found that the signature was not genuine.* 经过进一步的调查发现签名不是真迹. **2** (also **exam**) [C] testing of knowledge or ability by means of questions, practical exercises, etc 考试: *an examination in Physics* 物理考试 ○ *sit/take an examination*, ie have one's knowledge tested by a written examination 参加考试 ○ *pass/fail an examination*, ie be/not be successful in an examination 考试及格[不及格] ○ *an oral examination* 口试 ○ *an entrance examination*, eg to test an applicant wishing to enter a school, college, etc 入学考试 ○ [attrib 作定语] *an examination paper*, ie sheet(s) of paper with a list of questions set by an examiner 试卷. **3** [C] close inspection of sb/sth or inquiry into sth 检查; 查阅; 审查: *a medical examination by a doctor* 医生的诊察 ○ *an examination of business accounts* 对商业帐目的审查. **4** [C, U] (action of) questioning by a lawyer in a law court (在法庭上由律师进行的)讯问: *a fresh examination of the witness* 对证人的再次讯问 ○ *After further examination by the prosecution the witness was allowed to leave the court.* 证人经原告律师讯问后, 获准离开法庭. **5** (idm 习语) **under exami'nation** being examined 在检查中; 在调查中; 在审查中: *The prisoner is still under examination.* 囚犯仍在受审. ○ *The proposals are still under examination*, ie have not yet been approved. 提案仍在审查中.

ex·am·ine /ɪgˈzæmɪn; ɪgˈzæmɪn/ *v* [Tn, Tn·pr] **1 ~ sth/sb (for sth)** (**a**) look at carefully in order to learn about or from; inspect closely 仔细观察; 检查; 调查; 审查: *examine an old manuscript* 仔细检查旧手稿 ○ *examine facts, a theory, evidence, etc* 查验事实、理论、证据等 ○ *The detective examined the window frame for fingerprints.* 侦探仔细查看窗框, 寻找指纹. (**b**) inspect carefully (a patient or part of his body) to check for disease 诊察; 诊视: *have one's teeth examined for decay* 诊察龋齿 ○ *The doctor examined her patient carefully.* 那位女医生仔细诊察病人. **2 ~ sb (in/on sth)** (*fml* 文) test the knowledge or ability of sb by written or oral questions 考, 测验(某人): *examine students in mathematics/on their knowledge of mathematics* 考学生数学. **3** (*law* 律) question (sb) formally in order to get information; interrogate 询问, 盘问, 审问, 讯问(某人): *examine a witness in a court of law* 在法庭上讯问证人. Cf 参看 CROSS-EXAMINE. **4** (idm 习语) **need, etc one's head examined** ⇨ HEAD[1].

▷ **ex·am·inee** /ɪg,zæmɪˈni:; ɪg,zæməˈni/ *n* (*fml* 文) person being tested in an examination(2) 应考者; 被考者: *Ten of the examinees were failed.* 应考者有十名不及格.

ex·am·iner /ɪgˈzæmɪnə(r); ɪgˈzæmɪnɚ/ *n* **1** person who tests knowledge or ability 主考人: *He is one of the science examiners.* 他是理科主考人之一. **2** (idm 习语) **satisfy the examiners** ⇨ SATISFY.

ex·ample /ɪgˈzɑ:mpl; *US* -ˈzæmpl; ɪgˈzæmpl/ *n* **1** fact, event, etc that illustrates or represents a general rule 实例; 例证; 例子: *This dictionary has many examples of how words are used.* 这部词典有许多说明词语用法的实例. ○ *That outburst was a typical example of his lack of self-control.* 他那次发作是他缺乏自制力的典型事例. **2** specimen showing the quality of others in the same group or of the same kind 样品; 样本; 范例: *This church is a fine example of Norman architecture.* 这座教堂是典型的诺曼式建筑. ○ *This is a good example of Shelley's lyric poetry.* 这首诗是雪莱抒情诗的范例. ○ *It is a classic example of how not to design a new city centre.* 这对于设计新市中心是个最佳的反面教材. **3** [C, U] thing, person or quality that is worthy of imitation 榜样; 模范; 楷模: *She was an example to the rest of the class.* 她是全班的模范. ○ *His bravery should be an example to all of us.* 他的勇敢应作为我们大家学习的榜样. ○ *learn by example* 仿效. **4** warning 告诫; 警告: *Let this be an example* (ie May this punishment serve as a warning) *to you.* 你要以此为鉴戒. **5** (idm 习语) **follow sb's example/lead** ⇨ FOLLOW. **for example** (*abbr* 缩写 **eg**) by way of illustration 例如; 譬如: *I know many women who have a career and a family — Alison for example.* 我知道有许多妇女能事业家庭兼顾——艾莉森就是其中之一. **make an example of sb** punish (sb) as a warning to others 惩罚(某人)以警戒他人: *The headmaster decided to make an example of the pupil and expel him from the school.* 校长决定开除该生以儆效尤. **set (sb) an example/set a good, bad, etc example (to sb)** behave in a way worthy/not worthy of imitation (by sb) 树立好榜样[充当反面教员]: *The headmistress likes to arrive early at school to set (the other teachers) an example*, ie a good example. 那位女校长愿意早早到校, 以身作则(为其他教师树立好榜样).

ex·as·per·ate /ɪɡˈzæspəreɪt; ɪɡˋzæspəˌret/ *v* [Tn] irritate or annoy (sb) greatly 激怒, 触怒, 惹恼(某人): *That child exasperates me!* 那孩子真让我生气! ○ *She was exasperated at/by his stupidity.* 她因为他愚笨而发怒.

▷ **ex·as·per·at·ing** *adj* extremely annoying 使人极恼怒的; 使人发火的: *He's probably the most exasperating man I've ever met.* 他大概是我见过的最让人恼火的人. ○ *It's exasperating to run for a train and then miss it by half a minute.* 跑着赶火车, 却差半分钟没赶上, 真气人. **ex·as·per·at·ingly** *adv*.

ex·as·pera·tion /ɪɡˌzæspəˈreɪʃn; ɪɡˌzæspəˋreʃən/ *n* [U] state of being exasperated 愤怒; 恼怒; 恼火: *'Stop that noise,' he cried out in exasperation.* '不要发出那种噪音,'他愤怒地大喊.

ex·cav·ate /ˈekskəveɪt; ˋɛkskəˌvet/ *v* [Tn] **1** (*fml* 文) make (a hole or channel) by digging; remove (soil, etc) by digging 挖掘(洞或水道、河床); 掘出(土等): *excavate a trench* 挖壕沟. **2** uncover or extract by digging (esp sth from earlier times) 发掘(尤指古物): *excavate a buried city, a Greek vase* 发掘出一地下城市、一希腊花瓶.

▷ **ex·cava·tion** /ˌekskəˈveɪʃn; ˌɛkskəˋveʃən/ *n* **1** [U] activity of excavating 挖掘; 挖土; 发掘: *Excavation of the site will begin tomorrow.* 明天开始挖掘工作. **2** [C] **excavations** [pl] place that is being or has been excavated 挖掘的地方: *visit the excavations* 参观挖掘现场.

ex·cav·ator *n* person engaged in or machine used for excavating 挖掘者; 挖掘机: *excavators on an archaeological site* 考古场地上的挖掘者 ○ *mechanical excavators* 挖掘机.

ex·ceed /ɪkˈsiːd; ɪkˋsid/ *v* [Tn] (**a**) be greater or more numerous than (esp a quantity) 超过(尤指数量): *The price will not exceed £100.* 价格不会超过100英镑. ○ *The number admitted must not exceed 200.* 容纳的数目不得超过200. ○ *Their success exceeded all expectations*, ie was greater than anyone expected. 他们的成功出乎一切预料. (**b**) go beyond what is allowed, necessary or advisable 超出(所允许的、必需的或合理的)界线: *exceed the speed limit*, ie drive faster than is allowed 超速(超过驾驶速度限制) ○ *exceed one's instructions/authority*, ie do more than one has permission to do 越权.

▷ **ex·ceed·ingly** *adv* extremely; to an unusual degree 极端地; 非常; 极其: *an exceedingly difficult problem* 极其困难的问题.

ex·cel /ɪkˈsel; ɪkˋsɛl/ *v* (**-ll-**) **1** [Ipr] **~ in/at sth** be exceptionally good at sth 擅长: *excel in foreign languages* 擅长外语 ○ *The firm excels at producing cheap transistor radios.* 该公司以生产廉价晶体管收音机见长. **2** (idm 习语) **exˈcel oneself** do better than ever before 胜过过去: *His meals are always very good, but this time he's excelled himself.* 他做的饭菜一直很拿手, 但这次做得更好. ○ (*ironic* 反语) *So you've broken three windows today — you've really excelled yourself.* 那么, 你今天已经打碎三扇窗户了——真破了你以往的纪录了.

ex·cel·lence /ˈeksələns; ˋɛksl̩əns/ *n* **1** [U] **~ (in/at sth)** quality of being excellent; great merit 优秀; 卓越; 杰出: *a prize for excellence in furniture design* 家具设计优秀奖 ○ *known for excellence in/at all forms of sport* 因精于各项体育运动而知名. **2** [C] (*fml* 文) thing or quality in which a person excels 优点; 长处: *They do not recognize her many excellences.* 他们无视她的各种长处.

Ex·cel·lency /ˈeksələnsɪ; ˋɛksl̩ənsɪ/ *n* title given to ambassadors, governors, their husbands or wives, and some other officers and officials 阁下(对大使或总督本人或其配偶以及其他官员的敬称): *Your/His/Her Excellency* 阁下 ○ *His Excellency the French Ambassador* 法国大使阁下.

ex·cel·lent /ˈeksələnt; ˋɛksl̩ənt/ *adj* **1** very good; of very high quality 优秀的; 极好的; 卓越的; 杰出的: *an excellent meal* 精美的一餐 ○ *She speaks excellent French.* 她的法语说得非常漂亮. **2** (used to indicate approval or pleasure 用以表示赞同或愉快): *They won't be coming then? Excellent!* 那么他们不来了? 太好了!

▷ **ex·cel·lently** *adv*.

ex·cept[1] /ɪkˈsept; ɪkˋsɛpt/ *prep* **~ (for sb/sth); ~ (that...)** not including (sb/sth); but not 除了(某人[某事物])之外(表示所说的不包括在内): *The restaurant is open every day except Monday.* 这家饭店除星期一外, 每天都营业. ○ *Everyone except me got an invitation.* 除了我以外, 所有人都收到了请柬. ○ *I understand everything except why she killed him.* 我一切都明白, 只是不理解她为什么把他杀死了. ○ *I can answer all the questions except for the last.* 所有的题我都会答, 只是最后一题不会. ○ *The meal was excellent except for* (ie with the exception of) *the first course.* 这顿饭好极了, 只是第一道菜稍差. ○ *She remembered nothing (about him) except that his hair was black.* 她(对他)什么都不记得, 只记得他的头发是黑的. ○ *The two books are the same except (for the fact) that this one has an answer key at the back.* 除了这本书后面有问题答案以外, 这两本书完全一样.

ex·cept[2] /ɪkˈsept; ɪkˋsɛpt/ *v* **1** [esp passive 尤用于被动语态: Tn, Tn·pr] **~ sb/sth (from sth)** (*fml* 文) (often with a negative 常与否定词连用) leave sb/sth out; exclude sb/sth 将某人[某事物]除外; 不包括某人[某事物]: *Only children under five are excepted from this survey.* 这次调查仅仅不包括五岁以下的儿童. ○ *We all had to take part in the training run, with nobody excepted.* 我们大家都得参加跑步训练, 无人例外. ○ *the whole staff, not excepting the headmaster* 全体教职员工, 也包括校长. **2** (idm 习语) **present company excepted** ⇨ PRESENT[1].

ex·cep·tion /ɪkˈsepʃn; ɪkˋsɛpʃən/ *n* **1** [C, U] (an instance of) leaving out or excluding; person or thing that is not included 除外; 例外; 不包括在内的人或物: *Most of the buildings in this town are rather unattractive, but this church is an exception.* 这座城镇中大多数建筑物都不太好看, 但这座教堂是个例外. ○ *The children did well, the only exception being Jo, who failed.* 这些孩子考得都很好, 唯独乔不及格. ○ *All students without exception must take the English examination.* 所有的学生毫无例外, 都必须参加英语考试. ○ *I enjoyed all his novels with the exception of his last.* 他的小说我都爱看, 只是最后一部除外. **2** [C] thing that does not follow a rule 不合规则的事物: *an exception to a rule of grammar* 语法规则的一项例外. **3** (idm 习语) **the exception proves the ˈrule** (*saying* 谚) the excepting of some cases proves that the rule exists, or that it applies to all other cases 有例外则证明有规律: *All his family have red hair except him. He is the exception which proves the rule.* 他们全家除他以外头发都是红的. 正所谓有例外才证明有规律嘛. **make an exception (of sb/sth)** treat sb/sth as a special case 将某人[某事物]作为例外: *You must all be here at 8 am; I can make no exceptions*, ie I cannot excuse any of you. 你们都必须早晨八点钟到这里, 任何人都不能例外. **take exception to sth** object to sth; be offended by sth 反对某事物; 因某事物而生气: *He took great exception to what I said.* 他很反对我说的话. ○ *She took exception to having to wait outside in the rain.* 她得在雨中等候, 对此十分气愤.

E

▷ **ex·cep·tion·able** /-ʃənəbl; -ʃənəbl̩/ *adj* (*fml* 文) that sb can object to 可反对的: *There are no exceptionable scenes in the play.* 这出剧中没有能引起争议的情节.

ex·cep·tional /ɪkˈsepʃənl; ɪkˋsɛpʃənl̩/ *adj* very unusual; outstanding 异常的; 罕见的; 特殊的; 杰出的; 突出的: *This weather is exceptional for June.* 这种天气在六月份很罕见. ○ *show exceptional musical ability* 表现出非凡的音乐才能.

▷ **ex·cep·tion·ally** /-ʃənəlɪ; -ʃənl̩ɪ/ *adv* unusually; outstandingly 异常地; 罕见地; 特殊地; 杰出地; 突出地: *an exceptionally beautiful child* 特别漂亮的小孩.

ex·cerpt /ˈeksɜːpt; ˋɛksɝpt/ *n* [C] **~ (from sth)** passage, extract, from a book, film, piece of music, etc 书、电影、乐曲等的节录: *excerpts from a novel* 一部小说的摘录 ○ *I've seen a short excerpt from the film on television.* 我在电视上看过这部影片的片段.

ex·cess[1] /ɪkˈses; ɪkˋsɛs/ *n* **1** [sing] **an ~ of sth** (*derog* 贬) more than the reasonable, expected or moderate degree or amount of sth 过度; 过分; 过量; 过多: *an excess of enthusiasm, anger, emotion, zeal, etc* 过分的热情、愤怒、情感、热心等 ○ *An excess of fat in one's diet can lead to heart disease.* 饮食中脂肪过量能导致心脏病. **2** [U] going beyond the normal or accepted limits; immoderation 过火; 过头; 无节制: *Don't carry your anger to excess.* 不要肝火过盛. ○ *Luggage in excess of 100 kg will be charged extra.* 超过100公斤的行李要额外收费. **3** [C] amount by which sth is larger than sth else 超额的量; 过多的数: *She was charged an excess of £4 over the amount stated on the bill.* 向她索取的比帐单上显示的数额多出4英镑. **4** [U] (*esp Brit*) agreed sum taken by an insurance company from the total amount to be paid to an insured person who makes a claim 免赔额(保险公司从投保人要求索赔的总款额中扣除的规定数额): *You will have to pay the first £50 of the cost of repairing your damaged car as there is an excess of £50 on your policy.* 你的保险单列有50英镑免赔额, 所以你的汽车损坏修理费的头50英镑要由你付. **5 excesses** [pl] (*fml* 文) personal acts which go beyond the limits of good behaviour, or humanity 越轨的行为; 无人性的行为: *The excesses* (ie acts of cruelty) *committed by the occupying troops will never be forgotten.* 占领军犯下的灭绝人性的暴行, 人们是永远也不会忘记的. ○ *His excesses at parties are well known.* 尽人皆知他在聚会上十分放肆. **6** (idm 习语) **to exˈcess** to an extreme degree 过度; 过分; 无度: *He drinks to excess.* 他嗜酒无度.

▷ **ex·cess·ive** /ɪkˈsesɪv; ɪkˋsɛsɪv/ *adj* greater than what is normal or necessary; extreme 过分的; 过度的; 极度的: *excessive prices* 过高的价格 ○ *an excessive amount of alcohol* 过量的酒精 ○ *an excessive enthusiasm for sport* 对运动的狂热 **ex·cess·ively** *adv*.

ex·cess[2] /ˈekses; ˋɛksɛs/ *adj* [attrib 作定语] extra or additional (to the usual or permitted amount) 额外的; 附加的: *excess fare*, eg for travelling further than is allowed by one's ticket 补票费 ○ *A company which makes high profits must pay excess profits duty to the government.* 赢利高的公司须向政府交纳额外利得税.

□ ˌ**excess ˈbaggage** (also ˌ**excess ˈluggage**) amount of luggage that is over the weight that may be carried free on an aircraft 超重的行李.

ˌ**excess ˈpostage** amount charged to a person who receives a letter, etc which does not carry stamps of high enough value 欠资邮费.

ex·change[1] /ɪksˈtʃeɪndʒ; ɪksˋtʃendʒ/ *n* **1** [C, U] (action or process of) giving one thing or person in return for another 交换; 互换; 交流; 交易; 调换; 更换: *Is five apples for five eggs a fair exchange?* 用五个苹果换五个鸡蛋公平吗? ○ *The exchange of prisoners during a war is unusual.* 战时很少交换俘虏. ○ *the exchange of contracts*, ie the final stage of buying or selling a house 互换契约(买卖房屋的最后步骤) ○ *an exchange of glances* 互使眼色 ○ *an exchange of houses* 调换房屋 ○ *an exchange of gun-fire* 交火 ○ *He's giving her French lessons in exchange for* (ie as an exchange for) *her teaching him English.* 他教她法语, 她教他英语, 互教互学(作为交换条件). **2** [C] (angry) conversation or argument (愤怒的)谈话或争论: *bitter exchanges between MP's in parliament* 下议院议员在议会上的激烈争论. **3** [U] relation in value between kinds of money used in different countries 兑换; 兑换率: *What is the rate of exchange between the dollar and the pound?* 美元和英镑之间的兑换率是多少? ○ [attrib 作定语] *I want to change my dollars into pesetas — what is the exchange rate?* 我想把美元换成比塞塔 —— 兑换率是多少? **4 Exchange** [C] place where business people or financiers meet for business 交易所: *the ˈCorn Exchange* 谷物交易所 ○ *the ˈStock Exchange*, ie for the buying and selling of stocks, shares, etc 证券交易所. **5** = TELEPHONE EXCHANGE (TELEPHONE). **6** reciprocal visit between two (often young) people or groups from different countries (不同国家的团体或人, 常为青年之间的)互访, 交流: *be on, do, organize an exchange* 在、进行、组织互访 ○ *Sarah is going on an exchange to Paris to stay with Pierre, and he is coming to stay with her here in Scotland next year.* 萨拉将到巴黎作互访住在皮埃尔处, 而皮埃尔明年来苏格兰就住在她那里. ○ [attrib 作定语] *exchange students* 互派的留学生 ○ *exchange visits* 两国间的互访 ○ *She is an exchange teacher.* 她是出国的交流教师.

ex·change[2] /ɪksˈtʃeɪndʒ; ɪksˋtʃendʒ/ *v* **1 (a)** [Tn, Tn·pr] **~ A for B; ~ sth (with sb)** give or receive sth/sb (of the same kind or value) in place of another 交换; 互换; 调换; 更换: *He exchanged the blue jumper for a red one.* 他把蓝毛衣换成了红的. ○ *Ali exchanged seats with Ben.* 阿里与本调换了座位. ○ *The enemy countries exchanged prisoners.* 敌国间交换了俘虏. ○ *They exchanged hostages with each other.* 他们相互交换了人质. **(b)** [Tn] give sth and receive sth (from another person) in return 交换; 交易: *exchanging blows*, ie hitting each other 互相殴打 ○ *They exchanged glances*, ie looked at each other. 他们互相对视. ○ *The two men exchanged greetings*, ie Each greeted the other. 那两个男人互相问候. **2** (idm 习语) **exchange (angry, etc) ˈwords** quarrel; argue 争吵; 争论: *They exchanged angry words before the meeting but were finally persuaded to agree.* 他们在会议前争吵起来, 经劝说最后言归于好.

▷ **ex·change·able** /-əbl; -əbl̩/ *adj* that can be exchanged 可交换的; 可更换的; 可兑换的: *Sale goods in this shop are not exchangeable.* 本店货物售出概不退换.

ex·chequer /ɪksˈtʃekə(r); ɪksˋtʃɛkɚ/ *n* **1 the Exchequer** [sing] (*Brit*) government department in charge of public money 财政部: *The Chancellor of the Exchequer is the minister in charge of finance in Britain.* 英国财政大臣是负责财政的大臣. **2** [C] **(a)** public or national supply of money; treasury 公共财源; 国库. **(b)** (*often joc* 常作戏谑语) person's supply of money 个人的钱财: *There's nothing left in the exchequer this month.* 本月份本人国库空虚.

ex·cise[1] /ˈeksaɪz; ɪkˋsaɪz/ *n* [U] government tax on certain goods manufactured, sold or used within a country 国内货物税; 消费税: *the excise on beer/spirits/tobacco* 啤酒[烈性酒/烟草]消费税 ○ *customs and excise* 关税与国内货物税 ○ [attrib 作定语] *an excise officer*, ie an official employed in collecting excise 国内货物税务官. Cf 参看 CUSTOMS[1].

ex·cise[2] /ɪkˈsaɪz; ɪkˋsaɪz/ *v* [Tn, Tn·pr] **~ sth (from sth)** (*fml* 文) remove by, or as if by, cutting (esp a part of the body or a passage from a book) 切除(尤指身体的一部分); 删除(书中的一段): *The surgeon excised the lump from her breast.* 外科医生切除了她乳房的肿块. ○ *The censor insisted on excising the passage from the film.* 电影审查员坚持剪去影片的这一段.

▷ **ex·cision** /ɪkˈsɪʒn; ɪkˋsɪʒən/ *n* (*fml* 文) **1** [U] action of excising 切除; 删除: *the excision of a tumour* 肿瘤的切除. **2** [C] thing that is excised 被切除或删除之物: *The excisions have destroyed the literary value of the text.* 删除了这些就损害了原文的文学价值.

ex·cit·able /ɪkˈsaɪtəbl; ɪkˋsaɪtəbl̩/ *adj* (of a person, animal or temperament) easily excited (指人、动物或气质)易兴奋的, 易激动的: *an excitable child* 易兴奋的孩子 ○ *an excitable breed of dog* 一种易受刺激的狗 ○ *an excitable race of people* 容易冲动的民族.

▷ **ex·cit·ab·il·ity** /ɪkˌsaɪtəˈbɪlətɪ; ɪkˌsaɪtəˋbɪlətɪ/ *n* [U] quality of being excitable 易兴奋性; 易激动性.

ex·cite /ɪkˈsaɪt; ɪkˋsaɪt/ *v* **1** [Tn esp passive 尤用于被动语态, Tn·pr] cause strong feelings of eagerness, happiness, nervousness, etc in (a person or an animal) 使(人或动物)兴奋, 激动: *The children were very excited* *by the pantomime.* 孩子们看了童话剧非常兴奋. ○ *Don't excite yourself,* ie Keep calm. 不要激动. **2** [Tn, Tn·pr, Cn·t] **~ sb (to sth)** (*fml* 文) cause or bring about (sth) by arousing strong feelings in sb 刺激; 激起; 煽动; 鼓动: *excite a riot* 煽动暴乱 ○ *Agitators were exciting the people to rebel/to rebellion against their rulers.* 煽动者鼓动人民造反以反抗统治者. **3** [Tn, Tn·pr] **(a) ~ sth (in sb)** arouse (an emotion) in sb; cause (a response or reaction) in sb 激发某人的(情感); 引起某人的(回应或反应): *excite public suspicion* 引起大众怀疑 ○ *The recent discoveries have excited great interest among doctors.* 最近的多项发现引起医生们的极大兴趣. ○ *excite envy, admiration, greed, etc (in sb)* 引起(某人)羡慕、爱慕、贪念等. **(b)** arouse (sexual desire) 激发(性欲): *Some people are sexually excited by pornographic magazines.* 有的人看到色情杂志能激发起性欲. **4** [Tn] (*fml* 文) cause (part of the body) to be active 刺激(身体某部分): *drugs that excite the nervous system* 刺激神经系统的药物.

▷ **ex·cited** /ɪk'saɪtɪd; ɪk`saɪtɪd/ *adj* feeling or showing excitement 兴奋的; 激动的: *sexually excited* 性兴奋 ○ *The excited children forgot to take the presents to the party.* 孩子们兴奋得忘了把礼物带到聚会上了. ○ *It's nothing to get excited about.* 这没什么可值得激动的. **ex·cit·edly** *adv.*

ex·cit·ing *adj* causing great interest or enthusiasm 使人激动的; 令人兴奋的: *an exciting piece of work* 令人兴奋的工作 ○ *an exciting story* 使人激动的故事 ○ *an exciting discovery* 振奋人心的发现. **ex·cit·ingly** *adv.*

ex·cite·ment /ɪk'saɪtmənt; ɪk`saɪtmənt/ *n* **1** [U] state of strong emotion or feeling, esp one caused by sth pleasant 刺激; 激动; 兴奋: *The news caused great excitement.* 这消息令人极为兴奋. ○ *jumping about in excitement at the discovery* 因这一发现而兴奋得手舞足蹈. **2** [C] (*fml* 文) thing that excites; exciting incident, etc 令人兴奋的事物; 使人激动的事: *the excitements associated with a cruise around the world* 关于乘船周游世界的令人兴奋的事.

ex·claim /ɪk'skleɪm; ɪk`sklem/ *v* [I, Ipr, Tf] cry out suddenly and loudly from pain, anger, surprise, etc (因疼痛、愤怒、惊奇等)惊叫, 呼喊: *'What,' he exclaimed, 'Are you leaving without me?'* '怎么着,'他喊道, '你要把我丢下自己走吗?' ○ *He could not help exclaiming at how much his son had grown.* 他的儿子已长那么高了, 他不禁惊叫起来. ○ *He exclaimed that it was untrue.* 他大声说那不是事实.

ex·clama·tion /ˌekskləˈmeɪʃn; ˌɛkskləˋmeʃən/ *n* (short) sound(s) or word(s), expressing sudden surprise, pain, etc 呼喊; 惊叫; 叹词; 感叹语: *'Oh!', 'Look out!' and 'Ow!' are exclamations.* '啊!'、'小心!'、'哎哟!'都是感叹词语.

□ **excla'mation mark** (*US* **excla'mation point**) mark (!) written after an exclamation 叹号; 感叹号; 惊叹号(!). ⇨App 3 见附录 3.

ex·clam·at·ory /ɪk'sklæmətrɪ; *US* -tɔ:rɪ; ɪk`sklæmə,tɔrɪ/ *adj* (*fml* 文) of, using or containing an exclamation 呼喊的; 感叹的: *an exclamatory sentence* 感叹句.

ex·clude /ɪk'sklu:d; ɪk`sklud/ *v* **1** [Tn, Tn·pr] **~ sb/sth (from sth)** **(a)** prevent sb from entering somewhere, taking part in sth, etc; keep sb out 防止某人进入某处; 阻止某人参加某事等; 把某人排除在外: *exclude a person from membership of a society* 拒绝接纳某人入会 ○ *Women are often excluded from positions of authority.* 女子要想得到有权的职位往往遭到排斥. **(b)** prevent sth from getting in; keep sth out 防止某物进入; 将某物排斥在外: *All air must be excluded (from the bottle) if the experiment is to work.* 若要做好这一试验, 不得让空气进(到瓶子里)去. ○ *All draughts must be excluded from the room.* 这间屋子不可有风透进. **2** [Tn] reject (sth) as a possibility; ignore as a consideration 排除(某事)的可能性; 不予考虑: *The police have excluded robbery as a motive for the murder.* 警方已排除该谋杀案中有抢劫的动机. ○ *We must not exclude the possibility that the child has run away.* 我们不可排除这孩子离家出走的可能性. **3** [Tn] leave (sth) out; not include 将(某物)排除; 不包括: *lunch costs £5 per person, excluding drinks* 午餐费每人5英镑, 不包括饮料. ○ *That price excludes accommodation.* 那价钱不包括住宿.

ex·clu·sion /ɪk'sklu:ʒn; ɪk`skluʒən/ *n* **1** [U] **~ (of sb/sth) (from sth)** action of excluding; being excluded 排斥; 排除在外: *the exclusion of women from the temple* 妇女之被排斥于寺院之外. **2** (idm 习语) **to the exclusion of sb/sth** so as to exclude (all other members of a group) 排除(其他的一切): *He spent his spare time gardening, to the exclusion of all other interests.* 他把空余时间都用在园艺上了, 没有任何其他爱好.

ex·clus·ive /ɪk'sklu:sɪv; ɪk`sklusɪv/ *adj* **1 (a)** (of a group, society, etc) not readily admitting new members (esp if they are thought to be socially inferior); select (指群体、会社等)不愿接收新成员的(尤指对社会地位低下者); 精选的: *He is part of an exclusive social circle and belongs to an exclusive club.* 他所处的社交圈子很排外, 而且参加的又是个很排外的社团. **(b)** (of a high-class shop, goods sold in it, etc) not found elsewhere; reserved for the wealthy (指高级商店、货物等)罕见的, 高级的, 高档的: *exclusive styles, designs, articles* 高级的式样、设计、物品 ○ *an exclusive restaurant, private school* 为富人开设的饭店、私立学校. **2** reserved for or limited to the person(s) or group concerned 独有的; 独占的: *exclusive privileges of the aristocracy* 贵族独有的特权 ○ *an exclusive agency for the sale of Ford cars in this town* 这城镇的福特汽车包销商 ○ *The interview is exclusive to this magazine.* 本杂志得到独家访问权. **3** excluding all but the thing specified 唯一的: *Painting has not been her exclusive occupation.* 绘画并非她唯一的职业. **4** not admitting sth else; rejecting other considerations 排他的: *The two plans are mutually exclusive,* ie If you accept one you must reject the other. 这两个方案是相互抵触的. **5 ~ of sb/sth** not including sb/sth; not counting sb/sth 不包括某人[某事物]; 不把某人[某事物]算在内: *The ship has a crew of 57 exclusive of officers.* 这船上除高级船员外, 有57名普通船员. ○ *The price of the holiday is exclusive of accommodation.* 度假费用未包括住宿费.

▷ **ex·clus·ive** *n* [C] (also **exclusive story**) newspaper or magazine story given to and published by only one newspaper (报纸或杂志的)独家报道, 独家专文: *a Daily Mirror exclusive* 每日镜报独家报道.

ex·clus·ively *adv*: *This special offer has been exclusively designed for readers of this magazine.* 这一特价优惠是专为本杂志读者提供的.

ex·clus·ive·ness (also **ex·clus·iv·ity**) /ˌeksklu:'sɪvətɪ; ˌɛkskluˋsɪvətɪ/ *n* [U] quality of being exclusive 独特性: *The shop was proud of its exclusiveness.* 这商店因别具一格而沾沾自喜.

ex·com·mu·nic·ate /ˌekskə'mju:nɪkeɪt; ˌɛkskəˋmjunə,ket/ *v* [Tn] exclude (sb) as a punishment from the rights and privileges of membership of the Christian Church 将(某人)逐出基督教教会(剥夺教籍的惩罚).

▷ **ex·com·mu·nica·tion** /ˌekskəˌmju:nɪ'keɪʃn; ˌɛkskə,mjunəˋkeʃən/ *n* **1** [U] action of excommunicating or being excommunicated 逐出教会. **2** [C] example of this; official statement announcing this 逐出教会; 逐出教会的公告.

ex·cre·ment /'ekskrɪmənt; `ɛkskrɪmənt/ *n* [U] (*fml* 文) solid waste matter passed from the body through the bowels; faeces 粪便: *The pavement was covered in dogs' excrement.* 便道上满是狗屎.

ex·cres·cence /ɪk'skresns; ɪk`skrɛsn̩s/ *n* (*fml* 文) abnormal (ugly and useless) growth on an animal body or a plant 赘生物; 瘤; 赘疣: (*fig* 比喻) *The new office block is an excrescence on the landscape.* 这座新办公楼在这片风景中很碍眼.

ex·creta /ɪk'skri:tə; ɪk`skritə/ *n* [U] (*fml* 文) liquid and solid waste (excrement, urine, sweat) passed from the body 排泄物(粪、尿、汗): *the smell of excreta in the hospital ward* 医院病房里排泄物的气味.

ex·crete /ɪk'skri:t; ɛk`skrit/ *v* [Tn] (*fml* 文) (of an animal or a plant) pass out (waste matter, sweat, etc) from the system (指动物或植物)排泄或分泌(废物、汗等).

▷ **ex·cre·tion** /ɪk'skri:ʃn; ɪk`skriʃən/ *n* **(a)** [U] action of excreting 排泄; 分泌. **(b)** [C, U] that which is excreted 排泄物; 分泌物.

ex·cru·ci·at·ing /ɪk'skru:ʃɪeɪtɪŋ; ɪk`skruʃɪ,etɪŋ/ *adj* (of physical or mental pain) intense; acute (指肉体或精神痛苦)极度的, 剧烈的: *He has excruciating backache.* 他的背疼得很厉害. ○ *excruciating misery* 极大的苦难 ○

(*joc* 谑) *He's an excruciating bore.* 他是个非常讨厌的人. ○ *an excruciating concert* 十分糟糕的音乐会. ▷ **ex·cru·ci·at·ingly** *adv*: *an excruciatingly painful experience* 令人极为痛苦的经历.

ex·culp·ate /ˈekskʌlpeɪt; ˋɛkskʌl,pet/ *v* [Tn, Tn·pr] **~ sb (from sth)** (*fml* 文) free sb from blame; say that sb is not guilty 为某人开脱; 说某人无罪: *exculpate a person from a charge* 开脱对某人的指责 ○ *exculpate oneself from blame* 为自己辩解.

ex·cur·sion /ɪkˈskɜːʃn; *US* -ʒn; ɪkˋskɝʒən/ *n* (**a**) short journey, esp one made by a group of people together for pleasure 短程旅行; 远足: *go on/make a day excursion to the mountains*, ie there and back in one day 到山上游玩一天 ○ *Many excursions had been arranged by the holiday company.* 短程旅游原先多由度假服务公司安排的. ○ [attrib 作定语] *an excursion train* 游览火车 ○ *an excursion ticket*, ie one issued at a reduced fare 旅游特惠票. (**b**) short journey made for a particular purpose 短途行程: *a shopping excursion* 购物之行. ⇨Usage at JOURNEY 用法见 JOURNEY.

ex·cuse[1] /ɪkˈskjuːs; ɪkˋskjus/ *n* **~ (for sth/doing sth)** (true or invented) reason given to explain or defend one's behaviour; apology 理由; 解释; 辩护; 辩解; 借口; 道歉: *He's always making excuses for being late.* 他迟到总是有借口. ○ *There's no excuse for such behaviour.* 这种行为不可原谅. ○ *He made his excuses* (ie He apologized) *and left the meeting.* 他表示歉意后就离开了会场. ○ *Please offer/give them my excuses.* 请代我向他们致歉. ○ *I can't attend the meeting — would you make my excuses* (ie apologize and give my reasons for not attending), *please?* 我不能参加会议——你能替我道歉并解释一下吗? ○ (*fml* 文) *Those who are absent without (good) excuse* (ie without giving a (good) excuse) *will be dismissed.* 无故缺席者一律开除.

ex·cuse[2] /ɪkˈskjuːz; ɪkˋskjuz/ *v* **1** (**a**) [Tn, Tn·pr, Tsg] **~ sb/sth (for sth/doing sth)** forgive or overlook (a fault, etc); pardon sb/sth 宽恕或饶恕(过失等); 原谅某人[某事物]: *Please excuse my late arrival.* 请原谅我来晚了. ○ *Excuse me for being late.* 原谅我迟到了. ○ *Excuse my interrupting you.* 对不起, 打扰你一下. (**b**) [Tn, Tn·pr] **~ sb/sth (for sth/doing sth)** give reasons showing, or intended to show, that (a person or his actions) cannot be blamed 为(某人或某行为)辩解或辩白: *Nothing can excuse such rudeness.* 如此无礼决不可宽恕. ○ *She stood up, excused herself* (ie apologized for leaving) *and walked out of the meeting.* 她站起身来为中途离开道了歉, 然后走出会场. ○ *He excused himself for being late by saying that his car had broken down.* 他为迟到作辩解, 说他的汽车坏了. **2** [esp passive 尤用于被动语态: Tn, Tn·pr, Dn·n] **~ sb (from sth)** set sb free from a duty, requirement, punishment, etc 免除某人的责任、对其要求、惩罚等: *He was excused (from) piano practice.* 他获准不必练习钢琴. ○ *They may be excused (from doing) this exercise.* 他们可以免做这一练习. **3** (idm 习语) **excuse me** (**a**) (used as an apology when one interrupts, disagrees, disapproves or has to behave impolitely 用作打扰别人、表示不赞成、不同意或失礼时的道歉用语): *Excuse me, is anybody sitting here?* 请问, 这儿有人坐吗? ○ *Excuse me, but I don't think that's quite true.* 很抱歉, 我认为这与事实略有出入. (**b**) **excuse me?** (*esp US*) Please repeat what you said. 请再说一遍. **excuse/pardon my French** ⇨ FRENCH. **may I be excused?** (*euph* 婉 *Brit*) (used esp by schoolchildren) may I go to the toilet? (尤作小学生用语)我可以上厕所吗?

▷ **ex·cus·able** /ɪkˈskjuːzəbl; ɪkˋskjuzəbl̩/ *adj* that may be excused 可原谅的: *an excusable mistake* 可原谅的错误. **ex·cus·ably** /-əblɪ; -əblɪ/ *adv*.

NOTE ON USAGE 用法: **1** We say **Excuse me** to someone if we want to get his or her attention or before we do something that might disturb him or her, eg interrupt him/her, push him/her in a crowd, disagree with him/her 我们说 **Excuse me**, 是为了引起他人注意或因为可能打扰他人, 如打断别人谈话、在人群中推挤别人、不同意别人的意见: *Excuse me, can I get past, please?* 劳驾, 能让我过去吗? **2** We say **Sorry** or (formally) **I beg your pardon** when we need to apologize for something 我们说 **Sorry** 或(郑重其事时说) **I beg your pardon**, 是因为需要为某事道歉: *Sorry, did I tread on your toe?* 对不起, 我踩着你的脚了吧? ○ *I beg your pardon. I think you were next in the queue.* 对不起, 你原来是排在下一个的. In US English **Pardon me** and **Excuse me** are used for apologies. 在美式英语中, **Pardon me** 和 **Excuse me** 都用以表示道歉. **3** We say **Pardon?** when we did not hear what someone said and want them to repeat it. 若未听见某人刚说的话而请其重复时, 说 **Pardon?**. ☆ In this case **Sorry?** is also used in British English and **Excuse me?** or **Pardon me?** in US English. 在这种情况下, 用英式英语还可说 **Sorry?**, 而用美式英语则要说 **Excuse me?** 或 **Pardon me?**.

ex-directory /ˌeks dɪˈrektərɪ; ˌɛksdəˋrɛktərɪ/ *adj* (*US* **unlisted**) (of a telephone number) not listed in the telephone directory at the wish of the phone-owner (for reasons of security, privacy, etc) (指电话号码)未列入电话簿的(用户授意为安全、私用等而不列入者): *an ex-directory number* 未列入电话簿的电话号码 ○ *go ex-directory because of hoax telephone calls* 因有电话骚扰而不将电话号码列入电话簿中.

ex·ec·rable /ˈeksɪkrəbl; ˋɛksɪkrəbl̩/ *adj* (*fml* 文) very bad; terrible 极坏的; 糟透的; 恶劣的: *execrable manners, weather* 极度的无礼、恶劣的天气. ▷ **ex·ec·rably** /-blɪ; -blɪ/ *adv*.

ex·ec·rate /ˈeksɪkreɪt; ˋɛksɪ,kret/ *v* [esp passive 尤用于被动语态: Tn] (*fml* 文) express or feel hatred of (sb/sth); curse 憎恨, 厌恶(某人[某事物]); 咒骂; 诅咒. ▷ **ex·ec·ra·tion** /ˌeksɪˈkreɪʃn; ˌɛksɪˋkreʃən/ *n* [U, C].

ex·ecute /ˈeksɪkjuːt; ˋɛksɪ,kjut/ *v* [Tn] **1** (*fml* 文) carry out, perform (what one is asked or told to do) 执行; 实行; 履行; 完成: *execute sb's commands* 执行某人的命令 ○ *execute a plan, a piece of work, a purpose* 实行一计划、完成一工作、达到一目的. **2** (*law* 律) (**a**) put (sth) into effect 使(某事)生效; 实施: *execute a will* 依照遗嘱行事. (**b**) make (sth) legally valid 使(某事)有法律效力: *execute a legal document*, ie by having it signed, witnessed, sealed and delivered 使一法律文件生效(经签署、签名见证、封印、交付者). **3** kill (sb) as a legal punishment 将(某人)处死: *He was executed for treason.* 他因叛国罪已处死. ○ *execute a murderer* 处决一谋杀犯. **4** (*fml* 文) perform (sth) on the stage, at a concert, etc (在舞台上或音乐会中)演奏; 表演: *execute a dance step* 表演舞步 ○ *The piano sonata was badly executed.* 这首钢琴奏鸣曲演奏得很糟. **5** (*computing* 计) carry out (the instructions of a computer program) 执行(计算机程序的指令).

exe·cu·tion /ˌeksɪˈkjuːʃn; ˌɛksɪˋkjuʃən/ *n* **1** [U] carrying out or performance of a piece of work, plan, design, duty, etc 执行; 实行; 履行; 完成: *His original idea was good, but his execution of the scheme was disastrous.* 他的设想很好, 但实行起来却糟糕透顶. ○ *The plans were finally put into execution.* 这些计划终于得以实施. **2** [U] (*law* 律) action of carrying out the orders of a will 对遗嘱条款的执行: *The solicitor is proceeding with the execution of my mother's will.* 律师正着手执行我母亲的遗嘱. **3** [C, U] (act of) killing sb as a legal punishment 处死刑; 死刑: *execution by hanging* 以绞刑处死 ○ *five executions last year* 去年执行的五起死刑. **4** [U] (*fml* 文) skill in performing eg music 表演技巧(如音乐演奏): *The pianist's execution of the concerto was marvellous.* 那钢琴师弹的协奏曲神乎其技. **5** (idm 习语) **a stay of execution** ⇨ STAY *n*.

▷ **exe·cu·tioner** /ˌeksɪˈkjuːʃənə(r); ˌɛksɪˋkjuʃənɚ/ *n* public official who carries out a death sentence 死刑执行人; 行刑人.

ex·ec·ut·ive /ɪɡˈzekjʊtɪv; ɪɡˋzɛkjʊtɪv/ *adj* [usu attrib 通常作定语] **1** (esp in business) concerned with the management and carrying out of plans, decisions, etc (尤指企业中)经营管理的, 经营的, 经理的: *executive duties* 经营管理的职责 ○ *possess executive ability* 具有管理的才能. **2** having power to carry out decisions, laws, decrees, etc (对决策、法律、法令等)有执行权的, 行政的, 决策的: *executive authority* 行政当局 ○ *the executive branch of the Government* 政府的行政部门 ○ *the executive committee of a political party* 一政党的执行委员会 ○ *the executive head of State*, eg the President of the US 一国的行政首长(如美国的总统).

▷ **ex·ec·ut·ive** *n* **1** [CGp] person or group in a

business organization, trade union, etc with administrative or managerial powers（在企业、工会等中的）行政领导; 经理; 董事; 董事会: *a sales executive* 营业主任 ○ *She's an executive in a computer company.* 她是一家计算机公司的行政人员. ○ *The executive has/have been making decisions about the future of the company.* 领导层一直在研究公司未来的决策. ○ [attrib 作定语] *an executive briefcase* 行政人员公事包. **2** [C] (in the Civil Service) person who carries out what has been planned or decided（政府文职部门的）行政人员: [attrib 作定语] *executive officer* 行政主任. **3 the executive** [Gp] executive branch of a government 政府的行政部门.

ex·ec·utor /ɪɡˈzekjʊtə(r); ɪɡˋzɛkjətɚ/ *n* person who is appointed by the maker of a will to carry out the terms of the will（立遗嘱人指定的）遗嘱执行人.

ex·egesis /ˌeksɪˈdʒiːsɪs; ˌɛksəˋdʒisɪs/ *n* (*pl* **-ses** /-siz; -siz/) [U, C] (*fml* 文) explanation and interpretation of a written work, esp the Bible 诠释, 注解, 注释(尤指对《圣经》的文字).

ex·em·plary /ɪɡˈzemplərɪ; ɪɡˋzɛmplərɪ/ *adj* **1** serving as an example; suitable for imitation 用作模范的; 可作楷模的: *exemplary behaviour* 模范行为 ○ *an exemplary student* 模范学生. **2** (*fml* 文) serving as a warning 用作警戒的: *exemplary punishment* 警戒性的惩罚.

ex·em·plify /ɪɡˈzemplɪfaɪ; ɪɡˋzɛmpləˌfaɪ/ *v* (*pt, pp* **-fied**) [Tn] **1** be a typical example of (sth) 是(某事物)的典型: *This painting exemplifies the artist's early style.* 这幅画是该画家早期艺术风格的典型. **2** (*fml* 文) give an example of (sth); illustrate by example 举出(某事物)的例子; 举例说明: *exemplify the problems involved.* 举例说明所涉及的问题.

▷ **ex·em·pli·fica·tion** /ɪɡˌzemplɪfɪˈkeɪʃn; ɪɡˌzɛmpləfəˋkeʃən/ *n* **1** [U] exemplifying 举例说明; 示范. **2** [C] (*fml* 文) example 例证; 例子; 范例.

ex·empt /ɪɡˈzempt; ɪɡˋzɛmpt/ *adj* [pred 作表语] **~ (from sth)** free from an obligation, duty or payment; not liable 被免除义务或责任; 不用付款; 被豁免: *exempt from military service* 免服兵役 ○ *exempt from working overtime* 免于超时工作 ○ *goods exempt from tax* 免税货物 ○ *Children under 16 are exempt from prescription charges.* 16岁以下的儿童免付处方费.

▷ **ex·empt** *v* [Tn, Tn·pr] **~ sb/sth (from sth)** (*fml* 文) make sb/sth exempt 使某人[某事物]免除或豁免: *His bad eyesight exempted him from military service.* 他因视力不好而免服兵役. **ex·emp·tion** /ɪɡˈzempʃn; ɪɡˋzɛmpʃən/ *n* [U, C].

ex·er·cise[1] /ˈeksəsaɪz; ˋɛksɚˌsaɪz/ *n* **1** [U] use or practice (of the mind or esp the body) through effort or action（智力的）运用; (尤指)锻炼运动: *The doctor advised him to take more exercise.* 医生建议他多运动. ○ *Jogging is a healthy form of exercise.* 慢跑是有益健康的锻炼方式. ○ *Doing crosswords gives the mind some exercise.* 做纵横字谜游戏能锻炼脑筋. **2** [C] activity or task intended for physical or mental training 练习; 训练: *vocal, gymnastic, keep-fit, deep-breathing, etc exercises* 发音、体操、保健、深呼吸等练习 ○ *exercises for the piano, flute, harp, etc* 钢琴、长笛、竖琴等的练习 ○ *The teacher set her class a mathematics exercise for homework.* 那位女教师给班上布置数学的家庭作业. ○ [attrib 作定语] *an exercise book*, ie a book for writing in with soft covers and lined pages 练习本. **3** [U] **~ of sth** (effective) use or application（有效的）使用或应用: *The exercise of patience is essential in diplomatic negotiations.* 在外交谈判中, 重要的是要有耐性. ○ *the exercise of one's civil rights* 公民权利的行使 ○ *His stories showed considerable exercise of the imagination.* 他的故事颇具创意. **4** [C often *pl* 常作复数] series of movements or operations for training troops, etc（部队等的）操练, 演习: *military exercises* 军事操练 ○ (*fig* 比喻) *an exercise in diplomatic relations* 外交关系上的举动. **5 exercises** [pl] (*US*) ceremonies 典礼; 仪式: *graduation exercises* 毕业典礼 ○ *opening exercises*, eg speeches at the start of a conference 开幕仪式(如致开幕词).

ex·er·cise[2] /ˈeksəsaɪz; ˋɛksɚˌsaɪz/ *v* **1** [I] perform some kind of physical exercise（体能方面）锻炼, 运动: *He exercises twice a day.* 他每天锻炼两次. **2** [Tn, Tn·pr] **~ sb/sth (in sth)** give exercise[1](1) to sb/sth; train sb/sth (by means of exercises) 使某人[某物]得到锻炼; 训练某人[某物]: *Horses get fat and lazy if they are not exercised.* 马不训练就会增膘、变懒. ○ *Swimming exercises the whole body.* 游泳能使身体得到全面的锻炼. **3** [Tn] make use of (sth); employ 利用(某物); 使用; 运用: *exercise patience, tolerance, power, control, etc* 运用耐性、忍耐力、权力、控制力等 ○ *exercise one's rights as a citizen* 行使公民权 ○ *Teachers exercise authority over their pupils.* 教师经常管束学生. **4** [Tn usu passive 通常用于被动语态] (*fml* 文) worry or trouble (sb) 使(某人)担心、忧虑或烦恼: *This problem is exercising our minds very much at the moment.* 这一问题此刻使我们很伤脑筋. ○ *I am very much exercised about the education of my son.* 我对儿子的教育十分操心.

ex·ert /ɪɡˈzɜːt; ɪɡˋzɝt/ *v* **1** [Tn, Tn·pr] **~ sth (on sb/sth)** bring (a quality, skill, pressure, etc) into use; apply sth 用(某特质、技巧、压力等); 应用(某物): *He exerted all his influence to make them accept his plan.* 他用尽一切影响力使他们接受他的计划. ○ *Her husband exerted a lot of pressure on her to succeed.* 她丈夫殷切期望她能成功, 给了她很大的压力. **2** [Tn no passive 不用于被动语态] **~ oneself** make an effort 努力; 尽力: *You'll have to exert yourself more if you want to pass your exam.* 你若想考试及格, 就必须更加努力. ○ *He doesn't have to exert himself on my behalf.* 他不必为我费那么大力气.

ex·er·tion /ɪɡˈzɜːʃn; ɪɡˋzɝʃən/ *n* (**a**) [U] action of applying influence, etc 发挥; 运用; 行使; 施加: *Exertion of authority over others is not always wise; persuasion may be better.* 利用权力压服别人并非永远是上策, 运用说服方法或许更为可取. (**b**) [C, U] (instance of) great effort 努力; 尽力; 费力: *incapable of physical exertion* 体力上不能劳累的 ○ *He failed to lift the rock in spite of all his exertions.* 他虽然竭尽全力, 但仍未能将那石块搬起. ○ *Now that I'm 90, I find the exertions of travelling too great.* 我年届90岁, 出远门已力不从心.

ex·eunt /ˈeksɪʌnt; ˋɛksɪənt/ (*Latin* 拉) (as a stage direction 用作舞台说明) they leave the stage 他们退场: *exeunt Antony and Cleopatra* 安东尼和克娄巴特拉退场. Cf 参看 EXIT *v* 2.

ex gratia /ˌeks ˈɡreɪʃə; ɛksˋɡreʃə/ (*Latin* 拉) done or given as a favour; not from (esp legal) obligation 作为恩惠; 非出于(尤指法律上的)义务: *an ex gratia payment* 特惠金.

ex·hale /eksˈheɪl; ɛksˋhel/ *v* [I, Tn] (*fml* 文) **1** breathe (sth) out 呼出(某物): *She exhaled slowly to show her annoyance.* 她长吁着气以示厌烦. ○ *exhale air from the lungs* 从肺中呼出气来 ○ *exhale smoke* 吐出烟雾. **2** give off or expel (gas or vapour) 散发或排出(气体).

▷ **ex·hala·tion** /ˌekshəˈleɪʃn; ˌɛksəˋleʃən/ *n* (*fml* 文) **1** [C] act of exhaling 呼气; 排气. **2** [U, C] thing exhaled 被呼出或排出之物: *an exhalation of smoke* 排出的烟.

ex·haust[1] /ɪɡˈzɔːst; ɪɡˋzɔst/ *n* **1** [U] waste fumes, gases, steam, etc expelled from an engine or a machine（机器排出的）废气、蒸气等: *the smell of the exhaust* 排出的废气气味 ○ [attrib 作定语] *exhaust fumes* 排出的废气. **2** (also **exˈhaust-pipe**) [C] outlet or pipe through which these gases are sent out 排气口; 排气管: *My car needs a new exhaust.* 我的汽车该换排气管了. ⇨ illus at App 1 见附录1之插图, page xii.

ex·haust[2] /ɪɡˈzɔːst; ɪɡˋzɔst/ *v* [Tn] **1** [esp passive 尤用于被动语态] make (a person or an animal) very tired 使(人或动物)非常疲倦: *The long cycle ride exhausted her.* 她因长途骑车而疲惫不堪. ○ *He exhausted himself in the attempt.* 他因十分努力而筋疲力尽. **2** use (sth) up completely 用尽, 耗尽(某物): *exhaust one's patience, strength* 失去耐性、用尽力气 ○ *exhaust a money supply* 把钱用光. **3** make (sth) empty; take out the contents of 将(某物)弄空; 取出(所含之物): *exhaust a well* 将井汲干. **4** say, find out, all there is to say about (sth) 详尽论述(某事物): *I think we've just about exhausted that subject.* 我认为我们对这一问题已差不多是言无不尽了.

▷ **ex·hausted** /ɪɡˈzɔːstɪd; ɪɡˋzɔstɪd/ *adj* very tired 极其疲倦的: *I'm exhausted!* 我已筋疲力尽了! ○ *The exhausted troops surrendered.* 部队人困马乏结果投降了.

ex·haus·tion /ɪɡˈzɔːstʃən; ɪɡˋzɔstʃən/ *n* [U] **1** total loss of strength; extreme tiredness 筋疲力尽; 精疲力竭; 极度疲劳: *They were in a state of exhaustion after climbing the mountain.* 他们爬山以后筋疲力尽了. **2** (*fml* 文) action of using up completely 用尽; 耗尽; 枯竭: *the rapid exhaustion of the earth's natural resources* 地球上自

E

然资源的迅速枯竭.

ex·haust·ive /ɪɡˈzɔ:stɪv; ɪɡˋzɔstɪv/ *adj* very thorough; complete 彻底的; 详尽的; 完全的; 全面的: *an exhaustive enquiry, search* 彻底的调查、搜查. ▷ **ex·haust·ively** *adv*.

ex·hibit[1] /ɪɡˈzɪbɪt; ɪɡˋzɪbɪt/ *n* **1** object or collection of objects displayed for the public, eg in a museum 展览品; 陈列品: *a priceless exhibit* 一件极贵重的陈列品 ○ *The museum has some interesting new exhibits from India.* 博物馆新陈列一些有趣的印度展品. ○ *Do not touch the exhibits.* 请勿触摸展品. **2** document, object, etc produced as evidence in a lawcourt (当庭出示的)证件, 物证, 证据: *The first exhibit was a knife which the prosecution claimed was the murder weapon.* 当庭出示的第一件物证是一把刀, 据原告称是为谋杀凶器.

ex·hibit[2] /ɪɡˈzɪbɪt; ɪɡˋzɪbɪt/ *v* **1** (**a**) [Tn] show or display (sth) for the public (for pleasure, for sale, in a competition, in a lawcourt, etc) 当众显示或展出(某物): *exhibit flowers at a flower show* 在花展上展出花卉 ○ *documents exhibited in a lawcourt* 当庭出示的文件. (**b**) [I, Tn] (of an artist) present (works of art) for the public, esp in an art gallery (指艺术家)展出(艺术品)(尤指于美术馆): *The young painter has exhibited (his work) in several galleries.* 那年轻画家的作品已在几家美术馆中展出. **2** [Tn] (*fml* 文) show clearly that one possesses (a quality or feeling) 表现, 显示, 显出(某特质或感情): *He exhibited total lack of concern for the child.* 可以看出他对那孩子毫不关心. ○ *She exhibited great powers of endurance during the climb.* 她在攀登过程中表现出极大的耐力.

▷ **ex·hib·itor** *n* person who displays pictures, flowers, etc at a show (画展、花展等的)展出者, 参展者: *Nearly fifty exhibitors have provided pictures for the display.* 有近五十名参展者为画展提供了展品.

ex·hibi·tion /ˌeksɪˈbɪʃn; ˌɛksəˋbɪʃən/ *n* **1** [C] (**a**) collection of things shown publicly (eg works of art, industrial or commercial goods for advertisement) 展览品; 展览; 展览会: *Have you seen the Picasso exhibition?* ie exhibition of paintings by Picasso. 你参观过毕加索的画展吗? ○ [attrib 作定语] *one of the exhibition halls at the Frankfurt book fair* 法兰克福书展的展厅之一. (**b**) public display of animals, plants, flowers, etc (esp as shown in a competition for prizes) 动物、植物、花卉等的展览(尤指为获奖而参赛的). **2** (**a**) [sing] act of showing (a quality or feeling) (某特质或感情的)表现, 显示: *an exhibition of bad manners* 无礼的表现 ○ *The quiz was a good opportunity for the exhibition of his knowledge.* 这次测验是他显示知识的好机会. (**b**) [C] public demonstration of a skill (技术的)公开示范表演: *There's an exhibition of pottery-making at the fair.* 在集市场上有陶器制作的示范表演. ○ *a dancing exhibition* 舞蹈表演. ⇨Usage at DEMONSTRATION 用法见 DEMONSTRATION. **3** [C] (*Brit*) money allowance to a student from school or college funds for a number of years to pay for the costs of study 奖学金. **4** (idm 习语) **make an exhiˈbition of oneself** (*derog* 贬) behave foolishly or badly in public 当众出丑; 出洋相: *People at the party were embarrassed when Frank got drunk and made an exhibition of himself.* 弗兰克喝醉了, 出尽洋相, 使参加聚会的人很难为情.

▷ **ex·hi·bi·tioner** /-ʃənə(r); -ʃənɚ/ *n* (*Brit*) student who receives an exhibition(3) 获奖学金的学生.

ex·hibi·tion·ism /-ʃənɪzəm; -ʃənɪzəm/ *n* [U] **1** tendency to behave in a way intended to attract attention to oneself 表现癖: *She was embarrassed by his exhibitionism at the party.* 他在聚会上竭力表现自己使她感到很难堪. **2** (*fml* 文) offence of indecently exposing one's sexual organs in public 露阴癖(当众暴露自己性器官的猥亵行为).

ex·hibi·tion·ist /-ʃənɪst; -ʃənɪst/ *n* person who is given to exhibitionism 好自我表现的人; 有露阴癖的人: *Children are natural exhibitionists.* 儿童天生喜欢自我表现.

ex·hil·ar·ate /ɪɡˈzɪləreɪt; ɪɡˋzɪlə,ret/ *v* [Tn usu passive 通常用于被动语态] make (sb) feel very happy or lively 使(某人)愉快或活跃: *exhilarated by the news* 这消息使人高兴 ○ *We felt exhilarated by our walk along the beach.* 我们沿着海滩散步感到心旷神怡.

▷ **ex·hil·ar·at·ing** *adj* very exciting; causing happiness 使人兴奋的; 令人高兴的: *Our first parachute jump was an exhilarating experience.* 我们第一次跳伞感到兴奋莫名.

ex·hil·ara·tion /ɪɡˌzɪləˈreɪʃn; ɪɡ,zɪləˋreʃən/ *n* [U].

ex·hort /ɪɡˈzɔ:t; ɪɡˋzɔrt/ *v* [Tn, Tn·pr, Dn·t] **~ sb (to sth)** (*fml* 文) advise sb strongly or earnestly; urge sb 劝告, 规劝或告诫(某人): *The chairman exhorted the party workers to action.* 主席敦促党的工作人员采取行动. ○ *The teacher exhorted him to work hard.* 教师谆谆告诫他要用功.

▷ **ex·horta·tion** /ˌeɡzɔ:ˈteɪʃn; ˌɛɡzɔrˋteʃən/ *n* **1** [U] (*fml* 文) action of exhorting 劝告; 规劝; 告诫. **2** [C] earnest request; speech, etc that exhorts 诚恳的要求; 劝告; 告诫: *All his father's exhortations were in vain.* 他父亲的一切劝告都无效.

ex·hume /eksˈhju:m; *US* ɪɡˈzu:m; ɪɡˋzum/ *v* [Tn] take (a dead body) from the ground (for examination) 掘出(尸体)(以检验): *When the police exhumed the corpse they discovered traces of poison in it.* 警方掘出尸体, 发现有中毒的痕迹.

▷ **ex·hu·ma·tion** /ˌekshju:ˈmeɪʃn; *US* ˌeɡzu:-; ˌɛɡzuˋmeʃən/ *n* (*fml* 文) **1** [U] exhuming or being exhumed 掘尸. **2** [C] instance of this 掘尸.

exi·gency /ˈeksɪdʒənsɪ; ˋɛksədʒənsɪ/ *n* [C often *pl*, U 作可数名词时常作复数, 亦作不可数名词] (*fml* 文) (condition of) urgent need or demand; emergency 紧急的需要或要求; 紧急情况; 危急关头: *The people had to accept the harsh exigencies of war.* 人们要承受战乱的严酷现实.

▷ **exi·gent** /-dʒənt; -dʒənt/ *adj* (*fml* 文) **1** requiring immediate action; urgent 需要立即采取行动的; 紧急的: *an exigent set of circumstances* 一系列亟待处理的情况. **2** requiring much; exacting 苛求的; 苛刻的: *an exigent employer* 苛刻的雇主. **exi·gently** *adv*.

ex·igu·ous /eɡˈzɪɡjʊəs; ɪɡˋzɪɡjʊəs/ *adj* (*fml* 文) very small (in amount); scanty 稀少的; 少量的; 微小的: *an exiguous diet* 量少的规定饮食 ○ *the last of the old man's exiguous savings* 那老人微薄积蓄中的剩余部分.

ex·ile /ˈeksaɪl; ˋɛɡzaɪl/ *n* **1** [U] being sent away from one's native country or home, esp for political reasons or as a punishment; forced absence 流放; 放逐; 充军: *be/live in exile* 于流放中[过流放生活] ○ *go/be sent into exile* 流亡[遭放逐] ○ *a place of exile* 流放地. **2** [C] long stay away from one's country or home 长期去国或离家: *After an exile of ten years her uncle returned to Britain.* 她叔叔背井离乡十年后返回英国. **3** [C] person who lives away from his own country from choice or because he is forced to (自愿或被迫)去国者: *a tax exile*, ie a rich person who moves to another country where the rate of income tax is lower 迁往所得税率较低国家居住的富人 ○ *There were many French exiles in England after the Revolution.* 法国大革命后, 有许多法国人流亡英国.

▷ **ex·ile** *v* [esp passive 尤用于被动语态: Tn, Tn·pr] **~ sb (from ...)** send sb into exile 放逐某人: *exiled for life* 遭终生流放 ○ *She was exiled from her country because of her part in the plot against the government.* 她因参与反政府的阴谋而遭驱逐出国.

ex·ist /ɪɡˈzɪst; ɪɡˋzɪst/ *v* [I, Ipr] **1 ~ (in/on sth)** (**a**) be real or actual; have being 存在; 有: *Do you believe fairies exist?* ie that there are really fairies? 你相信真有小神仙吗? ○ *The idea exists only in the minds of poets.* 这种想法是诗人才有的. ○ *laws that have existed for hundreds of years* 已存在千百年的法规 ○ *Does life exist on Mars?* 火星上有生命吗? (**b**) be found; occur 被发现; 发生: *This plant exists only in Australia.* 这种植物只产于澳大利亚. **2 ~ (on sth)** continue living, esp with difficulty or with very little money; survive 生存(尤指有困难或钱很少); 活下来; 幸存: *We cannot exist without food or water.* 没有食物或水我们就不能生存. ○ *He exists on rice and water*, ie by eating rice and water. 他靠吃米饭和水过活. ○ *I can hardly exist on the wage I'm getting; there is no money for luxuries.* 我靠我挣的工资简直难以餬口, 根本无钱享受.

▷ **ex·ist·ence** /-əns; -əns/ *n* **1** [U] state or fact of existing 存在: *Do you believe in the existence of ghosts?* 你相信有鬼吗? ○ *This is the oldest Hebrew manuscript in existence*, ie that exists. 这是现存最早的希伯来语手稿. ○ *When did the world come into existence*, ie begin to exist? 世界是什么时候产生的? ○ *I was unaware of his* *existence until now.* 现在我才知道有他这么个人. **2** (**a**) [sing] manner of living, esp when this is difficult, boring, etc; way of living 生活(尤指艰苦、无聊等的生活); 生活方式: *We led a happy enough existence as children.* 我们小时候的生活过得很愉快. ○ *living a miserable existence miles from the nearest town* 在远离城镇的偏僻地区, 过着凄惨的日子. (**b**) [sing, U] continuance in life; survival 生存; 存活: *The peasants depend on a good harvest for their very existence*, ie for existence itself. 农民要靠丰收才能活命. ○ *They eke out a bare existence* (ie They scarcely manage) *on his low salary.* 他们靠他微薄的薪金勉强餬口. **3** (idm 习语) **the bane of sb's existence** ⇨ BANE.

ex·ist·ent /-ənt; -ənt/ *adj* (*fml* 文) existing; actual 存在的; 现有的; 现存的.

ex·ist·en·tial·ism /ˌegzɪˈstenʃəlɪzəm; ˌɛgzɪsˈtɛnʃəlˌɪzəm/ *n* (*philosophy* 哲) theory (deriving from Kierkegaard /ˈkɪəkəgɑːd; ˈkɪrkəˌgɑrd/ (1813-55), the Danish philosopher, and made popular by Sartre /ˈsɑːtrə; ˈsɑrtrə/ (1905-80), the French writer and philosopher) that man is a unique and isolated individual in a meaningless or hostile world, responsible for his own actions and free to choose his destiny 存在主义.

▷ **ex·ist·en·tial** /ˌegzɪˈstenʃəl; ˌɛgzɪsˈtɛnʃəl/ *adj* **1** (*fml* 文) of or relating to (esp human) existence (尤指人类)存在的; 与(人类)存在有关的. **2** of or relating to the theory of existentialism 存在主义的; 与存在主义有关的.

ex·ist·en·tial·ist /-ʃəlɪst; -ʃəlɪst/ *n, adj*: *He's an existentialist.* 他是存在主义者. ○ *He holds existentialist views.* 他持存在主义观点.

exit /ˈeksɪt, *also* ˈegzt; ˈɛksɪt, ˈɛgzɪt/ *n* **1** action of leaving; departure, esp that of an actor from the stage 离别; 离开; (尤指演员)退场: *The heroine makes her exit (from the stage).* 女主角退场. ○ *When his ex-wife arrived at the party he made a swift exit*, ie he left quickly. 在聚会上, 他的前妻来到时, 他匆匆离去. ○ [attrib 作定语] *an exit visa*, ie a stamp or signature on a passport giving permission to leave a particular country 出境签证. **2** way out (of a public building) (公共建筑物的)出口, 太平门: *There are four emergency exits in the department store.* 这百货公司有四个紧急出口. ○ [attrib 作定语] *The exit signs in cinemas are usually illuminated.* 电影院的出口标记通常都有照明. **3** point at which a road, etc turns off from a motorway or roundabout, allowing vehicles to leave (车辆可从高速公路或环状交叉路驶出的)出口, 出路: *At the roundabout, take the third exit.* 在环状交叉路口, 从第三条出路驶出. ○ *Leave the motorway at the Stokenchurch exit.* 在斯托肯彻切出口处驶离高速公路.

▷ **exit** *v* [I] **1** go out; (esp of an actor) leave (the stage) 出去; 离去; 退出; (尤指演员)退场: *At the end of the third scene the actress exits.* 该女演员于第三场结束时退场. ○ (*joc* 谑) *We exited from the party as soon as we could.* 我们在聚会上能抽得身时, 便鞠躬下台告辞而去. **2** (as a printed stage direction in plays) he or she leaves the stage (剧本中的舞台说明)他下场: *Exit Macbeth*. 麦克佩斯退场. Cf 参看 EXEUNT.

□ ˈ**exit poll** unofficial poll based on interviews with voters as they leave a polling station after voting 票站调查(在投票站外向刚投票者进行的访问).

exo- *comb form* 构词成分 external, outside or beyond 外部的; 外面的; 外: *exoskeleton* /ˈeksəʊskelɪtn; ˌɛkso-ˈskɛlətn̩/, ie external covering on an animal, eg the shell of a crab ○ *exogamous* /ekˈsɒgəməs; ɛksˈɑgəməs/, ie marrying outside one's religion, caste, etc.

ex·odus /ˈeksədəs; ˈɛksədəs/ *n* **1** [sing] **~ (from...) (to...)** (*fml or joc* 文或谑) departure of many people at one time (大批人同时之)离去: *the mass exodus of people to the sea and mountains for the summer holidays* 为度暑假游山玩水大批人外出 ○ *The play was so awful that there was a general exodus from the theatre at the interval.* 那剧十分糟糕, 在幕间休息时观众纷纷离去. **2 the Exodus** the departure of the Israelites from Egypt, in about 1300 BC 出埃及事(约公元前1300年以色列人离开埃及一事). **3 Exodus** title of the 2nd book of the Bible, which tells the story of this departure《出埃及记》(《圣经·旧约》中的第2卷).

ex of·fi·cio /ˌeks əˈfɪʃɪəʊ; ˌɛk səˈfɪʃɪˌo/ because of one's position, office or rank 由于职位或职权: *an ex officio member of the committee* 当然委员 ○ *present at the meeting ex officio* 依照职权而出席会议.

ex·on·er·ate /ɪgˈzɒnəreɪt; ɪgˈzɑnəˌret/ *v* [esp passive 尤用于被动语态: Tn, Tn·pr] **~ sb (from sth)** declare sb free from blame 宣布某人无罪过: *He was exonerated from all responsibility for the accident.* 已确定他无须对该事故负任何责任. ▷ **ex·on·era·tion** /ɪgˌzɒnəˈreɪʃn; ɪgˌzɑnəˈreʃən/ *n* [U].

ex·or·bit·ant /ɪgˈzɔːbɪtənt; ɪgˈzɔrbətənt/ *adj* (*fml* 文) (of a price, charge, etc) much too high or great; unreasonable (指价格、索价等)过高的, 过分的, 不合理的: *exorbitant rents* 过高的租金 ○ *The price of food here is exorbitant.* 这儿的食物价格太高. ▷ **ex·or·bit·ance** /-təns; -təns/ *n* [U] (*fml* 文). **ex·or·bit·antly** *adv*: *exorbitantly expensive* 过于昂贵.

ex·or·cize, -ise /ˈeksɔːsaɪz; ˈɛksɔrˌsaɪz/ *v* [Tn, Tn·pr] **~ sth (from sb/sth)** (*esp religion* 尤用于宗教) drive out or expel (an evil spirit) by prayers or magic 用祈祷或魔法驱逐或祛除(恶魔): *A priest exorcized the ghost from the house.* 教士将鬼从房屋中驱走. ○ (*fig* 比喻) *We gradually exorcized her feelings of panic and terror.* 我们帮助她渐渐消除惊恐的感觉.

▷ **ex·or·cism** /ˈeksɔːsɪzəm; ˈɛksɔrˌsɪzəm/ *n* [C, U] (instance of) exorcizing 驱除邪魔. **ex·or·cist** /ˈeksɔːsɪst; ˈɛksɔrˌsɪst/ *n* person who exorcizes 驱除邪魔者.

ex·otic /ɪgˈzɒtɪk; ɪgˈzɑtɪk/ *adj* **1** introduced from another country; not native 由外国引进的; 非本地的: *exotic houseplants* 引进的室内盆栽 ○ *monkeys and other exotic animals* 猴子及外来的其他动物 ○ *mangoes and other exotic fruits* 杧果及其他外国水果. **2** striking or attractive because colourful or unusual (因富色彩或式样奇特)醒目的, 吸引人的, 漂亮的: *exotic plumage* 别致的羽毛 ○ *exotic clothes* 奇装异服.

ex·pand /ɪkˈspænd; ɪkˈspænd/ *v* **1** [I, Ipr, Tn, Tn·pr] **~ (sth) (into sth)** (cause sth to) become greater in size, number or importance 使(某事物)变大, 扩大, 增大, 增加, 增强, 扩展: *Metals expand when they are heated.* 金属受热则膨胀. ○ *A tyre expands when you pump air into it.* 轮胎一打气就鼓起来. ○ *His modest business eventually expanded into a supermarket empire.* 他原先不大的生意后来扩展成了超级市场集团企业. ○ *Our foreign trade has expanded greatly in recent years.* 我国的对外贸易近年来已有极大发展. ○ *Why not try to expand your story into a novel?* 你怎么不把你的故事扩展成小说呢? **2** [I, Ipr] spread out; unfold 伸展; 伸开; 张开; 展开: *The petals of the flowers expanded in the sunshine.* 花瓣在阳光下张开了. ○ *His face expanded in a smile of welcome.* 他喜笑颜开地表示欢迎. Cf 参看 CONTRACT[3]. **3** [I] (of a person) become more friendly or talkative (指人)变得热情或愿意交谈: *The guests expanded a little when they'd had a glass or two of wine.* 客人们喝了一两杯酒以后, 就有说有笑了. **4** (phr v) **expand on sth** develop or give more of (a story, an argument, etc) 阐述或详述(某事, 故事, 论点等): *You mentioned the need for extra funding. Would you expand on that?* 你曾提到需要一笔额外资金. 你详细谈谈好吗?

□ **exˌpanded ˈmetal** sheet metal cut and stretched into a mesh used (esp) to reinforce concrete 拉制金属网(尤指用于加固混凝土者).

exˌpanded polyˈstyrene light packaging or insulation material made of air-filled plastic 多孔聚苯乙烯, 多孔塑料(用充气塑料制成的轻质包装或绝缘材料).

ex·panse /ɪkˈspæns; ɪkˈspæns/ *n* **~ (of sth)** wide and open area (of land, sea, etc) (陆地、海洋等的)广阔的区域: *the wide expanses of the Pacific* 浩淼的太平洋海域 ○ *the blue expanses of the sky* 广阔的蓝天 ○ *a broad expanse of brow* 宽阔的前额.

ex·pan·sion /ɪkˈspænʃn; ɪkˈspænʃən/ *n* [U] action of expanding; state of being expanded 扩大; 扩展; 膨胀: *the expansion of gases when heated* 气体受热时的膨胀 ○ *the expansion of his business interests* 他的商业利益的增加 ○ *the expansion of the school system* 学校机构的扩大.

▷ **ex·pan·sion·ism** /-ʃənɪzəm; -ʃənɪzəm/ *n* [U] belief in, or practice of, expansion, esp of one's territory or business 扩张主义, 扩展政策(尤指领土或企业): *Expansionism was advocated by many British politicians in the late 19th century.* 19世纪末, 英国许多政客鼓吹扩张主义. ○ *The owners of the firm feared the manager's* *vigorous expansionism.* 公司的股东都惧怕经理冒进的扩展政策. **ex·pan·sion·ist** /-ʃənɪst; -ʃənɪst/ *n* person who wishes esp a country or business to expand 扩张主义者; (企业中)赞成扩展政策者: [attrib 作定语] *Hitler's expansionist policies* 希特勒的扩张主义政策 ○ *expansionist business plans* 扩展企业的计划.

ex·pans·ive /ɪkˈspænsɪv; ɪkˈspænsɪv/ *adj* **1** able or tending to expand 可扩大或伸展的; 有扩大或伸展性的: *He greeted us with an expansive gesture* (eg he stretched his arms wide) *and a wide smile.* 他手舞足蹈笑逐颜开地迎接我们. **2** (of a person, his manner, etc) willing to talk a lot; unreserved (指人、态度等)健谈的, 豪爽的, 开朗的: *an expansive after-dinner speaker* 健谈的饭后演讲者 ○ *be in an expansive mood after a few drinks* 喝了几杯酒以后情绪高涨. ▷ **ex·pans·ively** *adv*. **ex·pans·ive·ness** *n* [U].

ex·pa·ti·ate /ɪkˈspeɪʃɪeɪt; ɪkˈspeʃɪˌet/ *v* [Ipr] **~ on/upon sth** (*fml* 文) write or speak at great length or in detail about a subject 详述; 细说; 阐述: *The chairman expatiated for two hours on his plans for the company.* 董事长用两小时阐述了公司的规划.

ex·pat·ri·ate /ˌeksˈpætrɪət; *US* -ˈpeɪt-; ɛksˈpetrɪɪt/ *n* person living outside his own country 居于国外的人; 侨民: *American expatriates in Paris* 居于巴黎的美国人 ○ [attrib 作定语] *expatriate Englishmen in Spain* 西班牙的英国侨民.

▷ **ex·pat·ri·ate** /-rɪeɪt; -rɪˌet/ *v* [Tn] cause (sb) to leave his native country; expel 使(某人)移居国外; 将(某人)逐出本国; 流放: *expatriated on suspicion of spying for the enemy* 涉嫌里通外国而被逐出本国.

ex·pect /ɪkˈspekt; ɪkˈspɛkt/ *v* **1 (a)** [Tn, Tn·pr, Tf, Tt, Tnt] **~ sth (from sb/sth)** think or believe that sth will happen or that sb/sth will come 预料, 预计, 期待, 盼望(某事物会发生或某人[某事物]会来到): *This is the parcel which we have been expecting (from New York).* 这是我们一直在期待的(从纽约来的)邮包. ○ *I expect (that) I will be back on Sunday.* 我预计星期日回来. ○ *You would expect that there would be/there to be strong disagreement about this.* 可以料到此事会有严重分歧. ○ *You can't expect to learn a foreign language in a week.* 不要指望一个星期就能学会一门外语. ○ *We expected him to arrive yesterday.* 我们原以为他昨天能到. **(b)** [Tn, Tn·pr] **~ sth (from sb)** hope and feel confident that one will receive sth (from sb) 期望, 盼望, 指望(从某人处)得到某事物: *I was expecting a present from her, so I was disappointed I didn't receive one.* 我原来一直盼望着能收到她送的礼物, 所以因得不到而失望. ○ *Don't expect any sympathy from me!* 不要指望能得到我的同情! ⇨Usage at WAIT[1] 用法见 WAIT[1]. **2** [Tn, Tn·pr, Tf, Tnt] **~ sth (from sb)** require sth (from sb), esp as a right or duty 要求(某人)某事物(尤指有权或有责任要求者): *The sergeant expects obedience from his men/that his men will obey him/his men to obey him.* 中士要士兵服从他的命令. ○ *I expect you to be punctual.* 我要求你准时. ○ *You will be expected to work on Saturdays.* 你们星期六要上班. **3** [Tn, Tf, Tt] (not in the continuous tenses 不用于进行时态) (*infml* 口 esp *Brit*) suppose (sth); assume 料想为(某事物); 认为; 猜想: *'Who has eaten all the cake?' 'Tom, I expect/I expect (that) it was Tom.'* '谁把蛋糕都吃光了?' '我想是汤姆[大概是汤姆]吧.' ○ *'Will you need help?' 'I don't expect so.'* '你需要帮忙吗?' '我想不必了.' ○ *'Will he be late?' 'I expect so.'* '他会迟到吗?' '我想会的.' **4** (idm 习语) **be expecting (a baby/child)** (*infml euph* 口, 婉) be pregnant 怀孕: *I hear Sally's expecting again.* 我听说萨莉又有身子了. **expect too ˈmuch (of sb)** believe or assume sb can do more than he can 对(某人)期望过高: *'I can't finish this job by Friday — you expect too much of me.'* '我星期五以前干不完这项工作——你对我期望过高了.' **(only) to be exˈpected** likely to happen; quite normal 可能发生; 相当正常: *A little tiredness after taking these drugs is to be expected.* 服下这些药后会有些疲倦. ○ *It is only to be expected your son will leave home eventually.* 儿子总归要离开家的, 这种事很难免.

▷ **ex·pect·ancy** /ɪkˈspektənsɪ; ɪkˈspɛktənsɪ/ *n* [U] state of expecting or hoping 预料; 预计; 期待; 盼望; 指望: *a look/feeling of expectancy* 期望的神色[心情] ○ *She went to meet him with an air of expectancy,* ie as if expecting him to bring sth. 她去见他时带着有所期待的神情. Cf 参看 LIFE EXPECTANCY (LIFE).

ex·pect·ant /ɪkˈspektənt; ɪkˈspɛktənt/ *adj* expecting (esp sth good); hopeful 期待的; 期望的; 怀有希望的: (*fml* 文) *children with expectant faces waiting for the pantomime to start* 眼巴巴地等候童话剧开演的儿童们. **ex·pect·antly** *adv*. **exˌpectant ˈmother** woman who is pregnant 怀孕的女人.

ex·pected *adj* [usu attrib 通常作定语] that is expected 预料的; 预期的; 期望的: *expected objections to the plan* 预料到的对该计划的反对意见.

ex·pecta·tion /ˌekspekˈteɪʃn; ˌɛkspɛkˈteʃən/ *n* **1** [U] **~ (of sth)** firm belief that sth will happen; hope of gaining sth/that sth will happen 预料; 预期; 期待; 期望: *There's no expectation of snow tonight.* 今晚预料无雪. ○ *The children waited patiently in expectation of* (ie expecting) *the magician.* 孩子们耐心地等待着魔术师. ○ *He has little expectation of winning a prize.* 他对获奖不抱什么希望. **2** [C usu *pl* 通常作复数] confident feelings (about sth) (对某事物)有信心的指望: *His parents have great expectations for his future.* 他父母对他的前途深寄厚望. ○ *She had high expectations of what university had to offer.* 她对大学所能给她提供的一切期望很高. ○ *The holiday was beyond all expectations*, ie better than was hoped for. 假日过得比预期的好得多. **3** (idm 习语) **aˌgainst/ˌcontrary to (all) expecˈtation(s)** quite different from what was expected 出乎意料; 意想不到: *a gold medal that was against all expectations* 出乎意料的一枚金质奖章. **ˌexpectation of ˈlife** years a person is expected to live 对某人的估计寿命. **fall short of sb's/not come up to (sb's) expecˈtations** be less good than was expected 未臻理想: *Unfortunately the restaurant he recommended fell far short of our expectations.* 遗憾的是他推荐的餐厅与我们心目中的相去甚远. ○ *His film performance didn't come up to expectations.* 他在影片中的演出有负众望.

ex·pect·or·ate /ɪkˈspektəreɪt; ɪkˈspɛktəˌret/ *v* [I, Tn] (*fml or medical* 文或医) send out (phlegm from the throat, blood from the lungs) by coughing; spit 吐或咯(痰、血、唾液等); 吐痰; 咯血; 吐唾液: *In cases of tuberculosis blood is expectorated.* 肺结核病有咯血症状.

▷ **ex·pect·or·ant** /-rənt; -rənt/ *n* medicine that helps sb to expectorate 祛痰剂: *The cough medicine contains an expectorant.* 咳嗽药中含有祛痰剂.

ex·pe·di·ent /ɪkˈspiːdɪənt; ɪkˈspidɪənt/ *adj* [usu pred 通常作表语] (of an action) useful, helpful or advisable for a particular purpose, though not necessarily fair or moral (指行动)有用, 有助益, 可取(但不一定合理或正当): *Since there was soon to be a general election, the Prime Minister decided that a change of policy was politically expedient.* 鉴于即将举行大选, 首相认为变通一下政策在政治上有利. ○ *actions that were expedient rather than principled* 非原则性的权宜手段.

▷ **ex·pe·di·ence** /-əns; -əns/ (also **ex·pe·di·ency** /-ənsɪ; -ənsɪ/) (*n* [U] suitability or usefulness for a purpose, though not necessarily fair or moral 适宜, 有用, 有利, 便利(但不一定合理或正当): *He acted from expediency, not from principle.* 他为求达到目的, 丧失了原则.

ex·pe·di·ent *n* means of achieving an aim, which may not be fair or moral 权宜之计, 应急手段(不一定合理或正当): *resort to various expedients to get the money together* 采取各种应急办法筹款.

ex·pe·di·ently *adv*.

ex·ped·ite /ˈekspɪdaɪt; ˈɛkspɪˌdaɪt/ *v* [Tn] (*fml* 文) help the progress of (work, business, etc); hasten or speed up 有助于(工作、业务等)的进展; 加快; 加速: *Please do what you can to expedite the building work.* 请尽量加快建筑工作.

ex·pedi·tion /ˌekspɪˈdɪʃn; ˌɛkspɪˈdɪʃən/ *n* **1 (a)** organized journey or voyage with a particular aim (为某目的而组织的陆路或水路的)远行; 探险; 考察: *send a party of people on an expedition* 派一队人去考察 ○ *go on an expedition to the North Pole* 到北极去探险 ○ *a hunting expedition* 狩猎之行 ○ (*joc* 谑) *a shopping expedition* 购物之行. **(b)** people, vehicles, ships, etc making this journey (进行远征、探险、考察等的)人或使用的车辆、船只等: *members of the Mount Everest expedition* 埃佛勒斯峰(即珠穆朗玛峰)探险队队员. **2** (*fml* 文) speed; promptness 迅速; 敏捷: *We carried out* *the captain's orders with all possible expedition.* 我们毫不迟疑地迅速执行船长的命令.

▷ **ex·pedi·tion·ary** /-ʃənərɪ; *US* -nerɪ; -ʃən,ɛrɪ/ *adj* [attrib 作定语] of or forming an expedition 远征的; 探险的; 考察的; 组成远征队等的: *an expeditionary force*, eg an army sent to take part in a war abroad 远征军(如到国外参战的军队).

ex·pedi·tious /ˌekspɪˈdɪʃəs; ˌɛkspɪˈdɪʃəs/ *adj* (*fml* 文) done with speed and efficiency 迅速而有效率的; 迅速完成的: *an expeditious response* 迅速的反应. ▷ **ex·pedi·tiously** *adv*: *We will carry out the enquiry as expeditiously as possible.* 我们将尽快进行调查.

ex·pel /ɪkˈspel; ɪkˈspɛl/ *v* (**-ll-**) [Tn, Tn·pr] **~ sb (from sth)** **1** force sb to leave (esp a country, school or club) 强迫(某人)离开(尤指国家、学校或会所); 驱逐; 赶走; 开除: *Following reports of drug-taking at a boarding-school, several senior boys have been expelled.* 自从某寄宿学校传出有人吸毒之后, 高年级有几个男生已被开除. ○ *Two attachés at the embassy were expelled from the country.* 大使馆的两名随员已驱逐出境. **2** send or drive (sth) out by force 用力排出或驱出(某物): *expel smoke from the lungs* 用力呼出肺里的烟 ○ *a fan in the kitchen for expelling cooking smells* 为排出烹调气味而安装于厨房中的电扇.

ex·pend /ɪkˈspend; ɪkˈspɛnd/ *v* [Tn, Tn·pr] **~ sth (on/upon sth/doing sth)** (*fml* 文) **1** spend, use (money, etc) in doing sth 花费, 使用(钱等)做某事: *expend time, effort and money on a project* 在一项目上花费时间、精力和金钱. **2** use (sth) up; exhaust 用光(某物); 耗尽: *expend all one's ammunition, stores, fuel* 用尽所有的弹药、储备、燃料.

▷ **ex·pend·able** *adj* (*fml* 文) that may be consumed, destroyed, etc to achieve a purpose 可消费的; 可消耗的; 可毁灭的: *In the Great War soldiers were considered expendable.* 在第一次世界大战中, 人们认为士兵是尽可牺牲的. ○ *In these conservation-conscious times, areas of grassland are no longer expendable.* 在人们意识到应当保护自然资源的这个时代, 草原已不容再受破坏了.

ex·pend·it·ure /ɪkˈspendɪtʃə(r); ɪkˈspɛndɪtʃɚ/ *n* **1** [U] action of spending or using 花费; 使用: *the expenditure of money on weapons* 购置武器的开支 ○ *expenditure of energy on a project* 在一项目上耗费的精力. **2** [C, U] amount (esp of money) spent (尤指金钱的)支出额: *an expenditure of £500 on new furniture* 购买新家具的 500 英镑开销 ○ *Limit your expenditure(s) to what is essential.* 你要把开销限制在必要的范围内. Cf 参看 RECEIPT 3.

ex·pense /ɪkˈspens; ɪkˈspɛns/ *n* **1** (**a**) [U] spending of money etc; cost 花费; 代价: *an expense of time, energy and cash* 时间、精力、现金的花费 ○ *He hired a plane, regardless of expense.* 他不惜代价, 租了一架飞机. ○ *Most children in Britain are educated at public expense.* 英国大多数儿童靠公费受教育. (**b**) [C] cause of spending 花费的原因: *An annual holiday is a big expense.* 一年一度的假日是一笔大开销. ○ *Running a car is a great expense.* 一辆汽车的经常开支很大. **2 expenses** [pl] money spent in doing a specific job, or for a specific purpose (做某工作或为某目的)花费的钱: *travelling expenses* 旅费 ○ *House repairs, holidays and other expenses reduced her bank balance to almost nothing.* 修房、度假和其他开销使她在银行的存款所剩无几. ○ *Who's meeting the expenses of your trip?* 谁为你支付旅费呢? **3** (idm 习语) **at sb's expense** (**a**) with sb paying 由某人付费: *We were entertained at the editor's expense.* 由编辑付钱招待我们. (**b**) at sb who has behaved foolishly, been tricked, etc 针对某人(因其举动愚蠢或受到捉弄等): *They had a good laugh* (ie were very amused) *at Sam's expense.* 他们嘲弄萨姆而乐不可支. **at great, little, no, etc exˈpense (to sb/oneself)** with a lot of, little, no, etc money being spent (by sb/oneself) (某人[自己])花费很大、花费很小、无花费等: *We can redecorate the room at little expense, if we use this old paint.* 我们要是用这种旧漆重新装饰这房间, 就不用花多少钱了. **at the expense of sth** with loss or damage to sth 在损失或损坏某事物的情况下: *He built up a successful business but it was all done at the expense of his health.* 他创建的企业很成功, 但这一切却损害了他的健康. **(all) expenses ˈpaid** with an employer, etc paying for everything (由雇主等)已付费用的: [attrib 作定语] *She's just returned from an all-expenses-paid trip to France.* 她刚由法国回来, 旅途一切费用由雇主支付. **go to/put sb to the expense of sth/doing sth** spend/cause sb to spend money on sth 在某事物上花钱或使某人花钱: *It's stupid to go to the expense of taking music lessons if you never practise.* 花钱上音乐课而从不练习是很愚蠢的. ○ *put sb to a lot of expense* 使某人破费极大. **no expense(s) ˈspared** with no regard for the cost 不惜费用: *I'm going to take you out to dinner, no expense spared.* 我带你出去用餐, 花费多少都无所谓. **spare no expense** ⇨ SPARE.

□ **exˈpense account** record of money spent by an employee in the course of his work (and later paid by his employer) 报销帐目(雇员工作上的开支记载, 事后由雇主偿付): *Whenever he buys petrol, he puts it on his expense account.* 他每次买汽油都记在报销帐目上.

ex·pens·ive /ɪkˈspensɪv; ɪkˈspɛnsɪv/ *adj* costing a lot (of money) 费用大的; 昂贵的: *an expensive car* 昂贵的汽车 ○ *Houses are very expensive in this area.* 这地区房价很高. ○ *It's too expensive for me to buy.* 太贵了, 我买不起. ▷ **ex·pens·ively** *adv*: *an expensively dressed lady* 穿着昂贵服装的女士.

ex·peri·ence /ɪkˈspɪərɪəns; ɪkˈspɪrɪəns/ *n* **1** [U] (process of gaining) knowledge or skill acquired from seeing and doing things 经验; 体验: *We all learn by experience.* 我们都从经验中学习. ○ *Does she have much experience of teaching?* 她教学经验丰富吗? ○ *He hasn't had enough work experience* (ie experience of work) *for the job.* 他做这项工作尚无足够经验. ○ *I know from experience that he'll arrive late.* 据我的经验之谈, 他要迟到的. **2** [C] event or activity that affects one in some way; event or activity that has given one experience(1) 经历; 阅历; 感受; 体会: *an unpleasant, a trying, an unusual, etc experience* 令人不快的、难堪的、不寻常等的经历 ○ *You must try some of her home-made wine — it's quite an experience!* ie it's very unusual. 你一定要尝尝她自制的葡萄酒——一饱口福! ○ *He had many interesting experiences while travelling in Africa.* 他在非洲旅行时, 有许多有趣的经历.

▷ **ex·peri·ence** *v* [Tn] have experience of (sth); feel 有(某事物)的经验; 经历; 感觉; 感受; 体验: *experience pleasure, pain, difficulty, great hardships, etc* 体验到愉快、痛苦、困难、苦难等 ○ *The child had never experienced kindness.* 这孩子从未受过善待. ○ *I don't think I've ever experienced real depression.* 我认为我从未体验过真正的情绪低落. **ex·peri·enced** *adj* having experience; having knowledge or skill as a result of experience 有经验的; 有阅历的; 有见识的; 熟练的: *an experienced nurse* 有经验的护士 ○ *He's experienced in looking after children.* 他有照料孩子的经验.

ex·peri·ment /ɪkˈsperɪmənt; ɪkˈspɛrəmənt/ *n* [C, U] (esp scientific 尤用于科学) test or trial done carefully in order to study what happens and gain new knowledge 实验; 试验: *perform/carry out/conduct an experiment* 进行试验 ○ *The researchers are repeating the experiment on rats.* 研究人员用老鼠反复做该试验. ○ *prove a theory by experiment* 通过试验证实一理论 ○ *learn by experiment* 通过试验学习 ○ (*fig* 比喻) *The play was staged as an experiment.* 这出剧已经试演.

▷ **ex·peri·ment** *v* [I, Ipr] **~ (on/upon sb/sth); ~ (with sth)** make an experiment 进行实验; 进行试验: *We experimented until we succeeded in mixing the right colour.* 我们不断进行实验, 直至将所需颜色调配成功. ○ *experiment upon animals* 用动物做实验 ○ *experiment with new methods* 实验新方法.

ex·peri·menta·tion /ɪkˌsperɪmenˈteɪʃn; ɪkˌspɛrəmɛnˈteʃən/ *n* [U] (*fml* 文) activity, process or practice of experimenting 实验; 试验: *Many people object to experimentation on animals.* 许多人反对用动物做实验. ○ [attrib 作定语] *experimentation methods* 实验方法.

ex·peri·mental /ɪkˌsperɪˈmentl; ɪkˌspɛrəˈmɛntl̩/ *adj* of, used for, using or based on experiments 实验的; 用于实验的; 用实验的; 以实验为基础的: *experimental methods* 实验方法 ○ *an experimental farm* 实验农场 ○ *an experimental physicist* 实验物理学家 ○ *experimental theatre* 实验剧场 ○ *The technique is still at the experimental stage. It hasn't been fully developed yet.* 这项技术仍处于实验阶段, 尚未完全成熟. ▷ **ex·peri·ment·ally** /-təlɪ; -tl̩ɪ/ *adv*: *We are using the substance experimentally at first.* 我们现在先试验性地使用这种物质.

ex·pert /ˈekspɜːt; ˋɛkspɝt/ *n* ~ **(at/in/on sth/doing sth)** person with special knowledge, skill or training in a particular field 专家; 能手: *an agricultural expert* 农业专家 ○ *an expert in psychology* 心理学专家 ○ *get the advice of the experts* 向专家请教 ○ *an expert at playing golf* 打高尔夫球的能手 ○ *an expert on ancient Greek vases* 古希腊花瓶专家.

▷ **ex·pert** *adj* ~ **(at/in/on sth/doing sth)** done with, having, or involving great knowledge or skill 熟练的; 老练的; 需有专门知识或技术的: *according to expert advice* 根据专家的意见 ○ *an expert rider* 熟练的骑手 ○ *an expert job* 需有专门知识的工作 ○ *He's expert at/in cooking good cheap meals.* 他善于烹制又好吃又便宜的饭菜. **ex·pertly** *adv*. **ex·pert·ness** *n* [U]: *The expertness of her driving surprised him.* 她驾驶技术熟练, 他感到很惊奇.

ex·pert·ise /ˌekspɜːˈtiːz; ˌɛkspɝˋtiz/ *n* [U] expert knowledge or skill, esp in a particular field 专门知识或技能(尤指在某一领域): *Customers will be impressed by the expertise of our highly trained employees.* 我们的雇员专业性强、训练有素, 保证顾客满意. ○ *We were amazed at his expertise on the ski slopes.* 他斜坡滑雪的技能使我们赞叹不已.

ex·pi·ate /ˈekspɪeɪt; ˋɛkspɪˌet/ *v* [Tn] (*fml* 文) accept punishment for (wrong one has done) and do something to show one is sorry; make up for 为(所犯罪过)受罚及补偿; 赎(罪); 抵偿: *expiate one's sin/a crime/one's guilt* 赎罪. ▷ **ex·pi·ation** /ˌekspɪˈeɪʃn; ˌɛkspɪˋeʃən/ *n* [U] (*fml* 文): *large sums paid to the family in expiation of the wrongs done to them* 为赎罪付给事主家人的巨额金钱.

ex·pire /ɪkˈspaɪə(r); ɪkˋspaɪr/ *v* [I] **1** (of sth that lasts a period of time) come to an end; become no longer in use (指延续一段时间的某事物)结束, 不再使用, 期满, 终止: *Our present lease on the flat expires next month.* 我们这套公寓的租约下月到期. ○ *When does your driving licence expire?* 你的驾驶执照何时到期? **2** (*esp medical* 尤用于医学) breathe out (air) 呼出(气). **3** (*dated fml* 旧, 文) die 死; 去世.

▷ **ex·pira·tion** /ˌekspɪˈreɪʃn; ˌɛkspəˋreʃən/ *n* [U] (*fml* 文) **1** ending, esp of the period when a contract, etc is in force 终止, 届期, 期满, 满期(尤指合同等的有效期): *the expiration of the lease, tenancy, agreement, contract, etc* 租约、租用、协议、合同等的期满. **2** (*esp medical* 尤用于医学) breathing out (of air) (空气的)呼出.

ex·piry /ɪkˈspaɪərɪ; ɪkˋspaɪrɪ/ *n* ~ **(of sth)** ending, esp of the period when a contract or agreement is in force 终止, 届期, 期满, 满期(尤指合同或协议的有效阶段): *the expiry of a driving licence, lease, credit card, contract, agreement, etc* 驾驶执照、租约、信用卡、合同、协议等的期满 ○ [attrib 作定语] *the expiry date* 终止日期.

ex·plain /ɪkˈspleɪn; ɪkˋsplen/ *v* **1** [Tn, Tw, Dn·pr] ~ **sth (to sb)** make sth plain or clear; give the meaning of sth 解释; 讲解; 说明; 阐明: *A dictionary explains the meaning of words.* 词典是解释词义的工具书. ○ *He explained his plan in some detail.* 他仔细地说明了自己的计划. ○ *Could you explain why you left?* 你能说说你为什么离开的吗? ○ *Please explain this problem to me.* 请把这个问题给我讲解一下. **2** [Tn, Tf, Tw, Dn·pr, Dpr·f, Dpr·w] ~ **sth (to sb)** give or be a reason for sth; account for sth 说明某事物的原因或理由; 为某事物辩解: *That explains his absence.* 那就是他缺席的原因. ○ *He explained that his train had been delayed.* 他解释说他乘坐的火车误点了. ○ *They explained what had happened.* 他们为所发生的事进行了辩解. ○ *She explained her conduct to her boss.* 她向老板说明了自己那种表现的原因. ○ *She explained to the children that the school had been closed.* 她向孩子们解释说学校已经关门了. ○ *The manager has explained to customers why the goods were late.* 经理已向顾客解释货物晚到的原因. **3** (idm 习语) **exˈplain oneself** (**a**) make one's meaning clear 把自己的意思解释清楚: *I don't understand your argument. Could you explain yourself a bit more?* 我不明白你的论点, 你能把意思再说清楚些吗? (**b**) give reasons for one's behaviour 为自己的行为作解释: *In recent weeks you've been late every day. Please explain yourself.* 近几个星期以来你每天都迟到. 请你说说原因. **4** (phr v) **explain sth away** give excuses why one should not be blamed for (a fault, mistake, etc) or why sth is not important 为(过失或错误等)辩解; 为某事物搪塞: *You will find it difficult to explain away your use of such offensive language.* 你使用这样无礼的语言是很难说得过去的. ○ *He explained away his late arrival by blaming it on the crowded roads.* 他辩称路上人多而把迟到一事推脱得一干二净.

ex·plana·tion /ˌekspləˈneɪʃn; ˌɛkspləˋneʃən/ *n* **1** [U] (process of) explaining 解释; 讲解; 说明; 阐述: *He left the room without explanation.* 他离开了房间而未加解释. ○ *I should say a few words (by way) of explanation.* 我应当说几句解释的话. ○ *Had he anything to say in explanation of his behaviour?* 他对自己的行为做过什么解释吗? **2** [C] statement, fact, circumstance, etc that explains sth 能说明某事物缘由的言语、事实、情况等: *That's not an adequate explanation.* 这并不足以说明问题. ○ *a satisfactory explanation of the mystery* 有关此奥秘的一种令人信服的解释 ○ *His explanations are always difficult to believe.* 他的说法总是很难令人相信.

ex·plan·at·ory /ɪkˈsplænətərɪ; *US* -tɔːrɪ; ɪkˋsplænəˌtɔrɪ/ *adj* [usu attrib 通常作定语] giving, serving or intended as an explanation 解释的; 说明的: *explanatory notes at the back of a book* 书后的注释.

ex·plet·ive /ɪkˈspliːtɪv; *US* ˈeksplətɪv; ˋɛksplɪtɪv/ *n* (*fml* 文) violent (often meaningless) exclamation said in anger, pain, etc; swear-word (愤怒、痛苦等时用的)叹词(常无意义); 咒骂语: *'Damn!' is an expletive.* '该死!'是咒骂语. ○ *He uttered several vigorous expletives when he dropped the iron on his foot.* 他的熨斗掉下砸在脚上, 他随口骂了几声.

ex·plic·able /ɪkˈsplɪkəbl, *also* ˈeksplɪkəbl; ˋɛksplɪkəbḷ, ɪkˋsplɪkəbḷ/ *adj* (*fml* 文) that can be explained 可解释的; 可说明的: *His behaviour is explicable in the light of his recent illness.* 他因近日患病, 这种表现是可以理解的. ○ *Scientists had maintained that the crop failure was not explicable.* 科学家认为作物歉收原因不明.

ex·plic·ate /ˈeksplɪkeɪt; ˋɛksplɪˌket/ *v* [Tn] (*fml* 文) explain and analyse (esp an idea, a statement or a work of literature) in detail 详细解说并分析(尤指想法、说法或文学作品): *explicate one's moral values* 详细阐述自己的道德标准.

ex·pli·cit /ɪkˈsplɪsɪt; ɪkˋsplɪsɪt/ *adj* **1** (**a**) (of a statement, etc) clearly and fully expressed (指说法等)明确而详细的: *He gave me explicit directions on how to get there.* 他清清楚楚地告诉我怎样到达那里. ○ *They gave explicit reasons for leaving.* 他们明确地说出了离开的原因. (**b**) (of a person) saying sth clearly, exactly and openly (指人)(说得)明确的, 直率的, 开诚布公的: *She was quite explicit about why she left.* 她对自己离去的原因直言不讳. **2** with nothing hidden or implied 毫不隐瞒的; 毫不含蓄的: *explicit sex scenes in the film* 影片中露骨的性爱镜头. ▷ **ex·pli·citly** *adv*: *She was explicitly forbidden to attend.* 清楚表明不准她参加. **ex·pli·cit·ness** *n* [U].

ex·plode /ɪkˈspləʊd; ɪkˋsplod/ *v* **1** [I, Tn] (cause sth to) burst with a loud noise; blow up (使某物)爆炸; 炸开: *When the boiler exploded many people were injured.* 因锅炉爆炸, 许多人受了伤. ○ *The firework exploded in his hand.* 那个爆竹在他手里响了. ○ *explode a bomb* 使一颗炸弹爆炸. Cf 参看 IMPLODE. **2** [I, Ipr] (**a**) (of feelings) burst out suddenly (指感情)迸发: *At last his anger exploded.* 他终于大发雷霆. (**b**) ~ **(with/in/into sth)** (of people) show sudden violent emotion (指人)冲动, 激动: *He exploded with rage, fury, jealousy, etc.* 他勃然大怒、暴跳如雷、妒火中烧等. ○ *She exploded into loud laughter.* 她突然大笑起来. **3** [I] (of a population, etc) increase suddenly or quickly (指人口等)突然或迅速增加: *the exploding world population* 激增的世界人口. **4** [Tn] destroy (a theory, an idea, etc) by showing it to be false 破除, 推翻(一理论、观念等)(揭示其谬误): *explode a superstition* 破除迷信 ○ *The myth that eating carrots improves your eyesight was exploded years ago.* 认为吃胡萝卜可以改善视力的海外奇谈, 多年前已祛除殆尽.

□ **exˌploded ˈdiagram** one showing the parts of a structure in their relative positions but slightly separated from each other 分解图.

ex·ploit[1] /ˈeksplɔɪt; ˋɛksplɔɪt/ *n* [C] brave or adventurous deed or action 英勇的或冒险的行为或事迹: *The daring exploits of the parachutists were much admired.* 跳伞者大胆的冒险动作令人赞叹不已. ○ (*joc* 谑) *I'm not interested in hearing about Bill's amorous exploits.* 我没兴

趣听比尔那些色胆包天的事. ⇨Usage at ACT[1] 用法见 ACT[1].

ex·ploit[2] /ɪk'splɔɪt; ɪk`splɔɪt/ *v* [Tn] **1** use, work or develop fully (esp mines and other natural resources) 利用或开发(尤指矿藏和其他自然资源): *exploit oil reserves, water power, solar energy, etc* 开发石油资源、开发水利资源、利用太阳能. **2** use (sb/sth) selfishly and unfairly for one's own advantage or profit 剥削或利用(某人[某事物]): *child labour exploited in factories* 在工厂中受剥削的童工 ○ *exploit a situation for one's own advantage* 趁着形势谋取私利 ○ *They exploited her generosity shamelessly.* 他们无耻地利用了她的慷慨.

▷ **ex·ploit·able** *adj* that can be exploited 可利用的; 可开发的; 可剥削的: *few exploitable coal-mines* 少量可开采的煤矿.

ex·ploita·tion /ˌeksplɔɪ'teɪʃn; ˌɛksplɔɪ`teʃən/ *n* [U] exploiting or being exploited 利用; 开发; 剥削: *full exploitation of oil wells* 充分利用油井资源 ○ *the exploitation of child labour* 对童工的剥削.

ex·plore /ɪk'splɔ:(r); ɪk`splɔr/ *v* **1** [I, Tn] travel into or through (a place, esp a country) in order to learn about it 踏勘; 勘探; 探测; 在(一地方, 尤指一国家)探险, 考察: *explore the Arctic regions* 到北极地区探险 ○ *Columbus discovered America but did not explore the new continent.* 哥伦布发现了美洲, 但没有考察这块新大陆. ○ *explore a castle* 探察一城堡 ○ *As soon as they arrived in the town they went out to explore.* 他们一到这座城镇就出外查看周围环境. **2** [Tn] examine (sth) thoroughly in order to test or find out about it (为测试或了解)仔细检查(某事物); 探索; 探究: *explore one's conscience* 良心省察 ○ *We explored several solutions to the problem.* 我们探讨了几种解决该问题的方法.

▷ **ex·plora·tion** /ˌeksplə'reɪʃn; ˌɛksplə`reʃən/ *n* **1** [U] activity of exploring 勘探; 探测; 探索; 探究: *the exploration of space* 对宇宙空间的探索 ○ *a voyage of exploration* 探险航行 ○ *detailed exploration of a subject* 对一题目的详细探讨. **2** [C] instance of this 勘探; 探测; 探索; 探究: *in the course of his explorations of the country* 在他对该国进行探索的过程中 ○ *an exploration of the subconscious mind* 对潜意识的探索.

ex·plor·at·ory /ɪk'splɒrətrɪ; *US* -tɔ:rɪ; ɪk`splɔrəˌtɔrɪ/ *adj* for the purpose of finding out sth 勘探的; 探测的; 探索的: *exploratory medical tests* 探索性的医学试验 ○ *an exploratory expedition up the Amazon river* 沿亚马孙河逆流而上的探险旅程.

ex·plorer /ɪk'splɔ:rə(r); ɪk`splɔrɚ/ *n* person who explores 勘探者; 探测者; 探险者; 探索者; 探究者: *Christopher Columbus was one of the great explorers.* 克里斯托弗·哥伦布是伟大的探险家.

ex·plo·sion /ɪk'spləʊʒn; ɪk`sploʒən/ *n* **1** (**a**) (loud noise caused by) sudden and violent bursting; exploding 爆裂(声); 爆炸(声): *a bomb explosion* 炸弹爆炸 ○ *gas explosions* 气体爆炸 ○ *The explosion was heard a mile away.* 那爆炸声一英里外都可听到. (**b**) sudden outburst (of anger, laughter, etc) (愤怒、笑声等的)迸发: *an explosion of rage* 大发雷霆. **2** great and sudden increase 激增: *a population explosion* 人口激增 ○ *the explosion of oil prices* 石油价格的急剧上涨.

ex·plos·ive /ɪk'spləʊsɪv; ɪk`splosɪv/ *adj* [esp attrib 尤作定语] **1** likely or easily able to explode 爆炸性的; 易爆炸的: *an explosive mixture of chemicals* 爆炸性化学混合物 ○ *explosive materials* 爆炸材料 ○ *Hydrogen is highly explosive.* 氢极易爆炸. **2** that arouses strong feelings or leads to violent outbursts 使人冲动的; 导致猛烈爆发的: *an explosive situation, issue* 一触即发的形势、极易引起争端的问题 ○ *Politics can be an explosive subject.* 政治问题容易引起激烈的争论. ○ *an explosive temper* 暴躁的脾气.

▷ **ex·plos·ive** *n* [C] substance that is likely or able to explode 爆炸物; 炸药: *Dynamite is an explosive.* 炸药是爆炸物. ○ *The bomb was packed with high explosive*, ie a substance that explodes with great force. 这炸弹装有烈性炸药.

ex·plos·ively *adv*.

ex·po·nent /ɪk'spəʊnənt; ɪk`sponənt/ *n* **1** person or thing that explains and supports a theory, belief, cause, etc (理论、信仰、事业等的)倡导者, 拥护者: *an exponent of free trade* 自由贸易的拥护者 ○ *Huxley was an exponent of Darwin's theory of evolution.* 赫胥黎是达尔文进化论的鼓吹者. **2** person able to perform skilfully a particular activity (某种活动的)能手: *the most famous exponent of mime* 最著名的哑剧表演大师 ○ *She's a practised exponent of the sport of water-skiing.* 她是滑水运动健将. **3** (*mathematics* 数) figure or symbol that shows how many times a quantity must be multiplied by itself 指数; 幂: *In* a^3, *the figure* ^{3} *is the exponent.* a^3 中的3是指数. ○ *In* x^n, *the symbol* ^{n} *is the exponent.* x^n 中的n是指数.

▷ **ex·po·nen·tial** /ˌekspəʊ'nenʃl; ˌɛkspo`nɛnʃəl/ *adj* (*mathematics* 数) **1** of or indicated by an exponent(3) 指数的; 幂的: 2^4 *is an exponential expression.* 2^4 是一个指数式. **2** produced or indicated by multiplying a set of numbers by themselves 由指数产生或表示的: *an exponential function* 指数函数 ○ (*fig* 比喻) *exponential* (ie more and more rapid) *growth* 越来越快的增长 ○ *an exponential curve*, eg on a graph indicating population increase 指数曲线(如人口增长示意图上的).

ex·po·nen·ti·ally /-ʃəlɪ; -ʃəlɪ/ *adv*: *increase exponentially.* 按指数增长.

ex·port[1] /'ekspɔ:t; `ɛksport/ *n* **1** [U] (business or action of) exporting 输出, 出口(的业务或活动): *a ban on the export of gold* 禁止黄金出口 ○ [attrib 作定语] *an 'export licence* 出口许可证 ○ *the 'export trade* 出口贸易 ○ *'export duties*, ie tax paid on exported goods 出口税. **2** [C usu *pl* 通常作复数] thing exported 出口物; 输出物: *Last year's exports exceeded imports in value.* 去年的出口价值超过进口. ○ *What are the chief exports of Botswana?* 博茨瓦纳的主要输出品是什么? Cf 参看 IMPORT[2].

ex·port[2] /ɪk'spɔ:t; ɪks`port/ *v* [I, Tn] send (goods) to another country for sale 输出; 出口: *This company has a large home market* (ie many buyers within the country) *but doesn't export.* 这家公司国内市场很大, 不做出口生意. ○ *India exports tea and cotton to many different countries.* 印度向许多国家出口茶叶和棉花. Cf 参看 IMPORT[1].

▷ **ex·porta·tion** /ˌekspɔ:'teɪʃn; ˌɛkspɔr`teʃən/ *n* [U] exporting of goods 输出; 出口: *articles for exportation abroad* 销往国外的物品 ○ *He manufactures paper for exportation only.* 他的工厂生产的纸张仅供出口.

ex·porter *n* person, company or country that exports goods 出口商; 出口公司; 出口国: *Argentina is a big exporter of beef products.* 阿根廷是牛肉制品的一大出口国. ○ *He is a successful exporter of diamonds.* 他是事业有成的钻石出口商.

ex·pose /ɪk'spəʊz; ɪk`spoz/ *v* **1** [Tn, Tn·pr] (**a**) uncover or make (sth) visible; display 显露或露出(某事物); 显示: *When he smiled he exposed a set of perfect white teeth.* 他笑时露出了一口漂亮的白牙. (**b**) **~ sth/sb/oneself (to sth)** uncover or leave sb/sth/oneself uncovered or unprotected 显露或暴露某人[某事物/自己]; 处于无遮蔽或不受保护的状态: *The soil was washed away by the flood, exposing bare rock.* 泥土被洪水冲走, 露出光秃秃的岩石. ○ *expose soldiers to unnecessary risks* 使士兵冒不必要的危险 ○ *expose one's skin to the sun* 使皮肤暴露于阳光下 ○ *The baby was left exposed to the wind and rain.* 婴儿被离弃于风雨之中. ○ (*fig* 比喻) *expose oneself to criticism, ridicule, mockery, etc* 遭受批评、嘲笑、嘲弄等. **2** [Tn] (**a**) make known (sth secret); reveal 揭露(秘密); 揭穿; 揭发; 揭破; 显露: *expose a plot, project, plan, etc* 揭露阴谋、方案、计划等 ○ *That unfortunate remark exposed his ignorance of the subject.* 他说了那句不妥的话, 暴露了自己对此事的无知. (**b**) make known (the guilt or wrongdoing) of (a secretly guilty person) 揭露(某人)的(不为人知的罪恶或过错); 揭穿; 揭发; 揭破: *expose crime, scandal, injustice, fraud, etc* 揭露罪行、丑闻、冤假错案、骗局等 ○ *expose a criminal, an impostor, a culprit, etc* 揭露罪犯、冒名顶替者、犯错误的人等. **3** [Tn, Tn·pr] (in photography) allow light to reach (film, etc) (摄影)使(软片等)曝光: *expose a reel of film* 使一卷软片曝光. **4** [Tn] **~ oneself** indecently show one's sexual organs in public 猥亵性公开裸露自己的性器官: *An old man was arrested for exposing himself to young children.* 有个老头向儿童裸露性器官而遭逮捕.

▷ **ex·posed** *adj* (of a place) not sheltered (from wind, weather, etc) (指地方)无遮蔽的; 不遮挡风雨的: *The cottage is in a very exposed position at the top of the hill.* 那小屋位于山顶毫无遮蔽之处.

ex·posé /ek'spəʊzeɪ; *US* ˌekspə'zeɪ; ˌɛkspə'ze/ *n* **1** short statement of a number of facts or beliefs（对事实或主张的）简短的陈述. **2** account of the facts of a situation, esp when these are shocking or have been kept deliberately secret 叙述, 报道(尤指令人震惊的或曾故意保密的): *The newspaper published an exposé of the film star's past life.* 报纸发表了该影星的逸闻. ○ *an exposé of corruption within the government* 揭露政府内部腐败情况的报道.

ex·posi·tion /ˌekspə'zɪʃn; ˌɛkspə'zɪʃən/ *n* (*fml* 文) **1** (**a**) [U] explaining or making clear by giving details 解释; 说明. (**b**) [C] instance of this; explanation of a theory, plan, etc 解释; 说明; 解说; (理论、计划等的)讲解: *an exposition of the advantages of nuclear power* 对核动力优越性的阐释. **2** [C] exhibition of goods, etc（货物等的）展出; 展览会; 博览会: *an industrial exposition* 工业博览会.

ex·pos·tu·late /ɪk'spɒstʃʊleɪt; ɪk'spɑstʃəˌlet/ *v* [I, Ipr] ~ **(with sb) (on/about sth)** (*fml* 文) make a protest (to sb); reason or argue (with sb), esp to persuade him not to do sth（向某人）提抗议;（与某人）讲道理或争论;（尤指）规劝, 劝戒: *They expostulated with him about the risks involved in his plan.* 他们指出他的计划有风险, 劝他放弃.

▷ **ex·pos·tu·la·tion** /ɪkˌspɒstʃʊ'leɪʃn; ɪkˌspɑstʃə'leʃən/ *n* [U, C] (making a) protest; reasoned persuasion, etc 抗议; 规劝; 劝戒: *My expostulation(s) had no effect.* 我提出的劝告毫无作用.

E

ex·pos·ure /ɪk'spəʊʒə(r); ɪk'spoʒɚ/ *n* **1** [U] action of exposing or state of being exposed 显露; 暴露; 揭露; 揭发; 曝光: *Exposure of the body to strong sunlight can be harmful.* 身体受烈日曝晒会造成损伤. ○ *The baby died of exposure*, ie as a result of being exposed to the weather. 那婴儿因曝露于室外而夭折. ○ *the exposure of his ignorance* 他的无知的暴露 ○ *The exposure of the plot against the President probably saved his life.* 揭发了反总统的阴谋可能救了他一命. ○ *the exposure of photographic film to light* 摄影软片的曝光. **2** [C] instance of exposing or being exposed (EXPOSE 2b) 揭露; 揭穿; 揭发; 揭破: *As a result of these exposures* (ie facts being made known to the public) *several ministers resigned from the government.* 这些问题揭发后, 有几个大臣辞职了. **3** action of exposing a film etc to the light（软片等的）曝光 ○ *An exposure of one-hundredth of a second will be enough*, ie Exposing the film for that length of time will make a good picture. 曝光百分之一秒就够了. ○ *How many exposures have you got left?* ie How many pictures remain on the camera film? 还剩下多少张底片没照? **4** [U] publicity (on television, in newspapers, etc)（电视、报纸等上的）宣传: *Her new film has had a lot of exposure on television recently.* 她的新影片最近在电视上做了大量宣传.

□ **ex'posure meter** (also **light meter**) device to measure illumination and to indicate how long a film should be exposed to light 曝光表.

ex·pound /ɪk'spaʊnd; ɪk'spaʊnd/ *v* [Tn, Tn·pr] ~ **sth (to sb)** (*fml* 文) explain or make sth clear by giving details 详加解释或详述某事物: *expound a theory* 详细解释一理论 ○ *He expounded his views on education to me at great length.* 他向我详细讲述了他的教育观点.

ex·press[1] /ɪk'spres; ɪk'sprɛs/ *adj* [attrib 作定语] **1** going, sent or delivered quickly（进行、传递或运送）迅速的: *express delivery* 快递 ○ *an express letter* 快信 ○ *an express messenger* 传送快件的信差. **2** clearly and definitely stated; explicit 清楚的; 明确的: *It was his express wish that you have his gold watch after he died.* 他的愿望很明确, 死后把金表留给你.

▷ **ex·press** *adv* by express delivery; by express train 用快邮递送; 乘快车: *The parcel was sent express.* 这包裹是用快邮寄的. ○ *travel express* 乘快车旅行.

ex·pressly *adv* **1** clearly; definitely 清楚地; 明确地: *You were expressly told not to touch my papers.* 已经明确地告诉过你不要动我的文件. **2** with a special purpose 特地; 专门: *a dictionary expressly compiled for foreign students of English* 专为学习英语的外国学生编纂的词典.

□ **ex'pressway** (also **'throughway**) *n* (*US*) = MOTORWAY: *a major accident on the expressway* 高速公路上的严重车祸. ⇨Usage at ROAD 用法见 ROAD.

ex·press[2] /ɪk'spres; ɪk'sprɛs/ *n* **1** [C] (also **ex'press train**) fast train that stops at few stations 快车: *the 8.00 am express to Edinburgh* 早上8点开往爱丁堡的快车. **2** [C] (*US*) company that delivers goods quickly 捷运公司. **3** [U] service provided by the post office, railways, road services, etc for carrying goods quickly（邮局、铁路、公路等部门提供的）快邮, 速递, 速运: *send goods by express* 特快货运.

ex·press[3] /ɪk'spres; ɪk'sprɛs/ *v* **1** [Tn, Tw, Dn·pr, Dpr·w] ~ **sth (to sb)** show or make known (a feeling, an opinion, etc) by words, looks, actions, etc（用语言、神色、动作等）表示或表达(感情、意见等): *The guests expressed their thanks before leaving.* 客人们临走前表示了谢意. ○ *His actions express his love more than any words could do.* 他用行动表示的爱胜过任何言语. ○ *He could not express his feelings of sadness to his mother.* 他不能向母亲表露出内心的悲痛. ○ *I can't express to you how grateful I am for your help.* 你对我的帮助, 我感激不尽. **2** [Tn] ~ **oneself** speak or write (clearly) what one thinks, feels, etc（清楚地）表达自己的意思: *Learning to express oneself well is an important part of education.* 学会把意思表达清楚是受教育的一个重要方面. ○ *He is still unable to express himself in English.* 他仍然不能用英语表达自己的意思. **3** [Tn, Tn·pr] ~ **sth (from/out of sth)** (*fml* 文) press or squeeze out (esp juices or oil) 压出或榨出(尤指汁液或油): *juice expressed from grapes* 自葡萄榨出的汁 ○ *milk expressed from a mother's breast* 从母亲乳房里挤出的乳汁. **4** [Tn] (*Brit*) send (a letter, parcel, etc) fast by special delivery 用快邮寄出(信、邮包等).

ex·pres·sion /ɪk'spreʃn; ɪk'sprɛʃən/ *n* **1** (**a**) [U] action or process of expressing (EXPRESS[3] 1) 表示; 表达: *She gave expression to her sadness*, ie said or showed how sad she was. 她流露出了悲伤之情. ○ *The school encourages free expression in art, drama and creative writing.* 学校鼓励师生在艺术、戏剧和文学创作上自由发挥. ○ *The scenery was beautiful beyond expression*, ie too beautiful to describe. 那景色妙不可言. ○ *The poet's anger finds expression* (ie a means of expressing itself) *in the last line of the poem.* 诗人在诗中最后一行把愤怒宣泄出来. (**b**) [C] (*fml* 文) instance or example of this 表示; 表达: *expressions of welcome to the queen* 对女王欢迎的表示 ○ *They greeted the president with many expressions of pleasure.* 他们兴高采烈地欢迎总统. **2** [C] look on a person's face that shows a mood or feeling 神色; 表情: *a happy expression* 愉快的神情 ○ *'I don't understand,' he said, with an expression of complete surprise (on his face).* '我不明白,'他说时(脸上)显出惊讶的神色. **3** [U] showing feeling for the meaning when playing music or speaking（演奏乐曲或说话时流露出的）感情: *recite a poem with expression* 带感情地朗读诗歌 ○ *She puts great expression into her violin playing.* 她的小提琴演奏感情充沛. **4** [C] word or phrase 词; 词语: *'Shut up' (meaning 'Stop talking') is not a polite expression.* '闭嘴'(意为'别说话')不是礼貌用语. ○ *slang expressions* 俚语. **5** [C] (*mathematics* 数) group of symbols expressing a quantity 式; 表达式: *$3xy^2$ is a mathematical expression.* $3xy^2$ 是数学式.

▷ **ex·pres·sion·less** *adj* not showing feelings, thoughts, etc（对感情、思想等）不流露的; 没有表情的; 呆板的: *an expressionless face, voice, tone, etc* 呆板的面孔、冷冰冰的声音、平淡的声调等 ○ *His recitation was almost expressionless.* 他的朗诵几乎毫无感情.

ex·pres·sion·ism /ɪk'spreʃənɪzəm; ɪk'sprɛʃənˌɪzəm/ *n* [U] style of painting, music, drama, film, etc which tries to express the artist's or writer's emotional experience rather than to show the physical world in a realistic way 表现主义. ▷ **ex·pres·sion·ist** /-ʃənɪst; -ʃənɪst/ *adj, n*: *of the expressionist school* 表现主义流派的 ○ *an expressionist film* 表现主义流派的影片 ○ *He's an expressionist.* 他是表现主义者.

ex·press·ive /ɪk'spresɪv; ɪk'sprɛsɪv/ *adj* **1** showing one's feelings or thoughts 表现感情或思想的; 富有表情的: *an expressive face, gesture* 富有表情的脸、姿势 ○ *an expressive piece of music* 抒情的乐曲. **2** [pred 作表语] ~ **of sth** (*fml* 文) expressing sth 表示或表达某事物: *a cry expressive of pain* 表示痛苦的呼叫 ○ *a look expressive of despair* 表示绝望的神情. ▷ **ex·press·ively** *adv*: *He reads his poems very expressively.* 他朗诵自己的诗感情充

沛. **ex·press·ive·ness** *n* [U].

ex·propri·ate /eks'prəʊprɪeɪt; ɛks'proprɪ,et/ *v* [Tn, Tn·pr] (*fml or law* 文或律) **1 ~ sth (from sb)** (**a**) take away (property, etc) for public use without payment to the owner 征用, 没收(财产等): *The new government expropriated his estate for military purposes.* 新政府将他的地产征作军用. (**b**) **~ sb (of sth)** dispossess sb in this way (以征用或没收的方式)剥夺某人的(财产等的)所有权: *She was expropriated (of her land).* 她的(土地的)所有权已遭剥夺. **2 ~ sth (from sb/sth)** take away (property, money, etc) illegally from the owners for one's own use (非法从物主处)取走(财物等)据为己有: *He expropriated the jewels from the bank's safe.* 他非法将他人的珠宝从银行保险箱中取走. ▷ **ex·pro·pri·ation** /ˌeksˌprəʊprɪ'eɪʃn; ɛksˌproprɪ'eʃən/ *n* [U, C].

ex·pul·sion /ɪk'spʌlʃn; ɪk'spʌlʃən/ *n* **~ (from ...)** **1** [U] action of expelling or being expelled 驱逐; 开除: *Expulsion from school is a harsh form of punishment.* 开除学籍是严厉的惩罚. ○ [attrib 作定语] *an expulsion order*, ie an official order expelling a person from a country 驱逐出境令. **2** [C] instance of this 驱逐; 开除: *There have been three expulsions from the school this year.* 今年学校已开除了三名学生.

ex·punge /ɪk'spʌndʒ; ɪk'spʌndʒ/ *v* [Tn, Tn·pr] **~ sth (from sth)** (*fml* 文) remove or wipe out (words, names, etc) from a list, book, etc (从名单、书等上)除去、删除或擦掉(词语、名字等): *Her name was expunged from the list.* 她的名字已从名册上除掉. ○ (*fig* 比喻) *He could not expunge the incident from his memory.* 他无法忘掉这件事.

ex·purg·ate /'ekspəgeɪt; 'ɛkspɚˌget/ *v* [Tn] remove (what are considered to be) improper or objectionable parts from (a book, etc) 从(书等中)删除(被认为)不当或令人反感的部分: *an expurgated edition of a novel* 一部小说的洁本. ▷ **ex·purga·tion** /ˌekspə'geɪʃn; ˌɛkspɚ'geʃən/ *n* [C, U].

ex·quis·ite /'ekskwɪzɪt, *also* ɪk'skwɪzɪt; 'ɛkskwɪzɪt, ɪk'skwɪzɪt/ *adj* **1** extremely beautiful or delicate; finely or skilfully made or done 优美的; 优雅的; 精致的; 制作精良的: *(an) exquisite painting* 极漂亮的画 ○ *exquisite workmanship* 精致的工艺 ○ *an exquisite piece of lace* 精美的花边. **2** (*fml* 文) (**a**) (of emotion) strongly felt; acute (指感情)感觉强烈的; 剧烈的: *exquisite joy, happiness, etc* 极大的愉快、幸福等 ○ *exquisite pain, agony, etc* 剧烈的疼痛、痛苦等. (**b**) (of power to feel) delicate; sensitive (指感觉、感受)敏锐的, 敏感的: *exquisite taste* 高尚的趣味 ○ *exquisite sensibility* 细腻的感情. ▷ **ex·quis·itely** *adv*. **ex·quis·ite·ness** *n* [U].

ex-service /ˌeks'sɜːvɪs; 'ɛks'sɝvɪs/ *adj* formerly belonging to the armed forces 退役的; 退伍的.

□ **ex-serviceman** /-mən; -mən/ (*pl* **-men** /-mən; -mən/), **ex-servicewoman** /-wʊmən; -ˌwʊmən/ (*pl* **-women** /-wɪmɪn; -ˌwɪmɪn/) *n* (*esp Brit*) person who was formerly in one of the armed services 退伍军人; 复员军人: *an ex-servicemen's organization* 退伍军人协会.

ext *abbr* 缩写 = **1** exterior; external. Cf 参看 INT 1. **2** extension (number) (eg of a telephone) 电话分机(号码): *ext 4299* 分机号码 4299.

ex·tant /ek'stænt; *US* 'ekstənt; 'ɛkstənt/ *adj* (esp of documents, etc) still in existence (尤指文件等)仍然存在的, 现存的: *the earliest extant manuscript of this poem* 此诗现存最早的原稿 ○ *an ancient but extant law* 一古老的但仍然有效的法律.

ex·tem·por·an·eous /ekˌstempə'reɪnɪəs; ɛkˌstɛmpə'renɪəs/ *adj* (*fml* 文) spoken or done without preparation; extempore 即席的; 无准备的. ▷ **ex·tem·por·an·eously** *adv*.

ex·tem·pore /ek'stempərɪ; ɪk'stɛmpərɪ/ *adj, adv* (spoken or done) without previous thought or preparation; impromptu 无准备的; 即席的: *an extempore speech* 即席讲话 ○ *speak extempore*, ie without notes 即席发言.

▷ **ex·tem·por·ize, -ise** /ɪk'stempəraɪz; ɪk'stɛmpəˌraɪz/ *v* [I] (*fml* 文) speak or perform extempore 即席讲话; 即兴表演: *He had to extemporize because he had forgotten to bring his notes.* 他因为忘了带讲稿, 只好即席发言. **ex·tem·por·iza·tion, -isation** /ɪkˌstempəraɪ'zeɪʃn; *US* -rɪ'z; ɪkˌstɛmpərə'zeʃən/ *n* [U, C].

ex·tend /ɪk'stend; ɪk'stɛnd/ *v* **1** [Tn] make (sth) longer or larger (in space or time) 使(某物)(在空间或时间上)更大, 更长, 伸长, 延长, 延展: *extend a fence, wall, railway, garden* 扩建篱笆、墙、铁路、花园 ○ *extend credit*, ie prolong the time for payment of a debt 延长信用期限 ○ *Can you extend your visit a few days longer?* 你能多停留几天吗? **2** [Tn, Tn·pr] lay or stretch out (the body or a limb) at full length 伸展, 舒展(肢体): *The gymnast extended her arms horizontally.* 那女子体操运动员双臂平伸. ○ *The bird extended its wings in flight.* 那鸟展翅飞翔. ○ *He extended his hand to* (ie offered to shake hands with) *the new employee.* 他主动与新雇员握手. **3** [Tn, Dn·n, Dn·pr] **~ sth (to sb)** offer or give sth 提供或给予某事物: *They extended the Queen a warm welcome.* 他们热烈欢迎女王. ○ *extend hospitality, an invitation, a greeting to sb* 款待、邀请、问候某人 ○ *They extended a warm welcome to her.* 他们向她表示热烈欢迎. **4** [In/pr] (of space, land, time, etc) reach or stretch; be continuous (指空间、土地、时间等)达到, 伸展, 伸延: *The road extends for miles and miles.* 这条路向远处绵延伸展. ○ *My garden extends as far as the river.* 我的花园一直伸展到河边. **5** [Tn, Tn·pr] cause (sth) to reach or stretch 使(某物)达到或伸展: *extend the ladder* 将梯子伸长 ○ *extend a cable between two posts* 在两根柱子间拉一条缆绳. **6** [Tn esp passive 尤用于被动语态] use or stretch the abilities or powers of (oneself, a person or an animal) to the greatest possible degree 使(自己、某人或某动物)竭尽全力: *Jim didn't really have to extend himself in the examination.* 吉姆这次考试大可不必那么拼命. ○ *The horse was fully extended by the long ride up the mountain.* 那匹马长途爬山已用尽力气了.

□ **extended 'family** family structure (as in parts of Africa) where uncles, aunts and cousins are regarded as close relatives, with an obligation to help and support each other 大家庭(数代同堂的家庭).

ex·ten·sion /ɪk'stenʃn; ɪk'stɛnʃən/ *n* **1** [U] process or action of extending (EXTEND 1,2,3); state of being extended 伸长; 延长; 延展; 伸展; 提供; 给予: *The extension of the garden will take several weeks.* 扩建花园需要几个星期. ○ *the extension of scientific knowledge* 科学知识的普及 ○ *the extension of a warm welcome* 给予热烈的欢迎. **2** [C] (**a**) **~ (to sth)** added part; addition; enlargement 增加的部分; 增加; 扩大: *build an extension to a hospital* 扩建一医院 ○ *Our extension is nearly finished.* 我们的扩建部分已接近完工. (**b**) **~ (of sth)** additional period of time 增加的一段时间; 延长期: *an extension of one's summer holidays* 暑假的延长 ○ *get an extension (of time)*, eg for paying a debt 获得延期(如偿债的宽限期) ○ *He's got an extension to finish writing his thesis.* 他获准延期交论文. **3** [C] telephone line leading from the main phone or switchboard to another room or office in a (large) building; its number 电话分机; 分机号码: *There are telephone extensions in every office.* 每间办公室都有电话分机. ○ *She has an extension in the kitchen and in the bedroom.* 她的厨房和卧室都有电话分机. ○ *'Extension 326, please.'* '请接326号分机.' **4** [U] (*medical or fml* 医或文) (**a**) action of stretching out a limb or finger (四肢或手指的)伸展: *Extension of the injured arm was painful.* 把受伤的胳膊伸展开是很疼的. (**b**) its position when stretched out 伸展开的姿势: *The leg is now at full extension.* 现在腿已伸直.

ex·tens·ive /ɪk'stensɪv; ɪk'stɛnsɪv/ *adj* **1** large in area; extending far 广大的; 广阔的: *an extensive view* 广阔的视野 ○ *extensive farming* 粗放的耕作 ○ *the extensive grounds of a country house* 农舍的宽敞庭院. **2** large in amount; wide-ranging 大量的; 广泛的: *extensive alterations to a building* 对一建筑物大规模的改建 ○ *Her knowledge of the subject is extensive.* 她这方面的学识很渊博. ▷ **ex·tens·ively** *adv*: *He has travelled extensively in Europe.* 他遍游欧洲各地. **ex·tens·ive·ness** *n* [U] (*fml* 文): *The extensiveness of his knowledge surprised them.* 他知识广博使他们很惊奇.

ex·tent /ɪk'stent; ɪk'stɛnt/ *n* **1** [U] length; area; range 长度; 面积; 范围: *From the roof we could see the full extent of the park.* 我们从屋顶可以一览公园的全景. ○ *I was amazed at the extent of his knowledge.* 我对他知识的渊博感到惊奇. ○ *The new race track is nearly six miles in extent.* 这条新跑道将近六英里长. **2** (idm 习语) **to**

E

some, what, such an, a certain, etc extent to the degree specified 达到某程度: *To some extent you are correct.* 在某种程度上你是正确的. ○ *To what extent can he be believed?* 可以相信他到什么程度? ○ *The carpet was badly stained, to such an extent that* (ie so much that) *you couldn't tell its original colour.* 这块地毯已经脏得辨认不出原来的颜色了. ○ *I agree with you to a certain extent, but...* 我在一定程度上同意你的意见, 但... ○ *He's in debt to the extent of £200.* 他负债达200英镑.

ex·tenu·ate /ɪk'stenjʊeɪt; ɪk`stɛnjʊ,et/ *v* [Tn] (*fml esp law* 文, 尤用于法律) make (wrongdoing) less serious (by providing an excuse) (提出借口或理由)使(罪过)的严重性减轻: *Nothing can extenuate such appalling behaviour.* 这种骇人听闻的行径罪无可恕. ○ *Because of extenuating circumstances* (ie facts taken into consideration that might be regarded as an excuse), *the court acquitted him of the crime.* 因考虑到情有可原, 法庭判他无罪.

▷ **ex·tenu·ation** /ɪk,stenjʊ'eɪʃn; ɪk,stɛnjʊ`eʃən/ *n* (*fml* 文) [U] action of extenuating; being extenuated 减轻罪责: *He pleaded poverty in extenuation of* (ie as an excuse for) *the theft.* 他以贫穷为借口请求为他犯的偷窃罪从轻量刑.

ex·ter·ior /ɪk'stɪərɪə(r); ɪk`stɪrɪɚ/ *adj* [usu attrib 通常作定语] on or coming from the outside; outer 外部的; 外来的; 外出的; 外面的; 外表的; 外界的: *paint the exterior walls of a house* 给房子的外墙刷油漆 ○ *exterior features of a building* 建筑物的外观. Cf 参看 INTERIOR.

▷ **ex·ter·ior** *n* **1** [sing] outward appearance or surface; outside 外貌; 外表; 外面; 外部: *The exterior of the building is very unattractive.* 这建筑物的外观很不起眼. ○ *a gentle man with a rough exterior* 外貌粗拙而性情温和的男子. **2** [C] scene set outside in a painting or play (绘画或戏剧的)外景.

ex·term·in·ate /ɪk'stɜːmɪneɪt; ɪk`stɝmə,net/ *v* [Tn] destroy completely (a race or group of people or animals); wipe out 彻底毁灭(一种族、一群人或动物); 消灭; 根除; 灭绝: *exterminate all the inhabitants of the village* 灭绝村中所有的生灵 ○ *exterminate rats to prevent the spread of disease* 为防止疾病传播而灭鼠.

▷ **ex·term·ina·tion** /ɪk,stɜːmɪ'neɪʃn; ɪks,tɝmə`neʃən/ *n* [U].

ex·ternal /ɪk'stɜːnl; ɪk`stɝnl/ *adj* **1** (of or for the) outside; situated on the outside of sth (esp the body) 外面的; 为外面的; 位于某物(尤指身体)外表的: *for external use only*, eg on a label on a skin cream 仅供外用(如皮肤膏的标记) ○ *All his injuries are external*, ie He hasn't been injured inside the body. 他受的伤都是外伤. **2** coming from outside (a place, sb's mind, etc) 来自(某地、某人思想意识等)外部的: *a tribe hardly affected by external influences* 几乎没受过外来影响的部落 ○ *This news programme only covers external events*, ie foreign news. 这一新闻节目只报道国外消息. Cf 参看 INTERNAL.

▷ **ex·ternal** *n* **1** [C] (*infml* 口) = EXTERNAL EXAMINER. **2 ex·tern·als** [pl] (*fml* 文) outward features or appearances 外观; 外貌: *Do not judge people by externals alone.* 不能仅以貌取人. ○ *the externals of religion*, ie acts and ceremonies (contrasted with inner and spiritual aspects) 宗教的外在形式(宗教行为和仪式, 区别于内在的和精神的方面).

ex·tern·al·ize, -ise /-nəlaɪz; -nl,aɪz/ *v* [Tn] (*fml* 文) make (sth) external 使(某事物)表面化: *externalize one's thoughts, emotions, etc* 使思想、感情等表露出来.

ex·tern·ally /ɪk'stɜːnəlɪ; ɪk`stɝnlɪ/ *adv*.

□ **ex,ternal 'evidence** evidence obtained from independent sources, not from what is being examined 外证.

ex,ternal exami'nation examination arranged by authorities outside the school, college, etc of the person(s) taking the examination 校外考试(由校外专家前来主持的考试).

ex,ternal e'xaminer (also **external**) person who conducts an external examination 校外主考人.

ex·tinct /ɪk'stɪŋkt; ɪk`stɪŋkt/ *adj* **1** (esp of a type of animal, etc) no longer in existence (尤指某种动物等)不再存在的; 绝种的; 灭绝的: *an extinct species* 已灭绝的物种 ○ *If we continue to destroy the countryside many more animals will become extinct.* 我们若继续破坏自然环境, 将会有更多的动物绝种. **2** (**a**) (of a volcano) no longer active (指火山)不再活跃的, 熄灭的, 死的. (**b**) (*fig rhet* 比喻, 修辞) (of feelings, beliefs, etc) dead (指感情、信仰等)消逝的, 破灭的: *Nothing could rekindle her extinct passion.* 她激情已逝, 无从心回意转.

ex·tinc·tion /ɪk'stɪŋkʃn; ɪk`stɪŋkʃən/ *n* [U] **1** action of making extinct; state of being extinct 灭绝; 绝种: *We may live to see the extinction of the whale.* 人类或许能亲眼见到鲸的灭绝. ○ *a tribe threatened by/with extinction* 受到绝种威胁的部落. **2** (*fml* 文) act of extinguishing 熄灭: *the extinction of a fire, a political movement, youthful hopes* 火的熄灭、政治运动的平息、青年人希望的幻灭.

ex·tin·guish /ɪk'stɪŋgwɪʃ; ɪk`stɪŋgwɪʃ/ *v* [Tn] **1** (**a**) cause (sth) to stop burning; put out 使(某物)熄灭; 扑灭: *Please extinguish your cigarettes.* 请将香烟熄灭. ○ *They tried to extinguish the flames.* 他们竭力要把火焰扑灭. (**b**) (*fig fml* 比喻, 文) end the existence of (hope, love, passion, etc) 使(希望、爱情、激情等)不复存在: *His behaviour extinguished the last traces of affection she had for him.* 他的这种行为使她对他的最后一丝爱慕之情荡然无存. **2** clear or pay off (a debt) 清偿(债务).

▷ **ex·ting·uisher** = FIRE EXTINGUISHER (FIRE).

ex·tirp·ate /'ekstəpeɪt; `ɛkstɚ,pet/ *v* [Tn] (*fml* 文) remove or destroy (sth) completely 根除或铲除(某事物): *extirpate social evils* 根除社会弊端 ○ *extirpate dissent, opposition, etc* 清除异端、对立面等. ▷ **ex·tirpa·tion** /,ekstə'peɪʃn; ,ɛkstɚ`peʃən/ *n* [U].

ex·tol /ɪk'stəʊl; ɪk`stol/ *v* (**-ll-**) [Tn, Tn·pr, Cn·n/a] **~sb (as sth)** (*fml* 文) praise (sb/sth) highly 赞颂, 颂扬(某人[某事物]): *extol the merits of small businesses* 赞扬小企业的优点 ○ *extol sb's virtues to the skies*, ie greatly 把某人的美德捧上天 ○ *extol sb as a hero* 把某人当作英雄来歌颂.

ex·tort /ɪk'stɔːt; ɪk`stɔrt/ *v* [Tn, Tn·pr] **~ sth (from sb)** obtain sth by violence, threats, etc 强夺; 强抢; 勒索; 敲诈: *extort money from sb* 勒索某人的金钱 ○ *The police used torture to extort a confession from him.* 警方对他严刑逼供.

▷ **ex·tor·tion** /ɪk'stɔːʃn; ɪk`stɔrʃən/ *n* **1** [U] action of extorting 强夺; 强抢; 勒索; 敲诈: *obtain money by extortion* 勒索金钱. **2** [C] instance of this 强夺; 强抢; 勒索; 敲诈. **ex·tor·tioner** /-ʃənə(r); -ʃənɚ/, **ex·tor·tion·ist** /-ʃənɪst; -ʃənɪst/ *ns* person who extorts 强夺者; 强抢者; 勒索者; 敲诈者: [attrib 作定语] *extortionist methods* 敲诈勒索的手段.

ex·tor·tion·ate /ɪk'stɔːʃənət; ɪk`stɔrʃənɪt/ *adj* (*derog* 贬) (of demands, prices) much too great or high; excessive (指要求、价格)过大的, 过高的, 过多的, 过分的: *The prices in this shop are extortionate.* 这家商店价格过高. ○ *They are asking an extortionate amount of money for their house.* 他们的房子要价太高. ▷ **ex·tor·tion·ately** *adv*: *They charged me extortionately for a simple job.* 他们为一件简单的工作敲我竹杠.

ex·tra /'ekstrə; `ɛkstrə/ *adj* more than or beyond what is usual, expected or necessary; additional 额外的; 外加的; 附加的: *extra pay for extra work* 额外工作的额外报酬 ○ *buy an extra pint of milk* 再买一品脱牛奶 ○ *The bus company provided extra buses because there were so many people.* 因为人太多, 公共汽车公司派出了加车. ○ *The football match went into extra time*, eg because of injury to players or a drawn score. 这场足球赛进入加时赛(如因运动员受伤或因比分持平).

▷ **ex·tra** *adv* **1** more than usually 超过一般地; 特别地; 格外; 分外: *an extra strong box* 加固的箱子 ○ *extra fine quality* 特别好的质量. **2** in addition 额外; 外加; 除外: *20% extra* 外加20% ○ *price £1.30, packing and postage extra* 价格1.30英镑, 包装和邮费另计.

ex·tra *n* **1** extra thing; thing that costs extra 额外的事物; 另外收费的事物: *Her school fees are £440 a term; music and dancing are extras.* 她的学费是每学期440英镑, 音乐和舞蹈课另外收费. **2** (in cinema, TV, etc) person employed and paid (usu by the day) for a minor part, eg in a crowd scene (电影、电视等的)临时演员(如扮演群众者): *We need hundreds of extras for the battle scenes.* 我们拍战斗场面需要上百的临时演员. **3** (in cricket) run scored otherwise than from a hit by the bat (板球的)额外得分(非击球所得的分). **4** special edition of a newspaper containing special or later news (报纸的)号外: *a late night extra* 晚间号外.

extra- *pref* 前缀 (with *adjs* 与形容词连用) **1** outside; beyond 在…之外; 越出; 超出: *extramarital* ○ *extrasensory*. **2** very; to an exceptional degree 非常; 格外: *extra-thin* ○ *extra-sensitive*.

ex·tract /ɪk'strækt; ɪk`strækt/ *v* [Tn, Tn·pr] **~ sth (from sb/sth) 1 (a)** take or get sth out, usu with effort or by force 取出; 拔出: *extract a cork from a bottle* 拔出瓶塞 ○ *have a tooth extracted* 拔牙. **(b)** obtain (money, information, etc) usu from a person unwilling to give it 获取(钱、消息等)(通常指获自不愿给予者); 强索: *extract a contribution from everyone* 硬要大家捐献 ○ *The police finally extracted the information after hours of questioning.* 警方经数小时盘问, 终于套得这一情报. ○ *It took me days to extract the truth from her.* 我用了几天时间才从她那儿打探出事实真相. **2** obtain (juices, etc) by crushing, pressing, etc 压出, 榨出(汁液等): *extract juice from oranges* 榨出橙子汁 ○ *extract oil from olives, sunflower seeds, etc* 榨出橄榄、葵花籽等的油. **3** select and present (passages, examples, words, etc) from a book, speech, etc 从书、讲话等中选取(段落, 例子, 词句等); 摘录; 选录: *poems extracted from a modern collection* 由一本当代诗集中摘选的诗篇 ○ *She extracted passages for the students to translate.* 她选了些短文让学生翻译.

▷ **ex·tract** /'ekstrækt; `ɛkstrækt/ *n* **1** [U, C] substance that has been extracted (EXTRACT 2) and concentrated 榨出物; 浓缩物; 精; 汁: *beef extract* 浓缩的牛肉汁 ○ *extract of malt* 麦芽精 ○ *yeast extract*, ie a savoury spread 酵母萃. **2** [C] passage selected (from a poem, book, film, piece of music, etc) (从诗歌、书、电影、乐曲等)精选的段落; 摘录; 选录; 选曲: *a short extract from a piano sonata* 钢琴奏鸣曲的选曲 ○ *an extract from a long poem* 长诗选萃 ○ *She read out extracts from his letters.* 她从他的信中挑了几段念出.

ex·trac·tion /ɪk'strækʃn; ɪk`strækʃən/ *n* **1 (a)** [U] action of extracting (EXTRACT 1a) 取出; 拔出; 强索: *the extraction of a tooth* 拔牙 ○ *the extraction of financial contributions* 硬性摊派捐款 ○ *the extraction of information* 打探消息 ○ [attrib 作定语] *an extraction process at a diamond mine* 钻石矿的开采过程. **(b)** [C] instance of extracting a tooth 拔牙: *He needs two extractions.* 他需要拔掉两颗牙齿. **2** [U] (*fml* 文) descent; parentage 血统; 出身; 家世: *an American of Hungarian extraction* 匈牙利血统的美国人.

ex·tractor /ɪk'stræktə(r); ɪk`stræktɚ/ *n* person or device that extracts (EXTRACT 2) (压榨汁液等的)人或装置; 榨取者; 榨汁机; 榨油机: *He makes fresh orange juice with an electric extractor.* 他用电动榨汁机榨取新鲜的橙汁. **ex'tractor fan** ventilator fan (in a kitchen, etc) for removing bad smells, etc (厨房等的)抽风扇, 排风扇. ⇨illus at FAN 见 FAN 之插图.

extra-curricular /ˌekstrəkə'rɪkjələ(r); ˌɛkstrəkə`rɪkjəlɚ/ *adj* [usu attrib 通常作定语] outside the regular course of work or studies at a school or college 课外的: *She's involved in many extra-curricular activities, such as music, sport and drama.* 她参加了许多课外活动, 如音乐、运动、戏剧.

ex·tra·dite /'ekstrədaɪt; `ɛkstrəˌdaɪt/ *v* [Tn] **1** give up or send back (sb accused or convicted of a crime) to the country where the crime was (said to be) committed 引渡(被告或罪犯): *The Spanish police have refused to extradite a man wanted for a bank robbery in France.* 西班牙警方拒绝引渡一个在法国抢劫银行而被通缉的人. **2** obtain (such a person) for trial or punishment 获得(被告或罪犯)的引渡. ▷ **ex·tra·di·tion** /ˌekstrə'dɪʃn; ˌɛkstrə`dɪʃən/ *n* [C, U]: *the extradition of war criminals* 对战犯的引渡.

extra-marital /ˌekstrə'mærɪtl; ˌɛkstrə`mærətl̩/ *adj* of (a married person's) sexual relationships outside marriage 婚外的: *have extra-marital relations with sb* 与某人有婚外的性关系 ○ *extra-marital affairs* 婚外的风流韵事.

ex·tra·mural /ˌekstrə'mjʊərəl; ˌɛkstrə`mjʊrəl/ *adj* [usu attrib 通常作定语] **1** (of university teaching, courses, etc) for people who are not full-time residential members of a university (指大学教学、课程等)为校外学生的: *extramural studies, lectures, courses, students* 大学校外课程的学习、大学校外课程的授课、大学的校外课程、大学校外课程部的学生 ○ *the extramural department of a university* 大学的校外课程部. **2** (of work, etc) not done as part of one's official (paid) duties (指工作等)业余的: *on an extramural basis* 在业余的基础上.

ex·trane·ous /ɪk'streɪnɪəs; ɪk`strenɪəs/ *adj* **~ (to sth) 1** not belonging to or directly connected with the subject or matter being dealt with 与正题无关的: *extraneous information* 无关的消息 ○ *extraneous material in a book* 书中的题外资料. **2** coming from outside 来自外部的; 外来的: *extraneous interference* 外来的干涉.

ex·tra·ord·in·ary /ɪk'strɔːdnrɪ; *US* -dənerɪ; ɪk`strɔrdn̩ˌɛrɪ/ *adj* **1** beyond what is ordinary; very unusual; remarkable 不平常的; 不普通的; 非常的; 格外的: *Her talents are quite extraordinary.* 她才华出众. ○ *extraordinary weather for the time of year* 一年中某段时间的反常天气 ○ *an extraordinary film about a highly gifted child* 关于一个天赋极高的孩子的出色影片. **2** [attrib 作定语] (*fml* 文) (of arrangements, meetings, etc) additional to what is usual or ordinary (指安排、会议等)特别的: *an extraordinary general meeting* 特别全会. **3** (used immediately after a *n* 紧接名词之后) (*fml* 文) (of an official) specially employed; additional to the usual one (指官员)特命的, 特派的: *envoy/ambassador extraordinary* 特使[特派大使]. ▷ **ex·tra·ord·in·ar·ily** /ɪk'strɔːdnrəlɪ; *US* -dənerəlɪ; ɪk`strɔrdn̩ˌɛrəlɪ/ *adv*: *extraordinarily beautiful, thoughtful, rude* 特别美丽的、周到的、粗野的.

ex·tra·pol·ate /ɪk'stræpəleɪt; ɪk`stræpəˌlet/ *v* [Tn, Tn·pr] **~ sth (from sth)** (*fml* 文) **1** (*mathematics* 数) calculate (an unknown quantity) approximately from known values or measurements (从已知的值或量)推算出(未知的量); 外推. **2** estimate (sth unknown) from facts that are already known 由已知事实估计(未知事物); 推断; 推知: *One can extrapolate the size of the building from the measurements of an average room.* 从一间屋子的量度可以推断出整座建筑物的大小. ▷ **ex·tra·pola·tion** /ɪkˌstræpə'leɪʃn; ɪkˌstræpə`leʃən/ *n* [U] **~ (from sth)** (*fml* 文): *He estimated his income tax bill by extrapolation from figures submitted in previous years.* 他从前几年的报税数字推算出自己应缴的所得税数额. ⇨illus at CHART 见 CHART 之插图.

extra-sensory per·cep·tion /ˌekstrəˌsensərɪ pə'sepʃn; ˌɛkstrə ˌsɛnsərɪ pɚ`sɛpʃən/ (*abbr* 缩写 **ESP**) (supposed) ability to perceive outside, past or future events without the use of the known senses 超感官知觉; 超感觉力: *He seems to know when his wife is away from home by some kind of extra-sensory perception.* 他凭某种超感觉力似乎知道妻子何时不在家.

ex·tra·ter·res·trial /ˌekstrətə'restrɪəl; ˌɛkstrətə`rɛstrɪəl/ *adj* of or from outside the earth and its atmosphere 地球和大气层外的; 来自天外的: *extraterrestrial life, beings, forces* 地球外的生命、生物、力量.

ex·tra·ter·rit·or·ial /ˌekstrəˌterɪ'tɔːrɪəl; ˌɛkstrəˌtɛrə`tɔrɪəl/ (also **ex·terri·tor·ial** /eksˌterɪ'tɔːrɪəl; ˌɛkstɛrɪ`tɔrɪəl/) *adj* (*fml* 文) (of an ambassador, etc) free from the laws of the country in which one lives (指大使等)不受所在国法律约束的, 治外法权的: *extraterritorial rights and privileges* 治外法权及其特权.

ex·tra·vag·ant /ɪk'strævəgənt; ɪk`strævəgənt/ *adj* **1** (in the habit of) using or spending too much; (of actions) showing this tendency (惯于)奢侈的, 挥霍的; (指行为)放纵的: *an extravagant man* 挥霍无度的人 ○ *extravagant tastes and habits* 奢侈的嗜好和习惯 ○ *an extravagant use of natural resources* 自然资源的滥用. **2** (of ideas, speech or behaviour) going beyond what is reasonable, usual or necessary (指想法、言行)放肆的, 越轨的, 过度的: *extravagant praise, behaviour, claims* 过分的赞扬、放肆的行为、过高的要求 ○ *pay extravagant compliments* 过分夸奖.

▷ **ex·tra·vag·ance** /-gəns; -gəns/ *n* **1** [U] being extravagant(1) 奢侈; 挥霍: *His extravagance explains why he is always in debt.* 他挥霍无度, 难怪总欠债. **2** [C] extravagant thing, act, statement, etc 奢侈品; 放纵的言行等: *I do not regard books as extravagances.* 我认为书不是侈奢品.

ex·tra·vag·antly *adv*: *extravagantly dressed* 衣着奢侈.

ex·tra·vag·anza /ɪkˌstrævə'gænzə; ɪkˌstrævə`gænzə/ *n* entertainment with elaborate and colourful costumes, scenery, etc (带有华丽服装、场景等的)娱乐表演: *a costly musical extravaganza on television* 电视上播出的

大场面音乐节目.

ex·treme /ɪk'stri:m; ɪk'strim/ *adj* **1** [attrib 作定语] as far away as possible (esp from the centre or beginning); remote 尽可能远的(尤指距中心或起点); 遥远的; 久远的: *in the extreme north of a country* 在一国的最北部 ○ *the extreme edge of the forest* 森林最远的边缘 ○ *in extreme old age* 极高的年龄. **2** [usu attrib 通常作定语] of the highest degree or intensity; greatest possible 程度或强度最高的; 最大可能的; 极度的: *show extreme patience, kindness, gentleness, etc* 表现出极为耐心、和蔼、温柔等 ○ *in extreme pain* 在极度的痛苦中 ○ (*fml* 文) *The extreme penalty of the law in some countries is the death penalty.* 有些国家的极刑是死刑. **3** (*often derog* 常作贬义) (of people and their opinions) far from moderate (指人和意见)偏激的, 极端的: *hold extreme views* 持偏激观点 ○ *a supporter of the extreme left/right*, ie a person who supports political views extreme left/right 极左[右]政治观点的拥护者 ○ *His ideas are too extreme for me.* 我认为他的思想太偏激了.

▷ **ex·treme** *n* [C usu *pl* 通常作复数] **1** feeling, condition, etc as far apart or as different from another as possible 极端不同的感情、状况等: *the extremes of misery and bliss* 悲惨与极乐天壤之别的境遇 ○ *Love and hate are extremes of passion.* 爱与恨是感情的两个极端. ○ *He was once terribly shy but now he's gone to the opposite extreme.* 他以前特别腼腆, 可现在却判若两人. **2** greatest or highest degree; either end of anything 最大程度; 最高程度; 极端: *He could not tolerate the extremes of heat in the desert.* 他忍受不住沙漠的酷热. **3** (idm 习语) **go, etc to ex'tremes** act or be forced to act in a way that is far from moderate or normal 走极端: *In the jungle, they were driven to extremes in order to survive.* 在丛林中, 他们为了生存被迫采取极端行动. **in the ex'treme** (*fml* 文) to the highest degree; extremely 极端; 极度: *This is inconvenient in the extreme.* 这极不方便.

ex·tremely *adv* (with *adjs* and *advs* 与形容词和副词连用) to a very high degree 极端; 极其; 非常: *That's extremely interesting.* 那极为有趣. ○ *I'm extremely sorry for the delay.* 对此延误, 我深感抱歉.

ex·trem·ist *n* (*usu derog* 通常作贬义) person who holds extreme(3) views (esp in politics) (尤指政治上) 偏激的人, 极端主义者: *When it comes to talking about patriotism, he's an extremist.* 一谈到爱国主义, 他就很偏激. ○ [attrib 作定语] *extremist policies* 极端主义的政策.

ex·trem·ism *n* [U] holding of such views 极端主义: *The council was often accused of extremism.* 人们常抨击该委员会是极端主义. ○ *the extremism of some feminists* 有些女权主义者所持的极端主义观点.

ex·trem·ity /ɪk'streməti; ɪk'strɛməti/ *n* **1** (**a**) [C] (*fml* 文) furthest point, end or limit of sth 极端; 末端; 极限; 尽头: *the extremities of the world* 世界的尽头. (**b**) **extremities** [pl] furthest parts of the human body, eg hands and feet (人的)肢体(如手和足): *Cold affects the extremities first.* 手和脚最先感到寒冷. **2** [sing] (*fml* 文) extreme degree (esp of misery, suffering, etc); great misfortune or distress 极度(尤指悲惨、痛苦等); 极大的不幸或危难: *reach an extremity of despair* 绝望已极 ○ *How can we help them in their extremity?* 我们怎样帮助他们摆脱困境呢? **3** [C usu *pl* 通常作复数] (*fml* 文) exceptionally cruel or violent behaviour 极端残暴的行为: *Both armies were guilty of extremities.* 两军都犯有残暴的罪行.

ex·tric·ate /'ekstrɪkeɪt; 'ɛkstrɪ,ket/ *v* [Tn, Tn·pr] **~ sb/sth (from sth)** (*fml* 文) set sb/sth free; release sb/sth 解脱某人[某物]; 释放某人[某物]: *The bird had to be extricated from the netting.* 要把小鸟从网中救出. ○ *extricate oneself from an unhappy love affair* 使自己摆脱不快的爱情纠葛.

ex·trinsic /ek'strɪnsɪk; ɛk'strɪnsɪk/ *adj* **~ (to sth)** (*fml* 文) (of qualities, values, etc) not belonging to or part of the real nature of a person or thing; coming from outside (指性质、价值等)非固有的, 外来的, 外在的: *extrinsic facts* 非本质的事实 ○ *information extrinsic to the situation* 与局势无关的消息. Cf 参看 INTRINSIC.

ex·tro·vert /'ekstrəvɜ:t; 'ɛkstrə,vɝt/ *n* **1** person more interested in what is happening around him than in his own thoughts and emotions 性格外向的人; 性格外倾的人: *Extroverts prefer lively conversation to brooding on the meaning of life.* 性格外向的人喜欢高谈阔论, 而不愿思索人生的意义. **2** (*infml* 口) lively, cheerful and sociable person 活跃、愉快、爱交际的人: *She's a good person to invite to a party because she's such an extrovert.* 最好把她邀来参加聚会, 因为她很爱交际. ○ [attrib 作定语] *extrovert behaviour* 性格外向的举止. Cf 参看 INTROVERT.

▷ **ex·tro·ver·sion** /,ekstrə'vɜ:ʃn; *US* -'vɜ:rʒn; ,ɛkstrə'vɝʒən/ *n* [U] (*fml* 文) state of being extroverted 外向性; 外倾.

ex·trude /ɪk'stru:d; ɪk'strud/ *v* [Tn, Tn·pr] **~ sth (from sth)** (*fml* 文) **1** force or squeeze out sth under pressure 压出, 挤出, 逐出(某物): *extrude glue from a tube* 从管里挤出胶水. **2** shape (metal, plastic, etc) by forcing it through a die (通过模具)将(金属、塑料等)挤压成形: *nylon extruded as very thin fibres* 挤压而成的细尼龙纤维. ▷ **ex·tru·sion** /ɪk'stru:ʒn; ɪk'struʒən/ *n* [C, U] (*fml* 文).

ex·uber·ant /ɪg'zju:bərənt; *US* -'zu:-; ɪg'zubərənt/ *adj* **1** (esp of people and their behaviour) overflowing with happiness and excitement; very lively and cheerful (尤指人和行为)兴高采烈的, 活跃的, 愉快的: *exuberant children at a fair* 在游乐场上兴高采烈的儿童 ○ *She gave an exuberant account of the party.* 她生动地介绍了那一聚会的情形. **2** (of plants, etc) growing vigorously; luxuriant (指植物等)茁壮的, 茂盛的; 繁茂的: *plants with exuberant foliage* 枝叶扶疏的植物 ○ (*fig* 比喻) *an exuberant imagination* 丰富的想像力.

▷ **ex·uber·ance** /-rəns; -rəns/ *n* [U] state or quality of being exuberant 兴高采烈; 活跃; 愉快; 茁壮; 茂盛: *the natural exuberance of young children* 幼儿固有的活泼 ○ *The speaker's exuberance enlivened a boring conference.* 讲演者谈笑风生, 使死气沉沉的会议顿添生气.

ex·uber·antly *adv*.

ex·ude /ɪg'zju:d; *US* -'zu:d; ɪg'zud/ *v* **1** [I, Ipr, Tn, Tn·pr] (*fml* 文) **~ (sth) (from/through sth)** (of drops of liquid, etc) come or pass out slowly; ooze out (指液滴等)缓慢流出, 渗出, 分泌出: *Sweat exudes through the pores.* 汗从毛孔中渗出. ○ *The hot sun made him exude sweat.* 烈日晒得他汗流浃背. **2** [Tn, Tn·pr] give out or radiate an air or feeling of (sth) 流露出对(某事物)的神态或感情: *exude cheerfulness* 流露出愉快的神情 ○ *He exudes confidence and energy.* 他信心十足、精力充沛. ▷ **ex·uda·tion** /,eksju:'deɪʃn; *US* ,eksu:-; ,ɛksu'deʃən/ *n* [U] (*fml* 文).

ex·ult /ɪg'zʌlt; ɪg'zʌlt/ *v* (*fml* 文) [I, Ipr, It] **~ (at/in sth)** get great pleasure from sth; rejoice greatly 从某事物中获得巨大的快乐; 狂喜: *exult at her sister's success* 对她姐姐的成功欣喜若狂 ○ *He obviously exulted in winning.* 他获胜后喜形于色. ○ *exulting to find that one has succeeded* 对自己的成功欢欣鼓舞. ▷ **ex·ult·ant** /-ənt; -nt/ *adj* **~ (at sth)** exulting; triumphant 欢欣的; 狂喜的; 欢跃的: *an exultant shout of victory* 胜利的欢呼声 ○ *exultant at one's success* 为自己的成功而欢欣鼓舞.

ex·ult·antly *adv: exultantly proud* 扬扬得意.

ex·ulta·tion /,egzʌl'teɪʃn; ,ɛgzʌl'teʃən/ *n* [U] **~ (at sth)** great happiness 狂喜; 大喜; 欢跃; 得意: *the exultaion of the winner* 获胜者的欢欣雀跃.

-ey ⇨-Y[1].

eye[1] /aɪ; aɪ/ *n* **1** (**a**) organ of sight 眼睛: *I can't see out of this eye.* 我这只眼看不见东西. ○ *She opened/closed her eyes.* 她睁开[闭上]眼睛. ○ *He is blind in one eye.* 他有一只眼失明. ○ *He lost an eye in the war.* 他在战争中瞎了一只眼睛. ○ [attrib 作定语] *The surgeon is performing an eye operation.* 医师正在做眼科手术. ⇨illus 见插图. (**b**) visible coloured part of this; iris 虹膜: *have blue eyes* 有蓝眼睛. **2** power of seeing; observation 视力; 眼力: *She has sharp eyes,* ie very good eyesight. 她视力极好. ○ *To her expert eye, the painting was terrible.* 她以内行的眼光看, 这幅画糟透了. ○ *His eyes fell upon* (ie he saw) *an advertisement in the magazine.* 他看到杂志上的一则广告上. **3** thing like an eye 似眼之物; 眼状物: *the eye of a needle,* ie the hole for the thread 针鼻儿(针上引线的孔) ○ *a hook and eye,* ie fastening with a hook and loop for a dress, etc 一副钩扣(系衣服的钩与环) ○ *the eye of a potato,* ie point from which a leaf bud will grow 马铃薯的芽眼 **4** (idm 习语) **a bird's eye view** ⇨BIRD. **the apple of sb's eye** ⇨APPLE. **as far as the eye can**

the eye 眼睛

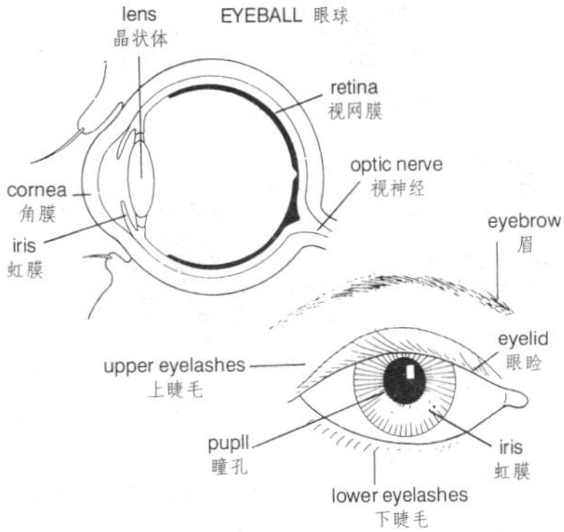

see ⇨ FAR[2]. **be all 'eyes** be watching intently 目不转睛地看; 全神贯注地看: *The children were all eyes as we opened the parcel.* 孩子们目不转睛地看着我们把包裹打开. **cast an eye/one's eye(s) over sb/sth** ⇨ CAST[1]. **catch sb's attention/eye** ⇨CATCH[1]. **clap/lay/set eyes on sb/sth** see sb/sth 看见某人[某物]: *I disliked the place the moment I clapped eyes on it.* 我一看见这个地方就讨厌. ○ *I hope I never set eyes on him again.* 我希望再也不要见到他了. **close one's eyes to sth** ⇨CLOSE[4]. **cry one's eyes/heart out** ⇨CRY[1]. **do sb in the 'eye** (*infml* 口) hurt or humiliate sb 伤害某人; 羞辱某人: *He certainly did his colleagues in the eye when he got the boss's approval.* 他得到老板的夸奖, 确也得罪了同事. **easy on the ear/eye** ⇨EASY[1]. **the evil eye** ⇨EVIL. **an ˌeye for an 'eye** a punishment as severe as the injury that was suffered; retaliation 以眼还眼; 报复: *The death penalty for murder works on the principle of an eye for an eye.* 犯谋杀罪处以死刑, 其原则是一命抵一命. **the eye of the 'storm** a relatively calm spot in the centre of a storm, esp a hurricane 台风眼. **the eye of the 'wind** (also **the wind's 'eye**) point from which the wind is blowing 起风处; 风眼. **sb's eyes are bigger than his 'stomach** (*saying* 谚) someone is too greedy in asking for or taking more food than he can eat 眼大肚小; 眼馋肚饱. **eyes 'right/'left/'front** (as a military command) turn the head and look to the right, etc (用作军令)向右看齐[向左看齐/向前看]. **feast one's eyes** ⇨FEAST. **find/lose favour with sb/in sb's eyes** ⇨FAVOUR[1]. **for 'sb's eyes only** only to be looked at, read, etc by the person specified 只给所指定的人看、读等: *The top secret file was marked 'For the President's eyes only'.* 在绝密档案上标有'只供总统亲阅'字样. **get one's 'eye/'hand in** (in ball games) become able, through practice, to follow with one's eyes the movement of the ball/to hit the ball accurately (在球戏中)通过锻炼能用眼跟上球的动向[准确击球]: *Now that she's got her eye in she plays an excellent game of tennis.* 她已能盯住球了, 所以网球打得很好. **give sb/get the (glad) 'eye** (*infml* 口) give sb/get inviting or amorous looks 向某人传送[看到传来的]诱人的或多情的眼色; 抛媚眼; 送秋波: *The woman at the next table was giving him the glad eye.* 坐在旁边桌子那儿的女子向他抛媚眼. **glance one's eye down/over/through sth** ⇨GLANCE. **a gleam in sb's eye** ⇨ GLEAM. **have an eye for sth** be a good judge of or have a proper sense of sth 对某事物有判断力或鉴赏力; 有眼力; 有眼光: *He has an eye for a bargain.* 他识便宜货. **have eyes in the back of one's 'head** observe everything (without seeming to do so) 脑袋后边长着眼睛; (留意到一切而不露声色): *How did you know I was behind you? You must have eyes in the back of your head.* 你怎么知道我在你后边? 你脑袋后面准是长眼睛了吧. **have/with an eye to sth/doing sth** have/having sth as one's aim or purpose 将某事作为自己的目标或目的: *He always has an eye to business,* ie looks for a chance of doing business. 他总是找机会做生意. ○ *He kept the customer talking with an eye to selling him something else.* 他引着顾客说个不停, 想再卖给人家一些别的东西. **have/with an eye for/on/to the main 'chance** look/looking for an opportunity for personal gain (esp to make money) 找便宜(尤指赚钱) **have, etc one's eyes on stalks** be looking at sth with fascination, astonishment, etc 着迷地、惊奇地...看着某事物 **have a roving eye** ⇨ROVE. **hit sb in the eye** ⇨HIT. **if you had half an eye** if you were not so dull and unobservant 假如你不是瞎了眼睛; 你要是稍微留意一下 **in the eyes of the 'law, 'world, etc** from the point of view of the law, etc; as the law, etc sees it 从法律等的角度看; 就法律等的观点而言: *In the eyes of the law she is guilty though few ordinary people would think so.* 从法律上说, 她有罪; 但一般人不见得这么看. **in the eyes of 'sb/in 'sb's eyes** in the opinion or estimation of sb 在某人的心目中; 在某人看来: *In your father's eyes you're still a child.* 在你父亲的眼里你仍是个孩子. **in one's mind's eye** ⇨MIND[1]. **in the public eye** ⇨ PUBLIC. **in the twinkling of an eye** ⇨TWINKLE. **keep a close eye/watch on sb/sth** ⇨CLOSE[1]. **keep an 'eye on sb/sth** make sure that sb/sth is safe, etc; look after sb/sth 照料某人[某事物]: *Keep an eye on the baby.* 照看一下这个婴儿. ○ *Could you keep an eye on my suitcase for a moment?* 你能给我照管一会儿手提箱吗? **keep an eye open/out (for sb/sth)** (*infml* 口) watch for sb/sth; look out for sb/sth 留心或注意某人[某事物]: *I've lost my ring — could you keep an eye out for it when you clean the house?* 我的戒指不见了 —— 你打扫房子时能留点儿神吗? **keep one's ears/eyes open** ⇨OPEN[1]. **keep one's 'eyes peeled/skinned (for sb/sth)** watch carefully; be observant 仔细观看; 留意: *The tramp always keeps his eyes peeled for coins lying on the ground.* 那流浪汉总是注意着寻找地上的硬币. ○ *Keep your eyes skinned for a campsite!* 留意找个宿营地! **keep a weather eye open** ⇨WEATHER[1]. **lift one's eyes** ⇨ LIFT. **(be unable to) look sb in the 'eye(s)/'face** (be unable to) look at sb steadily (because one feels ashamed, embarrassed, etc) (不能)直视某人(因觉得惭愧、尴尬等): *Can you look me in the eyes and say you did'nt break the window?* 你能正眼看着我说, 窗户不是你打碎的吗? **make ('sheep's) 'eyes at sb** look amorously at sb 向某人抛媚眼、送秋波: *The lovers were making sheep's eyes at each other over the table.* 恋人隔着桌子互送秋波. **meet sb's eye** ⇨MEET[1]. **meet the ear/eye** ⇨MEET[1]. **the mote in sb's eye** ⇨MOTE. **(all) ˌmy 'eye** (*infml* 口) (esp of sth said that is intended to deceive or mislead) completely untrue or nonsensical (尤指所说的话意在欺骗或使人误解)瞎说, 胡说: *She said she was only twenty-two — twenty-two my eye!* 她说她只有二十二岁 —— 二十二岁, 胡说八道! **the naked eye** ⇨NAKED. **never/not (be able to) take one's 'eyes off sb/sth** never/not (be able to) stop watching sb/sth 目不转睛地看着某人[某物]: *He couldn't take his eyes off the beautiful newcomer.* 他目不转睛地盯着那位新来的美人. **not believe one's ears/eyes** ⇨ BELIEVE. **not a dry eye in the house** ⇨DRY[1]. **one in the eye (for sb/sth)** (*infml* 口) hard or unkind rejection or defeat 惨败; 挫折: *If she gets the job, that's one in the eye for Peter: he was desperate to get it.* 假使她获得这份工作, 那对彼得是当头一棒; 他是拼命想得到这份工作的. **only have eyes for/have eyes only for sb** only be interested in or in love with (a specified person) 只对(某人)感兴趣; 只爱恋(某人): *It's no use asking Kim to go out with you; she only has eyes for Mark.* 你邀请金和你出去是白请, 她心目中只有马克. **Open one's/sb's eyes (to sth)** ⇨OPEN[2]. **out of the corner of one's eye** ⇨CORNER[1]. **pull the wool over sb's eyes** ⇨PULL[2]. **the scales fall from sb's eyes** ⇨ SCALE. **(not) see eye to 'eye with sb** (not) agree entirely; (not) have similar views (不)完全一致; (没)有相同的看法: *Jim and I have never seen eye to eye on this matter.* 我和吉姆对此事的意见从来就不一致. **see, etc sth with 'half any eye** see, etc sth at a glance 对某事物一目了然. **shut/close one's eyes to sth** refuse to see or take notice of sth 对某事物视而不见: *The government shuts its eyes to poverty.* 政府对贫穷问题置若罔闻. ○ *She closed her eyes to her husband's infidelities.* 她丈夫有不忠行为, 她却视而不见. **a sight for sore**

eyes ⇨SIGHT. **there is more in/to sb/sth than meets the eye** ⇨MEET[1]. **throw dust in sb's eyes** ⇨DUST[1]. **turn a blind eye** ⇨BLIND[1]. **under/before one's very ˈeyes** (**a**) in one's presence; in front of one 当着某人的面; 在某人面前: *'Ladies and gentlement! Before your very eyes I will cut this man in half,' said the magician.* '女士们、先生们! 我要当着你们大家把这个人一分为二,' 魔术师说. (**b**) without attempting to hide what one is doing 不想隐瞒自己所做的事: *He stole the stuff from under my very eyes.* 他当着我的面偷走的. **(be) up to one's ears/eyes/eyebrows/neck in sth** ⇨EAR. **the wind's eye** = THE EYE OF THE WIND. **with one's ˈeyes open** fully aware of what one is doing 充分了解自己所做之事: *I moved to this country with my eyes open; so I'm not complaining.* 我迁居到这个国家是心中有数的, 所以我并无怨言. ○ *He married her with her eyes wide open.* 他娶她时心里有底. **with one's ˈeyes shut/closed** without much effort; easily 没费多大力气; 轻易地: *He's cooked that meal so often he can do it with his eyes closed.* 他常做那种饭菜, 闭着眼也能做.

▷ **-eyed** (forming compound *adjs* 用以构成复合形容词) having an eye or eyes of the specified kind 有某种眼睛的: *a blue-eyed girl* ○ *a one-eyed man,* ie man with only one eye.

ˈeye·ful /fʊl; -ˌfʊl/ *n* **1** thing thrown or blown into one's eye 掷入、刮入或吹入眼中之物: *get an eyeful of sand* 眼里刮进沙子. **2** (*infml* 口) interesting or attractive sight 有趣的或诱人的景象: *She's quite an eyeful!* 她真是个美人! **3** (idm 习语) **have/get an eyeful (of sth)** (*infml* 口) have a good long look (at sth interesting, remarkable, unusual, etc) 好好看看(有趣的、美妙的、罕见的等物): *'Come and get an eyeful of this — there's a giraffe in the garden!'* '快来看哪——花园里有个长颈鹿!'

□ **ˈeyeball** *n* **1** round part of the eye within the eyelids and socket 眼珠; 眼球. ⇨illus 见插图. **2** (idm 习语) **ˌeyeball to ˈeyeball (with sb)** (*infml* 口) confronting a person closely; face to face 互相对视; 面对面: *We must discuss the situation eyeball to eyeball.* 我们要面对面地研究一下这种情况.

ˈeye-bath *n* small cup shaped to fit round the eye for holding lotion, etc in which to bathe the eye 洗眼器; 洗眼杯.

ˈeyebrow *n* **1** arch of hair above the human eye 眉; 眉毛: *pluck one's eyebrows* 拔眉毛. ⇨illus 见插图. ⇨ Usage at BODY 用法见 BODY. **2** (idm 习语) **raise one's eyebrows** ⇨RAISE. **up to one's ears/eyes/eyebrows/neck in sth** ⇨EAR. **ˈeyebrow pencil** make-up pencil used for darkening the eyebrows 眉笔.

ˈeye-catching *adj* striking and noticeable, esp because pleasant to look at 别人注目的; 令人注意的(尤指悦目者): *an eye-catching suit, hat, etc* 引人注目的服装、帽子等.

ˈeyeglass *n* lens (for one eye) to help poor eyesight (眼镜的)镜片; 单片眼镜: *The old man wore an eyeglass attached to a piece of ribbon.* 那老人戴着单片眼镜, 上面连结着一条丝带.

ˈeyelash (also **lash**) *n* hair, or one of the rows of hairs, on the edge of the eyelid 睫毛: *She was wearing false eyelashes,* ie artifical eyelashes, stuck to the eyelids. 她戴着假睫毛. ⇨illus 见插图.

ˈeyeless *adj* (*fml* 文) without eyes; without sight 无眼的; 无视力的.

ˈeye-level *adj* [usu attrib 通常作定语] level with a person's eyes when looking straight ahead (直视时)与眼睛相平的: *an eye-level grill* 与眼睛相平的铁栅栏.

ˈeyelid (also **lid**) *n* **1** upper or lower of two movable folds of skin that close to cover the eyeball 眼睑; 眼皮: *His eyelid is swollen.* 他眼皮肿了. ⇨illus 见插图. **2** (idm 习语) **not bat an eyelid** ⇨BAT[1].

ˈeye-liner (also **liner**) *n* cosmetic applied as a line round (part of) the eye 眼线液.

ˈeye-opener *n* event, etc that is enlightening or causes surprise 令人开眼界的或令人惊奇的事物: *My trip to India was quite an eye-opener.* 我的印度之行真令我大开眼界.

ˈeyepiece *n* lens at the end of a telescope or microscope through which the observer looks (望远镜或显微镜的)接目镜. ⇨illus at MICROSCOPE 见 MICROSCOPE 之插图.

ˈeye-shade *n* device worn above the eyes to protect them from strong light 遮光帽檐: *The tennis umpire wore an eye-shade.* 那网球裁判戴着遮光帽檐.

ˈeye-shadow *n* [C, U] type of cosmetic applied to the eyelids 眼影膏.

ˈeyesight *n* [U] power of seeing; ability to see 视力: *have good/bad/poor eyesight* 有良好的[很糟的/微弱的]视力.

ˈeyesore *n* ugly object; thing that is unpleasant to look at 丑陋的物品; 难看的东西: *That old block of flats is a real eyesore!* 那座旧公寓真不顺眼!

ˈeye-strain *n* [U] tired condition of the eyes (caused, eg by reading very small print, or in dim light) 眼睛疲劳(如因读小字或光线暗所致).

ˈeye-tooth *n* (*pl* **ˈeye-teeth**) **1** canine tooth in the upper (human) jaw, under the eye (人的)上犬齿. **2** (idm 习语) **cut one's ˈeye-teeth** acquire experience in the ways of the world 获得世事经验; 通晓世故: *He'll have to cut his eye-teeth before he gets promoted.* 他要有些阅历才可获提升. **give one's eye-teeth for sth** wish to possess or obtain sth very much 非常希望具有、占有或得到某物: *He'd give his eye-teeth to own a car like that.* 他巴不得有那样一辆汽车.

ˈeye-wash *n* [U] (**a**) liquid for bathing the eyes 洗眼药水 (**b**) (*infml* 口) thing said or done to deceive or create a false impression; nonsense 瞎扯; 瞎说; 胡说八道; 胡言乱语; 弄虚作假: *He pretends to care so much about his children, but it's all eyewash: he never even takes them out.* 他貌似很关心自己的孩子, 其实都是假象, 他从来不带他们出去.

ˈeyewitness *n* = WITNESS: [attrib 作定语] *an eyewitness account of a crime* 目击者对一罪行的叙述.

eye[2] /aɪ; aɪ/ *v* **1** [Tn, Tn·pr] (**a**) observe or watch (sb/sth) in the specified way 以所述方式观察或观看(某人[某事物]): *He eyed me with suspicion.* 他怀疑地看着我. ○ *They were ey(e)ing us jealously.* 他们忌妒地看着我们. (**b**) look at (sth) with longing 渴望地看(某物): *The children were ey(e)ing the sweets.* 孩子们眼巴巴地看着糖果. **2** (phr v) **eye sb up (and down)** (*infml* 口) look at sb amorously (in order to try to attract) 含情脉脉地看某人(以图吸引对方): *Did you see that creep eyeing up every woman at the party?* 你看见那个讨厌的傢伙了吗? 他对聚会上的每个女人都垂涎欲滴地打量不停.

eye·let /ˈaɪlɪt; ˈaɪlɪt/ *n* [C] small hole in cloth, in a sail, etc for a rope, etc to go through; metal ring round such a hole, to strengthen it (布、帆等上穿绳等用的)孔眼; (镶孔眼的)金属环.

eyrie (aslo **eyry, aerie, aery**) /ˈaɪərɪ; ˈɛrɪ/ *n* eagle's nest; nest of other birds of prey built high up among rocks 鹰巢; 建在岩石高处的其他猛禽的巢.

F f

F, f /ef; ɛf/ *n* (*pl* **F's, f's** /efs; ɛfs/) **1** the sixth letter of the English alphabet 英语字母表的第六个字母: *'Fabric' starts with an 'F'/F.* fabric一字以f字母开始. **2 F** (*music* 音) the fourth note in the scale of C major C大调音阶中的第四音或音符.

F *abbr* 缩写 = **1** (degree or degrees) Fahrenheit: *Water freezes at 32°F.* 水在32°F时结冰. Cf 参看 C *abbr* 缩写 2. **2** (in academic degrees) Fellow of: *FRCM*, ie Fellow of the Royal College of Music 皇家音乐学院会员. Cf 参看 A *abbr* 缩写 3. **3** (of lead used in pencils) fine.

f *abbr* 缩写 = **1** (also **fem**) (esp on forms) female (sex). **2** (also **fem**) (*grammar*) feminine (gender). **3** (*music* 音) loudly (Italian *forte*) 强, 大声(源自意大利文*forte*). Cf 参看 P 3.

FA /ˌef ˈeɪ; ˌɛf ˈe/ *abbr* 缩写 = (*Brit*) Football Association (英国)足球协会: *the FA Cup* (英国)足总杯.

fa (also **fah**) /fɑː; fɑ/ *n* (*music* 音) the fourth note in the sol-fa scale 唱名法音阶的第四音.

fab /fæb; fæb/ *adj* (*dated Brit sl* 旧, 俚) marvellous; fabulous(3) 极好的; 绝妙的.

Fa·bian /ˈfeɪbɪən; ˈfebɪən/ *n, adj* **1** (person) patiently planning to defeat the enemy gradually 耐心策划逐步消灭敌人的(人): *Fabian tactics* 耐心策划逐步消灭敌人的策略. **2** (*Brit*) (person) aiming to build socialism by means of gradual reform 以逐渐改革的方式建设社会主义为目标的(人); 费边式的: *the Fabian Society* 费边社.

fable /ˈfeɪbl; ˈfebḷ/ *n* **1** (**a**) [C] short story not based on fact, often with animals as characters, that conveys a moral 寓言: *Aesop's fables* 伊索寓言. (**b**) [U] such stories and legends considered as a group 寓言故事; 神话; 传说: *a land famous in fable* 以寓言故事闻名的国家. **2** [C, U] untrue statement(s) or account(s) 无稽之谈; 谎话; 胡扯: *distinguish fact from fable* 辨别虚实.

▷ **fabled** /ˈfeɪbld; ˈfebḷd/ *adj* famous in fables; legendary 寓言中有名的; 传说的.

fab·ric /ˈfæbrɪk; ˈfæbrɪk/ *n* **1** [C, U] type of cloth, esp one that is woven 织物: *woollen, silk, cotton, etc fabrics* 毛、丝、棉等的织物. **2** [sing] **the ~ (of sth)** (**a**) walls, floors and roof (of a building, etc) (建筑物等的)墙、地板和屋顶: *The entire fabric of the church needs renovation.* 这座教堂的全部结构需要维修翻新. (**b**) (*fig* 比喻) structure (of sth) (某事物的)结构: *the fabric of society* 社会的结构.

fab·ric·ate /ˈfæbrɪkeɪt; ˈfæbrɪˌket/ *v* [Tn] **1** invent (a false story) 编造(虚假的事); 虚构: *fabricate an excuse, an accusation, etc* 编造借口、捏造罪名 ○ *The reason he gave for his absence was obviously fabricated.* 他提出的缺席理由显然是瞎编的. **2** forge (a document) 伪造(文件): *a fabricated voting paper* 伪造的选票.

▷ **fab·rica·tion** /ˌfæbrɪˈkeɪʃn; ˌfæbrɪˈkeʃən/ *n* **1** [U] action or result of fabricating 编造、虚构、捏造、伪造的行为或结果: *That's pure fabrication!* 那纯粹是捏造的! **2** [C] thing that has been fabricated, eg a forged document or a false account of events 编造、虚构、捏造、伪造的事物(如伪造的文件或虚构的事情): *Her story was nothing but a series of fabrications.* 她说的完全都是编造的.

fab·ulous /ˈfæbjʊləs; ˈfæbjələs/ *adj* **1** incredibly great 极为巨大的: *fabulous wealth* 巨大的财富. **2** (*infml* 口) wonderful; marvellous 极好的; 绝妙的: *a fabulous performance* 精彩的表演. **3** [attrib 作定语] (*fml* 文) appearing in fables; legendary 寓言中的; 传说的; 神话的: *fabulous heroes, monsters, etc* 传奇式的英雄、妖怪等.

▷ **fab·ulously** *adv* incredibly 难以置信地: *fabulously rich* 难以置信地富有.

fa·çade /fəˈsɑːd; fəˈsɑd/ *n* **1** (*fml* 文) front (of a building) (建筑物的)正面. **2** (*fig* 比喻) outward appearance, esp a deceptive one 外表(尤指虚伪的): *a façade of indifference* 假装冷漠 ○ *Squalor and poverty lay behind the city's glittering façade.* 这城市表面繁华, 背后却肮脏和贫困.

face[1] /feɪs; fes/ *n* **1** front part of the head from the forehead to the chin 脸; 面孔: *a pretty, handsome, etc face* 漂亮的、英俊的...面孔 ○ *Go and wash your face.* 去把脸洗一洗. ○ *He was so ashamed that he hid his face in his hands.* 他羞愧得用手把脸蒙住. ○ *I saw many familiar/strange faces*, ie people whom I recognized/did not recognize. 我看见很多熟悉的[陌生的]面孔. **2** expression shown on a face 面部表情; 脸色: *a sad face* 悲伤的面容 ○ *smiling faces* 笑脸 ○ *She had a face like thunder*, ie She looked very angry. 她满面怒气. ○ *You are a good judge of faces*, ie You can judge a person's character by (the expression on) his face. 你很会根据人的相貌(表情)来判断人的性格. **3** (**a**) surface or side (of sth) (某事物的)表面, 面: *A cut diamond has many faces.* 经切割的钻石有很多晶面. ○ *They disappeared from/off the face of the earth*, ie totally disappeared. 他们从地面上消失了(全部消失了). ○ *The team climbed the north face of the mountain.* 那小队攀登山的北坡. (**b**) front or main side (of sth) (某事物的)正面, 主要的一面: *the face of a clock* 钟的面 ○ *He put the cards face down on the table.* 他把纸牌面向下放在桌上. (**c**) = COAL-FACE (COAL). (**d**) surface that is used for hitting, working, etc esp the striking-surface of a bat or the working-surface of a tool 用以打击、工作等的面(尤指球拍或工具的面). **4** = TYPEFACE (TYPE[2]). **5** (idm 习语) **be staring sb in the face** ⇨ STARE. **cut off one's nose to spite one's face** ⇨ NOSE[1]. **one's face falls** one's expression shows disappointment, dismay, etc 脸沉下来(表示失望、沮丧等): *Her face fell when she heard the news.* 她听到这个消息脸都沉下来了. **face to face (with sb/sth)** close to and looking at (sb/sth) 面对面地看(某人[某事物]): *His ambition was to meet his favourite pop star face to face.* 他心向往之的是要面对面地见见他心目中的流行曲歌星. ○ *The burglar turned the corner and found himself face to face with a policeman.* 盗贼一拐弯面对面地碰上个警察. ○ *The two rival politicians came/were brought face to face in a TV interview.* 那两个对立的政客面对面地一起接受电视访问. **fall flat on one's face** ⇨ FLAT[3]. **fly in the face of sth** ⇨ FLY[2]. **grind the faces of the poor** ⇨ GRIND. **have, etc egg on/all over one's face** ⇨ EGG[1]. **have the face (to do sth)** (*infml* 口) be bold or impudent enough 竟然有脸或胆敢(做某事): *How can you have the face to ask for more money when you do so little work?* 你干这么少工作还有脸多要钱? **have one's face lifted** have a face-lift(1) (做面部除皱纹)整容; 做面部拉皮手术. **in the face of sth** (**a**) in spite of sth 不顾某事物: *succeed in the face of danger* 不惧危险地完成 ○ *continue in the face of criticism* 不顾批评而继续干. (**b**) confronted by sth 面对某事物: *We are powerless in the face of such forces.* 面对这样强大的力量, 我们无能为力. **keep a straight face** ⇨ STRAIGHT[1]. **laugh in sb's face** ⇨ LAUGH. **laugh on the other side of one's face** ⇨ LAUGH. **a long face** ⇨ LONG[1]. **look sb in the eye/face** ⇨ EYE[1]. **lose face** ⇨ LOSE. **make/pull ˈfaces/a ˈface (at sb)** grimace (at sb); pull the face into amusing, rude, disgusted, etc expressions (对某人)做鬼脸, 扮怪相: *The schoolboy made a face at his teacher's back.* 那个男生对着教师的背后做个鬼脸. ○ *The clowns pulled funny faces.* 小丑扮出了可笑的鬼脸. **not just a pretty face** ⇨ PRETTY. **on the ˈface of it** (*infml* 口) judging by appearances 就表面判断: *On the face of it, he seems to be telling the truth though I suspect he's hiding something.* 表面上看, 他似乎说的是实话, 可我怀疑他有隐情. **plain as the nose on one's face** ⇨ PLAIN[1]. **put a bold, brave, good, etc ˈface on sth** accept (bad news, etc) courageously, pretending that it is not as bad as it is 装出满不在乎的样子面对(坏消息等): *Her exam results were disappointing but she tried to put a brave face on it.* 她的考试成绩令人失望, 但却装出若无其事的样子. **put one's ˈface on** (*infml joc* 口,

谑) apply make-up to one's face 往脸上涂化妆品. **save face** ⇨ SAVE[1]. **set one's face against sb/sth** be determined to oppose sb/sth 坚决反对某人[某事物]: *You shouldn't set your face against all forms of progress.* 你不应该硬是反对各种进步形式. **show one's face** ⇨ SHOW[2]. **shut/slam the door in sb's face** ⇨ DOOR. **shut one's mouth/face** ⇨ SHUT. **a slap in the face** ⇨ SLAP *n*. **till one is blue in the face** ⇨ BLUE[1]. **to sb's 'face** openly and directly so that sb can hear 当着某人的面: *I am so angry that I'll tell him to his face what I think of him.* 我气得要当面把我对他的想法告诉他. ○ *They called their teacher 'Fatty' but never to his face.* 他们把自己的老师叫作'胖子', 但却从未当面叫过. Cf 参看 BEHIND SB'S BACK (BACK[1]). **wipe sth off the face of the earth** ⇨ WIPE.

▷ **face·less** *adj* not known by name; with no clear character or identity 不知名的; 特性或身分不清楚的: *faceless civil servants* 不知名的公务员.

□ **'face-card** *n* = COURT-CARD (COURT).

'face-cloth (*Brit* also **'face-flannel**, **flannel**; *US* also **wash-cloth**) *n* small square of towelling material used for washing the face, hands, etc (洗脸、洗手等的)毛巾, 面巾, 手巾.

'face-cream *n* [U] cosmetic cream for the skin of the face 面霜; 面膏; 雪花膏.

'face-lift *n* **1** (also **'face-lifting**) operation in which the skin is tightened to smooth out wrinkles and make the face look younger (将面部皮肤拉紧以消除皱纹的)整容手术, 面部拉皮手术. **2** (*fig* 比喻) improvement in the appearance of sth; renovation (of a building, etc) 改善某事物的外观; (建筑物等的)翻新; 更新: *The town centre certainly needs a face-lift.* 市中心可真该装修一下了.

F

'face-pack *n* cream or paste applied to clean or refresh the skin on the face 面部洁霜; 洁肤膏.

'face-saver *n* thing that prevents sb from being embarrassed or losing dignity 保全某人面子的事物. **'face-saving** *adj* [usu attrib 通常作定语] acting as a face-saver 保全面子的: *a face-saving action, excuse, gesture* 保全面子的行动、借口、举动.

ˌface 'value **1** value printed or stamped on money or postage stamps 钱币或邮票的面值; 票面价值; 票面额. **2** (idm 习语) **take sth/sb at (its, his, etc) face value** assume that sth/sb is genuinely what it, he, etc appears to be 假定或认为某事物[某人]真如其显示的那样: *She seems friendly enough but I shouldn't take her at (her) face value.* 她好像够亲切的, 可是我不应该信以为真.

face[2] /feɪs; fes/ *v* **1** [Tn] have or turn the face towards (sb/sth); be opposite to 面对或面向(某人[某事物]); 正对; 朝: *Turn round and face me.* 转过身来面对着我. ○ *Who's the man facing me?* 面向着我的那个男人是谁? ○ *The window faces the street.* 那窗户面临着街道. ○ *The picture faces page 10.* 该图在第10页的对面. ○ *'Which way does your house face?' 'It faces south.'* '你的房子朝着那个方向?' '朝南.' **2** [Tn] meet (sb/sth) confidently or defiantly without trying to avoid sb/sth 毅然相对(某人[某事物]); 对付、应付某人[某事物]: *He turned to face his attackers.* 他转过身来对付那些攻击者. ○ (*fig* 比喻) *face dangers* 应付危险的事物 ○ *face one's responsibilities* 正视自己的责任 ○ *face facts*, ie accept the situation that exists 面对事实(承认现状). **3** [Tn] require the attention of (sb/sth); confront 要求(某人[某事物])的注意; 面临: *the problems that face the Government* 政府面临的难题. **4** [Tn, Tn·pr] **~ sth (with sth)** cover sth with a layer of different material 在某物上覆盖一层另一种材料: *face a wall (with plaster)* (用灰泥)涂墙壁. **5** (idm 习语) **about/left/right face** (*US*) = ABOUT/LEFT/RIGHT TURN (TURN[1]). **face a charge (of sth)/face 'charges** be forced to appear in court accused of sth 被控某事物须出庭受审: *face serious charges, a charge of shoplifting* 被控严重罪名、入店行窃之罪. **face the 'music** (*infml* 口) accept the criticisms, unpleasant consequences, etc that follow a decision or action of one's own 由于自己的决定或行动而接受批评、承担后果等: *You've been caught cheating — now you must face the music.* 你的骗局已经戳穿——这下子你得自食其果了. **let's 'face it** (*infml* 口) we must acknowledge that... 我们得承认...: *Let's face it, we won't win whatever we do.* 我们得承认, 怎么做都不行. **6** (phr v) **face up to sth** accept and deal with sth unpleasant or demanding honestly and bravely 诚实而勇敢地承认和处理令人不快的或困难的事物: *He must face up to the fact that he is no longer young.* 他应该勇于正视自己不再年轻这一事实. ○ *She's finding it difficult to face up to the possibility of an early death.* 她面临可能早逝而手足无措.

▷ **-faced** (forming compound *adjs* 用以构成复合形容词) with the specified type of face 有某种类型的面孔的: *red-faced* ○ *baby-faced*.

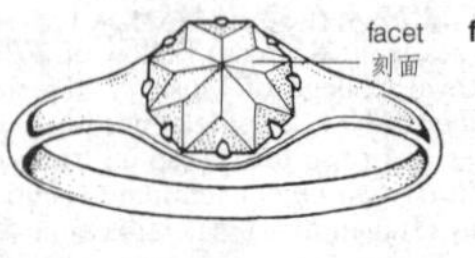

facet 刻面

fa·cet /ˈfæsɪt; ˈfæsɪt/ *n* **1** any of the many sides of a cut stone or jewel 宝石或首饰的小平面; 刻面. **2** aspect of a situation or problem 情况或问题的方面: *There are many facets to this question.* 这个问题有很多方面.

▷ **-faceted** (forming compound *adjs* 用以构成复合形容词) with the specified number of sides or aspects 有若干面或方面的: *many-faceted/multi-faceted*.

fa·cetious /fəˈsiːʃəs; fəˈsiʃəs/ *adj* (*usu derog* 通常作贬义) intended to be amusing, often inappropriately (常为不当地)引人发笑的, 诙谐的: *a facetious young man* 耍贫嘴的小伙子 ○ *She kept interrupting our discussion with facetious remarks.* 她不断用开玩笑的话干扰我们的讨论. ▷ **fa·cetiously** *adv*. **fa·cetious·ness** *n* [U].

fa·cia (also **fas·cia**) /ˈfeɪʃə; ˈfeʃə/ *n* **1** = DASHBOARD (DASH[1]). **2** board, etc with a name on it, put above the front entrance of a shop 商店入口处的店主名牌; 店号; 招牌.

fa·cial /ˈfeɪʃl; ˈfeʃəl/ *adj* of or for the face 面孔的; 面部用的: *a facial expression* 面部表情 ○ *a facial massage* 面部按摩.

▷ **fa·cial** *n* beauty treatment for the face 美容: *I've made an appointment for a facial next week.* 我已经预约了下星期去美容.

fa·cially /ˈfeɪʃəlɪ; ˈfeʃəlɪ/ *adv* as far as the face is concerned 在面孔方面: *She may resemble her father facially, but in other respects she's not at all like him.* 她尽管脸像父亲, 但其他方面却一点也不像.

fa·cile /ˈfæsaɪl; *US* ˈfæsl; ˈfæsl/ *adj* **1** (*usu derog* 通常作贬义) (**a**) [attrib 作定语] easily obtained or achieved (and so not highly valued) 容易得到的, 容易达到的(因而不受重视的): *a facile success, victory, etc* 轻易获得的成功、胜利等. (**b**) (of speech or writing) easily produced but superficial or of poor quality (指演说或写作)轻易完成但肤浅或质量差的: *a facile remark* 信口开河的话. **2** [attrib 作定语] (of a person) saying or doing things easily; fluent (指人)麻利的, 利落的: *a facile speaker* 能说会道的人.

fa·cil·it·ate /fəˈsɪlɪteɪt; fəˈsɪləˌtet/ *v* [Tn] (*fml* 文) (of an object, a process, etc but not of a person) make (sth) easy or less difficult (指物体、过程等, 但不用于指人)使(某事物)容易或减少困难: *It would facilitate matters if you were more co-operative.* 要是你再合作些就省事了.

▷ **fa·cil·ita·tion** /fəˌsɪlɪˈteɪʃn; fəˌsɪləˈteʃən/ *n* [U].

fa·cil·ity /fəˈsɪlətɪ; fəˈsɪlətɪ/ *n* **1** [U, sing] ability to learn or do things easily 容易学好或做好事物的能力: *have (a) great facility for (learning) languages* 有(学习)语言的天才 ○ *He plays the piano with surprising facility.* 他弹奏钢琴神乎其技. **2 facilities** [pl] circumstances, equipment, etc that make it possible, or easier, to do sth; aids 能够或易于做某事的环境、设备等; 辅助物: *'sports facilities*, eg running tracks, swimming pools 运动设施(如跑道、游泳池) ○ *'washing, 'postal, 'shopping, 'banking, etc facilities* 洗涤、邮政、购物、银行等设施 ○ *facilities for study*, eg libraries 有助学习的设施(如图书馆).

fa·cing /ˈfeɪsɪŋ; ˈfesɪŋ/ *n* **1** outer layer covering a surface (eg of a wall) 覆盖(如墙壁的)表面的覆饰; 饰面. **2** layer of material covering part of a garment either to decorate it in a different colour or to strengthen it 衣服上不同颜色的外层饰料或使之耐穿的补片: *a blue jacket with black facings* 有黑色饰料的蓝夹克.

fac·sim·ile /fæk'sɪməlɪ; fæk`sɪməlɪ/ *n* [U, C] exact copy or reproduction of writing, printing, a picture, etc (文字、印刷品、图画等的)精确的复制品, 模本, 传真: *reproduced in facsimile*, ie exactly 精确复制的 ○ [attrib 作定语] *a facsimile edition* 模真版.

fact /fækt; fækt/ *n* **1** [C] thing that is known to have happened or to be true or to exist 事实; 真相: *No one can deny the fact that fire burns.* 无人能否认火能燃烧的事实. ○ *Poverty and crime are facts.* 贫穷和犯罪是事实. ○ *He's resigned: I know it for a fact*, ie I know that it is really true. 他已经辞职了, 我知道这是真事. ○ (*infml* 口) *He came here yesterday, and that's a fact!* 他昨天来过, 是真的! Cf 参看 FICTION. **2** [C] thing that is believed or claimed to be true 认为或称为真实的事物: *I disagree with the facts on which your argument is based.* 我不同意你的论点所基于的论据. **3** [U] what is true; reality 真实的事物; 现实: *The story is founded on fact.* 这故事有真事作根据. ○ *It's important to distinguish fact from fiction.* 把现实与虚构区分开来是很重要的. **4** (idm 习语) **accessory before/after the fact** ⇨ ACCESSORY. **an accomplished fact** ⇨ ACCOMPLISH. **blink the fact** ⇨ BLINK. **as a matter of fact** ⇨ MATTER 1. **a ˌfact of ˈlife** thing that cannot be ignored, however unpleasant 生活的现实(尽管使人不快, 却不容忽视的事物): *We must all die some time: that's just a fact of life.* 我们终有一死, 这就是生活的现实. **the fact (of the matter) is (that)...; the fact remains (that)...** despite what has been said, the truth is... 虽然话是这么说, 但事实是...: *A holiday would be wonderful but the fact of the matter is (that) we can't afford one.* 有个假日好是真好, 可事实是我们花费不起. ○ *I agree that he tried hard but the fact remains that he has not finished the job in time.* 我承认他已尽力而为了, 但事实是他并未按时做完. **ˌfacts and ˈfigures** (*infml* 口) precise information 精确的资料; 准确的情报: *Before we make detailed plans, we need some more facts and figures.* 我们还需要更多的精确资料才能制定出详细计划. **the ˌfacts of ˈlife** (*euph* 婉) details of human sexuality, esp as told to children 性知识(尤指给儿童讲的). **the facts speak for themselves** the facts noted about a situation or an occurrence show what conclusions can be reached, without further interpretation or explanation 事实本身自明. **hard facts** ⇨ HARD[1]. **in ˈfact** in truth; really 事实上; 实际上; 其实: *For eight years she was in fact spying for the enemy.* 八年来她实际上一直为敌人做间谍工作. **in point of fact** ⇨ POINT[1].

□ **ˈfact-finding** *n* [U] discovering the truth about sth 揭示某事物的真相; 实情调查: [attrib 作定语] *a fact-finding mission, expedition, etc* 调查团、队等.

fac·tion /ˈfækʃn; `fækʃən/ *n* [C] (*usu derog* 通常作贬义) small united group within a larger one, esp in politics 大组织中的小派别, 派系(尤指政治上的): *rival factions within the party* 党内的对立派别.

▷ **fac·tious** /ˈfækʃəs; `fækʃəs/ *adj* **1** of or caused by faction 派系的; 由派性产生的. **2** fond of faction; quarrelsome 喜好派性的; 爱争吵的: *a factious individual* 派性强的人.

fac·ti·tious /fæk'tɪʃəs; fæk`tɪʃəs/ *adj* (*fml* 文) deliberately created or developed; unnatural; artificial 故意创造或发展的; 不自然的; 人为的: *factitious enthusiasm* 虚假的热情 ○ *a factitious demand for goods*, ie one created artificially by widespread advertising, etc 对货物需求的假相(由广泛宣传等人为造成的).

fac·tor /ˈfæktə(r); `fæktɚ/ *n* **1** fact, circumstance, etc that helps to produce a result 因素: *environmental factors* 环境因素 ○ *the factors that influenced my decision* 影响我做出决定的因素 ○ *an unknown factor*, ie sth unknown that is likely to influence a result 未知的因素(可能对结果造成影响的未知事物). **2** (*mathematics* 数) number, except 1, by which a larger number can be divided exactly 因数; 因子: *2, 3, 4 and 6 are factors of 12.* 2、3、4、6都是12的因数. **3** person or organization acting as a business agent (企业的)代理人, 代理商. **4** (*Scot* 苏格兰) land-agent; steward 地产经管人; 管家.

▷ **fac·tor·ize, -ise** /ˈfæktəraɪz; `fæktəˌraɪz/ *v* [Tn] (*mathematics* 数) find the factors of (a number) 分解(某数的)因数. **fac·tor·iza·tion, -isation** /ˌfæktəraɪˈzeɪʃn; *US* -rɪˈz-; ˌfæktərəˋzeʃən/ *n* [U].

fac·tor·ial /fæk'tɔːrɪəl; fæk`torɪəl/ *adj, n* (*mathematics* 数) (of the) product of a whole number and all those whole numbers below it 阶乘; 阶乘的; 因数的: *factorial 5 (represented as 5!)*, ie the product of 5 × 4 × 3 × 2 × 1 5的阶乘(记作5!, 为5×4×3×2×1的乘积).

fact·ory /ˈfæktərɪ; `fæktərɪ/ *n* building(s) in which goods are manufactured 工厂; 制造厂: [attrib 作定语] *ˈfactory workers* 工厂工人.

□ **ˈfactory farm** farm in which animals are kept and reared in a way designed to produce the maximum yield (of meat, young, milk, eggs, etc) 工厂化农场(为高产食用肉、奶、蛋等而饲养和繁殖牲畜和家禽的农场). **ˈfactory farming**.

ˈfactory ship ship to which ships in a fishing fleet bring their catch for processing, and often quick-freezing, while still at sea 捕捞加工船(在海上将捕获物急冻加工的渔船).

NOTE ON USAGE 用法: **Factory, mill, plant** and **works** all refer to industrial buildings or places but they indicate different products or processes. ☆ **factory**、**mill**、**plant**、**works**均指工业的建筑物或场所, 但其产品或加工程序则不尽相同. **Factory** is the most common word for the buildings where products are manufactured or assembled ☆ **factory**一词最为普通, 指产品生产或装配的工厂: *a car, shoe, bottle, etc factory* 汽车制造、制鞋、制瓶等工厂 ○ *factory workers* 工厂工人. **Works** suggests a larger group of buildings and machinery, generally not producing finished goods ☆ **works**意为较大的建筑物群及其机器设备, 一般并不生产成品: *a gasworks, ironworks* 煤气厂、钢铁厂. **Plant** is more common in US English and relates especially to industrial processes ☆ **plant**多用于美式英语, 尤为工业加工者: *a power, chemical plant* 发电厂、化工厂. **Mill** has the most limited meaning, relating to the processing of certain raw materials ☆ **mill**的意思最为狭窄, 限用于某些原材料的加工: *a paper/cotton/woollen/steel mill* 造纸[棉纺/毛纺/钢]厂.

fac·totum /fæk'təʊtəm; fæk`totəm/ *n* (*fml or joc* 文或谑) person employed to do all kinds of work 杂工; 打杂的: *a general factotum* 总勤杂工.

fac·tual /ˈfæktʃʊəl; `fæktʃʊəl/ *adj* based on or containing facts 根据事实的; 事实的; 真实的: *a factual account* 据实的报道. ▷ **fac·tu·ally** /-tʃʊəlɪ; -tʃʊəlɪ/ *adv*: *factually correct* 事实方面正确无误的.

fac·ulty /ˈfækltɪ; `fækltɪ/ *n* **1** [C] any of the powers of the body or mind 官能; 才能; 能力: *the faculty of sight* 视力 ○ *the mental faculties*, ie the power of reason 智力 ○ *be in possession of all one's faculties*, ie be able to see, hear, speak, understand, etc 具有各种官能(有视、听、说、理解等能力). **2** [sing] **~ of/for doing sth** particular ability for doing sth 做某事物的特殊才能: *have a great faculty for learning languages* 有学习语言的才能. **3** (**a**) [C] department or group of related departments in a university, etc (大学的)系, 科, 院: *the Faculty of Law, Science, etc* 法律学院、理学院. (**b**) [CGp] all the lecturers, etc in one of these (大学的某系、科、院的)全体教员: [attrib 作定语] *a faculty meeting* (大学的某系、科、院的)全体教员会议. (**c**) [CGp] (*US*) the whole teaching staff of a university, etc 大学等的全体教员.

fad /fæd; fæd/ *n* fashion, interest, preference, enthusiasm, etc that is not likely to last 流行的时尚、爱好、狂热等: *Will Tom continue to collect stamps or is it only a passing fad?* 汤姆还在集邮呢, 还是热劲已过?

▷ **fad·dish** *adj* (*derog* 贬) having peculiar likes and dislikes 有乖僻好恶的.

faddy *adj* (*infml derog* 口, 贬) faddish, esp about food (尤指对于食物)有乖僻好恶的. **fad·diness** *n* [U].

fade /feɪd; fed/ *v* **1** [I, Tn] (cause sth to) lose colour, freshness or vigour (使某事物)褪色, 凋落, 衰弱: *the fading light of evening* 傍晚渐暗的光 ○ *Will (the colour in) this material fade?* 这块料子(的颜色)褪色吗? ○ *Flowers soon fade when cut.* 花折下不久就会凋谢. ○ *She is fading fast*, ie is rapidly losing strength. 她身体很快就衰弱了. ○ *The strong sunlight had faded the curtains.* 强烈

F

的阳光把窗帘晒得褪了色. ○ *faded denims*, ie ones that have lost their original colour 褪了色的牛仔裤. **2** [I, Ipr, Ip] ~ **(away)** disappear gradually (from sight, hearing, memory, etc); become indistinct (从视野中、听力范围中、记忆中等)逐渐消失, 变得模糊不清: *As evening came, the coastline faded into darkness.* 夜晚降临时, 海岸线在黑暗中逐渐消失了. ○ *The sound of the cheering faded (away) in the distance.* 欢呼声在远处逐渐消失了. ○ *All memory of her childhood had faded from her mind.* 她对童年的一切记忆逐渐从脑海中消逝了. ○ *His hopes faded.* 他的希望渐渐破灭了. **3** (phr v) **fade away** (of people) disperse; die (指人)散开, 死亡: *The crowd just faded away.* 人群刚刚散去. ○ *She's fading away*, ie dying. 她已奄奄一息. **fade (sth) in/out** (*cinema or broadcasting* 电影或广播) (cause a picture to) increase/decrease gradually in sharpness; (cause the volume of sound to) become gradually audible/inaudible (使画面)清晰度逐渐增强[减弱]; (使音量)逐渐增大[减小]: *As the programme ended, their conversation was faded out.* 节目结束时, 他们的谈话声也逐渐消失了.

□ **'fade-in** *n* (*cinema or broadcasting* 电影或广播) gradual strengthening (of sounds, pictures, etc) (声音、画面等)逐渐清晰, 渐现, 渐显, 淡入.

'fade-out *n* (*cinema or broadcasting* 电影或广播) gradual weakening (of sounds, pictures, etc) (声音、画面等)逐渐模糊不清, 渐隐, 渐淡, 淡出.

fae·ces (*US* **fe·ces**) /'fi:si:z; 'fisiz/ *n* [pl] (*fml* 文) waste matter passed from the bowels 粪便.

▷ **faecal** (*US* **fecal**) /'fi:kl; 'fikl/ *adj* [usu attrib 通常作定语] (*fml* 文) of faeces 粪便的.

F

fag /fæg; fæg/ *n* **1** [sing, U] (*infml* 口) tedious and tiring job 沉闷而又吃力的工作: *I've got to tidy my room. What a fag!* 我得整理自己的房间. 真是累人的事. ○ *It's too much (of a) fag.* 这工作真叫人吃不消. **2** [C] (*Brit infml* 口) cigarette 香烟. **3** [C] (*Brit*) (formerly) junior boy at a public school performing certain duties for a senior boy (旧时)公学中为高年级男生服务的低年级男生. **4** [C] (*esp US*) = FAGGOT 3.

▷ **fag** /fæg; fæg/ *v* **(-gg-)** **1** [I, Ipr, Ip] ~ **(away) (at sth/at doing sth)** (*infml* 口) do very tiring work 做非常累的工作: *fagging (away) in the office, at her work* 在办公室辛勤工作、辛苦地做她的工作. **2** [I, Ipr] ~ **(for sb)** act as a fag(3) (for sb) 为(某高年级生)服务. **3** (phr v) **fag sb/sth out** (*infml* 口) make (a person or an animal) very tired 使(某人或某动物)极度疲劳: *Running soon fags me out.* 我很快就跑累了. ○ *He was completely fagged out*, ie exhausted. 他完全筋疲力尽了.

□ **'fag-end** *n* (*Brit infml* 口) **1** end of a cigarette after it has been smoked 香烟头; 烟蒂. **2** (*fig* 比喻) inferior or useless remnant; worthless part of anything 低劣或无用的剩余物; 无价值的部分: *He only heard the fag-end of their conversation.* 他只听到他们交谈中无足轻重的部分.

fag·got (*US* **fagot**) /'fægət; 'fægət/ *n* **1** bundle of sticks or twigs tied together for burning 枝条捆; 柴捆. **2** ball of chopped seasoned meat, etc cooked by baking or frying 烤的或煎的肉丸. **3** (also *esp US* **fag**) (*infml derog* 口, 贬) male homosexual 男同性恋者.

fah = FA.

Fahr·en·heit /'færənhaɪt; 'færən,haɪt/ *adj* of a temperature scale with the freezing-point of water at 32° and the boiling-point at 212° 华氏温度计的, 华氏的(冰点为32度, 沸点为212度): *The temperature today is seventy degrees Fahrenheit.* 今天气温是华氏七十度. ⇨ App 4, 5 见附录 4、5. Cf 参看 CENTIGRADE.

fai·ence /,faɪ'ɑ:ns; faɪ'ɑns/ *n* [U] decorated and glazed earthenware or porcelain 彩陶; 彩色瓷器.

fail /feɪl; fel/ *v* **1 (a)** [I, Ipr, Tn, Tt] ~ **(in sth)** be unsuccessful in (sth) 在(某事物)中失败: *If you don't work hard, you may fail.* 不努力就可能失败. ○ *I passed in maths but failed in French.* 我数学及格, 但法语不及格. ○ *He failed his driving-test.* 他驾驶测验不合格. ○ *She failed to reach the semi-finals.* 她未能进入半决赛. **(b)** [Tn] decide that (a candidate) is unsuccessful 评定(应考者)不及格: *The examiners failed half the candidates.* 主考者评定半数应试者不及格. Cf 参看 SUCCEED 1. **2** [It] forget, neglect or be unable (to do sth) 忘记、忽视或未能(做某事): *He never fails to write* (ie always writes) *to his mother every week.* 他每周都给母亲写信. ○ *She did not fail to keep* (ie She did keep) *her word.* 她没有食言. ○ *Your promises have failed to* (ie did not) *materialize.* 你没有信守诺言. **3** [I, Tn] not be enough for (sb); end or be lacking while still needed or expected by (sb) 不足; 短少; 缺乏: *The crops failed because of drought.* 由于干旱, 农作物歉收. ○ *Our water supply has failed (us).* 我们的水供应不足. ○ *Words fail me*, ie I cannot find words (to describe my feelings, etc). 我无法用言语来表达(自己的感情等). **4** [I] **(a)** (of health, eyesight, etc) become weak (指健康状况、视力等)衰退: *His eyesight is failing.* 他的视力渐渐衰退了. ○ *He has suffered from failing health/has been failing in health for the last two years.* 近两年来, 他的健康状况每况愈下. **(b)** stop working properly 失灵; 失去作用: *The brakes failed.* 煞车失灵了. **5** [I] become bankrupt 破产; 倒闭: *Several banks failed during the depression.* 有几家银行在不景气时期倒闭了.

▷ **fail** *n* **1** failure in an examination 考试不及格: *I had three passes and one fail.* 我考试三门及格一门不及格. **2** (idm 习语) **without 'fail** certainly, even though there may be difficulties; whatever happens; definitely 肯定; 一定; 必定: *I'll be there at two o'clock without fail.* 我两点钟一定到那里.

□ **'fail-safe** *adj* [attrib 作定语] (of equipment, machinery, etc) designed to compensate automatically for a breakdown or failure (指设备、机器等)设有自动保险装置的: *the fail-safe mechanism* 自动保险机械装置.

fail·ing[1] /'feɪlɪŋ; 'felɪŋ/ *n* weakness or fault (of character); shortcoming (性格中的)弱点, 缺陷, 短处: *We all have our little failings.* 我们都有小的缺点.

fail·ing[2] /'feɪlɪŋ; 'felɪŋ/ *prep* **1** if (sth) does not happen; without (sth) 如果(某事)不发生; 如果没有(某事物): *failing this*, ie if this does not happen 倘若此事不发生 ○ *failing an answer*, ie if no answer is received 若无答复. **2** if (sb) is not available 如果(某人)不在; 如果没有(某人): *Failing Smith, try Jones.* 要是史密斯不在, 就找琼斯.

fail·ure /'feɪljə(r); 'feljɚ/ *n* **1 (a)** [U] lack of success 失败; 不成功: *Failure in one examination should not stop you trying again.* 一次考试不及格不应妨碍你再试一次. ○ *The enterprise was doomed to failure.* 该企业注定要失败. ○ *All my efforts ended in failure*, ie were unsuccessful. 我所有的努力都失败了. **(b)** [C] instance of this 失败: *Success came after many failures.* 经多次失败后, 终于获得成功. **(c)** [C] person, attempt or thing that fails 失败的人、尝试或事物: *He was a failure as a teacher.* 他当过教师, 却不称职. ○ *Our new radio is an utter failure.* 我们的新收音机完全是个废物. **2 (a)** [U] state of being inadequate; not functioning as is expected or required 不足; 缺乏; 失灵; 故障: *a case of heart failure* 心力衰竭的患者 ○ *Failure of crops often results in famine.* 歉收常引起饥荒. **(b)** [C] instance of this 不足; 缺乏; 失灵; 故障: *'engine failures* 发动机故障 ○ *another crop failure* 农作物又一次歉收. **3 (a)** [U] ~ **to do sth** neglecting or forgetting to do sth 忽略或忘记做某事: *failure to comply with the regulations* 未遵守规则. **(b)** [C] ~ **to do sth** instance of this 忽略; 忘记: *repeated failures to appear in court* 多次未出庭.

faint[1] /feɪnt; fent/ *adj* **(-er, -est)** **1** that cannot be clearly perceived by the senses; indistinct; not intense in colour or sound or smell 微弱的; 模糊的; 暗淡的; 隐约的: *The sounds of music grew fainter in the distance.* 音乐的声音在远处逐渐模糊了. ○ *Only faint traces of the tiger's tracks could be seen.* 老虎的踪迹仅依稀可见. **2** (of ideas, etc) weak; vague (指想法等)模糊的, 不明确的: *There is a faint hope that she may be cured.* 她获治愈的希望渺茫. **3 (a)** (of physical abilities) lacking strength (指体力)无力的, 虚弱的: *in a faint voice* 以有气无力的声音 ○ *His breathing became faint.* 他的呼吸变得微弱了. **(b)** [pred 作表语] (of people) likely to lose consciousness; giddy (指人)易失去知觉; 昏眩: *She looks/feels faint.* 她看来[感到]快要晕倒了. **(c)** [pred 作表语] (of people) weak; exhausted (指人)无力, 精疲力竭: *The explorers were faint from hunger and cold.* 探险者们因饥寒交迫而委顿不堪. **4** (of actions, etc) weak; unlikely to have much effect (指动作等)无力的, 似无甚效果的: *a faint show of resistance* 软弱无力装装样子

的抵抗 ○ *make a faint attempt to do sth* 未尽全力尝试做某事. **5** (idm 习语) **damn sb/sth with faint praise** ⇨ DAMN[1]. **not have the 'faintest/'foggiest (idea)** (*infml* 口) not know at all 根本不知道: *'Do you know where she is?' 'Sorry, I haven't the faintest.'* '你知道她在哪里吗?' '对不起, 我一点也不知道.' ▷ **faintly** *adv*. **faint·ness** *n* [U].

□ ˌ**faint-'hearted** *adj* timid; not brave 怯懦的; 不勇敢的. ˌ**faint-'heartedly** *adv*. ˌ**faint-'heartedness** *n* [U].

faint[2] /feɪnt; fent/ *v* [I, Ipr] lose consciousness (because of heat, shock, loss of blood, etc) (因受热、受惊、失血等)失去知觉; 昏倒: *He fainted (from hunger).* 他(饿得)昏倒了.

▷ **faint** *n* **1** [sing] act or state of fainting 昏厥; 不省人事. **2** (idm 习语) **in a (dead) faint** (completely) unconscious (完全)失去知觉: *She fell to the ground in a dead faint.* 她昏倒在地, 全然不省人事.

fair[1] /feə(r); fɛr/ *adj* **1** (**a**) **~ (to/on sb)** treating each person, side, etc equally and according to the law, rules, etc; impartial (按照法律、规则等)公平地对待每个人、各方等; 公正的: *Our teacher isn't fair: he always gives the highest marks to his favourites.* 我们老师不公正, 总是给他喜欢的学生高分数. ○ *She deserves a fair trial.* 她应该得到公正的审判. ○ *The punishment was quite fair.* 这一惩罚十分公正. ○ *The ruling was not fair to everyone.* 这项裁决并非对每人都公正. (**b**) in accordance with what is deserved or expected or with existing rules 应得的; 合理的; 公道的: *a fair share, wage, price* 应得的一份、合理的工资、公道的价钱 ○ *It was a fair fight*, ie The rules of boxing were observed. 那是一场公正的拳击比赛(遵守拳击规则). ○ *It's not fair to give him the prize/not fair that he should be given the prize.* 让他获奖是不公正的. **2** (**a**) average; moderately good 中等的; 尚可的; 不错的: *There's a fair chance that we might win this time.* 这次我们颇有机会能赢. ○ *His knowledge of French is fair, but ought to be better.* 他法语还不错, 但应该再好些. (**b**) [attrib 作定语] (*infml* 口) quite large, long, etc 相当大的、相当长的等: *A fair number of people came along.* 来了不少人. **3** (**a**) (of the weather) good; dry and fine (指天气)好的; 晴朗的: *hoping for fair weather* 希望有好天气. (**b**) (of winds) favourable (指风)顺风的: *They set sail with the first fair wind.* 他们一有顺风就扬帆起航. **4** (of the skin or the hair) pale; light in colour (指皮肤或毛发)白皙的, 浅色的: *a fair complexion* 白皙的肤色 ○ *fair hair* 浅色的毛发. **5** (*arch* 古) beautiful 美丽的: *a fair maiden* 美丽的姑娘. ⇨Usage at BEAUTIFUL 用法见 BEAUTIFUL. **6** (idm 习语) **by ˌfair means or 'foul** somehow or other, whether by good or evil methods 千方百计; 不择手段: *She's determined to win, by fair means or foul.* 她决心要赢, 那怕是不择手段. **by one's ˌown fair 'hand** (*joc* 谑) by oneself 亲手; 亲自: *I hope you'll appreciate this: it's all done by my/mine own fair hand.* 希望你喜欢这件东西, 这是我亲手做的. **a fair 'cop** (*sl* 俚) legitimate arrest (usu made while the crime is being committed) 依法逮捕(通常为作案时). **a fair crack of the 'whip** (*infml* 口) reasonable chance to share in sth, to be successful, etc 分享某物、获得成功等的合理机会: *give him a fair crack of the whip* 给他一次应有的机会. **a fair/square deal** ⇨ DEAL[4]. **fair 'do/'dos/'do's** (*Brit infml* 口) (used esp as an *interj* 尤用作感叹语) fair treatment; fair shares 公平对待; 公平的份额: *Come on, fair dos — you've had a long go on the computer and now it's my turn.* 行了, 机会均等——你用计算机已经很长时间了, 现在该轮到我了. **fair 'game** person or thing that it is considered reasonable to chase, ridicule, etc 认为可追逐、嘲弄等的人或物: *The younger teachers were fair game for playing tricks on.* 那些年轻教师常是受作弄的对象. **(give sb/get) a fair 'hearing** opportunity of being listened to impartially, usu in a lawcourt 公平的申辩机会(通常指于法庭中). **fair 'play** equal treatment of both or all sides because of respect for the rules 尊重规则公平对待双方或各方: *determined to see fair play*, ie to see that no injustice is done 决心要让事情得到公正处理. **a fair 'question** question that is reasonable to ask (but often difficult to answer) 合理的问题(但常难以回答): *'If the proposals are obviously sensible, why do you oppose them?' 'That's a fair question.'* '这些建议若显然合理, 你为什么反对呢?' '这个问题倒是言之成理.' **fair's 'fair** (*infml* 口) (used as a protest or a reminder that) sb should be dealt with fairly (用以表示不满或提示)某人应受到公平对待: *'Come on, Sarah. Give me a bit more — fair's fair!'* '好了, 萨拉. 再给我一点——应当公平才是!' **a fair 'shake** (*US infml* 口) just or reasonable arrangement; fair chance 公正、合理的安排; 均等的机会. **have, etc (more than) one's fair share of sth** have, etc (more than) a usual or an expected amount of sth 得到(超过)通常得到的或期望得到的数量: *We got more than our fair share of rain on holiday.* 我们这次假期里遇到的雨天太多了. **in a fair way to do sth** likely to do sth 可能做某事物: *in a fair way to succeed* 可能成功. **in a fair way of 'business** having quite a large, successful, etc business 有相当大的、成功的…生意. **set 'fair** (of the weather) fine and with no sign of change (指天气)晴朗而无变化迹象. ▷ **fair·ness** *n* [U].

□ ˌ**fair 'copy** neat copy of a corrected document (修改后的)誊清本, 清稿: *Please make a fair copy of this letter.* 请把这封信誊写清楚.

ˌ**fair-'haired** *adj* with light-coloured or blond hair 浅色毛发的; 金色毛发的.

ˌ**fair-'minded** *adj* fair in judgement; not prejudiced 公正的; 不偏不倚的.

the 'fair sex (*dated or joc* 旧或谑) women 妇女.

ˌ**fair-to-'middling** (*infml* 口) *adj* slightly better than average 比一般稍好的.

ˌ**fair-weather 'friend** person who stops being a friend when one is in trouble 顺境中的朋友(不能共患难者).

fair[2] /feə(r); fɛr/ *adv* **1** in a fair[1](1) manner 公平地; 公正地; 正直地. **2** (idm 习语) **fair and 'square** (**a**) exactly on target 正中目标. (**b**) with no uncertainty or possibility of error, misunderstanding, etc 毋庸置疑; 无差错或误解等: *The blame rests fair and square on my shoulders.* 这一罪过着实地落在我的头上. **fair e'nough** (used esp as an *interj* 尤用作感叹语) (*infml* 口) (sometimes showing unwilling agreement) all right; I accept (有时用以表示勉强的同意)行, 好吧, 我接受. **play 'fair** play or act fairly, following rules or accepted standards (遵循规则或公认的标准)公平地比赛或行事: *Come on, you're not playing fair.* 得了吧, 你这样做不公平.

fair[3] /feə(r); fɛr/ *n* **1** market (esp for farm animals and farm products) held regularly in a particular place, often with entertainments 集市(尤指买卖牲口、农产品者, 在一固定地点定期举行, 常伴有娱乐表演). **2** large-scale exhibition of commercial and industrial goods (商品及工业产品的)大型展览会; 博览会: *a world fair* 世界博览会 ○ *a trade fair* 交易会. ⇨Usage at DEMONSTRATION 用法见 DEMONSTRATION.

□ **'fairground** *n* outdoor area where fun-fairs are held 露天游乐场.

fairly /ˈfeəlɪ; ˋfɛrlɪ/ *adv* **1** in a fair manner; honestly 公平地; 公正地; 诚实地: *You're not treating us fairly.* 你对我们不公正. **2** (before *adjs* and *advs* 用于形容词和副词之前) to a certain extent; moderately 相当地; 适度地: *This is a fairly easy book.* 这是相当浅易的书. ○ *We must leave fairly soon*, ie before very long. 我们得快些离开. **3** completely; actually 完全地; 简直: *Her suggestion fairly took me by surprise.* 她的建议真叫我大吃一惊. ○ *I fairly jumped for joy.* 我简直高兴得跳了起来. ○ *The time fairly raced by.* 时间过得真快. **4** (idm 习语) **fairly and squarely** = FAIR AND SQUARE (FAIR[2]).

NOTE ON USAGE 用法: The adverbs **fairly**, **quite**, **rather** and **pretty** can all mean 'moderately', 'to some extent' or 'not very' and are used to alter the strength of adjectives and adverbs. ☆ **fairly**、**quite**、**rather**、**pretty** 这几个副词均可表示'适度地'、'在某种程度上'或'不很'的意思, 常用以改变所修饰的形容词或副词的分量. **Fairly** is the weakest and **pretty** the strongest and most informal, but their effect is very much influenced by intonation. ☆ **fairly** 词义最弱而 **pretty** 词义最强, 也最通俗, 但词义的强弱受语调的影响很大. Generally, the more any of these adverbs is stressed, the more negative the sentence sounds. 一般说来, 这类副词读得越重, 句子听起来否定含义就越强. **1** When **rather** or **pretty** is used with a positive quality, it can sound enthusiastic ☆ **rather** 或 **pretty** 与褒义词连用时, 听起来心情愉快: *a rather/pretty good play* 一出相

F

当好的戏. With a negative or variable quality they express disapproval 这两个词与贬义词或可褒可贬的词连用时, 表示不赞成或不满意: *rather/pretty poor work* 相当差的工作 ○ *I'm rather/pretty warm.* 我很热. ○ *It's rather/pretty small/big.* 这可太小[大]了. **2 Fairly** is mostly used with positive qualities ☆ **fairly** 多与褒义词连用: *fairly tidy, spacious, friendly, etc* 挺整洁、宽敞、热情等 (compare 试比较: *rather untidy, cramped, unfriendly, etc* 很零乱、狭窄、冷淡等). **3** Only **rather** can be used with comparative expressions and **too** 只有 **rather** 可与比较级的词语和 **too** 连用: *The house is rather bigger than we thought.* 这所房子比我们想的大得多. ○ *These shoes are rather too small.* 这双鞋未免太小了. **4 Rather** and **quite** can precede the indefinite article when followed by an adjective + noun ☆ **rather** 和 **quite** 与'不定冠词+形容词+名词'连用时, 可置于不定冠词之前: *rather/quite a nice day* 十分晴朗的一天 ○ *a rather/quite/fairly/pretty nice day* 十分晴朗的一天. See also note on usage at QUITE 另见 QUITE 所附用法.

fair·way /ˈfeəweɪ; ˋfɛrˏwe/ *n* **1** part of a golf-course between the tee and the green, kept free of rough grass (高尔夫球场上的)平坦球道(球座和草坪间剪平的草地). ⇨illus at GOLF 见 GOLF 插图. Cf 参看 ROUGH³ 1. **2** channel that ships can sail through easily 航道; 水路.

fairy /ˈfeərɪ; ˋfɛrɪ/ *n* **1** small imaginary being with magical powers 小仙子; 小精灵: [attrib 作定语] *fairy voices, footsteps* 娇美的声音、轻巧的脚步. **2** (*sl derog* 俚, 贬) male homosexual 男同性恋者.

□ ˌ**fairy ˈgodmother** person who provides unexpected help 提供意外帮助的恩人.

ˈ**fairyland** /-lænd; -ˌlænd/ *n* **1** home of fairies 仙界; 仙国. **2** (*fig* 比喻) beautiful or enchanted place 仙境; 奇境: *The toy-shop is a fairyland for young children.* 玩具店就是幼儿的乐园.

ˈ**fairy lights** small coloured electric lights used as decoration (作装饰用的)彩色小灯.

ˈ**fairy story**, ˈ**fairy-tale** **1** story about fairies, magic, etc, usu for children 神话故事; 童话: [attrib 作定语] *Her marriage to the prince seemed like a fairy-tale romance.* 她与王子结婚, 这事像是神话中的爱情故事. **2** untrue or incredible story; falsehood 不真实的或不可信的事; 谎言: *'Now tell me the truth: I don't want any more of your fairy stories.'* '把真相告诉我, 我不想再听你胡诌了.'

fait ac·com·pli /ˌfeɪt əˈkɒmpliː; *US* əkɒmˈpliː; ˋfet ˌækɑmˋpli/ (*pl* **faits accomplis**) (*French* 法) thing already done, that cannot be undone and is therefore not worth arguing about 既成事实: *She married the man her parents disapproved of and presented them with a fait accompli.* 她所嫁的人她父母并不满意, 但这已是既成事实.

faith /feɪθ; feθ/ *n* **1** [U] **~ (in sb/sth)** trust; strong belief; unquestioning confidence 信任; 信仰; 信心: *put one's faith in God* 信仰上帝 ○ *Have you any faith in what he says?* 你相信他的话吗? ○ *I haven't much faith in this medicine.* 我对这种药没有多大信心. ○ *I've lost faith in that fellow,* ie I can no longer trust him. 我再也不相信那个家伙了. **2** [U, sing] strong belief, without proof, in God or in an established religion 宗教信仰: *a strong faith* 坚定的宗教信仰 ○ *lose one's faith* 失去对上帝的信仰 ○ *Faith is stronger than reason.* 宗教信仰比推理劝说更具威力. **3** [C] religion 宗教: *the Christian, Jewish and Muslim faiths* 基督教、犹太教和伊斯兰教. **4** (idm 习语) **break/keep faith with sb** break/keep one's promise to sb; be disloyal/loyal to sb 对某人不守信用[守信用]; 对某人不忠诚[忠诚]. **in good ˈfaith** with honest intentions 真诚地; 诚意地: *She signed the letter in good faith, not realizing its implications.* 她真心实意地在信上签了字, 没意识到其中另有含义. ○ *He bought the painting in good faith,* eg not realizing that it had been stolen. 他买这幅画时不虞内有跷蹊(如未想到是贼赃).

□ ˈ**faith-cure** *n* [C], ˈ**faith-healing** *n* [U] cure, etc that depends on faith rather than on medicines or other treatment 信仰疗法. ˈ**faith-healer** *n*.

faith·ful /ˈfeɪθfl; ˋfeθfəl/ *adj* **1 ~ (to sb/sth)** loyal (to sb/sth) (对某人[某事])忠实的: *a faithful friend* 忠实的朋友 ○ *faithful to his beliefs* 忠实于他的信仰 ○ *She was always faithful to her husband,* ie never had a sexual relationship with anyone else. 她对丈夫一直很忠诚. **2** [attrib 作定语] able to be trusted; conscientious 可信赖的; 认真的: *a faithful worker* 忠诚可靠的工作者 ○ *a faithful correspondent,* ie one who writes regularly 经常通信的人. **3** true to the facts; accurate 真实的; 正确的: *a faithful copy, description, account, etc* 精确的副本、描写、报道等.

▷ **the faith·ful** *n* [pl *v*] true believers (in a religion) (某宗教的)忠实信徒.

faith·fully /-fəlɪ; -fəlɪ/ *adv* **1** in a faithful manner 忠实地: *The old nurse had served the family faithfully for thirty years.* 老保姆为这个家庭忠实地服务了三十年. ○ *He followed the instructions faithfully.* 他严格遵守指令. **2** (idm 习语) **yours faithfully** ⇨ YOURS (YOUR). ⇨ Usage at YOUR 用法见 YOUR.

faith·ful·ness *n* [U].

faith·less /ˈfeɪθlɪs; ˋfeθlɪs/ *adj* not trustworthy; not loyal 不可靠的; 不忠实的: *a faithless friend, wife, ally, etc* 不忠实的朋友、妻子、盟邦等. ▷ **faith·lessly** *adv*. **faith·less·ness** *n* [U].

fake /feɪk; fek/ *n* (**a**) object (eg a work of art) that seems genuine but is not 赝品(如伪造的艺术品): *That's not a real diamond necklace, it's just a fake!* 那不是真钻石项链, 是假的! Cf 参看 COUNTERFEIT, FORGERY (FORGE²). (**b**) person who tries to deceive by pretending to be what he is not 骗子; 冒充者: *He looked like a postman but he was really a fake.* 他看上去像个邮递员, 但实际上是假冒的.

▷ **fake** *adj* not genuine 假的; 伪造的: *fake furs, jewellery, etc* 假的毛皮、珠宝等 ○ *a fake policeman* 假冒的警察.

fake *v* [Tn] **1** make (sth false) so that it seems genuine 伪造(某物): *He faked his father's signature.* 他伪造父亲的签字. ○ *Her whole story had been faked,* ie was completely untrue. 她的话全都是编造的. **2** pretend (sth); feign 假装(某事物); 佯装: *fake surprise, grief, illness* 装出吃惊、悲伤、患病的样子. **faker** *n*.

fakir /ˈfeɪkɪə(r); *US* fəˈk-; fəˋkɪr/ *n* **1** Hindu religious beggar regarded as a holy man (印度教中视为圣者的)托钵僧, 行者. **2** member of a Muslim holy sect who lives by begging (伊斯兰教的)托钵僧.

fal·con /ˈfɔːlkən; *US* ˈfælkən; ˋfælkən/ *n* small bird of prey 猎鹰.

▷ **fal·coner** *n* (**a**) person who trains falcons to hunt and kill other birds or animals for sport 训练猎鹰者. (**b**) person who keeps trained falcons 养猎鹰者.

fal·conry /-rɪ; -rɪ/ *n* [U] (**a**) sport of hunting with falcons 放鹰捕猎; 鹰猎. (**b**) art of breeding and training falcons 猎鹰饲养术; 猎鹰训练术.

fall¹ /fɔːl; fɔl/ *v* (*pt* **fell** /fel; fɛl/, *pp* **fallen** /ˈfɔːlən; ˋfɔlən/) **1** [I, Ipr, Ip] come or go down from force of weight, loss of balance, etc; descend or drop 落下; 跌落; 降落; 掉下: *The rain was falling steadily.* 雨不停地下着. ○ *The leaves fall in autumn.* 秋天树叶凋落. ○ *He slipped and fell ten feet.* 他失足自十英尺高处跌了下来. ○ *That parcel contains glass — don't let it fall.* 那包裹里有玻璃制品——别掉在地上. ○ *The book fell off the table onto the floor.* 那本书从桌上掉到地上. ○ *He fell into the river.* 他掉进河里了. ○ *I need a new bicycle lamp — my old one fell off and broke.* 我需要一个新的自行车车灯——旧的摔破了. **2** [I, Ipr] **~ (on/upon sb/sth)** come as if by dropping suddenly; descend 突然降临; 来临: *A sudden silence fell.* 突然静了下来. ○ *Darkness falls quickly in the tropics.* 热带地区天黑得很快. ○ *Fear fell upon them.* 他们突然感到很害怕. **3** [I, Ipr, Ip] **~ (down/over)** stop standing, esp suddenly; collapse 倒下(尤指突然间); 倒塌: *Many trees fell in the storm.* 在那场暴风雨中有许多树都倒了. ○ *He fell on his knees* (ie knelt down) *and begged for mercy.* 他跪下求饶. ○ *The toddler tried to walk but kept falling down.* 那小孩学着走路但老是跌跤. ○ *She fell over and broke her leg.* 她跌倒后摔折了腿. ○ (*fig* 比喻) *Six wickets fell* (ie Six batsmen in cricket were dismissed) *before lunch.* 午饭前有六个板球击球员被杀出局. **4** [Ipr] hang down 垂下; 低垂: *Her hair fell over her shoulders in a mass of curls.* 她的鬈发披在肩上. ○ *His beard fell to his chest.* 他的胡须垂到胸前. **5** [I] decrease in amount, number or intensity (数量、数目)下降; (强度)变弱: *Prices fell on the stock market.* 股市行情下跌. ○ *Her spirits fell* (ie She became sad) *at the bad news.* 她听到这坏消息后情绪很低落. ○ *Her voice fell as they entered the room.* 他们走进房间时她的声音低了下来. ○ *The temperature fell sharply in the night.* 夜间温度急剧下降. **6** [I, Ip] **~ (away/off)** slope downwards 向下倾斜: *Beyond the hill, the land falls (away) sharply towards the river.* 山那边地面呈陡坡向河边倾斜. **7** [I] **(a)** lose one's position, office or power; be defeated 失去地位、职位或权力; 垮台: *The government fell after the revolution.* 政府在那场革命之后垮台了. **(b)** die in battle; be shot 阵亡; 被击毙: *Half the regiment fell before the enemy onslaught.* 在敌军猛攻下, 这个团有一半人阵亡了. ○ *Six tigers fell to his rifle.* 他用步枪射倒了六只老虎. **(c)** (of a fortress, city, etc) be captured (指要塞、城市等)沦陷, 失守: *Troy finally fell (to the Greeks).* 特洛伊最终被(希腊人)攻陷. **8** [I] (*dated* 旧) sin; do wrong 犯罪; 堕落: *Eve tempted Adam and he fell.* 夏娃诱惑亚当, 结果他犯了罪. **9** [Ipr] **~ on/over sth** take the direction or position specified 朝某方向; 占据某位置: *Which syllable does the stress of this word fall on?* 这个字的重音是在哪个音节上? ○ *My eye fell on* (ie I suddenly saw) *a curious object.* 我突然看见一个奇怪的东西. ○ *A shadow fell over the room.* 有个影子映入室内. **10** [La, Ln, Ipr] **~ (into sth)** pass into a specified state; become 进入某种状态; 变成: *fall asleep* 入睡 ○ *The horse fell lame.* 那马瘸了. ○ *He fell silent.* 他静了下来. ○ *Has she fallen ill again?* 她又病了吗? ○ *When does the rent fall due?* ie When must it be paid? 租金何时到期? ○ *She fell an easy prey to his charm.* 她一下子被他迷住了. ○ *He fell into a doze*, ie began to doze. 他打起瞌睡来了. ○ *The house fell into decay.* 那房子腐朽了. **11** [I, Ipr] happen or occur; have as a date 发生; 适逢(一日期): *Easter falls early this year.* 今年的复活节来得早. ○ *Christmas Day falls on a Monday.* 今年的圣诞节是星期一. **12** [I, Ipr] be spoken 被说出: *I guessed what was happening from a few words she let fall*, ie from what she said. 我从她说的几句话中猜出发生什么事了. ○ *Not a word fell from his lips.* 他什么话也没说. **13** (For idioms containing **fall**, see entries for *ns, adjs*, etc 与 **fall** 搭配的其他习语见有关名词、形容词等的词条, 如 **fall in love (with sb)** ⇨ LOVE[1]; **fall flat** ⇨ FLAT[3].) **14** (phr v) **fall about** (*infml* 口) laugh uncontrollably 无法控制地大笑: *We all fell about (laughing/with laughter) when he did his imitation of the tea-lady.* 看到他模仿女勤杂工的样子, 我们全笑得前仰后合, 无法自制.

fall apart break; fall to pieces; disintegrate 破裂; 破碎; 散开: *My car is falling apart.* 我的汽车要散架了. ○ *Their marriage finally fell apart.* 他们的婚姻终于破裂了.

fall away (a) desert; leave 遗弃; 离开: *His supporters fell away as his popularity declined.* 在他声望下降时许多支持他的人都疏远了他. **(b)** disappear; vanish 消失: *In a crisis, old prejudices fall away and everyone works together.* 在危急关头, 大家就能捐弃前嫌, 同心协力.

fall back move or turn back; retreat 后退; 撤退; 退却: *The enemy fell back as our troops advanced.* 我军前进, 敌军后退. **fall back on sb/sth** (be able to) go to sb for support or use sth when in difficulty 有困难时(能)求助于某人, 依靠某事物: *At least we can fall back on candles if the electricity fails.* 停电时我们至少可以使用蜡烛. ○ *She's completely homeless — at least I have my parents to fall back on.* 她是真正无家可归 —— 我至少有父母可依靠.

fall behind (sb/sth) be overtaken (by sb/sth); fail to keep level (with sb/sth) 落后于(某人[某事物]): *The major world powers are afraid of falling behind in the arms race.* 世界各大强国均唯恐在军备竞赛中落后. ○ *France has fallen behind (Germany) in coal production.* 法国在产煤方面落后(于德国)了. **fall behind with sth** fail to pay for sth or to do sth for a period of time 逾期不为某事物付款或不做某事: *Don't fall behind with the rent, or you'll be evicted.* 不要逾期不缴房租, 否则会被逐出. ○ *I've fallen behind with my correspondence.* 我积压了许多信没回.

fall down be shown to be false or inadequate; collapse 显示不实或不足; 崩溃; 失败: *The plan fell down because it proved to be too expensive.* 这项计划因费用过高而告吹. **fall down on sth** (*infml* 口) fail to do sth properly or successfully 没有把某事做好: *fall down on one's promises* 未履行自己的诺言 ○ *He fell down on the job.* 他未能把这件工作做好.

fall for sb (*infml* 口) be attracted to sb; fall in love with sb 被某人所吸引; 爱上某人; 迷恋: *They met, fell for each other and got married six weeks later.* 他们俩一见倾心, 六个星期后就结了婚. **fall for sth** (*infml* 口) allow oneself to be persuaded by sth, esp unwisely 相信某事(尤指不智): *The salesman said the car was in good condition, and I was foolish enough to fall for it.* 推销员说这辆汽车状况良好, 而我那么傻竟然信以为真.

fall in collapse 塌陷; 倒塌: *The roof of the tunnel fell in.* 隧道顶部塌了下来. **fall (sb) in** (cause sb to) form a military formation; (cause sb to) go on parade (使某人)排成军事队形; (使某人)集合: *The sergeant ordered his men to fall in.* 中士命令士兵集合. **fall in with sb/sth (a)** meet sb by chance; join sb; become involved with sb/sth 偶遇某人; 与某人在一起; 与某人[某事物]牵涉在一起: *He fell in with bad company.* 他交上了损友. **(b)** agree to or show support for sb/sth 同意或支持(某人[某事物]): *She fell in with my idea at once.* 她立即同意了我的意见.

fall into sth (a) be able to be divided into sth 可分为: *The lecture series falls naturally into three parts.* 该系列讲座可自然分作三部分. **(b)** develop or acquire sth 养成; 染上: *fall into bad habits* 养成坏习惯. **(c)** be trapped by sth 落入圈套: *We played a trick on them and they fell right into it.* 我们设了个圈套, 他们就正好中计.

fall off decrease in quantity or quality 数量或质量下降: *Attendance at my lectures has fallen off considerably.* 听我讲课的人已大大减少了. ○ *It used to be my favourite restaurant but the standard of cooking has fallen off recently.* 那是我以前最喜欢的饭馆, 但近来烹饪水平已大不如前了.

fall on/upon sb/sth (a) attack sb/sth fiercely 猛烈攻击某人[某事物]: *Bandits fell on the village and robbed many inhabitants.* 土匪袭击了那座村庄, 抢劫了许多村民的财物. ○ (*fig* 比喻) *The children fell on the food and ate it greedily.* 孩子们争先恐后地抢到食物, 狼吞虎咽地吃起来. **(b)** be borne or incurred by sb 由某人承担或负担: *The full cost of the wedding fell on me.* 婚礼的全部费用都由我负担.

fall out happen; occur 发生: *We were pleased with the way things fell out.* 我们对事情的进展感到高兴. **fall (sb) out** (cause to) leave military formation; go or send (sb) off parade (使某人)离开军事队形, 解散: *The men fell out quickly after their march.* 士兵在列队行进之后, 很快便解散了. **fall out (with sb)** quarrel (with sb) (与某人)争吵: *They fell out with each other just before their marriage.* 他们就在举行婚礼之前吵了起来.

fall over sb/sth stumble or trip after hitting sb/sth with one's feet when walking, etc 在行走…时脚蹴到某人[某物]而打趔趄或跌倒. **fall over oneself** be very clumsy 动作笨拙: *He was an awkward child, always falling over himself and breaking things.* 他是个笨拙的孩子, 经常笨手笨脚地把东西摔破. **fall over oneself to do sth** (*infml* 口) be specially eager to do or achieve sth 想方设法做某事或获取某事物: *People were falling over themselves to be introduced to the visiting film star.* 人们千方百计地想把自己介绍给到访的影星.

fall through fail to be completed; come to nothing 落空; 成为泡影: *Our holiday plans fell through because of transport strikes.* 我们的假期计划因运输业工人罢工而成泡影.

fall to (doing sth) begin (to do sth) 开始(做某事): *They fell to (eating) with great gusto.* 他们开始津津有味地大吃起来. ○ *She fell to brooding about what had happened to her.* 她开始沉思默想自己的遭遇. **fall to sb (to do sth)** become the duty or responsibility of sb 成为某人的义务或责任: *It fell to me to inform her of her son's death.* 要把她儿子死亡的消息告诉她, 这责任落在了我的肩上.

fall under sth be classified among sth 列入某项下: *What heading do these items fall under?* 这几项应列在哪个标题下面?

▷ **the fallen** *n* [pl *v*] (*dated or fml* 旧或文) those killed in war 阵亡者.

□ **'fall-out** *n* [U] radioactive waste carried in the air after a nuclear explosion (核爆炸后大气中的)放射尘.

falling star = SHOOTING STAR (SHOOT[1]).

fall[2] /fɔːl; fɔl/ *n* **1** [C] act or instance of falling 落下; 跌落; 降落; 掉下: *I had a fall (from a horse) and broke my* *arm.* 我(从马上)跌下来把胳膊摔断了. ○ *That was a nasty fall.* 这一跤摔得不轻. **2** ~ **(of sth)** **(a)** [C] amount of sth that falls or has fallen 某物降落的数量: *a heavy fall of snow/rain* 一场大雪[大雨] ○ *a fall of rock(s)* 落下的岩石. **(b)** [C esp *sing* 尤作单数] distance through which sb/sth falls or descends 降落的距离; 落差: *a fall of twenty feet* 下落二十英尺 ○ *a twenty-foot fall* 二十英尺的落差. **3** [C] decrease in value, quantity, intensity, etc 价值、数量、强度等的降低: *a steep fall in prices* 价格的暴跌 ○ *a fall in the numbers attending* 出席人数的减少. **4** [sing] ~ **(of sth)** (esp political) defeat; collapse (尤指政治方面的)失败; 垮台: *the fall of the Roman Empire* 罗马帝国的灭亡 ○ *The fall of the Government resulted in civil war.* 政府倒台导致内战爆发. **5** [C] (*US*) = AUTUMN: *in the fall of 1970* 在1970年的秋季 ○ *several falls ago* 几年之前 ○ [attrib 作定语] *fall fashions* 秋季式样. **6** **(a)** [C] ~ **(from sth)** loss of innocence or a state of goodness 堕落; 变坏: *a fall from grace* 失宠. **(b)** **the Fall** [sing] (*Bible* 圣经) loss of mankind's innocence following the disobedience of Adam and Eve (亚当和夏娃偷食禁果后)人类的堕落. **7** [C] (usu *pl*, esp in geographical names 通常作复数, 尤用于地名中) large amount of water falling down from a height; waterfall 瀑布: *The falls upstream are full of salmon.* 该瀑布上流有许多大马哈鱼. ○ *Niagara Falls* 尼亚加拉瀑布. **8** (idm 习语) **pride comes/goes before a fall** ⇨ PRIDE. **ride for a fall** ⇨ RIDE[2].

fal·lacy /ˈfæləsɪ; ˋfæləsɪ/ *n* **1** [C] false or mistaken belief 错误的见解; 谬见: *It's a fallacy to suppose that wealth brings happiness.* 认为财富能带来幸福, 这是一种错误的见解. **2** [U] false reasoning or argument 错误的推论; 谬论: *a statement based on fallacy* 基于错误推理的说法.

▷ **fal·la·cious** /fəˈleɪʃəs; fəˋleʃəs/ *adj* misleading; based on error 令人误解的; 谬误的: *fallacious reasoning* 错误的推理. **fal·la·ciously** *adv.*

fallen *pp* of FALL[1].

fall guy /ˈfɔːl gaɪ; ˋfɔl ˌgaɪ/ (*esp US*) **(a)** = SCAPEGOAT. **(b)** person who is easily tricked or fooled 易上当的人; 易受愚弄的人.

fall·ible /ˈfæləbl; ˋfæləbl/ *adj* liable to make mistakes 易犯错误的: *We are fallible beings.* 我们都难免犯错误. ▷ **fal·lib·il·ity** /ˌfæləˈbɪlətɪ; ˌfæləˋbɪlətɪ/ *n* [U].

Fal·lo·pian tube /fəˌləʊpɪən ˈtjuːb; *US* ˈtuːb; fəˋlopɪənˋtub/ (*anatomy* 解) either of the two tubes along which egg-cells move from the ovaries to the womb 输卵管. ⇨illus at FEMALE 见 FEMALE 插图.

fal·low /ˈfæləʊ; ˋfælo/ *adj* (of land) ploughed but left unplanted to restore its fertility (指耕地)犁过而未耕种的, 休闲的: *allow land to lie fallow* 让耕地休闲.

▷ **fal·low** *n* [U] fallow land 休闲地; 休耕地.

fal·low deer /ˈfæləʊ dɪə(r); ˋfælo dɪr/ (*pl* unchanged 复数不变) small Eurasian deer with a brownish-yellow coat that has white spots in summer 黇鹿(欧亚地区产的一种小鹿, 毛皮呈棕黄色, 夏季有白斑).

false /fɔːls; fɔls/ *adj* **1** wrong; incorrect 错误的; 不正确的: *sing a false note* 唱错音符 ○ *'A whale is a fish. True or false?'* '鲸鱼是一种鱼. 对还是错?' **2** **(a)** not genuine; artificial 假的; 人造的: *false hair, teeth, etc* 假发、假牙. **(b)** sham; pretended 冒充的; 假装的: *false modesty* 假谦虚 ○ *false tears* 虚伪的眼泪. **(c)** [usu attrib 通常作定语] misleading; not what it appears 引起误会的; 与外观不符的: *a false sense of security*, ie feeling safe when one is really in danger 虚假的安全感 ○ *false economy* 不合算的节约 ○ *give a false impression of great wealth* 给人造成很富有的假象 ○ *hounds following a false scent* 沿着误入歧途的臭迹追踪的猎狗. **(d)** deliberately made incorrect in order to deceive 弄虚作假的; 伪造的: *false weights, scales, dice, etc* 假的砝码、天平、色子等 ○ *a false passport* 假护照 ○ *a false bottom*, ie the disguised bottom of a suitcase, etc concealing a secret compartment (手提箱等秘密藏物用的)假底. **3** deliberately meant to deceive; lying 有意欺骗的; 不诚实的; 虚妄的: *false evidence* 伪证 ○ *present false claims to an insurance company* 向保险公司提出伪造的索赔要求. **4** ~ **(to sb)** unfaithful; disloyal 不忠实的; 无信义的: *a false friend/lover* 不忠实的朋友[情人]. **5** [attrib 作定语] inaccurately named 命名不准确的: *the false acacia*, ie not really an acacia tree, despite its name 刺槐(非真正的金合欢树). **6** (idm 习语) **a false aˈlarm** warning or panic about sth which does not happen 虚假的警报; 虚惊: *The rumours of a petrol shortage turned out to be a false alarm.* 汽油短缺的谣传原来是一场虚惊. **(make) a false ˈmove** unwise or forbidden action that may have unpleasant consequences (可能带来不良后果的)不明智的或不允许的行为: *'One false move and you're a dead man,' snarled the robber.* 那强盗厉声叫道: '不许动, 不然就打死你.' **(make) a false ˈstart** **(a)** (in athletics) start made before the signal (eg for a race) has been given (运动中)抢在信号令前行动(如赛跑中的抢跑). **(b)** unsuccessful beginning 不顺利的开端: *After several false starts, she became a successful journalist.* 她开始时遇到几次挫折, 后来才成为能干的记者. **(take) a false ˈstep** (make) a wrong move or action 失足; 失策: *A false step could have cost the climbers their lives.* 爬山者一失足就会丧命. **in a false poˈsition** in circumstances which result in sb being misunderstood or acting against his principles 处于被人误解的地位; 处于违背自己的原则的境地. **on/under false preˈtences** pretending to be sb else or to have certain qualifications, etc in order to deceive 冒充某人或冒充有某资格以行骗: *obtaining money on false pretences* 以诈骗手段骗钱. **strike/sound a false ˈnote** say or do the wrong thing 说错话[做错事]: *He struck a false note when he arrived for the wedding in old clothes.* 他做错了一件事, 不该穿旧衣服去参加婚礼. **(sail) under false ˈcolours** **(a)** (of a ship) displaying a flag which it has no right to use (指船)挂着伪旗(航行). **(b)** pretending or appearing to be different from what one really is 冒充的; 披着伪装骗人的.

▷ **false** *adv* (idm 习语) **play sb ˈfalse** deceive or cheat sb 欺骗某人.

falsely *adv.*

false·ness *n* [U].

false·hood /ˈfɔːlshʊd; ˋfɔls·hʊd/ *n* (*fml* 文) **1** [C] untrue statement; lie 不实之辞; 谎言: *How can you utter such falsehoods?* 你怎能说出这种假话? **2** [U] telling lies; lying 说假话; 撒谎: *guilty of falsehood* 犯了说谎的错误.

fal·setto /fɔːlˈsetəʊ; fɔlˋsɛto/ *n* (*pl* ~**s**) [C, U] (man with an) unusually high voice, esp when singing (男子的)假(高音)嗓子, 用假高音嗓子的男子(尤指唱歌时): *sing falsetto* (男子)用假高音唱 ○ [attrib 作定语] *in a falsetto tone* (男子)用尖锐的假音调.

fals·ies /ˈfɔːlsɪz; ˋfɔlsɪz/ *n* [pl] (*infml* 口) pads or material to make the breasts seem larger 假乳房(用以使乳房显得丰满的衬垫).

fals·ify /ˈfɔːlsɪfaɪ; ˋfɔlsəˌfaɪ/ *v* (*pt, pp* **-fied**) [Tn] **1** alter (eg a document) falsely 窜改(如文件); 伪造: *falsify records, accounts, etc* 伪造记录、帐目等. **2** present (sth) falsely 歪曲(某事物): *falsify an issue, facts, etc* 歪曲问题、事实等. **3** prove (sth) to be false 证明(某事物)虚假: *falsify a theory* 证明一理论不成立.

▷ **falsi·fica·tion** /ˌfɔːlsɪfɪˈkeɪʃn; ˌfɔlsəfəˋkeʃən/ *n* **(a)** [U] falsifying or being falsified 窜改; 歪曲; 伪造; 证明为虚假. **(b)** [C] change made in order to deceive 窜改; 歪曲; 伪造.

fals·ity /ˈfɔːlsətɪ; ˋfɔlsətɪ/ *n* **(a)** [U] falsehood; error 谬误; 错误. **(b)** [C] instance of this 谬误; 错误.

fal·ter /ˈfɔːltə(r); ˋfɔltɚ/ *v* [I] **1** move, walk or act hesitantly, usu because of weakness, fear or indecision 摇晃, 蹒跚, 迟疑(通常因衰弱、恐惧或犹豫): *Jane walked boldly up to the platform without faltering.* 简沉着大胆地走上讲台. **2** **(a)** (of the voice) waver (指嗓音)颤抖: *His voice faltered as he tried to speak.* 他张口说话时, 声音发颤了. **(b)** speak hesitantly 结巴地说; 支吾地说: *The lecturer faltered after dropping his notes.* 那讲师讲稿掉了以后言语就结巴了. ▷ **fal·ter·ingly** /ˈfɔːltərɪŋlɪ; ˋfɔltərɪŋlɪ/ *adv.*

fame /feɪm; fem/ *n* [U] (condition of) being known or talked about by many people 名声; 名气; 声誉: *achieve fame and fortune* 获取名利 ○ *The young musician rose quickly to fame.* 那个年轻的音乐家很快就出了名. ▷ **famed** *adj* [pred 作表语] ~ **(for sth)**: *famed for their courage* 以他们的勇敢著称.

fa·mil·iar /fəˈmɪlɪə(r); fəˋmɪljɚ/ *adj* **1** [pred 作表语] ~ **with sth** having a good knowledge of sth 对某事物熟悉; 通晓: *facts with which every schoolboy is familiar* 小

学生都熟悉的事实 ○ *I am not very familiar with botanical names.* 我不太熟悉植物学方面的名称. **2 ~ (to sb)** well known (to sb); often seen or heard 为(某人)所熟知的; 经常见到或听到的: *facts that are familiar to every schoolboy* 小学生都熟悉的事实 ○ *the familiar scenes of one's childhood* 儿时常见的情景 ○ *the familiar voices of one's friends* 朋友的熟悉的声音. **3 ~ (with sb)** friendly and informal 友好的; 不拘礼节的: *She greeted them by their first names in a familiar way.* 她和他们打招呼时亲切地直呼其名. ○ *I'm on familiar terms with my bank manager.* 我与银行经理交情很好. **4 ~ (with sb)** too informal; more friendly and informal than is acceptable 过分亲密的; 冒失的: *The children are too familiar with their teacher.* 这帮小学生对老师过于随便.

▷ **fa·mil·iar** *n* close friend or spirit 密友; 挚友; (供女巫等差遣)的精灵: *a witch's familiar* 供女巫差遣的精灵. **fa·mil·iarly** *adv* in a familiar manner; informally 亲密地; 不拘礼节地: *William, familiarly known as Billy* 威廉, 昵称比利.

fa·mili·ar·ity /fəˌmɪlɪˈærətɪ; fəˌmɪlɪˋærətɪ/ *n* **1** [U] **~ with sth** good knowledge of sth (对某事物的)熟悉, 通晓: *His familiarity with the local languages surprised me.* 他对当地各种语言如此精通令我吃惊. **2** (**a**) [U] **~ (to/towards sb)** (esp excessively) friendly informality (尤指过分地)亲密而不拘礼仪: *You should not address your teacher with such familiarity.* 你不应该这样冒失地称呼老师. (**b**) [C usu *pl* 通常作复数] instance of this; act that lacks formality 冒失; 不拘礼节的行为: *Try to discourage such familiarities from your subordinates.* 不要让下属对你这样不拘礼节. **3** (idm 习语) **familiarity breeds conˈtempt** (*saying* 谚) knowing sb/sth very well may lead to a loss of respect, fear, etc 亲昵生狎侮(过分亲密易生侮慢之心).

fa·mili·ar·ize, -ise /fəˈmɪlɪəraɪz; fəˋmɪljəˌraɪz/ *v* [Tn·pr] **~ sb/oneself with sth** give sb/acquire a thorough knowledge of sth 使某人[自己]熟悉某事物: *familiarizing oneself with a foreign language, the use of a new tool, the rules of a game* 熟悉一门外语、新工具的用法、比赛的规则. ▷ **fa·mili·ar·iza·tion, -isation** /fəˌmɪlɪəraɪˈzeɪʃn; *US* -rɪˈz-; fəˌmɪljərəˋzeʃən/ *n* [U].

fam·ily /ˈfæməlɪ; ˋfæməlɪ/ *n* **1** (**a**) [CGp] group consisting of parents and their children 家; 家庭: *Almost every family in the village owns a television.* 村上几乎每家都有电视机. ○ *All my family enjoy skiing.* 我全家都喜欢滑雪. ○ *He's a friend of the family,* ie is known and liked by the parents and their children. 他是那家的朋友. (**b**) [CGp] group consisting of parents, their children and close relatives 家庭成员及关系密切的亲戚: *the Royal Family,* ie the children and close relatives of the Sovereign 王室 ○ *All our family came to our grandfather's eightieth birthday party.* 我们全家和所有的亲戚都来参加祖父的八十岁寿宴. (**c**) [attrib 作定语] suitable for all members of this group to enjoy together, regardless of age 适合全家大小一起欣赏的: *a family film* 适合全家大小一起看的电影 ○ *family entertainment* 适合全家大小一起参加的娱乐. **2** [CGp, U] person's children 子女: *Give my regards to Mr and Mrs Jones and family.* 代我向琼斯夫妇及其子女问好. ○ *Do they have any family?* 他们有儿女吗? ○ *They have a large family.* 他们子女很多. **3** (**a**) [CGp] all the people descended from a common ancestor 家族: *Some families have farmed in this area for hundreds of years.* 有些家族在该地区务农已达数百年. ○ *She comes from a famous family.* 她出生于名门望族. ○ [attrib 作定语] *the family estate* 家族的地产 ○ *the family jewels* 家传的珠宝. (**b**) [U] ancestry 家世; 世系: *a man of good family* 家世很好的人. **4** [C] (**a**) group of related genera of animals or plants (动植物的)科: *Lions belong to the cat family.* 狮子属于猫科动物. Cf 参看 PHYLUM, CLASS 7, ORDER[1] 9, GENUS 1, SPECIES 1. (**b**) group of things (eg languages) with common features and a common source 具有相同特征和同一来源的一组事物(如语言): *the Indo-European family of languages* 印欧语系. **5** (idm 习语) **(put sb/be) in the family way** (*infml* 口) (make sb/be) pregnant (使某人)怀孕的. **run in the ˈfamily** be a feature that keeps coming back in different generations of a family 为某家族中各代人呈现出的共有特征; 世代相传: *Red hair runs in his family.* 他家族的人头发都是红色的. **start a family** ⇨ START[2].

□ ˌ**family ˈcircle** friendly group of close relatives 家庭圈子(关系密切的亲戚).

ˌ**family ˈdoctor** general practitioner normally consulted by a family 家庭医生.

ˌ**family ˈlikeness** physical resemblance between members of a family 家庭成员间外貌的相像: *This must be your brother: I can see a family likeness.* 这位一定是你哥哥, 我看你们长得很像.

ˈ**family man** man who has a wife and children, and enjoys home life 有妻室儿女并喜欢家庭生活的男子.

ˈ**family name** surname 姓. ⇨Usage at NAME[1] 用法见 NAME[1].

ˌ**family ˈplanning** planning the number of children, intervals between births, etc in a family by using birth-control 计划生育.

ˌ**family ˈtree** diagram that shows the relationship between different members of a family 家谱; 家谱图. ⇨ App 8 见附录 8.

fam·ine /ˈfæmɪn; ˋfæmɪn/ *n* [C, U] (instance of) extreme scarcity of food in a region 饥荒: *a famine in Ethiopia* 埃塞俄比亚的饥荒 ○ *The long drought was followed by months of famine.* 久旱之后出现长达数月的饥荒.

fam·ished /ˈfæmɪʃt; ˋfæmɪʃt/ *adj* [usu pred 通常作表语] (*infml* 口) very hungry 非常饿: *When's lunch? I'm famished!* 什么时候吃午饭? 我都快饿死了!

fam·ous /ˈfeɪməs; ˋfeməs/ *adj* **1 ~ (for sth)** known to very many people; celebrated 出名的; 著名的: *Paris is a famous city.* 巴黎是著名的城市. ○ *New York is famous for its skyscrapers.* 纽约以其摩天大楼驰名. ○ *She is famous as a writer.* 她是著名的作家. **2** (*dated infml* 旧, 口) excellent 极好的: *We've won a famous victory.* 我们赢得了辉煌的胜利. **3** (idm 习语) **famous last words** (*joc catchphrase* 谑, 警语) (said when sb has made an important, optimistic, etc statement which may turn out to be untrue and which he may regret saying 有人说出重要的、胸有成竹之类的话, 但却可能不确而使说话的人自觉悔不该言, 此时用此词组).

▷ **fam·ously** *adv* (*infml* 口) extremely well 极好: *The two children got on famously.* 两个孩子相处得极好.

fan 扇子

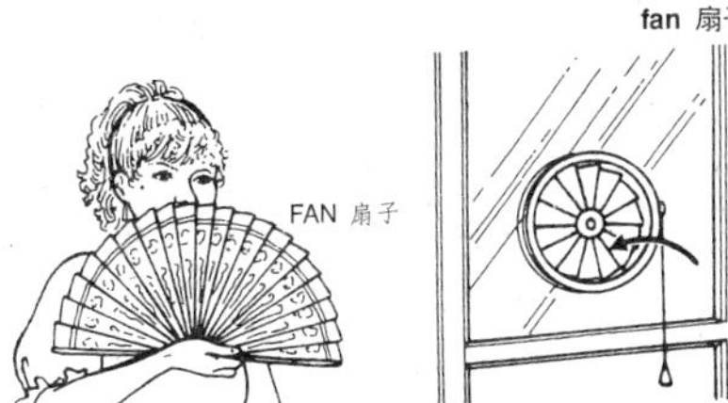

fan[1] /fæn; fæn/ *n* ⇨illus 见插图. **1** (**a**) object, often shaped like a semicircle, held in the hand and waved to create a current of cool air 扇子. (**b**) thing spread or shaped like a fan, eg the tail of a peacock 扇状物(如孔雀开屏状). **2** device with rotating blades, operated mechanically to create a current of cool air 电扇: *It's so hot — please turn the fan on.* 这么热——请把电扇打开.

□ ˈ**fan belt** belt driving the fan that cools the radiator of a car, etc 风扇皮带(带动汽车等散热器风扇的皮带). ⇨illus at App 1 见附录 1 插图, page xii.

ˈ**fan heater** device that blows hot air into a room 风扇式空气加热器.

fan[2] /fæn; fæn/ *v* (**-nn-**) **1** [Tn] make a current of air blow onto (sb/sth) with or as if with a fan 扇(某人[某物]): *cool one's face by fanning it with a newspaper* 用报纸扇风使脸凉快 ○ *fan a fire,* ie to make it burn more strongly 扇火. **2** [Tn] blow gently on (sb/sth) 徐徐吹在(某人[某物])上: *The breeze fanned our faces.* 微风轻轻吹在我们的脸上. **3** [Tn, Tn·p] **~ sth (out)** spread (esp playing-cards) in the form of a fan 展成扇形(尤指纸牌): *He fanned (out) the cards in his hand before playing.* 他出牌前先把纸牌在手里展成扇形. **4** (idm 习语) **fan the flames (of sth)** make (emotions, etc) stronger or (activity) more intense 煽动(情绪等); 使(行动)更为激烈: *Her wild behaviour merely fanned the flames of his jealousy.* 她那放肆的举动把他的妒火完全煽起. **5** (phr v) **fan out** (esp of soldiers) spread out from a central point (尤指士兵)作扇形散开: *The troops fanned out as they advanced.* 部队向前推进时呈扇形散开.

fan[3] /fæn; fæn/ *n* enthusiastic admirer or supporter of sth/sb 迷(某人[某事物]的热情崇拜者或拥护者): *football, jazz, cinema fans* 足球迷、爵士乐迷、影迷.
□ 'fan club organized group of a person's admirers 崇拜者俱乐部(由某人的崇拜者所组成的组织).
'fan mail letters from fans to the person they admire 崇拜者寄给心中偶像的信.

fan·atic /fəˈnætɪk; fəˈnætɪk/ *n* person who is too enthusiastic about sth, esp religion or politics 狂热者(尤指在宗教或政治方面): *a religious, political fanatic* 宗教狂、政治狂 ○ *model train fanatics* 对模型火车入迷的人. ▷ **fan·atic** (also **fan·at·ical** /-kl; -kl/) *adj* **~ (about sth)** obsessively enthusiastic 狂热的: *a fanatic jogger* 极喜欢慢跑的人 ○ *She's fanatical about keeping fit.* 她如醉如痴地注重健美. **fan·at·ic·ally** /-klɪ; -klɪ/ *adv*.
fan·aticism /-tɪsɪzəm; -təˌsɪzəm/ *n* [U, C] great or obsessive enthusiasm 狂热; 入迷.

fan·cier /ˈfænsɪə(r); ˈfænsɪɚ/ *n* (esp in compounds 尤用以构成复合词) person with a special interest in and love for sth 对某事物有特殊兴趣和爱好的人: *a 'dog-fancier* 玩赏狗的人 ○ *a 'pigeon-fancier* 喜爱养鸽子的人.

fan·ci·ful /ˈfænsɪfl; ˈfænsɪfəl/ *adj* **1** (of people) using the imagination rather than reason (指人)富于幻想的: *Children are very fanciful.* 儿童都很富于幻想. **2** (of things) designed or decorated in an odd but creative manner (指物)设计或装饰新颖奇特的. ▷ **fan·ci·fully** /-fəlɪ; -fəlɪ/ *adv*.

F

fancy[1] /ˈfænsɪ; ˈfænsɪ/ *n* **1** [U] power of the mind to imagine (esp unreal things) 想像力(尤指对非现实的事物): *the novelist's fancy* 小说家的想像力. **2** [C] thing imagined 想像之物: *Did I really hear someone come in, or was it only a fancy?* 我是真听到有人进来还是仅仅是幻觉而已? ○ *I have a fancy* (ie a vague idea) *that he will be late.* 我感觉他要迟到. **3** [sing] **~ (for sth)** desire; liking 渴望; 喜爱: *I have a fancy for some wine tonight.* 我今晚想喝点酒. **4** [C usu *pl* 通常作复数] small decorated cake 带装饰的小蛋糕: *fancies served with coffee* 佐咖啡的漂亮小蛋糕. **5** (idm 习语) **catch/take sb's fancy** please or attract sb 合某人的心意; 吸引某人: *She saw a dress in the shop window and it caught her fancy immediately.* 她看见商店橱窗里的一件连衣裙, 立刻觉得很合心意. **a flight of fancy** ⇨ FLIGHT[1]. **take a fancy to sb/sth** become fond of sb/sth, often without an obvious reason 喜欢上、爱上某人[某物](常无明显原因): *I've suddenly taken a fancy to detective stories.* 我突然喜欢上了侦探小说.
□ ˌ**fancy-'free** *adj* [usu pred 通常作表语] **1** not in love; not committed to anything 未在恋爱中; 不受束缚. **2** (idm 习语) **footloose and fancy-free** ⇨ FOOTLOOSE (FOOT[1]).

fancy[2] /ˈfænsɪ; ˈfænsɪ/ *adj* **1** [attrib 作定语] (esp of small things) brightly coloured; made to please the eye or taste (尤指小东西)色彩鲜艳的, 悦目的, 可口的: *fancy cakes/goods* 精美的蛋糕[物品]. **2** not plain or ordinary; unusual 有装饰的; 不寻常的; 精致的: *That's a very fancy pair of shoes!* 那是一双非常别致的鞋! **3** extravagant or exaggerated 过度的; 过分的: *fancy ideas, prices* 过分的想法、高昂的价格. **4** (*esp US*) (of food, etc) above average quality (指食物等)精选的, 精美的: *fancy vegetables* 精选的蔬菜. **5** [attrib 作定语] bred for particular points of beauty 因珍奇而特别培育的: *fancy dogs, pigeons, etc* 品种珍奇的狗、鸽子等.
□ ˌ**fancy 'dress** unusual costume, often historical or fantastic, worn at parties 聚会时所穿的奇装异服(常为有历史特色或别具一格的): [attrib 作定语] *a fancy dress ball* 化装舞会.
'**fancy man**, '**fancy woman** (*derog or joc infml* 贬或谑, 口) person's lover 情夫; 情妇; 情人.

fancy[3] /ˈfænsɪ; ˈfænsɪ/ *v* (*pt, pp* **fancied**) **1** [Tf] think or believe (sth); imagine 想; 以为; 想像: *I fancy (that) it's going to rain today.* 我看今天要下雨. ○ *He fancies she likes him.* 他以为她喜欢他. ○ *He fancied he heard footsteps behind him.* 他好像听到身后有脚步声. **2** [Tn] (*infml* 口) have a desire or wish for (sth); want 渴望或希望得到(某事物); 想要: *I fancy a cup of tea.* 我想来杯茶. ○ *What do you fancy for supper?* 你晚饭喜欢吃什么? **3** [Tn] (*Brit infml* 口) find (sb) attractive 喜爱(某人): *He rather fancies her.* 他很喜欢她. **4** [I, Tn, Tg, Tsg] (usu imperative, expressing surprise, disbelief, shock, etc 通常用于祈使句, 表示惊奇、不相信、震惊等): *Fancy that!* 多奇怪呀! ○ *Just fancy!* 真想不到! ○ *Fancy her being so rude!* 她竟如此放肆! ○ *Fancy never having seen the sea!* 竟然从未见过大海! **5** (idm 习语) **fancy oneself (as sth)** (*infml* 口) have a very high opinion of oneself; be conceited 自命不凡; 自负: *She rather fancies herself as a singer.* 她自以为是了不起的歌手.

fan·dango /fænˈdæŋgəʊ; fænˈdæŋgo/ *n* (*pl* **~es**) **1** (music for a) lively Spanish or S American dance 方丹戈舞(西班牙或南美的轻快舞蹈); 方丹戈舞曲. **2** nonsense 愚蠢的举动; 胡闹: *Politics before an election can be quite a fandango.* 选举前的政治活动简直可以说是胡闹一通.

fan·fare /ˈfænfeə(r); ˈfænˌfɛr/ *n* short ceremonial piece of music, usu played on trumpets 仪式上用的短曲(通常用小号吹奏): *A fanfare was played as the queen entered.* 女王驾到时, 小号奏起欢迎乐曲.

fang /fæŋ; fæŋ/ *n* **1** long sharp tooth, esp of dogs and wolves 长而尖的牙(尤指狗和狼的): *The dog growled and showed its fangs.* 那狗狺狺狂吠, 露出了尖牙. **2** snake's tooth with which it injects poison (蛇的)毒牙. **3** (idm 习语) **draw sb's/sth's teeth/fangs** ⇨ DRAW[2].

fan·light /ˈfænlaɪt; ˈfænˌlaɪt/ *n* small window above a door or another window 气窗(门或窗户上方的小窗).

fanny /ˈfænɪ; ˈfænɪ/ *n* **1** (*Brit* ⚠ *sl* 讳, 俚) female sex organs 屄; 女性生殖器. **2** (*sl* 俚 *esp US*) buttocks 屁股.

fan·tasia /fænˈteɪzɪə; *US* -ˈteɪʒə; fænˈteʒə/ *n* (also **fant·asy**) imaginative musical or other composition with no fixed form 幻想曲.

fan·tas·ize, -ise /ˈfæntəsaɪz; ˈfæntəˌsaɪz/ *v* [I, Ipr, Tf] **~ (about sth)** imagine or create a fantasy; daydream 想像; 幻想; 做白日梦: *He liked to fantasize that he had won a gold medal.* 他好想入非非, 觉得自己赢了一块金牌.

fant·astic /fænˈtæstɪk; fænˈtæstɪk/ *adj* **1** (**a**) wild and strange 荒诞的; 奇异的: *fantastic dreams, stories* 荒诞的梦、故事. (**b**) impossible to carry out; not practical 无法实现的; 不实际的: *fantastic schemes, proposals, etc* 不实际的计划、建议等. **2** (*infml* 口) marvellous; excellent 了不起的; 极好的: *She's a fantastic swimmer.* 她游泳游得非常好. ○ *You passed your test? Fantastic!* 你测验及格了? 太棒了! **3** (*infml* 口) very large; extraordinary 巨大的; 异乎寻常的: *Their wedding cost a fantastic amount of money.* 他们的婚礼花费了很大一笔钱. ▷ **fant·ast·ic·ally** /-klɪ; -klɪ/ *adv*: *You did fantastically well in the exam.* 你考得非常好.

fant·asy (also **phant·asy**) /ˈfæntəsɪ; ˈfæntəsɪ/ *n* **1** [U] imagination or fancy[1](2), esp when completely unrelated to reality 想像, 幻想(尤指完全脱离实际的): [attrib 作定语] *live in a fantasy world* 生活在幻想世界中. **2** [C] product of the imagination; wild or unrealistic notion 幻想出来的东西; 荒诞的或不现实的念头: *sexual fantasies* 性幻想 ○ *Stop looking for the perfect job — it's just a fantasy.* 别想找十全十美的工作了——那简直是幻想. **3** [C] = FANTASIA.

FAO /ˌef eɪ ˈəʊ; ˈɛf e ˈo/ *abbr* 缩写 = Food and Agriculture Organization (of the United Nations) (联合国)粮食及农业组织.

far[1] /fɑː(r); fɑr/ *adj* (**farther** /ˈfɑːðə(r); ˈfɑrðɚ/ or **further** /ˈfɜːðə(r); ˈfɝðɚ/, **farthest** /ˈfɑːðɪst; ˈfɑrðɪst/ or **furthest** /ˈfɜːðɪst; ˈfɝðɪst/) [attrib 作定语] **1** (*dated or fml* 旧或文) distant 远的; 远方的: *a far country* 远方的国家 ○ *to journey into far regions* 到远方去旅行. **2** more remote 较远的: *at the far end of the street* 在街的那一头 ○ *on the far bank of the river* 在河的彼岸 ○ *She's on the far right*, ie holds extreme right-wing views. 她持极右观点. **3** (idm 习语) **a far cry from sth/doing sth** (*infml* 口) a very different experience from sth/doing sth 与某事物[做某事物]大不相同: *Life on a farm is a far cry from what I've been used to.* 农场生活与我已过惯的日子迥然不同.
□ **the Far 'East** China, Japan and other countries of E

and SE Asia 远东(中国、日本及东亚与东南亚其他国家).

the Far 'West (*US*) the part of the USA near the Pacific coast 美国西部太平洋沿岸地区.

far[2] /fɑː(r); fɑr/ *adv* (**farther** /ˈfɑːðə(r); ˈfɑrðɚ/ or **further** /ˈfɜːðə(r); ˈfɝðɚ/, **farthest** /ˈfɑːðɪst; ˈfɑrðɪst/ or **furthest** /ˈfɜːðɪst; ˈfɝðɪst/) **1** (usu in questions and negative sentences 通常用于疑问句和否定句) (of space) at or to a great distance (指空间)远: *How far is it to London from here?* 从这里到伦敦有多远? (Cf 参看 *London's a long way from here.* 伦敦离这里很远.) ○ *How far have we walked?* 我们走了多远了? (Cf 参看 *We've walked only a short way.* 我们只走了一小段路程.) ○ *We didn't go far.* 我们没有走远. **2** (preceding particles and *preps* 用于小品词和介词前) (**a**) (of space) by a great distance (指空间)远: *far above the clouds* 远在云层之上 ○ *not far from here* 离这里不远 ○ *far beyond the bridge* 远在桥那边 ○ *Call me if you need me; I won't be far away/off.* 需要我时叫我一声, 我不到远处去. (**b**) (of time) a long way (指时间)久, 远: *far back in history* 在历史上久远的 ○ *as far back as 1902* 远在1902年 ○ *events that will happen far in the future* 很久以后将发生的事 ○ *We danced far into the night.* 我们跳舞跳到深夜. (**c**) (used within idioms 用于成语中) to a great extent 在很大程度上; 远远: *to live far beyond one's means* 过着远远入不敷出的生活 ○ *He's fallen far behind in his work.* 他的工作远远没有做完. **3** (preceding comparative *adjs* and *advs* 用于形容词或副词的比较级前) considerably; very much 很; 非常: *a far better solution* 好得多的解决办法 ○ *He runs far faster than his brother.* 他远比哥哥跑得快. **4** (idm 习语) **as far as** to the place mentioned, but no further 直至所提到之处为止: *I've read as far as the third chapter.* 我已读到第三章了. ○ *I'll walk with you as far as the post office.* 我陪你走到邮局. ○ *We'll go by train as far as London, and then take a coach.* 我们乘火车到伦敦, 然后换长途汽车. **as/so far as** (**a**) the same distance as 与…的距离相等: *We didn't go so far as the others.* 我们走得不如其他人远. (**b**) to the extent that; as much as 达到…的程度; 尽…; 就…: *So far as I know/As far as I can see, that is highly unlikely.* 就我所知[依我看]那是极不可能的. ○ *His parents supported him as far as they could.* 他父母竭尽全力抚养他. (**c**) (of progress) up to a specified point but not beyond (指进展)达到某一点为止: *We've got as far as collecting our data but we haven't analysed it yet.* 我们已收集了资料, 但尚未分析. **as/so far as in me 'lies** (*fml* 文) to the best of my ability; as much as I can 尽我所能; 尽我的力量. **as/so far as it, etc 'goes** to a limited extent, usu less than desirable 达到一定程度(通常并未如愿): *Your plan is a good one as far as it goes, but there are several points you've forgotten to consider.* 你的计划目前看来还算不错, 但有几点你忘了考虑进去. **as/so far as sb/sth is concerned** in the way, or to the extent, that sb/sth is involved or affected 就某人[某事物]而言: *The rise in interest rates will be disastrous as far as small firms are concerned.* 利率增加对小公司来说是大祸临头. ○ *The car is fine as far as the engine is concerned but the bodywork needs a lot of attention.* 这辆汽车发动机还不错, 但车身需要大修. ○ *As far as I'm concerned you can do what you like.* 对我个人来说, 你怎么做都可以. **as far as the eye can 'see** to the horizon 就视力所能及: *The prairies stretch on all sides as far as the eye can see.* 草原向四周伸展, 一望无际. **by 'far** (following comparative or superlative *adjs* or *advs*, preceding or following comparative or superlative expressions with *the* or *a* 与形容词或副词的比较级或最高级连用时, 置于这类词之后; 若这类词带有冠词the或a时, 则置于这类之前或之后均可) by a great amount …得多; 显然: *It is quicker by far to go by train.* 乘火车要快得多. ○ *She is the best by far/She is by far the best.* 她显然是最好的. **carry/take sth too, etc 'far** continue (doing) sth beyond reasonable limits 做得过分: *Don't be such a prude — you can carry modesty too far!* 别那么拘谨——你谦虚得太过分了! ○ *It's time to be serious; you've carried this joke far enough.* 该严肃些了, 这个玩笑你开得差不多了. **far/farther/further afield** ⇨ AFIELD. **far and a'way** (preceding comparative or superlative *adjs* 用于形容词的比较级或最高级之前) by a very great amount; very much 极; 非常: *She's far and away the best actress I've seen.* 她是我所见到的最好的演员. **far and 'near/'wide** everywhere; from or to a large area 到处; 四面八方: *They searched far and wide for the missing child.* 他们到处寻找失踪的小孩. ○ *People came from far and near to hear the famous violinist.* 人们从四面八方赶来听这位著名小提琴家的演奏. **far be it from me to do sth (but…)** (*infml* 口) I certainly don't want you to think I would do sth (but…) 我毫无做某事物的意思(但…): *Far be it from me to interfere in your affairs but I would like to give you just one piece of advice.* 我决无意干涉你的事, 但我只想给你提个建议. **far from doing sth** instead of doing sth (不但)不做某事物(反而…): *Far from enjoying dancing, he loathes it.* 他岂止不喜欢, 简直讨厌跳舞. **far from sth/from doing sth** not at all sth; almost the opposite of sth 毫不; 一点也不; 远非; 几乎与之相反: *The problem is far from easy*, ie is in fact very difficult. 这问题绝非易事. ○ *Your account is far from (being) true/is far from the truth.* 你所说远非事实. **far 'from it** (*infml* 口) certainly not; almost the opposite 当然不; 一点也不; 几乎相反: *'Are you happy here?' 'No, far from it; I've never been so miserable in my life.'* '你在这里愉快吗?' '一点也不愉快, 我从来没像现在这样难受过.' **few and far between** ⇨ FEW. **go as/so far as to do sth/as that, etc** be willing to go to extreme limits in dealing with sth 处理某事物时愿走极端; 甚至做到某地步: *I won't go so far as to say that he is dishonest*, ie I won't actually accuse him of dishonesty, even though I might suspect him of it. 我还不想说他不诚实(纵然我有所怀疑, 也不愿意这样指责他). **go 'far** (**a**) (of money) buy many goods, etc (指钱)可买许多东西: *A pound doesn't go very far* (ie You can't buy very much for a pound) *nowadays.* 现今一英镑已买不了多少东西了. (**b**) (of food, supplies, etc) be enough for what is needed; last (指食物、供应等)够用, 充足: *Four bottles of wine won't go far among twenty people.* 四瓶葡萄酒不够二十人喝. **go 'far/a long 'way** (of people) be very successful (指人)非常成功: *Someone as intelligent as you should go far.* 像你这样聪明的人一定很有作为. **go far/a long way towards sth/doing sth** help greatly in (achieving) sth 在(促成)某事物方面大有帮助: *Their promises don't go very far towards solving our present problems.* 他们的承诺对解决我们当前的问题没多大帮助. **go too 'far** behave in a way that is beyond reasonable limits 做得过分: *He's always been rather rude but this time he's gone too far.* 他总是很粗鲁, 但这次未免太过分了. **in so far as** to the extent that 到…的程度; 在…范围内: *This is the truth in so far as I know it.* 就我所知, 这是真实情况. **not far 'off/'out/'wrong** (*infml* 口) correct or almost correct 正确的; 几乎正确的: *Your guess wasn't far out.* 你猜得八九不离十了. **'so far** until now; up to this/that point, time, etc 迄今为止; 到这[那]点、时等为止: *So far the work has been easy but things may change.* 到目前为止, 这工作很容易, 但情况可能有变化. **ˌso 'far** (*infml* 口) only to a limited extent 仅到一定程度; 仅在有限的范围内: *I trust you only so far (and no further).* 我对你的信任只到这一程度. **ˌso far, so 'good** (*saying* 谚) up to now everything has been successful 到目前为止, 一切都很顺利.

□ **'far-away** *adj* [attrib 作定语] **1** distant; remote 远的; 遥远的: *far-away places* 遥远的地方. **2** dreamy, as if thinking of sth else 朦胧的; 恍惚的; 出神的: *You have a far-away look in your eyes.* 你眼中流露出恍惚的神情.

ˌfar-'fetched *adj* (*usu derog* 通常作贬义) **1** (of a comparison) strained; unnatural (指比拟)牵强的, 不自然的. **2** (*infml* 口) (of a story, an account, etc) exaggerated; incredible (指故事、叙述等)夸张的, 不可信的: *It's an interesting book but rather far-fetched.* 这本书很有趣, 只是太离奇了点.

ˌfar-'flung *adj* [usu attrib 通常作定语] **1** spread over a wide area; distributed widely 广泛的; 分布广的: *a far-flung network of contacts* 广泛的关系网. **2** distant 远的: *Her fame has reached the most far-flung corners of the globe.* 她已名扬四海.

ˌfar 'gone (*infml* 口) **1** very ill 病重: *The injured man was fairly far gone by the time the ambulance arrived.* 救护车到时那伤者已生命垂危. **2** very drunk 大醉: *You mustn't drive, you're too far gone!* 你喝得烂醉如泥, 不能开车!

ˈ**far-off** *adj* [attrib 作定语] remote 遥远的: *a far-off country* 遥远的国家.

ˌ**far-ˈreaching** *adj* likely to have a wide influence or many results 影响广泛的; 意义深远的: *far-reaching proposals* 意义深远的建议.

ˌ**far-ˈseeing** *adj* (*approv* 褒) seeing future problems and possibilities clearly and planning for them 目光远大的; 深谋远虑的; 远见卓识的.

ˌ**far-ˈsighted** *adj* **1** (*approv* 褒) (**a**) = FAR-SEEING. (**b**) (of ideas, etc) showing an awareness of future needs (指思想等)有远见的, 有先见之明的: *far-sighted changes in the organization* 这个组织中颇具远见的变革. **2** (*esp US*) = LONG-SIGHTED (LONG[1]).

farce /fɑːs; fɑrs/ *n* **1** (**a**) [C] funny play for the theatre based on unlikely situations and events 笑剧; 闹剧; 滑稽戏. (**b**) [U] plays of this type 笑剧、闹剧一类的剧目: *I prefer farce to tragedy.* 我喜欢笑剧而不喜欢悲剧. **2** [C] absurd and pointless proceedings 荒唐而无意义的行动: *The prisoner's trial was a farce.* 对那个囚犯的审讯简直是胡闹.

▷ **far·cical** /ˈfɑːsɪkl; ˋfɑrsɪkl/ *adj* absurd; ridiculous 荒谬的; 可笑的. **far·cic·ally** /-klɪ; -klɪ/ *adv*.

fare[1] /feə(r); fɛr/ *n* **1** money charged for a journey by bus, ship, taxi, etc (公共汽车、轮船、计程车等的)票价: *What is the bus fare to London?* 到伦敦的公共汽车费是多少? ○ *travel at half/full/reduced fare* 半价[全价/减价]票旅行 ○ *economy fares* 经济舱票价. **2** passenger who pays a fare, esp in a taxi (付费的)乘客; (尤指)计程车的乘客.

□ ˈ**fare-stage** *n* part of a bus route regarded as a unit in calculating the fare (公共汽车路线中的作为计算票价单位的)一段路程.

F

fare[2] /feə(r); fɛr/ *n* [U] food, esp when offered at a meal (used esp with the *adjs* shown) 食物; (尤指)饭菜(尤与下列形容词连用): *fine, simple, wholesome fare* 很好的、简单的、有益健康的食物.

fare[3] /feə(r); fɛr/ *v* [I] (*fml* 文) progress; get on 进展; 过日子: *How did you fare* (ie What were your experiences) *while you were abroad?* 你在国外时好吗(感受如何)?

fare·well /ˌfeəˈwel; ˋfɛrˋwɛl/ *interj* (*arch or fml* 古或文) **1** goodbye 再会; 再见: *Farewell until we meet again!* 下次再见! **2** (idm 习语) **(bid/say) farewell to sb/sth** (have) no more of sb/sth 不再(有某人[某事物]): *You can say farewell to seaside holidays as we once knew them.* 我们熟悉的海滨假日已可谓一去不复返了.

▷ **fare·well** *n* saying goodbye 辞行; 告别: *make one's last farewells* 作最后告别 ○ [attrib 作定语] *a farewell party, gift, speech* 送别宴会、辞行赠礼、告别演讲.

far·in·aceous /ˌfærɪˈneɪʃəs; ˌfærəˋneʃəs/ *adj* starchy or floury (含)淀粉的; (似)面粉的: *farinaceous foods*, eg bread, potatoes 含淀粉的食物(如面包、马铃薯).

farm[1] /fɑːm; fɑrm/ *n* **1** area of land, and the buildings on it, used for growing crops or raising animals 农田; 农场; 饲养场: *We've lived on this farm for twenty years.* 我们已在这农场住了二十年. ○ [attrib 作定语] *farm produce* 农产品 ○ *farm machinery* 农业机械. **2** farmhouse and the buildings near it 农舍及附近的建筑物: *get some eggs at the farm* 从农场弄些蛋. **3** place where certain fish or animals are raised (某些鱼或其他动物的)养殖场: *a trout-/mink-/pig-farm* 鳟鱼饲养场[貂饲养场/养猪场].

□ ˈ**farm-hand** *n* person who works as a labourer on a farm 农场工人.

ˈ**farmhouse** *n* farmer's house 农舍.

ˈ**farmstead** /ˈfɑːmsted; ˋfɑrmˌstɛd/ *n* farmhouse and the buildings near it 农舍及附近的建筑物.

ˈ**farmyard** *n* space enclosed by or next to farm buildings 农家的庭院.

farm[2] /fɑːm; fɑrm/ *v* **1** (**a**) [I] grow crops or rear animals 种田; 务农; 饲养动物: *He is farming in Africa.* 他在非洲务农. (**b**) [Tn] use (land) for this 耕种(土地): *She farms 200 acres.* 她耕种200英亩土地. (**c**) [Tn] breed (animals) on a farm 在农场饲养(动物): *farm beef cattle* 饲养肉牛. **2** (phr v) **farm sb out (to sb)** arrange for sb to be cared for by others 托别人照看(某人): *The children were farmed out to nannies at an early age.* 孩子们小时候由奶妈照看. **farm sth out (to sb)** send out or delegate (work) to be done by others 招人承包(工作): *We're so busy we have to farm out a lot of work.* 我们太忙, 许多工作得招人承包.

▷ **farmer** *n* person who owns or manages a farm 农场主人; 农人.

farm·ing *n* [U] profession of working on or managing a farm 务农; 经营农场: *take up farming* 开始务农 ○ *pig farming* 养猪 ○ [attrib 作定语] *farming subsidies, equipment* 农业津贴、设备.

far·rago /fəˈrɑːgəʊ; fəˋrɑgo/ *n* (*pl* **~s**; *US* **~es**) confused collection; mixture 杂烩; 混合物: *a farrago of useless bits of knowledge* 杂七杂八无用的知识.

far·rier /ˈfærɪə(r); ˋfærɪɚ/ *n* blacksmith who makes and fits horseshoes 蹄铁匠.

far·row /ˈfærəʊ; ˋfæro/ *v* [I] give birth to young pigs 产小猪: *When will the sow farrow?* 这头母猪何时产小猪?

▷ **far·row** *n* **1** number of young pigs born at the same time to one mother 一窝小猪. **2** giving birth to young pigs 产小猪: *Our sow had 15 at one farrow.* 我们的母猪一胎下了15个小猪.

fart /fɑːt; fɑrt/ *v* (⚠ 讳) **1** [I] send air from the bowels out through the anus 放屁. **2** (phr v) **fart about/around** (*sl* 俚) be silly; play the fool 愚蠢; 干蠢事: *Stop farting around and behave yourself!* 别胡来, 放规矩点!

▷ **fart** *n* (⚠ 讳) **1** releasing of air through the anus 放屁. **2** (*sl derog* 俚, 贬) person who is disliked or despised 讨厌的傢伙; 卑鄙的人.

farther /ˈfɑːðə(r); ˋfɑrðɚ/ *adj* (*comparative of* FAR[1] FAR[1] 的比较级) more distant in space, direction or time (在空间、方向或时间上)更远的: *on the farther bank of the river* 在河的彼岸 ○ *The cinema was farther down the road than I thought.* 电影院在路的另一端, 比我原来想的还远. ○ *Rome is farther from London than Paris is.* 罗马比巴黎离伦敦更远.

▷ **farther** *adv* (*comparative of* FAR[2] FAR[2] 的比较级) **1** at or to a greater distance in space or time; more remote (在空间或时间上)更远: *We can't go any farther without resting.* 我们要是不休息就再也走不动了. ○ *Looking farther forward to the end of the century*... 再向前展望到本世纪末.... **2** (idm 习语) **far/farther/further afield** ⇨ AFIELD.

NOTE ON USAGE 用法: **Further** is now more common than **farther** in British English. 在英式英语中, 现在 **further** 比 **farther** 用得更普遍. They can both be used in relation to distance 这两个词均可用以表示距离: *I can throw much further/farther than you.* 我扔得比你远得多. ○ *Bristol is further/farther than Oxford.* 布里斯托尔比牛津远. In US English **farther** is usually used in relation to distance. 在美式英语中 **farther** 通常用以表示距离. In British and US English only **further** can be used to indicate addition 在英式英语和美式英语中, 只有 **further** 可用以表示'更加'或'进一步'的意思: *Are there any further questions?* 还有问题吗? ○ *a College of Further Education* 进修学院.

farthest /ˈfɑːðɪst; ˋfɑrðɪst/ *adj* (*superlative of* FAR[1] FAR[1] 的最高级) **1** most distant in space, direction or time (在空间、方向或时间上)最远的, 最久的: *Go to the farthest house in the village and I'll meet you there.* 到村上最远的那座房子那儿去, 我在那里与你会面. **2** longest; most extended in space (在空间上)最长的, 伸展最远的: *The farthest distance I've run is ten miles.* 我跑过的最长的距离是十英里.

▷ **farthest** *adv* (*superlative of* FAR[2] FAR[2] 的最高级) **1** at or to the greatest distance in space or time; most remote (在空间或时间上)最远, 最久: *Who ran (the) farthest?* 谁跑得最远? ○ *It's ten miles away, at the farthest.* 最远不超过十英里. **2** to the highest degree or extent; most 达到最大程度或限度; 最: *She is the farthest advanced of all my students.* 她是我所有学生中学习最好的.

farth·ing /ˈfɑːðɪŋ; ˋfɑrðɪŋ/ *n* **1** former British coin worth one quarter of an old penny 英国旧时面值为四分之一便士的硬币. **2** (idm 习语) **not care/give a farthing** not care at all 毫不在乎.

fas·cia = FACIA.

fas·cin·ate /ˈfæsɪneɪt; ˋfæsṇˌet/ *v* [Tn] **1** attract or interest (sb) greatly 使(某人)着迷、神魂颠倒或极感兴趣: *The children were fascinated by the toys in the shop window.* 孩子们让商店橱窗里的玩具给吸引住了. **2**

take away power of movement from (eg an animal) by a strong light, etc 用强光照射等使(如动物)不能动弹: *The rabbit sat without moving, fascinated by the glare of our headlights.* 我们的车的前灯把兔子照得蹲在那里一动也不动.

▷ **fas·cin·at·ing** *adj* having great attraction or charm 吸引人的; 迷人的; 使人神魂颠倒的: *a fascinating voice, story, glimpse* 迷人的嗓音、故事、一瞥. **fas·cin·at·ingly** *adv*.

fas·cina·tion /ˌfæsɪˈneɪʃn; ˌfæsn̩ˋeʃən/ *n* **1** [U, C] fascinating quality; process of fascinating 魅力; 魔力; 入迷: *Stamp collecting holds a certain fascination for me.* 我特别喜爱集邮. ○ *The fascinations of the circus are endless.* 马戏表演非常吸引人. **2** [U, sing] state of being fascinated 着迷; 入迷: *a fascination for Chinese pottery* 对中国陶瓷的强烈爱好.

fas·cism (also **Fas·cism**) /ˈfæʃɪzəm; ˋfæʃˌɪzəm/ *n* [U] extreme right-wing dictatorial political system or views, esp (**Fascism**) as originally seen in Italy between 1922 and 1943 法西斯主义.

▷ **fas·cist** (also **Fas·cist**) /ˈfæʃɪst; ˋfæʃɪst/ *n* (*usu derog* 通常作贬义) person who supports fascism 法西斯主义者. — *adj* (*usu derog* 通常作贬义) extremely right-wing; reactionary 法西斯的; 极右的; 反动的: *a fascist state* 法西斯国家 ○ *fascist opinions* 极右的言论.

fash·ion /ˈfæʃn; ˋfæʃən/ *n* **1** [sing] manner or way of doing sth 样子; 方式: *He walks in a peculiar fashion.* 他走路的样子很怪. **2** [C, U] popular style (of clothes, behaviour, etc) at a given time or place 流行的式样; 时尚; 风尚; 风气: *dressed in the latest fashion* 穿着入时的 ○ *Fashions in art and literature are changing constantly.* 文艺的潮流总是日新月异. ○ [attrib 作定语] *a fashion show* 时装表演 ○ *fashion magazines* 时装杂志. **3** (idm 习语) **after a ˈfashion** to a certain extent, but not satisfactorily 达到一定程度(但尚未令人满意): *I can play the piano after a fashion.* 我多少会弹点钢琴. **after/in the fashion of sb** (*fml* 文) like sb; imitating the style of sb 像某人一样; 模仿某人的风格: *She paints in the fashion of Picasso.* 她模仿毕加索的绘画风格. **(be) all the ˈfashion/ˈrage** (be) the latest style or trend 流行(起来); (成为)时尚: *Suddenly, collecting antiques is all the fashion.* 收集古董突然盛行起来. **come into/be in ˈfashion** become/be popular 流行; 入时: *Long skirts have come into fashion again. Faded jeans are still in fashion too.* 长裙子又流行起来. 漂浅的牛仔裤也还很时髦. **go/be out of fashion** become/be unpopular as a style 不再流行; 过时.

▷ **fash·ion** *v* [Tn, Tn·pr] **~ A from B/B into A** give form or shape to sth; design or make sth 将某物做成某形状; 设计或制造某物: *fashion a doll (from a piece of wood)* (用木块)做成玩具娃娃 ○ *fashion a lump of clay into a bowl* 把黏土制成碗.

fash·ion·able /ˈfæʃnəbl; ˋfæʃənəbl̩/ *adj* **1** following a style that is currently popular 时兴的; 时髦的; 流行的: *fashionable clothes, furniture, ideas, ladies* 时髦的服装、家具、思想、女士 ○ *It is fashionable to have short hair nowadays.* 现在流行短发. **2** used or visited by people following a current fashion 时髦人物使用的或光顾的: *a fashionable hotel, resort, etc* 时髦人物常去的旅馆、胜地等.

▷ **fash·ion·ably** /-əblɪ; -əblɪ/ *adv* in a fashionable manner 时髦地; 流行地: *fashionably dressed* 穿得很时髦.

fast[1] /fɑ:st; *US* fæst; fæst/ *adj* **(-er, -est) 1 (a)** moving or done quickly; rapid 快的; 迅速的; 敏捷的: *a fast car, horse, runner*, ie one that can move at high speed 跑得很快的汽车、马、人. **(b)** happening quickly 迅速发生的; 短暂的: *a fast journey, trip, etc* 匆匆之行、一趟. **2** (of a surface) producing or allowing quick movement (指物体表面)可供快速运动的: *a fast road, pitch* 快速车道、平滑的球场. **3** (of a watch or clock) showing a time later than the true time (指钟表)走得过快的: *I'm early — my watch must be fast.* 我来早了——准是我的表快了. ○ *That clock's ten minutes fast.* 那钟快了十分钟. **4** (of photographic film) very sensitive to light, allowing a short exposure (指胶卷)感光快的, 曝光时间短的. **5** (*dated* 旧) (of a person) spending too much time and energy on pleasure and excitement; reckless (指人)耽于享乐的, 放荡的: *lead a fast life* 过放荡的生活. **6** (idm 习语) **fast and ˈfurious** (of games, parties, shows, etc) lively and energetic (指游戏、聚会、表演等)生动活泼的. **pull a fast one** ⇨ PULL[2].

▷ **fast** *adv* **1** quickly 快地; 迅速地: *Can't you run any faster than that?* 你不能跑得再快点吗? ○ *Night was fast approaching.* 黑夜转瞬而至. **2** (idm 习语) **run, etc as fast as one's legs can carry one** as fast as one is able 尽快地(跑等).

□ **fast ˈfood** food such as hamburgers, chips, etc that can be cooked easily, and is sold by restaurants to be eaten quickly or taken away 快餐食品: [attrib 作定语] *a fast food ˈcounter, ˈrestaurant* 快餐柜台、快餐店.

fast time (*US infml* 口) = SUMMER TIME (SUMMER).

fast[2] /fɑ:st; *US* fæst; fæst/ *adj* **1 (a)** [pred 作表语] firmly fixed or attached; secure 牢固; 坚固; 稳固的: *The post is fast in the ground.* 那柱子牢牢地埋在地里. ○ *make a boat fast*, ie moor it securely 把船系牢. **(b)** [attrib 作定语] (*dated* 旧) loyal; close 忠实的; 亲密的: *a fast friend/friendship* 忠实的朋友[牢不可破的友谊]. **2** (of colours) not likely to fade or run (指颜色)不褪色的. **3** (idm 习语) **hard and fast** ⇨ HARD[1].

▷ **fast** *adv* **1** firmly; securely; tightly 牢固地; 稳固地; 紧紧地: *be fast asleep*, ie sleeping deeply 酣睡 ○ *The boat was stuck fast in the mud.* 那船深深地陷在泥里. **2** (idm 习语) **hold fast to sth** continue to believe in (an idea, a principle, etc) resolutely or stubbornly 坚持(某种思想、原则等). **play fast and ˈloose (with sb/sth)** change one's attitude towards sb/sth repeatedly in an irresponsible way; trifle with sb/sth 对某人[某事物]反复无常; 玩弄: *Stop playing fast and loose with that girl's feelings — can't you see you're upsetting her?* 别玩弄那姑娘的感情——难道没看到你已经把她弄得心烦意乱了吗? **stand ˈfast/ˈfirm** not retreat, change one's views, etc 不后退; 不让步; 坚定不移. **thick and fast** ⇨ THICK.

fast[3] /fɑ:st; *US* fæst; fæst/ *v* [I] go without (certain kinds of) food, esp for religious reasons 禁食(某种食物); (尤指)斋戒: *Muslims fast during Ramadan.* 穆斯林在赖买丹月斋戒.

▷ **fast** *n* (period of) going without food 禁食(期); 斋戒(期): *a fast of three days* 禁食三日 ○ *break one's fast* 开斋 ○ [attrib 作定语] *fast days* 禁食的日子.

fasten /ˈfɑ:sn; *US* ˈfæsn; ˋfæsn̩/ *v* **1** [Tn, Tn·p] **(a) ~ sth (down)** secure or fix sth firmly 使某物牢固; 固定某物: *fasten (down) the lid of a box* 盖紧箱盖 ○ *Please fasten your seat-belts.* 请系好安全带. ○ *Have you fastened all the doors and windows?* 你把所有的门窗都关严了吗? **(b) ~ sth (up)** close or join sth 系住某物; 使某物联结在一起: *Fasten (up) your coat.* 把你的大衣系好. ○ *The tent flaps should be tightly fastened.* 帐篷的帘布应紧紧系住. **(c)** [Tn, Tn·pr, Tn·p] **~ sth (on/to sth); ~ A and B (together)** firmly attach sth to sth or two things together 将某物固定在另一物上; 将两物牢牢联结在一起: *fasten a lock on/to the door* 把门用锁锁好 ○ *fasten a brooch on a blouse* 把饰针别在衬衫上 ○ *fasten two sheets of paper (together) with a pin* 用大头针把两张纸别在一起 ○ (*fig* 比喻) *He fastened his eyes on me.* 他紧盯着我. ○ *They're trying to fasten the blame on others.* 他们想嫁祸于人. **2** [I, Ip] become closed or attached 关住; 闩住; 系牢; 扎牢: *The door fastens with a latch.* 这门是用撞锁锁住的. ○ *This dress fastens (up)* (ie has buttons, a zip, etc) *at the back.* 这件连衣裙是在背后系扣的. **3** (phr v) **fasten on sb/sth** take and use sb/sth for a particular purpose; seize on sb/sth 为某目的抓住并利用某人[某事物]; 抓牢某人[某事物]: *fasten on an idea* 坚持某种想法 ○ *He was looking for someone to blame and fastened on me.* 他正在找人派不是, 于是便推到我的身上.

▷ **fast·ener** /ˈfɑ:snə(r); *US* ˈfæs-; ˋfæsənɚ/, **fast·en·ing** /ˈfɑ:snɪŋ; *US* ˈfæs-; ˋfæsənɪŋ/ *ns* device that fastens sth 将某物固着的装置: *a zip fastener* 拉链.

fas·ti·di·ous /fəˈstɪdɪəs, fæ-; fæsˋtɪdɪəs/ *adj* **1** selecting carefully; choosing only what is good 仔细挑选的; 只选好的. **2** (*sometimes derog* 有时作贬义) hard to please; easily disgusted 难以取悦的; 爱挑剔的; 吹毛求疵的: *She is so fastidious about her food that I never invite her for dinner.* 她对食物过于挑剔, 因此我从不请她吃饭. ▷ **fas·ti·di·ously** *adv*. **fas·ti·di·ous·ness** *n* [U].

fast·ness[1] /ˈfɑ:stnɪs; *US* ˈfæs-; ˋfæstnɪs/ *n* [U] quality of

F

being fast²(2) 不褪色: *We guarantee the fastness of these dyes.* 我们担保这些染料不褪色.

fast·ness² /ˈfɑːstnɪs; US ˈfæs-; ˋfæstnɪs/ *n* fortified place that is easily defended; stronghold 堡垒; 要塞: *a mountain fastness* 山寨.

fat¹ /fæt; fæt/ *adj* (**-tter, -ttest**) **1** covered with or having a lot of fat 肥的: *fat meat* 肥肉. **2** (of the body) large in size; containing too much fat (指身体)肥胖的: *If you eat too much chocolate you'll get fat.* 吃巧克力太多会发胖. ⇨Usage 见所附用法. Cf 参看 THIN 2. **3** large; round 大的; 圆的: *a big fat apple* 又大又圆的苹果. **4** thick; well filled 厚的; 装满的: *a fat wallet*, ie one stuffed with banknotes 装满钞票的钱包. **5** rich; fertile 富饶的; 肥沃的: *fat lands* 肥沃的土地. **6** (*infml* 口) large in quantity 大量的: *a fat price, sum, profit, income, etc* 高价、巨额、暴利、优厚的收入 ○ *He gave me a nice fat cheque*, ie one for a lot of money. 他给了我一张数额很大的支票. **7** (idm 习语) **a fat lot (of good, etc)** (*infml ironic* 口, 反语) very little 很少: *A fat lot you care*, ie You don't care at all. 你根本就不在乎. ○ *A fat lot of good that did me*, ie It didn't help me at all. 对我一点帮助也没有.

▷ **fat·ness** *n* [U].

fat·ted /ˈfætɪd; ˋfætɪd/ *adj* (idm 习语) **kill the fatted calf** ⇨ KILL.

fat·tish *adj* rather fat 稍肥的; 略胖的.

□ **fat cat** (*infml* 口 *esp US*) person who is rich and powerful 有财有势的人; 大亨.

ˈ**fat-head** *n* (*infml* 口) stupid person 笨蛋; 傻瓜.

ˈ**fatstock** *n* [U] animals that are reared and fattened to be killed for food 肉畜(用作肉食的牲畜).

F

NOTE ON USAGE 用法: **Fat** is the most usual and direct adjective to describe people with excess flesh, but it is not polite ☆ **fat**是用以指人肥胖的最常用、最直接的形容词, 但含贬义: *That suit's too tight — it makes you look really fat.* 那套衣服太瘦——显得你很胖. More insulting are **flabby**, which suggests loose flesh, and **podgy**, used especially of fingers and hands. 贬义更强的词是**flabby**(指肌肉松弛)和**podgy**(尤指手指和手). To be polite we can use **plump**, suggesting slight or attractive fatness, or **stout**, indicating overall heaviness of the body. 较礼貌些可用**plump**(指稍胖或丰满)或**stout**(指身体胖得匀称). **Tubby** is often used in a friendly way of people who are also short, and **chubby** indicates pleasant roundness in babies and cheeks. ☆ **tubby**常用以指矮胖的人, 含亲切感, 而**chubby**则用于婴儿和脸颊, 意为圆胖而可爱. The most neutral term is **overweight**, while doctors use **obese** to describe people who are so overweight that they are unhealthy. 最无褒贬含义的词是**overweight**, 医生则用**obese**指胖得呈病态的人.

fat² /fæt; fæt/ *n* **1** [U] (**a**) white or yellow greasy substance found in animal bodies under the skin 脂肪; 肥肉: *This ham has too much fat on it.* 这火腿肥肉太多. (**b**) oily substance found in certain seeds 某些种子的油. **2** [C, U] fat from animals, plants or seeds, purified and used for cooking (食用的)动植物的油: *Vegetable fats are healthier than animal fats.* 植物油比动物油更有益于健康. ○ *Fried potatoes are cooked in deep fat.* 炸的马铃薯是用很多油炸的. **3** (idm 习语) **chew the fat/rag** ⇨ CHEW. **the fat is in the ˈfire** (*infml* 口) there will be a lot of trouble now 现在要出麻烦了. **live off/on the fat of the land** ⇨ LIVE². **run to ˈfat** (of persons) tend to gain weight; become fat (指人)发胖, 变胖.

fa·tal /ˈfeɪtl; ˋfetl/ *adj* **~ (to sb/sth)** **1** causing or ending in death 致命的: *a fatal accident* 致命的事故 ○ *fatal injuries* 致命伤. **2** causing disaster 灾难性的: *His illness was fatal to our plans*, ie caused them to fail. 他生病后我们的计划就落空了. ○ *a fatal mistake* 造成严重后果的错误. **3** (*fml* 文) fateful; decisive 命中注定的; 决定性的: *the fatal day/hour* 决定性的一日[时刻].

▷ **fa·tally** *adv* in a fatal manner 致命地; 灾难性地; 注定地: *Many people were fatally wounded during the bomb attacks.* 在轰炸期间许多人受了重伤.

fa·tal·ism /ˈfeɪtəlɪzəm; ˋfetl̩ˌɪzəm/ *n* [U] belief that events are decided by fate(1); acceptance of all that happens as inevitable 宿命论; 听天由命.

▷ **fa·tal·ist** /ˈfeɪtəlɪst; ˋfetl̩ɪst/ *n* person who believes in fate(1) or accepts everything as inevitable 宿命论者; 听天由命者.

fa·tal·istic /ˌfeɪtəˈlɪstɪk; ˌfetl̩ˋɪstɪk/ *adj* showing a belief in fate 宿命论的; 听天由命的: *a fatalistic person, attitude, outlook* 听天由命的人、态度、观点.

fat·al·ity /fəˈtæləti; feˋtælətɪ/ *n* **1** [C] death caused by accident or in war, etc (事故或战争等造成的)死亡: *There have been ten swimming fatalities* (ie Ten people have lost their lives while swimming) *this summer.* 今年夏季已有十人游泳遇溺. **2** [U] sense of being controlled by fate(1) 天数; 命中注定: *There was a strange fatality about their both losing their jobs on the same day.* 他们两人同一天失去工作, 真是天意叵测. **3** [U] fatal influence; deadliness 致死的作用; 致命性: *the fatality of certain diseases* 某些疾病之致命性.

fate /feɪt; fet/ *n* **1** [U] power believed to control all events in a way that cannot be resisted; destiny 命运; 天数; 定数: *I wanted to go to India in June, but fate decided otherwise.* 我本想六月去印度, 但天意难遂我愿. **2** [C] (**a**) person's destiny or future (人的)命运或未来: *The court met to decide our fate(s).* 法院开庭以决定我们的命运. ○ *I am resigned to my fate.* 我听天由命. (**b**) death or destruction 死亡; 毁灭: *He met his fate* (ie died) *bravely.* 他死得很英勇. **3** (idm 习语) **a ˌfate worse than ˈdeath** (*joc* 谑) very unpleasant experience 极不愉快的经历; 活受罪: *Having to watch their home movies all evening was a fate worse than death!* 整个晚上无可奈何地看他们的家庭电影真受罪! **tempt fate/providence** ⇨ TEMPT.

▷ **fate** *v* [only passive 只用于被动语态: Tf, Cn·t] destine 命中注定; 命该: *It was fated* (ie Fate decided) *that we would fail.* 我们注定要失败. ○ *He was fated to die in poverty.* 他注定在贫困中死去.

fate·ful /ˈfeɪtfl; ˋfetfəl/ *adj* [usu attrib 通常作定语] **1** important and decisive 重要的; 决定性的: *fateful events, moments* 决定性的事件、时刻 ○ *a fateful decision* 重大的决定. **2** causing or leading to great and usu unpleasant events 造成或导致重大的(通常指坏的)事情的: *His heart sank as he listened to the judge uttering the fateful words.* 他听到法官字字千钧的话, 顿时垂头丧气. ▷ **fate·fully** /-fəlɪ; -fəlɪ/ *adv*.

father¹ /ˈfɑːðə(r); ˋfɑðɚ/ *n* **1** male parent 父亲; 爸爸: *That baby looks just like her father!* 那婴儿真像她父亲. ○ *You've been (like) a father to me.* 您对我一直像父亲一样. ⇨App 8 见附录8. **2** (usu *pl* 通常作复数) ancestor 祖先: *the land of our fathers* 我们祖先的土地. **3** founder or first leader 创始人; 先驱; 鼻祖: *city fathers* 城市中德高望重的元老 ○ *the Pilgrim Fathers*, ie English Puritans among the first European settlers in the USA 美国的开国先驱(最早自欧洲移居美洲的英国清教徒) ○ *the Father of English poetry*, ie Chaucer 英国诗歌之父(乔叟). **4 Father** God 上帝; 圣父: *Our (Heavenly) Father* 我们的天父 ○ *God the Father* 上帝. **5** title of certain priests, esp those belonging to religious orders 神父. **6** (idm 习语) **be gathered to one's fathers** ⇨ GATHER. **the child is father of the man** ⇨ CHILD. **from ˌfather to ˈson** from one generation of a family to the next 家族中从一代人至另一代人: *The farm has been handed down from father to son since 1800.* 该农场自1800年起一直代代相传. **like ˌfather, like ˈson** (*saying* 谚) a son's character, actions, etc resemble, or can be expected to resemble, his father's 有其父必有其子. **old enough to be sb's mother/father** ⇨ OLD. **the wish is father to the thought** ⇨ WISH *n*.

▷ ˈ**fath·er·hood** *n* [U] state of being a father 作为父亲的身分: *The responsibilites of fatherhood are many.* 身为人父责任很重.

ˈ**fath·erly** *adj* like or typical of a father 父亲般的; 似父亲的: *fatherly advice* 慈父般的忠告.

□ ˌ**Father** ˈ**Christmas** old man with a red robe and a long white beard who symbolizes Christmas festivities 圣诞老人.

ˈ**father-figure** *n* older man who is respected because he guides and protects others (因指导、保护他人)受尊敬的男性长者.

ˈ**father-in-law** *n* /ˈfɑːðər ɪn lɔː; ˋfɑðɚɪnˌlɔ/ (*pl* **fathers-in-law**) father of one's husband or wife 岳父; 公公. ⇨App 8 见附录8.

ˈ**fatherland** *n* /-lænd; -ˌlænd/ country where one was born (used esp of Germany) 祖国(尤用以指德国).

ˌ**Father** ˈ**Time** old man, carrying a scythe and an hourglass, who symbolizes time 时间老人(手持大镰刀和沙漏象征时间的老人).

father[2] /ˈfɑːðə(r); ˋfɑðɚ/ *v* [Tn] **1** be the male parent of (sb); beget 做(某人的)父亲; (作为父亲)生育(子女): *father a child* (作为父亲)生个孩子. **2** (*fig* 比喻) create (sth); originate 发明(某物); 创始: *father a plan, an idea, a project, etc* 最先提出一项计划、一种思想、一项设计等. **3** (phr v) **father sb/sth on sb** say that sb is the father or originator of sb/sth 将某人说成是某人之父或某事物之创始人: *It's not my scheme; try fathering it on somebody else.* 这不是我的计策, 你去问问别人看是谁出的主意吧.

fathom /ˈfæðəm; ˋfæðəm/ *n* measure (6 feet or 1.8 metres) of the depth of water 英寻(水深量度单位, 合6英尺或1.8米): *The harbour is four fathoms deep.* 港深四英寻. ○ *The ship sank in twenty fathoms.* 该船下沉二十英寻. ⇨App 5 见附录5.

▷ **fathom** *v* [Tn] **1** measure the depth of (water) 测量(水的)深度. **2** understand or comprehend (sb/sth) fully 充分理解(某人[某事物]); 领悟: *I cannot fathom his remarks.* 我不能完全理解他的话. **3** (phr v) **fathom sth out** find a reason or explanation for sth 找出某事物的原因或理由: *Can you fathom it out?* 你能想出是怎么回事吗?

fathom·less *adj* (*rhet* 修辞) too deep to measure 深不可测的: *the fathomless ocean* 深不可测的海洋.

fa·tigue /fəˈtiːg; fəˋtig/ *n* **1** [U] great tiredness, usu resulting from hard work or exercise 疲乏; 疲劳; 疲倦: *We were all suffering from fatigue at the end of our journey.* 我们到旅程终点时全都累垮了. **2** [U] weakness in metals, etc caused by repeated stress (金属材料的)疲劳: *The aeroplane wing showed signs of metal fatigue.* 机翼显出有金属疲劳的现象. **3** [C] non-military duty of soldiers, such as cooking, cleaning, etc 士兵所承担的非军事性工作(如烹饪、清扫等): *Instead of training the men were put on fatigues/fatigue duty.* 那些士兵没有接受训练, 而是派去做杂务. **4 fatigues** [pl] (*US*) uniform worn for fatigue duty or when in battle (做杂务或打仗时穿的)制服.

▷ **fa·tigue** *v* [Tn] make (sb) very tired 使(某人)非常疲劳: *feeling fatigued* 感到疲劳 ○ *fatiguing work* 累人的工作.

fat·ted ⇨ FAT[1].

fat·ten /ˈfætn; ˋfætn̩/ *v* (**a**) [Tn, Tn·p] **~ sb/sth (up)** make sb/sth fat or fatter 使某人[某物]变胖或变肥: *fatten cattle for (the) market* 把牛养肥供应市场. (**b**) [I, Ip] **~ (up)** become fat or fatter 变得肥胖: *They're fattening up nicely.* 这些动物长膘情况良好.

fatty /ˈfætɪ; ˋfætɪ/ *adj* (**-ier, -iest**) (**a**) like fat 似脂肪般的. (**b**) containing a lot of fat 含脂肪多的; 肥的; 胖的: *fatty bacon* 很肥的腌猪肉.

▷ **fatty** /ˈfætɪ; ˋfætɪ/ *n* (*infml derog* 口, 贬) fat person 胖子.

fat·uous /ˈfætʃʊəs; ˋfætʃʊəs/ *adj* stupid and silly; foolish 蠢的; 傻的; 笨的: *a fatuous person, smile, remark* 笨人、傻笑、蠢话.

▷ **fa·tu·ity** /fəˈtjuːətɪ; *US* -ˈtuː-ətɪ; fəˋtuətɪ/ *n* **1** [U] state of being fatuous 愚昧. **2** [C] fatuous remark, act, etc 愚昧的言语、行动等.

fat·uously *adv*.

fat·uous·ness *n* [U].

fau·cet /ˈfɔːsɪt; ˋfɔsɪt/ *n* **1** tap for a barrel, etc (大桶等上的)龙头, 旋塞. **2** (*esp US*) any kind of tap (任何)龙头, 旋塞.

fault /fɔːlt; fɔlt/ *n* **1** [C] imperfection or flaw 缺点; 缺陷; 毛病; 瑕疵; 故障: *I like him despite his faults.* 虽然他有种种缺点, 但我仍然喜欢他. ○ *There is a fault in the electrical system.* 电路系统出了故障. ⇨Usage at MISTAKE[1] 用法见MISTAKE[1]. **2** [U] (responsibility for a) mistake or offence 过错; 过失: *'Whose fault is this?' 'Mine, I'm afraid.'* '这是谁的过错?''很抱歉, 是我的错.' **3** [C] incorrect serve in tennis, etc (网球等)发球失误. **4** [C] (place where there is a) break in the continuity of layers of rock, caused by movement of the earth's crust (地壳运动造成的)断层(处). **5** (idm 习语) **at fault** responsible for a mistake; in the wrong 有责任; 有错: *My memory was at fault.* 我记错了. **find fault** ⇨ FIND[1]. **to a** ˈ**fault** excessively 过分地; 过度地: *She is generous to a fault.* 她过分慷慨.

▷ **fault** *v* [Tn] discover a fault in (sb/sth) 发现(某人[某事物])有错、有缺陷等: *No one could fault his performance.* 他的演出无懈可击.

fault·less *adj*. **fault·lessly** *adv*.

faulty *adj* (**-ier, -iest**) having a fault or faults; imperfect 有缺点的; 有过失的; 不完善的: *a faulty switch* 有毛病的开关 ○ *a faulty argument* 有错误的论据. **fault·ily** *adv* in a faulty manner 有缺点地; 有过失地; 有错误地.

□ ˈ**faultfinding** *n* [U] (*usu derog* 通常作贬义) looking for faults in other people's work or behaviour 吹毛求疵; 挑剔.

faun /fɔːn; fɔn/ *n* (in Roman myths) god of the fields and woods, with goat's horns and legs but a human torso (罗马神话的)农牧神(躯干呈人形, 角、腿呈山羊形).

fauna /ˈfɔːnə; ˋfɔnə/ *n* [U, C] (*pl* **~s**) all the animals of an area or a period of time (某地区或某时期的)所有动物: *the fauna of East Africa* 东非的动物. Cf 参看 FLORA.

faux pas /ˌfəʊ ˈpɑː; ˋfoˋpɑ/ (*pl* **faux pas** /ˌfəʊpɑːz; ˋfo ˋpɑz/) (*French* 法) embarrassing mistake; indiscreet remark, etc 失态; 失言; 失礼.

fa·vour[1] (*US* **fa·vor**) /ˈfeɪvə(r); ˋfevɚ/ *n* **1** [U] liking; goodwill; approval (used esp with the *vs* shown) 喜爱; 宠爱; 好感; 欢心; 赞同(尤与下列动词连用): *win sb's favour* 获得某人的好感 ○ *look on a plan with favour*, ie approve of it 赞成一项计划. **2** [U] treating one person or group more generously or leniently than others; partiality 偏爱; 偏袒: *He obtained his position more by favour than by merit or ability.* 他因得宠而获此地位, 并非有何特长或本事. **3** [C] act of kindness beyond what is due or usual (used esp with the *vs* shown) 善行, 恩惠(尤与下列动词连用): *May I ask a favour of you* (ie ask you to do sth for me)? 请您帮个忙行吗? ○ *Do me a favour and turn the radio down while I'm on the phone, will you?* 劳驾, 我在打电话, 把收音机的声音调小点好吗? **4** [C] small token or badge worn to show that one supports sb/sth (供佩带的)标志或徽章(以示支持某人[某事物]): *Everyone at the rally wore red ribbons as favours.* 参加集会的人都系着红丝带作为支持大会的标记. **5 favours** [pl] (used of a woman offering herself freely to a man 用以指女子将自己献给某男子) pleasure through sexual intercourse 性交的快感: *bestow one's favours on sb* (指女子)使某人有性交的欢愉 ○ *be (too) free with one's favours* (指女子)(过分)随意性交. **6** (idm 习语) **be/stand high in sb's favour** ⇨ HIGH[3]. **be in/out of** ˈ**favour (with sb)**; **be in/out of sb's** ˈ**favour** have/not have sb's regard, approval, etc 得到[失去]某人的尊重、赞同等. **curry favour** ⇨ CURRY[2]. **find, lose, etc favour with sb/in sb's eyes** win/lose sb's approval 得[失]宠于某人; 获得[失去]某人的好感. **in favour of sb/sth** (**a**) in sympathy with sb/sth; in support of sb/sth 赞成某人[某事物]; 支持某人[某事物]: *Was he in favour of the death penalty?* 他赞成死刑吗? (**b**) (of cheques) payable to (the account of) sb/sth (指支票)以某人[某部门]为受款人: *Cheques should be written in favour of Oxfam.* 支票上请写明以牛津饥荒救济委员会为受款人. **in sb's favour** to the advantage of sb 对某人有利: *The exchange rate is in our favour today*, ie will benefit us when we change money. 今天的兑换率对我们有利. ○ *The court decided in his favour.* 法庭的判决对他有利. ○ *The decision went in his favour.* 这一判决对他有利. **without fear or favour** ⇨ FEAR[1].

fa·vour[2] (*US* **fa·vor**) /ˈfeɪvə(r); ˋfevɚ/ *v* [Tn] **1** support (sb/sth); prefer 支持(某人[某事物]); 喜爱: *Of the two possible plans I favour the first.* 在这两种可行方案中我赞成前者. **2** show a preference for (sb); treat (sb) with partiality 偏爱; 偏袒: *She always favours her youngest child (more than the others).* 她总是偏爱她最小的孩子. **3** (of events or circumstances) make (sth) possible or easy (指事情或情况)便于(某事物), 使(某事物)顺利: *The wind favoured their sailing at dawn.* 这风便于他们在黎明时航行. **4** (*dated* 旧) look like (sb); resemble (sb) in features 长得像(某人); 容貌像(某人): *You can see that she favours her father.* 她长得像她父亲. **5** (phr v) **favour sb with sth** (*dated or fml* 旧或文) do sth for sb; oblige(2) sb with sth 为某人做某事; 应某人要求做某事: *I should be grateful if you would favour me with an*

F

early reply. 若蒙早日赐复则不胜感谢.

fa·vour·able (*US* **fa·vor-**) /ˈfeɪvərəbl; ˈfevərəbl/ *adj* **1** (**a**) giving or showing approval 赞成的; 同意的; 嘉许的: *It's encouraging to receive a favourable report on one's work.* 工作得到好评是令人鼓舞的. (**b**) **~ (to/toward sb/sth)** tending to support sb/sth 倾向于支持某人[某事物]的: *Is he favourable to the proposal?* 他支持这项建议吗? (**c**) pleasing; positive 令人高兴的; 肯定的: *You made a favourable impression on the examiners.* 你给主考留下了很好的印象. ○ *We formed a very favourable impression of her.* 我们对她印象极好. **2 ~ (for sth)** helpful; suitable 有帮助的; 合适的: *favourable winds* 顺风 ○ *conditions favourable for skiing* 适合滑雪的条件.

▷ **fa·vour·ably** (*US* **fa·vor-**) /-əblɪ; -əblɪ/ *adv* in a favourable manner 赞成地; 同意地; 嘉许地: *speak favourably of a plan* 赞成一项计划 ○ *look favourably on sb* 赞许地看着某人.

fa·vour·ite (*US* **fa·vor-**) /ˈfeɪvərɪt; ˈfevərɪt/ *n* **~ (of sb)** **1** person or thing liked more than others 特别受喜爱的人或物: *These books are great favourites of mine.* 这些是我最喜爱的书. ○ *He is a favourite with his uncle/a favourite of his uncle's/his uncle's favourite.* 他伯伯特别喜爱他. **2 the favourite** (in racing) the horse, competitor, etc expected to win (竞赛中)认为会获胜的马、竞争者等: *The favourite came in third.* 那个最有希望获胜的却跑了个第三名.

▷ **fa·vour·ite** (*US* **fa·vor-**) *adj* [attrib 作定语] best liked 最喜欢的: *my favourite occupation, hobby, restaurant, aunt* 我最喜欢的消遣、嗜好、餐馆、姑母 ○ *Who is your favourite writer?* 你最喜欢哪位作家?

fa·vour·it·ism (*US* **-vor-**) /-ɪzəm; -ˌɪzəm/ *n* [U] (*derog* 贬) practice of giving unfair advantages to the people that one likes best 偏爱; 偏袒; 偏心: *Our teacher is guilty of blatant favouritism.* 我们老师有明显的偏心错误.

F

fawn[1] /fɔːn; fɔn/ *n* **1** [C] deer less than one year old (未满周岁的)幼鹿. Cf 参看 DOE, STAG 1. **2** [U] light yellowish brown 浅黄褐色: *a raincoat in fawn* 浅黄褐色的雨衣.

▷ **fawn** *adj* fawn-coloured 浅黄褐色的: *a fawn raincoat* 浅黄褐色的雨衣.

fawn[2] /fɔːn; fɔn/ *v* [I, Ipr] **~ (on sb)** **1** (of dogs) show affection by wagging the tail, pawing or licking sb, etc (指狗)(摇尾、用爪子抓或用舌舔等)表示亲热. **2** (*derog* 贬) try to win sb's approval by flattery or by obsequious behaviour 谄媚; 奉承; 巴结: *fawning behaviour, looks* 谄媚的举动、表情....

fax/fæks; fæks/*v* [Tn, Dn·n, Dn·pr] **~ sth (to sb)** send the copy of (a document, an illustration, etc) by an electronic system using telephone lines 用传真机(使用电话线路通过电子控制系统)传送(文件、图表等): *Please fax me the layout for the new catalogue.* 请用传真机把新目录的版面编排图样传送给我. *The plans were faxed to us by our New York office.* 这些设计图是我们的纽约办事处用传真机给我们传送来的.

▷ **fax** *n* (**a**) [U] system for sending such a copy 传真系统: *sent by fax* 由传真系统发送的 [attrib 作定语] *a fax machine* 传真机. (**b**) [C] copy sent in this way 传真件.

faze /feɪz; fez/ *v* [Tn] (*infml* 口 *esp US*) fluster (sb) 使(某人)紧张或慌张: *She's so calm; nothing seems to faze her.* 她很镇静, 遇事不慌.

FBI /ˌef biː ˈaɪ; ˌɛf bi ˈaɪ/ *abbr* 缩写 = (*US*) Federal Bureau of Investigation 联邦调查局: *head of the FBI* 联邦调查局的负责人 ○ *an FBI agent* 联邦调查局的调查员. Cf 参看 CIA.

FC *abbr* 缩写 = (*Brit*) Football Club 足球俱乐部: *Leeds United FC* 利兹联合足球俱乐部.

FCO /ˌef siː ˈəʊ; ˌɛf si ˈo/ *abbr* 缩写 = (*Brit*) Foreign and Commonwealth Office (combined in 1968) 外交和联邦事务部(1968年合并): *an official from the FCO* 外交和联邦事务部的官员. Cf 参看 FO.

FD /ˌef ˈdiː; ˌɛf ˈdi/ (also **Fid Def**) *abbr* 缩写 = (on British coins) Defender of the Faith (Latin *Fidei Defensor*) (英国硬币上的)保教者(源自拉丁文 *Fidei Defensor*).

fealty /ˈfiːəltɪ; ˈfiəltɪ/ *n* [C, U] (*arch* 古) (oath of) loyalty owed by a feudal tenant, etc to his lord (封建时代臣仆对主人的)效忠(的誓言): *take an oath of fealty* 宣誓(对封建领主的)效忠.

fear[1] /fɪə(r); fɪr/ *n* **1** (**a**) [U] emotion caused by the nearness or possibility of danger, pain, evil, etc 恐惧; 惧怕: *unable to speak from fear* 吓得说不出话来 ○ *overcome by fear* 被吓坏 ○ *feel, show no fear* 毫不畏惧、毫无惧色. (**b**) [C] this emotion caused by sth specific (因某事物产生的)畏惧: *a fear of heights* 对高处的恐惧 ○ *The doctor's report confirmed our worst fears.* 医生的报告证实了我们最为担心的事. ○ *overcome/dispel/allay sb's fears* 克服[消除/减轻]某人的恐惧心理. **2** (idm 习语) **for fear of sth/of doing sth; for fear (that/lest)...** in case; to avoid the danger of sth happening 惟恐; 以免(发生危险): *We spoke in whispers for fear of waking the baby/for fear (that) we might wake the baby.* 我们轻声谈话, 以免吵醒婴儿. **hold no fears/terrors for sb** not frighten sb 不能使某人感到害怕: *Hang-gliding holds no fears for her.* 她一点也不害怕悬挂式滑翔. **in fear and trembling** in a frightened or cowed manner 恐惧地; 胆怯地: *They went to the teacher in fear and trembling to tell her that they'd broken a window.* 他们战战兢兢地去告诉老师, 他们打破了一扇窗户. **in fear of sb/sth** in a state of fear about sb/sth 处于害怕某人[某事物]的状态: *The thief went in constant fear of discovery.* 那贼时刻都在担心被人发现. **in ˌfear of one's ˈlife** anxious for one's own safety 为自己的安全担忧. **ˌno ˈfear** (*infml* 口) (used when answering a suggestion) certainly not (用以回应别人的提议)当然不...: *'Are you coming climbing?' 'No fear!'* '你来爬山吗?' '我可不去!' **put the fear of God into sb** (*infml* 口) make sb very frightened 使某人非常恐惧. **there's not much fear of sth/that...** it is unlikely that sth will happen 某事不太可能发生: *There's not much fear of an enemy attack (taking place).* 敌人不太可能发动攻击. **without ˌfear or ˈfavour** (*fml* 文) showing impartial justice 公正的; 不偏不倚的.

▷ **fear·ful** /-fl; -fəl/ *adj* **1 ~ (of sth/of doing sth); ~ (that/lest...)** nervous and afraid 紧张而担心的: *fearful of waking the baby/fearful that we might wake the baby* 生怕把婴儿吵醒. **2** terrible; horrifying 可怕的; 可怖的: *a fearful railway accident* 火车失事惨剧. **3** (*infml* 口) very great; very bad 极端的: *What a fearful mess!* 简直是一塌糊涂! **fear·fully** /-fəlɪ; -fəlɪ/ *adv*. **fear·ful·ness** *n* [U].

fear·less *adj* **~ (of sth)** not afraid (of sth) (对某事物)不怕的; 无畏的: *a fearless mountaineer* 无畏的爬山者 ○ *fearless of the consequences* 不计后果的. **fear·lessly** *adv*. **fear·less·ness** *n* [U].

fear·some /ˈfɪəsəm; ˈfɪrsəm/ *adj* frightening in appearance 样子可怕的: *The battlefield was a fearsome sight.* 这战场的情景触目惊心. ○ (*fig* 比喻) *a fearsome task*, ie one that frightens by being difficult 令人望而却步的任务.

fear[2] /fɪə(r); fɪr/ *v* **1** (**a**) [Tn] be afraid of (sb/sth) 害怕(某人[某事物]); 惧怕: *fear death, illness* 怕死、怕生病 ○ *The plague was greatly feared in the Middle Ages.* 中世纪时这种瘟疫十分可怕. (**b**) [I, Tt] feel fear (about doing sth) (对做某事)感到害怕, 忧虑: *Never fear* (ie Don't worry), *everything will be all right.* 别害怕, 一切都会好的. ○ *She feared to speak in his presence.* 她怕在他的面前说话. **2** [Tn, Tf] have an uneasy feeling about or anticipation of (esp sth bad) 担心(尤指怕出事): *They feared the worst*, ie thought that the worst had happened or would happen. 他们担心的是最坏的情况(已经发生或可能发生). ○ *'Are we going to be late?' 'I fear so.'* '我们会迟到吗?' '我看要迟到.' ○ *I fear (that) he is going to die.* 我担心他快死了. **3** [Tn] (*arch or fml* 古或文) have respect and awe for 敬畏: *fear God* 敬畏上帝. **4** (phr v) **fear for sb/sth** be anxious or concerned about sb/sth 对某人[某事物]担忧或关心...: *I fear for her safety in this weather.* 在这种天气里我很担心她的安全.

feas·ible /ˈfiːzəbl; ˈfizəbl/ *adj* that can be done; practicable; possible 可做的; 可实行的; 可能的: *a feasible idea, suggestion, scheme, etc* 切实可行的主意、建议、计划等 ○ *It's not feasible to follow your proposals.* 按照你的建议去做是行不通的. ▷ **feas·ib·il·ity** /ˌfiːzəˈbɪlətɪ; ˌfizəˈbɪlətɪ/ *n* [U]: [attrib 作定语] *We should do a feasibility study before adopting the new proposals.* 我们在采用这些新建议之前应进行可行性研究. **feas·ibly** /-əblɪ; -əblɪ/ *adv*.

feast /fiːst; fist/ *n* **1** (**a**) unusually large or elaborate meal 盛宴; 宴会. (**b**) (*fig* 比喻) thing that pleases the mind or the senses with its richness or variety 赏心悦目的事物: *a feast of colours, sounds, etc* 赏心悦目的颜色、悦耳动听的声音. **2** religious festival celebrated with rejoicing 欢乐的宗教节日: *the feast of Christmas* 圣诞佳节.

▷ **feast** *v* **1 (a)** [I, Ipr] **~ (on sth)** enjoy a feast 宴饮; 参加宴会: *They celebrated by feasting all day.* 他们整天大吃大喝地庆祝. **(b)** [Tn, Tn·pr] **~ sb (with sth)** provide sb with a feast 设宴款待(某人); 宴请(某人): *They feasted their guests with delicacies.* 他们用美味佳肴款待客人. **2** (idm 习语) **feast one's eyes (on sb/sth)** enjoy the beauty of sb/sth 欣赏某人[某物]之美; 饱眼福: *She feasted her eyes on the beauty of the valley.* 她饱览那山谷的美景.

feat /fi:t; fit/ *n* successful completion of sth needing skill, strength or courage 技艺; 武艺; 功绩; 伟业: *brilliant feats of engineering* 工程上的伟绩 ○ *perform feats of daring* 表演惊险的技艺. ⇨Usage at ACT[1] 用法见 ACT[1].

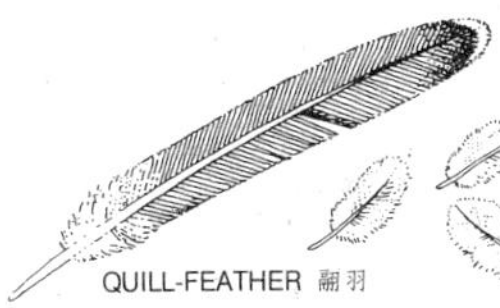

feather 羽毛

feather[1] /ˈfeðə(r); ˋfɛðɚ/ *n* **1** any of the many light fringed structures that grow from a bird's skin and cover its body 羽毛. ⇨illus 见插图. **2** (idm 习语) **birds of a feather** ⇨ BIRD. **(be) a ˈfeather in one's cap** an achievement, etc that one can be proud of 可引以自豪的成就等: *Winning the gold medal was yet another feather in her cap.* 夺得金牌是她又一值得骄傲的成就. **light as air/as a feather** ⇨ LIGHT[1]. **ruffle sb's feathers** ⇨ RUFFLE. **show the white feather** ⇨ SHOW[2]. **smooth sb's ruffled feathers** ⇨ SMOOTH[2]. **you could have knocked me down with a feather** ⇨ KNOCK[2].

▷ **feath·ery** /ˈfeðəri; ˋfɛðəri/ *adj* **1** light and soft like feathers 轻而软的; 似羽毛的: *feathery snowflakes* 羽毛般的雪片. **2** covered or adorned with feathers 长着羽毛的; 饰有羽毛的: *a feathery hat* 饰有羽毛的帽子.

□ ˌ**feather ˈbed** mattress stuffed with feathers 羽绒褥垫. ˌ**feather-ˈbed** *v* **(-dd-)** [Tn] make things easy for (sb), esp by helping financially; pamper 使(某人)安逸或予以方便(尤指资助); 娇养: *They have been so feather-bedded in the past that they can't cope with hardship now.* 他们一直娇生惯养, 所以现在过不了苦日子.

ˈ**feather-brained** *adj* (*derog* 贬) foolish; silly 愚蠢的; 没头脑的.

ˈ**featherweight** *n* **1** boxer weighing between 53.5 and 57 kilograms, next above bantamweight 次轻量级拳击手(体重在53.5至57公斤间, 高于最轻量级). **2 (a)** (*infml* 口) thing or person that is light in weight 重量轻的物或人. **(b)** (*infml derog* 口, 贬) thing or person of little merit or importance 微不足道的事物或人.

feather[2] /ˈfeðə(r); ˋfɛðɚ/ *v* **1** [Tn] cover or fit (sth) with feathers 将羽毛覆盖或装在(某物)上: *feather an arrow* 给箭装上翎. **2** [I, Tn] (in rowing) turn (one's oar) so that it passes flat just above the surface of the water (划船时)将(桨叶)持平(略出水面而与水面平行): *The crew feathered (their oars) for the last few yards of the race.* 在划船比赛到最后几码时, 全体队员回桨时把桨叶持平. **3** (idm 习语) **feather one's (own) ˈnest** (*usu derog* 通常作贬义) make oneself richer, more comfortable, etc, usu at sb else's expense 使自己更富足、更舒适等(通常指牺牲他人的利益); 中饱私囊. **tar and feather sb** ⇨ TAR[1] *v*.

fea·ture /ˈfi:tʃə(r); ˋfitʃɚ/ *n* **1 (a)** [C] one of the named parts of the face (eg nose, mouth, eyes) which together form its appearance 面部的一部分(如鼻、口、眼): *His eyes are his most striking feature.* 他面部最突出的部分是那双眼睛. ⇨illus at HEAD 见 HEAD 插图. **(b) features** [pl] face viewed as a whole 面貌; 容貌: *a woman of handsome, striking, delicate, etc features* 相貌漂亮、动人、秀气等的女子. **2** [C] distinctive characteristic; aspect 特征; 特色; 特点: *an interesting feature of city life* 城市生活的一个有趣特点 ○ *memorable features of the Scottish landscape* 苏格兰景色中令人难忘的特征 ○ *Many examples and extra grammatical information are among the special features of this dictionary.* 本词典别具特色, 诸如例证多及新增语法要点等. **3** [C] **(a) ~ (on sb/sth)** (in newspapers, television, etc) special or prominent article or programme (about sb/sth) (报纸、电视等中)(关于某人[某事物]的)特写或专题节目: *This magazine will be running a special feature on education next week.* 这一杂志下周要发表一篇关于教育的专题文章. **(b)** full-length film as part of a cinema programme (电影的)正片, 故事片: *the main feature following the cartoon* 动画片之后的正片 ○ [attrib 作定语] *a feature film* 故事片.

▷ **fea·ture** **1** *v* [Tn] give a prominent part to (sb/sth) 给(某人[某事物])以显著地位; 由(某人[某物])主演: *a film that features a new French actress* 由法国新女星主演的电影. **2** [Ipr] **~ in sth** have an important or prominent part in sth 在某事物中起重要作用或扮演主要角色: *Does a new job feature in your future plans?* 新的工作在你的未来计划中十分重要吗?

fea·ture·less *adj* without distinct features (FEATURE 2); uninteresting 无特色的; 无趣味的.

Feb /*in informal use* 俗读作 feb; fɛb/ *abbr* 缩写 = February: *18 Feb 1934* 1934年2月18日.

feb·rile /ˈfi:braɪl; ˋfibrəl/ *adj* (*fml* 文) **(a)** caused by a fever 发烧引起的: *a febrile cough* 发烧引起的咳嗽. **(b)** having a fever 发烧的: *a febrile patient* 发烧的病人.

Feb·ru·ary /ˈfebrʊəri; *US* -ʊeri; ˋfɛbrʊˌɛri/ *n* [U, C] (*abbr* 缩写 **Feb**) the second month of the year, next after January 二月.

For the uses of *February* see the examples at *April.* 关于 February 的用法见 April 词条中的示例.

fe·ces (*US*) = FAECES. ▷ **fe·cal** (*US*) = FAECAL (FAECES).

feck·less /ˈfeklɪs; ˋfɛklɪs/ *adj* (*derog* 贬) inefficient; irresponsible 效率低的; 不负责任的. ▷ **feck·lessly** *adv*. **feck·less·ness** *n* [U].

fec·und /ˈfi:kənd, ˈfekənd; ˋfikənd, ˋfɛkənd/ *adj* (*fml* 文) fertile; productive 肥沃的; 多产的; 丰饶的: (*fig* 比喻) *a fecund imagination* 丰富的想像力. ▷ **fe·cund·ity** /fɪˈkʌndətɪ; fɪˋkʌndətɪ/ *n* [U].

Fed /fed; fɛd/ *n* (*US infml* 口) member of the Federal Bureau of Investigation 联邦调查局成员.

fed *pt, pp* of FEED[1].

fed·eral /ˈfedərəl; ˋfɛdərəl/ *adj* **1** of a system of government in which several states unite, usu for foreign policy, etc, but retain considerable control over their own internal affairs 联邦制的: *federal unity* 联邦制的统一. **2** (within a federal system) relating to central rather than local or provincial government (联邦制中)联邦政府的: *The Trans-Canada highway is a federal responsibility.* 横跨加拿大的交通干线是由联邦政府管理的. **3 Federal** (*US*) supporting the union party in the US Civil War (美国南北战争中)拥护北部联邦的.

▷ **fed·eral·ism** /-ɪzəm; -ˌɪzəm/ *n* [U].

fed·eral·ist /ˈfedərəlɪst; ˋfɛdərəlɪst/ *n* supporter of federal union or power 联邦主义者.

fed·er·ally *adv* by the federal government 由联邦政府: *This development is federally funded.* 这一发展项目是由联邦政府资助的.

□ ˌ**Federal** ˌ**Bureau of Investiˈgation** (*abbr* 缩写 **FBI**) (in the USA) department responsible for investigating violations of federal law and protecting national security (美国的)联邦调查局.

fed·er·ate /ˈfedəreɪt; ˋfɛdəˌret/ *v* [I] (of states, organizations, etc) unite into a federation (指州、团体等)组成联邦, 结成同盟.

▷ **feder·a·tion** /ˌfedəˈreɪʃn; ˌfɛdəˋreʃən/ *n* **1** [C] union of states in which individual states retain control of many internal matters but in which foreign affairs, defence, etc are the responsibility of the central (federal) government 联邦. **2** [C] similarly organized union of societies, trade unions, etc (社团、工会等的)联合会. **3** [U] action of forming a federation 结成联邦政府; 联盟.

fed up /ˌfed ˈʌp; ˌfɛd ˋʌp/ *adj* [pred 作表语] **~ (about/**

F

with sb/sth) (*infml* 口) tired or bored; unhappy or depressed 厌倦; 厌烦; 不愉快; 沮丧: *What's the matter? You look pretty fed up.* 怎么啦? 你显得那么不高兴. ○ *I'm fed up with waiting for her to telephone.* 我等她的电话都等得不耐烦了.

fee /fiː; fi/ *n* **1** [C] (**a**) (usu *pl* 通常作复数) amount paid for professional advice or service, eg to private teachers, doctors, etc 服务费, 酬金(如付予私人教师、医生等的): *pay the lawyer's fees* 付律师费 ○ *a bill for school fees* 学费帐单. ⇨Usage at INCOME 用法见 INCOME. (**b**) amount paid to sit an examination, join a club, etc (考试的)报名费、(加入俱乐部的)会费等: *If you want to join, there's an entrance fee of £20 and an annual membership fee of £10.* 入会须缴入会费 20 英镑, 年费 10 英镑. **2** [U] (*law* 律) (**a**) rights (esp the right to bequeath) in property that one has inherited 不动产继承权(尤指遗赠权). (**b**) such property 继承的不动产.

feeble /ˈfiːbl; ˋfibl/ *adj* (**-r, -st**) (**a**) weak; faint 衰弱的; 虚弱的; 微弱的: *a feeble old man* 衰弱的老人 ○ *a feeble cry* 微弱的喊声. (**b**) (*derog* 贬) lacking force 无力的: *a feeble argument, attempt, gesture, excuse* 无力的论据、尝试、手势、辩解. ▷ **feeble·ness** *n* [U]. **feebly** /ˈfiːblɪ; ˋfiblɪ/ *adv*.

□ ˌ**feeble-ˈminded** *adj* having less than usual intelligence; mentally subnormal 弱智的; 低能的.

feed[1] /fiːd; fid/ *v* (*pt, pp* **fed** /fed; fɛd/) **1** (**a**) [Tn, Tn·pr] **~ sb/sth (on sth)** give food to (a person or an animal) 给(人或动物)食物; 喂; 喂养; 饲养: *She has a large family to feed.* 她要养活一大家人. ○ *Have the pigs been fed yet?* 猪已喂过了吗? ○ *Have you fed the chickens?* 你喂过鸡没有? ○ *The baby needs feeding.* 这婴儿需要喂了. ○ *The baby can't feed itself yet*, ie can't put food into its own mouth. 这婴儿还不会自己吃东西. ○ *What do you feed your dog on?* 你用什么喂狗? (**b**) [Dn·n, Dn·pr] **~ sth to sb/sth** give (a person or an animal) sth as food 给(人或动物)某物作为食物: *feed the baby some more stewed apple* 给婴儿多喂些炖苹果 ○ *feed oats to horses* 用燕麦喂马. **2** (**a**) [I, Ipr] **~ (on sth)** (of animals, or jokingly of humans) eat (指动物; 但若指人时为戏谑语)吃: *Have you fed yet?* 你吃过饭没有? ○ *The cows were feeding on hay in the barn.* 母牛正在牲口棚里吃干草呢. (**b**) [Tn] serve as food for (a person or an animal) 供(人或动物)作为食物: *There's enough here to feed us all.* 这里有足够的食物够我们大家吃的. **3** [Tn, Tn·pr] **~ A (with B)/~ B into A** supply (sth) with material; supply (material) to sth 给(某物)提供原料; 将(原料)提供给(某物): *The lake is fed by several small streams.* 这湖是由几条小溪的水汇聚而成的. ○ *feed the fire (with wood)* 往火里添柴 ○ *The moving belt feeds the machine with raw material/feeds raw material into the machine.* 传送带向机器输送原料[把原料输入机器中]. **4** [Tn] (in football, etc) send passes to (a player) (足球赛等)传球给(队友). **5** (idm 习语) **bite the hand that feeds one** ⇨ BITE[1]. **6** (phr v) **feed on sth** be nourished or strengthened by sth 受到某事物的滋养; 因某事物而助长: *Hatred feeds on envy.* 因妒生恨. **feed sb up** give extra food to sb to make him more healthy 给(某人)额外食物使其更健康: *You look very pale; I think you need feeding up a bit.* 你面色不好, 得多吃些东西保养一下.

□ ˈ**feeding-bottle** *n* bottle with a rubber teat for feeding liquid foods to young babies or animals 奶瓶.

feed[2] /fiːd; fid/ *n* **1** [C] meal, usu for animals or babies 一顿, 一餐(通常指给动物或婴儿的): *When is the baby's next feed?* 这孩子下顿什么时候喂? **2** [U] (**a**) food for animals 饲料: *There isn't enough feed left for the hens.* 母鸡的饲料不够了. (**b**) material supplied to a machine 供给机器的原料; 进料. **3** [C] pipe, channel, etc along which material is carried to a machine 输送原料至机器的管道、沟槽等; 进料管; 进料槽: *The petrol feed is blocked.* 汽油管堵了.

□ ˈ**feedbag** *n* (*US*) = NOSEBAG (NOSE[1]).

feed·back /ˈfiːdbæk; ˋfidˌbæk/ *n* [U] **1** information about a product, etc that a user gives back to its supplier, maker, etc 反馈信息: *We need more feedback from the consumer in order to improve our goods.* 我们需要从消费者那里多得到些反馈信息以提高产品质量. **2** return of part of the output of a system to its source, esp so as to modify the output 反馈: *The feedback from the computer enables us to update the program.* 计算机的反馈能使我们更新程序.

feeder /ˈfiːdə(r); ˋfidɚ/ *n* **1** (preceded by an *adj* 用于形容词之后) thing, esp an animal or a plant, that feeds in a specified way (以某种方式)进食或吸收养料者(尤指动植物): *a gross, dainty, greedy, etc feeder* 吃粗劣食物的、挑剔的、贪吃的…进食者. **2** (*Brit*) baby's bib or feeding-bottle 围嘴; 奶瓶. **3** subsidiary route or means of transport that links outside areas with the main route, service, etc 支路; 支线: [attrib 作定语] *a new feeder road for the motorway* 连接高速公路的新支线. **4** feeding apparatus in a machine 机器的进料装置; 进料器.

feel[1] /fiːl; fil/ *v* (*pt, pp* **felt** /felt; fɛlt/) **1** [Tn, Tw] explore or perceive (sth) by touching or by holding in the hands 摸, 触, 触摸(某物): *feel a rock, a piece of cloth, etc* 摸摸石头、布等 ○ *Can you feel the bump on my head?* 你能摸到我头上的肿块吗? ○ *Can you tell what this is by feeling it?* 你能摸出这是什么吗? ○ *Feel how rough this is.* 摸摸看这东西多粗糙. **2** [Tn, Tng, Tni] (not usu in the continuous tenses 通常不用于进行时态) be aware of or experience (sth physical or emotional); have the sensation of; sense 感觉到, 感受到, 体会到, 体验到(身体上或情绪上的情况); 有知觉; 觉得: *We all felt the earthquake tremors.* 我们都感觉到地震时的颤动. ○ *Can you feel the tension in this room?* 你能觉察出这房间里的紧张气氛吗? ○ *After the accident, she couldn't feel anything in her left leg*, ie it was numb. 出事以后, 她的左腿失去了知觉. ○ *I can feel a nail sticking into my shoe.* 我觉得有钉子扎进鞋里. ○ *I felt something crawl(ing) up my arm.* 我觉得有东西顺着我的胳膊向上爬. **3** [La] be in the specified physical, emotional or moral state 身体上、情绪上或精神上处于某种状态: *feel cold, hungry, comfortable, sad, happy, etc* 感到冷、饿、舒服、悲哀、快乐等 ○ *How are you feeling today?* 你今天身体好吗? ○ *You'll feel better after a good night's sleep.* 你好好睡上一觉就会好些. ○ *She felt betrayed.* 她觉得被人出卖了. ○ *I feel rotten about not taking the children out.* 我没带孩子出去觉得很不痛快. **4** [Ipr] **~ (to sb) (like sth/sb)** (not in the continuous tenses 不用于进行时态) give a sensation or an impression of sth or of being sth/sb 给人以某种感觉或印象: *The water feels warm.* 觉得出这水是温的. ○ *How does it feel to be alone all day?* 整日独自一人感觉如何? ○ *Nothing feels right in our new house.* 我们新房子里, 样样都觉得不对劲. ○ *This wallet feels to me like leather.* 我觉得这钱包像是皮的. ○ *It feels like rain*, ie seems likely to rain. 好像要下雨. ⇨Usage 见所附用法. **5** **~ as if .../as though ...** (not in the continuous tenses 不用于进行时态) have or give the impression that ... 仿佛觉得…: *I feel as if I'm going to be sick.* 我觉得我好像要生病了. ○ *My cold feels as though it's getting better.* 我的感冒好像好多了. ○ *It felt as though a great weight had been lifted from us.* 我们如释重负. **6** [Tn] be particularly conscious of (sth); be affected by 对(某事)特别敏感; 受…的影响: *He feels the cold a lot.* 他很怕冷. ○ *Of all the children, she felt her mother's death the most.* 在所有的子女中, 数她对母亲的去世感到最难过. ○ *We all felt the force of her arguments.* 我们都觉得她的论据很有力. ○ *Don't you feel the beauty of the countryside?* 你是不是觉得郊外的景色很美呀? **7** [I] be capable of sensation 能感觉; 有知觉: *The dead cannot feel.* 死人没有知觉. **8** [Tf, Cn·a, Cn·t] have as an opinion; consider; think; believe 认为; 以为; 想; 相信: *We all felt (that) our luck was about to turn.* 我们都认为快要转运了. ○ *She felt in her bones that she would succeed.* 她坚信自己能成功. ○ *I felt it advisable to do nothing.* 我认为最好什么也别做. ○ *He felt the plan to be unwise/felt that the plan was unwise.* 他认为这计划不当. **9** [I, Ipr, Ip] **~ (about) (for sb/sth)** search with the hands, the feet, a stick, etc (用手、足、杖等)寻找, 摸索, 探索: *He felt in his pocket for some money.* 他在口袋里摸着, 想找些钱. ○ *I had to feel about in the dark for the light switch.* 我得在黑暗中摸索着找电灯开关. ○ *She felt along the wall for the door.* 她沿着墙摸索着找门. **10** (idm 习语) **be/feel called to sth** ⇨ CALL[2]. ˌ**feel** ˈ**free** (*infml* 口) (said when giving permission 用以表示准许): *'May I use your phone?' 'Feel free.'* '我借用一下你的电话, 行吗?' '随便用吧.' ˌ**feel one's** ˈ**age** realize that one is growing old, as one becomes less strong or one's ideas are thought to be

F

old-fashioned（因体力渐弱或思想守旧）意识到自己老了: *My children's skill with computers really makes me feel my age!* 我的孩子使用电脑得心应手确使我觉得自己老了. **feel one's 'ears burning** think or imagine that others are talking about one 觉得耳朵在发烧(认为或猜想有人在谈论自己). **feel 'good** feel happy, confident, etc 感到愉快、有信心等: *It makes me feel good to know you like me.* 我知道你喜欢我, 感到很高兴. **feel (it) in one's 'bones (that...)** know or sense (sth) intuitively 凭直觉懂得或感到(某事物): *I know I'm going to fail this exam — I can feel it in my bones.* 我知道这次考试要不及格——我有这种直觉. **feel like sth/doing sth** think that one would like (to do/have) sth; want (to do) sth 想要(做)某事物: *I feel like (having) a drink.* 我想喝点酒. ○ *We'll go for a walk if you feel like it.* 你愿意的话, 咱们就去散散步. **feel one's oats** (*infml* 口) be in an energetic and lively mood and act accordingly 感到精神饱满. **feel one'self** feel fit and healthy 感到有精神: *I don't quite feel my'self today.* 我今天有些不舒服. **feel the 'pinch** (*infml* 口) (begin to) suffer from a lack of (esp) money (开始)感到缺乏(尤指钱): *The high rate of unemployment is making many families feel the pinch.* 失业率很高, 许多家庭感到日子不好过了. **feel/take sb's pulse** ⇨ PULSE[1]. **feel one's 'way** (a) move along carefully, eg in darkness, by touching walls, objects, etc (沿墙壁、物体等)摸索着走(如在黑暗中). (b) (*fig* 比喻) proceed cautiously 谨慎行事: *At this early stage of the negotiations both sides were still feeling their way.* 在这谈判的初始阶段, 双方尚十分谨慎. **look/feel small** ⇨ SMALL. **make one's presence felt** ⇨ PRESENCE. **11** (phr v) **feel for sb** have sympathy for sb 同情, 怜悯(某人): *I really felt for her when her husband died.* 她丈夫死了, 我十分同情她. **feel up to (doing) sth** consider oneself capable of (doing) sth 认为自己有能力做某事: *If you feel up to it, we could walk into town after lunch.* 你要是走得动, 咱们午饭后可以走到城里.

NOTE ON USAGE 用法: There are several verbs relating to the five senses of sight, smell, hearing, taste and touch. 有几个动词与视觉、嗅觉、听觉、味觉、触觉这五种感官有关. They are often used with the verb **can.** 这些动词常与**can**连用. Normally, only the simple tenses are used. 通常只用于简单时态. **1 See, smell, hear, taste** and **feel** indicate the experiencing of something through one of the senses ☆ **see**、**smell**、**hear**、**taste**、**feel**分别表示五种感官之一对某物的感知: *He saw a light in the window.* 他看见窗户里有灯光. ○ *I heard an explosion last night.* 我昨晚听到了爆炸声. ○ *I can smell gas.* 我闻到有煤气味. **2** These verbs can also indicate somebody's physical ability to perceive with the senses 这些动词还可用以表示某人的感官能力: *He can't see, hear, etc very well.* 他的视力、听力等不太好. **3 Look, smell, taste, sound** and **feel** are used to describe how somebody or something is experienced through one of the senses, usually in one of these patterns ☆ **look**、**smell**、**taste**、**sound**、**feel**可用以表示通过五官之一感知某人或某事物, 通常用于下列句型: **(a)** *She looks happy,* ie She's smiling. 她看上去很高兴. **(b)** *The wine tastes like water,* ie It's very weak. 这酒的味道像水一样. **(c)** *The singer sounds as though she's got a sore throat,* ie The sound of her voice suggests that she has a sore throat. 这歌手的声音听起来好像她嗓子疼. **4 Look, smell, listen, taste, feel** can indicate that somebody is making a deliberate effort to perceive something ☆ **look**、**smell**、**listen**、**taste**、**feel**可用以表示某人着意要感知某事物: **(a)** *'I can't see the spot.' 'Well look harder.'* '我看不到有斑点.' '再好好看看.' **(b)** *'I can't hear any music.' 'Listen carefully.'* '我听不出有音乐.' '再用心听听.' **(c)** *'I can't taste anything.' 'Try tasting this.'* '我尝不出有什么味道.' '再尝尝这个.' **5 Feel** and **look** can express the physical or emotional state of a person. ☆ **feel**和**look**可表示人的身体或情绪的状态. Here, the continuous tenses can be used 在这种情况下可用进行时态: *I feel sick, nervous, disappointed, etc.* 我感到不舒服、紧张、失望等. ○ *He was feeling tired so he didn't come to the party.* 他感到很累, 所以没来参加聚会. ○ *You're looking happy. Have you had good news?* 你看来很高兴. 有好消息吗?

feel[2] /fi:l; fil/ *n* [sing] **1** act of feeling 摸; 触; 触摸: *Let me have a feel.* 让我摸摸. **2 the feel** sense of touch 触觉: *rough, smooth, etc to the feel*, ie when touched or felt 摸起来感到粗糙、平滑等. **3 the feel (a)** sensation that sth gives when touching or being touched 触摸和被触摸时的感觉: *You can tell it's silk by the feel.* 你摸摸就知道是绸缎. ○ *She loved the feel of the sun on her skin.* 她喜欢太阳照射在皮肤上的那种感觉. **(b)** sensation created by a situation, etc (环境等给人造成的)感觉, 感受: *the feel of the place, the meeting, the occasion* 某地方、会议、场合的气氛的感受. **4** (idm 习语) **get the feel of sth/of doing sth** (*infml* 口) become familiar with (doing) sth 开始熟悉(做)某事: *You haven't got the feel of the gears in this car yet.* 你对这辆汽车的排挡还不熟悉. **have a feel for sth** (*infml* 口) have a sensitive appreciation or an easy understanding of sth 对某事物有敏锐的鉴赏力或很强的理解力: *He has a good feel for languages.* 他很有语感.

feeler /'fi:lə(r); 'filɚ/ *n* **1** long slender part in certain animals, esp insects, for testing things by touch 某些动物(尤指昆虫)的触须, 触角. **2** (idm 习语) **put out feelers** (*infml* 口) cautiously check the views of others 谨慎地试探别人的观点: *I'll try to put out some feelers to gauge people's reactions to our proposal.* 我想试探一下, 看看人们对我们建议的反应.

□ **'feeler gauge** one of a set of metal blades used for measuring gaps, etc 测隙规; 厚薄规.

feel·ing /'fi:lɪŋ; 'filɪŋ/ *n* **1** [U] ability to feel 知觉: *I've lost all feeling in my legs.* 我的双腿完全失去了知觉. **2 (a)** [C] **~ (of sth)** thing that is felt through the mind or the senses 感觉; 感触: *a feeling of hunger, well-being, discomfort, gratitude, joy, etc* 饥饿、健康愉快、不适、感激、快乐等的感觉. **(b)** [sing] **~ (of sth/that...)** vague notion or belief not based wholly on reason (并非完全基于理性的)模糊观念或想法; 预感: *a feeling of danger* 对危险的预感 ○ *I can't understand why, but suddenly I had this feeling that something terrible was going to happen.* 我说不清为什么, 但我忽然预感到要出事了. **(c)** [sing] attitude; opinion 态度; 看法: *The feeling of the meeting* (ie The opinion of the majority) *was against the proposal.* 与会的人大都反对此项提议. ○ *My own feeling is that we should buy it.* 我个人的看法是我们应该把它买下来. **3** [U] **(a)** sensitivity; appreciation 感受力; 鉴赏力: *He plays the piano with great feeling.* 他演奏钢琴时表现出极强的感受力. ○ *She hasn't much feeling for the beauty of nature.* 她对大自然的美缺少鉴赏力. **(b) ~ (for sb/sth)** sympathetic understanding (of sb/sth) (对某人[某事物]的)同情, 体谅: *You have no feeling for the sufferings of others.* 你对别人的痛苦漠不关心. **4** [C, U] strong emotion, esp of discontent, resentment, etc 激情(尤指不满、怨恨等): *The candidate's speech aroused strong feeling(s) on all sides.* 那位候选人的讲话激起了各方面的强烈不满. ○ *She spoke with feeling about the high rate of unemployment.* 她针对失业率之高慷慨陈辞. ○ *Feeling over the dismissal ran high*, ie There was much resentment, anger, etc about it. 对解雇事件群情鼎沸. **5 feelings** [pl] person's emotions rather than intellect (与理智相对而言的)感情: *The speaker appealed more to the feelings of her audience than to their reason.* 她演讲时并非靠以理服人而是要打动听众的感情. ○ *You've hurt my feelings*, ie You've offended me. 你伤了我的感情. **6** (idm 习语) **bad/ill 'feeling** resentment; dissatisfaction 恶感; 反感; 不满: *His rapid promotion caused much bad feeling among his colleagues.* 他获迅速提升在同事中引起很大的不满. **have mixed feelings about sb/sth** ⇨ MIXED. **no hard feelings** ⇨ HARD[1]. **one's better feelings/nature** ⇨ BETTER[1]. **relieve one's feelings** ⇨ RELIEVE. **a/that sinking feeling** ⇨ SINK[1]. **spare sb's feelings** ⇨ SPARE[2].

▷ **feel·ing** *adj* **1** sympathetic 有同情心的: *She is very feeling/is a very feeling person.* 她很有同情心. **2** [attrib 作定语] showing strong emotion; heartfelt 激动的; 衷心的: *a feeling remark* 恳切的言语. **feel·ingly** *adv* with deep emotion 激动地: *He spoke feelingly about his dismissal.* 他激动地谈到自己被解雇一事.

feet *pl* of FOOT[1].

feign /feɪn; fen/ *v* [Tn] pretend (sth) 假装, 冒充, 佯作(某事): *feign illness, madness, ignorance, etc* 装病、装疯、佯作无知 ○ *feigned innocence* 装出来的清白无辜.

F

feint[1] /feɪnt; fent/ *n* (in war, boxing, fencing, etc) pretended attack to distract an opponent's attention from the main attack (战争、拳击、击剑等中的)佯攻, 虚晃.
▷ **feint** /feɪnt; fent/ *v* [I] make a feint 佯攻; 虚晃.

feint[2] /feɪnt; fent/ *adj* [usu attrib 通常作定语] (of paper, etc) having faintly printed lines (指纸等)印有隐格线的: *a narrow feint pad*, ie one with narrowly-spaced faint lines 窄行隐格的拍纸簿.

feisty /ˈfi:stɪ; ˋfistɪ/ *adj* (**-ier**, **-iest**) (*US infml* 口) **1** (*approv* 褒) spirited; energetic; forceful 精神饱满的; 精力充沛的; 强有力的. **2** (*derog* 贬) irritable; quarrelsome 脾气坏的; 好争吵的: *a feisty old man* 脾气很坏的人.

feld·spar /ˈfeldspɑ:(r); ˋfɛld,spɑr/ (also **fel·spar** /ˈfelspɑ:(r); ˋfɛl,spɑr/) *n* [U] white or red mineral rock that contains aluminium and other silicates 长石.

fe·licit·ate /fəˈlɪsɪteɪt; fəˋlɪsə,tet/ *v* [Tn, Tn·pr] **~ sb (on sth)** (*fml* 文) congratulate sb 祝贺某人; 向某人道贺. ▷ **fe·licita·tion** /fə,lɪsɪˈteɪʃn; fə,lɪsəˋteʃən/ *n* [U, C usu *pl* 作不可数名词或可数名词, 后者通常作复数].

fe·licit·ous /fəˈlɪsɪtəs; fəˋlɪsətəs/ *adj* (*fml* 文) (esp of words) well-chosen; apt (尤指词语)经推敲的; 恰当的: *felicitous remarks* 恰如其分的言语 ○ *Her choice of music is felicitous.* 她选择的音乐很适当. ▷ **fe·licit·ously** *adv*.

fe·licity /fəˈlɪsətɪ; fəˋlɪsətɪ/ *n* (*fml* 文) **1** [U] great happiness 幸福; 快乐. **2** [C, U] (instance of a) pleasing style of speaking or writing (言语文字的)得当, 得体: *the many felicities of her language* 她言辞中妙语如珠 ○ *He expressed himself with great felicity.* 他表达自己的意思恰到好处.

F

fe·line /ˈfi:laɪn; ˋfilaɪn/ *adj, n* (of or like an) animal of the cat family 猫科动物; (似)猫科的: *walk with a feline grace* 轻巧地行走.

fell[1] *pt* of FALL[1].

fell[2] /fel; fɛl/ *adj* **1** (*arch* 古) fierce; destructive 凶猛的; 毁灭性的. **2** (idm 习语) **at one fell swoop** in a single deadly action 狠狠地一下子.

fell[3] /fel; fɛl/ *n* stretch of bare rocky moorland or hilly land in northern England (英格兰北部的)荒野, 沼泽地: *the Lakeland Fells* 莱克兰荒野.

fell[4] /fel; fɛl/ *v* [Tn] **1** cut down (a tree) 砍伐(树木). **2** knock down (sb) with a blow 击倒, 打倒(某人): *He felled his enemy with a single blow.* 他一拳就把敌人打倒了.

fel·la·tio /fəˈleɪʃiːəʊ; fəˋleʃio/ *n* [U] (*fml* 文) stimulation of the penis by sucking or licking 吮吸或舔阴茎之刺激.

fel·low /ˈfeləʊ; ˋfɛlo/ *n* **1** (esp *pl*, often in compounds 尤作复数, 常用以构成复合词) companion; comrade 同伴; 同志: *ˈplayfellows* ○ *ˈbedfellows* ○ *fellows in good fortune, misery* 共安乐、共患难的人 ○ *Her fellows share her interest in computers.* 她的同伴跟她一样对计算机感兴趣. **2** [attrib 作定语] of the same class, kind, etc 同阶层的; 同种的; 同类的: *a fellow member* 同一组织的成员 ○ *one's ,fellow-ˈcountrymen* 同胞. **3** (*esp Brit*) member of a learned society 学术团体的成员: *Fellow of the Royal Academy* 皇家学会会员. **4** member of the governing body of some colleges or universities (某些学院或大学的)董事. **5** (*esp US*) graduate student holding a fellowship (接受奖学金的)研究生. **6** (*fml or rhet* 文或修辞) one of a pair 一对中之一: *Here's one of my shoes, but where's its fellow?* 我的一只鞋在这里, 另一只在哪里呢? **7** (*infml* 口) man or boy; chap 男人; 男孩; 小伙子: *He's a nice fellow.* 他是个很好的人. ○ *Poor fellow!* 可怜的小伙子! ○ (*joc* 谑) *Where can a fellow* (ie Where can I) *get a bite to eat round here?* 我在附近什么地方能弄到点吃的? **8** (idm 习语) **be hail-fellow-well-met (with sb)** ⇨ HAIL.
□ **,fellow-ˈfeeling** *n* [U] sympathy with sb whose experience, etc one shares (对与自己经历等相同的人所产生的)同情.
,fellow-ˈtraveller *n* **1** person who sympathizes with the aims of a political party (esp the Communist Party) but is not a member (政党, 尤指共产党的)同路人. **2** person one is travelling with 旅伴.

fel·low·ship /ˈfeləʊʃɪp; ˋfɛlo,ʃɪp/ *n* **1** [U] friendly association with others; companionship 友谊; 交情: *enjoy fellowship with people* 喜欢与人交往 ○ *fellowship in misfortune* 患难之交. **2** (**a**) [C] group or society of people sharing a common interest or aim (有共同利益或目标的人组成的)团体, 协会, 联谊会. (**b**) [U] membership in such a group or society (团体、协会、联谊会的)会员资格: *admitted to fellowship* 获准入会. **3** [C] (*esp Brit*) position of a (college) fellow (学院中)董事的职位, 研究员的职位. **4** [C] award of money to a graduate student in return for some teaching, research assistance, etc 研究生的奖学金(作为助教、助研等工作之报酬): *We give three research fellowships a year.* 我们每年给三个研究生的奖学金.

fel·ony /ˈfelənɪ; ˋfɛlənɪ/ *n* [C, U] (*law* 律) serious crime, eg murder, armed robbery or arson 重罪(如谋杀、持械抢劫或放火): *a series of felonies* 一连串的重罪案 ○ *be convicted of felony* 被判犯有重罪.
▷ **felon** /ˈfelən; ˋfɛlən/ *n* person guilty of felony 重罪犯.

fe·loni·ous /fəˈləʊnɪəs; fəˋlonɪəs/ *adj* of or involving felony; criminal 重罪的; 犯重罪的.

fel·spar = FELDSPAR.

felt[1] *pt, pp* of FEEL[1].

felt[2] /felt; fɛlt/ *n* [U] wool, hair or fur, compressed and rolled flat into a thick cloth 毛毡: [attrib 作定语] *felt hats, slippers, etc* 毡帽、毡制拖鞋.
□ **,felt-ˈpen** *n* (also **,felt-ˈtip**, **,felt-tipped ˈpen**) pen with a tip made of felt 毡头笔.

fe·lucca /fəˈlʌkə; fəˋlʌkə/ *n* narrow ship with oars or sails or both, used on Mediterranean coasts (用桨或帆或两者皆用的)小船(用于地中海沿岸).

fem *abbr* 缩写 = female; feminine. Cf 参看 MASC.

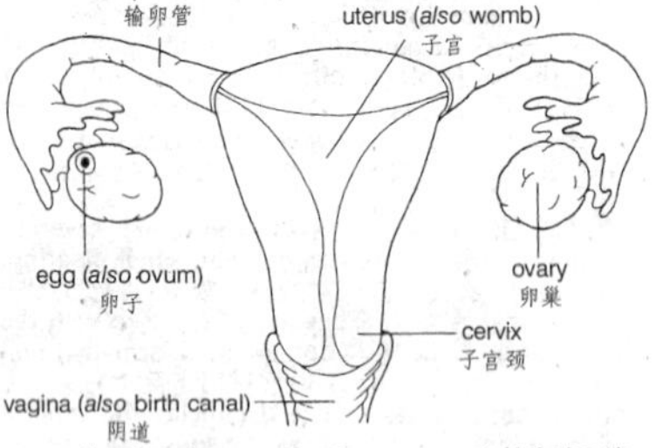

the female reproductive system 女性生殖系统

fe·male /ˈfi:meɪl; ˋfimel/ *adj* **1** (**a**) of the sex that can give birth to children or produce eggs 女的; 母的; 雌性的: *a female dog, cat, pig, etc* 母狗、母猫、母猪. (**b**) (of plants and flowers) producing fruit (指树木、花卉)结果实的, 雌性的, 有雌蕊的: *a female fig-tree* 雌性无花果树. **2** of or typical of women 妇女的; 女性的; 女性特有的: *female suffrage* 妇女选举权 ○ *the female mentality* 妇女心态. **3** (of a plug, socket, etc) having a hollow part designed to receive an inserted part (指插头、插座等)有内孔的, 凹的.
▷ **fe·male** *n* **1** female animal or plant 雌性的动物或植物. **2** (*often derog* 常作贬义) woman 女人: *Who on earth is that female he's with?* 跟他在一起的那个女人究竟是谁?

NOTE ON USAGE 用法: **1** (**a**) **Male** and **female** are nouns and adjectives used to indicate the sex of living things ☆ **male** 和 **female** 既可作名词也可作形容词, 用以表示生物的性别: *a male/female giraffe, bird, sardine, child, flower, etc* 公[母]长颈鹿、鸟、沙丁鱼; 男[女]孩子; 雄性的[雌性的]花等 ○ *The males in the herd protect the females and the young.* 兽群中的雄性动物保护雌性动物和幼崽. (**b**) When speaking of humans the adjectives **male/female** refer especially to the physical features of one sex or the other ☆ **male/female** 作形容词用于人时, 尤指男女的性别特征: *The male voice is deeper than the female.* 男性的嗓音比女性的低沉. ○ *the female figure* 女性的身材. (**c**) When speaking about occupations, we usually say: *a woman doctor/women doctors* (NOT *a female doctor/female doctors,* though we do say *a male doctor,* NOT *a man doctor).* 谈到男女的

职业, 通常说: a woman doctor / women doctors(不可说 a female doctor / female doctors, 但却一定要说 a male doctor, 而不可说 a man doctor). (**d**) The nouns **male**/**female** should not be used to refer to people (as opposed to their qualities, etc) ☆ **male/female** 作名词时不能用以指人. They can give offence, esp **female.** 用于指人时会引起反感, 尤其是 **female** 一词. We use **man/woman** instead 这时要用 **man** / **woman**: *Men have more body hair than women.* 男人的寒毛比女人的多. **2** (**a**) **Masculine** and **feminine** are adjectives used to describe the behaviour, appearance, etc considered normal or acceptable for humans of one sex or the other. ☆ **masculine** 和 **feminine** 为形容词, 用以描述所谓正常的或公认的男女之别, 如行为、外貌等. They can therefore be used of the 'opposite' sex: a man can be described as **feminine** but not **female** 形容男人可用 **feminine** 而不可用 **female**: *She dresses in a very feminine way.* 她穿得非常女性化. ○ *She has a deep masculine voice.* 她的声音像男人的那样低沉. (**b**) As nouns and adjectives **masculine** and **feminine** (as well as **neuter**) indicate grammatical gender. ☆ **masculine** 和 **feminine**(以及 **neuter**)作名词和形容词, 分别用以指语法中的阳性和阴性(以及中性).

fem·in·ine /ˈfemənɪn; ˋfɛmənɪn/ *adj* **1** of or like women; having the qualities or appearance considered characteristic of women 女性的; 女人般的; 具有女性气质或外貌特征的: *a feminine voice, figure, appearance* 女性的嗓声、体形、容貌. **2** (*grammar*) belonging to a class of words in English referring to female persons, animals, etc and often having a special form 阴性的: *'Lioness' is the feminine form of 'lion'.* lioness 是 lion 的阴性形式. ○ *The feminine form of 'count' is 'countess'.* count 的阴性形式是 countess.
▷ **fem·in·ine** *n* (*grammar*) feminine word or gender 阴性词; 阴性.
fem·in·in·ity /ˌfeməˈnɪnətɪ; ˌfɛməˋnɪnətɪ/ *n* [U] quality of being feminine 女子的气质. ➩Usage at FEMALE 用法见 FEMALE. Cf 参看 MASCULINE.

fem·in·ism /ˈfemɪnɪzəm; ˋfɛməˌnɪzəm/ *n* [U] (**a**) belief in the principle that women should have the same rights and opportunities (legal, political, social, economic, etc) as men 男女平等主义. (**b**) movement in support of this 争取女权运动.
▷ **fem·in·ist** /ˈfemɪnɪst; ˋfɛməˌnɪst/ *n* supporter of feminism 男女平等主义者; 争取女权主义者: *Suffragettes were among the first feminists in Britain.* 争取选举权的妇女是英国最早的男女平等主义者. ○ [attrib 作定语] *He has strong feminist opinions.* 他有强烈的男女平等思想.

femme fa·tale /ˌfæm fəˈtɑːl; ˌfæm fəˋtɑl/ (*pl* **femmes fatales** /ˌfæm fəˈtɑːl; ˌfæm fəˋtɑl/) (*French* 法) woman to whom a man feels irresistibly attracted, with dangerous or unhappy results 妖媚迷人的女子(为男子的祸患): *She was his femme fatale.* 她是他的红颜祸水.

fe·mur /ˈfiːmə(r); ˋfimɚ/ *n* (*pl* **~s** or **femora** /ˈfemərə; ˋfɛmərə/) (*anatomy* 解) thigh-bone 股骨. ➩illus at SKELETON 见 SKELETON 插图. ▷ **fem·oral** /ˈfemərəl; ˋfɛmərəl/ *adj.*

fen /fen; fɛn/ *n* **1** [C] area of low marshy land 沼地; 沼泽. **2 the Fens** [pl] low marshy areas in parts of East Anglia (英格兰东部的)沼泽地区. ➩illus at App 1 见附录1插图, pages xiv, xv.

fence[1] /fens; fɛns/ *n* **1** structure of rails, stakes, wire, etc, esp one put round a field or garden to mark a boundary or keep animals from straying 栅栏; 篱笆; 围墙. ➩illus at App 1 见附录1插图, page vi. **2** (idm 习语) **come down on one side of the fence or the other** ➩ SIDE[1]. **sit on the fence** ➩ SIT.
▷ **fence** *v* **1** [Tn] surround, divide, etc (sth) with a fence 用栅栏、篱笆、围墙等将(某物)围着或隔开等: *Farmers fence their fields.* 农人用篱笆把田地围起. ○ *His land was fenced with barbed wire.* 他的土地用铁丝网围着. **2** (phr v) **fence sb/sth in** (**a**) surround or enclose sb/sth with a fence 用栅栏、篱笆、围墙等围着或圈起某人[某物]: *The grounds are fenced in to prevent trespassing.* 庭院用栅栏围着以防外人进去. (**b**) restrict the freedom of sb 限制某人的自由: *She felt fenced in by domestic routine.* 她觉得自己完全被家务事束缚住了. **fence sth off** separate (one area from another) with a fence 用栅栏、篱笆、围墙等将(某处)隔开: *One end of the garden was fenced off for chickens.* 花园的一端已用篱笆隔开来养鸡.
fen·cing /ˈfensɪŋ; ˋfɛnsɪŋ/ [U] material used for making fences, eg wood, wire, etc 制做栅栏、篱笆、围墙等的材料(如木材、金属丝等).

fencing 击剑运动

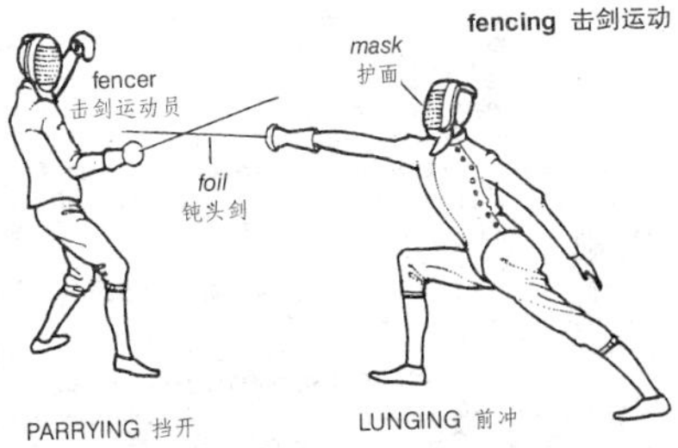

fence[2] /fens; fɛns/ *v* **1** [I] (*sport* 体) fight with a long slender sword (foil, épée or sabre) 击剑. **2** [I, Ipr] **~ (with sb/sth)** be evasive; avoid giving a direct answer to a question(er) 回避; 避免作正面回答: *Stop fencing with me — answer my question!* 别躲躲闪闪 —— 回答我的问题!
□ **fencer** *n* person who fences (FENCE[2] 1) 击剑运动员.
fencing *n* [U] art or sport of fighting with foils or other types of sword 击剑术; 击剑运动. ➩illus 见插图.

fence[3] /fens; fɛns/ *n* person who knowingly buys and resells stolen goods 买卖赃物的人.

F

fend /fend; fɛnd/ *v* (phr v) **fend for oneˈself** take care of or look after oneself; support oneself 照顾自己; 自谋生计; 独立生活: *It is time you left home and learnt to fend for yourself.* 你应该离家自立了. **fend sth/sb off** defend oneself from sth/sb; fight sth/sb off 抵御或抵挡某事物[某人]: *fend off a blow* 挡开一击 ○ *The minister had to fend off some awkward questions from reporters.* 部长需避开记者提出的某些尴尬的问题. ○ *He tried to kiss her but she fended him off.* 他想吻她, 但她把他挡开了.

fender /ˈfendə(r); ˋfɛndɚ/ *n* **1** metal frame placed around a fireplace to prevent burning coal, etc from falling out or young children from falling in 壁炉的栅栏. **2** mass of rope, piece of wood, rubber tyre, etc, hung on the side of a boat to prevent damage, eg when it is alongside a wharf or another boat 护舷垫(船舷悬挂的绳团、木块、轮胎等, 防碰损用). **3** (*US*) (**a**) mudguard (MUD) of a bicycle, etc (自行车等的)挡泥板. (**b**) = WING 4.

fen·nel /ˈfenl; ˋfɛnḷ/ *n* [U] herb with yellow flowers, used for flavouring food 茴香(用以调味).

feral /ˈfɪərəl; *US* ˈferəl; ˋfɪrəl/ *adj* (*fml* 文) (of animals) wild or savage, esp after escaping from captivity or from life as a pet (指动物)野的, 凶猛的(尤指捕后逃脱或豢养后逃脱者): *feral cats* 野猫.

fer·ment[1] /fəˈment; fɚˋmɛnt/ *v* [I, Tn] **1** (make sth) change chemically through the action of organic substances (esp yeast) (使某物)发酵: *Fruit juices ferment if they are kept a long time.* 果汁放置日久会发酵. ○ *When wine is fermented it gives off bubbles of gas.* 酒发酵时会放出气泡. **2** (*fig* 比喻) excite; stir up 激起; 煽动: *ferment trouble among the factory workers* 在工人中引起骚动.
▷ **fer·menta·tion** /ˌfɜːmenˈteɪʃn; ˌfɝmɛnˋteʃən/ *n* [U] (action or process of) fermenting 发酵: *Sugar is converted into alcohol through the process of fermentation.* 糖经发酵变成酒精. ○ *The fermentation of milk causes it to curdle.* 牛奶发酵会凝结起来.

fer·ment[2] /ˈfɜːment; ˋfɝmɛnt/ *n* **1** [C] substance, eg yeast, that causes sth to ferment 发酵剂; 酵母. **2** [U] (esp political or social) excitement or unrest (尤指政治或社会方面的)动荡不安: *The country was in (a state of) ferment.* 这个国家处于动荡不安之中.

fern /fɜːn; fɝn/ *n* [C, U] type of flowerless plant with feathery green leaves 蕨; 蕨类植物: *ferns growing in pots* 长在盆内的蕨类植物 ○ *hillsides covered in fern* 长满蕨

类植物的山坡 ○ *a spray of ornamental fern* 蕨类植物的枝状饰物. ▷ **ferny** *adj*.

fe·ro·cious /fəˈrəʊʃəs; fəˈroʃəs/ *adj* fierce, violent or savage 残忍的; 凶猛的; 野蛮的: *a ferocious beast* 猛兽 ○ *ferocious cruelty* 残酷的行为 ○ *a ferocious onslaught* 猛攻 ○ (*fig* 比喻) *a ferocious campaign against us in the press* 新闻界对我们的猛烈抨击. ▷ **fe·ro·ciously** *adv*: *snarling ferociously* 凶猛地咆哮.

fe·ro·city /fəˈrɒsətɪ; fəˈrɑsətɪ/ *n* **1** [U] fierceness; violence 凶恶; 残暴; 凶猛: *The lion attacked its victim with great ferocity.* 狮子凶猛地扑向猎物. **2** [C] fierce or savage act 凶猛的行为; 暴行.

fer·ret /ˈferɪt; ˋfɛrɪt/ *n* small animal of the weasel family, kept for driving rabbits from their burrows, killing rats, etc 雪貂(用以将兔从洞中逐出、捕鼠等). Cf 参看 ERMINE, WEASEL.

▷ **fer·ret** *v* **1** [I] (usu 通常作 **go ferreting**) hunt (rabbits, rats, etc) with ferrets 用雪貂捕猎(兔、鼠等). **2** [I, Ipr, Ip] **~ (about) (for sth)** (*infml* 口) search; rummage 搜寻; 翻找: *I spent the day ferreting (about) in the attic (for old photographs).* 我一整天都在阁楼上翻找(旧照片). **3** (phr v) **ferret sth out** (*infml* 口) discover sth by searching or asking questions thoroughly (通过搜查或仔细盘问)发现某事物; 查获; 侦破: *ferret out a secret, the truth, the facts, etc* 查明秘密、真相、事实等.

Ferris wheel /ˈferɪs wiːl; *US* hwiːl; ˋfɛrɪs ˌhwil/ (in fair-grounds, etc) large upright wheel revolving on a fixed axle and having seats hanging from its rim (游乐场等处的)摩天轮(在垂直转动的巨轮上挂有座位的游乐设施).

F

fer·ro·con·crete /ˌferəʊˈkɒŋkriːt; ˌfɛroˋkɑnkrit/ *n* [U] = REINFORCED CONCRETE (REINFORCE).

fer·rous /ˈferəs; ˋfɛrəs/ *adj* [attrib 作定语] containing or relating to iron 含铁的; 铁的: *ferrous and non-ferrous metals* 黑色及有色金属.

fer·rule /ˈferuːl; *US* ˈferəl; ˋfɛrəl/ *n* metal ring or cap placed on the end of a stick, an umbrella, etc to stop it splitting or wearing down (手杖、伞等顶端的)金属箍, 金属包头.

ferry /ˈferɪ; ˋfɛrɪ/ *n* **1** boat, hovercraft, etc that carries people and goods across a stretch of water 渡船: *The ferry leaves for France at one o'clock.* 渡船于一点钟开往法国. ○ *travel by ferry* 乘渡船 ○ [attrib 作定语] *the cross-channel ferry service* 摆渡服务. **2** place where such a service operates 渡口: *We waited at the ferry for two hours.* 我们在渡口等了两小时.

▷ **ferry** *v* (*pt, pp* **ferried**) [Tn, Tn·pr, Tn·p] transport (people or goods) by boat, aeroplane, etc, usu a short distance over a stretch of water, or regularly over a period of time (用船或飞机等)运送(人或货物)(通常指短程的或定期的): *ferry goods to the mainland* 将货物运往大陆 ○ *Can you ferry us across?* 你能渡我们过去吗? ○ *ferry the children to and from school* 接送孩子上学 ○ *planes ferrying food to the refugees* 给难民运送食物的飞机.

□ ˈ**ferry-boat** *n* boat used as a ferry 渡船.

ˈ**ferryman** /-mən; -mən/ *n* (*pl* **-men** /-mən; -mən/) person in charge of a (usu small) ferry 渡船主, 渡船工人(通常指小渡船的).

fer·tile /ˈfɜːtaɪl; *US* ˈfɜːrtl; ˋfɝtl/ *adj* **1** (of land/or soil) able to produce much; rich in nutrients (指土地)肥沃的, 富饶的: *The plains of Alberta are extremely fertile.* 艾伯塔平原极其肥沃. **2** (of plants or animals) able to produce fruit or young (指动植物)能结果实的, 能生育的. **3** (of seeds or eggs) capable of developing into a new plant or animal; fertilized (指籽、卵)能发芽的, 能孵的, 受精的. **4** (of a person's mind) full of new ideas; inventive (指人的头脑)主意多的, 有创造力的: *have a fertile imagination* 有丰富的想像力. Cf 参看 STERILE.

▷ **fer·til·ity** /fəˈtɪlətɪ; fɝˋtɪlətɪ/ *n* [U] state or condition of being fertile 肥沃; 多产; 丰富: *the fertility of the soil* 土地的肥沃 ○ *great fertility of mind* 丰富的智慧.

fer·til·ize, -ise /ˈfɜːtəlaɪz; ˋfɝtḷˌaɪz/ *v* [Tn] **1** introduce pollen or sperm into (a plant, an egg or a female animal) so that it develops seed or young 使(动植物)受孕, 受精, 受粉: *Flowers are often fertilized by bees as they gather nectar.* 蜜蜂采蜜时常使花受粉. **2** make (soil, etc) fertile or productive 使(土地等)肥沃, 多产: *fertilize the garden with manure* 给花园施肥.

▷ **fer·til·iza·tion, -isation** /ˌfɜːtəlaɪˈzeɪʃn; *US* -lɪˈz-; ˌfɝtḷəˋzeʃən/ *n* [U]: *successful fertilization by the male* 授精; 受胎.

fer·til·izer, -iser *n* [U, C] natural or artificial substance added to soil to make it more fertile 肥料; 化肥: *Get some more fertilizer for the garden.* 给花园再多施些肥料. ○ *Bone-meal and nitrates are common fertilizers.* 骨粉和硝酸盐是普通的肥料. Cf 参看 MANURE.

fer·vent /ˈfɜːvənt; ˋfɝvənt/ (also **fer·vid**) *adj* showing warmth and sincerity of feeling; enthusiastic; passionate 热诚的; 热情的; 热烈的; 强烈的: *a fervent farewell speech* 热情的告别演说 ○ *fervent love, hatred, etc* 强烈的爱、恨等 ○ *a fervent admirer* 痴心的倾慕者. ▷ **fer·vently** *adv*: *believe fervently in eventual victory* 坚信最后会取得胜利.

fer·vid /ˈfɜːvɪd; ˋfɝvɪd/ *adj* (*fml* 文) = FERVENT. ▷ **fer·vidly** *adv*.

fer·vour (*US* **fer·vor**) /ˈfɜːvə(r); ˋfɝvɚ/ *n* [U] strength or warmth of feeling; enthusiasm 热烈; 热诚; 热情: *speak with great fervour* 热情洋溢地说.

festal /ˈfestl; ˋfɛstḷ/ *adj* (*fml* 文) of a festival; gay and joyful 节日的; 欢乐的. Cf 参看 FESTIVE.

fes·ter /ˈfestə(r); ˋfɛstɚ/ *v* [I] **1** (of a cut or wound) become infected and filled with pus (指伤口)溃烂, 化脓: *a festering sore* 化脓的伤处. **2** (*fig* 比喻) (of feelings or thoughts) become more bitter and angry (指感情或思想)更加痛苦和愤怒: *The resentment festered in his mind.* 他心中的愤恨有增无已.

fest·ival /ˈfestəvl; ˋfɛstəvḷ/ *n* **1** (day or time of) religious or other celebration 节日; 节期; 喜庆日: *Christmas and Easter are Christian festivals.* 圣诞节和复活节是基督教的节日. ○ [attrib 作定语] *a festival atmosphere* 节日的气氛. **2** series of performances of music, drama, films, etc given periodically (音乐、戏剧、电影等的)会演: *the Edinburgh Festival* 爱丁堡艺术会演 ○ *a jazz festival* 爵士音乐会演.

fest·ive /ˈfestɪv; ˋfɛstɪv/ *adj* of or suitable for a feast or festival; joyous 欢宴的; 节日的; 欢乐的: *the festive season*, ie Christmas 欢乐的节日(即圣诞节) ○ *The whole town is in festive mood.* 全镇沉浸在节日的气氛之中. Cf 参看 FESTAL.

fest·iv·ity /feˈstɪvətɪ; fɛsˋtɪvətɪ/ *n* **1** [U] rejoicing; merry-making 欢宴; 欢庆; 欢乐: *The royal wedding was an occasion of great festivity.* 皇室婚礼是喜庆的盛事. **2** **festivities** [pl] festive, joyful events; celebrations 庆典; 喜庆: *wedding festivities* 结婚庆典.

fes·toon /feˈstuːn; fɛsˋtun/ *n* chain of flowers, leaves, ribbons, etc hung in a curve or loop as a decoration 花彩.

▷ **fes·toon** *v* [esp passive 尤用于被动语态: Tn, Tn·pr] **~ sb/sth (with sth)** decorate sb/sth with festoons 给某人[某物]饰以花彩: *a room festooned with paper streamers* 饰有纸带花彩的房间.

fetal ⇨ FOETUS.

fetch /fetʃ; fɛtʃ/ *v* **1** [Tn, Tn·pr, Tn·p, Dn·n, Dn·pr] **~ sb/sth (for sb)** go for and bring back sb/sth 接来(某人)[取来(某物)]: *Fetch a doctor at once.* 快去请医生来. ○ *Please fetch the children from school.* 请到学校把孩子接回来. ○ *The chair is in the garden; please fetch it in.* 椅子在花园里, 请把它搬进来. ○ *Should I fetch you your coat/fetch your coat for you from the next room?* 要我去隔壁房间把你的大衣拿来吗? **2** [Tn, Tn·pr] (*dated* 旧) cause (sth) to come out 使(某物)出来; 使发出: *fetched a deep sigh* 发出深深的叹息 ○ *fetch tears to the eyes* 使泪水涌上眼眶. **3** [Tn, Dn·n] (of goods) be sold for (a price) (指货物)售得, 卖得(某价钱): *The picture should fetch £2 000 at auction.* 这张画拍卖可得2 000英镑. ○ *Those old books won't fetch (you) much.* 这些旧书卖不了多少钱. **4** [Dn·n] (*infml* 口) give (a blow) to (sb) 给(某人)(一击): *She fetched him a terrific slap in the face.* 她狠狠地给了他一记耳光. **5** (idm 习语) **fetch and ˈcarry (for sb)** act like a servant (for sb); be busy with small duties 供(某人)差遣; 忙于杂务: *He expects his daughter to fetch and carry for him all day.* 他希望女儿终日听他支使. **6** (phr v) **fetch up** (*infml* 口) arrive at a certain place or in a certain position; land up 到达; 处于: *Where on earth have we fetched up now?* 我们现在究竟到哪里了?

fetch·ing /ˈfetʃɪŋ; ˋfɛtʃɪŋ/ *adj* (*dated infml* 旧, 口) attractive 迷人的; 吸引人的: *a fetching smile* 迷人的微笑 ○ *You look very fetching in that hat.* 你戴着这顶帽子显得格外动人. ▷ **fetch·ingly** *adv*.

fête /feɪt; fet/ *n* outdoor entertainment or sale, usu to raise money for a special purpose (室外举行的)游乐会, 义卖会: *the school/village/church fête* 学校[村民/教会]举办的义卖会.

▷ **fête** *v* [Tn esp passive 尤用于被动语态] honour or entertain (sb) in a special way 特别款待或招待(某人): *The queen was fêted wherever she went.* 女王不论走到哪里都受到盛情款待.

fetid /ˈfetɪd, ˈfiːtɪd; ˋfɛtɪd, ˋfitɪd/ *adj* smelling foul or unpleasant; stinking 有恶臭的; 臭的: *fetid air* 臭气.

fet·ish /ˈfetɪʃ; ˋfɛtɪʃ/ *n* **1** object that is worshipped, esp because a spirit is believed to live in it 物神(尤指认为有神灵寓于其中而受膜拜的). **2** (**a**) thing to which more respect or attention is given than is normal or sensible 受到过分崇拜或注意的东西: *He makes a fetish of his new car.* 他把自己的新汽车奉若神明. (**b**) object or activity that is necessary for or adds to an individual's sexual pleasure; fixation 能引起或增强个人性快感的物体或活动; 不正常的依恋; 固恋: *Women's underclothes are a common fetish.* 女人的内衣裤是常见的能引起性快感的恋物. ▷ **fet·ish·ism** *n* [U]: *magazines which cater to fetishism in men* 迎合男子异常性兴奋需要的杂志. **fet·ish·ist** *n*.

fet·lock /ˈfetlɒk; ˋfɛt,lɑk/ *n* part of a horse's leg above and behind the hoof, where a tuft of hair grows 球节(马蹄上生距毛的突起部分). ⇨illus at HORSE 见 HORSE 插图.

fet·ter /ˈfetə(r); ˋfɛtɚ/ *n* (usu *pl* 通常作复数) **1** chain put round the feet of a person or animal to limit movement 脚镣; (动物的)足械: *The prisoner was kept in fetters.* 犯人戴着脚镣. **2** (*fig* 比喻) thing that restricts or hinders 桎梏; 束缚; 羁绊: *the fetters of poverty* 贫困的束缚.

▷ **fet·ter** *v* [Tn] **1** put (sb) in fetters 给(某人)戴上脚镣. **2** restrict or hinder (sb) in any way 束缚或阻碍(某人): *I hate being fettered by petty rules and regulations.* 我讨厌受清规戒律的束缚.

fettle /ˈfetl; ˋfɛtl̩/ *n* (idm 习语) **in fine, good, etc ˈfettle** fit and cheerful 健壮而愉快: *The team are all in excellent fettle.* 队员们个个精神抖擞、神采奕奕.

fetus = FOETUS.

feud /fjuːd; fjud/ *n* long and bitter quarrel between two people, families or groups (两人、家族或团体间的)长期不和, 世仇: *a long-standing feud* 夙怨 ○ *Because of a family feud, he never spoke to his wife's parents for years.* 由于两家不和, 他已多年不与岳父母说话.

▷ **feud** *v* [I, Ipr] **~ (with sb/sth)** carry on a feud 长期争斗; 结世仇: *feuding neighbours* 长期不睦的邻居 ○ *The two tribes are always feuding (with each other).* 这两个部落一直争斗不休.

feudal /ˈfjuːdl; ˋfjudl̩/ *adj* of or according to the system as during the Middle Ages in Europe, under which people receive land and protection from the landowner and work and fight for him in return 封建的; 封建制度的: *feudal law* 封建制度的法律 ○ *the feudal barons* 封建贵族 ○ *The way some landowners treat their tenants today seems almost feudal.* 今天有些地主仍以近乎封建的方式对待佃农.

▷ **feud·al·ism** /-dəlɪzəm; -dl̩,ɪzəm/ *n* [U] (attitudes and structure of) the feudal system 封建制度; 封建主义. **feud·al·istic** /ˌfjuːdəˈlɪstɪk; ˌfjudl̩ˋɪstɪk/ *adj*.

fever /ˈfiːvə(r); ˋfivɚ/ *n* **1** [C, U] abnormally high body temperature, esp as a sign of illness 发烧; 发热: *He has a high fever.* 他发高烧. ○ *Aspirin can reduce fever.* 阿司匹林可以退烧. **2** [U] specified disease in which (a) fever occurs 热病: *yellow, typhoid, rheumatic, etc fever* 黄热病、伤寒、风湿热. **3** [sing] (state of) nervous excitement or agitation 兴奋; 激动: *He waited for her arrival in a fever of impatience.* 他激动不安地等待她到来. **4** (idm 习语) **at/to ˈfever pitch** at/to a high level of excitement 高度兴奋; 极为激动: *The speaker brought the crowd to fever pitch.* 演讲者激起群众高昂的情绪.

▷ **fe·vered** *adj* [attrib 作定语] **1** affected by or suffering from a fever 发烧的; 发热的: *She cooled her child's fevered brow.* 她给孩子滚烫的额头降温. **2** highly excited 激动的; 高度兴奋的: *a fevered imagination* 奔放的想像力.

fe·ver·ish /ˈfiːvərɪʃ; ˋfivərɪʃ/ *adj* **1** having a fever; caused or accompanied by a fever 发烧的; 发烧引起的; 伴有发烧的: *The child's body felt feverish.* 这孩子身上发烧. ○ *During her illness she had feverish dreams.* 她生病期间因发烧而做梦. **2** excited; restless 激动的; 焦躁不安的: *with feverish haste* 急匆匆地. **fe·ver·ishly** *adv* very quickly or excitedly 心急如焚地: *searching feverishly for her missing jewels* 心急火燎地寻找她丢失的珠宝.

few[1] /fjuː; fju/ *indef det, adj* [usu attrib 通常作定语] (**-er, -est**) **1** (used with *pl* [C] *ns* and a *pl v* 与复数可数名词和动词复数形式连用) not many 不多; 很少: *Few people live to be 100.* 很少有人活到一百岁. ○ *a man/woman of few words*, ie one who speaks very little 沉默寡言的人 ○ *There are fewer cars parked outside than yesterday.* 外面停的汽车比昨天少. ○ *The police found very few clues to the murderer's identity.* 警方对杀人凶手的线索所知甚少. ○ *There are very few opportunities for promotion.* 晋升的机会很少. ○ *The few houses we have seen are in terrible condition.* 我们见到的为数不多的几所房子都非常糟糕. ○ *There were too few people at the meeting.* 参加会议的人寥寥无几. ○ *Accidents on site are few.* 工地上事故不多. (Cf 参看 *There are few accidents on site*.) ⇨Usage at LESS 用法见 LESS. ⇨Usage at MUCH[1] 用法见 MUCH[1]. **2** (idm 习语) ˌ**few and** ˌ**far beˈtween** infrequent, with long periods of waiting involved 少的(要等候很久的): *The buses to our village are few and far between.* 到我们村的公共汽车很少. ○ *The sunny intervals we were promised have been few and far between.* 我们原可望能有几阵晴天, 结果却很稀少.

▷ **few** *indef pron* not many people, things, places, etc 很少的人、物、地方等. (**a**) (referring back 用以复指前文): *Of the 150 passengers, few escaped injury.* 150 名乘客中鲜有未受伤者. ○ *Few can deny the impact of his leadership.* 几乎没有人能否定他的领导作用. ○ (*saying* 谚) *Many are called but few are chosen.* 邀请的人多, 选上的人少. ○ *Hundreds of new records are produced each week but few (of them) get into the charts.* 每周推出数以百计的新唱片, 但(其中)没有几张能进人每周流行榜. (**b**) (referring forward 用以预指后文): *Few of us will still be alive in the year 2050.* 我们很少有人能活到 2050 年. ○ *The few who came to the concert enjoyed it.* 来听音乐会的少数几个人喜欢这场音乐会. ○ *We saw few of the sights as we were only there for two hours.* 我们在那里只待了两个小时, 因此没怎么游览.

the few *n* [pl *v*] the minority 少数: *a voice for the few* 代表少数人的意见.

few[2] /fjuː; fju/ **a few** *indef det* (used with *pl* [C] *ns* and *pl vs* 与复数可数名词和动词复数形式连用) a small number of; some 少数; 几个: *a few letters* 几封信 ○ *a few days ago* 几天前 ○ *He asked us a few questions.* 他问了我们几个问题. ○ *A few people are coming for tea.* 有几个人要来吃茶点. ○ *Only a few* (ie Not many) *students were awarded distinctions.* 只有几个学生获得优等成绩. ⇨Usage at MUCH[1] 用法见 MUCH[1].

▷ **a few** *indef pron* **1** a small number of people, things, places, etc; some 少数的人、物、地方等; 一些. (**a**) (referring back 用以复指前文): *I didn't get any cards yesterday but today there were a few.* 昨天我没收到贺卡, 但今天有几张. ○ *She's written hundreds of books but I've only read a few (of them).* 她写了几百部书, 但我只读了(其中的)几本. (**b**) (referring forward 用以预指后文): *A few of the seats were empty.* 有几个座位是空的. ○ *I recognized a few of the other guests.* 在其余的客人中, 我认识几位. **2** (idm 习语) **a good few; not a few** a considerable number; significantly many 相当多; 不少: *There were a good few copies sold on the first day.* 第一天就卖了许多本. ○ *Not a few of my friends are vegetarian.* 我朋友中不少人吃素. **ˈhave a few** (usu in the present perfect 通常用于现在完成时态) drink a sufficient amount of alcohol to make one drunk or almost drunk 已醉; 微醉: *I've had a few* (ie a few glasses of beer, whisky, etc) *already, actually.* 我喝了几杯, 其实已经醉了. ○ *She looks as if she's had a few.* 她像是有些醉了. **a few** *adv* a small but significant number 少量的一定数目: *a few more/less/too many* 再多几个[再少几个/多余了几个].

fey /feɪ; fe/ *adj* **1** (*Scot* 苏格兰) having a feeling of approaching death; able to foretell disaster 感到死期近的; 能预知灾难的. **2** having a strange whimsical charm 有稀奇古怪的魔力的. **3** (*derog* 贬) (of a person and his behaviour) not serious; frivolous (指人及其行为)不认真的, 轻浮的. ▷ **fey·ness** *n* [U].

fez /fez; fɛz/ *n* (*pl* **fezzes**) red felt hat with a flat top and a tassle but no brim, worn by men in certain Muslim countries (某些穆斯林国家男子戴的平顶无边的)红毡帽. ⇨illus at HAT 见 HAT 插图.

ff *abbr* 缩写 = **1** and the following (pages, lines, etc) 及其后的(页、行等): *early childhood, p 10 ff*, eg in the index of a book 童年时期, 自第10页起(如见于书目中). **2** (*music* 音) very loudly (Italian *fortissimo*) 极强的; 非常响的(源自意大利文 *fortissimo*). Cf 参看 PP 3.

fi·ancé (*fem* 阴性作 **fi·ancée**) /fɪˈɒnseɪ; *US* ˌfiːɑːnˈseɪ; ˌfiɑnˋse/ *n* man or woman to whom one is engaged to be married 未婚夫; 未婚妻: *his fiancée* 他的未婚妻 ○ *her fiancé* 她的未婚夫.

fi·asco /fɪˈæskəʊ; fɪˋæsko/ *n* (*pl* **~s**; *US* also **~es**) complete and ridiculous failure 彻底的失败; 惨败; 大出丑: *The party was a total fiasco because the wrong date was given on the invitations.* 那个聚会落得一场空, 因为请帖上的日期弄错了.

fiat /ˈfaɪæt; *US also* ˈfiːət; ˋfaɪæt, ˋfaɪət/ *n* [C, U] (*fml* 文) formal authorization, order or decree 谕; 命令; 法令: *The opening of a market stall is governed by municipal fiat.* 开设市场摊位受市政法令管制.

fib /fɪb; fɪb/ *n* (*infml* 口) untrue statement, esp about sth unimportant 谎言; (尤指无伤大雅的)小谎: *Stop telling such silly fibs.* 别说这种傻乎乎的谎话了. Cf 参看 LIE[1] *n*.
▷ **fib** *v* (**-bb-**) [I] say untrue things; tell a fib or fibs 说假话; 撒小谎: *Stop fibbing!* 别扯谎了! **fib·ber** *n* person who tells fibs 撒小谎的人: *You little fibber!* 你这个小骗子!

F

fibre (*US* **fiber**) /ˈfaɪbə(r); ˋfaɪbɚ/ *n* **1** [C] any of the slender threads of which many animal and plant tissues are formed (动植物的)纤维: *a cotton, wood, nerve, muscle fibre* 棉、木、神经、肌肉的纤维. **2** [U] material or substance formed from a mass of fibres 纤维质: *cotton fibre for spinning* 用以纺纱的棉纤维 ○ *The muscle fibre of this animal is diseased.* 这个动物的肌肉纤维产生了病变. ○ *Eating cereals and fruit will give you plenty of fibre in your diet.* 吃谷类食物和水果能多摄取纤维素. **3** [U] (**a**) texture or structure 质地; 结构: *material of coarse fibre* 粗糙的材料. (**b**) (*fig* 比喻) person's character 品格; 性情: *a woman of strong moral fibre* 道德观念强的女子.
▷ **fib·rous** /ˈfaɪbrəs; ˋfaɪbrəs/ *adj* like or made of fibres 似纤维的; 纤维制的.
□ ˈ**fibreboard** (*US* ˈ**fiber-**), ˈ**fibreglass** (*US* ˈ**fiber-**) *ns* [U] (also **glass fibre**) material made from glass fibres and resin, used for insulation and in making cars, boats, etc 玻璃纤维: [attrib 作定语] *a fibreglass racing yacht* 玻璃纤维赛艇.
fibre ˈ**optics** (*US* **fiber**) transmission of information by means of infra-red light signals along a thin glass fibre 光导纤维通讯.

fib·rosis /faɪˈbrəʊsɪs; faɪˋbrosɪs/ *n* [U] abnormal increase or development of fibrous tissue or muscle 纤维变性; 纤维化.

fib·ro·sitis /ˌfaɪbrəˈsaɪtɪs; ˌfaɪbrəˋsaɪtɪs/ *n* [U] inflammation of the fibrous tissue of the body, esp the muscles of the back, causing severe pain and stiffness 纤维织炎; 肌风湿病. Cf 参看 ARTHRITIS, RHEUMATISM.

fib·ula /ˈfɪbjʊlə; ˋfɪbjələ/ *n* (*pl* **fibulae** /-liː; -ˌli/) (*anatomy* 解) outer of the two bones between the knee and the foot 腓骨. ⇨illus at SKELETON 见 SKELETON 插图.

fickle /ˈfɪkl; ˋfɪkḷ/ *adj* often changing; not constant 易变的; 无常的: *fickle weather, fortune* 变化无常的天气、变幻莫测的命运 ○ *a fickle person, lover, etc*, ie not faithful or loyal 出尔反尔的人、用情不专的情人. ▷ **fickle·ness** *n* [U]: *the fickleness of the English climate* 英国气候之多变.

fic·tion /ˈfɪkʃn; ˋfɪkʃən/ *n* **1** [U] type of literature (eg novels, stories) describing imaginary events and people 小说: *works of fiction* 小说作品 ○ *He writes fiction.* 他是写小说的. ○ *Truth is often stranger than fiction.* 事实往往比小说更离奇. Cf 参看 NON-FICTION. **2** [C] thing that is invented or imagined and not strictly true 虚构的或想像出的事; 并非完全真实的事: *a polite fiction*, ie sth assumed to be true (though it may not be) for social reasons 冠冕堂皇的应酬话. Cf 参看 FACT.
▷ **fic·tional** /-ʃənl; -ʃənḷ/ *adj* of fiction; told as a story 小说的; 虚构的: *fictional characters* 虚构的人物 ○ *a fictional account of life on a farm* 描述农场生活的虚构情节.

fic·tion·al·ize, -ise /ˈfɪkʃənəlaɪz; ˋfɪkʃənəˌlaɪz/ *v* [Tn] write about (a true event) as if it were fiction or in the style of a fictional story, inventing some of the details, characters, etc 将(真实事情)编写成小说: *fictionalized history* 演义.

fic·ti·tious /fɪkˈtɪʃəs; fɪkˋtɪʃəs/ *adj* imagined or invented; not real 想像的; 虚构的; 假的: *The account he gives of his childhood is quite fictitious.* 他把童年往事说得很假. ○ *All the places and characters in my novel are entirely fictitious.* 我这篇小说中所有的地点和人物都是虚构的.

Fid Def /ˌfɪd ˈdef; ˌfɪd ˋdɛf/ *abbr* 缩写 = FD.

fiddle /ˈfɪdl; ˋfɪdḷ/ *n* **1** (*infml* 口) violin 小提琴. **2** (*sl* 俚) thing done dishonestly; swindle; fraud 骗局; 欺诈; 欺骗行为: *It's all a fiddle!* 完全是骗局! **3** (idm 习语) **be on the** ˈ**fiddle** (*sl* 俚) behave illegally, or dishonestly 干违法的或不正当的事. **fit as a fiddle** ⇨ FIT[1]. **play second** ˈ**fiddle (to sb/sth)** be treated as less important than another person, activity, etc 居次位; 当副手: *I have no intention of playing second fiddle to the new director, so I've resigned.* 我不想当新董事的副手, 所以辞职了. ○ *His family has had to play second fiddle to his political career.* 他因从政而把家庭置于次要地位.
▷ **fiddle** *v* **1** [I, Tn] (*infml* 口) play (a tune on) the violin 用小提琴演奏(曲调): *He learned to fiddle as a young boy.* 他自幼学小提琴. **2** [I, Ip] **~ (about/around)** play aimlessly; fidget or delay 胡混; 坐立不安; 拖拉; 耽误: *Stop fiddling (about) and do some work.* 别再瞎混了, 做点事吧. **3** [Ipr] **~ (about/around) with sth** play carelessly with sth in one's hands 胡乱摆弄: *She fiddled with her watch so much that it broke.* 她总胡乱摆弄手表, 结果把它弄坏了. **4** [Tn] (*infml* 口) falsify (accounts, etc); get (sth) by cheating 篡改(帐目等); 骗取(某物): *fiddle one's expenses* 虚报开支 ○ *He fiddled a free ticket for the match.* 他骗得一张那场比赛的免费入场券. **fid·dler** /ˈfɪdlə(r); ˋfɪdlɚ/ *n* **1** person who plays the violin 小提琴手. **2** (*infml* 口) person who cheats; swindler 骗子; 诈骗者. **fid·dling** /ˈfɪdlɪŋ; ˋfɪdlɪŋ/ *adj* [usu attrib 通常作定语] (*infml* 口) trivial; unimportant; petty 微不足道的; 无足轻重的; 小的: *fiddling little details* 琐碎的细节. **fid·dly** /ˈfɪdlɪ; ˋfɪdlɪ/ *adj* (*infml* 口) awkward to do or use 难弄的; 费事的; 不便使用的: *Changing a fuse is one of those fiddly jobs I hate.* 我最不愿意干换保险丝这类活儿了. ○ *This tin-opener is awfully fiddly.* 这把罐头刀很不好使.
□ ˈ**fiddlesticks** /ˈfɪdlstɪks; ˋfɪdḷˌstɪks/ *interj* (*dated* 旧) nonsense 胡扯; 废话.

fi·del·ity /fɪˈdelətɪ; *US* faɪ-; faɪˋdɛlətɪ/ *n* [U] **1 ~ (to sb/sth)** (**a**) loyalty; faithfulness 忠实; 忠贞; 忠诚: *fidelity to one's principles, religion, leader* 对自己的原则、宗教信仰、领袖的忠诚. (**b**) accuracy; truthfulness 精确; 真实; 确切: *fidelity to the text of the play* 忠实于剧本的原文 ○ *translate sth with the greatest fidelity* 极准确地翻译某材料. **2** quality or precision with which sound is reproduced (音响的)保真度: [attrib 作定语] *a high fidelity recording* 高保真的录音.

fid·get /ˈfɪdʒɪt; ˋfɪdʒɪt/ *v* [I, Ipr, Ip] **~ (about) (with sth)** make small restless movements, thus annoying other people 烦躁不安(惹人生厌): *Stop fidgeting!* 别坐立不安的! ○ *Hurry up, your father is beginning to fidget*, ie show signs of impatience. 快点, 你父亲有些不耐烦了. ○ *It's bad manners to fidget about (with the cutlery) at the table.* 用餐时摆弄刀叉玩儿是不雅的.
▷ **fid·get** *n* **1** [C] person who fidgets 烦躁不安的人: *You're such a fidget!* 你真是个坐不住的人! **2 the fidgets** [pl] restless movements 烦躁; 坐立不安: *I always get the fidgets during long meetings.* 会议开得长我就坐不住了.
fid·gety *adj* restless or inclined to fidget 烦躁的; 坐立不安的: *a fidgety child* 烦躁不安的孩子 ○ *Travelling in planes makes me fidgety.* 我一坐飞机就心神不安.

field[1] /fiːld; fild/ *n* **1** area of land (usu enclosed by a fence, hedge, etc) used for pasturing animals or cultivating crops 田; 地; 牧场: *working in the fields* 在田间干活 ○ *a fine field of wheat* 一片好麦田. **2** (usu in compounds 通常用以构成复合词) (**a**) wide area or expanse 辽阔的地方; 原野; 旷野: *an 'ice-field*, eg around the North Pole. (**b**) open space used for a specified purpose (作某用途的)场地, 场所: *a 'baseball, 'cricket, etc field*. **3** (usu in compounds 通常用以构成复合词) area from which minerals, etc are obtained 矿区; 产地: *'coalfields* ○ *'gold-fields* ○ *a new 'oilfield*. **4** range of a subject, an activity or an interest (某种学科、活动或兴趣的)领域, 范围, 界: *in the field of politics, art, science, music, etc* 在政治、艺术、科学、音乐等领域 ○ *That is outside my field*, ie not among the subjects I have studied. 那不在我所研究的范围之内. **5** (**a**) area or space within which a specified force can be felt 场(存在某种力的效应的范围或空间): *a magnetic 'field* 磁场 ○ *the earth's gravitational 'field*, ie the space in which the earth's gravity has an effect 地球引力场. (**b**) range over which sth can operate effectively 某物的有效作用范围: *the field of a telescope* 望远镜的视野 ○ *one's field of vision*, ie the area that one can see 视野 ○ *a gun with a good field of fire* 远射程的炮. **6** area or place where a battle is or was fought 战场: *the field of battle/'battlefield* 战场. **7** (*sport* 体) (**a**) all those taking part or competing in an event (比赛项目的)全体参赛者: *The field includes three world record holders.* 参赛者中包括三名世界记录保持者. (**b**) (in cricket and baseball) team that is not batting, with regard to their positions on the field (板球和棒球)守队: *bowling to a defensive field* 向守队投球. **8** (*computing* 计) one section of a record, representing a unit of information 字段; 信息组: *The firm's payroll has one field for gross pay and one for net pay.* 公司工资单上一部分是原工资, 一部分是实发工资. **9** (idm 习语) **hold the field (against sb/sth)** not be replaced (by sb/sth); remain dominant 不为(某人[某事物])所替代; 保持优势: *Einstein's ideas on physics have held the field for years.* 爱因斯坦的物理学理论多年来一直保持其权威性. **play the 'field** (*infml* 口 *esp US*) avoid committing oneself to one person, activity, etc 不对某一人做出承诺; 不承诺参加某一活动等. **take the 'field** (**a**) begin a war or battle 开始作战; 上阵. (**b**) (*sport* 体) go onto the playing area 开始比赛; 上场.

□ **'field-day** *n* **1** day on which military operations are practised 军事演习日. **2** day or period of great excitement and activity 振奋人心的重要日子或时期: *Whenever there's a government scandal the newspapers have a field-day.* 政府一有丑闻, 报界便紧张忙碌一阵. **3** (*esp US*) (**a**) sports day at a school, college, etc (学校等的)体育比赛日, 运动会. (**b**) day of outdoor scientific study 野外科研活动日.

'field-events *n* [pl] athletic sports other than races, eg jumping and discus-throwing 田赛(如跳高、跳远、掷铁饼). Cf 参看 TRACK EVENTS (TRACK).

'field-glasses *n* = glasses (GLASS 6).

'field hockey (*US*) = HOCKEY.

,Field 'Marshal officer of the highest rank in the British Army (英军的)陆军元帅. ⇨ App 9 见附录 9.

'field officer major or colonel in the army 陆军校级军官.

'field sports outdoor sports, eg hunting, fishing and shooting 野外运动(如打猎、钓鱼、射击).

'field-test *v* [Tn] test (sth) by using it in the conditions for which it is meant 对(某物)进行实地试验: *The equipment has all been field-tested.* 这些设备都已经过实地试验. — *n*: *undergo rigorous field-tests* 进行严格的现场试验.

'field-work *n* **1** [U] practical academic or social work done outside the laboratory or classroom 实地考察工作; 现场调查工作. **2** [C] temporary fortification made by troops 临时筑成的防御工事. **'field-worker** *n* person who helps in practical field-work 实地考察者; 现场调查者.

field[2] /fi:ld; fild/ *v* (**a**) [I, Tn] (in cricket and baseball) (stand ready to) catch and throw back (the ball) (板球和棒球)(准备)接或掷还(球), 守(球): *He fields well.* 他接球技术很好. ○ *She fielded the ball.* 她把球接住了. (**b**) [I] (in cricket and baseball) be (in) the team not batting (板球和棒球)任守方: *We're fielding first.* 我们先作守方. (**c**) [Tn] select (sb) to play in a game (of football, hockey, cricket, etc) (足球、曲棍球、板球等赛中)选派(某人)上场: *They're fielding a very strong side this season.* 他们本季派了一支很强的球队上场. (**d**) [Tn] (*fig* 比喻) deal successfully with (a series of questions, etc) 顺利处理(一系列问题): *The minister easily fielded all the journalist's awkward questions.* 部长轻而易举地一一回答了记者提出的棘手问题. ▷ **'fielder** *n* = FIELDSMAN. ⇨ illus at CRICKET 见 CRICKET 插图.

□ **'fieldsman** /-zmən; -zmən/ *n* (*pl* **-men** /-mən; -mən/) (in cricket, etc) member of the team not batting (板球、棒球等的)外场员, 外野手.

fiend /fi:nd; find/ *n* **1** evil spirit; devil 恶魔; 魔鬼: *the fiends of hell* 地狱的魔鬼. **2** (**a**) very cruel or spiteful person 恶魔般的人; 穷凶极恶的人. (**b**) person who causes mischief or annoyance 淘气的人; 讨厌的人: *Stop teasing her, you little fiend!* 别捉弄她了, 你这个小淘气鬼! **3** (*infml* 口) person who is fond of or strongly drawn to sth specified 耽于某事物者; 迷; 狂: *a fresh-'air fiend* 注重呼吸新鲜空气的人.

▷ **fiend·ish** *adj* **1** fierce or cruel 凶猛的; 残酷的: *a fiendish temper* 残暴的脾气. **2** (*infml* 口) clever and complicated 巧妙而复杂的: *a fiendish plot, plan, idea, etc* 巧妙而又复杂的构思、计划、主意等. **3** (*infml* 口) extremely bad, unpleasant or difficult 极坏的; 使人很不愉快的; 极其困难的: *fiendish weather* 恶劣的天气 ○ *a fiendish problem* 难题. **fiend·ishly** *adv* (*infml* 口) very; extremely 很; 极: *a fiendishly difficult puzzle* 极难解开的谜 ○ *It's fiendishly cold outside.* 外面冷极了.

fierce /fɪəs; fɪrs/ *adj* (**-r**, **-st**) **1** violent and angry 凶猛的; 凶狠的; 愤怒的: *fierce dogs, winds, attacks* 恶狗、强风、猛攻 ○ *look fierce/have a fierce look* 样子凶恶. **2** (**a**) intense 强烈的; 极度的: *fierce concentration, loyalty, hatred* 极端集中、忠诚、痛恨. (**b**) unpleasantly or uncontrollably strong 酷烈的; 激烈的: *fierce heat* 酷热 ○ *His plan met with fierce opposition.* 他的计划遭到激烈反对. ▷ **fiercely** *adv*. **fierce·ness** *n* [U].

fiery /'faɪərɪ; 'faɪrɪ/ *adj* [usu attrib 通常作定语] **1** (**a**) like or consisting of fire; flaming 似火的; 含火的; 燃烧着的: *fiery red hair* 赤色的毛发 ○ *a fiery sky* 火红的天空 ○ *fiery eyes*, ie angry and glaring 冒着怒火的目光. (**b**) very spicy; producing a burning sensation 味道强烈的; 辛辣的: *a fiery Mexican dish* 味道强烈的墨西哥菜 ○ *fiery liquor* 火辣辣的烈酒. **2** (**a**) (of a person, his character, etc) quickly or easily made angry (指人、性格等)暴躁的, 易怒的: *a fiery temper* 暴躁的脾气. (**b**) (of words, etc) intense; passionate (指言语等)激烈的, 充满激情的: *a fiery speech* 激昂的演说. (**c**) full of high spirits 情绪高涨的: *a fiery horse* 精神饱满的马. ▷ **fier·ily** /-rəlɪ; -rɪlɪ/ *adv*. **fier·iness** *n* [U].

fi·esta /fɪ'estə; fɪ'ɛstə/ *n* (**a**) religious festival in Spanish-speaking countries (西班牙语国家的)宗教节日. (**b**) any holiday or festival 节日; 假日.

FIFA /'fi:fə; 'fifə/ *abbr* 缩写 = International Association Football Federation (French *Fédération Internationale de Football Association*) 国际足球联合会(源自法文 *Fédération Internationale de Football Association*).

fife /faɪf; faɪf/ *n* small high-pitched musical instrument like a flute, used with drums in military music (军乐中与鼓合奏的)横笛: [attrib 作定语] *a fife and drum band* 笛鼓合奏的乐队.

fif·teen /ˌfɪf'ti:n; 'fɪf'tin/ *pron, det* 15; one more than fourteen 15, 十五(个). ⇨ App 4 见附录 4.

▷ **fif·teen** *n* **1** the number 15 ☆ 15; 十五. **2** team of Rugby Union players 橄榄球队.

fif·teenth /ˌfɪf'ti:nθ; 'fɪf'tinθ/ *pron, det* 15th; next after fourteenth 第15, 第十五(个). — *n* one of fifteen equal parts of sth 十五分之一.

For the uses of *fifteen* and *fifteenth* see the examples at *five* and *fifth*. 关于 fifteen 和 fifteenth 的用法见 five 和 fifth 词条中的示例.

fifth /fɪfθ; fɪfθ/ *pron, det* 5th; next after fourth 第5, 第五(个): *the fifth in line* 第五行 ○ *Today is the fifth (of March).* 今天是(三月)五号. ○ *the fifth book on the list* 书单上的第五本书 ○ *This is the fifth day of the conference.* 今天是会议的第五天. ○ *Edward V*, ie Edward the Fifth 爱德华五世. ⇨ App 4 见附录 4.

▷ **fifth** *n* one of five equal parts of sth 五分之一: *He gave her a fifth of the total amount.* 他给了她总量的五分

F

之一. ○ *They divided the money into fifths and took one fifth each.* 他们把钱分成五份, 每人拿了五分之一.

fifthly *adv* in the fifth position or place 在第五个位置或地点.

□ **a ˌfifth ˈcolumn** organized group of people working for the enemy within a country at war 第五纵队(战时在国内为敌人工作的组织).

fifty /ˈfɪftɪ; ˋfɪftɪ/ *pron, det* 50; one more than forty-nine 50, 五十(个). ⇨App 4 见附录4.

▷ **fif·tieth** /ˈfɪftɪəθ; ˋfɪftɪɪθ/ *pron, det* 50th; next after forty-ninth 第50, 第五十(个). — *n* one of fifty equal parts of sth 五十分之一.

fifty *n* **1** the number 50 ☆ 50; 五十. **2 the fifties** [pl] numbers, years or temperature from 50 to 59 从50到59的数目、年数或温度: *The total amount is in the fifties.* 总共五十多个. ○ *She was born in the fifties,* ie in the 1950's. 她生于五十年代. ○ *How warm is it today? It's in the (high/low) fifties.* 今天气温有多少度? 五十几度(不到六十度[五十度出头]). **3** (idm 习语) **in one's fifties** between the ages of 50 and 60 在50岁到60岁之间: *She's in her early/mid/late fifties.* 她五十刚出头[五十五岁左右/快六十岁了].

□ ˌ**fifty-ˈfifty** *adj, adv* (*infml* 口) shared or sharing equally between two 对半(的); 二一添作五: *divide the profits on a fifty-fifty basis,* ie take equal shares 平分利润 ○ *a fifty-fifty chance of winning,* ie an equal chance of winning or losing 胜负的可能性参半 ○ *We went fifty-fifty on dinner,* ie shared the cost equally. 我们平摊用餐费.

ˌ**fifty ˈpence** (also ˌ**fifty ˈp, 50p**) (*Brit*) (coin worth) fifty new pence 五十新便士(的硬币).

For the uses of *fifty* and *fiftieth* see the examples at *five* and *fifth*. 关于fifty和fiftieth的用法见five和fifth词条中的示例.

F

fig /fɪg; fɪg/ *n* **1** soft sweet fruit, full of small seeds and often eaten dried 无花果. **2** (also ˈ**fig-tree**) tree with broad leaves on which this grows 无花果树. **3** (idm 习语) **not care/give a ˈfig (for sb/sth)** not care at all; consider (sb/sth) valueless or unimportant 毫不理会; 认为(某人[某事物])毫无价值或微不足道: *I don't care a fig what others think of me.* 我毫不在乎别人对我有什么想法.

□ ˈ**fig-leaf** *n* leaf of a fig-tree, traditionally used for covering the genital organs of nude bodies in drawings, statues, etc 无花果树叶(传统上用作裸体画像、雕像等的阴部覆盖物).

fig *abbr* 缩写 = **1** figurative(ly). **2** figure; illustration: *see diagram at fig 3* 见图3的图解.

fight[1] /faɪt; faɪt/ *v* (*pt, pp* **fought** /fɔːt; fɔt/) **1 (a)** [I, Ipr] **~ (against/with sb/sth)** struggle against sb/sth using physical force, in a war, battle, etc 搏斗; 打架; 打仗; 作战: *soldiers training to fight* 为作战而受训的士兵 ○ *Do stop fighting, boys!* 别打了, 小伙子们! ○ *The two dogs were fighting over a bone.* 两只狗为一块骨头撕咬. ○ *Britain fought with* (ie as an ally of) *France against Germany in the last war.* 在第二次世界大战中, 英国与法国联合作战抗击德国. ○ *Have you been fighting with* (ie against) *your brother again?* 你又跟弟弟打架了吧? **(b)** [Tn] struggle thus against (sb) 与(某人)搏斗, 打架, 打仗, 作战: *We must fight the enemy.* 我们必须与敌人作战. ○ *The boxer has fought many opponents.* 该拳手已与许多对手交锋. **2** [Tn] engage in, take part in or carry on (a battle, etc) 打(仗); 进行(战斗等): *fight a war, duel, etc* 打仗、进行决斗 ○ *The government has to fight several by-elections in the coming months.* 政府要在数月内进行几次补选. **3** [Ipr, Tn] **~ (against) sth** strive to overcome, destroy or prevent sth 争取克服、战胜、摧毁或防止(某事物): *fight (against) poverty, oppression, ignorance* 与贫困、压迫、愚昧现象作斗争 ○ *fight an eviction notice* 努力与驱逐房客通知一事周旋 ○ *fight a fire* 救火. **4** [Ipr, Tn·pr] make (one's way) or achieve (sth) by fighting or effort (经奋斗或努力)开(路)或获得(某事物): *We had to fight (our way) through the crowded streets.* 我们得从街道上熙熙攘攘的人群中挤过去. ○ *They fought the bill through Parliament.* 他们极力争取使该法案在国会获得通过. **5** [I, Ipr] **~ (about/over sth)** quarrel or argue 争吵; 争论: *It's a trivial matter and not worth fighting about.* 区区小事不值得争吵. **6** (idm 习语) **fight like a ˈtiger** attack sb or defend oneself fiercely 极力攻击某人或保护自己: *She fought like a tiger to get what she wanted.* 她竭力争取自己想要的东西. **fight a losing ˈbattle (against sth)** struggle without (hope of) success to achieve or prevent sth 为获得或防止某事物而进行毫无成功希望的斗争: *Anyone who tries to resist the spread of new technology is fighting a losing battle.* 想阻止新技术传播的人注定要失败. **fight shy of sth/sb** be unwilling to undertake (a task) or confront sb; avoid sth/sb 不愿承担(某任务)或面对(某人); 避开某事物[某人]: *He was unhappy in his job for years but always fought shy of telling his boss.* 他多年来工作都很不愉快, 却始终未向老板启齿. **fight to the ˈfinish** fight until one side wins conclusively 战至分出胜负; 一决雌雄. **a ˌfighting ˈchance** small but distinct chance of success if a great effort is made 需经极大努力或许有成功的可能. **fighting ˈtalk/ˈwords** defiant statement or challenge showing that one is ready to fight for sth 挑衅的话; 挑战的言语. **live like fighting cocks** ⇨ LIVE[2]. **7** (phr v) **fight back** fight with renewed force and strength; show resistance or retaliation 反击; 回击; 抵抗: *After a disastrous first half the team fought back to level the match.* 该队在上半场惨败后重整旗鼓以求扳成平局. ○ *Don't let them bully you. Fight back!* 别让他们欺侮你. 把他们顶回去! **fight sth back/down** suppress (feelings, etc) 克制, 抑制(感情等): *fighting back tears* 强忍住眼泪 ○ *fighting down a sense of disgust* 抑制厌恶感. **fight for sth** strive to obtain or accomplish sth 争取获得或完成某事物: *fight for freedom, independence, human rights, etc* 争取自由、独立、人权等. **fight sb/sth off** resist or repel sb/sth by fighting 抵抗或击退某人[某事物]: *fighting off repeated enemy attacks* 击退敌人一次又一次的进攻 ○ *fight off a cold, a feeling of tiredness* 治愈感冒、驱除疲劳感. **fight sth out** settle (an argument, a dispute, etc) by fighting 通过斗争使(争论等)得到解决: *I can't help them to resolve their quarrel — they must fight it out between them.* 我无法帮助他们解决争论——他们得打出个结果来.

▷ **fighter** *n* **1** person who fights in war or in sport 战士; 战斗者; 游戏或比赛的参加者. **2** (*usu approv* 通常作褒义) person who does not yield without a struggle 斗士; 奋斗者: *She won't give up easily: she's a real fighter.* 她不会轻易放弃的, 她十分顽强. **3** fast military aircraft designed to attack other aircraft 战斗机; 歼击机: *a jet-ˈfighter* 喷气式战斗机 ○ [attrib 作定语] *fighter planes* 战斗机 ○ *a fighter pilot* 战斗机驾驶员.

fight·ing *n* [U]: *outbreaks of street fighting* 巷战的爆发.

fight[2] /faɪt; faɪt/ *n* **1** [C] act of fighting or struggling 战斗; 搏斗; 打架; 斗争: *a fight between two dogs* 两犬相争 ○ *the fight against poverty, crime, disease* 与贫困、犯罪行为、疾病所作的斗争 ○ *a prize fight,* eg in boxing 职业拳击赛 ⇨Usage at ARGUMENT 用法见ARGUMENT. **2** [U] desire or ability to fight or resist; determination 斗志; 战斗力; 决心: *In spite of many defeats, they still had plenty of fight left in them.* 他们尽管多次失败, 但仍有很强的战斗力. ○ *Losing their leader took all the fight out of them.* 他们失去了首领以后便丧失了斗志. **3** (idm 习语) **a fight to the ˈfinish** struggle, etc that continues until one side wins conclusively 决定胜负的战斗等. **pick a fight/quarrel** ⇨ PICK[3]. **put up a good, poor, etc ˈfight** fight with/without courage and determination 有[无]勇气和决心的战斗.

fig·ment /ˈfɪgmənt; ˋfɪgmənt/ *n* thing that is not real but only imagined (used esp in the expression shown) 想像中的事物, 虚构的事物(尤用于以下示例): *a figment of sb's imagination* 凭空想像出来的事物.

fig·ur·at·ive /ˈfɪgərətɪv; ˋfɪgjərətɪv/ *adj* (*abbr* 缩写 **fig**) (of words) used in an imaginative or a metaphorical way rather than literally (指言语)比喻的: *'He exploded with rage' shows a figurative use of the verb 'to explode'.* '他肺都气炸了,'一句中的'炸'字是比喻用法. ▷ **fig·ur·at·ively** *adv.*

fig·ure[1] /ˈfɪgə(r); *US* ˈfɪgjər; ˋfɪgjɚ/ *n* **1** [C] **(a)** written symbol for a number, esp 0 to 9 数字(尤指0至9): *Write the figure '7' for me.* 给我写个'7'字. ○ *He has an income of six figures/a six-figure income,* ie £100 000 or more. 他有六位数字的收入(至少为100 000英镑). **(b)** (usu *sing* 通常作单数) sum of money; price 金额; 价格: *We bought the house at a high/low figure,* ie for a high/low price. 我们以高[低]价买下了那所房子. **2** [C] **(a)** diagram or illustration 图解; 图表: *The figure on page 22* *shows a political map of Africa.* 第22页的插图是非洲的政区图. (**b**) geometrical shape enclosed by lines or surfaces 几何图形. **3** [C] decorative pattern or series of movements 装饰性的图案或系列动作: *The skater executed a perfect set of figures.* 那个滑冰的人做出了一套完美的花样动作. ○ [attrib 作定语] *figure-skating* 花样滑冰. **4** [C] representation of a person or an animal in drawing, painting, etc (绘画等中的)人或动物的像, 画像, 肖像: *The central figure in the painting is the artist's daughter.* 画中间的那个人是画家的女儿. **5** [C] human form, esp its appearance, what it suggests, and how it is seen by others 身材; (尤指)体态, 相貌: *have a good figure*, ie be slim, shapely, etc 身材苗条 ○ *I'm dieting to keep my figure*, ie in order not to get fatter. 我正在节食以保持身材不变(不发胖). ○ *I saw a figure approaching in the darkness.* 我看见黑暗中有个人影走近. ○ *He was once a leading figure in the community, but now he has become a figure of fun*, ie His influence was considerable but now he appears merely ridiculous. 他原是该社区的头面人物, 但现在成了人们取笑的对象. ○ *She's a fine figure of a woman*, ie pleasing in shape and appearance. 她身材苗条. **6 figures** [pl] arithmetic 算术: *Are you good at figures?* 你的算术好吗? **7** (idm 习语) **cut a fine, poor, sorry, etc 'figure** have a fine, etc appearance 出众、出丑、出洋相等. **facts and figures** ⇨ FACT. **put a figure on sth** quote a price or specify a number for sth 报价; 确定某物的数量: *It's impossible to put a figure on the number of homeless after the flood.* 水灾过后无家可归的人不计其数. **in round figures/numbers** ⇨ ROUND[1]. **single figures** ⇨ SINGLE.

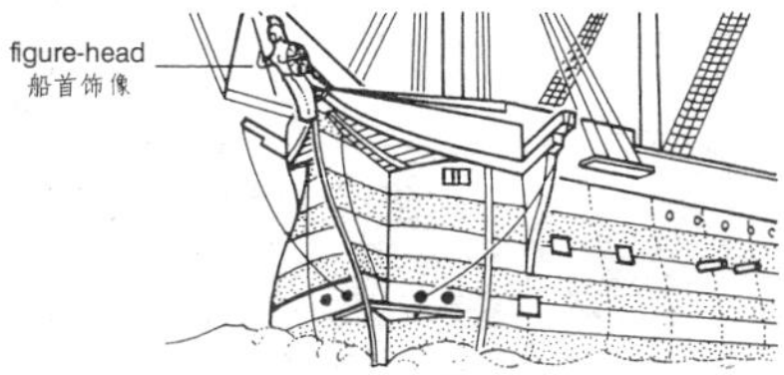

figure-head 船首饰像

□ **'figure-head** *n* **1** (esp formerly) large wooden carving, usu representing a human figure, placed at the prow of a ship (尤指旧时的)船首饰像, 破浪神的雕像. ⇨illus 见插图. **2** (*fig* 比喻) person in a high position but without any real authority 有名无实的首脑人物; 傀儡.

,figure of 'eight (*US* also **figure eight**) thing that resembles the number 8 in shape '8'字形: *skating figures of eight on the ice* 在冰上滑'8'字形.

figure of 'speech word or phrase used for vivid or dramatic effect and not literally 比喻: *I didn't really mean she was in outer space — it's just a figure of speech.* 我不是说她真在外层空间——这只是打个比方.

fig·ure[2] /ˈfɪgə(r); *US* ˈfɪgjər; ˈfɪgjɚ/ *v* **1** [I, Ipr] **~ (in sth)** appear or be mentioned, esp prominently 出现或被提及(尤指引人注目的): *a character that figures in many of her novels* 在她多部小说中出现的一个人物 ○ *She figured conspicuously in the public debate on the issue.* 她在该问题的公开辩论中很引人注目. **2** (**a**) [Tn, Tf] (*esp US*) think (sth); calculate 想(某事物); 估计: *I figured (that) you wouldn't come.* 我料想你不会来. ○ *It's what I figured.* 我是这样认为的. (**b**) [I] (used with *it* or *that* 与it或that连用) (*infml* 口) be likely or understandable 有可能; 可以理解: *'John isn't here today.' 'That figures, he looked very unwell yesterday.'* '约翰今天没来.' '怪不得, 他昨天就好像不太舒服.' **3** (phr v) **figure sth in** (*US*) include sth in one's calculations 将某事物包括在内; 计算在内: *Have you figured in the cost of food for our holiday?* 你把咱们度假的食物费用计算进去了吗? **figure on sth** (*US*) include sth in one's plans; rely on sth 计划; 指望: *I figure on being in New York in January.* 我计划一月份在纽约. **figure sb/sth out** (*esp US*) (**a**) come to understand sb/sth by thinking 理解某人[某事物]; 弄明白: *I've never been able to figure him out.* 我一直不能理解他. ○ *I can't figure out why he quit his job.* 我琢磨不透他为什么要辞掉工作. ○ *Have you figured out what's wrong with your car?* 你找出你汽车的毛病了吗? (**b**) discover sth by using arithmetic; calculate sth 演算出; 计算出: *Have you figured out how much the holiday will cost?* 你算出假期得花多少钱了吗?

fig·ur·ine /ˈfɪgəriːn; *US* ˌfɪgjəˈriːn; ˌfɪgjəˈrin/ *n* small ornamental statue, esp of a person 小塑像; (尤指)人的雕像.

fila·ment /ˈfɪləmənt; ˈfɪləmənt/ *n* **1** very thin strand or fibre, like a thread 细线; 细丝; 线状物. **2** thin wire in a light bulb that glows when electricity is passed through it (电灯泡的)灯丝. ⇨illus at BULB 见BULB插图.

filch /fɪltʃ; fɪltʃ/ *v* [Tn] (*infml* 口) steal (esp sth of small value) 偷(尤指不贵重的东西): *Who's filched my pencil?* 谁把我的铅笔拿走了?

file[1] /faɪl; faɪl/ *n* metal tool with a rough surface for cutting, smoothing or shaping hard substances 锉; 锉刀.

▷ **file** *v* **1** [Tn, Tn·pr, Cn·a] cut, smooth or shape (sth) with a file 用锉切削(某物): *file one's fingernails* 锉指甲 ○ *file sth smooth* 把某物锉光滑 ○ *file an iron bar in two* 把铁棒锉成两截. **2** (phr v) **file sth down** make sth smooth and smaller in size by using a file 将某物锉光滑、锉小. **fil·ings** /ˈfaɪlɪŋz; ˈfaɪlɪŋz/ *n* [pl] particles removed by a file 锉屑: *iron filings* 铁屑.

file[2] /faɪl; faɪl/ *n* **1** (**a**) any of various types of drawer, shelf, holder, cover, box, etc, usu with a wire or metal rod for keeping loose papers together and in order, for reference purposes (存放文件、公文、卷宗、档案等的)抽屉、架子、夹子、封皮、箱子等: *I need another file for my letters.* 我还需要一个存放信件的夹子. (**b**) file and its contents 存放文件等的用具及其中的文件; 档案; 卷宗: *Where's the file of our recent correspondence?* 我们近期的信件卷宗在哪里? ○ *have/open/keep a file on each member of staff* 有[设立/保管]每个职员的档案. **2** organized collection of related data or material in a computer (计算机)文件: *I can't access the file on your company because I've forgotten the code.* 我无法取出贵公司的文件, 因为我把代码忘了. **3** (idm 习语) **on file** kept in a file 存档; 归档: *We have all your particulars on file.* 我们已把你的全部资料存档.

▷ **file** /faɪl; faɪl/ *v* **1** [Tn, Tn·pr, Tn·p] **~ sth (away)** place sth in a file; store sth where it can be consulted 将某物归档: *file (away) letters in a drawer* 把信件归档放入抽屉中. **2** [Tn] send (sth) so that it may be recorded 送交(某物)以便备案; 提交: *file an application for divorce* 提交离婚申请书.

□ **'filing clerk** (*US* **file clerk**) person who files correspondence, etc and does general office tasks 档案管理员.

file[3] /faɪl; faɪl/ *n* **1** line of people or things one behind the other 排成行的人或物. **2** (idm 习语) **(in) Indian/single 'file** (in) one line, one behind the other (成)单行. Cf 参看 THE RANK AND FILE (RANK[1]).

▷ **file** *v* [I, Ipr, Ip] **~ in, out, off, past, etc** march or walk in the specified direction in a single line 排成单行沿某方向前进或行走: *The men filed onto the parade ground and past the general.* 士兵们排成单行进入阅兵场自将军面前走过.

filet /ˈfɪleɪ; fiˈle/ *n* (also **filet mignon** /ˌfɪleɪ ˈmiːnjɒn; fiˈle minˈjɔ̃/) (*US*) small tender piece of beef without bones, cut from a sirloin (牛的)里脊: *Two filets mignons, please.* 请来两份牛里脊.

fi·lial /ˈfɪlɪəl; ˈfɪlɪəl/ *adj* [usu attrib 通常作定语] of or expected from a son or daughter 子女的: *filial duty* 孝道.

fili·bus·ter /ˈfɪlɪbʌstə(r); ˈfɪlə,bʌstɚ/ *n* (*esp US*) **1** person who tries to delay or prevent the making of decisions in (esp parliamentary) meetings by making long speeches 以冗长的演说拖延或阻挠会议(尤指议会)做出决定的人. **2** such a speech 此种冗长的演说.

▷ **fili·bus·ter** *v* [I] (*esp US*) act as a filibuster (以冗长演说)拖延或阻挠: *filibustering tactics* 藉冗长演说来拖延的战术.

fili·gree /ˈfɪlɪgriː; ˈfɪlə,gri/ *n* [U] fine ornamental work using gold, silver or copper wire (用金丝、银丝或铜丝制成的)精工饰品: [attrib 作定语] *a filigree brooch* 银丝胸针 ○ *filigree ear-rings* 金丝耳环.

F

fil·ings ⇨ FILE[1].

fill[1] /fɪl; fɪl/ *v* **1** (**a**) [Tn, Tn·pr, Cn·a, Dn·n, Dn·pr] **~ sth (with sth); ~sth (for sb)** make sth full (of sth); occupy all of the space in sth 使某物充满(另一物); 装满; 填满: *fill a hole with sand, a tank with petrol, a hall with people* 用沙子把洞填满、把油箱注满汽油、大厅里挤满人 ○ *Smoke filled the room.* 房间里烟雾弥漫. ○ *The wind filled the sails*, ie made them swell out. 这阵风把帆吹得鼓鼓的. ○ (*fig* 比喻) *I am filled with admiration for your bravery.* 我由衷钦佩你英勇绝伦. ○ *fill a bucket full of water* 装满一桶水 ○ *Please fill this glass for me/fill me this glass.* 请把这个杯子给我斟满. (**b**) [I, Ipr] **~ (with sth)** become full 充满; 充塞: *The hall soon filled.* 那大厅不久就满了. ○ *The sails filled with wind.* 帆在风中张得鼓鼓的. **2** [Tn, Tn·pr] **~ sth (with sth)** block or plug (a hole, gap, etc) 填塞, 堵塞(洞、隙等): *A dentist often has to fill teeth.* 牙科医生常常给患者补牙. ○ *I must fill that crack in the wall.* 我得把墙上的那条裂缝填补好. **3** [Tn] (**a**) hold (a position) 任(某职): *She fills the post satisfactorily*, ie performs her duties well. 她非常尽职. (**b**) appoint sb to (a position) 派某人担任(某职): *The vacancy has already been filled.* 那空缺已有人补上了. **4** (idm 习语) **fill/fit the bill** ⇨ BILL[1]. **fill sb's shoes** take over sb's function, duties, etc and perform them satisfactorily 出色地接替某人的工作、职务等. **5** (phr v) **fill in (for sb)** take sb's place for a short time 临时接替某人; 暂代: *My partner is on holiday this week so I'm filling in (for him).* 我的合伙人本星期休假, 所以我暂代(他)一下. **fill sth in** (**a**) (*US* also **fill sth out**) add what is necessary to make sth complete 加入必要内容使某事物完备; 补充: *fill in an application form*, ie write one's name and other details required 填写申请表格. (**b**) fill sth completely 填满(某物): *The hole has been filled in.* 洞已填满. (**c**) spend (time) while waiting for sth (在等候某事物时)打发, 消磨(时间): *He filled in the rest of the day watching television.* 他看电视来打发当天剩下的时间. **fill sb 'in (on sth)** give sb full details (about sth) 向某人提供(关于某事物的)详情: *Can you fill me in on what has been happening?* 你能把发生的事情原原本本地告诉我吗? **fill 'out** become larger, rounder or fatter 变得更大、更圆、更胖: *Her cheeks began to fill out.* 她的脸胖起来了. ○ *He used to be a very thin child but he's filled out a lot recently.* 这孩子过去很瘦, 近来胖多了. **fill sth out** ⇨ FILL STH IN (a). **fill (sth) up** become or make completely full 充满; 填满; 装满: *The gutter has filled up with mud.* 沟槽里都是泥. ○ *fill up the tank with petrol* 把油箱装满汽油.

▷ **filler** *n* object or material used to fill a hole in sth or to increase the size of sth 填料; 填塞物.

□ **'filling station** = PETROL STATION (PETROL).

fill[2] /fɪl; fɪl/ *n* **1** [C] enough to fill sth 填满某物之量: *a fill of tobacco/petrol/oil* 一烟斗的烟丝[一桶汽油/一桶油]. **2** [U] **one's ~ (of sth/sb)** (*fml* 文) (**a**) as much as one can eat or drink 吃饱或喝足的量: *No more tea, thank you, I've had my fill.* 谢谢你, 不要再添茶了, 我已经喝足了. (**b**) as much as one can tolerate 能忍受的限度: *She decided she had had her fill of his cruelty.* 她认为自己已经受够了他的虐待.

fil·let /ˈfɪlɪt; ˋfɪlɪt/ *n* **1** [C, U] piece of meat or fish without bones 无骨的肉片或鱼片: [attrib 作定语] *a/some fillet steak* 一块[一些]里脊片. **2** [C] narrow band, ribbon, etc worn round the head to keep the hair in place or as an ornament 束发带; 头带.

▷ **fil·let** *v* [Tn] cut (meat or fish) into fillets 把(肉或鱼)切成片: *grilled filleted sole* 烤比目鱼片.

fill·ing /ˈfɪlɪŋ; ˋfɪlɪŋ/ *n* **1** [C] (process of putting in) material used to fill a hole in a tooth (补牙洞的)填料; 补牙: *I had to have two fillings at the dentist's today.* 我今天要请牙医给我补两颗牙. **2** [C, U] food put between slices of bread to make a sandwich, or between layers of cake, etc 馅: *a sponge cake with jam filling* 果酱馅饼.

fil·lip /ˈfɪlɪp; ˋfɪləp/ *n* **1** stimulus or incentive; encouragement 刺激; 激励; 鼓励: *an advertising campaign to give a much-needed fillip to sales* 刺激销路必不可少的广告运动. **2** quick flick made by pressing a finger against the thumb and then releasing it suddenly 弹指.

filly /ˈfɪlɪ; ˋfɪlɪ/ *n* young female horse 小母马. Cf 参看 COLT[1], MARE[1]1.

film[1] /fɪlm; fɪlm/ *n* **1** [C usu *sing* 通常作单数] **~ (of sth)** thin coating or covering on or over sth (某物上)薄薄的一层, 薄膜: *a film of dust* 一层灰尘 ○ *a film of oil on water* 水面上的一层油 ○ *a film of mist over the land* 笼罩大地的一层薄雾. **2** [C, U] roll or sheet of thin flexible light-sensitive material for use in photography 软片; 胶卷: *put a new film in one's camera* 在相机里装上新胶卷 ○ *expose/develop 50 feet of film* 使50英尺的软片曝光[冲洗50英尺的软片]. **3** [C] motion picture 电影: *What's your favourite film?* 你最喜欢哪部电影? ○ *My cousin is in films*, ie works in the film industry. 我表兄从事电影业.

▷ **filmy** *adj* (**-ier, -iest**) [usu attrib 通常作定语] thin and almost transparent 薄而近乎透明的: *a filmy cotton blouse* 极薄的棉质女衬衫.

□ **'film star** well-known cinema actor or actress 电影明星.

'film-strip *n* series of transparent still photographs that can be projected separately 幻灯片.

'film test photographic test to decide whether sb is suitable to act in films 试镜(以决定某人是否适合演电影).

film[2] /fɪlm; fɪlm/ *v* **1** (**a**) [Tn, Tng] make a film or motion picture of (a scene, story, etc) 将(一场面、故事等)拍成电影: *They're filming a new comedy.* 他们正在拍摄一部新的喜剧片. ○ *She filmed her children playing in the garden.* 她把她的孩子在花园嬉戏的镜头拍摄了下来. (**b**) [I] be engaged in doing this 从事电影拍摄: *They've been filming for six months.* 他们已经拍了半年电影. **2** (**a**) [Tn] cover (sth) with a thin coating or covering layer 给(某物)覆上一薄层: *Thin ice filmed the lake.* 湖上结了一层薄冰. (**b**) [Ip] **~ over** become covered in this way 覆上一薄层: *As she cried, her eyes filmed over.* 她哭得泪眼朦胧.

filter 过滤器

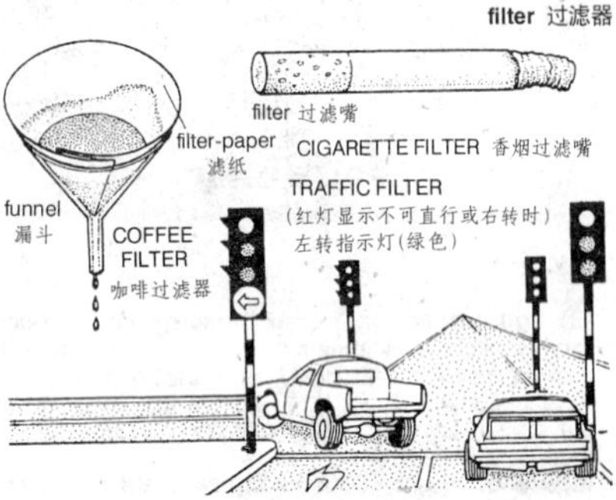

fil·ter /ˈfɪltə(r); ˋfɪltɚ/ *n* **1** device containing paper, sand, cloth, etc used to hold back any solid material or impurities in a liquid or gas passed through it 过滤器: *an oil filter* 滤油器 ○ *a coffee filter* 咖啡过滤器. ⇨illus 见插图. **2** screen (esp of coloured glass) that allows light only of certain wavelengths to pass through 滤光镜; 滤色镜: *I took this picture with a red filter.* 这张照片我是用红色滤光镜拍摄的. **3** device for suppressing certain electrical or sound waves (电波、声波的)滤波器. **4** (*Brit*) device that signals to show that traffic may turn left while other traffic waiting to go straight ahead or turn right is still stopped by a red traffic light (在红灯指示其他车辆不得直行或右转时)指示车辆左转的交通设施. ⇨illus 见插图.

▷ **fil·ter** *v* **1** [Tn] (**a**) pass (liquid, light, etc) through a filter 过滤(液体、光等): *It won't take long to filter the coffee.* 用不了多少时间就可以把咖啡过滤好. (**b**) purify (a liquid) by using a filter 滤清(液体): *All drinking water must be filtered.* 饮用水均须过滤净化. **2** [I, Ipr, Ip] **~ in, out, through, etc** (*fig* 比喻) pass or flow slowly in a specified direction; become known gradually 慢慢传开; 渗透: *New ideas are slowly filtering into people's minds.* 新思想逐渐深入人心. ○ *The news of the defeat started to filter through.* 战败的消息开始传出来. **3** [I] (*Brit*) (of traffic) turn left while other traffic waiting to go straight ahead or turn right is stopped by a red traffic light（指车辆）左转行驶（有红灯指示其他车辆不得直行或右转）.

□ **'filter-paper** *n* [U] porous paper for filtering liquids 滤纸.

'filter-tip *n* (cigarette one end of which contains a) filter for smoke（香烟的）过滤嘴；滤嘴香烟. **'filter-tipped** *adj*.

filth /fɪlθ; fɪlθ/ *n* [U] **1** disgusting dirt 肮脏；污物：*Look at the filth on your trousers!* 看你裤子上的脏东西！ **2** offensive and obscene words, literature, magazines, etc 下流的言语、文学、杂志等：*How can you read such filth?* 你怎么能看这种乌七八糟的东西？

▷ **filthy** *adj* (**-ier, -iest**) **1** (**a**) disgustingly dirty 污秽的；肮脏的：*a beggar dressed in filthy rags* 衣衫肮脏褴褛的乞丐. (**b**) obscene 猥亵的；淫秽的：*filthy language* 猥亵的语言. **2** (*infml* 口) (esp of weather) very unpleasant（尤指天气）恶劣的：*Isn't it a filthy day?* 今天天气糟透了！**filth·ily** *adv*. **filthi·ness** *n* [U].

filthy *adv* **1** in a filthy way 污秽地；淫秽地：*filthy dirty* 污秽不堪. **2** (*infml* 口) very 很；非常：*filthy rich* 非常富有. **3** (idm 习语) **filthy lucre** (*derog or joc* 贬或谑) money or financial gain 肮脏钱；不义之财.

fil·trate /ˈfɪltreɪt; ˋfɪltret/ *n* filtered liquid 经过滤的液体.

▷ **fil·tra·tion** /fɪlˈtreɪʃn; fɪlˋtreʃən/ *n* [U] process of filtering liquid, etc 过滤.

fin /fɪn; fɪn/ *n* **1** thin flat projecting part of a fish, used for swimming and steering 鳍. ⇨illus at FISH 见FISH插图. **2** thing shaped like this on eg an aircraft or a rocket that helps to keep it stable 鳍状物（如飞行器或火箭上的尾翅）. ⇨illus at AIRCRAFT 见AIRCRAFT插图.

fin·able ⇨ FINE[1].

fi·nal /ˈfaɪnl; ˋfaɪnḷ/ *adj* **1** [attrib 作定语] of the end; coming last 最终的；最后的：*the final chapter of a book* 书的最后一章. **2** [usu pred 通常作表语] (of a decision, etc) conclusive; decisive; that cannot be changed（指决定等）确定，决定性，不可变更：*The judge's ruling is final.* 法官的判决是不可改变的. ○ *I'm not coming, and that's final!* 我不来了，就这样定了！ **3** (idm 习语) **in the last/final analysis** ⇨ ANALYSIS. **the last/final straw** ⇨ STRAW.

▷ **fi·nal** *n* **1** (**a**) last of a series of contests or competitions 决赛：*the tennis finals* 网球决赛 ○ *the Cup Final*, ie the last in a series of esp football matches 优胜杯决赛（尤指足球）. (**b**) (usu *pl* 通常作复数) last set of university examinations 大学的毕业考试：*sit/take one's finals* 参加大学毕业考试 ○ *the law final(s)* 法律专业的毕业考试. **2** last edition of a day's newspaper（当天报纸的）最后发行的一版：*late night final* 晚间最后版.

fi·nal·ist /-nəlɪst; -nḷɪst/ *n* player who takes part in the final(s) of a competition 参加决赛者.

fi·nally /-nəlɪ; -nḷɪ/ *adv* **1** lastly; in conclusion 最后；总之：*Finally, I would like to say*... 最后，我想说.... **2** conclusively; decisively 确定地；决定性地：*We must settle this matter finally.* 我们必须彻底解决这一问题. **3** at last; eventually 最终；终于：*After a long delay the performance finally started.* 演出拖延很久，最后总算开始了.

fi·nale /fɪˈnɑːlɪ; *US* -ˈnælɪ; fəˋnælɪ/ *n* last part of a piece of music or a drama, etc 终曲，结局（音乐、戏剧等的最终部分）：*the grand finale of a pantomine* 童话剧的大结局.

fi·nal·ity /faɪˈnælətɪ; faɪˋnælətɪ/ *n* [U] quality or fact of being final 终结；定局：*She spoke with (an air of) finality*, ie gave the impression that there was nothing more to be said or done. 她以做结论式的口吻讲话.

fi·nal·ize, -ise /ˈfaɪnəlaɪz; ˋfaɪnḷˌaɪz/ *v* [Tn] put (sth) into final form; complete 使（某事物）达到最后形式；使完成：*finalize one's plans, arrangements, etc* 把计划、安排等确定下来. ▷ **fi·nal·iza·tion, -isation** /ˌfaɪnəlaɪˈzeɪʃn; *US* -lɪˈz-; ˌfaɪnələˋzeʃən/ *n* [U].

fin·ance /ˈfaɪnæns, fɪˈnæns; ˋfaɪnæns, fəˋnæns/ *n* **1** [U] management of (esp public) money 财务的管理；（尤指）财政：*an expert in finance* 财务专家 ○ *the Minister of Finance* 财政部长. **2** [U] ~ (**for sth**) money used or needed to support an undertaking 资金：*Finance for the National Health Service comes from taxpayers.* 国家卫生局的资金来自纳税人的税款. **3 finances** [pl] money available to a person, company or country（个人、公司或国家）可动用的钱，财源，财力：*Are the firm's finances sound?* 这家公司的财务状况可靠吗？

▷ **fin·ance** *v* [Tn esp passive 尤用于被动语态] provide money for (a project, etc); fund 为（某计划等）提供资金，提供款项：*The scheme is partly financed by a government grant.* 此计划有一部分是政府资助的.

□ **'finance company** (also **'finance house**) company that lends money for hire-purchase transactions 信贷公司，财务公司（贷款给分期付款者的公司）.

fin·an·cial /faɪˈnænʃl, fɪˈnæ-; faɪˋnænʃəl, fəˋnæ-/ *adj* concerning money and finance 财务的；金融的；财政的：*in financial difficulties*, ie short of money 处于财务困难之中 ○ *Tokyo and New York are major financial centres.* 东京和纽约是主要的金融中心. ▷ **fin·an·ci·ally** /-ʃəlɪ; -ʃəlɪ/ *adv*.

□ **fiˌnancial 'year** (*US* **fiscal year**) period of twelve months over which annual accounts and taxes are calculated 财政年度；会计年度.

fin·an·cier /faɪˈnænsɪə(r); *US* ˌfɪnənˈsɪər; ˌfɪnənˋsɪr/ *n* person engaged in financing businesses, etc on a large scale 财政家；金融家.

finch /fɪntʃ; fɪntʃ/ *n* (often in compounds 常用以构成复合词) any of several types of small songbird with short, stubby bills 雀科鸣鸟（任何一种短喙鸣鸟）：*a 'chaffinch* ○ *a 'goldfinch* ○ *a 'bullfinch*.

find[1] /faɪnd; faɪnd/ *v* (*pt, pp* **found** /faʊnd; faʊnd/) **1** [Tn, Tn·pr, Tn·p, Cn·a] discover (sth/sb) unexpectedly or by chance; come across 意外或偶然发现（某事物[某人]）；遇到；碰到：*Look what I've found.* 看我发现了什么. ○ *I found a £5 note on the pavement.* 我在人行道上捡到了一张5英镑的纸币. ○ *He woke up and found himself in hospital.* 他醒来发觉自己在医院里. ○ *I was disappointed to find you out* (ie that you were out) *when I called.* 我给你打电话时知道你不在，十分失望. ○ *We came home and found her asleep on the sofa.* 我们回到家，看到她在沙发上睡着了. **2** [Tn, Tn·pr, Dn·n, Dn·pr] ~ **sth/sb (for sb)** discover sth/sb by searching, inquiry or effort（经寻找、询问或努力）发现某事物[某人]：*After months of drilling, oil was found off the coast.* 经数月钻探，在沿海找到了石油. ○ *find a cure for cancer* 找到治疗癌症的方法 ○ *find an answer to a question* 找到问题的答案 ○ *I can find nothing new to say on this subject.* 对这个问题，我提不出什么新看法. ○ *Can you find me a hotel/find a hotel for me?* 你能给我找一家旅馆吗？ **3** [Tn, Dn·n, Dn·pr] ~ **sth/sb (for sb)** obtain or get back (esp sth/sb that was lost) 得到或找回（尤指丢失的某物[某人]）：*Did you find the pen you lost?* 你丢的笔找到了吗？ ○ *The missing child has not been found yet.* 失踪的孩子仍未找到. ○ *I'll help you find your shoes/find your shoes for you.* 我来帮你找鞋. **4** [Tn] succeed in obtaining (sth); provide or supply 得到（某事物）；提供；供给：*I keep meaning to write, but never seem to find (the) time.* 我一直想写，但似乎总是找不到时间. ○ *Who will find the money to pay for this trip?* 谁来筹措旅费？ **5** [Tf, Cn·a] discover (sth/sb) by experience (to be or do sth); become aware of（凭经验）发现（某事物[某人]）（为某事物或做某事物）；了解到：*I find (that) it pays to be honest.* 我认识到为人诚实终受益. ○ *How do you find your new job?* 你认为你的新工作怎么样？ ○ *She found it difficult to understand him/found him difficult to understand.* 她觉得很难理解他. ○ *We found the beds very comfortable.* 我们觉得这些床很舒服. ○ *We found him (to be) dishonest.* 我们认为他不诚实. **6** [Tn] arrive at (sth) naturally; reach（自然而然）达到；到达：*Water will always find its own level.* 水总会自行流平. ○ *The arrow found its mark.* 箭射中了目标. **7** [Tn] (used in a statement of fact, indicating that sth exists 用于对事实的陈述，说明某事物的存在)：*You'll find* (ie There is) *a teapot in the cupboard.* 碗橱里有个茶壶. ○ *These flowers are found* (ie exist, grow) *only in Africa.* 只有在非洲才有这类花. **8** [Cn·a] (*law* 律) decide and declare as a verdict 断定；裁决；宣判：*How do you find the accused?* 你如何裁决被告？ ○ *The jury found him guilty (of manslaughter).* 陪审团裁定他（误杀）罪名成立. **9** (idm 习语) **all 'found** (of wages) with free food and lodging included（指工资）附带免费食宿. **be found wanting** be shown to be not sufficiently reliable or capable of undertaking a task, etc 表现出不够可靠或能力不够. **find fault (with sb/sth)** look for and discover mistakes (in sb/sth); complain (about sb/sth) 找（某人[某事物]

的)错; 埋怨(某人[某事物]): *I have no fault to find with your work.* 我对你的工作没有说的. ○ *She's always finding fault (with me).* 她总是找(我的)茬儿. **find/lose favour with sb/in sb's eyes** ⇨ FAVOUR[1]. **find one's 'feet** (**a**) become able to stand, walk, etc steadily 能够站稳、走稳等: *After a six-week illness it took me some time to find my feet again.* 我病了六个星期, 痊愈后很长时间才能站稳. (**b**) become able to act independently and confidently 能够独立而有信心地行动: *I only recently joined the firm so I'm still finding my feet.* 我最近才加入这家公司, 因此还在摸索着干. **(not) find it in one's heart/oneself to do sth** (usu with *can/could* 通常与can/could连用) (not) be able to do sth because of kindness or consideration 由于善意或体谅而(不)能做某事物: *I cannot find it in myself to condemn a mother who steals for a hungry child.* 我不忍心责备为饥儿行窃的女人. ○ *Can you find it in your heart to apologize?* 你有诚意道歉吗? **'find oneself** discover one's true abilities, character and desires 发现自己真实的能力、性格和愿望: *At twenty-two, he's just beginning to find himself.* 他在二十二岁时才逐渐发现自己的实际才能. **find/meet one's match** ⇨ MATCH[2]. **find one's own level** find and associate with the people with whom one is morally, socially or intellectually equal 找到并结交道德观念、社会地位或知识层次与自己相当的人. **find/lose one's 'voice/'tongue** be able/unable to speak or express one's opinion 能够[不能够]说出或表达自己的意见: *Tell me what you think — or have you lost your tongue?* 告诉我你的想法——是否你有口难言? **find its way to...** reach a destination naturally 自然达到目的地: *Rivers find their way to the sea.* 江河径自流入海洋. **find one's way (to...)** discover the right route (to a place) 发现(到某处的)途径: *I hope you can find your way home.* 我希望你能找到回家的路. ○ *She couldn't find her way out of the building.* 她找不到走出大楼的路. **take sb as one 'finds him** accept sb as he is without expecting him to behave in a special way 认为某人就是如此, 并不期望他有其他表现: *We've only just returned from holiday so you must take us as you find us.* 我们刚刚度假回来, 所以你看我们就是这副样子. **10** (phr v) **find (sth) out** learn (sth) by study or inquiry (经研究或询问)获知(某事物): *Can you find out what time the train leaves?* 你能查问出火车什么时候开吗? **find sb out** discover sb who has done wrong, lied, etc 发现某人做错事、说谎等: *He had been cheating the taxman but it was years before he was found out.* 他一直欺骗税务局, 但多年之后才被查出. **find for/against sb** (*law* 律) give a verdict in favour of/against sb 做出对某人有利[不利]的裁决: *The jury found for the defendant.* 陪审团做了有利于被告的裁决.

▷ **finder** *n* **1** person who finds sth 找到某物的人: *Lost: one diamond ring. Finder will be rewarded.* 寻物: 遗失钻戒一枚, 寻得者将获重酬. **2** small telescope attached to a larger one used for locating an object for observation 寻星镜(附加在大望远镜上便于寻找观察目标的小望远镜). **3** (idm 习语) ˌ**finders 'keepers** (*saying* 谚) whoever finds sth has the right to keep it 谁找到归谁.

find·ing *n* (usu *pl* 通常作复数) **1** thing that is discovered as the result of an (official) inquiry (官方的)调查结果: *the findings of the Commission* 调查团的调查结果 ○ *The report's main finding is that pensions are inadequate.* 报告的主要内容是退休金不敷应用. **2** (*law* 律) decision or verdict of a court or jury 法庭或陪审团的判决或裁决.

find[2] /faɪnd; faɪnd/ *n* **1** thing or person that is found, esp sth/sb valuable or pleasing 发现或找到的物或人(尤指有用的): *Our new gardener was a marvellous find.* 我们找到了一个很出色的花匠. **2** act of finding sth/sb 发现; 找到: *an important archaeological find* 重要的考古发现 ○ *I made a great find in that second-hand bookshop yesterday.* 我昨天在旧书店找到一本很宝贵的书.

fine[1] /faɪn; faɪn/ *n* sum of money that must be paid as a punishment for breaking a law or rule 罚金; 罚款: *Offenders may be liable to a heavy fine.* 触犯者罚款很重.

▷ **fine** *v* [Tn, Tn·pr, Dn·n] **~ sb (for sth/doing sth)** punish sb by a fine 处某人以罚款: *fined for dangerous driving* 因危险驾驶而被罚款 ○ *The court fined him £500.* 法庭罚他500英镑.

fin·able /ˈfaɪnəbl; ˈfaɪnəbl̩/ *adj* (of an action) that is likely to be punished by a fine (指行为)应罚款的, 可罚款的: *a finable offence* 应罚款的过失.

fine[2] /faɪn; faɪn/ *adj* (**-r**, **-st**) **1** (**a**) of high quality 高质量的: *a fine painting* 精美的绘画 ○ *a very fine performance* 非常精彩的表演 ○ *fine food, clothes, material* 上好的食品、衣服、材料. (**b**) carefully and skilfully made; easily damaged; delicate 精制的; 易损坏的; 纤巧的: *fine workmanship* 精巧的手工 ○ *fine silk* 细绸. (**c**) good; beautiful; pleasing; enjoyable 好的; 美的; 漂亮的; 令人愉快的: *a fine view* 美丽的景色 ○ *We had a fine holiday in Switzerland.* 我们在瑞士度过了一个愉快的假期. ○ (*ironic* 反语) *This is a fine mess we're in!* 好一个乱摊子! **2** (of weather) bright; clear; not raining (指天气)晴朗的, 无云的, 无雨的: *It poured all morning, but turned fine later.* 下了一上午的瓢泼大雨, 后来才转晴. **3** made of very small grains or particles 颗粒微小的: *fine powder, flour, dust, etc* 细粉末、精制的面粉、微细的灰尘 ○ *Sand is finer than gravel.* 沙子比碎石细. **4** slender; thin 纤细的; 细小的: *fine thread* 细线 ○ *a pencil with a fine point* 很尖的铅笔. **5** (of metals) refined; pure (指金属)精炼的, 纯的: *fine gold* 纯金. **6** (**a**) difficult to perceive; subtle 难于察觉的; 细微的: *You are making very fine distinctions.* 你做的区分非常精细. (**b**) that can make delicate and careful distinctions 能辨别细微差别的: *a fine sense of humour* 敏锐的幽默感 ○ *a fine taste in art* 对艺术的细致的鉴赏力. **7** (of speech or writing) ornate; rhetorical; complimentary, esp in an insincere way (指语言或文字)词藻华丽的, 修辞的, 恭维的(尤指虚伪地): *His speech was full of fine words which meant nothing.* 他的讲话净是华而不实的词藻. **8** in good health; well; comfortable 健康的; 舒适的: *'How are you?' 'Fine, thanks.'* '你好吗?''很好, 谢谢!' **9** (*infml* 口) satisfactory 满意的: *I'm not very hungry — a small snack is fine for me.* 我不太饿——来点小吃就够了. **10** (idm 习语) **chance would be a fine thing** ⇨ CHANCE[1]. **the finer points (of sth)** the details or aspects of sth which can be recognized and appreciated only by those who understand or know it well 只有行家才能领悟和欣赏到的某些方面或细节: *I don't understand the finer points of snooker but I enjoy watching it on TV.* 我不太懂落袋台球游戏, 但我喜欢看电视里的这种节目. **get sth down to a fine 'art** (*infml* 口) learn to do sth perfectly 学会将某事物做得尽善尽美: *She's got the business of buying birthday presents down to a fine art.* 她对购买生日礼品的事非常在行. **not to put too fine a 'point on it** to speak plainly 直截了当地说: *I don't much like modern music — in fact, not to put too fine a point on it, I hate it.* 我不很喜欢现代音乐——说句老实话, 我其实很讨厌现代音乐. **one fine 'day** (in story-telling) on a certain day, in the past or in the future (讲故事用语)有一天(可指过去或将来).

▷ **finely** *adv* **1** well; splendidly 美好地; 华丽地: *finely dressed* 衣着华丽. **2** into small particles or pieces 微小地; 细微地: *finely chopped herbs* 剁得很碎的药草. **3** with precision; in a subtle way 准确地; 精巧细微地: *a finely tuned engine* 精确调整的发动机 ○ *The match was finely balanced.* 比赛双方刚好势均力敌.

fine·ness *n* [U].

□ **fine 'art** (also **the fine 'arts, art**) art or forms of art that appeal to the sense of beauty, eg painting, sculpture, etc 美术或美术的各种形式(如绘画、雕刻等): [attrib 作定语] *a fine-arts course* 美术课程.

fine-'tooth comb (idm 习语) **(go over, through, etc sth) with a fine-'tooth comb** (examine sth) closely and thoroughly 细心地, 彻底地(检查某事物): *Police experts are sifting all the evidence with a fine-tooth comb.* 警方专门人员仔仔细细地审查所有证据.

the fine print = THE SMALL PRINT (SMALL).

fine[3] /faɪn; faɪn/ *adv* **1** (*infml* 口) very well 很好: *That suits me fine.* 那对我很合适. **2** (in compounds 用以构成复合词) in a fine[2](1, 6) way 细微地; 精美地; 难于察觉地: *fine-'drawn* (ie subtle) *distinctions* 细微的区别 ○ *fine-spun*, ie delicate 精细的. **3** (idm 习语) **cut it/things 'fine** leave oneself only the minimum amount, esp of time 给自己剩下最小的量(尤指时间): *If we only allow five minutes for catching our train, we'll be cutting it too fine.* 假如我们只留五分钟的时间赶火车, 那么我们卡的时间就太紧了.

finery /ˈfaɪnərɪ; ˈfaɪnərɪ/ *n* [U] gay and elegant clothes or

F

decoration 华丽、优雅的服装或装饰: *court officials dressed in all their finery* 穿着华丽衣服的宫廷官员 ○ *The garden looks beautiful in its summer finery*, ie with its bright flowers, lawns, etc. 在夏日绚丽的景色中, 花园显得很美.

fin·esse /fɪˈnes; fəˈnɛs/ *n* **1** [U] skill in dealing with people or situations cleverly or tactfully 手段; 策略: *show finesse in averting a threatened strike* 在避免一触即发的罢工中显示出深谋大略 ○ *He wheedled money from his father with considerable finesse.* 他耍了个手腕儿花言巧语地从父亲那里得到了钱. **2** [C] (in card-games) attempt to win a trick(5) by playing a card that is not the highest one held (纸牌戏中)偷牌(打出手中并非最大的牌以赢得一墩的手法).

▷ **fin·esse** *v* [Tn] (in card-games) play (a card) as part of a finesse(2) (纸牌戏中)为偷牌打出(一张牌)而赢得一墩: *She succeeded in finessing her queen.* 她为偷牌打出Q而赢得一墩.

fin·ger[1] /ˈfɪŋɡə(r); ˈfɪŋɡɚ/ *n* **1** any of the five parts extending from each hand (ˈ*little finger*, ˈ*ring finger*, ˈ*middle finger*, ˈ*forefinger*/ˈ*index finger*, *thumb*); any of these except the thumb 手指(小指、无名指、中指、食指、拇指); 除拇指外的任何一个手指: *There are five fingers (or four fingers and one thumb) on each hand.* 每只手有五个手指. ⇨ illus at HAND 见HAND插图. ⇨ Usage at BODY 用法见BODY. **2** part of a glove that fits over a finger (手套的)手指部. **3** (*infml* 口) measure of alcohol in a glass, roughly equal to the width of one finger 指幅(对杯中酒类的度量, 约略等于一指宽): *He poured himself two fingers of whisky.* 他给自己倒了两指幅的威士忌. **4** (idm 习语) **be all ˌfingers and ˈthumbs** be clumsy or awkward with one's hands 笨手笨脚: *Can you thread this needle for me? I'm all fingers and thumbs today.* 你能替我穿针吗? 今天我手脚不灵. **burn one's fingers/get one's fingers burnt** ⇨ BURN[2]. **cross one's fingers** ⇨ CROSS[2]. **get, pull, etc a/one's ˈfinger out** (*infml* 口) stop being lazy; work faster 别再偷懒; 干快一些: *If you don't pull your finger out, you'll never get the job finished.* 你要是不快些, 就绝对干不完. **have a finger in every ˈpie** (*infml* 口) be involved in everything that is happening 参与或插手一切事情. **have/keep one's finger on the pulse** know all the latest news, developments, etc 充分了解或掌握最近的消息、情况等. **have, etc one's fingers in the till** (*infml* 口) steal money from one's place of work 从自己的工作部门偷钱: *be caught with one's fingers in the till* 在自己的工作部门偷钱时被捉住. ○ *He's had his fingers in the till for years.* 他偷工作部门的钱已多年. **lay a ˈfinger on sb/sth** touch sb/sth, however slightly (即使轻轻)触碰某人[某物]: *If you lay a finger on that boy* (ie harm him physically), *I'll never forgive you.* 你若碰这孩子一下, 我就决不饶你. **lift/raise a finger/hand** ⇨ LIFT. **point the finger** ⇨ POINT[2]. **put one's finger on sth** identify precisely or point out (an error, the cause of a problem, etc) 准确地看出或指出(错误、问题的所在): *I can't quite put my finger on the flaw in her argument.* 我看不出她的论点有何不妥. **put the finger on sb** (*sl* 俚) give imformation about (esp a criminal) to the police, etc 向警方等提供(尤指罪犯的)情况. **slip through sb's fingers** ⇨ SLIP[2]. **snap one's fingers** ⇨ SNAP. **sticky fingers** ⇨ STICKY. **twist sb round one's little finger** ⇨ TWIST. **work one's fingers to the bone** work very hard 非常努力地工作.

□ ˈ**finger-board** *n* piece of wood (on a guitar, violin, etc) where the strings are pressed against the neck of the instrument with the fingers to vary the tone (弦乐器的)指板.

ˈ**finger-bowl** *n* small bowl for rinsing the fingers during meals 洗指盆(用餐时涮手指用的小盆).

ˈ**finger-mark** *n* mark, eg on a wall, made by a (dirty) finger 指迹, 指痕(如脏手指留在墙上的): *leave finger-marks all over the shiny table* 在光亮的桌面上到处留下指印.

ˈ**finger-nail** *n* layer of nail(1) over the upper surface of the tip of a finger 手指甲.

ˈ**finger-plate** *n* glass, metal or plastic plate fastened on a door near the handle or keyhole to prevent finger-marks 指痕防护板(为防手指弄污而固定于门扶手或锁孔附近的玻璃、金属或塑料板).

ˈ**fingerprint** *n* mark made by the tip of a finger on a surface and used for identifying people, esp criminals 指纹: *take the prisoner's fingerprints* 取囚犯的指纹.

ˈ**finger-stall** *n* protective cover for an injured finger (保护受伤手指的)护指套.

ˈ**fingertip** *n* **1** extreme end of a finger 指端; 指尖. **2** (idm 习语) **have sth at one's ˈfingertips** be completely familiar with sth 对某事物了如指掌. **to one's ˈfingertips** in every way; completely; through and through 各方面; 完全; 彻底: *She's an artist to her fingertips.* 她是真正的艺术家.

fin·ger[2] /ˈfɪŋɡə(r); ˈfɪŋɡɚ/ *v* [Tn] **1** touch or feel (sth) with the fingers 触摸(某物): *She fingered the silk to feel its quality.* 她摸了摸这块绸料看质量如何. ○ *I don't like eating food that's been fingered by someone else.* 我不愿意吃别人摸过的食物. **2** play (a musical instrument) with the fingers 用手指拨弹(乐器). **3** (*sl* 俚) give information about (esp a criminal) to the police, etc 向警方报信(尤指关于罪犯的消息).

▷ **fin·ger·ing** /ˈfɪŋɡərɪŋ; ˈfɪŋɡərɪŋ/ *n* [U] method of using the fingers in playing a musical instrument or in typing; numbers on a printed piece of music showing this (演奏乐器或打字时的)指法; 乐谱上表示指法的数字: *a piano piece with tricky fingering* 指法很难的钢琴曲.

fin·icky /ˈfɪnɪkɪ; ˈfɪnɪkɪ/ (also **fin·ical** /ˈfɪnɪkl; ˈfɪnɪkl/, **fin·ick·ing** /fɪnɪkɪŋ; ˈfɪnɪkɪŋ/) *adj* **1** (*derog* 贬) too fussy about food, clothes, etc (对饮食、衣着等)过分挑剔的: *a finicky eater, dresser, etc* 对吃、穿等过分挑剔的人. **2** needing much attention to detail 需注意细节的: *This job is too finicky for me.* 我做不了这么细致的工作.

fin·ish /ˈfɪnɪʃ; ˈfɪnɪʃ/ *v* **1** (**a**) [I, Tn, Tg] come or bring (sth) to an end 结束, 完成(某事物): *Term finishes next week.* 下星期学期结束. ○ *finish one's work* 把工作做完 ○ *finish (reading) a book* 读完一本书. (**b**) [I] reach the end of a task or an activity 达到工作或活动的结束阶段: *Wait — I haven't finished yet.* 等一等——我还没有完呢. ○ *Two of the runners failed to finish.* 有两名赛跑者没有跑完全程. ○ *She was leading for part of the race but finally finished fourth.* 她在比赛中一度领先, 但最后得第四名. **2** [Tn, Tn·p] **~ sth (off/up)** eat, drink or use what is left of sth 把所剩之物吃完、喝完或用完: *We might as well finish (up) the cake; there isn't much left.* 咱们索性把蛋糕吃完吧, 也没剩多少了. **3** [Tn, Tn·p] **~ sth (off)** complete sth or make sth perfect 完成某事物; 使某事物臻于完美; 加工: *a beautifully finished wooden bowl* 加工精美的木碗 ○ *put the finishing touches to a work of art* 为艺术作品作最后的修饰 ○ *This blouse needs to be finished off before I can wear it.* 这件(女)衬衣还要再加一下工我才能穿. **4** [Tn, Tn·p] **~ sb (off)** (*infml* 口) exhaust sb completely 使某人筋疲力尽: *That bike ride absolutely finished me (off).* 我骑了一路自行车已筋疲力尽. **5** (phr v) **finish sb/sth off** (*infml* 口) destroy sb/sth 毁坏某人[某事物]: *That fever nearly finished him off.* 那次高烧险些要了他的命. ○ *The last bullet finished off the wounded animal.* 最后的那颗子弹结束了这受伤动物的性命. ○ (*fig* 比喻) *It would finish me off to see her with him.* 看见她和他在一起我简直活不了啦. **finish with sb/sth** (**a**) no longer be busy with sb; no longer be using sth 不再为某人忙碌; 不再使用某物: *Can you wait a minute? I haven't finished with Ann yet.* 你能稍等一下吗? 我和安还没完事呢. ○ *You'll be sorry by the time I've finished with you*, eg finished punishing you. 等我收拾完你(如惩罚完你), 你就后悔去吧. ○ *Please put the saucepan away if you've finished with it.* 你用完了那个长柄锅, 就把它收起来. (**b**) end a relationship with sb or a connection with sth 与某人断绝关系; 终止与某事物的联系: *She should finish with him — he treats her very badly.* 她应该和他断绝关系——他对她太不好了. ○ *I've finished with gambling — it's a waste of money.* 我已经戒赌了——赌博完全是浪费钱财. **finish (up) with sth** have sth at the end 以某事物作结尾: *We had a quick lunch and finished up with a cup of coffee/and a cup of coffee to finish up with.* 我们匆忙吃了午饭, 最后又喝了一杯咖啡. **finish up** (followed by an *adj* or *n* 后接形容词或名词) be at the end; end up 终结; 结束: *He could finish up dead or badly injured.* 他到头来不是死就是重伤.

▷ **fin·ish** *n* **1** [C] last part or end of sth 某事物的最后部分或结尾: *the finish of a race* 赛跑的终点 ○ *There*

F

were several close finishes during the competition, ie ones in which the leading competitors were close together at the end. 那几个参赛者在比赛临近结束时成绩极接近. **2** (**a**) [C, U] state of being finished or perfect 完成的或完美的状态: *furniture with a fine finish* 最后工序做得很细致的家具 ○ (*fig* 比喻) *His manners lack finish.* 他的仪态稍欠文雅. (**b**) [C] method, material or texture used for completing the surface of woodwork, etc 用于处理木器等表面的方法、材料或物质: *varnishes available in a range of finishes* 可以产生各种表面效果的漆料. **3** (idm 习语) **be in at the ˈfinish** be present at the end of sth 在某事物的终结时在场. **fight to the finish** ⇨ FIGHT[1]. **a fight to the finish** ⇨ FIGHT[2].

fin·isher *n* person or animal that finishes a race, etc 跑完赛程等的人或动物.

□ **ˈfinishing school** private (usu expensive) school where girls are taught how to behave in fashionable society 精修学校(教导女子在上流社会中仪态举止的私立学校, 通常学费极昂贵).

fin·ished /ˈfɪnɪʃt; ˋfɪnɪʃt/ *adj* **1** [pred 作表语] **~ (with sb/sth)** (*infml* 口) in a state of having completed sth or no longer dealing with sb/sth 完成某事物; 不再与某人[某事物]有联系: *I won't be finished for another hour.* 我还有一个小时才能完事. ○ *I'm not finished with you yet.* 我和你还有事未完. ○ *She decided she was finished with working for others.* 她决定不再为别人做事. **2** [pred 作表语] no longer effective; ruined 不再有效; 毁灭了: *The scandal means he's finished in politics.* 这一丑闻意味着他在政治上已身败名裂. ○ *Everything is finished between her and him.* 她和他已一刀两断了. **3** [usu attrib 通常作定语] made; completed 制造好的; 完成的: *the finished product, article, etc* 制成品、物件等.

fi·nite /ˈfaɪnaɪt; ˋfaɪnaɪt/ *adj* **1** having bounds; limited; not infinite 有限的; 有限制的; 有限度的: *Human knowledge is finite,* ie There are things we do not know. 人类的认识是有限的. **2** (*grammar*) of a verb form that agrees with its subject in person and number 限定的(在人称和数上与主语一致的动词形式的): *'Am', 'is', 'are', 'was' and 'were' are the finite forms of 'be'; 'be', 'being' and 'been' are the non-finite forms.* ☆ am、is、are、was、were是动词be的限定形式; be、being、been是非限定形式.

fink /fɪŋk; fɪŋk/ *n* (*US sl derog* 俚, 贬) **1** person who gives information to the police about criminals (向警方)通报罪犯情况的人. **2** person who continues to work while others are on strike 工贼(罢工时仍继续工作的人). **3** unpleasant or contemptible person 讨厌的人; 可鄙的人.

Finn /fɪn; fɪn/ *n* native of Finland 芬兰人.

▷ **Finn·ish** *n* [U] language of the Finns 芬兰语. — *adj* of the Finns or their language 芬兰人的; 芬兰语的.

fin·nan /ˈfɪnən; ˋfɪnən/ *n* (also ˌ**finnan ˈhaddock**) type of smoked haddock 熏鳕鱼.

fiord (also **fjord**) /fjɔːd; fjɔrd/ *n* long narrow inlet of the sea between high cliffs, as in Norway 峡湾(在悬崖峭壁之间的狭长海湾, 如挪威的).

fir /fɜː(r); fɝ/ *n* **1** [C] (also ˈ**fir-tree**) type of evergreen tree with leaves like needles on its shoots 枞; 冷杉. **2** [U] wood of this tree 此种树的木材.

□ ˈ**fir-cone** *n* fruit of the fir-tree 冷杉的球果.

fire[1] /ˈfaɪə(r); faɪr/ *n* **1** [U] burning that produces light and heat 火; 火焰; 燃烧: *man's discovery of fire* 人类对火的发现. **2** (**a**) [U] destructive burning 火灾; 失火: *Have you insured your house against fire?* 你的房子保火险了没有? (**b**) [C] instance of this 火灾; 失火: *forest fires* 森林火灾 ○ *a fire in the warehouse* 仓库失火. **3** (**a**) [C] burning fuel in a grate, furnace, etc for cooking food or heating a room 炉火: *make/build a fire* 生火 ○ *lay a fire,* ie put paper, wood, etc together for a fire, usu in a grate 准备生火 ○ *a blazing/roaring fire* 炽烈的[熊熊的]火. (**b**) [C] apparatus for heating rooms, etc 取暖装置: *a gas/electric fire* 煤气[电]暖炉. Cf 参看 HEATER (HEAT[2]), STOVE 2. **4** [U] shooting from guns 开火(枪炮的射击): *The soldiers kept up a steady fire.* 士兵们不停地射击. ○ *return sb's fire,* ie shoot back at sb 用枪炮向某人还击. **5** [U] strong emotion; angry or excited feeling; enthusiasm 激情; 愤怒或激动的感情; 热情: *His speech lacked fire,* ie was uninspiring. 他的讲话缺乏热情. **6** (idm 习语) **a ball of fire** ⇨ BALL[1]. **a baptism of fire** ⇨ BAPTISM. **between two ˈfires** being shot at from two directions 腹背受敌(受到两面夹攻). **catch fire** ⇨ CATCH[1]. **draw sb's fire** ⇨ DRAW[2]. **the fat is in the fire** ⇨ FAT[2]. ˌ**fire and ˈbrimstone** torture suffered in Hell as a result of God's anger 因触怒上帝在地狱中遭受的煎熬: (*fig* 比喻) *She was breathing fire and brimstone,* ie was furiously angry. 她火冒三丈. ˌ**fire and ˈsword** (*fml* 文) burning and killing, esp in war 杀人放火(尤指于战争中). **get on like a house on fire** ⇨ HOUSE[1]. **go through** ˌ**fire and ˈwater (for sb/sth)** endure great hardship and danger (for sb/sth) (为某人[某事物])冒极大危险及忍受巨大苦难, 赴汤蹈火. **hang fire** ⇨ HANG[1]. **have, etc many irons in the fire** ⇨ IRON[1]. **heap coals of fire on sb's head** ⇨ HEAP *v*. **hold one's ˈfire** stop shooting (for a period of time) 停止射击(一段时间) **make up a ˈfire** add wood, coal, etc to a fire to make it burn more strongly 在火上加木柴、煤等使其燃烧更旺. **no smoke without fire** ⇨ SMOKE[1]. **on ˈfire** (**a**) burning 燃烧: *The house is on fire!* 房子着火了! (**b**) (*fig* 比喻) burning with emotion, passion or sensation 感情激动的; 激情冲动的. **open fire** ⇨ OPEN[2]. **out of the frying-pan into the fire** ⇨ FRYING-PAN (FRY[1]). **play with ˈfire** take foolish and dangerous risks 玩火(进行愚蠢的冒险). **set fire to sth/set sth on fire** cause sth to start burning 使某物开始燃烧; 放火. **(not/never) set the ˈThames** /temz; tɛmz/ **on fire** (not) do sth remarkable (不)做惊人之举: *He's a good student, but he won't ever set the Thames on fire.* 他是好学生, 但也绝成不了大器. **set the world on fire** ⇨ WORLD. **under ˈfire** (**a**) being shot at 遭到射击: *come under intense fire* 受到枪炮猛烈攻击. (**b**) (*fig* 比喻) being criticized severely 受到严厉批评: *The government is under fire from all sides on its economic policy.* 政府在经济政策上受到各方的严厉批评.

□ ˈ**fire-alarm** *n* bell or other device that gives warning of a fire; sound made by this 火警报警器; 火警警报.

ˈ**firearm** *n* (usu *pl* 通常作复数) portable gun of any sort, eg a rifle, revolver, etc (便携式)枪枝(如步枪、左轮手枪等): *carry firearms* 携带枪枝.

ˈ**fire-ball** *n* **1** large bright meteor 火流星. **2** centre of an atomic explosion 原子弹爆炸的中心. **3** (*fig* 比喻) very energetic person 精力极充沛的人.

ˈ**fire-bomb** *n* bomb that burns fiercely after it explodes, causing destruction by fire; incendiary 燃烧弹.

ˈ**fire-box** *n* place where fuel is burned in a steam-engine or boiler (蒸气机或锅炉内燃料的)燃烧室.

ˈ**firebrand** *n* **1** piece of burning wood 燃烧的木块. **2** (*fig* 比喻) person who causes (esp social or political) trouble 引起(尤指社会的或政治的)动乱的人.

ˈ**fire-break** *n* strip of land cleared of trees to stop fire from spreading in a forest (森林中除掉树木以防止森林火蔓延的)防火带, 防火线.

ˈ**fire-brick** *n* type of brick made to withstand great heat, used in building grates, furnaces, chimneys, etc 耐火砖; 火砖.

ˈ**fire brigade** (*US* ˈ**fire department**) organized team of people trained and employed to extinguish fires 消防队; 消防处: *call out the fire brigade* 召唤消防队来.

ˈ**fire-clay** *n* [U] type of clay used to make fire-bricks 耐火黏土(制做耐火砖用的).

ˈ**firecracker** *n* (*esp US*) small firework that explodes with a cracking noise 鞭炮; 爆竹.

ˈ**firedamp** (also **damp**) *n* [U] gas in coal-mines, explosive when mixed in certain proportions with air; methane (煤矿中与一定比例的空气混合的)瓦斯; 沼气; 甲烷.

ˈ**firedog** *n* = ANDIRON.

ˈ**fire-drill** *n* [C, U] (practice of) what people must do to escape safely from a burning building, ship, etc 消防演习.

ˈ**fire-eater** *n* **1** person who appears to swallow fire as part of an entertainment act 表演吞火的人. **2** person who easily becomes angry or quarrelsome 易怒的人; 爱吵架的人.

ˈ**fire-engine** (also **appliance**) *n* special vehicle carrying equipment for fighting large fires 消防车.

ˈ**fire-escape** *n* special staircase or apparatus by which people may escape from a burning building, etc 可借以逃离火场的太平梯或机械装置.

'**fire extinguisher** (also **extinguisher**) portable metal container with water or a chemical mixture inside for putting out small fires 灭火器.

'**fire-fighter** *n* person who fights (esp forest) fires 消防人员(尤指护林的).

'**firefly** *n* type of winged insect that glows in the dark 萤火虫.

'**fire-guard** *n* protective metal frame or grating round a fire in a room (室内取暖炉的)炉挡.

'**fire-irons** *n* [pl] tools used for tending a fire, usu kept near the fireplace, eg poker, tongs, shovel, etc 火炉用具(如通条、火钳、铲子等).

'**firelight** *n* [U] light from a fire in a fireplace 壁炉发出的火光: *sitting in the firelight* 坐在壁炉周围.

'**fire-lighter** *n* [C, U] (piece of) inflammable material used to help start a fire in a grate 用于引火的易燃材料; 引火物.

'**fireman** /-mən; -mən/ *n* (*pl* **-men** /-mən; -mən/) **1** member of a fire brigade 消防队员. **2** person who tends the fire in a furnace, steam-engine, etc (熔炉、蒸气机等的)司炉工.

'**fireplace** *n* open space for a fire in a room, usu made of brick or stone and set into a wall 壁炉.

'**fire-plug** *n* (*esp US*) connection in a water-main for a fireman's hose; hydrant 消防栓.

'**fire-power** *n* [U] capacity to destroy, measured by the number and size of guns available 火力.

'**fireproof** *adj* that can resist great heat without burning, cracking or breaking 防火的; 耐火的: *a fireproof wall, door, etc* 防火墙、门等. — *v* [Tn] make (sth) fireproof 使(某物)防火.

'**fire-raising** *n* [U] deliberately setting fire to property, etc; arson 放火; 纵火. '**fire-raiser** *n*.

'**fireside** *n* (usu *sing* 通常作单数) part of a room beside the fireplace 壁炉旁: *sitting at the fireside* 坐在壁炉旁 ○ [attrib 作定语] *a fireside chair* 壁炉旁的椅子.

'**fire station** building for a fire brigade and its equipment 消防站.

'**fire-walking** *n* [U] (usu religious) ceremony of walking barefoot over very hot stones, ashes, etc as an act of faith 渡火(赤脚在灼热的石头、炭灰等之上行走, 通常为宗教仪式). '**fire-walker** *n*.

'**fire-watcher** *n* person who watches for fires, esp those caused by bombs during war 火灾警戒员(尤指空袭时的).

'**fire-water** *n* [U] (*infml* 口) strong alcoholic drink, eg whisky, gin, etc 烈酒(如威士忌、杜松子酒等).

'**firewood** *n* [U] wood used for lighting fires or as fuel 木柴.

'**firework** *n* [C] device containing chemicals that burn or explode spectacularly, used at celebrations or as a signal (庆典用或作信号用的)烟火: *set off* (ie explode) *a few fireworks* 燃放几个烟火. **2** '**fireworks** [pl] (**a**) display of fireworks 烟火表演. (**b**) (*fig* 比喻) display of anger, wit, etc 愤怒、机智等的表现: *Just you watch the fireworks when your father catches those boys!* 等你父亲抓住那几个男孩子的时候, 你就能看到他的火气有多大了!

fire[2] /'faɪə(r); faɪr/ *v* **1** [I, Ipr, Tn, Tn·pr] **~ (sth) (at sb/sth); ~ (sth) into sth** shoot with a gun (at sb/sth); shoot (a bullet) from a gun; shoot a bullet from (a gun) 用枪炮(向某人[某物])射击; 从枪中射出(子弹); 从(枪)中射出子弹: *'Fire!' ordered the captain.* '开火!'上尉命令道. ○ *The officer ordered his men to fire (at the enemy).* 军官命令士兵(向敌人)射击. ○ *The police fired (several rubber bullets) into the crowd.* 警察向人群射击(数发橡皮子弹). ○ *This weapon fires anti-aircraft missiles.* 这种武器是发射防空导弹的. ○ *He fired several shots (at the target).* 他向目标射出了几发子弹. ○ *fire (a pistol) into the air* (用手枪)向天空开枪 ○ *fire a 21-gun salute,* ie fire 21 shots from guns into the air as a sign of respect in a ceremony 鸣放21响礼炮. **2** [Tn·pr] **~ sth at sb** address (words) in quick succession at sb 对某人急速地连续说(话): *fire insults, questions, ideas, etc at sb* 对某人像发连珠炮似的说侮辱的话、提出问题、看法等. **3** [Tn] (*infml* 口) dismiss (an employee) from a job 解雇, 开除(雇员): *He was fired for stealing money from the till.* 他因从柜台抽屉偷钱而遭解雇. **4** [Tn] ignite or set fire to (sth) with the aim of destroying it (为焚毁)点火或纵火烧(某物): *fire a haystack* 点燃草堆. **5** [I] (of the explosive mixture in an engine) ignite (指发动机内的可燃气体混合物)点火; 发动: *The engine will not fire.* 这发动机发动不起来. ○ *The engine is only firing on three cylinders.* 这发动机只有三个汽缸工作. **6** [Tn, Tn·pr] **~ sb with sth; ~ sb into sth/doing sth** stimulate (the imagination); fill sb with (a strong emotion); inspire or excite sb to do sth 激发(想像力); 使某人充满(激情); 鼓励或鼓动某人做某事物: *Adventure stories fired his imagination.* 冒险小说激发起他的想像力. ○ *fire sb with enthusiasm, longing, desire, etc* 以热情、渴望、欲望等激励某人 ○ *The party leader's rousing speech fired the members into action.* 该党领袖令人振奋的讲话激发了党员行动起来. **7** [Tn] heat (an object made of clay) in an oven in order to harden and strengthen it (在窑内)烧制(陶瓷制品): *fire pottery, bricks, etc in a kiln* 在窑内烧陶瓷、砖瓦等. **8** (idm 习语) **working/firing on all cylinders** ⇨ CYLINDER. **9** (phr v) **fire away** (usu as a command 通常作命令语) (*infml* 口) begin asking questions; begin to speak 开始问问题; 开始说话: *'I've got a couple of questions I'd like to ask you.' 'Right, fire away.'* '我有几个问题想问你.' '好, 你说吧.' **fire sth off** shoot (a bullet) from a gun 从枪中射出(子弹): *fire off a few rounds, all one's ammunition, etc* 射出几发子弹、所有的弹药等.

▷ **-fired** (forming compound *adjs* 用以构成复合形容词) supplied by or using the specified fuel 使用某种燃料的: *gas-fired central heating* ○ *a coal-fired power station.*

fir·ing /'faɪərɪŋ; 'faɪrɪŋ/ *n* **1** [U] action of firing guns 开火; 开枪; 开炮; 射击: *There was continous firing to our left.* 在我们左翼有连续的射击. **2** [C, U] (act of) firing (FIRE[2] 7) a clay object (黏土制物的)焙烧: *It will take several firings to clear the shelves of all these pots.* 把这些架上的陶罐全都烧好要烧好几窑.

□ '**firing-line** *n* **1** front line of battle, nearest the enemy 火线(离敌人最近的前沿地带). **2** (idm 习语) **be in the 'firing line** be subject to criticism, blame, etc because of one's responsibilities or position (由于所负的责任或所处的地位)易受到批评、责备等: *She'll have to be careful now — she's directly in the firing-line of the new director.* 现在她要格外小心了 —— 她正在新主任的眼皮底下工作.

'**firing-squad** *n* [CGp] group of soldiers ordered to shoot a condemned person 行刑队(对判处死刑的犯人执行枪决的士兵): *He was sentenced to death by firing-squad.* 他被判枪决.

firm[1] /fɜːm; fɝm/ *adj* (**-er, -est**) **1** (**a**) not yielding when pressed; fairly hard 坚实的; 结实的; 坚硬的: *This wet ground is not firm enough to walk on.* 这块湿地不够坚实, 不能在上面走. ○ *firm soil* 坚硬的土壤 ○ *a firm cushion, mattress, sofa, etc* 结实的坐垫、床垫、沙发等 ○ *firm flesh/muscles* 结实的肌肉. (**b**) strongly fixed in place; secure or solid 牢固的; 稳固的; 坚固的: *firm foundations* 坚固的基础 ○ *a firm foothold* 稳固的立足点 ○ *firm concrete fencing* 坚固的混凝土围墙材料. **2** (of a movement) steady and strong; not weak or uncertain (指动作)稳定而有力的: *a firm handshake, grip, hold, etc* 有力的握手、紧抓、紧握. **3** not subject to change; definite 不易改变的; 肯定的; 坚定的: *a firm belief/believer in socialism* 对社会主义的坚定的信念[拥护者] ○ *a firm decision, date, arrangement, offer* 不改变的决定、确定的日期、不更改的排列方式、实盘 ○ *firm opinions, convictions, principles, etc* 坚定的意见、信念、原则等 ○ *firm news, evidence, information, etc* 可靠的新闻、证据、信息等 ○ *'Burnside' is the firm favourite to win the race,* ie the horse that is confidently expected to win. '伯恩赛德'是肯定会获胜的热门马. **4 ~ (with sb)** strong and consistent in attitude and behaviour; not easily persuaded to change one's mind; decisive 坚定的; 坚决的: *Parents must be firm with their children.* 父母对孩子一定要严格. ○ *exercise firm leadership, control, discipline, etc* 实行坚决的领导、严格的控制、严格的纪律等 ○ *'I don't want to be unkind,' he said in a firm voice.* '我不想发狠心,'他以坚定的口吻说. **5** [usu pred 通常作表语] **~ (against sth)** not lower than another currency, etc and possibly about to rise in price 稳定, 坚挺(不低于其他货币等而且有可能升值的): *The pound remained firm against the dollar, but fell against the yen.* 英镑对美元保持稳定, 但对日元则疲软. **6** (idm 习语)

be on firm 'ground be sure of one's facts; be secure in one's position, esp in a discussion 对事实确信无疑; 立场坚定(尤指在讨论中). **a firm 'hand** strong discipline or control 严明的纪律; 牢固控制: *That boy needs a firm hand to help him grow up.* 那个男孩需要严加管教才能有所长进. **have, etc a firm/tight hold on sth** ⇨ HOLD².

▷ **firm** *v* **1** [I, Ip, Tn, Tn·p] **~ (sth) (up)** (cause sth to) become firm (使某物)变得坚实、稳固: *firm (up) soil* 把土地弄得坚实. **2** (phr v) **firm sth up** (**a**) put sth into a final fixed form 使某物最后达到固定的形式或状态: *firm up a contract, deal, agreement, etc* 使合同、交易、协议等达成最后形式. (**b**) make (part of the body) firmer and less fatty 使(身体某部)更结实, 脂肪少: *Exercise will firm up your muscles.* 锻炼身体能使肌肉结实.

firm *adv* (idm 习语) **hold firm to sth** not abandon a principle, theory, etc 不放弃原则、理论等: *hold firm to one's beliefs, ideals, principles, etc* 坚持自己的信仰、理想、原则等. **stand fast/firm** ⇨ FAST².

firmly *adv* in a firm way 坚实地; 结实地; 坚固地; 稳固地; 坚定地; 稳定地: *The fence posts were fixed firmly in the ground.* 栅栏的立柱牢牢地固定在地上. ○ *The business was soon firmly established in the town.* 该商店不久即在城里稳固地建立起来. ○ *The suggestion was politely but firmly rejected by the chairman.* 主席婉言而果断地回绝了该建议.

firm·ness *n* [U].

firm² /fɜːm; fɝm/ *n* [CGp] (*esp infml* 尤作口语) business company 公司; 商行; 商号: *a firm of accountants* 会计师事务所 ○ *our firm has/have made 200 workers redundant* 我们公司已裁减200名雇员.

F

firma·ment /ˈfɜːməmənt; ˈfɝməmənt/ *n* **the firmament** [sing] (*arch* 古) the sky 天空; 苍天.

first¹ /fɜːst; fɝst/ *det* **1** (**a**) 1st; coming before all others in time, order, importance, etc 第一的; 最初的; 最早的; 最先的; 首要的: *the first public performance of the play* 该剧的首次公演 ○ *his first wife* 他的第一个妻子 ○ *their first baby* 他们的第一个孩子 ○ *her first job* 她的第一份工作 ○ *students in their first year at college* 学院一年级学生 ○ *at first light*, ie dawn 黎明 ○ *at the first* (ie earliest) *opportunity* 一有机会 ○ *the first signs that winter is approaching* 冬天来临的最初迹象 ○ *one's first impression/reaction* 最初的印象[反应] ○ *She won first prize in the competition.* 她在竞赛中获一等奖. ○ *King Edward I* (ie said as 'King Edward the First') 英王爱德华一世 ○ *go back to first* (ie basic) *principles* 回到基本的原则上 ○ *of the first importance* 最重要的 ○ *the first violins*, ie in an orchestra 第一小提琴手(管弦乐队中的) ○ *Your first duty is to your family.* 你的首要责任是照顾家庭. (**b**) never having happened or been experienced before 初次的: *It was the first time they had ever met.* 那是他们初次会面. ○ *his first real taste of success* 他对成功的初次真实感受. Cf 参看 LAST¹ 1. ⇨App 4 见附录4. **2** (idm 习语) **first/last/next but one, two, three, etc**: *Take the first turning but one* (ie the second turning) *on your left.* 在第二个路口向左转. ○ *I live in the last house but two* (ie the third house from the end) *in this street.* 我住在这条街上倒数第三座房子里. **first/last thing** ⇨ THING. **ˌfirst things 'first** (*saying* 谚) the most important or necessary duties or concerns must be dealt with before others 最重要的事要先做. (For other idioms containing **first**, see the entries for the other major words in each idiom 查阅含有**first**一词的其他习语, 见这类习语中含有其他主要词的词条, 如 **at first glance/sight** ⇨ GLANCE; **not have the first idea about sth** ⇨ IDEA.)

▷ **firstly** *adv* (in giving a list) to begin with (用于列举事项)首先, 第一: *The illness can develop in two ways: firstly, in cases of high blood pressure and secondly...* 这种病有两种情况: 第一, 由高血压引起; 第二....

□ **ˌfirst 'aid** treatment given to an injured person before a doctor comes 急救.

ˌfirst 'balcony = DRESS CIRCLE (DRESS).

ˌfirst 'base **1** first of the bases (BASE¹ 6) that must be touched in a game of baseball (棒球运动中的)一垒. **2** (idm 习语) **not get to first base (with sth)** (*infml* 口 *esp US*) not make a successful start (in a project); not even achieve the first step 不能顺利开始(一项计划); 连第一步也迈不出.

ˌfirst 'class **1** most comfortable accommodation in a train, ship, etc (火车、船等的)头等: *Smoking is not allowed in first class.* 头等舱中不准吸烟. ○ [attrib 作定语] *first-class carriages, compartments, seats, etc* 头等的车厢、车室、座位等. **2** class of mail most quickly delivered 第一类邮件(快件): *First class costs 5p more.* 第一类邮件贵5便士. ○ [attrib 作定语] *A first-class letter should arrive the following day.* 按第一类邮件投递的信应于次日到达. ○ *Ten first-class stamps, please.* 请来十张快信邮票. **3** in the best group or highest category; excellent 第一流的; 最好的; 最优的: *The entertainment provided was first class.* 提供的招待是一流的. ○ [attrib 作定语] *They can afford to eat at first-class restaurants.* 他们去得起一流的饭店. ○ *She got first-class results in her exams.* 她的考试成绩优异. ○ *They're first-class people — you'll like them.* 他们是大好人——你会喜欢他们的. — *adv* by the best or quickest form of transport or mail 以最好的和最快的方式运输或邮寄: *travel first class* 乘头等车[船/飞机]旅行 ○ *I sent the letter first class on Monday.* 星期一我已把信用快递寄出.

ˌfirst 'cousin = COUSIN.

ˌfirst-day 'cover envelope with a set of special stamps postmarked on the first day of issue 首日封.

ˌfirst de'gree least serious of three categories of murder or burn 第一级的, 第一度的(谋杀或烧伤、烫伤的三级分类中的最轻者): *He was charged with murder of the first degree/first-degree murder.* 他被控告一级谋杀罪. ○ *Hot coffee can give first-degree burns.* 热咖啡能造成一度烫伤.

'first finger finger next to the thumb; index finger 食指.

ˌfirst 'floor (usu 通常作 **the first floor**) **1** (*Brit*) floor immediately above the floor on ground level 二楼: [attrib 作定语] *a first-floor 'flat* 二楼的一套公寓. **2** (*US*) floor on ground level 一楼. ⇨ Usage at FLOOR¹ 用法见FLOOR¹.

ˌfirst-'footing *n* [U] (esp Scottish) custom or practice of waiting for the first person to enter a house in the New Year before celebrations can begin (尤指苏格兰的)等候进屋的第一个人以开始庆祝新年的习俗.

'first-fruit *n* (usu *pl* 通常作复数) **1** earliest agricultural produce, crops, etc of the season 一个季节中最早收获的农产品等. **2** (*fig* 比喻) first results of sb's work or efforts 某人工作或努力的最初成果.

ˌfirst 'gear lowest gear on a car, bicycle, etc 汽车、自行车等的最低挡.

ˌfirst'hand *adj* [attrib 作定语], *adv* gained or coming directly from the original source 第一手(的); 直接从来源处得到(的): *firsthand infor'mation* 第一手信息 ○ *experience sth firsthand* 亲身经历某事.

ˌfirst 'lady **1 the First Lady** (*US*) wife of the President of the USA; wife of a state governor 总统夫人; 州长夫人. **2** (usu *sing* 通常作单数) leading woman in a specified activity or profession 某活动或行业中首屈一指的女性: *recognized as the first lady of romantic fiction* 公认为浪漫主义小说的主要女作家.

'first name personal name or names given to sb at his birth, usu coming before a surname or family name 名字, 教名(通常置于姓前): *Mrs Thatcher's first name is Margaret.* 撒切尔夫人的名字叫玛格丽特. ○ [attrib 作定语] *We are all on first-name terms with our boss*, ie We call him by his first name (a sign of a friendly informal relationship). 我们和老板都以名相称(不冠姓, 显示关系密切不拘束). ⇨ Usage at NAME¹ 用法见NAME¹. Cf 参看 FORENAME, GIVEN NAME (GIVEN), CHRISTIAN NAME (CHRISTIAN).

ˌfirst 'night first public performance of a play, film, etc; opening night (戏剧、电影等的)首场演出, 首映夜场: *the first night of 'The Sound of Music'* '音乐之声'(又译'仙乐飘飘处处闻')首映夜场 ○ [attrib 作定语] *suffer from first-night 'nerves* 首演怯场.

ˌfirst of'fender person who has been found guilty of a crime for the first time 初犯.

'first officer officer second in command to a captain on a merchant ship (商船上的)大副.

the ˌfirst 'person **1** (*grammar*) set of pronouns and verb forms used by a speaker to refer to himself 第一人称代词和动词的搭配形式: *'I am' is the first person*

singular of the present tense of the verb 'to be'. I am是单数第一人称代词和动词to be的搭配形式. ○ [attrib 作定语] *'I', 'me', 'we' and 'us' are first-person pronouns.* I、me、we、us都是第一人称的代词. **2** style of story-telling in which the author writes or speaks as if telling the story personally 用第一人称叙述的文体: *Hemingway often writes in the first person.* 海明威常用第一人称写作.
ˌ**first-rate** *adj* excellent; of the best quality 第一流的; 优良的; 质量最佳的: *a ˌfirst-rate ˈmeal* 最好的饭菜 ○ *The food here is first-rate.* 这里的食品是第一流的. — *adv* in very good health; very fit 非常健康; 身体好: *feel first-rate* 身体极好.
first refusal right of deciding whether to accept or refuse sth before it is offered to others 优先取舍权(有先于他人对某事物取舍的权利): *If you ever decide to sell your car, I hope you'll give me (the) first refusal.* 你要是决定把汽车卖掉, 我希望你先让我考虑要不要, 我不要你再卖给别人.
ˈ**first school** (in Britain) school for children between the ages of 5 and 8 or 9 (英国)第一学校(5岁至8、9岁之间的儿童上的学校).
the ˌFirst World ˈWar (also **World War I**) the major international war of 1914-18, fought mainly in Europe 第一次世界大战(1914-1918).

first[2] /fɜːst; fɝst/ *adv* **1** (**a**) before anyone or anything else; at the beginning 第一; 最初; 最先: *Susan came into the room first.* 苏珊第一个来到屋子里. ○ *Who came first in the race?* ie Who won? 谁赛跑得第一? ○ *Ladies first,* ie said by a man, allowing a woman to enter a room, car, etc before he does. 女士先请(男子请女子先进屋、先上车等时说的话). (**b**) before another event or time 先; 首先: *First I had to decide what to wear.* 首先我得决定穿什么衣服. ○ *Think first, then act.* 先想清楚再行动. ○ *'Have some tea.' 'I'll finish my work first.'* '喝点茶吧.' '我先把工作做完再说.' Cf 参看 LAST[2]. **2** for the first time 第一次; 首次: *When did you first meet him?* 你第一次见他是什么时候? ○ *The play was first performed in Paris.* 此剧首次在巴黎公演. ○ *When he first arrived in this country, he couldn't speak any English.* 他刚到这个国家时, 一句英语也不会说. **3** (in giving a list) to begin with (用于列举事项)第一, 首先: *This method has two advantages: first it is cheaper and second(ly) it is quicker.* 这个方法有两个优点: 一是较便宜, 二是较迅速. ⇨ Usage 见所附用法. **4** in preference to sth else 宁愿; 宁可: *He said he'd resign first,* eg rather than compromise his principles. 他说他宁愿辞职(例如也不愿在原则上妥协). **5** (idm 习语) **at ˈfirst** at or in the beginning; initially 起初; 当初: *At first I thought he was shy, but then I discovered he was just not interested in other people.* 起初我还以为他很腼腆, 后来我才发觉他是不爱理人. ○ (*saying* 谚) *If at first you don't succeed, try, try again.* 一次不成功, 那就再接再厉地干下去. **come ˈfirst** be considered as more important than anything else 首先要考虑到的: *You know that your wife and children come first.* 你要知道首先要考虑的是你的妻子儿女. ˌ**first and ˈforemost** more than anything else; firstly and most importantly 比什么都重要; 首要的: *He does a bit of writing, but first and foremost he's a teacher.* 他也写一些文章, 但他主要是个教师. ˌ**first and ˈlast** (*fml* 文) taking everything into account; completely 考虑到一切因素; 完全地: *He was a real gentleman, first and last.* 从各方面来看, 他都是个正人君子. ˌ**first ˈcome, ˌfirst ˈserved** (*saying* 谚) people will be dealt with, seen, etc strictly in order of their arrival or application 先来后到. ˌ**first of ˈall** before (doing) anything else; initially; most importantly 首先; 最初; 首要: *First of all she just smiled, then she started to laugh.* 最初她只是微笑, 后来才放声大笑. ○ *Well, first of all we can't possibly spare the time.* 你看, 最主要的是我们实在抽不出时间. **first ˈoff** (*infml* 口) before anything else 首先: *First off, let's see how much it'll cost.* 首先, 让我们看看要花多少钱. **head first** ⇨ HEAD[1]. **last in, first out** ⇨ LAST[2]. **put sb/sth ˈfirst** consider sb/sth to be more important than anyone/anything else 把某人[某事物]放在首位: *put one's career, reputation, children first* 把事业、名誉、儿女放在首位. **see sb in hell first** ⇨ HELL.
□ ˈ**first-born** *n, adj* [attrib 作定语] (*dated* 旧) (child) born before other children; eldest (孩子中)头生的; 长子或长女: *their first-born son* 他们的长子.

NOTE ON USAGE 用法: When ordering items in a list, **first(ly), second(ly), third(ly),** etc are put at the beginning of the sentence or clause. 在列举项目时, 要将**first(ly)**、**second(ly)**、**third(ly)**等词置于句子或从句之首. They are usually followed by a comma. 在这些词后面通常用逗号. Some speakers prefer **first** to **firstly** 有些人说话时愿用**first**而不用**firstly**: *There are three reasons for my resignation. First(ly), I am dissatisfied with my wages; secondly, the hours are too long; and thirdly, there is little chance of promotion.* 我辞职有三个原因. 一是我对工资不满意; 二是工作时间太长; 三是几乎没有晋升机会. Alternatively, **first, second, third,** etc could be used. 在上述这类句子中也可使用**first**、**second**、**third**等.

first[3] /fɜːst; fɝst/ *n, pron* **1 the first** first person or thing mentioned or occurring (提到的或出现的)第一个人或事物: *Sheila was the first to arrive.* 希拉是第一个到达的. ○ *I'm the first in my family to go to university.* 我是我们家第一个上大学的. ○ *I'd be the first to admit* (ie I will most willingly admit) *I might be wrong.* 我愿第一个承认我可能错了. ○ *The first I heard about the firm closing down* (ie The first time I became aware of it) *was when George told me.* 我最初听到公司倒闭的消息是乔治告诉我的. **2** [C] (*infml* 口) notable achievement, event, etc never done or experienced before (以前从未有过的)显著成就、事件等: *a real first for the German team* 德国队的创举. **3** [C] **~ (in sth)** (*Brit*) university degree of the highest class (大学学位的)最高成绩, 优等: *She got a first in maths at Exeter.* 她在埃克塞特大学数学系毕业, 获一级荣誉学位. **4** [U] lowest gear on a car, bicycle, etc (汽车, 自行车等的)最低挡: *go up the hill in first gear* 挂一挡上山坡. **5** (idm 习语) **from the (very) ˈfirst** from the beginning 一开始: *I found the idea attractive from the first, and now I'm convinced its the only solution.* 一开始我就感到这主意很不错, 现在我深信这是唯一的解决方法. **from ˌfirst to ˈlast** from beginning to end; throughout 自始至终; 始终; 一贯.

firth /fɜːθ; fɝθ/ *n* (esp in Scotland) narrow inlet of the sea; part of a river when it flows into the sea (尤指苏格兰的)狭窄的海湾, 河流的入海口.

fiscal /ˈfɪskl; ˈfɪskl/ *adj* of or related to government money or public money, usu taxes 国库的; 公款的; (通常指)岁入的; 财政的: *the government's fiscal policy* 政府的财政政策.
□ **fiscal year** (*US*) = FINANCIAL YEAR (FINANCIAL).

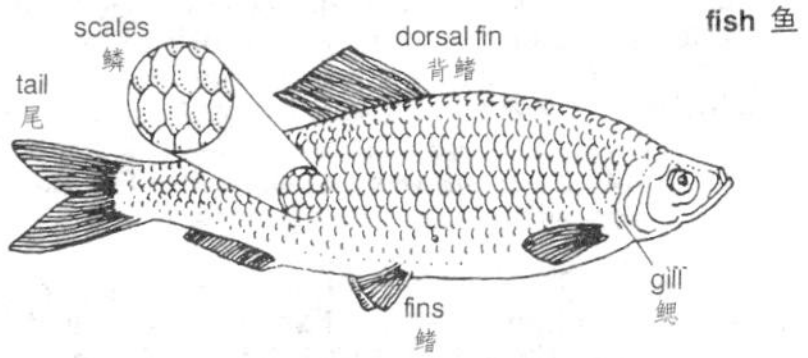

fish 鱼

fish[1] /fɪʃ; fɪʃ/ *n* (*pl* unchanged or **~es** 复数或不变或作 **fishes**) ⇨Usage 见所附用法. **1** [C] cold-blooded animal living in water and breathing through gills, with fins and a tail for swimming 鱼: *They caught several fish.* 他们捉到几条鱼. ○ *fishes, frogs and crabs* 鱼、青蛙和螃蟹 ⇨illus 见插图. **2** [U] flesh of fish eaten as food 鱼肉: *frozen, smoked, fresh, etc fish* 冻鱼、熏鱼、鲜鱼 ○ *boiled, fried, grilled, etc fish* 煮鱼、炸鱼、烤鱼 ○ *Fish was served after the first course.* 第一道菜之后就上了鱼. **3** (idm 习语) **a big fish** ⇨ BIG. **a cold fish** ⇨ COLD[1]. **a different kettle of fish** ⇨ DIFFERENT. **drink like a fish** ⇨ DRINK[2]. **a fine, etc kettle of fish** ⇨ KETTLE. **a ˌfish out of ˈwater** person who feels uncomfortable or awkward because he is in unfamiliar surroundings 离开水的鱼(因环境不熟悉而感到不舒服或尴尬的人): *With my working-class background I feel like a fish out of water among these high-society people.* 我出身于工人阶级, 在上流社会中感到很不自在. **have ˈbigger/ˈother fish to fry** have more important, interesting, etc things to do 另有要事或有兴趣的事要做. **neither fish, flesh nor**

good red herring (*saying* 谚) difficult to identify or classify; vague; ambiguous 难以识别或分类的; 非驴非马的; 不伦不类的. **an 'odd/a 'queer fish** (*infml* 口) eccentric person; person whom others find hard to understand 古怪的人; 难以理解的人: *He's a bit of an odd fish — he's never been out of his house for years.* 他这个人很古怪 —— 多年来深居简出. **play a 'fish** (when fishing with a rod and line) allow a fish to exhaust itself by forcing it to pull against the line (钓鱼时)让鱼拉钓线使之疲乏. **there are (plenty of) 'other fish in the sea; there are (plenty) 'more (good) fish in the sea** there are many other people/things that are as good as the one that has proved unsuccessful 海里的鱼有的是(这个不成, 好的人[事物]还有很多).

▷ **fishy** *adj* (**-ier, -iest**) **1** of or like a fish, esp in smell or taste 鱼的; 鱼味的; 鱼腥味的: *a fishy smell* 鱼腥味. **2** (*infml* 口) causing a feeling of doubt or suspicion 可疑的; 引起怀疑的: *There's something rather fishy going on here.* 这里有些事不大对头.

□ **ˌfish and 'chips** fish fried in batter and eaten with fried potato chips 软炸鱼加炸土豆条: *Fish and chips is getting very expensive now.* 现在软炸鱼加炸土豆条越来越贵了.

'fish cake small flat cake of cooked fish and mashed potato, usu covered with breadcrumbs 鱼饼(鱼、土豆泥, 通常裹以面包屑制成的饼).

ˌfish-eye 'lens wide-angled lens with a distorting effect 鱼眼镜头; 超广角镜头.

'fish-farm *n* area of water used to breed fish artificially 养鱼场.

ˌfish 'finger (*US* **ˌfish 'stick**) small oblong piece of fish covered with breadcrumbs or batter 鱼条(裹着面包屑或面糊的长方形鱼肉条).

'fish-hook *n* barbed metal hook for catching fish 鱼钩. ⇨ illus at HOOK 见 HOOK 插图.

'fish-kettle *n* oval pan used for boiling fish 椭圆形煮鱼锅.

'fish-knife *n* blunt knife with a broad blade used for eating fish (吃鱼用的)餐刀.

'fishmonger /-ˌmʌŋgə(r); -ˌmʌŋgər/ *n* (*Brit*) person whose job it is to sell fish in a shop (商店的)鱼贩: *buy fish at the fishmonger's/from the fishmonger* 从鱼贩那里买鱼.

fish-net *n* **1** [C] net used for catching fish 鱼网. **2** [U] fabric made with small holes 网眼织物: [attrib 作定语] *fish-net tights* 鱼网状裤袜.

'fish-slice *n* kitchen tool consisting of a broad flat blade that has slits in it and is attached to a long handle, used for turning or lifting food when cooking 煎鱼铲(铲面上带有长孔). ⇨ illus at KITCHEN 见 KITCHEN 插图.

'fishwife *n* **1** woman who sells fish 卖鱼妇. **2** (*derog* 贬) nagging abusive person (usu a woman) 粗俗爱骂街的人(通常指女人): *She was screaming like a fishwife!* 她像泼妇一样尖叫!

NOTE ON USAGE 用法: **1 Fish** as a countable noun has two plural forms: **fish** and **fishes**. ☆ **fish** 一词作可数名词时有两个复数形式: **fish** 和 **fishes**. **1 Fish** is the more usual form, used when referring to a mass of them in the water to be caught or seen 较普通的形式是 **fish**, 指水中可捕捉或可看见的鱼: *The number of fish in coastal waters has decreased.* 沿海鱼的数量已减少了. ○ *A lot of fish were caught during the competition.* 在比赛中捉到很多鱼. **2 Fishes** is used to refer to different species of fish ☆ **fishes** 的形式是用以指鱼的不同品种: *He studies in particular the fishes of the Indian Ocean.* 他专门研究印度洋的鱼类.

fish[2] /fɪʃ; fɪʃ/ *v* **1** (**a**) [I, Ipr] **~ (for sth)** try to catch fish with hooks, nets, etc (用鱼钩、鱼网等)捕鱼: *I often fish/go fishing at weekends.* 我常在周末去钓鱼. ○ *fishing for salmon* 捕大马哈鱼. (**b**) [Tn] try to catch fish in (an area of water) 在(某水域)中捕鱼: *fish a river, lake, etc* 在河中、湖中等捕鱼. **2** [Ipr] **~ for sth** search for sth, esp in an area of water or a hidden place 寻找某物(尤指于某水域或隐蔽处): *fish for pearls* 采集珍珠 ○ *Fishing (around) in the bag for the keys.* 在袋子里摸找钥匙. **3** (idm 习语) **fish in troubled waters** try to gain advantages for oneself from a disturbed state of affairs 混水摸鱼. **4** (phr v) **fish for sth** try to gain sth by indirect methods 设法用间接手段得到某事物: *fish for compliments, information, praise* 拐弯抹角获得恭维、情报、赞扬. **fish sth out (of sth)** take or pull sth out (of sth) esp after searching for it 经搜寻后从(某物)中拖出或拉出某物: *Several old cars are fished out (of the canal) every month.* 每月都从运河中打捞出几辆旧汽车来. ○ *He fished a length of string out of his pocket.* 他从口袋里掏出一条绳子.

▷ **fish·ing** *n* [U] catching fish as a job, sport, or hobby 捕鱼(为生、为娱乐或为业余爱好的): *deep-sea fishing* 深海捕鱼 ○ *Fishing is still the main industry there.* 捕鱼业仍为那里的主要行业. ○ [attrib 作定语] *a fishing boat* 渔船 ○ *a fishing ground* 渔场. **'fishing-line** *n* line[1](9a) with a hook attached for catching fish (系有钓钩的)钓线, 钓丝. **'fishing-rod** *n* (*US* **'fishing pole**) long wooden or (jointed) metal rod with a fishing-line attached to it 钓竿. **'fishing-tackle** *n* [U] equipment used in fishing 渔具.

fish·er·man /'fɪʃəmən; 'fɪʃərmən/ *n* (*pl* **-men**) person who catches fish, esp as a job but also as a sport or hobby 渔民, 渔夫, 钓鱼人(尤指作为职业者, 但也可指作为运动、娱乐或爱好者). Cf 参看 ANGLER (ANGLE[2]).

fish·ery /'fɪʃərɪ; 'fɪʃərɪ/ *n* **1** (usu *pl* 通常作复数) part of the sea where fish are caught commercially 渔场(商业捕鱼海域): *offshore fisheries*, ie at some distance from the coast 近海渔场. **2** business or industry of fishing 渔业: *the Ministry of Agriculture, Fisheries and Food* 农业、渔业和粮食部.

fish-plate /'fɪʃpleɪt; 'fɪʃˌplet/ *n* flat piece of iron joining one length of railway line to the next 鱼尾板(用于连接铁轨的结合板).

fis·sile /'fɪsaɪl; *US* 'fɪsl; 'fɪsḷ/ *adj* (*fml* 文) **1** capable of undergoing nuclear fission 可进行核裂变的. **2** tending to split or divide 易裂的; 易分开的: *fissile wood* 易裂的木材.

fis·sion /'fɪʃn; 'fɪʃən/ *n* [U] **1** splitting of the nucleus of an atom with the release of a large amount of energy 裂变: *nuclear fission* 核裂变. **2** (*biology* 生) splitting or division of biological cells as a method of reproduction 分裂生殖.

▷ **fis·sion·able** /-ʃənəbl; -ʃənəbḷ/ *adj* (of material) with a nucleus that can be split (指材料)可作核裂变的.

fis·si·par·ous /fɪ'sɪpərəs; fɪ'sɪpərəs/ *adj* reproducing by division of biological cells 分裂生殖的.

fis·sure /'fɪʃə(r); 'fɪʃər/ *n* long deep crack in rock or in the earth (岩石中或土地中的)深长裂缝.

fist /fɪst; fɪst/ *n* **1** hand when closed tightly with the fingers bent into the palm 拳; 拳头: *He struck me with his fist.* 他用拳头打我. ○ *He clenched his fists.* 他紧握拳头. ○ *She shook her fist at him*, ie as an angry threatening gesture. 她向他挥动拳头. ⇨Usage at BODY 用法见 BODY. **2** (idm 习语) **an iron fist/hand in a velvet glove** ⇨ IRON[1]. **the mailed fist** ⇨ MAIL[2]. **make money hand over fist** ⇨ MONEY.

▷ **fist·ful** /'fɪstfʊl; 'fɪstfʊl/ *n* number or quantity that can be held in a fist 可握在手中的数或量: *a fistful of ten-pound notes* 一把十英镑面额的纸币.

□ **fisticuffs** /'fɪstɪkʌfs; 'fɪstɪˌkʌfs/ *n* [pl] (*arch or joc* 古或谑) fighting with the fists 用拳殴打: *engage in fisticuffs* 以拳互殴.

fis·tula /'fɪstjʊlə; 'fɪstʃʊlə/ *n* **1** long pipelike ulcer with a narrow mouth 瘘管. **2** abnormal or surgically made passage in the body (身体中异常的或手术造成的)通道.

fit[1] /fɪt; fɪt/ *adj* (**-tter, -ttest**) **1** [usu pred 通常作表语] **~ for sb/sth; ~ to do sth** suitable or suited for sb/sth; well adapted for sb/sth; good enough for sb/sth 对某人[某事物]适宜; 合适; 适当: *a land fit for heroes to live in* 适合英雄生活的国土 ○ *The food was not fit for human consumption/not fit to eat*, ie was too bad to be eaten. 这食物不适宜人吃. **2** [usu pred 通常作表语] **~ to do sth** (*infml* 口) in such a condition as to be likely or ready to do or suffer sth specified 可能或准备做某事物; 可能或准备受罪: *They worked till they were fit to drop*, ie likely to collapse from exhaustion. 他们一直工作到快要累垮了. ○ *He's so angry that he's in no fit state to see anyone.* 他气成那个样子, 简直无法见人. ○ (used as an *adv* after a *v* and *to* + infinitive 用作副词, 在动词

及 to + 不定式之后) *He laughed fit to burst.* 他要笑破肚子了. ○ *His shouting was fit* (ie loud enough) *to wake the dead.* 他大喊大叫都要把死人吵醒了. **3 ~ (for sth/to do sth)** in good health, esp because of regular physical exercise 健康的(尤指因经常锻炼): *World-class athletes are extremely fit.* 具有国际水平的运动员体格非常好. ○ *He's been ill and isn't fit for work yet.* 他一直在生病, 尚不能工作. ○ *He keeps himself fit by running 5 miles every day.* 他每天跑5英里以保持身体健康. ○ *fighting fit,* ie in very good physical condition and ready for energetic action 健壮而精力充沛. ⇨ Usage at HEALTHY 用法见 HEALTHY. **4** (*fml* 文) suitable and right, usu according to accepted social standards 恰当的; 正当的; 得体的: *As George introduced Peter and Sarah it is only fit (and proper) that he should be best man at their wedding.* 因是乔治介绍彼得与萨拉相识的, 由他来作他们婚礼的男傧相是最合适的. **5** (idm 习语) **(as) ˌfit as a ˌfiddle** in very good physical condition 非常健康: *I felt as fit as a fiddle after my walking holiday.* 我经过假期徒步旅行, 身体极好. **see/think ˈfit (to do sth)** consider it correct, convenient or acceptable (to do sth); decide or choose 认为(做某事)为正当的、适宜的或得体的; 决定; 愿意: *The newspaper did not see fit to publish my letter.* 该报认为不宜发表我的信. ○ *Do as you think fit.* 你认为怎么做好就怎么做吧.

▷ **fit·ness** *n* [U] **1** condition of being physically fit 健康: *In many sports (physical) fitness is not as important as technique.* 在许多体育运动中, 体能没有技巧重要. **2 ~ for sth/to do sth** suitability for sth 适合某事物: *Her fitness for the job cannot be questioned.* 她能胜任这项工作, 这是无庸置疑的.

fit[2] /fɪt; fɪt/ *v* (**-tt-**, *pt, pp* **fitted**; *US also* **fit**) **1** (**a**) [I, Tn] be the right shape and size for (sb) 形状及大小对(某人)合适; 合身: *These shoes don't fit (me).* 这双鞋(我)穿着不合适. ○ *Her coat fits (her) exactly.* 她的大衣很合身. ○ *I can never get clothes to fit me.* 我总也买不到合身的衣服. ○ *a close-fitting dress* 紧身连衣裙 ○ *The key doesn't fit the lock.* 这把钥匙打不开这把锁. (**b**) [Tn·pr esp passive 尤用于被动语态] **~ sb for sth** try (clothing) on sb in order to adjust it to the right size and shape 试穿(衣服): *He went to the tailor's to be fitted for a coat.* 他去裁缝店试穿大衣. **2** (**a**) [Ipr, Ip] be of the right size to go somewhere 大小适合装入某处: *The cooker won't fit in/into your new kitchen.* 你的新厨房装不下这套炉具. ○ *The mask fitted tightly over his face.* 他用面具把脸蒙得严严的. ○ *a tightly-fitting mask* 严实的面具 ○ *The lift was so small that only three people could fit in.* 电梯很小, 只容得下三个人. (**b**) [Tn·pr, Tn·p] **~ sth into sth/in** find or have sufficient space or room for sth in a place 找到或尚有足够的地方容纳某物: *We can't fit any more chairs into the room.* 房间里没有地方多放椅子了. ○ *This card just fits nicely into that envelope.* 这张卡片正好能装进那个信封里. **3** [Tn, Tn·pr] **~ A (on/to B); ~ B with A** supply sth and fix or put it into place 安装或装置某物: *fit handles on the cupboards/fit the cupboards with handles* 给柜橱安装把手 ○ *The room was fitted with a new carpet.* 房间里铺上了新地毯. **4** [Tn, Tn·pr, Tn·p] **~ A (onto/to B); ~ A and B together** join one thing to another to make a whole 将一物装到另一物上: *fit the tail assembly to the fuselage* 把装配好的机尾安装到机身上 ○ *fit the pieces of a model kit together* 把模型的各个部件组装在一起. **5** [I, Tn] be in agreement with (sth); match or suit 与(某事物)相符; 相称; 相协调: *Something doesn't quite fit here.* 这里有些不太协调. ○ *All the facts certainly fit your theory.* 所有的事实都和你的说法相符. ○ *The punishment ought to fit the crime.* 罚需当罪. **6** [Tn, Tn·pr, Cn·t] **~ sb/oneself/sth for sth** make sb/oneself/sth suitable for a particular role or task 使某人[自己]胜任某职位或任务; 使某物适合某用途: *Am I really fitted for the role of director?* 我真能胜任董事一职吗? ○ *His experience fitted him for the job/to do the job.* 他有经验, 能胜任这项工作. **7** (idm 习语) **fill/fit the bill** ⇨ BILL[1]. **fit (sb) like a ˈglove** (**a**) fit the wearer perfectly in size or shape 某人穿着非常合身: *My dress fits (me) like a glove.* 我的连衣裙非常合身. (**b**) be very suitable and accurate 合适而准确; 恰如其分: *'Cautious' is a description that certainly fits the new president like a glove.* 用'谨小慎微'来形容新会长很恰当. **if the cap fits** ⇨ CAP. **8** (phr v) **fit sb/sth in; fit sb/sth in/into sth** succeed in finding time to see sb or to do sth 找到见某人或做某事物的时间: *I'll try and fit you in after lunch.* 我尽可能在午饭以后见你. ○ *I had to fit ten appointments into one morning.* 我要在一个上午里安排十个约会. **fit in (with sb/sth)** be a smoothly fitting part (of sth); be in harmony (with sb/sth) 与(某事物)相适应; 与(某人[某事物])相协调: *He's never done this type of work before; I'm not sure how he'll fit in (with the other employees).* 他以前从未做过这种工作, 我不知道他是否能(与其他雇员)配合好. ○ *Do these plans fit in with your arrangements?* 这些计划与你的安排一致吗? **fit sb/sth out/up (with sth)** supply sb/sth with the necessary equipment, clothes, food, etc; equip 供给某人[某事物]必要的设备、衣物、食品等; 装备: *fit out a ship before a long voyage* 为远航的轮船准备必需品 ○ *I'm getting the children fitted out with clothes for their new school.* 我在为孩子们准备到新学校去的衣服.

▷ **fit·ted** *adj* [attrib 作定语] **1** (of a carpet) cut so that it covers a floor completely and is fixed into place (指地毯)铺满地面而固定的. **2** (**a**) (of furniture) built to be fixed into a particular space (指家具)(按放置位置)定做的: *fitted cupboards* 定做的柜橱. (**b**) (of a room) having fitted furniture (指房间)有定做的家具的: *a fitted kitchen* 有固定设备的厨房. **3** (of a sheet) having sewn corners so that it fits tightly over a mattress (指床单)四角缝紧兜住床垫的.

fit·ter *n* **1** person whose job is to put together, adjust and repair machinery and equipment 装配工: *a gas fitter* 煤气装配工. **2** person whose job is to cut out, fit and alter clothes (负责剪裁、试样和修改服装的)裁缝.

fit[3] /fɪt; fɪt/ *n* [sing] (usu with a preceding *adj* 通常前面有形容词) way in which sth, esp a garment, fits 某物适合的样子; (尤指)合身: *The coat was a good, bad, tight, loose, etc fit.* 那件大衣很合身、不合身、很瘦、很宽松等.

fit[4] /fɪt; fɪt/ *n* **1** sudden attack of epilepsy or other disease with violent movements and loss of consciousness (癫痫的)发作; 痉挛; 昏厥: *an epileptic ˈfit* 癫痫发作. **2** sudden (usu short) attack of a minor illness (轻微疾病的)发作(通常为片刻的): *a fit of coughing* 一阵咳嗽 ○ *a ˈfainting fit* 一阵眩晕. **3** sudden burst of (usu uncontrollable) laughter, activity, etc (大笑、活动等的)突然爆发(通常指控制不住的): *a fit of laughter/(the) giggles* 一阵大笑[格格的笑] ○ *We were all in fits (of laughter)* (ie laughing uncontrollably) *at his jokes.* 他的笑话逗得我们前仰后合. ○ *a fit of energy, letter writing, spring-cleaning, etc* 一股干劲、猛写一阵信、一阵大扫除. **4** short period of an intense feeling (强烈感情的)突发, 冲动: *a fit of anger, rage, frustration, etc* 一股怒气、一阵怒火、一阵心烦. **5** (idm 习语) **by/in ˌfits and ˈstarts** in irregular bursts of activity over a period of time 一阵一阵地: *Because of other commitments I can only write my book in fits and starts.* 因为我有其他的事要做, 所以这本书只能时写时辍. **have/throw a ˈfit** (**a**) suffer a fit(1) 癫痫病发作; 痉挛; 昏厥. (**b**) (*infml* 口) be greatly shocked, alarmed, outraged, etc 震惊; 惊恐; 愤怒: *Your mother would have a fit if she knew you were here.* 你母亲要是知道你在这里准会非常生气.

▷ **fit·ful** /-fl; -fəl/ *adj* occurring in short periods, not regularly and steadily 一阵阵的; 不规则的; 不稳定的: *fitful bursts of energy* 一阵阵的干劲 ○ *a fitful night's sleep* 夜间时断时续的睡眠. **fit·fully** /-fəlɪ; -fəlɪ/ *adv.*

fit·ment /ˈfɪtmənt; ˋfɪtmənt/ *n* (usu *pl* 通常作复数) piece of furniture or equipment, esp one forming part of a unit or series 家具或设备(尤指一套中的一件): *kitchen fitments,* eg cupboards 厨房设备(如柜橱).

fit·ting[1] /ˈfɪtɪŋ; ˋfɪtɪŋ/ *adj* suitable for the occasion; right or proper 得体的; 恰当的; 适合的: *It was fitting that he should be here to receive the prize in person.* 他应该亲自来领奖才对.

fit·ting[2] /ˈfɪtɪŋ; ˋfɪtɪŋ/ *n* **1** (usu *pl* 通常作复数) small standard part or component 小型标准零件或配件: *electrical fittings* 电气配件 ○ *stainless-steel light fittings* 不锈钢灯具. **2** (usu *pl* 通常作复数) items, such as a cooker and shelves, that are fixed in a building but can be removed when the owner moves house (搬家时可移走的)装置(如炉具、橱架等). Cf 参看 FIXTURE 1, MOVABLES (MOVABLE). **3** process or occasion of having a garment fitted 试穿; 试衣: *a fitting for a wedding dress* 试

F

穿结婚礼服 ○ *costume fittings* 服装试穿.

five /faɪv; faɪv/ *pron, det* 5; one more than four 5, 五(个): *Look at page five.* 见第五页. ○ *Everyone took the exam, but only five passed.* 所有的人都参加了考试, 但只有五人及格. ○ *Five (of the students) passed.* 五个(学生)及格. ○ *There were five children at the party.* 聚会中有五个孩子. ○ *This shirt cost five pounds,* ie £5. 这件衬衣五英镑. ○ *He's five (years old) today.* 今天他五岁了. ⇨ App 4 见附录 4.

▷ **five** *n* the number 5 ☆ 5; 五: *a birthday card with a big five on it* 印有一个大大的'五'字的生日卡 ○ *a row of fives on the blackboard* 黑板上的一行'五'字 ○ *Five and five make ten.* 五加五等于十.

five- (in compounds 用以构成复合词) having five of the thing specified 五个: *a five-day week,* ie working five days out of seven, usu Monday to Friday ○ *a five-year contract* ○ *a five-sided figure.*

fiver /ˈfaɪvə(r); ˈfaɪvɚ/ *n* **1** (*Brit infml* 口) five pound note; £5 面值为五英镑的钞票; 5英镑: *Can I borrow a fiver?* 能借给我五英镑吗? **2** (*US infml* 口) five dollar note; $5 面值为五美元的钞票; 5 美元.

□ **five o'clock shadow** dark appearance on a man's chin and face caused by the slight growth of hair that has occurred since he shaved in the morning (早晨刮脸后)傍晚(又长出少许胡须)的容貌.

ˌ**five ˈpence** (also ˌ**five ˈp, 5p**) (*Brit*) (coin worth) five new pence 五便士; 面值为五便士的硬币.

ˈ**fivepenny** *adj* [attrib 作定语] (*Brit*) costing or worth five new pence 五便士的.

fives /faɪvz; faɪvz/ *n* [sing *v*] (*Brit*) game in which a ball is hit with gloved hands or a bat against the walls of a court 墙手球(一种球戏, 带着手套用手或用球拍向球场的墙上击球).

F

fix[1] /fɪks; fɪks/ *v* **1** [Tn·pr] fasten (sth) firmly to sth 将(某物)固定到另一物上; 安装: *fix a shelf to the wall* 把架子装在墙上 ○ *fix a post in the ground* 把杆子固定在地上 ○ (*fig* 比喻) *fix the blame on sb* 把过错推诿给某人 ○ *fix sb's name in one's mind,* ie make great efforts to remember it 牢记某人的名字. **2** [Tn·pr] **~ sth on sb/sth** direct (esp one's eyes) on sb/sth with steady attention 全神贯注于、(尤指)凝视某人[某物]: *Her eyes were fixed on the gun.* 她紧盯着那枝枪. ○ *fix one's thoughts/attention on what one is doing* 全神贯注地工作. **3** [Tn] decide (sth) definitely; set or determine 决定(某事物); 确定: *The time for our meeting has been fixed already.* 我们开会的时间已经确定了. ○ *We will fix the rent at £100 a week.* 我们要把租金定为每周 100 英镑. **4** [Tn] repair or mend (sth) 修理(某物): *My watch has stopped — it needs fixing.* 我的表停了 —— 需要修理了. **5** [Tn] put (sth) in order; adjust 整理(某事物); 调整: *Let me fix my hair* (ie brush and comb it) *and I'll be ready.* 我梳梳头, 马上就好. **6** [Tn, Tn·p] **~ sth (up)** arrange sth 安排某事物: *I'll fix (up) a meeting.* 我来安排会议. ○ *I could fix it up with Geoffrey.* 我可以和杰弗里商量一下, 把这事安排好. **7** [Tn] find out (the exact nature, position, time, etc of sth) 确定(某事物的真正性质、位置、时间等). **8** [Tn, Dn·n, Dn·pr] **~ sth (for sb)** (*esp US*) provide or prepare (esp food) 供给或准备(尤指食物): *He's just fixing a snack.* 他在准备一点小吃. ○ *Can I fix you a drink?* 我给你弄点饮料好吗? ○ *Let me fix supper for you.* 我去给你准备晚饭. **9** [Tn] treat (photographic film, dyed fabric, etc) with a chemical so that the colours do not change or fade (用化学药品)使(摄影底片、染过的织物等的颜色)固定不变, 定影. **10** [Tn esp passive 尤用于被动语态] (*infml* 口) influence the result or actions of (sth), by unfair or illegal means 作弊: *I knew the race was fixed.* 我知道这次比赛有鬼. ○ *The jury/judge had been fixed.* 有人操纵了陪审团[法官]. **11** [Tn] (*infml* 口) punish or kill (esp sb who has harmed one); get even with 惩罚或杀死(尤指伤害过自己的人); 报复: *I'll fix him so that he never bothers you again.* 我来收拾他, 叫他再也不能打扰你. **12** [I, Tn] (*sl* 俚) inject oneself with (a narcotic drug) 给自己注射(毒品). **13** (phr v) **fix on sb/sth** decide to have sb/sth; choose 决定要某人[某事物]; 选定; 确定: *They've fixed on Ashby as the new chairman.* 他们决定让阿什比做新的主席. ○ *Have you fixed on a date for the wedding?* 你们举行婚礼的日期确定了吗? **fix sth up** repair, redecorate, or adapt sth 修理、重新装饰或改装某物: *He fixed up the cottage before they moved in.* 他把农舍修整好, 他们才搬进去. **fix sb up (with sth)** (*infml* 口) arrange for sb to have sth; provide sb with sth 为某人安排某事物; 向某人提供某事物: *I'll fix you up with a place to stay.* 我来给你安排住处. ○ *She's got herself fixed up with a cosy flat.* 她弄到了一套舒适的公寓. **fix sb with sth** (*fml* 文) direct one's gaze, attention, etc at sb 凝视某人; 注视某人: *He fixed her with an angry stare.* 他怒目注视着她.

▷ **fixed** /fɪkst; fɪkst/ *adj* **1** already arranged and decided; not changing; set 已决定的; 确定不变的; 固定的: *fixed prices* 固定的价格 ○ *a fixed rate of interest* 固定的利率. **2** (of ideas, wishes, etc) held firmly and sometimes obsessively (指想法、愿望等)坚定的, 执着的, 固执的: *He had the fixed idea that a woman's place was in the home.* 他有个成见, 认为女人的天地是在家里. **3** [attrib 作定语] (of an expression on sb's face) not changing; intent (指表情)不变的, 专注的: *a fixed smile, glare, stare, etc* 呆板的微笑、眼睛一动不动的怒视、目不转睛的注视. **4** [pred 作表语] **~ for sth** (*infml* 口) provided or supplied with sth 供给或供应某物: *How are you fixed for money, food, time, etc?* 你的钱、食物、时间等是怎么来的? **5** (idm 习语) **(of) ˌno fixed aˈbode/adˈdress** (*law* 律) (having) no permanent place to live in 无固定住所[住址](的): *Lovejoy, of no fixed abode, was charged with murder.* 洛夫乔伊, 居无定所, 被控谋杀. **fix·edly** /ˈfɪksɪdlɪ; ˈfɪksɪdlɪ/ *adv* without altering one's gaze; intently 目不转睛地; 专注地: *stare fixedly at sb* 目不转睛地注视某人. **fixed ˈassets** permanent business assets, eg buildings and equipment 固定资产(如建筑物和设备). Cf 参看 CURRENT ASSETS (CURRENT[1]). **fixed ˈcosts** business costs that do not vary with the amount of work produced 固定成本(不随产量变化而变动的企业成本). ˌ**fixed ˈstar** star so far from the earth that it seems to have no movement 恒星.

fixer /ˈfɪksə(r); ˈfɪksɚ/ *n* **1** (*infml* 口) person who makes (usu illegal) arrangements 代为做(通常为非法的)安排的人. **2** (chemical) substance that fixes (FIX[1] 9) photographs or dyes 定影剂; 定色剂.

fix·ity /ˈfɪksɪtɪ; ˈfɪksətɪ/ *n* [U] **~ of sth** quality of being fixed; firmness 固定性; 稳定性: *She displayed great fixity of purpose.* 她目标始终如一.

fix[2] /fɪks; fɪks/ *n* **1** [C usu *sing* 通常作单数] (*infml* 口) awkward or difficult situation 尴尬的境地; 窘况; 困境: *be in/get oneself into a fix* 处于[使自己陷入]尴尬的境地. **2** [C] **(a)** action of finding the position of a ship, an aircraft, etc by taking measurements with a compass, etc (用罗盘对船只、飞行器等的)方位测定. **(b)** position found by these means 测出的方位. **3** [sing] (*infml* 口) thing arranged dishonestly 不光明正大的安排; 搞鬼; 勾当: *Her promotion was a fix, I'm sure.* 我敢肯定她的提升有鬼. **4** [C] (*sl* 俚) injection of a narcotic drug, eg heroin 注射麻醉品(如海洛因): *get oneself a fix* 给自己注射毒品.

fix·ated /fɪkˈseɪtɪd; ˈfɪkˌsetɪd/ *adj* [pred 作表语] **~ (on sb/sth)** having an abnormal emotional attachment (to sb/sth) (对某人[某事物])固恋, 异常依恋: *He is fixated on things that remind him of his childhood.* 他异常依恋那些使他回忆起童年生活的东西.

fixa·tion /fɪkˈseɪʃn; fɪksˈeʃən/ *n* **~ (on sb/sth)** unhealthy emotional attachment (to sb/sth); obsession (对某人[某事物])情感上不健康的依恋, 固恋: *a mother fixation* 对母亲的固恋 ○ *fixations about marriage* 对婚姻的固恋.

fix·at·ive /ˈfɪksətɪv; ˈfɪksətɪv/ *n* [C, U] **1** substance used for fixing (FIX[1] 9) photographic film, dye, etc, or for preventing perfume from evaporating too quickly 定影剂; 固色剂; 防(香料)挥发剂. **2** substance used for sticking things together or keeping things in position, esp false teeth or hair 固定剂(尤指粘假牙或假发的): *Dentures require a strong fixative.* 粘假牙需用强力固定剂.

fix·ture /ˈfɪkstʃə(r); ˈfɪkstʃɚ/ *n* **1** (usu *pl* 通常作复数) thing, such as a bath, water tank or toilet, that is fixed in a building and is not removed when the owner moves house (建筑物内的)固定装置(如澡盆、水箱、马桶等): *plumbing fixtures* 管道装置 ○ *The price of the house included many existing fixtures and fittings that were not to our taste.* 房价包括不合我们心意的许多固定装置和附

加设备. Cf 参看 FITTING[2] 2, MOVABLES (MOVABLE). **2** (day fixed or decided for a) sporting event 体育运动项目(已确定的比赛日期). **3** (*infml* 口) person or thing that is firmly established and appears unlikely to leave a place or position 地位稳固而不大可能离开某处或某职位的人; 固定于某处不大可能移动之物: *Professor Gravity now seems to have become an unwanted fixture in the college.* 格雷维蒂教授现在好像成了学院里的累赘.

fizz /fɪz; fɪz/ *v* [I] **1** (of a liquid) produce bubbles of gas; effervesce (指液体)冒泡, 起泡. **2** make a hissing or spluttering sound 发出嘶嘶声或噼啪声: *The match fizzed.* 火柴发出嘶嘶声.

▷ **fizz** *n* [U] **1** quality of having a lot of bubbles of gas in a liquid; effervescence 液体冒泡的性能; 起泡: *This lemonade has lost its fizz.* 这汽水跑气了. **2** fizzing sound 嘶嘶声或噼啪声: *the fizz of a firework* 烟火的嘶嘶声; (*infml* 口) drink, eg champagne, that has a lot of bubbles of gas 起泡的饮料(如香槟).

fizzle /ˈfɪzl; ˋfɪzl/ *v* **1** [I] make a weak fizzing sound 发出微弱的嘶嘶声. **2** (phr v) **fizzle out** end or fail in a weak or disappointing way 虎头蛇尾般结束或失败: *After a promising start, the project soon fizzled out.* 这项计划开始时很有希望, 但不久就失败了.

fizzy /ˈfɪzɪ; ˋfɪzɪ/ *adj* (**-ier, -iest**) (of a drink) having a lot of bubbles of gas that make a hissing sound; effervescent or carbonated (指饮料)有大量气泡因而嘶嘶作响的, 含二氧化碳的: *fizzy lemonade* 汽水. ▷ **fiz·zi·ness** *n* [U].

fjord = FIORD.

fl *abbr* 缩写 = floor: *Accounts Office 3rd fl* 四楼会计室.

flab /flæb; flæb/ *n* [U] (*infml derog* 口, 贬) soft loose fatty flesh on a person's body 人体上松弛的肌肉: *middle-age flab*, ie on people aged about 40-60 years 中年人的松弛的肌肉.

▷ **flabby** /ˈflæbɪ; ˋflæbɪ/ *adj* (**-ier, -iest**) (*derog* 贬) **1** (**a**) soft and loose; not strong or firm 松软的; 松弛的: *flabby muscles, thighs, flesh, etc* 松弛的肌肉、松软的大腿、松软的肉. (**b**) having soft loose fatty flesh 肥胖而肌肉松弛的: *He's getting fat and flabby because he doesn't have enough exercise.* 他因为缺少锻炼而日见肥胖肌肉松弛. ⇨Usage at FAT[1] 用法见 FAT[1]. **2** feeble and weak; ineffective 软弱无力的; 无效的: *flabby excuses* 软弱无力的托辞 ○ *a flabby argument, plot, speech, etc* 无力的论据、松散的情节、欠说服力的讲话. **flab·bily** *adv*. **flab·bi·ness** *n* [U].

flab·ber·gast /ˈflæbəgɑːst; *US* -gæst; ˋflæbɚˌgæst/ *v* [Tn usu passive 通常用于被动语态] (*infml* 口) overwhelm (sb) with shocked amazement: surprise very greatly 使(某人)目瞪口呆, 大吃一惊: *He was flabbergasted when he heard that his friend had been accused of murder.* 他听说朋友被控谋杀罪, 大吃一惊.

flac·cid /ˈflæksɪd; ˋflæksɪd/ *adj* (*fml* 文) soft and weak; loose and limp; not firm 软弱的; 松弛的; 不结实的. ▷ **flac·cid·ity** /flækˈsɪdətɪ; flækˋsɪdətɪ/ *n* [U].

flag[1] /flæg; flæg/ *n* **1** (usu oblong or square) piece of cloth with a particular design, that can be attached by one edge to a rope, pole, etc and used as a symbol of a country, party, etc or as a signal 旗: *The national flag of the United Kingdom is called the Union Jack.* 英国的国旗称作Union Jack. ○ *The ship was sailing under the Dutch flag*, ie the Dutch flag was flying from its mast. 那条船航行时悬挂着荷兰国旗. ○ *All the flags were flying at half-mast*, ie in honour of a famous dead person. 所有的旗帜都降半旗致哀. ○ *The guard waved his flag and the train left the station.* 列车长摇动手中的旗子, 火车随之开出车站. ○ *The white flag is a symbol of a truce or surrender.* 白旗表示停战或投降. ⇨illus 见插图. **2** small piece of paper or cloth attached to a stick or pin, esp one given to sb who contributes to a charity appeal 小纸旗或小布旗(尤指送给为慈善事业捐款者的): *children selling flags for a cancer research appeal* 为癌症研究募捐而售旗的孩子们. **3** sign displayed to show that a taxi is for hire (计程车表示可载客的)旗形牌. **4** (idm 习语) **a ˌflag of conˈvenience** flag of a foreign country under which a ship registers to avoid the taxes and certain regulations of the owner's home country 方便旗(船只为逃避本国捐税或避免履行某些规章而在他国注册所挂的该国国旗). **fly/show/wave the flag** make known one's support of or loyalty to one's country, party, movement, etc, esp in order to encourage others to do the same 表示对自己的国家、党派、运动等的拥护或忠诚. **keep the ˈflag flying** continue to support one's country or a set of principles 坚持拥护自己的国家或一套原则: *Our exporters proudly kept the flag flying at the international trade exhibition.* 在国际贸易展览会上, 我国的出口商为国争光.

▷ **flag** *v* (**-gg-**) **1** [Tn esp passive 尤用于被动语态] place a flag or flags on (sth); decorate with flags 悬旗于(某物); 用旗装饰: *The streets were flagged to celebrate the royal wedding.* 街上挂起了旗子, 庆祝皇室婚礼. **2** [Tn] mark (sth) for particular attention with a special mark or label (用特殊记号或标签)标出(某物, 以引起特别注意): *All the surnames in the list have been specially flagged so that the computer can print them out easily.* 名单上的姓氏都特别标出, 以便计算机容易打印出. **3** (phr v) **flag sth down** signal to (a moving vehicle) to stop, usu by waving one's arm 向(行驶的车辆)发出停车信号(通常指挥动手臂): *flag down a taxi* 挥手拦截计程车.

□ **ˈflag-day** *n* **1** (*US* **tag day**) day on which money is collected in public places for a charity, a small paper flag or sticker being given to those who contribute 售旗募捐日(该日于公共场所募捐, 捐款者获小纸旗或标贴). **2 Flag Day** (*US*) 14 June, anniversary of the day in 1777 when the Stars and Stripes became the national flag 美国国旗制定纪念日(6月14日, 为纪念1777年该日决定以星条旗为美国国旗).

ˈflag-pole *n* long pole on which a flag is flown 旗杆.

ˈflagship *n* **1** ship which has the commander of a fleet on board 旗舰. **2** (*fig* 比喻) most important of a group of products, projects, services, etc (一批产品、工程、服务设施等中)最重要者: *This dictionary is the flagship of Oxford's range of learners' dictionaries.* 本词典执牛津一系列学习者词典之牛耳.

ˈflagstaff *n* flag-pole 旗杆.

ˈflag-waving *n* [U] (esp excessive) expression of patriotic or group feeling(s) (尤指过激的)爱国情绪或宗派情绪: [attrib 作定语] *I didn't think much of that speech — it was just a flag-waving exercise*, ie one that did not deal with real issues. 我认为他的话无足轻重 —— 只不过是偏激的派性空话.

flag[2] /flæg; flæg/ *v* (**-gg-**) [I] **1** become tired, less active, or less interesting; weaken 变得疲倦、不活跃或乏味; 衰弱: *My strength, interest, enthusiasm, etc is flagging.* 我的力气、兴趣、热情等正在减退. **2** (esp of plants) become limp or feeble; hang down or droop (尤指植物)萎蔫, 枯萎: *Roses will flag in the summer heat.* 夏天炎热玫瑰就要枯萎.

flag[3] /flæg; flæg/ *n* = FLAGSTONE.

▷ **flagged** /flægd; flægd/ *adj* paved with flagstones 用石板铺成的: *a flagged terrace* 用石板铺成的台地.

flag[4] /flæg; flæg/ *n* type of plant with blade-like leaves, usu growing in wet land 菖蒲; 香蒲. Cf 参看 IRIS 2.

fla·gel·lant /ˈflædʒələnt; ˋflædʒələnt/ (*fml* 文) *n* person who whips himself or another person, either as a religious penance or to obtain or give sexual pleasure (为宗教苦行或为获得或给予性快感)鞭笞自己或他人者.

F

▷ **fla·gel·late** /ˈflædʒəleɪt; ˋflædʒə,let/ *v* [Tn] (*fml* 文) whip (sb or oneself), as a religious penance or for sexual gratification (作为宗教苦行或为满足性欲)鞭笞(某人或自己). **fla·gel·la·tion** /ˌflædʒəˈleɪʃn; ˌflædʒəˈleʃən/ *n*.

flagon /ˈflæɡən; ˋflæɡən/ *n* **1** large rounded bottle in which wine, cider, etc is sold, usu holding about twice as much as an ordinary bottle 大肚酒瓶(通常容量为普通酒瓶的两倍). **2** container with a handle, lip and lid for serving wine at a table (有把手、壶嘴、壶盖的)酒壶. **3** amount of liquid contained in a flagon 一个大肚酒瓶或酒壶的量: *drink a flagon of wine* 喝一大壶酒.

flag·rant /ˈfleɪɡrənt; ˋfleɡrənt/ *adj* (usu of an aciton) particularly bad, shocking and obvious (通常指行为)极坏的, 骇人听闻的, 公然的: *a flagrant breach of justice* 公然违反公正原则 ○ *flagrant violations of human rights* 对人权的粗暴践踏. ▷ **flag·rantly** *adv*.

flag·stone /ˈflæɡstəʊn; ˋflæɡ,ston/ (also **flag**) *n* flat piece of stone (usu square or oblong) for a floor, path or pavement 石板(通常为正方形或长方形, 用以铺室内地面、小径或边道).

flail /fleɪl; flel/ *n* tool consisting of a stick swinging from a long handle, used esp formerly to separate grain from chaff 连枷(有长柄的农具, 尤于旧时作打谷用).

▷ **flail** *v* **1** [I, Tn] (cause sth to) wave or swing about wildly (使某物)乱摇或乱摆: *The dying lamb fell, its legs flailing (about) helplessly.* 小羊快要死了, 倒在地上四条腿又踢又蹬. ○ *flail one's arms/hands above one's head* 将双臂[双手]举过头顶摇动. **2** [Tn] beat (sth) (as if) with a flail (似)用连枷打(某物).

flair /fleə(r); flɛr/ *n* **1** [sing, U] **~ for sth** natural ability to do sth well 天资; 天分: *He doesn't show much flair for the piano.* 他对弹钢琴没有什么天资. ○ *She has a real flair for languages*, ie is quick at learning them. 她真有学习语言的天分. **2** [U] original and attractive quality; stylishness 天生的吸引人的特质; 风度.

flak /flæk; flæk/ *n* [U] **1** guns shooting at enemy aircraft; fire from those guns 高射炮; 高射炮火: *run into heavy flak* 陷入密集的高射炮火中. **2** (*infml* 口) severe criticism 严厉的批评: *The plans for the new tax have come in for a lot of flak*, ie have been very strongly criticized. 新的税务计划遭到了猛烈抨击.

□ ˈ**flak jacket** heavy protective jacket reinforced with metal (衬有金属片的)防护衣; 避弹衣.

flake /fleɪk; flek/ *n* small thin layer or piece, esp one that has broken off a surface or object; small loose bit 小薄片(尤指从物体上剥落下来的); 小碎片: *Scrape off all the loose flakes of paint before redecorating.* 先把翘起来的漆皮刮掉再重新装修. ○ *snowflakes* 雪花 ○ *soap-flakes* 肥皂片.

▷ **flake** *v* **1** [I, Ip] **~ (off/away)** come or fall off in flakes 成片状剥落: *The paint on the walls is beginning to flake (off).* 墙上的漆开始剥落了. **2** [I, Tn] separate (usu food) into flakes (使)(通常为食物)成片: *flaked fish* 切成片的鱼. **3** (phr v) **flake out** (*infml* 口) collapse or fall asleep from exhaustion (因精疲力竭)瘫倒或入睡: *When I got home from the airport, I flaked out in the nearest armchair.* 我从机场回到家, 便一下瘫倒在离我最近的沙发上了.

flaky *adj* (**-ier**, **-iest**) made up of flakes; tending to break into flakes 由薄片组成的; 易分裂成薄片的: *flaky pastry* 酥饼. **fla·ki·ness** *n* [U].

flambé /ˈflɒmbeɪ; *US* flɑːmˈbeɪ; flɑmˋbe/ *adj* (*French* 法) (following *ns* 置于名词之后) (of food) covered with brandy or other spirit, set alight and served (指食物)浇上白兰地等酒类, 点燃后供食用的: *pancakes flambé* 带火焰的薄饼.

flam·boy·ant /flæmˈbɔɪənt; flæmˋbɔɪənt/ *adj* **1** (of a person or his character, manner, etc) showy, very confident and extravagant (指人或性格、举止等)爱炫耀的, 非常自信的, 奢华的: *rich flamboyant film stars* 阔绰而爱炫耀的电影明星 ○ *flamboyant gestures* 炫耀的姿态. **2** brightly coloured or decorated 艳丽的; 装饰华丽的: *flamboyant clothes* 华丽的服装. ▷ **flam·boy·ance** /-ˈbɔɪəns; -ˋbɔɪəns/ *n* [U]. **flam·boy·antly** *adv*.

flame[1] /fleɪm; flem/ *n* **1** [C, U] hot glowing portion of burning gas that comes from something on fire 火焰: *The curtains were enveloped in a sheet of flame.* 窗帘被火焰吞没. ○ *the tiny flame of a cigarette-lighter* 打火机小小的火焰 ○ *The house was in flames*, ie was on fire, burning. 房子失火了. ○ *An oil heater was knocked over and burst instantly into flames*, ie suddenly began to burn strongly. 油加热器碰倒了, 顿时燃起了一片大火. ○ *The whole hotel went up in flames* (ie was destroyed by fire) *in minutes.* 整个旅馆几分钟就烧毁了. ⇨illus at CANDLE 见CANDLE插图. **2** [C] bright light or brilliant colour, usu red or orange 明亮的光线或灿烂的颜色(通常指红色或橙色): *The flowering shrubs were a scarlet flame.* 花丛一片嫣红. **3** [C] (*rhet* 修辞) intense feeling, esp love 强烈的感情(尤指爱情): *the flame of passion* 激情的烈焰 ○ *A flicker of interest soon turned into the burning flames of desire.* 一丝情趣的星星之火未几演成了干柴烈火. **4** [C] (*infml* 口) person with whom one was once in love; sweetheart or lover (used esp in the expression shown) 旧情人, 情人, 爱人(尤用于以下示例): *an old flame* 老相好. **5** (idm 习语) **add fuel to the flames** ⇨ ADD. **fan the flames** ⇨ FAN[2]. **pour oil on the flames** ⇨ POUR.

□ ˈ**flame-thrower** *n* weapon that projects a stream of burning fuel 火焰喷射器; 喷火器.

flame[2] /fleɪm; flem/ *v* **1** [La, I] burn with a brighter flame 燃烧; 发出火焰: *The burning coals started to flame yellow and orange.* 燃烧着的煤开始发出了黄色与橙色的火焰. **2** [La, I, Ipr] glow or shine like (the colour of) flames; blaze 似火焰(的颜色)般地闪耀; 放光: *wooded hillsides that flame red in autumn* 长满树木的山坡, 在秋季红如火焰 ○ *a flaming sunset* 火红的晚霞 ○ *flaming red hair* 如火的红发 ○ *His face flamed (with anger/embarrassment).* 他(气得[窘得])面红耳赤.

▷ **flam·ing** *adj* [attrib 作定语] **1** passionate or violent 激情的; 激烈的; 暴躁的: *a flaming row/argument/temper* 激烈的争吵[激烈的争论/暴躁的脾气]. **2** (*infml* 口) (used to emphasize a judgement or comment) absolute; utter (用以加强判断或评论的语气)非常的, 十足的: *You flaming idiot!* 你这个大笨蛋!

fla·menco /fləˈmeŋkəʊ; fləˋmɛŋko/ *n* [C, U] (*pl* **~s**) (music for a) strongly rhythmical dance performed originally by Spanish gypsies 弗拉明柯舞(曲)(源于西班牙吉普赛人的节奏强烈的舞蹈).

fla·mingo /fləˈmɪŋɡəʊ; fləˋmɪŋɡo/ *n* (*pl* **~s**) long-legged wading-bird with a long neck and pink feathers 红鹳.

flam·mable /ˈflæməbl; ˋflæməbl̩/ *adj* easily set on fire; that can burn easily 易燃烧的: *Pyjamas made from flammable material have been removed from most shops.* 大部分商店都不再出售用易燃材料做的睡衣了. Cf 参看 INFLAMMABLE, NON-FLAMMABLE. ⇨Usage at INVALUABLE 用法见INVALUABLE.

flan /flæn; flæn/ *n* open pastry or sponge pie case containing a fruit, jam or savoury filling 果馅饼: *an apple flan* 苹果馅饼. Cf 参看 PIE, TART[2].

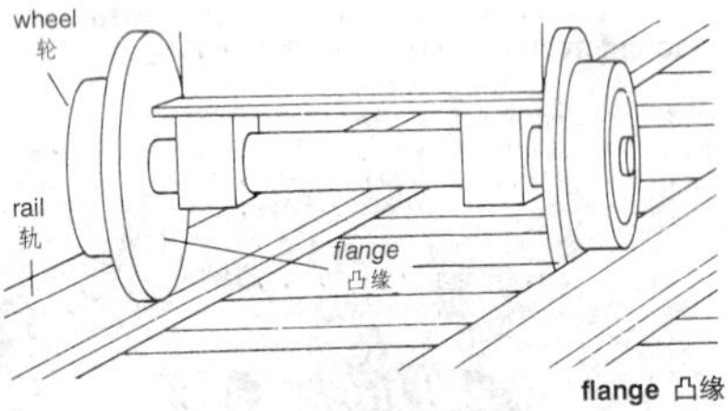

flange 凸缘

flange /flændʒ; flændʒ/ *n* raised outside edge, eg of a railway wheel, to hold it in place 凸缘; 法兰.

flank /flæŋk; flæŋk/ *n* **1** fleshy part of the side of an animal or person between the ribs and the hip 胁; 胁腹. ⇨illus at HORSE 见HORSE插图. **2** side of sth, eg a building or mountain 侧面(如建筑物或山的). **3** left or right side of an army or a body of troops (部队的)侧翼: *Our orders are to attack their left flank.* 我们的命令是攻击他们的左翼. ○ [attrib 作定语] *a flank attack* 侧翼攻击.

▷ **flank** *v* [Tn usu passive 通常用于被动语态] place (sb/sth) on each side of or at the side of sb/sth 置(某人[某物])于某人[某物]的两侧或一侧: *The prisoner was* *flanked by the two detectives*, ie There was a detective on each side of him. 那个囚犯夹在两名侦探的中间. ○ *The garden is flanked to the north with large maple trees.* 花园的北侧是一些高大的枫树.

flannel /ˈflænl; ˋflænl/ *n* **1** [U] type of soft loosely woven woollen cloth 法兰绒: [attrib 作定语] *flannel trousers* 法兰绒裤子. **2 flannels** [pl] men's trousers made of flannel 法兰绒男裤: *a pair of cricket flannels* 一条男用法兰绒板球裤. **3** = FACE-FLANNEL (FACE¹). **4** [U] (*infml* 口) wordy language that avoids talking about sth directly and is often intended to flatter 兜圈子的(常为奉承的)言语: *He gave me a lot of flannel but I still don't know the answer to my question.* 他说了很多恭维话, 我仍然不知道怎样解决我的问题.

▷ **flannel** *v* (**-ll-**; *US* **-l-**) [I] (*infml* 口) speak or write flannel(4) 说或写兜圈子的言语: *Stop flannelling and give a straight answer!* 别再兜圈子了, 直截了当地回答!

flan·nel·ette /ˌflænəˈlet; ˌflænlˋɛt/ *n* [U] type of soft cotton material 棉法兰绒; 绒布: [attrib 作定语] *flannelette night-gowns, sheets, pyjamas, etc* 绒布睡袍、床单、睡衣等.

flap¹ /flæp; flæp/ *n* **1 ~(of sth)** flat piece of material that covers an opening or hangs down (用以覆盖开口的或垂下的)扁平物: *the flap of an envelope* 信封的封盖 ○ *the flap of a tent, pocket, etc* 帐篷的帘、衣袋的盖 ○ *the flap of a table*, ie an extra hinged section that hangs down when not in use 桌子的活边(以铰链与桌面相连, 不用时可以垂下). **2** part of the wing on an aircraft that can be lifted in flight to change the aircraft's upward direction (飞行器的)襟翼. ⇨illus at AIRCRAFT 见AIRCRAFT插图. **3** action or sound of flapping; light blow, usu with something flat 拍打; 拍打声; 轻击(通常指用扁平物击打). **4** (idm 习语) **be in/get into a flap** (*infml* 口) be in/get into a state of agitation, confusion, nervous excitement, etc 处于忐忑不安、慌乱、紧张、激动等的状态: *I got into a real flap when I lost my keys.* 我丢了钥匙, 心里发慌.

flap² /flæp; flæp/ *v* (**-pp-**) **1** [I, Tn] (cause sth to) move, swing, wave, etc up and down or from side to side, usu making a noise (使某物)上下或左右移动、摆动、摇动等(通常发出声响): *The sails were flapping gently in the wind.* 船帆随风摆动. ○ *The bird flapped its wings and flew away.* 那鸟振翅飞去. **2** [Ipr, Tn·pr] (attempt to) give a light blow at (sth) with a flat object (用扁平物体)轻拍(某物): *flap at a fly with a cloth/flap a cloth at a fly* 用布来拍打苍蝇. **3** [I] (*infml* 口) become confused, excited or disturbed 困惑; 激动; 不安: *There's no need to flap!* 不必惊慌! **4** (phr v) **flap across, away, by, etc** (of a bird) fly in the specified direction by moving its wings (指鸟)振翅而飞: *The heron flapped slowly off across the lake.* 那白鹭振翅向湖对岸慢慢飞去.

flap·jack /ˈflæpdʒæk; ˋflæpˌdʒæk/ *n* **1** biscuit made from oats, butter and honey or syrup (用燕麦粉、黄油和蜂蜜或糖汁做的)饼干. **2** (*esp US*) thick pancake 厚煎饼.

flap·per /ˈflæpə(r); ˋflæpɚ/ *n* **1** broad flat device used for killing flies, etc (打苍蝇等的)拍子; 蝇拍. **2** (*dated infml* 旧, 口) fashionable and unconventional young woman of the 1920s (20世纪20年代的)不拘传统的时髦少女.

flare¹ /fleə(r); flɛr/ *v* **1** [I] burn brightly but briefly or unsteadily 燃烧; 闪耀: *The match flared in the darkness.* 火柴的光亮在黑暗中一闪. ○ *flaring gas jets* 闪耀着的煤气火焰. **2** [I] (*fig* 比喻) burst into sudden activity or anger (行动或愤怒)爆发: *Tempers flared at the conference.* 会上群情激奋. **3** (phr v) **flare up** (**a**) burn suddenly more intensely 火焰突然变旺: *The fire flared up as I put more logs on it.* 我加上了几块木柴, 火顿时旺起来. (**b**) reach a more violent state; suddenly become angry 达到更激烈的状态; 突然发怒: *Violence has flared up again.* 暴乱又起. ○ *He flares up at the slightest provocation.* 稍一激他, 他就大发脾气. (**c**) (of an illness) recur (指疾病)复发: *My back trouble has flared up again.* 我的后背又疼起来了.

▷ **flare** *n* **1** (usu *sing* 通常作单数) bright and unsteady or brief light or flame (耀眼而摇曳的)闪光或火焰: *the sudden flare of a torch in the darkness* 手电筒的光在黑暗中的一闪. **2** (device that produces a) flaring light used esp as a signal 闪光(装置)(尤指用作信号的): *The captain of the sinking ship used flares to attract the attention of the coastguard.* 轮船正在下沉, 船长向海岸巡逻队发出闪光信号求救.

□ ˈ**flare-path** line of lights on a runway to guide aircraft landing or taking off (供飞行器用的)照明跑道.

ˈ**flare-up** *n* **1** sudden burst of light or flame (光或火焰的)突然闪耀. **2** sudden outburst of strong or violent activity or feeling (激烈行动或情感的)爆发.

flare² /fleə(r); flɛr/ *v* [I, Ip, Tn esp passive 尤用于被动语态] (cause sth to) become wider at the bottom (使某物)底部变宽: *This skirt flares (out) at the hem.* 这条裙子的下摆张得很大. ○ *Her nostrils flared angrily.* 她气得鼻孔鼓了起来. ○ *flared trousers* 喇叭裤. Cf 参看 TAPER².

▷ **flare** *n* **1** gradual widening; flared shape 逐渐加宽; 喇叭状: *a skirt with a slight flare* 略成喇叭状的裙子. **2 flares** [pl] (*infml* 口) flared trousers 喇叭裤.

flash¹ /flæʃ; flæʃ/ *n* **1** [C] (**a**) sudden bright burst of light or flame 闪光; 闪烁: *a flash of lightning* 一道闪电. (**b**) (*fig* 比喻) sudden show of wit, understanding, etc (机智等的)显露; 恍然大悟: *a flash of inspiration, intuition, etc* 灵机一动、直觉的感触. **2** [C] = NEWS FLASH (NEWS). **3** [C, U] device or system that produces a brief bright light for taking photographs indoors or in poor light 闪光灯: *This camera has a built-in flash.* 这架照相机有内置闪光灯. ○ *I'll need flash for this shot; the light isn't good enough.* 我拍这张照片需用闪光灯, 这里光线不好. **4** [C] coloured stripe or patch of cloth worn as an emblem on a military uniform, eg on the shoulder (佩于军服上的)徽章(如肩章). **5** [C usu *sing* 通常作单数] (*infml* 口) brief showing of the sexual organs, esp by men; indecent exposure 瞬间展露性器官(尤指男子); 猥亵性暴露. **6** [attrib 作定语] (*infml derog* 口, 贬) expensive-looking, showy and usu not in good taste 花哨的; 炫耀的: *a flash sports car* 花里胡哨的跑车. **7** (idm 习语) **a ˌflash in the ˈpan** sudden brilliant success that lasts only a short time and is not repeated 昙花一现: *His first novel was a flash in the pan, and he hasn't written anything decent since.* 他的第一部小说如昙花一现, 此后他再没写出像样的东西. **in a/like a ˈflash** very quickly; at once; immediately 很快; 立刻; 立即: I'll be back in a flash. 我马上就回来. **quick as a flash** ⇨ QUICK.

□ ˈ**flashbulb** *n* bulb in a flash¹(3) 闪光灯泡.

ˈ**flash cube** set of four flashbulbs arranged as a cube for taking photographs one after the other 四连闪光灯(呈立方形, 四面各一闪光灯泡, 逐一使用).

ˈ**flash-flood** *n* sudden destructive flood of water 暴洪.

ˈ**flash-gun** *n* device that holds and operates the flashlight at the same time as the camera shutter opens 闪光操纵器, 闪光枪(与摄影机快门同步的闪光装置).

ˈ**flashlight** *n* **1** (device that produces a) brief bright light for taking photographs indoors or in poor light 摄影闪光(装置). **2** (*esp US*) = TORCH. **3** (source of) light used for signalling, eg in a lighthouse 闪光信号灯(如灯塔中的).

ˈ**flash-point** *n* **1** temperature at which the vapour above a liquid such as oil gives a brief flash, but does not catch fire, when a flame is brought near it 闪点; 燃点; 引火点. **2** (*fig* 比喻) point at which violence or anger breaks out (暴力事件或愤怒的)爆发点: *Community unrest is rapidly approaching the flashpoint.* 群众的不安定情绪已接近一触即发之势.

flash² /flæʃ; flæʃ/ *v* **1** (**a**) [I] give or send out a brief bright light 发出闪光: *Lightning flashed during the storm.* 暴风雨中闪电大作. ○ *A lighthouse was flashing in the distance.* 灯塔在远处发出闪烁的光. ○ (*fig* 比喻) *His eyes flashed angrily.* 他的眼睛怒火闪闪. (**b**) [Tn, Tn·pr] cause (sth) to shine briefly or suddenly 使(某物)短暂地或突然地发光: *flash a torch in sb's eyes/at sb* 用手电筒照某人的眼睛[照某人]. **2** [Tn, Tn·pr] (**a**) communicate with a light 用光联络: *flash a signal (to sb) with one's car headlights* 用汽车前灯(给某人)发信号. (**b**) send or reflect (sth) like a flash 如闪光般发出或反映出(某物): *Her eyes flashed anger and defiance (at everyone).* 她(看着大家,)眼中闪现着愤怒与轻蔑的神情. **3** [Tn] send (sth) by radio, television, etc (通过无线电、电视等)传送(某事物): *flash a message on the screen* 在屏幕上映出一信息. **4** [Tn, Tn·p] show or display (sth) briefly 短暂地显示或出示(某事物): *flash*

F

an identification card 出示一下身分证 ○ (*derog* 贬) *He's flashing his money around*, ie to try to gain the admiration of others. 他到处显示自己有钱. **5** [I] (*infml* 口) (esp of a man) show one's sexual organs briefly and indecently (尤指男子)猥亵性瞬间展露性器官. **6** (phr v) **flash along, by, past, through, etc** move very quickly in the specified direction 急速向某方向运动: *The train flashed by at high speed.* 火车疾驶而过. ○ (*fig* 比喻) *An idea flashed into her mind.* 她突然闪出一个念头. **flash back** (of one's thoughts) return to an earlier time (指某人的思想)回溯, 回顾, 回忆: *My mind flashed back to our previous meeting.* 我又想起了我们上次会面时的情景.

▷ **flasher** /ˈflæʃə(r); ˈflæʃɚ/ *n* **1** (*infml* 口) person who flashes (FLASH[2] 5) 猥亵性瞬间展露性器官的人. **2** (device that controls esp a) flashing light on a vehicle used to indicate which way the vehicle is turning (尤指)车辆转向闪光指示灯(的装置).

□ ˈ**flashback** *n* part of a film, play, etc that shows a scene earlier in time than the main story (电影的)闪回, 闪回镜头; (戏剧、小说等的)倒叙, 倒叙情节: *The events that led up to the murder were shown in a series of flashbacks.* 酿成谋杀案的各个环节是通过一系列倒叙手法来表现的.

ˈ**flash card** card on which a word or words are printed or written, used as a visual aid to learning 教学卡片(有单词或词语的直观教具).

flashy /ˈflæʃɪ; ˈflæʃɪ/ *adj* (**-ier**, **-iest**) attractive but usu not in good taste; showy 华丽而俗气的; 炫耀的: *flashy clothes, jewellery, etc* 花哨的服装、首饰等 ○ *a flashy car* 花里胡哨的汽车. ▷ **flash·ily** *adv*: *flashily dressed* 穿得花里胡哨.

flask /flɑːsk; *US* flæsk; flæsk/ *n* **1** (**a**) bottle with a narrow neck, esp one used in scientific laboratories for mixing or storing chemicals 细颈瓶; (尤指)烧瓶. (**b**) similarly shaped container for storing oil, wine, etc (装油、酒等的)细颈瓶. **2** (also ˈ**hip-flask**) small flat-sided bottle of metal or (often leather-covered) glass that is used for carrying alcoholic spirits in the pocket (小而扁的)金属酒瓶或(常为有皮套的)玻璃酒瓶(可装在衣袋里). **3** = VACUUM FLASK (VACUUM). **4** amount contained in a flask 一小酒瓶的容量: *drink a flask of wine, whisky, tea, etc* 喝下一小瓶葡萄酒、威士忌、茶等.

flat[1] /flæt; flæt/ *n* (*esp Brit*) (also *esp US* **apartment**) set of rooms (living-room, bedroom, kitchen, etc) for living in, usu on one floor of a building 公寓; 单元房; 一套房间: *a new block of flats* 一座新的公寓楼 ○ *They're renting a furnished flat on the third floor.* 他们租了四楼的一套带家具的房间. ○ *Many large old houses have now been converted into flats.* 许多旧的大房子都已改建成了单元房.

▷ **flat·let** /-lɪt; -lɪt/ *n* very small flat 小公寓.

flat[2] /flæt; flæt/ *adj* (**-tter**, **-ttest**) **1** smooth and level; even 平坦的; 平的: *a flat surface for writing on* 可以在上面写字的平面 ○ *The countryside is very flat here*, ie has no hills. 这一带农村地势平坦. **2** spread out on a single plane; extending at full length 平的; 平展的; 平伸的: *People used to think that the world was flat; now we know it is round.* 从前人们以为地球是平的, 现在知道是圆的. **3** with a broad level surface and little depth 浅的(从上到下距离短的): *a flat cap* 扁帽子 ○ *flat dishes, plates, etc* 浅碟子、盘子等 ○ *The cake was flat*, ie did not rise while cooking. 这蛋糕没发起来. **4** (of a tyre) not containing enough air, eg because of a puncture; deflated (指车胎)气不足的(如有穿孔), 撒气的. **5** dull; uninteresting; monotonous 枯燥的; 平淡无味的; 单调的: *speak in a flat voice* 用平淡的语调说 ○ *He felt a bit flat after his friends had gone.* 朋友们走了以后他觉得有些无聊. **6** not having much trade or business 生意清淡的; 萧条的; 不景气的: *The market has been flat today.* 今天市场上生意一直很清淡. **7** having a single price for a variety of goods or services (各种商品或服务)价格一律的或统一的: *a flat fare of 70p* 一律为70便士的票价 ○ *a flat rate* 统一收费率 ○ *flat-rate* (ie standard and fixed) *contributions* 定额捐款. **8** (of a carbonated or gaseous liquid) having lost its gas or effervescence (指充有二氧化碳气或含气的液体)走了气的, 跑了气的: *The lager tastes/has gone flat.* 这啤酒喝起来没有气[走气]了. **9** (of a battery) unable to supply any more electric current; run down (指电池)电用完了的. **10** (*music* 音) (half a tone) lower than true or correct pitch 降(半)音的: *B flat is a semitone below the note B.* 降B音比B音低半音. ○ *Your piano is flat; it needs tuning.* 你的钢琴的音低了, 该调一调了. Cf 参看 SHARP 12. **11** (**a**) [usu pred 通常作表语] (of pictures, photographs or colours) without contrast or shading; with no sense of depth or contrast (指图画、照片等)无景深, 无反差; (指颜色)无变化, 单调: *The colours used are flat and unvaried.* 使用的颜色既单调又无层次. ○ *His paintings are deliberately flat, it's part of his style.* 他作画刻意用单一色调, 这是他的一种风格. (**b**) (of paint) not glossy; matt (指油漆)无光泽的, 不发亮的. **12** absolute; unqualified 绝对的; 断然的; 直截了当的: [attrib 作定语] *give sb a flat denial/refusal* 对某人所指断然否认[断然拒绝某人]. **13** (of feet) not having normal raised arches (指脚)扁平的, 扁平足的. **14** (idm 习语) **and ˌthat's ˈflat** that's my final decision 这是我的最后决定: *I'm not going out with you and that's flat!* 我不跟你出去, 说定了! **be in/go into a flat spin**; **(as) flat as a pancake** completely flat 十分平坦或平淡: *The whole landscape looked as flat as a pancake.* 整个地形十分平坦. ○ *The surprise party turned out as flat as a pancake*, ie was very disappointing. 这次本想让大家感到惊奇的聚会到头来却十分扫兴.

▷ **flatly** *adv* **1** in a flat[2](5) manner 淡淡地; 无精打采地: *'Maybe,' he said flatly, 'I'll see.'* '也许吧,'他淡淡地说,'我考虑一下.' **2** in an outright, direct manner; positively; absolutely 直截了当地; 断然地; 绝对地: *The allegations were all flatly denied.* 这些指责遭到断然否认. ○ *Our request was flatly rejected.* 我们的请求遭到断然拒绝.

flat·ness *n* [U].

□ ˌ**flat-ˈbottomed** *adj* (of a boat) having a flat bottom and used in shallow water (指船)平底的.

ˈ**flatcar** *n* (*US*) railway carriage without a roof or raised sides, used for carrying freight (铁路上的)平车, 敞车, 平板货车.

ˈ**flat-fish** *n* type of fish with a flat body, eg plaice or sole 比目鱼(体形扁平的鱼, 如鲽或鳎).

ˌ**flat-ˈfooted** *adj* **1** having feet without normal raised arches 有扁平足的. **2** (*infml* 口) clumsy or awkward 笨手笨脚的: *His speed and skill makes other players look flat-footed.* 他速度快、技术好, 使其他运动员相形见绌.

ˈ**flat-iron** *n* heavy iron heated with coals or by the fire and used for pressing linen, etc 熨斗; 烙铁.

ˈ**flat racing** horse-racing over level courses without jumps (无障碍物的)平地赛马. Cf 参看 STEEPLECHASE 1.

ˌ**flat ˈspin** **1** fast, often uncontrollable, descent of an aircraft spinning nearly horizontally 平旋下坠(飞行器近平面旋转急速下降, 常因失控所致). **2** (idm 习语) **be in/go into a flat ˈspin** (*infml* 口) be/become very confused or agitated 惊慌失措.

flat[3] /flæt; flæt/ *adv* **1** lower than the true or correct pitch 低于正常的或准确的音: *She sings flat all the time.* 她总是唱低了音. **2** stretched out on one level; lying at full length 平坦地; 平伸地; 平躺地: *She lay flat on her back in the warm sunshine.* 她在温暖的阳光下平躺着. ○ *He knocked his opponent flat.* 他把对手打倒在地上. ○ *The earthquake laid the city flat*, ie demolished it, making all the buildings fall. 地震把这座城市夷为平地. **3** outright; positively; completely 直截了当; 断然; 完全: *My boss told me flat that I could not leave early.* 我的老板明确地告诉我不能早走. ○ *She went flat against my orders*, ie disobeyed or ignored them completely. 她全然无视我的命令. ○ *I'm flat broke*, ie have absolutely no money. 我一贫如洗. **4** (idm 习语) **fall flat** (of a joke, story, performance, etc) fail completely to produce the effect intended or expected (指笑话、故事、表演等)未达到预期的效果: *All my funny stories fell completely flat.* 我讲的有趣的故事都没有人觉得可笑. **fall flat on one's face** (*infml* 口) suffer a humiliating and undignified setback, esp after attempting sth that is too ambitious 遭到丢脸的挫折(尤指不自量力者). **flat/stony broke** ⇨ BROKE[2]. **flat ˈout** (**a**) as fast as possible; using all one's strength or resources 尽快地; 全力以赴地; 竭尽全力地: *running, working, training, etc flat out* 全速奔跑、竭尽全力地工作、全力以赴地训练. (**b**) exhausted 精疲力竭的; 疲惫的: *After running in the* *marathon, she was flat out for a week.* 她参加马拉松比赛后一星期都疲惫不堪. **in 10 seconds, 5 minutes, etc 'flat** in the period of time specified, but always implying an unexpectedly short period of time 才10秒钟、5分钟等: *I can change a tyre in 2 minutes flat.* 我只用两分钟就能换上一个轮胎. ○ *She was out of bed, dressed and at the breakfast table in 50 seconds flat.* 她起床、穿衣、坐到饭桌旁, 一共才用了50秒钟.

flat[4] /flæt; flæt/ *n* **1** [sing] **the ~ (of sth)** flat level part of sth (某物的)平面部分: *the flat of the hand* 手掌 ○ *the flat of a sword, a blade, an oar* 剑面、刀面、桨面 ○ *on the flat*, ie level, not uphill or downhill 在平面上(非上坡或下坡). **2** [C usu *pl* 通常作复数] level ground; stretch of low flat land, esp near water 平地; 低洼地(尤指近水的): *'mud flats* 泥塘 ○ *'salt flats* 盐田. **3 the flat** [sing] season of flat racing for horses 平地赛马季节. **4** [C] (*music* 音) flat²(10) note or sign flat symbol indicating this 降半音符号. ⇨illus at MUSIC 见MUSIC插图. Cf 参看 NATURAL 6, SHARP *n*. **5** [C] (*esp US infml* 口) flat²(4) tyre 撒了气的车胎. **6** movable upright section of stage scenery mounted on a frame 平面布景; 布景屏.

flat·ten /'flætn; 'flætn̩/ *v* **1** [I, Ip, Tn, Tn·p] **~ (sth) (out)** become or make (sth) flat 变平; 使(某物)变平: *The land flattens out near the coast.* 海岸附近地势变得很平坦. ○ *The graph flattens out gradually after a steep fall.* 图表上的曲线突降之后逐渐趋于平稳. ○ *a field of wheat flattened by storms* 因暴风雨而倒伏的一片小麦 ○ *flatten (out) a piece of metal by hammering it* 把一块金属砸平 ○ *flatten oneself against a wall to let people get by* 紧贴墙站直, 以便他人通过. **2** [Tn] (*fig* 比喻) defeat (sb) completely; depress or humiliate 彻底打败(某人); 使沮丧; 使丢脸: *He was totally flattened by her sarcasm.* 她说的挖苦话使他无地自容.

flat·ter /'flætə(r); 'flætɚ/ *v* **1** [Tn] praise (sb) too much or insincerely, esp in order to gain favour for oneself 恭维, 奉承, 讨好(某人): *If you flatter your mother a bit she might invite us all to dinner.* 你要是奉承你母亲几句, 说不定她会把我们全请去吃饭. **2** [Tn usu passive 通常用于被动语态] give a feeling of pleasure or honour to (sb) 使(某人)感到高兴或荣幸: *I was very flattered by your invitation to talk at the conference.* 承蒙你邀我在会上讲话, 深感荣幸. **3** [Tn] represent (sb) in a way that makes him seem better-looking than he really is 使(某人)显得(较其实际相貌)好看: (*ironic* 反语) *This photograph certainly doesn't flatter you*, ie It makes you look rather ugly. 这张相片实在不如你本人好看. **4** [no passive 不用于被动语态: Tn, Dn·f] **~ oneself (that...)** believe, usu mistakenly, that one has achieved sth or has certain abilities or good qualities 认为(通常指误以为)自己成就了某事物或有某种能力或优秀品质: *Do you really think he likes you? You flatter yourself!* 你真以为他喜欢你? 你那是自作多情! ○ *He flatters himself that he speaks French well.* 他自以为法语说得很好.

▷ **flat·terer** /'flætərə(r); 'flætərɚ/ *n* person who flatters 谄媚者; 奉承者: *Don't believe him — he's a real flatterer.* 别相信他——他纯粹是奉承.

flat·ter·ing /'flætərɪŋ; 'flætərɪŋ/ *adj* that flatters (FLATTER 3) a person 使一个人美过其实的: *That's a very flattering dress Ann's wearing.* 安穿着那条连衣裙显得更漂亮了.

flat·tery /'flætərɪ; 'flætərɪ/ *n* [U] insincere praise 奉承; 恭维话: *With a little flattery I might persuade him to do the job.* 我说几句好听的, 也许能说服他去做这工作. ○ (*saying* 谚) *Flattery will get you nowhere*, ie I will not be influenced by your flattering remarks. 你恭维奉承也无济于事.

flatu·lent /'flætjʊlənt; 'flætʃələnt/ *adj* **1** causing or suffering from gas in the stomach or digestive tract 使肠胃气胀的; 患肠胃气胀的. **2** (of a person's speech, behaviour, etc) pretentious or pompous (指言语、行为等)做作的, 浮夸的.

▷ **flatu·lence** /'flætjʊləns; 'flætʃələns/ *n* [U] **1 (a)** gas in the stomach or digestive tract 胃或肠中的气. **(b)** feeling of discomfort caused by this 肠胃气胀引起的不适: *suffer from flatulence* 患肠胃气胀病. **2** pretentiousness or pomposity 做作; 浮夸.

flaunt /flɔ:nt; flɔnt/ *v* [Tn] (*usu derog* 通常作贬义) show (sth considered valuable) in order to gain the admiration of other people 炫耀; 夸耀; 夸示: *flaunt one's new clothes, car, etc* 炫耀自己的新衣服、汽车等 ○ *He's always flaunting his wealth.* 他总是摆阔.

flaut·ist /'flɔ:tɪst; 'flɔtɪst/ (*US* **flut·ist** /'flu:tɪst; 'flutɪst/) *n* person who plays the flute, esp as a profession 吹笛者; (尤指)职业笛手.

fla·vour (*US* **fla·vor**) /'fleɪvə(r); 'flevɚ/ *n* **1** [U] taste and smell, esp of food 味道与气味(尤指食物的): *Adding salt to food improves the flavour.* 食物中加盐可以提味. **2** [C] distinctive or characteristic taste 特别的味道: *wines with a delicate flavour* 有清香味道的葡萄酒 ○ *six different flavours of ice-cream* 六种不同味道的冰激凌. **3** [C, U] special quality, characteristic or atmosphere 特性; 特色; 气氛: *The film retains much of the book's exotic flavour.* 这部电影保存了原著的许多异国情调.

▷ **fla·vour** (*US* **fla·vor**) *v* [Tn, Tn·pr] **~ sth (with sth)** give flavour to sth by adding herbs, spices, etc (加入香料、调味品等)给(某物)调味: *flavour a stew (with onions)* (加洋葱)给炖肉提味 ○ *meat strongly flavoured with pepper* 胡椒味很重的肉. **fla·vour·ing** (*US* **fla·vor·ing**) /'fleɪvərɪŋ; 'flevərɪŋ/ *n* [C, U] thing added to food to give it flavour 调味品; 调味香料: *This orange drink contains no artificial flavourings.* 这种橙汁饮品不含人工调味料. ○ *The soup needs more flavouring.* 这汤应该再加点调料. **-fla·voured** (*US* **-fla·vored**) (forming compound *adjs* 用以构成复合形容词) having a flavour of the specified kind 有某种味道的: *lemon-flavoured sweets.*

fla·vour·less (*US* **fla·vor·less**) *adj* having no flavour 无味的; 无滋味的.

flaw /flɔ:; flɔ/ *n* **1** crack or fault (in an object or in material); imperfection (物体或材料的)裂纹或缺陷, 瑕疵: *This vase would be perfect but for a few small flaws in its base.* 这花瓶底部没有那几个小斑点就十全十美了. **2** mistake that lessens the effectiveness or validity of sth 错误; 缺点: *an argument full of flaws* 错误百出的论点 ○ *a flaw in a contract* 合同中的一个漏洞. **3** weak part in sb's character (某人性格上的)缺陷: *Pride was the greatest flaw in his personality.* 傲慢是他品格上的最大缺陷.

▷ **flaw** *v* [Tn usu passive 通常用于被动语态] cause (sth) to have a flaw 使(某事物)有缺陷: *His reasoning can't be flawed.* 他的推理无懈可击. ○ *a flawed masterpiece*, ie a work of art that is very great despite its minor faults 有瑕疵的杰作.

flaw·less *adj* perfect 无瑕的; 完美的: *a flawless complexion* 无疵的面容 ○ *a flawless performance* 完美的表演. **flaw·lessly** *adv.*

flax /flæks; flæks/ *n* [U] **1** plant grown for its fibre and seeds 亚麻. **2** fibre from the stem of this plant, used to make linen 亚麻纤维.

▷ **flaxen** /'flæksn; 'flæksn̩/ *adj* (of hair) pale yellow (指毛发)淡黄色的: *a flaxen-haired child* 长着淡黄色头发的孩子.

flay /fleɪ; fle/ *v* [Tn] **1 (a)** remove the skin from (a dead animal) 剥(死动物)的皮. **(b)** whip violently and cruelly (用鞭子)毒打: *He was so angry he nearly flayed his horse alive*, ie He beat it so much that some of its skin came off and it almost died. 他气得几乎把马活活抽死. **2** (*fig* 比喻) criticize (sb/sth) severely 严厉批评(某人[某事物]).

flea /fli:; fli/ *n* **1** small jumping insect without wings that feeds on the blood of animals and humans 跳蚤; 虼蚤: *I must have been bitten by a flea, my arms are itchy.* 我一定是让跳蚤咬了, 胳膊很痒. ○ *The cat's got fleas.* 这猫长虼蚤了. **2** (idm 习语) **with a 'flea in one's ear** rebuked, reprimanded or humiliated after an attempt at sth (做某事以后)受到责难、批评或羞辱: *He burst into our meeting and got sent away with a flea in his ear.* 我们正在开会他闯了进来, 大家把他轰走了.

□ **'flea-bag** *n* (*sl* 俚) **1** (*Brit*) dirty or unpleasant person or animal 肮脏或令人讨厌的人或动物: *I hate the old lady next door — she's a real flea-bag.* 我讨厌隔壁的老太太——她纯粹是个邋遢鬼. **2** (*esp US*) cheap dirty hotel 廉价的肮脏旅馆.

'flea-bite *n* **1** bite of a flea 蚤咬. **2** small but annoying inconvenience 小麻烦.

'flea market (*infml* 口) open-air market that sells old and used goods at low prices 跳蚤市场(廉价出售旧物

F

的露天市场).

ˈ**flea-pit** *n* (*infml derog* 口, 贬) old and dirty cinema, theatre, etc 破旧肮脏的电影院、剧场等.

fleck /flek; flɛk/ *n* ~ **(of sth)** **1** very small patch or spot of a colour 斑点: *flecks of brown and white on a bird's breast* 小鸟胸部棕色和白色的斑点. **2** small particle or grain of sth 微粒: *flecks of dust, soot, dandruff* 灰尘的微粒、煤炱、头皮屑.

▷ **fleck** *v* [Tn·pr usu passive 通常用于被动语态] ~ **sth with sth** mark with flecks 使有斑点: *The sea was flecked with foam.* 大海上涌起点点泡沫.

fled *pt, pp* of FLEE.

fledged /fledʒd; flɛdʒd/ *adj* (of birds) having fully developed wing feathers for flying; able to fly (指鸟)羽翼丰满的, 会飞的.

fledge·ling (also **fledg·ling**) /ˈfledʒlɪŋ; ˈflɛdʒlɪŋ/ *n* **1** young bird that is just able to fly (刚会飞的)幼鸟. **2** inexperienced person 无经验的人.

flee /fli:; fli/ *v* (*pt, pp* **fled** /fled; flɛd/) **1** **(a)** [I, Ipr] ~ **(from sb/sth)** run or hurry away; escape (esp from danger, threat, etc) 逃跑; 逃避; 避开; (尤指遇到危险、威胁等)逃离: *The customers fled (from the bank) when the alarm sounded.* 警铃响起, 顾客纷纷(从银行)逃走. **(b)** [Tn] run away from (sb/sth) 逃避, 逃离(某人[某事物]): *During the civil war thousands of people fled the country.* 在内战期间成千上万的人逃离了这个国家. **2** [I] (*fml* 文) pass away quickly; vanish 迅速消散; 消失: *All hope had fled.* 一切希望都破灭了.

fleece /fli:s; flis/ *n* **1** [C] **(a)** woolly hair of a sheep or similar animal 绵羊之类动物的毛: *These sheep have fine thick fleeces.* 这些绵羊的毛又细又厚. ⇨illus at SHEEP 见 SHEEP 插图. **(b)** amount of wool cut from a single sheep at one time 从一只羊身上一次剪得的全部羊毛. **2** [U] type of fabric with a texture like fleece 像羊毛的纤维: *My warmest coat is lined with fleece.* 我那件最暖的大衣衬有绒毛里子.

F

▷ **fleece** *v* **1** [Tn, Tn·pr] ~ **sb (of sth)** (*infml* 口) take (a lot of money) from sb, esp by overcharging or tricking him 诈取某人(巨款); (尤指)敲竹杠: *Some local shops are really fleecing the holiday-makers (of their money).* 本地的一些商店简直是敲诈来度假的人(的钱). **2** [Tn] cut or shear the fleece from (a sheep) 剪羊毛.

fleecy *adj* (**-ier**, **-iest**) (appearing) woolly and fluffy (像)羊毛的: *fleecy clouds* 羊毛状的云彩.

fleet[1] /fli:t; flit/ *n* **1** **(a)** [C] group of warships, submarines, etc under one commander 舰队. **(b)** group of ships fishing together 捕鱼船队. **(c)** [CGp] (usu 通常作 **the fleet**) all the warships, submarines, etc of a country; navy 一国的全部战舰、潜水艇等; 海军. **2** [C] group of aircraft, buses, taxis, etc owned and operated by one organization or travelling together (同一机构的或同时运行的)机群、公共汽车队、计程车队等: *the company's new fleet of vans* 公司的新客货车队.

□ ˌ**fleet** ˈ**admiral** officer in the US navy of the highest rank (美国)海军五星上将. ⇨App 9 见附录 9.

fleet[2] /fli:t; flit/ *adj* (*dated* 旧) fast; light and quick in running 快速的; 脚步轻而跑得快的: *fleet of foot* 脚步快的 ○ *fleet-footed* 脚步快的. ▷ **fleet·ness** *n* [U].

fleet·ing /ˈfli:tɪŋ; ˈflitɪŋ/ *adj* passing quickly; lasting only a short time 飞逝的; 短暂的: *For a fleeting moment I thought the car was going to crash.* 刹那间我想到汽车要碰撞. ○ *We paid her a fleeting visit before leaving the country.* 我们出国前匆匆探望了她一次. ▷ **fleet·ingly** *adv*.

Fleet Street /ˈfli:t stri:t; ˈflit,strit/ **1** street in central London where several major newspapers have their offices 弗利特街(伦敦中心的街道, 为几家大报馆所在地, 旧译舰队街). **2** the press in general; London journalism 新闻界; 伦敦报界: *Fleet Street loves a good scandal.* 新闻界热衷于轰动性的丑闻.

flesh /fleʃ; flɛʃ/ *n* **1** [U] **(a)** soft substance between the skin and bones of animal bodies, consisting of muscle and fat 肉: *The trap had cut deeply into the rabbit's flesh.* 捕兽夹子紧紧夹住兔子的皮肉. **(b)** this as food (食用的)肉: *Tigers are flesh-eating animals.* 虎是肉食动物. **2** [U] soft pulpy part of fruits and vegetables, the part that is usu eaten 果肉; 蔬菜的可食部分. **3 the flesh** [sing] the (human) body contrasted with the mind or the soul (人的)肉体(与精神或灵魂相对): (*saying* 谚) *The spirit is willing but the flesh is weak,* ie Although sb may want to do sth, he is too lazy, tired, weak, etc actually to do it. 心有余而力不足. **4 the flesh** [sing] bodily or physical desire 肉欲; 情欲: *the pleasures/sins of the flesh* 满足肉欲的快感[放纵情欲的罪]. **5** (idm 习语) ˌ**flesh and** ˈ**blood** the human body or human nature with its emotions, weaknesses, etc 血肉之躯; 人性: *It was more than flesh and blood could bear.* 这是血肉之躯无法忍受的. **go the way of all flesh** ⇨ WAY[1]. **in the** ˈ**flesh** in physical bodily form; in person 活生生的; 亲自; 本人: *His appearance in the flesh ended the rumours about his death.* 他亲自露面使传说他死亡的谣言不攻自灭. ○ *I've got all her records but I've never seen her in the flesh.* 我有她的所有唱片, 却从未见过她本人. **make one's/sb's** ˈ**flesh crawl/creep** make one/sb feel nervous, frightened or filled with loathing 使自己[某人]感觉紧张、害怕或厌恶: *The mere sight of snakes makes my flesh creep.* 我一看见蛇就心惊肉跳. **neither fish, flesh nor good red herring** ⇨ FISH[1]. **one's** ˌ**own** ˌ**flesh and** ˈ**blood** close relatives in one's family 亲人; 近亲; 关系密切的亲属: *I'll have to go to my aunt's funeral — she was my own flesh and blood after all.* 我得参加我姑姑的葬礼——她是我的亲人哪. **one's pound of flesh** ⇨ POUND[1]. **a thorn in sb's flesh/side** ⇨ THORN. **the world, the flesh and the devil** ⇨ WORLD.

▷ **flesh** *v* (phr v) **flesh sth out** add more details or information to sth 充实(某事物); 增加细节或详情: *Your summary will need fleshing out before you present it.* 你的总结需要增加一些具体材料再交出.

fleshly *adj* (*fml* 文) of the body; sensual or sexual 肉体的; 肉欲的: *fleshly lusts* 肉欲.

fleshy *adj* **1** of or like flesh; rather plump (似)肉的; 多肉的; 肥胖的: *fleshy arms* 胖胳膊 ○ *a fleshy body* 肥胖的身体. **2** soft and pulpy 肉质的: *fleshy peaches* 肉质多的桃.

□ ˈ**flesh-pots** *n* [pl] **(a)** (places supplying) good food, wine, etc; luxurious living 美食、美酒等或供应此类食物的处所; 豪华的生活. **(b)** places, such as brothels, where sexual desires are satisfied 满足性欲的处所(如妓院).

ˈ**flesh-wound** *n* wound that breaks the skin but does not reach the bones or internal organs of the body 皮肉之伤; 轻伤.

fleur-de-lis (also **fleur-de-lys**) /ˌflɜ: də ˈli:; ˌflɝ dəˈli/ *n* (*pl* **fleurs-** /flɜ: də ˈli:; ˌflɝ də ˈli/) design representing a lily flower as used in heraldry, formerly the royal coat of arms of France 百合花形纹章; (旧时)法国王室纹章.

flew *pt* of FLY.

flex[1] /fleks; flɛks/ *n* (*esp Brit*) (*US* **cord**) [C, U] (length of) flexible insulated wire used for carrying an electric current to an appliance 花线; 皮线.

flex[2] /fleks; flɛks/ *v* **1** [Tn] bend or move (a limb, joint or muscle), esp in order to exercise one's body before an activity 弯曲或活动(四肢、关节或肌肉)(尤指准备活动): *flex one's knee, toes, muscles, etc* 曲膝、活动脚趾、活动肌肉. **2** (idm 习语) **flex one's** ˈ**muscles** show one's strength and power, esp as a warning or to display pride in oneself 显示力量(尤指表示警告或自豪).

flex·ible /ˈfleksəbl; ˈflɛksəbl/ *adj* **1** that can bend easily without breaking 易弯曲的; 柔韧的; 有弹性的: *flexible plastic tubing* 弹性塑料管. **2** **(a)** easily changed to suit new conditions 易适应新情况的; 可变通的; 灵活的: *Our plans are quite flexible.* 我们的计划十分灵活. **(b)** (of people) willing and able to change according to different circumstances; adaptable (指人)能随机应变的, 随遇而安的. ▷ **flex·ib·il·ity** /ˌfleksəˈbɪlətɪ; ˌflɛksəˈbɪlətɪ/ *n* [U]. **flex·ibly** /ˈfleksəblɪ; ˈflɛksəblɪ/ *adv*.

flexi·time /ˈfleksɪtaɪm; ˈflɛksə,taɪm/ *n* [U] system in which employees can start and finish work at different times each day, provided that each of them works a certain number of hours in a week or month 弹性工作时间制.

flib·ber·ti·gib·bet /ˌflɪbətɪˈdʒɪbɪt; ˈflɪbɚtɪ,dʒɪbɪt/ *n* irresponsible, silly and gossipy person 信口雌黄、愚蠢而饶舌的人.

flick /flɪk; flɪk/ *n* **1** [C] quick light blow, eg with a whip or the tip of a finger 快速轻击(尤指用鞭或指尖). **2**

[C] quick sharp movement; jerk 快而突然的动作: *He turned the pancake over with a strong flick of his wrist.* 他一抖腕子就把饼翻过来了. **3** **(a)** [C] (*dated infml* 旧, 口) cinema film 电影. **(b)** **the flicks** [pl] (*dated infml* 旧, 口) the cinema 电影院: *What's on at the flicks?* 电影院放映什么电影?

▷ **flick** *v* **1** [Tn, Tn·pr] **~ A (with B); ~ B (at A)** strike (sb/sth) with a flick; give a flick with (sth) (用某物)轻打(某人[某物]): *He flicked the horse with his whip/flicked his whip at the horse.* 他用鞭子轻轻抽马. **2** [Tn, Tn·p, Cn·a] **~ sth (off, on, etc)** moves sth with a flick (用快而轻的动作)移动某物: *flick the light switch (on),* ie turn on the light 轻按电灯开关(开灯) ○ *He flicked the knife open.* 他轻触一下把刀刃弹出. **3** [Ipr, Ip] move quickly and lightly 快而轻地移动: *The cow's tail flicked from side to side.* 牛尾巴轻轻地左右摇摆. **4** (phr v) **flick sth away; flick sth from/off sth** remove sth with a flick 轻轻地拂去某物; 弹掉; 抖掉: *The waiter flicked the crumbs off the table.* 服务员轻轻抖掉桌上的面包屑. **flick through (sth)** turn over the pages (of a book, etc) quickly, looking briefly at the contents 快速翻阅(书等); 浏览: *Sam flicked through a magazine while he waited.* 萨姆一边等着一边翻阅杂志.

□ **'flick-knife** *n* (*pl* **-knives**) (*US* **'switch-blade**) knife with a blade inside the handle that springs out quickly when a button is pressed 弹簧刀.

flicker /ˈflɪkə(r); ˋflɪkɚ/ *v* **1** **(a)** [I] (of a light or flame) burn or shine unsteadily (指灯光或火焰)闪烁, 摇曳: *All the lights flickered for a moment.* 所有的灯都闪了一会儿. **(b)** [Ipr] (*fig* 比喻) (of an emotion) be felt or seen briefly (指情感)稍纵即逝: *A slender hope still flickered within him.* 他心中仍闪出一线希望. ○ *A faint smile flickered across her face.* 她脸上闪过一丝微笑. **2** [I, Ipr] move back and forth lightly and quickly 轻而快地来回移动; 闪动: *flickering eyelids* 眨着的眼睛 ○ *The leaves flickered gently in the breeze.* 树叶在微风中摇曳.

▷ **flicker** *n* (usu *sing* 通常作单数) **(a)** flickering movement or light 闪动; 闪烁; 摇曳: *the flicker of pictures on the cinema screen* 银幕上闪动的画面. **(b)** (*fig* 比喻) faint and brief experience, esp of an emotion 微弱短暂的体验(尤指情感): *a flicker of hope, despair, interest, etc* 一线希望、一丝绝望情绪、微弱的兴趣.

flier (also **flyer**) /ˈflaɪə(r); ˋflaɪɚ/ *n* **1** pilot of an aircraft; airman 飞行器驾驶员; 飞行员. **2** person, animal, vehicle, etc that moves very quickly 动作敏捷的人或动物; 速度很快的车辆. **3** small advertising leaflet that is widely distributed 小张广告传单. **4** = HIGH-FLYER (HIGH).

flies /flaɪz; flaɪz/ *n* **the flies** [pl] space above the stage of a theatre, used for lights and storing scenery 舞台上方安装灯具及存放布景之处.

flight[1] /flaɪt; flaɪt/ *n* **1** [U] **(a)** action or process of flying through the air; ability to fly 飞行; 飞翔; 飞行的能力: *the age of supersonic flight* 超音速飞行的时代 ○ *The bird had been shot down in flight,* ie while flying. 这只鸟是在飞行中打下来的. **(b)** movement or path of a thing through the air (物体在空中的)飞行或路线: *the flight of an arrow, a dart, a missile, etc* 箭、标枪、导弹等的飞行. **2** [C] **(a)** journey made by air, esp in an aircraft on a particular route 空中的航行; (尤指飞机等的)航班: *a smooth, comfortable, bumpy, etc flight* 平稳的、舒服的、颠簸的空中航行 ○ *All flights have been cancelled because of fog.* 因为有雾所有航班都已取消. **(b)** aircraft making such a journey 班机: *We travelled aboard the same flight.* 我们搭乘同一班机. ○ *Flight number BA 4793 will arrive in London at 16.50.* 英国航空公司4793号班机于16时50分抵达伦敦. **3** [U, C] passage or journey through space 航天飞行; 宇宙飞行: *the history of manned space flight* 载人航天史. **4** [C] group of aeroplanes working as a unit 飞行队: *an aircraft of the Queen's flight* 女王专用机队的一架飞机. **5** [C] **~ (of sth)** number of birds, insects, etc flying together or of arrows released together (鸟、昆虫等的)群飞; (箭的)齐发: *a flight of geese* 一队飞雁 ○ *a flight of arrows* 齐发的箭. **6** [C] series of stairs between two floors or landings 一段楼梯或阶梯: *There was no lift and we had to climb six flights of stairs.* 没有电梯, 我们得爬六段楼梯. **7** [U] swift passage, esp of time 飞逝(尤指时间). **8** [C] **~ of sth** instance of sth very imaginative but usu not practical (想像力的)奔放: *wild flights of imagination* 想像联翩. **9** (idm 习语) **a flight of 'fancy** unrealistic idea, etc that exists only in sb's mind 悬想; 异想天开: *Her latest flight of fancy is to go camping in the Sahara desert!* 她最近心血来潮想到撒哈拉沙漠去野营! **in the first/top flight** taking a leading place; excellent of his/its kind 占先; 名列前茅; 同行[同类]中的优秀者: *She's in the top flight of journalists.* 她是出类拔萃的新闻工作者.

▷ **flight** *v* [Tn] (in cricket) give (the ball) a certain path through the air when bowling so as to deceive the batsman (板球中)使(球)沿某路线飞行(以迷惑击球员): *a well-flighted delivery* 漂亮的投球.

flight·less *adj* (of birds) not able to fly (指鸟)不会飞的.

□ **'flight-deck** *n* **1** (on a ship that carries aircraft) deck for the take-off and landing of aircraft (运载飞机的船舰上的)飞行甲板. **2** control room of a large aircraft, from which the pilot and crew fly the plane (大型飞行器的)驾驶舱.

ˌflight lieu'tenant officer in the Royal Air Force between the ranks of flying officer and squadron leader 皇家空军上尉. ⇨App 9 见附录9.

'flight path direction or course of an aircraft through the air (飞行器的)飞行方向或路线: *The flight paths of the aeroplanes crossed, with fatal results.* 飞机的航线互相交错铸成人命惨祸.

'flight-recorder *n* (also **black 'box**) electronic device in an aeroplane that records details of the flight 飞行记录仪; 黑盒.

'flight sergeant non-commissioned officer in the Royal Air Force next above sergeant 皇家空军上士. ⇨ App 9 见附录9.

'flight simulator device on the ground for training pilots by reproducing accurately all the conditions of flying 飞行模拟装置.

flight[2] /flaɪt; flaɪt/ *n* **1** [C, U] act or instance of fleeing or running away 逃; 逃避; 逃跑: *Many soldiers fell wounded in their flight from the defeat.* 许多士兵在溃逃中受伤. ○ (*fig* 比喻) *the flight of capital,* ie the sending of money out of a country during a financial crisis 资金外流(在财政危机时将资金转到国外). **2** (idm 习语) **put sb to 'flight** force sb to flee 迫使某人逃走: *The enemy was put to flight by the advancing army.* 部队向前进, 赶跑了敌人. **take (to) 'flight** flee; run away 逃走; 逃跑: *The gang took (to) flight when they heard the police car.* 那伙歹徒听到警车声便逃跑了.

flighty /ˈflaɪtɪ; ˋflaɪtɪ/ *adj* **(-ier, -iest)** (esp of a woman or her behaviour) changeable and unreliable; not serious (尤指女子或其行为)反复无常的, 轻浮的.

flimsy /ˈflɪmzɪ; ˋflɪmzɪ/ *adj* **(-ier, -iest)** **1** **(a)** (of cloth or material) light and thin (指布或材料)轻而薄的: *a flimsy dress* 薄的连衣裙. **(b)** not strong or solid enough for the purpose for which it is used 不结实的; 易损坏的: *a flimsy cardboard box* 不结实的纸箱. **2** (*fig* 比喻) weak or feeble; unconvincing 软弱无力的; 不足信的: *a flimsy excuse* 站不住脚的借口 ○ *The evidence against him is rather flimsy.* 对他不利的证据不足凭信.

▷ **flim·sily** /-ɪlɪ; -ɪlɪ/ *adv.*

flim·si·ness *n.*

flimsy *n* [C, U] (sheet of) very thin paper on which a copy of the typing is produced when it is put under carbon paper 打字纸.

flinch /flɪntʃ; flɪntʃ/ *v* **1** [I] move or draw back suddenly, from shock, fear or pain (因吃惊、害怕或疼痛)畏缩或退缩: *He listened to the jeers of the crowd without flinching.* 他毫不畏惧地听着群众的嘲笑. **2** [Ipr] **~ from sth/from doing sth** avoid thinking about or doing sth unpleasant 不想或不做某种不愉快的事: *We shall never flinch from (the task of) telling the people the whole truth.* 我们要把全部真相告诉人民, 决不推卸这种责任.

fling /flɪŋ; flɪŋ/ *v* (*pt, pp* **flung** /flʌŋ; flʌŋ/) **1** [Tn, Tn·pr, Tn·p] throw (sth) violently, angrily or hurriedly (猛力地、愤怒地或匆忙地)扔, 抛, 掷(某物): *fling a stone (at a window)* (朝窗户)扔石头 ○ *He flung the paper away in disgust.* 他厌恶地把报纸扔了. **2** [Tn·pr, Tn·p, Cn·a] put or push (sb/sth) somewhere quickly or roughly and forcefully (急速地或粗暴而猛烈地)将(某人[某物])放到或推向某处: *She flung the papers on the desk and left*

F

angrily. 她把文件往桌子上一摔便气冲冲地走了. ○ *He flung her to the ground.* 他把她推倒在地上. ○ *He was flung into prison,* ie put into prison roughly and perhaps without trial. 他被投入监狱. ○ *He flung open the door.* 他猛然推开了门. **3** [Tn·pr, Tn·p] move (oneself or part of one's body) suddenly or forcefully 突然或猛然移动(身体或身体的一部分): *She flung herself in front of a car.* 她猛然冲到汽车前面. ○ *He flung his arm out just in time to stop her falling.* 他急忙伸出手臂把她扶住, 她才没有跌倒. **4** [Tn, Tn·pr, Tn·p] **~ sth (at sb)** say or express sth (to sb) in a violent way 激昂地(对某人)说或表达某事物: *You must be certain of your facts before you start flinging accusations (around) (at people).* 必须对实情胸有成竹才能理直气壮地(到处)指责(别人). **5** (phr v) **fling oneself at sb** = THROW ONESELF AT SB (THROW). **fling oneself into sth** start or do sth with a lot of energy and enthusiasm (尽力而积极地)开始或做某事: *She flung herself into her new job.* 她全力投入新的工作. **fling off, out, etc** move angrily or violently in the specified direction 愤怒地或激烈地沿某方向冲去: *He flung out of the room.* 他愤怒地冲出房间. **fling sth on** get dressed hurriedly and carelessly 匆忙地穿上衣服: *She flung on her coat and ran to the bus-stop.* 她匆匆穿上大衣就向公共汽车站跑去.

▷ **fling** *n* **1** act or movement of flinging; throw 扔; 抛; 掷. **2** (*infml* 口) short period of enjoyment in some (often irresponsible) activity (used esp in the expressions shown) 一时的(常为放纵的)行乐(尤用于以下示例): *a last/final fling* 最后的行乐 ○ *have a/one's fling* 恣意行乐 ○ *I had a few flings* (ie casual love affairs) *in my younger days.* 我年轻时有些风流韵事. **3** type of energetic (esp Scottish) dance 充满活力的(尤指苏格兰的)舞蹈: *the Highland fling* 高地弗林格.

flint /flɪnt; flɪnt/ *n* **1** [U] very hard grey stone that can produce sparks when struck against steel 燧石; 火石: *This layer of rock contains a lot of flint.* 这一岩层中有大量燧石. ○ [attrib 作定语] *flint axes* 燧石斧 ○ (*fig* 比喻) *He has a heart like flint,* ie He is unfeeling and stubborn. 他铁石心肠. **2** [C] piece of this or of hard alloy used to produce sparks, eg in a cigarette lighter 打火石.

▷ **flinty** *adj* (**-ier, -iest**) **1** made of flint; very hard, like flint 燧石的; 燧石般坚硬的. **2** cruel; unyielding 冷酷的; 坚定不移的: *a flinty heart* 铁石心肠.

□ '**flintlock** *n* old-fashioned gun, in which the gunpowder is lit by a spark struck from a flint 火石簧扳枪.

flip /flɪp; flɪp/ *v* (**-pp-**) **1** [Tn, Tn·pr] toss (sth) with a sharp movement of the thumb and forefinger so that it turns over in the air (用拇指和食指)捻(某物)(使之在空中翻转): *flip a coin (in the air)* 捻硬币(抛向空中). **2** [Tn, Tn·p] **~ sth (over)** turn sth over quickly 快速地翻转某物: *flip the pages over* 很快地翻着书页. **3** [Tn, Tn·p] move (sth) with a quick sharp movement; flick (2) 快速猛然移动(某物): *He flipped the light on.* 他猛然开了灯. **4** [I] (*sl* 俚) become very angry, excited or enthusiastic 变得非常气愤、激动或热情: *My mother really flipped when I told her I was getting married.* 我把要结婚的消息告诉了母亲, 母亲非常激动. **5** (idm 习语) ˌ**flip one's** '**lid** (*infml* 口) lose one's self-control; go crazy 失去自制力; 发疯. **6** (phr v) **flip through sth** = FLICK THROUGH STH (FLICK).

▷ **flip** *n* quick light blow or movement, esp one that tosses sth 快而轻的打击或动作(尤指将某物抛出): *give a coin a flip* 把一枚硬币抛向空中.

flip *adj* (*infml* 口) glib; flippant 草率的; 轻率的: *a flip comment* 轻率的评论.

flip *interj* (expressing annoyance or great surprise 表示厌烦或惊讶).

flip·ping *adj, adv* (*Brit*) (used as a mild alternative to a swear-word 用作语气较轻的咒骂语): *I hate this flipping hotel!* 我讨厌这该死的旅馆! ○ *What flipping awful weather!* 多讨厌的天气!

□ '**flip-flop** (*US* **thong**) *n* type of open sandal with a strap that goes between the big toe and the next toe 夹趾拖鞋; 人字拖鞋: *a pair of flip-flops* 一双夹趾拖鞋. ⇨ illus at SANDAL 见 SANDAL 插图.

'**flip side** reverse side of a gramophone record, esp the side that does not have the main song or piece of music on it 唱片的反面(尤指没有主要歌曲或乐曲的一面).

flip·pant /'flɪpənt; 'flɪpənt/ *adj* not showing sufficient respect or seriousness 轻浮的; 轻率的: *a flippant answer, remark, attitude, etc* 漫不经心的回答、言语、态度等.

▷ **flip·pancy** /-ənsɪ; -ənsɪ/ *n* [U] (quality of) being flippant 轻浮; 轻率: *His flippancy makes it difficult to have a decent conversation with him.* 他玩世不恭, 很难正经地和他交谈.

flip·pantly *adv.*

flip·per /'flɪpə(r); 'flɪpɚ/ *n* **1** broad flat limb of certain sea animals (not fish) used for swimming (非鱼类海生动物的)鳍状肢: *Seals, turtles and penguins have flippers.* 海豹、海龟、企鹅均有鳍状肢. **2** either of a pair of flat rubber attachments worn on the feet and used to help in underwater diving and swimming (用于潜水和游泳的)橡胶蹼, 鸭脚板.

flirt /flɜːt; flɝt/ *v* [I, Ipr] **~ (with sb) 1** behave (towards sb) in a romantic or suggestive way but without serious intentions 调情: *It's embarrassing when they flirt like that in public,* ie with each other. 他们在大庭广众之中那样调情, 真让人难堪. ○ *He enjoys flirting (with the girls in the office).* 他爱(与办公室的女职员)调情. **2 ~ with sth (a)** pretend to be interested in sth; think about sth but not seriously 假装对某事物感兴趣; 对某事物想想而已: *I'm flirting with the idea of getting a job in China.* 我胡思乱想着要到中国去工作. **(b)** behave so casually that one's life is put in danger 举动轻率(罔顾自己的性命): *flirt with danger/death* 把危险[死亡]当儿戏.

▷ **flirt** *n* person who flirts with many people 与许多人调情的人: *They say he's a terrible flirt.* 据说他是调情色鬼.

flir·ta·tion /flɜː'teɪʃn; flɝ'teʃən/ *n* **1** [U] flirting 调情. **2** [C] **(a) ~ with sb** brief and frivolous romantic involvement 短暂的风流韵事: *carry on/have a flirtation with sb* 与某人一时风流. **(b) ~ with sth** superficial interest in sth 对某事物的淡薄的兴趣: *a brief flirtation with the idea of starting his own business* 想自己开业的短暂的念头.

flir·ta·tious /flɜː'teɪʃəs; flɝ'teʃəs/ *adj* **(a)** fond of flirting 爱调情的: *an attractive flirtatious young woman* 爱卖弄风情的年轻貌美的女子. **(b)** of or related to flirting 调情的; 与调情有关的: *flirtatious behaviour* 调情的举动.

flit /flɪt; flɪt/ *v* (**-tt-**) **1** [Ipr, Ip] fly or move lightly and quickly from one place to another 轻快地从一处飞到另一处; 掠过: *bees flitting (about) from flower to flower* 在花丛中飞来飞去的蜜蜂 ○ *He flits from one thing to another,* ie does not deal with anything seriously. 他做事总是三心二意. ○ (*fig* 比喻) *A thought flitted through my mind,* ie came suddenly but then quickly disappeared. 在我头脑中有一闪念. **2** [I] (*Brit infml* 口) move about from one house to another; move from one's home secretly ,esp in order to avoid paying debts, etc 频繁搬迁; 秘密离家(尤指为躲债等).

▷ **flit** *n* (*Brit infml* 口) act of flitting (FLIT 2) (used esp in the expression shown) (为躲债等)搬家, 离家(尤用于以下示例): *do a (moonlight) flit* (在夜半)秘密搬家.

float[1] /fləʊt; flot/ *v* **1 (a)** [I, Ipr] stay on or at the surface of a liquid and not sink; be held up in air or gas 漂浮; 飘: *Wood floats (in water).* 木头能漂浮(于水面). ○ *Try and float on your back.* 试试仰浮. **(b)** [Ipr] move without resistance in air, water or gas; drift slowly 漂流; 飘动: *A balloon floated across the sky.* 有个气球从空中飘过. ○ *The raft was floating gently down the river.* 筏子顺河水缓缓漂流. ○ (*fig* 比喻) *Thoughts of lazy summer afternoons floated through his mind.* 夏日懒洋洋的下午种种思绪在他脑海里浮想联翩. **2** [Tn, Tn·pr] bring (sth) to the surface of a liquid; cause (sth) to move on liquid or in air 使(某物)漂浮; 使(某物)漂流或飘动: *There wasn't enough water to float the ship.* 水不够深, 船浮不起来. ○ *float a raft of logs down the river* 使圆木筏顺河漂下 ○ *We waited for the tide to float the boat off the sandbank.* 我们等待涨潮, 让潮水把船浮起离开沙滩. **3** [Tn] suggest (a plan or project); present for acceptance or rejection 提出(计划、方案等); 交出(以供取舍): *Let me float a couple of ideas.* 让我来谈两三点意见仅供参考. **4** [I, Ipr, Ip] **~ (about/around (sth))** (*infml* 口) (of a person) move vaguely or aimlessly from place to place; do nothing in particular (指人)游荡, 无所事事: *My weekend was boring — I just floated about (the house) or watched TV.* 我的周末过得很无聊 —— 只是在屋子里

转转或者看看电视. **5** [Tn] start (a new business company) by selling shares in it to the public (以公开发行股票方式)开办(新公司). **6** (**a**) [Tn] allow the foreign exchange values of (a currency) to vary freely according to the value of other international currencies 使(某货币)的对外汇率浮动: *float the pound, dollar, yen, etc* 使英镑、美元、日元等的对外汇率浮动. (**b**) [I] (of a currency) find its own value in this way (指货币)随汇率浮动. **7** (phr v) **float about/around** (esp in the continuous tenses 尤用于进行时态) (**a**) (of a rumour) be heard or talked about a lot (指传闻)广为流传: *There's a rumour floating around of a new job in the unit.* 这个部门盛传有个新工作要聘人. (**b**) (of an object) be in an unspecified place (指物品)在未指出的某处: *Have you seen my keys floating about (anywhere)?* 你在什么地方见到我的钥匙了吗?

▷ **float·ing** *adj* [usu attrib 通常作定语] **1** not fixed, determined or committed 不固定的; 未决定的; 未承诺的: *a floating voter,* ie a person who is not committed to always voting for the same political party 浮动选民(未必总投同一政党选票者) ○ *floating population,* ie one in which people are constantly moving from one place to another 流动人口. **2** (*medical* 医) out of its normal position 游离的: *a floating kidney* 游离肾. ˌ**floating ˈcapital** money that is not invested or otherwise committed 流动资本. ˌ**floating ˈdock** large box-like structure that can be put under the water to allow a ship to enter it, and then floated to lift the ship out of water 浮船坞. ˈ**floating rib** (*anatomy* 解) rib that is not joined to the breastbone 浮肋.

float[2] /fləʊt; flot/ *n* **1** (**a**) light object made of cork, etc that stays on the surface of a liquid, esp one attached to a fishing-line (to indicate when the bait has been taken) or to a net (to support it in water) 漂浮物; (尤指)鱼漂, 浮子. (**b**) light buoyant object that non-swimmers can hold on to while learning to swim 浮板(学游泳用的). **2** floating hollow ball or other air-filled container, used to control the flow of water, petrol, etc into a tank 浮球(用以控制水、汽油等流量的). **3** structure that enables an aircraft to float on water 浮筒(使飞行器浮于水面的装置). **4** (**a**) lorry, cart or low platform on wheels, used for showing things in a procession (游行时载展品等的)卡车、大车或装有轮子的展台; 花车: *The club display was mounted on a huge float and paraded through the main street.* 俱乐部的展品装在大型花车上在大街上通过. (**b**) vehicle with a low flat base, used for transporting the thing specified 低矮的平板车: *a milk float* 运牛奶的平板车. **5** sum of money used for everyday business expenses or for giving change (企业的)日常零钱.

flock[1] /flɒk; flɑk/ *n* [CGp] **1 ~ (of sth)** group of sheep, goats or birds of the same kind, either kept together or feeding and travelling together (同一种的羊或鸟的)一群: *a flock of wild geese* 一群雁 ○ *flocks (of sheep) and herds (of cattle)* 羊群和牛群. **2** large crowd of people 人群; 群众: *People came in flocks to see the royal procession.* 人们蜂拥而至瞻望皇室人员外出时的仪仗队. **3** number of people in sb's care, esp Christian churchgoers under a priest (由某人照管的)一群人; (尤指同一牧师辖下的)全体教徒: *a priest and his flock* 牧师和他的教友.

▷ **flock** *v* [Ipr, Ip] gather, move, come or go together in great numbers 群集; 成群结队: *In the summer, tourists flock to the museums and art galleries.* 夏季游人成群结队到博物馆和艺术馆参观. ○ *Huge numbers of birds had flocked together by the lake.* 成群的鸟聚集在湖畔.

flock[2] /flɒk; flɑk/ *n* **1** [C usu *pl* 通常作复数] tuft of wool, cotton, hair, etc (羊毛、棉花、毛发等的)一束. **2** [U] soft material for stuffing cushions, mattresses, etc (填充靠垫、床垫等的)软质材料: [attrib 作定语] *a flock mattress* 软床垫 ○ *flock(ed) wallpaper,* ie with a raised pattern made of short tufts of material 植绒壁纸.

floe /fləʊ; flo/ *n* sheet of floating ice, usu on the sea 成片的浮冰(通常浮于海上的): *Ice-floes are a threat to shipping in the area.* 浮冰对这一带的航运是一种威胁.

flog /flɒg; flɑg/ *v* (**-gg-**) **1** [Tn] beat (sb) severely, esp with a rod or whip, as a punishment 重重责打(某人)(尤指用棍棒或鞭子): *The boy was cruelly flogged for stealing.* 那男孩偷东西挨了一顿毒打. **2** [Tn, Dn·n, Dn·pr] **~ sth (to sb)** (*Brit infml* 口) sell sth (to sb) 卖(给某人)某物: *We should be able to flog the car (to someone) for a good price.* 我们应该能把这辆汽车高价卖出. ⇨Usage at SELL 用法见SELL. **3** (idm 习语) ˌ**flog a dead ˈhorse** waste one's efforts on an activity or a belief that is already widely rejected or has long been accepted 鞭打死马(对已摒弃或认可的活动或信念徒费精力). ˌ**flog sth to ˈdeath** (*infml* 口) be so persistent or repetitive about sth that people lose interest in it 坚持或重复某事物而使人失去兴趣: *I hope he won't tell that joke again; he's flogged it to death already.* 但愿他别再讲那个笑话了, 已经老掉牙了.

▷ **flog·ging** *n* [C, U] (instance of) beating or whipping 打; 鞭笞.

flood[1] /flʌd; flʌd/ *v* **1** (**a**) [I, Tn] (cause a place that is usu dry to) be filled or overflow with water; inundate (使通常干燥的地方)灌满水; 淹没; 泛滥: *The cellar floods whenever it rains heavily.* 一下大雨地窖里就灌满了水. ○ *The river had burst its banks and flooded the valley.* 河水冲破堤岸, 淹没了山谷. (**b**) [Tn] (of rain) fill (a river, etc) so that it overflows (指雨水)使(河流等)泛滥: *streams flooded by violent storms* 因暴风雨而泛滥的河流. **2** [Ipr, Tn, Tn·pr] **~ (sth) (with sth)** cover or fill (sth) completely; spread into (sth) 铺满或充满(某物); 扩展到(某物): *A powerful light flooded (into) the grounds.* 有一道强光照进了庭院. ○ *The place was flooded with light.* 那地方十分光亮. **3** [Tn, Tn·pr] **~ sth (with sth)** fill (the carburettor of a motor engine) with too much petrol so that the engine will not start 使(汽车发动机的汽化器)溢流. **4** [Ipr, Ip, Tn] (*fig* 比喻) (of a thought or feeling) flow powerfully over (sb); surge over (sb) (指思想或感情)充溢, 涌现: *A great sense of relief flooded over him.* 他深感宽慰. ○ *Memories of his childhood came flooding back.* 他童年的往事涌上心头. **5** (idm 习语) ˌ**flood the ˈmarket** (cause sth to) be offered for sale in large quantities, often at a low price (使某物)充斥(常指廉价): *Japanese cars have flooded the American market.* 日本汽车已充斥美国市场. **6** (phr v) **flood in; flood into sth** come to or arrive at (a place) in great quantities or numbers 大量涌入(某处): *Applications flooded into the office.* 申请书像潮水般涌进办公室. **flood sb out** force sb to leave home because of a flood 大水迫使某人离家: *Half the village were flooded out by a burst water main.* 由于总水管破裂, 半数村民被迫离开了家. **flood sb/sth with sth** arrive in great quantities for sb/at sth 给某人大量的某事物; 大量的某事物涌向某处: *The office was flooded with complaints.* 办事处收到如洪水般涌至的投诉信件.

▷ **flood·ing** *n* [U] covering of an area of land that is usu dry with a lot of water, eg when a river overflows 泛滥: *Widespread flooding is affecting large areas of Devon.* 洪水泛滥, 淹没了德文郡的广大地区.

flood[2] /flʌd; flʌd/ *n* **1** (**a**) (coming of a) great quantity of water, esp over a place that is usu dry 大量的水; 洪水; 水灾: *The heavy rain caused floods in the houses by the river.* 这场大雨下得河边的房子里都进了水. ○ *There's a flood in the next valley.* 旁边的山谷被水淹了. (**b**) **the Flood** (*Bible*《圣经》) the one that was sent by God to punish mankind, as described in the Old Testament book of Genesis (《旧约·创世记》中所记载上帝借以惩罚人类的)洪水. **2 ~ (of sth)** great quantity or volume 多; 大批; 大量; 大: *a flood of anger, abuse, indignation, etc* 大发雷霆、大骂、满腔义愤 ○ *a flood of letters, refugees* 大量涌来的信件、难民 ○ *The child was in floods of tears,* ie was crying uncontrollably. 那孩子哭成了泪人儿. **3** flowing in of the tide from the sea to the land; rising tide 涨潮: *The tide is at the flood.* 正在涨潮. Cf 参看 EBB *n* 1. **4** (idm 习语) **in ˈflood** (of a river) overflowing (指河流)泛滥: *We can't cross the meadow there because the river is in flood.* 我们不能从那里穿过草地, 因为河水泛滥了.

□ ˈ**floodgate** *n* **1** gate that can be opened or closed to control the flow of water (水闸的)闸门. **2** (idm 习语) **open the floodgates** ⇨ OPEN[2].

ˈ**flood-tide** *n* rising tide 涨潮.

flood·light /ˈflʌdlaɪt; ˈflʌdˌlaɪt/ *n* (esp *pl* 尤作复数) large powerful light that produces a wide beam, used to light sports grounds, theatre stages, etc (运动场、舞台

等的)泛光灯, 强力照明灯: *a match played under floodlights* 在泛光灯下进行的比赛. ⇨illus at ASSOCIATION FOOTBALL 见 ASSOCIATION FOOTBALL 插图.

▷ **flood·light** *v* (*pt, pp* **floodlighted** or **floodlit** /-lɪt; -lɪt/) [Tn usu passive 通常用于被动语态] light (sth) using floodlights 用泛光灯照亮(某物): *The Acropolis is floodlit in the evenings.* 夜晚泛光灯把卫城照得通亮.

floor[1] /flɔ:(r); flɔr/ *n* **1** [C usu *sing* 通常作单数] surface of a room on which one stands, walks, etc (室内的)地面, 地板: *There weren't enough chairs so I had to sit on the floor.* 房间里的椅子不够, 我只好坐在地上. ○ *The bare concrete floor was cold on my feet.* 水泥地没铺地毯, 我的脚感到很凉. ○ [attrib 作定语] *5 000 square metres of floor space* 5 000平方米的房屋面积. **2** [C usu *sing* 通常作单数] bottom of the sea or ground surface of a cave, etc (海洋或洞穴等的)底: *the ocean, forest, valley, cave floor* 海洋的底、森林的地面、谷底、洞底. ⇨ Usage at EARTH 用法见 EARTH. **3** [C] all the rooms, etc on the same level in a building; level of storey of a building 同一层楼的所有房间等; 楼层: *Her office is on the second floor.* 她的办公室在三楼. ⇨Usage 见所附用法. **4 the floor** [sing] (**a**) part of an assembly hall where members sit, eg in the Houses of Parliament, US Congress, etc 议员席(如英国议会两院、美国国会等的): *speak from the floor* 在议员席上发言. (**b**) right to speak in such an assembly or meeting (在此种会议上的)发言权: *The floor is yours — you may present your argument.* 现在请您发言——尽请发表意见. **5** [C usu *sing* 通常作单数] area where a particular activity is undertaken 进行某种活动的场地: *the dance floor*, ie part of the floor of a night-club, etc where guests dance (夜总会等的)舞池 ○ *the factory/shop floor*, ie part of a factory where the ordinary workers (ie not the managers) work 车间. **6** [C] minimum level for wages or prices (工资或物价的)最低水平. **7** (idm 习语) **be/get in on the ground floor** ⇨ GROUND FLOOR (GROUND[1]). ˌ**hold the** ˈ**floor** speak to an audience, esp at great length or with determination, so that no one else has a chance to say anything 演说; (尤指)长篇演讲或慷慨陈辞(使他人无从插嘴): *She held the floor for over an hour.* 她发言占了一个多小时. ˌ**take the** ˈ**floor** (**a**) get up to speak or address an audience 起立发言或演讲: *I now invite the President to take the floor.* 现在请总统讲话. (**b**) get up and start to dance 起来跳舞: *She took the floor with her husband.* 她站起来和丈夫跳舞. **wipe the floor with sb** ⇨ WIPE.

▷ **floor·ing** *n* [U] material, eg boards or tiles, used for making floors 铺地面的材料(如木板或瓷砖).

□ ˈ**floor-board** *n* any of the long (wooden) planks or boards laid down to make a floor (铺地面的)木板.

ˈ**floor show** series of performances, eg of singing and dancing, presented in a night-club, bar, etc 一系列的表演(如夜总会、酒吧间等的唱歌、跳舞).

NOTE ON USAGE 用法: In British English the floor of a building at street level is the **ground floor** and the floor above that is the **first floor**. 在英式英语中, 楼房地面与街道相平的楼层叫**ground floor, ground floor**上面的一层叫**first floor**. ☆ In US English the street-level floor is the **first floor** and the one above is the **second floor**. 在美式英语中, 与街道相平的楼层叫**first floor**, 其上面的一层叫**second floor**.

floor[2] /flɔ:(r); flɔr/ *v* [Tn] **1** provide (a building or room) with a floor 为(建筑物或房间)铺设地面或地板. **2** knock down (sb) in a fight (在打斗或拳击中)打倒(某人): *He floored his opponent with a fine punch in the first round.* 他在第一局比赛中猛击一拳就把对手打倒在地. **3** (*infml* 口) defeat or confuse (sb) in an argument, discussion, etc (在辩论、讨论中等)驳倒或难倒(某人): *Tom was completely floored by two of the questions in the exam.* 试卷中有两个问题把汤姆难倒了.

floozie (also **floosie**) /ˈflu:zɪ; ˈfluzɪ/ *n* (*infml derog* 口, 贬) woman of low morals; prostitute 荡妇; 妓女.

flop /flɒp; flɑp/ *v* (**-pp-**) **1** [Ipr, Ip] move or fall clumsily, helplessly or loosely (笨拙地、不由自主地或松弛地)移动或落下: *The pile of books flopped noisily onto the floor.* 那摞书劈里啪啦地散落到地上. ○ *The fish we'd caught flopped around in the bottom of the boat.* 我们捕到的鱼在船底乱蹦. **2** [I, Ipr, Ip] hang or sway heavily and loosely (沉重地而不受束缚地)悬挂或摆动: *flopping stirrups* 垂着的马镫 ○ *Her hair flopped (about) over her shoulders.* 她的头发披散在肩上. **3** [I, Ipr, Ip] sit or lie down heavily and clumsily, because of tiredness (因疲劳)重重地、笨拙地坐下或躺下: *I'm ready to flop.* 我要累倒了. ○ *Exhausted, he flopped (down) into the nearest chair.* 他累得一下子坐到离他最近的小沙发上. **4** [I] (*infml* 口) (of a book, play, etc) fail totally; be unsuccessful (指书、戏剧等)彻底失败, 不成功.

▷ **flop** *n* **1** (usu *sing* 通常作单数) flopping movement or sound 笨拙的移动或凌乱的落下或这种声音. **2** (*infml* 口) total failure (of a book, play, etc) (书、戏剧等的)彻底失败: *Despite all the publicity, her latest novel was a complete flop.* 她的最新小说尽管广为宣传, 结果还是彻底失败.

flop *adv* with a flop 扑通一声: *fall flop into the water* 扑通一声掉进水里.

floppy *adj* (**-ier**, **-iest**) tending to flop; soft and flexible; falling loosely (笨拙地、不由自主地或松弛地)移动或落下的; 松软的; 松弛下垂的: *a floppy hat* 松软的帽子. — *n* (*infml* 口) = FLOPPY DISK. **floppy disk** (also **floppy**, **diskette**) (*computing* 计) flexible disk for recording and storing data in a form that a computer can read 软磁盘. ⇨illus at COMPUTER 见 COMPUTER 插图. Cf 参看 HARD DISK (HARD[1]).

flop-house /ˈflɒphaʊs; ˈflɑpˌhaʊs/ *n* (*US infml* 口) cheap lodging house or hotel; doss-house 廉价的寄宿处、旅馆或客栈.

flora /ˈflɔ:rə; ˈflɔrə/ *n* [pl] all the plants of a particular area or period of time (某地区或时代的)一切植物, 植物区系: *the flora of the Himalayas, the Palaeozoic era* 喜马拉雅山的、古生代的植物系. Cf 参看 FAUNA.

floral /ˈflɔ:rəl; ˈflɔrəl/ *adj* [usu attrib 通常作定语] (**a**) made of flowers 用花做的: *floral arrangements, tributes* 插花、敬献的鲜花. (**b**) decorated with flowers 用花装饰的: *floral wallpaper* 有花卉图案的壁纸.

florid /ˈflɒrɪd; *US* ˈflɔ:r-; ˈflɔrɪd/ *adj* **1** (*usu derog* 通常作贬义) elaborate and ornate; excessively decorated or colourful 华丽的; 过分装饰的; 过分艳丽的: *florid music, poetry, art, etc* 矫揉造作的音乐、诗、艺术等 ○ *a florid room, painting* 过分装饰的房间、过分艳丽的画. **2** (of a person's face) red in colour; ruddy (指人的面孔)红润的: *a florid complexion* 红润的面色.

florin /ˈflɒrɪn; *US* ˈflɔ:rɪn; ˈflɔrɪn/ *n* former British coin worth two shillings or one tenth of £1 (now ten pence) 英国旧币制中的硬币, 值二先令或十分之一镑(现值10便士).

flor·ist /ˈflɒrɪst; *US* ˈflɔ:r-; ˈflɔrɪst/ *n* person who has a shop that sells flowers 花商: *order a wreath from the florist* 从花店订购花圈 ○ *buy a bouquet at the florist's*, ie shop where flowers are sold 在花店买一束花.

floss /flɒs; *US* flɔ:s; flɔs/ *n* [U] **1** rough silk threads from the outside of a silkworm's cocoon (蚕茧外层的)粗丝. **2** (also ˈ**floss silk**) spun (but not twisted) silk thread used for embroidery 刺绣用的丝线.

flo·ta·tion /fləʊˈteɪʃn; floˈteʃən/ *n* [C, U] starting of a new company by selling shares in it to the public (公开发行股票)开办新公司.

flo·tilla /fləˈtɪlə; floˈtɪlə/ *n* (**a**) fleet of boats or small ships 船队; 小型舰队. (**b**) small fleet of warships 小舰队: *a destroyer flotilla* 驱逐舰的舰队.

flot·sam /ˈflɒtsəm; ˈflɑtsəm/ *n* [U] **1** parts of a wrecked ship or its cargo found floating in the sea (在海上漂浮的)遇难船只的残骸或货物. Cf 参看 JETSAM. **2** (idm 习语) ˌ**flotsam and** ˈ**jetsam** (**a**) people without homes or work or those who have had to leave their houses; vagrants and tramps or refugees 流离失所的人; 无业游民; 流浪者; 难民. (**b**) various unimportant objects; bits and pieces; odds and ends 无价值的东西; 零碎物品.

flounce[1] /flaʊns; flaʊns/ *v* [Ipr, Ip] move about in an exaggerated, and usu impatient and angry manner 大动作地走动(通常为不耐烦而愤怒地): *She flounced out of the room, swearing loudly.* 她大声地骂着离开了房间. ○ *children flouncing around in their party clothes* 穿着参加聚会的衣服到处乱跑的孩子们.

▷ **flounce** *n* (usu *sing* 通常作单数) sudden impatient movement of the body; jerk (身体突然发出的)不耐烦的动作, 猛然的动作: *with a flounce of the head* 脑袋猛

地一动.

flounce[2] /flaʊns; flaʊns/ *n* wide strip of cloth or lace sewn by its upper edge to a garment, eg a skirt 荷叶边(如裙子上的).

▷ **flounced** *adj* trimmed or decorated with flounces 镶荷叶边的: *a flounced frock* 镶荷叶边的连衣裙.

floun·der[1] /ˈflaʊndə(r); ˋflaʊndɚ/ *v* [I, Ipr, Ip] **1** move or struggle helplessly or clumsily; move with difficulty, as through mud or deep snow 笨拙地移动或挣扎; 艰难地移动(如在泥中或深雪中): *Anna couldn't swim and was left floundering (about/around) in the deep end of the swimming-pool.* 安娜不会游泳, 在游泳池的深水区里挣扎着. **2** hesitate or make mistakes when talking or when coming to a decision (说话或做决定时)犹豫或出错误: *I wasn't expecting the interviewer to ask about my private life and was left floundering for a while.* 我没想到主持面试的人问我私生活的事, 就犹豫了一下. ○ *flounder (on) through a badly prepared speech* 由于准备不充分而讲得错误百出.

floun·der[2] /ˈflaʊndə(r); ˋflaʊndɚ/ *n* small flat-fish that lives in the ocean and is eaten as food 鲆鲽.

flour /ˈflaʊə(r); flaʊr/ *n* [U] fine powder obtained by grinding grain, esp wheat or rye, and used for making bread, cakes, etc 谷物磨成的粉; (尤指)(小麦的)面粉, 黑麦粉.

▷ **flour** *v* [Tn] cover or sprinkle (sth) with flour 在(某物)上覆上或撒上面粉: *flour the pastry board* 在做点心的案板上撒上面粉.

floury /ˈflaʊərɪ; ˋflaʊrɪ/ *adj* of or like flour; covered with flour (似)面粉的; 覆有面粉的: *floury potatoes*, ie ones that are soft and fluffy 很面的土豆(柔软不脆的) ○ *She wiped her floury hands with a damp cloth.* 她用湿布擦去手上的面粉.

flour·ish /ˈflʌrɪʃ; ˋflʌrɪʃ/ *v* **1** [I] be successful, very active, or widespread; prosper 昌盛; 旺盛; 兴旺; 繁荣: *No new business can flourish in the present economic climate.* 在目前的经济气候中, 任何新生意都兴旺不起来. ○ *a flourishing squash club* 兴旺的壁球俱乐部. **2** [I] grow healthily; be well and active 健康成长; 茂盛; 健壮而活跃: *This species of flower flourishes in a warm climate.* 这种花在温暖的气候中长得茂盛. ○ *All the family are flourishing.* 全家人身体都很好. **3** [I, Ipr] (of ideas or people) be very active and influential (during the specified period) (指思想或人)(在某时期)活跃而有影响力: *In Germany the baroque style of art flourished in the 17th and 18th centuries.* 在德国, 巴罗克艺术风格在17和18世纪非常盛行. **4** [Tn] wave sth about in order to attract attention to it 挥舞某物(以引起注意): *He stormed into the office, flourishing a letter of complaint.* 他挥舞着一封投诉信冲进了办公室.

▷ **flour·ish** *n* (usu *sing* 通常作单数) **1** bold sweeping movement or gesture, used esp to attract attention 明显的大动作或手势(尤用以引起注意的): *He opened the door for her with a flourish.* 他潇洒地为她打开了门. **2** flowing curve, esp in handwriting or decoration 流畅的曲线(尤指书法或装饰方面的). **3** loud and elaborate piece of music; fanfare 响亮而细腻的乐曲; 小号曲: *A flourish of trumpets marked the Queen's arrival.* 小号奏出嘹亮的乐曲欢迎女王驾到.

flout /flaʊt; flaʊt/ *v* [Tn] disobey (sb/sth) openly and scornfully 公然藐视(某人[某事物]): *flout the law, (a) convention, the rules* 藐视法律、传统、规则等 ○ *flout sb's advice* 轻视某人的劝告.

flow /fləʊ; flo/ *v* (*pt, pp* **-ed**) **1** [I, Ipr, Ip] **(a)** (of a liquid) move freely and continuously (指液体)流动: *Her tears flowed freely (down her cheeks).* 她眼泪止不住地(顺着面颊)往下流. ○ *Most rivers flow into the sea.* 江河大多流入海洋. ○ *Blood suddenly started flowing out.* 突然流出血来. **(b)** move freely and continuously, esp within a closed system; circulate 畅通无阻(尤指在封闭系统内); 流通; 流传: *Keep the traffic flowing.* 保持交通畅通无阻. ○ *Electricity is flowing (in the circuit/wires).* 电在(电路[导线]中)流动. ○ *Blood flows round the body.* 血液在体内循环. ○ *In convection, hot currents flow upwards.* 在对流中热气流向上运动. **2** [I] (of speech or writing) proceed evenly and continuously (指讲话或写作)流畅: *Conversation flowed freely when the speaker invited discussion.* 演讲人请大家讨论, 于是人人畅所欲言. **3** [I, Ipr, Ip] fall or hang (down) loosely and freely 松散而无束缚地落下或垂下: *long flowing robes* 飘洒的长袍 ○ *Her hair flowed (down) over her shoulders.* 她长发垂肩. **4** [I, Ipr] **~ (with sth)** be available plentifully; be distributed freely 有的是; 大量供应; 取之不尽: *The party became lively when the drink began to flow.* 饮料开始大量供应, 聚会的气氛就活跃起来了. ○ *a land flowing with milk and honey*, ie place with rich natural resources 自然资源丰富的地方. **5** [I] (of the sea tide) come in; rise (指海潮)涨, 涨潮: *The tide began to flow and our footprints were covered.* 开始涨潮了, 潮水遮住了我们的脚印. Cf 参看 EBB 1. **6** (phr v) **flow in/into sth** arrive in a steady stream 不断涌入: *The election results flowed in throughout the night.* 通夜不断传来各项选举结果. ○ *Offers of help flowed into the office.* 人们接连不断地向办事处表示愿意提供帮助. **flow from sth** come or derive from sth; result from sth 源于某事物; 为某事物的结果: *Many benefits will flow from this discovery.* 这项发现将带来许多好处. **flow out (of sth)** leave in a steady stream 外流: *Profits are flowing out of the country.* 利润源源不断地流向国外. **flow over sb** take place without affecting sb (某事)发生而不影响某人: *Office politics just seem to flow over him.* 同事之间互相倾轧、勾心斗角的事似乎并未波及到他.

▷ **flow** *n* (usu *sing* 通常作单数) **1 ~ (of sth/sb)** (rate of a) flowing movement of sth/sb (某事物[某人]的)流动(量); 流量: *a steady flow of traffic* 川流不息的来往车辆 ○ *The government is trying to stop the increasing flow of refugees entering the country.* 政府正在设法阻止越来越多的难民流入本国. **2 ~ (of sth)** (rate of a) continuous stream or supply of sth 某事物的持续或连续供应(量): *cut off the flow of oil* 切断石油输送 ○ *the constant flow of information* 源源不断的信息. **3** even and continuous outpouring of words 口若悬河; 滔滔不绝: *I interrupted him while he was in full flow*, ie talking away strongly. 他正在高谈阔论, 我打断了他的话. **4** incoming tide 涨潮: *the ebb and flow of the sea* 海潮的涨落. **5** (idm 习语) **the ebb and flow (of sth)** ⇨ EBB *n*.

□ ˈ**flow chart** (also ˈ**flow diagram**) diagram showing the development of sth through the different stages or processes in a series 流程图.

flower /ˈflaʊə(r); ˋflaʊɚ/ *n* **1** part of a plant from which the seed or fruit develops, often brightly coloured and lasting only a short time 花; 花朵: *The plant has a brilliant purple flower.* 那棵植物开着一朵鲜艳的紫花. ⇨illus at App 1 见附录1插图, page ii. **2** plant grown for the beauty of its flowers; flower and its stem (供观赏的)开花植物; (带梗的)花: *arrange some flowers in a vase* 往花瓶里插花. **3** [sing] **the ~ of sth** (*rhet* 修辞) finest or best part of sth; prime or peak of sth 精华; 精粹; 精英; 鼎盛阶段: *the flower of the nation's youth* 该国青年的精英 ○ *in the flower of one's maturity/strength/youth* 正当成熟[身强力壮/年轻]的时候. **4** (idm 习语) **in/into** ˈ**flower** in/into the state of having the flowers open 处于[进入]开花期: *The roses have been in flower for a week.* 这些玫瑰花已经开了一星期了. ○ *The crocuses are late coming into flower.* 藏红花开花晚.

▷ **flower** *v* **1** [I] produce flowers; bloom 开花: *These plants will flower in the spring.* 这些植物到了春天就开花. ○ *a late-flowering chrysanthemum* 迟开的菊花. **2** [I] develop fully; mature or blossom 充分发展; 成熟; 繁荣: *Their friendship flowered while they were at college.* 他们的友谊在求学时已根深蒂固. **flowered** /ˈflaʊəd; ˋflaʊɚd/ *adj* [usu attrib 通常作定语] decorated with patterns of flowers 用花卉图案装饰的: *flowered wallpaper, cloth, curtains, etc* 有花卉图案的壁纸、布、帘等. **flower·ing** /ˈflaʊərɪŋ; ˋflaʊərɪŋ/ *n* (usu *sing* 通常作单数) **~ (of sth)** full development of (an idea, literary or political movement, etc) (思想、文学或政治运动等的)成熟发展: *the gradual flowering of modern democracy* 现代民主的日臻成熟.

flowery /ˈflaʊərɪ; ˋflaʊərɪ/ *adj* (**-ier, -iest**) **1** covered with or having a lot of flowers 有很多花的: *flowery fields* 有很多花的田野. **2** (of language, gestures or decoration) too elaborate or ornate (指语言、手势或装饰)矫揉造作的, 过分修饰的, 过于华丽的: *a flowery speech* 辞藻过分华丽的讲话.

flower·less *adj* not having or not producing flowers 无花的; 不开花的: *flowerless plants* 不开花的植物.

□ ˈ**flower-bed** *n* piece of ground in a garden or park,

specially prepared for growing flowers（花园或公园里的）花畦，花坛.
'flower children (also **'flower people**) (esp in the 1960s) (usu young) people supporting universal love and peace, and carrying flowers as a symbol of their beliefs（尤指20世纪60年代的）（通常为年轻的）戴花嬉皮士（主张博爱与和平，以花象征其信仰的人）.
'flower-girl *n* girl or woman who sells flowers in a market, etc 卖花女.
'flowerpot *n* container of plastic or earthenware, in which a plant is grown 花盆. ⇨illus at POT 见 POT 插图.
'flower power beliefs or cult of the flower children 戴花嬉皮士的信仰或崇拜.
'flower-show *n* exhibition at which flowers are displayed 花展.
flown *pp* of FLY².
fl oz *abbr* 缩写 = (*pl* unchanged or **fl ozs** 复数或不变或作 **fl ozs**) fluid ounce: *5 fl oz* 5液量盎司.
Flt Lt *abbr* 缩写 = Flight Lieutenant: *Flt Lt (Robert) Bell*（罗伯特·）贝尔空军上尉.
flu /fluː; flu/ *n* (*infml* 口) = INFLUENZA.
fluc·tu·ate /ˈflʌktʃʊeɪt; ˋflʌktʃʊˌet/ *v* [I, Ipr] ~ **(between A and B)** **1** (of a price, number, rate, etc) rise and fall; change irregularly（指价格、数量、比率、费用等）涨落，波动: *The price fluctuates between £5 and £6.* 价格在5英镑与6英镑之间波动. **2** (of an attitude or a state) change continually and irregularly; waver（指态度或状态）变化不定，动摇: *fluctuating opinions* 变化不定的意见. ▷ **fluc·tu·ation** /ˌflʌktʃʊˈeɪʃn; ˌflʌktʃʊˋeʃən/ *n* [C, U] ~ **(of/in sth)**: *wide fluctuations of temperature* 温度的巨大变化 ○ *fluctuations in the state of his health* 他健康状况时好时坏的变化.
flue /fluː; flu/ *n* channel, pipe, etc through which smoke, fumes or hot air pass from a boiler or oven, usu to a chimney 烟道；管道.
flu·ent /ˈfluːənt; ˋfluənt/ *adj* **1** (of a person) able to speak or write a language or perform an action smoothly, accurately and with ease（指人）语言流利的，文字流畅的，动作准确、轻松的: *a fluent speaker (of Spanish)*（西班牙语）说得流利的人 ○ *be fluent in speech* 讲话流利. **2** (of speech, a language or an action) expressed in a smooth and accurate way（指言语、语言）流利而通顺的；（指动作）灵活而准确的: *speak/write fluent Russian* 说[写]流利的俄语 ○ *fluent movements*, ie ones that are flowing and graceful 协调优美的动作.
▷ **flu·ency** /ˈfluːənsɪ; ˋfluənsɪ/ *n* [U] quality or condition of being fluent 流利；通顺；灵活而准确: *She speaks Swahili with great fluency.* 她说的斯瓦希里语非常流利.
flu·ently *adv*.
fluff /flʌf; flʌf/ *n* **1** [U] **(a)** soft feathery pieces of material shed by blankets, etc（毛毯等落下的）绒毛: *My best sweater is covered with fluff.* 我那件最好的毛衣上满是绒毛. **(b)** soft fur or down of animals or birds（禽兽的）绒毛. **2** [C] (*infml* 口) unsuccessful attempt at sth; mistake or blunder 未成功的尝试；错误；失误. **3** (idm 习语) **a bit of fluff** ⇨ BIT¹.
▷ **fluff** *v* **1** [Tn, Tn·p] ~ **sth (out/up)** shake sth into a soft full mass; puff or spread sth out lightly 抖开某物；抖松某物: *fluff up the pillows* 抖松枕头 ○ *The bird fluffed (out) its feathers.* 那鸟抖抖身子蓬开羽毛. **2** [Tn] (*infml* 口) be unsuccessful at doing (sth); perform (sth) badly; bungle 未做成（某事物）；将（某事）搞坏；出错: *fluff a stroke*, eg in golf 击球失误（如高尔夫球）○ *fluff one's lines in a play* 说错剧中台词 ○ *He really fluffed his exams.* 他的确考糟了.
fluffy *adj* (**-ier, -iest**) **1** like fluff; covered with fluff 似绒毛的；有绒毛的: *Most animals are soft and fluffy when first born.* 大多数动物刚出生时都很软，身上有绒毛. **2** soft, light and airy 蓬松的；松软的: *light and fluffy mashed potatoes* 松软的土豆泥. **fluf·fi·ness** *n* [U].
fluid /ˈfluːɪd; ˋfluɪd/ *adj* **1** able to flow freely, as gases and liquids do; not solid or rigid 流动的；流体的；不坚硬的: *a fluid substance* 流体. **2** not fixed; able to be changed 不固定的；可改变的: *fluid arrangements, ideas, opinions* 可改变的安排、思想、意见 ○ *The situation is still fluid.* 局势尚不稳定. **3** smooth and graceful in movement 动作灵活而优美的.
▷ **fluid** *n* [C, U] **1** any liquid substance 液体: *Drink plenty of fluids.* 多喝流质. ○ *There's some sort of sticky fluid on the kitchen floor.* 厨房的地上有一种发黏的液体. **2** (*chemistry* 化) fluid substance 流体；液.
flu·id·ity /fluːˈɪdətɪ; fluˋɪdətɪ/ *n* [U] quality or state of being fluid 流动性；流动状态.
□ **fluid ounce** (*abbr* 缩写 **fl oz**) liquid measure equal to one twentieth of an Imperial pint or one sixteenth of an American pint 液量盎司（英制等于十二分之一品脱，美制等于十六分之一品脱）. ⇨App 4, 5 见附录4、5.
fluke¹ /fluːk; fluk/ *n* (usu *sing* 通常作单数) (*infml* 口) thing that is accidentally successful; lucky stroke in a game 侥幸的成功；（在比赛中）侥幸击中: *Passing the exam was a real fluke — he didn't work for it at all.* 他考试及格实在是侥幸，因为他根本没下过功夫. ○ *That shot was a sheer fluke.* 那完全是靠侥幸击中的. ▷ **fluky** (also **flukey**) *adj*.
fluke² /fluːk; fluk/ *n* **1** either of the two flat triangular ends of an anchor 锚爪；锚钩. **2** either of the two lobes of a whale's tail 鲸的尾鳍.
fluke³ /fluːk; fluk/ *n* **1** flat-fish or flounder 比目鱼；鲆鲽. **2** parasitic worm found in the liver of a sheep（羊肝中的）肝蛭.
flum·mox /ˈflʌməks; ˋflʌməks/ *v* [Tn esp passive 尤用于被动语态] (*infml* 口) bewilder, confuse or disconcert (sb) 使（某人）迷惑、糊涂或仓皇失措: *The politician was completely flummoxed by the questions put to her.* 那位女政治家被问得十分狼狈.
flung *pt, pp* of FLING.
flunk /flʌŋk; flʌŋk/ *v* (*infml* 口 *esp US*) **1** [I, Tn] fail (an examination, academic course, etc) 使（考试、某学科的成绩等）不及格: *flunk biology* 生物学不及格. **2** [Tn] give a failing mark to (sb) 评定（某人）不及格: *be flunked in chemistry* 化学不及格. **3** (phr v) **flunk out** be dismissed from a school or college for failure 因成绩不及格而被学校除名.
flun·key (also **flunky**) /ˈflʌŋkɪ; ˋflʌŋkɪ/ *n* (*pl* ~**s** or **-kies**) (*infml derog* 口，贬) **1** servant in uniform（着制服的）男仆. **2** (*esp US*) person who does small unimportant tasks 打杂的人.
fluor·es·cence /flɔːˈresns; *US* flʊəˈr-; ˌflʊəˋrɛsn̩s/ *n* [U] property that a substance has of emitting light while being exposed to light or some other radiation of a shorter wavelength 荧光. Cf 参看 PHOSPHORESCENCE.
▷ **fluor·esce** *v* [I] send out light in this manner 放射荧光.
fluor·es·cent /-snt; -sn̩t/ *adj* **1** of, having or showing fluorescence 荧光的；有荧光的；显出荧光的: *fluorescent lighting* 荧光灯. **2** having a very bright glowing appearance because of fluorescence（因有荧光）发亮的: *wearing orange fluorescent clothing* 穿着橙色荧光服装.
□ **fluorescent 'lamp** electric light, usu in the form of a long strip, that gives off a fluorescent light 荧光灯；日光灯.
flu·or·ide /ˈflɔːraɪd; *US* ˈflʊər-; ˋflʊəˌraɪd/ *n* chemical compound of fluorine 氟化物.
▷ **flu·or·id·ate** /ˈflɔːrɪdeɪt; *US* ˈflʊər-; ˋflʊərəˌdet/ *v* [Tn] add traces of fluoride to (the water supply), esp to prevent tooth decay 在（饮水）中加氟（尤指为预防生龋齿）. **fluor·ida·tion** /ˌflɔːrɪˈdeɪʃn; *US* ˌflʊər-; ˌflʊərəˋdeʃən/ *n* [U].
flu·or·id·ize, -ise /ˈflɔːrɪdaɪz; *US* ˈflʊər-; ˋflʊərəˌdaɪz/ *v* [Tn] = FLUORIDATE. **flu·or·id·iza·tion, -isation** /ˌflɔːrɪdaɪˈzeɪʃn; *US* ˌflʊərɪdɪˈz-; ˌflʊərədɪˋzeʃən/ *n* [U] = FLUORIDATION.
flu·or·ine /ˈflɔːriːn; *US* ˈflʊər-; ˋflʊəˌrin/ *n* [U] (*chemistry* 化) element, a pale yellow gas that is both poisonous and corrosive 氟. ⇨App 10 见附录10.
flurry /ˈflʌrɪ; ˋflʌrɪ/ *n* **1** short sudden rush of wind or fall of rain, snow, etc 一阵风、雨、雪等: *light snow flurries/flurries of snow* 阵阵小雪. **2** ~ **(of sth)** sudden burst of intense activity; commotion（激烈活动的）爆发，骚动: *a flurry of activity/excitement* 一阵活动[激动] ○ *I'm always in a flurry* (ie confused and disorganized) *as deadlines get nearer.* 一接近最后期限我就忙乱不堪.
▷ **flurry** *v* (*pt, pp* **flurried**) [Tn usu passive 通常用于被动语态] confuse and disturb; fluster 使迷乱；使慌张: *Keep calm! Don't get flurried.* 镇静！不要慌.
flush¹ /flʌʃ; flʌʃ/ *n* **1** [C usu *sing* 通常作单数] **(a)** flow of blood to the face that causes a red colouring; blush 脸

红. (**b**) sudden rush of emotions, excitement, etc 感情、激情等的突发; 激动; 兴奋: *a flush of enthusiasm, anger, joy, etc* 一阵热情、怒火、喜悦等. **2** [sing] rush of water, esp for cleaning a toilet 冲水(尤指冲马桶): *Give the toilet a flush.* 冲一冲马桶. **3** [C] new fresh growth, esp of plants 新的成长; (尤指)萌发. **4** (idm 习语) **(in) the first/full flush of 'youth, etc** (in) the freshness or vigour of youth, etc; at its beginning/most fully developed stage 青春的初期[年轻力壮]; (在)初发[旺盛]阶段: *the first flush of manhood* 男子成年初期的精力 ○ *In the full flush of success, nothing was an obstacle.* 在成就如日中天时, 其势锐不可当.

flush[2] /flʌʃ; flʌʃ/ *v* **1** (**a**) [La, I] (of a person's face) become red because of a rush of blood to the skin; blush (指人的面部)变红, 发红: *Mary flushed crimson with embarrassment.* 玛丽羞得脸红了. (**b**) [Tn] (of illness, feelings, etc) cause (the face) to become red (指疾病、情感等)使(面部)变红: *Fever flushed his cheeks.* 他发烧满脸通红. **2** (**a**) [Tn] clean (esp a toilet or drain) with a rush of water (用水)冲洗(尤指马桶或下水道): *Please flush the toilet after you've used it.* 便后请冲水. (**b**) [I] (of a toilet) be cleaned in this way (指马桶)被冲洗: *The toilet won't flush properly*, ie it is blocked. 马桶冲不下去了(堵塞了). **3** (phr v) **flush sth away, down, through, etc** dispose of sth with a rush of water 用水将某物冲掉: *flush waste down a sink* 把残渣从洗涤槽冲走.

▷ **flushed** *adj* **~ (with sth)** very excited (by sth); filled with emotion (因某事物)非常激动的; 充满感情的: *flushed with success, pride, joy, etc* 因成功、得意、喜悦等而激动.

flush[3] /flʌʃ; flʌʃ/ *v* **1** (**a**) [Tn, Tn·pr] cause (birds) to fly suddenly, esp from undergrowth 使(鸟)突然飞起(尤指从矮树丛中): *flush a pheasant (from cover)* 惊起(躲藏着的)野鸡. (**b**) [I] (of birds) fly suddenly, esp from undergrowth (指鸟)突然飞起(尤指从矮树丛中). **2** (phr v) **flush sb out (of sth)** force sb to leave a hiding-place; drive sb out 迫使某人离开藏身处; 将某人赶出: *flush out spies, criminals, snipers, etc* 迫使间谍、罪犯、狙击手等离开藏身处.

flush[4] /flʌʃ; flʌʃ/ *n* (in card-games) set of cards held by a player, all of which belong to the same suit (纸牌戏)同花的一手牌, 清一色: *She won with a royal flush*, ie the five highest cards of a suit. 她以同花大顺(最大的同花顺次五张)获胜.

flush[5] /flʌʃ; flʌʃ/ *adj* **~ (with sth)** **1** completely level or even with another surface (与另一个面)完全齐平的: *flush fittings* 装置在同一平面上的组件 ○ *The door should be flush with the wall.* 门应该与墙在同一平面上. **2** [pred 作表语] (*infml* 口) having a lot of sth, esp money; well supplied 很多(尤指金钱); 充裕: *flush with funds* 金钱充足.

flus·ter /ˈflʌstə(r); ˋflʌstɚ/ *v* [Tn esp passive 尤用于被动语态] make (sb) nervous and confused 使(某人)慌张: *Don't get flustered!* 不要慌张!

▷ **flus·ter** *n* [sing] nervous agitated state 紧张; 焦虑: *all in a fluster* 心慌意乱.

flute[1] /flu:t; flut/ *n* wind instrument in the form of a pipe, with holes stopped by fingers or keys and a mouth-hole at the side 长笛: [attrib 作定语] *a flute solo* 长笛独奏. ⇨illus at App 1 见附录1插图, page x. ▷ **flut·ist** /ˈflu:tɪst; ˋflutɪst/ *n* (*US*) = FLAUTIST.

flute[2] /flu:t; flut/ *v* [Tn usu passive 通常用于被动语态] shape or carve long vertical grooves in (sth), as a decoration 制或刻垂直长凹槽于(某物)(作装饰): *fluted columns/pillars* 饰有凹槽的柱子.

▷ **flut·ing** *n* [U] series of such grooves cut in a surface for decoration (在平面上刻的装饰性的)一系列凹槽.

flut·ter /ˈflʌtə(r); ˋflʌtɚ/ *v* **1** (**a**) [I, Ipr] (of the wings of birds, butterflies, etc) move lightly and quickly (指鸟、蝴蝶等的翅膀)轻而快地抖动, 拍翅: *The wings of the bird still fluttered after it had been shot down.* 那鸟击落后翅膀仍在抖动. (**b**) [Tn] move (the wings) in this way 鼓(翼); 拍(翅膀): *The bird fluttered its wings in the cage.* 鸟在笼中拍着翅膀. **2** (**a**) [I, Ipr] move about in a quick irregular way 迅速而无规则地乱动; 飘动: *a flag fluttering from the mast-head* 在旗杆顶上飘扬着的旗帜 ○ *curtains fluttering in the breeze* 在微风中飘动的窗帘. (**b**) [Tn] move (sth) in this way 使(某物)迅速而无规则地动: *She fluttered her eyelashes (at me).* 她(朝我)眨眼睛. **3** [I] (of the heart) beat weakly and irregularly, esp because of nervous excitement (指心脏)微弱而无规律地跳动(尤指因紧张激动所致). **4** (idm 习语) ˌ**flutter the 'dovecotes** astonish, upset or alarm people who are used to a calm or conventional life 惊扰过惯平静或平凡生活的人们. **5** (phr v) **flutter about, around, across, etc** (**a**) fly in the specified direction with quick light movements of the wings 拍动翅膀飞(向某方向): *The wounded bird fluttered to the ground.* 那受伤的鸟拍着翅膀落到地上. ○ *A moth was fluttering round the lamp.* 有一只蛾子扑打着翅膀绕着灯飞. (**b**) move in the specified direction in a quick irregular way 迅速而无规则地(向某方向)运动: *autumn leaves fluttering to the ground* 飘摇落地的秋叶 ○ *She fluttered nervously about, going from room to room.* 她紧张不安地从这房间到那房间四处走动.

▷ **flut·ter** *n* **1** (usu *sing* 通常作单数) quick irregular movement 迅速而无规则的运动: *the flutter of wings* 翅膀的拍动 ○ *with a flutter of her long dark eyelashes* 她那长着又长又黑睫毛的眼睛一眨. **2** [sing] state of nervous or confused excitement 紧张; 慌乱: *in a flutter* 心绪不宁 ○ *all of a flutter* 突然一阵慌乱 ○ *The arrival of the first customer caused a flutter (of activity) in the shop.* 第一位顾客登门, 引起店中一阵慌乱. **3** [U] (**a**) dangerous vibration in part of an aircraft, esp the wings (飞行器的一部分, 尤指机翼的)危险的颤振. (**b**) rapid variation in the pitch or loudness of recorded sound 录音中的音高或音量的迅速变化. Cf 参看 wow[2]. **4** [C] (*Brit infml* 口) **~ (on sth)** small bet or gamble 小赌; 小赌注: *have a flutter (on a horse) at the races* 在赛马中(在一匹马上)下小赌注.

flu·vial /ˈflu:vɪəl; ˋfluvɪəl/ *adj* of or found in rivers 河流的; 河中的: *fluvial deposits of mud* 河中的淤泥.

flux /flʌks; flʌks/ *n* **1** [U] continuous change or succession of changes; unsettled state 连续的改变; 接连不断的变化; 不稳定的状态: *Organization of the company was then in a state of flux.* 当时公司的编制正处于不稳定状态. **2** [sing] **~ (of sth)** (rate of) flow or flowing (out); discharge 流(量); 流动(量); 流出(量): *a flux of neutrons* 中子通量 ○ *magnetic flux* 磁通量. **3** [C, U] substance used to help metals fuse together 焊剂; 助熔剂.

fly[1] /flaɪ; flaɪ/ *n* **1** type of insect with two wings, esp the house-fly 苍蝇; (尤指)家蝇. **2** (usu in compounds 通常用以构成复合词) any of several types of flying insect (会飞的)昆虫: *'dragonfly* ○ *'butterfly* ○ *'tsetse-fly*. **3** natural or artificial fly used as bait in fishing (用作钓饵的真的或假的)苍蝇. **4** (idm 习语) **die/fall/drop like 'flies** die or collapse in very large numbers 大批地死亡或倒下: *Men were dropping like flies in the intense heat.* 人们抵受不住酷热而纷纷倒下. **a/the 'fly in the ointment** person or thing that spoils an otherwise satisfactory situation or occasion 扫兴的人或事物. **a 'fly on the wall** hidden or unnoticed observer 隐蔽的或不引人注意的观察者: *I wish I could be a fly on the wall when they discuss my future.* 在他们讨论我的前途时, 我恨不得能偷偷旁观. **(there are) no flies on sb** (*infml* 口) sb is clever and not easily tricked 某人很机灵, 不易上当. **not harm/hurt a 'fly** be kind and gentle and unwilling to cause unhappiness 心地善良、文质彬彬、不愿引起不愉快: *Our dog may look fierce but he wouldn't hurt a fly.* 我们的狗别看样子凶, 其实很温顺.

□ **'fly-blown** *adj* **1** (of meat, etc) bad or unfit to eat, because contaminated by flies' eggs (指肉等)(因有蝇卵)腐败的, 不宜食用的. **2** (*fig* 比喻) in a bad condition; dirty or spoiled 破烂的; 肮脏的; 损坏的.

'flycatcher *n* type of bird that catches insects in the air 翔食雀.

'fly-fish *v* [I] fish using artificial flies as bait 以假蝇作饵钓鱼.

'fly-fishing *n* [U].

'fly-paper *n* [U, C] strip of sticky paper for catching flies 粘蝇纸.

'fly-spray *n* poisonous liquid sprayed from a container to kill flies 灭蝇喷雾剂.

'flyweight *n* **1** boxer of the lightest class, weighing between 48 and 51 kg 特轻量级拳击手(体重在48至51公斤者). **2** wrestler weighing between 48 and 51 kg 最

轻量级摔交选手(体重在48至51公斤者).

fly[2] /flaɪ; flaɪ/ *v* (*pt* **flew** /flu:; flu/, *pp* **flown** /fləʊn; flon/) **1** [I, Ipr, Ip] (of a bird or an insect) move through the air, using wings (指鸟或昆虫)飞, 飞翔: *watch the birds learn to fly* 看鸟学飞 ○ *A large bird flew past us.* 一只大鸟从我们这儿飞过. **2** [I, Ipr, Ip] (**a**) (of an aircraft or a spacecraft) move through air or space (指飞行器)飞行, 航行: *I can hear a plane flying overhead.* 我听到一架飞机正从上空飞过. (**b**) travel in an aircraft or a spacecraft 乘飞行器: *I'm flying (out) to Hong Kong tomorrow.* 明天我要乘飞机去香港. ⇨Usage at TRAVEL 用法见TRAVEL. **3** (**a**) [Tn] direct or control the flight of (an aircraft, etc) 驾驶或操纵(飞行器等): *Only experienced pilots fly large passenger aircraft.* 只有有经验的飞行员才能驾驶大型客机. (**b**) [Tn, Tn·pr, Tn·p] transport (goods or passengers) in an aircraft 用飞行器运送(货物或旅客): *Five thousand people were flown to Paris during the Easter weekend.* 在复活节的周末有五千人乘飞机去巴黎. ○ *He had flowers specially flown in for the ceremony.* 他特地为这一典礼空运来了鲜花. (**c**) [Tn] travel over (an ocean or area of land) in an aircraft 乘飞行器飞越(海洋或陆地): *fly the Atlantic* 飞越大西洋. **4** (**a**) [I, Ipr, Ip] go or move quickly; rush along 疾行; 快速地动; 急速前进: *The children flew to meet their mother.* 孩子们飞跑过去迎接妈妈. ○ *It's late — I must fly.* 太晚了——我得赶快走. ○ *The train flew by.* 列车飞驰而过. ○ *The dog flew down the road after the cat.* 狗在马路上飞跑着追赶猫. (**b**) [La, Ipr, Ip] move suddenly and with force 猛然移动: *A large stone came flying through the window.* 从窗外扔进来一块大石头. ○ *David gave the door a kick and it flew open.* 大卫一脚向门踹去, 那门猛地开了. (**c**) [I, Ip] (of time) pass very quickly (指时间)飞逝: *Doesn't time fly?* 时间过得真快呀! ○ *Summer has just flown (by).* 夏天一晃就过去了. **5** (**a**) [Tn] make (a kite) rise and stay high in the air 放(风筝). (**b**) [Tn] raise (a flag) so that it waves in the air 升(旗): *fly the Union Jack* 升起英国国旗. (**c**) [Ipr, Ip] move about freely; be carried about in the air 自由地移动; 在空中飘动: *Her hair was flying about (in the wind).* 她的头发随风飘动. **6** [I, Tn] (*rhet* 修辞) flee from (sb/sth) 从(某人[某物])之处逃走: *The robbers have flown (the country).* 抢劫犯逃到国外去了. **7** (idm 习语) **as the crow flies** ⇨ CROW[1]. **the bird has flown** ⇨ BIRD. **fly/show/wave the flag** ⇨ FLAG[1]. **fly 'high** be ambitious 胸怀大志. **fly in the face of sth** be contrary to sth; oppose sth 与某事物相悖; 反对某事物: *His version of events flies in the face of all the evidence.* 他对事件的说法与所有证据都不相符. **fly into a 'passion, 'rage, 'temper, etc** become suddenly very angry 勃然大怒. **fly a kite** (*Brit infml* 口) do or say sth in order to see how people will react, express their opinions, etc 试探舆论. **(go) fly a/one's kite** (*US infml* 口) (esp imperative 尤用于祈使句) go away and stop interfering or annoying sb 走开, 不再打扰某人. **fly/go off at a tangent** ⇨ TANGENT. **fly off the 'handle** (*infml* 口) become wildly angry 狂怒. **fly/go out of the window** ⇨ WINDOW. **keep the flag flying** ⇨ FLAG[1]. **let fly (at sb/sth) (with sth)** (**a**) shoot or throw sth (at sb/sth) violently (向某人[某物])猛烈射击, 猛掷某物: *He aimed carefully and then let fly*, ie fired. 他仔细瞄准之后便开了枪. (**b**) reproach or criticize (sb) angrily 愤怒地责备或批评(某人): *Furious at his deceit, she let fly at him with a stream of abuse.* 他欺骗人, 气得她把他大骂了一顿. **make the 'fur/'sparks fly** cause quarrelling or fighting 引起争吵或打斗: *The promotion of Russell instead of Sarah really made the sparks fly.* 因为提升了拉塞尔没提升萨拉, 这件事竟惹起了轩然大波. **pigs might fly** ⇨ PIG. **send sb/sth flying** ⇨ SEND. **send things flying** ⇨ SEND. **8** (phr v) **fly at sb** rush to attack sb 冲上去攻击某人.

□ **fly-away** /ˈflaɪəweɪ; ˈflaɪ ə,we/ *adj* **1** (esp of hair) loose and wispy; difficult to control (尤指毛发)松散而纤细的, 难以梳理的. **2** (*fig* 比喻) not sensible; frivolous or flighty 不合情理的; 轻率的; 轻浮的.

fly-by /ˈflaɪbaɪ; ˈflaɪ ,baɪ/ *n* (*pl* **'fly-bys**) flight, esp by a spacecraft, past a point or target 经某点或某目标的飞行(尤指宇宙飞行器): *a fly-by of Jupiter* 经过木星的飞行.

fly-by-night /ˈflaɪbaɪnaɪt; ˈflaɪ baɪ ,naɪt/ *n* (*pl* **fly-by-nights**) person who evades financial responsibility, esp debts, by (secretly) leaving; unreliable person 为躲债(偷偷)离去的人; 不可靠的人. — *adj* unreliable or dishonest, esp in financial and business matters 不可靠的; 不诚实的(尤指在财务及商业事务上): *a fly-by-night company* 无信誉的公司.

fly-half *n* (*pl* **fly-halves**) = STAND-OFF HALF (STAND).

'fly-past /-pɑ:st; *US* -pæst; -,pæst/ *n* (*Brit*) (*US* **'flyover**) ceremonial flight of aircraft, usu at low altitude, as part of a military display (阅兵式的)飞机编队飞行(通常为低空飞行).

fly[3] /flaɪ; flaɪ/ *n* **1** [C esp *pl* 尤作复数] (piece of material on a garment that contains or covers a) zip or buttoned opening, eg down the front of a pair of trousers 服装上盖住拉锁或钮扣的遮盖; 有拉锁或钮扣的开口(如裤子前面的): *John, your flies are/fly is undone!* 约翰, 你的拉锁开了! **2** [C] flap of material, eg canvas, at the entrance to a tent 帐篷的门帘(如帆布制的).

fly[4] /flaɪ; flaɪ/ *adj* (*infml* 口 *esp Brit*) not easily deceived; clever and sly 不易上当的; 机灵的; 精明的: *He's a very fly character.* 他是个很精明的人.

flyer = FLIER.

fly·ing /ˈflaɪɪŋ; ˈflaɪɪŋ/ *adj* moving by flight; able to fly 飞行的; 会飞的: *flying insects* 会飞的昆虫.

▷ **fly·ing** *n* [U] going in an aircraft for travel or sport 乘坐飞行器(旅行或运动): *I'm terrified of flying — I'd rather go by sea.* 我害怕坐飞机——我宁愿坐船.

□ **,flying 'buttress** (*architecture* 建) arched structure that supports the outside wall of a large building, esp a church 拱扶垛. ⇨illus at App 1 见附录1插图, page viii.

,flying 'colours **1** flags on display as a sign of victory or during a ceremony (象征胜利的或用于庆典的)旗帜. **2** (idm 习语) **with flying colours** with great and obvious success 大获全胜地: *She came through/passed her exams with flying colours.* 她考试成绩优异.

,flying 'column troops able to move rapidly and act independently 快速突击部队; 别动队.

,flying 'doctor (esp in Australia) doctor who travels in an aircraft to visit patients who live in distant or isolated places (尤指澳大利亚的)飞行医生(乘飞机到偏远地区出诊的).

'flying fish type of tropical fish that can rise and move forward above the surface of the water using its wing-like fins 飞鱼.

,flying 'fox type of large fruit-eating bat 狐蝠; 果蝠.

,flying 'jump (also **,flying 'leap**) forward jump/leap made while running quickly 助跑起跳.

'flying officer officer in the Royal Air Force between the ranks of pilot officer and flight lieutenant (英国皇家)空军中尉. ⇨App 9 见附录9.

,flying 'picket worker or group of workers on strike who are ready to travel quickly to different factories, etc to persuade other workers to join the strike 串联纠察员(可迅速到各工厂等动员一道罢工的工人).

,flying 'saucer (also **unidentified flying object**) spacecraft, shaped like a saucer or disc, that some people claim to have seen and that is believed to have come from another planet 飞碟; 不明飞行物.

'flying squad group of police officers who are always ready to move quickly, eg when a crime has occurred 机动警察队.

,flying 'start **1** start to a race in which the competitors are already running as they cross the starting line 行进间起跑(跑着通过起跑线). **2** (idm 习语) **get off to a flying start** begin sth well; have an initial advantage 开端很好; 一开始就占优势: *Our holiday got off to a flying start because the weather was good and the trains were on time.* 我们度假一开始就大吉大利, 天气很好, 火车也都准点.

,flying 'tackle (in Rugby football, etc) tackle made while running or jumping (在橄榄球等运动中)凌空抢球.

,flying 'visit very brief or hasty visit 短暂或匆忙的访问.

fly·leaf /ˈflaɪli:f; ˈflaɪ,lif/ *n* (*pl* **-leaves** /-li:vz; -,livz/) blank page at the beginning or end of a book (书刊前或后的)空白页.

fly·over /ˈflaɪəʊvə(r); ˈflaɪ,ovɚ/ *n* **1** (*Brit*) (*US* **overpass**) bridge which carries one road or railway

F

above another 立交桥. ⇨illus at App 1 见附录1插图, page xiii. **2** (*US*) = FLY-PAST (FLY[2]).

fly·sheet /ˈflaɪʃiːt; ˋflaɪ,ʃit/ *n* **1** additional outer cover for a tent to give protection from rain (盖在帐篷外面的)防雨布. **2** small pamphlet of two or four pages (两页或四页的)小册子.

fly·wheel /ˈflaɪwiːl; *US* -hwiːl; ˋflaɪ,hwil/ *n* heavy wheel revolving on a shaft to keep a machine operating at an even speed 飞轮; 惯性轮.

FM *abbr* 缩写 = **1** Field Marshal. **2** /ˌef ˈem; ˌɛf ˋɛm/ (*radio* 无) frequency modulation. Cf 参看 AM 1.

fm *abbr* 缩写 = fathom(s).

FO /ˌef ˈəʊ; ˌɛf ˋo/ *abbr* 缩写 = (*Brit*) (formerly 旧时) Foreign Office 外交部: *He used to work at the FO.* 他过去在外交部工作. Cf 参看 FCO.

foal /fəʊl; fol/ *n* **1** young of a horse or of a related animal, eg a donkey 驹子(如驴驹). **2** (idm 习语) **in/with foal** (of a female horse, etc) pregnant (指母马等)怀驹.

▷ **foal** *v* [I] give birth to a foal 产驹.

foam /fəʊm; fom/ *n* [U] **1 (a)** mass of small, usu white, air bubbles formed in or on a liquid 泡沫: *The breaking waves left the beach covered with foam.* 浪花弄得海滩都是泡沫. **(b)** frothy bubbles of saliva or perspiration 唾沫; 汗珠. **2** any of various chemical substances forming a thick bubbly mass and used for different purposes (化学物质的)厚层泡沫: ˈ*shaving foam* 剃须泡沫膏. **3** rubber or plastic in a spongy form, used to fill seats, cushions, etc 泡沫橡胶; 泡沫塑料: [attrib 作定语] *foam* ˈ*rubber* 泡沫橡胶.

▷ **foam** *v* [I, Ipr] form or send out foam; froth 起泡沫; 发出泡沫: *a glass of foaming beer* 一杯起泡沫的啤酒 ○ *The sick dog foamed at the mouth.* 那只病狗口吐白沫. ○ (*fig* 比喻) *After having to wait an hour the customer was foaming (at the mouth) with rage,* ie obviously very angry. 那顾客等了一小时后气得七窍生烟.

foamy *adj* full of or like foam 多泡沫的; 似泡沫的.

fob[1] /fɒb; fɑb/ *n* **1** chain or ribbon to which a pocket-watch is attached (怀表的)链或带. **2** ornament, esp a watch, hung from such a chain 怀表链上的饰物(尤指表). **3** ornament attached to a key-ring 钥匙环上的饰物.

fob[2] /fɒb; fɑb/ *v* **(-bb-)** (phr v) **fob sb off (with sth)** trick sb into being satisfied (with sth inferior, an excuse, etc) (用低劣的东西、用借口等)哄骗或搪塞某人: *I won't be fobbed off this time — I'm determined to say what I think.* 这次我可不上当了——我一定要把想法说出来. ○ *You can't fob an expert off with cheap imitations.* 用廉价的仿制品骗不了行家. **fob sth off on/onto sb** trick or deceive sb into buying or accepting sth inferior 哄骗某人购买或接受低劣的东西: *Don't try fobbing off last year's goods on me!* 别想拿去年的陈货来骗我!

fob /ˌef əʊ ˈbiː; ˋɛf ˌo ˋbi/ *abbr* 缩写 = (*commerce* 商) (of cargo) free on board (ie transported to the ship and loaded without the buyer paying extra) (指货物)船上交货价, 离岸价格.

focal /ˈfəʊkl; ˋfokḷ/ *adj* [attrib 作定语] of or at a focus 焦点的; 在焦点上的.

□ **focal ˈlength** (also **focal ˈdistance**) distance between the centre of a mirror or a lens and its focus 焦距.

ˈ**focal point** something that is the centre of interest or activity 感兴趣的或活动的中心: *Reducing unemployment is the focal point of the government's plans.* 减少失业人数是政府计划的重点.

fo'c's'le = FORECASTLE.

fo·cus /ˈfəʊkəs; ˋfokəs/ *n* (*pl* **~es** or **foci** /ˈfəʊsaɪ; ˋfosaɪ/) ⇨Usage at DATA 用法见 DATA. **1** [C] point at which rays (of light, sound, etc) meet or from which they appear to come (光、声等的)中心点, 源. **2** [C] point or distance at which (the outline of) an object is most clearly seen by the eye or through a lens 焦点; 焦距. **3** [C] adjustment or device on a lens to produce a clear image 聚焦; 调焦; 聚焦或调焦的装置: *The focus on my camera isn't working properly.* 我的照相机上的调焦装置有毛病. **4** [C usu *sing* 通常作单数] centre of activity, interest, etc 活动的中心; 使人感兴趣的所在: *Her beauty makes her the focus of attention.* 她长得漂亮, 很惹人注目. ○ *In tonight's programme our focus is on Germany.* 在今天晚上的节目中我们重点介绍德国. **5** (idm 习语) **be in ˈfocus; bring sth/come into focus** (cause sth to) be or become clearly seen or sharply defined (使某事物)清晰、明确或在焦点上: *Bring the object into focus if you want a sharp photograph.* 要照出清晰的照片, 就要把焦点对准物体. **be/go out of ˈfocus** not be or no longer be clearly seen, etc 模糊、不清楚或不在焦点上: *The children's faces were badly out of focus* (ie were very blurred) *in the photograph.* 照片上孩子们的面部非常模糊.

▷ **fo·cus** *v* **(-s-** or **-ss-) 1 (a)** [I] become able to see clearly 能够看清楚: *His eyes focused slowly in the dark room.* 他在那间黑屋子里眼睛慢慢地看清了东西. **(b)** [Tn, Tn·pr] **~ sth (on sth)** cause sth to be concentrated (at a point) 使某事物集中(于一点): *If you focus the sun's rays through a magnifying glass on a dry leaf, it will start to burn.* 用放大镜把阳光聚到干叶子上, 叶子就能燃烧. **(c)** [Tn, Tn·pr] **~ sth (on sth)** adjust the focus (2) of (a lens or the eye) 调整(透镜或眼睛)的焦点或焦距: *Focus your camera (on those trees).* 把照相机的焦距调准(把焦点集中在树上). **2 (a)** [I, Ipr] **~ (on sth)** concentrate (on sth) 集中(于某事物): *I'm so tired I can't focus (on anything) today.* 今天我太累了, 精神集中不起来. **(b)** [Tn, Tn·pr] **~ sth (on sth)** concentrate (one's attention, etc) on (sth) 将(注意力等)集中于(某事物): *Please focus your minds on the following problem.* 请集中考虑以下问题.

fod·der /ˈfɒdə(r); ˋfɑdɚ/ *n* [U] dried food, hay, etc for horses and farm animals (马及其他牲畜的)饲料, 草料, 秣.

foe /fəʊ; fo/ *n* (*fml or dated* 文或旧) enemy 敌人.

foetus (*US* **fetus**) /ˈfiːtəs; ˋfitəs/ *n* young human, animal, bird, etc that has developed within the womb or egg but has not yet been born or hatched 胎儿; 胚胎. Cf 参看 EMBRYO 1.

▷ **foetal** (*US* **fetal**) /ˈfiːtl; ˋfitḷ/ *adj* of or like a foetus (似)胚胎的: *She curled up her legs and arms into a foetal position,* ie like that of a foetus in the womb. 她像胎儿一样蜷曲起四肢.

fog /fɒg; *US* fɔːg; fɔg/ *n* **1 (a)** [U] thick cloud of tiny drops of water close to or just above land or sea; thick mist 雾: *Dense fog is covering roads in the north and visibility is very poor.* 浓雾笼罩了北部的公路, 能见度很低. ○ *Patches of fog will clear by mid-morning.* 早晨一过局部地区的雾气就能消散. **(b)** [C] instance or period of this 雾; 有雾时: *We get heavy fogs on this coast in winter.* 这里的海边冬季有浓雾. ⇨Usage 见所附用法. **2** [C, U] (area of) cloudiness on a photographic negative, etc, making the image unclear (摄影底片等上的)灰雾. **3** (idm 习语) **in a fog** puzzled and confused 困惑; 迷惑: *I'm in a complete fog about computer technology — I don't understand it at all.* 我对计算机技术如堕五里雾中——完全不懂.

▷ **fog** *v* **(-gg-) 1** [I, Ip, Tn, Tn·p] cover (sth) or become covered with fog 雾气笼罩(某物); 有雾气: *The windscreen has fogged (over/up).* 挡风玻璃让雾气遮住了. ○ *Steam has fogged the bathroom mirror.* 水蒸气把浴室里的镜子遮住了. **2 (a)** [Tn] cause cloudiness on (a photographic negative, etc) 使(摄影底片等上)产生灰雾: *Shut the door or the light will fog the film.* 把门关上, 不然亮光能使底片发灰. **(b)** [I] (of a photographic negative, etc) become cloudy (指摄影底片等)变灰. **3** [Tn] puzzle or confuse (sb) 使(某人)迷惑或困惑: *I'm a bit fogged by these instructions.* 这些说明把我搞得有些糊涂了. **4** [Tn] obscure or confuse (sth being discussed) 使(正在讨论的事物)变模糊或混淆不清: *complicated language that just fogs the real issues* 把实质问题弄得模糊不清的复杂的语言.

foggy *adj* **(-ier, -iest) 1** not clear because of fog; very misty 有雾的; 雾气蒙蒙的: *foggy weather* 有雾的天气 ○ *a foggy day* 雾天. **2** obscure; confused; vague 模糊的; 混乱的; 朦胧的: *His ideas on this subject are a bit foggy.* 他对这个问题的看法有些模糊. **3** (idm 习语) **not have the faintest/foggiest** ⇨ FAINT[1].

□ ˈ**fog-bank** *n* mass of dense fog on the sea 平流雾(海面上的浓雾); 雾堤.

ˈ**fog-bound** *adj* unable to travel or operate normally because of fog; trapped by fog 因雾而不能正常行进或运行的; 被雾困住的: *fog-bound planes, passengers* 因雾停飞的飞机、因雾滞留的旅客 ○ *a fog-bound airport, harbour* 因雾而关闭的机场、港口.

F

ˈfog-horn *n* instrument that makes a loud blaring noise to warn ships of danger when it is foggy 雾角; 雾号; 雾笛: (*joc or derog* 谑或贬) *He's got a voice like a fog-horn*, ie a loud, harsh voice. 他的嗓音像雾角(大而刺耳).

ˈfog-lamp *n* powerful light on the front of a car, etc for use in fog 雾灯(汽车等在雾天使用的前部强光灯).

NOTE ON USAGE 用法: **Fog, mist** and **haze** are all clouds of water vapour at ground level and above. ☆ **fog**、**mist**、**haze** 均为地面及地面以上的水蒸气. They indicate different degrees of thickness 这几个词表示的浓度有所不同: **fog** is the thickest and **haze** the least thick. ☆ **fog** 最浓, **haze** 最薄. **Haze** also occurs when it is very hot ☆ **haze** 在天气炎热时也会出现: *a heat-haze* 热天的薄雾. **Smog** is an unhealthy mixture of smoke and fog in the air of some industrial cities. ☆ **smog** 是在一些工业城市的空气中烟与雾的混合物, 是有害于健康的.

fogy (also **fogey**) /ˈfəʊgɪ; ˈfogɪ/ *n* (*pl* **-ies** or **~s**) person with old-fashioned ideas which he is unwilling to change 老顽固: *Come to the disco and stop being such an old fogey!* 来参加迪斯科舞会吧! 别再当老顽固了!

foible /ˈfɔɪbl; ˈfɔɪbl̩/ *n* small, usu harmless, peculiarity or weakness in a person's character (性格上的)小缺点, 怪癖(通常为无伤大雅的): *We all have our little foibles.* 我们人人都有些小缺点.

foil[1] /fɔɪl; fɔɪl/ *n* **1** [U] metal rolled or hammered into a very thin flexible sheet 箔: *tin, aluminium foil*, ie such as is wrapped round bars of chocolate 锡纸、铝箔(如包装巧克力的). **2** [C] person or thing that contrasts with, and so emphasizes, the qualities of another 陪衬; 衬托: *Her sparkling jewellery served as the perfect foil for her fine complexion.* 她戴着闪闪生辉的首饰, 更显得容貌姣好.

foil[2] /fɔɪl; fɔɪl/ *v* [Tn] prevent (sb) from carrying out a plan; prevent (a plan, etc) from succeeding; thwart; frustrate 阻止(某人)执行计划; 阻挠(计划等); 挫败: *He was foiled in his attempt to deceive us/His attempt to deceive us was foiled.* 他企图欺骗我们, 但没有得逞.

foil[3] /fɔɪl; fɔɪl/ *n* long thin light sword with a protective button on the point, used in fencing (FENCE[2]) (击剑运动的)钝头剑. ⇨illus at FENCING 见 FENCING 插图. Cf 参看 ÉPÉE, SABRE.

foist /fɔɪst; fɔɪst/ *v* (phr v) **foist sth on sb** force sb into accepting sth not wanted 迫使某人接受不想要的事物: *He's religious but he doesn't try to foist his beliefs on everyone.* 他是教徒, 但他不想把自己的信仰强加于人.

fold 折叠

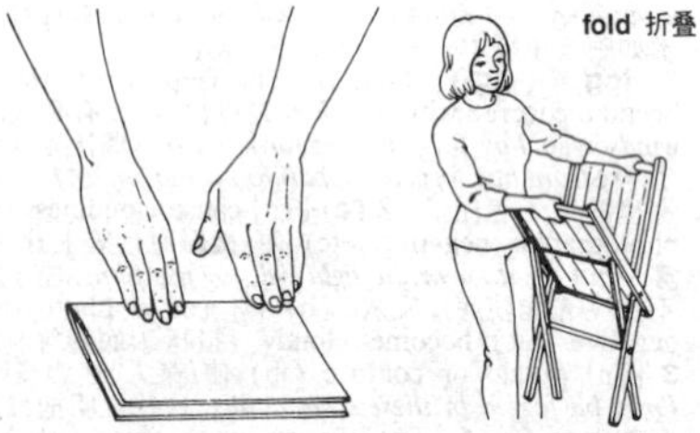

FOLD 折叠　　FOLD (UP) 折叠(起来)

fold[1] /fəʊld; fold/ *v* **1** (**a**) [Tn, Tn·pr, Tn·p] **~ sth (up)** bend or turn sth so that one part of it lies on another; close or flatten sth by pressing two parts of it together 折叠; 折叠收拢: *fold clothes (up) neatly* 把衣服叠整齐 ○ *a folded newspaper* 折叠起来的报纸 ○ *The bird folded its wings.* 那鸟收起了翅膀. ○ *Fold the letter (in two) before putting it in the envelope.* 把信(对)折起来再装入信封. (**b**) [I, Ip] **~ (up)** be able to be bent for storage, easy carrying, etc 能够折叠(以便储存、携带等): *This garden table folds (up) flat.* 这张庭园茶点桌可以折叠成平的. ○ *a folding chair, bed, bicycle, etc* 能折叠的椅子、床、自行车等. ⇨illus 见插图. **2** [Tn·pr] **~ A in B/~ B around A** cover or wrap sth in sth 将某物用另物遮住或包住: *Fold this glass bowl in newspaper/Fold newspaper round this glass bowl.* 把这个玻璃盆用报纸包好. **3** [I, Ip] **~ (up)** (*infml* 口) (**a**) cease to function; stop trading 停止运行; 停业: *The company folded (up) last week.* 那家公司上星期倒闭了. (**b**) cease to be performed 停止上演: *The play folded within a fortnight.* 那话剧演了两个星期就停演了. **4** (idm 习语) **fold one's ˈarms** bring one's arms together and cross them over one's chest 双臂在胸前合抱. **fold sb/sth in one's arms** hold sb/sth closely 抱住某人[某物]: *Father folded the tiny child in his arms.* 父亲把小孩儿抱在怀里. **fold one's ˈhands** bring or clasp one's hands together, eg when praying 十指交叉合掌(如祈祷时). **5** (phr v) **fold (sth) away** (cause sth to) become more compact for storage by folding (使某物)折叠收拢(以便存放): *The bed folds away (into the wall).* 那张床可以折叠收拢(到墙里面去). **fold sth in; fold sth into sth** (in cooking) mix one ingredient gently with another, usu with a spoon (烹饪)轻轻搅拌(通常用勺): *Fold in the beaten whites of two eggs.* 加进两个打散的蛋清后搅匀. **fold up** collapse because of pain or great laughter (因痛苦或大笑)倒下: *The boxer folded up in agony.* 那拳击手痛苦地倒下了. ○ *The comedian had the audience folding up.* 那个喜剧演员逗得观众笑得前仰后合.

▷ **fold** *n* **1** part of sth, esp fabric, that is folded or hangs as if folded 折叠的部分; (尤指)褶: *a dress hanging in loose folds* 有宽松褶的连衣裙. **2** mark or line made by folding; crease 折痕; 折线. **3** hollow among hills or mountains 山坳; 山谷; 山窝. **4** (*geology* 地质) bend in the line of rocks below the earth's surface that has been caused by movements in the earth's crust 褶皱.

□ **ˈfoldaway** *adj* that can be folded up or away for storage; collapsible 可折叠的: *a foldaway bed* 折叠床.

fold[2] /fəʊld; fold/ *n* **1** [C] area in a field surrounded by a fence or wall where sheep are kept for safety 羊栏. **2 the fold** [sing] group of people with the same (usu religious) beliefs 具有同一信仰(通常为宗教信仰)的人们. **3** (idm 习语) **return to the fold** ⇨ RETURN[1].

-fold *suff* 后缀 (with numbers forming *adjs* and *advs* 与数字结合构成形容词及副词) multiplied by; having the specified number of parts …倍; 有…部分: *tenfold* ○ *twofold*.

folder /ˈfəʊldə(r); ˈfoldɚ/ *n* cover for holding loose papers, etc, made of stiff material, esp cardboard, folded together 文件夹; 纸夹.

fo·li·age /ˈfəʊlɪɪdʒ; ˈfolɪɪdʒ/ *n* [U] (all the) leaves of a tree or plant; leaves with their stems and branches 植物的叶子(总称); 叶子及梗和枝: *a mass of green foliage* 茂密的绿叶 ○ *My flower arrangement needs more foliage.* 我的插花作品还得多要些枝叶.

fo·lio /ˈfəʊlɪəʊ; ˈfolɪ,o/ *n* (*pl* **~s**) **1** (**a**) [C] large sheet of paper folded once, making two leaves or four pages of a book 对折纸; 对开纸. (**b**) [C] book made of sheets folded in this way 对开本的书: *We have several early folios for sale.* 我们有几本早期的对开本书出售. (**c**) [U] largest size and format for a book 书的最大开本: *drawings published in folio* 以对开纸出版的画 ○ [attrib 作定语] *a folio volume* 一册对开本的书. **2** [C] (**a**) sheet of paper numbered on one side only 只在一面有页码的纸. (**b**) page number of a book 书的页码.

folk /fəʊk; fok/ *n* **1** (also *esp US* **folks**) [pl *v*] (**a**) people in general 人们: *Some old folk(s) have peculiar tastes.* 有些老人有特殊的爱好. ○ (sometimes used when talking to people in a friendly way 有时用于对人亲切谈话中) *Well, folks, what are we going to do today?* 喂, 各位, 今天咱们干什么? (**b**) people from a particular (part of a) country, or associated with a particular way of life 某一国家(的地区)的人们; 与某种生活方式有关的人们: *country folk* 乡下人 ○ *townsfolk* 城里人 ○ *farming folk* 从事农业劳动的人. **2 folks** [pl] (*infml* 口) (**a**) members of one's own family; relatives 家属; 亲戚: *How are your folks?* 你家里人好吗? (**b**) (*esp US*) parents 父母: *Have you ever met my folks?* 你见过我父母吗? **3** [attrib 作定语] = FOLK-MUSIC: *a folk concert* 民间音乐会.

□ **ˈfolk-dance** *n* (music for a) traditional dance of a community or country 民间舞(曲); 土风舞(曲).

ˈfolklore *n* [U] (study of the) traditions, stories, customs, etc of a community 民间传统; 民间故事; 民俗; 民俗学. **folklorist** /ˈfəʊklɔːrɪst; ˈfok,lɔrɪst/ *n* person who studies folklore, esp as an academic subject 民俗学研究者.

ˈ**folk-music** (also **folk**), ˈ**folk-song** *ns* music or song in the traditional style of a country 民间音乐; 民谣; 民歌.

ˈ**folk-tale** *n* popular story passed on in spoken form from one generation to the next 民间故事; 民间传说.

folksy /ˈfəʊksɪ; ˋfoksɪ/ *adj* (*infml* 口) simple in manners and customs; friendly and sociable; typical of ordinary people 朴实的; 亲切热情的; 平凡的.

foll *abbr* 缩写 = following.

fol·low /ˈfɒləʊ; ˋfɑlo/ *v* **1** (**a**) [I, Ip, Tn, Tn·pr] **~ sth (by/with sth)** (cause sth to) come, go or take place after (sb/sth else) (in space, time or order) (使某事物)(在空间、时间或顺序上)在(他人[他事物])之后, 来、去或发生; 跟随; 跟着: *The duckling followed its mother everywhere.* 小鸭子跟着鸭妈妈到处走. ○ *You go first and I'll follow (on) later.* 你先走, 我随后就到. ○ *Monday follows Sunday.* 星期一在星期日之后. ○ *One misfortune followed another.* 不幸的事情一件接着一件. ○ *The lightning was quickly followed by/with heavy thunder.* 闪电过后紧接着是响雷. ○ *You should follow your treatment with plenty of rest in bed.* 你应该在治疗之后好好卧床休息. (**b**) [Tn] go after (sb) in order to catch him; chase 追捕(某人); 追逐: *The police were following him.* 警察正在追捕他. **2** [Tn] go along (a road, path, etc) 沿着(道路等)而行: *Follow this road until you get to the corner, then turn left.* 沿着这条路走到拐角处, 然后向左转. **3** [Tn] (**a**) act according to (sth) 按照(某事物)去做; 听从; 采用: *follow the instructions* 按指示办事 ○ *follow sb's advice* 听从某人的劝告. (**b**) accept (sb/sth) as a guide, leader or example; copy 把(某人[某事物]) 当作指导、领导、榜样; 仿效: *follow the latest fashions* 赶时髦 ○ *follow the teachings of Muhammad* 遵照穆罕默德的教诲. **4** [Tn] carry on (sth) as one's particular job or trade; pursue 经营(某事物); 从事: *follow a legal career* 从事法律工作. **5** [I, Tn] understand (the explanation or meaning of sth); understand (the plot of a story) 明白(对某事物的解释或意思); 明白(故事的情节): *I don't follow.* 我不明白. ○ *I couldn't follow his argument at all.* 我根本不明白他的论点. **6** [Tn] pay close attention to (sth); watch or listen very closely 密切注意(某事物); 注视; 倾听: *The President's wife follows his every word.* 总统夫人总是注意听他说的话. ○ *The cat followed the mouse's movements carefully.* 那只猫紧盯着老鼠的动向. **7** [Tn] take an active interest in (sth) 对(某事物)产生浓厚的兴趣: *Have you been following the basketball tournament?* 你一直都在看篮球锦标赛吗? ○ *Millions of fans follow the TV soap operas devotedly.* 千百万观众非常着迷地收看这部电视连续剧. **8** [Tn] read (a text) while listening to the same text being spoken by sb else; read (a musical score) while listening to the music being performed 边听别人朗读边跟着阅读(文字); 边听正在演奏的乐曲边跟着读(乐谱): *Follow the text while I read it out to you.* 看着课文, 听我给你朗读. **9** (**a**) [I, Ipr, Ip, Tn] **~ (on) (from sth)** result from sth; happen as a consequence 由某事物引起; 随之发生: *Inevitably, a quarrel followed between the two sides.* 双方随后不可避免地争吵起来. ○ *Disease often follows (on from) starvation because the body is weakened.* 疾病的产生往往是由于饥饿的缘故, 这是因身体虚弱所致. (**b**) [I, Ipr] **~ (from sth)** happen as a necessary and logical consequence 必然发生: *I don't see how that follows (from what you've said).* (从你的话来看), 我不明白怎么会产生这样的结果. ○ *If a = b and b = c it follows that a = c.* 设 a = b, b = c, 则 a = c. ○ *She's not in the office but it doesn't necessarily follow that she's ill.* 她不在办公室, 并不见得就是病了. **10** [Tn] develop or happen in (a particular way) 按(某一方式)发展或发生: *His speech followed the usual pattern.* 他按照通常的方式讲话. **11** (idm 习语) **as follows** (used to introduce a list) 用以列举事项: *The main events were as follows: first, the president's speech, secondly the secretary's reply and thirdly, the chairman's summing-up.* 主要活动如下: 第一项, 总裁讲话; 第二项, 秘书做解答; 第三项, 主席做总结. **follow one's (own) ˈbent** do what one is interested in and enjoys doing 做自己感兴趣的事; 随心所欲. **follow the ˈcrowd** be content to do what most people do 随大溜: *Not wanting to make my controversial views known yet, I preferred to follow the crowd for a while.* 我还不想公开我那些会引起争论的观点, 宁可暂且随大溜. **follow sb's example/lead** do as sb else has done; accept and follow sb else's decision 仿效他人的做法[按照他人的决定行事]: *I don't want you to follow my example and rush into marriage.* 我不希望你效法我, 也仓促结婚. **follow (the) hounds** hunt foxes with a pack of hounds 带着一群猎犬去猎狐. **follow in sb's ˈfootsteps** do as sb else does; follow a similar occupation or life-style as sb else 效法他人; 从事与他人同样的职业或采取相同的生活方式: *She works in theatre, following in her father's footsteps.* 她继承父业, 也从事戏剧工作. **follow one's (own) ˈnose** (**a**) go straight forward 一直往前走: *The police station is a mile ahead up the hill — just follow your nose.* 警察局在前面一英里处的山坡上——一直往前走就行了. (**b**) act instinctively 凭本能或直觉行事; 凭直觉行事: *Since you don't know the language I can only suggest that you follow your nose.* 你既然不会这门语言, 我只能建议你见机行事. **follow ˈsuit** act or behave in the way that sb else has just done 照别人的方式去做; 学样: *One of the major banks has lowered its interest rates and the other banks are expected to follow suit.* 有一家大银行已降低了利率, 其他银行也准会照样做的. **to follow** (in a restaurant, etc) as the next course of a meal (在餐馆等)作为下一道菜: *To follow, we'll have peaches and cream, please.* 下一道, 请来个奶油蜜桃. **12** (phr v) **follow on** (of a side in cricket) bat again immediately after failing to get the necessary number of runs in the first innings (板球的一方)在第一局中得分不足后立即继续击球. **follow through** (in tennis, golf, etc) complete a stroke by continuing to move the racket, club, etc after hitting the ball (网球、高尔夫球等)击球后使球拍、球棒等完成顺势动作. **follow sth through** carry out or continue sth to the end; complete sth 将某事物进行到底; 完成某事物: *Starting projects is one thing, following them through is another.* 着手进行某项目是一回事, 而将之进行到底则是另一回事. **follow sth up** (**a**) take further action on sth; develop or exploit sth 对某事物采取进一步行动; 发展或利用某事物: *You should follow up your letter with a phone call.* 你应该写完信以后再跟着打个电话. (**b**) investigate sth closely 深入调查某事物: *follow up a lead, clue, rumour* 顺着头绪、线索、谣传进行调查.

▷ **fol·lower** *n* person who follows; supporter of a particular person, cause or belief 追随者; 拥护者; 信徒: *He's a follower, not a leader.* 他是追随者, 不是领导者. ○ *the followers of Mahatma Gandhi* 圣雄甘地的拥护者.

□ ˌ**follow-ˈon** *n* (in cricket) second innings of a team immediately following its first innings (板球中)一队于第一局结束后紧接着举行的第二局.

ˈ**follow-through** *n* (in tennis, golf, etc) final part of a stroke after the ball has been hit (网球、高尔夫球等)击球后的顺势动作.

ˈ**follow-up** *n* something done to continue or exploit what has already been started or done (对已开始或已完成的事物所做的)后续工作: *As a follow-up to the television series the BBC is publishing a book.* 英国广播公司在播放那部电视连续剧以后, 即将出版一部有关的书.

fol·low·ing /ˈfɒləʊɪŋ; ˋfɑloɪŋ/ *adj* **1** next in time 接着的: *It rained on the day we arrived, but the following day was sunny.* 我们到达的那天正下雨, 但次日天气晴朗. **2** about to be mentioned 下述的: *Answer the following question(s).* 回答下列问题.

▷ **fol·low·ing** *n* **1** [sing] group of supporters 一批支持者或拥护者: *Our party has a large following in the south.* 我党在南方有一大批拥护者. **2 the following** [sing or pl *v*] what follows or comes next 下列; 如下: *The following is of the greatest importance.* 下面一点最为重要. ○ *The following are extracts from the original article.* 下面是原文的节选.

fol·low·ing *prep* after (sth); as a result of 在(某事物)之后; 由于: *demonstrations following the murder of the union leader* 继工会领袖遭谋杀后引发的示威游行.

folly /ˈfɒlɪ; ˋfɑlɪ/ *n* **1** [U] **~ (to do sth)** foolishness; lack of wisdom 愚蠢; 愚笨: *an act of folly* 愚蠢之举 ○ *It's utter folly to go swimming in this cold weather.* 这么冷的天气还去游泳, 真是蠢透了. **2** [C] foolish or unwise act, idea or practice 愚蠢的行为、思想或做法: *You'll pay later for your follies.* 你以后要为你的愚蠢行动付出

代价的. **3** [C] very expensive ornamental building that serves no practical purpose 华而不实的建筑.

fo·ment /fəʊˈment; foˈmɛnt/ *v* [Tn] **1** arouse or increase (trouble or discontent) 引起或增加(麻烦或不满): *foment discord, ill feeling, civil disorder, etc* 引起不和、恶感、内乱等. **2** apply warmth and moisture to (a part of the body) to lessen pain or discomfort 热敷, 热罨(身体某部).

▷ **fo·men·ta·tion** /ˌfəʊmenˈteɪʃn; ˌfomɛnˈteʃən/ *n* **1** [U] act of fomenting 热敷. **2** [C] thing used for fomenting 热敷物; 热罨剂.

fond /fɒnd; fɑnd/ *adj* (**-er, -est**) **1** [attrib 作定语] (**a**) kind and loving; affectionate 慈爱的; 深情的: *a fond look, gesture, embrace, etc* 充满深情的目光、手势、拥抱等 ○ *fond eyes* 慈爱的目光. (**b**) foolishly loving; indulgent or doting 痴爱的; 溺爱的: *spoilt by fond parents* 被父母溺爱而惯坏的. **2** [pred 作表语] **~ of sb/(doing) sth** having a great liking for sb/(doing) sth 喜爱某人[(做)某事物]: *I've always been very fond of you.* 我一向非常喜欢你. ○ *fond of music, cooking, going to parties* 喜爱音乐、烹调、参加聚会 ○ *John's extremely fond of pointing out other people's mistakes*, ie He enjoys doing this constantly. 约翰特别喜欢挑剔别人的毛病. **3** [attrib 作定语] (of wishes or ambitions) hoped for, but not likely to be met or to come true; foolishly held (指愿望或抱负)不大可能实现的, 想入非非的: *fond hopes of success* 对于成功的美梦.

▷ **fondly** *adv* **1** lovingly; gently 亲爱地; 温柔地: *He held her hand fondly.* 他温柔地握着她的手. **2** in a foolishly optimistic way; naïvely 盲目乐观地; 天真地: *I fondly imagined that you cared.* 我天真地以为你很在乎呢.

F

fond·ness *n* [U] **~ (for sb/sth)** liking and affection 喜爱; 深情: *his fondness for his eldest grandchild* 他对长孙的钟爱.

fond·ant /ˈfɒndənt; ˈfɑndənt/ *n* [U, C] soft sweet made of flavoured sugar that melts in the mouth 一种软糖.

fondle /ˈfɒndl; ˈfɑndl̩/ *v* [Tn] touch or stroke (sb/sth) gently and lovingly; caress 爱抚, 抚弄(某人[某事物]); 抚摸: *fondle a baby, doll, kitten* 抚弄婴儿、娃娃、小猫.

fon·due /ˈfɒndjuː; ˈfɑndu/ *n* [C, U] **1** dish of melted cheese, mixed with wine and flavourings, into which pieces of bread are dipped (蘸面包片用的)融化的干酪(混以酒和调料). **2** dish of hot oil or sauce into which pieces of meat, seafood, etc are dipped (蘸肉、海鲜等用的)热油或沙司: *fish fondue* 蘸鱼用的汁.

font /fɒnt; fɑnt/ *n* **1** basin or vessel in a church, usu carved from stone, to hold water for baptisms; basin for holy water (教堂用的)洗礼盆, 圣水盆(通常为石雕的). **2** = FOUNT.

food /fuːd; fud/ *n* **1** (**a**) [U] any substance that people or animals eat or drink or plants take in to maintain life and growth (人或动物所需的)食物, 饮料; (植物所需的)养料: *a shortage of food in some countries* 有些国家的食物短缺. (**b**) [U] solid substance of this sort 固体食物: *We cannot survive for long without food and drink.* 我们没有食物和饮料就活不了多久. **2** [C] specific kind of food 食品: *breakfast food* 早餐食品 ○ *baby, health foods* 婴儿、保健食品 ○ *frozen, processed foods* 冷冻的、加工的食品. **3** (idm 习语) **food for ˈthought** something to think about seriously 需要认真考虑的事.

□ **ˈfood-chain** *n* series of living beings arranged so that each being feeds on the one below it in the series 食物链.

ˈfood poisoning (also *dated* 旧作 **ˈptomaine poisoning**) illness of the stomach caused by eating food that contains harmful bacteria 食物中毒.

ˈfood processor electrical appliance that mixes, slices or chops food 食品加工器.

ˈfoodstuff *n* any substance used as food 食物; 食品: *essential foodstuffs* 基本食物.

ˈfood value nutritional power of food, usu measured in vitamins, minerals, etc 食物营养价值(通常以含有的维生素、矿物质等来衡量): *Most sweet things don't have much food value.* 大多数甜食都没有什么营养价值.

fool[1] /fuːl; ful/ *n* **1** (*derog* 贬) person who acts unwisely; person lacking in good sense or judgement; idiot 蠢人; 傻瓜; 白痴: *What fools we were not to see the trap!* 我们没有看出那是个陷阱, 多么傻呀! ○ *And I was fool enough* (ie so stupid as) *to believe him.* 而我却相信他, 真够傻的了. **2** (formerly) man employed by a king, noble, etc to amuse others with jokes and tricks; clown or jester (旧时)(国王或贵族豢养的)小丑, 弄臣. **3** (idm 习语) **act/play the fool** behave irresponsibly or so as to amuse (and perhaps annoy) others 瞎胡闹; 逗乐; (有时指)把人惹恼. **be a fool for one's ˈpains** do sth for which one gets no reward or thanks 做费力不讨好的事. **be ˌno ˈfool; be ˌnobody's ˈfool** be a wise and clever person; not be easily deceived 为人精明; 不易上当. **a ˌfool and his ˌmoney are ˌsoon ˈparted** (*saying* 谚) a foolish person spends, or can be tricked into spending, all his money 傻瓜存不住钱. **(be sent/go on) a ˈfool's errand** (be sent/go on) a senseless or an unprofitable mission (被派去干[干])徒劳无功的或白费力气的差事. **(be/live in) a fool's ˈparadise** (be/live in) a state of (false) happiness that cannot last (处于[生活在]不能持久的)(虚幻的)乐境. **make a ˈfool of oneself/sb** behave foolishly/trick sb into behaving foolishly 使(自己[某人])出丑. **(the) ˌmore fool ˈsb** (used as an exclamation 用作感叹语) the person specified is especially unwise for behaving in the way he does 蠢极了. **(there is) ˌno fool like an ˈold fool** (*saying* 谚) the foolish behaviour of an older person seems even more foolish because he is expected to act more sensibly than a younger person 最傻的是老傻瓜. **not/never suffer fools gladly** ⇨ SUFFER.

▷ **fool** *v* **1** (**a**) [I, Ip] **~ (about/around)** behave stupidly or foolishly 干蠢事: *Stop fooling about with that knife or someone will get hurt.* 不要摆弄那把刀, 会伤人的. (**b**) [I] tease or joke; pretend 逗弄; 开玩笑: *I was only fooling when I said I'd lost your keys.* 我说把你的钥匙丢了, 只是逗你玩的. **2** [Tn] trick or deceive (sb) 哄骗, 欺骗(某人): *You can't/don't fool me!* 你休想[别]骗我! **3** (phr v) **fool about/around** waste time; be idle 虚度光阴; 胡混: *I was meant to be working on Sunday, but I just fooled around all day.* 星期日我本应工作的, 但却闲混了一整天.

□ **ˌApril ˈFool** person tricked on April Fool's Day (在愚人节)受愚弄的人.

April ˈFool's Day 1 April 愚人节(4月1日).

fool[2] /fuːl; ful/ *n* [C, U] (usu in compounds 通常用以构成复合词) cold light pudding of crushed cooked fruit mixed with cream or custard 一种用奶油或蛋奶沙司拌熟水果泥制成的凉布丁: *rhubarb fool* 大黄茎凉点心.

fool·ery /ˈfuːlərɪ; ˈfulərɪ/ *n* [U, C] foolish behaviour 愚蠢的行为.

fool·hardy /ˈfuːlhɑːdɪ; ˈfulˌhɑrdɪ/ *adj* (**-ier, -iest**) foolishly bold or rash; reckless 胆大妄为的; 有勇无谋的; 鲁莽的: *It was foolhardy (of him) to go swimming alone.* (他)独自一人去游泳真是鲁莽. ▷ **fool·har·di·ness** *n* [U].

fool·ish /ˈfuːlɪʃ; ˈfulɪʃ/ *adj* **1** (**a**) (of people) lacking good sense or judgement; silly 愚蠢的; 傻的: *She's a foolish interfering old woman!* 她是个瞎管闲事的老太太! ○ *And I was foolish enough to believe him!* 我真傻, 竟相信了他! ○ *It would be foolish (of us) to pretend that the accident never happened.* 要是装成没发生事故的样子, 那(我们)就太愚蠢了. (**b**) (of actions, statements, etc) showing a lack of good sense or judgement; unwise or stupid (指行为、言论等)缺乏头脑的, 欠妥的, 不明智的, 愚蠢的: *a foolish decision, comment, reply, etc* 不明智的决定、议论、答复等. **2** [usu pred 通常作表语] made to feel or look ridiculous and embarrassed; stupid 感到或显得荒唐而难堪; 愚蠢: *I felt very foolish having to stand up and give a speech.* 我必须站起来讲话, 感到很难为情. ○ *He's afraid of looking foolish in front of all his friends.* 他怕在所有朋友面前出洋相. **3** (idm 习语) **penny wise pound foolish** ⇨ PENNY. ▷ **fool·ishly** *adv*. **fool·ish·ness** *n* [U].

fool·proof /ˈfuːlpruːf; ˈfulˈpruf/ *adj* **1** not capable of going wrong or of being misunderstood; very plain and simple 不会错的; 不会引起误解的; 非常简单明了的: *a foolproof method, plan, scheme, etc* 万无一失的方法、计划、方案等. **2** not capable of going wrong or of being used wrongly; reliable and easy to operate 不会做错的; 不会用错的; 可靠而操作简便的: *a foolproof security system* 可靠的安全系统.

fools·cap /ˈfuːlskæp; ˈfulˌskæp/ *n* [U] large size of

writing or printing paper, about 330 × 200 (or 400) mm 大页纸(约为330 × 200或400mm大小).

the foot 脚

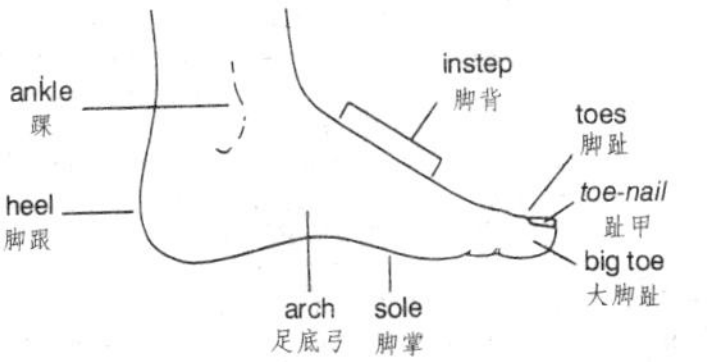

foot[1] /fʊt; fut/ *n* (*pl* **feet** /fi:t; fit/) **1** [C] lowest part of the leg, below the ankle, on which a person or animal stands 脚; 足: *He rose to his feet*, ie stood up. 他站起身来. ○ *walking round the house in bare feet*, ie not wearing socks, shoes, etc 光脚围着房子走 ○ [attrib 作定语] *a foot switch, brake, pump, etc*, ie operated by one's foot, not one's hand 脚踏开关、脚煞车、脚踏泵. ⇨illus 见插图. **2** [C usu *sing* 通常作单数] part of a sock, stocking, etc that covers the foot (袜子等的)足部. **3** [C] (*pl* **feet** or, in informal use and attributively, 用于口语或作定语时, 亦作 **foot**) (*abbr* 缩写 **ft**) measure of length: 12 inches (长度单位)英尺(12英寸): *We're flying at 35 000 feet.* 我们飞行的高度是35 000英尺. ○ *'How tall are you?' 'Five foot nine'*, ie five feet and nine inches. '你身高多少?' '五英尺九英寸.' ○ [attrib 作定语] *a 6-foot high wall* 6英尺高的墙. ⇨App 4,5 见附录4、5. **4** [sing] **the ~ of sth** (**a**) the lowest part of sth; base or bottom of sth (某物的)最下部, 底部: *at the foot of the stairs* 在楼梯底部 ○ *They camped at the foot of the mountain.* 他们在山脚下露营. ○ *at the foot of the page* 在该页的下端. (**b**) the lower end of a bed or grave 床或坟墓的尾端: *Spare blankets lay at the foot of each bed.* 每张床的尾端放有备用毛毯. **5** [U] (*arch* 古) manner of walking or moving 步态: *light/swift/fleet of foot* 步履轻盈[敏捷/如飞]. **6** [C] unit of rhythm in a line of poetry containing one stressed syllable and one or more unstressed syllables, as in the four divisions of *For 'men / may 'come / and 'men / may 'go* 音步(诗行中的节奏单位, 一个音步包括一个重读音节和一个或几个非重读音节, 如以下为四个音步: For 'men / may 'come / and 'men / may 'go. **7** (idm 习语) **be on one's 'feet** be standing 站着: *I've been on my feet all day.* 我站了一整天. **bind/tie sb hand and foot** ⇨ HAND[1]. **the boot is on the other foot** ⇨ BOOT. **catch sb on the wrong foot** ⇨ CATCH[1]. **cut the ground from under sb's feet** ⇨ GROUND[1]. **drag one's feet/heels** ⇨ DRAG[2]. **fall/land on one's 'feet** make a quick recovery after an illness, a business failure, etc, esp through good luck (病后、事业失败后等)迅速恢复(尤指侥幸). **find one's feet** ⇨ FIND. **from head to foot/toe** ⇨ HEAD[1]. **get/have a foot in the door** gain/have a first introduction to a profession, an organization, etc 初入一行业、机构等: *It's difficult to get a foot in the door of publishing.* 加入出版界是很难的. **get/have cold feet** ⇨ COLD[1]. **have feet of 'clay** have some basic weakness or fault 有某种根本的弱点或错误. **have the ball at one's feet** ⇨ BALL[1]. **have, etc one's/both feet on the 'ground** be sensible, realistic and practical 脚踏实地; 实事求是. **have a foot in both 'camps** have an interest in two different parties or sides, without a commitment to either 脚踩两只船. **have one foot in the grave** be so old or ill that one is not likely to live much longer 一只脚已踏进坟墓; 行将就木; 死期不远. **have two left feet** ⇨ LEFT[2]. **in one's stocking feet** ⇨ STOCKING. **itchy feet** ⇨ ITCHY (ITCH). **keep one's 'feet** keep one's balance, esp on a slippery surface; not fall 站稳脚跟(尤指在很滑的表面上); 不跌倒. **let the grass grow under one's feet** ⇨ GRASS[1]. **my 'foot!** (used to express scornful rejection of what sb has just said 用于对某人刚说过的话表示轻蔑的驳斥) nonsense! rubbish! 胡说八道! 没这回事! **on one's 'feet** completely recovered from an illness or a set-back (患病或遭受挫折后)完全复原: *After his wife's death it took him two years to get back on his feet.* 他妻子死后两年, 他才振作起来. ○ *Only our party's policies will put the country on its feet again.* 只有我们党的政策才会使国家恢复元气. **on foot** walking, rather than using any form of transport 步行: *We're going on foot, not by car.* 我们走着去, 不坐汽车. **the patter of tiny feet** ⇨ PATTER[2]. **pull the carpet/rug from under sb's feet** ⇨ PULL[2]. **put one's best foot forward** ⇨ BEST[1]. **put one's 'feet up** rest or relax in a chair or on a bed (esp, though not necessarily, with one's feet supported) 在椅子上或床上休息(尤指脚部垫起). **put one's 'foot down** be very firm in opposing sth which sb wishes to do 坚决反对某人想做的事: *Mother let us go to the party, but when it came to staying overnight, she put her foot down firmly.* 母亲允许我们去参加晚会, 但要说到过夜, 她可决不答应. **put one's 'foot in it** say or do sth that upsets, offends or embarrasses sb 说的话或做的事使人烦恼、得罪人或令人难堪. **put a foot wrong** (esp in negative sentences 尤用于否定句) make a mistake 做错事; 出错; 犯错: *I've never known him to put a foot wrong, no matter how delicate the issue.* 不论问题多么棘手, 我从没见他出过错. **rush/run sb (clean) off his 'feet** make sb work very hard or move about a lot, so making him exhausted 把某人累坏了; 使某人疲于奔命: *Before Christmas the shop assistants are rushed off their feet.* 圣诞节前店员忙得不可开交. **set foot in/on sth** enter or visit (a place); arrive 进入或参观(某地); 到达: *the first man to set foot on the moon* 第一个登上月球的人 ○ *Don't ever set foot in this house again!* 永远别再进这个门! **set sb/sth on his/its 'feet** make sb/sth independent 使某人[某事物]独立. **shake the dust off one's feet** ⇨ SHAKE[1]. **sit at sb's feet** ⇨ SIT. **stand on one's own (two) feet** be independent and able to take care of oneself 独立自主; 自立: *Now that you're growing up you must learn to stand on your own two feet.* 你既然已经长大成人, 就得学会独立生活. **start off on the right/wrong foot** ⇨ START[2]. **sweep sb off his feet** ⇨ SWEEP[1]. **take the weight off one's feet** ⇨ WEIGHT. **ten feet tall** pleased with and proud of oneself 沾沾自喜; 自鸣得意: *be/feel/look/seem ten feet tall* 表现出[感到/显得/似乎]得意扬扬. **under one's 'feet** disturbing one and being a nuisance 碍手碍脚; 讨厌: *The children are under my feet all day.* 孩子们整天烦我. **wait on sb hand and foot** ⇨ WAIT[1]. **walk sb off his feet** ⇨ WALK[1].

▷ **-footer** /fʊtə(r); 'futɚ/ (forming compounds 用以构成复合词) person or thing of the specified length, height or width 某一长度、高度、宽度的人或物: *a six-footer*, ie a person who is six feet tall or thing that is six feet wide or long.

□ ˌ**foot-and-'mouth (disease)** *n* [U] disease of cattle, etc which causes blisters on the mouth and feet (牛、羊等的)口蹄疫.

'**football** *n* (**a**) [C] large round or oval inflated ball, usu of leather 足球; 橄榄球. (**b**) [U] any of several outdoor games between two teams, played with such a ball 足球运动; 橄榄球运动. (**c**) [U] (*Brit*) = ASSOCIATION FOOTBALL (ASSOCIATION). ⇨App 4 见附录4. **footballer** *n* person who plays football, esp as a profession 足球运动员(尤指职业的). '**football pools** (also **the pools**) form of gambling in which sb tries to forecast the results of football matches 足球赛赌博.

'**foot-bridge** *n* narrow bridge for the use of people who are walking 步行桥; 人行桥.

'**footfall** *n* sound of sb walking; sound of a footstep 脚步声.

'**foot-fault** *n* (in tennis) act of breaking the rules by placing one's feet inside the back line when serving (网球)脚部违例, 脚部犯规(发球踏线犯规).

'**foothill** *n* [C usu *pl* 通常作复数] hill or low mountain at the base of a higher mountain or range of mountains 山麓小丘.

'**foothold** *n* **1** place where one's foot can be supported securely when climbing 立足处(攀登时脚踩的地方). **2** secure position in a business, profession, etc from which further progress may be made (在事业等方面可以进一步发展的)稳固地位: *gain a firm foothold in the industry* 在这一企业中取得稳固地位.

'**footlights** *n* [pl] row of lights along the front of the stage in a theatre 脚灯(舞台前面的一排灯). ⇨illus at

App 1 见附录1插图, page ix.

ˈ**footloose** *adj* (idm 习语) **footloose and fancy-ˈfree** without personal responsibilities or commitments; free to act as one pleases 无拘无束的; 自由自在的.

ˈ**footman** /-mən; -mən/ *n* (*pl* **-men**) male servant, usu in uniform, who admits visitors, serves food at table, etc (负责迎客、上菜等的)男仆(通常穿制服).

ˈ**footmark** *n* = FOOTPRINT.

ˈ**footnote** *n* additional piece of information at the bottom of a page in a book 脚注(列在一页末了的附注). ⇨App 3 见附录3.

ˈ**footpath** *n* = PATH 1.

ˈ**footplate** *n* metal platform on which the driver and fireman stand in a locomotive (机车上供司机和司炉站立的金属制的)平台.

ˈ**footprint** *n* [C usu *pl* 通常作复数] impression of a human or an animal foot on a surface; mark left by a foot 脚印; 足迹: *leave footprints in the snow* 在雪地上留下足迹 ○ *muddy footprints on the kitchen floor* 厨房地板上的泥脚印.

ˈ**foot-slog** *v* (**-gg-**) [I] (*infml* 口) walk for a long distance and so become very tired 因长途跋涉而步履维艰.

ˈ**footsore** *adj* having sore or tired feet, esp from walking a long way 脚疼的, 脚酸的(尤指因走长路而引起的): *footsore travellers* 走疼了脚的旅行者.

ˈ**footstep** *n* [C] **1** (**a**) (usu *pl* 通常作复数) sound or mark of a step taken when walking 脚步声; 足迹: *I heard his footsteps in the hall* 我听见大厅里有他的脚步声. (**b**) (distance covered by a) step taken when walking 脚步; 一步的距离. **2** (idm 习语) **follow in one's/sb's footsteps** ⇨ FOLLOW.

ˈ**footstool (also stool)** *n* low stool for resting the feet on when sitting in a chair 脚凳(坐时垫脚的矮凳).

ˈ**footway** *n* = FOOTPATH.

ˈ**footwear** *n* [U] anything worn on the feet, eg shoes and boots 鞋类(如鞋、靴).

ˈ**footwork** *n* [U] (**a**) manner of moving or using the feet in sports such as boxing or dancing (拳击或舞蹈的)步法. (**b**) (*fig* 比喻) ability to react quickly to sudden danger, new opportunities, etc 应变能力(对突发的危险、新机遇等做出敏捷反应的能力): *Thanks to agile footwork he always managed to escape his pursuers.* 他善于随机应变, 总能摆脱追踪他的人.

foot[2] /fʊt; fut/ *v* (idm 习语) **foot the ˈbill (for sth)** be responsible for paying the cost of sth 负责缴付费用; 付帐: *Who's going to foot the bill for all the repairs?* 谁来付所有的修理费? ˈ**foot it** (*infml* 口) walk; not travel by bus, etc 步行.

▷ **-footed** (forming compound *adjs* 用以构成复合形容词) having feet of the specified kind or number 有所述类型或数量的脚的: *bare-footed* ○ *flat-footed* ○ *four-footed.*

foot·age /ˈfʊtɪdʒ; ˋfutɪdʒ/ *n* [U] **1** length or distance measured in feet 以英尺量度的长度或距离. **2** length of film made for the cinema or TV (电影或电视的)片段: *The film contained some old newsreel footage.* 这部影片中有些旧新闻片的镜头.

foot·ing /ˈfʊtɪŋ; ˋfutɪŋ/ *n* [sing] **1** secure grip with the feet; balance 站稳; 平衡: *He lost his footing on the wet floor and fell.* 他在潮湿的地板上失去平衡而摔倒了. **2** basis on which sth is established 基础: *This enterprise is now on a firm footing and should soon show profits.* 现在这家企业基础稳固, 很快就会赢利. ○ *The army were put on a war footing*, ie were prepared for war. 这支军队是战时的编制(为战争作好准备). **3** position or status of sb/sth in relation to others; relationship 某人[某事物]与他人或其他事物相关的地位; 关系: *The workers want to be on an equal footing with/on the same footing as the managers.* 工人要求与经理地位平等.

footle /ˈfu:tl; ˋfutl/ *v* [I, Ip] **~ (about/around)** (*infml* 口) spend time aimlessly; do nothing in particular 虚度光阴; 闲混: *footle about all day* 整天瞎混.

▷ **foot·ling** /ˈfu:tlɪŋ; ˋfutlɪŋ/ *adj* unimportant; trivial 无足轻重的; 琐碎的: *footling little jobs* 鸡毛蒜皮的活儿.

foot·sie /ˈfʊtsɪ; ˋfutsɪ/ *n* (idm 习语) **play footsie with sb** (*infml* 口) touch sb's feet lightly with one's own feet, esp under a table, as a playful expression of affection or to arouse sexual interest 用脚轻碰某人的脚(尤指在桌下以示喜爱或用以调情).

fop /fɒp; fɑp/ *n* (*derog* 贬) man who is too concerned with his clothes and appearance; dandy 过于注意衣着与外表的男子.

▷ **fop·pish** *adj* of or like a fop (似)纨袴子弟的.

for[1] /fə(r); fɚ; *strong form* 强读式 fɔ:(r); fɔr/ *prep* **1** (indicating the person intended to receive or benefit from sth 表示接受某事物或从某事物中受益的人): *a letter for you* 给你的信 ○ *Are all these presents for me?* 这些礼物都是给我的吗? ○ *Save a piece for Mary.* 给玛丽留一块吧. ○ *Have you made a cup of tea for Mrs Watson?* 你给华生太太沏茶了吗? **2** (indicating purpose or function 表示目的或功能): *go for a walk* 去散步 ○ *It's a machine for slicing bread.* 这是切面包片的机器. ○ *Are you learning English for pleasure or for your work?* 你学英语是出于兴趣还是为了工作? ○ (*infml* 口) *What did you shout at him for?* ie Why did you shout at him? 你为什么朝他大声喊叫? ○ *For sales to* (ie In order that sales may) *increase, we must lower our prices.* 我们为了增加销售量, 必须把价格降低. **3** (indicating destination, aim or reason 表示目的地、目标或原因): *depart for home* 动身回家 ○ *head for the shore* 向岸边行进 ○ *Is this the train for Glasgow?* 这是开往格拉斯哥的火车吗? ○ *Passengers for Oxford must change at Didcot.* 前往牛津的旅客必须在迪德考特换车. ○ *She knew she was destined for a great future.* 她知道自己前程远大. ○ *It's a book for* (ie intended to be read by or to) *children.* 这是一本儿童读物. ○ *a chair for visitors* 来宾用的座椅 ○ *bicycles for sale or for hire* 供出售或出租的自行车. **4** in order to help or benefit (sb/sth) 有助于或有益于(某人[某事物]): *Would you please translate this letter for me?* 你给我翻译这封信行吗? ○ *What can I do for you?* 您想要什么? ○ *fighting for their country* 为其国家而战 ○ *Take some aspirin for* (ie to lessen the pain caused by) *your headache.* 你头痛吃点阿司匹林吧. ○ *The deputy manager ran the firm for* (ie instead of) *him while he was ill.* 在他生病期间, 副经理代他主持公司事务. **5** as the price, reward or penalty of sth 作为对某事物的代价、报酬或惩罚: *I bought a book for £3.* 我花3英镑买了一本书. ○ *She gave me their old TV for nothing.* 她把他们的旧电视机送给我了. ○ *He got a medal for bravery.* 他因勇敢而获得一枚奖章. ○ *You can go to prison for dangerous driving.* 鲁莽驾驶可导致入狱. **6** as the replacement of (sth else) 以取代(他事物): *exchange one's car for a new one* 用自己的汽车换一辆新的 ○ *Don't translate word for word.* 不要逐字硬译. **7** in defence or support of (sb/sth) 保卫、支持或拥护(某人[某事物]): *Are you for or against the new road scheme?* 你对修建新道路的计划是赞成还是反对? ○ *Three cheers for the winner!* 为获胜者三呼喝彩! ○ *We're petitioning for our right to keep a school in our village.* 我们为在村中保留一所学校这一权利进行请愿. ○ *I'm all for pubs being open all day.* 我完全赞成酒馆整日营业. **8** (**a**) as a representative of (sb/sth) 代表(某人[某事物]): *I am speaking for all the workers in this firm.* 我代表公司全体工作人员讲话. ○ *Who's the MP for Bradford?* 谁是代表布拉德福德的下院议员? (**b**) meaning (sth) 意为(某事物): *What's the 'S' for in A S Hornby?* 在A S Hornby中的S代表哪个字? ○ *Shaking your head for 'No' is not universal.* 世界上并非所有的人都用摇头来表示'不'. **9** (after a *v* 用于动词后) in order to obtain (sth) 为得到(某事物): *search for treasure* 寻宝 ○ *hope for a settlement* 希望得到和解 ○ *pray for peace* 为和平祈祷 ○ *fish for trout* 钓鳟鱼 ○ *ask the policeman for directions* 向警察问路 ○ *go to a friend for advice* 向朋友请教 ○ *There were 50 applicants for the post.* 有50人申请这个职位. **10** (after an *adj* 用于形容词后) considering what can be expected from (sb/sth) 就(某人[某事物])而言: *It's quite warm for January.* 就一月份来说, 天气相当暖和了. ○ *She's tall for her age.* 从她的年龄来看, 她个子算是高的. ○ *He's not bad for a beginner.* 就新手而论, 他已经很不错了. **11** (after a comparative *adj* 用于比较级的形容词之后) following (sth) 随(某事物)而来: *You'll feel all the better for a good night's sleep.* 你好好睡上一夜, 心情就好多了. ○ *This room would look all the better for a spot of paint.* 上一点油漆能让这房间增色不少. **12** as the equivalent of (sth); in return for (sth) 与(某事物)相对应; 作为对(某事物)的回报: *There's one bad apple for every three good* *ones.* 每四个苹果里就有一个坏的. ○ *You get a coupon for every 3 gallons of petrol.* 每买三加仑的汽油就可获得一张优惠券. **13** with regard to (sb/sth); concerning (sb/sth) 对于, 至于, 关于(某人[某事物]): *anxious for sb's safety* 为某人的安全担忧 ○ *ready for a holiday* 准备好去度假 ○ *eager for them to start* 急着要他们开始 ○ *Fortunately for us, the weather changed.* 我们真好运气, 天气变了. **14** because of (sth); on account of (sth) 因为, 由于(某事物): *famous for its cathedral* 以大教堂而闻名 ○ *for the following reasons* 由于以下的原因 ○ *Please take care of her for my sake.* 请为了我好好照顾她. ○ *I couldn't speak for laughing.* 我笑得说不出话来. ○ *He didn't answer for fear of hurting her.* 他没回答是怕伤她的感情. ○ *He gave me roses for my birthday.* 他送我玫瑰花来庆贺我的生日. **15** (**a**) (indicating a length of time 表示一段时间): *I'm going away for a few days.* 我要离开几天. ○ *He was in prison for twenty years.* 他在监狱中蹲了二十年. ○ *You said you would love me for ever.* 你说过你永远爱我. (**b**) (indicating that sth is intended to happen at the specified time 表示某事物在所述时间要发生): *a reservation for the first week in June* 六月第一周的预订 ○ *The appointment is for 12 May.* 约会定在5月12日. ○ *We're invited for 7.30.* 我们接到邀请, 时间为7点30分. (**c**) (indicating the occasion when sth happens 表示某事物发生的场合或时机): *I'm warning you for the last time — stop talking!* 我最后一次警告你——不要再说话了! ○ *I'm meeting him for the first time today.* 今天我要与他初次见面. **16** (indicating a distance 表示距离): *He crawled on his hands and knees for 100 metres.* 他爬行了100米. ○ *The road went on for miles and miles.* 这条路很长很长. **17** (**a**) (used after an *adj* and before a *n/pron* + infinitive 用于形容词之后和名词[代词]之前+不定式): *It's impossible for me to leave my family.* 我是不可能离开家的. ○ *It's useless for us to continue.* 我们继续下去是徒劳的. ○ (*fml* 文) *For her to have survived such an ordeal was remarkable.* 她居然能经得起这种磨难, 真了不起. ○ *It's customary for the women to sit apart.* 按习俗, 妇女要分开坐. ○ *His greatest wish was for his daughter to take over the business.* 他最大的心愿是让女儿接管公司. (**b**) (used after a *n* and before a *n/pron* + infinitive 用于名词之后和名词[代词]之前+不定式): *no need for you to go* 不需要你去 ○ *time for us to leave* 我们该动身的时间 ○ *a rush for them to finish* 他们需仓促完成. (**c**) (used after *too* + *adj* or *adj* + *enough* 用于too+形容词之后或形容词+enough之后): *The box is too heavy for me to lift.* 这个箱子太重了, 我提不动. ○ *Is it clear enough for you to read?* 这个清楚不清楚? 你能念吗? ○ *The coffee was too hot for her (to drink).* 咖啡太烫, 她没法喝. (**d**) (used before a *n/pron* + infinitive to show purpose or design 用于名词[代词]+不定式之前, 表示目的或意图): *letters for the manager to sign* 需要经理签字的信件 ○ *money for you to invest wisely* 你要看准机会投资的钱 ○ *I would give anything for this not to have happened.* 我宁愿付出任何代价, 也不愿出了这件事. ○ *It's not for me* (ie It is not my responsibility) *to say* 这不是由我来说的话. (**e**) (used after *more* with *than* 用于more与than结构之后): *Nothing could be more desirable than for them both to get jobs in Leeds.* 要是他俩都能在利兹找到工作, 那就再好不过了. ○ *Nothing would please me more than for her to win the next election.* 她若能在下次竞选中获胜, 我就再高兴不过了. **18** (idm 习语) **be 'for it** (*infml* 口) expect to be punished or to get into trouble 会受惩罚或惹出麻烦: *The headmaster saw me draw the picture on the blackboard — I'm for it now.* 校长看见我在黑板上画画, 这下子我可惹出麻烦了. **for 'all** despite; in spite of 尽管; 虽然: *For all his talk about sports cars and swimming-pools he's just an ordinary bank-clerk.* 别看他大谈昂贵的汽车跑车和私人游泳池, 其实他只不过是个银行的普通职员. ○ *For all you say, I think she's the best teacher we've got.* 不管你怎么说, 我仍然认为她是我们最好的老师. ○ *For all his wealth and fame, he's a very lonely man.* 他虽然又有钱又有名, 但很孤独. ○ *He has great power and wealth, but is still unhappy for all that.* 他有钱有势, 可尽管如此却并不快乐.

for[2] /fə(r); fɚ; *rare strong form* 罕, 强读式 fɔ:(r); fɔr/ *conj* (*dated or fml* 旧或文) (not used at the beginning of a sentence 不用于句首) because 因为; 由于: *We listened eagerly, for he brought news of our families.* 他给我们带来了家里的消息, 我们都迫不及待地听着. ○ *Prepare to alight, for we are almost there.* 我们马上就要到了, 准备下车吧.

for /ˌef əʊ ˈɑ:(r); ˌɛf o ˈɑr/ *abbr* 缩写 = (*commerce* 商) (of freight) free on rail (ie transported to the train and loaded without the buyer paying extra) (指运费)火车上交货价.

for·age /ˈfɒrɪdʒ; *US* ˈfɔ:r-; ˈfɔrɪdʒ/ *n* **1** [U] food for horses and cattle (牛马的)饲料. **2** [C usu *sing* 通常作单数] a search or hunt, esp for food 搜寻, 寻找(尤指寻找食物).

▷ **for·age** *v* [I, Ipr, Ip] **~ (for sth)**; **~ (about)** search or hunt for sth, esp food and supplies 搜寻或寻找某物(尤指食物及供应物): *One group left the camp to forage for firewood.* 一些人离开营地去寻找木柴. ○ *She foraged* (ie rummaged) *about in her handbag, but couldn't find her keys.* 她翻遍了手提包, 就是找不到钥匙.

□ **'forage crops** crops grown as food for horses and cattle (牛马的)饲料作物.

for·as·much as /ˌfɔ:rəzˈmʌtʃ əz; ˌfɔrəzˈmʌtʃ əz/ *conj* (*arch or law* 古或律) because; since; seeing that 因为; 由于; 鉴于.

foray /ˈfɒreɪ; *US* ˈfɔ:reɪ; ˈfɔre/ *n* **1** sudden attack, esp to obtain sth; raid 袭击(尤指为获得某物); 突袭: *go on/make a foray into enemy territory* 袭击敌占区. **2** brief but vigorous attempt to be involved in a different activity, profession, etc (对一新的活动、行业等)短暂而积极的改换尝试: *the company's first foray into the computer market* 该公司打入计算机市场的首次尝试.

▷ **foray** *v* [I] make a foray 袭击; 突袭.

for·bade (also **for·bad**) *pt* of FORBID.

for·bear[1] /fɔ:ˈbeə(r); fɔrˈbɛr/ *v* (*pt* **forbore** /fɔ:ˈbɔ:(r); fɔrˈbɔr/, *pp* **forborne** /fɔ:ˈbɔ:n; fɔrˈbɔrn/) [I, Ipr, Tt, Tg] **~ (from sth/doing sth)** (*fml* 文) refrain from doing or saying sth in a patient or self-controlled way 克制, 自制(不做或不说某事物): *her mother's gentle and forbearing character* 她母亲那温柔而宽容的性格 ○ *He could not forbear from expressing his disagreement.* 他忍不住要表达不同意见. ○ *He forbore to mention/mentioning the matter again.* 他克制住自己, 不再提及此事.

▷ **for·bear·ance** /fɔ:ˈbeərəns; fɔrˈbɛrəns/ *n* [U] (*fml* 文) patient self-control; tolerance 自制; 耐性: *show forbearance towards sb* 对某人有耐性 ○ *exercise forbearance in dealing with people* 宽以待人.

for·bear[2] = FOREBEAR.

for·bid /fəˈbɪd; fɚˈbɪd/ *v* (*pt* **forbade** /fəˈbæd; *US* fəˈbeɪd; fɚˈbed/ or **forbad** /fəˈbæd; fɚˈbæd/, *pp* **forbidden** /fəˈbɪdn; fɚˈbɪdn̩/) **1** (**a**) [Tsg, Dn·n, Dn·t] order (sb) not to do sth 禁止, 不准, 不许(某人)做某事: *I can't forbid you/your seeing that man again.* 我无法禁止你再和那个男人来往. ○ *She was forbidden access to the club.* 人家不允许她到那个俱乐部去. ○ *If you want to go, I can't forbid you.* 你想去, 我也拦不住你. ○ *He was forbidden to talk to her.* 不准他同她交谈. ○ *It is forbidden (for anyone) to smoke in this room.* 禁止(任何人)在本室吸烟. (**b**) [Tn, Tg] order that (sth) shall not be done; not allow 禁止(某事物); 不允许: *Her father forbade their marriage.* 她父亲不允许他们俩结婚. ○ *Photography is strictly forbidden in the cathedral.* 教堂内严禁摄影. ○ *forbidden subjects such as sex and politics* 禁止谈论的题目, 如性和政治 ○ *The law forbids building on this land.* 法律规定禁止在此处进行修建. **2** [Tn] make (sth) difficult or impossible; prevent or not allow 妨碍(某事); 阻止或不准: *Lack of space forbids further treatment of the topic here.* 因篇幅所限, 此处不便对本题作进一步阐述. **3** (idm 习语) **forˌbidden 'fruit** thing that is desired because it is disapproved of or not allowed 禁果(因受禁止而更想得到的东西). **forˌbidden 'ground** (**a**) area that one is not allowed to enter 禁区. (**b**) subject, activity, etc that is not allowed or approved of 不准涉及的或不认可的内容或活动等. **God/Heaven for'bid (that...)** (expressing a wish that sth may not happen 表示愿某事不要发生): *Heaven forbid that anything awful should have happened to her.* 但愿她不会出了大事.

▷ **for·bid·ding** *adj* looking unfriendly; stern; threatening 样子冷淡的; 严峻的; 令人生畏的: *a forbidding appearance, look, manner, etc* 冷酷的样子、神

情、态度等 ○ *a forbidding coastline*, ie one that looks dangerous险恶的海岸地形. **for·bid·dingly** *adv*.

for·bore *pt* of FORBEAR[1].

for·borne *pp* of FORBEAR[1].

force[1] /fɔ:s; fɔrs/ *n* **1** [U] (**a**) physical strength or power 力; 力量: *the force of the blow, explosion, collision, etc* 打击力、爆炸力、碰撞力 ○ *They used brute force to break open the door.* 他们靠蛮劲把门撞开了. (**b**) violent physical action 暴力; 武力: *The soldiers took the prisoners away by force.* 士兵们强行把犯人带走了. ○ *renounce the use of force* 放弃使用武力. **2** (**a**) [U] (intensity of) strength or power; influence 力量(的强度); 影响力: *the full force of her argument* 她的论据的全部力量 ○ *He overcame his bad habits by sheer force of will.* 他全凭毅力改掉了坏习惯. ○ *Through force of circumstances the plans had to be changed.* 情况所迫, 只得修改计划. (**b**) [C] person, thing, belief, etc with such strength or power; influence 具有此种力量的人、事物、信仰等; 影响: *She's a force to be reckoned with*, ie someone to be treated seriously. 她是不可忽视的力量. ○ *the two main political forces of left and right* 左派和右派两股主要的政治力量 ○ *powerful economic forces* 强大的经济实力 ○ *Is religion a force for good?* 宗教是诱导人们积德行善的力量吗? ○ *the forces of evil still at work today* 至今仍在作祟的邪恶势力. **3** [C, U] (in scientific use) measurable influence or intensity tending to cause movement (科技用语)力: *The force of gravity pulls things towards the earth's centre.* 地心吸力把物体吸向地心. **4** [C] (power of the) wind, rain or another of the natural elements 风、雨或其他自然现象(的力量): *fighting against the forces of nature* 与大自然作斗争. ⇨ Usage at STRENGTH 用法见STRENGTH. **5** [C usu *sing* 通常作单数] measure of wind strength 风力: *a force 9 gale* 9级风. **6** [CGp] group of people organized for a specified purpose 为某目的而组织起来的人: *a sales/labour force* 推销人员[劳动群众] ○ *Our work-force are completely dependable.* 我们的工作人员的能力完全可靠. **7** [CGp] organized body of armed and specially trained people 武装力量; 部队: *the police force* 警察部队 ○ *peace-keeping forces* 维持和平部队 ○ *the armed forces of a country*, ie the army, navy and air force 国家的武装力量(陆、海、空三军). **8** [U] (legal) authority (法律的)权威, 威力: *This decree has the force of law behind it.* 这一裁决有法律的力量作后盾. **9** (idm 习语) **break the force of sth** reduce or weaken the impact of sth such as a fall or blow 降低或减弱某事物(如下落或打击)的冲撞力: *The force of his fall was broken by the straw mats.* 草垫的缓冲作用减弱了他下跌的力量. **bring sth/come into 'force** (cause a law, rule, etc to) become effective or come into operation (使法律、规则等)生效, 开始执行: *When do the new safety rules come into force?* 新的安全规则何时生效? **(from/out of) force of 'habit** (because of) the tendency to do (some) things in a certain way from always having done so in the past (出于)习惯势力: *It's force of habit that gets me out of bed at 7.15 each morning.* 我每天早晨7点15分就起床, 这已成了习惯. **in 'force** (**a**) (of people) in large numbers (指人)大量的, 大批的: *The police were present at the demonstration in (full) force.* 警方派出大队人马在示威游行的现场戒备. (**b**) (of a law, rule, etc) effective or in operation (指法律、规则等)有效的, 现行的: *The new safety regulations are now in force.* 新的安全规则现已生效. **join forces** ⇨ JOIN.

force[2] /fɔ:s; fɔrs/ *v* **1** [Tn·pr, Cn·t] make (sb/oneself) do sth he/one does not want to do; compel; oblige 使(某人[自己])做不愿做的事; 强迫; 逼迫; 迫使: *force a confession out of sb* 逼某人招供 ○ *The thief forced her to hand over the money.* 强盗逼她把钱交出来. ○ *He forced himself to speak to her.* 他硬着头皮和她搭话. ○ *The president was forced into resigning/to resign.* 会长被迫辞职. **2** [Tn·pr, Tn·p] use physical strength to move (oneself) against resistance; use physical strength to move (sth) 靠体力使(自己)逆阻力而动; 用力使(某物)移动: *force one's way through a crowd* 挤过人群 ○ *force a way in/out/through* 挤入[出/过] ○ (*fig* 比喻) *The government forced the bill through Parliament.* 政府迫使议会通过该法案. ○ *force clothes into a bag* 硬把衣服塞进包里. **3** [Tn, Cn·a] break (sth) open using physical strength 用力打开(某物): *force (open) a door, lock, window, safe* 强行打开门、锁、窗户、保险柜. **4** [Tn] cause or produce (sth) by effort, esp when under stress 勉强促成或产生(某事物)(尤指迫于压力): *a forced smile/laugh*, ie not the natural result of amusement 强作笑脸[强装欢笑]. **5** [Tn] cause (fruit, plants, etc) to reach maturity earlier than is normal by keeping them under special conditions 使(果实、植物等)早熟. **6** (idm 习语) **force sb's 'hand** make sb do sth unwillingly or sooner than he intended 迫使某人勉强或提前做某事. **'force the issue** act so as to make an immediate decision necessary 为迫使立即做出必要的决定而采取行动. **force the 'pace** go very fast in a race, etc in order to tire the other competitors (在比赛等活动中为使对手疲劳)加快速度. **7** (phr v) **force sth back** try very hard not to show (an emotion) 极力不流露出(某种感情): *force back one's tears* 强忍着眼泪. **force sth down** (**a**) compel sb/oneself to swallow (food and drink) when he/one does not want to 强迫某人[自己]咽下(食物和饮料): *After being ill I didn't feel like eating but I managed to force something down.* 我病后不想吃东西, 不过还是勉强咽了一点. (**b**) compel (an aircraft) to land, eg because a bomb is found on board 迫使(飞机等)降落(如因发现机上有炸弹). **force sth on sb** make sb accept sth against his will 勉强某人接受某事物: *force one's ideas, company, attention on sb* 把自己的思想强加于人、硬要陪伴某人、硬要照料某人 ○ *Higher taxes were forced on the people.* 政府强行提高税收.

□ ˌ**forced 'labour** compulsory hard work, usu under harsh conditions 强迫劳动.

ˌ**forced 'landing** emergency landing that an aircraft has to make (飞行器的)紧急降落, 迫降.

ˌ**forced 'march** long emergency march made by troops 强行军.

force-feed /'fɔ:sfi:d; `fɔrs`fid/ *v* (*pp*, *pt* **force-fed** /'fɔ:sfed; `fɔrs`fɛd/) [Tn] compel (a person or an animal) to take food and drink 强迫(人或动物)进食及饮水: *All the prisoners on hunger strike had to be force-fed.* 所有绝食的犯人均需强迫进食.

force·ful /'fɔ:sfl; `fɔrsfəl/ *adj* strong and assertive 强有力的: (*approv* 褒) *a forceful speaker* 讲话有说服力的人 ○ *a forceful argument, speech, style of writing, etc* 有力的论据、言语、文体等. ▷ **force·fully** /-fəlɪ; -fəlɪ/ *adv*. **force·ful·ness** *n* [U].

force ma·jeure /ˌfɔ:s mæ'ʒɜ:(r); ˌfɔrs mɑ`ʒɝ/ (*French law* 法, 律) unforeseen circumstances, such as war, that excuses sb from keeping a promise, fulfilling a bargain, etc 不可抗力(难以预见的情况, 如战争, 借以原谅某人未能实践诺言、履行协议等).

force·meat /'fɔ:smi:t; `fɔrsˌmit/ *n* [U] finely chopped meat mixed with herbs, etc and used as stuffing, eg in a roast chicken 加香料的碎肉(如用作填充烤鸡的馅).

for·ceps /'fɔ:seps; `fɔrsəps/ *n* [pl] pincers or tongs used by dentists, surgeons, etc for gripping things (医生用的)钳子, 镊子: *a pair of forceps* 一把钳子 ○ [attrib 作定语] *a forceps delivery*, ie one in which the baby is delivered with the aid of forceps 产钳分娩.

for·cible /'fɔ:səbl; `fɔrsəbl̩/ *adj* [attrib 作定语] **1** done by or involving the use of physical force 用强力的: *make a forcible entry into a building* 强行进入一建筑物. **2** convincing and effective; forceful 有说服力的; 强有力的: *a forcible argument/reminder* 有说服力的论据[措辞强硬的催单]. ▷ **for·cibly** /-əblɪ; -əblɪ/ *adv*.

ford /fɔ:d; fɔrd/ *n* shallow place in a river where one can walk or drive across 河流中(可涉水或开车越过)的浅处.

▷ **ford** *v* [Tn] cross (a river) by walking or driving across a shallow part 从水浅处涉水或开车过(河). **ford·able** /-əbl; -əbl̩/ *adj* that can be forded 可以涉水而过的.

fore[1] /fɔ:(r); fɔr/ *adj* **1** [attrib 作定语] situated in the front part of a vehicle 在运输工具前部的: *in the fore part of the ship/plane/train* 在轮船[飞机/火车]的前部. Cf 参看 HIND[1]. **2** (idm 习语) **be/come to the fore** be/become prominent or important 作为[成为]突出的或重要的: *She's always to the fore at moments of crisis.* 她在危急关头总是挺身而出. ○ *After the election several new Members of Parliament came to the fore.* 大选后有几位新议员脱颖而出. **fore and 'aft** (**a**) at the bow (front) and stern (back) of a ship 在船首与船尾. (**b**) (of sails) set lengthwise on a ship or boat (指船帆)沿船体纵向悬挂.

▷ **fore** *adv* in, at or towards the front of a ship or aircraft 在船或飞行器的前部; 向着船或飞行器的前部.

fore *n* [U] front part (of a ship) (船的)前部.

fore[2] /fɔ:(r); fɔr/ *interj* (in golf) shout given to warn people that a player is about to hit the ball (高尔夫球运动中)前面注意(警告人们运动员即将击球的口令).

fore- *pref* 前缀 (with *ns* and *vs* 与名词及动词结合) **1** (of time or rank) before; in advance of (指时间或职位)前, 预先: *forefather* ○ *foreman* ○ *foretell*. **2** (of position) in front of (指位置)在前部: *foreground* ○ *foreshorten*.

fore·arm[1] /ˈfɔ:rɑ:m; ˋfɔr,ɑrm/ *n* part of the arm from the elbow to the wrist or fingertips 前臂. ⇨illus at HUMAN 见 HUMAN 插图.

fore·arm[2] /ˌfɔ:rˈɑ:m; fɔrˋɑrm/ *v* **1** [Tn usu passive 通常用于被动语态] prepare (oneself/sb) in advance for possible danger, attack, etc; arm beforehand 使(自己[某人])做好准备(以防危险、攻击等); 预先武装. **2** (idm 习语) **forewarned is forearmed** ⇨ FOREWARN.

fore·bear (also **for·bear**) /ˈfɔ:beə(r); ˋfɔr,bɛr/ *n* [C usu *pl* 通常作复数] person from whom one is descended; ancestor 祖宗; 祖先.

fore·bode /fɔ:ˈbəʊd; fɔrˋbod/ *v* [Tn] (*fml* 文) be a sign or a warning of (esp trouble) 预示(尤指坏事): *Her angry face forboded a confrontation.* 她一脸怒气预示将有一场冲突. ○ *These developments forebode disaster.* 这些情况预示着要有灾祸.

▷ **fore·bod·ing** *n* [C, U] **~ (that...)** strong feeling that danger or trouble is coming 要有危险或坏事的预感: *She had a sinister foreboding that the plane would crash.* 她有个不祥的预感, 飞机要失事. ○ *Thoughts about the future filled him with foreboding.* 他想到未来, 不寒而栗.

fore·cast /ˈfɔ:kɑ:st; *US* -kæst; fɔrˋkæst/ *v* (*pt, pp* **forecast** or **forecasted**) [Tn, Tf, Tw] tell in advance (what is expected to happen); predict with the help of information 预报; 预测: *forecast a fall in unemployment* 预测失业人数下降 ○ *forecast that it will rain tomorrow* 预报明天有雨 ○ *forecast what the outcome of the election will be* 预测选举结果.

▷ **fore·cast** *n* statement that predicts sth with the help of information 预测: *forecasts of higher profits* 利润将增加的预测 ○ *According to the (weather) forecast it will be sunny tomorrow.* (天气)预报说明天天晴. ○ *The forecast said there would be sunny intervals and showers.* 预报说晴间阵雨.

fore·caster *n* person who forecasts sth, esp sb whose job is to forecast the weather 预测者; (尤指)气象预报员.

fore·castle (also **fo'c's'le**) /ˈfəʊksl; ˋfoksl/ *n* part of the front of certain ships where the crew live and sleep 船首楼(某些船前部的水手舱).

fore·close /fɔ:ˈkləʊz; fɔrˋkloz/ *v* [I, Ipr, Tn] **~ (on sb/sth)** (of a bank, etc that has lent money for a mortgage) take possession of the property of (sb), usu because repayments have not been made (指已放出抵押贷款的银行等)取得(某人)的财产(通常因未偿付贷款): *The bank foreclosed (on the mortgage).* 该银行已取消(对该抵押品的)赎取权.

▷ **fore·clos·ure** /fɔ:ˈkləʊʒə(r); fɔrˋkloʒɚ/ *n* [C, U] (act of) foreclosing a mortgage 取消抵押品赎取权.

fore·court /ˈfɔ:kɔ:t; ˋfɔr,kɔrt/ *n* **1** large open area or courtyard in front of a building, esp the front of a filling station where petrol is sold (建筑物前面的)大片空地或院子(尤指汽车加油站前的加油处). **2** (in tennis, badminton, etc) part of the court between the service-line and the net (在网球、羽毛球等球场中)前场(自发球线至球网处).

fore·doomed /fɔ:ˈdu:md; fɔrˋdumd/ *adj* **~ (to sth)** intended (as if) by fate to be unsuccessful 注定失败的: *All attempts to revive the fishing industry were foredoomed to failure.* 千方百计振兴渔业注定徒劳无功.

fore·father /ˈfɔ:fɑ:ðə(r); ˋfɔr,fɑðɚ/ *n* [C usu *pl* 通常作复数] person from whom one is descended; ancestor, esp a male 祖宗, 祖先(尤指男性): *the religion of his forefathers* 他祖先的宗教信仰.

fore·fin·ger /ˈfɔ:fɪŋgə(r); ˋfɔr,fɪŋgɚ/ *n* finger next to the thumb; index finger 食指. ⇨illus at HAND 见 HAND 插图.

fore·foot /ˈfɔ:fʊt; ˋfɔr,fʊt/ *n* (*pl* **-feet** /-fi:t; -,fit/) either of the two front feet of a four-legged animal (四足动物的)前足.

fore·front /ˈfɔ:frʌnt; ˋfɔr,frʌnt/ *n* [sing] **the ~ (of sth)** the most forward or important position or place 最前部; 最重要之处: *in the forefront of my mind* 我首先考虑的 ○ *The new product took the company to the forefront of the computer software field.* 这一新产品面世后, 该公司在计算机软件领域中已处于领先地位.

fore·going /ˈfɔ:gəʊɪŋ; fɔrˋgoɪŋ/ *adj* [attrib 作定语] (*fml* 文) preceding; just mentioned 在前的; 刚提到的; 上述的: *the foregoing analysis, description, discussion, etc* 以上分析、描述、论述等.

▷ **the fore·going** *n* [sing or pl *v*] (*fml* 文) what has just been mentioned 刚提及的事物: *The foregoing have all been included in the proposals.* 以上各点均包括在建议中.

fore·gone /ˈfɔ:gɒn; *US* -gɔ:n; fɔrˋgɔn/ *adj* (idm 习语) **a ˌforegone conˈclusion** result that can be predicted with certainty 可预料的必然结果: *The outcome of the election is a foregone conclusion.* 选举结果已在预料之中.

fore·ground /ˈfɔ:graʊnd; ˋfɔr,graʊnd/ *n* **the foreground** [sing] (**a**) front part of a view, scene, picture, etc; part nearest the observer (景物、场景、画面等的)前部, 前景: *The red figure in the foreground is the artist's mother.* 画面前景中穿红衣服的人是画家的母亲. (**b**) (*fig* 比喻) position of greatest importance or prominence 最重要或最突出的位置: *These teachers are keeping education in the foreground of public attention.* 这些教师不断努力以使人人关心教育事业. Cf 参看 BACKGROUND 1,2.

fore·hand /ˈfɔ:hænd; ˋfɔr,hænd/ *adj* [attrib 作定语] (of a stroke in tennis, squash, etc) made with the palm of the hand turned towards one's opponent or towards the front of the court (指网球、壁球等的击球)正手打的: *a forehand volley* 正手拦击.

▷ **fore·hand** *n* **1** forehand stroke 正手击球. **2** (usu *sing* 通常作单数) (in tennis, squash, etc) the same side of a player as the hand in which he is holding the racket (指网球、壁球等运动中)运动员握拍的手的同一侧: *Hit the ball to her forehand.* 把球打到她握拍手的一边. Cf 参看 BACKHAND (BACK[2]).

fore·head /ˈfɒrɪd, *also* ˈfɔ:hed; *US* ˈfɔ:rɪd; ˋfɔrɪd/ (also **brow**) *n* part of the face above the eyebrows and below the hair 额. ⇨illus at HEAD 见 HEAD 插图.

for·eign /ˈfɒrən; *US* ˈfɔ:r-; ˋfɔrɪn/ *adj* **1** (**a**) of, in or from a country or an area other than one's own 外国的: *foreign languages, goods, students* 外国语、外国货、外国学生. (**b**) dealing with or involving other countries 外交的; 涉外的: *foreign affairs* 外交事务 ○ *foreign policy* 外交政策 ○ *foreign trade* 对外贸易 ○ *foreign aid*, ie money, etc given by one country to another in need 外国的援助. **2 ~ to sb/sth** (*fml* 文) not belonging naturally to sb/sth; alien to sb/sth; uncharacteristic of sb/sth 非某人[某事物]所固有的; 与某人[某事物]的本性相异: *Dishonesty is foreign to his nature.* 他的本性与弄虚作假格格不入. **3** (*fml* 文) coming or introduced from outside, usu by accident 来自外界的(通常指意外地): *a foreign body* (eg a hair or speck of dirt) *in the eye* 眼中的异物(如毛发或灰尘).

▷ **for·eigner** *n* **1** person from a country other than one's own 外国人. **2** person who is regarded as not belonging to a particular community; outsider or stranger 外人; 陌生人.

□ **the ˌForeign and ˈCommonwealth Office** (*abbr* 缩写 **FCO**) (*Brit*) the government department that deals with foreign affairs 外交和联邦事务部. Cf 参看 THE HOME OFFICE (HOME[1]).

foreign exˈchange (system of buying and selling) foreign money 外汇: [attrib 作定语] *the foreign exchange markets* 外汇市场.

ˌForeign ˈSecretary government minister in charge of the Foreign and Commonwealth Office 外交大臣.

fore·know·ledge /ˌfɔ:ˈnɒlɪdʒ; ˋfor,nɑlɪdʒ/ *n* [U] knowledge of sth before it happens or exists 预知; 预见.

fore·land /ˈfɔ:lənd; ˋfɔrlənd/ *n* piece of land that extends into the sea; cape or promontory 岬角; 海角.

fore·leg /ˈfɔ:leg; ˋfɔr,lɛg/ *n* either of the two front legs of a four-footed animal (四足动物的)前腿.

fore·lock /ˈfɔːlɒk; ˋfɔrˌlɑk/ *n* **1** piece of hair growing (and falling) over the forehead 额发. **2** (idm 习语) **touch, tug, etc one's ˈforelock** (formerly) raise a hand to one's forehead when meeting sb of higher social rank, usu as a sign of respect (旧时)(与地位高的人相见时)将一只手举至额头(通常指致敬).

fore·man /ˈfɔːmən; ˋfɔrmən/ *n* (*pl* **-men** /-mən; -mən/, *fem* 阴性作 **fore·wo·man** /-ˌwʊmən; -ˌwʊmən/, *pl* **-women** /-wɪmɪn; -ˌwɪmɪn/) **1** experienced worker who supervises and directs other workers 领班; 工头. **2** person who acts as the leader and spokesperson of a jury 陪审团团长.

fore·most /ˈfɔːməʊst; ˋfɔrˌmost/ *adj* **1** [attrib 作定语] most famous or important; best or chief 最著名的; 最重要的; 最好的; 主要的: *the foremost painter of his time* 在他那个时代里首屈一指的画家. **2** (idm 习语) **first and foremost** ⇨ FIRST[2].

▷ **fore·most** *adv* in the first position 居于首位: *She ranks foremost among the country's leading conductors.* 她在国内第一流指挥家中名列榜首.

fore·name /ˈfɔːneɪm; ˋfɔrˌnem/ *n* (*fml* 文) name preceding the family name; person's first or Christian name 名(在姓之前); 教名. ⇨App 7 见附录7. ⇨Usage at NAME[1] 用法见 NAME[1].

fore·noon /ˈfɔːnuːn; fɔrˋnun/ *n* (*Scot* and in official, eg electoral, notices 苏格兰, 用于官方通告中, 如选举通告) part of the day between sunrise and noon; morning 上午.

for·ensic /fəˈrensɪk; fəˋrɛnsɪk/ *adj* [attrib 作定语] of, related to or used in (courts of) law 法庭的; 与法庭有关的; 用于法庭的: *forensic medicine*, ie medical skill used to help with legal problems or police investigations 法医学.

F

fore·or·dain /ˌfɔːrɔːˈdeɪn; ˌfɔrɔrˋden/ *v* [usu passive 通常用于被动语态: Tn, Tf] (*fml* 文) (of God or fate) arrange or determine (sth) before it actually happens (指上帝或命运)注定: *It was foreordained that the company would suffer a spectacular collapse.* 这个公司注定要彻底垮台.

fore·play /ˈfɔːpleɪ; ˋfɔrˌple/ *n* [U] sexual activity such as caressing the sexual organs and kissing before sexual intercourse 性交之前的性活动(如抚摸性器官、亲吻).

fore·run·ner /ˈfɔːrʌnə(r); ˋfɔrˌrʌnɚ/ *n* person or thing that prepares the way for the coming of sb or sth else more important; sign of what is to follow 先驱者; 开路人; 先兆: *the forerunners of the modern diesel engine* 现代柴油机的前身.

fore·sail /ˈfɔːseɪl, *also* ˈfɔːsl; ˋfɔrˌsel/ *n* main sail on the front mast of a ship 前帆.

fore·see /fɔːˈsiː; fɔrˋsi/ *v* (*pt* **foresaw** /fɔːˈsɔː; fɔrˋsɔ/, *pp* **foreseen** /fɔːˈsiːn; fɔrˋsin/) [Tn, Tf, Tw] see or know that sth is going to happen in the future; predict 预见; 预知; 预料: *The difficulties could not have been foreseen.* 这些困难是无法预见的. ○ *He foresaw that the job would take a long time.* 他预见到做这件工作需要很长时间. ○ *They could not have foreseen how things would turn out.* 他们不可能预知事情的结果.

▷ **fore·see·able** /-əbl; -əbḷ/ *adj* that can be foreseen 可以预见的: *(in) the foreseeable future*, ie (during) the period of time (usu short) when one knows what is going to happen (在)可预见的将来.

fore·shadow /fɔːˈʃædəʊ; fɔrˋʃædo/ *v* [Tn] be a sign or warning of (sth to come or about to happen) 预示: *The increase in taxes had been foreshadowed in the minister's speech.* 部长的讲话中早已预示要提高税额.

fore·shore /ˈfɔːʃɔː(r); ˋfɔrˌʃɔr/ *n* (usu 通常作 **the foreshore**) [sing] part of the shore between the limits of high and low tides, or between the sea and land that is cultivated or built on (高潮线与低潮线之间的)海滩; (海水与已耕种或有建筑物的陆地之间的)海滨.

fore·shorten /fɔːˈʃɔːtn; fɔrˋʃɔrtṇ/ *v* [Tn] (in drawing) represent (an object) by shortening certain lines to give an effect of distance and perspective (绘画中)用透视法表现(所画对象).

fore·sight /ˈfɔːsaɪt; ˋfɔrˌsaɪt/ *n* [U] ability to see what one's future needs are likely to be; careful planning 先见之明; 精打细算: *The couple had the foresight to plan their retirement wisely.* 他们夫妇很有远见, 精心安排了退休后的生活. Cf 参看 HINDSIGHT.

fore·skin /ˈfɔːskɪn; ˋfɔrˌskɪn/ *n* loose fold of skin covering the end of the penis 包皮. ⇨illus at MALE 见 MALE 插图.

for·est /ˈfɒrɪst; *US* ˈfɔːr-; ˋfɔrɪst/ *n* **1** [C, U] (large area of land thickly covered with) trees, bushes, etc 森林(地带): *the dense tropical forests of the Amazon basin* 亚玛孙河流域茂密的热带森林 ○ *Very little forest is left unexplored nowadays.* 如今未经勘测的森林已是少之又少了. ○ [attrib 作定语] *forest animals, fires* 森林动物、森林火灾. **2** [C] (*fig* 比喻) dense mass of tall or narrow objects that looks like a forest 似森林般密集的细长物体: *a forest of television aerials* 林立的电视天线.

▷ **for·ested** *adj* covered in forest 覆盖树木如林的.

for·ester *n* **1** person who looks after a forest, eg by protecting the animals, planting new trees and guarding against fire 林务员; 守林人. **2** person who lives and works in a forest 在森林里居住及工作的人.

for·estry *n* [U] science and practice of planting, caring for, and managing forests 林学; 森林学.

fore·stall /fɔːˈstɔːl; fɔrˋstɔl/ *v* [Tn] act before (sb else) so as to prevent him from doing sth 抢在(别人)之前行动: *forestall a competitor, a rival, etc* 抢在竞争者、对手之前行动 ○ *I had my objection all prepared, but Stephens forestalled me.* 我已做好准备要提出反对意见, 不料斯蒂芬斯却抢先了一步.

fore·taste /ˈfɔːteɪst; ˋfɔrˌtest/ *n* ~ **(of sth)** small experience of sth before it actually happens; sample (在某事物到来之前的)浅尝; 样品: *a foretaste of the fierce conflict to come* 对未来的激烈冲突先尝到的滋味.

fore·tell /fɔːˈtel; fɔrˋtɛl/ *v* (*pt, pp* **foretold** /fɔːˈtəʊld; fɔrˋtold/) [Tn, Tf, Tw] (*fml* 文) tell (what will happen in the future); predict 预言; 预示; 预料: *No one could have foretold such strange events.* 谁也料不到有这些奇怪的事情. ○ *The gypsy had foretold that the boy would die.* 那吉普赛人曾经预言这男孩儿得夭折. ○ *You can't foretell how the war will end.* 这场战争的结局难以预料.

fore·thought /ˈfɔːθɔːt; ˋfɔrˌθɔt/ *n* [U] careful thought or planning for the future 深谋远虑: *With a little more forethought we could have bought the house we really wanted.* 我们当初若是稍微再多考虑一下, 也许就能买到我们真正想要的房子了.

fore·told *pt, pp* of FORETELL.

for·ever /fəˈrevə(r); fɚˋɛvɚ/ *adv* **1** (also **for ever**) for all time; always 永远: *I'll love you forever!* 我永远爱你! ○ *You'll never get that ball back — it's lost forever.* 你再也找不回那个球了——永远也找不回来了. ○ (*infml* 口) *It takes her forever* (ie an extremely long time) *to get dressed.* 她穿衣打扮得用半天时间. **2** (usu with *vs* in the continuous tenses 通常与进行时态的动词连用) at all times; constantly or persistently 总是; 不断地; 无休止地: *They are forever arguing.* 他们总是争吵. ○ *Why are you forever asking questions?* 你怎么老是问问题?

fore·warn /fɔːˈwɔːn; fɔrˋwɔrn/ *v* **1** [Tn, Tn·pr, Dn·f] ~ **sb (of sth)** warn sb before sth happens; advise sb (of possible dangers, problems, etc) 预先警告某人; 告诉某人(可能出现危险、问题等): *We had been forewarned of the risk of fire/that fire could break out.* 已经事先警告过我们有发生火灾的危险. **2** (idm 习语) **foreˌwarned is foreˈarmed** (*saying* 谚) knowledge of possible dangers, problems, etc allows one to prepare for them 有备无患.

fore·word /ˈfɔːwɜːd; ˋfɔrˌwɝd/ *n* short introduction to a book, printed at the beginning and usu written by a person other than the author (书的)前言, 序言(通常指并非作者写的). Cf 参看 PREFACE.

for·feit /ˈfɔːfɪt; ˋfɔrfɪt/ *v* [Tn] (have to) lose or give up (sth) as a consequence of or punishment for having done sth wrong, or in order to achieve sth (因做错事或为得到某事物)失去或放弃(另一事物): *Passengers who cancel their reservations will forfeit their deposit.* 旅客取消预订票者, 定金不予退还. ○ *He has forfeited the right to represent the people.* 已撤销他代表人民的资格. ○ *The couple forfeited their independence in order to help those less fortunate.* 这对夫妇把富裕出的钱都拿出来帮助那些受难的人.

▷ **for·feit** *n* **1** [C usu *sing* 通常作单数] thing (to be) paid or given up as a penalty or punishment (因受罚)丧失的东西; 罚金. **2** (a) **forfeits** [sing *v*] game in which a player gives up various articles if he makes a mistake and can have them back by doing sth ridiculous 罚物游

戏(输者交出小物品, 做滑稽表演后方可取回). (**b**) [C] article given up in this game 做此种游戏中交出的东西: *Give me your watch as a forfeit.* 你输了, 罚你把手表交给我.

for·feit *adj* [pred 作表语] **~ (to sb/sth)** (*fml* 文) (liable to be) lost, paid or given up as a forfeit (作为罚金或抵押品)(可能)失去, 交出: *All goods may be forfeit to the State in time of war.* 战时所有的货物都可能被国家征用.

for·feit·ure /ˈfɔːfɪtʃə(r); ˋfɔrfɪtʃɚ/ *n* [U] **~ (of sth)** (act of) forfeiting sth 丧失; 放弃; 没收: *(the) forfeiture of one's property* 放弃财产.

for·gather (also **fore·gather**) /fɔːˈgæðə(r); fɔrˋgæðɚ/ *v* [I] (*fml* 文) come together; meet socially 聚会.

for·gave *pt* of FORGIVE.

forge[1] /fɔːdʒ; fɔrdʒ/ *n* **1** workshop with a fire and an anvil where metals are heated and shaped, esp one used by a smith for making horseshoes 铁匠铺(尤指做马掌的). **2** (workshop, factory, etc with a) furnace for melting or refining metals 锻铁炉; 锻造车间或工厂.

forge[2] /fɔːdʒ; fɔrdʒ/ *v* [Tn] **1** (**a**) shape (sth) by heating it in a fire and hammering 锻造; 打铁: *forge a sword, a chain, an anchor, etc* 锻造剑、铁链、锚等. (**b**) (*fig* 比喻) create (usu a lasting relationship) by means of much hard work (靠艰苦工作)建立(通常为长期关系): *forge a bond, a link, an alliance, etc* 建立同盟、联系、联盟等 ○ *a friendship forged by adversity* 患难中建立起来的友谊. Cf 参看 WELD. **2** make an imitation or copy of (sth) in order to deceive people 伪造: *forge a banknote, will, signature, etc* 伪造钞票、遗嘱、签字等. Cf 参看 COUNTERFEIT *v*.

▷ **for·ger** *n* person who forges (FORGE[2] 2) money, a document, etc 伪造(钱币、文件等)的人. Cf 参看 COUNTERFEITER (COUNTERFEIT).

for·gery /ˈfɔːdʒərɪ; ˋfɔrdʒərɪ/ *n* **1** [U] (crime or act of) forging (FORGE[2] 2) a document, picture, signature, etc (文件、画、签字等的)伪造, 伪造罪, 伪造行为: *He spent 5 years in prison for forgery.* 他因伪造罪而坐了5年牢. **2** [C] document, signature, etc that has been forged 伪造的文件、签字等: *This famous painting was thought to be by Van Gogh, but it is in fact a forgery.* 人们以为这是凡·高的名画, 其实是赝品. Cf 参看 COUNTERFEIT.

for·ging *n* [C] piece of metal that has been forged (FORGE[2] 1a) or shaped under a press 锻件.

forge[3] /fɔːdʒ; fɔrdʒ/ *v* **1** [Ipr, Ip, Tn·pr] move forward steadily or gradually 稳步前进: *forge constantly onwards* 坚定不移地稳步前进 ○ *forge into the lead*, ie gradually overtake sb 稳步进入领先地位(逐步超越某人). **2** (phr v) **forge ahead** advance or progress quickly; take the leading position in a race, etc 高速前进; (在赛跑等运动中)进入领先地位: *One horse forged ahead, leaving the others behind.* 有一匹马跑在最前面, 把其他的马抛在后面.

for·get /fəˈget; fɚˋgɛt/ *v* (*pt* **forgot** /fəˈgɒt; fɚˋgɑt/, *pp* **forgotten** /fəˈgɒtn; fɚˋgɑtn̩/) **1** [Ipr, Tn, Tf, Tw, Tg] **~ about sth** (not used in the continuous tenses 不用于进行时态) fail to remember or recall (sth); lose the memory of (sth) 忘记(某事物); 遗忘: *He forgot (about) her birthday*, ie did not remember it at the proper time. 他把她的生日忘了. ○ *I've forgotten her name.* 我把她的名字忘了. ○ *Did you forget (that) I was coming?* 难道你忘了我要来吗? ○ *She forgot how the puzzle fitted together.* 她忘了那个拼图是怎么拼在一起的. ○ *I'll never forget seeing my daughter dance in public for the first time.* 我永远忘不了看着我女儿第一次当众跳舞的情景. **2** (**a**) [I, Tt] fail to remember to do sth; neglect 忘记(做某事); 忽视: *'Why didn't you buy any bread?' 'Sorry, I forgot.'* '你怎么没买面包呢?' '真抱歉, 我忘了.' ○ *Don't forget to feed the cat.* 别忘了喂猫. ○ *He forgot to pay me.* 他忘了付给我钱. (**b**) [Tn] fail to remember to bring, buy, etc (sth) or take care of (sth) 忘记带、购买、照料等(某事物): *I forgot my umbrella.* 我忘带伞了. ○ *Don't forget the waiter*, ie give him a tip. 别忘了给服务员小费. **3** [Ipr, Tn, Tf] **~ (about) sb/sth** stop thinking about sb/sth; not think about sb/sth; put sb/sth out of one's mind 忘掉或不再想某人[某事物]; 不把某人[某事物]放在心上: *Let's forget (about) our differences.* 咱们不要把彼此的分歧放在心上. ○ *Try to forget (all) about him.* 别再想他了. ○ *You can forget about a holiday this year — I've lost my job.* 你别再想今年去度假的事了 —— 我失业了. ○ *'How much do I owe you?' 'Forget it!'*, ie Don't bother to pay me back. '我欠你多少钱?' '算了吧!' ○ *The shop will accept cheques and credit cards, not forgetting* (ie and also) *cash, of course.* 这个商店可用支票和信用卡付帐, 当然也收现金. ○ *I was forgetting (that) David used to teach you.* 我几乎忘了大卫以前经常教你. **4** [Tn] **~ oneself** (**a**) behave without proper dignity 忘乎所以: *I'm afraid I forgot myself and kissed him wildly.* 当时我有些忘乎所以, 疯狂地吻着他. (**b**) act unselfishly 忘我; 无私: *Forget yourself and think of someone else for a change.* 别光想着你自己, 你也为别人想一次. **5** (idm 习语) **elephants never forget** ⇨ ELEPHANT. **forgive and forget** ⇨ FORGIVE.

▷ **for·get·ful** /-fl; -fəl/ *adj* **1** in the habit of forgetting; likely to forget 健忘的; 好忘记的: *Old people are sometimes forgetful.* 老人有时爱忘事. **2** [pred 作表语] **~ of sb/sth** not thinking about sth; neglectful of sb/sth 对某人[某事物]不考虑、疏忽: *be forgetful of one's duties* 玩忽职守. **for·get·fully** /-fəlɪ; -fəlɪ/ *adv*. **for·get·ful·ness** *n* [U].

forget-me-not /fəˈget mɪ nɒt; fɚˋgɛtmɪˌnɑt/ *n* small plant with tiny blue flowers 勿忘我(勿忘草属, 开蓝色小花).

for·give /fəˈgɪv; fɚˋgɪv/ *v* (*pt* **forgave** /fəˈgeɪv; fɚˋgev/, *pp* **forgiven** /fəˈgɪvn; fɚˋgɪvən/) **1** [Tn, Tn·pr, Dn·n] **~ sth; ~ sb (for sth/doing sth)** stop being angry or bitter towards sb or about sth; stop blaming or wanting to punish sb 原谅; 宽恕; 饶恕: *I forgave her a long time ago.* 我早已原谅她了. ○ *I cannot forgive myself for not seeing my mother before she died.* 母亲临终前我未去看她, 为这件事我永远不能原谅自己. ○ *She forgave him his thoughtless remark.* 她原谅了他说的轻率的话. ○ (*religion* 宗) *Forgive us our trespasses*, ie our sins. 请宽恕我们的罪孽吧! **2** [Tn, Tn·pr, Tsg] **~ sb (for doing sth)** (used in polite expressions to lessen the force of what the speaker says and in mild apologies 礼貌用语, 用以缓和语气并示歉意): *Forgive my ignorance, but what exactly are you talking about?* 请原谅我孤陋寡闻, 你说的到底是什么? ○ *Please forgive me for interrupting/my interrupting.* 对不起, 打搅了. **3** [Dn·n] say that sb need not repay (the money owed); not demand repayment from (sb) 免除(某人的债务); 不要求(某人)偿还: *Won't you forgive me such a small debt?* 这么小小的一笔债, 请你免了行吗? **4** (idm 习语) **forˌgive and forˈget** dismiss from one's mind all unkind feelings and the desire to blame and punish sb 不念旧恶; 不记某人的仇.

▷ **for·giv·able** /-əbl; -əbl̩/ *adj* that can be forgiven 可原谅的; 可宽恕的; 可饶恕的: *His harshness is forgivable.* 他很严厉, 但情有可原.

for·give·ness *n* [U] forgiving or state of being forgiven; willingness to forgive 原谅; 原谅的意愿: *He asked forgiveness for what he had done wrong.* 他请求原谅他的错误. ○ (*religion* 宗) *the forgiveness of sins* 对罪孽的宽恕 ○ *She is sympathetic and full of forgiveness.* 她富有同情心, 待人宽厚.

for·giv·ing *adj* ready and willing to forgive 宽容的; 宽恕的; 宽谅的: *kind forgiving parents* 慈爱而宽厚的父母 ○ *a forgiving nature* 宽容厚道的本性. **for·giv·ingly** *adv*.

forgo /fɔːˈgəʊ; fɔrˋgo/ *v* (*pt* **forwent** /fɔːˈwent; fɔrˋwɛnt/, *pp* **forgone** /fɔːˈgɒn; *US* -ˈgɔːn; fɔrˋgɔn/) [Tn] give up or do without (esp sth pleasant) 放弃或没有(尤指美好的事物)也行: *The workers agreed to forgo a pay increase for the sake of greater job security.* 工人们为了工作更保险, 同意放弃增加工资的要求.

for·got *pt* of FORGET.

for·got·ten *pp* of FORGET.

fork /fɔːk; fɔrk/ *n* **1** small implement with a handle and two or more points or prongs, used for lifting food to the mouth or holding things (esp meat) firmly while they are cut 叉子: *eat with a knife and fork* 使用刀叉吃东西. ⇨illus 见插图. **2** farm or gardening tool with a handle and prongs, used for digging the ground, lifting hay, etc 叉; 耙. ⇨illus 见插图. **3** (**a**) place where a road, river, tree branch, etc divides into two parts (路、河、树枝等的)分岔处, 岔口: *Go up to the fork and turn left.* 走到岔口处向左拐. (**b**) either of the two parts divided in this way 一个分岔: *Take the right fork.* 走右边

F

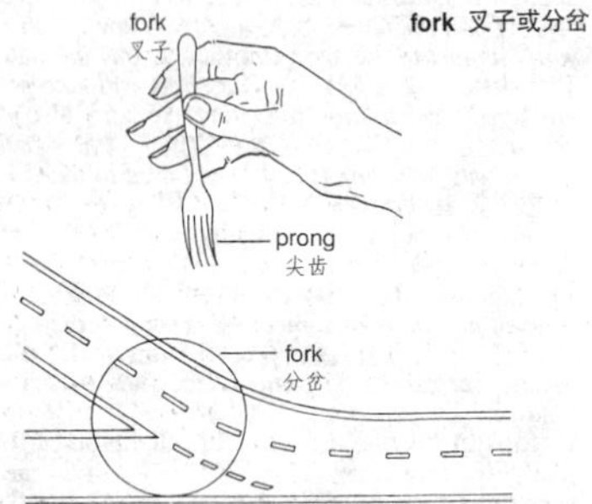

fork 叉子或分岔

的岔道. ⇨illus 见插图. **4** (usu *pl* 通常作复数) two metal supporting pieces into which a wheel on a bicycle or motor cycle is fitted (自行车或摩托车的)叉子. ⇨ illus at App 1 见附录1插图, page xiii. **5** thing shaped like a fork 叉状物: *a 'tuning-fork* 音叉.

▷ **fork** *v* **1** [Tn, Tn·pr, Tn·p] lift, dig, move, etc (sth) with a fork (用叉、耙)叉起, 挖掘, 移动(某物): *fork (over) the ground* 耙地 ○ *fork in manure*, ie dig it into the soil with a fork 用耙施粪肥. **2** [I] (**a**) (of a road, river, etc) divide into two parts (指路、河等)分为两条: *The road forks just beyond the village.* 过了这村, 这条路就分成两条. (**b**) (of a person) turn (left or right) at a fork (指人)在岔口处向(左或右)拐弯: *Fork left at the church.* 到了教堂向左拐. **3** (phr v) **fork out (sth)** (*infml* 口) pay (money), usu reluctantly 付(钱)(通常指不情愿地): *Why am I always forking out (money) on/for your school trips?* 为什么总是让我为你在学校的外出活动付钱?

forked *adj* divided into two (or more) parts; branched 叉状的; 分叉的: *the forked tongue of a snake* 蛇的叉状舌 ○ *a bird with a forked tail* 长着叉状尾的鸟 ○ *forked lightning* 叉状闪电.

□ **fork-lift 'truck** truck with a fork-like mechanical device on the front for lifting and moving heavy objects 叉车.

for·lorn /fəˈlɔːn; fɚˈlɔrn/ *adj* **1** lonely and unhappy; uncared for 孤独而凄凉的; 无人照顾的: *a forlorn child sitting on the street corner* 坐在街角没人照顾的孩子. **2** (of places) looking uncared for; wretched or forsaken (指地方)似无人管理的, 破烂的, 被离弃的: *deserted forlorn farmhouses* 弃置的破烂农舍. **3** (idm 习语) **a forlorn 'hope** plan or undertaking that is almost certain not to succeed 几乎不可能实现的计划或不可能成功的事情: *Going to their rescue in a rowing-boat is a bit of a forlorn hope.* 乘划艇去救他们, 希望不大. ▷ **for·lornly** *adv*. **for·lorn·ness** *n* [U].

form[1] /fɔːm; fɔrm/ *n* **1** [C, U] outward physical appearance of sb/sth; shape 某人[某物]的外形; 外貌; 样子; 形状: *a jelly mould in the form of a motor car* 做成汽车形状的果冻 ○ *We could just manage to see the form of an aircraft taking off in the fog.* 飞机在雾中起飞, 我们仅仅能看出它的轮廓. ○ *her slender graceful form* 她那苗条优美的体形. **2** [C] **~ (of sth)** specific type of arrangement or structure of sth; manner in which sth exists or appears; kind or variety 某事物的具体组成或结构; 某事物存在的或呈现的形式; 形态; 体制; 种类: *water in the form of ice* 水呈冰的形态 ○ *different forms of government* 各种政体 ○ *The training took the form of* (ie consisted of) *seminars and lectures.* 这种培训是以讨论与讲课的形式进行的. ○ *the form* (ie set order of words) *of the marriage service* 婚礼仪式. **3** [U] general structure and arrangement of sth created such as a musical composition or piece of writing, in contrast to its content (音乐及文学作品等的)形式, 体裁: *music in sonata form* 奏鸣曲 ○ *literary form* 文学体裁 ○ *This painting shows a good sense of form.* 这幅画的构图很好. **4** [C, U] (*grammar*) (particular) spelling or pronunciation of a word 字形; 字的发音: *The plural form of 'goose' is 'geese'.* goose 的复数形式是geese. ○ *The words 'elevator' and 'lift' are different in form but identical in meaning.* elevator与lift形式相异但意义相同. **5** [U] particular manner of behaving, speaking, or writing that is normally required or expected 礼貌; 礼节: *Although she is not entitled to attend the dinner, I think she should be invited as a matter of form*, ie because it is correct or polite. 尽管她没有资格参加这次晚宴, 我认为出于礼节还是应该邀请她. ○ *What is the form* (ie the correct thing to do)*?* 按理说该怎么做? **6** [U] (**a**) strength, fitness to compete with others, etc of an athlete, a horse, etc (运动员、马等的)竞技状态: *After six months training, the whole team is in superb form.* 全队经过六个月的训练竞技状态极佳. (**b**) record of the actions, behaviour, progress, etc of a person, team, etc (对个人或全队等的动作姿态、表现、进步情况等的)记录: *On present/current form, Spain will win tonight's match.* 就西班牙队目前的状态来看, 今晚的比赛他们能赢. ○ *Judging by recent form, he should easily pass the exam.* 从他最近的表现来看, 他应该很容易考及格. ○ *I've got no record of this horse's form.* 我没有这匹马的情况记录. **7** [U] person's feelings, humour or spirits 感情、幽默或精神状态: *They were both in fine/good form at dinner.* 晚餐时他们俩的精神都很好. **8** (*Brit sl* 俚) record of having been found guilty of crimes and (usu) of having received a prison sentence 犯罪记录(通常指曾入狱者); 前科: *He's got no form!* 他没有犯罪记录! **9** [C] class, esp in British private schools and some American private schools 年级(尤用于英国私立学校及美国部分私立学校的): *The youngest children are in the first form, the oldest in the sixth form.* 最小的儿童上一年级, 最大的上六年级. **10** [C] long wooden bench, usu without a back 长木凳. **11** [C] printed or typed piece of paper with questions, and spaces for answers 表格: *fill in an application form* 填申请表. **12** [C] place where a hare lives; lair (野兔的)窝, 窟. **13** (idm 习语) **bad/good 'form** (*dated* 旧) incorrect/correct social behaviour according to accepted standards 失礼的[有礼貌的]行为: *It is sometimes considered bad form to smoke between courses at a meal.* 在两道菜之间抽烟有时认为是失礼的. **a form of address** style of addressing sb in speech or writing 称呼: *What form of address should one use when writing to a bishop?* 给主教写信应该怎样称呼? **in any shape or form** ⇨ SHAPE[1]. **on/off 'form; in/out of 'form** in a good/bad state of fitness, ability, etc; performing as well as/not as well as usual 处于良好的[不佳的]竞技状态; 表现如常[不如平常]: *The team were on excellent form throughout the whole competition.* 这个队在整个比赛过程中一直处于极好的竞技状态. **on present form** ⇨ PRESENT[1]. **true to form** ⇨ TRUE.

▷ **-former** (forming compound *ns* 用以构成复合名词) child or young person in the specified form[1](9) at school 某年级的学生: *a sixth-former*.

form·less *adj* without a clear or definite shape or structure 形状或结构不清楚的; 无一定形状或结构的: *formless shadows, ideas, dreams* 模糊的影子、想法、梦. **form·lessly** *adv*.

form[2] /fɔːm; fɔrm/ *v* **1** (**a**) [Tn, Tn·pr] **~ sth (from sth)** give shape or structure to sth; fashion sth; produce sth 形成、构成、塑造或产生某事物: *form a bowl from clay* 用陶土做碗 ○ *form sentences and paragraphs* 构成句子与段落 ○ *The reservoir was formed by flooding the valley.* 这个水库是引水淹没山谷而形成的. ○ *The substances are formed from a mixture of liquids solidifying under pressure.* 这些材料是由几种液体混合在一起并加压使之凝固而成的. (**b**) [Ln] take a particular shape or structure; develop 成一定形状或结构; 发展; 成型. **2** [Ipr, Tn, Tn·pr] **~ (sb/sth) into sth** arrange(sb/sth) or be arranged in a certain order 将(某人[某事物])按一定顺序排列: *The children formed (into) a line/The teacher formed the children into a line.* 这些小学生排成了一排[老师让学生排成一排]. ○ *The volunteers formed (themselves into) three groups.* 志愿人员分成三组. **3** (**a**) [Tn, Tn·pr] **~ sth (from sth)** bring sth into existence; develop or organize sth 使某事物开始存在; 成立, 创立, 组织(某事物): *form a committee, society, company, etc* 成立委员会、协会、公司等 ○ *The Labour leader was asked to form a government.* 要求工党领袖组织政府. ○ (*fig* 比喻) *form an idea, impression, opinion, etc (of sb/sth)* 形成(对某人[某事物]的)想法、印象、意见等 ○

form a relationship 建立关系. (**b**) [Ipr] come into existence; take shape or develop 开始存在; 出现; 产生: *thunder clouds forming in the distance* 远处出现的雷雨云 ○ *Ice forms* (ie Water becomes solid) *at 0°C.* 水在0°C时结冰. ○ *A scab formed on his leg.* 他腿上结了个痂. **4** [Ln] be the material of (sth); be an essential part of (sth); constitute 成为(某事物的)材料; 成为(某事物的)基本部分; 构成: *His research formed the basis of his new book.* 他的研究成果是他这本新书的基础. ○ *Should the new department form part of the Faculty of Arts?* 这个新的系属文学院吗? ○ *The historical aspect formed the main theme of her essay.* 她的论文的主题是由历史观点贯穿起来的. **5** [Tn] instruct or train (sb/sth) 指导或训练(某人[某物]); 塑造; 养成: *a character formed by strict discipline* 靠严格的纪律培养起来的性格. **6** [Tn] produce (sth) as the particular spelling or pronunciation of a word 构成(字的某种拼写或发音形式): *form the plural of a noun by adding 's'* 在词尾加s构成名词的复数. **7** (phr v) **form (sb) up** move (sb) into position in lines, as on parade 将(某人)编入队伍: *The battalion formed up by companies on the barrack square.* 全营以连为单位在军营广场上列队.

formal /ˈfɔːml; ˋfɔrml̩/ *adj* **1** following accepted rules of behaviour; showing or expecting careful, serious behaviour, as eg on official occasions or in distant, not close, relationships 正式的; 正规的; 按规矩的; 有礼貌的; 庄重的; 文雅的: *She has a very formal manner.* 她举止端庄. ○ *a formal dinner, luncheon, dance, etc* 正式的晚餐、午餐、舞会等 ○ *formal dress* 礼服 ○ *'Request' is a more formal way of saying 'ask for'.* 用request一词比用ask for显得郑重. **2** regular or geometric in shape; symmetrical 形状整齐的; 成几何图形的; 匀称的: *formal gardens* 整齐的花园. **3** of the outward shape or appearance (in contrast to the content or substance) 外形的; 外观的; 形式上的: *There is only a formal resemblance between the two systems; they are in fact radically different.* 这两种体系只是在表面上有某种相似之处, 其实根本不同. **4** publicly declared and recognized as official 公开宣布的; 正式承认的: *a formal denial* 公开否认 ○ *a formal declaration of war* 正式宣战. **5** [attrib 作定语] (of education) officially given at a school, college, etc (指教育)正规的: *The job does not require any formal training.* 做这种工作不需要任何正规训练.

▷ **form·al·ism** /-məlɪzəm; -ml̩ˌɪzəm/ *n* [U] strict observance of external form, ceremony, technique, etc, often without concern for feeling or meaning, eg in art 形式主义: *creativity reduced to an empty formalism* 沦为空洞的形式主义的创造性.

form·ally /-məlɪ; -ml̩ɪ/ *adv*: *The new rates of pay have not been formally agreed.* 新的工资标准尚未正式同意.

form·al·de·hyde /fɔːˈmældɪhaɪd; fɔrˋmældəˌhaɪd/ *n* [U] (*chemistry* 化) strong-smelling colourless gas used as a preservative and disinfectant when dissolved in water 甲醛.

▷ **form·alin** /ˈfɔːməlɪn; ˋfɔrməlɪn/ *n* (*chemistry* 化) solution of formaldehyde in water, used as above 甲醛水溶液; 福尔马林.

form·al·ity /fɔːˈmælətɪ; fɔrˋmælətɪ/ *n* **1** [U] careful observance of rules, conventions, etc of language or behaviour (语言或行为)认真遵循规范、正统等: *At board meetings you have to get used to the formality of the language.* 参加董事会议必须习惯那种古板的语言. ○ *I found the formality of the occasion irritating.* 我觉得这种场合的繁文缛节十分讨厌. **2** [C] (**a**) action required by convention or law 传统上的或法律上的手续: *comply with all the necessary formalities* 遵照一切必需的礼仪 ○ *go through the legal formalities* 办理法律手续. (**b**) such an action which no longer has much real importance or meaning 形式; 例行公事: *They said the interview was just a formality/a mere formality, as they've already given me the job.* 他们说面试只是一种例行公事, 因为他们已经把工作给我了.

form·al·ize, -ise /ˈfɔːməlaɪz; ˋfɔrməˌlaɪz/ *v* [Tn] make (a plan, etc) official, esp by writing it down 使(计划等)成为正式的(尤指形成文字): *formalize the arrangements for the conference* 把会议的各项安排确定下来. ▷ **form·al·iza·tion, -isation** /ˌfɔːməlaɪˈzeɪʃn; ˌfɔrmələˋzeʃən/ *n* [U].

for·mat /ˈfɔːmæt; ˋfɔrmæt/ *n* **1** shape, size, binding, etc of a book (书的)版式, 开本, 装订方式: *It's the same book, but a new format.* 还是那本书, 但这是新的版式. **2** general arrangement, plan, design, etc of sth (某事物的)总体安排、计划、设计等: *The format of the meeting was such that everyone could ask a question.* 会议安排好可让每个人都能提一个问题. **3** arrangement or organization of data for processing or storage by a computer 格式.

▷ **for·mat** *v* (**-tt-**) [Tn] arrange (sth) in a particular format, usu for a computer 按一定方式安排(某事物); (通常指计算机)编排格式.

forma·tion /fɔːˈmeɪʃn; fɔrˋmeʃən/ *n* **1** [U] organizing and developing (of sth) (某事物的)组织, 形成, 构成: *the formation of a new government* 新政府的组成 ○ *the formation of national character* 民族特性的形成. **2** [C] thing that is formed, esp in a particular or characteristic way 形成物(尤指结构特殊的); 结构: *cloud, rock formations* 云层、岩层 ○ *new word formations* 新词的构成. **3** [U] particular arrangement or pattern 编排; 编队; 队形: *aircraft flying in formation* 编队飞行的飞机 ○ [attrib 作定语] *forˈmation flying* 编队飞行.

form·at·ive /ˈfɔːmətɪv; ˋfɔrmətɪv/ *adj* [attrib 作定语] having an important and lasting influence on the development of sb's character 对某人的性格的形成有重要长期影响的: *a child's formative years* 儿童性格的形成时期 ○ *formative influences in one's life* 一生中影响性格形成的因素.

for·mer /ˈfɔːmə(r); ˋfɔrmɚ/ *adj* [attrib 作定语] **1** of an earlier period or time 以前的: *the former world champion* 前世界冠军 ○ *my former landlady* 我以前的女房东 ○ *in former times* 以前 ○ *She's back to her former self again*, eg after an illness. 她又恢复了以前的样子(如病后). **2** being the first mentioned of two things or people 前者的(两者中先提到的): *The former option favours the married man.* 前一种选择对已婚男子有利. **3** (idm 习语) **a shadow of one's/its former self** ⇨ SHADOW.

▷ **the for·mer** *pron* the first mentioned of two things or people 前者: *If I had to choose between fish and chicken I'd prefer the former*, ie fish. 若让我在鱼和鸡之间选择其一, 我要前者(即鱼).

for·merly *adv* in earlier times; previously 以前; 从前: *The company formerly belonged to an international banking group.* 该公司以前隶属于一个国际银行集团. ○ *Namibia, formerly South West Africa* 纳米比亚, 旧称西南非洲. Cf 参看 LATTER.

For·mica /fɔːˈmaɪkə; fɔrˋmaɪkə/ *n* [U] (*propr* 专利名) hard heat-resistant plastic made into sheets for covering surfaces 福米加(贴于家具等表面的抗热硬塑料薄板).

formic acid /ˌfɔːmɪk ˈæsɪd; ˌfɔrmɪk ˋæsɪd/ colourless acid used in textile finishing, etc originally obtained from ants but now produced synthetically 甲酸; 蚁酸.

for·mid·able /ˈfɔːmɪdəbl; ˋfɔrmɪdəbl̩/ *adj* **1** causing fear or great anxiety; frightening; awesome 引起恐惧或不安的; 可怕的; 可畏的: *a formidable appearance, look, prospect* 可怕的外表、神情、景象. **2** difficult to deal with or overcome 难以应付的; 难以克服的: *formidable obstacles, opposition, debts* 难以逾越的障碍、难以克服的反对力量、难以偿还的债务 ○ *a formidable task* 艰巨的任务. **3** inspiring awe and respect because of excellence and strength; very impressive 极好极强的; 了不起的; 令人敬畏的; 惊人的: *a formidable athlete, competitor, list of qualifications* 杰出的运动员、强大的竞争对手、了不起的资历. ▷ **for·mid·ably** /-əblɪ; -əblɪ/ *adv*.

for·mula /ˈfɔːmjʊlə; ˋfɔrmjələ/ *n* (*pl* **~s** *or, in scientific use* 作科技用语, 复数作 **formulae** /-mjʊliː; -mjəˌli/) ⇨ Usage at DATA 用法见DATA. **1** [C] (**a**) (*chemistry* 化) set of symbols showing the elements that a substance is made of 分子式: *The formula for water is H_2O.* 水的分子式为H_2O. (**b**) (*mathematics or physics* 数或物) expression of a rule or relationship in algebraic symbols 公式: *the formula for converting gallons into litres* 加仑与升的换算公式. **2** [C] fixed arrangement of words, esp as used on social, legal or ceremonial occasions 套语, 惯用语(尤指社交、法律场合或仪式上使用的): *'How d'you do' and 'Excuse me' are social formulae.* '你好'和'对不起'是社交中的客套语. ○ *know the formula for*

F

addressing bishops 知道对主教的习惯称呼. **3** [C] list of ingredients or set of instructions for making sth, esp medicines and fuels 配方; 药方; 处方: *a formula for a new drug* 新药的配方. **4** [C] set of statements or plans that can be agreed on by two or more persons or groups (双方或各方同意的)方案, 计划: *Managers and workers are still working out a peace formula.* 劳资双方仍在商谈制订和解方案. **5** [C] **~ (for sth)** method, plan, or set of principles worked out to achieve a desired result (为达到预期目的而制订的)方法, 计划, 原则: *There is no sure formula for success.* 成功并无一定之规. ○ *a formula for a happy marriage* 美满婚姻的信条. **6** [U] classification of racing cars of a particular size, engine capacity, etc 方程式(根据汽车大小、发动机容量等对赛车的分级): [attrib 作定语] *Formula 1 racing cars* 一级方程式赛车. **7** [U] (*US*) artificial powdered milk for babies 人造婴儿奶粉.

▷ **for·mu·laic** /ˌfɔːmjʊˈleɪɪk; ˌfɔrmjəˈleɪk/ *adj* made up of set patterns of words 有固定用词格式的: *Anglo-Saxon poetry is formulaic.* 盎格鲁—撒克逊诗歌有固定的格式.

for·mu·late /ˈfɔːmjʊleɪt; ˈfɔrmjəˌlet/ *v* [Tn] **1** create (sth) in a precise form 将(某事物)形式固定格式: *formulate a rule, policy, theory, etc* 制定规则、制定政策、创立理论. **2** express (sth) clearly and exactly using particular words 确切地表达(某思想): *formulate one's thoughts carefully* 确切地阐述自己的思想 ○ *The contract was formulated in difficult legal language.* 该合同是用深奥的法律术语订立的.

▷ **for·mu·la·tion** /ˌfɔːmjʊˈleɪʃn; ˌfɔrmjəˈleʃən/ *n* **(a)** [U] action of formulating 格式化; 公式化; 确切的表达. **(b)** [C] result of this 公式; 确切的表达: *choose another formulation* 选择另一种表达方式.

F

for·nic·ate /ˈfɔːnɪkeɪt; ˈfɔrnɪˌket/ *v* [I] (*fml esp derog* 文, 尤作贬义) (of people not married to each other) have sexual intercourse (指无婚姻关系的人之间)性交; 通奸. ▷ **for·nica·tion** /ˌfɔːnɪˈkeɪʃn; ˌfɔrnɪˈkeʃən/ *n* [U].

for·sake /fəˈseɪk; fɚˈsek/ *v* (*pt* **forsook** /fəˈsʊk; fɚˈsʊk/, *pp* **forsaken** /fəˈseɪkən; fɚˈsekən/) [Tn] **1** (*fml* 文) give (sth) up; renounce 抛弃, 放弃(某事物): *forsake one's former habits* 抛弃旧习惯. **2** leave (sb), esp when one should be helping him; abandon or desert 离开(某人)(尤指应予帮助时); 遗弃; 舍弃: *forsake one's family and friends* 舍弃家人和朋友 ○ *a dreary forsaken beach in winter* 冬季人迹罕至的海滨.

for·swear /fɔːˈsweə(r); fɔrˈswɛr/ *v* (*pt* **forswore** /fɔːˈswɔː(r); fɔrˈswɔr/, *pp* **forsworn** /fɔːˈswɔːn; fɔrˈswɔrn/) (*fml* 文) **1** [Tn, Tg] (promise to) give up (sth); renounce (保证)放弃(某事物); 舍弃: *He had forsworn smoking.* 他已经戒烟了. **2** [Tn] **~ oneself** = PERJURE ONESELF (PERJURE).

for·sythia /fɔːˈsaɪθɪə; *US* fərˈsɪθɪə; fɚˈsɪθɪə/ *n* [U] bush with bright yellow flowers, blooming in the spring 连翘.

fort /fɔːt; fɔrt/ *n* **1** building(s) specially made or strengthened for the military defence of an area 要塞; 堡垒; 碉堡; 城堡. **2** (idm 习语) **hold the 'fort** have the responsibility or care of sth/sb in the absence of others 代他人尽责或替他人关照某人[某事物].

forte[1] /ˈfɔːteɪ; *US* fɔːrt; fɔrt/ *n* (usu *sing* 通常作单数) thing that sb does particularly well; strong point 某人擅长的事; 长处; 特长: *Mathematics was never my forte.* 数学一向非我所长.

forte[2] /ˈfɔːteɪ; ˈfɔrte/ *adj, adv* (*abbr* 缩写 **f**) (*music* 音) loud; (to be) played loudly 强音(的); 用强音演奏(的). Cf 参看 PIANO[1].

forth /fɔːθ; fɔrθ/ *adv part* **1** (*arch* 古) out from home, etc (离家等处)外出: *explorers who ventured forth to discover new lands* 冒险去发现新地域的探险家. **2** (*fml* 文) onwards; forwards 向前; 向前方: *from that day forth* 从那天起. **3** (idm 习语) **and (,so on and) 'so forth** and other things of the kind that have already been mentioned 等, 等等(表示列举未尽): *They discussed investments, the state of the economy and so forth.* 他们讨论了投资和经济状况等问题. **back and forth** ⇨ BACK[3].

forth·com·ing /ˌfɔːθˈkʌmɪŋ; ˈfɔrθˈkʌmɪŋ/ *adj* **1** [attrib 作定语] about to happen or appear in the near future 即将发生或出现的: *the forthcoming e'lections* 即将举行的选举 ○ *a list of forthcoming 'books*, ie those about to be published 即将出版的图书的目录. **2** [pred 作表语] (often with a negative 常与否定词连用) ready or made available when needed (需要时)现成, 可得到: *The money we asked for was not forthcoming.* 我们要的钱尚未得到. **3** [pred 作表语] ready to help, give information, etc 愿意帮忙或提供信息等: *The secretary at the reception desk was not very forthcoming.* 接待处的秘书不太主动.

forth·right /ˈfɔːθraɪt; fɔrθˈraɪt/ *adj* clear and honest in manner and speech; straightforward 言行坦诚的; 直率的: *He has a reputation for being a forthright critic.* 他是以直率著称的评论家. ○ *condemnation in the most forthright language* 直言不讳的谴责.

forth·with /ˌfɔːθˈwɪθ; *US* -ˈwɪð; fɔrθˈwɪθ/ *adv* (*fml* 文) immediately; at once 立刻; 立即; 即刻; 马上: *Mr Jones will be dismissed forthwith.* 琼斯先生即将被解职.

for·ti·eth ⇨ FORTY.

for·tify /ˈfɔːtɪfaɪ; ˈfɔrtəˌfaɪ/ *v* (*pt, pp* **-fied**) **1** [Tn, Tn·pr] **~ sth (against sth)** **(a)** strengthen (a place) against attack, by building walls, etc 防卫(某地)(筑围墙等): *fortify a town against invasion* 加强防卫一城镇以抵御敌人入侵 ○ *a fortified city* 设防的城市. **(b)** support or strengthen (sb) physically or morally (在物质或道义上)支持(某人): *Fortified against the cold by a heavy coat, he went out into the snow.* 他穿上御寒的大衣冒雪外出. ○ *fortify oneself by prayer and meditation* 通过祈祷和冥想增强自己的信念. **2** [Tn usu passive 通常用于被动语态] increase the nutritional value of (a variety of food) by adding vitamins (添加维生素)增加(食物的)营养价值: *cereal fortified with extra vitamins* 强化营养麦片.

▷ **for·ti·fica·tion** /ˌfɔːtɪfɪˈkeɪʃn; ˌfɔrtəfəˈkeʃən/ *n* **1** [U] fortifying; strengthening 加强防卫; 强化: *plans for the fortification of the city* 加强城市防御的计划. **2** [C usu *pl* 通常作复数] tower, wall, ditch, etc built to defend a place against attack 碉堡、围墙、战壕等防御进攻的建筑物: *These fortifications were all built during the last war.* 这些防御工事都是上次战争时修筑的.

□ **fortified 'wine** wine strengthened by adding strong alcohol 加度葡萄酒: *Port and madeira are fortified wines.* 波尔图酒和马德拉酒都是加度葡萄酒.

for·tis·simo /fɔːˈtɪsɪməʊ; fɔrˈtɪsəˌmo/ *adj, adv* (*abbr* 缩写 **ff**) (*music* 音) very loud; (to be) played very loudly 最强音(的); 用最强音演奏(的).

for·ti·tude /ˈfɔːtɪtjuːd; *US* -tuːd; ˈfɔrtəˌtud/ *n* [U] courage, endurance and self-control in facing pain, danger or difficulty (在痛苦、危险或困难面前表现出的)勇气、坚韧和自制力: *He bore the pain with great fortitude.* 他以极大的毅力忍受了痛苦.

fort·night /ˈfɔːtnaɪt; ˈfɔrtnaɪt/ *n* (usu *sing* 通常作单数) (*esp Brit*) **1** (period of) two weeks 两星期(的时间); 两周: *a fortnight's holiday* 两周的假期 ○ *a fortnight ago* 两星期前 ○ *a fortnight today/tomorrow/on Tuesday*, ie two weeks after the day specified 自今天[明天/星期二]起两周之后. **2** (idm 习语) **this day fortnight** ⇨ DAY.

▷ **fort·nightly** *adj, adv* (*esp Brit*) (happening) once a fortnight 每两星期(发生)一次(的): *a fortnightly flight to Brazil* 每两周飞往巴西一次的航班 ○ *go home fortnightly* 每两星期回家一次.

FORTRAN (also **Fortran**) /ˈfɔːtræn; ˈfɔrtræn/ *abbr* 缩写 = (*computing* 计) formula translation, a programming language used esp for scientific calculations 公式翻译(尤指用于科学计算的程序语言).

fort·ress /ˈfɔːtrɪs; ˈfɔrtrɪs/ *n* castle or large fort; town strengthened against attack 城堡或大的碉堡; 加强防御能力的城镇: *attempts to capture this well-protected fortress* 夺取这座坚固堡垒的多次进攻.

for·tu·it·ous /fɔːˈtjuːɪtəs; *US* -ˈtuː-; fɔrˈtuətəs/ *adj* (*fml* 文) happening by chance or coincidence 偶然发生的; 巧合的: *a fortuitous meeting* 偶然相遇.

for·tu·nate /ˈfɔːtʃənət; ˈfɔrtʃənɪt/ *adj* having, bringing or brought by good fortune; lucky 交好运的; 带来好运的; 好运带来的; 幸运的: *I was fortunate to have/in having a good teacher.* 我很幸运, 有位好老师. ○ *She's fortunate enough to enjoy good health.* 她身体好, 真有福气. ○ *Remember those less fortunate than yourselves.* 别忘了那些运气不如你们的人. ○ *It was very fortunate for him that I arrived on time.* 我按时到了, 算他走运. ○ *I made a fortunate choice and won!* 我幸亏选择得对, 结果赢了!

▷ **for·tu·nately** *adv* by good luck; luckily 运气好地; 幸运地; 幸亏: *I was late, but fortunately the meeting hadn't* *started.* 我迟到了，幸好会议还没开始。○ *Fortunately (for him) Mark quickly found another job.* 幸亏马克很快就找到了另一份工作.

for·tune /ˈfɔːtʃuːn; ˋfɔrtʃən/ *n* **1** [U] chance, esp regarded as a power affecting people's lives: (good or bad) luck 机会(尤指对人们生活有重要影响的); (好的或坏的)运气: *By a stroke* (ie instance) *of (good) fortune, he won the competition.* 他靠(好)运气在竞赛中获胜. ○ *be a victim of ill* (ie bad) *fortune* 成为恶运的牺牲品 ○ *I had the good fortune* (ie was lucky enough) *to be chosen for a trip abroad.* 我真幸运, 被选中出国旅行. **2** [C usu *pl* 通常作复数] event or change in the life of a person or in the progress of a country, business, etc (在人生中或在国家业务等的发展中的)事情或转变: *The party's fortunes were at their lowest level after the election defeat.* 该党在竞选失败后每况愈下. **3** [C] person's destiny or future; fate 个人的运气或前途; 命运: *At the fair a gypsy told (me) my fortune*, eg by looking at playing-cards or the lines on my hand. 有个吉卜赛人在游乐场上给我算过命. **4** [C] large amount of money 大笔的钱; 巨款: *That ring is worth/must have cost a fortune.* 那戒指很值钱. ○ *She inherited a large fortune.* 她继承了一大笔财产. ○ *He made a considerable fortune selling waste materials.* 他靠卖废料发了大财. **5** (idm 习语) **the fortune(s) of ˈwar** the good or bad luck one meets with in war 个人在战争中遇到的好运或恶运: *made homeless by the fortunes of war* 因战乱而无家可归. **a hostage to fortune** ⇨ HOSTAGE. **seek one's fortune** ⇨ SEEK. **a small fortune** ⇨ SMALL. **a soldier of fortune** ⇨ SOLDIER.

□ ˈ**fortune cookie** (*US*) thin biscuit, folded to hold a printed message (eg a proverb, prophecy or joke), served in Chinese restaurants 签语饼(中国餐馆飨客的小脆饼, 包着印有谚语、预言或笑话的小纸条).

ˈ**fortune-hunter** *n* (*derog* 贬) person who wants to marry sb for money 为追求钱财而与某人结婚的人.

ˈ**fortune-teller** *n* person who tells people's fortunes 算命者; 看相者.

forty /ˈfɔːtɪ; ˋfɔrtɪ/ *pron*, *det*, *n* 40; one more than thirty-nine 40, 四十(个). ⇨App 4 见附录 4.

▷ **for·ti·eth** /ˈfɔːtɪəθ; ˋfɔrtɪɪθ/ *pron*, *det* 40th; next after thirty-ninth 第40, 第四十(个). — *n* one of forty equal parts of sth 四十分之一.

forty *n* **1** [C] the number 40 ☆ 40; 四十. **2 the forties** [pl] numbers, years or temperature from 40 to 49 从40到49的数目、年数或温度. **3** (idm 习语) **in one's forties** between the ages of 40 and 50 在40岁到50岁之间.

□ **forty-ˈfive** (also **45**) *n* small record that is designed to be played on a record-player at 45 revolutions a minute (每分钟45转的)小唱片.

For the uses of *forty* and *fortieth* see the examples at *fifty*, *five* and *fifth*. 关于forty和fortieth的用法见fifty、five和fifth词条中的示例.

forum /ˈfɔːrəm; ˋfɔrəm/ *n* **1** (usu sing 通常作单数) place where important public issues can be discussed (讨论公共问题的)场所, 论坛: *The letters page serves as a useful forum for the exchange of readers' views.* 读者来信版是读者们交换意见的有益园地. **2** (in ancient Rome) public place where meetings were held (古罗马)集会的公共场所.

for·ward[1] /ˈfɔːwəd; ˋfɔrwəd/ *adj* **1** [attrib 作定语] (**a**) directed or moving towards the front 向前方的; 向前进的: *forward movement* 向前运动. (**b**) situated in front; near or at the front 位于前面的; 接近或在前面的: *forward ranks of troops* 军队队列的前几排 ○ *The forward part of the train is for first-class passengers only.* 火车的前部只是头等车厢. **2** (of plants, crops, etc) having progressed more than is normal or expected; (of children) having developed certain abilities earlier than normal; well advanced (指花草、农作物等)早熟的; (指儿童)发育早的; 早熟的: *The summer crops were forward this year.* 今年夏季农作物成熟得早. ○ *a forward child* 早熟的孩子. **3** [attrib 作定语] of or relating to the future 未来的; 与未来有关的: *forward planning* 对未来的计划 ○ (*commerce* 商) *forward buying*, ie buying goods at present prices for delivery later 预购. ⇨Usage at FORWARD[2] 用法见FORWARD[2]. **4** (**a**) ready and willing to be involved; eager 热心参与的; 急切的: *be forward in helping others* 热心助人的. (**b**) too eager; too bold in one's manner; presumptuous 过于急切的; (行为)过于大胆的; 冒昧的; 孟浪的; 莽撞的: *a forward young girl* 冒失的女孩子 ○ *I hope you'll apologize — that was a very forward thing to do.* 我希望你能道歉——那事你做得太莽撞了. Cf 参看 BACKWARD.

▷ **for·ward·ness** *n* [U] state of being forward[1](4b) 过于急切的行为; 胆大妄为; 冒昧; 莽撞: *Such forwardness is deplorable.* 像这样的胆大妄为应该受到指责.

for·ward[2] /ˈfɔːwəd; ˋfɔrwəd/ *adv* **1** (also **for·wards**) towards the front or end, into a prominent position 向前或向末端(到达一突出位置): *Move forward carefully or you'll slip.* 小心地往前走, 不然会滑倒. ○ *play a tape-recording forwards, not backwards* 将录音带向前转, 别向后倒 ○ *push one's way forward* 挤着往前走. Cf 参看 BACK[3] 1. **2** onward so as to make progress 向前; 前进: *an important step forward* 向前迈进的重要一步 ○ *We are not getting any further forward with the project.* 我们目前在该计划上没有什么进展. ○ *The project will go forward as planned.* 该工程将按计划进行. **3** towards the future; onwards in time 向着将来; 向着未来: *from this time forward* 从此以后 ○ *Look forward and consider the advantages of a larger house.* 从长远着想, 考虑一下大房子的好处. **4** (idm 习语) **backward(s) and forward(s)** ⇨ BACKWARDS (BACKWARD). **put one's best foot forward** ⇨ BEST[1]. **put the clock/clocks forward/back** ⇨ CLOCK[1].

□ ˈ**forward-looking** *adj* (*approv* 褒) concerned with the future; having modern ideas; progressive 有前途的; 有现代思想的; 进步的: *a young forward-looking company* 新兴的有发展前途的公司.

NOTE ON USAGE 用法: The suffix **-ward** means 'in the direction of' and forms adverbs and adjectives ☆ **-ward** 这一后缀意为'向着某方向', 用以构成副词和形容词: *forward, backward, westward, homeward, etc* 向前、向后、向西、向家里等. The suffix **-wards** has the same meaning but only forms adverbs ☆ **-wards** 与 **-ward** 意思相同但只能构成副词: *forwards, backwards, westwards, homewards, etc* 向前、向后、向西、向家里等. Compare 试比较: *They turned westward/westwards after crossing the river.* 他们过河以后向西拐了. *They travelled in a westward direction.* 他们往西走了. ○ *He leant forward/forwards to see better.* 他把身子向前探, 以便看得更清楚. *To move house requires forward planning.* 要搬家得先做好计划.

for·ward[3] /ˈfɔːwəd; ˋfɔrwəd/ *v* **1** (**a**) [I, Tn, Dn·n, Dn·pr] **~ sth (to sb)** send (a letter, etc) to a new address 将(信件等)投递到新地址; 转递: *please forward*, ie a note written on an envelope, a parcel, etc 请转递(写在信封、包裹上的字样) ○ *Please forward our post (to our new home) when we move.* 我们搬家后, 请将邮件转递(到我们的新住处). (**b**) [Tn, Dn·n, Dn·pr] **~ sth (to sb)** send or dispatch (esp goods or information) to a customer (向客户)发送或递送(尤指货物或信息): *forward a shipment of gloves* 发送一批手套 ○ *We have today forwarded you our new catalogue.* 我们今天已将新目录发送给你们了. **2** [Tn] help to advance or develop (sth); further 帮助促进或发展(某事物); 增进; 提高: *forward sb's plans, career, interests, etc.* 促使完成某人的计划、发展某人的事业、提高某人的利益.

□ ˈ**forwarding address** new address to which post is to be forwarded (邮件转递的)新地址: *He moved house without leaving a forwarding address.* 他搬家了, 没留下新地址.

ˈ**forwarding agent** person or company that forwards (FORWARD 1a) goods 转运行; 转运商.

for·ward[4] /ˈfɔːwəd; ˋfɔrwəd/ *n* attacking player near the front in football, hockey, etc (足球、曲棍球等的)前锋. Cf 参看 STRIKER 2.

for·went *pt* of FORGO.

fos·sil /ˈfɒsl; ˋfɑsl/ *n* **1** remains of a prehistoric animal or plant preserved by being buried in earth and now hardened like rock 化石: *This fossil may be over 2 million years old.* 这化石可能超过二百万年了. ○ [attrib 作定语] *fossil bones, shells, etc* 变成化石的骨、贝壳等. **2** (*infml derog* 口, 贬) person, esp an old one, who is unable to accept new ideas or adapt to new conditions 不能接受新思想或不能适应新情况的人(尤指老年人); 老顽固; 老古董: *Our literature teacher is an old fossil.* 我们的文学老师是个老顽固.

▷ **fos·sil·ize, -ise** /ˈfɒsəlaɪz; ˋfɑslˌaɪz/ *v* [I, Tn usu passive 通常用于被动语态] **1** (cause sth to) become a fossil (使某物)成为化石: *fossilized leaves* 成为化石的叶子. **2** (*fig* 比喻) make (sth) or become out of date or fixed 使(某事物)(变得)过时或固定不变: *old-fashioned fossilized attitudes* 落后的、固定不变的看法. **fos·sil·iza·tion, -isation** /ˌfɒsəlaɪˈzeɪʃn; *US* -lɪˈz-; ˌfɑsləˋzeʃən/ *n* [U].

□ ˈ**fossil fuel** fuel, eg coal or oil, formed from the decayed remains of prehistoric animals or plants 矿物燃料, 化石燃料(如煤或石油).

fos·ter /ˈfɒstə(r); *US* ˈfɔː-; ˋfɔstɚ/ *v* **1** [Tn] help the growth or development of (sth); encourage or promote 培养, 培育(某物); 鼓励; 促进: *foster an interest, attitude, impression, etc* 培养兴趣、滋长某种情绪、加深印象 ○ *foster the growth of local industries* 扶植地方工业. **2** [I, Tn] take care of and bring up (a child that is not legally one's own) 照顾, 抚养(法律上不属于自己的孩子); 领养; 收养: *People who cannot have a baby of their own sometimes foster (a child).* 不能生育的人有时领养别人的(孩子). Cf 参看 ADOPT 1.

▷ **fos·ter-** (forming compound *ns* 用以构成复合名词) with a family connection through fostering rather than of birth 通过收养而产生家庭关系的: *a ˈfoster-parent, -mother, -child, -son, -sister, etc* ○ *a ˈfoster-home.*

fought *pt, pp* of FIGHT.

foul[1] /faʊl; faʊl/ *adj* **1** having a bad smell or taste; dirty and disgusting 难闻的; 有恶味的; 污秽的; 令人厌恶的: *foul stagnant ponds* 臭烘烘的死水塘 ○ *a foul rubbish dump* 又脏又臭的垃圾堆 ○ *This medicine tastes foul!* 这药味让人恶心! **2** (**a**) unpleasant; dreadful 不愉快的; 可怕的: *'Go away! I've had a foul day at work.'* '走开! 我干了一天活儿够受的了.' ○ *His boss has a foul temper.* 他的老板的脾气很坏. (**b**) evil or wicked 邪恶的; 罪恶的: *a foul crime* 邪恶的罪行. **3** (of language) obscene and offensive; full of swear-words (指语言)猥亵的, 无礼的; 充满脏话的. **4** (of weather) very rainy and windy; stormy or rough (指天气)风雨大作的, 暴风雨的, 恶劣的: *The spring was foul this year — it was cold and wet for weeks.* 今春天气恶劣——一连几个星期又冷又潮湿. **5** (*sport* 体) (of an action) against the rules; unfair (指动作)犯规的, 不正当的: *a foul stroke* 犯规的一击. **6** (of a chimney, pipe, etc) blocked with waste, etc so that nothing can pass through (指烟囱、管道等)不通畅的, 阻塞的. **7** (idm 习语) **by fair means or foul** ⇨ FAIR[1]. **fall foul of sb/sth** have a confrontation or disagreement with sb/sth, esp the government or the authorities 与某人[某事物]冲突或不一致(尤指与政府或当局): *The police never caught him in any criminal activity but he eventually fell foul of the tax authorities.* 警方从未当场见到他有犯罪活动, 但他最终却与税务局惹上了官非.

▷ **foul** *n* (*sport* 体) action that is against the rules of a game (比赛中的)犯规行为: *That last foul (against/on Smith) lost us the match.* 最后那次(对史密斯)犯规使我们输了那场比赛.

foully /ˈfaʊllɪ; ˋfaʊllɪ/ *adv.*

foul·ness *n* [U].

□ ˌ**foul-ˈmouthed** *adj* using obscene and offensive language 用猥亵、无礼语言的: *a foul-mouthed ˈchild* 说脏话的孩子.

ˌ**foul ˈplay 1** action that is against the rules of a sport; unfair or illegal dealings (运动中的)犯规行为; 不正当的或违法的交易: *fresh evidence of foul play in financial dealings* 在财务方面违法的新证据. **2** criminal violence that leads to murder (导致谋杀的)犯罪暴力行为: *The police suspect foul play rather than suicide.* 警方怀疑是谋杀不是自杀.

foul[2] /faʊl; faʊl/ *v* **1** [Tn, Tn·p] **~ sth (up)** make sth dirty 弄脏某物: *Dogs are not permitted to foul* (ie excrete on) *the pavement.* 禁止狗在人行道上便溺. ○ *The factories are responsible for fouling up the air for miles around.* 这些工厂造成了很大范围的空气污染. **2** [I, Ip, Tn, Tn·p] **~ (sth) (up)** (cause sth to) become caught or twisted (in sth) (使某物)缠结; (与某物)缠住: *The ropes have fouled (up).* 绳子缠住了. ○ *My fishing-line got fouled (up) in an old net.* 我的钓丝跟旧鱼网缠在一起了. **3** [I, Tn] (*sport* 体) commit a foul against (another player) (对运动员)犯规: *He fouled the same player again in the second half.* 他在下半场对同一运动员再次犯规. **4** (idm 习语) **foul one's (own) nest** bring disgrace, etc to one's home, family, profession, country, etc (给自己的家庭、家人、职业、国家等)带来耻辱等. **5** (phr v) **foul sth up** (*infml* 口) spoil sth, usu by behaving in a thoughtless or foolish way; mess sth up 弄乱某事物(通常因粗心或愚蠢的行为所致); 搞糟: *Everything was just fine until Fred came along and fouled things up.* 本来一切都井井有条, 弗雷德一来就给搞得乱七八糟. ○ *The weather has really fouled up my holiday plans.* 我的假日安排因天气关系已全部打乱了.

▷ ˈ**foul-up** *n* (*infml* 口) spoiling or upsetting of arrangements, relationships, etc (安排、关系等的)混乱, 差错: *We'll finish the project on time if there are no more foul-ups.* 只要不再出差错, 我们就能按时完成计划.

found[1] *pt, pp* of FIND.

found[2] /faʊnd; faʊnd/ *v* **1** [Tn] (begin to) build (sth); establish (开始)建设(某物); 建立; 创建; 创立: *This settlement was founded in 1592.* 该居民点建立于1592年. ○ *The ancient Romans founded colonies throughout Europe.* 古罗马人在整个欧洲建立了殖民地. **2** [Tn] start or establish (an organization, institution, etc), esp by providing money 创办, 创建(组织、机构等)(尤指提供资金): *found a research institute, company, hospital, etc* 创办研究机构、公司、医院等. **3** [Tn·pr usu passive 通常用于被动语态] **~ sth on sth** base or construct sth on sth 将某事物建立在另一事物的基础上: *a novel founded on fact* 根据事实写成的小说 ○ *a morality founded on religious principles* 基于宗教原则的道德.

□ **founding ˈfather 1** person who establishes an institution, a popular movement, etc 创办机构、发起民众运动等的人; 创始人: *the founding fathers of modern linguistics* 现代语言学的创始人. **2 Founding Father** member of the body that in 1787 drew up the Constitution of the USA (1787年起草美国宪法的)制宪会议成员.

found[3] /faʊnd; faʊnd/ *v* **1** melt (metal) and pour it into a mould 熔化(金属)后注入模具; 熔铸. **2** make (an object) from metal in this way (用金属)铸造(物件).

founda·tion /faʊnˈdeɪʃn; faʊnˋdeʃən/ *n* **1** [U] act of founding (an institution, organization, etc) (机构、组织等的)建立, 创立, 创办: *the foundation of the university* 大学的创办. **2** [C] (**a**) (organization set up to provide) sums of money for research, charity, etc (为研究、慈善事业等提供的)基金, 基金会: *the Ford Foundation* 福特基金 ○ *You may be able to get support from an arts foundation.* 你可以从文艺基金会得到资助. (**b**) institution, eg a college or hospital, that is established by means of such a fund (用基金建立的)机构(如学院或医院). **3** [C usu *pl* 通常作复数] layer of bricks, concrete, etc forming the solid base of a building underground 地基; 房基; 基础: *lay the foundations of a building* 给建筑物奠基 ○ *The huge lorries shook the foundations of the house.* 大卡车驶过时, 连房基都震动了. **4** [C, U] principle, idea or fact on which sth is based; basis (作为某事的)基本原则、思想或事实; 基础: *lay the foundations of one's career* 奠定个人事业的基础 ○ *The political scandal shook the nation to its very foundations.* 这一政治丑闻从根本上动摇了该国家. ○ *The conclusions must have some solid foundation in reality.* 这些结论一定有些牢固的现实基础. ○ *That rumour has no foundation/is without foundation in fact.* 那谣言没有事实根据. **5** [U] (also **foundation cream**) cream put on the face before other make-up is applied 粉底霜(化妆品).

□ **founˈdation course** course taken at a college, etc that usu covers a wide range of subjects and prepares students for more advanced studies 基础课.

founˈdation-stone *n* large block of stone laid at a special ceremony to mark the founding of a public building 奠基石(在奠基典礼上放置的大石块, 标志公共建筑物开工).

founder[1] /ˈfaʊndə(r); ˋfaʊndɚ/ *n* person who founds or establishes sth 建立或创立某事物的人; 建立者; 缔造者: *founder of a city, institution, company, etc* 城市、机

构、公司等的创建人.
□ **founder-ˈmember** *n* one of the first and founding members of a society, an organization, etc (团体、组织等的)最初建立者; 发起人; 创始人.
founder[2] /ˈfaʊndə(r); ˋfaʊndɚ/ *v* **1** [I] (of a plan, etc) fail; break down (指计划等)失败, 垮掉: *The project foundered as a result of lack of finance.* 该项目因缺乏资金而告吹. **2** [I] (of a ship) fill with water and sink (指船)沉没: *The boat foundered on rocks near the harbour.* 船在港口附近触礁沉没. **3** [I] (esp of a horse) fall or stumble (尤指马)摔倒, 绊: *The mare foundered under the heavy load and collapsed in the road.* 那母马因负载过重而倒在路上.
found·ling /ˈfaʊndlɪŋ; ˋfaʊndlɪŋ/ *n* (*arch* 古) abandoned child of unknown parents who is found by sb 弃儿.
foundry /ˈfaʊndrɪ; ˋfaʊndrɪ/ *n* place where metal or glass is melted and moulded into articles of particular shapes 铸造厂; 玻璃厂.
fount[1] /faʊnt; faʊnt/ *n* **~ (of sth)** (*rhet or arch* 修辞或古) source or origin (of sth); fountain (某事物的)来源或根源; 泉: *the fount of all wisdom* 一切智慧的源泉.
fount[2] /faʊnt; faʊnt/ (also **font** /fɒnt; fɑnt/) *n* set of printing type of one style and size 一套(字体和字号相同的印刷用)活字.

fountain 喷泉

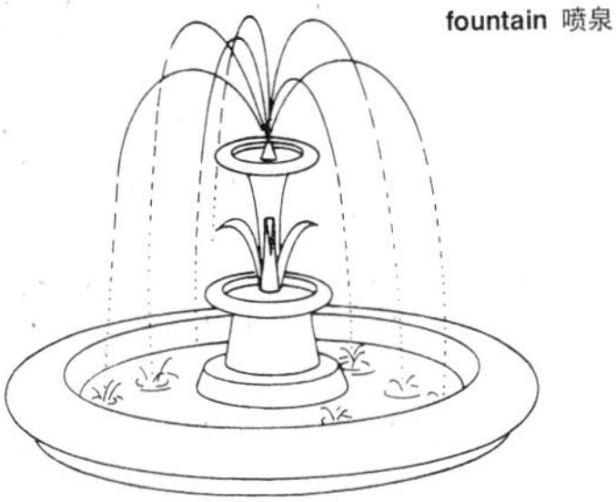

foun·tain /ˈfaʊntɪn; *US* -tn; ˋfaʊntṇ/ *n* **1** jet of water, esp one forced up into the air artificially as an ornament 喷水; (尤指人造的作装饰用的)喷泉: *The fountains of Rome are famed for their architectural beauty.* 罗马的喷泉以其建筑之美而著称. ○ *A fountain of water gushed from the broken fire hydrant.* 从损坏的消防栓里喷出水来. **2** = DRINKING FOUNTAIN (DRINK[2]). **3 ~ (of sth)** (*rhet or arch* 修辞或古) source or origin (of sth); fount (某事物的)来源或根源; 源泉: *the fountain of justice* 正义的源泉.
□ **ˈfountain-head** *n* origin or source 根源; 来源: *the fountain-head of power* 力量的根源.
ˈfountain-pen *n* pen with a container from which ink flows continuously to the nib 自来水笔.
four /fɔ:(r); fɔr/ *pron, det* **1** 4; one more than three 4, 四(个). ➪App 4 见附录4. **2** (idm 习语) **on all ˈfours** (of a person) with one's hands and knees (and usu also toes) on the ground (指人)双手和双膝(通常还用脚趾)着地, 趴着: *The baby was crawling about on all fours.* 婴儿那时正在满处爬. ➪illus at KNEEL 见KNEEL插图. **(be) on all fours (with sb/sth)** (be) the same in importance, function, etc (as sb/sth else) (重要性, 作用等)(与某人[某事物])相同, 一致.
▷ **four** *n* **1** the number 4 ☆ 4; 四. **2** group of four people or things 四个人或物的一组. **3** (crew of a) rowing-boat for four people 四人划行的船(员). **4** (in cricket) shot, scoring four runs, in which the ball crosses the boundary after having hit the ground (板球)得四分的一击.
four- (in compounds 用以构成复合词) having four of the thing specified 有四个...的: *a four-sided figure*.
fourth /fɔ:θ; fɔrθ/ *pron, det* 4th; next after third 第4, 第四(个). ➪App 4 见附录4. **fourthly** *adv* in the fourth position or place 在第四位. **the fourth diˈmension** the dimension of time 第四维(时间). **the ˌFourth of Juˈly** anniversary of the Declaration of Independence (1776) of the United States from Britain 美国独立纪念日(1776年7月4日). — *n* one of four equal parts of sth 四分之一.
□ **fourfold** /ˈfɔ:fəʊld; ˋfɔrˋfold/ *adj, adv* **1** four times as much or as many 四倍(的): *The population in this area has increased fourfold.* 该地区的人口已增加到四倍. **2** having four parts 有四部分(的).
ˌfour-in-ˈhand *n* coach or carriage pulled by four horses and driven by one person 驷马车(一人驾御四匹马拉的马车).
ˌfour-letter ˈword any of various short words, usu referring to sexual or other bodily functions, that are considered obscene or offensive 粗俗、下流的词; 脏话.
ˈfour-ply *adj* (of wool, wood, etc) having four strands or thicknesses (指毛线、木材等)四股的, 四层的.
ˌfour-ˈposter *n* (also **ˌfour-poster ˈbed**) (esp formerly) large bed with a tall post at each of the four corners to support curtains (尤指旧时)四柱大床(四角各有一柱以支撑幔帐的).
foursome /ˈfɔ:səm; ˋfɔrsəm/ *n* **1** four people joining together to play a game, esp golf 四人参加的游戏(尤指高尔夫球). **2** two couples undertaking a leisure activity together 两对男女一同参加的娱乐活动: *Let's make (up) a foursome and go out to a restaurant.* 咱们四个人(两对男女)一起下饭馆吧.
ˌfour-ˈsquare *adj* (**a**) square-shaped 方形的; 方的. (**b**) solidly based; steady or resolute 不动摇的; 坚定的; 坚决的; 果断的: *a four-square apˈproach to the problem* 对该问题的强硬态度.
ˌfour-wheel ˈdrive (of a vehicle in which) power is applied to all four wheels (指车辆)四轮驱动的.
For the uses of *four* and *fourth* see the examples at *five* and *fifth*. 关于four和fourth的用法见five和fifth词条中的示例.
four·teen /ˌfɔ:ˈti:n; fɔrˋtin/ *pron, det* 14; one more than thirteen 14, 十四(个). ➪App 4 见附录4.
▷ **four·teen** *n* the number 14 ☆ 14; 十四.
four·teenth /ˌfɔ:ˈti:nθ; fɔrˋtinθ/ *pron, det* 14th; next after thirteenth 第14, 第十四(个). — *n* one of fourteen equal parts of sth 十四分之一.
For the uses of *fourteen* and *fourteenth* see the examples at *five* and *fifth*. 关于fourteen和fourteenth的用法见five和fifth词条中的示例.
fowl /faʊl; faʊl/ *n* **1** [C] (*pl* unchanged or **~s** 复数或不变或作 **fowls**) domestic cock or hen 鸡: *We keep a few fowls and some goats.* 我们养了几只鸡和一些山羊. **2** [U] flesh of certain types of birds, eaten for food 禽肉; 鸡肉: *We had fish for the first course, followed by roast fowl and fresh vegetables.* 我们吃的第一道菜是鱼, 接着上的菜是烤禽肉和新鲜蔬菜. **3** [C] (*arch* 古) any bird 任何鸟类: *the fowls of the air* 飞禽. **4** (in compounds 用以构成复合词) bird of the type specified 某种禽鸟: *ˈwaterfowl* ○ *barnyard fowl* ○ *ˈwildfowl.*
▷ **fowl** *v* [I] (usu 通常作 **go ˈfowling**) hunt or snare wildfowl 猎捕野禽.
□ **ˈfowl pest** type of infectious disease among chickens, etc 家禽的瘟疫.
fox /fɒks; fɑks/ *n* **1** (**a**) [C] (*fem* 阴性作 **vixen** /ˈvɪksn; ˋvɪksṇ/) wild animal of the dog family, with reddish brown fur, a pointed face and a bushy tail 狐; 狐狸: *Hunting foxes is a peculiarly English sport.* 猎狐是英国特有的运动. ○ *The fox is known for its cleverness and cunning.* 狐狸的机敏和狡猾是人所共知的. ➪illus at App 1 见附录1插图, page iii. (**b**) [U] its skin and fur used to make coats, etc 狐皮. **2** [C] (*infml esp derog* 口, 尤作贬义) person who is clever and able to get what he wants by deceiving or manipulating others 狡猾的人; 老狐狸: *a crafty/sly old fox* 狡猾的老狐狸.
▷ **fox** *v* **1** [Tn] (**a**) be too difficult for (sb) to understand; baffle or confuse 使(某人)难以理解; 使困惑; 使迷惑: *He was completely foxed by her behaviour.* 他对她的所作所为大感迷惑. (**b**) trick (sb) by cunning; deceive (用诡计)骗(某人); 欺骗. **2** [Tn usu passive 通常用于被动语态] discolour (the pages of a book) with brown marks (生褐斑)使(书页)褪色: *This volume is foxed on the flyleaf.* 这卷书的空白页发黄了.
foxy /ˈfɒksɪ; ˋfɑksɪ/ *adj* (**-ier**, **-iest**) **1** crafty or deceitful; cunning 狡猾的; 骗人的; 狡诈的. **2** like a fox in appearance, ie reddish brown in colour or having a fox-like face 貌似狐狸的(即赤褐色的或面貌像狐狸

F

的). **3** (*sl approv* 俚, 褒 *esp US*) (of a woman) physically attractive; sexy (指女人)长得漂亮的, 性感的: *a foxy lady* 性感的女人.

□ ˈ**foxhole** *n* hole in the ground dug by soldiers as a shelter against enemy fire and as a firing-point 散兵坑.

ˈ**foxhound** *n* type of dog trained to hunt foxes 猎狐狗.

ˈ**fox-hunting** *n* [U] sport in which a fox is hunted by foxhounds and people on horses 猎狐(骑着马用猎狐狗猎狐的运动).

ˌ**fox-ˈterrier** *n* type of short-haired dog, formerly used to drive foxes out of their holes 猎狐㹴狗(旧时用以将狐狸从洞中赶出的).

fox·glove /ˈfɒksglʌv; ˋfɑksˌglʌv/ *n* tall plant with purple or white bell-shaped flowers growing up its stem 洋地黄; 毛地黄. ⇨illus at App 1 见附录1插图, page ii.

fox·trot /ˈfɒkstrɒt; ˋfɑksˌtrɑt/ *n* (music for a) formal dance with both slow and quick steps 狐步舞; 狐步舞曲.

▷ **fox·trot** *v* (**-tt-**) [I] dance the foxtrot 跳狐步舞.

foyer /ˈfɔɪeɪ; *US* ˈfɔɪər; ˋfɔɪɚ/ *n* entrance hall or large open space in a theatre, hotel, etc where people can meet or wait (剧场、旅馆等的)门厅, 休息厅: *I'll meet you in the foyer at 7 o'clock.* 我七点钟和你在门厅见面.

FPA /ˌef piː ˈeɪ; ˌɛf pi ˋe/ *abbr* 缩写 = (*Brit*) Family Planning Association 计划生育协会.

Fr *abbr* 缩写 = **1** (*religion* 宗) Father: *Fr (Paul) Black* (保罗·)布莱克神父. **2** French.

fr *abbr* 缩写 = franc(s): *fr18.50* 18.50 法郎.

fra·cas /ˈfrækɑː; *US* ˈfreɪkəs; ˋfrekəs/ *n* (*pl* unchanged 复数不变 /-kɑːz; -kɑz/; *US* **~es** /-kəsəz; -kəsɪz/) (usu *sing* 通常作单数) noisy quarrel, fight, or disturbance 大声争吵; 打闹; 骚乱: *The police were called in to break up* (ie stop) *the fracas.* 警察奉命去制止骚乱.

frac·tion /ˈfrækʃn; ˋfrækʃən/ *n* **1** small part, bit, amount, or proportion (of sth) (某物的)小部分, 一点儿, 少许, 片断: *The car stopped within a fraction of an inch of the wall.* 汽车在离墙不到一英寸的地方停住了. ○ *Could you move a fraction closer?* 你能不能稍微再挪近点儿? **2** precise division of a number, eg $\frac{1}{3}$, $\frac{5}{8}$, 0.76 分数, 小数(如 $\frac{1}{3}$、$\frac{5}{8}$、0.76).

▷ **frac·tional** /-ʃənl; -ʃənḷ/ *adj* **1** of or in fractions 部分的; 少许的; 片断的; 分数的; 小数的: *a fractional equation* 分数方程式. **2** very small; trivial or unimportant 极小的; 轻微的; 无足轻重的: *a fractional difference in prices* 微小的差价. **frac·tion·ally** /-ʃənəlɪ; -ʃənəlɪ/ *adv* to a very small degree; marginally 达极小程度地; 轻微地: *One dancer was fractionally out of step.* 有个跳舞人的舞步稍微有些不合拍.

frac·tious /ˈfrækʃəs; ˋfrækʃəs/ *adj* (esp of children) irritable; bad-tempered (尤指儿童)易怒的, 脾气坏的.

▷ **frac·tiously** *adv*. **frac·tious·ness** *n* [U].

frac·ture /ˈfræktʃə(r); ˋfræktʃɚ/ *n* (**a**) [C] instance of breaking (esp a bone) 折断; 断裂; 破裂; (尤指)骨折: *a fracture of the leg* 腿部骨折 ○ *He had several injuries, including three fractures.* 他多处受伤, 其中三处是骨折. ○ *a compound/simple fracture*, ie one in which the skin is/is not pierced by the broken bone 有创[单纯]骨折 ○ *a slight fracture in a pipe* 管道的裂缝. (**b**) [U] breaking or breakage, esp of a bone 折断; 断裂; 破裂; (尤指)骨折: *the site of fracture* 断裂的位置.

▷ **frac·ture** *v* [I, Tn] (cause sth to) break or crack (使某物)折断, 破碎: *Her leg fractured in two places.* 她的腿有两处骨折. ○ *suffer from a fractured pelvis* 出现骨盆骨折.

fra·gile /ˈfrædʒaɪl; *US* -dʒl; ˋfrædʒəl/ *adj* **1** easily damaged or broken; delicate 易受伤害的; 易碎的; 易损的: *fragile china/glass* 易碎的瓷器[玻璃器皿] ○ *a fragile plant* 娇嫩的植物 ○ (*fig* 比喻) *Human happiness is so fragile.* 人生幸福易逝. ○ *a fragile economy* 疲软的经济. **2** (*infml* 口) not strong and healthy; weak, eg because one has drunk too much alcohol 不强健的, 弱的(如因酗酒所致): *He's feeling a bit fragile after last night's party.* 他参加了昨晚的聚会以后, 现在觉得有些虚弱. Cf 参看 FRAIL. ▷ **fra·gil·ity** /frəˈdʒɪlətɪ; frəˋdʒɪlətɪ/ *n* [U].

frag·ment /ˈfrægmənt; ˋfrægmənt/ *n* **1** small part or piece broken off (sth) (某物的)碎片: *find several fragments of a Roman vase* 发现古罗马花瓶的几块残片. **2** separate or incomplete part (of sth) (某事物的)片断或不完整部分: *I heard only a fragment of their conversation.* 我只听到他们谈话的只言片语.

▷ **frag·ment** /frægˈment; frægˋmɛnt/ *v* [I, Tn] (cause sth to) break into small pieces or parts; split up (使某物)破碎或裂开; 分裂; 分离: *These bullets fragment on impact.* 这些子弹射中物体时爆炸成碎片. ○ (*fig* 比喻) *Ownership of the large estates is increasingly fragmented*, ie divided among several people. 大片地皮的产权逐渐分成若干份.

frag·ment·ary /ˈfrægməntrɪ; *US* -terɪ; ˋfrægmənˌtɛrɪ/ *adj* made up of small incomplete or unconnected parts 由小的、不完整的或无联系的部分组成的: *fragmentary evidence* 支离破碎的证据.

frag·menta·tion /ˌfrægmenˈteɪʃn; ˌfrægmɛnˋteʃən/ *n* [U]. **fragmenˈtation bomb** bomb designed to break up into many small pieces 杀伤炸弹(爆炸时成小碎片).

fra·grance /ˈfreɪgrəns; ˋfregrəns/ *n* (**a**) [C usu *sing* 通常作单数] pleasant or sweet smell; scent or perfume 好闻的或芳香的气味; 香; 香料: *Lavender has a delicate fragrance.* 薰衣草有淡淡的香味. (**b**) [U] quality of having a pleasant or sweet smell 芳香.

fra·grant /ˈfreɪgrənt; ˋfregrənt/ *adj* having a pleasant or sweet smell 有香味的; 芳香的: *fragrant herbs, flowers, etc* 香的药草、花等. ▷ **fra·grantly** *adv*.

frail /freɪl; frel/ *adj* **1** (of a person) physically weak or delicate (指人)体弱的, 虚弱的: *a frail child* 体弱的孩子 ○ *At 90, she's getting very old and frail.* 她90岁时渐渐非常衰老、虚弱. **2** easily broken; fragile 易破碎的; 易损的: *Careful: that chair's rather frail!* 小心点儿: 那把椅子不结实! **3** morally weak 道德观念薄弱的: *frail human nature* 易堕落的人性.

▷ **frailty** /ˈfreɪltɪ; ˋfreltɪ/ *n* **1** [U] physical weakness (身体)虚弱. **2** [C, U] (instance of) weakness in character or morals; fault or imperfection (性格)软弱; (道德观念)薄弱; 错误; 缺点: *She continued to love him despite his many frailties.* 尽管他有很多缺点, 但她仍爱他. ○ *human frailty* 人类的弱点.

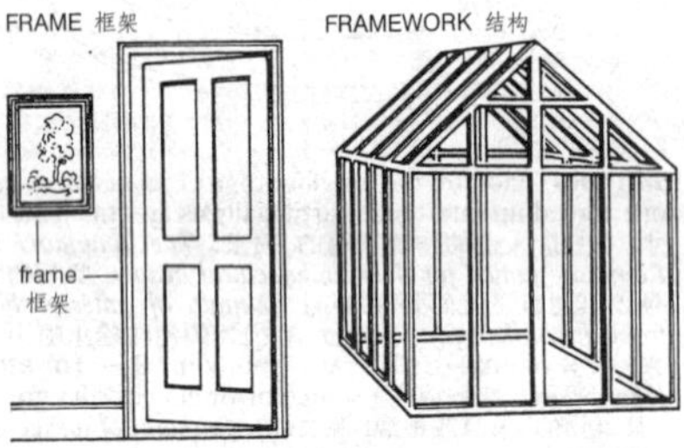

frame[1] /freɪm; frem/ *n* **1** border of wood, metal, etc in which a picture, door, pane of glass, etc is enclosed or set (木材、金属等做的)框架: *a picture frame* 画框 ○ *a window frame* 窗框. **2** rigid structure of a piece of furniture, building, vehicle, etc which makes its shape and forms a support for its parts (家具、建筑物、车辆等的)框架, 支架, 骨架: *the frame of a cupboard, bed, rucksack* 柜橱的框架、床的框架、帆布包的支架 ○ *the frame of an aircraft, a car, etc* 飞机、汽车等的框架. ⇨illus at App 1 见附录1插图, page xiii, ⇨illus 见插图. **3** (usu *pl* 通常作复数) structure of plastic, metal, etc that holds the lenses of a pair of glasses in place 眼镜框: *glasses with heavy black frames* 黑色粗框眼镜. ⇨illus at GLASS 见 GLASS 插图. **4** (usu *sing* 通常作单数) human or animal body; its form or structure (人或动物的)身体; 体形; 身体结构: *Sobs shook her slender frame.* 她抽泣着, 苗条的身体都在颤动. **5** general order or system that forms the background to sth (构成某事物背景的)规律或制度; 体制; 模式: *the frame of contemporary society* 现代社会的模式. **6** (**a**) any of the single photographs that make up a cinema film (影片的)一个镜头, 一个画面. (**b**) single picture in a comic strip (连环漫画中的)一幅画. **7** = COLD FRAME (COLD[1]). **8** (**a**) (in snooker, etc) triangular structure for positioning balls (落袋台球戏等)(摆放球的)三角框. (**b**) (in snooker, bowling, etc) single round of play (落袋台球

戏、地滚球戏等)一轮, 一局, 一回. **9** (idm 习语) **a frame of 'mind** particular state of one's mind or feelings; mood 心境; 心情; 情绪; 思想状态: *I'm not in the right frame of mind to start discussing money.* 我现在没心思来商量钱的问题. **a frame of 'reference** set of principles, standards or observations used as a basis for one's judgement, behaviour, etc (作为个人的判断、行为等的依据的)原则, 标准, 观点: *sociological studies conducted within a Marxist frame of reference* 以马克思主义观点指导的社会学研究.

□ **'frame-house** *n* house with a wooden frame covered with boards 木板房.

'framework *n* **1** structure giving shape and support 框架; 结构: *a bridge with a steel framework* 钢铁结构的桥梁. ⇨illus 见插图. **2** social order or system 社会的秩序或制度: *civil unrest which shook the framework of the old system* 动摇了旧制度的内乱. **3** set of principles or ideas used as a basis for one's judgement, decisions, etc (个人的判断、决定等所依据的)原则, 思想: *All the cases can be considered within the framework of the existing rules.* 一切情况都可依据现行的规章加以考虑.

frame[2] /freɪm; frem/ *v* **1** (**a**) [Tn] put or build a frame[1](1) round (sth) (给某物)镶框; (给某物)做框: *frame a photograph, painting, etc* 给照片、画等镶框. (**b**) [Tn esp passive 尤用于被动语态] serve or act as a frame[1](1) for (sb/sth) 形成(某人[某事])的框子: *He stood framed in the doorway to the hall.* 他站在门口, 堵住通向大厅的路. ○ *A dense mass of black hair framed his face.* 浓密的黑发衬托着他的面庞. **2** [Tn] express (sth) in words; compose or formulate (用文字)表达(某事); 创作; 拟定; 制定: *frame a question, argument, response, etc* 拟定问题、论点、回应等 ○ *frame a theory, plan, set of rules, etc* 创立理论、拟定计划、制定一套规章. **3** [Tn esp passive 尤用于被动语态] (*infml* 口) produce false evidence against (an innocent person) so that he appears guilty 诬陷; 陷害: *The accused man said he had been framed.* 被告说他受人陷害了.

□ **'frame-up** *n* (*infml* 口) situation in which false evidence is produced against an innocent person so that he appears guilty 诬陷; 诬告; 阴谋: *Don't you see — it was all a frame-up!* 难道你还不明白 —— 那都是诬陷!

franc /fræŋk; fræŋk/ *n* unit of currency in eg France, Belgium and Switzerland 法郎(如法国、比利时和瑞士的货币单位).

franch·ise /'fræntʃaɪz; ˋfræntʃaɪz/ *n* **1** [U] right to vote at public elections (公众选举的)投票权, 选举权: *system of universal adult franchise* 全体成年人都享有选举权的制度 ○ *Women were not given the franchise in Britain until the twentieth century.* 英国妇女直到二十世纪才获得选举权. **2** [C] formal permission to sell a company's goods or services in a particular area (正式授予在某地区销售某某公司的货物或经营某业务的)特权, 特许: *buy a fast-food, printing, etc franchise* 购买经营快餐、印刷等的特权 ○ *grant, withdraw a franchise* 授予、撤销特权.

▷ **franch·ise** *v* [Tn] grant a franchise(2) to (sb) 授予(某人)特权.

Fran·cis·can /fræn'sɪskən; frænˋsɪskən/ *n, adj* (friar or nun) of the Christian religious order founded by St Francis of Assisi 圣方济各会的(修士或修女).

Franco- *comb form* 构词成分 French; of France 法国的: *Franco-German history* ○ *Francophile*, ie (person who is) friendly towards France.

fran·co·phone /'fræŋkəʊfəʊn; ˋfræŋkə,fon/ *adj, n* French-speaking (person) 说法语的(人): *the francophone countries of West Africa* 非洲西部说法语的国家.

frank[1] /fræŋk; fræŋk/ *adj* **(-er, -est)** ~ **(with sb) (about sth)** showing thoughts and feelings openly; honest and direct in speech; plain and blunt 公开表达思想感情的; 言语真诚的; 坦率的; 坦白的; 直率的: *a frank reply, discussion, exchange of views, etc* 坦率的回答、讨论、交换意见等 ○ *To be (perfectly) frank with you, I think your son has little chance of passing the exam.* 说实在的, 我认为你儿子这次考试及格的希望不大.

▷ **frankly** *adv* **1** in a frank manner 坦率地; 坦白地; 直率地; 真诚地: *Tell me frankly what's wrong.* 老老实实告诉我出什么事了. **2** speaking honestly; to be truthful 说实话; 诚实地: *Frankly, I couldn't care less.* 说真的, 我毫不在乎. ○ *Quite frankly, I'm not surprised.* 坦白地说, 我并不感到意外. ⇨Usage at HOPEFUL 用法见 HOPEFUL.

frank·ness *n* [U]: *She spoke about her fears with complete frankness.* 她对自己的恐惧直言不讳.

frank[2] /fræŋk; fræŋk/ *v* [Tn] put a mark or a stamp on (a letter, etc) to show that postage has been paid or does not need to be paid 在(信件等)上做记号、加印记(以示邮资已付或免费邮寄).

□ **'franking-machine** *n* device that automatically franks letters, etc and counts up the total postal charges 自动邮资盖印机.

frank·furter /'fræŋkfɜ:tə(r); ˋfræŋkfɚtɚ/ (*US* **wiener**) *n* type of small smoked sausage 小熏肠.

frank·in·cense /'fræŋkɪnsens; ˋfræŋkɪn,sɛns/ *n* [U] type of sweet-smelling gum from a tree, burnt as incense 乳香(有香味的树脂, 可作燃香).

fran·tic /'fræntɪk; ˋfræntɪk/ *adj* **1** in an extreme state of emotion, esp fear or anxiety 情感的极度状态(尤指恐惧或焦急); 发狂的; 发疯的: *The child's parents were frantic when she did not return home on time.* 那孩子没有按时回家, 她父母都要急疯了. ○ *frantic with worry, anger, grief, etc* 愁得要命、气得要死、悲痛欲绝. **2** hurried and excited but disorganized; frenzied; desperate 慌乱不安的; 狂乱的; 疯狂的; 令人绝望的; 不顾一切的: *a frantic dash, rush, search, etc* 疯狂的撞击、冲击、搜查等 ○ *frantic activity* 不顾一切的行动. ▷ **fran·tic·ally** /-klɪ; -klɪ/ *adv*: *shouting frantically for help* 狂呼求救.

fra·ternal /frə'tɜ:nl; frəˋtɝnl/ *adj* (*esp rhet* 尤作修辞) of a brother or brothers; brotherly or friendly 兄弟的; 兄弟般的; 友好的: *fraternal love* 手足之情 ○ *fraternal greetings from fellow trade-unionists* 同行业工会会员的友好问候. ▷ **fra·tern·ally** /-nəlɪ; -nlɪ/ *adv*.

fra·tern·ity /frə'tɜ:nətɪ; frəˋtɝnətɪ/ *n* **1** [U] brotherly feeling; brotherhood 兄弟般的感情; 手足之情: *There is a strong spirit of fraternity among these isolated people.* 这些与世隔绝的人之间有强烈的兄弟般的情谊. **2** [CGp] group of people sharing the same profession or common interests or beliefs 有相同的职业、共同的爱好或信仰的群体; 同人; 同好: *the medical, banking, teaching, etc fraternity* 医务界、银行界、教育界等同人 ○ *the racing fraternity* 赛马界同好 ○ *the religious fraternity of St Benedict* 本笃会的教友. **3** [C] (*US*) group of male students at a university who form a social club 组成社团的大学男生群体. Cf 参看 SORORITY.

frat·ern·ize, -ise /'frætənaɪz; ˋfrætɚ,naɪz/ *v* [I, Ipr] ~ **(with sb)** become friendly with enemy soldiers, or with civilians of a former enemy country (与敌军士兵、原敌国百姓)建立友谊: *Soldiers who fraternize with the enemy will be punished.* 亲敌的士兵将受到惩罚. ○ *Army personnel are often forbidden to fraternize with the civilian population.* 军职人员常被禁止与平民百姓友好往来. ▷ **frat·ern·iza·tion, -isation** /,frætənaɪ'zeɪʃn; *US* -nɪ'z-; ,frætɚnɪˋzeʃən/ *n* [U].

frat·ri·cide /'frætrɪsaɪd; ˋfrætrə,saɪd/ *n* (**a**) [U] crime of killing one's brother or sister 杀害兄弟或姐妹罪. (**b**) [C] person who has done this 杀害兄弟或姐妹的人. ▷ **frat·ri·cidal** /,frætrɪ'saɪdl; ˋfrætrəˋsaɪdəl/ *adj*.

fraud /frɔ:d; frɔd/ *n* **1** [C, U] (act of) deceiving sb illegally in order to make money or obtain goods 欺骗(行为); 诈骗: *found guilty of fraud* 被裁定诈骗罪成立 ○ *Thousands of frauds are committed every year.* 每年有数以千计的诈骗案. **2** [C] person who deceives others by pretending to have abilities, skills, etc that he does not really have; impostor 骗子; 冒名顶替者: *This woman is a fraud — she has no medical qualifications at all.* 这女人是个骗子 —— 她根本没有行医的资格.

▷ **fraudu·lent** /'frɔ:djʊlənt; *US* -dʒʊ-; ˋfrɔdʒələnt/ *adj* **1** deceitful or dishonest 欺骗的; 诈骗的; 不诚实的; 不老实的: *a fraudulent display of sympathy* 假惺惺的同情. **2** obtained or done by fraud; involving fraud 骗得的; 骗来的; 涉及欺骗的: *fraudulent applications for shares* (ie type of investment) *in the new company* 以欺骗手段申请新公司的股票. **fraudu·lence** /'frɔ:djʊləns; *US* -dʒʊ-; ˋfrɔdʒələns/ *n* [U]. **fraudu·lently** /'frɔ:djʊləntlɪ; *US* -dʒʊ-; ˋfrɔdʒələntlɪ/ *adv*.

fraught /frɔ:t; frɔt/ *adj* **1** [pred 作表语] ~ **with sth** filled with sth; charged with sth 充满某事物; 注入某事物: *a situation fraught with danger* 充满危险的情况 ○ *a silence fraught with meaning* 意义无穷的沉默. **2** worried

F

or anxious; worrying 担心的; 烦恼的; 焦虑的; 令人忧虑的: *There's no need to look so fraught!* 用不着那么愁眉苦脸的. ○ *Next week will be particularly fraught as we've just lost our secretary.* 我们的秘书刚刚辞职, 下星期特别令人担心.

fray[1] /freɪ; fre/ *n* **the fray** [sing] (*rhet or joc* 修辞或谑) fight, contest or argument; lively or challenging action 打斗; 争吵; 争辩; 刺激的或挑战的行为: *ready/eager for the fray* 急欲争斗 ○ *enter/join the fray*, ie take part in a fight, quarrel, etc 参与打架、争吵等.

fray[2] /freɪ; fre/ *v* [I, Tn] **1** (cause sth to) become worn, so that there are loose threads, fibres or wires (使某物)磨损(致使线、纤维或丝松弛): *This cloth frays easily.* 这布太不经磨. ○ *Constant rubbing will fray even the thickest rope.* 再粗的绳子也经不住总磨. ○ *frayed shirt cuffs* 磨破的衬衫袖口. **2** (cause sth to) become strained and irritated (使某事物)变得令人紧张、急躁: *Nerves/Tempers began to fray in the heat.* 天热的时候人就容易神经紧张[脾气急躁]. ○ *Relations between us have become frayed through a series of misunderstandings.* 我们之间产生了一连串的误解, 因而关系紧张了.

frazzle /ˈfræzl; ˋfræzḷ/ *n* (idm 习语) **beaten, burnt, worn, etc to a ˈfrazzle** completely beaten, burnt, exhausted, etc 被打得一败涂地; 被烧成灰烬; 精疲力竭.

freak[1] /fri:k; frik/ *n* **1** (*infml derog* 口, 贬) person considered abnormal because of his behaviour, appearance, ideas, etc (因行为、相貌、思想等而被看作)不正常的人: *People think she's a freak just because she's religious.* 就因为她信教, 人们就把她当成怪人. **2** (*infml* 口) person with a specified interest or obsession; fan 有特别兴趣或着迷的人; 迷: *health/health-food freaks* 对健康[保健食品]着迷的人 ○ *a jazz freak* 爵士乐迷 ○ *an acid freak*, ie sb addicted to the drug LSD 有迷幻药瘾的人. **3** very unusual event or action 极不寻常的事或行为: *By some freak (of chance) I was overpaid this month.* 真稀奇, 这个月多给我钱了. ○ [attrib 作定语] *a freak accident, storm, etc* 反常的事故、暴风雨等. **4** (also ˌ**freak of ˈnature**) person, animal or plant that is abnormal in form 畸形的人、动物或植物.

▷ **freak·ish** *adj* unusual or abnormal; strange 不寻常的; 不正常的; 反常的; 奇怪的; 奇异的: *freakish weather* 反常的天气 ○ *freakish behaviour* 奇怪的行为. **freak·ishly** *adv*. **freak·ish·ness** *n* [U].

freaky *adj* unusual; weird; freakish 不寻常的; 不自然的; 怪诞的; 不正常的; 奇怪的; 奇异的.

freak[2] /fri:k; frik/ *v* (*infml* 口) **1** [I, Ip] **~ (out)** have an extreme reaction to sth 对某事物有极端强烈的反应: *My parents (really) freaked (out) when they saw my purple hair*, ie were shocked and angry. 我父母看见我的紫红头发, 大惊失色. ○ *When they told me I'd won a car, I absolutely freaked*, ie was extremely happy. 听说我赢得一辆小汽车, 简直欣喜若狂. **2** (phr v) **freak out (a)** temporarily lose control of oneself; go crazy; act abnormally, usu under the influence of drugs 暂时对自己失去控制, 发疯, 行为异常(通常为毒品所致): *This ordinary quiet guy just freaked out and shot ten people.* 这个平时温和的傢伙简直发疯了, 开枪打死了十个人. ○ *John's party was really wild — everyone freaked out (on drugs)*, ie hallucinated. 约翰搞的聚会真够疯狂的——大家都(因吸食毒品)神魂颠倒了. **(b)** adopt an unconventional style of life 采取不平常的生活方式. **freak sb out** make sb feel extreme pleasure or unease 使某人感到极度的欣喜或不安: *Listening to a good stereo system always freaks me out.* 我一听到好的立体声音乐就乐不可支.

□ ˈ**freak-out** *n* wild and extreme experience, esp one produced by drugs 疯狂、兴奋的感受(尤指因毒品所致).

freckle /ˈfrekl; ˋfrɛkḷ/ *n* (usu *pl* 通常作复数) one of the small light-brown spots on the human skin 雀斑; 斑点: *Ann's face and back are covered with freckles.* 安的脸上和背上长满了雀斑. Cf 参看 MOLE[1].

▷ **freckle** *v* [I, Tn] (cause skin to) become covered with freckles (使皮肤)生产斑或斑点: *Do you freckle easily?* 你容易长雀斑吗? ○ *the boy's freckled arms* 那男孩子长了雀斑的手臂.

free[1] /fri:; fri/ *adj* (**freer** /fri:ə(r); ˋfriɚ/, **freest** /fri:ɪst; ˋfriɪst/) **1 (a)** (of a person) not a slave or prisoner; allowed to move where one wants; having physical freedom (指人)(非奴隶或囚犯)自由的, 有人身自由的, 行动自由的: *After ten years in prison, he was a free man again.* 他坐了十年监狱, 又成了自由人. ○ *The convicts were pardoned and set free.* 那些囚犯获赦释放. ○ *The driver had to be cut free from the wreckage of his car.* 破开了汽车残骸才把司机解救出来. **(b)** (of an animal) not kept in a cage or tied up; able to move at will (指动物)不关在笼子里的, 不被拴住的, 可任意行动的: *In nature, all animals are wild and free.* 在自然界, 一切动物都是野生的, 自由自在的. ○ *The dog was chained, so how did it get free?* 狗拴着链子, 是怎么挣脱开的呢? ○ *An escaped tiger is roaming free in the town.* 有一只老虎跑出, 正在城里东逃西窜. **2** not fixed or held down; loose 不固定的; 不受牵制的; 松弛的: *the free end of the rope* 绳索松着的一端 ○ *Let the rope run free.* 把绳子放开. ○ *One of the wheels of the cart has worked (itself) free.* 马车的一个轮子松了. **3** clear; not blocked; unrestricted 通畅的; 无阻碍的; 不受限制的; 不受约束的: *Is the way/passage free?* 道路[通道]畅通吗? ○ *A free flow of water came from the pipe.* 水从管道里通畅地流了出来. ○ *The streets have been swept free of leaves.* 街上的落叶已打扫干净. **4** (of a country, its citizens and institutions) not controlled by a foreign government or the state itself (指国家及其公民和机关)不受外国政府或本国控制的, 自主的, 自由的: *This is a free country — I can say what I like.* 这是个自由的国家——我爱说什么就可以说什么. ○ *We might have a free press, but that doesn't mean all reporting is true and accurate.* 我们即使有新闻自由, 也并不意味着一切报道都真实可信、准确无误. **5 ~ (to do sth)** not controlled or restricted (by rules or conventions); permitted to do sth 不受(规章或习俗)控制的, 许可做某事物的: *free movement of workers within the European Community* 在欧洲共同体内部工人的自由流动 ○ *free access to secret information* 对机密资料的自由接触 ○ *You are free to come and go as you please.* 你来去自便. ○ *She's a free spirit*, ie a person not hampered by convention. 她是个无拘无束的人. **6** [pred 作表语] **~ from/of sth (a)** not harmed by sth dangerous; not spoilt by sth unpleasant 不受某危险事物伤害; 不受某不愉快事物影响: *free from harm, prejudice, pain* 不受伤害、无偏见、无痛苦 ○ *free of weeds, contamination, pollution, etc* 无杂草、传染、污染等. **(b)** not subject to certain rules, etc; unrestricted by sth 不受某规章等约束的; 不受某事物阻碍的: *a holiday free from all responsibilities* 摆脱一切责任的假期. **7 (a)** costing nothing 免费的: *free tickets for the theatre* 免费的戏票 ○ *Admission is free.* 免费入场. ○ *a free sample* 免费样品. **(b)** [pred 作表语] **~ (of sth)** not including, or not requiring, a specified payment, usu of tax or duty 免税: *a payment of £30 000 free of tax* 30 000英镑的免税付款 ○ *Delivery is free (of charge) if goods are paid for in advance.* 如预付货款就可免费送货. **8 (a)** (of a place) not occupied or being used; (of a time) not engaged or booked (指地方或时间)未占用的, 空着的, 闲着的: *Is that seat free?* 那座位有人吗? ○ *The bathroom's free now.* 洗澡间现在空着. ○ *Is there a time when the conference room is free?* 会议室有空着的时候吗? ○ *Friday afternoons are left free for revision.* 留出星期五下午的时间做复习. **(b)** (of a person) without engagements or things to do; not busy (指人)有空的, 闲着的: *I'm usually free in the afternoon.* 我通常下午有空. ○ *Are you free for lunch?* 你有空儿去吃午饭吗? **9** [pred 作表语] **~ with sth** giving sth easily and readily; generous with sth 大方; 慷慨: *He is very free with his time*, ie gives it willingly. 他毫不吝惜自己的时间. ○ *He's a bit too free with his compliments.* 他有点太爱恭维人. **10** (*derog* 贬) uncontrolled, often to the point of rudeness; too familiar 不约束的; 放肆的; 过于亲密的: *I don't like him — he is too free in his language and manner.* 我不喜欢他——他的言行太放肆. **11** (of a translation) expressing the meaning of the original loosely, not exactly (指译文)不拘泥原文的, 不确切的. Cf 参看 LITERAL 1a. **12** (*chemistry* 化) not combined with another element 未与其他元素化合的; 游离的: *free hydrogen* 游离氢. **13** (idm 习语) **feel free** ⇨ FEEL[1]. **(get sth) for ˈfree** without payment being required; for nothing 不要钱的; 白给的: *I got this ticket for free from sb who didn't want it.* 我这张票没花钱, 是别人不要的. **free and ˈeasy**

informal; relaxed 不拘束的; 不拘礼的; 轻松的: *The atmosphere in the office is quite free and easy.* 办公室的气氛很轻松. **free on 'board/'rail** (of goods) without charge for delivery to a ship/train (指货物)船[火车]上交货(价格). **get, have, etc a free 'hand** get, have, etc permission or an opportunity to do what one chooses and make one's own decisions, esp in a job 有自主权(尤指工作上): *My boss has given me a free hand in deciding which outside contractor to use.* 老板已经给了我自主权, 让我决定用哪家承包商. **give, allow, etc free 'play/'rein to sb/sth** give, etc complete freedom of movement or expression to sb/sth 给予...某人[某事物]行动或表达上的充分自由: *In this picture the artist certainly allowed his imagination free rein.* 艺术家在这幅画里任其想像力尽情奔驰. **have one's hands free/tied** ⇨ HAND[1]. **make sb free of sth** allow sb full use or enjoyment of sth 允许某人充分利用或享受某物; 随意使用: *He kindly made me free of his library for my research.* 他热情地让我随意使用他的书房做研究工作. **of one's own free will** without being ordered or forced 非强迫的; 自愿的: *I came here of my own free will.* 我是自愿到这里来的.

▷ **free** *adv* **1** without cost or payment; freely 无偿地; 免费地: *Children under five usually travel free on trains.* 五岁以下的儿童乘火车通常免费. **2** (idm 习语) **make free with sb/sth** treat sb/sth casually and without proper respect; use sth as if it belongs to oneself 对待某人[某事物]随便而不尊重; 任意使用他人之物: *He made free with all his girl-friend's money.* 他随便花女朋友的钱.

freely /'fri:lɪ; 'frilɪ/ *adv* **1** without any obstruction; in an unrestricted or uncontrolled manner 自由地; 毫无妨碍地; 不受阻挡地; 不受控制地; 无拘无束地: *Water flowed freely from the pipe.* 水从管道里通畅地流了出来. ○ *drugs that are freely available* 可随时买到的药物. **2** in an open and honest manner 开诚布公地; 坦诚地; 坦率地: *It may require courage to speak freely.* 要有勇气才能直言不讳. **3** willingly; readily 心甘情愿地; 自愿地: *I freely admit that I made a mistake.* 我欣然承认我犯了个错误. **4** in a generous and willing manner 大方地; 慷慨地; 爽快地: *Millions of people gave freely in response to the famine appeal.* 千百万人响应救灾呼吁而慷慨解囊.

□ **free 'agent** someone able to act as he pleases, because he is not responsible to anyone 可以按自己意愿行事的人: *I wish I were a free agent, but my contract binds me for three more years.* 我要是不受约束就好了, 可是我的合同还要约束我三年.

,free associ'ation (*psychology* 心) method of analysis in which a person says the first word that comes to his mind in response to one spoken by the analyst 自由联想.

,Free 'Church Church that does not follow the teaching or practices of established Churches such as the Roman Catholic or Anglican Church 独立教会.

,free 'enterprise operation of business and trade without government control 自由企业.

,free 'fall **1** movement through air or space under the force of gravity alone 自由降落. **2** part of a parachute jump before the parachute opens 降落伞张开前的降落.

'Freefone *n* [U] (*Brit*) system in which the person making a telephone call does not pay for the cost of the call 免费通话(打电话者不必付费的通话方式): *Ring the operator and ask for Freefone 8921.* 接通接线生, 然后要免费通话8921号.

'free-for-all *n* noisy fight or argument in which anyone present may join 在场者都可参加的争吵或辩论.

'free-hand *adj*, *adv* (done) by hand, without the use of an instrument, eg a ruler or compass 徒手(做)(的)(不使用仪器): *a free-hand sketch* 手画的略图 ○ *sketched free-hand* 徒手画略图.

,free-'handed *adj* generous, esp in spending or giving money 慷慨的(尤指花钱或给钱); 出手大方的.

'freehold *n*, *adj* (*law* 律) (having) complete ownership of property for an unlimited period of time 财产的完全保有(的). Cf 参看 LEASEHOLD (LEASE). **'freeholder** *n* person who owns land freehold 地产的完全保有者.

'free house (*Brit*) public house or inn not controlled by a brewery and therefore able to sell more than one brand of beer, etc (不受酿酒厂约束的)出售多种啤酒等的酒馆. Cf 参看 TIED HOUSE (TIE[2]).

,free 'kick (in football) kick taken without interference, as a penalty against the opposing team (足球)罚任意球.

'free lance /lɑ:ns; *US* læns; 'læns/ (also **freelancer**) *n* independent artist, writer, etc who earns his living by selling work to several employers (靠出卖作品为生的)自由艺术家、作家等: [attrib 作定语] *free-lance journalism* 自由新闻工作.

'free-lance *v* [I]: *I've free-lanced for several years.* 我做自由撰稿人已有几年了.

free-'living *adj* living for the pleasures of (esp) food and drink 沉溺于(尤指)吃喝享受的. **free-'liver** *n*.

free-'load *v* [I] (*infml* 口 *esp US*) take advantage of free food and lodging, etc without giving anything in return; sponge 占便宜; 揩油. **free-'loader** *n* person who free-loads; sponger 爱占便宜的人; 揩油的人.

,free 'love (*dated* 旧) agreed sexual relations without marriage 自由性爱.

freeman *n* **1** /-mæn; -mæn/ person who is not a slave 自由人(非奴隶). **2** /-mən; -mən/ person who has been given the freedom(5) of a city 荣誉市民: *made a freeman of the City of London* 被授予伦敦荣誉市民称号.

'free port port open to all traders, with no restrictions, taxes or import duties 自由港.

'Freepost *n* [U] (*Brit*) system in which postage costs are paid by the receiver (usu a business company) 免费邮递(由收信人, 通常为厂商, 付邮资的方式): *Reply to Publicity Department, FREEPOST, Oxford University Press, Oxford.* 回信免费邮寄至牛津牛津大学出版社宣传部.

,free-'range *adj* [attrib 作定语] produced by hens that are kept in natural conditions rather than in a battery(4) 放养的母鸡产的: *free-range 'eggs* 放养的母鸡产的蛋.

,free 'speech right to express (in public) opinions of any kind 言论自由.

,free-'standing *adj* not supported by or fixed to anything 无支撑物的; 不固于某物上的: *a free-'standing sculpture* 独立的雕塑.

'free-style *n* [U] **1** (**a**) swimming race in which any stroke may be used 自由泳比赛(可采用任何姿势). (**b**) type of swimming stroke, usu the crawl(*n* 2) 自由泳(通常指爬泳). **2** type of wrestling with few restrictions on the holds permitted (摔跤)自由式.

,free-'thinker *n* person who forms ideas independently of generally accepted religious teachings 自由思想者. **,free-'thinking** *adj*.

,free 'trade (system in which) trade is carried on between countries without import restrictions, eg tax and duty 自由贸易; 自由贸易制度.

,free 'verse poetry without a regular rhythm or rhyme 自由诗(无固定韵律的诗).

,free 'vote vote in parliament in which members do not have to follow party policy 自由投票(议员无须遵循党派的方针而进行的议会内投票).

'freeway *n* (*US*) = MOTORWAY (MOTOR). ⇨Usage at ROAD 用法见ROAD.

,free 'wheel (rear) wheel on a bicycle that continues to revolve when the pedals are not in use (自行车的)飞轮.

,free-'wheel *v* [I] **1** travel, usu downhill, by riding a bicycle without pedalling or driving a car without using engine power (自行车或汽车)滑行. **2** move or act freely or irresponsibly 自由地、不须负责地活动或行动: *I think I'll just free-wheel this summer and see what happens.* 我打算今年夏天尽情放任一下再说.

,free 'will **1** ability to decide one's own course of action 决定个人行动方针的能力; 自觉自愿: *I did it of my own free will*, ie acting voluntarily. 那是我自愿做的. **2** (belief in the) power to decide a course of action independently of God or fate 自由意志(不依靠上帝或命运而采取行动的决断力); 自由意志论. **,free-'will** *adj* voluntary 自愿的: *a ,free-will 'offering* 自愿的提供.

free[2] /fri:; fri/ *v* (*pt*, *pp* **freed** /fri:d; frid/) **1** [Tn, Tn·pr] **~ sth (from sth)** make (sb/sth) free; release or liberate 使(某人[某物])自由; 释放; 解放: *free the prisoner* 释放囚犯 ○ *free an animal from a trap* 把动物从陷阱中放出来. **2** [Tn·pr] **~ sb/sth of/from sth** take away sth unpleasant, unwanted, etc from sb/sth; rid sb/

sth of sth 使令人不快的、不需要的一类事物离开某人[某事物]; 使某人[某事物]摆脱某事物: *Relaxation exercises can free your body of tension.* 放松运动可以松缓身体的紧张. ○ *Try to free yourself from all prejudices.* 尽量消除一切偏见. **3** [Tn, Tn·pr] **~ sb/sth (from sth)** loosen sb/sth from sth that is preventing movement; disentangle or extricate sb/sth 使某人[某事物]摆脱妨碍活动的事物; 摆脱或脱离某人[某事物]: *It took hours to free the victims (from the collapsed building).* 用了很长时间才把遇难者(从倒塌的建筑物中)解救出来. ○ *Can you free the propeller from the weeds?* 你能把螺旋桨上的草除掉吗? **4** [Tn·pr, Cn·t] **~ sb/sth for sth** make sb/sth available for (a purpose or an activity) 使某人[某物]可用于(某一目的或活动): *The government intends to free more resources for educational purposes.* 政府想把更多的资源用于教育方面. ○ *Retiring early from his job freed him to join several local clubs.* 他早早退休, 摆脱了工作的羁绊而加入了当地的几个俱乐部.

-free *comb form* 构词成分 (forming *adjs* and *adv* 用以构成形容词和副词) without; free from 无; 免除: *carefree* ○ *duty-free* ○ *trouble-free*.

free·bie /ˈfriːbiː; ˋfribi/ *n* (*infml* 口 *esp US*) thing given away free 免费的物品; 赠品: *I got these mugs as freebies at the supermarket.* 我这些缸子是超级市场给的赠品.

free·dom /ˈfriːdəm; ˋfridəm/ *n* **1** [U] condition of being free; state of not being a prisoner or slave 自由: *After 10 years in prison, he was given his freedom.* 他坐了10年监狱以后又得到了自由. **2** (**a**) [U, C] **~ (of sth)** right (esp political) to act, speak, etc as one pleases without interference (随意行动、讲话等的, 尤指政治的)自由权: *freedom of speech, thought, worship, etc* 言论、思想、礼拜等的自由权 ○ *press freedom* 出版自由 ○ *preserve the freedoms of the trade-union movement* 保护工会运动的自由权. (**b**) [U] **~ (of sth)**; **~ (to do sth)** state of being unrestricted in one's actions; liberty 个人的行动自主; 自由: *freedom of action, choice, decision, etc* 行动、选择、决定等的自由 ○ *He enjoyed complete freedom to do as he wished.* 他享有完全按照自己的意愿行事的自由. **3** [U] **~ from sth** state of being without or not affected by the thing specified 无某事物的情况; 不受某事物影响的状态: *freedom from fear, pain, hunger, etc* 无恐惧、痛苦、饥饿等. **4** [sing] **the ~ of sth** unrestricted use of sth 随意使用某物的权利: *I gave him the freedom of my house and belongings.* 我让他随便使用我的房子和东西. **5** (idm 习语) **give, etc sb his ˈfreedom** agree to a divorce; allow one's husband/wife to leave without opposing him/her legally 同意离婚; 给予自由身分(允许丈夫[妻子]离去而不依法追究): *It seems foolish not to give Ann her freedom, if that's what she really wants.* 安要是真想离婚的话, 不同意她离就太蠢了. **give sb, receive, etc the freedom of the ˈcity** give, etc special rights of citizenship, esp as an honour for public services 授予荣誉市民权.

□ **ˈfreedom fighter** person belonging to a group that use violent means to overthrow the government and achieve the independence of their country 自由战士(用暴力推翻政府以使自己的国家独立的人).

Free·ma·son /ˈfriːmeɪsn; ˋfriˌmesn̩/ *n* member of an international secret society with the aims of offering mutual help and developing friendly relations among its members 共济会会员(旨在互相帮助、发展会员间友好关系的国际秘密组织的成员).

▷ **Free·ma·sonry** *n* [U] **1** system, practices and rites of the Freemasons 共济会的制度、活动及仪式. **2** **freemasonry** natural sympathy and unspoken understanding between people sharing similar interests 谅解; 默契: *the freemasonry of TV reporters, professional photographers, etc* 电视记者、职业摄影师等的默契.

free·sia /ˈfriːzɪə; *US* ˈfriːʒ-; ˋfriʒɪə/ *n* plant with fragrant yellow, pink, or white flowers 小苍兰(开黄色、粉色或白色花, 味香).

freeze /friːz; friz/ *v* (*pt* **froze** /frəʊz; froz/, *pp* **frozen** /ˈfrəʊzn; ˋfrozn̩/) **1** [I, Tn] (esp of water) change or be changed from liquid to solid by extreme cold (尤指水)结冰; 凝固: *Water freezes at 0°C.* 水在0°C时结冰. ○ *The severe cold froze the pond.* 天气寒冷池塘结了冰. Cf 参看 THAW. ⇨Usage at WATER[1] 用法见WATER[1]. **2** [I, Ip, Tn, Tn·p] **~ (sth) (up)** (cause sth to) become full of ice or hardened with ice (使某物)结满冰或由于结冰变硬: *The land itself freezes (up) in such low temperatures.* 温度这么低, 地都冻硬了. ○ *Our (water) pipes froze (up)* (ie were blocked with ice) *last winter.* 去年冬天, 我们的(水)管子冻了. ○ *The clothes were frozen on the washing-line.* 衣服在晾衣绳上冻住了. **3** [I] (used with *it* 与it连用) (of weather) be so cold that water turns to ice; be extremely cold (指天气)冷得使水结成冰, 严寒: *It's freezing outside!* 外面冷极了! ○ *It may freeze tonight, so make sure the plants are covered.* 今晚大概会有霜冻, 一定要把花草都遮盖好. **4** [I, Tn only passive 只用于被动语态] (cause a person or an animal to) be or feel very cold; (cause to) die from cold (使人或动物)冷或觉得很冷; (使)冻死: *Shut the window — I'm freezing!* 关上窗户——我冷极了! ○ *Two men froze to death/were frozen to death on the mountain.* 有两个人在山上冻死了. **5** [I, Tn] (of food, etc) be able to be preserved by being stored at a temperature below freezing-point; preserve (food, etc), in this way (指食物等)能冷冻储藏; 冷藏(食物等): *Some fruits don't freeze well at all.* 有些水果根本就不能冷藏. ○ *I'll buy extra meat and just freeze it.* 我要多买些肉冷藏起来. ○ *Strawberries don't taste nice if they've been frozen.* 草莓若冷冻就不好吃了. ○ *a packet of frozen peas* 一包冷藏豌豆. **6** [I, Tn] (cause a person or an animal to) stop suddenly; make or become unable to move, speak, or act, because of fear, shock, etc (使人或动物)突然停住; (因恐惧、震惊等)使得或变得不能活动、说话或行动; 惊呆; 吓呆: *Ann froze with terror as the door opened silently.* 门一声不响地开了, 把安吓呆了. ○ *The sudden bang froze us in our tracks.* 突然砰的一响, 顿时把我们惊呆了. **7** [Tn] hold (wages, prices, etc) at a fixed level officially for a period of time 稳定(工资、物价等): *freeze wages, prices, fares, etc* 稳定工资、物价、车费等. **8** [Tn] not allow (money or assets) to be used or exchanged, usu by government order 冻结(钱或资产): *freeze a society's funds* 冻结一团体的基金 ○ *frozen assets* 被冻结的资产. **9** (idm 习语) **freeze one's blood/make one's blood freeze** fill one with feelings of fear and horror 使充满害怕、恐怖的感觉: *The sight of the masked gunman made my blood freeze.* 我一看见那个持枪的蒙面人就吓得浑身冰凉. **10** (phr v) **freeze sb out** (*infml* 口) exclude sb from business or from society by harsh competition or unfriendly behaviour (以残酷的竞争或敌意的态度)将某人(从生意或团体中)逼走, 挤走: *Small shops are being frozen out by the big supermarkets.* 小铺子都要让大超级市场给挤垮了. **freeze (sth) over** (usu passive 通常用于被动语态) (cause sth to) become covered by ice (使某物)被冰封住: *The lake was frozen over until late spring.* 那湖全让冰封住了, 到晚春才解冻. **freeze (sth) up** (usu passive 通常用于被动语态) freeze (sth) so as to prevent normal use 冻住(某物)(以至妨碍正常使用): *The window has frozen up and I can't open it.* 窗户给冻上了, 我打不开.

▷ **freeze** *n* **1** (also **ˈfreeze-up**) period of weather during which temperatures are below freezing-point 冰冻期; 严寒期: *last year's big freeze* 去年的严寒期 ○ *After the last freeze-up we put insulation round the pipes.* 我们在上个冰冻期之后把管道用保温材料裹上了. **2** official fixing of wages, prices, etc for a period of time (官方对工资、物价等的)冻结: *a wage/price freeze* 工资[物价]冻结.

□ **ˈfreeze-dry** *v* (*pt, pp* **-dried**) [Tn] preserve (esp food) by freezing and then drying it in a vacuum 冷冻干燥保存(尤指食物).

ˈfreezing-point (also **freezing**) *n* [U] temperature at which a liquid, esp water, freezes 冰点; 凝固点: *The freezing-point of water is 0°C.* 水的冰点是0°C. ○ *Tonight the temperature will fall to 3 degrees below freezing.* 今夜的温度将降至冰点下3度. ⇨App 5 见附录5.

freezer /ˈfriːzə(r); ˋfrizɚ/ *n* **1** (also ˌ**deep ˈfreeze**) large refrigerator or room in which food is stored for a long time at a temperature below freezing point 冰柜; 冷藏室. **2** small compartment in a refrigerator for freezing ice and storing frozen food (冰箱里的)冷冻室.

freight /freɪt; fret/ *n* [U] goods transported by ships, aeroplanes, or trains (水运、空运、陆运的)货物: *send goods by air freight* 空运发货. ⇨Usage at CARGO 用法见CARGO.

▷ **freight** *v* **1** [Tn] transport (merchandise) as freight

运送(货物). **2** [Tn·pr] **~ sth with sth** load (a ship, etc) with freight 装货于(船等): *a barge freighted with bananas* 载着香蕉的驳船.

freighter *n* ship or aircraft that carries mainly freight 货船; 运输机.

□ **freight car** (*US*) = WAGON 2.

ˈ**freightliner** *n* (also **liner train, liner**) fast train carrying goods in special large containers that can be loaded and unloaded quickly and easily 集装箱列车; 货柜列车.

ˈ**freight train** (*US*) (*Brit* **goods train**) train that carries goods only 货运列车.

French /frentʃ; frɛntʃ/ *n* **1 the French** [pl *v*] the people who live in France 法国人: *The French are renowned for their cooking.* 法国人擅长烹饪. **2** [U] language spoken in France and parts of Belgium, Switzerland, and Canada 法语: *French is a Romance language.* 法语是罗曼语. **3** (idm 习语) **excuse/pardon my ˈFrench** (*infml euph* 口, 婉) excuse the swear-words I shall use 原谅我要说骂人的话了: *Excuse my French, but he's a bloody nuisance!* 别怪我骂人, 可他实在太不是东西! **take French ˈleave** leave one's work, duty, etc without permission 未经允许而脱离工作、岗位等; 擅离职守; 不辞而别.

▷ **French** *adj* of France, its people or its language 法国的; 法国人的; 法国语的: *the French countryside* 法国的乡村.

□ ˌ**French ˈbean** kidney or haricot bean, the pod and seeds of which are eaten as a vegetable 菜豆.

ˌ**French Caˈnadian** Canadian whose native language is French 以法语为母语的加拿大人.

ˌ**French ˈchalk** finely powdered talc, used as a marker, dry lubricant, etc 滑石粉.

ˌ**French ˈdressing** salad dressing of seasoned oil and vinegar 油和醋调成的色拉调料.

ˌ**French ˈfry** (*esp US*) = CHIP[1] 3.

ˌ**French ˈhorn** brass wind instrument with a long tube coiled in a circle and a wide bell 法国号(一种铜管乐器). ⇨illus at App 1 见附录1插图, page x.

ˌ**French ˈletter** (*infml* 口 *esp Brit*) contraceptive sheath; condom 避孕套; 阴茎套.

ˌ**French ˈloaf** (also ˌ**French ˈbread**) long thin loaf of crusty white bread 法国面包(长条状的). ⇨illus at BREAD 见 BREAD 插图.

ˈ**Frenchman** *n* (*pl* **-men** /-mən; -mən/) man of French birth or nationality 法国男人.

ˌ**French ˈpolish** varnish consisting of shellac and alcohol, painted onto wood to give a hard shiny surface 罩光漆. **French-polish** *v* [Tn] treat (wood) with French polish 给(木材)涂罩光漆.

ˌ**French ˈseam** seam on a garment, etc with the raw edges turned and sewn under 法式线缝; 来去线缝.

ˌ**French ˈwindow** (*US* also ˌ**French ˈdoor**) one of a pair of doors with long glass panes, usu opening onto a garden or balcony 落地窗(通常为通向花园或阳台的). ⇨illus at App 1 见附录1插图, page vii.

ˈ**Frenchwoman** *n* (*pl* **-women** /-wɪmɪn; -ˌwɪmɪn/) woman of French birth or nationality 法国女子.

fren·etic (also **phren·etic**) /frəˈnetɪk; frəˋnɛtɪk/ *adj* very excited; frenzied; frantic 非常激动的; 狂乱的; 发狂的: *frenetic activity* 疯狂的活动. ▷ **fren·et·ic·ally** /-klɪ; -klɪ/ *adv*.

frenzy /ˈfrenzɪ; ˋfrɛnzɪ/ *n* [sing, U] state of extreme excitement; extreme and wild activity or behaviour 极度激动的状态; 极度狂乱的活动或行为: *in a frenzy of zeal, enthusiasm, hate, etc* 疯狂的激情、热情、仇恨等 ○ *The speaker worked the crowd up into a (state of) frenzy.* 演讲者煽动起群众疯狂的情绪.

▷ **fren·zied** /ˈfrenzɪd; ˋfrɛnzɪd/ *adj* [usu attrib 通常作定语] wildly excited or agitated; frantic 狂乱的; 狂躁的; 发狂的: *The dog jumped at the intruder with frenzied barks.* 那狗狂吠着跳起扑向闯进来的人. ○ *the mob's frenzied attack* 暴徒的疯狂攻击. **fren·ziedly** *adv*.

fre·quency /ˈfriːkwənsɪ; ˋfrikwənsɪ/ *n* **1** [U] (**a**) rate of occurrence or repetition of sth, usu measured over a particular period of time (某事发生或重复的)频率: *Fatal accidents have decreased in frequency over recent years.* 近年来死亡事故发生的频率已经下降. ○ *the alarming frequency of computer errors* 计算机差错惊人的频密. (**b**) fact of being frequent or happening often 屡次; 频繁: *the frequency of premature births in this region* 该地区早产情况的频繁. **2** [C, U] rate at which a sound wave or radio wave vibrates; band or group of similar frequencies (声波或无线电波的)振动频率; 波段: *high-/low-frequency sounds* 高[低]频的声音 ○ *a musical note with a frequency of 256 vibrations per second* 振动频率为每秒256次的音调 ○ *In the evening this station changes frequency and broadcasts on another band.* 该电台晚上改变频率, 在另一波段播音.

fre·quent[1] /ˈfriːkwənt; ˋfrikwənt/ *adj* happening often; habitual 时常发生的; 惯常的: *the car manufacturer's frequent changes of models* 汽车制造厂产品型号的经常变换 ○ *His visits became less frequent as time passed.* 他渐渐地不常登门了.

▷ **fre·quently** *adv* often 时常; 经常: *Buses run frequently from the city to the airport.* 公共汽车频繁地从城市驶往机场.

fre·quent[2] /frɪˈkwent; frɪˋkwɛnt/ *v* [Tn] (*fml* 文) often go to or visit (a place) 常去, 常到(一地方): *He used to frequent the town's bars and night-clubs.* 他从前常去镇上的酒吧和夜总会.

fresco /ˈfreskəʊ; ˋfrɛsko/ *n* (*pl* **~s** or **~es** /-kəʊz; -koz/) picture painted in water-colour on a wall or ceiling before the plaster is dry (墙壁或天花板未干时绘制的)壁画: *The frescos in the Sistine Chapel are world-famous.* 西斯廷教堂的壁画举世闻名.

fresh /freʃ; frɛʃ/ *adj* (**-er, -est**) **1** (**a**) [usu attrib 通常作定语] new or different 新的; 不同的: *fresh evidence* 新的证据 ○ *a fresh piece of paper* 另一张纸 ○ *make a fresh start* 重新开始 ○ *fresh problems* 新问题 ○ *a fresh approach* (ie one that is original in a lively and attractive way) *to the difficulty* 解决困难的别开生面的方法. (**b**) made, obtained or experienced recently and not changed 新做的; 新得到的; 刚经历的: *fresh tracks in the snow* 雪地上的新痕迹 ○ *Their memories of the wedding are still fresh in their minds.* 他们至今对婚礼仍记忆犹新. **2** (**a**) (usu of food) newly made, produced, gathered, etc; not stale (通常指食物)新做的, 新出的, 新采的, 新鲜的: *fresh bread*, ie just baked 新烤的面包 ○ *fresh flowers, eggs, milk, etc* 新鲜的花、蛋、奶等. (**b**) (of food) not preserved in tins, with salt or by freezing (指食物)鲜的, 非罐头的, 未加盐的, 未冷冻的: *fresh vegetables, fruit, meat, etc* 鲜的蔬菜、水果、肉等. **3** (of clothes) not already used or worn; clean (指衣服)未经穿用的, 清洁的: *put on some fresh clothes* 穿几件新衣服. **4** (of water) not salty, stale or bitter; not sea water (指水)不咸的, 不腐的, 不苦的, 淡的. **5** (**a**) (of the air) clean and refreshing; pure (指空气)清洁的, 清新的, 纯净的: *Open the window and let in some fresh air.* 打开窗户放进些新鲜空气. ○ *play in the fresh air*, ie outside 在户外玩耍. (**b**) (of weather) rather cold and windy; (of the wind) cool and fairly strong (指天气)冷而有风的; (指风)凉飕飕的: *It's a bit fresh this morning, isn't it?* 今天早晨有点儿凉丝丝的吧? **6** [usu attrib 通常作定语] (**a**) (of colours) clear and bright; unfaded (指颜色)鲜明的, 鲜艳的, 未褪色的: *fresh colours in these old prints* 旧印刷物上的鲜艳色彩. (**b**) (of skin) clear and healthy (指皮肤)白净健康的: *a fresh complexion* 气色好的面容. **7** (of paint) just applied (指油漆)刚上的, 未干的: *Fresh paint — please do not touch.* 油漆未干——请勿触摸. **8** [usu pred 通常作表语] having renewed strength; refreshed and ready to tackle work, etc 又有活力; 又精神饱满: *I feel really fresh after my holiday.* 我度假之后真觉得又精神饱满了. **9** [pred 作表语] **~ from/out of sth** having just come from (a place) or having just had (a particular experience); straight from sth 刚从(某地)来; 刚有过(某一经历); 直接来自某事物: *students fresh from college* 刚从学校毕业的学生. **10** [pred 作表语] **~ (with sb)** (*infml* 口) too forward in behaviour or speech, esp in a sexual manner, with a person of the opposite sex (言行)过于卤莽(尤指对异性), 无礼, 放肆: *He then started to get fresh with me.* 他于是对我放肆起来. **11** (idm 习语) **break fresh/new ground** ⇨ GROUND[1]. **a breath of fresh air** ⇨ BREATH. **(as) fresh as a ˈdaisy** vigorous and lively or attractive, esp in a clean fresh way 生动活泼的, 有吸引力的(尤指以新的方式). **new/fresh blood** ⇨ BLOOD[1].

F

▷ **fresh** *adv* (idm 习语) **fresh out of sth** (*infml* 口 *esp US*) having just used all one's supplies of sth 刚刚(将储备的某物)用尽: *We're fresh out of eggs.* 我们刚把所有的鸡蛋都吃光了.

fresh- (forming compound *adjs* 用以构成复合形容词) newly; just 新近的; 刚刚的: *fresh-baked bread* ○ *fresh-cut flowers.*

fresher *n* (*Brit infml* 口) student in his/her first year at university or college 大学或学院一年级学生.

freshly *adv* (usu followed by past participles 通常后接过去分词) recently; newly 新近; 刚刚: *freshly picked strawberries* 新摘的草莓 ○ *freshly laid eggs* 刚生的蛋.

fresh·ness *n* [U].

□ ˈ**freshman** /-mən; -mən/ *n* (*pl* **-men** /-mən; -mən/) (*US*) student in his/her first year at college, high school or university 大学、学院或中学一年级的学生.

ˈ**freshwater** *adj* [attrib 作定语] from, of, living in or containing fresh (not salty or sea) water 来自淡水的; 淡水的; 生活于淡水的; 含淡水的: *freshwater fish* 淡水鱼 ○ *freshwater lakes* 淡水湖. Cf 参看 SALTWATER (SALT).

freshen /ˈfreʃn; ˋfrɛʃən/ *v* **1** [Tn, Tn·p] ~ **sth (up)** make sth fresh 使某物新鲜: *A good clean will really freshen (up) the house.* 好好收拾一下的确会使房子焕然一新. **2** [I] (of the wind) become strong and cool (指风)变得强而凉, 变得凉飕飕. **3** [Tn] (*US*) add (more liquid, esp alcohol) to a drink (往饮料中)添加(液体, 尤指酒): *Can I freshen your drink?* 我再给你添些酒好吗? **4** (phr v) **freshen (oneself) up** wash and make (oneself) look clean and tidy after a journey, before a meeting, etc (为自己)梳洗: *I'll just go and freshen (myself) up before the interview.* 我这就去梳洗打扮一番再去会面.

▷ **fresh·ener** /ˈfreʃnə(r); ˋfrɛʃənɚ/ *n* thing that freshens sth 使某物变得清新之物: *an* ˈ*air-freshener* 空气清新剂[器].

fret[1] /fret; frɛt/ *v* (**-tt-**) **1** [I, Ipr, Tn] ~ **(about/at/over sth)** (cause sb to) become unhappy, bad-tempered, or anxious about sth; worry (使某人)不愉快, 烦躁, 焦急, 发愁, 担心: *Don't fret, we'll get there on time.* 别着急, 我们能准时到那里. ○ *Fretting about it won't help.* 发愁于事无补. ○ *Babies often fret (themselves) when their mothers are not near.* 婴儿常常因母亲不在身边而哭闹. **2** [Tn] wear (sth) away by rubbing or biting 磨损, 咬坏(某物): *a horse fretting its bit* 咬嚼子的马 ○ *a fretted rope* 磨损的绳子.

▷ **fret** *n* [sing] state of irritation, worry 烦躁; 担忧: *be in a fret* 担忧.

fret·ful /-fl; -fəl/ *adj* irritable or complaining, esp because unhappy or worried 烦躁的, 发牢骚的(尤指因不愉快或烦恼): *a fretful child* 烦躁的孩子. **fret·fully** *adv*.

fret[2] /fret; frɛt/ *v* (**-tt-**) [Tn esp passive 尤用于被动语态] decorate (wood, etc) with patterns made by cutting or sawing 以刻出的或锯出的图案装饰(木制品等): *an elaborately fretted border* 回纹饰边.

□ ˈ**fretsaw** *n* narrow saw fixed in a frame, used for cutting designs in thin sheets of wood 线锯; 钢丝锯; 镂花锯.

ˈ**fretwork** *n* [U] ornamental work in a decorative pattern, esp wood cut into patterns with a fretsaw 回纹细工; 万字细工.

fret[3] /fret; frɛt/ *n* one of the bars or ridges on the finger-board of a guitar, etc, used as a guide for the fingers to press the strings at the correct place (吉他等指板上的)柱, 马, 品, 桥. ⇨illus at App 1 见附录1插图, page xi.

Freud·ian /ˈfrɔɪdɪən; ˋfrɔɪdɪən/ *adj* of or related to the theories of the Austrian psychiatrist Sigmund Freud (1856-1939) about the working of the human mind, esp his theories about subconscious sexual ideas or feelings (奥地利心理学家)弗洛伊德学说的, 与弗洛伊德学说有关的(尤指对性的潜在的意识或感觉的理论).

□ ˌ**Freudian** ˈ**slip** comment made accidentally by a speaker instead of what was originally intended, but which is considered to reveal his true thoughts 走嘴, 溜嘴(不留神而吐露的真心话).

Fri *abbr* 缩写 = Friday: *Fri 7 March* 3月7日星期五.

fri·able /ˈfraɪəbl; ˋfraɪəbḷ/ *adj* (*fml* 文) easily broken up or crumbled 易破的; 易碎的; 脆的: *friable soil* 松土. ▷ **fri·ab·il·ity** /ˌfraɪəˈbɪlətɪ; ˌfraɪəˋbɪlətɪ/ *n* [U].

friar /ˈfraɪə(r); ˋfraɪɚ/ *n* man who is a member of one of certain Roman Catholic religious orders, and who works with people in the outside world rather than living in retreat 托钵修士. Cf 参看 MONK.

▷ **fri·ary** /ˈfraɪərɪ; ˋfraɪərɪ/ *n* building in which friars live 男修道院.

fric·as·see /ˈfrɪkəsiː; ˌfrɪkəˋsi/ *n* [C, U] dish of pieces of cooked meat or poultry served in a thick white sauce 烹制后浇白色浓汁的肉块、鸡块等: *chicken fricassee* 白汁鸡块.

fric·at·ive /ˈfrɪkətɪv; ˋfrɪkətɪv/ *n, adj* (consonant) made by forcing air through an opening made narrow by bringing the tongue or lips near to another part of the mouth 由摩擦产生的(辅音): /f, v, θ/ *are fricatives.* /f/、/v/、/θ/是摩擦辅音.

fric·tion /ˈfrɪkʃn; ˋfrɪkʃən/ *n* **1** [U] (**a**) rubbing of one surface or thing against another 摩擦: *Friction between two sticks can create a fire.* 两个棍棒相互摩擦能起火. (**b**) resistance of one surface to another surface or substance that moves over it 摩擦力: *The force of friction affects the speed at which spacecraft can re-enter the earth's atmosphere.* 摩擦力能影响航天器返回地球大气层的速度. **2** [U, C] disagreement or conflict between people or parties with different views 人或党派之间不同观点的矛盾或冲突: *There is a great deal of friction between the management and the work force.* 劳资双方之间存在大量矛盾. ○ *conflicts and frictions that have still to be resolved* 仍须解决的冲突和摩擦.

Fri·day /ˈfraɪdɪ; ˋfraɪdɪ/ *n* [U, C] (*abbr* 缩写 **Fri**) the sixth day of the week, next after Thursday 星期五.

For the uses of *Friday* see the examples at *Monday.* 关于Friday的用法见 Monday 词条中的示例.

fridge /frɪdʒ; frɪdʒ/ *n* (*infml* 口) refrigerator 冰箱.

□ ˌ**fridge-**ˈ**freezer** *n* upright unit containing separate refrigerator and freezer compartments (冷藏室和冷冻室分开的)立式冰箱.

fried *pt, pp* of FRY.

friend /frend; frɛnd/ *n* **1** person one knows and likes, but who is not a relation 朋友: *He's my friend.* 他是我的朋友. ○ *We are all good friends.* 我们都是好朋友. ○ *I've known her for years, but she was never a friend.* 我认识她多年了, 但成不了朋友. **2** ~ **of/to sth** helper, supporter, or patron of sth 某事物的帮助者、支持者或赞助者: *a friend of the arts/the poor* 有助于艺术的人、帮助贫民的人 ○ *a friend of justice, peace, etc* 维护正义、和平等的人 ○ *You are invited to become a Friend of the Bristol Hospice*, ie to contribute money regularly. 邀请您作布里斯托尔末期病人安养所的赞助人. **3** person who is of the same country, group, etc as oneself; ally 同胞; 国人; 自己人; 同盟者: *Who goes there — friend or foe?* 谁在那里——是自己人还是敌人? ○ *At last, among friends, he was free to speak his mind.* 他终于向自己人倾诉衷肠. **4** thing that is very helpful or familiar 极有益或极熟悉的事物: *Honesty has always been his best friend.* 忠实可靠一向使他受益匪浅. ○ *Let's look it up in our old friend, the dictionary.* 让我们请教一下老朋友——字典吧. **5 Friend** member of the Society of Friends; Quaker (基督教)公谊会教友. **6** (*fml* 文) person being addressed in public 在公开场合对人的称呼: *Our friend from China will now tell us about her research.* 现在我们的中国朋友要向大家介绍她自己的研究情况. ○ *Friends, it is with great pleasure that I introduce...* 朋友们, 我很高兴地介绍... ○ *My learned friend*, ie used by a lawyer of another lawyer in a lawcourt 律师在法庭上的互称 ○ *My honourable friend*, ie used by a Member of Parliament to another Member of Parliament in the House of Commons 在下议院, 国会议员间的互称. **7** (idm 习语) **be/make** ˈ**friends (with sb)** be/become a friend (of sb) 是[成为](某人的)朋友; 交朋友: *They soon forgot their differences and were friends again*, ie after a quarrel. 他们不久就捐弃前嫌而重归于好. ○ *David finds it hard to make friends (with other children).* 戴维觉得(与别的孩子)交朋友是很难的事. **a** ˌ**friend in** ˈ**need (is a** ˌ**friend in**ˈ**deed)** (*saying* 谚) a friend who helps one when one needs help (is a true friend) 患难之交(是真交).

▷ **friend·less** *adj* without any friends 无朋友的.

friendly /ˈfrendlɪ; ˋfrɛndlɪ/ *adj* (**-ier**, **-iest**) **1** (**a**)

behaving in a kind and pleasant way; acting like a friend 和蔼可亲的; 朋友般的; 友爱的: *a friendly person* 和蔼可亲的人 ○ *The children here are quite friendly with one another.* 这里的孩子相互之间十分友爱. ○ *It wasn't very friendly of you to slam the door in his face.* 你冲着他摔门太伤和气了. ○ *friendly nations*, ie not hostile 友邦. (**b**) showing or expressing kindness and helpfulness 亲切的; 友好的: *a friendly smile, welcome, gesture, manner, etc* 亲切的微笑、亲切的欢迎、友好的表示、友好的态度 ○ *friendly co-operation* 亲密的合作. (**c**) of a relationship in which people treat each other as friends 和睦的; 融洽的: *friendly relations* 和睦的关系 ○ *on friendly terms with the boss* 与老板关系融洽. **2** not seriously competitive (竞争)不激烈的, 友好的: *a friendly game of football* 足球友谊赛 ○ *a friendly argument* 友好的争论 ○ *friendly rivalry* 友好的竞争.
▷ **friend·li·ness** *n* [U].
-friendly (in compound *adjs* 用以构成复合形容词) that is, or is intended to be, easy for the specified person to use 便于某人使用的: *a user-friendly computer system*.
□ **ˈfriendly match** (also **friendly**) game of football, etc that is not part of a serious competitive series (足球等的)友谊比赛: *There's a friendly between Leeds United and Manchester City next week.* 利兹联队和曼彻斯特市队下星期有一场友谊赛.
ˈFriendly Society (also **ˈProvident Society**) association formed to support its members when they are ill or old 互助会.

friend·ship /ˈfrendʃɪp; ˋfrɛndʃɪp/ *n* (**a**) [U] feeling or relationship between friends; state of being friends 友情; 友谊; 友爱: *There were strong ties of friendship between the members of the society.* 该团体的成员之间有牢固的友情. ○ *The aim of the conference is to promote international friendship.* 会议的目的是增进国际间的友谊. (**b**) [C] instance of this 友情; 友谊: *At school she formed a close friendship with several other girls.* 她在学校里与几个女同学建立起亲密的友谊. ○ *I've had many friendships, but never such an intimate one.* 我交过很多朋友, 但从没有如此密切.

frieze /fri:z; friz/ *n* [C] band of sculpture or decoration round the top of a wall or building 雕带; (墙头或建筑物上端的)带状装饰. ⇨illus at COLUMN 见COLUMN插图.

frig /frɪg; frɪg/ *v* (**-gg-**) (phr v) **frig about/around** (⚠ *infml* 讳, 口) waste time; mess about 浪费时间; 吊儿郎当: *I've been frigging about all day.* 我一整天吊儿郎当.

frig·ate /ˈfrɪgət; ˋfrɪgɪt/ *n* small fast naval escort-vessel (小型)护卫舰.

frig·ging /ˈfrɪgɪŋ; ˋfrɪgɪŋ/ *adj* [attrib 作定语] (⚠ *sl* 讳, 俚) (used to emphasise a judgement or comment 用以加强判断或评论的语气) utter; absolute; bloody 完全的; 十足的; 绝对的; 该死的: *You frigging idiot!* 你这个该死的大笨蛋!

fright /fraɪt; fraɪt/ *n* **1** (**a**) [U] feeling of sudden unpleasant fear 惊吓: *trembling with fright* 吓得发抖. (**b**) [C usu *sing* 通常作单数] instance of this 惊吓: *You gave me (quite) a fright suddenly coming in here like that.* 你那样突然走到这里, 真吓了我一大跳. ○ *I got the fright of my life*, ie I was extremely frightened. 我吓得要命. **2** [C usu *sing* 通常作单数] (*infml* 口) person or thing that looks ridiculous or unattractive 奇形怪状的或不起眼的人或物: *She thinks that dress is pretty — I think she looks a fright in it.* 她以为那件衣服挺漂亮——依我看她穿着像个丑八怪. **3** (idm 习语) **take fright (at sth)** be extremely frightened (by sth) (被某事物)惊吓, 受惊: *The animals took fright at the sound of the gun.* 那些动物受到枪声的惊吓.

frighten /ˈfraɪtn; ˋfraɪtn/ *v* **1** [Tn] fill (sb) with fear; make afraid; scare (使某人)感到恐惧; 使害怕; 惊吓: *Sorry, I didn't mean to frighten you.* 对不起, 我不是故意吓唬你的. ○ *Loud traffic frightens horses.* 车辆噪音使马受惊. **2** (idm 习语) **frighten/scare sb to ˈdeath/out of his ˈwits; frighten the ˈlife out of sb** frighten sb very much; terrify or startle sb 惊吓某人; 使某人恐怖或惊愕: *The child was frightened to death by the violent thunderstorm.* 那孩子让狂风暴雨吓得要命. ○ *You frightened the life out of me/frightened me out of my wits suddenly knocking on the window like that!* 你突然那样敲窗户真把我的魂儿都吓掉了. **frighten/scare the daylights out of sb** ⇨ DAYLIGHTS. **3** (phr v) **frighten sb/sth away/off** force or drive (a person or an animal) to run away by frightening him/it 将(人或动物)吓跑: *The alarm frightened the burglars away.* 警铃声把贼吓跑了. ○ *The children's shouts frightened off the birds.* 孩子们的喊声把鸟儿吓飞了. **frighten sb into/out of doing sth** cause sb to do/not to do sth by frightening him 吓得某人做[不敢做]某事: *News of the robberies frightened many people into fitting new locks to their doors.* 发生抢劫的消息把许多人吓得装上新门锁.
▷ **fright·ened** *adj* in a state of fear; afraid; scared 恐惧的; 害怕的; 受惊的: *Frightened children were calling for their mothers.* 受惊的孩子们呼喊着找妈妈. ○ *He looked very frightened as he spoke.* 他说话时显得非常恐惧. ○ *They're frightened of losing power.* 他们害怕失去权力.
fright·en·ing /ˈfraɪtnɪŋ; ˋfraɪtn̩ɪŋ/ *adj* causing fear; alarming 引起恐惧的; 惊恐的; 可怕的: *a frightening possibility, situation, development, etc* 引起恐惧的可能性、形势、发展等 ○ *It is frightening even to think of the horrors of nuclear war.* 核战争的恐怖状况连想都不敢想. **fright·en·ingly** *adv*: *The film was frighteningly realistic.* 该影片逼真得令人害怕.

fright·ful /ˈfraɪtfl; ˋfraɪtfəl/ *adj* **1** very unpleasant; dreadful 令人厌恶的; 令人惧怕的; 可怕的: *a frightful accident* 可怕的事故. **2** [attrib 作定语] (*infml* 口) (used to emphasize a statement) extreme; extremely bad (用以加强叙述的语气)极端的, 极坏的, 极糟的: *in a frightful rush* 极其匆促 ○ *They left the house in a frightful mess.* 他们离去时房子里乱七八糟.
▷ **fright·fully** /-fəlɪ; -fəlɪ/ *adv* (*infml* 口) very; awfully 非常; 很; 太; 极: *I'm frightfully sorry, but I can't see you today.* 太对不起了, 我今天不能见你.

fri·gid /ˈfrɪdʒɪd; ˋfrɪdʒɪd/ *adj* **1** very cold 寒冷的; 严寒的: *a frigid climate/zone* 严寒的气候[地区]. **2** (esp of a woman) not responsive sexually (尤指女人)性冷感的. **3** formal and unfriendly, esp in relationships with other people 郑重而冷淡的(尤指与他人的关系): *a frigid glance, look, etc* 冷淡的目光、神情等. ▷ **fri·gid·ity** /frɪˈdʒɪdətɪ; frɪˋdʒɪdətɪ/ *n* [U]. **fri·gidly** *adv*.

frill 饰边

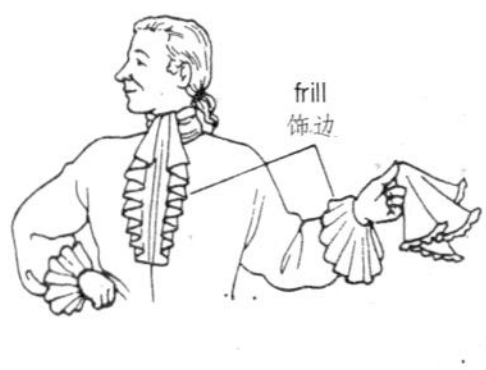

frill /frɪl; frɪl/ *n* **1** ornamental border on a garment or curtain, gathered or pleated at one edge (外衣或帘幕的)饰边, 褶边. ⇨illus 见插图. **2** (usu *pl* 通常作复数) (*fig* 比喻) additional item that is not essential for something but makes it more decorative (华而不实的)附加物: *a straightforward presentation with no frills* 直截了当、不加渲染的叙述.
▷ **frilled** *adj* decorated with frills (FRILL 1) 饰有褶边的: *a frilled blouse* 带褶边的女衬衫.
frilly /ˈfrɪlɪ; ˋfrɪlɪ/ *adj* having many frills (FRILL 1) 多饰边的; 多褶边的: *a frilly petticoat* 有很多褶边的衬裙.

fringe /frɪndʒ; frɪndʒ/ *n* **1** (*esp Brit*) (*US* **bang**) front hair cut so that it hangs over the forehead 垂在额前的短发; 刘海儿: *She has a fringe and glasses.* 她额前有刘海儿, 戴着眼镜. ⇨illus at HAIR 见HAIR插图. **2** decorative edge on a garment, rug, etc consisting of loose or hanging threads or cords (外衣、小地毯等的)饰边, 毛边, 穗子, 流苏. **3** outer edge of an area, group or activity (地方、群体或活动的)外围: *the fringe of a forest* 森林的边缘 ○ *on the fringes of society* 在社会的边缘 ○ *on the radical fringe of the party* (ie the part having views not held by most people) 党内意见偏激的一方 ○ [attrib 作定语] *fringe theatre*, ie that stages unconventional and experimental productions 实验剧院 ○ *a fringe meeting*, ie one which is not part of the main programme at a political conference (政治会议中的)小会议.

4 (idm 习语) **the lunatic fringe** ⇨ LUNATIC.

▷ **fringe** *v* **1** [Tn] make a fringe(2) for (sth); decorate with a fringe 给(某物)做穗; 以穗装饰: *fringe a shawl* 给围巾做穗. **2** (idm 习语) **be fringed by/with sth** have sth as a border 以某物做边界: *The estate was fringed with stately elms.* 那片地以挺拔的榆树为边界.

□ ˈ**fringe benefit** extra benefit, esp given to an employee in addition to salary or wages 额外津贴(尤指在工资之外付给雇员的); 附加福利: *The fringe benefits of this job include a car and free health insurance.* 这工作的附加福利包括一辆小汽车和免费健康保险.

frip·pery /ˈfrɪpərɪ; ˋfrɪpərɪ/ *n* **1** [U] unnecessary showy ornamentation, esp in clothing 无必要的炫耀装饰(尤指服装上的). **2** [C usu *pl* 通常作复数] cheap useless ornament 廉价而无用的装饰.

Fris·bee /ˈfrɪzbiː; ˋfrɪzbi/ *n* (*propr* 专利名) light plastic disc, shaped like a plate, thrown between players in a game 飞盘(一种碟形塑料盘, 供游戏者互相抛扔玩耍).

frisk /frɪsk; frɪsk/ *v* **1** [Tn] (*infml* 口) pass one's hands over (sb) in a search for hidden weapons, drugs, etc 搜查(某人)(寻找暗藏的武器、毒品等): *Everyone was frisked before getting on the plane.* 每个人都经过搜身才登上飞机. **2** [I, Ip] (of animals) run and jump playfully (指动物)欢快地跑跳: *lambs frisking (about) in the meadow* 在草地上跳来跳去的小羊.

▷ **frisk** *n* [sing] **1** (*infml* 口) act of frisking (FRISK 1) a person 搜身. **2** act of playfully jumping and running 欢跃; 欢快的跑跳.

frisky *adj* lively and energetic, wanting to enjoy oneself 活泼有力的; 爱玩耍的: *a frisky lamb* 欢蹦乱跳的小羊 ○ *I feel quite frisky this morning.* 我今天上午觉得精神挺足. **fris·kily** /-ɪlɪ; -ɪlɪ/ *adv*.

F

fris·son /ˈfriːsɒn; *US* friːˈsəʊn; friˋson/ *n* (*French* 法) sudden feeling or thrill, esp of excitement or fear 震颤, 战栗(尤指因激动或害怕): *a frisson of delight, horror, fear, etc* 喜悦、恐怖、惧怕等的战栗.

frit·ter[1] /ˈfrɪtə(r); ˋfrɪtɚ/ *v* (phr v) **fritter sth away (on sth)** waste (esp one's time or money) foolishly (on small useless things) (在无意义的小事上)愚蠢地浪费(尤指个人的时间或金钱): *fritter away time/energy* 浪费时间[精力] ○ *fritter away one's money on gambling* 在赌博上挥霍金钱.

frit·ter[2] /ˈfrɪtə(r); ˋfrɪtɚ/ *n* (usu in compounds 通常用以构成复合词) piece of fried batter, usu containing sliced fruit, meat, etc 油煎饼(通常有水果、肉等的馅): *banana fritters* 香蕉馅煎饼.

friv·ol·ous /ˈfrɪvələs; ˋfrɪvələs/ *adj* **1** (of people, their character, etc) not sensible or serious; foolish and light-hearted (指人、性格等)不明事理的, 不严肃的, 漫不经心的, 轻率的, 肤浅的: *At 18, he's still rather frivolous and needs to grow up.* 他到了18岁仍然很不懂事、很不成熟. ○ *frivolous comments, objections, criticisms, etc* 肤浅的评论、轻率的反对、不严肃的批评等. **2** (of activities) silly or wasteful (指活动)无聊的; 浪费的: *She thought that reading romantic novels was a frivolous way of spending her time.* 她认为看浪漫小说是虚度时光.

▷ **fri·vol·ity** /frɪˈvɒlətɪ; frɪˋvɑlətɪ/ *n* **1** [U] frivolous behaviour 轻浮的举止: *youthful frivolity* 年轻人的心浮气躁. **2** [C usu *pl* 通常作复数] frivolous activity or comment 无聊的活动或议论: *I can't waste time on such frivolities.* 我不能在这种无聊的事情上浪费时间.

friv·ol·ously *adv*.

frizz /frɪz; frɪz/ *v* [Tn] form (esp hair) into small tight curls 使(尤指毛发)鬈曲: *You've had your hair frizzed.* 你把头发鬈弯了.

▷ **frizz** *n* hair that has been frizzed 鬈发; 鬈毛.

frizzy *adj* (of hair) tightly curled; frizzed (指毛发)鬈紧的, 鬈曲的.

frizzle[1] /ˈfrɪzl; ˋfrɪzḷ/ *v* [I, Ip, Tn, Tn·p] **~ (sth) (up)** twist (hair) into small tight curls 使(毛发)鬈曲.

frizzle[2] /ˈfrɪzl; ˋfrɪzḷ/ *v* **1** [I, Tn] cook (food) with a sizzling noise 烹制(食物)发出吱吱声: *bacon frizzling in the pan* 在锅里煎得吱吱作响的腌肉. **2** [I, Ip, Tn, Tn·p] **~ (sth) (up)** burn or shrivel (food) by frying it over a very strong heat; scorch (用旺火将食物)炸焦, 炸缩, 烧焦: *The bacon is all frizzled up!* 腌肉都煎糊了!

fro /frəʊ; fro/ *adv* (idm 习语) **to and fro** ⇨ TO[3].

frock /frɒk; frɑk/ *n* **1** dress worn by women or girls 连衣裙; (小女孩的)整身衣裙: *All my frocks are for the summer.* 我的连衣裙都是夏天穿的. **2** long loose gown with sleeves, worn by monks 僧袍.

□ ˈ**frock-coat** *n* long coat worn (formerly) by men, now worn only on ceremonial occasions (旧时男子的)长礼服(现仅于典礼、仪式场合穿着).

FROG 青蛙 TOAD 蟾蜍

frog /frɒg; *US* frɔːg; frɔg/ *n* **1** type of small cold-blooded smooth-skinned animal that lives in water or on land and has very long back legs for jumping, and no tail 蛙; 青蛙: *the croaking of frogs* 蛙鸣. ⇨illus 见插图. **2** ornamental fastener on a garment, consisting of a button and a looped cord that fits over it 钮扣和钮袢. **3** **frog** (*infml offensive* 口, 蔑) French person 法国人. **4** (idm 习语) **have, etc a ˈfrog in one's throat** have a (usu temporary) loss or hoarseness of the voice (通常为暂时的)失音或嗓音嘶哑.

□ ˈ**frogman** /-mən; -mən/ *n* (*pl* **-men** /-mən; -mən/) swimmer with a rubber suit, flippers and an oxygen supply that enables him to work underwater for periods of time 蛙人.

frog-spawn /ˈfrɒgspɔːn; ˋfrɑg,spɔn/ *n* [U] soft almost transparent jelly-like mass of the eggs of a frog 蛙的卵块.

frog-march /ˈfrɒgmɑːtʃ; ˋfrɑg,mɑrtʃ/ *v* [Tn, Tn·pr, Tn·p] **1** force (sb) to move forward with the arms held tightly together behind the back 迫使(某人)(反剪双臂)前行: *All prisoners were frogmarched (out) into the compound.* 犯人都被迫反剪双臂(出来)进入院子. **2** carry (sb) face downwards with four people each holding an arm or a leg 蛙式抬运(某人)(使其面朝下由四人各持一肢抬行).

frolic /ˈfrɒlɪk; ˋfrɑlɪk/ *v* (*pt, pp* **frolicked**) [I, Ip] **~ (about)** play about in a lively happy way 嬉戏: *children frolicking about in the swimming-pool* 在游泳池里嬉戏的儿童.

▷ **frolic** *n* [sing] lively and enjoyable activity 欢乐的活动: *having a frolic in the garden* 在花园里开游乐会.

frol·ic·some /-səm; -səm/ *adj* merry; playful 欢快的; 爱逗着玩儿的: *a frolicsome kitten* 爱逗着玩儿的小猫.

from /frəm; frəm *strong form* 强读式 frɒm; frɑm/ *prep* **1** (indicating the place or direction from which sb/sth starts 表示某人[某物]出发的地方或方向): *go from Manchester to Leeds* 从曼彻斯特到利兹 ○ *a wind from the north* 从北方刮来的风 ○ *Has the train from London arrived?* 伦敦来的火车到了吗? ○ *She comes home from work at 7 pm.* 她下午7点下班回家. ○ *A child fell from the seventh floor of a block of flats.* 小孩儿从公寓的八楼上摔了下来. ○ *carpets stretching from to wall to wall*, ie from one wall to the opposite one 铺满地板的地毯(从地板一端铺到另一端). **2** (indicating the time at which sth starts 表示某事开始的时间): *I'm on holiday from 30 June.* 我从6月30日开始休假. ○ *It's due to arrive an hour from now.* 从现在起一个小时就该到了. ○ *We lived in Scotland from 1960 to 1973.* 我们从1960年到1973年住在苏格兰. ○ *There's traffic in the streets from dawn till dusk.* 从黎明到黄昏街上车辆川流不息. ○ *We're open from 8 am till 7 pm every day.* 我们每天由早8点到晚7点营业. ○ *He was blind from birth.* 他从出生就失明了. **3** (indicating who sent, gave or communicated sth 表示送、给予或传送某物的人): *a letter from my brother* 我兄弟来的信 ○ *a present from a friend* 朋友送的礼物 ○ *I had a phone call from Mary.* 我接到了玛丽的电话. ○ *the man from* (ie representing) *the Inland Revenue* 税务局的人. **4** (indicating where sb/sth originates or is stored 表示某人[某事物]的来源): *I'm from New Zealand.* 我是新西兰人. ○ *They come from the north.* 他们是北方人. ○ *the boy from the baker's* 面包房的小伙子 ○ *documents* *from the 16th century* 16世纪的文件 ○ *famous quotations from Shakespeare* 莎士比亚的名句 ○ *music from an opera* 歌剧选曲 ○ *draw water from a well* 从井中取水 ○ *powered by heat from the sun* 以太阳的热量为动力的. **5** (indicating distance between two places 表示两地间的距离): *10 miles from the coast* 距海岸10英里 ○ *100 yards from the scene of the accident* 离事故现场100码 ○ (*fig* 比喻) *Far from agreeing with him, I was shocked by his remarks.* 我很不同意他的意见, 听了他的话我很吃惊. **6** (indicating the lower limit of a range of numbers, prices, etc 表示数目、价格等的最低限度): *write from 10 to 15 letters daily* 每天写10到15封信 ○ *Tickets cost from £3 to £11.* 票价为3英镑至11英镑. ○ *Our prices start from £2.50 a bottle.* 我们的价格起码是2.50英镑一瓶. ○ *Salaries are from 10% to 50% higher than in Britain.* 薪金比在英国高10%到15%. **7** (indicating the state or form of sth/sb before a change 表示某事物[某人]改变之前的状态或形式): *Things have gone from bad to worse.* 事情已经越来越糟了. ○ *You need a break from routine.* 你需要从日常工作中脱身去休息一下. ○ *translate from English to Spanish* 从英语译成西班牙语 ○ *The bus fare has gone up from 35p to 40p.* 公共汽车的票价已由35便士涨到40便士. ○ *From being a librarian she is now an MP.* 她从一个图书馆管理员当上了如今的下议院议员. **8** (indicating the material from which sth is made, the material being changed in the process 表示制造某物的原料, 该原料在加工过程中有所改变): *Wine is made from grapes.* 葡萄酒是用葡萄酿造的. ○ *Steel is made from iron.* 钢是用铁炼成的. Cf 参看 OF 5, OUT OF 5. **9** (**a**) (indicating separation, removal, etc 表示分离、除去等): *separated from his mother for long periods* 与他母亲已分离很长时间 ○ *take the money from my purse* 从我钱包里把钱拿走 ○ *borrow a book from the library* 从图书馆借书 ○ *release sb from prison* 将某人从监狱释放 ○ *6 from 14 leaves 8.* 14减6剩8. (**b**) (indicating protection or prevention 表示保护或防止): *protect children from violence* 保护儿童免遭暴力侵犯 ○ *save a boy from drowning* 救一男孩使之免遭溺毙 ○ *Wild fruit kept us from dying of starvation.* 我们靠着野果才没饿死. ○ *prevent sb from sleeping* 不让某人睡着. **10** (indicating the reason, cause or motive 表示理由、原因或动机): *She felt sick from tiredness.* 她因疲劳而感到不舒服. ○ *suffer from cold and hunger* 受饥寒交迫之苦 ○ *She accompanied him from a sense of loyalty.* 她出于忠诚而伴随他. **11** considering (sth) 考虑到(某事物): *From the evidence we have heard so far...* 就我们所知的证据来说... ○ *From her looks I'd say she was Swedish.* 从她的相貌上看, 我敢说她是瑞典人. ○ *From what I heard last night we're going to need a new chairman.* 考虑到我昨晚听到的情况, 我们需要一个新主席了. ○ *You can tell quite a lot from the handwriting.* 从笔迹上能了解很多东西. **12** (used to make a distinction between two people, places or things 用以区别两人、两地或两事物): *Is Portuguese very different from Spanish?* 葡萄牙语和西班牙语的差别很大吗? ○ *I can't tell one twin from the other.* 我分不出双胞胎中谁是谁. ○ *How do you know a fake from the original?* 怎样识别赝品和真品呢? **13** (indicating a standpoint 表示立场、观点): *Seen from above the town covers a wide area.* 从高处下望, 这座城镇占地很广. ○ *From this angle it looks crooked.* 从这个角度看这是弯的. ○ *From a teacher's point of view this dictionary will be very useful.* 以教师的观点来看, 这部词典很有用. **14** (idm 习语) **from...on** starting at the specified time and continuing for an indefinite period 从所述的时间开始而延续的期间未定: *From now on you can work on your own.* 你从现在起可以独立工作了. ○ *From then on she knew she would win.* 她从那时起就知道自己会得胜. ○ *She never spoke to him again from that day on.* 她从那天以后就再也不和他说话了.

frond /frɒnd; frɑnd/ *n* leaf-like part of a fern or palm (蕨类或棕榈类的)叶.

front /frʌnt; frʌnt/ *n* **1** (esp **the front**) [sing] (**a**) most important part or side of sth; part or side that faces forward; most forward part of sth 正面; 前面: *The front of the building was covered with ivy.* 建筑物的前面爬满了常春藤. ○ *Put the statue so that the front faces the light.* 把雕像摆好, 让正面向着光. ○ *The front of the car has a dent in it.* 小汽车的前面有一个凹痕. ○ *The young boy spilt some juice down his front,* ie the clothes covering his chest. 那男孩把果汁洒在前襟上了. (**b**) position directly before or ahead; most forward position or place 正前方或前面的位置, 最靠前的位置或地方: *All eyes to the front as we pass the other competitors!* 我们超越对手时要目不斜视! ○ *The teacher made me move my seat to the front of the classroom.* 老师让我把座位挪到教室的最前面去坐. ○ *At the front of the house, someone had planted a beautiful garden.* 有人在房前种上了花, 成了个漂亮的花园. ○ *I prefer to travel in the front of the car,* ie next to the driver. 我愿意坐在汽车的前面(挨着司机). Cf 参看 BACK[1] 1. **2 the front** [sing] the land along the edge of the sea or a lake; promenade 海边; 湖边; 海滨: *walk along the (sea) front* 沿着海滨散步. **3 the front** [sing] (in war) area where fighting takes place; foremost line of an army (战争中)前线, 前沿: *be sent to the front* 被派往前线 ○ *serve at the front* 在前线服役. **4** [sing] outward appearance or show, esp of the specified type 外表或样子(尤指所述的类型): *Her rudeness is just a front for her shyness.* 她色厉内荏. ○ *put on/show/present a bold front* 装出一副大胆的样子 ○ *We might argue among ourselves, but against the management we must present a united front,* ie act and speak as a group. 我们内部不妨有争论, 但对付资方我们必须团结一致. **5** [sing] **a ~ for sth** (*infml* 口) something that serves to hide an illegal or a secret activity 非法或秘密活动的掩蔽物: *The jewellery firm is just a front for their illegal trade in diamonds.* 该珠宝公司不过是进行非法的钻石交易的幌子. **6** [C] (of weather) forward edge of an advancing mass of warm or cold air (指天气)(热或冷气团的)锋: *A cold front is moving in from the north.* 一股冷锋正从北方向这里移动. **7** [C] (usu with an *adj* or a *n* 通常与形容词或名词连用) specified area of activity 活动的范围或领域: *on the domestic, financial, education, etc front* 在国内、金融、教育等方面. **8** [sing] (esp in names 尤用于名称) organized and often aggressively active political group 有组织的、常有过激活动的政治团体: *the National Front* 民族阵线. **9** (idm 习语) **back to front** ⇨ BACK[1]. **eyes right/left/front** ⇨ EYE[1]. **in ˈfront; out ˈfront** part of a theatre where the audience sits 观众席. **in front** *adv* in a position further forward than but close to sb/sth 在某人[某物]前面: *a small house with a garden in front* 前面带花园的小房子 ○ *The children walked in twos with one teacher in front and one behind.* 孩子们排成两行走, 前后各有一位老师. ○ *The British car has been in front now for several minutes.* 英国汽车已领先数分钟. Cf 参看 BEHIND[2]. **in front of** *prep* (**a**) in a position further forward than but close to (sb/sth) 在(某人[某物])前面: *The car in front of me stopped suddenly and I had to brake.* 我前面那辆小汽车突然停住, 我只好刹车. ○ *The bus stops right in front of our house.* 公共汽车正停在我们房前. ○ *I keep the children's photographs in front of me on the desk.* 我把孩子们的照片放在书桌上, 摆在我面前. ○ *If you're phoning from outside London, dial 01 in front of the number.* 从伦敦以外的地方打来电话, 要先拨01再拨电话号码. Cf 参看 BEHIND[1]. ⇨Usage at BEFORE[2] 用法见 BEFORE[2]. (**b**) in the presence of (sb) 当(某人的)面: *The cheques must be signed in front of the cashier at the bank.* 必须当着银行出纳员的面签这些支票. ○ *Please don't talk about it in front of the children.* 请不要当着孩子们谈论那事. **up ˈfront** (*infml* 口) as payment in advance 提前付款; 先期付款: *We'll pay you half up front and the other half when you've finished the job.* 我们先付给你一半钱, 剩下的一半等你干完了再付.

▷ **front** *adj* [attrib 作定语] of or at (the) front(1) 前面的; 在前面的: *on the front page of the newspaper* 在报纸的头版 ○ *front teeth* 门齿 ○ *They keep the front room for visitors.* 他们把前面的房间留给客人. ○ *the front door,* ie the door that serves as the main entrance to a house 前门 ○ *the front seats of a bus* 公共汽车前面的座位.

front *v* **1** [Ipr, Tn] **~ (onto) sth** have the front facing or directed towards sth; face 面对; 直对; 面向: *hotels that front onto the sea* 面向大海的旅馆 ○ *Attractive gardens fronted the houses.* 这些房子的前面都有漂亮的花园. **2** [Tn usu passive 通常用于被动语态] provide (sth) with a front 用(某物)作正面: *The monument was fronted with stone.* 纪念碑的正面是石料做的. **3** [Tn] (*infml* 口) (**a**) serve as a leader or representative of (an organization) 作为(某组织的)领导人或代表.

F

(**b**) present (a television or radio programme) 主持(电视节目或广播节目): *Dan Davies has been chosen to front a new discussion programme.* 丹·戴维斯获任主持一个新的讨论节目.

□ **the ˌfront ˈbench** (either of the two rows of seats in the British Parliament occupied by the) leading members of the government and opposition (在英国议会中的两排)前座(的政府及反对党议员): *members on the front bench(es) opposite* 反对党前座议员 ○ [attrib 作定语] *the front-bench ˈspokesman on defence* 议会中谈论国防事务的前座发言人. **front-ˈbencher** *n* Member of Parliament entitled to sit on the front bench 前座议员.

the front line **1** line of fighting which is closest to the enemy 前线: [attrib 作定语] *front-line troops, units, etc* 前沿部队、单位等. **2** the most important, advanced or responsible position 最重要、最前面的或责任最重大的位置; 第一线: *in the front line of research* 处于研究工作的第一线.

ˈfront man (*infml* 口) **1** (person who acts as the) leader or representative of an organization 某组织的领导人或代表; 头面人物. **2** presenter of a television or radio programme (电视或广播的)节目主持人.

ˌfront-ˈpage *adj* [attrib 作定语] interesting or important enough to be printed on the front page of a newspaper 头版的: *front-page ˈnews* 头版新闻.

ˌfront ˈrunner person who seems most likely to succeed or win, eg in a race or contest 最有可能成功或获胜的人(如在比赛或竞争中); 领先者: *Who are the front runners in the Presidential contest?* 哪些人在总统竞选中最有可能获胜?

F

front·age /ˈfrʌntɪdʒ; ˋfrʌntɪdʒ/ *n* [C, U] extent of a piece of land or a building along its front, esp bordering a road or river 一块土地或一建筑物的正面的空地(尤指临街或沿河的): *For sale, shop premises with frontages on two streets.* 出售商业用房, 前有空地两面临街. ○ *a warehouse with good river frontage* 带有一片良好的临河空地的仓库.

frontal /ˈfrʌntl; ˋfrʌntl/ *adj* [attrib 作定语] **1** at, from, in, or of the front 靠正面的; 从正面的; 在正面的; 正面的: *a frontal view* 正面所见 ○ *a frontal attack*, ie one directed at the front or the main point 正面攻击 ○ *full frontal nudity*, ie complete nudity, showing the whole of the front of the body 正面全裸. **2** (*medical* 医) of a person's forehead 前额的: *frontal lobes* 额叶. **3** concerning a weather front(6) (天气)锋的: *a frontal system* 锋系.

fron·tier /ˈfrʌntɪə(r); *US* frʌnˈtɪər; frʌnˋtɪr/ *n* **1** [C] (**a**) **~ (between sth and sth)**; **~ (with sth)** border between two countries 国界; 边界: *the frontier between Austria and Hungary* 奥地利和匈牙利之间的边界. (**b**) land on either side of such a border 边疆; 边陲; 边境; 国境: [attrib 作定语] *a frontier zone* 边境地带 ○ *a frontier town* 边疆城镇 ○ *frontier disputes* 边界争端. **2** **the frontier** [sing] (*esp US*) extreme limit of settled land, beyond which the country is wild and undeveloped 已开发地区的边缘地带: *Beyond the frontier lay very real dangers.* 在开发地区以外十分危险. **3** **the frontiers** [pl] extreme limit, esp of knowledge about sth 极限(尤指有关某事物的知识的); 尖端; 边缘: *advance the frontiers of science* 拓展科学的领域 ○ *teach near the frontiers of one's subject*, ie give recently discovered information 讲授个人专业领域的新知识. ⇨Usage at BORDER 用法见 BORDER.

▷ **fron·tiers·man** /-zmən; -zmən/ *n* (*pl* **-men** /-mən; -mən/) man living on the frontier; one of the first settlers of an area 边疆居民; 边民; 拓荒者; 开拓者.

fron·tis·piece /ˈfrʌntɪspi:s; ˋfrʌntɪsˌpis/ *n* (usu *sing* 通常作单数) illustration at the beginning of a book, on the page opposite the title-page 卷首插图(在与书名页相对的一页上的).

frost /frɒst; *US* frɔ:st; frɔst/ *n* **1** (**a**) [U] weather condition in which the temperature falls below freezing-point, usu accompanied by the formation of frost(2) 严寒(气温在冰点以下, 通常伴有霜冻): *Young plants are often killed by frost.* 植物的幼苗常因严寒而冻死. ○ *a temperature of 10 degrees of frost*, ie 10 degrees Celsius below freezing-point 冰点下10摄氏度的气温. (**b**) [C] instance or period of this 严寒; 严寒期: *There was a heavy* (ie severe) *frost last night.* 昨夜有严重霜冻. ○ *early frosts*, ie in autumn 秋寒 ○ *late frosts*, ie in spring 春寒. **2** [U] dew or water vapour frozen into tiny white ice crystals that cover the ground, etc when the temperature falls below freezing-point 霜: *The windscreen was covered with frost.* 挡风玻璃上结了霜.

▷ **frost** *v* **1** [Tn] cover (sth) with frost 在(某物)上结霜: *frosted pavements* 结霜的人行道. **2** [Tn usu passive 通常用于被动语态] kill or damage (plants, etc) with frost *n* (1) 冻死或冻坏(植物等). **3** [Tn] (*esp US*) decorate (a cake, etc) with icing or frosting 用糖衣或糖霜装饰(糕饼等). **4** [Tn] make (glass) opaque by giving it a rough frostlike surface 使(玻璃)不透明(形成霜状粗糙表面): *frosted window panes* 磨砂窗户玻璃. **5** (phr v) **frost over/up** become covered with frost 结霜: *The car windscreen frosted over during the night.* 汽车的挡风玻璃在夜间结了霜.

□ **ˈfrost-bite** *n* [U] injury to the body, esp fingers, toes, ears, etc, caused by extreme cold 冻伤; 冻疮: *Two of the mountain climbers were suffering from frost-bite.* 有两个登山者冻伤了.

ˈfrost-bitten *adj* suffering from or affected by frost-bite 患冻疮的; 被冻伤的: *frost-bitten ears* 冻伤的耳朵.

ˈfrostbound *adj* (of the ground) made hard by frost (指地)冻硬的.

frost·ing /ˈfrɒstɪŋ; *US* ˈfrɔ:stɪŋ; ˋfrɔstɪŋ/ *n* [U] (*esp US*) = ICING.

frosty /ˈfrɒstɪ; *US* ˈfrɔ:stɪ; ˋfrɔstɪ/ *adj* (**-ier, -iest**) **1** (**a**) very cold; cold with frost 严寒的; 霜冻的: *frosty weather* 有霜冻的天气 ○ *It's sunny, but the air is frosty.* 虽然是晴天, 但空气很冷. (**b**) covered with frost 结霜的: *frosty fields* 结霜的田地. **2** (*fig* 比喻) cold and unwelcoming in manner; not friendly 冷若冰霜的; 不友好的: *a frosty look, response, welcome, etc* 冷若冰霜的表情、反应、迎接等. ▷ **frost·ily** /-ɪlɪ; ɪlɪ/ *adv*. **frosti·ness** *n* [U]: *a certain frostiness in her greeting* 在她的问候中略含冷淡之意.

froth /frɒθ; *US* frɔ:θ; frɔθ/ *n* [U] **1** mass of small bubbles, esp on the surface of a liquid; foam 泡(尤指液体表面上的); 泡沫: *I don't like beer with too much froth.* 我不喜欢泡沫太多的啤酒. **2** (*derog* 贬) light but worthless conversation, ideas, etc 空洞的交谈、思想等: *Their chatter was nothing but froth!* 他们聊天儿没别的, 全是废话!

▷ **froth** *v* **1** [Tn, Tn·p] **~ sth (up)** cause (a liquid) to foam 使(液体)起泡: *froth (up) a milk shake* 将含奶的饮料打起泡沫来. **2** [I, Ipr] have or produce froth 有泡沫、起泡沫; 发泡; 冒泡: *The water frothed as it tumbled down the rocks.* 水冲击在岩石上溅起了泡沫. ○ *Animals with rabies often froth at the mouth.* 患狂犬病的动物常常口吐白沫. ○ (*fig* 比喻) *He was so angry he was almost frothing at the mouth.* 他气得差点儿口吐白沫.

frothy *adj* (**-ier, -iest**) **1** full of or covered with froth 有泡沫的; 起泡沫的: *frothy beer* 有泡沫的啤酒 ○ *a frothy mixture of eggs and milk* 起泡儿的蛋奶混合物. **2** light and trivial 轻浮的; 浅薄的; 空洞的: *a novel written in a frothy style* 笔调轻浮的小说. **froth·ily** *adv*. **froth·iness** *n* [U].

frown /fraʊn; fraʊn/ *v* **1**[I, Ipr] **~ (at sb/sth)** bring the eyebrows together, so wrinkling the skin on one's forehead (to express anger, thought, worry, etc) 皱眉, 蹙额(以示生气、沉思、忧愁等): *What's wrong? Why are you frowning?* 出什么事了? 干什么皱着眉头? ○ *Peter frowned at the noise coming from the boys' bedroom.* 彼得听到从男孩子卧室传来的吵闹声便皱起眉头. ○ *She read through the letter, frowning at its contents.* 她把信看了一遍, 从头到尾双眉深锁. **2** (phr v) **frown on/upon sth** disapprove of sth 不赞成某事; 不许可; 不同意: *My parents always frown on late nights out.* 我父母向来不赞成深夜外出. ○ *Gambling is frowned upon by some church authorities.* 有些教会权力机关不许可赌博. ⇨Usage at SMIRK 用法见 SMIRK.

▷ **frown** *n* serious, angry, worried, etc look on the face causing lines on the forehead; expression of displeasure 皱眉; 蹙额; 不悦: *She looked up from her exam paper with a worried frown.* 她看完自己的试卷愁眉不展地抬起头来. ○ *I noticed a slight frown of disapproval on his face.* 我留意到他轻轻皱了一下眉, 露出不赞成的样子.

frowsty /ˈfraʊstɪ; ˋfraustɪ/ *adj* (*derog* 贬 *esp Brit*) (of the air conditions in a room) stale and stuffy (指房间里的空气)不流通的, 闷热的.

frowzy /ˈfraʊzɪ; ˋfraʊzɪ/ *adj* (*esp Brit*) **1** untidy or unclean in appearance; shabby 外表不整洁的; 邋遢的. **2** ill-smelling; stale and stuffy; musty 难闻的; 污浊闷热的; 霉臭的.

froze *pt* of FREEZE.

frozen *pp* of FREEZE.

FRS /ˌef ɑːr ˈes; ˌɛf ɑr ˋɛs/ *abbr* 缩写 = (*Brit*) Fellow of the Royal Society 皇家学会会员: *Charles May FRS* 皇家学会会员查尔斯·梅.

fruct·ify /ˈfrʌktɪfaɪ; ˋfrʌktəˌfaɪ/ *v* (*pt, pp* **-fied**) [I, Tn] (*fml* 文) (cause sth to) bear fruit or be fruitful (使某物)结果实或多产. ▷ **fruc·ti·fica·tion** /ˌfrʌktɪfɪˈkeɪʃn; ˌfrʌktəfəˋkeʃən/ *n* [U].

fruct·ose /ˈfrʌktəʊs, -əʊz; ˋfrʌktoz/ *n* type of sugar found in fruit juice, honey, etc 果糖(果汁、蜂蜜等中所含的糖).

fru·gal /ˈfruːgl; ˋfrugḷ/ *adj* (**a**) careful and thrifty, esp with money and food 节约的, 节俭的, 节省的(尤指对金钱和食物): *a frugal housekeeper* 节俭的管家. (**b**) of life in which such care is shown 生活俭朴的: *They lived a very frugal existence, avoiding all luxuries.* 他们生活非常俭朴, 力避奢华. (**c**) costing little; small in quantity 花费少的; 省钱的; 小量的: *a frugal meal of bread and cheese* 只有面包和奶酪的便餐. ▷ **fru·gal·ity** /fruˈgælətɪ; fruˋgælətɪ/ *n* [U]. **fru·gally** /-gəlɪ; -gḷɪ/ *adv*

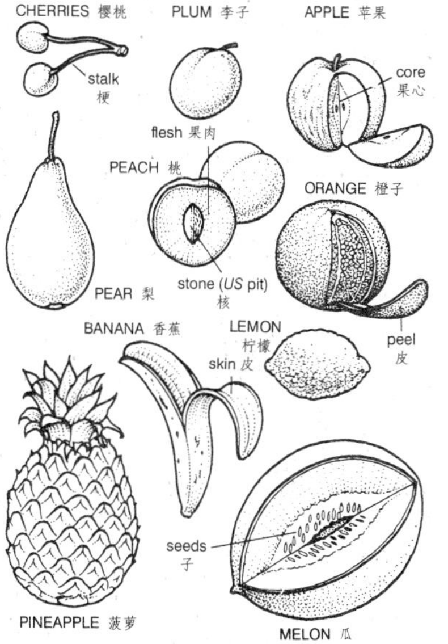

fruit 水果

fruit /fruːt; frut/ *n* **1** [C, U] fleshy seed-bearing part of a plant used as food; quantity of these 水果; 水果的量: *The country exports tropical fruit(s).* 该国出口热带水果. ○ *Is a tomato a fruit or a vegetable?* 蕃茄是水果还是蔬菜? ○ *Bananas, apples and oranges are all fruit.* 香蕉、苹果和橘子都是水果. ○ *This pudding has two pounds of fresh fruit in it.* 这个布丁里有两磅鲜果. ○ [attrib 作定语] ˈ*fruit juice* 果汁 ○ ˈ*fruit trees* 果树. ⇨illus 见插图. **2** [C] (*botany* 植) part of a plant, tree or bush in which the seed is formed 果实. **3** [C usu *pl* 通常作复数] any plant product used as food 可做食物的任何植物的产物: *the fruits of the earth*, ie vegetables, cereals, etc 农产品(蔬菜、谷物等). **4** (esp 尤作 **the fruits** [pl]) result or reward of an action, hard work, etc 成果; 结果; 产物: *enjoy the fruit(s) of one's labours* 享受自己的劳动成果. **5** [U] (also ˌ**dried** ˈ**fruit**) currants, raisins, or sultanas, used as food or in baking 干果. **6** (idm 习语) **bear fruit** ⇨ BEAR². **forbidden fruit** ⇨ FORBID.

▷ **fruit** *v* [I] produce fruit 结果实: *These apple trees have always fruited well.* 这些苹果树总是结很多苹果.

□ ˈ**fruit-cake** *n* **1** [C, U] cake containing dried fruit 含有干果的糕饼; 干果蛋糕. **2** (idm 习语) **nutty as a fruit-cake** ⇨ NUTTY (NUT).

ˈ**fruit-fly** *n* small fly that feeds on decaying plant matter, esp fruit 果蝇.

ˈ**fruit-knife** *n* small knife used for cutting and peeling fruit 水果刀.

ˈ**fruit machine** (*Brit*) (also *esp US* ˌ**one-armed** ˈ**bandit**) type of coin-operated gambling machine, often displaying symbols representing fruit 吃角子老虎(以硬币启动的赌具, 常以水果图案为显示符号).

ˌ**fruit** ˈ**salad** **1** (*esp Brit*) mixture of different types of fruit, cut up and served as a dessert 水果色拉; 水果杂拌. **2** (*US*) dish of small pieces of fruit set in jelly(1a) and served as a dessert 水果冻; 果冻.

fruit·erer /ˈfruːtərə(r); ˋfrutərɚ/ *n* (*esp Brit*) person who sells fruit, esp in a shop or stall 水果商贩.

fruit·ful /ˈfruːtfl; ˋfrutfəl/ *adj* **1** having many good results; productive or profitable; successful 硕果累累的; 多产的; 有利的; 成功的: *a fruitful experience, day's work, partnership* 丰富的经验、收获大的一日工作、成功的合作关系 ○ *fruitful areas of research* 硕果累累的研究领域. **2** producing a lot of fruit 果实结得多的. ▷ **fruit·fully** /ˈfruːtfəlɪ; ˋfrutfəlɪ/ *adv*. **fruit·ful·ness** /ˈfruːtfəlnɪs; ˋfrutfəlnɪs/ *n* [U].

fru·ition /fruːˈɪʃn; fruˋɪʃən/ *n* [U] fulfilment of hopes, plans, etc; getting what one wants or has worked for (希望、计划等的)实现; 完成: *After months of hard work, our plans came to/were brought to fruition.* 我们经过几个月的苦干, 终于实现了计划.

fruit·less /ˈfruːtlɪs; ˋfrutlɪs/ *adj* producing little or no result; unsuccessful 不结果实的; 无结果的; 不成功的; 无益的; 无效的: *a fruitless attempt* 无益的尝试 ○ *Our efforts to persuade her were fruitless — she didn't even listen.* 我们怎么劝她都没用——她连听都不听. ▷ **fruit·lessly** *adv*. **fruit·less·ness** *n* [U].

fruity /ˈfruːtɪ; ˋfrutɪ/ *adj* (**-ier**, **-iest**) **1** like fruit in smell or taste; containing a lot of fruit 果香的; 果味的; 含大量水果的: *a fruity wine* 果酒 ○ *a fruity dessert* 水果甜食. **2** (*infml* 口) funny in a crude and often sexually suggestive way (粗俗而常含色情内容)逗笑的: *a fruity joke, remark, story, etc* 色情的笑话、言语、故事等. **3** (*infml* 口) (of a voice, etc) rich and deep in tone or quality (指声音等)圆润而深沉的: *a fruity chuckle* 低沉的笑声.

frump /frʌmp; frʌmp/ *n* (*derog* 贬) person (usu a woman) who wears dull old-fashioned clothes 衣着不入时的人(通常指女子). ▷ **frump·ish** *adj*: *a frumpish outfit* 不时兴的衣装.

frus·trate /frʌˈstreɪt; *US* ˈfrʌstreɪt; ˋfrʌstret/ *v* [Tn] **1** (**a**) prevent (sb) from doing or achieving sth 阻止(某人)做成某事; 妨碍: *He had hoped to set a new world record, but was frustrated by bad weather.* 他本希望能创造新的世界纪录, 但因天气恶劣而未果. (**b**) make (efforts, etc) useless; defeat 使(努力等)无效; 失败: *Bad weather has frustrated plans to launch the spacecraft today.* 今日发射宇宙飞船的计划, 因天气恶劣而落空. **2** upset or discourage (sb) 扰乱或阻挠(某人); 使沮丧; 使灰心: *Mary was frustrated by the lack of appreciation shown of her work.* 玛丽因工作得不到赏识而灰心丧气.

▷ **frus·trated** *adj* **1** (**a**) [pred 作表语] discouraged; not satisfied 令人灰心; 令人沮丧; 令人不满: *As a nurse she got very frustrated, but being an administrator seems to suit her.* 她做护士很不顺心, 但当管理人员似乎倒很适合. (**b**) [attrib 作定语] unable to be successful in one's chosen career 失意的; 不得志的; 受挫的: *Film directors are sometimes frustrated actors.* 电影导演有时是不得志的演员. **2** not satisfied sexually 性欲上不满的.

frus·trat·ing *adj* annoying; discouraging 使人心烦的; 使人讨厌的; 使人灰心的; 使人沮丧的: *I find it frustrating that I can't speak other languages.* 我不会说别的语言, 感到惘然若失.

frus·tra·tion /frʌˈstreɪʃn; frʌsˋtreʃən/ *n* **1** [U] (state of) being frustrated 灰心; 沮丧; 不满; 失意; 受挫. **2** [C] instance of this; disappointment 灰心; 沮丧; 不满; 挫折; 失意; 失望: *Every job has its frustrations.* 每种工作都有

让人不称心的地方.

fry[1] /fraɪ; fraɪ/ *v* (*pt, pp* **fried** /fraɪd; fraɪd/) **1** [I, Tn] cook (sth) or be cooked in boiling fat or oil 油煎; 油炸: *fried chicken* 炸鸡 ○ *bacon frying in the pan* 在煎锅里煎着的腌肉. ⇨Usage at COOK 用法见 COOK. **2** (idm 习语) **have bigger/other fish to fry** ⇨ FISH[1].

□ ˈ**frying-pan** (*US* ˈ**fry-pan**) *n* **1** flat shallow pan with a long handle, used for frying food 长柄平底浅锅(煎锅). ⇨illus at PAN 见 PAN 插图. **2** (idm 习语) **out of the ˈfrying-pan into the ˈfire** from a bad situation to one that is worse 跳出油锅又入火坑; 愈来愈糟; 每况愈下.

ˈ**fry-up** *n* (*Brit*) (dish of) fried food, esp bacon, eggs, sausages, etc 油煎食品(菜肴)(尤指腌肉、蛋、香肠等): *We always have a fry-up for Saturday lunch.* 我们星期六的午饭总有一道油煎菜.

fry[2] /fraɪ; fraɪ/ *n* [pl *v*] **1** young or newly hatched fishes 小鱼; 鱼苗. **2** (idm 习语) ˈ**small fry** ⇨ SMALL.

fryer (also **frier**) /ˈfraɪə(r); ˋfraɪɚ/ *n* **1** large deep pan for frying food, esp fish 大而深的锅(用以炸食物、尤指鱼). **2** (*esp US*) small young chicken suitable for frying (适宜炸食的)雏鸡.

FT /ˌef ˈtiː; ˌɛf ˋti/ *abbr* 缩写 = (*Brit*) Financial Times (newspaper) 金融时报: *the FT (share) index* 金融时报(股票)指数.

Ft *abbr* 缩写 = (in names 用作名称) Fort: *Ft William*, eg on a map 威廉堡(如地图上的字样).

ft *abbr* 缩写 = (also *symb* 符号为 ') feet; foot: *11 ft* x (ie by) *6 ft* (11' x 6') 11英尺×6英尺 ○ *She was only 5 ft (tall).* 她只有5英尺(高). Cf 参看 IN, YD.

fuch·sia /ˈfjuːʃə; ˋfjuʃə/ *n* shrub with red, purple or white drooping flowers 倒挂金钟(灌木, 开红色、紫色或白色花, 悬垂呈倒挂钟状).

F

fuck /fʌk; fʌk/ *v* (⚠ *sl* 讳, 俚) **1** [I, Tn] have sexual intercourse with (sb) 与(某人)性交; 肏(某人). **2** [I, Tn] (esp imperative or as an *interj* in exclamations expressing extreme anger, annoyance or disgust 尤用于祈使句或用于感叹句中作感叹词, 表示极其愤怒、烦恼或憎恶): *Fuck (it)!* 他妈的! ○ *Fuck you — I don't care if I never see you again.* 滚你妈的蛋 —— 我这辈子也不想见你了. ○ *Fuck the bloody thing — it won't work.* 去他妈的倒霉玩意儿 —— 不管用. **3** (idm 习语) ˈ**fucking well** (used to emphasize an angry statement, esp an order 说气话时用以加强语气, 尤作命令用语) certainly; definitely 确实; 一定: *You're fucking well coming whether you want to or not.* 不管你想来不想来, 你是一定得来. **4** (phr v) **fuck aˈbout/aˈround** behave foolishly or unhelpfully 干愚蠢的或无谓的事; 胡闹: *Stop fucking around and come and give me a hand.* 别胡闹了, 过来给我帮个忙. **fuck sb about/around** treat sb badly or inconsiderately 亏待或不体谅某人: *This bloody company keeps fucking me about.* 这倒霉的公司一直亏待我. **fuck ˈoff** (esp imperative 尤用于祈使句) go away 走开; 滚. **fuck sth up** spoil or ruin sth 弄糟或毁坏某事物.

▷ **fuck** *n* (usu *sing* 通常作单数) (⚠ *sl* 讳, 俚) **1** act of sexual intercourse 性交. **2** (*sexist* 性别偏见) person, esp a woman, considered as a sexual partner 性交对象(尤指女子): *She's a good fuck.* 她是个床上的好伴. **3** (idm 习语) **not care/give a fuck (about sb/sth)** not care at all 毫不在乎: *He doesn't give a fuck about anyone else.* 他对别人毫不关心.

fucker *n* (⚠ *sl* 讳, 俚) (as a general term of abuse) fool; idiot (用作一般的辱骂用语)傻瓜, 笨蛋.

fuck·ing (⚠ *sl* 讳, 俚) *adj, adv* (used to add emphasis in expressions of anger, annoyance, etc 用以增强表示愤怒、烦恼等的语气): *I'm fucking sick of the whole fucking lot of you.* 你们他妈的真让我恶心.

□ ˌ**fuck-ˈall** *n* [U] (⚠ *sl* 讳, 俚) nothing at all 丝毫没有; 什么都没有: *You've done ˌfuck-ˈall today.* 你今天是屁事也没干. ○ [attrib 作定语] *He's fuck-all ˌuse as a ˈgoalkeeper.* 他当守门员屁事不顶.

fuck-up /ˈfʌkʌp; ˋfʌkˌʌp/ *n* (⚠ *sl* 讳, 俚) complete mess; disaster 一团糟; 一塌糊涂: *What a fuck-up!* 真是乱成一锅粥!

fuddle /ˈfʌdl; ˋfʌdḷ/ *v* [Tn esp passive 尤用于被动语态] confuse (sb/sth), esp with alcoholic drink 使(某人[某事])错乱(尤指因含酒精饮料所致): *in a fuddled state* 处于昏昏沉沉的状态 ○ *one's mind fuddled with gin* 喝杜松子酒喝得烂醉.

▷ **fuddle** *n* (usu *sing* 通常作单数) confused state 混乱: *My brain's in a fuddle.* 我的脑子糊里糊涂的.

fuddy-duddy /ˈfʌdɪdʌdɪ; ˋfʌdɪˌdʌdɪ/ *n* (*infml derog or joc* 口, 贬或谑) person who has old-fashioned ideas and habits 老脑筋; 老顽固; 老古董: *You're such an old fuddy-duddy!* 你这个老古董! ○ [attrib 作定语] *You and your fuddy-duddy ideas!* 你这个老脑筋!

fudge[1] /fʌdʒ; fʌdʒ/ *n* [U] soft sweet made of sugar, butter and milk, often with added flavourings (由糖、奶油和牛奶, 有时加香料制成的)软糖: *chocolate/walnut fudge* 巧克力[核桃]软糖.

fudge[2] /fʌdʒ; fʌdʒ/ *v* [Tn] (*infml* 口) **1** do (sth) clumsily or inadequately 胡乱地或敷衍地做(某事): *He had to fudge a reply because he didn't know the right answer.* 因为他不知道正确的答案, 只好胡编乱造一个. **2** misrepresent or falsify (sth); evade (sth) 歪曲或捏造(某事); 逃避(某事): *Our manager has been fudging the issue of bonus payments for months.* 我们的经理数月来一直回避发放奖金一事.

fuel /ˈfjuːəl; ˋfjuəl/ *n* **1** [U] (**a**) material burned to produce heat or power, eg wood, coal, oil, etc 燃料: *What sort of fuel do these machines need?* 这些机器需要哪种燃料? (**b**) material that produces nuclear energy 核燃料. **2** [C] any particular type of fuel 任何类型的燃料. **3** [C] (*fig* 比喻) thing that increases anger or other strong feelings (使愤怒或其他激情增强的)刺激因素: *His indifference was a fuel to her hatred.* 他无动于衷使她心中的怨恨火上加油. **4** (idm 习语) **add fuel to the flames** ⇨ ADD.

▷ **fuel** *v* (**-ll-**; *US* **-l-**) **1** [I] take in fuel 给(某物)加燃料: *All aircraft must fuel before a long flight.* 所有飞机均须先加油方能作长途飞行. **2** [Tn] supply (sth) with fuel 供给(某物)燃料: *fuelling a car with petrol* 给汽车加汽油 ○ (*fig* 比喻) *inflation fuelled by big wage increases* 因工资猛涨如火上浇油的通货膨胀.

fug /fʌg; fʌg/ *n* (usu *sing* 通常作单数); (*infml* 口) warm stuffy atmosphere, eg in a small or crowded room 热而污浊的空气(如在狭小的或拥挤的房间里): *Open the window — there's quite a fug in here.* 打开窗户吧 —— 这里的空气不新鲜了. ▷ **fuggy** *adj*.

fu·git·ive /ˈfjuːdʒətɪv; ˋfjudʒətɪv/ *n* **~ (from sb/sth)** person who is running away or escaping 逃跑者; 逃亡者: *fugitives from a country ravaged by war* 从饱受战争蹂躏的国家逃出的难民 ○ *a fugitive from justice* 逃犯.

▷ **fu·git·ive** *adj* **1** escaping; running away 逃亡的; 逃跑的: *a fugitive criminal* 逃跑的罪犯. **2** [usu attrib 通常作定语] (*fml* 文) lasting only a short time; fleeting 短暂的; 瞬间的; 转瞬即逝的: *fugitive thoughts, impressions, sensations, etc* 瞬间的想法、印象、感觉.

fugue /fjuːg; fjug/ *n* musical composition in which one or more themes are introduced and then repeated in a complex pattern 赋格曲.

-ful *suff* 后缀 **1** with *ns* and *vs* forming *adjs* 与名词和动词结合构成形容词; full of; having qualities of; liable to 充满...的; 有...性质的; 有...倾向的: *beautiful* ○ *masterful* ○ *forgetful*. **2** (with *ns* forming *ns* 与名词结合构成名词) amount that fills 充满...的量: *handful* ○ *mouthful*.

ful·crum /ˈfʊlkrəm; ˋfʌlkrəm/ *n* (*pl* **~s** or **fulcra** /ˈfʊlkrə; ˋfulkrə/) point on which a lever is supported 支撑杠杆的点; 支点. ⇨illus at LEVER 见 LEVER 插图.

ful·fil (*US* **ful·fill**) /fʊlˈfɪl; fulˋfɪl/ *v* (**-ll-**) [Tn] **1** perform (sth) or bring (sth) to completion 履行(某事); 使(某事)实现: *fulfil a promise, prophecy* 履行诺言、使预言实现. **2** satisfy (sth); answer 满足(某事); 符合: *fulfil a desire, prayer, hope, need, dream, etc* 满足欲望、实现祈愿、符合愿望、符合需要、符合理想 ○ *Does your job fulfil your expectations?* 你的工作符合你的预想吗? **3** satisfy the specific requirements of (sth) 满足(某事)的要求: *fulfil the terms of a contract* 满足合同条款的要求 ○ *fulfil the conditions of entry to a university* 具备某大学的入学条件. **4** perform (sth); do; obey fully 履行(某事); 做; 服从: *fulfil a duty, a command, an obligation, etc* 履行职责、服从命令、履行义务. **5 ~ oneself** fully develop one's abilities and character 充分发挥自己的能力和性格: *He was able to fulfil himself through music.* 他通过音乐能充分地发挥自己的才能.

▷ **ful·filled** *adj* satisfied; completely happy 满意的; 满足的; 十分愉快的: *He doesn't feel really fulfilled in his* *present job.* 他对目前的工作并非真正满意.

ful·fil·ment *n* [U] fulfilling or being fulfilled 满意; 满足.

full /fʊl; fʊl/ *adj* (**-er, -est**) **1 ~ (of sth/sb)** (**a**) holding or containing as much or as many as possible; completely filled 满的; 饱含的; 充满的: *drawers full to overflowing* 抽屉满得装不进东西 ○ *My cup is full.* 我的杯子是满的. ○ *The bin needs emptying; it's full of rubbish.* 垃圾箱该倒了, 垃圾都满了. ○ *The theatre is full, I'm afraid you'll have to wait for the next show.* 剧院已客满, 很抱歉你只能等下一场了. ⇨Usage at EMPTY[1] 用法见 EMPTY[1]. (**b**) having or containing much or many; crowded 充足的; 丰富的; 挤满的: *a lake full of fish* 有很多鱼的湖 ○ *a room full of people* 挤满人的房间 ○ *She's full of vitality.* 她充满活力. **2 ~ of sth** completely occupied in thinking about sth 头脑里充满某想法的; 只想着某事物的: *She was full of the news,* ie could not stop herself talking about it. 她满脑子都是那消息. **3 ~ (up)** having had enough to eat and drink 吃饱喝足: *No more thank you, I'm full up.* 不添了, 谢谢, 我已经吃饱喝足了. **4** [attrib 作定语] (**a**) complete; plentiful 全面的; 完整的; 详尽的; 充分的: *give full information, details, instructions, etc* 提供完整的资料、详尽的细节、全面的指导等. (**b**) complete; reaching specified or usual limits 完全的; 十足的; 达到(指定的或通常的)限度的: *The roses are in full bloom.* 玫瑰花正在盛开. ○ *I had to wait a full hour for the bus.* 我等公共汽车足足等了一小时. ○ *He got full marks* (ie the highest marks possible) *for his essay.* 他的文章得了满分. ○ *Her dress was a full three inches above the knee.* 她的连衣裙下摆离膝盖整整三英寸. **5** [usu attrib 通常作定语] plump; rounded 丰满的; 圆的: *a full figure* 胖体形 ○ *rather full in the face* 脸很胖. **6** (of clothes) fitting loosely or made with plenty of material (指衣服)宽松的, 肥大的: *a full skirt* 肥大的裙子 ○ *Please make this coat a little fuller across the back.* 请把这件大衣的后身放宽些. **7** (of a tone or voice) deep and mellow (指音调或嗓音)深沉圆润的. **8** (idm 习语) **at full 'stretch** to the limit of one's ability 达到个人能力的限度; 竭尽全力: *working at full stretch* 竭尽全力地工作. **at half/full cock** ⇨ COCK[2]. **come full 'circle** return to the starting point after a series of events, experiences, etc (事情、经历等)绕一圈回到原处. **come to a full 'stop** stop completely 停住: *The car came to a full stop at the traffic lights.* 汽车在交通信号灯处停住了. **draw onself up to one's full height** ⇨ DRAW[2]. **the first/full flush of youth, etc** ⇨ FLUSH[1]. **(at) full 'blast** at maximum power, activity, etc 以最大的力量、活力等: *going, talking, shouting full blast* 疾步行走、高声谈话、大声疾呼 ○ *An orchestra playing at full blast is a tremendous sound.* 管弦乐队全力演奏声音大得惊人. **full of 'beans/'life** having a lot of energy and vitality 精力旺盛. **full of the joys of spring** lively and light-hearted 活泼愉快. **(at) full length** with the body stretched out and flat 全身伸直: *lying full length on the sofa* 全身伸直躺在沙发上. **'full of oneself** (*derog* 贬) selfish and conceited 自私自利; 自以为是: *You're very full of yourself today, I must say.* 你今天太自以为是了, 我不得不说出来. **full of one's own im'portance** (*derog* 贬) thinking that one is very important 自负; 自高自大. **(at) full 'pelt/'tilt/'speed** with great speed or force 以极高的速度或极大的力量: *He drove full tilt into the lamppost.* 他车开得飞快, 撞上了路灯柱. **full speed/steam ahead** (proceeding) with as much speed and vigour as possible 全速前进; 竭尽全力. **give full/short measure** ⇨ MEASURE. **give sb/sth full play** give sb/sth complete freedom of action or expression 使某人[某事物]充分表现或发挥. **have one's hands full** ⇨ HAND[1]. **in full** completely; with nothing omitted 全部地; 全面地; 无省略地; 无遗漏地: *publish a report in full* 全文发表一份报告 ○ *write one's name in full,* eg John Henry Smith, *not* J H Smith 写全名(如写作 John Henry Smith, 不作 J.H. Smith). **in full 'cry** (of a pack of hunting hounds) barking together noisily as they chase their prey (指一群猎犬)追赶猎物时齐声狂吠: (*fig* 比喻) *The pop group raced for their car, pursued by fans in full cry.* 流行歌手朝着他们的汽车跑去, 后面跟着一群狂呼乱叫的歌迷. **in full play** fully operating or active 正在进行中; 正起劲. **in full sail** (of a ship) with all the sails spread or set (指船)张满帆. **in full 'swing** fully active 正起劲; 正活跃: *The party was in full swing when we arrived.* 我们到达时恰值聚会的高潮. **in full 'view (of sb/sth)** completely visible 全都看得见的: *He performed the trick in full view of the whole audience.* 他在全体观众都看得见的情况下变魔术. **to the 'full** to the greatest possible extent 达到尽可能大的程度; 充分地: *enjoy life to the full* 尽情享受人生的乐趣.

▷ **full** *adv* **1** exactly; directly 精确地; 直接地: *John hit him full in the face.* 约翰一下正打在他的脸上. **2** very 很; 非常: *as you know full well* 正如你十分了解的.

full·ness (also **ful·ness**) *n* [U] **1** completeness; being full(4b) 完整; 完全; 全部. **2** (idm 习语) **in the fullness of time** at the appropriate or right time; eventually 在适当的时候; 时机成熟时; 终于: *In the fullness of time they married and had children.* 他们到时候就结了婚, 生了孩子.

fully *adv* **1** completely; entirely 完全地; 全部地; 全面地; 十分地: *fully satisfied* 十分满意 ○ *She was fully dressed in five minutes.* 她用五分钟就已穿戴整齐了. ○ *I was fully expecting to lose my job, so this promotion has come as a complete surprise.* 我原先满以为会失业, 所以这次晋升完全出乎意料. **2** at least; the whole of 至少; 整整: *The journey will take fully two hours.* 此行至少要用两小时. **3** (idm 习语) **fully stretched** made to work, etc at the limits of one's capacities or talents 竭尽所能; 全力以赴. ,**fully-'fashioned** *adj* (of women's clothing) designed to fit the body closely (指女装)设计得完全合身的. ,**fully-'fledged** *adj* **1** (of a young bird) having grown all its feathers (指幼鸟)羽毛丰满的. **2** (*fig* 比喻) mature and well established 成熟的; 巩固的: *Computer science is now a fully-fledged academic subject.* 计算机科学目前已是一门成熟的学科.

'full back (in hockey, football, etc) defensive player near the goal (曲棍球、足球等的)后卫.

,**full-'blooded** *adj* **1** not of mixed race or breed 纯种的: *a* ,*full-blooded 'mare* 纯种母马. **2** vigorous and hearty 血气方刚的; 精神饱满的: *a* ,*full-blooded and* ,*passionate 'person* 既精神又热情的人 ○ (*fig* 比喻) *a* ,*full-blooded 'argument* 激烈的争论.

,**full-'blown** *adj* (esp of flowers) fully developed; quite open (尤指鲜花)盛开的, 怒放的: ,*full-blown 'roses* 盛开的玫瑰.

,**full 'board** the providing of bed and all meals, in a hotel, etc 全食宿(旅馆等提供住宿和全部伙食): *The price is £20 for bed and breakfast, £25 full board.* 住宿加早餐的价钱是 20 英镑, 全食宿 25 英镑. Cf 参看 HALF BOARD (HALF[3]).

,**full-'bodied** *adj* rich in quality, tone, etc 质地纯正的; 醇厚的; 浓烈的; 声调宏亮的; 雄浑的: *a* ,*full-bodied red 'wine* 醇厚的红葡萄酒.

,**full 'house** **1** theatre, cinema, etc with all its seats occupied 满座; 客满: *We have a full house tonight.* 我们今晚客满了. **2** (in poker) set of cards held by a player that consists of three cards of one value and two of another (扑克戏)由三张同点的及另两张同点的牌组成的一手牌. **3** (in bingo, etc) set of numbers needed to win (宾戈等赌博游戏)为获胜所需的一组号码.

,**full-'length** *adj* (**a**) (of a picture, mirror, etc) showing the whole (human) figure (指照片、镜子等)照出(人的)全身的. (**b**) not shortened; of the expected length 未缩短的; 未删节的; 全长的; 照原有长度的: *a* ,*full-length 'novel* 足本的小说 ○ *a* ,*full-length 'skirt,* ie one that reaches the ankles 全长裙(长及踝的).

,**full 'marks** maximum marks possible in an examination, etc (考试等的)满分: (*fig* 比喻) *I must say I give you full marks for your tactful handling of a difficult situation.* 你巧妙地处理了困难的局面, 我得给你打满分.

,**full 'moon** the moon in its fullest phase, with its whole disc illuminated; time when this occurs 满月; 望月. Cf 参看 NEW MOON (NEW).

,**full 'page** *adj* filling a complete page 全页的; 整版的: *a* ,*full page ad'vertisement* 整版篇幅的广告.

,**full-'scale** *adj* not reduced in size; the same size as the object itself; complete 原尺寸的; 与原物同样大小的; 实比的; 完全的; 全面的: *a* ,*full-scale 'drawing, 'plan, 'design, etc* 与原物同样大小的图画、全面的计划、实比的图样 ○ (*fig* 比喻) *a* ,*full-scale reorgani'zation of the department* 部门的全面大改组.

,**full 'stop** (also **full point,** *US* **period**) **1** punctuation

F

mark (.) used at the end of a sentence or an abbreviation 句号；句点. ⇨App 3 见附录3. **2** (used to indicate finality 用以表示定局) without further qualification 无斟酌余地: *I just think he is very unpleasant, full stop.* 我就是认为他很讨厌，没别的说的.
ˌ**full 'time** end of a game of football, etc (足球等比赛的)终场，结束.
ˌ**full-'time** *adj* for or during the whole of the working day or week 全(工作)日制的; 全(工作)周的: *a full-time 'job* 一份全日制的工作. — *adv* on a full-time basis 全日制地; 全周地: ˌ*work full-'time* 全日制工作. Cf 参看 PART-TIME (PART[1]).

fuller /ˈfʊlə(r); ˋfʊlɚ/ *n* person who cleans and thickens freshly woven cloth 漂洗工.
□ ˌ**fuller's 'earth** type of clay used for this process 漂白土; 漂土.

ful·min·ate /ˈfʌlmɪneɪt; *US* ˈfʊl-; ˋfʌlmə,net/ *v* [I, Ipr] ~ **(against sb/sth)** protest strongly and loudly 强烈抗议; 叱责.
▷ **ful·mina·tion** /ˌfʌlmɪˈneɪʃn; *US* ˌfʊl-; ˌfʌlməˋneʃən/ *n* **(a)** [U] fulminating 强烈抗议; 叱责. **(b)** [C] instance of this; bitter protest or criticism 强烈的抗议; 叱责; 激烈的反抗; 严厉的批评.

ful·some /ˈfʊlsəm; ˋfʊlsəm/ *adj* excessive and insincere 过分而虚伪的: *fulsome words, compliments, etc* 溢美之词、恭维等 ○ *be fulsome in one's praise* 假意称赞. ▷ **ful·somely** *adv*. **ful·some·ness** *n* [U].

fumble /ˈfʌmbl; ˋfʌmbl/ *v* **1** [I, Tn] touch or handle (sth) awkwardly or nervously (笨拙地或紧张地)摸索或处理(某事物): *He fumbled the ball and then dropped it.* 他笨手笨脚地漏接了球. **2** [Ipr] ~ **at/for/with sth** use the hands awkwardly in doing sth or in search of sth 笨手笨脚地做某事或寻找某物: *fumble in one's pocket for some coins* 笨手笨脚地在口袋里摸索几枚硬币 ○ *She fumbled with her notes and began to speak.* 她手忙脚乱地翻找讲稿, 然后开始讲话. ○ *fumble for the light switch* 摸索电灯开关 ○ (*fig* 比喻) *fumble for the right thing to say* 笨嘴拙舌地寻找恰当的话题. **3** [Ip] ~ **about/around** move about clumsily in doing sth or in search of sth 笨拙地四处乱走(做某事或寻找某物): *fumbling around in the dark* 在黑暗中瞎撞.
▷ **fumble** *n* [sing] act of fumbling 摸索; 笨拙的处理.

fume /fju:m; fjum/ *n* (usu *pl* 通常作复数) smoke, gas or vapour that smells strongly (气味强烈的)烟, 气, 汽: *petrol fumes* 强烈的汽油味 ○ *The air was thick with cigar fumes.* 空气里弥漫着雪茄的烟.
▷ **fume** *v* **1** [I, Ipr] ~ **(at sb/sth)** be very angry; show this anger 愤怒; 大怒; 发怒; 发火: *fume at the delay* 因耽搁而发怒 ○ *By the time we arrived an hour late she was fuming (with rage).* 我们晚到了一小时, 她正气得七窍生烟. **2** [I] emit or give off fumes 冒烟; 冒气: *The smouldering wreck fumed for days.* 燃烧的残骸冒了好几天的烟. **3** [Tn] treat (esp wood) with chemical fumes to darken it 用(化学药品的)烟雾处理(尤指木材)(使其颜色变深); 熏: *fumed oak* 熏栎木.

fu·mig·ate /ˈfju:mɪgeɪt; ˋfjumə,get/ *v* [Tn] destroy infectious germs, insects, etc in (sth) with the fumes of certain chemicals 用烟熏(某物)消毒: *The hospital wards were fumigated after the outbreak of typhus.* 发现斑疹伤寒以后, 医院的病房进行了烟熏消毒. ▷ **fu·miga·tion** /ˌfju:mɪˈgeɪʃn; ˌfjuməˋgeʃən/ *n* [U].

fun /fʌn; fʌn/ *n* [U] **1** enjoyment; pleasure 享乐; 快乐; 娱乐; 乐趣: *We had lots of fun at the fair today.* 我们今天在游乐场上玩得很高兴. ○ *It took all the fun out of the occasion when we heard that you were ill.* 我们一听说你病了, 欢乐的气氛一扫而光. ○ *What fun it will be when we all go on holiday together.* 我们大家一起去度假那可太有意思了. ○ *Have fun!* ie Enjoy yourself! 尽情玩儿吧! **2** source of this 有趣的事; 开心的事: *Sailing is (good/great) fun.* 帆船运动是一大乐趣. ○ *It's not much fun going to a party alone.* 独自一人去参加聚会没什么意思. **3** playfulness; good humour 滑稽; 幽默: *She's very lively and full of fun.* 她很活泼又很幽默. **4** [attrib 作定语] (*esp US*) amusing; providing pleasure 有趣; 逗笑: *a fun hat* 可笑的帽子. **5** (idm 习语) **(just) for 'fun/for the 'fun of it; (just) in 'fun** for amusement; not seriously; as a joke 取乐; 非认真地; 当笑话: *I'm learning to cook, just for the fun of it.* 我正在学做饭, 做着玩儿而已. ○ *He only said it in fun — he didn't really mean it.* 他只是说着玩儿——并非真是那个意思. **fun and 'games** (*infml* 口) light-hearted and playful activities 玩耍; 嬉戏: *That's enough fun and games! Let's get down to work.* 别再玩儿了! 咱们安下心来工作吧. **make fun of sb/sth** (cause people to) laugh at sb/sth, usu unkindly; ridicule sb/sth (使人)因某人[某事物]发笑(通常含恶意); 嘲笑某人[某事物]: *It's cruel to make fun of people who stammer.* 嘲笑口吃的人未免不近人情. **poke fun at sb/sth** ⇨ POKE[1].
□ **'fun-fair** (also **fair**) *n* collection of outdoor amusements, stalls and side shows, usu in a park 游乐场(露天的娱乐活动、摊位游戏、杂耍表演等, 通常于公园中).

func·tion /ˈfʌŋkʃn; ˋfʌŋkʃən/ *n* **1** special activity or purpose of a person or thing 作用; 功能; 机能; 职能; 职责: *to fulfil a useful function* 起到有益的作用 ○ *The function of the heart is to pump blood through the body.* 心脏的功能是把血液输往全身. ○ *It is not the function of this committee to deal with dismissals.* 处理解雇问题不是本委员会的职责. **2** important social event or official ceremony 重大的社交聚会; 典礼; 宴会: *Heads of state attend numerous functions every year.* 国家首脑每年要出席很多重大宴会. **3** (*mathematics* 数) quantity whose value depends on the varying values of others 函数: *X is a function of Y.* X是Y的函数. **4** any of the basic operations of a computer (计算机的任何基本的)功能: *What functions can this program perform?* 这一程序有哪些功能?
▷ **func·tion** *v* **1** [I] work; operate 起作用; 运转: *His brain seems to be functioning normally.* 他的大脑看来功能正常. ○ *This machine has stopped functioning,* ie is out of order. 这机器坏了. **2** [Ipr] ~ **as sth** work as sth; operate or perform the function(1) of the thing specified 起某物的作用; 具有某物的功能; 起到所述事物的作用: *The sofa can also function as a bed.* 这沙发也可以当床. ○ *Some English adverbs function as adjectives.* 英语中有些副词可作形容词用.
func·tional /-ʃənl; -ʃənl̩/ *adj* **1** of or having a function(1) or functions 功能的; 机能的; 职务上的; 有作用的; 有功能的: *a functional duty, title, office* 职责、职称、职能 ○ *a functional disorder,* ie illness caused when an organ of the body fails to perform its function 机能紊乱. **2** practical and useful; not decorative 实用的; 非装饰性的: *functional furniture, clothing, architecture* 实用的家具、衣服、建筑. **3** [pred 作表语] working; able to work 起作用; 运转; 能起作用; 能运转: *Is this machine functional?* 这机器能用吗? ○ *I'm hardly functional if I don't get eight hours' sleep!* 我要是不睡上八个小时就无法工作! **func·tion·ally** /-ʃənəlɪ; -ʃənəlɪ/ *adv*.
□ **'function key** (*computing* 计) key that causes an operation or sequence of operations to be performed 功能键; 操作键: *a special function key that displays the help menu* 显示求助项目单的特殊功能键.

func·tion·al·ism /ˈfʌŋkʃənəlɪzəm; ˋfʌŋkʃənl̩,ɪzəm/ *n* [U] principle in architecture, design, etc that the purpose and use of an object should determine its shape and construction 功能主义, 实用建筑主义(主张建筑物的形式和结构应取决于其用途).
▷ **func·tion·al·ist** /-ʃənəlɪst; -ʃənl̩ɪst/ *n, adj* (believer in the principle) of functionalism 功能主义的; 功能主义者.

func·tion·ary /ˈfʌŋkʃənərɪ; *US* -nerɪ; ˋfʌŋkʃən,ɛrɪ/ *n* (*often derog* 常作贬义) person with official duties 公务员; 官员: *a minor functionary* 小官.

fund /fʌnd; fʌnd/ *n* **1** [C] sum of money saved or made available for a particular purpose 专款; 基金: *a disaster/relief fund* 赈灾[救济]款 ○ *the church restoration fund* 教堂修缮基金. **2** [sing] stock or supply of sth 某事物的储备或蕴藏: *a fund of jokes, knowledge, experience, etc* 大量的笑话、知识、经验等. **3 funds** [pl] financial resources; money 资金; 现款: *government funds* 政府的资金 ○ *I'm short of funds so I'll pay you next week.* 我手头缺钱, 下星期再付给你吧. **4** (idm 习语) **in funds** having money to spend 有钱花.
▷ **fund** *v* [Tn] **1** provide (an institution, a project, etc) with money (为机构、项目等)拨款: *The government is funding another unemployment scheme.* 政府正为处理失业问题的另一计划拨款. **2** make (a debt) long-term at a fixed rate of interest 将(短期借款)转为有固定利息的长期借款.

F

fun·da·mental /ˌfʌndəˈmentl; ˌfʌndəˈmɛntl̩/ *adj* **1** (**a**) of or forming the basis or foundation of sth; essential 基本的; 基础的; 构成基础的; 根本的: *There are fundamental differences between your religious beliefs and mine.* 你我的宗教信仰根本不同. (**b**) serving as a starting-point; basic 作为起点的; 基本的: *the fundamental rules of mathematics* 数学的基本法则. **2** most important; central or primary 十分重要的; 主要的; 首要的: *His fundamental concern was for her welfare.* 他最关心的是她的幸福. ○ *The fundamental question is a political one.* 首要的问题是政治问题. **3** ~ (**to sth**) essential or necessary 根本的; 必要的: *Hard work is fundamental to success.* 必须苦干才能成功.

▷ **fun·da·mental** *n* (usu *pl* 通常作复数) basic rule or principle; essential part 基本规则; 基本原则; 基本原理; 基本部分: *the fundamentals of religion, philosophy, art, etc* 宗教、哲学、艺术等的基本原理.

fun·da·ment·ally /-təlɪ; -tlɪ/ *adv* basically 基本地; 基础地; 根本地: *Her ideas are fundamentally sound, even if she says silly things sometimes.* 即使她有时说些傻话, 她的想法基本上是好的.

fun·da·ment·al·ism /ˌfʌndəˈmentəlɪzəm; ˌfʌndəˈmɛntl̩ˌɪzəm/ *n* [U] (in Christian thought) belief that the Bible is literally true and should form the basis of religious thought or practice (基督教学说)原教旨主义, 基要主义(认为《圣经》的经文翔实无误, 应构成宗教的理论或实践的基础).

▷ **fun·da·ment·al·ist** /-ɪst; -ɪst/ *n* supporter of fundamentalism 原教旨主义者; 基要主义者: [attrib 作定语] *fundamentalist ideas* 原教旨主义思想.

fu·neral /ˈfjuːnərəl; ˋfjunərəl/ *n* **1** (usu religious) ceremony of burying or burning dead people (通常为宗教的)葬礼, 出殡: *When is his funeral?* 他的葬礼何时举行? ○ [attrib 作定语] *funeral rites* 葬礼 ○ *a funeral procession* 送葬的行列 ○ *a funeral march*, ie a sad and solemn piece of music suitable for funerals 送葬曲. **2** procession of people at a funeral 送葬人的行列. **3** (idm 习语) **it's/that's my, etc funeral** (*infml* 口) it's/that's my, etc particular and unpleasant responsibility 那是我自己的、某某人的...倒霉事: *'You're going to fail your exams if you don't work hard.' 'That's my funeral, not yours.'* '你要不努力, 考试就不会及格.' '倒霉是我自己的事, 跟你没关系.'

▷ **fu·ner·eal** /fjuːˈnɪərɪəl; fjuˋnɪrɪəl/ *adj* suitable for a funeral; gloomy; dismal 适于葬礼的; 忧郁的; 凄凉的; 阴沉的: *a funereal expression, atmosphere* 忧郁的表情、凄凉的气氛.

□ ˈ**funeral director** (*esp US*) = UNDERTAKER.

ˈ**funeral parlour** (*US* ˈ**funeral home**) place where dead people are prepared for burial or cremation 殡仪馆.

fun·gi·cide /ˈfʌndʒɪsaɪd; ˋfʌndʒəˌsaɪd/ *n* [C, U] substance that kills fungus 杀真菌剂.

fungus 真菌

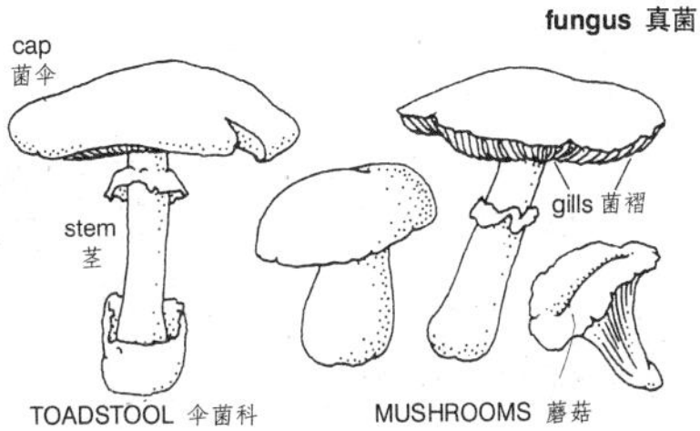

fungus /ˈfʌŋgəs; ˋfʌŋgəs/ *n* (*pl* **-gi** /-gaɪ, *also* -dʒaɪ; -gaɪ, -dʒaɪ/ or **~es** /-gəsɪz; -gəsɪz/) **1** (**a**) [C] any of various types of plant without leaves, flowers or green colouring-matter, growing on other plants or decaying matter 真菌; 蕈: *Mildew and mushrooms are fungi.* 霉和蘑菇都是真菌. ⇨illus 见插图. (**b**) [U] such plants as a group 真菌类植物丛: *The lawn was covered with fungus.* 草地上到处都是蘑菇. **2** [U] types of fungus harmful to plants, etc 对植物等有害的真菌: *The roses have fungus.* 玫瑰花长了真菌. ○ [attrib 作定语] *a fungus infection* 真菌感染.

▷ **fung·oid** /ˈfʌŋgɔɪd; ˋfʌŋgɔɪd/ *adj* of or like a fungus (似)真菌的: *fungoid growths* 真菌样生长物.

fung·ous /ˈfʌŋgəs; ˋfʌŋgəs/ *adj* of, like or caused by fungus (似)真菌的; 由真菌引起的: *fungous diseases* 由真菌引起的疾病.

fu·nicu·lar /fjuːˈnɪkjʊlə(r); fjuˋnɪkjələ˞/ *n* (also **funicular railway**) railway on a steep slope, with some cars being pulled up by a cable at the same time as others are lowered by it 缆索铁道.

funk /fʌŋk; fʌŋk/ *n* (*infml* 口) **1** [sing] (also **blue funk**) (state of) fear or anxiety 恐惧; 忧虑: *She was in a funk about changing jobs.* 她害怕变换工作. **2** [C] (*derog* 贬) coward 胆怯的人; 胆小鬼.

▷ **funk** *v* [Tn, Tg] avoid (sth/doing sth) because of fear (因恐惧)避开(某事物[做某事]): *He funked telling her he had lost his job.* 他不敢告诉她自己已经失业了.

funky /ˈfʌŋkɪ; ˋfʌŋkɪ/ *adj* (**-ier, -iest**) **1** (*sl* 俚) (of music, esp jazz) having a characteristic rhythm and expressiveness, like early blues music (指音乐, 尤指爵士乐)有独特节奏和表现力的(像早期布鲁斯乐曲). **2** (*infml approv* 口, 褒) very modern; fashionable 新式的; 新型的; 时髦的: *a funky car, party, hairstyle* 新型汽车、新式聚会、时髦发型.

fun·nel /ˈfʌnl; ˋfʌnl̩/ *n* **1** tube or pipe that is wide at the top and narrow at the bottom, used for pouring liquids, powders, etc into a small opening 漏斗: *I need a funnel to pour petrol into the tank.* 我需要一个漏斗把汽油灌进油箱. ⇨illus at FILTER 见FILTER插图. **2** metal chimney on a steam-engine, ship, etc, through which smoke escapes (蒸汽机、轮船等的)烟囱.

▷ **fun·nel** *v* (**-ll-**; *US* **-l-**) [Ipr, Ip, Tn, Tn·pr, Tn·p] (cause sth to) move through a funnel or a narrow space (使某物)通过漏斗或狭窄的空间: *funnel petrol into a can* 用漏斗把汽油注入罐中 ○ *The water funnelled through the gorge and out onto the plain.* 水穿过峡谷流到平原.

funny /ˈfʌnɪ; ˋfʌnɪ/ *adj* (**-ier, -iest**) **1** causing amusement, laughter, etc 有趣的; 可笑的: *funny stories* 好笑的故事 ○ *a funny man* 风趣的人 ○ *That's the funniest thing I've ever heard.* 那是我听说过的最可笑的事. **2** difficult to explain or understand; strange 难以解释的; 难以理解的; 奇怪的: *A funny thing happened to me today.* 今天我遇见个莫名其妙的事. ○ *That's funny — he was here a moment ago and now he's gone.* 真是怪事——他刚才还在这里, 转眼就走了. ○ *The engine's making a very funny noise.* 这发动机有一种很怪的声音. **3** (*infml* 口) (**a**) slightly unwell 稍感不适的; 稍不舒服的: *I feel a bit funny today — I don't think I'll go to work.* 我今天有点儿不舒服——不想上班去了. ○ *That drink has made me feel quite funny.* 我喝了那种饮料很不好受. (**b**) slightly insane; eccentric 轻度疯癫的; 古怪的: *a funny old lady* 古怪的女人 ○ *She went a bit funny after her husband died.* 她自丈夫死后就变得疯疯癫癫的. **4** (idm 习语) ˈ**funny business** (*infml* 口) sth that is illegal, suspicious or not approved of 非法的、可疑的或不认可的事物: *I want none of your funny business.* 我可不干那种非法的事. **funny ha-ˈha** (*infml* 口) = FUNNY 1. **funny peˈculiar** (*infml* 口) = FUNNY 2: *'He's a funny chap.' 'Do you mean funny ha-ha or funny peculiar?'* '他这家伙很有意思.' '你指的是有趣还是古怪?'

▷ **fun·nily** /-ɪlɪ; -ɪlɪ/ *adv* in a strange or odd way 奇怪地; 古怪的 (expressing surprise at a coincidence, etc 表示对巧合等的惊奇): *Funnily enough* (ie It so happened that) *I met her just yesterday.* 再没那么巧的了, 我昨天正碰见她.

fun·ni·ness *n* [U].

□ ˈ**funny-bone** *n* part of the elbow which has a very sensitive nerve, and which tingles unpleasantly when it is knocked 麻筋儿(肘端神经极敏感处, 碰撞时产生酥麻感).

fur /fɜː(r); fɝ/ *n* [U] **1** soft thick hair covering the bodies of certain animals (某些动物的)浓密的软毛: *The puppies haven't got much fur yet.* 小狗还没长出多少毛. **2** [U, C] animal skin(s) with fur on, esp as used for making clothes, etc 动物的毛皮(尤指做服装等用的): *a coat made of fur* 毛皮大衣 ○ *fine fox furs* 上等狐皮 ○ [attrib 作定语] *a fur coat* 毛皮大衣. **3** [C] garment made of fur 毛皮制成的衣服: *He gave her an expensive fur for her birthday.* 他送给她一件昂贵的毛皮衣服作生

日礼物. **4** [U] fabric made to look and feel like fur 外观和手感都像毛皮的织物. **5** [U] coating on a person's tongue during illness 舌苔. **6** [U] (*Brit*) (*US* **scale**) grey crusty coating that forms on the inside of a kettle, pipes, etc from water that contains lime 水锈; 水垢. **7** (idm 习语) **make the fur/sparks fly** ⇨ FLY².

▷ **fur** *v* (**-rr-**) [usu passive 通常用于被动语态: I, Ip, Tn, Tn·p] **~ (sth) (up)** (cause sth to) become covered with fur(5,6) 使(某物)生苔、生水锈: *a furred tongue/kettle* 长了苔的舌[生了水锈的壶].

furry /ˈfɜːrɪ; ˋfɝɪ/ *adj* (**-ier, -iest**) **1** of or like fur (似)毛皮的. **2** covered with fur 毛皮覆盖的; 生苔的; 生水锈的: *a furry toy* 毛茸茸的玩具.

fur *abbr* 缩写 = furlong(s).

fur·below /ˈfɜːbɪləʊ; ˋfɝbḷ,o/ *n* (usu *pl* 通常作复数) showy or unnecessary ornament (on a dress, etc) (连衣裙等的)花哨的或多余的装饰: *frills and furbelows* 褶边和花哨的装饰.

fur·bish /ˈfɜːbɪʃ; ˋfɝbɪʃ/ *v* [Tn, Tn·p] **~ sth (up)** polish, clean or renovate (esp sth that has not been used for a long time) 擦亮, 打扫, 整修(尤指很久没用的物品): *furbish up an antique sword* 擦亮一把古剑.

furi·ous /ˈfjʊərɪəs; ˋfjʊrɪəs/ *adj* **1 ~ (with sb)/(at sth)** full of violent anger 满腔愤怒的; 大发雷霆的: *She was absolutely furious (at his behaviour).* 她(对他的行为)大发雷霆. **2** violent; intense; unrestrained 猛烈的; 强烈的; 激烈的; 极度的: *a furious struggle, storm, debate* 激烈的斗争、猛烈的暴风雨、激烈的辩论 ○ *She drove off at a furious speed.* 她以飞快的速度开车走了. **3** (idm 习语) **fast and furious** ⇨ FAST¹. ▷ **furi·ously** *adv*.

furl /fɜːl; fɝl/ *v* **1** [Tn] roll up and fasten (a sail, a flag, an umbrella, etc) 卷紧, 收拢(帆、旗子、伞等). **2** [I] become furled 变成卷紧的或收拢的: *This fan doesn't furl neatly.* 这把扇子折不上了.

fur·long /ˈfɜːlɒŋ; *US* -lɔːŋ; ˋfɝlɔŋ/ *n* distance of 220 yards or 201 metres; one eighth of a mile 弗隆, 浪(长度单位, 相当于220码、201米或1/8英里). ⇨App 5 见附录5.

fur·lough /ˈfɜːləʊ; ˋfɝlo/ *n* [C, U] (permission for) absence from duty, esp that granted to civil servants, soldiers, etc working abroad 休假(许可)(尤指给予在国外工作的官员、士兵等的): *six months' furlough* 6个月的假期 ○ *going home on furlough* 休假回国.

fur·nace /ˈfɜːnɪs; ˋfɝnɪs/ *n* **1** enclosed fireplace for heating the water used to warm a building by means of pipes 暖气锅炉. **2** enclosed space or chamber for heating metal, glass, etc to a very high temperature 熔炉: *It's like a furnace in here — can we open a window?* 这里热得像个火炉——咱们打开窗户好吗?

fur·nish /ˈfɜːnɪʃ; ˋfɝnɪʃ/ *v* **1** [Tn, Tn·pr] **~ sth (with sth)** provide sth with furniture; put furniture in (a place) 为某物提供家具; 用家具布置(某地方): *furnish a house, a room, an office, etc* 用家具布置房子、房间、办公室等 ○ *a furnished flat*, ie one rented complete with its furniture 连同家具一起出租的公寓 ○ *The room was furnished with antiques.* 房间里摆着古董. **2** [Tn, Tn·pr, Dn·pr] **~ sb/sth with sth; ~ sth (to sb/sth)** supply or provide sb/sth with sth 为某人[某物]提供某事物: *furnish a village with supplies/furnish supplies to a village* 供应某村庄生活用品 ○ *furnish all the equipment for a major expedition* 为一大探险队提供全部装备 ○ *This scandal will furnish the town with plenty of gossip.* 这件丑事要在镇上惹出很多闲话.

▷ **fur·nish·ings** *n* [pl] furniture, equipment, fittings, etc in a room or house (房屋里的)家具与陈设等.

fur·ni·ture /ˈfɜːnɪtʃə(r); ˋfɝnɪtʃɚ/ *n* [U] movable articles, eg tables, chairs, beds, etc put into a house or an office to make it suitable for living or working in 家具. ⇨illus at App 1 见附录1插图, page xvi.

fur·ore /fjʊˈrɔːrɪ; ˋfjʊrɔr/ (*US* **furor** /ˈfjuːrɔːr; ˋfjʊrɔr/) *n* [sing] general uproar of admiration or anger 轰动; 骚动: *His last novel created a furore among the critics.* 他的最近一部小说在评论家中引起了轰动.

fur·rier /ˈfʌrɪə(r); ˋfʌrɪɚ/ *n* person who prepares or sells fur or fur clothing 毛皮加工者; 皮货商.

fur·row /ˈfʌrəʊ; ˋfʌro/ *n* **1** long narrow trench cut in the earth, esp by a plough 犁沟; 垄沟: *furrows ready for planting* 为播种而犁好的沟. Cf 参看 RIDGE 1, ⇨illus at PLOUGH 见 PLOUGH 插图. **2** groove resembling this, eg a deep wrinkle in the skin 类似的沟(如皮肤上的皱纹): *Deep furrows lined his brow.* 深深的皱纹布上他的额头. **3** (idm 习语) **plough a lonely furrow** ⇨ PLOUGH *v*.

▷ **fur·row** *v* [Tn esp passive 尤用于被动语态] make furrows in (sth) 犁; 使(某物)起皱纹: *newly furrowed fields* 刚犁过的田地 ○ *a forehead furrowed by old age and anxiety* 因年老和忧虑而起了皱纹的前额.

furry ⇨ FUR.

fur·ther /ˈfɜːðə(r); ˋfɝðɚ/ *adj* **1** more distant in space, direction or time; farther (空间、距离或时间上)更远的, 较远的: *The hospital is further down the road.* 医院在这条路上, 再往前走就到了. **2** additional; more 附加的; 更多的: *further volumes* 后续各卷 ○ *Have you any further questions?* 你还有问题吗? ○ *There is nothing further to be said.* 没有再多说的了. ○ *The museum is closed until further notice*, ie until another announcement about it is made. 博物馆现正闭馆, 开馆时间另行通知.

▷ **fur·ther** *adv* **1** at or to a greater distance in space or time; more remote; farther (在时间或空间上)距离更大地, 更远地: *It's not safe to go any further.* 再往远走就不安全了. ○ *Africa is further from England than France.* 非洲距离英国比距离法国远. ○ *Think further back into your childhood.* 想想你更小的时候, 回忆一下你的童年. **2** in addition; also 此外; 而且: *Further, it has come to my attention*... 此外, 我已注意到... **3** to a greater degree or extent 进一步地: *I must enquire further into this matter.* 我要进一步调查此事. ○ *I can offer you £50, but I can't go any further than that.* 我可以付给你50英镑, 不能再多了. **4** (idm 习语) **far/farther/further afield** ⇨ AFIELD. ⇨Usage at FARTHER 用法见 FARTHER.

fur·ther *v* [Tn] help the progress or development of (sth); promote 促进或推动(某事); 增进: *further sb's interests* 提高某人的兴趣 ○ *further the cause of peace* 推动和平事业.

fur·ther·ance /ˈfɜːðərəns; ˋfɝðərəns/ *n* [U] advancement of sb's interests, a cause, etc 某人兴趣的提高、某事业的促进等.

fur·ther·more /ˌfɜːðəˈmɔː(r); ˋfɝðɚ,mɔr/ *adv* in addition; moreover 此外; 再者; 而且.

fur·ther·most /-məʊst; -,most/ *adj* most distant in space or time; furthest (FURTHER 1) (在空间或时间上)相隔最远的.

□ ˌ**further eduˈcation** formal (but not university) education provided for people older than school age 继续教育(为超过中学学龄的人所设的正规教育, 但并非大学).

fur·thest /ˈfɜːðɪst; ˋfɝðɪst/ *adj, adv* = FARTHEST.

furt·ive /ˈfɜːtɪv; ˋfɝtɪv/ *adj* (**a**) done secretly and quietly so as not to be noticed 偷偷摸摸的; 鬼鬼祟祟的: *a furtive glance* 偷偷的一瞥 ○ *furtive movements* 诡秘的活动. (**b**) (of a person or his behaviour) sly or secretive, suggesting that one is guilty of sth or does not want to be noticed (指人或行为)躲躲闪闪的; 遮遮掩掩的. ▷ **furt·ively** *adv*. **furt·ive·ness** *n* [U].

fury /ˈfjʊərɪ; ˋfjʊrɪ/ *n* **1** [U] wild and violent anger 狂怒; 暴怒: *speechless with fury* 气得说不出话来. **2** [C] state or condition of extreme emotion, esp anger or excitement 愤怒; 激动: *He was in one of his uncontrollable furies.* 他怒不可遏. ○ *She flew into a fury when I wouldn't lend her any money.* 我不借给她钱, 她顿时勃然大怒. **3** [U] strength or violence of activity, weather, etc (活动、天气等的)激烈, 猛烈: *The fury of the storm abated.* 暴风雨的威力已经减弱. **4** [C] fiercely angry person, esp a woman or girl 狂怒的人(尤指女子); 泼妇. **5 the Furies** [pl] (in Greek mythology) goddesses with snakes instead of hair, sent from the underworld to punish crime (希腊神话中)复仇女神. **6** (idm 习语) **like fury** (*infml* 口) with great effort, speed, concentration, etc 努力; 飞快; 全神贯注: *He ran like fury to catch the bus.* 他拼命奔跑去追赶公共汽车.

furze /fɜːz; fɝz/ *n* [U] = GORSE.

fuse¹ /fjuːz; fjuz/ *n* **1** piece of easily burnt material (eg rope, paper) along which a spark moves to ignite a firework, bomb, etc so that it explodes 导火线; 导火索. **2** (*US* also **fuze** /fjuːz; fjuz/) device that makes a bomb, shell, etc explode either on impact or at a particular time 引信; 信管; 雷管: *The bomb had been set with a four-hour fuse.* 炸弹上装了一个四小时起爆的引信. **3** (idm 习语) **on a short fuse** ⇨ SHORT¹.

fuse² /fjuːz; fjuz/ *v* [I, Ipr, Ip, Tn, Tn·pr, Tn·p] **1** (cause

F

sth to) become liquid by means of heat（加热使某物）变成液体; 熔化; 熔融: *fuse metals (into a solid mass)* 使金属熔化(成为硬块). **2** join (sth) or become joined by means of heat（加热）连接某物; 熔合: *fuse two pieces of wire together* 熔合两根金属丝 ○ (*fig* 比喻) *The two companies are fused by their common interests.* 两公司因有共同利益而结合在一起.

▷ **fus·ible** /ˈfjuːzəbl; ˋfjuzəbl̩/ *adj* that can be melted or joined together 可熔化的; 可熔合的.

fuse[3] /fjuːz; fjuz/ *n* (in an electric circuit) short piece of wire that melts and breaks the circuit if the current exceeds a safe level 保险丝: *It looks as though you've blown a fuse*, ie caused it to melt. 看样子你把保险丝烧断了.

▷ **fuse** *v* **1** [I, Tn] (of an electric circuit) stop or cause to stop working because a fuse melts（指电路）因保险丝烧断而断电: *The lights have all fused.* 保险丝断了, 灯都灭了. ○ *I've fused all the lights.* 我把保险丝烧断了, 电灯全都灭了. **2** [Tn] put a fuse in (a circuit or an appliance)（在电路或电器上）安装保险丝.

□ ˈ**fuse-box** *n* small cupboard or box containing the fuses of an electrical system 保险丝盒.

ˈ**fuse wire** wire used in electrical fuses 作保险丝用的金属丝.

fu·sel·age /ˈfjuːzəlɑːʒ; *US* ˈfjuːsəlɑːʒ; ˋfjuzl̩,ɑʒ/ *n* body of an aeroplane, ie the part to which the engine(s), wings and tail are fitted（飞机的）机身. ⇨illus at AIRCRAFT 见 AIRCRAFT 插图.

fu·sil·ier /ˌfjuːzəˈlɪə(r); ˌfjuzl̩ˋɪr/ *n* **1** [C] (formerly) soldier armed with a light gun called a *musket*（旧时）配备轻滑膛枪的士兵. **2** (**a**) (also *esp US* **fu·sil·eer**) [C] soldier in certain infantry regiments 某些步兵团的士兵. (**b**) **Fusiliers** [pl] any of several infantry regiments formerly armed with light muskets 旧时以轻滑膛枪装备的步兵团: *the Royal Welsh Fusiliers* 皇家威尔士步兵团.

fu·sil·lade /ˌfjuːzəˈleɪd; *US* -sə-; ˌfjuzl̩ˋed/ *n* **1** continuous or simultaneous shooting of guns（枪炮的）连发, 齐射. **2** (*fig* 比喻) great outburst of questions, criticism, etc 连珠炮似的质问、批评等.

fu·sion /ˈfjuːʒn; ˋfjuʒən/ *n* [C, U] **1** the blending or uniting of different things into one, by melting, etc 熔合; 融合: *the fusion of copper and zinc to produce brass* 将铜和锌熔合以制造黄铜 ○ (*fig* 比喻) *a fusion of ideas* 不同思想的混合体. **2** union of atomic nuclei to form a heavier nucleus, usu with energy being released 聚变: *nuclear fusion* 核聚变.

fuss /fʌs; fʌs/ *n* **1** (**a**) [U] (esp unnecessary) nervous excitement or activity（尤指不必要的）神经质的激动或活动: *Stop all this fuss and get on with your work.* 别大惊小怪的闹了, 继续干你的活儿去吧. (**b**) [sing] display of excitement, worry, etc, esp over sth unimportant 无谓的激动、烦恼等: *Don't get into a fuss about nothing.* 别没事找事, 自寻烦恼. **2** [sing] angry scene 发怒的场面: *There will be a real fuss if you're caught stealing.* 你要是偷东西让人逮着, 那可真够你受的. **3** (idm 习语) **make, kick up, etc a fuss (about/over sth)** complain strongly 强烈地不满: *She's kicking up an awful fuss about the high rent.* 她大喊大叫地抱怨房租太高. **make a fuss of/over sb/sth** pay particular and often excessive attention to sb/sth 对某人[某事物]过于注意: *Don't make so much fuss over the children.* 不要对孩子照顾得太过分. ○ *A lot of fuss was made of the play, but it wasn't a success.* 对那出戏不厌其烦地精心计划, 到头来却并不成功.

▷ **fuss** *v* **1** [I, Ip] **~ (about)** be worried or excited, esp over small things 烦恼, 激动(尤指对小事): *Stop fussing and eat your food!* 别大惊小怪的, 吃你的东西吧! ○ *If you keep fussing about, we're sure to be late.* 你要是总瞎忙个没完, 我们非迟到不可. **2** [Tn] annoy or disturb (sb) 扰乱, 打搅(某人): *Don't fuss me while I'm driving.* 我开车时别打搅我. **3** [Ipr] **~ over sb** pay excessive attention to sb …过于注意某人: *He's always fussing over his grandchildren.* 他对孙儿们过于操心. **4** (idm 习语) **not be fussed (about sb/sth)** (*infml* 口) not care very much 不太关心; 不太注意; 不太在意: *'Where do you want to go for lunch?' 'I'm not fussed.'* '你想到哪儿去吃午饭?' '无所谓.'

□ ˈ**fusspot** *n* (*infml* 口) very fussy(1,2) person 非常挑剔的人.

fussy /ˈfʌsɪ; ˋfʌsɪ/ *adj* (**-ier, -iest**) (*usu derog* 通常作贬义) **1** nervously active or excited about small things（对小事）神经过敏的, 紧张不安的: *fussy parents* 过分操心的父母 ○ *a fussy manner* 紧张不安的举止. **2 ~ (about sth)** giving too much close attention to detail, etc and therefore difficult to please 挑剔的: *Our teacher is very fussy about punctuation.* 我们的老师对标点符号非常重视. ○ *Don't be so fussy (about your food).* 你别那么挑食. **3** (of clothes, design, etc) too full of detail or decoration（指服装、设计图样等）零碎儿太多的, 装饰太多的: *a fussy pattern* 过分装饰的式样. ▷ **fuss·ily** *adv.* **fussi·ness** *n* [U].

fus·tian /ˈfʌstɪən; *US* -tʃən; ˋfʌstʃən/ *n* [U] **1** thick strong coarse cotton cloth 厚而结实的粗棉布; 粗斜纹布: *a jacket (made) of fustian* 粗斜纹布(制成)的甲克 ○ [attrib 作定语] *a fustian jacket* 粗斜纹布甲克. **2** (*dated derog* 旧, 贬) talk that sounds impressive but is in fact empty and worthless; bombast 空洞无物的吹嘘; 夸夸其谈.

fusty /ˈfʌstɪ; ˋfʌstɪ/ *adj* (**-ier, -iest**) (*derog* 贬) **1** smelling old, stale or damp 腐臭的; 有霉湿味的: *a fusty room* 有潮湿味儿的房间 ○ *This blanket smells a bit fusty.* 这毯子有点儿发霉的味儿. **2** old-fashioned; not up-to-date 老式的; 不合潮流的: *a fusty old professor*, ie one who has learned much from books, etc but does not know about modern ideas 思想陈腐的老教授. ▷ **fusti·ness** *n* [U].

fu·tile /ˈfjuːtaɪl; *US* -tl; ˋfjutl̩/ *adj* producing no result; useless; pointless 无效的; 无用的; 无意义的: *a futile attempt/exercise* 无效的尝试[练习] ○ *Their efforts to revive him were futile.* 他们对他抢救无效. ○ *What a futile* (ie unnecessarily silly) *remark!* 纯属废话!

▷ **fu·til·ity** /fjuːˈtɪlətɪ; fjuˋtɪlətɪ/ *n* [U] uselessness; pointlessness 无效; 无用; 无益: *the futility of war* 战争的无谓.

fu·ture /ˈfjuːtʃə(r); ˋfjutʃɚ/ *n* **1** (**a**) [U] time that will come after the present 将来; 未来: *in the near/distant future*, ie soon/not soon 不久[很久]以后 ○ *Who knows what will happen in the future?* 谁知道将来会发生什么事? (**b**) [U] events that will happen then 以后将要发生的事: *History influences both the present and the future.* 历史既影响现在又影响将来. (**c**) [C] condition or state of sb/sth then 某人[某事物]今后的情况; 前途; 前景: *Her future is uncertain.* 她前途未卜. ○ *The future of this project will be decided by the government.* 该计划的前景将由政府决定. **2** [U] possibility of success, happiness, etc coming later; prospects 前途: *I gave up my job because there was no future in it.* 我的工作没有前途, 所以我不干了. **3 futures** [pl] (*commerce* 商) goods or shares (SHARE[1] 3) bought at agreed prices but delivered and paid for later 期货(交易). **4** (idm 习语) **in future** from this time onwards 从今以后; 今后: *Please be punctual in future.* 今后请准时.

▷ **fu·ture** *adj* [attrib 作定语] of or taking place in the future 将来的; 未来的; 将要发生的: *her future husband, job, prospects* 她未来的丈夫、工作、前途 ○ *future events* 未来的事情 ○ *a future life*, ie after death 来生.

fu·ture·less *adj* without hope for a (successful) future 无希望的; 无前途的: *a futureless career* 无前途的职业.

fu·tur·ism /ˈfjuːtʃərɪzəm; ˋfjutʃɚˌɪzəm/ *n* [U] movement in art and literature that abandoned tradition and sought to express the energy and growth of a modern mechanized life-style 未来主义, 未来派(主张打破传统的文艺运动, 追求表现现代机械化生活方式的力量与发展).

▷ **fu·tur·ist** *n, adj* (supporter) of futurism 未来主义的; 未来主义者; 未来派的(文艺家).

fu·tur·istic /ˌfjuːtʃəˈrɪstɪk; ˌfjutʃəˋrɪstɪk/ *adj* **1** looking suitable for the future or extremely modern; not traditional 合于未来的; 极新潮的; 非传统的: *futuristic design, furniture, housing* 新潮的设计、家具、房屋等. **2** of or relating to futurism 未来主义的; 与未来主义有关的.

fu·tur·ity /fjuːˈtjʊərətɪ; *US* -ˈtʊər-; fjuˋturətɪ/ *n* (**a**) [U] future time; the future 将来; 未来: *gazing into futurity* 展望未来. (**b**) [C often *pl* 常作复数] future events 将来的事.

fuzz[1] /fʌz; fʌz/ *n* [U] **1** mass of soft light particles; fluff 轻柔的物质; 绒毛: *A peach skin is covered with fuzz.* 桃

上有一层细毛. **2** short fine hair that sticks up 竖起来的短细的毛发.

fuzz[2] /fʌz; fʌz/ *n* [Gp] **the fuzz** (*sl* 俚) the police 警察.

fuzzy /ˈfʌzɪ; ˋfʌzɪ/ *adj* (**-ier**, **-iest**) **1** like fuzz; having a soft and fluffy texture 绒毛般的; 有柔软绒毛织物的; 毛茸茸的: *a fuzzy teddy bear, blanket, sweater* 毛茸茸的玩具熊、毯子、毛衣 ○ *fuzzy* (ie tightly curled) *hair* 有小卷的毛发. **2** blurred or indistinct, esp in shape or outline 模糊的, 不清楚的(尤指形状或轮廓): *These photographs have come out all fuzzy.* 这些照片照得都不清楚. ▷ **fuzz·ily** *adv*. **fuzzi·ness** *n* [U].

fwd *abbr* 缩写 = forward.

-fy ⇨ -IFY.

F

G g

G, g /dʒiː; dʒi/ *n* (*pl* **G's, g's** /dʒiːz; dʒiz/) **1** the seventh letter of the English alphabet 英语字母表的第七个字母: *'God' begins with (a) G/'G'.* God一字以G字母开始. **2 G** (*music* 音) the fifth note in the scale of C major C大调音阶中的第五音或音符.

g *abbr* 缩写 = **1** gram(s): *300g* 300克. **2** /dʒiː; dʒi/ (acceleration due to) gravity: *Spacecraft re-entering the earth's atmosphere are affected by g forces.* 航天器重返大气层是由于重力的作用.

gab /gæb; gæb/ *n* [U] (*infml* 口) **1** continuous, esp trivial, chatter (不断的)闲谈, 聊天(尤指琐事): *Stop your gab!* 别闲聊了! **2** (idm 习语) **the gift of the gab** ⇨ GIFT.

▷ **gab** *v* (**-bb-**) [I, Ip] **~ (on/away)** (*infml* 口) chatter about unimportant things 闲谈; 聊天: *They've been gabbing (away) on the phone for nearly an hour.* 他们通过电话聊天已经快一小时了.

gab·ar·dine (also **gab·er·dine**) /ˈgæbədiːn, ˌgæbəˈdiːn; ˋgæbɚˌdin, ˌgæbɚˋdin/ *n* (**a**) [U] strong cloth woven in a twill pattern 华达呢, 轧别丁(一种结实的斜纹布): [attrib 作定语] *a gabardine coat* 华达呢大衣. (**b**) [C] garment (esp a strong raincoat) made of this material 华达呢衣服; (尤指)华达呢雨衣.

gabble /ˈgæbl; ˋgæbl/ *v* (**a**) [I, Ip] **~ (on/away)** talk quickly and indistinctly 说话急促而含混不清: *Take your time and don't gabble!* 说话从容些, 不要快得叫人听不清! (**b**) [Tn, Tn·p] **~ sth (out)** say sth too quickly to be clearly understood 说话急促使人听不明白.

▷ **gabble** *n* [U] fast unintelligible speech 急促而含糊的话: *He speaks at such a gabble!* 他说话叽哩咕噜的!

gable /ˈgeɪbl; ˋgebl/ *n* triangular upper part of the side or end of a building, under a sloping roof 山墙; 三角墙. ⇨illus at App 1 见附录1插图, page vii.

▷ **gabled** /ˈgeɪbld; ˋgebld/ *adj* having one or more gables 有山墙的: *a gabled house/roof* 有山墙的房子[屋顶].

gad /gæd; gæd/ *v* (**-dd-**) (phr v) **gad about/around** (*infml derog* 口, 贬) go around from one place to another (usu in search of pleasure and excitement) 游荡(通常为寻欢作乐和寻求刺激): *While they gad about the world, their children are neglected at home.* 他们在世界各地游荡, 孩子在家无人照看.

□ ˈ**gadabout** *n* person who habitually gads about 惯于游荡的人.

gad·fly /ˈgædflaɪ; ˋgædˌflaɪ/ *n* **1** fly that stings horses and cattle 虻; 牛虻. **2** (*derog* 贬) annoying person, esp one who provokes others into action by criticism, etc 惹人讨厌的人(尤指用批评等手段怂恿别人采取行动者).

gadget /ˈgædʒɪt; ˋgædʒɪt/ *n* small mechanical device or tool 小机械; 小器具: *a complicated new gadget for opening tins* 复杂的新开罐器. ⇨Usage at MACHINE 用法见MACHINE.

▷ **gadgetry** *n* [U] gadgets collectively 小机械, 小器具(统称): *lots of modern gadgetry* 很多现代化的小机械.

Gaelic *n* [U], *adj* **1** /ˈgeɪlɪk; ˋgelɪk/ (language) of the Celtic people of Ireland (爱尔兰的)盖尔人的, 盖尔语. **2** /ˈgælɪk, *also* ˈgeɪlɪk; ˋgælɪk, ˋgelɪk/ (language) of the Celtic people of Scotland (苏格兰的)盖尔人的, 盖尔语.

gaff[1] /gæf; gæf/ *n* stick with an iron hook for pulling large fish out of the water 鱼叉(将鱼拉出水者).

▷ **gaff** *v* [Tn] seize (fish) with a gaff 用鱼叉叉(鱼).

gaff[2] /gæf; gæf/ *n* (idm 习语) **blow the gaff** ⇨ BLOW[1].

gaffe /gæf; gæf/ *n* social blunder; indiscreet act or remark 失礼; 失态; 失言: *He didn't realize what a gaffe he'd made.* 他没意识到自己已出乖露丑.

gaf·fer /ˈgæfə(r); ˋgæfɚ/ *n* (*infml* 口) **1** (*joc or derog* 谑或贬) old fellow 老头子: *That (old) gaffer going into the pub is 90 years old.* 走进酒店的那个老头子已经90岁了. **2** (*Brit sl* 俚) foreman (of a gang of workmen) 工头; 领班.

gag /gæg; gæg/ *n* **1** (**a**) thing, esp a piece of cloth, put in or over a person's mouth to prevent him from speaking or shouting 塞入口中或覆于口上的东西(尤指布)(使人不能说话或喊叫). (**b**) thing placed in a patient's mouth by a dentist, doctor, etc to keep it open 张口器(牙医等用的). (**c**) (*fig* 比喻) anything that restricts freedom of speech 限制言论自由的任何事物. **2** joke or funny story, esp as part of a comedian's act 笑话或滑稽故事; (尤指喜剧演员的)插科打诨: *a few rather feeble gags* 几个没什么趣的笑话.

▷ **gag** *v* (**-gg-**) **1** [Tn] (**a**) put a gag(1a) into or over the mouth of (sb); silence 塞住或捂住(某人)的嘴; 使缄默. (**b**) (*fig* 比喻) deprive (sb/sth) of free speech 剥夺(某人[某事物])的言论自由: *The new censorship laws are an attempt to gag the press.* 新的新闻审查法目的在于剥夺新闻界的言论自由. **2** [I, Ipr] **~ (on sth)** (*infml* 口) choke or retch 窒息; 作呕: *gagging on a piece of raw fish* 因吃一块生鱼而作呕. **3** [I] make jokes 插科打诨.

gaga /ˈgɑːgɑː; ˋgɑgɑ/ *adj* [usu pred 通常作表语] (*infml* 口) senile; slightly crazy 老朽; 疯疯癫癫: *He has gone quite gaga.* 他有点儿老糊涂了.

gage (*US*) = GAUGE.

gaggle /ˈgægl; ˋgægl/ *n* **1** flock (of geese) (鹅)群. **2** (*fig* 比喻) group of noisy or talkative people 一群(喧哗或多话的人): *a gaggle of tourists, schoolchildren, etc* 一群喧闹的游客, 小学生等.

gai·ety /ˈgeɪətɪ; ˋgeətɪ/ *n* [U] merriment; cheerfulness; being gay(2) 快乐; 欢乐; 愉快: *The colourful flags added to the gaiety of the occasion.* 彩旗给这次盛会增添了欢乐的气氛. Cf 参看 GAYNESS (GAY).

gaily ⇨ GAY.

gain[1] /geɪn; gen/ *n* **1** [U] increase in wealth; profit; advantage 财富的增加; 利润; 利益: *One man's loss is another man's gain.* 一人之失即是他人之得. ○ *We hope for some gain from our investment.* 我们希望投资有利可图. **2** [C] increase in amount or power; improvement 数量或力量的增加; 增进: *a gain in weight of two pounds* 体重增加两磅 ○ *Heavy gains were recorded on the Stock Exchange today.* 今日股票价格大幅上升.

▷ **gain·ful** /-fl; -fəl/ *adj* [usu attrib 通常作定语] profitable; bringing wealth 有利益的; 带来财富的: *gainful employment* 有报酬的工作. **gain·fully** *adv* profitably; usefully 有利益地; 有用地.

gain[2] /geɪn; gen/ *v* **1** (**a**) [Tn, Dn·n, Dn·pr] **~ sth (for sb)** obtain, win (esp sth wanted or needed) 获得, 赢得(尤指想要的或所需的事物): *gain possession* 获得所有权 ○ *gain access to secret information* 得以接触机密资料 ○ *gain sb's affections* 赢得某人的喜爱 ○ *I gained the impression that the matter had been settled.* 我得到的印象是事情已经解决了. ○ *His persistence gained him victory.* 他因坚持不懈而获胜. (**b**) [Tn] get more of (esp sth wanted or needed) 得到更多(尤指想要的或所需的事物); 增加: *gain experience, power, strength, weight* 增加经验、权势、力量、重量 ○ *Our campaign is gaining momentum.* 我们的运动在发展壮大. ○ *The plane rapidly gained height.* 飞机急速升高. **2** [Ipr] **~ by/from (doing) sth** benefit, profit from sth/doing sth 从某事物中获益、得到好处: *You can gain by watching how she works.* 看她怎样工作就可获益. **3** [Tn] reach (sth) (usu with effort) 达到, 到达(通常需经努力): *After swimming for an hour, he finally gained the shore.* 他游了一小时以后, 终于到达岸边. **4** [I, Tn] (of a watch or clock) go fast; become ahead of the correct time (指钟表)快: *My watch gains (by) several minutes a day.* 我的表一天快几分钟. **5** (idm 习语) **carry/gain one's point** ⇨ POINT[1]. **gain credence** ⇨ CREDENCE. **gain ˈground** make progress; begin to succeed 进步; 进展: *Your campaign is gaining ground.* 你们的运动不断取得进展. **gain/make up ground** ⇨ GROUND[1]. **gain/win sb's hand** ⇨ HAND[1]. **gain/win one's laurels** ⇨ LAUREL. **gain time** obtain extra time by making excuses, deliberately using slow methods, etc 拖延时间. **gain, get, etc the upper**

hand ⇨ UPPER. **nothing venture, nothing gain/win** ⇨ VENTURE. **stand to 'gain** ⇨ STAND. **6** (phr v) **gain in sth** obtain more of (a physical or an abstract quality) 更加; 增加: *gain in beauty, height, strength, weight, etc* 更加美丽、高、强、重等 ○ *gain in confidence, influence, knowledge, understanding, etc* 增加信心、影响、知识、谅解等. **gain on sb/sth** come closer to sb/sth, esp a rival or sth pursued 更接近某人[某事物](尤指对手或所追逐的事物); 赶上: *gain on the leader in a race* 在赛跑中赶上领先的人 ○ *The Socialists are gaining on the Conservatives in the opinion polls.* 民意测验显示社会党已逐渐赶上保守党.

gain·say /ˌgeɪnˈseɪ; ˌgenˋse/ *v* (*pt, pp* **gainsaid** /-ˈsed; -ˋsɛd/) [Tn] (*arch* 古) (usu in negative sentences or questions 通常用于否定句或疑问句) contradict (sb/sth); deny (sth) 反驳(某人[某事物]); 否认(某事物): *There's no gainsaying his honesty*, ie We cannot deny that he is honest. 他为人诚实无可否认.

gait /geɪt; get/ *n* [sing] manner of walking or running 步态; 步法: *with an unsteady gait* 脚步不稳.

gaiter /ˈgeɪtə(r); ˋgetɚ/ *n* covering of cloth, leather, etc for the leg from the ankle to below the knee (布、皮等的)绑腿: *a pair of gaiters* 一副绑腿.

gal /gæl; gæl/ *n* (*dated infml* 旧, 口) girl 姑娘.

gala /ˈgɑːlə; *US* ˈgeɪlə; ˋgelə/ *n* social, sporting or theatrical occasion with special features (社交、体育、戏剧等的)特别场合, 盛会: *a swimming gala* 游泳运动会 ○ [attrib 作定语] *a gala dinner, night, performance* 联欢宴会、晚会、演出会.

ga·lac·tic /gəˈlæktɪk; gəˋlæktɪk/ *adj* of a galaxy or the Galaxy 星系的; 银河系的.

gal·an·tine /ˈgælənti:n; ˋgælənˌtin/ *n* [U] white meat, boned, spiced, cooked in the form of a roll and served cold 肉卷(禽肉、小牛肉或猪肉等去骨加香料制成卷状, 冷食).

gal·axy /ˈgæləksɪ; ˋgæləksɪ/ *n* **1** [C] any of the large systems of stars in outer space 星系. **2 the Galaxy** [sing] (also **the Milky Way**) the system of stars that contains our solar system, seen as a luminous band in the sky 银河系; 银河. **3** [C] (*fig* 比喻) group of brilliantly talented people 一群杰出的人: *a galaxy of talent, beautiful women, film stars* 一群才子、美女、电影明星.

gale /geɪl; gel/ *n* **1** very strong wind (force 8 on the Beaufort Scale); storm (at sea) 大风(蒲福风级的8级); (海上的)风暴: *It's blowing a gale outside.* 外面刮着大风. ○ *The ship lost its masts in the gale.* 这船的桅杆都在风暴中刮掉了. ○ [attrib 作定语] *a gale warning* 大风警报 ○ *gale-force winds* 大风级的风. **2** (*fig* 比喻) noisy outburst 一阵喧闹: *gales of laughter* 阵阵笑声.

gall[1] /gɔ:l; gɔl/ *n* [U] **1** bitter liquid secreted by the liver; bile 胆汁. **2** (*fig* 比喻) bitter feeling; hatred or resentment 怨恨; 怨愤: *words full of venom and gall* 充满恶毒怨恨的话. **3** (*infml fig* 口, 比喻) impudence; impertinence 厚颜; 鲁莽: *Of all the gall!* ie What impudence! 脸皮真厚!

□ **'gall-bladder** *n* (*anatomy* 解) organ attached to the liver that stores and releases bile 胆囊. ⇨illus at DIGESTIVE 见DIGESTIVE插图.

'gallstone *n* hard mass forming in the gall-bladder and sometimes causing pain 胆石. Cf 参看 STONE 6.

gall[2] /gɔ:l; gɔl/ *n* sore place on an animal, esp a horse, caused by rubbing (of a harness, etc) (动物的)伤痛处(尤指马具等磨擦造成的).

▷ **gall** *v* [Tn] **1** cause pain to (an animal, part of the body, etc) by rubbing; chafe 使(动物、身体某部等)擦痛, 擦伤. **2** annoy (sb); humiliate 烦扰(某人); 侮辱: *It galled him to have to ask for a loan.* 他得向人借贷, 觉得甚为苦恼. **gall·ing** *adj* [usu pred 通常作表语] annoying; humiliating 烦恼; 羞辱: *It was galling to have to apologize to a man she detested.* 最为难堪的是她得向她讨厌的那个男的道歉.

gall[3] /gɔ:l; gɔl/ *n* unnatural growth on a tree produced by insects 虫瘿(树木受虫害而形成的畸形瘤状物). Cf 参看 OAK-APPLE (OAK).

gall *abbr* 缩写 = (*pl* unchanged or **galls** 复数或不变或作 **galls**) gallon(s): *petrol at 175p* (ie pence) *per gall* 汽油每加仑175便士.

gal·lant /ˈgælənt; ˋgælənt/ *adj* **1** (*fml or rhet* 文或修辞) brave 勇敢的; 英勇的: *a gallant knight, soldier, etc* 勇敢的骑士、战士等 ○ *a gallant deed, effort, struggle* 英勇的事迹、尝试、斗争. **2** fine; grand; stately 华丽的; 堂皇的; 壮丽的; 雄伟的: *a gallant ship* 豪华的船. **3** /*also* ˈgəˈlænt; gəˋlænt/ (of a man) giving special attention and respect to women (指男子)向女子献殷勤的.

▷ **gal·lant** /ˈgælənt, *also* gəˈlænt; ˋgælənt, gəˋlænt/ *n* fashionable young man, esp one who is attentive to women 时髦的青年男子(尤指向女子献殷勤的).

gal·lantly *adv*.

gal·lantry /ˈgæləntrɪ; ˋgæləntrɪ/ *n* **1** [U] bravery 勇气; 勇敢; 英勇: *a medal for gallantry* 勇敢勋章. **2** [U, C] special attentiveness (of a man) to women (男子)对女子的殷勤: *He won many hearts by his gallantry.* 他以殷勤热情赢得芳心无数.

gal·leon /ˈgælɪən; ˋgælɪən/ *n* large Spanish sailing-ship used from the 15th to the 17th century (用于15至17世纪的)西班牙大帆船.

gal·lery /ˈgælərɪ; ˋgælərɪ/ *n* **1** [C] room or building for showing works of art 美术品陈列室或展览馆: *a 'picture-gallery* 美术展览馆. **2** (**a**) [C] highest and cheapest seats in a theatre (戏院中票价最廉的)顶层楼座: *Four tickets for the gallery, please.* 请给我四张顶层楼座的票. (**b**) [Gp] people occupying these 顶层楼座的观众. **3** [C] raised covered platform or passage along an inner wall of a hall, church, etc (大厅、教堂等中沿内壁伸展的有檐的)廊台. **4** [C] covered walk or corridor partly open at one side; colonnade 走廊; 柱廊. **5** [C] long narrow room, esp one used for a particular purpose 狭长的房间(尤指有特殊用途的): *a 'shooting-gallery* 室内靶场. **6** [C] horizontal underground passage in a mine (矿坑中的)水平巷道. Cf 参看 SHAFT 7. **7** (idm 习语) **play to the 'gallery** behave in an exaggerated way to attract the attention of onlookers 以大动作吸引旁观者.

gal·ley /ˈgælɪ; ˋgælɪ/ *n* **1** (formerly) long flat ship, usu rowed by slaves or criminals; ancient Greek or Roman warship (旧时)平底大船(通常由奴隶或囚犯用浆划行的); (古代希腊或罗马的)战舰. **2** kitchen in a ship or an aircraft (船上或航空器上的)厨房. **3** long tray used by printers for arranging type 长形活字盘.

□ **'galley proof** (also **galley**) printed proof[1](4a) on a long slip of paper before it is divided into pages 长条校样(尚未分成单页者).

'galley-slave *n* **1** person forced to row in a galley (古代希腊或罗马的)被迫划桨的人. **2** (*fig* 比喻) person made to work like a slave 像奴隶般做苦工的人.

Gal·lic /ˈgælɪk; ˋgælɪk/ *adj* (**a**) of Gaul or the Gauls 高卢的; 高卢人的. (**b**) of the French people and their character 法国人及其性格的: *Gallic charm, sophistication, wit, etc* 法国人的魅力、世故、机智等.

▷ **Gal·li·cism** /ˈgælɪsɪzəm; ˋgæləˌsɪzəm/ *n* French word or expression used in another language (用于他国语言中的)法语词语: *'Déjà vu' is a Gallicism often used in English.* déjà vu是英语中常用的法语词语.

gal·li·vant /ˌgælɪˈvænt, ˈgælɪvænt; ˌgæləˋvænt, ˋgæləˌvænt/ *v* (phr v) **gallivant about** (*infml derog* 口, 贬) (usu in the continuous tenses 通常用于进行时态) go about from one place to another (usu in search of pleasure) 游荡(通常为寻欢作乐): *They should spend less time gallivanting about and more with their children.* 他们应少到各处游荡, 多用些时间照看子女.

gal·lon /ˈgælən; ˋgælən/ *n* measure for liquids; four quarts (4.5 litres) 加仑(液量单位, 合4夸脱或4.5升). ⇨App 5 见附录5.

gal·lop /ˈgæləp; ˋgæləp/ *n* **1** (**a**) [sing] fastest pace (of a horse, etc) with all four feet off the ground at each stride (马等的)飞跑, 奔驰: *He rode off at a gallop.* 他骑着马飞奔而去. ○ *at full gallop* (马)飞奔. Cf 参看 WALK[1] 1d. (**b**) [C] period of riding at this pace 骑马奔驰: *to go for a gallop* 骑马奔驰一番. **2** [sing] (*fig* 比喻) unusually fast speed 飞快: *to work at a gallop* 工作速度快.

▷ **gal·lop** *v* **1** (**a**) [I, Ipr, Ip] (of a horse, etc or a rider) go at a gallop (指马等或骑者)飞奔, 奔驰: *The frightened horse galloped away.* 受惊的马飞奔而去. ○ *I enjoy galloping over the fields.* 我喜欢骑着马在田野奔驰. ⇨ Usage at RUN[1] 用法见RUN[1]. (**b**) [Tn, Tn·pr, Tn·p] (of a rider) cause (a horse, etc) to go at a gallop (指骑者)使(马等)飞奔, 奔驰: *He galloped the horse along the track.* 他沿着跑道骑马奔驰. **2** (phr v) **gallop ahead (of sb)** progress rapidly 飞速前进: *Japan is galloping ahead in the race to develop new technologies.* 日本在发展新技术的竞争中突飞猛进. **gallop through sth** complete sth rapidly 急速做完某事物: *gallop through one's work, a lecture, a performance* 快马加鞭做完工作、讲完课、结束表演.

gal·lows /ˈgæləʊz; ˋgæloz/ (also **the gallows**) *n* (*pl* unchanged; usu *sing* with *sing v* 复数不变, 通常作单数, 与单数动词连用) wooden framework on which criminals are put to death by hanging 绞架: *to send a man to the gallows*, ie condemn him to death 把一男子送上绞架(处死).

□ **gallows ˈhumour** jokes about unpleasant things like death, disease, etc 伤感的幽默(有关死亡、疾病等不快事的笑话).

Gal·lup poll /ˈgæləp pəʊl; ˋgæləpˋpol/ assessment of public opinion by questioning a representative sample of people, esp in order to forecast voting at an election 盖洛普民意测验(尤指为预测大选的结果).

ga·lore /gəˈlɔː(r); gəˋlɔr/ *adv* (*usu approv* 通常作褒义) (following *ns* 用于名词之后) in plenty 很多: *to have books, food, friends, money galore* 有很多书、食物、朋友、金钱.

ga·loshes /gəˈlɒʃɪz; gəˋlɑʃɪz/ *n* [pl] rubber overshoes worn in wet weather (雨天用的)胶套鞋: *a pair of galoshes* 一双胶套鞋.

ga·lumph /gəˈlʌmf; gəˋlʌmf/ *v* (phr v) **~ up, down, etc** (*infml joc* 口, 谑) walk, run, etc noisily or clumsily 笨拙地走、跑等(或发出嘈声): *The children came galumphing into the house like a herd of elephants.* 孩子们像一群大象一样乱哄哄地闯进房子里.

gal·vanic /gælˈvænɪk; gælˋvænɪk/ *adj* **1** producing an electric current by chemical action (由化学作用)产生电流的: *a galvanic battery* 原电池 ○ *galvanic electricity* 动电. **2** (*fig* 比喻) sudden, jerky and dramatic (as if produced by an electric shock) 突然的、痉挛的和剧烈的(似被电击般的): *a galvanic effect, movement, smile* 突然而振奋的效果、动作、微笑.

gal·van·ize, -ise /ˈgælvənaɪz; ˋgælvə,naɪz/ *v* **1** [Tn] coat (iron) with zinc to protect it from rust 用锌镀(铁)(防锈): *a galvanized bucket, nail, hinge, etc* 镀锌的铁桶、钉子、铰链等 ○ *galvanized wire* 铅丝. **2** [Tn, Tn·pr] **~ sb (into sth/doing sth)** shock sb into action 激起某人行动起来: *The manager's arrival galvanized the workers into activity.* 经理一来, 工人闻风而动. ▷ **gal·van·iza·tion, -isation** /ˌgælvənaɪˈzeɪʃn; *US* -nɪˈzeɪ-; ˌgælvənəˋzeʃən/ *n* [U].

gam·bit /ˈgæmbɪt; ˋgæmbɪt/ *n* **1** opening move(s) in chess in which a player sacrifices a piece in order to win an advantage later (国际象棋的)开局让棋法. **2** (*fig* 比喻) opening move in any situation that is calculated to win an advantage 为获得优势采取的第一步行动: *His opening gambit at the debate was a direct attack on Government policy.* 他在辩论中的策略是先直接抨击政府的政策.

gamble /ˈgæmbl; ˋgæmbl/ *v* **1** (**a**) [I, Ipr] play games of chance, etc for money 赌博: *gamble at cards, on the horses, etc* 赌纸牌、马等 ○ *He spends all his time gambling in the casino.* 他把时间都消磨在赌场的赌博上. (**b**) [Tn, Tn·pr] **~ sth (on sth)** spend (money) by playing such games, etc 用(钱)赌博: *He gambled all his winnings on the last race.* 他把赢得的钱全压在最后一场赛马上了. **2** (phr v) **~ sth away** lose sth by gambling 赌博输掉某物: *gamble away all one's money* 把所有的钱都输光. **gamble in sth** risk money by investing in (a specified commodity) 对(某商品)作冒险投资: *gamble in oil (shares)* 做石油(股票)投机生意. **gamble on sth/doing sth** act in the hope of sth being successful, true, etc despite the risk of loss 不顾损失而冒险行动或碰运气: *gamble on (having) sb's support* 孤注一掷希望获得某人支持 ○ *I wouldn't gamble on the weather being fine.* 我可不指望天气能一直好下去.

▷ **gamble** *n* **1** act of gambling; undertaking with a risk of loss and a chance of profit 打赌; 投机; 冒险; 碰运气: *Setting up this business was a bit of a gamble.* 开办这样的公司有点冒险. **2** (idm 习语) **take a gamble (on sth)** gamble 赌博; 冒险而为: *The company took a gamble by cutting the price of their products, and it paid off*, ie was financially successful. 公司冒险将产品削价出售, 结果赢利.

gam·bler /ˈgæmblə(r); ˋgæmblɚ/ *n* person who gambles 赌博者: *a habitual gambler* 赌徒.

gamb·ling /ˈgæmblɪŋ; ˋgæmblɪŋ/ *n* [U] (**a**) playing games, etc for money 赌博; 赌钱: [attrib 作定语] *heavy gambling debts* 沉重的赌债. (**b**) taking risks for possible advantage 冒险; 投机: *to have a taste for gambling* 爱冒险.

gam·boge /gæmˈbuːʒ; *US* -ˈbəʊdʒ; gæmˋbodʒ/ *n* [U] (**a**) deep yellow resin used as colouring matter by artists 藤黄. (**b**) colour of this 橙黄色.

gam·bol /ˈgæmbl; ˋgæmbl/ *v* (**-ll-**) (*US* also **-l-**) [I, Ip] jump or skip about playfully (嬉戏地)跳跃, 蹦跳: *children/lambs gambolling (about/around)* (四处)嬉戏蹦跳的儿童[羊羔].

▷ **gam·bol** *n* act of gambolling 跳跃; 蹦跳.

game[1] /geɪm; gem/ *n* **1** [C] (**a**) form of play or sport with rules 游戏; 运动: *popular children's games* 儿童喜爱的游戏 ○ *a game of chance/skill* 一种碰运气的[赛技巧的]游戏. (**b**) instance of this 游戏; 运动: *to play a game of chess, football, hide-and-seek, etc* 下棋、踢足球、捉迷藏 ○ *Let's have a game of snooker.* 咱们打一局台球吧. ⇨Usage at SPORT 用法见 SPORT. **2 games** [pl] (**a**) athletics or sport as part of a school curriculum (学校的)体育活动: *Mary never played games at school.* 玛丽在学校从不参加体育活动. (**b**) (also **the Games**) (international) athletic contests (国际)体育比赛, 运动会: *the Olympic/Commonwealth/Highland ˈGames* 奥林匹克[英联邦/苏格兰高地]运动会. **3** [C] part of a game (eg tennis or bridge) that forms a scoring unit (网球或桥牌的)一局, 一盘, 一场: *We need another twenty points to make game*, ie in bridge. 我们需再打20分才够一局(桥牌). ○ *They lost the first game of the second set*, ie in tennis. 他们在第二盘中输了第一局(网球赛). ○ *(one) game all, two games all, etc*, ie each player or team has won one game, two games, etc 各赢一局、各赢两局等 ○ *Game, set and match (to…)*, ie The tennis match has been won (by…) 赢得这局、盘、场网球赛的是… ○ [attrib 作定语] *game ˈpoint*, ie stage in a competition when one point is needed to win the game (比赛中)决胜的一分. **4** [C] set of equipment for playing a game (游戏或运动的)器材: *My uncle always gives us a ˈboard game for Christmas.* 我叔叔每逢圣诞节总要送给我们一副棋. **5** [C] (usu *sing* 通常作单数) (*infml* 口) (**a**) secret and cunning plan; trick 诡计; 计谋; 花招: *So that's his (little) game!* ie Now I know what he has been planning. 原来那就是他的鬼点子! ○ *I wish I knew what her game is*, ie what she is planning to do. 但愿我知道她打的是什么主意. (**b**) type of activity or business 活动类型; 行业: *the ˈpublishing game* 出版业 ○ *the game of ˈpolitics* 政治工作 ○ *How long have you been in ˈthis game?* 你从事这一行业有多久了? **6** [U] (flesh of) wild animals or birds hunted for sport or food 猎物; 野兽或野禽的肉: [attrib 作定语] *game ˈpie* 野味馅饼. **7** (idm 习语) **beat sb at his own game** ⇨ BEAT[1]. **easy game** ⇨ EASY[1]. **fair game** ⇨ FAIR[1]. **fun and games** ⇨ FUN. **the ˌgame is not worth the ˈcandle** (*saying* 谚) the advantages to be gained from doing sth are not worth the trouble, expense, etc involved 不值得做; 得不偿失. **the game is ˈup** (usu said to or by a wrongdoer when he is caught 抓到做坏事者时说的话或做坏事者被抓到时的自语) your/our crime, trickery, etc has been discovered 事情已败露了; 你[我们]完蛋了. **a game that ˈtwo can ˈplay**; **ˈtwo can ˈplay at ˈthat game** (that is a) wrongdoing or trick that a victim can copy in return 那一套你会我也会. **give the ˈgame away** carelessly reveal a secret 不慎泄露秘密; 露马脚. **the luck of the game** ⇨ LUCK. **a mug's game** ⇨ MUG[2]. **the name of the game** ⇨ NAME[1]. **(be) ˌoff one's ˈgame** unable to play as well as usual 竞技状态不佳; 发挥失常. **(be) on the ˈgame** (*sl* 俚) involved in prostitution or thieving 卖淫; 行窃. **play a cat-and-mouse game with sb** ⇨ CAT[1]. **play the ˈgame** (**a**) play according to the rules 按规矩办事; 遵守规则. (**b**) (*fig* 比喻) act in a fair or honourable way 办事公道; 光明正大: *John only pretends to do his share of the work; he's just not playing the game.* 约翰只是装成做他那份工作, 实际上并不真心好好干. **play sb's game** act so as to further sb's plans intentionally or unintentionally 有意或无意地促进某人

的计划: *She didn't realize that by complaining she was only playing Peter's game.* 她未曾想发牢骚无形中反倒帮了彼得的忙. **a waiting game** ⇨ WAIT[1].

□ ˈ**game bird** bird that is hunted and killed for food or sport 可捕猎的鸟. ⇨illus at App 1 见附录1插图, page v.

ˈ**gamecock** *n* cock bred for cock-fighting 斗鸡.

ˈ**gamekeeper** *n* man employed to breed and protect game birds on an estate 猎禽看守人(繁殖和保护猎禽者).

ˈ**game reserve** area of land reserved for the breeding and protection of game[1](6) 猎物繁殖和保护区.

ˈ**gamesmanship** *n* [U] art of winning games by upsetting the confidence of one's opponent 比赛中藉挫伤对手自信心以取胜的策略.

ˈ**game-warden** *n* person employed to manage a game reserve (猎物繁殖与保护区的)管理员, 经理人.

game[2] /geɪm; gem/ *adj* **~ (for sth/to do sth)** eager and willing to undertake sth risky; brave 跃跃欲试的; 有冒险精神的; 勇敢的: *'Who'll climb up to get it?' 'I'm game (to try).'* '谁愿意爬上去把它拿下来?' '我来(试试).' ○ *He's always game for an adventure.* 他一向热衷于冒险. ▷ **gamely** *adv: fight, struggle, etc gamely,* ie bravely but perhaps unsuccessfully 暴虎冯河地战斗、斗争等(勇敢, 但未必成功).

game[3] /geɪm; gem/ *adj* (*dated infml* 旧, 口) lame; crippled (esp in the leg) 残疾的; (尤指)瘸的, 跛的: *He is game in the leg/has a game leg.* 他腿瘸[有一只瘸腿]. Cf 参看 GAMMY.

gam·ete /ˈgæmiːt; ˋgæmit/ *n* (*biology* 生) sexual cell able to unite with another in reproduction 配子. ▷ **gam·etic** /gəˈmetɪk; gəˋmɛtɪk/ *adj*.

gam·ing /ˈgeɪmɪŋ; ˋgemɪŋ/ *n* [U] (*dated or law* 旧或律) gambling 赌博: [attrib 作定语] *the Betting and Gaming Act* 赌博法 ○ *spending all night at the gaming tables* 在赌桌旁彻夜赌博.

gamma /ˈgæmə; ˋgæmə/ *n* the third letter of the Greek alphabet 希腊字母表的第三个字母.

G

□ ˌ**gamma ˈglobu·lin** /ˈglɒbjʊlɪn; ˋglɑbjʊlɪn/ (*medical* 医) form of protein, found in blood plasma, which gives protection against certain illnesses 丙种球蛋白; γ-球蛋白.

ˌ**gamma radiˈation** radioactivity consisting of gamma rays γ 辐射.

ˈ**gamma ray** (usu *pl* 通常作复数) ray of very short wavelength from radioactive materials γ 射线.

gam·mon /ˈgæmən; ˋgæmən/ *n* [U] (*esp Brit*) bacon from the hind leg or side of a pig 腌猪后腿: [attrib 作定语] *gammon rashers* 火腿肉片. Cf 参看 BACON, HAM[1], PORK.

gammy /ˈgæmɪ; ˋgæmɪ/ *adj* [usu attrib 通常作定语] (*infml* 口) (of a limb or joint) unable to function normally through pain or stiffness (指四肢或关节)(因疼痛或僵直)不能正常活动的, 瘸的, 跛的: *a gammy leg/knee* 不能正常活动的腿[膝]. Cf 参看 GAME[3].

gamut /ˈgæmət; ˋgæmət/ *n* **1 the gamut** [sing] complete range or scale (of sth) 全范围; 全部: *the whole gamut of human emotions from joy to despair* 人类情感包括欢乐及绝望之间的整个范围. **2** (idm 习语) **run the gamut (of sth)** experience or perform the complete range of sth 全过程: *In his short life he had run the entire gamut of crime, from petty theft to murder.* 他在短短的一生中, 从小偷小摸到杀人, 什么罪都犯过.

-gamy *comb form* 构词成分 (forming *ns* 用以构成名词) marriage or sexual union 结婚; 两性结合: *monogamy* ○ *polygamy*. ▷ **-gamous, -gamously** (forming *adjs* and *advs* 用以构成形容词和副词).

gamy /ˈgeɪmɪ; ˋgemɪ/ *adj* (of meat) having the strong flavour or smell of game[1](6) that has been kept for a long time (指肉)(野味经长久保存)气味强烈的, 有臭味的.

gan·der /ˈgændə(r); ˋgændɚ/ *n* **1** [C] male goose 雄鹅. **2** [sing] (*infml* 口) look, glance 看一眼; 一瞥: *have/take a gander at sth* 看某物一眼. **3** (idm 习语) **what's sauce for the goose is sauce for the gander** ⇨ SAUCE.

gang /gæŋ; gæŋ/ *n* [CGp] **1** organized group of criminals (罪犯有组织的)一帮, 一伙: *The gang are being hunted by the police.* 警方正在追捕这帮匪徒. Cf 参看 GANGSTER. **2** group of young people, usu males in their teens and early twenties, who are typically troublesome (闹事的青少年, 通常指男性)一群, 一伙: *The phone box was vandalized by a gang of youths.* 那电话亭被一群少年歹徒故意破坏了. ○ [attrib 作定语] *gang warfare,* ie fighting between rival gangs 打群架. **3** organized group of workers (工人有组织的)一队, 一组: *a gang of builders, roadmenders, etc* 一队建筑工、修路工等. **4** [sing] (*infml* 口) group of people who regularly associate together (经常来往的)一伙人: *The whole gang's here tonight.* 今晚伙伴们都在这里. ○ *Don't go around with that gang or you'll come to no good!* 别跟那伙人厮混在一起, 否则绝没有好下场. ○ (*esp US*) *Hi, gang!* 嘿, 伙计们!

▷ **gang** *v* (phr v) **gang together; gang up (with sb) (against sb)** (*derog* 贬) act together (with sb) (against sb) (和某人)合伙(对付他人). **gang up on sb** (*derog* 贬) join together to hurt or frighten sb 结伙伤害或恐吓某人: *bigger/older boys ganging up on smaller/younger ones* 高大的[年纪大的]小伙子结伙欺侮身材[年纪]较小的男孩. **ganger** /ˈgæŋə(r); ˋgæŋɚ/ *n* (*Brit*) foreman of a gang of workers 工头; 监工.

□ **gangland** *n* [sing] world of criminal gangs 犯罪集团的活动范围: [attrib 作定语] *gangland killings* 犯罪集团间的杀戮.

gang·ling /ˈgæŋglɪŋ; ˋgæŋglɪŋ/ (also **gan·gly** /ˈgæŋglɪ; ˋgæŋglɪ/) *adj* (of a person) tall, thin and awkward-looking (指人)瘦长而难看的: *a gangling youth* 瘦长而难看的青年.

gan·glion /ˈgæŋglɪən; ˋgæŋglɪən/ *n* (*pl* **~s** or **-lia** /-lɪə; -lɪə/) group of nerve cells from which nerve fibres radiate 神经节.

gang·plank /ˈgæŋplæŋk; ˋgæŋˌplæŋk/ *n* movable plank for walking into or out of a boat; (small) gangway (上下船用的)跳板.

gan·grene /ˈgæŋgriːn; ˋgæŋgrin/ *n* [U] decay and death of body tissue when the blood supply has been stopped 坏疽: *When gangrene set in, his foot had to be amputated.* 他的脚生了坏疽, 必须截除. ▷ **gan·gren·ous** /ˈgæŋgrɪnəs; ˋgæŋgrɪnəs/ *adj*.

gang·ster /ˈgæŋstə(r); ˋgæŋstɚ/ *n* member of a gang of armed criminals 匪徒; 歹徒: [attrib 作定语] *gangster films* 描写盗匪的影片.

gang·way /ˈgæŋweɪ; gæŋˌwe/ *n* **1** movable bridge for entering or leaving a ship (上下船用的)跳板. **2** (*Brit*) passage between two rows of seats in a theatre, concert-hall, etc (剧场、音乐厅等的)座间甬道, 过道. ▷ **gang·way** *interj* (used for telling people to get out of one's way 用以叫人让路).

ganja /ˈgændʒə; ˋgændʒə/ *n* [U] = CANNABIS.

gan·net /ˈgænɪt; ˋgænɪt/ *n* large sea-bird that catches fish by diving 塘鹅.

gantry /ˈgæntrɪ; ˋgæntrɪ/ *n* tall metal frame supporting a crane, signals on a railway or motorway, rocket-launching equipment, etc 金属台架; (起重的)龙门架; (铁路或高速公路的)信号机架; (火箭发射设备的)竖架.

gaol (*US* usu 美式英语通常作 **jail**) /dʒeɪl; dʒel/ *n* [C, U] prison 监狱: *The castle had been used as a gaol.* 那城堡曾用作监狱. ○ *be sent to gaol,* ie be imprisoned 入狱 ○ *spend a year in gaol* 入狱一年.

▷ **gaol** (*US* usu 美式英语通常作 **jail**) *v* [Tn, Tn·pr] **~ sb (for sth)** put sb in gaol 监禁某人: *He was gaoled for six months for his part in the robbery.* 他因参与抢劫监禁了六个月.

gaoler (*US* usu 美式英语通常作 **jailer, jailor**) /ˈdʒeɪlə(r); ˋdʒelɚ/ *n* person in charge of a gaol and the prisoners in it 监狱看守.

□ ˈ**gaolbird** (*US* usu 美式英语通常作 ˈ**jailbird**) *n* (*dated infml* 旧, 口) person (habitually) sent to prison 囚犯; 惯犯.

ˈ**gaolbreak** (*US* usu 美式英语通常作 ˈ**jail-break**) *n* escape from prison 越狱.

gap /gæp; gæp/ *n* **~ (in/between sth)** **1** opening or break in sth or between two things 缺口; 裂口; 豁口: *a gap in a fence, hedge, wall, etc* 篱笆、树篱、墙壁等的豁口 ○ *The road goes through a gap in/between the hills.* 公路从山间峡谷穿过. **2** unfilled interval of space (空间的)间隔: *a gap of five miles between towns* 镇与镇之间

相隔五英里 ○ (*fig* 比喻) *There were some unaccountable gaps in* (ie parts missing from) *his story.* 他讲的话有些地方连贯不起来. **3** unfilled interval of time; lapse (时间的)间隙, 间断: *a gap in the conversation* 谈话中的停顿 ○ *After a gap of 30 years the custom was reintroduced.* 这一风俗中断了30年后又兴起来了. ○ *a temporary job to fill the gap between school and university* 高中毕业到升入大学前这段时间的临时工作. **4** (*fig* 比喻) separation 分离: *a wide gap between the opinions of two people* 两人意见的巨大分歧. **5** (*fig* 比喻) deficiency which needs to be filled 需加填补的不足、缺陷或空白: *a gap in one's education* 个人受教育上的缺欠 ○ *There was a terrible gap in her life after her husband died.* 她在丈夫去世后生活中有过一段难堪的日子. ○ *a gap in the market*, ie absence of a type of article which people might wish to buy 市场上某货物的脱销. **6** (idm 习语) **bridge a/the gap** ⇨ BRIDGE. **a credibility gap** ⇨ CREDIBILITY. **the generation gap** ⇨ GENERATION.

□ **ˈgap-toothed** *adj* having teeth which are wide apart 牙齿间缝隙很大的.

gape /geɪp; gep/ *v* **1** [I, Ipr] **~ (at sb/sth)** (*often derog* 常作贬义) stare with an open mouth, usu in surprise 目瞪口呆地凝视: *Don't gape : it's rude!* 别张着嘴傻瞪着, 太不礼貌了! ○ *What are you gaping at?* 你目瞪口呆地看着什么? **2** [La, I] be or become open wide 张开; 张大: *A huge chasm gaped before them.* 他们面前有个巨大的裂痕. ○ *a gaping hole, wound, chasm* 很大的洞、伤口、裂隙 ○ *a shirt gaping open with a button missing* 丢一颗钮扣而敞开着的衬衫.

▷ **gape** *n* open-mouthed stare 张口凝视: *gapes of astonishment on the faces of the spectators* 观众目瞪口呆的惊讶表情.

gar·age /ˈgærɑːʒ, ˈgærɪdʒ; *US* gəˈrɑːʒ; gəˋrɑʒ/ *n* **1** building in which to keep one or more cars, vans, etc 汽车房; 汽车库; 汽车间: *a house with a separate/built-in garage* 另设[附设]汽车房的房子 ○ *a bus garage* 公共汽车车库. ⇨illus at App 1 见附录1插图, page vii. **2** (*Brit*) (*US* **ˈservice station**) roadside petrol station where vehicles can be serviced and repaired (兼作汽车维修等的)加油站: [attrib 作定语] *a garage mechanic* 加油站技工.

▷ **gar·age** *v* [Tn] put (a motor vehicle) in a garage 将(机动车辆)送入车房.

□ **garage sale** (*US*) = CAR-BOOT SALE (CAR).

garb /gɑːb; gɑrb/ *n* [U] (style of) clothing (esp as worn by a particular type of person) 服装, 服装式样(尤指某类人穿的): *military garb* 军装 ○ *a man in priest's garb/in the garb of a priest* 穿着牧师服装的人 ○ *in strange, unusual, odd, etc garb* 装束奇异、不寻常、古怪等.

▷ **garb** *v* [Tn usu passive 通常用于被动语态] dress (sb) in the stated way 穿某种服装: *a strangely garbed man* 衣着奇特的男子 ○ *women garbed in black* 穿黑衣的女子.

garb·age /ˈgɑːbɪdʒ; ˋgɑrbɪdʒ/ *n* **1** [U] (*esp US*) **(a)** waste material, esp domestic refuse 废物; (尤指家庭的)垃圾: [attrib 作定语] *garbage collection/disposal* 垃圾收集[处理] ○ *a garbage truck* 垃圾车. **(b)** place or receptacle for disposing of this 垃圾场; 垃圾箱: *Throw any left-over food in the garbage.* 把剩下的食物倒进垃圾箱里. **2** [U] (*fig infml* 比喻, 口) nonsense; rubbish 废话; 无聊的话: *You do talk a load of garbage!* 你的废话太多了! **3** [U] (*fig computing* 比喻, 计) meaningless or irrelevant data 无意义的或无关联的资料或数据. **4** (idm 习语) **garbage ˈin, garbage ˈout** (*infml* 口) (in computing) if you input wrong data, the output will also be wrong (计算机运算中)错进, 错出(若输入错误数据, 则输出亦为错误数据).

□ **ˈgarbage can** (*US*) = DUSTBIN.

garbled /ˈgɑːbld; ˋgɑrbḷd/ *adj* (of a message) confused or misleading (指信息)混乱的, 引起误解的: *The injured man was still groggy and could only give a garbled account of the accident.* 受伤的男子仍不很清醒, 只能含糊地说出事故的情形.

gar·den /ˈgɑːdn; ˋgɑrdṇ/ *n* **1** [C, U] (piece of) private ground used for growing flowers, fruit, vegetables, etc, typically with a lawn or other open space for recreation (私人的)花园、果园、菜园等园地: *We've only a small garden.* 我们的花园很小. ○ *a big house with a lot of garden* 有大片园地的大房子 ○ *a formal garden* 整齐的传统式花园 ○ *weeding the garden* 给菜园除草 ○ [attrib 作定语] *a garden wall* 花园的墙 ○ *garden flowers/plants* 园艺花卉[植物]. **2 gardens** [pl] public park 公园: *botanical/zoological gardens* 植物园[动物园]. **3** [C] place where refreshments are served out of doors 户外供应饮食的场所: *a beer/tea garden* 露天啤酒店[茶座]. **4** [sing] (*fig* 比喻) fertile region 沃土地区: *Kent is the garden of England.* 肯特郡是英格兰的肥田沃地. **5** (idm 习语) **a bear garden** ⇨ BEAR[1]. **common or garden** ⇨ COMMON[1]. **everything in the garden is ˈlovely** (*saying* 谚) everything is very satisfactory 样样满意. **lead sb up the garden path** ⇨ LEAD[3].

▷ **gar·den** *v* [I] cultivate a garden 从事园艺活动; 种植花木: *She's outdoors gardening every afternoon.* 她每天下午都在户外搞园艺. **gar·dener** /ˈgɑːdnə(r); ˋgɑrdnɚ/ *n* person who works in a garden, either for pay or as a hobby 园丁; 花匠; 园艺爱好者. **gar·dening** /ˈgɑːdnɪŋ; ˋgɑrdnɪŋ/ *n* [U] cultivating of gardens 园艺: *fond of gardening* 喜爱园艺 ○ [attrib 作定语] *gardening gloves, tools* 园艺用手套、工具.

□ **ˈgarden centre** place where plants, seeds, gardening equipment, etc are sold 花卉店(出售各种植物、种子、园艺工具等).

garden ˈcity, garden ˈsuburb city or suburb designed with many open spaces and planted with many trees (多空地、种有大量树木的)花园城市或市郊.

ˈgarden party formal social gathering on a lawn or in a garden, usu in the afternoon 游园会(通常在下午举行).

gar·denia /gɑːˈdiːnɪə; gɑrˋdinɪə/ *n* **1** tree or shrub with large white or yellow flowers, usu sweet-smelling 栀子. **2** its flower 栀子花.

gar·gan·tuan /gɑːˈgæntjʊən; gɑrˋgæntʃʊən/ *adj* enormous; gigantic 巨大的; 庞大的: *a gargantuan appetite, meal, person* 胃口极佳、丰盛的饭菜、巨人.

gargle /ˈgɑːgl; ˋgɑrgl/ *v* [I, Ipr] **~ (with sth)** wash the throat with liquid kept moving about by a stream of breath 含漱; 漱喉: *He always gargles (with salt water) before going to bed.* 他睡前总是(用盐水)漱口.

▷ **gargle** *n* **1** [C] liquid used for gargling 含漱剂; 漱口剂: *use a·gargle of salt water* 使用盐水含漱剂. **2** [sing] act of gargling 含漱; 漱口: *have a gargle with salt water* 用盐水漱口.

gar·goyle /ˈgɑːgɔɪl; ˋgɑrgɔɪl/ *n* stone or metal spout in the form of a grotesque human or animal figure, for carrying rain-water away from the roof of a church, etc (作怪异人形或动物形的)滴水嘴; (疏导雨水的)凸饰漏嘴.

gar·ish /ˈgeərɪʃ; ˋgɛrɪʃ/ *adj* unpleasantly bright; over-coloured or over-decorated, esp in a vulgar way 炫耀的, 过于艳丽的, 过分装饰的(尤指俗气的): *garish clothes, colours, lights* 花里胡哨的衣服、颜色、彩灯. ▷ **gar·ishly** *adv*: *garishly coloured, dressed, illuminated* 着色鲜艳的、穿着花哨的、照明炫耀的. **gar·ish·ness** *n* [U].

gar·land /ˈgɑːlənd; ˋgɑrlənd/ *n* circle of flowers, leaves or ribbons, worn (esp on the head or round the neck) or hung as a decoration 花环; 花冠; 花圈: *a garland of victory* 象征胜利的花环.

▷ **gar·land** *v* [usu passive 通常用于被动语态: Tn, Tn·pr] **~ sb (with sth)** put a garland or garlands on sb 给某人戴上花环或花冠: *garlanded with roses* 戴玫瑰花冠的.

gar·lic /ˈgɑːlɪk; ˋgɑrlɪk/ *n* [U] onion-like plant with strong taste and smell, used in cooking 蒜; 大蒜; 蒜头: *a clove of garlic* 一瓣蒜 ○ [attrib 作定语] *garlic butter, bread, sauce, etc*, ie flavoured with garlic 蒜蓉、蒜味面包、蒜汁. ⇨illus at ONION 见 ONION 插图.

▷ **gar·licky** *adj* (*infml* 口) smelling or tasting of garlic 蒜味的: *garlicky breath, food* 呼出的带蒜味的气息、有蒜味的食物.

gar·ment /ˈgɑːmənt; ˋgɑrmənt/ *n* **1** (*fml or joc* 文或谑) article of clothing (一件)衣服: *a strange shapeless garment that had once been a jacket* 用甲克改成的怪模怪样的衣服 ○ *his nether garments*, ie shorts, trousers, etc 他的裤子. **2** (*fig rhet* 比喻, 修辞) covering 覆盖: *In spring nature wears a new garment.* 春天, 大自然披上了新装.

gar·ner /ˈgɑːnə(r); ˋgɑrnɚ/ *v* [Tn, Tn·pr, Tn·p] **~ sth (from sth)**; **~ sth (in/up)** (*fml* 文) collect sth in and (usu) store it 收集并(通常)贮藏某物: *garner (in/up) the* *grain for the winter* 储粮以备过冬 ○ (*fig* 比喻) *garner knowledge, information, etc* 积累知识、搜集信息 ○ *facts garnered from various sources* 从各种渠道搜集到的资料.

gar·net /ˈgɑːnɪt; ˋgɑrnɪt/ *n* semi-precious gem of deep transparent red 石榴石(一种次宝石, 色深红而透明).

gar·nish /ˈgɑːnɪʃ; ˋgɑrnɪʃ/ *v* [Tn, Tn·pr] **~ sth (with sth)** decorate (food for the table) with small additional amounts of food 给(上餐桌的食物)加装饰: *fish garnished with slices of lemon* 用柠檬片作装饰的鱼 ○ *meat garnished with parsley, fresh vegetables, etc* 饰有香菜、新鲜蔬菜等的肉.

▷ **gar·nish** *n* vegetable, herb, etc used to decorate a dish of food or add to its flavour (作装饰或是提味用的)菜料: *a garnish of mixed herbs* 什锦装饰菜料.

gar·ret /ˈgærət; ˋgærɪt/ *n* room (often small, dark and unpleasant) on the top floor of a house (esp in the roof) 顶层房间; (尤指)阁楼: *a poor man living in a garret* 住在阁楼的穷人. Cf 参看 ATTIC.

gar·rison /ˈgærɪsn; ˋgærəsn̩/ *n* [CGp] troops stationed in a town or fort 卫戍部队; 守备部队; 警备部队: *Half the garrison is/are on duty.* 有半数卫戍部队在执勤. ○ [attrib 作定语] *garrison duty* 守备任务 ○ *a garrison town* 有驻防的城市.

▷ **gar·rison** *v* **1** [Tn, Tn·pr] **~ sth (with sb)** defend (a place) with or as a garrison 卫戍部队守备(某地): *The town was garrisoned with two regiments.* 该镇有两团士兵驻守. **2** [Tn·pr] **~ sb in/on sth** place (troops) as a garrison 派(部队)驻防: *A hundred soldiers were garrisoned in the town.* 派了一百名士兵在城里驻防.

gar·rotte (also **ga·rotte**, *US* also **ga·rote**) /gəˈrɒt; gəˋrɑt/ *v* [Tn] **1** execute (a condemned person) by strangling or throttling with a metal collar 用铁环绞死(判死刑的人). **2** strangle (sb) with wire or rope 勒死(某人).

▷ **gar·rotte** (also **ga·rotte**, *US* also **ga·rote**) *n* device used for garrotting (GARROTTE 1) 绞刑用的铁环.

gar·rul·ous /ˈgærələs; ˋgærələs/ *adj* talking too much, esp about unimportant things 喋喋不休的, 饶舌的(尤指对琐事): *becoming garrulous after a few glasses of wine* 喝了几杯酒后就唠唠叨叨 ○ *My garrulous neighbour had given away the secret.* 我那爱唠叨的邻居已把秘密泄露了.

▷ **gar·ru·lity** /gəˈruːlətɪ; gəˋrulətɪ/, **gar·rul·ous·ness** *ns* [U] talkativeness 絮叨; 饶舌; 多嘴.

gar·rul·ously *adv*.

gar·ter /ˈgɑːtə(r); ˋgɑrtɚ/ *n* **1** [C] (usu elastic) band worn round the leg to keep up a sock or stocking (通常为弹性的)袜带. **2 the Garter** [sing] badge or membership of the highest order of English knighthood 嘉德勋位(英国爵士的最高勋位); 嘉德勋章: *be awarded the Garter* 被授予嘉德勋位.

gas /gæs; gæs/ *n* (*pl* **gases**; *US* also **gasses**) **1** [C, U] air-like substance (ie not a solid or liquid) 气体: *Hydrogen and oxygen are gases.* 氢和氧都是气体. ○ *Air is a mixture of gases.* 空气是混合气体. ○ [attrib 作定语] *a gas balloon*, ie filled with gas 气球. **2** [U] **(a)** inflammable gas or mixture of gases used as fuel for heating, lighting or cooking 易燃气体, 混合气体(作取暖、照明或烹调用的燃料): *Is your central heating gas or electricity?* 你们的集中供热设备是煤气的还是用电的? ○ *Light the gas/Turn the gas on and we'll have a cup of tea.* 点上煤气, 咱们沏杯茶吧. ○ *butane/calor/coal/natural gas* 丁烷气[罐装石油气/煤气/天然气] ○ *cook on a low/medium/high gas*, ie on a gas cooker 在微火[中火/大火]上烹调(在煤气炉上) ○ [attrib 作定语] *a gas cooker, lighter* (ie cigarette lighter), *oven, ring, stove*, ie using gas as fuel 煤气炉、气体打火机、煤气烤箱、煤气炉环形喷火头、煤气炉. **(b)** gas (eg nitrous oxide) or mixture of gases used as an anaesthetic in surgery and dentistry 外科和牙科用作麻醉剂的气体(如一氧化二氮)或气体混合物: *I was given gas when they pulled my tooth out.* 给我拔牙时用了一氧化二氮. ○ *Did you have gas or an injection?* 你是用的麻醉气还是打的麻醉针? **(c)** poisonous gas (eg mustard gas) used in warfare (战争用的)毒气(如芥子气): [attrib 作定语] *a gas attack* 毒气攻击. **3** [U] (*US infml* 口) = PETROL. **4** [U] (*fig derog* 比喻, 贬) empty talk; boasting 空谈; 吹牛: *His long speech was nothing but gas and hot air.* 他的长篇大论只是吹牛和空话. **5** (idm 习语) **step on the gas** ⇨ STEP[1].

▷ **gas** *v* (**-ss-**) **1** [Tn] cause (sb) to breathe poisonous gas 使(某人)吸入毒气: *He was badly gassed in the war.* 他在战争中深受毒气伤害. ○ *She couldn't face the future, and gassed herself*, ie killed herself with gas. 她对未来感到绝望, 用煤气自杀了. **2** [I, Ipr] **~ (about sth)** (*infml derog* 口, 贬) talk for a long time without saying much that is useful 空谈; 瞎扯.

□ ˈ**gasbag** *n* (*infml derog* 口, 贬) talkative person 话痨.

ˈ**gas board** (*dated* 旧) (esp in Britain before the privatization of the gas supply) public body controlling the supply of gas for domestic and industrial use (尤指英国在煤气私有化前的)煤气供应局.

gas bracket pipe with one or more gas burners attached to a wall (装在墙上带喷嘴的)煤气管.

ˈ**gas chamber** room filled with gas for killing animals or people 毒气室(用以毒死动物或人的).

ˈ**gas cylinder** cylindrical metal container for storing gas 煤气罐.

ˌ**gas-ˈfired** *adj* using gas as fuel 以煤气为燃料的: *ˌgas-fired ˌcentral ˈheating* 以煤气为燃料的集中供热设备.

gas-fitter *n* worker who installs gas-fittings 煤气设备安装工.

ˈ**gas-fitting** *n* (usu *pl* 通常作复数) pipe, burner or other piece of apparatus for heating or lighting with gas 煤气装置.

ˈ**gasholder** *n* = GASOMETER.

ˈ**gas-lit** *adj* illuminated by light from burning gas 用煤气灯照明的.

ˈ**gas main** large pipe carrying gas from supplier to consumer 煤气总管道.

ˈ**gasman** /-mæn; -ˌmæn/ *n* (*pl* **-men**/-men; -ˌmɛn/) (*infml* 口) employee of a gas supply organization who checks gas meters and domestic gas apparatus (抄煤气表、检查设备的)煤气公司雇员.

ˈ**gas mask** breathing apparatus worn as protection against poison gas 防毒面具. ⇨illus at MASK 见 MASK 插图.

ˈ**gas meter** meter for measuring the amount of gas used 煤气表(计量煤气用量的仪表).

ˈ**gas poker** hollow metal rod connected to a gas supply, for lighting a coal fire 煤气引火棒(中空的金属棒, 与煤气源连接, 用以点燃煤炭).

ˈ**gas station** (*US*) = PETROL STATION (PETROL).

ˈ**gas tap** device for controlling the flow of gas from a pipe 煤气截门; 煤气阀.

ˈ**gasworks** *n* (*pl* unchanged 复数不变) [sing or pl *v*] place where gas for lighting and heating is manufactured 煤气厂.

gas·eous /ˈgæsɪəs, ˈgeɪsɪəs; ˋgæsɪəs/ *adj* like, containing or being gas 似气体的; 含气体的; 气体的: *a gaseous mixture* 气体混合物.

gash /gæʃ; gæʃ/ *n* **~ (in sth)** long deep cut or wound 长而深的切痕或伤口: *a nasty gash in the arm, leg, etc* 胳膊、腿等上深而长的伤口 ○ *make a gash in the bark of a tree with a knife* 用刀在树皮上割一道深而长的切口.

▷ **gash** *v* [Tn, Tn·pr] **~ sth (on/with sth)** make a gash in sth (在某物上)割一长而深的切口: *gash one's arm on a piece of broken glass* 胳膊被玻璃碎片划了一个大口子.

gas·ify /ˈgæsɪfaɪ; ˋgæsəˌfaɪ/ *v* (*pt, pp* **-fied**) [I, Tn] (cause sth to) change into gas (使某物)气化.

gas·ket /ˈgæskɪt; ˋgæskɪt/ *n* soft flat sheet or ring of rubber, card, etc used to seal a joint between metal surfaces to prevent steam, gas, etc from escaping 垫圈; 密封垫: *The engine had blown a gasket*, ie the gasket had suddenly let steam, etc escape. 发动机的一个垫圈失效了(蒸汽等逸出).

gasol·ine (also **gasol·ene**) /ˈgæsəliːn; ˋgæslˌin/ *n* [U] (*US*) = PETROL.

gaso·meter /gæˈsɒmɪtə(r); gæsˋɑmətɚ/ *n* (also ˈ**gas holder**) very large round tank in which fuel gas is stored and from which it is distributed through pipes 大型储煤气柜.

gasp /gɑːsp; gæsp/ *v* **1** [I, Ipr] **~ (at sth)**; **~ (for sth)** take one or more quick deep breaths with open mouth, because of surprise or exhaustion (因惊异或力竭)吸气, 喘气: *gasp like a fish out of water* 像鱼离开水似的大口

喘气 ○ *I gasped in/with astonishment at the magician's skill.* 那魔术师技艺惊人，我不禁倒抽一口凉气. ○ *The exhausted runner was gasping for air/breath.* 那人跑得疲惫已极，上气不接下气. **2** [Tn, Tn·p] **~ sth (out)** utter sth in a breathless way 喘着气说话: *She managed to gasp (out) a few words.* 她喘着气好不容易才说出了几个字来. **3** [I, Ipr] **~ (for sth)** (used in the continuous tenses 用于进行时态) (*infml* 口) want sth very much, esp sth to drink or smoke 很想要某物(尤指饮料或烟): *'Do you need a drink?' 'Yes, I'm gasping!'* '你要喝点什么吗?' '我巴不得能喝点!' ○ *I was gasping for a cigarette.* 我很想抽枝烟.

▷ **gasp** *n* **1** quick deep breath of pain, surprise, etc (因疼痛、惊异等引起的)深吸气，喘气: *give a sudden audible gasp* 突然大声地喘了一口气 ○ *There were gasps of horror from the spectators as he fell off the tightrope.* 他从绷紧的绳索上摔了下来，观众吓得直喘气. **2** (idm 习语) **at one's last gasp** ⇨ LAST[1].

gassy /ˈgæsɪ; ˋgæsɪ/ *adj* **(-ier, -iest)** **1** of, like or full of gas, esp in the form of bubbles in liquid (似)气体的，充满气体的(尤指液体中充满气泡): *Fizzy lemonade can be very gassy.* 有的汽水气很足. **2** (*infml derog* 口，贬) talkative, esp in a gossipy or boastful way 话多的(尤指闲话或大话): *a gassy old man,woman,etc* 爱絮叨的老头儿、老太婆等. ▷ **gas·si·ness** *n* [U].

gast·ric /ˈgæstrɪk; ˋgæstrɪk/ *adj* [attrib 作定语] (*medical* 医) of the stomach 胃的; 胃部的: *gastric ulcers* 胃溃疡 ○ *gastric juices* 胃液.

▷ **gast·ritis** /gæˈstraɪtɪs; gæsˋtraɪtɪs/ *n* [U] (*medical* 医) inflammation of the stomach 胃炎.

gastro-enteritis /ˌgæstrəʊˌentəˈraɪtɪs; ˌgæstroˌɛntəˋraɪtɪs/ *n* [U] (*medical* 医) inflammation of the stomach and intestines 胃肠炎.

gast·ro·nomy /gæˈstrɒnəmɪ; gæsˋtrɑnəmɪ/ *n* [U] art and science of choosing, cooking and eating good food 美食学; 美食法.

▷ **gast·ro·nomic** /ˌgæstrəˈnɒmɪk; ˌgæstrəˋnɑmɪk/ *adj* of gastronomy 美食学的; 美食法的: *Lyons, the gastronomic capital of France* 里昂，法国的美食之都. **gast·ro·nomi·cally** /-klɪ; -klɪ/ *adv*: *a gastronomically outstanding meal* 精美的饭菜.

gate /geɪt; get/ *n* **1** (**a**) movable barrier, usu on hinges, which closes an opening in a wall, fence or hedge 大门; 城门; 篱笆门: *a wooden, iron gate* 木门、铁门 ○ *the garden gate* 花园的门 ○ *the gates of the city* 城门. ⇨illus at App 1 见附录1插图, page vi. (**b**) opening closed by this; gateway 有大门的出入口; 大门口: *The carriage passed through the palace gates.* 马车穿过了宫殿的大门口. (**c**) similar movable barrier which controls a stream of water 闸门; 阀门: *a lock/sluice gate* 闸门[水闸]. **2** means of entrance or exit (for passengers at an airport or spectators at a sports ground) (飞机场或体育场的)进出口，站口，看台口: *The flight is now boarding at gate 16.* 本班机现在在第16号入口检票登机. **3** number of spectators at a sports event, esp a football match (体育比赛的)观众人数(尤指足球赛的): *a gate of ten thousand* 万人观众 ○ *a good/poor/large/small gate* 很多的[很少的/大量的/少量的]观众. **4** (also ˈ**gate money**) amount of money taken from tickets sold at a sports event, esp a football match 门票收入(尤指足球赛的): *Today's gate will be given to charity.* 今日的门票收入将捐献给慈善事业.

▷ **gate** *v* [Tn, Tn·pr] **~ sb (for sth)** (*Brit*) confine (a student) to college or school as a punishment 惩罚性禁止(学生)离校.

□ ˈ**gatecrash** (also **crash**) *v* [I, Tn] enter (a private social occasion) without paying or being invited (未付费或未受邀)擅自闯入，擅自出席(私人社交集会): *gatecrash a party* 擅自闯入一聚会. ˈ**gatecrasher** *n* person who gatecrashes 擅自参加者; 不速之客.

ˈ**gatehouse** *n* house built at or over a gate (eg at the entrance to a park or castle) 门房，门楼(如公园或城堡入口处的).

ˈ**gatekeeper** *n* keeper of a gatehouse 看门人; 管门人.

ˌ**gateleg** ˈ**table** (also ˌ**gatelegged** ˈ**table**) table with legs that can be moved out to support a folding top 折叠式桌子. ⇨illus at App 1 见附录1插图, page xvi.

ˈ**gatemoney** = GATE 4.

ˈ**gatepost** *n* **1** post on which a gate is hung or against which it is closed 门柱. **2** (idm 习语) **between you and me and the** ˈ**gatepost** (*infml* 口) in strict confidence 严格保密.

ˈ**gateway** *n* **1** way in and out that can be closed by a gate or gates 大门口: *Don't stand there blocking the gateway!* 别站在那儿挡着门口! **2** (usu *sing* 通常作单数) **~ to sth** (*fig* 比喻) (**a**) place through which one must go to reach somewhere else 门径; 关口: *The port of Dover is England's gateway to Europe.* 多佛港是英国进入欧洲的大门. (**b**) means of gaining sth desired 方法; 手段; 途径: *A good education can be the gateway to success.* 良好的教育是通往成功之路.

gât·eau /ˈgætəʊ; *US* gæˈtəʊ; gaˋto/ *n* (*pl* **~x** or **~s**) [C, U] large rich cream-cake often decorated with fruit, nuts, chocolate, etc 奶油大蛋糕(常饰有水果、坚果、巧克力等): *a (slice of) fresh cream gâteau* (一块)新鲜的奶油蛋糕.

gather /ˈgæðə(r); ˋgæðɚ/ *v* **1** (**a**) [I, Ipr, Ip, Tn, Tn·pr, Tn·p] **~ round (sb/sth); ~ sb/sth round (sb/sth)** come or bring sb/sth together in one place 聚集; 集合; 召集; 搜集: *A crowd soon gathered.* 很快聚集起一群人. ○ *Gather round* (ie Form a group round me) *and listen, children!* 孩子们，围拢过来听我说! ○ *a musical evening with the whole family gathered round the piano* 全家围在钢琴旁的音乐晚会. (**b**) [Tn, Tn·p] **~ sth (together/up)** bring together (objects) that have been spread about 收集，收拢(分散的东西): *Give me a moment to gather my notes together.* 给我些时间整理一下笔记. ○ *She gathered up her scattered belongings and left.* 她把自己的散乱物品收好就走了. **2** (**a**) [Tn, Tn·pr] **~ sth (from sth)** collect (plants, fruit, etc) from a wide area 搜集，采集(植物、水果等): *gather flowers, berries, nuts, etc* 采花、浆果、坚果等 ○ *gathering mushrooms in the fields* 在野地采集蘑菇 ○ (*fig* 比喻) *information gathered* (ie obtained) *from various sources* 从各处搜集的信息. (**b**) [Tn, Tn·p] **~ sth (in)** pick or cut and collect (crops) for storage 捡拾或收割(庄稼): *The harvest has been safely gathered in.* 庄稼已妥善收获完毕. **3** [Tn, Tn·pr, Tf] **~ sth (from sb/sth)** understand sth; conclude 理解某事物; 得出结论: *'Smith's resigned.' 'I gathered as much from the newspapers.'* '史密斯辞职了.' '我从报纸上也能看出他得辞职.' ○ *I gather you want to see the director.* 我猜想你要见经理. ○ *'She won't be coming.' 'So I gather.'* '她不来了.' '我也这么看.' ○ *I gathered from the way she replied that she wasn't very enthusiastic.* 从她的回答来看，她并不十分热心. **4** [Tn·pr, Tn·p] **~ sth round sb/sth; ~ sth up** pull (a garment) tighter to one's body 将(衣服)向身体收拢: *She gathered the shawl round her/round her shoulders.* 她用披肩把自己[肩头]裹紧. ○ *She gathered up her skirts and ran.* 她提起裙摆就跑了. **5** [Tn, Tn·p] **~ sth (in)** draw (a garment) together in folds or pleats (在衣服上)打褶子: *a skirt gathered (in) at the waist* 腰部打褶的裙子. **6** [I, Tn] increase (sth) 增加(某事物): *The darkness is gathering.* 夜色渐浓. ○ *in the gathering gloom of a winter's afternoon* 在冬天的一个下午，天色越来越暗 ○ *The car gathered speed.* 汽车速度逐渐加快了. **7** [Tn] (*fig* 比喻) bring (sth) together in order to make an effort; summon up 聚集或集中(某事物)以尽力; 鼓起; 唤起: *He gathered all his strength and swung the axe.* 他用尽全力抡起斧头. ○ *She sat trying to gather her thoughts before making her speech.* 她坐在那里努力集中思想准备发言. **8** (idm 习语) **be gathered to one's** ˈ**fathers** (*dated or rhet* 旧或修辞) die 死. **collect/gather one's wits** ⇨ WIT. **gather** ˈ**dust** be neglected or unused for a long time 长久忽略或久置不用. **a rolling stone gathers no moss** ⇨ ROLL[2].

▷ **gather** *n* fold or pleat in a garment (衣服上的)褶子.

gath·er·ing /ˈgæðərɪŋ; ˋgæðərɪŋ/ *n* meeting or coming together of people 集会; 人群的聚集: *a small family gathering* 家庭小聚会 ○ *a gathering of friends* 朋友的聚会.

GATT /gæt; gæt/ *abbr* 缩写 = General Agreement on Tariffs and Trade (signed in 1947) 关税及贸易总协定(1947年签订).

gauche /gəʊʃ; goʃ/ *adj* **1** socially awkward or clumsy 不善交际的; 不圆滑的: *I find him terribly gauche.* 我认为他太不圆通了. ○ *a gauche manner, person, remark* 不雅

G

的举止、人、言语. **2** (*fig* 比喻) (of literary or artistic work) clumsy (指文学或艺术作品)拙劣的, 不简练的: *a rather gauche style, technique, etc* 拙劣的文体、技艺等.
▷ **gauche·ness** /ˈɡəʊʃnɪs; ˋɡoʃnɪs/, **gaucherie** /ˈɡəʊʃərɪ; *US* ˌɡəʊʃəˈriː; ˌɡoʃəˋri/ *ns* [U] gauche behaviour 不文雅的举止.

gau·cho /ˈɡaʊtʃəʊ; ˋɡaʊtʃo/ *n* (*pl* **~s**) South American cowboy, esp one of Spanish and Indian descent 南美牧人; (尤指)加乌乔(西班牙人和印第安人的后裔).

gaudy /ˈɡɔːdɪ; ˋɡɔdɪ/ *adj* (**-ier, -iest**) (*derog* 贬) too bright and showy, esp in a vulgar way 花哨的; (尤指)俗气的: *gaudy decorations* 花哨的饰物 ○ *cheap and gaudy jewellery* 价廉而花哨的珠宝. ▷ **gaud·ily** /ˈɡɔːdɪlɪ; ˋɡɔdəlɪ/ *adv*. **gaudi·ness** /ˈɡɔːdɪnɪs; ˋɡɔdɪnɪs/ *n* [U].

gauge (*US* also **gage**) /ɡeɪdʒ; ɡedʒ/ *n* **1** [U, C] standard measure, esp of width or thickness 标准量度(尤指宽度或厚度): *the gauge of a sheet of metal* 金属板的厚度 ○ *What gauge of wire should we use for this job?* 我们干这活应该用多大号的铅丝? **2** [C] distance between rails on a railway or tramway (火车或电车轨道的)轨距: *standard gauge*, ie 4ft 8½ ins 标准轨距(4英尺8½英寸) ○ *narrow/broad gauge*, ie narrower/wider than standard 窄轨[宽轨] ○ [attrib 作定语] *a narrow-gauge railway* 窄轨铁路. **3** [C] instrument for measuring the amount or level of sth 计量器: *a petrol, pressure, rain, speed, etc gauge* 汽油量表、压力计、雨量计、速度计. **4** [C] fact or circumstance which one can use in estimating or judging; measure (用以作出估计或判断的)事实, 环境; 方法; 尺度: *Is a person's behaviour under stress a reliable gauge of his character?* 人在受到压力时的行为能作衡量其品性的可靠尺度吗?
▷ **gauge** *v* **1** [Tn] (**a**) measure (sth) esp accurately 测量(某物)(尤指精确地): *precision instruments which can gauge the diameter to a fraction of a millimetre* 可测出直径几分之一毫米的精密仪器. (**b**) make an estimate of (sth) 估计, 判定(某事物): *gauging the strength of the wind from the movement of the trees* 凭树的摇动估计风力. **2** [Tn, Tf, Tw] make a judgement about (sth) 判断(某事物): *trying to gauge reactions, sympathies, sentiments, etc* 试图判定各种反应、同情程度、观点等 ○ *It was difficult to gauge how people would respond.* 大家的反应如何难以估计. ○ *I gauged that it was not a good moment to speak to her.* 我认为那不是跟她说话的时机.

G

gaunt /ɡɔːnt; ɡɔnt/ *adj* **1** (of a person) made exceptionally thin by hunger or illness; haggard (指人)(因饥饿或疾病)憔悴的, 骨瘦如柴的: *the gaunt face of a starving man* 饿汉憔悴的面容. **2** (of a place) bare; desolate (指地方)不毛的, 荒凉的: *the gaunt landscape of the moon* 月球上荒凉的景色. ▷ **gaunt·ness** *n* [U].

gaunt·let¹ /ˈɡɔːntlɪt; ˋɡɔntlɪt/ *n* **1** metal glove forming part of a suit of armour, worn by soldiers in the Middle Ages (中世纪武士铠甲的)金属手套. **2** strong glove with a wide covering for the wrist, used for driving, fencing, etc (驾驶、击剑等用的)长手套, 防护手套: *motorcyclists with leather gauntlets* 戴着皮护手套的摩托车手. ⇨illus at GLOVE 见GLOVE插图. **3** (idm 习语) **pick up/take up the ˈgauntlet** accept a challenge 接受挑战: *He was quick to take up the gauntlet thrown down by the opposition.* 他立刻接受了对方提出的挑战. **throw down the ˈgauntlet** challenge sb to do sth 向某人提出挑战.

gaunt·let² /ˈɡɔːntlɪt; ˋɡɔntlɪt/ *n* (idm 习语) **run the ˈgauntlet** be exposed to danger, anger, or criticism 冒险; 受气; 受批评: *Before getting the proposals accepted, the government had to run the gauntlet of hostility from its own supporters.* 拥护政府的人对政府进行了尖锐的抨击之后, 这些建议才得以接受.

gauze /ɡɔːz; ɡɔz/ *n* [U] **1** thin, often transparent, fabric of cotton, silk, etc (丝或棉等的)薄纱: *a piece of (cotton, etc) gauze* 一块(棉等)薄纱 ○ [attrib 作定语] *a gauze curtain* 纱帘 ○ *a gauze patch applied to his wound* 敷在他伤口上的纱布. **2** netting made of very thin wire (极细的金属丝制的)纱网.
▷ **gauzy** *adj* of or like gauze 纱布的; 似薄纱的.

gave *pt* of GIVE.

gavel /ˈɡævl; ˋɡævḷ/ *n* small hammer used by an auctioneer or chairman as a signal for order or attention (拍卖者或主席用的)小槌: *bang, rap, etc one's gavel on the table* 用小槌在桌上猛击、敲打等.

ga·votte /ɡəˈvɒt; ɡəˋvɑt/ *n* (music for an) old French dance 古老的法国加伏特舞(曲).

gawk /ɡɔːk; ɡɔk/ *v* [I, Ipr] **~ (at sb/sth)** (*infml* 口) stare impolitely or stupidly; gawp 无礼地或呆呆地瞪眼看: *I hate being gawked at!* 我讨厌人家直瞪瞪地盯着我!

gawky /ˈɡɔːkɪ; ˋɡɔkɪ/ *adj* (**-ier, -iest**) (esp of a tall young person) awkward and clumsy (尤指高大的年轻人)笨手笨脚的, 笨拙的: *a shy gawky teenager* 腼腆而笨拙的年轻人. ▷ **gawk·ily** /ˈɡɔːkɪlɪ; ˋɡɔkɪlɪ/ *adv*. **gawki·ness** /ˈɡɔːkɪnɪs; ˋɡɔkɪnɪs/ *n* [U]: *Despite her gawkiness she was clearly going to be a beautiful woman one day.* 别看她高大笨拙, 总有一天她会出落为美女的.

gawp /ɡɔːp; ɡɔp/ *v* [I, Ipr] **~ (at sb/sth)** (*infml* 口) stare impolitely or stupidly; gawk 无礼地或呆呆地瞪眼看: *crowds of onlookers coming to gawp at the wreckage of the aircraft* 来看热闹的人望着失事飞机的残骸发愣. ⇨ Usage at LOOK¹ 用法见LOOK¹.

gay /ɡeɪ; ɡe/ *adj* **1** homosexual 同性恋的: *a gay person, club, bar* 搞同性恋爱的人、俱乐部、酒吧 ○ *I didn't know he/she was gay.* 我不知道他[她]是同性恋者. **2** happy and full of fun; light-hearted; cheerful 快乐的; 欢快的; 轻松的; 愉快的: *gay laughter, music* 欢快的笑声、音乐 ○ *The streets look gay with bright flags and coloured lights.* 街上旗帜鲜艳、彩灯缤纷, 显出一派欢乐景象. **3** [attrib 作定语] careless; thoughtless 轻率的; 不加思索的: *spending money with gay abandon* 挥霍钱财.
▷ **gaily** /ˈɡeɪlɪ; ˋɡelɪ/ *adv*: *the gaily decorated buildings* 装点得喜气洋洋的建筑物 ○ *She gaily announced that she was leaving the next day*, ie without having considered the trouble this would cause. 她轻率地宣布第二天就要走了(未考虑其后果).
gay *n* homosexual person 同性恋爱者.
gay·ness /ˈɡeɪnɪs; ˋɡenɪs/ *n* [U] homosexuality 同性恋. Cf 参看 GAIETY.

gaze /ɡeɪz; ɡez/ *v* **1** [I, Ipr] look long and steadily (at sb/sth), usu in surprise or admiration 久久地凝视, 注视(通常指因惊讶或赞赏): *She gazed at me in disbelief when I told her the news.* 我告诉她这消息时, 她以怀疑的目光注视着我. ○ *He just sat gazing into space/gazing through the window.* 他只是坐着茫然地望着[呆呆地望着窗外]. ⇨Usage at LOOK¹ 用法见LOOK¹. **2** [Ipr] **~ on/upon sb/sth** (*fml* 文) look at sb/sth 看某人[某事物]: *She was the most beautiful woman he had ever gazed upon.* 她是他所见过的最美丽的女子.
▷ **gaze** *n* [sing] long steady look 凝视; 端详: *Under his intense gaze she felt uncomfortable.* 他目不转睛地看着她, 使她觉得很不自在.

ga·zebo /ɡəˈziːbəʊ; ɡəˋzibo/ *n* (*pl* **~s**) small, usu hutlike, building designed to give a wide view of the surrounding country (供俯瞰景色的)小亭阁式建筑物, 凉亭, 观景阁.

gaz·elle /ɡəˈzel; ɡəˋzɛl/ *n* (*pl* unchanged or **~s** 复数或不变或作 **gazelles**) small, graceful antelope 瞪羚: *a herd of gazelle* 一群瞪羚.

gaz·ette /ɡəˈzet; ɡəˋzɛt/ *n* **1** official journal with public notices and lists of government, military, legal and university appointments (刊载政府、军事、法院、大学任命名单和告示的)公报. **2** (used in the titles of newspapers 用作报纸名称): *the Evening Gazette, London Gazette, etc* 《晚报》、《伦敦公报》.
▷ **gaz·ette** *v* (*esp Brit*) **1** [Tn usu passive 通常用于被动语态] publish or announce (sth) in an official gazette (在公报上)刊载或宣布(某事物): *His appointment was gazetted last week.* 上周在公报上宣布了对他的任命. **2** [usu passive 通常用于被动语态: Tn·pr, Cn·n] **~ sb to sth** appoint sb, esp to a military post 任命某人(尤指任军职): *He was gazetted to a new regiment.* 委派他赴一新团任职. ○ *He was gazetted captain.* 委派他任上尉.

gaz·ett·eer /ˌɡæzəˈtɪə(r); ˌɡæzəˋtɪr/ *n* index of geographical names 地名索引; 地名词典: *a world gazetteer* 世界地名词典.

ga·zump /ɡəˈzʌmp; ɡəˋzʌmp/ *v* [Tn usu passive 通常用于被动语态] (*Brit infml derog* 口, 贬) raise the price of property, esp a house, after accepting an offer from (a buyer) 抬价敲诈(尤指房产, 价格议定后再抬价): *We shan't be buying the house: we've been gazumped (by the owner).* 我们不想买那所房子了, 卖主变卦要敲诈我们.
▷ **ga·zumper** /ɡəˈzʌmpə(r); ɡəˋzʌmpɚ/ *n*.
ga·zump·ing /ɡəˈzʌmpɪŋ; ɡəˋzʌmpɪŋ/ *n* [U] (*Brit infml*

derog 口，贬）practice of gazumping buyers 抬价敲诈（尤指房产，价格议定后再抬价的行为）.

GB /ˌdʒiː ˈbiː; ˌdʒi ˋbi/ *abbr* 缩写 = Great Britain. ⇨ Usage at GREAT 用法见 GREAT.

GC /ˌdʒiː ˈsiː; ˌdʒi ˋsi/ *abbr* 缩写 = (*Brit*) George Cross (award to civilians for bravery): *be awarded the GC* 获乔治勋章 ○ *William Lawson GC* 乔治勋章获得者威廉·劳森. Cf 参看 VC 4.

GCE /ˌdʒiː siː ˈiː; ˌdʒi si ˋi/ *abbr* 缩写 = (*Brit*) General Certificate of Education : *have 9 GCEs* 有9门学科的普通教育证书 ○ *take GCE in 9 subjects* 参加9科普通教育证书考试 ○ *GCE O-level/A-level* 普通级［高级］普通教育证书. Cf 参看 CSE, GCSE.

GCSE /ˌdʒiː siː es ˈiː; ˌdʒi si ɛs ˋi/ *abbr* 缩写 = (*Brit*) General Certificate of Secondary Education. Cf 参看 CSE, GCE.

Gdn *abbr* 缩写 = (*pl* **Gdns**) (in street names 用作街道名称) Gardens: *7 Windsor Gdns* 温莎街7号.

GDP /ˌdʒiː diː ˈpiː; ˌdʒi di ˋpi/ *abbr* 缩写 = gross domestic product 国内生产总值. Cf 参看 GNP.

GDR /ˌdʒiː diː ˈɑː(r); ˌdʒi di ˋɑr/ *abbr* 缩写 = (formerly) German Democratic Republic (East Germany)（旧时）德意志民主共和国（东德）.

gear 传动装置

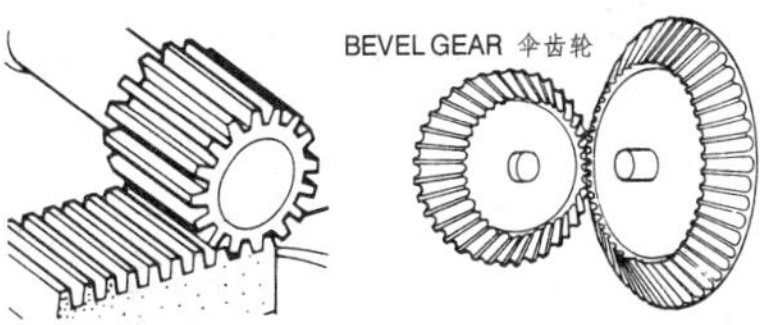

gear /ɡɪə(r); ɡɪr/ *n* **1** [U] equipment, clothing, etc needed for an expedition, a sport, etc（远征、运动等需用的）设备、装备、衣物等: *All his camping gear was packed in the rucksack.* 他的野营物品全都放在背囊里了. ○ *We're only going for two days; you don't need to bring so much gear!* 我们只去两天，你不用带那么多东西! ○ *wearing her party gear* 穿着她赴宴的衣服. **2** [sing] (esp in compounds 尤用以构成复合词) piece or set of apparatus or machinery for a particular purpose 仪器; 器械; 装置: *The landing-gear has jammed.* 着陆装置发生故障. ○ *winding gear for lifting heavy loads* 起重绞盘装置. **3** (**a**) [C often *pl* 常作复数] set of toothed wheels which fit into another set to transmit power from a vehicle's engine to its road wheels（机动车辆的）传动装置，排挡: *Careless use of the clutch may damage the gears.* 离合器使用不慎可能损坏传动装置. ○ *The car has four forward gears and one reverse gear.* 那汽车有四个前进挡和一个倒挡. ○ *The car started with a crashing of gears*, ie noise made by operating them badly. 那汽车开动时发出挂挡的咣当声（因操纵技术不佳所致）. ⇨illus at App 1 见附录1插图, page xiii. ⇨illus 见插图. (**b**) [U] particular position or setting of the gear mechanism 传动装置的某位置或组合状态; 排挡: *The car is in/out of gear*, ie has the gears engaged/disengaged. 汽车挂上挡［未挂挡］. ○ *low/bottom/first gear*, ie used for starting a vehicle or climbing a slope 低速挡［头挡/第一挡］（用于车辆起动或爬坡）○ *high/top gear*, ie used for high speeds 高速挡 ○ *change gear* 换排挡. **4** [U] (*fig* 比喻) degree of speed or efficiency 速度或效率的程度: *The party organization is moving into top gear as the election approaches.* 随着选举临近，党组织的活动也如火如荼. ○ *The athlete changed gear* (ie suddenly accelerated) *and shot ahead of the others.* 该运动员突然加速，冲到别人前面去了.

▷ **gear** *v* (phr v) **gear sth to/towards sth** adapt sth to a particular need or to an appropriate level or standard 对某事物加以调节以适合某种需要或达到某种水平或标准: *Industry must be geared to wartime needs.* 工业必须调整以适应战时需要. ○ *Our effort is geared to a higher level of production.* 我们调整力量将生产推向更高的水平. **gear down** (of a driver) change to a lower gear so as to have better control（指驾驶员）换至较低一挡以便操纵. **gear sth down (to sth)** reduce sth in force or intensity（在力量或强度上）减低某事物: *The period of exercise was geared down to ten minutes a day for men over 60.* 60岁以上的人的锻炼时间减低到每日十分钟. **gear up (for/to sth); gear sb/sth up (for/to sth)** become or make sb/sth ready (for sth)（为某事物）（使）某人［某事物］准备好: *The company's gearing up for the big export drive.* 公司正为大规模出口作好准备. ○ *I was all geared up* (ie excitedly ready) *to go on holiday, and now it's been cancelled.* 我兴致勃勃地做好去度假的准备，可是现在吹了. **gear·ing** /ˈɡɪərɪŋ; ˋɡɪrɪŋ/ *n* [U] set or arrangement of gears 齿轮装置; 传动装置: *The gearing of this machine is unusual.* 这机器的齿轮装置很特别.

□ ˈ**gearbox** *n* case that encloses a vehicle's gear mechanism（车辆的）变速箱，变速器. ⇨illus at App 1 见附录1插图, page xii.

ˈ**gear-change** *n* movement from one position of the gear mechanism to another 换挡; 变速: *a smooth gear-change* 平稳的变速.

ˈ**gear-lever**, ˈ**gear-stick** (*US* usu 美式英语通常作 ˈ**gearshift**) *ns* lever used to engage, disengage or change gear 变速杆. ⇨illus at App 1 见附录1插图, page xii, xiii.

ˈ**gearwheel** *n* toothed wheel in a set of gears 齿轮.

gecko /ˈɡekəʊ; ˋɡɛko/ *n* (*pl* **~s** or **~es**) small house lizard, found in warm countries 壁虎.

gee[1] /dʒiː; dʒi/ *interj* (also **gee-up**) /dʒiːˈʌp; ˋdʒiˋʌp/ (used for telling a horse, etc to start, go on or go faster 吆喝马等起行、前行或快行的用语).

▷ **gee** *v* (phr v) **gee sb/sth up** (*infml* 口) make sb/sth work or perform more quickly or efficiently 催促某人［某事物］更快地或更有效地工作.

gee-gee /ˈdʒiːdʒiː; ˋdʒidʒi/ *n* (used by and to small children) horse（儿语）马.

gee[2] /dʒiː; dʒi/ *interj* (also **gee whiz**) /ˌdʒiː ˈwɪz; ˌdʒi: ˋwɪz/ (*esp US*) (used to express surprise, admiration, etc 用以表示惊奇、赞赏等): *Gee, I like your new hat!* 嘿，我真喜欢你的新帽子!

geese *pl* of GOOSE.

geezer /ˈɡiːzə(r); ˋɡizɚ/ *n* (*infml* 口) man, esp an old one 人;（尤指）老头儿: *that old geezer over there* 那边的那个老头儿.

Geiger coun·ter /ˈɡaɪɡə kaʊntə(r); ˋɡaɪɡɚ ˌkaʊntɚ/ device for detecting and measuring radioactivity 盖革计数器（探测放射能量的仪器）.

gei·sha /ˈɡeɪʃə; ˋɡeʃə/ *n* Japanese girl trained to entertain men with conversation, dancing or singing（日本的）艺妓（陪男子谈话、表演歌舞者）.

gel /dʒel; dʒɛl/ *n* [C, U] (esp in compounds 尤用以构成复合词) semi-solid jelly-like substance 凝胶; 冻胶: *bath-gel, hair-gel*, ie jelly-like soap or shampoo 凝胶状皂、洗发液.

▷ **gel** *v* (**-ll-**) [I] **1** set into a jelly 形成胶体; 胶凝; 胶化: *This liquid gels faster in cold weather.* 这种液体天冷时凝结得快些. **2** (*fig* 比喻) take definite form 成形: *My ideas are beginning to gel.* 我的想法逐渐形成了.

gel·at·ine /ˈdʒelətiːn, -tɪn; ˋdʒɛlətin, -tɪn/ (also *esp US* **gel·atin** /ˈdʒelətɪn; ˋdʒɛlətn̩/) *n* [U] clear tasteless substance used for making jelly as food, manufacturing photographic film, etc 明胶; 凝胶.

▷ **ge·lat·in·ous** /dʒəˈlætɪnəs; dʒəˋlætənəs/ *adj* like jelly 明胶状的; 胶状的: *a gelatinous substance* 胶状物质.

geld /ɡeld; ɡɛld/ *v* [Tn] castrate (an animal) 阉割（动物）; 给（动物）去势或割除卵巢.

▷ **geld·ing** /ˈɡeldɪŋ; ˋɡɛldɪŋ/ *n* castrated animal, esp a horse 阉割过的动物（尤指马）. Cf 参看 STALLION.

gel·ig·nite /ˈdʒelɪɡnaɪt; ˋdʒɛlɪɡˌnaɪt/ *n* [U] powerful explosive made from nitric acid and glycerine 葛里炸药，爆炸胶（一种含有硝酸和甘油的炸药）.

gem /dʒem; dʒɛm/ *n* **1** precious stone or jewel, esp when cut and polished 宝石（尤指经切割打磨的）: *a crown studded with gems* 镶宝石的皇冠. **2** (*fig* 比喻) thing highly valued for beauty or some other special quality 宝物; 精华; 珍品; 美丽绝伦的事物: *This picture is the gem* (ie the best) *of the collection.* 这幅画是收藏的珍品. ○ *a gem of a place*, ie an excellent place 胜地 ○ *That restaurant is a little gem.* 那餐厅是个小乐园. ○ *She's a real gem!* 她美如仙子!

G

□ **'gemstone** *n* precious or semi-precious stone, esp before cutting into shape 宝石或次宝石(尤指未经琢磨成形的).

Gem·ini /ˈdʒemɪnaɪ, -ni; ˋdʒɛmə,naɪ/ *n* **1** [U] the third sign of the zodiac, the Twins 双子宫(黄道第三宫). **2** [C] person born under the influence of this sign 属双子宫星座的人. ▷ **Gem·in·ean** *n, adj.* ⇨Usage at ZODIAC 用法见 ZODIAC. ⇨illus at ZODIAC 见 ZODIAC 插图.

gen /dʒen; dʒɛn/ *n* [U] **~ (on sth)** (*dated Brit infml* 旧, 口) information 情报; 资料; 消息: *Give me the gen on this new project.* 把这新项目的资料给我.

▷ **gen** *v* **(-nn-)** (phr v) **gen (sb) up (on sth)** (*dated Brit infml* 旧, 口) obtain information or provide (sb) with information (about sth) 获得情报; 给某人(关于某事物的)资料: *He is fully genned up on the new project.* 他充分了解新工程的情况.

Gen *abbr* 缩写 = General: *Gen (Stanley) Armstrong* (史坦雷·)阿姆斯特朗将军.

gen·darme /ˈʒɒndɑːm; ˋʒɑndɑrm/ *n* member of a military force employed on police duties, esp in France and French-speaking countries 宪兵(尤指法国及法语国家中的).

▷ **gen·darm·erie** /ʒɒnˈdɑːmərɪ; ʒɑnˋdɑrmərɪ/ *n* **1** [pl *v*] whole body of gendarmes 宪兵(总称). **2** [C] headquarters of a body of gendarmes 宪兵队队部; 宪兵司令部.

gen·der /ˈdʒendə(r); ˋdʒɛndɚ/ *n* [C, U] **1** (*grammar*) (in certain languages) classification of a noun or pronoun as masculine or feminine (某些语言的)性(名词或代词分为阳性和阴性): *There are three genders in German: masculine, feminine and neuter.* 德语中有三性: 阳性、阴性和中性. ○ *In French the adjective must agree with the noun in number and gender.* 法语中形容词必须在数和性上与名词一致. **2** (*fml* 文) sexual classification; sex (生理上的)性别分类, 性: *the male and female genders* 男性和女性.

gene /dʒiːn; dʒin/ *n* (*biology* 生) unit in a chromosome which controls heredity 基因: *a dominant/recessive gene* 显性[隐性]基因 ○ *have sth in one's genes*, ie have an inherited quality 在遗传基因中具有某种性质.

genea·logy /ˌdʒiːnɪˈælədʒɪ; ˌdʒinɪˋælədʒɪ/ *n* **1** [U] study of family history, showing who the ancestors of particular people were and how they were related to each other 家谱学; 宗谱学. **2** [C] (diagram showing a) particular person's ancestry 家谱; 宗谱.

▷ **genea·lo·gical** /ˌdʒiːnɪəˈlɒdʒɪkl; ˌdʒinɪəˋlɑdʒɪkl/ *adj* concerned with tracing family descent 家谱的; 宗谱的: *a genealogical expert* 家谱学家 ○ *genealogical evidence, proof, records, etc* 家谱关系证据、证明、记录等 ○ *a genealogical table/tree*, ie a diagram with branches showing a family's ancestry 家谱表[家系图]. **genea·lo·gic·ally** /-klɪ; -klɪ/ *adv*.

genea·lo·gist /ˌdʒiːnɪˈælədʒɪst; ˌdʒinɪˋælədʒɪst/ *n* student of or expert in genealogy 家谱学的研究者; 家谱学家.

gen·era *pl* of GENUS.

gen·eral /ˈdʒenrəl; ˋdʒɛnərəl/ *adj* **1 (a)** affecting all or most people, places or things 普遍的; 全面的: *a general lowering of standards* 标准的全面降低 ○ *The announcement was met with general rejoicing.* 该项宣布受到普遍的欢迎. ○ *a matter of general interest, concern, etc* 公众感兴趣、关心等的事情 ○ *Once quite rare, they are now in general use*, ie used by most people. 那些东西一度非常罕见, 现在已普遍使用. ○ *That man's a general nuisance*, ie to most people at most times. 那男子处处招人讨厌. ○ *the general public*, ie the majority of (ordinary) people 人民大众 ○ *a general meeting, strike, etc* 全体会议、总罢工 ○ *The bad weather has been fairly general*, ie has affected most areas. 这恶劣的天气影响大部分地区. ○ *The general impression was* (ie Most people thought) *that it had improved.* 普遍认为情况已有改善. **(b)** [attrib 作定语] not limited to one part or aspect of a person or thing or to a particular time; overall 整体的(不局限于一人, 一事或一时); 总的: *There is still some weakness in the legs, but her general condition is good.* 她双腿仍有些软弱无力, 但总的情况尚好. ○ *The opening chapter gives a general overview of the subject.* 开篇第一章是对主题的概述. ○ *The old building was in a general state of decay/disrepair.* 这古老建筑物整体上已残破了[失修]. **2 (a)** not specialized in subject matter 非专门的; 一般的; 普遍的: *a general degree* 普通学位 ○ *general knowledge, sciences, studies, etc* 一般的知识、科学、研究等 ○ *We kept the conversation/discussion fairly general.* 我们谈话[讨论]的内容一直相当广泛. **(b)** [attrib 作定语] not specialized or limited in range of work, use, activity, etc 非专门的或不局限于某工作、用途、活动等范围的: *a general hospital* 综合医院 ○ *the general reader* 一般读者 ○ *a general factotum*, ie servant or assistant able to do all kinds of work 杂务总管. **3** [usu attrib 通常作定语] normal; usual 正常的; 常规的; 通常的: *The general practice in such cases is to apply for a court order.* 处理这类案件的常规做法是请求法院发出指令. ○ *a general principle* (ie one true of most cases) *to which there may be several exceptions* 可能有若干例外的一般原则 ○ *In the general way of things* (ie Usually) *not much happens here.* 通常此地不多见. **4** showing the chief aspects of sth; not detailed; vague 大致的; 不详细的; 笼统的: *His description was too general to be of much use.* 他的描述很笼统, 用处不大. ○ *My general impression was that it was quite good.* 大致上我觉得那相当好. ○ *bear a general resemblance to sb/sth* 与某人[某事物]大致相似 ○ *speak/write in general terms* 措辞笼统地说[写]. **5** [attrib 作定语] (often in titles with a capital letter and following the *n* 常作大写, 用于头衔, 置名词之后) chief; head 总的; 首席的: *the general manager* 总经理 ○ *the Attorney, Inspector, Governor, Secretary, etc General* 首席检察官、监察长、总督、总书记. **6** (idm 习语) **as a general 'rule** in most cases 在通常情况下; 一般而言. **be caviare to the general** ⇨ CAVIARE. **in 'general** mainly; mostly; usually 总的说来; 大体上; 通常: *In general her work has been good, but this essay is dreadful.* 总的说来, 她的作品不错, 不过这篇文章糟透了.

▷ **gen·eral** *n* army officer of very high rank, esp an officer in the British Army below the rank of field marshal 将军; (尤指英国的)陆军上将: *a four-star general*, ie in the US army 四星上将(美国陆军) ○ [attrib 作定语] *General Roberts* 罗伯茨上将. ⇨App 9 见附录 9. **gen·eral·ship** /ˈdʒenrəlʃɪp; ˋdʒɛnərəl,ʃɪp/ *n* [U] skill and leadership (as) of a general, esp in battle 将军的才能, 将才(尤指作战中表现出的).

□ **ˌGeneral Aˈssembly** main meeting of representatives (of the United Nations, etc) (联合国等的)代表大会.

ˌGeneral Cerˌtificate of Eduˈcation (*abbr* 缩写 **GCE**) (certificate for passing) any of a range of examinations taken in Britain at the age of 16+ (在英国为16岁以上的人参加的)普通教育证书(的考试). Cf 参看 ADVANCED LEVEL (ADVANCE²), A/S LEVEL, ORDINARY LEVEL (ORDINARY).

ˌGeneral Cerˌtificate of ˌSecondary Eduˈcation (*abbr* 缩写 **GCSE**) (certificate for passing) any of a range of examinations introduced in Britain in the late 1980s to replace both the Ordinary level GCE and the CSE 普通中等教育证书(的考试)(在英国80年代末采用, 以取代普通教育和中等教育的普通级考试). Cf 参看 A/S LEVEL, CERTIFICATE OF SECONDARY EDUCATION, GENERAL CERTIFICATE OF EDUCATION.

ˈgeneral ˈdealer person who trades in all kinds of goods 杂货商.

ˌgeneral eˈlection national parliamentary election 大选; 普选. Cf 参看 BY-ELECTION.

ˌgeneral headˈquarters (*abbr* 缩写 **GHQ**) main centre of military organization and supplies 总司令部.

ˌGeneral ˈPost Office (*abbr* 缩写 **GPO**) **(a)** (formerly in Britain) national organization of postal services (now called the Post Office) (旧时英国的)邮政总局(现称邮政局). **(b)** (*Brit*) main post office in a town 市邮政局.

ˌgeneral ˈpractice (*Brit*) medical treatment of all types of illness within the community (as opposed to hospital work or specialization in treating a particular sort of disease) 全科医师的业务(在社区中医治各科疾病的, 有别于医院的或专科的). **ˌgeneral pracˈtitioner** (*abbr* 缩写 **GP**) (*Brit*) doctor who is in general practice 全科医师.

ˌgeneral-ˈpurpose *adj* [attrib 作定语] that has a variety of uses 多用途的; 多功能的: *a ˌgeneral-purpose ˈfarm vehicle* 多用农业机动车.

ˌgeneral ˈstaff officers assisting a military commander at headquarters (司令部的)全体参谋.

G

gen·er·al·is·simo /ˌdʒenrəˈlɪsɪməʊ; ˌdʒɛnərəlˈɪsə,mo/ *n* (*pl* **~s**) commander of combined military and naval and air forces, or of combined armies 大元帅; 三军总司令; 联军总指挥.

gen·er·al·ity /ˌdʒenəˈrælətɪ; ˌdʒɛnəˈrælətɪ/ *n* **1** [C] general statement, esp one that is vague or indefinite 概述: *speak in generalities* 泛泛地说 ○ *Unfortunately the treaty is full of generalities, and fails to get down to specifics.* 遗憾的是条约很笼统, 订得不具体. **2 the generality** [pl *v*] (*fml* 文) majority or greater part; most 主体; 大多数; 大部分: *The generality of Swedes are blond.* 瑞典人大部分是金发的. **3** [U] quality of being general 一般性; 普遍性: *a rule of great generality*, ie one with few exceptions 极具普遍性的规则(鲜有例外者).

gen·er·al·ize, -ise /ˈdʒenrəlaɪz; ˋdʒɛnərəl,aɪz/ *v* **1** [I, Ipr, Tn, Tn·pr] **~ (about sth); ~ (sth) (from sth)** draw (a general conclusion) from particular examples or evidence (从某些事例或证据中)归纳, 概括出(一般性结论): *You cannot generalize about the effects of the drug from one or two cases.* 不能根据一两个病例就得出该药是否有效的结论. ○ *generalize a conclusion from a set of facts* 从一些事实中归纳出一项结论. **2** [I, Ipr] **~ (about sth)** make general statements for which there is little evidence 大体上说; 概括; 推想(没什么根据): *Europeans, if I may generalize, are all...* 倘若我可以大致说说的话, 欧洲人都... ○ *Perhaps you oughtn't to generalize about that.* 也许你不该对那事一概而论.

▷ **gen·er·al·ized, -ised** *adj* **1** widespread; general(1a) 广泛的; 普遍的; 全面的: *Use of this drug is now fairly generalized.* 这种药现在用得相当普遍. **2** not specific; general(1b) 非具体的; 整体的: *a sort of generalized malaise* 全身不适.

gen·er·al·iza·tion, -isation /ˌdʒenrəlaɪˈzeɪʃn; *US* -lɪˈz-; ˌdʒɛnərələˈzeʃən/ *n* [C, U] (statement based on) generalizing 归纳; 概括; 推想(的说法): *a speech full of sweeping generalizations* 高度概括的讲话.

gen·er·ally /ˈdʒenrəlɪ; ˋdʒɛnərəlɪ/ *adv* **1** by most people; widely 普遍地; 广泛地: *He is generally popular.* 他广受欢迎. ○ *The plan was generally welcomed.* 该计划大受欢迎. **2** in a general sense; without regard to details 一般意义上; 不考虑细节: *Generally speaking, it's quite a fair settlement.* 大致上说, 这样解决很恰当. **3** usually 通常地: *I generally get up early.* 我平常起得很早. ⇨Usage at HOPEFUL 用法见 HOPEFUL.

gen·er·ate /ˈdʒenəreɪt; ˋdʒɛnə,ret/ *v* [Tn] cause (sth) to exist or occur; produce 使(某物)存在或发生; 产生: *generate heat, electricity, power, etc* 产生热、电、动力等 ○ *hatred generated by racial prejudice* 种族偏见引起的仇恨 ○ *grammatical rules for generating sentences* 造句的语法规则.

gen·era·tion /ˌdʒenəˈreɪʃn; ˌdʒɛnəˈreʃən/ *n* **1** [U] (**a**) production 产生; 发生: *the generation of electricity by steam or water-power* 蒸汽或水力发电 ○ *the generation of heat by friction* 摩擦生热. (**b**) (*biology* 生) production of living beings, esp offspring; procreation 繁殖; (尤指)生育后代. **2** [C] single stage in a family history (家史中的)一代: *a family party at which all three generations were present*, ie children, parents and grandparents 三代同堂的家庭聚会 ○ *experience handed down from generation to generation* 世代相传的经验. **3** [C, Gp] all people born at about the same time 代(大致在同一时期内出生的所有人): *My generation behaves differently from my father's and grandfather's.* 我这一代人和我父辈及祖辈表现不同. ○ [attrib 作定语] *a first-, second-, third-, etc generation American*, ie sb who himself or whose parents or grandparents, etc emigrated to America 第一、第二、第三等代美国人(本人或其父母或其祖父母等移居美国者). **4** [C] average period, usu considered to be 25-30 years, in which children grow up to become full adults 一代人的期间, 代(通常认为是从儿童长到成年人的25-30年间): *a generation ago* 一代人之前 ○ *within one generation* 在一代人的期间内. **5** [C] single stage in the development of a type of product (产品类型的)代: *the new generation of supersonic airliners* 新一代的超音速客机 ○ [attrib 作定语] *third-generation robots* 第三代机器人.

□ **the geneˈration gap** difference in attitude, or lack of understanding, between young people and older people 代沟(两代人之间态度的差异或隔阂).

gen·er·at·ive /ˈdʒenərətɪv; ˋdʒɛnə,retɪv/ *adj* **1** able to produce; productive 能生产的; 有生产力的: *generative processes* 生产过程 ○ *a generative grammar*, ie one which gives rules for accounting for all possible sentences in a language 生成语法(对一语言中可能出现的所有句子提供规则的语法). **2** (*biology* 生) concerned with reproduction 生殖的: *generative organs* 生殖器官.

gen·er·ator /ˈdʒenəreɪtə(r); ˋdʒɛnə,retɚ/ *n* **1** (*Brit*) (*US* **dynamo**) machine for producing electrical energy 发电机: *The generator has started up/broken down.* 发电机已开动[出现故障]. **2** machine or apparatus that produces steam, gas, vapour, etc (蒸汽、煤气等的)发生器. **3** person who generates or originates 生产者; 生殖者; 创始者: *a generator of new ideas* 新思想的创立者.

gen·eric /dʒɪˈnerɪk; dʒəˋnɛrɪk/ *adj* shared by or including a whole group or class; not specific 属的; 类的; 一般的: *The generic term for wine, spirits and beer is 'alcoholic beverages'.* 葡萄酒、烈性酒、啤酒的通称是酒类饮料. ▷ **gen·er·ic·ally** /dʒɪˈnerɪklɪ; dʒəˋnɛrɪklɪ/ *adv*.

gen·er·os·ity /ˌdʒenəˈrɒsətɪ; ˌdʒɛnəˋrɑsətɪ/ *n* **1** [U] quality of being generous 慷慨; 大方; 宽容. **2** [C] generous act 慷慨或宽容的行为.

gen·er·ous /ˈdʒenərəs; ˋdʒɛnərəs/ *adj* (*approv* 褒) **1** giving or ready to give freely 慷慨的; 大方的: *generous with one's money/in giving help* 用钱大方的[慷慨助人的] ○ *It was generous of you to share your food with me.* 你把食物与我分享, 真慷慨. **2** given freely; plentiful 慷慨给予的; 大量的; 丰富的: *a generous gift, offer, increase* 丰厚的礼物、慷慨的提议、大量的增加 ○ *a generous helping of potatoes* 一大份马铃薯. **3** free from meanness or prejudice; magnanimous 心地高尚的; 无偏见的; 宽宏大量的: *a generous mind, spirit, etc* 高尚的心、精神等 ○ *A wise ruler is generous in victory.* 贤明的统治者在胜利时能宽宏大量. ▷ **gen·er·ously** *adv*: *Please give generously.* 请慷慨施予. ○ *a dress cut generously*, ie using plenty of material 用料多的连衣裙.

gen·esis /ˈdʒenəsɪs; ˋdʒɛnəsɪs/ *n* (*pl* **geneses** /ˈdʒenəsi:z; ˋdʒɛnəsiz/) **1** (*fml* 文) beginning; starting-point; origin 起源; 开端; 创始: *the genesis of civilization* 文明的起源. **2 Genesis** (*Bible* 圣经) the first book of the Old Testament, describing the creation of the world 《创世记》(《旧约》首卷).

G

gen·etic /dʒɪˈnetɪk; dʒəˋnɛtɪk/ *adj* of genes; of genetics 基因的; 遗传学的: *genetic information, material, etc* 遗传信息、物质等.

▷ **gen·et·ic·ally** /-klɪ; -klɪ/ *adv*: *genetically determined, linked, etc* 由基因决定的、与遗传有关的.

gen·eti·cist /dʒɪˈnetɪsɪst; dʒəˋnɛtə,sɪst/ *n* specialist in genetics 遗传学家.

gen·et·ics /dʒɪˈnetɪks; dʒəˋnɛtɪks/ *n* [sing *v*] scientific study of the ways in which characteristics are passed from parents (or, in plants, from parent stock) to their offspring 遗传学.

□ **geˌnetic ˈcode** system of storage of genetic information in chromosomes 遗传密码.

geˌnetic ˌengiˈneering deliberate changes made to hereditary features by altering the structure or position of individual genes 遗传工程.

gen·ial /ˈdʒi:nɪəl; ˋdʒinɪəl/ *adj* **1** kindly; pleasant; sociable 和蔼的; 亲切的; 友好的: *a genial person, manner, smile* 和蔼可亲的人、举止、微笑. **2** (of climate) mild; warm; favourable to growth (指气候)温和的, 温暖的, 利于生长的: *the genial air of the Pacific Islands* 太平洋岛屿上温暖的空气.

▷ **geni·al·ity** /ˌdʒi:nɪˈælətɪ; ˌdʒinɪˋælətɪ/ *n* **1** [U] quality of being genial 和蔼; 亲切; 友好. **2** [C] genial act, look or remark 和蔼可亲的行为、表情或言语.

geni·ally /ˈdʒi:nɪəlɪ; ˋdʒinɪəlɪ/ *adv*.

genie /ˈdʒi:nɪ; ˋdʒinɪ/ *n* (*pl* **~s** or **genii** /ˈdʒi:nɪaɪ; ˋdʒinɪ,aɪ/) (in Arabian stories) spirit or goblin with strange powers (阿拉伯故事中的)神怪, 妖怪.

gen·ital /ˈdʒenɪtl; ˋdʒɛnətl/ *adj* [attrib 作定语] (*medical or fml* 医或文) of animal reproduction or reproductive organs (动物)生殖的, 生殖器的: *the genital area* 阴部 ○ *genital stimulation* 生殖器的刺激.

▷ **gen·it·als** /ˈdʒenɪtlz; ˋdʒɛnətlz/ (also **gen·it·alia** /ˌdʒenɪˈteɪlɪə; ˌdʒɛnɪˋtelɪə/) *n* [pl] (*fml* 文) external sex organs 外生殖器.

gen·it·ive /ˈdʒenətɪv; ˋdʒɛnətɪv/ *n* (*grammar*) special form of a noun, a pronoun or an adjective used (in certain inflected languages) to indicate or describe esp possession 属格, 所有格(某些屈折语中的一种格, 尤用以表示属有关系). Cf 参看 POSSESSIVE *n* 2.

▷ **gen·it·ive** *adj* of or in the genitive 属格的; 所有格的: *The genitive forms of the pronouns 'I', 'we' and 'she' are 'my/mine', 'our/ours' and 'her/hers'.* 代词I、we、she的所有格形式是my / mine、our / ours、her / hers.

genius /ˈdʒi:nɪəs; ˋdʒinjəs/ *n* (*pl* **geniuses**) **1** (**a**) [U] exceptionally great mental or creative ability 天才; 创造力: *a man of genius* 才子 ○ *It is rare to find such genius nowadays.* 这样的天才现在非常罕见. (**b**) [C] person who has this ability 天才人物: *Einstein was a mathematical genius.* 爱因斯坦是数学天才. ○ *He is hard-working and able, but no genius.* 他勤奋、能干, 但决非天才. **2** [sing] **a ~ for (doing) sth** exceptional natural ability for sth 对(做)某事物的天生的非凡才能: *have a genius for languages, making friends, saying the wrong thing* 有学语言的、交朋友的、说错话的本事. **3** [sing] **the ~ (of sth)** (**a**) guardian spirit (of a person, a place or an institution) 守护神. (**b**) (*fml* 文) special character, spirit or principles of a language, a period of time, an institution, a nation, etc (语言、时代、制度、民族等的)特点, 特征, 精神, 原则: *the genius of the English language, of the age* 英语语言的、时代的特点. **4** (idm 习语) **one's good/evil ˈgenius** person or spirit supposed to have a strong influence on one for good or for evil 对自己好坏有极大影响的人或神魔: *Blame it on my evil genius!* 都怪我中了邪魔了!

geno·cide /ˈdʒenəsaɪd; ˋdʒɛnə,saɪd/ *n* [U] deliberate extermination of a nation or race of people 种族灭绝.

genre /ˈʒɑ:nrə; ˋʒɑnrə/ *n* particular style or kind, esp of works of art or literature grouped according to their form or subject matter 种类; 类型; (尤指按形式或主题划分的文艺作品的)风格, 体裁: *The novel and short story are different genres.* 长篇小说和短篇故事是不同的类别.

□ **ˈgenre-painting** *n* [U] style of painting that shows scenes, etc from ordinary life 世态画, 风俗画(以日常生活为题材的).

G

gent /dʒent; dʒɛnt/ *n* **1** [C] (*infml or joc* 口或谑) gentleman 先生; 绅士: *This way, please, gents!* 先生, 请这边走! **2 gents** [pl] (esp in shops) men (尤用于商店中)男子: *a gents' hairdresser, outfitter, etc* 男宾理发师、出售男子服装的商店. **3 a/the Gents** [usu sing *v* 通常与单数动词连用] (*Brit infml* 口) public lavatory for men 男厕所: *Where's the Gents?* 男厕所在哪儿?

gen·teel /dʒenˈti:l; dʒɛnˋtil/ *adj* **1** (*derog* 贬) polite or refined in an affected or exaggerated way (做作或过分显示)文雅的, 有礼貌的, 有教养的: *She is too genteel for words!* 她说话太咬文嚼字了! **2** (*dated* 旧) of the upper social classes 上流社会的: *living in genteel poverty*, ie trying to maintain the style of upper-class living, though too poor to do so 过穷酸的上流社会生活. ▷ **gen·teelly** /dʒenˈti:llɪ; dʒɛnˋtillɪ/ *adv*.

gen·tian /ˈdʒenʃn; ˋdʒɛnʃən/ *n* [C, U] plant with blue flowers that grows in mountainous districts 龙胆属植物(长于山地, 开紫蓝色花).

□ ˌ**gentian ˈviolet** dye used as an antiseptic, esp in the treatment of burns 龙胆紫(用作杀菌剂, 尤用于治疗烧伤、烫伤者).

gen·tile /ˈdʒentaɪl; ˋdʒɛntaɪl/ *n, adj* (person who is) not Jewish 非犹太人(的).

gen·til·ity /dʒenˈtɪlətɪ; dʒɛnˋtɪlətɪ/ *n* [U] (*approv or ironic* 褒或反语) genteel manners and behaviour; social superiority 文雅风度; 彬彬有礼; 高贵的社会地位或身分: *He thinks fine clothes are a mark of gentility.* 他认为衣着讲究是身分高贵的标志.

gentle /ˈdʒentl; ˋdʒɛntl/ *adj* (**-r** /ˈdʒentlə(r); ˋdʒɛntlɚ/, **-st** /ˈdʒentlɪst; ˋdʒɛntlɪst/) **1** (**a**) mild; kind; careful; not rough, violent or severe 温和的; 慈祥的; 小心的; 温柔的; 文雅的; 轻轻的: *a gentle person, manner, voice, look* 温和的人、举止、声音、样子 ○ *a doctor who is gentle with his hands* 手法轻巧的医师 ○ (*sexist* 性别偏见) *the gentle* (ie female) *sex* 女性 ○ *be gentle with animals, children, etc* 对动物、儿童等温和 ○ *Be gentle with my best china!* 对我最心爱的瓷器要轻拿轻放! (**b**) (of weather, temperature, etc) mild; temperate (指天气、温度等)温和的, 暖和的: *a gentle breeze* 和风 ○ *gentle rainfall* 细雨 ○ *a gentle heat* 温暖. **2** not steep or abrupt 不陡峭的; 和缓的: *a gentle slope* 缓坡. **3** (*dated* 旧) (of a family) with good social position (指家庭)门第高的, 上层阶级的: *of gentle birth* 出身名门的.

▷ **gen·tle·ness** /ˈdʒentlnɪs; ˋdʒɛntl̩nɪs/ *n* [U].

gently /ˈdʒentlɪ; ˋdʒɛntlɪ/ *adv* **1** in a gentle(1a) manner 温和地; 慈祥地; 温柔地; 文雅地; 轻轻地: *handle sth gently* 轻拿轻放某物 ○ *speak to sb gently* 对某人轻声细语地谈话 ○ *The beach slopes gently to the sea.* 沙滩缓缓伸展入海. **2** (idm 习语) **easy/gently does it** ⇨ EASY[2].

□ **ˈgentlefolk** *n* [pl *v*] (*dated* 旧) people belonging to respected upper-class families 出身名门的人; 上流人士.

gen·tle·man /ˈdʒentlmən; ˋdʒɛntl̩mən/ *n* (*pl* **-men** /-mən; -mən/) **1** [C] (*approv or ironic* 褒或反语) man who is polite and shows consideration for the feelings of other people; man who always acts in an honourable way 绅士; 先生; 君子: *Thank you. You're a real gentleman.* 谢谢. 您真是君子. ○ *He's no gentleman!* 他可不是正人君子! Cf 参看 LADY. **2** (**a**) **gentlemen** [pl] (*fml* 文) (as a polite form of address to men 用作对男性的尊称): *Gentlemen of the jury!* 陪审团诸位先生! ○ *Ladies and gentlemen!* eg when beginning a speech. 女士们、先生们! (**b**) [C] (as a polite way of referring to a man 用作对男子的尊称): *There's a gentleman at the door.* 门外有位先生. ⇨Usage at LADY 用法见LADY. **3** [C] (*dated* 旧) man of wealth and social position, esp one who does not work for a living 富绅; (尤指无需谋生的)富贵闲人: *a country gentleman* 乡间富绅 ○ [attrib 作定语] *a gentleman farmer*, ie one who owns a farm, but does no manual work himself 乡绅(有农场而不参加体力劳动者).

▷ **gen·tle·manly** *adj* (*approv* 褒) of or like a gentleman(1) 绅士风度的; 似绅士的: *of gentlemanly appearance* 绅士风貌的 ○ *gentlemanly behaviour* 绅士般的举止.

□ **a** ˌ**gentleman's aˈgreement** agreement that cannot be enforced by law but depends on the mutual trust and good faith of those involved 君子协定; 绅士协定.

ˌ**gentleman-at-ˈarms** *n* (*Brit*) one of the sovereign's bodyguard (君主或国王的)侍卫.

gen·tle·wo·man /ˈdʒentlwʊmən; ˋdʒɛntl̩,wʊmən/ *n* (*pl* **-women** /-wɪmɪn; -,wɪmɪn/) (*arch* 古) lady 女士.

gentry /ˈdʒentrɪ; ˋdʒɛntrɪ/ *n* [pl *v*] (usu 通常作 **the gentry**) people of good social position next below the nobility 绅士; 上等人.

▷ **gent·rify** /ˈdʒentrɪfaɪ; ˋdʒɛntrɪ,faɪ/ *v* (*pt, pp* **-fied**) [Tn] (*infml* 口) restore and smarten (a house, an area, etc) to make it suitable for middle-class residents 将(房子、地方等)翻修和装饰(以适合中产阶级的人居住).

genu·flect /ˈdʒenju:flekt; ˋdʒɛnjʊ,flɛkt/ *v* [I] (*fml* 文) bend the knee, esp in worship 屈膝, 下跪(尤指礼拜).

▷ **genu·flex·ion** /ˌdʒenju:ˈflekʃn; ˌdʒɛnjʊˋflɛkʃən/ *n* [C, U].

genu·ine /ˈdʒenjʊɪn; ˋdʒɛnjʊɪn/ *adj* **1** real; truly what it is said to be; not fake or artificial 真的; 名副其实的; 非伪造的; 非人工的: *a genuine Rubens*, ie a painting definitely by Rubens himself, not by an imitator 鲁宾斯的亲笔画 ○ *a genuine pearl* 一颗天然珍珠. **2** (*fig* 比喻) sincere; honest 真诚的; 诚实的: *She seems genuine but can I trust her?* 她似乎很诚实, 但我可以信赖她吗? ▷ **genu·inely** *adv*: *genuinely sorry* 真抱歉. **genu·ine·ness** *n* [U].

genus /ˈdʒi:nəs; ˋdʒinəs/ *n* (*pl* **genera** /ˈdʒenərə; ˋdʒɛnərə/) **1** (*biology* 生) group of animals or plants within a family(4), often itself subdivided into several species(1) (动植物的)属. Cf 参看 PHYLUM, CLASS 7, ORDER[1] 9. **2** (*infml* 口) kind; type 类; 种; 型.

geo- *comb form* 构词成分 of the earth 地球的; 土地的: *geoˈcentric* ○ *geˈography* ○ *geˈology*.

geo·cent·ric /ˌdʒi:əʊˈsentrɪk; ˌdʒioˋsɛntrɪk/ *adj* **1** having the earth as its centre 以地球为中心的: *a geocentric view of the universe* 以地球为中心的宇宙观. **2** measured from the centre of the earth 自地心测量的.

geo·graphy /dʒɪˈɒgrəfɪ; dʒiˋɑgrəfɪ/ *n* **1** [U] scientific study of the earth's surface, physical features, divisions, climate, products, population, etc 地理学: *physical/political/social geography* 自然[政治/社会]地理学 ○ [attrib 作定语] *a geography book, student, lecture* 研究地理的书、学生、讲座. **2** [sing] **the ~ (of sth)** (*infml*

口) arrangement of the features of a place (某处的)地形, 地势: *getting to know the geography of a neighbourhood, house, kitchen, etc*, ie where things are in relation to each other 了解邻居的环境、房屋的布局、厨房的安排等.

▷ **geo·grapher** /dʒɪˈɒɡrəfə(r); dʒiˋɑɡrəfɚ/ *n* student of or expert in geography 地理学研究者或专家.

geo·graph·ical /ˌdʒɪəˈɡræfɪkl; ˌdʒiəˋɡræfɪkḷ/ *adj* of or relating to geography 地理(学)的; 关于地理(学)的: *geographical features, research* 地理特征、研究. **geo·graph·ic·ally** /-klɪ; -klɪ/ *adv*.

geo·logy /dʒɪˈɒlədʒɪ; dʒiˋɑlədʒɪ/ *n* [U] scientific study of the earth's crust, rocks, strata, etc and of the history of its development 地质学: [attrib 作定语] *a geology course, department, field-trip* 地质课程、系、考察旅行.

▷ **geo·lo·gical** /dʒɪəˈlɒdʒɪkl; ˌdʒiəˋlɑdʒɪkl/ *adj* of or relating to geology 地质(学)的; 有关地质(学)的: *a geological age, formation* 地质年代、结构. **geo·lo·gic·ally** /-klɪ; -klɪ/ *adv*.

geo·lo·gist /dʒɪˈɒlədʒɪst; dʒiˋɑlədʒɪst/ *n* student of or expert in geology 地质学研究者或专家.

geo·metry /dʒɪˈɒmətrɪ; dʒiˋɑmətrɪ/ *n* [U] branch of mathematics dealing with the properties and relations of lines, angles, surfaces and solids 几何(学): [attrib 作定语] *a geometry set*, ie a collection of the instruments needed for drawing geometric figures 一套几何学绘图仪.

▷ **geo·met·ric** /dʒɪəˈmetrɪk; ˌdʒiəˋmɛtrɪk/ (also **geo·met·rical** /-ɪkl; -ɪkḷ/) *adj* of geometry; of or like the lines, figures, etc used in geometry 几何(学)的; (似)几何线条、图形等的: *a geometric design* 几何图形设计. **geo·met·ric·ally** /-klɪ; -klɪ/ *adv*. **geometric progression** ordered set of numbers in which each is multiplied or divided by a fixed number to produce the next, as 1, 3, 9, 27, 81 几何级数; 等比级数. Cf 参看 ARITHMETIC PROGRESSION (ARITHMETIC).

geo·phys·ics /ˌdʒɪəʊˈfɪzɪks; ˌdʒioˋfɪzɪks/ *n* [sing *v*] scientific study of the physics of the earth, eg its magnetism, meteorology 地球物理学. ▷ **geo·phys·ical** /ˌdʒɪəʊˈfɪzɪkl; ˌdʒioˋfɪzɪkḷ/ *adj*. **geo·physi·cist** /ˌdʒɪəʊˈfɪzəsɪst; ˌdʒioˋfɪzɪsɪst/ *n*.

geo·pol·it·ics /ˌdʒɪəʊˈpɒlətɪks; ˌdʒioˋpɑlətɪks/ *n* [sing *v*] study of how politics is affected by geographical factors 地理政治学; 地缘政治学.

▷ **geo·pol·it·ical** /ˌdʒɪəʊpəˈlɪtɪkl; ˌdʒiopəˋlɪtɪkḷ/ *adj* of geopolitics 地理政治(学)的; 地缘政治(学)的.

George /dʒɔːdʒ; dʒɔrdʒ/ *n* (idm 习语) **by George!** (*dated* 旧 *Brit*) (used as an exclamation of surprise or approval 用作表示惊奇或赞成的感叹语).

□ ˌ**George** ˈ**Cross**, ˌ**George** ˈ**Medal** (*Brit*) decorations for bravery awarded esp to civilians 乔治勋章(表彰平民勇敢行为者).

geor·gette /dʒɔːˈdʒet; dʒɔrˋdʒɛt/ *n* [U] thin silky dress-material 乔其纱.

Geor·gian /ˈdʒɔːdʒən; ˋdʒɔrdʒən/ *adj* (*Brit*) of the time of the British kings George I - IV (1714-1830) 乔治一世至四世时代(1714-1830)的: *a Georgian house* 乔治王朝时代的房子 ○ *Georgian furniture* 乔治王朝时代的家具.

ge·ra·nium /dʒəˈreɪnɪəm; dʒəˋrenɪəm/ *n* garden plant with red, pink or white flowers 老鹳草, 天竺葵(园艺植物, 开红色、粉红色或白色花).

ge·ri·at·rics /ˌdʒerɪˈætrɪks; ˌdʒɛrɪˋætrɪks/ *n* [sing *v*] branch of medicine dealing with the diseases and care of old people 老年医学; 老年病学; 老年保健学.

▷ **ge·ri·at·ric** /ˌdʒerɪˈætrɪk; ˌdʒɛrɪˋætrɪk/ *adj* of or relating to geriatrics 老年医学的; 老年病学的; 老年保健学的: *the geriatric ward of a hospital* 医院中的老年人病房.

ge·ri·at·ri·cian /ˌdʒerɪəˈtrɪʃn; ˌdʒɛrɪəˋtrɪʃən/ *n* doctor specializing in geriatrics 老年医学专家; 老年病学专家; 老年保健学专家.

germ /dʒɜːm; dʒɝm/ *n* **1** [C] portion of a living organism capable of becoming a new organism; embryo of a seed 胚芽; 芽孢; 胚. **2** [C] micro-organism, esp one capable of causing disease 微生物; 细菌; (尤指)病菌: *Disinfectant kills germs.* 消毒剂可杀菌. ○ [attrib 作定语] *germ warfare*, ie the use of harmful bacteria as a weapon of war 细菌战. **3** [sing] **the ~ of sth** (*fig* 比喻) beginning from which sth may develop (某物的)发端, 起源, 萌芽: *the germ of an idea* 一种想法的发端.

□ ˌ**germ** ˈ**warfare** = BIOLOGICAL WARFARE (BIOLOGICAL).

Ger·man /ˈdʒɜːmən; ˋdʒɝmən/ *adj* of Germany, its culture, its language or its people 德国的; 德国文化的; 德语的; 德国人的: *German industry, traditions, grammar* 德国工业、德意志传统、德语语法.

▷ **Ger·man** *n* **1** [C] German person 德国人; 德意志人. **2** [U] language spoken in Germany, Austria and part of Switzerland 德语(德国、奥地利和瑞士部分地区通行的语言).

Ger·manic /dʒəˈmænɪk; dʒɚˋmænɪk/ *adj* having German characteristics 有德国(人)特点的; 德语的; 日耳曼(人、民族、语族)的: *Germanic features, attitudes* 德国人特征、态度 ○ *the Germanic languages*, ie the group including German, Dutch, English, etc 日耳曼诸语言(包括德语、荷兰语、英语等).

□ ˌ**German** ˈ**measles** (also **ru·bella**) (*infml* 口) mild contagious disease causing red spots all over the body 风疹.

ˌ**German** ˈ**shepherd** (*US*) = ALSATIAN.

ger·mane /dʒəˈmeɪn; dʒɚˋmen/ *adj* [pred 作表语] **~ (to sth)** (*fml* 文) relevant 有关: *remarks that are germane to the discussion* 与讨论有关的言语.

ger·mi·cide /ˈdʒɜːmɪsaɪd; ˋdʒɝməˌsaɪd/ *n* [C, U] substance used for killing germs 杀菌剂. ▷ **ger·mi·cidal** /ˌdʒɜːmɪˈsaɪdl; ˌdʒɝməˋsaɪdḷ/ *adj*.

ger·minal /ˈdʒɜːmɪnl; ˋdʒɝmənḷ/ *adj* in the earliest stage of development 处于萌芽状态的; 初级阶段的: *in a germinal form* 处于初级形式.

ger·min·ate /ˈdʒɜːmɪneɪt; ˋdʒɝməˌnet/ *v* [I, Tn] (cause sth to) start growing (使某物)发芽, 萌芽: *The cabbages germinated within a week.* 白菜一星期内就发芽了. ○ *to germinate cabbages, beans, etc* 使白菜、豆子等发芽.

▷ **ger·mina·tion** /ˌdʒɜːmɪˈneɪʃn; ˌdʒɝməˋneʃən/ *n* [U] germinating; sprouting 发芽; 萌芽.

ge·ron·to·logy /ˌdʒerɒnˈtɒlədʒɪ; ˌdʒɛrənˋtɑlədʒɪ/ *n* [U] scientific study of old age and the process of growing old 老年学(对年老和衰老的研究).

ger·ry·man·der /ˈdʒerɪmændə(r); ˋdʒɛrɪˌmændɚ/ *v* [Tn] (*derog politics* 贬, 政) arrange the boundaries of or divide (an area) for voting in order to give unfair advantages to one party in an election (为使某政党在选举中取得优势)不公正地将(某地区)划成或分成选区.

▷ **ger·ry·man·der** *n* [C] such a rearrangement 对选区做出的不公正重新划分.

ger·ry·man·der·ing *n* [U] making such a rearrangement 对选区作不公正的重新划分: *There has been some gerrymandering.* 对选区已作出某些不公正的重新划分.

ger·und /ˈdʒerənd; ˋdʒɛrənd/ *n* = VERBAL NOUN (VERBAL).

Ge·stapo /geˈstɑːpəʊ; gəˋstɑpo/ *n* **the Gestapo** [Gp] German secret police of the Nazi regime 盖世太保(德国纳粹时期的秘密警察).

gesta·tion /dʒeˈsteɪʃn; dʒɛsˋteʃən/ *n* **1 (a)** [U] carrying or being carried in the womb between conception and birth 怀孕; 妊娠: [attrib 作定语] *Elephants have a gestation period of about 624 days.* 象的怀孕期大约为624日. **(b)** [sing] period of time taken by this 怀孕期; 妊娠期. **2** [U] (*fig* 比喻) development of an idea, a work of art, etc (思想、艺术作品等的)酝酿, 孕育.

ges·ticu·late /dʒeˈstɪkjʊleɪt; dʒɛsˋtɪkjəˌlet/ *v* [I] move the hands or arms (usu rapidly) instead of speaking or to emphasize one's words 做手势(通常为迅速地)示意或强调: *He was gesticulating wildly at me, but I could not understand what he was trying to tell me.* 他使劲向我做手势, 可是我不明白他的意思.

▷ **ges·ticu·la·tion** /dʒeˌstɪkjʊˈleɪʃn; ˌdʒɛstɪkjəˋleʃən/ *n* **1** [U] gesticulating 做手势; 做示意动作. **2** [C] movement used in this 手势; 示意动作: *wild gesticulations* 明显的手势.

ges·ture /ˈdʒestʃə(r); ˋdʒɛstʃɚ/ *n* **1** [C, U] expressive movement of a part of the body, esp the hand or head 姿势; 手势: *make a rude gesture* 做出粗野的姿势 ○ *with a gesture of despair* 用表示绝望的姿势 ○ *communicating by gesture* 用手势表达. **2** [C] (*fig* 比喻) action showing one's (usu friendly) intentions or attitude 示意的或

表明态度的(通常为友好的)动作或姿势: *a gesture of sympathy* 同情的态度 ○ *The invitation was meant as a friendly gesture.* 那邀请是友好的表示.

▷ **ges·ture** *v* **1** [I] make expressive movements 做表意的动作: *to gesture with one's hands* 做手势. **2** [Tn, Tn·pr, Tf, Dpr·f, Dpr·t] **~ sth (to sb)** convey sth by making gestures 以姿势表示某意: *She gestured her disapproval.* 她用姿势表示不赞成. ○ *He gestured (to me) that it was time to go.* 他向我示意该走了. ○ *He gestured to them to keep quiet*, ie told them to do so by making gestures. 他示意要他们保持安静.

get /get; gɛt/ *v* (**-tt-**, *pt* **got** /gɒt; gɑt/, *pp* **got**; *US* **gotten** /ˈgɒtn; ˈgɑtn̩/)

▸ RECEIVING OR OBTAINING 接到或得到 **1** [Tn no passive 不用于被动语态] receive (sth) 收到, 接到(某物): *I got a letter from my sister this morning.* 今晨我接到妹妹的信. ○ *Did you get my postcard?* 你收到我的明信片了吗? ○ *What did you get for Christmas?* 你收到什么圣诞节礼物了吗? ○ *He gets* (ie earns) *£25 000 a year.* 他每年收入25 000英镑. ○ *This room gets very little sunshine.* 这房间没什么阳光. ○ *Schoolteachers get long holidays.* 中小学教师有长假. ○ *He got* (ie was hit by) *a bullet in the thigh.* 他大腿中弹. ○ *She got a shock when she saw the telephone bill.* 她看到电话帐单大吃一惊. ○ *I got the impression that he was bored with his job.* 我得到的印象是他对工作感到厌倦. **2** [no passive 不用于被动语态: Tn, Dn·n, Dn·pr] (**a**) **~ sth (for oneself/sb)** obtain sth 得到某事物: *Where did you get* (ie buy) *that skirt?* 你那条裙子是从哪儿买的? ○ *Did you manage to get tickets for the concert?* 你弄到音乐会的票了吗? ○ *She opened the door wider to get a better look.* 她为了看得更清楚, 把门开大了一些. ○ *Try to get some sleep.* 去睡一会儿吧. ○ *He doesn't look as though he gets enough exercise.* 他似乎缺乏锻炼. ○ *Johnson got* (ie won) *the gold medal in the 100 metres.* 约翰逊获得百米金牌. ○ *She's just got* (ie been appointed to) *a job with a publishing company.* 她刚得到在出版公司的工作. ○ *Why don't you get (yourself) a flat of your own?* 你为什么不弄套房子? ○ *Have you remembered to get your mother a birthday present/to get a birthday present for your mother?* 记得给你母亲买生日礼物了吗? (**b**) **~ sb/sth (for oneself/sb)** fetch sb/sth 接(某人); 取(某物): *Go and get a dictionary and we'll look the word up.* 去拿词典来, 我们查查这个字. ○ *Somebody get a doctor! I think this woman's had a heart attack.* 谁去把医生找来! 我看这女人心脏病发作了. ○ *I have to go and get my mother* (ie collect her in a car) *from the station.* 我要到车站接母亲. ○ *Could you get me that book (down) from the top shelf?* 请你把最高一格的那本书给我取(下)好吗? ○ *Can I get you a drink/get a drink for you?* 我给您弄点什么喝好吗? **3** [no passive 不用于被动语态: Tn, Tn·pr] **~ sth (for sth)** obtain or receive (an amount of money) by selling sth (卖某物)得到或收到(钱): *'How much did you get for your old car?' 'I got £800 (for it).'* '你的旧汽车卖了多少钱?' '卖了800英镑.' **4** [Tn no passive 不用于被动语态] receive (sth) as a punishment 受到(某种)惩罚: *He got ten years* (ie was sentenced to ten years in prison) *for armed robbery.* 他因械劫罪被判十年徒刑. **5** [Tn no passive 不用于被动语态] (**a**) be able to receive broadcasts from (a particular television or radio station) 收听或收看到(某电视台或电台的)节目: *We can't get Channel 4 on our television.* 我们的电视机收看不到第4频道的节目. (**b**) be connected with (sb) by telephone (与某人)接通电话: *I wanted to speak to the manager but I got his secretary instead.* 我想找经理说话, 可是接电话的是他的秘书. **6** [Tn no passive 不用于被动语态] regularly buy (a newspaper) 定期买(报纸): *Do you get 'The Times' or the 'Guardian'?* 你经常买《泰晤士报》还是《卫报》? **7** [Tn no passive 不用于被动语态] become infected with (an illness); suffer from or be affected by (a pain, etc) 感染(某病); 患(病); 受(疼痛等)侵袭: *get bronchitis, flu, measles, etc* 患支气管炎、流感、麻疹等 ○ *She gets* (ie regularly suffers from) *bad headaches.* 她经常头痛. **8** [Tn no passive 不用于被动语态] achieve or be awarded (the specified examination grade, class of degree, etc) (考试)达到(某等级); 获授予(某学位): *She got a first in English at Oxford.* 她在牛津大学学习英文, 获优等学位.

G

▸ REACHING OR BRINGING TO A PARTICULAR STATE OR CONDITION 达到或使处于某状态或情况 **9** (**a**) [La] reach the specified state or condition; become 达到某状态或情况; 变得: *get angry, bored, hungry, worried, etc* 发怒、生厌、饥饿、不安 ○ *get fat, fit, thinner, etc* 发胖、健康、变瘦 ○ *It/The weather is getting colder.* 天气渐冷. ○ *She's getting better*, eg after her illness. 她渐渐好了(如病后). ○ *You'll get wet if you go out in the rain without an umbrella.* 雨天外出不带伞会淋湿的. ○ *You'll soon get used to the climate here.* 你很快就会习惯这里的气候. ○ *We ought to go; it's getting late.* 我们该走了, 天越来越晚了. ⇨Usage at BECOME 用法见BECOME. (**b**) [La, Cn·a] cause oneself to be in the specified state or condition 使自己处于某状态或情况: *get dressed/undressed*, ie put one's clothes on/take one's clothes off 穿上[脱下]衣服 ○ *They plan to get married in the summer.* 他们打算夏天结婚. ○ *She's upstairs getting (herself) ready (to go out).* 她在楼上(更衣)准备(外出). (**c**) (used in place of *be* with a past participle to form passive constructions 代替be, 与过去分词连用构成被动结构): *Do you think the Tories will get* (ie be) *re-elected?* 你认为保守党能再次当选吗? ○ *I wouldn't go there after dark; you might get* (ie be) *mugged.* 天黑之后我就不到那里去了, 怕有人抢劫. **10** [Cn·a] cause (sb/sth) to be or become 使(某人[某事物]为)成: *She soon got the children ready for school.* 她很快帮孩子做好上学的准备. ○ *I must get the dinner ready*, ie prepare it. 我得把饭做好. ○ *Don't get your new trousers dirty!* 别把你的新裤子弄脏! ○ *Don't let the incident get you upset.* 别为这事烦恼. ○ *Do you think you'll get the work finished on time?* 你认为你的工作可以如期完成吗? ○ *He got his wrist broken*, ie broke it accidentally. 他扭伤了手腕. ○ *I couldn't get the car started this morning.* 今晨我无法把汽车发动起来. ○ *Go and get your hair cut!* 你去理理发去! ○ *She got her fingers caught in the door.* 她的手指让门给夹了.

▸ MAKING SOMETHING HAPPEN 使某事发生 **11** [Cn·g] bring (sb/sth) to the point at which he/it is doing sth 使(某人[某事物])做某事: *Can you really get that old car going again?* 你真能让那辆旧汽车再跑起来? ○ *It's not hard to get him talking; the problem is stopping him!* 让他说话不难, 难的是说开了止不住他! **12** [Cn·t] cause, persuade, etc (sb/sth) to do sth 使, 说服...(某人[某事物])做某事: *I couldn't get the car to start* (ie make it start) *this morning.* 今早我无法把汽车发动起来. ○ *He got* (ie persuaded) *his sister to help him with his homework.* 他说服他姐姐帮他做家庭作业. ○ *You'll never get him to understand.* 谁也无法让他明白. ○ *I can't get her to talk at all.* 我简直无法叫她说话.

▸ REACHING THE POINT WHERE ONE DOES SOMETHING 做起某事来 **13** (**a**) [Tg] reach the stage at which one is doing sth; start doing sth 做起某事来; 开始做某事: *I got talking to her/We got talking.* 我和她谈起话来了[我们谈起话来了]. ○ *We got chatting and discovered we'd been at college together.* 我们聊起天来才发现我们原是校友. ○ *get working on a problem* 开始研究某问题 ○ *You have an hour to clean the whole house — so get scrubbing!* 你只有一个小时来打扫整座房子——快开始擦洗吧! (**b**) [It] reach the point at which one feels, knows, is, etc sth 开始感觉到、认识、成为...某事物: *You'll like her once you get to know her.* 你一旦了解她, 就喜欢她了. ○ *How did you get to know* (ie discover or learn) *that I was here?* 你怎么知道我在这里? ○ *One soon gets to like it here.* 谁都会很快就喜欢这里的. ○ *She's getting to be an old lady now.* 她现在可算是位老妇人了. ○ *After a time you get to realize that these things don't matter.* 你过些时候就知道这些事无关紧要. ○ *His drinking is getting to be a problem.* 他酗酒越来越成问题了. ○ *Your mother will be furious if she gets to hear of this.* 你母亲若知此事定会怒不可遏. **14** [It] (*esp US*) have the chance or opportunity to do sth; manage to do sth 有做某事的时机; 设法做某事: *Did you get to see the Louvre while you were in Paris?* 你在巴黎时有机会参观罗浮宫吗? ○ *One day we'll both get to see New York.* 总有一天我俩都有机会看看纽约. ○ *When do I get to go to a movie?* 我什么时候才可以去看场电影?

▸ MOVING OR CAUSING TO MOVE 移动或使移动 **15** (**a**) [Ipr, Ip] move to or from a specified point or in a specified direction, sometimes with difficulty 到或离开某处或沿某方向移动(有时有困难): *The bridge was destroyed so we couldn't get across* (ie cross) *the river.* 桥已毁坏, 我们无法过河. ○ *She got back into bed.* 她回到床上. ○ *She got down from the ladder.* 她从梯子上下来. ○ *He got into the car.* 他钻进汽车里. ○ *Can you get over the wall?* 你能爬过那堵墙吗? ○ *We didn't get* (ie go) *to bed till 3 am.* 我们凌晨3时才上床睡觉. ○ *I'm getting off* (ie leaving the train) *at the next station.* 我下站下(火车). ○ *Where have they got to?* ie Where are they? 他们到什么地方去了? ○ *Please let me get by*, ie pass. 请让我过去. ○ *We must be getting home; it's past midnight.* 我们得回家了, 已经半夜了. (**b**) [Tn·pr, Tn·p] cause (sb/sth) to move to or from a specified point or in a specified direction, sometimes with difficulty 使(某人[某事物])到或离开(某处)或沿某方向移动(有时有困难): *The general had to get his troops across the river.* 将军要使其部队过河. ○ *We couldn't get the piano through the door.* 我们无法将钢琴搬过这道门. ○ *He's drunk again; we'd better call a taxi and get him home.* 他又醉了, 最好叫辆计程车把他送回家去. ○ *I can't get the lid on/off.* 我盖不上[取不下]盖子. (**c**) [Ipr, Ip] **~ to/into...; ~ in** arrive at or reach a place or point 来到或到达某地或某点: *We got to London at 7 o'clock.* 我们7点到达伦敦. ○ *The train gets into Glasgow at 6 o'clock in the morning.* 火车早晨6点到达格拉斯哥. ○ *You got in/home very late last night.* 昨夜你回来[回家]很晚. ○ *What time did you get here?* 你什么时候到这里的? ○ *I haven't got very far with the book I'm reading.* 那本书我还没读多少呢. **16** [Tn no passive 不用于被动语态] travel by (bus, taxi, plane, etc); take (a bus, etc) 乘(公共汽车、计程车、飞机等): *We're going to be late; let's get a taxi.* 我们要迟到了, 坐计程车吧. ○ *'How do you come to work?' 'I usually get the bus.'* '你怎么来上班的?' '一般坐公共汽车.'

▸ OTHER MEANINGS 其他意义 **17** [Tn, Dn·n, Dn·pr] **~ sth (for oneself/sb)** prepare (a meal) 准备(饭菜): *Don't disturb your mother while she's getting (the) dinner.* 你母亲做饭时不要打搅她. ○ *I have to go home and get the children their supper/get supper for the children.* 我得回去给孩子做晚饭. **18** [Tn, Tn·pr] (**a**) catch or seize (sb/sth) 抓住或捕获(某人[某物]): *He was on the run for a week before the police got him.* 他逃跑一周后警方才逮住他. ○ *get sb by the arm, scruff of the neck, throat, wrist, etc* 抓住某人的胳膊、脖子的后部、喉咙、手腕等. (**b**) catch and harm, injure or kill (sb), often in revenge for sth 捉住并伤害或杀死(某人)(常指报复): *She fell overboard and the sharks got her.* 她从船上跌落水中, 被鲨鱼咬了. ○ *He thinks the Mafia are out to get him.* 他意识到黑手党要来报复他. ○ *I'll get you for that, you bastard!* 我早晚要跟你算那笔帐, 你这坏蛋! (**c**) hit or wound (sb) 击中或伤(某人): *Where did the stone get you?* 那石头砸到你哪儿了? ○ *The bullet got him in the neck.* 子弹击中他的颈部. ○ *I got him on the back of the head with a crowbar.* 我一撬棍打在他头的后部. **19** [Tn no passive 不用于被动语态] (*infml* 口) (**a**) understand (sb/sth) 理解(某人[某事物]): *I don't get you/your meaning.* 我不明白你的意思. ○ *She didn't get the joke.* 她没理解那个笑话. ○ *I don't get it; why would she do a thing like that?* 我不明白她为什么要做那种事. (**b**) hear (sth) 听见(某事物): *I didn't quite get what you said.* 我没听清楚你说的话. **20** [Tn no passive 不用于被动语态] (*infml* 口) confuse or puzzle sb 使某人迷惑或困惑; 难住某人: *'What's the capital of Luxembourg?' 'I don't know; you've got me there!'* '卢森堡的首都叫什么?' '我不知道, 这你可难住我了!' **21** [Tn no passive 不用于被动语态] annoy or irritate (sb) 使(某人)烦恼或恼怒: *It really gets me when she starts bossing people around.* 她颐指气使地对人, 真叫我厌恶.

22 (idm 习语) **be getting 'on** (**a**) (of a person) be/becoming old (指人)老, 变老: *Grandma's getting on a bit and doesn't go out as much as she used to.* 奶奶年事日高, 不像从前那样常出门了. (**b**) (of time) be/becoming late (指时间)晚, 渐迟: *The time's getting on; we ought to be going.* 时间渐晚, 我们该走了. **be getting on for...** be near to or approaching (the specified time, age or number) 接近(某时刻、年龄或数目): *It must be getting on for midnight.* 八成已经半夜了. ○ *He must be getting on for eighty!* 他一定快八十了! **sb can't/couldn't get over sth** (*infml* 口) sb is/was shocked, surprised, amused, etc by sth 某人因某事物而震惊、惊异、觉得有趣等: *I can't get over that shirt he was wearing.* 我觉得他穿的那件衬衣真可笑. ○ *I can't get over how rude she was.* 她很粗野, 我仍心有余悸. **get a'long/a'way/'on (with you)** (*infml* 口) (used to express disbelief or to rebuke sb gently 用以表示不相信或温和的反驳): *'How old are you?' 'I'm forty.' 'Get along with you! You don't look a day over thirty-five!'* '你多少岁了?' '四十岁了.' '别瞎说了, 你看上去顶多三十五岁!' **get a'way from it all** (*infml* 口) have a short holiday in a place that is totally different from where one usu lives 到异地度短假. **get (sb) anywhere/somewhere/nowhere** (*infml* 口) (cause sb to) achieve something/nothing or to make progress/no progress (使某人)有所成就[毫无成就]或[有进展/无进展]: *After six months' work on the project, at last I feel I'm getting somewhere.* 那计划我搞了半年, 终于觉得有所进展. ○ *Are you getting anywhere with your investigations?* 你的调查有进展吗? **'get there** achieve one's aim or complete a task by patience and hard work (耐心而努力地)达到目的或完成任务: *I'm sure you'll get there in the end.* 我相信你最终能成功. ○ *Writing a dictionary is a long and difficult business but we're getting there.* 编写词典是费时费事的工作, 但我们一定能成功. **how selfish, stupid, ungrateful, etc can you 'get?** (*infml* 口) (used to express surprise, disbelief or disapproval that sb has been so selfish, etc 用以表示对某人自私等的惊讶、不相信或不赞成): *He wouldn't even lend me ten pence; how mean can you get?* 他连十便士都不肯借给我, 你看他有多小气? **there's no getting away from sth; one can't get away from sth** one has to admit the truth of (sth unpleasant) 只好承认或接受(不愉快的事实): *There's no getting away from the fact that the country's economy is suffering.* 国家经济疲软, 这一事实无法回避. (For other idioms containing **get**, see entries for *ns, adjs,* etc 与 **get** 搭配的其他习语见有关名词、形容词等的词条, 如 **get sb's goat** ⇨ GOAT; **get square with sb** ⇨ SQUARE[1].)

23 (phr v) **get a'bout** (also **get a'round**) (be able to) move from place to place (能)各处走动: *He's getting about again after his accident.* 他在事故过后, 渐渐又能走动了. ○ *She doesn't get around much these days.* 近来她不大各处走动. **get a'bout/a'round/'round** (of news, a rumour, etc) spread from person to person; circulate (指消息、谣言等)传播, 流传: *The news of her resignation soon got about.* 她辞职的消息不久就传开了.

get a'bove oneself have too high an opinion of oneself 自视甚高; 自高自大: *She's been getting a bit above herself since winning her award.* 她获奖以来, 渐渐有点骄傲了.

get (sth) a'cross (to sb) (cause sth to) be communicated or understood (使某事)传播或为人理解: *Your meaning didn't really get across.* 你的意思别人并未真正理解. ○ *He's not very good at getting his ideas across.* 他不善于表达思想.

get a'head (of sb) progress (beyond sb) 领先(于某人): *She's keen to get ahead in her career.* 她热望在事业上出人头地. ○ *By doing extra homework, he soon got ahead of his class-mates.* 他靠多做家庭作业, 很快在班上名列前茅.

get a'long (**a**) (usu in the continuous tenses 通常用于进行时态) leave a place 离开某地: *It's time we were getting along.* 是我们该走的时候了. (**b**) = GET ON (a). (**c**) = GET ON (b). **get along with sb; get a'long (together)** have a harmonious or friendly relationship with sb; get on with sb 与某人合得来; 与某人和睦相处: *Do you get along with your boss?/Do you and your boss get along?* 你跟老板合得来吗? ○ *We get along just fine.* 我们关系很好. **get along with sth** = GET ON WITH STH.

get around (**a**) = GET ABOUT. (**b**) ⇨ GET ABOUT/AROUND/ROUND. **get around sb** = GET ROUND SB. **get around sth** = GET ROUND STH. **get around to sth/doing sth** = GET ROUND TO STH/DOING STH.

'get at sb (*infml* 口) (**a**) (usu in the continuous tenses 通常用于进行时态) criticize sb repeatedly; nag sb 不断指责某人; 数落某人: *He's always getting at his wife.* 他老

是责怪妻子. ○ *She feels she's being got at.* 她觉得自己一再受人数落. (**b**) influence sb, esp unfairly or illegally 对某人施加影响(尤指不公地或不合法地): *One of the witnesses had been got at*, eg bribed. 有一证人已被收买. **get at sb/sth** gain access to sb/sth; reach sb/sth 接近某人[某事物]; 到达某人[某物]处: *The files are locked up and I can't get at them.* 卷宗锁起来了, 我无法取出. **get at sth** (**a**) learn, discover or find out sth 知悉、发现或查明(某事物): *The truth is sometimes difficult to get at.* 有时真相不易搞清. (**b**) (*infml* 口) (no passive; used only in the continuous tenses and usu in questions 不用于被动语态, 仅用于进行时态, 通常用于疑问句) suggest sth indirectly; imply sth 意指; 暗指: *What exactly are you getting at?* 你究竟指的是什么意思?

get aˈway have a holiday 去度假: *We're hoping to get away for a few days at Easter.* 我们盼着复活节休息几天. **get away (from...)** succeed in leaving a place 得以离开某地: *I won't be able to get away (from the office) before 7.* 我7时以前离不开(办公室). **get away (from sb/...)** escape from sb or a place 逃离或摆脱开(某人或某地): *Two of the prisoners got away (from their captors).* 有两个犯人逃走了. **get away with sth** (**a**) steal sth and escape with it 偷携某物潜逃: *Thieves raided the bank and got away with a lot of money.* 盗贼抢劫银行, 掠走了大批现款. (**b**) receive (a relatively light punishment) 受到(较轻的惩罚): *For such a serious offence he was lucky to get away with a fine.* 他犯了那么严重的过失, 却侥幸只交罚款了事. (**c**) (also **get away with doing sth**) (*infml* 口) not be punished for sth 不因某事受惩罚: *If you cheat in the exam you'll never get away with it.* 考试作弊必予追究. ○ *Nobody gets away with insulting me like that.* 这样侮辱我的人, 我是不会放过的.

get ˈback return, esp to one's home 返回; (尤指)回家: *What time did you get back last night?* 昨晚你是什么时候回来的? ○ *We only got back from our holidays yesterday.* 我们昨天才度假回来. **get sth back** obtain sth again after having lost it; recover sth 失而复得; 重新得到: *She's got her old job back.* 她已重新获得从前那份工作. ○ *I never lend books; you never get them back.* 我的书决不外借, 因为总是有去无回. **get back (in)** (of a political party) return to power after having lost it (指政党)重新执政: *The Democrats hope to get back (in) at the next election.* 民主党人希望在下次选举中重新执政. **get back at sb** (*infml* 口) take revenge on sb; retaliate against sb (向某人)复仇, 报复: *I'll find a way of getting back at him!* 我早晚想法报复他! **get back to sb** speak or write to sb again later, esp in order to give a reply 以后再对某人说或给某人写信(尤指作复): *I hope to get back to you on the question of costs by next week.* 我希望下星期再回答你费用的问题. **get back to sth** return to sth 回到某事物上: *Could we get back to the original question of funding?* 我们可以回到最初有关集资的问题上吗?

get ˈbehind (with sth) not proceed at the necessary rate; not produce sth at the right time 落后; 误时; 拖延: *I'm getting behind (with my work).* 我(工作)落后了. ○ *He got behind with his payments for the car.* 他拖欠买汽车的车款.

ˈget by be considered good, smart, etc enough; be accepted 好; 行; 过得去; 获得认可: *I have no formal clothes for the occasion. Perhaps I can get by in a dark suit?* 我没有适合那种场合的礼服, 也许穿深色西服还行吧? ○ *He should just about get by in the exam.* 他这次考试应该能勉强及格. **get by (on sth)** manage to live, survive, etc (using the specified resources); manage; cope (靠某物)勉强维生; 设法维持; 对付: *How does she get by on such a small salary?* 她靠那么一点儿薪水怎么过活? ○ *He gets by on very little money.* 他靠着很少的钱过日子.

ˈget down (of children) leave the table after a meal (指儿童)饭后离桌. **get sb ˈdown** (*infml* 口) make sb depressed or demoralized (使某人)沮丧或情绪低落: *This wet weather is getting me down.* 这种阴湿天气使我打不起精神. ○ *Don't let the incident get you down too much.* 别让这事搅得你过于烦恼了. **get sth down** (**a**) swallow sth, usu with difficulty 吞咽某物(通常为费力地): *The medicine was so horrible I could hardly get it down.* 那药这么难吃, 我好不容易才咽下去. (**b**) note or record sth; write sth down 记下或录下; 写下: *Did you get his telephone number down?* 你记下他的电话号码了吗? **get down to sth/doing sth** begin to do sth; give serious attention to sth; tackle sth 开始做某事; 重视某事物; 认真处理某事: *get down to business* 开始办正事 ○ *It's time I got down to some serious work.* 我该认真干点正事了.

get in (**a**) (of a train, etc or a passenger) arrive at its destination (指火车等或乘客)到达目的地: *The train got in late.* 火车到站误点了. ○ *What time does your flight get in?* 你乘的班机什么时候到? ○ *When do you normally get in from work?* 你平时下班几点到家? **get ˈin**; **get into sth** be elected to a political position 被选任一政治职务: *The Tory candidate stands a good chance of getting in.* 保守党候选人很有当选可能. ○ *Labour got in* (ie won the election) *with a small majority.* 工党以微弱多数票在选举中获胜. ○ *She first got into Parliament* (ie became an MP) *in 1959.* 她1959年第一次获选进入议会. **get (sb) in**; **get (sb) into sth** (cause sb to) be admitted to a school, university, etc, esp after taking an examination (使某人)被接纳入学; (尤指)考取: *He took the entrance exam but didn't get in.* 他参加了入学考试但未被录取. ○ *She's got into Durham to read law.* 她考上达勒姆大学学法律. ○ *She usually gets her best pupils into university.* 她教的最好的学生通常都能考上大学. **get sb in** call sb to one's house to perform a service 请某人到家中服务: *We'll have to get a plumber in to mend that burst pipe.* 我们得请管子工来修理那根爆裂的管子. **get sth in** (**a**) collect or gather sth 收集或收获某物: *get the crops, harvest, etc in* 收获作物、庄稼等. (**b**) buy a supply of sth 购某物供陆续使用: *get coal in for the winter* 买煤以备过冬 ○ *Remember to get in some beers for this evening!* 记住为今日的晚会买些啤酒! (**c**) manage to do or say sth 设法做或说某事: *I got in an hour's gardening between the showers.* 阵雨间歇时我抽空整理了一小时花园. ○ *She talks so much that it's impossible to get a word in.* 她说个没完, 别人休想插话. **get in on sth** (*infml* 口) take part in (an activity) 参加(一活动): *She's keen to get in on any discussions about the new project.* 她一心想参加有关新计划的讨论. **get in with sb** (*infml* 口) (try to) become friendly with sb, esp in order to gain an advantage (极力)对某人亲近; (尤指)拉关系, 讨好: *Have you noticed how he's trying to get in with the boss?* 你注意到他现在多巴结老板了吗? ○ *He got in with a bad crowd at university.* 他在大学里和一帮坏人厮混.

get into sb (*infml* 口) (of a feeling) affect, influence or take control of sb (指感情)影响或控制某人: *I don't know what's got into him recently; he's become very bad-tempered.* 不知道他最近怎么了, 脾气变得坏极了. **get into sth** (**a**) put on (a garment), esp with difficulty 穿上(衣服等)(尤指费力地): *I can't get into these shoes; they're too small.* 这双鞋太小了, 我穿不进去. (**b**) start a career in (the specified profession) 开始从事(某职业): *get into accountancy, journalism, publishing, etc* 从事会计、新闻、出版等工作. (**c**) become involved in sth; start sth 参与某事; 开始某事: *get into an argument, a conversation, a fight (with sb)* (和某人)争论、谈话、斗殴. (**d**) acquire or develop sth 得到或形成某事物: *get into bad habits* 染上恶习. (**e**) become familiar with sth; learn sth 熟悉某事物; 学会某事物: *I haven't really got into my new job yet.* 我还未真正熟悉新工作. (**f**) (*infml* 口) develop a taste or liking for or an interest in sth 产生对某事物的爱好或兴趣: *I'm really getting into jazz these days.* 近来我喜爱上爵士乐了. ○ *How did she get into* (ie start taking) *drugs?* 她是怎么吸起毒来的? **get (oneself/sb) into sth** (cause oneself/sb to) pass into or reach (the specified state or condition) (使自己[某人])进入或达到(某种状态或情形): *get into a fury, rage, temper, etc* 愤怒、勃然大怒、发脾气 ○ *He got into trouble with the police while he was still at school.* 他还在上学时就惹是生非与警方纠缠了. ○ *She got herself into a real state* (ie became very anxious) *before the interview.* 她还未面试就紧张极了.

get (sb) ˈoff (**a**) (cause sb to) leave a place or start a journey (使某人)离开某地或出发: *We got off immediately after breakfast.* 我们吃完早餐就动身了. ○ *get the children off to school* 打发孩子上学. (**b**) (cause sb to) fall asleep (使某人)入睡: *I had great difficulty getting off to sleep last night.* 昨夜我翻来覆去难以入睡.

○ *She got the baby off (to sleep) by rocking it.* 她摇着婴儿哄他入睡. **get off (sth)** leave (work) with permission 下班: *I normally get off (work) at 5.30.* 我通常是5点30分下班. ○ *Could you get off (work) early tomorrow?* 明天你可以提前下班吗? **get off sth** stop discussing (a particular subject) 不再讨论(某事): *Please can we get off the subject of dieting?* 我们别讨论节食了行吗? **get sth off** send sth by post 邮寄某物: *I must get these letters off by the first post tomorrow.* 我这些信必须随明天首批邮件寄出. **get sth off (sth)** remove sth from sth 从某物上移去某物: *Her finger was so swollen that she couldn't get her ring off.* 她手指肿得褪不下戒指来. **get off (with sth)** escape or nearly escape injury in an accident (在事故中)幸免于难或无大恙: *She was lucky to get off with just a few bruises.* 她幸免于难, 只是有几处擦伤. **get (sb) off (with sth)** (*infml* 口) (cause sb to) escape or nearly escape punishment (使某人)免受惩罚或获得从轻发落: *A good lawyer might be able to get you off.* 请位好律师有可能使你免受追究. ○ *He got off with a small fine.* 他交了一小笔罚款了事. ○ *She was lucky to get off with a suspended sentence.* 她侥幸被判缓刑. **get off with sb**; **get 'off (together)** (*Brit infml* 口) have a sexual or romantic experience with sb 和某人有性关系或谈恋爱: *Steve got off with Tracey/Steve and Tracey got off (together) at Denise's party.* 史蒂夫和特蕾西在丹尼斯的聚会中搞上了.

get 'on (**a**) (also **get a'long**) (esp followed by an *adv* or used in questions after *how* 后尤接副词或用于疑问句的how之后) perform or fare in a particular situation; make progress 过日子; 进展; 进步: *Our youngest son is getting on well at school.* 我们的小儿子功课很有进步. ○ *How did you get along in your driving test?* 你的驾驶考试进展如何? ○ *How are you getting along these days?* ie Is your life enjoyable, successful, etc at the moment? 近来生活如何? (**b**) be successful in one's life or career 出人头地: *Parents are always keen for their children to get on.* 父母总是热望子女有出息. ○ *She's ambitious and eager to get on (in the world).* 她雄心勃勃, 一心要(在世上)出人头地. (**c**) (also **get along**) manage or cope 对付; 应付: *I simply can't get along without a secretary.* 我没有秘书简直一筹莫展. ○ *We can get on perfectly well without her.* 我们没有她也能干得很好. **get 'on to sb** (**a**) contact sb by telephone or letter (打电话或通信)与某人联系: *If you wish to lodge a complaint you'd better get on to the manager.* 你有什么不满最好找经理提. (**b**) become aware of sb's presence or activities; detect or trace sb 意识到某人的存在或活动; 侦查或追踪某人: *He had been stealing money from the company for years before the police got on to him.* 警方追查到他时, 他偷公司的钱已有多年了. (**c**) begin to discuss (a new subject) 开始讨论(新课题): *It's time we got on to the question of costs.* 我们该讨论费用问题了. **get on with sb**; **get 'on (together)** have a friendly relationship with sb; get along with sb 与某人关系良好; 与某人和睦相处: *She's never really got on with her sister/She and her sister have never really got on.* 她和妹妹一向合不来. ○ *They don't get on at all well together/with one another.* 他们彼此极不和. ○ *Our new manager is very easy to get on with.* 我们的新经理非常随和. **get on with sth** (**a**) (also **get along with sth**) (esp followed by an *adv* or used in questions after *how* 后尤接副词或用于疑问句的how之后) make progress with a task 取得进展: *How's your son getting on with his French?* 你儿子的法语学得好吗? ○ *I'm not getting on very fast with this job.* 我这份工作进展不太快. (**b**) continue doing sth, esp after an interruption 继续做某事(尤指中断后): *Be quiet and get on with your work.* 安静下来, 继续做你们的工作.

get 'out become known 泄露: *The secret got out.* 秘密泄露了. ○ *If the news gets out there'll be trouble.* 消息若泄露, 必将有后患. **get (sb) out** (in cricket) be dismissed or dismiss sb (板球中)出局, 使某人出局: *How did Gatting get out?* 加廷是怎么出局的? ○ *If England can get Richards out they might win the match.* 英格兰队要是能使理查兹出局, 他们就可能赢. **get sth out** (**a**) produce or publish sth 生产; 出版: *Will we get the new dictionary out by the end of the year?* 咱们的新词典能在年底出版吗? (**b**) say or utter sth with difficulty 勉强说出某事: *She managed to get out a few words of thanks.* 她勉为其难地说出了几句道谢的话. **get out (of sth)** leave a place, esp in order to visit places, meet people, etc 出外走动(尤指参观、会友等): *You ought to get out (of the house) more.* 你应该多出去走走. ○ *We love to get out into the countryside at weekends.* 我们周末爱到郊外去玩儿. **get out of sth/doing sth** (**a**) avoid (a responsibility or duty); not do sth that one ought to do 逃避(责任或义务); 不做分内事: *I wish I could get out of (going to) that meeting.* 但愿我能不(去)参加那个会议. ○ *Don't you dare try and get out of the washing-up!* 你敢逃避洗碗碟! (**b**) (cause sb to) abandon, lose or give up (a habit, routine, etc) (使某人)放弃、停止或戒除(习惯、常规等): *I can't get out of the habit of waking at six in the morning.* 我早上一到六点就醒, 这习惯改不掉了. ○ *Smoking is a habit she can't get out of.* 她抽烟成瘾, 戒不掉了. **get sth out of sb** extract or obtain sth from sb, esp by force 从某人处抽取或获得某物(尤指强迫): *The police have got a confession out of her,* ie have made her confess. 警方逼她招了供. ○ *Just try getting money out of him!* ie He is very mean. 你试试看, 叫他掏腰包! **get sth out of sb/sth** gain or obtain sth from sb/sth 从某人[某事物]处得到或获得: *She seems to get a lot out of life.* 她生活似乎十分丰富. ○ *I never get much from his lectures.* 我听他的课从未得到过什么教益. ○ *She always gets the best out of people.* 她一向善于用人.

get over sth overcome, surmount or master sth 克服; 战胜; 掌握: *She can't get over her shyness.* 她克服不掉羞怯感. ○ *I can't get over* (ie I'm still amazed by) *how much your children have grown.* 我一直在想你的孩子竟长这么大了. ○ *I think the problem can be got over without too much difficulty.* 我认为问题不太难解决. **get over sth/sb** return to one's usual state of health, happiness, etc after an illness, a shock, the end of a relationship with sb, etc 恢复常态(如病后、受惊之后、结束与某人的某种关系后等): *He was disappointed at not getting the job, but he'll get over it.* 他因没有得到那份工作而大失所望, 不过他能想得开. ○ *He never got over the shock of losing his wife.* 他失去妻子后便一蹶不振. ○ *I was still getting over Peter when I met and fell in love with Harry.* 我与彼得情思未断之际, 却遇上了哈里又生恋情. **get sth over (to sb)** make sth clear to sb; communicate sth to sb 向某人讲清某事; 向某人表达某事: *She didn't really get her meaning over to her audience.* 她并未真正把意思向听众讲清楚. **get sth over (with)** (*infml* 口) complete sth unpleasant but necessary 完成或结束必须做的讨厌事: *She'll be glad to get the exam over (and done) with.* 考试结束后她就高兴了.

get round ⇨ GET ABOUT/AROUND/ROUND. **get round sb** (also **get around sb**) (*infml* 口) persuade sb to agree to sth or to do sth which he first opposed 说服某人同意或做其原先反对的事: *She knows how to get round her father.* 她知道怎么哄她爸爸同意. **get round sth** (also **get around sth**) (**a**) tackle sth successfully; overcome sth 顺利应付某事; 克服某事: *Do you see a way of getting round the problem?* 你有解决这问题的办法吗? (**b**) evade or avoid (a law, regulation, etc) without acting illegally; circumvent sth 规避, 回避, 躲避(法律、规则等)(但不违法): *A clever lawyer might find ways of getting round that clause.* 高明的律师也许能找到回避那一条款的办法. **get round to sth/doing sth** (also **get around to sth/doing sth**) finally do sth after dealing with other matters; find the necessary time to do sth (处理完其他事以后)终于能做某事; 找出时间做某事: *I'm very busy at the moment but I hope to get round to answering your letter next week.* 我现在很忙, 希望下周能抽出时间给你回信.

get through sth (**a**) use up or consume (the specified quantity or amount of sth) 用完, 消耗掉(一定量的某物): *She gets through forty cigarettes a day.* 她一天抽四十枝香烟. ○ *We got through a fortune while we were on holiday!* 我们度假花了一大笔钱! (**b**) (manage to) do or complete sth (设法)做或完成某事: *I've got through a lot of correspondence today.* 今天我处理了一大批信件. ○ *Let's start; there's a lot of work to get through/to be got through.* 开始吧, 有大批工作要做呢. **get (sb) 'through (sth)** (help sb to) be successful in or pass (an examination, a test, etc) (帮助某人)(考试、测验等)及格: *Tom failed but his sister got through.* 汤姆不及格, 但他妹妹及格了. ○ *She got all her pupils through French 'A' Level.* 在她的帮助下, 所有学生的法语高级考试都及

G

格了. **get (sth) 'through (sth)** (cause sth to) be officially approved or accepted (使某事物)正式通过或被采纳: *Do you think the Bill will get through (Parliament)?* 你认为那议案(议会)能通过吗? ○ *get a proposal through a committee* 使委员会接受一项建议. **get 'through (to sb)** (**a**) reach (sb) 到达(某人处): *Thousands of refugees will die if these supplies don't get through (to them).* 数以千计的难民若得不到这些救济物品,(他们)就要死亡. (**b**) make contact (with sb), esp by telephone (与某人)联系(尤指通电话): *I tried ringing you several times yesterday but I couldn't get through (to you).* 昨天我给你打了几次电话, 可是都没(和你)接通. **get 'through (to sth)** (of a player or team) reach the next stage of a competition (指运动队或队员)进入下一阶段比赛: *Everton have got through to the final.* 埃弗顿队已进入决赛. **get 'through to sb** make sb understand the meaning of what one is saying; communicate with sb 所说的话使某人理解; 与某人沟通: *I find her impossible to get through to.* 我发觉无法跟她沟通思想. ○ *Try to get through to him that he's wasting his life in that job.* 设法让他明白做那种工作是浪费生命. **get through with sth** finish or complete (a job, task, etc) 完成(工作、任务等): *As soon as I get through with my work I'll join you.* 我工作一做完就来找你们.
get to doing sth reach the point where one does sth; begin to do sth 开始或着手做某事: *He got to thinking that she perhaps wouldn't come after all.* 他已意识到也许她根本不来了. **'get to sb** (*infml* 口) annoy, anger, or affect sb 使某人恼怒或生气; 影响某人: *Her constant nagging is beginning to get to him.* 她不停地唠叨惹得他生起气来.
get sb/sth together assemble or collect (people or things) 聚集(人); 收集(物品): *Rebel leaders hastily tried to get an army together.* 叛乱首领急于想纠集起一支军队. ○ *Could you get your things together? We're leaving in five minutes!* 你能不能把自己的东西收拾好? 再过五分钟我们就要动身了! **get together with sb**; **get to'gether** meet with sb for social purposes or to discuss sth 参加社交聚会; 开会讨论某事: *The management should get together with the union/The management and the union should get together to discuss their differences.* 劳方与资方应该开会[劳资双方应该开会]讨论彼此间的分歧. ○ *We must get together for a drink some time.* 我们得找个时间聚聚喝上一杯.
get up (**a**) stand after sitting, kneeling, etc; rise 站起; 起来: *The class got up when the teacher came in.* 老师进来时全班起立. ○ *He got up slowly from the armchair.* 他慢慢从单人沙发上站起身来. (**b**) (of the sea or wind) increase in force or strength; become violent (指海浪或风)变猛烈: *The wind is getting 'up.* 风越刮越大了. **get (sb) up** (cause sb to) get out of bed (使某人)起床: *What time do you get up (in the morning)?* 你(早上)什么时候起床? ○ *She always gets up early.* 她一向早起. ○ *Could you get me up* (ie wake me) *at 6.30 tomorrow?* 你明天早晨6点30分叫醒我好吗? **get oneself/sb up** (often passive 常用于被动语态) arrange the appearance of sb/sth in the specified way 以某方式打扮某人[某物]: *She was got up* (ie dressed) *as an Indian princess.* 把她打扮成了印度公主. **get sth up** (**a**) arrange or organize sth 安排或组织某事物: *We're getting up a party for her birthday.* 我们要给她开生日庆祝会. (**b**) acquire a knowledge of sth; study sth 获得某事物的知识; 研究某事物: *She's busy getting up the American constitution for tomorrow's exam.* 她忙着温习美国宪法, 准备明天的考试. **get up to sth** (**a**) reach (the specified point) 达到(某程度): *We got up to page 72 last lesson.* 上一课我们学到第72页. (**b**) be occupied or busy with (esp sth surprising or undesirable) 做着或忙于(尤指令人惊奇的或不好的事): *What on earth will he get up to next?* 下一步他究竟要要什么花样? ○ *He's been getting up to his old tricks again!* 他又要重施故技了.
□ **get-at-able** /ˌgetætəbl; ˌgɛtˋætəbl/ *adj* [usu pred 通常作表语] (*infml* 口) that can be reached; accessible 能达到; 易获得: *We've got a spare suitcase but it's not very get-at-able.* 我们有个多余的手提箱, 但是不太容易拿出来.
'getaway *n* escape, esp after committing a crime 逃跑(尤指犯罪后): *make one's getaway* 逃跑 ○ [attrib 作定语] *a getaway car*, ie one used to escape in 逃跑用的汽车.
'get-together *n* (*infml* 口) social gathering 聚会; 联欢会: *We're having a little get-together to celebrate David's promotion.* 我们为戴维的晋升开一个小型庆祝会.
'get-up *n* (*infml* 口) set of clothes, esp an unusual one; costume 一套衣服, 服装(尤指特别的装束): *She wears the most extraordinary get-ups.* 她穿着最不寻常的衣裳. ○ *He looked absurd in that get-up.* 他穿着那套衣服看上去怪模怪样的.
ˌget-up-and-'go *n* [U] (*infml* 口) quality of being energetic and forceful 干劲; 进取精神: *She's got lots of get-up-and-go.* 她干劲十足.

geum /ˈdʒiːəm; ˋdʒiəm/ *n* kind of small garden plant with red or yellow flowers 水杨梅(矮小的园艺植物, 开红色或黄色花).

gey·ser *n* **1** /ˈgaɪzər; ˋgaɪzɚ/ column of hot water or steam sent up from the ground at intervals, caused by the heating of water deep in the Earth 间歇泉. **2** /ˈgiːzə(r); ˋgizɚ/ (*Brit*) apparatus formerly used for heating large amounts of water (usu by gas) in a kitchen or bathroom (旧时厨房或浴室中通常燃煤气的)热水器.

ghastly /ˈgɑːstlɪ; *US* ˈgæstlɪ; ˋgæstlɪ/ *adj* (**-ier, -iest**) **1** [usu attrib 通常作定语] causing horror or fear 可怕的; 恐怖的: *a ghastly accident, experience, fright, murder* 可怕的事故、经历、惊吓、谋杀. **2** (*infml* 口) very bad; distasteful 极坏的; 糟透的; 令人反感的: *a ghastly error, mess, mistake, etc* 极大的过失、混乱、错误等 ○ *Her hairdo and make-up look positively ghastly!* 她的发型和脂粉看上去真令人恶心! ○ *What a ghastly man!* 多讨厌的人! **3** [usu pred 通常作表语] ill; upset 有病; 不适; 苦恼: *I feel ghastly; I shouldn't have drunk so much!* 我觉得很不舒服, 我不该喝那么多! ○ *I felt ghastly about refusing, but I had no alternative.* 我觉得要加以拒绝很不是滋味, 但我别无他途. **4** (*fml* 文) very pale and death-like in appearance 苍白的; 死一般的: *You look ghastly; are you all right?* 你脸色很难看, 是不舒服了吗? ○ *She had a ghastly pallor.* 她脸色苍白难看. ○ *His face was a ghastly white.* 他脸色苍白. ▷ **ghast·li·ness** *n* [U].

ghat (also **ghaut**) /gɔːt; gɔt/ *n* **1** (in India) flight of steps leading down to a landing place on a river bank or lakeside (印度的)(河边或湖边供人上下的)台阶. **2** (usu *pl* 通常作复数) (also **burning 'ghat**) level area at the top of a river ghat on which Hindus cremate their dead 河边火葬地(河边台阶顶部平台, 为印度人火化尸体处). **3** mountain pass in India (印度的)山隘, 山路.

ghee /giː; gi/ *n* [U] purified semi-liquid butter used in Indian cooking (印度烹饪用的半流质的)精炼奶油.

gher·kin /ˈgɜːkɪn; ˋgɝkɪn/ *n* small green cucumber for pickling (做泡菜的)小黄瓜.

ghetto /ˈgetəʊ; ˋgɛto/ *n* (*pl* **~s**) **1** (formerly in some countries) Jewish quarter of a town (旧时某些国家的)城市中的犹太人区. **2** (*often derog* 常作贬义) area of a town lived in by any minority national or social group, typically crowded and with poor housing conditions 少数民族居住区; 贫民区: *the clearance of slum ghettos to make way for new housing developments* 为建筑新住宅区而对贫民区的拆除 ○ *a rich people's ghetto*, ie an area in a town where rich people live, surrounded by poorer people (贫民区中的)富人区.
▷ **ghet·to·ize, -ise** *v* [Tn] (*derog* 贬) put (sb/sth) into a separate limited category, artificially cut off from others 将(某人[某事物])置于隔离的有限范围内. **ghet·to·iza·tion, -isation** /ˌgetəʊaɪˈzeɪʃn; *US* -əʊɪˈz-; ˌgɛtoəˋzeʃən/ *n* [U].
□ **'ghetto blaster** large and powerful portable radio and cassette player 大功率手提式大型收音录音机.

ghost /gəʊst; gost/ *n* **1** spirit of a dead person appearing to sb who is still living 鬼; 幽灵: *The ghost of Lady Margaret is supposed to haunt this chapel.* 据说玛格丽特女士的鬼魂常在这个礼拜堂出没. ○ *I don't believe in ghosts*, ie don't believe that they exist. 我不相信有鬼. ○ *He looked as if he had seen a ghost*, ie looked very frightened. 他那副惊骇的样子就像见到了鬼似的. **2** [sing] **~ of sth** (*fig* 比喻) very faint, slight amount or trace of sth 某事物的一点点; 朦胧的痕迹; 隐约的一丝: *The ghost of a smile* (ie a very faint smile) *played round her lips.* 她嘴角上露着一丝微笑. ○ *You haven't a ghost of a chance*, ie You have no chance. 你毫无机会. **3** faint secondary image on a television screen (电视屏幕

上的)重影, 重像. **4** (idm 习语) **give up the ˈghost** (**a**) die 死. (**b**) (*joc* 谑) fail to work or to make an effort 失效; 不能使用; 不再努力: *The car seems to have given up the ghost.* 看来这汽车算是报销了. **lay a ˈghost** (**a**) exorcise an evil spirit 驱除魔鬼: *The ghost has been laid and will not return to haunt you again.* 那鬼魂已经祛除, 不会再回来缠着你了. (**b**) (*infml* 口) finally overcome a previous failure which seemed impossible to recover from 终于洗雪前次似无可挽回的失败: *Her gold-medal victory laid the ghost of her shock defeat in the European Championships.* 她在欧洲锦标赛中的惨败终因她夺得金牌的胜利而雪耻.

▷ **ghost** *v* [Ipr, Tn] **~ (for) sb** act as a ghost-writer for sb 给某人捉刀; 为人代笔: *He ghosts for a number of sports personalities who 'write' newspaper columns.* 他给一些为报纸专栏'写'文章的体育界名人做捉刀人. ○ *her ghosted memoirs*, ie written by someone else 她那由别人代笔的回忆录.

ghostly /ˈgəʊstlɪ; ˋgostlɪ/ *adj* (**-ier, -iest**) of or being a ghost; like a ghost in appearance or sound 鬼的; (外貌或声音)像鬼的: *a ghostly voice whispering in sb's ear* 在某人耳边低语的幽灵般的声音 ○ *ghostly shapes of bats flitting about in the dark* 黑暗中蝙蝠飞翔的鬼影.

ghost·li·ness *n* [U]: *the ghostliness of the ship's outline* 幽灵般的船影.

□ **ˈghost story** story about ghosts, intended to frighten the reader 鬼怪故事.

ˈghost town town whose former inhabitants have all left 废弃的城镇.

ˈghost-write *v* [I, Ipr, Tn esp passive 尤用于被动语态] **~ sth (for sb)** write (material) for sb else and allow him to publish it under his own name 代人写作; 为人捉刀写(材料): *a ghost-written newspaper column* 代人捉刀的报纸专栏. **ˈghost-writer** *n* person who does this 捉刀人; 代笔者.

ghoul /guːl; gul/ *n* **1** (in stories) spirit that robs graves and feeds on the corpses in them (故事中的)盗墓食尸鬼. **2** (*derog* 贬) person with an unnaturally strong interest in death, disaster and other unpleasant things 以死亡、灾难等恶事为乐的人: *these ghouls who come and stare at road accidents* 来看交通事故惨状引以为乐的好事者.

▷ **ghoul·ish** /ˈguːlɪʃ; ˋgulɪʃ/ *adj* of or like a ghoul; very unpleasant; gruesome 食尸鬼似的; 极为讨厌的; 令人毛骨悚然的: *ghoulish behaviour, laughter, stories* 凶残的行为、狞笑、恐怖故事.

GHQ /ˌdʒiː eɪtʃ ˈkjuː; ˌdʒi etʃ ˋkju/ *abbr* 缩写 = General Headquarters: *orders received from GHQ* 总司令部发来的命令.

GI /ˌdʒiː ˈaɪ; ˋdʒiˋaɪ/ *n* enlisted soldier of the US army 美国现役陆军士兵.

□ **ˌGI ˈbride** foreign woman who marries a US soldier on duty abroad 美国军人在国外服役时娶的外国女子.

gi·ant /ˈdʒaɪənt; ˋdʒaɪənt/ *n* **1** (in fairy-tales and myths) person of human shape but enormous size and strength (often cruel and stupid) (童话和神话故事中的)巨人(常为残酷和愚蠢的). **2** unusually large person, animal, plant, business organization, etc 巨人, 巨物(异常大的动植物、商业组织等): *His son is a giant of 6 feet already.* 他的儿子已是6英尺高的大个子了. ○ *He's the giant of* (ie the tallest person) *the family.* 他是家中个子最高的. ○ *What a giant of a tree!* 多高大的树哇! ○ *the multinational oil giants* 跨国大石油公司 ○ [attrib 作定语] *a giant cabbage* 大洋白菜 ○ *a cabbage of giant size* 巨大的洋白菜. **3** (*fig* 比喻) person of unusually great ability or genius 能力或才智超群的伟人: *Shakespeare is a giant among poets/the giant of poets.* 莎士比亚是诗人中的大文豪.

▷ **giant·ess** /ˈdʒaɪəntes; ˋdʒaɪəntəs/ *n* female giant 女巨人.

□ **giant ˈpanda** = PANDA.

ˈgiant-size (also **ˈgiant-sized**) *adj* very large; larger than usual 非常大的; 特大的: *a giant-sized packet of detergent* 特大号包装的洗涤剂.

gib·ber /ˈdʒɪbə(r); ˋdʒɪbɚ/ *v* [I, Ipr, Ip] **~ (away/on) (about sth/at sb)** (**a**) (of a monkey or a frightened person) talk quickly or make meaningless sounds (指猴子或受惊吓的人)快速地说或发出无意义的声音: *monkeys gibbering at one another in the tree-tops* 在树梢上叽哩咕噜乱叫的猴子 ○ *He cowered in the corner, gibbering with terror.* 他蜷缩在角落里, 吓得喃喃自语. (**b**) (*derog* 贬) talk a lot without seeming to say anything important 说得多而无什么意义; 瞎扯: *What's he gibbering away about?* 他在胡扯些什么? ○ *a gibbering idiot* 胡言乱语的白痴.

▷ **gib·ber·ish** /ˈdʒɪbərɪʃ; ˋdʒɪbərɪʃ/ *n* [U] meaningless sounds; unintelligible talk; nonsense 无意义的声音; 含混不清的谈话; 胡说: *Don't talk gibberish!* 别胡扯!

gib·bet /ˈdʒɪbɪt; ˋdʒɪbɪt/ *n* **1** (*arch* 古) gallows 绞刑架; 绞台. **2** upright post with a projecting arm from which in former times the bodies of executed criminals were hung (旧时罪犯受绞刑后吊尸体的)示众架.

gib·bon /ˈgɪbən; ˋgɪbən/ *n* long-armed ape of south-east Asia 长臂猿(产于东南亚). ⇨illus at APE 见 APE 插图.

gibe (also **jibe**) /dʒaɪb; dʒaɪb/ *v* [I, Ipr] **~ (at sb/sth)** jeer at or mock sb/sth; make fun of sb/sth 讥笑、嘲弄、戏弄或取笑某人[某事物]: *It's easy enough for you to gibe at them, but could you do any better?* 笑话人家很容易, 可是你能做得更好吗?

▷ **gibe** (*US* **jibe**) *n* **~ (about/at sb/sth)** taunt; mocking remark; cruel joke 嘲弄; 嘲讽; 挖苦人的笑话: *a cruel, malicious, nasty, etc gibe* 刻薄的、恶意的、恶毒的...嘲弄 ○ *cheap gibes about her fatness* 对她的肥胖所作的粗俗的嘲笑.

gib·lets /ˈdʒɪblɪts; ˋdʒɪblɪts/ *n* [pl] edible organs (heart, liver, etc) of a bird, taken out and usu cooked separately (禽类可供食用的)内脏, 杂碎(心、肝等).

giddy /ˈgɪdɪ; ˋgɪdɪ/ *adj* (**-ier, -iest**) **1** (**a**) [usu pred 通常作表语] having the feeling that everything is turning round and that one is going to fall 头晕; 眩晕: *I feel giddy; I must sit down.* 我觉得头晕, 得坐下来. ○ *have a giddy feeling* 有眩晕的感觉 ○ (*fig* 比喻) *giddy with their first business success* 为商业上初次成功而飘飘然. (**b**) [usu attrib 通常作定语] causing such a feeling 令人眩晕的; 头昏眼花的; 头晕的: *travel at a giddy speed* 以令人目眩的速度行进 ○ *look down from a giddy height* 从令人眩晕的高处俯视 ○ (*fig* 比喻) *Life then was a succession of giddy triumphs*, ie exciting but not stable or lasting. 那时的生活可谓人间得意、千红万紫, 盛极一时. **2** [usu attrib 通常作定语] (*dated derog* 旧, 贬) too fond of excitement and pleasure; not serious 热衷于刺激和欢乐的; 轻浮的; 不严肃的: *a giddy girl, who will never settle down to anything serious* 永远安不下心来做正经事的轻浮女孩. **3** [attrib 作定语] (*dated* 旧) (used to add emphasis to certain exclamations 用以加强某些感叹词语的语气): *Oh my giddy aunt!* 哦, 我的好姑姑! ○ *That really is the giddy limit!* 那真是最大限度了!

▷ **gid·dily** /ˈgɪdɪlɪ; ˋgɪdɪlɪ/ *adv*: *stagger giddily round the room* 在房间各处摇摇摆摆地走.

gid·di·ness /ˈgɪdɪnɪs; ˋgɪdɪnɪs/ *n* [U] giddy feeling 眩晕感; 头晕; 头昏.

gift /gɪft; gɪft/ *n* **1** thing given willingly without payment; present 礼物; 赠品: *a kind, generous, small, etc gift* 使人感到亲切的、慷慨的、小小的...礼物 ○ *a birthday, Christmas, wedding, etc gift* 生日、圣诞、结婚等礼品 ○ *a gift to charity* 慈善捐赠 ○ *a gift of chocolates, flowers, etc* 巧克力、鲜花等礼物. **2 ~ (for sth/doing sth)** natural talent or ability 天赋; 禀赋; 才能: *I've always been able to learn languages easily; it's a gift.* 我学习语言一向是轻而易举, 这是天分. ○ *He has many outstanding gifts.* 他多才多艺. ○ *have a gift for music* 有音乐天才 ○ *the gift of making friends easily* 善于交友的才能 ○ (*ironic* 反语) *a gift for doing/saying the wrong thing* 天生的做错事[说错话]的本事. **3** (usu *sing* 通常作单数) (*infml* 口) (**a**) unusually cheap purchase; bargain 便宜货; 合算的交易: *At that price it's an absolute gift!* 那个价钱, 纯粹是白给! (**b**) (*fig* 比喻) thing that is very easy or too easy to do 轻而易举的事; 过分容易的事: *Their second goal was a real gift.* 他们得的第二分真是易如反掌. ○ *That exam question was an absolute gift!* 那道试题纯粹是白送分! ○ *It was a gift of a question.* 解答那一道题不费吹灰之力. ○ [attrib 作定语] *a gift question* 一道白送分的题. **4** (idm 习语) **a gift from the ˈgods** advantageous thing that is unearned and unexpected 非劳动所得; 意外所得: *To have such an easy examination paper was a gift from the gods.* 碰到这样容易的考卷, 那是老天爷的恩赐. **the gift of the ˈgab** (*sometimes derog* 有时作贬义) the ability to speak fluently and

G

eloquently 口才; 辩才. **God's gift to sb/sth** ⇨ GOD. **in the gift of sb** which sb has the right or power to give or grant 由某人授予或准予: *a post in the sovereign's gift*, ie one which the sovereign has the right to appoint a person to 君主授予的职位. **look a gift horse in the ˈmouth** (usu with negatives 通常与否定词连用) refuse or criticize sth that is given to one for nothing 拒受馈赠; 受礼而加挑剔.

▷ **gif·ted** /ˈgɪftɪd; ˋgɪftɪd/ *adj* **1 ~ (at/in sth)** having a great deal of natural ability or talent 有天才的; 有天赋的: *a gifted artist, pianist, etc* 有天赋的艺术家、钢琴家等 ○ *gifted at singing, writing, etc* 有唱歌、写作等天资的 ○ *gifted in art, music, etc* 有艺术、音乐等天才的. **2** very intelligent or talented 悟性高的; 聪颖的; 天才的: *gifted children* 聪慧的儿童.

□ ˈ**gift box**, ˈ**gift pack** box or pack specially designed to contain a gift 礼物盒; 礼物包装.

ˈ**gift shop** shop that specializes in selling articles suitable as gifts 礼品商店.

ˈ**gift token**, ˈ**gift voucher** token or voucher that can be exchanged in a shop for goods of a certain value 礼券.

ˈ**gift-wrap** *v* [Tn usu passive 通常用于被动语态] wrap (an article) in a shop ready for presentation as a gift (商店中)将(某物)包装成礼品状. ˈ**gift-wrapping** *n* [U] special paper, etc used for wrapping a gift 礼物包装纸等.

gig /gɪg; gɪg/ *n* **1** small light two-wheeled carriage pulled by one horse 单马双轮轻便马车. **2** (*infml* 口) engagement to play jazz or pop music, esp for a single night (爵士乐或流行音乐的)特约演奏(尤指一夜的).

gi·gantic /dʒaɪˈgæntɪk; dʒaɪˋgæntɪk/ *adj* of very great size or extent; immense 巨大的; 庞大的: *a gigantic person, with a gigantic appetite* 胃口极大的大高个儿 ○ *a problem of gigantic proportions* 重大的问题 ○ *a gigantic effort, improvement, success, etc* 巨大的努力、改进、成功等. ▷ **gi·gant·ic·ally** /dʒaɪˈgæntɪklɪ; dʒaɪˋgæntɪklɪ/ *adv*: *gigantically successful* 非常成功的.

G

giggle /ˈgɪgl; ˋgɪgl̩/ *v* [I, Ipr] **~ (at sb/sth)** laugh lightly in a nervous or silly way 咯咯笑; 傻笑: *Stop giggling, children; this is a serious matter.* 孩子们, 别傻笑了, 这是严肃的事情. ○ *giggling at one of her silly jokes* 让她那拙劣的笑话逗得咯咯笑.

▷ **giggle** *n* **1** [C] laugh of this kind 咯咯笑; 傻笑: *There was a giggle from the back of the class.* 从教室后面传来咯咯的笑声. **2** [sing] (thing which provides) amusement 娱乐; 提供娱乐的事物: *What a giggle!* 多有意思的玩意儿! ○ *Today's lesson was a bit of a giggle.* 今天的课真有趣. ○ *I only did it for a giggle.* 我做那事只是为了取乐. **3 the giggles** [pl] continuous uncontrolled laughter of this kind (esp by young girls) 持续的, 放纵的笑(尤指女孩): *get the giggles* 发出咯咯笑声 ○ *She had a fit of the giggles.* 她咯咯地笑了一阵.

gig·gly /ˈgɪglɪ; ˋgɪglɪ/ *adj* (*often derog* 常作贬义) **1** inclined to giggle 爱傻笑的: *a giggly schoolgirl* 爱傻笑的女学生. **2** having the sound or quality of giggling 咯咯笑的; 傻笑的: *giggly laughter* 咯咯的笑声.

NOTE ON USAGE 用法: **1 Snigger** (*US* **snicker**) indicates childish and disrespectful laughing at something regarded as unusual or improper ☆ **snigger**(美式英语作 **snicker**) 指对异常的或不当的事发出幼稚的、不尊重的笑声: *What are you sniggering at? Haven't you seen people kissing before?* 你们笑什么? 没见过接吻吗? **2 Giggle** is also childish. ☆ **giggle** 也指发出幼稚的笑声. It is often uncontrolled (a **fit of giggling/(the) giggles**) and is either in response to something silly or a nervous reaction 这一词常指失去控制的笑(a **fit of giggling / (the) giggles** 一阵傻笑), 或因无聊琐事引起或为神经质的反应: *The children couldn't stop giggling at the teacher's high-pitched voice.* 教师的嗓音很高, 孩子们都不禁咯咯地笑起来. ○ *She giggled nervously when the judges congratulated her on her costume.* 评判员赞赏她的服装, 她神经质地笑了起来.

gig·olo /ˈʒɪgələʊ; ˋʒɪgə,lo/ *n* (*pl* **~s**) **1** professional male dancing partner who may be hired by wealthy women 舞男; (有钱女子雇的)男舞伴. **2** (*derog* 贬) paid male companion or lover of a wealthy older woman (有钱的年长妇女雇的)男伴或情人.

gild /gɪld; gɪld/ *v* [Tn] **1** cover (sth) with gold-leaf(3) or gold-coloured paint 覆金箔于(某物); 涂金色于(某物): *gild a picture-frame* 给画框涂上金色. **2** (*fig rhet* 比喻, 修辞) make (sth) bright as if with gold 使(某物)如金子般生光: *white walls of houses gilded by the morning sun* 金色晨光照耀下的房子的白墙. **3** (idm 习语) **gild the ˈlily** try to improve what is already satisfactory 给百合花贴金(尽力改进本已合意的事物). **gild the ˈpill** make (sth) unpleasant but necessary seem attractive 苦药裹糖衣(将讨厌的但必要的事物弄得吸引人).

▷ **gilded** *adj* [attrib 作定语] wealthy and of the upper-classes 富有的; 上层阶级的: *the gilded youth* (ie young people) *of the Edwardian era* 爱德华时代的富贵年轻人.

gilder /ˈgɪldə(r); ˋgɪldɚ/ *n* person who gilds things 金饰工人.

gild·ing /ˈgɪldɪŋ; ˋgɪldɪŋ/ *n* [U] **1** applying of gilt to sth 在某物上覆金箔或涂金色. **2** material with which things are gilded; surface made by such material 饰金用的或金色的材料; 金饰或金色的表面.

gill[1] /gɪl; gɪl/ *n* (usu *pl* 通常作复数) **1** opening on the side of a fish's head through which it breathes 鳃. ⇨illus at FISH 见 FISH 插图. **2** any of the thin vertical sheets on the underside of a mushroom (蘑菇的)菌褶. ⇨illus at FUNGUS 见 FUNGUS 插图. **3** (*infml joc* 口, 谑) area of skin under a person's ears and jaw (人的)腮: *be/go green/white about the gills*, ie look pale with fear or sickness 脸色发青[苍白](受惊吓或因病).

gill[2] /dʒɪl; dʒɪl/ *n* one quarter of a pint (liquid measure) 及耳(液量单位, 合四分之一品脱). ⇨App 5 见附录 5.

gil·lie /ˈgɪlɪ; ˋgɪlɪ/ *n* man or boy attending sb shooting or fishing for sport in Scotland (苏格兰)伺候渔猎运动者的仆人或男孩.

gilt /gɪlt; gɪlt/ *n* **1** [U] gold (or sth resembling gold) applied to a surface in a thin layer (覆于物体表面的)薄层的金(或似金的物质): [attrib 作定语] *a gilt brooch* 镀金胸针. **2 gilts** [pl] (*finance* 财) gilt-edged securities 金边证券. **3** (idm 习语) **take the gilt off the ˈgingerbread** do or be sth which makes a situation or achievement less attractive or worthwhile (做出)使情况或成就失色的事物.

□ ˌ**gilt-ˈedged** *adj* (*finance* 财) not risky; secure 金边的; 保险的; 安全的: *ˌgilt-edged seˈcurities/ˈshares/ˈstock*, ie investments that are considered safe and sure to produce interest 金边证券[股分/股票](可靠、安全、确保获利的).

gim·bals /ˈdʒɪmblz; ˋdʒɪmbl̩z/ *n* [pl] pivoting device for keeping instruments (eg a compass) horizontal in a moving ship, etc 平衡环, 水平环(使仪表, 如罗盘, 保持水平位置的仪器).

gim·crack /ˈdʒɪmkræk; ˋdʒɪm,kræk/ *adj* [attrib 作定语] worthless; flimsy; badly made 无价值的; 不结实的; 粗制滥造的: *gimcrack ornaments* 劣质的饰物.

gim·let /ˈgɪmlɪt; ˋgɪmlɪt/ *n* small T-shaped tool for boring a screw hole in a piece of wood 螺丝锥; 木钻; 手钻: (*fig* 比喻) *eyes like gimlets*, ie sharp eyes which seem to penetrate with their look 锐利如锥的目光.

gim·mick /ˈgɪmɪk; ˋgɪmɪk/ *n* (*often derog* 常作贬义) unusual, amusing, etc thing whose only purpose is to attract attention, and which has little or no value or importance of its own (为引人注意而无甚价值或不重要的)异常的或有趣的事物; 小玩意儿; 花招: *a promotional/publicity/sales gimmick* 推销的[宣传的/兜售的]噱头 ○ *a flashy expensive car with all sorts of gimmicks like self-winding windows* 装置有各式小革新如自动升降窗的豪华昂贵汽车.

▷ **gim·mickry** /ˈgɪmɪkrɪ; ˋgɪmɪkrɪ/ *n* [U] (*derog* 贬) (use of) gimmicks 花招; 小玩意儿: *There is too much advertising gimmickry.* 广告花招太多了.

gim·micky /ˈgɪmɪkɪ; ˋgɪmɪkɪ/ *adj*.

gin[1] /dʒɪn; dʒɪn/ *n* **1** trap or snare for catching animals (诱捕动物的)陷阱, 圈套. **2** (also **cotton gin**) machine for separating raw cotton from its seeds 轧棉机; 轧花机.

gin[2] /dʒɪn; dʒɪn/ *n* [U, C] colourless alcoholic drink distilled from grain or malt and flavoured with juniper berries, often used in cocktails 杜松子酒: *pink gin*, ie with angostura 苦味杜松子酒(加安古苦味汁的) ○ *I'll have a gin and tonic*, ie with tonic water. 我要一杯掺奎宁水的杜松子酒.

□ **gin 'rummy** type of rummy (a card-game) for two players 金兰姆(一种双人牌戏).

gin·ger /'dʒɪndʒə(r); 'dʒɪndʒɚ/ *n* [U] **1** (plant with a) hot-tasting spicy root used as a flavouring 姜: *crystallized ginger* 糖姜 ○ *ground, root, stem ginger* 姜粉、姜丝、蜜饯姜. **2** liveliness; spirit; energy 活力; 精神; 精力: *The football team needs a bit more ginger in it.* 这支足球队需要些活力. **3** light reddish-yellow colour 姜黄色: *His hair was a bright shade of ginger.* 他的头发带一点姜黄色.

▷ **gin·ger** *adj* **1** [attrib 作定语] flavoured with ginger 姜味的: *ginger cake* 姜汁饼. **2** of the colour ginger 姜黄色的: *ginger hair, whiskers, eyebrows, etc* 姜黄色的头发、络腮胡子、眉毛等 ○ *a ginger cat* 姜黄色的猫.

gin·ger *v* (phr v) **ginger sb/sth up** make sb/sth more vigorous or lively 使某人[某事物]有活力、活跃或有生气: *Some dancing would ginger up the party.* 跳跳舞就可以使聚会活跃起来. ○ *The Prime Minister appointed some new ministers to ginger up her administration.* 首相任命一些新大臣以增强她现届政府的活力.

gin·gery /'dʒɪndʒərɪ; 'dʒɪndʒərɪ/ *adj* (somewhat) like ginger (有点)似姜的; 姜味的: *a gingery flavour* 姜味 ○ *a gingery colour* 姜黄色.

□ **ginger-'ale, ginger-'beer** *ns* [U] types of non-alcoholic fizzy drink flavoured with ginger 姜味汽水.

'gingerbread *n* [U] **1** ginger-flavoured treacle cake or biscuit 姜味饼. **2** (idm 习语) **take the gilt off the gingerbread** ⇨ GILT.

'ginger group group within a larger group (esp in a political party) urging a more active or livelier policy 活跃的或激进的集团(尤指政党中的).

'ginger-nut, 'ginger-snap *ns* types of ginger-flavoured biscuit 姜味薄脆饼.

gin·gerly /'dʒɪndʒəlɪ; 'dʒɪndʒɚlɪ/ *adv* with great care and caution to avoid causing harm or making a noise 极谨慎地(以免造成伤害或发出声响): *Gingerly he opened the door of the rat's cage.* 他小心翼翼地打开鼠笼的门.

▷ **gin·gerly** *adj* cautious 小心翼翼的; 轻手轻脚的: *She sat down in a gingerly manner.* 她轻轻地坐下.

ging·ham /'gɪŋəm; 'gɪŋəm/ *n* [U] cotton or linen cloth with a striped or check pattern 条纹的或方格的棉布或亚麻布: [attrib 作定语] *a gingham dress* 方格连衣裙.

gin·giv·itis /ˌdʒɪndʒɪ'vaɪtɪs; ˌdʒɪndʒə'vaɪtɪs/ *n* [U] (*medical* 医) inflammation of the gums 龈炎.

gin·seng /'dʒɪnseŋ; 'dʒɪnsɛŋ/ *n* [U] (plant with a) sweet-smelling root used esp in alternative medicine 人参; 西洋参.

gipsy = GYPSY.

gir·affe /dʒɪ'rɑ:f; *US* dʒə'ræf; dʒə'ræf/ *n* (*pl* unchanged or **~s** 复数或不变或作 **giraffes**) African animal with a very long neck and legs and dark patches on its coat 长颈鹿(产于非洲).

gird /gɜ:d; gɝd/ *v* (*pt, pp* **girded** or **girt** /gɜ:t; gɝt/) **1** [Tn, Tn·pr] **~ sth (with sth)** (*arch* 古) surround sth 围绕某物: *Trees girded the dark lake.* 树木环绕着那阴暗的湖. ○ *a sea-girt island* 四面环海的岛. **2** [Tn·pr] **~ sb (with sth)** (*arch* 古) clothe sb 给某人穿衣; 供某人以衣服: *He girded himself with armour for the battle.* 他穿好铠甲准备战斗. **3** (idm 习语) **gird (up) one's 'loins** (*rhet or joc* 修辞或谑) prepare for action 准备行动. **4** (phr v) **gird sth on** (*arch* 古) fasten sth on, esp with a belt 将某物束紧, 扎住, 缠好(尤指用带子): *He girded on his sword.* 他系上宝剑.

girder /'gɜ:də(r); 'gɝdɚ/ *n* long strong iron or steel beam used for building bridges and the framework of large buildings (桥梁和大建筑物的)主梁, 大梁.

girdle[1] /'gɜ:dl; 'gɝdl/ *n* **1** cord or belt fastened round the waist to keep clothes in position 腰带. **2** (*rhet* 修辞) thing that surrounds sth else 围绕物: *a girdle of green fields round a town* 城镇四周绿色的田野. **3** (*anatomy* 解) connected ring of bones in the body 带; 环状骨: *the pelvic girdle* 骨盆带. **4** (*dated* 旧) corset 束腹紧身衣.

▷ **girdle** *v* [Tn, Tn·pr, Tn·p] **~ sth (about/around) (with sth)** (*rhet* 修辞) surround sth 围绕某事物: *a village girdled with green fields* 绿色田野环绕的村庄 ○ *an island girdled about by deep blue water* 蓝色的深水域环绕着的岛.

girdle[2] /'gɜ:dl; 'gɝdl̩/ *n* (*Scot* 苏格兰) = GRIDDLE.

girl /gɜ:l; gɝl/ *n* **1** [C] (**a**) female child 女孩; 姑娘: *a baby girl* 女婴 ○ *a little girl of six (years old)* 六岁女童 ○ *Good morning, girls and boys!* 孩子们, 早上好! (**b**) daughter 女儿: *Their eldest girl's getting married.* 他们的长女就要结婚了. **2** [C] (**a**) young, usu unmarried, woman 年轻女子(通常指未婚者): *a girl in her teens or early twenties* 十几岁或二十岁出头的姑娘 ○ *He was eighteen before he started going out with girls.* 他十八岁才开始交女朋友. (**b**) woman of the specified type 某种类型的女人: *She's the new girl in the office, so give her any help she needs.* 她是办公室的新人, 她有什么需要就多帮帮忙. ○ *the old girl who owns the sweet shop* 这家糖果店的女掌柜 ○ *I'm a career girl*, ie I concentrate on my career rather than getting married, etc. 我是事业心强的女人(注重事业而不思结婚等). **3** [C] (usu in compounds 通常用以构成复合词) female worker 女工作人员: *an office-girl, a shop-girl, a telephone-girl, etc.* **4** (man's) girl-friend (男子的)女朋友: *taking his girl home to meet his parents* 带女朋友回家见父母. **5 girls** [pl] (*infml often joc* 口, 常作戏谑语) (used for addressing a group of women of any age, by market-salesman, popular entertainers, etc 市场推销员、受欢迎的演员等用以称呼任何年龄的妇女). **6 the girls** [pl] female friends of any age (任何年龄的)女性朋友: *a night out with the girls* 与女朋友外出的夜晚.

▷ **girl·hood** /'gɜ:lhʊd; 'gɝlhʊd/ *n* [U] state or time of being a girl 少女时期: *She spent her girlhood in Africa.* 她的少女时代是在非洲度过的. ○ [attrib 作定语] *my girlhood ambitions* 我在少女时代的抱负.

girlie (also **girly**) /'gɜ:lɪ; 'gɝlɪ/ *adj* [attrib 作定语] (*often derog* 常作贬义) containing erotic pictures of young women 有年轻女子的色情图片的: *girlie magazines, calendars, etc* 有美女艳照的杂志、日历等.

girl·ish /'gɜ:lɪʃ; 'gɝlɪʃ/ *adj* of, for or like a young girl 女孩子的; 少女的; 为少女的; 少女般的: *girlish games, behaviour, laughter* 女孩子的游戏、举止、笑声. **girl·ishly** /'gɜ:lɪʃlɪ; 'gɝlɪʃlɪ/ *adv*.

□ **girl 'Friday** young woman with a wide range of office duties 办公室中任多种职责的年轻女助理.

'girl-friend *n* female companion, esp a man's regular (and possibly sexual) partner (男子的)女朋友, 情人.

Girl 'Guide (*Brit* also **Guide**, *US* **Girl 'Scout**) member of an organization for girls (equivalent to the Boy Scouts) which aims to develop practical skills, self-reliance and helpfulness 女童子军. Cf 参看 SCOUT 2.

giro /'dʒaɪrəʊ; 'dʒaɪro/ *n* (*pl* **~s**) (*commerce* 商) **1** [U, C] system for transferring money directly from one bank account or post-office account to another (银行或邮局间的)直接转帐制度: *Money has been credited to your account by bank giro.* 钱已由银行直接转帐入你的帐户. ○ *I'll pay by giro*, ie using the giro system. 我用直接转帐支付. ○ *The British Post Office giro system is called the National Giro/Girobank.* 英国邮局直接转帐制度称为全国邮政通汇转帐制. ○ [attrib 作定语] *a (bank) giro credit, payment, transfer, etc* (银行)直接转帐贷项、直接转帐付款、直接转帐 ○ *a giro account*, ie a special account for paying through the giro system 直接转帐帐户 ○ *a giro cheque*, ie for use with a giro account 直接转帐支票. **2** [C] (*Brit*) giro cheque, esp one issued by the government to pay social security benefit 直接转帐支票(尤指政府支付社会保障金的): *My giro hasn't arrived this week.* 我的直接转帐支票这星期还未汇到.

girt *pt, pp* of GIRD.

girth /gɜ:θ; gɝθ/ *n* **1** [U, C] (**a**) distance round sth of approximately cylindrical shape (近似圆柱体的)围长: *a tree 1 metre in girth/with a girth of 1½ metres* 干围1米[1½ 米]的树. (**b**) waist measurement of a person (人的)腰围, 腰身: *His girth is 1½ metres.* 他的腰身为1½米. ○ *a man of enormous girth* 腰围粗大的男子. **2** [C] (*US* **cinch**) leather or cloth band or strap fastened tightly round the body of a horse, etc to keep the saddle in place (马等的)肚带, 腰带.

gist /dʒɪst; dʒɪst/ *n* **the gist** [sing] main point or general meaning (of sth spoken or written) 主旨; 要点; 大意: *get* (ie understand) *the gist of an argument, a conversation, a book* 理解一场辩论、一次谈话、一部书的主旨.

give[1] /gɪv; gɪv/ *v* (*pt* **gave** /geɪv; gev/, *pp* **given** /'gɪvn; 'gɪvən/)

G

▸ CAUSING SOMEBODY OR SOMETHING TO HAVE OR RECEIVE 给予 **1** [Dn·n, Dn·pr] **~ sth to sb** cause sb to receive, hold, have or own sth 给某人某物: *I gave each of the boys an apple.* 我给男孩每人一个苹果. ○ *I gave an apple to each of the boys.* 我给每个男孩一个苹果. ○ *Each of the boys was given an apple.* 给了每个男孩一个苹果. ○ *An apple was given to each of the boys.* 每个男孩都得到一个苹果. ○ *She gave her mother the tickets/gave the tickets to her mother to look after.* 她把票交给母亲保管. ○ *Can I give you* (ie Would you like) *another slice of cake?* 要不要再来一块蛋糕? ○ *She was given a new heart* (ie had a heart transplant) *in an eight-hour operation.* 经八小时的手术给她移植了一颗新的心脏. ○ *He gave the old lady his arm* (ie allowed the old lady to lean on his arm) *as they crossed the road.* 他让老太太挽着他的胳膊过马路. ○ *I've just been given a £2 000 pay rise.* 我刚获得2 000英镑的加薪. **2** (**a**) [Dn·n, Dn·pr] **~ sth to sb** cause sb to have sth as a present 送给某人某礼物: *What are you giving (to) your brother for his birthday?* 你弟弟生日你打算送他什么? ○ *I'm giving all my friends books for Christmas.* 我在圣诞节要向所有的朋友赠书. ○ *Have you given the waiter a tip?* 你给侍者小费了吗? (**b**) [I, Ipr, Tn, Tn·pr] **~ (sth) to sth** contribute (money) to sth, esp a charity 捐赠(钱财)(尤指给慈善事业): *Handicapped children need your help — please give generously.* 残疾儿童需要您的帮助——请慷慨解囊. ○ *Please give generously to famine relief.* 请为饥荒赈款慷慨捐赠. ○ *Many people regularly give money to charity.* 很多人经常为慈善事业捐款. **3** [Dn·n] allow (sb/sth) to have sth 允许(某人[某事物])有某事物: *They gave me a week to make up my mind.* 他们允许我有一周的时间作决定. ○ (*infml* 口) *I give their marriage six months at the very most.* ie I think that it will last only six months. 我认为他们的婚姻顶多能维持半年. ○ *She wishes that she'd been given the chance to go to university.* 她想以前要是有机会上大学就好了. ○ *She wants a job that gives her more responsibility.* 她想得到一份责任更大的工作. ○ *What gives you the right to tell me what to do?* 你有什么权力指使我做事? **4** [Tn·pr, Dn·n] **~ (sb) sth for sth** pay (the specified amount of money) to (sb) in order to have sth 付给(某人)(某钱数)购买某物: *Do you mean to tell me you gave £1 500 for that pile of scrap metal!* 难道说你花了1 500英镑买了那堆破铜烂铁! ○ *How much will you give me for my old car?* 你肯出多少钱买我那辆旧车? **5** [Tn, Dn·n, Dn·pr] **~ sth (to sb)** cause (sb) to have sth; provide or supply (sb) with sth 使(某人)有某事物; 供给或供应(某人)某事物: *The sun gives (us) warmth and light.* 太阳供给我们光和热. ○ *You may be called to give evidence at the trial.* 法庭可能传你去作证. ○ *She gives private lessons to supplement her income.* 她给私人授课以贴补收入. ○ *She gave me a lift as far as the station.* 她让我坐她的车顺便送我到车站. ○ *He gives the impression of not caring a damn.* 他给人的印象是满不在乎. ○ *Could you give me your honest opinion of the book?* 你对这书有何意见可否直率提出? ○ *What gave you the idea that I didn't like you?* 你怎么以为我不喜欢你呢? ○ *They gave the name Roland to their first child.* 他们给自己的第一个孩子起名为罗兰. **6** [Tn, Dn·n, Dn·pr] **~ sth to sb/sth** devote (time, thought, etc) to sb/sth 将(时间、思想等)用于某人[某事物]: *I've given the matter a lot of thought/given a lot of thought to the matter.* 我对这事已反复思考过. ○ *The government should give top priority to rebuilding the inner cities.* 政府应该优先重建城内旧中心区.

▸ CAUSING SOMEBODY TO SUFFER 使遭受 **7** [Dn·n, Dn·pr] **~ sth to sb** cause sb to undergo (the specified punishment, esp a period of time in prison) 使某人承受(某种惩罚, 尤指监禁): *The judge gave him a nine-month suspended sentence.* 法官判处他9个月监禁, 缓期执行. ○ *The headmaster gave the boys a scolding.* 校长训斥了那些男生. **8** [Dn·n, Dn·pr] **~ sth to sb** infect sb with (an illness) 传染给某人(疾病): *You've given me your cold/given your cold to me.* 你把感冒传染给我了.

▸ COMMUNICATING 传达 **9** [Dn·n] (used in the imperative 用于祈使句) offer (sth) to sb as an excuse or explanation 向某人提出(某事)作为借口或解释: *Don't give me that rubbish about having a headache; I know you don't want to go to the party.* 别跟我扯什么头痛来当借口, 我知道你不想赴会. **10** [Dn·n] make (a telephone call) to sb 给某人打(电话): *I'll give you a ring tomorrow.* 明天我给你打电话. **11** [Dn·n] admit the truth of (sth) to sb; grant 向某人承认(某事)属实; 同意: *This government has a good record on inflation, I give you that, but what is it doing about unemployment?* 政府抑制通胀有方, 此话不假, 可是对失业问题又怎么处理呢?

▸ PERFORMING OR PROVIDING 表现、表演或举办 **12** [Tn] perform or present (a play, concert, etc) in public 表演或演出(戏剧、音乐会等): *give a poetry reading, a song recital, etc* 表演诗朗诵、举行独唱会 ○ *How many performances of the play are you giving?* 这剧你们要演多少场? ○ *The play was given its first performance in June 1923.* 这剧于1923年6月首次公演. ○ *The Prime Minister will be giving a press conference tomorrow morning.* 首相明日上午举行记者招待会. **13** [Tn] provide (a meal, party, etc) as a host 作东道主举办(宴会、聚会等): *I'm giving a dinner party next Friday evening; would you like to come?* 下星期五晚上我举行宴会, 您肯赏光吗? **14** [Tn] carry out or perform (an action) 做(某动作): *She gave a shrug of her shoulders.* 她耸了耸肩膀. ○ *He gave a start and woke up suddenly.* 他突然惊醒. **15** [Dn·n] perform (the specified action) on (sb/sth) 对(某人[某物])施(某动作): *give sb a kick, push, shove, etc* 踢某人一脚、推某人一把、挤某人一下 ○ *give sb a punch on the nose* 在某人鼻子上打一拳 ○ *She gave him a kiss.* 她吻了他一下. ○ *Do give your shoes a polish before you go out.* 出门前把皮鞋擦亮.

▸ UTTERING OR DECLARING 出声或宣布 **16** [Tn] utter (the specified sound) 发出(某声音): *give a groan, laugh, sigh, yell, etc* 发出一声呻吟、笑一笑、叹一口气、大喊一声 ○ *He gave a strangled cry and fell to the floor.* 他发出一声受扼的叫喊, 随即倒在地板上. **17** [Dn·n] (used in the imperative 用于祈使句) ask (people) to drink a toast to (sb) 请(大家)为(某人)干杯: *Ladies and gentlemen, I give you his Royal Highness, the Prince of Wales.* 女士们, 先生们, 请为威尔士亲王殿下干杯. **18** [Cn·a] (esp of a referee, an umpire, etc in sport) declare that (sb/sth) is in the specified condition or position (尤指体育运动的裁判等)宣布, 判: *The umpire gave the batsman out (leg before wicket).* 裁判裁定击球员(用腿截球违例)出局.

▸ OTHER MEANINGS 其他意义 **19** [Dn·n] produce (the specified feeling) in (sb) 使(某人)产生(某感觉): *All that heavy lifting has given me a pain in the back.* 我一直抬那些重东西, 现在腰都痛了. ○ *Why don't you go for a walk? It'll give you an appetite for your lunch.* 你怎么不出去散散步? 散散步午饭时就有食欲了. **20** [I] bend or stretch under pressure 在压力下弯曲或伸长: *The branch began to give under his weight.* 他身体的重量把树枝压弯了. ○ (*fig* 比喻) *Unless one side gives, the strike could go on until Christmas.* 除非有一方让步, 否则罢工很可能继续到圣诞节. **21** (combines with a *n* in many fixed expressions, where *give* and the *n* together have the same meaning as a *v* related in form to the *n* 与名词结合构成give + n形式的许多固定词组, 具有与该名词相应的动词同样的词义, 如 *give sb a surprise = surprise sb*): *Let me give you a piece of advice*, ie advise you. 我给你提个建议吧. ○ *Her acting has given pleasure to* (ie pleased) *millions (of people)*. 她的表演给千百万人带来娱乐享受. ○ *The news gave us rather a shock*, ie rather shocked us. 这消息使我们颇为震惊. ○ *I trust that you can give an explanation for* (ie explain) *your extraordinary behaviour?* 我认为你一定能对自己的不寻常行为作出解释吧? ○ *We will give you all the help* (ie help you in every way) *we can.* 我们一定尽力帮助你. (For other similar expressions, see entries for the *ns* 其他类似固定词组见有关名词词条, 如 *give one's approval to sth* ⇨ APPROVAL; *give one's permission* ⇨ PERMISSION.)
22 (idm 习语) **sb doesn't/couldn't give a damn, a hoot, etc (about sb/sth)** (*infml* 口) sb does not care at all (about sb/sth) 某人(对某人[某事物])满不在乎, 无所谓: *He couldn't give a damn whether he passes the exam or not.* 他对考试及格与否满不在乎. **ˌgive and**

ˈ**take** be mutually tolerant and forgiving within a relationship 相互容让: *For a marriage to succeed, both partners must learn to give and take.* 要使婚姻美满, 双方必须懂得互相迁就. ˈ**give it to sb** (*infml* 口) attack, criticize or rebuke sb severely 猛烈攻击、批评或驳斥某人: *The boss will really give it to you if you miss the deadline for the job.* 要是到期完不成工作, 老板就要给你点厉害. **give me sth/sb** (*infml* 口) (used to show that one prefers the thing or person specified to sth/sb mentioned previously 用以表示宁取某事物或某人, 而不取先提及的某事物[某人]): *I can't stand modern music; give me Bach and Mozart every time!* ie I shall always prefer Bach and Mozart. 我受不了现代音乐, 还是喜欢巴赫和莫扎特的作品! **give or take sth** the specified amount, time, etc more or less (数量、时间等)或多或少: *'How long will it take us to get to Oxford?' 'About an hour and a half, give or take a few minutes.'* '到牛津要多久?' '大约一个半小时, 上下差不了几分钟.' **give sb to believe/understand (that)...** (often passive 常用于被动语态); (*fml* 文) cause sb to believe/understand sth 使某人相信[明白]某事物: *I was given to understand that she was ill.* 我获悉她生病了. **What** ˈ**gives?** (*infml* 口) What is happening? 出什么事了? (For other idioms containing **give**, see entries for *ns, adjs*, etc 与 **give** 搭配的其他习语见有关名词、形容词等的词条, 如 **give ground** ⇨ GROUND[1]; **give rise to sth** ⇨ RISE[1].)

23 (phr v) **give sb away** (in a marriage ceremony) lead the bride to the bridegroom and 'give' her to him (婚礼中)将新娘交与新郎: *The bride was given away by her father.* 由父亲把新娘交与新郎. **give sth away** (**a**) give sth free of charge 免费送出某物; 赠送: *He gave away most of his money to charity.* 他把大部分钱都捐赠给慈善事业了. ○ (*infml* 口) *These watches are only a pound each; we're almost giving them away!* 这些手表每块只卖一英镑, 我们差不多等于白送! (**b**) distribute or present sth 分发或赠与某物: *The mayor gave away the prizes at the school sports day.* 市长在学校运动会上颁发奖品. (**c**) not use or take (a chance, an opportunity, etc) through carelessness 由于大意而未利用或抓住(时机、机会等): *They gave away their last chance of winning the match.* 他们坐失赢得比赛的最后机会. **give sth/sb away** reveal sth/sb intentionally or unintentionally; betray sth/sb 有意或无意地泄露某事物或出卖某人: *She gave away state secrets to the enemy.* 她将国家机密泄露给敌人了. ○ *His broad Liverpool accent gave him away*, ie revealed who he really was. 他那很重的利物浦口音把他自己暴露了.

give sb back sth; give sth back (to sb) (**a**) return sth to its owner 将某事物归还原主: *Could you give me back my pen/give me my pen back?* 你把我那枝笔还给我好吗? (**b**) allow sb to have or enjoy sth again 使某人恢复或享受某事物: *The operation gave him back the use of his legs.* 他手术后双腿恢复了功能.

give sth for sth exchange or sacrifice (much) for sth 交换某事物; (多)作出牺牲以换取某事物: *I'd give a lot for the chance to go to India.* 我宁可多作牺牲也要争取到去印度的机会.

give sth forth (*fml or joc* 文或谑) produce or emit sth 产生或发出某物: *The engine gave forth a grinding noise, then stopped.* 发动机发出一阵轧轧声, 随即停了下来.

give sth in hand over sth to sb who is authorized to receive it 将某事物呈交给某人: *Please give your examination papers in (to the teacher) when you've finished.* 考卷答完后请上交(给老师). **give** ˈ**in (to sb/sth)** allow oneself to be defeated or overcome (by sb/sth) (向某人[某事物])屈服, 让步, 投降: *The rebels were forced to give in.* 叛乱者被迫投降. ○ *She's a gutsy player, she never gives in.* 她是个勇敢的选手, 从不屈服. ○ *The authorities showed no signs of giving in to the kidnapper's demands.* 当局对绑架者的要求丝毫没有让步的迹象.

give sth off send out or emit sth 送出或发出某物: *The cooker is giving off a funny smell.* 锅里冒出一股怪味. ○ *This fire doesn't seem to be giving off much heat.* 这炉火好像不大热.

give on to sth have a view of sth; lead directly to sth 有某物的景致; 朝向某物: *The bedroom windows give on to the street.* 卧室的窗户面向街道. ○ *This door gives on to the hall.* 这门是通往大堂的.

give ˈ**out** (**a**) come to an end; be exhausted 用完; 消耗尽; 精疲力竭: *After a month their food supplies gave out.* 过了一个月, 他们的食物已消耗殆尽. ○ *Her patience finally gave out.* 她终于失去了耐性. (**b**) (of an engine, a motor, etc) stop working; break down (指发动机等)停止运转, 停机, 出故障: *One of the plane's engines gave out in mid-Atlantic.* 飞机在大西洋中部飞行时, 其中一个发动机出了故障. **give sth out** (**a**) distribute or hand out sth 分发或散发某物: *The teacher gave out the examination papers.* 教师发了考卷. (**b**) send out or emit sth 送出或发出某物: *The radiator is giving out a lot of heat.* 散热器释放出很多热量. (**c**) (often passive 常用于被动语态) announce or broadcast sth 宣布或广播某事: *The news of the President's death was given out in a radio broadcast.* 总统逝世的消息已在电台上播出了. ○ *It was given out that the President had been shot.* 据称总统受到枪击.

give over (doing sth) (*infml* 口) (used esp in the imperative or with a verb in the *-ing* form 尤用于祈使句或与动词ing形式连用) stop doing sth 停止做某事: *Give over, can't you? I can't work with you chattering away like that.* 到此为止吧, 行吗? 你这样聊下去我就没法工作了. ○ *Give over complaining!* 别发牢骚了! **give oneself over to sth** sink into (the specified state); devote oneself completely to sth 沉溺于(某种状态); 完全献身于某事物: *After his wife's death, he seemed to give himself over to despair.* 他妻子死后, 似乎万念俱灰. ○ *In her later years she gave herself over to writing full-time.* 她晚年专事写作. **give sth over to sth** (usu passive 通常用于被动语态) use sth specifically for sth 专为某事而使用某物: *The village hall is given over to civic functions and meetings.* 村子的礼堂专作举行庆典和会议之用. ○ *The period after supper was given over to games.* 晚饭后是游戏时间.

give ˈ**up** abandon an attempt to do sth 放弃做某事的尝试: *They gave up without a fight.* 他们不战而降. ○ *She doesn't give up easily.* 她做任何事都不轻易放弃. ○ *I give up; tell me what the answer is.* 我认输, 告诉我答案吧. **give sb up** (**a**) no longer hope for or expect the arrival or recovery of sb 对某人的到来、康复或寻回不再抱希望或不再期待: *There you are at last! We'd given you up.* 你终于来了! 我们还以为你不来呢! ○ *The doctors had given her up but she made a remarkable recovery.* 医生们已放弃了治愈她的希望, 而她却恢复得很好. (**b**) stop having a relationship with sb 与某人断绝关系: *Why don't you give him up?* 你怎么不和他一刀两断呢? **give sth up** stop doing or having sth; renounce sth 停止做某事; 放弃持有某物; 宣布放弃某事物: *You ought to give up smoking; I gave it up last year.* 你应该戒烟, 我去年就戒掉了. ○ *She didn't give up her job when she got married.* 她未因结婚而放弃工作. **give oneself/sb up (to sb)** no longer avoid or protect oneself/sb from being captured; surrender 投案; 自首; 出首; 投降: *After a week on the run he gave himself up (to the police).* 他经过一周的逃亡以后(向警方)投案了. **give sth up (to sb)** hand sth over to sb else 将某物交与他人: *He had to give his passport up to the authorities.* 他得把护照交给当局. ○ *He gave up his seat to a pregnant woman*, ie stood up to allow her to sit down. 他把座位让给一个孕妇. **give up on sb** (*infml* 口) no longer believe that sb is going to be successful; lose hope in sb 不再相信某人会成功; 对某人失望.

□ ˈ**give-away** *n* (*infml* 口) **1** thing that is given to sb without charge 赠品. **2** look, remark, etc that unintentionally reveals a secret 无意中泄露秘密的表情、言语等: *The expression on her face was a (dead) give-away.* 她脸上的表情(完全)暴露了她的秘密.

give[2] /gɪv; gɪv/ *n* **1** [U] quality of bending or stretching under pressure; elasticity 延展性; 弹性; 弹力: *This rope has too much give in it.* 这条绳子弹性太大. ○ *Don't worry if the shoes seem a bit tight at first; the leather has plenty of give in it.* 这鞋刚穿时要是有点紧没关系, 这种皮子很有延展性. **2** (idm 习语) ˌ**give and** ˈ**take** (**a**) willingness to be mutually tolerant and forgiving within a relationship 互相忍让; 互相迁就: *If the dispute is to be resolved there must be some give and take.* 若要争执获得解决, 双方就要互相让步. ○ [attrib 作定语] *Marriage is a give-and-take affair.* 婚姻是互谅互让的事.

G

(**b**) exchange 交换: *the lively give and take of ideas*, ie willingness to make concessions or compromises 活跃的思想交流(乐于迁就或妥协).

given /ˈgɪvn; ˋgɪvən/ *adj* **1** [esp attrib 尤作定语] specified or stated 所述的; 确定的; 规定的: *all the people in a given area* 某地区内所有的人 ○ *They were to meet at a given time and place.* 他们要在规定的时间和地点会晤. **2** (idm 习语) **be given to sth/doing sth** be in the habit of doing sth 有做某事的习惯: *She's much given to outbursts of temper.* 她老爱发脾气. ○ *He's given to going for long walks on his own.* 他习惯于独自散步走很长的路.

▷ **given** *prep* taking (sth) into account 考虑到(某事物): *Given the government's record on unemployment, their chances of winning the election look poor.* 鉴于政府在解决失业问题上成绩不佳, 他们在选举中获胜机会似乎不大. ○ *Given her interest in children/Given that she is interested in children, I am sure teaching is the right career for her.* 考虑到她喜欢孩子, 我可以肯定教书是最适合她的职业.

□ **ˈgiven name** (*esp US*) = CHRISTIAN NAME (CHRISTIAN). ⇨Usage at NAME[1] 用法见 NAME[1].

giver /ˈgɪvə(r); ˋgɪvɚ/ *n* one who gives 给与者; 施赠者: *a cheerful, generous, regular giver* 快乐的、慷慨的、经常性的捐赠者.

giz·zard /ˈgɪzəd; ˋgɪzɚd/ *n* **1** pouchlike part in which a bird grinds up food before digesting it in its stomach (鸟的)砂囊, 胗. **2** (idm 习语) **stick in one's craw/gizzard/throat** ⇨ STICK[2].

glacé /ˈglæseɪ; *US* glæˈseɪ; glæˋse/ *adj* [attrib 作定语] (of fruits) preserved in sugar (指水果)糖渍的, 蜜饯的.

gla·cial /ˈgleɪsɪəl; *US* ˈgleɪʃl; ˋgleʃəl/ *adj* **1** (*geology* 地质) (**a**) of the Ice Age 冰期的; 冰川期的; 冰河时代的; 冰河期的: *the glacial era/epoch/period*, ie the time when much of the northern hemisphere was covered by ice 冰期(亦称'冰川期'、'冰河时代'或'冰河期'). (**b**) caused by glaciers 冰川造成的: *glacial deposits*, ie rocks deposited by a moving glacier 冰川沉积 ○ *glacial flow*, ie movement of a glacier 冰川运动. **2** very cold; like ice 寒冷的; 冰冷的: *glacial winds, temperatures, etc* 寒风、低温 ○ *the glacial waters of the Arctic* 北极寒冷的水域. **3** (*fig* 比喻) icy in manner; showing no sign of human emotion 冷若冰霜的; 不流露情感的: *a glacial smile, manner, silence* 冷冷的微笑、举止、沉默 ○ *glacial indifference, politeness* 冷漠、冷淡的礼貌. ▷ **gla·ci·ally** *adv*.

G

gla·ci·ation /ˌgleɪsɪˈeɪʃn; ˌglesɪˋeʃən/ *n* [U] (*geology* 地质) covering with glaciers or sheets of ice 冰蚀: *the effects of glaciation* 冰川作用.

gla·cier /ˈglæsɪə(r); ˋgleʃɚ/ *n* mass of ice, formed by snow on mountains, moving slowly down a valley 冰川; 冰河.

glad /glæd; glæd/ *adj* (**-dder**, **-ddest**) **1** [pred 作表语] (**a**) **~ (about sth/to do sth/that...)** pleased; delighted 高兴; 喜悦: *'I passed the test.' 'I'm so glad!'* '我考试及格了.''我真高兴!' ○ *I'm glad about your passing the test.* 你考及格了, 我很高兴. ○ *I'm glad to hear he's feeling better.* 听说他身体好些了, 我很高兴. ○ *I'm glad he's feeling better.* 他身体好些了, 我很高兴. (**b**) **~ (about/of sth); ~ (to do sth/that...)** relieved 令人宽慰; 使人安心: *I'm so glad I didn't agree to do it; it would have got me into serious trouble.* 幸而我没同意做那事, 要不然惹的麻烦就大了. (**c**) **~ of sth** grateful for sth 为某事而感激: *I'd be glad of* (ie I'd like) *your help/a cup of tea.* 你若能帮忙[给我一杯茶]本人十分感激. (**d**) **~ to do sth** willing and eager to do sth 愿意并热切要做某事: *I'd be glad to lend you the money.* 我很乐意借给你钱. ○ *If you'd like me to help you, I'd be only too glad to.* 若要我帮忙, 我十分乐意相助. **2** [attrib 作定语] (**a**) causing or bringing joy 令人高兴的; 给人带来喜悦的: *glad news/tidings* 好消息[喜讯] ○ *a glad day, moment, etc* 令人高兴的日子、时刻等. (**b**) (*rhet* 修辞) expressing joy 快乐的; 欣喜的: *the children's glad laughter* 儿童们快乐的笑声. **3** (idm 习语) **I would be glad if...** (*ironic* 反语) (used instead of a direct command 用作间接命令): *I'd be glad if you would go away!* ie Go away! 你要是能走开, 我感激不尽. **ˈglad rags** (*infml* 口) clothes for a festive occasion 庆祝场合穿的衣服: *put on one's glad rags* 穿上节日盛装.

▷ **glad·den** /ˈglædn; ˋglædn̩/ *v* [Tn] make (sb) glad or happy 使(某人)高兴或快乐: *gladden sb's heart*, ie make sb feel happy 使某人心花怒放.

gladly *adv* **1** happily; gratefully 快乐地; 欣然: *She suggested it, and I gladly accepted.* 那是她提出的建议, 我欣然接受了. **2** willingly 乐意地; 情愿地: *I wouldn't gladly go through that unpleasant experience again.* 我再也不愿领教那种令人不快的经历. **3** (idm 习语) **not/never suffer fools gladly** ⇨ SUFFER.

glad·ness *n* [U] joy; happiness 高兴; 快乐; 欢乐.

glad·some /-səm; -səm/ *adj* (*arch* 古) joyful 高兴的; 快乐的.

□ **ˌglad-ˈhand** *v* [Tn] (*infml often derog* 口, 常作贬义) greet (sb) enthusiastically but often insincerely 热情欢迎(某人)(但常为假意).

glade /gleɪd; gled/ *n* open space in a forest; clearing 森林中的空地.

gla·di·ator /ˈglædɪeɪtə(r); ˋglædɪˌetɚ/ *n* (in ancient Rome) man trained to fight with weapons at public shows in an arena (古罗马)(在竞技场用武器作打斗表演的)斗士.

▷ **gla·di·at·or·ial** /ˌglædɪəˈtɔːrɪəl; ˌglædɪəˋtɔrɪəl/ *adj* of gladiators 斗士的: *a gladiatorial combat, show, etc* 斗士的格斗、表演等.

gla·di·olus /ˌglædɪˈəʊləs; ˌglædɪˋoləs/ *n* (*pl* **-li** /-laɪ; -laɪ/ or **~es**) plant with long thin pointed leaves and spikes of brightly-coloured flowers 唐菖蒲属植物(叶长而尖, 花朵鲜艳).

glam·our (*US* also **glamor**) /ˈglæmə(r); ˋglæmɚ/ *n* [U] **1** attractive or exciting quality which sb/sth has, and which seems out of reach to others (某人[某事物]独特的)魅力, 吸引力: *Now that she's an air hostess, foreign travel has lost its glamour for her.* 她当上了空中小姐, 到国外旅行对她已失去吸引力. ○ *hopeful young actors and actresses dazzled by the glamour of Hollywood* 在好莱坞电影业光怪陆离的诱惑之下有前途的年轻演员. **2** attractive beauty, usu with sex appeal 迷人的美(通常指性感的): *a girl with lots of glamour* 性感迷人的女郎 ○ [attrib 作定语] (*dated* 旧) *a glamour girl/boy* 迷人的女郎[小伙子].

gla·mor·ize, -ise /-məraɪz; -məraɪz/ *v* [Tn] make (sth) seem more attractive or exciting than it really is 使(某事物)比其实际更吸引人或更激动人心: *Television tends to glamorize acts of violence.* 电视往往渲染暴力. **glam·or·iza·tion, -isation** /ˌglæməraɪˈzeɪʃn; *US* -rɪˈz-; ˌglæmərɪˋzeʃən/ *n* [U].

▷ **glam·or·ous** /-mərəs; -mərəs/ *adj* full of glamour 富有魅力的; 美丽动人的: *glamorous film stars* 富有魅力的影星. **glam·or·ously** *adv*: *glamorously dressed* 穿着美丽动人.

glance /glɑːns; *US* glæns; glæns/ *v* **1** [Ipr] take a quick look 瞥一眼; 看一下: *She glanced shyly at him and then lowered her eyes.* 她羞怯地偷看了他一下, 随即垂下眼帘. ○ *glance at one's watch* 看一下手表 ○ *glance round a room* 环视一下房间 ○ *I glanced up to see who had come in.* 我抬头瞥了一眼看是谁进来了. **2** [Ipr] **~ at/down/over/through sth** read sth quickly or superficially 迅速地或草草地读: *glance at the newspapers* 浏览报纸 ○ *glance down a list of names* 匆匆看一名单 ○ *glance over/through a letter* 草草读一信. **3** [Ipr] **~ at sth** (*fig* 比喻) deal with sth in a superficial way; refer briefly to sth 草草处理某事; 简略提及某事: *a book, an article, etc that only glances at a problem, question, topic, etc* 仅仅简略提及某问题、疑难、题目等的书、文章等. **4** [Tn, Tn·pr] (in cricket) deflect (the ball) with the bat (板球中)将(球)击偏: *glance the ball down to fine leg* 将球击偏斜飞至击球员左后方场地. **5** [I] (used esp in the continuous tenses 尤用于进行时态) (of bright objects) flash (指光亮物体)闪烁, 闪耀: *glancing lights* 闪烁的灯光 ○ *water glancing in the sunlight* 在阳光下闪闪生光的水面. **6** (idm 习语) **glance one's eye down/over/through sth** (*infml* 口) take a very quick, superficial look at sth 匆匆或草草看某物一眼: *glance one's eye over the newspaper* 浏览一下报纸. **7** (phr v) **glance off (sth)** (of sth that strikes) be deflected off (sth) (指击打之物)被弹离(某物): *The ball glanced off the goal post into the net.* 球撞到球门柱上斜飞入网. ○ *The tree was so hard that the blows of the axe simply glanced off.* 那树硬得劈不动, 简直把斧子震得滑向一边.

▷ **glance** *n* **1 ~ (at sb/sth)** quick look 一瞥: *take/have/cast a glance at the newspaper headlines* 看一眼[浏览/瞥一眼]报纸的大标题 ○ *We exchanged glances*, ie looked quickly at each other. 我们迅速地互相打量了一下. ○ *a brief, casual, fleeting, furtive, timid glance* 短促的、不经意的、一闪即逝的、偷偷的、怯生生的一瞥 ○ *She walked off without a glance in my direction.* 她扬长而去, 都不朝我这儿看一眼. ○ (*fig* 比喻) *Before the end of the programme, let's take a glance at* (ie refer briefly to) *the sports news.* 在节目结束之前, 让我们简要谈谈体育新闻. **2** (idm 习语) **at a (single) 'glance** with one look 看一眼: *He could tell at a glance what was wrong with the car.* 他一眼就能看出汽车有什么毛病. **at first glance/sight** when seen or examined (often quickly) for the first time 乍看之下: *At first glance the problem seemed easy.* 乍一看问题似乎很容易解决. ○ *They fell in love at first sight.* 他们一见钟情.

glan·cing /ˈglɑːnsɪŋ; ˋglænsɪŋ/ *adj* [attrib 作定语] that is deflected rather than striking with full force (未正面击中)偏斜的: *strike sb a glancing blow* 给某人一击而打偏.

gland /glænd; glænd/ *n* (*anatomy* 解) organ that separates from the blood those substances that are to be used by or removed from the body 腺: *a snake's poison glands* 蛇的毒腺 ○ *sweat glands* 汗腺 ○ *suffer from swollen glands*, eg the salivary glands in the throat 患腺体肿胀(如咽部的唾液腺) ○ *have an overactive/underactive adrenal, pituitary, thyroid, etc gland* 肾上腺、垂体腺、甲状腺等机能亢进[减退].

▷ **glandu·lar** /ˈglændjʊlə(r); *US* -dʒʊ-; ˋglændʒələ˞/ *adj* of, like or involving a gland or glands 腺的; 似腺的; 与腺有关的. **glandular fever** infectious disease causing swelling of the lymph glands 腺热.

glare[1] /gleə(r); glɛr/ *n* **1** [U] strong unpleasant dazzling light 耀眼的光: *avoid the glare of the sun, of car headlights, etc* 避开耀眼的阳光、汽车前灯的强光. **2** [C] angry or fierce look; fixed look 怒视; 恶狠狠的注视; 凝视: *give sb a hostile glare* 含敌意地注视某人. **3** (idm 习语) **the ˌglare of puˈblicity** constant attention from newspapers, television, etc 经常在报纸、电视等上报道的; 受公众注目: *The hearings were conducted in the full glare of publicity.* 那审讯是在公众密切关注下进行的.

glare[2] /gleə(r); glɛr/ *v* **1** [I, Ipr, Ip] **~ (down)** shine with a dazzling, unpleasant light 发出眩目而令人不快的强光: *The searchlights glared, illuminating the prison yard.* 探照灯发出强光, 照亮监狱场地. ○ *the sun glaring (down) mercilessly from a clear sky* 透过晴空太阳正毒. **2** [I, Ipr] **~ (at sb/sth)** stare angrily or fiercely 怒目而视; 恶狠狠地盯视: *He didn't shout or swear, but just glared silently at me.* 他不喊不骂, 只是默默地怒视着我. **3** (idm 习语) **glare defiance at sb/sth** stare at sb/sth with angry defiance 愤怒而轻蔑地瞪着某人[某物].

▷ **glar·ing** /ˈgleərɪŋ; glɛrɪŋ/ *adj* **1** dazzling 令人目眩的: *glaring lights* 耀眼的灯光. **2** angry; fierce 生气的; 凶狠的: *glaring eyes* 怒目. **3** [usu attrib 通常作定语] (*fig* 比喻) that cannot or should not be ignored; gross 不能或不应忽视的; 明显的: *a glaring abuse, error, injustice, omission* 明显的滥用、错误、不公、疏漏. **glar·ingly** *adv*.

glasnost /ˈglæznɒst; ˋglæznɑst/ *n* [U] (*Russian* 俄) (in the former Soviet Union) greater openness and frankness in public affairs (前苏联)(在公众事务上较大的)公开, 开放.

glass 玻璃杯

glass /glɑːs; *US* glæs; glæs/ *n* **1** [U] hard brittle, usu transparent, substance (as used in windows) 玻璃: *cut oneself on broken glass* 让碎玻璃割伤 ○ *reinforced, toughened, frosted glass* 强化、韧化、磨砂玻璃 ○ *a sheet/pane of glass* 一块[面]玻璃 ○ *as smooth as glass* 如玻璃般平滑 ○ [attrib 作定语] *glass jars*, ie made of glass 广口玻璃瓶 ○ *a glass factory*, ie where glass is made 玻璃制造厂. **2** [C] (**a**) (often in compounds 常用以构成复合词) drinking vessel made of glass 玻璃杯: *a beer, brandy, sherry, whisky, etc glass* 啤酒、白兰地酒、雪利酒、威士忌酒等的酒杯 ○ *a wineglass* 葡萄酒杯. ⇨illus 见插图. (**b**) contents of this 玻璃杯中所盛之物: *Could I have a glass of water, please?* 请给我来杯水, 可以吗? **3** [U] vessels and articles made of glass 玻璃器皿: *All our glass and china is kept in the cupboard.* 我们所有的玻璃和陶瓷器皿都放在柜橱里. ○ *several areas under glass*, ie covered with glasshouses or glass-filled frames for growing plants 玻璃温室里的几处地方. **4** [sing] protecting cover made of glass in a watch-case, picture or photo frame, fire alarm, etc 玻璃保护面(如表蒙子、图画或照片的镜框、火灾警报器的保护罩等): *In case of emergency, break the glass and press the button.* 遇到紧急情况时, 击碎玻璃罩并揿下按钮. **5 glasses** (also **spectacles**, *infml* 口语亦作 **specs**) [pl] pair of lenses in a frame that rests on the nose and ears (used to help a person's eyesight or protect the eyes from bright sunlight) 眼镜: *She wears glasses.* 她戴眼镜. ○ *a new pair of glasses* 一副新眼镜 ○ *dark, strong, reading, long-distance, etc glasses* 墨镜、度数大的眼镜、花镜、近视镜 ○ [attrib 作定语] *Where's my glasses case?* 我的眼镜盒在哪儿呢? ⇨illus 见插图. **6 glasses** (also **'field-glasses**) [pl] binoculars for outdoor use (户外用的双筒的)望远镜. **7** [C usu *sing* 通常作单数] mirror; looking-glass 镜子: *He looked in the glass to check that his tie was straight.* 他对着镜子看领带是否系正. **8 the glass** [sing] barometer 气压计; 晴雨表: *The glass* (ie atmospheric pressure) *is falling.* 气压在下降. **9** (idm 习语) **raise one's glass to sb** ⇨ RAISE.

GLASSES (*also* SPECTACLES) 眼镜

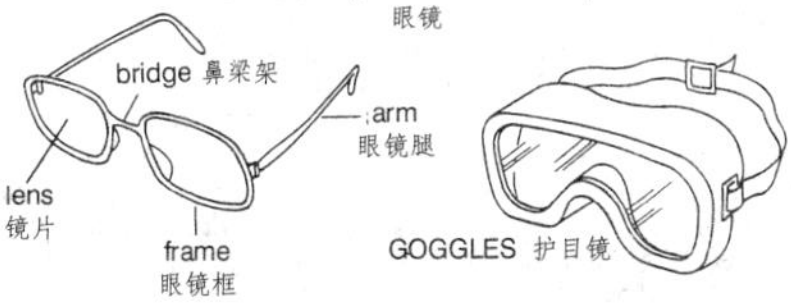

▷ **glass** *v* (phr v) **glass sth in/over** cover sth with (a roof or wall of) glass 给某物加玻璃(的罩、顶或壁): *a glassed-in veranda* 镶玻璃的阳台.

glass·ful /-fʊl; -ˌfʊl/ *n* as much as a drinking-glass will hold 一玻璃杯的量.

□ **'glass-blower** *n* worker who blows molten glass to shape it into bottles, etc 玻璃吹制工.

glass 'fibre = FIBREGLASS.

'glasshouse *n* **1** (**a**) building with glass sides and roof, for growing plants; greenhouse 温室. (**b**) (*Brit infml* 口) military prison 军人监狱. **2** (idm 习语) **people in glasshouses shouldn't throw stones** ⇨ PEOPLE.

'glassware /-weə(r); -ˌwɛr/ *n* [U] articles made of glass 玻璃制品; 玻璃器皿.

'glassworks *n* (*pl* unchanged 复数不变) [sing or pl *v*] factory where glass is manufactured 玻璃制造厂.

glassy /ˈglɑːsɪ; ˋglæsɪ/ *adj* (**-ier, -iest**) **1** like glass 像玻璃的: *a glassy sea*, ie smooth and shiny 光滑如镜的海面 ○ *Be careful of the icy pavement; it's really glassy*, ie slippery. 小心人行道上有冰, 路面可真滑. **2** (*fig* 比喻) with no expression; lifeless 无表情的; 无生气的: *glassy eyes* 神情呆滞的眼睛 ○ *a glassy look/stare* 木然的样子[呆视]. ▷ **glass·ily** *adv*. **glass·iness** *n* [U].

□ **ˌglassy-'eyed** *adj*: *a ˌglassy-eyed 'look, 'stare, etc* 眼神呆滞的样子、凝视等.

glauc·oma /glɔːˈkəʊmə; glɔˋkomə/ *n* [U] eye disease causing gradual loss of sight 青光眼; 绿内障.

glaze /gleɪz; glez/ *v* **1** [Tn] fit sheets or panes of glass into (sth) 装玻璃于(某物); 给(某物)镶嵌玻璃: *glaze a*

G

window, house, etc 给窗户、房子等安装玻璃. **2** [Tn, Tn·pr, Tn·p] **~ sth (with sth)**; **~ sth (over)** cover sth with a thin shiny transparent surface 给某物覆上薄而亮的透明表面: *glazed pottery, porcelain, bricks, etc*, ie covered with a liquid which when baked gives a hard glass-like surface 上釉的陶器、瓷器、砖等 ○ *Glaze the pie with beaten egg.* 在馅饼上涂上打匀的蛋液使表面发亮. **3** (phr v) **glaze over** (of the eyes) become dull and lifeless (指眼睛)变呆滞, 变得无生气: *After six glasses of vodka his eyes glazed over and he remembered nothing more.* 他喝了六杯伏特加之后, 眼神发呆, 什么都再也记不住了.

▷ **glaze** *n* [C, U] (**a**) (substances used to give a) thin shiny transparent surface to pottery, porcelain, etc 釉: *The vase was sold cheaply because of a fault in the glaze.* 那花瓶因釉面有残已廉价售出. (**b**) (beaten egg, sugar, etc used to give a) shiny attractive surface to a pie, flan, etc (在馅饼等上面涂的)蛋液、糖液等或(因而生成的)光面.

glazed *adj* dull and lifeless, esp with expressionless eyes 呆滞无神的; (尤指)无眼神的: *the glazed faces/expressions of the survivors* 生还者木然呆滞的面孔[表情] ○ *eyes glazed with boredom* 厌倦无神的眼睛.

glaz·ier /ˈɡleɪzɪə(r); *US* -ʒər; ˋɡleʒɚ/ *n* person who fits glass into the frames of windows, etc 装玻璃的工人.

GLC /ˌdʒiː el ˈsiː; ˌdʒi ɛl ˋsi/ *abbr* 缩写 = (*Brit*) (formerly) Greater London Council (旧时)大伦敦市政会.

gleam /ɡliːm; ɡlim/ *n* **1** (**a**) [C] brief appearance of light 闪光: *A few faint gleams of sunshine lit up the gloomy afternoon.* 有几束隐约的阳光使阴暗的下午有些明亮. ○ *the sudden gleam of a match in the darkness* 黑暗中突然出现擦亮火柴的闪光. (**b**) [sing] soft diffused light, usu reflected 柔弱散漫的光; (通常指)反光: *the gleam of moonlight on the water* 水面上泛漾的月光 ○ *the gleam of polished brassware in the firelight* 因炉火的光照在擦亮的铜器上而产生的反光. **2** [sing] (*fig* 比喻) brief show of some quality or emotion (某种品质或情感的)闪现, 表露: *a serious book with an occasional gleam of humour* 偶有幽默片段的严肃的书 ○ *a gleam of hope in an apparently hopeless situation* 在看来绝望时闪现的一线希望 ○ *a man with a dangerous gleam in his eye*, ie with a threatening look 眼露凶光的男子. **3** (idm 习语) **a gleam in sb's eye** (*infml* 口) person or thing that is expected at some time in the future but is thought about with pleasure or desire 令人向往的人或事物: *The plans for the new town hall were then still only a gleam in the architect's eye.* 当时有关新市政大厅的计划还仅仅是那建筑师酝酿中的意念.

▷ **gleam** *v* **1** [I, Ipr] shine softly 发出柔和的光: *He had polished the table-top until it gleamed.* 他把桌面擦得很亮. ○ *moonlight gleaming on the water* 在水面上泛漾的月光 ○ *water gleaming in the moonlight* 在月光下反射微光的水面 ○ *a cat's eyes gleaming in the dark* 在黑暗中闪烁的猫眼 ○ (*fig* 比喻) *anticipation, excitement, etc gleaming in their eyes* 在他们眼睛里流露着期待、激动等的神情. **2** [Ipr] **~ with sth** (*fig* 比喻) (of the face or eyes) show the specified emotion (指面部或眼睛)表露某种情感: *eyes gleaming with anticipation, excitement, etc* 流露着期待、激动等神情的眼睛. **gleam·ing** /ɡliːmɪŋ; ɡlimɪŋ/ *adj*: *gleaming white teeth* 晶莹皓齿.

glean /ɡliːn; ɡlin/ *v* **1** [I, Tn] gather (grain left in a field by harvest workers) 拾(收割者落在地里的谷物). **2** [Tn, Tn·pr, Tf] **~ sth (from sb/sth)** (*fig* 比喻) obtain (news, facts, information, etc) usu from various sources, in small quantities and with effort 搜集(消息、资料、情报等)(通常指来源广、零碎而费力): *glean a few bits of information from overhearing various conversations* 从旁边听到的谈话中搜集点滴信息 ○ *From what people said, I managed to glean that he wasn't coming.* 我从别人说话中总算弄清楚他不来了.

▷ **gleaner** *n* person who gleans 拾谷人; 搜集消息、资料、情报等的人.

glean·ings *n* [pl] (*usu fig* 通常作比喻) gleaned items 收集到的零星事物: *a gossip column put together with a few gleanings from cocktail-party conversations* 鸡尾酒会闲话拾零专栏.

glee /ɡliː; ɡli/ *n* **1** [U] **~ (at sth)** feeling of great delight which makes one (want to) laugh, caused by sth good experienced by oneself, or sth bad that happens to sb else 欣喜; 幸灾乐祸: *The children laughed with glee at the clown's antics.* 孩子们让小丑的滑稽动作逗得哈哈大笑. ○ *He rubbed his hands with glee at the prospect of their defeat.* 他眼看着他们行将失败, 快乐得直搓手. ○ *She couldn't disguise her glee at their discomfiture.* 他们受挫, 她不禁喜形于色. **2** [C] song for three or four voices singing different parts in harmony (三部或四部的)重唱歌曲: [attrib 作定语] *a glee club*, ie a group of people who sing such songs 合唱团.

▷ **glee·ful** /-fl; -fəl/ *adj* full of glee; joyous 欣喜的; 快乐的; 欢喜的: *gleeful faces, laughter* 快乐的面孔、笑声. **glee·fully** /-fəlɪ; -fəlɪ/ *adv*.

glen /ɡlen; ɡlɛn/ *n* narrow valley, esp in Scotland or Ireland 狭谷, 幽谷(尤指苏格兰或爱尔兰的).

glib /ɡlɪb; ɡlɪb/ *adj* (**-bber, -bbest**) (*derog* 贬) speaking or spoken fluently and without hesitation, but not sincerely or trustworthily 能说会道的; 油嘴滑舌的: *a glib talker, salesman, etc* 油嘴滑舌的谈话者、推销员等 ○ *a glib remark, speech, etc* 八面锋的言语、演说等 ○ *glib arguments, excuses, etc* 诡辩的论据、借口等 ○ *have a glib tongue* 有巧舌如簧的嘴. ▷ **glibly** *adv*. **glib·ness** *n* [U].

glide /ɡlaɪd; ɡlaɪd/ *v* [I, Ipr, Ip] **1** move along smoothly and continuously 滑行; 滑动; 滑翔: *So graceful was the ballerina that she just seemed to glide.* 那芭蕾舞女演员翩跹起舞, 宛如滑翔. ○ *skiers gliding across the snow* 穿越雪地滑行的滑雪人 ○ *a snake gliding along the ground* 在地上蜿蜒滑行的蛇 ○ *Silently the boat glided past.* 那船悄然滑行而过. ○ *She glided by unnoticed.* 她悄悄地溜过. ○ (*fig* 比喻) *The days just glided by.* 时光悄悄地流逝. **2** fly without engine power (either in a glider or in an aeroplane with engine failure) (滑翔机或飞机发动机有故障时)滑行, 滑翔: *The pilot managed to glide down to a safe landing.* 驾驶员设法使飞机滑行下降安全着陆.

▷ **glide** *n* (**a**) [sing] gliding movement 滑行; 滑动; 滑翔: *the graceful glide of a skater* 滑冰者优美的滑行动作. (**b**) [C] (*phonetics* 语音) gradual change of a speech sound made by moving (esp) the tongue from one position to another 音渡; 过渡音: *a palatal glide* 颚音的音渡.

glider /ˈɡlaɪdə(r); ˋɡlaɪdɚ/ *n* light aircraft that is used for gliding 滑翔机.

glid·ing *n* [U] sport of flying in gliders 滑翔运动. Cf 参看 HANG-GLIDING (HANG).

glim·mer /ˈɡlɪmə(r); ˋɡlɪmɚ/ *v* [I] send out a weak unsteady light 发出微弱的闪光: *lights (faintly) glimmering in the distance* 远方明灭不定的(微弱)灯光.

▷ **glim·mer** *n* **1** weak faint unsteady light 微弱的闪光: *a glimmer of light through the mist* 透过薄雾隐约闪现的微光. **2** (*fig* 比喻) small sign (of sth) (某事物的)隐约的迹象: *a glimmer of hope* 一线希望 ○ *not the least glimmer of intelligence* 一点智慧也没有.

glim·mer·ing /ˈɡlɪmərɪŋ; ˋɡlɪmərɪŋ/ *n* glimmer 微光; 迹象: *We begin to see the glimmerings of a solution to the problem.* 我们开始看到问题可望解决的迹象.

glimpse /ɡlɪmps; ɡlɪmps/ *n* **1** (usu *sing* 通常作单数) **~ (at sth)** short look 一瞥; 一看: *a quick glimpse at the newspaper headlines* 对报纸大标题匆匆的看一遍 ○ *One glimpse at himself in the mirror was enough.* 让他照着镜子瞧上自己一眼就够了. **2** (idm 习语) **catch sight/a glimpse of sb/sth** ⇨ CATCH[1].

▷ **glimpse** *v* [Tn] get a quick look at (sb/sth) 匆匆看一下(某人[某物]): *glimpse someone between the half-drawn curtains* 从半掩的窗帘夹缝中瞥见某人.

glint /ɡlɪnt; ɡlɪnt/ *v* [I] **1** give out small, bright flashes of light 闪闪发光: *She thought the diamond was lost until she saw something glinting on the carpet.* 她以为那颗钻石已丢失, 后来看见地毯上有东西闪闪发光遂失而复得. **2** (of sb's eyes) sparkle and indicate a particular emotion (指某人的眼睛)闪现某种神色: *eyes glinting with mischief* 流露出调皮神色的眼睛.

▷ **glint** *n* **1** flash of light, esp as reflected from a hard shiny surface 光泽; (尤指光亮硬物的)反光: *His eye caught the glint of a revolver among the bushes.* 他一眼看到灌木丛中有手枪的反光. **2** sparkle in sb's eye indicating a particular emotion (眼神里某种情感的)闪露, 闪现: *a glint of anger* 愤怒的目光 ○ *He had a wicked glint in his eye*, ie suggesting mischievousness. 他的眼里

G

闪现着调皮的神情. ○ *before you were a glint in your father's eye*, ie before you were conceived 还没有你的时候(你还未成胎儿时).

gliss·ade /glɪˈseɪd; *US* -ˈsɑ:d; glɪˋsad/ *v* [I, Ipr, Ip] **1** (in mountaineering) slide on the feet down a steep slope of ice or snow (usu with the support of an ice-axe) (登山运动中)从覆有冰雪的陡坡上滑下(通常用破冰斧支撑). **2** (in ballet) make a sliding step (芭蕾舞中)作滑步动作.
▷ **gliss·ade** *n* such a slide or step 滑步.

glis·sando /glɪˈsændəʊ; glɪˋsando/ *n* (*pl* **-di** /-di:; -di/ or **~s**) (*music* 音) (in playing an instrument or singing) effect of sliding quickly up or down a scale, without separating the notes (演奏或演唱中)滑奏, 滑唱: *a series of glittering glissandi on the piano* 钢琴演奏中一系列明快的滑奏.

glis·ten /ˈglɪsn; ˋglɪsn̩/ *v* [I, Ipr] **~ (with sth)** (esp of wet or polished surfaces) shine brightly; sparkle (尤指潮湿的或光洁的物体表面)闪闪发光, 发亮, 闪耀: *dew-drops glistening in the grass* 草丛中晶莹的露珠 ○ *grass glistening with dew-drops* 有晶莹露珠的草 ○ *eyes, faces, bodies, etc glistening with tears, sweat, oil* 晶莹的泪眼、汗珠闪闪的面孔、油光发亮的身体.

glit·ter /ˈglɪtə(r); ˋglɪtɚ/ *v* **1** [I, Ipr] **~ (with sth)** shine brightly with little sharp flashes of light; sparkle 闪烁; 闪耀; 闪光: *stars glittering in the frosty sky* 寒空中闪烁的星星 ○ *a necklace glittering with diamonds* 闪闪生辉的钻石项链. **2** (idm 习语) ˌ**all that** ˌ**glitters is not** ˈ**gold** (*saying* 谚) what looks good on the outside may not really be so 闪闪发光的东西不一定都是金子(外表好不见得真好).
▷ **glit·ter** *n* [U] **1** brilliant, sparkling light 灿烂的光辉: *the glitter of decorations on a Christmas tree* 圣诞树上饰物的璀灿光华. **2** (*fig* 比喻) (superficial) attractiveness (外表的)诱惑力, 吸引力: *the glitter of a show-business career* 演艺事业的诱惑力.
glit·ter·ati /ˌglɪtəˈrɑ:tɪ; ˌglɪtəˋrɑtɪ/ *n* [pl] (*sl* 俚) fashionable people 时髦人物.
glit·ter·ing /ˈglɪtərɪŋ; ˋglɪtərɪŋ/ *adj* (**a**) sparkling 闪光的; 闪耀的. (**b**) (*fig* 比喻) spectacularly excellent, opulent or successful 绝妙的; 富丽的; 成功的: *a glittering occasion attended by the whole of high society* 上流人士济济一堂的盛会 ○ *the glittering prizes*, ie things most desired in life 人生追求的目标 ○ *A glittering career had been predicted for her in the Civil Service.* 她在政府的文职机关任职前途无量.
glit·tery /ˈglɪtərɪ; ˋglɪtərɪ/ *adj* glittering 闪闪发光的; 绝妙的; 富丽的; 成功的: *little glittery eyes* 亮晶晶的小眼睛 ○ *a glittery occasion* 富丽堂皇的场面.

glitz /glɪts; glɪts/ *n* [U] (*sl* 俚) showy glamour; glitter(2) 浮华; 诱惑力; 吸引力. ▷ **glitzy** *adj*: *The film star's wedding was a glitzy affair.* 那位影星的婚礼是堂皇的盛事.

gloam·ing /ˈgləʊmɪŋ; ˋglomɪŋ/ *n* **the gloaming** [sing] (*arch* 古) twilight 黄昏; 薄暮.

gloat /gləʊt; glot/ *v* [I, Ipr] **~ (about/over sth)** express or feel selfish delight at one's own success or good fortune or sb else's failure 沾沾自喜; 得意扬扬; 幸灾乐祸: *Stop gloating — just because you won the game!* 别因为赢了就扬扬得意! ○ *It's nothing to gloat about.* 没有什么可幸灾乐祸的. ○ *a miser gloating over his gold* 望着自己的金子而沾沾自喜的守财奴. ▷ **gloat·ingly** *adv*.

global /ˈgləʊbl; ˋglobl̩/ *adj* **1** covering or affecting the whole world; world-wide 全球性的; 全世界的: *a global tour* 环球旅行 ○ *global warfare* 世界大战. **2** covering the whole of a group of items, etc 包括一切的: *a global definition, rule* 总的定义、规则. ▷ **glob·ally** /-bəlɪ; -bəlɪ/ *adv*.

globe /gləʊb; glob/ *n* **1** [C] small spherical model of the earth showing the continents and usu also countries, rivers, cities, etc 地球仪. **2 the globe** [sing] the earth 地球; 世界: *travel (all) round the globe* 环球旅行. **3** [C] thing shaped like a sphere 球状物; 球体: *The oil-lamp needs a new globe*, spherical lampshade. 这油灯需配个新的圆灯罩. ○ *The silvery globe of the moon sank towards the horizon.* 银盘似的月亮朝地平线落去.
□ **globe** ˈ**artichoke** = ARTHICHOKE 1.
ˈ**globe-fish** *n* fish able to inflate itself into the shape of a globe 河豚.
ˈ**globe-trot** *v* (**tt**) [I] (*infml* 口) travel through many countries seeing as many different things as possible 周游世界. ˈ**globe-trotter** *n* (*infml* 口) person who does this 周游世界者.

the globe 地球

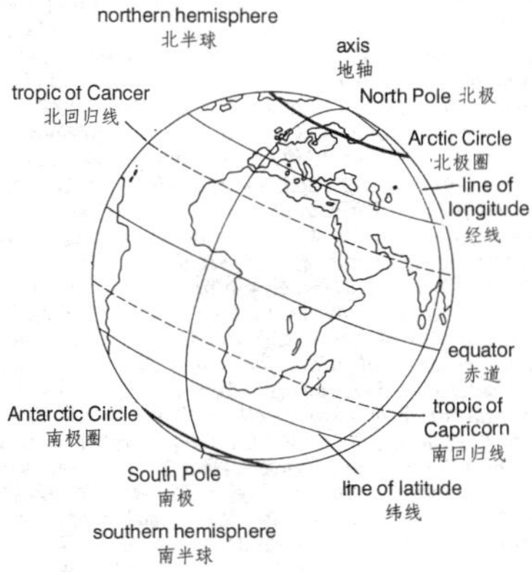

glob·ule /ˈglɒbju:l; ˋglɑbjʊl/ *n* tiny drop or ball, esp of liquid or a melted solid 小滴, 小球体(尤指液体或熔化的固体): *globules of wax from a candle* 蜡滴.
▷ **globu·lar** /ˈglɒbjʊlə(r); ˋglɑbjəlɚ/ *adj* shaped like a globe or ball; spherical 球形的; 球体的; 圆的.

glock·en·spiel /ˈglɒkənspi:l; ˋglɑkənˌspil/ *n* musical instrument consisting of metal bars of varying length which produce notes when struck with two light hammers 钟琴(用两小槌敲击长短不同的金属棒而发声).

gloom /glu:m; glum/ *n* **1** [U] near darkness 昏暗; 阴暗: *In the gathering gloom it was hard to see anything distinctly.* 光线越来越暗, 什么东西都看不清. **2** [U, sing] feeling of sadness and hopelessness 忧郁; 忧愁; 失望: *The news cast a deep gloom over the village.* 这消息使全村笼罩着一片愁云惨雾.
▷ **gloomy** /ˈglu:mɪ; ˋglumɪ/ *adj* (**-ier, -iest**) **1** dark or unlighted, esp in a way that is depressing or frightening 阴暗的, 黑暗的(尤指使人沮丧或恐惧): *a gloomy corner, passage, room, house* 黑暗的角落、过道、屋子、房子 ○ *a gloomy day*, ie with dark clouds and dull light 阴沉沉的一天. **2** (that makes people feel) sad and depressed (使人感到)忧愁的, 沮丧的: *a gloomy outlook, prospect, etc* 悲观的看法、前景等 ○ *What are you so gloomy about? Cheer up!* 你为什么情绪这么低落? 振作起来吧! ○ *a gloomy face, expression, voice, person* 忧伤的面孔、表情、声音、人. **gloom·ily** /-ɪlɪ; -ɪlɪ/ *adv*. **gloomi·ness** *n* [U].

glor·ify /ˈglɔ:rɪfaɪ; ˋglɔrəˌfaɪ/ *v* (*pt, pp* **-fied**) [Tn] **1** (*derog* 贬) make (sth/sb ordinary or bad) appear better or more noble than it/he really is 吹捧; 美化: *a book which glorifies the horrors of war* 美化战争恐怖的书. **2** (**a**) (*arch* 古) praise (sb/sth) highly; make glorious 颂扬或赞美(某人[某事物]); 使光荣或荣耀: *an ancient epic glorifying the hero's deeds in battle* 歌颂战斗英雄业绩的古代史诗. (**b**) (*Bible* 圣经) worship (sb) 崇拜: *glorify God* 归荣耀与上帝.
▷ **glori·fica·tion** /ˌglɔ:rɪfɪˈkeɪʃn; ˌglɔrəfəˋkeʃən/ *n* [U] glorifying or being glorified 美化; 颂扬; 赞美; 崇拜.
glori·fied *adj* [attrib 作定语] (*derog* 贬) ordinary but described in a way that makes it seem very desirable 吹捧的; 吹嘘的; 浮夸的: *a 'holiday cottage' which is only a glorified barn* 把谷仓美其名曰'度假别墅'.

glori·ous /ˈglɔ:rɪəs; ˋglɔrɪəs/ *adj* **1** having, worthy of or bringing great fame or glory 荣誉的; 光荣的; 显赫的; 荣耀的: *a glorious deed, victory, etc* 光荣的业绩、胜利等 ○ *the glorious days, years, reign, etc of Elizabeth I* 英国女王伊丽莎白一世光辉的日子、年代、朝代等 ○ *die a glorious death*, ie esp in battle for one's country 死得光

G

荣(尤指为国捐躯). **2** beautiful; splendid; magnificent 美丽的; 灿烂的; 瑰丽的: *a glorious day, sunset, view, prospect* 美丽的日子、日落、景色、前景 ○ *glorious colours* 绚丽的色彩 ○ *It's been really glorious today*, ie warm and sunny. 今天真是个风和日丽的好天. **3** (*infml* 口) very pleasant; enjoyable 非常愉快的; 令人快乐的: *have a glorious time* 过得非常愉快 ○ *What glorious fun!* 多么有趣啊! **4** [attrib 作定语] (*ironic* 反语) dreadful 糟糕的; 极度的: *a glorious mess, muddle, etc* 极度的混乱、杂乱等. ▷ **glori·ously** *adv*.

glory /ˈglɔːrɪ; ˋglɔrɪ/ *n* **1** [U] high fame and honour won by great achievements 光荣; 荣誉: *glory won on the field of battle* 战场上赢得的荣誉 ○ *a proud father basking in his son's reflected glory*, ie sharing the fame achieved by his son 因儿子的荣耀其父感到骄傲 ○ *Our team didn't exactly cover itself with glory today*, eg was heavily defeated. 我队今天未能真正载誉而归(如遭惨败). ○ *The regiment's motto was 'Death or Glory'.* 该团队的座右铭是'誓死争取荣誉'. **2** [U] (*Bible* 圣经) worship, adoration and thanksgiving 崇敬; 赞美; 赞颂; 感恩: *'Glory to God in the highest.'* '在至高之处荣耀归与神.' **3** [U] beauty; splendour 美丽; 壮丽: *the glory of a sunset, a summer's day, etc* 美丽的日落、夏日等 ○ *the countryside in all its glory* 气象万千的郊野. **4** [C, U] special cause for pride, respect or honour 产生骄傲、崇敬或荣耀的原因: *One of the glories of the British heritage is the right to a fair trial.* 英国人引以自豪的传统之一是有获得公正审判的权利. **5** (idm 习语) **go to ˈglory** (*dated euph* 旧, 婉) die 死; 上天堂; 归天. **cover oneself with glory** ⇨ COVER[1].

▷ **glory** *v* [Ipr] **~ in sth** (*approv or derog* 褒或贬) take (too much) pleasure or pride in sth 对某事物(过分)得意; 因某事物而自豪: *glory in one's freedom, success, etc* 为自己的自由、成功等而骄傲 ○ *military leaders who seem to glory in slaughter* 仿佛以杀戮为荣的军事领导人.

□ **ˈglory-hole** *n* (*Brit infml* 口) room, cupboard or drawer where belongings can be thrown untidily until needed 可乱放杂物的房间、橱柜或抽屉.

G

gloss[1] /glɒs; glɔs/ *n* [U, sing] **1** (**a**) brightness or shine on a smooth surface 平滑表面上的光泽或光亮: *With this polish you can give a good high gloss to the wood.* 使用这种上光蜡可使木器表面极为平滑光亮. ○ *the gloss on sb's hair* 某人头发的光泽. (**b**) (often in compounds 常用以构成复合词) substance (eg make-up) designed to give such a shine 用以产生光泽的物质(如化妆品): *ˈlip-gloss* 透明唇膏 ○ [attrib 作定语] *gloss paint*, ie paint which, when dry, has a hard shiny surface 光泽涂料 ○ *gloss photographs* 光面照片 ○ *a gloss finish*, ie a shiny surface (after painting, processing, etc) 上光. (**c**) gloss paint 清漆; 光泽涂料: *a tin of gloss* 一罐清漆. Cf 参看 MATT. **2** (*fig* 比喻) deceptively good appearance 虚假的外表; 虚饰: *acquire a pleasing social gloss*, ie attractive manners, etc 培养社交中体面的风度 ○ *the gloss and glitter of Hollywood* 好莱坞的虚荣与豪华 ○ *a gloss of respectability*, ie cover for a life of secret wrongdoing 道貌岸然的假象. Cf 参看 VENEER 2.

▷ **gloss** *v* (phr v) **gloss over sth** treat sth briefly, or in a superficial or an incomplete way, so as to avoid embarrassing details 简略地、浮皮潦草地或敷衍地处理某事(以求避开难堪的细节): *gloss over the awkward facts* 掩饰令人尴尬的事实.

glossy *adj* (**-ier, -iest**) smooth and shiny 光滑的; 光亮的: *glossy hair, photographs* 有光泽的毛发、照片 ○ *glossy magazines/periodicals*, ie printed on high-quality glossy paper, with many photographs, coloured illustrations, etc (esp fashion magazines) 用有光纸印刷的杂志[期刊](尤指时装杂志). **gloss·ily** /-ɪlɪ; -ɪlɪ/ *adv*. **glossi·ness** *n* [U].

gloss[2] /glɒs; glɔs/ *n* **~ (on sth)** **1** explanatory comment added to a text; brief definition 注释; 简明注解: *a gloss on a word, phrase, etc* 单词、短语等的注释. **2** explanation; interpretation 解释; 阐释: *The minister has put a different gloss on recent developments in the Middle East.* 部长对中东局势的最新发展作了另一番解释.

▷ **gloss** *v* [Tn] give an explanation or a brief definition of (a word); add a gloss to (a text) 对(一词)作解释或简要释义; 给(一段文字)作注释: *a difficult word that needs to be glossed* 需加注释的难词.

gloss·ary /ˈglɒsərɪ; ˋglɑsərɪ/ *n* list of technical or special words (esp those occurring in a particular text) explaining their meanings (注释)词汇表, 术语或专门词语汇编, 集注(尤指针对某篇文字的). Cf 参看 VOCABULARY 3.

glot·tis /ˈglɒtɪs; ˋglɑtɪs/ *n* (*anatomy* 解) opening between the vocal cords in the upper part of the windpipe 声门.

▷ **glot·tal** /ˈglɒtl; ˋglɑtl/ *adj* of the glottis 声门的. **ˌglottal ˈstop** speech sound produced by a complete closure of the glottis, followed by an explosive release of breath 喉塞音; 声门闭塞音.

gloves 手套

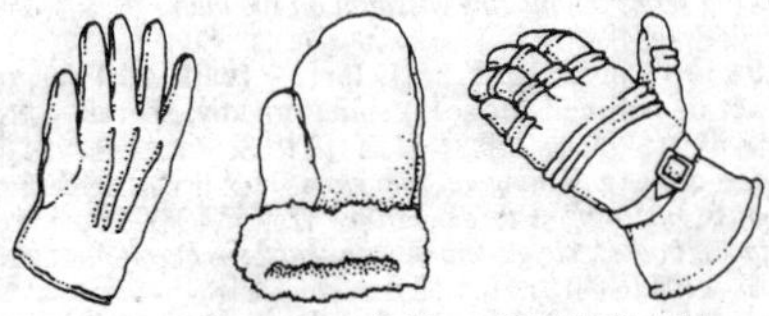

GLOVE 手套 MITTEN 连指手套 GAUNTLET 长手套

glove /glʌv; glʌv/ *n* **1** covering of leather, knitted wool, etc for the hand, usu with separated fingers 手套(通常指分指的): *a pair of gloves* 一副手套 ○ *rubber gloves for washing up* 洗涤用的胶皮手套 ○ *strong leather gardening gloves* 园艺用的厚皮手套 ○ *batting gloves* 击球用的手套. ⇨illus 见插图. **2** (idm 习语) **fit like a glove** ⇨ FIT[2]. **the gloves are off** sb is ready for a fight 做好战斗准备. **hand in glove** ⇨ HAND. **handle, etc sb with kid gloves** ⇨ KID[1]. **an iron fist/hand in a velvet glove** ⇨ IRON[1]. ▷ **gloved** *adj* [usu attrib 通常作定语]: *a gloved hand* 戴着手套的手.

□ **ˈglove compartment** compartment in a car in front of the passenger's or driver's seat for holding small articles (汽车中乘客或司机座位前放小物件的)贮物箱或隔间. ⇨illus at App 1 见附录1插图, page xii.

ˈglove puppet kind of puppet worn on the hand and worked by the fingers 手套式木偶(套在手上用手指操纵的). ⇨illus at PUPPET 见 PUPPET 插图.

glow /gləʊ; glo/ *v* **1** [I] send out light and heat without flame 发出光和热; 燃烧(无焰): *glowing embers, charcoal, etc* 灼热的余烬、木炭等 ○ *glowing metal in a furnace* 熔炉中炽热的金属 ○ *A cigarette glowed in the dark.* 黑暗中有枝香烟发着光. **2** [I, Ipr] **~ (with sth)** be, look or feel warm or red (eg after exercise or because excited) 发红, 发热, 显得红, 觉得热(如运动之后或情绪激动): *her glowing cheeks* 她发红的双颊 ○ *glowing with health, pride, etc* 红光满面、神气活现. **3** [I, Ipr] **~ (with sth)** be strongly or warmly colourful 色彩强烈; 绚丽夺目: *The countryside glowed with autumn colours.* 郊野焕发出斑斓的秋色.

▷ **glow** *n* [sing] **1** dull light 暗淡的光: *The fire cast a warm glow on the walls.* 炉火映在墙上呈现一片融融红光. **2** warm look or feeling 发热的样子或感觉: *cheeks with a rosy/healthy glow* 绯红的双颊[容光焕发]. **3** feeling of satisfaction 满足的心情: *the special glow you get from a truly unselfish act* 从真正的无私行为中体验到的特殊喜悦.

glow·ing *adj* [usu attrib 通常作定语] giving enthusiastic praise 热情赞扬的; 热烈的: *a glowing account, report, etc* 热情的叙述, 报道等 ○ *describe sth in glowing colours, terms, phrases, etc*, ie praise sth strongly 热烈赞扬某事物. **glow·ingly** *adv*.

□ **ˈglow-worm** *n* insect of which the wingless female gives out a green light at its tail 萤火虫.

glower /ˈglaʊə(r); ˋglaʊɚ/ *v* [I, Ipr] **~ (at sb/sth)** look in an angry or a threatening way 怒目而视; 愠然作色: *He sat glowering at his opponent.* 他坐在那里怒视着对手. ○ (*fig* 比喻) *the glowering sky*, ie with dark clouds 阴沉的天空. ▷ **glower·ingly** /ˈglaʊərɪŋlɪ; ˋglaʊərɪŋlɪ/ *adv*.

gluc·ose /ˈgluːkəʊs; ˋglukos/ *n* [U] form of sugar (eg dextrose) found in fruit-juice, easily turned into energy by the human body 葡萄糖; 右旋糖.

glue /gluː; glu/ *n* [U, C] thick sticky liquid used for joining things 胶; 胶水: *mend a broken cup with glue* 用胶粘补破杯 ○ *He sticks to her like glue*, ie never leaves her. 他如胶似漆地寸步不离开她. Cf 参看 ADHESIVE *n*, CEMENT 2.

▷ **glue** *v* **1** [Tn, Tn·pr, Tn·p] **~ A (to/onto B); ~ A and B (together)** stick or join a thing or things with glue 用胶水将物体粘合: *glue wood (on)to metal* 将木头粘到金属上 ○ *glue two pieces of wood together* 将两块木料粘合在一起. **2** (idm 习语) **glued to sth** (*infml* 口) continually close to sth; unwilling to leave sth 紧附于, 不愿离开, 似胶般固着于(某事物): *He's glued to the television*, ie watching it with close interest. 他目不转睛地看着电视. ○ *with his ear glued to the keyhole*, ie listening hard to a conversation in another room 他耳朵紧贴在钥匙孔上(偷听室内谈话).

gluey /ˈgluːɪ; ˋgluɪ/ *adj* sticky; like glue 胶粘的; 似胶的.

□ **ˈglue-sniffing** *n* [U] practice of breathing in the fumes of certain types of glue for their intoxicating effect 吸胶毒(为获兴奋效果而吸入某些类型的胶的气体).

glum /glʌm; glʌm/ *adj* **(-mmer, -mmest)** (*infml* 口) gloomy; sad 忧郁的; 闷闷不乐的: *glum expressions, faces, features* 忧伤的神情、面孔、相貌. ▷ **glumly** *adv*: *'Another rainy day,' he remarked glumly.* '又是一个雨天,' 他闷闷不乐地说. **glum·ness** *n* [U].

glut /glʌt; glʌt/ *v* **(-tt-)** [Tn, Tn·pr] **1 ~ sth (with sth)** supply sth with much more than is needed 超量供应某事物: *glut the market with cheap apples from abroad* 进口过量的廉价苹果供应市场. **2 ~ oneself (with/on sth)** fill oneself (by eating too much); gorge oneself 吃得过饱; 大吃: *glut oneself with rich food, on cream buns* 大吃油腻食物、奶油面包 ○ (*fig* 比喻) *glutted with pleasure* 纵情享乐.

▷ **glut** *n* (usu *sing* 通常作单数) situation in which supply exceeds demand; excess 供过于求; 供应过剩: *a glut of fruit, of American films, of talent* 水果、美国影片、人材供过于求.

glu·ten /ˈgluːtn; ˋglutn̩/ *n* [U] sticky protein substance that is left when starch is washed out of flour 面筋; 麸质; 谷胶.

▷ **glu·tin·ous** /ˈgluːtənəs; ˋglutənəs/ *adj* of or like gluten; sticky (似)面筋的; 黏的; 胶质的: *a glutinous substance* 胶性物质 ○ (*fig* 比喻) *the film's glutinous* (ie excessive) *sentimentality* 这部影片的缠绵悱恻.

glut·ton /ˈglʌtn; ˋglʌtn̩/ *n* **1** person who eats too much 贪吃的人; 吃得过多的人: *You've eaten the whole pie, you glutton!* 你把整块馅饼都给吃了, 你这贪吃鬼! **2 ~ for sth** (*infml* 口) person always ready for more (of sth difficult or unpleasant) 甘愿承受更多困难、不快事物的人: *a glutton for punishment, (hard) work, etc* 对惩罚、(艰苦的)工作等无所畏惧的人.

▷ **glut·ton·ous** /ˈglʌtənəs; ˋglʌtn̩əs/ *adj* very greedy for food 贪吃的; 贪嘴的. **glut·ton·ously** *adv*.

glut·tony /-tənɪ; -tn̩ɪ/ *n* [U] habit or practice of eating (and drinking) too much 贪吃; 大吃八喝.

gly·cer·ine /ˈglɪsəriːn; ˋglɪsəˌrin/ (*US* **gly·cer·in** /-rɪn; -rɪn/) *n* [U] thick sweet colourless liquid made from fats and oils, used in medicines, toilet products and explosives 甘油; 丙三醇.

GM /ˌdʒiː ˈem; ˌdʒi ˋɛm/ *abbr* 缩写 = (*Brit*) George Medal: *be awarded the GM* 获授予乔治勋章 ○ *John Green GM* 乔治勋章获得者约翰·格林.

gm (also **gr**) *abbr* 缩写 = (*pl* unchanged or **gms, grs** 复数或不变或作 **gms**、**grs**) gram(s); gramme(s): *10 gm* 10克.

GMT /ˌdʒiː em ˈtiː; ˌdʒi ɛm ˋti/ *abbr* 缩写 = Greenwich Mean Time. Cf 参看 BST.

gnarled /nɑːld; nɑrld/ *adj* **1** (of trees) twisted and rough; covered with knobs (指树木)扭曲粗糙的, 多节瘤的: *a gnarled oak, branch, trunk* 多节瘤的橡树、树枝、树干. **2** (of hands or fingers) twisted, with swollen joints and rough skin; deformed (指手或手指)关节扭曲肿胀及皮肤粗糙的, 变形的: *hands gnarled with age* 经年操劳而骨节嶙峋的手.

gnash /næʃ; næʃ/ *v* [Tn] (*usu fig* 通常作比喻) grind (one's teeth) together as a sign of great emotion (因情绪激动)咬或磨(牙): *I was gnashing my teeth with/in rage*, ie was extremely angry. 我咬牙切齿愤怒已极.

▷ **gnash·ers** *n* [pl] (*joc sl* 谑, 俚) teeth 牙齿.

gnat /næt; næt/ *n* small two-winged fly that stings; small mosquito 蚋; 蠓; 蚊.

gnaw /nɔː; nɔ/ *v* **1** [Ipr, Tn] **~ (at) sth** bite sth hard continually until it is worn away 不断地啃, 咬, 啮硬物(直至啃掉、咬去、啮断): *a dog gnawing (at) a bone* 啃着骨头的狗 ○ *a boy gnawing his fingernails* 咬着指甲的男孩. **2** [Ipr, Ip, Tn] **~ (at) sb/sth** (*fig* 比喻) cause sb/sth continual distress and torment 使某人苦恼; 使某事物受折磨: *fear and anxiety gnawing (at) one's heart* 心中受着恐惧和不安的折磨 ○ *the gnawing pains of hunger* 饥饿引起的绞痛 ○ *guilt gnawing (away) at one's conscience* 使良心不安的罪愆. **3** (phr v) **gnaw sth away/off** destroy sth gradually by gnawing 啃掉或咬坏某物: *Rats gnawed off the lid of the box.* 老鼠啃坏了箱盖.

gneiss /naɪs; naɪs/ *n* [U] (*geology* 地质) coarse-grained rock of quartz, feldspar and mica 片麻岩.

gnome /nəʊm; nom/ *n* **1** (in stories) creature like a small human being living under the ground (often guarding treasure) (故事中的)守护神, 地精(常作守卫宝藏者). **2** model of such a creature used as an ornament in a garden 守护神塑像(用作花园中的饰物). **3** (*usu derog* 通常作贬义) powerful international banker 势力雄厚的国际银行家: *the gnomes of Zürich* 苏黎世的国际银行家们.

gnomic /ˈnəʊmɪk; ˋnomɪk/ *adj* (*fml* 文) (of a remark, etc) mysteriously brief and obscure (指言语等)(出奇地)简短而晦涩的. ▷ **gnom·ic·ally** /-klɪ; -klɪ/ *adv*.

GNP /ˌdʒiː en ˈpiː; ˌdʒi ɛn ˋpi/ *abbr* 缩写 = gross national product: *The country's GNP has risen by 10% this year.* 今年国家的国民生产总值增长了10%. Cf 参看 GDP.

gnu /nuː; nu/ *n* (*pl* unchanged or **~s** 复数或不变或作 **gnus**) (also **wildebeest**) large thickset African antelope 角马(产于非洲).

go[1] /gəʊ; go/ *v* (*3rd pers sing pres t* **goes** /gəʊz; goz/, *pt* **went** /went; wɛnt/, *pp* **gone** /gɒn; *US* gɔːn; gɔn/). ⇨ Usage at BEEN 用法见 BEEN.

▸ MOVEMENT 动作 (Senses 1, 2, 3, 4, 5 and 6 refer esp to movement *away from* the place where the speaker or writer is or a place where he imagines himself to be. 1、2、3、4、5、6各义尤指从说话的人或书写的人所在之处离去的动作, 或从其想像所处之处离去的动作.) **1** (**a**) [I, Ipr, Ip] move or travel from one place to another 去: *Are you going (there) by train or by plane?* 你坐火车去还是乘飞机去(那儿)? ○ *She went into her room and shut the door behind her.* 她进入自己的房间, 关上了门. ○ *I have to go to London on business tomorrow.* 明天我要到伦敦去办事. ○ *I think you ought to go to/to go and see* (ie consult) *the doctor.* 我认为你应当去找医生看看病. ○ *Would you go and get me a glass of water?* 你去给我倒杯水来好吗? ○ *She has gone to see her sister this weekend.* 她本周末看姐姐去了. ○ *We're going to France for our holidays this year.* 我们今年要去法国度假. ○ *She has gone to China*, ie is now in China or is on her way there. 她到中国去了. ○ *He goes to work by bus.* 他坐公共汽车上班. ○ *Go away and leave me alone!* 走开, 别打搅我! ○ *Are you going home for Christmas?* 你回家过圣诞节吗? ⇨Usage at AND 用法见 AND. (**b**) [I] leave one place in order to reach another; depart 离去: *I must go/be going now.* 我现在得走了. ○ *They came at six and went at nine.* 他们六时来的, 九时走的. ○ *Has she gone yet?* 她走了吗? ○ *When does the train go?* 火车什么时候开? ○ *She's been gone an hour*, ie She left an hour ago. 她已离开一个小时. (**c**) [I, Ipr] **~ (to sth) (with sb)** move or travel with sb to a particular place or in order to be present at an event 与某人去某处: *I went to the cinema with Denise last night.* 昨晚我和丹尼斯去看电影了. ○ *Dave's having a party tonight; are you going (to it)?* 戴夫今晚举行晚会, 你去吗? ○ *Who are you going with?* 你和谁一起去? ○ *I'll be going with Keith.* 我和基思一起去. ○ *His dog goes everywhere with him.* 他的狗总跟着他. **2** [Ipr] **~ to sth** (**a**) (usu without *a* or *the* 通常不与a或the连用) move or travel to (the place specified) for the purpose esp associated with it 为某目的去某处: *go to hospital*, ie for medical treatment 去医院(治疗) ○ *go to prison*, ie be sent there for having committed a crime 进监狱(因犯罪) ○ *go to market*, ie to sell one's produce 上市场(卖货). (**b**) (usu without *a* or *the* 通常不与a或

the 连用) attend (a place), esp regularly 参加, 出席(尤指经常地): *go to church, school* 上教堂去做礼拜、上学 ○ *Did you go to* (ie study at) *university?* 你上过大学吗? **3** [Ipr] (**a**) **~ for sth** (also used with the *-ing* form of a *v* 与动词-ing形式运用) leave a place or travel to a place to take part in an activity or carry out an action 离开某处或去某处参加活动或进行活动: *go for a walk, swim, run, etc* 去散步、游泳、跑步等 ○ *Annie's not in; she's gone for a walk.* 安妮不在家, 她出去散步了. ○ *Shall we go for a drink* (ie at a pub or bar) *this evening?* 今晚我们去喝酒好吗? ○ *go fishing, hiking, jogging, sailing, pot-holing, etc* 去钓鱼、远足、慢跑、做帆船运动、探岩洞等 ○ *I have to go shopping this afternoon.* 今天下午我得去买东西. (**b**) **~ on sth** leave a place with the purpose of undertaking sth 离开某处去做某事: *go on a journey, an outing, a trip, a cruise, (a) safari* 去旅行、郊游、短途旅行、乘船旅游、狩猎旅行 ○ *Richard isn't at work this week; he's gone on holiday.* 理查德本周不上班, 他去度假了. ○ *After leaving college she went on a secretarial course.* 她从学院毕业以后又学习秘书课程. **4** [I] move or travel in the specified way or over a specified distance 以某方式移动或经过某距离: *That car is going too fast.* 那辆汽车开得太快了. ○ *We had gone about fifty miles when the car broke down.* 我们开出约五十英里汽车就抛锚了. ○ *We still have five miles to go*, ie until we reach our destination. 我们还要走五英里. **5** (used with the *-ing* form of a *v* to show that sb/sth moves in the specified way or that sb/sth is doing sth while moving 与动词-ing形式连用, 表示某人[某事物]以某方式移动或在移动中做某事物): *The car went careering off* (ie careered off) *the road into a ditch.* 汽车猛地冲出公路跌进沟里. ○ *The train went chugging* (ie chugged) *up the hill.* 火车轰隆隆地爬上山去. ○ *She went sobbing* (ie was sobbing as she went) *up the stairs.* 她抽抽搭搭地上楼去了. **6** [I, Ipr] be sent or passed on 发送; 传递: *Will this letter go by tonight's post?* 这信今晚能邮走吗? ○ *Such complaints must go through the proper channels.* 这种意见应当通过适当渠道反映. ○ *I want this memo to go to all departmental managers.* 这份备忘录要送交各部门的经理. **7** [La, I, Ipr, Ip] **~ (from...) to...** extend or lead from one place to another 从一地伸展或通向另一地: *The roots of this plant go deep.* 这种植物的根系扎得很深. ○ (*fig* 比喻) *Differences between employers and workers go deep.* 雇主和工人间的分歧很大. ○ *Does this road go to London?* 这条公路通往伦敦吗? ○ *I want a rope that will go from the top window to the ground.* 我要一条绳, 其长度能自最上一扇窗户垂到地面. ○ *Our garden goes down as far as the river.* 我们的花园一直延伸到河边.

G

▸ POSITION 位置 **8** (**a**) [I, Ipr] have as a usual or proper position; be placed 放, 置, 摆, 在(通常的或应在的位置): *This dictionary goes on the top shelf.* 这部词典放在最上一格. ○ *Where do you want the piano to go?* ie Where shall we put it? 你想把钢琴放在哪儿? ○ *'Where does this teapot go?' 'In that cupboard.'* '这把茶壶放在什么地方?' '放到那个柜橱里.' (**b**) [I, Ipr, Ip] be contained (in sth); fit (in sth) 被容纳(在某事物中); 装(进某物中): *This key won't go in (the lock).* 这把钥匙插不进(那把锁中). ○ *My clothes won't all go into that tiny suitcase.* 那个小衣箱装不下我所有的衣物. (**c**) [I, Ipr] (of a number) be contained in another number, esp without a remainder (指数)包含在另一数中(尤指无余数): *3 into 12 goes 4*, ie is contained in 12 four times 3除12得4 ○ *7 into 15 won't go/7 won't go into 15* 7除不尽15.

▸ ACTIVITY 行动 **9** [I] (used with *advs*, or in questions after *how* 与副词连用, 或在疑问句中用于how之后) take place or happen in the way specified; turn out; progress 发生; 出现; 结果; 进行: *'How did your holiday go?' 'It went (very) well.'* '你假日过得好吗?' '过得很好.' ○ *The election went badly for the Conservatives.* 选举结果对保守党不利. ○ *Did everything go smoothly?* 一切进行得顺利吗? ○ *The meeting went better than we had expected.* 会议开得比我们预料的好. ○ *How's it going?/How are things going?* ie Is your life pleasant, enjoyable, etc at the moment? 一切可好(日子过得怎么样)? ○ *The way things are going the company will be bankrupt by the end of the year.* 从事态发展来看, 公司年底就要破产. **10** [I] (esp in commands 尤用于命令语句) start an activity 开始某行动: *I'll say 'One, two, three, go!' as a signal for you to start.* 我喊'一、二、三、开始!'你就开始. **11** [I] (of a machine, etc) function; work; operate (指机器等)运行, 工作, 运转: *This clock doesn't go.* 这钟不走了. ○ *Is your watch going?* 你的表走吗? ○ *This machine goes by electricity.* 这机器是电动的.

▸ STATE 状态 **12** [La, Ln] pass into the specified condition; become 进入某状态; 变为: *go bald, blind, mad, pale, bankrupt* 变秃、变瞎、变疯、变苍白、破产 ○ *Her hair is going grey.* 她的头发日见花白. ○ *This milk has gone sour.* 这牛奶馊了. ○ *Fish soon goes bad* (ie rotten) *in hot weather.* 天热时鱼坏得快. ○ *The children went wild with excitement.* 孩子欣喜若狂. ○ *Britain went Labour* (ie changed politically by electing a Labour government) *in 1945.* 1945年英国转由工党执政. ⇨ Usage at BECOME 用法见BECOME. **13** [La] be or live habitually in the specified state or manner 处于某状态; (以某方式)生活: *She cannot bear the thought of children going hungry.* 她想到儿童挨饿就受不了. ○ *You'd better go armed*, ie carry a weapon. 你最好带上武器. **14** (used with a negative past participle to show that an action does not take place 与否定式过去分词连用, 表示某动作未发生): *Her absence went unnoticed*, ie was not noticed. 没有人注意到她缺席. ○ *Police are worried that many crimes go unreported*, ie are not reported to them. 警方不安的是很多罪行无人报案.

▸ SOUND 声音 **15** [I, Ipr] **~ like sth** (used esp in questions after *how* 尤用于疑问句中的how之后) (of a piece of music or writing) have a certain tune or wording (指一篇乐曲或文字)有某种基调或措辞: *How does that song go?* 那首歌是怎么唱的? ○ *The national anthem goes like this...* 国歌是这样唱的... ○ *I forget how the next line goes.* 我忘记下一行是什么了. ○ *The story goes that she poisoned her husband/She poisoned her husband, or so the story goes*, ie It is said that she poisoned him. 故事说她把丈夫毒死了. **16** (**a**) [Ln] make the specified sound 发出某种声音: *The clock went 'tick-tock, tick-tock'.* 钟发出嘀嗒嘀嗒的声音. ○ *The gun went 'bang'.* 枪砰的一声响了. ○ *Cats go 'miaow.'* 猫的叫声是'喵喵'. (**b**) [Ipr] make the specified movement 做某种动作: *She went like this with her hand.* 她用手这样比划着. **17** [I] be sounded as a signal or warning 发出信号或警告的声响: *The whistle goes at the end of the match.* 比赛结束时哨声响了. ○ *No one may leave the classroom until the bell goes.* 铃响以前任何人均不得离开教室. ○ *If the fire-alarm goes, staff should assemble outside the building.* 火警警报响时全体人员应到楼外集合.

▸ COMING TO AN END 结束 **18** [I] cease to exist; disappear; vanish 不再存在; 消失; 消散: *Has your headache gone yet?* 你头痛好了吗? ○ *I rubbed hard but the stain just wouldn't go.* 我使劲擦也擦不掉那污迹. ○ *I left my bike outside the shop and when I came out again it had gone*, ie somebody had taken it. 我把自行车放在商店外面, 等我出来时已不翼而飞了. **19** [I] (used after *must, have to* or *can* 用于must、have to或can之后) be thrown away, rejected or dismissed 被扔掉、驳回或辞退: *The old settee will have to go.* 那个长靠椅该扔掉了. ○ *He's incompetent; he'll have to go.* 他不称职, 得辞掉他. **20** [I] get worse; be lost 变坏; 丧失: *His sight is going.* 他的视力在衰退. ○ *Her hearing went* (ie She became deaf) *in her seventies.* 她70多岁时耳聋了. ○ *His mind is going*, ie He is becoming senile. 他心智日衰. **21** [I] become damaged or stop functioning properly 受损; 不起作用: *My jumper has gone* (ie has worn into holes) *at the elbows.* 我的毛衣肘部已磨坏. ○ *I was driving into town when my brakes went*, ie failed. 我正开车进城时, 制动器失灵了. ○ *This light bulb has gone.* 这灯泡不亮了. ○ *Her voice has gone*, ie She cannot speak properly, eg because she has a sore throat. 她嗓子哑了. **22** [I] (*euph* 婉) die 死: *Old Mrs Davis has gone.* 戴维斯老太太去世了. **23** [I, Ipr, It] **~ (on sth)** (of money) be spent or used up (指钱)花掉, 用光: *I don't know where the money goes!* 我不知道钱都花到什么地方去了. ○ *All* *her earnings go on clothes.* 她挣来的钱都花在衣服上了. ○ *Most of my salary goes on/in (paying) rent.* 我薪水的大部分都用来付房租了. ○ *The money will go to finance a new community centre.* 这些钱将用来资助一个新社区中心. **24** [I, Ipr] **~ (to sb) (for sth)** be sold 卖; 售: *These socks are going at £1 a pair.* 这些短袜每双卖1英镑. ○ *The new dictionary is going well,* ie A lot of copies of it are being sold. 这部新词典销路很好. ○ *We shan't let our house go for less than £50 000.* 我们的房子低于50 000英镑不卖. ○ *The antique table went to the lady in the pink hat.* 这张古董桌子卖给那位戴粉红色帽子的女士了.

▸ COMMANDS 命令 **25** (used in negative commands with a *v* in the *-ing* form to tell sb not to do sth 用于否定命令句, 与动词-ing形式连用, 告诉某人不要做某事): *Don't go getting yourself into trouble!* 别自找麻烦! **26** (*infml* 口 *esp US*) (used in commands with a *v* in the infinitive without *to* to send sb away angrily 用于命令句, 与不带to的动词不定式连用, 表示愤怒地打发某人走开): *Go jump in a lake!* 滚开!

▸ OTHER MEANINGS 其他意义 **27** [It] contribute; help 促成; 有助于: *This all goes to prove my theory.* 这一切均有助于证明我的说法. ○ *The latest unemployment figures go to show that government policy isn't working.* 最新的失业统计数字表明政府的政策行不通. ○ *What qualities go to make a successful businessman?* 企业家要具备什么素质才能出人头地? **28** [I] (*infml* 口) (only in the continuous tenses 只用于进行时态) be available 现成可用; 可得到: *There simply aren't any jobs going in this area.* 这地区简直没有工作可找. ○ *Is there any tea going?* ie Can I have some tea? 有茶吗? **29** [I] (of time) pass; elapse (指时间)过去, 消逝: *Hasn't the time gone quickly?* 时间过得太快了吧? ○ *There are only two days to go before the election,* ie It takes place in two days' time. 离选举只有两天了. **30** [Ipr, Ip] be willing to pay a certain amount of money for sth 愿付某数额的钱购买某物: *He's prepared to pay £2 500 for the car but I don't think he'll go any higher.* 他准备付2 500英镑买这辆汽车, 我想他不会再多付了. ○ *I'll go to £2 500 but no higher.* 我愿出2 500英镑, 不能再多了. **31** [Tn no passive 不用于被动语态] (in the game of bridge) declare or bid (桥牌戏中)叫牌: *go two spades, three no trumps, etc* 叫二黑桃、三无王等. **32** (**a**) (used with *to* or *into* + a *n* in many expressions to show that sb/sth has reached the state indicated by the *n* 与to或into加名词连用可构成许多固定词组, 表示某人[某事物]已达到该名词所示的状态, 如 *She went to sleep,* ie began to sleep 她去睡觉了; *The company has gone into liquidation,* ie become bankrupt 公司已破产; for similar expressions see entries for *ns* 类似固定词组见有关名词词条, 如 **go to pot** ⇨ POT.) (**b**) (used with *out of* + a *n* in many expressions to show that sb/sth is no longer in the state indicated by the *n* 与out of加名词连用可构成许多固定词组, 表示某人[某事物]不再处于该名词所示的状态, 如 *Flared trousers have gone out of fashion,* ie are no longer fashionable 喇叭裤已不再流行; for similar expressions see entries for *ns* 类似固定词组见有关名词词条, 如 **go out of use** ⇨ USE.)

33 (idm 习语) ˈ**anything goes** (*infml* 口) anything that sb says or does is accepted or allowed, however shocking or unconventional it may be 无论什么事情(不管多么惊人或不寻常)都有可能: *Almost anything goes these days.* 现在简直无奇不有. **as people, things, etc go** in comparison with the average person, thing, etc 就一般情况而论: *Twenty pounds for a pair of shoes isn't bad as things go nowadays,* ie considering how much shoes usually cost. 一双鞋卖二十英镑, 就目前情况而论还算可以. **be going on (for) sth** be near to or approaching (the specified time, age or number); be getting on for sth 快到或接近(某时刻、年龄或数目): *It must be going on (for) midnight.* 现在一定快半夜了. ○ *There were going on for* (ie nearly) *fifty people at the party.* 参加聚会的将近五十人. ○ *He must be going on for ninety.* 他准有九十岁了. ○ *She's sixteen, going on seventeen.* 她十六岁, 快十七岁了. **be going to do sth** (**a**) (used to show what sb is intending or planning to do in the future 用以表示某人打算做某事): *We're going to spend our holidays in Wales this year.* 今年我们打算到威尔士度假. ○ *We're going to buy a house when we've saved enough money.* 我们打算攒够钱买所房子. (**b**) (used to indicate sth that is about to happen or is likely to happen in the future 用以表示某事物即将发生或很可能发生): *I'm going to be sick.* 我要病了. ○ *I'm going to be twenty next month.* 下个月我就二十岁了. ○ *I'm going to tell you a story.* 我来给你讲个故事. ○ *Look at those black clouds; there's going to be a storm.* 瞧那些乌云, 眼看要有暴风雨了. **enough/something/sth to be going ˈon with** something that is sufficient or adequate for the time being 暂敷所需; 足够目前之用: *'How much money do you need?' '£50 should be enough to be going on with.'* '你需要多少钱?' '50英镑暂时够了.' ○ *I can't lend you the whole amount now, but I can give you something to be going on with.* 我现在不能全部如数借给你, 不过可以给你些应急. ○ *Here's a cup of tea to be going on with; we'll have something to eat later.* 先喝杯茶垫垫底儿, 咱们等一会再吃东西. **go all ˈout for sth; go all out to ˈdo sth** make a very great effort to obtain sth or do sth 竭尽全力以获得某事物或做某事: *The Labour Party are going all out for victory in/going all out to win the election.* 工党全力以赴争取选举获胜. (phr v) **go and do sth** (used esp to express anger that sb has done sth foolish 尤用于表示因某人做了蠢事而恼怒): *Trust him to go and mess things up!* 他就是那样, 总把事情弄得一团糟! ○ *Why did you (have to) go and upset your mother like that?* 你为什么让你母亲那样伤心? **go for ˈnothing** be wasted or in vain 浪费; 白费: *All her hard work has gone for nothing.* 她的艰苦工作尽付东流. **go ˈon (with you)** (used to rebuke sb gently or to express disbelief 用以婉言反驳某人或表示不相信): *'How old are you?' 'I'm forty.' 'Go on with you — you don't look a day over thirty.'* '你多少岁了?' '四十了.' '去你的吧 —— 你看起来绝对不超过三十岁.' **go ˈto it** (used esp in the imperative to encourage sb to do sth 尤用于祈使句, 以鼓励某人做某事) give energy and time to doing sth; make a special effort to do sth 用精力和时间做某事; 特别努力做某事: *Go to it, John! You know you can beat him.* 约翰, 干吧! 你知道你比他强. ○ *We went to it and got the job done quickly.* 我们一努力, 工作很快就做完了. **here ˈgoes/here we ˈgo** (*infml* 口) (used to show that one is about to do sth, esp sth new, exciting or risky 用以表示即将做某事, 尤指新的、令人兴奋的或冒险的事物): *Well, here goes — wish me luck!* 那么, 看我的吧 —— 祝我走运吧! **(have) a lot, plenty, not much, nothing, etc ˈgoing for one** (have) many, not many, etc advantages (有)很多有利条件、没(有)什么有利条件等: *You're young, intelligent, attractive: you've got a lot going for you!* 你年轻、聪明、漂亮, 有很多有利条件! ˌ**no ˈgo** (*infml* 口) not possible, permissible or desirable 不可能; 不可以; 不可取: *I tried to get him to increase my salary but it was clearly no go.* 我已尽力让他给我增加薪水, 但显然行不通. **there goes sth** (*infml* 口) (used to show regret that sth has been lost 用以表示因失去某物而感到惋惜): *They've scored again — there go our chances of winning* (ie we are now certain to lose) *the match.* 他们又得分了 —— 这场比赛我们赢不了了. **there sb ˈgoes (again)** (*infml* 口) (used to show annoyance, exasperation or resignation that sth said or done before has been, or is about to be, repeated 用以对说过的或做过的某事物竟然再次出现而表示厌烦、愤怒或无可奈何): *There you go again, prying into other people's affairs!* 你又来探听人家的事了! **to ˈgo** (*US infml* 口) (of cooked food sold in a restaurant or shop) to take away and eat elsewhere (指饭馆或商店出售的熟食)外卖的: *Two pizzas to go!* 来两份外卖的意大利饼! **what/whatever ˌsb says, ˈgoes** (*infml* 口) the specified person has total authority and must be obeyed 某人说了算: *My wife wanted the kitchen painted white, and what she says, goes.* 我妻子想把厨房刷成白色, 她说了算. ˌ**where does sb ˌgo from ˈhere?** (esp of sb who is in a difficult situation) what action should sb take next (esp in order to improve the situation he is in)? (尤指处于困境的人)下一步该怎么办?: *Sales are down; redundancies are inevitable: where does the company go from here?* 销售量下降、裁员势在必行, 公司何去何从? ˌ**who goes ˈthere?** (used by a sentry to order sb to say who he is 哨兵喝问对方身分的用语): *Halt, who goes*

G

there? 站住, 什么人? (For other idioms containing **go**, see entries for *ns*, *adjs*, etc 与 **go** 搭配的其他习语见有关名词、形容词等的词条, 如 **go bananas** ⇨ BANANA; **go haywire** ⇨ HAYWIRE.)

34 (phr v) **go a'bout (a)** ⇨ GO ROUND/AROUND/ABOUT. **(b)** (of a boat) change direction; tack (指船)改变航向, 抢风调向. **go about sth** continue to do sth; keep busy with sth 继续做某事物; 忙于某事物: *go about one's daily routine* 忙于日常事务 ○ *Despite the threat of war, people went about their work as usual.* 尽管战争一触即发, 人们仍像平时一样工作. **go about sth/doing sth** start to work at sth; approach or tackle sth; set about sth 开始做某事物; 处理某事物; 着手于某事物: *You're not going about the job in the right way.* 你处理此事的方法不对. ○ *How should I go about finding a job?* 我应该怎样着手寻找工作? **go about with sb** ⇨ GO ROUND/AROUND/ABOUT WITH SB.

go after sb chase or pursue sb 追逐或追踪某人: *He went after the burglars.* 他追赶那些盗贼. **go after sb/sth** try to get or obtain sb/sth 设法得到某人[某事物]: *He goes after* (ie tries to attract sexually) *every woman he meets.* 他对女人见一个追一个. ○ *We're both going after the same job.* 我们俩都谋求得到这份工作.

go against sb be unfavourable to sb 对某人不利: *The jury's verdict went against him.* 陪审团裁断他有罪. ○ *The war is going against us.* 这场战争对我们很不利. **go against sb/sth** resist or oppose sb/sth 抵抗或反对某人[某事物]: *Don't go against your parents/your parents' wishes.* 不要违背父母的意愿. ○ *He went against the advice of his colleagues and resigned.* 他不顾同事的劝告辞了职. **go against sth** be opposed or contrary to sth; conflict with sth 反对或违反某事; 与某事冲突: *Paying for hospital treatment goes against her socialist principles.* 付给医院医疗费是有违她的社会主义原则的. ○ *His thinking goes against all logic.* 他的思维完全不合逻辑.

go a'head be carried out; take place 进行; 发生: *Despite the bad weather the fête will go ahead.* 尽管天气不好, 游乐会照常举行. ○ *The building of the new bridge will go ahead as planned.* 新桥的修建将按计划进行. **go a'head (with sth)** begin to do sth without hesitation 毫不迟疑地开始做某事物: *'May I start now?' 'Yes, go ahead.'* '我现在可以开始吗?' '可以, 开始吧.' ○ *The government intends to go ahead with its privatization plans.* 政府拟推行私有化计划.

go a'long (a) (used esp after *as* 尤用于as之后) proceed with an activity; continue 进行下一项活动; 继续: *You may have some difficulty at first but you'll find it easier as you go along.* 初时可能有些困难, 继续做下去就会觉得容易多了. ○ *He made the story up as he went along.* 他说的内容是现讲现编的. **(b)** progress; develop 进展; 发展: *Things are going along nicely.* 事情进展得很好. **go a'long with sb/sth** agree with sb/sth; accept sth 与某人[某事]意见一致; 赞同某事物: *I can't go along with you on that point.* 在那一点上我无法同意你的意见. ○ *I don't go along with her views on nuclear disarmament.* 我不同意她在核裁军问题上的看法.

go around ⇨ GO ROUND/AROUND/ABOUT. **go around with sb** ⇨ GO ROUND/AROUND/ABOUT WITH SB.

go at sb attack sb 攻击某人: *They went at each other furiously.* 他们互相猛烈攻击. **go at sth** make great efforts to do sth; work hard at sth 努力做某事物: *They went at the job as if their lives depended on it.* 他们拼命做这项工作.

go a'way (a) leave a place 走开; 离开: *We're going away for a few days*, eg for a holiday. 我们要外出几天(如度假). **(b)** disappear; fade 消失; 散去; 变淡: *The smell still hasn't gone away.* 气味尚未消失.

go 'back (to...) return 返回: *The children have to go back to school next week.* 下周孩子们要返校了. ○ *This toaster is going back* (ie must be taken back) *to the shop — it doesn't work properly.* 这个面包片加热器得退回商店——有毛病. **go 'back (to sth) (a)** return to an earlier point in space or time (在空间或时间上)回到先前某点: *How far does your memory go back?* 你能回忆起多久以前的事情? ○ *Once you have taken this decision, there will be no going back*, ie you will not be able to change your mind. 一旦作出这个决定, 就不能改变主意. ○ *Can I go back to what you said at the beginning of the meeting?* 我可以再提你在会议开始时所说的事情吗? ○ *To trace the origins of the Irish problem, we have to go back over three hundred years.* 要探讨爱尔兰问题的起因就要追溯到三百多年以前. **go back on sth** fail to keep (a promise); change one's mind about sth 食言; 改变对某事的主意: *He never goes back on his word.* 他从不食言. **go back to sth/doing sth (a)** start doing sth that one had stopped doing 重做某事物; 重操旧业: *She's decided to go back to teaching.* 她已决定重新执教. **(b)** have existed since (a specified time) or for (a specified period) 自(某时候)起已存在; 已存在(某时期): *His family goes back to the time of Queen Elizabeth I.* 他的家族渊源可回溯到伊丽莎白女王一世的时代. ○ *How far does the tradition go back?* 这传统有多久的历史了?

go be'fore exist or happen in an earlier time 存在或发生于早一些的时间: *The present crisis is more than any that have gone before.* 目前的危机比以前发生过的都严重. **go before sb/sth** be presented to sb/sth for discussion, decision or judgement 送交某人[某部门]讨论、决定或裁断: *My application goes before the planning committee next week.* 我的申请下星期提交计划委员会审批.

go beyond sth exceed sth 超过(某事物): *This year's sales figures go beyond all our expectations*, ie are much better than we thought they would be. 今年的销售额之高完全超出我们的预料. ○ *The matter has gone beyond a joke*, ie has become too serious to be amusing. 这事可不是闹着玩儿的.

go 'by (of time) pass; elapse (指时间)过去, 消逝: *As time goes by my memory seems to get worse.* 随着时间的流逝, 我的记忆力似乎越来越差. ○ *The weeks went slowly by.* 一星期一星期慢慢过去了. **'go by sth (a)** be guided or directed by sth 遵照或依照某事物: *I shall go entirely by what my solicitor says*, ie I shall follow his advice. 我要完全按照律师的建议去做. ○ *That's a good rule to go by.* 那是要遵守的好规则. **(b)** form an opinion or a judgement from sth (根据某事物)形成意见或做出判断: *Have we enough evidence to go by?* 我们有足以做出判断的证据吗? ○ *It's not always wise to go by appearances.* 根据表面现象看问题有时是不可取的. ○ *If past experience is anything to go by, the plane will be late.* 过去的经验要是还靠得住的话, 这飞机会晚点的.

go 'down (a) fall to the ground 倒在地上: *She tripped and went down with a bump.* 她绊了一下, 猛地跌倒在地上. **(b)** (of a ship, etc) sink (指船等)沉没: *Hundreds died when the liner went down.* 班轮沉没时, 有数百人罹难. **(c)** (of the sun and moon) disappear beneath the horizon; set (指日、月)落下, 没入地平线以下: *We sat and watched the sun go down.* 我们坐着观看日落. **(d)** (of food and drink) be swallowed (指食物和饮料)咽下: *This pill just won't go down*, ie I can't swallow it. 这个药丸我简直咽不下去. ○ *A glass of wine would go down very nicely*, ie I would very much like one. 有杯葡萄酒就太好了. **(e)** be reduced in size, level, etc (体积、水平等)减小, 降低: *The swelling has gone down a little.* 肿块已小了一些. ○ *The flood waters are going down.* 洪水渐退. **(f)** (of prices, the temperature, etc) become lower; fall (指价格、温度等)减低, 下降: *The price of petrol is going down/Petrol is going down (in price).* 汽油价正在下跌. **(g)** (of the wind) become less strong or violent (指风)减弱, 减缓: *We waited for the wind to go down.* 我们等待风势减弱. **(h)** (*infml* 口) decrease in quality; deteriorate 质量下降; 恶化: *This neighbourhood has gone down a lot recently.* 此处的邻居素质最近差多了. **go 'down (from...)** leave a university (esp Oxford or Cambridge) at the end of a term or after finishing one's studies 学期结束时或完成学业后离开大学(尤指牛津或剑桥): *She went down (from Cambridge) in 1984.* 她于1984年(自剑桥)大学毕业. **go 'down (in sth)** be written (in sth); be recorded or remembered (in sth) (在某处)写上; (在某事物中)记着: *It all goes down* (ie She writes it all) *in her notebook.* 那些全都记在她的笔记本里了. ○ *He will go down in history as a great statesman.* 他将作为伟大的政治家而载入史册. **go 'down (to sb)** be defeated by sb, esp in a match or contest 被某人击败(尤指在比赛或竞赛中): *Connors went down (to Becker) by three sets to one.* 康纳斯以三负一胜输(给贝克尔)了. **go down (to...) (from...)** go from one place to another, esp from the north of Britain to London, or from a city or large town to a smaller place 从一处到另一处(尤指从英国北部到伦敦或从大城镇到小地方): *We're going down to London next week.* 下周我们南下去伦敦. ○ *They've gone down to Brighton for a couple of days.* 他们已南下到布赖顿市住两天. **go down (with sb)** (used with *advs* or in questions after *how* 与副词连用或用于疑问句中的how之后) (of a remark, performance, etc) be received by sb in the specified way (指言语、表演等)被某人以某方式接受: *Her speech went down well (with the conference).* 她的讲话很受(大会)赞许. ○ *His plays have gone down badly in America.* 他的剧本在美国不受欢迎. ○ *Rude jokes don't go down too well with* (ie are disapproved of by) *the vicar.* 教区牧师对粗鄙的笑话颇不以为然. **go down to sth** reach or extend as far as (the specified time or period) 达到或延续到(某时间或时期): *This volume only goes down to* (ie only deals with the period up to) *1945.* 这一卷涉及的时间仅至1945年. **go down with sth** become ill with (an illness) 患(某病): *Our youngest boy has gone down with mumps.* 我们的小儿子得了腮腺炎.

go for sb attack sb 攻击某人: *She went for him with a carving knife.* 她持切肉刀攻击他. ○ (*fig* 比喻) *The newspapers really went for him over his defence of terrorism.* 报章对他偏袒恐怖主义行为大加抨击. **go for sb/sth** (**a**) apply to sb/sth 应用或适用于某人[某事物]: *What I said about Smith goes for you, too.* 我说的关于史密斯的话也适用于你. ○ *Britain has a high level of unemployment — but the same goes for many other countries.* 英国失业率很高——但许多国家也如此. (**b**) go to fetch sb/sth 去找来某人[某事物]: *Shall I go for a doctor?* 我去请医生来好吗? ○ *She's gone for some milk.* 她取牛奶去了. (**c**) be attracted by sb/sth; like or prefer sb/sth 被某人[某事物]吸引; 喜欢某人[某事物]: *She goes for tall slim men.* 她喜欢瘦高个子的男子. ○ *I don't go much for modern art.* 我对现代艺术不很欣赏. **go for sth** (**a**) choose sth 选择某事物: *I think I'll go for the fruit salad.* 我想我还是要水果色拉吧. (**b**) attempt to have or achieve sth 想要取得或成就某事: *She's going for the world record in the high jump.* 她想创造跳高世界纪录.

go 'in (**a**) (of the sun or moon) disappear behind a cloud (指日或月)被云遮住: *The sun went in and it grew colder.* 太阳进入云层而天气转冷. (**b**) (of a batsman in cricket) go to the wicket at the start of one's innings (指板球戏中的击球员)入场击球, 开始一局比赛: *Who's going in next?* 下一局谁上场击球? **go in for sth** (**a**) take (an examination) or take part in (a competition) 参加(考试或比赛): *She's going in for the Cambridge First Certificate.* 她将参加剑桥初级证书考试. ○ *Which events is he going in for at the Olympics?* 他参加奥林匹克运动会的什么项目? (**b**) choose sth as one's career 选择某事作职业: *Have you ever thought of going in for teaching?* 你考虑过以教书为职业吗? **go in for sth/doing sth** have sth as an interest or a hobby 将某事物当作兴趣或爱好: *go in for golf, stamp-collecting, growing orchids* 爱好打高尔夫球、集邮、种植兰花 ○ *She goes in for a lot of sport.* 她很喜欢运动.

go into sth (**a**) (of a vehicle) make (violent) contact with sth; hit sth (指车辆)撞到某物上: *The car skidded and went into a tree.* 汽车打滑, 撞到树上. (**b**) join (an organization), esp in order to have a career in it; enter sth 参加(一组织)(尤指为业); 进入某事物: *go into the Army, the Church, Parliament* 从军、当神职人员、当国会议员 ○ *go into banking, publishing, teaching, etc* 从事银行业、出版业、教学等 ○ *When did Britain go into Europe* (ie join the EEC)*?* 英国是何时加入欧洲经济共同体的? (**c**) (of a vehicle or driver) start the specified movement (指车辆或驾驶员)开始某动作: *The lorry went into a spin on a patch of ice.* 卡车在一片冰地上打滑了. ○ *The plane went into a nosedive.* 飞机开始俯冲. (**d**) begin to act or behave in the way specified 开始以某方式行动或表现: *He went into a long explanation of the affair.* 他对那件事长篇大论地解释起来. ○ *She went into hysterics.* 她歇斯底里大发作. ○ *She went into fits/peals of laughter.* 她发出阵阵笑声. (**e**) examine or investigate sth carefully 仔细检查或调查某事物: *We need to go into the question of costs.* 我们需要研究一下费用问题. ○ *I don't want to go into the minor details now.* 我现在不想涉及枝节问题. ○ *The problem will need a lot of going into.* 这问题需进行大量调查. ○ *The matter is being gone into.* 事情正在调查中. (**f**) (of resources, time, etc) be spent or used to do sth (指资源、时间等)消耗或用以做某事物: *More government money needs to go into rebuilding the inner cities.* 政府需动用更多经费重建旧城区. ○ *Years of work have gone into the preparation of this dictionary.* 这部词典的筹备工作已进行了多年.

go 'off (**a**) (of an actor) leave the stage (指演员)退场, 下场: *Hamlet goes off stage left.* 哈姆雷特从舞台左侧退下. (**b**) be fired; explode 开火; 爆炸: *The gun went off by accident.* 那枪走火了. ○ *The bomb went off in a crowded street.* 炸弹在熙来攘往的街道上爆炸了. (**c**) make a sudden loud noise; be sounded 突然发出巨响; 发出声音: *The thieves ran away when the burglar alarm went off.* 防盗警报器一响, 盗贼立刻逃走了. (**d**) (of electric power, a light, etc) stop functioning or operating (指电力)中断; (指电灯等)熄灭: *Suddenly the lights went off.* 灯光突然熄灭了. ○ *The heating goes off at night.* 供暖设备在夜间停止运作. (**e**) (*infml* 口) fall asleep 入睡: *Hasn't the baby gone off yet?* 孩子睡着了吗? (**f**) become unfit to eat or drink; go bad 变得不适于食用或饮用; 变坏: *This milk has gone off*, ie has turned sour. 这牛奶已变质. (**g**) become worse in quality; deteriorate 质量变坏; 恶化: *Her books have gone off in recent years.* 近年来她写的书质量下降了. (**h**) (used with *advs* or in questions after *how* 与副词连用或用于疑问句中的how之后) take place or happen in the way specified; go 以某种方式进行或发生: *The performance went off well.* 演出很成功. ○ *How did the concert go off?* 音乐会开得如何? **go off sb/sth** lose interest in sb; lose one's taste for sth 对某人失去兴趣; 对某事物感到乏味: *Jane seems to be going off Peter.* 简好像对彼得日趋冷淡. ○ *I've gone off beer.* 我不爱喝啤酒了. **go off with sb** leave one's husband, wife, lover, etc in order to have a relationship with sb else 离开丈夫、妻子、情人等另结新欢: *He went off with his best friend's wife.* 他与至友之妻逃之夭夭了. ○ *She went off with the milkman.* 她与送牛奶的人私奔了. **go off with sth** leave a place with sth that does not belong to one 携非己之物而去: *He went off with £10 000 of the company's money.* 他拐走公司10 000英镑. ○ *Who's gone off with my pen?* 谁把我的钢笔拿走了?

go 'on (**a**) (of an actor) walk onto the stage (指演员)上场, 发场: *She doesn't go on till Act 2.* 她要到第二幕才出场. (**b**) (of a sportsman) join a team as a substitute during a match (指运动员)在比赛中上场替换他人: *Allen went on (in place of Lineker) just before half-time.* 就在上半场结束前, 艾伦上场(替换莱恩克). (**c**) (of a bowler in cricket) begin to bowl (板球戏中的投球手)开始投球: *Dilley went on (to bowl) after tea.* 茶点过后, 迪理上场投球. (**d**) start to function; be lit 开始运作; 点亮: *Why won't the heating go on?* 为什么供暖设备停了? ○ *Suddenly all the lights went on.* 突然所有的灯都亮了. (**e**) (of time) pass; elapse; go by (指时间)过去, 流逝, 经过: *She became more and more talkative as the evening went on.* 夜渐深, 她的话也渐渐多起来. ○ *Things will improve as time goes on.* 随着时间的推移, 情况会改善的. (**f**) (esp in the continuous tenses 尤用于进行时态) take place; happen 发生; 出现: *What's going on here?* 这儿出什么事了? ○ *There must be a party going on next door.* 隔壁准是在举行聚会. (**g**) (of a situation or state of affairs) continue without changing (指情况或状态)继续下去而无变化: *The present state of affairs cannot be allowed to go on.* 目前的情况不得再继续下去了. ○ *How much longer will this hot weather go on (for)?* 这样炎热的天气还要持续多久? ○ *We* (ie Our relationship) *can't go on like this — we seem to be always arguing.* 我们不能老是这样了——好像我们总在争吵. (**h**) continue speaking, after a short pause (经短暂停顿后)继续说: *She hesitated for a moment, and then went on.* 她迟疑了一下, 然后接着说. (**i**) used to encourage or dare sb to do sth 用以鼓励或鼓动某人做某事: *Go on! Have another drink.* 来呀! 再喝一杯. **go on sth** (**a**) begin to receive (payments from the State because one is unemployed) or to take (a medicine) 开始领取(失业补助金); 开始服用(药物): *go on social se'curity/the 'dole* 开始领取社会保障金[失业救济金] ○ *go on the 'pill*, ie start using contraceptive pills 开始服用避孕药丸.

G

(**b**) (used with the negative or in questions 与否定词连用或用于疑问句) base an opinion or a judgement on sth 以某事物为依据形成意见或判断: *The police don't have much evidence to go on.* 警方没有什么证据作凭借. **go 'on (about sb/sth)** talk about sb/sth for a long time (esp in a boring or complaining way) 长时间谈某人[某事物](尤指抱怨或令人生厌): *She does go on sometimes!* 她有时就是爱唠叨! ○ *I know you don't like my smoking, but there's no need to go on about it.* 我知道你不喜欢我抽烟, 可也没有必要老唠叨这事. **go 'on (at sb)** complain to sb about his behaviour, work, etc; criticize sb; nag sb 埋怨或责怪(某人的行为、工作等); 挑剔某人; 数落某人: *She goes on at her husband continually.* 她老是数落自己的丈夫. **go 'on (with sth)** continue an activity, esp after a pause or break 继续进行某活动(尤指停顿之后): *He paused to take a sip of water, and then went on (with his story).* 他停下来呷了一口水, 然后继续讲(他的事). ○ *If we don't finish painting the kitchen today, we can go on with it tomorrow.* 要是今天厨房粉刷不完, 明天可以接着干. **go on doing sth** continue an activity without stopping 不停地从事某活动: *go on coughing, crying, laughing, talking, etc* 不停地咳嗽、哭泣、笑、谈话等 ○ *You can't go on working without a break.* 人不能不停地工作而不休息. ○ *If you go on drinking like this you'll make youself ill.* 你这样喝个没完, 要喝出毛病来的. **go on to sth** pass from one item to the next 从一项目转移至下一项目: *Let's go on to the next item on the agenda.* 我们讨论议程表上的下一项吧. **go on to do sth** do sth after completing sth else 完成一事后接着做某事: *After attacking the Government's economic policy, he went on to describe how the Labour Party would reduce unemployment.* 他抨击了政府的经济政策之后, 接着讲述工党降低失业率的计划.

go 'out (**a**) leave one's house to go to social events 出门参加社交活动: *She goes out a lot.* 她经常参加社交活动. ○ *He goes out drinking most evenings.* 晚上他差不多都到外边喝酒. (**b**) (of the tide) move away from the land; ebb (指潮汐)退潮, 落潮. (**c**) stop work; strike 停止工作; 罢工: *Are we likely to gain anything by going out (on strike)?* 我们罢工能得到什么好处吗? (**d**) be sent 送出; 发出; 派出: *Have the invitations gone out yet?* 请帖发出去没有? (**e**) (of a programme) be broadcast on radio or television (指节目)在电台或电视台上播放或播送: *The first episode goes out next Friday evening at 8.00 pm.* 下星期五晚上8时播出第一集. (**f**) (of news, information, etc) be announced or published (指新闻、信息等)宣布, 发布, 发表, 刊登: *Word went out that the Prime Minister had resigned.* 传说首相已经辞职. (**g**) become unfashionable or cease to be used 不流行; 过时; 停止使用: *Flared trousers went out years ago.* 喇叭裤多年前就不时兴了. (**h**) stop burning or shining; be extinguished 不再燃烧或发光; 熄灭: *The fire has gone out.* 火已熄灭. ○ *There was a power cut and all the lights went out.* 因停电所有的灯都熄灭了. (**i**) end; finish 结束; 终止: *The year went out with blizzards and gales.* 在暴风雪中送走了一年. **go 'out (of sth)** be eliminated from a competition, contest, etc (在比赛、竞赛等中)被淘汰: *She went out in the first round of the tournament/went out of the tournament in the first round.* 她在比赛的第一轮比赛中遭淘汰. **go 'out (to...)** leave one's native country and go to a distant one 出国: *Our daughter went out to Australia ten years ago.* 我们的女儿十年前出国到澳大利亚去了. **go out of sb/sth** (of a quality or feeling) no longer be present in sb/sth; disappear from sb/sth (指素质或情感)在某人[某事物]中不复存在: *All the fight seemed to go out of him.* 他似乎再无斗志. ○ *The heat has gone out of the argument.* 辩论已不那么激烈了. **go out to sb** (of feelings) be offered or extended to sb (指感情)给与或倾注于某人: *Our hearts/sympathies go out to relatives of the victims.* 我们很同情受害者的亲属. **go out with sb; go 'out (together)** (*infml* 口) (esp of a young person) spend time with sb and have a romantic or sexual relationship with him (尤指年轻人)与某人谈恋爱或有性关系: *Terry has been going out with Sharon for six weeks.* 特里和沙伦相恋有六个星期了. ○ *Sharon and Terry have been going out (together) for six weeks.* 沙伦和特里两人谈情说爱已经有六个星期了.

go 'over (used with *advs* or in questions after *how* 与副词连用或用于疑问句中的how之后) be received in the specified way 以某种方式接受: *How did her speech go over?* 人们对她的演讲反应如何? **go over sth** (**a**) look at sth carefully; inspect sth 仔细检查某事物; 察看某事物: *The surveyor went over the house thoroughly and advised us not to buy it.* 房屋鉴定人彻底察看了房子以后, 劝我们不要买. (**b**) examine the details of sth; check sth 检查某事物的细节; 核对某事物: *You'll have to go over these figures again, they don't add up.* 你必须再核对一下这些数字, 总数不符. ○ *Go over your work carefully before you hand it in.* 交作业前要仔细检查一下. (**c**) study or review sth carefully; rehearse or revise sth 仔细研究或温习某事物; 演习或修订某事物: *He went over the events of the day in his mind*, ie thought about them carefully. 他对白天发生的事情细加反思. ○ *She went over her lines before the first night of the play.* 她在该剧首演前又练习了一次台词. (**d**) clean sth, esp thoroughly 将某物弄干净(尤指彻底地): *She went over the room with a duster.* 她用抹布把房间擦得干干净净. **go over (to...)** move from one (usu distant) place to another 从一处(通常为远处)到另一处: *Many of the Irish went over to America during the famine.* 很多爱尔兰人在饥荒期间迁徙到了美国. **go over to sb/sth** (*broadcasting* 播) transfer to (a different reporter, studio, etc) 转换至(另一记者、演播室等): *We are now going over to the news desk for an important announcement.* 现在我们转至新闻部, 宣布一项重要消息. **go over to sth** change from one side, opinion, habit, system, etc to another (从一边、一见解、一习惯、一体系等)转至(另一方面): *Two Conservative MPs went over to the Liberals.* 有两名保守党议员转至自由党一边. ○ *She's gone over to a milder brand of cigarettes.* 她已改吸另一牌子味道较淡的香烟.

go 'round (**a**) go by a longer route than usual 走弯路; 绕道: *The main road was flooded so we had to go round by narrow country lanes.* 公路干线遭水淹没, 我们只得择乡间小径绕行. (**b**) (of a number or quantity of sth) be enough for everyone to have a share (指某物的数或量)足够每人一份: *There aren't enough chairs to go round.* 椅子不够坐. ○ *Is there enough food to go round?* 食物够每人一份吗? **go round/around/about** (**a**) (used with an *adj*, or a *v* in the *-ing* form 与形容词或动词-ing形式连用) move from place to place; move in society 四处活动; 在交际方面活跃: *She goes about barefoot.* 她光着脚四处走. ○ *It's unprofessional to go round criticizing your colleagues.* 四处活动批评同事是不符合职业道德的. (**b**) (of a rumour, story, etc) pass from person to person; circulate (指传言、故事等)流传, 传播: *There's a rumour going round that Sue and David are having an affair.* 有谣传称休和戴维关系暧昧. (**c**) (of an illness) spread from person to person in a group or community (指疾病)传染, 流行: *There's a lot of flu going round at the moment.* 现在流感传染很广. **go round (to...)** visit sb or a place (usu within the same town, city, etc) 访问某人或参观某处(通常在同一市镇等): *I'm going round to my parents' (house) later.* 我打算以后到父母(家)那儿看看. **go round/around/about with sb** be often in the company of sb 经常与某人来往: *He goes round with a bunch of thugs.* 他经常和一帮流氓厮混.

go 'through (**a**) (of a law, bill, etc) be officially approved or accepted (指法律、法案等)被正式通过或接受: *The bill went through*, ie was passed by Parliament. 该法案已正式通过. ○ *As soon as my divorce goes through, we'll get married.* 一俟我的离婚申请获准, 我们就结婚. (**b**) be successfully completed 顺利完成: *The deal did not go through.* 这笔交易未谈成. **go through sth** (**a**) wear a hole in sth 磨穿某物: *I've gone through the elbows of my sweater.* 我的毛衣的肘部都磨破了. (**b**) study or examine sth closely or systematically, esp in order to find sth 仔细或系统地研究或检查(尤为寻找、发现某事物): *I always start the day by going through my mail.* 我总是每天一早就仔细查阅我的邮件. ○ *I've gone through all my pockets but I can't find my keys.* 我把所有的口袋儿都找遍了, 就是找不到我的钥匙. ○ *She went through the company's accounts, looking for evidence of fraud.* 她仔细审核公司的帐目, 查找欺骗作弊的证据. (**c**) discuss, study or review sth in detail 详细讨论、研究、检讨或审核某事物: *Let's go through the arguments* again. 我们再研究一下这些论据吧. ○ *Could we go through* (ie rehearse) *Act 2 once more?* 我们重排一次第二幕的戏好吗? **(d)** take part in sth; perform sth 参加某事; 履行某事: *Certain formalities have to be gone through before one can emigrate.* 必须办妥某些手续方可移居他国. **(e)** experience, endure or suffer sth 经历、忍受或遭受某事物: *She's gone through a bad patch* (ie a difficult or an unhappy time) *recently.* 她最近经历了一段困难时期. ○ *He's amazingly cheerful considering all that he's gone through.* 鉴于他经历过的种种遭遇, 他的乐天达观令人惊叹. **(f)** (of a book) be published in (the specified number of editions) (指书)发行(若干版): *The dictionary has gone through ten editions.* 本词典已发行了十版. **(g)** use up or consume sth; get through sth 用光或消耗某物; 做完某事物: *I seem to be going through a lot of money at the moment.* 目前我花钱似乎很多. **go through with sth** do what is necessary to complete or take (a course of action) 做必要的事以完成或采取(某行动): *She decided not to go through with* (ie not to have) *the abortion.* 她决定不做流产. ○ *He's determined to go through with the marriage despite his parents' opposition.* 他不顾父母的反对决心举办这桩婚事.

go to sb be given to, awarded to or inherited by sb 给予或奖给某人; 为某人所继承: *Proceeds from the concert will go to charity.* 音乐会的收入将捐赠给慈善事业. ○ *The first prize went to the youngest child in the class.* 一等奖授予了班里年龄最小的学生. ○ *The estate went to the eldest son.* 该地产归长子继承.

go together ⇨ GO WITH SB, GO WITH STH.

go towards sth be used as part of the payment for sth; contribute to sth 作为对某事物的部分付款; 有助于或促成某事物: *This money can go towards the new camera you're saving up for.* 你正攒钱买新照相机, 这笔钱可派上用场.

go ˈunder (a) sink below the surface of the sea 沉没海中. **(b)** (*infml* 口) become bankrupt; fail 破产; 失败: *The firm will go under unless business improves.* 生意若无起色, 公司非垮不可.

go ˈup (a) (of the curtain on the stage of a theatre) be raised (指幕布)升起: *The curtain goes up on* (ie is raised to show) *a suburban living-room.* 幕布升起, 展现的是市郊住宅的起居室. **(b)** be built 兴建: *New office blocks are going up everywhere.* 到处都在兴建新的办公楼群. **(c)** be destroyed by fire or an explosion; be blown up 烧毁; 炸毁: *The whole building went up in flames.* 整座建筑物在大火中焚毁. **(d)** become higher in price, level, etc; rise (价格、水平等)上升, 增长: *The price of cigarettes is going up/Cigarettes are going up (in price).* 香烟价上涨了[香烟涨价了]. ○ *Unemployment has gone up again.* 失业人数又上升了. **go ˈup (to...)** begin one's studies at a university (esp at Oxford or Cambridge) 进大学(尤指进牛津或剑桥): *She went up (to Cambridge) in 1977.* 她于1977年进入(剑桥)大学. **go up (to...) (from...)** go from one place to another, esp from a smaller place to London or from the south to the north of Britain 从一处到另一处(尤指从小地方到伦敦或从英国南部到北部): *We're going up to London next weekend.* 下周末我们上伦敦去. ○ *When are you next going up to Scotland?* 下次你什么时候北上苏格兰?

go with sb; ˈgo together (*sl* 俚) have sb as a boyfriend or girlfriend; have sex with sb 交男朋友或女朋友; 和某人有性关系: *He goes with a different woman every week.* 他一星期换一个女人. ○ *Are Kevin and Tracey going together?* 凯文和特蕾西在谈恋爱吗? **go with sth** be included with or as a part of sth 包括在某事物中; 附属于某事物: *A new car goes with the job.* 获这份工作还附带一辆新汽车. ○ *Do the carpet and curtains go with* (ie Are they included in the price of) *the house?* 房价中包括地毯和窗帘吗? **go with sth; go together (a)** combine well with sth; harmonize with sth 与某事物配合良好; 与某事物协调: *Her blouse doesn't go with her skirt/Her blouse and skirt don't go (together).* 她的衬衫和裙子不协调. ○ *I need some new shoes to go with these trousers.* 我需要双新鞋来配这条裤子. ○ *White wine goes well* (ie is suitable to drink) *with fish.* 吃鱼最适合喝白葡萄酒. **(b)** exist at the same time or in the same place as sth; be commonly found together 同时或同地存在; 相伴共存: *Disease often goes with poverty/Disease and poverty often go together.* 疾病与贫穷常相伴而生.

go without (sth) (used esp after *can*, *could* and *have to* 尤用于can、could、have to之后) endure the lack of sth; manage without sth 忍受某事物的缺乏; 没有某事物也可应付: *I had to go without breakfast this morning as I was in a hurry.* 我今早很匆忙, 只好不吃早饭了. ○ *How long can a human being go* (ie survive) *without food?* 人不吃东西能活多久? ○ *She went without sleep for three days.* 她三天没睡觉了.

□ **ˈgo-ahead** *n* **the go-ahead** [sing] permission to do sth (对做某事物的)许可: *We've got the go-ahead from the council/The council have given (us) the go-ahead to start building.* 我们已得到市政会的准许[市政会已准许我们]开工建筑. — *adj* willing to try new methods; enterprising; progressive 愿意尝试新方法的; 有进取精神的; 进步的: *a go-ahead company, school, person* 勇于创新的公司、进步的学校、上进的人.

ˈgo-between *n* person who acts as a messenger or negotiator between two people; intermediary 信使; 调解人; 媒人; 中间人: *act as a go-between* 作中间人.

ˈgo-by *n* (idm 习语) **give sb the ˈgo-by** (*infml* 口) ignore sb; snub sb 漠视某人; 冷落某人: *She gave me the go-by in the street yesterday.* 她昨天在街上不理睬我.

ˈgo-getter *n* (*infml* 口) person who is successful by being energetic and ambitious 有干劲和雄心的成功者: *He's a real go-getter!* 他真是个实干家!

ˌgo-ˈslow *n* type of industrial protest in which employees deliberately work more slowly than usual 怠工.

go[2] /gəʊ; go/ *n* (*pl* **goes** /gəʊz; goz/) **1** [C] person's turn to play in a game (游戏中)轮到某人的机会: *Whose go is it?* 该谁了? ○ *It's your go.* 该你了. **2** [U] (*infml* 口 *esp Brit*) energy; vitality 精力; 活力; 生气: *She's full of/She's got a lot of go!* 她干劲冲天! **3** [C] (*infml* 口) attack of an illness (疾病的)侵袭, 发作: *He's had a bad go of flu.* 他得过很重的流感. **4** (idm 习语) **at one ˈgo** in one single attempt 一下子; 一举: *He blew out all the candles on his birthday cake at one go.* 他一口气吹灭了生日蛋糕上所有的蜡烛. **be all ˈgo** (*Brit infml* 口) be very busy; be full of activity 繁忙; 活动多: *It's all go in the office today.* 今天办公室里忙得不可开交. **be on the ˈgo** (*infml* 口) be very active or busy 非常活跃或繁忙: *I've been on the go all week.* 我整个星期一直都很忙. **have a ˈgo (at sth/doing sth)** (*infml* 口) make an attempt to do sth 企图, 尝试(做某事): *He had several goes at the high jump before he succeeded in clearing it.* 他跳高时试跳了几次才跳过去. ○ *I'll have a go at mending your bike today.* 我今天修修你的自行车. **make a go of sth** (*infml* 口) make a success of sth 使某事物成功: *She's determined to make a go of her new career.* 她决心在新事业上有所成就.

goad /gəʊd; god/ *n* **1** pointed stick for making cattle, etc move on (赶牲畜用的)尖头棒. **2** (*fig* 比喻) thing urging a person to action 刺激或激励人行动的事物: *motivated by the twin goads of punishment and reward* 受赏与罚的双重因素所促使的.

▷ **goad** *v* **1** [Tn, Tn·pr] **~ sb/sth (into sth/doing sth)** (*fig* 比喻) continually provoke or annoy (a person or an animal) 不断招惹或激怒(人或动物): *Stop goading the poor beast!* 别再招惹那可怜的动物了. ○ *His persistent questions finally goaded me into an angry reply/into replying angrily.* 他三番五次地问问题惹得我回答时也没有好气. ○ *trying to goad these lazy fellows into action* 尽力驱使这些懒人行动. **2** (phr v) **goad sb on** continually urge and encourage sb to do sth 不断催促或鼓励某人做某事: *goaded on by fierce ambition* 为强烈的野心所驱使.

goal /gəʊl; gol/ *n* **1 (a)** (in football, hockey, etc) pair of posts with a crossbar, between which the ball has to be kicked, hit, etc in order to score (足球、曲棍球等的)球门: *He headed the ball into an open goal,* ie one temporarily unprotected by the goalkeeper. 他乘虚把球顶入球门. ○ *Who is keeping goal/is in goal* (ie is goalkeeper) *for Arsenal?* 谁给阿森纳队守球门? ⇨illus at ASSOCIATION FOOTBALL (ASSOCIATION) 见 ASSOCIATION FOOTBALL (ASSOCIATION)插图. **(b)** point scored when the ball goes into the goal 进球得的分: *score/kick a goal* 得[踢进一球得]一分 ○ *win by three goals to one* 以三比一获胜 ○ *score an own goal,* ie knock the ball into one's

G

own goal (by accident), thus giving a point to the other team, or (*fig*) do sth that harms oneself 误将球踢进己方球门(白送对方一分或比喻做某事害了自己). **2** (*fig* 比喻) object of one's efforts; target 努力的对象; 目标: *pursue, reach, attain, etc one's goal in life* 追求、达到、实现…人生的目标 ○ *The company has set itself some stiff* (ie high) *production goals for this year.* 公司今年定下很高的生产指标. ○ *Their goal was to eradicate smallpox.* 他们奋斗的目标是消灭天花.

▷ **goal·less** /ˈɡəʊllɪs; ˋgollɪs/ *adj* [usu attrib 通常作定语] with no goal scored (足球、曲棍球等)未得分的: *a goalless draw* 零比零的平局.

□ ˈ**goal-area** *n* (in soccer) marked rectangular area in front of a goal (足球的)球门区. ➪illus at ASSOCIATION FOOTBALL (ASSOCIATION) 见 ASSOCIATION FOOTBALL (ASSOCIATION) 插图.

ˈ**goalkeeper** (also *infml* 口语亦作 **goalie** /ˈɡəʊlɪ; ˋgolɪ/) *n* player who stands in goal and tries to prevent the other team from scoring 守门员. ➪illus at HOCKEY 见 HOCKEY 插图.

ˈ**goal-kick** *n* (in soccer) kick by the defending side to put the ball back into play after the attacking side has sent it over the goal-line (足球的)球门球.

ˈ**goal-line** *n* either of the pair of lines marking the two ends of a pitch 端线.

goal-mouth *n* area immediately in front of a goal: 球门口(正对球门前的区域) [attrib 作定语] *an exciting match with a lot of goal-mouth incidents* 在球门口有许多险球的一场扣人心弦的比赛.

ˈ**goal-post** *n* **1** either of the two upright posts which together with the crossbar form a goal 球门柱: *a cracking shot which hit the goal-post* 射中球门柱的一个漂亮的球. ➪illus at RUGBY 见 RUGBY 插图. **2** (idm 习语) **move the goal-posts** ➪ MOVE².

goat 山羊

goat /ɡəʊt; got/ *n* **1** small lively horned animal with long hair 山羊: *goat's milk* 羊奶 ○ *climb like a mountain goat*, ie very nimbly 像山羊般敏捷地爬. Cf 参看 BILLY-GOAT, NANNY-GOAT. ➪illus 见插图. **2** (*sl* 俚) unpleasant old man, esp one who is sexually active 讨厌的老头; (尤指)老色鬼: *Let go, you randy old goat!* 放开我, 你这老色鬼! **3** (idm 习语) **act/play the (giddy) ˈgoat** (*infml* 口) behave frivolously or irresponsibly 举止轻浮或不负责任. **get sb's ˈgoat** (*infml* 口) greatly irritate or annoy sb 激怒或惹恼某人. **separate the sheep from the goats** ➪ SEPARATE².

▷ **goatee** /ɡəʊˈtiː; goˈti/ *n* man's small pointed beard like the tuft of hair on a goat's chin 山羊胡子(男子下巴上的小撮尖形胡须).

□ ˈ**goatherd** *n* person who looks after a flock of goats 牧羊人; 羊倌.

ˈ**goatskin** *n* (**a**) [U] leather made from the skin of a goat 山羊皮: [attrib 作定语] *a goatskin bag, purse, etc* 山羊皮包、山羊皮钱包. (**b**) [C] bottle made of this 山羊皮囊: *a goatskin filled with wine* 装着酒的山羊皮囊.

ˈ**goat's cheese** cheese made from goat's milk 山羊奶酪.

gob¹ /ɡɒb; gɑb/ *n* (*infml* 口) lump or drop of slimy substance (esp saliva, etc from the mouth) (黏性物质的)团, 块, 滴; (尤指)唾液等: *Gobs of grease/spittle ran down his chin.* 一滴滴的油[口水]顺着他的下巴流下.

▷ **gob** *v* (-bb-) [I] (*infml* 口) spit 吐.

gob² /ɡɒb; gɑb/ *n* (*Brit sl offensive* 俚, 蔑) mouth 嘴: *Shut your gob!* ie Be quiet. 闭上你的嘴!

□ ˈ**gob-stopper** *n* (*Brit*) large ball-shaped sweet 大糖球.

gob·bet /ˈɡɒbɪt; ˋgɑbɪt/ *n* (*infml* 口) **1** lump or chunk, esp of food 团、块或片(尤指食物). **2** (*fig* 比喻) short extract from a text 短小的引文; 摘录: *learn and quote gobbets of poetry* 背诵和引用诗段.

gobble¹ /ˈɡɒbl; ˋgɑbḷ/ *v* **1** [I, Tn, Tn·p] ~ **sth (up/down)** eat sth fast, noisily and greedily (leaving nothing behind) 狼吞虎咽(一点不剩): *Eat slowly and don't gobble!* 慢点吃, 别狼吞虎咽的! ○ *gobble one's food (down) in a hurry* 匆匆忙忙吞(下)食物 ○ *gobble up all the cakes* 大口吃光所有的蛋糕. **2** (phr v) **gobble sth up** (*infml* 口) use sth up quickly; swallow 很快用完; 吞没: *The rent gobbles up half his earnings.* 租金一项就占去他一半的收入. ○ *Small family businesses are often gobbled up by larger firms.* 家庭小商业遭到大公司的吞并.

gobble² /ˈɡɒbl; ˋgɑbḷ/ *v* [I] (**a**) (of a male turkey) make its characteristic sound (指雄火鸡)咯咯叫. (**b**) (of a person) make such a sound when speaking quickly, angrily, etc (指人)(说话急、愤怒时等)发出咯咯声.

▷ **gobble** *n* sound made by a male turkey (雄火鸡的)咯咯叫声.

gob·bler /ˈɡɒblə(r); ˋgɑblɚ/ *n* (*US*) male turkey 雄火鸡.

gobble·de·gook (also **gobble·dy·gook**) /ˈɡɒbldɪɡuːk; ˋgɑbḷdɪˌguk/ *n* [U] (*infml* 口) difficult or pompous language use by specialists; jargon 费解或浮夸的术语; 行话: *Civil Service documents are often written in gobbledegook that ordinary people cannot understand.* 政府部门的文件中常使用术语, 普通人看不懂.

go-between /ˈɡəʊ bɪtwiːn; ˋgobəˌtwin/ *n* messenger or negotiator for two people or groups who do not or cannot meet 信使; 调解人; 媒人; 中间人: *In some countries marriages are arranged by go-betweens.* 在有些国家, 缔结婚姻要靠媒妁之言.

gob·let /ˈɡɒblɪt; ˋgɑblɪt/ *n* glass, metal, etc drinking-vessel (for wine) with a stem and base, but no handle (玻璃、金属等的)高脚(酒)杯. ➪illus at GLASS 见 GLASS 插图.

gob·lin /ˈɡɒblɪn; ˋgɑblɪn/ *n* (in fairy stories) small ugly mischievous manlike creature (童话故事中)(丑陋而调皮的)小妖精, 小妖怪.

go-cart /ˈɡəʊkɑːt; ˋgoˌkɑrt/ *n* (*esp US*) light handcart 轻便手推车. Cf 参看 GO-KART.

god /ɡɒd; gɑd/ *n* **1** [C] being or spirit that is believed to have power over nature and control over human affairs 神: *Mars was the Roman god of war.* 马尔斯是罗马的战神. ○ *a feast/sight (fit) for the gods*, ie which is exceptionally fine 精美绝伦的宴席[美景]. **2 God** [sing] (in various religions, esp Christianity, Judaism and Islam) the Supreme Being, creator and ruler of the universe (在各种宗教中, 尤指基督教、天主教、犹太教和伊斯兰教中的)上帝, 天主, 主, 真主, 宇宙的创造者和主宰: *God the Father, God the Son and God the Holy Ghost*, ie the Holy Trinity in the Christian religion 圣父、圣子、圣灵(基督教中的三位一体) ○ *I swear by Almighty God* (ie very solemnly) *that the evidence I shall give*… 我对全能的神发誓, 我提出的证据… ○ *As God is my witness* (ie I solemnly swear), *that's the truth!* 上帝为我作证, 一切属实! ○ *He likes to play God*, ie behave as if he could control people and events. 他以上帝自居(控制人与事). **3** [C] (**a**) person greatly admired or adored 极受崇敬的人: *To people of their generation Kennedy was a god.* 对他们这一代人来说, 肯尼迪是他们崇拜的偶像. (**b**) thing to which too much attention is given 过分注意的事物: *Money is his god.* 金钱是他的命. **4 the gods** [pl] gallery seats high up in a theatre (剧院中的)最高楼座: *sitting in the gods* 坐在最高楼座. **5** (idm 习语) **an act of God** ➪ ACT¹. **for God's, etc sake** ➪ SAKE. **for the love of ˈGod, etc** ➪ LOVE¹. **God alˈmighty/God in ˈheaven/good ˈGod/(oh) (my) God** (used to express surprise, horror, etc 用以表示惊异、恐怖等): *God, what a stupid thing to do!* 天哪, 多么愚蠢的事呀! **God/goodness/Heaven knows** ➪ KNOW. **God/Heaven forbid** ➪ FORBID. **God/Heaven help sb** ➪ HELP¹. **God's gift to sb/sth** (*often ironic* 常作反语) sb/sth that seems specially created to be useful to or enjoyed by a group of people, an industry, etc 上帝恩赐的人[事物](给大家、企业等): *He seems to think he's God's gift to women.* 似乎他认为自己是上帝赐给女人的宝贝. **God willing** (used to express the wish that one will be able to do as one intends or plans 用以表示但愿事情能如愿): *I'll be back next week, God willing.* 如一切顺利，我下周就回来. **honest to God/goodness** ⇨ HONEST. **in 'God's name** (used when asking angry or surprised questions 用于疑问句，表示气愤或惊讶): *What in God's name was that huge bang?* 究竟是什么砰的一声响? **in the lap of the gods** ⇨ LAP[1]. **a man of God** ⇨ MAN. **please God** ⇨ PLEASE. **put the fear of God into sb** ⇨ FEAR[1]. **thank God, etc** ⇨ THANK. **a tin god** ⇨ TIN. **to God/goodness/Heaven** (used after a *v* to express a strong hope, wish, etc 用于动词之后，表示强烈的希望、愿望等): *I wish to God he'd turn that radio down!* 我真希望他把收音机的音量调低些! **,ye 'gods** (*dated or joc* 旧或谑) (used to express surprise 用以表示惊讶).

□ **'godchild, 'god-daughter, 'godson** *ns* person for whom sb takes responsibility as a godparent 教子; 教女.

'god-damn(ed) (*US* **god·dam** /'gɒdæm; `gɑd'dæm/) *adj, adv* (⚠ *infml* 讳，口) (used for adding force to an expression 用以加强语气): *Where's that god-damned pen?* 那枝该死的钢笔哪儿去了? ○ *There's no need to be so goddam rude!* 没必要那么粗鲁!

'godfather, 'godmother, 'godparent *ns* person who promises when a child is baptized to see that it is brought up as a Christian 教父; 教母.

'god-fearing *adj* living a good life; sincerely religious 敬畏上帝的; 正直善良的; 虔诚的.

'god-forsaken *adj* (of places) dismal; wretched (指地方)冷落的，偏僻的，凄凉的: *a god-forsaken little town in the middle of nowhere* 荒野中一座凄凉的小镇.

'god·like *adj* like God or a god in some quality 如神的; 上帝般的: *his godlike beauty* 他那神人般的容貌.

God's 'acre (*arch* 古) churchyard 教堂墓地.

god-awful /'gɒdɔːfl; `gɑd 'ɔfəl/ *adj* (*infml* 口) extremely bad; terrible 糟透的; 极坏的: *What a god-awful day I've had!* 我这天真倒霉!

god·dess /'gɒdɪs; `gɑdɪs/ *n* **1** female god, eg in Greek and Latin mythology 女神(如希腊和罗马神话中的): *Diana, the goddess of hunting* 戴安娜，狩猎女神. **2** female person greatly adored or admired 极受崇敬的女子: *screen goddesses*, ie female film stars 银幕女明星.

god·head /'gɒdhed; `gɑdhɛd/ *n* **the Godhead** [sing] (*fml* 文) God 上帝: *worshipping the Godhead* 崇敬上帝.

god·less /'gɒdlɪs; `gɑdlɪs/ *adj* not respecting or believing in God; wicked 无神的; 不敬奉上帝的; 邪恶的. ▷ **god·less·ness** *n* [U].

godly /'gɒdlɪ; `gɑdlɪ/ *adj* (**-lier, -liest**) loving and obeying God; deeply religious 热爱和崇敬上帝的; 虔诚的. ▷ **god·li·ness** *n* [U].

go·down /'gəʊdaʊn; `go,daʊn/ *n* (in Asia) warehouse (亚洲的)仓库，货栈.

god·send /'gɒdsend; `gɑd,sɛnd/ *n* unexpected piece of good luck; sth welcome because it gives great help in time of need (意外的)好运; (因及时应需)令人喜出望外的事物: *The rent was due, so your cheque came as an absolute godsend!* 租金已到期，你的支票来到真是喜从天降!

god·speed /,gɒd'spiːd; `gɑd,spid/ *interj, n* (*arch* 古) (used when wishing sb success on a journey, etc 用以祝某人一路平安等): *We bade/wished her godspeed*, ie said farewell to her. 我们祝她一路顺风.

goer /'gəʊə(r); `goɚ/ *n* **1** (*infml* 口) lively or enterprising person 活跃的人; 有进取心的人. **2** (*sexist* 性别偏见) woman or girl who enjoys having sex frequently with different men 喜欢与并非同一男子常有性关系的女子: *She's a real goer — she'll do anything with anyone!* 她是个十足的骚货——人尽可夫，什么事都干得出来!

▷ **-goer** (only in compounds 只用以构成复合词) person who regularly goes to or attends the specified place or event 常去某地或参加某活动的人: *'cinema-/'concert-/'theatre-goers* ○ *He's a regular church-goer.* 他按时到教堂做礼拜.

go-getter ⇨ GO[1].

goggle /'gɒgl; `gɑgl/ *v* [I, Ipr] **~ (at sb/sth)** look (at sb/sth) with wide round bulging eyes 瞪圆眼睛看(某人[某事物]): *He goggled at her in surprise.* 他惊奇地睁大眼睛看着她. ○ *a frog with goggling eyes* 两眼瞪得鼓鼓的青蛙.

□ **'goggle-box** *n* (*Brit infml* 口) TV set 电视机.

'goggle-eyed *adj* with staring, prominent or wide-open eyes 瞪大眼睛的; 眼珠突出的; 瞠目而视的.

goggles /'gɒglz; `gɑglz/ *n* [pl] large round spectacles with flaps at the sides to protect the eyes from wind, dust, water, etc (worn by racing motorists, frogmen, skiers, etc) (赛车驾驶员、蛙人、滑雪者等戴的防风、尘、水等的)护目镜: *a pair of goggles* 一副护目镜. ⇨ illus at GLASSES (GLASS) 见 GLASSES (GLASS) 插图.

go·ing /'gəʊɪŋ; `goɪŋ/ *n* **1** [sing] act of leaving a place; departure 离去; 离开: *We were all sad at her going.* 她一走我们都很难过. **2** [U] condition or state of the ground, a road, a race-track, etc for walking, riding on, etc (地面、道路、跑道等的)路面条件或情况: *The path was rough going.* 这小道崎岖难走. ○ *The going* (ie The surface of the race-track) *at Newmarket is soft today.* 今天纽马基特的跑道湿软. **3** [U] rate of progress, travel, etc 进展、行进等的速率: *It was good going to reach London by midday.* 那次行进速度很快，到中午已抵达伦敦. ○ *She was a company director before she was 25; that's not bad going!* 她不到25岁就当上公司主管，升得可真快! **4** (idm 习语) **comings and goings** ⇨ COMING. **get out, go, leave, etc while the ,going is 'good** leave a place or stop doing sth while conditions are still favourable or while it is still easy to do so 趁情况有利时离开; 急流勇退; 及时脱身: *Life here is getting more difficult all the time — let's go while the going's good.* 这里的生活越来越困难了——趁现在好走，咱们还是走吧. **heavy going** ⇨ HEAVY.

▷ **go·ing** *adj* (idm 习语) **a ,going con'cern** an active and prosperous business, institution, etc 活跃和繁荣的企业、机构等. **the ,going 'rate (for sth)** the usual amount of money paid for goods or services at a particular time (某段时间内为商品或服务所付的)一般的费用或酬金: *The going rate for freelance work is £5 an hour.* 自由职业者的现行酬金是每小时5英镑.

□ **,going-'over** *n* (*pl* **goings-over**) **1** (*infml* 口) act of examining, cleaning or repairing sth thoroughly 对某物彻底的检查、清理或检修: *The document will need a careful going-over before we make a decision.* 我们要对文件仔细审阅后再作决定. ○ *I gave the car a thorough going-over.* 我把汽车彻底检修了一遍. **2** (*sl* 俚) beating or thrashing 痛打; 鞭挞: *The thugs gave him a real going-over.* 那帮流氓把他着实打了一顿.

,goings-'on *n* [pl] (*infml* 口) unusual or surprising happenings or events 不寻常的或令人惊奇的现象或事情: *There were some strange goings-on next door last night.* 昨夜隔壁有些异常.

goitre (*US* **goi·ter**) /'gɔɪtə(r); `gɔɪtɚ/ *n* [U] large swelling of the throat caused by disease of the thyroid gland 甲状腺肿.

go-kart /'gəʊkɑːt; `go ,kɑrt/ *n* small low racing car with an open framework 小型竞赛汽车. Cf 参看 GO-CART.

gold /gəʊld; gold/ *n* **1** [U] precious yellow metal used for making coins, ornaments, jewellery, etc 金; 黄金: *prospecting for gold* 勘探黄金 ○ *coins made of solid gold* 足金金币 ○ *pure gold* 纯金 ○ *5-, 18-, 22-carat gold* 5、18、22开金 ○ *payment in gold* 用黄金支付 ○ [attrib 作定语] *gold bars, bullion, etc* 金条、金块 ○ *a gold bracelet, ring, watch, etc* 金手镯、金戒指、金表 ○ *a gold medal*, ie one given usu as first prize 金质奖章. ⇨ App 10 见附录10. **2** [U] (*rhet* 修辞) money in large sums; wealth 大批金钱; 财富: *a miser and his gold* 守财奴及其财富. **3** [U, C] colour of this metal 金色: *hair of shining gold* 闪着金光的毛发 ○ *the reds and golds of the autumn trees* 秋天树木斑斓的火红色与金黄色 ○ [attrib 作定语] *gold lettering* 金字. **4** [C] (*sport* 体) gold medal 金质奖章: *win a/the gold* 获得金牌. **5** (idm 习语) **all that glitters is not gold** ⇨ GLITTER. **(as) good as gold** very well-behaved 表现很好的: *The children were as good as gold while you were out.* 你不在时孩子都乖极了. **a heart of gold** ⇨ HEART. **strike gold/oil** ⇨ STRIKE[2]. **worth one's/its weight in gold** ⇨ WORTH.

□ **'gold-digger** *n* (*derog* 贬) girl or woman who uses her sexual attractions to get money from men 以色相诱骗男子钱财的女子.

'gold-dust *n* [U] gold in the form of powder 沙金; 金泥; 金粉: *Good electricians are like gold-dust round here*, ie are very rare and sought-after. 好的电工在这一带如

G

凤毛麟角.

ˈ**gold-field** *n* district in which gold is found in the ground 金矿区; 黄金产地.

ˌ**gold ˈfoil** (also ˌ**gold-ˈleaf**) = LEAF 3.

ˌ**gold ˈmedallist** winner of a gold medal 金质奖章获得者.

ˈ**gold-mine** *n* **1** place where gold is mined 金矿. **2** (*fig* 比喻) any source of wealth; prosperous business 富源; 繁荣的企业: *This shop is a regular gold-mine.* 这家商店日进斗金.

ˌ**gold-ˈplate** *n* [U] articles (spoons, dishes and other vessels) made of gold 金制器皿(匙、盘等容器).

ˈ**gold-rush** *n* rush to a newly discovered gold-field 淘金热(涌向新的金矿区的热潮).

ˈ**goldsmith** *n* person who makes articles of gold 金匠.

ˈ**gold standard** economic system in which the value of money is based on that of gold 金本位制.

golden /ˈgəʊldən; ˋgoldn/ *adj* **1** of gold or like gold in value or colour 金的; 金色的; 贵重如黄金的: *a golden crown, ring, etc* 金皇冠、金戒指 ○ *golden hair, sand, light* 金黄色的头发、沙子、光. **2** [usu attrib 通常作定语] precious; fortunate 珍贵的; 幸运的: *golden days*, ie a specially happy period in sb's life 黄金时代(一生中特别幸福的时期) ○ *a golden opportunity*, ie an excellent one which should not be missed 良机. **3** (idm 习语) **a golden handshake** (usu large) sum of money given to a senior member of a company, etc when he leaves (公司等给高级职员的)(通常为大笔的)退职金, 遣散费. **kill the goose that lays the golden egg** ⇨ KILL. **silence is golden** ⇨ SILENCE.

□ ˌ**golden ˈage** period in the past when commerce, the arts, etc flourished 黄金时代, 全盛时期(商业、艺术等曾兴盛的时期): *The Elizabethan period was the golden age of English drama.* 伊丽莎白时期是英国戏剧的黄金时代. ○ *looking back to a past golden age* 回顾过去的黄金时代.

ˌ**golden ˈeagle** large golden-brown eagle of northern parts of the world 金雕(产于北半球). ⇨illus at App 1 见附录1插图, page iv.

golden jubilee (celebration of a) 50th anniversary 50周年纪念(庆典). Cf 参看 DIAMOND JUBILEE (DIAMOND), SILVER JUBILEE (SILVER).

the ˌ**golden ˈmean** principle of moderation; balance between too much and too little of sth 中庸之道: *find the golden mean between drunkenness and total abstinence* 在酗酒与绝对禁酒之间寻找一个居中之道.

ˌ**golden ˈrule** very important principle which should be followed when performing a particular task 重要的原则; 金科玉律: *The golden rule in playing tennis is to watch the ball closely.* 打网球最重要的一点就是紧盯着球.

ˌ**Golden ˈSyrup** (*propr* 专利名) kind of pale yellow refined treacle 金黄糖浆.

golden wedding 50th anniversary of a wedding 金婚纪念(结婚50周年纪念). Cf 参看 DIAMOND WEDDING (DIAMOND), SILVER WEDDING (SILVER).

gold·finch /ˈgəʊldfɪntʃ; ˋgold,fɪntʃ/ *n* bright-coloured song-bird with yellow feathers on its wings 金翅(鸣禽, 翼羽呈黄色).

gold·fish /ˈgəʊldfɪʃ; ˋgold,fɪʃ/ *n* small esp orange or red fish (a type of carp) kept in bowls and ponds 金鱼.

golf /gɒlf; gɑlf/ *n* [U] outdoor game in which the player tries to hit a small hard ball into a series of 9 or 18 holes using as few strokes as possible 高尔夫球运动: *play a round of golf* 打一场高尔夫球. ⇨App 4 见附录4. ⇨ illus 见插图.

▷ **golfer** *n* person who plays golf 打高尔夫球者.

□ ˈ**golf ball** **1** ball used in golf 高尔夫球. **2** small metal sphere with raised letters on it, used in some electric typewriters 球形字头(某些电动打字机上有凸形字母的金属球). Cf 参看 DAISY WHEEL (DAISY).

ˈ**golf-club** *n* stick used for striking the ball in golf 高尔夫球棒. ˈ**golf club** (**a**) association whose members play golf 高尔夫球会. (**b**) grounds and club-house where they meet and play 高尔夫球场地及会所.

ˈ**golf-course** (also ˈ**golf-links**) *n* area of land where golf is played 高尔夫球场.

Go·li·ath /gəˈlaɪəθ; gəˋlaɪəθ/ *n* (*rhet* 修辞) giant 歌利亚(巨人).

gol·li·wog /ˈgɒlɪwɒg; ˋgɑlɪ,wɑg/ (also **golly** /ˈgɒlɪ; ˋgɑlɪ/) *n* black-faced doll with thick stiff hair 头发又浓又硬的黑脸玩偶.

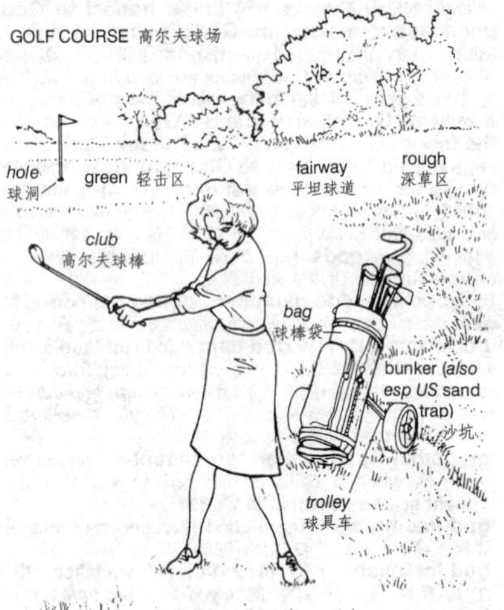

golf 高尔夫球运动

golly /ˈgɒlɪ; ˋgɑlɪ/ *interj* (*infml* 口) (used to express surprise 用以表示惊奇).

go·loshes = GALOSHES.

-gon *comb form* 构词成分 (forming *ns* 用以构成名词) figure with a specified number of angles 有若干角的图形: *octagon, polygon, etc.*

▷ **-gonal** /-gənəl; -gənḷ/ *comb form* 构词成分 (forming *adjs* 用以构成形容词) of or in the shape of such a figure 有若干角形的: *octagonal, polygonal, etc.*

gonad /ˈgəʊnæd; ˋgɑnæd/ *n* male or female organ (eg testis or ovary) in which reproductive cells are produced 性腺, 生殖腺(如睾丸、卵巢).

gondola (威尼斯)平底舟

gon·dola /ˈgɒndələ; ˋgɑndələ/ *n* **1** long flat-bottomed boat with high peaks at each end, used on canals in Venice (威尼斯运河上行驶的)长形平底舟. **2** cabin suspended from an airship or a balloon or from a cable-railway (飞艇、气球或缆索铁路的)吊舱, 吊篮, 缆车. **3** set of shelves (in a self-service shop) for displaying goods (自助商店中的)商品陈列架.

▷ **gon·do·lier** /ˌgɒndəˈlɪə(r); ˌgɑndəˋlɪr/ *n* man who propels a gondola(1) (威尼斯运河上划平底舟的)船夫.

gone[1] *pp* of GO.

gone[2] /gɒn; *US* gɔːn; gɔn/ *adj* **1** [pred 作表语] past; departed 过去; 离去: *Gone are the days when you could buy a three-course meal for under £1.* 一顿饭吃三道菜不到1英镑, 这日子一去不复返了. **2** (used after a phrase expressing time in weeks or months 用于表示星期或月的时间短语之后) having been pregnant for the specified period of time 已怀孕一段时间的: *She's seven months gone.* 她已有七个月的身孕. **3** (idm 习语) **be gone on sb** (*infml* 口) be very much in love with sb; be infatuated with sb 与某人热恋; 迷恋某人: *It's a pity Peter's so gone on Jane.* 彼得如此迷恋简, 真遗憾.

ˌ**going,** ˌ**going,** ˈ**gone** (said by an auctioneer to show that bidding must stop because an item has been sold 拍卖商用语, 表示某物售出而停止出价).

▷ **gone** *prep* later than; past (in time) 晚于; (时间上)已过: *It's gone six o'clock already.* 现在已过了六点钟.

goner /ˈgɒnə(r); *US* ˈgɔːn-; ˋgɔnɚ/ *n* (*infml* 口) person or thing that is dead, ruined or doomed 死亡的、毁灭的或劫数难逃的人或事物: *When his parachute failed he thought he was a goner.* 他的降落伞打不开了, 他想他算完了.

gong /gɒŋ; gɔŋ/ *n* **1** metal disc that gives a resonant note when struck with a stick, used esp as a musical instrument or as a signal for meals (in a hotel, etc) 锣: *beat/sound a gong* 敲[鸣]锣 ○ *Do I hear the dinner gong?* 是开饭的锣声吗? **2** (*Brit infml* 口) (esp military) medal (尤指军功的)奖章, 勋章.

gonna /ˈgɒnə; ˋgɑnə/ (*infml* 口 *esp US*) going to 将要: *We're gonna win.* 我们要赢了.

go·nor·rhoea (also **go·nor·rhea**) /ˌgɒnəˈrɪə; ˌgɑnəˋriə/ *n* [U] contagious venereal disease which causes a painful discharge from the sexual organs 淋病.

goo /guː; gu/ *n* [U] (*infml* 口) **1** sticky wet substance 湿黏物质: *a baby's face covered in goo* 婴儿黏糊糊的脸. **2** (*fig derog* 比喻, 贬) sentimentality 多愁善感.

▷ **gooey** /ˈguːɪ; ˋguɪ/ (**gooier, gooiest**) *adj* (*infml* 口) **1** sticky 黏的: *a gooey face* 黏糊糊的脸. **2** (*fig derog* 比喻, 贬) sentimental 多愁善感的: *gooey words, music* 伤感的言词、音乐.

good[1] /gʊd; gʊd/ *adj* (**better** /ˈbetə(r); ˋbɛtɚ/, **best** /best; bɛst/) **1** of high quality; of an acceptable standard; satisfactory 好的; 优质的; 符合标准的; 令人满意的: *a good lecture, performance, harvest* 好的演讲、表演、收成 ○ *good pronunciation, behaviour, eyesight* 好的发音、行为、视力 ○ *a good* (eg sharp) *knife* 快的刀 ○ *Is the light good enough to take photographs?* 光线适合照相吗? ○ *The car has very good brakes.* 这辆汽车的刹车很灵. ○ *Her English is very good.* 她的英语很好. **2** (**a**) **~ (at sth)** (often used with names of occupations or with *ns* derived from *vs* 常与职业名称或动词派生的名词连用) able to perform satisfactorily; competent 表现令人满意的; 有能力的: *a good teacher, hairdresser, poet, etc* 优秀的教师、理发师、诗人等 ○ *good at mathematics, languages, describing things* 擅长数学、语言、叙事 ○ *a good loser*, ie one who doesn't complain when he loses 输得起的人. (**b**) [pred 作表语] **~ with sth/sb** capable when using, dealing with, etc sth/sb 善于使用某物、处事、待人或用人: *good with one's hands*, eg able to draw, make things, etc 手巧(如会画、会做东西等) ○ *He's very good with children*, ie can look after them well, amuse them, etc. 他很会照看孩子. **3** (**a**) morally acceptable; virtuous 有道德的; 高尚的: *a good deed* 合乎道德的行为 ○ *try to lead a good life* 努力过高尚的生活. (**b**) (esp of a child) well-behaved (尤指儿童)守规矩的, 乖的: *Try to be a good girl.* 要做个乖女孩. **4 ~ (to sb)** willing to help others; kind 乐于助人的; 好心的; 仁慈的: *You were a good girl to help in the shop.* 你帮店里干活儿, 是个好姑娘. ○ *He was very good to me when I was ill.* 我生病时他帮了我的大忙. ○ *Would you be good enough to carry this for me?* 劳驾给我拿着这个行吗? **5** pleasant; agreeable; welcome 快乐的; 愉快的; 随和的; 令人喜悦的: *The firm has had good times and bad times.* 这公司经历过顺境和逆境. ○ *What good weather we're having!* 天气多好哇! ○ *Have you heard the good news about my award?* 你听到我获奖的好消息了吗? ○ *It's good to be home again.* 重返家园, 令人快慰. **6** (of food) fit to be eaten; not yet rotting or rotten (指食物)适合食用的, 未腐败的: *good eggs, fruit, etc* 新鲜的鸡蛋、水果等 ○ *Separate the good meat from the bad.* 把鲜肉和腐肉分开. **7** [usu attrib 通常作定语] not diseased; healthy; strong 无病的; 健康的; 强健的: *good teeth and bones* 健康的牙齿和骨骼 ○ *Would you speak into my good ear, I can't hear in the other one.* 请对着我这只没毛病的耳朵说, 那只耳朵听不见. **8** (of money) not fake or false; genuine (指钱)非伪造的, 真的: *This note is counterfeit, but that one's good.* 这张钞票是假的, 那张是真的. ○ (*fig* 比喻) *I gave good money for that camera, and it turned out to be worthless.* 我买那架照相机可真花了一大笔钱, 结果却不能用. **9** [attrib 作定语] (of clothes, etc) used only for more formal or important occasions (指衣服等)仅用于庄重的或重要的场合的: *My one good suit is at the cleaner's.* 我那套讲究的衣服还在洗衣店里呢. ○ *Wear your good clothes to go to church.* 要穿上像样的衣服去做礼拜. **10** [attrib 作定语] thorough; complete; sound 彻底的; 完全的; 着实的: *give sb a good beating, scolding, telling-off, etc* 给某人一顿痛打、痛骂、痛斥等 ○ *go for a good long walk* 好好地散散步 ○ *We had a good laugh at that.* 那件事情叫我们笑个痛快. **11** [usu attrib 通常作定语] amusing 有趣的; 好玩的: *a good story, joke, etc* 有趣的故事、笑话等 ○ *'That's a good one!' she said, laughing loudly.* '这个真有意思!'她大笑着说. **12 ~ (for sb/sth)** beneficial; wholesome 有益的; 有益健康的: *the good* (ie clean, refreshing) *mountain air* 山中清新的空气 ○ *Is this kind of food good for me?* 这种食物对我身体有益吗? ○ *Sunshine is good for your plants.* 你的花草要多晒太阳. ○ *This cream is good for* (ie soothes and heals) *burns.* 这种油膏治烧伤和烫伤很管事儿. **13 ~ (for sth/to do sth)** suitable; appropriate 适合的; 相宜的: *a good time for buying a house/to buy a house* 买房子的适当时机 ○ *This beach is good for swimming but bad for surfing.* 这个海滨适于游泳而不适于冲浪. ○ *She would be good for the job.* 她做这工作很合适. **14 ~ for sth** (**a**) (of a person or his credit) such that he will be able to repay (a sum lent) (指人或其信贷)有偿还(借款)能力的: *He/His credit is good for £5 000.* 他[凭他信用]可获贷款5 000英镑. (**b**) having the necessary energy, fitness, durability, etc 有必要的精力、健康条件、忍耐力等的: *You're good for* (ie will live) *a few years yet.* 你还能活几年呢. ○ *This car's good for many more miles.* 这辆汽车还能行驶很多英里. (**c**) valid for sth 有效的: *The return half of the ticket is good for three months.* 回程票三个月内有效. **15** (used in greetings 用于问候): *Good morning/afternoon/evening!* 你好! **16** (*fml* 文) (used as a polite, but more often patronizing, form of address or description 用作敬称或客气的描述, 但多含屈尊俯就之意): *my good sir, man, friend, etc* 我的好先生、好人、好朋友等 ○ *How is your good lady* (ie your wife) *?* 尊夫人好吗? **17** [attrib 作定语] (used as a form of praise 用作赞语): *Good old Fred!* 忠厚的弗雷德! ○ *Good man! That's just what I wanted.* 好心人! 那正是我想要的. **18** [attrib 作定语] (used in exclamations 用于感叹句): *Good Heavens!* 天哪! ○ *Good God!* 上帝呀! **19** (with *a* 与a连用) [attrib 作定语] (**a**) great in number, quantity, etc (数目、数量等)很大的, 很多的: *a good many people* 很多人 ○ *We've come a good* (ie long) *way/distance.* 我们是远道而来的. (**b**) (used with expressions of measurement, quantity, etc 与表示量度、数量等的短语连用) not less than; rather more than 不少于; 稍多于: *We waited for a good hour.* 我们足足等了一小时. ○ *It's a good three miles to the station.* 离车站至少三英里. ○ *She ate a good half of the cake.* 那个蛋糕她整整吃了一半. **20** (idm 习语) **as good as** almost; practically 几乎; 实际上: *He as good as said I'm a liar*, ie suggested that I was a liar without actually using the word 'liar'. 他无异于说我撒谎(只是未用'撒谎'一词罢了. ○ *The matter is as good as settled.* 这事等于解决了. **good and...** (*infml* 口) completely 完全; 彻底: *I won't go until I'm good and ready.* 我完全准备好了才去. **a good ˈfew** a considerable number (of); several 相当多(的); 几个: *'How many came?' 'A good few.'* '来了多少?''很不少.' ○ *There are still a good few empty seats.* 还有好几个空位子. **ˌgood for ˈsb, ˈyou, ˈthem, etc** (*infml* 口) (used when congratulating sb 用以祝贺某人) sb, etc did well 某人干得好: *She passed the exam? Good for her!* 她考试及格了? 真行! (For other idioms containing **good**, see entries for other major words in each idiom 查阅其他含有**good**一词的习语, 见该习语中含有其他主要词的词条, 如 **(as) good as gold** ⇨ GOLD; **in good time** ⇨ TIME[1].)

▷ **good** *adv* (*US infml* 口) well 好好地: *Now, you listen to me good!* 喂, 你好好听我说!

□ **good ˈfaith** honest or sincere intention 诚实; 真挚; 善意: *I don't doubt your good faith.* 你是好意, 我并不怀疑.

ˈgood-for-nothing *n, adj* [attrib 作定语] (person who is) worthless, lazy, etc 无用的(人); 懒惰的(人): *Where's that good-for-nothing son of yours?* 你那个废物儿子在哪儿呢?

ˌGood ˈFriday the Friday before Easter, commemorating

the Crucifixion of Christ 耶稣受难日(复活节前的星期五, 纪念耶稣被钉死在十字架上).

ˌ**good-ˈhearted** *adj* kind 好心肠的; 仁慈的.

ˌ**good ˈhumour** cheerful mood or state of mind 愉快的心情或心态: *a meeting marked by good humour and friendliness* 充满愉快和友好气氛的会议 ○ *a man of great good humour* 脾气极好的男子. ˌ**good-ˈhumoured** *adj* cheerful; amiable 愉快的; 和蔼可亲的.

ˌ**good ˈlooks** pleasing appearance (of a person) 好看的相貌; (人的)漂亮的外表. ˌ**good-ˈlooking** *adj* (esp of people) having a pleasing appearance (尤指人)漂亮的, 好看的: *She's terribly good-looking.* 她非常漂亮. ○ *a ˌgood-looking ˈhorse* 一匹好看的马. ⇨Usage at BEAUTIFUL 用法见 BEAUTIFUL.

ˌ**good ˈnature** kindness and friendliness of character 温顺的性情; 和蔼. ˌ**good-ˈnatured** *adj* having or showing good nature 温顺的; 和蔼的: *a ˌgood-natured ˈperson, disˈcussion* 温顺的人、温和的讨论气氛.

ˌ**good-ˈneighbourliness** *n* [U] friendly relations with or a friendly attitude towards one's neighbours 友好的睦邻关系或态度.

ˌ**good ˈsense** soundness in judgement; practical wisdom 判断的准确性; 处理问题的智慧.

ˌ**good-ˈtempered** *adj* not easily irritated or made angry 脾气好的; 不爱生气的.

good[2] /gʊd; gud/ *n* **1** [U] that which is morally right or acceptable 有道德的事; 善: *the difference between good and evil* 善恶之分 ○ *Is religion always a force for good?* 宗教一向是诲人从善的力量吗? **2** [U] that which gives benefit, profit, advantage, etc 好处、利益、益处等: *work for the good of one's country* 为国家利益工作 ○ *I'm giving you this advice for your own good.* 我劝你是为你好. ○ *Do social workers do a lot of good?* 社会工作者的贡献大吗? Cf 参看 DO-GOODER (DO[1]). **3 the good** [pl v] virtuous people 高尚的人: *a gathering of the good and the great* 贤人伟人荟萃. **4** (idm 习语) **be no/not much/any/some ˈgood (doing sth)** be of no, not much, etc value 没有、没什么…好处: *It's no good (my) talking to him.* (我)同他谈没有用. ○ *Was his advice ever any good?* 他的建议有什么价值吗? ○ *This gadget isn't much good.* 这小机械没什么用处. ○ *What good is it asking her?* 问她有什么好处? **do (sb) ˈgood** benefit sb 有益于(某人): *Eat more fruit: it will do you good.* 多吃水果, 对你有好处. ○ *This cough medicine tastes nice but it doesn't do much good*, ie isn't very effective. 这咳嗽药不难吃, 但作用不大. ○ (*usu ironic* 通常作反语) *Much good may it do you*, ie You won't get much benefit from it. 但愿对你大有好处(其实对你没什么好处). **for ˈgood (and ˈall)** permanently; finally 永久; 永远; 决定性地: *She says that she's leaving the country for good*, ie intending never to return to it. 她说她要永远离开这个国家. **to the ˈgood** (used to describe sb's financial state) in credit (用以记述某人的财务状况)盈余: *We are £500 to the good*, ie We have £500 more than we had. 我们盈余500英镑. **up to no ˈgood** (*infml* 口) doing sth wrong, mischievous, etc 做坏事; 淘气; 恶作剧: *Where's that naughty child now? I'm sure he'll be up to no good wherever he is.* 那调皮孩子哪儿去了? 我看, 他到哪儿也做不出好事来.

good·bye /ˌgʊdˈbaɪ *also* ˌgʊˈbaɪ; gudˈbaɪ/ *interj, n* **1** (used when leaving or being left by sb 用于离别时): *say 'Goodbye!' to sb* 向某人说'再见' ○ *We said our goodbyes* (ie said 'Goodbye!' to each other) *and left.* 我们彼此道别然后离去. **2** (idm 习语) **kiss sth goodbye/kiss goodbye to sth** ⇨ KISS.

good·ish /ˈgʊdɪʃ; ˈgudɪʃ/ *adj* [attrib 作定语] **1** quite good; not the best 尚好的; 差强人意的: *a goodish pair of shoes* 一双不错的鞋. **2** fairly/quite large or great 颇大的; 相当大的: *walk a goodish distance, eat a goodish amount* 走相当远的路、吃得颇多.

goodly /ˈgʊdlɪ; ˈgudlɪ/ *adj* (**-ier, -iest**) **1** (*arch* 古) handsome; pleasant to look at 漂亮的; 好看的: *a goodly man* 漂亮的男子 ○ *a goodly sight* 悦目的景色. **2** [attrib 作定语] (*fml* 文) large (in amount) (数量)大的, 相当多的: *a goodly sum of money* 一大笔钱.

good·ness /ˈgʊdnɪs; ˈgudnɪs/ *n* **1** [U] quality of being good; virtue; kindness (to sb) 善良; 美德; (对某人的)好意: *praise God for his goodness and mercy* 赞美上帝的仁慈和怜悯 ○ *In spite of the bad things he's done I still believe in his essential goodness.* 尽管他做了坏事, 我仍然相信他本质是善良的. ○ *her goodness to her old parents* 她对年迈双亲的孝心. **2** [U] quality that nourishes sb/sth or helps growth (滋养某人[某事物]或助其成长的)养分, 精华: *Much of the goodness in food may be lost in cooking.* 食物在烹调中可能失去许多养分. ○ *Brown bread is full of goodness.* 黑面包富于营养. ○ *soil with a lot of goodness in it* 含大量养分的土壤. **3** [sing] (*euph* 婉) (used in exclamations instead of 'God' 用于感叹句, 代替 God 一词): *Goodness, what a big toy!* 嚯, 多大的玩具呀! ○ *Thank goodness!* ie expressing relief 谢天谢地! ○ *For goodness' sake!* ie expressing protest 看在老天爷的分上!(表示抗议) ○ *My goodness!/Goodness me!/Goodness gracious (me)!* ie expressing surprise 天哪!(表示惊异). **4** (idm 习语) **God/goodness/Heaven knows** ⇨ KNOW. **have the goodness to do sth** (*fml* 文) (used when requesting sb to do sth 用于请求某人做某事): *Have the goodness to step this way, please.* 劳驾, 请这边走. **honest to God/goodness** ⇨ HONEST. **to God/goodness/Heaven** ⇨ GOD.

goods /gʊdz; gudz/ *n* [pl] **1** movable property 动产: *stolen goods* 赃物. **2** things for sale; merchandise 货物; 商品: *cheap, expensive, low-quality, high-quality, etc goods* 便宜的、昂贵的、劣质的、优质的…货物 ○ *cotton, leather, woollen, etc goods* 棉织、皮革、毛纺等商品 ○ *electrical goods* 电器商品. **3** (*Brit*) (*US* **freight**) things carried by rail (contrasted with passengers) (火车运载的)货物: [attrib 作定语] *a goods train, wagon, etc*, ie not for passengers 铁路货车、货车车厢. ⇨Usage at CARGO 用法见 CARGO. **4** (idm 习语) **come up with/deliver the ˈgoods** (*infml* 口) carry out or complete a task as expected, or fulfil a promise 如约实现; 如期完成; 履行诺言: *Under the terms of the agreement the union undertook to get the men back to work, but it was unable to deliver the goods*, ie the men stayed on strike. 根据协议工会负责让工人回去上班, 但却未能如愿(工人坚持罢工). **sb's ˌgoods and ˈchattels** (*law* 律) sb's personal belongings 某人的全部财物; 全部动产. **the ˈgoods/a (nice) piece of ˈgoods** (*dated infml* 旧, 口) excellent or sexually desirable person 出色人物; 性感的人. **price oneself/one's goods out of the market** ⇨ PRICE *v*.

□ **goods train** = FREIGHT TRAIN.

good·will /ˌgʊdˈwɪl; ˈgudˈwɪl/ *n* [U] **1** friendly, co-operative or helpful feeling 好意; 善意; 友善; 亲善: *a policy, spirit, etc of goodwill in international relations* 国际关系中的亲善政策、精神等 ○ *show goodwill to/towards sb* 对某人表示善意 ○ *Given goodwill on both sides I'm sure we can reach agreement.* 若双方均有诚意, 我确信我们能达成一致意见. **2** (financial value attached to the) good reputation of an established business (企业的)信誉; 商誉; 商誉的经济价值: *The goodwill is being sold together with the shop.* 商店连同其商誉一并出售.

goody /ˈgʊdɪ; ˈgudɪ/ *n* (*infml* 口) **1** (*usu pl* 通常作复数) (**a**) pleasant thing to eat; sweet, cake, etc 好吃的东西; 糖果、点心等: *Too many goodies will make you sick.* 好吃的东西吃得太多也要伤身体. (**b**) desirable thing 想要的东西: *I can now afford a new car, holidays abroad and lots of other goodies.* 现在我能买得起新汽车, 能到外国度假还能买很多好东西. **2** hero (of a book, film etc); good person (小说、电影等中的)主人公; 好人: *Is he one of the goodies or one of the baddies?* 他是好人还是坏人?

▷ **goody** (also **goody ˈgumdrops**) *interj* (*infml* 口) (used esp by children, for expressing pleasure and excitement 尤作儿童用语, 表示愉快和激动).

goody-goody /ˈgʊdɪ gʊdɪ; ˈgudɪˈgudɪ/ *n, adj* (*pl* **goody-goodies**) (*derog* 贬) (person) who behaves so as to appear very virtuous and respectable 假正经的(人); 伪善的(人).

gooey ⇨ GOO.

goof /gu:f; guf/ *n* (*infml* 口) **1** silly or stupid person 傻瓜; 笨蛋. **2** stupid error 愚蠢的错误: *Sorry, that was a bit of a goof on my part!* 对不起, 那是我的疏忽!

▷ **goof** *v* (*infml* 口 *esp US*) **1** [I, Tn] fail to do (sth) properly; make a mess (of) 搞糟, 弄坏或弄乱(某事物): *She had a great chance, but she goofed again*, ie failed to

G

take the opportunity. 她原有个极好的机会，可是她又错过了. ○ *The actor goofed his lines.* 那演员把台词弄乱了. **2** (phr v) **goof about/around/off** behave stupidly or irresponsibly; mess around 愚蠢地或不负责任地行事; 乱搞.

goofy *adj* (**-ier, -iest**) (*infml* 口) silly; stupid; crazy 愚蠢的; 傻的; 疯的.

googly /ˈguːglɪ; ˋguglɪ/ *n* (in cricket) ball bowled as if to turn in a particular direction after bouncing, that actually turns the opposite way (板球戏的)曲球(先向一方, 继而转向相反方向的球).

goon /guːn; gun/ *n* (*infml* 口) (**a**) stupid or crazy person 傻子; 狂人. (**b**) (*US*) person employed to threaten or attack people (雇佣的)打手.

goose /guːs; gus/ *n* (*pl* **geese** /giːs; gis/) **1** (**a**) [C] web-footed water bird larger than a duck 鹅. ⇨illus at App 1 见附录1插图, page v. (**b**) (*masc* 阳性作 **gander** /ˈgændə(r); ˋgændɚ/) [C] female of this bird 雌鹅. (**c**) [U] the flesh of the goose served as food 鹅肉: [attrib 作定语] *goose-liver pâté* 鹅肝酱. **2** (*dated* 旧) foolish or gullible person, esp female 傻瓜, 笨蛋(尤指女性): *You silly goose!* 你这笨蛋! **3** (idm 习语) **all sb's geese are ˈswans** (used when describing sb who overestimates or exaggerates the good qualities of other people 用以比喻某人过高估计或夸大他人的优点). **cook sb's goose** ⇨ COOK *v*. **kill the goose that lays the golden eggs** ⇨ KILL. **not say 'boo' to a goose** ⇨ SAY. **what's sauce for the goose is sauce for the gander** ⇨ SAUCE.

□ **ˈgoose-flesh** *n* [U] (also **ˈgoose-pimples** [pl]) condition in which the skin is temporarily raised into little lumps, caused by cold or fear 鸡皮疙瘩.

ˈgoose-step *n* [sing] (*derog* 贬) way of marching without bending the knees 正步.

goose·berry /ˈgʊzbərɪ; *US* ˈguːsberɪ; ˋgus,bɛrɪ/ *n* **1** (bush with a) green, smooth, sour but edible berry (used for jam, tarts, etc) 醋栗树; 醋栗(用以做果酱、果馅糕点等): [attrib 作定语] *gooseberry jam* 醋栗果酱. **2** (*infml* 口) unwanted third person present when two people (esp lovers) wish to be alone together 不知趣的第三者(夹在两人之间, 尤指情侣间者): *I didn't wish to play gooseberry*, ie be the unwanted person. 我可不想当不识趣的人.

□ **gooseberry ˈfool** dessert made from crushed gooseberries and cream 奶油醋栗泥.

go·pher /ˈgəʊfə(r); ˋgofɚ/ *n* burrowing rat-like N American animal 囊地鼠(产于北美).

Gor·dian knot /ˈgɔːdɪən ˈnɒt; ,gɔrdɪən ˋnɑt/ *n* **1** difficult or seemingly impossible problem or task 戈尔迪之结(棘手的问题或艰巨的任务). **2** (idm 习语) **cut the Gordian ˈknot** solve a problem by forcefully direct but unorthodox methods 用快刀斩乱麻的方式解决问题.

gore[1] /gɔː(r); gɔr/ *n* [U] (*esp rhet* 尤作修辞) (mainly in descriptions of fighting) thickened blood from a cut or wound (主要用于描写战斗)伤口处凝固的血, 血污: *a film with too much gore*, ie scenes of bloodshed 流血场面过多的电影. Cf 参看 GORY.

gore[2] /gɔː(r); gɔr/ *v* [Tn] pierce or wound (a person or an animal) with a horn or tusk (用角或长牙)刺或戳伤(人或动物): *gored to death by an angry bull* 被愤怒的公牛抵死.

gore[3] /gɔː(r); gɔr/ *n* wedge-shaped section of a garment, an umbrella or a sail (衣服、伞或帆上的)三角形布.

▷ **gored** /gɔːd; gɔrd/ *adj* made with gores 有三角形布的: *a gored skirt* 用细长三角形布片缝制的裙子.

gorge[1] /gɔːdʒ; gɔrdʒ/ *n* **1** narrow steep-sided valley, usu with a stream or river 峡谷(通常夹有河溪): *the Rhine gorge* 莱茵峡谷. **2** (*dated* 旧) throat; gullet 咽喉: *a fish bone stuck in his gorge* 卡在他咽部的鱼刺. **3** (idm 习语) **make sb's ˈgorge rise** fill sb with anger or disgust; sicken sb 使某人愤怒、厌恶或作呕: *The sight of so many starving children made his gorge rise.* 他看到这么多儿童挨饿十分气愤.

gorge[2] /gɔːdʒ; gɔrdʒ/ *v* [I, Ipr, Tn, Tn·pr] **~ (oneself) (on/with sth)** eat greedily; fill (oneself) 贪婪地吃; 填饱: *gorging (herself) on cream-cakes* 大吃奶油蛋糕.

gor·geous /ˈgɔːdʒəs; ˋgɔrdʒəs/ *adj* **1** (*infml* 口) giving pleasure and satisfaction; wonderful 令人愉快而满意的; 极好的: *a gorgeous meal* 好吃的饭菜 ○ *gorgeous weather* 宜人的天气. **2** (*infml* 口) very beautiful 非常漂亮的: *gorgeous hair* 十分好看的头发. **3** [usu attrib 通常作定语] (*esp rhet* 尤作修辞) richly coloured; magnificent 绚丽的; 辉煌的; 壮丽的: *walls hung with gorgeous tapestries* 挂着绚丽挂毯的墙壁. ▷ **gor·geously** *adv*: *gorgeously dressed, decorated, etc* 穿得、装饰得…华丽.

Gor·gon /ˈgɔːgən; ˋgɔrgən/ *n* **1** (in Greek myth) any of three snake-haired sisters whose looks turned to stone anyone who saw them (希腊神话中的)戈耳工(蛇发三姐妹之一, 见到者皆化为石头). **2 gorgon** (*fig* 比喻) domineering, frightening or repulsive woman 专横的、可怕的或令人憎恶的女人: *Her step-mother, who hated her, was an absolute gorgon.* 她的继母是个专横跋扈的女人, 很恨她.

Gor·gon·zola /,gɔːgənˈzəʊlə; ,gɔrgənˋzolə/ *n* [U] rich creamy blue-veined Italian cheese 戈尔贡佐拉干酪(意大利干酪, 乳脂丰富, 有蓝色花纹).

gor·illa /gəˈrɪlə; gəˋrɪlə/ *n* very large powerful African ape 大猩猩(产于非洲). ⇨illus at APE 见 APE 插图.

gor·mand·ize, -ise /ˈgɔːməndaɪz; ˋgɔrmən,daɪz/ *v* [I] (*fml derog* 文, 贬) eat greedily for pleasure 大吃八喝.

▷ **gor·mand·izer, -iser** *n* person who does this 大吃八喝的人.

gorm·less /ˈgɔːmlɪs; ˋgɔrmlɪs/ *adj* (*Brit infml* 口) stupid; foolish 愚蠢的; 傻的: *What a gormless thing to do!* 多么愚蠢的事! ○ *a gormless fellow* 笨傢伙. ▷ **gorm·lessly** *adv*. **gorm·less·ness** *n* [U].

gorse /gɔːs; gɔrs/ *n* (also **furze, whin**) [U] yellow-flowered evergreen shrub with sharp thorns, growing on heaths and wasteland 荆豆(常绿灌木, 有刺、开黄花, 生于荒野).

gory /ˈgɔːrɪ; ˋgɔrɪ/ *adj* (**-ier, -iest**) **1** (*esp rhet* 尤作修辞) covered with gore[1] 沾满血污的. **2** full of violence and bloodshed 充满暴力和血腥的: *a gory battle, fight, film, spectacle, etc* 血肉横飞的战斗、打斗、影片、场面等 ○ (*fig* 比喻) *'Have you heard about their divorce?' 'Spare us the gory* (ie sensational) *details.'* '你们听说他们离婚的事了吗?' '可别跟我们提那些骨肉相残的细节.'

gosh /gɒʃ; gɑʃ/ *interj* (*infml euph* 口, 婉) (used as a mild alternative to 'God' to express surprise or strong feeling 用以替代God的委婉说法, 表示惊异或强烈情感): *Gosh, I'm hungry!* 啊呀, 我饿极了! ○ *I said I'd do it and, by gosh, I did!* 我说过我要做那件事, 上天作证, 我还真做了!

gos·ling /ˈgɒzlɪŋ; ˋgɑzlɪŋ/ *n* young goose 幼鹅.

gos·pel /ˈgɒspl; ˋgɑspl/ *n* **1** (*Bible* 圣经) (**a**) **the Gospel** [sing] (the life and teaching of Jesus as recorded in) the first four books of the New Testament 圣经新约四福音书; 福音(记载于福音书中的耶稣生平及其教导): *preach the Gospel* 传布福音. (**b**) [C] any one of these books 新约四福音书之一: *the Gospel according to St John* 约翰福音 ○ *St John's Gospel* 约翰福音 ○ [attrib 作定语] *the gospel message, story, etc* 福音信息、故事等. **2** [C usu *sing* 通常作单数] set of principles 原则; 主义; 信条: *spreading the gospel of hard work* 宣传努力工作的原则 ○ *the gospel according to which one lives* 生活的准则 ○ *Health of body and mind is my gospel.* 保持身心健康是我的信条. **3** [U] (*infml* 口) the truth (esp of an unlikely story or a rumour) 真事(尤指貌似不实的事或传言): *Is that gospel?* 那是真的吗? ○ *You can take this as absolute gospel*, ie should believe it. 你应该相信这是千真万确的. ○ [attrib 作定语] *gospel truth*, ie completely reliable 完全可信的事实. **4** [U] religious music of black American origin in a popular or folk style 福音音乐(源于美国黑人歌曲宗教音乐, 有流行歌曲或民歌风格): [attrib 作定语] *gospel singers* 福音歌曲演唱者.

gos·samer /ˈgɒsəmə(r); ˋgɑsəmɚ/ *n* [U] **1** fine silky substance of webs made by small spiders, floating in calm air or spread over grass, etc 蛛丝; 游丝. **2** (*fig esp rhet* 比喻, 尤作修辞) soft light delicate material 轻而软的精细材料: *a veil spun of the finest gossamer* 精纺的面纱 ○ [attrib 作定语] *the gossamer wings of a fly* 薄如轻纱的蝇翅.

gos·sip /ˈgɒsɪp; ˋgɑsəp/ *n* **1** [U] (*derog* 贬) casual talk about the affairs of other people, typically including rumour and critical comments 闲言碎语; 流言蜚语: *Don't believe all the gossip you hear.* 那些道听途说的话

不可尽信. ○ *She's too fond of idle gossip.* 她太爱听飞短流长的话了. ○ *It's common gossip that they're having an affair,* ie Everyone is saying so. 大家都说他们之间关系暧昧. **2** [U] (*often derog* 常作贬义) informal writing about people and social events, eg in letters or newspapers 随笔; 漫谈: [attrib 作定语] *the gossip column,* ie of a newspaper 漫谈专栏(报纸上的) ○ *a gossip columnist/writer,* ie a writer of such material 写漫谈专栏的作家. **3** [C] conversation including gossip 闲言闲语的谈话: *have a good gossip with a friend, neighbour, etc* 和朋友、邻居等聊闲天. **4** [C] (*derog or joc* 贬或谑) person fond of gossip 爱传播流言蜚语的人: *You're nothing but an old gossip!* 你这个专门搬弄是非的老傢伙!

▷ **gos·sip** *v* [I, Ipr] **~ (with sb) (about sth)** talk gossip 传播流言蜚语; 说长道短: *I can't stand here gossiping all day.* 我可不能整天站在这里闲聊下去. ⇨ Usage at TALK[1] 用法见 TALK[1].

gos·sipy /ˈgɒsɪpɪ; ˋgɑsəpɪ/ *adj*: *a gossipy letter* 聊闲天的信.

got *pt, pp* of GET.

Gothic /ˈgɒθɪk; ˋgɑθɪk/ *adj* **1** of the Goths (Germanic people who invaded the Roman Empire) 哥特人的, 哥特族的(指曾入侵罗马帝国的一支日耳曼民族). **2** (*architecture* 建) of or in a style common in W Europe from the 12th to the 16th centuries and characterized by pointed arches, arched roofs, tall thin pillars, etc 哥特式建筑的(12至16世纪流行于西欧的建筑风格, 以尖拱、拱顶、细长柱等为特点): *a Gothic church, cathedral, arch, window* 哥特式教堂、大教堂、拱门、窗户. **3** of or in an 18th-century style of literature which described romantic adventures in mysterious or frightening settings 哥特派的, 哥特风格的(18世纪的一种文学风格, 通常描述有神秘或恐怖气氛的爱情故事): *Gothic novels, horror* 哥特式的小说、恐怖. **4** (of printing type) with pointed letters made up of thick lines and sharp angles, as formerly used for German (指字体)哥特字体的: *Gothic lettering, type, etc* 哥特字体的字、字体等.

G

▷ **Gothic** *n* [U] (**a**) Gothic language 哥特语. (**b**) Gothic type 哥特字体: *printed in Gothic* 用哥特字体印刷的.

gotta /ˈgɒtə; ˋgɑtə/ (*infml* 口 *esp US*) (have) got to 必须; 只好: *I gotta/I've gotta go.* 我得走了.

got·ten (*US*) *pp* of GET.

gou·ache /gʊˈɑːʃ; gʊˋɑʃ/ *n* [U] type of thick watercolour paint; method of painting pictures using this material 水粉画; 水粉画法.

Gouda /ˈgaʊdə; *US also* ˈguːdə; ˋgaʊdə, ˋgudə/ *n* [U] type of mild-flavoured Dutch cheese 豪达干酪(一种淡味的荷兰干酪).

gouge /gaʊdʒ; gaʊdʒ/ *n* tool with a sharp semicircular edge for cutting grooves in wood 半圆凿; 弧口凿.

▷ **gouge** *v* (**a**) [Tn, Tn·pr] **~ sth (in sth)** make (a hole) in sth roughly or destructively 在某物上胡乱地或破坏性地凿(洞): *A maniac had gouged several holes in the priceless painting.* 有个狂徒在那幅价值连城的画上乱凿了几个洞. (**b**) (phr v) **gouge sth out** remove sth by digging into a surface with a sharp tool, one's fingers, etc (用利器或手指等在物体表面上抠、挖、掘等)除去某物: *gouge out a narrow groove* 凿出窄槽 ○ *gouge out a stone from a horseshoe* 从马掌中抠出石块 ○ *gouge sb's eyes out* 挖出某人的眼睛.

gou·lash /ˈguːlæʃ; ˋgulæʃ/ *n* [C, U] dish of Hungarian origin consisting of stewed beef seasoned with paprika 匈牙利红烩牛肉.

gourd /gʊəd; gʊrd/ *n* **1** (large hard-skinned fleshy fruit of a) type of climbing or trailing plant 葫芦科植物; 葫芦. **2** bottle or bowl consisting of the dried skin of this fruit (用葫芦果壳制的)罐或瓢: *a wine gourd* 酒葫芦.

gour·mand /ˈgʊəmənd; ˋgʊrmənd/ *n* (*often derog* 常作贬义) lover of food; glutton 喜欢吃喝的人; 贪吃的人.

gour·met /ˈgʊəmeɪ; ˋgʊrme/ *n* person who enjoys and is expert in the choice of fine food, wines, etc 美食家; 美酒美食专家: [attrib 作定语] *gourmet restaurants,* ie serving fine food 菜肴精美的餐馆.

gout /gaʊt; gaʊt/ *n* [U] disease causing painful swellings in joints, esp toes, knees and fingers 痛风.

▷ **gouty** *adj* suffering from gout 患痛风病的.

Gov *abbr* 缩写 = **1** Governor: *Gov (Stephen) King* (史蒂芬·)金总督. **2** (also **Govt**) Government 政府; 内阁.

gov·ern /ˈgʌvn; ˋgʌvən/ *v* **1** [I, Tn] rule (a country, etc); control or direct the public affairs of (a city, country, etc) 统治(国家等); 控制, 支配, 治理, 管辖(城市、国家等)的公共事务: *In Britain the Queen reigns, but elected representatives of the people govern the country.* 在英国, 女王是君主而治理国家的却是民选的代表. **2** [Tn] prevent the expression of (a strong emotion); control 抑制, 控制(强烈感情)的表露: *govern one's feelings, passion, temper, etc* 控制住感情、激情、脾气等. **3** [Tn] influence (sth/sb) decisively; determine 支配某事物[某人]; 决定: *Self-interest governs all his actions.* 他的所作所为皆取决于一己之利. ○ *The law of supply and demand governs the prices of goods.* 供求规律决定商品的价格. ○ *I will be governed by you,* ie will do as you suggest. 我愿秉承您的意旨. **4** [Tn] (*grammar*) (esp of a *v* or *prep*) require the object to be in (a particular grammatical case) (尤指动词或介词)要求宾语处于(语法上的某格): *In Latin, several verbs govern the dative.* 在拉丁语中, 有些动词要求与格的宾语.

▷ **gov·ern·ing** /ˈgʌvənɪŋ; ˋgʌvənɪŋ/ *adj* [attrib 作定语] having the power or right to govern 有统治、控制或治理权力的: *the governing body of a school, college, etc* 学校、学院等的行政部门.

gov·ern·ance /ˈgʌvənəns; ˋgʌvənəns/ *n* [U] (*fml or rhet* 文或修辞) governing; government(1) 统治; 控制; 支配; 治理: *the governance of Britain* 对英国的统治.

gov·ern·ess /ˈgʌvənɪs; ˋgʌvənɪs/ *n* (esp formerly) woman employed to teach young children in their home (usu living as a member of the household) (尤指旧时)家庭女教师(通常似家庭成员般一起生活): *act, serve as (a) governess to a family* 给一家庭当、做家庭女教师.

gov·ern·ment /ˈgʌvənmənt; ˋgʌvənmənt/ *n* **1** [U] governing; power to govern 统治; 控制; 支配; 统治权: *If we do not have strong government, there will be rioting and anarchy.* 我们若不加强控制就会出现动乱和无政府状态. ○ *weak, ineffectual, corrupt, etc government* 软弱的、无能的、腐败的…治理. **2** [U] method or system of governing (统治或治理的)方式, 政体, 体制: *Democratic government gradually took the place of an all-powerful monarchy.* 民主政体逐渐取代了有无上权力的君主政体. ○ *liberal, totalitarian, parliamentary, etc government* 自由主义的、极权主义的、议会式的…政体. **3** (often 常作 **the Government**) [CGp] body of persons governing a state 政府; 内阁: *lead, form a government* 领导、组织政府 ○ *Foreign governments have been consulted about this decision.* 这一决定曾征询过他国政府的意见. ○ *She has resigned from the Government,* ie from her job as a minister. 她已辞去大臣职位. ○ *The Government* (ie its members) *are discussing the proposal.* 内阁官员正在讨论该议案. ○ *The Government* (ie collectively) *welcomes the proposal.* 政府欢迎该建议. ○ [attrib 作定语] *a government department, grant, publication* 政府的部门、拨款、出版物 ○ *government policies, money, ministers* 政府的政策、国帑、部长 ○ *government-controlled industries,* ie those controlled by the government 政府控制的企业. **4** (idm 习语) **in government** being the government; governing 执政; 统治; 治理: *The Labour Party was in government from 1964 to 1970.* 工党从1964年到1970年执政.

▷ **gov·ern·mental** /ˌgʌvnˈmentl; ˌgʌvənˋmentl/ *adj* of or connected with government 政府的; 与政府有关的: *governmental institutions* 政府机构.

□ ˌ**Government** ˈ**House** official residence of the Governor (of a province, etc) 州长的或省长等的官邸.

gov·ernor /ˈgʌvənə(r); ˋgʌvənɚ/ *n* **1** (**a**) person appointed to govern a province or state (esp a colony abroad) 省长; 州长; (尤指海外殖民地的)总督: *a provincial governor* 省长. (**b**) elected head of each state in the USA (美国的)州长: *the Governor of New York State* 纽约州州长. **2** (**a**) head of an institution 机构首脑: *a prison governor* 监狱长 ○ *the governor of the Bank of England* 英格兰银行总裁. (**b**) member of a governing body 行政机构的成员: *the board of governors of a school, college, hospital, etc* 学校、学院、医院等的董事会. **3** (*Brit infml* 口) (**a**) (also **guv·nor** /ˈgʌvnə(r); ˋgʌvnɚ/) person having power or authority over the speaker, eg an employer or a father 顶头上司(如雇主或父亲): *I shall have to ask permission from the/my governor.*

我需求得顶头上司的允许. **(b)** (also **guv** /gʌv; gʌv/, **guv·nor**) (used by a man when addressing another man, esp one of higher social status 用作男子对男子的称谓, 尤用于社会地位比自己高的人): *Can I see your ticket, guvnor?* 先生, 我能看看您的票吗? **4** (*engineering* 工) mechanism that controls automatically the speed, temperature, etc of a machine 机器上自动调速、调温等装置.

□ ˌ**Governor-ˈGeneral** *n* official representative of the Crown, in a Commonwealth country (英联邦国家的)总督(英王的官方代表): *the Governor-General of Canada* 加拿大总督.

Govt *abbr* 缩写 = Gov 2.

gown /gaʊn; gaʊn/ *n* **1** woman's dress, esp a long one for special occasions 女服(尤指于特殊场合穿的长服): *a ˈball-gown* 舞会长服 ○ [attrib 作定语] *a gown shop* 女礼服商店. **2** loose flowing robe worn to indicate profession or status (eg by a judge, lawyer, teacher, member of a university) (表示职业或地位的)长服(如法官、律师、教师、大学成员所穿的): *a BA gown* 学士服. **3** garment worn over clothes to protect them, eg by a surgeon 罩衣(如外科医生穿的).

▷ **gowned** /gaʊnd; gaʊnd/ *adj* wearing a (legal or academic) gown 穿着(法律界或学术界的)长服的.

GP /ˌdʒiː ˈpiː; ˌdʒi ˋpi/ *abbr* 缩写 = general practitioner: *consult your local GP* 请教你当地的全科医生.

Gp Capt *abbr* 缩写 = Group Captain: *Gp Capt (Tom) Fletcher* (汤姆·)弗莱彻空军上校.

GPO /ˌdʒiː piː ˈəʊ; ˌdʒi pi ˋo/ *abbr* 缩写 = (*Brit*) General Post Office: *The GPO is very busy at Christmas.* 圣诞节时邮政总局十分繁忙.

GR *abbr* 缩写 = (eg on coins) King George (Latin *Georgius Rex*) (如铸于硬币上的)乔治王(源自拉丁文 *Georgius Rex*). Cf 参看 ER.

gr *abbr* 缩写 = **1** = GM. **2** gross: *gr income £15 000* 总收入15 000英镑.

grab /græb; græb/ *v* **(-bb-) 1 (a)** [I, Tn, Tn·pr] **~ sth (from sb/sth)** grasp sth suddenly or roughly; snatch sth selfishly or rudely 抢; 抓; 抢夺; 攫取: *Don't grab!* 不要抢! ○ *He grabbed my collar and pulled me towards him.* 他抓住我的领子把我拉到他面前. ○ *He just grabbed the bag from my hand and ran off.* 他抢走我手中的提包就跑了. **(b)** [Tn] (*fig* 比喻) take (an opportunity, etc) eagerly 热切地抓住(机会等): *When I gave him the chance, he grabbed it at once.* 我给他这一机会, 他立刻抓住不放. **2** [Ipr] **~ at sb/sth** (attempt to) seize sb/sth eagerly or desperately 热切地或拼命地(企图)抓住或捉住某人[某事物]: *He grabbed at the boy, but could not save him from falling.* 他想抓住那男孩儿, 然而那孩子还是跌倒了. ○ (*fig* 比喻) *grabbing at any excuse to avoid an unpleasant task* 胡乱找个借口以逃避不喜欢的任务. **3** [Tn] (*infml joc* 口, 谑) have or take (sth) esp in a casual or hasty manner 取或拿(某物)(尤指随便地或匆匆地): *Grab a seat and make yourself at home.* 随便找个地方坐, 别客气. ○ *Let's grab a quick sandwich and watch TV.* 咱们赶快吃个三明治就去看电视吧. **4** [Tn] (*sl* 俚) impress (sb); excite 给(某人)留下深刻的印象; 使激动或兴奋: *'How does this music grab you?' 'It doesn't grab me at all.'* '这音乐你喜欢吗?' '一点都不喜欢.'

▷ **grab** *n* **1** [sing] sudden (attempt to) snatch 猛然(去)抓: *make a grab at sth* 猛地去抓某物. **2** [C] (*engineering* 工) mechanical device for picking up and holding sth to be lifted or moved 抓具; 抓斗. **3** (idm 习语) **up for ˈgrabs** (*US infml* 口) available for anyone to take 任何人皆可得到的: *The job is up for grabs. Why don't you apply now?* 那工作谁都可以争取. 你怎么不现在就申请呢?

grab·ber *n* selfish person always trying to get things for himself 贪得无厌的人.

grace /greɪs; gres/ *n* **1** [U] quality of simple elegant beauty (esp in smoothly controlled movement) 优美(尤指动作顺畅协调): *the grace with which a ballerina leaps into the air* 芭蕾舞女演员腾空起舞的优美姿势. **2** [U] God's mercy and favour towards mankind; influence and result of this 上帝对人类的慈悲和恩典; 天恩的应验: *By the grace of God their lives were spared.* 蒙上帝恩宠, 他们免于一死. ○ *Did he die in a state of grace?* ie strengthened and inspired by God, esp after having been pardoned and given the Sacraments. 他临终是否曾蒙主感召?(尤指受到宽恕后行圣礼) ○ (*saying* 谚) *There, but for the grace of God, go I/we,* ie sth equally bad might have happened to me/us. 你瞧, 若非天恩眷顾, 我[我们]也难幸免. **3** [U] extra time allowed to renew a licence, pay an insurance premium, etc after the day when it is due 宽限; 缓期: *have a couple of days' grace* 有一两天的宽限期 ○ *Payment is due today, but I gave her a week's grace,* ie an extra week to pay. 今天付款到期, 但我给了她一个星期的宽限. **4** [U] favour; goodwill 恩惠; 善意: *He had been the king's favourite, and his sudden fall from grace surprised everyone.* 他本是国王的幸臣, 一朝失宠众人无不感到意外. ○ *an act of grace,* ie freely given, not taken as a right 恩惠(迳自施予的, 并非受者有此权利). **5** [C usu *pl* 通常作复数] pleasing accomplishment 风度; 魅力; 长处; 才艺: *well-versed in the social graces* 社交风度潇洒的. **6** [U, C] short prayer of thanks before or after a meal (饭前或饭后的)谢恩祈祷: *Father said (a) grace.* 父亲做了饭前谢恩祈祷. **7 His/Her/Your Grace** [C] (used as a title when speaking to or of an archbishop, a duke or a duchess 用作称呼或提及大主教、公爵、公爵夫人、女公爵的尊称): *Good morning, Your Grace!* 大人, 早上好! ○ *Their Graces, the Duke and Duchess of Kent* 肯特公爵及公爵夫人阁下. **8 the Graces** [pl] (in Greek myth) three beautiful sister goddesses who gave beauty, charm and happiness to humans (希腊神话中)美惠三女神(赐予人类美丽、魅力和快乐者). **9** (idm 习语) **airs and graces** ⇨ AIR[1]. **have the grace to do sth** be polite enough to do sth 出于礼貌而做某事: *He might have had the grace to say he was sorry!* 他本可以出于礼貌说声抱歉的嘛! **in sb's good ˈgraces** approved of and favoured by sb 为某人赞同和喜爱: *I'm not in her good graces at the moment.* 我此刻尚未讨得她的欢心. **a saving grace** ⇨ SAVE[1]. **with (a) bad/good ˈgrace** reluctantly and rudely/willingly and cheerfully 勉强而粗鲁地[欣然而情愿地]: *She apologized with (a) bad grace.* 她很勉强地道了歉. ○ *They withdrew their objections with as good a grace as they could manage.* 他们极力装出情愿的样子撤回了反对意见. **year of grace** ⇨ YEAR.

▷ **grace** *v* **1** [Tn] decorate or adorn (sth) 修饰或装扮(某物): *Fine paintings graced the walls of the room.* 这些精美的绘画使四壁生辉. **2** [Tn, Tn·pr] **~ sb/sth (with sth)** give honour or dignity to sb/sth 给某人[某事物]以荣耀或光彩: *The Queen is gracing us with her presence.* 女王莅临使我们不胜荣幸. ○ *The occasion was graced by the presence of the Queen.* 女王驾临使场面增辉.

grace·ful /ˈgreɪsfl; ˋgresfəl/ *adj* **1** showing a pleasing beauty of form, movement or manner (形式、动作或举止)优雅的, 优美的: *a graceful dancer* 绰约多姿的跳舞者 ○ *a graceful leap* 优美的跳跃 ○ *the graceful curves of the new bridge* 新桥的美丽曲线. **2** pleasing in both style and attitude; polite and considerate 得体的; 礼貌而周到的: *His refusal was worded in such a graceful way that we could not be offended.* 他婉言谢绝, 无损于我们颜面. ▷ **grace·fully** /-fəlɪ; -fəlɪ/ *adv.*

grace·less /ˈgreɪslɪs; ˋgreslɪs/ *adj* **1** without grace or elegance 不优美的; 不文雅的: *a room cluttered with ugly graceless furniture* 零乱地摆着丑陋不雅的家具的房间. **2** ungracious; rude 不雅观的; 粗鲁的: *graceless behaviour* 不雅的举止 ○ *a graceless remark, refusal, etc* 无礼的言词、拒绝等. ▷ **grace·lessly** *adv.* **grace·less·ness** *n* [U].

gra·cious /ˈgreɪʃəs; ˋgreʃəs/ *adj* **1 ~ (to sb)** (of persons and behaviour) kind, polite and generous (esp to sb who is socially inferior) (指人及其行为)和善的, 有礼貌的, 大方的, (尤指)礼贤下士的: *a gracious lady, hostess, etc* 落落大方的女士, 女主人等 ○ *a gracious manner, reply, invitation, smile* 殷勤的态度、回复、邀请、微笑 ○ *He was most gracious to everyone, smiling and thanking them.* 他对大家彬彬有礼, 向他们微笑、道谢. ○ *It was gracious of the Queen to speak to the elderly patients.* 女王和蔼可亲地慰问年老的病人. **2** [attrib 作定语] (*fml* 文) (used as a polite term for royal people or their acts 用作对皇族及其行为的敬语): *her gracious Majesty the Queen* 女王陛下 ○ *by gracious permission of Her Majesty* 蒙女王陛下恩准. **3 ~ (to sb)** (of God)

G

merciful（指上帝）仁慈的: *He is kind and gracious to all sinners who repent.* 他对忏悔的罪人一概慈悲为怀. **4** [usu attrib 通常作定语] marked by luxury, elegance and leisure 奢华的; 优美的; 雍容华贵的: *gracious living* 豪华的生活. **5** (*dated* 旧) (used in exclamations expressing surprise 用于感叹句, 表示惊异): *Good(ness) gracious!* 天哪! ○ *Gracious me!* 天哪! ▷ **gra·ciously** *adv*. **gra·cious·ness** *n* [U].

grada·tion /grəˈdeɪʃn; grəˈdeʃən/ *n* **1** [U, C] gradual change from one thing to another（从一事物到另一事物的）渐变: *Note the subtle gradation of/in colour in this painting.* 注意这幅画中色彩的细微变化. **2** [C] any of the stages or steps into which sth is divided（事物划分的）阶段, 等级: *It was hard to understand all the minute gradations of their bureaucracy.* 很难弄清楚他们那套官僚体制全部细微的等级分别. **3** [C] mark showing a division on a scale 刻度: *the gradations on a thermometer* 温度计上的刻度.

grade[1] /greɪd; gred/ *n* **1** step, stage or degree of rank, quality, etc; level of classification（官阶、质量等的）等级, 品级; 阶段; 程度: *a person's salary grade*, ie level of pay 某人的薪金级别 ○ [attrib 作定语] *high/low-grade civil servants, milk, pigs, materials* 等级高[低]的公务员、奶品、猪、材料 ○ *Grade A potatoes are the best in quality.* 甲等马铃薯是质量最好的. **2** (**a**) mark given in an examination or for school work（考试或作业的）分数, 评分等级: *Pupils with 90% or more are awarded Grade A.* 满90分的学生评为甲等. ○ *She got excellent grades in her exams.* 她考试成绩优异. (**b**) level of (esp musical) skill at which a pupil is tested（学生受测试的）技巧水平（尤指音乐方面）: *He's got Violin Grade 6*, ie has passed a test at that level of skill. 他的小提琴6级考试及格了. **3** (*US*) division of a school based on the age of the pupils; pupils in such a division 年级;（按年级划分的）小学生: *My son's in the third grade.* 我儿子上小学三年级. **4** (*US*) = GRADIENT. **5** (idm 习语) **make the ˈgrade** (*infml* 口) reach the required or expected standard; succeed 达到要求的或预期的标准; 成功. **on the ˈup/ˈdown grade** getting better/worse 逐渐好转[恶化]: *Business is on the up grade.* 生意日渐兴隆.

□ **ˈgrade crossing** (*US*) = LEVEL CROSSING (LEVEL[1]). **ˈgrade school** (*US*) = PRIMARY SCHOOL (PRIMARY). **ˈgrade teacher** (*US*) teacher in a grade school 小学教师.

grade[2] /greɪd; gred/ *v* **1** [esp passive 尤用于被动语态: Tn, Tn·pr, Cn·n] **~ sth/sb by/according to sth; ~ sth/sb from sth to sth** arrange sth/sb in order by grades or classes, ie assessed and marked with the standard or grade obtained 将某事物[某人]按级分类或分等: *The potatoes are graded by/according to size.* 马铃薯按大小分等级. ○ *Eggs are graded from small to extra-large.* 鸡蛋从小的到特大的分成了等级. **2** [Tn, Cn·n] (*esp US*) mark (written work); give (a student) a mark 给（书面作业）评分; 给（学生）分数: *The term papers have been graded.* 期末考卷已评完分数了. ○ *A student who gets 90% is graded A.* 凡得90分的学生列为甲等. **3** [Tn] make (land, esp for roads) more nearly level by reducing the slope（用削减斜度的办法）使（地面, 尤指路面）接近水平.

gra·di·ent /ˈgreɪdɪənt; ˈgredɪənt/ *n* degree of slope, as on a road, railway, etc（公路, 铁路等的）坡度, 斜率: *a steep gradient* 陡峭的坡度 ○ *a hill with a gradient of 1 in 4 (or 25%)* 坡度为1:4（或25%）的山岗.

grad·ual /ˈgrædʒʊəl; ˈgrædʒʊəl/ *adj* (**a**) taking place by a series of small changes over a long period; not sudden 逐渐的; 渐变的: *gradual decline, progress, etc* 逐渐的衰落、进步等 ○ *a gradual increase, decrease, recovery* 逐渐的增加、减少、恢复. (**b**) (of a slope) not steep（指斜坡）不陡峭的, 和缓的: *a gradual rise, fall, incline, etc* 渐起、渐落、渐降.

▷ **gradu·ally** /-dʒʊlɪ; -dʒʊlɪ/ *adv* in a gradual way; by degrees 逐渐地; 逐步地: *Things gradually improved.* 情况已逐渐改善.

grad·ual·ness *n* [U].

gradu·ate[1] /ˈgrædʒʊət; ˈgrædʒʊɪt/ *n* **1 ~ (in sth)** person who holds a degree (esp the first or bachelor's) from a university or polytechnic 有学位（尤指学士学位）的人; 大学毕业生: *a graduate in law, history, etc* 法律学、历史学等学士 ○ *a law graduate* 法律系毕业生 ○ *a graduate of Oxford/an Oxford graduate* 牛津大学毕业生 ○ [attrib 作定语] *a graduate student*, ie one studying for a master's or doctor's degree 研究生. Cf 参看 POSTGRADUATE, UNDERGRADUATE. **2** (*US*) person who has completed a course at an educational institution 毕业生: *a high-school graduate* 高中毕业生 ○ [attrib 作定语] *a graduate nurse*, ie one from a college of nursing 护士学校毕业的护士.

gradu·ate[2] /ˈgrædʒʊeɪt; ˈgrædʒʊˌet/ *v* **1** [I, Ipr] **~ (in sth) (at/from sth)** (**a**) complete a course for a degree（学完一学位课程）毕业: *graduate in law, history, etc at Oxford* 毕业于牛津大学法律系、历史系等 ○ *She graduated from Cambridge with a degree in law.* 她毕业于剑桥大学, 获法学学士学位. (**b**) (*US*) complete an educational course（学完一教育课程）毕业: *She's just graduated from the School of Cookery.* 她刚从烹饪学校毕业. **2** [Tn, Tn·pr] **~ sb (from sth)** (*esp US*) give a degree, diploma, etc to sb 授予某人学位、毕业文凭等: *The college graduated 50 students from the science department last year.* 这所学院去年有50名理科毕业生. **3** [Tn esp passive 尤用于被动语态] divide (sth) into graded sections 将（某事物）分成等级或阶段: *In a graduated tax scheme the more one earns, the more one pays.* 按照累进税制, 收入多者多纳税. **4** [esp passive 尤用于被动语态: Tn, Tn·pr] **~ sth (in/into sth)** mark sth into regular divisions or units of measurement 给某物划分度数: *a ruler graduated in both inches and centimetres* 有英制和公制两种刻度的尺. **5** [Ipr] **~ (from sth) to sth** (*fig approv* 比喻, 褒) make progress; move on (from sth easy or basic) to sth more difficult or important 进步; 进展; 进而做较难或较重要之事: *Our son has just graduated from a tricycle to a proper bicycle.* 我们的儿子刚刚从骑三轮自行车过渡到骑普通自行车了.

▷ **gradu·ation** /ˌgrædʒʊˈeɪʃn; ˌgrædʒʊˈeʃən/ *n* **1** [U] (**a**) graduating at a university, etc（大学等）毕业: *students without jobs to go to after graduation* 毕业后工作无着的大学生. (**b**) ceremony at which degrees, etc are conferred（大学的）毕业典礼, 授学位典礼: [attrib 作定语] *graduˈation ceremony, day, etc* 大学毕业典礼、毕业日. **2** [C] gradation(3) 刻度; 分等级: *The graduations are marked on the side of the flask.* 烧瓶侧面有刻度标志.

□ **ˌgraduated ˈpension** pension in which the contributions paid (while working) and the size of pension (after retirement) are related to the amount of salary earned 累进退休金（在职时预付的退休积累基金和退休金的多寡同薪金额相关）: [attrib 作定语] *a graduated pension scheme* 累进退休金制度.

Graeco- (also *esp US* **Greco-**) *comb form* 构词成分 Greek; of Greece 希腊的: *Graeco-Roman.*

graf·fiti /grəˈfiːtɪ; grəˈfitɪ/ *n* [pl] drawings or writing on a public wall, usu humorous, obscene or political（在公共墙壁上涂写的）图画或文字（通常含幽默、猥亵或政治内容）.

graft[1] /grɑːft; *US* græft; græft/ *n* **1** piece cut from a living plant and fixed in a cut made in another plant, to form a new growth; process or result of doing this 接穗; 嫁接: *A healthy shoot should form a strong graft.* 健康的嫩枝可作强壮的接穗. **2** (*medical* 医) piece of skin, bone, etc removed from a living body and attached to another body or another part of the same body, usu to replace unhealthy or damaged tissue; process or result of doing this（皮肤、骨骼等的）移植物, 移植: *a ˈskin graft* 移植的皮肤.

▷ **graft** *v* [Tn, Tn·pr, Tn·p] **~ sth onto sth; ~ sth in/on** attach sth as a graft（将某物作为移植物）移植, 嫁接: *graft one variety of apple onto another* 把一种苹果树嫁接到另一种苹果树上 ○ *New skin had to be grafted on.* 需移植新皮肤. ○ (*fig* 比喻) *trying to graft some innovations onto an outdated system* 试将某些改革引进到一落伍的体制中.

graft[2] /grɑːft; *US* græft; græft/ *n* [U] **1** (*esp US*) (**a**) use of illegal or unfair means (esp bribery) to gain an advantage in business, politics, etc 行贿; 贿赂: *graft and corruption* 行贿和贪污. (**b**) profit obtained in this way 行贿得到的利益. **2** (*Brit*) hard work 艰巨的工作: *Hard graft is the only way to succeed in business.* 艰苦奋斗是在事业上成功的唯一途径.

▷ **graft** *v* **1** [I] (*esp US*) practice graft[2](1a) 行贿; 贿赂. **2** [I, Ip] **~ (away)** (*Brit*) work hard 努力工作: *grafting (away) all day* 苦干终日. **grafter** *n* hard worker 努力工作的人.

grail /greɪl; grel/ *n* (usu 通常作 **the Holy Grail**) plate or cup used by Jesus at the Last Supper, in which one of his followers is said to have received drops of his blood at the Crucifixion 圣盘, 圣杯(耶稣在最后的晚餐所用的, 据称在耶稣被钉于十字架上时其门徒曾用以承接耶稣的血滴).

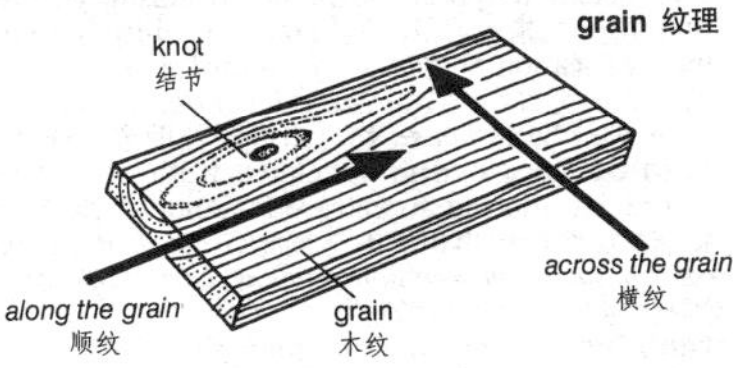

grain /greɪn; gren/ *n* **1** [U] (*esp commerce* 尤用于商业) small hard seeds of food plants such as wheat, rice, etc 谷物: [attrib 作定语] *America's grain exports* 美国的谷物出口. **2** [C] single seed of such a plant 谷粒: *a few grains of rice in a bowl* 碗中的几颗米粒. ➪illus at CEREAL 见CEREAL插图. **3** [C] tiny hard bit 小的硬粒: *a grain of sand, gold, etc* 沙粒、金粒. **4** [C] smallest unit of weight in various measuring systems, $\frac{1}{7000}$ lb or 0.065 gm 格令(重量的最小单位, 等于$\frac{1}{7000}$磅或0.065克): *The analysis showed a few grains of arsenic in the solution.* 分析显示溶液中有几格令的砷. ➪App 5 见附录5. **5** [C] (*fig* 比喻) very small amount 少量; 微量: *There isn't a grain of* (ie any) *truth in it.* 那事无丝毫真实性. **6** [U] (**a**) (surface) texture produced by particles (微粒形成的)质地(表面): *a stone of fine/medium/coarse grain*, ie containing small/medium/large particles 质地细的[不粗不细的/粗的]石头. (**b**) pattern made by the lines of fibres in wood, or of layers in rock, coal, etc (木、石、煤等的)纹理: *cut a piece of wood along/across the grain* 把木头顺着木纹[对着横纹]截断. ➪illus 见插图. (**c**) rough appearance of a photographic print, as if made up of small particles of light and dark (照片的)颗粒. **7** (idm 习语) **(be/go) against the 'grain** (be) contrary to one's nature or inclination 与自己的性格、意愿格格不入: *It really goes against the grain to have to go into the office at weekends*, ie I do not like it. 我真不愿意周末还要上班.

▷ **-grained** (forming compound *adjs* 用以构成复合形容词) having a grain(3,6) of the specified kind 有某种硬粒[颗粒/质地/纹理]的: *coarse-grained* ○ *fine-grained*.

grainy *adj* (esp of a photograph) having a noticeable grain(6) (尤指照片)有明显颗粒的.

gram (also **gramme**) /græm; græm/ *n* (*abbr* 缩写 **g**) metric unit of weight 克(重量单位). ➪App 5 见附录5.

-gram *comb form* 构词成分 (forming *ns* 用以构成名词) **1** metric unit of weight 克(重量单位): *milligram, kilogram*. **2** thing written or drawn 写出或画出的东西: *telegram*.

gram·mar /ˈgræmə(r); ˋgræmɚ/ *n* **1** [U] (study or science of) rules for forming words and combining them into sentences 语法; 语法学: *a good understanding of grammar* 精通语法 ○ *the rules of English grammar* 英语语法规则 ○ *transformational grammar* 转换语法. Cf 参看 MORPHOLOGY, SYNTAX. **2** [C] book containing a description of such rules for a particular language 语法书: *I'm writing a grammar of modern English.* 我在写现代英语的语法书. ○ *I want to buy a French grammar.* 我想买法语语法书. **3** [U] person's knowledge and use of a language 个人对一种语言的掌握: *I'm trying to improve my grammar.* 我在努力提高语言能力. ○ *use bad grammar* 遣词造句不当 ○ (*infml* 口) *Is that grammar* (ie correct usage)? 这词语通吗?

▷ **gram·mar·ian** /grəˈmeərɪən; grəˋmɛrɪən/ *n* expert in grammar 语法学家.

□ **'grammar school** **1** type of secondary school which provides academic (contrasted with technical) courses 文法学校(教授文化课程而非技术课程者). **2** (*US*) = PRIMARY SCHOOL (PRIMARY).

gram·mat·ical /grəˈmætɪkl; grəˋmætɪkḷ/ *adj* of, about or in accordance with the rules of grammar 语法的; 符合语法规则的: *a grammatical treatise* 语法论文 ○ *a grammatical error* 语法错误 ○ *That sentence is not grammatical.* 那个句子语法不通. ▷ **gram·mat·ic·ally** /-klɪ; -klɪ/ *adv*: *grammatically irregular* 语法上不规则的.

gramme /græm; græm/ *n* = GRAM.

gramo·phone /ˈgræməfəʊn; ˋgræmə,fon/ *n* (*dated* 旧) = RECORD-PLAYER (RECORD[1]): [attrib 作定语] *a gramophone record* 唱片.

gram·pus /ˈgræmpəs; ˋgræmpəs/ *n* **1** large dolphin-like sea animal 逆戟鲸. **2** (*infml* 口) person who breathes noisily 呼吸声粗重的人.

gran /græn; græn/ *n* (*Brit infml* 口) grandmother 祖母; 外祖母; 奶奶; 姥姥.

gran·ary /ˈgrænərɪ; ˋgrænərɪ/ *n* **1** building where grain is stored 谷仓; 粮仓: (*fig* 比喻) *The Mid-West is America's granary*, ie region producing much wheat, corn, etc. 美国的中西部地区是个粮仓. **2** [attrib 作定语] (*Brit*) (of bread) containing whole grains of wheat (指面包)全麦的: *a granary loaf* 全麦的面包.

grand /grænd; grænd/ *adj* (**-er**, **-est**) **1** magnificent; splendid; big; of great importance (also in names of places, buildings, etc) 宏伟的; 壮丽的; 大的; 伟大的; 重大的(也用于地名、建筑物名等): *We dined in grand style.* 我们的宴会非常隆重. ○ *It's not a very grand house, just a little cottage.* 那不是深宅大院, 只不过是个小农舍. ○ *a grand occasion, procession* 盛大的场面、浩浩荡荡的队伍 ○ *make a grand entry/exit*, eg on the stage, in a way that attracts the attention of everyone 隆重登场[退场](如在舞台上) ○ *the Grand Cańyon* 科罗拉多大峡谷 ○ *The Grand Hotel* 大旅馆. **2** (*usu derog* 通常作贬义) dignified; imposing; proud; self-important 尊严的; 威严的; 骄傲的; 自负的: *put on a grand air/manner*, ie pretend to be important 摆出一副了不起的样子[架势] ○ *make a grand gesture*, ie a generous act intended to make a great impression 故作豪爽的举动(旨在给人以好印象) ○ *She loves to play the grand lady.* 她喜爱装扮贵妇人. **3** (*dated infml or Irish* 旧, 口或爱尔兰) very fine; excellent 极好的; 美妙的: *It's grand weather!* 天气真好! ○ *It's a grand day today!* 今天是个好天! ○ *I feel grand*, ie very well. 我觉得好极了. ○ *have a grand* (ie very enjoyable) *time* 过得很愉快 ○ *You've done a grand job.* 你干得很出色. **4 Grand** [attrib 作定语] (used in the title of very high-ranking people 用作对官阶很高的人的尊称): *The Grand Vizier* 大维齐(穆斯林国家旧时的首席大臣). **5** (idm 习语) **a/the ˌgrand old ˈman (of sth)** man long and highly respected in a particular field 元老, 老前辈(某一领域中长期备受尊敬的人): *the grand old man of the English theatre* 英国戏剧泰斗.

▷ **grand** *n* **1** (*pl* unchanged 复数不变) (*sl* 俚) $1000; £1000 1000美元; 1000英镑: *It'll cost you 50 grand!* 那要5万元! **2** grand piano 大钢琴; 平台式钢琴: *a concert grand* 音乐会用的大钢琴.

grandly *adv*: *live rather grandly* 生活相当豪华 ○ *gesture grandly* 做出大动作的手势.

grand·ness *n* [U].

□ **ˌgrand ˈduke** hereditary ruler of various European countries 大公(欧洲各国的世袭统治者).

ˌgrand fiˈnale /fɪˈnɑːlɪ; fɪˋnɑlɪ/ last part of a theatrical or similar performance, in which all the performers reassemble on stage (戏剧之类演出的)终场(演员全部再次登台).

ˌgrand ˈjury (in the US) jury that has to decide whether there is enough evidence against an accused person for him to be tried (美国的)大陪审团.

ˈgrand master **1** chess champion 国际象棋大师. **2 ˈGrand Master** head of an order of knighthood, group of Freemasons, etc (骑士团或共济会等的)大头领.

the ˌGrand ˈNational annual horse-race at Liverpool, England, with high fences to jump (在英国利物浦举行一年一度的)越野障碍赛马.

ˌgrand ˈopera opera in which there are no spoken parts, everything being sung 大歌剧(全部为演唱, 无说白者).

ˌgrand ˈpiano large piano with horizontal strings 大钢琴; 平台式钢琴. ➪illus at App 1 见附录1插图, page xi.

Grand Prix /ˌgrɑːn ˈpriː; ˌgrɑnˋpri/ (*French* 法) any of a

G

series of races for the international motor-racing championship 国际汽车大奖赛中的任何一场比赛.

ˌ**grand** ˈ**slam** (*sport* 体) (**a**) victory in every single part of a contest, or in all the main tournaments in a year 全胜(比赛中每场皆胜或在全年的主要联赛上每战皆胜). (**b**) (in cards, esp bridge) winning all 13 tricks in a hand (牌戏中, 尤指桥牌的)大满贯(全赢13墩牌).

ˈ**grandstand** *n* large building with rows of seats for spectators at races, sports meetings, etc 大看台. Cf 参看 STAND[1] 7.

ˌ**grand** ˈ**total** complete total when other totals have been added together 总计; 共计.

ˌ**grand** ˈ**tour** (in former times) tour of the chief towns, countries, etc of Europe, considered as completing the education of a wealthy young person (旧时)(英国富家子弟教育中, 到欧洲大陆观光的)大旅行(为学业的必经阶段).

grand- (forming compound *ns* indicating family relationships 用以构成复合名词, 表示家族关系).

□ ˈ**grandchild** (*pl* **-children**), ˈ**granddaughter**, ˈ**grandson** *ns* daughter or son of one's child (外)孙女或(外)孙子. ⇨App 8 见附录8.

ˈ**grandfather**, ˈ**grandmother**, ˈ**grandparent** *ns* **1** father or mother of either of one's parents (外)祖父或(外)祖母. ⇨App 8 见附录8. **2** (idm 习语) **teach one's grandmother to suck eggs** ⇨ TEACH.

ˈ**grandfather clock** clock worked by weights in a tall wooden case 落地式大摆钟.

grand-dad (also **gran·dad**) /ˈgrændæd; ˋgrænˌdæd/ *n* (*Brit infml* 口) = GRANDFATHER (GRAND-).

gran·dee /grænˈdiː; grænˋdi/ *n* (formerly) Spanish or Portuguese nobleman of high rank (旧时)(西班牙或葡萄牙的)大公.

grand·eur /ˈgrændʒə(r); ˋgrændʒɚ/ *n* [U] **1** greatness; magnificence; impressiveness 伟大; 壮丽; 壮观: *the grandeur of the Swiss alps* 瑞士的山上草场的壮丽景色. **2** (idm 习语) **delusions of grandeur** ⇨ DELUSION.

G

gran·di·loquent /grænˈdɪləkwənt; grænˋdɪləkwənt/ *adj* (*fml derog* 文, 贬) using or being a pompous style of speech, full of words which ordinary people do not understand 言语夸张的; 卖弄词藻的; 文体浮华而晦涩的: *a grandiloquent speaker, speech* 浮夸的演讲人、演说. ▷ **gran·di·loquence** /-əns; -əns/ *n* [U].

gran·di·ose /ˈgrændɪəʊs; ˋgrændɪˌos/ *adj* (*usu derog* 通常作贬义) planned on a large scale; (intended to seem) imposing 庞大的; 浮夸的: *a grandiose building, style, etc* 华而不实的建筑、风格等 ○ *She had some grandiose* (ie overambitious) *plan to start up her own company.* 她有个野心勃勃的大计划, 想独立创办公司.

grandma /ˈgrænmɑː; ˋgrænmɑ/ *n* (*infml* 口) = GRANDMOTHER (GRAND-).

grandpa /ˈgrænpɑː; ˋgrænpɑ/ *n* (*infml* 口) = GRANDFATHER (GRAND-).

grange /greɪndʒ; grendʒ/ *n* country house with farm buildings attached 庄园大宅.

gran·ite /ˈgrænɪt; ˋgrænɪt/ *n* [U] hard, usu grey, stone used for building 花岗岩; 花岗石.

granny (also **gran·nie**) /ˈgrænɪ; ˋgrænɪ/ *n* (*infml* 口) = GRANDMOTHER (GRAND-).

□ ˈ**granny flat** (*infml* 口) flat for an old person, esp in a relative's house 老奶奶套间(供老人住的一套房间, 尤指于亲戚家中者).

ˈ**granny knot** reef knot (REEF) that is incorrectly tied, so that it easily comes undone 反平结(反向打的平结, 易松开).

grant /grɑːnt; grænt/ *v* **1** (**a**) [Tn, Dn·n] agree to give or allow (what is asked for) 同意给予或允许(所求): *grant a favour, request, etc* 答应帮忙、请求等 ○ *They granted him permission to go.* 他们准许他去. ○ *The minister granted journalists an interview.* 部长答应接见记者. (**b**) [Dn·n, Dn·pr] **~ sth (to sb)** give sth formally or legally 正式或依法给予某物: *These lands were granted to our family in perpetuity.* 这些土地依法永远归我们家族所有. ○ *She was granted a pension.* 她得到了养老金. **2** [Tn, Tf, Dn·f] (*fml* 文) agree or admit (that sth is true) 同意或承认(某事属实): *grant the truth of what sb says* 承认某人所说属实 ○ *I grant he's been ill, but that doesn't excuse him.* 我承认他是病了, 但是那也不能原谅他. ○ *I grant you she's a clever woman, but I wouldn't want to work for her.* 我同意你说的, 她很精明, 可是我不想为她工作. **3** (idm 习语) **take sb/sth for ˈgranted** be so familiar with sb/sth that one no longer appreciates his/its full value 因熟悉某人[某事物]而觉察不出其真正价值: *He never praises his wife: he just takes her for granted.* 他从不夸妻子, 只是觉得她一切理当如此. **take sth for ˈgranted** assume sth to be true 认为某事属实: *I take it for granted you have read this book.* 我认为你一定读过这本书.

▷ **grant** *n* **~ (to do sth/towards sth)** thing given for a particular purpose, esp money from the government 授予物; (尤指政府的)拨款: *student grants*, ie to pay for their education 学生助学金 ○ *award sb a research grant* 给某人研究经费 ○ *You can get a grant to repair/towards the repair of your house.* 你可以得到补助金来修缮住房.

granted *adv* (used to admit the truth of a statement before introducing a contrary argument 用以肯定某事物属实, 然后提出相反的论据): *Granted, it's a splendid car, but have you seen how much it costs!* 的确, 那汽车很漂亮, 可你看过价钱了吗?

granu·lar /ˈgrænjʊlə(r); ˋgrænjəlɚ/ *adj* **1** like, containing or consisting of small hard pieces 似粒状的; 含颗粒的; 小粒的: *a granular substance* 粒状物质. **2** rough to the touch or in appearance 表面粗糙的: *a granular surface, texture, etc* 粗糙的表面、质地等.

granu·late /ˈgrænjʊleɪt; ˋgrænjəˌlet/ *v* [I, Tn esp passive 尤用于被动语态] (cause sth to) form into grains or have a granular surface or texture (使某物)形成颗粒, 表面呈微粒状或有颗粒状的质地.

□ ˌ**granulated** ˈ**sugar** sugar in the form of small crystals 砂糖.

gran·ule /ˈgrænjuːl; ˋgrænjʊl/ *n* small hard piece; small grain(3) 小颗粒; 小硬粒: *instant-coffee granules* 速溶咖啡微粒.

grape /greɪp; grep/ *n* **1** green or purple berry growing in clusters on vines, used for making wine or eaten as fruit 葡萄: *a bunch of grapes* 一串葡萄 ○ [attrib 作定语] *grape juice* 葡萄汁. ⇨illus 见插图. **2** (idm 习语) **sour grapes** ⇨ SOUR.

□ ˈ**grape-shot** *n* [U] (formerly) cluster of small iron balls fired together from a cannon (旧时)(用炮发射的)葡萄弹.

ˈ**grape-sugar** *n* [U] dextrose or glucose, a type of sugar found in ripe grapes and other kinds of fruit 葡萄糖.

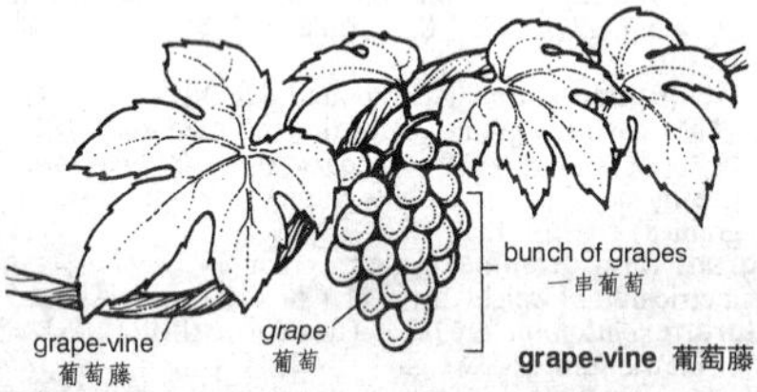

grape-vine 葡萄藤

ˈ**grape-vine** *n* **1** type of vine on which grapes grow 葡萄藤. ⇨illus 见插图. **2** (usu 通常作 **the grape-vine**) [sing] (*fig* 比喻) means by which news is passed on from person to person, eg in an office, a school or a group of friends 消息的传播途径(如在办公室、学校、朋友间): *I heard on the grape-vine that Jill is to be promoted.* 我听人说吉尔就要提升了.

grape·fruit /ˈgreɪpfruːt; ˋgrepˌfrut/ *n* (*pl* unchanged or **~s** 复数或不变或作 **grapefruits**) large round yellow citrus fruit with acid juicy flesh 葡萄柚: [attrib 作定语] ˈ*grapefruit juice* 葡萄柚汁.

graph /grɑːf; *US* græf; græf/ *n* (*mathematics* 数) (diagram consisting of a) line or lines (often curved) showing the variation of two quantities, eg the temperature at each hour 图表; 坐标图; 曲线图: *the rising graph of crime statistics* 罪案统计数字上升的曲线图. ⇨illus at CHART 见 CHART 插图.

□ ˈ**graph paper** paper with squares of equal size, used for drawing graphs 方格纸; 坐标纸.

-graph *comb form* 构词成分 (forming *ns* 用以构成名词) **1** instrument that writes or records 书写或记录用具: *telegraph* ○ *pantograph* ○ *phonograph*. **2** writing, record or drawing 书写; 记录; 图画: *autograph* ○ *monograph* ○ *photograph* ○ *lithograph*.
▷ **-graphic(al)** *comb form* 构词成分 (forming *adjs* from *ns* ending in *-graph* or *-graphy* 和以 -graph, -graphy 结尾的名词构成形容词).

graphic /ˈgræfɪk; ˋgræfɪk/ *adj* **1** [attrib 作定语] of visual symbols (eg lettering, diagrams, drawings) 文字的; 书写的; 图表的; 绘画的: *a graphic artist* 书画艺术家 ○ *graphic displays* 图表展示 ○ *the graphic arts* 书画艺术. **2** (of descriptions) giving one a clear detailed picture in the mind; vivid (指描写)形象的; 生动的: *a graphic account of a battle* 对一场战斗的生动记述 ○ *She kept telling us about her operation, in the most graphic detail.* 她一直绘声绘色地给我们讲她手术的细节.
▷ **graph·ic·ally** /-klɪ; -klɪ/ *adv* **1** by writing or diagrams 以书写; 以图表. **2** (*fig* 比喻) vividly 生动地.
graph·ics *n* [pl] lettering, drawings, etc 文字; 绘图: *computer graphics* 计算机制图.

graph·ite /ˈgræfaɪt; ˋgræfaɪt/ *n* [U] soft black substance (a form of carbon) used in making lead pencils, in lubrication, and for slowing down neutrons in atomic reactors 石墨.

grapho·logy /græˈfɒlədʒɪ; græˋfɑlədʒɪ/ *n* [U] scientific study of handwriting, esp to determine the writer's personality 笔体学(尤用以推测书写者的性格).
▷ **grapho·lo·gist** /-dʒɪst; -dʒɪst/ *n* expert in this 笔体学家.

-graphy *comb form* 构词成分 (forming *ns* 用以构成名词) **1** indicating a form of writing, representation, etc 表示书写、表现等的形式: *calligraphy* ○ *photography*. **2** indicating an art or a descriptive science 表示某种艺术或描述性的学科: *choreography* ○ *geography*.
▷ **-grapher** *comb form* 构词成分 (forming *ns* 用以构成名词) person who does such an activity 从事该项活动的人: *photographer* ○ *geographer*.

grapnel 多爪锚

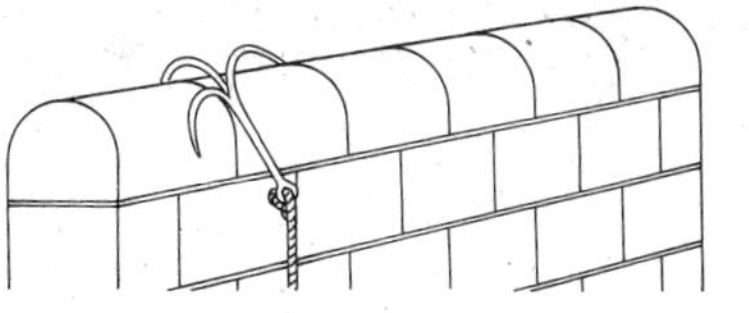

grap·nel /ˈgræpnəl; ˋgræpnəl/ *n* (*nautical* 海) **1** (formerly) instrument with hooks for holding an enemy ship in order to climb on board (旧时)多爪钩(用以钩住敌船的工具). **2** hooked anchor for holding a boat still, esp in a lake, river, etc 多爪锚. ⇨illus 见插图.

grapple /ˈgræpl; ˋgræpl/ *v* [I, Ipr] **~ (with sb/sth)** **1** seize (an opponent) firmly and try to fight 扭住(对手)格斗; 扭打: *She grappled with her assailant but he got away.* 她与袭击者扭打而他却逃走了. **2** (*fig* 比喻) work hard to overcome (a difficulty) 努力克服(困难): *He has been grappling with the problem for a long time.* 他长期以来一直努力解决该问题.
□ **ˈgrappling-iron** *n* grapnel 多爪钩; 多爪锚.

grasp /grɑːsp; US græsp; græsp/ *v* **1** [Tn] **(a)** seize (sb/sth) firmly with hand(s), finger(s), teeth, etc 抓住或咬住(某人[某物]): *She grasped the rope and pulled herself up.* 她抓住绳子攀了上去. ○ *He grasped my hand warmly*, ie to shake it. 他热情地跟我握手. ○ *He grasped her firmly by the arm.* 他紧紧地抓住她的胳膊. **(b)** (*fig* 比喻) take advantage of (sth); not lose 利用(某事物); 抓紧: *grasp an opportunity* 抓住机会. **2** [Tn, Tw] understand (sth) fully 全面理解(某事); 全面领会: *I don't think you've quite grasped the seriousness of the situation.* 我认为你对情况的严重性理解得还不透彻. ○ *She never could grasp how to do it.* 她始终弄不明白该怎样做. **3** (idm 习语) **grasp the ˈnettle** deal with a difficult matter firmly and boldly 坚定果断地处理棘手的事情. **4** (phr v) **grasp at sth** try to seize sth 尽力抓住某物: *grasp at a swinging rope* 尽力抓住摇摆的绳子 ○ (*fig* 比喻) *grasp at an opportunity* 抓住时机.
▷ **grasp** *n* (usu *sing* 通常作单数) **1** **(a)** hold; grip 抓住; 把握: *Take a firm grasp of the handle and pull.* 抓住把手用力拉. **(b)** (*fig* 比喻) power; control 力量; 权力; 支配; 控制: *in the grasp of powerful emotions he could not control* 在他难以控制的强烈感情支配下 ○ *They had fled to America, and were beyond the grasp of their enemies.* 他们逃到美洲, 摆脱了敌人的控制. **2** understanding 理解; 理解力; 领会; 掌握: *difficulties within/beyond sb's grasp* 某人能[不能]理解的困难 ○ *She has a good grasp of the subject.* 她对该学科有深刻的了解.

grasp·ing /ˈgrɑːspɪŋ; US ˈgræspɪŋ; ˋgræspɪŋ/ *adj* greedy for money, possessions, etc; avaricious 贪财的; 贪心的; 贪婪的: *a grasping miser, capitalist, etc* 贪得无厌的守财奴、资本家等. ▷ **grasp·ingly** *adv*.

grass[1] /grɑːs; US græs; græs/ *n* **1** [U] various kinds of common wild low-growing plants of which the thin green leaves and stalks are eaten by cattle, horses, sheep, etc 草; 牧草: *a blade* (ie leaf) *of grass* 一片草叶 ○ *a meadow covered with/planted with grass* 长着[种着]草的草地 ○ [attrib 作定语] *grass seed* 草籽 ○ *a grass skirt*, ie made of long dried grass, as worn in the S Pacific 草裙(以长干草制成, 南太平洋地区人穿用). **2** [C] any species of this plant (including, in botanical use, cereals, reeds and bamboos) 禾本科植物(植物学的用语, 包括谷类、芦苇、竹): *a study of different grasses* 对各种草的研究. **3** [U] ground covered with grass; lawn; pasture 草地; 草坪; 牧场: *Don't walk on the grass.* 勿踏草坪. ○ *mow the grass* 割草 ○ *cattle put out to grass*, ie put in a field to eat the grass 在田野里牧放的牛. **4** [U] (*sl* 俚) marijuana 大麻. **5** [C] (*Brit sl usu derog* 俚, 通常作贬义) (used by criminals 罪犯用语) person who informs the police of criminal activities and plans 告密者. **6** (idm 习语) **the grass is (always) greener on the other ˌside (of the fence)** (*saying* 谚) (said of people who never seem satisfied and always think that others have a better situation than they have 用以指永不知足的人, 总以为别人的境况比自己的好). **(not) let the grass grow under one's feet** (not) delay in getting sth done 做事(不)拖拉. **put sb out to ˈgrass** (*infml* 口) force sb to retire, esp because of old age 迫使某人退休(尤指因年老). **a snake in the grass** ⇨ SNAKE.
▷ **grassy** *adj* (**-ier**, **-iest**) covered with grass 长满草的: *a grassy meadow* 草地.
□ **grass·land** /-lænd; -lənd; -ˌlænd/ *n* [U] (also **grass·lands** [pl]) land covered with grass, esp as used for grazing 草原; 草地; (尤指)草场.
ˌgrass ˈroots (*esp politics* 尤用于政治) ordinary people in society, as opposed to those who make decisions 平民百姓(与决策者相对): *We must not forget about the grass roots.* 我们绝不能忘记民众. ○ *dissatisfaction at the grass roots* 群众的不满 ○ [attrib 作定语] *grass-roots opposition to the party's policy* 民间对那政党的政策的抗拒.
ˈgrass snake small harmless type of snake 游蛇(无毒小蛇).
ˌgrass ˈwidow (*often joc* 常作戏谑语) woman whose husband is temporarily absent 与丈夫暂时分开的女人.

grass[2] /grɑːs; US græs; græs/ *v* **1** **(a)** [Tn, Tn·p] **~ sth (over)** cover sth with turf 以草皮覆盖某物. **(b)** [Tn] (*US*) feed (animals) with grass 以草喂(动物). **2** [I, Ipr] **~ (on sb)** (*Brit sl usu derog* 俚, 通常作贬义) (used by criminals 罪犯用语) inform the police of sb's criminal plans or activities 向警方告密; 出卖: *If anyone grasses on us, his life won't be worth living!* 谁要是出卖我们, 他就别想活了!

grass·hop·per /ˈgrɑːshɒpə(r); US ˈgræs-; ˋgræsˌhɑpɚ/ *n* **1** jumping insect that makes a shrill chirping noise 蝗虫; 蚂蚱; 蚱蜢. **2** (idm 习语) **knee-high to a grasshopper** ⇨ KNEE-HIGH (KNEE).

grate[1] /greɪt; gret/ *n* (metal frame for holding coal, etc in a) fireplace 壁炉; 炉条; 炉箅子.

grate[2] /greɪt; gret/ *v* **1** [esp passive 尤用于被动语态: Tn, Tn·pr] **~ sth (into sth)** rub sth into small pieces, usu against a rough surface; rub small bits off sth 磨碎某物; 擦碎; 从某物上磨下碎屑: *Grate the carrot finely/into small pieces.* 把胡萝卜擦成细丝[末]. ○ *grated* *cheese, carrot, etc* 磨碎的干酪、胡萝卜等 ○ *Grate the nutmeg into the mixture/over the pudding.* 把肉荳蔻磨碎放入混合料中[撒在布丁上]. **2 (a)** [I] make a harsh noise by rubbing (因磨擦)发出噪音: *The hinges grated as the gate swung back.* 大门自动关上时, 合叶发出吱嘎的响声. **(b)** [I, Ipr] **~ (on sb/sth)** (*fig* 比喻) have an irritating effect (on a person or his nerves) (对人或神经)起刺激作用: *His voice grates (on my ears).* 他的嗓音刺(我的)耳(朵). ○ *His bad manners grate on my nerves.* 他没有礼貌让我心烦. ○ *It's her ingratitude that grates on me.* 是她忘恩负义把我惹火了.

▷ **grater** *n* device with a rough surface for grating food 礤床(把食物擦成丝的器具): *a nutmeg grater* 擦肉豆蔻的礤床儿.

grat·ing *adj* irritating 刺耳的; 令人烦躁的: *her grating voice* 她刺耳的嗓音. **grat·ingly** *adv*.

grate·ful /ˈgreɪtfl; ˋgretfəl/ *adj* **1 ~ (to sb) (for sth); ~ (that...)** feeling or showing appreciation for sth good done to one, for sth fortunate that happens, etc; thankful 感激的; 感谢的: *I am grateful to you for your help.* 我感谢你的帮助. ○ *I was grateful that they didn't ask me.* 我感到庆幸的是他们没有问我. **2** (*dated* 旧) pleasant; agreeable; comforting 令人愉快的; 宜人的; 使人感到舒服的: *trees that afford a grateful shade* 遮阴凉的树木. **3** (idm 习语) **be grateful/thankful for small mercies** ⇨ SMALL.

▷ **grate·fully** /-fəlɪ; -fəlɪ/ *adv* in a thankful manner 感激地; 感谢地: *I offered help, and she accepted gratefully.* 我主动提出帮助, 她十分领情.

grat·ify /ˈgrætɪfaɪ; ˋgrætə,faɪ/ *v* (*pt, pp* **-fied**) (*fml* 文) **1** [Tn esp passive 尤用于被动语态] give pleasure or satisfaction to (sb) 使(某人)高兴或满意: *I was most gratified at/by/with the outcome of the meeting.* 我对会议的结果感到极其满意. ○ *It gratified me to hear of your success.* 获悉你取得成功我甚感欣慰. ○ *I was gratified that they appreciated what I did for them.* 使我感到欣慰的是, 我为他们做的事他们很领情. **2** [Tn] give (sb) what is desired; indulge 满足(某人)所欲; 纵容: *gratify a person's whims* 满足一人的奇想 ○ *To gratify my curiosity, do tell me what it is.* 为满足我的好奇心, 你一定得告诉我那是什么.

▷ **grati·fica·tion** /ˌgrætɪfɪˈkeɪʃn; ˌgrætəfəˋkeʃən/ *n* (*fml* 文) **1** [U] gratifying or being gratified; state of being pleased or satisfied 喜悦; 满意; 满足: *the gratification of knowing one's plans have succeeded* 得知计划实现后的喜悦 ○ *sexual gratification* 性满足. **2** [C] thing that gives one pleasure or satisfaction 令人高兴或满意的事物: *one of the few gratifications of an otherwise boring job* 枯燥的工作中少有的一项乐趣.

grati·fy·ing *adj* **~ (to do sth/that...)** (*fml* 文) pleasing; satisfying 令人高兴的; 令人满意的: *It is gratifying to see one's efforts rewarded.* 看到自己的努力有所收获是令人高兴的. **grati·fy·ingly** *adv*.

grat·ing /ˈgreɪtɪŋ; ˋgretɪŋ/ *n* framework of wooden or metal bars, either parallel or crossing one another, placed across an opening, eg a window, to prevent people or animals from climbing through or to allow air to flow easily 格栅; 栅栏; 格子.

gra·tis /ˈgreɪtɪs; ˋgretɪs/ *adv* without payment; free 不付款地; 免费地: *be admitted to the exhibition gratis* 免费参观展览.

grat·it·ude /ˈgrætɪtjuːd; *US* -tuːd; ˋgrætə,tud/ *n* [U] **~ (to sb) (for sth)** being grateful; thankfulness 感激; 感谢: *She felt eternal gratitude to him for saving her life.* 她终生感激他的救命之恩. ○ *I owe you a debt of gratitude for what you've done.* 对你所做的事, 我欠你一份人情债.

gra·tu·it·ous /grəˈtjuːɪtəs; *US* -ˈtuː-; grəˋtuətəs/ *adj* (*fml derog* 文, 贬) done, given or acting unnecessarily, purposely and without good reason 无必要的; 故意的; 无正当理由的: *a gratuitous insult* 无端的侮辱 ○ *a gratuitous lie/liar* 胡诌[胡诌的人] ○ *scenes of gratuitous violence on TV* 电视节目中多此一举的暴力场面. ▷ **gra·tu·it·ously** *adv*. **gra·tu·it·ous·ness** *n* [U].

gra·tu·ity /grəˈtjuːətɪ; *US* -ˈtuː-; grəˋtuətɪ/ *n* **1** (*fml* 文) money given to sb who has done one a service; tip 报酬; 小帐; 小费. **2** (*Brit*) money given to a retiring employee 养老金; 退休金.

grave[1] /greɪv; grev/ *adj* **(-r, -st)** **1** (*fml* 文) (of situations, etc) needing careful consideration; serious (指情况等)需认真考虑的, 严重的, 严峻的: *This could have grave consequences.* 这会造成严重后果. ○ *grave news, danger, etc* 重要的新闻、严重的危险 ○ *There is a grave risk of flooding.* 有闹水灾的极大危险. ○ *a sick person in a grave condition* 危重病人 ○ *a situation that is graver/more grave than expected* 超出预料的严峻形势 ○ *a grave mistake, error, etc* 严重的错误、过失等. **2** (of people) serious or solemn in manner (指人)严肃的, 一本正经的: *He looked grave. 'Is there anything wrong?' I asked.* 他表情严肃. '是出事了吗?' 我问. ▷ **gravely** *adv*: *gravely ill* 病情严重 ○ *If you think that, you are gravely mistaken.* 你若是那样想, 就大错特错了.

grave[2] /greɪv; grev/ *n* **1** hole dug in the ground for a dead body; mound of earth or monument over it 墓穴; 坟墓; 坟头; 墓碑: *strewing flowers on her grave* 往她墓上撒花. **2 the grave** [sing] (*rhet* 修辞) death; being dead 死亡: *from the cradle to the grave*, ie from birth till death 由生至死 ○ *Is there life beyond the grave*, ie after death? 死后还有生命吗? **3** (idm 习语) **dig one's own grave** ⇨ DIG[1]. **from the cradle to the grave** ⇨ CRADLE. **have one foot in the grave** ⇨ FOOT[1]. **turn in one's ˈgrave** (*saying* 谚) of a person who is already dead, likely to be offended or angry 死后不得安生: *You can't go out dressed like that. It's enough to make your grandmother turn in her grave!* 你千万别穿戴成那样子出去. 那会让你祖母躺在坟里也不得安生.

□ **ˈgravestone** *n* stone on top of or at the head of a grave, with the name, etc of the person buried there 墓碑. ⇨illus at app 1 见附录1插图, page viii.

ˈgraveyard *n* burial ground; cemetery 墓地; 坟场; 公墓.

grave[3] /grɑːv; grɑv/ *n* (also ˌ**grave ˈaccent**) mark placed over a vowel to indicate how it is to be sounded (as in French *mère*) 钝音符.

gravel /ˈgrævl; ˋgrævl̩/ *n* [U] small stones, as used to make the surface of roads and paths 砾石; 石子; 沙砾: *a load of gravel* 一车砾石 ○ [attrib 作定语] *a gravel path* 石子路 ○ *a gravel pit*, ie from which gravel is dug 砾石采掘场.

▷ **gravel** *v* **(-ll-;** *US also* **-l-)** [Tn esp passive 尤用于被动语态] cover (sth) with gravel 用砾石铺(某物): *gravel a road* 以石子铺路 ○ *a gravelled path* 砾石铺成的小路.

grav·elly /ˈgrævəlɪ; ˋgrævəlɪ/ *adj* **1** (full) of gravel (多)砂砾的: *This gravelly soil is well drained and good for growing root crops.* 这沙土地利于排水, 适于种植块根作物. **2** (*fig esp approv* 比喻, 尤作褒义) (of a voice) deep and rough (指声音)低沉而沙哑的.

graven /ˈgreɪvn; ˋgrevən/ *adj* [pred 作表语] **~ (in/on sth)** (*arch* 古) carved 雕刻: (*fig* 比喻) *graven on* (ie permanently fixed in) *my memory* 铭刻在我心中.

□ ˌ**graven ˈimage** (*Bible* 圣经) idol 雕像; 偶像.

grav·ing dock /ˈgreɪvɪŋ dɒk; ˋgrevɪŋ dɑk/ *n* dry dock in which the outside of a ship's hull may be cleaned 干船坞(清理船外壳的场所).

grav·it·ate /ˈgrævɪteɪt; ˋgrævə,tet/ *v* [Ipr] **~ towards/to sb/sth** move towards or be attracted to sb/sth, gradually and irresistibly; turn to sb/sth (逐渐地、不由自主地)移向某人[某事物], 受某人[某事物]吸引; 转向某人[某事物]: *When this beautiful girl arrived, all the men in the room gravitated towards her.* 这美貌的姑娘一到, 全屋的男人都让她吸引住了. ○ *The conversation gravitated to sport.* 谈话的内容转到了运动方面.

▷ **grav·ita·tion** /ˌgrævɪˈteɪʃn; ˌgrævəˋteʃən/ *n* [U] force of attraction; gravity(1) 吸引力; 万有引力; 地心引力: *effects of gravitation on bodies in space* 太空中万有引力对星体的影响. **grav·ita·tional** /-ʃənl; -ʃənəl/ *adj*: *a gravitational field* 引力场.

grav·ity /ˈgrævətɪ; ˋgrævətɪ/ *n* [U] **1** force that attracts objects in space towards each other, and on the earth pulls them towards the centre of the planet, so that things fall to the ground when dropped 万有引力; 地心引力; 重力. **2 (a)** importance (of a worrying kind); seriousness (令人忧虑的)重要性; 严重性: *I don't think you realize the gravity of the situation.* 我认为你没有意识到局势的严重. ○ *For an offence of this gravity, imprisonment is the usual punishment.* 对这种重大罪行通常处以监禁. ○ *news of considerable, unusual, etc gravity* 相当重要、非常重要等的新闻. **(b)** solemnity 严

肃; 庄严: *behave with due gravity in a court of law, at a funeral, etc* 在法庭、葬礼等场合表现应有的庄重态度 ○ *a twinkle in his eye which belied the gravity of his demeanour* (他)眼睛一眨, 借以掩盖他的严肃态度.

gravy /ˈgreɪvɪ; ˋgrevɪ/ *n* [U] **1** juice that comes from meat while it is cooking; sauce made from this 肉汁; 调味肉汁. **2** (*sl* 俚 *esp US*) unearned or unexpected money (or profit) 不劳而获的或意外得到的钱财(或利益); 飞来福.

□ ˈ**gravy-boat** *n* vessel in which gravy is served at table 盛肉汁的器皿.

ˈ**gravy train** (*sl* 俚 *esp US*) means of getting a lot of money without much effort (eg through corruption) 轻易捞到大量钱财的手段(如贪污、舞弊): *be/get on the gravy train* 大把捞钱.

gray /greɪ; gre/ *adj, n, v* (*esp US*) = GREY.

graze[1] /greɪz; grez/ *v* **1** [I, Ipr] **~ (in/on sth)** (of cattle, sheep, etc) eat growing grass (指牛、羊等)吃青草: *cattle grazing in the fields* 在田野里吃青草的牛. **2** (**a**) [Tn, Tn·pr] **~ sth (in/on sth)** put (cattle, etc) in a field to eat grass (在田野里)放牧(牛等): *graze sheep* 牧羊. (**b**) [Tn] use (grassland) to feed cattle, etc 用(草地)养牛等.

▷ **gra·zier** /ˈgreɪzɪə(r); ˋgreʒɚ/ *n* **1** person who farms grazing animals 畜牧者. **2** (*Austral* 澳) sheep-farmer 养羊者.

□ ˈ**grazing land** /lænd; ˌlænd/ land used for grazing cattle 牧牛场.

graze[2] /greɪz; grez/ *v* **1** [Tn, Tn·pr] **~ sth (against/on sth)** touch and scrape the skin from sth 擦去某物的皮; 擦破: *graze one's arm, leg, etc against/on a rock* 岩石擦破胳膊、腿等的皮 ○ *I fell and grazed my knee.* 我跌倒了, 擦破了膝盖上的皮. **2** [I, Tn, Tn·pr] **~** (sth) **(against/along sth)** touch or scrape (sth) lightly while passing (经过时)触及或轻擦(某物); 磨擦; 蹭: *Our bumpers just grazed* (ie touched each other) *as we passed.* 我们错车时保险杠互相蹭了一下. ○ *A bullet grazed his cheek.* 子弹擦伤了他的面颊. ○ *a missile which flies so low that it almost grazes the tops of the hedgerows* 低得几乎擦树篱而过的子弹 ○ *The car's tyres grazed (against) the kerb.* 汽车轮胎蹭到路边石.

▷ **graze** *n* raw place where the skin is scraped 皮肤擦伤之处; 擦伤.

grease /gri:s; gris/ *n* [U] **1** animal fat that has been softened by cooking or heating (炼出的)动物油脂: *The grease from pork can be used for frying.* 猪肉炼出的油可用来煎炸食物. **2** any thick semi-solid oily substance 脂膏; 滑脂: *axle-grease*, ie used to lubricate axles 轴用润滑脂 ○ *He smothers his hair with grease*, eg hair-oil. 他用发蜡擦头发. ○ [attrib 作定语] *Grease marks or spots can be removed with liquid detergent.* 油迹或油污可用洗涤液除去.

▷ **grease** *v* **1** [Tn] put or rub grease on or in (esp parts of a machine) 在(尤指机器部件)上涂油或擦油. **2** (idm 习语) **grease sb's** ˈ**palm** (*infml* 口) bribe sb 贿赂某人; 打点. **greaser** *n* (*Brit*) person who greases machinery, eg a ship's engines 涂油工人; 擦拭工人.

□ ˈ**grease-gun** *n* device for forcing grease into the parts of an engine, a machine, etc 注油枪(将润滑油注入发动机等的部件之用具).

ˈ**grease-paint** *n* [U] coloured make-up used by actors (演员用的)化装油彩.

ˌ**grease-proof** ˈ**paper** paper that does not let grease pass through it, and is used esp for cooking or wrapping food in 耐油纸(尤指用于烹调食物或包裹食物的).

greasy /ˈgri:sɪ; ˋgrisɪ/ *adj* (**-ier, -iest**) **1** (**a**) covered with grease; slippery 涂有油脂的; 沾有油脂的; 滑的: *greasy fingers* 沾着油脂的手指 ○ *a greasy road* 滑的路. (**b**) producing an excessive amount of oily secretions 多脂的; 油性的: *greasy skin/hair* 油性的皮肤[头发]. (**c**) (*derog* 贬) containing or cooked with too much fat or oil 油腻的: *greasy food* 油腻的食物. **2** (*fig infml derog* 比喻, 口, 贬) (of people or their behaviour) insincerely flattering and smooth; unctuous (指人或其行为)油滑的, 谄媚的, 虚情假意的: *He greeted me with a greasy smile.* 他皮笑肉不笑地和我打了招呼. ▷ **greas·ily** /-ɪlɪ; -əlɪ/ *adv*. **greasi·ness** *n* [U].

great /greɪt; gret/ *adj* (**-er, -est**) **1** (**a**) [attrib 作定语] well above average in size, extent or quantity 大的; 巨大的; 非常的; 很多的: *The great ship sank below the waves.* 巨轮在滚滚浪涛中沉没. ○ *a great expanse of forest* 广阔的森林 ○ *dive to a great depth* 潜到极深处 ○ *all creatures great and small* 大大小小的生物 ○ *A great crowd had turned up.* 来了一大群人. ○ *People had turned up in great numbers.* 来了成批的人. ○ *The great majority (of people)* (ie Most people) *approve.* 大多数人赞成. (**b**) far away in space or time 距离遥远的; 时间久远的: *He lives a great distance away.* 他住得很远. ○ *That was a great while ago.* 那是很久以前的事了. (**c**) [usu attrib 通常作定语] exceptional in degree or intensity; considerable (程度或强度)异乎寻常的; 格外的; 相当的: *of great value, importance, relevance, significance, etc* 价值、重要性、关系、意义等颇大的 ○ *He described it in great detail.* 他描述得相当详细. ○ *Take great care to do it properly.* 要格外用心地把这事做好. ○ *You have my greatest* (ie very great) *sympathy.* 我非常同情你. ○ *be in great demand*, ie much wanted 需求甚大. (**d**) in a very good state of health, morale or well-being; fine 健康的; 精神好的; 安宁的; 平安的; 好的: *I feel great today!* 我今天觉得精神好极了! ○ *in great form*, ie very fit and active 精力充沛 ○ *in great spirits*, ie very cheerful 心情很愉快. (**e**) [attrib 作定语] with very good or bad effects 有极好的或极坏的效果的: *It's a great relief to know you're safe.* 知你平安无事才放下心来. ○ *You've been a great help.* 你帮了大忙. ○ *the greatest disaster that has ever befallen us.* 我们遭受的最严重的灾难. ⇨Usage at BIG 用法见 BIG. **2** (**a**) of remarkable ability or quality; outstanding 伟大的; 杰出的: *a great man, artist, musician, etc* 伟人、伟大的艺术家、伟大的音乐家 ○ *her great deeds* 她的伟大事迹 ○ *No one would deny that Beethoven's symphonies are great masterpieces.* 人人都认为贝多芬的交响乐是伟大的杰作. ○ *the world's greatest novelist* 世界最杰出的小说家. (**b**) [attrib 作定语] of high rank or status 级别高的; 地位高的: *a great lady* 贵妇人 ○ *the great powers*, ie important and powerful countries 强国 ○ *Alexander the Great* 亚历山大大帝. (**c**) (*infml* 口) very remarkable; splendid 非常的; 非凡的; 出众的; 绝妙的; 了不起的: *He's great!* 他真了不起! ○ *She's the greatest!* 她真是不得了! ○ *It's great that you can come!* 你能来太好了! ○ *What a great party!* 这聚会真棒! ○ *He scored a great goal.* 他射入的一球真绝. (**d**) (*infml* 口) **~ (to do sth)** very enjoyable or satisfactory 非常愉快的; 令人满意的: *We had a great time in Majorca.* 我们在马霍卡玩儿得真痛快. ○ *It's great to know you!* 认识您很高兴! ○ *It's great to have met you!* 与您会面令人十分愉快! **3** (**a**) **~ for sth** (*infml* 口) very suitable for sth; ideal or useful for sth 对某事物极适合的; 对某事物理想的或有用的: *This little gadget's great for opening tins.* 这小玩意儿开罐头挺好用. ○ *These are great shoes for muddy weather.* 这种鞋在雨天泥泞的地上走最合适. (**b**) [pred 作表语] **~ at sth** (*infml* 口) clever or skilful at sth 擅长某事; 精于某事: *She's great at tennis, chess, etc.* 她对网球、象棋什么的都擅长. (**c**) (*ironic* 反语) (used to express exasperation, scorn, etc 用以表示恼怒、愤怒、轻蔑、嘲笑等): *Oh great, I've missed the bus again!* 真倒霉, 我又没赶上公共汽车! ○ *You've been a great help, you have!* 你可帮大忙了, 帮倒忙! **4** [attrib 作定语] (**a**) important; noteworthy 重要的; 显著的; 值得注意的: *The princess was getting married, and everyone was in town for the great occasion.* 公主那时即将成婚, 人人都在首都等待这一盛典. ○ *As the great moment approached, she grew more and more nervous.* 她因那重要时刻渐近而越来越紧张. (**b**) unequalled; excellent 无比的; 无双的; 极好的: *She had a great chance/opportunity, but she let it slip.* 她曾有个绝好的机会, 但没抓住. (**c**) **the great** the most important 最重要的: *The great advantage of this metal is that it doesn't rust.* 这种金属最大的优点是不生锈. **5** [attrib 作定语] fully deserving the name of; beyond the ordinary 名符其实的; 真正的; 不一般的; 不寻常的: *We are great friends.* 我们是真正的朋友. ○ *I've never been a great reader*, ie I do not read much. 我读书不多. ○ *He's a great one for complaining*, ie He constantly complains. 他是个抱怨大王(他总抱怨). **6** [attrib 作定语] (*infml* 口) (used to intensify another *adj* of size, etc 用以加强表示体积等另一形容词的词义) very 非常; 很: *What a great big idiot!* 纯粹的大傻瓜! ○ *You great fat pig!* 你这大肥猪! ○ *That's a great thick slice of cake!* 那是一大块蛋糕哇! **7** [attrib 作定语] (used to name the larger of two

G

types, species, etc 用以指称两类、两种生物等之较大者): *the great auk*, ie contrasted with the little auk 大海雀(与小海雀相对). **8** (added to words for relatives beginning with *grand-* to show a further stage in relationship 冠于以grand-起首的表示亲属的词之前，以示更高或更低一辈的亲属关系): *one's ˌgreat-ˈgrandfather*, ie one's father's or mother's grandfather 某人之曾祖父(或外曾祖父) ○ *one's ˌgreat-ˈgrandson*, ie the grandson of one's son or daughter 某人的曾孙. ⇨ App 8 见附录8. **9** (*dated infml* 旧，口) (in exclamations of surprise 用于惊叹句中): *Great Scott!* 哎呀! ○ *Great heavens!* 天哪! **10** (idm 习语) **be no great shakes** (*infml* 口) not be very good, efficient, suitable, etc 并非很好；不太有效；不怎么适合；没什么了不起: *She's no great shakes as an actress.* 她不是什么名角儿. **going great guns** (*infml* 口) proceeding vigorously and successfully 顺利；成功. **a good/great deal** ⇨ DEAL[2]. **great and small** rich and poor, powerful and weak, etc 贫富、强弱等: *Everyone, great and small, is affected by these changes.* 所有的人，无论高低贵贱都受这些变革的影响. **make great/rapid strides** ⇨ STRIDE. **of great price** very valuable 很有价值的；很贵重的. **your need is greater than mine** ⇨ NEED.

▷ **great** *n* **1** (usu *pl* 通常作复数) (*infml* 口) person of outstanding ability 高手；名家: *one of boxing's all-time greats* 一位空前的拳击高手. **2 the great** [pl v] great (2) people 大人物；显要人物；要人: *a fashionable affair attended by all the great and the good*, ie important and influential people 显要人物都出席的社交盛事.

greatly *adv* much; by much 很；非常: *We were greatly amused.* 我们很快乐. ○ *The reports were greatly exaggerated.* 报告被严重夸大了. ○ *I revere him greatly.* 我很尊敬他.

great·ness *n* [U]: *achieve greatness in one's lifetime* 一生颇有建树.

□ **the ˌGreat ˈBear** large constellation near the North Pole 大熊座. Cf 参看 THE LITTLE BEAR (LITTLE[1]).

ˌGreat ˈBritain (*abbr* 缩写 **GB**) (also **Britain**) England, Wales and Scotland 英格兰、威尔士和苏格兰.

great ˈcircle circle drawn round a sphere in such a way that one of its diameters passes through the centre of the sphere 大圆(球体被通过球心的直径所截得的圆).

ˈgreatcoat *n* heavy (esp military) overcoat (尤指军用的)厚大衣.

the ˌGreat ˈLakes five large lakes in N America between Canada and the US 五大湖(加拿大与美国之间的五个大湖).

ˌGreater ˈLondon administrative area that includes inner London and the outer suburbs 大伦敦(包括伦敦市及郊区).

the Great ˈWar (*dated* 旧) World War I, 1914-18 第一次世界大战(1914-1918).

NOTE ON USAGE 用法: **Britain** or **Great Britain (GB)** consists of the geographical areas of England, Scotland and Wales. 不列颠或大不列颠(GB)由英格兰、苏格兰和威尔士的地域组成. It is often also used to refer to the political state, officially called the **United Kingdom of Great Britain and Northern Ireland** and usually abbreviated to the **United Kingdom** or the **UK**. 这一名称也常用以表示行政上的国家，官方称为大不列颠及北爱尔兰联合王国，通常简称为联合王国或UK. ☆ The **British Isles** are the islands of Britain and Ireland. 不列颠群岛包括不列颠和爱尔兰等岛屿. There is no noun in British English commonly used to refer to the nationality of the people of Britain; instead the adjective is used 在英式英语中没有表示英国人国籍的通用名词而用形容词: *She's British.* 她是英国人. ○ *The British are said to have an unusual sense of humour.* 据说英国人有一种特殊的幽默感. **Britisher** is used in American English. ☆ **Britisher** 用于美式英语. **Briton** is found in newspaper, etc reports of incidents concerning British people and in statistical information. ☆ **Briton** 见于报刊等涉及英国人的报道及统计资料. It is also used of the early inhabitants of Britain ☆ **Briton**也用以指不列颠早期的居民: *10 Britons in hijacked plane* 被劫持飞机上的10个英国人 ○ *According to the latest surveys many Britons suffer from heart disease.* 据最近调查显示，许多英国人患心脏病. ○ *the ancient Britons* 古代不列颠人.

greaves /gri:vz; grivz/ *n* [pl] pieces of armour worn (esp formerly) to protect the shins 护胫，胫甲(尤用于旧时).

grebe /gri:b; grib/ *n* water bird similar to a duck but without webbed feet 鸊鷉.

Gre·cian /ˈgri:ʃn; ˈgriʃən/ *adj* (suggestive) of the art or culture of ancient Greece (带有)古希腊艺术或文化的: *a Grecian* (ie an ancient Greek) *urn* 古希腊的瓮 ○ *his handsome Grecian profile* 他那古希腊式俊美的侧面脸形.

greed /gri:d; grid/ *n* [U] ~ **(for sth)** (*derog* 贬) **1** excessive desire for food, esp when one is not hungry 贪食(尤指不饥饿时). **2** excessive and selfish desire for wealth, power, etc 贪心；贪婪: *the greed with which large companies swallow up their smaller competitors* 大公司为吞并与之竞争的小公司而怀有的贪心 ○ *consumed with greed and envy* 充满贪婪和嫉妒.

▷ **greedy** *adj* (**-ier, -iest**) ~ **(for sth)** filled with greed or desire 贪吃的；贪心的；贪婪的；渴望的；热望的: *a greedy little boy* 贪吃的小男孩 ○ *not hungry, just greedy* 饿倒是不饿，只是贪吃罢了 ○ *looking at the cakes with greedy eyes* 眼巴巴地看着蛋糕 ○ *greedy for power* 贪图权力的 ○ *greedy for information* 渴求信息的. **greed·ily** *adv*. **greedi·ness** *n* [U].

Greek /gri:k; grik/ *adj* of Greece or its people or language 希腊的；希腊人的；希腊语的.

▷ **Greek** *n* **1** [C] member of the people living in ancient or modern Greece 希腊人. **2** [U] their language 希腊语. **3** (idm 习语) **it's all ˈGreek to me** (*infml saying* 口，谚) it's impossible to understand 全然不懂；一窍不通.

green[1] /gri:n; grin/ *adj* (**-er, -est**) **1** of the colour between blue and yellow in the spectrum; of the colour of growing grass, and the leaves of most plants and trees 绿色的；青色的: *as green as grass* 像青草般绿的 ○ *fresh green peas* 鲜嫩的豌豆. ⇨ illus at SPECTRUM 见SPECTRUM插图. **2** covered with grass or other plants 长着青草或其他植物的: *green fields, hills, etc* 绿色的田野、山丘等. **3** (**a**) (of fruit) not yet ripe (指水果)未成熟的；生的；青的: *green bananas* 青香蕉 ○ *apples too green to eat* 生得不能吃的苹果. (**b**) (of wood) not yet dry enough for use (指木头)未干燥的，潮的: *Green wood does not burn well.* 潮木头不好烧. (**c**) (of tobacco) not dried (指烟草)未干的. **4** (*infml* 口) immature; inexperienced; easily fooled 未成熟的；无经验的；易受愚弄的: *a green young novice* 无经验的年轻新手 ○ *You must be green to believe that!* 你真幼稚，竟然相信那个! **5** [usu pred 通常作表语] (of the complexion) pale; sick-looking (指面色)苍白，带病容: *The passengers turned quite green with sea-sickness.* 旅客们由于晕船而脸色发青. **6** [pred 作表语] extremely envious 非常嫉妒: *I was absolutely green (with envy) when I saw his splendid new car.* 我看到他那辆漂亮的新汽车就非常眼红. **7** (*fig rhet* 比喻，修辞) flourishing; full of vigour; fresh (used esp in the expressions shown) 旺盛的；精力充沛的；新鲜的(尤用于下列示例): *live to a green old age* 老当益壮 ○ *keep sb's memory green*, ie not allow sb (dead) to be forgotten 对(逝去的)某人永记不忘. **8** [usu attrib 通常作定语] (*esp politics* 尤用于政治) (favouring the party that is) particularly concerned about protecting the environment and the plants and animals that grow in it 特别关注保护环境及野生动植物的；拥护有此主张的党派的: *green politics* 主张保护环境的政见. **9** (idm 习语) **give sb/get the green ˈlight** (*infml* 口) give sb/get permission to do sth 准许某人[获准]做某事；开绿灯. **the grass is greener on the other side** ⇨ GRASS[1].

▷ **green·ish** /ˈgri:nɪʃ; ˈgrinɪʃ/ *adj* somewhat green 浅绿色的: *a greenish-yellow tinge* 黄中透绿的色彩.

green·ness *n* [U].

□ **ˈgreenback** *n* (*US infml* 口) US banknote 美钞.

ˌgreen ˈbelt area of open land around a city, where building is strictly controlled 环城绿化地带.

ˌgreen-eyed ˈmonster [sing] (*rhet* 修辞) envy; jealousy 嫉妒.

ˈgreenfinch *n* finch with green and yellow feathers 绿金翅.

ˌgreen ˈfingers (*infml* 口) skill in gardening 园艺技能: *Mother has green fingers.* 母亲有园艺技术.

ˈgreenfly *n* (*pl* unchanged 复数不变) any of various kinds of small insects (*aphids*) that are harmful to plants 蚜虫.

ˈ**greengage** /-geɪdʒ; -ˌgedʒ/ *n* type of small yellowish-green plum 青梅.

ˈ**greengrocer** *n* (*Brit*) shopkeeper selling vegetables and fruit 蔬菜水果商人; 果菜商.

ˈ**greenhouse** *n* building with sides and roof of glass, used for growing plants that need protection from the weather 温室; 暖房. ˈ**greenhouse effect** gradual warming of the earth's atmosphere, thought to be caused by increased carbon dioxide in the air 温室效应(地球大气层逐渐变暖, 认为是空气中二氧化碳增加所致).

ˌ**Green ˈPaper** preliminary report of government proposals, for discussion 绿皮书(政府提案的初步报告, 供讨论). Cf 参看 WHITE PAPER (WHITE[1]).

the ˈGreen Party (in Britain) political party whose aims are to protect the countryside, atmosphere, etc from pollution and other dangers (英国)绿党(以保护郊野、大气等免遭污染, 免受危害为宗旨的政党).

ˌ**green ˈpound** value of the pound as a currency exchange for agricultural produce in the EEC 绿色英镑(欧洲共同体的农产品交易币值).

green ˈsalad salad made chiefly from lettuce and other raw green vegetables 绿色拉(主要以莴苣和其他生的绿色蔬菜制成).

green ˈtea light-coloured tea made from incompletely fermented leaves 绿茶.

ˈ**greenwood** *n* (*arch* 古) forest in summer 夏季之树林; 绿林.

green[2] /gri:n; grin/ *n* **1** [U, C] green colour 绿色: *the green of the English countryside in spring* 春天英国郊野呈现青葱的颜色 ○ *curtains of bright emerald green* 浅翠绿色的帘子 ○ *a picture in greens and blues*, ie with various shades of green and blue 以不同深浅的绿色和蓝色绘成的画. **2** [U] green clothes 绿色的衣服: *a girl dressed in green* 穿绿衣的女孩. **3 greens** [pl] (**a**) vegetables with large edible green leaves, eg cabbage, spinach 绿色蔬菜(如洋白菜、菠菜). (**b**) (*US*) vegetation; greenery 植物; 绿叶; 绿树: *Christmas greens*, eg branches of fir and holly for decoration 圣诞节的绿色植物(如供装饰用的枞树和冬青的树枝). **4** [C] area of land with grass growing 草地; 绿地: *the village ˈgreen*, ie public or common land 公有的或共有的土地 ○ *a ˈbowling-green*, ie for the game of bowls 草地滚球场. **5** [C] area with grass cut short surrounding a hole on a golf-course 高尔夫球场上球洞周围剪短的草地: *a ˈputting-green* 轻击区 ○ *the 13th ˈgreen* 第13轻击区. ⇨ illus at GOLF 见 GOLF 插图. **6 Green** [C] (usu *pl* 通常作复数) member of a green[1](8) political party 绿党党员.

green·ery /ˈgri:nərɪ; ˈgrinərɪ/ *n* [U] attractive green foliage, either on growing plants or cut for decoration (长着的或采下做装饰的)漂亮的绿叶: *The hall looks more festive with all that greenery in pots.* 花盆里的绿叶使大厅显得节日气氛更浓.

green·horn *n* inexperienced and easily deceived person 无经验易受骗的人; 涉世不深的人.

green-room *n* room in a theatre, TV studio, etc where the performers can relax (设于剧场、电视演播室等中的)演员休息室.

Green·wich Mean Time /ˌgrenɪdʒ ˈmi:n taɪm; ˈgrɪnɪdʒ ˈmin ˌtaɪm/ (*abbr* 缩写 **GMT**) (also **Universal Time**) time on the line of 0° longitude (which passes through Greenwich, London), used as a basis for calculating time throughout the world 世界时(也叫格林威治时间或格林尼治时间).

greet /gri:t; grit/ *v* **1** (**a**) [Tn, Tn·pr] **~ sb (with sth)** give a conventional sign or word of welcome or pleasure when meeting sb or receiving a (guest) 欢迎; 迎接; 致意; 问候: *He greeted me in the street with a friendly wave of the hand.* 他在街上向我亲切地挥手致意. ○ *greeting her guests at the door* 在门口迎接她的客人. (**b**) [Tn·pr esp passive 尤用于被动语态] **~ sth with sth** receive sth with a particular reaction 对某事做出某种反应: *The news was greeted by/with cheering, booing, etc.* 对这消息欢呼喝彩、嘘声四起等. ○ *This appointment was greeted with relief, dismay, etc.* 这一委任使人欣慰、怅惘等. **2** [Tn] (of sights and sounds) be suddenly seen or heard by (sb) (指景象和声音)突然被(某人)看见或听见: *the view that greeted us at the top of the hill* 在山顶上收入我们眼底的景色.

▷ **greet·ing** *n* **1** first words used on seeing sb or in writing to sb; expression or act with which sb is greeted 招呼; 书信开端的称呼; 问候; 欢迎: *'Hello!' and 'Dear Sir' are greetings.* '喂'和'敬启者'都是招呼用语. ○ *exchange, send greetings* 互致、致以问候 ○ [attrib 作定语] *a ˈgreetings card*, ie a decorative card sent at Christmas, on sb's birthday, etc 贺卡(圣诞节、某人生日等时赠送的装饰性卡片). **2** (idm 习语) **the season's greetings** ⇨ SEASON.

greg·ari·ous /grɪˈgeərɪəs; grɪˈgɛrɪəs/ *adj* **1** liking to be with other people 爱交际的. **2** (*biology* 生) (of animals, birds, etc) living in groups or communities (指动物、鸟等)群居的、共生的. ▷ **greg·ari·ously** *adv*. **greg·ari·ous·ness** *n* [U].

Greg·or·ian /grɪˈgɔ:rɪən; grɪˈgɔrɪən/ *adj*.

□ **Greˌgorian ˈcalendar** system now in general use of arranging the months in the year and the days in the month, introduced by Pope Gregory XIII (1502-85) 格雷果里历(由教皇格雷果里十三世提倡, 至今通用的历法); 阳历. Cf 参看 JULIAN CALENDAR.

Greˌgorian ˈchant kind of medieval church music named after Pope Gregory I (540-604) 格列高利圣咏(以教皇格列高利一世之名命名的中世纪圣歌).

grem·lin /ˈgremlɪn; ˈgrɛmlɪn/ *n* imaginary mischievous creature supposed to cause mechanical or other failure (好捣乱的)小精灵(据信可使机械或其他东西失灵): *The gremlins have got into the computer again.* 捣乱的小精灵又钻进计算机里了.

gren·ade /grəˈneɪd; grɪˈned/ *n* small bomb thrown by hand or fired from a rifle 手榴弹; 枪榴弹: *a ˈhand-grenade* 一颗手榴弹 ○ [attrib 作定语] *a grenade attack* 榴弹攻击.

gre·na·dier /ˌgrenəˈdɪə(r); ˌgrɛnəˈdɪr/ *n* (formerly) soldier who threw grenades; (now) soldier in the Grenadiers (or Grenadier Guards), a British infantry regiment (旧时)掷弹兵; (现今)英国近卫步兵团的士兵.

grew *pt* of GROW.

grey (also *esp US* **gray**) /greɪ; gre/ *adj* **1** (**a**) of the colour between black and white; coloured like ashes, slate, lead, etc 灰色的; 灰白的: *grey eyes, hair, etc* 灰色的眼睛、头发等 ○ *a grey suit* 灰色西装. (**b**) [usu pred 通常作表语] having grey hair 有灰色头发; 有花白头发: *She has turned quite grey recently.* 她近来头发多已斑白. ○ *I'm going grey.* 我的头发开始白了. (**c**) dull; cloudy 灰暗的; 阴沉的: *a grey day* 阴沉的一天. **2** (*fig* 比喻) (**a**) depressing; monotonous 郁闷的; 单调乏味的: *a grey existence* 单调乏味的生活 ○ *Life seemed grey and pointless after she'd gone.* 她走后生活显得既单调又无意义. (**b**) (*derog* 贬) having no life or attractive features; anonymous 无生气的; 不突出的; 无名的: *a government department run by little grey men* 由无名之辈掌管的政府部门.

▷ **grey** (also *esp US* **gray**) *n* **1** [U, C] grey colour 灰色: *a suit of dark/light/medium grey* 深[浅/中]灰色的西装. **2** [U] grey clothes 灰色衣服: *dressed in grey* 身穿灰色衣服.

grey (also *esp US* **gray**) v [I, Tn] (cause sth to) become grey (使某物)变成灰色: *He/His hair has greyed a lot.* 他[的]头发多已花白. ○ *He was 50 and greying.* 他那时50岁头发就渐白了. ○ *Worry had greyed her hair.* 她愁白了头发.

grey·ish (also *esp US* **gray·ish**) *adj* somewhat grey 略带灰色的; 浅灰的.

□ ˌ**grey ˈarea** aspect, topic, etc that does not fit into a particular category, and is therefore difficult to deal with 灰色区域(不易归类故难以处理的方面、题目等): *When the rules for police procedure were laid down, a lot of grey areas remained.* 警方的程序规章定立后, 遗留下许多难以处理的灰色区域.

ˈ**greybeard** *n* (*rhet* 修辞) old man 老人.

ˌ**grey-ˈheaded** *adj* with grey hair; old 有白发的; 老的.

ˈ**grey matter** (**a**) material of the brain (脑的)灰质. (**b**) (*fig infml* 比喻, 口) intelligence 智力; 脑筋: *a boy without much grey matter* 脑筋不够用的男孩.

grey·hound /ˈgreɪhaʊnd; ˈgreˌhaʊnd/ *n* large thin fast-running dog used in racing 灵猩(身驱瘦长、善跑之狗, 用于比赛): [attrib 作定语] *ˈgreyhound racing* 赛狗. ⇨ illus at App 1 见附录 1 插图, page iii.

G

grid /ɡrɪd; ɡrɪd/ *n* **1** framework of crossing or parallel metal or wooden bars; grating (金属的或木的)格子; 栅栏: *a 'cattle-grid*, ie one covering a ditch to prevent cattle from straying onto a main road, etc 牲口栅子(置于沟渠上者, 以防牲口走上公路). **2** (**a**) network of lines, esp crossing at right angles 网格; (尤指)方格: [attrib 作定语] *New York is laid out on a grid pattern.* 纽约展示在网格图上. (**b**) network of squares on a map, numbered for reference (地图上的)坐标方格: [attrib 作定语] *the grid reference of a place on a map* 地图上某地的坐标方格数字. ⇨illus at MAP 见MAP插图. **3** system of electric-power cables or gas-supply lines for distributing power evenly over a large area 输电网; 煤气输送网: *the National Grid*, ie the network of electricity supply in Britain (英国)国家输电网. **4** pattern of lines marking the starting-places on a car-racing track 赛车跑道上标志起点的平行线.

griddle /'ɡrɪdl; 'ɡrɪdl/ *n* (*Scot* 苏格兰作 **girdle**) circular iron plate heated for cooking flat cakes (烤饼用的)烤盘.

grid·iron /'ɡrɪdaɪən; 'ɡrɪd,aɪɚn/ *n* **1** framework of metal bars used for cooking meat or fish over an open fire (置于明火上烧烤肉或鱼用的)烤架. **2** (*US*) field for American football (the area of play being marked by a pattern of parallel lines) 橄榄球场.

grief /ɡri:f; ɡrif/ *n* **1** [U] **~ (over/at sth)** deep or violent sorrow 忧伤; 悲伤: *driven almost insane by grief over/at his death* 因他死去而悲伤得几乎发狂 ○ *die of grief* 忧伤而死. **2** [C] event causing such feelings 引起忧伤、悲伤的事; 伤心事: *His marriage to someone outside their faith was a great grief to his parents.* 他娶了异教徒是他父母的一大伤心事. **3** (idm 习语) **come to 'grief** (*infml* 口) (**a**) end in failure 终归失败; 以失败告终: *All his little schemes for making money seem to come to grief.* 他为赚钱而耍的花招儿看来都要失败. (**b**) have an accident; fall down, crash, etc 出事故; 遭意外; 跌倒; 碰撞等: *Several pedestrians had come to grief on the icy pavement.* 几个行人在结冰的人行道上滑倒了. **good 'grief!** (*infml* 口) (exclamation of surprise and (usu mild) dismay 表示惊奇和(通常为轻度的)惊恐的感叹语).

□ **grief-stricken** *adj* overcome by deep sorrow 极度悲伤的: *trying to console the grief-stricken relatives* 尽力劝慰悲痛欲绝的亲属.

griev·ance /'ɡri:vns; 'ɡrivəns/ *n* **~ (against sb)** real or imagined cause for complaint or protest (used esp with the *vs* shown) 委屈, 苦衷, 牢骚, 不满, 怨恨(尤与下列示例中动词连用): *inviting the members to air* (ie express) *their grievances* 请成员们诉说苦衷 ○ *He'd been harbouring/nursing a grievance against his boss.* 他一直对老板心怀不满. ○ *Management agreed to settle the workers' grievances.* 资方同意处理工人的申诉.

grieve /ɡri:v; ɡriv/ *v* (*fml* 文) **1** [Tn] cause great sorrow to (sb) 使(某人)极为悲伤: *Your mother is very grieved by your refusal to return home.* 你离家不归, 你母亲极为伤心. ○ *It grieves me to hear how disobedient you've been.* 听说你很不听话, 使我感到非常难过. ○ *It grieves me to have to say it, but* (ie It is regrettably true that) *you have only yourself to blame.* 我是万不得已才说的, 但你是咎由自取. **2** (**a**) [I, Ipr] **~ (for sb); ~ (over/about sb/sth)** feel a deep sorrow because of loss (因失去而)感到悲痛: *Their daughter died over a year ago, but they are still grieving.* 他们的女儿死去已一年多了, 但他们现在仍很悲痛. ○ *grieve for one's (dead, lost) child* 为(死去的、失去的)孩子伤心 ○ *grieve over the death of sb* 为某人之死而悲哀. (**b**) [Ipr] **~ at/about/over sth** feel deep regret (about sth) (对某事)感到非常后悔、懊悔: *It's no use grieving about past errors.* 为以往的错误懊悔于事无补.

griev·ous /'ɡri:vəs; 'ɡrivəs/ *adj* **1** causing grief or suffering 令人伤心或痛苦的: *grievous news, losses, wrongs* 令人伤心的消息、损失、错误. **2** (*fml* 文) (of sth bad) severe; serious (指坏事)剧烈的, 严重的: *grievous pain, wounds, etc* 剧痛、重伤等 ○ *a grievous error, fault, sin, crime, etc* 严重的错误、过失、罪过、罪行等. ▷ **griev·ously** *adv*: *If you think that, you are grievously in error.* 你要是那样想, 你可就大错特错了.

□ ,**grievous** ,**bodily** '**harm** (*law* 律) (*abbr* 缩写 **GBH**) serious injury caused by a criminal attack 严重的身体伤害; 重伤.

grif·fin /'ɡrɪfɪn; 'ɡrɪfɪn/ (also **grif·fon**, **gry·phon** /'ɡrɪfən; 'ɡrɪfən/) *n* mythical creature with the head and wings of an eagle and a lion's body (神话中的)狮身鹰首兽.

grill /ɡrɪl; ɡrɪl/ *n* **1** (**a**) device on a cooker that directs heat downwards for cooking meat, toasting bread, etc (热力自上而下的)烤架: *an electric grill* 电烤架 ○ *an eye-level grill* 平视烤架 ○ *Put it under the grill for a minute to brown the top.* 放在烤架下烤一分钟把上部烤成金黄色. ○ [attrib 作定语] *a grill pan* 焙盘. (**b**) gridiron (for cooking on) (热力自下而上的)烤架. (**c**) dish of meat, etc cooked directly over or under great heat 一盘烤肉等: *a mixed grill*, ie grilled steak, liver, bacon, etc served together 什锦烤肉. (**d**) (also '**grill-room**) room in a hotel or restaurant where such dishes are cooked and served (旅馆或饭店的)烤肉餐室: *Let's meet in the first-floor grill-room.* 咱们在二楼烤肉餐室见面. **2** = GRILLE.

▷ **grill** *v* **1** (**a**) [I, Tn, Dn·n] be cooked or cook (sth) over or under great heat 烧烤, 炙烤(食物): *grilled steak* 烤肉排 ○ *I'll grill you some fish.* 我来给你烤些鱼. ⇨ Usage at COOK 用法见COOK. (**b**) [I, Tn] (*infml* 口) expose (oneself) to great heat 使(自己)暴露于高温下; 烤: *sit grilling (oneself) in front of a fire, in the sun, under a sun-ray lamp, etc* 坐着烤火、晒太阳、烤紫外线灯等. **2** [Tn] (*fig infml* 比喻, 口) question (sb) intensively and for a long time, often hostilely 盘问(某人): *The police grilled him (with non-stop questions) for over an hour.* 警方(以连串的问题)盘问了他一个多小时.

grille (also **grill**) /ɡrɪl; ɡrɪl/ *n* protective screen of metal bars or wires (用金属棒或金属丝做的)保护屏, 隔板, 格栅: *The bank clerk peered at the customer through/from behind the grille.* 银行的职员从格栅后面看着顾客. ○ *Ensure that the grille is in place while the machinery is in operation.* 机器运转时一定要放好安全网罩.

grim /ɡrɪm; ɡrɪm/ *adj* (**-mmer, -mmest**) **1** very serious and unsmiling in appearance 非常严肃的; 无笑容的: *a grim face, look, etc* 严肃的面孔、神情等 ○ *He looked grim; I could tell something was wrong.* 他表情严肃, 我知道可能出事了. **2** severe; unrelenting 严厉的; 严峻的; 不懈的; 无情的: *their grim day-to-day struggle for survival* 他们为生存日日进行的坚苦挣扎. **3** unpleasant; depressing 令人不愉快的; 令人沮丧的: *grim news* 令人不快的消息 ○ *We face the grim prospect of still higher unemployment.* 我们面对失业率进一步增高前景堪虑. **4** determined in spite of fear 坚定而无畏的: *a grim smile* 大无畏的微笑. **5** containing disturbing or horrific material 含不快或恐怖内容的: *a grim little tale of torture and murder* 有折磨凶杀内容的恐怖小故事. **6** (of a place) depressingly plain; gloomy (指地方)极简陋的, 令人沮丧的: *the grim walls of the prison* 监狱中令人郁闷的四壁. **7** [pred 作表语] (*infml* 口) ill 生病; 不舒服: *I feel pretty grim.* 我觉得有点儿不舒服. **8** [usu pred 通常作表语] (*infml* 口) very bad or unpleasant 很坏; 令人厌恶: *I've seen her so-called paintings; they're fairly grim, I can tell you!* 我看见过她那所谓的画; 一点儿都不好, 真的! **9** (idm 习语) **like grim 'death** with great determination or perseverance in spite of difficulties 坚定地; 不懈地: *He held on to the branch like grim death.* 他紧紧抓住树枝不松手. ○ *She stuck to her task like grim death.* 她百折不挠地执行任务. ▷ **grimly** *adv*: *grimly determined* 毫不动摇的. **grim·ness** *n* [U].

grim·ace /ɡrɪ'meɪs; *US* 'ɡrɪməs; 'ɡrɪməs/ *n* ugly twisted expression (on the face), expressing pain, disgust, etc or intended to cause laughter (表示痛苦、厌恶等或欲引人发笑的)怪相, 鬼脸: *make/give a grimace of pain* 作出[露出]痛苦的怪相.

▷ **grim·ace** *v* [I, Ipr] **~ (at sb/sth)** make grimaces 作怪相; 作鬼脸: *She grimaced in/with distaste at the thought of it.* 她一想到那个就厌恶得作怪相. ⇨Usage at SMIRK 用法见SMIRK.

grime /ɡraɪm; ɡraɪm/ *n* [U] dirt, esp in a layer on a surface 尘垢(尤指表面上的一层); 污垢: *the soot and grime of a big manufacturing town* 大工业城市的煤烟与尘垢 ○ *a face covered with grime and sweat* 满是污垢和汗水的脸.

▷ **grime** *v* [Tn esp passive 尤用于被动语态] make (sb/sth) dirty 将(某人[某物])弄脏: *a face grimed with dust* 沾有灰尘的脸.

grimy /ˈgraɪmɪ; ˋgraɪmɪ/ *adj* (**-ier, -iest**) covered with grime 沾满污垢的: *grimy hands, windows* 沾满污垢的手、窗户.

grin /grɪn; grɪn/ *v* (**-nn-**) **1** [I, Ipr] **~ (at sb)** smile broadly, so as to show the teeth, expressing amusement, foolish satisfaction, contempt, etc 露齿而笑(表示高兴、愚蠢的满足、轻蔑等); 咧着嘴笑; 龇着牙笑: *He grinned at me, as if sharing a secret joke.* 他朝我龇牙一笑, 好像彼此会心领略一个笑话. ○ *grin with delight* 高兴得露齿一笑 ○ *grin from ear to ear*, ie very broadly 咧着大嘴笑. **2** [Tn] express (sth) by grinning 露齿笑着表示(某事): *He grinned his approval.* 他咧嘴一笑表示赞成. **3** (idm 习语) **grin and ˈbear it** endure pain, disappointment, etc without complaining 毫无怨言地忍受痛苦、挫折等.

▷ **grin** *n* act of grinning 露齿笑: *a broad, foolish, silly, etc grin* 咧着嘴的、愚蠢的、傻气的...一笑 ○ *With a nasty grin on his face he took out a knife.* 他狞笑着掏出了刀子.

grind /graɪnd; graɪnd/ *v* (*pt, pp* **ground** /graʊnd; graʊnd/) **1** (a) [Tn, Tn·pr, Tn·p] **~ sth (down/up) (to/into sth)** crush sth to very small pieces or to powder between millstones, the teeth, etc or using an electrical or a mechanical apparatus 磨碎; 磨成粉状; 碾碎; 咬碎; 嚼碎: *The elephant grinds its food with/between its powerful molars.* 象用其强有力的臼齿嚼碎食物. ○ *grind coffee beans* 磨咖啡豆 ○ *grind corn (down/up) into flour* 将谷磨成粉 ○ *grind sth to dust, to (a fine) powder, etc* 将某物磨成末、(细)粉等. (b) [I, Ipr, Ip] **~ (down) (to/into sth)** be able to be crushed finely 可磨细: *The corn grinds easily.* 谷物容易磨成粉. ○ *It won't grind down any finer than this.* 不能磨得比这个再细了. (c) [Tn] (*US*) mince (meat) 绞碎(肉): *ground beef* 绞碎的牛肉. **2** [Tn, Tn·pr] **~ sth (from sth)** produce sth by crushing 经磨碎而制成某物: *grind flour from corn* 将谷物磨成面粉. **3** [esp passive 尤用于被动语态: Tn, Tn·p] **~ sb (down)** (*fig* 比喻) treat sb extremely harshly; oppress sb 虐待某人; 压迫某人: *people ground (down) by poverty, taxation, tyranny, etc* 受贫困、苛税、暴政等折磨的人民 ○ *tyrants who grind down the poor* 压榨穷人的暴君. **4** [Tn, Tn·pr] **~ sth (on/with sth)** polish or sharpen sth by rubbing it on or with a rough hard surface 磨光某物; 将某物磨锋利; 磨快: *grind a knife, lens, etc on a stone, etc* 在石头等上磨刀、镜片等. **5** [Tn, Tn·pr, Tn·p] **~ sth (together)**; **~ sth in/into sth** press or rub sth firmly and often noisily 挤压或磨擦某物(常发出声音): *He ground his teeth (together) in frustration.* 他因失败而把牙咬得咯咯响. ○ *dirt that had become ground into the surface* 落在物体表面的尘土 ○ (*fig* 比喻) *grind one's heel into the fragments*, ie crush them very hard 用脚跟把破片碾碎. **6** [I, Ip] **~ (away)** make a harsh noise (as if) from friction 发出(似)摩擦之声; 发出刺耳声: *The old engine ground and shuddered.* 那台陈旧的发动机抖动着发出摩擦的声音. **7** [Tn] work (sth) by turning a handle (转动摇柄)开动(某物): *grind a coffee-mill, barrel-organ* 摇咖啡磨、筒风琴. **8** [I, Ipr, Ip] **~ (away) (at sth)** (*infml* 口) work or study hard and long 刻苦工作或学习; 苦干; 用功: *grind away at one's studies* 刻苦学习. **9** (idm 习语) **grind the faces of the ˈpoor (into the ˈdust)** (*rhet* 修辞) deliberately cause poor people to suffer more than necessary, taking pleasure in doing so 以压迫穷人为乐. **grind to a ˈhalt/ˈstandstill** (a) (of a vehicle) stop slowly and noisily (指车辆)伴有噪音缓缓停住. (b) (*fig* 比喻) (of a process) gradually stop (指过程)逐渐停止: *The strike brought industry grinding to a halt.* 由于罢工生产逐渐停顿下来. **have an axe to grind** ⇨ AXE. **10** (phr v) **grind on** continue for a long time boringly and monotonously 烦人、乏味地继续下去: *The speaker ground on, oblivious of his listeners' boredom.* 演说者唠唠叨叨, 没注意到听众的厌烦情绪. **grind sth out** (a) produce sth by turning a handle (经转动摇柄)产生某物: *grind out music from a barrel-organ* 摇动筒风琴奏出音乐. (b) (*derog* 贬) play (music) heavily, tediously or monotonously 沉闷地、单调地或乏味地演奏(乐曲): *The jukebox ground out an incessant stream of pop music.* 自动电唱机没完没了地放送流行乐曲. (c) (*derog* 贬) produce (books, stories, etc) with sustained but uninspired effort 无灵感却费力硬写(书、小说等): *He has been grinding out cheap romantic stories at the rate of one a week.* 他一直以每周一篇的速度生拼硬凑廉价的浪漫小说.

▷ **grind** *n* [sing] **1** act of grinding 磨; 碾. **2** size of ground particles 磨细的程度: *a coarse grind* 粗磨. **3** (*infml* 口) long, steady, tiring or monotonous effort (physical or mental) 长时间的、令人疲劳厌倦的(体力的或脑力的)劳动; 苦事: *a long uphill grind in a cycle race* 自行车比赛中的一大段上坡路 ○ *Marking examination papers is a real grind.* 批改试卷的确是个苦事.

grind·ing *adj* **1** making a harsh noise (as if) from friction 发出(似)摩擦声的; 刺耳的: *The car screeched to a halt with grinding brakes.* 汽车停住时发出刺耳的刹车声. **2** (idm 习语) **bring sth/come to a grinding ˈhalt** (*infml* 口) (cause sth to) stop completely (使某物)停住, 停稳. **grinding ˈpoverty** (*rhet* 修辞) extreme poverty that causes suffering 贫苦不堪.

□ **grindstone** /ˈgraɪndstəʊn; ˋgraɪnd,ston/ *n* **1** stone shaped like a wheel, turned on an axle, against which one holds knives or other tools to sharpen them 砂轮. **2** (idm 习语) **keep one's/sb's nose to the grindstone** ⇨ NOSE[1].

grinder /ˈgraɪndə(r); ˋgraɪndɚ/ *n* **1** thing that grinds, eg a molar tooth; apparatus for grinding 起研磨作用之物(如臼齿); 研磨的装置; 研磨机: *a ˈcoffee-grinder* 磨咖啡机. **2** (in compounds 用以构成复合词) person who grinds 做研磨工作的人; 做摇转工作的人: *a ˈknife-grinder* ○ *an ˈorgan-grinder*, ie sb who plays a barrel-organ.

grip /grɪp; grɪp/ *v* (**-pp-**) **1** [I, Tn] take and keep a firm hold of (sth/sb) 紧抓(某物[某人]); 紧握: *The frightened child gripped its mother's hand.* 受惊的孩子紧抓住他母亲的手. ○ *The brakes failed to grip* (ie engage with and stop the wheels) *and the car ran into a wall.* 汽车刹车失灵撞在墙上了. **2** [Tn esp passive 尤用于被动语态] (*fig* 比喻) seize the attention, imagination, etc of (sb) 吸引(某人)的注意力、想像力等: *an audience gripped by a play* 受戏剧吸引的观众 ○ *gripped by/with fear* 吓住.

▷ **grip** *n* **1** [sing] **~ (on sb/sth)** (a) action of gripping; firm hold 紧抓; 紧握: *take a grip on a rope* 抓紧绳索 ○ *I let go/released my grip and he ran away.* 我一松手他就跑了. ○ *The climber relaxed her grip and fell.* 攀登者手一松跌了下去. ○ (*fig* 比喻) *The play's exciting at first, but in the third act it loses its grip on one's attention.* 那剧一开始很精彩, 但到第三幕就没看头儿了. (b) way or power of gripping 紧握的方式; 紧握力: *a grip like iron, like a vice, like a bulldog, etc* 像钢铁般、像老虎钳般、像斗牛犬般夹住或咬住不放 ○ *tyres which give (a) good grip on the road* 能紧贴着路面的车胎. (c) (*fig* 比喻) force that paralyses or disables 造成瘫痪或伤残的因素: *the icy grip of winter* 冬季严寒的破坏力 ○ *people in the grip of disease, despair, etc* 疾病缠身、陷于绝望等的人们. **2** [C] part that is to be gripped; handle 把手; 柄: *a wooden, metal, etc (hand-)grip* 木、金属等(手)柄. **3** [C] wire pin with two prongs for keeping hair tidy; hair-grip 发卡; 发夹. **4** [C] (*US*) large strong bag with handles 手提包: *a leather grip* 皮制手提包. **5** (idm 习语) **come/get to grips with sb/sth** (a) seize (an opponent) and begin to fight 抓住(对手)搏斗起来; 扭打: *She was unable to get to grips with her assailant.* 她无力与袭击她的人扭打. (b) (*fig* 比喻) begin to deal with (a problem, challenge, etc) 开始应付(难题、挑战等). **get/keep/take a ˈgrip/ˈhold on oneself** (*infml* 口) gain control of oneself and improve one's behaviour (eg after being afraid, lazy, out of control, etc) 恢复自制力并改进行为(如不再胆怯、懒惰、失态等). **lose one's grip** ⇨ LOSE.

grip·ping *adj* exciting; holding the attention 令人激动的; 吸引人注意力的: *a gripping account, film, story, etc* 吸引人的报告、电影、故事等 ○ *gripping yarns* 扣人心弦的奇谈. **grip·pingly** *adv*.

gripe[1] /graɪp; graɪp/ *v* [I] feel or cause sudden sharp pain in the stomach or intestines 感到或引起腹或肠绞痛: *a griping pain in the stomach* 胃痉挛 ○ *medicine to take when your stomach gripes* 胃疼时服用的药.

▷ **the gripes** *n* [pl] (*infml* 口) sharp pain in the intestines, etc 肚子疼.

□ **ˈgripe-water** *n* [U] medicine to cure stomach or intestinal pain in babies 治疗小儿腹痛的药.

gripe[2] /graɪp; graɪp/ *v* [I, Ipr] ~ **(about sb/sth)** (*infml derog* 口, 贬) complain (about sb/sth); grumble (habitually) 抱怨(某人[某事物]); (惯于)发牢骚: *He keeps griping about having no money.* 他不断地抱怨自己没钱.

▷ **gripe** *n* (*infml* 口) **1** [C] complaint; expression of discontent 牢骚; 怨言; 不平; 不满: *Bring all your gripes to the boss.* 你跟老板发牢骚去. **2** (*derog* 贬) [sing] act of complaining 发牢骚: *He likes to have a good gripe from time to time.* 他时常爱发上一通牢骚.

grisly /ˈgrɪzlɪ; ˋgrɪzlɪ/ *adj* causing horror or terror; ghastly 恐怖的; 可怕的: *the grisly remains of the half-eaten corpses* 尸体被吃掉一半的恐怖残骸.

grist /grɪst; grɪst/ *n* **1** [U] (*arch* 古) grain to be ground 待磨的谷物. **2** (idm 习语) **grist to the/sb's ˈmill** useful or profitable, esp in addition to or as a contribution to sth larger 有益的或有利的东西(尤指对某事物的补充或补助): *I never refuse odd jobs to supplement my income — it's all grist to the mill.* 我为增加收入, 对于做零活总是来者不拒——多多益善.

gristle /ˈgrɪsl; ˋgrɪsl/ *n* [U] tough unappetizing tissue (esp cartilage) in meat 肉中难吃的硬组织(尤指软骨): *I can't eat this meat — it's all gristle*, ie full of gristle. 这肉不能吃——净是软骨.

▷ **gristly** /-lɪ; -lɪ/ *adj* like or full of gristle 似软骨的; 满是软骨的.

grit /grɪt; grɪt/ *n* [U] **1** tiny hard bits of stone, sand, etc 细石子、沙粒等: *spread grit on icy roads* 往结冰的路上撒沙子 ○ *I've got some grit/a piece of grit in my shoe.* 我的鞋里进了沙子. **2** quality of courage and endurance 勇气和毅力: *Mountaineering in a blizzard needs a lot of grit.* 在暴风雪中登山需要极大的勇气和毅力.

▷ **grit** *v* (**-tt-**) **1** [Tn] cover (sth) with grit; spread grit on (esp icy roads) 以沙砾覆盖(某物); 撒沙砾于(尤指结冰的道路)上. **2** (idm 习语) **grit one's ˈteeth** (**a**) keep one's jaws tight together 咬紧牙关. (**b**) (*fig* 比喻) summon up one's courage and determination 鼓起勇气下定决心: *When things get difficult, you just have to grit your teeth and persevere.* 遇到困难只需咬紧牙关坚持下去.

gritty *adj* (**-ier, -iest**) full of grit 多沙的; 刚强的: *cheap gritty bread* 牙碜的廉价面包 ○ *a gritty fighter* 坚强的战士. **grit·ti·ness** *n* [U].

grits /grɪts; grɪts/ *n* [pl] coarse oatmeal 粗燕麦粉.

grizzle /ˈgrɪzl; ˋgrɪzl/ *v* (*infml derog* 口, 贬) [I] ~ **(about sth)** (esp of children) keep complaining (about sth) in a whining way (尤指儿童)哭着不停地抱怨(某事): *Stop grizzling!* 别哭哭啼啼地缠磨人!

▷ **grizzly** *adj* grizzling or inclined to grizzle (爱)哭着抱怨的.

grizzled /ˈgrɪzld; ˋgrɪzld/ *adj* grey(-haired) 灰色(毛发)的.

grizzly /ˈgrɪzlɪ; ˋgrɪzlɪ/ *n* (also ˌ**grizzly ˈbear**) large fierce grey-brown bear of N America 灰熊(产于北美). ⇨illus at BEAR 见BEAR插图.

Gro *abbr* 缩写 = (in street names) Grove 用于街道名称: *6 Lime Gro* 莱姆林阴道6号.

groan /grəʊn; gron/ *v* **1** [I, Ipr] ~ **(at sb/sth)**; ~ **(with sth)** make a deep sad sound when in pain, or to express despair, disapproval or distress 呻吟; 叹息: *'I've been hit,' he groaned*, ie said with a groan. '打中我了,' 他呻吟道. ○ *She groaned with pain.* 她痛苦地呻吟. ○ *The audience groaned at his terrible jokes.* 他讲的笑话很糟, 听众发出了不满的叹息声. **2** (**a**) [I, Ipr] ~ **(with sth)** (of things) make a noise like that of groaning (指东西)发出似呻吟的声音: *The ship's timbers groaned during the storm.* 船骨在暴风雨中吱咯作响. (**b**) [Ipr] ~ **with sth** (*fig* 比喻) be heavily laden with sth 受到某物的重压; 装满或堆满某物: *a table groaning with food* 布满食物的桌子. **3** [I, Ipr, Ip] ~ **(on) (about/over sth)** (*derog* 贬) complain irritably; moan 气愤地发牢骚; 抱怨: *She's always groaning on about how much work she has to do.* 她总抱怨自己得干很多活儿. **4** [Ipr] ~ **beneath/under sth** (*fig esp rhet* 比喻, 尤作修辞) suffer or be oppressed by sth 受苦; 受某事之迫: *poor people groaning beneath/under the weight of heavy taxes* 在苛税重压下的贫民. **5** (idm 习语) ˌ**groan ˈinwardly** feel like groaning at sth but remain silent 暗中叫苦: *She groaned inwardly as she saw the fresh pile of work on her desk.* 她看到自己办公桌上又是一堆要处理的东西就暗自叫苦.

▷ **groan** *n* **1** deep sound made when in pain, etc 呻吟; 叹息: *the groans of an injured man* 伤者的呻吟 ○ *give a groan of dismay* 发出气馁的呻吟 ○ *The chair gave a groan as he sat down in it.* 他往下一坐, 椅子就发出了响声. **2** (usu *sing* 通常作单数) (*fig infml* 比喻, 口) person or thing that makes people groan 令人呻吟、叹息的人或事物: *a joke, story, person that is a bit of a groan* 令人叹息的笑话、故事、人.

groats /grəʊts; grots/ *n* [pl] (crushed) grain, esp oats, that has had the outer covering removed 去壳(压碎的)谷物(尤指燕麦); 燕麦片.

gro·cer /ˈgrəʊsə(r); ˋgrosɚ/ *n* shopkeeper who sells food in packets, tins or bottles and general small household goods 杂货商: *Go down to the grocer's* (ie grocer's shop) *and get me some sugar.* 去杂货店给我买点儿糖来.

▷ **gro·cer·ies** *n* [pl] things sold by a grocer 杂货.

gro·cery *n* **1** [U] grocer's trade 杂货业: [attrib 作定语] *a grocery store* 杂货店. **2** [C] (*esp US*) grocer's shop 杂货店.

grog /grɒg; grɑg/ *n* [U] (*nautical or infml* 海或口) drink of spirits (esp rum) mixed with water 烈酒(尤指朗姆酒)与水混合的饮料.

groggy /ˈgrɒgɪ; ˋgrɑgɪ/ *adj* (**-ier, -iest**) weak and dizzy (after illness, shock, lack of sleep, etc); unsteady (生病、震惊、睡眠不足等之后)虚弱的、眩晕的; 不稳的: *The attack of flu left her feeling very groggy.* 她患流感后非常虚弱. ○ *He's still groggy from the anaesthetic.* 他用过麻药, 现在仍眩晕无力. ▷ **grog·gily** *adv.* **grog·gi·ness** *n* [U].

groin /grɔɪn; grɔɪn/ *n* **1** (*anatomy* 解) lower part of the abdomen, where the tops of the legs meet, containing the sexual organs 阴部: *She kicked her attacker in the groin.* 她踢着了袭击者的阴部. ⇨illus at HUMAN 见HUMAN插图. **2** (*architecture* 建) curved edge where two arches supporting a roof meet 穹棱; 穹窿交接线. **3** (*US*) = GROYNE.

grom·met /ˈgrɒmɪt; ˋgrɑmɪt/ (also **grum·met** /ˈgrʌmɪt; ˋgrʌmɪt/) *n* ring-shaped piece of metal or other strong material used to strengthen a hole (eg in a piece of fabric) (用以加固孔眼的)环, 圈(如织物上的金属扣眼).

groom /gru:m; grum/ *n* **1** person in charge of horses 马夫. **2** = BRIDEGROOM.

▷ **groom** *v* **1** (**a**) [Tn] clean and look after (horses), esp by brushing 刷洗, 照看(马). (**b**) [I, Tn] (of an ape, a monkey, etc) clean the fur and skin of (another or itself) (指猿、猴等)把(另一猿、猴或自身)的毛皮弄干净: *a female ape grooming her mate* 为一猿把毛皮弄干净的母猿. **2** [esp passive 尤用于被动语态: Tn, Tn·pr, Cn·n/a] ~ **sb (for/as sth)** (*infml* 口) select, prepare and train (a young person) for a particular career, etc 挑选、培养、训练(年轻人)从事某职业等: *groomed for stardom by ambitious parents* 由望子成龙的父母培养作演员 ○ *He had been groomed for a career in the Civil Service/groomed as a future civil servant.* 他受过公务员职业培训. **groomed** *adj* (usu preceded by an adv 通常用于副词之后) having the stated appearance of dress, hairstyle and general neatness 穿着打扮一贯整洁的; 干净利落的: *She is always perfectly groomed.* 她总是浑身上下干净利落.

groove /gru:v; gruv/ *n* **1** long narrow cut or depression in the surface of hard material 沟; 槽; 纹: *a groove for a sliding door* 滑动门的槽. ⇨illus 见插图. **2** spiral cut on a gramophone disc for the needle or stylus 唱片上的纹

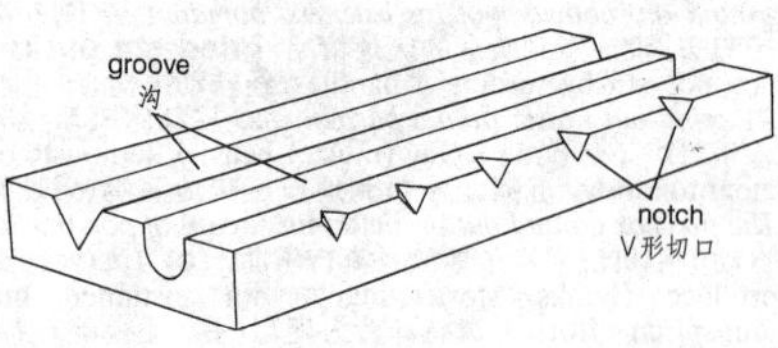

路: *The needle has jumped several grooves.* 唱针跳过了几道纹路. **3** (idm 习语) **get into/be stuck in a groove** become set in a particular way of life 养成某种生活习惯.

▷ **grooved** *adj* having a groove or grooves 有沟的; 有槽的; 有纹的.

groovy /ˈgru:vɪ; ˋgruvɪ/ *adj* (*dated sl* 旧, 俚) attractive or excellent, esp because fashionable or modern 吸引人的, 绝妙的(尤指因流行或时髦).

grope /grəʊp; grop/ *v* **1** [Ipr, Ip] **~ (about) (for/after sth)** feel or search about (for sth) as one does in the dark 摸索; 探索: *grope about in the dark* 在黑暗中摸索 ○ *grope for the door-handle, light-switch, etc* 摸索着找门把手、电灯开关等 ○ (*fig* 比喻) *a tricky question which left him groping for an answer* 迫使他搜寻答案的棘手问题 ○ *scientists groping blindly after the secrets of the atom* 茫然探索原子奥秘的科学家们. **2** [I, Tn] (*infml derog* 口, 贬) (attempt to) touch or fondle (sb) sexually (企图)猥亵(某人). **3** (phr v) **grope (one's way) across, along, past, etc (sth)** make one's way in the stated direction by feeling or searching 摸索着向某方向走: *grope one's way along a darkened corridor* 在黑暗的走廊里摸索着走.

▷ **grop·ingly** *adv* in the manner of sb who gropes 摸索着; 探索着.

gross[1] /grəʊs; gros/ *n* (*pl* unchanged or **~es** 复数或不变或作 **grosses**) (*esp commerce* 尤用于商业) twelve dozen; 一罗(12打; 144个): *two gross of best apples* 两罗优等苹果 ○ *sell sth by the gross/in grosses* 按罗出售某物. ⇨App 4 见附录 4.

gross[2] /grəʊs; gros/ *adj* (**-er, -est**) **1** repulsively fat 过于肥胖的; 太胖的: *a gross person* 过胖的人 ○ *He's not just fat. He's positively gross!* 他不只是胖. 他是过于肥胖! **2** (*fml* 文) not refined; vulgar; coarse 不雅的; 粗俗的; 粗野的: *gross behaviour, language, manners* 粗鲁的行为、语言、举止 ○ *indulging in the grosser pleasures* 迷恋低级庸俗的娱乐. **3** [usu attrib 通常作定语] (*esp law fml* 尤用于法律, 文) glaringly obvious; flagrant 显而易见的; 显然恶劣的: *gross negligence, indecency, vice, etc* 显然的疏忽、下流、不道德等 ○ *a gross error, injustice, etc* 明显的错误、不公等. **4** [attrib 作定语] total; whole 全部的; 整个的; 总的; 毛的: *gross weight, profit, etc* 毛重、毛利等 ○ *sb's gross income*, ie before deduction of tax, etc 某人的总收入(未扣除税等的). Cf 参看 NET[2] 1. **5** (idm 习语) **in (the) gross** in a general or large-scale way rather than in detail 一般地; 大体上; 不详细地.

▷ **gross** *v* [Tn, Tn·p] **~ sth (up)** make sth as a total amount 总共赚得: *Her last film grossed* (ie earned) *a million pounds.* 她拍最后一部影片总共赚了一百万英镑. ○ *work out the grossed-up interest on a loan* 计算出贷款的总利息.

grossly *adv* (of sth bad) extremely (指坏事)极度地, 十分地, 非常: *grossly fat, extravagant, unfair, exaggerated* 极胖的、奢侈的、不公平的、夸张的.

gross·ness *n* [U] coarseness; vulgarity 粗野; 粗俗.

□ ˌ**gross** ˌ**national** ˈ**product** (*abbr* 缩写 **GNP**) annual total value of goods produced, and services provided, in a country 国民生产总值.

grot·esque /grəʊˈtesk; groˋtɛsk/ *adj* **1** strangely distorted so as to arouse fear or laughter; fantastic 因变得古怪而可怕或可笑的; 奇形怪状的: *tribal dancers wearing grotesque masks* 部落中戴着古怪面具的跳舞的人. **2** (*art* 美术) combining human, animal and plant forms in a fantastic design 奇异风格的(由人、动植物混合组成之图案的). **3** ridiculously exaggerated or unreasonable; absurd 荒谬地夸张的或无理的; 荒唐的: *a grotesque distortion of the truth* 对事实的无理歪曲 ○ *It's grotesque to expect a person of her experience to work for such little money.* 想让有她那样经验的人为这点儿钱工作真是可笑. **4** offensively incongruous 扞格不入的; 极不协调的: *the grotesque sight of an old man trying to flirt with a young girl* 老头儿极力与少女调情那种离谱的样子.

▷ **grot·esque** *n* **1** [C] with fantastic or incongruous clothes, make-up, features, etc 衣着、打扮、五官等古怪、不协调的样子. **2 the grotesque** [sing] grotesque style used in a painting, carving, etc (绘画、雕刻等所采用的)奇异风格.

grot·esquely *adv.*

grot·esque·ness *n* [U].

grotto /ˈgrɒtəʊ; ˋgrato/ *n* (*pl* **~-es** or **~-s**) cave, esp one made artificially as a garden shelter 洞穴; (尤指花园中的)人工洞室.

grotty /ˈgrɒtɪ; ˋgratɪ/ *adj* (**-ier, -iest**) (*infml* 口) unpleasant 令人不愉快的; 不舒服的; 可恶的: *a grotty little man living in a grotty little room in a grotty part of town* 在城里一个讨厌的地方的一间讨厌的屋子里住着一个讨厌的男子 ○ *I feel pretty grotty*, ie unwell. 我身体不大舒服.

grouch /graʊtʃ; graʊtʃ/ *v* [I, Ipr] **~ (about sth)** (*derog* 贬) complain 发牢骚; 抱怨: *Stop grouching about everything!* 别再事事都抱怨了!

▷ **grouch** *n* **1** (**a**) [sing] **~ (about sth)** (*derog* 贬) fit of bad-tempered complaining 大发牢骚: *He's always having a grouch about something.* 他总是发脾气抱怨这个抱怨那个. (**b**) [C] **~ (against sth/sb)** complaint 牢骚; 抱怨: *One of my main grouches against the council is that they don't run enough buses.* 我对市议会不满, 主要是投入营运的公共汽车不够用. **2** [C] (*derog* 贬) sulky discontented person 爱发牢骚的人: *You're nothing but an old grouch!* 你就是个爱发牢骚的老傢伙! **grouchy** *adj* (**-ier, -iest**) sullenly discontented 愠怒的; 不满的: *in a grouchy mood* 怀着不满情绪.

ground[1] /graʊnd; graʊnd/ *n* **1 the ground** [sing] solid surface of the earth (esp contrasted with the air above) 地面(尤指与空中相对): *sit on the ground* 坐在地上 ○ *He slipped off the ladder and fell to the ground.* 他从梯子上滑了下来摔在地上. ○ *The aircraft hadn't enough power to get off the ground*, ie take off. 那架飞机的升空动力不足. ○ [attrib 作定语] *at ground level* 在地平面. **2** [U] (**a**) area or distance on the earth's surface; land 地面上的区域或距离; 土地: *have more ground than one's next-door neighbour* 土地比邻居的多 ○ *buy up some ground for building on* 购置地皮以供建筑之用 ○ *The land near the border is disputed ground.* 靠近边界的土地是有争议的地区. ○ *measure the ground between two points* 测量地面上两点间的距离. (**b**) soil; earth 泥土; 土地: *solid, marshy, stony, etc ground* 坚硬的土地、沼泽地、多石的地. ⇨Usage at EARTH 用法见 EARTH. **3** (esp in compounds 尤用以构成复合词) (**a**) [C] piece of land (often with associated buildings) used for a particular purpose 场地: *a ˈfootball, ˈcricket, ˈsports, recreˈation ground* ○ *a paˈrade-ground* ○ *a ˈplayground* ○ *The cheers of the fans echoed round the ground as the team appeared.* 球队刚一上场, 球迷的欢呼声立即响遍全场. (**b**) **grounds** [pl] large area of land or sea used for the stated purpose (作某用途的)地域或水域: *ˈfishing, ˈhunting grounds* 渔场、猎场. **4 grounds** [pl] land or gardens round a building, often enclosed with walls, hedges or fences 建筑物四周的土地或花园(常用墙或篱围起); 庭园: *The house has extensive grounds.* 这房子四周的庭园宽阔. ○ *the grounds of Buckingham Palace* 白金汉宫的花园. **5** [U] (*fig* 比喻) area of interest, discussion, etc 兴趣、讨论等的范围: *They managed to cover quite a lot of ground in a short programme.* 他们设法在一个短小的节目中包罗了多方面的内容. ○ *go over the same ground*, ie discuss a familiar topic 讨论熟悉的题目 ○ *trying to find some common ground between the two sides*, ie points on which they can agree 努力找出双方一致之处 ○ *You're on dangerous ground when you criticize his daughter*, ie because he will react angrily. 你批评他的女儿就要惹出是非了(因为他生气). **6** [C esp *pl* 尤作复数] **~ (for sth/doing sth/to do sth)** reason(s) or justification for saying, doing or believing sth 说、做或相信某事的原因或理由: *You have no grounds for complaint/for complaining.* 你没有抱怨的理由. ○ *If you continue to behave like this you will give them/provide them with grounds for dismissing you.* 你照这样下去就让他们找到辞退你的理由了. ○ *Desertion is a ground* (ie legally sufficient reason) *for divorce.* 被配偶遗弃是离婚的充足理由. ○ *They had no grounds to arrest him.* 他们没有理由逮捕他. ○ *I had to retire on medical grounds/on the grounds of ill health*, ie because I was ill. 我因健康的缘故不得已才退休了. ○ *Her claim was disallowed on the ground(s) that she had not paid her premium.* 她要求赔款遭到拒绝, 原因是她事先没有交纳保险费. ○ *On what grounds do you make that accusation?* 你根据什么提出那项控告? ⇨Usage at REASON[1] 用法见 REASON[1].

7 [C] surface on which a design is painted, printed, cut, etc; undecorated part; background（印刷、雕刻等的）版面, 底子; 背景: *a design of pink roses on a white ground* 白底粉红玫瑰的花样. **8** [U] bottom of the sea 海底: *The ship touched ground a few yards from the shore.* 船在距海岸几码处搁浅了. **9 grounds** [pl] ground coffee beans after they have been brewed 烘烤后再磨碎的咖啡豆. **10** (idm 习语) **above 'ground** above the surface of the earth 地面之上; 地上. **be on firm ground** ⇨ FIRM[1]. **below 'ground** beneath the surface of the earth 地面之下; 地下: *Their missile silos are below ground.* 他们的导弹发射井在地下. **break fresh/new 'ground** introduce or discover a new method, system, etc; innovate 引进或发现新方法、制度等; 改革; 革新. **cut the ground from under sb's 'feet** spoil sb's plan, argument, defence, etc by anticipating it（预先采取措施）破坏某人的计划、论据、答辩等; 挖墙脚; 拆台. **forbidden ground** ⇨ FORBID. **gain/make up ground (on sb/sth)** get gradually closer to sb/sth going in the same direction as oneself 逐渐追及某人[某事物]: *The police car was gaining ground on the robbers.* 警车逐渐追上劫匪. ○ (*fig* 比喻) *How can we make up ground on our competitors?* 我们怎样才能赶上竞争对手? **get off the 'ground** (of activities, enterprises, etc) make a successful start（指活动、事业等）顺利开始. **give/lose 'ground (to sb/sth)** (**a**) retreat 撤退. (**b**) get gradually less far ahead of sb/sth going in the same direction 被追上来的某人[某事物]逐渐赶上: *The leader is losing ground as the rest of the runners accelerate.* 领先者在其余赛跑者加速时就逐渐失去了优势. ○ (*fig* 比喻) *The gas lamp gradually lost ground to* (ie was replaced by) *electric lighting.* 电灯逐步取代了煤气灯. **go/run to earth/ground** ⇨ EARTH. **have/keep a/one's ear to the ground** ⇨ EAR[1]. **have, etc one's/both feet on the ground** ⇨ FOOT[1]. **hold/keep/stand one's 'ground** maintain one's claim, intention, argument, etc; not yield or give way 坚持主张、意图、论点等; 不屈服; 不让步. **keep both/one's feet on the ground** ⇨ FOOT. **on the 'ground** amongst ordinary people 在普通人中: *There's a lot of support for our policies on the ground.* 我们的政策在一般群众中得到普遍拥护. **prepare the ground (for sth)** make the development of sth possible or easier 使某事物能够或容易发展: *Early experiments with military rockets prepared the ground for space travel.* 早年对军用火箭进行的实验为发展航天技术奠定了基础. **run sb/sth into the 'ground** (*infml* 口) wear sb/sth out completely; exhaust sb/sth 使某人精疲力竭; 耗尽某物: *By working 13 hours a day she is running herself into the ground.* 她一天工作13小时, 眼看就要累垮了. ○ *Unable to afford a new car, we had to run the old one into the ground.* 我们因为买不起新汽车, 只得把那辆旧的用坏为止. **shift/change one's 'ground** change the basis of one's argument, claim, etc 改变论点、主张等的依据; 改变观点: *Just when you think you've proved him wrong, he shifts his ground.* 你刚以为你已经证实他错了, 他就改变观点了. **suit sb down to the ground** ⇨ SUIT[2]. **thin on the ground** ⇨ THIN. **to the 'ground** (of destroying, demolishing, etc) completely; utterly（指毁坏、拆除等）全部, 完全: *The building was burned to the ground.* 该建筑物已全部焚毁.

□ **'ground-bait** *n* [U] food thrown to the bottom of a river, lake, etc by an angler to attract fish（钓鱼人投入水底的）诱饵.

'ground control personnel, system or equipment (stationed on the ground) whose job is to ensure the safe flight of aircraft or spacecraft（保证飞行器安全飞行的）地面导航人员、系统或设备.

'ground crew people at an airfield whose job is to repair, refuel, etc aircraft（机场的）地勤人员.

ˌground 'floor 1 floor of a building at ground level, not upstairs 建筑物与地面相平的一层; 一楼: [attrib 作定语] *at ground-floor level* 与一楼地面相平 ○ *a ˌground-floor 'flat* 一楼的单元. ⇨Usage at FLOOR[1] 用法见FLOOR[1]. **2** (idm 习语) **be/get in on the ground 'floor** (*infml* 口) join an enterprise at its beginning（在一企业开创时）加入其中.

'ground-nut *n* = PEANUT.

'ground-plan *n* (drawing representing the) lay-out of a building at ground level 建筑物的一楼平面设计(图).

'ground-rent *n* [U, C] rent paid for the use of land leased for building（租用建筑用地的）地租.

'ground rule (usu *pl* 通常作复数) basic principle 基本原则: *The new code of conduct lays down the ground rules for management-union relations.* 新的管理章程为劳资关系确定了基本的原则.

'groundsheet *n* waterproof sheet spread on the ground, eg under bedding in a tent 铺于地面的防水布（如帐篷内铺在被褥下者）.

'groundsman /-mən; -mən/ *n* person who maintains a sports ground 运动场管理员.

'ground speed speed of an aircraft relative to the ground（飞行器的）地速. Cf 参看 AIR SPEED (AIR[1])

'ground staff 1 people at a sports ground whose job is to maintain the condition of grass, equipment, etc 运动场管理人员. **2** = GROUND CREW.

'ground swell 1 heavy slow-moving waves caused by a distant or recent storm or earthquake 长涌浪（由远方或刚过去的暴风或地震引起的移动缓慢的巨浪）. **2** (*fig* 比喻) rapidly developing general feeling or opinion 迅速高涨的情绪或舆论声势: *Opinion polls have detected a ground swell of support for the Socialists.* 民意测验表明拥护社会党的情绪高涨.

'groundwork *n* [U] **~ (for sth)** preparatory work that provides the basis for sth 为某事打基础的准备工作.

ground[2] /graʊnd; graund/ *v* **1** (**a**) [I, Ipr, Tn, Tn·pr] **~ (sth) (in/on sth)** (of a ship) touch the sea bottom; cause (a ship) to do this（指船）触海底, 搁浅; 使(船)触海底、搁浅: *Our ship grounded in shallow water/on a sandbank.* 我们的船在浅水中[在沙滩上]搁浅. (**b**) [Tn esp passive 尤用于被动语态] require or force (an aircraft) to stay on the ground 要求或迫使(飞行器)停留在地面; 停飞: *All aircraft at London Airport were grounded by fog today.* 因今天有雾, 伦敦机场的所有飞机都被迫停飞. **2** [Tn] (*esp US*) = EARTH *v*. **3** (idm 习语) **ground arms** (of soldiers) lay (esp rifles) on the ground（指士兵）将(尤指步枪)放在地上; 放下武器. **4** (phr v) **ground sb in sth** give sb good teaching or basic training in (a subject)（在某学科上）给某人良好的教导或基本训练: *She grounded her pupils well in arithmetic.* 她给自己的学生打下良好的算术基础. **ground sth on sth** base beliefs, etc on sth 将信仰等建立于某事物的基础上: *ground one's arguments on facts* 以事实为根据来立论 ○ *a well-grounded theory* 有坚实基础的理论.

▷ **ground·ing** *n* [sing] **~ (in sth)** teaching of the basic elements of a subject 对某学科基本要素的教授; 基础; 底子: *a thorough grounding in grammar* 对基础语法的透彻教授.

ground[3] *pt, pp* of GRIND: *ˌground 'rice*, ie reduced to a fine powder 米粉 ○ *ˌground 'glass*, ie made non-transparent by rubbing the surface to make it rough 毛玻璃.

ground·less /'graʊndlɪs; 'graundlɪs/ *adj* without foundation or good reason 无根据的; 无理由的: *groundless anxiety, rumours, allegations* 无理由的焦虑、无根据的谣言、无根据的供述 ○ *Our fears proved groundless.* 我们感到恐惧是毫无道理的. ▷ **ground·lessly** *adv*.

ground·sel /'graʊnsl; 'graunsl/ *n* [U] weed with yellow flowers, sometimes used as food for certain cage-birds 千里光（开黄花的草, 有时用作某些笼养鸟的食物）.

group /gru:p; grup/ *n* [CGp] **1** number of people or things gathered, placed or acting together, or naturally associated 群; 团体; 组; 类: *a group of girls, trees, houses, etc* 一群女孩子、一片树林、一片房子 ○ *A group of us are going up to London for the day.* 我们有些人要去伦敦一天. ○ *people standing about in groups* 一群一群在各处站着的人 ○ *an 'age group*, ie people of the same age 年龄组（年龄相同的人）○ *Our di'scussion group is/are meeting this week.* 我们的讨论小组本周开会. ○ *a 'drama group*, ie small club for acting 戏剧小组 ○ *the Germanic group of languages* 日耳曼语系 ○ *What 'blood group are you?* 你是什么血型? ○ [attrib 作定语] *a group ac'tivity*, ie done by people in a group 集体活动. **2** set of jointly-controlled business companies, eg as the result of a merger（公司联营的）集团: *a 'newspaper group* 报业集团 ○ *the 'Burton Group* 伯顿集团 ○ [attrib 作定语] *the group sales director* 集团的销售董事. **3** set of

G

musicians performing pop music together 流行音乐的乐团.

▷ **group** *v* [I, Ipr, Ip, Tn, Tn·pr, Tn·p] **~ (sb/sth) (round sb/sth); ~ (sb/sth) (together)** gather or form (sb/sth) into a group or groups 使(某人[某事物])集合、聚集、成群、成组或归类: *The police grouped (themselves) round the demonstrators.* 警察围聚在示威者的四周. ○ *Group together in fours!* 每四人一组!

groupie /ˈgru:pɪ; ˋgrupɪ/ *n* (*infml* 口) keen supporter (esp a young girl) who follows pop groups to concerts given on tour (在流行音乐乐团巡回演出时到处尾随的)歌迷(尤指少女).

group·ing *n* set of individuals with sth in common, esp acting together within a larger organization 小集团(尤指大组织中行动一致的): *various anti-leadership groupings within the party* 党内形形色色的反领导小集团.

□ ˈ**group captain** officer in the British air force between the ranks of wing commander and air commodore (英国)空军上校. ⇨App 9 见附录 9.

group practice set of doctors who work jointly, use the same premises, etc 集体开业.

ˌ**group** ˈ**therapy** form of treatment in which people with similar psychological problems meet together to discuss them 集体疗法(使有同一心理症状的病人在一起讨论病情的方法).

grouse[1] /graʊs; graʊs/ *n* (*pl* unchanged 复数不变) (**a**) [C] small dark bird of northern hilly areas, shot for sport and food 松鸡; 松鸡类: [attrib 作定语] ˈ*grouse shooting on the moors of Scotland and northern England* 在苏格兰与英格兰北部之松鸡猎场上猎松鸡. ⇨illus at App 1 见附录 1 插图, page v. (**b**) [U] its flesh as food 松鸡肉: *roast grouse* 烤松鸡肉.

grouse[2] /graʊs; graʊs/ *v* (*infml usu derog* 口, 通常作贬义) [I, Ipr] **~ (about sb/sth)** grumble; complain 抱怨; 发牢骚: *He's always grousing about the work-load.* 他总是抱怨工作量大.

▷ **grouse** *n* complaint 怨言; 牢骚: *If you've got any grouses, you'd better tell me about them.* 你若有什么不满就跟我说.

grove /grəʊv; grov/ *n* group of trees; small wood 树丛; 小树林: *an olive grove* 橄榄树丛.

grovel /ˈgrɒvl; ˋgrɑvl̩/ *v* (**-ll-**; *US* **-l-**) (*derog* 贬) **1** [I, Ipr] **~ (to/before sb)** lie or crawl with the face downwards in a show of humility or fear 趴伏, 匍匐(作谦卑或恐惧状): *Those who wished a favour of the emperor had to grovel on hands and knees before him.* 凡希望受到皇帝恩宠的人都要拜倒在他面前. **2** (*fig* 比喻) [I, Ipr] **~ (to sb) (for sth)** behave with a show of humility or shame 带着谦卑或羞愧的样子行事: *You will just have to grovel to the bank manager for a loan.* 你只得低声下气地向银行经理借贷. **3** (phr v) **grovel about/around** move about on one's hands and knees; crawl about 四处爬行; 爬来爬去: *grovelling around under the table looking for a pin* 在桌子下爬来爬去寻找一根针.

▷ **grov·el·ling** /ˈgrɒvəlɪŋ; ˋgrɑvlɪŋ/ *adj* excessively humble; abject 过分谦逊的; 可鄙的: *a grovelling apology* 低声下气的道歉.

grow /grəʊ; gro/ *v* (*pt* **grew** /gru:; gru/, *pp* **grown** /grəʊn; gron/) **1** [La, I] increase in size or quantity; become greater (体积或数量的)增加; 变大: *How tall you've grown!* 你都长这么高了! ○ *A growing child needs plenty of sleep.* 正发育的孩子必须睡眠充足. ○ *She wants to let her hair grow*, ie not have it cut short. 她要留头发. ○ *You must invest if you want your business to grow.* 要想使生意扩大, 必须投资. **2** [I, Ipr] **~ (from sth) (into sth)** develop, esp into a mature or an adult form 生长; 发育(尤指成熟或成年): *Rice does not grow in a cold climate.* 稻在寒冷的气候下不能生长. ○ *Plants grow from seeds.* 植物是由种子发育而成的. ○ *Tadpoles grow into frogs.* 蝌蚪能长成蛙. ○ (*fig* 比喻) *grow in stature, wisdom, etc* 提高名望、增长智慧. **3** [La] become (gradually) (逐渐)变成; 渐变: *grow old(er), rich(er), etc* 变得年纪大(些)、富(些)等 ○ *grow small(er), weak(er), etc* 变得年纪小(些)、弱(些)等 ○ *It began to grow dark.* 天渐渐黑了. ○ *I grew tired of waiting, and left.* 我等得不耐烦了就走了. **4** [Tn, Tn·pr] **~ sth (from sth)** cause or allow sth to grow 使某物生长; 种植: *grow roses* 种玫瑰 ○ *grow a beard* 蓄胡须 ○ *grow onions from seed* 用种子种洋葱. **5** [It] reach the point or stage at which one does the specified thing 达到做某事的程度或地步: *He grew increasingly to rely on her.* 他越来越依赖她了. ○ *She has a hot temper, but you will soon grow to like her.* 她脾气躁, 但不久你就会喜欢她了. **6** (idm 习语) **big, etc oaks from little acorns grow** ⇨ OAK. **let the grass grow under one's feet** ⇨ GRASS[1]. **(not) grow on trees** be (not) plentiful, easily obtained, etc (不)多, 易获得等: *Don't spend so much — money doesn't grow on trees, you know.* 别花这么多 —— 钱不是容易挣的. **7** (phr v) **grow away from sb** come to have a less close, less easy relationship with sb 与某人逐渐疏远、不太融洽: *a teenage girl growing away from her mother* 跟自己的母亲逐渐疏远的少女. **grow into sth** (no passive 不用于被动语态) (**a**) become sth (gradually, with the passage of time) 渐渐成为或变得: *She is growing into a beautiful young woman.* 她渐渐出落成美丽的姑娘. ○ *He has grown into an old miser.* 他已经变成老守财奴了. (**b**) become big enough to fit (clothes) 长得大以适合于(衣服): *The coat is too big for him now, but he will grow into it.* 这上衣他现在穿还太大, 等他长大些再穿就合适了. (**c**) become accustomed to (a new job, role or activity) 变得习惯于(新工作、角色、或活动): *She is a good actress, but still needs time to grow into the part she is playing.* 她是个好演员, 但仍需要时间去熟悉她要扮演的角色. **grow on sb** (no passive 不用于被动语态) (**a**) become more firmly established in sb 对某人的影响变得更深: *a habit that grows on you if you are not careful* 若不在意就变成根深蒂固的习惯. (**b**) come to have a greater attraction for sb; win the liking of sb 渐渐对某人产生更大的吸引力; 赢得某人的喜爱: *a book, piece of music, etc that grows on you* 渐渐把人迷住的书、乐曲等. **grow out of sth** (**a**) become too big to wear sth 长得高大而不能穿某物: *grow out of one's clothes* 长得高大致使穿不下自己原来的衣服. (**b**) become too old for sth and stop doing it 年龄增长不再做某事: *grow out of children's games, etc* 年龄大了不再做儿童游戏等. (**c**) (no passive 不用于被动语态) have sth as a source 由某事物而产生: *My interest in the art of India grew out of the time I spent there during the war.* 战争时期我在印度时对其艺术产生了兴趣. **grow up** (**a**) (of people or animals) reach the stage of full development; become adult or mature (指人或动物)长大; 成年; 成熟: *She's growing up fast.* 她长得很快. ○ *Oh, grow up!* ie Behave in a more mature way. 噢, 别那么不懂事了(表现得成熟些吧)! Cf 参看 GROWN UP (GROWN). (**b**) develop 发展: *A close friendship gradually grew up between them.* 他们之间的友谊日益亲密.

▷ **grower** *n* (usu in compounds 通常用以构成复合词) **1** person who grows things 种植者: *a* ˈ*fruit-grower* 种果木者 ○ ˈ*rose-growers* 种玫瑰者. **2** plant that grows in a certain way 以某种方式生长的植物: *a quick grower* 早熟植物.

grow·ing *adj* increasing 增长中的; 发展中的: *his growing indifference to her* 他对她的逐渐冷淡 ○ *a growing problem* 越来越大的问题 ○ *a popular club with a growing membership* 会员不断增多、广受欢迎的俱乐部. ˈ**growing pains** (**a**) pains in the limbs of young children, popularly believed to be caused by rapid growth 发育期痛(儿童或少年的四肢疼痛, 一般认为系因发育迅速所致). (**b**) (*fig* 比喻) problems arising while a new enterprise is developing 新事业发展过程中所产生的问题: *The business is still suffering from growing pains.* 该企业在发展中仍面临许多难题.

growl /graʊl; graʊl/ *v* **1** [I, Ipr] **~ (at sb/sth)** (of animals or thunder) make a low threatening sound (指动物或雷)作低沉的怒吼声; 作狺狺的叫声; 作隆隆声: *The dog growled at the intruder.* 狗向闯入者狺狺狂吠. ○ *The thunder growled in the distance.* 雷在远处隆隆地响. ○ (*fig* 比喻) *He's in a really bad mood today, growling at* (ie speaking angrily to) *everyone.* 他今天情绪很坏, 跟谁说话都动气. **2** [Tn, Tn·p] **~ sth (out)** say sth in a low threatening voice 以低声的威胁口吻说某事: *He growled out an answer.* 他低声威胁着回答.

▷ **growl** *n* low threatening sound or remark 低沉而吓人的声音; 低声说的带威胁口吻的话.

grown /grəʊn; gron/ *adj* [attrib 作定语] adult; mature 长大的; 成年的; 成熟的: *a grown man* 成人 ○ *a* *full-grown/fully grown elephant* 发育成熟的象. Cf 参看 GROW 2.

□ ˌ**grown ˈup** adult; mature 长大的; 成年的; 成熟的: *What do you want to be when you're grown up?* 你长大了想做什么? ○ [attrib 作定语] *his ˌgrown-up ˈson* 他成年的儿子 ○ *Try to behave in a more grown-up way.* 要尽量表现得成熟些. **grown-up** /ˈgrəʊnʌp; ˈgronˌʌp/ *n* adult person (contrasted with a child) 成年人(与儿童相对).

growth /grəʊθ; groθ/ *n* **1** [U] **(a)** (process of) growing; development 生长(过程); 发展: *the rapid growth of plants, of hair, of inflation, of the economy* 植物的迅速生长、毛发的迅速生长、通货膨胀的迅速加剧、经济的迅速发展 ○ *Lack of water will stunt the plant's growth.* 缺水会影响植物的生长. ○ *a phenomenon of comparatively recent growth*, ie that has developed recently 近期产生的现象 ○ [attrib 作定语] *a growth industry*, ie one which is developing faster than most others 发展特别快的行业. **(b)** ~ **(in/of sth)** increase 增加; 增长: *the recent growth in/of violent crime* 近期暴力罪行的增加. **2** [U] increase in economic activity, profitability, etc 经济活动、收益等的增加: *The government has decided to go for growth*, ie a policy of increased production, spending, etc. 政府已决定促进经济发展. ○ [attrib 作定语] *Japan's growth rate* 日本的增长率. **3** [sing] thing that grows or has grown 生长物; 长成物: *a thick growth of weeds* 杂草丛生 ○ *a week's growth of beard* 长了一星期的胡须. **4** [C] abnormal or diseased formation in the body (eg a tumour or cancer) 体内不正常的或有病变的生长物(如肿瘤或癌); 瘤; 癌: *a (non-)malignant growth* 恶[良]性肿瘤.

groyne (*US* **groin**) /grɔɪn; grɔɪn/ *n* structure of wood, stone or concrete, built to prevent sand and pebbles from being washed away by the sea, the current of a river, etc 防波堤; 折流坝. ⇨illus at COAST 见 COAST 插图.

grub[1] /grʌb; grʌb/ *n* **1** [C] larva of an insect 蛴螬; 蛆. **2** [U] (*infml* 口) food 食物: *Grub's up!* ie The meal is ready! 吃饭了!

grub[2] /grʌb; grʌb/ *v* **(-bb-)** **1** [I, Ipr, Ip] ~ **(around/about) (for sth)** **(a)** dig or poke at the soil; search (for sth) by digging 挖土; 掘土; 挖掘寻找; 发掘: *pigs grubbing around/about in the bushes* 在树丛中到处乱拱的猪 ○ *a dog grubbing for a bone* 从土里刨骨头的狗. **(b)** (*fig* 比喻) search for (esp information) intently but usu unmethodically (急切地但通常为不得法地)查找(尤指资料): *He found what he wanted by grubbing around in the library.* 他在图书馆乱翻一通终于找到了需要的资料. **2** (phr v) **grub sth up/out** dig sth up 将某物挖出: *birds grubbing up worms* 刨虫子的鸟 ○ *grub out a dead tree* 挖出死树.

grubby /ˈgrʌbɪ; ˈgrʌbɪ/ *adj* **(-ier, -iest)** (*infml* 口) dirty; unwashed 肮脏的; 不洁的: *grubby hands* 脏手 ○ (*fig* 比喻) *a grubby* (ie unsavoury) *scandal* 丑闻. ▷ **grubbi·ness** *n* [U].

grudge /grʌdʒ; grʌdʒ/ *v* [Tn, Tg, Tsg, Dn·n, Dn·pr] ~ **sth (to sb)** feel resentful about sth; do or give sth very unwillingly 怨恨某事物; 勉强做某事或给某物: *He grudges every penny he has to spend.* 他每花一便士都非常吝惜. ○ *I grudge paying so much for such inferior goods.* 我不愿花这么多钱买次品. ○ *He grudges her earning more than he does.* 他嫉妒她挣的比他多. ○ *I don't grudge him his success*, ie I admit he deserves it. 我认为他成功是理所当然的. ○ *She would grudge a penny even to the poorest beggar*, ie She is very mean. 她连给最穷的乞丐一个便士都舍不得.

▷ **grudge** *n* ~ **(against sb)** feeling of ill-will, envy, resentment, spite, etc 恶意; 嫉妒; 怨恨; 遗憾: *I bear him no grudge.* 我对他没有怨恨. ○ *He has a grudge against me.* 他对我有恶意. ○ *He has been harbouring/nursing a grudge against me.* 他一直对我心怀嫉妒. ○ [attrib 作定语] *a grudge fight*, ie when one boxer, etc has a grudge against the other 彼此结怨的拳手互斗.

grudging *adj* unwilling; reluctant 不情愿的; 勉强的: *a grudging admission* 勉强的承认 ○ *grudging praise* 不情愿的赞扬. **grudgingly** *adv*: *The boss grudgingly raised my salary.* 老板很不情愿地给我加了薪.

gruel /ˈgru:əl; ˈgruəl/ *n* [U] simple dish made of oatmeal, etc boiled in milk or water (以牛奶或水煮燕麦片等制成的)简便食物; 麦片粥.

gru·el·ling (*US* **gruel·ing**) /ˈgru:əlɪŋ; ˈgruəlɪŋ/ *adj* severe; exhausting 严厉的; 使人筋疲力竭的: *a gruelling climb, race, trial, ordeal, etc* 使人筋疲力竭的攀登、竞赛、审讯、考验等.

grue·some /ˈgru:səm; ˈgrusəm/ *adj* filling one with horror or disgust; frightful 令人恐怖的; 讨厌的; 可怕的: *After the slaughter, the battlefield was a gruesome sight.* 经过这场厮杀, 战场上一派触目惊心的惨状. ▷ **grue·somely** *adv*. **grue·some·ness** *n* [U].

gruff /grʌf; grʌf/ *adj* (of a person, his voice or behaviour) rough; surly (指人、其声音或行为)粗野的, 粗暴的: *Beneath his gruff exterior he's really very kind-hearted.* 他外表粗鲁, 心地却十分善良. ▷ **gruffly** *adv*. **gruff·ness** *n* [U].

grumble /ˈgrʌmbl; ˈgrʌmbḷ/ *v* **1** [I, Ipr] ~ **(at/to sb) (about/at/over sth)** complain or protest in a bad-tempered way 发怨言; 鸣不平: *Stop grumbling! You've got nothing to complain about.* 别抱怨了! 你没什么可抱怨的. ○ *Why grumble at me about your own stupid mistakes?* 你自己犯了愚蠢的错误, 为什么向我抱怨? ○ *grumble at one's low pay/at being badly paid* 抱怨待遇低[差]. **2** [I, Ip] ~ **(away)** make a deep continuous sound 发生低沉、连续的声音: *thunder grumbling (away) in the distance* 远方隆隆的雷声 ○ *the sound of one's stomach grumbling* 肚子咕咕的叫声 ○ (*fig* 比喻) *a grumbling* (ie intermittently painful) *appendix* 间歇性疼痛的阑尾.

▷ **grumble** *n* **1** complaint 怨言; 牢骚: *a person full of grumbles* 牢骚满腹的人 ○ *I don't want to hear another grumble from you.* 我不愿再听到你的怨言了. **2** rumble 隆隆声; 辘辘声: *a distant grumble of thunder* 远方雷声隆隆.

grumbler /ˈgrʌmblə(r); ˈgrʌmblɚ/ *n* person who grumbles 埋怨者; 发牢骚的人: *He's a dreadful grumbler.* 他是特别爱发牢骚的人.

grum·met /ˈgrʌmɪt; ˈgrʌmɪt/ *n* = GROMMET.

grumpy /ˈgrʌmpɪ; ˈgrʌmpɪ/ *adj* **(-ier, -iest)** (*infml* 口) bad-tempered; surly 脾气坏的; 脾气暴躁的. ▷ **grump·ily** /-ɪlɪ; -ɪlɪ/ *adv*. **grumpi·ness** *n* [U].

grunt /grʌnt; grʌnt/ *v* **1** [I] **(a)** (of animals, esp pigs) make a low rough sound from deep in the throat (指动物, 尤指猪)作哼哼声. **(b)** (of people) make a similar sound expressing pain, boredom, irritation, etc or indicating inattention or distraction (指人)发类似的哼声(表示痛苦、厌烦、恼怒等或表示没注意、走神儿): *He grunted as the bullet hit him.* 子弹击中他时他疼得哼出声来. ○ *I asked him what he thought, but he just grunted.* 我问他在想什么, 他只哼了一声. ○ *grunting with pain, pleasure, etc* 因痛苦、满足等而哼哼. **2** [Tn, Tn·pr] ~ **sth (to sb)** utter sth in a grunting way 咕噜着或哼哼着说某事: *She grunted some incomprehensible reply.* 她咕噜着回答了些令人费解的话.

▷ **grunt** *n* low rough sound made by an animal or a person (动物或人发出的)咕噜声; 哼哼声: *give a grunt of approval, pain, pleasure, etc* 发出表示赞成、痛苦、满足等的哼声.

gruy·ère /ˈgru:jeə(r); gruˈjɛr/ *n* [U] type of pale firm cheese with large holes 格鲁耶尔干酪.

gry·phon /ˈgrɪfən; ˈgrɪfən/ *n* = GRIFFIN.

G-string /ˈdʒi:strɪŋ; ˈdʒiˌstrɪŋ/ *n* narrow piece of cloth (worn esp by female dancers) that covers the sexual organs and is held up by a string round the hips G字带(遮挡阴部的窄布条, 用绳系于臀部, 尤指女舞蹈演员用的).

GT /ˌdʒi: ˈti:; ˌdʒi ˈti/ *abbr* 缩写 = (of cars) large tourer (Italian *gran turismo*) (指汽车)大型轿车(源自意大利文 *gran turismo*).

Gt *abbr* 缩写 = Great: *Gt Britain* 大不列颠; 英国.

guano /ˈgwɑ:nəʊ; ˈgwɑno/ *n* [U] dung from sea-birds, poultry, etc, used as fertilizer 海鸟、家禽等的粪(用作肥料).

guar·an·tee[1] /ˌgærənˈti:; ˌgærənˈti/ *n* **1 (a)** ~ **(against sth)** promise (usu in writing) that certain conditions agreed to in a transaction will be fulfilled (交易的)保证, 保证书: *The watch comes with a year's guarantee*, ie a promise to repair it free for a year after purchase. 这手表保修一年. ○ *It's still under guarantee* (ie The guarantee is still valid), *so the manufacturer will repair it.* 保证书还有效, 所以厂家会给修理的. ○ *provide a* *guarantee against rust* 保不生锈 ○ *You have our guarantee!* 我们给你产品保证! ○ *The Soviets were demanding certain guarantees about verification before signing the treaty.* 苏联人要求得到有关核实的某些保证后才签约. (**b**) **~ (of sth/that...)** promise given by one person to another that he will be responsible for seeing that sth is done (eg payment of a debt by another person) 担保, 保证(如另一人偿还债务): *give a guarantee of (one's/sb's) good behaviour* 对(自己的[某人的])良好品行给予保证. (**c**) document, property, etc offered as security for carrying out the conditions in a guarantee (作为保证物的)契据、财产等; 抵押品: *'What guarantee can you offer?' 'I can offer my house as a guarantee.'* '你用什么做抵押?' '我可以拿房子抵押.' Cf 参看 SECURITY 3. **2** person who promises to be responsible for seeing that sth is done 保证人; 担保人: *Are you willing to be a guarantee of your friend's good behaviour,* ie undertake to make sure that he behaves himself properly? 你愿担保你朋友品行良好吗? ○ *be sb's guarantee for a loan from the bank* 做某人从银行贷款的保证人. **3 ~ (of sth/that...)** (*infml* 口) thing that makes an event likely to happen 担保(某事可能发生)的事物: *Blue skies are not a guarantee of continuing fine weather.* 蔚蓝的天空不一定担保天气持续晴朗. ○ *There's no guarantee she won't reject them all,* ie She may well do so. 不能保证她不会全盘否定.

guar·an·tee² /ˌgærənˈti:; ˌgærənˈti/ *v* **1** [Tn, Tf, Tt, Cn·a usu passive 通常用于被动语态, Cn·t usu passive 通常用于被动语态, Dn·n, Dn·pr] **~ sth (to sb)** promise sth with certainty (to sb) (向某人)担保某事物; 保证: *We cannot guarantee the punctual arrival of trains in foggy weather.* 我们不能保证火车在雾天正点到达. ○ *I can guarantee it's true — I saw it myself.* 我能保证那是真的——我亲眼看见的. ○ *We guarantee to deliver within a week.* 我们保证一周内送到. ○ *This food is guaranteed additive-free,* ie The manufacturer officially promises that it contains no additives. 该食品保证不含添加剂. ○ *We guarantee you delivery within one day.* 我们担保你在一日内收到. **2** [Tn, Tf, Tt] undertake to be legally responsible for (sth/doing sth) 承诺对(某事[做某事])负法律责任; 保证; 担保: *guarantee sb's debts/the payment of sb's debts* 为某人的债务作保[担保某人偿还债务] ○ *guarantee that the debts will be paid* 保证付清债务 ○ *guarantee to pay debts* 保证还债. **3** [Tn, Tn·pr] **~ sth (against sth)** undertake to pay the cost of repairs resulting from a fault in (an article which has been bought) 承担(所购物品)的修理费: *a clock guaranteed for one year against mechanical failure or faulty workmanship* 对机械故障或制造缺陷有一年保修的钟. **4** [Tn] make (an event) likely to happen 使(事情)很可能发生: *His turning up will guarantee the success of the meeting.* 他一出席, 会议便成功在望. **5** (idm 习语) **be guaranteed to do sth** (*infml ironic* 口, 反语) be certain to do sth 必定做某事; 准做某事: *It's guaranteed to rain when you want to go out.* 你想出门, 天准下雨.

guar·antor /ˌgærənˈtɔ:(r); ˈgærəntɔr/ *n* (*law* 律) person who gives a guarantee(1b, 2) 保证人; 担保人.

guar·anty /ˈgærəntɪ; ˈgærəntɪ/ *n* (*law* 律) guarantee¹(1) 保证; 保证书.

guard¹ /gɑ:d; gɑrd/ *n* **1** [U] state of watchfulness against attack, danger or surprise 警戒; 看守; 守望: *a soldier, sentry, etc on guard,* ie at his post, on duty 担任警戒的士兵、哨兵等 ○ *The escaped prisoner was brought back under (close) guard,* ie (closely) guarded. 在严密的戒备下将逃犯押回. ○ *policemen keeping guard outside the building* 在建筑物外面守备的警察 ○ [attrib 作定语] *guard duty* 警卫任务 ○ *a guard dog,* ie kept to guard a building, etc 警卫犬. **2** [U] position of readiness to defend oneself, eg in boxing, fencing, bayonet-drill 防御姿势(如在拳击、剑术、劈刺中): *drop/keep up one's guard* 未作出[保持]防御姿势 ○ (*fig* 比喻) *an awkward question which got through/penetrated the minister's guard* 突破部长防范的尴尬问题. **3** [C] (**a**) person (esp a soldier or policeman) who watches over sb or sth 警卫(尤指士兵、警察): *The prisoner slipped past the guards on the gate and escaped.* 犯人从大门口的警卫身旁溜过逃走了. ○ *a se'curity guard,* ie one responsible for protecting property, a building, its grounds, etc against entry by intruders, burglars, etc 守卫者 ○ *'border guards* 边防战士. (**b**) (*esp US*) (*Brit* **warder**) person who watches over prisoners in gaol 监狱看守. **4** (**a**) **the guard** [Gp] group of soldiers who protect buildings, etc 警卫队: *the changing of the guard,* ie replacing of one such group by another, eg at Buckingham Palace 换岗(如白金汉宫之更换警卫) ○ *The guard are being inspected today.* 警卫队今天要接受检阅. ○ *double the guard (in an emergency),* ie have twice the usual number of sentries on duty 派双岗(在紧急情况下派两倍于平时数目的哨兵上岗). (**b**) [CGp] body of soldiers with the duty of protecting, honouring or escorting sb 卫士队; 仪仗队: *On his arrival the president inspected the guard of honour.* 总统抵达时, 检阅了仪仗队. **5 the Guards** [pl] (in Britain and some other countries) regiments whose original duty was to protect the sovereign (英国和某些国家的)禁卫军; 警卫部队: *the Royal 'Horse Guards* 禁卫骑兵队 ○ [attrib 作定语] *a Guards officer* 禁卫队军官. **6** [C] (*Brit*) person in charge of a railway train 列车长. **7** [C] (esp in compounds 尤用以构成复合词) (part of an) article or apparatus designed to prevent injury or loss 保护器; 防护罩; 防卫物: *Ensure the guard is in place before operating the machine.* 将防护罩确实放好后再开机器. ○ *a 'fire-guard,* ie in front of a fireplace ○ *a 'mudguard,* ie over the wheel of a bicycle, etc. **8** (idm 习语) **mount guard** ⇨ MOUNT. **off/on one's 'guard** unprepared/prepared for an attack, a surprise or a mistake 失去[保持]警惕: *be on one's guard against saying the wrong thing* 提防说错话 ○ *put sb on his guard* 使某人提防 ○ *The lawyer's seemingly innocent question caught the witness off his guard.* 那个律师提出的似乎无关痛痒的问题, 把证人问得措手不及. **stand 'guard (over sb/sth)** act as a sentry 站岗; 守卫: *Four soldiers stood guard over the coffin.* 四个士兵守卫灵柩.

□ **'guardhouse** *n* building with the same function as a guardroom 卫兵室; 禁闭室.

'guard-rail *n* protective rail, eg to prevent people falling off a staircase or to separate them from dangerous traffic 护栏.

'guardroom *n* room for soldiers on guard or for keeping military prisoners 卫兵室; 禁闭室.

'guardsman /-mən; -mən/ *n* (*pl* **-men** /-mən; -mən/) soldier in the Guards 禁卫队之士兵.

'guard's van (*Brit*) (*US* **caboose**) carriage in which the guard on a train travels 守车(火车上警卫人员乘坐的车厢).

guard² /gɑ:d; gɑrd/ *v* **1** [Tn] (**a**) keep (sb/sth) safe from danger, theft, etc; protect 保卫; 保护: *soldiers guarding the president* 总统的卫兵 ○ *A dragon guarded the treasure.* 有条龙守护着财宝. ○ (*fig* 比喻) *a woman who jealously guarded her reputation* 小心地保护自己名誉的妇人. (**b**) watch over (sb) and prevent him from escaping 看守(某人)并防其逃跑: *guard prisoners closely* 对犯人严加看守. **2** (phr v) **guard against sth** use care and caution to prevent sth 预防某事物: *guard against disease* 预防疾病 ○ *They've been doing very well, but they should guard against over-confidence,* ie not become over-confident. 他们一直干得挺好, 但应防止过于自信.

▷ **guarded** *adj* (of statements, etc) cautious (指言论等)谨慎的: *a guarded reply* 谨慎的回答 ○ *be guarded in what one says* 言语谨慎. **guard·edly** *adv.*

guard·ian /ˈgɑ:dɪən; ˈgɑrdɪən/ *n* **1** one who guards or protects sth 保护者; 保卫者; 维护者: *The police are guardians of law and order.* 警察是维护法纪的人. ○ *a self-appointed guardian of public morality* 自封的卫道士. **2** (*law* 律) person who is legally responsible for sb who cannot manage his own affairs, eg an orphaned child 保护人; 监护人.

▷ **'guardi·an·ship** *n* [U] position or office of a guardian 监护人的职责.

□ **ˌguardian 'angel** **1** spirit that supposedly protects and guides a person or place 守护天使. **2** person who behaves like this 守护者.

guava /ˈgwɑ:və; ˈgwɑvə/ *n* (tropical tree with a) fruit having a light yellow skin and pink or white edible flesh 番石榴树, 番石榴(生长于热带).

gu·ber·na·torial /ˌgu:bənəˈtɔ:rɪəl; ˌgubərnəˈtɔrɪəl/ *adj* (*fml* 文) (in US, Nigeria, etc) of a (state) governor (美

国、尼日利亚等)州长的.

gudgeon /ˈgʌdʒən; ˋgʌdʒən/ *n* small freshwater fish used as bait 鮈(小型淡水鱼, 可作钓饵).

guelder rose /ˌgeldə ˈrəuz; ˋgɛldɚˌroz/ shrub with round bunches of white flowers 绣球花(灌木、开白花).

guer·rilla (also **guer·illa**) /gəˈrɪlə; gəˋrɪlə/ *n* person (not a member of a regular army) engaged in fighting in small secret groups 游击队员: *urban guerrillas*, ie those who fight in towns only 城市游击队员 ○ [attrib 作定语] *guerrilla war/warfare*, ie fought on one side or both sides by guerrillas 游击战.

guess /ges; gɛs/ *v* **1** (**a**) [I, Ipr, Tn, Tf, Tw, Tnt] **~ (at sth)** give an answer, form an opinion or make a statement about (sth) without calculating or measuring and without definite knowledge 猜想; 估计; 臆测; 推测: *You don't know. You're just guessing!* 你不知道. 你只管猜! ○ *guess at an answer* 猜答案 ○ *guess right/wrong* 猜对[错] ○ *'Can you guess her age/guess how old she is?' 'I'd guess that she's about 30/guess her to be about 30.'* '你能猜出她的年龄吗?' '我估计她大概30岁.' (**b**) [Tn, Tf, Tw no passive 不用于被动语态] do this correctly 猜出; 猜着; 猜中: *She guessed the answer straight away.* 她马上就猜中了答案. ○ *I knew by her smile that she had guessed what I was thinking.* 我从她的微笑知道她猜着了我在想什么. ○ *You'll never guess how they got in!* 你永远也猜不透他们是怎么进去的! **2** [no passive 不用于被动语态: Tn, Tf] (*infml* 口 *esp US*) suppose (sth); consider likely 推测(某事); 认为可能: *I guess you're feeling tired after your journey.* 我想你在旅行之后一定感到很疲劳. ○ *'Will you be there?' 'I guess so.'* '你那时能在那里吗?' '我想可能在.' **3** (idm 习语) **keep sb ˈguessing** (*infml* 口) keep sb uncertain about one's plans, etc 使别人对自己的计划等犹豫不定.

▷ **guess** *n* **1 ~ (at sth); ~ (that...)** opinion formed by guessing 猜测; 猜想: *have/make a guess (at sth)* (对某事)加以猜想 ○ *If I might hazard a guess, I'd say she was about 30.* 要是让我猜的话, 我说她大概30岁. ○ *My guess is that it will rain soon.* 我猜一会儿要下雨. ○ *Your guess is as good as mine*, ie I do not know. 我跟你一样都不知道. ○ *I'll give you three guesses!* ie The answer is fairly obvious and you should guess it easily. 我让你猜三次(你显然一猜就能猜中)! **2** (idm 习语) **ˈanybody's guess** fact that no one can be sure about 无人能说得准的事: *What will happen is anybody's guess!* 要发生什么事, 谁也说不准! **at a ˈguess** making a guess 依猜测: *'How old is she?' 'At a guess, about 30.'* '她有多大年纪?' '凭猜测, 大概30岁.' **an educated guess** ⇨ EDUCATE.

□ **guess·tim·ate** /ˈgestɪmət; ˋgɛstəmət/ *n* (*infml* 口) estimate made by combining guessing with reasoning (凭猜测的)估计; 瞎估计; 瞎猜.

ˈ**guesswork** *n* [U] guessing 猜测; 臆断: *obtain an answer by pure guesswork* 全凭猜测得出答案.

guest /gest; gɛst/ *n* **1** person invited to visit one's house or being entertained at one's expense 宾客; 客人: *We are expecting guests this weekend.* 我们本周末要来客人. ○ *He invited her to be his guest for the evening at the theatre.* 他邀请她晚上去看戏. ○ *an uninvited guest* 不速之客 ○ *the guest of honour* (ie most important guest) *at a banquet* 宴会上的贵宾. **2** person staying at a hotel, boarding house, etc 住在旅馆、寄宿处等的人; 旅客: *This hotel has accommodation for 500 guests.* 这旅馆能接待500位客人. ○ *a paying guest*, ie one living in a private house, but paying as if in a hotel 寄宿客(住于私人家中如住旅馆一样付费者). **3** visiting performer taking part in an entertainment 客串演员; 特约演出者: *tonight's guests on the chat show* 今晚谈天说地节目的特约嘉宾 ○ [attrib 作定语] *a guest artist, singer, conductor, etc* 特约艺术家、歌唱家、指挥等. **4** person specially invited to visit a place, participate in a conference, etc 受特别邀请访问某地、参加某会议等的人; 特邀来宾: *The scientists are visiting this country as guests of the government.* 这些科学家获该国政府特别邀请正在进行访问. ○ [attrib 作定语] *a guest speaker* 特邀演讲者. **5** (idm 习语) **be my ˈguest** (*infml* 口) (used as a response to a request 用作请求的答语) please do 请便; 随便: *'May I see the newspaper?' 'Be my guest!'* '我可以看这份报吗?' '随便!'

▷ **guest** *v* [I, Ipr] **~ (on sth)** (*infml* 口) appear as a guest(3) on a television or radio programme (在电视或广播节目中)客串.

□ ˈ**guest-house** *n* boarding house 高级寄宿舍; 宾馆; 招待所.

ˈ**guest-night** *n* evening on which members of a club or other society may invite guests (俱乐部等社团)招待来宾的夜晚; 来宾之夜.

ˈ**guest-room** *n* bedroom kept for the use of guests 供宾客用的寝室; 客房.

guf·faw /gəˈfɔː; gəˋfɔ/ *v* (*derog* 贬) [I] give a noisy laugh 哄笑; 大笑.

▷ **guf·faw** *n* such a laugh 哄笑; 大笑: *let out a loud guffaw* 发出哄然大笑.

guid·ance /ˈgaɪdns; ˋgaɪdṇs/ *n* [U] guiding or being guided; leadership; direction 引导; 领导; 指导: *be under sb's guidance* 在某人的指导下 ○ *parental guidance*, ie guidance by parents 受父母指教 ○ *child guidance*, ie (system of) help given to children with social or psychological problems 儿童指导(制度)(对与人交往或心理方面有问题的儿童给予帮助) ○ [attrib 作定语] *a missile guidance system* 导弹制导系统.

guide /gaɪd; gaɪd/ *n* **1** person who shows others the way, esp a person employed to point out interesting sights on a journey or visit 向导; (尤指)导游: *I know the place well, so let me be your guide.* 我熟悉那地方, 我来当你们的向导. ○ *The tour guide gave a running commentary from the front of the coach.* 导游在旅游车的前部向游客作连续的现场解说. ○ *We engaged a guide to show us the way across the mountians.* 我们雇了个向导带领我们翻山越岭. **2** thing that helps one form an opinion, make a calculation, etc 有助于形成意见、作出估计等的事物; 有指导意义的事物: *The essay needn't be too long; as a rough guide, you should write about three pages.* 论文不必过长, 大致应写三页左右. **3** adviser; person or thing that directs or influences one's behaviour 指导者; 指导或影响个人行为的人或事: *His elder sister had been his guide, counsellor and friend.* 他姐姐过去一直指导他, 给他出主意, 是他的朋友. ○ *Instinct is not always a good guide.* 凭本能行事不一定都对. **4 ~ (to sth)** (**a**) (also ˈ**guidebook**) book for travellers, tourists, etc with information about a place (旅行、游览等)指南: *a guide to Italy, to the British Museum, etc* 意大利旅行指南、大英博物馆参观要览. (**b**) book giving information about a subject 入门书: *a guide to French wines* 法国酒类手册 ○ *a gardening guide* 园艺入门. **5 Guide** = GIRL GUIDE (GIRL).

□ ˈ**guide-dog** *n* dog trained to guide a blind person 导盲犬.

ˈ**guide-line** *n* (usu *pl* 通常作复数) advice (usu from sb in authority) on policy (政策的)指导方针: *drawing up guide-lines on prices and incomes* 拟订物价和收入的指标 ○ *follow the guide-lines closely* 遵循指导方针.

guide² /gaɪd; gaɪd/ *v* **1** [Tn, Tn·pr, Tn·p] **~sb (to...)** (go with sb and) show the way (to a place) 引导; 指导; 领导: *If you haven't a compass, use the stars to guide you.* 倘若没有指南针, 可利用星辰引路. ○ *I guided him to his chair.* 我把他领到他的座位上去. **2** [Tn] direct (sb); influence 指导(某人); 影响: *Be guided by your sense of what is right and just.* 做事要有是非观念和正义感.

▷ **guided** *adj* [usu attrib 通常作定语] accompanied or led by a guide 有指导的; 有向导的: *a guided tour/visit* 有向导指引的观光[访问]. ˌ**guided** ˈ**missile** rocket (for use in war) which can be guided to its destination while in flight by electronic devices 导弹.

guild /gɪld; gɪld/ *n* [CGp] society of people with similar interests and aims, esp one of the associations of craftsmen or merchants in the Middle Ages 协会; 行会; (尤指中世纪的)基尔特: *the guild of barber-surgeons* 理发师——外科医生同业公会 ○ *the Townswomen's Guild* 城市妇女协会.

□ ˌ**guild-ˈhall** (**a**) hall in which members of a guild met in the Middle Ages (中世纪同业公会的)会馆. (**b**) **the ˈGuild-hall** hall of the Corporation of the City of London, used for banquets, receptions, etc 伦敦市政厅.

guilder /ˈgɪldə(r); ˋgɪldɚ/ *n* (also **gulden**) unit of money in the Netherlands 荷兰盾(荷兰货币单位).

guile /gaɪl; gaɪl/ *n* [U] deceit; cunning 欺诈; 狡猾: *a man full of guile* 奸诈的人 ○ *get sth by guile* 诈取某物. ▷ **guile·ful** /-fl; -fəl/ *adj*. **guile·fully** /-fəlɪ; -fəlɪ/ *adv*.

guile·less *adj*. **guile·lessly** *adv*.

guil·le·mot /ˈgɪlɪmɒt; ˋgɪlə,mɑt/ *n* (type of) northern sea-bird with black and white plumage and a long narrow beak 海鸽, 海鸠(北方海鸟, 长有黑色和白色羽毛, 嘴狭长).

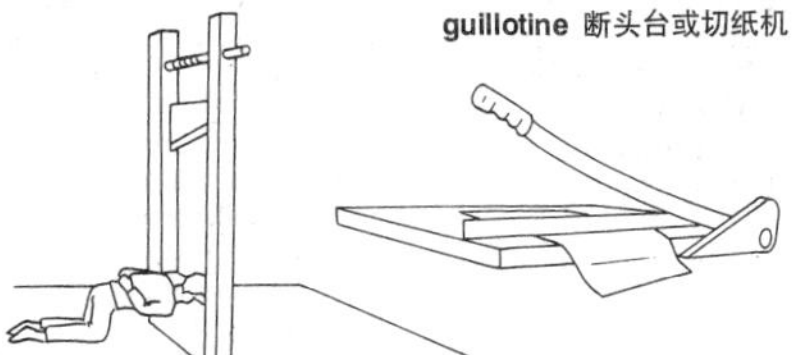

guillotine 断头台或切纸机

guil·lot·ine /ˈgɪləti:n; ˋgɪlə,tin/ *n* **1** machine of French origin for cutting people's heads off, consisting of a heavy blade which slides in grooves and is dropped from a height (源于法国的)断头台. **2** machine with a long blade for cutting or trimming large quantities of paper (eg in book-binding) or for cutting metal 切纸机(如用于书籍装订者); (金属)截切机. ⇨illus 见插图. **3** (*fig Brit politics* 比喻, 政) setting of a time limit for discussion of a bill in Parliament so as to prevent it being obstructed by too much debate (议会中)截止辩论的时限. Cf 参看 CLOSURE 2.

▷ **guil·lot·ine** *v* [Tn] use the guillotine on (sb/sth) 用断头台处死(某人); 用切纸机或切截机切割(某物); (议会中)截止辩论(某事).

guilt /gɪlt; gɪlt/ *n* [U] **1** (*law* 律) condition or fact of having done wrong 有罪, 罪状: *The police established his guilt beyond all doubt.* 警方确凿地认定他有罪. **2** blame or responsibility for wrongdoing 责任; 罪责: *find out where the guilt lies*, ie who is to blame 找出罪责之所在(何人之过) ○ *Guilt was written all over her face*, ie She was obviously to blame. 她的罪过都写在脸上了(显而易见她有罪). **3** anxiety or unhappiness caused by the knowledge of having done wrong 不安; 内疚: *racked by feelings of guilt because he had not done enough to help his sick friend* 因朋友生病未尽力帮助而内疚 ○ [attrib 作定语] *a guilt complex* 犯罪情结.

▷ **guilt·less** *adj* **~ (of sth)** innocent; without guilt 无辜的; 无罪的: *guiltless of the offence* 无罪.

guilty *adj* (**-ier**, **-iest**) **1 ~ (of sth)** (*esp law* 尤用于法律) having done wrong; being to blame (for sth) 有罪的; 犯罪的; (对某事)有罪责的: *plead guilty to a crime* 认罪 ○ *The verdict of the jury was 'not guilty'*, ie innocent. 陪审团裁决无罪. ○ *be found guilty of negligence* 被判犯有玩忽职守罪 ○ *the guilty party*, ie person to blame 有罪者. **2** showing or feeling guilt 表现有罪的; 感觉有罪的: *look guilty* 显出有罪的样子 ○ *I feel guilty about visiting her so rarely.* 我因极少去看望她而感到惭愧. ○ *guilty looks* 感到有罪的表情 ○ *a guilty conscience*, ie conscience troubled by feelings of guilt 内疚. **guilt·ily** /-ɪlɪ; -əlɪ/ *adv*: *She looked up guiltily as I came in.* 我进来时, 她内疚地抬起了头. **guilti·ness** *n* [U].

guinea /ˈgɪnɪ; ˋgɪnɪ/ *n* (formerly in Britain) (gold coin worth the) sum of 21 shillings (now £1.05), used in stating professional fees (eg legal, medical), prices, etc (英国旧时的)基尼(金币, 值21先令, 现值1.05英镑, 用于计算专业人员的收费, 如律师、医生等的费用): *the 2 000 Guineas*, ie a British horse race with an original prize of this amount 2 000基尼(最初奖金为这一数目的英国赛马).

guinea-fowl /ˈgɪnɪfaʊl; ˋgɪnɪ faʊl/ *n* (*pl* unchanged 复数不变) bird of the pheasant family, with dark grey feathers spotted with white, often used as food 珠鸡(常供食用).

guinea-pig /ˈgɪnɪpɪg; ˋgɪnɪ pɪg/ *n* **1** short-eared animal like a big rat, often kept as a pet 天竺鼠, 豚鼠(常作宠物). **2** person or animal used in medical or other experiments 供医学或其他实验用的人或动物: *local residents who were unwitting guinea-pigs in the government's nuclear power programme* 在政府核电计划中因不知就里而成为实验品的当地居民.

Guin·ness /ˈgɪnɪs; ˋgɪnɪs/ *n* [U, C] (*propr* 专利名) kind of dark bitter beer; glass of this 吉尼斯黑啤酒; 一杯吉尼斯黑啤酒: *a pint of draught Guinness* 一品脱散装吉尼斯黑啤酒.

guise /gaɪz; gaɪz/ *n* **1** (*arch* 古) style of dress 装束: *in the guise of a knight* 作骑士装束. **2** outward manner or appearance, esp put on in order to conceal the truth 态度; 相貌; (尤指)伪装: *under the guise* (ie pretence) *of friendship* 以友谊为掩饰 ○ *an ancient tale which appears in various guises in several European languages* 以几种欧洲语言叙述的一个古老故事.

gui·tar /gɪˈtɑ:(r); gɪˋtɑr/ *n* (usu) six-stringed musical instrument, plucked with the fingers or a plectrum 吉他; 六弦琴: *strum a guitar* 漫不经心地弹吉他 ○ *a classical/an electric/a Spanish guitar* 古典[电/西班牙]吉他. ⇨ illus at App 1 见附录1插图, page i.

▷ **gui·tar·ist** /gɪˈtɑ:rɪst; gɪˋtɑrɪst/ *n* guitar player 吉他手.

gulch /gʌltʃ; gʌltʃ/ *n* (*US*) deep narrow rocky valley 峡谷.

gul·den /ˈgʊldən; ˋgʊldən/ *n* (*pl* unchanged or **~s** 复数或不变或作 **guldens**) = GUILDER.

gulf /gʌlf; gʌlf/ *n* **1** part of the sea almost surrounded by land 海湾: *the Gulf of Mexico* 墨西哥湾. **2** (**a**) (*rhet* 修辞) deep hollow in the ground; chasm; abyss 沟壑; 深坑; 深渊: *a yawning gulf opened up by an earthquake* 地震造成的裂缝. (**b**) **~ (between A and B)**; **~ (in sth)** (*fig* 比喻) area of difference; division (in opinions, etc) 鸿沟; (意见等的)分歧: *The gulf between the two leaders cannot be bridged*, ie Their opinions are so far apart that they cannot be reconciled. 两位领导人之间的鸿沟难以逾越.

□ **the 'Gulf Stream** warm current flowing across the Atlantic Ocean from the Gulf of Mexico towards Europe 墨西哥湾流(从墨西哥湾横过大西洋, 流向欧洲的暖流).

gull[1] /gʌl; gʌl/ (also **'seagull**) *n* any of several types of large long-winged sea-bird with usu white and grey or black feathers 鸥. ⇨illus at App 1 见附录1插图, page v.

gull[2] /gʌl; gʌl/ *v* [Tn, Tn·pr] **~ sb (into/out of sth)** (*arch* 古) cheat sb (so that he has to do or give up sth); deceive sb 欺骗某人(以使其不得不做或放弃某事物); 欺诈某人.

▷ **gull** *n* (*arch* 古) person who is easily deceived; simpleton 易受欺骗的人; 笨人; 傻子.

gul·let /ˈgʌlɪt; ˋgʌlɪt/ *n* food passage from the mouth to the stomach; throat 食道; 咽喉: *a bone stuck in one's gullet* 卡在喉咙里的骨头. ⇨illus at DIGESTIVE 见 DIGESTIVE 插图.

gull·ible /ˈgʌləbl; ˋgʌləbḷ/ *adj* willing to believe anything or anyone; easily deceived 轻信的; 易受欺骗的: *He must have been pretty gullible to fall for that old trick.* 他准是有点儿傻, 才落入那惯用的圈套. ▷ **gull·ib·il·ity** /ˌgʌləˈbɪlətɪ; ˌgʌləˋbɪlətɪ/ *n* [U]. **gull·ibly** /-əblɪ; -əblɪ/ *adv*.

gully /ˈgʌlɪ; ˋgʌlɪ/ *n* **1** narrow channel cut or formed by rain-water, eg on a hillside, or made for carrying water away from a building (山腰等地的)水冲沟; 壑; 溪谷; 沟渠. **2** (in cricket) close fielding position between cover point and slip (板球)(后卫与外场员之间的)防守位置.

gulp /gʌlp; gʌlp/ *v* **1** [Tn, Tn·p] **~ sth (down)** swallow (food or drink) quickly or greedily 快速或贪婪地吞咽(食物或饮料): *gulp one's food* 狼吞虎咽地吃东西 ○ *gulp down a cup of tea* 一口气喝下一杯茶. **2** [I] make a swallowing motion 吞咽; 咽: *She gulped nervously, as if the question bothered her.* 她紧张地咽了一下, 似乎那问题把她难住了. **3** [Tn, Tn·p] **~ sth (in)** breathe (air) deeply, (as if) to recover from partial suffocation 深呼吸; 喘大气; 喘长气: *She crawled onto the river bank and lay there gulping in air.* 她爬上河岸, 躺在那里喘着大气. **4** (phr v) **gulp sth back** prevent (the expression of emotion) by swallowing (以吞咽动作)抑制(感情的流露); 咽下; 咽回: *She gulped back her tears and tried to smile.* 她咽下眼泪, 强作笑容.

▷ **gulp** *n* **1** act of gulping 吞咽: *swallow/sob with loud gulps* 大声吞咽[抽泣]. **2** mouthful, esp of sth liquid 一大口(尤指液体): *a gulp of cold milk* 一大口冷牛奶. **3** (idm 习语) **at a 'gulp** with one gulp 一口气吞下: *empty*

G

a glass at a gulp 一口气喝完一杯.

gum[1] /gʌm; gʌm/ *n* (usu *pl* 通常作复数) firm pink flesh at the base of the teeth 齿龈; 牙龈; 牙床: *The dog bared its gums at me.* 狗呲着牙冲我叫. ⇨illus at TOOTH 见 TOOTH 插图.

□ **gumboil** /ˈgʌmbɔɪl; ˈgʌm,bɔɪl/ *n* boil or abscess on the gums 龈溃疡; 龈脓肿.

gum[2] /gʌm; gʌm/ *n* **1** [U] (**a**) sticky substance which oozes from certain trees, used for making glue 树胶; 树脂. (**b**) glue used for sticking light things (eg paper) together 胶(用以粘轻的东西, 如纸). **2** [U] = CHEWING-GUM (CHEW). **3** (also ˈ**gum-drop**) [C] transparent sweet made of a firm jelly-like substance 透明软糖: *fruit gums* 水果软糖. **4** [C] = GUM-TREE.

▷ **gum** *v* (**-mm-**) **1** [Tn, Tn·pr, Tn·p] **~ A to/onto B; ~ A and B together; ~sth (down)** spread gum on the surface of sth; stick (one thing to another) with gum 在(某物表面)上涂胶; 用胶粘(一物于另一物): *gum (the edges of) a piece of paper* 往一页纸(的边)上涂胶 ○ *gum down the flap of an envelope* 用胶粘住信封的盖口 ○ *gum paper to/onto card* 把纸粘在厚纸板上 ○ *Cut out two pieces of cardboard and gum them together.* 割两块硬纸板, 再把它们粘在一起. **2** (idm 习语) **gum up the ˈworks** (*infml* 口) make a machine or system unable to operate 使机器不能开动; 使制度不能实行; 弄坏; 搞乱. **3** (phr v) **gum sth up** fill sth with a sticky substance and stop it moving 将某物粘牢.

ˈ**gummy** *adj* (**-ier, -iest**) sticky 黏的.

□ ˈ**gumboot** *n* rubber boot that extends up the leg 长统橡胶靴.

ˈ**gum-tree** *n* **1** eucalyptus tree 树胶树. **2** (idm 习语) **up a ˈgum-tree** (*infml* 口) in difficulties 有困难; 在困境.

gum[3] /gʌm; gʌm/ *n* [U] (*Brit infml euph* 口, 婉) (used in oaths, etc, esp in N England 用于誓语、咒语等中, 尤用于北英格兰) God 上帝: *By gum!* 我向上帝发誓!

gumbo /ˈgʌmbəʊ; ˈgʌmbo/ *n* [U] (*US*) thick soup made with the vegetable okra (用秋葵荚做的)浓汤.

gump·tion /ˈgʌmpʃn; ˈgʌmpʃən/ *n* [U] (*infml* 口) common sense and initiative; qualities likely to bring success 常识与进取精神; 魄力: *He's a nice enough lad, but he doesn't seem to have much gumption.* 他是个不错的小伙子, 但好像没有什么进取心.

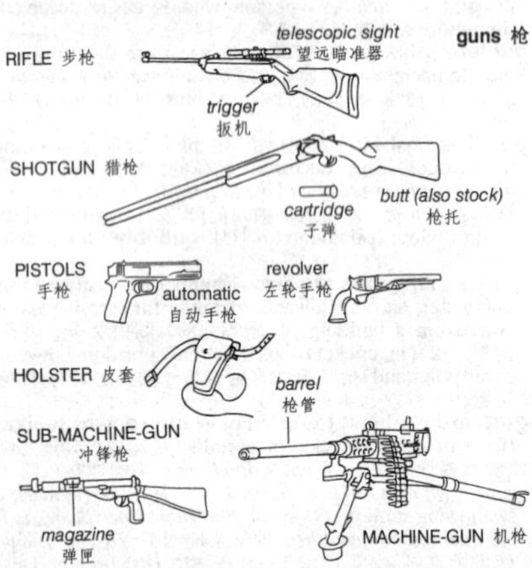

gun /gʌn; gʌn/ *n* **1** [C] any kind of firearm that fires bullets or shells from a metal tube 炮; 枪: *Look out, he's got a gun!* 小心, 他拿着枪呢! ○ *a warship with 16-inch guns* 装有16英寸口径大炮的军舰 ○ *maˈchine-guns* 机关枪. ⇨illus 见插图. **2 the gun** [sing] signal to begin a race, given with a starting pistol (用发令枪发出的)起跑信号; 发令枪声: *Wait for the gun!* 等着发令枪响! **3** [C] tool that forces out a substance for injecting; device for fixing sth 喷射用具; 用以固定某物的装置: *a ˈgrease-gun* 注油枪 ○ *a ˈstaple-gun* U钉枪. **4** [C] person using a sporting gun as a member of a shooting party 猎手. **5** [C] (*US infml* 口) gunman 杀手; 枪手: *a hired gun* 雇佣枪手. **6** (idm 习语) **going great guns** ⇨ GREAT. **jump the gun** ⇨ JUMP[2]. **spike sb's guns** ⇨ SPIKE *v*. **stick to one's guns** ⇨ STICK[2].

▷ **gun** *v* (**-nn-**) **1** (idm 习语) **be gunning for sb** (*infml* 口) be looking for an opportunity to attack or criticize sb 寻找机会攻击或批评某人. **2** (phr v) **gun sb down** (*infml* 口) shoot sb, esp so as to kill or seriously injure him 射倒某人(尤指使之伤亡).

□ ˈ**gunboat** *n* small warship carrying heavy guns or long-range missiles 炮艇. ˌ**gunboat diˈplomacy** (*fig* 比喻) diplomacy backed by the threat of force 炮舰外交(以武力威胁作后盾之外交政策).

ˈ**gun-carriage** *n* wheeled support of a big gun, or part on which a gun slides when it recoils 炮架.

ˈ**gun cotton** cellulose material impregnated with nitric acid, used as an explosive 强棉药; 硝化棉(用作炸药).

ˈ**gun dog** dog trained to help in the sport of shooting (eg by collecting shot birds) 猎犬.

ˈ**gunfire** *n* [U] firing of a gun or guns 炮火.

ˈ**gunman** /-mən; -mən/ *n* (*pl* **-men** /-mən; -mən/) man who uses a gun to rob or kill people 持枪抢劫或杀人的歹徒: *terrorist gunmen* 极可怕的持枪歹徒.

ˈ**gun-metal** *n* [U] alloy of copper and tin or zinc 炮铜; 青铜(铜与锡或锌的合金): [attrib 作定语] *gun-metal grey*, ie a dull blue-grey colour 铁灰色(暗蓝灰色).

ˈ**gunpoint** *n* (idm 习语) **at ˈgunpoint** while threatening or being threatened with a gun 在枪口威胁下: *rob a bank at gunpoint* 用枪威胁抢劫银行.

ˈ**gunpowder** *n* [U] explosive powder used in guns, fireworks, blasting, etc 火药.

ˈ**gunroom** *n* room in a large country house, in which sporting guns are kept (乡村大宅中的)藏枪室.

ˈ**gun-runner** *n* person engaged in the secret and illegal importation of firearms into a country, eg to help a revolt 私运军火者(如以帮助叛乱). ˈ**gun-running** *n* [U] activity of a gun-runner 私运军火.

ˈ**gunshot** *n* (**a**) [C] shot fired from a gun (射出的)炮弹或枪弹: *the sound of gunshots* 枪炮声. [attrib 作定语] *gunshot wounds* 枪炮造成的伤口. (**b**) [U] range of a gun (枪或炮的)射程: *be out of/within gunshot* 射程以外[内].

ˈ**gunsmith** *n* person who makes and repairs small firearms 造枪及修枪工人.

gunge /gʌndʒ; gʌndʒ/ *n* [U] (*Brit infml* 口) unpleasant messy semi-liquid substance 恶心人的半流质脏东西: *What's this horrible gunge in the bottom of the bucket?* 水桶底部黏乎乎怪恶心人的东西是什么?

gun·ner /ˈgʌnə(r); ˈgʌnɚ/ *n* **1** (in the British army) soldier in the artillery (英国陆军)炮兵: *Gunner Jones* 炮兵琼斯. **2** (in the British navy) warrant officer in charge of a battery of guns (英国海军)枪炮士官长. ⇨ App 9 见附录 9.

▷ **gun·nery** /ˈgʌnərɪ; ˈgʌnərɪ/ *n* [U] operation of large military guns 枪炮操作与射击: [attrib 作定语] *gunnery practice* 射击演习 ○ *the gunnery officer* 射击指挥官.

gun·wale /ˈgʌnl; ˈgʌnḷ/ *n* (*nautical* 海) upper edge of the side of a boat or small ship 舷缘(小船船舷的上缘).

gurgle /ˈgɜːgl; ˈgɝgl/ *n* bubbling sound like water flowing from a narrow-necked bottle (esp that made by babies when happy) 汩汩声(似水自窄颈瓶内流出的); (尤指婴儿高兴时发出的)咯咯声: *gurgles of delight* 咯咯的笑声.

▷ **gurgle** *v* [I] make this sound 作汩汩声; 作咯咯声: *The water gurgled as it ran down the plug-hole.* 水汩汩地从塞孔中流下去. ○ *The baby was gurgling happily.* 那婴儿高兴得发出咯咯声.

Gurkha /ˈgɜːkə; ˈgʊrkə/ *n* member of a regiment in the British or Indian army made up of soldiers from Nepal 廓尔喀兵(英国或印度陆军中由尼泊尔籍士兵组成的团之成员).

guru /ˈgʊruː; *US* gəˈruː; gəˈru/ *n* **1** Hindu spiritual leader 古鲁(印度的宗教领袖). **2** (*fig infml* 比喻, 口) respected and influential teacher or authority (受尊敬、有影响力的)教师或权威.

gush /gʌʃ; gʌʃ/ *v* **1** [I, Ipr, Ip] **~ (out) (from sth)** flow or pour out suddenly in great quantities (突然大量地)流出, 泻出, 涌出: *gushing water* 涌出的水 ○ *oil gushing* *out (from a well)* （从井中）涌出的石油 ○ *blood gushing from a wound* 自伤口涌出的血. **2** [I, Ipr] **~ over sb/sth** (*fig derog* 比喻, 贬) talk with excessive enthusiasm 滔滔不绝地说; 过分热心地说: *Don't gush!* 别唠唠叨叨说个没完! ○ *a young mother gushing over a baby* 喋喋不休地谈着婴儿的年轻母亲.

▷ **gush** *n* (esp *sing* 尤作单数) sudden outflow or outburst 涌出; 迸发: *a gush of oil, anger, enthusiasm* 石油的涌出、怒火的迸发、热情的奔放.

gusher *n* oil-well with a strong natural flow (so that pumping is not needed) 喷油井(自动流出的油井).

gush·ing *adj*: *gushing compliments* 滔滔不绝的赞扬话. **gush·ingly** *adv*.

gus·set /ˈɡʌsɪt; ˋɡʌsɪt/ *n* (usu triangular or diamond-shaped) piece of cloth inserted in a garment to strengthen or enlarge it 为加固或加大衣服而插接于衣服中的布块(通常为三角形或菱形).

gust /ɡʌst; ɡʌst/ *n* (**a**) sudden violent rush of wind （突然的）一阵狂风: *the wind blowing in gusts* 刮起阵阵的狂风 ○ *fitful gusts of wind* 阵阵的狂风. (**b**) (*fig* 比喻) outburst of feeling 感情的迸发: *a gust of temper* 大发脾气.

▷ **gust** *v* [I] (of the wind) blow in gusts （指风）劲吹, 猛刮: *winds gusting up to 60 mph* 风速达每小时60英里的狂风.

gusty *adj* (**-ier**, **-iest**) with wind blowing in gusts 有阵阵狂风的: *a gusty day, wind* 刮阵阵狂风的一天、阵阵强劲的风.

gusto /ˈɡʌstəʊ; ˋɡʌsto/ *n* [U] (*infml* 口) enthusiastic vigour in doing sth 做某事的兴致; 热忱: *singing the choruses with great gusto* 兴致勃勃地合唱.

gut /ɡʌt; ɡʌt/ *n* **1 guts** [pl] (*infml* 口) (**a**) internal organs of the abdomen （腹腔的）内脏: *a pain in the guts* 肚子疼. (**b**) (*fig* 比喻) essential (mechanical) parts of sth 某物的重要(机械)部分: *remove the guts of a clock* 除去钟的机芯. **2 guts** [pl] (*fig infml* 比喻, 口) courage and determination 勇气与决心; 胆量; 魄力: *a man with plenty of guts* 很有魄力的人 ○ *have the guts to do sth* 有胆量做某事. **3** [C] (**a**) (*anatomy* 解) lower part of the alimentary canal; intestine 消化道的下段; 肠: *dissecting a frog's gut* 解剖蛙的肠. (**b**) (*infml* 口) abdomen; stomach 肚子; 胃: *his huge beer gut*, ie made fat by drinking beer 他的大啤酒肚. **4 guts** [sing or pl *v*] (*infml* 口) person who eats a lot 饭量大的人: *He's a real greedy guts.* 他真是贪吃的大肚汉. **5** [U] thread made from the intestines of animals, used surgically for sewing wounds, and for violin and tennis-racket strings; catgut 肠线(用作外科的缝合线及小提琴和网球拍的弦). **6** (idm 习语) **hate sb's guts** ⇨ HATE. **slog/sweat one's ˈguts out** (*infml* 口) work very hard, to the point of exhaustion 拼命干.

▷ **gut** *v* (**-tt-**) [Tn] **1** take the guts out of (a fish, etc) 取出(鱼等)的内脏. **2** destroy the inside or contents of (a building, room, etc) 毁坏(建筑物、房间等)的内部或内部的东西: *a warehouse gutted by fire* 内部为火焚毁的仓库.

gut *adj* [attrib 作定语] instinctive rather than based on thought 本能的、非理性的: *a gut feeling/reaction* 本能的感觉[反应].

gut·less *adj* cowardly 怯懦的; 胆小的.

gutsy /ˈɡʌtsɪ; ˋɡʌtsɪ/ *adj* (**-ier**, **-iest**) (*infml* 口) full of courage and determination 充满勇气和决心的: *a gutsy fighter* 坚定无畏的战士.

gutta-percha /ˌɡʌtəˈpɜːtʃə; ˋɡʌtəˋpɝtʃə/ *n* [U] rubber-like substance made from the juice of various Malayan trees 杜仲胶; 古塔波胶.

gutter[1] /ˈɡʌtə(r); ˋɡʌtɚ/ *n* **1** long (usu semicircular) metal or plastic channel fixed under the edge of a roof to carry away rain-water 排水檐沟; 天沟. ⇨illus at App 1 见附录1插图, page vii. **2** (**a**) (channel at the) side of a road, next to the kerb 路边沟; 排水沟; 阴沟: *cigarette packets thrown into the gutter* 扔在阴沟里的香烟盒. (**b**) **the gutter** [sing] (*fig* 比喻) poor or debased state of life 贫苦低级的生活: *the language of the gutter*, ie vulgar language 粗鄙的语言 ○ *He picked her out of the gutter and made her a great lady.* 他使她脱离贫苦生活, 并成为贵妇.

▷ **gut·ter·ing** /ˈɡʌtərɪŋ; ˋɡʌtərɪŋ/ *n* [U] system of gutters 排水系统.

□ ˈ**gutter press** (*derog* 贬) newspapers that print a lot of sensational stories, scandal, etc 低级趣味的报纸.

ˈ**guttersnipe** /-snaɪp; -ˌsnaɪp/ *n* (*derog* 贬) poor, badly-dressed, badly-behaved child 衣衫褴褛、行为恶劣的贫儿.

gutter[2] /ˈɡʌtə(r); ˋɡʌtɚ/ *v* [I] (of a candle) burn fitfully, as if about to go out （指蜡烛）忽明忽暗(似要熄灭).

gut·tural /ˈɡʌtərəl; ˋɡʌtərəl/ *adj* (of a sound) (seeming to be) produced in the throat （指声音）(似)喉间发出的: *a low guttural growl* 用喉音低声嘟囔 ○ *guttural consonants* 软颚辅音.

guv, guv·nor ⇨ GOVERNOR[3].

guy[1] /ɡaɪ; ɡaɪ/ *n* rope or chain used to keep sth steady or secured, eg to hold a tent in place （帐篷等的）支索; 牵索; 拉索.

□ ˈ**guy rope** such a rope 用作支索等的绳子.

guy[2] /ɡaɪ; ɡaɪ/ *n* **1** (*infml* 口) man 男人; 傢伙; 小伙子: *He's a great guy.* 他是个了不起的小伙子. ○ *the guys at the office* 办公室的男同事 ○ *her guy*, ie boy-friend, husband, etc 她那个男朋友[丈夫] ○ *Come on, (you) guys, let's get going!* 快点吧, 你们这些小伙子, 咱们动手干吧! **2** figure in the form of a man, dressed in old clothes, burned in Britain on 5 November in memory of Guy Fawkes 盖伊(英国盖伊·福克斯的模拟像, 着旧时衣服, 每逢11月5日焚烧, 称'福克斯日').

▷ **guy** *v* [Tn] (*fml* 文) ridicule (sb/sth), esp by comic imitation 嘲弄(某人[某事物])(尤指以滑稽模拟像的方式).

guzzle /ˈɡʌzl; ˋɡʌzl̩/ *v* [I, Ip, Tn, Tn·p] **~ (away); ~ sth (down/up)** (*infml* 口) eat or drink sth greedily 无节制地吃或喝某物; 滥吃; 狂饮: *He's always guzzling.* 他总是大吃大喝的. ○ *guzzle beer* 狂饮啤酒 ○ *The children guzzled down all the cakes.* 孩子们大吃一通, 把蛋糕都吃光了.

▷ **guz·zler** /-zlə(r); -zl̩ɚ/ *n* person who guzzles 大吃大喝的人.

gybe (*US* **jibe**) /dʒaɪb; dʒaɪb/ *v* [I] (*nautical* 海) change direction when the wind is behind, by swinging the sail from one side of a boat to the other （顺风时将船帆自一舷转向另一舷以）改变方向.

gym /dʒɪm; dʒɪm/ *n* (*infml* 口) **1** [C] gymnasium 体育馆; 健身房: *exercises in the gym* 在健身房的锻炼. **2** [U] gymnastics, esp at school 体操(尤指学校中的): *I don't like gym.* 我不喜欢体操. ○ [attrib 作定语] *gym-shoes*, ie esp plimsolls 运动鞋(尤指橡胶底帆布面的) ○ *a gym mistress* 体育课女教师.

□ ˈ**gym-slip** (also **slip**) *n* sleeveless tunic worn in Britain by some girls as part of school uniform （英国女生的）无袖制服.

gym·khana /dʒɪmˈkɑːnə; dʒɪmˋkɑnə/ *n* public competitive display of horse-riding or vehicle-driving 马术比赛, 汽车驾驶比赛.

gym·nas·ium /dʒɪmˈneɪzɪəm; dʒɪmˋnezɪəm/ *n* (*pl* **~s** or **-ia** /-zɪə; -zɪə/) room or hall with apparatus for physical exercise 健身房; 体育馆.

gym·nast /ˈdʒɪmnæst; ˋdʒɪmnæst/ *n* expert in gymnastics 体育家; 体操运动员.

gym·nastic /dʒɪmˈnæstɪk; dʒɪmˋnæstɪk/ *adj* of physical exercises and training 体育的; 体操的.

▷ **gym·nast·ics** *n* [pl] (forms of) exercises performed to develop the muscles or fitness or to demonstrate agility 体操; 体能训练: (*fig* 比喻) *mental gymnastics*, ie mental agility, elaborate reasoning 智力训练.

gyn·ae·co·logy (*US* **gyne-**) /ˌɡaɪnəˈkɒlədʒɪ; ˌɡaɪnɪˋkɑlədʒɪ/ *n* [U] scientific study and treatment of diseases and disorders of the female reproductive system 妇科学; 妇科.

▷ **gyn·ae·co·lo·gical** (*US* **gyne-**) /-kəˈlɒdʒɪkl; -kəˋlɑdʒɪkl/ *adj*.

gyn·ae·co·lo·gist (*US* **gyne-**) *n* expert in gynaecology 妇科学家.

gyp /dʒɪp; dʒɪp/ *n* (idm 习语) **give sb ˈgyp** (*Brit infml* 口) (**a**) scold or punish sb very severely 痛骂或严惩某人. (**b**) cause sb much pain 使某人很痛苦: *My rheumatism's been giving me gyp.* 我的风湿病使我一直很痛苦.

gypsum /ˈdʒɪpsəm; ˋdʒɪpsəm/ *n* [U] mineral (calcium sulphate) from which plaster of Paris is made, also used as fertilizer 石膏.

gypsy (also **gipsy**, **Gypsy**) /ˈdʒɪpsɪ; ˋdʒɪpsɪ/ *n* member of a wandering, originally Asiatic, people who live in caravans 吉卜赛人: (*fig* 比喻) *I've never lived in one place for long; it must be the Gypsy in me,* ie my desire to wander round the world. 我从未在任何一个地方长住过，一定是我合该周游世界. ○ [attrib 作定语] *a gypsy camp* 吉卜赛营地 ○ *the gypsy life,* ie wandering from place to place 吉卜赛式的生活(到处流浪).

gyrate /ˌdʒaɪˈreɪt; *US* ˈdʒaɪreɪt; ˋdʒaɪret/ *v* [I] move around in circles or spirals; revolve 旋转; 回旋.
▷ **gyra·tion** /ˌdʒaɪˈreɪʃn; dʒaɪˋreʃən/ *n* [U, C] act of revolving 旋转; 回旋.

gyro /ˈdʒaɪərəʊ; ˋdʒaɪro/ *n* (*pl* ~ **s**) (*infml* 口) = gyroscope.

gyro·scope /ˈdʒaɪrəskəʊp; ˋdʒaɪrəˌskop/ *n* device containing a wheel which, when its spins fast, always maintains the same orientation regardless of any movement of the supporting structure, often used in ships' stabilizers 陀螺仪; 回转仪. ▷ **gyro·scopic** /ˌdʒaɪrəˈskɒpɪk; ˌdʒaɪrəˋskɑpɪk/ *adj*: *a gyroscopic compass* 陀螺罗盘.

G

H h

H, h /eɪtʃ; etʃ/ *n* (*pl* **H's, h's** /ˈeɪtʃɪz; ˋetʃɪz/) the eighth letter of the English alphabet 英语字母表的第八个字母: *'Hat' begins with (an) H/'H'.* hat一字以h字母开始. Cf 参看 AITCH.

H /eɪtʃ; etʃ/ *abbr* 缩写 = (of lead used in pencils) hard (指铅笔中的铅心)硬的: *an H/an HH/a 2H pencil* 硬度为H［HH/2H］的铅笔. Cf 参看 B, HB.

ha /hɑː; hɑ/ *interj* **1** (used to express surprise, joy, triumph, suspicion, etc 用以表示惊奇、快乐、得意、疑惑等) **2** (also **ha! ha!**) (used in print to indicate laughter; when spoken used ironically 书写或印刷中用以表示大笑声; 用于口头时含讥讽之意). ▷ **ha** *v* (idm 习语) **hum and ha** ⇨ HUM.

ha *abbr* 缩写 = hectare(s).

hab·eas cor·pus /ˌheɪbɪəs ˈkɔːpəs; ˋhebɪəs ˋkɔrpəs/ (also **writ of habeas corpus**) (*law* 律) order requiring a person to be brought before a judge or into court, esp to investigate the right of the authorities to keep him in prison 人身保护状(要求将某人移送法院处理的令状, 尤指为调查有关当局将其拘禁是否合法).

hab·er·dasher /ˈhæbədæʃə(r); ˋhæbɚˌdæʃɚ/ *n* **1** (*Brit*) shopkeeper who sells small articles for sewing such as pins, cotton, buttons, zips, etc 经营缝纫用小商品(如针、线、钮扣、拉链等)的店主. **2** (*US*) shopkeeper who sells men's clothing 经营男子服装的店主.

▷ **hab·er·dash·ery** *n* **1** [U] goods sold by a haberdasher (英)缝纫用小商品; (美)(作为商品的)男子服装. **2** [C] haberdasher's shop (英)出售缝纫用小商品的商店; (美)出售男子服装的商店.

habit /ˈhæbɪt; ˋhæbɪt/ *n* **1** (**a**) [C] thing that a person does often and almost without thinking, esp sth that is hard to stop doing 习惯: *He has the irritating habit of smoking during meals.* 他有边吃饭边抽烟那让人讨厌的习惯. ○ *It's all right to borrow money occasionally, but don't let it become a habit.* 偶尔借点钱倒没什么, 只是不要成为一种习惯. (**b**) [U] usual behaviour 惯常的行为; 习性; 脾性: *I only do it out of habit.* 我做这事只是出于习惯. **2** [C] long garment worn by a monk or nun 修道士或修女所穿的长袍. **3** (idm 习语) **be in/fall into/get into the habit of doing sth** have/acquire the habit of doing sth 有［养成］做某事的习惯: *He's not in the habit of drinking a lot.* 他不习惯于多喝酒. ○ *I've got into the habit of switching on the TV as soon as I get home.* 我已养成一到家就打开电视机的习惯. **break sb/oneself of a habit** succeed in getting sb/oneself to give a habit up 使某人［自己］改掉某种习惯. **a creature of habit** ⇨ CREATURE. **fall/get into bad ˈhabits** acquire bad habits 养成坏习惯. **fall/get out of the habit of doing sth** lose the habit of doing sth 去掉做某事的习惯: *I've got out of the habit of having a cooked breakfast.* 我已不再保持早餐吃热食的习惯. **force of ˈhabit** ⇨ FORCE[1]. **kick the habit** ⇨ KICK[1]. **make a habit/practice of sth/doing sth** develop the habit of (doing) sth 形成做某事的习惯: *I make a habit of never lending money to strangers.* 我自己立下个规矩, 从来不把钱借给生人.

□ ˈ**habit-forming** *adj* causing addiction 成为习惯的; 上瘾的: *habit-forming drugs* 成瘾性毒品.

hab·it·able /ˈhæbɪtəbl; ˋhæbɪtəbl̩/ *adj* suitable for living in 适于居住的: *This house is no longer habitable.* 这所房子已经不能住人了. ▷ **hab·it·ab·il·ity** /ˌhæbɪtəˈbɪlətɪ; ˌhæbɪtəˋbɪlətɪ/ *n* [U].

hab·itat /ˈhæbɪtæt; ˋhæbəˌtæt/ *n* natural environment of an animal or a plant; home (动物或植物的)自然环境; 栖息地: *This creature's (natural) habitat is the jungle.* 这种动物的(天然)栖息地是丛林.

hab·ita·tion /ˌhæbɪˈteɪʃn; ˌhæbəˋteʃən/ *n* **1** [U] inhabiting or being inhabited 居住: *houses unfit for (human) habitation* 不适于(人)居住的房子. **2** [C] (*fml* 文) place to live in; house or home 住处; 住房; 家宅: *wildlife undisturbed by human habitations* 因无人在附近居住而未受搅扰的野生动物.

ha·bit·ual /həˈbɪtʃʊəl; həˋbɪtʃʊəl/ *adj* **1** [attrib 作定语] regular; usual 惯常的; 通常的: *his habitual place at the table* 他惯常坐在桌旁的位子. **2** done constantly or as a habit 经常做的; 习以为常的: *their habitual moaning* 他们那经常不断的呻吟. **3** [attrib 作定语] doing sth by habit 由于习惯而做某事的: *a habitual drunkard, cinema-goer, etc* 日久成瘾的酗酒者、电影院常客.

▷ **hab·itu·ally** /-tʃʊəlɪ; -tʃʊəlɪ/ *adv* usually; regularly 通常地; 惯常地: *Tom is habitually late for school.* 汤姆上学经常迟到.

ha·bitu·ate /həˈbɪtʃʊeɪt; həˋbɪtʃʊˌet/ *v* [Tn·pr] **~ sb/oneself to sth** (*fml* 文) accustom sb/oneself to sth 使某人［自己］习惯于某事物: *habituate oneself to* (ie get used to) *hard work, a cold climate* 使自己习惯于艰苦的工作、寒冷的气候.

ha·bi·tué /həˈbɪtʃʊeɪ; həˋbɪtʃʊˌe/ *n* (*French* 法) person who visits a place regularly 常客: *a habitué of the Café Royal* 皇家小餐馆的常客.

ha·ci·enda /ˌhæsɪˈendə; ˌhɑsɪˋɛndə/ *n* (in Spanish-speaking countries) large landed estate with a house (说西班牙语的国家的)大庄园.

hack[1] /hæk; hæk/ *v* **1** [Ipr] **~ at sth/sb** strike heavy cutting blows at sth/sb 猛砍或猛劈某物［某人］: *He hacked (away) at the branch until it fell off.* 他朝着树枝(不停地)砍, 直到砍下为止. ⇨Usage at CUT[1] 用法见CUT[1]. **2** [Tn] kick (sth) roughly 狠踢, 乱踢(某物): *hack the ball/sb's shin* 照着球［某人的小腿］狠踢. **3** [I] cough harshly 咳嗽(发出刺耳声音). **4** (phr v) **hack sth off (sth)** remove sth with rough heavy blows 砍掉某物: *hack a leg off the carcass* 从动物的尸体上砍下一只腿. **hack one's way across, out of, through, etc, sth** make a path by hacking at sth 从某物中劈出一条路来: *We hacked our way through the undergrowth.* 我们披荆斩棘在矮树丛中前进.

▷ **hack** *n* **1** act of chopping 砍; 劈. **2** kick with the toe of a boot 用靴头踢.

□ **hacking cough** short dry persistent cough (短促而持续的)干咳.

ˈ**hack-saw** *n* saw with a short narrow blade in a frame, used for cutting metal 弓锯, 钢锯(用于切割金属).

hack[2] /hæk; hæk/ *v* [I, Ipr, Tn] **~ (into) (sth)** (*computing infml* 计, 口) gain unauthorized access to (the contents of a computerized storage system, eg a database) 私自存取(计算机化存储系统, 如数据库中的资料).

▷ **hacker** *n* (*infml* 口) **1** person whose hobby is programming or using computers 计算机迷. **2** person who hacks (HACK[2]) 私自存取计算机中资料者.

hack[3] /hæk; hæk/ *n* **1** horse for ordinary riding or one that may be hired 日常骑用的马; 供出租的马. **2** person paid to do hard and uninteresting work, esp as a writer 受雇从事辛苦而乏味之工作的人; (尤指)雇佣文人: *a publisher's hack* 受雇于出版商的文人 ○ [attrib 作定语] *a hack journalist* 受雇佣的记者 ○ *hack work* 雇佣工作. **3** (*US infml* 口) (**a**) taxi 计程车. (**b**) taxi driver 计程车司机.

▷ **hack** *v* [I, Ip] **1** (*Brit*) ride on horseback at an ordinary pace, esp along roads (以普通速度)骑马(尤指沿路骑行): *go hacking* (以普通速度)骑马. **2** (*US infml* 口) drive a taxi 驾驶计程车.

hackles /ˈhæklz; ˋhækl̩z/ *n* [pl] **1** long feathers on the neck of the domestic cock, etc or hairs on the neck of a dog (雄鸡等家禽颈上的)长羽毛; (狗的)颈部的毛. **2** (idm 习语) **make sb's ˈhackles rise/raise sb's ˈhackles** make sb angry 激怒某人. **with one's ˈhackles up** angry and ready to fight 怒气冲冲地要动武.

hack·ney car·riage /ˈhæknɪ kærɪdʒ; ˋhæknɪ ˌkærɪdʒ/ (also **hackney cab**) (*dated* 旧 *Brit*) taxi 计程车.

hack·neyed /ˈhæknɪd; ˋhæknɪd/ *adj* (of a phrase, saying, etc) used so often that it has become trite and dull (指词语、言辞等)陈腐的, 老生常谈的.

had *pt, pp* of HAVE.

had·dock /ˈhædək; ˈhædək/ *n* (*pl* unchanged 复数不变) [C, U] sea-fish like cod but smaller, used for food 黑线鳕(海鱼,用作食物).

Hades /ˈheɪdi:z; ˈhediz/ *n* [sing] (in Greek mythology) place where the spirits of the dead go; the underworld (希腊神话中的)冥府, 阴间.

hadji (also **hajji**) /ˈhædʒɪ; ˈhædʒi/ *n* Muslim who has been to Mecca as a pilgrim 去麦加朝拜过的伊斯兰教徒.

haem·ato·logy (also *esp US* **hem-**) /hi:məˈtɒlədʒɪ; ˌhiməˈtɑlədʒɪ/ *n* [U] scientific study of the blood and its diseases 血液学. ▷ **haem·ato·lo·gist** (also *esp US* **hem-**) *n*.

haem(o)- (also *esp US* **hem(o)-**) *comb form* 构词成分 of blood 血液的: *haematology* ○ *haemophilia*.

hae·mo·globin (also *esp US* **hem-**) /ˌhi:məˈgləʊbɪn; ˌhiməˈglobɪn/ *n* [U] substance carrying oxygen in the red blood-cells of vertebrates 血红蛋白.

hae·mo·philia (also *esp US* **hem-**) /ˌhi:məˈfɪlɪə; ˌhiməˈfɪlɪə/ *n* [U] disease, usu inherited, that causes the sufferer to bleed severely from even a slight injury, because the blood fails to clot normally 血友病.

▷ **hae·mo·phil·iac** (also *esp US* **hem-**) /ˌhi:məˈfɪlɪæk; ˌhiməˈfɪlɪˌæk/ *n* person who suffers from haemophilia 血友病患者.

haem·or·rhage (also *esp US* **hem-**) /ˈhemərɪdʒ; ˈhɛmə,rɪdʒ/ *n* **1** [U] (esp heavy) bleeding (尤指大量的)出血. **2** [C] escape of blood 失血.

▷ **haem·or·rhage** *v* [I] bleed heavily; undergo a haemorrhage 大出血.

haem·or·rhoids (also *esp US* **hem-**) /ˈhemərɔɪdz; ˈhɛmə,rɔɪdz/ (also **piles**) *n* [pl] swollen veins at or near the anus 痔(内痔或外痔).

haft /hɑ:ft; *US* hæft; hæft/ *n* handle of an axe, a knife, etc (斧、刀等的)柄.

hag /hæg; hæg/ *n* (*derog* 贬) ugly old woman or witch 丑老太婆; 巫婆.

hag·gard /ˈhægəd; ˈhægəd/ *adj* looking tired and unhappy, esp from worry, lack of sleep, etc 憔悴的, 形容枯槁的(尤因忧愁或缺觉等所致): *a haggard face* 枯槁的脸 ○ *He looks haggard.* 他显得很憔悴.

hag·gis /ˈhægɪs; ˈhægɪs/ *n* [C, U] Scottish dish made from sheep's heart, lungs and liver 用羊的心、肺及肝制成的苏格兰食品: *Would you like some more haggis?* 再吃点苏格兰羊杂碎好吗?

H

haggle /ˈhægl; ˈhægl/ *v* [I, Ipr] **~ (with sb) (over/about sth)** argue (esp about the price, etc when agreeing upon the terms of a sale or other transaction) 争论; (尤指)讨价还价: *It's not worth haggling over a few pence.* 为几便士争论不休实在不值得.

ha·gio·graphy /ˌhægɪˈɒgrəfɪ; ˌhægɪˈɑgrəfɪ/ *n* [U, C] **1** writing about the lives of saints 圣徒传记. **2** biographical writing that is too full of praise for its subject 充满溢美之辞的传记.

hag·rid·den /ˈhægrɪdn; ˈhæg,rɪdn̩/ *adj* **1** troubled by bad dreams 受噩梦惊扰的. **2** very worried 非常苦恼的: *a hagridden look* 愁眉苦脸的样子.

ha-ha /ˈhɑ:hɑ:; ˈhɑ,hɑ/ *n* ditch with a wall or fence in it, forming a boundary to a park or garden without interrupting the view (有墙或篱筑于其间的)壕沟(作公园或花园的边界而不致妨碍视线).

hail[1] /heɪl; hel/ *n* **1** [U] frozen rain falling in a shower 雹; 冰雹. **2** [sing] (*fig* 比喻) thing coming in great numbers and with force 来得又多又猛的事物: *a hail of bullets, blows, curses* 一阵弹雨、乱打、乱骂.

▷ **hail** *v* **1** [I] fall as hail in a shower 下雹: *It is hailing.* 正在下雹. **2** [I, Ip, Tn, Tn·p] **~ (sth) down (on sb)** (*fig* 比喻) come or send (sth) down hard and fast 迅而猛地落下; 使(某事物)迅而猛地落下: *Stones hailed down on them.* 石头像雹子一样落在他们身上. ○ *They hailed curses down on us.* 他们大骂了我们一通.

□ ˈ**hailstone** *n* (usu *pl* 通常作复数) small ball of hail 雹粒.

ˈ**hailstorm** *n* period of heavy hail 雹暴.

hail[2] /heɪl; hel/ *v* **1** [Tn] (**a**) call to (a person or ship) in order to attract attention 招呼(人或船): *within* ˈ*hailing distance*, ie close enough to be hailed 在可以招呼的距离内. (**b**) signal to (a taxi, etc) to stop 打信号示意(计程车等)停下. **2** [Cn·n/a] **~ sb/sth as sth** enthusiastically acknowledge sb/sth as sth 热情地承认某人[某事物]为...: *crowds hailing him as king, as a hero* 拥他为王、赞他为英雄的群众 ○ (*fig* 比喻) *The book was hailed as a masterpiece/as masterly.* 这本书被誉为杰作. **3** [Ipr] **~ from...** originate from (a place) 来自(某地): *She hails* (ie comes) *from India.* 她来自印度. ○ *Where does the ship hail from?* ie Which is her home port? 这条船是从哪里开出来的(船籍港是何处)? **4** (idm 习语) **be** ˌ**hail-fellow-well-**ˈ**met (with sb)** be very friendly or too friendly (with people, esp strangers) (与人, 尤指生人)十分友好或过于亲昵.

▷ **hail** *interj* (*arch* 古) welcome! 欢迎!: *Hail, Caesar!* 凯撒大帝万岁! — *n* [U] (idm 习语) **within** ˈ**hail** close enough to be hailed 在招呼能及的地方.

hair /heə(r); hɛr/ *n* **1** (**a**) [C] one of the fine thread-like strands that grow from the skin of people and animals (人或动物的)毛发(指单根): *two blonde hairs on his coat collar* 留在他外衣领子上的金发女子的两根头发 ○ *There's a hair in my soup.* 我的汤里有根毛. (**b**) [U] mass of these, esp on the human head 毛发; (尤指)头发: *have one's* ˈ*hair cut* 理发 ○ *have long, black hair* 长着一头长、黑发 ○ *a cat with a fine coat of hair* 长着一身好毛的猫. (**c**) [C] thread-like growth on the stems and leaves of some plants (某些植物的茎和叶上长的)茸毛. **2** (idm 习语) **(by) a** ˈ**hair/a** ˌ**hair's** ˈ**breadth** (by) a very small amount or distance (以)极少的数量或极短的距离: *She won by a* ˈ*hair.* 她以微弱的优势获胜. ○ *We escaped by a hair's* ˈ*breadth.* 我们从九死一生的险境中逃出. ○ [attrib 作定语] *a* ˌ*hair's-breadth e*ˈ*scape* 九死一生的逃亡. **get/have sb by the short hairs** ⇨ SHORT[1]. **get in sb's** ˈ**hair** be a burden to or annoy sb 给某人添麻烦; 惹恼某人. **a/the hair of the** ˈ**dog (that** ˈ**bit you)** (*infml* 口) another alcoholic drink to cure the effects of drink 可解酒的另一种酒. **hang by a hair/a thread** ⇨ HANG[1]. **(not) harm, etc a hair of sb's** ˈ**head** (not) injure sb, even in the slightest way (不)损某人一根毫毛. **have a good, etc head of hair** ⇨ HEAD[1]. **keep your** ˈ**hair on** (*catchphrase* 警语) don't become angry; remain calm 别发火; 保持冷静. **let one's** ˈ**hair down** (*infml* 口) relax after a period of being formal (不再拘谨之后)放松一下. **make sb's** ˈ**hair curl** (*infml* 口) horrify sb 使某人感到惊骇: *The clothes some young people wear nowadays really make your hair curl.* 现今有些年轻人穿的衣服的确令人惊诧. **make one's** ˈ**hair stand on end** fill one with fright or horror 使人毛骨悚然. **neither hide nor hair of sb/sth** ⇨ HIDE[2]. **not turn a** ˈ**hair** not show fear, dismay, surprise, etc when such a reaction might be expected 竟然一点也不畏惧、惊慌、惊奇等. **split hairs** ⇨ SPLIT. **tear one's hair** ⇨ TEAR[2].

▷ **-**ˈ**haired** (in compound *adjs* 用以构成复合形容词) with hair of the specified kind 有某种毛发的: *a* ˌ*curly-haired* ˈ*girl*.

hair·less *adj* without hair; bald 无毛发的; 秃的.

hairy *adj* (**-ier, -iest**) **1** of or like hair (似)毛发的. **2** having much hair 多毛的: *a hairy chest* 长有许多毛的胸部. **3** (*sl* 俚) difficult; unpleasant 困难的; 令人不快的: *Driving on icy roads can be pretty hairy.* 在结冰的道路上开车有时真使人心惊胆战. **hairi·ness** *n* [U].

□ ˈ**hairbrush** *n* brush for the hair 发刷; 毛刷. ⇨illus at BRUSH 见 BRUSH 插图.

ˈ**haircloth** *n* cloth made of a mixture of fabric and animal's hair 马尾衬; 毛布.

ˈ**haircut** *n* **1** cutting the hair 理发: *You ought to have a haircut.* 你该理发了. **2** style in which hair is cut 发式; 发型: *That's a nice haircut.* 那个发式很漂亮.

ˈ**hair-do** *n* (*pl* **~s**) (*infml* 口) style or process of arranging (esp a woman's) hair 发式, 发型, 做头发(尤指女子的): *She has a new hair-do.* 她的头发式样很新.

ˈ**hairdresser** *n* person whose business is to arrange and cut hair 美发师; 理发师. Cf 参看 BARBER. ˈ**hairdressing** *n* [U].

ˈ**hair-drier** (also ˈ**hair-dryer**) *n* device for drying the hair by blowing hot air over it (吹干头发用的)吹风机.

ˈ**hair-grip** (also **grip**) *n* (*Brit*) flat clip with two ends close together, used for holding the hair in place 发夹.

ˈ**hair-line** *n* **1** edge of a person's hair round the face 发型正面的轮廓线. **2** (*fig* 比喻) very thin line 极细的线:

[attrib 作定语] *a* ˌ*hair-line* ˈ*crack*/ˈ*fracture* 细小的裂纹[裂缝].

ˈ**hair-net** *n* net for keeping the hair in place 发网.

ˈ**hair-oil** *n* oil for dressing the hair 发油.

ˈ**hair-piece** *n* false hair worn to increase the amount of a person's natural hair 假发.

ˈ**hairpin** *n* U-shaped pin for keeping the hair in position U形发夹. ˌ**hairpin** ˈ**bend** very sharp bend in a road, esp a very steep road (尤指在很陡的道路上的)急转弯处.

ˈ**hair-raising** *adj* terrifying 使人毛发悚立的; 吓人的.

ˈ**hair-restorer** *n* [C, U] substance used to promote growth of hair 生发剂.

ˌ**hair** ˈ**shirt** shirt made of rough cloth and therefore uncomfortable, worn by penitents or ascetics 粗毛布衬衫(忏悔者或苦行者穿的).

ˈ**hair-slide** (also **slide**) *n* (*Brit*) clip for keeping the hair in position 发夹.

ˈ**hair-splitting** *n* [U] making small unimportant distinctions 作过于琐细的分辨.

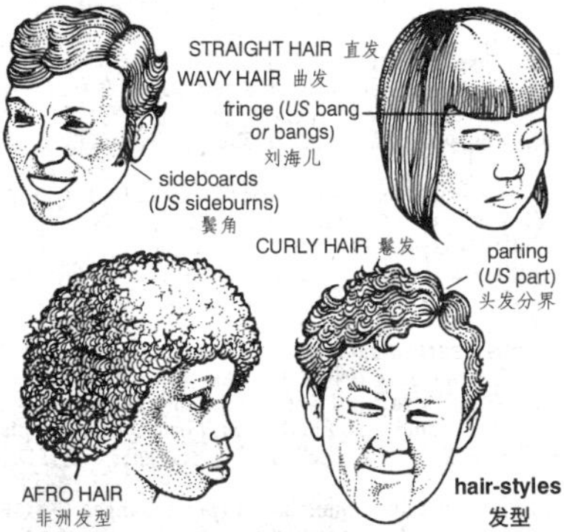

hair-styles
发型

ˈ**hair-style** *n* particular way of arranging or cutting the hair 发式; 发型. ⇨illus 见插图. ˈ**hair-stylist** *n* hairdresser 美发师; 理发师.

ˈ**hair-trigger** *n* trigger that causes a gun to fire at the very slightest pressure (枪的)微力扳机.

hair·spring /ˈheəsprɪŋ; ˋhɛrˌsprɪŋ/ *n* fine spring in a watch, controlling the balance-wheel (表的)游丝(控制摆轮的细小弹簧).

hake /heɪk; hek/ *n* (*pl* unchanged 复数不变) [C, U] fish of the cod family, used as food 鳕鱼(可食).

halal (also **hal·lal**) /hɑːˈlɑːl; həˋlɑl/ *v* [Tn] kill (animals for meat) as prescribed by Muslim law (按伊斯兰教教规的规定)宰杀(肉畜).

▷ **halal** *n* [U] meat prepared in this way (伊斯兰教的)合法肉食.

hal·cyon /ˈhælsɪən; ˋhælsɪən/ *adj* (*dated or rhet* 旧或修辞) peaceful and happy 太平而幸福的: *the halcyon days of youth* 青春的好年华.

hale /heɪl; hel/ *adj* (idm 习语) **hale and** ˈ**hearty** (esp of an old person) strong and healthy (尤指老年人)健壮的; 矍铄的.

half[1] /hɑːf; *US* hæf; hæf/ *n* (*pl* **halves** /hɑːvz; *US* hævz; hævz/) **1** either of two equal or corresponding parts into which a thing is divided 半; 一半: *I broke the chocolate into halves — here's your half.* 我把巧克力掰成两半——这一半给你. ○ *John and Liz shared the prize money between them — John used his half to buy a word processor.* 约翰和利兹二人把奖金分了——约翰用他分到的那一半奖金购买了文字处理机. ○ *Two halves make a whole.* 两个一半就是整个. ○ *The second half of the book is more exciting than the first.* 这本书的后半部比前半部更精彩. ○ *two and a half ounces, hours, miles* 两盎司半、两个半小时、两英里半. ⇨Usage at ALL[1] 用法见 ALL[1]. **2** either of two (usu equal) periods of time into which a sports match, concert, etc is divided (体育比赛、音乐会等的)半场: *No goals were scored in the first half.* 上半场未能进球. **3** half-price ticket, esp for a child, on a bus or train (公共汽车或火车的)半票(尤指儿童票): *Two and two halves to the city centre, please.* 劳驾, 买去市中心的两张全票和两张半票. **4** = HALF-BACK (HALF[2]): *playing (at) left half* 打左前卫. **5** (*infml* 口 *esp Brit*) half a pint (esp of beer) 半品脱(尤指啤酒): *Two halves of bitter, please.* 请来两份半品脱苦啤酒. **6** (idm 习语) **and a** ˈ**half** (*infml* 口) of more than usual importance, excellence, size, etc 非同小可的; 非常出色的; 特大的: *That was a game and a half!* 那场比赛十分精彩! **one's better half** ⇨ BETTER[1]. **do nothing/not do anything by** ˈ**halves** do everything one is engaged in completely and thoroughly 做任何事情都力求完全彻底: *He's not a man who does things by halves — either he donates a huge sum to a charity or he gives nothing.* 他这个人做事一不做二不休——向慈善事业捐款不捐则已, 一捐就是一大笔. **break, chop, cut, tear, etc sth in** ˈ**half** cause sth to become separated into two parts by breaking, chopping, cutting, tearing, etc 把某物破、劈、切、撕…成两半: *I once saw a man tear a telephone directory in half.* 我有一次看见一个人把电话簿撕成了两半. **go half and** ˈ**half/go** ˈ**halves (with sb)** share the cost (of sth) equally 均摊(某物的)费用: *That was an expensive meal — let's go halves.* 那顿饭花了不少钱——费用咱们均摊吧. **the** ˈ**half of it** (*infml* 口) the most important part 最重要的部分: *You don't know the half of it.* 你不了解那最重要的部分. **how the other half lives** (knowledge or experience of a) way of life of a different social group, esp one much richer or poorer than oneself 另一类人的生活方式(尤指与自己贫富悬殊的人的); 对另一类人的生活方式的了解或体验: *He's been lucky all his life and has never had to find out how the other half lives.* 他享了一辈子的福, 从来不知道穷人生活的滋味.

NOTE ON USAGE 用法: **Quarter, half** and **whole** can all be nouns ☆ **quarter**、**half**、**whole** 均可用作名词: *Cut the apple into quarters.* 把苹果切成四瓣儿. ○ *Two halves make a whole.* 两个一半就是整个. **Whole** is also an adjective ☆ **whole** 亦为形容词: *I've been waiting here for a whole hour.* 我在这儿等了整整一个钟头. **Half** is also a determiner ☆ **half** 亦为限定词: *Half the work is already finished.* 这项工作已完成了一半. ○ *They spent half the time looking for a parking space.* 他们用了一半时间寻找停车场. ○ *Her house is half a mile down the road.* 她的房子位于沿此路往前走半英里的地方. It can be used as an adverb 这个词可作副词使用: *This meal is only half cooked.* 这顿饭煮得半生不熟.

half[2] /hɑːf; *US* hæf; hæf/ *indef det* **1** amounting to or forming a half 半; 一半: *half the men* 一半人员 ○ *half an hour/a half-hour*, ie thirty minutes 半小时 ○ *half a pint/a half-pint* 半品脱 ○ *half a dozen/a half-dozen*, ie six 半打(六个) ○ *He has a half share in the firm.* 他持有该公司的一半股分. ○ *Half the fruit was bad.* 水果有一半是坏的. Cf 参看 ALL[1], BOTH[1]. ⇨Usage at ALL[1] 用法见 ALL[1]. **2** (idm 习语) **half a minute, second, tick, etc** (*infml* 口) a short time 一会儿: *I'll be ready in half a minute.* 我马上就准备好. **half past** ˈ**one,** ˈ**two, etc**; *US* **half after** ˈ**one,** ˈ**two, etc** thirty minutes after (any hour on the clock) (一点半、两点半…). **half** ˈ**one,** ˈ**two, etc** (*Brit infml* 口) = HALF PAST ONE, TWO, ETC.

▷ **half** *indef pron* **1** quantity or amount that constitutes a half 半数: *Half of six is three.* 六的一半是三. ○ *Half of the plums are rotten.* 半数的李子腐烂了. ○ *Half of the money is mine.* 这钱的一半是我的. ○ *I only need half.* 我只需要半数. ○ *Out of 36 children, half passed.* 在36个儿童中, 有半数合格. **2** (idm 习语) **too clever, etc by** ˈ**half** far too clever, etc 太聪明等.

□ ˌ**half-and-**ˈ**half** *adj* [usu pred 通常作表语] being half one thing and half another 此物彼物各一半: *'How do you like your coffee?' 'Half-and-half* (ie Half coffee and half milk), *please.'* '您要什么样的咖啡?' '请来一样一半(即一半咖啡一半牛奶).'

ˈ**half-back** *n* (position of a) player between the forwards and the full back in football, hockey, etc (足球、曲棍球等的)中卫, 中卫队员.

ˌ**half** ˈ**board** provision of bed, breakfast and one main meal at a hotel, etc 半膳宿(在旅馆等处住宿并可享用早餐及一顿主餐). Cf 参看 FULL BOARD (FULL).

ˈ**half-brother** *n* brother with only one parent in common with another 同父异母或同母异父的兄弟.

ˈ**half-caste** (also ˈ**half-breed**) *n* (*sometimes derog* 有时作贬义) person of mixed race 混血儿.

ˌ**half ˈcock 1** position of the hammer of a gun when pulled half-way back (枪的)半击发状态(击锤向后拉到行程一半的位置上). **2** (idm 习语) **go off at half ˈcock** (of an event) fail because of being only half ready or badly prepared (指事情)因时机不成熟或未做好准备而未成功.

ˌ**half-ˈcrown** *n* (also ˌ**half a ˈcrown**) (*Brit*) (before 1971) coin or amount of 2½ shillings (1971年以前的)2先令6便士的硬币或金额.

ˌ**half ˈholiday** day of which the afternoon is taken as a holiday 半天休假日(下午为休假时间).

ˌ**half-ˈhourly** *adj*, *adv* (done or occurring) every thirty minutes 每半小时(做或发生)一次(的): *a half-hourly news bulletin* 每半小时发布一次的新闻简报 ○ *The buses run half-hourly.* 公共汽车每半小时一班.

ˌ**half-ˈlength** *adj* (of a portrait) of the upper half of a person (指肖像)上半身的.

ˈ**half-life** *n* time taken for the radioactivity of a substance to fall to half its original value 半衰期(某物质的放射性元素由原有量衰减到一半所需的时间).

ˈ**half-light** *n* [sing] dim imperfect light 灰暗的光; 半明半暗的光.

ˌ**half-ˈmast** *n* (idm 习语) **at half-mast** (**a**) (of a flag) half-way up a mast, as a mark of respect for a dead person (指旗)下半旗(以示哀悼): *Flags were (flown) at half-mast everywhere on the day of the king's funeral.* 国王安葬那天各处都下了半旗. (**b**) (*joc* 谑) (of full-length trousers) too short, so that the ankles are seen (指长裤)太短以致露出了脚踝的.

half ˈmoon 1 moon when only half its disc is illuminated 半月(月亮只现出一半). **2** time when this occurs 出现半月的时候. **3** object shaped like a half moon 半月形的物体.

half nelson /ˌhɑːf ˈnelsn; ˌhæfˈnɛlsən/ hold in wrestling with an arm under the opponent's arm and behind his back (摔跤时)侧面肩下握颈.

ˈ**half-note** *n* (*US*) = MINIM.

ˌ**half ˈpay** reduced pay given to sb who is not fully employed but not yet retired 半薪(支付给半退职员工的).

H

halfpenny /ˈheɪpnɪ; ˈhepnɪ/ *n* (*pl* usu **halfpennies** for separate coins, **halfpence** /ˈheɪpəns; ˈhepəns/ for a sum of money 复数通常作 **halfpennies** 或 **halfpence**, 指硬币作 **halfpennies**, 指币值作 **halfpence**) (*Brit*) obsolete coin, either (before 1971) one worth half a penny, or (after 1971) a smaller one worth half a (new) penny 半便士硬币(废用的硬币, 1971年以前面值为半便士, 1971年改为较小的硬币后, 面值为新币半便士).

halfpennyworth /ˈheɪpnɪwɜːθ; ˈhepənɪˌwɝθ/ (*Brit* **ha'p'orth**) *n* amount this would buy; very small amount 半便士能买到的东西; 极小数量.

ˌ**half-ˈprice** *adv* at half the usual price 以半价: *Children are (admitted) half-price.* 儿童半价(入场).

ˌ**half-seas-ˈover** *adj* [pred 作表语] (*dated infml* 旧, 口) half drunk 半醉不醒.

ˈ**half-sister** *n* sister with only one parent in common with another 同父异母或同母异父的姐妹.

ˌ**half-ˈsize** *adj* half the usual or regular size 半号尺码(按一般尺码减半).

ˌ**half-ˈterm** *n* short holiday half-way through a school term (学校的)期中假.

ˌ**half-ˈtime** *n* [sing] interval between the two halves of a game of football, hockey, etc (足球、曲棍球等比赛上下半场间的)中场休息: *The score at half-time was 2-2.* 上半场结束时比分为2比2. ○ [attrib 作定语] *the ˌhalf-time ˈscore* 上半场结束时的得分.

ˈ**half-tone** *n* **1** black-and-white illustration (eg in a book) in which light and dark shades are reproduced by small and large dots 网目版画. **2** (*US*) = SEMITONE.

ˈ**half-track** *n* vehicle, esp one for carrying troops, with wheels at the front and tracks (TRACK 7) at the back 半履带式车(前为车轮, 后为履带, 尤指军车).

ˈ**half-truth** *n* statement that gives only a part of the truth, and is intended to mislead 半真半假的陈述(内容真真假假, 意在误导对方).

ˌ**half-ˈway** *adj*, *adv* **1** situated between and at an equal distance from two places 位于中途(的); 半路上(的): *reach the half-ˈway point* 到达中间地点 ○ *meet ˌhalf-ˈway* 半路上相遇. **2** (idm 习语) **a ˌhalf-way ˈhouse** compromise between opposite attitudes, plans, etc (对立的态度、方案等的)折衷, 妥协. **meet sb half-way** ⇨ MEET[1].

ˈ**half-wit** *n* stupid or foolish person 笨人; 傻子. ˌ**half-ˈwitted** *adj*.

ˌ**half-ˈyearly** *adj*, *adv* (done or occurring) every half year 每半年(做或发生)一次(的): *meetings held at ˌhalf-yearly ˈintervals* 每隔半年举行一次的会议.

half[3] /hɑːf; *US* hæf; hæf/ *adv* **1** to the extent of half 半: *half full* 半满. **2** partly 部分地: *half cooked* 半生不熟的 ○ *half built* 部分建成的 ○ *I'm half inclined to agree.* 我比较同意. **3** (idm 习语) ˌ**half as ˌmany, ˌmuch, etc aˈgain** an increase of 50% of the existing number, amount, etc 在现有数目, 数量等上加50%: *There aren't enough chairs for the meeting — we need half as many again.* 供开会用的椅子数量不够——需要再增加一半. ○ *I'd like the photograph enlarged so that it's half as big again.* 我想把这张照片放大一半. ˌ**not ˈhalf** (**a**) (*infml* 口) not at all 一点也不: *It's ˌnot half ˈbad, your new flat*, ie I like it. 你这套新公寓很不错(我很喜欢). (**b**) (*sl* 俚) to the greatest possible extent 极其; 非常: *He didn't half swear*, ie He swore violently. 他大骂特骂. ○ *'Was she annoyed?' 'Not half!'*, ie She was extremely annoyed. '她很生气吗?''生气极了.'

□ ˌ**half-ˈbaked** *adj* (*infml* 口) stupid; foolish 笨的; 愚蠢的: *a ˌhalf-baked iˈdea* 愚蠢的想法.

ˌ**half-ˈcrazed** = CRAZED.

ˌ**half-ˈhardy** *adj* (of plants) able to grow in the open air at all times except in severe frost (指植物)半耐寒的(除严冬时节外一直可在户外生长的).

ˌ**half-ˈhearted** *adj* lacking enthusiasm; feeble 缺乏热情的; 不热心的; 无精打采的. ˌ**half-ˈheartedly** *adv*.

ˌ**half-ˈtimbered** *adj* (of a building) having walls of a wooden framework filled in with brick, stone or plaster (指建筑物)半木结构的(墙壁为木架加砖、石或灰泥筑成的).

hal·ibut /ˈhælɪbət; ˈhæləbət/ *n* (*pl* unchanged 复数不变) [C, U] large flat sea-fish used as food 大比目鱼(可食).

hal·ide /ˈheɪlaɪd; ˈhælaɪd/ *n* (*chemistry* 化) chemical compound of a halogen with another element or radical 卤化物.

hal·it·osis /ˌhælɪˈtəʊsɪs; ˌhæləˈtosɪs/ *n* [U] breath that smells unpleasant 口臭.

hall /hɔːl; hɔl/ *n* **1** (also ˈ**hallway**) [C] space or passage on the inside of the main entrance or front door of a building 门厅; 正门走廊: *Leave your coat in the hall.* 把你的大衣放在门厅里. **2** [C] building or large room for meetings, meals, concerts, etc 开会、用餐、音乐演出等用的建筑物或厅堂: *the Town ˈHall* 市政厅 ○ *ˈdance halls* 舞厅. **3** (**a**) [C] = HALL OF RESIDENCE. (**b**) [U] (in colleges at some English universities) large room for meals (英国一些大学各学院的)食堂: *dine in hall* 在学院食堂用餐. **4** [C] (in England) large country house, esp one that belongs to the chief landowner in the district (英国)大的庄园府第(尤指属于该地区最大之地主者). **5** (idm 习语) **Liberty Hall** ⇨ LIBERTY.

□ ˌ**hall of ˈresidence** (also **hall**) building for university students to live in (大学的)学生宿舍.

ˈ**hall-stand** *n* piece of furniture in the hall of a house, for hats, coats, umbrellas, etc 衣帽架.

ˈ**hallway** *n* **1** = HALL 1. **2** (*esp US*) corridor 走廊.

hal·lal = HALAL.

hal·le·lu·jah = ALLELUIA.

hal·liard = HALYARD.

hall·mark /ˈhɔːlmɑːk; ˈhɔlˌmɑrk/ *n* **1** mark used for indicating the standard of gold, silver and platinum on articles made of these metals (金、银及铂的制品上打的)纯度印记. **2** (*fig* 比喻) distinctive feature, esp of excellence 特点, 特征(尤指优良事物所具有者): *Attention to detail is the hallmark of a fine craftsman.* 能工巧匠的特点是一丝不苟.

▷ **hall·mark** *v* [Tn] stamp (sth) with a hallmark 给(某物)打上纯度标记.

hallo (also **hello, hullo**) /həˈləʊ; həˈlo/ *interj* (used in greeting, or to attract attention or express surprise, or to answer a telephone call 用作打招呼、引起注意、表示惊讶或接电话的招呼声: *Hello, how are you?* 嘿, 你好吗? ○ *Hallo, can you hear me?* 哎, 你听得见我说的话吗? ○ *Hullo, hullo, hullo, what's going on here?* 喂, 喂, 喂, 这里出了什么事了? ○ *Hallo, is that Oxford 56767?* 喂, 是牛津区56767吗?

▷ **hallo** (also **hello, hullo**) *n* (*pl* **~s**) the cry 'hallo' 打招呼或惊讶时发出的'嘿'、'哎'、'喂'等声音: *He gave me a cheery hallo.* 他高兴地向我打了一下招呼.

hal·loo /həˈluː; həˈlu/ *interj, n* cry used to urge on hounds or to attract attention (嗾狗追逐的叫声)嘿; (引起注意的呼语)哎.

▷ **hal·loo** *v* [I] shout 'halloo', esp to hounds 叫'嘿'(尤用以嗾狗).

hal·low /ˈhæləʊ; ˋhælo/ *v* [Tn usu passive 通常用于被动语态] make (sb/sth) holy; honour as holy 使(某人[某事物])成为神圣; 尊崇: *ground hallowed by sacred memories* 因在宗教上有纪念意义而视为神圣的土地.

Hal·low·e'en /ˌhæləʊˈiːn; ˌhæloˋin/ *n* 31 October, the eve of All Saints' Day 万圣节前夕(10月31日).

hal·lu·cin·ate /həˈluːsɪneɪt; həˋlusn̩ˌet/ *v* [I] imagine one is seeing or hearing sth when no such thing is present 在幻觉中看见或听见某事物: *Drug addicts often hallucinate.* 吸毒成瘾的人常常产生幻觉.

hal·lu·cina·tion /həˌluːsɪˈneɪʃn; həˌlusn̩ˋeʃən/ *n* **1** [C, U] illusion of seeing or hearing sth when no such thing is actually present 幻觉; 幻视; 幻听: *suffer from/have hallucinations* 产生[有]幻觉. **2** [C] thing seen or heard in this way 幻觉中的看到或听到的事物.

▷ **hal·lu·cin·at·ory** /həˈluːsɪnətrɪ, həˌluːsɪˈneɪtərɪ; *US* həˈluːsɪnətɔːrɪ; həˋlusn̩əˌtorɪ/ *adj* of or causing hallucinations 幻觉中的; 引起幻觉的: *a hallucinatory experience/drug* 幻觉中的体验[致幻药].

hal·lu·cin·ogen /həˈluːsɪnədʒen; həˋlusənədʒɛn/ *n* drug caus-ing hallucinations 致幻剂; 幻觉剂. ▷ **hal·lu·cin·ogenic** /həˌluːsɪnəˈdʒenɪk; həˌlusənəˋdʒɛnɪk/ *adj*.

halo /ˈheɪləʊ; ˋhelo/ *n* (**~es** or **~s**) (also **au·re·ola, au·re·ole**) **1** (in paintings, etc) circle of light shown round or above the head of a sacred figure (绘画等作品中)(环绕圣像头上的)光轮, 光环. **2** = CORONA.

hal·ogen /ˈhælədʒən; ˋhælədʒən/ *n* (*chemistry* 化) any of the chemical elements fluorine, chlorine, bromine and astatine which form salts by simple union with a metal 卤素: [attrib 作定语] *halogen lamps/headlights* 卤素灯[前灯].

halt /hɔːlt; hɔlt/ *n* **1** (**a**) [sing] temporary stop; interruption of progress 暂停; 停顿: *Work was brought/came to a halt when the machine broke down.* 机器出了毛病, 工作便停顿下来. (**b**) [C] (esp of soldiers) short stop on a march or journey (尤指军队)暂停行进, 途中休息. **2** [C] (*Brit*) place on a railway line where local trains stop, but where there are no station buildings (供慢车使用而无车站建筑物的)铁路小站. **3** (idm 习语) **bring sth/come to a grinding halt** ⇨ GRIND. **call a halt** ⇨ CALL². **grind to a halt/standstill** ⇨ GRIND.

▷ **halt** *v* [I, Tn] (cause sb/sth to) stop temporarily (使某人[某事物])暂停: *Platoon, halt!* 全排注意, 立定! ○ *The officer halted his troops for a rest.* 军官下令部队停下来休息.

hal·ter /ˈhɔːltə(r); ˋhɔltɚ/ *n* **1** rope or leather strap put round the head of a horse for leading or fastening it 笼头(套在马头上用以驭马或系马的绳子或皮条). **2** rope used for hanging a person 绞索. **3** (also **halter-neck**) style of woman's dress with the top held up by a strap passing round the back of the neck, leaving the back and shoulders bare (用带绕过颈后的)袒肩露背连衣裙.

halt·ing /ˈhɔːltɪŋ; ˋhɔltɪŋ/ *adj* [usu attrib 通常作定语] slow and hesitant, as if lacking in confidence 迟疑不决的; 犹豫的: *speak in a halting voice* 结结巴巴地说 ○ *a halting reply* 吞吞吐吐的回答 ○ *a toddler's first few halting steps* 孩子初学走路时那蹒跚的几步. ▷ **halt·ingly** *adv*: *speak haltingly* 犹豫地说.

halve /hɑːv; *US* hæv; hæv/ *v* [Tn] **1** divide (sth) into two equal parts 把(某物)对半分: *halve an apple* 把一个苹果分成两半. **2** reduce (sth) by a half 把(某物)减半: *The latest planes have halved the time needed for crossing the Atlantic.* 最新型号的飞机把飞越大西洋所需的时间减少了一半.

halves *pl* of HALF¹.

hal·yard (also **hal·liard**) /ˈhæljəd; ˋhæljɚd/ *n* rope for raising or lowering a sail or flag (帆和旗的)升降索.

ham /hæm; hæm/ *n* **1** (**a**) [C] upper part of a pig's leg, salted and dried or smoked for food 火腿: *several hams hanging on hooks* 挂在钩上的几只火腿. (**b**) [U] meat from this 火腿肉: *a slice of ham* 一片火腿 ○ [attrib 作定语] *a ham sandwich* 火腿三明治. Cf 参看 BACON, GAMMON, PORK. **2** [C] (esp of animals) back of the thigh; thigh and buttock (尤指动物)后腿, 股部和臀部. **3** [C] (*sl* 俚) person who acts or performs badly 拙劣的表演者: *He's a terrible ham.* 他的表演糟透了. ○ [attrib 作定语] *ham actors/acting* 蹩脚的演员[演出]. **4** [C] (*infml* 口) operator of an amateur radio station 业余无线电台的操作者: *a radio ham* 业余无线电台的收发报员.

▷ **ham** *v* (**-mm-**) [I, Ip, Tn, Tn·p] **~ (it/sth) (up)** (*sl* 俚) act in a deliberately artifical or exaggerated way; overact 以做作或夸张的方式作表演; 表演过火: *Do stop hamming!* 不要再做戏了吧! ○ *The actors were really hamming it up to amuse the audience.* 这些演员为博观众一粲, 表演得实在太过火了.

□ ˌ**ham-ˈfisted,** ˈ**ham-ˌhanded** *adjs* (*infml derog* 口, 贬) clumsy in using the hands 笨手笨脚的.

ham·burger /ˈhæmbɜːɡə(r); ˋhæmbɝɡɚ/ *n* **1** (also **burger**) [C] flat round cake of minced beef, usu fried and eaten with onions, often in a bread roll 汉堡牛肉饼; 汉堡包. **2** [U] (*US*) = MINCE *n*.

ham·let /ˈhæmlɪt; ˋhæmlɪt/ *n* small village, esp one without a church 小村庄(尤指无教堂的).

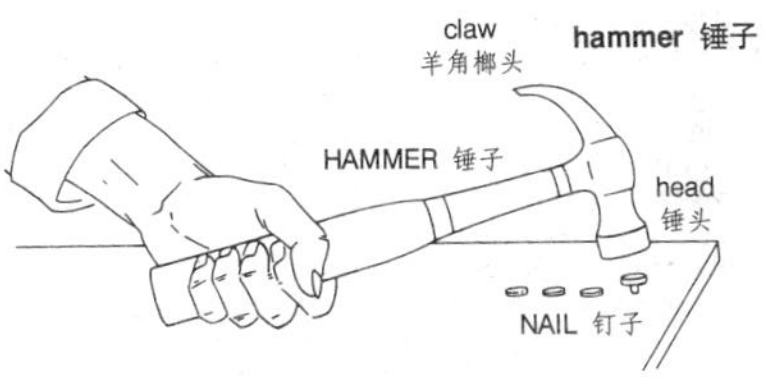

ham·mer¹ /ˈhæmə(r); ˋhæmɚ/ *n* **1** [C] tool with a heavy metal head at right angles to the handle, used for breaking things, driving nails in, etc 锤子; 榔头. ⇨illus 见插图. **2** [C] any of the parts of a piano that strike the strings (钢琴的)音锤. **3** [C] part of the firing device of a gun that explodes the charge (枪炮的)击铁(为引爆装置之一部分). **4** [C] instrument like a small wooden hammer used by an auctioneer to indicate with a rap that an article is sold (拍卖人用的)小木槌. **5** (**a**) [C] (in athletics) metal ball attached to a wire for throwing (体育)链球. (**b**) **the hammer** [sing] event in which this is thrown 掷链球比赛. **6** [C] (*anatomy* 解) bone in the ear (耳的)锤骨. **7** (idm 习语) **be/go at it/each other** ˈ**hammer and** ˈ**tongs** (of two people) argue or fight violently and noisily (指两人)激烈地争吵或打斗: *We could hear the neighbours going at each other hammer and tongs.* 我们可以听见邻居大吵大闹的声音. **come/go under the** ˈ**hammer** be sold at auction 被拍卖: *This painting came under the hammer at Christie's today.* 这幅画今天由克里斯蒂拍卖行拍卖了.

□ **hammer and sickle** symbols of the industrial worker and the peasant, used as the emblem of the USSR (代表产业工人和农民的)锤子镰刀图案(用作前苏联国徽).

ham·mer² /ˈhæmə(r); ˋhæmɚ/ *v* **1** [I, Ip, Tn] hit or beat (sth) with a hammer or as if with a hammer 锤打或似用锤般敲打(某物): *I could hear him hammering (away) in the house next door.* 我可以听见他在隔壁屋子里(不停地)锤打东西. ○ *hammer a sheet of copper* 把铜片锤平. **2** [Ipr] **~ at/on sth** strike sth loudly 打击某物发出大的声音: *hammer at the door*, ie with one's fists, a stick, etc 咚咚敲门(用拳头、棍棒等) ○ *He hammered on the table with his fist.* 他用拳头捶打桌子. **3** [Tn] (*infml* 口)

defeat (sb) utterly 彻底击败(某人): *Manchester United were hammered 5-1.* 曼彻斯特联队以1比5惨败. **4** [phr v] **hammer away at sth** work hard at sth 努力做某事: *hammer away at a difficult problem* 刻苦钻研一难题. **hammer sth down, off, etc** cause sth to fall down, etc by hammering 把某物锤倒、锤掉等: *hammer the door down* 将门锤倒. **hammer sth flat, straight, etc** make sth flat, etc by hammering 把某物锤平、锤直等. **hammer sth home** (**a**) hammer (a nail) in fully 把(钉子)锤打到位. (**b**) stress (a point, an argument, etc) so that it is fully understood 强调(某一点、某一论点等). **hammer sth in** force sth inwards by hammering 用锤将某物敲入: *hammer a nail in/hammer in a nail* 钉钉子. **hammer sth into sb** force sb to learn sth by repeating it many times 向某人反复灌输某事物: *They have had English grammar hammered into them.* 他们强制自己反复学习英语语法. **hammer sth into sth** (**a**) force sth to enter sth by hammering 将某物敲进或钉进某处: *hammer a nail into a wall* 把钉子敲进墙里. (**b**) fashion sth by hammering (esp metal) 把某物(尤指金属)锤成某种形状: *hammer copper into pots and pans* 把铜板锻造成罐子和盆子. **hammer sth out** (**a**) remove (a dent, etc) by hammering 用锤敲去(凹痕等). (**b**) devise (a plan, solution, etc): achieve sth by great effort 想出(方案、解决办法等); 竭力做成某事: *After much discussion the negotiators hammered out a compromise settlement.* 双方经多次谈判达成一项折衷的解决办法.

▷ **ham·mer·ing** /ˈhæmərɪŋ; ˋhæmərɪŋ/ *n* **1** noisy beathing or striking, esp with a hammer 击打(尤指用锤)的声音. **2** (*infml* 口) total defeat 彻底的失败: *Our team took a terrible hammering.* 我们队一败涂地.

ham·mock /ˈhæmək; ˋhæmək/ *n* bed made of canvas or rope netting, suspended by cords at the ends, used esp on board ship 吊床.

ham·per[1] /ˈhæmpə(r); ˋhæmpɚ/ *n* **1** large basket with a hinged lid, esp one containing food, wine, etc (有带铰链的盖子的)大篮子(尤指盛有食物、酒等的). **2** (*esp Brit*) box or parcel containing food, wine, etc sent as a gift (装有食品、酒等礼物的)盒子或包裹: *a Christmas hamper* 圣诞礼物篮.

ham·per[2] /ˈhæmpə(r); ˋhæmpɚ/ *v* [Tn] prevent the free movement or activity of (sb); hinder (sb/sth) 束缚(某人); 妨碍(某人[某事物]): *Our progress was hampered by the bad weather.* 我们前进时受到了恶劣天气的阻碍.

H

ham·ster /ˈhæmstə(r); ˋhæmstɚ/ *n* small rat-like rodent kept as a pet, with pouches in its cheeks for carrying grain 仓鼠(供玩赏的一种小鼠, 有颊囊可携谷粒).

ham·string /ˈhæmstrɪŋ; ˋhæm,strɪŋ/ *n* **1** any of the five tendons at the back of the human knee 腘绳肌腱. **2** thick tendon at the back of an animal's hock (动物跗关节后部的)大肌腱.

▷ **ham·string** *v* (*pt, pp* **hamstringed** or **hamstrung** /ˈhæmstrʌŋ; ˋhæm,strʌŋ/) [Tn] **1** cripple (a person or an animal) by cutting the hamstring(s) 割断腿筋使(人或动物)瘸腿. **2** (fig 比喻) destroy the activity or efficiency of (sb/sth) 使(某人[某事物])难以动作或难有作为: *The project was hamstrung by lack of funds.* 这个计划因缺乏资金而难以实现.

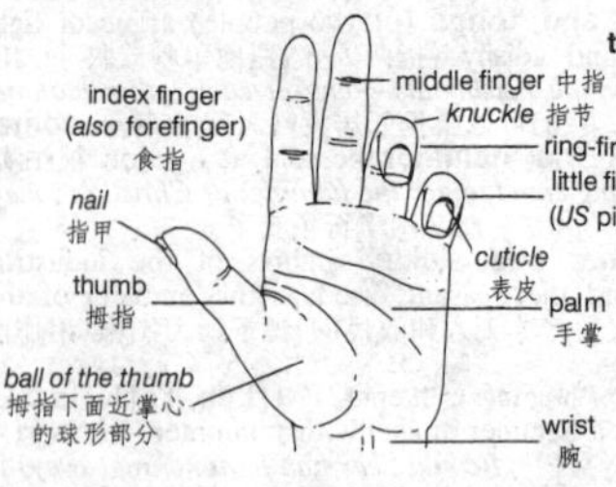

the hand 手

hand[1] /hænd; hænd/ *n* **1** [C] end part of the human arm below the wrist 手: *take/lead sb by the hand* 拉着某人的手[牵着某人的手走] ○ *have one's hands in one's pockets* 双手插在衣袋里. ⇨illus 见插图. **2 a hand** [sing] (*infml* 口) active help 积极的帮助: *Give (me) a hand with the washing-up.* 帮(我)洗洗餐具吧. ○ *Do you want/need a hand?* 你需要帮忙吗? **3** [C] pointer on a clock, dial, etc (时钟、仪表等的)指针: *the ˈhour/ˈminute/ˈsecond hand of a watch* 表的时[分/秒]针. **4** [C] (**a**) manual worker on a farm or in a factory, dockyard, etc (农场或工厂、船坞等的)从事体力劳动的工人; 劳工: *ˈfarm-hands* 农场工人. (**b**) member of a ship's crew 船员: *All hands* (ie All seamen are needed) *on deck!* 所有船员都到甲板上来! **5** [sing] skill in using the hands 手艺; 技能: *He has a light hand with pastry,* ie makes it well. 他很会做糕点. **6** [C] (**a**) set of cards dealt to a player in a card-game (纸牌戏中拿到的)一手牌: *have a good, bad, poor, etc hand* 拿到一手好、坏、糟...牌. (**b**) one round in a game of cards (纸牌戏的)一局: *Let's play one more hand.* 我们再打一局吧. **7** [sing] style of handwriting 书法: *He has/writes a good/legible hand.* 他字写得好[清楚]. **8** [sing] (*dated or fml* 旧或文) promise to marry 许婚: *He asked for her hand.* 他向她求婚. ○ *She gave him her hand (in marriage).* 她同意嫁给他. **9** [C] unit of measurement, about four inches (10.16 cm), used for measuring the height of a horse 一手之宽(约四英寸, 即10.16厘米, 用以量马的高度). **10** (idm 习语) **all ˌhands to the ˈpump** (*saying* 谚) everyone must help 人人都该出把力: *We've an urgent job on this week, so it's (a case of) all hands to the pump.* 我们本周有紧急任务, 所以人人都该出把力. **at first, second, etc ˈhand** directly/indirectly from the original source 直接、间接...地: *I only heard the news at second hand.* 我只是间接听到这个消息的. **(close/near) at ˈhand** (**a**) near; close by 在附近; 在手头: *He lives close at hand.* 他住在附近. (**b**) (*fml* 文) about to happen 即将发生: *Your big moment is at hand.* 你的重大时刻即将到来. **at sb's hands** from sb 出自某人之手: *I did not expect such unkind treatment at your hands.* 我没想到你如此刻薄. **be a dab, an old, a poor, etc hand (at sth)** have (or lack) the specified skill or experience 有(或缺乏)某种技能或经验: *He's an old hand* (ie very experienced) *at this game.* 他是玩这种游戏的老手(很有经验). ○ *I was never much of a hand* (ie never very good) *at cookery.* 我从来不是干烹饪的好手(未做过好饭菜). **bind/tie sb hand and ˈfoot** (**a**) tie sb's hands and feet together 捆住某人的手脚. (**b**) (*fig* 比喻) take away sb's freedom of action 使某人不能行动自如. **a bird in the hand is worth two in the bush** ⇨ BIRD. **bite the hand that feeds one** ⇨ BITE[1]. **blood on one's hands** ⇨ BLOOD[1]. **bring sb/sth up by hand** rear (a person or an animal) by feeding from a bottle 用奶瓶喂养(人或动物): *The lamb had to be brought up by hand.* 这只小羊要用奶瓶喂养. **by ˈhand** (**a**) by a person, not a machine 用手而不用机器; 以手工: *made by hand* 手工制作的. (**b**) by a messenger (not through the post) 由传递者(非经邮局): *The note was delivered by hand.* 这封短信经由专人送交. **by one's own fair hand** ⇨ FAIR[1]. **cap in hand** ⇨ CAP. **change hands** ⇨ CHANGE[1]. **the dead hand of sth** ⇨ DEAD. **the devil makes work for idle hands** ⇨ DEVIL[1]. **eat out of sb's hand** ⇨ EAT. **fall, etc into sb's, etc ˈhands** be taken or obtained (esp by an enemy) 落入某人(尤指敌人)之手; 为某人所获得: *The town fell into enemy hands.* 该城已落到敌人手中. ○ *I would hate my diary to get into the wrong hands.* 我不愿意别人看我的日记. **a firm hand** ⇨ FIRM[1]. **fold one's hands** ⇨ FOLD[1]. **force sb's hand** ⇨ FORCE[2]. **from ˌhand to ˈhand** from one person to another 从一人之手转到另一人之手: *Buckets of water were passed from hand to hand to put the fire out.* 人们一桶又一桶传递着水以便把火扑灭. **gain/win sb's hand** (*fml* 文) make sb promise to marry one 获得某人本人对婚事的应允. **gain, get, etc the upper hand** ⇨ UPPER. **get one's eye/hand in** ⇨ EYE[1]. **get, have, etc a free hand** ⇨ FREE[1]. **give sb/get a big hand** ⇨ BIG. **give one's ˈhand on sth** (*fml* 文) take sb's hand and clasp it when agreeing to sth 紧握某人的手表示同意某事物. **(be) ˌhand in ˈglove (with sb)** working in close association 密切合作: *He was found to be hand in glove with the enemy.* 已发现他跟敌人勾结在一起. **ˌhand in ˈhand** (**a**) holding each other's hand 手拉手. ⇨illus at ARM 见ARM插图. (**b**) (*fig* 比喻) closely associated; linked together 密切关联的; 连在一起的: *War and suffering go* *hand in hand.* 战争和苦难是同时并存的. **ˌhand over ˈhand** using one's hands alternately (as when climbing) 双手交替使用(如攀登时). **ˌhands ˈoff (sth/sb)** (*infml* 口) don't touch (sth/sb); don't interfere 不许触及(某物[某人]); 不许干涉: *ˌHands off my ˈsandwiches!* 别动我的三明治! **ˌhands ˈup (a)** (said when addressing a group of people) raise one hand (eg to show agreement or to answer a question) (对大家说的话)举手(举一只手, 如用以表示同意或准备回答问题): *Hands up, anyone who knows the answer.* 能回答的举手. **(b)** raise both hands (eg to show that one is surrendering) 举手(举双手, 如表示投降): *Hands up and drop your gun!* 举起手来, 把抢放下! **ˌhand to ˈhand** (of fighting) involving physical contact with one's opponent 短兵相接; 肉搏: [attrib 作定语] *hand-to-hand combat* 肉搏战. **have/take a hand in sth** participate in sth; be partly responsible for sth 参与或介入某事物; 对某事物有一定责任: *I bet he had a ˈhand in it.* 我敢说他一定参与了此事. **have one's ˈhands free/tied** be/not be in a position to do as one likes 可以[不能]自行其是. **have one's ˈhands full** be so busy that one cannot undertake anything else 忙得腾不出手来; 无暇兼顾. **have sb in the palm of one's hand** ⇨ PALM[1]. **have time on one's hands/time to kill** ⇨ TIME[1]. **have, etc the whip hand** ⇨ WHIP. **a heavy hand** ⇨ HEAVY. **a helping hand** ⇨ HELP[1]. **hold sb's ˈhand** comfort or help sb in a sad or difficult situation 安慰或帮助某人(减轻痛苦或摆脱困境). **hold ˈhands (with sb)** sit, walk, etc beside another person with hands linked, usu as a sign of affection 与别人手拉手地坐着、行走等(通常含有爱意): *two lovers holding hands* 手拉着手的一对恋人. **in ˈhand (a)** in one's possession and available for use 在手中(持有); 在手头(随时可用): *I still have some money in hand.* 我手中还有些钱. ○ *Cash in hand, £37.25.* 手头现金共37.25英镑. **(b)** in control 在控制下: *We have the situation well in hand.* 我们完全控制住了局面. **(c)** receiving attention and being dealt with 得到照顾并在处理之中: *the job in hand* 正在办理的工作 ○ *The work is in hand and will soon be completed.* 这工作在进行中, 不久即可完成. **in one's/sb's ˈhands** in one's/sb's possession, control or care 在本人的[某人的]支配、控制、照料或监护之下: *The affair is no longer in my hands.* 这事已不归我管了. ○ *Put the matter in the hands of a solicitor.* 把这事交给律师去办. **in capable, good, etc ˈhands** being well managed, etc 在妥善的管理等中: *I've left the department in Bill's very efficient hands.* 我已把这个部门交由非常得力的比尔去管理. **an iron fist/hand in a velvet glove** ⇨ IRON[1]. **join hands** ⇨ JOIN. **keep one's ˈhand in** retain one's skill by practice 藉练习以保持熟练程度: *I like to play tennis regularly, just to keep my hand in.* 我喜欢经常打打网球, 以免技术生疏. **know (a place) like the back of one's hand** ⇨ KNOW. **lay one's ˈhands on sb/sth (a)** find sb/sth 找到某人[某物]: *The book's here somewhere, but I can't lay my hands on it just now.* 那本书就放在这儿的什么地方, 但我现在就是找不到. **(b)** (*infml* 口) catch sb/sth 捉住某人[某物]: *If I ever lay my hands on the thief, he'll be sorry.* 我要是什么时候抓到了那个贼, 有他好受的. **(c)** (of a priest) put the hands on the head of sb, to bless, confirm or ordain him (指牧师)对某人行按手礼(将双手按在某人的头上表示祝福、对其施行坚信礼或授予圣职). **lend a hand** ⇨ LEND. **lift/raise a finger/hand (to do sth)** ⇨ LIFT. **lift/raise a/one's ˈhand against sb** threaten or attack sb 威胁或攻击某人. **live from ˌhand to ˈmouth** satisfy only one's present basic needs (esp for food) 仅能满足眼前的基本需要(尤指食物方面的需要): [attrib 作定语] *a hand-to-mouth existence* 仅能糊口的生活. **make money hand over fist** ⇨ MONEY. **many hands make light work** (*saying* 谚) a task is soon completed if many people help 人多好办事. **not do a hand's ˈturn** not do any work 什么工作也不做: *He never does a hand's turn around the house — his wife does everything.* 家里的事儿他从来都不做——一切都由妻子操劳. **off one's ˈhands** no longer one's responsibility 不再承担责任: *They'll be glad to get their son off their hands.* 他们再不必为儿子操心, 感到很高兴. **offer one's hand** ⇨ OFFER. **on either/every ˈhand** (*fml* 文) on both/all sides 在两[每一]边; 在两个[各个]方面. **on ˈhand** available 现有(随时可用). **on one's ˈhands** resting on one as a responsibility 由本人照管; 由本人处理; 由本人负责: *I have an empty house on my hands,* eg one for which I want to find a buyer or tenant. 我手中有一所空房子要处理(如想找买家或租客). **on the ˈone hand... on the ˈother (hand)...** (used to indicate contrasting points of view, opinions, etc 用以引导出相互矛盾的观点、意见等). **out of ˈhand (a)** out of control; undisciplined 无法控制; 无纪律: *The football fans have got completely out of hand.* 那些足球迷已经完全失去控制. **(b)** at once; without further thought 立即; 不假思索地: *The proposal was rejected out of hand.* 这个建议当即遭到了拒绝. **ˌout of one's ˈhands** no longer under one's control 不再受本人控制: *I can't help you, I'm afraid — the matter is out of my hands.* 我爱莫能助, 很抱歉——此事已非我力所能及. **overplay one's hand** ⇨ OVERPLAY. **ˌplay into sb's ˈhands** do sth that is to (an opponent's) advantage 做有利于(对手)的蠢事; 让(对手)占便宜. **put one's ˌhand in one's ˈpocket** be ready to spend or give money 伸手掏腰包(准备花钱或付款). **putty in sb's hands** ⇨ PUTTY. **see, etc sb's hand in sth** notice sb's (esp unfriendly or harmful) influence in sth 注意到某人对某事物的(尤指坏的)影响: *Do I detect your hand in this?* 你在这件事情上起的作用, 能瞒得了我吗? **set one's hand to sth** (*dated or fml* 旧或文) sign (esp a formal document) 签署(尤指正式文件): *set one's hand to a treaty* 在条约上签字. **shake sb's hand/shake hands/shake sb by the hand** ⇨ SHAKE[1]. **show one's hand/cards** ⇨ SHOW[2]. **a show of hands** ⇨ SHOW[1]. **sit on one's hands** ⇨ SIT. **sleight of hand** ⇨ SLEIGHT. **take one's courage in both hands** ⇨ COURAGE. **ˌtake sb in ˈhand** take control of sb in order to improve his behaviour 管教某人: *Those dreadful children need to be taken in hand.* 那些讨厌的孩子需要加以管教. **take the law into one's own hands** ⇨ LAW. **take one's life in one's hands** ⇨ LIFE. **take matters into one's own hands** ⇨ MATTER[1]. **throw one's ˈhand in** (*infml* 文) abandon sth in which one is engaged 从正在做的某事中退出; 放弃某事物. **time hangs/lies heavy on one's hands** ⇨ TIME[1]. **to ˈhand (a)** within reach; readily available 在手头; 随时可用: *I don't have the information to hand.* 我手头没有现成的资料. **(b)** (*commerce* 商) received 收到: *Your letter is to hand,* ie has reached me and is receiving attention. 来函敬悉. **try one's hand** ⇨ TRY[1]. **turn one's hand to sth** (be able to) undertake sth (能够)担任某工作: *She can turn her hand to all sorts of jobs.* 她能做各种工作. **wait on sb hand and foot** ⇨ WAIT[1]. **wash one's hands of sb/sth** ⇨ WASH[2]. **win hands down** ⇨ WIN. **wring one's hands** ⇨ WRING.

▷ **-handed** (in compound *adjs* 用以构成复合形容词) **1** having hands as specified 有某类型手的: *big-handed.* **2 (a)** using the specified hand usually, in preference to the other 常用某只手的(而不常用另一只手): *right-handed people.* **(b)** made by or for the specified hand 用某只手做的; 为某只手做的: *a left-handed blow* ○ *a one-handed catch.*

hand·ful /ˈhændfʊl; ˋhændfʊl/ *n* (*pl* **-fuls**) **1** [C] **~ (of sth)** as much or as many as can be held in one hand 一把: *pick up a handful of sand* 抓起一把沙子. **2** [sing] **~ (of sb/sth)** small number 少数; 少量: *a handful of people* 少数几个人. **3 a handful** [sing] (*infml* 口) person or animal that is difficult to control 难控制的人或动物: *That young lad is quite a handful,* ie is lively and troublesome. 那个小伙子真难管束(活泼而淘气).

□ **ˈhandbag** (*US* **purse**) *n* small bag for money, keys, etc, carried esp by women (装钱、钥匙等的)小手提包(尤指女用的). ⇨illus at LUGGAGE 见 LUGGAGE 插图.

ˈhand-baggage *n* [U] (*US*) = HAND-LUGGAGE.

ˈhandball *n* [U] any of several games in which players throw a ball to each other or hit it (usu with a gloved hand) against a wall 手球运动.

ˈhand-barrow *n* light two-wheeled barrow (两轮的)手推车.

ˈhandbill *n* printed advertisement or announcement distributed by hand 传单.

ˈhandbook *n* small book giving useful facts; guidebook 手册; 指南: *a car handbook* 汽车手册 ○ *a handbook of wild flowers* 野生花卉手册. Cf 参看 MANUAL *n* 1.

ˈ**handbrake** *n* (in a motor vehicle) brake operated by hand, used when the vehicle is stationary (机动车的)手刹车, 手闸: *Don't drive with the handbrake on.* 手闸扳上时不可开车. ⇨illus at App 1 见附录1插图, page xii.

ˈ**handcart** *n* = CART 1.

ˈ**handclap** *n* [sing] clapping of the hands 拍手; 鼓掌: *give sb a slow handclap*, ie clap slowly and rhythmically to show impatience 对某人缓慢而有节奏地鼓掌(表示不耐烦).

ˈ**handcuffs** *n* [pl] pair of metal rings joined by a chain, for fastening round the wrists of prisoners 手铐: *The prisoner wore (a pair of) handcuffs.* 犯人戴着(一副)手铐. ⇨illus at SHACKLE 见SHACKLE插图. ˈ**handcuff** *v* [esp passive 尤用于被动语态: Tn, Tn·pr] **~ sb (to sth/sb)** put handcuffs on sb 给某人戴手铐: *The demonstrator had handcuffed herself to the railings.* 有个示威的妇女把自己铐在栏杆上.

ˈ**hand-grenade** *n* grenade thrown by hand 手榴弹.

ˈ**hand-gun** *n* (*esp US*) gun that is held and fired with one hand; pistol 手枪.

ˌ**hand-ˈheld** *adj* held in the hand 手提式的; 便携式的: *film taken with a ˌhand-held ˈcamera* 用手提式摄影机拍摄的影片.

ˈ**handhold** *n* thing that a climber may grip, eg on a rock face 攀登者可以抓牢的东西(如岩石上的).

ˈ**hand-luggage** (*US* ˈ**hand-baggage**) *n* [U] luggage that is light enough to be carried by hand 手提行李.

ˌ**handˈmade** *adj* made by hand 手工制的: ˌ*handmade ˈpottery* 手工制作的陶器. Cf 参看 MACHINE-MADE (MACHINE).

ˈ**handmaid** (also ˈ**handmaiden**) *n* (*arch* 古) female servant 女仆; 侍女.

ˌ**hand-ˈpicked** *adj* carefully chosen 仔细挑选的; 精选的.

ˈ**handrail** *n* narrow rail for holding as a support, eg when going up or down stairs 扶手(如楼梯的). ⇨illus at STAIR 见STAIR插图.

ˈ**handsaw** *n* saw used with one hand only 手锯.

ˈ**handshake** *n* **1** shaking of sb's hand with one's own, as a greeting, etc 握手. **2** (idm 习语) **a ˌgolden ˈhandshake** ⇨ GOLDEN.

ˌ**hands-ˈon** *adj* [attrib 作定语] practical 亲身实践的; 实习的: *have ˌhands-on exˈperience of a computer keyboard* 有操作计算机的实际经验.

ˈ**handspring** *n* somersault in which a person lands first on his hands and then on his feet 手翻; 前手翻腾越.

ˈ**handstand** *n* balancing on one's hands with one's feet in the air 手倒立: *do a handstand* 做手倒立动作.

ˈ**handwriting** *n* [U] **1** writing with a pen, pencil, etc 书写. **2** person's particular style of this 书法; 笔迹: *I can't read his handwriting.* 我看不懂他的笔迹.

ˈ**handwritten** *adj* written by hand (ie not printed or typed) 手写的: *Letters of application must be handwritten.* 申请信必须手写.

hand² /hænd; hænd/ *v* **1** [Tn·p, Dn·n, Dn·pr] **~sth (to sb)** give or transfer sth with one's hand or hands 交; 递: *He handed round the biscuits.* 他把饼干传递过去. ○ *Please hand me that book.* 请把那本书递给我. ○ *She handed it to the boy.* 她把它交给了那个男孩子. **2** (idm 习语) **hand/give sb sth on a plate** ⇨ PLATE¹. **3** (phr v) **hand sth down (to sb)** (**a**) pass sth on by tradition, inheritance, etc 传递某物; 把某物往下传: *stories handed down from generation to generation* 代代相传的故事 ○ *Most of my clothes were handed down to me by my older brother.* 我的衣服大多是我哥哥传给我的. (**b**) (*esp US*) announce sth formally or publicly 正式宣布某事物; 颁布某事物: *hand down a budget, legal decision, verdict* 公布预算、判决、裁定. **hand sth in (to sb)** bring or give sth; offer or submit sth 交来、交上、提交或呈交某物: *Hand in your examination papers now, please.* 请把试卷交上来. ○ *She handed in her resignation.* 她提交了辞呈. **hand sth on (to sb)** send or give sth to another person 将某物送交或转交他人: *Please hand on the magazine to your friends.* 请把这本杂志传给你的朋友们看. **hand sth out (to sb)** distribute sth 分发或分配某物: *Relief workers were handing out emergency rations (to the survivors).* 救济人员在(向生还者)分发紧急配给品. **hand (sth) over (to sb)** transfer (a position of authority or power) to sb 把(权位或权力)移交给某人: *I am resigning as chairman and handing over to my deputy.* 我现在辞去主席职位, 交由我的副手接替. ○ *hand over power to an elected government* 把权力移交给经选举产生的政府. **hand sb over to sb** (esp at a meeting, on TV, etc or on the telephone) let sb listen or speak to another person (尤指在会议、电视等中或在电话里)让某人听另一个人的讲话或与另一个人谈话: *I'm handing you over now to our home affairs correspondent.* 现在请听本台记者报道的国内新闻. **hand sb/sth over (to sb)** deliver sb/sth, esp to authority 把某人[某物]交出(尤指交给当局): *They handed him/their weapons over to the police.* 他们把他[武器]交给了警方. **hand it to sb** (*infml* 口) (always with *must* or *have (got) to* 需与must或have (got) to连用) give sb the praise that he deserves 给某人以应得的赞扬; 肯定某人的优点: *You've got to hand it to her — she's damned clever.* 你不能不佩服她——她简直聪明到了极点.

□ ˈ**hand-me-downs** (also ˈ**reach-me-downs**) *n* [pl] used or unwanted things (esp clothes) that are given to another person, esp a younger brother or sister 某人用旧的或不要的而传给他人的东西(尤指留给弟弟妹妹用的衣物): *I don't want your old hand-me-downs!* 我不要你那些用过了的旧东西!

ˈ**hand-out** *n* **1** (esp) food, money or clothes given free to a needy person 施舍物(尤指食物、金钱或衣物). **2** (**a**) leaflet, etc distributed free of charge 免费散发的印刷品. (**b**) prepared statement given, eg by a politician, to newspaper men (政治家等对报界发表的)声明. (**c**) duplicated sheet containing examples, etc distributed by a teacher 教师分发给学生的讲义等.

ˈ**hand-over** *n* (period of) transfer, esp of power or responsibility (尤指权力或职责的)移交(时期).

han·di·cap /ˈhændɪkæp; ˈhændɪˌkæp/ *n* **1** thing that makes progress or success difficult 不利的因素; 障碍. **2** physical or mental disability 生理上或智力上的缺陷; 残疾; 智力低下: *Deafness can be a serious handicap.* 耳聋有时算是严重的缺陷. **3** (**a**) race or competition in which the competitors are given disadvantages in order to make their chances of success more equal 让步(加诸某些参赛者的不利因素以平衡获胜机会的比赛). (**b**) disadvantage given in this way, eg a weight to be carried by a horse 让步中对某些参赛者设置的障碍(如赛马时给马增加负重). **4** number of strokes by which a golfer normally exceeds par for the course 在高尔夫球赛中, 参赛一方超过标准杆数的击球次数.

▷ **han·di·cap** *v* (**-pp-**) [Tn esp passive 尤用于被动语态] give or be a disadvantage to (sb) 对(某人)设置不利条件; 被施加不利条件: *be handicapped by a lack of education* 因文化水平低而吃亏. **han·di·capped** *adj* suffering from a serious physical or mental disability 有生理缺陷的; 弱智的; 残疾的. **the han·di·capped** *n* [pl v] handicapped people 有生理缺陷者; 弱智者; 残疾人: *a school for the severely handicapped* 残疾人学校.

han·di·craft /ˈhændɪkrɑːft; *US* -kræft; ˈhændɪˌkræft/ *n* [U, C] work that needs both skill with the hands and artistic skill, eg needlework, pottery, woodwork 手工艺(如缝纫、制陶、木工); 手工艺品: *an exhibition of handicraft(s)* 手工艺品展览.

handi·work /ˈhændɪwɜːk; ˈhændɪˌwɝk/ *n* [U] **1** work done by the hands 手工; 手工制品. **2** (*often ironic* 常作反语) thing done by a particular person 某人做的东西: *Is that drawing on the board your handiwork, Clare?* 克莱尔, 那板上的画儿是你的大作吗?

hand·ker·chief /ˈhæŋkətʃɪf, *also* -tʃiːf; ˈhæŋkɚtʃɪf, -tʃif/ *n* (*pl* **~s** or **handkerchieves** /-tʃiːvz; -ˌtʃivz/) (usu square) piece of cloth or paper tissue for blowing the nose into, wiping the face, etc 手帕; 手绢; 纸巾.

handle /ˈhændl; ˈhændl/ *n* **1** part of a tool, cup, bucket, door, drawer, etc, by which it may be held, carried or controlled (工具、杯、桶、门、抽屉等的)柄, 把, 把手, 拉手. **2** fact that may be taken advantage of 可能被利用的事实; 把柄; 可乘之机: *His indiscretions gave his enemies a handle to use against him.* 他不够慎重予敌人以反对他的可乘之机. **3** (*sl* 俚) title 头衔: *have a handle to one's name*, ie have a title, eg 'Sir' or 'Lord' 姓名带有头衔(如爵士或勋爵). **4** (idm 习语) **fly off the handle** ⇨ FLY².

▷ **handle** *v* **1** [Tn] touch (sth) with or hold (sth) in the hand(s) (用手)触, 摸, 拿, 抓(某物): *Gelignite is dangerous stuff to handle.* 葛里炸药是不可随便触碰的危险材料. ○ *Wash your hands before you handle food.* 洗完手再拿食物. ○ *Fragile — handle with care.* 易碎品——小心轻放. **2** [Tn] deal with, manage or control (people, a situation, a machine, etc) 对付、管理或控制(人、情况、机器等): *An officer must know how to handle his men.* 当军官的应懂得怎样统率士兵. ○ *This port handles 100 million tons of cargo each year.* 这个港口每年货物吞吐量达1亿吨. ○ *I was impressed by her handling of the affair.* 我觉得她对此事的处理很了不起. **3** [I] (with an *adv* 与副词连用) (esp of a vehicle) be able to be operated in the specified way (尤指机动车)可用某方式操纵: *This car handles well.* 这辆汽车开起来真灵便. **4** [Tn] treat (a person or an animal) as specified (以某方式)对待(人或动物): *The speaker was roughly handled by the mob.* 演说者受到暴民的粗暴对待. **5** [Tn] buy and sell (sth) 买卖(某物): *This shop does not handle such goods.* 这家商店不经营这类商品. **6** [Tn] discuss or write about (a subject) 论及(某一题目). **hand·ler** /ˈhændlə(r); ˈhændlɚ/ *n* person who trains and controls an animal, esp a police-dog 训练和管理动物的人; (尤指)警犬训练员.

-handled (in compound *adjs* 用以构成复合形容词) having a handle of the specified type 有某类型把手的: *a ˌbone-handled ˈknife.*

□ **ˈhandlebar** *n* (usu *pl* 通常作复数) bar with a handle at each end, for steering a bicycle, etc (自行车等的)把手. ⇨illus at App 1 见附录1插图, page xiii. **ˌhandlebar mouˈstache** thick moustache with curved ends 翘八字胡.

hand·some /ˈhænsəm; ˈhænsəm/ *adj* **1 (a)** (of men) good-looking (指男子)好看的, 漂亮的, 相貌堂堂的, 英俊的. **(b)** (of women) having a fine figure and a strong dignified appearance (指女子)健美而端庄的, 标致的: *I would describe her as handsome rather than beautiful.* 我认为她是健美而不是貌美. **(c)** of fine appearance 美观的: *a handsome horse, building, car* 漂亮的马、建筑物、汽车. ⇨Usage at BEAUTIFUL 用法见 BEAUTIFUL. **2** (of gifts, behaviour, etc) generous (指礼物、行为等)慷慨的, 大方的: *a handsome present* 出手大方的礼物. **3** considerable 可观的: *a handsome profit, price, fortune, etc* 相当大的利润、相当高的价格、相当好的运气. **4** (idm 习语) **ˌhandsome ˈis as ˌhandsome ˈdoes** (*saying* 谚) a person's quality can only be judged from his behaviour, not from his appearance 行为美才是真美. ▷ **hand·somely** *adv*: *She was handsomely rewarded for her efforts.* 她由于自己的努力而获得了相当大的报酬. **hand·some·ness** *n* [U].

handy /ˈhændɪ; ˈhændɪ/ *adj* **(-ier, -iest) 1** (of gadgets, etc) convenient to handle or use; useful (指小器具等)便于拿取的, 便于使用的, 有用的: *A good tool-box is a handy thing to have in the house.* 家里有一个好的工具箱就方便多了. **2** [pred 作表语] conveniently placed for being reached or used 近便; 便当: *Our flat is very handy for the schools.* 我们的住所离学校很近, 非常方便. ○ *Always keep a first-aid kit handy.* 手边要经常有个急救箱. **3** [usu pred 通常作表语] clever with one's hands 手巧: *He's handy about the house.* 他修理房子手很巧. **4** (idm 习语) **ˌcome in ˈhandy** be useful some time or other 迟早有用: *My extra earnings came in very handy.* 我的额外收入可备我不时之需. ○ *Don't throw that cardboard box away — it may come in handy.* 不要把那个纸盒丢掉——可能用得着. ▷ **hand·ily** *adv*: *We're handily placed for* (ie within a short distance of) *the shopping centre.* 我们距离购物中心不远, 非常方便. **handi·ness** *n* [U].

□ **handyman** /ˈhændɪmæn; ˈhændɪmæn/ *n* (*pl* **-men** /-men; -mɛn/) person who is clever at doing household repairs, etc or who is employed to do odd jobs 善于干家庭中修修补补的活儿的人; 受雇干零碎杂活的人.

hang[1] /hæŋ; hæŋ/ *v* (*pt, pp* **hung** /hʌŋ; hʌŋ/; in senses 5 and 9 用于下述第5义和第9义时作 **hanged**) **1 (a)** [Ipr, Ip, Tn, Tn·pr, Tn·p] be supported, or support (sth) from above, esp so that the lower end is free 悬挂; 吊: *A towel hung from the rail.* 栏杆上搭着条毛巾. ○ *Hang your coat (up) on that hook.* 把你的外衣挂在那个挂钩上. ○ *She was hanging her washing (out) on the line.* 她正在把洗好的衣服晾在绳子上. **(b)** [Ipr, Ip] (of material, clothing, etc) drape or fall as specified (指织物、衣服等)挂着或垂吊着的某种样子: *The curtains were hanging in folds.* 窗帘成褶状下垂. ○ *How does the dress hang at the back?* 这件连衣裙后身合适吗? **2** [I, Tn] be left hanging, or leave (sth) hanging, until ready for eating 晾挂风干(以便食用): *How long has this meat (been) hung for?* 这肉晾了多久了? **3 (a)** [I, Tn] be fastened, or fasten (sth), to a wall esp in an exhibition 固定在墙上; (尤指)展览: *His portrait (was) hung above the fireplace.* 他的肖像挂在壁炉的上方. ○ *Her paintings hang in the National Gallery.* 她的一些绘画作品在国家美术馆里展出. **(b)** [Tn·pr esp passive 尤用于被动语态] **~ sth with sth** decorate sth with (pictures, ornaments, etc) 用(图画、饰物等)装饰某物: *The rooms were hung with tapestries.* 这些房间都装饰着挂毯. **4** [Tn] stick (wallpaper) to a wall 将壁纸贴在墙上. **5 (a)** [Tn, Tn·pr] kill (sb/oneself) by hanging from a rope around the neck, esp as capital punishment 上吊; 绞死(某人); (尤指)处以绞刑: *He was hanged for murder.* 他因犯谋杀罪而被处以绞刑. ○ *She hanged herself from the rafters.* 她悬梁自尽了. **(b)** [I] be killed in this way as a punishment 被处以绞刑: *You can't hang for such a crime.* 你犯的这种罪不可能被处以绞刑. **6** [Tn] fasten (a door or gate) to hinges so that it swings freely 给(门)安装铰链. **7** [Ipr, Ip, Tn] (cause sth to) droop or bend downwards (使某物)下垂或弯曲下垂: *The dog's tongue was hanging out.* 这条狗把舌头伸在外面. ○ *Children hung* (ie were leaning) *over the gate.* 孩子们扒在大门上. ○ *She hung her head in shame.* 她羞愧得低下了头. **8** [Ipr] **~ (above/over sth/sb)** remain in the air 悬浮于空中: *Smog hung in the sky (over the city).* (城市)上空烟雾弥漫. **9** [Tn] (*infml* 口) damn (sth) 骂(某事物)该死、见鬼、岂有此理等: *Do it and hang the expense!* 无论花多少钱也要干! ○ *Hang it all, they hardly know each other!* 真见鬼, 他们彼此不太认识! ○ *I'm hanged if I know* (ie I don't know at all) *what to do.* 我根本不知道该怎样办. **10** (idm 习语) **go hang** (*sl* 俚) (used to express defiance or lack of concern 用以表示蔑视或不关心) be damned 被骂该死、见鬼去、去他妈的等: *He can go hang for all I care.* 见他的鬼吧, 我才不在乎哩. **hang by a ˈhair/a (single) ˈthread** (of a person's fate, etc) depend on sth small (指人的命运等)系于一发, 千钧一发. **hang ˈfire (a)** (of a gun) be slow in firing (指枪炮)迟发, 滞火. **(b)** be slow in taking action or making progress 行动迟缓; 进展慢: *The project had hung fire for several years because of lack of funds.* 这个项目由于缺少资金而推迟了许多年. **hang in the ˈbalance** (of events) have reached a critical point, where the result may go either way (指事情)发展到关键性阶段或紧要关头. **hang on sb's ˈlips/ˈwords/on sb's every ˈword** listen attentively to sb 注意听某人讲话[不放过某人讲的每一个字]. **let it all hang ˈout** (*sl catchphrase* 俚, 警语) be completely uninhibited 无拘无束. **one may/might as well be hanged/hung for a ˌsheep as (for) a ˈlamb** (*saying* 谚) if the penalty for a more serious offence is no greater than that for a less serious one, one might as well continue to commit the more serious one 偷小羊是死罪, 偷大羊也是死罪(若重罪不重罚, 则犯轻罪者索性犯重罪). **a peg to hang sth on** ⇨ PEG. **(and) thereby hangs a tale** there is an interesting (often surprising) story or piece of further information about what has just been mentioned 这里面还有个有趣的(常为令人惊奇的)故事哩; 这里面还大有文章. **time hangs/lies heavy on one's hands** ⇨ TIME[1]. **with one' tongue hanging out** ⇨ TONGUE. **11** (phr v) **hang aˈbout/aˈround (...)** (*infml* 口) be standing about (a place), doing nothing definite; not move away 无所事事地待在(某处); 荡来荡去: *unemployed people hanging about (the ˈstreets)* (街上)闲荡着的失业者. **hang back (from sth)** show unwillingness to do sth; hesitate 不情愿做某事; 犹豫: *She volunteered to help but he was afraid and hung ˈback.* 她自愿帮忙, 可是他却畏避而不愿接受. **hang ˈon (a)** grip sth firmly 紧紧握住某物: *ˌHang on ˈtight — we're off!* 握紧了——我们出发了! **(b)** (*infml* 口) wait for a short time 稍等: *Hang ˈon a minute — I'm nearly ready.* 稍等片刻——我这就完. **(c)** (*infml* 口) (on the telephone) not replace the receiver (打电话时)不挂断: *The line was engaged and the operator asked if I'd like to hang ˈon.* 电话占线

H

了，话务员问我是否愿意等一下(别挂断电话). **hang on sth** depend on sth 依赖某事物: *A great deal hangs on this decision.* 这个决定关系重大. **hang on to sth** (**a**) hold sth tightly 抓紧某物: *ˌHang on to that ˈrope and don't let go.* 抓紧那根绳子，不要松手. (**b**) (*infml* 口) keep sth; not sell or give sth away 保留某物; 不把某物卖掉或给别人: *I should ˌhang on to those old ˈphotographs — they may be valuable.* 我要保存那些旧照片——可能很有价值. **hang ˈout** (*infml* 口) visit a place often; have one's home 常去某处; 居住: *Where does he hang out these days?* 他这些日子里都在什么地方来着? **hang sth out** put (washing) on a clothes-line so that it can dry (在绳上)晾干(衣服等): *He ˌhung out her ˈblouses.* 他把她的衬衫晾在绳子上了. **hang toˈgether** (**a**) (of people) support or help one another (指人)团结一致, 互相帮助. (**b**) (of statements) be consistent (指说法)一致, 相符: *Their accounts of what happened don't hang together.* 他们对于所发生的事的说法互相之间有矛盾. **hang ˈup (on sb)** (*infml* 口) end a telephone conversation by replacing the receiver 挂断电话. **be/get hung ˈup (about/on sb/sth)** (*sl* 俚) be emotionally upset or inhibited 心烦意乱; 不自在: *She's really hung up on that guy.* 她对那个小伙子确已神魂颠倒. **be/get hung ˈup (by sth)** be delayed by some difficulty (因某种困难)被拖延.

▷ **hang·ing** *n* **1** [U, C] death by hanging 绞死; 绞刑: *sentence sb to death by hanging* 判处某人绞刑 ○ *There were two hangings here today.* 今天此地有两起绞刑. **2** **hangings** [pl] curtains, draperies, etc hung on walls 墙壁上的悬挂物; 窗帘; 帷幔.

□ **hanger-on** /ˌhæŋgər ˈɒn; ˈhæŋɚ ˈɑn/ *n* (*pl* **hangers-on** /ˌhæŋəz ˈɒn; ˈhæŋɚz ˈɑn/) (*usu derog* 通常作贬义) person who tries to become or appear friendly with others, esp in the hope of personal gain 竭力讨好他人的人(尤指为谋取私利者): *The great actor was surrounded by his usual crowd of hangers-on.* 这位大演员的周围经常有些前呼后拥的人.

hang-gliding 悬挂式滑翔运动

ˈhang-gliding *n* [U] sport of flying while hanging from a frame like a large kite controlled by one's own movements 悬挂式滑翔运动(吊在一个如同大风筝的框架下面，由自身动作控制飞行). Cf 参看 GLIDING (GLIDE). **ˈhang-glider** *n* frame used in this sport 悬挂式滑翔机.

hangman /-mən; -mən/ *n* (*pl* **-men** /-mən; -mən/) person whose job is to hang people condemned to death (绞刑的)行刑人, 刽子手.

ˈhang-out *n* (*sl* 俚) place where one lives or which one visits often 住处; 常去的地方.

ˈhang-up *n* (*sl* 俚) emotional inhibition or problem 情绪上的困扰或问题: *She's got a real hang-up about her freckles.* 她因生有雀斑而感到十分苦恼.

hang[2] /hæŋ; hæŋ/ *n* [sing] **1** way in which sth hangs 悬挂的方式; 下垂的样子: *the hang of a coat, skirt, etc* 大衣、裙子等下垂的样子. **2** (idm 习语) **get the hang of sth** (*infml* 口) (**a**) learn how to operate or do sth 熟悉某物的用法; 掌握做某事的方法: *I'm trying to get the hang of the new telephone system.* 我正在练习掌握新型的电话机的用法. (**b**) grasp the meaning of sth said or written 弄清言语或文字的意义: *I didn't quite get the hang of his argument.* 我不太了解他那论点的含义. **not care/give a ˈhang (about sth/sb)** (*infml* 口) not care at all 毫不在乎.

hangar /ˈhæŋə(r); ˈhæŋɚ/ *n* large shed in which aircraft are kept 飞机棚; 飞机库.

hang·dog /ˈhæŋdɒg; ˈhæŋˌdɔg/ *adj* [attrib 作定语] (of sb's look) sly and ashamed, as if guilty (指人的外表)(似因负疚)躲躲闪闪的, 鬼鬼祟祟的: *his hangdog expression* 他那羞愧的表情.

hanger /ˈhæŋə(r); ˈhæŋɚ/ *n* **1** (also ˈ**clothes-hanger**, ˈ**coat-hanger**) curved piece of wood, plastic or wire with a hook, used for hanging up a garment 衣架. **2** loop or hook on or by which sth is hung (挂东西的)环子, 挂钩.

hang·nail /ˈhæŋneɪl; ˈhæŋˌnel/ (also **ag·nail** /ˈægneɪl; ˈægˌnel/) *n* (soreness caused by) torn skin near the root of a finger-nail (指甲根上的)倒刺, 甲刺(所产生的痛感).

hang·over /ˈhæŋəʊvə(r); ˈhæŋˌovɚ/ *n* **1** unpleasant after-effects of drinking too much alcohol 宿醉(过量饮酒后的不适反应): *The next morning he was suffering from/had a hangover.* 他过量饮酒后第二天早上感到不适. **2** thing left from an earlier time 遗留物: *This procedure is a hangover from the old system.* 这样的程序是从旧制度那里沿袭下来的.

hank /hæŋk; hæŋk/ *n* coil or length of wool, thread, etc (毛线、棉线等的)一束, 一卷, 一把: *wind a hank of wool into balls* 把一卷毛线缠成线团.

hanker /ˈhæŋkə(r); ˈhæŋkɚ/ *v* [Ipr, It] **~ after/for sth/to do sth** have a strong desire for sth 渴求某事物: *hanker after wealth* 渴求财富 ○ *hanker to become famous* 渴望成名.

▷ **hanker·ing** *n* **~ (after/for sth)** strong desire 强烈的念头: *have a hankering for a cigarette* 很想吸烟.

hanky /ˈhæŋkɪ; ˈhæŋkɪ/ *n* (*infml* 口) handkerchief 手帕.

hanky-panky /ˌhæŋkɪ ˈpæŋkɪ; ˈhæŋkɪ ˈpæŋkɪ/ *n* [U] (*infml* 口) **1** dishonest dealing; trickery 不老实的行为; 骗人的把戏. **2** naughty (esp sexual) behaviour 调戏的(尤指性方面的)举动.

Han·sard /ˈhænsɑːd; ˈhænˌsɑrd/ *n* [sing] official report of the proceedings of the British Parliament 英国议会议事录.

han·som /ˈhænsəm; ˈhænsəm/ *n* (also ˌ**hansom ˈcab**) old type of horse-drawn carriage with two wheels, for carrying two passengers inside, having the driver's seat high at the back outside, and the reins going over the roof 汉萨姆马车(旧式的双轮双座马车，车夫的座位高踞车后，缰绳越过车顶).

hap·haz·ard /hæpˈhæzəd; ˌhæpˈhæzɚd/ *adj* without plan or order; random 无计划的; 无秩序的; 任意的: *books piled on shelves in a haphazard fashion* 乱七八糟地堆在书架上的书籍. ▷ **hap·haz·ardly** *adv*.

hap·less /ˈhæplɪs; ˈhæplɪs/ *adj* [attrib 作定语] (*arch or rhet* 古或修辞) unlucky; unfortunate 不走运的; 不幸的: *our hapless hero* 我们这不幸的男主人公 ○ *a hapless fate* 不幸的命运.

ha'p'orth /ˈheɪpəθ; ˈhepɚθ/ *n* (*Brit infml* 口) = HALFPENNY-WORTH (HALF).

hap·pen /ˈhæpən; ˈhæpən/ *v* **1** (**a**) [I] occur (by chance or otherwise); take place (偶然地或必然地)出现; 发生: *How did the accident happen?* 事故是怎么发生的? ○ *What happened next?* 后来怎么啦? ○ *I'd stay if they promoted me, but I can't see that happening.* 假若他们提升我，我就留下来，但我看那是不可能的. (**b**) [Ipr] **~ to sb/sth** be the experience or fate of sb/sth 成为某人[某事物]的体验或命运; 临到某人[某事物]头上: *If anything happens to him* (ie If he has an accident), *let me know.* 万一他有什么不测，就请通知我. ○ *What's happened to my clothes?* ie Do you know where they are? 我的衣服到哪里去了? **2** have the (good or bad) fortune (to do sth); chance 碰巧; 恰巧; 恰好: *She happened to be out/It happened that she was out when he called.* 他打电话时，她恰巧不在家. ⇨Usage at APPEAR 用法见 APPEAR. **3** [Ipr] **~ on sth** (*fml* 文) find sth by chance 偶然发现某事物: *I happened on just the thing I'd been looking for.* 我偶然发现了我一直在寻找的东西. **4** (idm 习语) **accidents will happen** ⇨ ACCIDENT. **as it happens/happened** by coincidence or chance 碰巧; 偶然: *We met her only yesterday, as it happens.* 我们只是在昨天才与她偶然相遇.

▷ **hap·pen·ing** /ˈhæpənɪŋ; ˈhæpənɪŋ/ *n* (**a**) (usu *pl* 通常作复数) thing that happens; event; occurrence 发生的事; 事情; 事件: *There have been strange happenings here lately.* 这里近来发生了一些怪事. (**b**) special event, esp a spontaneous theatrical performance 特殊的事; (尤指)戏剧的即兴表演.

NOTE ON USAGE 用法: Compare **happen, occur** and **take place.** 试比较 **happen**、**occur**、**take place** 这三个词语. **Happen** and **occur** refer to accidental or unplanned events; **occur** is more formal than **happen** ☆ **happen** 和 **occur** 指偶然发生的或未经筹划的事件; **occur** 比 **happen** 文雅些: *The accident happened/occurred at about 9.30.* 事故发生在9点30分左右. **Happen** can also indicate one event resulting from another ☆ **happen** 亦可指某件事是由另一事引起的: *What happened when you told him the news?* (ie What did he do?) 你告诉他这消息时, 他有何反应? **Take place** suggests that an event is/was planned ☆ **take place** 指的事情是有计划的: *The funeral took place on 24 April at 3 pm.* 葬礼已于4月24日下午3时举行.

happy /ˈhæpɪ; ˋhæpɪ/ *adj* (**-ier, -iest**) **1 ~ (about/in/with sth/sb)** feeling or expressing pleasure, contentment, satisfaction, etc 有愉快、满意、满足等感受或表现的; 快乐的; 幸福的: *a happy marriage, scene, memory, child, ending (to a book, etc)* 美满的婚姻、欢喜的场面、愉快的回忆、幸福的孩子、(书等的)圆满的结尾 ○ *I won't be happy until I know she's safe.* 我只有在知道她平安无事之后才会感到高兴. ○ *Are you happy in your work/with your life?* 你对工作[对生活]是否满意? **2** (in greetings) full of joy (祝愿用语)快乐的: *Happy birthday!* 祝你生日快乐! ○ *Happy Christmas!* 祝你圣诞节快乐! **3** [pred 作表语] **~ to do sth** (*fml* 文) pleased to do sth 乐于做某事: *I am happy to be of service.* 我很愿意提供帮助. **4** fortunate; lucky 幸运的; 运气好的: *He is in the happy position of never having to worry about money.* 他真有福气, 从来不需要为金钱之事操心. **5** (of words, ideas, behaviour, etc) well suited to the situation; pleasing (指言语、思想、行为等)恰如其分的, 令人满意的: *That wasn't a very happy choice of words.* 那样的措辞并不十分恰当. **6** (idm 习语) **(as) happy as the day is ˈlong/as a ˈsandboy/as ˈLarry** very happy 非常快乐. **a happy eˈvent** the birth of a child 弄璋或弄瓦之喜. **a/the happy ˈmedium** thing that achieves a satisfactory avoidance of excess; balance between extremes 中庸之道; 折衷办法: *be/find/seek a happy medium* 是[找/寻求]一个折衷办法. **many happy reˈturns (of the ˈday)** (used as a greeting to sb on his or her birthday 用作生日的祝词).

▷ **hap·pily** *adv* **1** contentedly 满足地; 幸福地: *They lived happily ever after.* 此后他们一直生活得很幸福. **2** fortunately 幸运地: *Happily this never happened.* 幸好这事从未发生. **3** appropriately 妥当地: *His message was not very happily worded.* 他的通知在措辞上有些欠妥.

hap·pi·ness *n* [U].

□ ˌ**happy-go-ˈlucky** *adj* accepting events cheerfully as they happen; carefree 乐天的; 无忧无虑的: *She goes through life in a happy-go-lucky fashion.* 她一向乐天知命.

hara-kiri /ˌhærəˈkɪrɪ; ˋhɑrəˋkɪrɪ/ *n* [U] ritual suicide using a sword to cut open one's stomach, formerly practised by Japanese Samurai to avoid dishonour when they believed they had failed in their duty 切腹, 剖腹(旧时日本武士在自知任务失败时为免受屈辱的自杀手段).

har·angue /həˈræŋ; həˋræŋ/ *n* long, loud, serious and usu angry speech 长篇大论、慷慨激昂、郑重其事且通常为义愤填膺的演讲.

▷ **har·angue** *v* [I, Tn] give a harangue to (sb) 对(某人)作慷慨激昂的演讲: *haranguing the troops before a battle* 临作战时向士兵作慷慨激昂的讲话.

har·ass /ˈhærəs; *US* həˈræs; həˋræs/ *v* [Tn] **1** trouble and annoy (sb) continually 不断打扰、骚扰(某人): *Political dissidents complained of being harassed by the police.* 持不同政见者申诉他们受到警方的不断骚扰. ○ *He always looks harassed*, ie tired and irritated by constant worry. 他老是愁眉苦脸的. **2** make repeated attacks on (an enemy) 不断骚扰(敌人).

▷ **har·ass·ment** *n* [U] harassing or being harassed 烦扰; 骚扰.

har·bin·ger /ˈhɑːbɪndʒə(r); ˋhɑrbɪndʒɚ/ *n* **~ (of sb/sth)** (*rhet* 修辞) person or thing that announces or shows that sb/sth is coming 预告者; 先驱; 前兆: *The crowing of the cock is a harbinger of dawn.* 鸡啼报晓. ○ *The cuckoo is a harbinger of spring.* 布谷鸟预告春天的来临.

har·bour (*US* **har·bor**) /ˈhɑːbə(r); ˋhɑrbɚ/ *n* [C, U] **1** place of shelter for ships 港; 港口; 港湾: *Several boats lay at anchor in the harbour.* 港湾里停泊着几只船. ○ *We reached (the) harbour at sunset.* 日落时我们抵达了港口. **2** (*fig* 比喻) place of safety or shelter 避难处; 庇护所.

▷ **har·bour** (*US* **har·bor**) *v* **1** [Tn] give shelter to (a criminal, etc); protect; conceal 庇护(罪犯等); 保护; 藏匿: *be convicted of harbouring a wanted man* 因窝藏被通缉者而被定罪 ○ *Dirt harbours germs.* 污垢中藏有病菌. **2** [Tn] keep (sth) secretly in one's mind 心怀(某事物): *harbour a grudge, suspicions, thoughts of revenge, etc* 心怀怨恨、疑虑、报复的念头等. **3** [I, Ipr] (of a sailor or ship) shelter in a harbour (指水手或船只)在港内停留.

har·bour·age (*US* **-bor-**) /ˈhɑːbərɪdʒ; ˋhɑrbərɪdʒ/ *n* [U] shelter 庇护.

□ ˈ**harbour-master** *n* official in charge of a harbour 港务监督.

hard[1] /hɑːd; hɑrd/ *adj* (**-er, -est**) **1** not soft or yielding to the touch or easily cut; solid; firm 硬的; 坚实的; 坚固的: *ground made hard by frost* 冻硬的土地 ○ *Their bodies were hard and muscular after much training.* 他们经过长期锻炼, 身体又结实又强壮. Cf 参看 SOFT. **2 ~ (for sb) (to do sth)** difficult to do or understand or answer; not easy 难做的; 难懂的; 难答的; 困难的: *a hard task, book, language* 艰巨的任务、难读的书、难学的语言 ○ *She found it hard to decide.* 她感到难以决定. ○ *Whether it's true or not is hard to tell.* 很难说究竟是真的还是假的. ○ *It's hard for old people to change their ways.* 老年人很难改变自己的习惯. ○ *You are hard to please/a hard person to please.* 你这个人, 很难讨你欢心[是个很难讨你好的人]. **3** (**a**) requiring much effort of body or mind; tough 费力的; 费神的; 艰难的: *It's hard work shifting snow.* 清除积雪是很吃力的工作. ○ *Some hard bargaining is called for.* 需要进行艰难的谈判. ○ *We must take a hard look at our finances.* 我们应该密切注意财务问题. (**b**) [attrib 作定语] showing much effort; energetic 辛苦的; 努力的: *a hard worker* 努力工作的人. (**c**) of or like a strict or extreme political faction (政治斗争中)持强硬态度的, 不妥协的, 不让步的: *the hard left/right* 持强硬态度的左派[右派]. **4** forceful; violent; harsh 有力的; 猛烈的; 严厉的: *hard knocks* 猛烈的打击 ○ *hard words* 严厉的言辞. **5** causing unhappiness, discomfort or pain; difficult to endure 困苦的; 难以忍受的: *have a hard childhood* 童年生活很艰苦 ○ *be given/have a hard time*, ie experience difficulties, misfortunes, etc 过苦日子(经受艰难, 不幸等) ○ *in these hard times*, ie when life is difficult because of poverty, unemployment, etc 当此困苦时期(由于贫穷、失业等原因而感到生计艰难的时期). **6** (of the weather) severe (指天气)凛冽的: *a hard winter/frost* 严冬[寒]. **7** (esp of a person) unfeeling; unsympathetic; harsh (尤指人)硬心肠的, 冷酷无情的, 严厉的: *a hard father*, ie one who treats his children severely 严父. **8** (of sounds or colours) unpleasant to the ear or eye; harsh (指声音)刺耳的; (指色彩)刺目的: *a hard voice* 刺耳的声音. **9** (of consonants) sounding sharp, not soft (指辅音)硬音的: *The letter 'g' is hard in 'gun' and soft in 'gin'.* g这个字母在gun字中是硬音, 在gin字中是软音. **10** (of drinks) strongly alcoholic (指酒)酒精含量高的: *hard liquor* 烈酒 ○ (*joc* 谑) *a drop of the hard stuff*, ie alcoholic drink 一点酒. **11** (idm 习语) **be hard on sb** (**a**) treat or criticize sb severely 严格对待或严厉批评某人: *Don't be too hard on her — she's very young.* 别对她太严了——她还小呢. (**b**) be unfair to sb 对某人不公平: *The new law is a bit hard on those who were born abroad.* 新法令对那些在国外出生的人有点不够公平. **drive a hard bargain** ⇨ DRIVE[1]. ˌ**hard and ˈfast** (of rules, etc) that cannot be altered to fit special cases; inflexible (指规则等)不能变通的, 不容更改的: *hard and fast regulations, categories* 硬性的规章制度、分类方法 ○ *This distinction isn't hard and fast.* 这样的分类并非是一成不变的. **(as) hard as ˈnails** (of a person) without sentiment or sympathy; hard-hearted (指人)冷酷无情的, 铁石心肠的. **(as) hard as ˈstone** very hard or firm 极硬的; 坚如磐石的: *The ground is as hard as stone after the drought.* 长期干旱之后土地硬得就像石头一样. **hard ˈat it** working hard 努力工作. **hard ˈfacts** accurate information, not expressions of opinion, etc 客观事实(而不是意见、看

法等). **hard ˈgoing** difficult to understand or enjoy; boring 难懂的; 难欣赏的; 令人厌烦的: *I'm finding this book very hard going.* 我觉得这本书十分难懂. **hard ˈlines; hard, etc luck (on sb)** (*infml* 口) (used as an exclamation or a sympathetic comment on sb's misfortune 用作叹词或当提及某人的不幸时用以表示同情): *You failed your driving test, I hear — hard lines!* 听说你驾驶执照考试没及格 —— 真不走运! ○ *Its hard luck on those who were beaten in the first round of the competition.* 那些在第一轮比赛中就遭到失败的人真倒霉. **a hard-ˈluck story** version of events told by sb wanting sympathy (为博取同情而诉说的)不幸事. **a hard/tough nut to crack** ⇨ NUT. **ˌhard of ˈhearing** rather deaf 听觉不灵的: *TV subtitles for the hard of hearing* 电视中为听力差的观众加设的字幕. **the hard/soft sell** ⇨ SELL *n*. **hard to ˈtake** difficult to accept without annoyance, grief or bitterness (令人气恼、悲伤或痛苦因而)难以接受的: *I find his attitude very hard to take.* 我觉得他的态度实在难以忍受. **the ˈhard way** using the most difficult or least convenient method to do or achieve sth 采用最困难或最麻烦的方法(做或实现某事物): *do sth/find out/learn/grow up the hard way* 以吃力的方式或以高昂的代价做某事[调查/学习/成长]. **make hard ˈwork of sth** make an activity seem more difficult than it is 用笨法子做某事. **no hard ˈfeelings** no resentment or bitterness 没有嫌隙; 没有恶感: *We were enemies once, but there are no hard feelings between us now.* 我们曾经是仇人, 但现在彼此已不存芥蒂. **play hard to ˈget** (*infml* 口) try to increase one's status and desirability by not readily accepting an offer or invitation, esp from the opposite sex 不轻易接受别人(尤指异性)给予的好处或邀请以提高身价. **take a hard line (on/over sth)** remain fixed and uncompromising in one's attitude, policy, etc 奉行强硬路线; 持强硬态度. **too much like hard ˈwork** (of an activity) too demanding or wearisome to undertake (指活动)太费劲, 太累人: *I don't want to go for a walk on such a hot day — it's too much like hard work for me.* 我不想在这样的大热天里去散步 —— 我简直吃不消. ▷ **hard·ness** *n* [U].

□ **ˈhardback** *n* [C, U] book bound in a stiff cover 精装书: *Hardbacks are expensive.* 精装书很贵. ○ *My novel has just appeared in hardback.* 我的小说刚出精装本. ○ [attrib 作定语] *a hardback book* 精装书. Cf 参看 PAPERBACK (PAPER).

ˈhardboard *n* [U] stiff board made of compressed and treated wood-pulp 硬质纤维板(由木浆经加压处理后制成).

ˌhard ˈcash coins and notes (ie not a cheque or promise to pay later) 现金; 现款.

ˌhard ˈcopy (*computing* 计) printed material produced by a computer or from a microfilm, etc and able to be read without a special device 硬拷贝(由计算机打印或由缩微胶卷等复制的文件, 可不藉专门设备进行阅读).

ˈhard core (**a**) rubble, broken bricks, etc (used for foundations, roadmaking, etc) (用作地基、路基等的)碎石、碎砖等. (**b**) central, basic or most enduring part (of a group, etc) (某一组织等的)中坚力量, 基干部分, 最坚定的一部分人: *the hard core of the opposition* 在反对党内的中坚分子.

hard court tennis court with a hard surface, not of grass 硬地网球场(非草地的).

ˌhard ˈcover stiff binding for a book (书的)精装封面: [attrib 作定语] *ˌhard-cover ˈbooks* 精装书.

ˌhard ˈcurrency currency that is not likely to fall suddenly in value 硬通货(其价值较为稳定).

ˌhard ˈdisk (*computing* 计) rigid disk, capable of holding more data than a floppy disk (FLOP) 硬磁盘.

ˌhard ˈdrug drug that is strong and likely to lead to addiction 硬性毒品(性烈且易成瘾): *Heroin and cocaine are hard drugs.* 海洛因和可卡因都是容易上瘾的烈性毒品. Cf 参看 SOFT DRUG (SOFT).

ˌhard-ˈheaded *adj* not sentimental; practical 不感情用事的; 讲求实际的: *a ˌhard-headed ˈrealist* 清醒的现实主义者.

ˌhard-ˈhearted *adj* lacking in feeling or sympathy; unkind 硬心肠的; 无情的.

ˌhard ˈlabour (imprisonment with) heavy physical labour as a punishment 劳役; 苦役: *be sentenced to ten years' hard labour* 被判处服十年劳役.

ˌhard-ˈline *adj* uncompromising in one's beliefs or policies 立场坚定的; 奉行强硬路线的: *a ˌhard-line ˈsocialist* 立场坚定的社会主义者. **ˌhard-ˈliner** *n*: *socialist hard-liners* 社会主义者中的强硬派.

ˌhard-ˈnosed *adj* (*infml* 口 *esp US*) tough and unyielding 顽强的; 不屈的: *a ˌhard-nosed ˈbusinessman* 实打实的生意人.

ˌhard ˈporn very obscene pornography 赤裸裸的色情描绘; 黄色书刊、图画等.

ˌhard ˈsauce (*esp US*) butter and sugar creamed with a flavouring (eg vanilla, rum or brandy) and served with plum pudding, etc 黄油甜酱(将黄油和糖搅成乳脂状加上香精、朗姆酒或白兰地等调料制成, 可配合干果布丁等食用).

ˌhard ˈshoulder strip of ground with a hard surface beside a motorway where vehicles may stop in an emergency 硬质路肩(高速公路旁供车辆紧急停车使用的表面坚硬的狭长路段). ⇨illus at App 1 见附录1插图, page xiii.

ˈhard-top *n* car with a metal roof 硬顶小轿车(有金属顶篷的).

ˈhardware *n* [U] (**a**) metal tools and household implements, eg pans, nails, locks; ironmongery 五金制品(如锅、钉、锁); 五金. (**b**) heavy machinery or weapons 重型机器; 重武器: *military hardware* 重型军事装备. (**c**) (*computing* 计) mechanical and electronic parts of a computer 硬件(计算机的机械及电子部件). Cf 参看 SOFTWARE (SOFT).

ˌhard ˈwater water containing mineral salts that prevent soap from lathering freely and produce a hard coating inside pipes, tanks, etc 硬水.

ˈhardwood *n* [U] hard heavy wood from a deciduous tree, eg oak, teak, beech 硬木(如橡木、柚木、山毛榉木等): [attrib 作定语] *hardwood doors, floors, etc* 硬木房门、地板等. Cf 参看 SOFTWOOD.

hard[2] /hɑːd; hɑrd/ *adv* **1** with great effort, energy or concentration; strenuously; intently 努力地; 费劲地; 费神地; 辛苦地; 热切地: *work, think, pull, push, etc hard* 努力工作、悉心思考、用力拉、使劲推 ○ *try hard to succeed* 争取成功. **2** with difficulty; with a struggle 困难地; 辛劳地: *enjoy a hard-earned rest* 享受以辛勤工作赢得的喘息机会 ○ *Our victory was hard won.* 我们的胜利来之不易. **3** severely; heavily 严重的; 猛烈的: *freezing/raining/snowing hard* 严寒[下大雨/下大雪]. **4** at a sharp angle 呈锐角: *Turn hard left.* 向左急转. **5** (idm 习语) **be hard ˈput (to it) (to do sth)** find it difficult 难以: *He was hard put (to it) to explain her disappearance.* 他难以说明她为什么不见了. **be hard ˈup** be short of money 缺钱. **be hard up for sth** have too few of sth; need sth 缺少某事物; 需要某事物: *He's hard up for ideas.* 他没有主意. **die hard** ⇨ DIE[2]. **hard by (sth)** (*arch* 古) near by 在附近: *ˌhard by the ˈriver* 在河边 ○ *There was an inn hard ˈby.* 附近有个客栈. **hard ˈdone by** unfairly treated 受到不当的或不公正的对待: *She feels (she's been) rather hard done by.* 她觉得(自己)有点委屈. **hard on sth** (*fml* 文) soon after sth 紧接某事物之后: *His death followed hard on hers.* 他在她死后不久也死了. **hard on sb's ˈheels** closely following sb 紧跟某人: *He ran ahead, with the others hard on his heels.* 他在前面跑, 其他人紧随其后. **hit sb/sth hard** ⇨ HIT[1]. **take sth hard** be very grieved or upset by sth 因某事而极度悲伤或烦恼: *When their child died they took it very hard.* 他们的孩子死时他们痛苦不堪.

□ **ˌhardˈbitten** *adj* (of people) made tough by bitter experience (指人)经过磨练而变得坚强的.

ˌhard-ˈboiled *adj* **1** (of eggs) boiled until solid inside (指蛋)煮老的. **2** (*infml* 口) (of people) callous; tough; unsentimental (指人)无情的, 强硬的, 无动于衷的.

ˌhard-ˈhitting *adj* not sparing the feelings of others; vigorous; direct 令人难堪的; 强有力的; 直截了当的: *a ˌhard-hitting ˈspeech* 措辞激烈的演说.

ˌhard-ˈpressed *adj* **1** closely pursued 被紧紧催逼的. **2** very busy 忙得不可开交的.

ˌhard-ˈwearing *adj* able to stand much wear and use 耐穿的; 耐用的: *a ˌhard-wearing maˈterial* 经久耐用的材料.

ˌhard-ˈworking *adj* working with care and energy 尽心尽力的; 努力工作的.

harden /ˈhɑːdn; ˈhɑrdn̩/ *v* **1** (**a**) [I, Tn] (cause sth to) become hard, strong, unyielding, etc (使某事物)变硬、变坚强、变坚定等: *The varnish takes a few minutes to harden.* 清漆几分钟就能变硬. ○ *Attitudes to the strike have hardened on both sides.* 双方对罢工所持的态度更加强硬了. ○ *For her own good, you must harden your heart*, ie not allow yourself to show love, pity, etc. 替她着想, 你不能心软(不要流露自己的爱、同情等). **(b)** [esp passive 尤用于被动语态: Tn, Tn·pr] **~ sb (to sth)** make sb less sensitive (to sth) 使某人(对某事)麻木不仁或毫不在乎: *a hardened criminal*, ie one who shows no sign of shame or repentance 怙恶不悛的罪犯 ○ *He became hardened to the suffering around him.* 他对周围的苦难现象已经见怪不怪了. **2** (phr v) **harden (sth) off** (cause young plants, esp seedlings to) become strong enough for planting outside (使幼小植物, 尤指幼苗)增强耐受能力以备露天种植.

hardly /ˈhɑːdlɪ; ˋhɑrdlɪ/ *adv* **1** only just; scarcely 刚刚; 仅仅: *I hardly know her.* 我不怎么认识她. ○ *We had hardly begun/Hardly had we begun our walk when it began to rain.* 我们刚一举步就下起雨来了. ○ *I'm so tired I can hardly* (ie only with difficulty) *stay awake.* 我疲倦得简直昏昏欲睡. **2** (used to suggest that sth is improbable, unlikely or unreasonable 用以表示某事未必能发生、不大可能发生或不合情理): *He can hardly* (ie cannot possibly) *have arrived yet.* 他大概还没有到. ○ *You can hardly expect me to lend you money again.* 你可别指望我再借给你钱. **3** almost no; almost not 几乎没有; 几乎不: *There's hardly any coal left.* 几乎没有煤了. ○ *Hardly anybody* (ie Very few people) *came.* 几乎没有什么人来. ○ *He hardly ever* (ie very seldom) *goes to bed before midnight.* 他很少在午夜以前就寝. ○ *I need hardly say* (ie It is almost unnecessary for me to say) *that I was very upset.* 无庸赘言, 我心乱如麻. ⇨Usage at ALMOST 用法见 ALMOST.

hard·ship /ˈhɑːdʃɪp; ˋhɑrdʃɪp/ *n* **1** [U] severe suffering or discomfort; privation 苦难; 困苦; 贫困: *bear/suffer great hardship* 遭受[经受]巨大的苦难. **2** [C] circumstance causing this 艰难情况: *During the war we suffered many hardships.* 我们在战争期间吃了许多苦头.

hardy /ˈhɑːdɪ; ˋhɑrdɪ/ *adj* **(-ier, -iest) 1** able to endure cold or difficult conditions; tough, robust 耐寒的; 能吃苦的; 强壮的; 坚强的: *A few hardy people swam in the icy water.* 有几个不怕冷的人在冰冷的水里游泳. **2** (of a plant) that can grow in the open air all through the winter (指植物)可在露天过冬的, 耐寒的. ▷ **hardi·ness** *n* [U].

□ ˌ**hardy** ˈ**annual 1** annual plant strong enough to be grown in the open air 耐寒的一年生植物. **2** (*fig joc* 比喻, 谑) subject that is mentioned or discussed regularly 周期性地提出来的老问题.

hare /heə(r); hɛr/ *n* **1** fast-running mammal that lives in fields, like a rabbit but larger, with long ears and a divided upper lip 野兔. Cf 参看 LEVERET. ⇨illus at App 1 见附录1插图, page iii. **2** (idm 习语) ˌ**mad as a March** ˈ**hare** ⇨ MAD. ˌ**run with the** ˌ**hare and** ˌ**hunt with the** ˈ**hounds** try to remain friendly with both sides in a dispute 两面讨好. ˌ**raise/**ˌ**start a** ˈ**hare** introduce a subject for discussion to stimulate conversation or to divert people's minds from the main subject 提出一个问题以引起议论或转移人们对主要问题的注意.

▷ **hare** *v* [Ipr, Ip] run very fast 奔跑: *He hared off* (ie ran away at great speed) *down the street.* 他沿街飞奔而去.

□ ˈ**hare-brained** *adj* foolish; crazy 愚蠢的; 疯狂的: *a hare-brained scheme, person* 愚蠢的计划、人.

ˌ**hare**ˈ**lip** *n* condition in which a person's (usu upper) lip is deformed at birth, with a vertical split in it 兔唇; 唇裂.

hare·bell /ˈheəbel; ˋhɛrˌbɛl/ (*Scot* 苏格兰作 **bluebell**) *n* wild plant with blue bell-shaped flowers and round leaves 圆叶风铃草.

harem /ˈhɑːriːm; *US* ˈhærəm; ˋhɛrəm/ *n* **1** separate part of a traditional Muslim house in which the women live 穆斯林传统住宅中女眷居住的内室或闺房. **2** women living in this 穆斯林闺房中的女眷.

hari·cot /ˈhærɪkəʊ; ˋhærɪˌko/ *n* (also ˌ**haricot** ˈ**bean**) white dried seed of a type of bean plant, eaten as a vegetable 扁豆.

hark /hɑːk; hɑrk/ *v* **1** [I] (*arch* 古) listen 听. **2** (phr v) **hark at sb** (*infml joc* 口, 谑) (usu imperative 通常用于祈使语气) listen to sb (implying that the previous speaker is being arrogant, silly, etc) 听某人的(暗指刚才说话的人讲得放肆、愚蠢等): *Just hark at him! Who does he think he is?* 听听他的! 看他自以为是何许人也? **hark back (to sth)** mention again or remember an earlier subject, event, etc 重新提到或想起原先的问题、旧事等: *To hark back to what we were discussing earlier...* 回到我们原来的议题上来....

har·le·quin /ˈhɑːlɪkwɪn; ˋhɑrləkwɪn/ *n* (formerly) comic character in pantomime, usu dressed in a costume of many colours and wearing a mask (旧时)童话剧中的滑稽角色(通常身穿杂色衣服, 头戴面具).

▷ **har·le·quin** *adj* [usu attrib 通常作定语] gaily coloured 色彩鲜艳的.

har·le·quin·ade /ˌhɑːlɪkwɪˈneɪd; ˌhɑrləkwɪnˋed/ *n* part of a pantomime in which a harlequin plays the main part (童话剧中以滑稽角色为主的)丑角戏.

har·lot /ˈhɑːlət; ˋhɑrlət/ *n* (*arch or derog* 古或贬) prostitute 妓女; 娼妓.

harm /hɑːm; hɑrm/ *n* **1** [U] damage; injury 损害; 伤害: *He meant no harm*, ie did not intend to hurt or upset anyone. 他并无恶意. ○ *A few late nights never did anyone any harm.* 熬几个晚上对任何人绝无害处. **2** (idm 习语) ˌ**come to** ˈ**harm** (usu negative 通常用于否定式) be injured physically, mentally or morally 身体上、精神上或道义上受到损害: *I'll go with her to make sure she comes to no harm.* 我要和她同去以免她受到伤害. ˌ**do more** ˌ**harm than** ˈ**good** have an effect which is more damaging than helpful 弊大于利: *If we interfere, it may do more harm than good.* 倘若我们进行干预, 那可能弊多利少. **out of harm's way** in a safe place 在安全的地方: *Put that vase out of harm's way so the children can't break it.* 把那只花瓶放在安全的地方, 免得孩子们打碎了. **there is no harm in (sb's) doing sth/it does no harm (for sb) to do sth** nothing is lost by doing sth (and some good may result from it) 做某事并无害处(反而可能带来某些好处): *He may not be able to help but there's no harm in asking him.* 他可能帮不了忙, 但是求他一下倒也无妨.

▷ **harm** *v* **1** [Tn] cause harm to (sb/sth) 损害或伤害(某人[某事物]): *an event which has harmed relations between the two countries* 危及两国关系的事件 ○ *Were the hostages harmed?* 人质受到伤害了没有? **2** (idm 习语) **not harm/hurt a fly** ⇨ FLY[1].

harm·ful /ˈhɑːmfl; ˋhɑrmfəl/ *adj* **~ (to sb/sth)** causing harm 有害的; 可致损伤的: *the harmful effects of smoking* 吸烟的害处 ○ *Smoking is harmful to your health.* 吸烟有害于健康. **harm·fully** /ˈhɑːmfəlɪ; ˋhɑrmfəlɪ/ *adv*.

harm·less *adj* **1** not able or likely to cause harm 无害的; 不会引起损伤的: *harmless snakes* 无毒的蛇. **2 (a)** (*infml* 口) unlikely to be difficult or unpleasant; inoffensive 不至于令人为难或不快的; 无恶意的: *harmless fun* 并无恶意的玩笑 ○ *He's a harmless enough chap.* 他是个好好先生. **(b)** innocent 无辜的: *The bomb blast killed several harmless passers-by.* 那颗炸弹炸死了几个无辜的过路人. **harm·lessly** *adv*. **harm·less·ness** *n* [U].

har·monic /hɑːˈmɒnɪk; hɑrˋmɑnɪk/ *n* (*music* 音) higher note produced (eg by the vibration of a string) when a note is played that has a fixed relation to it 泛音.

▷ **har·monic** *adj* of or full of harmony 和声的: *harmonic tones/overtones* 和音[泛音].

har·mon·ica /hɑːˈmɒnɪkə; hɑrˋmɑnɪkə/ *n* = MOUTH-ORGAN (MOUTH[1]).

har·mo·ni·ous /hɑːˈməʊnɪəs; hɑrˋmonɪəs/ *adj* **1** free from disagreement or ill feeling 和谐的; 和睦的: *a harmonious community, relationship, atmosphere* 和睦的社会、关系、气氛. **2** arranged together in a pleasing, orderly way 协调的; 调和的: *a harmonious group of buildings* 协调的建筑群 ○ *harmonious colour combinations* 调和的色彩组合. **3** sweet-sounding; tuneful 音调优美的; 悦耳的: *harmonious sounds* 美妙的声音. ▷ **har·mo·ni·ously** *adv*.

har·mo·nium /hɑːˈməʊnɪəm; hɑrˋmonɪəm/ *n* musical instrument with a keyboard (like an organ), in which notes are produced by air pumped through metal reeds 簧风琴(类似风琴的键盘乐器, 依靠空气使金属簧片振动而发音).

har·mon·ize, -ise /ˈhɑːmənaɪz; ˋhɑrməˌnaɪz/ *v* **1** [I,

H

Ipr, Tn, Tn·pr] **~ (sth) (with sth)** be or make (sth) harmonious (使某事物)和谐, 协调: *colours that harmonize well*, ie together produce a pleasing artistic effect 极为调和的各种颜色(整体上产生悦目的艺术效果) ○ *The cottages harmonize well with the landscape.* 这些村舍与周围风景显得十分协调. ○ *It would be sensible if we could harmonize our plans (with yours).* 假定我们能使自己的计划(与你们的)协调起来, 那就切合实际了. **2** (*music* 音) (**a**) [Tn, Tn·pr] **~ sth (with sth)** add notes to (a melody) to produce harmony 为(乐曲)配和声. (**b**) [I, Ipr] **~ (with sb)** sing in harmony with another singer or singers (与其他歌唱者)用和声唱: *That group harmonizes well.* 那一组用和声演唱得很出色. ▷ **har·mon·iza·tion, -isation** /ˌhɑːmənaɪˈzeɪʃn; *US* -nɪˈz-; ˌhɑrmənɪˈzeʃən/ *n* [U, C].

har·mony /ˈhɑːmənɪ; ˈhɑrmənɪ/ *n* **1** [U] agreement (of feelings, interests, opinions, etc) (感情、兴趣、意见等)相符, 一致: *working towards harmony in international affairs* 致力使国际事务协调一致. **2** [C, U] (instance of a) pleasing combination of related things 协调; 匀称: *the harmony of colour in nature* 自然界色彩的协调 ○ *The designer's aim is to produce a harmony of shape and texture.* 设计者的目标是要使外观与材料的特性两者统一起来. **3** (**a**) [U] (*music* 音) (study of the) combination of different notes at the same time to produce chords 和声(学): *The two sang in harmony.* 这两人用和声演唱. (**b**) [C] sweet or melodious sound 美妙动听的声音; 乐声. Cf 参看 CONCORD, DISCORD. **4** (idm 习语) **in harmony (with sb/sth)** agreeing; matching 协调一致; 相配: *live together in perfect harmony*, ie peacefully and happily 住在一起十分融洽 ○ *His tastes are in harmony with mine.* 他的爱好与我的相同.

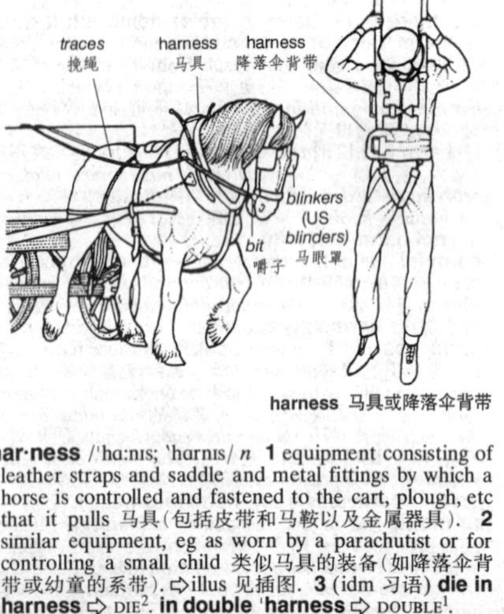

harness 马具或降落伞背带

har·ness /ˈhɑːnɪs; ˈhɑrnɪs/ *n* **1** equipment consisting of leather straps and saddle and metal fittings by which a horse is controlled and fastened to the cart, plough, etc that it pulls 马具(包括皮带和马鞍以及金属器具). **2** similar equipment, eg as worn by a parachutist or for controlling a small child 类似马具的装备(如降落伞背带或幼童的系带). ⇨illus 见插图. **3** (idm 习语) **die in harness** ⇨ DIE[2]. **in double ˈharness** ⇨ DOUBLE[1].

▷ **har·ness** *v* **1** [Tn, Tn·pr] **~ sth (to sth)** put a harness on (a horse, etc); attach (a horse, etc) by a harness 给(马等)上挽具; 套(马等): *harness a horse to a wagon* 把马套到四轮马车上. **2** [Tn] control and use (a natural force) to produce electrical power, etc 控制及利用(自然界的力量)以产生电能等: *harness a river, a waterfall, the sun's rays as a source of energy* 利用河水、瀑布、太阳光作为能源.

harp /hɑːp; hɑrp/ *n* large upright musical instrument with strings stretched on a triangular frame and played with the fingers 竖琴. ⇨illus at App 1 见附录1插图, page xi.

▷ **harp** *v* (phr v) **harp on (about) sth** talk repeatedly and tiresomely about sth 唠叨; 对某事物絮聒不休: *She's always harping on (about) my faults.* 她对我的错误老是唠叨个没完.

harp·ist *n* person who plays the harp 竖琴弹奏者.

har·poon /hɑːˈpuːn; hɑrˈpun/ *n* missile like a spear with a rope attached, thrown by hand or fired from a gun, used for catching whales, etc 鱼叉(状若梭镖, 系于绳上, 用手掷出或用炮射出, 用以捕鲸等).

▷ **har·poon** *v* [Tn] strike (sth) with a harpoon 用鱼叉叉(某物).

harp·si·chord /ˈhɑːpsɪkɔːd; ˈhɑrpsɪˌkɔrd/ *n* musical instrument similar to a piano, but with strings that are plucked mechanically 拨弦键琴(似钢琴的一种乐器, 有弦, 用机械拨奏).

harpy /ˈhɑːpɪ; ˈhɑrpɪ/ *n* **1** (in Greek mythology) cruel monster with a woman's head and body and a bird's wings and claws (希腊神话中的)鸟身女妖(凶残的怪物, 头部及身躯似女人, 生有鸟翼与鸟爪). **2** cruel greedy hard-hearted woman 残酷无情、贪婪成性的女子.

har·ri·dan /ˈhærɪdən; ˈhærədən/ *n* bad-tempered old woman 脾气暴躁的老妇人; 老泼妇.

har·rier /ˈhærɪə(r); ˈhærɪɚ/ *n* **1** hound used for hunting hares 猎兔犬. **2** cross-country runner 越野赛跑者. **3** type of falcon 鹞.

har·row /ˈhærəʊ; ˈhæro/ *n* heavy frame with metal spikes or discs dragged over ploughed land to break up lumps of earth, cover seeds, etc 耙.

▷ **har·row** *v* **1** [I, Tn] pull a harrow over (land) 耙(地). **2** [Tn] distress (sb) greatly 使(某人)极其痛苦. **har·row·ing** /ˈhærəʊɪŋ; ˈhæroɪŋ/ *adj* very distressing 令人极其伤心的: *a harrowing experience, story, film* 极其痛苦的经历、令人肠断的故事、催人泪下的电影.

harry /ˈhærɪ; ˈhærɪ/ *v* (*pt, pp* **harried**) [Tn] **1** annoy (sb) with repeated requests, questions, etc; harass (以不断地要求、询问等方式)打扰, 烦扰(某人); 使烦恼: *harried by press reporters wanting a story* 受到渴望获得报道材料的新闻记者的打扰. **2** raid and plunder (sth) repeatedly 不断袭扰和打劫(某处): *The Vikings harried the English coast.* 北欧海盗曾不断骚扰英国沿海地区.

harsh /hɑːʃ; hɑrʃ/ *adj* (**-er, -est**) **1 ~ (to sb/sth)** unpleasantly rough or sharp, esp to the senses 粗糙而使人不舒服的; (尤指)刺激人感官的: *a harsh texture, voice, light, colour* 毛糙的织物、刺耳的声音、刺目的光线、耀眼的颜色 ○ *be harsh to the ear/eye/touch* 刺耳[刺目/扎手]. **2** stern; cruel; severe 严酷的; 无情的; 严厉的: *a harsh judge, judgement, punishment* 严厉的法官、判决、处罚. ▷ **harshly** *adv*: *be harshly treated* 受到严厉对待. **harsh·ness** *n* [U].

hart /hɑːt; hɑrt/ *n* (*pl* unchanged or **~s** 复数或不变或作 **harts**) adult male of (esp red) deer; stag (长成的)公鹿(尤指红鹿). Cf 参看 HIND[2].

har·te·beest /ˈhɑːtəbiːst; ˈhɑrtəˌbist/ *n* large African antelope with curving horns 麋羚(非洲的大羚羊, 有弯角).

harum-scarum /ˌheərəm ˈskeərəm; ˈhɛrəmˈskɛrəm/ *adj* (*infml* 口) (of a person or his behaviour) wild and reckless (指人或其行为)莽撞的, 冒失的.

har·vest /ˈhɑːvɪst; ˈhɑrvɪst/ *n* **1** (**a**) [C] cutting and gathering of grain and other food crops 收割; 收获. (**b**) [C, U] season when this is done 收获季节; 收获期: *Farmers are very busy during (the) harvest.* 在收获季节里农民非常忙碌. (**c**) [C] (amount of the) crop obtained 收成; 收获量: *gather in the harvest* 收庄稼 ○ *a succession of good harvests* 连续的好收成 ○ *This year's wheat harvest was poor.* 今年小麦收成不好. **2** [C] (*fig* 比喻) consequences of any action 结果: *reap the harvest of* (ie be rewarded for) *one's hard work* 获得辛勤劳动的成果.

▷ **har·vest** *v* [I, Tn] gather (a crop); reap 收割(庄稼); 收获: *The farmers are out harvesting (the corn).* 农民们在地里收割(作物). **har·ves·ter** *n* **1** person who harvests crops; reaper 收割庄稼的人; 收获者. **2** machine for cutting and gathering grain, esp the type that also binds the grain into sheaves or threshes the grain 收割机; (尤指兼能捆扎或脱粒的)联合收割机. Cf 参看 COMBINE[2] 2.

□ ˌ**harvest ˈfestival** service of thanksgiving in Christian churches after the harvest has been gathered 秋收感恩礼拜(基督教教会于收获后所举行的仪式); 秋收感恩节.

ˌ**harvest ˈhome** (*esp Brit*) celebration organized by farmers for their workers after the harvest has been gathered 收获节祝宴(收获后农场主人为雇工举行的家宴).

ˌ**harvest ˈmoon** full moon nearest to the autumn equinox (22 or 23 September) 9月22日或23日秋分前后的满月.

has ⇨ HAVE.

has-been /ˈhæz biːn; ˋhæzˏbɪn/ *n* (*infml derog* 口, 贬) person or thing that is no longer as famous, successful, popular, etc as formerly 已经不如过去那样有名、有为、走红等的人或事物; 过时的人或事物.

hash¹ /hæʃ; hæʃ/ *n* **1** [U] (dish of) cooked meat cut into small pieces and recooked 回锅肉丁. **2** [C] mixture or jumble; re-used material 混杂(物); 大杂烩; 再次使用的材料. **3** (idm 习语) **make a hash of sth** (*infml* 口) do sth badly 把某事物搞得一团糟. **settle sb's hash** ⇨ SETTLE².

▷ **hash** *v* [Tn, Tn·p] **~ sth (up) 1** chop (meat) into small pieces 把(肉)切成小块; 把(肉)剁碎. **2** (*sl* 俚) make a mess of sth; do sth badly 把某事物弄糟; 做坏某事物: *I'm sorry I hashed up the arrangements.* 对不起, 我把整个安排给打乱了.

hash² /hæʃ; hæʃ/ *n* [U] (*infml* 口) = HASHISH.

hash·ish /ˈhæʃiːʃ; ˋhæʃiʃ/ (also **hash**) *n* [U] top leaves and tender parts of the hemp plant dried for smoking or chewing as a narcotic drug 哈希什(从印度大麻提出的可供吸食或咀嚼的麻醉品). Cf 参看 CANNABIS, MARIJUANA.

hasp /hɑːsp; *US* hæsp; hæsp/ *n* part of a fastening for a door, window, etc consisting of a hinged metal strip that fits over a staple and is secured by a padlock (门窗等的)搭扣(包括一带有铰链的金属条及一U形环, 套上后可用挂锁锁住).

hassle /ˈhæsl; ˋhæsl̩/ *n* [C, U] (*infml* 口) (**a**) difficulty; struggle 困难; 斗争: *Changing trains with all that luggage was a real hassle.* 带着那么多行李换乘火车真是件麻烦事. (**b**) argument; quarrel 争辩; 争吵: *Do as you're told and don't give me any hassle!* 叫你怎么做就怎么做, 别跟我多嘴!

▷ **hassle** *v* (*infml* 口) **1** [I, Ipr] **~ (with sb)** argue; quarrel 争辩; 争吵. **2** [Tn] harass (sb); bother; jostle 不断打扰(某人); 烦扰; 搅扰: *Don't keep hassling me!* 别老烦我!

has·sock /ˈhæsək; ˏhæsək/ *n* thick firm cushion for kneeling on, esp in church 厚实的跪垫(尤指教堂用的).

haste /heɪst; hest/ *n* **1** [U] quickness of movement; hurry 急忙; 匆忙: *Why all the haste?* 为什么这么匆忙? **2** (idm 习语) **in haste** quickly 匆忙地. **make haste** (*dated or fml* 旧或文) act quickly; hurry 赶快; 赶紧. **marry in haste, repent at leisure** ⇨ MARRY. ˌ**more** ˌ**haste,** ˌ**less** ˈ**speed** (*saying* 谚) one makes more real progress if one does things less hurriedly 欲速则不达. **with all speed/haste** ⇨ SPEED.

hasten /ˈheɪsn; ˋhesn̩/ *v* **1** [Ipr, Ip, It] move or act with speed; hurry 急忙; 赶快: *He hastened (away) to the office.* 他急急忙忙到办公室去了. ○ *I have important news for you — good news, I hasten to add.* 我有重要消息要告诉你——是好消息, 我得赶紧补充一句. **2** [Tn] cause (sth) to be done or to happen earlier 催促; 促进: *Artificial heating hastens the growth of plants.* 人工供暖能促进植物生长.

hasty /ˈheɪstɪ; ˋhestɪ/ *adj* (**-ier, -iest**) (**a**) said, made or done quickly or too quickly; hurried 急急忙忙的; 过于匆忙的; 仓促完成的: *a hasty departure, meal, farewell* 匆匆忙忙的离去、用餐、告别 ○ *hasty words that are soon regretted* 脱口而出旋即后悔的话. (**b**) [usu pred 通常作表语] **~ (in doing sth/to do sth)** (of a person) acting quickly; too fast (指人)仓促从事, 草率: *You shouldn't be too hasty in deciding to get married.* 在婚姻大事上你不该过于轻率. ▷ **hast·ily** /-ɪlɪ; -lɪ/ *adv.* **hasti·ness** *n* [U]

hat /hæt; hæt/ *n* **1** covering made to fit the head, usu with a brim, worn out of doors 帽子(通常指有檐的): *put on/take off one's hat* 戴[脱]帽. Cf 参看 BONNET. **2** (*infml* 口) symbol of a person's official position 官职的象征: *wear two hats*, ie have two official or professional roles 身兼两职. **3** (idm 习语) **at the drop of a hat** ⇨ DROP¹. **I'll eat my hat** ⇨ EAT. ˌ**keep sth under one's** ˈ**hat** keep sth secret 对某事物保密. **knock sb/sth into a cocked hat** ⇨ KNOCK². ˌ**my** ˈ**hat** (used as an exclamation of astonishment or disbelief 用以表示惊讶或不信). **old hat** ⇨ OLD. ˌ**out of a/the** ˈ**hat** picked at

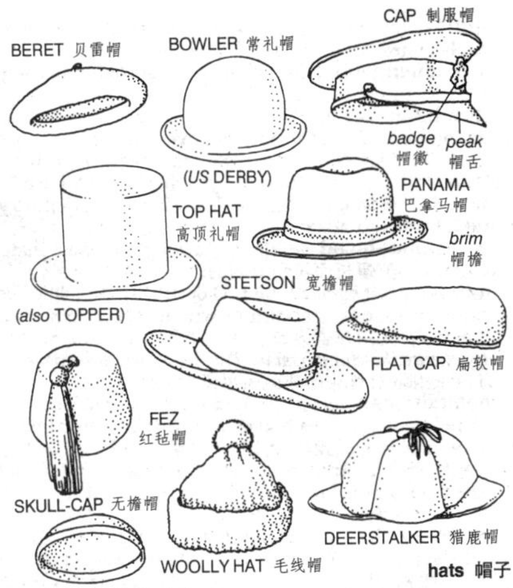

hats 帽子

random 随意挑选的: *Prizes went to the first three out of the hat.* 奖品为随意挑选出来的前三人所得. **pass the hat round** ⇨ PASS². **take one's hat off to sb** acknowledge admiration for sb 向某人脱帽致敬; 对某人表示钦佩: *I must say I take my hat off to him — I never thought he would get into the first team.* 我得说我对他真是敬佩——我从未想到他能参加甲队. **talk through one's hat** ⇨ TALK².

▷ **hat·less** *adj* not wearing a hat 不戴帽子的.

hat·ter /ˈhætə(r); ˋhætɚ/ *n* **1** person who makes or sells hats 制帽者; 帽商. **2** (idm 习语) **mad as a hatter** ⇨ MAD.

□ ˈ**hatband** *n* band of ribbon, etc round a hat just above the brim 帽带(帽檐上的一圈由丝等做成的带子).

ˈ**hat-pin** *n* long pin used to fasten a hat to the hair 帽针(将帽子别在头发上的长别针).

ˈ**hat trick** (**a**) (in cricket) taking of three wickets by the same bowler with three successive balls (板球运动)投球手连续三次击倒三柱门: *take a hat trick* (一人)连续三次击倒三柱门. (**b**) three similar successes achieved by one person in another sport or activity (其他运动或活动中)一人连续三次取胜的成绩: *score a hat trick of goals* (一人)连进三球.

hatch¹ /hætʃ; hætʃ/ *n* **1** (**a**) opening in a door, floor or ceiling (门、地板或天花板上的)开口. (**b**) (also ˈ**hatch·way**) opening in a ship's deck through which cargo is lowered or raised (船的甲板上装卸货物的)舱口: *under hatches*, ie below deck 在甲板下. (**c**) opening in a wall between two rooms, esp a kitchen and dining-room, through which dishes, etc are passed 两室之间的小窗口(尤指厨房和餐厅之间的, 用以传递菜肴等). (**d**) door in an aircraft or a spacecraft (飞机或宇宙飞船上的)舱门. **2** movable cover over any of these openings 各种开口的活动门; 舱口盖. **3** (idm 习语) ˌ**down the** ˈ**hatch** (*infml* 口) (said before esp drink is swallowed) down the throat 干杯.

hatch² /hætʃ; hætʃ/ *v* **1** [I, Ip] **~ (out)** (**a**) (of a young bird or fish, etc) emerge from an egg (指小鸟、小鱼等)(从卵中)孵出: *The chicks/caterpillars/grubs have hatched ('out).* 小鸡[毛虫/小蛆]孵出来了. (**b**) (of an egg) produce a young bird, etc (指蛋)孵化: *When will the eggs hatch ('out)?* 这些蛋什么时候孵化? **2** [Tn, Tn·p] **~ sth (out)** (**a**) cause (sth) to emerge from an egg 孵出(某物): *The hen hatches (out) her young by sitting on the eggs.* 母鸡伏在蛋上孵小鸡. (**b**) cause (eggs) to produce young birds, etc 使(蛋)孵化; 孵(蛋). **3** [Tn, Tn·p] **~ sth (out/up)** think out and produce (a plot, plan, etc) 策划(阴谋); 拟订(计划): *What mischief are those children hatching ('up)?* 那些孩子在琢磨什么鬼花样?

▷ **hatch·ery** *n* place for hatching eggs, esp of fish 孵卵处; (尤指鱼的)孵化场: *a* ˈ*trout hatchery* 鳟鱼孵化场. Cf 参看 INCUBATOR (INCUBATE).

H

hatch[3] /hætʃ; hætʃ/ *v* [Tn] mark (a surface) with close parallel lines 在(某一平面)上标出影线.
▷ **hatch·ing** *n* [U] lines drawn or engraved in this way 影线.

hatch·back /ˈhætʃbæk; ˋhætʃ,bæk/ *n* car with a large sloping back, hinged at the top, that opens like a door (带上掀式斜背的)小轿车. ⇨illus at CAR 见 CAR 插图.

hatchet /ˈhætʃɪt; ˋhætʃɪt/ *n* **1** light short-handled axe 短柄小斧. ⇨illus at AXE 见 AXE 插图. **2** (idm 习语) **bury the hatchet** ⇨ BURY.
□ ˈ**hatchet-faced** *adj* having a long face and sharp features 面部瘦长而棱角分明的.
ˈ**hatchet job** (*infml* 口 *esp US*) destructive or malicious attack on sb, esp in speech or writing 对某人的诋毁或恶毒攻击(尤指在言语或文字上): *Two newspapers did a very effective hatchet job on the Prime Minister's achievements.* 有两家报纸对首相的成就极尽诋毁之能事.
ˈ**hatchet man** (*infml* 口) (**a**) person employed to discredit and remove opponents or to carry out criminal tasks 受雇从事诋毁及除掉对手之活动的人; 受雇执行罪恶使命的人. (**b**) person employed to reduce staff and expenditure in a firm, etc 企业等中执行裁减人员及费用之事务的雇员.

hatch·way /ˈhætʃweɪ; ˋhætʃ,we/ *n* = HATCH[1] 1.

hate /heɪt; het/ *v* **1** (**a**) [Tn] feel hatred towards (sb/sth) 憎恨, 憎恶(某人[某事物]): *My cat hates dogs.* 我的猫与狗极不睦. ○ *her hated rival* 她所憎恨的对手. (**b**) [Tn, Tt, Tnt, Tg, Tsg] strongly dislike (sb/sth) 讨厌, 厌恶(某人[某事物]): *I hate fried food.* 我厌恶煎炸食品. ○ *I hate delays/to be delayed/being delayed.* 我对耽搁时间很反感. ○ *She hates anyone listening when she's telephoning.* 她讨厌别人听着她打电话. (**c**) [Tt, Tnt, Tg] (*infml* 口) be reluctant; regret 不愿; 遗憾: *I hate to trouble you.* 我不愿麻烦你. ○ *I would hate you to think I didn't care.* 很遗憾你认为我漠不关心. **2** (idm 习语) ˌ**hate sb's** ˈ**guts** (*infml* 口) dislike sb intensely 对某人恨之入骨.
▷ **hate** *n* (**a**) [U] strong dislike; hatred 憎恨; 厌恶: *feel hate for sb* 对某人感到厌恶 ○ *a look (full) of hate* (充满)敌意的目光. (**b**) [C] (*infml* 口) hated person or thing 所恨的人或事物: *one of my pet hates* 我所恨之入骨者之一 ○ *Plastic flowers are a particular hate of mine.* 塑料花是我特别厌恶的东西.

hate·ful /ˈheɪtfl; ˋhetfəl/ *adj* **~ (to sb)** causing sb to feel hatred or strong dislike; detestable; very unpleasant 可恨的; 可恶的; 讨厌的; 令人厌恶的: *a hateful person, remark, deed* 可恶的人、言语、行为 ○ *All tyranny is hateful to us.* 我们对一切暴政都深恶痛绝. ▷ **hate·fully** /-fəlɪ; -fəlɪ/ *adv*. **hate·ful·ness** *n* [U].

hat·red /ˈheɪtrɪd; ˋhetrɪd/ *n* [U] **~ (for/of sb/sth)** very strong dislike; hate 仇恨; 憎恨: *feel hatred for the enemy* 对敌人怀着仇恨 ○ *He looked at me with hatred.* 他以憎恨的眼光望着我. ○ *She has a profound hatred of fascism.* 她对法西斯主义怀有深仇大恨.

hat·ter ⇨ HAT.

haughty /ˈhɔːtɪ; ˋhɔtɪ/ *adj* (**-ier**, **-iest**) (of a person or his manner) arrogant while despising others; proud and disdainful (指人或态度)高傲自大的, 倨傲不逊的: *The nobles treated the common people with haughty contempt.* 贵族对待平民趾高气扬不可一世. ▷ **haught·ily** /-ɪlɪ; -ɪlɪ/ *adv*. **haughti·ness** *n* [U].

haul /hɔːl; hɔl/ *v* **1** [I, Ipr, Ip, Tn, Tn·pr, Tn·p] pull or drag (sth) with effort or force 用力拖或拉(某物): *sailors hauling (away) (on the ropes)* 拽着(绳索)(不放)的水手 ○ *elephants hauling logs* 拖运木材的象 ○ *haul a car out of the mud* 把小汽车从烂泥里拽出来 ○ *They hauled the boat up the beach.* 他们把船拖上岸. ⇨Usage at PULL[2] 用法见 PULL[2]. **2** [Tn] transport (sth) by lorry, etc 用卡车等运送(某物). **3** (idm 习语) ˌ**haul sb over the** ˈ**coals** (*infml* 口) reprimand sb severely 严厉斥责某人: *I was hauled over the coals for being late.* 我因迟到而受到了严厉的训斥. **4** (phr v) **haul sb up (before sb)** (*infml* 口) bring sb to be tried or reprimanded 把某人带上来审问或训斥: *He was hauled up before the local magistrates for disorderly conduct.* 他因妨害治安被送交地方法官究办.
▷ **haul** *n* **1** act of hauling 拖; 拉; 运送. **2** (usu *sing* 通常作单数) distance to be travelled 移动的距离: *short/medium/long haul aircraft* 短程[中程/远程]运输飞机 ○ *Our camp is only a short haul from here.* 我们的营地近在咫尺. **3** (**a**) quantity of fish caught in a net at one time 一网的捕鱼量: *The fishermen had a good haul.* 渔民捕得满满一网鱼. (**b**) (*fig* 比喻) amount gained by effort 经努力获得的数量: *The thief got away with a huge haul.* 那个贼偷走了大量财物. **4** (idm 习语) **a long haul** ⇨ LONG[1].

haul·age /ˈhɔːlɪdʒ; ˋhɔlɪdʒ/ *n* [U] **1** transport of goods 货运: *the road haulage industry*, ie the business of transporting goods by road in lorries, etc 公路货运业 ○ *a haulage contractor* 货物承运者. **2** money charged for this 货物运费: *How much is haulage?* 运费是多少?

haul·ier /ˈhɔːlɪə(r); ˋhɔljɚ/ *n* (*Brit*) (*US* **hauler**) person or firm whose trade is transporting goods by road 公路运输业者; 公路运输行.

haunch /hɔːntʃ; hɔntʃ/ *n* **1** (usu *pl* 通常作复数) (in man and animals) fleshy part of the buttock and thigh (人和动物)臀部和腿部多肉的部分: *The dog was sitting on its haunches.* 那狗蹲着. **2** leg and loin of deer, etc as food (鹿等供食用的)腰腿肉: *a haunch of venison* 鹿的腰腿肉.

haunt /hɔːnt; hɔnt/ *v* [Tn] **1** (of ghosts) visit (a place) regularly (指鬼魂)常出没于(某处): *a haunted house* 经常闹鬼的房子 ○ *A spirit haunts the castle.* 那座城堡中常有幽灵出现. **2** be in (a place) very often 常到(某处): *This is one of the cafés I used to haunt.* 这是我以前常去的一家咖啡馆. **3** return repeatedly to the mind of (sb) 经常浮现于(某人)脑际: *a haunting melody* 萦绕心头的曲调 ○ *a wrongdoer haunted by fear of discovery* 经常提心吊胆怕被人发现的作恶者 ○ *The memory still haunts me.* 那回忆仍然萦回在我的脑际.
▷ **haunt** *n* (often *pl* 常作复数) place visited frequently by the person or people named (某某人)常去之处: *This pub is a favourite haunt of artists.* 这家小酒店是艺术家们喜欢光顾的地方. ○ *revisit the haunts of one's youth*, ie the places where one spent one's time then 重游年轻时的旧地.

haute cou·ture /ˌəʊt kuːˈtjʊə(r); ˌot kuˋtur/ (*French* 法) leading companies making fashionable clothes, or their products; high fashion 最具有影响力的时装制作公司; 此类公司制作的时装; 高级时装式样.

haute cuis·ine /ˌəʊt kwɪˈziːn; ˌot kwɪˋzin/ (*French* 法) high-class cookery 高级烹饪术.

haut·eur /əʊˈtɜː(r); oˋtɝ/ *n* [U] (*fml* 文) haughtiness 傲慢; 自大.

Hav·ana /həˈvænə; həˋvænə/ *n* cigar made in Cuba 哈瓦那雪茄(产于古巴).

have[1] /həv; həv; *strong form* 强读式 hæv; hæv/ ⇨ Detailed Guide 6.2, 6.3 见词条使用详细说明 6.2、6.3. *aux v* ⇨Usage at HAVE[3] 用法见 HAVE[3]; (used with the *past participle* to form perfect tenses 与过去分词连用构成完成时态): *I've finished my work.* 我已经做完工作了. ○ *He's gone home, hasn't he?* 他已经回家去了, 是吗? ○ *Have you seen it? Yes I have/No I haven't.* 你看见了吗? 看见了[没看见]. ○ *He'll have had the results by then.* 他到时候会有结果的. ○ *She may not have told him yet.* 她可能还没有告诉他. ○ *Had they left before you got there?* 你到达那里时他们已经离开了吗? ○ *She'd fallen asleep by that time, hadn't she?* 那时她早已睡着了, 是吗? ○ *If I hadn't seen it with my own eyes I wouldn't have believed it.* 我要不是亲眼看见, 还可能不相信呢. ○ *Had I known that* (ie If I had known that), *I would never have come.* 我要是早知道, 我绝对不来.

have[2] /hæv; hæv/ *v* ⇨Usage at HAVE[2,3] 用法见 HAVE[2,3]. (*Brit* also **have got**) (not used in the continuous tenses 不用于进行时态).
▸ POSSESSING 有 **1** (Cf 参看 *my, your, his, her, its, our, their*) (**a**) [Tn] possess or own (sth) 有, 据有(某物): *He has a house in London and a cottage near the sea.* 他在伦敦有一所房子, 在海边还有一个小屋. ○ *Do you have any pets?* 你有什么宠物吗? ○ *They've got two cars.* 他们有两辆小汽车. ○ *How many glasses have we got?* 我们有多少个玻璃杯? ○ *Do you have/Have you got a 50p piece?* 你有没有一枚50便士的硬币? (**b**) [Tn, Tn·pr, Cn·a] possess or display (a mental quality or physical feature) 有, 具有(某种精神素质或生理特点): *You must have a lot of courage.* 你可真有胆量. ○ *She has a good memory.* 她的记性很好. ○ *Giraffes have long necks.* 长颈鹿的脖子很长. ○ *The house has* (ie contains) *three bedrooms.* 这所房子有三间卧室. ○ *You've got a cut*

on your chin. 你下巴上有一道伤口. ○ *have a tooth loose/missing* 有一颗牙齿松了[掉了]. **2** [Tn] (indicating a relationship 表示某种关系): *I have two sisters.* 我有两个姐姐. ○ *They have four children.* 他们有四个孩子. ○ *Does he have any friends?* 他有朋友吗? **3** [Tn] (be able to) make use of or exercise (sth) (有能力)利用或运用(某事物): *She has no real power.* 她没有实权. ○ *I don't have the authority to send them home.* 我无法打发他们回家. ○ *I haven't as much responsibility as before.* 我不再担负过去那样多的责任了. ○ *Have you got time to phone him?* 你有时间给他打电话吗?

▸ EXPERIENCING 体验或经历 **4** [Tn] experience or feel (sth); keep in the mind (used esp with the *ns* shown) 体验或感到(某事物); 心存, 心怀(尤与下列名词连用): *I have no doubt* (ie I am sure) *that you are right.* 我肯定你说得对. ○ *She had the impression that she had seen him before.* 她觉得以前见过他. ○ *Do you have any idea where he lives?* 你知道他住在哪里吗? ○ *What reason have you (got) for thinking he's dishonest?* 你凭什么认为他不诚实? **5** [Tng] experience the results of sb's actions 经受(某人的行动所产生的结果): *We've got people phoning up from all over the world.* 我们接到人们从世界各地打来的电话. ○ *They have orders coming in at the rate of 30 an hour.* 他们每小时接到30份定单. **6** [Tn] suffer from (an illness or a disease) 患(病); 遭受(病痛): *She's got appendicitis.* 她得了阑尾炎. ○ *He says he has a headache.* 他说他头痛. ○ *Have you got problems at work?* 你工作中有问题吗? ○ *How often do you have a bad back?* 你多长时间腰痛一次?

▸ SHOWING OR DISPLAYING 表现或显示 **7** [Tnt] show or demonstrate (a quality) by one's actions 以行动表现或显示(某种品性): *He has the impudence to take things behind my back!* 他背着我拿东西真不害臊! ○ *Surely she didn't have the nerve to say that to him?* 她真的没有勇气对他说那件事吗? ○ (*fml* 文) *Would you have the goodness* (ie Please be good or kind enough) *to help me with my cases?* 劳驾帮我拿拿箱子好吗?

▸ TAKING OR ACCEPTING SOMEBODY 吸收或接纳某人 **8** [Tn] (sometimes in the *-ing* form to indicate an intention or arrangement for the future 有时以 -ing 的形式表示意向或打算) attend to the needs of (sb/sth) for a limited period; take care of; look after 满足(某人[某事物])一时之需; 关照; 看管: *Are you having the children tomorrow afternoon?* 明天下午你照料孩子吗? ○ *We've had the neighbours' dog while they're away.* 邻居出门时把狗交给我们看管. ○ *We usually have my mother* (ie staying in our house) *for a month in the summer.* 我们在夏天往往请母亲来住上一个月. **9** [Cn·n/a] take or accept (sb) in a specified function 吸收或接受(某人)担负某种责任: *We'll have Jones as our spokesman.* 我们让琼斯做我们的代言人. ○ *Who can we have as treasurer?* 我们能让谁掌管财务呢?

▸ OTHER MEANINGS 其他意义 **10** [Tn, Tn·pr, Tn·p] be holding or displaying (sb/sth) in a specified way (以某种方式)抓住或展示(某人[某事物]): *She's got him by the collar.* 她抓住他的衣领. ○ *Why did you have your back to the camera?* 你为什么背对着照相机? ○ *He had his head down as he walked out of the court.* 他走出法庭时耷拉着脑袋. **11** [Tn, Tnt] be aware of (sth) as a duty or necessity 对(某事物)觉得有责任或有必要: *He has a lot of homework (to do) tonight.* 他今晚有许多家庭作业(要做). ○ *I must go — I have a bus to catch.* 我该走了——我得赶上公共汽车. ○ *She's got a family to feed.* 她要养活一家人. **12** (idm 习语) **ˈhave it (that)...** claim to be a fact that...; say that... 断言...; 说...: *Rumour has it that we'll have a new manager soon.* 据说我们不久就要来一位新经理. **have (got) it/that ˈcoming** can expect unpleasant consequences to follow 注定; 活该: *It was no surprise when he was sent to prison — everyone knew he had it coming (to him).* 果不其然他进了监狱——大家都清楚(他)得有这么一天. **have it ˈin for sb** (*infml* 口) intend to punish or do sth unpleasant to sb 意图惩罚某人; 跟某人过不去: *She's had it in for him ever since he called her a fool in public.* 自从他当众说她是蠢货以来, 她就一直想治治他. **have it ˈin one (to do sth)** (*infml* 口) be capable (of sth); have the ability (to do sth) 有(某一方面)的能力; 有能力(做某事): *Do you think she's got it in her to be a dancer?* 你认为她是舞蹈家的材料吗? **13** (phr v) **have sth in** have a stock of sth in one's home, etc 家里等存有某物: *Have we got enough food in?* 我们存的食物够不够? **have sth on** be wearing sth 穿着; 戴着: *She has a red jacket on.* 她穿着一件红色的短上衣. ○ *He's got a tie on today.* 他今天系着一条领带. **have sth on sb** (*infml* 口) (no passive 不用于被动语态) have (evidence) to show that sb is guilty of a crime, etc 有(证据)表明某人有罪等: *Have the police got anything on him?* 警方有证据证明他有罪吗? **have sb/sth to oneself** be able to use, enjoy, etc sb/sth without others 可独自使用某人[某物]; 得以独享: *With my parents away I've got the house to myself.* 由于我父母不在, 我可以独自使用这所房子.

NOTE ON USAGE 用法: When indicating possession, the most commonly used verb in British English is **have got** (in present tense forms) 在表示'有'的意思时, 英式英语中最常用的动词是**have got**(用现在时态): *'Have you got any pets?' 'Yes, I've got three rabbits and a tortoise.'* '你有什么宠物吗?' '有, 我有三只兔子和一只乌龟.' In US English (and commonly in tenses other than the present in British English) **have** is used 在美式英语中, 用**have**表示'有'(在英式英语, **have**表示'有'时一般不用于现在时态, 但常用于其他时态): *I have an apartment in downtown Manhattan.* 我在曼哈顿中心区有一套住房. ○ *I haven't got a car now but I'll have one next week.* 我现在没有汽车, 但是下星期就能有一辆. **Have** when used in the present tense in British English is more formal than **have got** ☆ **have** 在英式英语中用于现在时态, 比用 **have got** 显得郑重: *I have no objection to your proposal.* 我对你的提议没有异议. In British English **have got**, indicating possession, behaves like an auxiliary verb and a *pp* 在英式英语中, **have got** 表示'有'的意思时, 其用法如同一个助动词加一个过去分词: *'Have you got a computer?' 'Yes, I have.'* '你有计算机吗?' '有.' In US English questions and negatives are formed with **do** 在美式英语中, 与 **do** 连用可构成疑问式和否定式: *'Do you have a computer?' 'Yes I do.'* '你有计算机吗?' '我有.' This construction is common in British English in tenses other than the present 这种结构在英式英语中多用于除现在式以外的其他时态: *I didn't have any money so I couldn't get a newspaper.* 我当时没有钱, 所以没能买报纸. It is also increasingly found in the present tense. 这种用法现亦逐渐多见于现在时态.

have³ /hæv; hæv/ *v* ⇨Usage 见所附用法.

▸ PERFORMING AN ACTION 做某动作 **1** [Tn] (**a**) perform (the action indicated by the following *n*) for a limited period (以有限的时间)从事, 进行(由后接之名词所表示的动作): *have a swim, walk, ride, etc* (Cf 参看 *go for a swim, walk, ride, etc*) 游泳、散步、骑马 ○ *have a wash, rest, talk* 洗一洗、歇一歇、谈一谈 ○ *Let me have a try.* 让我试一下. ○ *She usually has a bath in the morning.* 她早上通常要洗个澡. (**b**) consume (sth) by eating, drinking, smoking, etc 消费(某物); 吃、喝或吸(烟)等: *have breakfast/lunch/dinner* 吃早饭[午饭/晚饭] ○ *I usually have a sandwich for lunch.* 我午饭时通常吃块三明治. ○ *We have coffee at 11.* 我们11点钟喝咖啡.

▸ RECEIVING OR UNDERGOING 接受或经受 **2** [Tn] (**a**) (not used in the continuous tenses 不用于进行时态) receive (sth); experience 接受(某物); 体验: *I had a letter from my brother this morning.* 今早我收到哥哥的来信. ○ *She'll have an accident one day.* 她总有一天要出事. ○ *I had a shock when I heard the news.* 我听到这个消息时感到震惊. (**b**) undergo (sth) 经受(某事物): *I'm having treatment for my lumbago.* 我腰痛正在治疗中. ○ *She's having an operation on her leg.* 她的腿正在动手术. **3** [Tn] experience (sth) 经历(某事物): *We're having a wonderful time, holiday, party.* 我们玩得、假期过得、聚会举办得有意思极了. ○ *I've never had a worse morning than today.* 我哪一天早上也不像今天早上这样倒霉. ○ *They seem to be having some difficulty in starting the car.* 他们在启动这辆小汽车时似乎遇到了一些困难.

▸ PRODUCING 生产或产生 **4** [Tn] give birth to (sb/sth); produce 生(孩子[小动物]); 生产; 产生: *My wife's having a baby.* 我妻子怀孕了. ○ *Our dog has had puppies twice already.* 我们的狗已经生了两窝小狗了. ○ *have a good effect/result/outcome* 产生良好的效果[结果/成果] ○ *His paintings had a strong influence on me as a student.* 他的画儿对我这个学生产生了很大的影响.

▸ CAUSING OR ALLOWING SOMETHING TO HAPPEN 使或让某事发生 **5** [Cn·i no passive 不用于被动语态] order or arrange (that sb does sth) 命令或安排(某人做某事): *I'll have the gardener plant some trees.* 我要让园丁种些树. ○ *Have the driver bring the car round at 4.* 让司机4点钟把汽车开来. **6** (**a**) (used with a *n* + past participle 与名词+过去分词连用) cause sth to be done 使某事物予以处理: *Why don't you have your hair cut?* 你为什么不理发? ○ *They're going to have their house painted.* 他们准备把房子粉刷一下. ○ *We're having our car repaired.* 我们的汽车正在修理. (**b**) (used with a *n* + past participle 与名词+过去分词连用) suffer the consequences of another person's action 承受、蒙受他人行为之后果: *He had his pocket picked,* ie Something was stolen from his pocket. 他的口袋被掏了(衣袋中有东西被窃). ○ *She's had her wallet taken.* 她的钱包被人拿走了. ○ *Charles I had his head cut off.* 查理一世遭斩首. ○ *They have had their request refused.* 他们的请求遭到拒绝. (**c**) [Tn, Cn·g] (used in negative sentences, esp after *will not, cannot,* etc 用在否定句中, 尤用于will not、cannot等之后) allow or tolerate (sth) 允许或容忍(某事物): *I cannot have such behaviour in my house.* 我不能容忍家中有这种行为. ○ *She won't have boys arriving late.* 她不允许这些男孩子迟到. **7** (**a**) [Cn·g no passive 不用于被动语态] cause sb to do sth 使某人做某事: *She had her audience listening attentively.* 她使听众听得入神. ○ *The film had us all sitting on the edges of our seats with excitement.* 这部影片让我们大家激动不已. (**b**) [Cn·a no passive 不用于被动语态] cause sb to be in a certain state 使某人处于某种状态: *The news had me worried.* 我听了这消息十分不安. **8** [no passive 不用于被动语态: Tn·pr, Tn·p] cause (sb) to come in a specified direction as a visitor, guest, etc 邀请(某人)来访、来作客等: *We're having friends (over) for dinner.* 我们请朋友们来吃饭. ○ *We had her up here last term to give a lecture.* 我们上学期请她上这里来讲过课.

H

▸ OTHER MEANINGS 其他意义 **9** [Tn] (*infml* 口) (**a**) (esp passive 尤用于被动语态) trick (sb); deceive 蒙骗(某人); 欺骗: *I'm afraid you've been had.* 看来你上当了. (**b**) win an advantage over (sb); beat 胜过(某人); 击败: *She certainly had me in that argument.* 她在辩论中确实把我驳倒了. ○ *You had me there!* 还是你行! **10** [Tn] (⚠ *sl* 讳, 俚) (esp of a man) have sexual intercourse with (sb) (尤指男人)与(某人)性交: *Have you had her yet?* 你跟她发生过性关系吗? **11** (idm 习语) **have ˈhad it** (*sl* 俚) (**a**) not be going to receive or enjoy sth 将得不到或享受不到某事物: *If he was hoping for a lift home I'm afraid he's had it.* 他要是想搭乘便车回家, 我看是吹了. (**b**) be going to experience sth unpleasant 将吃苦头: *When they were completely surrounded by police they realized they'd had it.* 警察把他们团团围住, 他们知道要有罪受了. **have it ˈoff/aˈway (with sb)** (⚠ *sl* 讳, 俚) have sexual intercourse with sb 与某人性交: *She was having it off with a neighbour while her husband was away on business.* 她在丈夫出差时跟邻居发生了性关系. **what ˈhave you** (*infml* 口) other things, people, etc of the same kind 诸如此类的事物、人等: *There's room in the cellar to store unused furniture and what have you.* 地下室里有地方存放不用的家具之类的东西. **12** (phr v) **have sb back** allow (a spouse, etc from whom one is separated) to return 允许(分手的配偶等)返回: *I'll never have her back.* 我决不与她复合. **have sth back** receive sth that has been borrowed, stolen, etc from one 收回(被借走、偷走等之)某物: *Let me have it back soon.* 早些把东西还给我. ○ *You can have your files back after we've checked them.* 等我们检查完你的文件就退还给你.

have sb in have sb working in one's house 召某人到家里来干活儿: *We had the builders in all last week.* 上星期我们请建筑工人到家里来干了一星期.

have sb ˈon (*infml* 口) persuade sb of the truth of sth, usu to make fun of him 哄骗某人(通常意在戏弄): *You really won all that money on a horse? You're not having me on?* 你当真在一匹马上投注就赢了那么多的钱吗? 你不是在骗我吧?

have sth ˈout cause sth to be removed, etc 将某物去掉等: *have a tooth, one's appendix, one's tonsils out* 拔掉一颗牙齿、切除阑尾、割除扁桃腺. **have sth out (with sb)** settle (a dispute, etc) by open (often angry) discussion 通过公开的(常为愤愤的)辩论以解决(争端等): *After weeks of silent hostility they've at last had it out with each other.* 他们经过几个星期的暗斗之后, 彼此终于谈开了.

have sb ˈup (for sth) (*infml* 口) (esp passive 尤用于被动语态) cause sb to be accused of a crime, etc in a lawcourt 使某人出庭受审: *He was had up for exceeding the speed limit.* 他因超速行驶而遭控告.

NOTE ON USAGE 用法: **Have** is used as an auxiliary verb (**have**[1]) and as two separate main verbs (**have**[2] and **have**[3]). ☆ **have** 可用作助动词(**have**[1]), 也可用作两个独立的主要动词(**have**[2] 和 **have**[3]). ☆ Except for the negative forms **haven't**, **hasn't** and **hadn't**, the following written and spoken forms are common to all three verbs 除否定形式 **haven't**、**hasn't**、**hadn't** 外, 这三个动词具有以下共同的书写和读音形式: **have** (*pres t* with *I, you, we, they*) **have** (现在时态, 与 I、you、we、they 连用) /həv, əv, v; həv, əv, v/, *strong form* 强读式 /hæv; hæv/; written contractions 缩写式 **I've** /aɪv; aɪv/, **you've** /juːv; juv/, **we've** /wiːv; wiv/, **they've** /ðeɪv; ðəv/; negative 否定式 **haven't** /ˈhævnt; ˋhævn̩t/. **has** (*pres t* with *he, she, it*) **has** (现在时态, 与 he、she、it 连用) /həz, əz, s, z; həz, əz, s, z/, *strong form* 强读式 /hæz; hæz/; written contractions 缩写式 **he's** /hiːz; hiz/, **she's** /ʃiːz; ʃiz/, **it's** /ɪts; ɪts/, **Jack's** /dʒæks; dʒæks/, **Sam's** /sæmz; sæmz/; negative 否定式 **hasn't** /ˈhæznt; ˋhæzn̩t/. **had** (*pt*) /həd, əd, d; həd, əd, d/, *strong form* 强读式 /hæd; hæd/; written contractions 缩写式 **I'd** /aɪd; aɪd/, **we'd** /wiːd; wid/, **she'd** /ʃiːd; ʃid/, etc; negative 否定式 **hadn't** /ˈhædnt; ˋhædn̩t/. **had** (*pp*) /hæd; hæd/. When **have**[2] refers to a regular state or habitual feature, etc, negatives and questions are formed with **do** in both British and US English ☆ **have**[2] 用于指经常性的状态或习惯性的特征等时, 在英式英语和美式英语中都与 **do** 连用, 构成否定式和疑问式: *People don't have central heating in their houses in my country.* 在我国, 一般人家里没有集中供热设备. ○ *Does the referee have the power to send him off the field?* 裁判员有权勒令他退场吗? However, when **have**[2] refers to a specific object, fact or feature, etc, British speakers tend to form negatives and questions without an auxiliary verb (informally they use **have got**), while US speakers invariably form them with **do** 然而当 **have**[2] 特指某物体、某事实或某性状等时, 在构成否定式和疑问式中, 英国人一般不使用助动词(口语中用 **have got**), 而美国人则一律使用 **do**: (*Brit*) *We haven't (got) many wine glasses.* 我们的酒杯不多. ○ (*US*) *We don't have many wine glasses.* 我们的酒杯不多. ○ (*Brit*) *Have you got a £1 coin?* 你有一枚1英镑的硬币吗? ○ (*US,* and sometimes *Brit*) *Do you have a £1 coin?* 你有一枚1英镑的硬币吗? As regards **have**[3], British and US speakers form negatives and questions in the same way — with **do** 至于 **have**[3], 英国人和美国人均以同样的方式(加 **do**)构成否定式和疑问式: *She didn't have any letters last week.* 她上周没有收到任何信件. ○ *Did this have a good effect?* 这有效吗? Note that, as a general rule, the continuous tenses can be used with **have**[3] but not with **have**[2]. 注意: 一般说来, **have**[3] 可用于进行时态, 而 **have**[2] 不能用于进行时态. As a present tense form of the auxiliary, **has** is often contracted to **'s** ☆ **has** 用作现在时态的助动词时, 常缩写为 **'s** /s, z; s, z/, 如 *She's gone to Scotland.* 她到苏格兰去了. But **has** is seldom reduced in this way when it is a part of a main verb, except in set phrases 但 **has** 用作主要动词时, 则很少使用缩写形式, 只有一些惯用语例外, 如: *He's no head for heights.* 他攀高就头晕. ○ *She's no right to say that.* 她没有权利说那话.

haven /ˈheɪvn; ˋhevən/ *n* **1** place of safety or rest; refuge

安全的地方; 憩息处; 避难所: *Terrorists will not find a safe haven here.* 恐怖分子在这里将找不到安身之处. **2** (*dated* 旧) harbour 港.

haver /ˈheɪvə; ˋhevɚ/ *v* [I] **1** keep changing one's mind; hesitate 犹豫; 迟疑. **2** (*esp Scot* 尤用于苏格兰) talk foolishly 说胡话.

hav·er·sack /ˈhævəsæk; ˋhævɚˌsæk/ *n* strong (usu canvas) bag carried on the back or over the shoulder 背包(通常为帆布的). Cf 参看 RUCKSACK.

have to /ˈhæv tə, ˈhæf tə; ˋhæf tə/ *modal v* (*3rd pers sing pres t*) **has to** /ˈhæz tə, ˈhæs tə; ˋhæs tə/, *pt* **had to** /ˈhæd tə, *also* ˈhæt tə; ˋhæd tə/) (negative sentences and questions usu formed with *do* 构成否定和疑问句时通常须加do) **1** (indicating obligation 表示义务或责任): *I have to type letters and answer the phone.* 我又得用打字机打信, 又得接电话. ○ *He has to pass an examination before he can start work.* 他须考试及格, 才能开始工作. ○ (*fml* 文) *Have we to make our own way to the conference?* 我们必须亲自到那里去开会吗? ○ *You don't have to knock — just walk in.* 你不必敲门——进来就是了. ○ *They don't have to have finished the work before I arrive.* 他们无须在我到达之前完成此项工作. ○ *Does she have to stay at home every night?* 她每天晚上都得待在家里吗? ○ *Did you have to pay a fine?* 你必须交付罚金吗? ⇨Usage 1 at MUST 见 MUST 所附用法第1项. **2** (indicating advice or recommendation 表示劝告或建议): *You simply have to get a new job.* 你只须找个新工作. ⇨Usage 2 at MUST 见 MUST 所附用法第2项. **3** (drawing a logical conclusion 得出合乎逻辑的结论): *There has to be a solution.* 一定会有解决的办法. ○ *This has to be part of the original manuscript.* 这一定是原稿的一部分. ⇨Usage 3 at MUST 见 MUST 所附用法第3项. **4** (idm 习语) **have/has got to** (*Brit infml* 口) (**a**) (indicating obligation 表示义务或责任): *I've got to go to work by bus tomorrow.* 我明天得坐公共汽车去上班. ○ *Why have you got to take these tablets?* 你为什么要吃这些药片? ○ *You haven't got to take flowers but many people do.* 你不必非带花去不可, 但是许多人都带着花去. ⇨Usage 1 at MUST 见 MUST 所附用法第1项. (**b**) (indicating advice or recommendation 表示劝告或建议): *You've got to try this new recipe — it's delicious.* 你应该试试这种新烹饪法——味道好极了. ⇨Usage 2 at MUST 见 MUST 所附用法第2项.

havoc /ˈhævək; ˋhævək/ *n* [U] **1** widespread damage; great destruction (大范围的)破坏; (巨大的)毁坏: *The floods created havoc.* 洪水造成了巨大的灾害. **2** (idm 习语) **make havoc of sth; play/wreak havoc with sth** damage or upset sth 破坏或扰乱某事物: *The bad weather played havoc with our plans.* 天气恶劣把我们的计划打乱了.

haw[1] /hɔː; hɔ/ *n* red berry of the hawthorn bush 山楂果.

haw[2] /hɔː; hɔ/ *v* (idm 习语) **hum and haw** ⇨ HUM.

hawk[1] /hɔːk; hɔk/ *n* **1** strong swift bird of prey with sharp eyesight 鹰; 隼. **2** (*politics* 政) person who favours aggressive policies in foreign affairs '鹰派'人物(对外事务上持强硬路线者). Cf 参看 DOVE[1] 2.

▷ **hawk·ish** *adj* (*politics* 政) favouring aggressive policies rather than negotiation and compromise 坚持强硬政策的(不谈判、不妥协的). **hawk·ish·ness** *n* [U].

□ ˌ**hawk-ˈeyed** *adj* **1** having very good eyesight 目光犀利的. **2** (of a person) watching closely and carefully (指人)观察力强的.

hawk[2] /hɔːk; hɔk/ *v* [Tn, Tn·p] **~ sth (about/around)** **1** offer (goods) for sale by going from house to house, street to street, etc 沿街叫卖(货物). **2** (*fig* 比喻) spread (news) by talking 散布(消息): *Who's been hawking gossip about?* 是谁在散布流言蜚语?

▷ **hawker** *n* person who hawks goods 走街串巷的小贩.

haw·ser /ˈhɔːzə(r); ˋhɔzɚ/ *n* thick heavy rope or thin steel cable, used for mooring or towing a ship 缆索, 钢丝绳(系船或拖船用的).

haw·thorn /ˈhɔːθɔːn; ˋhɔˌθɔrn/ *n* thorny shrub or tree with white, red or pink blossom and small dark red berries 山楂树: [attrib 作定语] *a hawthorn hedge* 山楂树篱.

hay /heɪ; he/ *n* [U] **1** grass cut and dried for use as animal food (用作饲料的)干草: *make hay*, ie turn it over to be dried by the sun 制干草(进行翻晒). **2** (idm 习语) **hit the hay/sack** ⇨ HIT[1]. **make hay of sb/sth** destroy sb/sth; throw sb/sth into confusion 搞垮某人[某事物]; 使某人[某事物]陷于混乱: *She made hay of my argument.* 她把我的论点搅得乱七八糟. **make hay while the ˈsun shines** (*saying* 谚) make good use of opportunities, favourable conditions, etc while they last 善于利用时机、有利条件等.

□ ˈ**hay fever** allergic illness affecting the nose and throat, caused by pollen or dust 枯草热(由花粉或尘埃引起鼻部和咽喉发炎的变态反应症).

ˈ**hay-fork** *n* two-pronged fork for turning or lifting hay (有两个长齿的)干草叉.

ˈ**haymaking** *n* [U] cutting grass and spreading it to dry 制干草(割草并翻晒). ˈ**hay-maker** *n* **1** person or machine employed in making hay 制干草的工人或机器. **2** (*infml* 口 *esp US*) powerful swinging blow with the fist 挥拳猛击.

ˈ**haystack** (also ˈ**hayrick**) *n* **1** large pile of hay firmly packed for storing, with a pointed or ridged top (捆扎妥当便于贮存的)大干草垛(顶端呈尖形或脊形). **2** (idm 习语) **a needle in a haystack** ⇨ NEEDLE.

hay·wire /ˈheɪwaɪə(r); ˋheˌwaɪr/ *adj* (idm 习语) **be/go haywire** (*infml* 口) be/become disorganized or out of control 乱糟糟的; 失去控制的: *Since I dropped it on the floor my watch has gone completely haywire.* 我的表掉在地板上以后, 就完全乱了套.

hazard /ˈhæzəd; ˋhæzɚd/ *n* **1 ~ (to sb/sth)** (thing that can cause) danger; risk 危险; 有危险的事物; 风险: *Smoking is a serious health hazard.* 吸烟严重危及健康. ○ *Wet roads are a hazard to drivers.* 道路湿滑会对司机构成危险. **2** obstacle on a golf-course (高尔夫球场上的)障碍物.

▷ **hazard** *v* [Tn] **1** expose (sth) to danger; risk 使(某事物)遭受危险; 使…冒风险: *Rock-climbers are hazarding their lives.* 岩石上的攀登者在冒生命的危险. **2** venture to make (sth); suggest tentatively 冒险做出(某事物); 试探性地提出: *I don't know where he is but I could hazard a guess.* 我不知道他在那里, 但我可以猜猜看.

haz·ard·ous *adj* dangerous; risky 危险的; 冒险的: *hazardous work, conditions* 危险的工作、情况 ○ *The journey was hazardous.* 旅途十分艰险. **haz·ard·ously** *adv*.

haze[1] /heɪz; hez/ *n* [C, U] **1** thin mist 薄雾; 霾. ⇨Usage at FOG 用法见 FOG. **2** (*fig* 比喻) mental confusion or uncertainty 迷糊; 疑惑: *I/My mind was in a complete haze.* 我完全糊涂了.

▷ **haze** *v* (phr v) **haze over** (**a**) become covered with a thin mist 为薄雾所笼罩. (**b**) lose focus; become dreamy 变模糊; 变朦胧: *His eyes hazed over when he thought of her.* 他想起她来时, 眼前一片模糊.

haze[2] /heɪz; hez/ *v* [Tn] (*US*) harass (sb) by making him perform humiliating jobs; bully; persecute 使(某人)出丑; 欺凌; 为难.

hazel /ˈheɪzl; ˋhezl/ *n* bush or small tree with small edible nuts 榛树(灌木, 结小的坚果, 可食). ⇨illus at App 1 见附录1插图, page i.

▷ **hazel** *adj* (esp of eyes) reddish or light yellowish brown (尤指眼睛)红褐色的, 浅黄褐色的.

□ ˈ**hazel-nut** *n* edible nut of the hazel 榛子(可食). ⇨ illus at NUT 见 NUT 插图.

hazy /ˈheɪzɪ; ˋhezɪ/ *adj* (**-ier, -iest**) **1** misty 有薄雾的: *We couldn't see far because it was so hazy.* 雾气蒙蒙妨碍了我们的视线. **2** not clear; vague 模糊的; 朦胧的: *hazy memories* 模糊不清的记忆. **3** (of a person) rather confused; uncertain (指人)困惑的, 没有把握的: *I'm a bit hazy about what to do next.* 我不太清楚下一步该做什么. ▷ **haz·ily** *adv*: *remember sth hazily* 隐隐约约地想起某事物. **hazi·ness** *n* [U].

HB /ˌeɪtʃ ˈbiː; ˌetʃ ˋbi/ *abbr* 缩写 = (of lead used in pencils) hard black (ie medium hard) (指铅笔芯)硬黑(即硬度适中): *an HB pencil* 一支HB的铅笔. Cf 参看 B, H.

H-bomb /ˈeɪtʃ bɒm; ˋetʃˌbɑm/ *n* hydrogen bomb 氢弹.

he /hiː; hi/ ⇨Detailed Guide 6.2. *pers pron* 人称代词 (used as the subject of a *v* 用作动词的主体) **1** male person or animal mentioned earlier or being observed now 他; (指雄性动物)它: *'Where's your brother?' 'He's in Paris.'* '你哥哥在哪里?''他在巴黎.' ○ *Look! He* (ie The man we are watching) *is climbing the fence.* 瞧啊!

他(我们看见的那个人)在爬栅栏. **2** (male or female) person (男性或女性)人: (*fml* 文) *If a member wishes to bring a guest into the club, he must sign the visitors' book.* 会员欲携宾客前来俱乐部者, 须在来宾簿上登记. ○ (*saying* 谚) *He who* (ie Anyone who) *hesitates is lost.* 优柔寡断者必然有失(当断不断, 必受其乱). Cf 参看 HIM.
▷ **he** *n* [sing] male animal 雄性动物: *What a sweet puppy! Is it a he or a she?* 多可爱的小狗哇! 是公的还是母的?

he- (forming compound *ns* 用以构成复合名词) male 雄性: *a* ˈ*he-goat.*
□ ˈ**he-man** /-mæn; -mæn/ *n* (*pl* **-men** /-men; -mɛn/) strong virile man 男子汉.

NOTE ON USAGE 用法: Frequently, **he, him** and **his** are used to refer to a member of a group which includes both males and females ☆ **he**、**him**、**his** 经常用以指称有男有女的人群中的一人: *Everybody knows what he wants.* 人人都知道自己想要的是什么. ○ *A good teacher always prepares his lessons well.* 好的教师每次备课都很充分. Many people think that this discriminates against women and the use of **he or she, him or her,** etc is becoming more common. 许多人认为这种用法是对女性的歧视, 而逐渐多用 **he or she**、**him or her** 等表达. In writing, **he/she, s/he** or **(s)he** can be used 书面上可写作 **he/she**、**s/he** 或 **(s)he**: *Everybody knows what's best for him or herself.* 人人都知道对自己最有利的是什么. ○ *If in doubt, ask your doctor. He/She can give you further information.* 你若有疑问, 可以问问医生. 他(她)会向你作进一步的说明. ○ *When a baby cries, it means that s/he is tired, hungry or just unhappy.* 幼儿哭叫, 就是他困了、饿了或是不高兴了. In informal language **they, them,** or **their** can be used 在口语中可使用 **they**、**them** 或 **their**: *Everybody knows what they want.* 人人都知道自己想要的是什么. Alternatively, the sentence can be rephrased, using a plural noun 变通一下说法, 可以改变句子的措辞, 使用复数名词: *Babies cry when they are tired.* 幼儿困了就哭. Note that, to save space in this dictionary, we use **he/him/his** when referring to 'sb' (somebody) in definitions, although the person may be either female or male. 注意: 本词典为节省篇幅, 释义中凡涉及'sb'(somebody)时, 均使用 **he/him/his**, 其所指可为男性或女性. This is usually made clear by the examples which follow such definitions. 在这类释义之后, 通常备有例证以分清性别.

HE *abbr* 缩写 = **1** (on labels, notices, etc) high explosive (标签、警告等用语)高爆炸药, 烈性炸药. **2** /ˌeɪtʃˈiː; ˌetʃˈi/ His/Her Excellency 阁下(用作间接称谓): *HE the British Ambassador* 英国大使阁下 ○ *HE Governor Robert Mount* 罗伯特·蒙特总督阁下 ○ (*infml* 口) *HE is coming.* 阁下即将驾到.

the head 头部

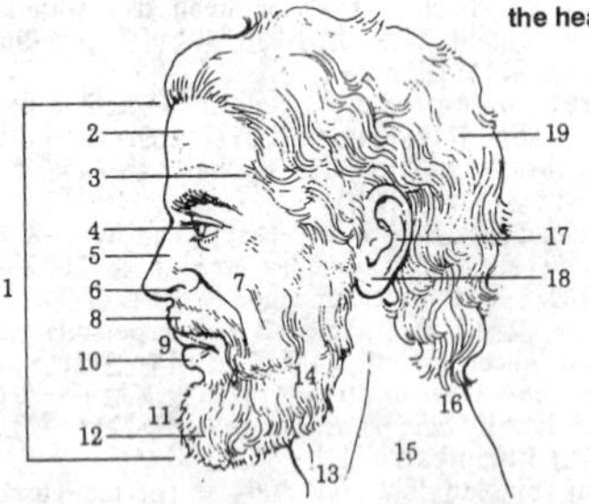

1 face 脸
2 forehead 额 (*also* brow)
3 temple 太阳穴
4 eye 眼睛
5 nose 鼻子
6 nostril 鼻孔
7 cheek 面颊
8 moustache 须 (*US* mustache)
9 mouth 嘴
10 lip 嘴唇
11 chin 颏
12 beard 胡子
13 throat 喉咙
14 jaw 颌
15 neck 脖子
16 nape of the neck 颈背
17 ear 耳
18 ear lobe 耳垂
19 hair 头发

head[1] /hed; hɛd/ *n* **1** (**a**) [C] part of the body containing the eyes, nose, mouth and brain 头; 头部: *He fell and hit his head.* 他摔着了脑袋. ○ *The ball hit her on the head.* 那球打在她头上了. ○ *My head aches.* 我头痛. ⇨ illus 见插图. (**b**) **a head** [sing] this as a measure of length 一个头部之长度(量度单位): *The Queen's horse won by a head.* 女王的马以一马头之距领先获胜. ○ *Tom is taller than John by a head.* 汤姆比约翰高一个头. **2** [C] (*infml* 口) headache 头痛: *I've got a terrible head this morning.* 我今早头痛得厉害. **3** [C] ability to reason; intellect; imagination; mind 理解力; 智力; 想像力; 头脑: *Use your head*, ie Think. 动动脑筋. ○ *The thought never entered my head.* 我从来没有过这种想法. **4** [sing] mental ability or natural talent as specified 某方面的才智或天资: *have a good head for business, figures, etc* 很有经商、计算等的天才 ○ *have no head for heights*, ie feel giddy and frightened in high places, eg on top of a cliff 登高(如身临悬崖之上)会头晕和胆怯. **5 heads** [sing *v*] side of a coin with the head of a person on it 漫面(硬币有人头像的一面): *We tossed a coin* (eg to decide sth by chance) *and it came down heads.* 我们把硬币一掷(如以此法决定某事), 落下后是漫面朝上. Cf 参看 TAILS (TAIL 6). **6** (**a**) **a head** [sing] individual person 一人: *dinner at £15 a head* 每人15英镑的饭菜. (**b**) [pl *v*] individual animal in a herd or flock (禽兽群中的)头, 只: *50 head of cattle* 50头牛. **7** [C] thing like a head in form or position, eg the flattened end of a pin etc, the striking or cutting part of a tool, the mass of leaves or flowers at the top of a stem 形状或位置似头之物(如大头针等之平端、工具之打击或切割部分、植物茎梗顶部之叶或花): *the head of a nail, hammer, axe, etc* 钉子、锤子、斧子等的头 ○ *cut off the dead heads (of the roses)* 把枯萎了的(玫瑰)花从茎梗上割掉 ○ *a cabbage-head* 一棵洋白菜. **8** [C] foam on the top of poured beer, etc (倒出的啤酒等上面的)泡沫. **9** [C] device on a tape-recorder that touches the moving magnetic tape and converts the electrical signals into sound (录音机的)磁头. **10** [C] top part of a boil or swelling on the skin 疖子或皮肤上的脓肿的隆起部分: *The pimple came to a head before bursting.* 丘疹长成脓包后才破裂. **11** [C usu *sing* 通常作单数] top or highest part 上端; 顶端: *the title at the head of the page* 该页上端的标题 ○ *stand at the head of the stairs* 站在台阶的顶部 ○ *at the head of the poll*, ie having received most votes in an election 获得最多的选票. **12** [C] more important or prominent end 较重要或较突出的一端: *My father took his place at the head of the table.* 我父亲坐在上首. ○ *Place the pillows at the head of the bed.* 把枕头放置在床头. ○ *the head of the lake*, ie where a river enters it 湖的源头(河水流入该湖之处). **13** [sing] (**a**) leading part in a procession or army; front (行列或军队的)领头部分, 前列: *be at the head of a queue* 位居排头 ○ *march at the head of the regiment* 在团队的前排行进. (**b**) (*fig* 比喻) chief position 领导地位: *be at the head of one's profession* 在本专业中居领先地位. **14** [C] (**a**) chief person of a group or organization, etc 某集体或组织等的领导人: *the head of the family* 家长 ○ *a meeting of the heads of government* 政府首脑会议 ○ *a gathering of the crowned heads* (ie kings or queens) *of Europe* 欧洲各国国王的聚会 ○ [attrib 作定语] *head waiter* 服务员的领班 ○ *head office*, ie chief place of a business 总公司. (**b**) (also **Head**) chief person in a school or college; headmaster or headmistress (中小学或学院的)领导人, 校长: *Report to the Head immediately!* 马上报告校长! **15** [C usu *sing* 通常作单数] (**a**) mass of water kept at a certain height (eg for a water-mill or a hydro-electric power station) (保持一定高度的)水头(如用作水磨或水电站之动力的); 水的落差; 水压. (**b**) confined body of steam for exerting pressure 蒸气压力: *They kept up a good head of steam.* 他们把蒸气压力保持在所需的水平上. **16** [C usu *sing* 通常作单数] (in place names) promontory; cape (用于地名)岬, 海角: *Beachy Head* 比奇角. **17** [C] main division in a lecture, an essay, etc; heading (演讲、文章等的)主要部分, 标题: *a speech arranged under five heads* 分为五个部分的讲话. **18** (idm 习语) **above/over one's** ˈ**head** too difficult to understand 难以理解: *The lecture was/went way above my head.* 这演讲太深奥, 我理解不了. **bang, etc one's head against a brick** ˈ**wall** (*infml* 口) continue vainly trying to achieve sth in spite of several unsuccessful attempts 以头撞墙(尽管屡次失败, 仍然枉费心机地试图做成某事); 徒劳

无益. **be/stand head and ˈshoulders above sb/sth** be very much better, cleverer, etc than (others) 比(他人)好、聪明…得多; 鹤立鸡群. **bite sb's head off** ⇨ BITE[1]. **bother one's head/oneself about sth** ⇨ BOTHER. **bring sth/come to a ˈhead** bring sth to/reach a climax 使某事物达到顶点: *The atmosphere in the office had been tense for some time but this latest dismissal brought matters to a head.* 办事处的气氛已紧张一段时日, 而最近解雇员工一事使事态的发展达到了顶点. **bury one's head in the sand** ⇨ BURY. **by a short head** ⇨ SHORT[1]. **drive sth into sb's head** ⇨ DRIVE[1]. **drum sth into sb/sb's head** ⇨ DRUM[2]. **from ˌhead to ˈfoot/ˈtoe** over the whole length of one's body 从头到脚; 全身: *The children were covered in mud from head to toe.* 孩子们全身沾满了污泥. Cf 参看 FROM TOP TO TOE (TOP[1]). **get it into one's head that…** understand fully…; realize… 充分了解到…; 认识到…: *I wish he'd get it into his head that exams are important.* 但愿他能认识到考试是至关重要的. **give sb his ˈhead** let sb move or act freely 让某人随意而为. **go to one's ˈhead** (**a**) (of alcoholic drink) make one dizzy or slightly drunk (指酒)上头, 使人有醉意: *The whisky went straight to my head.* 威士忌酒喝得我晕头转向. (**b**) (of success) make one conceited or too confident (指成功)使人自负或过于自信: *All that praise has really gone to her head.* 那些赞扬的确冲昏了她的头脑. **harm, etc a hair of sb's head** ⇨ HAIR. **have eyes in the back of one's head** ⇨ EYE[1]. **have a good, etc head of ˈhair** have a full, etc covering of hair on the head 有一头浓密等的头发. **have a good ˈhead on one's shoulders** have practical ability, common sense, etc 有实际才能、常识等. **have one's head in the ˈclouds** have one's thoughts far away; be day-dreaming 想入非非; 做白日梦. **have one's ˈhead screwed on (the right way)** (*infml* 口) be sensible 头脑清醒. **have a level head** ⇨ LEVEL[1]. **have a swollen head** ⇨ SWELL. **have, etc a thick head** ⇨ THICK. **head ˈfirst** (**a**) (plunging, etc) with one's head before the rest of one's body (跳水等)头在前的: *She fell head first down the stairs.* 她摔倒了, 一头栽下楼梯. (**b**) with too much haste; rashly 仓促地; 轻率地. **head over ˈheels** (**a**) rolling the body over in a forward direction 向前翻跟斗. (**b**) completely 完全地: *She's head over heels in ˈlove (with him).* 她深深地爱上了(他). **ˌheads I ˈwin, ˌtails you ˈlose** (*saying* 谚) I win whatever happens 正面我赢, 反面你输(反正都是我赢; 我赢定了). **heads or ˈtails?** said when spinning a coin to decide sth by chance 要正面还是反面? (旋转钱币决定某事物时说的). **ˈheads will roll (for sth)** some people will be punished (because of sth) 有些人(因某事)要倒霉. **heap coals of fire on sb's head** ⇨ HEAP *v*. **hit the nail on the head** ⇨ HIT[1]. **hold one's ˈhead high** show pride in one's achievements, worth, ability, etc; not feel ashamed 为自己的成就、价值、才干等而骄傲; 无愧于人. **hold a pistol to sb's head** ⇨ PISTOL. **in one's ˈhead** in one's memory (not in writing) 在记忆中(而不是写下的): *How do you keep all those telephone numbers in your head?* 你是怎样把那些电话号码都记住的? **keep one's ˈhead** remain calm in a crisis (在危机中)保持镇定. **keep one's head above water** stay out of debt, difficulty, etc 未举债、未陷入困境等: *I'm managing to keep my head above water, though I'm not earning much.* 我尽管收入不多, 却能设法不欠债. **keep one's ˈhead down** avoid danger or distraction 避免危险; 防止分心. **knock sb's block/head off** ⇨ KNOCK[2]. **knock your/their heads together** ⇨ KNOCK[2]. **laugh, scream, etc one's ˈhead off** (*infml* 口) laugh, scream, etc loudly 大笑、大叫等. **like a bear with a sore head** ⇨ BEAR[1]. **lose one's ˈhead** ⇨ LOSE. **make head or ˈtail of sth** understand sth 理解某事物: *I can't make head (n)or tail of these instructions.* 我对这说明书摸不着头脑. **need, etc (to have) one's ˈhead examined** (*infml* 口) show oneself to be stupid or crazy 需要检查一下脑子; 冒傻气: *He swims in the sea in winter — he ought to have his head examined!* 他冬天在海里游泳——真是冒傻气! **not right in the/one's head** ⇨ RIGHT[1]. **off one's ˈhead** (*infml* 口) crazy; very foolish 精神错乱的; 愚不可及的: *He's (gone) off his head!* 他发疯了! **off the top of one's head** ⇨ TOP[1]. **an old head on young shoulders** ⇨ OLD. **on sb's/one's (own) head be it** sb/one will be responsible for any unpleasant consequences 某人[自己]将承担一切后果: *You wanted to try this new route, not me, so on your head be it.* 是你要试一试这条新路线的, 与我无关, 所以该由你负责. **ˌover sb's ˈhead** to a position of authority higher than sb (升)至比某人高的职位; 超越某人: *I couldn't help feeling jealous when she was promoted over my head.* 她获提升后职位比我高, 我压抑不住忌妒的心情. ○ *When her boss refused to listen to her she went over his head to the managing director.* 领班拒不听取她的意见, 她就越过他去找总经理. **a price on sb's head** ⇨ PRICE. **put one's head in the noose** allow oneself to be caught 自投罗网; 找死. **put our/your/their ˈheads together** exchange ideas or advice; consult together 交流思想; 交换意见; 合议: *I'm sure we can solve the problem if we all put our heads together.* 我相信, 只要我们大家集思广益, 就能使问题迎刃而解. **put sth into sb's ˈhead** make sb believe sth; suggest sth to sb 使某人相信某事物; 向某人提出某事物: *Who's been putting such ideas into your head?* 是谁给你出的这个主意? **put sth out of one's ˈhead** stop thinking about sth; give up (a plan, etc) 不再考虑某事物; 放弃(计划等): *You'd better put the idea of marriage out of your head.* 你最好打消结婚的念头. **put sth out of sb's/one's ˈhead** make sb/one forget sth 使某人[自己]忘掉某事物: *An interruption put it quite out of my head.* 一打岔我就把这事全忘了. **scratch one's head** ⇨ SCRATCH[1]. **shake one's head** ⇨ SHAKE[1]. **(do sth) standing on one's ˈhead** (*infml* 口) (do sth) very easily (做某事)轻而易举: *She could pass the exam standing on her head.* 她不费吹灰之力就可以考及格. **stand/turn sth on its ˈhead** reverse the expected order of sth 颠倒某事物预期的秩序: *She stood our argument on its head.* 她驳倒了我们的论点. **take it into one's head to do sth/that…** decide (esp sth unexpected or foolish) 决定做(尤指不该做的事或蠢事); (错误地)认定: *She suddenly took it into her head to dye her hair green.* 她突然心血来潮要把头发染成绿色. ○ *He's taken it into his head that I'm spreading rumours about him.* 他一直认为我在散播关于他的谣言. **talk one's/sb's head off** ⇨ TALK[2]. **turn sb's ˈhead** make sb conceited 使某人骄傲自满: *The success of his first novel completely turned his head.* 他第一部小说很成功, 便得意忘形了. **two heads are better than ˈone** (*saying* 谚) two people working together achieve more than one person working alone 两个脑袋总比一个脑袋强; 三个臭皮匠胜过诸葛亮. **weak in the head** ⇨ WEAK.

▷ **-headed** (in compound *adjs* 用以构成复合形容词) having a head or heads as specified 有某种样子的头的: *a bald-headed man.*

head·less *adj* having no head 无头的.

□ **ˈheadache** *n* **1** continuous pain in the head 头痛: *suffer from headaches* 患头痛 ○ *have a splitting headache* 头痛得要命. **2** person or thing that causes worry 令人头痛的人或事物: *Their son is a constant headache to them.* 他们的儿子老是给他们惹麻烦.

ˈheadband *n* strip of material worn around the head 束发带.

ˈheadboard *n* upright panel along the head of a bed 床头板. ⇨illus at App 1 见附录1插图, page xvi.

ˈhead cheese (*US*) = BRAWN 2.

ˈhead-dress *n* ornamental covering or band worn on the head (装饰用的)头巾; 头饰.

ˈheadgear *n* [U] hat, cap or head-dress 帽子; 头巾; 头饰.

ˈhead-hunter *n* **1** member of a tribe that collects the heads of its enemies as trophies 收集敌人首级作为战利品的部落人. **2** person or firm paid to find and recruit staff at a senior level 物色、招聘高级人才的人或公司.

ˈhead-hunting *n* [U].

ˈheadlamp *n* = HEADLIGHT.

headland /ˈhedlənd; ˈhɛdˌlænd/ *n* high piece of land that juts into the sea; promontory 岬角(突入海中的高地). ⇨illus at COAST 见COAST插图.

ˈheadlight *n* (**a**) lamp at the front of a motor vehicle or railway engine (汽车或火车头的)头灯, 前灯. ⇨illus at App 1 见附录1插图, page xii. (**b**) beam from this 汽车或火车头前灯射出的光线: *Driving without headlights at* *night is illegal.* 夜晚行车不开亮头灯是违法的.

ˈ**headline** *n* **1** [C] line of words printed in large type at the top of a page, esp in a newspaper 书刊(尤指报纸)页首的大字标题: [attrib 作定语] *headline news* 头版头条新闻. **2 the headlines** [pl] brief summary on TV or radio of the most important items of news (电视或无线电广播中的)新闻内容提要. **3** (idm 习语) **hit/make/reach the ˈheadlines** become important or much-publicized news 成为重要新闻; 大事宣扬的新闻.

ˈ**headlong** *adv, adj* [attrib 作定语] **1** with the head first 头在前(的): *fall headlong* 倒栽葱. **2** in a hasty and rash way 迅急莽撞(的): *rush headlong into danger* 不顾一切地迎着危险冲上去.

ˈ**headman** /-mæn; -mæn/ *n* (*pl* **-men** /-men; -mɛn/) chief man of a village, tribe, etc (村子、部落等的)首领; 村长; 酋长; 头人.

headˈmaster, headˈmistress *ns* principal man or woman in a school, responsible for organizing it (中小学的)校长.

ˌ**Head of ˈState** (*pl* **Heads of State**) chief public representative of a country, who may also be the head of government 一国民众的领导人(亦可为政府之首脑).

ˌ**head-ˈon** *adj, adv* (**a**) with the front parts of two vehicles colliding (两辆机动车)正面相撞(的): *a ˌhead-on ˈcrash* 迎头相撞的事故 ○ *The lorries crashed head-ˈon.* 两辆卡车迎面撞个正着. (**b**) with the front part of a vehicle hitting a stationary object (汽车)正面撞及固定物体(的): *The car hit the tree head-ˈon.* 汽车迎面撞到树上. ○ (*fig* 比喻) *tackle a problem head-ˈon,* ie without trying to avoid it 正视某问题加以解决(不回避问题).

ˈ**headphones** *n* [pl] radio or telephone receivers held over the ears by a band fitting over the head; earphones 头戴式受话器; 耳机: *a pair of headphones* 一副耳机.

ˌ**headˈquarters** *n* [sing or pl *v*] (*abbr* 缩写 **HQ**) place from which an organization is controlled 总部; 司令部; 指挥部; 大本营: *The firm's headquarters are in London.* 总公司设在伦敦.

ˈ**head-rest** *n* thing that supports the head of a person sitting down, eg in a car (座位上的)头垫, 头枕(如汽车中的). ⇨illus at App 1 见附录1插图, page xii.

ˈ**headroom** *n* [U] overhead space, esp above a vehicle; clearance 头上空间(尤指机动车的上方); 净空高度: *There is not enough headroom for buses to go under this bridge.* 这座桥梁下面的净空高度不够, 公共汽车不能通行.

ˈ**headscarf** *n* (*pl* **-scarves**) scarf tied round the head, usu with a knot under the chin, worn instead of a hat 头巾.

ˈ**head-set** *n* headphones 头戴式受话器; 耳机.

ˈ**headship** *n* position of headmaster or headmistress (中小学)校长的职位: *apply for a headship* 申请担任校长职务.

ˈ**head-shrinker** *n* (*sl* 俚) psychiatrist 精神病医师或专家.

ˌ**head ˈstart** advantage given or gained at an early stage 先起步所处的有利地位; 先起步的优势: *Being already able to read gave her a head start over the other pupils.* 她已识字, 因而比其他学生在学习上领先一步.

ˈ**headstone** *n* piece of stone placed to mark the head of a grave 墓碑.

ˈ**head-waters** *n* [pl] tributary stream or streams forming the sources of a river 河源的支流; 源头.

ˈ**headway** *n* [U] progress, esp in difficult circumstances 进步, 进展(尤指在困难条件下所取得者): *We are making little headway with the negotiations.* 我们在谈判中没有取得什么进展. ○ *The boat made slow headway against the tide.* 那船逆着潮水缓慢地前进.

ˈ**head wind** wind blowing from directly in front 顶头风; 逆风. Cf 参看 TAIL WIND (TAIL).

ˈ**headword** *n* word forming a heading, eg the first word, in heavy type, of a dictionary entry 首词(标题或起首用的词, 如词典词条中用粗体刊出的第一个词).

head[2] /hed; hɛd/ *v* **1** [Tn] (**a**) be at the front or top of (sth) 在(某事物)的前部或顶部: *head a procession* 在队伍的前列 ○ *Smith's name headed the list.* 史密斯的名字在名单的最上端. (**b**) be in charge of or lead (sth) 主管或领导(某事物): *head a rebellion, government, delegation* 领导叛乱、政府、代表团. **2** [Tn esp passive 尤用于被动语态] give a heading to (a letter, etc) 给(信等)加上信头、标题等: *The chapter was headed 'My Early Life'.* 这一章的标题是'我早年的生活'. **3** [Ipr, Ip] move in the specified direction 朝某方向行进: *Where are you heading/headed?* 你往哪儿走? ○ *head south, back to camp, away from the town, towards home, etc* 朝南、回营地、城外、家里等的方向走. **4** [Tn] strike (the ball) with one's head in football (足球比赛中)用头顶(球). **5** (idm 习语) **head/top the bill** ⇨ BILL[1]. **6** (phr v) **head for ...** move towards (a place) 向(某处)行进: *The boat was heading for some rocks.* 那船正驶向礁石. ○ *He headed straight for the bar.* 他径直朝酒吧间走去. ○ (*fig* 比喻) *Is the world heading for disaster?* 世界正面临灾难吗? **head sb/sth off** get in front of sb/sth so as to turn him/it back or aside 当头拦阻某人[某物](使其折返或转向): *head off enemy troops, reporters, an angry mob, etc* 拦截敌军、拦阻记者、拦住气势汹汹的暴徒 ○ *head off a flock of sheep,* ie to prevent them from going the wrong way 拦阻羊群(以防其走错方向) ○ (*fig* 比喻) *head off* (ie prevent or forestall) *a quarrel* 防止争吵.

header /ˈhedə(r); ˈhɛdɚ/ *n* **1** (*infml* 口) dive or fall (esp into water) with the head first 头部向下跳水或跌落(尤指入水): *take a header into the swimming-pool* 头先入水跳入游泳池. **2** (in football) act of hitting the ball with the head (足球运动中)用头顶球.

head·ing /ˈhedɪŋ; ˈhɛdɪŋ/ *n* word or words put at the top of a page, section of a book, etc as a title (书籍等篇页、章节上端的)标题.

head·strong /ˈhedstrɒŋ; *US* -strɔːŋ; ˈhɛdˌstrɔŋ/ *adj* obstinately determined to do things in one's own way without listening to others; self-willed 刚愎自用的; 固执任性的.

heady /ˈhedɪ; ˈhɛdɪ/ *adj* (**-ier, -iest**) **1** (**a**) (of alcoholic drinks) likely to make people drunk quickly; potent (指酒精饮料)易使人醉的, 烈性的: *a heady wine* 易使人醉的酒. (**b**) having a quick effect on the senses; very exciting 迅速作用于感官的; 兴奋的: *a heady perfume* 气味扑鼻的香水 ○ *the heady days of one's youth* 年轻时使人陶醉的日子. **2** (**a**) (of a person) excited and acting rashly (指人)激动得忘乎所以的: *be heady with success* 因成功而得意忘形. (**b**) (of an action) done impulsively or rashly (指行为)一时冲动的, 鲁莽冒失的.

heal /hiːl; hil/ *v* **1** [I, Ip, Tn] **~ (over/up)** (cause sth to) become healthy again (使某物)康复: *The wound healed slowly.* 伤口愈合得很慢. ○ *The cut soon healed over/up, but it left a scar.* 伤口不久就愈合了, 但却留下了伤疤. ○ *the healing powers of sleep* 睡眠的治疗作用 ○ *The wound is not yet healed,* ie has not yet been covered by new skin. 伤口尚未愈合(尚未长出新皮). **2** (**a**) [Tn] cause (sth) to end; make easier to bear 使(某事物)完结; 使好受一些: *heal a quarrel* 平息一场争吵 ○ *Time heals all sorrows.* 时间可化解一切忧伤. (**b**) [Tn, Tn·pr] **~ sb (of sth)** (*arch* 古) restore sb to health; cure sb (of a disease) 使某人康复; 治愈某人(的疾病): *The holy man healed them of their sickness.* 那位神职人员治好了他们的疾病.

▷ **healer** *n* person or thing that heals 进行治疗的人或物: *Time is a great healer.* 时间就是良药.

health /helθ; hɛlθ/ *n* [U] **1** condition of a person's body or mind 人的身体或精神状况; 健康状况: *have poor health* 身体不好 ○ *be in/enjoy the best of health* 身体非常好 ○ *Exercise is good for the health.* 锻炼身体有益于健康. ○ *Your (very) good health!* eg said when drinking a toast to sb 祝你健康! (如向某人敬酒时之用语) ○ [attrib 作定语] *health insurance/care* 健康保险[保健] ○ *He retired early for health reasons.* 他由于健康上的原因而提前退休. **2** state of being well and free from illness 健康: *be restored to health* 恢复健康 ○ *be bursting with health and vitality* 身体健康、精神抖擞. **3** (idm 习语) **a clean bill of health** ⇨ CLEAN[1]. **drink sb's health; drink a health to sb** ⇨ DRINK[2]. **in rude health** ⇨ RUDE. **propose a toast/sb's health** ⇨ PROPOSE.

▷ **health·ful** /ˈhelθfl; ˈhɛlθfəl/ *adj* (*fml* 文) good for the health 有益于健康的.

□ ˈ**health centre** (*Brit*) headquarters of a group of local medical services 地方医疗服务中心; 卫生院.

ˈ**health farm** place where people go in order to try to improve their health by dieting, exercising, etc 健身场.

ˈ**health food** (often *pl* 常作复数) natural food, usu free

of artificial substances, that is thought to be especially good for the health 保健食品(天然的、通常不加人造物质的食物): [attrib 作定语] *a health food restaurant, shop, etc* 供应保健食品的餐馆、商店等.

'**health service** public service providing medical care 公共医疗卫生服务.

'**health visitor** (*Brit*) nurse who visits sick or old people at their homes (上门访视病人或老年人的)护理人员.

healthy /ˈhelθɪ; ˋhɛlθɪ/ *adj* (**-ier, -iest**) **1** having good health; well and able to resist disease 健康的; 强健的: *a healthy child, animal, tree* 健康的孩子、健壮的动物、茁壮的树木 ○ (*fig* 比喻) *a healthy bank balance* 相当多的银行存款余额. **2** likely to produce good health 可能对健康有益的: *a healthy climate, lifestyle, environment* 宜于健康的气候、生活方式、环境. **3** indicating good health 显示健康的: *have a healthy appetite* 胃口好. **4** natural and beneficial 自然产生并有益处的: *The child showed a healthy curiosity.* 那孩子有好奇心, 这是好现象. ○ *She has a healthy respect for her rival's talents.* 她很明智, 没有轻视对手的才能. ▷ **health·ily** *adv*. **healthi·ness** *n* [U]

NOTE ON USAGE 用法: **1 Healthy** and **fit** both indicate that a person is physically strong and rarely suffers from any physical illness. ☆ **healthy** 和 **fit** 这两个词均表示人身体强健, 很少生病. **Healthy** also refers to the conditions which are good for somebody's health, or the outward signs of somebody having good health ☆ **healthy** 亦指有益于健康的条件, 或健康人的外部征象: *They have very healthy children.* 他们的孩子都很健康. ○ *This damp climate isn't very healthy.* 这种潮湿的气候对健康不太有利. ○ *She has a healthy appetite.* 她胃口很好.· **2 Fit** suggests that someone is in good physical condition particularly as a result of taking regular exercise ☆ **fit** 指人的身体状况良好, 尤因经常锻炼所致: *'How do you stay so fit?' 'I go to keep-fit classes.'* '你是怎样保持健康的?' '我经常上健身课.' **3 Well** generally refers to somebody's health on a particular occasion. ☆ **well** 一般指人在特定场合下身体良好. It is used in answer to inquiries about health 这个词常用以回答有关健康的询问: *He's been quite ill. I hope he gets well soon.* 他病得很厉害, 但愿他不久能好. ○ *I think I'll go to bed. I don't feel at all well.* 我要睡觉去了. 我感到很不舒服. ○ *'How are you?' 'Very well, thank you.'* '你好吗?' '很好, 谢谢你的问候.'

heap /hi:p; hip/ *n* **1** number of things or mass of material lying piled up 堆: *a heap of books, sand, rubbish* 一堆书、沙、垃圾 ○ *clothes left in heaps on the ground* 丢弃在地上的一堆堆的衣服 ○ *The building was reduced to a heap of rubble.* 那建筑物已成了一片瓦砾. ○ (*fig* 比喻) *She collapsed on the floor in a heap.* 她蜷作一团瘫倒在地上. **2 heaps** [pl] **~ (of sth)** (*infml* 口) great number or amount; plenty 大量; 许多: *We have heaps of time.* 我们有很多时间. ○ *She's been there heaps of times.* 她去过那里许多次了. ○ *I've got heaps to tell you.* 我有很多话要跟你说. **3** (*infml joc* 口, 谑) motor car that is old and in poor condition 破旧的汽车. **4** (idm 习语) **heaps better, more, older, etc** (*infml* 口) much better, etc 好、多、旧…得多: *Do have a second helping — there's heaps more.* 再吃一些吧——东西多着呢.

▷ **heap** *v* **1** [Tn, Tn·p] **~ sth (up)** put (things) in a pile 堆积(物品): *heap (up) stones to form a dam* 把石头堆成一道堤坝 ○ (*fig* 比喻) *heap up riches* 积聚财富 ○ *a heaped spoonful of flour* 满满的一匙面粉. **2** [Tn·pr] **~ sth on sb/sth; ~ sb/sth with sth** load or place sth in a pile on sb/sth 在某物中装满某物; 给予某人大量的某事物: *heap food on one's plate/heap one's plate with food* 在盘中盛满食物 ○ (*fig* 比喻) *heap praises, insults, etc on sb* 对某人大加赞扬、侮辱等. **3** (idm 习语) **heap coals of 'fire on sb's head** make sb feel remorse for treating one badly by treating him well in return 对某人以德报怨而使之愧悔.

hear /hɪə(r); hɪr/ *v* (*pt, pp* **heard** /hɜ:d; hɝd/) **1** [I, Tn, Tng, Tni] perceive (sounds) with the ears 听见(声音): *She doesn't/can't hear very well,* ie is rather deaf. 她听觉不灵. ○ *We listened but could hear nothing.* 我们留心听, 却什么也没有听见. ○ *Have you ever heard that song sung in Italian?* 你听过用意大利语唱的那首歌曲吗? ○ *I heard someone laughing.* 我听见有人笑. ○ *Did you hear him go out?* 你听见他走出去了吗? ○ *He was heard to groan.* 有人听见他在呻吟. **2** [Tn, Tw] listen or pay attention to (sb/sth) 听, 聆听, 谛听, 倾听(某人的声音[某事物]): *You're not to go — do you hear me!* 你不要走——听我的话! ○ *We'd better hear what they have to say.* 我们还是听听他们要说些什么吧. ⇨Usage at FEEL[1] 用法见 FEEL[1]. **3** [Tn] listen to and try (a case) in a lawcourt 审理(案件): *The court heard the evidence.* 法庭听取了证词. ○ *Which judge will hear the case?* 哪位法官(将)审理这案件? **4** [I, Tn, Tf] be told or informed about (sth) 听说或得知(某事物): *You sing very well, I hear.* 听说你唱得好极了. ○ *Have you heard the news?* 你听到那消息了吗? ○ *I heard (that) he was ill.* 我听说他病了. ○ *I've heard (say) that it's a good film.* 听说那是部好影片. **5** [Tn] grant (a prayer) 答允(所祈求的事物). **6** (idm 习语) ˌ**hear!** '**hear!** (used to express agreement and approval 用以表示同意和赞成). **hear/see the last of sb/sth** ⇨ LAST[1]. **hear a 'pin drop** hear the slightest noise 听得见最细小的声音: *The audience was so quiet you could have heard a pin drop.* 观众静得连别针落地的声音也能听见. **hear tell of sth** hear people talking about sth 听人说起某事物: *I've often heard tell of such things.* 我时常听人说起这类事情. **listen to/hear reason** ⇨ REASON. **make one's voice heard** ⇨ VOICE. **not/never hear the end of sth** not be finished with sth as the subject of discussion or matter that affects one (议论到的或涉及自身的某事物)未结束: *If we don't give her what she wants we'll never hear the end of it.* 我们若不满足她的要求, 这事就没完没了了. **7** (phr v) **hear about sth** be given information about sth 听到关于某事物的消息: *I've only just heard about his dismissal.* 我刚听到他遭解雇的事. ○ *You will hear about this* (ie will receive a formal rebuke about it) *later.* 这件事你就等瞧吧(要受到严厉斥责). **hear from sb** receive a letter, telephone call, etc from sb 接到某人的来信、电话等: *How often do you hear from your sister?* 你多长时间接到你姐姐一次信? **hear of sb/sth** be told about or have knowledge of sb/sth 听到或知道某人[某事物]的情况: *I've never heard of the place.* 我从未听说过那个地方. ○ *She disappeared and was never heard of again.* 她不知去向了, 再未听到她的消息. **not 'hear of sth** (usu with *will* or *would* 通常与 will 或 would 连用) refuse to allow sth 不允许某事: *He wouldn't hear of my walking home alone.* 他不许我单独一人走回家. ○ *I can't let you pay my debts — I won't hear of such a thing.* 我不能让你替我还债——我不同意此事. **hear sb out** listen until sb has finished saying what he wants to say 把某人要讲的话听完: *I know you don't believe me but please hear me out!* 我知道你不信我的话, 但是请听我把话说完!

▷ **hearer** /ˈhɪərə(r); ˋhɪrɚ/ *n* person who hears sth, esp a member of an audience 听者; (尤指)一名听众或观众.

hear·ing /ˈhɪərɪŋ; ˋhɪrɪŋ/ *n* **1** [U] ability to hear; sense(1) with which sound is perceived 听力; 听觉: *Her hearing is poor,* ie She is rather deaf. 她的听觉不灵(她耳朵有点背). **2** [U] distance within which one can hear 听力可以达到的距离: *He said so in my hearing,* ie in my presence so that I could hear. 他当着我的面说的这番话. ○ *Please keep within hearing (distance),* ie stay near enough to hear. 请保持在听得见的距离内. **3** [C] **(a)** opportunity to be heard 说话或申辩的机会: *be given a fair hearing* 获得公平的申辩机会 ○ *I never gained a hearing,* ie Nobody was willing to listen to me. 我一直没有机会说话(谁也不愿听). **(b)** trial of a case in a lawcourt, esp before a judge without a jury 开审; 审讯; (尤指无陪审团的)听讯: *The defendant's family were present at the hearing.* 被告家属在审讯时旁听. **4** (idm 习语) **hard of hearing** ⇨ HARD[1].

□ '**hearing-aid** *n* small device that amplifies sound and helps a deaf person to hear 助听器: *have/wear a hearing-aid* 有[戴]助听器.

hearken /ˈhɑ:kən; ˋhɑrkən/ *v* [I, Ipr] **~ (to sb/sth)** (*arch* 古) listen 聆听; 谛听; 倾听.

hear·say /ˈhɪəseɪ; ˋhɪrˌse/ *n* [U] things one has heard another person or other people say, which may or may not be true; rumour 道听途说; 谣言: *You shouldn't believe that — it's just hearsay.* 你不该相信那话——那

不过是道听途说罢了. ○ [attrib 作定语] *hearsay evidence* 传闻证据.

hearse /hɜːs; hɝs/ *n* vehicle for carrying a coffin at a funeral 灵车; 柩车.

heart /hɑːt; hɑrt/ *n* **1** [C] (**a**) hollow muscular organ that pumps blood through the body 心; 心脏: *His heart stopped beating and he died soon afterwards.* 他心脏停止了跳动, 随即死亡. ○ [attrib 作定语] *have heart trouble/disease* 患心脏病 ○ *a heart hospital* 心脏专科医院. ⇨ illus at RESPIRE 见 RESPIRE 插图. (**b**) part of the body where this is 心脏的部位: *He pressed her hand against his heart.* 他把她的一只手按在自己胸部心脏的地方. **2** [C] centre of a person's thoughts and emotions, esp of love; ability to feel emotion 内心; 衷心; 心灵; 心肠; (尤指)爱心: *I have everything my heart desires.* 我心满意足. ○ *She knew it in her heart.* 她心里明白. ○ *He has a kind heart.* 他心肠好. ○ *The princess captured the hearts of the nation.* 那位公主赢得了全体国民的心. **3** [U] enthusiasm 热心; 热情: *I want you to put more heart into your singing.* 我希望你在唱的时候多带点感情. **4** [C] (**a**) central, innermost or most important part of sth 某事物的中心; 核心部分; 要点; 实质: *in the heart of the forest* 在森林中央 ○ *get to the heart of the matter, subject, mystery* 把握住事情、问题、难解事物的实质. (**b**) inner compact part of a cabbage, lettuce, etc (洋白菜、莴苣等的)菜心. **5** (**a**) [C] thing shaped like a heart, esp a regular red shape used to represent a heart, eg to symbolize love or on a playing-card 心形物; (尤指象征爱情的或纸牌上的)红心, 红桃. (**b**) **hearts** [sing or pl *v*] suit of playing-cards marked with these 一组红桃牌: *the ten of hearts* 红桃十点 ○ *Hearts is/are trumps.* 红桃是王牌. ⇨illus at PLAYING-CARD 见 PLAYING-CARD 插图. (**c**) [C] playing-card of this suit 红桃牌: *play a heart* 打出红桃牌. **6** [C] (used as a term of endearment 用作亲昵语) beloved person 心爱的人: *dear heart* 心肝宝贝儿. **7** (idm 习语) **after one's own 'heart** of exactly the type one likes best 正合某人心意: *He likes good wine too — he's obviously a man after my own heart.* 他也喜欢好酒——真是与我臭味相投了. **at 'heart** in one's real nature; basically 内心里; 基本上: *I'm a country girl at heart.* 我实际上是个乡下姑娘. **bare one's heart/soul** ⇨ BARE[2]. **break sb's/one's 'heart** make sb/one feel very sad 使某人[自己]很伤心: *It breaks my heart to see him crying.* 我见他在哭, 感到难过极了. ○ *It broke her heart when he left.* 他离开时她心都碎了. **by 'heart** from memory 凭记性: *learn/know a poem by heart* 记住[能背出]一首诗. **a change of heart** ⇨ CHANGE[2]. **close/dear/near to sb's 'heart** of deep interest and concern to sb 使某人很感兴趣; 为某人深切关注: *This subject is very close to my heart.* 这题目使我很感兴趣. **cross my heart** ⇨ CROSS[2]. **cry one's eyes/heart out** ⇨ CRY[1]. **do one's 'heart good** cause one to feel encouraged, cheerful, etc 使人感到鼓舞、欢欣等: *It does my heart good to see the children enjoying themselves.* 我看到孩子们玩得很高兴, 心中非常愉快. **eat one's heart out** ⇨ EAT. **find it in one's heart/oneself to do sth** ⇨ FIND[1]. **from the (bottom of one's) 'heart** sincere(ly) 衷心(的); 真诚(的): *This advice comes from the heart.* 这个劝告是真心实意的. **give one's heart to sb/sth** come to love sb/sth 爱上某人[某事物]. **have sth at 'heart** be anxious to support or defend sth 很关心某事物; 亟欲支持或维护某事物: *He has your welfare at heart*, ie wants you to be happy, etc. 他非常关心你的幸福. **have a 'heart** (*infml* 口) be sympathetic or kind; show mercy 发慈悲; 做好事. **have the heart (to do sth)** (usu in negative sentences or questions with *can* or *could* 通常在否定句或疑问句中与 can 或 could 连用) be cruel or unfeeling enough (to do sth) 忍心(做某事): *I hadn't the heart to refuse.* 我不忍心拒绝. **have one's heart in one's 'boots** be very gloomy and depressed 极为悲观消沉. **have one's heart in one's 'mouth** be badly frightened 非常惊恐: *My heart was in my mouth.* 我吓得要命. **have one's 'heart in the right place** have true or kind feelings 怀有真情或善意. **have one's heart set on sth** = SET ONE'S HEART/HOPES ON STH. **heart and 'soul** enthusiastically; energetically 满腔热情地; 全力地: *devote oneself heart and soul to one's work* 全心全意地致力于工作. **one's heart 'bleeds for sb** (*often ironic* 常作反语) one pities or feels sorry for sb 怜悯或同情某人. **one's heart goes out to sb** one feels compassion for sb 同情或怜悯某人. **a heart of 'gold** a very kind nature 非常善良的本性; 好心肠: *He sometimes seems bad-tempered but really he's got a heart of gold.* 他有时显得脾气暴躁, 而实际上却心地善良. **a heart of 'stone** a pitiless and unfeeling nature 冷酷无情的本性; 铁石心肠. **one's heart is in sth** one is enthusiastic about sth 热心于某事物: *I want her to take the exam again but her heart's not in it.* 我想让她重考一次, 她却掉以轻心. **one's heart sinks** one feels disappointed 感到失望: *When I saw the pile of dirty dishes, my heart sank.* 我看到那一堆肮脏的餐具时, 感到很扫兴. **in good 'heart** in good condition or spirits 兴致勃勃(地); 兴高采烈的. **in one's ˌheart (of 'hearts)** in one's inmost feelings 在内心深处: *He knew in his heart that he was doing the wrong thing.* 他心里明白自己做的是错事. **lose heart** ⇨ LOSE. **lose one's heart to sb/sth** ⇨ LOSE. **open one's heart/mind to sb** ⇨ OPEN[2]. **search one's heart/conscience** ⇨ SEARCH *v*. **set one's heart on (having/doing) sth** want sth greatly 渴望某事物. **sick at heart** ⇨ SICK. **sob one's heart out** ⇨ SOB. **strike fear, etc into sb/sb's heart** ⇨ STRIKE[2]. **take 'heart (at sth)** become encouraged or more confident 鼓足勇气; 增强信心. **take sth to 'heart** be much affected or upset by sth 深受某事物困扰; 因某事物而烦恼: *I took your criticism very much to heart.* 我听到你的批评受到很大震动. **to one's heart's con'tent** as much as one wishes 尽情地. **wear one's heart on one's sleeve** ⇨ WEAR[2]. **with ˌall one's 'heart/one's whole 'heart** completely; sincerely 全心全意地; 真心实意地: *I hope with all my heart that you succeed.* 我衷心希望你成功. **young at heart** ⇨ YOUNG.

▷ **-hearted** (in compound *adjs* 用以构成复合形容词) having feelings or a nature as specified 有某种心情或天性的: *kind-hearted* ○ *faint-hearted*.

heart·less *adj* unkind; without pity 无情的; 残忍的. **heart·lessly** *adv*. **heart·less·ness** *n* [U].

□ **'heartache** *n* [U, C] great sorrow 痛心; 悲痛.

'heart attack sudden illness with irregular and violent beating of the heart 心脏病的突然发作: *have/suffer a heart attack* 心脏病突然发作. Cf 参看 CORONARY THROMBOSIS (CORONARY).

'heartbeat *n* pulsating movement of the heart or the sound it makes 心搏; 心跳声: *Your heartbeat is quite normal.* 你的心跳得很正常.

'heart-break *n* [C, U] (cause of) very great unhappiness 很大的不幸; 造成很大不幸的原因: *She's had her share of heart-break(s).* 她也有她自己的伤心事.

'heart-breaking *adj*.

'heart-broken *adj* (of a person) feeling great sadness (指人)极其伤心的: *He was heart-broken when she left.* 她离开时他伤心已极.

'heartburn *n* [U] burning sensation in the lower part of the chest, caused by indigestion 胃灼热, 烧心(系因消化不良所致).

'heart failure sudden failure of the heart to function properly 心力衰竭.

'heartfelt *adj* deeply felt; sincere 衷心的; 真诚的: *heartfelt sympathy/thanks* 由衷的同情[感谢].

heartland /ˈhɑːtlænd; ˈhɑrtˌlænd/ *n* central or most important part of an area 心脏地带; 中心区域: *Germany's industrial heartland* 德国的工业中心.

ˌheart-'lung machine machine that can temporarily perform the functions of the heart and lungs, esp during a surgical operation 人工心肺机(临时代替心脏和肺脏功能的机器, 尤用于外科手术时).

'heart-rending *adj* very distressing 使人极为悲痛的: *a heart-rending sight, scream, appeal* 令人心碎的情景、尖叫、哀诉.

'heart-searching *n* [U] examination of one's own feelings and motives 省察; 反省: *After much heart-searching they decided to separate.* 他们考虑再三之后, 决定分开.

'heartsick *adj* sad and dejected 沮丧的.

'heart-strings *n* [pl] deepest feelings of love or pity 最深厚的爱或同情; 心弦: *play upon sb's heart-strings*, ie move him emotionally 拨动某人心弦(使其感动).

'heart-throb *n* (*infml* 口) attractive person who arouses strong feelings of love; sweetheart 迷恋的对象; 心爱的人: *He's my heart-throb.* 他是我的心上人. ○ *He's a real heart-throb.* 他真有魅力.

ˌ**heart-to-ˈheart** *n* frank conversation about personal matters 谈心: *have a heart-to-heart with sb* 与某人谈心 ○ [attrib 作定语] *a ˌheart-to-heart ˈchat* 促膝谈心.

ˈ**heart-warming** *adj* causing feelings of happiness and pleasure 令人感到幸福愉快的: *a heart-warming reunion, gesture, gift* 令人欣喜的团聚、表示、礼物.

hearten /ˈhɑːtn; ˋhɑrtn̩/ *v* [Tn esp passive 尤用于被动语态] make (sb) feel cheerful and encouraged 使(某人)欢欣鼓舞: *We are much heartened by the latest developments.* 最近的事态发展使我们受到很大的鼓舞.
▷ **hearten·ing** *adj*: *heartening news* 振奋人心的消息. **hearten·ingly** *adv*.

hearth /hɑːθ; hɑrθ/ *n* **1** (**a**) floor of a fireplace (壁炉的)炉床: *a fire burning in the hearth* 在炉床里燃烧的火. (**b**) area in front of this 炉前区域; 壁炉边: *slippers warming on/by the hearth* 放在壁炉边烤着的拖鞋. **2** (*fig* 比喻) home 家: *a longing for hearth and home* 渴望家庭的温暖.
□ ˈ**hearthrug** *n* rug laid in front of a fireplace 壁炉前的地毯.

heart·ily /ˈhɑːtɪlɪ; ˋhɑrtɪlɪ/ *adv* **1** with obvious enjoyment and enthusiasm; vigorously 尽情地; 热心地; 痛快地: *laugh, sing, eat, etc heartily* 开怀大笑、纵情歌唱、大吃特吃. **2** very; truly 极其; 确实: *be heartily glad, pleased, relieved, upset, etc* 极其高兴、愉快、轻松、不安等 ○ *I'm heartily sick of this wet weather.* 我非常讨厌这种潮湿的天气.

hearty /ˈhɑːtɪ; ˋhɑrtɪ/ *adj* (**-ier, -iest**) **1** [usu attrib 通常作定语] showing warm and friendly feelings; enthusiastic 亲切友好的; 热诚的; 衷心的: *a hearty welcome, reception, greeting, etc* 热烈的欢迎、热情的接待、亲切的问候 ○ *give one's hearty approval and support to a plan* 竭诚地赞同并支持一项计划. **2** (*sometimes derog* 有时作贬义) loud and (too) cheerful 喧闹而(过分)快活的: *a hearty person, laugh* (过于)开心的人、纵情的大笑. **3** [attrib 作定语] large 大的: *eat a hearty breakfast* 吃一顿丰盛的早餐 ○ *have a hearty appetite* 胃口很好. **4** (esp of older people) strong and healthy (尤指老人)健壮的. **5** (idm 习语) **hale and hearty** ⇨ HALE.
▷ **hearti·ness** *n* [U].
hearty *n* **1** hearty person, esp one who is fond of sport 强健者; (尤指)体育爱好者. **2** (idm 习语) **my hearties** (*dated infml* 旧, 口) (used as a form of address, esp among sailors) 用作称呼语(尤于水手之间): *Heave ho, my hearties!* 伙伴们, 用力呀!

heat[1] /hiːt; hit/ *n* **1** [U] (**a**) high temperature; hotness 高温; 热: *feel the heat of the sun's rays* 感到阳光的热力 ○ *This fire doesn't give out much heat.* 这个炉子的火不旺. (**b**) hot weather 炎热天气: *suffer from the heat* 经受炎热天气之苦 ○ *Never go out in the heat* (ie at the hottest time) *of the day without a hat.* 在白天最热的时候出门不能不戴帽子. **2** [U] (*fig* 比喻) intense feeling, esp of anger or excitement 强烈的感情; (尤指)愤怒或激动: *speak with considerable heat* 颇为激动地说 ○ *in the heat of the argument* 在激烈辩论中 ○ *This topic generates a lot of heat.* 这个话题会引起群情激奋. ○ *He tried to take the heat out of the situation*, ie reduce the tension. 他竭力让局面缓和下来. **3** [C] preliminary contest, the winners of which take part in further contests or the final 预赛(获胜者可参加复赛或决赛): *be eliminated in the first heat* 在第一场预赛中被淘汰. **4** (idm 习语) **be on heat**; *US* **be in heat** (of female mammals) be in the time or condition of sexual excitement and ready for mating (指雌性哺乳动物)发情. **in the ˌheat of the ˈmoment** while (temporarily) very angry, excited, upset, etc 在(一时)盛怒、激动、心烦意乱等中.
□ ˈ**heat barrier** limit on the speed of aircraft, etc caused by heat resulting from air friction 热障(因摩擦生热使飞行器等受到的速度限制).
ˈ**heat rash** itchy red rash caused by blockage of the sweat glands in hot weather 痱子.
ˈ**heat shield** device on a spacecraft that protects it against excessive heat, esp when it re-enters the earth's atmosphere 热屏蔽(宇宙飞船上的隔热层, 尤于重返地球大气层时, 可防止飞船过热受损).
ˈ**heat-stroke** *n* [U] sudden illness caused by too much exposure to heat or sun 中暑.
ˈ**heatwave** *n* time of unusually hot weather 酷暑时期; 热浪.

heat[2] /hiːt; hit/ *v* [I, Ip, Tn, Tn·p] **~ (sth) (up)** (cause sth to) become hot or warm (使某物)变热或变暖: *The office will soon heat up.* 办公室很快就会暖和起来. ○ *Heating these offices is expensive.* 这些办公室的供暖费用很高. ○ *The pie has already been cooked — it just needs heating up.* 馅饼是熟的 —— 只需热热就可以了. ○ *Is it a heated swimming-pool?* 这是温水游泳池吗?
▷ **heated** *adj* (of a person or discussion) angry; excited (指人或讨论)愤怒的, 激烈的: *a heated argument* 激烈的辩论. **heatedly** *adv*.
heater *n* device for supplying warmth to a room or for heating water 供热装置; 加热器; 炉子: *a gas heater* 煤气暖炉 ○ *a water-heater* 热水器 ○ *The heater in my car doesn't work properly.* 我汽车里的暖气设备出了点毛病. Cf 参看 FIRE[1] 3, STOVE 2.
heat·ing *n* [U] means or system of supplying heat 加热法; 供热系统; 暖气设备: *Switch the heating on — I'm cold!* 把暖气打开吧 —— 我冷! ○ [attrib 作定语] *heating costs* 暖气费.

heath /hiːθ; hiθ/ *n* **1** [C] area of flat uncultivated land, esp one covered with shrubs; moorland 荒地(尤指灌木丛生之处); 荒野. **2** [C, U] small evergreen shrub that grows on a heath 石楠属常绿灌木. Cf 参看 HEATHER.

heathen /ˈhiːðn; ˋhiðən/ *n* **1** person who does not believe in any of the world's chief religions, esp one who is neither Christian, Muslim nor Jew; pagan 不信世界上任何主要宗教的人; (尤指基督教、伊斯兰教、犹太教以外的)异教徒: [attrib 作定语] *heathen customs* 异教徒的风俗. **2** (*infml* 口) wild or bad-mannered person 未开化的人; 行为不端的人: *Some young heathen has vandalized the bus shelter.* 有几个坏小子故意损坏了公共汽车候车亭.
▷ **hea·then·ish** /ˈhiːðənɪʃ; ˋhiðənɪʃ/ *adj* of or like heathens; barbarous 异教徒的; 似异教徒的; 野蛮的.

heather /ˈheðə(r); ˋhɛðɚ/ *n* [U] low evergreen plant or shrub with small purple, pink or white bell-shaped flowers, common on moorland 帚石楠(常绿小乔木或灌木, 开紫色、粉红色或白色的钟形小花, 常见于欧洲荒野). Cf 参看 HEATH 2.

Heath Rob·in·son /ˌhiːθ ˈrɒbɪnsən; ˌhiθ ˋrɑbɪnsən/ (of equipment) absurdly complicated and unlikely to work (指设备)结构复杂古怪而未必中用的: [attrib 作定语] *a Heath Robinson contraption* 稀奇古怪而不实用的玩意儿.

heave /hiːv; hiv/ *v* (*pt, pp* **heaved** or, esp in nautical use, **hove** /həʊv; hov/亦作 **hove** /həʊv; hov/, 尤作航海用语) **1** (**a**) [Tn·pr, Tn·p] lift or drag (sth heavy) with great effort (用力)举起, 提升, 拖动, 拉动(重物): *We heaved the wardrobe up the stairs.* 我们用力把衣柜搬上楼了. (**b**) [I, Ipr] **~ (at/on sth)** pull (at a rope, etc) 拉(绳等): *heave (away) at the capstan* 转动绞盘 ○ *'Heave ho!' cried the sailors as they raised the anchor.* '用力绞呀!' 水手们起锚时吆喝道. **2** [Tn, Tn·pr, Tn·p] (*infml* 口) throw (esp sth heavy) 扔(尤指重物): *heave a brick through a window* 把砖从窗口扔过去 ○ *heave sth overboard* 把某物抛到船外. **3** [Tn] utter (sth) with effort (口中用力)发出(声音): *heave a sigh of relief/a groan* 如释重负地舒一口气[发出呻吟声]. **4** [I] rise and fall regularly (有规律地)起伏, 升降: *his heaving chest* 他那起伏的胸部. **5** [I, Ip] **~ (up)** be violently sick; vomit 恶心; 呕吐. **6** (idm 习语) ˌ**heave in ˈsight** become visible 进入视野: *A ship hove in sight.* 一艘船出现了. **7** (phr v) ˌ**heave (sth) ˈto** (of a ship) stop; cause (a ship) to stop without anchoring or mooring (指船)停住; 使(船)停住(未下锚亦未使用系绳): *The vessel/We hove to.* 船[我们(这艘船)]停了. ○ *We hove the vessel to.* 我们把船停住了.
▷ **heave** *n* [C, U] (act of) heaving 举; 提; 拖; 拉; 扔; 起伏; 升降: *with a mighty heave*, ie a strong pull or throw 猛地一拉(或使劲一扔) ○ *the steady heave of the waves* 波浪不停的起伏.

heaven /ˈhevn; ˋhɛvən/ *n* **1** [sing] (without *a* or *the* 不用 a或 the) place believed to be the home of God and the angels and of good people after death 天国; 天堂: *ascend into/go to heaven* 升入[进]天堂. **2** (also **Heaven**) [sing] God; Providence 上帝; 天帝; 神; 老天

H

爷: *It was the will of Heaven.* 这是天意. ○ *If that's the way he treats his friends, heaven help his enemies!* 假若这就是他的待友之道, 那他的敌人可就更遭殃了! **3** [U, C] place or state of very great happiness 极乐(世界): *She was in heaven when he kissed her.* 他吻她时, 她飘飘欲仙了. ○ *Sitting here with you is heaven.* 跟你一起坐在这里, 其乐无穷. ○ *If there's a heaven on earth, this is it!* 人间若有天堂, 非此莫属! **4 the heavens** [pl] the sky, as seen from the earth 天; 天空: *Rain fell from the heavens all day long.* 整天都下着雨. **5** (idm 习语) **for God's/goodness'/Heaven's sake** ⇨ SAKE. **God/Heaven forbid** ⇨ FORBID. **God/Heaven help sb** ⇨ HELP[1]. **God in Heaven** ⇨ GOD. **God/goodness/Heaven knows** ⇨ KNOW. **(Good) ˈHeavens!**; **ˌHeavens aˈbove!** (used to express surprise 用以表示惊讶). **the heavens opened** it began to rain heavily 大雨倾盆. **move heaven and earth** ⇨ MOVE[2]. **seventh heaven** (*infml* 口) state of great happiness 极乐; 欢天喜地: *Just give him a bucket and spade and he's in seventh heaven!* 只要给他一个桶子和一把铲子, 他就高兴极了! **smell, etc to high heaven** ⇨ HIGH[1]. **to God/goodness/Heaven** ⇨ GOD.

▷ **heaven·ward** /-wəd; -wɚd/ (also **heaven·wards** /-wədz; -wɚdz/) *adv* towards heaven 朝天空; 向天国.

□ ˌ**heaven-ˈsent** *adj* happening at a most favourable time; very lucky 最合时宜的; 吉祥如意的: *a ˌheaven-sent opporˈtunity* 天赐良机.

heav·enly /ˈhevnlɪ; ˋhɛvənlɪ/ *adj* **1** [attrib 作定语] of or from heaven; divine 天国的; 来自天国的; 神的; 神圣的: *a heavenly angel, vision* 天使、天国幻景. **2** [attrib 作定语] of the sky 天上的: *heavenly bodies*, ie the sun, moon, stars, etc 天体(日、月、星等). **3** (*infml* 口) very pleasing 令人愉快的; 非常合意的: *This cake is heavenly.* 这块糕饼好极了.

Heavi·side layer /ˌhevɪsaɪd ˈleɪə(r); ˈhɛvɪˌsaɪd ˋleɚ/ (*physics* 物) part of the earth's atmosphere that reflects medium-frequency waves 亥维赛层, 海氏层, E电离层(地球大气中反射中频电波的大气层). Cf 参看 IONOSPHERE (ION).

heavy /ˈhevɪ; ˋhɛvɪ/ *adj* (**-ier**, **-iest**) **1** having weight (esp great weight); difficult to lift or move 重的; 难以抬起、举起或移动的: *How heavy is it?* ie How much does it weigh? 这个东西有多重? ○ *Lead is a heavy metal.* 铅是重金属. ○ *The box is too heavy for me to carry.* 这箱子太重了, 我搬不动. **2** (**a**) of more than the usual size, amount, force, etc 超出一般规模、数量、力量等的: *heavy guns, artillery*, ie of the largest type 重炮 ○ *a heavy* (ie abundant) *crop* 丰收 ○ *Traffic on the roads is heaviest at weekends.* 周末的交通最为繁忙. ○ *Fighting was heavy.* 战斗很激烈. ○ *suffer heavy casualties/losses* 遭受重大伤亡[损失] ○ *have heavy expenses* 花销很大 ○ *a heavy frost* 厚厚的霜 ○ *have a heavy cold* 患重感冒 ○ *heavy* (ie loud) *breathing* 大声的呼吸 ○ *a heavy sleeper*, ie one who is difficult to wake 睡得很死的人 ○ *a heavy drinker/smoker*, ie one who drinks/smokes a lot 酒[烟]瘾极大的人. (**b**) [usu attrib 通常作定语] full of activity; busy 活动多的; 繁忙的: *a very heavy day, programme, schedule* 有很多活动的一天、节目单、日程表. (**c**) [pred 作表语] **~ on sth** (*infml* 口) using large quantities of sth 用量很大; 大量: *My car is rather heavy on petrol.* 我的汽车很费油. ○ *Don't go so heavy on the sauce!* 沙司不要加得太多! **3** falling or striking with force (落下或打击)沉重的: *a heavy blow, fall of snow* 重重的一击、一场大雪 ○ *heavy rain, seas* 大雨、汹涌的海浪. **4** (**a**) dense; solid 浓密的; 坚实的: *a heavy mist* 浓雾 ○ *heavy bread*, ie doughy from not having risen 未发起的面包. (**b**) (of the ground) muddy and sticky; hard to work or travel over (指土地)泥泞的, 难耕或难行的: *heavy soil* 难耕的土地 ○ *The going was heavy at the racecourse.* 马场地面泥泞难跑. **5** (**a**) (of food) difficult to digest (指食物)难消化的: *a heavy meal* 不易消化的饭菜. (**b**) (*fig* 比喻) serious 严肃的; 认真的; 庄重的: *the heavier newspapers* 理论性较强的报纸. (**c**) (*derog* 贬) (of a person, book, style,etc) serious and tedious; dull (指人、书、风格等)严肃而沉闷的, 单调乏味的: *This article is/makes heavy reading.* 这篇文章读起来枯燥乏味. **6** stern 严厉的; 苛刻的: *He can be very heavy with/on his children.* 他有时对子女很严厉. **7** (of a person's appearance or way of moving) clumsy or ungraceful (指人的外貌或动作)笨拙的, 不雅的: *heavy features* 粗眉大眼. **8** drowsy 昏昏欲睡的: *be heavy with sleep/wine* 睡觉睡[喝酒喝]昏了头. **9** (of the sky) dark with clouds (指天空)阴沉沉的. **10** (*sl* 俚 *esp US*) dangerous; threatening 危险的; 令人惊恐不安的: *a heavy scene* 令人惊恐不安的场面. **11** sad 沉痛的: *a heavy heart* 沉重的心情. **12** (idm 习语) ˌ**heavy ˈgoing** difficult or boring 困难的; 令人厌烦的: *She's heavy going*, ie hard to talk to in an easy, friendly way. 她不好说话(很难随便亲切交谈). ○ *I find the work heavy going.* 我觉得这工作很难. **a heavy hand** harsh or firm control 严厉的或强硬的管理或控制手段: *He runs his department with a heavy hand.* 他采取强硬措施管理所属部门. **make heavy ˈweather of sth** make a task more difficult than it really is 将某事弄得比实际困难. **take a heavy toll/take its toll** ⇨ TOLL[1].

▷ **heav·ily** *adv*: *a heavily loaded lorry* 重载的卡车 ○ *smoke/drink heavily* 大量抽烟[饮酒] ○ *be heavily taxed* 被征重税 ○ *heavily armed terrorists* 全副武装的恐怖分子 ○ *rely heavily on sb* 依赖某人 ○ *He fell heavily and twisted his ankle.* 他摔了一大跤, 扭伤了脚踝. ○ *She lost heavily at cards.* 她玩牌输了很多钱. **heavi·ness** *n* [U].

heavy *adv* (idm 习语) **lie heavy on sth** ⇨ LIE[2]. **time hangs/lies heavy on one's hands** ⇨ TIME.

heavy *n* **1** villainous or serious role or actor in a play, film, etc 戏剧、电影等中的反派或庄重角色; 扮演反派或庄重角色的演员. **2** (*sl* 俚) big strong man employed as a bodyguard, etc (受雇任保镖等的)魁伟强壮的人: *a gangster protected by his heavies* 有打手护卫着的匪徒.

□ ˌ**heavy-ˈduty** *adj* intended to withstand hard use, bad weather, etc 耐用的; 经受得起恶劣天气等的: *a ˌheavy-duty ˈbattery, ˈtyre* 耐久的电池、轮胎.

ˌ**heavy-ˈhanded** *adj* **1** clumsy; awkward 笨拙的; 粗劣的: *ˌheavy-handed interˈference, ˈcompliments, ˈhumour* 粗手粗脚的干涉、笨口拙舌的恭维、毫无意趣的幽默. **2** oppressive 暴虐的; 压制的: *a heavy-handed regime* 暴虐无道的政权. ˌ**heavy-ˈhandedly** *adv*. ˌ**heavy-ˈhandedness** *n* [U].

ˌ**heavy-ˈhearted** *adj* sad 心情沉重的; 悲伤的.

ˌ**heavy ˈhydrogen** isotope of hydrogen with atoms twice the normal weight 重氢.

ˌ**heavy ˈindustry** industry producing metal, large machines, etc 重工业.

ˌ**heavy-ˈladen** *adj* carrying a heavy load 重载的.

ˌ**heavy ˈwater** water whose molecules consist of two heavy hydrogen atoms and one ordinary oxygen atom 重水.

ˈ**heavyweight** *n* **1** boxer weighing 79.3kg or more; next above light-heavyweight 重量级拳击手(体重79.3公斤以上, 仅高于次重量级): [attrib 作定语] *a heavyweight contest* 重量级拳击比赛. **2** person of more than average weight 超过平均体重的人. **3** (*fig* 比喻) person of great influence or importance 有影响的人物; 要人: *a literary heavyweight* 文坛巨匠.

Heb·raic /hiːˈbreɪɪk; hiˋbre·ɪk/ *adj* of the Hebrew language or people 希伯来语的; 希伯来人的.

Heb·rew /ˈhiːbruː; ˋhibru/ *n* **1** [C] member of a Semitic people in ancient Palestine 希伯来人. **2** [U] (**a**) language of the Hebrews 希伯来语. (**b**) modern form of this used esp in Israel 现代希伯来语(尤用于以色列). Cf 参看 YIDDISH. ▷ **Heb·rew** *adj*.

heck /hek; hɛk/ *interj*, *n* (*infml euph* 口, 婉) (used to express mild annoyance or surprise or for emphasis 用以表示轻度的懊恼或惊讶, 或用以加强语气) hell: *Oh heck, I'm going to be late.* 糟糕, 我要迟到了. ○ *We had to wait a heck of a long time.* 我们可等了很长时间.

heckle /ˈhekl; ˋhɛkl̩/ *v* [Tn] interrupt and harass (a speaker) at a public meeting with troublesome questions and rude remarks (在公开场合)诘问, 质问, 诘责, 诘难(发言者): *The Socialist candidate was heckled continuously.* 社会党候选人不断受到诘问. ▷ **heck·ler** /ˈheklə(r); ˋhɛklɚ/ *n*.

hec·tare /ˈhekteə(r), ˈhektɑː(r); ˋhɛktɛr/ *n* (*abbr* 缩写 **ha**) measure of area in the metric system, equal to 100 ares or 10 000 square metres (2.471 acres) 公顷(合100公亩或10 000平方米或2.471英亩). ⇨App 5 见附录5.

hec·tic /ˈhektɪk; ˋhɛktɪk/ *adj* with much confused activity and excitement; very busy 忙乱的; 忙碌的: *hectic last-minute preparations* 最后关头忙碌的准备工作 ○ *lead a hectic life* 过忙忙碌碌的生活 ○ *Today was hectic.* 今天

忙得不亦乐乎. ▷ **hec·tic·ally** /-klɪ; -kəlɪ/ *adv*.

hect(o)- *comb form* 构词成分 hundred 一百: *hectare* ○ *hectogram*. ⇨App 11 见附录11.

hec·to·gram /ˈhektəgræm; ˈhɛktəˌgræm/ *n* unit of mass in the metric system, equal to 100 grams 百克(100克).

hec·tor /ˈhektə(r); ˈhɛktɚ/ *v* [Tn] try to frighten (sb) by bullying 威吓(某人): *a hectoring tone of voice* 威吓的口气.

he'd /hiːd; hid/ ⇨ Detailed Guide 6.3 见词条使用详细说明6.3. *contracted form* 缩约式 **1** he had ⇨ HAVE. **2** he would ⇨ WILL¹, WOULD².

hedge /hedʒ; hɛdʒ/ *n* **1** row of bushes or shrubs planted close together and forming a boundary for a field, garden, etc 树篱: *a privet hedge* 女贞树篱. ⇨illus at App 1 见附录1插图, page vii. **2** ~ **(against sth)** means of defence against possible loss 防止可能造成损失的手段: *buy gold as a hedge* (ie to protect one's money) *against inflation* 为防通货膨胀而购买黄金.

▷ **hedge** *v* **1** [Tn] put a hedge round (a field, garden, etc) 在(田地、花园等)周围设置树篱. **2** [I] make or trim hedges 栽种或修整树篱. **3** [I] avoid giving a direct answer to a question; refuse to commit oneself 避免正面答复; 拒绝承诺: *Answer 'yes' or 'no' — stop hedging!* 回答'是'或'不是'——不要再闪烁其词了! **4** (idm 习语) ˌ**hedge one's** ˈ**bets** protect oneself against loss or error by not committing oneself to a single course of action, opinion, etc 两面下注(以防损失); 骑墙; 脚踏两只船: *hedge one's bets by backing both teams to win the game* 下赌注于比赛双方的队以保万无一失. **5** (phr v) **hedge sb/sth about/around (with sth)** restrict or limit sb/sth 限制某人[某事物]: *My life is hedged about with petty regulations.* 我的生活受到一些琐细的条条框框的限制. **hedge sb in** restrict the freedom of sb 限制某人的自由.

□ ˈ**hedge-hop** *v* (**-pp-**) [I] fly an aircraft very low, eg when spraying crops (驾飞机)低空飞行(如喷洒农药时).

ˈ**hedgerow** *n* row of bushes, etc forming a hedge 一排树篱.

ˈ**hedge-sparrow** (also **sparrow**) *n* small brown bird common in Europe and America 篱雀(褐色小鸟, 常见于欧洲和美洲).

hedge·hog /ˈhedʒhɒg; *US* -hɔːg; ˈhɛdʒˌhɑg/ *n* small insect-eating animal covered with stiff spines, that rolls itself up into a ball to defend itself 刺猬. ⇨illus at App 1 见附录1插图, page iii.

he·don·ism /ˈhiːdənɪzəm; ˈhidnˌɪzəm/ *n* [U] (behaviour based on the) belief that pleasure should be the main aim in life 享乐主义; 享乐主义的行为.

▷ **he·don·ist** *n* believer in hedonism 享乐主义者.

he·don·istic /ˌhiːdəˈnɪstɪk; ˌhidəˈnɪstɪk/ *adj*.

heebie-jeebies /ˌhiːbɪ ˈdʒiːbɪz; ˈhibi ˈdʒibiz/ *n* [pl] (*infml* 口) feeling of discomfort or nervous fear 惶恐不安; 神经紧张: *Being alone in the dark gives me the heebie-jeebies.* 我独自待在黑暗处就感到心慌.

heed /hiːd; hid/ *v* [Tn, Tw] (*fml* 文) pay attention to (advice, etc); take notice of (sth) 注意或听从(劝告等); 留心(某事物): *heed a warning* 注意一项警告 ○ *heed what sb says* 留心听某人说.

▷ **heed** *n* **1** [U] (*fml* 文) careful attention 注意; 留心. **2** (idm 习语) **pay heed** ⇨ PAY². **take heed (of sth)** note sth carefully and act accordingly 听从: *Take heed of your doctor's advice.* 听医生的话吧. **heed·ful** /-fl; -ˌful/ *adj* [usu pred 通常作表语] ~ **(of sth/sb)** (*fml* 文) attentive 注意; 留心: *You should be more heedful of advice.* 你应该多听人劝. **heed·less** *adj* [usu pred 通常作表语] ~ **(of sth/sb)** (*fml* 文) disregarding; inattentive 不加注意; 不予理会: *heedless of danger* 忽视危险. **heed·lessly** *adv*.

hee-haw /ˈhiː hɔː; ˈhiˌhɔ/ *n* cry of donkey 驴叫声.

heel¹ /hiːl; hil/ *n* **1** (**a**) back part of the human foot 足跟. ⇨illus at FOOT 见FOOT插图. (**b**) part of a sock, stocking, etc covering this (袜子等的)踵部, 后跟. (**c**) part of a boot or shoe supporting this (鞋、靴的)后跟. ⇨illus at SHOE 见SHOE插图. **2** thing like a heel in shape or position 外形或位置似踵部之物: *the heel of the hand*, ie the front part next to the wrist 手掌根(手掌近腕部分). **3** (*sl* 俚) dishonourable man; rogue; villain 无耻之徒; 恶棍; 坏蛋. **4** (idm 习语) **an/one's Achilles' heel** ⇨ ACHILLES. **at/on sb's** ˈ**heels; on the heels of sth** following closely after sb/sth 紧跟在某人[某事物]后面: *The thief ran off with an angry crowd at his heels.* 那小偷在前面跑, 一群愤怒的人在后面紧追. ○ *Famine often follows on the heels of war.* 战争过后常闹饥荒. **bring sb/sth to** ˈ**heel/come to** ˈ**heel** (**a**) (force sb to) submit to discipline and control (迫使某人)服从纪律和管束: *The rebels have been brought to heel.* 反叛者被压制住了. (**b**) (cause a dog to) come close behind its owner (让狗)紧跟在主人后面: *I'm training my dog to come to heel.* 我在训练我的狗让它紧跟着我. **cool one's heels** ⇨ COOL². **dig one's heels/toes in** ⇨ DIG¹. ˌ**down at** ˈ**heel** (**a**) (of shoes) with the heels worn down by wear (指鞋)后跟磨掉的. (**b**) (of a person) untidy and poorly dressed; shabby (指人)邋遢的, 衣衫褴褛的, 穿着寒酸的. **drag one's feet/heels** ⇨ DRAG². **hard on sb's heels** ⇨ HARD². **head over heels** ⇨ HEAD¹. **hot on sb's heels** ⇨ HOT. **kick one's heels** ⇨ KICK¹. ˌ**kick up one's** ˈ**heels** behave excitedly (esp to show joy at freedom) 欢蹦乱跳(尤为表现无束缚之轻松愉快). **show a clean pair of heels** ⇨ SHOW². ˌ**take to one's** ˈ**heels** run away 逃走: *We took to our heels and ran.* 我们拔腿就跑. **tread on sb's heels** ⇨ TREAD. ˌ**turn on one's** ˈ**heel** turn sharply round and go in the opposite direction 急转身回头走. **under the heel of sb** dominated by sb 受某人支配.

▷ **heel** *v* [Tn] repair the heel of (a shoe, etc) 给(鞋等)修后跟: *These shoes need soling and heeling.* 这鞋需上鞋底和修后跟.

-heeled (forming compound *adjs* 用以构成复合形容词) with heels of the specified type 有某种后跟的: *ˌhigh-heeled ˈshoes*.

□ ˈ**heel bar** small shop or counter in a large shop where shoes are repaired quickly 小型快速修鞋店; 大商店中的快速修鞋部.

heel² /hiːl; hil/ *v* [I, Ip] ~ **(over)** (of a ship) lean over to one side (指船)倾侧: *The boat heeled over in the strong wind.* 船在大风吹袭下倾到了一边.

hefty /ˈheftɪ; ˈhɛftɪ/ *adj* (**-ier, -iest**) (*infml* 口) **1** (of a person) big and strong (指人)身高体壮的. **2** [usu attrib 通常作定语] (**a**) (of a thing) large and heavy (指物)又大又重的: *a hefty suitcase* 又大又沉的衣箱. (**b**) powerful 有力的: *deal sb a hefty blow* 给予某人重重的一击. (**c**) (*fig* 比喻) extensive; substantial 大量的; 可观的: *She earns a hefty salary.* 她的薪水很高. ▷ **heft·ily** *adv*: *a heftily-built fellow* 高大健壮的人.

he·ge·mony /hɪˈgemənɪ; *US* ˈhedʒəməʊnɪ; ˈhɛdʒəˌmonɪ/ *n* [U, C] (*fml* 文) leadership, esp by one state in a group of states 领导权; 支配权; (尤指国家集团中的)霸权.

Heg·ira (also **Hej·ira**) /ˈhedʒɪrə, hɪˈdʒaɪərə; hiˈdʒaɪrə/ *n* **the Hegira** [sing] Muhammad's flight from Mecca to Medina in AD 622, from which date the Muslim era is reckoned 公元622年穆罕默德从麦加到麦地那之逃亡; 伊斯兰教纪元.

heifer /ˈhefə(r); ˈhɛfɚ/ *n* young cow, esp one that has not yet had a calf 小母牛(尤指未曾生育的). Cf 参看 COW¹ 1.

heigh-ho /ˌheɪ ˈhəʊ; ˈheˈho/ *interj* (used to express disappointment, boredom, etc 用以表示失望、厌烦等).

height /haɪt; haɪt/ *n* **1** (**a**) [U, C] measurement from the bottom to the top of a thing or from head to foot of a standing person 高度; 身高: *What is the height of the mountain?* 这山有多高? ○ *State your height*, ie how tall are you. 说出你身高多少. ○ *He is two metres in height.* 他身高二米. ⇨App 4 见附录4. ⇨illus at DIMENSION 见DIMENSION 插图. (**b**) [U] being tall 高: *She can see over the wall because of her height.* 她个子高, 能看到墙的那一边. **2** [C, U] distance (of an object or a position) above ground or sea-level (物体或位置的)高度, 海拔: *fly at a height of 6 000 metres (above sea-level)* 在(海拔)6 000米的高度上飞行 ○ *The aircraft was gaining height.* 飞机在不断升高. **3** [C esp *pl* 尤作复数] high place or area 高处; 高地: *be afraid of heights* 畏高. **4** [sing] main point or highest degree of sth 顶点; 极度: *the height of summer* 盛夏时节 ○ *The storm was at its height.* 风暴正猛. ○ *the height of folly* 愚不可及 ○ *be dressed in the height of fashion* 穿着最时髦的衣服 ○ *the height of one's ambition* 最大的抱负. **5** (idm 习语) **draw oneself up to one's full height** ⇨ DRAW².

NOTE ON USAGE 用法: **Height** can be ☆ **height** 可指 **1** the vertical measurement of a person or object 人或物体的垂直高度: *Please state your height.* 请说出你的身高. ○ *What's the height of that wall?* 那堵墙有多高? or **2** the distance of somebody or something from ground/sea-level 某人或某物高于地面[海面]的距离: *The climber fell from a great height.* 攀登者从极高的地方坠落下来. ○ *The aircraft was flying at a height of 2 000 feet.* 飞机在2 000英尺的高空飞行. The adjective **tall** relates to sense 1 and is used mainly of people, trees and buildings 形容词**tall**同1义, 主要用于指人、树及建筑物: *How tall are you/is the building/tree?* 你[这座建筑物/那棵树]有多高? **High** relates to senses 1 and 2 (but is not used for the vertical measurement of people) ☆ **high** 同1和2义(但不可用于指人的身高): *How high is that jump?* 要跳过的那障碍物有多高? ○ *That poster is too high — nobody can read it.* 那海报贴得太高了——谁也看不清楚.

heighten /ˈhaɪtn; ˋhaɪtn̩/ *v* [I, Tn] (cause sth to) become higher or more intense (使某事物)提高, 加强: *heightening tension* 越来越紧张的情况 ○ *her heightened colour,* ie the increased colour in her face, eg caused by emotion 她那绯红的脸庞(如因激动所致) ○ *music to heighten the dramatic effect* 藉以提高戏剧效果的配乐.

hein·ous /ˈheɪnəs; ˋhenəs/ *adj* very wicked 极凶恶的: *a heinous crime, criminal* 十恶不赦的罪行、罪犯. ▷ **hein·ously** *adv*. **hein·ous·ness** *n* [U].

heir /eə(r); ɛr/ *n* **~ (to sth)** person with the legal right to receive property, etc when the owner dies 继承人: *be heir to a large fortune, a title, the throne* 是大笔财产、头衔、王位的继承人 ○ *She made her stepson (her) heir.* 她让丈夫与前妻生的儿子做自己的继承人.

▷ **heir·ess** /ˈeərɪs, eəˈres; ˋɛrɪs/ *n* female heir, esp one who inherits great wealth 女继承人(尤指继承大笔财产者).

□ ˌ**heir apˈparent** (*pl* **heirs apparent**) heir whose legal right cannot be cancelled by the birth of another with a stronger claim 确定继承人(其继承权不因其他人之出生而受影响).

ˌ**heir preˈsumptive** (*pl* **heirs presumptive**) heir who may lose his legal right if another heir with a stronger claim is born 推定继承人(其继承权可能因其他人之出生而丧失).

heir·loom /ˈeəlu:m; ˋɛrˈlum/ *n* (usu valuable) object that has been handed down in a family for several generations (通常为贵重的)祖传遗物, 传家宝: *That clock is a family heirloom.* 那个座钟是祖传下来的.

heist /haɪst; haɪst/ *n* (*sl* 俚 esp US) robbery; burglary 抢劫; 盗窃.

▷ **heist** *v* [Tn] (*sl* 俚 esp US) rob or steal (sth) 抢劫, 盗窃(某物).

Hej·ira = HEGIRA.

held *pt, pp* of HOLD.

hel·ical /ˈhelɪkl, *also* ˈhi:lɪkl; ˋhɛlɪkəl, ˋhilɪkəl/ *adj* like a helix 螺旋形的.

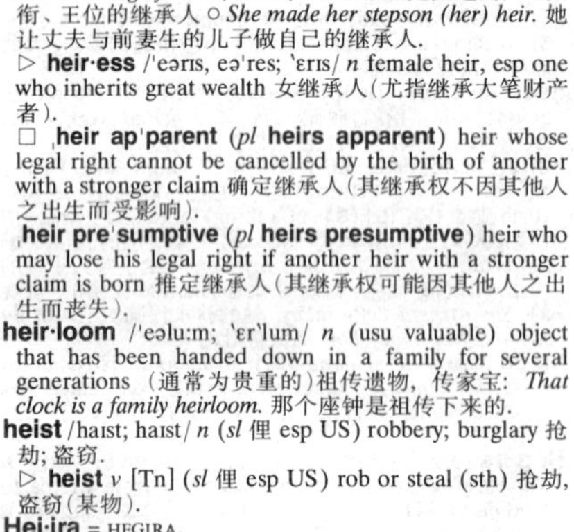

helicopter 直升飞机

heli·cop·ter /ˈhelɪkɒptə(r); ˋhɛlɪˌkɑptɚ/ *n* type of aircraft with horizontal revolving blades or rotors, able to take off and land vertically and remain stationary in the air 直升飞机: *rescued from the sea by (a) helicopter* 用直升飞机从海上救起的 ○ [attrib 作定语] *a helicopter pilot* 直升飞机驾驶员. ⇨illus 见插图.

he·lio·trope /ˈhi:lɪətrəʊp; ˋhilɪəˌtrop/ *n* **1** [C, U] plant with small sweet-smelling purple flowers 天芥菜属植物(开芳香之紫色小花). **2** [U] light purple colour 浅紫色.

heli·port /ˈhelɪpɔ:t; ˋhɛlɪˌpɔrt/ *n* place where helicopters take off and land 直升飞机机场; 直升飞机航站.

he·lium /ˈhi:lɪəm; ˋhilɪəm/ *n* [U] chemical element, a light colourless gas that does not burn, used in airships 氦. ⇨App 10 见附录10.

he·lix /ˈhi:lɪks; ˋhilɪks/ *n* (*pl* **helices** /ˈhi:lɪsi:z; ˋhɛlɪˌsiz/) spiral, either like a corkscrew or flat like a watch-spring 螺旋: *Some biological molecules have the form of a helix.* 有些生物分子呈螺旋状.

hell /hel; hɛl/ *n* **1** [sing] (without *a* or *the* 不与a或the连用) place believed in some religions to be the home of devils and of wicked people after death 地狱. **2** [U, C] state or place of great suffering or wickedness; very unpleasant experience 苦痛的境况; 受苦受难的地方; 极不愉快的经历: *suffer hell on earth* 受人间地狱之苦 ○ *She made his life (a) hell.* 她使他活受罪. ○ *The journey was absolute hell.* 一路上吃尽了苦头. **3** [U] (*infml* 口) (used as an exclamation of annoyance or surprise or for emphasis 用作感叹词, 表示恼怒或惊讶, 或用以加强语气): *Oh hell, I've broken it!* 啊, 真倒霉, 我把它弄坏了! ○ *Bloody hell!* 真该死! ○ *Oh go to hell!* 见鬼去吧! ○ *Who the hell is he?* 他究竟是谁? ○ *What the hell* (ie It doesn't matter), *I can go tomorrow instead.* 没关系, 我可以改在明天去. **4** (idm 习语) **a/one hell of a...** (also **a helluva** /ˈheləvə; ˋhɛləvə/) (*sl* 俚) (**a**) (used for emphasis 用以加强语气): *one hell of a row,* ie a dreadful row 大吵大闹. (**b**) very 非常: *It's a hell of a long way.* 路远极了. ○ *He's a helluva (nice) guy.* 他是个呱呱叫的(好)人. **all ˈhell broke/was let loose** suddenly there was great noise and confusion 突然之间闹翻天. **beat/knock hell out of sb/sth** (*infml* 口) hit sb/sth very hard 猛击某人[某物]. **a cat in hell's chance** ⇨ CAT[1]. **for the ˈhell of it** (*infml* 口) just for fun 仅为取乐: *steal a car for the hell of it* 为了好玩而偷汽车. **give sb ˈhell** (*infml* 口) scold, punish or harass sb 申斥、惩罚或骚扰某人: *The boss really gave me hell today.* 老板今天着实数落了我一通. ○ *This tooth is giving me hell,* ie is very painful. 我这颗牙很疼. **hell for ˈleather** as quickly as possible 尽快地: *drive, ride, run, etc hell for leather* 尽快地驾驶、骑、跑等. **(come) ˌhell or high ˈwater** no matter what the difficulties 不管有什么困难. **like a bat out of hell** ⇨ BAT[1]. **like ˈhell** (**a**) (*infml* 口) (used for emphasis 用以加强语气): *drive like hell,* ie very fast 飞快地驾驶. (**b**) (*sl ironic* 俚, 反语) (used before a clause 用于从句前) not at all 绝不: *'You can pay.' 'Like hell I will* (ie I certainly will not)*!'* '你可以给钱的.' '我才不给呢!' **not have a hope in hell** ⇨ HOPE *n*. **play hell with sth/sb** (*infml* 口) seriously upset sth/sb 给某事物[某人]造成极大麻烦: *That curry is playing hell with my insides!* 我吃了咖喱食物, 肚子真不舒服! **raise Cain/hell/the roof** ⇨ RAISE. **the road to hell is paved with good intentions** ⇨ ROAD. **see sb (damned) in ˈhell first** (*infml* 口) (used when emphatically rejecting a suggestion 用于断然拒绝某项提议时): *Lend him money? I'll see him in hell first.* 把钱借给他? 绝对不行. **there will be/was ˈhell to pay** (*infml* 口) sb will be/was punished severely 某人将受到[受到了]严惩: *There'll be hell to pay if we're caught.* 我们要是被抓住就有罪受了. **to hell with sb/sth** damn sb/sth 某人[某事物]该死: *To hell with the lot of you, I'll do what I please!* 你们全都见鬼去吧, 我爱怎么着就怎么着!

▷ **hell·ish** *adj* **1** of or like hell (似)地狱的. **2** (*infml* 口) extremely unpleasant 极不愉快的: *His schooldays were hellish.* 他的学生时代苦不堪言. — *adv* (*infml* 口) extremely 极端地: *hellish expensive* 贵得要命. **hell·ishly** *adv* **1** very badly 极恶劣地: *be hellishly treated* 受到极其恶劣的对待. **2** (*infml* 口) extremely 极端地: *a hellishly difficult problem* 极其困难的问题.

□ ˌ**hell-ˈbent** *adj* [pred 作表语] **~ on sth** recklessly determined to do sth 不顾一切而要做某事: *He seems hell-bent on drinking himself to death.* 他拼命喝酒, 似乎连命都不要了.

ˈ**hell-cat** *n* spiteful or furious woman 恶妇; 泼妇.

he'll /hi:l; hil/ *contracted form* 缩约式 he will ⇨ WILL[1].

Hel·lene /ˈheli:n; ˋhɛlin/ *n* **1** native of modern Greece 现今的希腊人. **2** person of genuine Greek race in ancient times 古希腊人.

▷ **Hel·lenic** /heˈli:nɪk; *US* heˈlenɪk; hɛˋlɛnɪk/ *adj* of the ancient or modern Greeks, their arts, culture, etc (古,

今)希腊人的, 希腊艺术、文化等的.

Hel·len·istic /ˌhelɪˈnɪstɪk; ˌhɛlɪˈnɪstɪk/ *adj* of the Greek language and culture of the 4th-1st centuries BC (公元前4世纪至公元前1世纪的)希腊语言和文化的.

hello = HALLO.

hel·luva /ˈheləvə; ˋhɛləvə/ ⇨ HELL 4.

helm /helm; hɛlm/ *n* **1** handle or wheel for moving the rudder of a ship or boat 舵柄; 舵轮: (*fig* 比喻) *the helm of state*, ie government of a country 政府. Cf 参看 TILLER. **2** (idm 习语) **at the ˈhelm** at the head of an organization, etc; in control 担任某一组织等的领导人; 掌权.

□ **ˈhelmsman** (/-zmən; -zmən/) *n* (*pl* **-men** /-mən; -mən/) person who steers a ship 舵手; 操舵人. Cf 参看 STEERSMAN (STEER[1]).

hel·met /ˈhelmɪt; ˋhɛlmɪt/ *n* protective head-covering such as that worn by firemen, miners, motor-cyclists, policemen and sportsmen, and by soldiers when they are fighting 头盔. ⇨illus at AMERICAN FOOTBALL (AMERICAN) 见AMERICAN FOOTBALL (AMERICAN)插图.

▷ **hel·meted** *adj* wearing or provided with a helmet 戴头盔; 备有头盔的.

help[1] /help; hɛlp/ *v* **1** [I, Ipr, It, Tn, Tn·pr, Tn·p, Cn·t, Cn·i] **~ (sb) (with sth)** be of use or service to (sb); make it easier for (sb) to do sth; aid; assist 帮助(某人); 协助(某人)做某事; 援助; 救助: *Help! I'm stuck.* 帮帮忙吧! 我卡住了. ○ *May I help with the washing-up?* 我帮你洗餐具好吗? ○ *Your advice helped (me) a lot.* 你的意见对我大有帮助. ○ *We must all help each other.* 我们都应该互相帮助. ○ *A man is helping the police with their enquiries.* 有一男子在协助警方进行调查. ○ *Please help me up/down the stairs with this heavy case*, ie help me to carry it up/down. 请帮我把这只沉重的箱子搬上[下]楼. ○ *Would it help you to know* (ie if I told you) *that...?* 如果我告诉你..., 对你会有帮助吗? ○ *This charity aims to help people to help themselves.* 这一慈善团体的宗旨是帮助人们实行自助. ○ *I helped (him) (to) find his things.* 我帮(他)找东西. **2** (**a**) [Tn, Tn·pr] **~ oneself/sb (to sth)** serve oneself/sb with food, drink, etc 为自己[某人]取食品、饮料等: *Help yourself (to a cigarette).* 请随便用(香烟)吧. ○ *May I help you to some more meat?* 再给你来点肉好吗? (**b**) [Tn·pr] **~ oneself to sth** take sth without permission 擅自拿取: *He's been helping himself to my stationery.* 他未经许可一直用我的文具. **3** [I, It, Tn] make it easier for sth to happen 促进; 促成: *This latest development doesn't exactly help (matters).* 这一最新情况对事情并没有真正好处. ○ *drugs that help to take away pain* 能止痛的药 ○ *stiffer measures to help fight terrorism* 有助打击恐怖活动的更为强硬的措施. **4** (idm 习语) **can/could (not) help (doing) sth** can/could (not) prevent or avoid sth (不)能防止或避免某事物: *It can't/couldn't be helped*, ie There was no way of avoiding it and we must accept that. 这是不可避免的. ○ *Can I help it* (ie Is it my fault) *if people don't read the instructions?* 人家不看使用说明书, 我又有什么办法呢? ○ *He can't help having big ears.* 他总是忍不住要打听别人的事. ○ *I wouldn't live there; well, not if I could help it.* 我可不愿在那儿生活, 嗳, 要是有别的办法我才不住那儿呢. ○ *We can't help thinking he's still alive.* 我们总是认为他还活着. ○ *She burst out laughing; she couldn't help it/herself*, ie could not stop herself. 她突然大笑起来, 无法克制自己. ○ *Don't tell him more than you can help*, ie more than you must. 能不告诉他的, 就别告诉他. ○ *She never does more work than she can help*, ie She does as little as possible. 她做工作, 能少做就少做. **God/Heaven ˈhelp sb** (used when expressing fears for sb's safety 用于对某人的安全表示担心时): *God help you* (ie You will be in trouble) *if the teacher finds out!* 要是老师发现了, 可够你受的! **help a lame dog over a stile** give help to sb who is in difficulty or trouble 助某人渡过难关. **a ˌhelping ˈhand** assistance 帮助; 援助: *give/lend (sb) a helping hand* 帮(某人)忙. **so ˈhelp me (God)** I swear it 我发誓; 老天爷作证: *I never stole the money, so help me (I didn't)!* 钱决不是我偷的, 老天爷可以作证! **5** (phr v) **help sb off/on with sth** help sb to take off/put on (a garment) 帮某人脱[穿](衣服): *Can I help you on with your coat?* 我帮你把大衣穿上好吗? **help (sb) ˈout** help sb esp in a difficult situation or a crisis 帮助某人(尤指摆脱困境或危难): *He's always willing to help (us) out when we're short of staff.* 我们职员人手不足时, 他总是急人之难.

▷ **helper** *n* person who helps 帮忙者; 助手.

help·ing *n* portion of food at a meal (饭菜的)一份, 一客: *take a third helping* 吃第三份食物 ○ *She had two generous helpings of pie.* 她吃了两客分量很足的馅饼.

help[2] /help; hɛlp/ *n* **1** [U] helping or being helped 帮助; 协助; 援助; 救助: *Thank you for all your kind help.* 谢谢你各方面的热心帮助. ○ *Can I be of (any) help to you?* 我能帮你忙吗? ○ *The map wasn't much help.* 这地图用处不大. ○ *She came to our help*, ie helped us. 她来帮助我们了. **2** [sing] **a ~ (to sb)** person or thing that helps 帮忙者; 帮手; 有助益的事物: *The servants were more of a hindrance than a help (to me).* 这些用人(对我来说)帮不上忙反而是累赘. ○ *Her advice was a great help.* 她的劝告大有益处. ○ (*ironic* 反语) *You're a great help* (ie no help at all), *I must say!* 老实不客气地说, 你净帮倒忙! **3** [C] person employed to help with the housework 用人; 仆人: *The help hasn't come this morning.* 仆人今早没有来. **4** [C] way of avoiding or preventing sth (used esp in the expression shown) 避免或防止某事物的方法(尤用于以下示例): *There's no help for it.* 没法子了.

▷ **help·ful** /-fl; -fəl/ *adj* giving help; useful 有帮助的; 有用的: *a helpful person, suggestion, map* 有用的人、建议、地图 ○ *He's always very helpful to his mother.* 他一向都是他母亲的得力帮手. **help·fully** /-fəlɪ; -fəlɪ/ *adv.* **help·ful·ness** *n* [U].

help·less *adj* **1** unable to act without help; needing the help of others 不能自立的; 需要他人帮助的: *a helpless baby, invalid, drunkard* 要人照顾的婴儿、伤残者、喝醉的人 ○ *be helpless with laughter* 笑得全身无力. **2** without help; defenceless 无助的; 无保护的: *Without their weapons they were helpless.* 他们没有武器便不能自卫. **help·lessly** *adv.* **help·less·ness** *n* [U].

help·mate /ˈhelpmeɪt; ˋhɛlpˌmet/ *n* helpful partner or companion, esp a husband or wife 可以依靠的伴侣; (尤指)丈夫或妻子.

helter-skelter /ˌheltə ˈskeltə(r); ˋhɛltəˋskɛltə/ *adv* in disorderly haste 忙乱地.

▷ **helter-skelter** *n* tall tower at a fun-fair, etc with a spiral track outside it that people slide down on mats (游乐场等处的)螺旋滑梯.

helve /helv; hɛlv/ *n* handle of a weapon or tool, esp an axe (武器或工具的)柄(尤指斧柄).

hem[1] /hem; hɛm/ *n* edge of a piece of cloth which has been turned under and sewn or fixed down (布的)折边, 卷边, 滚边: *I took the hems of my dresses up to make them shorter.* 我把我的连衣裙都改短了.

▷ **hem** *v* (**-mm-**) **1** [Tn] make a hem on (sth) 给(某物)镶边, 缝边: *hem a skirt, handkerchief, etc* 镶裙子、手帕等的边. **2** (phr v) **hem sb about/around** (esp passive 尤用于被动语态) surround sb 包围某人: *be hemmed about by obstacles* 被障碍物团团围住. **hem sb in** surround and restrict the movement of sb; confine sb 包围某人; 限制某人的行动; 约束某人: *The enemy troops were hemming us in.* 敌军把我们包围了. ○ (*fig* 比喻) *He felt hemmed in by convention.* 他感到受清规戒律的束缚.

□ **ˈhem-line** *n* lower edge of a dress or skirt (衣裙的)下摆, 底边: *lower/raise the hem-line*, ie make a skirt, etc longer/shorter 把下摆放低[提高](把裙子等改长[短]). **ˈhem-stitch** *n* [U] ornamental stitching used esp on hems 花饰线迹; 抽丝线迹. — *v* [Tn] decorate (sth) with such stitching 用加饰线或抽丝法在(某物)上加饰边.

hem[2] /hem; hɛm/ (also **h'm** /hm; hm/) *interj* (used to call attention or express doubt or hesitation) 用以唤起注意或表示怀疑或犹豫.

▷ **hem** *v* (**-mm-**) [I] say *hem*; hesitate while speaking 发'嗯'声; 说话时犹豫.

hemi·sphere /ˈhemɪsfɪə(r); ˋhɛməsˌfɪr/ *n* **1** half a sphere 半球. **2** any half of the earth, esp as divided by the equator (**the Northern/Southern hemisphere**) or by a line passing through the poles (**the Eastern hemisphere**, ie Europe, Africa, Asia, Australia, and **the Western hemisphere**, ie N and S America) (地球的)半球(尤指按赤道划分之南[北]半球或按通过极地之经线划分之东半球——即欧洲、非洲、亚洲、澳洲和西半球——即南北美洲). ⇨illus at GLOBE 见GLOBE插图. **3** (*anatomy* 解) either half of the cerebrum (大脑

的)半球.
▷ **hemi·spher·ical** /ˌhemɪˈsferɪkl; ˌhɛməˈsfɛrɪkl/ *adj* shaped like a hemisphere 半球形的.

hem·lock /ˈhemlɒk; ˈhɛmlɑk/ *n* **1** [C, U] poisonous plant with small white flowers 毒芹(有毒, 开小白花). **2** [U] poison made from this plant 由毒芹提取的毒药.

hem(o)- ⇨ HAEM(O)-.

hemp /hemp; hɛmp/ *n* [U] **1** plant from which coarse fibres are obtained for making rope and cloth 大麻. **2** narcotic drug made from this plant 大麻制的麻醉剂. Cf 参看 CANNABIS, HASHISH, MARIJUANA.
▷ **hempen** /ˈhempən; ˈhɛmpən/ *adj* made of hemp 大麻制的: *a hempen rope* 麻绳.

hen /hen; hɛn/ *n* **1** female of the common domestic fowl 母鸡. ⇨illus at App 1 见附录1插图, page v. **2** female of any of several types of bird 雌禽: *a ˈguinea-hen* 雌珍珠鸡 ○ [attrib 作定语] *a hen ˈpheasant* 雌雉. Cf 参看 COCK.
□ **ˈhen-coop** *n* cage for keeping poultry in 家禽笼.
ˈhen-house *n* small building for fowls to roost in 家禽棚舍.
ˈhen-party *n* (*infml* 口) party for women only 女性的聚会. Cf 参看 STAG-PARTY (STAG).
ˈhenpecked *adj* (*infml* 口) (of a husband) nagged by a fussy and domineering wife (指丈夫)受妻子摆布的, 怕老婆的, 惧内的.

hence /hens; hɛns/ *adv* **1** from this time 从此时起: *a week hence*, ie in a week from now 从现在起一星期后. **2** for this reason 因此: *I fell off my bike yesterday — hence the bruises.* 我昨天骑自行车摔倒了——所以青一块、紫一块的. **3** (*arch* 古) from here 从此处.
□ **henceforth** /ˌhensˈfɔːθ; ˌhɛnsˈfɔrθ/ (also **henceforward** /ˌhensˈfɔːwəd; ˌhɛnsˈfɔrwɚd/) *adv* (*fml* 文) from this time on; in future 从今以后; 今后: *Henceforth I expect you to be punctual for meetings.* 我希望你今后准时到会.

hench·man /ˈhentʃmən; ˈhɛntʃmən/ *n* (*pl* **-men** /-mən; -mən/) faithful follower or political supporter who always obeys the orders of his leader (对领导者唯命是从的)忠实的追随者或政治上的支持者: *the dictator and his henchmen* 独裁者及其亲信.

henna /ˈhenə; ˈhɛnə/ *n* [U] **1** reddish-brown dye used esp on the hair 散沫花染剂(一种棕红色的染料, 尤用以染发). **2** tropical plant from which this dye is obtained 散沫花(热带植物, 可制染剂).
▷ **hennaed** /ˈhenəd; ˈhɛnəd/ *adj* dyed with henna 用散沫花染剂染过的.

H

hep·at·itis /ˌhepəˈtaɪtɪs; ˌhɛpəˈtaɪtɪs/ *n* [U] inflammation of the liver 肝炎.

hep·ta·gon /ˈheptəgən; *US* -gɒn; ˈhɛptəˌgɑn/ *n* geometric figure with seven sides and angles 七边形; 七角形. ▷ **hep·ta·gonal** /hepˈtægənl; hɛpˈtægənl/ *adj*.

her[1] /hɜː(r); hɝ/ ⇨Detailed Guide 6.2 见词条使用详细说明 6.2. *pers pron* 人称代词 (used as the object of a *v* or of a *prep*; also used independently and after *be* 用作动词或介词的宾语, 亦可单用及置于 be 之后) female person or animal mentioned earlier or being observed now 她; (指雌性动物时用)它: *We're going to call her Diana.* 我们打算称呼她为黛安娜. ○ *Please give her my regards.* 请代我问候她. ○ *The manager will be free soon — you can wait for her here.* 经理一会儿就有空了——你可以在这儿等候她. ○ (*infml* 口) *That must be her now.* 那位一定就是她了. ○ (*fig* 比喻) *I know that ship well — I've often sailed in her.* 那只船我很熟——因为我经常乘坐. Cf 参看 SHE, ⇨Usage at HE 用法见 HE.

her[2] /hɜː(r); hɝ/ ⇨Detailed Guide 6.2 见词条使用详细说明 6.2. *possess det* of or belonging to a female person or animal mentioned earlier 她的; (指雌性动物时用)它的: *Mary's mother is dead but her father is still alive.* 玛丽的母亲去世了, 她父亲依然健在. ○ *Jane's here, I think — isn't that her coat?* 我想简在这儿——那不是她的大衣吗? ○ *Fiona has broken her leg.* 菲奥纳把腿摔折了.
▷ **hers** /hɜːz; hɝz/ *possess pron* of or belonging to her 她的: *If this isn't Susan's book that one must be hers.* 假若这本书不是苏珊的, 那末那本书就一定是她的了. ○ *My mother has a lot of hats so I borrowed one of hers.* 我母亲帽子很多, 所以我向她借了一顶. ⇨Usage at HE 用法见 HE.

her·ald /ˈherəld; ˈhɛrəld/ *n* **1** (formerly) person who made important announcements and carried messages from a ruler (旧时)传令官, 使者, 信使. **2** person or thing that announces or shows that sb/sth is coming 报信者; 先兆: *In England the cuckoo is the herald of spring.* 在英国, 杜鹃鸟预告春天的来临. **3** (*Brit*) official who keeps records of families that have coats of arms (COAT) 司宗谱纹章的官员.
▷ **her·ald** *v* [Tn, Tn·p] **~ sb/sth (in)** announce the approach of sb/sth 宣布某人[某事物]即将来临: *This invention heralded (in) the age of the computer.* 这项发明宣告了计算机时代的到来.
her·aldic /heˈrældɪk; hɛˈrældɪk/ *adj* of heralds or heraldry 司宗谱纹章官员的; 纹章(学)的: *heraldic arms, devices, etc* 盾徽、纹章图案等.
her·aldry *n* [U] study of the coats of arms and the history of old families 纹章学.

herb /hɜːb; *US* ɜːrb; ɝb/ *n* (**a**) plant with a soft stem that dies down to the ground after flowering 草本植物. (**b**) plant of this kind whose leaves or seeds, etc are used in medicines and perfumes or for flavouring food 药草, 芳草(叶或种子等可制成药和香料, 或用作调味品): *Sage, mint and dill are all herbs.* 鼠尾草、薄荷、莳萝均为药草. ○ [attrib 作定语] *a herb garden* 芳草园.
▷ **herbal** /ˈhɜːbl; *US* ˈɜːrbl; ˈɝbl/ *adj* [usu attrib 通常作定语] of herbs used in medicine or for flavouring 药草的; 芳草的: *herbal remedies* 药草治疗法. — *n* book containing descriptions of these 草本植物志; 药草书.
herb·al·ist /ˈhɜːbəlɪst; *US* ˈɜːrb-; ˈɝblɪst/ *n* person who grows, sells or specializes in herbs for medical use 药草栽培者; 药草商; 药草专家; 草药医生.

herb·aceous /hɜːˈbeɪʃəs; *US* ɜːr-; ɝˈbeʃəs/ *adj* of or like herbs 草本的; 草质的.
□ **herˌbaceous ˈborder** flower-bed in a garden with plants that flower year after year (花园中种有多年生花草的)花坛.

herb·age /ˈhɜːbɪdʒ; *US* ˈɜːr-; ˈɝbɪdʒ/ *n* [U] herbs collectively, esp as pasture for cattle, etc; grass and other field plants 草本植物(总称); (尤指)牧草; 草类.

herbi·cide /ˈhɜːbɪsaɪd; *US* ˈɜːr-; ˈɝbəˌsaɪd/ *n* substance that is poisonous to plants, used to destroy weeds, etc 除草剂.

herbi·vore /ˈhɜːbɪvɔː(r); *US* ˈɜːr-; ˈɝbəˌvɔr/ *n* animal that feeds on plants 食草动物. Cf 参看 CARNIVORE.
▷ **herbi·vor·ous** /hɜːˈbɪvərəs; *US* ɜːr-; ɝˈbɪvərəs/ *adj* (of animals) feeding on plants (指动物)食草的.

her·cu·lean /ˌhɜːkjʊˈliːən; hɝˈkjulɪən/ *adj* having or needing very great strength 力大无比的; 十分费力的: *a herculean task* 艰巨的任务.

herd /hɜːd; hɝd/ *n* **1** [C] number of animals, esp cattle, feeding or staying together 兽群; 牧群; (尤指)牛群: *a herd of cows, deer, elephant(s), etc* 一群牛、鹿、象等. **2 the herd** [sing] (*usu derog* 通常作贬义) large number of people; mob 人群; 群氓: *the common herd* 普通民众 ○ *He preferred to stick with the herd* (ie do the same as everyone around him) *so as not to be noticed.* 他愿随大溜以免引人注目.
▷ **herd** *v* **1** [Ipr, Ip, Tn·pr, Tn·p] move or drive (sb/sth) forward as a herd in the specified direction (某人[某物])成群地移动; 驱赶成群的(某人[某物]): *The prisoners were herded (together) onto the train.* 一群囚犯被驱赶着押送上了火车. **2** [Tn] look after (sth) in a herd 牧放(兽群): *a shepherd herding his flock* 正在放牧的牧羊人.
□ **herdsman** /-mən; -mən/ *n* (*pl* **-men** /-men; -mɛn/) person who looks after a herd of animals 牧人.
herd instinct instinct in people or animals to behave and think like the majority 群集本能(人或动物在行为和思维上与大多数求同的本能).

here /hɪə(r); hɪr/ *adv* **1** (**a**) (with a *v* or after a *prep* 与动词连用或用于介词之后) in, at or to this position or place 在这里; 向这里: *I live here.* 我住在这里. ○ *We leave here tomorrow.* 我们明天离开此地. ○ *Fill it up to here.* 把它装到此处为止. ○ *Let's get out of here.* 我们离开这里吧. ○ *Put the box here.* 把盒子放在这里. ○ *Come (over) here.* 到这来吧. (**b**) (placed for emphasis at the beginning of a sentence and followed by the finite *v* if the subject is a *n*, but not if the subject is a *pers pron* 为加强语气可置于句首, 若主语为名词则限定动词紧接here之后, 若主语为人称代词则限定动词不紧接here之后): *Here comes the bus!* 公共汽车来了! ○ *Here* *it comes!* 它来了! ○ *Here are the others!* 其余的在这里! ○ *Here they are!* 他们到了! ○ *Here we are* (ie We've arrived)! 我们到了! **2** at this point (in an activity, a series of events or a situation) (在一项活动、一连串事件或一种情况中)在这一点上: *Here the speaker paused to have a drink.* 这时演讲人停下来喝了一口水. **3** (used for emphasis immediately after a *n* or informally before a *n* 用以加强语气, 可紧接名词之后, 在口语中可置于名词之前): *My friend here saw it happen.* 我这朋友就看见了它是怎样发生的. ○ (*infml* 口) *What do you make of this here letter?* 你对这封来信有什么看法? **4** (idm 习语) ˌ**here and** ˈ**there** in various places 在各地; 各处. **here below** (*rhet* 修辞) on earth (contrasted with being in heaven) 在尘世间: *Life goes on for those of us who remain here below.* 对于我们凡人来说, 生活依旧. ˌ**here** ˈ**goes** (*infml* 口) (used to announce that one is about to do something exciting, risky, etc 用以宣布令人兴奋、具有冒险性等的举动). **here's to sb/sth** (used when drinking to a person's health or to the success of an enterprise, etc 用于敬酒时祝某人健康或祝事业等成功): *Here's to the bride!* 敬新娘一杯! ○ *Here's to your future happiness!* 祝你将来幸福! ˌ**here, there and** ˈ**everywhere** in many different places; all around 在许多地方; 到处. **neither** ˌ**here nor** ˈ**there** not important; irrelevant 无关紧要的; 不相干的: *The fact that I don't like your fiancé is neither here nor there — what matters is what you feel.* 我不喜欢你那未婚夫, 这是题外话 —— 问题在于你意下如何.

▷ **here** *interj* **1** (used to call attention to sth or as a command 用以唤起对某事物的注意或用作命令): *Here, let me carry it.* 嘿, 让我来搬. **2** (used as a reply in a roll-call 用作点名时的答语) I am present 到; 有.

□ **hereabouts** /ˌhɪərəˈbaʊts; ˌhɪrəˋbaʊts/ (also **hereabout**) *adv* (*fml* 文) near this place; around here 在附近; 在这一带.

hereafter /ˌhɪərˈɑːftə(r); *US* -ˈæf-; hɪrˋæftɚ/ *adv* (*fml* 文) **1** (in legal documents, etc) from now on; following this (用于法律文件等)自此以后, 此后. **2** in future 在将来. — *n* **the hereafter** [sing] the future; life after death 将来; 死后的生命.

hereby /ˌhɪəˈbaɪ; hɪrˋbaɪ/ *adv* (*fml* 文) by this means; as a result of this 以此方式; 由此.

herein /ˌhɪərˈɪn; hɪrˋɪn/ *adv* (*fml* 文) in this place or document 于此处; 于此文件中.

hereof /ˌhɪərˈɒv; hɪrˋɑv/ *adv* (*arch* 古) of this 关于此点.

hereto /ˌhɪəˈtuː; hɪrˋtu/ *adv* (*arch* 古) to this 至此.

heretofore /ˌhɪətuːˈfɔː(r); ˌhɪrtəˋfɔr/ *adv* (*fml* 文) until now; formerly 直到此时; 在此之前; 前此.

herewith /ˌhɪəˈwɪð, -ˈwɪθ; hɪrˋwɪθ/ *adv* (*fml* 文) (esp in commercial use) with this (letter, etc) (尤用于商业函件)同此(函等): *Please fill in the form enclosed herewith.* 请填写随函附上之表格.

her·ed·it·ary /hɪˈredɪtrɪ; *US* -terɪ; həˋrɛdəˌtɛrɪ/ *adj* **1** passed on from parent to child, or from one generation to following generations 遗传的; 世代相传的: *hereditary characteristics, features, beliefs* 遗传而来的特性、有遗传特点的相貌、世代沿袭的信仰 ○ *The disease is hereditary.* 这种病有遗传性. **2** holding a position by inheritance 继承的; 世袭的: *a hereditary ruler* 世袭的统治者.

her·ed·ity /hɪˈredətɪ; həˋrɛdətɪ/ *n* [U] (**a**) passing on of physical or mental characteristics from parents to children遗传: [attrib 作定语] *heredity factors* 遗传因素. (**b**) such characteristics in a particular person 某人来自遗传的特征: *part of one's heredity* 来自遗传的部分特征.

her·esy /ˈherəsɪ; ˋhɛrəsɪ/ *n* **1** [C] belief or opinion that is contrary to what is generally accepted, esp in religion 异端(尤指宗教方面的): *the heresies of the early Protestants* 早期新教徒的异端邪说. **2** [U] holding of such an opinion 持异端邪说: *be guilty of heresy* 犯有异端罪.

▷ **her·etic** /ˈherətɪk; ˋhɛrətɪk/ *n* person who is guilty of heresy or who supports a heresy 犯异端罪者; 持异端观点者.

her·et·ical /hɪˈretɪkl; həˋrɛtɪkḷ/ *adj* of heresy or heretics 异端的; 持异端观点者的: *heretical beliefs* 异端观点. **her·et·ic·ally** *adv.*

her·it·able /ˈherɪtəbl; ˋhɛrətəbḷ/ *adj* (*law* 律) **1** (of property, etc) that can be inherited (指财产等)可继承的. **2** (of a person) able to inherit (指人)有继承权的.

her·it·age /ˈherɪtɪdʒ; ˋhɛrətɪdʒ/ *n* [C usu *sing* 通常作单数] **1** things such as works of art, cultural achievements and folklore that have been passed on from earlier generations 文化遗产(如祖辈遗留下来的艺术作品、文明成果及民俗): *our literary heritage* 我们的文学遗产 ○ *These ancient buildings are part of the national heritage.* 这些古建筑是民族遗产的一部分. **2** (*dated or fml* 旧或文) property that has been or may be inherited by an heir 遗产; 继承物.

herm·aph·rod·ite /hɜːˈmæfrədaɪt; hɝˋmæfrəˌdaɪt/ *n* person or animal that has both male and female sexual organs or characteristics 两性人; 阴阳人; 雌雄同体的动物. Cf 参看 BISEXUAL. ▷ **herm·aph·rod·itic** /hɜːˌmæfrəˈdɪtɪk; hɝˌmæfrəˋdɪtɪk/ *adj.*

her·metic /hɜːˈmetɪk; hɝˋmɛtɪk/ *adj* tightly closed so that air cannot escape or enter; completely airtight 不透气的; 密封的. ▷ **her·met·ic·ally** /-klɪ; -klɪ/ *adv*: *hermetically sealed containers* 密封容器.

her·mit /ˈhɜːmɪt; ˋhɝmɪt/ *n* person (esp a man in early Christian times) who has withdrawn from society and lives completely alone; recluse (尤指早期基督教的)隐居修道士; 隐士; 遁世者.

▷ **her·mit·age** /-ɪdʒ; -ɪdʒ/ *n* place where a hermit or a group of hermits lives 隐居处; 修道院.

her·nia /ˈhɜːnɪə; ˋhɝnɪə/ *n* [U, C] rupture, esp one caused by a part of the bowel being pushed through a weak point of the muscle wall of the abdomen 疝; 突出.

hero /ˈhɪərəʊ; ˋhɪro/ *n* (*pl* **~es**) **1** person who is admired by many for his noble qualities or his bravery 英雄; 豪杰: *receive a hero's welcome*, ie such as is given to returning heroes 受到如同英雄凯旋一般的欢迎 ○ *He died a hero/a hero's death*, ie died while doing sth very brave or noble. 他死得英勇. ○ *You're my hero*, ie I admire you greatly. 你是我心中的偶像. **2** chief male character in a story, poem, play, etc (小说、诗歌、戏剧等中的)男主角, 男主人公: *the hero of the novel* 该小说的男主人公. Cf 参看 VILLAIN.

▷ **hero·ine** /ˈherəʊɪn; ˋhɛro·ɪn/ *n* female hero 女主角; 女主人公.

hero·ism /ˈherəʊɪzəm; ˋhɛroˌɪzəm/ *n* [U] brave and noble conduct; courage 英雄行为; 英勇精神: *an act of great heroism* 大无畏的举动.

□ ˈ**hero-worship** *n* [U] excessive devotion to a person one admires 个人崇拜; 英雄崇拜. — *v* (**-pp-**) [Tn] be excessively devoted to (sb) 崇拜(某人): *pop-stars hero-worshipped by their fans* 为歌迷们所崇拜的流行歌星.

heroic /hɪˈrəʊɪk; hɪˋro·ɪk/ *adj* **1** (**a**) having the characteristics of a hero; very brave 有英雄气概的; 英勇的: *heroic deeds* 英勇事迹. (**b**) of heroes 英雄的: *heroic myths* 英雄的故事. **2** of a size larger than in real life 大于真人或实物的: *a statue on a heroic scale* 大于真人的塑像. ▷ **hero·ic·ally** /-klɪ; -klɪ/ *adv.*

hero·ics *n* [pl] **1** talk or behaviour that is excessively dramatic 夸张的言语或行为: *There is no need to indulge in such heroics.* 根本没有必要这样肆意夸张. **2** = HEROIC VERSE.

□ **he**ˌ**roic** ˈ**verse** (also **he**ˌ**roic** ˈ**couplets**) verse form used in epic poetry, with lines of ten syllables and five stresses, in rhyming pairs 英雄诗体(用于史诗或叙事诗, 每行十个音节, 五个音步, 每两行押韵).

heroin /ˈherəʊɪn; ˋhɛro·ɪn/ *n* [U] narcotic drug made from morphine, used medically to cause sleep or relieve pain, or by drug addicts 海洛因; 二乙酰吗啡.

hero·ine ⇨ HERO.

heron /ˈherən; ˋhɛrən/ *n* water-bird with a long neck and long legs that lives in marshy places 鹭. ⇨illus at App 1 见附录1插图, page v.

▷ **her·onry** *n* place where herons breed 鹭群繁殖处.

her·pes /ˈhɜːpiːz; ˋhɝpiz/ *n* [U] (*medical* 医) virus disease that causes blisters on the skin 疱疹.

□ ˌ**herpes** ˈ**simplex** simple and painless form of herpes 单纯性疱疹(无痛).

ˌ**herpes** ˈ**zoster** = SHINGLES.

Herr /heə(r); hɛr/ *n* (*pl* **Herren** /ˈherən; ˋhɛrən/) German word for *Mr*; title of a German man 先生(德语词, 相当于英语的 Mr).

her·ring /ˈherɪŋ; ˋhɛrɪŋ/ *n* (*pl* unchanged or **~s** 复数或不变或作 **herrings**) **1** [U, C] N Atlantic fish, usu swimming in very large shoals, used for food 鲱(产于北

H

大西洋，通常成大群游动，可食): *a catch of mackerel and herring* 捕捉鲭鱼和鲱鱼 ○ *a couple of fresh herring (s)* 几条鲜鲱鱼 ○ [attrib 作定语] *herring fishermen* 捕鲱的渔人. **2** (idm 习语) **neither fish, flesh nor good red herring** ⇨ FISH[1]. **a red herring** ⇨ RED[1].

□ ˈ**herring-bone** *n* [U] zigzag pattern used in stitching and weaving 人字形图案(用于缝纫和纺织). ⇨illus at PATTERN 见 PATTERN 插图.

ˈ**herring gull** large N Atlantic gull with dark wing-tips 银鸥(产于北大西洋, 体大, 翼端呈黑色).

hers ⇨ HER[2].

her·self /hɜːˈself; hɚˋsɛlf/ *reflex, emph pron* 反身、强调代词 (only taking the main stress in sentences when used emphatically 仅用以加强语气时方读重音) **1** (*reflex* 反身) (used when the female doer of an action is also affected by it 用作女性、雌性动物的或事物的反身代词): *She ˈhurt herself.* 她伤了自己. ○ *She must be ˈproud of herself.* 她一定为自己而骄傲. **2** (*emph* 强调) (used to emphasize the female subject or object of a sentence 用以强调句中为女性或雌性的主语或宾语): *The Prime Minister herˈself was at the meeting.* (女)首相亲自莅临会议. ○ *She told me the news herˈself.* 这消息是她亲口告诉我的. ○ *I saw Jane herˈself in the supermarket.* 我在超级市场看见简本人了. **3** (idm 习语) **(all) by herˈself** (**a**) alone 单独地: *She lives by herself.* 她独身一人生活. (**b**) without help 独力地: *She can mend the fridge by herself.* 她能自己修理冰箱. ⇨Usage at HE 用法见 HE.

hertz /hɜːts; hɝts/ *n* (*pl* unchanged 复数不变) (*abbr* 缩写 **Hz**) unit of frequency, equal to one cycle per second 赫(兹)(频率单位, 等于每秒一周).

he's /hiːz; hiz/ ⇨Detailed Guide 6.3 见词条使用详细说明 6.3. *contracted form* 缩约式 **1** he is ⇨ BE. **2** he has ⇨ HAVE.

hes·it·ant /ˈhezɪtənt; ˋhɛzətənt/ *adj* tending to be slow in speaking or acting because of uncertainty or unwillingness 犹豫的; 踌躇的; 迟疑的: *a hesitant reply, manner, voice, speaker* 犹疑不决的回答、举棋不定的样子、结结巴巴的声音、说话吞吞吐吐的人 ○ *I'm rather hesitant about signing this.* 我不大愿意签这个字.

▷ **hes·it·ancy** /-ənsɪ; -ənsɪ/ *n* [U] state or quality of being hesitant 犹豫; 踌躇; 迟疑.

hes·it·antly *adv*.

hes·it·ate /ˈhezɪteɪt; ˋhɛzəˌtet/ *v* **1** [I, Ipr] **~ (at/about/over sth)** be slow to speak or act because one feels uncertain or unwilling; pause in doubt 犹豫; 踌躇; 迟疑; (因有疑虑而)停顿: *She replied without hesitating.* 她毫不犹豫地作了回答. ○ *She hesitated before replying.* 她犹豫了一下才回答. ○ *He's still hesitating about joining/over whether to join the expedition.* 他对是否参加考察队仍拿不定主意. ○ *He hesitates at nothing.* 他从不优柔寡断. ○ *I'd hesitate before accepting such an offer.* 我得先斟酌一下, 才能决定是否接受这样的提议. **2** [It] be reluctant 不情愿: *I hesitate to spend so much money on clothes.* 我舍不得把这么多钱花在穿衣服上. ○ *Don't hesitate to tell us if you have a problem.* 你有问题就直截了当地告诉我们.

▷ **hes·ita·tion** /ˌhezɪˈteɪʃn; ˌhɛzəˋteʃən/ *n* **1** [U] state of hesitating 犹豫; 踌躇; 迟疑; 不情愿: *She agreed without the slightest hesitation.* 她毫不犹豫地同意了. ○ *There's no room for hesitation.* 没有踌躇的余地. **2** [C] instance of hesitating 犹豫; 踌躇; 迟疑; 不情愿: *His frequent hesitations annoyed the audience.* 他三番五次欲言又止, 听众已感到厌烦.

hes·sian /ˈhesɪən; *US* ˈheʃn; ˋhɛʃən/ *n* [U] strong coarse cloth of hemp or jute; sack-cloth 一种结实的粗麻布(由大麻或黄麻制成); 麻袋布.

het /het; hɛt/ *adj* (phr v) **(be/get) het up (about/over sth)** (*infml* 口) (of a person) upset; excited (指人)烦躁的; 激动的: *What are you getting so het up about?* 你为什么这样激动?

hetero- *comb form* 构词成分 other; different 异的; 杂的: *heterogeneous* ○ *heterosexual*. Cf 参看 HOMO-.

het·ero·dox /ˈhetərədɒks; ˋhɛtərəˌdɑks/ *adj* not conforming with accepted standards or beliefs 异端的: *a heterodox opinion, person* 非正统见解、持非正统观点的人. Cf 参看 ORTHODOX, UNORTHODOX. ▷ **het·ero·doxy** *n* [U, C].

het·ero·gen·eous /ˌhetərəˈdʒiːnɪəs; ˌhɛtərəˋdʒinɪəs/ *adj* made up of different kinds; varied in composition 由不同种类组成的; 成分混杂的: *the heterogeneous population of the USA*, ie of many different races 由不同种族组成的美国人口. Cf 参看 HOMOGENEOUS.

▷ **het·ero·gen·eity** /-dʒɪˈniːətɪ; -dʒəˋniətɪ/ *n* [U].

het·ero·gen·eously *adv*.

het·ero·sexual /ˌhetərəˈsekʃʊəl; ˌhɛtərəˋsɛkʃʊəl/ *adj* feeling sexually attracted to people of the opposite sex 异性恋的. Cf 参看 BISEXUAL, HOMOSEXUAL.

▷ **het·ero·sexual** *n* heterosexual person 异性恋者.

het·ero·sexu·al·ity /ˌhetərəˌsekʃʊˈælətɪ; ˌhɛtərəˌsɛkʃʊˋælətɪ/ *n* [U].

heur·istic /hjʊəˈrɪstɪk; hjʊˋrɪstɪk/ *adj* (of a method of teaching) that helps or allows a learner to discover and learn things for himself (指教学法)启发式的.

▷ **heur·ist·ics** *n* [U] method of solving problems by evaluating past experience and moving by trial and error to a solution 启发法; 探索法.

hew /hjuː; hju/ *v* (*pt* **hewed**, *pp* **hewed** or **hewn** /hjuːn; hjun/) **1** [Tn, Tn·pr] chop or cut (sth/sb) with an axe, sword, etc (用斧、刀剑等)砍, 劈(某物[某人]): *hewing wood* 劈木 ○ *He hewed his enemy to pieces.* 他将敌人劈成数段. **2** [Tn, Tn·p] **~ sth (down)** cause sth to fall by chopping 砍倒或劈倒某物: *hewing (down) trees* 将树伐倒. **3** [Tn] shape (sth) by chopping 将(某物)砍成或劈成某种形状: *roughly hewn timber* 粗劈的木材. **4** [I, Ipr, Ip] **~ (away) (at/among sth)** aim cutting blows at sth 砍向某物: *He was hewing away at the trunk of the tree.* 他不停地照着树干砍去. **5** (phr v) **hew sth across, through, etc (sth)** make sth by chopping 开辟某物: *They hewed a path through the jungle.* 他们在丛林中开辟出一条路. **hew sth away, off, etc** remove sth by chopping 砍掉某物: *hew off dead branches* 砍去枯枝. **hew sth out** make sth by hard work 努力做成某事物: *hew out a career for oneself* 奋力开创一番事业.

▷ **hewer** *n* person who hews, esp one who cuts out coal in a mine 砍伐者; (尤指)采煤工人.

HEW *abbr* 缩写 = (*US*) Department of Health, Education and Welfare 卫生、教育和福利部.

hex(a)- *comb form* 构词成分 having or made up of six of sth 含有数量为六的某事物; 由数量为六的某事物组成: *hexagon* ○ *hexameter*.

hexa·gon /ˈheksəgən; *US* -gɒn; ˋhɛksəˌgɑn/ *n* geometric figure with six sides and angles 六边形; 六角形.

▷ **hexa·gonal** /heksˈægənl; hɛksˋægənḷ/ *adj* six-sided 六边形的; 六角形的.

hexa·meter /hekˈsæmɪtə(r); hɛksˋæmətɚ/ *n* line of verse with six metrical feet 有六个韵步的诗行.

hey /heɪ; he/ *interj* **1** (also **hi**) (used to call attention or express surprise or inquiry 用以唤起注意或表示惊讶或疑问): *Hey, come and look at this!* 喂, 来瞧瞧这个! **2** (idm 习语) **hey presto** (said by a conjuror as he completes a trick successfully, or by sb commenting on or announcing sth that has been done surprisingly easily or quickly 魔术师将戏法变成功时的用语或人们用以评论或表达某事完成得出奇地容易或迅速): *I just turned the piece of wire in the lock and hey presto, the door opened.* 我把金属丝伸到锁孔里一拧, 嘿, 那门就开了.

hey·day /ˈheɪdeɪ; ˋheˌde/ *n* [sing] time of greatest success, prosperity, power, etc 最成功、最繁荣、最强盛等的时期: *She was a great singer in her heyday.* 她在自己的黄金时代是个了不起的歌唱家. ○ *Steam railways had their heyday in the 19th century.* 19 世纪是蒸汽机车的全盛时期.

HF /ˌeɪtʃ ˈef; ˌetʃ ˋɛf/ *abbr* 缩写 = (*radio* 无) high frequency. Cf 参看 LF.

HG *abbr* 缩写 = His/Her Grace 阁下, 大人, 夫人(用于他称): *HG the Duke/Duchess of Kent* 肯特公爵[公爵夫人]阁下.

HGV /ˌeɪtʃ dʒiː ˈviː; ˌetʃ dʒi ˋvi/ *abbr* 缩写 = (*Brit*) heavy goods vehicle, eg a lorry, bus, etc 大型载货机动车(如卡车、公共汽车等): *have an HGV licence* 有大型运货卡车牌照.

HH *abbr* 缩写 = **1** His/Her Highness 殿下(用于他称): *HH the Prince/Princess of Wales* 威尔斯亲王[王妃]殿下. **2** His Holiness 陛下(用于他称): *HH the Pope* 教皇陛下.

hi /haɪ; haɪ/ *interj* (*infml* 口) **1** (*esp US*) = HALLO: *Hi there!* 喂! **2** (*Brit*) = HEY.

hi·atus /haɪˈeɪtəs; haɪˋetəs/ *n* **1** gap in a series or sequence, making it incomplete; break in continuity 裂隙; 缺漏; 脱漏; 间断. **2** (*linguistics* 语言) break between two vowels coming together but not in the same syllable 元音分立, 母音分读(相邻两单元音分开, 不连成一音节).

hi·bern·ate /ˈhaɪbəneɪt; ˋhaɪbɚˌnet/ *v* [I] (of animals) spend the winter in a state like deep sleep (指动物)冬眠, 蛰伏. ▷ **hi·berna·tion** /ˌhaɪbəˈneɪʃn; ˌhaɪbɚˋneʃən/ *n* [U]: *go into hibernation* 进入冬眠状态.

hi·bis·cus /hɪˈbɪskəs; *US* haɪ-; haɪˋbɪskəs/ *n* plant or shrub with large brightly coloured flowers, grown esp in tropical countries 木槿.

hic·cup (also **hic·cough**) /ˈhɪkʌp; ˋhɪkʌp/ *n* **1** (**a**) [C] sudden involuntary stopping of the breath with a sharp gulp-like sound, often recurring at short intervals 嗝; 呃逆: *give a loud hiccup* 打一个响嗝. (**b**) **hiccups** [pl] persistent repetition of these 连续的打嗝: *She laughed so much she got (the) hiccups.* 她笑得直打嗝. **2** [C] (*infml* 口) temporary small problem or stoppage 暂时性的小问题; 暂时的停顿: *There's been a slight hiccup in our mailing system.* 我们的邮政系统临时出了一点小问题.

▷ **hic·cup** (also **hic·cough**) *v* [I] make a hiccup(1) 打嗝; 打呃.

hick /hɪk; hɪk/ *n* (*infml derog* 口, 贬 *esp US*) **1** awkward or foolish country person; bumpkin 乡巴佬; 土包子. **2** [attrib 作定语] provincial; not sophisticated 乡下的; 土头土脑的: *a hick town* 小乡镇.

hickey /ˈhɪkɪ; ˌhɪkɪ/ *n* (*US infml* 口) **1** gadget; device 小机械; 小装置. **2** pimple; blemish 丘疹; 瑕疵.

hick·ory /ˈhɪkərɪ; ˋhɪkərɪ/ *n* (**a**) N American tree with edible nuts 山核桃树(产于北美, 果实可食). (**b**) its hard wood 山核桃木: [attrib 作定语] *a hickory walking-stick* 山核桃木的手杖.

hide[1] /haɪd; haɪd/ *v* (*pt* **hid** /hɪd; hɪd/, *pp* **hidden** /ˈhɪdn; ˋhɪdn̩/) **1** (**a**) [Tn, Tn·pr, Tn·p] prevent (sth/sb/oneself) from being seen; put or keep out of sight 隐藏(某事物[某人/自己]); 隐蔽: *The sun was hidden by the clouds.* 太阳被云遮住了. ○ *The trees hid the house from view.* 树木把房屋遮挡住了. ○ *He hid the gun in his pocket.* 他把枪藏在衣袋里. ○ *She's hidden my book (away) somewhere.* 她把我的书藏起来了. (**b**) [I, Ipr, Ip] be or get out of sight; be or become concealed 躲藏; 隐匿: *Quick, run and hide!* 快, 赶紧跑, 躲起来! ○ *The child was hiding behind the sofa.* 那孩子藏在沙发后面了. ○ (*fig* 比喻) *She hid behind a false identity.* 她以假身分作掩护. ○ *The wanted man hid (away) in the forest.* 那受通缉的男子躲进了森林里. **2** [Tn, Tn·pr] **~ sth (from sb)** prevent sth from being known; keep sth secret 隐瞒(某事物); 掩盖(某事物): *She tried to hide her feelings.* 她尽力不使感情外露. ○ *The future is hidden from us.* 未来是我们难以预卜的. ○ *His words had a hidden meaning.* 他话里有话. **3** (idm 习语) **cover/hide a multitude of sins** ⇨ MULTITUDE. **hide one's ˌlight under a ˈbushel** hide one's talents, abilities or good qualities because of modesty, etc 不展才; 不露锋芒.

▷ **hide** *n* (*Brit*) (*US* **blind**) place where naturalists, hunters, etc can watch wild animals or birds without being seen by them 隐蔽观察处(博物学家、猎人等暗地观察野生鸟兽之处).

hid·ing *n* [U] (idm 习语) ˌ**go into**/ˌ**come out of** ˈ**hiding** hide/reveal oneself 躲藏起来[从躲藏处出来]. **in** ˈ**hiding** hidden 隐藏的: *He stayed in hiding for a year.* 他隐藏了一年.

□ **hide-and-seek** /ˌhaɪdnˈsiːk; ˋhaɪdn̩ˋsik/ *n* [U] children's game in which one player hides and the others try to find him 捉迷藏游戏.

ˈ**hide-out** (*US* also ˈ**hideaway**) *n* hiding-place for people (人的)藏身处: *a guerrilla hide-out in the mountains* 山里游击队的隐藏处.

ˈ**hiding-place** *n* place where sb/sth is or could be hidden (人或物的)隐藏处.

hide[2] /haɪd; haɪd/ *n* **1** [C] animal's skin, esp when bought and sold or used for making sth 兽皮; (尤指)皮革: *boots made of buffalo hide* 水牛皮制的靴子. **2** [U] (*infml joc* 口, 谑) human skin 人的皮肤. **3** (idm 习语) **have, etc a hide/skin like a rhinoceros** ⇨ RHINOCEROS. **neither hide nor** ˈ**hair of sb/sth** no trace of sb/sth 无某人[某物]的踪迹: *I've not seen hide nor hair of him all week.* 我整星期连他的影子都没看见. **save one's hide** ⇨ SAVE[1]. **tan sb's hide** ⇨ TAN.

hide·bound /ˈhaɪdbaʊnd; ˋhaɪdˌbaʊnd/ *adj* (*derog* 贬) not willing to consider new ideas, methods, etc; too conventional and narrow-minded 对新的思想、方法等格格不入的; 守旧的; 思想偏狭的: *hidebound views, bureaucrats* 守旧的观点、官僚 ○ *a society hidebound by convention* 墨守成规的社会.

hid·eous /ˈhɪdɪəs; ˋhɪdɪəs/ *adj* filling the mind with horror; very ugly; frightful 令人惊骇的; 极其丑陋的; 可怕的: *a hideous crime, face, noise, creature* 邪恶的罪行、丑陋的面孔、吓人的声音、可怕的怪物 ○ (*infml* 口) *I think the colour scheme they've chosen is hideous.* 我觉得他们选用的颜色配合起来难看极了. ▷ **hid·eously** *adv*: *be hideously deformed* 严重畸形. **hid·eous·ness** *n* [U].

hid·ing[1] ⇨ HIDE[1].

hid·ing[2] /ˈhaɪdɪŋ; ˋhaɪdɪŋ/ *n* **1** (*infml* 口) beating; thrashing 打; 鞭打: *His dad gave him a good hiding.* 他爸爸给他一顿好打. **2** (idm 习语) **on a** ˌ**hiding to** ˈ**nothing** (*infml* 口) with no chance at all of succeeding 毫无成功希望.

hie /haɪ; haɪ/ *v* (*pt* **hied**, *pres part* **hieing** or **hying**) [Ipr, Tn·pr] **~ oneself to sth** (*arch or joc* 古或谑) go quickly 快走: *Hie (thee) to thy chamber.* 你撒开丫子回屋去吧.

hier·archy /ˈhaɪərɑːkɪ; ˋhaɪəˌrɑrkɪ/ *n* system with grades of authority or status from the lowest to the highest 等级制度: *She's high up in the management hierarchy.* 她在管理阶层中地位很高. ○ *There is a hierarchy in the classification of all living creatures.* 一切生物均可按等级分类.

▷ **hier·arch·ical** /ˌhaɪəˈrɑːkɪkl; ˌhaɪəˋrɑrkɪkl̩/ *adj* of or arranged in a hierarchy 等级制的; 按等级划分的: *a hierarchical society, system, organization, etc* 有等级之分的社会、体系、组织等.

hiero·glyph /ˈhaɪərəglɪf; ˋhaɪərəˌglɪf/ *n* **1** picture or symbol of an object, representing a word, syllable or sound, as used in ancient Egyptian and other writing 象形字(如古埃及等所用的). **2** written symbol with a secret or hidden meaning 秘密的或另有含义的书写符号.

▷ **hiero·glyphic** /ˌhaɪərəˈglɪfɪk; ˌhaɪərəˋglɪfɪk/ *adj* of or written in hieroglyphs (用)象形文字(写成)的; (用)秘密的书写符号(写成)的.

hiero·glyphics *n* [pl] hieroglyphs 象形文字: *deciphering Egyptian hieroglyphics* 译解古埃及的象形文字 ○ *His writing is so bad it just looks like hieroglyphics to me.* 他写的糟透了, 对我来说就像天书一样.

hi-fi /ˈhaɪfaɪ; ˌhaɪˋfaɪ/ *adj* [usu attrib 通常作定语] (*infml* 口) = HIGH FIDELITY (HIGH): *hi-fi records, tapes, radios* 高保真度的唱片、录音带、收音机.

▷ **hi-fi** *n* [C, U] (*infml* 口) hi-fi equipment 高保真度的音响设备: *You must hear my new hi-fi.* 你务必要听听我这套新的高保真度音响设备.

higgledy-piggledy /ˌhɪgldɪ ˈpɪgldɪ; ˋhɪgldɪˋpɪgldɪ/ *adv, adj* [usu pred 通常作表语] (*infml* 口) without order; completely mixed up 杂乱无章; 乱七八糟: *Files were scattered (all) higgledy-piggledy about the office.* 办公室里文件乱七八糟地满处都是.

high[1] /haɪ; haɪ/ *adj* (**-er**, **-est**) **1** (**a**) (of things) extending far upwards; having a relatively big distance from the base to the top (指物)高的: *a high fence, forehead, mountain* 高的栅栏、额头、山 ○ *high heels* 高跟 ○ *How high is Mt Everest?* 埃佛勒斯峰(即珠穆朗玛峰)有多高? (**b**) having a specified distance from the base to the top 有某一高度的: *knee-high boots* 齐膝高的靴子 ○ *The wall is six feet high.* 这墙高六英尺. (**c**) situated far above the ground or above sea level 离地面或海拔很高的: *a high ceiling, shelf* 高的天花板、搁板 ○ *fly at a high altitude* 在高空飞行. (**d**) being above the normal level 超过正常高度的: *a jersey with a high neck* 高领紧身针织套衫. (**e**) (of a physical action) performed at or reaching a considerable distance above ground (指动作)在距离地面相当高处进行的或达到相当高度的: *a high dive, kick* 高台跳水、踢高球. ⇨Usage at HEIGHT 用法见 HEIGHT. Cf 参看 LOW. **2** [usu attrib 通常作定语] ranking above others in importance or quality 高级的: *a high official* 高级官员 ○ *a man of high standing* 身分高的人 ○ *refer a case to a higher court* 将案件提交上级法院处理 ○ *high society*, ie the upper classes 上流社会 ○ *I have this information on the highest authority.* 我有最高当局的这一方面资料. **3** (**a**) above the normal; extreme; intense 超乎寻常的; 极度的; 强烈的: *a high price, temperature, fever, speed, wind, living standard* 高价、高温、高烧、高速、大风、高的生活水平 ○ *high voltage, blood pressure, praise* 高电压、高血压、高度的赞扬 ○ *The cost in terms of human life was high.* 人命的损失很大. ○ *I have high hopes of passing the exam.* 我考试极有希望能及格. ○ *A high degree of accuracy is needed.* 需要有高度的准确性. ○ *be in high spirits*, ie be very cheerful 兴高采烈 ○ *a high Tory*, ie one holding traditional Conservative opinions 坚持保守党传统观点的人. (**b**) of great value 价值高的; 数值大的: *play for high stakes* 豪赌 ○ *My highest card is a ten.* 我最大的牌是十点. (**c**) [attrib 作定语] extravagant; luxurious 奢侈的; 铺张的: *indulge in high living* 奢靡无度 ○ *enjoy the high life* 过奢侈生活. (**d**) [usu attrib 通常作定语] (of aims, ideas, etc) morally good; noble; virtuous (指目标、思想等)高尚的, 崇高的, 有道德的: *have high ideals* 具有崇高的理想 ○ *a woman of high principle* 有崇高道德原则的女子. (**e**) [usu attrib 通常作定语] very favourable 极讨人喜欢的; 极有利的: *have a high opinion of/high regard for sb* 极赞许某人. (**f**) [attrib 作定语] (most) enjoyable (最)令人愉快的: *the high point of the evening* 晚会的高潮. **4** (of a sound) at or near the top of the musical scale; not deep or low (指声音)尖利的, 高音调的: *the high voice of a child* 孩子的尖利的嗓音 ○ *The note was too high for him.* 这音符太高, 他唱不了. **5** [attrib 作定语] (of time) fully reached (指时间)已届时的, 全盛的: *high noon* 正午 ○ *high summer*, ie the middle of the summer 盛夏. **6** (of a gear) allowing greater speed of a vehicle in relation to its engine speed (指变速器)高挡的: *You can change into a higher gear now you're going faster.* 你既然已加快了速度, 就可以换上高挡了. **7** [pred 作表语] (of meat, etc) beginning to go bad (指肉等)开始变质: *Some game-birds are kept until they are high before cooking.* 有些猎获的飞禽一直保存到开始变质才烹制. **8** [usu pred 通常作表语] **~ (on sth)** (*infml* 口) under the influence of (esp drugs or alcohol) 受到(尤指麻醉品或酒精饮料)影响: *be/get high on cannabis* 因吸食大麻而神魂恍惚. **9** (idm 习语) **be/get on one's ˌhigh ˈhorse** (*infml* 口) act haughtily 趾高气扬; 盛气凌人. **have/give sb a ˈhigh old time** (*infml* 口) enjoy oneself/entertain sb in a very exuberant or jolly way 玩得很痛快[使某人玩得很痛快]. **hell or high water** ⇨ HELL. **ˌhigh and ˈdry** (of a ship) stranded; aground (指船)触礁, 搁浅: (*fig* 比喻) *He left her high and dry in a strange country without any money.* 他把她遗弃在异国他乡, 身无分文, 处于困境. **ˌhigh and ˈmighty** (*infml* 口) arrogant; haughty 倨傲不逊的; 盛气凌人的: *There's no need to be/get so high and mighty with me!* 用不着对我摆架子! **ˌhigh days and ˈholidays** festivals and special occasions 节日和假日. **ˌhigh ˈjinks** (*infml* 口) noisy and mischievous fun 狂欢作乐; 胡闹. **a high/low profile** ⇨ PROFILE. **high/about time** ⇨ TIME[1]. **in ˌhigh ˈdudgeon** angry and indignant 极其愤怒: *He stalked off in high dudgeon.* 他极其愤怒地昂首阔步走开了. **in ˌhigh ˈplaces** among people of power and influence 在有权势的人当中: *She has friends in high places.* 她有一些很有势力的朋友. **smell, stink, etc to high ˈheaven** (*infml* 口) (**a**) have a strong unpleasant smell 发恶臭. (**b**) seem to be very dishonest, corrupt, etc 极不诚实的、极腐败的等: *The whole scheme stinks to high heaven — don't get involved in it.* 整件事十分卑鄙龌龊——可别陷了进去.

□ **ˈhigh-born** *adj* of noble birth 出身高贵的.

ˌhigh ˈchair infant's chair with long legs and an attached tray, for use at meals (幼童吃饭时坐的)高脚椅(附有托盘). ⇨illus at App 1 见附录1插图, page xvi.

ˌHigh ˈChurch section of the Church of England that emphasizes ritual and the authority of bishops and priests 高派教会(英国国教之一派, 注重仪式以及主教和牧师的权威). **ˌHigh-ˈChurchman** /-mən; -mən/ *n* (*pl* **-men** /-mən; -mən/).

ˌhigh-ˈclass *adj* **1** of high quality; excellent 高级的; 上等的: *a ˌhigh-class ˈrestaurant* 高级餐厅. **2** of high social class 上流社会的.

ˌhigh ˈcolour unusually red complexion 发红的脸色.

ˌHigh Comˈmission embassy of one Commonwealth country in another (英联邦中一国派驻另一国的)高级专员公署. Cf 参看 CONSULATE[1]. **ˌHigh Comˈmissioner** head of this (equivalent to an ambassador) (英联邦中一国派驻另一国的)高级专员(相当于大使).

ˌHigh ˈCourturt (also **ˌHigh Court of ˈJustice**) supreme court for civil cases (审理民事案件的)高等法院.

ˌhigher ˈanimals, ˈplants, etc animals, plants, etc that are highly developed and have a complex structure 高级动物、植物等(进化程度高、构造复杂者).

ˌhigher eduˈcation education and training at universities, polytechnics, etc 高等教育.

ˌhigh exˈplosive very powerful explosive with a violent shattering effect 高爆炸药; 烈性炸药.

high-falutin /ˌhaɪ fəˈluːtn; ˌhaɪfəˈlutn̩/ *adj* (*infml* 口) pompous; pretentious 浮夸的; 矫饰的: *high-falutin ideas, language* 妄自尊大的思想、浮夸的语言.

ˌhigh fiˈdelity (also **ˈhi-fi**) reproduction of sound (by radios, record-players, tape-recorders, etc) that is of high quality, with little or no distortion of the original sound (收音机、电唱机、录音机等复制声音的)高保真度.

ˌhigh-ˈflown *adj* (of language, etc) extravagantly grand and pretentious (指语言等)浮夸的, 言过其实的.

ˌhigh-ˈflyer (also **high-flier**) *n* person with the ability or ambition to be very successful 有能耐的人; 有抱负的人; 野心勃勃的人. **ˌhigh-ˈflying** *adj*.

ˌhigh ˈfrequency (*abbr* 缩写 **HF**) radio frequency of 3 to 30 megahertz 高频(指无线电频率由3至30兆赫).

ˌHigh ˈGerman standard written and spoken German 高地德语(书面和口头使用的标准德语).

ˌhigh-ˈgrade *adj* of high quality 高级的; 优质的: *ˌhigh-grade ˈpetrol* 高级汽油.

ˌhigh-ˈhanded *adj* using power or authority without considering the opinions and wishes of others 专横的; 高压的: *a ˌhigh-handed ˈperson, ˈaction* 专横的人、做法. **ˌhigh-ˈhandedly** *adv*. **ˌhigh-ˈhandedness** *n* [U].

the ˈhigh jump **1** athletic contest of jumping as high as possible, over an adjustable horizontal bar 跳高(比赛): *enter for the high jump* 参加跳高比赛. **2** (idm 习语) **be for the high jump** (*infml* 口) be likely to be severely punished 可能遭受严厉惩罚: *If you're caught stealing you'll be for the high jump.* 偷东西被人抓住就要受到严厉的惩罚.

ˈhighland /-lənd; -lənd/ *adj* **1** of or in mountainous regions 高地的; 高原(地区)的. **2 Highland** of or in the Scottish Highlands 苏格兰高地的: *Highland cattle* (苏格兰出产的)高原牛 ○ *Highland dress* (苏格兰的)高地人服装. — *n* **1** [C usu *pl* 通常作复数] mountainous part of a country 高原地区; 山岳地带. **2 the Highlands** [pl] the mountainous part of Scotland 苏格兰高地. ⇨ illus at App 1 见附录1插图, pages xiv, xv. **ˈhighlander** *n* person who lives in the Scottish Highlands 苏格兰高地人.

ˌHighland ˈfling lively Scottish dance 高地舞(一种轻快的苏格兰舞蹈).

ˌhigh-ˈlevel *adj* [usu attrib 通常作定语] (of negotiations, etc) involving very senior people (指谈判等)高层次的, 高级别的: *ˌhigh-level ˈtalks, ˈconferences, etc* 高阶层的会谈、会议等.

ˌhigh-level ˈlanguage computer language that is close to ordinary language and usu not machine-readable 高级语言(接近日常语言的计算机语言, 通常并非机器可读的).

ˈhigh life (in W Africa) popular style of music and dance (非洲西部的)一种流行的音乐舞蹈形式.

high-minded /ˌhaɪ ˈmaɪndɪd; ˈhaɪˈmaɪndɪd/ *adj* having or showing a noble and virtuous character 情操高尚的; 思想境界高的. **ˌhigh-ˈmindedly** *adv*. **ˌhigh-ˈmindedness** *n* [U].

ˌhigh-ˈoctane *adj* (of petrol) having a high percentage of a certain octane and thus of good quality (指汽油)高辛烷值的, 优质的.

ˌhigh-ˈpitched *adj* **1** (of sounds) shrill; high in pitch[3] (3a) (指声音)尖锐的, 声调高的: *a ˌhigh-pitched ˈwhine* 尖声的哀叫. **2** (of roofs) steeply sloping (指屋顶)坡度

大的,陡的.

ˌhigh-ˈpowered *adj* [usu attrib 通常作定语] **1** (of things) having great power (指事物)强有力的: *a ˌhigh-powered ˈcar, ˈrifle, ˈengine* 马力很大的汽车、火力很强的步枪、大功率的发动机. **2** (of people) forceful and energetic (指人)劲头很足的,精力旺盛的: *high-powered business executives* 干劲十足的商务行政人员.

ˌhigh ˈpressure **1** condition of the atmosphere with pressure above average 高压的; 高气压的: *a ridge of high pressure* 高压脊. **2** energetic activity and effort 积极的行动; 极大的努力: *work at high pressure* 极其紧张地工作 ○ [attrib 作定语] *ˌhigh-pressure* (ie aggressive and persistent) *ˈsalesmanship* 强行推销术.

ˌhigh-ˈpriced *adj* expensive 高价的; 昂贵的.

ˌhigh ˈpriest chief priest 大祭司: (*fig* 比喻) *the high priest of modern technology* 现代技术的权威.

ˌhigh-ˈprincipled *adj* honourable 光明正大的: *a ˌhigh-principled ˈperson, ˈdeed* 光明正大的人、行为.

ˌhigh-ˈranking *adj* of high rank; senior 级别高的; 显要的: *a ˌhigh-ranking ˈarmy officer* 高级军官.

ˈhigh-rise *adj* [attrib 作定语] (of a building) very tall, with many storeys (指建筑物)高层的: *a high-rise office block* 高层办公大楼. — *n* such a building 高层大楼.

ˈhigh road main road 大路; 公路干线: (*fig* 比喻) *take the high road* (ie the most direct way) *to happiness* 走上幸福的康庄大道.

ˈhigh school (*esp US*) secondary school; school providing more advanced education than a primary or middle school 中学; 高中.

the ˌhigh ˈsea (also **the high seas**) the open seas beyond the legal control of any one country 公海.

ˌhigh ˈseason time of year when most visitors regularly come to a resort, etc (旅游活动的)旺季: *Hotels usually raise their prices in (the) high season.* 在旅游旺季,旅馆通常提高收费.

ˈhigh-sounding *adj* (of language, etc) pretentious; high-flown (指语言等)夸张的,言过其实的.

ˌhigh-ˈspeed *adj* [usu attrib 通常作定语] (that can be) operated at great speeds (适于)高速操作的: *ˌhigh-speed ˈtrains*.

ˌhigh-ˈspirited *adj* **1** lively and cheerful; vivacious 兴高采烈的; 活泼愉快的. **2** (of a horse) frisky (指马)活蹦乱跳的.

ˈhigh spot (*infml* 口) outstanding event, memory, etc; most important feature 突出的事件、记忆等; 最重要的特点: *The excursion was the high spot of our holiday.* 我们那个假日的最大乐趣是远足.

ˈhigh street (esp in names) main street of a town, with shops, etc (尤用于街名)大街(市镇的主要街道): *Oxford High Street* 牛津大街 ○ [attrib 作定语] *high-street banks, shops, etc* 主要大街上的银行、商店等.

ˌhigh ˈtable table on a raised platform where the most important people at a public dinner or in a college sit to eat 聚餐会上或学院里为最显要人士特设的置于较高平台上的餐桌.

ˌhigh ˈtea (*Brit*) early evening meal of cooked food, usu with tea 傍晚茶(傍晚用的膳食,通常有茶).

ˌhigh-ˈtech *adj* (*infml* 口) **1** involving high technology 高技术的. **2** (of interior design, etc) imitating styles more common in industry, etc (指室内装饰等)仿工业等中的常见式样的.

ˌhigh techˈnology advanced technological development 高技术.

ˌhigh ˈtension high voltage 高电压: [attrib 作定语] *ˌhigh-tension ˈcables* 高压电缆.

ˌhigh ˈtide (**a**) tide when at its highest level 高潮. (**b**) time when this occurs 高潮时期.

ˌhigh ˈtreason treason against one's country or ruler 叛国罪; 叛逆罪.

ˈhigh-up *n* (*infml* 口) person of high rank 上面(居高位的人,上级).

ˌhigh ˈwater = HIGH TIDE. **ˌhigh-ˈwater mark** **1** mark showing the highest level reached by the sea or by flood waters 高水位线(标明海水或洪水所达到的最高水位). **2** (*fig* 比喻) highest point of achievement 成就的顶点.

ˌhigh ˈwire high tightrope 绷紧的绳索.

high² /haɪ; haɪ/ *n* **1** high or highest level or number (最)高水平; (最)高数值: *Profits reached a new high last year.* 去年所获得的利润达到了一个新的最高点. **2** area of high barometric pressure; anticyclone 高(气)压区; 反气旋: *A high over southern Europe is bringing fine sunny weather to all parts.* 欧洲南部上空的反气旋给各地区带来了晴朗的好天气. **3** (*sl* 俚) feeling of extreme pleasure or excitement caused by a drug 由麻醉品引起的快感. **4** (idm 习语) **on ˈhigh** (**a**) in a high place 在高处: *The climbers gazed down from on high.* 攀登者从高处向下眺望. (**b**) in heaven 在天上: *God on high* 天上的神 ○ *The disaster was seen as a judgement from on high.* 这一灾难被视为上天的惩罚.

high³ /haɪ; haɪ/ *adv* **1** at or to a high position or level 高; 高高地: *An eagle circled high overhead.* 一只鹰在高空盘旋. ○ *I can't jump any higher.* 再高些我就跳不了啦. ○ *He never got very high in the company.* 他在公司里所担任的职务,从来就不是很高的. ○ *aim high*, ie be ambitious 胸怀大志 ○ *pay high*, ie pay a high price 付出高价. **2** (of sound) at or to a high pitch (指声音)音调高: *I can't sing that high.* 我唱不了那么高的调门儿. **3** (idm 习语) **be/stand ˌhigh in sb's ˈfavour** be well regarded by sb 为某人所赏识. **fly high** ⇨ FLY². **ˌhigh and ˈlow** everywhere 到处: *I've searched high and low for my lost pen.* 我到处寻找丢失的钢笔. **hold one's head high** ⇨ HEAD¹. **play ˈhigh** play a card of high value 打出一张大牌. **ride high** ⇨ RIDE². **run ˈhigh** (**a**) (of the sea) have a strong current with a high tide (指大海)波涛汹涌. (**b**) (esp of feelings) be intense (尤指情绪)高涨: *Passions ran high as the election approached.* 选举日期临近,人们情绪很高涨.

high·ball /ˈhaɪbɔːl; ˋhaɪˌbɔl/ *n* (*US*) drink of spirits mixed with soda water, ginger ale, etc and served with ice in a tall glass 混有汽水、姜汁麦芽酒等的酒精饮料(加有冰块,盛于高杯内).

high·boy /ˈhaɪbɔɪ; ˋhaɪˌbɔɪ/ *n* (*US*) = TALLBOY.

high·brow /ˈhaɪbraʊ; ˋhaɪˌbraʊ/ *n* (*often derog* 常作贬义) person who has or is thought to have superior intellectual and cultural tastes 博学而兴趣高雅的人; 风雅之士. ▷ **high·brow** *adj*: *highbrow drama, books, interests* 格调高雅的戏剧、书籍、兴趣. Cf 参看 LOWBROW, MIDDLE-BROW (MIDDLE).

high·light /ˈhaɪlaɪt; ˋhaɪˌlaɪt/ *n* **1** best, most interesting or most exciting part of something 最有意思或最精彩的部分: *The highlight of our tour was seeing the palace.* 我们旅游中最有意思的活动就是参观宫殿. ○ *The highlights of the match will be shown on TV tonight.* 比赛的最精彩场面将在今晚的电视节目中播放. **2** (usu *pl* 通常作复数) (**a**) light or bright part of a picture, photograph, etc (绘画、摄影等作品中的)光亮部分,亮部. (**b**) bright tint in the hair 头发上有光泽的浅色.

▷ **high·light** *v* [Tn] **1** give special attention to (sth); emphasize 对(某事物)予以特别的注意; 强调: *a TV programme highlighting the problems of the unemployed* 着重反映失业问题的电视节目. **2** bleach or tint (parts of the hair) so that it reflects the light 将(部分头发)染成浅色使之有光泽.

high·lighter *n* marker pen used to draw attention to a written or printed word by covering it with a transparent colouring (作记号用的)亮光笔.

highly /ˈhaɪlɪ; ˋhaɪlɪ/ *adv* **1** to an unusually great extent; very 高度地; 非常: *a highly amusing film* 非常有趣的影片 ○ *be highly probable, contagious, inflammable* 极有可能、易传染、易燃烧 ○ *The goods on display are all very highly priced.* 所展出的物品都是非常昂贵的. **2** very favourably 极为赞许: *think highly of sb*, ie have a high opinion of sb 极其赞赏某人 ○ *speak highly of sb*, ie praise sb 称赞某人.

□ **ˌhighly-ˈstrung** *adj* (of a person) very sensitive and nervous; easily upset (指人)十分敏感的,紧张不安的,容易激动的.

high·ness /ˈhaɪnɪs; ˋhaɪnɪs/ *n* [C] (usu 通常作 **Highness**) title used in speaking to or of a member of the royal family 殿下,阁下(用作对皇室成员的尊称): *His/Her/Your Royal Highness* 殿下(或阁下) ○ *Their Royal Highnesses the Duke and Duchess of Kent* 肯特公爵和公爵夫人阁下.

high·way /ˈhaɪweɪ; ˋhaɪˌwe/ *n* **1** (*esp US*) main public road 公路; 交通要道. **2** direct route by air, sea or land (空中、水上或陆上的)直接航线或路线: (*fig* 比喻) *We are on the highway to progress.* 我们在走向进步.

□ **ˌHighway ˈCode** (*Brit*) set of official rules for users

H

of public roads; book containing these 公路法规(汇编). ⇨Usage at ROAD 用法见 ROAD.

ˈ**highwayman** /-mən; -mən/ *n* (*pl* **-men** /-mən; -ˌmən/) (formerly) man, usu armed and on horseback, who robbed travellers on public roads (旧时)拦路抢劫的强盗(通常骑马持械).

hi·jack /ˈhaɪdʒæk; ˋhaɪˌdʒæk/ *v* [Tn] **1** seize control of (a vehicle, esp an aircraft) in order to force it to go to a new destination, to take its passengers hostage or to steal its cargo 劫持(交通工具, 尤指飞行器): *The plane was highjacked while on a flight to Delhi.* 该机在飞往德里的途中遭到劫持. **2** steal (goods) from a vehicle 抢劫(载运中的货物).

▷ **hi·jack** *n* instance of hijacking 劫持交通工具之事件. **hi·jacker** *n* person who hijacks a vehicle 劫持交通工具的人.

hi·jack·ing *n* [C, U]: *prevent (a) hijacking* 防止(一场)劫持事件.

hike /haɪk; haɪk/ *n* **1** long walk, esp in the country, taken for pleasure or exercise 远足, 徒步旅行(尤指在乡间进行者): *go on a ten-mile hike* 作一次十英里的徒步旅行. Cf 参看 RAMBLE 1. **2** (*infml* 口) rise in prices, costs, etc (价格、价值等的)提高, 增加: *The union demands a 7% wage hike.* 工会要求提高工资7%.

▷ **hike** *v* **1** [I] go for a long walk 作远足旅行; 作徒步旅行: *a hiking holiday* 作远足活动的假日. **2** [Tn, Tn·p] **~ sth (up)** (*infml* 口) (*esp US*) raise (prices, etc) 提高(价格等): *hike(up) an insurance claim* 提高保险索赔金额. **hiker** *n* person who hikes 远足者; 徒步旅行者.

hil·ari·ous /hɪˈleərɪəs; həˋlɛrɪəs/ *adj* (**a**) extremely amusing; very funny 十分有趣的; 非常滑稽的: *a hilarious account of their camping holiday* 对他们在假日里进行野营活动的引人入胜的记述. (**b**) noisily merry 欢闹的: *a hilarious party* 狂欢会.

▷ **hil·ari·ously** *adv*: *be hilariously funny* 滑稽可笑.

hil·ar·ity /hɪˈlærətɪ; həˋlærətɪ/ *n* [U] loud laughter; great amusement 欢笑; 狂欢: *The announcement was greeted with much hilarity and mirth.* 这一项宣布引起了热烈的欢呼声.

hill /hɪl; hɪl/ *n* **1** natural elevation on the earth's surface, not as high or rugged as a mountain 山冈; 小山: *a range of hills* 一列山丘 ○ *The house is on the side of a hill.* 那所房子坐落在山坡上. **2** slope in a road, etc (道路等的)斜坡: *push one's bike up a steep hill* 推着自行车上陡坡. **3** (esp in compounds 尤用以构成复合词) heap of earth; mound 土堆; 土墩: *an ˈanthill* ○ *a ˈmolehill*. **4** (idm 习语) **a hill of ˈbeans** (*US infml* 口) thing of little value 没有多大价值的东西: *It's not worth a hill of beans*, ie It is worth very little. 这一钱不值. **old as the hills** ⇨ OLD. **over the ˈhill** (*infml* 口) (of a person) past one's prime; old (指人)巅峰时期已过, 人老珠黄. **up ˌhill and down ˈdale** everywhere 到处: *We've been chasing up hill and down dale trying to find you.* 我们在到处找你呢.

▷ **hilly** /ˈhɪlɪ; ˋhɪlɪ/ *adj* having many hills 多小山的; 多斜坡的: *hilly countryside* 丘陵地带. **hil·li·ness** *n* [U].

□ ˈ**hillside** *n* sloping side of a hill (小山的)山坡. ˈ**hilltop** *n* top of a hill (小山的)山顶.

hill-billy /ˈhɪl bɪlɪ; ˋhɪlˌbɪlɪ/ *n* **1** [C] (*US infml usu derog* 口, 通常作贬义) unsophisticated person from a remote rural area, esp the mountains in the south-eastern US 乡巴佬; (尤指)美国东南部的山里人. **2** [U] folk music like that of the southern US (类似美国南部曲调的)民间音乐.

hil·lock /ˈhɪlək; ˋhɪlək/ *n* small hill; mound 小丘; 土墩.

hilt /hɪlt; hɪlt/ *n* **1** handle of a sword, dagger, etc (刀剑、匕首等的)柄. ⇨illus at SWORD 见 SWORD 插图. **2** (idm 习语) **(up) to the ˈhilt** completely 完全地; 彻底地: *be up to the hilt in debt* 债台高筑 ○ *be mortgaged up to the hilt*, ie have an extremely high mortgage 抵押到极高的数额 ○ *I'll support you to the hilt.* 我完全支持你.

him /hɪm; hɪm/ *pers pron* 人称代词 (used as the object of a *v* or of a *prep*; also used independently or after *be* 用作动词或介词的宾语, 亦可单独使用或用于 be 之后) male person or animal mentioned earlier or being observed now 他; 它(用以指雄性动物): *When did you see him?* 你是什么时候看见他的? ○ *I'm taller than him.* 我比他高. ○ (*infml* 口) *That's him over there.* 那边那个人就是他. ○ *Oh, not ˈhim again!* 噢, 可别再是他了! ⇨Usage at HE 用法见 HE.

him·self /hɪmˈself; hɪmˋsɛlf/ *reflex, emph pron* 反身、强调代词 (only taking the main stress when used emphatically 只在强调时才读主要重音) **1** (*reflex* 反身) (used when the male doer of an action is also affected by it 用作男性或雄性的反身代词): *He ˈcut himself.* 他割伤了自己. ○ *Peter ought to be aˈshamed of himself.* 彼得应该感到惭愧. **2** (*emph* 强调) (used to emphasize the male subject or object of a sentence 用以加强句中男性或雄性主语或宾语的语气): *The doctor said so himˈself.* 医生亲口这样说的. ○ *Did you see the manager himˈself?* 你见到经理本人了吗? **3** (idm 习语) **(all) by himˈself** (**a**) alone (他)单独地, 独自地: *He lives all by himself in that large house.* 他独自一人住在那所大房子里. (**b**) without help (他)独力地: *John managed to repair his car by himself.* 约翰设法独力修理自己的汽车. ⇨Usage at HE 用法见 HE.

hind[1] /haɪnd; haɪnd/ *adj* **1** (of things in pairs) situated at the back (指成对的事物)后面的, 在后的: *a dog's hind legs* 狗的后腿. Cf 参看 FORE[1]. **2** (idm 习语) **on one's hind ˈlegs** (*joc* 谑) on one's feet; standing 站着; 站立: *Get up on your hind legs and do some work!* 站起来干点活儿吧! **talk the hind legs off a donkey** ⇨ TALK[2].

▷ ˈ**hind·most** *adj* (*dated* 旧) **1** furthest behind 最后面的. **2** (idm 习语) **the devil take the hindmost** ⇨ DEVIL[1].

□ ˌ**hind**ˈ**quarters** *n* [pl] back parts of a four-legged animal including the back legs (四腿动物的)臀部和后腿. ⇨illus at HORSE 见 HORSE 插图.

hind[2] /haɪnd; haɪnd/ *n* (*pl* unchanged or **~s** 复数或不变或作 **hinds**) female deer, esp red deer 雌鹿; (尤指)红雌鹿. Cf 参看 DOE, HART.

hinder /ˈhɪndə(r); ˋhɪndɚ/ *v* [Tn, Tn·pr] **~ sb/sth (from sth/doing sth)** prevent the progress of sb/sth; obstruct or delay sb/sth 阻碍、妨碍某人[某事物]的进展; 阻挠或耽搁某人[某事物]: *hinder sb (from working)* 妨碍某人(工作) ○ *hinder sb in his work* 阻挠某人的工作 ○ *Production was hindered by lack of materials.* 由于缺乏原料, 生产陷于停顿.

Hindi /ˈhɪndiː; ˋhɪndi/ *adj, n* [U] (of) one of the official languages of India, spoken esp in N India 印地语(印度官方语言之一, 主要通行印度北部); 印地语的.

hind·rance /ˈhɪndrəns; ˋhɪndrəns/ *n* **1 ~ (to sth/sb)** thing or person that hinders 起妨碍作用的事物或人: *Some kitchen gadgets are more of a hindrance than a help.* 有些灵巧的炊具非但没有用处反而碍事. **2** (idm 习语) **without let or hindrance** ⇨ LET[3].

hind·sight /ˈhaɪndsaɪt; ˋhaɪndˌsaɪt/ *n* [U] wisdom about an event after it has occurred 事后的觉悟; 事后的聪明: *We failed, and with (the benefit of) hindsight I now see where we went wrong.* 我们失利了, 事后一想, 我终于明白了错在哪里. Cf 参看 FORESIGHT.

Hindu /ˌhɪnˈduː; *US* ˈhɪnduː; ˋhɪndu/ *n* person, esp of N India, whose religion is Hinduism 印度人; (尤指印度北部的)印度斯坦人(信奉印度教).

▷ **Hindu** *adj* of the Hindus 印度人的; 印度斯坦人的.

Hin·du·ism /ˈhɪnduːɪzəm; ˋhɪnduˌɪzəm/ *n* [U] Indian religion, philosophy and social system characterized by belief in reincarnation, worship of several gods and the caste system 印度教(印度的宗教、哲学及社会体系, 其特点为相信轮回转世, 崇拜几位天神, 实行种姓制度).

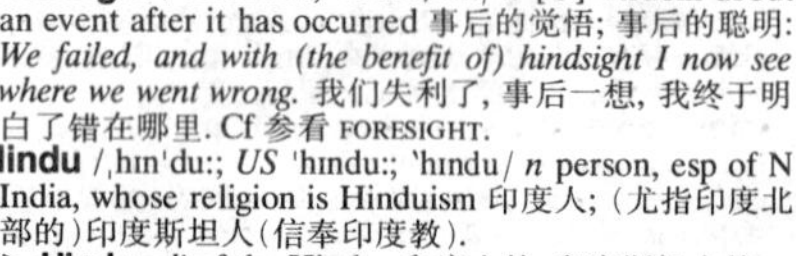

hinge 铰链

hinge /hɪndʒ; hɪndʒ/ *n* piece of metal, etc on which a lid, door, or gate turns or swings as it opens and closes 铰链; 合叶: *take the door off its hinges and rehang it* 把门从铰链上卸下重装 ○ *The gate hinges need oiling — they're squeaking.* 大门的铰链吱吱响 —— 该上油了. ⇨illus 见插图.

▷ **hinge** *v* **1** [I, Tn esp passive 尤用于被动语态] be

attached or attach (sth) by a hinge or hinges 用铰链连接(某物); 给(某物)装上铰链: *The rear door hinges/is hinged at the top so that it opens upwards.* 后面的门是在顶部铰接上的, 以便可以向上开. **2** (phr v) **hinge on sth** depend on sth 依赖某事物: *Everything hinges on the outcome of these talks.* 一切均将取决于这些会谈的结果.

hint /hɪnt; hɪnt/ *n* **1** subtle way of indicating to sb what one is thinking or what one wants; indirect suggestion 暗示; 示意; 间接的提示: *a strong, broad, gentle, delicate, etc hint* 强烈的、明白的、轻微的、微妙的…示意 ○ *She coughed to give him the hint that he should go.* 她咳了一声, 向他暗示他该走了. **2** slight indication; trace 细微的迹象; 线索: *There was more than a hint of sadness in his voice.* 他的声音里有许多哀伤的成分. ○ *The calm sea gave no hint of the storm that was coming.* 平静的海上没有一点迹象显示暴风雨即将来临. **3** small piece of practical information or advice; tip 在实际方面给予的指点; 忠告; 注意事项: *helpful hints for plant lovers* 对植物爱好者的有益忠告. **4** (idm 习语) **drop a hint** ⇨ DROP². **take a 'hint** understand and do what has been indirectly suggested 领会示意并付诸行动: *I thought they'd never go — some people just can't take a hint!* 我以为他们是永远也不会走的 —— 有些人根本就不明白别人的暗示.

▷ **hint** *v* [Ipr, Tn, Dn·pr, Dpr·f] **~ at sth; ~ sth (to sb)** suggest sth slightly or indirectly 稍微地或间接地提及某事物: *The possibility of an early election has been hinted at.* 已经有迹象表明可能提前进行选举. ○ *She has already hinted (to me) that I've won the prize.* 她已经(向我)暗示说我得到了这个奖.

hin·ter·land /ˈhɪntəlænd; ˈhɪntɚ,lænd/ *n* (usu *sing* 通常作单数) **1** area lying inland from the coast or away from a river 内陆地区; 内地; 腹地. **2** part of a country that is served by a port or some other centre (由某一港口或某些其他中心城市供应物资的)内陆贸易区.

hip¹ /hɪp; hɪp/ *n* part on either side of the body below the waist where the bone of a person's leg is joined to the trunk 臀部; 髋部: *He stood with his hands on his hips.* 他两手叉腰站立着. ○ *I'm quite wide round/in the hips.* 我的臀部很大. ○ *break one's hip*, ie break the top of one's thigh-bone 股骨端部折断. ○ [attrib 作定语] *the hip-bone* 髋骨 ○ *one's hip measurement* 臀部的尺寸.

▷ **-hipped** (forming compound *adjs* 用以构成复合形容词) having hips of the specified size, shape, etc 有某种尺寸、形状等之臀部的: *a large-hipped girl.*

□ **'hip-bath** *n* portable tub in which one sits immersed up to the hips 轻便浴盆(坐入后臀部浸于水中).

'hip-flask *n* small bottle for spirits, with flat or curved sides for carrying in the hip-pocket 小酒瓶(呈扁平或弧形, 可放在裤子的后袋里携带).

ˌhip-'pocket *n* trouser pocket just behind the hips 裤子后部的口袋儿.

hip² /hɪp; hɪp/ (also **'rose-hip**) *n* berry-like fruit of the wild rose, red when ripe 野蔷薇的果实(状若浆果, 成熟时呈红色).

hip³ /hɪp; hɪp/ *interj* (idm 习语) **hip, hip, hurrah/hurray** (used as a cheer to express general satisfaction or approval 表示满意或赞同的欢呼声).

hip⁴ /hɪp; hɪp/ *adj* (*dated sl* 旧, 俚) fashionable; trendy; up-to-date 时髦的; 赶时髦的; 新式的.

hip·pie (also **hippy**) /ˈhɪpɪ; ˈhɪpɪ/ *n* (esp in the late 1960s) person who rejects organized society and established social habits and who joins others in adopting an unconventional way of life, style of dress, etc (尤指20世纪60年代晚期的)嬉皮士(与社会现实格格不入的人, 常成群结伙实行与众不同的生活方式、着奇装异服等). Cf 参看 BEATNIK.

hippo /ˈhɪpəʊ; ˈhɪpo/ *n* (*pl* **~s**) (*infml* 口) = HIPPOPOTAMUS.

Hip·po·cratic oath /ˌhɪpəkrætɪk ˈəʊθ; ˌhɪpə,krætɪk ˈoθ/ oath to observe the medical code of ethical and professional behaviour, sworn by doctors when they become qualified 医生在取得行医资格时保证遵守医生道德守则的誓言.

hip·po·drome /ˈhɪpədrəʊm; ˈhɪpə,drom/ *n* **1** (esp in names) dance-hall or music-hall; theatre or cinema (尤用于专名)舞厅或音乐厅, 剧院或电影院: *the Brighton Hippodrome* 布赖顿剧院. **2** (in ancient Greece or Rome) course for horse or chariot races (古希腊或古罗马)赛马场, 战车竞赛场

hippopotamus 河马

hip·po·pot·amus /ˌhɪpəˈpɒtəməs; ˌhɪpəˈpɑtəməs/ *n* (*pl* **-muses** /-məsɪz; -məsɪz/ or **-mi** /-maɪ; -maɪ/) (also **hippo**) large African river animal with short legs and thick dark skin 河马(产于非洲). ⇨illus 见插图.

hippy = HIPPIE.

hire /ˈhaɪə(r); haɪr/ *v* **1** [Tn, Tn·pr] **~ sth/sb (from sb)** obtain the use of sth or the services of sb temporarily and esp for a short period of time, in return for payment 租用(某物); 雇用(某人): *hire a bicycle, hall, wedding-dress* 租自行车、礼堂、结婚礼服 ○ *a hired car* 租用的汽车 ○ *a hired assassin* 受雇的刺客 ○ *hire a dozen men to dig a ditch* 雇十二个人挖沟. **2** [Tn, Tn·pr, Tn·p] **~ sth (out) (to sb)** allow the temporary use of sth, in return for payment 出租某物: *We hire out our vans by the day*, ie at a cost of a certain amount per day. 我们按日出租客货车(按日计租). ⇨Usage at LET² 用法见 LET².

▷ **hire** *n* [U] **1** hiring 租用; 雇用; 出租: *have the hire of a car for a week* 租用汽车一星期 ○ *bicycles for hire, £1 an hour* 自行车出租, 每小时1英镑 ○ *pay for the hire of a hall* 付会堂租金 ○ *This suit is on hire.* 这套衣服是供租用的. ○ [attrib 作定语] *a car hire firm* 汽车出租公司 ○ *a hire car* 供租用的汽车. **2** payment for hiring sth/sb 租金; 工钱: *work for hire* 当雇工. **3** (idm 习语) **ply for hire** ⇨ PLY².

hire·able /ˈhaɪərəbl; ˈhaɪrəbl/ *adj* (of an object) that may be hired (指物件)出租的, 可租用的.

hire·ling /ˈhaɪəlɪŋ; ˈhaɪrlɪŋ/ *n* (*usu derog* 通常作贬义) person whose services may be hired 可被雇用的人.

□ **ˌhired 'hand** (*US*) person hired to work as a labourer on a farm (农场的)雇工.

ˌhire-'purchase *n* [U] (*Brit*) (*abbr* 缩写 **hp**) (*US* **in'stalment plan**) method of purchase by which the buyer pays for an article in instalments, is allowed to use it immediately and becomes the owner of it after a certain number of instalments have been paid 分期付款购买方式: *We're buying a TV on hire-purchase.* 我们以分期付款方式购买一台电视机. ○ [attrib 作定语] *a hire-purchase agreement* 分期付款购物协议.

hir·sute /ˈhɜːsjuːt; *US* -suːt; ˈhɝsut/ *adj* (*fml* 文) (esp of a man) covered with hair; hairy; shaggy (尤指男子)多毛发的, 毛发蓬乱的: (*joc* 谑) *You're looking very hirsute, Richard — are you growing a beard?* 理查德, 瞧你一脸的胡子 —— 是不是在留胡子了?

his /hɪz; hɪz/ ⇨Detailed Guide 6.2 见词条使用详细说明 6.2. *possess det* of or belonging to a male person or animal mentioned earlier 他的; 它的(用于雄性动物): *James has sold his car.* 詹姆斯把汽车卖了. ○ *He claims it was 'his idea.* 他声称这是他的主意. ○ *His speech on unemployment was well received.* 他那关于失业问题的演讲受到了欢迎.

▷ **his** *possess pron* of or belonging to him 他的; 它的(用于雄性动物): *My address is No 22 Laburnum Close so his must be No 26.* 我的地址是拉布耐姆巷22号, 所以他的地址一定是26号. ○ *Learning to ski has always been an ambition of his.* 他一直渴望滑雪. ⇨Usage at HE 用法见 HE.

His·panic /hɪˈspænɪk; hɪsˈpænɪk/ *adj* **1** of Spain and Portugal 西班牙和葡萄牙的. **2** of Spain and other Spanish-speaking countries 西班牙及其他说西班牙语国家的.

hiss /hɪs; hɪs/ *v* **1** [I, Ipr] **~ (at sb/sth)** make a sound like that of a long 's' 发出'嘶'声: *The steam escaped with a loud hissing noise.* 蒸汽发出很大的嘶嘶声冒了出

H

来. ○ *A fire hisses if water is thrown on it.* 把水浇到火上, 火就发出嘶嘶声. ○ *The goose hissed at me angrily.* 那鹅愤怒地向我发出嘶嘶声. **2** (**a**) [Ipr, Tn] **~ (at) sb/sth** make this sound to show disapproval of sb/sth 发嘘声(表示不赞成或不满意某人[某事物]): *hiss (at) a new play* 向一出新戏发出嘘声. (**b**) [Tn] say (sth) with an angry hissing voice 带着愤怒的嘶嘶声说出(某事): *'Stay away from me!' she hissed.* '去你的吧!'她带着愤怒的嘶嘶声嚷道. **3** (phr v) **hiss sb off (sth)** (of an audience) force (a performer or speaker) to leave (the stage, etc) by hissing in disapproval (指观众或听众)用嘘声把(演出者或演讲者)轰下(台等): *The politician was hissed off (the platform).* 人们用嘘声把那政客轰下了台.

▷ **hiss** *n* hissing sound '嘶'声; 嘘声: *The crowd greeted the performers with boos and hisses.* 观众向演出者发出一片嘘声.

his·tam·ine /ˈhɪstəmiːn; ˋhɪstəmin/ *n* [U] (*medical* 医) chemical compound that is present in all body tissues and causes (usu unpleasant) reactions in people with certain allergies 组胺.

his·to·gram /ˈhɪstəɡræm; ˋhɪstə͵ɡræm/ *n* = BAR CHART (BAR[1]).

his·to·logy /hɪˈstɒlədʒɪ; hɪsˋtɑlədʒɪ/ *n* [U] scientific study of animal and plant tissues 组织学.

his·tor·ian /hɪˈstɔːrɪən *or, rarely* 罕读作 ɪˈs-; hɪsˋtorɪən/ *n* person who studies or writes about history 历史学家; 史学工作者.

his·toric /hɪˈstɒrɪk *or, rarely* 罕读作 ɪˈs-; *US* -ˈstɔːr-; hɪsˋtɔrɪk/ *adj* famous or important in history 历史上著名的或重要的: *the historic spot on which the first pilgrims landed in America* 初期的英国移民登上美洲大陆的具有历史意义的地点 ○ *This is a(n) historic occasion*, ie will be regarded as a significant event in history. 这是具有重大历史意义的时刻. ○ *historic times*, ie those of which the history is known and recorded 有历史记载的时期.

□ **his͵toric ˈpresent** (*grammar*) simple present tense used when describing events in the past to make the description more vivid 历史现在时态(在叙述过去的事情时, 为求生动而使用的现在时态).

his·tor·ical /hɪˈstɒrɪkl *or, rarely* 罕读作 ɪˈs-; *US* -ˈstɔːr-; hɪsˋtɔrɪkl/ *adj* [usu attrib 通常作定语] **1** concerning past events 历史(上)的: *historical records, research* 历史记载、研究. **2** based on the study of history 以对历史的研究为基础的; 依据历史科学的: *We have no historical evidence for it.* 我们缺乏可以证明这一点的史学根据. ○ *It's a historical fact.* 这是历史事实. **3** (**a**) that have actually occurred or existed (as contrasted with legend or fiction) 真实的, 有史可稽的(别于传说或虚构的故事): *historical* (ie real, not imaginary) *events, people* 历史上的(即真实的, 非虚构的)事件、人物. (**b**) (of a book, film, etc) dealing with real events in history (指书、影片等)历史题材的: *a historical novel* 历史小说. ▷ **his·tor·ic·ally** /-klɪ; -klɪ/ *adv*: *The book is historically inaccurate.* 该书内容与史实不符.

his·tory /ˈhɪstrɪ; ˋhɪstrɪ/ *n* **1** (**a**) [U] study of past events, esp the political, social and economic development of a country, a continent or the world 历史学: *a student of Russian history* 俄国史学者 ○ *ancient/medieval/modern history* 古代[中古/近代]史. (**b**) this as a subject at school or university 历史(课程): *a degree in history and geography* 历史和地理学位 ○ [attrib 作定语] *my history teacher* 我们的历史老师. **2** [U] past events, esp when considered as a whole 历史(尤指将过去的事件作为整体看待时): *Throughout history men have waged war.* 自有历史以来就有战争. ○ *a people with no sense of history* 没有历史感的民族. **3** [C] systematic description of past events 历史(对过去事件的系统叙述): *writing a new history of Europe* 撰写一部新的欧洲史 ○ [attrib 作定语] *Shakespeare's history plays* 莎士比亚的历史剧. **4** [C usu sing 通常作单数] series of past events or experiences connected with an object, a person or a place (某物的)来历; (某人的)经历; (某地的)沿革: *This house has a strange history.* 这所房子有一段奇怪的来历. ○ *sb's medical history*, ie record of his past illnesses 某人的病历(其过去患病的纪录) ○ *There is a history of heart disease in my family.* 我家有患心脏病的家族病史. ○ *He has a history of violent crime.* 他有暴力犯罪的记录. **5** [U] (*infml* 口) fact, event, etc that is no longer relevant or important 不复相关或不再重要的事实、事件等: *They had an affair once, but that's ancient history now.* 他们曾经有过一段暧昧关系, 但现在那已成为遥远的过去了. **6** (idm 习语) **make/go down in ˈhistory** be or do sth so important or unusual that it will be recorded in history 成为或开创历史的新篇章: *a discovery that made medical history* 载入医学史册的重大发现.

his·tri·onic /͵hɪstrɪˈɒnɪk; ͵hɪstrɪˋɑnɪk/ *adj* **1** (*usu derog* 通常作贬义) very theatrical in manner; excessively dramatic; affected 做作的; 过分戏剧化的; 不自然的: *histrionic behaviour* 装腔作势. **2** (*fml* 文) of acting or the theatre 表演的; 戏剧的: *her histrionic talents* 她的表演天才.

▷ **his·tri·on·ic·ally** /-klɪ; -klɪ/ *adv* (*usu derog* 通常作贬义): *wave one's arms around histrionically* 装模作样地朝各方挥动手臂.

his·tri·on·ics *n* [pl] (*usu derog* 通常作贬义) theatrical manners or behaviour, esp when exaggerated in order to impress others 装腔作势的态度或举止(尤指为表现自己): *indulge in histrionics* 一味装腔作势.

hit[1] /hɪt; hɪt/ *v* (**-tt-**, *pt, pp* **hit**) **1** (**a**) [I, Tn, Tn·pr, Dn·n] **~ sb/sth (with sth)** strike sb/sth with a blow, missile, etc 打、打击、击中或命中某人[某物]: *hit the nail with the hammer* 用锤子钉钉子 ○ *She hit him on the head with a book.* 她用书打他的头. ○ *I was hit by a falling stone.* 我被落下的石块击中了. ○ *The car was hit by a grenade.* 手榴弹击中了汽车. ○ *He's been hit* (ie wounded) *in the leg by a sniper's bullet.* 狙击手的子弹打伤了他的腿部. ○ *All her shots hit the target.* 她射击全部命中目标. ○ (*fig* 比喻) *The family likeness really hits you*, ie is very noticeable. 这家人彼此相像之处, 一眼就能看出来. ○ *He hit himself a nasty blow on the head.* 他的脑袋撞得这一下很重. (**b**) [Tn] come against (sth/sb) with force 撞、撞击或碰撞(某物[某人]): *The lorry hit the lamp-post with a crash.* 卡车嘭的一声撞到路灯柱上了. (**c**) [Tn, Tn·pr] **~ sth (on/against sth)** knock (part of the body) against sth 使(身体部位)磕碰某物: *He hit his forehead (against the wall) as he fell.* 他摔倒时, 额头磕着了(墙). ⇨Usage 见所附用法. **2** (**a**) [Tn, Tn·pr] drive (a ball, etc) forward by striking it with a bat or club (用球拍或球棒)击(球等): *hit a ball over the fence* 把球击过围栏. (**b**) [Tn] (in cricket) score (runs) in this way (板球)击球得分: *He's already hit two sixes*, ie scored two boundaries worth six runs each. 他已经击中球获两个六分(两次击球到边界线, 每次得六分). **3** [Tn] have a bad or sudden effect on (a person, thing or place); cause to suffer; affect 对(某人、某事物或某地)产生不良的或意外的影响; 使痛苦; 殃及: *How will the new law hit the unemployed?* 新颁布的法令将使失业者遭受什么样的打击? ○ *The rent increase will hit the pockets of the poor.* 租金的提高将加重穷人的负担. ○ *Rural areas have been worst hit by the strike.* 受罢工影响最严重的是乡村地区. ○ *News of the disaster hit the Stock Exchange around noon.* 大约中午时分, 发生灾祸的消息引起了股票市场的动荡. **4** [Tn] (**a**) find (sth sought), esp by chance 发现(所寻之物, 尤指无意之中): *Follow the footpath and you'll eventually hit the road.* 沿这条小径走终究会见到大路的. (**b**) (*infml* 口) arrive in or at (a place) 到达(某地); 在(某地): *When does the new show hit town?* 新戏什么时候可在城里演出? (**c**) achieve (sth); reach 达到(某事物); 至: *I can't hit the high notes.* 我唱不了高音. ○ *The yen hit a record high in trading today.* 在今日的交易中, 日元已升值到历史的最高水平. **5** [Tn] (*infml* 口) encounter (sth); experience 遇到(某事物); 经历: *If you go now, you're likely to hit the rush hour.* 你要是现在走, 可能正赶上交通拥挤的时刻. ○ *hit a snag, problem, etc* 遇到障碍、问题等 ○ *Everything was going well but then we hit trouble.* 起初一切都进行得很顺利, 可是后来我们遇到了麻烦. **6** [Tn] (*infml* 口) attack (sb/sth); raid 攻击(某人[某事物]); 袭击: *hit the enemy when they least expect it* 乘敌不备时予以攻击. **7** (idm 习语) **hit the ˈbottle** (*infml* 口) drink too much alcohol regularly 经常酗酒: *After she died he began to hit the bottle.* 她死之后, 他开始酗酒. **hit the ˈceiling/ˈroof** (*infml* 口) become suddenly very angry 勃然大怒. Cf 参看 GO THROUGH THE ROOF (ROOF). **hit the ˈdeck** (*US infml* 口) (**a**) fall to the ground 落到地上; 摔倒在地. (**b**) get out of bed 起床. (**c**) get ready

H

for action 准备行动. **hit/knock sb for six** deal a severe blow to sb; affect deeply 给予某人以沉重打击; 使深受影响: *He was knocked completely for six by his sudden dismissal.* 他突然遭解雇因而受到沉重的打击. **hit sb/sth ˈhard** affect sb/sth badly 对某人[某事物]产生不利的影响: *Television has hit the cinema industry very hard.* 电视的出现沉重地打击了电影业. ○ *Old people are hardest hit by the rising cost of living.* 生活费用上升, 老年人最受影响. **hit the ˈhay/ˈsack** (*infml* 口) go to bed 上床睡觉; 就寝. **hit/make/reach the headlines** ⇨ HEADLINES (HEAD[1]). **hit/strike home** ⇨ HOME[3]. **hit sb in the ˈeye** be very obvious to sb 对某人来说是显而易见的. **hit it** = HIT THE NAIL ON THE HEAD. **hit it ˈoff (with sb)** (*infml* 口) have a good and harmonious relationship (with sb); get on well (与某人)关系良好; 和睦相处. **hit the ˈjackpot** make a lot of money unexpectedly 意外地得到一大笔钱. **hit/kick a man when he's down** ⇨ MAN. **hit/miss the mark** ⇨ MARK[1]. **hit the nail on the ˈhead** express the truth precisely; guess correctly 一针见血; 猜中. **hit/touch a nerve** ⇨ NERVE. **hit/strike the right/wrong note** ⇨ NOTE[1]. **hit the ˈroad**; *esp US* **hit the ˈtrail** (*infml* 口) start on a journey 上路; 出发. **8** (phr v) **hit at sb/sth** aim a blow at sb/sth 对准某人[某物]打去. **hit back (at sb/sth)** reply forcefully to (esp verbal) attacks; retaliate 反击(尤指言语方面); 报复: *In a TV interview she hit back at her critics.* 她在接受电视采访时, 反驳了那些批评者的观点. **hit sb/sth off** (*infml* 口) describe sb/sth briefly and accurately (in words) (用言语或文字)简洁而精确地描述某人[某事物]. **hit on/upon sth** think up (a plan, solution, etc) unexpectedly and by inspiration; find sth by luck 偶然地、灵机一动地想出(方案、解决办法等); 无意中发现某事物: *She hit upon a good title for her new novel.* 她突然灵机一动, 为自己的新小说想出了一个很好的书名. **hit out (at sb/sth)** attack sb/sth vigorously or violently with words or blows 猛烈抨击或打击某人[某事物]: *In a rousing speech the President hit out against the trade union.* 主席在一次言辞激烈的讲话中对工会进行了严厉的批评. **not know what hit one** ⇨ KNOW.

□ ˌ**hit-and-ˈrun** *adj* [attrib 作定语] (**a**) (of a motorist) causing an accident and driving away immediately so as not to be identified (指机动车驾驶人)肇事后逃走的. (**b**) (of a road accident) caused by a driver who does not stop to help, call an ambulance, etc (指交通事故)驾驶人肇事后不顾而去的.

ˌ**hit-or-ˈmiss** (also ˌ**hit-and-ˈmiss**) *adj* done haphazardly or carelessly; liable to error; random 偶然做出的; 漫不经心的; 容易出错的; 随意的: *Long-term planning is always rather a hit-or-miss affair.* 凡是定长远的计划都难免出偏差.

NOTE ON USAGE 用法: **Hit** is used in a more general way than **strike** or **beat.** ☆ **hit** 比 **strike** 或 **beat** 用得广. A person, an animal or a thing can be **hit** by a hand or by an object held or thrown. 用手、用手执物或投掷物击打人、动物或物品均可为 **hit.** ☆ When used with this meaning, **strike** is more formal than **hit.** 在用于以上意义时, **strike** 比 **hit** 较为文雅. One can **hit** or **strike** a person with the intention of hurting them 这两个词均可表示有意地伤害对方: *She hit/struck him hard on the face.* 她用力地打他耳光. One can also **hit** or **strike** a person or thing accidentally 这两个词还可以表示施之于人或物的意外的动作: *The car hit/struck a lamp-post.* 汽车撞到路灯柱上了. In addition we can **hit** or **strike** things with a purpose 此外, 可用 **hit** 或 **strike** 表示含有某目的而击打物品: *hit/strike a nail with a hammer* 用锤子钉钉子. **Beat** means 'hit repeatedly'. ☆ **beat** 意为'接连地打'. We cannot **beat** people or things accidentally 不可用 **beat** 表示意外地施于人或物的动作: *He was beaten to death by thugs.* 他被暴徒殴打致死. ○ *beat eggs, a carpet, a drum* 打蛋、拍打地毯、击鼓.

hit[2] /hɪt; hɪt/ *n* **1** (**a**) act of hitting; blow or stroke 打; 打击: *That was a clever hit!* 那一击妙极了! ○ *a direct hit on an enemy ship* 对准敌舰的一击. (**b**) point scored by a shot, etc that reaches its target 命中目标; 得分: *a final score of two hits and six misses* 两次击中六次未中的最后分数. **2** ~ **at sb** (*fig* 比喻) sarcastic comment made to or about sb 对某人的嘲讽; 关于某人的嘲讽话: *That last remark was a hit at me.* 最后的话是对我的讽刺. **3** person or thing that is very popular; success 红极一时的人物或事物; 成功: *He's a hit with everyone.* 大家都喜欢他. ○ *Her new film is quite a hit.* 她的新影片十分成功. ○ *They sang their latest hit.* 他们唱了最新流行歌曲. ○ [attrib 作定语] *hit songs, records* 流行歌曲、歌曲唱片. **4** (idm 习语) **make a hit (with sb)** (*infml* 口) make a very favourable impression (on sb) 给予(某人)极其良好的印象: *You've made quite a hit with Bill.* 比尔觉得你人很好.

□ ˈ**hit list** (*sl* 俚) list of people who are to be killed or against whom some action is being planned 预谋杀害或对付的人的名单.

ˈ**hit man** (*sl* 俚 esp US) hired assassin; person who is paid to kill another person 职业杀手; 被人收买充当刺客的人.

ˈ**hit parade** list of best-selling popular records; record charts 最畅销的流行歌曲唱片目录; 唱片曲目集锦.

hitch /hɪtʃ; hɪtʃ/ *v* **1** [I, Ipr, Tn, Tn·pr] get (free rides) in other people's cars as a way of travelling (免费)搭乘他人之车; 搭便车: *hitch round Europe* 沿途搭便车周游欧洲 ○ *hitch a ride to London on a lorry* 免费搭乘卡车去伦敦 ○ *Can I hitch a lift with you as far as the station?* 我可以搭乘你的便车到车站吗? Cf 参看 HITCH-HIKE. **2** [Tn·pr, Tn·p] fasten (sth) to sth with a loop, hook, etc (用环、钩等)套住, 钩住(某物): *hitch a horse to a fence* 把马栓在栅栏上 ○ *hitch a rope round a branch* 把绳子绕系在树枝上 ○ *a car with a trailer hitched on (to it) at the back* 背后挂着一辆拖车的汽车. **3** (idm 习语) **get ˈhitched** (*dated sl* 旧, 俚) get married 结婚. **4** (phr v) **hitch sth up** pull (esp one's clothes) up with a quick movement 急速拉起(尤指自己的衣服): *He hitched up his trousers before sitting down.* 他把裤子往上拉起, 然后坐下. ○ *She hitched up her skirt so as not to get it wet.* 她把裙子往上提起, 免得弄湿了.

▷ **hitch** *n* **1** temporary difficulty or problem; snag 暂时的困难或问题; 意外障碍: *The ceremony went off without a hitch.* 典礼进行得很顺利. ○ *The launch was delayed by a technical hitch.* 由于技术上出现临时故障而发射延期. **2** sudden pull or push 急拉; 急推. **3** any of various types of noose or knot 绳套; 索结: *a clove hitch* 卷结.

□ ˈ**hitch-hike** *v* [I, Ipr] travel by obtaining free rides in other people's cars 免费搭乘他人之车: *hitch-hike through France to Spain* 沿途搭便车经法国前往西班牙. ˈ**hitch-hiker** *n*.

hither /ˈhɪðə(r); ˈhɪðɚ/ *adv* **1** (*arch* 古) to or towards this place 到此处; 向此处. **2** (idm 习语) ˌ**hither and ˈthither** in various directions 到处; 各处; 四面八方: *blown hither and thither by the wind* 被风刮得到处都是的.

hith·erto /ˌhɪðəˈtu:; ˌhɪðɚˈtu/ *adv* (*fml* 文) until now 迄今; 至今: *a woman referred to hitherto as Mrs X* 迄今称之为X夫人的女子 ○ *a hitherto unknown species of moth* 至今尚不知属何种类的蛾.

HIV /ˌeɪtʃ aɪ ˈvi:; ˌetʃˌaɪˈvi/ *abbr* 缩写 = human immunodeficiency virus (the virus that causes AIDS) 人体免疫缺损病毒(艾滋病病毒): *HIV positive* 人体免疫缺损病毒检验呈阳性反应.

hive /haɪv; haɪv/ *n* **1** (**a**) (also ˈ**bee·hive**) box or other container for bees to live in 蜂箱; 蜂房. ⇨illus at BEE 见 BEE 插图. (**b**) bees living in a hive 蜂房内的蜂群. **2** place full of busy people 人群纷纷攘攘的地方; 繁忙的场所: *a hive of activity/industry* 喧闹的[繁忙的]活动场所.

▷ **hive** *v* **1** [Tn] place (bees) in a hive 使(蜂群)进入蜂箱: *hive a swarm* 把一群蜜蜂引入蜂箱. **2** [I] (of bees) enter or live in a hive (指蜂群)进入蜂箱, 集居于蜂箱内. **3** (phr v) **hive off** become separate from a large group; form an independent body 从一大的组织中分离出来; 建立独立的单位. **hive sth off (to/into sth)** transfer (work) to another section or firm; make (part of an organization) independent 将(工作)转移到其他部门或机构办理; 使(机构的某部分)独立: *hive off parts of a nationalized industry to private ownership* 将部分国营工业私有化.

hives /haɪvz; haɪvz/ *n* [pl] skin disease with itchy red patches; nettle-rash 荨麻疹.

hiya /ˈhaɪjə; ˋhaɪjə/ *interj* (*US infml* 口) (used as a greeting 用作招呼语).

h'm = HEM[2].

HM *abbr* 缩写 = Her/His Majesty 陛下(用于他称): *HM the Queen* 女王陛下.

HMG *abbr* 缩写 = Her/His Majesty's Government 女王[国王]陛下政府: (*infml* 口) *HMG should be kept informed.* 须经常向女王陛下政府报告情况.

HMI /ˌeɪtʃ em ˈaɪ; ˌetʃ ɛm ˋaɪ/ *abbr* 缩写 = (*Brit*) Her/His Majesty's Inspector (of schools) 皇家督学: *a visit from (the) HMI* 督学所进行的视察.

HMS /ˌeɪtʃ em ˈes; ˌetʃ ɛm ˋɛs/ *abbr* 缩写 = (*Brit*) (for warships only) Her/His Majesty's Ship (仅用于战舰)皇家海军舰艇: *HMS Apollo* 皇家海军阿波罗号. Cf 参看 USS.

HMSO /ˌeɪtʃ em es ˈəʊ; ˌetʃ ɛm ɛs ˋo/ *abbr* 缩写 = (*Brit*) Her/His Majesty's Stationery Office 皇家文书局.

HNC /ˌeɪtʃ en ˈsiː; ˌetʃ ɛn ˋsi/ *abbr* 缩写 = (*Brit*) Higher National Certificate (a qualification recognized by many UK technical and professional bodies) 国家高级合格证书: *have the HNC in electrical engineering* 执有电机工程的国家高级合格证书 ○ *go on/do an HNC course* 为获国家高级合格证书学习必修课程.

HND /ˌeɪtʃ en ˈdiː; ˌetʃ ɛn ˋdi/ *abbr* 缩写 = (*Brit*) Higher National Diploma (a qualification in technical subjects equal to a bachelor's degree without honours) 国家高等技术教育毕业文凭: *have the HND in fashion design* 执有时装设计的国家高等技术教育毕业文凭 ○ *go on/do an HND course* 为获得国家高等技术教育证书学习必修课程.

ho /həʊ; ho/ *interj* **1** (used to express surprise, scorn, admiration, amusement, etc 用以表示惊奇、嘲笑、赞美、欢愉等) **2** (used to draw attention to sth 用以引起对某事物的注意): *Land ho!* 啊, 陆地!

hoar /hɔː(r); hɔr/ *adj* (*dated* 旧) = HOARY 1: *a hoar-headed old man* 白发苍苍的老人.

hoard /hɔːd; hɔrd/ *n* carefully collected and guarded store of money, food or other treasured objects (钱财、食物或其他珍贵物品的)储藏, 积存: *a miser's hoard* 守财奴储藏的财宝 ○ *a squirrel's hoard of nuts* 松鼠储藏的坚果.

▷ **hoard** *v* [I, Tn, Tn·p] **~ sth (up)** collect (sth in quantity) and store it away 积聚并储藏(某物): *People found hoarding (food) during the famine were punished.* 在饥荒时期屯积(食物)的人受到了惩罚. ○ *hoard up treasure* 储藏财宝. **hoarder** *n* person who hoards 贮藏者.

hoard·ing /ˈhɔːdɪŋ; ˋhɔrdɪŋ/ *n* **1** (*Brit*) (*US* **ˈbillboard**) large board used for displaying advertisements 大广告牌. **2** temporary fence of light boards around a building site, etc 建筑工地等周围用轻木板临时搭起的围栏.

hoar-frost /ˈhɔː frɒst; *US* -frɔːst; ˋhɔrˌfrɔst/ *n* [U] white frost; frozen dew on grass, leaves, roofs, etc 白霜; 草、叶子、房顶等上面的霜.

hoarse /hɔːs; hɔrs/ *adj* (**a**) (of the voice) sounding rough and harsh (指嗓音)粗哑的, 嘶哑的. (**b**) (of a person) having a hoarse voice (指人)声音沙哑的: *He shouted himself hoarse.* 他把嗓子都喊哑了. ▷ **hoarsely** *adv*. **hoarse·ness** *n* [U].

hoary /ˈhɔːrɪ; ˋhɔrɪ/ *adj* (**-ier, -iest**) **1** (also **hoar**) (esp of hair) grey or white with age (尤指毛发)因年老而变灰或变白的. **2** very old 古老的; 陈旧的: *a hoary old joke* 老掉牙的笑话. ▷ **hoari·ness** *n* [U].

hoax /həʊks; hoks/ *n* mischievous trick played on sb for a joke 恶作剧; 戏弄: *The fire-brigade answered the emergency call but there was no fire — it was all a hoax.* 消防队接到报警电话后采取了行动, 但是并没有火灾——这完全是一场恶作剧. ○ [attrib 作定语] *a hoax phone call* 恶作剧的电话.

▷ **hoax** *v* [Tn, Tn·pr] **~ sb (into doing sth)** deceive sb as a joke 开玩笑骗某人; 戏弄某人: *I was hoaxed into believing their story.* 我上了当, 还以为他们的玩笑是真的呢. **hoaxer** *n*.

hob /hɒb; hɑb/ *n* (**a**) flat heating surface for a pan, kettle, etc on the top of a cooker 炉盘(炉具上部供放置锅、壶等以加热的平面). (**b**) (esp formerly) flat metal shelf at the side of a fireplace, where a pan, kettle, etc can be heated (尤指旧时)(壁炉侧面供锅、壶等加温用的)平面金属架.

hobble /ˈhɒbl; ˋhɑbl̩/ *v* **1** [I, Ipr, Ip] walk with difficulty because the feet or legs hurt or are disabled; walk lamely; limp 跛行; 蹒跚; 一瘸一拐地走: *The old man hobbled along (the road) with the aid of his stick.* 那老汉拄着拐杖一瘸一拐地走着. ➪Usage at SHUFFLE 用法见 SHUFFLE. **2** [Tn] tie together two legs of (a horse, etc) to prevent it from going far away 捆缚(马等)之两腿(以防走失).

▷ **hobble** *n* [sing] limping way of walking 跛行; 蹒跚.

hobby /ˈhɒbɪ; ˋhɑbɪ/ *n* favourite activity that a person does for pleasure and not as his regular business (业余)爱好; 嗜好: *My hobby is stamp-collecting/collecting stamps.* 我爱好集邮.

hobby-horse /ˈhɒbɪ hɔːs; ˋhɑbɪˌhɔrs/ *n* **1** long stick with a horse's head, used as a toy 马头杆子(玩具); 竹马. **2** subject that a person likes to discuss; favourite topic of conversation (讨论、交谈中)喜爱的话题: *You've got me onto* (ie talking about) *one of my favourite hobby-horses.* 你把我引到我喜爱的一个话题上来了.

hob·gob·lin /hɒbˈgɒblɪn; ˋhɑbˌgɑblɪn/ *n* (in folklore) mischievous little creature; ugly and evil spirit; goblin (民间传说中的)淘气的小妖精, 鬼怪, 妖怪.

hob·nail /ˈhɒbneɪl; ˋhɑbˌnel/ *n* short nail with a heavy head used for the soles of heavy shoes (钉在笨重靴鞋底部的)平头钉: [attrib 作定语] *hobnail boots* 带有平头钉的靴子.

▷ **hob·nailed** *adj* (of boots, etc) fitted with hobnails (指靴等)装有平头钉的.

hob-nob /ˈhɒb nɒb; ˋhɑbˌnɑb/ *v* (**-bb-**) [I, Ipr, Ip] **~ (with sb)**; **~ (together)** (*sometimes derog* 有时作贬义) spend time (with sb) in a friendly way; associate (with sb) (与某人)过从甚密, 交往密切: *I've seen you two hob-nobbing (together) a lot recently.* 近来我总看见你们俩(在一起)拉拉扯扯. ○ *hob-nob with the rich and famous* 与有钱财有名望的人交往密切.

hobo /ˈhəʊbəʊ; ˋhobo/ *n* (*pl* **~s** or **~es** /-bəʊz; -boz/) (*esp US*) (**a**) unemployed worker who wanders from place to place 流动的失业工人; 无业游民. (**b**) tramp; vagrant 流浪者; 漂泊者.

Hob·son's choice /ˌhɒbsnz ˈtʃɔɪs; ˋhɑbsn̩zˋtʃɔɪs/ situation in which a person must accept what is offered because there is no alternative other than taking nothing at all 无可选择的选择; 没有选择余地的局面.

hock[1] /hɒk; hɑk/ *n* middle joint of an animal's hind leg 跗关节. ➪illus at HORSE 见 HORSE 插图.

hock[2] /hɒk; hɑk/ *n* [U, C] type of German white wine 霍克酒(德国产的一种白葡萄酒): *a fine dry hock* 美味的干霍克酒.

hock[3] /hɒk; hɑk/ *v* [Tn] (*sl* 俚) give (an object of some value) as security for the repayment of a loan; pawn 典当; 抵押.

▷ **hock** *n* (*sl* 俚) **1** [U] state of being pawned 抵押: *get sth out of hock* 把抵押的某物赎回. **2** (idm 习语) **in hock** (**a**) pawned 在抵押中: *Her jewellery is all in hock.* 她当掉了所有的首饰. (**b**) in prison 在监狱里; 在关押中. (**c**) in debt 欠着债: *I'm in hock to the tune of* (ie I owe a total of) *£5 000.* 我负债总数达 5 000 英镑.

hockey (*US* field hockey)
曲棍球运动

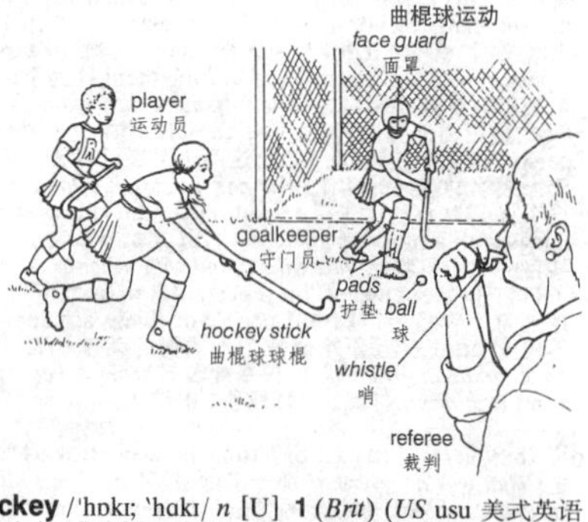

hockey /ˈhɒkɪ; ˋhɑkɪ/ *n* [U] **1** (*Brit*) (*US* usu 美式英语通常作 **ˈfield hockey**) game played on a field by two teams of eleven players each, with curved sticks and a small hard ball 曲棍球. ➪illus 见插图. **2** (*US*) = ICE

HOCKEY (ICE).
□ 'hockey stick 1 long stick curved at the bottom, used to hit the ball in hockey 曲棍球球棍. 2 (idm 习语) **jolly hockey sticks** ⇨ JOLLY.

hocus-pocus /ˌhəʊkəs ˈpəʊkəs; ˈhokəsˈpokəs/ *n* [U] talk or behaviour designed to draw one's attention away from what is actually happening; trickery; deception 旨在转移他人注意力的言谈或举止; 花招; 骗术.

hod /hɒd; hɑd/ *n* **1** light open box attached to a pole, used by builders for carrying bricks, etc on the shoulder (建筑工人挑砖等用的连在扁担上的)轻便无盖挂斗. **2** container for coal used in the home; coal-scuttle (家用)煤斗; 煤桶.

hodge·podge = HOTCHPOTCH.

hoe /həʊ; ho/ *n* long-handled tool with a blade, used for loosening the soil and removing weeds 耘锄.
▷ **hoe** *v* (*pres p* **hoeing**, *pt, pp* **hoed**) (**a**) [Tn] loosen (ground) with a hoe 用耘锄整(地): *hoe the soil, the flower beds, etc* 松土、平整花坛. (**b**) [Tn, Tn·p] **~ sth (up)** remove (weeds) with a hoe 用锄除(草). (**c**) [Tn] remove weeds from around (crops, plants, etc) with a hoe 用锄为(庄稼、花草等)除去周围的杂草: *hoeing the lettuces* 锄去生菜周围的杂草.

hog /hɒg; *US* hɔ:g; hɔg/ *n* **1** pig reared for meat, esp a castrated male pig 猪(供食用的, 尤指阉过的公猪). Cf 参看 BOAR, SOW[1]. **2** (*infml* 口) selfish or greedy person 自私的或贪婪的人. **3** (idm 习语) **go the whole hog** ⇨ WHOLE.
▷ **hog (-gg-)** [Tn] (*infml* 口) take more than one's fair share of (sth); use (sth) selfishly, excluding others 多占(某事物); 自私地占用(某物): *hog (the middle of) the road*, ie drive near the middle of the road so that others cannot overtake 占路(中)(即紧挨道路中线驾驶使其他车辆无法超越) ○ *hog the bathroom*, ie spend a long time in it preventing others from using it 占用浴室(使别人无法使用) ○ *hog the fire*, ie sit in front of it so that others do not feel the heat 霸占烤火位置(坐的位置挡住他人烤火) ○ *Stop hogging the biscuits and pass them round!* 别把持着饼干不放, 传给大家!
hog·gish *adj* greedy and selfish 自私而贪婪的.
□ 'hog-wash *n* [U] nonsense; bilge 胡说; 废话.

hog·manay /ˈhɒgməneɪ; ˌhagməˈne/ *n* (usu 通常作 **Hogmanay**) (*Scot* 苏格兰) last day of the year and the celebrations that occur on it, esp in Scotland 除夕(尤指苏格兰的).

hogs·head /ˈhɒgzhed; *US* ˈhɔ:g-; ˈhɔgzˌhɛd/ *n* **1** large barrel for beer 大啤酒桶. **2** liquid or dry measure, about 50 gallons in Britain, 62 gallons in the US 液量或干量单位(在英国约合50加仑, 在美国约合62加仑).

hoick /hɔɪk; hɔɪk/ *v* [Tn·pr, Tn·p] (*infml* 口) lift or bring (sth) in the specified direction, esp with a jerk 提起或拉动(某物)(尤指猛然地): *She hoicked her bike onto the car roof.* 她猛地一下把自行车举到汽车顶上. ○ *He tried to hoick the meat out of the tin with a fork.* 他试着用叉子把罐头里的肉使劲叉出来.

hoi pol·loi /ˌhɔɪ pəˈlɔɪ; ˈhɔɪpəˈlɔɪ/ [pl] **the hoi polloi** (*derog* 贬) the common people; the masses 民众; 老百姓; 乌合之众.

hoist /hɔɪst; hɔɪst/ *v* **1** [Tn, Tn·pr, Tn·p] raise (sth) by means of ropes, special apparatus, etc (用绳索、专门器械等)提升(某物): *hoist a flag, the sails* 升旗、帆 ○ *hoisting crates aboard ship* 将板条箱吊上船 ○ *hoist in the boats*, ie raise them from the water up to the deck 将小船从水面吊至甲板上 ○ *The fireman hoisted the boy (up) onto his shoulders.* 消防队员把那男孩举到自己的双肩上. **2** (idm 习语) **(be) hoist with one's own petard** /peˈtɑ:d; pɪˈtard/ (be) caught or injured by what one intended as a trick for others 自食其果; 害人反害己.
▷ **hoist** *n* **1** (usu *sing* 通常作单数) pull or push up; lift 吊起; 举起; 提升: *Give me a hoist (up)*, eg when climbing a wall. 往上推我一下(如爬墙时). **2** apparatus for hoisting things 起重器械.

hoity-toity /ˌhɔɪtɪ ˈtɔɪtɪ; ˈhɔɪtɪˈtɔɪtɪ/ *adj* (*infml derog* 口, 贬) behaving in an arrogant way as if one thinks one is superior to others; haughty 傲慢的; 自以为高人一等的: *a hoity-toity person, manner* 傲慢的人、态度.

hokum /ˈhəʊkəm; ˈhokəm/ *n* [U] (*infml* 口 *esp US*) **1** poor or crude theatrical writing 乏味或粗劣的戏剧作品: *a piece of second-rate hokum* 一个二流的乏味剧本. **2** nonsense 胡说: *talking complete hokum* 废话连篇.

hold[1] /həʊld; hold/ *v* (*pt, pp* **held** /held; hɛld/) **1** [Tn, Tn·pr] take and keep or support (sb/sth) in one's arms, hands, teeth, etc 拿住, 抓住, 抱住, 咬住, 托住, 支撑住(某人[某物]): *The girl was holding her father's hand.* 那女孩抓住她父亲的手. ○ *The lovers held each other tight.* 这一对情侣紧紧地搂抱着. ○ *They were holding hands*, ie holding each other's hands. 他们手握着手. ○ *She was holding an umbrella.* 她拿着一把伞. ○ *She held me by the sleeve.* 她抓住我的袖子. ○ *She was holding the baby in her arms.* 她抱着婴儿. ○ *He held the rope in his teeth as he climbed the tree.* 他爬树时用牙齿咬着绳子. **2** [Tn] (**a**) bear the weight of (sb/sth); support 承受(某人[某物])的重量; 支承: *Is that branch strong enough to hold you/your weight?* 那树枝经得住你[你的重量]吗? (**b**) restrain or control (sb/sth) 约束或控制(某人[某事物]): *Try to hold the thief until the police arrive.* 设法看管好这个小偷, 等警察到来. ○ *The dam gave way; it was not strong enough to hold the flood waters.* 水坝坍塌了; 它不够坚固, 挡不住洪水. **3** [Tn·pr, Tn·p, Cn·a] keep (oneself/sb/sth) in the specified position or condition 使(自己[某人/某物])保持在某一位置或某种状况: *The wood is held in position by a clamp.* 木头用钳夹固定住了. ○ *Hold your head up.* 把头抬起来. ○ *Hold your arms out.* 把手臂伸出来. ○ *It took three nurses to hold him down while they gave him the injection.* 给他打针时, 用了三个护士才把他按住. ○ *She held out her hand to take the rope.* 她伸手去抓那根绳子. ○ *Hold yourself still for a moment while I take your photograph.* 你不要动, 我给你拍照. **4** (**a**) [I] remain secure or in position 保持稳定或固定: *How long will the anchor hold?* 这锚能稳住多久? ○ *I don't think the shelf will hold if we put anything else on it.* 我看再放上其他东西那架子就不稳了. (**b**) remain unchanged; last 持续; 维持: *How long will this fine weather hold?* 这样的好天气能维持多久? ○ *If their luck holds, they could still win the championship.* 他们假若能继续交好运, 还能获得冠军. (**c**) continue to be true or valid 继续适用; 继续有效: *The offer I made to you last week still holds.* 上星期我向你提供的建议仍然有效. ○ *The argument still holds.* 该论据仍然站得住脚. **5** [Tn] (of the wheels of a car, etc) maintain a grip of (a corner, road, etc) (指汽车等的轮子)贴紧, 咬住(拐角、道路等): *My new car holds the road well.* 我的新汽车贴路性能很好. **6** [Tn] have enough space for (sth/sb); contain 可容纳(某物[某人]); 包含: *This barrel holds 25 litres.* 这个桶能装25升. ○ *Will this suitcase hold all my clothes?* 这只衣箱装得下我所有的衣物吗? ○ *I don't think the car will hold you all.* 我看这辆汽车坐不下你们这些人. ○ *My brain can't hold so much information at one time.* 我脑子一下子记不住这么多信息. ○ (*fig* 比喻) *Who knows what the future holds for us?* 谁能知道我们未来会如何? **7** [Tn] defend (sth) against military attack; keep possession of 守卫(某物); 据守: *hold a fort, garrison, etc* 据守堡垒、要塞等 ○ *The town was held against frequent enemy attacks.* 该城抵御了敌人一次又一次的进攻. ○ *The Tory candidate held the seat, but with a greatly reduced majority.* 保守党的候选人保住了席位, 然而在得票上所占的优势却大为减少. **8** [Tn, Cn·n] keep (sb) and not allow him to leave 拘留(某人): *Police are holding two men in connection with last Thursday's bank robbery.* 警方拘留了两名与上星期四的银行劫案有关的人. ○ *The terrorists are holding three men hostage.* 恐怖分子把三个人扣为人质. ○ *He was held prisoner throughout the war.* 他在战争期间一直被囚禁着. **9** [Tn] have ownership of (sth); possess 握有(某事物); 占有: *An American conglomerate holds a major share in the company.* 一家美国的大联合企业持有该公司的大部分股分. **10** [Tn] have the position of (sth); occupy 担任(某职位); 占据: *She has now held the post of Prime Minister longer than anyone else this century.* 她现在当首相任期之长在本世纪是前所未有的. ○ *How long has he held office?* 他已任职多长时间了? **11** [Tn] have (sth) as sth one has gained 获得, 博得, 赢得, 持有(某事物): *She holds the world record for the long jump.* 她保持着跳远世界纪录. **12** [Tn] keep (sb's attention or interest) by being interesting 使(某人的注意力或兴趣)不减: *A good teacher must be able to hold her pupils' attention.* 优秀的教师一定能吸引住学生. **13** [Tn] have (a belief, an opinion, a view, etc) 怀有, 持有(某种信念、见解、观点

H

等): *He holds strange views on religion.* 他对宗教问题持有奇怪的看法. ○ *I hold the view that the plan cannot work.* 我认为那个计划不可行. **14** [Tf, Cn·a, Cn·t] (*fml* 文) believe, consider or regard 相信; 认为; 视作: *I hold that the government's economic policies are mistaken.* 我认为政府的经济政策是错误的. ○ *I hold the parents responsible for their child's behaviour.* 我认为父母应对子女的行为负责. ○ *I hold him to be a fool.* 我认为他是个傻瓜. **15** [Tn] cause (a meeting, conference, etc) to take place 召开, 举行(会议、大会等): *The meeting will be held in the community centre.* 会议将在社区活动中心举行. ○ *We hold a general election every four or five years.* 我们每四五年举行一次大选. ○ *The Motor Show is usually held in October.* 汽车展览会通常在十月份举行. **16** [Tn] (**a**) (of a ship or an aircraft) continue to move in (a particular direction) (指船只或飞行器)继续朝(某一方向)航行: *The ship is holding a south-easterly course.* 船只继续朝东南方向航行. (**b**) (of a singer) continue to sing (a note) (指歌唱者)继续唱(某音符): *hold a high note* 持续唱着高音. **17** [I, Tn] wait until the person one has telephoned is ready to speak 等对方接电话: *Mr Crowther's extension is engaged at the moment; will you hold (the line)?* 克劳瑟先生的电话分机正占着线呢, 您稍等一下好吗? **18** (idm 习语) **hold 'good** remain true or valid 仍然适用; 仍然有效: *The same argument doesn't hold good in all cases.* 同一论点并非对所有情况都适用. **'hold it** (*infml* 口) (used to ask sb to wait, or not to move 用以请求某人等候或不要活动): *Hold it a second — I don't think everyone's arrived yet.* 稍等片刻吧 —— 我看人还没有到齐呢. **there is no holding sb** sb cannot be prevented from doing sth 什么也拦不住某人做某事: *Once she gets onto the subject of politics there's no holding her.* 她一谈起政治, 就没完没了. (For other idioms containing **hold**, see entries for *ns, adjs*, etc 与 **hold** 搭配的其他习语见有关名词、形容词等的词条, 如 **hold the fort** ⇨ FORT; **hold sb/sth dear** ⇨ DEAR.)

19 (phr v) **hold sth against sb** (*infml* 口) allow sth to influence one's judgement or opinion of sb 让某事物影响自己对某人的评价或看法: *He's afraid that his criminal record will be held against him when he applies for jobs.* 他担心自己有前科不好找工作. ○ *I don't hold it against him that he votes Conservative.* 我并不因为他投了保守党的票而对他有看法.

H

hold 'back (from sth) hesitate to act or speak because of fear or reluctance (因恐惧或不情愿而在言行上)退缩, 踌躇: *She held back, not knowing how to break the terrible news.* 她踌躇着, 不知该怎样宣布这一坏消息. ○ *She held back from telling him what she thought of him.* 她要把自己对他的看法告诉他, 但又觉得难以启齿.

hold sb 'back prevent the progress or development of sb 阻止或妨碍某人的进步或发展: *Do you think that mixed-ability teaching holds the brighter children back?* 你认为混合能力组教学会阻碍聪明儿童的进步吗? **hold sb/sth back** prevent sb/sth from advancing; control or restrain sb/sth 阻止、阻挡、控制或限制某人[某事物]: *The police cordon was unable to hold back the crowd.* 警方的警戒线阻挡不住人群. ○ *The dam was not strong enough to hold back the flood waters.* 水坝不太坚固, 挡不住洪水. **hold sth back** (**a**) not release or grant sth; withhold sth 扣住、保留或抑制某事物: *hold back information* 不走漏消息 ○ *I think he's holding sth back; he knows more than he admits.* 我认为他有所隐瞒, 他知道的比他承认的要多. (**b**) not express or reveal (an emotion); control sth 不表现或不流露(感情); 抑制某事物: *She just managed to hold back her anger.* 她总算抑制住了自己的愤怒情绪. ○ *He bravely held back his tears.* 他强忍着不让眼泪流出来.

hold sb 'down control the freedom of sb; oppress sb 限制某人的自由; 压制某人: *The people are held down by a vicious and repressive military regime.* 人民受着凶恶而专制的军政权的压迫. **hold sth 'down** (**a**) keep sth at a low level; keep sth down 使某事物保持低水平; 压住某事物: *The rate of inflation must be held down.* 通货膨胀率必须控制在低水平上. (**b**) (be competent enough to) remain in (a job) for some time (有足够的能力)保持(职位)到一定时候: *He couldn't hold down a job after his breakdown.* 他病倒以后, 工作也就保不住了. ○ *What's the longest she's held down a job?* 她任职时间最长的是什么工作?

hold 'forth speak pompously and lengthily about sth 夸夸其谈地、滔滔不绝地讲述某事: *He loves holding forth on any subject once he has an audience.* 不管是什么问题, 只要有人听, 他就爱大发议论.

hold sth/oneself in restrain, control or check sth/oneself 限制、控制或抑制某事物[自己]: *hold in one's feelings, temper, anger, etc* 克制感情、忍住脾气、压住怒火 ○ *He's incapable of holding himself in.* 他克制不住自己的感情.

hold 'off (**a**) (of rain, a storm, etc) not occur; be delayed (指雨、风暴等)未发生, 延迟: *The rain held off just long enough for us to have our picnic.* 雨一时下不起来, 我们有足够的时间吃完野餐. (**b**) restrain oneself from doing sth, esp attacking sb 约束自己而不做某事(尤指不攻击他人): *Let's hope the gunmen will hold off for the duration of the cease-fire.* 但愿持枪歹徒在停火期间能约束自己的行动. **hold sb/sth off** resist (an attack or advance by sb) 阻止或挡住(某人的进攻或前进): *Though outnumbered, they held off (repeated attacks by) the enemy.* 尽管寡不敌众, 他们还是抵挡住了敌人(一次又一次的进攻). **hold off sth/doing sth** delay sth 推迟某事物: *Could you hold off (making) your decision until next week?* 你可以推迟到下星期再做决定吗?

hold 'on (**a**) (*infml* 口) (usu in the imperative 通常用于祈使语气) wait or stop 等一下; 停住: *Hold on a minute while I get my breath back.* 停一停, 让我喘口气. (**b**) survive in a difficult or dangerous situation; hang on 历经危难而不死; 坚持住: *They managed to hold on until help arrived.* 他们设法坚持住直到有救援到来. ○ *I don't think I can hold on much longer.* 我觉得自己坚持不了多长时间了. **hold sth on** keep sth in position 将某物固定住: *These nuts and bolts hold the wheels on.* 这些螺帽和螺栓把轮子固定住了. ○ *This knob is only held on by sellotape.* 这个旋钮只是用透明胶带固定住的. **hold on (to sb/sth)** keep grasping or gripping sb/sth; not let go of sb/sth 抓住或握住某人[某物]: *He held on (to the rock) to stop himself slipping.* 他紧紧抓住(岩石)以免自己往下滑. ○ *hold on to one's hat on a windy day* 在大风天按住自己的帽子. **hold on to sth** (*infml* 口) not give or sell sth to sb else; keep or retain sth 不把某物给予或售予他人; 保留或保有某物: *You should hold on to your oil shares.* 你应该继续保留着石油股分. ○ *I'd hold on to that house for the time being; house prices are rising sharply at the moment.* 目前我不能出让那所房子, 此刻房价正在急剧上涨.

hold 'out (**a**) last; remain 维持; 保持: *We can stay here for as long as our supplies hold out.* 我们的供应品能维持多久, 我们就能在这里呆多久. ○ *I can't hold out* (ie retain my urine) *much longer; I must find a toilet.* 我憋不住了(要小便), 得找个厕所. (**b**) resist an attack 抵抗; 抵御: *They held out bravely against repeated enemy bombing.* 敌人轮番轰炸, 他们仍英勇地抵抗. **hold sth out** offer (a chance, hope, possibility, etc) 提供(机会); 带来(希望); 使有(可能): *The forthcoming talks hold out the hope of real arms reductions.* 即将举行的会谈给实现真正的裁军带来了希望. ○ *Doctors hold out little hope of her recovering.* 医生帮助她康复的希望甚微. **hold out for sth** (*infml* 口) deliberately delay reaching an agreement in the hope of gaining sth 故意拖延达成协议以谋求某事物: *Union negotiators are holding out for a more generous pay settlement.* 工会代表故意拖延谈判以争取达成大幅度增加工资的解决方案. **hold out on sb** (*infml* 口) refuse to give information, etc to sb 拒绝给予某人信息等; 瞒着: *I'm not holding out on you. I honestly don't know where he is.* 我不是故意瞒着你.我的确不知道他在哪里.

hold sth 'over (often passive 常用于被动语态) postpone or defer sth 延缓或推迟某事物: *The matter was held over until the next meeting.* 此事推迟到下次会议解决.

'hold to sth not abandon or change (a principle, an opinion, etc); remain loyal to sth 不放弃或不改变(原则、观点等); 忠于某事物: *She always holds to her convictions.* 她始终坚持自己的信念. ○ *beliefs that were firmly held to* 严格遵守的信条. **hold sb to sth** make sb keep (a promise) 使某人遵守(诺言): *He promised her a honeymoon in Paris when they got married, and she held him to it.* 他们结婚时, 他答应她到巴黎度蜜月, 她要求他遵守诺言. ○ *We must hold the contractors to* (ie not allow them to exceed) *their estimates.* 我们必须使承包

者遵照他们的预算办事(不许超支).

hold to'gether (**a**) remain whole 保持完整: *The car's bodywork scarcely holds together.* 这汽车的车身简直都要散架了. (**b**) remain united 保持团结: *The Tory party always holds together in times of crisis.* 保守党在紧要关头总是能团结一致. **hold sth together** cause sth to remain together; unite sth 使某事物不散开或团结一致: *The country needs a leader who will hold the nation together.* 该国需要一个能使全国团结的领袖.

hold sb/sth up (**a**) put sb/sth forward as an example 举某人[某事物]作为范例: *She's always holding up her children as models of behaviour.* 她总标榜自己的子女是良好品行的榜样. (**b**) obstruct or delay the progress of sb/sth 阻碍或延误某人[某事物]: *Road-works on the motorway are holding up traffic.* 高速公路上的道路施工影响了交通. ○ *My application was held up by the postal strike.* 我的申请书由于邮政部门罢工而延误了. ○ *Our flight was held up by fog.* 我们的班机因有雾而停航. **hold up sth** rob sth using the threat of force or violence 以武力或暴力威胁抢劫: *hold up a bank, post office, etc* 抢劫银行、邮局等 ○ *Masked men held up a security van in South London yesterday.* 蒙面歹徒昨天在伦敦南部抢劫了一辆护卫车.

hold with sth (used in negative sentences or in questions 用于否定句或疑问句中) agree with or approve of sth 同意或赞成某事物: *I don't hold with his views on education.* 我不同意他在教育问题上的观点. ○ *Do you hold with nudity on the stage?* 你赞成在舞台上作裸体表演吗?

□ **'hold-up** *n* (**a**) stoppage or delay 停顿或延搁: *a hold-up on the motorway* 高速公路上的交通阻塞 ○ *We should arrive in half an hour, barring hold-ups.* 若无交通阻塞, 我们半小时后可到达. (**b**) robbery by armed robbers 持械抢劫: *After the hold-up, the gang made their getaway in a stolen car.* 匪徒们打劫后, 乘一辆盗来的汽车逃走了.

hold[2] /həʊld; hold/ *n* **1** (**a**) [sing] act or manner of holding sb/sth; grasp; grip 拿; 抓; 抱; 咬; 托; 支撑: *She kept a firm hold of her little boy's hand as they crossed the road.* 横过马路时, 她紧紧地牵着她那小男孩的手. ○ *He lost his hold on the rope.* 他未能抓住绳索. (**b**) [C] particular way of holding an opponent, etc 抓紧对手等的某种方式; 擒拿(法): *wrestling holds* 摔跤中的擒拿法. **2** [sing] **~ (on/over sb/sth)** influence 影响: *He has a tremendous hold over his younger brother.* 他对他弟弟很有影响. **3** [sing] **~ (on sb/sth)** power or control of sb/sth 左右某人[某事物]的能力; 对某人[某事物]的控制: *The military has tightened its hold on the country.* 军方加强了对这个国家的控制. **4** [C] place where a climber can put his hands or feet when climbing 攀登者可手攀或脚踏之处: *There are very few holds on the cliff face.* 峭壁的正面可供手攀或脚踏的地方很少. Cf 参看 FOOTHOLD (FOOT). **5** (idm 习语) **catch, get, grab, seize, take, etc 'hold of sb/sth** take sb/sth in the hands 抓住、拿住、握住某人[某物]: *I threw the rope and he caught hold of it.* 我把绳子扔了过去, 他一把就抓住了. ○ *I managed to grab hold of the jug before it fell.* 我设法抓住了那个罐子才未跌落. **get hold of sb/sth** (*infml* 口) (**a**) find and use sth 找到某物以供使用: *Do you know where I can get hold of a second-hand carpet cleaner?* 你知道我在哪里可以弄到旧的地毯除尘器吗? ○ *Wherever did you get hold of that idea?* 你那想法究竟是从哪里来的? (**b**) contact or find sb 与某人联系; 找到某人: *I've been trying to get hold of her for days but she's never at home.* 我找了她好几天, 她始终不在家.

hold[3] /həʊld; hold/ *n* hollow part of a ship below the deck, where cargo is stored 货舱.

hold·all /'həʊldɔːl; 'hold,ɔl/ (*US* **'carry-all**) *n* large (usu soft) bag for holding clothes, etc when travelling (装衣物用的)大旅行袋(通常为软包).

holder /'həʊldə(r); 'holdɚ/ *n* (often forming compound *ns* 常用以构成复合名词) **1** person who holds sth; person who has sth at his disposal or in his possession 拿住、抓住、握住、抱住、托住某物的人; 持有或占有某物者: *an account-holder* 帐户持有人 ○ *a licence-holder* 领有执照者 ○ *a ticket-holder* 持票人 ○ *the holder of the world record/the world record-holder* 世界纪录保持者 ○ *holders of high office* 居高位者 ○ *the holder of a French passport* 持有法国护照者. **2** thing that supports or holds sth 支承或用以握持某物之物: *a pen-holder* 钢笔杆 ○ *a cigarette-holder* 香烟嘴 ○ *a plant pot holder* 花盆架.

hold·ing /'həʊldɪŋ; 'holdɪŋ/ *n* **1** land held by a tenant 佃户租种的土地. **2** (often *pl* 常作复数) thing owned, such as land, stocks, shares, etc; personal property 所有物(如土地、债券、股分等); 私有财产: *She has a 40% holding* (ie share) *in the company.* 她有公司的40%股分.

□ **'holding company** company formed to hold the shares of other companies, which it then controls 控股公司(持有其他公司的多数股权因而对这些公司有控制权的公司).

hole /həʊl; hol/ *n* **1** [C] (**a**) sunken or hollow place in a solid mass or surface; cavity 洞; 孔; 坑; 洞穴: *a hole in a tooth* 龋齿的洞 ○ *roads full of holes* 满是坑洼的道路. (**b**) opening through sth; gap 开口; 裂口: *The prisoner escaped through a hole in the wall.* 那囚犯从墙上的缺口处逃走了. ○ *I've worn holes in my socks.* 我把袜子穿破了. ○ *My socks are in holes/full of holes*, ie worn so much that holes have formed. 我的袜子破了. ○ *a hole in the heart*, ie a defect at birth in the membrane of the heart 先天性心膜缺损. **2** [C] (**a**) animal's burrow (动物的)巢穴: *a 'mouse hole* 鼠洞 ○ *a fox's hole* 狐穴. (**b**) (usu *sing* 通常作单数) (*fig infml* 比喻, 口) small, dark or unpleasant room, flat, district, etc 狭小、阴暗或简陋的房间、住所、区域等: *Why do you want to live here — it's a dreadful hole!* 你为什么要住在这里——这小地方简直糟透了. **3** [sing] (*sl* 俚) awkward or difficult situation 窘境; 困境: *be in (a bit of) a hole* 感到(有点)为难. **4** [C] (*sport* 体) (**a**) hollow or cavity into which a ball, etc must be hit in various games (多种游戏中将球等击入的)洞或孔: *an ,eighteen-hole 'golf-course* 有十八个洞的高尔夫球场. (**b**) (in golf) section of a golf-course between a tee and a hole; point scored by a player who reaches the hole with the fewest strokes (高尔夫球)由球座到球洞的一段距离, 以最少杆数进球所得的分数: *win the first hole* 在第一洞时领先. **5** (idm 习语) **have an ace in the hole** ⇨ ACE. **a hole in the 'wall** very small dingy shop, café, etc, esp in a row of buildings 狭小而昏暗的店铺、小餐馆等(尤指设于成排建筑物中的). **make a hole in sth** (*infml* 口) use a large amount of (one's money, supplies, etc) 大量耗费(金钱、供应品等): *The hospital bills made a big hole in his savings.* 医疗费已用掉了他一大笔存款. **money burns a hole in sb's pocket** ⇨ MONEY. **pick holes in sth** ⇨ PICK[3].

▷ **hole** *v* **1** [Tn] make a hole or holes in (sth) 在(某物)上打洞或穿孔: *The ship was holed by an iceberg.* 冰山把船撞出了窟窿. **2** [I, Ip, Tn] **~ (out)** (in golf, etc) hit (the ball) into a hole (高尔夫球等)击(球)入洞: *She holed out from forty yards.* 她从四十码远的地方把球打入洞中. **3** (phr v) **hole up** (also **be holed up**) (*sl* 俚 *esp US*) hide oneself 躲藏: *The gang (was) holed up in the mountains somewhere.* 那帮匪徒躲在山中某处.

□ **,hole-and-'corner** *adj* [usu attrib 通常作定语] (*derog* 贬) (of an activity) secret because dishonest or illegal; underhand (指活动)偷偷摸摸的, 见不得人的, 不光明正大的: *a hole-and-corner affair, business, method* 鬼鬼祟祟的事情、交易、方法.

holi·day /'hɒlədeɪ; 'hɑlə,de/ *n* **1** (**a**) day of rest, recreation or festivity, when no work is done 假日; 节日: *Sunday is a holiday in Christian countries.* 在基督教国家中星期天是假日. (**b**) (*esp Brit*) (also *esp US* **vacation**) (often *pl* 常作复数) period of time away from everyday work, used esp for travel, recreation and rest 假期: *the school holidays* 学校的假期 ○ *the Christmas holidays* 圣诞节假期 ○ *We're going to Spain for our summer holiday(s).* 我们打算去西班牙度暑假. ○ *I'm taking two weeks' holiday.* 我正在休假两星期. ○ *I'm entitled to 20 days' holiday a year.* 我每年有20天假期. ○ [attrib 作定语] *a holiday resort, brochure* 度假胜地、手册. **2** (idm 习语) **a busman's holiday** ⇨ BUSMAN (BUS). **high days and holidays** ⇨ HIGH[1]. **on 'holiday/on one's 'holidays** having a holiday 在休假: *The typist is away on holiday this week.* 打字员本周休假.

▷ **holi·day** *v* (*esp Brit*) (also *esp US* **vacation**) [I, Ipr, Ip] spend a holiday 度假: *They're holidaying on the west coast.* 他们正在西海岸度假.

□ **'holiday camp** (also **'holiday centre**) (*esp Brit*)

H

place with accommodation and organized amusements for people on holiday 度假中心(提供膳宿及有组织的娱乐活动的假日去处).

ˈ**holiday-maker** *n* person who is on holiday 度假者: *The plane was full of holiday-makers.* 飞机上满是度假的乘客.

NOTE ON USAGE 用法: **Holiday, vacation** and **leave** all indicate a period of absence from work or duty. ☆ **holiday**、**vacation**、**leave** 均指不工作、不上课或不值班的期间. There are differences between British and American usage. 这几个词的用法在英美之间有所不同. **1 Holiday** is used in both Britain and the US to mean a single day without work because of a religious or national festival 因宗教节日或国家喜庆而停止工作的单日假, 英美两国均用 **holiday** 表示之: *Friday is a holiday in Muslim countries.* 在伊斯兰教国家中星期五是假日. ○ *The shops are closed tomorrow because it is a bank holiday.* 明天是法定假日, 商店停止营业. ○ *In this country New Year's Day is a national holiday.* 在这个国家里, 元旦是全国性的假日. **2 Holiday** is used in Britain and **vacation** in the US when talking about the regular period of time taken away from work each year 指每年中的例行休假期间, 英国用 **holiday**, 美国则用 **vacation**: *Where are you going for your summer holidays/vacation?* 你打算去哪里度暑假? ○ *I was on holiday/vacation last month.* 我上个月休假了. **3** In Britain **vacation** is used mainly for the period of time when universities and lawcourts do not work 在英国, **vacation** 主要用以指大学和法院放假期间: *in Britain the long vacation is from June to October* 在英国, 长的假期是从六月到十月. **4 Leave** means permission given to an employee to be absent from work for a special reason ☆ **leave** 指雇员因有某种理由而获准的休假: *She's been given sick/compassionate/maternity leave.* 她获准休病假[事假/产假]. ○ *They've refused him leave of absence.* 他们不准他休假. ○ *He's taken unpaid leave for a month.* 他请了一个月的停薪假. **5 Leave** also means the period away from official duties of those working overseas, eg soldiers and diplomats ☆ **leave** 亦指派往海外工作的人员(如军人和外交人员)的假期: *He gets home leave every two years.* 他每两年有一次探亲假.

holier-than-thou /ˌhəʊlɪə ðən ˈðaʊ; ˌholɪɚ ðən ˈðaʊ/ *adj* (*infml derog* 口, 贬) thinking that one is more virtuous than others; self-righteous 自以为品格高人一等的; 自以为是的: *a holier-than-thou preacher, attitude* 好为人师的说教者、态度.

ho·li·ness /ˈhəʊlɪnɪs; ˈholɪnɪs/ *n* **1** [U] state of being holy or sacred 神圣. **2 His/Your Holiness** title used of or to the Pope 陛下, 圣座(对教皇的尊称).

hol·ler /ˈhɒlə(r); ˈhɑlɚ/ *v* [I, Tn] (*infml* 口 esp US) shout (sth); yell 喊出(某事物); 叫喊.

hol·low /ˈhɒləʊ; ˈhɑlo/ *adj* **1** having a hole or empty space inside; not solid 空的; 中空的: *a hollow tree, ball* 中空的树、球. **2** sunken; deeply set 凹的; 凹陷的: *hollow cheeks* 凹陷的双颊 ○ ˌ*hollow-*ˈ*eyed from lack of sleep* 由于睡眠不足而双眼凹陷的. **3** [usu attrib 通常作定语] (of sounds) echoing, as if coming from a hollow place (指声音)似由空腔中发出而生共鸣的, 重浊的: *a hollow groan* 低沉的呻吟. **4** (*fig* 比喻) (**a**) false; insincere 虚伪的; 缺乏诚意的: *a hollow promise* 空洞的诺言 ○ *hollow* (ie forced and cynical) *laughter* 虚伪的笑声 ○ *His words rang hollow.* 他的话听起来缺乏诚意. (**b**) without real value; worthless 无真正价值的; 不足道的: *hollow joys and pleasures*, ie not giving true happiness 空欢喜 ○ *win a hollow victory* 表面上获胜. **5** (idm 习语) **beat sb hollow** ⇨ BEAT[1]. **have hollow legs** (*Brit joc* 谑) have a large appetite 胃口很大.

▷ **hol·low** *n* (**a**) sunken place, esp a small valley 凹陷处; (尤指)小山谷: *a wooded hollow* 树木繁茂的小山谷. (**b**) hole or enclosed space within sth 洞; 孔; 围以某物之处: *She held the small bird in the hollow of her hand.* 她把那小鸟握在掌心里.

hol·low *v* **1** [Tn, Tn·p] ~ **sth (out)** form (sth) into a hollow shape 使(某物)成为中空形状或变成凹形: *river banks hollowed out by rushing water* 由于激流冲刷而凹陷了的河岸. **2** (phr v) **hollow sth out** form sth by making a hole in sth else 在一物上挖洞形成某物; 挖成某物: *hollow out a nest in a tree trunk* 在树干上凿巢.

hol·lowly *adv*.

hol·low·ness *n* [U].

holly /ˈhɒlɪ; ˈhɑlɪ/ *n* (**a**) [C] evergreen shrub with hard shiny sharp-pointed leaves and, in winter, red berries 冬青(常绿灌木, 叶尖而硬, 有光泽, 冬季结红色浆果). (**b**) [U] its branches used for Christmas decorations (用作圣诞节饰物的)冬青树枝.

hol·ly·hock /ˈhɒlɪhɒk; ˈhɑlɪˌhɑk/ *n* tall garden plant with brightly coloured flowers 蜀葵(高株园艺植物, 花鲜艳). ⇨illus at App 1 见附录1插图, page ii.

holm-oak /ˈhəʊm əʊk; ˈhom ok/ *n* = ILEX 2.

holo·caust /ˈhɒləkɔːst; ˈhɑləˌkɔst/ *n* (**a**) [C] large-scale destruction, esp by fire; great loss of human life 大规模的毁灭(尤指由火灾造成的); 大批的人的死亡: *fear a nuclear holocaust* 惧怕核灾难. (**b**) **the Holocaust** [sing] the mass killing of Jews by the Nazis before and during World War II (第二次世界大战之前及大战期间, 纳粹对犹太人的)大屠杀.

holo·gram /ˈhɒləgræm; ˈhɑləˌgræm/ *n* (*physics* 物) photographic representation that gives a three-dimensional image when suitably lit 全息图; 全息照相.

holo·graph /ˈhɒləgrɑːf; *US* -græf; ˈhɑləˌgræf/ *n* document that is handwritten by the author 亲笔文件.

hols /hɒlz; hɑlz/ *n* (*Brit infml* 口) holidays (HOLIDAY 1b) 假期.

hol·ster /ˈhəʊlstə(r); ˈholstɚ/ *n* leather case for a pistol, usu fixed to a belt or saddle (手枪的)皮套(通常固定于腰带或鞍子上). ⇨illus at GUN 见 GUN 插图.

holy /ˈhəʊlɪ; ˈholɪ/ *adj* (**-ier, -iest**) **1** (**a**) associated with God or with religion; of God 与神或宗教有关的; 神的; 上帝的: *the Holy Bible/Scriptures* 圣经. (**b**) regarded as sacred; consecrated 视为神圣的; 神圣化的: *holy ground* 神圣的土地 ○ *holy water*, ie water blessed by a priest 圣水(牧师祝福过的水) ○ *a holy war*, ie one fought to defend what is sacred 圣战(为捍卫神圣事业的战斗). **2** devoted to the service of God; morally and spiritually pure 献身于神或上帝的; 圣洁的; 心地纯洁的: *a holy man* 献身于上帝的人 ○ *live a holy life* 过圣洁的生活. **3** (idm 习语) **a holy** ˈ**terror** (*infml* 口) (**a**) (*joc* 谑) naughty or cheeky child 淘气的或鲁莽的孩子. (**b**) formidable or dominating person 难对付的或操纵人的人.

□ **the Holy** ˈ**City** Jerusalem 圣城(耶路撒冷).

Holy Communion = COMMUNION 1.

the Holy ˈ**Father** the Pope 教皇.

the Holy Ghost = THE HOLY SPIRIT.

the Holy Grail ⇨ GRAIL.

the ˈ**Holy Land** **1** country west of the river Jordan, revered by Christians as the place where Christ lived 圣地(位于约旦河西岸, 基督生活过的地方, 基督徒奉之为神圣土地). **2** any region revered in non-Christian religions (基督教以外的)宗教圣地.

ˌ**the holy of** ˈ**holies** (**a**) sacred inner chamber of a Jewish temple 至圣所(犹太圣殿的内殿). (**b**) (*fig often joc* 比喻, 常作戏谑语) sacred place 神圣的地方: *To the children, their father's study was the holy of holies.* 在这些孩子的眼里, 父亲的书房是最神圣的地方.

holy orders ⇨ ORDER.

the Holy ˈ**See** **1** the papal court; the Vatican 罗马教廷; 梵蒂冈. **2** the office of the pope; the papacy 教皇的职位; 教皇的权力.

the Holy ˈ**Spirit** (also **the Holy** ˈ**Ghost**) the Third Person in the Trinity; God acting spiritually 圣灵.

ˈ**Holy Week** week before Easter Sunday 复活节前的一周.

Holy ˈ**Writ** holy writings, esp the Bible 圣典; (尤指)《圣经》: *You shouldn't treat the newspapers as if they were Holy Writ.* 你不应该把报上说的话奉若神明.

hom·age /ˈhɒmɪdʒ; ˈhɑmɪdʒ/ *n* [U] (*fml* 文) things said or done to show great respect; tribute to a person or his qualities (used esp with the *vs* shown) 深表敬意的言行, 褒扬某人或某品德的事物(尤与下列句中动词连用): *They stood in silent homage round her grave.* 他们站立在她的墓的周围向她默哀. ○ *Many came to do the dead man homage.* 很多人前来向死者致哀. ○ *We pay homage to the genius of Shakespeare.* 我们对莎士比亚的天才表示敬仰.

Hom·burg /ˈhɒmbɜːɡ; ˈhɑmbɝɡ/ *n* man's soft felt hat with a narrow curled brim and a lengthwise dent in the top 洪堡毡帽(男用软毡帽, 帽边狭窄呈卷形, 帽顶有纵向凹坑).

home[1] /həʊm; hom/ *n* **1** (**a**) [C, U] place where one lives, esp with one's family 家: *The nurse visits patients in their homes.* 护士对病人进行家访. ○ *He left home* (ie left his parents and began an independent life) *at sixteen.* 他在十六岁时离开了家(离开双亲独立生活). ○ [attrib 作定语] *my home address* 我家的地址. (**b**) [C] house, flat, etc 房子、住所等: *Homes for Sale*, eg on an estate agent's notice. 房屋待售(如房地产经纪人之告示上所标明者). ○ [attrib 作定语] *a home improvement grant* 房屋改进装修补助金. (**c**) [C] (*infml* 口) place where an object is stored 存物处: *I must find a home for all these tins.* 我得找个地方存放这些罐头. **2** [C, U] district or country where one was born or where one has lived for a long time or to which one feels attached 家乡; 故乡; 老家: *She was born in London, but she now looks on Paris as her home.* 她生在伦敦, 但现在把巴黎看成是她的家乡. ○ *She lives a long way from home.* 她远远地离开故乡在外地生活. ○ *He left India for home*, ie for his own country. 他离开印度回国去了. **3** [C] (**a**) institution for people needing care or rest 为需要照顾或休息的人们设立的机构: *a children's home* 儿童之家 ○ *a home for the blind* 盲人院 ○ *an old people's home* 老年人之家. (**b**) institution providing accommodation for workers 为工人提供膳宿服务的机构: *a sailor's home* 海员之家. **4** [C] (**a**) place where an animal or a plant is native or most common; habitat (动植物的)生息地, 栖息处: *The tiger's home is in the jungle.* 老虎生活在丛林里. (**b**) place from which sth originates 发源地; 发祥地: *Greece is the home of democracy.* 希腊是民主的发祥地. **5** [U] (**a**) (in sport and in various games) place where a player is safe, cannot be caught, etc (体育活动及各种游戏中)安全、不会被捉住等之处. (**b**) finishing point in a race (赛跑的)终点. **6** (idm 习语) **at home** (**a**) in the house, flat, etc 在家里: *Is there anybody at home?* 有人在家吗? (**b**) at one's ease, as if in one's own home (像在自己家里一样)自在, 无拘束: *Make yourself at home!* 不要拘束! ○ *They always make us feel very much at home.* 他们总是使我们感到非常自在. (**c**) (of football matches, etc) played in the town, etc to which the team belongs (指足球比赛等)在主场进行的: *Is our next match at home or away?* 我们下一场比赛是在主场进行呢, 还是在客场进行? (**d**) (*fml* 文) expecting and ready to receive visitors 期待并准备接待来访者: *Mrs Hill is not at home to anyone except close relatives.* 希尔夫人不会客, 但近亲除外. **at home in sth** familiar and relaxed with sth 熟练掌握某事物; 驾轻就熟: *Is it difficult to feel at home in* (ie confident when using) *a foreign language?* 精通一门外语难不难? **charity begins at home** ⇨ CHARITY. **close/near to home** close to the point at which one is directly affected 即将受到触及; 临到自己头上: *Her remarks were embarrassingly close to home.* 她说的那些话很露骨而使人感到很尴尬. ○ *The threat of war is coming steadily nearer to home.* 战争的威胁正在一步步地临近. **eat sb out of house and home** ⇨ EAT. **an Englishman's home is his castle** ⇨ ENGLISHMAN (ENGLISH). **a ˈhome bird** person who likes to spend as much time as possible at home because he is happiest there 喜欢待在家里的人. **a ˌhome from ˈhome** place where one is as happy, comfortable, etc as in one's own home 像自己家里一样惬意、舒适等的处所: *You will find our hotel a true home from home!* 本旅社将使你感到宾至如归! **a ˌhome ˈtruth** unpleasant fact about a person told to him by sb else (从他人那里听到的有关自己的)不愉快的事实: *It's time you listened to a few home truths about yourself.* 你该听一些逆耳之言了. **one's spiritual home** ⇨ SPIRITUAL. **there's no place like home** ⇨ PLACE[1]. **when he's, it's, etc at ˈhome** (*joc* 谑) (used facetiously to emphasize a question 用以加强疑问句的诙谐语气): *Who's Gloria Button when she's at home?* 那位格洛丽亚·巴顿是何许人也?

▷ **home·less** *adj* having no home 无家的: *homeless families* 无处安身的家庭. **the home·less** *n* [pl *v*] homeless people 无家可归的人们: *provide emergency accommodation for the homeless* 向无家可归者提供食宿紧急救助. **home·less·ness** *n* [U].

home·ward /ˈhəʊmwəd; ˈhomwɚd/ *adj*, *adv* going towards home 回家去(的); 回家乡去(的); 回国去(的): *the homeward journey* 回程 ○ *We're homeward bound.* 我们回家去.

home·wards /-wədz; -wɚdz/ *adv* towards home 向家; 向家乡; 向本国: *travel homewards* 踏上回家的路途. ⇨ Usage at FORWARD[2] 用法见 FORWARD[2].

□ **ˌhome-ˈbrewed** *adj* (of beer, etc) made at home (contrasted with beer from a brewery) (指啤酒等)家酿的(以别于啤酒厂酿制的).

the ˌHome ˈCounties the counties round London 伦敦周围各郡. ⇨ illus at App 1 见附录1插图, pages xiv, xv.

ˌhome-ˈcured *adj* (of food, esp bacon) treated by smoking, salting, etc (指食品, 尤指熏咸肉)用烟熏、盐腌等方法制成的.

ˌhome ecoˈnomics study of household management 家政学.

ˈhome farm farm worked by the owner of an estate on which there are other farms 由地产主人自家经营的农场(以别于其出租的农场).

the ˌhome ˈfront the civilians (in a country at war) (战时的)后方民众.

ˌhome-ˈgrown *adj* (of food, esp fruit and vegetables) grown in one's own country, garden, etc (指食物, 尤指水果和蔬菜)本国、本地、自家的园子等产的: *Are these lettuces home-grown or did you buy them in the market?* 这些生菜是自家种的呢, 还是你在市场上买的? ○ (*fig* 比喻) *The team includes several foreign players because of the shortage of ˌhome-grown ˈtalent.* 由于本国人才缺乏, 该队尚有几名外籍队员.

the ˌHome ˈGuard (formerly) British volunteer army formed in 1940 to defend the country against invaders (旧时)地方军(1940年英国为抗击侵略者保卫国家而成立的志愿部队).

ˌhome ˈhelp person whose job is to help others with housework, etc, esp one employed by a local authority to help the elderly, disabled, etc in this way (帮助料理家务等的)佣人; (尤指受雇于地方当局帮助老年人、伤残者等料理家务等的)家庭服务员.

ˈhomeland /-lænd; -ˌlænd/ *n* **1** one's native country 祖国; 故乡. **2** (usu *pl* 通常作复数) any of the areas reserved for black people in the Republic of S Africa 南非共和国的黑人定居地.

ˌhome-ˈmade *adj* made at home 家里做的: *a ˌhome-made ˈcake* 自制糕饼 ○ *Home-made jam is usually better than the kinds you buy in the shops.* 自制的果酱通常要比从商店里买的好吃.

the ˈHome Office British Government department dealing with law and order, immigration, etc in England and Wales (英国的)内政部(负责处理英格兰和威尔士的治安、移民等问题). Cf 参看 THE FOREIGN AND COMMONWEALTH OFFICE (FOREIGN).

ˌHome ˈRule government of a country or region by its own citizens 地方自治.

ˌhome ˈrun (in baseball) hit that allows the batter to run round all the bases without stopping (棒球)本垒打.

ˌHome ˈSecretary Government minister in charge of the Home Office (英国)内政大臣.

ˈhomesick *adj* sad because one is away from home 想家的; 患怀乡病的: *He was homesick for Italy.* 他思念祖国意大利. **ˈhomesickness** *n* [U]: *suffer from homesickness when abroad* 旅居国外而苦苦思念故国.

ˈhomespun *adj* **1** made of yarn spun at home 家里纺的. **2** plain and simple 朴素的; 简单的: *homespun remedies for minor ailments* 一般小病的简易疗法 ○ *sensible homespun advice* 明智而实际的劝告. — *n* homespun fabric 家里纺的布; 土布.

homestead /ˈhəʊmsted; ˈhomˌstɛd/ *n* **1** house with the land and outbuildings round it, esp a farm 包括周围土地及附属房屋的家宅; (尤指)带农场的家宅. **2** (*US*) land given to a person by the State on condition that he lives on it and cultivates it 国家分给个人定居并进行开垦的土地. **homesteader** *n* (*US*) person who lives on a homestead 有宅地的人; 在分到的土地上定居并进行开垦的人.

the home ˈstraight (also *esp US* **the home ˈstretch**) (**a**) last part of a race, near the finishing-line (赛跑的)最后一段路程. (**b**) (*fig* 比喻) last part of an undertaking,

H

etc, when it is nearly completed (任务等的)最后部分, 最后阶段.

'**homework** *n* [U] **1** work that a pupil is required to do away from school (学生的)家庭作业, 课外作业: *The teacher gave us an essay (to do) for our homework.* 老师给我们布置的家庭作业是写一篇作文. **2** (*fig infml* 比喻, 口) work done in preparation for a meeting, etc (会议等的)准备工作: *The politician had clearly not done his homework*, ie found out all he needed to know about a particular topic. 那位政治家显然还没有完成会前的准备工作.

home[2] /həʊm; hom/ *adj* [attrib 作定语] **1** (**a**) of or connected with one's home 家的; 家庭的: *have a happy home life* 过幸福的家庭生活 ○ *home comforts* 家庭生活的种种享受. (**b**) done or produced at home 家里做成的; 家里制造的: *home cooking* 家常饭菜 ○ *home movies* 家里自拍的影片. **2** in one's own country; not foreign; domestic 本地的; 本国的; 国内的: *home industries* 本地工业 ○ *the home market* 国内市场 ○ *home news* 国内新闻. **3** (*sport* 体) played on or connected with one's own ground 在本地或主方赛场举行的: *a home match, win, defeat* 在主场举行的比赛、获得的胜利、遭到的失败 ○ *the home team*, ie the one playing at home 主队 ○ *playing in front of their home crowd* (主队)在本地群众面前的比赛.

home[3] /həʊm; hom/ *adv* **1** at, in or to one's home or country 在家; 到家; 向家; 在家乡; 到家乡; 向家乡; 在国内; 到国内; 向国内: *Is he home yet?* 他到家了吗? ○ *She's on her way home.* 她正在回家的路上. ○ *He went home.* 他回家去了. ○ *Will the Spanish authorities send him home for trial?* 西班牙当局要把他押送回国审讯吗? ○ (*US*) *stay home*, ie stay at home 待在家里. **2** to the point aimed at; as far as possible 正中目标; 尽可能地: *drive a nail home* 把钉子钉到头儿. **3** (idm 习语) **be, etc nothing to write home about** ⇨ WRITE. **bring home the 'bacon** (*infml* 口) achieve sth successfully 成就某事物. **bring sth 'home to sb** make sb realize sth fully 使某人彻底了解某事物: *The television pictures brought home to us all the plight of the refugees.* 我们从电视上知道了难民所处的一切困境. **come 'home (to sb)** become fully (and often painfully) clear 完全(常为令人痛苦地)明白. **come home to 'roost** (of words) take effect upon the person who has said them (指言语)应验到说出者本人身上. **drive sth home** ⇨ DRIVE[1]. **drive the point home** ⇨ DRIVE[1]. **hit/strike 'home** (of remarks, etc) have the intended (often painful) effect (指言语等)产生预期的(常为令人痛苦的)效果, 击中要害: *I could see from her expression that his sarcastic comments had hit home.* 从她的表情中我可以看出他那些挖苦人的话已经触及她的痛处. **(be) home and 'dry** safe and successful, esp after a difficult time 大功告成而能完好无损的(尤指经历过困难). **invalid sb home** ⇨ INVALID[2] *v*. **press sth home** ⇨ PRESS[2]. **romp home/in** ⇨ ROMP. **till the cows come home** ⇨ COW[1]. **when one's ship comes home/in** ⇨ SHIP[1].

□ '**home-coming** *n* [C, U] arrival at home (esp of sb who has been away for a long time) 返回家中, 还乡, 归国(尤指离别很久之后).

H

home[4] /həʊm; hom/ *v* **1** [I] (of a trained pigeon) fly home (指信鸽)飞回自己的窝, 归巢. **2** (phr v) **home in (on sth)** be directed or move towards sth 对准某事物; 朝某事物运动: *The torpedo homed in on its target.* 鱼雷射向目标. ○ *Pop fans are homing in on the concert site from miles around.* 流行歌曲的爱好者纷纷从四面八方向音乐会的举办地点聚集.

homely /'həʊmlɪ; 'homlɪ/ *adj* (**-ier, -iest**) **1** (*approv* 褒 *esp Brit*) (**a**) simple and plain 简单的; 平常的: *a homely woman* 朴素的女子. (**b**) making sb feel comfortable 使人感到舒适的: *a homely place, atmosphere* 宾至如归的地方、气氛. **2** (*US derog* 贬) (of a person's appearance) not good-looking; plain (指人的外貌)不好看的; 相貌平平的. ▷ **homeli·ness** *n* [U].

homeo·path, homeo·pathy *ns* (*US*) = HOMOEOPATH (HOMOEOPATHY), HOMOEOPATHY.

Ho·meric /həʊ'merɪk; ho'mɛrɪk/ *adj* of the writings or heroes of Homer 荷马史诗的; 荷马史诗中的人物的.

homey /'həʊmɪ; 'homɪ/ *adj* (**-mier, -miest**) (*US infml* 口) = HOMY.

hom·icide /'hɒmɪsaɪd; 'hɑmə,saɪd/ *n* **1** [U] killing of one person by another 杀人: *be accused of homicide* 被控犯有杀人罪. Cf 参看 MURDER. **2** [C] person who kills another 杀人者.

▷ **hom·icidal** /,hɒmɪ'saɪdl; ,hɑmə'saɪdl/ *adj* of homicide 杀人的: *have homicidal tendencies* 有杀人的倾向 ○ *a homicidal maniac* 杀人狂.

hom·ily /'hɒmɪlɪ; 'hɑmlɪ/ *n* **1** (*often derog* 常作贬义) long and boring talk from sb on the correct way to behave, etc 有关规矩等问题的冗长而令人厌倦的说教: *preach/give/deliver a homily* 进行说教. **2** (*fml* 文) sermon 讲道. ▷ **ho·mi·letic** /,hɒmɪ'letɪk; ,hɑmə'lɛtɪk/ *adj*.

hom·ing /'həʊmɪŋ; 'homɪŋ/ *adj* [attrib 作定语] **1** (of a pigeon) having the instinct or trained to fly home from a great distance (指鸽子)有自远处飞返原地的本能或训练的. **2** (of a torpedo, missile, etc) fitted with an electronic device that enables it to find and hit a target (指鱼雷、导弹等)自动寻的的, 自动导引: *'homing devices* 自动导引装置.

homo- *comb form* 构词成分 the same 同; 相同: *homosexual* ○ *homophone* ○ *homogeneous*. Cf 参看 HETERO-.

hom·oe·opathy (*US* **homeo-**) /,həʊmɪ'ɒpəθɪ; ,homɪ'ɑpəθɪ/ *n* [U] treatment of a disease by very small amounts of drugs that, if given to a healthy person, would produce symptoms like those of the disease itself 顺势疗法.

▷ **hom·oeo·path** (*US* **homeo-**) /'həʊmɪəpæθ; 'homɪə,pæθ/ *n* person who practises homoeopathy 采用顺势疗法的医生.

hom·oe·opathic (*US* **homeo-**) /,həʊmɪə'pæθɪk; ,homɪə'pæθɪk/ *adj*: *homoeopathic remedies, treatment, medicines, etc* 顺势疗法、顺势治疗、顺势治疗所用的药物.

homo·gen·eous /,hɒmə'dʒi:nɪəs; ,hɑmə'dʒinɪəs/ *adj* formed of parts that are all of the same type 由同类部分组成的. Cf 参看 HETEROGENEOUS.

▷ **homo·gen·eity** /,hɒmədʒɪ'ni:ətɪ; ,hɑmədʒə'niətɪ/ *n* [U] quality of being alike 同种; 同质.

homo·gen·ize, -ise /hə'mɒdʒənaɪz; hə'mɑdʒə,naɪz/ *v* [Tn] **1** treat (milk) so that the particles of fat are broken down and the cream is blended with the rest 对(牛奶)作均质处理(将脂肪微粒搅碎使奶油分布均匀). **2** make (sth) homogeneous 使(某物)成分均匀.

homo·graph /'hɒməgrɑ:f; *US* -græf; 'hɑmə,græf/ *n* word spelt like another word but with a different meaning or pronunciation 同形异义词(写法相同而意义或读音不同者), 如 *bow*[1]/bəʊ; bo/, *bow*[2] /baʊ; baʊ/.

hom·onym /'hɒmənɪm; 'hɑmə,nɪm/ *n* word spelt and pronounced like another word but with a different meaning 同形同音异义词(写法和读音相同而意义不同者), 如 *see*[1], *see*[2].

homo·phone /'hɒməfəʊn; 'hɑmə,fon/ *n* word pronounced like another word but with a different meaning or spelling 同音异义词, 同音异形词(读音相同而意义或写法不同者), 如 *some, sum* /sʌm; sʌm/; *knew, new* /nju:; nju/.

Homo sa·pi·ens /,həʊməʊ 'sæpɪenz; ,homo 'sæpɪɛnz/ (*Latin* 拉) modern man regarded as a species 智人.

homo·sexual /,hɒmə'sekʃʊəl; ,homə'sɛkʃʊəl/ *adj* sexually attracted only to people of the same sex as oneself 同性恋的: *homosexual relationships, tendencies* 同性恋关系、癖好. Cf 参看 HETEROSEXUAL, BISEXUAL.

▷ **homo·sexual** *n* homosexual person 同性恋者. Cf 参看 LESBIAN.

homo·sexu·al·ity /,hɒməsekʃʊ'ælətɪ; ,homə,sɛkʃʊ'ælətɪ/ *n* [U] condition of being homosexual 同性恋.

homy (*US* **homey**) /'həʊmɪ; 'homɪ/ *adj* (**-ier, -iest**) (*approv* 褒) like home; cosy 像家一样的; 舒适惬意的.

Hon *abbr* 缩写 = **1** /ɒn; ɑn/ Honorary: *the Hon Sec*, ie Honorary Secretary 义务秘书 ○ *the Hon Treasurer* 义务司库. **2** Honourable: *the Hon Emily Smythe* 埃米莉·斯迈思阁下. Cf 参看 RT HON.

hone /həʊn; hon/ *n* stone used for sharpening the cutting edges of tools, etc (磨工具等的刀口用的)磨石.

▷ **hone** *v* [Tn] sharpen (sth) on a hone 在磨石上把(某物)磨锋利.

hon·est /'ɒnɪst; 'ɑnɪst/ *adj* **1** (**a**) (of a person) telling the truth; not cheating or stealing (指人)诚实的, 老实的: *an honest witness, businessman* 可靠的证人、商人. (**b**) (of a statement) frank, sincere and direct (指陈述)坦白的, 真诚的, 直率的: *give an honest opinion* 提出坦诚的意见 ○ *Do you like my dress? Please be honest!* 你喜欢我的连衣裙吗? 请说真话! (**c**) showing or resulting from an honest mind 显示心地诚实的; 由诚意产生的: *an honest face* 一副诚实的面孔 ○ *He looks honest enough, but can we trust him?* 他看起来倒挺诚实, 但我们能信得过他吗? ○ *She's never done an honest day's work* (ie worked hard and conscientiously) *in her life.* 她一辈子从来没有实实在在地(努力而认真地)干过一天活儿. **2** (of wages, etc) fairly earned (指工资等)以正当手段挣得的: *make an honest living* 靠正当的收入生活. **3** (of actions, etc) sincere but undistinguished (指行为等)踏实而平平的. **4** (idm 习语) **earn/turn an honest ˈpenny** earn money by working hard and fairly 以正当的手段凭努力工作挣钱. **honest to ˈGod/ˈgoodness** (*infml* 口) truthfully 实在地: *Honest to goodness, I didn't do it.* 老天爷可以作证, 我没有做过这件事. **make an honest ˈwoman of sb** (*dated joc* 旧, 谑) marry sb after having had a sexual relationship with her 与某女人发生性关系后娶其为妻. **to be (quite) ˈhonest (about it/with you)** (*catchphrase* 警语) (used to emphasize that one is speaking frankly 用以强调所言出自真心): *To be honest, I don't think we have a chance of winning.* 说实话, 我认为我们没有获胜的可能.

▷ **hon·est** *adv* (*infml* 口) truthfully 实在地: *It wasn't me, honest!* 说实话, 那不是我!

hon·estly *adv* **1** in a truthful and fair way 以公平而正当的方式: *deal honestly with sb* 与某人公平交易. **2** (used for emphasis 用以加强语气) really 的确: *I don't honestly know.* 我的确不知道. ○ *Honestly, that's all the money I've got!* 我的的确确只有这点钱了! **3** (used to show disapproval and impatience 用以表示不赞成和不耐烦): *Honestly! What a fuss!* 真是大惊小怪!

□ ˌ**honest-to-ˈgoodness** *adj* [attrib 作定语] plain and simple; genuine; straightforward 实打实的; 真正的; 率直的: *a bit of honest-to-goodness hard work* 一点真正吃力的工作.

hon·esty /ˈɒnəstɪ; ˈɑnəstɪ/ *n* [U] **1** quality of being honest; truthfulness 诚实; 老实; 正直; 实在. **2** plant with purple flowers and flat round semi-transparent seed-pods 缎花属植物(开紫花, 有扁圆形半透明的种子荚). **3** (idm 习语) **in all ˈhonesty** honestly 诚实地; 实在地: *I can't in all honesty* (ie if I must be honest) *deny it.* 我确实不能否认这一点.

honey /ˈhʌnɪ; ˈhʌnɪ/ *n* **1** [U] (**a**) sweet sticky yellowish substance made by bees from nectar 蜂蜜. (**b**) its colour 蜜色: *honey-coloured hair* 蜜色的毛发. **2** [U] sweetness; pleasantness 甜蜜; 甜美. **3** [C] (*infml* 口 *esp US*) (**a**) (used to address or refer to a person one likes or loves 用作爱称): *You look great tonight, honey!* 亲爱的, 你今晚真漂亮! ○ *Our baby-sitter is an absolute honey.* 我们的临时保姆好极了. (**b**) thing that is excellent or delightful 出类拔萃的事物; 讨人喜欢的东西: *That computer game's a honey.* 那电脑游戏真好玩儿.

▷ **hon·eyed** /ˈhʌnɪd; ˈhʌnɪd/ *adj* (of words) sentimental and flattering (指词语)亲切而讨好的; 甜言蜜语的.

□ ˈ**honey-bee** *n* ordinary type of bee that lives in hives 蜜蜂.

honeycomb /ˈhʌnɪkəʊm; ˈhʌnɪˌkom/ (also **comb**) *n* **1** [C, U] wax structure of six-sided cells made by bees for holding their honey and eggs 蜂巢: *a piece of honeycomb* 一块蜂巢. **2** [C] pattern or arrangement of six-sided sections 蜂巢形图案; 蜂巢状排列形式. ˈ**honeycombed** *adj* **~ (with sth)** filled with holes, tunnels, etc 蜂巢状的; 多孔的; 多洞的; 多孔道的: *The Rock of Gibraltar is honeycombed with caves.* 直布罗陀岩山上有许多洞穴.

hon·ey·dew /ˈhʌnɪdjuː; ˈhʌnɪˌdju/ *n* [U] sweet sticky substance found on leaves and stems in hot weather 树蜜(树叶和树茎在天气炎热时分泌的带甜味的黏汁).

□ ˌ**honeydew ˈmelon** cultivated variety of melon with pale skin and sweet green flesh 蜜瓜; 白兰瓜.

hon·ey·moon /ˈhʌnɪmuːn; ˈhʌnɪˌmun/ *n* **1** holiday taken by a newly married couple 蜜月: *They went to Italy for their honeymoon.* 他们去意大利度蜜月. ○ *We're on our honeymoon.* 我们正在度蜜月. **2** (*fig* 比喻) period of enthusiastic goodwill at the start of an undertaking, a relationship, etc 事业、关系等之初始的热火时期: [attrib 作定语] *The honeymoon period for the new government is over, and they must now start to tackle the country's many problems.* 新政府建立之初的那一阵子热劲已经过去了, 现在得着手解决国家的众多问题了.

▷ **hon·ey·moon** *v* [I, Ipr] spend a honeymoon 度蜜月: *They are honeymooning in Paris.* 他们正在巴黎度蜜月. **hon·ey·mooner** *n*.

hon·ey·suckle /ˈhʌnɪsʌkl; ˈhʌnɪˌsʌkl/ *n* [U] climbing shrub with sweet-smelling yellow or pink flowers 忍冬(蔓生灌木, 开黄色或粉红色的花, 气味芳香).

honk /hɒŋk; hɔŋk/ *n* **1** cry of the wild goose 雁叫声. **2** sound made by a car horn, esp of the old-fashioned type 汽车喇叭的鸣声(尤指旧式的).

▷ **honk** *v* [I, Ipr, Tn, Tn·pr] **~ (sth) (at sb/sth)** (cause sth to) make a honk (使某物)发出雁叫似的声音, 发汽车喇叭声: *the honking cry of migrating geese* 大雁的鸣叫声 ○ *The driver honked (his horn) at me to get out of the way.* 司机按汽车喇叭叫我让路.

honky-tonk /ˈhɒŋkɪ tɒŋk; ˈhɑŋkɪ ˌtɑŋk/ *n* (*infml* 口) **1** [U] type of ragtime music played on a piano 杭基汤克音乐(用钢琴演奏的名为雷格泰姆的爵士音乐): [attrib 作定语] *a honky-tonk rhythm* 杭基汤克节奏. **2** [C] cheap night-club 低级夜总会.

hon·or·ar·ium /ˌɒnəˈreərɪəm; ˌɑnəˈrɛrɪəm/ *n* (*pl* **~s**) voluntary payment made for professional services for which a fee is not normally paid or required by law (自愿赠予的)酬金, 谢礼.

hon·or·ary /ˈɒnərərɪ; *US* ˈɒnərerɪ; ˈɑnəˌrɛrɪ/ *adj* [usu attrib 通常作定语] **1** (of a degree, rank, etc) given as an honour (指学位、级别等)荣誉的: *be awarded an honorary doctorate, title* 被授予荣誉博士学位、头衔. **2** (in titles 称谓中作 **Honorary**, *abbr* 缩写 **Hon**) (of a position or its holder) unpaid (指职位或任职者)无报酬的, 名誉的: *the honorary (post of) President* 名誉会长 ○ *the Honorary Secretary Mrs Hill* 义务秘书希尔夫人.

honor, hon·or·able (*US*) = HONOUR, HONOURABLE.

hon·or·ific /ˌɒnəˈrɪfɪk; ˌɑnəˈrɪfɪk/ *n*, *adj* (expression) indicating respect for the person being addressed, esp in Oriental languages 表示敬意的(用语); (尤指东方语言中的)敬语(的).

hon·our[1] (*US* **honor**) /ˈɒnə(r); ˈɑnə/ *n* **1** [U, sing] source of pride and pleasure; privilege 光荣; 荣幸: *the seat of honour at the head of the table* 上首席位 ○ *It is a great honour to be invited.* 承蒙邀请, 十分荣幸. **2** [U] (**a**) good personal character; strong sense of what is morally right 节操; 正义感: *a man of honour* 品德高尚的人 ○ *Honour demands that he should resign.* 为了保持气节, 他应该辞职. (**b**) reputation for greatness, good behaviour, truthfulness, etc 荣誉; 名誉; 信誉: *fight for the honour of one's country* 为祖国的荣誉而战 ○ *My honour is at stake.* 我的名誉利害攸关. **3** [U] great respect; high public regard 崇敬; 公众表示的敬意: *They stood in silence as a mark of honour to her.* 他们肃立向她致敬. **4** [sing] **an ~ to sth/sb** a person or thing that brings credit to sth/sb 给某事物[某人]增光的人或事物: *She is an honour to her profession.* 她是同行的光荣. **5** [C usu *pl* 通常作复数] thing given as a distinction or mark of respect, esp an official award for achievement or bravery 作为荣誉或尊敬的标志而授予之事物(尤指为表扬成绩或英勇行为而正式授予的): *bury a person with full military honours*, ie with a special ceremony to honour the dead soldier 以隆重的军葬礼埋葬死者 ○ *Birthday/New Year Honours*, ie titles, decorations, etc awarded in Britain by the Sovereign on his or her birthday or on 1 January each year 英国国王或女王在其诞辰或元旦之日授予的荣誉称号、勋章等. **6 honours** [pl] specialized course for a university degree or high level of distinction reached in it (大学)荣誉学位课程, 优等成绩: [attrib 作定语] *an honours degree course in French literature* 法国文学荣誉学位课程. **7 your/his/her Honour** [sing] (used to or about certain judges or people of importance as a title of respect 用作对某些法官或显要人士的尊称): *I plead innocent, your Honour.* 我不认罪, 法官大人. **8** [C esp *pl* 尤作复数] (in card-games) any of the cards of highest value (纸牌戏中)最大点数的牌: *hold five spades to* (ie of which the highest is) *an honour* 手中有五张黑桃, 其中有一张大牌. **9** [U] (in golf) right of driving off first (高尔夫球

H

的)先打权: *It's 'your honour, partner.* 伙伴, 该你先打. **10** (idm 习语) **a debt of honour** ⇨ DEBT. **do sb 'honour** (*fml* 文) show respect for sb 向某人表示敬意或致敬: *Fifty heads of state attended the Queen's coronation to do her honour.* 五十位国家元首参加了女王的加冕典礼, 向女王表示敬意. **do sb an honour; do sb the honour (of doing sth)** (*fml* 文) give sb a privilege 给某人以特权; 使某人有特殊的荣幸: *You do us a great honour by attending.* 你肯光临使我们感到无比荣幸. ○ *Will you do me the honour of dining with me?* 可否赏光与我一起吃饭? **do the 'honours** (*infml* 口) act as host or hostess; perform some social duty or small ceremony 尽主人之谊; 履行某种社交责任; 执行某种小礼仪: *Who's going to pour the tea — shall I do the honours?* 谁管斟茶——我来斟好吗? **have the honour (of sth)** (*fml* 文) be granted the privilege specified 获得某种特权; 获得某种特殊的荣幸: *May I have the honour of this dance?* 可以赏光和我跳这个舞吗? ○ *To whom do I have the honour of speaking?* 能跟您谈话十分荣幸, 请问尊姓大名? **(there is) honour among 'thieves** (*saying* 谚) criminals often have their own standards of behaviour that they live by 罪犯往往也有赖以生存的行为准则; 盗亦有道. **honours are 'even** the contest is level 比赛打成平局: *Both teams have won the same number of games so honours are even between them.* 两队积分相同, 比赛结果不分胜负. **(in) honour 'bound (to do sth)** required to do sth as a moral duty but not by law 道义上应做某事的; 理应做的(非硬性规定的): *I feel honour bound to attend because I promised I would.* 我觉得不参加不大好, 因为是我答应过的事. **in honour of sb/sth; in sb's/sth's honour** out of respect for sb/sth 出于对某人[某事物]的敬意: *a ceremony in honour of those killed in battle* 为纪念阵亡将士而举行的仪式. **on one's honour (to do sth)** under a moral obligation (to do sth) 在道义的促使下(做某事). **on my 'honour** I swear it 我发誓; 我以人格担保: *I promise I'll pay you back, on my honour.* 我以人格担保, 一定把钱还给你. **a point of honour** ⇨ POINT[1]. **put sb on his, etc 'honour** make sb promise solemnly to do sth 使某人郑重承诺做某事. **one's word of honour** ⇨ WORD.

□ **'honours list** (*Brit*) list of people given titles, decorations, etc by the Sovereign (国君授予称号、勋章等的)荣誉名册.

H **hon·our**[2] (*US* **hon·or**) /ˈɒnə(r); ˈɑnɚ/ *v* **1** [Tn, Tn·pr] **~ sb/sth (with sth)** show great respect for sb/sth; give public praise and distinction to sb 向某人[某事物]致敬; 表扬某人; 给某人以荣誉: *I feel highly honoured by your trust.* 我得到您的信任, 感到十分荣幸. ○ (*fml* 文) *Will you honour me with a visit?* 如蒙造访则荣幸之至. **2** [Tn] (*commerce* 商) accept and pay (sth) when due 承认(某事物)并如期支付款项; 承兑: *honour a cheque/bill/draft* 承兑支票[票据/汇票].

hon·our·able (*US* **hon·or·able**) /ˈɒnərəbl; ˈɑnərəbl/ *adj* **1** deserving, bringing or showing honour 光荣的; 荣耀的; 应享受荣誉的: *an honourable person, deed, calling* 声誉卓著的人[光荣的事迹/体面的职业] ○ *conclude an honourable peace* 缔结体面的和约 ○ *do the honourable thing by resigning* 以辞职的行动保持名节. **2** (in titles 称谓中作 **the Honourable**, *abbr* 缩写 **Hon**) **(a)** (title given to certain high officials 对某些高级官员的尊称). **(b)** (title used in Parliamentary debates by members of Parliament when speaking of or to each other 议会辩论中用作议员之间的尊称): *my Honourable friend, the member for Chester* 切斯特市议员阁下. Cf 参看 RIGHT HONOURABLE (RIGHT[2]). **(c)** (title given to the children of peers below the rank of marquis 对侯爵以下贵族子女的尊称): *the Honourable Mrs Craig Holmes* 克雷格·霍尔姆斯夫人阁下. ▷ **hon·our·ably** /-əblɪ; -əblɪ/ *adv*: *acquit oneself honourably* 表现得光明正大.

Hons /ɒnz; ɑnz/ *abbr* 缩写 = Honours (in Bachelor degrees) 学士学位的: *Jim West BSc (Hons)* 吉姆·威斯特理学士(优等学位) ○ *a degree with Hons* 荣誉学位 ○ *degree class: Hons 2(i)* 学位等级: 二等甲级.

Hon Sec /ˌɒn ˈsek; ˌɑn ˈsɛk/ *abbr* 缩写 = Honorary Secretary.

hooch /huːtʃ; hutʃ/ *n* [U] (*US infml* 口) (esp cheap or illegally made) alcoholic liquor (尤指便宜的或非法酿造的)酒.

hood[1] /hʊd; hʊd/ *n* **1 (a)** covering for the head and neck, often fastened to a coat, etc, so that it can hang down at the back, or be detached, when not in use 风帽, 兜帽(通常连在外衣等上, 蒙住头部及颈部, 不用时可垂在背后或取下). **(b)** garment of coloured silk, fur, etc similar to a hood and worn over a university gown to show the degree held by the wearer 学位服垂布(用有色丝绸、毛皮等制成, 披于学位服外的学位标志). **2** thing resembling a hood in shape or use 形状或用途似风帽之物: *The robbers all wore hoods to hide their faces.* 那些劫匪都戴着面罩蒙着脸. **3 (a)** (*Brit*) folding waterproof top of a motor car, carriage, pram, etc (汽车、马车、婴儿车等的)折叠式车篷: *In fine weather I can drive my car with the hood down.* 天气好时我可以敞着顶篷开车. **(b)** cover placed over a machine to protect it or sb using it (机器的)安全罩, 防护罩: *a soundproof hood for the computer printer* 计算机打印机的隔音罩. **4** (*US*) = BONNET 3.

▷ **hooded** *adj* **1** having a hood 有兜帽的; 有罩的; 有篷盖的: *a hooded raincoat* 有兜帽的雨衣. **2** wearing a hood 戴着兜帽的: *hooded monks* 戴兜帽的修道士.

hood[2] /hʊd; hʊd/ *n* (*US sl* 俚) = HOODLUM 2.

-hood *suff* 后缀 (with *ns* or *adjs* forming *ns* 与名词或形容词结合构成名词) **1** state or condition of ...的状态或状况: *childhood* ○ *brotherhood* ○ *falsehood*. **2** group of ...的集体: *priesthood*.

hood·lum /ˈhuːdləm; ˈhudləm/ *n* **1** destructive and rowdy youth 为非作歹的青年; 小流氓. **2** violent criminal; gangster 暴徒; 歹徒.

hoo·doo /ˈhuːduː; ˈhudu/ *n* (*pl* **~s**) (*esp US*) **~ (on sb/sth)** person or thing that brings or causes bad luck; jinx 带来厄运的人或物; 不祥的人或物: *My car seems to have a hoodoo on it — it keeps breaking down.* 我的汽车好像中了邪了——老是出故障.

▷ **hoo·doo** *v* [Tn] (*esp US infml* 口) make (sb) unlucky 使(某人)倒霉.

hood·wink /ˈhʊdwɪŋk; ˈhʊdˌwɪŋk/ *v* [Tn, Tn·pr] **~ sb (into doing sth)** deceive sb; trick sb 欺骗某人; 哄某人上当: *I was hoodwinked into buying fake jewels.* 我受骗买了假珠宝.

hooey /ˈhuːɪ; ˈhuɪ/ *n* [U], *interj* (*sl* 俚) false or foolish talk; nonsense 瞎话; 废话; 胡说八道: *That's a lot of hooey!* 那都是胡说八道! ○ *What hooey!* 废话!

hoof /huːf; huf/ *n* (*pl* **~s** or **hooves** /huːvz; huvz/) **1** horny part of the foot of a horse, an ox or a deer (马、牛、或鹿的)蹄. ⇨ illus at HORSE 见 HORSE 插图. **2** (idm 习语) **on the 'hoof** (of cattle) alive (指牛)活的: *bought on the hoof and then slaughtered* 买活牛然后宰杀.

▷ **hoof** *v* (idm 习语) **'hoof it** (*sl* 俚) go on foot 步行: *The last bus had gone so we had to hoof it home.* 末班公共汽车已经开走了, 我们只好走回家.

hoo-ha /ˈhuː hɑː; ˈhuˌhɑ/ *n* [U, sing] (*infml* 口) noisy or excited protest, esp about sth unimportant; commotion; fuss 大吵大闹(尤指为小事); 小题大作: *The photo caused a real hoo-ha.* 那张照片竟激起了一场轩然大波. ○ *What are they making such a hoo-ha about?* 他们这样吵吵闹闹是怎么回事? ○ *There was a terrific hoo-ha (going on) about who should pay.* 对谁该付款这区区小问题争吵得不可开交.

hook 钩子

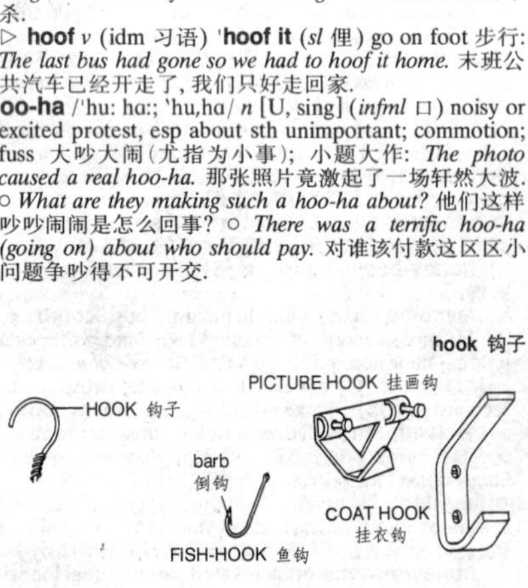

hook[1] /hʊk; hʊk/ *n* **1** curved or bent piece of wire, plastic, etc for catching hold of sth or for hanging sth on 钩子; 吊钩; 挂钩: *a 'fish-hook* 鱼钩 ○ *a 'crochet hook* 钩针 ○ *Hang your towel on a hook.* 把你的毛巾挂在挂钩上吧. **2** (esp in compounds 尤用以构成复合词) curved tool for cutting (grain, etc) or for chopping (branches) 镰刀;(砍树枝用的)弯刀: *a 'reaping-hook ○ a 'billhook.* **3** thing shaped like a hook, eg a sharp bend in a river, etc or a curving point of land 钩状物; 河曲; 陆地弯曲处: *the Hook of Holland* 荷兰钩. **4** (**a**) (in cricket or golf) type of stroke that hooks (HOOK[2] 4a) the ball (板球或高尔夫球)击出曲线球. (**b**) (in boxing) short blow with the elbow bent (拳击)用钩拳击打: *a left hook to the jaw* 照着下颌的一击左钩拳. **5** (idm 习语) **by ˌhook or by 'crook** by one means or another, no matter what happens 用种种方法; 千方百计. **ˌhook, line and 'sinker** entirely; completely 完全地; 全部地: *What I said was untrue but he fell for it/swallowed it* (ie believed it) *hook, line and sinker.* 我所说的并非实话, 他却完全信以为真. **off the 'hook** (of a telephone receiver) not replaced, thus preventing incoming calls (指电话听筒)未挂上(以防有电话打进): *He left the phone off the hook so that he wouldn't be disturbed.* 他不把电话听筒挂上, 以免受到打扰. **(let sb/get) off the 'hook** (*infml* 口) out of difficulty or trouble 脱离困境; 免除烦恼: *She was winning easily, but then she started to get careless and let her opponent off the hook*, ie allowed her to avoid being defeated. 她赢得很顺利, 可是跟着就大意起来了, 对手转忧为喜. **sling one's hook** ⇨ SLING *v*.

□ ˌ**hook and 'eye** small metal hook and loop which together form a fastening for clothes, etc (衣服等上的)钩眼扣: *a row of hooks and eyes* 一行钩眼扣.

'**hook-nose** *n* nose with a curved shape; aquiline nose 鹰钩鼻. '**hook-nosed** *adj*.

hook[2] /hʊk; hʊk/ *v* **1** (**a**) [I, Ipr, Tn, Tn·pr] **~ (sth) (on/onto/over/round sth)** (cause sth to) be fastened with or as if with a hook or hooks 钩住(某物): *These two pieces of the chain hook together.* 这两个链环套在一起. ○ *a dress that hooks/is hooked at the back* 从背面用钩眼扣扣住的连衣裙 ○ *hook the caravan (on)to the car* 把有篷的拖车跟汽车挂上 ○ *My shirt got hooked on a thorn.* 一根刺儿挂着了我的衬衣. (**b**) [Tn] catch (sth) with a hook 用钩子钩住(某物): *hook a large fish* 钓着一条大鱼 ○ (*fig joc* 比喻, 谑) *hook a husband/wife* 嫁人[娶妻]. **2** [Tn] make (sth) into the form of a hook 把(某物)弯成钩状: *hook one's finger* 屈指. **3** [Tn] (*sl* 俚) steal (sth) 偷窃(某物). **4** [Tn] (*sport* 体) (**a**) hit (a ball) in a curving path or with a curving stroke 击出(曲线球); 以弧线击(球). (**b**) (in Rugby football) kick (the ball) backwards in a scrum(1) (橄榄球)并列争球时钩射(球). **5** (idm 习语) **be hooked (on sb)** (*sl* 俚) be in love (with sb) 爱上(某人). **be/get hooked (on sth)** (*sl* 俚) be/become addicted (to sth); be/become completely committed (to sth) 迷上(某事物); 完全陷于(某事物)之中: *get hooked on heroin, gambling, television* 吸海洛因[赌博/看电视]上了瘾 ○ *She's completely hooked on the idea of a camping holiday.* 她一心想着来个野营度假. **6** (phr v) **hook sth/sb up** fasten (a garment) by means of hooks and eyes 用钩眼扣扣好(衣服): *hook up a dress* 把连衣裙上的钩眼扣扣好 ○ *Please will you hook me up* (ie fasten my dress up) *at the back?* 请你替我把后背的钩眼扣扣上好吗?(扣好连衣裙) **hook (sth) up (with sth)** link broadcasting facilities for special transmissions 连接无线电设备以播送特别节目; 联播: *The BBC is hooked up with Australian television by satellite.* 英国广播公司通过卫星与澳大利亚电视实行联播.

▷ **hooked** *adj* (**a**) curved like a hook 像钩一样弯曲的: *a hooked nose, beak* 钩形鼻、喙. (**b**) having a hook or hooks 有钩的.

□ '**hook-up** *n* link between two or more radio or television stations for the transmission of the same programme (广播电台或电视台的)联播: *a satellite hook-up between the major European networks* 欧洲各主要电视网之间的卫星联播.

hookah /'hʊkə; 'hʊkə/ (also **hubble-bubble**) *n* pipe used esp in Arab countries for smoking tobacco, with a long flexible tube to a container of water which cools the smoke as it is drawn through it (尤指阿拉伯国家用的)水烟袋.

hooker /'hʊkə(r); 'hʊkɚ/ *n* **1** (*sl* 俚 *esp US*) prostitute 妓女. **2** player in the front row of a scrum in Rugby football, who tries to hook[2](4) the ball (橄榄球并列争球时位于前排的)钩射队员.

hookey (also **hooky**) /'hʊkɪ; 'hʊkɪ/ *n* (idm 习语) **play 'hookey** (*sl* 俚 *esp US*) stay away from school, etc without permission; play truant 逃学; 旷课.

hook·worm /'hʊkwɜ:m; 'hʊkˌwɝm/ *n* (**a**) [C] worm that infests the intestines of men and animals 钩虫. (**b**) [U] disease caused by this 钩虫病.

hoo·li·gan /'hu:lɪgən; 'hulɪgən/ *n* disorderly and noisy young person who often behaves in a violent and destructive way; young thug or ruffian 小流氓; 阿飞: *acts of vandalism committed by football hooligans* 足球迷小流氓破坏公物的行为. ▷ **hoo·li·gan·ism** /-ɪzəm; -ˌɪzəm/ *n* [U].

hoop /hu:p; hup/ *n* **1** circular band of wood, metal, etc (木头、金属等做的)箍, 圈, 环: *a barrel bound with iron hoops* 加有铁箍的桶. **2** large ring used at a circus for riders or animals to jump through (马戏团中供骑手或动物穿越的)大圈. **3** large (usu wooden) ring used (esp formerly) as a child's toy (尤指旧时)儿童游戏用的大环子(通常为木质的). **4** (in croquet) small iron arch fixed in the ground, through which balls are hit (槌球戏中的)铁拱门. **5** (idm 习语) **put sb/go through the 'hoops** make sb/be made to endure a test or an ordeal 使某人经受考验或磨练.

▷ **hoop** *v* [Tn] bind or encircle (a barrel, etc) with hoops 用箍箍(桶等).

hoop-la /'hu:p lɑ:; 'hupˌlɑ/ *n* [U] game in which players try to throw rings over objects in order to win them as prizes 投环套物游戏(套中则获得该物).

hoo·poe /'hu:pu:; 'hupu/ *n* bird with a large fan-like crest and striped wing and tail feathers 戴胜(鸟名, 有大的扇状冠, 翼部及尾部的羽毛带有条纹).

hooray /hʊ'reɪ; hʊ're/ *interj* = HURRAH.

hoot /hu:t; hut/ *n* **1** cry of an owl 猫头鹰的叫声. **2** sound made by a vehicle's horn, factory siren, etc 车辆的喇叭、工厂汽笛等的鸣响声. **3** shout expressing disapproval or scorn 表示反对或轻蔑的喊叫声: *His suggestion was greeted with hoots of laughter.* 他的建议引起了阵阵嗤笑. **4** (*infml* 口) (**a**) loud laugh of delight and amusement 哈哈大笑. (**b**) thing that causes this 令人捧腹的事物: *What a hoot!* 真可笑! ○ *She looked an absolute hoot!* 她看起来十分可笑! **5** (idm 习语) **not care/give a hoot/two hoots** (*infml* 口) not care at all 毫不在乎.

▷ **hoot** *v* **1** [I, Ipr] **~ (at sb/sth)** make a hoot or hoots (猫头鹰)鸣叫; (车辆的喇叭、工厂汽笛等)鸣响; 嘘叫: *the eery sound of an owl hooting* 猫头鹰那怪异恐怖的叫声 ○ *The driver hooted at the sheep in the road.* 那司机按汽车喇叭把道路上的羊轰走. ○ *The crowd was hooting and jeering at the speaker.* 人群发出嘘叫声嘲笑那个演说者. ○ *He hooted with laughter.* 他哈哈大笑. **2** [Tn] make scornful hoots at (sb); greet with jeers 向(某人)发出轻蔑的喝叫声: *hoot a bad actor* 向蹩脚演员叫倒好. **3** [Tn, Tn·pr] **~ sth (at sb/sth)** sound (a horn) 鸣(喇叭): *The driver hooted his horn (at us).* 司机(冲着我们)鸣喇叭. **4** (phr v) **hoot sth/sb down/off; hoot sb off sth** reject sth or drive sb away (from a place) by jeering 以讥笑声拒绝某事物; 以嘘叫声把某人(从某处)轰走: *The proposal was hooted down.* 人们嘘叫着拒绝了这项建议. ○ *hoot a speaker off (a platform)* 把一个发言人轰下(台)去. **hooter** *n* **1** (*esp Brit*) siren or steam whistle, esp as a signal for work to start or stop at a factory, etc 汽笛; (尤指工厂等发出上下班信号的)汽笛. **2** (*dated* 旧 *esp Brit*) car horn 汽车喇叭. **3** (*Brit sl* 俚) nose 鼻子.

Hoover /'hu:və(r); 'huvɚ/ *n* (*propr* 专利名) vacuum cleaner 真空吸尘器.

▷ **hoover** *v* [Tn] clean (a carpet, etc) with a vacuum cleaner 用真空吸尘器吸干净(地毯等): *hoover the rug, floor, hall, whole house* 用真空吸尘器吸干净小地毯、地板、大厅、整个房子.

hooves *pl* of HOOF.

hop[1] /hɒp; hɑp/ *v* (**-pp-**) **1** [I, Ipr, Ip] (**a**) (of a person) move by jumping on one foot (指人)单足跳跃, 单足跳行: *He had hurt his left foot and had to hop along.* 他左脚受伤了, 不得不单足跳行. (**b**) (of an animal or a bird) move by jumping with both or all feet together (指鸟兽)双足或齐足跳行: *Several frogs were hopping about on the lawn.* 有几只青蛙在草地上跳来跳去. **2** [Tn] cross

H

(a ditch, etc) by jumping 跳过(沟等). **3** [Ip] **~ across/over (to...)** (*infml* 口) make a short quick trip to a place 作短途短期旅行: *I'm hopping over to Paris for the weekend.* 我要去巴黎度周末. **4** (idm 习语) **hop it** (*sl* 俚) go away 走开: *Go on, hop it!* 快点走开! ○ *When the burglar heard their car he hopped it out of the window.* 那窃贼听到他们汽车的声音就从窗口逃走了. **hopping 'mad** (*infml* 口) very angry 极其愤怒的; 暴跳如雷的. **5** (phr v) **hop in/into sth; hop out/out of sth** get into/out of (a car) 上[下](汽车): *Hop in, I'll give you a lift to the station.* 上车吧, 我开车送你去车站. **hop on/onto sth; hop off (sth)** jump (esp quickly) onto/off (a bus, etc) 跳(尤指急忙地)上[下](公共汽车等).

▷ **hop** *n* **1** act of hopping; short jump, esp on one leg (单足或齐足)跳跃; 短距离跳跃(尤指单足). **2** (*infml* 口) short flight or one stage in a long-distance flight 短距离飞行; (长距离飞行中的)一段航程: *the long flight across the Atlantic, then the final hop from New York to Boston* 先是横越大西洋的长距离飞行, 最后从纽约飞到波士顿 ○ *We flew from London to Bombay in one hop.* 我们从伦敦直接飞到孟买. **3** (*infml* 口) informal dance party (非正式的)舞会: *Are you coming to the hop tonight?* 今晚你来跳舞吗? **4** (idm 习语) **on the 'hop** (*infml* 口) active; busy 活跃的; 忙碌的: *I've been on the hop all day.* 我一天到晚忙得团团转. **(catch sb) on the 'hop** unprepared; taken by surprise 乘人不备的; 猝不及防的: *You've caught me on the hop, I'm afraid — give me five minutes to get ready.* 你弄得我措手不及——给我五分钟准备一下吧.

□ **hopped-up** /ˌhɒpt ˈʌp; ˌhɑpt ˈʌp/ *adj* (*US sl* 俚) **1** excited, esp by drugs 兴奋的(尤因毒品所致). **2** supercharged 增压的; 功率增大了的: *a ˌhopped-up ˈengine* 增压发动机.

hop² /hɒp; hɑp/ *n* **(a)** [C] climbing plant with flowers growing in clusters 葎草. **(b) hops** [pl] dried flowers of this plant, used for giving a bitter flavour to beer (干的)葎草, 忽布花, 啤酒花(用以增加啤酒苦味的). ▷ **hop·per** *n* = HOP-PICKER.

□ **'hop-field** (also **hop-garden**) *n* field in which hops are grown 啤酒花藤栽培园.

'hop-picker *n* worker or machine employed to pick hops 采摘啤酒花的工人或机器.

'hop-pole *n* tall pole for supporting wires on which hop plants are trained to grow (用以架线供啤酒花藤攀缘生长的)杆子.

hope /həʊp; hop/ *n* **1** [C, U] **~ (of/for sth); ~ (of doing sth/that...)** desire for sth to happen, combined with the expectation that it will 希望; 期望: *cherish a/the hope that he will recover* 希望他恢复健康 ○ *a ray of hope*, ie a slight hope 一线希望 ○ *Our hopes for fine weather were not disappointed.* 我们盼望天气好, 这倒并未落空. ○ *We've set/pinned all our hopes on you.* 我们全指望你了. ○ *She has (high) hopes* (ie is very confident) *of winning.* 她对胜利充满信心. ○ *Don't give up hope yet.* 不要就此失去信心. ○ *There is not much hope that they are/hope of their being still alive.* 他们仍然活着的希望不大. ○ *All hope (of finding them) was abandoned and the search was called off.* (找到他们的)一切希望都已化为泡影, 因而搜寻工作停止了. **2** [C usu *sing* 通常作单数] person, thing or circumstance that encourages hope 使人抱有希望的人、事物或情况: *You are my last hope; if you can't help, I'm ruined.* 你是我最后的希望, 你要是帮不了我, 我就完了. ○ *Does our only hope of survival lie in disarmament?* 我们求生的唯一希望就在于裁军吗? **3** (idm 习语) **be beyond hope** have no chance of succeeding, recovering, etc (成功、痊愈等)毫无希望. **build up/raise sb's hopes** encourage sb to expect better fortune, etc 使某人抱有希望: *Don't raise his hopes too much.* 不要让他存有奢望. **dash/shatter sb's hopes** cause sb to lose hope 使某人失望; 使某人的希望破灭: *All our hopes were dashed by the announcement.* 这事宣布后, 我们的一切希望都落空了. **a forlorn hope** ⇨ FORLORN. **have a hope (of doing sth)** have a chance of succeeding, recovering, etc 有(成功、痊愈等的)希望: *He has no hope of winning.* 他没有希望获胜. **hold out (some, not much, little, no, etc) hope (of sth/that...)** provide (some, etc) reason to expect sth 对(某事物)抱(一些)希望: *The doctors held out no hope of recovery.* 医生们对痊愈不抱希望. **in the hope of sth/that...** because of the wish for sth/that... 怀着...的希望: *I called in the hope of finding her at home.* 我希望她能在家才给她打的电话. **live in hope; live in hope(s) of sth** ⇨ LIVE². **not have a hope in hell** have no chance at all 不抱任何希望. **not a 'hope; ˌsome 'hope!** (there is) no chance at all (that that will happen) 毫无指望: *'He might turn up with the cash.' 'Some hope!'* '他也许会带钱来.' '那是妄想!'

▷ **hope** *v* [I, Ipr, Tf, Tt] **~ (for sth) 1 (a)** desire and expect (sth) or feel confident (about sth) 希望, 期待(某事物); (对某事物)有信心: *We haven't heard from him for weeks but we're still hoping (for a letter).* 我们已经有好几个星期没有听到他的消息了, 但是仍然在盼望着(能有信来). ○ *I hope to announce the winner shortly.* 我希望马上宣布胜利者的名字. **(b)** wish (sth); desire 但愿(某事物); 想望: *'Will it rain tomorrow?' 'I hope not/so.'* '明天会下雨吗?' '但愿不会下[能下].' ○ *We hope (that) you're well.* 我们希望你健康. **2** (idm 习语) **ˌhope against 'hope (that)...** continue to hope for sth even though it is very unlikely 对某事物仍抱一线希望. **ˌhope for the 'best** hope for a favourable result 希望获得好结果.

□ **'hope chest** (*US*) = BOTTOM DRAWER (BOTTOM).

NOTE ON USAGE 用法: Compare **hope** and **wish** as verbs. 试比较作为动词的 **hope** 和 **wish**. **1 Hope (that)** indicates a desire relating to the past, present or future ☆ **hope (that)** 指与过去、现在或未来有关的希望: *I hope you weren't late.* 我希望你没有迟到. ○ *I hope you're ready.* 我希望你已经准备好了. ○ *We hope you'll be very happy.* 我们希望你非常幸福. **Wish (that)** expresses regret about the past, present or future ☆ **wish (that)** 表达的是过去、现在或将来发生的令人遗憾的事: *I wish I hadn't gone to that party*, ie but I went. 我那时要是不去参加聚会就好了(但是我去了). ○ *I wish I could speak Chinese*, ie but I can't. 我要是会说汉语该多好(但是我不会说). ○ *I wish I was going on holiday next month*, ie but I'm not. 我要是下个月去度假多好哇(但是我不能去). **2 Hope** and **wish** can also be used with an infinitive, in which case their meanings are closer. ☆ **hope** 和 **wish** 亦可与不定式连用, 此时两者意义较为接近. *She hopes to get a job overseas* means she has a strong desire to get one and there's a good possibility that she will. ☆ She hopes to get a job overseas(她希望找个海外的工作)意为她有此强烈愿望并极有可能实现. *She wishes to get a job overseas* is a formal way of saying that she wants to get one. ☆ She wishes to get a job overseas(她盼望找个海外的工作)是表达她有此愿望的郑重说法.

hope·ful /ˈhəʊpfl; ˈhopfəl/ *adj* **1** [usu pred 通常作表语] **~ (of/about sth); ~ (that...)** (of a person) having hope (指人)抱有希望: *be hopeful about the future* 对未来充满希望 ○ *I feel hopeful of success/that we shall succeed.* 我对成功[我们将获得成功]抱有希望. **2** (of a sign, situation, etc) giving hope; likely to be favourable or successful; promising (指征兆、情况等)有希望的, 顺利的, 有前途的: *The future does not seem very hopeful.* 前途似乎有点不妙.

▷ **hope·ful** *n* person who hopes or seems likely to succeed 抱有希望的人; 有望获得成功的人: *the young hopefuls, lined up before the judges* 在评判员面前排成行的雄心勃勃的年轻人 ○ *Many a young hopeful went to Hollywood.* 许多满怀希望的青年涌至好莱坞. **hope·fully** *adv* **1** in a hopeful way 抱有希望地: *'I'm sure we'll find it,' he said hopefully.* '我肯定我们能找到它,' 他信心十足地说. **2** it is to be hoped; let us hope 可望; 我们可以指望: *Hopefully, we'll arrive before dark.* 我们可望天黑以前到达. **hope·ful·ness** *n* [U].

NOTE ON USAGE 用法: There is a group of adverbs and adverbial phrases (eg **frankly, obviously, to begin with**) which can be used in two distinct ways 有些副词和副词性词组(如 **frankly**、**obviously**、**to begin with** 等)可以有两种迥然不同的用法: **1** They may modify the whole sentence 可以用作全句的修饰语: *Frankly, you are wrong.* 说实在的, 你错了. ○ *Obviously, I'd prefer a better job.* 明说了吧, 我想找个更好的工作. ○ *To begin with, I don't like his attitude.* 第一

点，我不喜欢他的态度. **2** They may simply modify the verb 可以单纯用作动词的修饰语: *He spoke frankly* (= in a frank way) *about his past life.* 他坦率地讲述了他过去的生活. ○ *He pointed very obviously at the woman in the fur coat.* 他显然指的是那个穿着毛皮大衣的女子. ○ *I liked it in America to begin with.* 我起初是喜欢美国的这一点的. Other examples are **generally, hopefully, personally, really, sadly, seriously, thankfully.** 属于这一类的还有**generally**、**hopefully**、**personally**、**really**、**sadly**、**seriously**、**thankfully**等. Some careful speakers use **hopefully** only in pattern 2, but its use in pattern 1 is now widely accepted. 有些用词严谨的人使用**hopefully**仅限于第二式，但第一式的用法现已广为接受.

hope·less /ˈhəʊplɪs; ˈhoplɪs/ *adj* **1** most unlikely to improve, succeed, be settled, etc; causing despair 没有希望的; 令人绝望的: *a hopeless situation, struggle, attempt, etc* 没有希望的局势、斗争、尝试等 ○ *It's hopeless trying to convince her.* 要说服她是没有希望的. ○ *Most of the students are making good progress but Jeremy seems a hopeless case,* ie he cannot or will not learn anything. 大多数学生进步都很快，但杰里米却似乎无可救药. **2 ~ (at sth)** (*infml* 口) (of a person) lacking in ability or skill; incompetent (指人)无能的, 无技巧的, 不能胜任的: *a hopeless cook, teacher, etc* 滥竽充数的厨子、教员等 ○ *He's hopeless at maths.* 他对数学一窍不通. ▷ **hope·lessly** *adv*: *a hopelessly ill patient* 身患绝症的病人 ○ *be hopelessly lost* 完全失去踪影 ○ *be hopelessly in love, in debt* 堕入情网、债台高筑不能自拔. **hope·less·ness** *n* [U].

hop·per[1] /ˈhɒpə(r); ˈhɑpɚ/ *n* (**a**) V-shaped structure for holding (esp) grain or coal, with an opening at its base through which the contents can pass into a mill, furnace, etc below (碾磨机、熔炉等的)漏斗, 送料斗. (**b**) any similar device for feeding materials into a machine, etc (向机器等供料的)漏斗状装置.

hop·per[2] /ˈhɒpə(r); ˈhɑpɚ/ *n* any hopping insect, eg a flea 蹦跳的昆虫(如跳蚤).

hop·scotch /ˈhɒpskɒtʃ; ˈhɑpˌskɑtʃ/ *n* [U] children's game of hopping into and over squares marked on the ground in order to retrieve a stone thrown into one of these squares 跳房子, 跳间(一种儿童游戏).

horde /hɔːd; hɔrd/ *n* (*sometimes derog* 有时作贬义) very large group (esp of people); huge crowd; throng 大群, 大帮(尤指人); 人群: *hordes of fans, tourists, football supporters, shoppers, etc* 大群的狂热爱好者、旅游者、足球迷观众、购物者等 ○ *There were hordes of people at the jumble sale.* 废旧货物拍卖场上人山人海. ○ *Fans had descended on the concert hall in their hordes,* ie in large numbers. 大群的歌迷一窝蜂地涌向音乐厅. ○ *The plains were overrun by Tartar hordes.* 这些平原上散布着鞑靼人的游牧部落.

ho·ri·zon /həˈraɪzn; həˈraɪzn̩/ *n* **1 the horizon** [sing] the line at which the earth and sky appear to meet 地平线: *The sun sank below the horizon.* 太阳已落到地平线下. ○ *A ship appeared on the horizon.* 在天水交接处出现了一艘船. **2** [C usu *pl* 通常作复数] (*fig* 比喻) limit of a person's knowledge, experience, interest, etc (知识、经验、兴趣等的)范围, 见识, 眼界: *a woman of narrow horizons* 眼界狭小的女子 ○ *Travel broadens one's horizons.* 旅行可开阔人的眼界. **3** (idm 习语) **on the hoˈrizon** about to happen; just becoming apparent; imminent 即将发生的; 已露端倪的; 临近的: *There's trouble on the horizon.* 很快就会出事.

ho·ri·zontal /ˌhɒrɪˈzɒntl; US ˌhɔːr-; ˌhɔrəˈzɑntl̩/ *adj* parallel to the horizon; flat; level 与地平线平行的; 平的; 水平的: *a horizontal line* 水平线. ⇨illus at VERTICAL 见VERTICAL插图.
▷ **ho·ri·zontal** *n* [C, sing] horizontal line, bar, etc 水平的线、条、杠等: *He shifted his position from the horizontal.* 他在单杠上变换了姿势.
ho·ri·zont·ally /-təlɪ; -tl̩ɪ/ *adv*: *Lay it horizontally on the floor.* 把它平放在地板上.

hor·mone /ˈhɔːməʊn; ˈhɔrmon/ *n* (**a**) substance produced within the body of an animal and carried by the blood to an organ which it stimulates to assist growth, etc; similar substance produced by a plant and transported in the sap 激素; 荷尔蒙: [attrib 作定语] *hormone deficiency, imbalance* 激素缺乏、失调. (**b**) synthetic substance that has a similar effect 合成激素.
▷ **hor·monal** /hɔːˈməʊnl; hɔrˈmonl̩/ *adj* of a hormone or hormones 激素的; 荷尔蒙的.

horn /hɔːn; hɔrn/ *n* **1** (**a**) [C] bony outgrowth, usu curved and pointed and one of a pair, on the heads of cattle, deer, rams and various other animals (牛、鹿、羊等动物的)角. ⇨illus at SHEEP 见SHEEP插图. (**b**) [U] hard smooth substance of which this is made 角质. **2** [C] any of the various wind instruments with a trumpet-shaped end (乐器中的)号: *a French ˈhorn* 法国号 ○ *a ˈhunting horn* 猎号. **3** [C] device for sounding a warning signal 示警装置: *a ˈcar horn* 汽车喇叭 ○ *sound the horn to alert a cyclist* 向骑自行车的人鸣喇叭示警 ○ (*joc* 谑) *He's got a voice like a ˈfog-horn.* 他嗓音像雾号, 又粗又响. **4** [C] thing resembling an animal's horn, eg the projection on the head of a snail 像动物的角之物(如蜗牛的触角). **5** [C] either of the ends of the crescent moon (新月的)钩尖. **6** (idm 习语) **draw in one's horns** ⇨ DRAW[2]. **on the horns of a diˈlemma** faced with a choice betwen things that are equally undesirable 进退维谷. **take the bull by the horns** ⇨ BULL[1].
▷ **horn** *v* (phr v) **horn in (on sth)** (*sl* 俚) join in (an attractive or a profitable undertaking, etc) without being invited; intrude 强行介入(有吸引力的或有利可图的事情等); 闯入.
horned *adj* (often in compound *adjs* 常用以构成复合形容词) having horns, esp of the specified type 有角的; (尤指)有某种角的: *horned cattle* 有角的牛 ○ *long-horned cattle* 长着长角的牛.
horn·less *adj* without horns 无角的.
horn·like *adj* **1** similar to a horn(1a) in shape 角状的. **2** hard like horn(1b) 坚硬似角的.
horny *adj* (**-ier, -iest**) **1** made of horn 角制的. **2** made hard and rough, eg by hard work 坚硬而粗糙的(如因做粗活儿所致): *horny hands* 粗硬起茧的双手. **3** (*sl* 俚) sexually aroused 引起性欲的: *feeling horny* 欲火中烧.
□ **ˈhornbill** *n* tropical bird with a hornlike growth on its beak 犀鸟.
horn of plenty = CORNUCOPIA.
ˈhorn-rimmed *adj* (of spectacles) with frames made of a material like horn (指眼镜)仿角质镜架的.

horn·beam /ˈhɔːnbiːm; ˈhɔrnˌbim/ *n* type of tree with smooth grey bark and hard tough wood, often used in hedges 鹅耳枥(树, 皮光滑, 灰色, 木质坚韧, 常用以构筑树篱).

hor·net /ˈhɔːnɪt; ˈhɔrnɪt/ *n* **1** large type of wasp that can give a severe sting 大黄蜂; 马蜂. **2** (idm 习语) **a ˈhornet's nest** attacks, criticism or abuse from several people, or angry quarrelling (一些人的)攻击、批评或辱骂; 愤怒的争吵: *His letter to the newspaper about racialism in schools has stirred up a real hornet's nest.* 他给报纸写的关于学校中存在种族歧视现象的信件引起了很大的麻烦.

horn·pipe /ˈhɔːnpaɪp; ˈhɔrnˌpaɪp/ *n* **1** lively dance usu performed by one person and traditionally associated with sailors 角笛舞. **2** music for such a dance 角笛舞曲.

horo·scope /ˈhɒrəskəʊp; US ˈhɔːr-; ˈhɔrəˌskop/ *n* **1** forecast of a person's future based on a diagram showing the relative positions of the planets, etc at a particular time, eg the time of his birth 占星术: *read one's horoscope* 根据占星术算命. Cf 参看 ASTROLOGY, ZODIAC. **2** such a diagram, made by an astrologer 天宫图.

hor·rend·ous /hɒˈrendəs; hɔˈrɛndəs/ *adj* (*infml* 口) horrifying; horrific 可怕的; 令人吃惊的: *horrendous queues, prices, clothes* 令人吃惊的长队、价格、衣服 ○ *That colour scheme is horrendous.* 那样的色彩设计真让人吃惊. ▷ **hor·rend·ously** *adv*: *horrendously expensive* 贵得惊人的.

hor·rible /ˈhɒrəbl; US ˈhɔːr-; ˈhɔrəbl̩/ *adj* **1** causing horror 可怕的; 令人恐惧的: *a horrible crime, nightmare, death* 骇人听闻的罪行、叫人心惊胆颤的恶梦、令人恐惧的死亡. **2** (*infml* 口) very unpleasant 令人极不愉快的: *horrible weather, food, people* 糟糕的天气、难吃的食物、极不友好的人 ○ *It tastes horrible.* 这味道很不好. ○ *Don't be so horrible (to me).* 别那么(让我)讨厌. ▷ **hor·ribly** /-əblɪ; -əblɪ/ *adv*: *horribly burnt* 严重烧伤的 ○ *He died horribly and in great pain.* 他死得非常可怖、非

常痛苦.

hor·rid /ˈhɒrɪd; *US* ˈhɔːrɪd; ˋhɔrɪd/ *adj* **1** terrible; frightful; horrible 可怕的; 恐怖的; 令人惊恐的: *horrid cruelty, crimes* 骇人听闻的残暴行为、罪行. **2** (*infml* 口) very unpleasant 令人极不愉快的: *horrid weather, food, children* 糟糕的天气、难吃的食物、讨厌的孩子 ○ *Don't be so horrid to your little sister.* 别对你的小妹妹那么厉害. ▷ **hor·ridly** *adv.* **hor·rid·ness** *n* [U].

hor·rific /həˈrɪfɪk; hɔˈrɪfɪk/ *adj* **1** causing horror; horrifying 令人恐惧的; 可怕的: *a horrific crash, murder* 令人心惊胆颤的相撞事故、谋杀. **2** (*infml* 口) excessive; causing horror 过分的; 吓人的: *horrific prices* 过高的价格. ▷ **hor·rif·ic·ally** /-klɪ; -klɪ/ *adv* (*infml* 口): *The hotel was horrifically expensive.* 这旅馆收费高得吓人.

hor·rify /ˈhɒrɪfaɪ; *US* ˈhɔːr-; ˋhɔrə,faɪ/ *v* (*pt, pp* **-fied**) [Tn] fill (sb) with horror; shock greatly 使(某人)恐惧或受惊吓; 使震惊: *We were horrified by what we saw.* 我们看到后很害怕. ▷ **hor·ri·fy·ing** *adj*: *a horrifying sight, experience* 怵目惊心的景象、使人震惊的经历 ○ (*infml* 口) *I find their ignorance horrifying.* 我感到他们简直愚昧到了极点. **hor·ri·fy·ingly** *adv.*

hor·ror /ˈhɒrə(r); *US* ˈhɔːr-; ˋhɔrɚ/ *n* **1** [U] feeling of intense fear or dismay; terror 恐怖; 恐惧; 惊恐: *I recoiled in horror from the snake.* 那条蛇把我吓得直往后缩. ○ *To her horror she saw him fall.* 她看见他跌下而惊恐万状. ○ *I have a/this horror of being trapped in a broken lift.* 我常害怕电梯有故障会把我困于其中. **2** [U] (**a**) feeling of intense dislike; hatred 强烈的厌恶; 憎恶; 痛恨: *I have a deep horror of cruelty.* 我对残暴的行为深恶痛绝. (**b**) horrifying nature 恐怖的性质或实况: *It's hard to appreciate the full horror of life in a prison camp.* 战俘营中骇人听闻的生活惨状外人是很难完全体验到的. **3** [C] thing or person that causes hatred or fear 讨厌的事物或人; 令人感到恐怖的事物或人: *the horrors of war* 战争的惨状. **4** [C] (*infml* 口) bad or mischievous person, esp a naughty child 坏蛋; 恶作剧的傢伙; (尤指)顽皮的孩子: *Her son is a right little horror.* 她的儿子是个不折不扣的小淘气. **5 the horrors** [pl] (*infml* 口) fit of depression or nervousness, etc 抑郁症或神经过敏等之发作: *Having to address an audience always gives me the horrors.* 在大庭广众面前讲话, 我总是感到非常紧张.

▷ **hor·ror** *adj* [attrib 作定语] designed to entertain by arousing pleasurable feelings of horror, shock, etc 以恐怖、惊吓等为刺激以资娱乐的: *horror films/stories/comics* 恐怖影片[故事/连环图画].

H

horrors *interj* (*usu joc* 通常作戏谑语) used to express fear or dislike 用以表示恐惧或厌恶: *Oh horrors! Not another invitation to tea with Aunt Muriel!* 哎哟! 可别再应邀去缪里尔大婶那里参加茶会了!

□ ˈ**horror-stricken** (also ˈ**horror-struck**) *adj* overcome with horror; very shocked 受惊吓的; 惊恐万状的.

hors de com·bat /ˌɔː də ˈkɒmbɑː; ˋɔrdəˋkambɑ/ (*French* 法) unable to continue fighting because one is wounded 因受伤而不能继续战斗的; 丧失战斗力的: (*fig* 比喻) *I can't play you at squash this week — I'm hors de combat with a twisted ankle.* 本星期我不能和你打壁球了——我的脚踝扭伤了.

hors-d'oeuvre /ˌɔːˈdɜːvrə; *US* -ˈdɜːv; ɔrˈdɝv/ *n* (*pl* unchanged or **-d'oeuvres** 复数或不变或作 **hors-d'oeuvres**) food served at the beginning of a meal as an appetizer (餐前的)开胃小吃.

horse /hɔːs; hɔrs/ *n* **1** (**a**) [C] large four-legged animal with a flowing mane and tail, used for riding on or to carry loads, pull carts, etc 马. ⇨illus 见插图. Cf 参看 COLT[1], FILLY, FOAL, GELDING (GELD), MARE, STALLION. (**b**) [C] adult male horse; stallion (未阉过的)成年公马. (**c**) [Gp, U] mounted soldiers; cavalry 骑马的军人; 骑兵: *a detachment of horse* 骑兵小分队. **2** [C] = VAULTING HORSE (VAULT[2]). **3** [C] frame on which sth is supported 支架: *a ˈclothes-horse* 衣架. **4** [U] (*sl* 俚) heroin 海洛因. **5** (idm 习语) **be/get on one's high horse** ⇨ HIGH[1]. **back the wrong horse** ⇨ BACK[4]. **change/swap horses in midˈstream** transfer one's preference for or trust in sb/sth to another in the middle of an undertaking 在做一件事的中途对某人[某事物]做出重大变动. **a dark horse** ⇨ DARK[2]. **drive a coach and horses through sth** ⇨ DRIVE[1]. **eat like a horse** ⇨ EAT. **flog a dead horse** ⇨ FLOG. **(straight) from the horse's ˈmouth** (of advice, information) given by sb who is directly involved or very reliable (指劝告、情报等)来自直接参与者的, 从可靠的人那里获得的. **hold one's ˈhorses** (*infml* 口) wait a moment; restrain one's impatience, enthusiasm, etc 等一下; 忍耐、控制自己的热情等. **you can ˌtake, etc a horse to ˈwater, but you ˌcan't make him ˈdrink** (*saying* 谚) you can give a person the opportunity to do sth but he may still refuse to do it 牵马到水边易, 逼马饮水难(即使给某人机会, 他也不一定利用). **lock, etc the stable door after the horse has bolted** ⇨ STABLE[2]. **look a gift horse in the mouth** ⇨ GIFT. **put the cart before the horse** ⇨ CART. **a willing horse** ⇨ WILLING.

horse 马

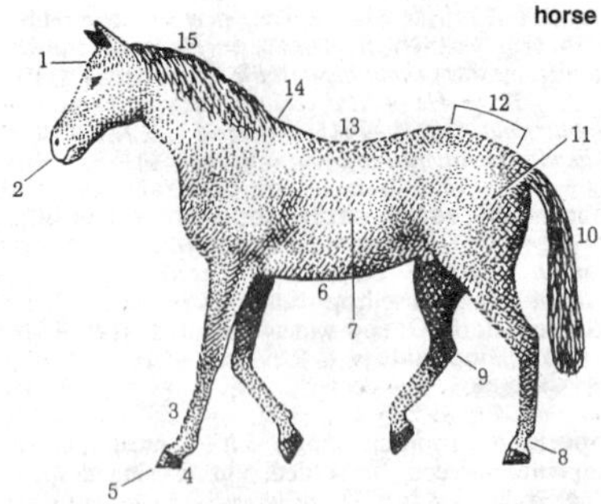

1 forelock 额发
2 muzzle 吻突
3 shank 胫
4 pastern 系部
5 hoof 蹄
6 belly 腹部
7 flank 胁
8 fetlock 球节
9 hock 跗关节
10 tail 尾
11 croup 臀部
12 hindquarters 臀部和后腿
13 back 脊背
14 withers 马肩隆
15 mane 鬃

▷ **horse** *v* (phr v) **horse about/around** (*infml* 口) act in a noisy rough playful way 哄闹; 捣蛋.

□ ˌ**horse-and-ˈbuggy** *adj* [attrib 作定语] (*US infml* 口) of times before motorized vehicles; old-fashioned 机动车发明以前的; 马车时代的; 老式的: (*fig* 比喻) *ˌhorse-and-buggy eduˈcational methods* 旧式教育方法.

ˈ**horseback** *n* (idm 习语) **on** ˈ**horseback** mounted on a horse 骑着马的: *riding on horseback* 骑马. — *adv, adj* [attrib 作定语] (*esp US*): *Do you like to ride horseback?* 你喜欢骑马吗? ○ *horseback riding* 骑马.

ˈ**horse-box** *n* closed vehicle for transporting a horse 运马用的棚车.

ˌ**horse-ˈchestnut** *n* **1** large tree with widely spreading branches and tall clusters of white or pink flowers 七叶树, 马栗(高大乔木, 树枝扩展很大, 顶生白色或粉红色花簇). ⇨illus at App 1 见附录1插图, page i. **2** its reddish-brown nut 七叶树的红褐色坚果.

ˈ**horseflesh** *n* [U] **1** (also ˈ**horsemeat**) flesh of a horse, used as food (供食用的)马肉. **2** horses collectively 马(总称): *He's a good judge of horseflesh.* 他是个相马能手.

ˈ**horse-fly** *n* any of various large insects that bite horses, cattle, etc 叮咬马、牛等的大昆虫; 虻; 马蝇.

ˈ**Horse Guards** (*Brit*) cavalry brigade of troops guarding the sovereign 皇家骑兵卫队.

ˈ**horsehair** *n* [U] hair from the mane or tail of a horse, used esp for padding furniture, etc 马鬃, 马尾毛(尤用作家具等的垫料).

ˈ**horse laugh** loud coarse laugh 哈哈大笑.

ˈ**horseman** /-mən; -mən/ *n* (*pl* **-men** /-mən; -mən/, *fem* 阴性作 ˈ**horsewoman**) rider on horseback, esp a skilled one 骑马者; (尤指)骑手. ˈ**horsemanship** *n* [U] art of or skill in riding horses 骑术; 马术.

ˈ**horseplay** *n* [U] rough noisy fun or play 喧闹的娱乐.

ˈ**horse-race** *n* race between horses with riders 赛马.

ˈ**horse-racing** *n* [U] ⇨App 4 见附录4.

ˈ**horse sense** (*infml* 口) basic common sense; ordinary wisdom 常识; 一般的见识.

ˈ**horseshoe** (also **shoe**) *n* **1** U-shaped piece of iron nailed to the bottom of a horse's hoof and regarded as a symbol of good luck 马蹄铁；马掌；马蹄铁吉祥物. **2** thing having this shape 马蹄铁形物: *Stand in a horseshoe facing me.* 面向我排成半圆形站着. ○ [attrib 作定语] *a horseshoe bend* 马蹄铁形弯曲.

'horse-trading *n* [U] (*esp US*) shrewd bargaining; clever business dealing 精明的讨价还价；手段精明的交易.

'horsewhip *n* whip used for driving horses 马鞭. — *v* **(-pp-)** [Tn] beat (sb) with a horsewhip 用马鞭鞭打(某人).

'horsewoman *n* (*pl* **-women**) woman rider on horseback, esp a skilled one 骑马的女子；(尤指)女骑手: *a fine horsewoman* 出色的女骑手.

horse·power /'hɔ:spaʊə(r); 'hɔrs,paʊɚ/ *n* (*pl* unchanged 复数不变) (*abbr* 缩写 **hp**) unit for measuring the power of an engine, etc (550 foot-pounds per second, about 750 watts) 马力(功率单位, 1马力等于每秒钟把550磅重的物体提高1英尺所作的功, 约为750瓦): [attrib 作定语] *a twelve horsepower engine* 一台十二马力的发动机.

horse-rad·ish /'hɔ:s rædɪʃ; 'hɔrs,rædɪʃ/ *n* [U] (plant with a) hot-tasting root which is grated to make a cold sauce 辣根(植物)；辣根(辣根的根, 磨碎后可制成调味汁): [attrib 作定语] *roast beef with horse-radish sauce* 浇有辣根沙司的烤牛肉.

horsy /'hɔ:sɪ; 'hɔrsɪ/ *adj* **1** of or like a horse 马的；似马的: *He had a long, rather horsy face.* 他的脸很长, 有点像马的脸. **2** interested in or involved with horses and horse-racing; showing this in one's dress, conversation, etc 喜爱马和赛马的；(在衣着、谈吐等方面)与马和赛马有关的: *She comes from a very horsy family.* 她出生于一个爱马的家庭.

hor·ti·cul·ture /'hɔ:tɪkʌltʃə(r); 'hɔrtɪ,kʌltʃɚ/ *n* [U] art of growing flowers, fruit and vegetables; gardening 园艺；园艺学.

▷ **hor·ti·cul·tural** /,hɔ:tɪ'kʌltʃərəl; ,hɔrtɪ'kʌltʃərəl/ *adj*: *a horticultural show, society, expert* 园艺展览、协会、专家. **hor·ti·cul·tur·ist** /,hɔ:tɪ'kʌltʃərɪst; ,hɔrtɪ'kʌltʃərɪst/ *n* person who practises horticulture; skilled gardener 园艺家；园艺学家.

hos·anna /həʊ'zænə; ho'zænə/ *interj*, *n* shout of praise and worship to God 和散那(赞美和崇敬上帝的呼喊声).

hose[1] /həʊz; hoz/ (also **'hose-pipe**) *n* [C, U] flexible tube made of rubber, plastic or canvas and used for directing water onto fires, gardens, etc 软管(橡皮、塑料或帆布制成, 用以输水救火、浇花等): *a length of hose* 一段软管 ○ *The firemen played their hoses on* (ie directed them at) *the burning building.* 消防队员用水龙向失火的建筑物喷水. ⇨illus at App 1 见附录1插图, page vii.

▷ **hose** *v* [Tn, Tn·p] **~ sth/sb (down)** wash or water sth/sb using a hose 用软管洗或浇某物[某人]: *hose the flower-beds* 用软管输水浇花坛里的花 ○ *hose down the car* 用软管输水冲洗汽车.

hose[2] /həʊz; hoz/ *n* [pl *v*] **1** (esp in shops 尤用于商店中) stockings, socks and tights 长统袜；短袜；裤袜. **2** garment covering the body from the waist to the knees or feet, formerly worn by men; breeches (旧时男子穿的)紧身裤, 齐膝短裤: *doublet and hose* 男式紧身上衣和紧身裤.

ho·sier /'həʊzɪə(r); *US* -ʒər; 'hoʒɚ/ *n* (*dated or fml* 旧或文) person who sells stockings and socks 卖袜子的商人.

▷ **ho·si·ery** /'həʊzɪərɪ; *US* 'həʊʒərɪ; 'hoʒərɪ/ *n* [U] (esp in shops 尤用于商店中) stockings, socks and knitted or woven underwear (袜子及内衣等)针织品: [attrib 作定语] *the hosiery department* 针织品部.

hos·pice /'hɒspɪs; 'hɑspɪs/ *n* **1** (**a**) hospital for dying people 末期病人安养所. (**b**) home for very poor people in need of food and shelter 救济院. **2** (*arch* 古) house where travellers could stay and rest, esp one kept by a religious order 旅客招待所(尤指宗教团体办的).

hos·pit·able /hɒ'spɪtəbl, *also* 'hɒspɪtəbl; hɑ'spɪtəbl, 'hɑspɪtəbl/ *adj* **~ (to/towards sb)** (of a person) pleased to welcome and entertain guests; giving hospitality (指人)乐于接待客人的, 好客的: *She is always hospitable to visitors from abroad.* 她总是殷勤招待外宾. ▷ **hos·pit·ably** /-əblɪ; -əblɪ/ *adv*.

hos·pital /'hɒspɪtl; 'hɑspɪtl/ *n* institution providing medical and surgical treatment and nursing care for ill or injured people 医院: *go to hospital*, ie as a patient 去医院看病 ○ *I'm going to the hospital to visit my brother.* 我要去医院看望我的哥哥. ○ *be admitted to/be taken to/be released from/be discharged from hospital* 入[出]院 ○ *The injured were rushed to hospital in an ambulance.* 救护车把伤者火速送往医院. ○ *He died in hospital.* 他死在医院里. ○ *I've never been in hospital*, ie as a patient. 我从未住过院. ○ [attrib 作定语] *a hospital nurse* 医院护士 ○ *receive hospital treatment* 在医院接受治疗. ⇨Usage at SCHOOL[1] 用法见SCHOOL[1].

▷ **hos·pit·al·ize, -ise** *v* [Tn esp passive 尤用于被动语态] send or admit (sb) to hospital 将(某人)送入医院；准予(某人)住院治疗. **hos·pit·al·iza·tion, -isation** /,hɒspɪtəlaɪ'zeɪʃn; *US* -lɪ'z-; ,hɑspɪtəlɪ'zeʃən/ *n* [U]: *a long period of hospitalization* 很长的住院治疗时期.

hos·pit·al·ity /,hɒspɪ'tælətɪ; ,hɑspɪ'tælətɪ/ *n* [U] friendly and generous reception and entertainment of guests or strangers, esp in one's own home 殷勤待客；好客: *Thank you for your kind hospitality.* 谢谢你的盛情款待. ○ [attrib 作定语] *a hospitality room, suite, coach*, ie one reserved for the use of guests in a hotel, TV studio, etc (旅馆、电视台等的)迎宾室、套间、大轿车.

host[1] /həʊst; host/ *n* **1 ~ of sb/sth** large number of people or things 大群, 众多, 许多(人或事物): *He has hosts of friends.* 他有很多朋友. ○ *I can't come, for a whole host of reasons.* 由于种种原因, 我来不了. **2** (*arch* 古) army 军队.

host[2] /həʊst; host/ *n* **1** (*fem* 阴性作 **hostess** /'həʊstɪs; 'hostɪs/) person who receives and entertains one or more other people as guests (待客的)主人: *I was away so my son acted as host.* 我那时不在家, 所以由我的儿子招待客人. ○ *Mr and Mrs Hill are such good hosts.* 希尔先生和夫人招待客人真周到. ○ [attrib 作定语] *the host nation*, eg for an international conference, etc 东道国, 主办国(如主办召开国际会议等). **2** (*fem* 阴性作 **hostess**) compère of a television programme, etc (电视节目等的)主持人: *Your host on tonight's show is Max Astor.* 今晚表演节目的主持人是马克斯·阿斯特. **3** (*dated or joc* 旧或谑) landlord of an inn; publican 旅店老板；酒店老板: *mine host* 我住的旅店的老板. **4** animal or plant on which a parasite lives 寄主, 宿主(寄生物所寄生的动植物): [attrib 作定语] *host organisms* 寄主. **5** (idm 习语) **be/play host to sb** receive and entertain sb as a guest (作为主人)招待或款待某人: *The college is (playing) host to a group of visiting Russian scientists.* 这所学院接待了一批来访的俄国科学家.

▷ **host** *v* [Tn] act as host at (an event) or to (a person) 主办或主持(某活动)；作为主人招待(某人): *Which country is hosting the Games this year?* 今年的运动会由哪国主办? ○ *Hosting our show this evening is the lovely Gloria Monroe.* 我们今晚的演出由美丽的格洛丽亚·门罗主持.

host[3] /həʊst; host/ *n* **the Host** [sing] the bread that is blessed and eaten at Holy Communion (在圣餐中经祝祷而食用的)圣饼.

host·age /'hɒstɪdʒ; 'hɑstɪdʒ/ *n* **1** person held as a captive by one or more others who threaten to keep, harm or kill him unless certain demands are met 人质: *The hijackers kept the pilot on board the plane as (a) hostage.* 劫机者把飞机驾驶员扣留在飞机上作为人质. **2** (idm 习语) **a ,hostage to 'fortune** (*fml* 文) person or thing that one acquires and may then suffer by losing, esp a husband or wife or child 希望得到的但需蒙受可能失去之痛苦的人或事物(尤指配偶或子女). **take/hold sb 'hostage** seize/keep sb as a hostage 抓住[扣押]某人作为人质: *The gunman is holding two children hostage in the building.* 持枪歹徒把两个孩子扣押在这座建筑物里当作人质.

hos·tel /'hɒstl; 'hɑstl̩/ *n* building in which (usu cheap) food and lodging are provided for students, certain groups of workers, the homeless, travellers, etc (为学生、某些工人、无家者、旅客等提供膳宿的)寄宿舍, 招待所(通常收费低廉): *a youth hostel* 青年招待所.

▷ **hos·tel·ler** (*US* **hos·teler**) /'hɒstələ(r); 'hɑstl̩ɚ/ *n* person who travels around staying in youth hostels (沿途投宿青年招待所的)旅行者.

hos·telry /'hɒstəlrɪ; 'hɑstl̩rɪ/ *n* (*arch or joc* 古或谑) inn; public house 客栈；旅店: *Why don't we adjourn to the*

H

local hostelry? 我们怎么不搬到本地旅馆去住呢?

host·ess /ˈhəʊstɪs; ˋhostɪs/ *n* **1** woman who receives and entertains one or more other people as guests (待客的)女主人. **2** woman employed to welcome and entertain people at a night-club, etc, or to provide information at an exhibition, etc (夜总会等的)女招待; (展览会等的)女解说员. **3** = AIR-HOSTESS (AIR[1]). **4** female compère of a television programme, etc (电视节目等的)女主持人. Cf 参看 HOST 2.

hos·tile /ˈhɒstaɪl; *US* -tl; ˋhɑstḷ/ *adj* **1** ~ **(to/towards sb/sth)** (**a**) showing strong dislike or enmity; very unfriendly 显示极厌恶的; 含敌意的; 极不友好的: *a hostile crowd, glance, review, reception* 怀有敌意的群众、一瞥、评论、接待 ○ *She found his manner towards her distinctly hostile.* 她觉得他对她的态度极不友好. (**b**) [usu pred 通常作表语] showing rejection of sth; opposed to sth 对某事物持否定态度; 反对某事物: *be hostile to reform* 反对改革. **2** of an enemy; warlike 敌人的; 敌方的; 敌对的: *hostile aircraft* 敌机. ▷ **hos·tilely** *adv.*

hos·til·ity /hɒˈstɪlətɪ; hɑsˋtɪlətɪ/ *n* **1** [U] ~ **(to/towards sb/sth)** (**a**) being hostile (to sb/sth); antagonism; enmity 敌对; 对抗; 敌意: *feelings of hostility* 敌对情绪 ○ *feel no hostility towards anyone* 对任何人均无敌意 ○ *show hostility to sb/sth* 对某人[某事物]表示敌意. (**b**) opposition; rejection 反对; 否决: *His suggestion met with some hostility.* 他的建议遭到某种程度的反对. **2** **hostilities** [pl] acts of war; fighting 战争行动; 战斗: *at the outbreak of hostilities* 战争爆发时 ○ *suspend hostilities*, ie stop fighting 停战.

hot /hɒt; hɑt/ *adj* (**-tter**, **-ttest**) **1** (**a**) having a relatively or noticeably high temperature; giving off heat 热的; 烫的: *a hot day, meal* 热天、热的饭菜 ○ *hot weather, water* 炎热的天气、热水 ○ *Cook in a very hot oven.* 放在炽热的烤箱里烹调. ○ *This coffee is too hot to drink.* 这咖啡太烫, 不能喝. Cf 参看 COLD[1], WARM[1]. (**b**) (of a person) feeling heat (指人)感到热的: *I am/feel hot.* 我很热. (**c**) causing the sensation of heat 使人感到热的: *be in a hot sweat* 热得出汗. **2** (of spices, etc) producing a burning sensation to the taste (指调味品等)辣的, 辛辣的: *a hot curry* 辛辣的咖喱 ○ *Pepper and mustard are hot.* 胡椒和芥末都是辣的. **3** intense; fiery; passionate 强烈的; 激烈的; 热烈的: *have a hot temper*, ie be easily angered 脾气暴躁 ○ *in the hottest part of the election campaign* 在竞选活动最激烈的部分 ○ *The current debate about privatization is likely to grow hotter in the coming weeks.* 目前这场关于私有化的争论在未来几周内可能愈演愈烈. **4** (**a**) (of the scent in hunting) fresh and strong (指猎物的臭迹)新鲜而强烈的. (**b**) (of news) fresh, very recent and usu sensational (指新闻)新鲜、及时且通常为引起轰动的: *a hot tip* 最新秘闻 ○ *a story that is hot off the press*, ie has just appeared in the newspapers 刚见报的轰动新闻. **5** (*infml* 口) (of a competitor, performer or feat) very skilful or impressive (指竞赛者、表演者或技艺)技术高明的, 令人赞叹的. **6** (*sl* 俚) (of goods) stolen and difficult to dispose of because of determined efforts made by the police to recover them (指物品)(因警方极力查找)难于销赃的: *This painting is too hot to handle.* 这幅画不好销赃. **7** (of music, esp jazz) rhythmical and emotional; stirring (指音乐, 尤指爵士乐)节奏感强、情绪激昂的, 扣人心弦的. **8** (*sl* 俚) radioactive 放射性的. **9** (*infml* 口) (in children's games, etc) very near the object sought; very close to guessing correctly (儿童游戏等)快找到目标的, 快猜中的: *You're getting really hot!* 你快猜着了! **10** (idm 习语) **be hot at/in/on sth** (*infml* 口) be skilled, gifted or knowledgeable in sth 有某方面的技艺、才能或知识: *I'm good at history but not so hot at arithmetic.* 我的历史成绩不错, 但算术不太好. **be hot on sb** (*infml* 口) be infatuated with sb; admire sb 迷恋某人; 爱慕某人. **be in/get into hot ˈwater** (*infml* 口) be in/get into trouble or disgrace 惹来麻烦或羞辱. **blow hot and cold** ⇨ BLOW[1]. **go/sell like hot ˈcakes** sell quickly or in great numbers or quantity 畅销; 卖得快; 卖得多: *The new portable computers are going like hot cakes.* 新的便携式计算机卖得很快. **hot ˈair** (*infml* 口) empty or boastful talk 空话; 大话. **(all) hot and ˈbothered** (*infml* 口) harassed because of fear, the pressure of work, the need to hurry, etc (因恐惧或担忧、工作有压力、紧迫等)心急火燎的. **(too) hot for sb** (*infml* 口) (too) difficult for sb to cope with 某人感到(太)难应付或处理: *When the pace got too hot for him, he disappeared.* 他感到跟不上时, 便溜之大吉了. ○ *They're making things very hot for her*, ie making her life difficult or dangerous. 他们逼得她走投无路. **(be) hot on sb's ˈheels** following sb very closely 紧跟某人; 接踵而来. **(be) hot on sb's ˈtracks/ˈtrail; (be) hot on the trail (of sth)** (*infml* 口) pursuing sb or searching for sth so closely that one has almost caught him or found it 紧追某人几至将其逮获; 彻底搜寻某物接近于发现目标. **a hot poˈtato** (*infml* 口) thing or situation that is difficult or unpleasant to deal with 棘手的或讨厌的事物或情况: *The racial discrimination issue is a political hot potato.* 种族歧视问题是政治上的棘手问题. **the ˈhot seat** (*infml* 口) the vulnerable position of a person who has important responsibilities and must face criticism, answer questions, etc 因身负重任而须面对批评、回答问题等之难堪处境. **a hot spot** (*infml* 口) difficult or dangerous situation; place where (eg political) trouble is likely 困难的或危险的情况; 可能(如在政治上)出事之处; 热点. **hot ˈstuff** (*sl* 俚) (**a**) person or thing of first-rate quality 第一流的人或事物: *She's really hot stuff at tennis.* 她可真是网球好手. (**b**) sexually attractive person 性感的人. **hot under the ˈcollar** (*infml* 口) angry, indignant or embarrassed 愤怒的; 愤慨的; 尴尬的. **like a cat on hot bricks** ⇨ CAT[1]. **not so/too/that ˈhot** (*infml* 口) not well; not good 不太好; 不怎么好: *'How do you feel?' 'Not so hot.'* '你觉得怎么样?' '不过如此.' ○ *Her exam results aren't too hot.* 她考得不太好. **piping hot** ⇨ PIPING. **strike while the iron is hot** ⇨ STRIKE[2].

▷ **hot** *v* (**-tt-**) (phr v) **hot up** (*infml* 口) become more exciting or critical; intensify; increase 变得更兴奋或更紧急; 增强; 增加: *With only a week to go before the election things are really hotting up.* 还有一个星期就要进行选举, 一切越来越紧张了.

hotly *adv* (**a**) passionately; excitedly; angrily 热烈地; 激动地; 愤怒地: *a hotly debated topic* 热烈辩论的话题 ○ *Recent reports in the press have been hotly denied.* 有关方面极力否认新闻界最近的报道. ○ *'Nonsense!' he replied hotly.* '胡说!' 他怒气冲冲地答道. (**b**) closely and determinedly 紧紧地; 坚决地: *a hotly contested match* 争夺激烈的比赛 ○ *The pickpocket ran off, hotly pursued by the police.* 那扒手望风而逃, 警察紧追不舍.

□ **hot-ˈair balloon** = BALLOON 2.

ˈhotbed *n* **1** bed of earth heated by rotting manure to help plants to grow (用粪肥发酵产生热量的)温床. **2** (*fig* 比喻) ~ **of sth** place where sth evil or undesirable is able to develop easily and freely (有利于坏事物滋生发展的)温床: *a hotbed of vice, crime, intrigue, etc* 罪恶、犯罪、阴谋活动等的温床.

ˌhot-ˈblooded *adj* (**a**) easily angered; excitable 易怒的; 易激动的. (**b**) passionate; ardent 热情的; 热烈的: *a ˌhot-blooded ˈlover* 感情炽热的爱人.

ˈhot cake (*US*) = PANCAKE.

ˌhot cross ˈbun sweet bun (usu containing currants) marked with a cross and eaten toasted on Good Friday 十字面包(通常为带葡萄干的甜面包, 表面有十字图案, 于耶稣受难节烤热食用).

ˌhot ˈdog **1** hot sausage served in a soft bread roll, often with onions and mustard 热狗(中间夹有热香肠并常佐以碎洋葱和芥末的长圆面包). **2** (*US infml* 口) (used as an *interj* to express pleasure or surprise 用作叹词, 表示高兴或惊讶).

hot ˈfavourite competitor most fancied to win a race, etc 竞赛等活动中众望所归的热门参赛者.

ˌhotˈfoot *adv* in great haste; quickly and eagerly 匆忙地; 急忙地: *The children came running hotfoot when they heard tea was ready.* 孩子们听说茶点已准备好了, 便赶紧跑过来. — *v* (idm 习语) **ˈhotfoot it** (*infml* 口) walk or run hurriedly and eagerly 急走; 急跑: *We hotfooted it down to the beach.* 我们急急忙忙地赶到沙滩.

ˌhot ˈgospeller (*infml often derog* 口, 常作贬义) eager and enthusiastic preacher 热心的传教者; 狂热的鼓吹者.

ˈhothead *n* person who often acts too hastily or rashly; impetuous person 性急的人; 急躁的人; 容易冲动的人. **ˌhot-ˈheaded** *adj* rash; impulsive; impetuous 性急的; 容易冲动的; 急躁的. **ˌhot-ˈheadedly** *adv.*

ˌhot-ˈheadedness *n* [U].

ˈhothouse *n* heated building, usu made of glass, used for growing delicate plants in; greenhouse 温室; 暖房.

ˈhot line direct and exclusive communication link between heads of government, eg those of Moscow and Washington 热线(政府首脑之间, 如莫斯科与华盛顿的首脑之间, 直通的通迅专线).

ˌhot ˈmoney funds moved frequently from one financial centre to another by speculators seeking high interest rates and the greatest opportunity for profit 投机者为追求高利率及最大获利机会而由一金融中心转移到另一金融中心的频繁流动的资金; 国际游资.

ˈhotplate *n* flat heated metal surface on a cooking stove, etc used for cooking food or keeping it hot (炉灶等上的金属的)加热板(用以烹制食物或使之保温).

ˈhotpot *n* stew of meat and vegetables cooked in the oven in a dish with a lid 炖或焖的肉和蔬菜.

ˈhot rod (*sl* 俚) motor vehicle modified to have extra power and speed (经改装而使功率加大的)高速汽车.

ˈhotshot *n* (*US infml* 口) person who is skilful or talented in a showy or aggressive way 卖弄技艺的人; 艺高而自负的人: [attrib 作定语] *a hotshot young lawyer* 好展才的年轻律师.

ˌhot ˈspring spring¹(2) of naturally hot mineral water 温泉.

ˌhot-ˈtempered *adj* easily becoming very angry 性情暴躁的.

ˌhot-ˈwater bottle container, usu made of rubber, that is filled with hot water and put in a bed, etc to warm it 热水袋.

hotch·potch /ˈhɒtʃpɒtʃ; ˋhɑtʃˏpɑtʃ/ (also **hodge·podge** /ˈhɒdʒpɒdʒ; ˋhɑdʒˏpɑdʒ/) *n* (usu *sing* 通常作单数) number of things mixed together without order; confused jumble 杂乱的一堆东西; 乱七八糟的混杂物: *His essay was a hotchpotch of other people's ideas.* 他的文章是把别人的想法拼凑在一起的大杂烩.

ho·tel /həʊˈtel; hoˋtɛl/ *n* building where rooms and usu meals are provided for people in return for payment 旅社; 旅馆: *staying at/in a(n) hotel* 住旅馆. Cf 参看 INN.

▷ **ho·tel·ier** /həʊˈtelɪə(r), -lɪeɪ; *US* ˌhəʊtelˈjeɪ; ˌhotɛlˋje/ *n* person who owns or manages a hotel 旅馆老板; 旅馆经理.

hound /haʊnd; haʊnd/ *n* **1** type of dog used in hunting; foxhound 猎犬; 猎狐狗: *The hounds lost the scent of the fox.* 这些猎犬失去了狐狸的臭迹. **2** (idm 习语) **follow hounds** ⇨ FOLLOW. **ride to hounds** ⇨ RIDE². **run with the hare and hunt with the hounds** ⇨ HARE.

▷ **hound** *v* **1** [Tn] pursue (sb) relentlessly and energetically (esp in order to obtain sth); harass 无情而竭力地追逼(某人)(尤指为了获得某物); 烦扰; 纠缠: *be hounded by reporters, one's creditors, the press* 受到记者的纠缠、债主的追逼、新闻界的烦扰. **2** (phr v) **hound sb/sth down** find sb/sth after a persistent chase 穷追某人[某物]直至达到目的; 追寻到某人[某物]. **hound sb out (of sth/...)** force sb to leave (sth/a place) 强迫某人离开(某事物[某地]): *He was hounded out of his job by jealous rivals.* 他受到忌妒他的竞争者的算计而被迫离职.

hour /ˈaʊə(r); aʊr/ *n* **1** [C] twenty-fourth part of a day and night; 60 minutes 小时: *The film starts at 7.30 and lasts two hours.* 影片7点30分开演, 演两个小时. ○ *work a forty-hour week* 每周工作四十小时 ○ *a three hours' journey/a three-hour journey* 三小时的旅程. ⇨App 5 见附录5. **2** (**a**) [C] number of hours past midnight, eg 1 o'clock, 2 o'clock, etc, as indicated by a clock, watch, etc 钟点; 点钟(如一点钟、两点钟等): *The clock strikes the hours but not the half-hours.* 这个钟是正点打点而不是半小时打点. (**b**) **hours** [pl] (*fml* 文) (used when calculating time according to the 24-hour clock 用于24小时计时制): *It's eighteen hundred hours*, ie 6 pm. 现在是十八点整(下午6点). ○ *It's twenty-one thirty hours*, ie 9.30 pm. 现在是二十一点三十分(晚上9点30分). **3** **hours** [pl] fixed period of time for work, use of facilities, etc (工作、设施等的)固定时间: *hours of business* 营业时间 ○ *Office hours are from 9 am to 5 pm.* 办公时间从上午9点到下午5点. ○ *Doctors work long hours.* 医生的工作时间很长. **4** [C usu *sing* 通常作单数] period of about an hour, usu set aside for a specified purpose 约一小时的时间(通常指作某用途的): *a long lunch hour* 很长的午餐时间. **5** [C] distance that can be travelled in an hour 一小时的行程: *London's only two hours away.* 到伦敦只需两小时. **6** [C] point in time 某一时刻: *He came at the agreed hour.* 他在约定时间来到了. ○ *Who can be ringing us at this late hour?* 谁能在这么晚的时间给我们打电话呢? **7** [C usu *sing* 通常作单数] indefinite period of time 不确定的一段时间: *the country's finest hour* 乡村中最好的时间 ○ *She helped me in my hour of need.* 她在我需要的时候帮助了我. **8** (idm 习语) **ˌafter ˈhours** after a period of regular business, etc 下班后: *Staff must stay behind after hours to catch up on their work.* 下班后工作人员需要留下来把工作赶完. **at/till ˈall hours** at/till any time, however unsuitable or inconvenient 在[到]任何时候(不管多么不适宜或不方便)亦在所不惜: *She stays out till all hours*, ie very late. 她在外面一直呆到很晚的时候. ○ *He's inclined to telephone at all hours of the day or night.* 他不分白天黑夜, 想打电话就打. **at the eˌleventh ˈhour** at the last possible moment; only just in time 在最后的时刻; 刚刚来得及: *The president's visit was called off at the eleventh hour.* 总裁的这次访问到时取消了. ○ [attrib 作定语] *an eˌleventh-hour deˈcision* 犹未为晚的决定. **the early hours** ⇨ EARLY. **keep late, early, regular, etc ˈhours** go to bed or work late, early, for a normal and regular period of time, etc 作息时间较正常的或规定的时间等为晚、为早等. **on the ˈhour** at exactly 1 o'clock, 2 o'clock, 3 o'clock, etc 在某一正点: *My appointment was for 9 am and I arrived on the hour*, ie at 9 am precisely. 我的约会时间定在上午9点, 我到达时9点整. ○ *The London bus departs every hour on the hour.* 伦敦的公共汽车每小时零分开出一趟. **ˌout of ˈhours** (**a**) before or after one's regular work time 在工作时间之外. (**b**) (*esp Brit*) during times when alcohol may no longer be sold in bars 在酒吧间不再售酒的时候. **the small hours** ⇨ SMALL. **one's waking hours** ⇨ WAKE¹.

▷ **hourly** /ˈaʊəlɪ; ˋaʊrlɪ/ *adv* **1** every hour 每小时(一次): *This medicine is to be taken hourly.* 这药每小时服一次. **2** at any time 随时: *We're expecting news hourly.* 我们时刻期待着消息. — *adj* **1** done or occurring every hour 每小时一次的: *an hourly bus service* 每小时一班的公共汽车 ○ *Trains leave at hourly intervals.* 列车每隔一小时开出一趟. **2** calculated by the hour 按钟点计算的: *be paid on an hourly basis* 按钟点获取报酬. **3** continual; frequent 不断的; 频繁的: *live in hourly dread of being discovered* 时时刻刻担心被人发觉.

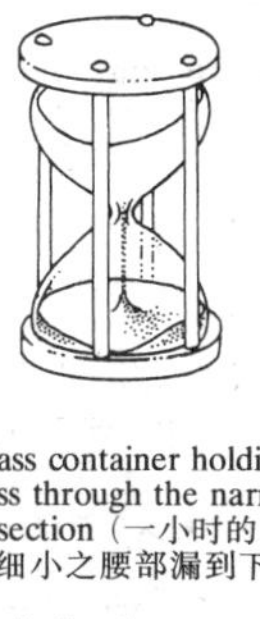

hourglass 沙漏

□ **ˈhourglass** *n* glass container holding fine sand that takes an hour to pass through the narrow gap from the upper to the lower section (一小时的)沙漏(玻璃漏壶, 内盛细沙由上部经细小之腰部漏到下部, 于一小时后漏尽).

ˈhour-hand *n* small hand on a clock or watch, indicating the hour (钟表的)时针.

houri /ˈhʊərɪ; ˋhʊrɪ/ *n* beautiful young woman of the Muslim paradise (伊斯兰教)天堂的美女.

house¹ /haʊs; haʊs/ *n* (*pl* **~s** /ˈhaʊzɪz; ˋhaʊzɪz/) **1** [C] (**a**) building made for people to live in, usu for one family or for a family and lodgers 房子; 住宅. ⇨illus at App 1 见附录1插图, pages vi, vii. (**b**) (usu *sing* 通常作单数) people living in such a building 住在一所房子中的人们; 家人: *Be quiet or you'll wake the whole house!* 安静点吧, 别把全家人都吵醒了! **2** [C] (in compounds 用以构成复合词) building made or used for some special purpose or for keeping animals or goods in 为某种目的而建造的房子; 用作某目的的建筑物; (动物的)棚, 舍;

(储物的)库, 房: *an 'opera-house* ○ *a 'schoolhouse* ○ *a 'hen-house* ○ *a 'store-house.* **3** [C] (**a**) building in which a religious community or a section of a boarding-school or college lives 宗教会所; (学校中包膳食的)寄宿舍. (**b**) (group of pupils in) each of the divisions of a day-school for competitive purposes, esp sport 日校学生为进行比赛(尤指体育)而分的组; 组成竞赛小组的学生. **4** (usu 通常作 **House**) [C] (building used by a) group of people who meet to discuss or pass laws 议院(大楼): *the ˌHouse of 'Commons/'Lords* 下[上]议院 ○ *the ˌHouses of 'Parliament* 议会 ○ *This house condemns the Prime Minister's action*, eg said in a debate. 本议会谴责首相所采取的行动(如在辩论中宣称). **5 the House** [sing] (*infml* 口) (**a**) (*Brit*) the House of Commons or the House of Lords 下议院或上议院: *enter the House*, ie become an MP 进入议院(当议员). (**b**) (*Brit*) the Stock Exchange 证券交易所. (**c**) (*US*) the House of Representatives 众议院. **6** [C] business firm 商业机构: *a fashion house* 时装商店 ○ *a banking house* 银行 ○ [attrib 作定语] *house style*, ie written style established by a newspaper, publishing firm, etc 报刊、出版社等自己的文字风格. **7** (usu 通常作 **House**) [C] royal family or dynasty 皇族; 王朝: *the House of Windsor*, ie the British Royal Family 英国王室. **8** [C] (**a**) (usu *sing* 通常作单数) audience in a theatre, concert hall, etc (剧院、音乐厅等的)观众, 听众: *Is there a doctor in the house?* 观众中有医生吗? (**b**) theatre, etc building 剧场等娱乐场所(指建筑物): *a full house*, ie with every seat occupied 客满 ○ *an orchestra playing to packed houses*, ie full concert halls 为座无虚席的全场听众演出的管弦乐队. (**c**) performance in a theatre, etc (戏剧等的)演出场次: *The second house starts at 8 o'clock.* 第二场演出8点钟开始. **9** [C] each of the twelve parts into which the heavens are divided in astrology 占星术中把天分成的十二个部分之一; 黄道十二宫之一. **10** (idm 习语) **bring the 'house down** make an audience laugh or applaud loudly 使观众或听众欢声或掌声如雷. **eat sb out of house and home** ⇨ EAT. **get on like a 'house on fire** (*infml* 口) (of people) quickly become very friendly; have an agreeable and cheerful relationship (指人)很快就亲热起来或关系融洽. **a half-way house** ⇨ HALF-WAY (HALF²). **keep 'house** manage the affairs of a household 管理家务. **keep open house** ⇨ OPEN¹. **the lady of the house** ⇨ LADY. **master in one's own house** ⇨ MASTER¹. **move house** ⇨ MOVE². **not a dry eye in the house** ⇨ DRY¹. **on the 'house** paid for by the pub, firm, etc; free 由店家、公司等负担费用; 免费: *The landlord gave us a drink on the house.* 店主免费请我们喝酒. **put/set one's (own) 'house in order** organize one's own affairs efficiently 把自己的事情处理得井井有条. **safe as houses** ⇨ SAFE¹. **set up 'house (together)** live together as man and wife 过夫妻生活.

▷ **'house·ful** /-fʊl; -ˌfʊl/ *n* as much or as many as a house can contain or accommodate 整座房子所容纳的量: *have a houseful of guests* 有整座房子的客人.

□ **'house-agent** *n* = ESTATE AGENT (ESTATE).

ˌhouse 'arrest detention in one's own house, not in prison 软禁: *be (kept) under house arrest* 受到软禁.

'houseboat *n* boat, usu stationary on a river, equipped as a place to live in 用于居住的船; 水上住宅.

'house-bound *adj* unable to leave one's house, eg because of illness 不能离家的(如因病).

'housebreaking *n* [U] entering a building without right or permission in order to commit a crime 私自入室图谋不轨; 破门入屋. **'housebreaker** *n.*

'housecoat *n* woman's long dress-like garment for informal wear in the house (女子在家穿的)宽松长袍.

'housecraft *n* [U] theory and practice of running a home 家政(学).

'house-dog *n* dog kept to guard a house 看家狗; 守门犬.

'house-father *n* man in charge of children in an institution, esp a children's home (儿童设施, 尤指儿童福利院的)男舍监, 男管理员.

'house-fly *n* (*pl* **-flies**) common fly found in and around houses 苍蝇.

'housekeeper *n* person (esp a woman) employed to manage a household 管家(尤指女性). **'housekeeping** *n* [U] **1** management of household affairs 家务管理. **2** money allowed for this 家务开支.

'house lights lights in the auditorium of a theatre, cinema, etc (剧院、电影院等的)观众席照明灯.

'housemaid *n* woman servant in a house, esp one who cleans rooms, etc (尤指清扫房间等的)女仆, 女用人.

housemaid's 'knee inflammation of the kneecap, caused by kneeling too much (因经常用跪着姿势而引起的)髌前滑囊炎.

'houseman /-mən; -mən/ *n* (*pl* **-men** /-mən; -mən/) (*Brit*) (*US* **intern** /'ɪntɜːn; 'ɪntɝn/) resident junior doctor at a hospital, etc 驻院实习医生.

'house-martin *n* bird that builds its nest of mud in the walls of houses and in cliffs 家燕(筑巢于房屋的墙上和峭壁上的燕子).

'housemaster *n* (*fem* 阴性作 **'housemistress**) teacher in charge of a house(3a) at a boarding-school (寄宿学校的)舍监.

'house-mother *n* woman in charge of children in an institution, esp a children's home (儿童设施, 尤指儿童福利院的)女舍监, 女管理员.

ˌhouse of 'cards **1** tower-like structure built by balancing playing-cards against and on top of each other 搭成屋形的纸牌. **2** (*fig* 比喻) scheme, etc that is likely to collapse 不大可行的计划等.

the ˌHouse of 'Commons (also **the 'Commons**) (**a**) the assembly of elected representatives of the British or the Canadian Parliament (英国或加拿大议会中的)下议院, 众议院. (**b**) the building where they meet 下议院大楼. Cf 参看 THE HOUSE OF LORDS.

ˌHouse of 'God (*fml* 文) church or chapel 教堂.

the ˌHouse of 'Lords (also **the 'Lords**) (**a**) the assembly of members of the nobility and bishops in the British Parliament (英国议会中的)上议院, 贵族院. (**b**) the building where they meet 上议院大楼. Cf 参看 THE HOUSE OF COMMONS.

the ˌHouse of ˌRepre'sentatives the assembly of elected representatives in the central government of the USA, Australia and New Zealand (美国、澳大利亚和新西兰的中央政府所设之)众议院. Cf 参看 CONGRESS 2, SENATE 1.

'house party group of guests staying at a country house, etc 留宿于乡村府第等中的宾客们.

'house physician doctor living in a hospital as a member of its staff 驻院内科医师.

'house-proud *adj* giving great attention to the care and appearance of one's home 对家事格外关心的; 热衷于美化家庭的.

'house-room *n* [U] (idm 习语) **not give sb/sth 'house-room** not want to have sb/sth in one's house, etc 家中不留某人(某物): *I wouldn't give that table house-room.* 我才不要那张桌子呢.

the ˌHouses of 'Parliament (**a**) the House of Commons and the House of Lords, regarded together (包括上、下两院的)议会. (**b**) the group of buildings in London where these two assemblies meet (伦敦的)议会大厦.

'house-sparrow (also **sparrow**) *n* common grey and brown bird 家雀. ⇨illus at App 1 见附录1插图, page iv.

'house surgeon surgeon living in a hospital as a member of its staff 驻院外科医师.

ˌhouse-to-'house *adj* [attrib 作定语] calling at each house in turn 挨家挨户的: *The police made house-to-house enquiries.* 警方进行了逐户调查.

'house-tops *n* (idm 习语) **(proclaim, shout, etc sth) from the 'house-tops** (announce sth) publicly so that many people know about it 公开(宣布或宣扬某事物); 公之于世.

'house-trained *adj* (of pet cats, dogs, etc) trained not to defecate and urinate inside the house (指猫、狗等宠物)经训练不在室内便溺的: (*fig joc* 比喻, 谑) *His manners were appalling before he got married, but his wife soon got him house-trained.* 他以前很没规矩, 婚后不久妻子就把他管教好了.

'house-warming *n* party given to celebrate the move into a new home 庆祝乔迁的宴会: [attrib 作定语] *have/throw a house-warming party* 举行乔迁宴会.

'housewife *n* (*pl* **-wives**) woman whose occupation is looking after her family, cleaning the house, etc, and who usu does not have full-time paid work outside the home 家庭主妇; 家庭妇女. ˈ**housewifely** *adj* of a housewife 家庭主妇的: *housewifely skills* 主妇的持家本领. ˈ**housewifery** /-wɪfərɪ; -ˌwaɪfrɪ/ *n* [U] work of a housewife 家务; 家政.

ˈ**housework** *n* [U] work done in a house, eg cleaning and cooking 家务劳动(如打扫卫生和烹调食品).

house[2] /haʊz; haʊz/ *v* [Tn] **1** (**a**) provide permanent or temporary accommodation for (sb) 给(某人)房子住; 给(某人)房子用: *be poorly housed* 被安排住条件差的房子 ○ *We can house you if the hotels are full.* 假若旅馆已客满, 我们可以留你住宿. (**b**) provide shelter for (an animal) 给(动物)栖身的处所. **2** store (goods, etc) 储存(货物等): *house one's old books in the attic* 把旧书存放在阁楼上. **3** enclose or contain (a part or fitting), esp in order to protect it 将(零部件或器材)覆盖或遮蔽起来: *The gas meter is housed in the cupboard under the stairs.* 煤气表安装在楼梯底下的柜橱里.

house·hold /ˈhaʊshəʊld; ˈhausˌhold/ *n* **1** all the people (family, lodgers, etc) living together in a house 同住在一所房子里的人(家人、房客等); 一家人; 家庭: *I grew up as part of a large household.* 我是在一个大家庭里长大的. ○ [attrib 作定语] *household* (ie domestic) *expenses, duties, goods* 家庭的开销、事务、用品. **2** (idm 习语) **a** ˌ**household** ˈ**name**/ˈ**word** name of a person or thing that has become very well known because it is so often used 家喻户晓的名字或名称: *The product was so successful that its name became a household word.* 这一产品非常成功, 其名称已经家喻户晓.

▷ ˈ**house·holder** *n* /-həʊldə(r); -ˌholdɚ/ **1** person who rents or who owns and occupies a house (ie not a person who lives in a hotel, etc) 住户; 房主. **2** head of a household 家长; 户主.

□ ˌ**household** ˈ**troops** soldiers employed to guard the sovereign 王室禁卫军.

hous·ing /ˈhaʊzɪŋ; ˈhaʊzɪŋ/ *n* **1** [U] houses, flats, etc, considered collectively; accommodation 房屋、住宅等(总称); 住处: *More housing is needed for old people.* 需要为老年人提供更多的住宅. ○ [attrib 作定语] *poor housing conditions* 恶劣的居住条件. **2** [U] providing accommodation for people 供给住房: [attrib 作定语] *the council's housing policy* 市建住房政策. **3** [C] hard casing that protects machinery, etc 机器等的防护外壳或外罩: *a car's rear axle housing* 汽车的后轴套.

□ ˈ**housing association** society formed by a group of people with the aim of building and providing housing at reasonable cost and without making a profit 房屋协会(非牟利的团体, 旨在以廉宜的费用建房和提供住宅).

ˈ**housing estate** area in which a number of houses for living are planned and built together 统建的住宅区.

hove ⇨ HEAVE.

hovel /ˈhɒvl; *US* ˈhʌvl; ˈhʌvl̩/ *n* (*derog* 贬) small house that is unfit to live in; very poor and squalid dwelling 不适于居住的小屋; 简陋肮脏的住所.

hover /ˈhɒvə(r); *US* ˈhʌvər; ˈhʌvɚ/ *v* [I, Ipr, Ip] **1** (of birds, etc) remain in the air in one place (指鸟等)翱翔, 盘旋: *a hawk hovering above/over its prey* 在猎物头顶上盘旋的一只鹰 ○ *There was a helicopter hovering overhead.* 有一架直升飞机在头顶上盘旋. **2** (**a**) (of a person) wait in a timid and uncertain manner (指人)彷徨, 踌躇: *I can't work with you hovering over me like that.* 你那样缠着我磨磨唧唧, 我实在没法工作了. ○ *She's always hovering around the place annoying people.* 她老是在周围转来转去打搅别人. ○ *He hovered about outside, too afraid to go in.* 他在外面犹豫徘徊, 因过于胆怯而不敢进去. (**b**) remain near sth or in an uncertain state 留在某事物近旁; 维持某种不确定状态: *hovering between life and death* 处于生死之间 ○ *a country hovering on the brink of war* 陷于战争边缘的国家.

□ ˈ**hovercraft** *n* (*pl* unchanged 复数不变) vehicle that is capable of moving over land or water while supported on a cushion of air made by jet engines 气垫飞行器, 悬浮运载工具(藉喷气发动机所产生的气垫支持, 可在陆地或水面的上方运行); 气垫船; 悬浮车.

how /haʊ; haʊ/ *interrog adv* **1** in what way or manner 怎样; 怎么; 如何: *How is the word spelt?* 这个字怎么拼? ○ *Tell me how to spell it.* 告诉我怎么拼. ○ *How did you escape?* 你是怎样脱逃的? ○ *Tell us how you escaped.* 告诉我们你是怎样脱逃的. ○ *How are things going* (ie Is your life good or bad) *at the moment?* 你现在情况怎么样(生活得好不好)? **2** in what state of health; in what condition 健康状况怎么样; 情况如何: *How are the children?* 孩子们身体好吗? ○ *How is* (ie What is your opinion of) *your job?* 你的工作怎么样? **3** (used before an *adj* or *adv* 后接形容词或副词) to what extent or degree 到什么程度; 到何种地步; 多少; 多么: *How old is she?* 她有多大年纪了? ○ *How long did you wait?* 你等了多长时间了? ○ *How often do you go swimming?* 你多久去游泳一次? ○ *How fast can she run?* 她能跑多快? ○ *How much money have you got?* 你有多少钱? **4** (used in exclamations to comment on extent or degree 用于感叹句中, 当言及所达到的状况或程度时): *How dirty that child is.* 那孩子多脏啊. ○ *How kind of you to help.* 有你的帮助真是太好了. ○ *How pale she looks.* 她看上去多么苍白啊. ○ *How well he plays the violin.* 他小提琴拉得多好啊. ○ *How he snores!* ie He snores very loudly. 他鼾声真大! **5** (idm 习语) ˌ**and**ˈ **how!** (*infml* 口) (used to agree strongly and sometimes ironically 用以表示极为赞同, 有时为反语): *'He's done very well, hasn't he?' 'And how!'* '他干得好极了, 对吗?' '那还用说!' **how about?** (used to make a suggestion 用以提出建议): *How about going for a walk?* 去散散步好吗? ○ *How about a hot bath?* 洗个热水澡怎么样? ˌ**how's** ˈ**that?** (**a**) what is the explanation for that? 那是怎么回事? (**b**) (used when asking sb's opinion of sth 用于征询某人对某事物的意见时): *How's that for punctuality?* 你对遵守时间有什么看法? (**c**) (used by the fielding side in cricket to ask the umpire if the batsman is out or not 板球运动中防守一方向裁判员询问击球手是否出局的用语).

▷ **how** *conj* (*infml* 口) the/any way in which 怎样; 如何: *She described to me how he ran up to her and grabbed her handbag.* 她向我讲述了他是怎样跑到她跟前抢走她的手提包的. ○ *I can dress how I like in my own house!* 我在自己家里想穿什么就穿什么!

hovercraft 气垫船

how·dah /ˈhaʊdə; ˈhaʊdə/ *n* seat, usu with a canopy, for riding on the back of an elephant or a camel 象轿, 驼轿(架在象或骆驼的背上供人乘骑的通常带有篷盖的座位).

how·ever /haʊˈevə(r); haʊˈɛvɚ/ *adv* **1** (used before an *adj* or *adv* 后接形容词或副词) to whatever extent or degree 无论如何; 不管多么: *You won't move that stone, however strong you are.* 不管你力气多大, 也休想搬动那块石头. ○ *She leaves her bedroom window open, however cold it is.* 无论天气多么冷, 她都敞着卧室的窗户. ○ *He will never succeed however hard he tries.* 不论他怎样努力, 都不会获得成功. ○ *However short the journey is, you always get something to eat on this airline.* 不管航程多么短, 这一班机上都有些吃的. **2** (used to comment on a previously stated fact 用于言及既成事实时表示转折) although sth is, was or may be true; nevertheless 然而; 不过; 仍然: *She felt ill. She went to work, however, and tried to concentrate.* 她病了. 然而她照旧去上班, 并且尽力集中精神工作. ○ *His first response was to say no. Later, however, he changed his mind.* 他最初的反应是不同意. 可是后来他改变了主意. ○ *I thought those figures were correct. However, I have recently heard they were not.* 我原以为那些数字正确无误. 不过我最近听说并不正确. ⇨ Usage at ALTHOUGH 用法见 ALTHOUGH.

▷ **how·ever** *conj* in any way; regardless of how 无论以何种方式; 不管怎样: *You can travel however you like.* 你可以随心所欲地去旅行. ○ *However I approached the problem, I couldn't find a solution.* 这一问题我不管怎样都无法解决.

how·ever *interrog adv* (expressing surprise 表示惊奇) in what way; by what means 究竟怎样; 到底以什么方式: *However did you get here without a car?* 没有汽车你究竟是怎样来的呢? ○ *However does he manage to write music when he is so deaf?* 他聋成这个样子, 究竟是怎样从事作曲的呢?

how·it·zer /ˈhaʊɪtsə(r); ˋhaʊɪtsɚ/ *n* short gun for firing shells at a high angle and at short range 榴弹炮.

howl /haʊl; haʊl/ *n* **(a)** long loud wailing cry of a dog, wolf, etc (狗、狼等的)尖利的长嚎, 嗥叫. **(b)** loud cry of a person expressing pain, scorn, amusement, etc (表示疼痛、轻蔑、高兴等的)高声叫喊: *let out a howl of laughter, agony, rage* 发出狂笑、哀号、怒吼声 ○ (*fig* 比喻) *The proposed changes caused howls of protest from the public.* 拟议中的改革引起公众一片抗议的呼声. **(c)** similar noise made by a strong wind, an electrical amplifier, etc (狂风、电力扬声器等的)啸鸣.

▷ **howl** *v* **1** [I, Ipr] make a howl 尖声嚎叫; 嗥叫; 大声叫喊; 啸鸣: *wolves howling in the forest* 在森林中嗥叫的狼 ○ *howl in agony* 哀叫 ○ *howl with laughter* 高声大笑 ○ *The wind howled through the trees.* 风呼啸着穿过树林. **2** [I] weep loudly 大声哭: *The baby howled all night.* 那婴儿哇哇地哭了一夜. **3** [Tn] utter (sth) with a howl 吼叫着说出(某事): *'I hate you all!' she howled.* '我恨你们所有的人!' 她吼叫着说. ○ *The crowd howled its displeasure.* 人群怒吼着表示不满. **4** (phr v) **howl sb down** (of an audience, etc) prevent a speaker from being heard by shouting scornfully (指听众等)以表示轻蔑的吼叫声压倒讲演者的声音, 把讲演者轰下台.

howler /ˈhaʊlə(r); ˋhaʊlɚ/ *n* (*dated infml* 旧, 口) foolish and obvious mistake, esp in the use of words 愚蠢而明显的错误(尤指措辞): *schoolboy howlers* 小学生的用词错误.

howl·ing /ˈhaʊlɪŋ; ˋhaʊlɪŋ/ *adj* [attrib 作定语] (*infml* 口) very great; extreme 极大的; 极端的: *a howling success* 极大的成功 ○ *Shut the door — there's a howling draught in here!* 把门关上吧 —— 这儿穿堂风太大!

hoy·den /ˈhɔɪdn; ˋhɔɪdn̩/ *n* (*fml derog* 文, 贬) girl who behaves in a wild noisy manner 撒野的女孩子; 胡闹的姑娘. ▷ **hoy·den·ish** /-dənɪʃ; -dənɪʃ/ *adj*.

hp (also **HP**) /ˌeɪtʃ ˈpi:; ˌetʃ ˋpi/ *abbr* 缩写 = **1** (*Brit*) hire-purchase: *buy a new television on (the) hp* 用分期付款方式购买一台新电视机. **2** horsepower (of an engine).

H

HQ /ˌeɪtʃ ˈkju:; ˌetʃ ˋkju/ *abbr* 缩写 = headquarters: *see you back at HQ* 咱们回到总部见面 ○ *police HQ* 警察总局.

hr *abbr* 缩写 = (*pl* **hrs**) hour: *fastest time 1 hr* 最快班次1小时 ○ *The train leaves at 15.00 hrs.* 列车15点整发车. Cf 参看 MIN 2.

HRH /ˌeɪtʃ ɑ:(r) ˈeɪtʃ; ˌetʃ ɑr ˋetʃ/ *abbr* 缩写 = His/Her Royal Highness 殿下(用于他称): *HRH the Duke of Edinburgh* 爱丁堡公爵殿下 ○ (*infml* 口) *HRH was there.* 殿下在那儿呢.

hub /hʌb; hʌb/ *n* **1** central part of a wheel from which the spokes radiate 轮毂. ⇨illus at App 1 见附录1插图, page xiii. **2** (*fig* 比喻) central point of activity, interest or importance (活动、兴趣或要务的)中心: *a hub of industry, commerce, etc* 工业、商业等中心 ○ *He thinks that Boston is the hub of the universe.* 他认为波士顿是世界的中心.

□ ˈ**hub-cap** *n* round metal cover over the hub of a car wheel (汽车的)毂盖. ⇨illus at App 1 见附录1插图, page xii.

hubble-bubble /ˈhʌbl bʌbl; ˋhʌbl̩ˌbʌbl̩/ *n* (*infml* 口) = HOOKAH.

hub·bub /ˈhʌbʌb; ˋhʌbʌb/ *n* [sing, U] **(a)** loud confused noise, eg of many voices; din 喧嚷; 喧闹; 嘈杂声. **(b)** disturbance; uproar 混乱; 骚乱; 闹哄哄.

hubby /ˈhʌbɪ; ˋhʌbɪ/ *n* (*Brit infml* 口) husband 丈夫.

hub·ris /ˈhju:brɪs; ˋhjubrɪs/ *n* [U] (*fml* 文) arrogant pride 傲慢.

huckle·berry /ˈhʌklbərɪ; *US* -berɪ; ˋhʌkl̩ˌbɛrɪ/ *n* **1** low shrub common in N America 越橘树(北美常见的灌木). **2** its small dark-blue berry 越橘(越橘树的深蓝色小浆果).

huck·ster /ˈhʌkstə(r); ˋhʌkstɚ/ *n* person who sells goods in the street; hawker 沿街叫卖的小贩.

huddle /ˈhʌdl; ˋhʌdl/ *v* **1** [Ipr, Ip, Tn·pr esp passive 尤用于被动语态, Tn·p esp passive 尤用于被动语态] (cause sb/sth to) crowd or be heaped together, esp in a small space (使某人[某物])聚集在一起(尤指在某狭小空间内): *sheep huddling (up) together for warmth* 挤在一起取暖的羊 ○ *We all huddled around the radio to hear the news.* 我们大家围聚在收音机旁听新闻广播. ○ *The clothes lay huddled up in a pile in the corner.* 衣服乱成一团, 堆放在角落里. **2** (phr v) **~ up (against/to sb/sth)** curl one's body up into a small space; snuggle 把身子蜷成一团; 蜷缩: *Tom was cold so he huddled up against the radiator.* 汤姆感到冷, 所以他挨着散热器把身子缩成一团.

▷ **huddle** *n* **1** number of people or things close together without order 挤作一团的人; 杂乱地堆在一起的东西: *People stood around in small huddles, sheltering from the rain.* 人们三五成群地挤在一起避雨. ○ *Their clothes lay in a huddle on the floor.* 他们的衣服杂乱地堆在地板上. **2** (idm 习语) **go into a** ˈ**huddle (with sb)** (*infml* 口) hold a private or secret conference 进行私下商议; 举行秘密会议.

hue[1] /hju:; hju/ *n* (*fml* 文) colour; variety or shade of colour 颜色; 色彩; 色调; 色度: *birds of many different hues* 各种不同颜色的鸟 ○ *Add orange paint to get a warmer hue.* 加些橙色颜料使之略呈暖色.

▷ **-hued** /hju:d; hjud/ (forming compound *adjs* 用以构成复合形容词) having the specified colour 有某种颜色的: ˈ*dark-hued* ○ ˈ*many-hued*.

hue[2] /hju:; hju/ *n* (idm 习语) ˌ**hue and** ˈ**cry** general alarm or loud public protest; outcry (示警的)喊叫; (公众的)大声抗议或反对; 呐喊: *A terrific hue and cry was raised against the new tax proposals.* 人们大声疾呼抗议新的税收计划.

huff[1] /hʌf; hʌf/ *n* (usu *sing* 通常作单数) fit of bad temper or annoyance (used esp in the expressions shown) 一阵恼火(尤用于以下示例): *be in a huff* 发怒 ○ *get/go into a huff* 发怒 ○ *go off in a huff* 愤然走开.

▷ **huff·ish**, **huffy** *adjs* **(a)** in a bad temper 怒气冲冲的. **(b)** easily offended 易生气的. **huff·ily** *adv*.

huff[2] /hʌf; hʌf/ *v* [I] **1** blow; puff 吹气; 喷气. **2** (idm 习语) ˌ**huff and** ˈ**puff** **(a)** breathe heavily because one is exhausted 气喘吁吁: *When I got to the top I was huffing and puffing.* 我到达顶端时累得直喘. **(b)** show one's annoyance in a self-important or threatening way without actually achieving anything 恼怒(表现出自命不凡的或虚张声势的样子).

hug /hʌg; hʌg/ *v* **(-gg-)** [Tn] **1** put the arms round (sb/sth) tightly, esp to show love 紧紧抱住(某人[某物]); (尤指示爱)拥抱, 搂抱. **2** (of a bear) squeeze (sb/sth) between its front legs (指熊)用两只前腿抱住(某人[某物]). **3** (of a ship, car, etc) keep close to (sth) (指船只、汽车等)紧挨着(某物): *hug the shore, kerb* 贴近岸边、路缘 ○ *tyres that help a vehicle to hug the road* 能贴紧路面的车辆轮胎. **4** fit tightly round (sth) 紧紧箍在(某物)上: *a figure-hugging dress* 紧身连衣裙. **5** cling firmly to and take pleasure in (opinions) 坚持并乐于信守(某观点): *hug one's cherished beliefs* 坚持自己所抱的信念.

▷ **hug** *n* strong clasp with the arms, esp to show love; tight embrace 紧紧的拥抱(尤指为示爱); 紧搂: *She gave her mother an affectionate hug.* 她紧紧拥抱着她的母亲.

huge /hju:dʒ; hjudʒ/ *adj* very large in size or amount; enormous 极大的; 巨大的: *a huge elephant* 巨大的象 ○ *Canada is a huge country.* 加拿大是个幅员广大的国家. ○ *have a huge appetite* 胃口很大 ○ *huge debts, profits* 巨额的债务、利润.

▷ **hugely** *adv* enormously, very much 极大地; 非常: *be hugely successful* 非常成功 ○ *enjoy oneself hugely* 过得十分愉快.

huge·ness *n* [U].

hugger-mugger /ˈhʌgə mʌgə(r); ˋhʌgɚˌmʌgɚ/ *adj, adv* **1** secret(ly) 秘密(的). **2** confused(ly); in disorder 混乱(的); 乱糟糟(的).

▷ **hugger-mugger** *n* [U] **1** secrecy 秘密. **2** confusion 混乱.

Hu·gue·not /ˈhju:gənəʊ; ˋhjugəˌnɑt/ *n* (formerly) French Protestant (旧时)法国基督教新教徒.

huh /hʌ; hʌ/ *interj* (used to express scorn, disgust, enquiry, etc 用以表示轻蔑、厌恶、疑问等): *You think* *you know the answer, huh?* 你以为你知道那答案吗，嗯？

hulk /hʌlk; hʌlk/ *n* **1** body of an old ship which is no longer in use（废弃的旧船的）船体: *rotting hulks on the beach* 在海滩上的腐烂的船体. **2** very large and usu clumsy person or thing 很大的而且通常为很笨的人或物.
▷ **hulk·ing** *adj* [attrib 作定语] (*infml* 口) (of a person or thing) very big or heavy and usu awkward or clumsy（指人或物）很大的，很重的，（通常指）很笨拙的: *a hulking great brute of a man* 彪形蠢汉.

hull[1] /hʌl; hʌl/ *n* body of a ship 船体; 船身: *a fully-loaded tanker with its hull low in the water* 船身没入水中的满载的油船. ⇨illus at CATAMARAN, YACHT 见 CATAMARAN 和 YACHT 插图.

hull[2] /hʌl; hʌl/ *n* **1** outer covering of some fruits and seeds, esp the pods of peas and beans（某些水果和种子的）外壳，（尤指）豆荚. **2** cluster of leaves on a strawberry, raspberry, etc（草莓、悬钩子等的）花萼.
▷ **hull** *v* [Tn] remove the hulls of (peas, beans, fruit, etc) 除去（豌豆、大豆、水果等）的荚、壳、皮.

hul·la·ba·loo /ˌhʌləbəˈlu:; ˈhʌləbəˌlu/ *n* (*pl* **~s**) (usu *sing* 通常作单数) continuous loud noise, esp of people shouting; uproar; din（尤指人的）持续的吵闹声，喧闹，嘈杂: *make a hullabaloo (about sth)*（为某事物）大吵大闹.

hullo = HALLO.

hum /hʌm; hʌm/ *v* (**-mm-**) **1** (**a**) [I] make a low steady continuous sound like that made by bees 发嗡嗡声（如蜜蜂的声音）. (**b**) [I] utter a slight sound, esp of hesitation 发嗯嗯声（尤表示犹豫）. (**c**) [I, Ip, Tn, Tn·pr] **~ (sth) (to sb)** sing (a tune) with closed lips 哼（曲子）: *She was humming (away) to herself.* 她在低声哼唱. ○ *I don't know the words of the song but I can hum it to you.* 我不知道这首歌的歌词，但我可以哼给你听. **2** [I, Ipr] (*infml* 口) be in a state of activity 活跃: *make things hum* 使事情显得有生气 ○ *The whole place was humming (with life) when we arrived.* 我们到达时，到处是繁忙的景象. **3** [I] (*sl* 俚) smell unpleasantly 发出臭味. **4** (idm 习语) **ˌhum and ˈha**; **ˌhum and ˈhaw** (*infml* 口) take a long time to make a decision; hesitate 踌躇再三; 迟疑: *We hummed and ha'd for ages before deciding to buy the house.* 我们犹豫了很久，才决定买这所房子.
▷ **hum** *n* (usu *sing* 通常作单数) **1** humming sound, esp of an insect; indistinct murmur, esp of many voices（尤指昆虫的）营营声，嗡嗡声；（尤指混杂的）模糊而连续的声音: *the hum of bees, of distant traffic, of machines* 蜜蜂的嗡嗡声、远处车辆的呜呜声、机器的隆隆声 ○ *the hum of conversation in the next room* 隔壁房间里嗡嗡的谈话声. **2** (*sl* 俚) bad smell 臭味.
hum *interj* (used to indicate hesitation 用以表示犹豫).
□ **ˈhumming-bird** *n* any of various types of tropical bird, usu very small and brightly coloured, that make a humming sound by vibration of the wings 蜂鸟（产于热带，通常体小而色彩鲜艳，双翼鼓动时发嗡嗡声）.
ˈhumming-top *n* top[3](1) that makes a humming sound when it spins 响簧陀螺（旋转时发嗡嗡声）.

hu·man /ˈhju:mən; ˈhjumən/ *adj* **1** of or characteristic of man (contrasted with God, animals or machines) 人的，显示人的本性的（以别于神的、动物的或机器的）: *a human skull* 人的头盖骨 ○ *human anatomy, affairs, behaviour* 人体解剖学、人的事情、人的行为 ○ *a terrible loss of human life* 人命的巨大损失 ○ *This food is not fit for human consumption.* 这种食物不宜人类食用. ○ *We must allow for human error.* 我们应该考虑到有人为的错误. ○ *Even she makes mistakes occasionally — she's only human.* 即便是她偶尔犯一些错误——她也是人哪. **2** (*approv* 褒) having or showing the better qualities of man; kind; good 有良好品性的; 有人情的; 好心肠的: *She'll understand and forgive; she's really quite human.* 她是能谅解的，她是个大好人. **3** (idm 习语) **the milk of human kindness** ⇨ MILK[1]. **to err is human** ⇨ ERR.
▷ **hu·man** *n* = HUMAN BEING.
hu·man·kind /ˌhju:mənˈkaɪnd; ˈhjumənˌkaɪnd/ *n* [U] (*fml* 文) = MANKIND.
hu·manly *adv* **1** in a human way 以人的方式; 人道地; 有人性地. **2** by human means; within human ability 用人力; 在人力所能及的范围: *The doctors did all that was humanly possible.* 医生们已尽了最大的力量了.

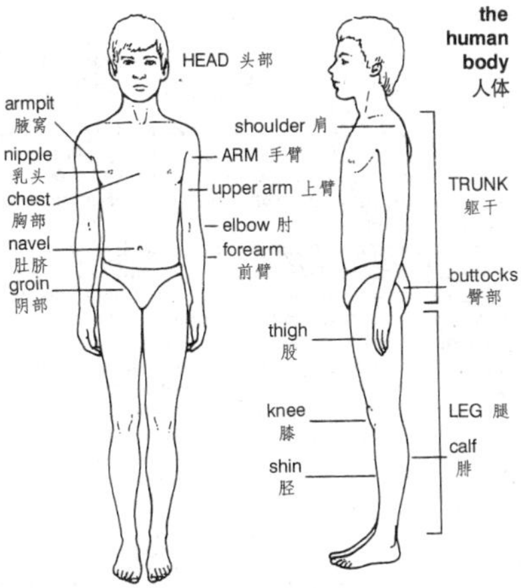

□ **ˌhuman ˈbeing** man, woman or child; person 男人、女人或孩子; 人.
ˌhuman ˈinterest aspect of a newspaper story, etc that interests people because it describes the experiences, feelings, etc of individuals（报纸报道等中描写个人的遭遇、感情等的）人情世故.
ˌhuman ˈnature general characteristics and feelings common to all people 人性: *You can't change human nature.* 人的本性难移.
the ˌhuman ˈrace human beings collectively; mankind 人（总称）; 人类. ⇨Usage at MAN[1] 用法见 MAN[1].
ˌhuman ˈrights rights which it is generally thought that every living person should have, eg the right to freedom, justice, etc 人权.

hu·mane /hju:ˈmeɪn; hjuˈmen/ *adj* **1** having or showing sympathy, kindness and understanding 富于同情心的; 仁慈的; 能体谅人的: *a humane person, act, penal system* 富于同情心的人、古道热肠的行为、合乎人道的刑罚体系 ○ *humane killing* 动物无痛屠宰（法）. **2** [attrib 作定语] (*dated fml* 旧，文) (of areas of learning) tending to civilize（指学科）促进文明或教化的: *humane studies* 人文学科. ▷ **hu·manely** *adv*.
□ **ˌhumane ˈkiller** instrument for the painless killing of animals 无痛屠宰机（屠宰牲畜家禽等的）.

hu·man·ism /ˈhju:mənɪzəm; ˈhjumənˌɪzəm/ *n* [U] **1** (**a**) system of beliefs that concentrates on common human needs and seeks rational (rather than divine) ways of solving human problems 人道主义. (**b**) study of mankind and human affairs (contrasted with theological subjects) 人本主义（研究人的事情，以别于神学的研究）. **2** literary culture (esp in the Renaissance) based on Greek and Roman learning 人文主义（基于希腊和罗马学术思想的文学思潮，尤指文艺复兴时代的）.
▷ **hu·man·ist** /ˈhju:mənɪst; ˈhjumənɪst/ *n* supporter of humanism 人道主义者; 人本主义者; 人文主义者.
hu·man·istic /ˌhju:məˈnɪstɪk; ˌhjuməˈnɪstɪk/ *adj*.

hu·man·it·ar·ian /hju:ˌmænɪˈteərɪən; hjuˌmænəˈtɛrɪən/ *adj* concerned with improving the lives of mankind and reducing suffering, esp by social reform 人道主义的; 主张改善人的生活、减轻苦难的（尤指以社会改良为手段）; 博爱的; 慈善的: *humanitarian deeds, ideals, work* 人道主义的行为、理想、工作.
▷ **hu·man·it·ar·ian** *n* humanitarian person 人道主义者; 博爱者; 慈善家.
hu·man·it·ar·ian·ism /-ɪzəm; -ɪzəm/ *n* [U].

hu·man·ity /hju:ˈmænətɪ; hjuˈmænətɪ/ *n* **1** [U] human beings collectively; the human race; people 人（总称）; 人类: *crimes against humanity* 戕害人类罪. ⇨Usage at MAN[1] 用法见 MAN[1]. **2** [U] being humane; kind-heartedness 人道; 仁慈: *treat people and animals with humanity* 以仁慈之心对待人和动物. **3** [U] human nature; being human 人性. **4 humanities** [pl] subjects of study concerned with human culture, esp literature, language, history and philosophy 人文学科(尤指文学、语言、历史和哲学).

hu·man·ize, -ise /ˈhju:mənaɪz; ˋhjumə,naɪz/ *v* [Tn] **1** make (sth) human 使(某事物)具有人的属性; 将(某事物)人格化: *animal characters humanized in cartoons* 在动画片中人性化了的动物角色. **2** make (sb) humane 使(某人)变得人道、仁慈、文明: *have a humanizing influence on a barbaric system* 对不文明的制度产生教化作用. ▷ **hu·man·iza·tion, -isation** /ˌhju:mənaɪˈzeɪʃn; *US* -nɪˈz-; ˌhjumənəˋzeʃən/ *n* [U].

humble /ˈhʌmbl *or, rarely, US* 罕, 美亦读作 ˈʌm-; ˋhʌmbḷ, ˋʌmbḷ/ *adj* (**-r** /-blə(r); -blɚ/, **-st** /-blɪst; -blɪst/) **1** (of a person or his words or actions) having or showing a low or modest opinion of one's own importance; not proud (指人或其言行)谦虚的: *my humble apologies* 鄙人的道歉 ○ *in my humble opinion* 依拙见. **2** (**a**) (of a person, his position in society, etc) low in rank; unimportant (指人、其社会地位等)低下的, 卑微的: *men of humble birth* 出身卑微的人 ○ *a humble occupation* 低贱的职业. (**b**) (of a thing) not large or elaborate; poor (指事物)简陋的, 低劣的: *a humble home, meal, offering* 简陋的家、简单的饭菜、小惠. **3** (idm 习语) **eat humble pie** ⇨ EAT.

▷ **humble** *v* [Tn] make (sb/sth/oneself) humble; lower the rank or self-importance of 使(某人[某事物/自己])变得卑微; 降低...的地位或自满情绪: *humble one's enemies* 挫敌人的锐气 ○ *humble sb's pride* 打掉某人的傲气 ○ *humble oneself before God* 在上帝面前表示卑微 ○ *a humbling experience* 使人谦虚的经历.

hum·bly /ˈhʌmblɪ *or, rarely, US* 罕, 美亦读作 ˈʌm-; ˋhʌmblɪ, ˋʌm-/ *adv*: *beg most humbly for forgiveness* 卑躬屈膝地祈求宽恕 ○ *live humbly* 过卑贱的生活 ○ *humbly born*, ie of a poor or an unimportant family 出身卑贱的.

hum·bug /ˈhʌmbʌg; ˋhʌm,bʌg/ *n* **1** [U] dishonest behaviour or talk that is intended to deceive people and win their support or sympathy (为骗取支持或同情的)花招, 谎话. [C] dishonest and deceitful person 骗子. **2** [C] (*Brit*) hard boiled sweet, usu flavoured with peppermint 一种硬糖果(通常带薄荷味).

▷ **hum·bug** *v* (**-gg-**) [Tn, Tn·pr] **~ sb (into/out of sth/doing sth)** deceive or trick sb; cheat sb 欺诈或哄骗某人.

hum·dinger /ˌhʌmˈdɪŋə(r); ˌhʌmˋdɪŋɚ/ *n* (*sl* 俚) excellent or remarkable person or thing 很了不起的人或事物: *His girl-friend is a real humdinger.* 他的女朋友真了不起. ○ *We had a humdinger of an argument.* 我们着实地争论了一次.

H

hum·drum /ˈhʌmdrʌm; ˋhʌm,drʌm/ *adj* lacking excitement or variety; dull; monotonous 平淡的; 单调的; 乏味的: *humdrum chores* 乏味的日常杂务 ○ *Her life is humdrum.* 她的生活平平淡淡.

hu·merus /ˈhju:mərəs; ˋhjumərəs/ *n* (*pl* **humeri** /ˈhju:məraɪ; ˋhjumə,raɪ/) (*anatomy* 解) bone in the upper arm, from shoulder to elbow 肱骨. ⇨illus at SKELETON 见SKELETON 插图.

hu·mid /ˈhju:mɪd; ˋhjumɪd/ *adj* (of the air or climate) containing moisture; damp (指空气或气候)潮湿的, 湿润的: *humid heat, atmosphere* 湿热、潮湿的空气.

▷ **hu·mid·ify** /hju:ˈmɪdɪfaɪ; hjuˋmɪdə,faɪ/ *v* (*pt, pp* **-fied**) [Tn] make (the air, etc) damp 使(空气等)湿润. **hu·midi·fier** *n* device for keeping the air moist in a room, etc 增湿器.

hu·mid·ity /hju:ˈmɪdətɪ; hjuˋmɪdətɪ/ *n* [U] degree of moisture, esp in the air; dampness 湿度(尤指空气中的); 潮湿.

hu·mi·li·ate /hju:ˈmɪlɪeɪt; hjuˋmɪlɪ,et/ *v* [Tn] make (sb) feel ashamed or disgraced; lower the dignity or self-respect of 使(某人)感到羞耻或不光彩; 使丧失尊严或自尊: *He felt humiliated by her scornful remarks.* 他听到她那些嘲讽的话而感到屈辱. ○ *a country humiliated by defeat* 因战败而受辱的国家. ▷ **hu·mi·li·at·ing** *adj*: *a rather humiliating experience* 不怎么光彩的经历. **hu·mi·li·ation** /hju:ˌmɪlɪˈeɪʃn; hju,mɪlɪˋeʃən/ *n* [C, U]: *suffer public humiliation* 当众受辱.

hu·mil·ity /hju:ˈmɪlətɪ; hjuˋmɪlətɪ/ *n* [U] humble attitude of mind; modesty 谦虚的态度; 谦逊: *a person of great humility* 很谦虚的人 ○ *I say this in all humility*, ie without wishing to appear boastful. 我说的决不过分(无意夸张).

hum·mock /ˈhʌmək; ˋhʌmək/ *n* low hill or hump in the ground; hillock 小丘; 小山.

hu·mor·ist /ˈhju:mərɪst; ˋhjumərɪst/ *n* person who is known for his humorous writing or talk 幽默作家; 谈吐诙谐的人.

hu·mor·ous /ˈhju:mərəs; ˋhjumərəs/ *adj* having or showing a sense of humour; amusing; funny 幽默的; 诙谐的; 滑稽的: *a humorous writer, remark* 幽默的作家、话语 ○ *see the humorous side of a situation* 看到事情中滑稽的一面. ▷ **hu·mor·ously** *adv*.

hu·mour (*US* **hu·mor**) /ˈhju:mə(r); ˋhjumɚ/ *n* **1** [U] quality of being amusing or comic 幽默; 诙谐; 滑稽: *a story full of humour* 非常幽默的故事 ○ *recognize the humour of a situation* 看出某处境之可笑. **2** [U] ability to appreciate things, situations or people that are comic; ability to be amused 幽默感: *She lacks humour.* 她缺乏幽默感. ○ *He has a good sense of humour.* 他很有幽默感. **3** [U, sing] (*fml* 文) person's state of mind; mood; temper 人的精神状态; 心情; 脾气: *be in (an) excellent humour* 情绪很好 ○ *I'll do it when the humour takes me.* 我心情好时就去做. **4** [C] (*arch* 古) any of the four liquids (blood, phlegm, choler, melancholy) in the body that were once thought to determine a person's mental and physical qualities 四种体液(血液、黏液、胆汁、忧郁液)之一种(曾认为可对人的性情和健康起决定作用). **5** (idm 习语) ˌ**out of** ˈ**humour** (*dated fml* 旧, 文) in a bad mood 心情不好.

▷ **hu·mour** (*US* **hu·mor**) *v* [Tn] keep (sb) happy or contented by accepting or agreeing to his wishes, even if they seem unreasonable 迁就, 迎合(某人): *It's always best to humour him when he's in one of his bad moods.* 他心境不好的时候, 最好还是迁就他.

-humoured (*US* **-humored**) (forming compound *adjs* 用以构成复合形容词) having or showing the specified mood 有某种情绪的: *good-humoured* ○ *ill-humoured*.

hu·mour·less (*US* **hu·mor·less**) *adj* lacking a sense of humour 缺乏幽默感的: *a humourless person, style of writing* 无幽默感的人、无风趣的文风.

hump /hʌmp; hʌmp/ *n* **1** (**a**) round projecting part on the back of a camel, etc (骆驼等的)峰. ⇨illus at CAMEL 见CAMEL 插图. (**b**) deformity on a person's back, where there is an abnormal curvature of the spine (人的)驼背. **2** rounded raised mound of earth, etc (圆形的)土墩, 小丘, 冈: *a dangerous hump in the road* 道路上危险的隆起物. **3** (idm 习语) **give sb the** ˈ**hump** (*Brit infml* 口) make sb feel depressed or annoyed 使某人感到沮丧或烦恼. **over the** ˈ**hump** past the most difficult part (of a task, etc) 渡过(任务等的)最艰难阶段或完成最困难部分.

▷ **hump** *v* **1** [Tn, Tn·p] **~ sth (up)** form sth into a hump 使某物隆起: *hump up the bedclothes* 隆起被子. **2** [Tn·pr, Tn·p] carry (sth) on one's shoulder or back 扛或背(某物): *I don't enjoy humping heavy furniture around all day.* 一天到晚扛重家具我可受不了. ⇨Usage at CARRY 用法见CARRY. **3** [Tn] (⚠ *sl* 讳, 俚) have sexual intercourse with (sb) 与(某人)性交.

□ ˈ**humpback** *n* = HUNCHBACK (HUNCH). ˈ**humpbacked** *adj* = HUNCHBACKED (HUNCH). ˌ**humpback** ˈ**bridge** small bridge with an arch that rises and falls steeply 驼峰桥; 弓形桥.

humph /hʌmpf, həh; hʌmpf/ *interj* (light grunting sound usu made with the lips closed and used to express doubt or dissatisfaction 通常为双唇闭拢发出的轻微的哼声, 用以表示怀疑或不满).

hu·mus /ˈhju:məs; ˋhjuməs/ *n* [U] rich dark organic material formed by the decay of dead leaves, etc and essential to the fertility of soil 腐殖质.

Hun /hʌn; hʌn/ *n* **1** member of one of the Asiatic peoples who ravaged Europe in the 4th and 5th centuries AD 匈奴人. **2** (*derog offensive* 贬, 蔑) German 德国人.

hunch /hʌntʃ; hʌntʃ/ *n* idea based on intuition or instinct and not on evidence 基于直觉的想法: *He had a hunch that she was lying.* 他凭直觉认为她说的是谎话. ○ *play/follow one's hunch*, ie act according to one's intuition 凭直觉行事.

▷ **hunch** *v* [Tn, Tn·p] **~ sth (up)** bend forward (part of the body, esp the back and shoulders) into a rounded shape 把(身子)弯成弓状(尤指弯背、耸肩): *Stand straight, don't hunch your shoulders!* 站直了, 别耸肩! ○

She sat all hunched up over the small fire. 她蜷起身子坐在小火炉前.

□ ˈ**hunchback** (also ˈ**humpback**) *n* **1** rounded part on a person's back where there is an abnormal curvature of the spine; hump (人的)驼背. **2** person with such a deformity 驼背的人; 驼子. ˈ**hunchbacked** (also ˈ**humpbacked**) *adj* having such a hump on the back 驼背的.

hun·dred /ˈhʌndrəd; ˈhʌndrəd/ *pron, det* (after *a* or *one* or an indication of quantity 用于a、one或含有数量意义的词之后) 100; one more than ninety-nine 100, 一百(个): *one, two, three, etc hundred* 一百、二百、三百 ○ *a few hundred* 几百 ○ *There were a/one hundred (people) in the room.* 房间里有一百人. ○ *I could give you a hundred reasons for not going.* 我可以给你说出一百个不去的理由. ○ *This antique is worth several hundred pounds.* 这件古物值几百镑. ○ *If I've said it once, I've said it a hundred times.* 这件事我不但说过, 而且已经说过上百次了. ○ *He's a hundred (years old) today.* 他今天一百岁了. ⇨ App 4 见附录4.

▷ **hun·dred** *n* (after *a* or *one*, a number or an indication of quantity 用于a、one、数词或含有数量意义的词之后) the number 100 ☆ 100; 一百: *How many hundreds are there in a thousand?* 一千里有多少个一百? ○ *Her coat cost hundreds (of pounds).* 她的大衣值好几百(镑). ○ *There are hundreds (of people)* (ie very many) *who need new housing.* 有许许多多人需要新的住房. ○ *The cake was decorated with a large (one) hundred.* 这块蛋糕上面装饰着一个很大的'(一)百'字样.

hundred- (in compounds 用以构成复合词) having one hundred of the thing specified 有一百个...的: *a hundred-year lease*.

hun·dredth /ˈhʌndrətθ; ˈhʌndrədθ/ *pron, det* 100th; next after ninety-ninth 第100, 第一百(个). — *n* one of one hundred equal parts of sth 百分之一.

□ ˈ**hundredfold** *adj, adv* **1** one hundred times as much or as many 百倍(的). **2** having one hundred parts 一百分(的).

ˈ**hundredweight** *n* (*pl* unchanged 复数不变) (*abbr* 缩写 **cwt**) one twentieth of one ton; 112 lb (in US 100 lb) 英担(一吨的二十分之一, 英国为112磅, 美国为100磅). ⇨ App 5 见附录5.

hung *pt, pp* of HANG.

□ ˌ**hung-ˈover** *adj* [pred 作表语] (*infml* 口) having a hangover 酗酒之后感到不适: *I feel a bit hung-over this morning.* 今天早上我因宿醉而略感不适.

ˌ**hung ˈparliament** parliament in which no party has a clear majority 任何政党均未能占明显多数席位的议会.

hun·ger /ˈhʌŋgə(r); ˈhʌŋgɚ/ *n* **1** [U] (**a**) state of not having enough to eat; lack of food 饿; 饥饿: *He died of hunger.* 他饿死了. (**b**) desire for food 食欲: *satisfy one's hunger* 解饿. **2** [sing] **~ for sth** (*fig* 比喻) strong desire for sth 渴望某事物: *have a hunger for adventure* 渴望冒险.

▷ **hun·ger** *v* **1** [I] (*arch* 古) feel a lack of or desire for food 饥饿. **2** (phr v) **hunger for/after sth/sb** have a strong desire for sth/sb; long for sth/sb 渴望得到某事物[某人]: *She hungered for his love.* 她渴望得到他的爱.

□ ˈ**hunger march** long walk undertaken by unemployed people to make others aware of their sufferings (失业者的)反饥饿游行.

ˈ**hunger strike** refusal to take food, esp by a prisoner, as a form of protest 绝食抗议(尤指囚犯的): *be/go on (a) hunger strike* 进行绝食抗议. ˈ**hunger striker**.

hun·gry /ˈhʌŋgrɪ; ˈhʌŋgrɪ/ *adj* (**-ier**, **-iest**) **1** (**a**) suffering from weakness, pain, etc because of lack of food; starving 饥饿的; 挨饿的: *the hungry masses* 饥民. (**b**) feeling a desire for food 感到饿的: *Let's eat soon — I'm hungry!* 咱们早点儿吃吧——我饿了! **2** [pred 作表语] **~ for sth** (*fig* 比喻) in need of sth; feeling a strong desire for sth 需要某事物; 渴望得到某事物: *The orphan was hungry for affection.* 这孤儿渴望得到爱. **3** [usu attrib 通常作定语] showing hunger 显出饥饿样子的: *He had a hungry look.* 他面有饥色. **4** [attrib 作定语] causing hunger 引起饥饿的: *Haymaking is hungry work.* 割草晾晒的活儿很累, 干一会儿就饿了. **5** (idm 习语) **go ˈhungry** remain unfed 挨饿: *Thousands are going hungry because of the failure of the harvest.* 由于收成不好, 成千上万的人在挨饿. ○ *I'd rather go hungry than eat that!* 我宁可挨饿也不吃那种东西! ▷ **hun·grily** /ˈhʌŋgrəlɪ; ˈhʌŋgrɪlɪ/ *adv*.

hunk /hʌŋk; hʌŋk/ *n* **1** large piece (esp of food) cut from a larger piece (切下的)大块, 大片(尤指食物): *a hunk of bread, cheese, meat* 一大块面包、干酪、肉. **2** (*sl usu approv* 俚, 通常作褒义) big strong man, esp an attractive one 高大健壮的男子; (尤指)富于魅力的男子.

hunk·ers /ˈhʌŋkəz; ˈhʌŋkɚz/ *n* [pl] (*infml* 口) haunches 臀部; 屁股: *on one's hunkers*, ie in a squatting position 蹲着.

hunt[1] /hʌnt; hʌnt/ *v* **1** [I, Tn] chase (wild animals or game) and try to kill or capture them, for food or sport 打猎; 猎取(野生禽兽): *go hunting* 去打猎 ○ *Wolves hunt* (ie pursue their prey) *in packs.* 狼是成群猎食的. **2** [I, Ipr, Ip, Tn] **~ (for sth/sb)** search for (sth/sb); try to find (sth/sb) 搜索(某物[某人]); 试图找到(某物[某人]): *hunt for a lost book* 寻找一本失去的书 ○ *I've hunted everywhere but I can't find it.* 我到处都找遍了, 就是找不到. ○ *Police are hunting an escaped criminal.* 警方正在追捕逃犯. **3** [Tn·pr, Tn·p] drive or chase (sth) away; pursue (sth) with hostility 赶走, 驱逐(某物); 追逐, 追击(某物): *hunt the neighbour's cats out of the garden* 把邻居的猫赶出花园. **4** [Tn] (*Brit*) (**a**) (in fox-hunting) follow the hounds through or in (a district) (猎狐活动中)随猎狗通过或进入(某区域): *hunt the country* 在郊野猎狐. (**b**) use (a horse or hounds) in hunting 用(马或猎狗)打猎. (**c**) act as master or huntsman of (a pack of hounds) 带(一群猎狗)打猎. **5** (idm 习语) **run with the hare and hunt with the hounds** ⇨ HARE. **6** (phr v) **hunt sb/sth down** pursue sb/sth until he/it is found 对某人[某物]穷追到底: *hunt down a criminal* 追捕罪犯. **hunt sth out** search for sth (esp an object that has been put away or is no longer in use) until it is found 找出(尤指闲置或不复使用之物): *hunt out an old diary* 找出一本旧日记. **hunt sth up** search for sth (esp sth hidden and difficult to find) 寻找某物(尤指隐蔽而不易发现的): *hunt up references in the library* 在图书馆里查找参考资料.

▷ **hunter** *n* **1** (often in compounds 常用以构成复合词) person who hunts 狩猎者; 猎人: *hunters of big game in Africa* 捕猎非洲大猎物的人 ○ *ˈbargain-hunters in the sales*. **2** horse used in hunting 狩猎用的马. **3** watch with a metal cover over the glass face 猎用表(表蒙子上有金属护罩).

hunt·ing *n* [U] chasing and capturing or killing of wild animals, etc as a sport; (esp in Britain) fox-hunting 狩猎运动; (尤指英国的)猎狐运动: [attrib 作定语] *a ˈhunting jacket* 猎人装 ○ *a ˈhunting crop* 猎鞭.

hunting-ground *n* **1** place where one hunts for sth 猎场. **2** (idm 习语) **a happy, etc hunting-ground (for/of sb)** favourable place, etc where sb may do or observe or acquire what he wants (某人)可随意而为的大好去处: *Crowded shops are a happy hunting-ground for pick-pockets.* 拥挤不堪的商店是扒手行窃最得手的地方.

hunt·ress /ˈhʌntrɪs; ˈhʌntrɪs/ *n* (*dated* 旧) woman hunter 狩猎的女子; 女猎人.

NOTE ON USAGE 用法: **1** In British English **go hunting** refers to the sport of chasing and killing foxes with dogs while on horseback. 在英式英语中, **go hunting** 指骑马带狗猎狐的体育活动. The riders in charge of the hunt are called **huntsmen** and the event is a **hunt.** 这种骑马猎狐者叫 **huntsmen**, 这种猎狐活动叫 **hunt**. ☆ A **hunter** chases big game, eg lions, elephants, etc. ☆ **hunter** 指以大猎物(如狮、象等)为目标的狩猎者. **Shooting** is the killing of game birds, deer and other animals for sport. ☆ **shooting** 指猎杀野鸟、鹿及其他动物的体育活动. **2** In US English **hunting** relates to the shooting of deer or game birds by a **hunter.** 在美式英语中, **hunting** 指 **hunter** 猎杀鹿或野鸟.

hunt[2] /hʌnt; hʌnt/ *n* **1** [C] (often in compounds 常用以构成复合词) act of hunting wild animals; chase 打猎: *a ˈfox-hunt*. **2** [C usu *sing* 通常作单数] act of looking for sth; search 寻找; 搜索: *I had a good hunt for that key.* 那把钥匙我找了好一阵子. ○ *He found it after a long hunt.*

H

他找了很长时间才把它找到. ○ *The police are on the hunt for further clues.* 警方正进一步寻找线索. ○ *The hunt is on for the culprit.* 正在搜捕该罪犯. **3** (*esp Brit*) (**a**) [CGp] group of people who regularly hunt foxes, etc with horses and hounds (经常骑马带狗猎狐等的)打猎队伍. (**b**) [C] district in which they hunt (可作猎狐活动的)猎区, 猎场.

hunts·man /ˈhʌntsmən; ˋhʌntsmən/ *n* (*pl* **-men** /-mən; -mən/) **1** man who hunts wild animals, esp foxes 猎人; (尤指)猎狐的人. **2** man in charge of the hounds during a hunt 猎狐时管理猎犬的人.

hurdle /ˈhɜːdl; ˋhɝdḷ/ *n* **1** (**a**) [C] (in athletics or horse-racing) each of a series of upright frames to be jumped over in a race (体育或赛马用的)栏架, 跳栏: *five furlongs over hurdles* 五弗隆(即1 100码)跨栏比赛 ○ [attrib 作定语] *a ˈhurdle-race* 跨栏赛. ⇨illus 见插图. (**b**) **hurdles** [pl] race over these 跨栏赛: *He won the 400 metres hurdles.* 他在400米跨栏赛中获胜. **2** [C] (*fig* 比喻) difficulty to be overcome; obstacle 难关; 障碍: *I've passed the written test; the interview is the next hurdle.* 我书面考试已经及格了, 下一个难关是面试. **3** [C] portable oblong frame with bars used for making temporary fences (eg for sheep pens) (长方形的便携式)临时围栏(如羊栏).

▷ **hurdle** *v* [I] (in athletics) run in a hurdle-race (体育竞赛中)进行跨栏赛. **hurd·ler** /ˈhɜːdlə(r); ˋhɝdlɚ/ *n* person who runs in hurdle-races 跨栏运动员.

hurdy-gurdy /ˈhɜːdɪ gɜːdɪ; ˋhɝdɪˌgɝdɪ/ *n* **1** portable musical instrument with a droning sound, played by turning a handle 手摇风琴. **2** (*infml* 口) = BARREL-ORGAN (BARREL).

H

hurl /hɜːl; hɝl/ *v* [Tn, Tn·pr, Tn·p] **1** throw (sth/sb/oneself) violently; fling 用力扔(某物); 用力摔(某人); 猛扑: *rioters hurling stones at the police* 向警察扔石子的暴徒 ○ *He hurled himself into his work.* 他完全扑在工作上. ○ *She was hurled to her death.* 她被人砸死了. **2** (*fig* 比喻) utter (sth) with force; shout; yell 大声说出(某事); 叫喊; 叫嚷: *hurl insults at sb* 厉声辱骂某人.

hurl·ing /ˈhɜːlɪŋ; ˋhɝlɪŋ/ (also **hur·ley** /ˈhɜːlɪ; ˋhɝlɪ/) *n* [U] Irish ball game similar to hockey 爱尔兰式曲棍球戏.

hurly-burly /ˈhɜːlɪ bɜːlɪ; ˋhɝlɪˌbɝlɪ/ *n* [U] noisy and energetic activity (esp of many people together) 骚乱; 闹腾.

hur·rah /hʊˈrɑː; huˋrɑ/ (also **hur·ray**, **hoo·ray** /hʊˈreɪ; huˋre/) *interj* **1** ~ **(for sb/sth)** (used to express joy, approval, etc 用以表示欢喜、赞成等): *Hurrah for the holidays!* 好哇, 放假啦! **2** (idm 习语) **hip, hip, hurrah/hurray** ⇨ HIP[3].

▷ **hur·rah** (also **hur·ray**) *n* shout of 'hurrah' 叫好声; 欢呼声.

hur·ric·ane /ˈhʌrɪkən; *US* -keɪn; ˋhʌrɪˌken/ *n* **1** storm with a violent wind, esp a West Indian cyclone 飓风; (尤指西印度群岛的)旋风. **2** wind of 73 miles per hour or more (每小时风速73英里以上的)风暴: [attrib 作定语] *gales of hurricane force* 十二级的大风. Cf 参看 CYCLONE, TYPHOON.

□ ˈ**hurricane lamp** (also ˈ**storm-lantern**) type of lamp with glass sides to protect the flame from the wind 防风灯.

hurry /ˈhʌrɪ; ˋhʌrɪ/ *n* **1** [U] need or wish to get something done quickly; eager haste 匆忙; 急忙: *In his hurry to leave, he forgot his passport.* 他急急忙忙动身的时候, 忘了带护照. ○ *There's no hurry, so do it slowly and carefully.* 不必赶时间, 要慢慢细心地做. ○ *What's the hurry?* 忙什么呀? ○ *Why all the hurry?* 为什么这样匆匆忙忙? **2** (idm 习语) **in a** ˈ**hurry** (**a**) quickly; hastily 迅速地; 匆忙地: *She dressed in a hurry.* 她迅速穿好衣服. (**b**) eager; impatient 急切; 赶紧: *He was in a hurry to leave.* 他急于离开. (**c**) (*infml* 口) (usu with a negative 通常与否定词连用) soon; readily 立刻; 乐意地; 轻易地: *I shan't invite him again in a hurry — he behaved very badly.* 我实在不愿意再邀请他——他的举止太不像话. ○ *She won't forget that in a hurry.* 她不会一下子就忘的. **in no** ˈ**hurry/not in any** ˈ**hurry** (**a**) not eager or under pressure to act 不急于行动; 不着忙: *I don't mind waiting — I'm not in any particular hurry.* 我可以等着——我没有什么急事儿. (**b**) unwilling 不愿意: *I'm in no hurry to see him again.* 我不愿再见到他.

▷ **hurry** *v* (*pt, pp* **hurried**) **1** (**a**) [I, Ipr, Ip] do sth or move quickly or too quickly; rush 迅速地或仓促地做某事或移动; 赶紧: *Don't hurry; there's plenty of time.* 别忙, 有的是时间. ○ *It's no use trying to make her hurry.* 想催她快点是没用的. ○ *He picked up his bag and hurried off along the platform.* 他拿起提包急急忙忙地沿着站台走了. ○ *Hurry along, children!* 孩子们, 赶快! (**b**) [Tn, Tn·pr, Tn·p] make (sb) do sth or move quickly or too quickly 使(某人)迅速地或仓促地做某事或移动; 催(某人): *We're late; I must hurry you.* 咱们迟到了, 我必须催你一下. ○ *They hurried him into hospital.* 他们催他上医院. ○ *I was hurried into making an unwise decision.* 我在催逼之下草率地做出了不智的决定. **2** [Tn, Tn·p] ~ **sth (along/up)** hasten the progress of sth 使某事加快; 催促某事物: *This work needs care; it mustn't be hurried.* 这活儿需要细心, 催不得. ○ *A good meal should never be hurried.* 美食不应狼吞虎咽. **3** (phr v) **hurry up** (*infml* 口) move more quickly or too quickly; do sth more quickly 加快地或仓促地移动; 快些做某事: *I wish the train would hurry up and come.* 我希望列车快点开来. ○ *Hurry up and get ready — we're waiting!* 快点准备好——我们在等着呢! **hurry sb/sth up** make sb/sth do sth or move quickly or too quickly; speed sth up 使某人[某事物]迅速地或仓促地做某事或移动; 使某事物加快速度: *He's a good worker but he needs hurrying up.* 他工作做得好, 只是需要督促. **hur·ried** *adj* done quickly or too quickly 匆匆赶完的; 仓促完成的: *a hurried meal* 匆匆吃完的一顿饭 ○ *write a few hurried lines* 草草写几行字. **hur·riedly** *adv*: *We had to leave rather hurriedly.* 我们只好匆匆离去.

hurt /hɜːt; hɝt/ *v* (*pt, pp* **hurt**) **1** (**a**) [I, Tn] cause physical injury or pain to (sb/oneself, a part of the body, an animal, etc) 使(某人[自己]、身体的某个部位、动物等)受伤或受肉体痛苦: *Did you hurt yourself?* 你把自己弄伤了吗? ○ *Are you badly hurt?* 你伤得厉害吗? ○ *She was more frightened than hurt.* 她受惊较之受伤更为严重. ○ *He hurt his back when he fell.* 他跌倒时背部受了伤. (**b**) [I] feel or cause pain 感到或引起疼痛: *My leg hurts.* 我腿疼. ○ *My shoes hurt; they're too tight.* 我的鞋太紧, 穿着脚疼. ○ *It hurts when I move my leg.* 我的腿一动就疼. ⇨Usage at WOUND[1] 用法见 WOUND[1]. **2** [Tn] cause mental pain to (a person, his feelings); distress; upset 使(某人)精神痛苦; 伤(某人)心; 伤(感情); 使烦恼: *These criticisms have hurt him/his pride deeply.* 这些批评使他很伤心[使他的自尊心受到了伤害]. ○ *It hurts/I am hurt not to have been invited.* 没有邀请我, 我很不痛快. ○ *I hope we haven't offended him; he sounded rather hurt on the phone.* 但愿我们没有得罪他, 他在电话里的声音像是受了委屈. **3** [Tn] have a bad effect on (sth); harm 对(某事物)有不良影响; 损害: *Sales of the product have been seriously hurt by the adverse publicity.* 该产品受到了反面宣传, 销量大受影响. **4** (idm 习语) **it, etc won't/wouldn't hurt (sb/sth) (to do sth)** (*esp ironic* 尤作反语) it, etc will/would not cause harm or inconvenience 不会有什么害处或不便: *It won't hurt to postpone the meeting.* 不妨把开会时间往后延. ○ *A bit of weeding wouldn't hurt (this garden).* 有一点杂草(对这个花园来说)也无所谓. ○ *It wouldn't hurt (you) to say sorry for once.* 说一声对不起(于你)没有什么不好. **not harm/hurt a fly** ⇨ FLY[1].

▷ **hurt** *n* **1** [U, sing] ~ **(to sth)** mental pain or suffering 精神上的痛苦或创伤: *The experience left me with a feeling of deep hurt.* 这段经历给我心灵上留下了严重的创伤. ○ *It was a severe hurt to her pride.* 这严重地伤害了她的自尊心. **2** [C] physical injury or pain 肉体

上的伤害或痛苦. **hurt·ful** /-fl; -fəl/ *adj* **~ (to sb)** causing (esp mental) suffering; unkind 使人(尤指精神上)痛苦的; 刻薄的: *hurtful remarks* 伤人感情的言语 ○ *She can be very hurtful sometimes.* 她有时是很刻薄的. **hurt·fully** /-fəlɪ; -fəlɪ/ *adv*. **hurt·ful·ness** *n* [U].

hurtle /ˈhɜːtl; ˈhɝtl/ *v* [Ipr, Ip] move violently, noisily or with great speed in the specified direction 猛力地或飞快地朝某方向运动(有时发出声响): *During the gale roof tiles came hurtling down.* 在暴风中屋顶的瓦片哗啦啦地落了下来. ○ *The van hurtled round the corner.* 客货车疾驶转过街角. ○ *She slipped and went hurtling downstairs.* 她一失足咕噜噜跌下楼梯.

hus·band /ˈhʌzbənd; ˈhʌzbənd/ *n* **1** man to whom a woman is married 丈夫: *her new husband* 她的新婚丈夫 ○ *He'll make someone a very good husband.* 谁要嫁给他那就太幸福了. ⇨App 8 见附录8. **2** (idm 习语) ˌ**husband and** ˈ**wife** married couple 夫妇: *They lived together as husband and wife for years.* 他们结为夫妇共同生活了很多年.

▷ **hus·band** *v* [Tn] (*fml* 文) use (sth) sparingly and economically; try to save 节省地使用(某事物); 节约: *husband one's strength, resources* 节省体力、资源.

hus·bandry /ˈhʌzbəndrɪ; ˈhʌzbəndrɪ/ *n* [U] (*fml* 文) **1** farming 农牧业: *animal husbandry* 畜牧业. **2** management of resources 对资源的管理: *Through careful husbandry we survived the hard winter.* 通过精打细算, 我们终于熬过了严冬.

hush /hʌʃ; hʌʃ/ *v* **1** (**a**) [I] become silent 安静下来: *Hush!* ie Be quiet! 肃静! (**b**) [Tn, Tn·pr] make (sb) silent or calm; quieten (sb) 使(某人)安静下来或平静下来: *He hushed the baby to sleep.* 他把婴儿哄得安然入睡. **2** (phr v) **hush sth up** prevent sth from becoming generally known, esp sth shameful 防止某事物(尤指丑闻)张扬出去: *The government hushed the affair up to avoid a public outcry.* 当局对此事秘而不宣, 以免引起公众抗议.

▷ **hush** *n* [U, sing] stillness; silence 安静; 寂静: *in the hush of the night* 在夜的寂静中 ○ *There was a sudden deathly hush.* 突然间周围像死一般寂静.

□ ˌ**hush-**ˈ**hush** *adj* (*infml* 口) very secret or confidential 非常秘密的; 机密的: *a hush-hush affair* 秘事 ○ *His job is very hush-hush.* 他的工作是很保密的.

ˈ**hush-money** *n* [U] money paid to prevent sth scandalous from becoming known publicly 封口钱, 遮羞费(为防止丑事张扬的贿赂).

husk /hʌsk; hʌsk/ *n* **1** dry outer covering of certain seeds and fruits, esp grain (某些种子和果实的)外壳, 外皮(尤指谷类的): *rice in the husk*, ie brown rice, with the husks not removed 稻谷. Cf 参看 BRAN, CHAFF. **2** (*fig* 比喻) worthless outside part of anything (任何东西的没有价值的)外层部分.

▷ **husk** *v* [Tn] remove the husk(s) from (seeds or fruit) 除去(种子或果实)的外壳.

husky[1] /ˈhʌskɪ; ˈhʌskɪ/ *adj* (**-ier, -iest**) **1** (of a person or voice) dry in the throat; sounding slightly hoarse (指人或嗓音)喉咙发干的, 沙哑的: *I'm still a bit husky after my recent cold.* 我最近患过感冒, 声音还有些哑. **2** (*infml* 口) (of a person) big and strong (指人)高大强壮的; 魁梧的. ▷ **husk·ily** *adv*: *speak huskily* 以嘶哑的声音说. **huski·ness** *n* [U].

husky[2] /ˈhʌskɪ; ˈhʌskɪ/ *n* strong breed of dog with a thick coat, used in the Arctic for pulling sledges 爱斯基摩狗(强壮的厚毛狗, 在北极地区用来拖曳雪橇).

hus·sar /hʊˈzɑː(r); hʊˈzɑr/ *n* soldier of a cavalry regiment, carrying light weapons 轻骑兵.

hussy /ˈhʌsɪ; ˈhʌsɪ/ *n* (*dated derog* 旧, 贬) **1** bold cheeky girl 粗野的女子. **2** sexually immoral woman 淫荡的女子; 荡妇: *You brazen hussy!* 你这个不要脸的婊子!

hust·ings /ˈhʌstɪŋz; ˈhʌstɪŋz/ *n* [pl] **the hustings** the political campaigning leading up to a parliamentary election, eg canvassing votes and making speeches (议会选举前的)竞选活动(如拉选票和演讲): *Most politicians will be at/on the hustings in the coming week.* 大多数政治家将在下周展开竞选活动.

hustle /ˈhʌsl; ˈhʌsl/ *v* **1** [Tn·pr, Tn·p] push (sb) roughly and hurriedly; jostle; shove 推搡(某人); 猛推; 挤撞: *The police hustled the thief out of the house and into their van.* 警察把那个窃贼推搡出房子又推进囚车里. ○ *The thief was hustled off (to gaol).* 那窃贼被推推搡搡(进入监房). **2** [Tn, Tn·pr] **~ sb (into sth/doing sth)** make sb act quickly and without time to consider things 催促(某人); 催赶(某人): *I was hustled into (making) a hasty decision.* 我在催逼之下匆匆地做出决定. **3** [I] hurry; push one's way 匆忙; 挤撞着走: *people hustling and bustling all around us* 在我们的周围熙来攘往的人. **4** [Tn] (*infml* 口 *esp US*) sell or obtain (sth) by energetic (and sometimes deceitful) activity 竭力地(有时以欺诈手段)兜售或获取(某事物). **5** [I] (*US sl* 俚) work as a prostitute 卖淫.

▷ **hustle** *n* [U] busy energetic activity 忙碌; 奔忙: *I hate all the hustle (and bustle) of Saturday shopping.* 我讨厌星期六买东西那么挤来挤去的.

hust·ler /ˈhʌslə(r); ˈhʌslɚ/ *n* **1** (*infml* 口 *esp US*) person who hustles (HUSTLE 4) 竭力地(有时以欺诈手段)兜售或获取某物的人. **2** (*US sl* 俚) prostitute 妓女; 男妓.

hut /hʌt; hʌt/ *n* small roughly-built house or shelter, usu made of wood or metal 简陋的小房子, 棚, 舍(通常为木头或金属建造的). Cf 参看 SHED[1].

▷ **hut·ment** /ˈhʌtmənt; ˈhʌtmənt/ *n* group of huts, esp for soldiers 一片简陋的小房子; (尤指军队的)营房.

hut·ted having huts 有简陋小房子的: *a hutted camp* 有简陋小房子的兵营.

hutch /hʌtʃ; hʌtʃ/ *n* box or cage with a front of wire netting, esp one used for keeping rabbits in 正面有铁丝网的箱或笼; (尤指)兔笼.

hy·acinth /ˈhaɪəsɪnθ; ˈhaɪəˌsɪnθ/ *n* plant with sweet-smelling bell-shaped flowers, growing from a bulb 风信子. ⇨illus at App 1 见附录1插图, page ii.

hy·aena = HYENA.

hy·brid /ˈhaɪbrɪd; ˈhaɪbrɪd/ *n* **1** animal or plant that has parents of different species or varieties 杂交生成的动植物; 杂种动物; 杂交植物: *A mule is a hybrid of a male donkey and a female horse.* 骡子是公驴和母马交配而生的杂种动物. **2** thing made by combining two different elements, esp a word with parts from different languages (不同成分的)混合物, 合成物; (尤指由不同语言成分构成的)混合词.

▷ **hy·brid** *adj* **1** produced as a hybrid; cross-bred 杂交产生的; 杂种的: *a hybrid animal, plant* 由杂交生成的动物、植物. **2** composed of unrelated parts 混合的; 合成的; 混成的.

hy·brid·ize, -ise /-aɪz; -ˌaɪz/ *v* **1** [I] (of animals or plants) produce hybrids; interbreed (指动植物)产生杂交品种, 杂交. **2** [Tn] cause (animals or plants) to produce hybrids; cross-breed 使(动植物)产生杂交品种; 使杂交.

hy·dra /ˈhaɪdrə; ˈhaɪdrə/ *n* **1** (in Greek mythology) snake-like monster with many heads that grew again if they were cut off (希腊神话中的)蛇怪(长着许多头, 斩去后能重新长出). **2** (*fig* 比喻) thing that is hard to get rid of; recurring problem 难以除掉的事物; 一再出现的问题.

hy·dran·gea /haɪˈdreɪndʒə; haɪˈdrendʒə/ *n* shrub with white, pink or blue flowers growing in large round clusters 绣球花(有白色、粉红色或蓝色大花球).

hy·drant /ˈhaɪdrənt; ˈhaɪdrənt/ *n* pipe (esp in a street) with a nozzle to which a hose can be attached, for drawing water from a water-main to clean streets, put out fires, etc (尤指街道上的)给水栓, 消防栓.

hy·drate /ˈhaɪdreɪt; ˈhaɪdret/ *n* chemical compound of water with another substance 水合物.

▷ **hy·drate** /ˈhaɪdreɪt, haɪˈdreɪt; ˈhaɪdret/ *v* **1** [I] combine chemically with water 与水结合; 水合. **2** [Tn] cause (a substance) to absorb water 使(某物质)吸入水分. **hy·dra·tion** /haɪˈdreɪʃn; haɪˈdreʃən/ *n* [U].

hy·draulic /haɪˈdrɔːlɪk; haɪˈdrɔlɪk/ *adj* **1** of water moving through pipes 通过水管流动之水的. **2** operated by the movement of liquid 用水力驱动的: *a hydraulic lift* 液压升降机 ○ *hydraulic brakes* 液压制动器 ○ *a hydraulic engineer*, ie one concerned with the use of water in this way 水利工程师. **3** hardening under water 水硬的; 在水中凝固的: *hydraulic cement* 水硬水泥.

▷ **hy·draul·ic·ally** /-klɪ; -klɪ/ *adv*.

hy·draul·ics *n* [sing or pl *v*] science of using water to produce power 水力学.

hydr(o)- *comb form* 构词成分 **1** of water or liquid 水的; 液体的: *hydroelectricity*. **2** combined with hydrogen

H

氢化的: *hydrochloric*.

hy·dro·car·bon /ˌhaɪdrəˈkɑːbən; ˌhaɪdroˈkɑrbən/ *n* any of a class of compounds of hydrogen and carbon that are found in petrol, coal and natural gas 烃; 碳氢化合物.

hy·dro·chloric /ˌhaɪdrəˈklɒrɪk; *US* -ˈklɔːr-; ˌhaɪdrəˈklɔrɪk/ *adj* containing hydrogen and chlorine 含氢和氯的: ˌ*hydrochloric* ˈ*acid* 盐酸.

hy·dro·elec·tric /ˌhaɪdrəʊɪˈlektrɪk; ˌhaɪdroɪˈlɛktrɪk/ *adj* (**a**) using water-power to produce electricity 使用水力发电的: *a hydroelectric plant* 水力发电厂. (**b**) (of electricity) produced by the pressure of rushing water (指电)水力发出的: *hydroelectric power* 水电力. ▷ **hy·dro·elec·tric·ally** /-klɪ; -klɪ/ *adv*. **hy·dro·elec·tri·city** /ˌhaɪdrəʊˌɪlekˈtrɪsətɪ; ˌhaɪdroɪˌlɛkˈtrɪsətɪ/ *n* [U].

hy·dro·foil /ˈhaɪdrəfɔɪl; ˈhaɪdrəˌfɔɪl/ *n* **1** boat equipped with a device which raises the hull out of the water when the boat is moving, enabling it to travel fast and economically 水翼船. **2** such a device 水翼.

hy·dro·gen /ˈhaɪdrədʒən; ˈhaɪdrədʒən/ *n* [U] (*chemistry* 化) gas that has no colour, taste or smell and is the lightest substance known, combining with oxygen to form water 氢. ⇨App 10 见附录10.

□ ˈ**hydrogen bomb** (also ˈ**H-bomb**) immensely powerful type of bomb which explodes when the nuclei of hydrogen atoms fuse 氢弹.

ˌ**hydrogen peˈroxide** = PEROXIDE 2.

hy·dro·meter /ˌhaɪˈdrɒmɪtə(r); haɪˈdrɑmətə/ *n* scientific instrument that measures the density of liquids 液体比重计.

hy·dro·phobia /ˌhaɪdrəˈfəʊbɪə; ˌhaɪdrəˈfobɪə/ *n* [U] **1** abnormal fear of water and of drinking, esp as a symptom of rabies in humans 恐水(尤指恐水病的症状). **2** rabies, esp in humans (尤指人患的)恐水病, 狂犬病.

hy·dro·plane /ˈhaɪdrəpleɪn; ˈhaɪdrəˌplen/ *n* **1** light motor boat with a flat bottom, that can travel fast over the surface of the water 机动平底快艇. **2** device on a submarine enabling it to rise or descend (控制潜艇升降的)水平舵.

hy·dro·pon·ics /ˌhaɪdrəˈpɒnɪks; ˌhaɪdrəˈpɑnɪks/ *n* [sing *v*] art of growing plants without soil in water or sand to which chemical food is added 溶液栽培; 水培; 营养栽培; 无土栽培.

hy·dro·ther·apy /ˌhaɪdrəʊˈθerəpɪ; ˌhaɪdrəˈθɛrəpɪ/ *n* [U] treatment of disease and abnormal physical conditions by exercising the body in water and applying water internally 水疗法.

hy·ena (also **hy·aena**) /haɪˈiːnə; haɪˈinə/ *n* flesh-eating animal of Africa and Asia, like a wolf, with a howl that sounds like wild laughter 鬣狗(产于非洲和亚洲, 似狼, 食肉, 叫声似狂笑).

hy·giene /ˈhaɪdʒiːn; ˈhaɪdʒin/ *n* [U] study and practice of cleanliness as a way of maintaining good health and preventing disease 卫生(学): *Wash regularly to ensure personal hygiene.* 要经常洗澡以保证个人卫生. ○ *In the interests of hygiene, please do not smoke in this shop.* 请勿在本店吸烟以利健康.

▷ **hy·gienic** /haɪˈdʒiːnɪk; *US* ˌhaɪdʒɪˈenɪk; *US also* haɪˈdʒenɪk; ˌhaɪdʒɪˈɛnɪk, haɪˈdʒɛnɪk/ *adj* free from germs that cause disease; clean 卫生的; 清洁的: *hygienic conditions* 卫生的环境. **hy·gien·ic·ally** /-klɪ; -klɪ/ *adv*.

hy·men /ˈhaɪmən; ˈhaɪmən/ *n* (*anatomy* 解) piece of skin-like tissue partly closing the external opening of the vagina of a virgin girl or woman 处女膜.

hymn /hɪm; hɪm/ *n* song of praise, esp one praising God sung by Christians 赞美诗, 圣歌(尤指基督徒为颂扬上帝而唱的).

▷ **hymn** *v* [Tn] praise (God) in hymns 唱圣歌赞颂(上帝).

hym·nal /ˈhɪmnəl; ˈhɪmnəl/ (also ˈ**hymn·book**) *n* book of hymns 赞美诗集.

hype /haɪp; haɪp/ *n* [C, U] (*sl* 俚) (piece of) misleading and exaggerated publicity 天花乱坠的宣传报道: *The public were not fooled by all the hype the press gave the event.* 新闻界言过其实的种种报道并没有愚弄得了公众.

▷ **hype** *v* (phr v) **hype sth up** (*sl* 俚) publicize sth in a wildly exaggerated way 言过其实地宣传某事物: *The movie has been hyped up far beyond its worth.* 这部影片被吹得离了谱了. **hyped up** *adj* (*sl* 俚) **1** exaggerated 夸张的; 言过其实的. **2** (of a person) stimulated (as if) by drugs (指人)(似)因毒品刺激而变得兴奋的.

hyper- *pref* 前缀 (with *adjs* and *ns* 与形容词和名词结合) to an excessive degree; above; over 过度; 在...上; 高于: *hypercritical* ○ *hypersensitive* ○ *hypertension*. Cf 参看 OVER-.

hy·per·act·ive /ˌhaɪpə(r)ˈæktɪv; ˌhaɪpəˈæktɪv/ *adj* (esp of a child) abnormally and excessively active; unable to relax (尤指儿童)活跃得反常的, 多动的. ▷ **hy·per·ac·tiv·ity** /ˌhaɪpəræk'tɪvətɪ; ˌhaɪpəæk'tɪvətɪ/ *n* [U]

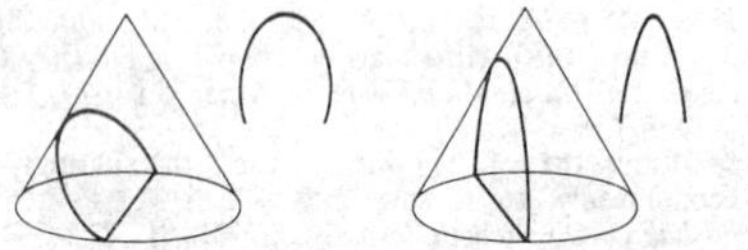

PARABOLA 抛物线 HYPERBOLA 双曲线

hy·per·bola /haɪˈpɜːbələ; haɪˈpɝbələ/ *n* (*geometry* 几) curve produced when a cone is cut by a plane that makes a larger angle with the base than the side of the cone makes 双曲线. ⇨illus 见插图. ▷ **hy·per·bolic** /ˌhaɪpəˈbɒlɪk; ˌhaɪpəˈbɑlɪk/ *adj*.

hy·per·bole /haɪˈpɜːbəlɪ; haɪˈpɝbəlɪ/ *n* [U, C] exaggerated statement that is made for special effect and is not meant to be taken literally, eg *I've invited millions of people to my party* 夸张(修辞手段, 如我请来赴宴的人成千上万). ▷ **hy·per·bol·ical** /ˌhaɪpəˈbɒlɪkl; ˌhaɪpəˈbɑlɪkəl/ *adj*.

hy·per·crit·ical /ˌhaɪpəˈkrɪtɪkl; ˈhaɪpəˈkrɪtɪkl/ *adj* too critical, esp of small faults 批评苛刻的; (尤指)吹毛求疵的. ▷ **hy·per·crit·ic·ally** /-klɪ; -klɪ/ *adv*.

hy·per·mar·ket /ˈhaɪpəmɑːkɪt; ˈhaɪpəˌmɑrkɪt/ *n* (*Brit*) very large self-service shop, selling a wide range of goods and offering a number of services (eg hairdressing), usu situated outside a town 巨型超级市场(采取自选购物方式, 经营范围极广并提供多种服务, 如美发等, 通常设于城区之外).

hy·per·sens·it·ive /ˌhaɪpəˈsensətɪv; ˌhaɪpəˈsɛnsətɪv/ *adj* **1 ~ (to/about sth)** extremely sensitive emotionally (情绪上)过敏的. **2 ~ (to sth)** abnormally sensitive to certain drugs, etc (对某些药物等)有过敏反应的. ▷ **hy·per·sens·it·iv·ity** /ˌhaɪpəˌsensəˈtɪvətɪ; ˌhaɪpəˌsɛnsəˈtɪvətɪ/ *n* [U].

hy·per·ten·sion /ˌhaɪpəˈtenʃn; ˌhaɪpəˈtɛnʃən/ *n* [U] (*medical* 医) **1** abnormally high blood pressure 高血压. **2** great emotional tension 精神过度紧张.

hy·phen /ˈhaɪfn; ˈhaɪfən/ *n* short line (-) used to join two words together (as in *ex-wife*; *co-operated*; *long-legged*; *a ten-dollar bill*) or to show that a word has been divided into parts, eg between the end of one line and the beginning of the next 连接号(-)(用以将两词连接为一个复合词, 如ex-wife、co-operated、long-legged、a ten-dollar bill中者, 或将词分解为其组成之部分, 如移行时所见). ⇨App 3 见附录3.

▷ **hy·phen**, **hy·phen·ate** /ˈhaɪfəneɪt; ˈhaɪfənˌet/ *vs* [Tn] join or write (words) with a hyphen 用连接号连接或分割(词语). **hy·phena·tion** /ˌhaɪfəˈneɪʃn; ˌhaɪfəˈneʃən/ *n* [U].

hyp·no·sis /hɪpˈnəʊsɪs; hɪpˈnosɪs/ *n* [U] state like deep sleep in which a person's actions may be controlled by another person 催眠状态: *put a person under hypnosis* 对某人施催眠术.

▷ **hyp·notic** /hɪpˈnɒtɪk; hɪpˈnɑtɪk/ *adj* **1** of or producing hypnosis or a similar condition 催眠(术)的; 有催眠或类似催眠作用的: *be in a hypnotic trance* 在受催眠状态中. **2** (of a drug) producing sleep (指药物)安眠的. — *n* hypnotic drug or influence 催眠药物或催眠作用; 安眠药或安眠效果.

hyp·not·ism /ˈhɪpnətɪzəm; ˈhɪpnəˌtɪzəm/ *n* [U] production or practice of hypnosis 催眠; 催眠术.

hyp·not·ist /ˈhɪpnətɪst; ˈhɪpnətɪst/ *n* person who

produces hypnosis in another person or who practices hypnosis 催眠术士.

hyp·not·ize, -ise /ˈhɪpnətaɪz; ˋhɪpnə,taɪz/ *v* [Tn] **1** produce hypnosis in (sb) 对(某人)施催眠术. **2** (*fig* 比喻) fascinate (sb); chaam 使(某人)精神恍惚; 使着迷: *He was hypnotized by her beauty.* 他见她艳丽动人而神魂颠倒.

hypo /ˈhaɪpəʊ; ˋhaɪpo/ *n* (*pl* **~s**) (*infml* 口) = HYPODERMIC *n*.

hyp(o)- *pref* 前缀 under; beneath 在...下; 低于; 次于: *hypodermic* ○ *hypothesis*.

hy·po·chon·dria /ˌhaɪpəˈkɒndrɪə; ,haɪpəˋkɑndrɪə/ *n* [U] abnormal and unnecessary anxiety about one's health (过分关心自己的健康而引起的病态的过虑)疑病症, 忧郁症.

▷ **hy·po·chon·driac** /-drɪæk; -drɪ,æk/ *n* person who suffers from hypochondria 疑病症患者. Cf 参看 VALETUDINARIAN. — *adj* of or suffering from hypochondria (患)疑病症的.

hy·po·crisy /hɪˈpɒkrəsɪ; hɪˋpɑkrəsɪ/ *n* [U] practice of misrepresenting one's real character, opinions, etc, esp by pretending to be more virtuous than one really is; insincerity 伪善; 虚伪.

▷ **hy·po·crite** /ˈhɪpəkrɪt; ˋhɪpə,krɪt/ *n* person who pretends to have opinions which he does not have or to be what he is not 伪善者; 伪君子.

hy·po·crit·ical /ˌhɪpəˈkrɪtɪkl; ,hɪpəˋkrɪtɪkḷ/ *adj* of hypocrisy or a hypocrite 伪善的; 虚伪的; 伪善者的; 伪君子的: *hypocritical behaviour, people* 伪善的行为、人. **hy·po·crit·ic·ally** /-klɪ; -klɪ/ *adv*.

hy·po·dermic /ˌhaɪpəˈdɜːmɪk; ,haɪpəˋdɝmɪk/ *adj* (**a**) (of drugs, etc) injected beneath the skin (指药物等)皮下注射的. (**b**) (of a syringe) used for such injections (指注射器)供皮下注射使用的: *a hypodermic needle* 皮下注射器针头.

▷ **hy·po·dermic** *n* **1** (also *infml* 口语亦作 **hypo**) hypodermic syringe 皮下注射器. **2** hypodermic injection 皮下注射.

□ ˌ**hypodermic syˈringe** (also **syringe**) syringe with a hollow needle used for injecting a liquid beneath the skin, taking blood samples, etc 皮下注射器. ⇨illus at INJECTION 见 INJECTION 插图.

hy·po·ten·use /haɪˈpɒtənjuːz; *US* -tənuːs; haɪˋpɑtṇ,us/ *n* (*geometry* 几) side opposite the right angle of a right-angled triangle (直角三角形的)斜边, 弦. ⇨illus at TRIANGLE 见 TRIANGLE 插图.

hy·po·ther·mia /ˌhaɪpəˈθɜːmɪə; ,haɪpəˋθɝmɪə/ *n* [U] (*medical* 医) condition of having an abnormally low body-temperature 体温过低.

hy·po·thesis /haɪˈpɒθəsɪs; haɪˋpɑθəsɪs/ *n* (*pl* **-ses** /-siːz; -,siz/) idea or suggestion that is based on known facts and is used as a basis for reasoning or further investigation (根据已知事实提出并有待于进一步论证或研究的)假说, 假设: *put sth forward as a hypothesis* 提出一种假说 ○ *prove/disprove a hypothesis* 证明某种假设正确[不正确].

▷ **hy·po·thes·ize, -ise** /haɪˈpɒθəsaɪz; ,haɪˋpɑθə,saɪz/ *v* [I, Tn, Tf] form a hypothesis; assume (sth) as a hypothesis 假设; 假定(某事物).

hy·po·thet·ical /ˌhaɪpəˈθetɪkl; ,haɪpəˋθɛtɪkḷ/ *adj* of or based on a hypothesis; not necessarily true or real (基于)假设的; 未必是事实的. **hy·po·thet·ic·ally** /-klɪ; -klɪ/ *adv*.

hys·ter·ec·tomy /ˌhɪstəˈrektəmɪ; ,hɪstəˋrɛktəmɪ/ *n* [C, U] (*medical* 医) surgical operation for removing a woman's womb 子宫切除(术).

hys·teria /hɪˈstɪərɪə; hɪsˋtɪrɪə/ *n* [U] (**a**) wild uncontrollable emotion or excitement, with eg laughter, crying or screaming 歇斯底里; 癔病: *crowds of football supporters gripped by mass hysteria* 众多歇斯底里的球迷. (**b**) disturbance of the nervous system, esp with emotional outbursts 精神错乱(尤指有情绪发作之表现者).

▷ **hys·ter·ical** /hɪˈsterɪkl; hɪsˋtɛrɪkḷ/ *adj* **1** caused by hysteria 因患歇斯底里而引起的: *hysterical laughter, weeping, screaming, etc* 歇斯底里的大笑、大哭、大叫等 ○ *hysterical behaviour* 歇斯底里的表现. **2** suffering from hysteria 患歇斯底里的: *hysterical fans at a rock concert* 摇滚音乐会的狂热听众. **3** (*infml* 口) very amusing 极可笑的; 极有趣的. **hyster·ic·ally** /-klɪ; -klɪ/ *adv*: *laughing hysterically* 狂笑 ○ (*infml* 口) *It was hysterically funny.* 这太可笑了.

hy·sterics /hɪˈsterɪks; hɪsˋtɛrɪks/ *n* [pl] **1** fit of hysteria 歇斯底里的发作: *go into hysterics* 歇斯底里发作 ○ (*infml* 口) *Your mother would have hysterics* (ie be very angry and upset) *if she knew you were using her car.* 你母亲要是知道你用了她的汽车, 一定大发雷霆. **2** (*infml* 口) wild uncontrolled laughter 无法控制的狂笑: *She had the audience in hysterics.* 她把观众逗得捧腹大笑.

Hz *abbr* 缩写 = hertz. Cf 参看 KHz.

I i

I, i[1] /aɪ; aɪ/ *n* (*pl* **I's, i's** /aɪz; aɪz/) **1** the ninth letter of the English alphabet 英语字母表的第九个字母: *'Idiot' begins with an I/'I'.* 'idiot' 一字以 i 字母开始. **2** (idm 习语) **dot one's/the i's and cross one's/the t's** ⇨ DOT *v*.

I[2] /aɪ; aɪ/ *pers pron* 人称代词 (used as the subject of a *v* 用作动词的主体) person who is the speaker or writer 我(说话者或写作者称自己): *I think I'd like a bath.* 我想洗个澡. ○ *When he asked me to marry him I said yes.* 他向我求婚, 我答应了. Cf 参看 ME.

I *abbr* 缩写 = Island(s); Isle(s): *CI*, ie (the) Channel Islands, eg in an address 海峡群岛(如用于地址中) ○ *I* (ie Isle) *of Man*, eg on a map 马恩岛(如地图上的标记). Cf 参看 Is *abbr* 缩写.

I (also **i**) *symb* 符号 Roman numeral for 1 罗马数字的 1.

-ial *suff* 后缀 (with *ns* forming *adjs* 与名词结合构成形容词) characteristic of 有…特性的: *dictatorial* ○ *managerial* ○ *editorial*. ▷ **-ially** (forming *advs* 用以构成副词): *officially*.

iam·bus /aɪˈæmbəs; aɪˋæmbəs/ *n* (*pl* **~es** or **-bi** /-baɪ; -baɪ/) (also **iamb** /ˈaɪæm, ˈaɪæmb; ˋaɪ,æm, ˋaɪ,æmb/) metrical foot in poetry consisting of one short or unstressed syllable followed by one long or stressed syllable 抑扬格(诗的韵步, 每一短音节或非重读音节接以一长音节或重读音节组成一步).

▷ **iambic** /aɪˈæmbɪk; aɪˋæmbɪk/ *adj* of or using iambuses 抑扬格的; 用抑扬格的: *iambic feet* 抑扬格的音步, 如 I ˈsaw three ˈships come ˈsailing ˈby. **iamb·ics** *n* [pl] lines of poetry in iambic metre 用抑扬格律写的诗句.

-ian (also **-an**) *suff* 后缀 **1** (with proper *ns* forming *ns* and *adjs* 与专有名词结合构成名词和形容词): *Bostonian* ○ *Brazilian* ○ *Shakespearian* ○ *Libran*. **2** (with *ns* ending in *-ics* forming *ns* 与 -ics 结尾的名词结合构成名词) specialist in 专长于…: *optician* ○ *paediatrician*.

-iana (also **-ana**) *suff* 后缀 (with proper *ns* forming uncountable *ns* 与专有名词结合构成不可数名词) collection of objects (esp publications), facts, anecdotes, etc relating to 涉及…方面的事实、轶事、物品(尤指出版物)的收藏品; …集选; …文献汇编: *Victoriana* ○ *Mozartiana* ○ *Americana*.

-iatrics *comb form* 构词成分 (forming *ns* 用以构成名词) medical treatment of 对…的医疗: *paediatrics*. ▷ **-iatric**, **-iatrical** (forming *adjs* 用以构成形容词). Cf 参看 -IATRY.

-iatry *comb form* 构词成分 (forming *ns* 用以构成名词) healing or medical treatment of 对…的治疗: *psychiatry*. ▷ **-iatric** (forming *adjs* 用以构成形容词). Cf 参看 -IATRICS.

IBA /ˌaɪ biː ˈeɪ; ˌaɪ bi ˋe/ *abbr* 缩写 = (*Brit*) Independent Broadcasting Authority 独立广播局. Cf 参看 BBC, ITV.

ibex /ˈaɪbeks; ˋaɪbɛks/ *n* (*pl* unchanged or **~es** 复数或不变或作 **ibexes**) type of mountain goat with long curved horns 巨角塔尔羊(角长而曲).

ib·idem /ˈɪbaɪdem; ɪˋbaɪdɛm/ *adv* (*Latin* 拉) (*abbr* 缩写 **ibid**) in the same book, article, passage, etc (previously mentioned) 在同一书、同一文章、同一段落等之中(同上或同前).

ibis /ˈaɪbɪs; ˋaɪbɪs/ *n* wading bird like a heron with a long curved beak, found in warm climates 鹮(涉禽, 似鹭, 喙长而曲, 产于温带).

-ible ⇨ -ABLE.

IBM /ˌaɪ biː ˈem; ˌaɪ bi ˋɛm/ *abbr* 缩写 = International Business Machines (a large computer company) 国际商用机器公司(一家大型计算机公司): *work for IBM* 在国际商用机器公司工作.

i/c /ˌaɪ ˈsiː; ˌaɪ ˋsi/ *abbr* 缩写 = in charge (of); in command (of) 负责; 主管; 指挥: (*infml* 口) *Who's i/c ticket sales?* 谁是负责卖票的?

-ic /-ɪk; -ɪk/ *suff* 后缀 **1** (with *ns* forming *adjs* and *ns* 与名词结合构成形容词和名词) of or concerning …的; 关于…的: *poetic* ○ *scenic* ○ *Arabic*. **2** (with *vs* ending in *-y* forming *adjs* 与以 y 结尾的动词结合构成形容词) that performs the specified action 表示该动词所指动作或行为的: *horrific* ○ *specific*. ▷ **-ical** /-ɪkl; -ɪkl/ (forming *adjs* 用以构成形容词): *comical*. **-ically** /-ɪklɪ; -ɪklɪ/ (forming *advs* 用以构成副词): *economically*.

NOTE ON USAGE 用法: Both **-ic** and **-ical** form adjectives from nouns ☆ **-ic** 和 **-ical** 型的形容词都是由名词派生的: *scene/scenic*; *sociology/sociological*. Some nouns form pairs of adjectives with both **-ic** and **-ical** which have different meanings 有些名词可派生出成对的有 **-ic** 和 **-ical** 这两种词尾的形容词, 但意义各异: *history/historic* (of great significance 指有重大意义的)/ *historical* (belonging to history 属于历史的); *economy/ economic* (concerned with the economy 有关经济的)/ *economical* (not wasteful 不浪费的). Other examples are 其他例子有 *comic/comical*, *politic/political*, *classic/ classical*, *poetic/poetical*. Sometimes the pairs are almost synonymous 有时这成对的形容词几乎同义: *rhythmic/ rhythmical*. Note that the adverb is derived from the **-ical** form 注意副词是由 **-ical** 型派生的: *comically, poetically, rhythmically, etc.*

ICBM /ˌaɪ siː biː ˈem; ˌaɪ si bi ˋɛm/ *abbr* 缩写 = intercontinental ballistic missile 洲际弹道导弹. Cf 参看 IRBM, MRBM.

ice[1] /aɪs; aɪs/ *n* **1** [U] (**a**) water frozen so that it has become solid 冰: *pipes blocked by ice in winter* 冬天因结冰堵塞的管子. (**b**) sheet or layer of this 冰层: *Is the ice thick enough for skating?* 这冰的厚度能禁得住在上边滑冰吗? **2** [C] (**a**) = WATER ICE (WATER): *Can I have a strawberry-ice?* 给我一份草莓雪糕行吗? (**b**) portion of ice-cream 一份冰激凌: *Two ˈchoc-ices, please.* 请来两份巧克力冰激凌. **3** (idm 习语) **be skating on thin ice** ⇨ SKATE[1]. **ˌbreak the ˈice** do or say sth to remove or reduce awkwardness or tension, esp at a first meeting or at the start of a party, etc 说或做某事以消除或缓解偈促或紧张的气氛(尤指初次相会或聚会开始时). **ˌcut no ˈice (with sb)** have little or no effect or influence; be unconvincing 无作用; 无影响; 不足以令人信服: *His excuses cut no ice with me.* 他的辩解不足以说服我. **on ˈice** (**a**) (of wine, etc) kept cold by being surrounded by ice (指果酒)冰镇的. (**b**) (*fig* 比喻) in reserve for later use or consideration 留待后用; 留待考虑. (**c**) (of entertainment, etc) performed by skaters (指娱乐等)由滑冰者表演的, 冰上进行的: *Cinderella on ice* 在冰上演出的灰姑娘. (**d**) (*infml* 口) absolutely certain 绝对肯定; 有绝对把握: *The deal's on ice.* 这项交易绝无问题.

□ **ˈice age** period when much of the northern hemisphere was covered with glaciers 冰期; 冰川期; 冰河时代.

ˈice-axe (also *esp US* **ice-ax**) *n* axe used by mountaineers for cutting steps and holds in ice 冰镐(登山运动员用的). ⇨illus at AXE 见 AXE 插图.

ˌice-ˈblue *adj*, *n* [U] (of a) very pale blue colour 淡蓝色(的).

ˈice-bound *adj* surrounded by ice or unable to function because of ice 被冰封住的; 因冰封受阻而不能运作的: *an ice-bound ship, harbour* 冰封的船、港口.

ˈicebox *n* (**a**) box with ice in, used for keeping food cool; freezing compartment of a refrigerator (里面置冰以冷藏食物的)冰箱; (电冰箱中的)冷冻室. (**b**) (*esp US*) = REFRIGERATOR.

ˈice-breaker *n* strong ship designed to break a passage through ice 破冰船.

ˈice-cap *n* permanent covering of ice, esp in polar regions 冰冠(尤指极地的).

ˌice-ˈcold *adj* as cold as ice; very cold 冰冷的; 极冷的: *an ˌice-cold ˈdrink* 一份冷饮.

ˌice-ˈcream /ˌaɪsˈkriːm; *esp US* ˈaɪskriːm; ˋaɪsˋkrim/ *n* [C, U] (portion of) frozen food made from sweetened and flavoured cream or custard 冰激凌: *a/some strawberry ice-cream* 一份[些]草莓冰激凌.

ˈ**ice-cube** *n* small cube of ice made in a mould in the refrigerator, for drinks, etc (在电冰箱中制备, 加于饮料中用的)小冰块.

ˌ**ice ˈdancing** art or sport of dancing on ice-skates 冰上舞蹈.

ˈ**ice-fall** *n* very steep part of a glacier, like a frozen waterfall 冰川的陡峭部分(状如结成冰的瀑布).

ˈ**ice-field** *n* large area of floating ice, esp in polar regions 冰原(浮于海面的大冰块, 尤指极地的).

ˈ**ice-floe** *n* large sheet of floating ice (大块的)浮冰: *In spring the ice-floes break up.* 春天浮冰碎裂了.

ˈ**ice-free** *adj* (of a harbour) free from ice (指港口等)不冻的.

ˈ**ice hockey** (*US* **hockey**) form of hockey played on ice by two teams of skaters, using long sticks to hit a hard rubber disc 冰球运动.

ˌ**ice ˈlolly** (*US* **Popsicle**) flavoured ice on a small stick 冰棍; 冰棒; 棒冰.

ˈ**ice-pack** *n* bag filled with ice, used medically to cool parts of the body, esp the head 冰袋(医疗上作局部降温用, 尤指敷于头部的).

ˈ**ice-pick** *n* tool for breaking ice 碎冰锥.

ˈ**ice-rink** *n* specially prepared sheet of ice, often indoors, for skating, playing ice hockey, etc 冰场(供滑冰、打冰球等用的, 常指室内的).

ˈ**ice-show** *n* variety entertainment performed by skaters on an ice-rink 冰上表演.

ˈ**ice-skate** *n* boot fitted with a thin metal blade for skating on ice 冰鞋. ⇨illus at SKATE 见SKATE插图. — *v* [I] skate on ice 滑冰. ˈ**ice-skating** *n* [U].

ˈ**ice-tray** *n* small tray divided into sections for making ice-cubes (冰箱内用以制小冰块的)冰格.

ˈ**ice-water** *n* (*esp US*) water made very cold and used for drinking (供饮用的)冰水.

ice[2] /aɪs; aɪs/ *v* **1** [Tn] make (esp a liquid) very cold 使(尤指液体)凉; 冰镇: *iced water/beer* 冰水[冰镇啤酒]. **2** [Tn] cover (a cake) with sugar icing (在糕饼上)挂糖衣, 滚糖霜. **3** (phr v) ˌ**ice (sth) ˈover/ˈup** cover (sth) or become covered with ice 冰覆盖着(某物); 结冰: *The pond (was) iced over during the cold spell.* 寒流期间池塘都封冻了. ○ *The wings of the aircraft had iced up.* 机翼上结了一层冰.

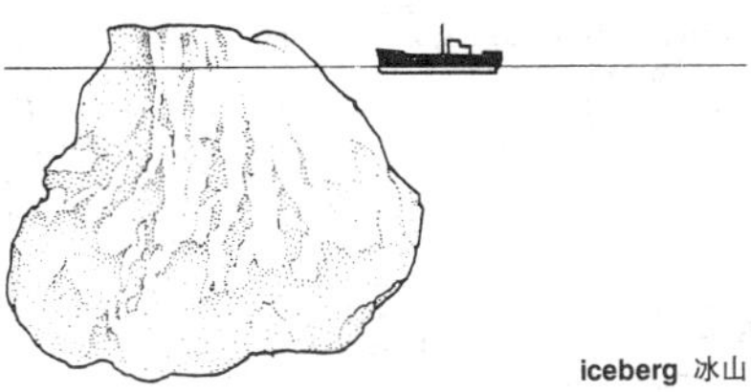

iceberg 冰山

ice·berg /ˈaɪsbɜːg; ˋaɪsˌbɝg/ *n* **1** huge mass of ice floating in the sea 冰山(海上飘浮的巨大冰块). ⇨illus 见插图. **2** (*fig* 比喻) unemotional person 冷若冰霜的人. **3** (idm 习语) **the tip of the iceberg** ⇨ TIP[1].

ich·neu·mon /ɪkˈnjuːmən; *US* -ˈnuː-; ɪkˋnumən/ (also **ichˈneumon-fly**) *n* small insect that lays its eggs in or on the larva of another insect 姬蜂(小昆虫, 产卵于另一昆虫之蛹中或蛹上).

ICI /ˌaɪ siː ˈaɪ; ˌaɪ si ˋaɪ/ *abbr* 缩写 = Imperial Chemical Industries 帝国化学工业公司: *work for ICI* 在帝国化学工业公司工作.

icicle /ˈaɪsɪkl; ˋaɪsɪkl̩/ *n* pointed piece of ice formed by the freezing of dripping water 冰柱, 冰锥, 冰溜(滴水凝成的冰条).

icing /ˈaɪsɪŋ; ˋaɪsɪŋ/ (*US* **frosting**) *n* [U] mixture of sugar, egg-white, flavouring, etc for covering and decorating cakes 用糖、蛋白、香料等混制的混合物(覆于糕饼上): *chocolate icing* 巧克力糖衣.

□ ˈ**icing sugar** finely powdered sugar used esp for icing (制甜食用的)糖粉.

icon (also **ikon**) /ˈaɪkɒn; ˋaɪkɑn/ *n* (in the Orthodox Church) painting, carving, etc of a holy person, itself regarded as sacred (东正教的)圣像.

icono·clast /aɪˈkɒnəklæst; aɪˋkɑnəˌklæst/ *n* **1** person who attacks popular beliefs or established customs 反对传统信仰或习俗的人. **2** (formerly) person who destroyed religious images (旧时)破坏宗教偶像的人. ▷ **icono·clasm** /aɪˈkɒnəklæzəm; aɪˋkɑnəˌklæzəm/ *n* [U]. **icono·clastic** /aɪˌkɒnəˈklæstɪk; aɪˌkɑnəˋklæstɪk/ *adj*.

-ics *suff* 后缀 (forming *ns* 用以构成名词) science, art or activity of ... 的学科、艺术或活动: *aesthetics* ○ *athletics* ○ *graphics* ○ *acrobatics* ○ *dramatics*.

icy /ˈaɪsɪ; ˋaɪsɪ/ *adj* (**-ier**, **-iest**) **1** very cold; as cold as ice 寒冷的; 冰冷的: *icy winds* 凛冽的风. **2** covered with ice 结满冰的; 冰封的: *icy roads* 冰霜覆盖的道路. **3** (*fig* 比喻) very cold and unfriendly in manner (态度)冷漠的, 冷冰冰的, 不友好的: *an icy welcome, voice, stare* 冷淡的欢迎、声音、凝视. ▷ **icily** /ˈaɪsɪlɪ; ˋaɪsɪlɪ/ *adv*. **ici·ness** *n* [U].

id /ɪd; ɪd/ *n* (*psychology* 心) part of the mind relating to a person's unconscious instincts and impluses 伊德, 本我(指人的无意识的本能和冲动之源的那一部分精神). Cf 参看 EGO 1, SUPEREGO.

I'd /aɪd; aɪd/ *contracted form* 缩约式 **1** I had ⇨ HAVE. **2** I would ⇨ WILL[1], WOULD[2].

ID /ˌaɪ ˈdiː; ˋaɪ ˋdi/ *abbr* 缩写 = (*esp US*) identification; identity: *an ID card* 身分证.

-ide *suff* 后缀 (*chemistry* 化) (with *ns* 与名词结合) compound of a particular chemical element (某些化学元素的)化物: *chloride* ○ *sulphide*.

idea /aɪˈdɪə; aɪˋdɪə/ *n* **1** [C] plan, etc formed by thinking; thought 构想; 思想; 主意: *He's full of good ideas.* 他足智多谋. ○ *That's an* (ie a good) *idea.* 那是个(好)主意. **2** [U, sing] mental impression 印象; 感想: *This book gives you some idea/a good idea of life in ancient Greece.* 这本书可以使你对古希腊人的生活有一些认识[有深入的了解]. **3** [C] opinion; belief 意见; 信念: *He has some very strange ideas.* 他有一些奇怪的想法. **4** [U, sing] vague notion or fancy; feeling that sth is likely 模糊的想法; 想像; 认为某事很有可能发生的感觉: *He had no idea she was like that.* 他万万没想到她是那样的. ○ *Have you any idea what time it is?* 你知道现在几点钟了吗? ○ *I have an idea it's going to rain.* 我看要下雨了. **5 the idea** [sing] the aim or purpose 目的; 目标: *The idea of the game is to get all your pieces to the other side of the board.* 这个游戏的目标是要把所有的棋子全走到棋盘的另一边. **6** (used in exclamations to indicate that what has been suggested is stupid, shocking, etc 认为提出的事情愚蠢、耸人听闻等而表示惊叹时用): *The idea of it!* 真糊涂! ○ *What an idea!* 这叫什么主意呀! **7** (idm 习语) **buck one's ideas up** ⇨ BUCK[2]. **get the iˈdea** understand 理解: *Do you get the idea?* 你明白了吗? **get the idea that...** form the impression that... 形成...的印象: *Where did you get the idea that she doesn't like you?* 你是从哪儿得来的这个印象, 说她不喜欢你呢? **give sb ideas** give sb expectations or hopes which may not be realized 使某人抱不切实际的希望: *Don't give her ideas — you know how difficult it is to get into films.* 别让她空抱希望吧——你知道跻身影界有多难哪. **have no iˈdea** not know; be incompetent 不知道; 无能力: *He has no idea how to manage people.* 他根本不知道如何做人事工作. **not have the first idea about sth** know nothing at all about sth 对某事一无所知. **one's idea of sth** what one thinks of as representing sth 对某事物的看法. **run away with the idea that...** (*infml* 口) (often used in the negative imperative 常用于否定的祈使句中) be misled by or accept a false idea 误以为; 接受某错误的想法: *Don't run away with the idea that this job is going to be easy.* 别以为这工作是轻而易举的. **the young idea** ⇨ YOUNG.

ideal /aɪˈdɪəl; aɪˋdɪəl/ *adj* **1** satisfying one's idea of what is perfect; most suitable 理想的; 完美的; 最合适的: *ideal weather for a holiday* 度假的理想天气 ○ *He's the ideal husband for her.* 他是她理想的丈夫. **2** existing only in the imagination or as an idea; unrealistic and so not likely to be achieved 想像的; 空想的; 不切实际的: *ideal plans for reform* 不切实际的改革计划 ○ *ideal happiness* 想像的幸福 ○ *in an ideal world* 在理想的世界里.

▷ **ideal** *n* **1** [C usu *sing* 通常作单数] person or thing regarded as perfect 完美的人或事物: *She's looking for a job, but hasn't found her ideal yet.* 她在找工作, 但还未找到最理想的. **2** [C usu *pl* 通常作复数] standard of perfection 完美境界的标准: *He finds it hard to live up to his ideals.* 他认为很难按自己的理想办事.

ideally /aɪˈdɪəlɪ; aɪˈdɪəlɪ/ *adv*: *She's ideally suited to the job.* 她最适合做这项工作. ○ *Ideally, everyone would be given equal opportunities.* 最理想的是, 人人都能有平等的机会.

ideal·ism /aɪˈdɪəlɪzəm; aɪˈdɪəl,ɪzəm/ *n* [U] **1** forming, pursuing or believing in ideals (IDEAL *n* 2), esp unrealistically 理想主义(尤指不切实际地追求或信奉的理想): *Idealism has no place in modern politics.* 在当代政治生活中, 理想主义根本行不通. **2** (esp in art and literature) imaginative treatment of objects or ideas in an ideal and often unrealistic way (尤指文艺方面的)观念主义(以理想的、常为不现实的方法对待事物或思想). Cf 参看 CLASSICISM, ROMANTICISM (ROMANTIC). **3** (*philosophy* 哲) belief that ideas are the only things that are real or about which we can know anything 唯心论; 观念论; 理念论. Cf 参看 REALISM.

▷ **ideal·ist** /aɪˈdɪəlɪst; aɪˈdɪəlɪst/ *n* person who has high ideals and tries (often in an unrealistic way) to achieve them 理想主义者; 空想家; 唯心论者. **ideal·istic** /ˌaɪdɪəˈlɪstɪk; aɪ,dɪəlˈɪstɪk/ *adj*. **ideal·istic·ally** /ˌaɪdɪəˈlɪstɪklɪ; aɪ,dɪəlˈɪstɪklɪ/ *adv*.

ideal·ize, -ise /aɪˈdɪəlaɪz; aɪˈdɪəl,aɪz/ *v* [Tn] consider or represent (sb/sth) as perfect or ideal 将(某人[某事物])理想化; 将(某人[某事物])视为理想的; 作理想化的反映或描述: *an idealized account of village life* 对乡村生活作理想化的描述. ▷ **ideal·iza·tion, -isation** /aɪ,dɪəlaɪˈzeɪʃn; *US* -lɪˈz-; aɪ,dɪələˈzeʃən/ *n* [U, C].

ident·ical /aɪˈdentɪkl; aɪˈdɛntɪkl/ *adj* **1 the ~** [attrib 作定语] the same 同一的: *This is the identical room we stayed in last year.* 这是我们去年住过的(同一间)房间. **2 ~ (to/with sb/sth)** similar in every detail; exactly alike 完全相同的; 一模一样的: *They're wearing identical clothes.* 他们穿着完全相同的衣服. ○ *Their clothes are identical.* 他们的衣服完全一样. ○ *This picture is identical to one my mother has.* 这张照片和我母亲的那张一模一样. ▷ **ident·ic·ally** /-klɪ; -klɪ/ *adv*.

□ **iˌdentical ˈtwins** twins born from a single egg and therefore of the same sex and very similar in appearance 同卵双生(同性双胎)(由一个受精卵发育而成, 性别相同, 外貌酷似).

identi·fy /aɪˈdentɪfaɪ; aɪˈdɛntə,faɪ/ *v* (*pt, pp* **-fied**) **1** [Tn, Cn·n/a] **~ sb/sth as sb/sth** show, prove, etc who or what sb/sth is; recognize sb/sth (as being the specified person or thing) 确认、证明某人[某事物]; 鉴别出(系某人或某物): *Can you identify your umbrella among this lot?* 你能在这些伞中认出你自己的那一把吗? ○ *She identified the man as her attacker.* 她认出那个男人就是袭击过她的人. **2** [Tn·pr] **~ sth with sth** consider sth to be identical with sth; equate two things 认为某事物与另事物等同: *One cannot identify happiness with wealth.* 幸福和财富不能混为一谈. **3** (phr v) **identify (oneself) with sb/sth** give support to sb/sth; be associated with sb/sth 支持某人[某事物]; 与某人[某事物]有关联: *He refused to identify himself/become identified with the new political party.* 他拒绝与那个新政党来往. **identify with sb** regard oneself as sharing the characteristics or fortunes of sb; take sb as a model 与某人认同; 以某人为模式: *I found it hard to identify with any of the characters in the film.* 我对这部影片里的任何角色都难以认同.

▷ **iden·ti·fica·tion** /aɪ,dentɪfɪˈkeɪʃn; aɪ,dɛntəfəˈkeʃən/ *n* [U] **1** (process of) identifying or being identified 验明; 鉴别: *The identification of the accident victims took some time.* 验明事故遇难者身分的工作费了不少时间. **2** (*abbr* 缩写 **ID**) means of proving who one is; official papers that do this 身分证明; 身分证明书: *Can I see some identification, please?* 请给我看看你的身分证件行吗? **iˌdentifiˈcation parade** number of people, including one suspected of a crime, arranged in a row for viewing by witnesses who may be able to identify the suspect 供辨认嫌疑犯的一排人(其一为嫌疑犯, 供目击者辨认).

Iden·ti·kit /aɪˈdentɪkɪt; aɪˈdɛntɪkɪt/ *n* (*propr* 专利名) set of pictures of different features that can be fitted together to form the face of a person (esp sb wanted by the police) with the help of descriptions given by people who have seen him 容貌拼具(一整套各种类型的口、鼻、眼等图片, 可根据亲眼见过的人之描述, 用以拼制出某人的面部像, 尤指警方欲寻找者).

iden·tity /aɪˈdentətɪ; aɪˈdɛntətɪ/ *n* **1** [C, U] who or what sb/sth is 本身; 本体; 身分: *There is no clue to the identity of the thief.* 没有确定窃贼身分的线索. ○ *The cheque will be cashed on proof of identity.* 这张支票凭身分证件兑现. ○ *This is a clear case of mistaken identity*, eg when the wrong person is arrested by mistake. 这显然是个误认的案例(如捕错人). **2** [U] (state of) exact likeness or sameness 相同(性); 一致(性).

□ **iˈdentity card** (also **ID card** /ˌaɪˈdi: kɑ:d; ˌaɪ ˈdi ˌkɑrd/), **iˈdentity disc** card or disc, often with a photograph, carried or worn by sb to show who he is 身分卡, 身分证章(通常有相片, 供本人携带或佩带).

ideo·gram /ˈɪdɪəgræm; ˈɪdɪə,græm/ (also **ideo·graph** /ˈɪdɪəgrɑ:f; *US* -græf; ˈɪdɪə,græf/) *n* **1** symbol used in a writing system that represents the idea (rather than the sounds forming the name) of a thing, eg Chinese characters 表意文字(不表声)(如汉字). **2** any sign or symbol for sth 表意的符号或标志: *In this dictionary the ideogram* ⚠ *is used to mean 'taboo'.* 在本词典中, 用⚠符号表示避讳语. ▷ **ideo·graphic** /ˌɪdɪəˈgræfɪk; ˌɪdɪəˈgræfɪk/ *adj*.

ideo·logy /ˌaɪdɪˈɒlədʒɪ; ˌaɪdɪˈɑlədʒɪ/ *n* [C, U] (set of) ideas that form the basis of an economic or political theory or that are held by a particular group or person 思想(体系); 思想意识: *Our ideologies differ.* 我们的思想不同. ○ *according to Marxist, bourgeois, monetarist, etc ideology* 根据马克思主义的、资产阶级的、货币主义等的思想体系. ▷ **ideo·lo·gical** /ˌaɪdɪəˈlɒdʒɪkl; ˌaɪdɪəˈlɑdʒɪkl/ *adj*. **ideo·lo·gically** /-klɪ; -klɪ/ *adv*.

idi·ocy /ˈɪdɪəsɪ; ˈɪdɪəsɪ/ *n* **1** [U] **(a)** extreme stupidity 极端愚蠢: *It's sheer idiocy to go climbing in such bad weather.* 在这样恶劣的天气里去爬山简直是愚蠢到家了. **(b)** state of being an idiot; imbecility 白痴; 极度低能. **2** [C] extremely stupid act, remark, etc 极端愚蠢的行为、言论等.

idio·lect /ˈɪdɪəlekt; ˈɪdɪə,lɛkt/ *n* (*linguistics* 语言) total amount of a language that any one person knows and uses 个人言语(个人所认识和使用的某语言的总汇): *Is the word 'psychosis' part of your idiolect?* 在你的个人言语中使用 psychosis 这个词吗?

idiom /ˈɪdɪəm; ˈɪdɪəm/ *n* **1** [C] phrase or sentence whose meaning is not clear from the meaning of its individual words and which must be learnt as a whole unit 习语; 成语; 惯用语, 如 *give way, a change of heart, be hard put to it*: *The English language has many idioms.* 英语有很多惯用语. **2** [U] **(a)** language or dialect of a people or country 某民族或某国家之语言或方言: *the French idiom* 法语. **(b)** use of language that is typical of or natural to speakers of a particular language (操某语言者典型的或自然的)语言用法. **(c)** use of language peculiar to a period or an individual (某时期或某人特有的)语言用法: *Shakespeare's idiom* 莎士比亚的语言风格.

▷ **idio·matic** /ˌɪdɪəˈmætɪk; ˌɪdɪəˈmætɪk/ *adj* **(a)** in accordance with the particular nature or structure of a language, dialect, etc 符合某一语言或方言等的习惯或特点的: *She speaks fluent and idiomatic French.* 她说得一口又流利又地道的法语. **(b)** containing an idiom or idioms 含有习语的: *an idiomatic expression, language* 固定词组、成语多的语言. **idio·mat·ic·ally** /-klɪ; klɪ/ *adv*.

idio·syn·crasy /ˌɪdɪəˈsɪŋkrəsɪ; ˌɪdɪəˈsɪŋkrəsɪ/ *n* person's particular way of thinking, behaving, etc that is clearly different from that of others (个人独有的)习性、癖好、气质: *One of her little idiosyncrasies is always washing in cold water.* 她有个怪习惯, 就是洗什么都爱用冷水. ▷ **idio·syn·cratic** /ˌɪdɪəsɪŋˈkrætɪk; ˌɪdɪosɪŋˈkrætɪk/ *adj*.

idiot /ˈɪdɪət; ˈɪdɪət/ *n* **1** (*infml* 口) very foolish person; fool 蠢人; 笨蛋; 傻瓜: *What an idiot I was to leave my suitcase on the train!* 我真笨, 竟把手提箱落在火车上了! **2** person with very limited intelligence who cannot think or behave normally 白痴; 呆子: *an idiot since birth* 天生的白痴.

▷ **idi·otic** /ˌɪdɪˈɒtɪk; ˌɪdɪˈɑtɪk/ *adj* stupid 十分愚蠢的; 白痴般的: *Don't be idiotic!* 别那么傻了! **idi·ot·ic·ally** /-klɪ;

-klɪ/ *adv*.

idle /ˈaɪdl; ˋaɪdl̩/ *adj* (-r, -st) **1** (**a**) doing or having no work; not employed 闲散的; 不工作的或没有工作的: *Many people were idle during the depression.* 在那萧条时期, 很多人都无事可做. (**b**) not active or in use 闲置的: *The factory machines lay idle during the workers' strike.* 在工人罢工期间, 工厂的机器都闲置着. **2** (of time) not spent in doing sth (指时间)空闲的: *We spent many idle hours just sitting in the sun.* 我们在太阳地里呆呆坐了好几个钟头. **3** (of people) avoiding work; lazy (指人)无所事事的, 懒散的, 懒惰的: *an idle, useless student* 懒散、不成器的学生. **4** [usu attrib 通常作定语] worthless or having no special purpose or effect; useless 无价值的; 徒然的; 无效的; 无用的: *an idle threat/promise* 说说而已的恐吓[允诺] ○ *idle curiosity/gossip/speculation* 无聊的好奇[闲言碎语/胡思乱想] ○ *It's idle to expect help from him.* 指望他帮助只会是一场空. **5** (idm 习语) **the devil makes work for idle hands** ⇨ DEVIL[1].

▷ **idle** *v* **1** [I, Ip] **~ (about)** do nothing; waste time; be idle 无所事事; 浪费时光; 闲荡: *Stop idling and help me clean up.* 别游手好闲的, 来帮我打扫打扫吧. **2** [I] (of an engine) run slowly in neutral gear or without doing work (指发动机)挂空挡, 空转. **3** (phr v) **idle sth away** waste (time) 虚度(光阴): *idle away the hours watching TV* 把时间浪费在看电视上. **idler** /ˈaɪdlə(r); ˋaɪdlɚ/ *n*.

idle·ness *n* [U].

idly /ˈaɪdlɪ; ˋaɪdlɪ/ *adv*.

idol /ˈaɪdl; ˋaɪdl̩/ *n* **1** image of a god, often carved in stone, wood, etc and used as an object of worship 神像(常为石雕、木刻等供顶礼膜拜用). **2** person or thing that is greatly loved or admired 受崇拜与热爱的人或物: *As an only child he was the idol of his parents.* 他是独生子, 是父母的宠儿. ○ *The Beatles were the pop idols of the 60's.* 披头士乐队是六十年代人们崇拜的偶像.

id·ol·ater /aɪˈdɒlətə(r); aɪˋdɑlətɚ/ (*fem* 阴性作 **id·ol·at·ress** /aɪˈdɒlətrɪs; aɪˋdɑlətrɪs/) *n* person who worships an idol or idols 偶像崇拜者.

▷ **id·ol·at·rous** /aɪˈdɒlətrəs; aɪˋdɑlətrəs/ *adj* (**a**) worshipping idols 崇拜偶像的. (**b**) of or like the worship of idols (似)偶像崇拜的: *an idolatrous love of material wealth* 对物质财富极度的爱慕. **id·ol·at·rously** /-lɪ; -lɪ/ *adv*.

id·ol·atry /aɪˈdɒlətrɪ; aɪˋdɑlətrɪ/ *n* [U] (**a**) worship of idols 偶像崇拜. (**b**) too much devotion or admiration 盲目崇拜: *He supports his local team with a fervour that borders on idolatry.* 他是本地队的球迷, 狂热得到了近乎盲目崇拜的程度了.

id·ol·ize, -ise /ˈaɪdəlaɪz; ˋaɪdl̩,aɪz/ *v* [Tn] (**a**) treat (sb/sth) as an idol 将(某人[某物])当作偶像崇拜. (**b**) love or admire (sb/sth) very much 极度喜爱或仰慕(某人[某事物]): *idolize a pop group* 十分喜爱某流行乐团.

▷ **id·ol·iza·tion, -isation** /ˌaɪdəlaɪˈzeɪʃn; ˌaɪdl̩aɪˋzeʃən/ *n* [U] idolizing or being idolized 偶像化; 奉为神圣; 盲目崇拜.

idyll /ˈɪdɪl; *US* ˈaɪdl; ˋaɪdl̩/ *n* **1** short piece of poetry or prose that describes a happy and peaceful scene or event, esp of country life 描述欢愉恬静情景的短诗或短文; (尤指)田园诗. **2** simple pleasant scene or event 轻松欢乐的情景或事情.

▷ **idyllic** /ɪˈdɪlɪk; *US* aɪˈd-; aɪˋdɪlɪk/ *adj* like an idyll; peaceful and pleasant 田园诗般的; 田园风光的; 平和欢畅的: *an idyllic setting, holiday, marriage* 田园风光的环境、恬静愉快的假日、和谐美满的婚姻. **idyllic·ally** /-klɪ; -klɪ/ *adv*: *idyllically happy* 悠然自得.

ie /ˌaɪ ˈiː; ˌaɪ ˋi/ *abbr* 缩写 = that is to say; in other words (Latin *id est*) 亦即, 也就是, 换言之(源自拉丁文 *id est*): *Hot drinks, ie tea and coffee, are charged for separately.* 热饮, 即茶和咖啡, 另计. ⇨Usage at VIZ 用法见 VIZ.

-ie ⇨ -Y[2].

if /ɪf; ɪf/ *conj* **1** on condition that; supposing 假如; 如果; 倘若; 要是. (**a**) (used with the present and present perfect tenses for highly predictable situations 与现在时态和现在完成时态连用表示预料到的情况): *I'll only stay if you offer me more money.* 假若你肯多给钱, 我就留下. ○ *If you have finished eating you may leave the table.* 你要是吃完了, 就可以离席了. ○ *If (it is) necessary I will come at 6.* 如有必要, 我6点钟来. ○ *You can stay to dinner if you like.* 你愿意的话, 可以留下一起吃饭. ○ *If anyone calls tell them I'm not at home.* 有人来电话, 就说我不在家. ○ (*fml* 文) *If the patient should vomit, turn him over with his head to the side.* 倘若病人要呕吐, 就帮他翻过身来, 头侧向一边. (**b**) (used with a past tense for imaginary situations 与过去时态连用表示假想的情况): *If you learned to type you would easily find a job.* 假使你学过打字, 就容易找工作了. ○ *If he were here I could explain to him myself.* 要是他在这里, 我就可以亲自向他解释了. ○ *If I was a man they would have given me the job.* 我要是男的, 这份工作就准给我了. ○ *Would she tell us the truth if we asked her?* 我们问她, 她会告诉我们实情么? ○ *If you liked* (ie With your approval) *I could ask my brother to look at your car.* 你要同意的话, 我可以叫我弟弟来给你检查一下汽车. ○ *They would have been here by now if they'd caught the early train.* 他们要是赶上了早班火车, 现在都该到这儿了. ○ *I wouldn't have believed it possible, if I hadn't seen it happen.* 要不是亲眼目睹, 我决不会相信能有这种事. ⇨ Usage at UNLESS 用法见 UNLESS. **2** when(ever) 无论何时; 当: *If metal gets hot it expands.* 金属遇热则膨胀. ○ *She glares at me if I go near her desk.* 我一走近她的办公桌, 她就瞪我. **3** (used with *will* and *would* as the first part of a sentence when making a polite request 与will和would连用, 作复合句的前部, 用以提出请求显得客气): *If you will sit down for a few moments* (ie Please sit down and) *I'll tell the manager you're here.* 请稍坐, 我这就通知经理说您来了. ○ *If you would care to leave your name, we'll get in touch as soon as possible.* 请留下您的名字, 我们尽快和您联系. **4** (used after *ask, know, find out, wonder,* etc to introduce alternatives 用于ask、know、find out、wonder等之后, 以引导含不同可能性的情况) whether 是否: *Do you know if he's married?* 他结婚没结婚, 你知道吗? ○ *I wonder if I should wear a hat.* 我不知道该不该戴帽子. ○ *He couldn't tell if she was laughing or crying.* 他弄不清她是笑还是哭. ○ *Listen to the tune — see if you can remember the words.* 请听这曲子——看你能不能想得起歌词来. **5** (used after *vs* or *adjs* expressing feelings 用于表示情感的动词或形容词之后): *I am sorry if I'm disturbing you.* 很抱歉, 打搅您了. ○ *I'd be grateful if you would keep it a secret.* 如予保密, 无任感激. ○ *Do you mind if I switch the radio off?* 我可以关掉收音机吗? **6** (also **even if**) (used when admitting that sth may be true or may happen 用于承认某事可能属实或可能发生) although 即使; 纵然; 虽然: *If he said that, he didn't expect you to take it personally.* 即使他是那样说的, 他也并不是针对你个人而言的. ○ *Even if you saw him pick up the money, you can't be sure he stole it.* 就算你看见是他拾起的钱, 你也不能肯定钱就是他偷的. **7** (used before an *adj* to introduce a contrast 用于形容词之前, 以引导一对比情况) although also 虽然; 尽管: *It was thoughtless if well-meaning.* 用意虽好, 考虑欠周. ○ *He's a real gentleman, if a little pompous at times.* 他可是个正人君子, 虽然有时略显得傲慢了些. **8** (used to express surprise, astonishment, dismay, etc 用以表示意外、惊奇、沮丧等): *If it isn't my old friend Bob Thomson — what a coincidence!* 这不是我的老朋友鲍勃·汤姆森吗——真巧哇! ○ *If that's not the best idea I've heard in a long time!* 很久没听到过这么好的意见了啊! ○ *If he hasn't gone and got into trouble with the police!* 他竟然跟警方惹上了麻烦! **9** (used before *you think, ask, remember, etc* to invite sb to listen to one's opinion 用于you think、ask、remember等之前, 请对方听自己的意见): *If you ask me, she's too scared to do it.* 依我说, 她是吓得不敢去做. ○ *If you think about it, those children must be grown-up by now.* 想想吧, 那些孩子现在一定都长大成人了. ○ *If you remember, Mary was always fond of animals.* 记得吗, 玛丽一向喜欢动物. **10** (idm 习语) **ˌif and ˈwhen** (used to express uncertainty about a possible event in the future 用以表示怀疑将来的事能否发生): *If and when we ever meet again I hope he remembers to thank me.* 倘若我们再有见面之时, 希望他不会忘记谢我. **if ˌI were ˈyou; if ˌI was/were in ˈyour shoes/place** (used to introduce a piece of advice to sb 用以引导出劝告某人的话): *If I were you I'd start looking for another job.* 我要是你, 就去另找工作了. ○ *If I were in your shoes, he'd soon know what I thought of him.* 若是我处在你的地位, 他很快就会知道我对他的看法了. **if ˈanything** (used to express a tentative opinion or after a negative statement to say that the opposite is true 用以表达无把握的看法，或用于否定的话语之后，表示所说的是反话) if anything definite can be said, this is it 若能稍有把握地说出来，其实是这样: *I'd say he was more like his father, if anything.* 若非要说出像谁不可来，我倒认为他略微像他父亲. ○ *He's not thin — if anything he's rather on the plump side.* 他可不瘦——按说还算有点胖呢. **if ˈnot** (**a**) (used after *if* and a *v* in the present or present perfect tense 用于 if + 动词(现在时态或现在完成时态)之后) otherwise 要不; 不然: *I'll go if you're going — if not I'd rather stay at home.* 你去我就去，否则我宁可待在家里. ○ *If you've finished we can have a coffee — if not, you'd better keep working.* 你要是完事了，咱们可以喝杯咖啡——不然的话，你最好接着干下去. (**b**) (used after a *yes/no* question to give a promise, warning, etc 用于 yes/no 疑问句之后，表示许诺、告诫等): *Are you ready? If not, I'm going without you.* 准备好了吗？要不，我就自己去了. **if ˈonly** (**a**) (used to express a wish with reference to present or future time 用以表示对现时或未来的愿望): *If only I were rich.* 但愿我很富. ○ *If only I could swim.* 要是我会游泳该多好. ○ *If only I knew her name.* 我要是知道她的名字就好了. ○ *If only it would stop raining.* 真希望雨能停. ○ *If only they would tell me what they've decided.* 但愿他们能把决定告诉我. (**b**) (used to express a wish that past events had been different 用以表示与过去事实相反的愿望): *If only he'd remembered to buy some fruit.* 他当时要是记得买些水果来该多好. ○ *If only I had gone by taxi.* 假若我是乘计程车去的就好了. **only if** (when used at the beginning of a sentence, making the *v* in the following clause precede its subject 用于句首，后接从句主谓倒装) only on condition that 只要; 只有: *Only if a teacher has given permission is a student allowed to enter this room.* 只有得到教师的允许，学生才可以进这间屋. ○ *Only if the red light comes on is there any danger to employees.* 只要红灯一亮，就表示有危及职工的险情.

▷ **if** *n* (*infml* 口) **1** uncertainty 不确定的事; 无把握的事: *If he wins — and it's a big if — he'll be the first Englishman to win for twenty years.* 假使他赢了——是否能赢还是一大疑问——他将是二十年来第一个获胜的英国人. **2** (idm 习语) ˌ**ifs and ˈbuts** reservations; arguments against sth 保留意见; 对某事物的辩解: *Now I'm not having any ifs and buts — it's cold showers for everyone before breakfast tomorrow.* 好了，不要跟我讨价还价——明天早饭前大家都要用冷水淋浴.

NOTE ON USAGE 用法: Both **if** and **whether** are used in reporting questions which invite yes/no answers or offer a choice between alternatives ☆ **if** 和 **whether** 均用于间接疑问句，要求回答 yes/no 或提供选择: *('Do you want a drink?') He asked whether/if we wanted a drink.* ('你们想喝点东西吗?')他问我们是否要喝点东西. ○ *He didn't know whether/if we should write or phone.* 他不知道我们是写信好呢还是打电话好. **Whether** (NOT **if**) can be followed by an infinitive ☆ **whether** 后面可接不定式(**if** 不可这样用): *I'm not sure whether to resign or stay on.* 我拿不准主意是辞职还是留任. After a preposition **whether** must be used 在介词之后只能用 **whether**: *It depends on whether the letter arrives in time.* 这取决于信是否来得及时. **Whether** is also used when the clause it begins is the subject of a sentence ☆ **whether** 还可用以引导主语从句: *Whether they win or lose is all the same to me.* 他们是赢是输于我都一样. **Whether** (NOT **if**) can be immediately followed by 'or not' ☆ **whether** 后面可直接用 or not(**if** 不可这样用): *I'll be happy whether or not I get the job* (compare 试比较: *I'll be happy whether/if I get the job or not* 我能不能得到那份工作都一样高兴).

-ify (also **-fy**) *suff* 后缀 (with *ns* and *adjs* forming *vs* 与名词和形容词结合构成动词) make or become 使得; 变成: *solidify* ○ *speechify*.

ig·loo /ˈɪɡlu:; ˋɪɡlu/ *n* (*pl* **~s**) small dome-shaped house built by Eskimos from blocks of hard snow as a temporary shelter (爱斯基摩人用坚硬雪块砌成的临时栖身用的)拱形圆顶小屋.

ig·ne·ous /ˈɪɡnɪəs; ˋɪɡnɪəs/ *adj* (*geology* 地质) (of rocks) formed by molten matter (esp from volcanoes) that has become solid (指岩石)火成的(尤指火山喷出的).

ig·nite /ɪɡˈnaɪt; ɪɡˋnaɪt/ *v* [I, Tn] (cause sth to) catch fire (使某物)燃烧，着火; 点火; 点燃: *Petrol ignites very easily.* 汽油易燃. ○ *He struck a match and ignited the fuse.* 他划了根火柴，点着了导火索.

▷ **ig·ni·tion** /ɪɡˈnɪʃn; ɪɡˋnɪʃən/ *n* **1** [U] causing sth to catch fire 着火; 点火; 发火. **2** [C] electrical mechanism that ignites the mixture of explosive gases in a petrol engine (汽油发动机的)发火装置，点火装置，点火开关: *switch/turn on the ignition* 打开点火开关.

ig·noble /ɪɡˈnəʊbl; ɪɡˋnobl̩/ *adj* not honourable in character or purpose; shameful 卑鄙的; 不光彩的; 可耻的: *an ignoble person, action* 卑鄙的人、行为. ▷ **ig·nobly** /-nəʊblɪ; -ˋnoblɪ/ *adv*.

ig·no·miny /ˈɪɡnəmɪnɪ; ˋɪɡnəˌmɪnɪ/ *n* [U] (esp public) shame or humiliation; disgrace (尤指公开的)耻辱，污辱，不名誉，不体面，丑行: *the ignominy of defeat* 战败的耻辱.

▷ **ig·no·mi·ni·ous** /ˌɪɡnəˈmɪnɪəs; ˌɪɡnəˋmɪnɪəs/ *adj* shameful or humiliating; causing disgrace 耻辱的; 屈辱的; 丢脸的: *an ignominious defeat* 可耻的失败. **ig·no·mi·ni·ously** *adv*.

ig·nor·amus /ˌɪɡnəˈreɪməs; ˌɪɡnəˋreməs/ *n* (*pl* **~es** /-sɪz; -sɪz/) ignorant person 无知的人.

ig·nor·ance /ˈɪɡnərəns; ˋɪɡnərəns/ *n* [U] **~ (of sth)** lack of knowledge or information (about sth) (对某事物)无知: *We are in complete ignorance of your plans.* 我们对你的计划一无所知. ○ *If he did wrong it was only through ignorance.* 要是他做错了，那也只是出于无知.

ig·nor·ant /ˈɪɡnərənt; ˋɪɡnərənt/ *adj* **1** (**a**) **~ (of sth)** knowing little or nothing; lacking education or information; unaware 无知的; 愚昧的; 没有学识的; 不知道的: *He's not stupid, just ignorant.* 他并不蠢，只是无知罢了. ○ *To say you were ignorant of the rules is no excuse.* 说自己不知道规则是不能成为借口的. (**b**) showing or resulting from lack of knowledge 显示无知的; 由无知而产生的: *an ignorant stare, look, etc* 茫然的凝视、样子等. **2** (*infml* 口) rude through lack of knowledge about good manners 不识礼的; 粗野的; 没有礼貌的: *His ignorant behaviour at the dinner table caused much embarrassment.* 他在餐桌上举止粗鲁，在座的人颇为难堪. ▷ **ig·nor·antly** *adv*.

ig·nore /ɪɡˈnɔ:(r); ɪɡˋnɔr/ *v* [Tn] **1** take no notice of (sb/sth) 忽视(某人[某事物]): *You've been ignoring me.* 你一直不把我放在眼里. ○ *I can't ignore his rudeness any longer.* 他粗暴无礼，我再也不能不闻不问了. ○ *ignore criticism* 忽视批评. **2** deliberately refuse to greet or acknowledge (sb) 对(某人)故意不打招呼、不予承认或不予理睬: *I said hello to her, but she ignored me completely!* 我向她打招呼，可她根本不理我!

iguana /ˈɪɡwɑ:nə; ɪˋɡwɑnə/ *n* type of large tree-climbing lizard of tropical America 鬣鳞蜥(产于热带美洲的攀木大蜥蜴).

ikon = ICON.

il- ⇨ IN-[2].

ilex /ˈaɪleks; ˋaɪlɛks/ *n* (*pl* **~es**) **1** (*botany* 植) (plant of the) genus of trees that includes holly 冬青属; 冬青属植物. **2** (also **holm-oak**) type of evergreen oak-tree with leaves like holly 圣栎(一种常青栎树，叶似冬青).

ilk /ɪlk; ɪlk/ *n* (idm 习语) **of that/the same/his, her, etc ilk** (*infml joc* 口，谑) of that, the same, his, etc kind, sort or type 那一类[同一种/他、她…那类]: *I can't stand him, or any others of that/his ilk.* 他这类人的行为我无法忍受.

ill[1] /ɪl; ɪl/ *adv* (esp in compounds 尤用以构成复合词) **1** badly; wrongly 坏; 恶劣地: *an ˌill-written ˈbook* 写得很差劲的书 ○ *Their children are ill ˈcared for,* ie neglected. 他们的孩子疏于照料. Cf 参看 WELL[3] 1a. **2** unfavourably; unkindly 不利地; 不友好地; 坏: *speak/think ill of sb* 说某人坏话[对某人不怀好感]. Cf 参看 WELL[3] 1b. **3** only with difficulty; scarcely 困难地; 几乎不: *We can ill afford the time or money for a holiday.* 我们简直连度假的时间或金钱都没有. **4** (idm 习语) **augur well/ill for sb/sth** ⇨ AUGUR. **bode well/ill** ⇨ BODE. **deserve well/ill of sb** ⇨ DESERVE. ˌ**ill at ˈease** uncomfortable; embarrassed 不舒服; 困窘; 侷促. **wish sb well/ill** ⇨ WISH *v*.

□ ˌ**ill-adˈvised** *adj* unwise 不明智的; 考虑欠周的: *an ˌill-advised ˈmeeting* 考虑欠周的会晤. **ill-advisedly** /ˌɪlədˈvaɪzɪdlɪ; ˋɪlədˋvaɪzɪdlɪ/ *adv*.

ˌ**ill-asˈsorted** *adj* badly matched; mixed 不配合的; 不相称的: *an ill-assorted collection of shoes* 杂七杂八的一堆鞋 ○ *They make an ˌill-assorted ˈcouple*, ie don't seem well suited to each other. 他们俩不很般配.

ˌ**ill-ˈbred** *adj* badly brought up; badly behaved; rude 教养不好的; 粗野的; 无礼的: *an ˌill-bred ˈchild* 没有教养的孩子. Cf 参看 WELL-BRED (WELL[3]). ˌ**ill ˈbreeding** bad manners 恶劣的教养; 粗野; 无礼.

ˌ**ill-conˈsidered** *adj* not carefully or sufficiently thought about 考虑欠周的; 不谨慎的; 不妥的: *an ˌill-considered ˈact* 不明智的举动.

ˌ**ill-deˈfined** *adj* **1** not accurately described 不清楚的; 含混的; 不分明的; 不明确的: *an ˌill-defined ˈjob* 内容不明确的工作. **2** not distinct in outline 轮廓不鲜明的: *an ill-defined lump of rock on the horizon* 天边一处轮廓不清的岩影.

ˌ**ill-disˈposed** *adj* **~ (towards sb/sth)** (*fml* 文) not friendly or pleasant; not favouring 不友好的; 不喜欢的; 无好感的: *She's very ill-disposed towards her neighbours.* 她对左邻右舍概无好感. Cf 参看 WELL-DISPOSED (WELL[3]).

ˌ**ill-ˈfated** *adj* bringing or having bad luck or misfortune 带来不幸的; 注定倒霉的: *an ill-fated expedition* 运气不佳的远征.

ˌ**ill-ˈfavoured** *adj* (*fml* 文) (esp of people) unattractive in appearance; ugly (尤指人)丑陋的, 其貌不扬的, 难看的.

ˌ**ill-ˈfounded** *adj* not based on fact or truth 无根据的; 凭空的; 毫无理由的: *ˌill-founded ˈclaims, asˈsumptions, suˈspicions, etc* 毫无理由的索赔、凭空的臆断、无根据的怀疑.

ˌ**ill-ˈgotten** *adj* (*dated or joc* 旧或谑) obtained dishonestly 非法得来的; 来路不正的: *ˌill-gotten ˈgains* 不义之财.

ˌ**ill-ˈjudged** *adj* not well timed; unwise 判断不当的; 不合时宜的; 不明智的: *an ˌill-judged ˈrescue attempt* 时机选择不当的营救行动.

ˌ**ill-ˈmannered** *adj* having bad manners; rude 无礼貌的; 举止粗鲁的.

ˌ**ill-ˈnatured** *adj* bad-tempered; unkind 脾气坏的; 粗暴的; 不厚道的; 不仁慈的: *an ˌill-natured ˈperson, ˈcomment* 脾气恶劣的人、恶意的评语.

ˌ**ill-ˈomened**, ˌ**ill-ˈstarred** *adjs* (*rhet* 修辞) unlucky 不吉利的; 倒霉的; 不幸的.

ˌ**ill-ˈtimed** *adj* done or happening at a wrong or unsuitable time 不合时宜的; 不适时的: *Our visit was ill-timed — my mother had guests already.* 我们探望母亲很不是时候——她家里已经来了客人. Cf 参看 WELL-TIMED (WELL[3]).

ˌ**ill-ˈtreat**, ˌ**ill-ˈuse** *vs* [Tn] treat or use (sb/sth) unkindly or badly 虐待, 折磨(某人[某物]): *ill-treat one's dog* 虐待自己的狗. ˌ**ill-ˈtreatment**, ˌ**ill-ˈusage** *ns* [U].

ill[2] /ɪl; ɪl/ *adj* **1** (*US* usu 美式英语通常作 **sick**) [usu pred 通常作表语] physically or mentally unwell; sick (身体上或精神上)不适, 不健康, 有病: *He's been ill for two weeks.* 他病了两个星期了. ○ *She fell ill/was taken ill suddenly.* 她突然病了. ⇨Usage at SICK 用法见 SICK. **2** [attrib 作定语] (**a**) not good; bad 不好的; 不良的; 坏的; 糟糕的: *ill health* 不健康 ○ *people of ill repute*, ie with a bad reputation 名声不好的人. (**b**) harmful; intending harm 有害的; 邪恶的: *suffer no ill effects* 未受坏影响. (**c**) unkind; resentful 不友好的; 敌意的; 怨恨的: *bear sb no ill will* 对某人不存恶意 ○ *You ought to apologize and show there is no ill feeling between you.* 你应当道歉, 表明你们之间并无恶感. **3** [attrib 作定语] not favourable 不利的; 不吉的: *ill luck* 恶运 ○ *a bird of ill omen*, ie one thought to bring bad luck 不祥之鸟. **4** (idm 习语) **it's an ˌill ˈwind (that blows nobody any good)** (*saying* 谚) few things are so bad that they don't offer some good to sb 世上鲜有绝对的坏事; 害于此者利于彼.

▷ **ill** *n* (*fml* 文) **1** [U] harm; evil 伤害; 恶行; 邪恶: *I wish him no ill.* 我对他并无恶感. **2** [C usu *pl* 通常作复数] problem; misfortune 困难; 不幸; 苦恼: *the various ills of life* 人生种种苦难.

I'll /aɪl; aɪl/ *contracted form* 缩约式 I will ⇨ WILL.

il·legal /ɪˈliːɡl; ɪˈliɡl/ *adj* against the law; not legal 不合法的; 违法的.

▷ **il·leg·al·ity** /ˌɪlɪˈɡæləti; ˌɪliˈɡæləti/ *n* **1** [U] state of being illegal 不合法; 违法. **2** [C] illegal act 非法行为.

il·leg·ally /-ɡəli; -ɡḷɪ/ *adv*: *an illegally parked car* 违章停放的汽车.

il·legible /ɪˈledʒəbl; ɪˈlɛdʒəbl/ (also **unreadable**) *adj* difficult or impossible to read; not legible 难以辨认的; (字迹)模糊的; 不能辨识的: *an illegible signature* 难以辨认的签字. ▷ **il·legib·il·ity** /ɪˌledʒəˈbɪləti; ɪˌlɛdʒəˈbɪləti/ *n* [U]. **il·legibly** /-əbli; -əblɪ/ *adv*.

il·le·git·im·ate /ˌɪlɪˈdʒɪtɪmət; ˌɪlɪˈdʒɪtəmɪt/ *adj* **1** born of parents not married to each other; not legitimate by birth 非婚生的; 私生的: *an ˌillegitimate ˈchild* 私生儿 ○ *She's illegitimate.* 她是私生女. **2** not allowed by the law or by the rules 法律不容的; 规则不许可的; 非法的: *illegitimate use of company property* 对公司财产的盗用. **3** (of a conclusion in an argument, etc) not logical (指辩论等的结论)不合逻辑的, 不合理的. ▷ **il·le·git·im·acy** /ˌɪlɪˈdʒɪtɪməsi; ˌɪlɪˈdʒɪtəməsɪ/ *n* [U]. **il·le·git·im·ately** *adv*.

il·lib·eral /ɪˈlɪbərəl; ɪˈlɪbərəl/ *adj* (*fml* 文) **1** (**a**) not tolerant; narrow-minded 不能容让的; 心胸狭隘的: *illiberal attitudes* 偏执的看法. (**b**) lacking culture 缺乏文化素养的; 粗鄙的: *an illiberal upbringing* 不良的教养. **2** mean or stingy; not generous 吝啬的; 小气的; 不大方的: *illiberal helpings of food* 添加的分量少的食物. ▷ **il·lib·er·al·ity** /ɪˌlɪbəˈræləti; ɪˌlɪbəˈræləti/ *n* [U]. **il·li·ber·ally** /-rəli; -rəlɪ/ *adv*.

il·li·cit /ɪˈlɪsɪt; ɪˈlɪsɪt/ *adj* (**a**) not allowed by law; illegal 法律不许可的; 违禁的; 非法的: *the illicit sale of drugs* 毒品的非法贩卖. (**b**) not approved by the normal rules of society 违反社会规则的; 不正当的: *an illicit relationship* 不正当的关系. ▷ **il·li·citly** *adv*.

il·lit·er·ate /ɪˈlɪtərət; ɪˈlɪtərɪt/ *adj* **1** (**a**) not able to read or write 不会读或不会写的; 不识字的: *an illiterate child* 不识字的孩子. Cf 参看 UNLETTERED. (**b**) showing such ignorance 文字不通的: *an illiterate letter*, ie one that contains many mistakes of spelling and grammar 文字不通的信. **2** (**a**) showing little or no education 缺乏教育的; 教育程度很低的: *You must be illiterate if you've never heard of Marx.* 要是你连马克思这个人都从未听说过, 那么你一定是没有受过教育的了. (**b**) ignorant in a particular field (对某一领域)无知的, 外行的: *be scientifically illiterate* 科盲.

▷ **il·lit·er·acy** /ɪˈlɪtərəsi; ɪˈlɪtərəsɪ/ *n* [U] state of being illiterate 文盲; 缺乏教育; 无知: *Illiteracy is a major problem in some developing countries.* 在一些发展中国家, 文盲是个大问题.

il·lit·er·ate *n* illiterate person 文盲; 无知的人.

ill·ness /ˈɪlnɪs; ˈɪlnɪs/ *n* **1** [U] state of being ill in body or mind; lack of health 病; 疾病; 不健康: *We've had a lot of illness in the family.* 我们家的人患过很多病. **2** [C] type or period of illness 患的病; 患病期间: *serious illnesses* 重病 ○ *recovering after a long illness* 久病之后逐渐康复.

il·lo·gical /ɪˈlɒdʒɪkl; ɪˈlɑdʒɪkl/ *adj* **1** without reason or logic; not sensible 没有道理的; 不合逻辑的; 悖于理的; 乖戾的: *It seems illogical to change the timetable so often.* 时间表变动得如此频繁, 似乎没有什么道理. **2** contrary to the rules of logic 与逻辑相违的: *an illogical conclusion* 不合逻辑的结论. ▷ **il·lo·gic·al·ity** /ɪˌlɒdʒɪˈkæləti; ɪˌlɑdʒɪˈkæləti/ *n* [C, U]. **il·lo·gic·ally** /-kli; -klɪ/ *adv*.

il·lu·min·ate /ɪˈluːmɪneɪt; ɪˈlumə,net/ *v* [Tn] **1** provide (sth) with light 照明, 照亮, 照射(某物): *a football pitch illuminated with floodlights* 用泛光灯照亮的足球场. **2** decorate (sth) with bright lights for a special occasion 用灯装饰(某物): *illuminate a street, building, etc* 用彩灯装饰街道、建筑物等. **3** (esp formerly) decorate (a book) with gold, silver and bright colours, usu by hand (尤指旧时)用金色、银色或鲜艳色彩装饰(书)(通常为手工制作): *an illuminated manuscript* 装饰过的手稿. **4** (*fml* 文) make (sth) clear; help to explain 阐明(某事物); 解释清楚; 启发: *illuminate a difficult passage in a book* 解释书中难懂的段落.

▷ **il·lu·min·at·ing** *adj* particularly revealing or helpful 富有启发性的; 很有助益的: *an illuminating analysis, talk, etc* 很有启发的分析、谈话等.

il·lu·mina·tion /ɪˌluːmɪˈneɪʃn; ɪˌluməˈneʃən/ *n* **1** [U] illuminating or being illuminated; (source of) light 照明; 照度; 光(源). **2 illuminations** [pl] (*Brit*) bright colourful lights used to decorate a town for a special occasion 彩灯; 灯饰: *the Christmas illuminations in the* *high street* 大街上的圣诞节彩灯. **3** [C usu *pl* 通常作复数] coloured decoration, usu painted by hand, in an old book (旧书上的)彩饰, 图案花饰(通常为手工制作的).

il·lu·sion /ɪˈluːʒn; ɪˈluʒən/ *n* **1** (**a**) [C] false idea, belief or impression; delusion 错误的观念; 幻觉; 错觉: *I have no illusions about my ability*, ie I know that I am not very able. 我对自己的能力如何颇有自知之明(我知道自己的能力不很强). ○ *We're left with few illusions about our ally.* 我们的处境已不容我们对盟友再存多少幻想了. (**b**) [U] state of mind in which one is deceived in this way 幻觉; 错觉: *You think that, do you? Pure illusion!* 你是那么想的吗? 纯粹是错觉! **2** [C] thing that a person wrongly believes to exist; false perception 幻想中的事物; 错觉: *an optical illusion* 光幻视 ○ *In the hot sun the surface of the road seems wet, but that is only an illusion.* 路面在烈日之下像是湿的, 然而这仅仅是错觉. **3** (idm 习语) **be under an/the illusion (that...)** believe wrongly 误信: *I was under the illusion that he was honest until he was caught stealing some money.* 他偷钱当场被人抓住, 在此之前我一直误以为他是个老实人.

▷ **il·lu·sion·ist** /-ʒənɪst; -ʒənɪst/ *n* person who does clever tricks on stage that deceive the audience; conjurer 魔术师; 幻术师.

il·lus·ive /ɪˈluːsɪv; ɪˈlusɪv/, **il·lus·ory** /ɪˈluːsərɪ; ɪˈlusərɪ/ *adjs* based on illusion; deceptive 幻觉的; 虚假的; 骗人的.

il·lus·trate /ˈɪləstreɪt; ˋɪləstret/ *v* [Tn] **1** supply (sth) with pictures, diagrams, etc 为(某物)作插图或图表: *illustrate a book, magazine, lecture* 给书、杂志、讲义作插图 ○ *a well-illustrated textbook* 有精美插图的教科书. **2** (**a**) explain or make (sth) clear by examples, diagrams, pictures, etc (用示例、图表等)说明, 阐明(某事物): *To illustrate my point I have done a comparative analysis.* 为说明我的观点, 我做了对比分析. (**b**) be an example of (sth) 表明或显示为(某事物)的例证: *This behaviour illustrates your selfishness.* 你的行为说明你很自私.

▷ **il·lus·tra·tion** /ˌɪləˈstreɪʃn; ˌɪləsˋtreʃən/ *n* **1** [U] illustrating or being illustrated 作插图; 图解; 图示; 示例; 举例说明: *the art of book illustration* 书籍的插图艺术 ○ *Illustration is often more useful than definition for showing what words mean.* 用图解或示例解释词义往往比用定义解释更清楚. **2** [C] drawing, diagram or picture in a book, magazine, etc 书或杂志上的图画、图表、照片: *colour illustrations* 彩色插图. **3** [C] example used to explain sth (说明某事物用的)示例, 实例, 例证.

il·lus·trat·ive /ˈɪləstrətɪv; *US* ɪˈlʌs-; ɪˋlʌstrətɪv/ *adj* serving as an example or illustration 作为例证或图解的; 作说明用的; 解说性的: *an illustrative quotation* 说明性的引文 ○ *That outburst was illustrative of her bad temper.* 这一通发作适足说明她脾气坏.

il·lus·trator *n* person who draws and paints pictures for books, etc 为书制作插图的人.

il·lus·tri·ous /ɪˈlʌstrɪəs; ɪˋlʌstrɪəs/ *adj* very famous and distinguished 著名的; 杰出的; 卓越的. ▷ **il·lus·tri·ously** *adv.*

ILO /ˌaɪ el ˈəʊ; ˌaɪ ɛl ˈo/ *abbr* 缩写 = International Labour Organization 国际劳工组织.

im- ⇨ IN-¹, IN-².

I'm /aɪm; aɪm/ *contracted form* 缩约式 I am ⇨ BE.

im·age /ˈɪmɪdʒ; ˋɪmɪdʒ/ *n* **1** (**a**) [C] copy of the shape of a person or thing, esp one made in stone or wood; statue 像, 肖像, 偶像(尤指木、石雕刻的): *carved images* 雕像. (**b**) [sing] (*arch* 古) close likeness 极相像: *According to the Bible, God created man in his image.* 据《圣经》所叙, 上帝按自己的形象创造了人. **2** [C] mental picture or idea 心目中的形象或概念: *I have this image of you as always being cheerful.* 在我的心目中, 你的样子总是兴高采烈的. **3** [C] general impression that a person, firm, product, etc gives to the public; reputation (人、公司、产品等给公众的)总印象; 形象; 声誉: *How can we improve our (public) image?* 我们怎样才能改善自己(在公众心目中)的形象? **4** [C] figure of speech; simile; metaphor 意象; 比喻; 明喻; 隐喻: *a poem full of startling images* 充满惊人意象的诗. **5** [C] appearance of sb or sth when seen in a mirror or through the lens of a camera 映像; 影像; 镜像. **6** (idm 习语) **be the (very/living/spitting) image of sb/sth** (*infml* 口) be or look exactly like sb/sth 极像某人[某事物]: *She's the (spitting) image of her mother.* 她长得活像她妈妈.

▷ **im·agery** /ˈɪmɪdʒərɪ; ˋɪmɪdʒərɪ/ *n* [U] **1** use of figurative language to produce pictures in the minds of readers or hearers 形象化的描叙; 意象: *poetic imagery* 诗的意象. **2** statues; images as a group 像, 画像, 塑像, 雕像, 偶像(总称).

imag·in·able /ɪˈmædʒɪnəbl; ɪˋmædʒɪnəbl/ *adj* that can be imagined 可想像的; 想像得到的: *We had the greatest difficulty imaginable getting here in time.* 我们为了及时赶到此地, 经历了可能想见的最大的困难.

imag·in·ary /ɪˈmædʒɪnərɪ; *US* -ənerɪ; ɪˋmædʒəˌnerɪ/ *adj* existing only in the mind or imagination; not real 想像中的; 假想的; 虚构的; 幻想的: *imaginary fears* 想像中的恐惧.

imag·ina·tion /ɪˌmædʒɪˈneɪʃn; ɪˌmædʒəˋneʃən/ *n* **1** (**a**) [U, C] ability to form mental images or pictures 想像力: *He hasn't much imagination.* 他缺乏想像力. ○ *Her talk captured* (ie gripped and stimulated) *the imagination of the whole class.* 她的谈话吸引了全班的同学, 激发了他们的想像力. (**b**) [C] part of the mind that does this 想像: *In my imagination, I thought I heard her calling me.* 我在想像中彷彿听到她在呼唤我. **2** [U] use of this ability in a practical or creative way 想像力的运用: *His writing lacks imagination.* 他的写作缺乏想像力. ○ *Use your imagination to find an answer.* 运用你的想像力来寻找答案. **3** [U] thing experienced in the mind and not in reality 想像出来的事物; 幻想物: *I can't have seen a ghost — it must have been imagination.* 我看到的不可能是鬼——一定是幻想的东西吧. ○ *Is it my imagination or have you lost a lot of weight?* 是我的错觉呢, 还是你真的瘦了许多? **4** (idm 习语) **the mind/imagination boggles** ⇨ BOGGLE. **not by any/by no stretch of the imagination** ⇨ STRETCH *n*.

▷ **imag·in·at·ive** /ɪˈmædʒɪnətɪv; *US* -əneɪtɪv; ɪˋmædʒəˌnetɪv/ *adj* having or showing imagination 富于想像力的; 爱想像的: *an imaginative child, writer, production* 有想像力的孩子、富于想像力的作家、体现出想像力的产品. **imag·in·at·ively** *adv.*

ima·gine /ɪˈmædʒɪn; ɪˋmædʒɪn/ *v* **1** [Tn, Tf, Tw, Tg, Tsg, Cn·a, Cn·pr, Cn·t] form a mental image of (sth) 想像, 设想(某事物): *Imagine a house with a big garden.* 设想有一所带大花园的房子. ○ *Imagine that you are in London.* 想像一下你正在伦敦吧. ○ *Can you imagine what it would be like to live without electricity?* 你能想像出生活中没有电会是一幅什么样的情景吗? ○ *She imagined walking into the office and telling everyone what she thought of them.* 她想像自己走进办公室, 对每个人都说出自己对他们的看法. ○ *Imagine yourself (to be) rich and famous.* 想像一下你又有钱, 又有名的情况. **2** [Tf, Tw, Tg, Tsg] think of (sth) as probable or possible 料想, 设想, 想到(某事物): *I can't imagine that anyone cares what I do.* 我想不出谁会关心我的所作所为. ○ *I can't imagine living* (ie don't think I shall ever live) *anywhere but England.* 我很难设想能到英国以外的地方去生活. ○ *Would you ever have imagined him/his becoming a politician?* 你怎能料想到他竟当上政治家了? **3** [Tn, Tf] suppose (sth); assume 猜想(某事物); 认为: *I imagine (that) he'll be there.* 我猜他会到那儿去.

imam /ɪˈmɑːm; ɪˋmɑm/ *n* **1** person who leads the prayers in a mosque 伊玛目(清真寺内率领伊斯兰教徒作礼拜的人). **2 Imam** title of various Muslim religious leaders 伊玛目(伊斯兰教领袖的头衔).

im·bal·ance /ˌɪmˈbæləns; ɪmˋbæləns/ *n* lack of balance or proportion; inequality 不平衡; 不均衡; 失衡; 失调: *The current trade deficit indicates a serious imbalance between our import and export trade.* 当前的贸易赤字表明我们的进出口贸易严重失调.

im·be·cile /ˈɪmbəsiːl; *US* -sl; ˋɪmbəsḷ/ *n* (**a**) (esp adult) person with abnormally low intelligence (尤指成年人)低能者, 弱智者. (**b**) (*infml* 口) stupid or silly person; fool 蠢人; 傻瓜.

▷ **im·be·cile, im·be·cilic** *adjs* [usu attrib 通常作定语] stupid; foolish 愚蠢的; 傻的: *an imbecile remark* 愚蠢的言语 ○ *imbecile behaviour* 愚笨的举止.

im·be·cil·ity /ˌɪmbəˈsɪlətɪ; ˌɪmbəˋsɪlətɪ/ *n* **1** [U] stupidity 愚蠢. **2** [C] stupid act, remark, etc 愚蠢的行为、言语等.

im·bibe /ɪmˈbaɪb; ɪmˋbaɪb/ *v* **1** [I, Tn] (*fml or joc* 文或谑) drink (sth, esp alcohol) 喝, 饮(尤指酒类): *Are you imbibing?* 你正在喝酒吗? **2** [Tn] (*fig* 比喻) take in or absorb (sth) 吸收或接受(某事物): *imbibe fresh air, knowledge* 吸入新鲜空气、接受知识.

im·bro·glio /ɪmˈbrəʊlɪəʊ; ɪmˋbroljo/ *n* (*pl* **~s** /-z; -z/) complicated, confused or embarrassing situation, esp a political or an emotional one 错综复杂的局面, 纠缠不清的关系, 尴尬的处境(尤指政治上的或感情上的).

im·bue /ɪmˈbju:; ɪmˋbju/ *v* [Tn·pr esp passive 尤用于被动语态] **~ sb/sth with sth** (*fml* 文) fill or inspire sb/sth with (feelings, etc) 使(某人[某事物])充满或激起(感情等): *imbued with patriotism, ambition, love, etc* 充满爱国主义精神、雄心勃勃、满怀爱心 ○ *politicians imbued with a sense of their own importance* 自以为举足轻重的政治家们.

IMF /ˌaɪ em ˈef; ˌaɪ ɛm ˋɛf/ *abbr* 缩写 = International Monetary Fund 国际货币基金组织.

im·it·ate /ˈɪmɪteɪt; ˋɪməˌtet/ *v* [Tn] **1** copy the behaviour of (sb/sth); take or follow as an example 学(某人[某物])的样; 仿效: *Decide what you want to do; don't just imitate others.* 想做什么自己决定, 不要一味学别人的样. **2** copy the speech, actions, dress, etc of (sb); mimic 模仿(某人的言谈、举止、衣着等): *He's very clever at imitating his friends.* 他非常擅长于模仿朋友的言行. **3** be like (sb/sth); look like 与(某人[某事物])相似; 好像: *The stage was designed to imitate a prison cell.* 舞台设计成牢房的样子.

▷ **im·it·ator** *n* person who imitates (esp other people) 模仿(尤指他人)的人.

im·ita·tion /ˌɪmɪˈteɪʃn; ˌɪməˋteʃən/ *n* **1** [C] thing produced as a copy of the real thing 仿制品; 仿造品; 赝品: *That's not an original Rembrandt, it's an imitation.* 这不是伦勃朗的真品, 是件赝品. ○ [attrib 作定语] *imitation leather, jewellery, etc*, ie material made to look like leather, jewellery, etc 人造革、假珠宝. **2** [U] imitating 仿; 效: *learn sth by imitation* 通过模仿学习某事物 ○ *The house was built in imitation of a Roman villa.* 这所房子是仿罗马别墅式的建筑. **3** [C] impersonation or mimicking of a person's speech or behaviour 扮演或模仿某人的言谈举止: *an entertainer who does hilarious imitations of politicians' voices* 专门学政治家讲话作滑稽模拟表演的演员.

im·it·at·ive /ˈɪmɪtətɪv; *US* -teɪtɪv; ˋɪməˌtetɪv/ *adj* copying or following a model or example 模仿的; 仿效的; 模拟的: *His style of public speaking is imitative of the prime minister.* 他的演讲风格是模仿首相的. ○ *Sculpture is an imitative art*, ie it copies people, things, etc from real life. 雕刻是模仿的艺术(模刻真实生活中的人、物等).

im·macu·late /ɪˈmækjʊlət; ɪˋmækjəlɪt/ *adj* (*approv* 褒) **1** perfectly clean and tidy; spotless 整洁的; 无污迹的; 无瑕的: *an immaculate uniform* 整洁的制服. **2** right in every detail; having no mistakes 精确的; 无误的: *an immaculate performance* 完美的演出. ▷ **im·macu·lately** *adv*: *immaculately dressed* 衣着整洁.

□ **the Imˌmaculate Conˈception** Roman Catholic teaching that the Virgin Mary was without sin from the moment of her conception 无原罪始胎, 始胎无玷(天主教会信条, 谓圣母马利亚自怀孕之始即无原罪).

im·man·ent /ˈɪmənənt; ˋɪmənənt/ *adj* **~ (in sth)** **1** (*fml* 文) (of qualities) naturally present; inherent (指特性)天生的, 内在的, 固有的: *He believed that beauty was not something imposed, but something immanent.* 他认为美丽不是外在的而是内在的. **2** (of God) permanently present throughout the whole universe (指上帝)无处不在的. ▷ **im·man·ence** /-əns; -əns/ *n* [U].

im·ma·ter·ial /ˌɪməˈtɪərɪəl; ˌɪməˋtɪrɪəl/ *adj* **1 ~ (to sb)** not important; irrelevant 不重要的; 不相干的: *The cost is immaterial.* 成本微不足道. ○ *It is immaterial (to me) whether he stays or leaves.* 他的去留(对我)无所谓. **2** without physical form or substance 非物质的; 非实体的; 无形的: *as immaterial as a ghost* 虚无如鬼魂.

im·ma·ture /ˌɪməˈtjʊə(r); *US* -tʊər; ˌɪməˋtʊr/ *adj* **1** not sensible in behaviour or in controlling one's feelings; less mature than one would expect (行为或控制感情)不成熟的, 不够老练的: *He's very immature for his age.* 就他的年龄来说, 他还很不成熟. **2** not (yet) fully developed or grown (尚)未充分成长的; 发育(尚)未完全的: *immature plants* 幼嫩的植物. ▷ **im·ma·tur·ity** /ˌɪməˈtjʊərətɪ; *US* -tʊər-; ˌɪməˋtʊrətɪ/ *n* [U].

im·meas·ur·able /ɪˈmeʒərəbl; ɪˋmɛʒərəbḷ/ *adj* that cannot be measured, esp because of largeness in size or extent 不可计量的, 无限的, 无比的(尤指因体积或程度之大): *the immeasurable depths of the universe* 宇宙的无限深广. ▷ **im·meas·ur·ably** /-blɪ; -blɪ/ *adv*: *Your presence has enriched our lives immeasurably.* 有你在, 我们的生活无比丰富. ○ *The task seems immeasurably difficult.* 任务似乎极为艰巨.

im·me·di·ate /ɪˈmi:dɪət; ɪˋmidɪɪt/ *adj* **1** (**a**) happening or done at once 立即的; 即刻的: *I want an immediate reply.* 我要求立即答复我. ○ *The response of the people to the famine appeal was immediate.* 人们对救济饥荒的吁求立刻作出了回应. ○ *take immediate action* 立刻采取行动. (**b**) [usu attrib 通常作定语] existing at the present time 目前的; 当前的: *Our immediate concern is for/with the families of those who died.* 我们当务之急是安抚死者的家属. **2** [attrib 作定语] nearest in time, space or relationship (在时空上、关系上)最接近的, 紧接的: *What are your plans for the immediate future?* 你最近有什么计划? ○ *There's no post office in the immediate neighbourhood.* 附近没有邮局. ○ *his immediate predecessor* 他的前任 ○ *one's immediate family*, ie parents, children, brothers and sisters 直系亲属(父母、子女、兄弟、姐妹). **3** [attrib 作定语] with nothing coming in between; direct 直接的: *The immediate cause of death is unknown.* 造成死亡的直接原因不明.

▷ **im·me·di·acy** /-əsɪ; -əsɪ/ (also **im·me·di·ate·ness**) *n* [U] closeness or reality of sth, so that one feels directly involved or has to deal with it at once 直接性; 即时性; 直观性; 实感性; 迫切性: *the immediacy of the war, as seen on television* 战争的实感, 一如电视上所见 ○ *the immediacy of the problem* 问题的紧迫性.

im·me·di·ately *adv* **1** at once; without delay 立刻; 马上; 当即; 毫不耽搁: *She answered almost immediately.* 她几乎当下就答复了. ○ *The purpose may not be immediately evident.* 这种目的不一定显而易见. **2** being nearest in time or space; directly (在时空上)最接近地, 直接地: *in the years immediately after the war* 战后最初的几年 ○ *fix the lock immediately below the handle* 把锁直接安在把手下方. **3** directly or very closely 直接地; 紧接地: *the houses most immediately affected by the motorway* 最直接受高速公路影响的房子. — *conj* (*esp Brit*) as soon as; the moment that 即刻; 一...就...: *I recognized her immediately I saw her.* 我一看见她就立刻认出她来了.

im·me·mor·ial /ˌɪməˈmɔ:rɪəl; ˌɪməˋmorɪəl/ *adj* (*fml or rhet* 文或修辞) **1** going back beyond the reach of human memory or written records (因年代久远)人类无法追忆的或文字记录所不及的. **2** (idm 习语) **from/since time immemorial** ⇨ TIME.

im·mense /ɪˈmens; ɪˋmɛns/ *adj* extremely large 巨大的; 广大的: *immense difficulties, problems, possibilities, etc* 巨大的困难、问题、可能性等 ○ *of immense importance* 极为重要的.

▷ **im·mensely** *adv* to a very great extent; extremely 极大地; 无限地; 极端地: *immensely popular, rich, successful, etc* 极其流行、富有、成功等 ○ *They enjoyed the film immensely.* 他们非常喜欢这部影片.

im·mens·ity /ɪˈmensətɪ; ɪˋmɛnsətɪ/ *n* [U] largeness; great size 巨大; 广大: *the immensity of the universe* 宇宙的浩瀚无垠.

im·merse /ɪˈmɜ:s; ɪˋmɝs/ *v* [Tn, Tn·pr] **1 ~ sth (in sth)** put sth under the surface of a liquid 使某物浸没于液体中: *Immerse the plant (in water) for a few minutes.* 把那棵植物(在水里)浸泡几分钟. **2 ~ oneself (in sth)** involve oneself deeply (in sth); absorb oneself 使自己沉浸(于某事物); 使自己深陷于或专心于: *be immersed in thought, one's business, a book* 沉思、埋首事务、专心读书 ○ *He immersed himself totally in his work.* 他埋首于工作.

▷ **im·mer·sion** /ɪˈmɜ:ʃn; *US* -ʒn; ɪˋmɝʒən/ *n* [U] **1** immersing; being immersed 沉浸; 浸沉. **2** baptism by putting the whole body under water 洗礼; 浸礼.

immersion heater electric heater fixed inside a hot-water tank in a home 浸入式加热器(家庭用的).

im·mig·rate /ˈɪmɪgreɪt; ˋɪməˌgret/ *v* [I, Ipr] **~ (to/into...)** enter a foreign country in order to live there permanently 移入(外国定居). Cf 参看 EMIGRATE.

▷ **im·mig·rant** /ˈɪmɪgrənt; ˋɪməgrənt/ *n* person who has come to live permanently in a foreign country (自外国移入的)移民: *Irish immigrants* 来自爱尔兰的移民 ○

illegal immigrants 非法移民 ○ [attrib 作定语] *the immigrant population* 外来的移民人口.

im·mig·ra·tion /ˌɪmɪˈgreɪʃn; ˌɪməˋgreʃən/ *n* **1** [U, C] (instance of) moving of people from one country to come to live in another country permanently 移民: *restrictions on immigration* 对外来移民的限制 ○ [attrib 作定语] *immigration officials* (处理外来移民的)移民局官员 ○ *immigration controls* (对外来的)移民管制. **2** [U] (also **immiˈgration control**) control point at an airport, sea terminal, etc at which the passports and other documents of people wanting to come into a country are checked (设于机场、港口等的)移民局检查站(负责检查入境者的护照及有关文件): *go/pass through immigration* 通过移民局检查.

im·min·ent /ˈɪmɪnənt; ˋɪmənənt/ *adj* (esp of unpleasant events) about to happen; likely to happen very soon (尤指不愉快的事件)即将发生的, 临近的, 逼近的: *no warning of imminent danger* 没有即将发生危险的警告 ○ *An announcement of further cuts in government expenditure is imminent.* 最近将发布进一步削减政府开支的公告.
▷ **im·min·ence** /-əns; -əns/ *n* [U]: *the imminence of nuclear war* 核战迫近的危险. **im·min·ently** *adv*.

im·mob·ile /ɪˈməʊbaɪl; *US* -bl; ɪˋmobl̩/ *adj* **1** unable to move or be moved 不能活动的; 不能移动的: *Her illness has made her completely immobile.* 她病得完全失去了活动能力. **2** not moving 不活动的; 静止的: *The deer stood immobile among the trees.* 那只鹿一动不动地站在树丛里.
▷ **im·mob·il·ity** /ˌɪməˈbɪləti; ˌɪmoˋbɪləti/ *n* [U] state of being immobile 静止(状态); 固定; 不能动.

im·mob·il·ize, -ise /ɪˈməʊbəlaɪz; ɪˋmobl̩ˌaɪz/ *v* [Tn] **1** prevent (sth) from moving or operating normally 使(某物)不动、固定或不能正常运作: *A whole tank regiment was completely immobilized by enemy air attacks.* 敌军的空袭将整个坦克团完全钳制住了. ○ *This alarm immobilizes the car.* 这种警报一发出, 汽车就停止不动了. ○ *The firm has been immobilized by a series of strikes.* 公司因一连串的罢工而陷于瘫痪. **2** keep (a patient, a broken limb, etc) completely still, in order to help recovery 固定(病人、断肢等)以助复元. **im·mob·il·iza·tion, -isation** /ɪˌməʊbəlaɪˈzeɪʃn; *US* -lɪˈz-; ɪˌmobl̩əˋzeʃən/ *n* [U].

im·mod·er·ate /ɪˈmɒdərət; ɪˋmɑdərɪt/ *adj* too extreme or excessive; not moderate 过度的; 无节制的; 极端的; 不适度的: *immoderate eating/drinking habits* 无节制的大吃[大喝]的习惯. ▷ **im·mod·er·ately** *adv*.

im·mod·est /ɪˈmɒdɪst; ɪˋmɑdɪst/ *adj* **1** indecent or not proper; not modest, esp concerning sexual behaviour 不雅的; 不端庄的; (尤指)猥亵的, 下流的: *an immodest dress* 过分暴露的连衣裙 ○ *immodest talk, behaviour, etc* 不雅的谈话、举动等. **2** showing or expressing too high an opinion of oneself; conceited 自高自大的; 自负的: *If I may be immodest for a moment, let me tell you about the latest book that I've written.* 恕我出言无状, 请姑且容我谈谈新近的拙著. ▷ **im·mod·estly** *adv*. **im·mod·esty** *n* [U].

im·mol·ate /ˈɪməleɪt; ˋɪməˌlet/ *v* [Tn] (*fml* 文) kill (sb) as a sacrifice 杀(某人)作祭品. ▷ **im·mola·tion** /ˌɪməˈleɪʃn; ˌɪməˋleʃən/ *n* [U].

im·moral /ɪˈmɒrəl; *US* ɪˈmɔːrəl; ɪˋmɔrəl/ *adj* **1** not following accepted standards of morality; not moral 不道德的; 邪恶的: *It's immoral to steal.* 盗窃是不道德的. **2** not following accepted standards of sexual behaviour 放荡的; 猥亵的: *Some people still think it is immoral to have sex before marriage.* 有些人仍然认为婚前的性行为是不道德的. ○ *an immoral young man* 不正经的年轻男子 ○ *immoral earnings*, eg from prostitution 不干净的收入(如卖淫得来的).
▷ **im·mor·al·ity** /ˌɪməˈræləti; ˌɪməˋræləti/ *n* [U] immoral behaviour 不道德; 淫荡: *a life of immorality* 淫荡的生活.
im·mor·ally /-rəlɪ; -rəlɪ/ *adv*: *behave immorally* 淫荡地; 邪恶地; 不正经地; 猥亵地. Cf 参看 AMORAL.

im·mor·tal /ɪˈmɔːtl; ɪˋmɔrtl̩/ *adj* **1** living for ever; not mortal 不朽的; 永世的: *The soul is immortal.* 灵魂不灭. **2** (**a**) famous for ever; that will be remembered for ever 流芳百世的; 万古流芳的; 名垂千古的: *the immortal Shakespeare* 不朽的莎士比亚. (**b**) that will last for a long time or for ever; unfading 永存的; 永世的; 不泯的: *immortal fame/glory* 不朽的名声[荣耀].
▷ **im·mor·tal** *n* (usu *pl* 通常作复数) **1** person of lasting fame 不朽的人物; 千古流芳之士: *Beethoven is regarded as one of the immortals of classical music.* 贝多芬被认为是不朽的古典音乐大师. **2** immortal being, esp a god of ancient Greece and Rome 永生不朽者(尤指古代希腊和罗马的神).
im·mor·tal·ity /ˌɪmɔːˈtæləti; ˌɪmɔrˋtæləti/ *n* [U] state of being immortal 不朽; 永存: *man's belief in immortality* 人类对永生的信念.
im·mor·tal·ize, -ise /ɪˈmɔːtəlaɪz; ɪˋmɔrtl̩ˌaɪz/ *v* [Tn] give endless life or fame to (sb/sth) 使(某人[某事物])不朽、永生、永存、名垂千古: *Wigan pier, as immortalized in George Orwell's book 'The Road to Wigan Pier'* 因乔治·奥韦尔的《通向威根码头之路》一书而永享盛名的威根码头.

im·mov·able /ɪˈmuːvəbl; ɪˋmuvəbl̩/ *adj* **1** that cannot be moved; impossible to move; fixed 不可移动的; 固定的: *an immovable stone column* 岿然不动的石柱 ○ (*law* 律) *immovable property*, eg buildings and land 不动产(如建筑物和土地). **2** not changing; steadfast; firm 不变的; 坚定不移的; 牢固的: *immovable in purpose, intent, etc* 目标、意图等坚定不移的. ▷ **im·mov·ably** /-əblɪ; -əblɪ/ *adv*.

im·mune /ɪˈmjuːn; ɪˋmjun/ *adj* [usu pred 通常作表语] **1** ~ (**to/against sth**) that cannot be harmed by a disease or illness, either because of inoculation or through natural resistance 有免疫力(因接种疫苗或自发的): *I'm immune to smallpox as a result of vaccination.* 我种过牛痘了, 所以对天花有免疫力. **2** ~ (**to sth**) not affected by sth; not susceptible to sth 不受某事物影响; 不易感受某事物: *immune to criticism, abuse, opposition, etc* 不为批评、漫骂、反对等所动摇. **3** ~ (**from sth**) protected or exempt from sth (对某事物)免除, 豁免: *immune from additional taxes* 免纳附加税 ○ *immune from prosecution* 免予起诉.
▷ **im·mun·ity** /ɪˈmjuːnəti; ɪˋmjunəti/ *n* [U] **1** ~ (**to/against sth**) ability to resist infection, disease, etc 免疫力: *immunity to measles* 对麻疹的免疫力 ○ *This vaccine will give you immunity for two years.* 接种这种疫苗可有两年的免疫力. **2** ~ (**to sth**) ability to be unaffected by sth 不受某事物影响的能力: *immunity to criticism* 不受批评的影响. **3** ~ (**from sth**) ability to be protected or exempt from sth 受保护; 免除; 豁免: *immunity from prosecution* 免予起诉 ○ *diplomatic immunity* 外交豁免权.
im·mun·ize, -ise /ˈɪmjʊnaɪz; ˋɪmjʊˌnaɪz/ *v* [Tn, Tn·pr] ~ **sb** (**against sth**) make sb immune (to a disease or infection), esp by injecting him with a vaccine 使某人免疫(尤指通过注射疫苗): *Have you been immunized (against smallpox) yet?* 你接种过(抗天花)疫苗没有? Cf 参看 INOCULATE, VACCINATE. **im·mun·iza·tion, -isation** /ˌɪmjʊnaɪˈzeɪʃn; *US* -nɪˈz-; ˌɪmjʊnəˋzeʃən/ *n* [U, C]: *government plans for (a) mass immunization against measles* 政府的大规模麻疹免疫注射计划.
im·muno·logy /ˌɪmjʊˈnɒlədʒɪ; ˌɪmjʊˋnɑlədʒɪ/ *n* [U] scientific study of protection against and resistance to infection 免疫学.

im·mure /ɪˈmjʊə(r); ɪˋmjʊr/ *v* [Tn] (*fml* 文) imprison (sb); shut in 监禁(某人); 禁闭: *immured in a cold dungeon* 监禁在冰冷的地牢中 ○ *He immured himself in a small room to work undisturbed.* 他自己关在小屋里埋头工作, 以免受到骚扰.

im·mut·able /ɪˈmjuːtəbl; ɪˋmjutəbl̩/ *adj* (*fml* 文) that cannot be changed; that will never change 不可改变的; 永恒不变的: *an immutable decision* 不可更易的决定 ○ *immutable principles/laws* 永恒不变的原则[规律]. ▷ **im·mut·ab·il·ity** /ɪˌmjuːtəˈbɪləti; ɪˌmjutəˋbɪləti/ *n* [U]. **im·mut·ably** /-əblɪ; -əblɪ/ *adv*.

imp /ɪmp; ɪmp/ *n* **1** small devil or evil spirit 小魔鬼; 小恶魔. **2** mischievous child 顽童; 小淘气: *What a little imp you are!* 你这个淘气包!

im·pact /ˈɪmpækt; ˋɪmpækt/ *n* **1** [U] (**a**) hitting of one object against another 撞击; 冲击; 碰撞: *the impact of a collision* 碰撞时的冲击 ○ *The bomb exploded on impact*, ie at the moment of collision. 炸弹在撞击时立即爆炸. (**b**) force with which one object hits another 撞击力; 冲击力: *He collapsed under the full impact of the blow.* 他受到重击而倒下. **2** [C usu *sing* 通常作单数] ~ (**on/**

upon sb/sth) strong impression or effect on sb/sth 对某人[某事物]的强烈的印象或巨大的影响: *Her speech made a tremendous impact on everyone.* 她的演说对大家震动很大. ○ *the impact of new methods, technology, etc on modern industry* 新方法、新技术等对现代工业的巨大影响.

▷ **im·pact** /ɪmˈpækt; ɪmˋpækt/ *v* **1** [I, Tn] press, drive or wedge (sth) firmly into sth; press, etc (two things) together 将(某物)压入或插入另一物; (将两物)挤、压、塞...到一起. **2** [Ipr, Tn] **~ (on) sth** (*esp US*) have an effect on sth 对某事物有影响. **im·pac·ted** *adj* (of a tooth) wedged in the jaw so that it cannot grow through the gum normally (指牙齿)阻生的: *an impacted wisdom tooth* 阻生智齿.

im·pair /ɪmˈpeə(r); ɪmˋpɛr/ *v* [Tn] weaken or damage (sth) 削弱或损害(某事物): *Loud noise can impair your hearing.* 巨大的噪音有损听觉. ○ *Today's attack has seriously impaired attempts to achieve peace in the area.* 今日发动的攻击严重损害了在该地区谋求和平的努力. ○ *impaired vision* 受损的视力. ▷ **im·pair·ment** *n* [U].

im·pala /ɪmˈpɑːlə; ɪmˋpɑlə/ *n* (*pl* unchanged or **~s** 复数或不变或作 **impalas**) type of African antelope 黑斑羚(产于非洲).

im·pale /ɪmˈpeɪl; ɪmˋpel/ *v* [Tn, Tn·pr] **~ sb/sth (on sth)** pierce sb/sth with a sharp-pointed object 用尖物刺(某人[某物]): *In former times, prisoners' heads were impaled on pointed stakes.* 从前的人把监犯的头钉在尖桩上. ▷ **im·pale·ment** *n* [U].

im·palp·able /ɪmˈpælpəbl; ɪmˋpælpəbḷ/ *adj* (*fml* 文) **1** that cannot be touched or felt physically 触摸不着的; 感觉不到的: *impalpable darkness, horror, fear* 无形的黑暗、恐怖、害怕. **2** not easily understood or grasped by the mind 难以理解的; 不易意会的.

im·panel = EMPANEL.

im·part /ɪmˈpɑːt; ɪmˋpɑrt/ *v* (*fml* 文) **1** [Tn, Tn·pr] **~ sth (to sth)** give (a quality) to sth 将(某性质)给予或赋予某事物: *Her presence imparted an air of elegance (to the ceremony).* 她一出席(给仪式)增添了高雅的气氛. ○ *impart spin to a cricket ball* 使板球增加旋转力. **2** [Tn, Dn·pr] **~ sth (to sb)** make known (information) to sb; reveal sth 将(情况)通知或告知某人; 透露某事物: *I have no news to impart (to you).* 我没有消息可告诉你.

im·par·tial /ɪmˈpɑːʃl; ɪmˋpɑrʃəl/ *adj* not favouring one person or thing more than another; fair or neutral 不偏不倚的; 公正的; 中立的: *an impartial judge, judgement* 公正的法官[判决]. Cf 参看 PARTIAL 2. ▷ **im·par·ti·al·ity** /ˌɪmˌpɑːʃɪˈæləti; ˌɪmpɑrʃɪˋælətɪ/ *n* [U]: *They showed complete impartiality in discussing these sensitive issues.* 在讨论这些敏感的问题时, 他们完全不偏不倚. **im·par·ti·ally** /-ʃəlɪ; -ʃəlɪ/ *adv*: *treat prisoners impartially* 公正地对待犯人.

im·pass·able /ɪmˈpɑːsəbl; *US* -ˈpæs-; ɪmˋpæsəbḷ/ *adj* (of a road, route, etc) impossible to travel on or over (指道路、路线等)不能通行的, 不能超越的: *country lanes that are often impassable in winter* 在冬天经常不能通行的乡间小路 ○ *roads made impassable by fallen trees* 因有倒伏的树木而不能通行的道路.

im·passe /ˈæmpɑːs; *US* ˈɪmpæs; ˋɪmpæs/ *n* difficult position or situation from which there is no way out; deadlock 绝境; 僵局; 停顿: *The negotiations had reached an impasse, with both sides refusing to compromise.* 由于双方都不肯妥协, 谈判陷入僵局.

im·pas·sioned /ɪmˈpæʃnd; ɪmˋpæʃənd/ *adj* showing strong deep feeling 充满激情的; 热烈的: *an impassioned plea for mercy* 希望获得宽恕的热切恳求.

im·pass·ive /ɪmˈpæsɪv; ɪmˋpæsɪv/ *adj* showing no sign of feeling 无动于衷的; 无表情的; 不动声色的: *an impassive expression* 冷漠的表情. ▷ **im·pass·ively** *adv*: *The accused sat impassively as the judge sentenced him to ten years in prison.* 法官宣布对被告判以十年徒刑, 被告木木然坐着毫无反应. **im·pass·ive·ness, im·pass·iv·ity** /ˌɪmpæˈsɪvəti; ˌɪmpæˋsɪvətɪ/ *ns* [U].

im·pa·tient /ɪmˈpeɪʃnt; ɪmˋpeʃənt/ *adj* **1** (**a**) **~ (at sth/with sb)** unable to deal calmly with sth/sb or to wait for sth; easily irritated by sb/sth; not patient 不耐烦的; 无耐性的: *Don't be so impatient! The bus will be here soon.* 别那么不耐烦! 公共汽车马上就来了. ○ *You're too impatient with her; she's only a child.* 你对她太缺乏耐心, 她只不过是个孩子. (**b**) showing a lack of patience 表示不耐烦的; 焦躁的: *another impatient glance at his watch* 又一次不耐烦地看了看他的手表. **2** [pred 作表语] **~ (to do sth); ~ (for sth)** very eager to do sth or for sth to happen; anxious 热切(要做某事或期待某事): *Many graduates are impatient to become managers.* 很多人毕了业就迫不及待想当经理. ○ *impatient for the summer holidays to come* 热切盼望暑假到来. **3** [pred 作表语] **~ of sth** (*fml* 文) intolerant of sth 对某事物不能忍受: *impatient of delay* 对耽搁时间不能容忍. ▷ **im·pa·tience** /ɪmˈpeɪʃns; ɪmˋpeʃəns/ *n* [U]: *the government's growing impatience with the unions* 政府对工会的容忍已逐渐接近极限. **im·pa·tiently** *adv*: *We sat waiting impatiently for the film to start.* 我们干坐着, 焦躁地等着电影开场.

im·peach /ɪmˈpiːtʃ; ɪmˋpitʃ/ *v* **1** [Tn, Tn·pr] **~ sb (for sth)** accuse (a public official or politician) of committing a serious crime, esp one against the State 控告(公职人员或政治家)犯罪(尤指有害国家的); 弹劾: *The committee decided to impeach the President.* 委员会决定弹劾总统. ○ *impeach a judge for taking bribes* 控告法官受贿. **2** [Tn] (*fml* 文) raise doubts about (sth); question 对(某事物)怀疑; 提出异议: *impeach sb's motives* 怀疑某人的动机.

▷ **im·peach·able** *adj* (of a crime) for which a public official or politician can be impeached (指罪行)可提出控告或弹劾的: *an impeachable offence* 可弹劾的过失.

im·peach·ment *n* [U].

im·pec·cable /ɪmˈpekəbl; ɪmˋpɛkəbḷ/ *adj* free from mistakes; excellent or faultless 无错误的; 极好的; 无瑕疵的: *Your English is impeccable!* 你的英语十分好! ○ *impeccable behaviour, manners, style, etc* 完美的品行、礼貌、风格等. ▷ **im·pec·cably** /-blɪ; -blɪ/ *adv*: *He was impeccably dressed for the occasion.* 他的穿着在那种场合非常得体.

im·pe·cu·ni·ous /ˌɪmpɪˈkjuːnɪəs; ˌɪmpɪˋkjunɪəs/ *adj* (*fml* 文) having little or no money 一贫如洗的; 不名一文的. ▷ **im·pe·cu·ni·ously** *adv*. **im·pe·cu·ni·ous·ness** *n* [U].

im·ped·ance /ɪmˈpiːdəns; ɪmˋpidṇs/ *n* [U] resistance of an electric circuit to the flow of alternating current 阻抗.

im·pede /ɪmˈpiːd; ɪmˋpid/ *v* [Tn] hinder or obstruct the progress or movement of (sb/sth) 阻碍, 妨碍, 阻止(某人[某事物]): *The development of the project was seriously impeded by a reduction in funds.* 由于基金削减工程进度严重受阻.

im·pedi·ment /ɪmˈpedɪmənt; ɪmˋpɛdəmənt/ *n* **1 ~ (to sb/sth)** person or thing that hinders or obstructs the progress or movement of sth 妨碍、阻碍某事物进展或活动的人或物: *The main impediment to growth was a lack of capital.* 影响发展的主要障碍是缺乏资本. **2** physical disability of a specified type; defect 身体上的某类残疾; 缺陷: *a speech impediment*, eg a lisp or a stammer 言语障碍(如口齿不清或口吃).

im·pedi·menta /ɪmˌpedɪˈmentə; ˌɪmpɛdəˋmɛntə/ *n* [pl] (*fml or joc* 文或谑) baggage and other supplies that slow down an army on a long journey 妨碍军队长途行进的行李、装备等重负: *He came with his wife, six children, four dogs and various other impedimenta.* 他来时携妻子、六个孩子、四条狗以及各式各样的累赘什物.

im·pel /ɪmˈpel; ɪmˋpɛl/ *v* (**-ll-**) [Tn, Tn·pr, Cn·t] **~ sb (to sth)** force or urge sb to do sth 推动、推进、驱策或敦促某人做某事物: *Impelled by feelings of guilt, John wrote to apologize.* 约翰有感愧疚, 于是写信道歉. ○ *The President's speech impelled the nation to greater efforts.* 总统的讲话激励国民更加努力. ○ *I felt impelled to investigate the matter further.* 我觉得自己有责任对事情作进一步调查. Cf 参看 COMPEL.

im·pend·ing /ɪmˈpendɪŋ; ɪmˋpɛndɪŋ/ *adj* [esp attrib 尤作定语] about to happen; imminent 即将发生的; 迫在眉睫的; 行将到来的: *his impending arrival, departure, retirement, visit, etc* 他即将到达、离去、退休、出访等.

im·pen·et·rable /ɪmˈpenɪtrəbl; ɪmˋpɛnətrəbḷ/ *adj* **1 ~ (to sth)** that cannot be entered, passed through, etc 不能通过的; 不可穿越的; 透不过的: *an impenetrable jungle, swamp, fortress, etc* 无法通过的丛林、无法经过的沼泽、不可逾越的要塞 ○ *impenetrable darkness, fog, etc*, ie that cannot be seen through 一片漆黑、浓雾重锁 ○ (*fig* 比喻) *his impenetrable ignorance* 无法启迪的愚昧. **2** impossible to understand or solve 不可理解的; 无法解决的: *an impenetrable difficulty, mystery, problem, etc*

无可克服的困难、难解之谜、百思莫解的问题 ○ *This history book is completely impenetrable to me.* 这本历史书我完全看不懂. ▷ **im·pen·et·rab·il·ity** /ɪm,penɪtrə'bɪlətɪ; ɪm,pɛnətrə'bɪlətɪ/ *n* [U]. **im·pen·et·rably** /-blɪ; -blɪ/ *adv*.

im·pen·it·ent /ɪm'penɪtənt; ɪm'pɛnətənt/ *adj* (*fml* 文) not sorry for or ashamed of one's misdoings; not penitent 不知悔悟的; 不觉羞耻的. ▷ **im·pen·it·ence** /-əns; -əns/ *n* [U]. **im·pen·it·ently** *adv*.

im·per·at·ive /ɪm'perətɪv; ɪm'pɛrətɪv/ *adj* **1** [usu pred 通常作表语] very urgent or important; needing immediate attention 紧急; 重要; 需要立即处理: *It is imperative that we make a quick decision.* 我们要尽快做出决定. **2** expressing a command; authoritative 命令式的; 必须服从的; 专断的; 权威的: *an imperative tone of voice that had to be obeyed* 必须服从的命令腔调. **3** (*grammar*) of the verb form that expresses a command 祈使的: *'Go!' is in the imperative mood.* 'Go!' 是祈使语气的句子. Cf 参看 INDICATIVE, INFINITIVE, SUBJUNCTIVE.

▷ **im·per·at·ive** *n* **1** (*grammar*) (verb in the) mood[2] that expresses a command 祈使语气(的动词): *In 'Go away!' the verb is in the imperative.* 在'Go away!'中用的是祈使语气的动词. ○ *'Go!' is an imperative.* 'Go!'是祈使语气的动词. **2** thing that is essential or urgent 必要的事; 紧急的事; 必须履行的责任; 需要; 必要性: *Survival is our first imperative.* 我们当务之急是设法生存下来. ○ *a moral imperative* 道德上的责任.

im·per·at·ively *adv*.

im·per·cept·ible /,ɪmpə'septəbl; ,ɪmpɚ'sɛptəbl/ *adj* that cannot be noticed or felt because so small, slight or gradual (因细小、轻微、渐变)觉察不出的, 感觉不到的, 些微的: *an imperceptible change in temperature* 温度的难以察觉的变化 ○ *an almost imperceptible shift of opinion* 几乎觉察不到的意见上的改变. ▷ **im·per·cept·ibly** /-əblɪ; -əblɪ/ *adv*: *Almost imperceptibly her expression changed.* 她的表情有些变化, 但轻微得几乎觉察不到.

im·per·fect /ɪm'pɜ:fɪkt; ɪm'pɝfɪkt/ *adj* **1** faulty or defective; not perfect 有缺点的; 有瑕疵的; 残缺的; 不完美的: *an imperfect copy* 残本 ○ *imperfect knowledge, understanding, etc of sth* 对某事物的不完备的知识、不透彻的理解等. **2** [attrib 作定语] (*grammar*) of the verb tense that expresses incomplete action in the past (more usually called *continuous* or *progressive*) 动词的过去未完成时态(通常多称过去进行时态): *the imperfect tenses in French* 法语的过去未完成时态.

▷ **im·per·fect** *n* **the imperfect** [sing] (*grammar*) (verb in the) tense that expresses incomplete action in the past; continuous aspect (表示过去未完成行为的)过去未完成时态(的动词); 进行体: *'I was speaking' is in the imperfect.* 'I was speaking'是过去未完成时态.

im·per·fec·tion /,ɪmpə'fekʃn; ,ɪmpɚ'fɛkʃən/ *n* **1** [U] being imperfect 不完美: *My father never tolerated imperfection.* 我父亲要求一切事情非尽善尽美不可. **2** [C] fault or defect that makes sb/sth imperfect; blemish 缺点; 瑕疵: *The only slight imperfection in this painting is a scratch in the corner.* 这幅画唯一的小疵是在角落里有一道划痕. ○ *the house's structural imperfections* 房子结构上的缺陷.

im·per·fectly *adv*.

im·per·ial /ɪm'pɪərɪəl; ɪm'pɪrɪəl/ *adj* **1** [usu attrib 通常作定语] (**a**) of an empire or its ruler(s) 帝国的; 帝王的; 皇帝的: *the imperial palace, guards, servants* 皇宫、皇家卫士、皇帝的侍从 ○ *imperial power, trade* 皇权、帝国的贸易. (**b**) like or characteristic of such rulers; majestic 至高无上的; 帝王般的; 威严的: *with imperial generosity* 宽宏大量地. **2** [attrib 作定语] belonging to a legal non-metric system of weights and measures formerly used in the United Kingdom for all goods and still used for certain goods 英制的(非公制的度量衡制, 旧时用于所有物品, 现仍用于某些物品): *an imperial pint, gallon, pound, etc* 英制品脱、加仑、磅等. ▷ **im·per·ially** /-rɪəlɪ; -rɪəlɪ/ *adv*.

im·peri·al·ism /ɪm'pɪərɪəlɪzəm; ɪm'pɪrɪəl,ɪzəm/ *n* [U] (*usu derog* 通常作贬义) (belief in the) policy of extending a country's power and influence in the world through diplomacy or military force, and esp by acquiring colonies 帝国主义; 帝国主义政策.

▷ **im·peri·al·ist** /ɪm'pɪərɪəlɪst; ɪm'pɪrɪəlɪst/ *n* (*usu derog* 通常作贬义) person who supports or believes in imperialism 帝国主义者: [attrib 作定语] *imperialist policies* 帝国主义政策.

im·peri·al·istic /ɪm,pɪərɪə'lɪstɪk; ɪm,pɪrɪəl'ɪstɪk/ *adj*.

im·peril /ɪm'perəl; ɪm'pɛrəl/ *v* (**-ll-**; *US also* **-l-**) [Tn] (*fml* 文) put (sb/sth) in danger; endanger 使(某人[某事物])陷于危险; 危及: *The security of the country had been imperilled.* 国家安全处于危险之中.

im·peri·ous /ɪm'pɪərɪəs; ɪm'pɪrɪəs/ *adj* (*fml* 文) proud and arrogant; domineering; expecting obedience 傲慢的; 飞扬跋扈的; 专横的: *an imperious look, command, gesture* 飞扬跋扈的样子、专横的命令、傲慢的姿势. ▷ **im·peri·ously** *adv*: *The envoys were dismissed imperiously.* 傲慢地令各国使者散去. **im·peri·ous·ness** *n* [U].

im·per·ish·able /ɪm'perɪʃəbl; ɪm'pɛrɪʃəbl/ *adj* (*fml* 文) that will not decay; that will never disappear 不腐烂的; 不灭的: *imperishable goods* 不腐烂的商品 ○ (*fig* 比喻) *imperishable glory* 不朽的光荣.

im·per·man·ent /ɪm'pɜ:mənənt; ɪm'pɝmənənt/ *adj* (*fml* 文) not permanent; temporary 非永久的; 暂时的. ▷ **im·per·man·ence** /-əns; -əns/ *n* [U].

im·per·meable /ɪm'pɜ:mɪəbl; ɪm'pɝmɪəbl/ *adj* (of a substance) not allowing a liquid to pass through (指物质)不容液体渗透的, 不透水的: *an impermeable membrane* 不渗透的膜. Cf 参看 PERMEABLE (PERMEATE).

im·per·miss·ible /,ɪmpə'mɪsəbl; ,ɪmpɚ'mɪsəbl/ *adj* (*fml* 文) not allowed or permitted 不允许的; 不许可的.

im·per·sonal /ɪm'pɜ:sənl; ɪm'pɝsnl/ *adj* **1** (*usu derog* 通常作贬义) not influenced by, showing or involving human feelings 不受个人情感影响的; 冷淡的; 没有人情味的; 不牵涉个人感情的: *a vast impersonal organization* 庞大而无人情味的组织 ○ *a cold impersonal stare* 冷冷的凝视 ○ *Giving people time to get to know one another will make the meeting less impersonal.* 让大家有时间互相了解一下, 会议的气氛就能亲切些. **2** (*usu approv* 通常作褒义) not referring to any particular person; objective 非特指某一个人的; 客观的: *an impersonal discussion* 客观的讨论. ▷ **im·per·son·ally** /-sənəlɪ; -snəlɪ/ *adv*.

im·per·son·ate /ɪm'pɜ:səneɪt; ɪm'pɝsn,et/ *v* [Tn] **1** pretend to be (another person) in order to entertain others 扮演, 饰演(他人): *He can impersonate many well-known politicians.* 他能饰演许多著名政治家的角色. **2** imitate the behaviour of (another person) in order to deceive others 模仿, 假冒(他人)(借以行骗): *He was caught trying to impersonate a military officer.* 他企图冒充军官, 但当场被抓获.

▷ **im·per·sona·tion** /ɪm,pɜ:sə'neɪʃn; ,ɪmpɝsn'eʃən/ *n* [C, U]: *He does some brilliant impersonations of the president.* 他扮演总统有些地方十分出色.

im·per·son·ator *n* person who impersonates other people (模仿他人的)演员; 扮演他人的人; 假冒他人的人: *a famous female impersonator*, ie a man who impersonates women on the stage 著名的男扮女装的演员.

im·per·tin·ent /ɪm'pɜ:tɪnənt; ɪm'pɝtnənt/ *adj* **~ (to sb)** not respectful; rude 不礼貌的; 粗鲁的; 不敬的: *impertinent remarks* 粗鲁的言语 ○ *an impertinent child* 没有礼貌的孩子 ○ *It would be impertinent to suggest that he was always wrong.* 说他从无是处未免不够礼貌. ▷ **im·per·tin·ence** /-əns; -əns/ *n* [C usu *sing*, *U* 作可数名词时通常作单数, 亦作不可数名词]: *I've had enough of your impertinence.* 你太没礼貌, 我已经受够了. **im·per·tin·ently** *adv*.

im·per·turb·able /,ɪmpə'tɜ:bəbl; ,ɪmpɚ'tɝbəbl/ *adj* not easily troubled or worried; calm 不易受搅扰的; 不易发愁的; 冷静的: *She was one of those imperturbable people who never get angry or upset.* 她是那种从不生气也不烦恼的人. ▷ **im·per·turb·ab·il·ity** /,ɪmpə,tɜ:bə'bɪlətɪ; ,ɪmpɚ,tɝbə'bɪlətɪ/ *n* [U]. **im·per·turb·ably** /-əblɪ; -əblɪ/ *adv*.

im·per·vi·ous /ɪm'pɜ:vɪəs; ɪm'pɝvɪəs/ *adj* **~ (to sth)** **1** not allowing water, gas, etc to pass through 不容液体、气体等透过的; 不能渗透的: *This material is impervious to rain-water.* 这种材料防雨. **2** not affected or influenced by sth 不受某事物影响的; 无动于衷的: *impervious to criticism, argument, fear* 对批评我行我素的、对争论不闻不问的、将恐惧置之度外的.

im·pe·tigo /,ɪmpɪ'taɪgəʊ; ,ɪmpɪ'taɪgo/ *n* [U] type of

contagious skin disease that causes crusty yellow sores 脓疱病(一种传染性皮肤病).

im·petu·ous /ɪmˈpetʃʊəs; ɪmˋpɛtʃuəs/ *adj* acting or done quickly and with little thought or care; rash or impulsive 轻率的; 鲁莽的; 冲动的: *an impetuous young man* 易冲动的年轻人 ○ *impetuous behaviour* 鲁莽的行为 ○ *It would be foolish and impetuous to resign over such a small matter.* 为这样的小事辞职未免愚蠢而轻率了. ▷ **im·petu·os·ity** /ɪmˌpetʃʊˈɒsətɪ; ˌɪmpɛtʃuˋɑsətɪ/ *n* [U]. **im·petu·ously** *adv*.

im·petus /ˈɪmpɪtəs; ˋɪmpətəs/ *n* **1** [U, sing] **~ (to sth/to do sth)** thing that encourages a process to develop more quickly 推动; 刺激; 促进: *The treaty gave (a) fresh impetus to trade.* 这条约使双方的贸易又推进了一步. **2** [U] force with which sth moves 推动力.

im·pi·ety /ɪmˈpaɪətɪ; ɪmˋpaɪətɪ/ *n* **(a)** [U] lack of respect, esp for God and religion 不敬, 不恭(尤指对上帝和宗教). **(b)** [C usu *pl* 通常作复数] act, remark, etc showing a lack of such respect 不敬的行为、言论等(尤指对上帝和宗教).

im·pinge /ɪmˈpɪndʒ; ɪmˋpɪndʒ/ *v* [Ipr] **~ on/upon sth** (*fml* 文) have an effect on sth 对某事物起作用或有影响: *In his sleepy state, the sound of a car driving up to the house scarcely impinged on his consciousness.* 他困得那副样子, 连汽车朝那房子开去时发出的声音都没能使他清醒.

im·pi·ous /ˈɪmpɪəs; ˋɪmpɪəs/ *adj* (*fml* 文) showing a lack of respect, esp for God and religion; not pious 不敬的, 不恭的(尤指对上帝和宗教). ▷ **im·pi·ously** *adv*.

imp·ish /ˈɪmpɪʃ; ˋɪmpɪʃ/ *adj* of or like an imp; mischievous (似)顽童的; 顽皮的; 恶作剧的. ▷ **imp·ishly** *adv*. **imp·ish·ness** *n* [U].

im·plac·able /ɪmˈplækəbl; ɪmˋplækəbl̩/ *adj* that cannot be changed or satisfied 不能变动的; 无法平息或安抚的: *implacable hatred, fury, opposition* 无法消解的仇恨、愤怒、对立 ○ *an implacable enemy, rival, etc* 势不两立的敌人、竞争对手等. ▷ **im·plac·ably** /-əblɪ; -əblɪ/ *adv*: *implacably opposed to the plan* 坚决反对该计划.

im·plant /ɪmˈplɑːnt; *US* -ˈplænt; ɪmˋplænt/ *v* [Tn, Tn·pr] **~ sth (in sth)** **1** deliberately introduce or fix (ideas, etc) into a person's mind 灌输, 注入(思想等): *implant religious beliefs in young children* 向青少年灌输宗教信仰. **2** insert (tissue, etc) into a part of the body 在身体某部植入、埋置、嵌入(组织等); 移植: *In this operation the surgeons implant a new lens (in the eye).* 医生在这次手术中给病人(眼球)植入了新的水晶体.

▷ **im·plant** /ˈɪmplɑːnt; *US* -plænt; ˋɪmˌplænt/ *n* [C] thing that has been implanted in the body (植入身体中的)移植物.

im·planta·tion /ˌɪmplɑːnˈteɪʃn; *US* -plænt-; ˌɪmplænˋteʃən/ *n* [U].

im·plaus·ible /ɪmˈplɔːzəbl; ɪmˋplɔzəbl̩/ *adj* unlikely to be true; not convincing 不像真实的; 难以置信的; 说服不了人的: *an implausible story, excuse, theory, etc* 不像真实的故事、不可信的借口、悖于情理的说法. Cf 参看 PLAUSIBLE.

im·ple·ment[1] /ˈɪmplɪmənt; ˋɪmpləmənt/ *n* tool or instrument 工具; 器具: *farm implements* 农具 ○ *Man's earliest implements were carved from stone and bone.* 人类最早的工具是用石头和骨头制成的. ➪Usage at MACHINE 用法见 MACHINE.

im·ple·ment[2] /ˈɪmplɪment; ˋɪmpləˌmɛnt/ *v* [Tn] put (sth) into effect; carry out 使(某事物)生效; 履行; 实施; 贯彻: *implement plans, policies, a programme of reforms, etc* 执行计划、政策、改革计划等. ▷ **im·ple·menta·tion** /ˌɪmplɪmenˈteɪʃn; ˌɪmpləmɛnˋteʃən/ *n* [U].

im·plic·ate /ˈɪmplɪkeɪt; ˋɪmplɪˌket/ *v* [Tn, Tn·pr] **~ sb (in sth)** show that sb is involved in sth, esp a crime 显示某人牵连于某事(尤指罪行); 涉及: *His enemies tried to implicate him (in the murder).* 他的仇人竭力想把他牵扯进谋杀案中. ○ *He was deeply implicated* (ie involved) *in the plot.* 他与该阴谋牵涉颇深.

im·plica·tion /ˌɪmplɪˈkeɪʃn; ˌɪmplɪˋkeʃən/ *n* **1** [C, U] **~ (for sb/sth)** thing that is suggested or implied; thing not openly stated 含意; 暗示; 暗指: *Study the implications of the president's statement.* 研究总统声明的含义. ○ *The new report has far-reaching implications for the future of broadcasting.* 这一新报告对广播业的前途有些意味深长的暗示. ○ *Failure to say 'No' may, by implication, be taken to mean 'Yes'.* 没表示否定, 其含义可能理解为是肯定的. **2** [U] involving or being involved, esp in a crime 卷入, 牵连(尤指于罪行中): *The trial resulted in the implication of several major figures in the organization.* 审讯结果表明这个组织中几个主要人物都牵连在案.

im·pli·cit /ɪmˈplɪsɪt; ɪmˋplɪsɪt/ *adj* **1 ~ (in sth)** implied, but not expressed directly; not explicit 含蓄的; 不直接表明的; 不明确的: *implicit assumptions* 含蓄的假定 ○ *an implicit threat* 暗示的恫吓 ○ *obligations which are implicit in the contract* 合同中未直接载明的责任. **2** unquestioning and absolute 无疑问的; 绝对的: *I have implicit faith in your abilities.* 我完全相信你的能力. ▷ **im·pli·citly** *adv*: *trust sb implicitly* 绝对信任某人.

im·plode /ɪmˈpləʊd; ɪmˋplod/ *v* [I, Tn] (cause sth to) burst or collapse inwards (使某事物)向心聚爆, 内爆: *The light bulb imploded.* 这灯泡是向内侧爆裂的. Cf 参看 EXPLODE 1. ▷ **im·plo·sion** /ɪmˈpləʊʒn; ɪmˋploʒən/ *n* [C, U].

im·plore /ɪmˈplɔː(r); ɪmˋplɔr/ *v* [Tn, Dn·t] ask or beg (sb) earnestly; beseech 恳求或乞求(某人); 哀求: *'Help me,' he implored.* '救救我吧,'他哀求道. ○ *implore sb's forgiveness, mercy, etc* 乞求某人原谅、宽恕等 ○ *They implored her to stay.* 他们恳求她留下. ➪Usage at ASK 用法见 ASK. ▷ **im·plor·ing** *adj*: *She gave him an imploring look.* 她以哀求的眼神看着他. **im·plor·ingly** *adv*.

im·ply /ɪmˈplaɪ; ɪmˋplaɪ/ *v* (*pt, pp* **implied**) **1** [Tn, Tf] suggest (sth) indirectly rather than state it directly; hint 含有...的意思; 暗示; 暗指: *His silence implied agreement.* 他沉默不语意味着同意了. ○ *implied criticism* 暗含的批评 ○ *I don't wish to imply that you are wrong.* 我无意暗示你错了. **2** [Tn] suggest (sth) as a logical consequence; entail 必然包含(某事物); 使(某事物)必然产生或有必要: *Freedom does not necessarily imply responsibility.* 自由不一定包含着责任. ○ *The fact she was here implies a degree of interest.* 她当时在场, 这一事实就意味着她有一定程度的兴趣. Cf 参看 INFER.

im·pol·ite /ˌɪmpəˈlaɪt; ˌɪmpəˋlaɪt/ *adj* rude; not polite 粗鲁的; 不礼貌的: *Some people still think it is impolite for men not to stand up when a woman comes into the room.* 有些人仍然认为妇女进屋时男子不起立是有失礼貌的. ▷ **im·pol·itely** *adv*. **im·pol·ite·ness** *n* [U].

im·pol·itic /ɪmˈpɒlətɪk; ɪmˋpɑlətɪk/ *adj* (*fml* 文) not wise; not politic 不明智的; 不当的; 失策的: *It might be impolitic to refuse his offer.* 谢绝他的好意未免失策.

im·pon·der·able /ɪmˈpɒndərəbl; ɪmˋpɑndərəbl̩/ *adj* of which the effect or importance cannot be measured or estimated (作用或重要性)无法衡量的, 无法估计的.

▷ **im·pon·der·able** *n* (usu *pl* 通常作复数) thing, eg a quality or an emotion, that is imponderable 无法估量的事物(如性质或感情): *the great imponderables of love and power* 爱情与权力, 极难衡量的事物.

im·port[1] /ɪmˈpɔːt; ɪmˋpɔrt/ *v* [Tn, Tn·pr] **~ sth (from...)**; **~ sth (into...)** bring (goods, ideas, etc) from a foreign country into one's own country 进口, 输入, 引进(货物、思想等): *The country has to import most of its raw materials.* 这个国家原料大部分靠进口. ○ *cars imported from Japan* 从日本进口的汽车 ○ *meat imported (into the United Kingdom)* 进口(到英国)的肉 ○ *the latest pop music imported from America* 从美国传入的最新流行乐曲. Cf 参看 EXPORT[2].

▷ **im·porta·tion** /ˌɪmpɔːˈteɪʃn; ˌɪmpɔrˋteʃən/ *n* [U, C]: *a ban on the importation of drugs* 禁止毒品进口的法令.

im·porter *n* person, company, etc that imports goods or services 从事进口商品或服务的人或公司: *the country's largest importer of tobacco* 全国最大的烟草进口商.

im·port[2] /ˈɪmpɔːt; ˋɪmpɔrt/ *n* **1** [C esp *pl* 尤作复数] imported goods, services, etc 进口货; 引进的劳务等: *Britain's food imports (from the rest of the world)* 英国(从世界各地)进口的食物 ○ *restrict cheap foreign imports* 限制廉价外国进口货. **2** [U] action of importing goods 进口; 输入; 引入: *the import of coal* 煤炭的进口 ○ *tariffs on the import of manufactured goods* 工业品的进口税 ○ [attrib 作定语] *import controls* 进口管制. Cf 参看 EXPORT[1].

im·port[3] /ɪmˈpɔːt; ɪmˋpɔrt/ *v* [Tn, Tn·pr] **~ sth (to sb)** (*fml* 文) mean or convey sth (to sb) (对某人)意味着某事物或传达某事物: *What did these developments import to them?* 这些新情况对他们来说意味着什么呢?

▷ **im·port** /ˈɪmpɔːt; ˋɪmpɔrt/ *n* (*fml* 文) **1** [U]

importance or significance 重要性; 意义: *matters of no great import* 无关宏旨的事. **2** [sing] meaning (of sth), esp when not directly stated (某事物的)意思(尤指未直接说明的): *the hidden import of his speech* 他话中的言外之意.

im·port·ant /ɪmˈpɔːtnt; ɪmˋpɔrtn̩t/ *adj* **1 ~ (to sb/sth)** very serious and significant; of great value or concern 重要的; 重大的; 非常有价值的: *an important decision, announcement, meeting* 重要的决定、宣布、会议 ○ *It is vitally important to cancel the order immediately.* 最重要的是要立即取消这一定单. ○ *It is important that students (should) attend/for students to attend all the lectures.* 所有的课学生都应该去听, 这是很重要的. ○ *They need more money now but, more important, they need long-term help.* 目前他们需要更多的钱, 不过更重要的是他们需要长期的援助. ○ *It's important to me that you should be there.* 你应该在场, 这对我来说很重要. **2** (of a person) having great influence or authority; influential (指人)有很大影响或权威的: *She was clearly an important person.* 她显然是个有影响的人. ○ *It's not as if he was very important in the company hierarchy.* 他在公司的领导层中似乎无多大权力.

▷ **im·port·ance** /-tns; -tn̩s/ *n* **1** [U] **~ (to sb/sth)** being important; significance or value 重要性; 重大; 有价值: *the importance of industry to the economy* 工业对经济的重要性 ○ *They attached very great importance to the project*, ie They considered it to be very important. 他们对这项目极为重视. ○ *a matter of the utmost political importance* 有重大政治意义的事情 ○ *These issues now assume even greater importance.* 这些问题现在就显得更加重要了. **2** (idm 习语) **full of one's own importance** ⇨ FULL.

im·port·antly *adv*: *strut about importantly* 神气十足地昂首阔步 ○ *More importantly, can he be depended on?* 更重要的是, 可以依靠他吗?

im·por·tun·ate /ɪmˈpɔːtʃʊnət; ɪmˋpɔrtʃənɪt/ *adj* (*fml* 文) persistent, esp in making requests or demands 坚持的(尤指提出请求或要求时): *an importunate beggar* 缠着讨要的乞丐. ▷ **im·por·tun·ately** *adv*. **im·por·tun·ity** /ˌɪmpɔːˈtjuːnətɪ; ˌɪmpɚˋtjunətɪ/ *n* [U, C esp *pl* 作不可数名词或可数名词, 后者尤作复数]: *irritated by his constant importunities* 被他没完没了的强求所激怒.

im·por·tune /ˌɪmpɔːˈtjuːn; ˌɪmpɔrˋtjun/ *v* (*fml* 文) **1** [Tn, Tn·pr, Dn·t] **~ sb (for sth)** ask sb persistently (for sth), usu in an annoying manner; beg or demand insistently 一再向某人要求(某事物)(尤指令人厌烦): *importune one's creditors for an extension of the borrowing period/to extend the borrowing period* 再三乞求债权人延长借贷期限. **2** [I, Tn] (of a prostitute) attempt to attract (clients) (指妓女或男妓)拉(客): *arrested for importuning* 因拉客被捕.

im·pose /ɪmˈpəʊz; ɪmˋpoz/ *v* **1** [Tn, Tn·pr] **~ sth (on sb/sth)** (**a**) place (a penalty, tax, etc) officially on sb/sth 加(惩罚等)于某人; 对某物课(税): *impose a fine, sentence, term of imprisonment, etc* 罚款、判处刑期、予以监禁 ○ *impose a further tax on wines and spirits* 对果酒及烈性酒进一步加税. (**b**) place (sth unwelcome or unpleasant) on sb/sth; inflict sth 将(不愉快的、不受欢迎的事物)强加于某人[某事物]: *impose one's rule (on a people)* 将统治强加(于一民族) ○ *impose restrictions, limitations, restraints, etc (on trade)* (对贸易)强行管制、限制、约束等. **2** [Tn, Tn·pr] **~ sth (on sb)** try to make sb accept (an opinion or a belief); inflict sth 使某人接受(意见或信仰); 将某事物强加于: *She imposed her ideas on the group.* 她竭力把自己的想法强加于全组的人. **3** [Tn, Tn·pr] **~ oneself/sth (on sb)** force sb to accept (oneself, one's company, etc) 强迫某人接纳(自己等); 硬要与某人在一起: *She'd never think of imposing herself.* 她决不想勉强别人接纳自己. ○ *He imposed his presence on us for the weekend.* 他硬要跟我们一起过周末. **4** (phr v) **impose on/upon sb/sth** win a favour from sb, esp by using undue pressure 赢得某人的欢心, 占某人便宜(尤指施加不当的压力): *I hope it's not imposing on you/your hospitality, but could I stay to dinner?* 我可以在您这儿吃顿饭吗? 不过希望不要使您为难[觉得我不知趣].

▷ **im·pos·ing** *adj* impressive in appearance or manner; grand (外表或举止)壮观的; 令人印象深刻的: *an imposing façade, building, person, personality* 宏伟的外观、雄伟的建筑、威严的人、突出的个性. **im·pos·ingly** *adv*.

im·posi·tion /ˌɪmpəˈzɪʃn; ˌɪmpəˋzɪʃən/ *n* **~ (on sb/sth)** **1** [U] action of imposing 强加; (税等的)征收; (惩罚等的)施加: *The imposition of the tax on books caused a sharp rise in price.* 对书籍课税造成书价急剧上涨. **2** [C] unfair or unpleasant thing that sb is obliged to accept 被迫接受的不公正、不愉快的事物: *I'd like to stay if it's not too much of an imposition(on you).* 要是不致(给你)添太多的麻烦的话, 我倒是愿意留下.

im·poss·ible /ɪmˈpɒsəbl; ɪmˋpɑsəbl̩/ *adj* **1** that cannot be done or exist; not possible 不可能做到或存在的; 不可能的: *It's impossible for me to be there before 8.00p.m.* 要我晚上8点之前赶到那儿是根本办不到的. ○ *It is virtually impossible to predict the future accurately.* 精确预言未来的事实际上是办不到的. ○ *an almost impossible task* 几乎无法完成的任务 ○ *It's an impossible story*, ie it cannot be believed. 这不可能是真事. **2** very difficult to bear; hopeless 难以忍受的; 无希望的: *an impossible situation* 绝境 ○ *Their son is impossible*, eg He is very badly behaved. 他们的儿子无可救药(他品行极坏).

▷ **im·poss·ib·il·ity** /ɪmˌpɒsəˈbɪlətɪ; ˌɪmpɑsəˋbɪlətɪ/ *n* [U, C]: *the impossibility of any improvement* 无改进之可能 ○ *a logical impossibility* 逻辑上不可能的事.

the im·poss·ible *n* [sing] thing that cannot be achieved 不可能做到的事情: *ask for, want, attempt, do the impossible* 要求、想要、尽力做、做不可能办到的事物.

im·poss·ibly /-əblɪ; -əblɪ/ *adv*: *impossibly difficult* 极其困难.

im·postor /ɪmˈpɒstə(r); ɪmˋpɑstɚ/ *n* person pretending to be sb else, usu in order to deceive others 冒名顶替的人(通常为行骗).

im·pos·ture /ɪmˈpɒstʃə(r); ɪmˋpɑstʃɚ/ *n* [C, U] (*fml* 文) (action of) deliberately deceiving by pretending to be sb else 冒名顶替(行骗).

im·pot·ent /ˈɪmpətənt; ˋɪmpətənt/ *adj* **1** [usu pred 通常作表语] unable to take effective action; powerless or helpless 不能采取有效行动; 无能为力: *Without the chairman's support, the committee is impotent.* 没有主席的支持, 委员会是无能为力的. **2** (of men) unable to have sexual intercourse or reach an orgasm (指男子)阳痿的, 不能性交的, 不能达到性高潮的.

▷ **im·pot·ence** /-əns; -əns/ *n* [U] being impotent 无能为力; 阳痿: *political impotence* 政治上的无能 ○ *fear of impotence* 对阳痿的恐惧.

im·pot·ently *adv*.

im·pound /ɪmˈpaʊnd; ɪmˋpaʊnd/ *v* [Tn] **1** take legal possession of (sth) 依法没收, 扣押(某物): *impound goods, property, belongings, etc* 扣留货物、财产、财物等. **2** put (an illegally parked car or a stray animal) in a pound(2) until it is claimed 将(违章停放的汽车或走失的动物)暂存待领.

im·pov·er·ish /ɪmˈpɒvərɪʃ; ɪmˋpɑvərɪʃ/ *v* [Tn] **1** make (sb) poor 使(某人)贫困: *an elderly impoverished writer* 穷困的老作家. **2** make (sth) poorer or worse in quality 使(某物)贫瘠或恶化: *Heavy rain and excessive use have impoverished the soil.* 这土地因遭暴雨侵蚀及使用过度已贫瘠不堪. ○ *Our lives would have been greatly impoverished if we had not known our dear friend.* 若不是得识我们这位好朋友, 我们的生活一定十分不妙. ▷ **im·pov·er·ish·ment** *n* [U].

im·prac·tic·able /ɪmˈpræktɪkəbl; ɪmˋpræktɪkəbl̩/ *adj* impossible to put into practice; not practicable 不能实行的: *an impracticable scheme* 行不通的计划. ▷ **im·prac·tic·ab·il·ity** /ɪmˌpræktɪkəˈbɪlətɪ; ˌɪmpræktɪkə-ˋbɪlətɪ/ *n* [U]. **im·prac·tic·ably** /-əblɪ; -əblɪ/ *adv*.

im·prac·tical /ɪmˈpræktɪkl; ɪmˋpræktɪkl̩/ *adj* **1** not sensible, useful or realistic 不切实际的; 无用的; 不现实的: *It was impractical to think that we could build the house in one month.* 以为我们用一个月的时间就能把房子盖好, 这种想法不切合实际. **2** not skilled at doing practical work 不善做实际工作的: *an academically clever but totally impractical young man* 学有专长但毫无实际工作能力的年轻男子. ▷ **im·prac·tic·ality** /ɪmˌpræktɪˈkælətɪ; ɪmˌpræktɪˋkælətɪ/ *n* [U, C]. **im·prac·tic·ally** /-klɪ; -klɪ/ *adv*.

im·preca·tion /ˌɪmprɪˈkeɪʃn; ˌɪmprɪˋkeʃən/ *n* (*fml* 文) oath or curse 起誓; 诅咒: *mutter imprecations* 低声诅咒.

im·pre·cise /ˌɪmprɪˈsaɪs; ˌɪmprɪˋsaɪs/ *adj* not exact or accurate; not correctly or clearly stated; not precise 不精

确的; 不确切的; 不明确的; 不准确的: *imprecise thoughts, statements, measurements* 含混的想法、不确切的说法、不精确的量度. ▷ **im·pre·cisely** *adv*. **im·pre·ci·sion** /ˌɪmprɪˈsɪʒn; ˌɪmprɪˋsɪʒən/ *n* [U]: *imprecision in his use of legal terms* 他在法律术语的使用上之不确.

im·preg·nable /ɪmˈpregnəbl; ɪmˋprɛgnəbḷ/ *adj* (**a**) so strong and well-constructed that it cannot be entered or captured 坚固得不能进入或无法占领的: *an impregnable fortress* 坚不可摧的要塞. (**b**) (*fig* 比喻) so strong that it cannot be overcome or broken down 无法征服的; 压不倒摧不垮的: *impregnable arguments, defences, reserve* 驳不倒的论点、有理有据的辩护、无法改变的拘谨. ▷ **im·preg·nab·il·ity** /ɪmˌpregnəˈbɪlətɪ; ˌɪmprɛgnəˋbɪlətɪ/ *n* [U]. **im·preg·nably** /-əblɪ; -əblɪ/ *adv*.

im·preg·nate /ˈɪmpregneɪt; *US* ɪmˈpreg-; ɪmˋprɛgnet/ *v* **1** [Tn, Tn·pr] **~ sth (with sth)** (**a**) cause (one substance) to be filled in every part with another substance; saturate sth 使(一物质)中充满另一物质; 使某物浸透或饱和: *water impregnated with salt* 饱和的盐水. (**b**) cause sth to be affected or influenced in every part by sth 使某事物的各方面受他事物的作用或影响: *The drawing is impregnated with the artist's personality.* 这幅画充分体现了作者的个性. **2** [Tn] (*fml* 文) fertilize (an egg or ovum) with sperm or pollen; make pregnant 使(卵)受精; 使怀孕; 使妊娠.

im·pres·ario /ˌɪmprɪˈsɑːrɪəʊ; ˌɪmprɪˋsɑrɪˌo/ *n* manager or director of a ballet, concert, theatre or opera company (芭蕾舞剧团、音乐会、剧院或歌剧团的)经理或指挥.

im·press /ɪmˈpres; ɪmˋprɛs/ *v* **1** [Tn, Tn·pr] **~ sb (with sth)** have a favourable effect on sb; make sb feel admiration and respect 给予某人深刻印象; 使某人钦佩而起敬: *The sights of the city never fail to impress foreign tourists.* 外国游客无一不对该市留有深刻印象. ○ *The girl impressed her fiancé's family with her liveliness and sense of humour.* 姑娘又活泼又富幽默感, 未婚夫家人十分喜欢她. ○ *We were most impressed with/by your efficiency.* 你的工作效率很高, 我们极为钦佩. **2** [Tn·pr] **~ sth on/upon sb** fix sth in sb's mind; make sb keenly aware of sth 使某人铭记某事物; 使某人深深意识到某事物: *His words impressed themselves on my memory.* 他的话铭刻在我的记忆里. ○ *The manager impressed on his office staff the importance of keeping accurate records.* 经理让办公室职员认识到做精确记录的重要性. **3** [Tn, Tn·pr] **~ sth (in/on sth)** press sth hard into a soft surface, leaving a mark 用硬物压入软物表面而留下痕迹; 盖印: *designs impressed on/in wax* 在蜡板上压印出的图样.

▷ **im·press** /ˈɪmpres; ˋɪmprɛs/ *n* (*fml* 文) mark left by pressing sth hard, eg a seal, into a soft surface 压痕, 印记(如印章的印记).

impression 印记

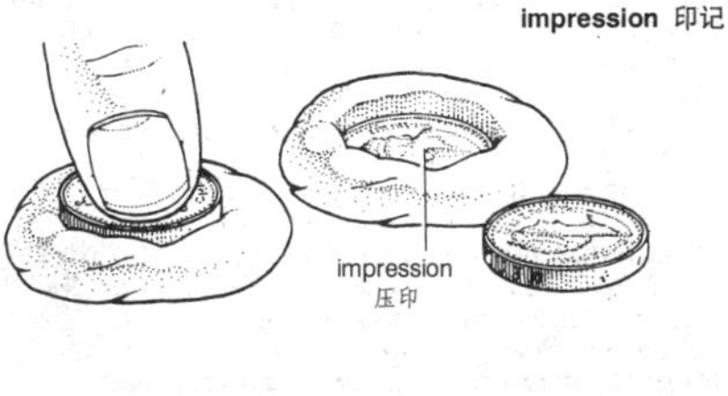

im·pres·sion /ɪmˈpreʃn; ɪmˋprɛʃən/ *n* **1 ~ (on sb)** deep lasting effect on the mind or feelings of sb 印象; 感想: *His first speech as president made a strong impression on his audience.* 他当会长后的第一次演讲给听众留下了深刻的印象. ○ *create an unfavourable impression* 产生不利的影响. **2** (esp *sing* 尤作单数) **~ (of sth/doing sth/that...)** (unclear or uncertain) idea, feeling or opinion (不清晰的或不确切的)想法, 感觉, 看法: *My general impression was that he seemed a pleasant man.* 我总的印象是他似乎很和蔼可亲. ○ *I had the distinct impression that I was being followed.* 我清楚地感觉到有人跟踪我. ○ *one's first impressions of* (ie one's immediate reaction to) *the new headmaster* 对新校长的初步印象 ○ *He gives the impression of being a hard worker/that he works hard*, ie It seems as if he works hard. 他给人的印象是工作很努力. ○ *'I always thought you were a nurse.' 'I wonder how you got that impression?'* '我一向以为你是护士呢.' '不知道你这个想法从何而来?' **3** appearance or effect of sb/sth 某人[某事物]的外貌、影响或作用: *The room's lighting conveys an impression of spaciousness.* 这个房间的照明给人以宽敞的感觉. **4 ~ (of sb)** funny imitation of the behaviour or way of talking of a well-known person (对名人言谈举止的)滑稽的模仿: *The students did some marvellous impressions of the teachers at the end-of-term party.* 在期末联欢会上, 学生模仿教师惟妙惟肖令人捧腹. **5** mark left by pressing an object hard into a surface 将一物压在另一物上留下的印记: *the impression of a leaf in a fossil* 化石中一片叶子留下的痕迹. ⇨illus 见插图. **6** reprint of a book made with few or no alterations to its contents (书的)重印, 再次印刷(内容无甚更动或不作更动): *the fifth impression* 第五次印刷. Cf 参看 EDITION 2. **7** (idm 习语) **be under the impression that...** have the (usu mistaken) idea that... 有某种(通常指错误的)想法...: *I was under the impression that you were coming tomorrow.* 我以为你明天才来呢.

▷ **im·pres·sion·ism** /-ʃənɪzəm; -ʃənˌɪzəm/ *n* (usu 通常作 **Impressionism**) [U] style of painting developed in France in the late 19th century that creates the general impression of a subject by using the effects of colour and light, without realistic detail 印象主义, 印象派(绘画风格, 19 世纪下半叶兴于法国, 主张用颜色及光线效果对物体作总体化描绘, 不着眼于实体细节). **im·pres·sion·ist** /-ʃənɪst; -ʃənɪst/ *n* **1** (usu 通常作 **Impressionist**) artist who paints in the style of Impressionism 印象派画家. **2** person who does impressions (IMPRESSION 4) of other people 用滑稽方式模仿名流的人. — *adj* (usu 通常作 **Impressionist**) of or relating to the style of Impressionism 印象派的; 印象主义的: *Impressionist painters, works, exhibitions* 印象派画家、作品、画展. **im·pres·sion·istic** *adj* giving a general idea rather than specific facts or detailed knowledge 给人以一般印象的; 不涉及事实或细节的: *a purely impressionistic description of the incident* 对事情作的纯凭印象的描叙.

im·pres·sion·able /ɪmˈpreʃənəbl; ɪmˋprɛʃənəbḷ/ *adj* easily influenced or affected 易受影响的: *children at an impressionable age* 处在易受外界影响年龄期的儿童 ○ *impressionable young people* 易受影响的年轻人. ▷ **im·pres·sion·ab·il·ity** /ɪmˌpreʃənəˈbɪlətɪ; ɪmˌprɛʃənəˋbɪlətɪ/ *n* [U].

im·press·ive /ɪmˈpresɪv; ɪmˋprɛsɪv/ *adj* having a strong effect on sb, esp through size, grandeur, or importance 给人以深刻印象的(尤指因巨大、壮观或重要): *an impressive ceremony, building, speech, performance* 令人难忘的仪式、建筑、讲话、演出 ○ *His collection of paintings is most impressive.* 他的绘画收藏令人叹为观止. ▷ **im·press·ively** *adv*. **im·press·ive·ness** *n* [U].

im·prim·atur /ˌɪmprɪˈmeɪtə(r), -ˈmɑːtə(r); ˌɪmprɪˋmetɚ/ *n* (**a**) official permission to print a book, esp as given by the Roman Catholic Church 准予印行令(尤指天主教会颁发的). (**b**) (*fig* 比喻) permission or approval 批准; 认可; 同意: *give the scheme one's imprimatur* 对计划表示同意.

im·print /ɪmˈprɪnt; ɪmˋprɪnt/ *v* [Tn·pr] **~ sth in/on sth** (**a**) press (sth hard) onto a surface, leaving an impression or mark 将(硬物)压在某物上留下痕迹; 压印; 印: *imprint one's hand in soft cement* 在未凝固的水泥上压手印. (**b**) (*fig* 比喻) fix sth firmly in sb's mind 铭记: *details imprinted on his memory/mind* 铭记于他的记忆中[头脑中]的细节详情.

▷ **im·print** /ˈɪmprɪnt; ˋɪmprɪnt/ *n* **1 ~ (in/on sth)** mark made by pressing or stamping a surface 印迹; 痕迹: *the imprint of a foot in the sand* 沙滩上的足迹. **2** (usu *sing* 通常作单数) **~ (on sb/sth)** lasting characteristic mark or effect 持久的特征、标志或影响: *Her face bore the deep imprint of suffering.* 她的脸上带着受过苦难的深深的痕迹. **3** name and address of the publisher, usu printed on the title-page of a book 出版者的名称和地址(通常印在书名页上).

im·print·ing /ɪmˈprɪntɪŋ; ɪmˋprɪntɪŋ/ *n* [U] learning process in which young animals recognize and have a strong attachment to members of their own species, esp their mothers 铭印, 铭记, 印随(幼小动物的学习形式, 指辨识同类并产生牢固的依附行为, 尤指依附其母).

im·prison /ɪmˈprɪzn; ɪmˋprɪzn̩/ *v* [esp passive 尤用于被动语态: Tn, Tn·pr] **~ sb (in sth)** put or keep sb in or as if in prison 监禁某人; 似监禁般束缚某人: *Several of the rioters were imprisoned for causing a disturbance.* 有几个暴乱者因制造动乱被关押在狱. ○ *conditions in which young mothers feel virtually imprisoned in their own homes* 年轻的母亲感到的居家如坐牢一般的处境.

▷ **im·pris·on·ment** /-mənt; -mənt/ *n* [U] state of being imprisoned 关押; 监禁; 坐牢: *sentenced to one year's, ten years', life, etc imprisonment* 被判处一年、十年、终身监禁等.

im·prob·able /ɪmˈprɒbəbl; ɪmˋprɑbəbl̩/ *adj* not likely to be true or to happen; not probable 不大可能是真实的; 未必会发生的; 不大可能的: *an improbable idea, event, result* 不切实际的想法、未必会发生的事情、不太可能有的结果 ○ *It is very/most improbable that the level of unemployment will fall.* 失业率几无可能下降.

▷ **im·prob·ab·il·ity** /ɪmˌprɒbəˈbɪlətɪ; ɪmˌprɑbəˋbɪlətɪ/ *n* (**a**) [U] state of being improbable 不大可能; 未必能发生: *the improbablity of his being recaptured* 对他再行拘捕之不大可能. (**b**) [C] event that is improbable 不大可能的事; 未必能发生的事: *Don't worry about such improbabilities as floods and earthquakes.* 像洪水、地震这类不大可能发生的事, 就不要担心了.

im·prob·ably /-əblɪ; -əblɪ/ *adv*.

im·promptu /ɪmˈprɒmptju:; *US* -tu:; ɪmˋprɑmptu/ *adj*, *adv* (done) without preparation, rehearsal or thought in advance 事先无准备(的); 临时(的); 即兴(的); 即席(的): *an impromptu speech, news conference, performance, etc* 即席讲话、临时召开的记者招待会、即兴表演 ○ *He spoke impromptu.* 他临时发了言.

▷ **im·promptu** *n* musical composition, etc that is or appears to be improvised 即兴曲: *an impromptu by Schubert* 舒伯特的即兴曲.

im·proper /ɪmˈprɒpə(r); ɪmˋprɑpɚ/ *adj* **1** wrong or incorrect 错误的; 不正确的: *improper use of a tool, word, drug, etc* 工具、词、药等的误用. **2** not suited or appropriate to the situation or circumstances; unseemly or indecent 不适合的; 不适当的; 不相宜的; 不得体的; 下流的: *Laughing and joking are considered improper behaviour at a funeral.* 在葬礼上发笑或开玩笑是失礼的行为. **3** dishonest; irregular 不正当的; 不诚实的; 不正规的: *improper business practices* 不正当的商业行为. Cf 参看 PROPER. ▷ **im·properly** *adv*.

□ **improper ˈfraction** numerical fraction in which the value above the line is greater than the value below the line 假分数, 如 $\frac{720}{63}$. Cf 参看 PROPER FRACTION (PROPER).

im·pro·pri·ety /ˌɪmprəˈpraɪətɪ; ˌɪmprəˋpraɪətɪ/ *n* (*fml* 文) (**a**) [U] indecent or unsuitable behaviour; dishonest practice 下流的或不适当的行为; 不正当的做法: *The investigation revealed no impropriety.* 调查表明没有不正当的做法. (**b**) [C] instance of this 下流的或不适当的行为.

im·prove /ɪmˈpru:v; ɪmˋpruv/ *v* **1** [I, Tn] (cause sth to) become better (使某事物)改进, 改善: *His work is improving slowly.* 他的工作在慢慢改进. ○ *Her health is gradually improving*, ie after an illness. 她的健康状况逐渐好转. ○ *The Post Office aims to improve its quality of service.* 邮局锐意改善服务质量. ○ *The fertility of the soil has been greatly improved by the use of pesticides.* 土壤施用杀虫剂后肥力大增. ○ *He studied harder to improve his French.* 他更加努力提高法语水平. ○ *a new improved washing-powder* 经改进的新型洗衣粉. **2** (phr v) **improve on/upon sth** achieve or produce sth of a better standard or quality than sth else 改进或生产出比某物更好的事物: *The German girl improved on her previous best performance in the 100 metres.* 那个德国姑娘在100米比赛中刷新了自己以往最好的成绩. ○ *This achievement has never been improved on.* 这个成就从未有人超过.

▷ **im·prove·ment** *n* **1** [C, U] **~ (on/in sth)** action or process of improving; state of being improved 改进; 改善; 改良: *cause a distinct/significant/marked improvement in working conditions* 使工作环境有明显的[重大的/显著的]改善 ○ *a slight, gradual, etc improvement in the weather* 天气的轻微的、逐渐的…好转 ○ *This year's car is an improvement on* (ie is better than) *last year's model.* 今年的汽车是去年型号的改进型. ○ *There is room for further improvement in your English.* 你的英语尚有进一步提高的余地. **2** [C] addition or alteration that improves sth or adds to its value (改进某事物或提高其价值的)增加或修改: *home improvements* 住宅的装修 ○ [attrib 作定语] *a road improvement scheme* 道路改善计划.

im·prov·id·ent /ɪmˈprɒvɪdənt; ɪmˋprɑvədənt/ *adj* (*fml* 文) not preparing for future needs; wasteful 不顾及将来需要的; 浪费的: *improvident spending habits* 不为将来打算的花钱习惯. ▷ **im·prov·id·ence** /-əns; -əns/ *n* [U]. **im·prov·id·ently** *adv*.

im·pro·vise /ˈɪmprəvaɪz; *US also* ˌɪmprəˈvaɪz; ˋɪmprə-ˌvaɪz, ˌɪmprəˋvaɪz/ *v* [I, Tn] **1** compose or play (music), speak or act without previous preparation (即兴地或即席地)创作、演奏、讲话、表演等: *The pianist forgot his music and had to improvise (the accompaniment).* 弹钢琴的人把乐谱忘了, 只好即兴伴奏. ○ *an improvised speech* 即席的演讲. **2** make (sth) from whatever is available, without preparation (临时就现有的条件)做(某事物): *As we've not got the proper materials, we'll just have to improvise.* 我们没有弄到合适的材料, 只好临时凑合了. ○ *a hastily improvised meal* 匆匆拼凑的一顿饭.

▷ **im·pro·visa·tion** /ˌɪmprəvaɪˈzeɪʃn; *US also* ɪmˌprɒvəˈzeɪʃn; ˌɪmprəvaɪˋzeʃən, ɪmˌprɑvəˋzeʃən/ *n* [U, C].

im·pru·dent /ɪmˈpru:dnt; ɪmˋprudn̩t/ *adj* (*fml* 文) not wise or discreet; not prudent 不智的; 不谨慎的; 轻率的: *It would be imprudent (of you) to resign from your present job before you are offered another.* (你)还没有得到新的工作就辞去现有的工作太不慎重了. ▷ **im·pru·dence** /-ns; -n̩s/ *n* [U]. **im·pru·dently** *adv*.

im·pud·ent /ˈɪmpjʊdənt; ˋɪmpjʊdənt/ *adj* very rude and disrespectful 粗鲁的; 放肆的; 无礼的; 不尊重的: *an impudent child, grin, question* 粗俗的孩子、笑、问题.

▷ **im·pud·ence** /-əns; -əns/ *n* [U] being impudent; impudent behaviour or speech 粗鲁; 放肆; 无礼的言行: *I've had enough of your impudence!* 你这样放肆, 我已经受够了!

im·pud·ently *adv*.

im·pugn /ɪmˈpju:n; ɪmˋpjun/ *v* [Tn] (*fml* 文) express doubts about (sth) 对(某事物)表示怀疑: *impugn sb's motives, actions, morals, etc* 怀疑某人的动机、行为、品行等.

im·pulse /ˈɪmpʌls; ˋɪmpʌls/ *n* **1** (**a**) [C] **~ (to do sth)** sudden urge to act without thinking about the results 凭冲动行事(未顾及后果); 突如其来的念头: *He felt an irresistible impulse to jump.* 他突然有个无法抗拒的冲动, 想跳下去. ○ *check/curb/resist an impulse* 抑制[约束/遏止]冲动. (**b**) [U] tendency to act in this way 好冲动行事: *a man of impulse* 易冲动的人. **2** [C] push or thrust; stimulus; impetus 推动; 冲力; 刺激; 推动力: *give an impulse to industrial expansion* 促进工业的扩展. **3** [C] stimulating force in a nerve or an electric circuit that causes a reaction 神经冲动; 电路脉冲: *nerve impulses* 神经冲动. **4** (idm 习语) **on impulse** suddenly and without previous thinking or planning 一时冲动: *On impulse, I picked up the phone and rang my sister in Australia.* 我一时心血来潮, 拿起话筒就给在澳大利亚的妹妹打了个电话.

□ **ˈimpulse buying** buying goods on impulse 凭冲动购买货物.

im·pul·sion /ɪmˈpʌlʃn; ɪmˋpʌlʃən/ *n* [C] **~ (to do sth)** (*fml* 文) strong urge (to do sth) (做某事的)强烈欲望: *the impulsion to break away and make a new life* 想脱离开, 去过一种新生活的强烈欲望.

im·puls·ive /ɪmˈpʌlsɪv; ɪmˋpʌlsɪv/ *adj* (of people or their behaviour) marked by sudden action that is undertaken without careful thought (指人或人的行为)凭冲动的, 易冲动的, 由冲动造成的: *an impulsive man, comment, decision, departure* 易冲动的人、一时冲动的评语、在冲动中做出的决定、在冲动下离去. ▷ **im·puls·ively**: *react, behave impulsively* 冲动地反应、表现. *adv*. **im·puls·ive·ness** *n* [U].

im·pun·ity /ɪmˈpju:nətɪ; ɪmˋpjunətɪ/ *n* (idm 习语) **with impunity** with freedom from punishment or injury 不受惩罚或伤害: *You cannot break the law with impunity.* 违法者必受惩罚.

im·pure /ɪmˈpjʊə(r); ɪmˋpjʊr/ *adj* **1** (*dated* 旧) morally wrong, esp in one's sexual behaviour 道德败坏的; (尤指)淫猥的: *impure thoughts, motives, actions* 淫秽的想

法、动机、举动. **2** not clean; dirty or contaminated 不洁的; 肮脏的; 污染的. **3** not consisting of one substance, but mixed with another substance of poorer quality 不纯的; 有杂质的: *impure metals* 不纯的金属.

▷ **im·pur·ity** /ɪmˈpjʊərətɪ; ɪmˈpjʊrətɪ/ *n* **1** [U] state or quality of being impure 不纯; 不洁; 淫秽. **2** [C] substance present in another substance that makes it of poor quality 杂质: *remove impurities from silver* 去除银中的杂质.

im·pute /ɪmˈpju:t; ɪmˈpjut/ *v* [Tn·pr] **~ sth to sb/sth** (*fml* 文) put the responsibility for sth on sb/sth; attribute sth to sb/sth 将某事物的责任加之于某人[某事物]; 将某事物归因于或归咎于某人[某事物]: *He imputed the failure of his marriage to his wife's shortcomings.* 他把婚姻的失败归咎于妻子的缺点.

▷ **im·puta·tion** /ˌɪmpju:teɪʃn; ˌɪmpjuˈteʃən/ *n* [U, C] (*fml* 文) action of imputing; accusation 归罪; 归咎; 非难: *imputation of guilt* 归罪.

in[1] /ɪn; ɪn/ *adv part* (For special uses with many *vs* 与动词搭配的特殊用法, 如 *come in, give in,* see the *v* entries 见有关动词词条.) **1** (to a position) within a particular area or volume (指位置)在里面, 在内: *The top drawer is the one with the cutlery in.* 最上面的抽屉是放刀叉的. ○ *I'm afraid I can't drink coffee with milk in.* 我不能喝搀牛奶的咖啡. ○ *She opened the bedroom door and went in.* 她打开卧室的门走了进去. ○ *The children were playing by the river when one of them slipped and fell in.* 孩子们在河边玩耍, 突然其中一个滑了一跤跌进河里. ○ *The door opened and in walked my father.* 门一开, 父亲进来了. **2** (of people) at home or at a place of work (指人)在家或在工作处: *Nobody was in when we called.* 我们打过电话, 可是屋里没有人. ○ *She's usually in by seven o'clock.* 她通常七点钟就到家了. ○ *I'm afraid the manager isn't in today.* 经理今天不在. Cf 参看 OUT 2. **3** (of trains, buses, etc) at the station or terminus (指火车、公共汽车等)在站上或在总站: *The train was in when we got to the station.* 我们赶到车站时, 火车已停在站上了. ○ *It's due in* (ie It should arrive) *at 6 o'clock.* 这班车应在6点钟到达. **4** (of farm animals or crops) brought to the farm from the fields (指家畜或农作物)从田野弄回农场: *The cows will be in for milking soon.* 奶牛一会儿就赶回来等待挤奶. ○ *We need help to get the wheat in.* 我们需要人手来帮助抢收小麦. **5** (of the tide) at or towards its highest point on land (指潮汐)上涨或处最高点: *It's one o'clock. The tide must be in.* 一点钟了. 潮水准已涨上来了. ○ *Is the tide coming in or going out?* 现在是涨潮还是落潮? ○ (*fig* 比喻) *My luck's in — I won a new car in a raffle.* 我的运气来了 —— 在有奖抽彩中我得了一辆新汽车. **6** (of letters, cards, etc) delivered to the destination; received (指信件、名信片等)投递到, 收到: *Applications must be in by 30 April.* 申请书必须在4月30日以前交来. ○ *Entries should be in on Monday morning.* 参加者名单应在星期一上午交来. **7** fashionable; popular 时髦; 入时; 流行: *Miniskirts are (coming) in again.* 超短裙又(快)时兴了. **8** (of fruit, fish, etc) on sale or obtainable (指水果、鱼等)上市, 当令, 可买到: *Strawberries are never in for long.* 草莓上市的时间从来就不长. ○ *Do you have any fresh salmon in at the moment?* 现在有新鲜大马哈鱼卖吗? **9** elected to office 当选; 执政: *Labour came in after the war.* 战后工党开始执政. ○ *The club president has been in since 1979.* 俱乐部主任是自1979年选任的. **10** (*sport* 体) **(a)** (in cricket, baseball, etc) batting (板球、垒球等)击球: *England were in first.* 英国队首先击球. ○ *He had only been in for 10 minutes when Jones bowled him out.* 他击球才十分钟就被琼斯投球杀出局. **(b)** (in tennis, badminton, etc) (of a ball, etc) having landed inside the line (网球、羽毛球等)(指球)落在界内: *Her service was in.* 她发球落入界内. **(c)** (of the ball in football, hockey, etc) between and behind the goalposts (指足球、冰球等的球)在球门柱之间或入门: *It's in — we've got a goal!* 球进了 —— 我们射门得分! Cf 参看 OUT 16. **11** (of a coal or wood fire) burning (指煤火或柴火)燃烧: *The fire was still in when we got home.* 我们到家时, 煤火还在燃烧. **12** (idm 习语) **be in for sth** (*infml* 口) **(a)** be about to experience (esp sth unpleasant) 即将体验到(尤指不愉快的事物): *He's in for a nasty shock/surprise!* 他就要碰上一件非常糟糕而震惊[意外]的事了! ○ *I'm afraid we're in for a storm.* 看来我们要赶上暴雨了. **(b)** having agreed to take part in sth 同意参加某事: *Are you in for this game of whist?* 这场惠斯特桥牌你参加吗? ○ *I'm in for the 1000 metres.* 我参加一千米赛跑. **be/get in on sth** (*infml* 口) participate in sth; have a share or knowledge of sth 参与某事; 对某事知情: *I'd like to be in on the scheme.* 我很想参与这项计划. ○ *Are you in on her secret?* 你知道她的秘密吗? **be (well) ˈin with sb** (*infml* 口) be (very) friendly with sb (and likely to benefit from the friendship) 同某人亲密(且可能从中获益): *He's well in with the boss.* 他和老板关系很密切. **have (got) it ˈin for sb** (*infml* 口) want to take revenge on sb; bear ill will towards sb 欲向某人报复; 对某人不怀好意: *That teacher has always had it in for me.* 那位老师总想跟我过不去. **ˌin and ˈout (of sth)** sometimes in and sometimes out (of a place) 时进时出(于某处): *He's been in and out of hospital* (ie often ill and in hospital) *all year.* 他一整年经常入院出院.

▷ **in-** (forming compound *ns* 用以构成复合名词) **1** (*infml* 口) popular and fashionable 流行和时髦: *It's the in-thing to do at the moment.* 这是目前最时兴的做法了. ○ *the in-place to go* 大家一时爱去的地方. **2** shared by or appealing to a small group (小圈子内)分享的或感兴趣的: *an in-joke* 一则内部笑话.

□ **ˈin-tray** *n* tray for holding letters, etc that are waiting to be read or answered 收文盘(放置待阅或待复信件的). Cf 参看 OUT-TRAY (OUT).

in[2] /ɪn; ɪn/ *prep* (For special uses with many *ns* and *vs* 与名词和动词搭配的特殊用法, 如 *in place, in memory of, end in sth,* see the *n* and *v* entries 见有关名词和动词词条.) **1** (indicating place 表示地方) **(a)** at a point within the area or volume of (sth) 在(某事物)的范围内的一点上: *the highest mountain in the world* 世界上最高的山 ○ *a country in Africa* 非洲的一个国家 ○ *She lives in a small village in France.* 她住在法国的一个小乡村里. ○ *the biggest shop in town* 镇上最大的商店 ○ *islands in the Pacific Ocean* 太平洋上的岛屿 ○ *children playing in the street* 在街上玩耍的孩子 ○ *not a cloud in the sky* 天上一朵云彩也没有 ○ *swimming in the pool* 在池中游泳 ○ *standing in the corner of a room* 站在房间的角落里 (Cf 参看 *standing at the corner of the street*) ○ *It's in a drawer.* 在抽屉里. ○ *I read about it in the newspaper.* 那件事我是在报上看到的. ○ *Can you see the dog in the picture?* 你看见画里的狗了吗? **(b)** within the shape of (sth); enclosed by 在(某物)的形体或范围中; 在...之内; 在...之中: *lying in bed* 躺在床上 (Cf 参看 *sitting on the bed*) ○ *sitting in a chair,* ie an armchair 坐在单座沙发上 ○ *Leave the key in the lock.* 钥匙就留在锁孔里吧. ○ *a cigarette in her mouth* 她嘴里叼着的香烟 ○ *What have you got in your hand/pocket?* 你手[口袋]里有什么东西? **2** (indicating movement 表示移动) into (sth) 进入(某物): *He dipped his pen in the ink.* 他把钢笔往墨水里蘸了蘸. ○ *Throw it in the fire.* 把它扔到火里去吧. ○ *She got in her car and drove off.* 她进入汽车里把车开走了. **3** during (a period of time) 在(某段时间)内: *in the twentieth century* 在二十世纪 ○ *in 1999* 在1999年 ○ *in spring, summer, etc* 在春天、夏天等 ○ *in March* 在三月里 (Cf 参看 *on 18 March*) ○ *in the morning/afternoon/evening* 在上午[下午/晚上] ○ *It happened in the past.* 这是过去发生的事情. ⇨Usage at TIME[2] 用法见 TIME[2]. **4 (a)** after (a maximum length of time) 在(一整段时间)之后: *return in a few minutes, hours, days, months, etc* 过几分钟、几小时、几天、几个月...之后回来 ○ *It will be ready in a week.* 一周之后即准备妥当. ○ *She learnt to drive in three weeks,* ie After 3 weeks she could drive. 她用了三个星期学会了开车. **(b)** (used after a negative or *first, last,* etc 用于否定词之后或 first、last 等词之后) during; for 在某段时间内: *I haven't seen him in years.* 我多年没见到他了. ○ *It's the first/only letter I've had in 10 days.* 这是我10天中收到的第一封[唯一的一封]信. **5** forming the whole or part of (sth); contained within 构成(某事物)的整体或部分; 包含在...之内: *seven days in a week* 一星期有七天 ○ *eight pints in a gallon* 一加仑有八品脱 ○ *There's a cover charge included in the total.* 帐单总额里包括服务费. ○ *I recognize his father in him,* ie His character is partly similar to his father's. 我看到他身上有他父亲的某些气质. **6** (indicating ratio 表示比率): *a slope/gradient of one in five* 1:5的坡度[倾斜度] ○ *taxed at the rate of 15p in the pound* 以每镑纳15便士的税率课税 ○ *One in ten said they preferred their old* *brand of margarine.* 有十分之一的人说比较喜欢老牌子的人造黄油. **7** wearing (clothes, colours, etc) 穿戴(衣物等): *dressed/clothed in rags* 穿着[衣着]褴褛 ○ *the man in the hat* 戴着帽子的男子 ○ *the woman in white* 穿着白色衣服的女子 ○ *in uniform, mourning, disguise, armour* 穿着制服、带着孝、戴着伪装、披着铠甲 ○ *in high-heeled shoes* 穿着高跟鞋 ○ *in a silk shirt* 穿着绸衬衫. **8** (indicating physical surroundings, circumstances, etc 表示具体的环境、情况等): *go out in the rain, sun, cold, etc* 冒着雨、顶着太阳、冒着寒冷等外出. **9** (indicating the state or condition of sb/sth 表示某人[某事物]的状态或状况): *in order* 整齐 ○ *in a mess* 乱七八糟 ○ *in good repair* 保养良好 ○ *in poor health* 健康欠佳 ○ *in a rage* 愤怒之中 ○ *in a hurry* 匆忙地 ○ *in fun* 开玩笑地 ○ *in poverty* 在穷困中 ○ *in ruins* 呈废墟状态 ○ *in anger*, ie angrily 愤怒地. **10** (indicating form, shape, arrangement or quantities 表示形式、形状、安排或数量): *a novel in three parts* 分为三部分的一本小说 ○ *stand in groups* 成群地站着 ○ *sit in rows* 成排地坐着 ○ *her hair in a pony-tail* 她那梳成马尾状的头发 ○ *curtains hanging in folds* 挂着的打着褶儿的窗帘 ○ *Tourists queue in (their) thousands to see the tomb.* 游客数以千计排着长队参观陵墓. **11** (indicating the medium, means, material, etc 表示媒体、手段、材料等): *speak in English* 用英语说 ○ *write a message in code* 用密码写一条消息 ○ *written in biro, ink, pencil, etc* 用圆珠笔、墨水、铅笔等写的 ○ *printed in italics, capitals, etc* 用斜体字、大写字体等印刷的 ○ *say it in a few words* 用几句话来说 ○ *speak in a loud voice* 大声地说 ○ *pay in cash* 用现金支付 (Cf 参看 *by cheque*). **12** (used to introduce the name of a particular person 用以引出某人姓名): *We have lost a first-rate teacher in Jim.* 我们失去了吉姆这位一流的教师. ○ *You've got a real trouble-maker in Wilkins.* 你们有个威金斯这个货真价实的捣乱分子. ○ *You will always find a good friend in me*, ie I will always be a good friend to you. 我永远是你的好朋友. **13** with reference to (sth); regarding 在(某)方面; 关于; 至于: *He's behind the others in reading but a long way ahead in arithmetic.* 他在阅读方面不如别人, 但算术却遥遥领先. ○ *lacking in courage* 缺乏勇气 ○ *equal in strength* 强度一样 ○ *a country rich/poor in minerals* 矿藏丰富[贫乏]的国家 ○ *blind in one eye* 一目失明 ○ *three feet in length, depth, diameter, etc* 长度、深度、直径…为三英尺. **14** (indicating sb's occupation, activity, etc 表示某人的职业、活动等): *in the army/navy/air force* 在陆军[海军/空军]服役 ○ *in business, insurance, computers, journalism, etc* 从事商业、保险业、计算机业、新闻业等 ○ *He's been in politics* (ie a politician) *all his life.* 他一生从政. ○ *killed in action*, ie While fighting as a soldier 阵亡 ○ *In* (ie While) *attempting to save a child from drowning, she nearly lost her own life.* 她在抢救溺水的孩子时, 自己几乎丧了命. **15** (idm 习语) **in that** /ɪn ðət; ɪn ðət/ (never taking stress 不可重读)for the reason that; because 基于…的理由; 因为: *Privatization is thought to be beneficial in that it promotes competition.* 私营化的优点在于能促进相互竞争.

in[3] /ɪn; ɪn/ *n* (idm 习语) **the ins and outs (of sth)** the details and complexities (of an activity or a procedure) (活动或程序的)细节, 始末, 详情: *know all the ins and outs of a problem* 熟悉问题的来龙去脉 ○ *He's been here for years; he should know the ins and outs of the job by now.* 他在这里已经很多年了, 现在理应熟悉工作的各种方面了.

in-[1] (also **im-**) *pref* 前缀 **1** (with *vs* forming *ns* and *vs* 与动词结合构成名词和动词) in; on 在内; 向内; 在上: *intake* ○ *imprint*. **2** (with *ns* forming *vs* 与名词结合构成动词) put into a certain state or condition 置于某状态或条件中: *inflame* ○ *imperil*.

in-[2] (also **il-, im-, ir-**) *pref* 前缀 (forming *adjs, advs* and *ns* 用以构成形容词、副词、名词) not 不; 非; 无: *infinite* ○ *illogical* ○ *immorally* ○ *irrelevance.* ⇨Usage at UN- 用法见 UN-.

-in /ɪn; ɪn/ (forming compound *ns* 用以构成复合名词) (*becoming dated* 渐旧) (added to another word (usu a *v*) to indicate an activity in which many people participate 附于另一词(通常为动词)后, 表示有很多人参加的活动): *a 'sit-in* ○ *'teach-ins*.

in *abbr* 缩写 = (*pl* unchanged or **ins** 复数或不变或作 **ins**) (also *symb* 符号为 ″) inch: *4 in* × (ie by) *2 in (4″ × 2″)* 4英寸×2英寸(4″ × 2″) ○ *He is 6 ft 2 in (tall).* 他身高6英尺2英寸. Cf 参看 FT, YD.

in·ab·il·ity /ˌɪnəˈbɪlətɪ; ˌɪnəˈbɪlətɪ/ *n* [U] **~ (to do sth)** lack of power, skill or ability; being unable 无力; 无能; 无技术; 不能: *his inability to understand mathematics* 他在理解数学方面能力之差.

in·ac·cess·ible /ˌɪnækˈsesəbl; ˌɪnækˋsɛsəbl/ *adj* **~ (to sb)** very difficult or impossible to reach, approach, or be contacted (by sb); not accessible 难达到的; 不可及的; 不易进入的; 不可接触的: *an inaccessible mountain retreat* 很难抵达的山间僻静处 ○ *His busy schedule made him completely inaccessible to his students.* 他的时间排得很满, 学生根本无法和他接触. ○ (*fig* 比喻) *philosophical theories that are inaccessible to* (ie cannot be understood by) *ordinary people* 普通人无法理解的哲学理论. ▷ **in·ac·cess·ib·il·ity** /ˌɪnækˌsesəˈbɪlətɪ; ˌɪnækˌsɛsəˈbɪlətɪ/ *n* [U]. **in·ac·cess·ibly** /ˌɪnækˈsesəblɪ; ˌɪnækˋsɛsəblɪ/ *adv*.

in·ac·cur·ate /ɪnˈækjərət; ɪnˋækjərɪt/ *adj* having errors; not correct or accurate 有错误的; 不正确的; 不精确的: *an inaccurate report, statement, description, etc* 失实的报道、说法、叙述等.

▷ **in·ac·cur·acy** /ɪnˈækjərəsɪ; ɪnˋækjərəsɪ/ *n* (**a**) [U] being inaccurate 不准确; 不正确; 误差: *an unacceptable level of inaccuracy* 误差达无法容许的程度. (**b**) [C] inaccurate statement; mistake or error 不准确的说法; 错误; 差错: *There are so many inaccuracies in this report that it will have to be written again.* 这份报告错误百出, 须重写.

in·ac·cur·ately *adv*.

in·ac·tion /ɪnˈækʃn; ɪnˋækʃən/ *n* [U] lack of action; doing nothing; idleness 无行动; 无作为; 不活跃; 懒散.

in·act·ive /ɪnˈæktɪv; ɪnˋæktɪv/ *adj* **1** not (physically) active; idle 不活动的; 不活跃的; 懒散的: *If you weren't so inactive you wouldn't be so fat!* 你要是好动一些也不至于这么胖! ○ *Some animals are inactive during the daytime.* 有些动物白天不活动. **2** not working or operating any more; not in use 不再工作的; 不再运行的; 不再使用的: *an inactive machine* 停用的机器. **3** not participating fully (in a club, etc) 参加(俱乐部等)活动不踊跃的: *inactive members of the music society* 音乐协会内不积极参加活动的会员. ▷ **in·ac·tiv·ity** /ˌɪnækˈtɪvətɪ; ˌɪnækˋtɪvətɪ/ *n* [U]: *A holiday need not mean inactivity.* 放假不一定就是不进行活动.

in·ad·equate /ɪnˈædɪkwət; ɪnˋædəkwɪt/ *adj* **1** not sufficient or enough; not good enough for a particular purpose 不充分的; 不足的; 不够好的: *The safety precautions are totally inadequate.* 这些安全措施完全不合格. ○ *inadequate supplies, income, preparation* 不足的供应品、收入、准备. **2** not sufficiently able or confident to deal with a difficult situation 不足胜任的; 信心不足的: *feel inadequate when faced by a difficult problem* 面对难题觉得力不从心.

▷ **in·ad·equacy** /ɪnˈædɪkwəsɪ; ɪnˋædəkwəsɪ/ *n* **1** [C, U] (instance or example of) being inadequate 不充分; 不足; 不胜任: *the inadequacy of our resources* 我们资源的不足 ○ *realize one's personal inadequacy* 认识自己的不足. **2** [C] fault or failing; weakness 毛病; 缺陷; 弱点: *the inadequacies of the present voting system* 现行选举制度的弊病.

in·ad·equately /ɪnˈædɪkwətlɪ; ɪnˋædəkwɪtlɪ/ *adv*.

in·ad·miss·ible /ˌɪnədˈmɪsəbl; ˌɪnədˋmɪsəbl/ *adj* that cannot be allowed or admitted, esp in a court of law 不允许的, 不许可的, 不能承认的(尤指在法庭上): *inadmissible evidence* 不能采纳的证据. ▷ **in·ad·miss·ib·il·ity** /ˌɪnədˌmɪsəˈbɪlətɪ; ˌɪnədˌmɪsəˈbɪlətɪ/ *n* [U]. **in·ad·miss·ibly** /ˌɪnədˈmɪsəblɪ; ˌɪnədˋmɪsəblɪ/ *adv*.

in·ad·vert·ent /ˌɪnədˈvɜːtənt; ˌɪnədˋvɝtn̩t/ *adj* (of actions) done without thinking or not deliberately (指行动)漫不经心的, 非故意的, 无意的: *an inadvertent slip, omission, etc* 不经意的失误、遗漏等.

▷ **in·ad·vert·ence** *n* [U].

in·ad·vert·ently *adv* by accident; unintentionally 偶然地; 非故意地; 无意地: *She inadvertently telephoned the wrong person.* 她无意中打错了电话.

in·ad·vis·able /ˌɪnədˈvaɪzəbl; ˌɪnədˋvaɪzəbl/ *adj* [usu pred 通常作表语] unwise; not sensible 不明智; 不可取; 失策: *It is inadvisable to have too much sugar in your diet.* 饮食中糖分太多是不可取的. ▷ **in·ad·vis·ab·il·ity** /ˌɪnədˌvaɪzəˈbɪlətɪ; ˌɪnədˌvaɪzəˈbɪlətɪ/ *n* [U].

in·ali·en·able /ɪn'eɪlɪənəbl; ɪn'elɪənəbl̩/ *adj* [usu attrib 通常作定语] (*fml* 文) that cannot be taken away 不可剥夺的; 不能让与的: *inalienable rights* 不可剥夺的权利.

in·ane /ɪ'neɪn; ɪn'en/ *adj* without meaning; silly or stupid 无意义的; 愚蠢的: *an inane remark, question, etc* 无聊的言语、问题等 ○ *inane conversation* 无意义的谈话.

▷ **in·anely** *adv*: *They grinned inanely.* 他们咧嘴傻笑.

in·an·ity /ɪ'nænətɪ; ɪn'ænətɪ/ *n* **(a)** [U] being inane 无意义; 愚蠢. **(b)** [C] inane remark or act 无意义的或愚蠢的言行.

in·an·im·ate /ɪn'ænɪmət; ɪn'ænəmɪt/ *adj* **1** not alive, esp in the way that humans and animals are 无生命的: *A rock is an inanimate object.* 石头是无生命的物体. **2** lacking energy and vitality; dull 无精力的; 无生气的; 单调的: *inanimate conversation* 沉闷的谈话.

in·ap·plic·able /ɪn'æplɪkəbl, *also* ˌɪnə'plɪkəbl; ɪn'æplɪkəbl̩, ˌɪnə'plɪkəbl̩/ *adj* **~ (to sb/sth)** that is not relevant or cannot be applied 不相干的; 不适用的: *The rules seem to be inapplicable to this situation.* 这些规则似乎不适用于这种情况. ▷ **in·ap·plic·ab·il·ity** /ɪnˌæplɪkə'bɪlətɪ, *also* ˌɪnəˌplɪkə'bɪlətɪ; ˌɪnæplɪkə'bɪlətɪ, ˌɪnəˌplɪkə'bɪlətɪ/ *n* [U]. **in·ap·plic·ably** /ɪn'æplɪkəblɪ, *also* ˌɪnə'plɪkəblɪ; ɪn'æplɪkəblɪ, ˌɪnə'plɪkəblɪ/ *adv*.

in·ap·pro·pri·ate /ˌɪnə'prəʊprɪət; ˌɪnə'proprɪɪt/ *adj* **~ (to/for sb/sth)** not suitable or appropriate (for sb/sth) (对某人[某事物])不恰当的, 不适合的: *an inappropriate comment, name, moment* 不当的评语、名称、时刻 ○ *clothes inappropriate to the occasion* 不适合这种场合的衣物 ○ *It seems inappropriate for us to intervene at this stage.* 我们在此阶段介入似不甚妥. ▷ **in·ap·pro·pri·ately** *adv*: *inappropriately dressed for the funeral* 参加葬礼时衣着不当. **in·ap·pro·pri·ate·ness** *n* [U].

in·apt /ɪn'æpt; ɪn'æpt/ *adj* not relevant, appropriate or useful 不相干的; 不合适的; 无用的: *an inapt remark, question, translation* 不恰当的言语、问题、翻译.

▷ **in·ap·ti·tude** /ɪn'æptɪtju:d; *US* -tu:d; ɪn'æptəˌtud/ *n* [U] **~ (for sth)** lack of ability or suitability (for sth) 无能力; 不合适.

in·apt·ness *n* [U] being inapt 不相干; 不合适; 无用.

in·ar·ticu·late /ˌɪnɑ:'tɪkjʊlət; ˌɪnɑr'tɪkjəlɪt/ *adj* **1** unable to express one's words, ideas or feelings clearly 不善表达思想感情的: *a clever but inarticulate mathematician* 聪明但不善言辞的数学家. **2** not clearly or well expressed 表达得不清楚的; 含糊其辞的: *an inarticulate speech, essay, sound* 含糊不清的讲话、文章、声音 ○ *speaking in an inarticulate mumble* 叽哩咕噜地说着. **3** not expressed as spoken words 非言语表达的: *Her actions were an inarticulate cry for help.* 她的行动是无言的呼救. ▷ **in·ar·ticu·lately** *adv*. **in·ar·ticu·late·ness** *n* [U].

in·as·much as /ˌɪnəz'mʌtʃ əz; ˌɪnəz'mʌtʃ əz/ *conj* (*fml* 文) since; because; to the extent that 因为; 由于; 鉴于; 至...限度: *He is a Dane inasmuch as he was born in Denmark, but he became a British citizen at the age of 30.* 他按其出生在丹麦来说是丹麦人, 但他在30岁时成了英国公民.

in·at·ten·tion /ˌɪnə'tenʃn; ˌɪnə'tɛnʃən/ *n* [U] **~ (to sb/sth)** lack of attention; neglect 不注意; 不经心; 疏忽: *work marred by inattention to detail* 因忽略了细节而嫌美中不足的作品.

▷ **in·at·tent·ive** /ˌɪnə'tentɪv; ˌɪnə'tɛntɪv/ *adj* **~ (to sb/sth)** not paying attention (to sb/sth); not attentive 不注意的; 不经心的; 疏忽的: *inattentive to the needs of others* 漠视他人需要. **in·at·tent·ively** *adv*. **in·at·tent·ive·ness** *n* [U].

in·aud·ible /ɪn'ɔ:dəbl; ɪn'ɔdəbl̩/ *adj* not loud enough to be heard; not audible (因声音低)听不见的: *speak in an almost inaudible voice* 用低得难以听到的声音说话. ▷ **in·aud·ib·il·ity** /ɪnˌɔ:də'bɪlətɪ; ˌɪnɔdə'bɪlətɪ/ *n* [U]. **in·aud·ibly** /ɪn'ɔ:dəblɪ; ɪn'ɔdəblɪ/ *adv*.

in·aug·ural /ɪ'nɔ:gjʊrəl; ɪn'ɔgjərəl/ *adj* [attrib 作定语] of or for an inauguration 就职的; 就任的; 开幕的; 创始的: *an inaugural speech, lecture, meeting, etc* 就职演说、首次讲课、开幕典礼.

in·aug·ur·ate /ɪ'nɔ:gjʊreɪt; ɪn'ɔgjəˌret/ *v* **1** [Tn, Cn·n/a] **~ sb (as sth)** introduce (a new public official or leader) at a special ceremony 为(新官员或领袖)举行就职典礼: *inaugurate the President* 为总统举行就职典礼 ○ *He will be inaugurated as president in January.* 他将在一月就任总裁. **2** [Tn] mark the beginning of (an organization or undertaking) or open (a building, an exhibition, etc) with a special ceremony 为(组织或工程的创立或开工)举行仪式; 为(建筑物、展览会等)举行落成或开幕仪式: *inaugurate a conference, an organization, a scheme, etc* 为会议开幕、组织成立、计划创始举行仪式 ○ *The city library was inaugurated by the mayor.* 市长主持了市图书馆的落成仪式. **3** [Tn] be the beginning of (sth); introduce 开创, 创始, 引进(某事物): *Concorde inaugurated a new era in aeroplane travel.* 协和式飞机开创了空中旅行的新纪元.

▷ **in·aug·ura·tion** /ɪˌnɔ:gjʊ'reɪʃn; ɪnˌɔgjə'reʃən/ *n* [C, U] (act of) inaugurating or being inaugurated 就职; 就职典礼; 开幕式; 落成典礼: *the President's inauguration* 总统就职典礼 ○ [attrib 作定语] *the President's inauguration speech* 总统就职演说.

in·aug·ur·ator *n* person who inaugurates sth 典礼主持人; 创始人.

in·aus·pi·cious /ˌɪnɔ:'spɪʃəs; ˌɪnɔ'spɪʃəs/ *adj* having signs which show that future success is unlikely; not favourable 不吉的; 不祥的; 不利的: *an inauspicious occasion, event, meeting, etc* 预兆不祥的情况、事件、会面等. ▷ **in·aus·pi·ciously** *adv*. **in·aus·pi·cious·ness** *n* [U].

in·board /'ɪnbɔ:d; 'ɪnˌbɔrd/ *adj*, *adv* (situated) within the sides of or towards the centre of a boat or aircraft (处于)船或飞行器的内部(的); 向船或飞行器的中心(的): *an inboard motor* 舷内机.

in·born /ˌɪn'bɔ:n; ɪn'bɔrn/ *adj* existing in a person or animal from birth; natural; innate 天生的; 先天的; 生来的: *an* ˌ*inborn* ˌ*talent for* '*music* 天赋的音乐才能.

in·bred /ˌɪn'bred; ɪn'brɛd/ *adj* **1** natural; innate 天生的; 先天的: *an* ˌ*inbred* ˌ*sense of* '*duty* 天生的责任感. **2** produced by inbreeding 同系交配产生的: *The long nose on these dogs is an* ˌ*inbred characte*'*ristic.* 这些狗的长鼻子是同系交配的特点.

▷ **in·breed·ing** /'ɪnbri:dɪŋ; 'ɪnˌbridɪŋ/ *n* [U] breeding among closely related people or animals 人或动物的近亲繁殖; 同系交配: *deformities caused by inbreeding* 近亲繁殖造成的畸形.

in-built /ˌɪn'bɪlt; 'ɪn'bɪlt/ *adj* = BUILT-IN (BUILD).

Inc (also **inc**) /ɪŋk; ɪŋk/ *abbr* 缩写 = (*US*) Incorporated: *Manhattan Drugstores Inc* 曼哈顿药物杂物有限公司. Cf 参看 LTD, PLC.

in·cal·cul·able /ɪn'kælkjʊləbl; ɪn'kælkjələbl̩/ *adj* **1** too large or great to be calculated 不可计算的; 极大的; 不可估量的; 无数的: *do incalculable harm to sb's reputation* 严重损害某人的声誉. **2** that cannot be predicted; uncertain 无法预料的; 难以确定的: *a person of incalculable moods* 喜怒无常的人. ▷ **in·cal·cul·ably** /-əblɪ; -əblɪ/ *adv*.

in·can·des·cent /ˌɪnkæn'desnt; ˌɪnkən'dɛsn̩t/ *adj* glowing or shining when heated 白炽的; 白热的. ▷ **in·can·des·cence** /-sns; -sn̩s/ *n* [U].

□ ˌ**incan**ˌ**descent** '**lamp** electric lamp with a heated filament that gives off white light 白炽灯.

in·canta·tion /ˌɪnkæn'teɪʃn; ˌɪnkæn'teʃən/ *n* **(a)** [C] series of words used as a magic spell or charm 符咒; 咒语; 魔法: *chant incantations to the evil spirits* 向恶魔念符咒. **(b)** [U] saying or use of these 念符咒; 用魔法.

in·cap·able /ɪn'keɪpəbl; ɪn'kepəbl̩/ *adj* **1** [pred 作表语] **~ of sth/doing sth** not able to do sth 不能做某事: *The children seem to be totally incapable of working quietly by themselves.* 这些孩子简直完全不能静静地自己做功课. ○ *incapable of telling a lie*, ie too honest to do so 不会说谎(极诚实而不说谎) ○ *incapable of sympathy* 不能同情人. **2** unable to do anything well; helpless; not capable 什么事都做不好的; 不能胜任的; 无能的: *As a lawyer she's totally incapable.* 她当律师完全不合格. **3** (idm 习语) **drunk and incapable** ⇨ DRUNK. ▷ **in·cap·ab·il·ity** /ɪnˌkeɪpə'bɪlətɪ; ˌɪnkepə'bɪlətɪ/ *n* [U]. **in·cap·ably** *adv*.

in·ca·pa·cit·ate /ˌɪnkə'pæsɪteɪt; ˌɪnkə'pæsəˌtet/ *v* [Tn, Tn·pr] **~ sb (for sth/from doing sth)** **1** make sb unable (to do sth); weaken or disable sb 使某人不能(做某事); 使某人孱弱或伤残: *be incapacitated by an accident* 在事故中致残 ○ *Poor health incapacitated him for work/from working all his life.* 他身体不好, 一辈子不能工作. **2** deprive sb of the legal ability (to do sth);

I

disqualify sb 使某人无合法的能力(做某事); 取消某人的资格.

in·ca·pa·city /ˌɪnkəˈpæsətɪ; ˌɪnkəˋpæsətɪ/ *n* [U] **~ (to do sth); ~ (for sth/doing sth)** lack of ability and necessary strength (to do sth); weakness or inability 无能力(做某事); 孱弱; 无能: *his increasing incapacity for work* 他对工作日渐不能胜任 ○ *society's incapacity to deal with the growing numbers of the elderly* 社会对人口老化问题之无能为力.

in·car·cer·ate /ɪnˈkɑːsəreɪt; ɪnˋkɑrsəˌret/ *v* [Tn, Tn·pr] **~ sb (in sth)** (*fml* 文) put sb in prison 将某人监禁: *He was incarcerated (in the castle dungeon) for years.* 他被多年监禁(在古堡的地牢里). ▷ **in·car·cera·tion** /ɪnˌkɑːsəˈreɪʃn; ɪnˌkɑrsəˋreʃən/ *n* [U].

in·carn·ate /ɪnˈkɑːneɪt; ɪnˋkɑrnet/ *adj* (following *ns* 用于名词之后) **1** in the physical form of a human being 人体化的; 化身的: *The guards were sadistic beasts and their leader was the devil incarnate.* 那些警卫都是残暴的野兽, 他们的首领是个魔鬼的化身. **2** (of ideas, qualities, etc) appearing in a human form (指思想、性质等)拟人化的, 具体化的: *virtue incarnate* 贞洁的化身.

▷ **in·carn·ate** /ˈɪnkɑːneɪt; ɪnˋkɑrnet/ *v* [Tn] (*fml* 文) **1** give human form to (sth) 赋予(某事物)人的形体; 将(某事物)人格化. **2** put (an idea, a quality, etc) into real or physical form 使(概念, 品质等)具体化或形象化. **3** (of a person) be a living form of (a quality) (指人)为(某特质)的体现: *He incarnates all the qualities of a successful manager.* 他表现出了事业有成的经理人员所具有的一切品质.

in·carna·tion /ˌɪnkɑːˈneɪʃn; ˌɪnkɑrˋneʃən/ *n* **1** [C] person that prominently displays a particular quality (突出表现某种品质的)典型人物, 化身: *She's the very incarnation of goodness.* 她是美德的化身. **2** [C, U] (instance of) being alive in human form 化身: *the nine incarnations of Vishnu* 护持神的九个化身 ○ *He believed he had been a prince in a previous incarnation.* 他相信他前生是王子. **3 the Incarnation** [sing] (in Christianity) the act of God becoming a man in Jesus (基督教)道成肉身(神以耶稣基督的身分化为人).

in·cau·tious /ɪnˈkɔːʃəs; ɪnˋkɔʃəs/ *adj* acting or done without enough care or thought; not cautious; rash 不谨慎的; 粗心的; 轻率的. ▷ **in·cau·tiously** *adv*.

in·cen·di·ary /ɪnˈsendɪərɪ; *US* -dɪerɪ; ɪnˋsɛndɪˌɛrɪ/ *adj* **1** designed to set buildings, etc on fire 放火的; 纵火的: *an incendiary bomb, device, attack* 燃烧弹、喷火器、火攻. **2** tending to create public disturbances or violence 煽动的: *an incendiary speech* 煽动性演说.

▷ **in·cen·di·ary** *n* bomb that causes a fire 燃烧弹.

in·cense[1] /ˈɪnsens; ˋɪnsɛns/ *n* [U] (smoke from a) substance that produces a pleasant smell when burnt, used esp in religious ceremonies 香(尤指宗教仪式上用的); (香冒出的)烟.

in·cense[2] /ɪnˈsens; ɪnˋsɛns/ *v* [Tn esp passive 尤用于被动语态] make (sb) very angry 使(某人)大怒; 激怒(某人): *The decision to reduce pay levels incensed the work-force.* 降低工资的决定激怒了工人. ○ *He felt deeply incensed by/at the way he had been treated.* 他受到那样的待遇感到非常愤怒.

in·cent·ive /ɪnˈsentɪv; ɪnˋsɛntɪv/ *n* [C, U] **~ (to do sth)** thing that encourages sb to do sth; stimulus 激励某人做某事的事物; 刺激; 奖励: *the offer of cash incentives* 现金奖励的提供 ○ *an incentive to work harder* 对更加努力工作的刺激 ○ *They don't try very hard, but then there's no incentive.* 他们不太卖力气, 不过却也没给他们奖励. ○ [attrib 作定语] *an incentive scheme* 鼓励方案.

in·cep·tion /ɪnˈsepʃn; ɪnˋsɛpʃən/ *n* [sing] (*fml* 文) start or beginning of sth 开始; 开端: *He had been director of the project since its inception.* 这项工作从一开始他就是负责人.

in·cess·ant /ɪnˈsesnt; ɪnˋsɛsnt/ *adj* not stopping; continual 不停的; 连续的; 不断的: *a week of almost incessant rain* 雨差不多没有停过的一个星期 ○ *an incessant stream of visitors* 络绎不绝的参观人流. ▷ **in·cess·antly** *adv*: *complain incessantly* 不停地抱怨.

in·cest /ˈɪnsest; ˋɪnsɛst/ *n* [U] sexual intercourse between people who are too closely related to marry, eg brother and sister or father and daughter 乱伦, 血亲相奸(如兄妹或父女之间).

▷ **in·ces·tu·ous** /ɪnˈsestjʊəs; *US* -tʃʊəs; ɪnˋsɛstʃʊəs/ *adj* **1** involving incest; guilty of incest 乱伦的; 犯乱伦罪的: *an incestuous relationship* 乱伦的关系. **2** (*derog* 贬) of a group of people that have close relationships with one another and do not include people outside their group 小集团的; 小圈子的: *Theatre people are a rather incestuous group, I find.* 我觉得戏剧工作者的小圈子针插不进. **in·ces·tu·ously** *adv*.

inch /ɪntʃ; ɪntʃ/ *n* **1** (*abbr* 缩写 **in**) measure of length equal to 2.54 cm or one twelfth of a foot 英寸(1英尺等于12英寸, 1英寸等于2.54厘米): *a pile of books 12 inches high* 一摞厚达12英寸的书. ⇨App 4,5 见附录4、5. **2** small amount or distance 少量; 短距离: *He escaped death by an inch.* 他险些丧了命. ○ *We argued for an hour but he wouldn't budge* (ie change his attitude or ideas) *an inch.* 我们争论了一个钟头, 但他毫无回旋余地. **3** amount of rain or snow that would cover a surface one inch deep (一英寸厚的)降雨或降雪量: *Three inches of rain fell in Manchester last night.* 曼彻斯特市昨夜降雨三英寸. **4** (idm 习语) **by inches** only just 差一点儿; 险些儿; 几乎: *The car missed me by inches.* 那辆汽车差一点儿撞着我. **every inch (a)** the whole area 整个地方: *The police examined every inch of the house for clues.* 警方为寻找线索彻底检查了整所房子. **(b)** completely; entirely 完全地; 整个地: *He looked every inch a gentleman.* 他看上去完全是正人君子. ˌ**give sb an** ˈ**inch (and he'll** ˌ**take a** ˈ**mile/**ˈ**yard)** (*saying* 谚) if you surrender a little to sb, he will increase his demands greatly 得寸进尺. ˌ**inch by** ˈ**inch** very slowly and in small steps; by degrees 慢慢地; 逐步地; 一点一点地: *They climbed the steep mountain inch by inch.* 他们一点一点地攀上那座陡峭的山. **within an inch of sth/doing sth** very close to sth/doing sth 对某事物[做某事]间不容发; 差一点儿: *He came within an inch of being killed.* 他差一点儿被弄死. ▷ **inch** *v* [I, Ipr, Ip, Tn·pr, Tnp] **~ (sth) forward, past, through, etc (sth)** move (sth) slowly and carefully in the specified direction 使(某物)朝某方向慢慢移动: *inch the car forward* 开车慢慢前行 ○ *He inched (his way) through the narrow passage.* 他慢慢地穿过狭窄的通道.

in·cho·ate /ɪnˈkəʊeɪt, ˈɪnkəʊeɪt; ɪnˋkoɪt/ *adj* (*fml* 文) just begun and therefore not fully formed or developed 刚开始的; 未完全成形的; 未充分发展的: *inchoate ideas, attitudes, wishes, etc* 初步的想法、态度、愿望等.

in·cid·ence /ˈɪnsɪdəns; ˋɪnsədəns/ *n* [sing] **1 ~ of sth** extent to which sth happens or has an effect 事情发生或具有影响的程度; 发生率; 影响范围: *This area has a high incidence of crime, disease, unemployment, etc.* 这个地区的犯罪率、发病率、失业率等很高. **2** way in which a ray of light strikes a surface 光线向物体表面的照射; 入射: *the angle of incidence* 入射角.

in·cid·ent[1] /ˈɪnsɪdənt; ˋɪnsədənt/ *n* **1** event or happening, often of minor importance 事情, 发生的事(常指小事): *He could remember every trivial incident in great detail.* 他能把每件小事的细节都记得很清楚. **2** hostile military activity between countries, opposing forces, etc (国际间或敌对力量等之间的)敌对行动, 军事冲突: *border incidents* 边境事件. **3** [C, U] public disturbance, accident or violence 骚乱; 事故; 暴力事件: *The demonstration proceeded without incident.* 游行示威进行时没有出事. ⇨Usage at OCCURRENCE 用法见OCCURRENCE.

in·cid·ent[2] /ˈɪnsɪdənt; ˋɪnsədənt/ *adj* [pred 作表语] **~ to/upon sb/sth** (*fml* 文) forming a natural or expected part of sb/sth; naturally connected with sb/sth 伴随某人[某事物]而来; 与某人[某事物]自然联系: *the risks incident to the life of a test pilot* 试飞员免不了要冒的生命危险 ○ *responsibilities incident upon one as a parent* 为父母者自然要承担的责任.

in·cid·ental /ˌɪnsɪˈdentl; ˌɪnsəˋdɛntl/ *adj* **1** small and relatively unimportant; minor 小的而较不重要的; 次要的: *incidental expenses* 杂费. **2** accompanying, but not a major part of sth; supplementary 伴随的; 补充的; 附属的: *incidental music for a play* 戏剧的配乐. **3** [pred 作表语] **~ (to sth)** liable to occur because of sth or in connection with sth 易伴随发生; 因相关而产生: *the risks that are incidental to exploration* 探险时容易遇到的危险 ○ *additional responsibilities that are incidental to the job* 做这项工作要承担的额外责任. **4** occurring by chance in connection with sth else (伴随某事)偶然发生的.

▷ **in·cid·ent·ally** /-tlɪ; -tlɪ/ *adv* **1** (used to introduce sth additional that the speaker has just thought of 说话者用以引入临时想到补充要说的事情) by the way 顺便提一句: *Some people, and incidentally that includes Arthur, just won't look after themselves properly.* 有些人, 比如说阿瑟吧, 就是不能好好自理. **2** in an incidental way 偶然地; 不经意地.

in·cin·er·ate /ɪnˈsɪnəreɪt; ɪnˋsɪnəˌret/ *v* [Tn] destroy (sth) completely by burning; burn to ashes 将(某物)烧成灰烬; 焚毁; 火化.

▷ **in·cin·era·tion** /ɪnˌsɪnəˈreɪʃn; ˌɪnsɪnəˋreʃən/ *n* [U].

in·cin·er·ator /ɪnˈsɪnəreɪtə(r); ɪnˋsɪnəˌretɚ/ *n* furnace or enclosed container for burning rubbish, etc (烧垃圾等的)焚化炉.

in·cipi·ent /ɪnˈsɪpɪənt; ɪnˋsɪpɪənt/ *adj* (*fml* 文) in its early stages; beginning to happen 初始的; 早期的; 刚出现的: *signs of incipient tooth decay* 早期龋齿的征象.

in·cise /ɪnˈsaɪz; ɪnˋsaɪz/ *v* [Tn] (**a**) make a cut in (a surface) 切, 切开(物体表面). (**b**) carve designs into (a surface); engrave 在(某物表面)上雕刻.

▷ **in·cision** /ɪnˈsɪʒn; ɪnˋsɪʒən/ *n* [C, U] (act or instance of) cutting, esp by a surgeon into the flesh for an operation 切, 切开, 切割, 切口(尤指外科手术): *make a deep incision in the thigh* 在大腿上深切一刀.

in·cis·ive /ɪnˈsaɪsɪv; ɪnˋsaɪsɪv/ *adj* clear and precise; direct or sharp 清晰而精确的; 直接的; 尖锐的: *incisive comments, criticism, advice, etc* 中肯的评论、批评、劝告等 ○ *an incisive mind* 敏锐的头脑. ▷ **in·cis·ively** *adv*. **in·cis·ive·ness** *n* [U].

in·cisor /ɪnˈsaɪzə(r); ɪnˋsaɪzɚ/ *n* one of the eight sharp cutting teeth at the front of the mouth 门齿; 切牙. ⇨ illus at TOOTH 见 TOOTH 插图.

in·cite /ɪnˈsaɪt; ɪnˋsaɪt/ *v* **1** [Tn·pr, Dn·t] **~ sb (to sth)** urge or persuade sb to do sth by making him very angry or excited 煽动或鼓动某人做某事: *incite the workers to violence/against the government* 煽动工人暴动[反对政府] ○ *The captain was accused of inciting other officers to mutiny.* 该上尉被控煽动军官叛变. **2** [Tn] create or cause (sth) 制造或引起(某事件): *incite a riot/breach of the peace* 制造动乱[妨害治安事端].

▷ **in·cite·ment** *n* [U, C] **~ (to sth)** action that incites certain behaviour 煽动; 鼓励: *incitement to defy authority* 煽动反对当局.

in·ci·vil·ity /ˌɪnsɪˈvɪlətɪ; ˌɪnsəˋvɪlətɪ/ *n* (*fml* 文) **1** [U] lack of politeness 无礼貌. Cf 参看 UNCIVIL. **2** [C] impolite act or remark 无礼的言行.

incl *abbr* 缩写 = including; inclusive: *total £29.53 incl tax* 连税在内总额 29.53 英镑.

in·clem·ent /ɪnˈklemənt; ɪnˋklɛmənt/ *adj* (*fml* 文) cold and stormy; bad 严寒的; 狂风暴雨的; 恶劣的: *inclement weather* 恶劣的天气. ▷ **in·clem·ency** /-ənsɪ; -ənsɪ/ *n* [U].

in·clina·tion /ˌɪŋklɪˈneɪʃn; ˌɪnkləˋneʃən/ *n* **1** [C, U] **~ (to/for/towards sth); ~ (to do sth)** feeling that makes sb want to behave in a particular way; disposition 倾向; 意向; 意愿: *I have little inclination to listen to you all evening.* 我可不愿意一晚上都听你说话. ○ *She is not free to follow her own inclination in the matter of marriage.* 她的婚姻不能自主. **2** [C] **~ to sth; ~ to be/do sth** event that regularly happens; tendency 经常发生的事; 趋向; 趋势: *He has an inclination to stoutness/to be fat.* 他有发福[发胖]的趋势. ○ *The car has an inclination to stall on cold mornings.* 这辆汽车天冷时早晨常常熄火. **3** (**a**) [U] degree of sloping; slant 倾斜度; 坡度; 倾斜. (**b**) [C] sloping surface; slope 坡面; 斜面; 斜坡: *a small inclination just beyond the trees* 就在树丛那边的一片小坡地. **4** [C usu *sing* 通常作单数] bending or bowing movement 弯曲的动作; 弯腰: *an inclination of his head* 他点了点头.

in·cline¹ /ɪnˈklaɪn; ɪnˋklaɪn/ *v* **1** [Ipr] **~ towards sth** lean or slope in the direction of sth 向某物的方向倾斜: *The land inclines towards the shore.* 地面向海岸倾斜. **2** [Tn] bend (usu a part of the body) forward 向前弯(通常为身体局部); 弯腰; 点头: *She inclined her head in prayer.* 她低下头祈祷. **3** (*fml* 文) (**a**) [Tn·pr, Cnt] **~ sb towards sth** persuade sb to do sth; cause a certain tendency in sb; influence sb 说服某人做某事; 使某人有某倾向; 对某人施加影响: *His love of languages inclined him towards a career as a translator.* 他对语言的热爱促使他从事翻译工作. ○ *His sincerity inclines me to trust him.* 他很真诚, 不由得我不信任他. (**b**) [Ipr] **~ to/towards sth** have a physical or mental tendency towards sth (身体上或思想上)有某种倾向; 倾向于; 易于: *He inclines to laziness.* 他爱偷懒. ○ *She inclines towards depression.* 她动不动就情绪低落.

▷ **in·clined** *adj* [pred 作表语] **1 ~ (to do sth)** wanting to behave in a particular way; disposed 想以某种方式行事; 准备做某事: *I'm inclined to trust him.* 我比较信任他. ○ *We can go for a walk, if you feel so inclined.* 你要是愿意的话, 咱们去散散步吧. **2 ~ to do sth** having a tendency to be/do sth; likely to be/do sth 有某种倾向; 很有可能做某事: *He's inclined to be lazy.* 他爱偷懒. ○ *The car is inclined to stall when it's cold outside.* 这辆汽车天冷时爱熄火. **3 ~ to do sth** (used to make what is said sound less strong) holding a particular opinion (用以使语气和缓)持某种意见: *I'm inclined to believe he's innocent.* 我颇以为他是无辜的. ○ *Generally speaking, I'm inclined to agree with you.* 总的说来, 我比较同意你的意见. **4** having a natural ability in a specified subject 有某方面的天赋: *Louise is very musically inclined.* 路易丝很有音乐天赋.

□ **inˌclined ˈplane** plane whose angle to the horizontal is less than 90° 斜面(与水平面构成小于 90° 夹角的平面).

in·cline² /ˈɪŋklaɪn; ˋɪnklaɪn/ *n* sloping surface; slope 斜面; 斜坡: *a gentle/steep incline* 缓的[陡的]斜坡.

in·close = ENCLOSE.

in·clos·ure = ENCLOSURE.

in·clude /ɪnˈklu:d; ɪnˋklud/ *v* **1** [Tn, Tg] have (sb/sth) as part of a whole 包括, 包含(某人[某事物]): *The conference delegates included representatives from abroad.* 大会代表中有来自海外的代表. ○ *The tour included a visit to the Science Museum.* 旅游项目中包括参观科学博物馆. ○ *Does the price include VAT?* 这价钱是否已包括增值税在内? ○ *Your duties include checking the post and distributing it.* 你的职责是检查和发送邮件. **2** [Tn, Tn·pr] **~ sb/sth (in/among sth)** make sb/sth part of a larger group or set 使(某人[某事物])成为整体中的一部分: *include an article (in a newspaper)* (在报纸上)登一篇文章 ○ *We all went, me/myself included,* ie I was among those who went. 大家都去了, 我也在内. ○ *Detailed instructions are included in the booklet.* 小册子中有详细说明.

▷ **in·clud·ing** /ɪnˈklu:dɪŋ; ɪnˋkludɪŋ/ *prep* having (sb/sth) as a part 包括(某人[某事物])在内: *£57.50, including postage and packing* 57.50 英镑, 包括邮费及包装费在内 ○ *The band played many songs, including some of my favourites.* 乐队演奏了许多歌曲, 包括几首我最喜爱的. ○ *Sales up to and including last month amounted to £10 000.* 销售额至上月底为止达 10 000 英镑.

in·clu·sion /ɪnˈklu:ʒn; ɪnˋkluʒən/ *n* [U] **~ (in sth)** including or being included 包括; 包含: *the inclusion of the clause in the contract* 合同中该条款包括在内.

in·clus·ive /ɪnˈklu:sɪv; ɪnˋklusɪv/ *adj* **1 ~ (of sth)** including sth; including much or all 包括或包含某事物的; 包括许多或全部的: *The price is £800, inclusive of tax.* 价格 800 英镑, 连税在内. ○ *inclusive terms*, ie with no extra charges, eg at a hotel 一应费用(一切包括在内, 不再额外收费, 如旅馆中的). **2** (following *ns* 置于名词之后) including the limits stated 包括所述的限度: *from Monday to Friday inclusive* 从星期一至星期五, 共五日 ○ *pages 7 to 26 inclusive* 7-26 页, 包括第 7 页及第 26 页. ▷ **in·clus·ively** *adv*.

in·cog·nito /ˌɪŋkɒɡˈni:təʊ; *US* ɪŋˈkɒɡnətəʊ; ɪnˋkɑgnɪˌto/ *adj* [pred 作表语], *adv* with one's true identity hidden; in disguise 隐瞒个人真实身分; 伪装: *He didn't want to be recognized, so he travelled incognito.* 他不想被人认出, 所以出行时隐瞒身分.

▷ **in·cog·nito** *n* (*pl* **~s**) pretended identity 假身分.

in·co·her·ent /ˌɪŋkəʊˈhɪərənt; ˌɪnkoˋhɪrənt/ *adj* **1** not clear or logical 不清楚的; 不合逻辑的: *an incoherent explanation* 不合逻辑的解释. **2** not expressed clearly 表达不清的: *talk incoherent gibberish* 语无伦次地胡扯. ▷ **in·co·her·ence** /-əns; -əns/ *n* [U]. **in·co·her·ently** *adv*. Cf 参看 COHERENT (COHERE).

in·com·bust·ible /ˌɪŋkəmˈbʌstəbl; ˌɪnkəmˋbʌstəbl̩/ *adj* (*fml* 文) that cannot be burnt 不能燃烧的.

in·come /ˈɪŋkʌm; ˋɪnˌkʌm/ *n* [C, U] money received over a certain period, esp as payment for work or as interest on investments 收入(某一段时间所得，尤指工作报酬或投资收益): *a family with two incomes*, eg when the husband and wife both do paid work 有双份收入的家庭(如夫妻皆工作) ○ *Tax is payable on all income over £2 000.* 收入超过2 000英镑者征收所得税. ○ *high/low income groups* 高[低]收入阶层 ○ *a useful source of income for the charity* 用作慈善事业的能解决问题的收入来源.

□ ˈ**income tax** tax payable according to the level of one's income 所得税: *reduce the standard rate of income tax* 降低所得税的标准税率. Cf 参看 CAPITAL LEVY (CAPITAL²).

NOTE ON USAGE 用法: **1 Income** is the most general word for money we receive from work, investments, etc. 用以指从工作、投资等所得的钱, **income**是最通用词. It can be **earned** or **unearned income.** 这个词可指挣来的收入, 也可指并非挣来的收入. **2 Pay** is a general word for money we regularly receive from an employer for work done. ☆ **pay**一般用以指雇主定期付给的工资. **Pay-day** is the day of the week/month when this money is received. ☆ **pay-day** 指每星期[每月]领取工资的日子. **3 Wages** are paid weekly (sometimes daily) and usually in cash. ☆ **wages** 按星期(有时按日)发放, 通常为现款. They are based on an hourly, daily or weekly rate or on a certain amount of work done. ☆ **wages**按小时、日、星期计算或按完成一定的工作量计算. **Wage-earners** are usually manual workers ☆ **wage-earners**通常指体力劳动者: *A postman's wages are £180 per week.* 邮递员的工资为每周180英镑. **4** A **salary** is paid monthly, often directly into a bank account. ☆ **salary**按月支付, 常直接拨入领取者的银行帐户内. The amount of **salary** received is quoted at a yearly rate ☆ **salary**的收入, 是指一年的收入: *a salary of £12 000 a year/per annum* 每年12 000英镑的薪水. Professional people and those who work in offices receive a **salary** 专业人员和在办公室工作的人员领取**salary**: *The company is offering a salary of £20 000 per annum.* 这家公司招聘职员, 年薪为20 000英镑. **5** A **fee** is a payment to a lawyer, doctor, etc for professional services ☆ **fee**是付给律师、医生等的报酬: *I thought the accountant's fee rather high.* 我认为那个会计师收费很高.

in·com·ing /ˈɪnkʌmɪŋ; ˈɪn,kʌmɪŋ/ *adj* [attrib 作定语] **1** coming in 正来临的: *the incoming tide* 涨潮 ○ *incoming* (ie enemy) *artillery fire* (敌人)发射来的炮火 ○ *incoming telephone calls* 打进来的电话 ○ *incoming passengers* 来到的旅客. **2** recently elected or appointed; new or succeeding 新选的; 新任的; 新来的; 继任的: *the incoming president* 新任总裁.

in·com·men·sur·able /ˌɪŋkəˈmenʃərəbl; ˌɪnkəˈmenʃərəbl/ *adj* [usu pred 通常作表语] (also **in·com·men·sur·ate**) **~ (with sb/sth)** (*fml* 文) that cannot be judged or measured by the same standard (as sb/sth) (与某人[某事物])不能用同一标准鉴定或衡量.

in·com·men·sur·ate /ˌɪŋkəˈmenʃərət; ˌɪnkəˈmɛnʃərət/ *adj* [usu pred 通常作表语] (*fml* 文) **1 ~ (to/with sth)** not in proportion to sth; inadequate 不相称; 不成比例; 不足: *His abilities are incommensurate to the task.* 他的能力和他担负的任务不相称. **2** = INCOMMENSURABLE.

in·com·mode /ˌɪŋkəˈməʊd; ˌɪnkəˈmod/ *v* [Tn] (*fml* 文) inconvenience or trouble (sb) 给(某人)带来不便; 打扰(某人).

▷ **in·com·mo·di·ous** /ˌɪŋkəˈməʊdɪəs; ˌɪnkəˈmodɪəs/ *adj* (*fml* 文) uncomfortable, usu because too small; inconvenient 不舒适的(通常因过小); 不方便的. **in·com·mo·di·ously** *adv*.

in·com·mu·nic·able /ˌɪŋkəˈmju:nɪkəbl; ˌɪnkəˈmjunɪkəbl/ *adj* that cannot be communicated 不能传达的; 不可交流的.

in·com·mu·nic·ado /ˌɪŋkəˌmju:nɪˈkɑ:dəʊ; ˌɪnkəˌmjunɪˈkɑdo/ *adj* [pred 作表语], *adv* without being allowed to communicate with other people 不许可与他人接触: *The prisoner was held incommunicado.* 那监犯被禁不得与他人接触.

in·com·par·able /ɪnˈkɒmprəbl; ɪnˈkɑmprəbl/ *adj* too good, great, etc to have an equal; beyond comparison 无比的; 无双的; 不可比拟的: *incomparable singing, hospitality, food* 无与伦比的歌唱、殷勤招待、食物. ▷ **in·com·par·ab·il·ity** /ɪnˌkɒmpərəˈbɪlətɪ; ɪnˌkɑmpərəˈbɪlətɪ/ *n* [U]. **in·com·par·ably** /ɪnˈkɒmprəblɪ; ɪnˈkɑmprəblɪ/ *adv*.

in·com·patible /ˌɪŋkəmˈpætəbl; ˌɪnkəmˈpætəbl/ *adj* **1 ~ (with sb)** not able to live or work happily with sb (与某人)不能和谐相处的, 合不来的: *temperamentally, sexually, socially incompatible* 脾气不相投、性生活不和谐、社交上合不来 ○ *I've never seen such an incompatible couple.* 我从来没有见过这么不般配的一对儿. **2 ~ (with sth)** not consistent or in logical agreement with sth (与某物)不一致的, 不相符的, 不相配的: *behaviour that is totally incompatible with the aims of the society* 与社团目标完全背道而驰的行为. ▷ **in·com·pat·ib·il·ity** /ˌɪŋkəmˌpætəˈbɪlətɪ; ˌɪnkəmˌpætəˈbɪlətɪ/ *n* [U, C].

in·com·pet·ent /ɪnˈkɒmpɪtənt; ɪnˈkɑmpətənt/ *adj* **1** not having or showing the necessary skills to do sth successfully 不胜任的; 不称职的: *I suppose my application has been lost by some incompetent bureaucrat.* 我估计我的申请书不知道让哪个无能的官僚给弄丢了. ○ *criticized for his incompetent handling of the problem* 他因处理该问题无能而受到批评. **2** not (esp legally) qualified 无资格的(尤指法律方面): *incompetent to judge* 无资格作裁决.

▷ **in·com·pet·ence** /-əns; -əns/ *n* [U] lack of skill or ability to do a task successfully 不胜任; 不称职: *He was dismissed for incompetence.* 他因不称职而遭辞退.

in·com·pet·ent *n* incompetent person 不能胜任的人; 不称职的人.

in·com·pet·ently *adv*.

in·com·plete /ˌɪŋkəmˈpli:t; ˌɪnkəmˈplit/ *adj* not having all its parts; not complete 不完全的; 不完整的; 不完备的: *an incomplete set of results* 一组不完整的答数. ▷ **in·com·pletely** *adv*. **in·com·plete·ness** *n* [U].

in·com·pre·hens·ible /ɪnˌkɒmprɪˈhensəbl; ˌɪnkɑmprɪˈhɛnsəbl/ *adj* that cannot be understood; not comprehensible 无法理解的; 难于领悟的: *technical expressions that are incomprehensible to ordinary people* 普通人难以理解的技术用语. ▷ **in·com·pre·hens·ib·il·ity** /ɪnˌkɒmprɪˌhensəˈbɪlətɪ; ˌɪnkɑmprɪˌhɛnsəˈbɪlətɪ/ *n* [U]. **in·com·pre·hens·ibly** /-səblɪ; -səblɪ/ *adv*.

in·com·pre·hen·sion /ɪnˌkɒmprɪˈhenʃn; ˌɪnkɑmprɪˈhɛnʃən/ *n* [U] failure to understand sth 不理解; 不领悟: *Her explanations were met with blank incomprehension.* 大家对她的解释茫然不解.

in·com·press·ible /ˌɪŋkəmˈpresəbl; ˌɪnkəmˈprɛsəbl/ *adj* that cannot be compressed; unyielding 不可压缩的; 不屈的: *incompressible gases/liquids* 不可压缩的气体[液体].

in·con·ceiv·able /ˌɪŋkənˈsi:vəbl; ˌɪnkənˈsivəbl/ *adj* **1** (*infml* 口) very difficult to believe 难以置信的: *It seems inconceivable that the accident could have happened so quickly.* 这一事故发生得这么快, 简直不可思议. **2** that cannot be imagined; not conceivable 不可想像的; 匪夷所思的: *the inconceivable vastness of space* 宇宙难以想像的广漠.

▷ **in·con·ceiv·ably** *adv* in a way that is very difficult to believe or understand 难以置信地; 不可思议地: *The task proved inconceivably more difficult than we had imagined.* 任务的困难程度超过我们的想像, 确实难以置信.

in·con·clus·ive /ˌɪŋkənˈklu:sɪv; ˌɪnkənˈklusɪv/ *adj* not leading to a definite decision, conclusion or result 非决定性的; 非结论性的; 无结果的: *inconclusive arguments, discussions, evidence, etc* 无结果的辩论、非决定性的讨论、无效的证据. ▷ **in·con·clus·ively** *adv*. **in·con·clus·ive·ness** *n* [U].

in·con·gru·ous /ɪnˈkɒŋgrʊəs; ɪnˈkɑŋgrʊəs/ *adj* strange because not in harmony with the surrounding features; out of place 不协调的; 不和谐的; 不一致的: *slow traditional methods that seem rather incongruous in this modern technical age* 与当今技术时代相比显得格格不入的缓慢的传统方法.

▷ **in·con·gru·ity** /ˌɪŋkɒŋˈgru:ətɪ; ˌɪnkɑŋˈgruətɪ/ *n* **1** [U] state of being incongruous 不协调; 不和谐; 不一致: *the apparent incongruity of a scientist having a simple religious faith* 身为科学家而有单纯的宗教信仰那种明显的不协调. **2** [C] something that is incongruous 不协调的或不一致的事物.

in·con·gru·ously *adv*.

in·con·sequent /ɪnˈkɒnsɪkwənt; ɪnˈkɑnsəˌkwɛnt/ *adj* **1** not following logically 不合逻辑的; 不连贯的. **2** = INCONSEQUENTIAL. ▷ **in·con·sequence** /ɪnˈkɒnsɪkwəns; ɪnˈkɑnsəˌkwɛns/ *n* [U]. **in·con·sequently** *adv*.

in·con·sequen·tial /ɪnˌkɒnsɪˈkwenʃl; ˌɪnkɑnsəˈkwɛnʃəl/ *adj* (also **in·con·sequent**) trivial or irrelevant; not important 琐细的; 不相干的; 不重要的: *inconsequential details, events, questions* 琐碎的细节、事情、问题. ▷ **in·con·sequen·tially** /-ʃəlɪ; -ʃəlɪ/ *adv*.

in·con·sid·er·able /ˌɪŋkənˈsɪdrəbl; ˌɪnkənˈsɪdrəbl̩/ *adj* small in size or value; not worth considering 微小的; 价值低的; 不值得考虑的: *a not inconsiderable sum of money*, ie a large sum of money 数额不小的一笔钱.

in·con·sid·er·ate /ˌɪŋkənˈsɪdərət; ˌɪnkənˈsɪdərɪt/ *adj* not caring about the feelings of other people; thoughtless; not considerate 不体贴别人的; 不替别人着想的; 考虑不周的: *How could you have been so inconsiderate?* 你怎么能这样不顾别人呢? ○ *inconsiderate behaviour, remarks* 欠考虑的举动、言语. ▷ **in·con·sid·er·ately** *adv*. **in·con·sid·er·ate·ness** *n* [U].

in·con·sist·ent /ˌɪŋkənˈsɪstənt; ˌɪnkənˈsɪstənt/ *adj* **1** [usu pred 通常作表语] **~ (with sth)** not in harmony (with sth); containing parts that do not agree with one another 不和谐; 不一致; 不协调: *Such behaviour is inconsistent with her high-minded principles.* 这样的行为与她情操高尚的原则是格格不入的. ○ *His account of the events was inconsistent.* 他对那些事情的说法前后矛盾. **2** not staying the same; changeable 反复无常的; 易变的: *He is inconsistent in his loyalty: sometimes he supports us, sometimes he's against us.* 他并非一贯忠心耿耿, 有时支持我们, 有时反对我们.

▷ **in·con·sist·ency** /-ənsɪ; -ənsɪ/ *n* (**a**) [U] quality of being inconsistent 不一致; 不一贯; 前后矛盾; 反复无常: *inconsistency in the standard of his work* 他的工作好坏的前后不一. (**b**) [C] instance of this 不一致; 不一贯; 前后矛盾; 反复无常: *She noticed several minor inconsistencies in his argument.* 她觉察到他的论点有几处略微有些自相矛盾.

in·con·sist·ently *adv*.

in·con·sol·able /ˌɪŋkənˈsəʊləbl; ˌɪnkənˈsoləbl̩/ *adj* that cannot be comforted 不能安慰的; 无法慰藉的: *inconsolable grief* 无法抚慰的悲伤 ○ *The children were inconsolable when their father died.* 这些孩子因丧父而悲伤不已. ▷ **in·con·sol·ably** /-əblɪ; -əblɪ/ *adv*: *weep inconsolably* 伤心欲绝地哭泣.

in·con·spicu·ous /ˌɪŋkənˈspɪkjʊəs; ˌɪnkənˈspɪkjuəs/ *adj* not very noticeable or obvious; not conspicuous 不引人注目的; 不显眼的; 不显著的: *a small inconspicuous crack in the vase* 花瓶上一道不明显的小裂纹 ○ *The newcomer tried to make herself as inconspicuous as possible*, ie tried to avoid attention. 那个新来的人极力使她自己不惹人注意. ▷ **in·con·spicu·ously** *adv*. **in·con·spicu·ous·ness** *n* [U].

in·con·stant /ɪnˈkɒnstənt; ɪnˈkɑnstənt/ *adj* (*fml* 文) **1** (of people) having feelings and intentions that change often; not faithful (指人)反复无常的, 不忠的: *an inconstant lover* 爱情不专的人. **2** having a quantity or value that changes; not fixed (数量或价值)有变化的, 不固定的. ▷ **in·con·stancy** /-ənsɪ; -ənsɪ/ *n* [U, C].

in·con·test·able /ˌɪŋkənˈtestəbl; ˌɪnkənˈtɛstəbl̩/ *adj* that cannot be disputed or disagreed with 无可争辩的; 不能不同意的: *an incontestable fact* 无可争辩的事实. ▷ **in·con·test·ably** /-əblɪ; -əblɪ/ *adv*.

in·con·tin·ent /ɪnˈkɒntɪnənt; ɪnˈkɑntənənt/ *adj* **1** unable to control the bladder or bowels in passing waste matter from the body 失禁的: *People often become incontinent when they get very old.* 人老了就往往有内急失禁现象. **2** lacking self-control, esp in sexual matters 缺乏自制力的(尤指性方面). ▷ **in·con·tin·ence** /-əns; -əns/ *n* [U].

in·con·tro·vert·ible /ˌɪŋkɒntrəˈvɜːtəbl; ˌɪnkɑntrəˈvɝtəbl̩/ *adj* so obvious and certain that it cannot be disputed or denied 无可辩驳的; 不容否认的: *incontrovertible evidence* 确凿无疑的证据. ▷ **in·con·tro·vert·ib·il·ity** /ɪnˌkɒntrəvɜːtəˈbɪlətɪ; ˌɪnkɑntrəˌvɝtəˈbɪlətɪ/ *n* [U]. **in·con·tro·vert·ibly** /ˌɪŋkɒntrəˈvɜːtəblɪ; ˌɪnkɑntrəˈvɝtəblɪ/ *adv*: *incontrovertibly true* 千真万确.

in·con·veni·ence /ˌɪŋkənˈviːnɪəns; ˌɪnkənˈvinjəns/ *n* (**a**) [U] trouble, difficulty or discomfort 不方便; 麻烦; 打扰; 困难; 不适: *He apologized for the inconvenience he had caused.* 他为打扰了人家而道歉. ○ *put sb to, suffer great inconvenience* 给某人带来、遇到极大的不便. (**b**) [C] person or thing that causes inconvenience 造成不便的人或事物: *Having to change trains is a small inconvenience.* 换乘火车多少有些不便. ○ *put up with slight inconveniences* 忍受些少不便.

▷ **in·con·veni·ence** *v* [Tn] cause inconvenience to (sb/sth) 给(某人[某事物])带来不便; 麻烦; 打扰: *The companies were greatly inconvenienced by the postal delays.* 邮件延误给这些公司造成极大不便.

in·con·veni·ent /ˌɪŋkənˈviːnɪənt; ˌɪnkənˈvinjənt/ *adj* causing trouble, difficulty or discomfort; awkward 不方便的; 打扰的; 造成困难的; 让人不舒服的; 为难的: *They arrived at an inconvenient time — we had just started the meal.* 他们来得很不是时候——我们刚开始吃饭. ○ *Living such a long way from the shops can be very inconvenient.* 住得离商店这么远有时候非常不便. ▷ **in·con·veni·ently** *adv*.

in·corp·or·ate /ɪnˈkɔːpəreɪt; ɪnˈkɔrpəˌret/ *v* **1** (**a**) [Tn, Tn·pr] **~ sth (in/into sth)** make sth part of a whole; include 将某事物包括进去; 包含: *Many of your suggestions have been incorporated in the new plan.* 你的建议多已纳入新计划中. (**b**) [Tn] have (sth) as part of a whole 将(某事物)作为整体的一部分; 合并: *The new car design incorporates all the latest safety features.* 汽车的新设计具备最新安全措施的一切特点. **2** [Tn] (*US*) form a legal corporation(2b) 组成公司: *We had to incorporate the company for tax reasons.* 鉴于税务原因, 我们得组成公司. ○ *a company incorporated in the USA* 在美国组建的公司.

▷ **in·corp·or·ate** /ɪnˈkɔːpərət; ɪnˈkɔrpərɪt/ *adj* formed into a corporation; incorporated 合成一体的; 组成公司的.

in·corp·or·ated /ɪnˈkɔːpəreɪtɪd; ɪnˈkɔrpəˌretɪd/ *adj* (*US*) (*abbr* 缩写 **Inc**) (following the name of a company 置于公司名称之后) formed into a legal organization 组成法人组织的: *Nelson Inc* 纳尔逊公司.

in·corp·ora·tion /ɪnˌkɔːpəˈreɪʃn; ɪnˌkɔrpəˈreʃən/ *n* [U] incorporating or being incorporated 包含; 合并; 组成公司.

in·cor·por·eal /ˌɪŋkɔːˈpɔːrɪəl; ˌɪnkɔrˈpɔrɪəl/ *adj* (*fml* 文) without a body or material form 非实体的; 无形体的.

in·cor·rect /ˌɪŋkəˈrekt; ˌɪnkəˈrɛkt/ *adj* **1** not correct or true 不正确的; 错误的; 不真实的: *an incorrect answer* 不正确的答案 ○ *incorrect conclusions* 错误的结论. **2** not according to accepted standards; improper 不合公认准则的; 不正当的: *incorrect behaviour* 不端的行为. ▷ **in·cor·rectly** *adv*: *answer incorrectly* 回答得不正确. **in·cor·rect·ness** *n* [U].

in·cor·ri·gible /ɪnˈkɒrɪdʒəbl; *US* -ˈkɔːr-; ɪnˈkɔrɪdʒəbl̩/ *adj* (of people or their faults) that cannot be corrected or improved (指人或毛病)无法改好的, 不可救药的, 难以矫正的: *an incorrigible liar, gambler, gossip, etc* 不可救药的撒谎的人、赌徒、是非小人等 ○ *incorrigible habits* 难改的积习. ▷ **in·corri·gib·il·ity** /ɪnˌkɒrɪdʒəˈbɪlətɪ; ɪnˌkɔrɪdʒəˈbɪlətɪ/ *n* [U]. **in·cor·ri·gibly** /ɪnˈkɒrɪdʒəblɪ; ɪnˈkɔrɪdʒəblɪ/ *adv*.

in·cor·rupt·ible /ˌɪŋkəˈrʌptəbl; ˌɪnkəˈrʌptəbl̩/ *adj* **1** unable to be corrupted morally, eg with bribes (道德上)不受腐蚀的(如不受贿): *Judges should be incorruptible.* 法官应当廉洁. **2** that cannot decay or be destroyed 不腐的; 不可摧毁的. ▷ **in·cor·rupt·ib·il·ity** /ˌɪŋkəˌrʌptəˈbɪlətɪ; ˌɪnkəˌrʌptəˈbɪlətɪ/ *n* [U]. **in·cor·rupt·ibly** /ˌɪŋkəˈrʌptəblɪ; ˌɪnkəˈrʌptəblɪ/ *adv*.

in·crease[1] /ɪnˈkriːs; ɪnˈkris/ *v* [I, Ipr, Tn, Tn·pr] **~ (sth) (from A) (to B)** become or make (sth) greater in number, quantity, size, etc 增加, 增大(数目、数量、体积等): *The population has increased from 1.2 million 10 years ago to 1.8 million now.* 人口从10年前的120万已增加到现在的180万. ○ *The rate of inflation has increased by 2%.* 通货膨胀率已增长了2%. ○ *increased profits* 增加的利润 ○ *He increased his speed to overtake the lorry.* 他加大速度以超过前面的货车.

▷ **in·creas·ingly** /ɪnˈkriːsɪŋlɪ; ɪnˈkrisɪŋlɪ/ *adv* more and more 越来越多地; 逐渐增加地: *increasingly difficult, important, popular* 日益困难的、重要的、普及的 ○ *Increasingly, people are realizing that our basic problems are not economic ones.* 人们越来越认识到我们的根本

I

问题并非经济问题.

in·crease[2] /ˈɪŋkriːs; ˋɪnkris/ *n* **1** [C, U] **~ (in sth)** amount by which sth increases 增加的量: *Greater spending on education is expected to lead to a large increase in the number of students.* 希望在教育上多投资以期多收学生. ○ *an increase of nearly 50% over/on last year* 比去年增加近50% ○ *a wage increase* 工资增加额 ○ *Some increase in working hours may soon be needed.* 也许不久需将工时延长一些. **2** (idm 习语) **on the ˈincrease** (*infml* 口) increasing 正在增长: *The number of burglaries in the area seems to be on the increase.* 这一地区的入室盗窃案件似有增无已.

in·cred·ible /ɪnˈkredəbl; ɪnˋkrɛdəbḷ/ *adj* **1** impossible to believe 不可相信的: *What an incredible story!* 这件事真不可相信! **2** (*infml* 口) difficult to believe; amazing or fantastic 难以置信的; 不可思议的; 惊人的; 奇异的: *He earns an incredible amount of money.* 他挣钱多得惊人. ○ *We had an incredible* (ie extremely good) *holiday!* 我们度过了一个极愉快的假日. ○ *She's an incredible actress.* 她是个了不起的演员.

▷ **in·cred·ib·il·ity** /ɪnˌkredəˈbɪlətɪ; ˌɪnkrɛdəˋbɪlətɪ/ *n* [U].

in·cred·ibly /ɪnˈkredəblɪ; ɪnˋkrɛdəblɪ/ *adv* **1** to a great degree; extremely or unusually 非常地; 极端地; 异乎寻常地: *incredibly hot weather* 极热的天气. **2** in a way that is difficult to believe; amazingly 难以置信地; 惊人地: *Incredibly, no one had ever thought of such a simple idea before.* 真是难以相信, 这样简单的主意竟没有人想到过.

in·credu·lous /ɪnˈkredjʊləs; *US* -dʒuːl-; ɪnˋkrɛdʒələs/ *adj* not willing or able to believe; showing disbelief 不肯轻信的; 不能相信的; 表示怀疑的: *an incredulous look, stare, gaze, etc* 怀疑的神情、注视、逼视等. ▷ **in·credu·lity** /ˌɪŋkrɪˈdjuːlətɪ; *US* -ˈduː-; ˌɪnkrəˋdulətɪ/ *n* [U]: *an expression of shock and utter incredulity* 愕然而十分怀疑的神情. **in·credu·lously** *adv*.

in·cre·ment /ˈɪŋkrəmənt; ˋɪnkrəmənt/ *n* increase, esp in money paid as a salary; added amount 增加; 增长; (尤指)加薪; 增加量: *Your salary will be £12 000 a year, with annual increments of £500.* 你的年薪为12 000英镑, 每年增加500英镑. ▷ **in·cre·mental** /ˌɪŋkrəˈmentl; ˌɪnkrəˋmɛntḷ/ *adj*: *incremental increases* 递增的量. **in·cre·ment·ally** /-təlɪ; -təlɪ/ *adv*.

in·crim·in·ate /ɪnˈkrɪmɪneɪt; ɪnˋkrɪməˌnet/ *v* [Tn] make (sb) appear to be guilty of wrongdoing 使(某人)显得有罪: *She refused to make a statement to the police in case she incriminated herself.* 她拒绝向警方作陈述以免受连累. ○ *incriminating evidence* 可显示有罪的证据.

▷ **in·crim·ina·tion** /ɪnˌkrɪmɪˈneɪʃn; ɪnˌkrɪməˋneʃən/ *n* [U].

in·crim·in·at·ory /ɪnˈkrɪmɪnətrɪ, -neɪtərɪ; ɪnˋkrɪmənəˌtorɪ/ *adj* tending to incriminate sb 可显示某人有罪的.

in·crusta·tion /ˌɪnkrʌˈsteɪʃn; ˌɪnkrʌsˋteʃən/ *n* **1** [U] formation of a hard outer covering; encrusting 结皮; 形成硬壳. **2** [C] hard outer covering or layer, esp one that forms gradually 硬壳, 外层(尤指逐渐形成的): *incrustations of barnacles on the hull* 藤壶附在船身上形成坚硬的外层.

in·cub·ate /ˈɪŋkjʊbeɪt; ˋɪŋkjəˌbet/ *v* **1** (**a**) [I, Tn] keep (eggs) warm, usu by sitting on them, until they hatch 孵(卵); 孵化: *a bird incubating (her eggs)* 正在孵卵的鸟. (**b**) [I] (of eggs) be kept warm until ready to hatch (指卵)孵化. **2** [I, Tn] (*medical or biology* 医或生) (of bacteria, etc) develop under favourable conditions, esp heat; cause (bacteria, etc) to develop (指细菌等)培养; 使(细菌等)繁殖: *Some viruses incubate very rapidly.* 有些病毒繁殖得很迅速. ○ *incubate germs in a laboratory* 在实验室中培养细菌. **3** [I, Tn] (*fig* 比喻) (cause sth to) develop slowly and patiently (使某事物)逐渐发展, 酝酿: *plans for revolution that had long been incubating in their minds* 他们心中酝酿已久的革命计划.

▷ **in·cuba·tion** /ˌɪŋkjʊˈbeɪʃn; ˌɪnkjəˋbeʃən/ *n* **1** [U] hatching (of eggs) 孵卵; 孵化: *artificial incubation*, ie hatching by artificial warmth 人工孵化. **2** [C] (also **incuˈbation period**) (**a**) (*medical* 医) period between being infected with a disease and the appearance of the first symptoms (传染病的)潜伏期. (**b**) (*fig* 比喻) (period for) developing plans, etc (计划等的)酝酿(期).

in·cub·ator /ˈɪŋkjʊbeɪtə(r); ˋɪŋkjəˌbetɚ/ *n* boxlike apparatus for hatching eggs by artificial warmth or for rearing small, weak babies (esp those born prematurely) 孵化器; 恒温育婴箱(尤指培育早产婴儿的). Cf 参看 HATCHERY (HATCH[2]).

in·cubus /ˈɪŋkjʊbəs; ˋɪŋkjəbəs/ *n* (*pl* **~es** or **-bi** /-baɪ; -ˌbaɪ/) (**a**) male evil spirit formerly supposed to have sex with a sleeping woman 梦淫妖(传说与熟睡女子交合的妖魔). Cf 参看 SUCCUBUS. (**b**) (*rhet* 修辞) thing (eg an approaching examination, an unpaid debt) that oppresses sb like a nightmare 给某人造成巨大压力的事物(似恶梦中所见的可怕事物, 如临近的考试、未清偿的债务).

in·cul·cate /ˈɪnkʌlkeɪt; *US* ɪnˈkʌl-; ɪnˋkʌlket/ *v* [Tn, Tn·pr] **~ sth (in/into sb)**; **~ sb with sth** (*fml* 文) fix (ideas, principles, etc) firmly in sb's mind, esp by repetition 向某人灌输(思想、原则等)(尤指反复地): *inculcate in young people a respect for the law* 向年轻人灌输尊重法制的思想 ○ *inculcate young people with a respect for the law* 用尊重法制的思想反复教育年轻人.

in·cum·bent /ɪnˈkʌmbənt; ɪnˋkʌmbənt/ *adj* **1** [pred 作表语] **~ on/upon sb** (*fml* 文) necessary as part of sb's duty 有责任; 有义务; 必须履行: *It is incumbent upon all users of this equipment to familiarize themselves with the safety procedure.* 凡使用这种设备的人都应熟悉安全程序. **2** [usu attrib 通常作定语] holding the specified official position; current 现任的; 在职的: *the incumbent president* 现任总裁.

▷ **in·cum·bent** *n* person holding an official position, esp in the church 现任者, 在职者(尤指神职): *the present incumbent of the White House*, ie the US President 现任美国总统. **in·cum·bency** /-ənsɪ; -ənsɪ/ *n* position of an incumbent 现任职位.

incur /ɪnˈkɜː(r); ɪnˋkɝ/ *v* (**-rr-**) [Tn] cause oneself to suffer (sth bad); bring upon oneself 遭受; 蒙受; 招致; 引起; 带来: *incur debts, great expense, sb's anger* 负上债、须付巨额费用、惹某人生气.

in·cur·able /ɪnˈkjʊərəbl; ɪnˋkjʊrəbḷ/ *adj* that cannot be cured 不能治愈的; 无可救药的; 不可矫正的: *incurable diseases, habits* 不治之症、无法矫正的习惯.

▷ **in·cur·able** *n* person with an incurable disease 患不治之症的人: *a home for incurables* 绝症病人收容所.

in·cur·ably /-əblɪ; -əblɪ/ *adv*: *incurably ill, stupid, optimistic* 病重得、愚蠢得、乐观得到头了.

in·curi·ous /ɪnˈkjʊərɪəs; ɪnˋkjʊrɪəs/ *adj* (*fml* 文) having no curiosity; not inquisitive 无好奇心的; 不追根究底的.

in·cur·sion /ɪnˈkɜːʃn; *US* -ʒn; ɪnˋkɝʒən/ *n* (*fml* 文) **~ (into/on/upon sth)** **1** sudden attack on or invasion of a place (not usu made in order to occupy it permanently) (对某地的)袭击, 侵犯(通常指非永久性的侵占): *repel a sudden incursion of enemy troops (into/on one's territory)* 击退敌军(对领土)的突然入侵. **2** (*fig* 比喻) inconvenient interruption of sb's time, privacy, etc; intrusion (对某人的时间、私生活等的)扰乱, 打扰: *I resent these incursions into/upon my leisure time.* 屡次侵占我的闲暇时间, 我很反感.

in·curved /ˌɪnˈkɜːvd; ɪnˋkɝvd/ *adj* curved inwards; bent into a curve 向内弯曲的; 弯成曲线的.

Ind *abbr* 缩写 = (*politics* 政) Independent (candidate) 独立的(候选人): *Tom Lee (Ind)* 汤姆·李(独立候选人).

in·debted /ɪnˈdetɪd; ɪnˋdɛtɪd/ *adj* **~ to sb (for sth)** owing money or gratitude to sb 负债的; 感激的; 欠情的: *be (deeply, greatly, etc) indebted to sb for his help, advice, encouragement, etc* (深深地、非常地等)感激某人的帮助、建议、鼓励等. ▷ **in·debted·ness** *n* [U].

in·de·cent /ɪnˈdiːsnt; ɪnˋdisṇt/ *adj* **1** (of behaviour, talk, etc) offending against accepted standards of decency or morality; obscene (指行为、谈话等)不礼貌的, 粗野的, 下流的, 猥亵的: *That short skirt of hers is positively indecent.* 她那条短裙实在是不雅观. **2** [usu attrib 通常作定语] improper; undue 不合适的; 不适当的: *leave a party in indecent haste*, ie too early or too soon to be polite 在聚会中匆匆离去而失礼. Cf 参看 DECENT.

▷ **in·de·cency** /-nsɪ; -ṇsɪ/ *n* **1** [U] being indecent; indecent behaviour 失礼; 粗鲁; 不体面; 下流; 有伤风化的行为: *arrested by the police for gross indecency*, eg indecent exposure 因猥亵行为遭警方拘留(如猥亵露体). **2** [C] indecent act, gesture, expression, etc 下流的

动作、姿势、表情等.
in·de·cently *adv*.
□ **in,decent ex'posure** crime of showing one's sexual organs in public 猥亵露体(当众裸露性器官的犯罪行为).
in·de·ci·pher·able /ˌɪndɪˈsaɪfrəbl; ˌɪndɪˈsaɪfrəbḷ/ *adj* that cannot be deciphered 不可破译的; 不可辨识的: *an indecipherable code, signature, scribble, etc* 不可破译的密码、难以辨识的签字、潦草莫辨的字迹.
in·de·ci·sion /ˌɪndɪˈsɪʒn; ˌɪndɪˈsɪʒən/ *n* [U] **~ (about sth)** state of being unable to decide; hesitation 优柔寡断; 犹豫不决: *He stood outside the door in an agony of indecision.* 他站在门外, 不知如何是好, 非常难受.
in·de·cis·ive /ˌɪndɪˈsaɪsɪv; ˌɪndɪˈsaɪsɪv/ *adj* (**a**) not final or conclusive 非最终的; 非决定性的: *an indecisive battle, answer, meeting* 非决定性的战斗、答复、会议. (**b**) unable to make decisions; hesitating; uncertain 无能力作决定的; 迟疑不决的; 不肯定的: *He's too indecisive to make a good leader.* 他优柔寡断, 当不了好领导. ▷ **in·de·cis·ively** *adv*.
in·dec·or·ous /ɪnˈdekərəs; ɪnˈdɛkərəs/ *adj* (*fml* 文) not in accordance with dignity, good manners or good taste 不合礼仪的; 失礼的; 不雅观的: *forced to make a hasty and indecorous departure without his trousers* 他被迫离去, 慌忙中未穿裤子十分不雅. ▷ **in·dec·or·ously** *adv*.
in·dec·orum /ˌɪndɪˈkɔːrəm; ˌɪndɪˈkɔrəm/ *n* [U] (*fml* 文) improper or undignified behaviour; lack of decorum 不当的或不礼貌的行为; 不雅的举止.
in·deed /ɪnˈdiːd; ɪnˈdid/ *adv* **1** truly; really; certainly 的确; 实在地; 确实. (**a**) (used to emphasize an affirmative reply 用以强调一肯定答复的语气): *'Did he complain?' 'Indeed he did.'* '他抱怨了吗?' '他当然抱怨了.' ○ *'Do you agree?' 'Yes indeed!'* '你同意了?' '当然同意了!' (**b**) (intensifying an *adj*, an *adv* or a *n* in an exclamation 在感叹句中加强形容词、副词或名词的语气): *That is indeed remarkable! That is indeed a remarkable thing!* 那可真了不起! 那真是了不起的事情! **2** (used after *very* + *adj* or *adv* to emphasize a statement, description, etc 用于 very + 形容词或副词之后以强调陈述、描述等部分的语气) really 真正地; 实在地: *Thank you very much indeed!* 确实非常感激您! ○ *I was very sad indeed to hear about it.* 我听到这件事, 确实非常难过. ○ *a very big elephant indeed* 很大的大象. **3** (*fml* 文) in fact 事实上; 实际上; 其实: *I don't mind. Indeed, I am delighted to help.* 我不在乎. 其实, 我很乐于帮忙. ○ *I was annoyed, indeed furious, over what happened.* 出了这件事我很不痛快, 实际上是愤怒已极. **4** (as a comment or response 用作评语或回应语) (**a**) (expressing surprise, but not disbelief 表示惊讶, 但并非不信): *'I saw a ghost!' 'Indeed? Where was it?'* '我看见鬼了!' '真的吗? 在哪儿呢?' (**b**) (expressing disbelief and even scorn 表示不相信甚或轻蔑之意): *'A ghost indeed! I've never heard anything so ridiculous!'* '真是鬼! 我可从没听说过这种荒谬的事!' (**c**) (showing interest of a critical or an ironical kind 表示挑剔的或反语的兴味): *'When will the weather improve?' 'When, indeed!'* '天气什么时候能好转?' '什么时候? 没时候!'
in·de·fat·ig·able /ˌɪndɪˈfætɪgəbl; ˌɪndɪˈfætɪgəbḷ/ *adj* (*fml approv* 文, 褒) never giving up or stopping in spite of tiredness or difficulty; tireless 不顾疲倦的; 不畏困难的; 不屈不挠的; 不懈的: *indefatigable workers* 不知疲倦的工作者 ○ *an indefatigable campaigner for civil rights* 不屈不挠的民权运动人士.
in·de·fens·ible /ˌɪndɪˈfensəbl; ˌɪndɪˈfɛnsəbḷ/ *adj* that cannot be defended, justified or excused 无法防守的; 无可辩解的; 不可原谅的: *indefensible behaviour, rudeness, harshness, etc* 不可原谅的行为、粗暴表现、苛刻态度. ▷ **in·de·fens·ibly** /-əblɪ; -əblɪ/ *adv*: *indefensibly rude* 粗鲁得不可原谅.
in·de·fin·able /ˌɪndɪˈfaɪnəbl; ˌɪndɪˈfaɪnəbḷ/ *adj* that cannot be defined 不能下定义的; 不能解释的; 轮廓不清的: *an indefinable air of mystery* 不可言状的神秘气氛. ▷ **in·de·fin·ably** /-əblɪ; -əblɪ/ *adv*.
in·def·in·ite /ɪnˈdefɪnət; ɪnˈdɛfənɪt/ *adj* **1** not clearly defined or stated; vague 不确定的; 不明确的; 模糊的: *He has rather indefinite views on the question.* 他对该问题的看法颇暧昧. ○ *He gave me an indefinite answer*, ie neither 'yes' nor 'no'. 他给我的答复模棱两可. **2** lasting an unspecified time 无限期的; (时间)不确定的: *She'll be away for an indefinite period.* 她将离开一段时间, 何时回来未定. ▷ **in·def·in·itely** *adv*: *You may have to wait indefinitely.* 你可能得无限期地等下去.
□ **in,definite 'article** (*grammar*) the word 'a' or 'an' 不定冠词, 即 a 或 an. Cf 参看 DEFINITE ARTICLE (DEFINITE).
in·del·ible /ɪnˈdeləbl; ɪnˈdɛləbḷ/ *adj* (of marks, stains, ink, etc) that cannot be rubbed out or removed (指记号、污迹、墨迹等)擦不掉的, 难以去除的: *an indelible pencil*, ie one that makes such marks 笔迹擦不掉的铅笔 ○ (*fig* 比喻) *indelible shame* 雪洗不掉的耻辱 ○ *an indelible memory* 无法磨灭的记忆. ▷ **in·del·ibly** /-əblɪ; -əblɪ/ *adv*.
in·del·ic·ate /ɪnˈdelɪkət; ɪnˈdɛləkət/ *adj* (*fml often euph* 文, 常作委婉语) (of a person, his speech, behaviour, etc) lacking in tact or refinement; rather rude or embarrassing (指人及言行等)不圆通的, 不文雅的, 颇粗鲁或令人难堪的: *indelicate remarks* 粗鄙的言语 ○ *It was indelicate of you to mention her marriage problems.* 你提到她的婚姻难题, 这很失礼.
▷ **in·del·ic·acy** /-kəsɪ; -kəsɪ/ *n* **1** [U] being indelicate 不圆通; 不文雅; 颇粗鲁或令人难堪. **2** [C] indelicate act, remark, etc 不圆通或不文雅的言行.
in·dem·nify /ɪnˈdemnɪfaɪ; ɪnˈdɛmnəˌfaɪ/ *v* (*pt, pp* **-fied**) **1** [Tn, Tn·pr] **~ sb (from/against sth)** (*law or commerce* 律或商) promise to compensate sb for any harm he may suffer 保证赔偿或补偿某人可能受到的损失: *indemnify sb against harm, damage, loss, etc* 向某人承担其万一受到伤害、损害、损失等时的赔偿. **2** [Tn, Tn·pr] **~ sb (for sth)** (*fml* 文) repay sb (for sth) (为某事物)向某人赔偿, 补偿: *I undertook to indemnify them for expenses incurred on my behalf.* 我负责偿还他们为我而用的全部花费.
▷ **in·dem·ni·fica·tion** /ɪnˌdemnɪfɪˈkeɪʃn; ɪnˌdɛmnəfəˈkeʃən/ *n* (*fml* 文) **1** [U] indemnifying or being indemnified 赔偿; 补偿; 获得保障. **2** [C] thing given or received as compensation or repayment 赔偿物; 补偿金.
in·dem·nity /ɪnˈdemnətɪ; ɪnˈdɛmnətɪ/ *n* **1** [U] **~ (against/for sth)** guarantee against damage or loss; compensation for these (为防遭伤害或损失的)保障, 保险, 补偿, 赔偿: [attrib 作定语] *an indemnity fund* 赔偿基金. **2** [C] money, goods, etc given as compensation for damage or loss (为所遭伤害或损失而提供的)赔偿物、钱、货物等: *The victorious nations are demanding huge indemnities from their former enemies.* 战胜国要求战败国交付巨额赔款.
in·dent /ɪnˈdent; ɪnˈdɛnt/ *v* **1** [Tn] make a mark or set of marks (as if) by cutting into the edge or surface of (sth) (在物体边缘或面上)造成凹陷、凹坑或缺口: *an indented* (ie very irregular) *coastline* 犬牙交错的海岸线. **2** [I, Tn] start (a line of print or writing) further in from the margin than the other lines 缩进(排印或书写一行的前端); 缩排; 缩格书写: *Please indent the first line of each paragraph.* 请于每段第一行缩格书写. **3** [Ipr] **~ (on sb) for sth** (*commerce* 商 *esp Brit*) make an official order for goods or stores 订购; 订货: *indent on the firm for new equipment*, ie place an order for which the firm will pay 为公司订购新设备(订货由公司付款).
▷ **in·dent** /ˈɪndent; ˈɪndɛnt/ *n* (*commerce* 商 *esp Brit*) official order for stores or equipment (货物或设备)订货, 定单.
in·denta·tion /ˌɪndenˈteɪʃn; ˌɪndɛnˈteʃən/ *n* **1** [U] indenting (INDENT 1, 2) or being indented 作凹坑或锯齿状; 缩进排印或书写. **2** [C] (**a**) **~ (in sth)** mark made by indenting 凹陷; 凹坑; 缺口: *the deep indentations of the Norwegian coastline* 挪威海岸线的犬牙交错状. (**b**) space left at the beginning of a line of print or writing (排印或书写的)行首空格.
in·den·tures /ɪnˈdentʃəz; ɪnˈdɛntʃəz/ *n* [pl] (esp formerly) written contract according to which an apprentice works for and is trained by a particular employer (尤指旧时的)师徒合同.
▷ **in·den·ture** *v* [Tn, Tn·pr] **~ sb (to sb)** contract sb to work as an apprentice 与某人签订师徒合同将之收为学徒: *His son was indentured to the local blacksmith.* 他的儿子拜当地的铁匠为师签订了师徒合同.
in·de·pend·ence /ˌɪndɪˈpendəns; ˌɪndɪˈpɛndəns/ *n* [U] **~ (from sb/sth)** state of being independent 独立; 自主; 自立: *young people who want independence from their*

parents 不想依赖父母的年轻人 ○ [attrib 作定语] *independence celebrations*, eg of a newly independent country 独立庆典(如新独立的国家的).

□ **Inde'pendence Day** 4 July, celebrated in the US as the anniversary of the day in 1776 on which the American colonies declared themselves independent of Britain 美国独立纪念日(7月4日，美国国庆日，纪念1776年脱离英国而独立之日).

in·de·pend·ent /ˌɪndɪˈpendənt; ˌɪndɪˋpɛndənt/ *adj* **1 ~ (of sb/sth)** not dependent (on other people or things); not controlled (by other people or things) 独立的; 自主的; 自立的: *old enough to be independent of one's parents* 年岁已大不必依赖父母 ○ *She never borrows anything; she's far too independent for that.* 她从不向别人借东西，她很有独立性. ○ *Barbados was once a British colony, but now it's independent.* 巴巴多斯曾是英国的殖民地，现已独立. **2 ~ (of sb/sth)** not connected with each other; separate 不相关联的; 单独的; 独自的; 分开的: *Two independent investigators have reached virtually the same conclusions.* 两个调查人员各自做出的结论简直完全一致. **3** financed by private rather than government money 靠私人而非政府资助的; 私立的: *independent television* 私营电视台 ○ *the independent sector in education* 私立的教育机构 ○ *independent schools* 私立学校. **4** not depending for its validity or operation on the thing(s) involved (不依附所涉及的事物)本身有效的或有作用的: *independent evidence, proof, etc* 独立的证词、证据等. **5** not unfairly influenced by the people who are involved; impartial 未受有关的人影响的; 无偏见的: *an independent witness, observer, etc* 无偏见的证人、观察者等 ○ *We demand an independent inquiry into the government's handling of the affair.* 我们要求对政府处理该事的情况作独立的调查.

▷ **in·de·pend·ent** *n* (*abbr* 缩写 **Ind**) (*politics* 政) MP, candidate, etc who does not belong to a political party 无党派的议员、候选人等: *stand as an independent* 作为无党派候选人.

in·de·pend·ently *adv*: *Scientists in different countries, working independently of each other, have come up with very similar results.* 各国科学家各自独立进行研究都得到了非常相似的结果.

□ ˌ**independent** ˈ**means** private income sufficiently large for one not to have to rely financially on anyone else 足以自给自足、不必依赖他人的个人收入: *a woman of independent means* 靠个人收入生活的女子.

in·des·crib·able /ˌɪndɪˈskraɪbəbl; ˌɪndɪˋskraɪbəbḷ/ *adj* too bad or good to be described (好得或坏得)难以形容的: *indescribable squalor* 难以描述的污秽. ▷ **in·des·crib·ably** /-əblɪ; -əblɪ/ *adv*: *indescribably beautiful, awful, filthy, etc* 美丽得、糟糕得、肮脏得…无法形容.

in·des·truct·ible /ˌɪndɪˈstrʌktəbl; ˌɪndɪˋstrʌktəbḷ/ *adj* that cannot be destroyed 不可毁灭的; 不能损坏的: *Furniture for young children needs to be indestructible.* 幼儿用的家具须不易损坏. ○ (*fig joc* 比喻，谑) *I'm pretty indestructible; it takes more than a bout of flu to lay me low.* 我身体很壮，得一次流感不致于躺下. ▷ **in·des·truct·ib·il·ity** /ˌɪndɪˌstrʌktəˈbɪlətɪ; ˌɪndɪˌstrʌktəˋbɪlətɪ/ *n* [U].

in·de·term·in·able /ˌɪndɪˈtɜːmɪnəbl; ˌɪndɪˋtɝmɪnəbḷ/ *adj* (*fml* 文) that cannot be decided or settled 无法决定的; 无法解决的.

in·de·term·in·ate /ˌɪndɪˈtɜːmɪnət; ˌɪndɪˋtɝmənɪt/ *adj* (**a**) not fixed or exact; vague; indefinite 不固定的; 不确切的; 未限定的; 模糊的: *a sort of indeterminate colour, half-way between grey and brown* 一种介于灰色与棕色之间说不清的颜色. (**b**) (*mathematics* 数) of no fixed value 数值不定的; 未定元的: *an indeterminate quantity* 不定量. ▷ **in·de·term·in·acy** /-nəsɪ; -nəsɪ/ *n* [U].

in·dex /ˈɪndeks; ˋɪndɛks/ *n* (*pl* **~es** 复数作 **indexes**; in sense 2, **~es** or **indices** /ˈɪndɪsiːz; ˋɪndəˌsiz/ 用于下述第2义时复数作 **indexes** 或 **indices**; in sense 3, **indices** 用于下述第3义时复数作 **indices**) **1** (**a**) list of names or topics referred to in a book, etc, usu arranged at the end in alphabetical order 索引. (**b**) (also ˈ**card index**) set of names, book titles, etc filed on cards, usu in alphabetical order (eg in a library) 卡片索引(如图书馆中的). **2** (**a**) figure showing the relative level of prices or wages compared with that of a previous date (物价或工资的)指数: *the cost-of-ˈliving index* 生活费用指数. (**b**) **~ (of sth)** (*fig* 比喻) thing that is a sign of sth else, esp because it increases or decreases proportionately; measure 标志; 表征; 量度: *The increasing sale of luxury goods is an index of the country's prosperity.* 奢侈商品销售量日增是该国繁荣的标志. **3** (*mathematics* 数) small number or letter showing how many times a quantity is to be multiplied by itself; exponent 指数; 幂: *In* $b^{3n} + x$, *3 and n are indices.* 在 $b^{3n} + x$ 式中, 3 和 n 是指数.

▷ **in·dex** *v* **1** (**a**) [Tn] make an index for (sth) 为(某事物)编索引: *The book is not well indexed.* 这部书索引做得不好. (**b**) [Tn, Tn·pr] **~ sth (in sth)** enter sth in an index 将某事物编入索引: *index all the quoted names in a book* 把书中提到的所有人名编入索引. **2** [Tn, Tn·pr] **~ sth (to sth)** link (wages, pensions, etc) to increases in prices, etc 将(工资、养老金等)与物价等的上涨相联系.

in·dexa·tion /ˌɪndekˈseɪʃn; ˌɪndɛkˋseʃən/ *n* [U] indexing (INDEX *v* 2) of wages, pensions, etc (工资、养老金等的)调整指数, 指数化.

□ ˈ**index finger** *n* finger next to the thumb, used for pointing 食指. ⇨illus at HAND 见 HAND 插图.

ˈ**index-linked** *adj* (of wages, pensions, etc) increased according to increases in the cost of living (指工资、养老金等)按生活指数调整的.

In·dian /ˈɪndɪən; ˋɪndɪən/ *n, adj* **1** (native or inhabitant) of the Republic of India 印度共和国的(土著或居民); 印度的; 印度人. **2** = AMERICAN INDIAN (AMERICAN): *an Indian ceremony, encampment* 印第安人的仪式、营地. **3** (idm 习语) **Indian/single file** ⇨ FILE[3]. **an** ˌ**Indian** ˈ**summer** (**a**) period of calm dry sunny weather in late autumn 小阳春, 秋老虎(深秋时平和、干燥、阳光充足的天气). (**b**) (*fig* 比喻) period of late success or improvement 迟来的成功或改进时期.

□ ˌ**Indian** ˈ**club** bottle-shaped object for use in juggling, gymnastic exercises, etc 瓶状棒(用于杂耍、体操等的).

ˌ**Indian** ˈ**corn** maize 玉蜀黍; 玉米.

ˌ**Indian** ˈ**hemp** = CANNABIS.

ˌ**Indian** ˈ**ink** thick black ink, used esp for drawing 墨; 墨汁.

india·rub·ber /ˌɪndɪəˈrʌbə(r); ˌɪndɪəˋrʌbɚ/ *n* piece of rubber for removing pencil or ink marks; eraser (擦掉字迹用的)橡皮.

in·dic·ate /ˈɪndɪkeɪt; ˋɪndəˌket/ *v* **1** (**a**) [Tn, Tf, Tw, Dn·pr, Dpr·f, Dpr·w] **~ sth (to sb)** show sth, esp by pointing 指示; 指出; 标示: *a sign indicating the right road to follow* 指示应走道路的标记 ○ *With a nod of his head he indicated to me where I should sit.* 他点头示意我应坐的地方. (**b**) [Tn, Tf, Tw] be a sign of (sth); suggest the possibility or probability of 象征(某事物); 表明或暗示…的可能性: *A red sky at night indicates fine weather the following day/indicates that the following day will be fine.* 晚上天边红预示明朝天气好. (**c**) [Tn] give (the specified reading or measurement) on a scale 在仪表盘上显示出(某读数、量度): *The speedometer was indicating 95 mph.* 速度计指示着每小时95英里. **2** [Tn, Tf, Tw, Dn·pr, Dpr·f, Dpr·w] **~ sth (to sb)** state sth briefly or indirectly (简要或间接)表示某事物: *The minister has indicated that he may resign next year.* 该大臣已示意他明年可能辞职. ○ *She has not indicated how she proposes to react.* 她未表示打算做何回应. **3** [Tn esp passive 尤用于被动语态] show the need for or advisability of (sth); call for 显示需要(某事物); 显示(某事物)可取; 要求: *With the government's failure to solve the problem of unemployment, a fresh approach is indicated.* 鉴于政府未能处理好失业问题, 有必要采取新的措施. ○ *a diagnosis of advanced cancer indicating an emergency operation* 诊断为晚期癌症, 急需动手术. **4** [I, Tf] signal that one's vehicle is going to change direction 发出改变行车方向的信号: *Why don't you indicate!* 你为什么不打信号! ○ *He indicated that he was turning right, but then he turned left!* 他发出右转信号, 却突然向左转了!

▷ **in·dica·tion** /ˌɪndɪˈkeɪʃn; ˌɪndəˋkeʃən/ *n* **1** [U] indicating or being indicated 指示; 指标; 象征; 预示. **2** [C, U] **~ (of sth/doing sth)**; **~ (as to sth/that…)** remark, gesture, sign, etc that indicates sth 表示某种意

思的言语、姿势、记号等: *She gave no indication of having heard us.* 看不出她听见我们的声音了. ○ *Can you give me some indication as to your intentions?* 你究竟是什么用意, 能向我透露一点吗? ○ *There are indications that the situation may be improving.* 有迹象表明情况可能好转.

in·dic·at·ive /ɪnˈdɪkətɪv; ɪnˈdɪkətɪv/ *adj* **1** (*grammar*) stating a fact or asking questions of fact 陈述的: *the indicative mood* 陈述语气. Cf 参看 IMPERATIVE 3, INFINITIVE, SUBJUNCTIVE. **2** [pred 作表语] **~ of sth/that...** (*fml* 文) showing or suggesting sth 表示或暗示某事物: *Is a large head indicative of high intelligence?* 头部大是不是表示智慧高? ○ *Their failure to act is indicative of their lack of interest/indicative that they have no interest in the problem.* 他们没采取行动, 表明他们对这个问题不感兴趣.

in·dic·ator /ˈɪndɪkeɪtə(r); ˈɪndəˌketɚ/ *n* **1** person or thing that points out or gives information (eg a pointer or needle on a machine showing speed or pressure, etc) 指示者; 指示器; 指针: *Litmus paper can be used as an indicator of the presence of acid in a solution.* 石蕊试纸可用以测试溶液是否含酸. **2** board giving up-to-date information about times of arrival or departure of trains, aircraft, etc (表示火车、飞机等往来时刻的)指示牌: *a ˈtrain indicator* 列车时刻指示牌 ○ *an arˈrivals indicator* 到达时刻指示牌. **3** device (esp a flashing light) on a vehicle showing that it is about to change direction (车辆的)方向指示装置(尤指闪动的灯光): *a ˈtraffic-indicator* 方向指示器 ○ *His left-hand/right-hand indicator is flashing.* 他的左[右]信号灯在闪动. ⇨illus at App 1 见附录1插图, page xii.

in·di·ces *pl* of INDEX.

in·dict /ɪnˈdaɪt; ɪnˈdaɪt/ *v* [Tn, Tn·pr] **~ sb (for sth)** (*law* 律) accuse sb officially (of sth); charge sb (就某事)控告、起诉或告发某人: *He was indicted for murder/on three counts of murder.* 他被控杀人[三项谋杀罪].

▷ **in·dict·able** *adj* for which one may be indicted 可被控告或起诉的: *indictable offences*, ie that may be tried by a jury 可起诉的刑事罪(可由陪审团裁决的).

in·dict·ment *n* **1** [C] (a) **~ (against sb)** written statement that indicts sb 起诉书; 诉状: *bring in an indictment against sb* 控告某人. (b) **~ of sb/sth** (*fig* 比喻) reason for condemning sb/sth 谴责某人[某事物]的原因: *The rise in delinquency is an indictment of our society and its values.* 为非作歹现象有增无已, 这是对我们的社会及其价值观的控诉. **2** [U] indicting or being indicted 控诉; 控告.

in·dif·fer·ence /ɪnˈdɪfrəns; ɪnˈdɪfrəns/ *n* [U] **~ (to sb/sth)** state of being indifferent; absence of interest, feeling or reaction 漠不关心; 冷淡; 无兴趣、感觉或反应: *He treated my request with indifference.* 他对我的请求置若罔闻. ○ *It's a matter of complete indifference to me*, ie I do not care about it. 这件事对我来说完全无所谓. ○ *her indifference to their appeals* 她对他们的请求所抱的漠不关心的态度.

in·dif·fer·ent /ɪnˈdɪfrənt; ɪnˈdɪfrənt/ *adj* **1** [usu pred 通常作表语] **~ (to sb/sth)** having no interest in sb/sth; neither for nor against sb/sth; not caring about sb/sth 不感兴趣; 不置可否; 漠不关心; 满不在乎: *How can you be indifferent to the sufferings of starving people?* 你怎能对饥民的疾苦无动于衷呢? ○ *explorers indifferent to the dangers of their journey* 把征途上的危险置之度外的探险家. **2** of rather low quality or ability 质量或能力低的: *an indifferent book, wine, meal* 质量低劣的书、果酒、饭食 ○ *a very indifferent athlete* 极差的运动员. ▷ **in·dif·fer·ently** *adv*: *He nodded indifferently.* 他漠然地点点头. ○ *The team played indifferently today.* 今天这个队表现很糟.

in·di·gen·ous /ɪnˈdɪdʒɪnəs; ɪnˈdɪdʒənəs/ *adj* **~ (to sth)** (*fml* 文) belonging naturally (to a place); native 本地的; 土产的; 当地的; 土生土长的: *Kangaroos are indigenous to Australia.* 袋鼠产于澳大利亚. ○ *the indigenous language, culture, etc*, ie of the people regarded as the original inhabitants of an area 本地的语言、文化等.

in·di·gent /ˈɪndɪdʒənt; ˈɪndədʒənt/ *adj* (*fml* 文) poor 贫穷的.

▷ **in·di·gence** /-əns; -əns/ *n* [U] (*fml* 文) poverty 贫穷.

in·di·gest·ible /ˌɪndɪˈdʒestəbl; ˌɪndəˈdʒɛstəbl̩/ *adj* difficult or impossible to digest 难消化的; 不能消化的: *Fried onions can be indigestible.* 炸洋葱有时很难消化. ○ (*fig* 比喻) *indigestible statistics*, ie hard to understand 难懂的统计资料. ▷ **in·di·gest·ib·il·ity** /ˌɪndɪˌdʒestəˈbɪlətɪ; ˌɪndəˌdʒɛstəˈbɪlətɪ/ *n* [U].

in·di·ges·tion /ˌɪndɪˈdʒestʃən; ˌɪndəˈdʒɛstʃən/ *n* [U] (pain from) difficulty in digesting food 不消化; 消化不良症: *suffer from indigestion* 患消化不良症 ○ *have an attack of indigestion* 消化不良发作 ○ [attrib 作定语] *indigestion pills/tablets*, ie taken to cure indigestion 治消化不良的药丸[药片].

in·dig·nant /ɪnˈdɪɡnənt; ɪnˈdɪɡnənt/ *adj* **~ (with sb)/(at/over/about sth)** angry and scornful, esp at injustice or because of undeserved blame, etc 愤慨的, 愤怒的(尤指对不公正或冤屈之事): *She was most indignant with me when I suggested she might try a little harder.* 我建议她不妨再努力一些, 她竟大为恼火. ○ *He was terribly indignant at what he saw as false accusations.* 他认为那些指责皆属不实之词, 因而十分气愤. ▷ **in·dig·nantly** *adv*.

in·dig·na·tion /ˌɪndɪɡˈneɪʃn; ˌɪndɪɡˈneʃən/ *n* [U] **~ (against sb)/(at/over/about sth)** anger caused by sth thought to be unjust, unfair, etc (对不公正的事激起的)愤慨, 愤怒: *general indignation at the sudden steep rise in bus fares* 公共汽车票价突然猛增激起的公愤 ○ *arouse sb's indignation* 激起某人的愤懑 ○ *Much to my indignation, he sat down in my seat.* 我生气的是他坐在我的座位上. ○ *righteous indignation*, ie which one considers appropriate and justified (but others usu do not) 仗义的愤慨(自觉义愤填膺而别人通常不这样认为的).

in·dig·nity /ɪnˈdɪɡnətɪ; ɪnˈdɪɡnətɪ/ *n* **1** [U] rude or unworthy treatment causing shame or loss of respect 侮辱; 轻蔑: *be subjected to indignity and humiliation* 受到侮慢和羞辱. **2** [C] thing said or done that humiliates sb 侮辱性的言行: *The highjackers inflicted all kinds of indignities on their captives.* 劫持者对人质百般侮辱.

in·digo /ˈɪndɪɡəʊ; ˈɪndɪˌɡo/ *n* [U] **1** deep blue dye (obtained from plants) 靛, 靛青, 靛蓝(自植物中提取的颜料). **2** its colour (in the spectrum between blue and violet) 靛蓝色: *a tropical night sky of deepest indigo* 靛蓝色的热带夜空. ⇨illus at SPECTRUM 见 SPECTRUM 插图.

in·dir·ect /ˌɪndɪˈrekt, -daɪˈr-; ˌɪndəˈrɛkt, -daɪˈr-/ *adj* **1** not going in a straight line; circuitous 非直接的; 间接的; 迂回的: *an indirect route* 迂回的路线 ○ *indirect lighting*, ie by reflected light 间接照明(利用反光的). **2** avoiding direct or explicit mention of a topic; allusive 闪烁其词的; 不直截了当的: *make an indirect reference to sth* 暗示某事 ○ *an indirect answer to a question* 对问题的非正面回答. **3** not primary or immediate; not directly aimed at sth; secondary 非直接相关的; 次要的: *an indirect cause, reason, result* 次要的原因、理由、结果. Cf 参看 DIRECT.

▷ **in·dir·ectly** *adv*. **in·dir·ect·ness** *n* [U].

□ ˌ**indirect ˈobject** (*grammar*) additional object of certain verbs which refers to the person or thing that an action is done to or for, eg *him* (= *to him*) in *Give him the money* 间接宾语(如在 Give him the money 一句中的 him 即是, him = to him). Cf 参看 OBJECT[1] 5.

ˌ**indirect ˈquestion** (*grammar*) question in indirect speech 间接疑问句.

ˌ**indirect ˈspeech** (also **reported speech**) (*grammar*) reporting of what sb has said (as compared with direct reproduction of sb's words) 间接引语: *In indirect speech, 'He said, "I will come"' becomes 'He said he would come.'* '他说: "我要来."'在间接引语中变成'他说他要来.'

ˈ**indirect tax** tax that is not paid directly to the government but as an extra amount added to the price of certain goods 间接税(非直接向政府缴纳的, 而是将之加在某些商品的销售价上).

in·dis·cern·ible /ˌɪndɪˈsɜːnəbl; ˌɪndɪˈsɝnəbl̩/ *adj* that cannot be discerned 不能识别的; 辨别不清的: *an indiscernible difference* 难以辨别的差异.

in·dis·cip·line /ɪnˈdɪsɪplɪn; ɪnˈdɪsəplɪn/ *n* [U] lack of discipline; unruliness 无纪律; 缺乏管教; 无秩序.

in·dis·creet /ˌɪndɪˈskriːt; ˌɪndɪˈskrit/ *adj* too open in what one says or does; lacking tact or caution 不稳重的; 不审慎的; 轻率的; 不策略的: *Don't tell her any secrets; she's so indiscreet.* 什么秘密都不要告诉她, 她很不稳重. ○ *One indiscreet remark at the wrong moment could ruin* *the whole plan.* 若时机不当，一言不慎，可能毁掉整个计划.

▷ **in·dis·creetly** *adv.*

in·dis·cre·tion /ˌɪndɪˈskreʃn; ˌɪndɪˈskreʃən/ *n* **1** [U] indiscreet conduct; lack of discretion 轻率的行为；不谨慎的言行. **2** [C] (**a**) indiscreet remark or act 轻率的言行. (**b**) offence against social conventions (违反社会准则的)过失: *committing youthful indiscretions* 犯年轻人的不检点的错误.

in·dis·crim·in·ate /ˌɪndɪˈskrɪmɪnət; ˌɪndɪˈskrɪmənɪt/ *adj* (**a**) **~ (in sth)** acting without careful judgement 不加鉴别的；不加分析的: *indiscriminate in his choice of friends* (他)择友不慎重. (**b**) given or done without careful judgement, or at random 不加鉴别的；任意而为的: *indiscriminate praise* 随意的夸奖 ○ *indiscriminate bombing of enemy targets*, eg that might kill civilians as well as damage military sites 对敌方狂轰滥炸(如既毁军事据点，又祸及平民). ▷ **in·dis·crim·in·ately** *adv.*

in·dis·pens·able /ˌɪndɪˈspensəbl; ˌɪndɪˈspɛnsəbl̩/ *adj* **~ (to sb/sth); ~ (for sth/doing sth)** that cannot be dispensed with; absolutely essential 不可缺少的；必需的: *Air, food and water are indispensable to life.* 空气、食物、水皆为生命不可或缺者. ○ *A good dictionary is indispensable for learning a foreign language.* 学习外语离不开好的词典.

in·dis·posed /ˌɪndɪˈspəʊzd; ˌɪndɪˈspozd/ *adj* [pred 作表语] **1** (*often euph* 常作委婉语) (slightly) ill 有(小)病: *She has a headache and is indisposed.* 她患头疼，略感不适. **2** [pred 作表语] **~ to do sth** (*fml* 文) not inclined or willing to do sth 不想做或无意做某事: *I felt indisposed to help him.* 我不愿意帮助他.

▷ **in·dis·posi·tion** /ˌɪndɪspəˈzɪʃn; ˌɪndɪspəˈzɪʃən/ *n* [C, U] **1** (*often euph* 常作委婉语) slight illness; ill health 微恙；不健康. **2 ~ to do sth** (*fml* 文) feeling of unwillingness or disinclination to do sth 不乐意或不情愿做某事.

in·dis·put·able /ˌɪndɪˈspju:təbl; ˌɪndɪˈspjutəbl̩/ *adj* that cannot be disputed or denied 不可争辩的；不容置疑的；无可否认的. ▷ **in·dis·put·ably** *adv*: *indisputably the best tennis player in the world* 世界上无疑最好的网球运动员.

in·dis·sol·uble /ˌɪndɪˈsɒljʊbl; ˌɪndɪˈsɑljʊbl̩/ *adj* (*fml* 文) that cannot be dissolved or broken up; firm and lasting 不可溶解的；不可分解的；牢固持久的: *indissoluble bonds of friendship between the two men* 这两个人之间牢不可破的友谊 ○ *The Roman Catholic Church regards marriage as indissoluble.* 天主教会认为婚姻关系是不容解除的. ▷ **in·dis·sol·ub·il·ity** /ˌɪndɪˌsɒljʊˈbɪlətɪ; ˌɪndɪˌsɑljʊˈbɪlətɪ/ *n* [U]. **in·dis·sol·ubly** /ˌɪndɪˈsɒljʊblɪ; ˌɪndɪˈsɑljʊblɪ/ *adv*.

in·dis·tinct /ˌɪndɪˈstɪŋkt; ˌɪndɪˈstɪŋkt/ *adj* not distinct; vague 不清楚的；模糊的: *indistinct speech* 含糊的讲话 ○ *indistinct sounds, memories* 不清晰的声音、记忆. ▷ **in·dis·tinctly** *adv*. **in·dis·tinct·ness** *n* [U].

in·dis·tin·guish·able /ˌɪndɪˈstɪŋgwɪʃəbl; ˌɪndɪˈstɪŋgwɪʃəbl/ *adj* **~ (from sth)** that cannot be identified as different or distinct; (virtually) identical 不能区别的；无法辨别的；(实际上)完全相同的: *Its colour makes the moth indistinguishable from the branch it rests on.* 这蛾子停在树枝上，其颜色和树枝几不可辨. ▷ **in·dis·tin·guish·ably** /-əblɪ; -əblɪ/ *adv*.

in·dium /ˈɪndɪəm; ˈɪndɪəm/ *n* [U] (*chemistry* 化) soft silvery metallic element found in small quantities in zinc ores and used to make transistors 铟 ⇨App 10 见附录 10.

in·di·vidual /ˌɪndɪˈvɪdʒʊəl; ˌɪndəˈvɪdʒʊəl/ *adj* **1** [attrib 作定语] (esp after *each* 尤用于 each 之后) single; separate 单独的；个别的: *Each individual person is responsible for his own arrangements.* 每人均须对自己的计划负责. **2** [usu attrib 通常作定语] (**a**) of or for one person 一个人的；供一个人用的: *food served in individual portions* 按一人一份儿供给的食物 ○ *It is difficult for a teacher to give individual attention to children in a large class.* 教师在人数多的班上很难对各个学生都照顾到. (**b**) by or from one person 靠个人的；来自个人的: *an individual effort, contribution, etc* 个人的努力、贡献等. Cf 参看 COLLECTIVE. **3** [usu attrib 通常作定语] characteristic of a single person, animal, plant or thing; particular (人、动植物或事物)独特的，特有的: *an individual style of dress* 个人的衣着风格 ○ (*approv* 褒) *He writes in a very individual way*, ie an original way, not derived or imitative 他的写作方法别具一格(有独创方式，不沿袭或模仿他人).

▷ **in·di·vidual** *n* **1** single human being 个人: *the rights of an/the individual compared with those of society as a whole* 针对社会整体权利而言的个人权利. **2** (*infml* 口) person of the specified sort 有某种特点的人: *a pleasant, unpleasant, etc individual* 和蔼可亲的、讨人厌的...人 ○ *What a strange individual!* 多怪的傢伙! **3** (*approv or derog* 褒或贬) unusual or eccentric person 不寻常的或古怪的人: *He's quite an individual!* 他是个十足的怪人!

in·di·vidu·ally /-dʒʊəlɪ; -dʒʊəlɪ/ *adv* separately; one by one 分别地；各个地；各自地: *speak to each member of a group individually* 对组里每个人逐个地说.

in·di·vidu·al·ism /ˌɪndɪˈvɪdʒʊəlɪzəm; ˌɪndəˈvɪdʒʊəlˌɪzəm/ *n* [U] **1** feeling or behaviour of a person who likes to do things his/her own way, regardless of what other people do (不管别人怎样做)只按个人方法行事的感觉或行为；我行我素. **2** theory that favours free action and complete liberty of belief for each individual person (contrasted with the theory that favours the supremacy of the state) 个人主义.

▷ **in·di·vidu·al·ist** /-əlɪst; -əlɪst/ *n* **1** person who behaves with individualism(1) 我行我素的人: *a rugged individualist* 豪爽的自行其是的人. **2** supporter of the theory of individualism(2) 个人主义者.

in·di·vidu·al·istic /ˌɪndɪˌvɪdʒʊəˈlɪstɪk; ˌɪndəˌvɪdʒʊəlˈɪstɪk/ *adj* of individualism or its principles 我行我素的；个人主义的. **in·di·vidu·al·ist·ic·ally** /-klɪ; -klɪ/ *adv*.

in·di·vidu·al·ity /ˌɪndɪˌvɪdʒʊˈælətɪ; ˌɪndəˌvɪdʒʊˈælətɪ/ *n* **1** [U] all the characteristics that belong to a particular person and that make him/her different from others 个性；个人特征: *a man of marked individuality* 个性突出的男子 ○ *the individuality of sb's work, style, etc* 某人工作、风格等的特色. **2** [U] state of separate existence 个人: *The state often presents a threat to individuality.* 国家的利益往往对个人自由构成威胁. **3 individualities** [pl] individual tastes, preferences, etc 个人的趣味、爱好等: *cater for different people's individualities* 迎合人们各式各样的爱好.

in·di·vidu·al·ize, -ise /ˌɪndɪˈvɪdʒʊəlaɪz; ˌɪndəˈvɪdʒʊəlˌaɪz/ *v* **1** [Tn] give an individual, a distinct or a personal character to (sth); characterize; personalize 使(某事物)个性化、具有个人特色或个体化: *Does your style of writing individualize your work?* 你的写作风格是否体现在你的作品中了? ○ *Prisoners try to individualize their cells by hanging up pictures, etc.* 监犯在牢房里挂上了画片等东西，都想营造些个人气氛. ○ *individualized writing paper*, ie made for a particular person with his/her address, etc printed on it 私人用笺(印有私人地址等的). **2** [I, Tn] treat (sth) separately; specify; particularize 对(某事物)个别对待；指明；个别列举.

in·di·vis·ible /ˌɪndɪˈvɪzəbl; ˌɪndəˈvɪzəbl̩/ *adj* that cannot be divided 不可分割的. ▷ **in·di·vis·ib·il·ity** /ˌɪndɪˌvɪzɪˈbɪlətɪ; ˌɪndəˌvɪzəˈbɪlətɪ/ *n* [U]. **in·di·vis·ibly** /ˌɪndɪˈvɪzəblɪ; ˌɪndəˈvɪzəblɪ/ *adv*.

Indo- *comb form* 构词成分 Indian; of India 印度人；印度的: *the Indo-Pakistan border.*

□ **Indo-European** /ˌɪndəʊˌjʊərəˈpi:ən; ˌɪndoˌjurəˈpiən/ *adj* of the family of languages spoken originally in Europe and parts of western Asia (including eg English, French, German, Latin, Greek, Swedish, Hindi, etc) 印欧语系的(最初在欧洲和西亚部分地区说的语言，包括英语、法语、德语、拉丁语、希腊语、瑞典语、印地语等)

in·doc·trin·ate /ɪnˈdɒktrɪneɪt; ɪnˈdɑktrɪnˌet/ *v* [Tn, Tn·pr, Cn·t] **~ sb (with sth/against sb/sth)** (*usu derog* 通常作贬义) cause sb to have (a particular set of beliefs), esp by teaching which excludes any other points of view 向某人灌输(学说或信仰)(尤指排斥其他观点的): *teachers who indoctrinate children with antisocial theories* 向儿童灌输反社会学说的教师 ○ *a religious organization which indoctrinates young people against their parents/to disobey their parents* 向年轻人灌输反对父母[不听父母话]的思想的宗教组织.

▷ **in·doc·trina·tion** /ɪnˌdɒktrɪˈneɪʃn; ɪnˌdɑktrɪˈneʃən/ *n* [U] **~ (with/in/against sth)** indoctrinating 灌输: *indoctrination of prisoners* 对监犯进行的思想灌输 ○ *indoctrination of converts in the ways of their new religion*

向新皈依者灌输教义.

in·dol·ent /ˈɪndələnt; ˈɪndələnt/ *adj* (*fml* 文) lazy; inactive 懒惰的; 不活跃的; 不活动的. ▷ **in·dol·ence** /-əns; -əns/ *n* [U]. **in·dol·ently** *adv*.

in·dom·it·able /ɪnˈdɒmɪtəbl; ɪnˈdɑmətəbl/ *adj* (*fml approv* 文, 褒) that cannot be subdued or defeated; unyielding 不可屈服的; 不可战胜的: *indomitable courage* 大无畏的勇气 ○ *an indomitable will* 不屈不挠的意志. ▷ **in·dom·it·ably** /-əblɪ; -əblɪ/ *adv*.

in·door /ˈɪndɔ:(r); ˈɪn,dɔr/ *adj* [attrib 作定语] carried on or situated inside a building; used in or suitable for the inside of a building 在室内进行的或放置的; 使用于或适用于室内的: *indoor games, photography, activities* 室内游戏、摄影、活动 ○ *an indoor swimming-pool* 室内游泳池 ○ *indoor clothes* 室内用的衣物. Cf 参看 OUTDOOR.

in·doors /,ɪnˈdɔ:z; ˈɪnˈdɔrz/ *adv* in or into a building 在室内; 往室内: *go/stay indoors* 进[留在]屋内 ○ *kept indoors all week by bad weather* 天气恶劣, 整个星期足不出户. Cf 参看 OUTDOORS.

in·dorse = ENDORSE.

in·drawn /,ɪnˈdrɔ:n; ˈɪnˈdrɔn/ *adj* [attrib 作定语] drawn in, esp inhaled 吸入的(尤指吸气): *All that betrayed his surprise was a sharply indrawn breath.* 他大大吸了一口气, 无意中流露出他吃了一惊.

in·dub·it·able /ɪnˈdju:bɪtəbl; *US* -ˈdu:-; ɪnˈdubɪtəbl/ *adj* (*fml* 文) that cannot be doubted; without doubt 不容置疑的; 无可怀疑的. ▷ **in·dub·it·ably** /-əblɪ; -əblɪ/ *adv*: *That is indubitably the best course of action.* 那无疑是上策.

in·duce /ɪnˈdju:s; *US* -du:s; ɪnˈdus/ *v* **1** [Cn·t] **(a)** persuade or influence (sb) to do sth 劝诱或促使(某人)做某事: *We couldn't induce the old lady to travel by air.* 我们无法劝说那位老太太坐飞机去. **(b)** lead or cause (sb) to do sth 导致或使得(某人)做某事: *What induced you to do such a stupid thing?* 是什么促使你做出这等蠢事来的? **2** [Tn] **(a)** bring (sth) about; cause 引起或诱发(某事); 产生; 造成: *illness induced by overwork* 过劳造成的疾病. **(b)** (*medical* 医) cause (a woman) to begin (childbirth) by means of drugs 用药物为(孕妇)催产: *an induced labour* 催生 ○ *We'll have to induce her.* 我们得给她引产.

▷ **in·duce·ment** *n* [C, U] **~ (to do sth)** **(a)** that which persuades; incentive 引诱; 鼓励; 刺激; 诱因: *They have little inducement to work harder.* 他们没有什么更加努力工作的好处. **(b)** (*euph* 婉) bribe; bribery 收买; 贿赂: *offer sb an inducement* 向某人行贿.

in·du·cible *adj* that can be induced 可诱导的; 可诱发的.

in·duct /ɪnˈdʌkt; ɪnˈdʌkt/ *v* [Tn, Tn·pr, Cn·n/a] **~ sb (to/into/as sth)** install sb formally or with ceremony in a position or an office; admit sb as a member of sth 使某人正式就职; 吸收某人为成员: *induct sb to/into the priesthood/as a priest* 使某人就任牧师职位[任职牧师].

in·duc·tion /ɪnˈdʌkʃn; ɪnˈdʌkʃən/ *n* [U] **1 ~ (into sth/as sb/sth)** inducting or being inducted; initiation 就职; 接纳会员; 成为会员: *the induction of new employees into their jobs* 新雇员参加工作 ○ *his induction as a priest* 他之就任牧师 ○ [attrib 作定语] *an induction course*, ie to give a new employee, entrant, etc general knowledge of future activities, requirements, etc 入门课(向新雇员、新成员等介绍情况、要求等). **2** inducing 诱导; 引发; 催产: *the induction of labour*, ie in childbirth 引产(接生时的). **3** method of logical reasoning which obtains or discovers general laws from particular facts or examples 归纳法. Cf 参看 DEDUCTION 1. **4** (*physics* 物) production of an electric or a magnetic state in an object (eg a circuit) by bringing an electrified or a magnetic object close to but not touching it, or by varying a magnetic field 电磁感应. **5** (*engineering* 工) drawing a fuel mixture into the cylinder(s) of an internal combustion engine 吸气, 进气(内燃机汽缸吸进油与空气混合物的工作过程): [attrib 作定语] *a fuel-induction system* 燃油进气系统.

□ **inˈduction-coil** *n* (*physics* 物) transformer for producing a high voltage from a low voltage 感应线圈.

inˈduction motor (*physics* 物) type of electric motor in which a magnetic field is created that produces an electric current 感应电动机.

in·duct·ive /ɪnˈdʌktɪv; ɪnˈdʌktɪv/ *adj* **1** (of logic, mathematics) based on induction (指逻辑学、数学)归纳的, 归纳法的: *inductive reasoning* 归纳推理. **2** (*physics* 物) of magnetic or electrical induction 电磁感应的. ▷ **in·duct·ively** *adv*.

in·dulge /ɪnˈdʌldʒ; ɪnˈdʌldʒ/ *v* **1 (a)** [Tn, Tn·pr] **~ oneself/sb (with sth)** allow oneself/sb to have whatever one/he likes or wants 放纵自己[某人]: *They indulge their child too much; it's bad for his character.* 他们过分纵容孩子, 这对孩子的性格有不良影响. ○ *I'm really going to indulge myself tonight with a bottle of champagne.* 今天晚上我可真要放纵一下自己, 喝他一瓶香槟. **(b)** [Tn] (*fml* 文) allow (sb) to proceed without interrupting or hindering him 容许或迁就(某人)做要做的事: *If you will indulge me for one moment* (ie allow me to continue to speak), *I think I can explain the matter to you.* 你要是容我把话说完, 我想我可以把此事给你解释清楚. **2** [Tn] satisfy (a perhaps unwarranted or illicit desire) 满足(可能为不正当的或不应有的愿望): *Will you indulge my curiosity and tell me how much it cost?* 你能不能满足我的好奇心, 告诉我那值多少钱? ○ *She indulges his every whim.* 她对他的怪念头有求必应. **3** [I, Ipr] **~ (in sth)** allow oneself to enjoy the pleasure of sth 让自己尽情享受某事物: *I shall forget about dieting today. I'm just going to indulge*, ie eat and drink what I like. 今天我要把节食计划置之脑后, 想吃什么就吃什么. ○ *indulge in (the luxury of) a long hot bath* (奢侈地)享受一下泡在浴缸里洗上半天热水澡的美滋味.

▷ **in·dul·gent** /-ənt; -ənt/ *adj* inclined to indulge 放纵的; 纵容的: *indulgent parents*, ie parents who allow their children to have or do anything 纵容子女的父母. **in·dul·gently** *adv*.

in·dul·gence /ɪnˈdʌldʒəns; ɪnˈdʌldʒəns/ *n* **1** [U] state of being allowed whatever one wants 放纵; 纵容: *a life of (self-)indulgence*, ie gratifying oneself (自我)放纵的生活 ○ *If I may crave your indulgence for one moment*... 祈蒙俯允赐时片刻.... **2** [U] **~ in sth** (habit of) satisfying one's own desires 放纵, 任性(的习惯): *Constant indulgence in bad habits brought about his ruin.* 他长期耽于恶习, 结果毁了自己. **3** [C] thing in which a person indulges 嗜好; 爱好: *A cigar after dinner is my only indulgence.* 饭后一枝雪茄是我唯一的嗜好. **4 (a)** [U] (in the Roman Catholic Church) granting of freedom from punishment for sin (天主教会的)特赦; 赦免; 免罪. **(b)** [C] instance of this 特赦; 赦免; 免罪: *selling indulgences* 出售赎罪券.

in·dus·trial /ɪnˈdʌstrɪəl; ɪnˈdʌstrɪəl/ *adj* **1** [attrib 作定语] of or engaged in industry 工业的; 产业的; 从事工业的: *industrial workers* 产业工人 ○ *industrial development* 工业发展. **2** for use in industry 用于工业的: *industrial diamonds* 工业用金刚石. **3** having many well-developed industries 工业发达的: *an industrial country, society, etc* 工业发达的国家、社会等 ○ *the industrial areas of England* 英格兰的工业地区.

▷ **in·dus·tri·al·ism** /-ɪzəm; -,ɪzəm/ *n* social system in which large industries have an important part 工业主义, 产业主义(以大型工业为主的社会体制).

in·dus·tri·al·ist /-ɪst; -ɪst/ *n* owner of a large industrial firm 工业家; 实业家.

in·dus·tri·al·ize, -ise /-aɪz; -,aɪz/ *v* [Tn] develop (a country or an area) extensively with industries 使(国家或地区)工业化: *the industrialized nations* 工业化国家.

in·dus·tri·al·iza·tion, -isation /ɪn,dʌstrɪəlaɪˈzeɪʃn; *US* -lɪz-; ɪn,dʌstrɪələˈzeʃən/ *n* [U].

in·dus·tri·ally /-əlɪ; -əlɪ/ *adv*.

□ **in,dustrial ˈaction** refusing to work normally; striking 工业行动; 怠工; 罢工: *take industrial action*, ie strike 采取工业行动(罢工).

in,dustrial ˈalcohol alcohol for industrial use (not for drinking) 工业用酒精(非饮用的).

in,dustrial diˈspute disagreement between workers and management 劳资纠纷.

in,dustrial eˈstate area of land, usu on the edge of a town, containing factories 工业区(通常位于市郊). Cf 参看 TRADING ESTATE (TRADE[2]).

in,dustrial reˈlations dealings between employers and employees 劳资关系: *setting up a combined workers/management committee to foster good industrial relations* 为促进良好的劳资关系建立劳资联合委员会.

the In,dustrial Revoˈlution development of Britain

and other western nations into industrial societies in the 18th and 19th centuries 工业革命, 产业革命(18及19世纪英国及其他西方国家转变为工业社会的发展过程).

in·dus·tri·ous /ɪnˈdʌstrɪəs; ɪnˋdʌstrɪəs/ *adj* hard-working; diligent 勤劳的; 勤奋的; 勤勉的. ▷ **in·dus·tri·ously** *adv*. **in·dus·tri·ous·ness** *n* [U].

in·dus·try /ˈɪndəstrɪ; ˋɪndəstrɪ/ *n* **1** [C, U] (**a**) (branch of) manufacture or production 制造或生产(的部门); 工业; 企业; 行业: *Britain's coal industry* 英国的煤炭工业 ○ *heavy industry*, ie producing large goods, eg steel or cars 重工业 ○ *nationalized industries* 国有化工业. (**b**) commercial undertaking that provides services (行)业(提供服务的商业性部门): *the catering, hotel, tourist, entertainment, etc industry* 饮食、旅馆、旅游、娱乐等(行)业. **2** [U] (*fml* 文) quality of being hard-working 勤奋; 勤劳: *praise sb for his industry* 赞扬某人勤奋 ○*The industry of these little ants is wonderful to behold.* 这些小蚂蚁很勤奋, 看起来多奇妙. **3** (idm 习语) **a captain of industry** ⇨CAPTAIN.

in·ebri·ated /ɪˈniːbrɪeɪtɪd; ɪnˋibrɪˌetɪd/ *adj* [usu pred 通常作表语] (*fml or joc* 文或谑) drunk; intoxicated 喝醉; 醉醺醺: (*fig* 比喻) *inebriated* (ie uncontrollably excited) *by his success* 他因成功而陶醉.

▷ **in·ebri·ate** /ɪˈniːbrɪət; ɪnˋibrɪɪt/ *adj*, *n* (*fml* 文) habitually drunk (person) 醉醺醺的; 酒徒; 酒鬼.

in·ebri·ation /ɪˌniːbrɪˈeɪʃn; ɪnˌibrɪˋeʃən/ *n* [U] (*fml or joc* 文或谑) drunkenness 醉; 酒醉.

in·ed·ible /ɪnˈedɪbl; ɪnˋɛdəbl̩/ *adj* (*fml* 文) not suitable to be eaten 不宜食用的; 不能吃的: *The fish was quite inedible.* 这种鱼完全不宜食用. Cf 参看 UNEATABLE.

in·ef·fable /ɪnˈefəbl; ɪnˋɛfəbl̩/ *adj* (*fml* 文) too great to be described in words 不可言喻的; 难用言语表达的; 不可言状的: *ineffable joy, beauty, etc* 难以形容的喜悦、美丽等. ▷ **in·ef·fably** /-əblɪ; -əblɪ/ *adv*.

in·ef·fect·ive /ˌɪnɪˈfektɪv; ˌɪnəˋfɛktɪv/ *adj* not producing the required effect(s) 不起作用的; 无效果的; 效果不佳的: *use ineffective methods* 使用无效的方法 ○ *She is totally ineffective as a teacher*, ie She cannot teach satisfactorily. 她当老师全然不称职. ▷ **in·ef·fect·ively** *adv*. **in·ef·fect·ive·ness** *n* [U].

in·ef·fec·tual /ˌɪnɪˈfektʃʊəl; ˌɪnəˋfɛktʃʊəl/ *adj* lacking confidence and unable to get things done; without effect 信心不足而又无能为力的; 无效的; 不起作用的: *make ineffectual attempts to do sth* 徒然尝试做某事 ○ *ineffectual as a leader, teacher, etc* 作领袖、作教师等不能胜任的 ○*a well-meaning but ineffectual person* 心有余而力不足的人. ▷ **in·ef·fec·tu·ally** /-tʃʊəlɪ; -tʃʊəlɪ/ *adv*.

in·ef·fi·cient /ˌɪnɪˈfɪʃnt; ˌɪnəˋfɪʃənt/ *adj* **1** (of a machine, process, etc) not producing adequate results; wasteful (指机器、方法等)无效率的, 无效果的, 效率低的, 不经济的: *an inefficient system, method, use of resources, etc* 不经济的体制、方法、资源利用等. **2** (of a person) wasting time, energy, etc in what one does, and therefore failing to do it well or quickly enough (指人)做事效率低的, 能力差的, 不称职的: *dismissed for being inefficient* 因效率低遭辞退 ○ *an inefficient management, administration, body of workers, etc* 效率低的经理人员、行政机构、一群工人等. ▷ **in·ef·fi·ci·ency** /-nsɪ; -ənsɪ/ *n* [U]: *dismissed for inefficiency* 因能力差遭解雇. **in·ef·fi·ci·ently** *adv*.

in·el·astic /ˌɪnɪˈlæstɪk; ˌɪnɪˋlæstɪk/ *adj* not flexible or adaptable; unyielding 无弹性的; 无适应性的; 无伸缩性的: (*fig* 比喻) *This timetable is too inelastic. You must allow for possible modifications.* 这个时间表太死了, 你总得留有余地吧.

in·el·eg·ant /ˌɪnˈelɪɡənt; ɪnˋɛləɡənt/ *adj* not graceful or refined; ugly 不优美的; 不雅的; 不精致的; 丑陋的: *an inelegant gesture, reply* 有失风雅的姿势、答复. ▷ **in·el·eg·ance** /-əns; -əns/ *n* [U]. **in·el·eg·antly** *adv*.

in·el·igible /ɪnˈelɪdʒəbl; ɪnˋɛlɪdʒəbl̩/ *adj* **~ (for sth/to do sth)** not having the appropriate or necessary qualifications (for sth) 不合格的; 无资格的: *ineligible for the job, for promotion* 无资格做该项工作、晋升 ○ *Any person under the age of 18 is ineligible for benefit.* 未满18岁者无资格领取补助金. ▷ **in·el·igib·il·ity** /ɪnˌelɪdʒəˈbɪlətɪ; ɪnˌɛlɪdʒəˋbɪlətɪ/ *n* [U].

in·eluct·able /ˌɪnɪˈlʌktəbl; ˌɪnɪˋlʌktəbl̩/ *adj* (*fml* 文) that cannot be escaped from 不可避免的; 难免的: *the victim of ineluctable fate* 难逃厄运的牺牲品. ▷ **in·eluct·ably** /-əblɪ; -əblɪ/ *adv*.

in·ept /ɪˈnept; ɪnˋɛpt/ *adj* (**a**) **~ (at sth/doing sth)** completely unskilful (at sth) 不熟练的; 不擅长的: *I've never heard anyone so inept at making speeches.* 我从未听说过有这样不会讲话的人. ○ *His inept handling of a minor problem turned it into a major crisis.* 他处理不善使小事变大了. (**b**) said or done at the wrong time; not appropriate or tactful 不合适的; 不恰当的; 不策略的: *an inept remark* 不当的言语.

▷ **in·ept·it·ude** /ɪˈneptɪtjuːd; *US* -tuːd; ɪnˋɛptəˌtud/ *n* (**a**) [U] quality of being inept 不熟练; 不适宜. (**b**) [C] inept action, remark, etc 不当的言行等.

in·eptly *adv*.

in·equal·ity /ˌɪnɪˈkwɒlətɪ; ˌɪnɪˋkwɑlətɪ/ *n* (**a**) [U] lack of equality in size, degree, circumstances, etc, esp unfair difference in rank, wealth, opportunity, etc (大小、程度、环境等)不均等, 不平等, 不平衡, 不等量(尤指等级、财富、机会等的不公平差异): *fight against political, racial, etc inequality* 反对政治的、种族的...不平等. (**b**) [C] instance of this 不平等; 不均等; 不平衡: *Inequalities in wealth cause social unrest.* 贫富不均可造成社会动荡.

in·equit·able /ɪnˈekwɪtəbl; ɪnˋɛkwɪtəbl̩/ *adj* (*fml* 文) unjust; unfair 不公正的; 不公平的: *an inequitable division of the profits* 利润之不公平分配. ▷ **in·equit·ably** /-əblɪ; -əblɪ/ *adv*.

in·equity /ɪnˈekwətɪ; ɪnˋɛkwətɪ/ *n* (*fml* 文) (**a**) [U] injustice or unfairness 不公正; 不公平: *the inequity of the system* 制度的不公正. (**b**) [C] instance of this 不公正; 不公平.

in·erad·ic·able /ˌɪnɪˈrædɪkəbl; ˌɪnɪˋrædɪkəbl̩/ *adj* (esp of sth bad) that cannot be got rid of; firmly and deeply established (尤指坏事)不能根除的, 根深蒂固的, 积重难返的: *ineradicable faults, failings, prejudices, etc* 不能根除的缺点、过失、成见等. ▷ **in·erad·ic·ably** /-əblɪ; -əblɪ/ *adv*.

in·ert /ɪˈnɜːt; ɪnˋɝt/ *adj* **1** without power to move or act 无行动或活动能力的: *She lay there inert; I thought she must be dead.* 她躺在那儿一动不动, 我想她一定死了. ○ (*physics* 物) *inert matter* 惰性物质. **2** (*derog* 贬) heavy and slow in action, thought, etc; without vigour 迟钝的; 迟缓的; 呆滞的: *an inert management team* 死气沉沉的管理阶层. ▷ **in·ertly** *adv*. **in·ert·ness** *n* [U].

□ **iˌnert ˈgas** gas (eg helium, neon) that does not react chemically with other substances 惰性气体.

in·er·tia /ɪˈnɜːʃə; ɪnˋɝʃə/ *n* [U] **1** (*usu derog* 通常作贬义) (**a**) lack of vigour; lethargy 无活力; 迟钝: *I'm unable to throw off this feeling of inertia.* 我无法摆脱这种懒散的感觉. (**b**) tendency to remain unchanged 惰性; 保守: *Because of the sheer inertia of the system many badly needed reforms were never introduced.* 纯粹是由于制度本身有惰性, 很多事急需改革却从未实行. **2** (*physics* 物) property of matter by which it remains in a state of rest or, if in motion, continues moving in a straight line, unless acted upon by an external force 惯性.

▷ **in·er·tial** /ɪˈnɜːʃl; ɪnˋɝʃəl/ *adj* of or by inertia 惯性的: *a missile's inertial guidance system* 导弹惯性制导系统.

□ **iˌnertia ˈreel** type of reel round which one end of a safety-belt is wound so that the belt will tighten automatically over the wearer if it is pulled suddenly 惯性卷筒(安全带伸缩装置, 突然受力时可自动绷紧以保护使用者).

iˌnertia ˈseat-belt seat-belt incorporating an inertia reel 惯性卷筒式座位安全带.

iˌnertia ˈselling (*esp Brit*) sending of goods to a person who has not ordered them, in the hope that he will not refuse them and will therefore later have to pay for them 惯性销售(将货物送至未订购者处, 希不遭退货而成交, 事后清帐).

in·es·cap·able /ˌɪnɪˈskeɪpəbl; ˌɪnəˋskepəbl̩/ *adj* that cannot be avoided; inevitable 不可逃避的; 不可避免的; 难免的; 免不了的: *be forced to the inescapable conclusion that he is a liar* 只能做出舍此无他的结论, 他撒谎了. ▷ **in·es·cap·ably** /-əblɪ; -əblɪ/ *adv*.

in·es·tim·able /ɪnˈestɪməbl; ɪnˋɛstəməbl̩/ *adj* (*fml* 文) too great, precious, etc to be estimated (因过大、过于贵重等)难以估量的, 无法评价的: *The value of your assistance is inestimable.* 阁下鼎力相助之功不可胜言. ▷ **in·es·tim·ably** /-əblɪ; -əblɪ/ *adv*.

in·ev·it·able /ɪnˈevɪtəbl; ɪnˋɛvətəbl̩/ *adj* **1** that cannot be avoided; that is sure to happen 不可避免的; 必然发生的; 难免的: *an inevitable disaster* 不可避免的灾难 ○ *It seems inevitable that they'll lose.* 看来他们的败局是势不可免了. **2** [attrib 作定语] (*infml often joc* 口, 常作戏谑语) so frequently seen, heard, etc that it is familiar and expected 在意料中的; 熟悉的; 惯常的: *a tourist with his inevitable camera* 惯常带着照相机的游客.
▷ **in·ev·it·ab·il·ity** /ɪnˌevɪtəˈbɪlətɪ; ˌɪnɛvətəˋbɪlətɪ/ *n* [U].
the in·ev·it·able *n* [sing] that which is inevitable 不可避免的事物; 必然性: *accept the inevitable* 承受不可避免的事物.
in·ev·it·ably /-əblɪ; -əblɪ/ *adv* as is or was sure to happen 不可避免地; 必然地: *The train was inevitably delayed by the accident.* 火车不可避免地受到这事故的耽误.

in·ex·act /ˌɪnɪgˈzækt; ˌɪnɪgˋzækt/ *adj* not exact or precise 不准确的; 不精确的; 不严谨的: *Weather forecasting is an inexact science.* 天气预报是一门模糊的科学.
▷ **in·ex·act·it·ude** /ˌɪnɪgˈzæktɪtjuːd; *US* -tɪtuːd; ˌɪnɪgˋzæktəˌtud/ *n* (**a**) [U] being inexact 不准确; 不精确. (**b**) [C] instance of this 不准确; 不精确: (*joc euph* 谑, 婉) *a terminological inexactitude*, ie a lie 术语误差(即谎言).

in·ex·cus·able /ˌɪnɪkˈskjuːzəbl; ˌɪnɪkˋskjuzəbl̩/ *adj* too bad to be excused 不可原谅的; 不可宽恕的; 不可辩解的: *inexcusable conduct, delays, inefficiency* 不可原谅的行为、耽搁、低效率. ▷ **in·ex·cus·ably** /-əblɪ; -əblɪ/ *adv*: *inexcusably rude, late, etc* 粗暴得、迟迟未到...难以容忍.

in·ex·haust·ible /ˌɪnɪgˈzɔːstəbl; ˌɪnɪgˋzɔstəbl̩/ *adj* that will always continue; that cannot be used up 无穷尽的; 用不完的: *an inexhaustible supply of sth* 某物源源不绝的供应 ○ *My patience is not inexhaustible*, ie I will eventually become angry or impatient. 我的耐心是有限度的. ▷ **in·ex·haust·ibly** /-əblɪ; -əblɪ/ *adv*.

in·ex·or·able /ɪnˈeksərəbl; ɪnˋɛksərəbl̩/ *adj* continuing unstoppably; relentless 不可阻挡的; 坚持不懈的; 无情的: *inexorable demands, pressures, etc* 无可变更的要求、无情的压力 ○ *the inexorable march of progress* 势不可挡的进展. ▷ **in·ex·or·ab·il·ity** /ɪnˌeksərəˈbɪlətɪ; ɪnˌɛksərəˋbɪlətɪ/ *n* [U]. **in·ex·or·ably** /ɪnˈeksərəblɪ; ɪnˋɛksərəblɪ/ *adv*.

in·ex·pedi·ent /ˌɪnɪkˈspiːdɪənt; ˌɪnɪkˋspidɪənt/ *adj* (*fml* 文) not serving a useful purpose; unwise; not expedient 不合宜的; 失策的; 不明智的: *It would be inexpedient to inform them at this stage.* 在目前阶段就通知他们很不妥当. ▷ **in·ex·pedi·ency** /-ənsɪ; -ənsɪ/ *n* [U].

in·ex·pens·ive /ˌɪnɪkˈspensɪv; ˌɪnɪkˋspɛnsɪv/ *adj* low priced; not expensive 价廉的; 不贵的. ▷ **in·ex·pens·ively** *adv*.

in·ex·peri·ence /ˌɪnɪkˈspɪərɪəns; ˌɪnɪkˋspɪrɪəns/ *n* [U] ~ **(in sth)** lack of experience 无经验; 缺乏经验: *failure due to inexperience* 因无经验而失败 ○ *You must forgive my inexperience in these matters.* 我在这些事情上没有经验, 你得多包涵.
▷ **in·ex·peri·enced** *adj* ~ **(in sth)** lacking experience 无经验的; 缺乏经验的: *inexperienced in love, business, negotiation* 在恋爱、经商、谈判方面无经验.

in·ex·pert /ɪnˈekspɜːt; ˌɪnɪkˋspɝt/ *adj* ~ **(at sth)** unskilled 不熟练的; 无技巧的: *inexpert advice, guidance, etc* 不在行的劝告、指导等. ▷ **in·ex·pertly** *adv*: *an inexpertly executed stroke* 不熟练地一击.

in·ex·pi·able /ɪnˈekspɪəbl; ɪnˋɛkspɪəbl̩/ *adj* (*fml* 文) (of an offence) so bad that nothing one can do can make up for it; that cannot be expiated (指罪过)不能自赎的, 不可抵偿的.

in·ex·plic·able /ˌɪnɪkˈsplɪkəbl; ˌɪnɪkˋsplɪkəbl̩/ *adj* that cannot be explained 无法解释的: *an inexplicable phenomenon* 神秘莫测的现象. ▷ **in·ex·plic·ab·il·ity** /ˌɪnɪkˌsplɪkəˈbɪlətɪ; ˌɪnɪkˌsplɪkəˋbɪlətɪ/ *n* [U]. **in·ex·plic·ably** /ˌɪnɪkˈsplɪkəblɪ; ˌɪnɪkˋsplɪkəblɪ/ *adv*: *Inexplicably, she never turned up.* 令人不解的是, 她从未露面.

in·ex·press·ible /ˌɪnɪkˈspresəbl; ˌɪnɪkˋsprɛsəbl̩/ *adj* too great to be expressed in words 无法用言语表达的: *inexpressible sorrow, anguish, joy, etc* 难以形容的悲哀、痛苦、喜悦等. ▷ **in·ex·press·ibly** /-əblɪ; -əblɪ/ *adv*: *inexpressibly sad* 悲伤得无法用言语表达.

in·ex·tin·guish·able /ˌɪnɪkˈstɪŋgwɪʃəbl; ˌɪnɪkˋstɪŋgwɪʃəbl̩/ *adj* (*fml* 文) that cannot be extinguished or put out 不能熄灭或扑灭的: *the inextinguishable flame of liberty* 不可扑灭的自由之火 ○ (*fig* 比喻) *inextinguishable hope, love, desire, etc* 不可遏止的希望、爱情、欲望等. ▷ **in·ex·tin·guish·ably** /-əblɪ; -əblɪ/ *adv*.

in ex·tremis /ˌɪnɪkˈstriːmɪs; ˌɪnɪkˋstrimɪs/ (*Latin* 拉) **1** (*fml* 文) (as a last resort when) in an emergency 在紧急关头; 应变措施: *This alarm button is only to be used in extremis.* 此警报按钮只在紧急情况下使用. **2** (*religion* 宗) (in the Roman Catholic Church) about to die (天主教会用语)临终: *administer the last sacrament to sb in extremis* 给临终的人傅油.

in·ex·tric·able /ˌɪnɪkˈstrɪkəbl, ɪnˈekstrɪkəbl; ɪnˋɛkstrɪkəbl̩/ *adj* **1** so closely linked that separation is impossible 无法分开的: *In the Middle Ages, philosophy and theology were inextricable.* 在中世纪, 哲学与神学是不分的. **2** that cannot be escaped from 不能逃避的: *inextricable difficulties* 无法避免的困难. ▷ **in·ex·tric·ably** *adv*: *Her career was inextricably linked with his.* 她的事业是和他的事业紧密联系在一起的.

inf *abbr* 缩写 = below; further on (in a book, etc) (Latin *infra*) 在下面, (书等的)下文(源自拉丁文 *infra*). Cf 参看 SUP *abbr* 缩写.

in·fal·lible /ɪnˈfæləbl; ɪnˋfæləbl̩/ *adj* **1** incapable of making mistakes or doing wrong 不会犯错误的; 不可能错的; 无过失的: *None of us is infallible.* 我们无人不犯错误. **2** extremely accurate 极准确的; 极精确的: *a journalist with an infallible nose* (ie instinct) *for a story* 触角敏锐的新闻记者. **3** never failing; always effective 绝对可靠的; 永远有效的; 万无一失的: *an infallible remedy, cure, method, test* 万无一失的处方、妙药、方法、试验.
▷ **in·fal·lib·il·ity** /ɪnˌfæləˈbɪlətɪ; ɪnˌfæləˋbɪlətɪ/ *n* [U] **1** complete freedom from the possibility of being wrong 绝对正确; 断无错误: *the doctrine of Papal infallibility* 教皇无谬说的教义. **2** absolute certainty of effectiveness 绝对有效: *I can't claim infallibility for this method.* 我不敢说这方法绝对有效.
in·fal·libly /-əblɪ; -əblɪ/ *adv* **1** in a manner that cannot fail 不可能错地; 万无一失地: *infallibly accurate* 绝对准确. **2** without exception; always 毫无例外地; 总是; 永远: *Every day she arrives, infallibly, five minutes late. I could time my watch by her!* 她每天晚到五分钟, 从无例外, 我都能依照她来对表!

in·fam·ous /ˈɪnfəməs; ˋɪnfəməs/ *adj* **1** ~ **(for sth)** well-known as being wicked or immoral; notorious 声名狼藉的; 恶名昭著的: *an infamous traitor* 臭名昭彰的叛徒 ○ *a king infamous for his cruelty* 以残暴而臭名远扬的国王. **2** (*fml* 文) wicked; disgraceful 邪恶的; 无耻的; 丢脸的: *his infamous treatment of her* 他对她恶毒的虐待.
▷ **in·fam·ously** *adv*.
in·famy /ˈɪnfəmɪ; ˋɪnfəmɪ/ *n* (*fml* 文) **1** (**a**) [U] infamous behaviour; wickedness 丑事; 邪恶. (**b**) [C] wicked act 恶行: *guilty of many infamies* 罪恶多端. **2** [U] public dishonour or disgrace 臭名; 恶名; 丢脸; 耻辱: *His name will live in infamy*, ie He will always be held in disgrace. 他的名字将与耻辱共存.

in·fancy /ˈɪnfənsɪ; ˋɪnfənsɪ/ *n* [U] **1** (**a**) state or period of being an infant; early childhood 婴儿期; 幼儿期: *in early infancy* 在婴儿时期. (**b**) (*Brit law* 律) period before one reaches the age of 18; minority 未成年(未满 18 岁者). **2** (*fig* 比喻) early stage of development or growth (发展或生长的)初期: *The project was cancelled while it was still in its infancy.* 这项目尚处于初期阶段时就取消了.

in·fant /ˈɪnfənt; ˋɪnfənt/ *n* **1** child during the first few years of life 婴儿; 幼儿: *infants, older children and adults* 幼儿、大孩子和成人 ○ [attrib 作定语] *our infant ˈson* 我们的幼小的儿子 ○ *infant ˈvoices* 童声 ○ *infant morˈtality rate*, ie percentage of children that die in the first few years of life 幼儿死亡率 ○ *an ˈinfant teacher*, ie one who teaches infants 幼儿教师 ○ (*fig* 比喻) *In its first general election, the infant* (ie newly-formed) *Social Democratic Party won few seats.* 新成立的社会民主党初次参加大选所得席位无几. **2** (*Brit law* 律) person under the age of 18; minor 未成年人(18 岁以下者).
□ ˌ**infant ˈprodigy** unusually talented child that shows signs of genius from an early age 神童.
ˈ**infant ˌschool** (part of a) primary school for children up to the age of 7 幼儿学校(为七岁以下儿童设置的).

in·fanti·cide /ɪn'fæntɪsaɪd; ɪn'fæntə,saɪd/ *n* **1** [U] (**a**) crime of killing an infant 杀婴(杀害婴儿的罪行): *commit infanticide* 犯杀婴罪. (**b**) (formerly) custom among some people of killing unwanted new-born children (旧时)有些人将不想要的新生儿杀掉的风俗. **2** [C] person who kills an infant 杀害婴儿的人.

in·fant·ile /'ɪnfəntaɪl; 'ɪnfən,taɪl/ *adj* **1** [usu attrib 通常作定语] of infants or infancy 婴儿(期)的; 幼儿(期)的: *infantile diseases* 幼儿疾病. **2** (*derog* 贬) (esp of older children or adults) childish (尤指大孩子或成年人)孩子气的, 幼稚的: *infantile behaviour* 孩子气的行为.

▷ **in·fant·il·ism** /ɪn'fæntɪlɪzəm; ɪn'fæntəl,ɪzəm/ *n* [U] (of older children and adults) mentally and physically underdeveloped state (指大孩子和成年人)幼稚病, 幼稚型(生理和智力发育不良的状态).

□ ˌ**infantile pa'ralysis** (*dated* 旧) poliomyelitis 小儿麻痹症(脊髓灰质炎).

in·fan·try /'ɪnfəntrɪ; 'ɪnfəntrɪ/ *n* [U, Gp] soldiers who fight on foot 步兵: *We have less infantry and armour than the enemy.* 我们的步兵和装甲兵均比敌军的少. ○ *The infantry is/are defending well.* 步兵防守甚佳. ○ [attrib 作定语] *an infantry regiment* 步兵团. Cf 参看 CAVALRY.

□ '**infantryman** /-mən; -mən/ *n* (*pl* **-men**) soldier in an infantry regiment 步兵团的士兵; 步兵.

in·fatu·ated /ɪn'fætʃʊeɪtɪd; ɪn'fætʃʊ,etɪd/ *adj* **~ (with/by sb/sth)** (*usu derog* 通常作贬义) (temporarily) filled with an intense but usu foolish love (一时地)热恋着的, (通常指)痴情的: *It's no use talking to him: he's completely infatuated.* 跟他谈也没用, 他已完全堕入情网. ○ *She's infatuated by his good looks.* 她迷恋上他那俊俏的外貌了. ○ (*fig* 比喻) *He's so infatuated with the idea that he can't talk about anything else.* 他让那个想法迷住了, 一谈话就是那件事.

▷ **in·fatu·ation** /ɪn,fætʃʊ'eɪʃn; ɪn,fætʃʊ'eʃən/ *n* [U, C] **~ (with/for sb/sth)** being infatuated 热恋; 痴情; 迷恋: *His infatuation with her lasted six months.* 他对她迷恋了半年. ○ *This is only a passing infatuation, not to be taken too seriously.* 这仅仅是一时的恋情, 不必过于认真. ○ *develop an infatuation for sb* 逐渐迷恋上某人.

in·fect /ɪn'fekt; ɪn'fɛkt/ *v* [esp passive 尤用于被动语态: Tn, Tn·pr] **~ sb/sth (with sth)** **1** cause sb/sth to have a disease; contaminate sb/sth 使某人[某物]传染、感染; 污染某人[某事物]: *The laboratory animals had been infected with the bacteria.* 实验室的动物都已受到这种细菌的感染. ○ *an infected wound* 受到感染的伤口 ○ *Clean the infected area with disinfectant.* 把受感染的部分用消毒剂消毒. ○ *Police have sealed off infected areas of the country.* 警方已将全国各感染区封锁了. **2** (*fig derog* 比喻, 贬) fill (sb's mind) with undesirable ideas 用坏思想感染(某人的思想): *a mind infected with racial prejudice* 受到种族偏见影响的头脑. **3** (*fig approv* 比喻, 褒) fill (sb's mind or spirit) with happy and positive ideas or feelings 用快乐的、好的思想感情感染(某人的心灵): *Her cheerful spirits and bubbling laughter infected the whole class*, ie They became happy too. 她那快乐的情绪和爽朗的笑声感染了全班.

in·fec·tion /ɪn'fekʃn; ɪn'fɛkʃən/ *n* **1** [U] **~ (with sth)** (**a**) becoming ill through contact with bacteria, etc 传染; 感染; 侵染: *be exposed to infection* 处于受感染范围 ○ *the infection of the body with bacteria* 身体受细菌侵染. (**b**) (*fig derog* 比喻, 贬) filling the mind with undesirable ideas 头脑中充斥着坏思想: *the infection of young people with dangerous ideologies* 危险的思想意识对年轻人的影响. **2** [C] disease caused by a micro-organism 传染病: *spread/pass on an infection* 传播[传染]某种病 ○ *People catch all kinds of infections in the winter.* 冬天人们易患多种传染病. ○ *an airborne/a waterborne infection* 由空气[水]传播的传染病. Cf 参看 CONTAGION.

in·fec·tious /ɪn'fekʃəs; ɪn'fɛkʃəs/ *adj* **1** (of a disease) caused by bacteria, etc that are passed on from one person to another (指疾病)传染的, 感染的: *Flu is highly infectious.* 流感的传染性很强. **2** [usu pred 通常作表语] (of a person) in danger of infecting others (with a disease) (指人)能传染他人(疾病): *While you have this rash you are still infectious.* 身上还有这种疹子, 就仍然有传染性. **3** (*fig approv* 比喻, 褒) quickly influencing others; likely to spread to others 有感染力的; 易传播给他人的: *infectious enthusiasm* 有感染力的热情 ○ *an infectious laugh* 有感染作用的笑声. ▷ **in·fec·tiously** *adv*: *laugh infectiously* 笑得富有感染力. **in·fec·tious·ness** *n* [U]. Cf 参看 CONTAGIOUS.

in·fer /ɪn'fɜː(r); ɪn'fɝ/ *v* (**-rr-**) [Tn, Tn·pr, Tf] **~ sth (from sth)** reach (an opinion) from facts or reasoning; conclude sth (根据事实或推理)推断, 推定(一想法); 得出某事物的结论: *It is possible to infer two completely opposite conclusions from this set of facts.* 从这些事实中可能推断出两种截然相反的结论. ○ *Am I to infer (from your remarks) that you think I'm not telling the truth?* (从你的话中)看来你认为我没说实话? Cf 参看 IMPLY.

▷ **in·fer·ence** /'ɪnfərəns; 'ɪnfərəns/ *n* **1** [U] process of inferring 推论; 推理; 推断: *If he is guilty then by inference so is she*, ie This conclusion follows logically from the same set of facts. 如果他有罪, 可推断出她也有罪. **2** [C] **~ (from sth) (that...)** that which is inferred; conclusion 结论; 推断结果: *Is that a fair inference (to draw) from his statement?* 从他的说法中得出这种结论恰当吗? ○ *She'd begun spending a lot of money, and the obvious inference was that she'd stolen it.* 她花起钱来大手大脚了, 事情很明显, 钱是偷来的.

in·fer·en·tial /,ɪnfə'renʃl; ,ɪnfə'rɛnʃəl/ *adj* that may be inferred 可以推断的: *inferential proof* 由推论得出的证据. **in·fer·en·tially** /-ʃəlɪ; -ʃəlɪ/ *adv*.

in·ferior /ɪn'fɪərɪə(r); ɪn'fɪrɪɚ/ *adj* **~ (to sb/sth)** low(er) in rank, social position, importance, quality, etc (等级、社会地位、重要性、质量等)(较)低的, 次要的, 低等的, 差的: *A captain is inferior to a major.* 上尉的级别低于少校. ○ *be socially inferior* 社会地位低下 ○ *make sb feel inferior* 使某人自惭形秽 ○ *inferior goods, workmanship* 次货、劣等手艺. Cf 参看 SUPERIOR.

▷ **in·ferior** *n* person who is inferior (in rank, etc) (级别等)低于他人者; 下级; 下属: *one's social inferior* 社会地位不如自己的人 ○ *We should not despise our intellectual inferiors.* 我们不应轻视智力不如我们的人.

in·feri·or·ity /ɪn,fɪərɪ'ɒrətɪ; US -'ɔːr-; ɪn,fɪrɪ'ɔrətɪ/ *n* [U] state of being inferior 下级; 下属; 低人一等: *feelings of inferiority* 自卑感.

□ **inferi'ority complex** (*psychology* 心) state of mind in which sb feels less important, clever, admired, etc than other people, and often tries to compensate for this by boasting and being aggressive 自卑感; 自卑情结. Cf 参看 SUPERIORITY COMPLEX (SUPERIOR).

in·fernal /ɪn'fɜːnl; ɪn'fɝnl/ *adj* **1** (*rhet* 修辞) (**a**) of hell 阴间的; 地狱的: *the infernal regions* 阴间. (**b**) devilish; abominable 魔鬼般的; 地狱似的: *infernal cruelty* 恶魔般的残忍. **2** [attrib 作定语] (*infml* 口) annoying; tiresome 讨厌的; 可恶的: *That infernal telephone hasn't stopped ringing all day!* 那讨厌的电话整天响个不停! ○ *an infernal nuisance* 很可恶的事. ▷ **in·fern·ally** /-nəlɪ; -nlɪ/ *adv*: *infernally rude* 粗鲁得讨人厌.

in·ferno /ɪn'fɜːnəʊ; ɪn'fɝno/ *n* (*pl* **~s** /-z; -z/) **1** place or situation like hell, esp in being full of horror and confusion 地狱似的处境(尤指一片恐怖和混乱): *the inferno of war* 战争的恐怖景象. **2** (place affected by a) large destructive fire 毁灭性的大火(殃及之处): *The place was a blazing, raging, roaring, etc inferno.* 那地方是一片熊熊的、滚滚的、咆哮的...火海.

in·fer·tile /ɪn'fɜːtaɪl; US -tl; ɪn'fɝtl/ *adj* not fertile; barren 贫瘠的; 不结果实的; 不能生育的: *infertile land* 贫瘠的土地 ○ *an infertile couple*, ie unable to have children 不能生育的夫妇. ▷ **in·fer·til·ity** /,ɪnfə'tɪlətɪ; ,ɪnfɚ'tɪlətɪ/ *n* [U].

in·fest /ɪn'fest; ɪn'fɛst/ *v* [usu passive 通常用于被动语态: Tn, Tn·pr] **~ sth (with sth)** (*derog* 贬) (of pests, vermin, insects, etc) live in (a place) persistently and in large numbers (指有害的鸟兽昆虫等)大批孳生出没, 遍布, 侵扰(某处): *a warehouse infested by rats* 有大批老鼠出没的仓库 ○ *clothing infested with lice* 爬满虱子的衣服 ○ *a garden infested with weeds* 杂草丛生的花园.

▷ **in·festa·tion** /,ɪnfe'steɪʃn; ,ɪnfɛs'teʃən/ *n* [C, U] (instance of) infesting or being infested (指有害的鸟兽昆虫等)大批出没, 侵扰, 骚扰: *an infestation of cockroaches* 蟑螂的侵扰.

in·fi·del /'ɪnfɪdəl; 'ɪnfədl/ *n* (*arch derog* 古, 贬) person with no belief in a religion, esp in what is considered to be the true religion 不信宗教者, 无宗教信仰之人(尤指没有正统宗教信仰者).

in·fi·del·ity /,ɪnfɪ'delətɪ; ,ɪnfə'dɛlətɪ/ *n* [C, U] (*fml* 文) (act of) disloyalty or unfaithfulness, esp adultery 背信;

不忠实;(尤指)通奸: *willing to forgive her husband's little infidelities* 愿意原谅丈夫的些微不忠行为.

in·field /ˈɪnfiːld; ˈɪnˌfild/ *n* **the infield** **1** (**a**) [sing] (in cricket) part of the ground near the wicket (板球)内场(靠近三柱门的场地). (**b**) [pl *v*] fielders stationed there (板球)内场全体球员. **2** (**a**) [sing] (in baseball) area within the diamond(4) (棒球)内场, 内野(垒与垒围线之内的场地). (**b**) [pl *v*] fielders stationed there (棒球)全体内野手或内场手. Cf 参看 OUTFIELD.

▷ **in·fielder** *n* person fielding in the infield 内野手; 内场手.

in·fight·ing /ˈɪnfaɪtɪŋ; ˈɪnˌfaɪtɪŋ/ *n* [U] **1** (in boxing) fighting in which the opponents are very close to or holding on to each other (拳击)接近战. **2** (*fig infml* 比喻, 口) fierce competition between rivals (eg involving intrigue, betrayal, etc) 对手间的激烈竞争(如事涉阴谋、出卖等): *I gather a lot of political infighting went on before he got the top job.* 我看他一定经历了政治上诸多明争暗斗才获此高位.

in·fill /ˈɪnfɪl; ˈɪnfɪl/ (also **in·fill·ing**) *n* [U] **1** act of filling gaps (eg in a row of buildings) 填空隙(如一排建筑物之间). **2** material used to fill a hole or gap (eg in a wall) 填充物(用以填实洞穴或空隙的, 如在墙上).

in·filt·rate /ˈɪnfɪltreɪt; ɪnˈfɪltret/ *v* **1** [I, Ipr] **~ (through sth) (into sth)** (of liquids, gases, etc) pass slowly by filtering; penetrate (指液体、气体等)渗透, 透入: *The thick fog seemed to have infiltrated through the very walls into the room.* 浓雾好像透过墙壁进到房间里. ○ (*fig* 比喻) *the depths of the ocean, where no light can infiltrate* 海洋的深处, 光线射不进去. **2** [Tn·pr] **~ A into B/~ B with A** cause sth to pass slowly by filtering it into sth else 使某物慢慢渗人或透入他物: *infiltrate poison into the water-supply/infiltrate the water-supply with poison* 把毒药慢慢渗入水源. **3** [Ipr, Tn] **~ (through sth) (into sth)** (*esp military or politics* 尤用于军事或政治) enter (sth) stealthily without being noticed 悄悄进入; 潜入: *troops infiltrating through enemy lines into occupied territory* 通过敌人封锁线潜入占领区的部队 ○ *Our entire organization had been infiltrated by enemy agents.* 敌特已打入我们整个组织. **4** [Tn·pr] (*esp military or politics* 尤用于军事或政治) **~ sb/sth into sth; ~ sth with sb/sth** introduce sb/sth stealthily into sth 暗中使某人[某事物]进入: *infiltrate spies into a country* 派间谍进入某国家 ○ *infiltrate an organization with one's own men* 派自己的人混入某组织.

▷ **in·filt·ra·tion** /ˌɪnfɪlˈtreɪʃn; ˌɪnfɪlˈtreʃən/ *n* **1** [U] **~ (of sth)** (into sth) infiltrating or being infiltrated 渗入; 渗透: *infiltration of poisonous chemicals into the water-supply* 有毒化学药品向水源的渗入. **2 ~ (of sb/sth into sth); ~ (of sth with sb/sth)** (*esp military or politics* 尤用于军事或政治) (**a**) [U] infiltrating of people, ideas, etc (人员、思想等的)渗入, 潜入, 混入: *the infiltration of spies, troops, etc into an area, organization, etc* 特务、部队等向某地区、某组织等的潜入 ○ *the infiltration of an organization with one's agents* 己方代理人向某组织的渗入. (**b**) [C] instance of this 渗透活动; 渗透战术.

in·filt·rator /ˈɪnfɪltreɪtə(r); ɪnˈfɪlˌtretɚ/ *n* person who infiltrates 潜入或渗入的人: *left-wing infiltrators* 左翼潜入分子.

in·fin·ite /ˈɪnfɪnət; ˈɪnfənɪt/ *adj* (**a**) without limits; endless 无限的; 无穷的: *infinite space* 无限的空间. (**b**) that cannot be measured, calculated or imagined; very great 无法衡量的; 无法估计的; 难以想像的; 极大的: *the infinite goodness of God* 上帝无限的恩惠 ○ *have infinite faith/an infinite amount of faith in sb* 对某人绝对的信心 ○ *a painting restored with infinite care* 经极度精心修复的画 ○ *You need infinite patience for this job.* 做这项工作要有极大的耐心.

▷ **the Infinite** *n* [sing] (*rhet* 修辞) God 上帝.

in·fin·itely *adv* **1** to an infinite degree 无限地; 无穷地; 极其: *The particles in an atom are infinitely small.* 原子里的粒子极小. **2** (esp with comparatives 尤与比较级连用) very much 远; 甚: *infinitely better, taller, wiser, etc (than sb/sth else)* (比某人[某事物])好、高、聪明...得多 ○ *infinitely preferable (to sb/sth else)* 远胜(于某人[某事物]).

in·fin·it·es·imal /ˌɪnfɪnɪˈtesɪml; ˌɪnfɪnəˈtɛsəml/ *adj* extremely small 极小的; 极少的: *an infinitesimal increase* 微增. ▷ **in·fin·it·es·im·ally** /-məlɪ; -mlɪ/ *adv*.

in·fin·it·ive /ɪnˈfɪnətɪv; ɪnˈfɪnətɪv/ *n* (*grammar*) **1** basic form of a verb, without inflections, etc (in English used with or without *to*, as in *he can go*; *ask him to go*) (动词)原形, 不定式(无语尾变化等, 在英语中的用法为带to或不带to, 如he can go、ask him to go): *a verb in the infinitive* 原形动词 ○ [attrib 作定语] *the infinitive form* 不定式的形式. **2** (idm 习语) **split an infinitive** ⇨ SPLIT.

in·fin·it·ude /ɪnˈfɪnɪtjuːd; *US* -tuːd; ɪnˈfɪnəˌtud/ *n* (*fml* 文) (**a**) [U] state of being endless or boundless; boundless number or extent 无穷; 无极; 无限; 无限量; 无穷数: *the infinitude of God's mercy* 上帝的慈悲无量. (**b**) [C] infinite number, quantity or extent 无限的数量或程度: *an infinitude of small particles* 无数的微小粒子.

in·fin·ity /ɪnˈfɪnətɪ; ɪnˈfɪnətɪ/ *n* **1** [U] state of being endless or boundless; infinite nature 无穷; 无极; 无限; 大自然: *the infinity of space* 空间的无限. **2** [U] infinite distance or point in space 空间中无限远的距离或点: *gaze into infinity*, ie vaguely into the distance 向茫茫远方望去 ○ *Parallel lines meet at infinity.* 平行线永不相交. **3** [U] (*mathematics* 数) number larger than any other that can be thought of (expressed by the symbol ∞); infinite quantity 无穷大, 无穷(符号为 ∞): *Multiply y by infinity.* 以无穷数乘y. ⇨App 4 见附录4. **4** [sing] indefinitely large amount 无限大的量: *an infinity of stars, of troubles, of things to do* 星星、麻烦、要做的事无限多.

in·firm /ɪnˈfɜːm; ɪnˈfɝm/ *adj* **1** physically weak (esp from old age or illness) 体弱的, 虚弱的, 衰弱的(尤指因年迈或疾病): *walk with infirm steps* 迈着虚弱的步子行走. **2 ~ of sth** (*fml* 文) without strength of sth 欠缺某方面的力量: *infirm of purpose, will, etc*, ie not purposeful, not resolute 目的不明确、意志不坚强.

▷ **the in·firm** *n* [pl *v*] infirm people 体弱的人: *support for the aged and infirm* 援助年老的人和体弱的人.

in·firm·ity /ɪnˈfɜːmətɪ; ɪnˈfɝmətɪ/ *n* [C, U] (particular form of) weakness 体弱; 虚弱; 衰弱: *Old age and infirmity had begun to catch up with him.* 他开始显出年老体衰的样子了. ○ *infirmity of purpose* 意志薄弱 ○ *Deafness and failing eyesight are among the infirmities of old age.* 耳聋眼花是年老体衰的现象.

in·firm·ary /ɪnˈfɜːmərɪ; ɪnˈfɝmərɪ/ *n* **1** hospital 医院. **2** (in a school or some other institution) room used for people who are ill or injured (学校或其他机构的)医务室.

in·flame /ɪnˈfleɪm; ɪnˈflem/ *v* [Tn, Tn·pr] **~ sb/sth (with/to sth)** cause sb/sth to become angry or over-excited 使某人[某物]愤怒或激动: *a speech that inflamed the crowd with anger/to a high pitch of fury* 激起听众愤怒的[使群众怒不可遏的]演说.

▷ **in·flamed** *adj* **~ (by/with sth)** **1** (of a part of the body) red, hot and sore (eg because of infection) (指身体某部)发炎的, 红肿热痛的(如因感染): *inflamed eyes* 红肿的眼睛 ○ *an inflamed boil* 发炎的疖子 ○ *a nose inflamed by an infection* 受感染而红肿的鼻子. **2** (*fig* 比喻) roused to anger, indignation, etc 惹怒的; 愤怒的; 激动的: *inflamed by sb's words* 被某人的话惹得怒火中烧 ○ *inflamed with passion* 情绪激动.

in·flam·mable /ɪnˈflæməbl; ɪnˈflæməbl/ *adj* **1** that can be set on fire 可燃的; 易燃的: *Petroleum — Highly inflammable*, eg on a notice 汽油——易燃品(如告示牌上的字样). Cf 参看 NON-FLAMMABLE. ⇨Usage at INVALUABLE 用法见INVALUABLE. **2** (*fig infml* 比喻, 口) easily excited or aroused 易激动的; 易激怒的: *a man with an inflammable temper* 脾气暴躁的男子.

in·flam·ma·tion /ˌɪnfləˈmeɪʃn; ˌɪnfləˈmeʃən/ *n* [C, U] condition in which a part of the body is red, swollen and sore or itchy, esp because of infection 炎症; 发炎: *(an) inflammation of the lungs, liver, etc* 肺、肝等的炎症.

in·flam·mat·ory /ɪnˈflæmətrɪ; *US* -tɔːrɪ; ɪnˈflæməˌtorɪ/ *adj* **1** (*derog* 贬) tending to make people angry or over-excited 使人激愤的; 煽动感情的: *inflammatory remarks, speeches, words, etc* 煽动性的言论、演说、言词等. **2** of, being or tending to produce inflammation 炎性的; 发炎的: *an inflammatory condition of the lungs* 肺部发炎.

in·flate /ɪnˈfleɪt; ɪnˈflet/ *v* **1** (**a**) [Tn, Tn·pr] **~ sth (with sth)** fill (a tyre, balloon, etc) with air or gas 使(轮胎、气球等)充气、膨胀: *a fully inflated tyre* 气充得很足的

I

轮胎. (**b**) [I] become filled with air or gas; swell 充满气体; 膨胀; 胀大: *With a supply of compressed air the large balloon inflated in a matter of seconds.* 大气球注入压缩空气后, 几秒钟就充足了气. **2** [Tn] (*fig* 比喻) cause (sb's self-opinion) to become too great 使某人自视甚高; 骄傲; 得意: *flattery that would inflate the most modest person's ego* 把最谦虚的人也能吹捧得趾高气扬的恭维. **3** [I, Tn] (*finance* 财) take action to increase the amount of money in circulation in (an economy) so that prices rise 物价上涨; 使通货膨胀. Cf 参看 DEFLATE, REFLATE.

▷ **in·flat·able** /-əbl; -əbl̩/ *adj* that can be or must be inflated 可充气的; 必须充气的; 可膨胀的: *an inflatable dinghy* 充气筏.

in·flated *adj* **1** filled with air, gas, etc 充气的. **2** (*derog* 贬) exaggerated 夸张的; 言过其实的: *an inflated opinion of oneself* 自视过高 ○ *inflated language*, ie full of impressive words, but little meaning 浮夸的语言. **3** (of prices) raised artificially or as a result of financial inflation (指价格)人为抬高的, 因通货膨胀而上涨的.

in·fla·tion /ɪnˈfleɪʃn; ɪnˋfleʃən/ *n* [U] **1** process of inflating (INFLATE 1a); being inflated 充气; 膨胀. **2** rise in prices resulting from an increase in the supply of money, credit, etc 通货膨胀; 物价上涨: *control/curb inflation* 控制[遏制]通货膨胀 ○ *galloping* (ie severe and rapid) *inflation* 失控通胀. **in·fla·tion·ary** /ɪnˈfleɪʃnrɪ; *US* -nerɪ; ɪnˋfleʃən,ɛrɪ/ *adj* of, caused by or causing financial inflation 通货膨胀的; 由通货膨胀引起的; 引起通货膨胀的: *the inflationary spiral*, ie economic situation in which prices and wages rise in turn as the supply of money is increased 恶性通货膨胀(因流通货币增加导致工资与物价交互上涨的现象) ○ *inflationary wage claims* 通货膨胀引起的增加工资的要求.

in·flect /ɪnˈflekt; ɪnˋflɛkt/ *v* [Tn] **1** (*grammar*) change the ending or form of (a word) to show its grammatical function in a sentence 使词尾屈折, 使词尾变化(以示其在句中之语法功能): *Most English verbs are inflected with '-ed' in the past tense.* 英语大多数动词过去式词尾均变化为 -ed 的形式. **2** make (the voice) higher or lower in speaking 使(说话的声音)变高或变低: *By inflecting the voice more one can hold the attention of an audience.* 讲话声音有些抑扬变化可以吸引住听众的注意力.

▷ **in·flected** *adj* (of a language) having many inflected words (指语言)有许多屈折变化词语的: *Latin is a more inflected language than English.* 拉丁语比英语词尾变化多.

in·flec·tion (also **in·flex·ion**) /ɪnˈflekʃn; ɪnˋflɛkʃən/ *n* **1** (*grammar*) (**a**) [U] inflecting (词尾的)屈折变化; 词尾变化. (**b**) [C] suffix used to inflect a word (eg *-ed, -ing*) (词形变化的)后缀, 屈折尾缀(如 -ed、-ing). **2** [U] rise and fall of the voice in speaking (说话声音的)抑扬变化. Cf 参看 INTONATION, STRESS 3.

▷ **in·flec·tional** /-ʃənl; -ʃənl̩/ *adj* of or being inflections 词尾变化的; 屈折变化的: *inflectional endings/forms*, eg *-ed* 屈折变化的词尾[形式](如 -ed).

in·flex·ible /ɪnˈfleksəbl; ɪnˋflɛksəbl̩/ *adj* (**a**) that cannot be bent or turned 不可弯曲的; 不能转变的: *made of an inflexible plastic* 用硬塑料制成. (**b**) (*fig* 比喻) that cannot be changed, influenced, etc; unyielding 不可改变的; 不受影响的; 不屈的: *an inflexible will, determination, purpose, etc* 不可动摇的意志、决心、目的等 ○ *an inflexible attitude, rule, system* 不可改变的态度、规则、制度. ▷ **in·flex·ib·il·ity** /ɪn,fleksəˈbɪlətɪ; ɪn,flɛksəˋbɪlətɪ/ *n* [U]. **in·flex·ibly** /-əblɪ; -əblɪ/ *adv*.

in·flict /ɪnˈflɪkt; ɪnˋflɪkt/ *v* **1** [Tn, Tn·pr] **~ sth (on sb)** cause (a blow, penalty, etc) to be suffered (by sb) 使(某人)遭受(打击、惩罚等): *inflict a severe wound on sb* 使某人受重创 ○ *inflict a crushing defeat on the enemy* 把敌军打得一败涂地. **2** [Tn·pr] **~ sb/sth on sb** (*infml often joc* 口, 常作戏谑语) force sb to accept one's unwelcome presence 硬要某人接待自己: *apologize for inflicting oneself/one's company on sb* 为叨扰某人而道歉 ○ *My uncle is inflicting himself on* (ie visiting) *us again this weekend.* 本周末我的叔叔又要不请自来了.

▷ **in·flic·tion** /ɪnˈflɪkʃn; ɪnˋflɪkʃən/ *n* (**a**) [U] inflicting or being inflicted 施加; 蒙受: *the unnecessary infliction of pain and suffering* 带来不必要的痛苦和苦难. (**b**) [C] thing inflicted; painful or troublesome experience 施加的事物; 痛苦的或苦恼的经历.

in-flight /,ɪnˈflaɪt; ˋɪnˋflaɪt/ *adj* [usu attrib 通常作定语] occurring or provided during the flight of an aircraft (飞行器)飞行中发生的, 飞行中供应的: *,in-flight reˈfuelling, enterˈtainment* 空中加油、飞行中提供的娱乐活动.

in·flor·es·cence /,ɪnflɔːˈresəns; ,ɪnfloˋrɛsn̩s/ *n* (*botany* 植) arrangement of a plant's flowers on the stem; collective flower of a plant 花序; 花(一植物上花的总称).

in·flow /ˈɪnfləʊ; ˋɪn,flo/ *n* **1** [U] flowing in 流入. **2** [C, U] (**a**) that which flows in 流入物; 流入量: *an inflow of 25 litres per hour* 每小时25升的流入量 ○ [attrib 作定语] *an inflow pipe* 注入管道. (**b**) (*fig* 比喻) influx 注入; 流入; 涌入: *an inflow of cash, capital, etc* 现款、资金等的流入.

in·flu·ence /ˈɪnflʊəns; ˋɪnflʊəns/ *n* **1** [U] **~ (on sth)** power to produce an effect; action of natural forces 影响力; 作用: *the influence of the moon (on the tides), of the climate (on agricultural production), etc* 月球(对潮汐)的作用、气候(对农业生产)的影响. **2** (**a**) [sing] **~ (on sb/sth)** (exercising of) power to affect sb's actions, character or beliefs through example, fear, admiration, etc 感化(力); 影响(力); 支配(力): *the influence of parents on their children* 父母对子女的影响 ○ *have a good, bad, beneficial, harmful, civilizing, pernicious, etc influence on sb's behaviour, character, etc* 对某人行为、性格等有良好的、恶劣的、有利的、有害的、感化性的、邪恶的 ... 影响 ○ *a young ruler under the influence of his chief minister* 受总理大臣左右的年轻统治者 ○ *escape sb's influence* 避开某人的势力范围. (**b**) [C] **~ (on sb/sth)** person, fact, etc that exercises such power 有影响的人或事物: *Those so-called friends of hers are a bad influence on her.* 她那些所谓的朋友对她的影响很坏. ○ *Religion has been an influence for good in her life.* 宗教信仰一直引导她向善. ○ *We are subject to many influences.* 我们都受着多方的影响. ○ *The influences at work in this case* (ie factors causing it to develop in a particular way) *are hard to disentangle.* 在此事中起作用的种种因素很难缕析得清楚. **3** [U] **~ (over sb/sth)** power to control sb's behaviour 支配力; 控制力: *His parents no longer have any real influence over him.* 他的父母对他不再有任何真正的约束力了. **4** [U] **~ (with sb)** ability to obtain favourable treatment from sb, usu by means of acquaintance, status, wealth, etc 权力; 势力; 权势: *use one's influence (with sb)* 利用(与某人的关系的)影响力 ○ *She has great influence with the manager and could no doubt help you.* 她对经理很有影响力, 无疑能帮你忙. **5** (idm 习语) **under the ˈinfluence (of ˈalcohol)** (*fml or joc* 文或谑) (showing signs of) having had too much to drink 酒喝得太多; 有点醉: *be charged with driving under the influence* 被控酒后开车.

▷ **in·flu·ence** *v* **1** [Tn] have an effect or influence on (sb/sth); cause (sb/sth) to act, behave, think, etc in a particular way 影响(某人[某事物]); 对(某人[某事物])起作用: *the belief of astrologers that planets influence human character* 星相家认为星体能影响人的性格的信念 ○ *I don't want to influence you either way, so I won't tell you my opinion.* 我不想对你有任何影响, 所以我不告诉你我的看法. ○ *It's clear that her painting has been influenced by Picasso.* 她的画显然受了毕加索的影响. **2** [Cn·t] cause or persuade (sb) to do sth 支配或左右(某人)做某事: *What influenced you to behave like that?* 你是受了什么支配而那样做的?

in·flu·en·tial /,ɪnflʊˈenʃl; ,ɪnflʊˋɛnʃəl/ *adj* **1 ~ (in sth/doing sth)** having influence; persuasive 有影响的; 有说服力的: *factors that are influential* (ie have an important effect) *in reaching a decision* 对做出决定有影响(有重要作用)的因素 ○ *an influential speech* 有说服力的演说. **2** having the status, wealth, etc that enables one to persuade others to do sth 有地位、财富等的(因而能影响他人做某事): *a committee of influential businessmen, union leaders, etc* 由有权势的商界人士、工会领袖等组成的委员会.

in·flu·enza /,ɪnflʊˈenzə; ,ɪnflʊˋɛnzə/ *n* [U] (*fml* 文) (also *infml* 口语作 **flu** /fluː; flu/) infectious virus disease causing fever, muscular pain and catarrh 流行性感冒; 流感.

in·flux /ˈɪnflʌks; ˋɪn,flʌks/ *n* **~ (into...)** arrival of people or things, esp suddenly and in large numbers or quantities （人或事物的）注入，涌入，汇集: *frequent influxes of visitors* 来访的人纷至沓来 ○ *an influx of wealth* 财富的大量汇集.

in·form /ɪnˈfɔːm; ɪnˈfɔrm/ *v* **1** [Tn, Tn·pr, Dn·f] **~ sb (of/about sth)** give sb knowledge (of sth); tell sb 通知或报告某人（某事）；告诉某人: *'Some money is missing.' 'Have you informed the police?'* '有些钱不见了.' '你报告警方了吗？' ○ *Keep me informed (of/about what happens).* 有事随时通知我. ○ *inform oneself of the facts,* ie find out all that needs to be known 使自己了解事实 ○ *He informed the police that some money was missing.* 他向警方报案说有些钱不见了. **2** [Ipr] **~ against/on sb** (*law* 律) give evidence or make an accusation against sb (to the police) （向警方）告发或检举某人: *One of the criminals informed against/on the rest of the gang.* 有一罪犯告发了同党. **3** [Tn] (*fml* 文) give (sth) its essential features; pervade 赋予（某事物）其特征；贯穿；遍及: *the sense of justice which informs all her writings* 体现在她所有写作中的那种正义感.

▷ **in·form·ant** /-ənt; -ənt/ *n* **1** person who gives information 提供消息或情报的人: *The journalist did not want to reveal the identity of his informant.* 那个新闻工作者不想透露消息提供人的身分. **2** (*linguistics* 语言) native speaker of a language who helps a scholar make an analysis of the language 发音合作人（为语言学者分析语言提供资料的说本地话的人）.

in·formed *adj* having or showing knowledge 有知识的；见闻广的；了解情况的: *an informed critic, member of the public, etc* 掌握情况的评论家、公众等 ○ *informed criticism* 有见地的批评 ○ *an informed guess,* ie based on some knowledge 有根据的猜测.

in·former *n* person who informs, esp against a criminal or fugitive 告密者，告发者，检举人（尤指告发罪犯或逃犯的）.

in·formal /ɪnˈfɔːml; ɪnˈfɔrml/ *adj* **1** not formal; without formality 非正式的；非正规的；不拘礼节的；不讲究形式的: *an informal* (ie friendly) *manner, tone, atmosphere, person* 友好的态度、语调、气氛、人 ○ *an informal* (ie not official) *arrangement, gathering, meeting, occasion, visit* 非正式的安排、聚会、会晤、场合、访问. **2** (of dress, behaviour, etc) chosen to show personal taste rather than follow social conventions of formality （指衣着、举止等）按个人爱好选择的，不依从社会习俗的，日常的. **3** (of language, speech, writing) conversational in style (and marked (*infml*) in this dictionary) （指语言、讲话、文字）口语体的（本词典中以（*infml* 口）标示）: *an informal letter* 用口语体写的信. Cf 参看 COLLOQUIAL, SLANG.

▷ **in·form·al·ity** /ˌɪnfɔːˈmælətɪ; ˌɪnfɔrˈmælətɪ/ *n* **1** [U] being informal 非正式；不拘礼节；衣着随便；口语体. **2** [C] informal act 不拘礼节的举动.

in·form·ally /ɪnˈfɔːməlɪ; ɪnˈfɔrmlɪ/ *adv*: *They told me informally* (ie unofficially) *that I had got the job.* 他们非正式地告诉我，我已获得那份工作.

in·forma·tion /ˌɪnfəˈmeɪʃn; ˌɪnfɚˈmeʃən/ *n* [U] **1** informing or being informed 通知；告知: *For your information* (ie This is sth you may wish to know), *the library is on the first floor.* 谨奉告，图书馆在二楼. ○ (*ironic* 反语) *I'm perfectly able to look after myself, for your information.* 我完全能够自己照顾自己，特此奉告. ○ (*fml* 文) *My information is that* (ie I have been told that) *they have all left.* 据我所知，他们已经走了. **2 ~ (on/about sb/sth)** facts told, heard or discovered (about sb/sth) （关于某人[某事物]的）情报，消息，资料: *give, pass on, receive, obtain, seek, find, collect, etc information (on/about sb/sth)* 供给、传递、收到、获得、寻找、发现、搜集等（关于某人[某事]的）消息 ○ *For further information please write to...* 欲知详情，请写信致... ○ *a useful bit/piece of information* 一份很有价值的情报 ○ [attrib 作定语] *an information bureau, desk, etc* 新闻局、询问处. **3** (idm 习语) **a mine of information** ⇨ MINE[2].

□ **inforˈmation science** (also **inforˈmation technology**) study or use of processes (esp computers, telecommunications, etc) for storing, retrieving and sending information of all kinds (eg words, numbers, pictures) 资料学，信息学，情报学（研究或使用各种信息的学科，如文字、数字、图像之存储、检索和发送，尤指用计算机、电信等手段进行的）.

in·form·at·ive /ɪnˈfɔːmətɪv; ɪnˈfɔrmətɪv/ *adj* giving much information; instructive 提供大量资料或信息的；授予知识的: *an informative book, film, lecture, speaker* 令人大开眼界的书、影片、讲座、演讲者.

infra /ˈɪnfrə; ˈɪnfrə/ *adv* (*Latin fml* 拉，文) further on (in a book, etc); below （书等的）下文，在下面: *see infra* 参看下文. Cf 参看 VIDE.

□ ˌ**infra** ˈ**dig** /dɪg; dɪg/ [pred 作表语] (*infml often joc* 口，常作戏谑语) beneath one's dignity; demeaning 有失尊严；有失身分: *Dancing in the street is rather infra dig for a bank manager!* 一个银行经理在街上跳舞，那是颇失身分的!

ˌ**infra-ˈred** *adj* of the (invisible, heat-giving) rays below the red in the spectrum 红外线的. Cf 参看 ULTRAVIOLET.

ˈ**infrastructure** *n* (**a**) subordinate parts, installations, etc that form the basis of a system, an organization or an enterprise (eg of an army) （组成一制度、企业或组织如军队的）基础结构，基础设施. (**b**) (*economics* 经) stock of fixed capital equipment in a country (eg roads, railways, power-stations, water supply, etc) 基础设施，基础结构（国家的固定基本设备，如公路、铁路、发电站、供水装置等）.

infra- *pref* 前缀 (with *adjs* 与形容词结合) below 在下: *infra-red.* Cf 参看 ULTRA-.

in·frac·tion /ɪnˈfrækʃn; ɪnˈfrækʃən/ *n* (*fml* 文) (**a**) [U] breaking of a rule, law, etc （对规则、法律等的）违背，违犯. (**b**) [C] instance of this 犯规；违法: *a minor infraction of the rules* 轻微的犯规.

in·fre·quent /ɪnˈfriːkwənt; ɪnˈfrikwənt/ *adj* not frequent; rare 不频发的；不经常的；罕见的: *infrequent visits, performances, etc* 少有的拜访、演出等. ▷ **in·fre·quency** /-kwənsɪ; -kwənsɪ/ *n* [U]. **in·fre·quently** *adv*.

in·fringe /ɪnˈfrɪndʒ; ɪnˈfrɪndʒ/ *v* **1** [Tn] (**a**) break (a rule, an agreement, etc) 违反，违背（规则、协议等）: *infringe the regulations, a copyright agreement, etc* 违反规则、版权协定等. (**b**) interfere with (sth); violate 干涉；干扰；侵犯；侵害: *infringe sb's liberty, rights, etc* 干扰某人的自由、侵犯某人的权利. **2** [Ipr] **~ on/upon sth** affect sth so as to limit or restrict it; encroach on 侵犯；侵入；侵害: *infringe upon the rights of other people* 侵害他人权利.

▷ **in·fringe·ment** /-mənt; -mənt/ *n* (**a**) [U] infringing or being infringed 违反；触犯；侵害；侵犯: *laws subject to frequent infringement* 经常触犯的法规. (**b**) [C] instance of this 违反；触犯；侵害；侵犯: *an infringement of the highway code, of copyright, of sb's privacy* 违反公路法、侵犯版权、侵犯某人的隐私权.

in·furi·ate /ɪnˈfjʊərɪeɪt; ɪnˈfjʊrɪˌet/ *v* [Tn] make (sb) extremely angry 使（某人）大怒；激怒（某人）: *I was infuriated by/with their constant criticism.* 他们没完没了地批评把我给气坏了.

▷ **in·furi·at·ing** *adj* that infuriates 使人大怒的: *infuriating delays* 让人感到愤怒的耽搁. **in·furi·at·ingly** *adv*: *Infuriatingly, I just missed my plane.* 真气人，我刚刚误了飞机.

in·fuse /ɪnˈfjuːz; ɪnˈfjuz/ *v* **1** [Tn·pr] **~ sth into sb/sth; ~ sb/sth with sth** put (a quality) into sb/sth; fill sb/sth with (a quality) 将（某特性）灌输给或注入某人[某事物]；使某人[某事物]获得（某特性）: *infuse new life, energy, etc into the workers* 使工人获得新的活力、力量等 ○ *infuse the workers with new life, energy, etc* 使工人获得新的活力、力量等. **2** (**a**) [Tn] soak (tea or herbs) in a liquid (usu hot water) to extract flavour or ingredients for a drink or medicine （草药）泡（茶）；泡制. (**b**) [I] (of tea or herbs) undergo this process （指茶叶或药草）被浸泡: *Don't drink the tea until it has finished infusing.* 茶泡好再喝.

in·fu·sion /ɪnˈfjuːʒn; ɪnˈfjuʒən/ *n* **1** [U] **~ of sth (into sb/sth)** infusing a quality or being infused into sb/sth 注入；灌输；浸泡；泡制: *infusion of new life (into the enterprise)* （给企业）注入新的活力 ○ *This company needs an infusion of new blood,* ie needs new employees to give it vigour. 这家公司需要注进新的血液（需要新雇员给公司以活力）. **2** (**a**) [U] infusing of tea, herbs, etc or being infused （茶叶、草药等的）沏，泡. (**b**) [C] liquid made by infusing 沏、泡或浸后的液体.

in·geni·ous /ɪnˈdʒiːnɪəs; ɪnˈdʒinjəs/ *adj* (**a**) **~ (at sth/doing sth)** (of a person) clever at finding new or simple solutions for complex problems （指人）善于用新

的或简单的方法解决复杂问题的; 心灵手巧的: *So you fitted that wire through that little hole there: that's very ingenious!* 那么说是你把金属线穿过那个小孔的了, 真灵巧! ○ *ingenious at solving difficult crossword puzzles* 善于破解困难的纵横填字谜. (**b**) (of a thing) original in design and well suited to its purpose (指物件)设计独特而精巧的: *an ingenious device, gadget, etc* 精巧的装置、小机械等. (**c**) (of an idea) very clever and original (指主意)别出心裁的, 奇妙的: *an ingenious plan, method, solution, etc* 别出心裁的计划、方法、解决办法等.
▷ **in·geni·ously** *adv*.

in·genu·ity /ˌɪndʒɪˈnju:ətɪ; *US* -ˈnu:-; ˌɪndʒəˈnuətɪ/ *n* [U] cleverness and originality in solving problems 心灵手巧; 善于发明创造.

in·génue /ˈænʒeɪnju:; *US* ˈændʒənu:; ˈændʒəˌnu/ *n* simple innocent girl, esp as portrayed in plays, films, etc 天真无邪的少女(尤指戏剧、电影等的人物): [attrib 作定语] *an ingénue role* 天真少女的角色.

in·genu·ous /ɪnˈdʒenjʊəs; ɪnˈdʒɛnjʊəs/ *adj* (*fml* 文) not attempting to deceive or conceal; open; innocent 不欺骗的; 不隐瞒的; 坦率的; 天真无邪的: *an ingenuous smile* 纯真的微笑. ▷ **in·genu·ously** *adv*. **in·genu·ous·ness** *n* [U].

in·gest /ɪnˈdʒest; ɪnˈdʒɛst/ *v* [Tn] (*fml* 文) **1** take (food, etc) into the body, typically by swallowing 咽下, 吞下(食物等). **2** (*fig* 比喻) take (sth) in; absorb 获取(某事物); 摄取: *ingest information* 获取信息.

ingle-nook /ˈɪŋgl nʊk; ˈɪŋglˌnʊk/ *n* small opening beside a wide old-fashioned fireplace in which one can sit close to the fire 壁炉隅(壁炉旁边供近火而坐的角落).

in·glori·ous /ɪnˈglɔ:rɪəs; ɪnˈglorɪəs/ *adj* **1** shameful; ignominious 可耻的; 不光彩的; 不名誉的: *an inglorious defeat* 可耻的失败 ○ *a new play which suffered the inglorious fate of being taken off after only three days* 一出新剧, 只上演三天就遭撤换的不光彩结局. **2** [usu attrib 通常作定语] (*rhet* 修辞) unknown; obscure 不出名的; 默默无闻的: *an inglorious name* 不见经传的名字. ▷ **in·glori·ously** *adv*.

in·go·ing /ˈɪŋgəʊɪŋ; ˈɪnˌgoɪŋ/ *adj* [attrib 作定语] going in 进入的; 进来的: *the ingoing* (ie new) *tenant of a flat* 公寓里新来的房客.

in·got /ˈɪŋgət; ˈɪŋgət/ *n* (usu brick-shaped) lump of metal esp gold and silver, cast in a mould 铸块, 锭(尤指金、银铸锭).

in·grained /ɪnˈgreɪnd; ɪnˈgrend/ *adj* **1** (of habits, tendencies, etc) deeply fixed; thorough (指习惯、习性等)根深蒂固的, 一成不变的: *ingrained prejudices, suspicions, assumptions, etc* 由来已久的成见、怀疑、臆见等. **2** (of dirt, stains, etc) going deeply into a substance, and therefore difficult to clean off (指尘土、污迹等)积深而难于清除的: *deeply ingrained dirt* 积聚得很深的污垢.

I

in·gra·ti·ate /ɪnˈgreɪʃɪeɪt; ɪnˈgreʃɪˌet/ *v* [no passive 不用于被动语态: Tn, Tn·pr] (*fml derog* 文, 贬) **~ oneself (with sb)** (attempt to) gain the favour of sb by flattering him, doing things that will please him, etc (竭力)取悦某人(靠奉承或做某事等): *She tried to ingratiate herself with the director, in the hope of getting promotion.* 她竭力巴结主任希望得到提升.
▷ **in·gra·ti·at·ing** *adj* (*derog* 贬) attempting to please, flatter or gain favour 讨好的; 迎合的; 奉承的: *an ingratiating smile* 阿谀奉承的微笑. **in·gra·ti·at·ingly** *adv*.

in·grat·it·ude /ɪnˈgrætɪtju:d; *US* -tu:d; ɪnˈgrætəˌtud/ *n* [U] lack of gratitude 忘恩负义.

in·gre·di·ent /ɪnˈgri:dɪənt; ɪnˈgridɪənt/ *n* **1** any of the foods that are combined to make a particular dish (烹调用的)材料, 原料, 成分: *the ingredients of a cake* 蛋糕的原料 ○ *Mix all the ingredients in a bowl.* 将原料放在盆里调匀. **2** (*fig* 比喻) any of the qualities of which sth is made 因素; 要素; 组分; 成分: *the ingredients of a/sb's character, of success, of happiness, etc* 某人性格的一方面、成功的要素、幸福的因素.

in·gress /ˈɪŋgres; ˈɪngrɛs/ *n* [U] (*fml* 文) going in; (right of) entrance 进入; 进入的权利: *a means of ingress* 进入的手段. Cf 参看 EGRESS.

in-group /ˈɪn gru:p; ˈɪnˌgrup/ *n* (*usu derog* 通常作贬义) group within an organization or in society that behaves in an exclusive way and gives favoured treatment to its own members; clique 小圈子, 自己人团体, 小集团(有排他性质、对自己成员优予对待之组织或社团).

in·grow·ing /ˈɪngrəʊɪŋ; ˈɪnˌgroɪŋ/ *adj* [usu attrib 通常作定语] growing inwards 向内生长的: *an ingrowing toenail*, ie one growing into the flesh 向肉里生长的脚指甲.

in·habit /ɪnˈhæbɪt; ɪnˈhæbɪt/ *v* [Tn] live in (sth); occupy 居住于(某处); 占据; 栖居于: *an island inhabited only by birds* 只有鸟类栖息的岛.
▷ **in·hab·it·able** *adj* that can be lived in 可居住的; 可栖居的.
in·hab·it·ant /-ənt; -ənt/ *n* person or animal living in a place (某地的)居民, 住户, 栖息的动物: *the local inhabitants* 当地居民 ○ *the oldest inhabitants of the island* 岛上最早的栖息者.

in·hale /ɪnˈheɪl; ɪnˈhel/ *v* [I, Tn, Tn·pr] **~ sth (into sth)** (**a**) breathe sth in 吸入某物: *inhale deeply* 作深吸气 ○ *Inhale! Exhale!* ie breathe in; breathe out 吸气! 呼气! ○ *miners who have inhaled coal dust into their lungs* 肺里吸入煤尘的矿工. (**b**) take (tobacco smoke) into the lungs 吸(烟); 抽(烟): *Smokers who inhale are likely to become addicted to nicotine.* 吸烟的人容易对尼古丁上瘾. ▷ **in·haler** *n* device that emits medicine in a fine spray to be inhaled, eg by sb with asthma 吸入器(人工呼吸装置).

in·har·mo·ni·ous /ˌɪnhɑ:ˈməʊnɪəs; ˌɪnhɑrˈmonɪəs/ *adj* (*fml* 文) not harmonious 不协调的; 不和谐的; 不和睦的. ▷ **in·har·mo·ni·ously** *adv*. **in·har·mo·ni·ous·ness** *n* [U].

in·her·ent /ɪnˈhɪərənt, -ˈher-; ɪnˈhɪrənt, -ˈhɛr-/ *adj* **~ (in sb/sth)** existing as a natural or permanent feature or quality of sb/sth 内在的; 固有的; 本来的: *an inherent distrust of foreigners* 天生对外国人的不信任 ○ *an inherent weakness in a design* 设计本身存在的弱点 ○ *the power inherent in the office of President* 总统任内固有的权力. ▷ **in·her·ently** *adv*: *a design which is inherently weak* 有内在缺陷的设计.

in·herit /ɪnˈherɪt; ɪnˈhɛrɪt/ *v* [Tn, Tn·pr] **~ sth (from sb)** **1** receive (property, a title, etc) as a result of the death of the previous owner 继承(财产、头衔等): *a youngman inheriting an estate, a title, etc (from his father)* 继承(父亲的)地产、头衔等的年轻人 ○ *She inherited a little money from her grandfather.* 她从祖父处继承了一小笔钱财. **2** derive (qualities, etc) from an ancestor 因遗传而获(特性等): *She inherited her mother's good looks and her father's bad temper.* 她生来就有母亲的美貌和父亲的坏脾气. **3** (*fig* 比喻) receive (sth) from a predecessor 从前任接过(某事物): *This government has inherited many problems from the previous one.* 上届政府遗留给本届政府很多问题.
▷ **in·her·it·ance** /-əns; -əns/ *n* **1** [U] **~ (of sth) (from sb/sth)** inheriting (sth from sb) 继承; 遗传: *The title passes by inheritance to the eldest son.* 这头衔按世袭传给长子. ○ (*fig* 比喻) *the inheritance of good looks from one's parents* 得自父母遗传的美貌 ○ [attrib 作定语] *inheritance tax* 遗产税. **2** [C] **~ (from sb)** what is inherited 继承或遗传之物; 遗产; 遗赠物: *When she was 21 she came into* (ie received) *her inheritance.* 她21岁时获得遗产. ○ (*fig* 比喻) *a bitter dispute which left an inheritance of ill-feeling* 留下恶感的激烈争辩. Cf 参看 LEGACY.
in·her·itor *n* person who inherits 继承人.

in·hibit /ɪnˈhɪbɪt; ɪnˈhɪbɪt/ *v* **1** [Tn, Tn·pr] **~ sb (from sth/doing sth)** prevent sb from doing sth that should be natural or easy to do 使某人不能做轻易可做的事: *Shyness inhibited him from speaking.* 他因害羞而说不出话来. **2** [Tn] hinder or prevent (a process or an action) 阻碍或抑制(某过程或行动): *an enzyme which inhibits a chemical reaction* 抑制化学反应的酶.
▷ **in·hib·ited** *adj* (**a**) (of people) unable to relax or express one's feelings in a natural and spontaneous way (指人)拘谨的, 不能自然表达感情的: *She's too inhibited to laugh at jokes about sex.* 她很拘谨, 听到性爱笑话也不笑. (**b**) (of behaviour) not relaxed or spontaneous (指举止)不轻松的, 不自然的: *a nervous inhibited laugh* 紧张而矜持的笑. **in·hib·it·edly** *adv*.
in·hibi·tion /ˌɪnhɪˈbɪʃn, ˌɪnɪˈb-; ˌɪnhɪˈbɪʃən, ˌɪnɪˈb-/ *n* **1** [U] inhibiting or being inhibited 抑制; 阻止; 禁止; 受抑制: *Inhibition of natural impulses may cause psychological*

problems. 压抑自然的冲动可能会引起心理上的问题. **2** [C] inability to act naturally or spontaneously 抑制力: *Alcohol weakens a person's inhibitions*, ie makes him behave more naturally. 酒精能削弱人的抑制力. ○ (*infml* 口) *She had no inhibitions about asking for more*, ie did so without hesitation. 她毫无顾忌, 要求再多给她一些.

in·hos·pit·able /ˌɪnhɒˈspɪtəbl; ɪnˈhɑspɪtəbl̩/ *adj* (**a**) (of people) not giving a friendly or polite welcome to guests (指人)待客不殷勤的, 不好客的: *It was inhospitable of you not to offer her a drink.* 你未给她饮品是待客不周. (**b**) (*fig* 比喻) (of places) not giving shelter; unpleasant to be in (指地方)无遮蔽处的, 荒凉的: *an inhospitable coast* 荒凉的海岸. ▷ **in·hos·pit·ably** *adv*.

in·hu·man /ɪnˈhjuːmən; ɪnˈhjumən/ *adj* lacking normal human qualities of kindness, pity, etc; extremely cruel or brutal 无人性的; 无同情心的; 野蛮的; 残酷的: *inhuman behaviour, treatment, etc* 野蛮的行为、非人的待遇 ○ *That man is an inhuman monster!* 那人是残暴的恶魔! ○ *It was inhuman to refuse him permission to see his wife.* 不容许他去看自己的妻子是太不近人情了.
▷ **in·hu·man·ity** /ˌɪnhjuːˈmænətɪ; ˌɪnhjuˈmænətɪ/ *n* [U] inhuman conduct or behaviour 无人性; 野蛮; 不近人情; 不人道: *man's inhumanity to man* 人对人的残忍.

in·hu·mane /ˌɪnhjuːˈmeɪn; ˌɪnhjuˈmen/ *adj* insensitive to the suffering of others; cruel 对受难者无动于衷的; 不人道的; 残忍的: *inhumane treatment of animals, prisoners, the mentally ill, etc* 对动物、囚犯、精神病人等的残酷对待 ○ *an inhumane law, policy, decision, etc* 不人道的法律、政策、决定等. ▷ **in·hu·manely** *adv*: *animals slaughtered inhumanely* 遭残忍方法宰杀的动物.

in·im·ical /ɪˈnɪmɪkl; ɪnˈɪmɪkl̩/ *adj* [usu pred 通常作表语] **~ (to sb/sth)** (*fml* 文) **1** unfriendly; hostile 不友好; 含敌意: *countries that are inimical to us/to our interests* 对我们不友好的[有损我国利益的]国家. **2** tending to prevent or discourage sth; harmful 对某事物不利; 有害: *actions that are inimical to friendly relations between countries* 对国家间友好关系有害的行动. ▷ **in·imic·ally** /-kəlɪ; -klɪ/ *adv*.

in·im·it·able /ɪˈnɪmɪtəbl; ɪnˈɪmətəbl̩/ *adj* impossible to imitate; too good, clever, etc to imitate 不能模仿的; 妙处难学的: *Frank Sinatra's inimitable style of singing* 弗兰克·西纳特拉无人能模仿的演唱风格. ▷ **in·im·it·ably** /-əblɪ; -əblɪ/ *adv*.

ini·quit·ous /ɪˈnɪkwɪtəs; ɪˈnɪkwətəs/ *adj* **1** (*fml* 文) very wicked or unjust 极邪恶的; 极不公正的: *an iniquitous system, regime, etc* 罪恶的制度、政权等. **2** (of a price, charge, etc) unfairly or ridiculously high (指价格、费用等)不公道的, 高得出奇的: *Have you seen this bill? It's iniquitous!* 你看见这份帐单了吗? 简直是漫天要价!
▷ **ini·quit·ously** *adv*.
ini·quity /ɪˈnɪkwətɪ; ɪˈnɪkwətɪ/ *n* **1** (**a**) [U] (*rhet* 修辞) wickedness and unjustness 邪恶; 罪恶; 不公正: *He regards the city as a place where all forms of iniquity are practised.* 他认为该城是万恶丛集的渊薮. (**b**) [C] wicked and unjust act 邪恶的及不公正的行为. **2** (idm 习语) **a den of iniquity/vice** ⇨ DEN.

ini·tial /ɪˈnɪʃl; ɪˈnɪʃəl/ *adj* [attrib 作定语] of or at the beginning; first 开始的; 最初的; 第一个的: *the initial letter of a word* 一个字起首的字母 ○ *in the initial stages* (ie at the beginning) *(of sth)* 某事的创始阶段 ○ *My initial reaction was to refuse.* 我最初的反应是予以拒绝.
▷ **ini·tial** *n* (usu *pl* 通常作复数) initial letter (of a name) (姓名的)首字母: *George Bernard Shaw was well-known by his initials GBS.* 人们对萧伯纳姓名的首字母GBS非常熟悉. ○ *Sign your name and initials*, ie your surname and the initial letters of your other names. 请签上您的姓及名字的首字母.
ini·tial *v* (**-ll-**; *US* usu 美式英语通常作 **-l-**) [I, Tn] mark or sign (sth) with one's initials 用姓名的首字母签名或作标记: *Initial here, please.* 请在这儿签上姓名首字母. ○ *initial a note, document, treaty, etc* 用名字的首字母签署便条、文件、条约等.
ini·tially /-ʃəlɪ; -ʃəlɪ/ *adv* at the beginning; at first 最初; 开头; 首先: *She came initially to spend a few days, but in the end she stayed for a whole month.* 起先她只打算来待几天, 但后来却住了整整一个月.

ini·ti·ate /ɪˈnɪʃɪeɪt; ɪˈnɪʃɪˌet/ *v* **1** [Tn] (*fml* 文) put (a scheme, etc) into operation; cause (sth) to begin 开始实施(计划等); 发起, 创始, 开始(某事物): *initiate plans, schemes, social reforms, etc* 开始实施计划、方案、社会改革等 ○ (*law* 律) *initiate proceedings against sb*, ie prosecute sb 起诉某人. **2** [Tn, Tn·pr] **~ sb (into sth)** (**a**) admit or introduce sb to membership of a group, etc, often by means of a special ceremony 接纳或介绍某人加入某团体等(常通过某种仪式): *initiate sb into a religious sect, secret society, etc* 介绍某人加入某教派、秘密会社等. (**b**) give sb elementary instruction (in sth) or secret knowledge (of sth) 向某人传授(某事物的)基本要领或秘密知识: *an older woman who had initiated him into the mysteries of love* 让他初尝云雨情的年长女子.
▷ **ini·ti·ate** /ɪˈnɪʃɪət; ɪˈnɪʃɪɪt/ *n* person who has (just) been initiated into a group 经介绍(刚)加入某组织的人.
the ini·ti·ated /ɪˈnɪʃɪeɪtɪd; ɪˈnɪʃɪˌetɪd/ *n* [pl *v*] people who share special knowledge, secrets, etc known only to a few 掌握仅为少数人知道的专门知识和秘密的人: *the government's secret defence committee, known to the initiated as DefCom* 政府的秘密防御委员会, 知情人都称之为DefCom.
ini·ti·ation /ɪˌnɪʃɪˈeɪʃn; ɪˌnɪʃɪˈeʃən/ *n* [U] **1 ~ (of sth)** (*fml* 文) bringing sth into effect; starting 开始实施; 开始; 创始; 发起: *the initiation of an investigation* 调查的开始. **2 ~ (into sth)** initiating or being initiated (into sth) 入会; 加入, 被接纳加入(某事物): [attrib 作定语] *an initiation ceremony* 入会仪式.

ini·ti·at·ive /ɪˈnɪʃətɪv; ɪˈnɪʃɪətɪv/ *n* **1** [C] action taken to resolve a difficulty 为解决困难而采取的行动: *It is hoped that the government's initiative will bring the strike to an end.* 希望政府采取的行动可以结束罢工. **2 the initiative** [sing] power or right to take action 采取行动的力量或权利; 主动权: *The initiative has passed to us.* 主动权已转到我方. ○ *Because of the general's indecisiveness, our armies have lost the initiative to the enemy.* 由于将军未能当机立断, 我军已丧失对敌采取行动的主动权. **3** [U] (*approv* 褒) capacity to see what needs to be done and enterprise enough to do it, esp without others' help 主动性; 自发性; 积极性: *a man who lacks the initiative to be a leader* 缺乏当领导人应具备的主动精神的人 ○ *The child showed/displayed great initiative in going to fetch the police.* 那孩子极为主动地把警察找来了. ○ [attrib 作定语] *an initiative test* 自发的试验. **4** [C] power or right of ordinary citizens to make proposals for new laws (as in Switzerland) (普通公民提出新法规倡议的)创制权(如瑞士的). **5** (idm 习语) **on one's own iˈnitiative** without anyone else ordering one to do sth, or suggesting that one should do it 主动地; 自发地; 积极地: *In the absence of my commanding officer, I acted on my own initiative.* 指挥官不在场, 我主动见机行事. **take the initiative** take the first step in an undertaking, esp one that encourages others to act 带头; 倡导; 发起: *It's up to this country to take the initiative in banning nuclear weapons.* 这个国家应该主动提出禁止核武器.

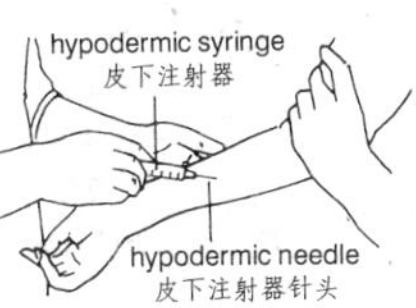

injection 注射

in·ject /ɪnˈdʒekt; ɪnˈdʒɛkt/ *v* **1** [Tn, Tn·pr] **~ sth (into sb/sth); ~ sb/sth (with sth)** force (a drug or other liquid) into sb/sth with a syringe or similar implement 给某人[某物]注射(药物或其他液体): *a drug that can be injected or taken by mouth* 可供注射或口服的药 ○ *inject penicillin into sb/sb's arm, leg, etc* 给某人[某人的胳膊、腿等部位]注射青霉素 ○ *inject sb/sb's arm, leg, etc with penicillin* 给某人[某人的胳膊、腿等部位]注射青霉素 ○ *inject foam into a cavity wall* 向空心墙内注入泡沫填料. **2** [Tn, Tn·pr] **~ sth (into sb/sth)** (*fig* 比

喻) introduce (new thoughts, feelings, etc) into sb/sth 向某人[某事物]介绍, 引进(新思想、感情等): *inject a few new ideas into the project* 在这个项目中加入些新构想 ○ *Try to inject a bit of enthusiasm into your performance.* 你要尽力在演出中倾注一点热情.

▷ **in·jec·tion** /ɪn'dʒekʃn; ɪn'dʒɛkʃən/ *n* **~ (of sth) (into sb/sth)** **1** [U] injecting 注射: *The morphine was administered by injection.* 那吗啡是注射进去的. ○ [attrib 作定语] *a fuel-injection system* 燃料喷射系统. **2** [C] instance of this 注射; 注入: *a lethal injection of the drug* 药品的致死量注射 ○ *a course of injections* 注射疗程 ○ *If you're going abroad, have you had your injections yet?* 你不是要出国吗, 打过防疫针没有? ○ *The firm would be revitalized by an injection of new funds.* 该公司重新注入资金即可复苏.

in·ju·di·cious /ˌɪndʒu:'dɪʃəs; ˌɪndʒu'dɪʃəs/ *adj* (*fml* 文) not appropriate or tactful 不合适的; 不策略的: *injudicious remarks* 不适当的言语 ○ *Now would be an injudicious moment to ask for a rise.* 现在要求加薪不是时候. ▷ **in·ju·di·ciously** *adv*. **in·ju·di·cious·ness** *n* [U].

in·junc·tion /ɪn'dʒʌŋkʃn; ɪn'dʒʌŋkʃən/ *n* (*fml* 文) official order, esp a written order from a lawcourt, demanding that sth shall or shall not be done 命令, 指令, 禁令, 禁制令(尤指法院发出的): *The government has sought an injunction preventing the paper from publishing the story.* 政府已申请禁制令, 禁止该报发表此事.

in·jure /'ɪndʒə(r); 'ɪndʒɚ/ *v* [Tn] hurt (sb); harm 伤害(某人); 损害: *injure oneself (by falling)* (跌倒)受伤 ○ *be slightly/seriously/badly injured in the crash* 在事故中受的伤很轻[很严重/很重] ○ (*fig* 比喻) *injure one's health (by smoking, drinking, etc)* (因吸烟、饮酒等)损害健康 ○ *malicious gossip which seriously injured her reputation* 严重损害了她名誉的恶毒的流言蜚语.

▷ **in·jured** *adj* **1** wounded; hurt 受伤的; 受损害的: *an injured man* 受伤的男子 ○ *an injured leg* 受伤的腿. **2** treated unfairly; wronged 受不公正对待的; 受委屈的: (*law* 律) *the injured party*, ie person who has been wronged 被害者. **3** offended 受触犯的: *an injured look, voice, etc* 不痛快的样子、声音等. **the in·jured** *n* [pl *v*] people injured (in an accident, battle, etc) (在事故、战斗等中)受伤的人: *counting the dead and injured* 统计伤亡人数 ○ *All 14 injured were later discharged from hospital.* 受伤的14人其后全部出院. ○ [attrib 作定语] *on the injured list*, ie the list of people injured 在受伤者的名单上. ⇨Usage at WOUND¹ 用法见 WOUND¹.

in·juri·ous /ɪn'dʒʊərɪəs; ɪn'dʒurɪəs/ *adj* (*fml* 文) **1 ~ (to sb/sth)** causing or likely to cause injury; harmful (很可能)造成伤害的; 有害的: *Smoking is injurious to the health.* 吸烟对健康有害. **2** wrongful; insulting 不正当的; 侮辱的: *injurious treatment by sb* 受某人的亏待 ○ *injurious remarks* 伤人的话.

I

in·jury /'ɪndʒərɪ; 'ɪndʒərɪ/ *n* **~ (to sb/sth)** **1** [U] (**a**) physical harm to a living being (对生物体的)伤害, 损害: *Excessive dosage of this drug can result in injury to the liver.* 这种药使用过量会损害肝脏. ○ *a person prone to injury*, ie one who is easily or often injured 易受损伤的人. (**b**) (*fig* 比喻) damage (to sb's feelings, reputation, etc) (对感情、名誉等的)损害: *injury to one's pride* 自尊心的挫伤. **2** [C] instance of harm to one's body or reputation (对身体或名誉的)伤害, 损害: *In the crash he suffered severe injuries to the head and arms.* 在事故中他头部和双臂受了重伤. ○ *an eye injury* 眼睛受伤 ○ (*fig* 比喻) *injuries to one's reputation* 对个人名声的败坏. **3** (idm 习语) **add insult to injury** ⇨ ADD. **do sb/oneself an 'injury** (*often joc* 常作戏谑语) cause sb/oneself (physical) harm 使(某人[自己])受(身体的)伤害: *If you try and lift that suitcase you'll do yourself an injury!* 要提起那只箱子, 你就要受伤了!

□ **'injury time** (*sport* 体) time added on by the referee at the end of a (football, rugby, etc) match, if the game has been interrupted because of injuries to players 受伤延长比赛时间(足球、橄榄球等因运动员受伤耽搁的时间, 裁判员在比赛之末准予相应追加).

in·just·ice /ɪn'dʒʌstɪs; ɪn'dʒʌstɪs/ *n* **1** [U] lack of justice 非正义; 不公正; 无道义: *a fierce opponent of injustice* 反抗非正义行为的顽强斗士. **2** [C] unjust act, etc 不正义的行为等. **3** (idm 习语) **do sb an in'justice** (**a**) judge sb unfairly 冤枉某人; 待某人不公: *In saying this you do her an injustice.* 你这样说就冤枉她了. (**b**) (*fig* 比喻) fail to show sb's true merits 未能反映某人的真正优点或长处: *His latest novel does him an injustice*, ie does not show how well he can write. 他的小说新作未能反映出他的才华.

ink /ɪŋk; ɪŋk/ *n* **1** [U, C] coloured liquid for writing, drawing and printing 墨水; 油墨: *written in ink* 用墨水写的 ○ *different coloured inks* 不同颜色的墨水 ○ [attrib 作定语] *an ink blot* 墨水渍 ○ *a pen-and-ink drawing* 钢笔画. **2** [U] black liquid produced by cuttlefish, squids, etc (乌贼、鱿鱼等分泌的)墨汁.

▷ **ink** *v* **1** [Tn] cover (sth) with ink (for printing) 给(某物)上油墨(以印刷): *ink the roller of a duplicating machine* 给复印机的油墨辊上油墨. **2** (phr v) **ink sth in** write or draw over (a pencilled word, outline, etc) with ink (在铅笔字、略图等上)用墨水加描.

inky /'ɪŋkɪ; 'ɪŋkɪ/ (**-ier, -iest**) *adj* **1** made dirty with ink 用墨水弄脏的: *inky fingers* 沾有墨水的手指. **2** black like ink 墨汁般黑的; 漆黑的: *the inky darkness of a moonless night* 无月之夜的一片黑暗.

□ **'ink-bottle** *n* bottle in which ink is sold 墨水瓶.

'ink-pad (also **pad**) *n* pad for ink used on rubber stamps 印台.

'ink-pot *n* pot for holding ink 墨水瓶.

'inkstand *n* stand for one or more ink-bottles 墨水瓶架.

'ink-well *n* ink-pot that fits into a hole in a desk 墨水池(嵌入写字台上的墨水瓶).

ink·ling /'ɪŋklɪŋ; 'ɪŋklɪŋ/ *n* [sing] **~ (of sth/that...)** slight knowledge (of sth secret or not previously known); hint (对秘密的或以前不知道的事物)略知; 暗示: *Can you give me some inkling of what is going on?* 现在有什么情况, 你能告诉我一点儿吗? ○ *The first inkling I had that all was not well was when the share prices began to fall.* 股票价格一跌落, 我就开始察觉到情况有些不妙.

in·laid *pt, pp* of INLAY.

in·land /'ɪnlənd; 'ɪnlənd/ *adj* [usu attrib 通常作定语] **1** (**a**) situated in the interior of a country, not by the sea or by a frontier 内陆的; 内地的: *inland areas, towns, waterways, etc* 内陆的地区、城镇、水路等. Cf 参看 COASTAL (COAST¹). (**b**) (of a sea) (almost) surrounded by land or islands (指海)(几乎)被陆地或岛屿包围的: *an inland sea such as the Caspian* 如里海那样的内海. **2** (*commerce* 商 *esp Brit*) carried on or obtained inside a country 国内的: *inland trade*, ie domestic trade, as opposed to imports and exports 国内贸易(与进出口贸易相对).

▷ **in·land** /ˌɪn'lænd; 'ɪnˌlænd/ *adv* in or towards the interior 在内地; 在内陆; 向内地; 向内陆: *They live inland.* 他们住在内地. ○ *move further inland* 更深入地向内地迁移.

□ **ˌInland 'Revenue** (in Britain) government department responsible for collecting taxes (英国)税务局. Cf 参看 INTERNAL REVENUE SERVICE (INTERNAL).

in-laws /'ɪn lɔ:z; 'ɪnˌlɔz/ *n* [pl] (*infml* 口) relatives by marriage 姻亲; 亲家: *All my in-laws live far away.* 我的姻亲全都住得很远.

in·lay /ˌɪn'leɪ; ɪn'le/ *v* (*pt, pp* **inlaid** /ˌɪn'leɪd; ɪn'led/) [esp passive 尤用于被动语态: Tn, Tn·pr] **~ A (with B); ~ B (in/into A)** make a design on (a surface) by putting pieces of wood, metal, etc into it in such a way that the resulting surface is smooth; insert (pieces of wood, metal, etc) in this way 镶; 嵌入; 镶饰: *ivory inlaid with gold* 镶金牙雕 ○ *gold inlaid into ivory* 牙雕上的金饰.

▷ **in·laid** *adj* **1** embedded in a substance 镶嵌的; 嵌饰的: *a floor with inlaid tiles* 嵌花砖的地板. **2** decorated with inlaid designs 有嵌饰图案的: *an inlaid floor* 嵌花地板.

in·lay /'ɪnleɪ; 'ɪnˌle/ *n* [C, U] **1** design or pattern made by inlaying 嵌镶装饰或图案: *a wooden jewel-box with (a) gold inlay* 镶金木质首饰盒. **2** (in dentistry) (method of making a) solid filling of gold, plastic, etc for a hole in a tooth (牙科)(金、塑料等的)镶体, 镶补术.

in·let /'ɪnlet; 'ɪnˌlɛt/ *n* **1** strip of water extending into the land from the sea or a lake, or between islands 湾, 水湾(江河湖海伸入陆地或岛屿间的水域). **2** opening to allow esp liquid to enter 入口, 进口(尤指供液体进入

的): *the fuel inlet* 燃料入口 ○ [attrib 作定语] *an inlet pipe* 输入管道. **3** something put in, eg a piece of material inserted into a garment to make it larger 衬入物, 嵌入物(如填入衣服中的).

in loco par·entis /ɪn ˌləʊkəʊ pəˈrentɪs; ɪn,lokopəˋrɛntɪs/ (*Latin* 拉) acting for or instead of a parent; having the responsibility of a parent 代替父或母; 代尽人父或人母之责: *I stand towards her in loco parentis.* 我对她代尽其父母亲的责任.

in·mate /ˈɪnmeɪt; ˋɪnmet/ *n* one of a number of people living together, esp in a hospital, prison or some other institution 同住在一起的人(尤指医院、监狱或其他机构中的).

in me·moriam /ˌɪn məˈmɔːrɪəm; ˌɪnməˋmɔrɪ,æm/ (*Latin* 拉) (used in epitaphs, on gravestones, etc 用于悼念诗文、墓碑志文等中) in memory of sb; as a memorial to sb 纪念某人; 作为对某人之纪念.

in·most /ˈɪnməʊst; ˋɪn,most/ *adj* [attrib 作定语] **1** most inward; furthest from the surface 最内的; 最深的: *the inmost recesses of the cave* 洞穴的最深处. **2** (*fig* 比喻) most private or secret 纯粹私人的; 最秘密的: *my inmost thoughts, feelings, etc* 我心灵深处的思想、感情等.

inn /ɪn; ɪn/ *n* (*Brit*) public house or small old hotel where lodgings, drink and meals may be had, now usu in the country 客栈, 小而旧的旅馆(现多指乡村的). Cf 参看 HOTEL.

□ **ˈinnkeeper** *n* person who manages an inn 上述客栈或旅馆的老板.

ˌInn of ˈCourt (building occupied by) any of four law societies in London having the exclusive right of admitting people to the rank of barrister in England 律师学院(所属的建筑物)(伦敦四个法律学院之任何一所, 又译作律师协会. 此四所学院或协会是唯一有权授予讼务律师资格的组织).

inn·ards /ˈɪnədz; ˋɪnɚdz/ *n* [pl] (*infml* 口) **1** stomach and/or bowels 胃; 肠; 肠胃: *a pain in my innards* 我肚子疼. **2** any inner parts 内部部件: *To mend this engine I'll have to have its innards out.* 要修理这部发动机, 我得拆下里面的部件.

in·nate /ɪˈneɪt; ɪˋnet/ *adj* (of a quality, feeling, etc) in one's nature; possessed from birth (指特质、感情等)天生的, 先天的, 固有的, 天赋的: *innate ability, beauty, etc* 天生的才能、丽质等 ○ *an innate desire* 固有的欲望.

▷ **in·nately** *adv* naturally 自然地; 天然地; 天生地: *innately honest* 天生诚实.

in·ner /ˈɪnə(r); ˋɪnɚ/ *adj* [attrib 作定语] **1** (of the) inside 内部的; 里面的: *an inner room* 内室. Cf 参看 OUTER. **2** (of feelings) unexpressed (指感情)内心的, 未表达出来的: *If she had inner doubts, it was not apparent to anyone else.* 她若心中生疑亦不形之于色. **3** (idm 习语) **the ˌinner ˈman/ˈwoman (a)** (*rhet* 修辞) a person's mind or soul 人的精神或灵魂. **(b)** (*joc* 谑) one's appetite 胃; 食欲: *satisfy the inner man/woman* 喂饱肚子.

▷ **in·ner·most** /-məʊst; -,most/ *adj* [attrib 作定语] most inward; inmost 最内的; 最深的: *the innermost depths of a forest* 密林深处 ○ *encouraging her to express her innermost feelings* 鼓励她表达个人内心深处的感情.

□ **ˌinner ˈcircle** small, often secretive, controlling group of people within an organization 核心集团(组织内部少数人, 常为不公开的人物组成的有权力的小集团).

ˌinner ˈcity oldest parts of a city, at or near its centre (近市中心的)旧城区: [attrib 作定语] *ˌinner-city ˈslums, deˈcay, ˈhousing problems* 旧城区的贫民窟、衰败、住房问题.

ˌinner ˈlane = INSIDE LANE (INSIDE).

ˌinner ˈtube inflatable rubber tube inside a tyre (轮胎的)内胎.

in·nings /ˈɪnɪŋz; ˋɪnɪŋz/ *n* (*pl* unchanged 复数不变) **1** (in cricket) time during which a team or single player is batting (板球的)局, 回合(一球队或一队员击球的时间): *England made 300 runs in their first innings.* 英格兰队在最初几局里获300分. **2** (idm 习语) **have had a good ˈinnings** (*Brit infml* 口) have had a long and happy life 一生幸福且长寿.

▷ **inn·ing** *n* (*pl* **~s**) (in baseball) time during which one team is batting; division of a game in which both teams have a turn to bat (棒球的)局, 回合(比赛两队各攻守一次的时间).

in·no·cent /ˈɪnəsnt; ˋɪnəsn̩t/ *adj* **1 ~ (of sth)** not guilty (of wrongdoing) 无辜的; 无罪的; 清白的: *They have imprisoned an innocent man.* 他们监禁了一个无辜的男子. ○ *innocent of a crime, a charge, an accusation* 未犯某罪、被指控的罪、被指责的事. **2** [attrib 作定语] suffering harm although not involved 无辜受害的; 被殃及的: *an innocent bystander* 无端受害的旁观者 ○ *innocent victims of the bomb blast* 炸弹下的无辜牺牲者. **3** harmless; innocuous 无害的; 无恶意的: *innocent amusement, enjoyment, etc* 无害的娱乐、享受等 ○ *It was a perfectly innocent question. Why get so worked up about it?* 那纯粹是无所谓的问题. 何必那么激动? **4** knowing nothing of evil or wrong 天真无邪的; 纯真的; 单纯的: *as innocent as a new-born babe* 像初生婴儿般纯洁. **5** foolishly simple 头脑简单的; 愚钝的: *Don't be so innocent as to believe everything the politicians tell you.* 别那么幼稚, 以为政客说的一切都是可信的. **6** [pred 作表语] **~ of sth** (*fml* 文) lacking sth 没有或缺少某事物: *a bare room, innocent of any decoration* 空荡荡的房间, 了无装饰.

▷ **in·no·cence** /-sns; -sn̩s/ *n* [U] **~ (of sth)** quality or state of being innocent(1, 4, 5) 无辜; 清白; 天真纯洁; 愚钝: *do sth in all innocence*, ie without any evil intention or knowledge 做事无私心杂念 ○ *She protested her innocence*, ie kept saying she was innocent. 她坚称自己无罪. ○ *Children lose their innocence as they grow older.* 童稚的天真随着年龄的增长而消逝.

in·no·cent *n* innocent person, esp a young child 天真无邪的人(尤指小孩).

in·no·cently *adv.*

in·nocu·ous /ɪˈnɒkjʊəs; ɪˋnɑkjuəs/ *adj* (*fml* 文) **1** causing no harm 无害的; 无毒的: *innocuous snakes, drugs* 无毒的蛇、无害的药品. **2** not intended to offend 无意得罪人的: *a fairly innocuous remark, statement, etc* 无伤大雅的言语、说法等. ▷ **in·nocu·ously** *adv.* **in·nocu·ous·ness** *n* [U].

in·nov·ate /ˈɪnəveɪt; ˋɪnə,vet/ *v* [I] make changes; introduce new things 革新; 改革; 创新; 引入新事物: *prepared to innovate in order to make progress* 为取得进步准备革新.

▷ **in·nova·tion** /ˌɪnəˈveɪʃn; ˌɪnəˋveʃən/ *n* **(a)** [U] innovating 革新; 改革; 创新; 引入新事物: *a period of innovation* 革新时期. **(b)** [C] instance of this; new technique, idea, etc 新方法、新技术、新思想等: *one innovation after another* 一个又一个的革新项目 ○ *technical innovations in industry* 工业中的技术革新.

in·nov·at·ive /ˈɪnəveɪtɪ; ˋɪnə,vetɪv/ (also **in·nov·at·ory** /ˌɪnəˈveɪtərɪ; ˋɪnə,vetərɪ/) *adj* (*approv* 褒) introducing or using new ideas, techniques, etc 革新的; 有革新精神的; 采用新思想、新技术的: *an innovative firm* 革故鼎新的商行.

in·nov·ator /ˈɪnəveɪtə(r); ˋɪnə,vetɚ/ *n* person who innovates 革新者; 创新者.

in·nu·endo /ˌɪnjuːˈendəʊ; ˌɪnjuˋɛndo/ *n* [C, U] (*pl* **~es** /-z; -z/) (*derog* 贬) indirect reference (usu suggesting sth bad or discreditable about sb) 影射; 暗射: *There have been too many unpleasant innuendoes in this debate and not enough facts.* 在这场辩论中据实而争者少, 含沙射影者多, 令人生厌. ○ *He had been subject to a campaign of innuendo in the press.* 他一直受到新闻界指桑骂槐的影射.

In·nuit (also **In·uit**) /ˈɪnuːɪt, -njuː-; ˋɪnjuɪt/ *n* (*pl* unchanged 复数不变) = ESKIMO.

in·nu·mer·able /ɪˈnjuːmərəbl; *US* ɪˈnuː-; ɪˋnumərəbl̩/ *adj* too many to be counted 无数的; 数不清的. ➪Usage at INVALUABLE 用法见 INVALUABLE.

in·nu·mer·ate /ɪˈnjuːmərət; ɪnˋjumərɪt/ *adj* without a basic knowledge of mathematics; unable to count or do sums 不懂数学的; 不会数数的; 不会计算的; 数学盲的.

▷ **in·nu·mer·acy** /-rəsɪ; -rəsɪ/ *n* [U] state of being innumerate 无数学基本知识; 数学盲: *the problem of innumeracy and illiteracy among young people* 年轻人中的数学盲和文盲的问题.

in·ocu·late /ɪˈnɒkjʊleɪt; ɪnˋɑkjə,let/ *v* [Tn, Tn·pr] **~ sb (with sth) (against sth)** inject sb with a mild form of a disease, so that he will not catch the disease itself (给某人)接种, 作预防注射, 打预防针: *inoculate sb (with a vaccine)* 给某人注射疫苗 ○ *inoculate sb against cholera*

给某人注射霍乱预防针. Cf 参看 IMMUNIZE (IMMUNE), VACCINATE.

▷ **in·ocu·la·tion** /ɪˌnɒkjʊˈleɪʃn; ɪnˌɑkjəˈleʃən/ *n* ~ **(with sth) (against sth)** (**a**) [U] inoculating or being inoculated 接种; 预防注射. (**b**) [C] instance of this 接种; 预防注射: *have inoculations against cholera and yellow fever* 进行霍乱和黄热病的防疫注射.

in·of·fens·ive /ˌɪnəˈfensɪv; ˌɪnəˈfɛnsɪv/ *adj* not giving offence; not objectionable 不触犯人的; 不招人讨厌的: *an inoffensive remark, person* 不讨人嫌的话、人. ▷ **in·of·fens·ively** *adv*. **in·of·fens·ive·ness** *n* [U].

in·op·er·able /ɪnˈɒpərəbl; ɪnˈɑpərəbl̩/ *adj* **1** (of tumours, etc) that cannot be cured by a surgical operation (指肿瘤等)不能动手术的, 手术无法治愈的. **2** (*fml* 文) that cannot be made to work; not practicable 不能实行的; 行不通的; 不实用的: *an inoperable solution to a problem* 不能解决问题的办法.

in·op·er·at·ive /ˌɪnˈɒpərətɪv; ɪnˈɑpərətɪv/ *adj* (of laws, rules, etc) not working or taking effect; invalid (指法律、规则等)不生效的, 无效的, 不起作用的: *a bus, train, air service that is inoperative* 停止运作的公共汽车、铁路、航空服务 ○ *This rule is inoperative until further notice.* 此规则何时生效待通知.

in·op·por·tune /ˌɪnˈɒpətjuːn; *US* -tuːn; ˌɪnɑpɚˈtun/ *adj* (esp of time) not appropriate or convenient (尤指时间)不合适的, 不方便的: *at an inopportune moment* 在不当的时刻. ▷ **in·op·por·tunely** *adv*: *arrive inopportunely* 到达得不是时候.

in·or·din·ate /ɪnˈɔːdɪnət; ɪnˈɔrdn̩ɪt/ *adj* (*fml* 文) beyond proper or normal limits; excessive 超出适当或正常限度的; 无节制的; 过度的: *the inordinate demands of the tax collector* 税收员过分的要求 ○ *inordinate delays* 过分的拖延. ▷ **in·or·din·ately** *adv*: *inordinately fond of sth* 过分喜爱某事物.

in·or·ganic /ˌɪnɔːˈɡænɪk; ˌɪnɔrˈɡænɪk/ *adj* **1** not composed of living substances 无生物的; 无机的: *Rocks and minerals are inorganic.* 岩石和矿物都是无机物. **2** (*fig* 比喻) not the result of natural growth; artificial 非自然生长的; 人造的: *an inorganic form of society* 一种非由自然发展而形成的社会形式. Cf 参看 ORGANIC 2. ▷ **in·or·gan·ic·ally** /-klɪ; -klɪ/ *adv*.

□ ˌ**inorganic** ˈ**chemistry** branch of chemistry that deals with substances which do not contain carbon 无机化学. Cf 参看 ORGANIC CHEMISTRY (ORGANIC).

in-patient /ˈɪn peɪʃnt; ˈɪnˌpeʃənt/ *n* person who lives in hospital while receiving treatment 住院病人.

in·put /ˈɪnpʊt; ˈɪnˌpʊt/ *n* ~ **(into/to sth)** **1** (**a**) [U] action of putting sth in 放入; 投入; 输入: *the input of additional resources into the project* 给这项工程额外注入的资金. (**b**) [C, U] that which is put in 投入物: *an input of energy (to a system)* (向某系统的)能量输入 ○ *electrical input* 电的输入. (**c**) [C] place in a system where this happens 输入端. **2** (*computing* 计) (**a**) [U] putting of data into a computer for processing or storage 数据输入(以备处理或存储). (**b**) [C, U] data that is put in 输入的数据. (**c**) [C] place in a computer where this is done 输入端: [attrib 作定语] *an input key, code, level* 输入键、代码、电平. Cf 参看 OUTPUT 3.

▷ **in·put** *v* (**-tt-**, *pt*, *pp* **input** or **inputted**) [Tn, Tn·pr] ~ **sth (into/to sth)** (*computing* 计) put (data) into a computer 将(数据)输入计算机. Cf 参看 OUTPUT *v*.

□ ˈ**input circuit** (*computing* 计) circuit that controls input 输入电路; 输入回路.

ˈ**input device** (*computing* 计) equipment by which data is transferred from a memory store to a computer 输入装置; 输入设备.

in·quest /ˈɪŋkwest; ˈɪnkwɛst/ *n* ~ **(on/into sth)** **1** official inquiry to discover facts, esp about a death which may not have been the result of natural causes 审问, 审理(尤指调查疑为非自然死亡者的死因). **2** (*infml* 口) discussion about sth which has been unsatisfactory (对不满意的事进行的)事后讨论: *hold an inquest on the team's performance in the match* 对球队在比赛中的表现进行评议.

in·qui·et·ude /ɪnˈkwaɪətjuːd; *US* -tuːd; ɪnˈkwaɪəˌtud/ *n* [U] (*fml* 文) uneasiness of mind; anxiety 不安; 忧虑.

in·quire (also **en·quire**) /ɪnˈkwaɪə(r); ɪnˈkwaɪr/ *v* (*fml* 文) **1** [Tn, Tn·pr, Tw] ~ **sth (of sb)** ask to be told sth (by sb) 询问: *inquire sb's name* 询问某人的姓名 ○ *'How are you?' she inquired.* '你好吗?'她问道. ○ *inquire where to go, how to do sth, etc* 询问一下到哪儿去, 如何做某事等 ○ *She inquired of me most politely whether I wished to continue.* 她非常有礼貌地问我是否想继续下去. **2** [I, Ipr] ~ **(about sb/sth)** ask for information 打听消息: *'How much are the tickets?' 'I'll inquire.'* '票价多少钱?' '我去打听一下.' ○ *inquire at the information desk* 在询问处查问 ○ *inquire about trains to London* 查询到伦敦去的车次. **3** (phr v) **inquire after sb** ask about sb's health or welfare 问好; 问候; 问安: *People called to inquire after the baby.* 大家打电话来打听婴儿的情形. **inquire into sth** try to learn the facts about sth; investigate sth 调查; 查问; 究问: *We must enquire further into the matter.* 我们须进一步调查此事.

▷ **in·quirer** /ɪnˈkwaɪərə(r); ɪnˈkwaɪrɚ/ *n* person who inquires 调查者; 查问者.

in·quir·ing /ɪnˈkwaɪərɪŋ; ɪnˈkwaɪrɪŋ/ *adj* [usu attrib 通常作定语] **1** showing an interest in learning 爱询问的; 爱打听的: *an inquiring mind* 爱探索的头脑. **2** suggesting that information is needed 探询的; 追究的: *an inquiring look* 追究的神情. **in·quir·ingly** *adv*.

in·quiry (also **en·quiry**) /ɪnˈkwaɪərɪ; *US* ˈɪnkwərɪ; ˈɪnkwərɪ/ *n* **1** (**a**) [C] ~ **(about/concerning sb/sth)** (*fml* 文) request for help or information (about sb/sth) 请求帮助; 询问: *In answer to your recent inquiry, the book you mention is not in stock.* 您近日询问的书暂时无货, 谨此奉复. ○ *I've been making (some) inquiries* (ie trying to find out) *about it.* 我一直在(多方)打听这件事. ○ [attrib 作定语] *an inquiry desk/office* 问讯台[处]. (**b**) **inquiries** [pl] place from which one can get information 问讯处: *'How do I apply for this licence?' 'You want inquiries.'* '怎样申请许可证?' '你得到问讯处打听.' ○ *directory inquiries*, ie giving information about telephone numbers 电话号码查询台. **2** [U] (*fml* 文) asking; inquiring 问询; 调查; 查询: *learn sth by inquiry* 经查询得知某事 ○ *The police are following several lines of inquiry.* 警方正沿几条线索进行调查. ○ *On inquiry* (ie Having asked) *I found it was true.* 我经打听方知事情属实. **3** [C] ~ **(into sth)** investigation 调查; 查究: *hold an official inquiry* 进行正式调查 ○ *call for a public inquiry into safety standards* 要求公开调查安全情况.

□ **inˈquiry agent** private detective 私人侦探.

in·quisi·tion /ˌɪnkwɪˈzɪʃn; ˌɪnkwəˈzɪʃən/ *n* **1 the Inquisition** (also **the Holy ˈOffice**) [sing] organization appointed by the Roman Catholic Church to suppress heresy (esp from the 15th to the 17th century) (天主教镇压异教徒的)异端裁判所, 宗教法庭(尤指15至17世纪的). **2** [C] ~ **(into sth)** (*fml or joc* 文或谑) investigation or interrogation, esp one that is severe and looks closely into details 调查, 查究, 盘问(尤指严格而详细的): *I was subjected to a lengthy inquisition into the state of my marriage and the size of my bank balance.* 有关方面就我的婚姻状况以及银行存款余额对我进行了详细的调查.

in·quis·it·ive /ɪnˈkwɪzətɪv; ɪnˈkwɪzətɪv/ *adj* (too) fond of inquiring into other people's affairs (太)好打听别人的事情的: *'What's that you're hiding?' 'Don't be so inquisitive!'* '你藏什么东西呢?' '别那么爱管闲事!' ▷ **in·quis·it·ively** *adv*. **in·quis·it·ive·ness** *n* [U].

in·quis·itor /ɪnˈkwɪzɪtə(r); ɪnˈkwɪzətɚ/ *n* investigator, esp an officer of the Inquisition 调查人(尤指天主教的宗教法庭审判官).

▷ **in·quis·it·or·ial** /ɪnˌkwɪzɪˈtɔːrɪəl; ɪnˌkwɪzəˈtɔrɪəl/ *adj* of or like an inquisitor (似)审判官的. **in·quis·it·ori·ally** /-rɪəlɪ; -rɪəlɪ/ *adv*.

in·road /ˈɪnrəʊd; ˈɪnˌrod/ *n* (esp *pl* 尤作复数) **1** ~ **(into sth)** sudden attack on another's territory; raid 突然侵袭他人领地; 突袭: *inroads into enemy territory* 突袭敌国领土. **2** (idm 习语) **make inroads into/on sth** gradually use up or consume more and more of sth; lessen the amount of sth available 消耗某物: *Hospital bills had made deep inroads into her savings.* 住院的花销用去她一大笔积蓄. ○ *Already the children had made considerable inroads on the food.* 孩子们早已吃掉不少食物.

in·rush /ˈɪnrʌʃ; ˈɪnˌrʌʃ/ *n* (usu *sing* 通常作单数) rushing in (of sth); sudden arrival in large numbers 涌入; 冲入; 大量突然抵达: *an inrush of air, water, etc* 空气、水等流入 ○ *an inrush of tourists, visitors, etc* 纷至沓来的游客、

观光的人等.

in·sa·lu·bri·ous /ˌɪnsəˈluːbrɪəs; ˌɪnsəˈlubrɪəs/ *adj* (*fml* 文) unhealthy 有损健康的; 不卫生的: *insalubrious alleys and slums* 卫生条件恶劣的陋巷和贫民窟.

in·sane /ɪnˈseɪn; ɪnˈsen/ *adj* not sane; mad; senseless 精神失常的; 疯狂的; 愚蠢的: *an insane person* 精神错乱的人 ○ *an insane desire, idea, decision, policy* 疯狂的欲望、想法、决定、政策.
▷ **the in·sane** *n* [pl *v*] insane people 精神错乱的人: *an institution for the insane* 精神病院.
in·sanely *adv*: *insanely jealous* 忌妒得发狂.
in·san·ity /ɪnˈsænətɪ; ɪnˈsænətɪ/ *n* [U] madness; being mad 疯狂; 精神错乱: *a plea of insanity*, ie a plea in a court of law that a crime was due to the defendant having a mental disorder 精神失常的抗辩(在法庭上被告的辩护, 称作案时精神失常).
□ **insane asylum** (*dated* 旧) = MENTAL HOME (MENTAL).

in·san·it·ary /ɪnˈsænɪtrɪ; *US* -terɪ; ɪnˈsænəˌtɛrɪ/ *adj* not sanitary 不卫生的: *insanitary living conditions* 不卫生的生活环境.

in·sa·ti·able /ɪnˈseɪʃəbl; ɪnˈseʃəbl̩/ *adj* **~ (for sth)** that cannot be satisfied; very greedy 不能满足的; 极贪心的: *Another cake? You're insatiable!* 再来一块蛋糕? 你可真贪得无厌! ○ *an insatiable appetite, curiosity, desire, thirst (for knowledge), etc* 永不满足的食欲、好奇心、欲望、(求知)如渴之欲等 ○ *a politician who is insatiable for power* 权欲心重的政客. ▷ **in·sa·ti·ably** /-ʃəblɪ; -ʃəblɪ/ *adv*.

in·sa·ti·ate /ɪnˈseɪʃɪət; ɪnˈseʃɪɪt/ *adj* (*fml* 文) never satisfied 永不满足的.

in·scribe /ɪnˈskraɪb; ɪnˈskraɪb/ *v* [Tn, Tn·pr, Cn·n] **~ A (on/in B)/~ B (with A)** write (words, one's name, etc) on or in sth, esp as a formal or permanent record 在某物上写, 题(词语、名字等)(尤指作正式的或永久性的记录): *inscribe verses on a tombstone/inscribe a tombstone with verses* 在墓碑上题诗 ○ *inscribe one's name in a book/inscribe a book with one's name* 在书上签名 ○ *The book was inscribed 'To Cyril, with warmest regards.'* 这本书题有'西里尔惠存, 谨致最亲切的问候'的字样.
▷ **in·scrip·tion** /ɪnˈskrɪpʃn; ɪnˈskrɪpʃən/ *n* words written on sth, cut in stone (eg on a monument) or stamped on a coin or medal 题名, 题字, 铭文(写、刻或压印于某物上的, 如纪念碑、硬币或勋章): *an illegible inscription carved on the doorpost* 刻在门柱上的已模糊不清的字迹 ○ *What does the inscription say?* 这碑文记叙的是什么?

in·scrut·able /ɪnˈskruːtəbl; ɪnˈskrutəbl̩/ *adj* that cannot be understood or known; mysterious 不可理解的; 不可知的; 神秘的: *the inscrutable ways of Providence* 不可思议的天道 ○ *his inscrutable face*, ie which does not show what he is thinking 他那神秘莫测的面孔(看不出他在想什么). ▷ **in·scrut·ab·il·ity** /ɪnˌskruːtəˈbɪlətɪ; ɪnˌskrutəˈbɪlətɪ/ *n* [U]. **in·scrut·ably** /ɪnˈskruːtəblɪ; ɪnˈskrutəblɪ/ *adv*.

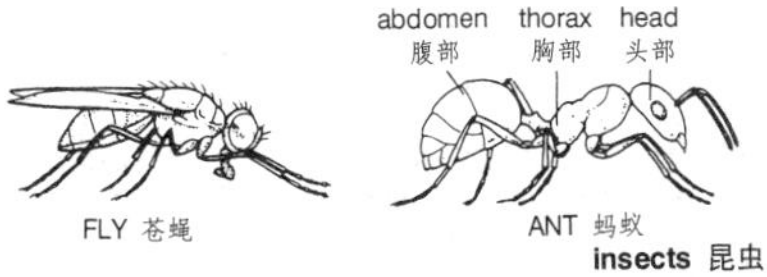

insects 昆虫

in·sect /ˈɪnsekt; ˈɪnsɛkt/ *n* **1** type of small animal (eg an ant, a fly, a wasp) having six legs, no backbone and a body divided into three parts (head, thorax and abdomen) 昆虫: [attrib 作定语] *an insect bite* 昆虫咬伤. ⇨illus 见插图. **2** (in incorrect but common usage 不确切的通俗用法) any small, crawling creature (eg a spider) 爬行的小动物(如蜘蛛).
▷ **in·sect·icide** /ɪnˈsektɪsaɪd; ɪnˈsɛktəˌsaɪd/ *n* [C, U] substance used for killing insects (eg DDT) 杀虫剂, 杀虫药(如滴滴涕): [attrib 作定语] *an insecticide spray, powder, etc* 灭虫喷雾剂、粉剂等. Cf 参看 PESTICIDE. **in·sect·icidal** /ɪnˌsektɪˈsaɪdl; ɪnˌsɛktəˈsaɪdl̩/ *adj*.
in·sect·ivore /ɪnˈsektɪvɔː(r); ɪnˈsɛktəˌvɔr/ *n* animal that eats insects 食虫动物. **in·secti·vor·ous** /ˌɪnsekˈtɪvərəs; ˌɪnsɛkˈtɪvərəs/ *adj* that eats insects 食虫的: *Swallows are insectivorous.* 燕子以虫为食.

in·sec·ure /ˌɪnsɪˈkjʊə(r); ˌɪnsɪˈkjʊr/ *adj* **1** not secure or safe; not providing good support; that cannot be relied on 不保险的; 不安全的; 不牢固的; 不稳定的; 不可靠的: *have an insecure hold/grip on sth*, eg when climbing 未抓牢某物(如攀登时) ○ (*fig* 比喻) *an insecure arrangement, plan, etc* 不可靠的安排、计划等 ○ *an insecure job*, ie from which one may be dismissed at any time 不稳固的工作(随时有被解雇的可能) ○ *insecure evidence*, ie not reliable enough to convict sb in a court of law 不可靠的证据(即不足以在法庭上给被告定罪的). **2 ~ (about sb/sth)** not feeling safe or protected; lacking confidence 缺乏安全感的; 感到无保障的; 信心不足的: *an insecure person* 缺乏安全感的人 ○ *She feels very insecure about her marriage.* 她对自己的婚姻缺乏信心. ▷ **in·sec·urely** *adv*: *insecurely fastened* 固定得不很牢靠. **in·sec·ur·ity** /ˌɪnsɪˈkjʊərətɪ; ˌɪnsɪˈkjurətɪ/ *n* [U]: *suffer from feelings of insecurity* 感到不安全.

in·sem·in·ate /ɪnˈsemɪneɪt; ɪnˈsɛməˌnet/ *v* [Tn] put sperm into (a female, esp a female animal) either naturally or artificially 使(尤指动物)受精(自然受精或人工授精): *inseminate a cow* 使母牛受精.
▷ **in·sem·ina·tion** /ɪnˌsemɪˈneɪʃn; ɪnˌsɛməˈneʃən/ *n* [U] inseminating 受精.

in·sens·ate /ɪnˈsenseɪt; ɪnˈsɛnset/ *adj* (*fml* 文) **1** without the power to feel or experience 无感觉的; 无感知能力的: *insensate rocks* 顽石. **2** unfeeling, esp in a foolish way 无情的; (尤指)蠢笨无情的: *insensate rage, cruelty, etc* 无理性的狂怒、残忍等. ▷ **in·sens·ately** *adv*.

in·sens·ib·il·ity /ɪnˌsensəˈbɪlətɪ; ˌɪnsɛnsəˈbɪlətɪ/ *n* [U] (*fml* 文) **1** unconsciousness 无知觉; 无意识: *lying in a state of drugged insensibility* 用药后一直躺着, 毫无知觉. **2 ~ (to sth)** (**a**) lack of physical feeling (肉体上)无感觉: *insensibility to pain, cold, etc* 对疼痛、寒冷等无感觉. (**b**) (*derog* 贬) lack of ability to respond emotionally (情感上)缺乏反应能力: *insensibility to art, music, beauty, etc* 对艺术、音乐、美等无欣赏能力. (**c**) (*derog* 贬) indifference 漠不关心; 冷淡: *He showed total insensibility to the animal's fate.* 他对那个动物的命运漠不关心.

in·sens·ible /ɪnˈsensəbl; ɪnˈsɛnsəbl̩/ *adj* (*fml* 文) **1** unconscious as the result of injury, illness, etc (因伤、病等)昏迷不醒的, 失去知觉的: *knocked insensible by a falling rock* 被落石击中而失去知觉. **2** [pred 作表语] **~ (of sth)** without knowledge (of sth); unaware 一无所知; 未觉察到: *be insensible of (one's) danger* 对(自己)面临的危险懵然无知 ○ *I'm not insensible how much I owe to your help.* 你帮了我这许多忙, 我不是不知道的. **3** [pred 作表语] **~ (to sth)** not able to feel (sth); insensitive(2) 无知觉; 无感觉: *insensible to pain, cold, etc* 对疼痛、寒冷等无感觉. **4** [attrib 作定语] (of changes) too small or gradual to be noticed; imperceptible (指变化)(因细微或缓慢)不易觉察的, 感觉不到的: *by insensible degrees* 不知不觉地. ▷ **in·sens·ibly** /-əblɪ; -əblɪ/ *adv*.

in·sens·it·ive /ɪnˈsensətɪv; ɪnˈsɛnsətɪv/ *adj* **1** not realizing or caring how other people feel, and therefore likely to offend them 未意识到或不顾及他人的感受的(因而易触犯他人): *It was rather insensitive of you to mention his dead wife.* 你也太粗心了, 竟然提起他已故的妻子来. **2 ~ (to sth)** not able to feel sth 无感觉的; 麻木不仁的: *insensitive to pain, cold, etc* 对疼痛、寒冷等无感觉 ○ (*fig* 比喻) *He's insensitive to criticism.* 他对批评毫无反应. ▷ **in·sens·it·ively** *adv*. **in·sens·it·iv·ity** /ɪnˌsensəˈtɪvətɪ; ɪnˌsɛnsəˈtɪvətɪ/ *n* [U].

in·sep·ar·able /ɪnˈseprəbl; ɪnˈsɛprəbl̩/ *adj* **~ (from sb/sth)** that cannot be separated 不可分的; 分不开的: *Rights are inseparable from duties.* 权利和职责是分不开的. ○ *inseparable* (ie extremely close) *friends* 形影不离的朋友. ▷ **in·sep·ar·ab·il·ity** /ɪnˌseprəˈbɪlətɪ; ɪnˌsɛprəˈbɪlətɪ/ *n* [U]. **in·sep·ar·ably** /ɪnˈseprəblɪ; ɪnˈsɛprəblɪ/ *adv*.

in·sert /ɪnˈsɜːt; ɪnˈsɝt/ *v* [Tn, Tn·pr] **~ sth (in/into/between sth)** put, fit, place sth into sth or between two things 插入、放入、置入或嵌于某物或某两物间: *insert an additional paragraph in an essay, an advertisement in a* newspaper, etc 在文章中加插一个段落、在报上刊登一段广告 ○ *insert a key into a lock* 把钥匙插进锁中 ○ *Insert your fingers between the layers and press them apart.* 把手指插入两层之间, 用力将之分开.

▷ **in·sert** /ˈɪnsɜːt; ˋɪnsɝt/ *n* **~ (in sth)** thing inserted (esp an additional section in a book, newspaper, etc) 插入物(尤指书、报等的插页): *an eight-page insert* 八页的附加页.

in·ser·tion /ɪnˈsɜːʃn; ɪnˋsɝʃən/ *n* **1** [U] **~ (into sth)** inserting or being inserted 插入; 放入; 置入: *the insertion of a coin into a slot* 往投币孔塞进一枚硬币. **2** [C] thing inserted, eg an announcement or advertisement put in a newspaper 插入物(如在报纸上刊登的启事或广告).

in-service /ˈɪnsɜːvɪs; ˋɪnˈsɝvɪs/ *adj* [attrib 作定语] carried out while actually working at a job 在职期间进行的; 不脱产的: *the in-service training of teachers* 教师在职培训.

in·set /ˈɪnset; ˋɪnˌset/ *n* additional thing put in, esp a small picture, map, diagram, etc within the border of a printed page or of a larger picture 添入物(尤指一页印刷品或大图中插入或套印的小图).

▷ **in·set** *v* (**-tt-**, *pt, pp* **inset**) [Tn, Tn·pr] **~ sth (into sth)** put sth in as an inset 嵌入; 插入: *For an explanation of the symbols see the key, inset left.* 有关各符号的意义请见左边附表.

in·shore /ˌɪnˈʃɔː(r); ˋɪnˌʃɔr/ *adj* [usu attrib 通常作定语] (of sth at sea) close to the shore (指海上某物)近海岸的, 向陆的: *an ˌinshore ˈcurrent* 近滨流 ○ *ˌinshore ˈfisheries* 近海渔场. ▷ **in·shore** *adv*: *fishing inshore or out at sea* 沿海或出海捕鱼.

in·side[1] /ɪnˈsaɪd; ˋɪnˈsaɪd/ *n* **1** (**a**) [C usu *sing* 通常作单数] inner side or surface; part within 里面; 背面; 内侧; 内部: *The inside of the box was lined with silk.* 那盒子用丝做衬里. ○ *This cup is stained on the inside.* 这杯子的内侧有积垢. ○ *chocolates with a creamy inside* 有奶油心的巧克力 ○ *Which paint is suitable for the inside of a house?* 房子内部刷什么漆合适? ○ *The room had been locked from/on the inside.* 这房间已从里面锁上了. ○ *The insides of the cylinders must be carefully cleaned.* 汽缸内部必须仔细清理干净. (**b**) [sing] part of a road or track nearest to the inner side of a curve (道路或跑道)转弯处的内侧, 内圈, 里道: *Daley Thomson is coming up on the inside.* 戴利·汤姆森正从里圈赶上来了. (**c**) [sing] side of a pavement or footpath that is furthest away from the road (人行道)远离车道的一侧, 内侧: *Walk on the inside to avoid the traffic fumes.* 在人行道的内侧走, 避开车辆的废气. Cf 参看 OUTSIDE[1]. **2** [sing] (also **in·sides** /ɪnˈsaɪdz; ɪnˋsaɪdz/ [pl]) (*infml* 口) stomach and bowels 肠胃: *a pain in his inside* 他肚子痛 ○ *My insides are crying out for food.* 我饿得肚子直叫. **3** (idm 习语) ˌ**inside** ˈ**out** (**a**) with the normal inner side on the outside 里面朝外: *wearing his socks inside out* 他把袜子穿反了. ○ *Turn the blouse inside out before drying it.* 把衬衫翻过来再干衣. ○ *My umbrella has blown inside out.* 我的雨伞给吹得翻过去了. ⇨illus at BACK[1] 见 BACK[1] 插图. (**b**) thoroughly; completely 彻底地; 完全地: *know a subject inside out* 非常熟悉某问题 ○ *turn a cupboard, drawer, etc inside out*, ie search thoroughly by emptying it and looking through its contents 把碗橱、抽屉等里面的东西全倒出来彻底翻找. **on the inˈside** (**a**) within a group or an organization so that one has direct access to information, etc 处于集团或组织内部因而知内情: *The thieves must have had someone on the inside to help them break in.* 那伙盗贼一定有内应, 协助他们闯了进去. (**b**) (of motorists, motor vehicles, etc) using the lane that is furthest away from the centre of the road or motorway (指开汽车的人或机动车辆等)使用内车道: *The driver behind me tried to overtake on the inside.* 我后面的驾驶员想从内车道超过我.

▷ **in·side** *adj* [attrib 作定语] **1** forming the inner part of sth; not on the outer side 内部的; 里面的; 内侧的: *He kept his wallet in an ˌinside ˈpocket.* 他把钱包放在里面的口袋里. ○ *What does your inside leg* (ie from the crutch to the inner side of the foot) *measure?* 你的腿从内侧量有多长? ○ *the inside pages of a newspaper* 报纸中间的各版 ○ *choosing to run on the inside track* 选择在内跑道跑. **2** told or performed by sb who is in a building, a group or an organization 从内部得到的; 得自内线的: *Acting on inside information, the police were able to arrest the gang before the robbery occurred.* 警方根据匪徒内部情报, 在劫案发生前把他们一网打尽. ○ *The robbery appeared to have been an inside job.* 这抢劫案看来是内部的人干的.

in·sider /ɪnˈsaɪdə(r); ɪnˋsaɪdɚ/ *n* person who, as a member of a group or an organization, is able to obtain information not available to others 内部的人; 知情人. **inˌsider ˈdealing** (also **inˌsider ˈtrading**) buying or selling with the help of information known only by those connected with the business 内幕交易.

□ ˌ**inside ˈlane** section of a road or motorway where the traffic moves more slowly 内车道: *After overtaking you should move back into the inside lane.* 超车后应回到内车道行驶.

ˌ**inside ˈleft**, ˌ**inside ˈright** player (in football, etc) in the forward line who is immediately to the left/right of the centre-forward (足球等的)左内锋, 右内锋.

in·side[2] /ɪnˈsaɪd; ɪnˋsaɪd/ (also *esp US* **in·side of**) *prep* **1** on or to the inner side of (sb/sth); within 在或往(某人[某物])里面: *go inside the house* 走进房子里 ○ *put it inside its cage* 把它放到笼子里去 ○ *Inside the box there was a gold coin.* 盒子里面曾有一块金币. ○ *You'll feel better with a good meal inside you*, ie when you've eaten a good meal. 你好好吃上一顿饭, 就会觉得好些. Cf 参看 OUTSIDE[2]. **2** (of time) in less than (sth) (指时间)少于: *The job is unlikely to be finished inside (of) a year.* 这工作一年之内不见得能完成.

▷ **in·side** *adv* **1** on or to the inside 在或向里面: *The coat has a detachable lining inside.* 这件大衣有活里儿. ○ *She shook it to make certain there was nothing inside.* 她把它摇了摇, 想知道里面确实没有东西. ○ *The guests had to move inside* (ie indoors) *when it started to rain.* 外面下起雨来, 客人只好都回到屋里. **2** (*sl* 俚) in prison 在监狱里; 在押.

in·si·di·ous /ɪnˈsɪdɪəs; ɪnˋsɪdɪəs/ *adj* (*fml derog* 文, 贬) spreading or acting gradually and unnoticed but with harmful effects 隐伏的; 潜在的; 暗中为害的: *an insidious disease* 潜伏的疾病 ○ *insidious jealousy* 暗暗产生的忌妒. ▷ **in·si·di·ously** *adv*: *He had insidiously wormed his way into her affections.* 他已神不知鬼不觉地逐渐赢得了她的爱情. **in·si·di·ous·ness** *n* [U].

in·sight /ˈɪnsaɪt; ˋɪnˌsaɪt/ *n* **~ (into sth)** **1** (**a**) [U] (*approv* 褒) ability to see into the true nature (of sth); deep understanding 洞察力; 深刻的了解: *a person of insight* 有洞察力的人 ○ *show insight into human character* 表现出对人性的深刻了解. (**b**) [C] instance of this 洞察力; 深刻的了解: *a book full of remarkable insights* 很有真知灼见的书. **2** [C] (sudden) perception or understanding of the true nature (of sth) (突然的)领悟, 猛省: *She was given an unpleasant insight into what life would be like as his wife.* 她恍然大悟嫁给他就要过那种日子, 心里十分难过. ○ *have/gain an insight into a problem* 对某问题豁然开朗.

▷ **in·sight·ful** /-fʊl; -fəl/ *adj* (*approv* 褒) showing insight 富有洞察力的; 有深刻见解的: *an insightful remark* 有真知灼见的言语.

in·sig·nia /ɪnˈsɪgnɪə; ɪnˋsɪgnɪə/ *n* [pl] (**a**) symbols of rank or authority, eg the crown and sceptre of a king or queen 官阶识别符号, 象征(如国王或王后的王冠及权杖): *the insignia of office* 官职的标记. (**b**) identifying badge of a military regiment, squadron, etc 军队、航空队等的标记、标志.

in·sig·ni·fic·ant /ˌɪnsɪgˈnɪfɪkənt; ˌɪnsɪgˋnɪfəkənt/ *adj* having little or no value, use, meaning or importance 无价值的; 无用的; 无意义的; 不重要的; 无足轻重的: *The rate has fallen by an insignificant* (ie too small to be important) *amount.* 比率虽有下降, 但微不足道. ○ *an insignificant-looking little man who turned out to be the managing director* 一个其貌不扬的男人, 却原来是总经理. ▷ **in·sig·ni·fic·ance** /-kəns; -kəns/ *n* [U]: *reduced to insignificance* 削弱到无足轻重的程度. **in·sig·ni·fic·antly** *adv*.

in·sin·cere /ˌɪnsɪnˈsɪə(r); ˌɪnsɪnˋsɪr/ *adj* not sincere 不真诚的; 不诚恳的. ▷ **in·sin·cerely** *adv*. **in·sin·cer·ity** /ˌɪnsɪnˈserətɪ; ˌɪnsɪnˋserətɪ/ *n* [U].

in·sinu·ate /ɪnˈsɪnjʊeɪt; ɪnˋsɪnjʊˌet/ *v* **1** [Tn, Dn·pr, Tf, Dpr·f] **~ sth (to sb)** suggest sth (to sb) unpleasantly and indirectly (向某人)旁敲侧击示意某事物: *What are you insinuating?* 你旁敲侧击, 究竟指的是什么? ○ *Are* *you insinuating that I am a liar?* 你绕来绕去是否暗指我撒谎? **2** [Tn·pr] **~ sth/oneself into sth** (*fml* 文) place sth/oneself smoothly and stealthily into sth 使某事物[自己]悄然潜入某事物中: *insinuate one's body/person into a narrow opening* 使自己的身体[自己]小心翼翼地钻入狭窄的孔隙中 ○ (*fig derog* 比喻, 贬) *insinuate oneself into sb's favour*, ie ingratiate oneself with sb 巧妙地逐渐取得某人的宠信.

▷ **in·sinu·ation** /ɪnˌsɪnjʊˈeɪʃn; ɪnˌsɪnjuˈeʃən/ *n* (**a**) [U] insinuating 旁敲侧击; 巧妙地进入; 巴结: *blacken sb's character by insinuation* 含沙射影地贬低某人的品格. (**b**) [C] **~ (that...)** thing that is insinuated; indirect suggestion 影射; 暗示的批评; 讨好的委婉话; 谀词: *I object to your (unpleasant) insinuations!* 我讨厌你那些(令人不快的)拐弯抹角的话!

in·sipid /ɪnˈsɪpɪd; ɪnˋsɪpɪd/ *adj* (*derog* 贬) **1** having almost no taste or flavour 无味道的: *insipid food* 无味道的食物. **2** (*fig* 比喻) lacking in interest or vigour 乏味的; 无生气的: *painted in pale, insipid colours* 涂有灰暗的、死气沉沉的颜色 ○ *an insipid performance of the symphony* 交响乐团乏味的演奏 ○ *a good-looking but insipid young man* 外貌好看而无情趣的小伙子. ▷ **in·sip·id·ity** /ˌɪnsɪˈpɪdətɪ; ˌɪnsɪˋpɪdətɪ/ (also **in·sipid·ness**) *n* [U]. **in·sipidly** *adv*.

in·sist /ɪnˈsɪst; ɪnˋsɪst/ *v* **1** [I, Ipr, Tf] **~ (on sth)** demand (sth) forcefully, not accepting a refusal 坚持或坚决要求(某事物): *'You really must go!' 'All right, if you insist.'* '你真得走了!' '好吧, 你一定要我走, 我就走.' ○ *I insist on your taking/insist that you take immediate action to put this right.* 我坚决要求你立刻采取行动把事情处理好. **2** [Ipr] **~ on sth/doing sth** require or demand (the specified thing), refusing to accept an alternative 一定要(某事物); 坚决主张: *I always insist on wholemeal bread.* 我一贯主张要吃全麦面包. ○ (*fig* 比喻) *She will insist on getting up early and playing her radio loud*, ie She always does this, annoyingly. 她老是一大早起来就把收音机音量开得很大. **3** [Ipr, Tf] **~ on sth** state or declare sth forcefully, esp when other people oppose or disbelieve one 坚持说, 固执地声称(尤指别人反对或不信时): *She kept insisting on her innocence/insisting that she was innocent.* 她坚持说她是清白的.

▷ **in·sist·ent** /-ənt; -ənt/ *adj* **~ (about/on sth); ~ (that...)** tending to insist; not allowing refusal or opposition 坚持的; 不容拒绝或反对的: *She's a most insistent person; she won't take 'no' for an answer.* 她是个说一不二的人, 决不容别人反对. ○ *You mustn't be late; he was most insistent about that.* 你万不可迟到, 他对这一点最严格. ○ (*fig* 比喻) *this job's insistent demands* 此工作之硬性要求 ○ (*fig* 比喻) *the insistent* (ie constantly and noticeably repeated) *horn phrase in the third movement of the symphony* 交响乐第三乐章中反复突出的号音. **in·sist·ence** /-əns; -əns/ *n* [U] **~ (about/on sth); ~ (that...)**. **in·sist·ently** *adv*.

in situ /ˌɪn ˈsɪtjuː; ɪnˋsaɪtju/ (*Latin* 拉) in its original or proper place 在原处; 在原位置.

in·so·far as /ˌɪnsəˈfɑːr əz; ˌɪnsəˋfɑr əz/ = IN SO FAR AS (FAR).

in·sole /ˈɪnsəʊl; ˋɪnˌsol/ *n* inside surface of the bottom of a shoe 鞋的内底; 鞋垫.

in·sol·ent /ˈɪnsələnt; ˋɪnsələnt/ *adj* **~ (to/towards sb)** extremely rude, esp in expressing contempt 粗鲁的; 粗野的; 无礼的; 侮慢的: *insolent children, remarks, behaviour* 无礼的儿童、言语、举止.

▷ **in·sol·ence** /-əns; -əns/ *n* [U] **~ (to/towards sb)** being insolent 粗野; 无礼; 傲慢; 侮辱: *That's enough of your insolence, boy!* 不要再放肆了, 小伙子! ○ *dumb insolence*, ie expressed by behaviour rather than verbally 无声的侮慢(用行为而非言语表达的).

in·sol·ently *adv*.

in·sol·uble /ɪnˈsɒljʊbl; ɪnˋsɑljəbl̩/ *adj* **1** (of substances) that cannot be dissolved; not soluble (指物质)不能溶解的. **2** (*fig* 比喻) that cannot be solved or explained 不能解决的; 不能解释的: *an insoluble problem, mystery, riddle, etc* 不能解决的问题、无法解释的奥秘、不解之谜.

in·solv·ent /ɪnˈsɒlvənt; ɪnˋsɑlvənt/ *adj* unable to pay debts; bankrupt 无力偿付债务的; 破产的.

▷**in·solv·ency** /-ənsɪ; -ənsɪ/ *n* [U].

in·solv·ent *n* insolvent person 无力偿付债务的人; 破产者.

in·som·nia /ɪnˈsɒmnɪə; ɪnˋsɑmnɪə/ *n* [U] inability to sleep 失眠; 失眠症: *suffer from insomnia* 患失眠症.

▷ **in·som·niac** /ɪnˋsɒmnɪæk; ɪnˋsɑmnɪæk/ *n* person who finds it difficult to go to sleep 失眠者; 失眠症患者.

in·so·much /ˌɪnsəʊˈmʌtʃ; ˌɪnsoˋmʌtʃ/ *adv* **~ as...** because of the fact that...; to the degree or extent that...; inasmuch as... 因为; 由于; 鉴于; 至如此程度: *This statement was important insomuch as it revealed the extent of their knowledge.* 这一陈述显示了他们了解情况之多, 因而十分重要.

in·sou·ci·ance /ɪnˈsuːsɪəns; ɪnˋsusɪəns/ *n* [U] (*fml* 文) state of being unconcerned, esp in a light-hearted way; nonchalance 无忧无虑; 满不在乎; 漠不关心; 漫不经心.

▷ **in·sou·ci·ant** /-sɪənt; -sɪənt/ *adj*.

Insp *abbr* 缩写 = Inspector (esp in the police force): *Chief Insp (Paul) King* 总巡官(保罗·)金.

in·spect /ɪnˈspekt; ɪnˋspɛkt/ *v* **1** [Tn] (**a**) examine (sth) closely 检查(某事物): *The customs officer inspected my passport suspiciously.* 海关官员颇为怀疑地检查了我的护照. (**b**) visit (sth) officially to see that rules are obeyed, that work is done properly, etc 视察(某事物): *inspect a school, factory, regiment, etc* 视察学校、工厂、团队等. **2** [Tn·pr] **~ sb/sth for sth** examine sb/sth in order to detect the presence of sth 检查; 查看; 察看; 审视: *inspect sb/sb's head for lice, dandruff, etc* 检查某人头部有无头虱、头皮屑等 ○ *inspect an object for fingerprints* 察看一物件以寻找指纹.

▷ **in·spec·tion** /ɪnˈspekʃn; ɪnˋspɛkʃən/ *n* **1** [U] inspecting or being inspected 检查; 视察: *On inspection* (ie When inspected) *the notes proved to be forgeries.* 经检查发现钞票是伪造的. ○ *after inspection (of the factory) for signs of inefficiency* 视察(工厂)有无效率低的迹象之后. **2** [C] instance of this 检查; 视察: *carry out frequent inspections* 进行经常性检查.

in·spector /ɪnˈspektə(r); ɪnˋspɛktɚ/ *n* **1** official who inspects eg schools, factories, mines 检查员; 视察员; 巡视员; 稽查员; 检验员; 督学. **2** (*Brit*) police officer between the ranks of chief-inspector and sergeant (警察)巡官: *Inspector Davies* 戴维斯巡官. **3** official who examines bus or train tickets to ensure that they are valid (公共汽车或火车的)查票员.

▷ **in·spect·or·ate** /ɪnˈspektərət; ɪnˋspɛktərət/ *n* [CGp] inspectors collectively 视察人员(总称); 视察团: *the primary schools inspectorate* 小学督学团.

□ **inˌspector of ˈtaxes** (also **ˈtax inspector**) official who examines statements of people's income and decides the tax to be paid on it 税务稽查员.

in·spira·tion /ˌɪnspəˈreɪʃn; ˌɪnspəˋreʃən/ *n* **1** [U] **~ (to do sth)** stimulation of the mind, feelings, etc to do sth beyond a person's usual ability, esp creative ability in art, literature, music, etc; state or quality of being inspired 灵感: *Wordsworth found (his) inspiration in/drew (his) inspiration from the Lake District scenery. It was a great source of inspiration to him.* 华兹华斯从风景优美的英格兰湖区获得灵感. 那地方是他灵感的巨大源泉. ○ *Her work shows real inspiration.* 她的作品表现出她很有灵感. ○ *I sat down to write my essay, but found I was completely without inspiration*, ie could think of nothing to write. 我坐下来写文章, 可是发觉自己毫无灵感(想不出写什么). ○ (*saying* 谚) *Genius is 10% inspiration and 90% perspiration*, ie hard work. 天才是10%的灵感加上90%的勤奋. **2** [C] **~ (to/for sb)** person or thing that causes this state 鼓舞或激励人的人或事物: *This woman's an inspiration to all of us*, ie is so excellent that she inspires us. 这一女子就是鼓舞我们大家的人. **3** [C] (*infml* 口) (sudden) good idea resulting from such a state (心血来潮的)妙计, 好主意, 灵机: *I've just had an inspiration: why don't we try turning it the other way!* 我突然想到一个好主意, 我们何不试试向相反的方向转一转呢!

▷ **in·spira·tional** /-ʃənl; -ʃənl̩/ *adj* providing inspiration 启发灵感的; 鼓舞或激励人的: *an inspirational piece of writing* 一篇鼓舞人心的文字.

in·spire /ɪnˈspaɪə(r); ɪnˋspaɪr/ *v* **1** [Tn, Tn·pr, Cn·t] **~ sb (to sth)** fill sb with the ability or urge to do, feel, etc sth beyond his usual ability, esp to write, paint, compose, etc 赋予某人灵感(尤指写作、绘画、作曲

等); 启示; 启迪: *His noble example inspired the rest of us to greater efforts.* 他那高尚的榜样激发我们大家更加努力. ○ *The Lake District scenery inspired Wordsworth to write his greatest poetry.* 英格兰湖区的美景给了华兹华斯灵感而创作出他最伟大的诗篇. **2** [Tn, Tn·pr] **~ sb (with sth)/~ sth (in sb)** fill sb with thoughts, feelings or aims 激励或鼓舞某人: *Our first sight of the dingy little hotel did not inspire us with much confidence/inspire much confidence in us.* 我们一见到那旅店昏暗肮脏, 心里就很不痛快. ○ *inspire hope, loyalty, enthusiasm, etc in sb* 燃起某人的希望、唤起某人的忠诚、激起某人的热情 ○ *gloomy statistics which inspired panic in the stock market/among the stockbrokers* 在证券市场[证券经纪人]中引起恐慌的令人沮丧的统计数字.

▷ **in·spired** *adj* (*approv* 褒) **1** filled with creative power 有创作力的: *an inspired poet, artist, etc* 有创作力的诗人、艺术家等. **2** full of a spirit that leads to outstanding achievements 有雄心壮志的: *act like a man/woman inspired* 表现得像是很有雄心壮志的人. **3** produced (as if) by or with the help of inspiration 受灵感启示的; (仿佛)得自灵感的: *an inspired work of art* 得自灵感的艺术作品 ○ *an inspired effort* 由灵感产生的力量 ○ *an inspired guess*, ie made by intuition rather than logic, but usu correct 凭灵感的猜测(靠直觉而不靠逻辑, 但往往正确).

in·spir·ing /ɪnˈspaɪərɪŋ; ɪnˋspaɪrɪŋ/ *adj* **1** that inspires (sb to do sth) 鼓舞人的: *an inspiring thought* 鼓舞人心的想法. **2** (usu with negatives 通常与否定词连用) (*infml* 口) filling one with interest and enthusiasm 使人感兴趣的; 吸引人的: *a book on a not very inspiring subject* 题材并不十分令人感兴趣的书.

Inst *abbr* 缩写 = Institute; Institution.

inst /ɪnst; ɪnst/ *abbr* 缩写 = (*dated or fml commerce* 旧或文, 商) instant (of this month) 本月的: *your letter of the 6th inst* 您本月6日的信.

in·stab·il·ity /ˌɪnstəˈbɪlətɪ; ˌɪnstəˋbɪlətɪ/ *n* [U] lack of stability 不稳定; 不稳固: *mental instability*, ie liability to fits of madness 精神不稳定 ○ *the inherent instability of this chemical*, eg one which may blow up or catch fire 这种化学药品固有的不稳定性(如易爆炸或着火).

in·stall (*US* also **in·stal**) /ɪnˈstɔːl; ɪnˋstɔl/ *v* **1** [Tn, Tn·pr] **~ sth (in sth)** fix equipment, furniture, etc in position for use, esp by making the necessary connections with the supply of electricity, water, etc 安装, 设置(设备、家具等): *install a heating or lighting system (in a building)* (在建筑物中)安装暖气或照明设备 ○ *I'm having a shower installed.* 我正在安装淋浴设备. **2** [Tn, Tn·pr] **~ sb/oneself (in sth)** settle sb/oneself in a place 将某人安顿或安置于某处[在某处安顿下来]: *be comfortably installed in a new home* 在新居舒适地安顿下来 ○ *She installed herself in her father's favourite armchair.* 她坐在她父亲最喜欢坐的单座沙发上. **3** [Tn, Tn·pr] **~ sb (in sth)** place sb in a new position of authority with the usual ceremony (以例行仪式)使某人就新职: *install a priest (in office)* 使一牧师就职.

▷ **in·stalla·tion** /ˌɪnstəˈleɪʃn; ˌɪnstəˋleʃən/ *n* **1** (**a**) [U] installing or being installed 安装; 设置; 就职: *Installation requires several days.* 安装工程需时数日. ○ *the installation of the new vice-chancellor* 大学校长的就职 ○ [attrib 作定语] *installation costs/charges* 安装费. (**b**) [C] instance of this 安装; 设置; 就职: *carry out several installations* 实施几项安装工程. **2** [C] (**a**) that which is installed 安装物; 装置; 设备: *a heating installation* 取暖装置. (**b**) site housing military equipment 军事设施: *attacking the enemy's missile installations* 攻击敌人的导弹设施.

in·stal·ment (*US* usu 美式英语通常作 **in·stall·ment**) /ɪnˈstɔːlmənt; ɪnˋstɔlmənt/ *n* **1** any one of the separate but connected parts in which a story is presented over a period of time (一故事分段连载或连播等的)一集: *a story that will appear in instalments* 分段连载的故事 ○ *Don't miss the next instalment!* 下期续载, 切勿错过! **2** **~ (on sth)** any one of the parts of a payment spread over a period of time (分期付款的)一期付款: *pay for a house by monthly instalments* 按月分期付款买房 ○ *keep up the instalments* (ie maintain regular payments) *on the house* 为买该房按时分期付款.

□ **inˈstalment plan** (*esp US*) = HIRE PURCHASE (HIRE).

in·stance /ˈɪnstəns; ˋɪnstəns/ *n* **1 ~ (of sth)** particular occurrence of sth that happens generally or several times; example; case 例子; 实例; 事例: *I can quote you several instances of her being deliberately rude.* 我可以给你举出她故意粗暴待人的几个例子. ○ *In most instances* (ie Mostly) *the pain soon goes away.* 在多数情况下, 这种疼痛很快就消失. **2** (idm 习语) **at the instance of sb** (*fml* 文) at sb's (urgent) request or suggestion 应某人之(紧急)请求或建议. **for ˈinstance** as an example; for example 例如; 比如: *Several of his friends came: Ben, Carol and Mike, for instance.* 他的几个朋友来了, 比如本、卡罗尔、麦克. **in the ˈfirst instance** (*fml* 文) at the beginning; intially 首先; 第一: *In the first instance I was inclined to refuse, but then I reconsidered.* 起初我想拒绝, 但后来还是重新考虑了. **in ˈthis instance** on this occasion; in this case 在这种情况下.

▷ **in·stance** *v* [Tn] give (sth) as an example 举(某事物)为例.

in·stant[1] /ˈɪnstənt; ˋɪnstənt/ *adj* **1** [usu attrib 通常作定语] coming or happening at once 立即的; 立刻的: *a new book that was an instant success* 一出版就大获成功的新书 ○ *feel instant relief after treatment* 医治后随即感到舒服了 ○ *instant hot water*, ie as soon as the tap is turned on 瞬间致热的水(一开龙头水就热). **2** (of food preparations) that can very quickly and easily be made ready for use (指食品的制备)调制快速方便的, 速成的: *instant coffee*, ie made by adding hot water or milk to a powder 速溶咖啡. **3** (*abbr* 缩写 **inst**) (*dated commerce* 旧, 商) (after dates 用于日期之后) of the present month 本月的: *in reply to your letter of the 9th inst* 兹复本月9日来函. **4** [attrib 作定语] (*fml* 文) urgent 紧急的; 急迫的: *attend to sb's instant needs* 满足某人紧急的需要 ○ *in instant need of help* 在需要紧急援助时.

▷ **in·stantly** *adv* at once; immediately 立刻; 马上; 瞬即: *an instantly recognizable face* 一眼就可以认得出来的面孔. — *conj* as soon as 一…就…: *Tell me instantly he arrives.* 他一到就告诉我.

in·stant[2] /ˈɪnstənt; ˋɪnstənt/ *n* (esp *sing* 尤作单数) **1** precise point of time 当时: *Come here this instant!* ie at once! 马上到这里来! ○ *He left (at) that (very) instant.* 他立刻离开了. ○ *leave on the instant of six o'clock*, ie not a second later than six 六时整离开 ○ *I recognized her the instant (that)* (ie as soon as) *I saw her.* 我一眼就认出是她. **2** short space of time; moment 顷刻; 刹那; 瞬间; 片刻: *I shall be back in an instant.* 我马上就回来. ○ *Help came not an instant too soon.* 援助来得正是时候. ○ *Just for an instant I thought he was going to refuse.* 我脑中有一闪念, 以为他要拒绝了.

in·stant·an·eous /ˌɪnstənˈteɪnɪəs; ˌɪnstənˋtenɪəs/ *adj* happening or done immediately 即时的; 瞬间的: *Death was instantaneous*, eg in a fatal accident. 当即死去(如在致命事故中). ▷ **in·stant·an·eously** *adv*.

in·stead /ɪnˈsted; ɪnˋstɛd/ *adv* as an alternative or replacement 代替; 更换: *We've no coffee. Would you like tea instead?* 我们没有咖啡了. 改喝茶好么? ○ *It will take days by car, so let's fly instead.* 开车去要好几天呢, 咱们还是坐飞机去吧. ○ *Stuart was ill so I went instead.* 斯图尔特病了, 所以换了我去.

□ **instead of** *prep* as an alternative or replacement to (sb/sth) 作为(某人[某事物])的替换: *Let's play cards instead of watching television.* 咱们玩纸牌吧, 别看电视了. ○ *We sometimes eat rice instead of potatoes.* 我们有时候吃大米, 不吃土豆. ○ *Instead of Graham, it was Peter who moved in.* 搬进来的不是格雷厄姆, 而是彼得.

in·step /ˈɪnstep; ˋɪnˌstɛp/ *n* (**a**) upper surface of the human foot between the toes and the ankle 脚背. ⇨illus at FOOT 见 FOOT 插图. (**b**) part of a shoe, etc covering this (鞋等的)覆盖脚背的部分; 鞋面. ⇨illus at SHOE 见 SHOE 插图.

in·stig·ate /ˈɪnstɪɡeɪt; ˋɪnstəˌɡet/ *v* [Tn] cause (sth) to begin or happen; initiate 使(某事物)开始或发生; 鼓动; 唆使; 煽动; 怂恿: *instigate a strike, strike action, etc* 煽动罢工、罢工行动等 ○ *The minister has instigated a full official inquiry into the incident.* 部长已开始正式全面调查这一事件.

▷ **in·sti·ga·tion** /ˌɪnstɪˈɡeɪʃn; ˌɪnstəˋɡeʃən/ *n* [U] instigating or being instigated 发起; 鼓动; 唆使; 煽动; 怂恿: *At his instigation we concealed the facts from the authorities*, ie He encouraged us to do so. 我们受他的怂恿向当局隐瞒了事实.

in·stig·ator /ˈɪnstɪgeɪtə(r); ˋɪnstəˌgetɚ/ *n* person who instigates (esp sth bad) 发起者; (尤指)教唆者, 煽动者, 挑动者: *the instigators of violence in our society* 在我们社会中那些鼓吹使用暴力的人.

in·stil (*US* **in·still**) /ɪnˈstɪl; ɪnˋstɪl/ *v* **(-ll-)** [Tn, Tn·pr] **~ sth (in/into sb)** cause sb gradually to acquire (a particular desirable quality) 逐渐使某人获得(某种可取的品质); 逐步灌输: *instilling a sense of responsibility (in/into one's children)* 逐步培养(孩子的)责任感. ▷ **in·stilla·tion** /ˌɪnstɪˈleɪʃn; ˌɪnstɪˋleʃən/ *n* [U].

in·stinct /ˈɪnstɪŋkt; ˋɪnstɪŋkt/ *n* **~ (for sth/doing sth); ~ (to do sth)** [U, C] **1** natural inborn tendency to behave in a certain way without reasoning or training 本能: *Birds learn to fly by instinct.* 鸟会飞是出自本能. ○ *Birds have the instinct to learn to fly.* 鸟有飞的本能. **2** natural feeling that makes one choose to act in a particular way 直觉: *When I saw the flames I acted on instinct and threw a blanket over them.* 我看见火焰时便凭直觉把一张毯子扑在火焰上. ○ *My first instinct was to refuse, but later I reconsidered.* 最初我凭直觉加以拒绝, 但后来又重新考虑了. ○ *have an instinct for survival* 有求生的直觉 ○ *Trust your instincts and marry him!* 要相信你的直觉, 就嫁给他吧! ○ *I'm afraid I gave way to my worst instincts and hit him.* 真遗憾, 我一时任性打了他. ○ *The sight of the helpless little boy aroused her maternal instinct(s).* 她看见那孤苦无助的小男孩激发了她的母性. ○ (*ironic* 反语) *have an instinct for doing or saying the wrong thing* 有做错事或说错话的本领 ○ (*fig* 比喻) *I'm afraid he lacks the killer instinct*, ie ability to be ruthless. 我看他不够心狠手辣.

▷ **in·stinc·tive** /ɪnˈstɪŋktɪv; ɪnˋstɪŋktɪv/ *adj* based on instinct; not coming from training or based on reasoning 凭本能的; 天生的; 直觉的: *an instinctive fear of fire* 天生怕火 ○ *an instinctive dislike of sb* 对某人出自直觉的讨厌 ○ *an instinctive reaction* 本能的反应. **in·stinc·tively** *adv*: *I instinctively raised my arm to protect my face.* 我本能地抬起手臂护着脸.

in·sti·tute[1] /ˈɪnstɪtjuːt; *US* -tuːt; ˋɪnstəˌtut/ *n* (building that contains a) society or organization for a special (usu social, professional or educational) purpose 会; 社; 学会; 协会; 会址; 会所; 社址: *the Working Men's institute* 工人会馆 ○ *the Institute of Chartered Surveyors* 特许土地测量师学会.

in·sti·tute[2] /ˈɪnstɪtjuːt; *US* -tuːt; ˋɪnstəˌtut/ *v* (*fml* 文) **1** [Tn] establish or start (an inquiry, a custom, a rule, etc) 建立, 设立, 制定(习俗、规则等); 开始, 着手(调查等): *institute legal proceedings against sb* 起诉某人 ○ *Police have instituted inquiries into the matter.* 警方已就此事展开调查. **2** [Tn] place (sb, esp a clergyman) officially in a new post with a formal ceremony 以正式仪式授予(某人, 尤指牧师)新职位.

in·sti·tu·tion /ˌɪnstɪˈtjuːʃn; *US* -tuːʃn; ˌɪnstəˋtuʃən/ *n* **1** [U] instituting (INSTITUTE[2] 1,2) or being instituted 建立; 设立; 制定; 任命: *the institution of rules, customs, etc* 规则的制定、习俗的形成 ○ *institution of a bishop/of sb as a bishop* 主教的授职[授某人以主教之职]. **2** [C] (building of an) organization for helping people with special needs, eg an orphanage, a home for old people 慈善机关, 社会福利机构(如孤儿院、养老院): *living in an institution* 住在收容所. **3** [C] long-established custom, practice or group (eg a club or society) 由来已久的风俗、习惯或团体(如俱乐部或会社): *Marriage is a sacred institution.* 婚姻制度是神圣的. ○ *Drinking tea at 4 pm is a popular British institution.* 下午4点钟吃茶点是英国人很流行的习惯. **4** [C] (*infml usu approv or joc* 口, 通常作褒义或作戏谑语) person who is a very familiar figure in some activity or place (在某活动上或在某处的)知名人士, 闻人, 名流: *My uncle has become quite an institution at the club!* 我叔叔在俱乐部里已是颇有名气的人物了!

▷ **in·sti·tu·tional** /-ʃənl; -ʃənḷ/ *adj* of, from or connected with an institution 由来已久的; 习已为常的; 公共机构的; 慈善机关的; 知名人士的: *institutional food* 老一套的食物 ○ *old people in need of institutional care* 需慈善机关照顾的老年人. **in·sti·tu·tion·al·ize, -ise** /-ʃənəlaɪz; -ʃənḷˌaɪz/ *v* **1** [Tn] make (sth) into an institution(3) 使(某事物)制度化. **2** [Tn] place (sb) in an institution(2) 将(某人)收容在社会福利机构的. **3** [Tn esp passive 尤用于被动语态] cause (sb) to become accustomed to living in an institution, esp so as to lose self-reliance 使(某人)习惯于生活在收容所(尤指因而失去自立能力). **in·sti·tu·tion·al·iza·tion, -isation** /ˌɪnstɪˌtjuːʃənəlaɪˈzeɪʃn; *US* -lɪˈz; ˌɪnstəˌtjuʃənələˋzeʃən/ *n* [U].

in·struct /ɪnˈstrʌkt; ɪnˋstrʌkt/ *v* **1** [Tn, Tn·pr] **~ sb (in sth)** teach sb a school subject, a skill, etc 教授某人学校课目; 传授某人技巧: *instruct a class (in history), recruits (in drill), etc* 教某班级(历史)、训练新兵(操练). ➪ Usage at TEACH 用法见 TEACH. **2** [Tn·pr, Dn·w, Dn·t] **~ sb (about sth)** give orders or directions to sb 向某人下命令或指示; 指导: *instruct sb about his duties* 向某人交待其责任 ○ *They haven't instructed us where to go.* 他们还未指示我们到何处去. ○ *I've instructed them to keep the room locked.* 我已吩咐他们那房间要上锁. ➪ Usage at ORDER[2] 用法见 ORDER[2]. **3** [Dn·f esp passive 尤用于被动语态] (*esp law* 尤用于法律) inform 通知; 告知: *We are instructed by our clients that you owe them £300.* 我们的委托人通知我们说你欠他们300英镑. **4** [Tn] (*law* 律) employ (a solicitor or barrister) to act on one's behalf 聘用(事务律师或讼务律师)代表自己: *Who are the instructing solicitors* (ie solicitors who are employing a barrister to act) *in this case?* 谁是此案中聘请讼务律师的事务律师?

▷ **in·structor** *n* person who instructs; trainer 教员; 教练; 指导员: *a driving instructor* 驾驶教练.

in·struc·tion /ɪnˈstrʌkʃn; ɪnˋstrʌkʃən/ *n* **1** [U] **~ (in sth)** process of teaching; knowledge or teaching given (对知识的)教授, 传授; (传授的)知识; 教导: *In this course, students receive instruction in basic engineering.* 在本课程中, 学生能学到基础工程学的知识. **2** [C] **~ (to do sth/that...)** **(a)** order or direction given 命令; 指令; 指示: *leave, give detailed instructions* 留下、给予详细指令 ○ *understand, carry out an instruction* 理解、执行命令. **(b)** (*computing* 计) word, code, etc that, when input into a computer, makes it perform a particular operation (输入计算机的)指令. **3 instructions** [pl] **~ (to do sth/that...)** statements telling sb what he should or must do 用法说明; 操作指南; 吩咐; 命令: *follow the instructions on a tin of paint, in a car repair manual, etc* 依照颜料桶上的用法说明、按照汽车维修手册的操作指示 ○ *My instructions are that I am not to let anyone in*, ie I have been ordered not to. 我得到吩咐不让任何人入内. ○ *instructions to a lawyer* 给律师的指示.

▷ **in·struc·tional** /-ʃənl; -ʃənḷ/ *adj* giving instruction; educational 教学的; 有教育内容的: *instructional films* 教学影片.

in·struc·tive /ɪnˈstrʌktɪv; ɪnˋstrʌktɪv/ *adj* (*approv* 褒) giving much useful information 提供丰富知识的; 有益的: *instructive books* 有教育意义的书 ○ *The minister's visit to the prison was not instructive.* 这个牧师这次探监没有什么有益的贡献. ▷ **in·struc·tively** *adv*.

in·stru·ment /ˈɪnstrʊmənt; ˋɪnstrəmənt/ *n* **1** implement or apparatus used in performing an action, esp for delicate or scientific work 器具; 器械; 仪器: *a surgical instrument*, eg a scalpel 外科器械(如手术刀) ○ *an optical instrument*, eg a microscope 光学仪器(如显微镜) ○ *instruments of torture* 刑具. **2** apparatus for producing musical sounds, eg a piano, violin, flute or drum 乐器(如钢琴、小提琴、笛或鼓): *learning to play an instrument* 学习演奏乐器 ○ *the instruments of the orchestra* 演奏管弦乐的乐器. **3** measuring device giving information about the operation of an engine, etc or in navigation (发动机等或航海、航空中用的)测量仪器, 仪表: *a ship's instruments* 船用测量仪器 ○ [attrib 作定语] *an instrument panel* 仪表盘. ➪ Usage at MACHINE 用法见 MACHINE. **4 (a) ~ of sb/sth** person used and controlled by another person, organization, etc, often without being aware of it 受人利用或控制的人(常为不自觉的): *We humans are merely the instruments of fate.* 我们人类只不过是天命的工具. **(b) ~ of sth** person or thing that brings sth about 促成某事的人或物: *The organization he had built up eventually became the instrument of his downfall.* 他创建起来的组织到头来却成为促使他倒台的根本原因了. **5 ~ (of sth)** formal (esp legal) document 正式的(尤指合法的)文件、文书: *The king signed the instrument of abdication.* 国王签署了逊位的文告.

▷ **in·stru·menta·tion** /ˌɪnstrʊmenˈteɪʃn; ˌɪnstrəmɛnˋteʃən/ *n* [U] **1** arrangement of music for instruments 为器乐的

编曲: *The instrumentation is particularly fine.* 这首器乐曲编得特别细致. **2** instruments (INSTRUMENT 3) 测量仪器; 仪表: *monitoring the spacecraft's instrumentation* 监控宇航器的检测仪表.

in·stru·mental /ˌɪnstrʊˈmentl; ˌɪnstrəˈmɛntl̩/ *adj* **1** [pred 作表语] **~ in doing sth** being the means of bringing sth about 作为促成某事物之手段; 有帮助; 起作用: *Our artistic director was instrumental in persuading the orchestra to come and play for us.* 我们的艺术指导大费唇舌请来管弦乐队为我们演出. **2** of or for musical instruments 乐器的; 为器乐用的: *instrumental music* 器乐曲.

▷ **in·stru·ment·al·ist** /-təlɪst; -tl̩ɪst/ *n* player of a musical instrument 乐器演奏者. Cf 参看 VOCALIST (VOCAL).

in·stru·ment·al·ity /ˌɪnstrʊmenˈtælətɪ; ˌɪnstrəmɛnˈtælətɪ/ *n* [U] (*fml* 文) condition of being instrumental(1); means 手段; 工具: *by the instrumentality of sb*, ie by means of sb 借助于某人.

in·sub·or·din·ate /ˌɪnsəˈbɔːdɪnət; ˌɪnsəˈbɔrdn̩ɪt/ *adj* disobedient; rebellious 不服从的; 反抗的; 犯上的.

▷ **in·sub·or·dina·tion** /ˌɪnsəˌbɔːdɪˈneɪʃn; ˌɪnsəˌbɔrdn̩ˈeʃən/ *n* (**a**) [U] being insubordinate 不服从; 违抗; 犯上: *gross/rank insubordination* 不折不扣的忤逆行为. (**b**) [C] instance of this 不服从; 违抗; 犯上.

in·sub·stan·tial /ˌɪnsəbˈstænʃl; ˌɪnsəbˈstænʃəl/ *adj* **1** not solid or real; imaginary 非实体的; 非实质的; 非实在的; 非真实的; 幻想的: *an insubstantial vision, figure, creature* 虚幻的景象、人物、生物. **2** not firmly or solidly made; weak (做得)不坚固的, 不坚实的, 薄弱的: *Early aircraft were insubstantial constructions of wood and glue.* 早期的飞行器是木头和胶粘合的脆弱机器. ○ (*fig* 比喻) *an insubstantial argument, accusation, claim, etc* 无真凭实据的争论、指控、索赔要求等.

in·suf·fer·able /ɪnˈsʌfrəbl; ɪnˈsʌfrəbl̩/ *adj* **1** too extreme to be tolerated; unbearable 过于偏激而不能容忍的; 难以忍受的: *insufferable insolence* 令人不堪忍受的侮慢. **2** (of a person) extremely annoying and unpleasant, esp because of conceit (指人)令人嫌憎的, 令人厌恶的(尤指因自负): *He really is insufferable!* 他真可恶! ▷ **in·suf·fer·ably** /-əblɪ; -əblɪ/ *adv*.

in·suf·fi·cient /ˌɪnsəˈfɪʃnt; ˌɪnsəˈfɪʃənt/ *adj* **~ (for sth/to do sth)** not sufficient 不充足的; 不充分的; 不足的; 不够的: *The case was dismissed because of insufficient evidence.* 该案因证据不足而撤销. ▷ **in·suf·fi·ciency** /-ʃnsɪ; -ʃənsɪ/ *n* [U]. **in·suf·fi·ciently** *adv*.

in·sular /ˈɪnsjʊlə(r); *US* -sələr; ˈɪnsələ˞/ *adj* **1** of an island 岛的; 岛上的: *an insular climate, way of life* 海岛的气候、生活方式. **2** (*derog* 贬) narrow-minded and avoiding contact with others 偏狭的; 不愿与他人接触的: *an insular attitude* 偏狭的态度 ○ *insular habits and prejudices* 狭猛的习性和偏见.

▷ **in·su·lar·ity** /ˌɪnsjʊˈlærətɪ; *US* -səˈl-; ˌɪnsəˈlærətɪ/ *n* [U] state of being insular(2) 偏狭性.

in·su·late /ˈɪnsjʊleɪt; *US* -səl-; ˈɪnsəˌlet/ *v* **1** [I, Ipr, Tn, Tn·pr] **~ (sth) (from/against sth) (with sth)** protect (sth) by covering it with a material that prevents sth (esp heat, electricity or sound) from passing through 使(某事物)隔离或绝缘(尤指对热量、电流或声音): *material which insulates well* 绝缘性能良好的材料 ○ *insulate pipes from loss of heat with foam rubber* 用泡沫橡胶封裹管道以防热量损失. **2** [Tn·pr] **~ sb/sth from/against sth** (*fig* 比喻) protect sb/sth from the unpleasant effects of sth 使某人[某物]与不良影响隔绝: *children carefully insulated from harmful experiences* 受到细心保护免受不良影响的孩子们 ○ *Index-linked pay rises insulated them against inflationary price increases.* 与生活指数挂钩的工资增长使他们免受通货膨胀带来的损失.

▷ **in·su·lated** *adj* protected in this way (受到)绝缘的, 隔热的, 隔音的: *an insulated wire*, ie to avoid an electric shock 绝缘电线 ○ *a well-insulated house*, ie to avoid loss of heat 隔热性能良好的房子.

in·su·lat·ing *adj* giving this kind of protection (提供)绝缘的, 隔热的, 隔音的: *insulating materials* 绝缘材料.

in·su·la·tion /ˌɪnsjʊˈleɪʃn; *US* -səˈl-; ˌɪnsəˈleʃən/ *n* [U] (**a**) insulating or (state of) being insulated 隔离; 隔绝; 绝缘; 隔热; 隔音: *Foam rubber provides good insulation.* 泡沫橡胶隔绝性能良好. (**b**) materials used for this 绝缘、隔热或隔音等的材料: *pack the wall cavity with insulation* 用隔热材料填充壁腔.

in·su·lator /ˈɪnsjʊleɪtə(r); *US* -səl-; ˈɪnsəˌletə˞/ *n* substance or device for insulating, esp a porcelain support for bare electric wires and cables 绝缘、隔热或隔音等的物质或装置; (尤指)绝缘子.

□ **ˈinsulating tape** tape used for covering joins in electrical wires, preventing the possibility of an electrical shock 绝缘胶带; 电线胶布.

in·su·lin /ˈɪnsjʊlɪn; *US* -səl-; ˈɪnsəlɪn/ *n* [U] substance (a hormone) produced in the pancreas, controlling the absorption of sugar by the body 胰岛素: [attrib 作定语] *People suffering from diabetes have to have insulin injections, because they cannot produce their own.* 患糖尿病的人需注射胰岛素, 因为病人本身不能分泌胰岛素.

in·sult /ɪnˈsʌlt; ɪnˈsʌlt/ *v* [Tn] speak or act in a way that hurts or is intended to hurt the feelings or dignity of (sb); be extremely rude to (sb) 侮辱; 辱骂; 侮慢: *I felt most insulted when they made me sit at a little table at the back.* 他们让我坐到尽里头的一张小桌旁, 我觉得受到极大侮辱.

▷ **in·sult** /ˈɪnsʌlt; ˈɪnsʌlt/ *n* **1 ~ (to sb/sth)** remark or action that insults 侮辱; 辱骂; 侮慢: *She hurled insults at the unfortunate waiter.* 她大骂那个倒霉的服务员. ○ *Don't take it as an insult if I go to sleep during your speech; I'm very tired.* 要是你讲着话时我睡着了, 可别以为是不敬, 我太累了. **2** (idm 习语) **add insult to injury** ⇨ ADD. **a calculated insult** ⇨ CALCULATE. **an insult to sb's inˈtelligence** task, explanation, etc that is too easy, foolish, etc to be worthy of sb's attention 对某人智慧的侮辱(指任务、解释等容易得不值某人一顾).

in·sult·ing *adj* uttering or being an insult 出言不逊的; 侮辱的; 无礼的: *He was most insulting to my wife.* 他对我的妻子非常粗野无礼. ○ *insulting remarks, behaviour* 侮辱性的言语、行为.

in·su·per·able /ɪnˈsuːpərəbl *or, in British use*, 英式英语读作 -ˈsjuː-; ɪnˈsupərəbl̩/ *adj* (*fml* 文) (of difficulties) that cannot be overcome (指困难)不能克服的: *insuperable barriers, obstacles, etc* 不可逾越的障碍、阻碍等. Cf 参看 INSURMOUNTABLE. ▷ **in·su·per·ably** /-əblɪ; -əblɪ/ *adv*.

in·sup·port·able /ˌɪnsəˈpɔːtəbl; ˌɪnsəˈpɔrtəbl̩/ *adj* (*fml* 文) unbearable; too bad to be endured 不能忍受的; 难以容忍的: *insupportable behaviour, rudeness, etc* 不能容忍的行为、粗暴等.

in·sur·ance /ɪnˈʃɔːrəns; *US* -ˈʃʊər-; ɪnˈʃʊrəns/ *n* **1** [U, sing] **~ (against sth)** (contract made by a company or society, or by the state, to provide a) guarantee of compensation for loss, damage, sickness, death, etc in return for regular payment 保险(契约): *People without insurance had to pay for their own repairs.* 未投保者需自付修理费. ○ *an insurance against theft, fire, etc* 盗窃保险、火险 ○ *household, personal, etc insurance* 家庭、人身保险等 ○ [attrib 作定语] *an insurance company*, ie one that provides this 保险公司 ○ *an insurance salesman* 保险公司推销员. **2** [U] business of providing such contracts 保险业: *Her husband works in insurance.* 她丈夫在保险业工作. **3** [U] payment made by or to such a company, etc 保险费: *When her husband died, she received £50 000 in insurance.* 她丈夫去世后, 她得到50 000英镑的保险金. **4** [C, U] **~ (against sth)** (*fig* 比喻) any measure taken as a safeguard against loss, failure, etc 保险措施; (预防损失、失败等的)安全保障: *He's applying for two other jobs as an insurance against not passing the interview for this one.* 他还申请了另外两份工作, 以防这份工作面试不合格.

□ **inˈsurance broker** person whose business is providing insurance 保险经纪人.

inˈsurance policy contract between the company insuring and the insured person 保险单: (*fig* 比喻) *They regard nuclear weapons as an insurance policy against conventional attack.* 他们认为有核武器是防止遭常规武器进攻的保障.

inˈsurance premium one of the regular sums paid in order to be insured (定期交付的)保险费.

in·sure /ɪnˈʃɔː(r); *US* ɪnˈʃʊər; ɪnˈʃʊr/ *v* **1** [Tn, Tn·pr] **~ sb/sth (against sth)** make a contract that promises to pay sb an amount of money in case of accident, injury, death, etc, or damage to or loss of sth 保险; 投保: *insure oneself/one's life for £50 000* 为自己投 50 000 英镑的人寿保险 ○ *insure one's house against fire* 为自己的房子保火险. **2** (*esp US*) = ENSURE.

▷ **the in·sured** *n* [sing or pl *v*] person or people to whom payment will be made in the case of loss, etc 被保险人; 保户; 投保人.

in·surer /ɪn'ʃɔːrə(r); *US* ɪn'ʃʊərər; ɪn'ʃʊrɚ/ *n* person or company undertaking to make payment in case of loss, etc 承保人; 保险公司.

in·sur·gent /ɪn'sɜːdʒənt; ɪn'sɝdʒənt/ *adj* [usu attrib 通常作定语] in revolt; rebellious 起义的; 叛乱的; 造反的: *insurgent troops* 叛军 ○ *an insurgent mob* 暴民.

▷ **in·sur·gent** *n* rebel soldier 叛乱士兵: *an attack by armed insurgents* 武装叛乱士兵发起的攻击.

in·sur·mount·able /ˌɪnsə'maʊntəbl; ˌɪnsɚ'maʊntəbl/ *adj* (*fml* 文) (of obstacles, difficulties, etc) that cannot be overcome (指障碍、困难等)无法超越的, 不能克服的: *The problems are not insurmountable.* 问题不是无法解决的. Cf 参看 INSUPERABLE.

in·sur·rec·tion /ˌɪnsə'rekʃn; ˌɪnsə'rɛkʃən/ *n* **1** [U] sudden, usu violent, action taken by (part of) the population to try to remove the government 起义; 暴动; 叛乱; 造反. **2** [C] instance of this; revolt 起义; 暴动; 叛乱; 造反.

▷ **in·sur·rec·tion·ist** /-ʃənɪst; -ʃənɪst/ *adj* of or taking part in an insurrection 起义的; 暴动的; 参加叛乱的.

int *abbr* 缩写 = **1** interior; internal. Cf 参看 EXT 1. **2** international.

in·tact /ɪn'tækt; ɪn'tækt/ *adj* undamaged; complete 无损伤的; 完整的: *a box recovered from an accident with its contents intact* 从事故中抢救出来的箱子, 里面的东西完好无损 ○ *He can scarcely survive this scandal with his reputation intact.* 他经此丑闻名誉很难不受损.

in·taglio /ɪn'tɑːlɪəʊ; ɪn'tɑljo/ *n* (*pl* **~s** /-z; -z/) **1** [U] (process or technique of) carving deeply into stone or metal 凹雕; 凹刻; 凹雕术. **2** [C] (gem with a) figure or design made by cutting into the surface 凹纹图形; 刻有凹纹图形的宝石.

in·take /'ɪnteɪk; 'ɪnˌtek/ *n* **1** (**a**) [U] process of taking liquid, gas, etc into a machine, etc 吸入, 纳入(液体、气体等). (**b**) [C] place where liquid, etc enters (液体等的)进入口: *the fuel intake* 燃油进入口 ○ [attrib 作定语] *an intake pipe* 吸入管. **2** (**a**) [C, U] quantity, number, etc of people entering or taken in (during a particular period) (一定时期内)进入或纳入的人数: *an annual intake of 100 000 men for military service* 每年征召 100 000 人入伍服役 ○ *Intake in state primary schools is down by 10%.* 公立小学入学人数下降了10%. (**b**) [CGp] such people 新进入或纳入的人: *This year's intake seems/seem to be quite bright.* 今年新招入的人看来十分聪明.

in·tan·gible /ɪn'tændʒəbl; ɪn'tændʒəbl/ *adj* **1** that cannot be clearly or definitely understood or grasped; indefinable 难以捉摸的; 难以理解的; 无法确定的: *The old building had an intangible air of sadness about it.* 那座古老建筑物周围笼罩着说不出的凄凉气氛. **2** (*commerce* 商) (of a business asset) that has no physical existence (指企业资产)无形的: *the intangible value of a good reputation* 良好商誉的无形价值. ▷ **in·tan·gib·il·ity** /ɪnˌtændʒə'bɪlətɪ; ɪnˌtændʒə'bɪlətɪ/ *n* [U]. **in·tan·gibly** *adv*.

in·te·ger /'ɪntɪdʒə(r); 'ɪntədʒɚ/ *n* (*mathematics* 数) whole number (contrasted with a *fraction*) 整数(fraction 之对): *1, 2 and 3 are integers; $\frac{3}{4}$ is not an integer.* 1、2、3 是整数, $\frac{3}{4}$ 不是整数.

in·teg·ral /'ɪntɪgrəl; 'ɪntəgrəl/ *adj* **1** **~ (to sth)** necessary for completeness 构成整体所必需的: *The arms and legs are integral parts of the human body; they are integral to the human body.* 手臂和腿是人体的组成部分, 是构成完整的人体必不可少的. **2** [usu attrib 通常作定语] having or containing all parts that are necessary for completeness; whole 具备构成整体所必需的所有部分的; 完整的: *an integral design* 完整的设计. **3** [usu attrib 通常作定语] included as part of the whole, rather than supplied from outside 作为整体的一部分的(并非来自外部的): *a machine with an integral power source* 有内置电源的机器. **4** (*mathematics* 数) of or being an integer; made up of integers 整数的; 由整数组成的; 积分的. ▷ **in·teg·rally** /-grəlɪ; -grəlɪ/ *adv*.

□ ˌ**integral** '**calculus** (*mathematics* 数) branch of calculus concerned with finding out the sum total of a lot of extremely small numbers, and with applying this knowledge to calculating areas, volumes, etc 积分学. Cf 参看 DIFFERENTIAL CALCULUS (DIFFERENTIAL).

in·teg·rate /'ɪntɪgreɪt; 'ɪntəˌgret/ *v* **1** [Tn, Tn·pr] **~ sth (into sth); ~ A and B/~ A with B** combine sth in such a way that it becomes fully a part of sth else (将某事物与另一事物结合)构成整体: *integrating private schools into the state education system* 将私立学校纳入国家教育体系 ○ *The buildings are well integrated with the landscape/The buildings and the landscape are well integrated.* 这些建筑物和周围的自然景物相融合, 浑然一体. **2** [I, Tn, Tn·pr] **~ (sb) (into sth/with sth)** (cause sb to) become fully a member of a community, rather than remaining in a separate (esp racial) group (使某人)与社区融合(尤指种族间): *foreign immigrants who don't integrate well* 未能完全融入当地社会的外国移民 ○ *integrating black people into a largely white community* 使黑人融合进以白人为主的社区. Cf 参看 SEGREGATE.

▷ **in·teg·rated** /-tɪd; -tɪd/ *adj* with various parts fitting well together 各部分配合好的; 综合的; 完整的: *an integrated transport scheme*, eg including buses, trains, taxis, etc 综合联运计划(如公共汽车、火车、计程车等) ○ *an integrated personality*, ie sb who is psychologically stable 统合性格(即其人心理状态稳定).

in·teg·ra·tion /ˌɪntɪ'greɪʃn; ˌɪntə'greʃən/ *n* [U] **~ (into sth)** integrating or being integrated 结合; 综合; 融合: *the integration of black children into the school system in the Southern States of America* 美国南方各州准许黑人儿童进入白人学校之事. Cf 参看 SEGREGATION (SEGREGATE).

□ ˌ**integrated** '**circuit** very small electronic circuit(2b) made of a single small piece of semiconductor material (eg a silicon chip), designed to replace a conventional electric circuit of many parts 集成电路.

in·teg·rity /ɪn'tegrətɪ; ɪn'tɛgrətɪ/ *n* [U] **1** quality of being honest and morally upright 诚实而正直: *He's a man of integrity; he won't break his promise.* 他为人诚实正直, 决不食言. ○ *personal, commercial, intellectual, etc integrity* 为人的、商业上的、做学问的...诚实正直. **2** condition of being whole or undivided 完整; 整体: *respect, preserve, threaten, etc a nation's territorial integrity* 尊重、保持、威胁...国家领土的完整.

in·tegu·ment /ɪn'tegjʊmənt; ɪn'tɛgjəmənt/ *n* (*fml* 文) (usu natural) outer covering, eg a skin, husk, rind or shell (通常指天然的)覆盖物, 外皮(如皮肤、果壳、果皮或甲壳).

in·tel·lect /'ɪntəlekt; 'ɪntlˌɛkt/ *n* **1** [U] power of the mind to reason and acquire knowledge (contrasted with feeling and instinct) 智力, 思维能力, 领悟力, 理解力(与感情及本能相对): *a man of (great) intellect* (极)具聪明才智的人 ○ *Intellect distinguishes humans from other animals.* 人类与禽兽之别在于人具有思维能力. **2** [C] person of high intelligence and reasoning power 有高智慧和推理能力的人: *He was one of the most formidable intellects of his time.* 他是该时代的盖世奇才.

in·tel·lec·tual /ˌɪntɪ'lektʃʊəl; ˌɪntl'ɛktʃʊəl/ *adj* **1** [usu attrib 通常作定语] of the intellect 智力的; 理智的: *the intellectual faculties* 智能. **2** of, interested in or able to deal with things of the mind (eg the arts, ideas for their own sake) rather than practical matters 思维的, 善思考的, 能运用聪明才智的(如艺术、思想等方面, 并非指实际事情): *intellectual people* 善思考的人 ○ *intellectual interests, pursuits, etc* 需用脑力的爱好、研究等.

▷ **in·tel·lec·tual** *n* intellectual person 知识分子; 脑力劳动者: *a play, book, etc for intellectuals* 以知识分子为对象的剧、书等.

in·tel·lect·tu·ally *adv*.

in·tel·li·gence /ɪn'telɪdʒəns; ɪn'tɛlədʒəns/ *n* **1** [U] power of learning, understanding and reasoning; mental ability 学习、理解和推理的能力; 智力; 脑力: *a person of high, great, average, little, low intelligence* 智力高的、有智慧的、智力中等的、无头脑的、智能低下的人 ○ *When the water pipe burst, she had the intelligence to turn off the water at the main.* 水管裂开时, 她很有头脑, 连忙把总水门关上了. **2** (**a**) [U] information, esp of military value 情报, 信息(尤指有军事价值的): *an intelligence-gathering satellite* 搜集情报的卫星 ○ [attrib 作定语] *the* *government's Secret Intelligence Service*, ie organization that gathers such information, esp by spying 政府的秘密情报部门. (**b**) [Gp] people engaged in gathering such information 情报人员: *Intelligence has/have reported that the enemy is planning a new attack.* 情报人员报告说敌军正在策划发动新攻势.

▷ **in·tel·li·gent** /-dʒənt; -dʒənt/ *adj* having or showing intelligence 聪明的; 有才智的; 有头脑的: *an intelligent child* 聪明的孩子 ○ *an intelligent expression on sb's face* 某人脸上聪慧的神情 ○ *intelligent questions, answers, remarks, etc* 巧妙的问题、回答、言语等 ○ *take an intelligent interest in sth* 对某事物产生琢磨的兴趣. **in·tel·li·gently** *adv*.

□ **in'telligence test** test to measure sb's mental ability 智力测验. Cf 参看 APTITUDE TEST (APTITUDE).

in·tel·li·gent·sia /ɪn,telɪ'dʒentsɪə; ɪn,tɛlə'dʒɛntsɪə/ *n* **the intelligentsia** [Gp] (*usu approv or derog* 通常作褒义或作贬义) those people within a community who are of high intelligence and concern themselves with matters of culture, learning, etc; intellectuals as a class 知识界; 知识阶层.

in·tel·li·gible /ɪn'telɪdʒəbl; ɪn'tɛlɪdʒəbl/ *adj* that can be (easily) understood 可(易)理解的: *intelligible speech* 明白易懂的讲话 ○ *a muddled explanation which was scarcely intelligible* 难以理解的胡涂解释.

▷ **in·tel·li·gib·il·ity** /ɪn,telɪdʒə'bɪlətɪ; ɪn,tɛlɪdʒə'bɪlətɪ/ *n* [U] quality of being intelligible 可理解性.

in·tel·li·gibly *adv*.

in·tem·per·ate /ɪn'tempərət; ɪn'tɛmpərɪt/ *adj* (*fml* 文) showing lack of self-control 无节制的; 放纵的: *intemperate habits*, ie esp excessive drinking of alcohol 无节制的习惯(尤指纵酒) ○ *His intemperate* (ie thoughtlessly angry or rude) *remarks got him into trouble.* 他言语肆无忌惮, 惹出了是非. ▷ **in·tem·per·ance** /-pərəns; -pərəns/ *n* [U]. **in·tem·per·ately** *adv*.

in·tend /ɪn'tend; ɪn'tɛnd/ *v* **1** (**a**) [Tn, Tf, Tt, Tnt, Tg, Cn·n/a, Dn·n] **~ sth (as sth)** have (a particular purpose or plan) in mind; mean 打算; 意欲; 想要: *I meant it to be an informal discussion, but it didn't turn out as I intended (it should).* 我本想随便商量一下, 结果事与愿违. ○ *It's not what I intended (it to be).* 那并不是我的本意. ○ *I hear they intend to marry/intend marrying.* 听说他们要结婚了. ○ *I intended to do it, but I'm afraid I forgot.* 我本有意去做, 但很遗憾, 我忘记了. ○ *I don't intend to listen to this rubbish any longer!* 我再也不想听这种无稽之谈了! ○ *I intended it as a joke.* 我不过说笑罢了. ○ *He intends you no harm*, ie does not plan to harm you. 他对你并无恶意. (**b**) [Tf, Tnt] have (sth) as a fixed plan or purpose for sb else 为某人定下计划或目标: *I intend that you shall take over the business.* 我有意让你接管公司. ○ *I intend you to take over.* 我打算让你来接管. ○ *You weren't intended* (ie supposed) *to hear that remark.* 你按说不应该听那些话. **2** [Dn·pr] **~ sth for sb** plan that sb should receive or be affected by sth 为某人准备某事物; 要使某人受某事物的影响: *I think the bomb was intended for* (ie planned to harm) *me.* 我认为那颗炸弹是要炸我的. **3** [Cn·n/a] **~ sth as sth** plan that sth should be or become sth 打算使某事物成为另一事物: *Was that remark intended as* (ie supposed to be) *a joke?* 那句话是不是当作笑话说的? **4** [Tn·pr] **~ sth by sth** plan that sth should have the specified meaning 欲使某事物具有某意义; 意指; 意谓: *What did he intend by that remark?* 他说那话是什么意思?

▷ **in·ten·ded** /-dɪd; -dɪd/ *adj* **1** [attrib 作定语] planned; meant; desired 计划的; 打算的; 意欲的: *the intended meaning, result, effect, purpose* 原来的意思、想要的结果、预期的效果、原有的目的. **2 ~ for sb/sth** [pred 作表语] planned or designed for sb/sth 为(某人[某事物])计划或设计: *a book, course, programme, etc intended for children, adults, beginners, etc* 为儿童、成人、初学者等而写的书、开设的课程、编排的节目等 ○ *water (not) intended for drinking* (非)饮用水.

in·tense /ɪn'tens; ɪn'tɛns/ *adj* (**-r, -st**) **1** (of sensations) very great or severe; extreme (指感觉)强烈的, 剧烈的, 极度的: *intense heat, pain, etc* 酷热、剧痛. **2** (of emotions, etc) very strong (指感情等)强烈的, 热烈的: *intense interest, anger, jealousy, convictions, etc* 浓厚的兴趣、盛怒、极端的忌妒、强烈的信念. **3** (of people) highly emotional (指人)热情的, 易动感情的.

▷ **in·tensely** *adv*.

in·tens·ify /-sɪfaɪ; -sə,faɪ/ *v* (*pt, pp* **-fied**) [I, Tn] (cause sth to) become more intense or intensive (使某事物)变得更强烈、剧烈或尖锐; 加剧: *Her anger intensified.* 她更加生气了. ○ *The terrorists have intensified their bombing campaign.* 恐怖分子增加了炸弹爆炸活动. **in·tensi·fica·tion** /ɪn,tensɪfɪ'keɪʃn; ɪn,tɛnsəfə'keʃən/ *n* [U]. **in·tensi·fier** /ɪn'tensɪfaɪə(r); ɪn'tɛnsə,faɪɚ/ *n* (*grammar*) word (esp an *adj* or *adv*, eg *so, such, very*) that strengthens the meaning of another word 强调成分(尤指形容词或副词, 如so、such、very, 起加强另一词词义的作用).

in·tens·ity /-sətɪ; -sətɪ/ *n* [U] **1** state or quality of being intense 强烈; 剧烈; 紧张: *work with greater intensity* 更加紧张地工作. **2** strength of emotion (感情的)强烈程度, 深刻程度: *I didn't realize the intensity of people's feelings on this issue.* 我没有意识到这一问题能引起群情激奋.

in·tens·ive /ɪn'tensɪv; ɪn'tɛnsɪv/ *adj* **1** (**a**) concentrating all one's effort on a specific area 集中的; 密集的: *intensive bombardment of a town* 密集轰击某城镇 ○ *intensive farming*, ie aimed at producing large quantities of food by concentrating labour and care in small areas 集约耕作(旨在小块土地上集中劳力精耕细作以获高产的方法). (**b**) involving hard work concentrated into a limited amount of time 在有限时间内紧张工作的: *They teach you English in an intensive course lasting just a week; it's quite an intensive few days!* 他们用一周时间教速成英语课程, 那几天可真紧张! **2** extremely thorough 彻底的: *An intensive search failed to reveal any clues.* 经过彻底搜查未发现任何线索. **3** (*grammar*) giving force and emphasis 加强语气的: *In 'It's a bloody miracle!', 'bloody' is used as an intensive word.* 在'It's a bloody miracle!'一句中, 'bloody'是用作加强语气的词.

▷ **in·tens·ive** *n* (*grammar*) intensive word; intensifier 增强语气的词; 强调成分.

-intensive (forming compound *adjs* 用以构成复合形容词) using or requiring a lot of the stated thing 集约的; 密集的: *a capital-intensive/labour-intensive industry.*

in·tens·ively *adv*.

□ **in,tensive 'care** (part of a hospital giving) constant attention in the treatment of seriously ill patients (医院中对重病人的)特别护理(病房): *The accident victims are in/have been taken into intensive care.* 事故受害者在特别护理中[已送进特别护理病房].

in·tent[1] /ɪn'tent; ɪn'tɛnt/ *adj* **1** (of looks, attention, etc) full of eager interest and concentration (指神情、注意力等)专心的, 渴望的, 热切的: *watch with an intent gaze, look, expression, etc* 以专心致志的目光、样子、神情等看着. **2** [pred 作表语] **~ on/upon sth/doing sth** (**a**) having the stated firm intention 热中; 坚决: *He's intent on getting promotion, and no one's going to stop him!* 他一心一意想得到晋升, 谁也劝阻不了他. (**b**) occupied in doing sth with great concentration 专心; 专注: *I was so intent (up)on my work that I didn't notice the time.* 我专心工作, 没有留意时间. ▷ **in·tently** *adv*: *I listened intently to what she had to say.* 我聚精会神地听她说话. **in·tent·ness** *n* [U].

in·tent[2] /ɪn'tent; ɪn'tɛnt/ *n* **1** [U] **~ (to do sth)** (*esp law* 尤用于法律) intention; purpose 意图; 意向; 目的: *act with criminal intent* 带犯罪意图行事 ○ *fire a weapon with intent to kill* 蓄意开枪杀人 ○ *arrest sb for loitering with intent*, ie for apparently intending to commit a crime 因某人闲荡有犯罪意图而予扣留. **2** (idm 习语) **to all intents (and purposes)** in all important respects; virtually 在一切重要方面; 实际上: *Although there was still a faint heartbeat, he was to all intents and purposes dead.* 他虽然仍有隐隐心搏, 但从身体各方面看已经死亡.

in·ten·tion /ɪn'tenʃn; ɪn'tɛnʃən/ *n* **1** (**a**) [C, U] **~ (of doing sth/that...)** that which one proposes or plans to do 意图; 意向; 目的; 打算: *What are your intentions?* ie What do you plan to do? 你有什么打算? ○ *She's keeping her intentions to herself*, ie not telling anyone what she plans to do. 她对自己的意图秘而不宣. ○ *I came with the/every intention of staying, but now I've decided to leave.* 我来时一心想留下, 但现在我已决定离开. ○ *My intention was to stay.* 我原意要留下. ○ *I have no intention of coming* (ie I shall certainly not come) *to this terrible place again!* 我再也不想到这个糟糕的地方

来了. ○ (*dated* 旧) *Peter asked the young man if his intentions were honourable*, ie if he intended to marry his daughter, whom he was courting. 彼得问那年轻人是否真心实意要娶他的女儿. (**b**) [U] (*fml* 文) intending 有意; 蓄意: *I'm sorry I offended you; it wasn't my intention.* 对不起, 我冒犯您了, 但决不是有意的. **2** [C] purpose or aim; meaning 意图; 目的; 意思: *What do you think was the author's intention in this passage?* 你认为作者写这一段的用意是什么? **3** (idm 习语) **the road to hell is paved with good intentions** ⇨ ROAD. **with the best of intentions** ⇨ BEST[3].

▷ **-intentioned** (forming compound *adjs* 用以构成复合形容词) having the specified intentions 有某种意图的: *ill-intentioned* ○ *well-intentioned*.

in·ten·tional /ɪnˈtenʃənl; ɪnˋtɛnʃənl/ *adj* done on purpose; not accidental; intended 存心的; 故意的; 蓄意的: *If I hurt your feelings, it was not intentional.* 我若伤了你的感情, 那并不是有意的. ○ *an intentional foul in football* 足球赛中的故意犯规.

▷ **in·ten·tion·ally** /-ʃənəlɪ; -ʃnəlɪ/ *adv* deliberately 故意地; 蓄意地; 存心地: *I would never intentionally hurt your feelings.* 我决不会有意伤害你的感情.

in·ter /ɪnˈtɜː(r); ɪnˋtɝ/ *v* (**-rr-**) [Tn] (*fml* 文) put (a corpse) in a grave or tomb; bury 埋葬(尸体). Cf 参看 INTERMENT.

inter- *pref* 前缀 (with *vs, ns* and *adjs* 与动词、名词、形容词结合) **1** between; from one to another 在...之间; 在...之内; 由此至彼: *interleave* ○ *interface* ○ *international.* **2** together; mutually 共同; 互相; 彼此: *interconnect* ○ *interlink*.

in·ter·act /ˌɪntərˈækt; ˌɪntɚˋækt/ *v* **1** [I, Ipr] **~ (with sth)** act or have an effect on each other 相互作用; 相互影响: *chemicals that interact to form a new compound* 相互作用形成新化合物的化学物质 ○ *ideas that interact* 相互影响的想法. **2** [I, Ipr] **~ (with sb)** (of people) act together or co-operatively, esp so as to communicate with each other (指人)一起活动或互相合作(尤指为互相联系): *a sociologist studying the complex way in which people interact (with each other) at parties* 研究人们在聚会中互相交往的复杂方式的社会学家.

▷ **in·ter·ac·tion** /-ˈækʃn; -ˋækʃən/ *n* (**a**) [U] **~ (among/between sb/sth); ~ (with sb/sth)** interacting; co-operation 一起活动; 合作; 配合: *Increased interaction between different police forces would improve the rate of solving crimes.* 加强警察队伍之间的相互配合可改善处理罪案的效率. (**b**) [C] instance of this 一起活动; 合作; 配合.

in·ter·act·ive /-ˈæktɪv; -ˋæktɪv/ *adj* **1 ~ (with sb/sth)** (of two or more people or things) interacting (指至少两个人或物)一起活动或互相合作的: *The psychotherapy is carried out in small interactive groups.* 这种心理治疗是在一起活动的小组之间进行的. **2** (*computing* 计) allowing a continuous two-way transfer of information between a computer and the person using it 交互式的; 人机对话的.

inter alia /ˌɪntər ˈeɪlɪə; ˌɪntɚˋelɪə/ (*Latin* 拉) among other things 除了其他事物之外.

in·ter·breed /ˌɪntəˈbriːd; ˌɪntɚˋbrid/ *v* [I, Ipr, Tn, Tn·pr] **~ (sth) (with sth)** (cause individuals of different species to) breed together, so producing a hybrid (使)杂交繁殖, 生育杂种: *These two types of dog can interbreed/be interbred (with each other).* 这两种类型的狗可以杂交繁殖.

in·ter·cede /ˌɪntəˈsiːd; ˌɪntɚˋsid/ *v* (*fml* 文) **1** [I, Ipr] **~ (with sb) (for/on behalf of sb)** plead (with sb) to be merciful (to sb) (为他人)(向某人)求情: *We have interceded with the authorities on behalf of people unfairly imprisoned there*, ie asked them to release the prisoners. 我们代表含冤系狱的人向当局求情(予以释放). **2** [I, Ipr] **~ (between A and B)** act as an intermediary (between two people, groups, countries that cannot agree), trying to help them settle their differences (在两人、两集团、两国之间)调解, 调停, 斡旋.

▷ **in·ter·ces·sion** /ˌɪntəˈseʃn; ˌɪntɚˋsɛʃən/ *n* (**a**) [U] interceding 求情; 调解; 调停; 斡旋. (**b**) [C] plea on behalf of sb 代某人求情.

in·ter·cept /ˌɪntəˈsept; ˌɪntɚˋsɛpt/ *v* [Tn] stop or catch (sb travelling or sth in motion) before he or it can reach a destination 中途阻止或拦截(某人[某物]): *Reporters intercepted him as he tried to leave by the rear entrance.* 他想从后门溜走, 记者把他截住了. ○ *Effective defence is a matter of intercepting their missiles before they can reach us.* 有效的防卫是不待对方导弹击中我们而先行将其拦截. ○ *The police had been intercepting my mail*, ie reading it before it was delivered. 警方一直截查我的邮件.

▷ **in·ter·cep·tion** /ˌɪntəˈsepʃn; ˌɪntɚˋsɛpʃən/ *n* (**a**) [U] intercepting 中途阻止或拦截. (**b**) [C] instance of this 中途阻止或拦截.

in·ter·ceptor /-tə(r); -tɚ/ *n* person or thing that intercepts (esp a fast military plane which attacks incoming bombers) 进行中途阻止或拦截的人或物; (尤指)截击机.

in·ter·change /ˌɪntəˈtʃeɪndʒ; ˌɪntɚˋtʃendʒ/ *v* **1** [Tn, Tn·pr] **~ sth (with sb)** (of two people, etc) give sth to and receive sth from each other; exchange (指两人等)交换事物, 互换: *We interchanged partners; he danced with mine, and I danced with his.* 我们交换了舞伴; 他和我的舞伴跳, 我和他的舞伴跳. **2** [Tn, Tn·pr] **~ sth/sb (with sth/sb)** put each of two things or people in the other's place 使两人或两物相互易位: *interchange the front and rear tyres of a car* 把汽车的前后轮胎对调 ○ *interchange the front tyres with the rear ones* 把前轮胎和后轮胎互相调换. **3** [I, Tn] (cause sth to) alternate (使某事物)交替变化: *the city's brightly-lit Christmas decorations, with their constantly interchanging colours* 市里圣诞节五彩缤纷的装饰, 颜色不断变幻.

▷ **in·ter·change** /ˈɪntətʃeɪndʒ; ˋɪntɚˌtʃendʒ/ *n* **1** (**a**) [U] interchanging 交换; 互换: *a regular interchange of letters* 经常通信. (**b**) [C] instance of this 交换; 互换. **2** [C] junction (eg on a motorway) where vehicles leave or join a road without crossing other lines of traffic 立体交叉道(如高速公路上的).

in·ter·change·able /ˌɪntəˈtʃeɪndʒəbl; ˌɪntɚˋtʃendʒəbl̩/ *adj* **~ (with sth)** that can be interchanged, esp without affecting the way in which sth works 可交换的, 可互换的, 可交替的(尤指不影响操作的): *a machine with interchangeable parts* 零件可替换的机器 ○ *True synonyms are entirely interchangeable (with one another).* 真正的同义词是完全可以(彼此)互换的. **in·ter·change·ably** *adv*.

inter-city /ˌɪntəˈsɪtɪ; ˌɪntɚˋsɪtɪ/ *adj* [usu attrib 通常作定语] (of fast transport) operating between cities, esp without making stops on the way (指高速运输)市际间的, (尤指)直达的: *an inter-city train, coach, etc* 市际直通火车、长途汽车等 ○ *an inter-city air shuttle* 市际班机.

▷ **inter-city** *n* (**a**) [U] such a service 市际交通服务: *travel by inter-city* 乘坐市际交通工具. (**b**) [C] (*infml* 口) such a train, coach, etc 往返市际间的火车、长途汽车等: *catch the inter-city* 赶乘市际火车.

in·ter·col·le·gi·ate /ˌɪntəkəˈliːdʒɪət; ˌɪntɚkəˋlidʒɪɪt/ *adj* existing or done between colleges 学院之间的; 大学之间的: *intercollegiate games, debates, etc* 大学校际运动会、辩论会等.

in·ter·com /ˈɪntəkɒm; ˋɪntɚˌkɑm/ *n* system of communication by means of microphones and loudspeakers, as used on an aircraft, in a large building (eg a factory), etc 内部通话系统或设备(用话筒及扩音器在飞行器、工厂等大建筑物内进行通话的): *make an announcement on/over the intercom* 用内部通话设备宣布 ○ [attrib 作定语] *an intercom system* 内部通话设备.

in·ter·com·mun·ic·ate /ˌɪntəkəˈmjuːnɪkeɪt; ˌɪntɚkəˋmjunəˌket/ *v* **1** [I, Ipr] **~ (with sb)** communicate with one another; give messages to each other 互通消息; 互相联系: *The lack of a common language made it very difficult to intercommunicate (with each other).* 缺乏共同语言很难(相互)联系. **2** [I, Ipr] **~ (with sth)** (also **interconnect**) (of two or more rooms, compartments, etc) have a means (eg door or corridor) of passing from one to another (指房间、隔间等)相通(如经门或过道): *We had intercommunicating rooms.* 我们的房间是通间. ▷ **in·ter·com·mu·nica·tion** /ˌɪntəkəˌmjuːnɪˈkeɪʃn; ˌɪntɚkəˌmjunəˋkeʃən/ *n* [U].

in·ter·com·mu·nion *n* [U] mutual communion, esp between different Churches, eg Catholic and Orthodox 互相交往(尤指教会间, 如天主教与东正教之间的).

in·ter·con·nect /ˌɪntəkəˈnekt; ˌɪntɚkəˋnɛkt/ *v* [I, Ipr] **~ (with sth)** **1** be connected with each other 互相连接; 互相联系: *It's strange how people's lives interconnect.* 人

们的生活是如何互相联系在一起的, 真是不可思议. **2** = INTERCOMMUNICATE 2.

▷ **in·ter·con·nected** /-tɪd; -tɪd/ *adj* **~ (with sth)** that have a connection (with one another); not independent (彼此)有联系的; 相互依存的: *I see these two theories as somehow interconnected.* 我认为这两种理论在某种程度上是互相关联的.

in·ter·con·nect·ing *adj* [attrib 作定语] joining two or more things together 将事物联结在一起的; 互相连接的: *an interconnecting corridor* 相连接的走廊.

in·ter·con·nec·tion /-ˈnekʃn; -ˈnɛkʃən/ *n* (**a**) [U] connecting two or more things together 相互联结. (**b**) [C] mutual connection between two or more things 相互联系.

in·ter·con·tin·ental /ˌɪntəˌkɒntɪˈnentl; ˌɪntɚˌkɑntəˈnɛntəl/ *adj* between continents 洲际的; 洲与洲之间的: *intercontinental travel* 洲际旅行.

□ **ˌinterconti ˌnental balˌlistic ˈmissile** (*abbr* 缩写 **ICBM**) missile capable of being fired a very long distance, from one continent to another, and typically having a nuclear warhead 洲际弹道导弹.

in·ter·course /ˈɪntəkɔːs; ˈɪntɚˌkɔrs/ *n* [U] **~ (with sb); ~ (between sb and sb)** (*fml* 文) **1** = SEXUAL INTERCOURSE (SEXUAL). **2** dealings with people, nations, etc (与人、国家等的)交往, 交际: *a shy person who avoids all human intercourse* 避免一切人际关系的害羞的人.

in·ter·de·nom·ina·tional /ˌɪntədɪˌnɒmɪˈneɪʃənl; ˌɪntɚdɪˌnɑməˈneʃənl/ *adj* common to or shared by different religious denominations, eg Methodist, Baptist, Catholic 各不同宗教派别(如循道公会、浸礼会、天主教)间所共有的; 超宗派的.

in·ter·de·part·mental /ˌɪntəˌdiːpɑːtˈmentl; ˌɪntɚdiˌpɑrtˈmɛntl/ *adj* of or done by more than one department 各系、部门等之间的. ▷ **in·ter·de·part·ment·ally** /-təlɪ; -tlɪ/ *adv*.

in·ter·de·pend·ent /ˌɪntədɪˈpendənt; ˌɪntɚdɪˈpɛndənt/ *adj* depending on each other 互相依赖的; 互相依存的: *All nations are interdependent in the modern world.* 当今世界上所有国家都是互相依存的. ▷ **in·ter·de·pend·ence** /-əns; -əns/ *n* [U]. **in·ter·de·pend·ently** *adv*.

in·ter·dict /ˌɪntəˈdɪkt; ˌɪntɚˈdɪkt/ *v* [Tn] (*fml* 文) **1** (*esp law* 尤用于法律) prohibit (an action); forbid the use of (sth) 禁止(某行动); 禁用(某物). **2** (in the Roman Catholic Church) forbid sb from taking part in church services and receiving Communion (天主教)禁止某人参加礼拜及领圣体.

▷ **in·ter·dict** /ˈɪntədɪkt; ˈɪntɚˌdɪkt/ *n* (*fml* 文) (**a**) (*law* 律) prohibition from doing sth by an official order of the court (法庭的)强制令, 禁令. (**b**) (in the Roman Catholic Church) order forbidding sb from taking part in church services, etc (天主教)不准某人参加礼拜等之禁令, 褫夺教权的禁令.

in·ter·dic·tion /ˌɪntəˈdɪkʃn; ˌɪntɚˈdɪkʃən/ *n* [C, U] (instance of) interdicting 禁止; 禁用; 禁令; 褫夺教权.

in·ter·dis·cip·lin·ary /ˌɪntəˈdɪsɪplɪnərɪ; ɪntɚˌdɪsəˈplɪnərɪ/ *adj* of or covering more than one area of study 各学科间的; 跨学科的: *interdisciplinary studies* 跨学科研究 ○ *an interdisciplinary course, qualification, degree, etc* 多学科课程、资格、学位等.

in·ter·est[1] /ˈɪntrəst; ˈɪntrɪst/ *n* **1** [U, sing] **~ (in sb/sth)** state of wanting to learn or know (about sb/sth); curiosity; concern 兴趣; 好奇心; 关心: *feel, have, show, express (an) interest in sb or sth* 对某人或某事物觉得有、有、表现有、表示有兴趣 ○ *a topic that arouses, provokes, stimulates, etc a lot of interest* 能引起、激起、唤起...很大兴趣的话题 ○ *Now he's grown up he no longer takes any interest in his stamp collection: he's lost all interest in it.* 他已经长大了, 对集邮不再感兴趣了, 完全失去了兴趣了. ○ *do sth (just) for interest/out of interest/for interest's sake*, ie (just) to satisfy a desire for knowledge (纯粹)因为有兴趣[从兴趣出发/为了兴趣]而做某事(以满足求知欲). **2** [U] quality that arouses concern or curiosity; power to hold one's attention 引起关心或好奇心的性质; 趣味; 吸引力: *The subject may be full of interest to you, but it holds no interest for me.* 这个问题即使你兴味盎然, 我也是兴味索然. ○ *Suspense adds interest to a story.* 故事中的悬疑情节更加引人入胜. **3** [C] thing with which one concerns oneself or about which one is enthusiastic 令人感兴趣的事物; 爱好: *a person of wide, varied, narrow, limited interests* 兴趣广泛、多样、狭窄、有限的人 ○ *Her main interests in life are music, tennis and cooking.* 她生活中的主要爱好是音乐、网球和烹饪. **4** [C usu *pl* 通常作复数] advantage; benefit 好处; 利益; 福利: *look after, protect, safeguard, etc one's own interests*, ie make sure that nothing is done to one's disadvantage 照顾、保护、保卫...自己的利益 ○ *He has your best interests at heart*, ie is acting for your advantage. 他处处为你的利益着想. **5** [C usu *pl* 通常作复数] **~ (in sth)** legal right to share in sth (eg a business), esp in its profits (某事物中的)合法权益(如企业中的)(尤指利润): *He has considerable business interests.* 他有很多企业股分. ○ *American interests in Europe*, eg capital invested in European countries 美国在欧洲的权益(如在欧洲各国的投资) ○ *sell one's interest in a company* 把自己在某公司的股分售出. **6** [C] **~ (in sth)** personal connection with sth from which one may benefit, esp financially 利害关系(尤指财务上的): *If a Member of Parliament wishes to speak about a company with which he is connected, he must declare his interest.* 下院议员若想谈论与其有关的公司的事, 则必须申明他和该公司的利益关系. **7** [U] **~ (on sth)** (*finance* 财) money charged for borrowing money, or paid to sb who invests money 利息: *pay interest on a capital sum* 付一笔资金的利息 ○ *the rate of interest*, ie payment made by the borrower expressed as a percentage of capital 利率 ○ *interest at 10%* 利率为10% ○ [attrib 作定语] *the interest rate* 利率 ○ *an interest-free loan*, ie on which one does not have to pay interest 无息贷款. **8** [C usu *pl* 通常作复数] (*often derog* 常作贬义) group of people engaged in the same business, etc or having sth in common (企业等的)同行; 有共同之处的人: *landed interests*, ie landowners 土地所有者 ○ *Powerful business interests* (ie large business firms collectively) *are influencing the government's actions.* 强有力的企业集团影响着政府采取的措施. ○ [attrib 作定语] *influential interest groups* 有影响的有共同利益的各集团. **9** (idm 习语) **in sb's interest(s)** for or to sb's advantage 为某人的利益; 对某人有好处; 有利于某人: *sth that is not in the public interest* 不符合公众利益的事 ○ *It would be in your interests to accept.* 接受下来对你有利. **in the interest(s) of sth** for the sake of sth 为某事物的缘故: *In the interest(s) of safety, no smoking is allowed.* 为了安全, 严禁吸烟. **a vested interest** ⇨ VEST[2]. **(repay, return, etc sth) with interest** (**a**) (*finance* 财) (give back a sum of money) adding a percentage of interest 加息(还款). (**b**) (*fig infml* 比喻, 口) (respond to an action, good or bad, by doing it to the doer) with added force 加重回报: *return a blow, a kindness with interest* 重重回击、加倍报答好意.

in·ter·est[2] /ˈɪntrəst; ˈɪntrɪst/ *v* [Tn, Tn·pr] **~ oneself/sb (in sth)** (**a**) cause oneself/sb to give one's/his attention (to sth) or to be concerned (about sth) 使自己[某人]注意、关心或感兴趣: *a topic that interests me greatly* 使我大感兴趣的题目 ○ *Having lost his job, he'd begun to interest himself in local voluntary work.* 他失业后便开始关注地方的志愿工作了. ○ *It may interest you to know that she's since died.* 你可能不知道吧, 她后来死了. (**b**) arouse sb's desire to do, buy, eat, etc sth 引起某人要做、买、吃等的欲望: *Can I interest you in our latest computer?* 我给您介绍一下我们最新的计算机好吗?

▷ **in·ter·es·ted** /-tɪd; -tɪd/ *adj* **1 ~ (in sth/sb)** showing curiosity or concern (about sb or sth) (对某人或某事物)感兴趣的, 关心的: *Are you interested in history?* 你喜欢历史吗? ○ *I tried to tell him about it, but he just wasn't interested.* 我想把这件事告诉他, 可他简直不感兴趣. ○ *interested listeners* 感兴趣的听众 ○ *an interested look* 显出好奇的样子 ○ *I shall be interested to know what happens.* 我很想知道情况会怎样. **2 ~ (in sth)** in a position to obtain an advantage (from sth); not impartial 处于获利益的地位的; 有关系的: *As an interested party* (ie sb likely to profit), *I was not allowed to vote.* 因为其中有我的利益, 所以我不得投票.

in·ter·est·ing *adj* holding the attention; arousing curiosity 有趣的; 引起兴趣的: *interesting people, books, conversation* 有趣的人、书籍、谈话. **in·ter·est·ingly** *adv*: *She was there but her husband, interestingly, wasn't.* 她在那儿, 有趣的是她丈夫却没在那里.

I

NOTE ON USAGE 用法: The adjective **interested** can mean ☆ **interested**这一形容词的意思有两个 **1** 'desiring to learn or know (about something)' '(对某事)想知道的': *I am very interested in local history.* 我很想了解本地的历史. **2** 'having an involvement (in something)' '(与某事)有牵连的': *The lawyer invited the interested parties to discuss the problem.* 律师邀请有关的当事人一起商讨问题. **Uninterested** relates to sense 1 ☆ **uninterested**涉及第1义: *She seemed completely uninterested in what I had to tell her about my new job.* 我想把我新工作的事告诉她, 她好像丝毫不感兴趣. **Disinterested** relates to sense 2 ☆ **disinterested**涉及第2义: *In financial matters it is important to get disinterested advice,* ie from somebody who is not directly involved. 在财务方面, 要征询与之无利益关系者的意见, 这是十分重要的.

in·ter·face /ˈɪntəfeɪs; ˋɪntɚˌfes/ *n* **1** surface common to two areas 界面; 分界面. **2** (*computing* 计) electrical circuit linking one device with another and enabling data coded in one format to be transmitted in another 接口(连接两装置的电路, 可使数据从一种代码转换成另一种代码). **3** (*fig* 比喻) place where two subjects, etc meet and affect each other (两学科等的)相接触并相互影响之处: *at the interface of art and science* 在艺术与科学的交汇处 ○ *at the art/science interface* 在艺术[科学]交接处.

in·ter·fere /ˌɪntəˈfɪə(r); ˌɪntɚˋfɪr/ *v* **1** [I, Ipr] **~ (in sth); ~ (between sb and sb)** concern oneself with or take action affecting sb else's affairs without the right to do so or being invited to do so 干涉; 介入; 干预: *Don't interfere in matters that do not concern you!* 不要干预与你无关的事! ○ *It's unwise to interfere between husband and wife.* 夫妻间的事最好不要管. **2** [Ipr] **~ with sth** (**a**) handle, adjust, etc sth without permission, esp so as to cause damage (未得允许)摆弄; (尤指)弄坏: *Who's been interfering with the clock? It's stopped.* 是谁摆弄这钟来着? 已经不走了. (**b**) obstruct sth wholly or partially; prevent sth from being done or carried out properly 阻碍; 妨碍; 妨害: *interfere with sb else's plans* 妨碍某人的计划 ○ *Don't allow pleasure to interfere with duty.* 不要让娱乐妨碍了职责. **3** [Ipr] **~ with sb** (**a**) distract or hinder sb 干扰或妨碍某人: *Don't interfere with him while he's working.* 他工作的时候不要打搅他. (**b**) (*Brit euph* 婉) assault sb sexually (在性方面)侵犯某人: *The police reported that the murdered child had not been interfered with.* 警方报告说被害儿童没有遭到性侵犯.

▷ **in·ter·fer·ence** /ˌɪntəˈfɪərəns; ˌɪntɚˋfɪrəns/ *n* [U] **1 ~ (in/with sth)** interfering 干涉; 干预; 摆弄; 妨碍; (性的)侵犯: *I don't want any interference from you!* 我用不着你来干涉! **2** (**a**) (*radio* 无) prevention of clear reception because a second signal is being transmitted on a wavelength close to the first 干扰: *interference from foreign broadcasting stations* 外来广播电台的干扰. (**b**) (*computing* 计) presence of unwanted signals in a communications circuit 干扰. (**c**) (*sport* 体 *esp US*) (in ice hockey, American football, etc) unlawful obstruction of an opposing player (冰球, 美国橄榄球等)阻挡犯规.

in·ter·fer·ing *adj* [attrib 作定语] likely to concern oneself annoyingly with other people's affairs, to try to control what they do, etc 好干涉的; 爱管闲事的: *She's an interfering old busybody!* 她是个爱管闲事的女人!

in·ter·feron /ˌɪntəˈfɪərɒn; ˌɪntɚˋfɪˌrɑn/ *n* [U] type of protein produced by the body cells when attacked by a virus which acts to prevent the further development of the virus 干扰素.

in·terim /ˈɪntərɪm; ˋɪntərɪm/ *n* (idm 习语) **in the interim** during the time that comes between; meantime 在其间; 在其时: *'My new job starts in May.' 'What are you doing in the interim?'* '我的新工作五月开始.' '这期间你干什么呢?'

▷ **in·terim** *adj* [attrib 作定语] existing or in force only for a short time; temporary; provisional 暂时的; 临时的: *interim arrangements, measures, proposals, etc* 临时的安排、措施、建议等 ○ *an interim loan, payment, etc* 临时的借贷、付款等 ○ *an interim report,* ie one made before the main or final report 期中报告.

in·ter·ior /ɪnˈtɪərɪə(r); ɪnˋtɪrɪɚ/ *n* **1** [C usu *sing* 通常作单数] inner part; inside 内部; 里面: *the interior of a house* 房子的内部 ○ *a house with a classical exterior and a modern interior* 外表古色古香而内部装饰现代化的房子 ○ [attrib 作定语] *an interior room* 内室 ○ *an interior-sprung mattress,* ie with springs inside 弹簧床垫 ○ (*fig* 比喻) *an interior monologue,* ie sb's thoughts, eg as recorded in a novel 内心独白(如小说中的). Cf 参看 EXTERIOR. **2 the interior** [sing] inland part of a country or continent 内地; 腹地; 内陆: *the jungles of the interior of Africa* 非洲内地的丛林 ○ *explorers who penetrated deep into the interior* 深入腹地的探险者. **3 the Interior** [sing] domestic affairs of a country, as dealt with by its government (in the UK, the responsibility of the Home Office) 内政, (国家的)内务(在英国指内政部的事务): *the Department/Minister of the Interior* 内政部[大臣].

□ **inˌterior ˈdecorator** person who decorates the inside of a house or other building with paint, wallpaper, etc 室内装饰工匠.

inˌterior deˈsign planned choice of style, colour, furnishing, etc for the inside of a house, flat, etc 室内设计.

inˌterior deˈsigner person who is expert in this 室内设计师.

in·ter·ject /ˌɪntəˈdʒekt; ˌɪntɚˋdʒɛkt/ *v* [Tn, Tn·pr, Tf] **~ sth (into sth)** make (a sudden remark) that interrupts what sb else is saying 突然插入(言语); 打断(别人的话): *If I may interject a note of caution into the discussion...* 请容我在讨论中插句话, 要注意... ○ *When I brought up the question of funding, he quickly interjected that it had been settled.* 我刚提出筹集基金的问题, 他急忙插嘴说问题已经解决了.

▷ **in·ter·jec·tion** /ˌɪntəˈdʒekʃn; ˌɪntɚˋdʒɛkʃən/ *n* (*grammar*) word or phrase used as an exclamation (eg *Oh!, Hurray!* or *For goodness sake!*) 叹词, 感叹语(如'啊!''好哇!'或'看在老天爷的面上!').

in·ter·lace /ˌɪntəˈleɪs; ˌɪntɚˋles/ *v* [I, Ipr, Tn, Tn·pr] **~ (sth) (with sth)** (cause things to) be joined by weaving or lacing together; cross (one thing with another) as if woven (使东西)编结, 交织; 使(物与另一物)交错: *interlacing branches* 交错的树枝 ○ *interlace sb's hair with ribbons* 用缎带把某人的头发编扎起来.

in·ter·lard /ˌɪntəˈlɑːd; ˌɪntɚˋlɑrd/ *v* [Tn·pr] **~ sth with sth** (*rhet often derog* 修辞, 常作贬义) mix (ordinary writing, speech, etc) with unusual or striking expressions, eg quotations or foreign phrases 使(一般的文字、话语等)夹杂生僻的或惊人的词语(如语录或外来语): *essays liberally interlarded with quotations from the poets* 大量掺杂诗人名句的文章.

in·ter·leave /ˌɪntəˈliːv; ˌɪntɚˋliv/ *v* [Tn, Tn·pr] **~ B (between A)/~ A (with B)** insert (extra pages, usu blank ones) between the pages of a book 在书页间加(页, 通常为空白页): *The exercise book has plain pages interleaved between its lined ones/has lined pages interleaved with plain ones.* 横格练习簿的页间已插入空白页.

in·ter·line /ˌɪntəˈlaɪn; ˌɪntɚˋlaɪn/ *v* [Tn, Tn·pr] **~ sth (with sth) 1** put an extra layer of material between the fabric of (a garment) and its lining in order to give firmness or extra warmth (在衣服的面与里之间)加内衬: *interline a coat (with wool, acrylic fibre, etc)* 在大衣内加(毛的、丙稀酸纤维等的)内衬. **2** (also **in·ter·lin·eate** /ˌɪntəˈlɪnɪeɪt; ˌɪntɚˋlɪnɪˌet/) write or print additional material between the lines of (a text) 在(正文)的字行间加写或加印: *interline a book with notes, glosses, etc* 在书中做评注、注解等.

▷ **in·ter·lin·ing** /ˈɪntəlaɪnɪŋ; ˋɪntɚˌlaɪnɪŋ/ *n* (usu *sing* 通常作单数) material used to interline a garment 做内衬的材料; 衬布.

in·ter·lin·ear /ˌɪntəˈlɪnɪə(r); ˌɪntɚˋlɪnɪɚ/ *adj* (written or printed) between the lines of a text 在行间(书写或印刷)的.

in·ter·link /ˌɪntəˈlɪŋk; ˌɪntɚˋlɪŋk/ *v* [I, Ipr, Tn, Tn·pr] **~ (sth) (with sth)** (**a**) link (sth) (with sth) 将(某物)(与他物)连结: *chains which interlink/are interlinked* 互相连结的链子. (**b**) (*fig* 比喻) connect (sth) or be connected closely (with sth) 将(某物)(与他物)相连或相接: *transport systems that interlink with each other* 互相衔接的交通运输系统 ○ *destinies that are interlinked* 休戚与共的命运.

in·ter·lock /ˌɪntəˈlɒk; ˌɪntɚˋlɑk/ *v* [I, Ipr, Tn, Tn·pr] **~**

(sth) (with sth) fit (things which are joined together) firmly so they do not come apart 使(东西)结合、连接、连锁、互锁: *a system of interlocking parts* 各部分互相结合的设备 ○ *two pieces of machinery, pipe, etc that interlock* 互相连接的两个机械、管子等 ○ *They walked along holding hands, their fingers interlocked.* 他们手指交错, 携手而行. ○ *interlock one pipe with another* 把一根管子和另一根管子连接起来.

▷ **in·ter·lock** /ˈɪntəlɒk; ˋɪntɚ,lɑk/ *n* **1** [C] (*computing* 计) device used in a logic circuit to prevent certain operations from occurring unless preceded by certain events 互锁设备. **2** [U] machine-knitted fabric with fine stitches 双罗纹针织品.

in·ter·loc·utor /ˌɪntəˈlɒkjʊtə(r); ˌɪntɚˋlɑkjətɚ/ *n* (*fml* 文) person taking part in a conversation or discussion 参加对话或讨论的人: *my interlocutor*, ie the person talking to me 我的对话者(与我谈话的人).

in·ter·loper /ˈɪntələʊpə(r); ˌɪntɚˋlopɚ/ *n* person who is present in a place where he does not belong, interferes in sth which is not his affair, etc; intruder 闯入者; 干涉他人事务者: *Security guards were stationed at the door to deal with any interlopers.* 门口已设警卫人员以阻止闯入的人.

in·ter·lude /ˈɪntəlu:d; ˋɪntɚ,lud/ *n* **1** (**a**) short period of time separating the parts of a play, film, etc; interval (戏剧、电影等的)中间休息, 幕间休息: *There will now be a 15-minute interlude.* 现在有15分钟的中间休息. (**b**) piece performed during this 中间休息时演出的节目: *a musical interlude* 音乐插曲. **2** period of time coming between two events 两事件间的时间: *a brief interlude of peace between two wars* 两场战争之间的短暂的和平. **3** event or phase of a different kind occurring in the middle of something 某事过程中发生的事件或片段: *a comic interlude*, ie during a serious drama or during sb's life 幽默插曲(幕间的或某人生活中的). ⇨Usage at BREAK[2] 用法见 BREAK[2].

in·ter·marry /ˌɪntəˈmærɪ; ˌɪntɚˋmærɪ/ *v* (*pt, pp* **-ried**) [I, Ipr] **~ (with sb)** **1** (of racial, religious, etc groups) become connected by marriage with other groups (指不同种族、宗教等的人)通婚: *blacks intermarrying with whites* 与白人通婚的黑人 ○ *Catholics intermarrying with Protestants* 和基督教徒通婚的天主教徒. **2** marry sb within one's own family or group (家族或群体内部)通婚: *cousins who intermarry (with one another)*, eg in a royal family 通婚的堂表兄弟姐妹(如在皇族中).

▷ **in·ter·mar·ri·age** /ˌɪntəˈmærɪdʒ; ˌɪntɚˋmærɪdʒ/ *n* [U] such marriage (种族、宗教、家族之间的)通婚.

in·ter·me·di·ary /ˌɪntəˈmi:dɪərɪ; *US* -dɪerɪ; ˌɪntɚˋmidɪ,ɛrɪ/ *n* **~ (between sb and sb)** person who acts as a means of communication between two or more others 中间人; 调解人; 斡旋人: *They disliked each other too much to meet, so they conducted all their business through an intermediary.* 他们彼此交恶不愿相见, 有事均通过中间人处理.

▷ **in·ter·me·di·ary** *adj* acting in such a way 居间的; 中间人的; 调解的: *play an intermediary role in a dispute* 在一场争吵中起调停人的作用.

in·ter·me·di·ate /ˌɪntəˈmi:dɪət; ˌɪntɚˋmidɪɪt/ *adj* **~ (between A and B)** (**a**) situated or coming between two people, things, etc in time, space, degree, etc (时间、空间、程度等)介于(两人、物等)之间的, 居间的: *at an intermediate point, level, stage, etc* 在中间的一点、水平、阶段等 ○ *The pupa is at an intermediate stage of development; it is intermediate between the egg and the adult butterfly.* 蛹是蝴蝶发育的中间阶段, 介于卵和成虫之间. (**b**) between elementary and advanced 中级的: *an intermediate course, book, level* 中级的课程、书、水平. ▷ **in·ter·me·di·ately** *adv*.

□ **interˌmediate-range (balˌlistic) ˈmissile** missile (typically nuclear) designed to attack targets between long-range and short-range 中程(弹道)导弹(多为核导弹).

in·ter·ment /ɪnˈtɜ:mənt; ɪnˋtɝmənt/ *n* (*fml* 文) [C, U] burying of a dead body 埋葬; 安葬. Cf 参看 INTER.

in·ter·mezzo /ˌɪntəˈmetsəʊ; ˌɪntɚˋmɛtso/ *n* (*pl* **~s** or **-zzi** /-tsɪ; -tsɪ/) (*music* 音) (**a**) short composition to be played between the acts of a drama or an opera, or one that comes between the main movements of a symphony or some other large work 幕间插曲; 间奏曲. (**b**) short instrumental piece in one movement 单乐章的短小的器乐曲: *two intermezzi by Brahms* 布拉姆斯的两首单乐章的短小的器乐曲.

in·ter·min·able /ɪnˈtɜ:mɪnəbl; ɪnˋtɝmɪnəbl̩/ *adj* (*usu derog* 通常作贬义) going on too long, and usu therefore annoying or boring 持续得过长的(通常指使人恼怒或厌烦): *an interminable argument, debate, sermon, etc* 没完没了的争论、辩论、说教等. ▷ **in·ter·min·ably** /-əblɪ; -əblɪ/ *adv*: *We had to wait interminably.* 我们只好干等着.

in·ter·mingle /ˌɪntəˈmɪŋgl; ˌɪntɚˋmɪŋgl̩/ *v* [I, Ipr, Tn, Tn·pr] **~ (sb/sth) (with sb/sth)** (cause people, ideas, substances, etc to) mix together (使人、思想、物质等)混合: *Oil and water will not intermingle.* 油和水不相融合. ○ *a busy trading port, where people of all races intermingle (with each other)* 一个繁忙的贸易港口, 各种族的人(相互)混在一起 ○ *a book which intermingles fact with fiction* 事实和虚构情节交织的书.

in·ter·mis·sion /ˌɪntəˈmɪʃn; ˌɪntɚˋmɪʃən/ *n* [C, U] period of time during which sth stops before continuing; interval; pause 暂停; 中间休息; 幕间休息: *a short intermission halfway through a film* 电影放映中途的短暂休息 ○ *The fever lasted five days without intermission.* 连续发烧五天. ⇨Usage at BREAK[2] 用法见 BREAK[2].

in·ter·mit·tent /ˌɪntəˈmɪtənt; ˌɪntɚˋmɪtn̩t/ *adj* continually stopping and then starting again; not constant 断续的; 间歇的: *intermittent flashes of light from a lighthouse* 灯塔发出的一闪一灭的光 ○ *intermittent bursts of anger, energy, interest, etc* 一阵一阵的怒气、精力、兴趣等 ○ *an intermittent fever* 间歇热. ▷ **in·ter·mit·tently** *adv*.

in·ter·mix /ˌɪntəˈmɪks; ˌɪntɚˋmɪks/ *v* [I, Ipr, Tn, Tn·pr] **~ (sb/sth) (with sb/sth)** (cause people, things, ideas, etc to) mix together; intermingle (使人、物、思想等)混合.

▷ **in·ter·mix·ture** /ˌɪntəˈmɪkstʃə(r); ˌɪntɚˋmɪkstʃɚ/ *n* [C, U] (instance of) intermixing 混合: *a confusing intermixture of fact and fiction* 事实和虚构情节杂乱的大混合.

in·tern[1] /ɪnˈtɜ:n; ɪnˋtɝn/ *v* [Tn, Tn·pr] **~ sb (in sth)** put sb (eg a terrorist or sb from an enemy country) in prison, a camp, etc, esp during a war and without trial 将某人(如恐怖分子或敌国的人)拘留、扣押(于监狱、拘留营等, 尤指战时不经审讯的).

▷ **in·ternee** /ˌɪntɜ:ˈni:; ˌɪntɝˋni/ *n* person who is interned (在上述情况下)被拘留者.

in·tern·ment /ɪnˈtɜ:nmənt; ɪnˋtɝnmənt/ *n* [U]: *the internment of enemy aliens* 对敌国侨民的拘留 ○ [attrib 作定语] *an internment camp* 拘留营.

in·tern[2] (also **in·terne**) /ˈɪntɜ:n; ˋɪntɝn/ *n* (*US*) (*Brit* **ˈhouseman**) young doctor who is completing his training by living in a hospital and acting as an assistant physician or surgeon there 住院实习医生.

in·ternal /ɪnˈtɜ:nl; ɪnˋtɝnl̩/ *adj* **1** of or on the inside 内部的; 在内部的: *the internal workings of a machine* 机器内部的运转 ○ *holding an internal inquiry* (ie within an organization) *to find out who is responsible* 进行内部调查, 找出应对此事承担责任的人 ○ (*mathematics* 数) *an internal angle*, eg one of the three inside a triangle 内角. Cf 参看 EXTERNAL. **2** (*medical* 医) of the inside of the body 体内的: *internal organs* 内脏 ○ *internal medicine*, ie medical study of the interior of the body 内科学 ○ (*infml* 口) *She's been having some internal problems.* 她一直有些内科疾病. **3** of the mind, but not outwardly expressed 内心的; 精神的: *wrestling with internal doubts* 疑虑重重心神不定. **4** (of examinations, etc) set and marked within a school, university, college, etc (指考试等)校内的: *an internal examiner*, ie one who marks papers from his own college, etc 校内主考人. **5** of political, economic, etc affairs within a country, rather than abroad; domestic 国内的; 内政的: *internal trade, revenue, etc* 国内贸易、税收等. **6** (derived from) within the thing itself (得自)本身的: *a theory which lacks internal consistency*, ie of which the parts do not fit together 缺乏内部一致性的理论 ○ *internal evidence*, eg of when a book was written 内在证据(如从书中可知悉其写作时间).

▷ **in·tern·al·ize, -ise** /-nəlaɪz; -nl̩aɪz/ *v* [Tn] (*psychology* 心) make (attitudes, behaviour, language, etc) fully part of one's nature or mental capacity, by learning or

unconsciously assimilating them 使(态度、看法、行为、语言等经学习或同化)内在化(成为本性或主观意识).
in·tern·al·iza·tion, -isation /ɪn,tɜ:nəlaɪ'zeɪʃn; *US* -lɪ'z-; ɪn,tɝnələ'zeʃən/ *n* [U, C].

in·tern·ally /-nəlɪ; -nl̩ɪ/ *adv*: *medicine that is not to be taken internally*, ie not swallowed 不可内服的药 ○ *a theory which is not internally consistent* 不能自圆其说的理论.

□ **in,ternal com'bustion** process by which power is produced by the explosion of gases or vapours inside a cylinder (as in a car engine) 内燃(由气缸内气体膨胀产生动力的方法, 如汽车的发动机的): [attrib 作定语] *an internal-combustion engine* 内燃机.

Internal Revenue Service (*US*) government department responsible for collecting domestic taxes 国内税务署. Cf 参看 INLAND REVENUE (INLAND).

in·ter·na·tional /ˌɪntə'næʃnəl; ˌɪntɚ'næʃənl̩/ *adj* of, carried on by or existing between two or more nations 国际的; 国际间进行的: *international sport, trade, law* 国际体育运动、国际贸易、国际法 ○ *an international agreement, conference, flight* 国际协定、会议、航班 ○ *an international call*, ie a telephone call to another country 国际电话 ○ *an international incident*, ie a crisis between two or more nations 国际事件 ○ *a pianist with an international reputation* 享有国际声誉的钢琴家.

▷ **in·ter·na·tional** *n* **1** (*sport* 体) (**a**) contest involving teams from two or more countries 国际比赛: *the France-Scotland Rugby international* 法国对苏格兰的橄榄球赛. (**b**) player who takes part in an international contest 国际比赛选手: *a retired Welsh Rugby international* 退休的威尔士橄榄球队国际选手. **2** **International** any of four socialist or communist associations for workers of all countries, formed in 1864, 1889, 1919 and 1938 第一国际(1864 年)、第二国际(1889 年)、第三国际(1919 年)或第四国际(1938 年).

in·ter·na·tion·al·ize, -ise /ˌɪntə'næʃnəlaɪz; ˌɪntɚ'næʃənl̩-ˌaɪz/ *v* [Tn] bring (sth) under the combined control or protection of all or many nations; make international 将(某事物)置于国际共管之下; 使国际化: *Should the Suez and Panama Canals be internationalized?* 苏伊士运河和巴拿马运河应归国际共管吗? **in·ter·na·tion·al·iza·tion, -isation** /ˌɪntəˌnæʃnəlaɪ'zeɪʃn; *US* -lɪ'z-; ˌɪntɚˌnæʃənl̩ə-'zeʃən/ *n* [U].

in·ter·na·tion·ally /-nəlɪ; -nl̩ɪ/ *adv*: *an internationally known pianist* 国际知名的钢琴家.

In·ter·na·tion·ale /ˌɪntənæʃə'nɑ:l; ˌɪntɚˌnæʃə'nɑl/ *n* **the Internationale** [sing] (revolutionary) socialist song《国际歌》.

in·ter·na·tion·al·ism /ˌɪntə'næʃnəlɪzəm; ˌɪntɚ'næʃənl̩-ˌɪzəm/ *n* [U] belief in the need for friendly co-operation between nations 国际主义.

▷ **in·ter·na·tion·al·ist** /-ʃnəlɪst; -ʃənəlɪst/ *n* person who supports or believes in internationalism 国际主义者.

in·terne = INTERN².

in·ter·ne·cine /ˌɪntə'ni:saɪn; ˌɪntɚ'nisaɪn/ *adj* causing destruction to both sides 两败俱伤的: *internecine strife, war, conflict, etc* 两败俱伤的争斗、战争、冲突等.

in·ter·pel·late /ɪn'tɜ:peleɪt; *US* ˌɪntər'peleɪt; ˌɪntɚ'pɛlet/ *v* [Tn] (in some parliaments, eg the French and Japanese) question (a government Minister) about a matter of government policy, thus interrupting parliamentary proceedings (在某些议会中如法国和日本)(就政府政策)质询(部长或大臣)而中断议会议程.

▷ **in·ter·pel·la·tion** /ɪn,tɜ:pə'leɪʃn; ɪn,tɝpə'leʃən/ *n* [C, U] (instance of) interpellating (议会中就政府政策向部长或大臣提出的)质询.

in·ter·pen·et·rate /ˌɪntə'penɪtreɪt; ˌɪntɚ'pɛnə,tret/ *v* [I, Tn] penetrate (each other), esp so as to lose individuality; spread through (sth) thoroughly in each direction 互相渗透(尤指因而失去原有特性); 贯穿; 扩散: *two cultures, originally distinct, which have so interpenetrated (each other) as to become virtually a single culture* 两种起源截然不同的文化互相渗透以致实际上已融为一体.

▷ **in·ter·pen·et·ra·tion** /ˌɪntəˌpenɪ'treɪʃn; ˌɪntɚˌpɛnə-'treʃən/ *n* [C, U] (instance of) interpenetrating or being interpenetrated 渗透; 贯穿; 扩散.

in·ter·per·sonal /ˌɪntə'pɜ:sənl; ˌɪntɚ'pɝsənl̩/ *adj* existing or done between two people 人与人之间的; 人际的: *ˌinterpersonal re'lations* 人际关系.

in·ter·plan·et·ary /ˌɪntə'plænɪtrɪ; *US* -terɪ; ˌɪntɚ'plænə-ˌtɛrɪ/ *adj* between planets 行星间的: *an interplanetary flight* 在行星间的航行.

in·ter·play /'ɪntəpleɪ; 'ɪntɚ,ple/ *n* [U] **~ (of A and B/ between A and B)** way in which two or more things have an effect on each other; interaction 相互作用; 相互影响; 互相合作; 一起活动: *the subtle interplay of colours* (ie their combined effect) *in Monet's painting* 莫奈绘画中的色彩的相互掩映 ○ *the interplay between generosity and self-interest which influences people's actions* 影响人的行为的慷慨与私利两者的相互作用.

In·ter·pol /'ɪntəpɒl; 'ɪntɚ,pol/ *n* [Gp] International Police Commission, an organization through which national police forces can co-operate with each other 国际刑事警察组织.

in·ter·pol·ate /ɪn'tɜ:pəleɪt; ɪn'tɝpə,let/ *v* [Tn, Tn·pr] **~ sth (into sth)** (*fml* 文) **1** make (a remark, etc) which interrupts a conversation, speech, etc 插入(言语等): *If I may interpolate a comment, before you continue your speech...* 很抱歉打断你的演讲, 请让我插句话.... **2** add (sth) to a text, book, etc, sometimes misleadingly (在文章、书等中)插入文字等(有时指篡改): *Close inspection showed that many lines had been interpolated into the manuscript at a later date.* 经仔细检查发现不少字句是后来添写进原手稿中去的.

▷ **in·ter·pola·tion** /ɪn,tɜ:pə'leɪʃn; ɪn,tɝpə'leʃən/ *n* (**a**) [U] interpolating or being interpolated 插入言语、文字或篡改. (**b**) [C] thing interpolated 插入的言语或文字.

in·ter·pose /ˌɪntə'pəʊz; ˌɪntɚ'poz/ *v* (*fml* 文) **1** [Tn, Tn·pr] **~ sb/sth (between A and B)** place sb/sth between others 使某人[某事物]介入二者之间: *He interposed his considerable bulk* (ie body) *between me and the window, so that I could not see out.* 他个头很大, 夹在我和窗户之间, 我看不见外边的东西了. **2** [I, Tn] interrupt, esp by making (a remark) 打断谈话; (尤指)插入(言语): *'But how do you know that?' he interposed.* '那么你是怎么知道那件事的呢?'他插嘴问道.

▷ **in·ter·posi·tion** /ˌɪntəpə'zɪʃn; ˌɪntɚpə'zɪʃən/ *n* (*fml* 文) (**a**) [U] interposing or being interposed 介入; 打断谈话; 插嘴. (**b**) [C] thing interposed 插入物; 插入的话.

in·ter·pret /ɪn'tɜ:prɪt; ɪn'tɝprɪt/ *v* **1** [Tn] (**a**) explain (sth which is not easily understandable) 解释; 说明: *interpret a difficult text, an inscription, sb's dream, etc* 解释一篇难懂的文字、一篇铭文、某人的梦等. (**b**) make clear or bring out the intended meaning of (a character, composition, etc) 表明或体现(人物、作品等)的内涵: *interpret a role in a play* 表演剧中某角色 ○ *interpret a piece of music*, ie as player or conductor 演奏一首乐曲(任演奏者或指挥) ○ *Poetry helps us to interpret life.* 诗歌有助于我们阐发人生的意义. **2** [Cn·n/a] **~ sth as sth** understand sth in a particular way 理解; 了解: *'How would you interpret his silence?' 'I would interpret it as a refusal.'* '你认为他的沉默是什么意思?' '我认为意思是拒绝.' **3** [I, Ipr] **~ (for sb)** give a simultaneous spoken translation from one language to another 作口译: *Will you please interpret for me?* 请你为我翻译一下好吗? Cf 参看 TRANSLATE.

▷ **in·ter·preta·tion** /ɪn,tɜ:prɪ'teɪʃn; ɪn,tɝprɪ'teʃən/ *n* (**a**) [U] interpreting 解释; 说明; 表明; 体现; 理解; 口译. (**b**) [C] result of this; explanation or meaning 解释; 翻译; 含义: *the conductor's controversial interpretation of the symphony* 该指挥对那交响乐曲值得商榷的理解 ○ *These facts allow of/may be given many possible interpretations.* 这些事实容或[可以]作多种解释. ○ *What interpretation would you put/place on them?* ie How would you explain them? 你对这些作何解释?

in·ter·pret·at·ive /ɪn'tɜ:prɪtətɪv; ɪn'tɝprɪtətɪv/ *adj* (*Brit*) (also *esp US* **in·ter·pret·ive** /ɪn'tɜ:prɪtɪv; ɪn'tɝprɪtɪv/) of or concerning interpretation 解释的; 说明的; 表明的; 体现的; 理解的; 口译的: *the pianist's considerable interpretative skills* 那个弹钢琴的人深刻理解原作而表现的演奏技巧.

in·ter·preter *n* person who gives a simultaneous translation of words spoken in another language 作口译的人. Cf 参看 TRANSLATOR (TRANSLATE).

in·ter·pret·ing *n* [U] activity of an interpreter 口译.

in·ter·ra·cial /ˌɪntə'reɪʃl; ˌɪntɚ'reʃəl/ *adj* between or involving different races 种族间的: *interracial conflict, harmony, cooperation, etc* 种族间的冲突、和谐、合作等.

in·ter·reg·num /ˌɪntəˈregnəm; ˌɪntɚˈrɛgnəm/ *n* (*pl* **~s** or **-na** /-nə; -nə/) **1** (**a**) period when a state has no normal or lawful ruler, esp at the end of a sovereign's reign and before the appointment of a successor (国家无正常统治者或合法统治者的)空位期(尤指一君主的统治权结束而继任者尚未执政的时期). (**b**) period in an organization when no appointed head or leader is in charge, after the resignation or death of the previous one, until a new appointment is made (一组织的新旧领导人交替间的)空位期(旧任辞职或死亡, 新任未定之际). **2** (*fig* 比喻) interval or pause; gap in continuity 间歇; 停顿; 中断期间.

in·ter·re·late /ˌɪntərɪˈleɪt; ˌɪntɚrɪˈlet/ *v* [I, Ipr, Tn, Tn·pr] **~ (sth) (with sth)** (cause parts, etc to) be connected very closely so that they have an effect on each other (使各部分等)紧密联系(而相互作用): *Many would say that crime and poverty interrelate/are interrelated (with one another).* 很多人都说犯罪与贫穷是密切相关的.

▷ **in·ter·re·lated** *adj* mutually related 相互联系的; 相互关联的: *a complex network of interrelated parts* 由相互关联的部分组成的复杂网络.

in·ter·re·la·tion /ˌɪntərɪˈleɪʃn; ˌɪntɚrɪˈleʃən/, **in·ter·re·la·tion·ship** *ns* [U, C] **~ (of A and B/between A and B)** mutual relationship 相互关系.

in·ter·rog·ate /ɪnˈterəgeɪt; ɪnˈtɛrəˌget/ *v* [Tn, Tn·pr] **~ sb (about sth)** question sb aggressively or closely and for a long time (长时间)讯问、审问、盘问或质问某人: *interrogate a prisoner* 审问犯人 ○ *He refused to be interrogated about his friends.* 盘问关于他朋友的事, 他拒不回答.

▷ **in·ter·roga·tion** /ɪnˌterəˈgeɪʃn; ɪnˌtɛrəˈgeʃən/ *n* [C, U] (instance of) interrogating or being interrogated 讯问; 审问; 盘问; 质问: *several interrogations by police officers* 由警察主持的几次审问 ○ *The prisoner gave way under interrogation.* 犯人受审而招供了. ○ [attrib 作定语] *interrogation techniques* 审问的技巧.

in·ter·rog·ator *n* person who interrogates 讯问者; 审问者; 质问者.

in·ter·rog·at·ive /ˌɪntəˈrɒgətɪv; ˌɪntəˈrɑgətɪv/ *adj* **1** (*fml* 文) asking or seeming to ask a question; inquiring 讯问的; 疑问的; 探问的: *an interrogative look, glance, remark, etc* 疑问的神情、目光、言语等 ○ *in an interrogative tone, manner, etc* 疑问的口吻、态度等. **2** (*grammar*) used in questions 用于疑问句的: *interrogative pronouns, determiners, adverbs*, eg *who, which, why* 疑问代词、疑问限定词、疑问副词(如who、which、why).

▷ **in·ter·rog·at·ive** *n* (*grammar*) interrogative word, esp a pronoun or determiner 疑问词(尤指代词或限定词). **in·ter·rog·at·ively** *adv*.

in·ter·rog·at·ory /ˌɪntəˈrɒgətrɪ; *US* -tɔːrɪ; ˌɪntəˈrɑgəˌtɔrɪ/ *adj* (*fml* 文) interrogative(1) 讯问的; 疑问的; 探问的: *in an interrogatory tone, voice, manner, etc* 以疑问的口吻、声音、态度等.

in·ter·rupt /ˌɪntəˈrʌpt; ˌɪntəˈrʌpt/ *v* **1** [Tn] break the continuity of (sth) temporarily 暂时中断或中止(某事物): *Trade between the two countries was interrupted by the war.* 两国间贸易因战争而中断. ○ *We interrupt this programme to bring you a news flash.* 我们中断节目, 报告新闻快讯. **2** [I, Ipr, Tn, Tn·pr] **~ (sb/sth) (with sth)** (*derog* 贬) stop (sb) speaking, etc or (sth) happening by speaking oneself or by causing some other sort of disturbance 打断(某人)讲话; 打岔; 打扰: *Don't interrupt (me) while I'm busy!* 我正忙着, 不要打搅我! ○ *Don't interrupt the speaker now; he will answer questions later.* 现在不要打断他的话, 他稍后再回答问题. ○ *Hecklers interrupted her speech with jeering.* 诘问者的嘲笑打断了她的讲话. **3** [Tn] destroy the uniformity of (sth) 打破(某事物)的同一性或均衡性: *a vast flat plain interrupted only by a few trees* 只有几棵树的广阔平原. **4** [Tn] obstruct (sth) 阻碍(某事物): *These new flats will interrupt our view of the sea.* 这些新公寓将遮住我们眺望海景的视野.

▷ **in·ter·rupter** *n* person or thing that interrupts 造成中断、中止、打搅或阻碍的人或事物.

in·ter·rup·tion /ˌɪntəˈrʌpʃn; ˌɪntəˈrʌpʃən/ *n* (**a**) [U] interrupting or being interrupted 中断; 中止; 阻碍. (**b**) [C] instance of this; thing that interrupts 中断; 中止; 阻碍; 阻断物; 障碍物: *Numerous interruptions have prevented me from finishing my work.* 我屡遭搅扰以致工作未能完成.

in·ter·sect /ˌɪntəˈsekt; ˌɪntɚˈsɛkt/ *v* **1** [Tn esp passive 尤用于被动语态] divide (sth) by going across it 横断, 横切, 横穿(某物): *a landscape of small fields intersected by hedges and streams* 有绿篱和小溪纵横交错分成许多小块的田野景色. **2** [I, Ipr, Tn] **~ (sth) (with sth)** (of lines, roads, etc) meet and go past (another or each other) forming a cross shape (指线条、道路等)相交, 交叉: *The lines AB and CD intersect at E.* 直线AB与直线CD相交于E点. ○ *The line AB intersects the line CD at E.* 直线AB与直线CD相交于E点. ○ *How many times do the road and railway intersect (with one another) on this map?* 在这张地图上公路与铁路(彼此)相交共有多少次?

▷ **in·ter·sect·ing** *adj* that intersect 相交的; 交叉的: *intersecting lines* 相交的线.

in·ter·sec·tion /ˌɪntəˈsekʃn; ˌɪntɚˈsɛkʃən/ *n* **1** [U] intersecting or being intersected 横断; 横切; 相交; 交叉. **2** [C] point where two lines, etc intersect 交点. **3** [C] place where two or more roads intersect; crossroads 交叉路口; 十字路口.

in·ter·sperse /ˌɪntəˈspɜːs; ˌɪntɚˈspɝs/ *v* [Tn·pr] **~ B among/between/in/throughout A; ~ A with B** vary sth by placing other things at irregular intervals among it 散置; 散布; 点缀: *intersperse flower-beds among/between the trees* 树与树之间点缀着花坛 ○ *a landscape of trees interspersed with a few flower-beds* 树丛间有几个花坛的景致 ○ *a day of sunshine interspersed with occasional showers* 间中有阵雨而充满阳光的一天.

in·ter·state /ˌɪntəˈsteɪt; ˌɪntɚˈstet/ *adj* [usu attrib 通常作定语] between states, esp in the USA 州与州间的, 州际的(尤指美国的): *ˌinterstate ˈrivalry, ˈtensions, ˈhighways* 州际竞争、紧张关系、公路.

in·ter·stel·lar /ˌɪntəˈstelə(r); ˌɪntɚˈstɛlɚ/ *adj* between the stars 星与星间的; 星际的: *interstellar matter*, eg the masses of gas between stars 星际物质(如星间的气团) ○ *interstellar communication* 星际通讯. Cf 参看 STELLAR.

in·ter·stice /ɪnˈtɜːstɪs; ɪnˈtɝstɪs/ *n* (usu *pl* 通常作复数) **~ (of/between/in sth)** (*fml* 文) very small gap or crack 裂隙; 缝隙; 空隙: *The interstices between the bricks let in cold air.* 冷空气透过砖缝进入室内.

in·ter·tribal /ˌɪntəˈtraɪbl; ˌɪntɚˈtraɪbl/ *adj* between tribes 种族间的; 部落间的: *intertribal wars* 部落间的战争.

in·ter·twine /ˌɪntəˈtwaɪn; ˌɪntɚˈtwaɪn/ *v* [I, Ipr, Tn, Tn·pr] **~ (sth) (with sth)** be twisted so as to become joined; twist (things) so as to join them 缠结在一起; 使(东西)缠绕在一起: *Their fingers intertwined.* 他们的手指在一起勾着. ○ *His fingers intertwined with hers.* 他的手指勾着她的手指. ○ *They intertwined their fingers.* 他们把手指勾在一起. ○ *He intertwined his fingers with hers.* 他用手指勾着她的手指. ○ (*fig* 比喻) *Our fates seemed inextricably intertwined*, ie linked. 我们的命运好像紧密相连, 难分难解.

in·ter·val /ˈɪntəvl; ˈɪntɚvl/ *n* **1 ~ (between sth)** (**a**) time between two events (两事件中的)间隔时间: *the interval between a flash of lightning and the sound of thunder* 闪电和雷声之间的间隙 ○ *go out, and return after an interval of half an hour* 出去, 隔半小时再回来. (**b**) space between two or more things (物体之间的)间隔空间: *They planted trees in the intervals between the houses.* 他们在房子与房子之间种上了树. **2** (*Brit*) short period of time separating parts of a play, film, concert, etc (戏剧、电影、音乐会等的)幕间休息, 中间休息: *an interval of 15 minutes after the second act* 第二幕之后的十五分钟幕间休息. **3** pause; break in activity 停顿; 中断: *an interval of silence to show respect for the dead* 向死者致敬的片刻默哀 ○ *He returned to work after an interval in hospital.* 他住院一段时间以后又回来上班了. ⇨Usage at BREAK[2] 用法见 BREAK[2]. **4** (esp *pl* 尤作复数) limited period during which sth occurs (某事发生的)一段时间: *sunny/showery intervals*, ie non-continuous periods of sunshine/rain 间中放晴[有雨]的一段一段时间 ○ *She's delirious, but has lucid intervals.* 她神志昏乱, 但时而清醒. **5** (*music* 音) difference in pitch between two notes 音程: *an interval of one octave* 一个八度音程. **6** (idm 习语) **at intervals** (**a**) with time between 每隔…时间; 间或; 不时; 时而: *At intervals she would stop for a rest.* 她不时停下来休息. ○ *He comes back to see us at regular intervals.* 他每隔一段时间就回

来看看我们. ○ *The runners started at 5-minute intervals.* 赛跑的人每隔五分钟出发一批. **(b)** with spaces between 每隔…距离: *The trees were planted at 20 ft intervals.* 这些树是每隔20英尺栽种一棵的.

in·ter·vene /ˌɪntəˈviːn; ˌɪntɚˈvin/ *v* (*fml* 文) **1** [I] (of time) come or be between (指时间)进入, 介入, 在其间: *during the years that intervened* 这期间的若干年里. **2** [I] (of events, circumstances) happen in such a way as to hinder or prevent sth from being done (指事情、情形)发生(以致阻碍某事): *I will come if nothing intervenes.* 假若没有别的事, 我一定来. ○ *We should have finished harvesting, but a storm intervened.* 我们本可以收割完, 但却遇上了暴风雨. **3** [I, Ipr] **~ (in sth/ between A and B)** (of people) interfere so as to prevent sth happening or to change the result (指人)干涉, 干预, 调停, 调解, 斡旋: *When rioting broke out, the police were obliged to intervene.* 暴乱发生时, 警察有责任干预. ○ *intervene in a dispute, quarrel, etc* 调解纠纷、争吵等 ○ *intervene between two people who are quarrelling* 在吵架的两人间作调解 ○ *I intervened on her behalf to try and get the decision changed.* 我为她力争以求改变决定.

▷ **in·ter·ven·ing** *adj* coming between 发生于其间的: *When she came back, she found that much had changed in the intervening years.* 她回来后发现这几年有了很大的变化.

in·ter·ven·tion /ˌɪntəˈvenʃn; ˌɪntɚˈvɛnʃən/ *n* **~ (in sth)** [C, U] (instance of) interfering or becoming involved, eg to prevent sth happening 干涉, 干预, 介入(如阻止某事发生): *armed intervention by one country in the affairs of another* 一国对另一国内政的武力干涉 ○ *He had been saved from death as if by divine intervention*, ie as though God had taken action to save him. 他得以死里逃生似有神助. **in·ter·ven·tion·ist** /-ʃənɪst; -ʃənɪst/ *n* person in favour of intervening in the affairs of other countries 干涉主义者; 主张干预的人: [attrib 作定语] *interventionist policies* 干涉主义政策.

in·ter·view /ˈɪntəvjuː; ˈɪntɚˌvju/ *n* **~ (with sb)** **1** meeting at which sb (eg sb applying for a job) is asked questions to find out if he is suitable 面试; 面谈: *a job interview* 招聘面试 ○ *I've got an interview with National Chemicals.* 我已获全国化学制品公司邀约面试. ○ *Applicants will be called for interview in due course.* 申请者将于适当时候获邀约面谈. ○ [attrib 作定语] *an interview panel* 面试小组. **2** meeting at which a reporter, etc asks sb questions in order to find out his views (记者等的)采访, 交谈, 晤谈: *a TV interview* 电视采访 ○ *I never give interviews.* 我从不接受采访. ○ *In an exclusive interview with David Frost, the former president made many revelations.* 前总裁在接受戴维·弗罗斯特独家采访时透露了不少内幕情况. **3** meeting between two people to discuss important matters, usu rather formally (两人之间)会谈, 晤谈, 商谈, 面谈: *a careers interview* 职业前途面谈 ○ *I asked for an interview with my boss to discuss my future.* 我请求和老板谈谈我的未来.

▷ **in·ter·view** *v* **1** [I, Tn, Tn·pr] **~ sb (for sth)** conduct an interview with sb (eg a job applicant) 对某人进行面试或面谈(如对求职者): *I'm interviewing all this afternoon.* 今天整个下午我都要进行面试. ○ *interview a number of candidates* 对一些候选人进行面谈 ○ *We interviewed 20 people for the job.* 为这份工作我们对20人进行了面试. **2** [Tn, Tn·pr] **~ sb (about sth)** (of a reporter, etc) ask sb questions in an interview (指记者等)采访, 访问: *interview the Prime Minister (about government policy)* (就政府政策)采访首相.

in·ter·viewee /ˌɪntəvjuːˈiː; ˌɪntɚvjuˈi/ *n* person who is interviewed (面试中)受审核者; 被接见者; 被采访者.

in·ter·viewer /ˈɪntəvjuːə; ˈɪntɚˌvjuɚ/ *n* person who conducts an interview 主持面试者; 接见者; 采访者.

in·ter·weave /ˌɪntəˈwiːv; ˌɪntɚˈwiv/ *v* (*pt* **-wove** /-ˈwəʊv; -ˈwov/, *pp* **-woven** /-ˈwəʊvn; -ˈwovən/) **1** [I, Ipr, Tn, Tn·pr] **~ (sth) (with sth)** be woven or weave (sth) together 交织; 编结; 编织; 将某物交织在一起: *threads that interweave (with one another)* 合股的线 ○ *interweave wool with cotton/wool and cotton* 棉毛交织. **2** [usu passive 通常用于被动语态: Tn, Tn·pr] **~ sth (with sth)** (*fig* 比喻) **(a)** join (two or more lives, etc) together so that they seem to be no longer separate or independent 使(至少两个生命等)结合(成一体或密不可分): *Our lives are interwoven.* 我们的命运已经结合在一起了. ○ *Your destiny is interwoven with mine.* 你的命运已和我的命运结合在一起了. **(b)** combine different features in writing, artistic creation, etc 将(写作、艺术创作等的不同特点)混在一起: *primitive dance rhythms interwoven with folk melody* 混有民间曲调的原始舞蹈节奏.

in·test·ate /ɪnˈtesteɪt; ɪnˈtɛstet/ *adj* [usu pred 通常作表语] (*law* 律) not having made a will before death occurs 无遗嘱: *die intestate* 死时没有留下遗嘱.

▷ **in·test·acy** /ɪnˈtestəsɪ; ɪnˈtɛstəsɪ/ *n* [U] (*law* 律) condition of being intestate (死亡时)无遗嘱.

in·test·ine /ɪnˈtestɪn; ɪnˈtɛstɪn/ *n* (usu *pl* 通常作复数) long tube in the body which helps to digest food and carries it from the stomach to the anus 肠: *a pain in the intestines* 由肠疾患引起的疼痛 ○ *Food passes from the stomach to the small intestine and from there to the large intestine.* 食物由胃进入小肠再进入大肠. Cf 参看 ABDOMEN. ⇨illus at DIGESTIVE 见 DIGESTIVE 插图.

▷ **in·test·inal** /ɪnˈtestɪnl *or, in British use*, 英式英语读作 ˌɪntesˈtaɪnl; ɪnˈtɛstɪnḷ/ *adj* of the intestines 肠的: *intestinal disorders* 肠疾.

in·tim·ate[1] /ˈɪntɪmət; ˈɪntəmɪt/ *adj* **1 ~ (with sb)** **(a)** having or being a very close and friendly relationship 亲密的; 密切的: *intimate friends* 密友 ○ *an intimate friendship* 亲密的友情 ○ *We had been intimate* (ie very close friends) *for some time.* 我们曾经是极要好的朋友. **(b)** (*euph* 婉) having a sexual relationship, esp outside marriage 有性关系的(尤指婚外的): *She was accused of being intimate with several men.* 有人说她与几个男人关系暧昧. **2** likely or intended to encourage close relationships, esp sexual ones, typically by being small, quiet and private 便于有亲昵关系的(尤指性关系, 因环境范围小、幽静、无人打扰): *an intimate restaurant, atmosphere* 适宜幽会的餐厅、气氛. **3** private and personal 私人的; 个人的: *tell a friend the intimate details of one's life* 把自己生活中的隐私告诉朋友 ○ *an intimate diary*, ie one in which sb records private experiences, thoughts, emotions, etc 私人日记. **4** [attrib 作定语] (*fml* 文) (of knowledge) detailed and obtained by deep study or long experience (指知识)精通的, 详尽的: *an intimate knowledge of African religions* 对非洲宗教的广博知识. **5** (idm 习语) **be/get on intimate ˈterms (with sb)** (come to) know sb very well and be friendly with him (渐渐)熟悉某人且关系密切: *We're not exactly on intimate terms, but we see each other fairly often.* 我们虽算不上关系密切, 但还常见面.

▷ **in·tim·acy** /ˈɪntɪməsɪ; ˈɪntəməsɪ/ *n* **1** [U] **(a)** state of being intimate; close friendship or relationship 亲密; 亲切; 亲昵; 关系密切. **(b)** (*euph* 婉) sexual activity 性行为. **2 intimacies** [pl] (*rhet* 修辞) intimate actions, eg caresses or kisses 亲昵行为(如爱抚、接吻).

in·tim·ate *n* intimate friend 至交; 知己; 密友; 挚友: *Sir Reginald, known to his intimates as 'Porky'.* 雷金纳德爵士, 他的至交都叫他'胖子'.

in·tim·ately *adv*.

in·tim·ate[2] /ˈɪntɪmeɪt; ˈɪntəˌmet/ *v* [Tn, Tf, Tw, Dn·pr, Dpr·f, Dpr·w] **~ sth (to sb)** (*fml* 文) make sth known (to sb), esp discreetly or indirectly 将某事透露(给某人); (尤指谨慎地或间接地)示意; 暗示: *He intimated his wishes with a slight nod of his head.* 他微微颔首示意. ○ *She has intimated (to us) that she no longer wishes to be considered for the post.* 她已(向我们)透露希望不再考虑让她担任该职. ○ *The judge has not intimated (to the jury) whether they will be allowed to reach a majority verdict.* 法官没有指示(陪审团)他们可否达成大多数裁定.

▷ **in·tima·tion** /ˌɪntɪˈmeɪʃn; ˌɪntəˈmeʃən/ *n* (*fml* 文) **(a)** [U] intimating 透露; 示意; 暗示. **(b)** [C] **~ (of sth/ that…)** something intimated; hint; notification 透露的事; 暗示; 通知: *He has given us no intimation of his intentions/what he intends to do.* 他没有向我们透露他的意图.

in·tim·id·ate /ɪnˈtɪmɪdeɪt; ɪnˈtɪməˌdet/ *v* [Tn, Tn·pr] **~ sb (into sth/doing sth)** frighten sb (in order to make him do sth) 恐吓, 威胁(某人做某事): *intimidate a witness (into silence, into keeping quiet, etc)*, eg by threatening him 恐吓目击证人(迫使其不出声、保持缄默等).

▷ **in·tim·id·at·ing** *adj* frightening, esp because of

seeming difficulty or impossibility 吓人的, 令人惊恐的(尤指因为看似很困难或不可能): *The intimidating bulk of Mt Everest rose up before the climbers.* 登山者面前耸立着险峻的埃佛勒斯峰(即珠穆朗玛峰).

in·tim·ida·tion /ɪnˌtɪmɪˈdeɪʃn; ɪnˌtɪməˈdeʃən/ *n* [U] intimidating or being intimidated 恐吓; 威胁: *give way to intimidation* 向所受的威胁让步 ○ *keep people in order by intimidation* 用恫吓手段迫使人们就范.

in·tim·ida·tory /ɪnˌtɪmɪˈdeɪtərɪ; ɪnˈtɪməˌdetərɪ/ *adj* tending to intimidate 恐吓的; 威胁的: *intimidatory tactics* 恫吓手法.

into /ˈɪntə; ˈɪntə, *before vowels and finally* 元音前及句末读作 ˈɪntu:; ˈɪntu/ *prep* **1** (**a**) (moving) to a point within (an enclosed space or volume) 进入; 到...里面: *Come into the house.* 到房子里来. ○ *Throw it into the fire.* 把它扔进火里. ○ *go into town* 进城 ○ *She dived into the swimming-pool.* 她头向下跳进游泳池里. ○ (*fig* 比喻) *He turned and walked off into the night.* 他转身走开, 消失在夜幕中. ○ *put money into an account* 把钱存入帐户. Cf 参看 OUT OF. (**b**) in the direction of (sth) 朝; 向; 对着: *Speak clearly into the microphone.* 对着话筒说清楚些. ○ *Driving into the sun, we had to shade our eyes.* 车朝着有太阳的方向开, 我们只好遮挡着眼睛. (**c**) to a point at which one hits (sb/sth) 触及或撞上(某人[某物]): *I nearly ran into a bus when it stopped suddenly in front of me.* 前面一辆公共汽车突然停住, 我险些撞上. ○ *A lorry drove into a line of parked cars.* 一辆卡车撞上了一排停着的汽车. **2** until a point during (sth) 在(某过程)中直到某一点: *He carried on working long into the night.* 他一直工作到深夜. ○ *She didn't get married until she was well into middle age.* 她步入中年以后才结婚. ○ *We're usually into May before the weather changes.* 我们这儿的天气到五月份才有变化. **3** (**a**) (indicating a change in form as the result of an action 指因一行动而产生在形式上的变化): *turn the spare room into a study* 把空房改成书房 ○ *cut the paper into strips* 把纸裁成小条 ○ *fold the napkin into a triangle* 把餐巾折成三角形 ○ *collect the rubbish into a heap* 把垃圾堆在一起. Cf 参看 OUT OF. (**b**) (indicating a change to a specified condition or action 指改变成某种情况或行动): *frighten sb into submission* 威逼某人屈从 ○ *shocked into a confession of guilt* 吓得承认有罪 ○ *She came into power in 1979.* 她于1979年掌权. (See *n* entries for similar examples 类似示例见有关名词词条.) **4** (used to express division in mathematics 用以表示数学的'除'): *5 into 25 = 5.* 5除25等于5. **5** (idm 习语) **be into sth** (*infml* 口) be enthusiastic about sth in which one takes an active interest 对某事物很有兴趣; 非常喜欢: *be (heavily) into yoga, science fiction, stamp collecting* (极)喜爱瑜伽、科幻小说、集邮.

in·tol·er·able /ɪnˈtɒlərəbl; ɪnˈtɑlərəbl/ *adj* too bad to be borne or endured 无法忍受的; 难以容忍的: *intolerable heat, noise, etc* 无法忍受的炎热、嘈杂声等 ○ *intolerable insolence, behaviour, etc* 不能容忍的侮慢、行为等 ○ *This is intolerable: I've been kept waiting for three hours!* 太不像话了, 让我一直等了三个小时! ▷ **in·tol·er·ably** /-əblɪ; -əblɪ/ *adv*: *intolerably rude* 粗鲁得难以忍受.

in·tol·er·ant /ɪnˈtɒlərənt; ɪnˈtɑlərənt/ *adj* ~ **(of sb/sth)** (*usu derog* 通常作贬义) not tolerant 不容忍的: *intolerant of opposition* 不容反对. ▷ **in·tol·er·ance** /-əns; -əns/ *n* [U]: *religious intolerance* 宗教上的不容异说. **in·tol·er·antly** *adv*.

in·tona·tion /ˌɪntəˈneɪʃn; ˌɪntoˈneʃən/ *n* **1** [U] intoning 吟诵; 吟唱: *the intonation of a prayer* 祈祷文的吟诵. **2** (**a**) [C, U] rise and fall of the pitch of the voice in speaking, esp as this affects the meaning of what is said 语音的抑扬; 语调; 音调: *In English, some questions have a rising intonation.* 英语中有些疑问句需用升调. ○ *a change of intonation* 语调的变化 ○ [attrib 作定语] *intonation patterns* 语调类型. Cf 参看 INFLECTION 2, STRESS 3. (**b**) [C] slight accent in speaking (说话时稍含民族的、地方的或个人的)口音: *speak English with a Welsh intonation* 说英语稍带威尔士口音. **3** [U] (*music* 音) quality of playing or singing in tune (演奏或唱歌中的)调音: *The violin's intonation was poor.* 这个小提琴的调音不准.

in·tone /ɪnˈtəʊn; ɪnˈton/ *v* **1** [I, Tn] recite (a prayer, psalm, etc) in a singing tone 吟诵, 吟唱(祈祷文、赞美诗等). **2** [Tn] (*fig* 比喻) say (sth) in a solemn voice 用庄重的语调说(话).

in toto /ɪnˈtəʊtəʊ; ɪnˈtoto/ (*Latin fml* 拉, 文) totally; altogether 完整地; 完全地; 全部地.

in·tox·ic·ant /ɪnˈtɒksɪkənt; ɪnˈtɑksəkənt/ *n* intoxicating substance, esp alcoholic drink 醉人的物质(尤指酒类饮料).

in·tox·ic·ate /ɪnˈtɒksɪkeɪt; ɪnˈtɑksəˌket/ *v* (*fml* 文) **1** [esp passive 尤用于被动语态: Tn, Tn·pr] ~ **sb (with sth)** cause sb to lose self-control as a result of the effects of a drug, a gas, or (esp alcoholic) drink (用药物、气体或饮料, 尤指酒)使某人失去自制力; 使醉: *He'd been in the bar all night and was thoroughly intoxicated.* 他整夜泡在酒吧里, 烂醉如泥. **2** [Tn·pr usu passive 通常用于被动语态] ~ **sb with sth** (*fig* 比喻) excite sb greatly, beyond self-control 使某人兴奋得不能自制: *intoxicated by success, by a sense of power, etc* 因成功、觉得威风等而欣喜若狂 ○ *intoxicated with joy, with the fresh air* 为欢乐、清新空气所陶醉.

▷ **in·toxi·ca·tion** /ɪnˌtɒksɪˈkeɪʃn; ɪnˌtɑksəˈkeʃən/ *n* [U] state of being intoxicated, esp drunkenness 极度兴奋; (尤指)酒醉.

intra- *pref* 前缀 (with *adjs* 与形容词结合) on the inside; within 在内部; 在内: *intramuscular* ○ *intramural*.

in·tract·able /ɪnˈtræktəbl; ɪnˈtræktəbl/ *adj* (*fml* 文) not easily controlled or dealt with; hard to manage 难控制的; 难对付的; 难处理的: *intractable children* 难管教的儿童 ○ *an intractable problem* 伤脑筋的问题. ▷ **in·tract·ab·il·ity** /ɪnˌtræktəˈbɪlətɪ; ˌɪntræktəˈbɪlətɪ/ *n* [U]. **in·tract·ably** /ɪnˈtræktəblɪ; ɪnˈtræktəblɪ/ *adv*.

in·tra·mural /ˌɪntrəˈmjʊərəl; ˌɪntrəˈmjʊrəl/ *adj* **1** intended for full-time students living within a college 为大专住校生而设的: *intramural courses, studies, staff* 大专院校的校内课程、学业、教职工. **2** (*US*) between teams or players from the same school 校内运动队间或选手间的: *an intramural game, league* 校内比赛、校内运动队联合会.

in·tra·mus·cu·lar /ˌɪntrəˈmʌskjʊlə(r); ˌɪntrəˈmʌskjələ/ *adj* (*medical* 医) within a muscle or muscles 肌肉内的: *an intramuscular injection* 肌肉注射.

in·trans·igent /ɪnˈtrænsɪdʒənt; ɪnˈtrænsədʒənt/ *adj* (*fml derog* 文, 贬) unwilling to change one's views or be co-operative; stubborn 固执己见的; 不愿合作的; 顽固的: *Owing to their intransigent attitude we were unable to reach an agreement.* 由于他们态度僵硬, 我们无法达成协议. ▷ **in·trans·igence** /-əns; -əns/ *n* [U]. **in·trans·igently** *adv*.

in·trans·it·ive /ɪnˈtrænsətɪv; ɪnˈtrænsətɪv/ *adj* (*grammar*) (of verbs) used without an object (指动词)不及物的. Cf 参看 TRANSITIVE. ▷ **in·trans·it·ively** *adv*.

in·tra·state /ˌɪntrəˈsteɪt; ˌɪntrəˈstet/ *adj* (existing) within one state, esp of the USA (存在于)州内的(尤指美国): *intrastate highways* 州内公路.

intra-uterine /ˌɪntrəˈju:təraɪn; ˌɪntrəˈjutəraɪn/ *adj* (*medical* 医) within the uterus 子宫内的.

□ ˌ**intra-uterine deˈvice** (*abbr* 缩写 **IUD**) (also **coil**) loop or spiral inserted in the uterus as a contraceptive 子宫内避孕器; 避孕环.

in·tra·ven·ous /ˌɪntrəˈvi:nəs; ˌɪntrəˈvinəs/ *adj* (*medical* 医) within a vein or veins 静脉内的: *an intravenous injection*, ie into the bloodstream 静脉注射. ▷ **in·tra·ven·ously** *adv*.

in·trench = ENTRENCH.

in·trepid /ɪnˈtrepɪd; ɪnˈtrɛpɪd/ *adj* (*esp rhet* 尤作修辞) fearless; brave 无畏的; 勇敢的: *our intrepid hero* 我们的无畏的英雄.

▷ **in·trep·id·ity** /ˌɪntrɪˈpɪdətɪ; ˌɪntrəˈpɪdətɪ/ *n* [U] fearlessness 无畏.

in·trep·idly /ɪnˈtrepɪdlɪ; ɪnˈtrɛpɪdlɪ/ *adv*.

in·tric·ate /ˈɪntrɪkət; ˈɪntrəkɪt/ *adj* made up of many small parts put together in a complex way, and therefore difficult to follow or understand 错综复杂的: *an intricate piece of machinery* 一部复杂的机器 ○ *a novel with an intricate plot* 情节错综复杂的小说 ○ *the intricate windings of a labyrinth* 迷宫中扑朔迷离的路线 ○ *an intricate design, pattern, etc* 复杂的设计、图案等.

▷ **in·tric·acy** /ˈɪntrɪkəsɪ; ˈɪntrəkəsɪ/ *n* (**a**) [U] quality of being intricate 错综复杂. (**b**) **intricacies** [pl] intricate things, events, etc 错综复杂的事物: *unable to follow the intricacies of the plot* 难以理解情节中复杂的关系.

in·tric·ately /-ətlɪ; -ətlɪ/ *adv*.

in·trigue /ɪnˈtri:g; ɪnˋtrig/ *v* **1** [I, Ipr] **~ (with sb) (against sb)** make and carry out secret plans or plots to do sth bad 搞阴谋诡计: *She was intriguing with her sister against her mother.* 她和妹妹串通捣鬼跟母亲作对. ○ *Some of the members had been intriguing to get the secretary dismissed.* 有些人一直搞鬼想让老板把秘书解雇. **2** [Tn, Tn·pr] **~ sb (with sth)** arouse sb's interest or curiosity 激起某人的兴趣或好奇心: *What you say intrigues me; tell me more.* 你说的很有意思, 多给我讲些吧. ○ *intrigue sb with an exciting story, a piece of news, etc* 以使人兴奋的故事、新闻等引起某人的兴趣.

▷ **in·trigue** /ˈɪntri:g, ɪnˈtri:g; ˋɪntrig, ɪnˋtrig/ *n* **1** [U] making of secret plans to do sth bad; conspiracy 密谋策划; 阴谋: *a novel of mystery and intrigue* 有神秘和阴谋情节的小说. **2** [C] (**a**) secret plan to do sth bad 阴谋; 密谋. (**b**) secret arrangement 秘密安排: *amorous intrigues* 偷情.

in·tri·guer /ɪnˈtri:gə; ɪnˋtrigɚ/ *n* person who intrigues (INTRIGUE 1) 搞阴谋诡计的人.

in·tri·guing *adj* full of interest, esp because unusual; fascinating 饶有兴味的(尤指因稀奇); 迷人的: *What an intriguing story!* 多么引人入胜的故事啊!

in·trinsic /ɪnˈtrɪnsɪk, -zɪk; ɪnˋtrɪnsɪk, -zɪk/ *adj* (of a value or quality) belonging naturally; existing within, not coming from outside (指价值或性质)固有的, 内在的, 本质的: *a man's intrinsic worth*, eg arising from such qualities as honour and courage, rather than how much he owns, etc 一个人的内在价值(如正义感、勇敢等品质, 而不在财富多寡) ○ *the intrinsic value of a coin*, ie the value of the metal in it, usu less than the value of what it will buy 一硬币的本身价值(即所含金属的价值, 通常低于用其所购物品的价值). Cf 参看 EXTRINSIC. ▷ **in·trins·ic·ally** /-klɪ; -klɪ/ *adv*: *He is not intrinsically bad.* 他本质并不坏.

intro /ˈɪntrəʊ; ˋɪntro/ *n* (*pl* **~s**) (*infml* 口) introduction 介绍: *I'd like an intro to that girl you were talking to!* 我想请你把我介绍给刚才你和她说话的那姑娘! ○ (*music* 音) *There's an intro of eight bars before you come in.* 你在八小节的前奏之后加入.

in·tro·duce /ˌɪntrəˈdju:s; *US* ˈdu:s; ˌɪntrəˋdus/ *v* **1** [Tn, Tn·pr] **~ sb (to sb)** make sb known formally to sb else by giving the person's name, or by giving each person's name to the other 把某人介绍给另外的人; 使相互认识; 引见: *Allow me to introduce my wife.* 让我介绍一下, 这是我太太. ○ *I don't think we've been introduced*, ie and therefore I do not know your name. 我想我们未曾彼此介绍过(因此不知您怎么称呼). ○ *I was introduced to the president at the party.* 在聚会上有人把我介绍给总裁了. **2** [Tn, Tn·pr] **~ sth (to sb)** announce and give (details of a speaker or broadcast, programme, etc) to listeners or viewers (向听众或观众)宣布并介绍(演讲者或广播、节目等的细节): *The next programme is introduced by Mary Davidson.* 下一个节目由玛丽·戴维森主持. **3** [Tn] present (sth new) formally for discussion 提出(新问题)供讨论: *introduce a Bill before Parliament* 向议会提出法案. **4** [Tn·pr] **~ sb to sth** (**a**) lead sb up to the main part of sth 引导或带领某人接触某事物的主体: *The first lecture introduces new students to the broad outlines of the subject.* 第一堂课是让新同学概括地了解这一科目. ○ *It was she who first introduced me to the pleasures of wine-tasting.* 是她第一个让我领略到参加品酒会的乐趣. (**b**) cause sb to start using or experiencing sth 使某人开始采用或体验某事物: *introduce young people to alcohol, tobacco, drugs, etc* 教年轻人喝酒、抽烟、吸毒等. **5** [Tn, Tn·pr] **~ sth (in/into sth)** bring sth into use or operation for the first time 初次投入使用或运作; 引进; 推行; 采用: *The company is introducing a new family saloon this year.* 公司准备今年推出一种新型家庭轿车. ○ *introduce computers (into schools)* (使学校)采用计算机 ○ *introduce a ban on smoking in public places* 推行在公共场所禁止吸烟的规则. **6** [Tn, Tn·pr] **~ sth (into sth)** (*fml* 文) put sth (into sth) 将某物放或插(入某物): *introduce a hypodermic needle into a vein* 将一皮下注射针头插入静脉 ○ (*fig* 比喻) *introduce a subject into a conversation* 在谈话中加进一话题. **7** [Tn] begin (a piece of music, book, play, etc) 作为(一段音乐、一本书、一场戏等)的开头: *A slow theme introduces the first movement.* 第一乐章以缓慢的主旋律开始.

in·tro·duc·tion /ˌɪntrəˈdʌkʃn; ˌɪntrəˋdʌkʃən/ *n* **1** [C, U] **~ (to sb)** formal presentation of one person to another, in which each is told the other's name (正式的)介绍; 引见: *It is time to make introductions all round*, ie introduce many people to one another. 是大家互相介绍的时候了. ○ *a person who needs no introduction*, ie who is already well-known 不需作介绍的人(大家都知道的) ○ *a letter of introduction*, ie which tells sb who you are, written by a mutual acquaintance 介绍信. **2** [C] (**a**) **~ (to sth)** something that leads up to the main part of sth (eg an explanatory article at the beginning of a book) 引至主要部分的事物(如书中的序言): *a short, brief, detailed, general, long, etc introduction* 短序、简短的序言、绪论、前言、长的序言 ○ *The introduction explains how the chapters are organized.* 前言部分说明各章的编排情况. Cf 参看 PREFACE. (**b**) **~ (to sth)** textbook for people beginning a subject 入门(初级读物): *'An Introduction to Astronomy'* 《天文学入门》. **3** [sing] **~ to sth** first experience of sth 对某事物的初次经历或体验: *his introduction to modern jazz* 他对现代爵士音乐的初次接触. **4** [U] bringing into use or operation for the first time 初次投入使用或运作; 引进; 推行; 采用: *the introduction of new manufacturing methods* 新的制造方法的采用. **5** [C] **~ (in/into sth)** thing introduced, esp a new animal or plant species 引进的事物(尤指新动植物品种); 引种: *The rabbit is a relatively recent introduction in Australia.* 兔子在澳洲是较为近期引进的动物. **6** [C] (*music* 音) short section at the beginning of a musical composition, leading up to the main part 前奏; 导奏: *an eight-bar introduction* 八小节组成的前奏.

in·tro·duct·ory /ˌɪntrəˈdʌktərɪ; ˌɪntrəˋdʌktərɪ/ *adj* acting as an introduction(2) 引导的; 序言的: *some introductory remarks by the chairman* 主席的开场白 ○ *an introductory chapter* 序篇.

in·tro·spect /ˌɪntrəˈspekt; ˌɪntrəˋspɛkt/ *v* [I] (*fml* 文) examine or be concerned with one's own thoughts, feelings and motives 反省; 内省.

▷ **in·tro·spec·tion** /ˌɪntrəˈspekʃn; ˌɪntrəˋspɛkʃən/ *n* [U] introspecting 反省; 内省.

in·tro·spect·ive /-ˈspektɪv; -ˋspɛktɪv/ *adj* (**a**) inclined to introspect 好反省的; 好内省的: *an introspective person* 好自我反省的人. (**b**) characteristic of sb who does this 反省的; 内省的: *in an introspective mood* 以反省的心情 ○ *introspective writing* 反思的文字.

in·tro·vert /ˈɪntrəvɜ:t; ˋɪntrəˌvɝt/ *n* person who is more interested in his own thoughts and feelings than in things outside himself, and is often shy and unwilling to speak or join in activities with others (思想感情等)内向的人. Cf 参看 EXTROVERT.

▷ **in·tro·ver·ted** /ˌɪntrəˈvɜ:tɪd; ˌɪntrəˋvɝtɪd/ *adj* having the quality of an introvert (思想感情等方面)内向的.

in·tro·ver·sion /ˌɪntrəˈvɜ:ʃn; *US* -ˈvɜ:rʒn; ˌɪntrəˋvɝʒən/ *n* [U] state of being introverted (思想感情等的)内向.

in·trude /ɪnˈtru:d; ɪnˋtrud/ *v* [I, Ipr, Tn·pr] **~ (oneself) on/upon sb/sth; ~ (oneself/sth) into sth** (*esp fml* 尤作文雅语) put (oneself/sth) into a place or situation where one/it is unwelcome or unsuitable 闯入; 侵入; 打搅; 侵扰: *I don't wish to intrude, but could I talk to you for a moment?* 我无意打扰您, 不过我可以跟您谈一会儿吗? ○ *I felt as though I was intruding on their private grief.* 他们正伤心时, 我觉得我好像骚扰了他们. ○ *If I could intrude a note of seriousness into this frivolous conversation...* 我真想说一句, 叫他们谈话放严肃些....

▷ **in·truder** *n* person or thing that intrudes, esp sb who enters another's property illegally 闯入的人或物(尤指非法进入属于他人的地方的).

in·tru·sion /ɪnˈtru:ʒn; ɪnˋtruʒən/ *n* **~ (on/upon/into sth)** (**a**) [U] intruding 闯入; 侵入; 打搅; 侵扰: *guilty of intrusion upon sb's privacy* 侵犯某人的隐私. (**b**) [C] instance of this 闯入; 侵入; 打搅; 侵扰: *This newspaper article is a disgraceful intrusion into my private life.* 报纸上这篇文章是对我私生活的侵扰, 这种做法很不光彩.

▷ **in·trus·ive** /ɪnˈtru:sɪv; ɪnˋtrusɪv/ *adj* intruding 闯入的; 侵入的; 打搅的; 侵扰的: *intrusive neighbours* 打扰人的邻居 ○ *the intrusive 'r' often heard between vowel sounds*, eg in 'law and order' 元音之间常听到的外加音 r(如在 law and order 中的).

in·tuit /ɪn'tju:ɪt; *US* 'tu:-; ɪn'tuɪt/ *v* [I, Tn, Tf] (*fml* 文) sense (sth) by intuition 凭直觉感知(某事物): *incapable of intuiting (sb's intentions, feelings, etc)* 不善于凭直觉了解(某人的意图、感情等).

in·tu·ition /ˌɪntju:'ɪʃn; *US* -tu-; ˌɪntu'ɪʃən/ *n* (*often approv* 常作褒义) **1** [U] (power of) understanding things (eg a situation, sb's feelings) immediately, without the need for conscious reasoning or study 直觉; 直觉力: *know sth by intuition* 凭直觉了解某事物 ○ *Nobody told me where to find you. It was sheer intuition.* 没有人告诉我到哪儿去找你. 我纯粹是凭直觉找到你的. ○ *Intuition told me you were here.* 我凭直觉知道你在这儿. **2** [C] **~ (about sth/that...)** piece of knowledge gained by this power 凭直觉感知的信息: *I had a sudden intuition about the missing jewels.* 我凭直觉突然对失去的珠宝有所感知. ○ *I had an intuition that we would find them there.* 我有一种直觉, 我们可以在那里找到他们. ○ *My intuitions proved correct.* 我的直觉确实是正确的.

▷ **in·tu·it·ive** /ɪn'tju:ɪtɪv; *US* 'tu:-; ɪn'tuɪtɪv/ *adj* (**a**) of or coming from intuition 直觉的; 来自直觉的: *intuitive knowledge* 凭直觉知道 ○ *an intuitive feeling (about sb), approach (to sth), assessment (of sth), etc* (对某人)直觉的感觉、(对某事)直觉的态度、(对某事物)直觉的评价. (**b**) possessing intuition 有直觉力的: *Are women more intuitive than men?* 女子比男子的直觉力更强吗? **in·tu·it·ively** *adv*: *He seemed to know intuitively how to do it.* 他似乎凭直觉知道如何做.

in·tu·mes·cence /ˌɪntju:'mesns; *US* -tu:-; ˌɪntu'mɛsn̩s/ *n* [U, C] (*medical* 医) (process or condition of) swelling 隆起; 肿胀; 肿块; 疙瘩.

In·uit = INNUIT.

in·und·ate /'ɪnʌndeɪt; 'ɪnʌnˌdet/ *v* **1** [Tn, Tn·pr] **~ sth (with sth)** (*fml* 文) cover sth with water by overflowing; flood 泛滥; 淹没: *When the river burst its banks the fields were inundated.* 河岸决堤后, 田地遭洪水淹没. **2** [esp passive 尤用于被动语态: Tn, Tn·pr] **~ sb (with sth)** (*fig* 比喻) give or send sb so many things that he can hardly deal with them all; overwhelm 给予或交予某人很多事物使之难以应付; 使某人不胜负荷: *We were inundated with enquiries.* 查询的人很多, 我们应接不暇.

▷ **in·unda·tion** /ˌɪnʌn'deɪʃn; ˌɪnʌn'deʃən/ *n* [C, U] (*fml* 文) (instance of) flooding 泛滥; 淹没.

in·ure /ɪ'njʊə(r); ɪn'jur/ *v* [usu passive 通常用于被动语态: Tn, Tn·pr] **~ oneself/sb (to sth)** (*fml* 文) accustom oneself/sb (usu to sth unpleasant) 使自己[某人]习惯于(通常指厌恶的事物): *After living here for years I've become inured to the cold climate.* 我在此地居住多年, 已习惯寒冷的气候. ○ *One cannot inure oneself altogether to such malicious criticism.* 谁也不能总是忍受这种恶意批评.

in·vade /ɪn'veɪd; ɪn'ved/ *v* **1** (**a**) [I, Ipr, Tn, Tn·pr] **~ (sth) (with sth)** enter (a country or territory) with armed forces in order to attack, damage or occupy it 武装进入(一国或一领地); 侵犯; 侵入; 侵略: *He ordered the army to invade at dawn.* 他命令军队拂晓侵入该国. ○ *Alexander the Great invaded India with a large army.* 亚历山大大帝曾率领大军入侵印度. (**b**) [Tn esp passive 尤用于被动语态] (*fig* 比喻) enter (sth) in large numbers, esp so as to cause damage; crowd into 涌入(某事物)(尤指为破坏); 侵袭: *The cancer cells may invade other parts of the body.* 癌细胞可能侵袭身体的其他部分. ○ *a city invaded by tourists* 游客大批涌入的城市 ○ *a mind invaded with worries, anxieties, etc* 充满烦恼、焦虑等的心境. **2** [Tn] interfere with (sth); intrude on 干扰(某事物); 侵扰: *invade sb's rights, privacy, etc* 侵犯某人的权利、隐私权等.

▷ **in·vader** *n* person or thing that invades 侵入的人或物; 武装进入者; 侵犯者.

in·valid[1] /ɪn'vælɪd; ɪn'vælɪd/ *adj* **1** not properly based or able to be upheld by reasoning 无适当根据的; 无道理的; 站不住脚的: *an invalid argument, assumption, claim, etc* 站不住脚的论据、没有根据的假定、没有道理的要求. **2** not usable; not officially acceptable (because of an incorrect detail or details); not legally recognized 无用的; 不能正式接受的; 法律上不承认的; 无效的: *A passport that is out of date is invalid.* 护照过期是无效的. ○ *an invalid will* 无效的遗嘱 ○ *declare a marriage invalid* 宣布一婚姻在法律上无效.

▷ **in·val·id·ate** /ɪn'vælɪdeɪt; ɪn'væləˌdet/ *v* [Tn] make (sth) invalid 使(某事物)无效或作废: *faulty logic which invalidated her argument* 造成她的论据不能成立的错误逻辑. **in·val·ida·tion** /ɪnˌvælɪ'deɪʃn; ɪnˌvælə'deʃən/ *n* [U] (action of) making sth invalid 无效; 作废: *The making of false statements could result in the invalidation of the contract.* 提供虚假资料可能导致合同失效. **in·va·lid·ity** /ˌɪnvə'lɪdətɪ; ˌɪnvə'lɪdətɪ/ *n* [U] state of being invalid 无根据; 无道理; 无用; 无效: *the invalidity of his passport* 他的护照之无效.

in·valid[2] /'ɪnvəlɪd, 'ɪnvəli:d; 'ɪnvəlɪd/ *n* person weakened through illness or injury; one who suffers from ill health for a very long time 病弱者; 伤残者; 久病者: *He has been an invalid all his life.* 他终身残废. ○ [attrib 作定语] *her invalid mother, father, etc* 她那长期抱病的母亲、父亲等 ○ *an invalid diet*, ie one planned for an invalid 伤病残者的规定饮食 ○ *an invalid chair*, ie one with wheels on for moving an invalid easily 轮椅.

▷ **in·valid** *v* **1** (idm 习语) **invalid sb 'home** send sb (esp a soldier) home (esp from abroad) because of ill health (因健康恶劣)遣送某人(尤指士兵)回家(尤指回国). **2** (phr v) **invalid sb out (of sth)** cause sb to leave (esp the armed forces) because of ill health (因健康恶劣)使某人离去, (尤指)退役: *He was invalided out of the army because of the wounds he received.* 他因负伤而退役.

in·val·id·ism /-ɪzəm; -ˌɪzəm/ *n* [U] long-lasting ill health 久病体弱: *a life of invalidism* 久病的一生.

in·va·lid·ity /ˌɪnvə'lɪdətɪ; ˌɪnvə'lɪdətɪ/ *n* [U] state of being an invalid 病弱; 伤残; 久病: [attrib 作定语] *an invalidity pension* 伤病残补助金.

in·valu·able /ɪn'væljʊəbl; ɪn'væljuəbl̩/ *adj* **~ (to sb/sth)** of value too high to be measured; extremely valuable 价值高得无法估量的; 极宝贵的: *an invaluable collection of paintings* 珍品画的收藏 ○ *invaluable help, advice, etc* 宝贵的帮助、意见等 ○ *Your help has been invaluable to us.* 你对我们的帮助是非常宝贵的.

NOTE ON USAGE 用法: A few adjectives have misleading 'negative' affixes such as *in-* or *-less*. 有几个形容词带有貌似'否定'的词缀, 如 in- 或 -less. **1 Invaluable** means 'extremely valuable'. ☆ **invaluable** 意思是'极有价值的'. It is not the opposite of **valuable,** which is **valueless** (or **worthless**). 这个词并不是 **valuable** 的反义词, **valuable** 的反义词是 **valueless**(或 **worthless**). **2 Priceless** means 'too valuable to be priced', ie 'having a very high price'. ☆ **priceless** 意思是'贵重得无法定出价格的', 即'价格非常高的'. **3 Innumerable** and **numberless** mean 'too many to be counted' or 'very numerous'. ☆ **innumerable** 和 **numberless** 意思是'多得数不清的'或'极多的'. **4 Flammable** and **inflammable** have the same meaning (opposite: **non-flammable**). ☆ **flammable** 和 **inflammable** 意思一样, 是'易燃的'(反义词是: **non-flammable** '不易燃的').

in·vari·able /ɪn'veərɪəbl; ɪn'vɛrɪəbl̩/ *adj* never changing; always the same; constant 永不变的; 始终如一的; 恒定的: *an invariable pressure, temperature, amount* 恒定的压力、温度、数量 ○ *a noun with an invariable plural* 复数形式不变的名词 ○ *his invariable courtesy* 他那一贯的谦恭有礼. ▷ **in·vari·ab·il·ity** /ɪnˌveərɪə'bɪlətɪ; ɪnˌvɛrɪə'bɪlətɪ/ *n* [U]. **in·vari·ably** /ɪn'veərɪəblɪ; ɪn'vɛrɪəblɪ/ *adv*: *She invariably* (ie always) *arrives late.* 她老是迟到.

in·va·sion /ɪn'veɪʒn; ɪn'veʒən/ *n* (**a**) [U] invading or being invaded 侵略; 侵犯: *suffer invasion by enemy forces* 遭受敌军的侵犯 ○ *the invasion of Poland by Germany in 1939* 1939年德国对波兰的侵略. (**b**) [C] instance of this 侵略; 侵犯: *an outrageous invasion of privacy* 对隐私权的粗暴侵犯.

in·vas·ive /ɪn'veɪsɪv; ɪn'vesɪv/ *adj* tending to spread harmfully 有扩散危害的; 扩散性的; 蔓延性的: *invasive cancer cells* 扩散性癌细胞.

in·vect·ive /ɪn'vektɪv; ɪn'vɛktɪv/ *n* [U] (*fml* 文) violent attack in words; abusive language 猛烈抨击; 咒骂: *a speech full of invective* 大张挞伐的讲话 ○ *let out a stream of invective* 破口大骂.

in·veigh /ɪn'veɪ; ɪn've/ *v* [Ipr] **~ against sb/sth** (*fml* 文) attack sb or sth violently in words 痛骂; 痛斥; 猛烈抨击: *inveigh against God, destiny, the elements, the* *system* 亵渎上帝、咒骂命运、诅咒天气、抨击该制度.

in·veigle /ɪnˈveɪgl; ɪnˈvegl/ *v* [Tn·pr] **~ sb into sth/doing sth** persuade sb to go somewhere or do sth by using flattery and deception 引诱; 诱惑; 哄骗: *She inveigled him into the house and robbed him while he slept.* 她把他骗进房子, 趁他睡着时偷走了他的东西. ○ *He inveigled them into buying a new car, even though they didn't really want one.* 他诱惑他们买了一辆新汽车, 其实他们并不真正需要.

in·vent /ɪnˈvent; ɪnˈvɛnt/ *v* [Tn] **1** make or design (sth that did not exist before); create by thought 发明; 创造: *Laszlo Biro invented the ball-point pen.* 拉斯洛·拜罗发明了圆珠笔. Cf 参看 DISCOVER 1. **2** (*often derog* 常作贬义) make up or think of (esp sth that does not exist or is not true) 虚构; 捏造; 胡编: *Use an invented name, such as Anytown, not a real one.* 瞎编个名字吧, 比方叫'A城'吧, 别用真名. ○ *Can't you invent a better excuse than that?* 你就不能编造一个高明些的借口吗?

▷ **in·vent·ive** /ɪnˈventɪv; ɪnˈvɛntɪv/ *adj* **1** [attrib 作定语] of or for invention 发明的; 创造的: *using one's inventive powers* 发挥自己的发明创造才能. **2** (*approv* 褒) having or showing the ability to invent things and think originally 善于发明创造的; 具有创造性思考能力的: *an inventive mind* 有发明创造力的头脑 ○ *an inventive design* 独创性的设计.

in·ventor *n* person who invents things 发明者; 发明家; 创造者.

in·ven·tion /ɪnˈvenʃn; ɪnˈvɛnʃən/ *n* **1** [U] (**a**) action of inventing 发明; 创造; 虚构; 捏造: *the invention of radio by Marconi* 马可尼对无线电的发明 ○ *a story of one's own invention*, ie invented by oneself 自己杜撰的故事. (**b**) capacity for inventing 发明或创造的才能; 虚构或捏造的能力. (**c**) (*euph* 婉) making up of untrue or unreal things; lying 虚构; 捏造; 造假; 撒谎: *I'm afraid he is guilty of a good deal of invention.* 我看他撒了很多谎. **2** [C] thing that is invented 发明物: *the scientific inventions of the 20th century* 20世纪的科技发明. **3** (idm 习语) **necessity is the mother of invention** ⇨ NECESSITY.

in·vent·ory /ˈɪnvəntrɪ; *US* -tɔːrɪ; ˈɪnvən,torɪ/ *n* detailed list, eg of goods, furniture, jobs to be done 详细目录, 清单(如商品、家具、要做的事的单子): *keep/make a full, complete, careful inventory (of sth)* 记录[开列](某事物的)详尽的、完整的、仔细的清单.

▷ **in·vent·ory** *v* (*pt, pp* **-ried**) [Tn] make an inventory of (sth); put in an inventory 列出(某事物)的清单; 编入目录: *inventory the contents of a house* 列出房子内各项物品的清单 ○ *These items have not been inventoried yet.* 这些物品尚未编入目录.

in·verse /ˌɪnˈvɜːs; ɪnˈvɝs/ *adj* [usu attrib 通常作定语] reversed in position, direction or relation (位置、方向或关系)相反的, 反向的: *The number of copies the paper sells seems to be in ˌinverse ˈratio/proˈportion to the amount of news it contains*, ie The more news, the fewer copies it sells. 这种报纸的销售量似乎与刊登的新闻多寡成反比(新闻越多, 销售量越少).

▷ **in·verse** /ˈɪnvɜːs; ɪnˈvɝs/ *n* **the inverse** [sing] **1** (*esp mathematics* 尤用于数学) inverted state 反数; 倒数: *The inverse of 2 ($\frac{2}{1}$) is $\frac{1}{2}$.* 2(即 $\frac{2}{1}$)的倒数是 $\frac{1}{2}$. **2** direct opposite 相反; 颠倒; 反面: *This is the inverse of his earlier proposition.* 这和他早些时候提的建议截然相反.

in·versely /ɪnˈvɜːslɪ; ɪnˈvɝslɪ/ *adv*: *inversely proportional to each other* 互成反比.

in·ver·sion /ɪnˈvɜːʃn; *US* ɪnˈvɜːrʒn; ɪnˈvɝʒən/ *n* [U, C] (**a**) inverting or being inverted; instance of this 倒置; 倒转; 颠倒: *(an) inversion of word order* 词序的倒装. (**b**) (*music* 音) (arrangement of a) chord[1] with a different note in the first or basic position 转位; 转回: *A chord of C major with E in the bass is in the 1st inversion.* 用E做最低音的C大调主和弦是第一转位.

invert /ɪnˈvɜːt; ɪnˈvɝt/ *v* [Tn] put (sth) upside down or in the opposite order, position or arrangement 使(某物)倒置、倒转或颠倒: *invert a glass* 把玻璃杯倒过来 ○ *invert the word order in a sentence* 颠倒句中的词序.

□ **inˌverted ˈcommas** (*Brit*) quotation-marks, ie ' ' or " " 引号(' '或" "). ⇨App 3 见附录3.

inˌverted ˈsnob (*derog* 贬) person who unnecessarily finds fault with things of good quality or things which suggest wealth or social superiority; one who wishes to prove that he is not a snob 反面势利眼(对高级物品横加挑剔的人; 想证明自己并非势利眼的人). **inˌverted ˈsnobbery** attitude or behaviour of such a person 反面势利眼的态度或行为.

in·ver·teb·rate /ɪnˈvɜːtɪbreɪt; ɪnˈvɝtə,bret/ *n, adj* (animal) not having a backbone or spinal column 无脊椎的(动物): *Molluscs, insects and worms are all invertebrates.* 软体动物、昆虫、蠕虫都是无脊椎动物.

in·vest /ɪnˈvest; ɪnˈvɛst/ *v* **1** [I, Ipr, Tn, Tn·pr] **~ (sth) (in sth/with sb)** use (money) to buy shares, property, etc, in order to earn interest or bring profit 投资; 投资于: *The best time to invest is now.* 现在是投资的最佳时机. ○ *invest £1 000 (in government bonds)* 投资1 000英镑(于公债) ○ *invest (one's money) in a business enterprise* 把(自己的钱)投资于一企业 ○ *invest (money) with a firm* 向一公司投资. **2** [Tn·pr] **~ sth in sth/doing sth** give (time, effort, etc) to a particular task, esp in a way that involves commitment or self-sacrifice 为某任务付出(时间、精力等)(尤指涉及承诺或自我牺牲的): *invest one's time in learning a new language* 花时间学习一种新语言 ○ *invest all one's efforts in passing an exam* 为考试及格而全力以赴 ○ *She's invested a lot of emotional energy in that business.* 她为那事费尽心血. **3** [Ipr] **~ in sth** (*infml* 口) buy sth expensive but useful 购买价钱高的有用之物: *I'm thinking of investing in a new car.* 我打算花一笔钱买辆新汽车. **4** [Tn·pr, Cn·n/a] **~ sb (with sth/as sth)** (*fml* 文) confer a rank, an office or power on sb 授予某人官阶、职位或权力: *The governor has been invested with full authority to act.* 总督已获全权进行处理. ○ *Prince Charles was invested as Prince of Wales in 1969.* 查尔斯王子于1969年受封为威尔士亲王. **5** [Tn·pr] **~ sb/sth with sth** (*fml* 文) cause sb/sth to have a quality 赋予某人[某事物]以某种性质: *The crimes committed there invested the place with an air of mystery and gloom.* 在那里发生罪案后, 该地笼罩上一种阴森诡秘的气氛. **6** [Tn] (*dated* 旧) surround (a fort, town, etc) with armed forces 包围(要塞、城镇等).

▷ **in·vest·ment** *n* **1** [U] **~ (in sth)** investing of money 投资: *make a profit by careful investment* 谨慎投资以赚取利润. **2** [C] **~ (in sth)** (**a**) sum of money that is invested 投资额: *an investment of £500 in oil shares* 金额为500英镑的石油股分投资. (**b**) company, etc in which money is invested 接受投资的公司等: *Those oil shares were a good investment*, ie have been profitable. 那些石油股票是有利可图的投资. **3** = INVESTITURE.

in·vestor *n* person who invests money 投资者.

in·vest·ig·ate /ɪnˈvestɪgeɪt; ɪnˈvɛstə,get/ *v* **1** [I, Tn, Tw] find out and examine (all the facts about sth) in order to obtain the truth 调查; 侦查: *The police were baffled, and Sherlock Holmes was called in to investigate.* 警方被难住了, 于是请福尔摩斯前来侦查. ○ *Scientists are investigating to find out the cause of the crash/are investigating how the crash occurred.* 科学家们正在调查失事的原因[事故是如何发生的]. ○ *The police are investigating the murder.* 警方正在调查那起凶杀案. **2** [Tn] find out detailed facts about (sb or his character) by questioning, observation, etc 审问; 审查: *Applicants for government posts are always thoroughly investigated before being appointed.* 申请担任政府公职的人总要经过彻底审查才能受到委任. **3** [Tn] try to discover (sth) by detailed study, research, etc 详细研究; 调查; 查明: *investigate the market for a product, ways of increasing profits, etc* 对某商品、增加利润的方法等作市场调查 ○ *We might be able to help you; I'll investigate the possibilities.* 我们也许能帮助你, 我要研究一下这种可能性. **4** [I] (*infml* 口) make a brief check 作简短的检查: *'What was that noise outside?' 'I'll just go and investigate.'* '外面是什么声音?' '我去查看一下.'

▷ **in·vest·iga·tion** /ɪnˌvestɪˈgeɪʃn; ɪnˌvɛstəˈgeʃən/ *n* (**a**) [U] investigating or being investigated 调查研究: *The matter is under investigation.* 事情正在调查中. ○ *It is subject to investigation*, ie It must be investigated. 那事得进行调查. (**b**) [C] **~ (into sth)** instance of this 调查研究: *Scientists are conducting an investigation into the causes of the accident.* 科学家们就事故的原因正展开调查. ○ *carry out fresh investigations* 重新调查.

in·vest·ig·at·ive /ɪnˈvestɪgətɪv; *US* -geɪtɪv; ɪnˈvɛstə,getɪv/,

in·vest·ig·at·ory /ɪnˈvestɪgeɪtərɪ; *US* -gətɔːrɪ; ɪnˈvɛstəgə-ˌtorɪ/ *adjs* of or concerned with investigating 调查的; 侦查的; 审问的; 审查的: *investigative/investigatory methods used by the police* 警方采取的调查方式 ○ *investigative journalism*, ie in which reporters try to uncover important facts of public interest which have been concealed 调查性质的新闻报道(记者追查并揭露被掩饰的公众关心的重要事实).

in·vest·ig·ator /ɪnˈvestɪgeɪtə(r); ɪnˈvɛstəˌgetɚ/ *n* person who investigates 调查者; 侦查员; 审阅者; 审查者: *accident investigators who find out the causes of air crashes* 飞机失事原因的事故调查人员 ○ *insurance investigators* 保险事故调查人员.

in·vest·it·ure /ɪnˈvestɪtʃə(r); *US* -tʃʊər; ɪnˈvɛstətʃɚ/ (also **in·vest·ment**) *n* [U, C] ceremony of conferring an office, a rank or power on sb 对某人授职、授衔或授权的仪式: *the investiture of the Prince of Wales* 册封威尔士亲王的仪式.

in·vet·er·ate /ɪnˈvetərət; ɪnˈvɛtərɪt/ *adj* (*derog* 贬) **1** (of bad feelings, habits, etc) that have lasted a long time and seem likely to continue (指恶感、陋习等)根深蒂固的, 由来已久的: *inveterate hatred, prejudice, drunkenness, etc* 根深蒂固的仇恨、由来已久的偏见、长醉不醒的状态. **2** (of people) habitually doing the specified bad thing; addicted (指人)有恶习的, 成瘾的: *an inveterate smoker, drinker, gambler, liar, etc* 积习已久的烟鬼、酒徒、赌棍、撒谎家等. ▷ **in·vet·er·ately** *adv*.

in·vidi·ous /ɪnˈvɪdɪəs; ɪnˈvɪdɪəs/ *adj* likely to cause resentment or unpopularity (esp because it is or seems to be unjust) 易招怨恨的, 引起不满的(尤因不公正): *an invidious comparison, distinction, argument, etc* 招人反感的对比、区分、论证等 ○ *You put me in an invidious position by asking me to comment on my colleague's work.* 你要我评论同事的工作, 这无异置我于招人怨尤的境地. ▷ **in·vidi·ously** *adv*. **in·vidi·ous·ness** *n* [U].

in·vi·gil·ate /ɪnˈvɪdʒɪleɪt; ɪnˈvɪdʒəˌlet/ *v* [I, Ipr, Tn] ~ **(at sth)** (*Brit*) be present during (an examination) to make sure that it is properly conducted, that no cheating occurs, etc (在考场上)监考: *invigilate (at) a history exam* 监考历史.

▷ **in·vi·gila·tion** /ɪnˌvɪdʒɪˈleɪʃn; ɪnˌvɪdʒɪˈleʃən/ *n* [C, U] (instance of) invigilating or being invigilated 监考: *pupils under invigilation* 在监考中应考的学生.

in·vi·gil·ator /ɪnˈvɪdʒɪleɪtə(r); ɪnˌvɪdʒɪˈletɚ/ *n* person who invigilates 监考人.

in·vig·or·ate /ɪnˈvɪgəreɪt; ɪnˈvɪgəˌret/ *v* [I, Tn] make (sb) feel more lively and healthy 使(某人)感觉健壮有精神: *I feel invigorated by all this fresh air!* 空气很清新, 我觉得精神焕发!

▷ **in·vig·or·at·ing** *adj* that invigorates 使人健壮; 使人有精神的: *an invigorating climate, morning, swim, walk* 使人爽快的气候、早晨、游泳、散步. **in·vig·or·at·ingly** *adv*.

in·vin·cible /ɪnˈvɪnsəbl; ɪnˈvɪnsəbḷ/ *adj* too strong to be overcome or defeated 不能克服的; 不可战胜的; 不能征服的: *an invincible army* 不可战胜的军队 ○ (*fig* 比喻) *an invincible will* 坚强的意志. ▷ **in·vin·cib·il·ity** /ɪnˌvɪnsəˈbɪlətɪ; ɪnˌvɪnsəˈbɪlətɪ/ *n* [U]: *the apparent invincibility of their forces* 他们部队的凛然不可侵犯的气概. **in·vin·cibly** /ɪnˈvɪnsəblɪ; ɪnˈvɪnsəblɪ/ *adv*.

in·vi·ol·able /ɪnˈvaɪələbl; ɪnˈvaɪələbḷ/ *adj* (*fml* 文) that must not be violated or dishonoured 不可侵犯的; 不可违背的; 不可亵渎的: *The people possess inviolable rights.* 人民享有不可侵犯的权利. ○ *an inviolable oath, law, treaty* 不容违背的誓言、法律、条约. ▷ **in·vi·ol·ab·il·ity** /ɪnˌvaɪələˈbɪlətɪ; ɪnˌvaɪələˈbɪlətɪ/ *n* [U]. **in·vi·ol·ably** /ɪnˈvaɪələblɪ; ɪnˈvaɪələblɪ/ *adv*.

in·vi·ol·ate /ɪnˈvaɪələt; ɪnˈvaɪəlɪt/ *adj* [usu pred 通常作表语] ~ **(from sth)** (*fml* 文) that has not been or cannot be violated or harmed 未受侵犯; 不可侵犯; 未受破坏; 不可破坏: *The treaty remained/stood inviolate*, ie was not broken. 没有违反该条约的现象. ○ *They considered themselves inviolate from attack.* 他们认为自己是不可侵犯的.

in·vis·ible /ɪnˈvɪzəbl; ɪnˈvɪzəbḷ/ *adj* **1** ~ **(to sb/sth)** that cannot be seen; not visible 看不见的; 不可见的: *distant stars that are invisible to the naked eye*, ie that cannot be seen except with a telescope or binoculars 肉眼看不到的遥远的星球. **2** [usu attrib 通常作定语] (*commerce* 商) in the form of services (eg banking, insurance, tourism, etc) rather than goods or raw materials 服务业形式的(如银行、保险、旅游等); 非贸易的; 无形的: *invisible exports/trade* 无形输出[贸易]. ▷ **in·vis·ib·il·ity** /ɪnˌvɪzəˈbɪlətɪ; ˌɪnvɪzəˈbɪlətɪ/ *n* [U]. **in·vis·ibly** /ɪnˈvɪzəblɪ; ɪnˈvɪzəblɪ/ *adv*.

□ **inˌvisible ˈink** ink which, when used for writing, cannot be seen until specially treated, eg by heat 隐形墨水(需经特殊处理方可显现字迹, 如加热).

inˌvisible ˈmending repair of woven materials, etc by interweaving threads so that the repair is hardly noticeable 织补.

in·vite /ɪnˈvaɪt; ɪnˈvaɪt/ *v* **1** [Tn, Tn·pr, Dn·t] ~ **sb (to/for sth)** (**a**) ask sb in a friendly way to go somewhere or do sth (朋友般地)邀请, 约请: *'Are you coming to the party?' 'No, I haven't been invited.'* '你来参加聚会吗?' '不, 我没有受到邀请.' ○ *invite sb for/to dinner/to have dinner* 请某人吃饭 ○ *invite sb home/to one's house* 邀请某人到家中作客 ○ *invite sb to a party/to come to a party* 邀请某人参加聚会. (**b**) ask sb formally to go somewhere or do sth (正式地)邀请, 约请: *Candidates will be invited for interview early next month.* 下月初将约请候选人面试. ○ *I've been invited to give a talk at the conference.* 我已受邀在大会上发言. **2** [Tn, Tn·pr] ~ **sth (from sb)** ask for (comments, suggestions, etc) 请求、要求或征求(意见、建议等): *After his speech he invited questions and comments (from the audience).* 他讲完话后请听众提问题和意见. **3** [Tn] act so as to be likely to cause (sth bad) usu without intending to 引起, 招致(坏的事物)(通常并非本意): *Leaving your car unlocked is just inviting trouble!* 汽车不锁上纯粹是自找麻烦! ○ *behaviour that is sure to invite criticism, hostility, ridicule, etc* 肯定招致批评、敌视、嘲笑等的行为. **4** [Tn, Cn·t] attract (sb/sth); tempt 吸引(某人[某事物]); 引诱: *Cover the jam! It's sure to invite the wasps.* 盖上果酱瓶! 要不准得招黄蜂. ○ *Leaving the windows open is inviting thieves to enter.* 窗户不关犹如开门揖盗. **5** (phr v) **invite sb along** ask sb to accompany one 邀某人作伴. **invite sb away** ask sb to go away with one, eg on holiday 邀某人同行(如度假). **invite sb back** (**a**) ask sb to return with one to one's home 邀某人回自己家里(作客): *Shall we invite them back after the theatre?* 看完戏我们把他们邀回家去好吗? (**b**) ask sb who has been one's host to come to one's home as a guest 回请(被人请后, 还请对方). **invite sb down** ask sb to come for a visit at some distance, esp in the country or by the sea 邀请某人自远方来(尤指到乡间或海滨): *They've invited us down to their country cottage for the weekend.* 他们邀请我们到他们的乡间小屋去度周末. **invite sb in** ask sb to enter a room, house, etc 请某人进入房间、房子等. **invite sb out** ask sb to come out with one for a walk, a ride, entertainment, etc, esp for the purpose of courting 邀请某人一同出外散步、骑马、开车、娱乐等(尤指为谈情说爱). **invite sb over/round** ask sb to visit one's home 邀请某人到家中作客: *I've invited the Smiths round for drinks next Friday.* 我已邀请史密斯一家下周五来家中小酌. **invite sb up** ask sb to come upstairs 请某人上楼来.

▷ **in·vita·tion** /ˌɪnvɪˈteɪʃn; ˌɪnvəˈteʃən/ *n* **1** [U] inviting or being invited 邀请: *a letter of invitation* 邀请信 ○ *Admission is by invitation only.* 凭请柬入场. **2** [C] ~ **(to sth/to do sth)** request to go or come somewhere, or do sth 敦请某人去或来某处或做某事: *send out invitations to a party* 发出宴会请帖 ○ *I gladly accepted their invitation to open the fête.* 我愉快地接受了他们的邀请, 为义卖会主持开幕式. ○ [attrib 作定语] *an invitation card* 请帖. **3** [C usu *sing* 通常作单数] ~ **to sb/sth (to do sth)** that which tempts or encourages sb to do sth 引诱、鼓励或怂恿(某人做某事)的事物: *An open window is an invitation to burglars/an invitation to crime.* 窗户开着会引贼入室[引发窃案].

in·vite /ˈɪnvaɪt; ˈɪnvaɪt/ *n* (*infml* 口) invitation, eg to a party 邀请(如赴宴): *Did you get an invite?* 你接到邀请了吗?

in·vit·ing /ɪnˈvaɪtɪŋ; ɪnˈvaɪtɪŋ/ *adj* tempting; attractive 诱人的; 动人的: *an inviting look, smell, prospect, idea* 诱人的样子、气味、前景、主意 ○ *an inviting smile, place, meal* 动人的微笑、吸引人的场所、诱人的美餐. **in·vit·ingly** *adv*.

in vitro /ˌɪnˈviːtrəʊ; ɪnˈvitro/ (*Latin* 拉) (*biology* 生) (of the fertilization of an egg) by artificial means outside the body of the mother (指卵子受精)在母体外(人工授精): ˌ*in vitro fertiliˈzation* 体外受精 ○ *an egg fertilized in vitro* 体外受精的卵子.

in·voca·tion ⇨ INVOKE.

in·voice /ˈɪnvɔɪs; ˈɪnvɔɪs/ *n* ~ **(for sth)** (*commerce* 商) list of goods sold or services provided with the price(s) charged, esp sent as a bill 发票; 发货清单; 服务费用清单: *make out an invoice for the goods* 开发货清单.

▷ **in·voice** *v* (*commerce* 商) **1** [Tn] make a list of (such goods) 开(货物)的发票: *invoice the orders, goods, etc* 开定单、货物等的发票. **2** [Tn, Tn·pr] ~ **sb (for sth)**/~ **sth to sb** send such a list to sb, esp as a request for payment 给某人开发票(尤指要求付款的): *invoice sb (for an order, for goods, etc)* 给某人开(定单、货物等的)发票.

in·voke /ɪnˈvəʊk; ɪnˈvok/ *v* (*fml* 文) **1** [Tn] use (sth) as a reason for one's action 援用(某事物)为行动依据或理由: *The government has invoked the Official Secrets Act in having the book banned.* 政府援引国家机密保密法以禁该书. **2** [Tn] (**a**) call upon (God, the power of the law, etc) for help or protection 祈求(上帝)的保佑; 求助于(法律的力量等). (**b**) summon (sth) up (as if) by magic (似)用法术召唤(某事物): *invoke evil spirits* 用法术召来恶鬼. **3** [Tn, Tn·pr] ~ **sth (on/upon sb/sth)** beg for sth (as if) by praying (似)以祷告祈求某事物: *invoke help, assistance, etc in a desperate situation* 在走投无路时祈祷求救、求助等 ○ *invoke vengeance (up)on one's enemies* 求神降祸给敌人.

▷ **in·voca·tion** /ˌɪnvəˈkeɪʃn; ˌɪnvəˈkeʃən/ *n* ~ **(to sb)** (**a**) [U] invoking or being invoked 援用; 求助于神或法律; 用法术召唤; 祷告祈求. (**b**) [C] instance of this 援用; 求助于神或法律; 用法术召唤; 祷告祈求.

in·vol·un·tary /ɪnˈvɒləntrɪ; *US* -terɪ; ɪnˈvɑlənˌtɛrɪ/ *adj* done without intention; done unconsciously 非有意的; 无意的; 无意识的; 不自觉的: *an involuntary movement of surprise*, eg jumping when startled 因吃惊而引起的不自觉的动作(如吓得跳起来). Cf 参看 VOLUNTARY[1].

▷ **in·vol·un·tar·ily** /ɪnˈvɒləntrəlɪ; *US* ɪnˌvɒlənˈterəlɪ; ɪnˈvɑlənˌtɛrəlɪ/ *adv*. **in·vol·un·tari·ness** *n* [U].

in·vol·ute /ˈɪnvəluːt; ˈɪnvəˌlut/ (also **in·volu·ted**) *adj* **1** complex or intricate 复杂的; 纷繁的. **2** (*botany* 植) (esp of leaves or petals in bud and of shells) curling inwards at the edges (尤指叶片或花蕾的瓣及甲壳)边缘向内卷曲的, 内卷的, 内旋的. ▷ **in·volu·tion** /ˌɪnvəˈluːʃn; ˌɪnvəˈluʃən/ *n* [U, C].

in·volve /ɪnˈvɒlv; ɪnˈvɑlv/ *v* **1** [Tn, Tg, Tsg] make (sth) necessary as a condition or result; entail 使(某事物)成为必要条件或结果; 需要: *The scheme involves computers.* 这一设计离不开计算机. ○ *The job involved me/my living in London.* 工作需要我住在伦敦. **2** [Tn] include or affect (sb/sth) in its operation 包括, 包含, 牵涉, 牵连(某人[某事物]): *The strike involved many people.* 许多人参加了罢工. ○ *a situation in which national security is involved* 涉及国家安全的形势. **3** [Cn·pr] (**a**) ~ **sb/sth in (doing) sth** cause sb/sth to take part in (an activity or a situation) 使某人[某事物]参与某活动或陷入某情况: *Don't involve me in solving your problems!* 你解决你的问题, 不要把我拉进去! (**b**) ~ **sb/sth in sth** bring sb/sth into (a difficult situation) 使某人[某事物]陷入(困境): *involve sb in expense, a lot of trouble* 使某人破费、招惹许多麻烦 ○ *He was involved in a heated argument.* 他参与了一场激烈的争论. (**c**) ~ **sb in sth** show sb to be concerned in (a crime, etc) 表明某人与(某罪行等)有关联: *The witness's statement involves you in the robbery.* 证人的证词表明你与劫案有涉.

▷ **in·volved** *adj* **1** complicated in thought or form (思想或形式上)复杂的: *an involved sentence, explanation, style of writing, etc* 复杂的句子、解释、文体等. **2** (**a**) ~ **(in sth)** concerned (with sth) (与某事物)有关联的: *be/become/get involved in politics, criminal activities, etc* 与政治、犯罪活动等有关联. (**b**) ~ **(with sb)** (closely) connected (with sb) (与某人)有(密切)关系的: *become emotionally involved with sb* 与某人感情缠绵 ○ *He sees her often but doesn't want to get too involved.* 他常与她来往, 但不愿缱绻难分.

in·volve·ment *n* [U, C].

in·vul·ner·able /ɪnˈvʌlnərəbl; ɪnˈvʌlnərəbḷ/ *adj* **1** ~ **(to sth)** that cannot be wounded, hurt or damaged by attack 不能伤害的; 不能攻破的: *a fortification that is invulnerable to attack* 固若金汤的防御工事. **2** (*fig* 比喻) secure; safe 安全的; 保险的: *in an invulnerable position* 立于不败之地. ▷ **in·vul·ner·ab·il·ity** /ɪnˌvʌlnərəˈbɪlətɪ; ɪnˌvʌlnərəˈbɪlətɪ/ *n* [U].

in·ward /ˈɪnwəd; ˈɪnwərd/ *adj* **1** situated within; inner (esp in the mind or spirit) 内部的; 里面的; (尤指)内心的, 精神的: *inward thoughts, feelings, doubts, etc* 内心的思想、感情、怀疑等 ○ *sb's inward nature* 某人的心性. **2** turned towards the inside 向内的: *an inward curve* 向内的弧. Cf 参看 OUTWARD.

▷ **in·ward** (also **in·wards**) *adv* **1** towards the inside 向内: *toes turned inwards* 内曲的脚趾. **2** into or towards the mind or soul 进入内心或灵魂; 向内心或灵魂: *thoughts turned inwards* 转向内省的思想 ○ *be inward-looking*, ie introvert 性格内向. ⇨Usage at FORWARD[2] 用法见 FORWARD[2].

in·wardly *adv* **1** in mind or spirit 内心或精神方面: *inwardly grateful, relieved, etc* 内心铭感的、解脱的等 ○ *grieve inwardly*, ie not show one's grief 内心痛苦(不表露出来). **2** (idm 习语) **groan inwardly** ⇨ GROAN.

in·ward·ness *n* [U] spiritual quality 本性; 心性; 灵性: *the true inwardness of Christ's teaching* 基督教训的真谛.

iod·ine /ˈaɪədiːn; *US* -daɪn; ˈaɪəˌdaɪn/ *n* [U] **1** (*chemistry* 化) non-metallic element found in sea water and seaweed 碘. ⇨App 10 见附录 10. **2** solution of this used as an antiseptic 碘酒; 碘酊.

iod·ize, -ise /ˈaɪədaɪz; ˈaɪəˌdaɪz/ *v* [Tn] treat (a substance) with iodine or a compound of iodine 用碘酒或碘剂处理(某物).

IOM *abbr* 缩写 = Isle of Man 马恩岛.

ion /ˈaɪən; *US also* ˈaɪɒn; ˈaɪɒn/ *n* (*chemistry or physics* 化或物) electrically charged particle resulting from the breakdown of atoms through solution in water and making this solution a conductor of electricity 离子.

▷ **ion·ize, -ise** /ˈaɪənaɪz; ˈaɪənˌaɪz/ *v* [I, Tn esp passive 尤用于被动语态] be converted or convert (sth) into ions 电离; 使(某物)电离成离子. **ion·iza·tion, -isation** /ˌaɪənaɪˈzeɪʃn; *US* -nɪˈz-; ˌaɪənəˈzeʃən/ *n* [U].

-ion (also **-ation**, **-ition**, **-sion**, **-tion**, **-xion**) *suff* 后缀 (with *vs* forming *ns* 与动词结合构成名词) action or condition of ... 的动作或状态: *confession* ○ *hesitation* ○ *competition*.

Ionic /aɪˈɒnɪk; aɪˈɒnɪk/ *adj* (*architecture* 建) of the type of column(1) in ancient Greek architecture having scrolls on the capital[1](3) 爱奥尼亚柱式的(古希腊建筑风格, 柱顶有涡卷形装饰). Cf 参看 CORINTHIAN 2, DORIC.

iono·sphere /aɪˈɒnəsfɪə(r); aɪˈɑnəˌsfɪr/ *n* [sing] set of layers of the earth's atmosphere that reflect radio waves round the earth 电离层. Cf 参看 HEAVISIDE LAYER, STRATOSPHERE.

iota /aɪˈəʊtə; aɪˈotə/ *n* **1** the Greek letter I, i 希腊字母 I, i. **2** (*fig* 比喻) (esp in negative expressions 尤用于否定式) smallest amount 极少量: *not an iota of truth* (ie no truth at all) *in the story* 所说的没有一点真事.

IOU /ˌaɪ əʊ ˈjuː; ˈaɪˌoˈju/ *n* (*infml* 口) (*abbr* of *I owe you* I owe you 的缩写) signed paper acknowledging that one owes the sum of money stated 借据; 欠条: *give sb an IOU for £20* 给某人开具借款 20 英镑的字据.

IOW *abbr* 缩写 = Isle of Wight 怀特岛.

IPA /ˌaɪ piː ˈeɪ; ˈaɪˌpiˈe/ *abbr* 缩写 = International Phonetic Alphabet/Association 国际音标; 国际语音学协会.

ipso facto /ˌɪpsəʊ ˈfæktəʊ; ˈɪpsoˈfækto/ (*Latin* 拉) (*fml* 文) by that very fact 就该事实而论: *He was an outstanding pupil and, ipso facto, disliked by the rest of the class.* 他是优秀的学生, 正因为这个缘故, 全班都不喜欢他.

IQ /ˌaɪ ˈkjuː; ˌaɪ ˈkju/ *abbr* 缩写 = intelligence quotient (a comparative measure of a person's intelligence) 智商: *have a high/low IQ* 智商高[低] ○ *an IQ of 120* 智商 120.

ir- ⇨ IN-[2].

IRA /ˌaɪ ɑːr ˈeɪ; ˌaɪ ɑr ˈe/ *abbr* 缩写 = Irish Republican Army 爱尔兰共和军: *an IRA attack* 爱尔兰共和军的攻击 ○ *a member of the IRA* 爱尔兰共和军成员.

iras·cible /ɪˈræsəbl; ɪˈræsəbḷ/ *adj* (*fml* 文) (of a person) easily made angry (指人)易怒的, 性情暴躁的.

▷ **iras·cib·il·ity** /ɪˌræsəˈbɪlətɪ; ɪˌræsəˈbɪlətɪ/ *n* [U] tendency to become angry; angry behaviour 易怒; 性情暴躁.
iras·cibly /ɪˈræsəblɪ; ɪˈræsəblɪ/ *adv*.

ir·ate /aɪˈreɪt; aɪˈret/ *adj* (*fml* 文) angry 发怒的; 愤怒的. ▷ **ir·ately** *adv*.

IRBM /ˌaɪ ɑː biː ˈem; ˌaɪ ɑr bi ˈɛm/ *abbr* 缩写 = intermediate-range ballistic missile 中程弹道导弹. Cf 参看 ICBM, MRBM.

ire /ˈaɪə(r); aɪr/ *n* [U] (*fml* 文) anger 愤怒.

iri·des·cent /ˌɪrɪˈdesnt; ˌɪrəˈdɛsn̩t/ *adj* (*fml* 文) **1** showing colours like those of the rainbow 彩虹色的. **2** changing colour as its position changes (因位置改动)变色的: *jewels sparkling with iridescent colours* 闪烁着奇光异彩的珠宝. ▷ **iri·des·cence** /-ˈdesns; -ˈdɛsn̩s/ *n* [U].

iri·dium /ɪˈrɪdɪəm; ɪˈrɪdɪəm/ *n* [U] (*chemistry* 化) hard white metallic element of the platinum group 铱. ⇨App 10 见附录10.

iris /ˈaɪərɪs; ˈaɪrɪs/ *n* **1** (*anatomy* 解) coloured part round the pupil of the eye 虹膜. ⇨illus at eye 见 EYE 插图. **2** any of various types of tall plant with sword-shaped leaves and large bright flowers 鸢尾属植物(株高, 叶呈剑状, 花大色艳). Cf 参看 FLAG[4]. ⇨illus at App 1 见附录1插图, page ii.

Ir·ish /ˈaɪərɪʃ; ˈaɪrɪʃ/ *adj* of Ireland, its culture, language or people 爱尔兰的; 爱尔兰文化的; 爱尔兰语的; 爱尔兰人的: *the Irish Republic*, ie Eire 爱尔兰共和国.
▷ **Ir·ish** *n* **1 the Irish** [pl] the Irish people 爱尔兰人. **2** (also **Erse**) [U] the Celtic language of Ireland 爱尔兰凯尔特语.
□ ˌ**Irish** ˈ**coffee** hot coffee mixed with whiskey and having thick cream on top 爱尔兰咖啡(掺威士忌和浓奶油的热咖啡).
ˈ**Irishman** /-mən; -mən/, ˈ**Irishwoman** *ns* (*pl* **-men** /-mən; -mən/, **-women** /-ˌwɪmɪn; -ˌwɪmɪn/) native of Ireland 爱尔兰人.
ˌ**Irish** ˈ**setter** (also **red setter**) type of dog with a silky reddish-brown coat 爱尔兰猎狗(被毛光滑, 呈红棕色).
ˌ**Irish** ˈ**stew** stew of mutton boiled with onions and other vegetables 炖羊肉(加洋葱及其他蔬菜).

irk /ɜːk; ɝk/ *v* [Tn] (esp in constructions with *it* 尤与 it 连用) be tiresome to (sb); annoy 使(某人)厌烦; 使烦恼: *It irks me to see money being wasted.* 我看着浪费金钱就讨厌. ○ *It irked him that she had thought of it first.* 她竟先想到那件事, 为此他很不痛快.
▷ **irk·some** /ˈɜːksəm; ˈɝksəm/ *adj* tiresome; annoying 令人厌烦的; 令人烦恼的: *an irksome task* 令人厌烦的工作 ○ *irksome complaints* 令人厌恶的牢骚.

iron 熨斗或烙铁

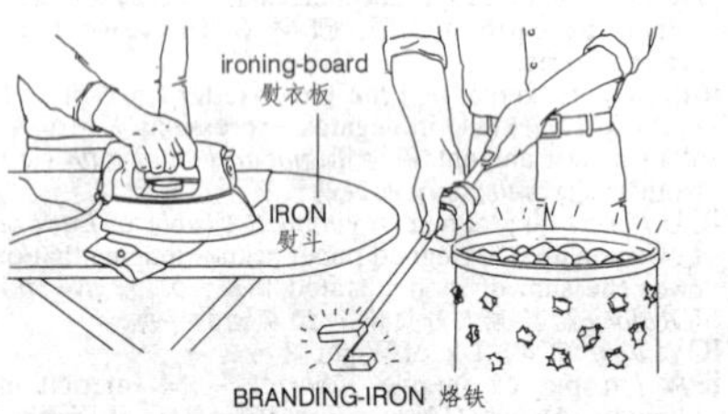

iron[1] /ˈaɪən; *US* ˈaɪərn; ˈaɪɚn/ *n* **1** [U] (*chemistry* 化) common hard silver-white metallic element capable of being magnetized and used in various forms 铁: *cast iron* 铸铁 ○ *wrought iron* 熟铁 ○ *scrap iron* 废铁 ○ *as hard as iron* 铁一般的坚硬 ○ [attrib 作定语] *iron ore*, ie rock containing iron 铁矿石 ○ *an iron bar, gate, railing*, ie made of iron 铁棒、铁门、铁栏. ⇨App 10 见附录10. **2** [C] implement with a smooth flat base that can be heated to smooth clothes, etc 熨斗: *a* ˈ*steam-iron* 蒸汽熨斗. ⇨illus 见插图. **3** [C] (esp in compounds 尤用以构成复合词) tool made of iron 铁制的工具: ˈ*fire-irons*, ie poker, tongs, etc used at a fireplace ○ *a* ˈ*branding-iron*, eg for marking cattle, etc. ⇨illus 见插图. **4** [C] golf-club with an iron or steel head (高尔夫球的)铁头球棒. Cf 参看 WOOD 4. **5** [C usu *pl* 通常作复数] metal splint or support worn on the leg (腿上用的)金属夹板或夹具. **6 irons** [pl] fetters 镣铐: *put/clap sb in irons*, ie fasten his wrists and ankles in chains 给某人戴上镣铐. **7** [U] a preparation of iron as a tonic 铁质补剂. **8** [U, esp attrib 尤作定语] (*fig* 比喻) (showing) physical strength or moral firmness or harshness 坚强; 刚强; 坚定; 冷酷: *have an iron constitution*, ie very good health 有钢铁般的强壮体魄 ○ *a man of iron* 铁汉 ○ *have a will of iron/an iron will* 有钢铁般的意志 ○ *impose an iron rule*, ie rule very strictly 施以铁腕. **9** (idm 习语) **an** ˌ**iron** ˌ**fist**/ˌ**hand in a** ˌ**velvet** ˈ**glove** an appearance of gentleness concealing severity, determination, etc 外柔内刚. **have many, etc irons in the fire** have many resources available or be involved in many undertakings at the same time 有多种现成手段; 同时参与很多事务. **rule with a rod of iron** ⇨ RULE. **strike while the iron is hot** ⇨ STRIKE[2].
□ **the** ˈ**Iron Age** the prehistoric period following the Bronze Age, when iron began to be used for making tools and weapons 铁器时代.
the ˌ**Iron** ˈ**Curtain** (*fig* 比喻) the frontier separating the former USSR and other communist countries of Eastern Europe from the West, seen by the West as a barrier to information and trade 铁幕(从西方观点看前苏联及东欧共产党国家与西方之间在信息、贸易等方面的屏障): *life behind the Iron Curtain* 铁幕后的生活 ○ [attrib 作定语] *Iron Curtain countries*, ie countries of the former Soviet bloc 铁幕国家(即前苏联集团各国).
ˈ**iron foundry** foundry where cast iron is produced 铸铁厂.
ˌ**iron-**ˈ**grey** *adj*, *n* (of the) colour of freshly broken cast iron 铁灰色(的): ˌ*iron-grey* ˈ*hair* 铁灰色的毛发.
ˌ**iron** ˈ**lung** metal case fitted over the whole body, except the head, to provide a person with prolonged artificial respiration by the use of mechanical pumps 铁肺; 人工呼吸器.
ˈ**iron-mould** (*US* **-mold**) *n* [U] brown mark caused by iron-rust or an ink-stain 铁锈迹; 墨迹.
ˌ**iron** ˈ**rations** small supply of (esp tinned) food to be used only in an emergency (by troops, explorers, etc) (部队或探险人员等的)应急口粮(尤指罐头食品).
ˈ**ironstone** *n* [U] **1** (also ˌ**ironstone** ˈ**china**) type of hard-wearing white pottery 硬质陶器; 坚质陶器. **2** hard iron ore 铁矿石.
ˈ**ironware** /-weə(r); -ˌwɛr/ *n* [U] (esp domestic) articles made of iron (尤指家用的)铁制用具.
ˈ**ironwork** *n* [U] things made of iron, eg gratings, rails, railings 铁制品(如格栅、铁轨、栏杆).
ˈ**ironworks** *n* [pl, usu sing *v* 通常与单数动词连用]; (*Brit*) place where iron is smelted or where heavy iron goods are made 钢铁厂.

iron[2] /ˈaɪən; *US* ˈaɪərn; ˈaɪɚn/ *v* **1** [I, Ip, Tn] smooth (clothes, etc) with an iron[1](2) (用熨斗)熨平(衣物等): *This material irons well/easily*, ie the creases come out quickly. 这种材料很好熨. ○ *She was ironing (away) all evening.* 她整个晚上都在熨衣服. ○ *I prefer to iron my shirts while they are still damp.* 我喜欢在衬衫尚潮湿时熨烫. **2** (phr v) **iron sth out** (**a**) remove sth by ironing 用熨烫方法去除某物: *iron out creases* 把皱褶熨平. (**b**) (*fig* 比喻) resolve sth by discussion 通过商讨解决: *iron out misunderstandings, problems, difficulties, etc* 消除误会、解决问题、排除困难.
▷ **iron·ing** *n* [U] **1** action of smoothing clothes with an iron 熨烫. **2** clothes that need to be or have just been ironed 待烫的衣物; 刚熨好的衣物: *do the ironing* 熨衣服.
□ ˈ**ironing-board** *n* padded board, usu fitted with adjustable legs, on which clothes are ironed 熨衣板. ⇨ illus at IRON 见 IRON 插图.

ironic /aɪˈrɒnɪk; aɪˈrɑnɪk/ (also **iron·ical** /aɪˈrɒnɪkl; aɪˈrɑnɪkl/) *adj* using or expressing irony; full of irony 用反语的; 有很多反语的; 讽刺的: *an ironic expression, smile, remark etc*, ie one showing that you do not expect to be taken seriously or literally 揶揄的表情、微笑、言语等 ○ *His death gave an ironic twist to the story*, eg because he died before he could enjoy the money he had stolen. 他这一死使整件事啼笑皆非(如偷了钱未及享用即已一命呜呼).

▷ **iron·ic·ally** /-klɪ; -klɪ/ *adv* **1** in an ironic manner 用反语或讽刺的方式: *He smiled ironically.* 他微笑中带有讽刺意味. **2** it seems ironic (that) 具有讽刺意味的(是…): *Ironically, most people came to watch the match on the day it poured with rain.* 老天爷好像成心捉弄人, 很多人前来看比赛却偏偏下起瓢泼大雨.

iron·mon·ger /ˈaɪənmʌŋɡə(r); ˋaɪɚn,mʌŋɡɚ/ *n* (*Brit*) (*US* ˈ**hardware dealer**) dealer in tools, household implements, etc 五金商人. ▷ ˈ**iron·mon·gery** /-mʌŋɡərɪ; -,mʌŋɡərɪ/ *n* [U] (*Brit*) (*US* **hardware**).

irony /ˈaɪərənɪ; ˋaɪrənɪ/ *n* **1** [U] expression of one's meaning by saying the direct opposite of one's thoughts in order to be emphatic, amusing, sarcastic, etc 反语; 反话: *'That's really lovely, that is!' he said with heavy irony.* '那真是可爱极了, 真的!' 他故意说反话. **2** [U, C] situation, event, etc that is desirable in itself but so unexpected or ill-timed that it appears to be deliberately perverse 有讽刺意味的情况、事情等(其本身未始不可取, 但因出人意料或来非其时而似故意乖违): *the irony of fate* 命运的嘲弄 ○ *He inherited a fortune but died a month later; one of life's little ironies.* 他继承一笔遗产后一个月就死了, 有点时乖命蹇吧.

ir·ra·di·ate /ɪˈreɪdɪeɪt; ɪˋredɪ,et/ *v* (*fml* 文) **1** [Tn, Tn·pr] **~ sth (with sth)** send rays of light upon sth; subject sth to sunlight, ultraviolet rays or radioactivity 照耀某物; (用阳光、紫外线或放射线)照射某物. **2** [Tn·pr esp passive 尤用于被动语态] **~ sth with sth** (*fig* 比喻) light up or brighten sth 使某事物生辉; 焕发: *faces irradiated with joy* 闪露着喜悦之光的脸.

ir·ra·tional /ɪˈræʃənl; ɪˋræʃənl̩/ *adj* **1** not guided by reason; illogical or absurd 没有道理的; 不合逻辑的; 荒谬的: *irrational fears, behaviour, arguments* 荒唐无稽的恐惧、行为、论据. **2** not capable of reasoning 无理性的: *behave like an irrational animal* 表现得像无理性的野兽. ▷ **ir·ra·tion·al·ity** /ɪ,ræʃəˈnælətɪ; ɪ,ræʃəˋnælətɪ/ *n* [U]. **ir·ra·tion·ally** /ɪˈræʃnəlɪ; ɪˋræʃənl̩ɪ/ *adv*.

ir·re·con·cil·able /ɪˈrekənsaɪləbl, ɪ,rekənˈsaɪləbl; ɪˋrɛkən,saɪləbl/ *adj* (*fml* 文) **~ (with sb/sth)** (**a**) (of people) that cannot be reconciled (指人)不能和解的. (**b**) (of ideas, actions) that cannot be brought into harmony with each other (指思想、行动)不能调和的: *We can never agree — our views are irreconcilable.* 我们永远不能一致——彼此的看法无法调和. ▷ **ir·re·con·cil·ably** /-əblɪ; -əblɪ/ *adv*.

ir·re·cov·er·able /,ɪrɪˈkʌvərəbl; ,ɪrɪˋkʌvərəbl̩/ *adj* (*fml* 文) that cannot be recovered or remedied 无法挽回的; 不能治愈的; 无法补救的: *suffer irrecoverable losses*, eg in business 遭受无法挽回的损失(如在商业中). ▷ **ir·re·cov·er·ably** /-əblɪ; -əblɪ/ *adv*.

ir·re·deem·able /,ɪrɪˈdiːməbl; ,ɪrɪˋdiməbl̩/ *adj* **1** (*finance* 财) (**a**) (of government annuities, bonds, shares, etc) that cannot be terminated by repayment (指政府年金, 债券、股票等)不能藉偿还而终止的. (**b**) (of paper money) that cannot be exchanged for money in coins (指纸币)不能兑成硬币的. **2** (*fml* 文) that cannot be restored, reclaimed or saved 不能恢复的; 不能收回的; 不能挽救的: *an irredeemable loss, misfortune, etc* 不能挽救的损失、不幸等. ▷ **ir·re·deem·ably** /-əblɪ; -əblɪ/ *adv* (*fml* 文).

ir·re·du·cible /,ɪrɪˈdjuːsəbl; *US* -ˈduːs-; ,ɪrɪˋdusəbl̩/ *adj* (*fml* 文) **1** that cannot be reduced or made smaller 不能减低的; 不能缩小的: *Expenditure on road repairs has been cut to an irreducible minimum.* 修路费已削减到不能再减的最低限度了. **2** that cannot be made simpler 不可简化的: *a problem of irreducible complexity* 复杂性不可简化的问题. ▷ **ir·re·du·cibly** /-əblɪ; -əblɪ/ *adv*.

ir·re·fut·able /,ɪrɪˈfjuːtəbl, *also* ɪˈrefjʊtəbl; ,ɪrɪˋfjutəbl, ɪˋrɛfjutəbl̩/ *adj* (*fml* 文) that cannot be proved false 驳不倒的: *an irrefutable argument* 无法反驳的论点 ○ *irrefutable evidence, proof, etc* 无法推翻的证据、证明等. ▷ **ir·re·fut·ably** /-əblɪ; -əblɪ/ *adv*: *irrefutably the greatest living violinist* 当今无可争议的最伟大的小提琴家.

ir·regu·lar /ɪˈregjʊlə(r); ɪˋrɛgjəlɚ/ *adj* **~ (in sth)** **1** not regular in shape, arrangement, etc; uneven (形状)不规则的; (安排)无规律的; 不平坦的: *a coast with an irregular outline*, eg with many bays, inlets, etc 曲折的海岸线(如有很多的海湾等). **2** not happening, coming, going, etc regularly; varying or unequal (发生、来、去等)无规律的; 变化的; 不均等的: *an irregular pulse* 不均匀的脉搏 ○ *occur at irregular intervals* 不定期发生 ○ *be irregular in attending class* 听课次数不定. **3** contrary to the rules or to what is normal or established 不规则的; 不合常规的; 非正规的: *an irregular practice, situation* 不合常规的做法、情况 ○ *keep irregular hours*, eg get up and go to bed at unusual times 不守常时(如不于正常时间起床和入睡) ○ *His behaviour is highly irregular.* 他的行为很不规矩. **4** (*grammar*) not inflected in the usual way 不规则(变化)的: *'Child' has an irregular plural, ie 'children'.* Child 一词的复数形式不规则, 即 children. ○ *irregular verbs* 不规则动词. ⇨App 2 见附录 2. **5** (of troops) not belonging to the regular armed forces (指部队)非正规的.

▷ **ir·regu·lar** *n* (usu *pl* 通常作复数) member of an irregular military force 非正规军成员.

ir·regu·lar·ity /ɪ,regjʊˈlærətɪ; ,ɪrɛgjəˋlærətɪ/ *n* **1** [U] state or quality of being irregular 不整齐; 不平坦; 无规律; 不规则; 不合常规. **2** [C] thing that is irregular 不整齐、不平坦、无规律、不规则或不合常规的事物: *the irregularities of the earth's surface* 地球表面的凹凸不平 ○ *There were some irregularities in the accounts*, eg figures that were not correct. 帐目中有些出入(如数字不确).

ir·regu·larly *adv*.

ir·rel·ev·ant /ɪˈreləvənt; ɪˋrɛləvənt/ *adj* **~ (to sth)** not connected (with sth); not relevant (to sth) (与某事物)不相关的, 无关系的; 不切题的: *irrelevant remarks* 不相关的言语 ○ *What you say is irrelevant to the subject.* 你说的话不切题.

▷ **ir·rel·ev·ance** /-əns; -əns/ *n* [U] state of being irrelevant 不相关; 无关系; 不切题.

ir·rel·ev·ancy /-ənsɪ; -ənsɪ/ *n* **1** [U] = IRRELEVANCE. **2** [C] irrelevant remark, question, etc 不相干的言语、问题等: *Let us ignore these irrelevancies.* 咱们不必管这些不相干的事.

ir·rel·ev·antly *adv*.

ir·re·li·gious /,ɪrɪˈlɪdʒəs; ,ɪrɪˋlɪdʒəs/ *adj* feeling no interest in, or feeling hostile to, religion; irreverent 漠视宗教的; 敌视宗教的; 不虔敬的: *an irreligious act, person* 反宗教的行为、人.

ir·re·me·di·able /,ɪrɪˈmiːdɪəbl; ,ɪrɪˋmidɪəbl̩/ *adj* (*fml* 文) that cannot be remedied or corrected 无可救药的; 不能补救的; 无法改正的: *an irremediable loss, mistake* 无法补救的损失、错误. ▷ **ir·re·me·di·ably** /-əblɪ; -əblɪ/ *adv*.

ir·re·mov·able /,ɪrɪˈmuːvəbl; ,ɪrɪˋmuvəbl̩/ *adj* that cannot be removed 不能移动的; 不能除去的.

ir·re·par·able /ɪˈrepərəbl; ɪˋrɛpərəbl̩/ *adj* (of a loss, an injury, etc) that cannot be put right, restored or repaired (指损失、伤害等)不可弥补的, 无法恢复的, 不能修补的: *irreparable damage, harm, etc* 无法修复的损坏、无可弥补的伤害. ▷ **ir·re·par·ably** /-əblɪ; -əblɪ/ *adv*.

ir·re·place·able /,ɪrɪˈpleɪsəbl; ,ɪrɪˋplesəbl̩/ *adj* that cannot be replaced if lost or damaged (若失掉或损坏时)不能替代的: *an irreplaceable antique vase, the only one of its kind* 一件举世无双、独一无二的古花瓶.

ir·re·press·ible /,ɪrɪˈpresəbl; ,ɪrɪˋprɛsəbl̩/ *adj* that cannot be held back or controlled 不能抑制的; 不能控制的: *irrepressible laughter, envy, high spirits, etc* 情不自禁的笑声、羡慕、高昂情绪等 ○ *You cannot keep her quiet for long; she's irrepressible!* 想让她多安静会儿可办不到, 她总是欢蹦乱跳的! ▷ **ir·re·press·ibly** /-əblɪ; -əblɪ/ *adv*.

ir·re·proach·able /,ɪrɪˈprəʊtʃəbl; ,ɪrɪˋprotʃəbl̩/ *adj* free from blame or fault 无可指责的; 无过失的: *irreproachable conduct* 无可指责的行为. ▷ **ir·re·proach·ably** /-əblɪ; -əblɪ/ *adv*.

ir·res·ist·ible /,ɪrɪˈzɪstəbl; ,ɪrɪˋzɪstəbl̩/ *adj* **1** too strong to be resisted (强大得)不可抵抗的: *an irresistible temptation, urge, impulse, etc* 无法抗拒的诱惑、强烈愿望、冲动等 ○ *His arguments were irresistible.* 他的论据是无从反驳的. **2** too delightful or attractive to be resisted (因讨人喜爱或吸引人)使人不能自己的: *On such a hot day, the sea was irresistible*, ie We couldn't resist the desire to swim in it. 天这么热, 我们不禁要下海游泳. ○ *With her beauty, wit and charm, he found her irresistible.* 她漂亮、聪明、帅气, 他不由得一见倾心. ▷ **ir·res·ist·ibly** /-əblɪ; -əblɪ/ *adv*.

ir·res·ol·ute /ɪˈrezəluːt; ɪˋrɛzə,lut/ *adj* (*fml* 文) feeling or showing uncertainty; hesitating 优柔寡断的; 犹豫不决的. ▷ **ir·res·ol·utely** *adv.* **ir·res·olu·tion** /ɪˌrezəˈluːʃn; ˌɪrɛzəˋluʃən/ *n* [U].

ir·re·spect·ive /ˌɪrɪˈspektɪv; ˌɪrɪˋspɛktɪv/ **irrespective of** *prep* not taking account of or considering (sth/sb) 不顾或不考虑(某事物[某人]): *The laws apply to everyone irrespective of race, creed or colour.* 法律适用于所有的人, 不分种族、信仰或肤色.

ir·re·spons·ible /ˌɪrɪˈspɒnsəbl; ˌɪrɪˋspɑnsəbl̩/ *adj* (of people, actions, etc) not showing a proper sense of responsibility (指人、行为等)不负责任的, 没有责任感的: *an irresponsible child* 没有责任感的孩子 ○ *irresponsible behaviour* 不负责任的行为 ○ *It is irresponsible of you not to prepare students for their exams.* 你不帮助学生准备考试就是不负责. Cf 参看 RESPONSIBLE 4. ▷ **ir·re·spons·ib·il·ity** /ˌɪrɪˌspɒnsəˈbɪlətɪ; ˌɪrɪˌspɑnsəˋbɪlətɪ/ *n* [U]. **ir·re·spons·ibly** /-əblɪ; -əblɪ/ *adv.*

ir·re·triev·able /ˌɪrɪˈtriːvəbl; ˌɪrɪˋtrivəbl̩/ *adj* (*fml* 文) that cannot be retrieved or remedied 不可挽回的; 不能补救的: *an irretrievable loss* 不可弥补的损失 ○ *The breakdown of their marriage was irretrievable.* 他俩婚姻破裂, 已无法和好如初. ▷ **ir·re·triev·ably** /-əblɪ; -əblɪ/ *adv.*

ir·rev·er·ent /ɪˈrevərənt; ɪˋrɛvərənt/ *adj* feeling or showing no respect for sacred things (对神圣之物)不敬的. ▷ **ir·rev·er·ence** /-əns; -əns/ *n* [U]. **ir·rev·er·ently** *adv.*

ir·re·vers·ible /ˌɪrɪˈvɜːsəbl; ˌɪrɪˋvɝsəbl̩/ *adj* that cannot be reversed or revoked; unalterable 不能反转的; 不能撤销的; 不能更改的: *He suffered irreversible brain damage in the crash.* 他在事故中大脑受伤无法治愈. ▷ **ir·re·vers·ibly** /-əblɪ; -əblɪ/ *adv.*

ir·re·voc·able /ɪˈrevəkəbl; ɪˋrɛvəkəbl̩/ *adj* (*fml* 文) that cannot be changed or revoked; final 不能改变的; 不能撤回的; 不能取消的; 最后确定性的: *an irrevocable decision, judgement, etc* 不可改变的决定、判决等 ○ (*finance* 财) *an irrevocable letter of credit* 不可撤销信用证. ▷ **ir·re·voc·ably** /-əblɪ; -əblɪ/ *adv.*

ir·rig·ate /ˈɪrɪgeɪt; ˋɪrəˌget/ *v* [Tn] **1** supply (land or crops) with water (by means of streams, reservoirs, channels, pipes, etc) 灌溉(田地或作物): *irrigate desert areas to make them fertile* 灌溉荒芜地区使之肥沃. **2** (*medical* 医) wash (a wound, etc) with a constant flow of liquid 冲洗(伤口等).

▷ **ir·rig·able** /ˈɪrɪgəbl; ˋɪrɪgəbl̩/ *adj* that can be irrigated 可灌溉的; 可冲洗的.

ir·riga·tion /ˌɪrɪˈgeɪʃn; ˌɪrəˋgeʃən/ *n* [U]: [attrib 作定语] *an irrigation project* 灌溉工程 ○ *irrigation canals* 灌溉渠.

ir·rit·able /ˈɪrɪtəbl; ˋɪrətəbl̩/ *adj* easily annoyed or made angry; touchy 急躁的; 易怒的; 暴躁的. ▷ **ir·rit·ab·il·ity** /ˌɪrɪtəˈbɪlətɪ; ˌɪrətəˋbɪlətɪ/ *n* [U]. **ir·rit·ably** /-əblɪ; -əblɪ/ *adv.*

ir·rit·ant /ˈɪrɪtənt; ˋɪrətənt/ *adj* causing irritation; irritating 有刺激性的; 刺激的: *a substance that is irritant to sensitive skins* 对敏感的皮肤有刺激性的物质.

▷ **ir·rit·ant** *n* (**a**) substance that irritates, eg pepper in the nose 刺激物(如呛到鼻子里的胡椒). (**b**) (*fig* 比喻) thing that annoys 令人烦恼的事物: *The noise of traffic is a constant irritant to city dwellers.* 车辆的噪音对城市居民是永无止境的骚扰.

ir·rit·ate /ˈɪrɪteɪt; ˋɪrəˌtet/ *v* [Tn] **1** make (sb) angry, annoyed or impatient 使(某人)愤怒、烦恼或急躁: *irritated by/at the delay* 受耽搁而恼怒 ○ *It irritates me to have to shout to be heard.* 我得大嚷大叫别人才能听见, 我为此十分不快. **2** (**a**) (*biology* 生) cause discomfort to (a part of the body) 使(身体某部)不适; 刺激: *Acid irritates the stomach lining.* 酸能刺激胃黏膜. (**b**) make sore or inflamed 使疼痛或发炎: *The smoke irritates my eyes.* 烟熏得我眼睛发痛.

▷ **ir·rita·tion** /ˌɪrɪˈteɪʃn; ˌɪrəˋteʃən/ *n* (**a**) [U] irritating or being irritated 愤怒; 烦恼; 急躁; 刺激; 疼痛; 发炎. (**b**) [C] instance of this 愤怒; 烦恼; 急躁; 刺激; 疼痛; 发炎.

ir·rup·tion /ɪˈrʌpʃn; ɪˋrʌpʃən/ *n* [C] (*fml* 文) **~ (into sth)** sudden and violent entry; bursting in 突然冲人; 闯入: *the irruption of a noisy group of revellers* 参加欢宴的喧闹人群一涌而人.

is ⇨ BE.

Is *abbr* 缩写 = Island(s); Isle(s): *(the) Windward Is*, ie Islands 向风群岛 ○ *(the) British Is*, ie Isles 不列颠群岛. Cf 参看 I *abbr* 缩写.

ISBN /ˌaɪ es biː ˈen; ˌaɪ ɛs bi ˋɛn/ *abbr* 缩写 = International Standard Book Number 国际标准图书编号: *ISBN 0 19 861131 5*, eg on the cover of a book ISBN 0 19 861131 5 (如印于书皮上的字样).

ISD /ˌaɪ es ˈdiː; ˌaɪ ɛs ˋdi/ *abbr* 缩写 = international subscriber dialling 国际电话用户拨号服务.

-ise ⇨ -IZE.

-ish *suff* 后缀 **1** (with *ns* forming *adjs* and *ns* 与名词结合构成形容词和名词) (language or people) of the specified nationality 某国家或某民族(语言或民族): *Danish* ○ *Irish*. **2** (with *ns* forming *adjs* 与名词结合构成形容词) (*esp derog* 尤作贬义) of the nature of; resembling ...性的; ...一样的; 像...似的: *childish* ○ *bookish* ○ *stand-offish*. **3** (with *adjs* 与形容词结合) somewhat; approximately 稍为...的; 有点儿...的: *reddish* ○ *twentyish*. ▷ **-ishly** (with sense 2 forming *advs* 按上述第2义构成副词).

is·in·glass /ˈaɪzɪŋglɑːs; *US* -glæs; ˋaɪzɪŋˌglæs/ *n* [U] clear white jelly from the air bladders of some freshwater fish, used for making jellies, glue, etc 鱼胶(用鱼鳔制成, 可制果冻及胶水等).

Is·lam /ɪzˈlɑːm; *US* ˈɪslɑːm; ˋɪsləm/ *n* **1** [U] Muslim religion, based on the teaching of the prophet Muhammad 伊斯兰教; 回教. **2** [sing] all Muslims; all the Muslim world (全体)伊斯兰教徒, 回教徒; 伊斯兰世界. ⇨ Usage at CHRISTIAN 用法见 CHRISTIAN. ▷ **Is·lamic** /ɪzˈlæmɪk; *US* ɪsˈlɑːmɪk; ɪsˋlɑmɪk/ *adj.*

is·land /ˈaɪlənd; ˋaɪlənd/ *n* **1** (*abbrs* 缩写 **I, Is**) piece of land surrounded by water 岛: *a group of tropical islands* 在热带的一些岛上 ○ [attrib 作定语] *The Shetlanders are an island race.* 设得兰人是岛屿民族. **2** = TRAFFIC ISLAND (TRAFFIC).

▷ **is·lander** *n* person living on an island, esp a small or an isolated one 岛民, 岛上居民(尤指小岛或孤岛上的).

isle /aɪl; aɪl/ *n* (*abbrs* 缩写 **I, Is**) (esp in poetry and proper names 尤用于诗歌和专有名词中) island 岛: *the Isle of Wight* 怀特岛 ○ *the British Isles* 不列颠群岛.

▷ **is·let** /ˈaɪlɪt; ˋaɪlɪt/ *n* small island 小岛.

ism /ˈɪzəm; ˋɪzəm/ *n* (*usu derog* 通常作贬义) any distinctive doctrine or practice 主义; 学说; 制度: *behaviourism and all the other isms of the twentieth century* 二十世纪的行为主义及一切其他学说.

-ism *suff* 后缀 **1** (with *vs* ending in *-ize* forming *ns* 与以 -ize 结尾的动词结合构成名词): *baptism* ○ *criticism*. **2** (**a**) (with *ns* forming *ns* 与名词结合构成名词) showing qualities typical of 表现有...的典型特征、特性或状态: *heroism* ○ *Americanism*. (**b**) (with proper *ns* forming uncountable *ns* 与专有名词结合构成不可数名词) doctrine, system or movement 主义、学说、体系或运动: *Buddhism* ○ *Communism*. (**c**) (with *ns* 与名词结合) medical condition or disease 病的状态; 疾病: *alcoholism*. (**d**) (with *ns* 与名词结合) practice of showing prejudice or discrimination because of 因...的偏见或歧视: *sexism* ○ *racism*.

isn't ⇨ BE.

is(o)- *comb form* 构词成分 equal 相同; 相等: *isobar* ○ *isometric*.

ISO /ˌaɪ es ˈəʊ; ˌaɪ ɛs ˋo/ *abbr* 缩写 = International Standardization/Standards Organization 国际标准化组织. Cf 参看 ASA 2, BSI.

iso·bar /ˈaɪsəbɑː(r); ˋaɪsəˌbɑr/ *n* line on a map, esp a weather chart, joining places with the same atmospheric pressure at a particular time 等压线.

isol·ate /ˈaɪsəleɪt; ˋaɪsl̩ˌet/ *v* [Tn esp passive 尤用于被动语态, Tn·pr] **1 ~sb/sth (from sb/sth)** put or keep sb/sth entirely apart from other people or things; separate sb/sth 使某人[某事物]与他人他事物完全隔离; 孤立某人[某事物]: *isolate a problem*, ie in order to deal with it separately 将一问题剔出(以便单独处理) ○ *When a person has an infectious disease, he is usually isolated (from other people).* 人患传染病时通常要(与他人)隔离. ○ *Several villages have been isolated by heavy snowfalls.* 下过大雪后有几个村子与外界隔绝了. **2 ~ sth (from sth)** (*chemistry* 化) separate (a single substance, germ, etc) from its combination with others 将(某物质、细菌等)从其种群中离析或分离出来:

Scientists have isolated the virus causing the epidemic. 科学家们已分离出引起这种流行病的病毒.

▷ **isol·ated** *adj* **1** separate; single or unique 隔离的; 分离的; 孤立的; 单独的; 独一无二的: *an isolated outbreak of smallpox* 局部地区的天花病突发 ○ *an isolated case, instance, occurrence, etc* 个别的事例、例子、现象等. **2** standing alone; solitary 孤立的; 孤独的: *an isolated building* 独立的建筑物 ○ *lead an isolated existence*, eg as a lighthouse-keeper 过着与世隔绝的生活(如灯塔看守人).

isola·tion /ˌaɪsəˈleɪʃn; ˌaɪslˋeʃən/ *n* [U] **1 ~ (from sb/sth)** isolating or being isolated 隔离; 脱离; 分离; 孤立. **2** (idm 习语) **in isolation (from sb/sth)** separately; alone 单独地; 独自地; 个别地: *examine each piece of evidence in isolation*, ie without considering the others 分别审查每一证据(不考虑与其他证据的关系) ○ *Looked at in isolation, these facts are not encouraging.* 孤立地看, 这些事实并不乐观.

□ **isoˈlation hospital, isoˈlation ward** hospital or ward for people with infectious diseases 隔离病院; 隔离病房.

isola·tion·ism /ˌaɪsəˈleɪʃənɪzəm; ˌaɪslˋeʃənɪzm/ *n* [U] **~ (from sth)** policy of not participating in the affairs of other countries or groups 孤立主义.

▷ **isola·tion·ist** /-ʃənɪst; -ʃənɪst/ *n, adj* (person) supporting isolationism 孤立主义的; 孤立主义者.

iso·met·ric /ˌaɪsəˈmetrɪk; ˌaɪsəˋmɛtrɪk/ *adj* **1** having equal dimensions and measurements 有相等的量度的; 等量的. **2** (in physiology) (of muscle action) contracting and developing tension while the muscle is prevented from shortening (生理学上)(指肌肉运动)提高肌张力而肌肉不缩短的. **3** (of a drawing, etc) without perspective, so that lines along the three axes are of equal length (指图样等)等长的, 等角的, 等距的.

iso·morph /ˈaɪsəmɔːf; ˋaɪsəˌmɔrf/ *n* substance or organism with the same form or structure as another 同形体; 同晶体. ▷ **iso·morphic** /ˌaɪsəˈmɔːfɪk; ˌaɪsəˋmɔrfɪk/ (also **iso·morph·ous** /ˌaɪsəˈmɔːfəs; ˌaɪsəˋmɔrfəs/) *adj*.

isos·celes /aɪˈsɒsəliːz; aɪˋsɑslˌiz/ *adj* (*geometry* 儿) (of a triangle) having two sides equal in length (指三角形)二等边的, 等腰的. ⇨ illus at TRIANGLE 见 TRIANGLE 插图.

iso·therm /ˈaɪsəθɜːm; ˋaɪsəˌθɝm/ *n* line on a map joining places that have the same average temperature 等温线.

iso·tope /ˈaɪsətəʊp; ˋaɪsəˌtop/ *n* one of two or more forms of a chemical element with different atomic weight and different nuclear properties but the same chemical properties 同位素: *radioactive isotopes*, ie unstable forms of atoms used in medicine and industry 放射性同位素(用于医学和工业).

issue /ˈɪʃuː, ˈɪsjuː; ˋɪʃu/ *n* **1 (a)** [U] outgoing; outflow 放出; 发出; 流出: *the place/point of issue* 发出地[点]. **(b)** [sing] instance of flowing out 放出; 发出; 流出: *an issue of blood*, eg from a wound 流血(如自伤口流出). **2 (a)** [U] supply and distribution of items for use or sale 发出; 分发: *buy new stamps on the day of issue* 于邮票发行日购买新邮票 ○ *the issue of rifles and ammunition to troops* 发给部队枪枝弹药 ○ *the issue of a new edition of this dictionary* 这部词典的新版本的出版. **(b)** [C] number, quantity or set of items supplied and distributed at one time 一次发出、分发的数量或一套: *a special issue of stamps/banknotes/shares* 特别发行的邮票[钞票/股票] ○ *emergency issues of blankets to refugees* 向难民紧急发放的毛毯. **(c)** [C] one of a regular series of publications (出版物的)期号: *the July issue*, eg of a magazine 七月号(如杂志的). **3** [sing] (*fml* 文) result or outcome 结果; 结局: *await the issue* 等待结果 ○ *bring a campaign to a successful issue* 使一活动获得良好结果. **4** [C] important topic for discussion; point in question 重要的议题; 争论点; 争端: *a vital, political, topical, etc issue* 重大的、政治的、时事的...问题 ○ *debate an issue* 辩论一问题 ○ *raise a new issue* 提出新议题 ○ *evade/avoid the issue* 回避该问题 ○ *confuse the issue* 混淆该问题. **5** [U] (*law* 律) children considered as part of one's family 子女; 子孙: *die without issue*, ie childless 身故无后. **6** (idm 习语) **(the matter, point, etc) at issue** (the matter, point, etc) being discussed or debated 讨论或争议中的(问题、争论点等): *What's at issue here is the whole future of the industry.* 争论的焦点是这个行业总的前景. **force the issue** ⇨ FORCE². **make an issue (out) of sth** treat (a minor matter) as if it needed serious discussion like a major matter (像对待大事一样)处理(小事): *It's only a small disagreement — let's not make an issue of it.* 那仅仅是个小小的分歧——咱们别小题大作了. **take issue with sb (about/on/over sth)** proceed to disagree or argue with sb (about sth) (就某事)向某人提出异议或与某人争论.

▷ **issue** *v* (*fml* 文) **1** [Ipr, Ip] **~ from sth**; **~ out/forth (from sth)** come, go or flow out 出来; 出去; 流出: *blood issuing from a wound* 从伤口流出的血 ○ *smoke issuing (forth) from a chimney* 从烟囱中冒出的烟. **2** [Tn, Tn·pr] **~ sth (to sb)/sb with sth** supply or distribute sth to sb for use 将某物发给、供给或分配给某人使用: *issue visas to foreign visitors* 给外国游客签证 ○ *issue warm clothing to the survivors* 给幸存者分发御寒衣物 ○ *issue them with warm clothing* 发给他们御寒衣物. **3** [Tn] publish (books, articles, etc) or put into circulation (stamps, banknotes, shares, etc) 出版或发表(书、文章等); 发行(邮票、钞票、股票等). **4** [Tn, Tn·pr] **~ sth (to sb)** send sth out; make sth known 发出; 颁布; 公布: *issue orders, instructions, etc* 发布命令、指示等 ○ *The minister issued a statement to the press.* 部长向新闻界发表声明. **5** [Ipr] **~ from sth** (*fml* 文) result or be derived from sth 由某事物得出或产生.

-ist *suff* 后缀 **1** (with *vs* ending in *-ize* forming *ns* 与以 -ize 结尾的动词结合构成名词): *dramatist* ○ *publicist*. **2** (with *ns* ending in *-ism* 与以 -ism 结尾的名词结合) believer in; practiser of ...的信仰者; ...主义者; ...实行者: *atheist* ○ *socialist*. **3** (with *ns* forming *ns* 与名词结合构成名词) person concerned with 从事...的人; ...专业人员: *physicist* ○ *motorist* ○ *violinist*.

NOTE ON USAGE 用法: Both **-ist** and **-ite** form nouns indicating people who have certain beliefs. ☆ **-ist** 和 **-ite** 都可用以构成名词, 指有某种信仰的人. **-ist** suggests a strong belief in a theory, religion, etc ☆ **-ist** 指对某学说、宗教等有坚定信念的人: *She's a convinced Marxist, Buddhist, etc.* 她是坚定的马克思主义者、佛教徒等. Nouns with **-ite** generally indicate a follower of someone or a member of a group. ☆ **-ite** 型的名词一般指某人的追随者或某集团的成员. They are often used in a derogatory way 这类名词常用于贬义: *a committee full of Unionites, Thatcherites, etc* 主要由工会成员、撒切尔夫人的支持者等组成的委员会.

isth·mus /ˈɪsməs; ˋɪsməs/ *n* (*pl* **~es**) narrow strip of land joining two larger areas of land that would otherwise be separated by water 地峡: *the Isthmus of Panama* 巴拿马地峡.

it¹ /ɪt; ɪt/ *pers pron* 人称代词 (used as the subject or object of a *v* or after a *prep* 用作动词的主体或宾语或用于介词之后) **1 (a)** animal or thing mentioned earlier or being observed now 它: *'Where's your car?' 'It's in the garage.'* '你的汽车在哪儿呢?' '在车库里'. ○ *Did you hit it?* 你打中了吗? ○ *Fill a glass with water and dissolve this tablet in it.* 倒杯水把药片放进去溶解了. ○ *We've got £500. Will it be enough for a deposit?* 我们有 500 英镑了. 够不够作押金的? **(b)** baby, esp one whose sex is not known or unimportant 他(指婴儿, 尤指性别不详或无所谓时): *Her baby's due next month. She hopes it will be a boy.* 她怀的孩子该下月出生. 她希望是个男孩儿. ○ *The baby next door kept me awake. It cried all night.* 隔壁的孩子吵得我睡不着觉. 他整夜哭个没完. **2** fact or situation already known or implied (已知的或暗含的)事实或情况: *When the factory closes, it* (ie this event) *will mean 500 redundancies.* 工厂一旦关闭, 那就意味着要有 500 人遭遣散. ○ *Yes, I was at home on Sunday. What about/of it?* 是啊, 我星期天在家来着. 怎么了? **3** (used to identify a person 用以确定一人的身分): *It's the milkman.* 那是送牛奶的. ○ *It's Peter on the phone.* 是彼得打来的电话. ○ *Was it you who put these books on my desk?* 是你把这些书放到我桌上的吗? **4** (idm 习语) **this/that is ˈit (a)** this/that is what is required 这[那]正是所需要的: *We've been looking for a house for months and I think this is it.* 我们找房子已经找了好几个月了, 我看这所就是我们要找的. **(b)** this/that is the reason for the lack of success 这[那]正是未能成功的原因: *That's just it — I can't work when you're making so* *much noise.* 原因就在这里——你弄出这么大的声音，我工作不了. (**c**) this/that is the end 这[那]就是终结: *I'm afraid that's it — we've lost the match.* 我看到此为止了——这场比赛我们已经输了.

▷ **its** /ɪts; ɪts/ *possess det* of or belonging to a thing, an animal or a baby 它的, 他的(指事物、动物或幼儿): *We wanted to buy the table but its surface was damaged.* 我们想买那张桌子, 可惜桌面残了. ○ *Have you any idea of its value?* 你知道这东西的价值吗? ○ *The dog was howling — its paw was hurt.* 那条狗在嗥叫——它的爪子受伤了. ○ *The baby threw its food on the floor.* 那个小孩儿把食物扔到地上了.

it² /ɪt; ɪt/ *pron* **1** (used in the normal subject or object position to indicate that a longer subject or object has been placed at the end of a sentence 作长的主语或宾语的先行代词): *It appears that the two leaders are holding secret talks.* 两位领导人好像在举行秘密会谈. ○ *Does it matter what colour it is?* 是什么颜色有关系吗? ○ *It's impossible (for us) to get there in time.* (我们)不可能及时赶到那里. ○ *It's no use shouting.* 叫喊并没有用. ○ *She finds it boring staying/to stay at home.* 她觉得待在家中很无聊. ○ *I find it strange that she doesn't want to travel.* 她竟不想旅游, 我觉得很奇怪. **2** (used in the normal subject position to make a statement about time, distance or weather 指时间、距离或天气时作句中主语): *It's ten past twelve.* 现在十二点十分. ○ *It's our anniversary.* 今天是我们的周年纪念. ○ *It's two miles to the beach.* 离海滨有两英里远. ○ *It's a long time since they left.* 他们走后很久了. ○ *It was raining this morning.* 今晨下雨来着. ○ *It's quite warm at the moment.* 现在天气很暖和. ○ *It's stormy out at sea.* 海上有风暴. **3** circumstances or conditions; things in general 环境或情况; 泛指的事物: *If it's convenient I can see you tomorrow.* 要是方便的话, 我明天可以见你. ○ *It's getting very competitive in the car industry.* 汽车工业方面的竞争日益加剧. **4** (used to emphasize any part of a sentence 用以强调句中任何部分): *It's 'Jim who's the clever one.* 聪明的是吉姆. ○ *It's 'Spain that they're going to on holiday.* 他们假日要去的地方是西班牙. ○ *It was three weeks 'later that he heard the news.* 三个星期以后他才听到这消息.

IT /ˌaɪ ˈtiː; ˌaɪ ˋti/ *abbr* 缩写 = (*computing* 计) Information Technology.

ita /ˌaɪ tiː ˈeɪ; ˌaɪ ti ˋe/ *abbr* 缩写 = initial teaching alphabet (a partially phonetic system used to teach reading) 启蒙教学字母.

It·al·ian /ɪˈtæliən; ɪˋtæljən/ *adj* of Italy, its culture, language or people 意大利的; 意大利文化的; 意大利语的; 意大利人的.

▷ **It·al·ian** *n* native of Italy 意大利人.

It·ali·an·ate /ɪˈtæljəneɪt; ɪˋtæljənˌet/ *adj* of Italian style or appearance 意大利风格的; 意大利式的.

it·alic /ɪˈtælɪk; ɪˋtælɪk/ *adj* **1** (of printed letters) sloping forwards (指印刷字母)斜体的: *This sentence is in italic type.* 本句是用斜体字印刷的. Cf 参看 ROMAN 3. **2** of or for a compact pointed style of handwriting (书写)斜体的: *write in italic script* 用斜体写 ○ *an italic pen-nib* 写斜体字用的钢笔尖.

▷ **it·al·icize, -ise** /ɪˈtælɪsaɪz; ɪˋtæləˌsaɪz/ *v* [Tn] print (sth) in italic type 用斜体字印刷(某物).

it·alics *n* [pl] printed italic letters 印刷的斜体字母: *Examples in this dictionary are in italics.* 本词典中的示例均为斜体字. ⇨App 3 见附录3.

Italo- *comb form* 构词成分 Italian; of Italy 意大利的: *the Italo-Swiss frontier.*

itch /ɪtʃ; ɪtʃ/ *n* **1** [C usu *sing* 通常作单数] feeling of irritation on the skin, causing a desire to scratch 痒: *suffer from, have, feel an itch* 觉得痒. **2** [sing] **~ for sth/to do sth** (*infml* 口) restless desire or longing 热望; 渴望: *have an itch for adventure* 渴望冒险 ○ *She cannot resist the/her itch to travel.* 她巴不得要去旅行. **3** (idm 习语) **the seven-year 'itch** (*joc infml* 谑, 口) the desire for new sexual experience that is thought to be felt after about seven years of marriage 七年之痒(据认为结婚约七年后会有喜新厌旧之感).

▷ **itch** *v* **1** [I] have or cause an itch 发痒: *scratch where it itches* 搔痒处 ○ *Scratch yourself if you itch!* 觉得痒就挠挠! ○ *Are your mosquito bites still itching?* 蚊子咬的地方还痒吗? **2** [Ipr, It] **~ for sth/to do sth** (*infml* 口) feel a strong restless desire for sth 渴望; 热望: *pupils itching for the lesson to end* 盼着下课的学生 ○ *I'm itching to tell you the news!* 我巴不得要把这消息告诉你! **3** (idm 习语) **have an itching 'palm** be greedy for money 贪财.

itchy *adj* (**-ier** /ˈɪtʃɪə(r); ˋɪtʃɪɚ/, **-iest** /ˈɪtʃɪɪst; ˋɪtʃɪɪst/) **1** having or producing irritation on the skin 发痒的: *an itchy scalp*, eg caused by dandruff 发痒的头皮(如因有头皮屑). **2** (idm 习语) **(get/have) itchy feet** (*infml* 口) (feel a) restless desire to travel or move from place to place 渴望各处走动. **itchi·ness** *n* [U].

it'd /ˈɪtəd; ˋɪtəd/ *contracted form* 缩约式 **1** it had ⇨ HAVE. **2** it would ⇨ WILL¹, WOULD².

-ite *suff* 后缀 (with proper *ns* forming *ns* 与专有名词结合构成名词) follower or supporter of 追随者; 支持者: *Labourite* ○ *Thatcherite.* ⇨Usage at -IST 用法见 -ist.

item /ˈaɪtəm; ˋaɪtəm/ *n* **1** single article or unit in a list, etc 条款; 项目: *the first item on the agenda* 议事日程上的第一项 ○ *number the items in a catalogue* 给目录中各条目编号. **2** single piece of news 一则或一条新闻: *There's an important news item/item of news in today's paper.* 今天报上有一则重要新闻.

▷ **item** *adv* (used to introduce each of several articles in a list 逐条列举时用以起首) also (还有)一项: *item, one chair; item, two carpets, etc* 一项, 椅子一把; 还有一项, 地毯两张等.

item·ize, -ise /ˈaɪtəmaɪz; ˋaɪtəmaɪz/ *v* [Tn] give or write every item of (sth) 逐项列出或记载: *an itemized list, account, bill, etc* 分项开列的清单、记载帐目、帐单等.

it·er·ate /ˈɪtəreɪt; ˋɪtəˌret/ *v* [Tn, Tn·pr, Tf, Tw, Dpr·f, Dpr·w] **~sth (to sb)** (*fml* 文) say sth again and again; make (an accusation, a demand, etc) repeatedly 反复说某事; 一再提出(指责、要求等). Cf 参看 REITERATE. ▷ **it·era·tion** /ˌɪtəˈreɪʃn; ˌɪtəˋreʃən/ *n* [U].

it·in·er·ant /aɪˈtɪnərənt, ɪˈtɪnərənt; aɪˋtɪnərənt, ɪˋtɪnərənt/ *adj* [usu attrib 通常作定语] travelling from place to place 巡回的; 流动的: *an itinerant musician, entertainer, preacher, etc* 巡回音乐家、演员、牧师等.

it·in·er·ary /aɪˈtɪnərərɪ, ɪˈtɪnərərɪ; *US* -rerɪ; aɪˋtɪnəˌrɛrɪ, ɪˋtɪnəˌrɛrɪ/ *n* plan for, or record of, a journey; route 旅行的计划或记录; 旅行路线: *keep to, depart from, follow one's itinerary* 按照、离开、根据自己的旅行计划.

-ition ⇨ -ION.

-itis *suff* 后缀 (with *ns* forming uncountable *ns* 与名词结合构成不可数名词) **1** (*medical* 医) inflammatory disease of …炎症; …炎: *appendicitis* ○ *tonsillitis.* **2** (*infml esp joc* 口, 尤作戏谑语) excessive interest in or exposure to 过分沉迷于…; …迷、癖或狂: *World Cup-itis.*

it'll /ˈɪtl; ˋɪtl/ *contracted form* 缩约式 it will ⇨ WILL¹.

ITN /ˌaɪ tiː ˈen; ˌaɪ ti ˋɛn/ *abbr* 缩写 = (*Brit*) Independent Television News 独立电视新闻公司: *news at 10 on ITN* 独立电视新闻公司10点钟的新闻.

its ⇨ IT¹.

it's /ɪts; ɪts/ *contracted form* 缩约式 **1** it is ⇨ BE. **2** it has ⇨ HAVE.

itself /ɪtˈself; ɪtˋsɛlf/ *reflex, emph pron* 反身、强调代词 (only taking the main stress in sentences when used emphatically 只在句中表示强调时方重读) **1** (*reflex* 反身) (used when the animal, thing, etc causing the action is also affected by it 用以复指施动的动物、事物等): *The wounded horse could not ˌraise itself from the 'ground.* 那受伤的马自己站不起来了. ○ *The committee decided to aˌward itself a 'pay increase.* 委员会决定给委员本身加薪. **2** (*emph* 强调) (used to emphasize an animal, a thing, etc 用以强调动物、事物等以加强语气): *The name it'self sounds foreign.* 这名字本身听起来就很陌生. **3** (idm 习语) **by it'self** (**a**) automatically 自动地: *The machine will start by itself in a few seconds.* 机器在几秒钟后会自动开启. (**b**) alone 独自地; 单独地: *The statue stands by itself in the square.* 广场上孤零零地立着这座雕像.

ITT /ˌaɪ tiː ˈtiː; ˌaɪ ti ˋti/ *abbr* 缩写 = International Telephone and Telegraph Corporation 国际电话电报公司: *work for ITT* 为国际电话电报公司工作.

ITV /ˌaɪ tiː ˈviː; ˌaɪ ti ˋvi/ *abbr* 缩写 = (*Brit*) Independent Television 独立电视公司: *watch a film on ITV* 看独立电视公司播放的影片 ○ *an ITV documentary* 独立电视公司的记录片. Cf 参看 BBC, IBA.

-ity *suff* 后缀 (with *adjs* forming *ns* 与形容词结合构成名词): *purity* ○ *oddity*.

IUD /ˌaɪ juː ˈdiː; ˌaɪ ju ˈdi/ (also **IUCD** /ˌaɪ juː siː ˈdiː; ˌaɪ ju si ˈdi/) *abbr* 缩写 = intra-uterine (contraceptive) device.

I've /aɪv; aɪv/ *contracted form* 缩约式 I have ⇨ HAVE.

-ive *suff* 后缀 (with *vs* forming *ns* and *adjs* 与动词结合构成名词和形容词) (person or thing) having a tendency to or the quality of 有...倾向的或有...性质的(人或事物): *explosive* ○ *captive* ○ *descriptive*.

iv·ory /ˈaɪvərɪ; ˈaɪvərɪ/ *n* **1** [U] creamy-white bone-like substance forming the tusks of elephants, walruses, etc 象牙; (海象等的)长牙: [attrib 作定语] *an ivory statuette* 象牙制的小雕像. **2** [C] object made of this 象牙制品: *a priceless collection of ivories* 象牙的稀世珍品收藏. **3** [U] colour of ivory 象牙色的; 乳白色的: [attrib 作定语] *an ivory skin, complexion, etc* 乳白色的皮肤、面色等 ○ *ivory-coloured silk* 乳白色的丝绸. **4** (idm 习语) **an ˌivory ˈtower** place or situation where people retreat from the unpleasant realities of everyday life and pretend that these do not exist 象牙塔(对日常生活中烦恼的现实视而不见者的退身之所或处境): *live in an ivory tower* 生活在象牙塔中 ○ [attrib 作定语] *lead an ˌivory-tower eˈxistence* 过象牙塔式的生活.

ivy /ˈaɪvɪ; ˈaɪvɪ/ *n* [U] any of various types of climbing evergreen plant, esp one with dark shiny five-pointed leaves 常春藤: [attrib 作定语] *an ivy leaf* 常春藤叶.

▷ **ivied** /ˈaɪvɪd; ˈaɪvɪd/ *adj* covered with ivy 爬满常春藤的: *ivied walls* 长满常春藤的墙壁.

□ **ˌIvy ˈLeague** group of traditional universities in the eastern US with a reputation for high academic standards and social prestige 常春藤联盟(美国东部有高度学术水平和社会声誉的名牌大学的通称).

-ize, -ise *suff* 后缀 (with *ns* and *adjs* forming *vs* 与名词和形容词结合构成动词) **1** become or make like 成为...; 使像...; 使...化: *dramatize* ○ *miniaturize*. **2** act or treat with the qualities of 以...方式处理或对待: *criticize* ○ *deputize*. **3** place in 置于: *containerize* ○ *hospitalize*. ▷ **-ization**, **-isation** (forming *ns* 用以构成名词): *immunization*. **-izationally**, **-isationally** (forming *advs* 用以构成副词): *organizationally*.

NOTE ON USAGE 用法: **1** In some words ending with the sound /aɪz; aɪz/ **-ize** and **-ise** are equally acceptable spellings 有些字的字尾读音为/aɪz; aɪz/, 其拼写法作 **-ize** 和 **-ise** 均可: *emphasize/emphasise*, *criticize/criticise*. **-ise** is more common in British than in US English. ☆ **-ise** 的拼法在英式英语中比在美式英语中常见. In this dictionary both spellings are shown when both are possible. 在两种拼法皆可时, 本词典将之一并列出. **2** There are some words which, because of their origin, are always spelt with **-ise** 有些字, 因字源关系, 一向拼作 **-ise**: *advertise* (*US* also *advertize*), *advise*, *comprise*, *despise*, *exercise*, *etc*. **3** Some people criticize the over-use of **-ize** or **-ise** to form words such as *burglarize* (= 'burgle') or *hospitalize* (= 'send to hospital'). 有些人批评滥用 **-ize** 或 **-ise** 造字的现象, 如burglarize (= burgle) 或 hospitalize (= send to hospital).

J j

J, j /dʒeɪ; dʒe/ *n* (*pl* **J's, j's** /dʒeɪz; dʒez/) the tenth letter of the English alphabet 英语字母表的第十个字母: *'Joker' begins with (a) J/'J'.* joker 一字以j字母开始.

J *abbr* 缩写 = joule(s).

jab /dʒæb; dʒæb/ *v* (**-bb-**) **1** [I, Ipr, Ip, Tn, Tn·pr] **~ (at sb/sth) (with sth); ~ sb/sth (with sth)** poke or push at sb/sth roughly, usu with sth sharp or pointed 捅, 刺, 戳, 猛击(某人[某物])(通常指用利器或尖物): *He kept jabbing (away) at the paper cup with his pencil.* 他用铅笔(不停地)戳着纸杯. ○ *a blackbird jabbing at a worm*, ie using its beak 啄食蠕虫的黑鹂 ○ *He jabbed at his opponent*, eg of a boxer aiming a quick blow. 他猛击对手(如拳击手以快拳出击). ○ *She jabbed me in the ribs with her elbow.* 她用肘顶我的肋部. **2** (phr v) **jab sth into sb/sth** force sth into sb/sth 使某物捅或刺某人[某物]: *He jabbed his elbow into my side.* 他用肘猛顶我的腰. **jab sth out** force or push sth out by jabbing 戳出某物: *Be careful with that umbrella — you nearly jabbed my eye out!* 小心那把伞——你差一点把我的眼睛戳出来! ⇨Usage at NUDGE 用法见 NUDGE.

▷ **jab** *n* (**a**) sudden rough blow or thrust, usu with sth pointed 捅; 刺; 戳; 猛击: *a jab in the arm* 刺在手臂上的一下. (**b**) (*infml* 口) injection or inoculation 注射; 打针; 接种: *Have you had your cholera jabs yet?* 你打霍乱预防针了吗?

jab·ber /ˈdʒæbə(r); ˈdʒæbɚ/ *v* **1** [I, Ip] **~ (away/on)** talk rapidly in what seems to be a confused manner 急促而含混不清地说话: *Listen to those children jabbering away!* 你听那些孩子叽叽喳喳地说个没完! **2** [Tn, Tn·p] utter (words, etc) rapidly and indistinctly 急促而含混不清地说(话等): *He jabbered out what I assumed was an apology.* 他叽叽咕咕地说了些我认为像是道歉的话.

▷ **jab·ber** *n* [U] jabbering; chatter 急促而含混不清的话; 唠叨: *the jabber of monkeys* 猴子吱吱的叫声.

jabot /ˈʒæbəʊ; ʒæˈbo/ *n* ornamental frill on the front of a woman's blouse or a man's shirt (衬衫胸部的)装饰褶边.

jack[1] /dʒæk; dʒæk/ *n* **1** (usu portable) device for raising heavy weights off the ground, esp one for raising the axle of a motor vehicle so that a wheel may be changed (通常指便携式)起重器, 千斤顶(尤指更换机动车车轮时用的). **2** ship's flag flown to show nationality 船上表示国籍的旗子: *the Union Jack*, ie the flag of the United Kingdom 英国国旗. **3 Jack** familiar form of the name *John* 杰克(约翰的昵称). **4** (also **knave**) (in a pack of playing-cards) card between the ten and the queen (纸牌中的)杰克, J(介于王后与十点之间): *the jack of clubs* 梅花J. **5** (in the game of bowls) small white ball towards which bowls are rolled (滚球戏中)作靶子的小白球. **6** (idm 习语) **before you can/could say Jack Robinson** ⇨ SAY. **every man jack** ⇨ MAN. **a jack of ˈall trades** person who can do many different kinds of work but not necessarily well 博而不精的人.

□ **Jack ˈFrost** (*joc* 谑) frost considered as a person (拟人化的)霜: *Look what pretty patterns Jack Frost has painted on the windows.* 瞧霜大哥在窗户上绘制了多么美丽的图案.

ˈjack-in-office *n* (*derog* 贬) self-important official 自命不凡的官吏.

ˈjack-in-the-box *n* (*pl* **-boxes**) toy in the form of a box with a figure inside that springs up when the lid is opened 玩偶盒(开盒盖时其中的玩偶能跳起).

ˌjack-o'-ˈlantern *n* pumpkin with holes cut in it so that it looks like a face, used as a lantern (by placing a candle inside) for fun 南瓜灯笼(在南瓜上挖成人面形窟窿, 内点蜡烛).

ˈjack-rabbit *n* large hare of Western N America 杰克兔(北美西部产的大野兔).

Jack ˈtar (also **tar**) (*dated nautical* 旧, 海) sailor 水手; 水兵.

jack[2] /dʒæk; dʒæk/ *v* (phr v) **jack sth in** (*sl* 俚) leave sth readily; abandon (work, etc) 打算离开; 放弃(工作等): *I can't concentrate any more. I'm going to jack it in.* 我再也无法集中精神了. 我不打算干了. **jack sth up** (**a**) raise sth using a jack[1](1) 用千斤顶顶起某物: *to jack up a car* 用千斤顶把汽车顶起. (**b**) (*fig infml* 比喻, 口) increase (salary, payment, etc); raise 增加(薪金, 报酬等); 提高: *It's time you jacked up my allowance.* 您该给我增加点儿零用钱了. (**c**) (*infml* 口) arrange or organize sth that is in disorder 把凌乱的事物安排好或料理好: *Everything's falling apart; the whole system needs jacking up.* 一切都乱了, 整个系统有待整顿.

jackal /ˈdʒækɔːl; *US* -kl; ˈdʒækl/ *n* wild animal of Africa and Asia that is related to the dog 胡狼, 豺(产于亚非).

jack·an·apes /ˈdʒækəneɪps; ˈdʒækəˌneps/ *n* (*pl* unchanged 复数不变) (*dated* 旧) impertinent fellow; mischievous child 无礼的傢伙; 顽童: *Come here, you young jackanapes!* 过来, 你这个小淘气鬼!

jack·ass /ˈdʒækæs; ˈdʒækˌæs/ *n* **1** male ass 公驴. **2** (*fig infml* 比喻, 口) foolish person 愚蠢的人; 笨蛋.

jack·boot /ˈdʒækbuːt; ˈdʒækˌbut/ *n* **1** tall boot, esp one worn by certain soldiers 长统靴(尤指某些军人穿的). **2** (*fig* 比喻) military oppression; tyranny 军事压迫; 暴政: *under the jackboot of a dictatorial regime* 在专制制度的暴政下.

jack·daw /ˈdʒækdɔː; ˈdʒækˌdɔ/ *n* bird of the crow family (noted for stealing small bright objects) 寒鸦, 穴鸟(以偷取明亮的小东西而闻名).

jacket 短上衣

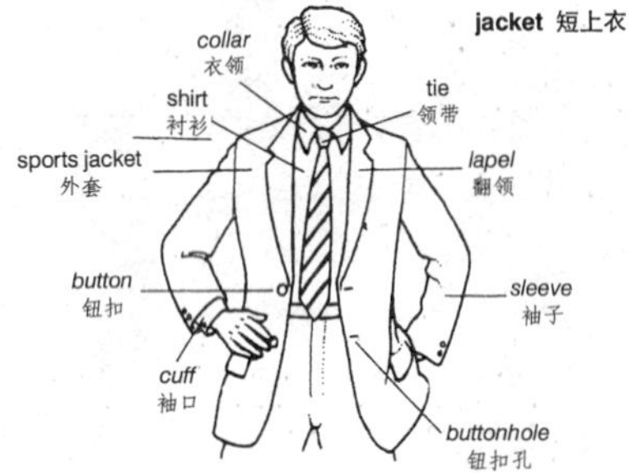

jacket /ˈdʒækɪt; ˈdʒækɪt/ *n* **1** short coat with sleeves 短上衣; 夹克: *a tweed jacket* 花呢上衣. ⇨illus 见插图. **2** outer cover round a boiler, tank, pipe, etc to reduce loss of heat (锅炉、槽、管等的)保温套: *a water jacket*, ie cover used to cool an engine (发动机的)冷却套. **3** (also **ˈdust-jacket**) loose paper cover for a hardback book (精装书的)护封. **4** (of a potato) skin (指马铃薯)皮: [attrib 作定语] *jacket poˈtatoes*, ie potatoes baked without being peeled 带皮烤熟的土豆.

jack-knife /ˈdʒæknaɪf; ˈdʒækˌnaɪf/ *n* (*pl* **-knives** /-naɪvz; -ˌnaɪvz/ **1** large pocket-knife with a folding blade (可放衣袋内的)大折刀. **2** (*sport* 体) dive in which the body is first bent double and then straightened 屈体跳水.

▷ **jack-knife** *v* [I] (esp of an articulated lorry) bend sharply in the middle into a V-shape, usu as the result of an accident (尤指铰接的货车)弯成V字形(通常因交通事故所致): *A heavy lorry has jack-knifed on the motorway, causing long delays.* 一辆重型铰接货车在高速公路上撞成V字形, 耽搁了很长时间.

jack·pot /ˈdʒækpɒt; ˈdʒækˌpɑt/ *n* **1** (in various games, esp poker) stake or prize that continues to be added to until won (多种游戏中, 尤指扑克)累积的赌注(逐渐增加直到赌赢为止). **2** (idm 习语) **hit the jackpot** ⇨ HIT[1].

Ja·co·bean /ˌdʒækəˈbɪən; ˌdʒækəˈbiən/ *adj* of the reign of the English king, James I (1603-25) 英王詹姆斯一世时期的(1603-1625年): *Jacobean 'literature, 'architecture, 'furniture, etc* 英王詹姆斯一世时期的文学、建筑、家具等.

Jac·ob·ite /ˈdʒækəbaɪt; ˋdʒækəˌbaɪt/ *n* supporter of the English king James II (reigned 1685-88) after his overthrow, or of his descendants who claimed the throne 英王詹姆斯二世(1685-1688年在位)被推翻后的遗民或拥戴其后裔复辟的人: [attrib 作定语] *the first Jacobite rebellion* 英王詹姆斯二世追随者的第一次叛乱.

Ja·cuzzi /dʒəˈku:zɪ; dʒəˋkuzɪ/ *n* (*propr* 专利名) bath with underwater jets of water that massage the body 按摩浴缸(水下喷水可起按摩作用).

jade[1] /dʒeɪd; dʒed/ *n* [U] **1** hard, usu green, stone from which ornaments, etc are carved 玉; 翡翠: [attrib 作定语] *a jade vase, necklace, etc* 翡翠花瓶、项链等 ○ *jade-green eyes* 碧绿的眼睛. **2** ornaments, etc made of jade 玉制的饰物等: *a collection of Chinese jade* 收藏的一批中国玉器.

jade[2] /dʒeɪd; dʒed/ *n* **1** tired or worn-out horse 疲惫的马; 衰老的马. **2** (*dated derog or joc* 旧, 贬或谑) woman 女子: *You saucy little jade!* 你这个糟女人!

jaded /ˈdʒeɪdɪd; ˋdʒedɪd/ *adj* (*derog or joc* 贬或谑) tired and lacking zest, usu after too much of sth 疲倦的, 缺乏热情的(尤指因厌倦): *looking jaded after an all-night party* 在通宵欢聚之后显得疲惫不堪 ○ (*fig* 比喻) *a jaded appetite* 吃腻了的胃口.

jag /dʒæg; dʒæg/ *n* (*infml* 口) **1** bout of heavy drinking; spree 一阵痛饮; 欢闹. **2** period of concentrated activity, strong emotion, etc 一阵精神集中的活动、感情激动等.

jagged /ˈdʒægɪd; ˋdʒægɪd/ *adj* with rough, uneven, often sharp, edges; notched 边缘不整齐的(常为锐利的); 有V形缺口的: *jagged rocks* 犬牙交错的岩石 ○ *a piece of glass with a jagged edge* 边缘参差不齐的玻璃.

jag·uar /ˈdʒægjʊə(r); ˋdʒægjʊˌɑr/ *n* large spotted member of the cat family inhabiting parts of central America 美洲豹; 美洲虎.

jail = GAOL.

ja·lopy /dʒəˈlɒpɪ; dʒəˋlɑpɪ/ *n* (*infml* 口) battered old car 破旧的汽车.

jam[1] /dʒæm; dʒæm/ *n* **1** [U] sweet substance made by boiling fruit with sugar until it is thick, usu preserved in jars, etc 果酱: *He spread some strawberry jam on his toast.* 他把草莓酱涂在烤面包片上. **2** [C] type of this 果酱: *recipes for jams and preserves* 果酱和蜜饯的制作方法. **3** (idm 习语) **money for jam/old rope** ⇨ MONEY.

▷ **jammy** /ˈdʒæmɪ; ˋdʒæmɪ/ *adj* (**-ier, -iest**) (*infml* 口) **1** covered with jam 涂有果酱的: *Don't wipe your jammy fingers on the table-cloth.* 你别在桌布上擦沾了果酱的手指. **2** (*Brit infml* 口) (**a**) lucky 幸运的: *You jammy so-and-so!* 你这个幸运的傢伙! (**b**) easy 容易的: *This is one of the jammiest jobs I've ever had.* 这是我干过的最轻松的工作.

jam[2] /dʒæm; dʒæm/ *v* (**-mm-**) **1** [esp passive 尤用于被动语态: Tn·pr, Tn·p] **~ sb/sth in, under, between, etc sth; ~ sb/sth in** (**a**) squeeze sb/sth (into a space) so that he/it cannot move out 将某人[某物]塞(进某空间)不能出来: *sitting in a railway carriage, jammed between two fat men* 坐在火车里夹在两个胖子中间出不来 ○ *The ship was jammed in the ice.* 轮船卡在冰中间无法驶出. ○ *Don't park there — you'll probably get jammed in.* 别把汽车停在那里——有可能夹在里面开不出来. (**b**) thrust sth forcibly or clumsily into a space 将某物硬塞入某处: *The newspapers were so tightly jammed in the letter-box he could hardly get them out.* 报纸紧紧塞在信箱里, 他很难取出来. ○ *He jammed his key into the lock.* 他把钥匙卡在锁里了. **2** [I, Tn, Tn·p] **~ sth (up)** (cause sth to) become immovable or unworkable because sth has stuck (使某物)因被卡住而不能动弹或发生故障: *The key turned halfway and then jammed.* 钥匙转了一半就卡住了. ○ *There's something jamming (up) the lock.* 有什么东西把锁卡住了. **3** [Tn, Tn·p] **~ sth (up)** crowd (an area, etc) so as to block; obstruct 堵塞(某地方等); 阻塞: *The holiday traffic is jamming the roads.* 假日的车辆堵塞了道路. ○ *a river jammed up with logs* 被圆木堵塞了的河流 ○ *a corridor jammed full of people and luggage* 挤满了人和行李的走廊. **4** [Tn] (*broadcasting* 播) make (a message, programme, etc) difficult to understand by sending out a signal at the same time (发射无线电波)干扰(信息、节目等): *The government tried to jam the guerrillas' transmissions.* 政府设法干扰游击队的无线电通讯. **5** (phr v) **jam sth on** apply (esp brakes) suddenly and forcibly 急拉, 猛踩(尤指制动器): *As soon as she saw the child in the road, she jammed on her brakes.* 她一见路上有个小孩, 便猛踩刹车.

▷ **jam** *n* **1** crowding together of people, things, etc so that movement is difficult or impossible; congestion 拥挤; 拥塞: *a 'traffic jam in a town* 城里的交通堵塞 ○ *a 'log-jam on a river* 河面上的圆木堵塞. **2** failure or stoppage of a system, machine, etc caused by jamming (系统、机器等卡住造成的)失灵或停顿: *a jam in the dispatch department* 发送部门的文件积压. **3** (*infml* 口) difficult or embarrassing situation 困难的处境; 窘况: *How am I going to get out of this jam?* 我怎样才能摆脱困境呢? ○ *be in/get into a jam* 陷入困境.

□ **'jam session** performance of improvised jazz 爵士乐的即兴演奏.

jamb /dʒæm; dʒæm/ *n* vertical post at the side of a doorway, window frame, fireplace, etc (门、窗、壁炉等的)侧柱.

jam·boree /ˌdʒæmbəˈri:; ˌdʒæmbəˋri/ *n* **1** large party; celebration 大聚会; 庆祝会. **2** large rally of Scouts or Guides 童子军的大会.

jam-packed /ˌdʒæmˈpækt; ˋdʒæmˋpækt/ *adj* [usu pred 通常作表语] (*infml* 口) **~ (with sb/sth)** very full or crowded 挤满; 拥挤: *a stadium jam-packed with spectators* 挤满观众的体育馆.

Jan /*in informal use* 俗读作 dʒæn; dʒæn/ *abbr* 缩写 = January: *1 Jan 1932* 1932年1月1日.

jangle /ˈdʒæŋgl; ˋdʒæŋgl/ *v* **1** [I, Ip, Tn] (cause sth to) make a harsh metallic noise (使某物)发出刺耳的金属撞击声: *The fire-alarm kept jangling (away).* 火警报警器响个不停. **2** (phr v) **jangle on sth** irritate (nerves, etc) by making an unpleasant noise 发出噪声刺激(神经等): *Her voice jangles on my ears.* 她的声音我觉得很刺耳.

▷ **jangle** *n* [sing] harsh, usu metallic, noise 刺耳的声音(通常指金属声).

jan·itor /ˈdʒænɪtə(r); ˋdʒænətɚ/ *n* (*US*) = CARETAKER.

Janu·ary /ˈdʒænjʊərɪ; *US* -jʊerɪ; ˋdʒænjuˌɛrɪ/ *n* [U, C] (*abbr* 缩写 **Jan**) the first month of the year, coming before February 一月.

For the uses of *January* see the examples at *April.* 关于January的用法见April词条中的示例.

ja·pan /dʒəˈpæn; dʒəˋpæn/ *n* hard shiny black varnish 黑色亮漆.

▷ **ja·pan** *v* [Tn usu passive 通常用于被动语态] (**-nn-**) cover (esp sth made of wood or metal) with japan 在(尤指木制品或金属制品)上涂黑色亮漆.

jape /dʒeɪp; dʒep/ *n* (*dated infml* 旧, 口) joke played on sb 玩笑; 嘲弄.

ja·pon·ica /dʒəˈpɒnɪkə; dʒəˋpɑnɪkə/ *n* ornamental type of quince tree, with red flowers 贴梗海棠(装饰用的植物, 开红花).

jar[1] /dʒɑ:(r); dʒɑr/ *n* **1** (**a**) cylindrical container, usu made of glass 广口瓶: *I keep my paint-brushes in old 'jam jars.* 我把画笔存放在旧果酱瓶里. ⇨ illus at POT 见POT插图. (**b**) this and its contents 广口瓶及其所盛之物或量: *a jar of plum jam* 一瓶梅子酱. **2** tall vessel with a wide mouth, usu cylindrical, with or without handles 罐子; 坛子; 缸: *large jars of olive oil* 大罐子的橄榄油 ○ *a 'wine-jar* 酒缸. **3** (*Brit infml* 口) glass (of beer) (啤酒)杯: *We're going down to the pub for a few jars.* 我们打算去酒馆喝几杯啤酒.

jar[2] /dʒɑ:(r); dʒɑr/ *v* (**-rr-**) **1** [I, Ipr] **~ (on sb/sth)** have a harsh or an unpleasant effect 有不舒服或不愉快的感觉: *His tuneless whistling jarred on my nerves.* 我听到他吹着不和谐的口哨声感到心烦意乱. **2** [I, Ipr] **~ (with sth)** be out of harmony; clash 不和谐; 不一致; 冲突; 抵触: (*fig* 比喻) *Her comments on future policy introduced a jarring note to the proceedings.* 她对未来政策的评论是与会议议程唱反调. ○ *His harsh criticism jarred with the friendly tone of the meeting.* 他批评得十分尖刻, 与会议中的友好气氛很不协调. **3** [Tn] give a sudden or painful shock to (sb/sth); jolt 使(某人)受震动而疼痛; 使(某物)震动, 动摇: *He jarred his back badly when he fell.* 他这一跌, 背部摔得很重. **4** (phr v) **jar against/on sth** strike sth with a harsh unpleasant sound 撞击某物发出刺耳的声音: *The ship jarred against the quayside.* 船撞在码头上发出刺耳的声音.

▷ **jar** *n* [sing] **1** unpleasant sound or vibration 令人不快的声音或颤动: *The side of the boat hit the quay with a grinding jar.* 船舷撞到码头发出刺耳的声音. **2** sudden unpleasant shock; jolt 令人难受的猛然震动; 颠簸: *He gave his back a nasty jar when he fell.* 他这一跌, 背部摔得很厉害.

jar·gon /ˈdʒɑ:gən; ˋdʒɑrgən/ *n* [U] (*often derog* 常作贬义) technical or specialized words used by a particular group of people and difficult for others to understand 术语; 行话; 切口: *scientific jargon* 科学术语 ○ *She uses so much jargon I can never understand her explanations.* 她用的术语太多, 我怎么也听不懂她的讲解.

jas·mine /ˈdʒæsmɪn; *US* ˈdʒæzmən; ˋdʒæzmən/ *n* [U] shrub with white or yellow sweet-smelling flowers 茉莉.

jas·per /ˈdʒæspə(r); ˋdʒæspɚ/ *n* [U] red, yellow or brown semi-precious stone 碧玉(一种次宝石, 呈红色、黄色或褐色).

jaun·dice /ˈdʒɔ:ndɪs; ˋdʒɔndɪs/ *n* [U] **1** disease caused by an excess of bile in the blood which makes the skin and the whites of the eyes become abnormally yellow 黄疸. **2** (*fig* 比喻) state of mind in which one is jealous, spiteful or suspicious 忌妒; 怨恨; 猜疑: *Do I detect a touch of jaundice* (ie a slight hint of jealousy, etc) *in that remark?* 我听出那话里有点儿忌妒之意吧?

▷ **jaun·diced** *adj* affected by jealousy, spite, etc; bitter 受忌妒、怨恨、猜疑等影响的: *a jaundiced mind, opinion, outlook, etc* 有偏见的思想、看法、观点等 ○ *He has rather a jaundiced view of life.* 他对生活有点儿怨天尤人的看法.

jaunt /dʒɔ:nt; dʒɔnt/ *n* short journey, made for pleasure 短途游览: *She's gone on a jaunt into town.* 她到城里游逛去了.

jaunty /ˈdʒɔ:ntɪ; ˋdʒɔntɪ/ *adj* (**-ier**, **-iest**) feeling or showing cheerfulness and self-confidence; sprightly 扬扬得意的; 轻松愉快的: *wear one's hat at a jaunty angle*, ie tipped to one side, as a sign of high spirits, etc 歪戴着帽子, 得意扬扬. ▷ **jaun·tily** *adv*: *swagger jauntily* 神气活现大摇大摆地走. **jaun·ti·ness** *n* [U].

javelin 标枪

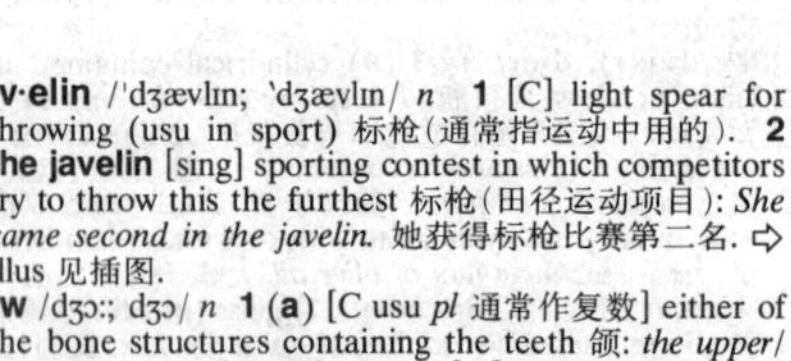

J

jav·elin /ˈdʒævlɪn; ˋdʒævlɪn/ *n* **1** [C] light spear for throwing (usu in sport) 标枪(通常指运动中用的). **2 the javelin** [sing] sporting contest in which competitors try to throw this the furthest 标枪(田径运动项目): *She came second in the javelin.* 她获得标枪比赛第二名. ⇨ illus 见插图.

jaw /dʒɔ:; dʒɔ/ *n* **1** (**a**) [C usu *pl* 通常作复数] either of the bone structures containing the teeth 颌: *the upper/lower jaw* 上[下]颌. (**b**) **jaws** [pl] the mouth with its bones and teeth 口部, 嘴(包括颌骨及牙齿): *The crocodile's jaws snapped shut.* 鳄鱼的嘴啪的一声合上了. ○ (*fig* 比喻) *into/out of the jaws of death*, ie into/out of great danger 陷入[摆脱]险境. (**c**) [sing] lower part of the face; lower jaw 脸的下部; 下颌; 下巴: *a handsome man with a strong square jaw* 长着一副结实的方下巴的漂亮男子 ○ *The punch broke the boxer's jaw.* 这一拳捣坏了那个拳击手的下巴. ⇨illus at HEAD 见 HEAD 插图. **2 jaws** [pl] narrow mouth of a valley, channel, etc (山谷、水道等的)狭窄入口: *the jaws of a gorge, canyon, etc* 峡谷等的口. **3 jaws** [pl] part of a tool, machine, etc that grips or crushes things (工具、机器等的)钳夹部分, 夹紧装置: *the jaws of a vice* 虎钳口. ⇨illus at VICE 见 VICE 插图. **4** [U, C] (*infml* 口) (**a**) long dull talk, usu giving moral advice 冗长的话(通常指说教). (**b**) gossip; talkativeness 流言蜚语; 饶舌. **5** (idm 习语) **one's ˈjaw drops** (*infml* 口) one shows sudden surprise or disappointment 吃惊; 失望: *My jaw dropped when I saw how much the meal had cost.* 我看到那顿饭要花这么多钱真大吃一惊.

▷ **jaw** *v* (*infml* 口) **1** [I, Ipr, Ip] **~ (on) (at sb)** talk at length about sb's faults, behaviour, etc (对某人的错误、行为等)喋喋不休地说. **2** [I, Ip] **~ (on)** gossip 说闲话.

□ **ˈjaw-bone** *n* either of the two bones forming the lower jaw in most mammals 下颌骨.

jay /dʒeɪ; dʒe/ *n* noisy European bird with brightly coloured feathers 松鸦(产于欧洲, 羽毛鲜艳, 喜鸣叫).

jay-walk /ˈdʒeɪ wɔ:k; ˋdʒe ˌwɔk/ *v* [I] walk carelessly across or along town streets without paying enough attention to traffic or traffic signals 无视交通规则任意行走. ▷ **ˈjay-walker** *n*.

jazz /dʒæz; dʒæz/ *n* **1** [U] music of American Negro origin, characterized by the use of improvisation and strong, often syncopated, rhythms 爵士乐: *traditional jazz* 传统爵士乐 ○ *modern jazz* 现代爵士乐 ○ [attrib 作定语] *jazz music/musicians* 爵士乐曲[乐师] ○ *a ˈjazz band* 爵士乐队. **2** [U] (*sl derog* 俚, 贬) pretentious talk; nonsense 假大空; 废话: *Don't give me that jazz!* 别跟我胡扯! **3** (idm 习语) **and all that jazz** (*sl usu derog* 俚, 通常作贬义) and similar things 以及类似的东西: *She lectured us about the honour of the school and all that jazz.* 她给我们讲了学校的荣誉还有一大堆这类的事情.

▷ **jazz** *v* **1** [Tn, Tn·p] **~ sth (up)** play or arrange (music) in the style of jazz 用爵士乐风格演奏(乐曲); 将(乐曲)改编为爵士乐: *a jazzed-up version of an old tune* 被改编为爵士乐的古老曲调. **2** (phr v) **jazz sth up** make sth more lively 使某事物更有生气: *jazz up a party, a magazine, a dress* 使聚会、杂志、连衣裙显得富有生气.

jazzy *adj* (*infml* 口) **1** of or like jazz (似)爵士乐的. **2** flashy or showy 绚丽的; 花哨的: *jazzy clothes, colours, etc* 绚丽的衣物、颜色等 ○ *a jazzy sports car* 花哨的跑车.

jeal·ous /ˈdʒeləs; ˋdʒɛləs/ *adj* **1** feeling or showing fear or resentment of possible rivals in love or affection 忌妒的; 妒忌的: *a jealous husband* 好忌妒的丈夫 ○ *jealous looks* 忌妒的样子. **2 ~ (of sb/sth)** feeling or showing resentment of sb's advantages, achievements, etc; envious 妒羡的; 羡慕的: *He was jealous of Tom/of Tom's success.* 他妒羡汤姆[汤姆的成就]. **3 ~ (of sth)** anxiously protective (of one's rights, belongings, etc); possessive (对自己的权利、所有物等)精心守护的, 占有的: *keeping a jealous eye on one's property* 精心保护自己的财产 ○ *She's jealous of her privileges.* 她极为珍视自己的特权.

▷ **jeal·ously** *adv*.

jeal·ousy /ˈdʒeləsɪ; ˋdʒɛləsɪ/ *n* (**a**) [U] being jealous 忌妒; 妒羡: *a lover's jealousy* 情人的忌妒. (**b**) [C] instance of this; act or remark that shows a person to be jealous 忌妒, 妒羡, 羡慕(的言行): *She grew tired of his petty jealousies.* 她越来越讨厌他那种心胸狭窄的忌妒行为. Cf 参看 ENVY[1].

jeans /dʒi:nz; dʒinz/ *n* [pl] trousers of strong cotton for informal wear 牛仔裤: *She was wearing a pair of tight blue jeans.* 她穿着蓝色紧身牛仔裤.

Jeep /dʒi:p; dʒip/ *n* (*propr* 专利名) small sturdy motor vehicle with four-wheel drive 吉普车.

jeer /dʒɪə(r); dʒɪr/ *v* [I, Ipr, Tn] **~ (at sb/sth)** laugh at or mock (sb/sth) 嘲笑, 嘲弄(某人[某事物]): *a jeering crowd* 起哄的人群 ○ *jeer at a defeated opponent* 嘲弄被击败的对手 ○ *They jeered (at) the speaker.* 他们讥笑发言的人.

▷ **jeer** *n* jeering remark; taunt 揶揄的言语; 嘲讽: *He ran off, their jeers ringing in his ears.* 他一跑了之, 耳边仍回响着他们的冷嘲热讽.

jeer·ing *n* [U]: *He had to face the jeering of his classmates.* 他只得面对同学们的奚落.

Je·ho·vah /dʒɪˈhəʊvə; dʒɪˋhovə/ *n* (*Bible* 圣经) name of God used in the Old Testament 耶和华(《圣经·旧约》中对上帝的称呼).

□ **Jehovah's 'Witness** member of a religious organization which believes that the end of the world is near and that everyone will be damned except its own members 耶和华见证人(相信世界末日在即的一种教派的教徒, 认为除该教教徒外, 一切人都将受到惩罚).

JEEP 吉普车

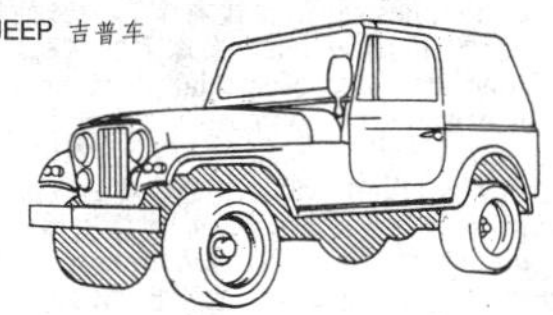

PICK-UP (*also* PICK-UP TRUCK) 轻型小货车

je·june /dʒɪ'dʒu:n; dʒɪ'dʒun/ *adj* (*fml* 文) **1** (of writings) dull and uninteresting; unsatisfying to the mind (指文字)枯燥无味的, 言之无文的. **2** childish; unsophisticated 幼稚的; 不懂世故的.

Jek·yll and Hyde /ˌdʒekl ən 'haɪd; ˌdʒɛkl ən 'haɪd/ single person with two personalities, one good (*Jekyll*) and one bad (*Hyde*) 有善恶双重人格的人: *I'd never have expected him to behave like that; he's a real Jekyll and Hyde.* 我从来没有想到他会那样, 他真是有善恶双重人格.

jell /dʒel; dʒɛl/ *v* [I] **1** become like jelly; set 成胶状; 凝结: *This strawberry jam is still runny: I can't get it to jell.* 这草莓酱还是太稀, 凝结不起来. **2** (*fig* 比喻) take shape; become definite 定形; 明确化: *My ideas are beginning to jell.* 我的想法逐渐明确了.

jelly /'dʒelɪ; 'dʒɛlɪ/ *n* **1** (**a**) [U, C] clear (fruit-flavoured) food substance made of liquid set with gelatine, usu prepared in a mould, which shakes when moved 果冻: *Can I have some more jelly, please?* 请再给我点果冻行吗? ○ *All the strawberry jellies had been eaten.* 草莓冻都吃光了. ○ (*fig* 比喻) *She went into the interview room, her legs shaking like jelly*, ie She was so nervous that she was unsteady. 她走进面试室, 两腿抖得像果冻一样颤颤巍巍. ○ [attrib 作定语] *a jelly mould* 果冻模子. (**b**) [U] savoury food like this made from the juices of meat and gelatine 肉冻. **2** [U] type of jam made of strained fruit juice and sugar (滤过的果汁和糖制成的)果酱: *blackcurrant jelly* 黑醋栗果酱. **3** [U] jelly-like substance 果冻状物: *petroleum jelly* 矿脂.

▷ **jel·lied** *adj* [usu attrib 通常作定语] set in jelly; prepared in jelly; like jelly 胶凝的; 做成冻子的; 胶冻状的: *jellied eels* 鳗冻.

□ **'jelly baby** small fruit-flavoured sweet in the shape of a baby, made from gelatine 胶糖娃娃(娃娃形状的果味凝胶软糖).

'jellyfish *n* (*pl* unchanged or **~es** 复数或不变或作 **jellyfishes**) sea animal with a jelly-like body and stinging tentacles 水母; 海蜇.

jemmy /'dʒemɪ; 'dʒɛmɪ/ (*US* **jimmy** /'dʒɪmɪ; 'dʒɪmɪ/) *n* short heavy steel bar used by burglars to force open doors and windows (窃贼撬门窗用的)短铁撬, 铁撬棍.

je ne sais quoi /ʒə nə seɪ 'kwɑ:; ʒə nə se 'kwɑ/ (*French* 法) (usu pleasing) quality that is difficult to describe (通常指好的)难以描述的特性: *His new play has a certain je ne sais quoi.* 他的这出新戏有些地方真是妙不可言.

jeop·ard·ize, -ise /'dʒepədaɪz; 'dʒɛpɚdˌaɪz/ *v* [Tn] cause (sth) to be harmed, lost or destroyed; put in danger 使(某事物)受到伤害、损失或破坏; 使陷于险境: *The security of the whole operation has been jeopardized by one careless person.* 整个作业的安全让一个粗心大意的人给破坏了.

jeop·ardy /'dʒepədɪ; 'dʒɛpɚdɪ/ *n* (idm 习语) **in jeopardy** in danger of harm, loss or destruction 处于受伤害、受损失或受破坏的危险境地: *A fall in demand for oil tankers has put/placed thousands of jobs in the shipbuilding industry in jeopardy.* 油轮需求量下降使造船业成千上万的工作职位受到威胁.

jer·boa /dʒɜ:'bəʊə; dʒɚ'boə/ *n* small rat-like animal of Asia and the N African deserts with long hind legs and the ability to jump well 跳鼠(产于亚洲和非洲北部的沙漠, 后腿长, 善跳).

je·re·miad /ˌdʒerɪ'maɪæd; ˌdʒɛrə'maɪæd/ *n* (*fml* 文) long, sad and complaining story of troubles, misfortunes, etc 悲伤的长篇故事; 血泪史.

jerk /dʒɜ:k; dʒɝk/ *n* **1** sudden pull, push, start, stop, twist, lift or throw 突然的拉、推、开始、停止、拧、抬或扔: *He gave his tooth a sharp jerk and it came out.* 他猛一使劲把牙拔了下来. ○ *The bus stopped with a jerk.* 公共汽车骤然停住了. **2** sudden involuntary twitch of a muscle or muscles (肌肉的) 反射: *a jerk of an eyelid* 眼皮的一跳. **3** (*infml derog* 口, 贬) foolish person 蠢人.

▷ **jerk** *v* **1** [Tn·pr, Tn·p] pull (sth/sb) suddenly and quickly in the specified direction 猛拉(某物[某人]): *He jerked the fishing-rod out of the water.* 他猛然从水中挑起鱼竿. ○ *She jerked her hand away when he tried to touch it.* 他刚要摸她的手, 她一下子就把手缩了回去. **2** [I, Ipr, Ip, Tn, Tn·pr, Tn·p] (cause sth/sb to) move with a short sudden action or a series of short uneven actions (使某物[某人])猛然一动或颤动: *His head keeps jerking.* 他直晃脑袋. ○ *The train jerked to a halt.* 火车猛然停住了. ○ *She jerked upright in surprise.* 她惊讶得跳了起来. ○ *Try not to jerk the camera when taking a photograph.* 拍照时照相机不要晃. ○ *He jerked his head towards the door.* 他猛然把头扭向大门. **3** (phr v) **jerk (oneself) off** (⚠ *sl* 讳, 俚) (of a man) masturbate (指男子)手淫. **jerk sth out** utter sth in an abrupt nervous manner 紧张而断断续续地说出某事: *jerk out a request, an apology, etc* 结结巴巴地提出请求、道歉等.

jerky *adj* (**-ier**, **-iest**) making abrupt starts and stops; not moving or talking smoothly 忽动忽停的; 颠簸不稳的; 结结巴巴的: *The toy robot moved forward with quick jerky steps.* 玩具机器人一颠一颠地走得很快. ○ *his jerky way of speaking* 他讲话时结结巴巴的样子. **jerk·ily** /-ɪlɪ; -əlɪ/ *adv*. **jerki·ness** *n* [U].

jer·kin /'dʒɜ:kɪn; 'dʒɝkɪn/ *n* short close-fitting jacket without sleeves, worn by men or women (男用或女用的)坎肩.

jerry-build /'dʒerɪbɪld; 'dʒɛrɪˌbɪld/ *v* [I, Tn] (*derog* 贬) build (houses, etc) quickly and cheaply without concern for quality 偷工减料地建造(房屋等).

▷ **'jerry-builder** *n* person who builds in this way 偷工减料的营造商.

'jerry-building *n* [U].

'jerry-built *adj*: *jerry-built houses* 偷工减料建成的房屋.

jer·ry·can /'dʒerɪkæn; 'dʒɛrɪˌkæn/ *n* type of large flat-sided metal container used for storing or carrying liquids, usu petrol or water 扁平金属罐(贮存或运送汽油、水等液体用的).

Jer·sey /'dʒɜ:zɪ; 'dʒɝzɪ/ *n* type of light-brown cow that produces creamy milk 泽西乳牛(浅棕色, 乳中含脂率高).

jer·sey /'dʒɜ:zɪ; 'dʒɝzɪ/ *n* (*pl* **~s**) **1** (also **jumper, pullover, sweater**) [C] close-fitting knitted (esp woollen) garment without fastenings, usu worn over a shirt or blouse 针织(尤指毛织)紧身套衫(通常穿在衬衣外面): *a thick green jersey* 厚的绿色套头毛衣. **2** (also **jersey-wool**) [U] soft fine knitted woollen fabric used for making clothes 优级细毛纱.

jest /dʒest; dʒɛst/ *n* **1** thing said or done to cause amusement; joke 玩笑; 笑话. **2** (idm 习语) **in jest** in fun; not seriously 开玩笑地; 不严肃地: *His reply was taken half seriously, half in jest.* 他的答复看来是半开玩笑半认真的. ○ (*saying* 谚) *Many a true word is spoken in jest.* 玩笑话里有许多是真话.

▷ **jest** *v* [I, Ipr] **~ (with sb) (about sth)** make jokes (to sb) (about sth); speak or act without seriousness (跟某人)(以某事)开玩笑; 以不严肃的态度说话或做事: *Stop jesting and be serious for a moment!* 别开玩笑了, 严肃一会儿吧! ○ *Don't jest about such important matters!* 这么重要的事情可不要当儿戏! **jester** *n* (formerly) man whose job was to make jokes to amuse a court or noble household (旧时)(宫廷或贵族豢养的)弄臣, 小

丑: *the court/king's/queen's jester* 宫廷的[国王的/王后的]弄臣.

Jes·uit /ˈdʒezjʊɪt; US ˈdʒeʒəwət; ˋdʒɛʒʊɪt/ *n* **1** member of the Society of Jesus, a Roman Catholic religious order 耶稣会会士(天主教修会的). **2** (*derog* 贬) person who deceives others, or fails to tell the (whole) truth, to achieve his ends 弄虚作假的人.

▷ **Jesu·it·ical** /ˌdʒezjʊˈɪtɪkl; US ˌdʒeʒʊ-; ˌdʒɛʒʊˋɪtɪkl/ *adj* (*derog* 贬) involving deception or dishonesty 狡诈的; 虚伪的: *a Jesuitical scheme, reply* 诡诈的阴谋、回答.

Jesus /ˈdʒi:zəs; ˋdʒizəs/ *n* = CHRIST.

jet[1] /dʒet; dʒɛt/ *n* **1** (also **jet aircraft**) aircraft powered by a jet engine 喷气式飞机: *The accident happened as the jet was about to take off.* 喷气式飞机正要起飞时出了事故. ○ *travel by jet* 乘喷气式飞机 ○ [attrib 作定语] *a jet fighter, airliner, etc* 喷气式战斗机、班机等 ○ *the age of jet travel* 乘喷气机的时代. **2** (**a**) strong narrow stream of gas, liquid, steam or flame, forced out of a small opening 喷射流: *The pipe burst and jets of water shot across the kitchen.* 管子破了, 水从厨房的这边喷到那边. (**b**) narrow opening from which this comes 喷嘴; 喷射口: *clean the gas jets on the cooker* 把煤气炉的喷嘴弄干净.

▷ **jet** *v* (**-tt-**) **1** [I, Ipr, Ip] (*infml* 口) travel by jet airliner 乘喷气式飞机: *politicians who constantly jet around the world* 乘喷气式飞机往来于世界各地的政治家. **2** (phr v) **jet (sth) from/out of sth; jet (sth) out** (cause sth to) come out in a jet or jets (使某物)喷出: *Flames jetted out (of the nozzles).* 火焰(从喷嘴中)喷出来了.

□ ˈ**jet engine** engine that gives forward movement by sending out a high-speed jet of hot gases, etc at the back 喷气发动机. ⇨illus at AIRCRAFT 见 AIRCRAFT 插图.

ˈ**jet lag** delayed physical effects of tiredness, etc felt after a long flight by plane, esp when there is a great difference in the local times at which the journey begins and ends 喷气飞行时差反应(长途飞行后延缓的身体疲劳反应, 尤因两地时差悬殊所致). ˈ**jet-lagged** *adj* affected by jet lag 有喷气飞行时差反应的.

ˌ**jet-proˈpelled** *adj* powered by jet engines 喷气推进的. ˌ**jet proˈpulsion** [U].

the ˈ**jet set** rich fashionable social group who travel about the world for business or pleasure 喷气机阶层(乘喷气机往来于世界各地公干或旅游的有钱人): *I see she's joining the jet set!* 我看她是进入了喷气机阶层. ˈ**jet-setter** *n* member of the jet set 喷气机阶层的成员.

jet[2] /dʒet; dʒɛt/ *n* [U] hard black mineral that can be polished brightly and is used for jewellery 煤玉, 黑玉(黑色矿物, 质硬, 可抛光用作饰物).

□ ˌ**jet-ˈblack** *adj, n* [U] (of a) deep glossy black 煤玉色(的); 黑而亮(的): *ˌjet-black ˈhair, ˈeyebrows, etc* 黑油油的头发、眉毛等.

jet·sam /ˈdʒetsəm; ˋdʒɛtsəm/ *n* [U] **1** goods thrown overboard from a ship in distress to lighten it; such goods washed up ashore 遇难船只为减轻重量而抛弃的货物; 冲到岸上的这类物品. Cf 参看 FLOTSAM. **2** (idm 习语) **flotsam and jetsam** ⇨ FLOTSAM.

J

jet·tison /ˈdʒetɪsn; ˋdʒɛtəsn̩/ *v* [Tn] **1** throw or eject (unwanted goods or material) from a ship in distress, or from an aeroplane, a spacecraft, etc 从遇难船中或从飞机、宇宙飞船等上投弃(物品): *The first-stage vehicle is used to launch the rocket and is then jettisoned in the upper atmosphere.* 第一级运载火箭是用来发射火箭的, 进入高层大气后即抛掉. **2** abandon or reject (sth that is not wanted) 放弃或拒绝(不想要的事物): *to jettison a plan, an idea, a theory, etc* 放弃一计划、想法、理论等.

jetty /ˈdʒetɪ; ˋdʒɛtɪ/ *n* stone wall or wooden platform built out into a sea, river, etc as a breakwater or landing-place for boats 防波堤; 突堤; 码头. Cf 参看 PIER.

Jew /dʒu:; dʒu/ *n* person of the Hebrew people or religion 犹太人; 犹太教徒.

▷ **Jew·ess** /ˈdʒu:ɪs; ˋdʒuɪs/ *n* (*sometimes offensive* 有时作轻蔑语) Jewish woman 犹太女子.

Jew·ish /ˈdʒu:ɪʃ; ˋdʒuɪʃ/ *adj* of the Jews 犹太人的: *the local Jewish community* 当地的犹太人社区.

Jewry /ˈdʒʊərɪ; ˋdʒurɪ/ *n* **1** [Gp] Jewish people collectively 犹太人(总称): *world Jewry* 世界上的犹太人. **2** [U] Jewish religion or culture 犹太人的宗教或文化. ⇨ Usage at CHRISTIAN 用法见 CHRISTIAN.

□ ˌ**Jew's** ˈ**harp** small musical instrument held between the teeth with a projecting metal strip that is struck with a finger 单簧口琴(含在齿间, 用手指拨奏外伸的金属片).

jewel /ˈdʒu:əl; ˋdʒuəl/ *n* **1** (**a**) precious stone (eg a diamond or a ruby) 宝石(如钻石或红宝石). (**b**) ornament with such a stone or stones set in it 镶有宝石的装饰品; 珠宝: [attrib 作定语] *a jewel thief* 盗珠宝的窃贼. **2** small precious stone, or piece of special glass, used in the machinery of a watch or compass (手表或罗盘内的)宝石轴承: *a watch with 17 jewels* 17钻的手表. **3** person or thing that is greatly valued 受珍视的人或物: *He's always saying his wife is a real jewel.* 他总说他的妻子是至宝. ○ *a painting by Goya, the brightest jewel in his collection of art treasures* 戈雅的画, 他所收藏的艺术珍品中最光彩夺目的一颗明珠.

▷ **jew·elled** (US **jew·eled**) *adj* decorated with or having jewels 饰以宝石的; 镶宝石的: *a jewelled ring, dagger, snuff-box, etc* 镶宝石的戒指、匕首、鼻烟壶等.

jew·el·ler (US **jew·eler**) *n* person who sells, makes or repairs jewellery or watches 出售、制造或修理珠宝饰物或钟表的人.

jew·el·lery (also **jew·elry**) /ˈdʒu:əlrɪ; ˋdʒuəlrɪ/ *n* [U] ornaments, eg rings and necklaces, esp made of a valuable metal and sometimes set with jewels 珠宝; 首饰.

□ ˈ**jewel box**, ˈ**jewel case** box for keeping jewels in 珠宝盒; 首饰盒.

Jez·ebel /ˈdʒezəbl, -bel; ˋdʒɛzəbl̩, -bɛl/ *n* (*derog* 贬) shameless scheming woman 无耻而诡计多端的女子.

jib[1] /dʒɪb; dʒɪb/ *n* **1** small triangular sail in front of the mainsail 主帆前的小三角帆; 艏帆. ⇨illus at YACHT 见 YACHT 插图. **2** projecting arm of a crane 起重机的臂. **3** (idm 习语) **the cut of his jib** ⇨ CUT[2].

□ ˈ**jib-boom** *n* pole to which the lower part of a jib(1) is fastened 艏斜帆桁.

jib[2] /dʒɪb; dʒɪb/ *v* (**-bb-**) **1** [I] (of a horse, etc) stop suddenly; refuse to go forwards (指马等)突然停步, 逡巡不前. **2** [I, Ipr] **~ (at sth/doing sth)** (*fig* 比喻) refuse to proceed with (an action); be reluctant to do or accept sth 拒绝继续进行(活动); 不愿做或不愿接受某事物: *He jibbed when he heard how much the tickets would cost.* 他一知道票价就不想买了. ○ *The staff don't mind the new work schedule but they would jib at taking a cut in wages.* 全体工作人员对新工作时间表倒不介意, 但不同意削减工资.

jibe **1** = GIBE. **2** (US) = GYBE.

jiffy /ˈdʒɪfɪ; ˋdʒɪfɪ/ *n* [C] (*infml* 口) moment 一会儿: *I'll be with you in a couple of jiffies*, ie very soon. 我一会儿就来.

jig /dʒɪg; dʒɪg/ *n* **1** (music for a) quick lively dance 吉格舞; 吉格舞曲. **2** device that holds a piece of work in position and guides the tools that are working on it 夹具.

▷ **jig** *v* (**-gg-**) **1** [I] dance a jig 跳吉格舞. **2** [I, Ip, Tn, Tn·p] (cause sb/sth to) move up and down in a quick jerky way (使某人[某物])急速颠簸: *jigging up and down in excitement* 兴奋得又蹦又跳 ○ *to jig a baby (up and down) on one's knee* 把婴儿放在膝上(上下)颠动.

jig·ger /ˈdʒɪgə(r); ˋdʒɪgɚ/ *n* small measure for alcoholic drinks; small glass holding this amount (量酒的)小量器; (盛此量的)小玻璃杯.

jig·gered /ˈdʒɪgəd; ˋdʒɪgɚd/ *adj* [pred 作表语] (*infml* 口) **1** (*dated* 旧) (used as a mild expression of surprise, anger, etc 用以表示轻度的惊奇、愤怒等): *Well I'm jiggered!* 哪有这种事! **2** exhausted 精疲力竭: *I was completely jiggered.* 我完全累垮了.

jiggery-pokery /ˌdʒɪgərɪ ˈpəʊkərɪ; ˋdʒɪgərɪˋpokərɪ/ *n* [U] (*infml* 口 *esp Brit*) secret and mischievous or dishonest behaviour; mischief or trickery 捣鬼; 欺骗: *He began to suspect that some jiggery-pokery was going on.* 他怀疑有人在暗中捣鬼.

jiggle /ˈdʒɪgl; ˋdʒɪgl/ *v* [I, Tn] (*infml* 口) (cause sth to) move lightly and quickly from side to side or up and down (使某物)很快地左右或上下移动: *jiggling in time to the music* 随着音乐摇摆 ○ *jiggle a key in a lock* 轻轻转动锁里的钥匙.

jig·saw /ˈdʒɪgsɔ:; ˋdʒɪgˌsɔ/ *n* **1** (also ˈ**jigsaw puzzle**) picture, map, etc pasted on cardboard or wood and cut

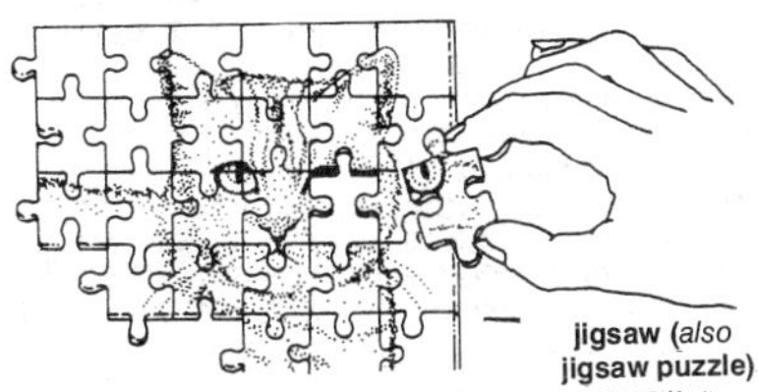

jigsaw (*also* **jigsaw puzzle**) 拼图游戏

into irregular shapes that have to be fitted together again 拼图玩具: *do a jigsaw* 做拼图游戏 ○ *Have you finished the jigsaw yet?* 你拼好那个拼图了吗? ○ (*fig* 比喻) *a complex jigsaw of interlocking social and economic factors* 相关联的社会和经济因素的相互交错. ⇨illus 见插图. **2** mechanically operated fretsaw 锯曲线机; 线锯; 镂花锯.

ji·had /dʒɪˈhɑːd; dʒɪˈhɑd/ *n* holy war fought by Muslims against those who reject Islam 圣战(穆斯林对异教徒之战).

jilt /dʒɪlt; dʒɪlt/ *v* [Tn] leave (a man or woman) with whom one has had a close emotional relationship, esp suddenly and unkindly 抛弃或遗弃(情人): *a jilted lover* 被抛弃的恋人.

Jim Crow /ˌdʒɪm ˈkrəʊ; ˈdʒɪmˈkro/ (*US derog offensive* 贬, 蔑) Black; negro 黑人: [attrib 作定语] *Jim Crow laws*, ie ones unfair to Black Americans 黑人法(对美国黑人不公正的法律) ○ *Jim Crow schools, buses, etc*, ie for American Blacks only, and usu of poor quality 黑人学校、公共汽车等(仅为美国黑人提供的, 通常质量低劣).

jim-jams /ˈdʒɪmdʒæmz; ˈdʒɪmˌdʒæmz/ *n* **the jim-jams** [pl] (*sl* 俚) feelings of extreme nervousness; the jitters 神经极度紧张: *Steady on: you're giving me the jim-jams!* 沉住气, 你弄得我神经紧张!

jimmy (*US*) = JEMMY.

jingle /ˈdʒɪŋgl; ˈdʒɪŋgl/ *n* **1** [sing] metallic ringing or clinking sound, as of coins, keys or small bells (金属发出的)叮当声(如硬币、钥匙或小铃的声音): *the jingle of coins in his pocket* 他衣袋里硬币的叮当声. **2** [C] short simple rhyme or song that is designed to attract attention and be easily remembered, esp one used in advertising on radio or television (吸引人又易记的)简短的韵文或歌曲(尤指广播或电视广告中的): *an advertising jingle* 广告顺口溜.

▷ **jingle** *v* [I, Tn] (cause sth to) make a gentle ringing or clinking sound (使某物)发出叮当声: *The coins jingled in his pocket.* 他衣袋里的硬币叮当作响. ○ *the sound of jingling bracelets and bangles* 手镯、脚镯的叮当声 ○ *Stop jingling your keys like that!* 别把钥匙弄得叮当乱响!

jin·go·ism /ˈdʒɪŋgəʊɪzəm; ˈdʒɪŋgoˌɪzəm/ *n* [U] (*derog* 贬) extreme and unreasonable belief that one's own country is best, together with a warlike attitude towards other countries 极端爱国主义(主张对外实行战争政策).

▷ **jin·go·ist** /ˈdʒɪŋgəʊɪst; ˈdʒɪŋgoɪst/ *n* person who has such a belief 极端爱国主义者.

jin·go·istic /ˌdʒɪŋgəʊˈɪstɪk; ˌdʒɪŋgoˈɪstɪk/ *adj*: *ˌjingoistic reˈmarks* 极端爱国主义的言论.

jink /dʒɪŋk; dʒɪŋk/ *v* [I, Ipr, Ip] (*infml* 口) move quickly or suddenly with sharp turns, usu to avoid being caught; dodge 急转; (通常指)躲闪, 避开.

▷ **jink** *n* **1** quick turning movement 急转弯: *a sharp jink to the right* 向右的急转弯. **2** (idm 习语) **high jinks** ⇨ HIGH[1].

jin·nee /dʒɪˈniː; dʒɪˈni/ (also **djinn, jinn** /dʒɪn; dʒɪn/) *n* (*pl* **jinn**) **1** (in Muslim mythology) spirit with supernatural power which is able to appear in human and animal forms 镇尼(穆斯林神话中的精灵, 能变成人形和动物). **2** = GENIE.

jinx /dʒɪŋks; dʒɪŋks/ *n* (usu *sing* 通常作单数) **~ (on sb/sth)** (*infml* 口) (person or thing that is thought to bring) bad luck (to sb/sth); curse 厄运; 不祥的人或事物; 祸根: *There's a jinx on/Someone's put a jinx on this car: it's always giving me trouble.* 这辆汽车上有什么妨人的东西, 总给我找麻烦.

▷ **jinx** *v* [Tn usu passive 通常用于被动语态] (*infml* 口) bring bad luck to (sb/sth) 给(某人[某事])带来厄运: *I've been jinxed!* 我一直走背运! ○ *I think this computer must be jinxed — it's always breaking down.* 这计算机一定闹鬼了——总出毛病.

jit·ter /ˈdʒɪtə(r); ˈdʒɪtɚ/ *v* [I] (*infml* 口) feel nervous; behave nervously 感到神经紧张; 举止不自然: *jittering with fright* 吓得神经紧张.

▷ **the jit·ters** *n* [pl] (*infml* 口) feelings of extreme nervousness; the jim-jams 神经极度紧张: *give sb/have/get the jitters* 使某人极为紧张 ○ *I always get the jitters before I go on stage.* 我登台之前总是感到紧张.

jit·tery /ˈdʒɪtərɪ; ˈdʒɪtərɪ/ *adj* (*infml* 口) nervous; frightened 神经紧张的; 害怕的.

□ **ˈjitterbug** *n* performer of a lively popular dance of the 1940s to swing music 跳吉特巴舞的人. — *v* [I] perform such a dance 跳吉特巴舞.

jive /dʒaɪv; dʒaɪv/ *n* (usu 通常作 **the jive**) [sing] fast lively form of music with a strong beat; dance done to this 摇摆乐(节拍强烈、快而活泼的音乐); 摇摆舞.

▷ **jive** *v* [I] dance to jive music 跳摇摆舞.

Jnr (also **Jr, Jun**) *abbr* 缩写 = (*esp US*) Junior: *John F Davis Jnr*, ie to distinguish him from his father with the same name 小约翰·F·戴维斯(因父子同名, 用以区别其父). Cf 参看 SEN 3.

Job /dʒəʊb; dʒob/ *n* (idm 习语) **the patience of job** ⇨ PATIENCE.

□ **ˌJob's ˈcomforter** person who increases the unhappiness or distress of the person he is attempting to comfort 给被安慰的人增加痛苦或烦恼的人.

job /dʒɒb; dʒɑb/ *n* **1** regularly paid position or post 职业; 职位: *Thousands of workers lost their jobs when the factory closed.* 那家工厂一倒闭, 成千的工人都失业了. ○ *He got a part-time job as a gardener.* 他找到个兼职工作, 当花匠. ○ *Should she give up her job when she has a baby?* 她有小孩之后, 要辞去工作吗? ○ *The government is trying to create new jobs.* 政府正设法提供新的就业机会. ⇨Usage at TRADE[1] 用法见 TRADE[1]. **2** piece of work; task or assignment 工作; 任务: *The shipyard is working on three different jobs*, ie building three ships. 该造船厂正在造三艘船. ○ *They've done a fine job (of work) sewing these curtains.* 他们把缝窗帘这项工作干得挺好. ○ *pay sb by the job*, ie separately for each job done 按件计酬 ○ *Writing a book was a more difficult job than he'd thought.* 写书这工作可比他原来想像的难得多. ○ *It was quite a job* (ie a difficult task) *finding his flat.* 找到他的寓所可不是件容易事. ⇨Usage at WORK[1] 用法见 WORK[1]. **3** (usu *sing* 通常作单数) responsibility or function of sb/sth 责任; 职责: *It's not my job to lock up!* 上锁不是我分内的事. ○ *It's the job of the church to help people lead better lives.* 帮助人们生活得好些是教会的责任. **4** (*infml* 口) thing that is completed; product 成品; 产品: *Your new car is a neat little job, isn't it?* 你这辆新汽车很精巧哇, 是吧? **5** (*infml* 口) criminal act, esp theft; dishonest or unfair action 罪行(尤指盗窃); 欺骗; 不正当的行为: *He got three years for a job he did in Leeds.* 他在利兹犯盗窃罪被判三年徒刑. **6** (idm 习语) **do the ˈjob/ˈtrick** (*infml* 口) succeed in doing what is required or desired 起作用; 奏效: *This extra strong glue should do the job nicely.* 这种超强度胶应该管用. **give sb/sth up as a bad ˈjob** (*infml* 口) decide that one can no longer help sb or be concerned for sb/sth because there seems no hope of success (因无成效)决定不再帮助某人或不再关心某人[某事]: *His parents have given him up as a bad job.* 他父母对他已不抱希望了. ○ *After waiting an hour for the bus she decided to give it up as a bad job.* 她等了一小时公共汽车后就决定不再等了. **a good ˈjob** (*infml* 口) (used as a comment on actions or events 用作对行动或事情的评语) a fortunate state of affairs 幸运之事: *She's stopped smoking, and a good job too!* 她戒烟了, 真是好事! ○ *It's a good job you were there to help — we couldn't have managed without you.* 多亏你来帮忙——不然我们真没法办. **have a devil of a job doing sth** ⇨ DEVIL[1]. **jobs for the ˈboys** (*infml* 口) the giving of paid employment to favoured groups, usu

J

friends or relations 将有薪工作给予亲信(通常指亲友). **just the 'job/'ticket** (*infml approv* 口, 褒) exactly what is wanted or needed 正是想要的: *Thanks for lending me your big lawn-mower. It was just the job for the long grass.* 多谢你借给我大割草机. 割高草正需要这个. **make a bad, excellent, good, poor, etc job of sth** do sth badly, well, etc 将某事做坏、做好等: *Mark's a difficult child and I think they're making a good job of bringing him up.* 马克是个不听话的孩子, 我看他们现在对他的培养方面做得不错. ○ *You've certainly made an excellent job of the kitchen*, eg decorating it. 你把厨房弄得太棒了(如装修). **make the best of a bad job** ⇨ BEST[3]. **on the 'job (a)** working; at work 正在工作; 上班: *lie down/go to sleep on the job*, ie not work energetically and continuously 工作时无精打采、时干时停 ○ [attrib 作定语] *on-the-job training*, ie training given to workers at their place of work 岗位培训(在工作人员的工作处进行培训). **(b)** (*Brit sl* 俚) having sexual intercourse 正在性交. **out of a 'job** unemployed 失业: *He was out of a job for six months.* 他已失业半年了.

▷ **job·less** *adj* unemployed 失业的; 无职业的. **the jobless** *n* [pl *v*] people who are unemployed 失业的人: *The government's new scheme is designed to help the jobless.* 政府制定了协助失业者的新计划. **job·less·ness** *n* [U].

□ **'jobcentre** *n* (*Brit*) (*Brit* also *dated* 旧亦作 **Labour Exchange**) government office displaying information about available jobs 政府职业介绍所.

'job creation process of providing opportunities for paid work, esp for those who are currently unemployed 提供就业机会(尤指为一时无工作的人): [attrib 作定语] *a job-creation 'scheme, 'project, 'programme, etc* 提供就业机会的计划、方案、安排等.

'job description written description of the exact responsibilities of a job 工作职责说明.

job 'lot mixed collection of articles, esp of poor quality, offered together for sale 物品(尤指次品)的混合搭配销售.

'job satisfaction fulfilment gained from doing one's job 完成工作的满足感.

'job sharing arrangement by which two or more people are employed on a part-time basis to do work that would otherwise have been done by one person working full-time 一工分做制(两人或两人以上分时做一份工作的制度).

job·ber /ˈdʒɒbə(r); ˋdʒɑbɚ/ *n* (*Brit*) (formerly) trader on the Stock Exchange who buys and sells shares without dealing directly with the public (旧时)股票经纪人.

job·bery /ˈdʒɒbərɪ; ˋdʒɑbərɪ/ *n* [U] (*derog* 贬) use of unfair or corrupt methods in order to gain a financial or political advantage 营私舞弊; 假公济私; 贪污渎职.

job·bing /ˈdʒɒbɪŋ; ˋdʒɑbɪŋ/ *adj* [attrib 作定语] doing single, specific (and esp small) pieces of work for payment 做零工的; 做散工的: *a jobbing printer, gardener, etc* 承印零星印刷品的商人、打零工的花匠.

J

jockey[1] /ˈdʒɒkɪ; ˋdʒɑkɪ/ *n* (*pl* **~s**) person who rides a horse, usu a professional competing in races 骑师; (通常指)职业赛马骑师.

jockey[2] /ˈdʒɒkɪ; ˋdʒɑkɪ/ *v* (phr v) **jockey for sth** manoeuvre to gain (an advantage, a favour, etc) 用计谋获取(利益、好处等): *jockey for position, power, favours, etc* 用计谋获得职位、权力、好处等. **jockey sb into/out of sth** persuade sb by skilful management or unfair manoeuvring to do/give up sth 用巧妙的方法或诡计说服某人做[放弃]某事: *They jockeyed Fred out of his position on the board.* 他们设法欺骗弗雷德放弃在董事会的职位.

jock-strap /ˈdʒɒkstræp; ˋdʒɑkˌstræp/ *n* close-fitting undergarment worn by sportsmen to support or protect the genitals (男运动员用的)下体护身, 护裆.

joc·ose /dʒəʊˈkəʊs; dʒoˋkos/ *adj* (*dated fml* 旧, 文) humorous; playful 诙谐的; 开玩笑的. ▷ **joc·osely** *adv*. **joc·os·ity** /dʒəʊˈkɒsətɪ; dʒoˋkɑsətɪ/ *n* [U].

joc·ular /ˈdʒɒkjʊlə(r); ˋdʒɑkjəlɚ/ *adj* **1** meant as a joke; humorous 滑稽的; 诙谐的: *jocular remarks* 诙谐的言语. **2** fond of joking; playful 爱开玩笑的; 嬉戏的: *a jocular fellow* 爱开玩笑的傢伙. ▷ **jocu·lar·ity** /ˌdʒɒkjʊˈlærətɪ; ˌdʒɑkjəˋlærətɪ/ *n* [U]. **joc·ularly** *adv*: *Philip, jocularly known as Flip* 菲利普, 被戏称为'费力跑'.

joc·und /ˈdʒɒkənd; ˋdʒɑkənd/ *adj* (*dated* 旧) merry; cheerful 欢乐的; 愉快的. ▷ **joc·und·ity** /dʒəʊˈkʌndətɪ; dʒoˋkʌndətɪ/ *n* [U].

jodh·purs /ˈdʒɒdpəz; ˋdʒɑdpɚz/ *n* [pl] trousers worn for horse-riding, loose above the knee and close fitting from the knee to the ankle 马裤: *a pair of jodhpurs* 一条马裤.

jog /dʒɒg; dʒɑg/ *v* **(-gg-) 1** [Tn] push or knock (sb/sth) slightly 轻推或轻碰(某人[某物]): *Don't jog me, or you'll make me spill something!* 别碰我, 不然我就把东西弄洒了. **2** [I] (usu 通常作 **go jogging**) run slowly and steadily for a time, for physical exercise 慢跑(作为运动): *He goes jogging every evening.* 他每天晚上都作慢跑. ⇨Usage at RUN[1] 用法见RUN[1]. **3** [Ipr, Ip] move unsteadily, esp up and down, in a shaky manner 不平稳地移动; (尤指)颠簸: *The wagon jogged along (a rough track).* 马车(沿凹凸不平的小路)颠簸前行. **4** [I] (of a horse) move at a jogtrot (指马)颠跑. **5** (idm 习语) **jog sb's memory** help sb to recall sth 唤起某人记起某事: *This photograph may jog your memory.* 这照片能引起你的回忆. **6** (phr v) **jog along/on** continue in a steady manner, with little or no excitement or progress 持续而缓慢地进行; 无起色或无大进展: *For years the business just kept jogging along.* 多年来生意仅仅是平平而已.

▷ **jog** *n* [sing] **1** slight push, knock or shake; nudge 轻推; 轻碰; 轻摇; 以肘轻触: *He gave the pile of tins a jog and they all fell down.* 他轻轻一碰, 那些罐子就都倒了. ○ (*fig* 比喻) *give sb's memory a jog* 给某人提个醒. **2** spell of jogging as exercise (为锻炼的)短时慢跑: *Are you coming for a jog tomorrow morning?* 明天早晨你来慢跑吗?

jog·ger /ˈdʒɒgə(r); ˋdʒɑgɚ/ *n* person who jogs for exercise (为锻炼)慢跑的人.

jog·ging /ˈdʒɒgɪŋ; ˋdʒɑgɪŋ/ *n* [U].

□ **'jogtrot** *n* slow regular trot 慢而有规律的行走; 缓行.

joggle /ˈdʒɒgl; ˋdʒɑgl/ *v* [I, Ip, Tn, Tn·p] (cause sb/sth to) move or shake slightly, usu up and down (使某人[某物])轻轻颠动, 摇动.

john /dʒɒn; dʒɑn/ *n* (*US sl* 俚) toilet 厕所: *go to the john* 去厕所.

John Bull /ˌdʒɒn ˈbʊl; ˋdʒɑn ˋbʊl/ (*dated* 旧) the English nation; typical Englishman 英国; 典型的英国人.

johnny /ˈdʒɒnɪ; ˋdʒɑnɪ/ *n* (*Brit*) **1** (*dated infml* 旧, 口) man; fellow 男子; 傢伙. **2** (*sl* 俚) condom 男用避孕套; 阴茎套: *a rubber johnny* 橡胶避孕套.

joie de vivre /ˌʒwɑ: də ˈvi:vrə; ˌʒwɑdəˋvivr/ (*French* 法) cheerful enjoyment of life 生活的乐趣: *full of joie de vivre* 充满生活乐趣.

join /dʒɔɪn; dʒɔɪn/ *v* **1** [Tn, Tn·pr, Tn·p] **~ sth onto sth/on; ~ A to B; ~ A and B (together/up)** fasten one thing to another; connect or combine two things 连结; 结合; 联合: *Two extra carriages were joined onto the train/joined on at York.* 列车在约克又挂上了两节车厢. ○ *join one section of pipe to the next* 把一段管道与相邻的管道连接起来 ○ *join two sections of pipe together* 把两条管子接在一起 ○ *The island is joined to the mainland by a bridge.* 岛上有座桥与大陆相连. ○ (*fig* 比喻) *join two people (together) in marriage*, ie make them man and wife 使二人结为夫妻. **2** [I, Ipr, Ip, Tn] **~ up with sb/sth; ~ up** meet and unite with (sb/sth) to form one group or thing 与(某人[某物])会合或相聚: *the place where the rivers join* 河流的汇合处 ○ *The firm joined up with a small delivery company to reduce costs.* 该商行与一家小运输公司合并以降低成本. ○ *The M62 joins up with the M1/The M62 and the M1 join up south of Leeds.* 62号高速公路与1号高速公路在利兹以南会合. ○ *The two groups of walkers joined up for the rest of the holiday.* 两组步行度假者会合一起度过剩下的假期. ○ *The road joins the motorway at Newtown.* 该路在纽敦与高速公路连接. **3** [Tn] come into the company of (sb); meet 与(某人)在一起、会面或相见: *I'll join you in a minute.* 我马上就来找你. ○ *Ask him to join us for lunch.* 请他和我们一起吃午饭. ○ *Mary has just joined her family in Australia.* 玛丽不久前刚和她的家人在澳大利亚团聚. ○ *They joined* (ie got on) *the train at Watford.* 他们在沃特福德上的火车. **4** [I, Tn] become a member of (sth); become an employee in (sth) 参加(某组织); 加入(某处任职): *Membership is free, so join today!* 免交会费, 今天

就参加吧！○ *join a union, choir, club, etc* 参加工会、唱诗班、俱乐部等 ○ *join the army, navy, police, etc* 加入陆军、海军、警务部门等. **5 (a)** [Tn] take part in (sth); take one's place in (sth) 参与(某事); 在(某事)中占一位置: *join a demonstration, procession, queue, etc* 参加游行、加入一长列、排队. **(b)** [Ipr, Tn·pr] **join (with) sb in doing sth/to do sth; ~ together in doing sth/to do sth** take part with sb in an activity 与某人一起参加活动: *Mother joins (with) me in sending you our best wishes.* 我母亲和我一起向你表示美好的祝愿. ○ *The class all joined together to sing 'Happy Birthday' to the teacher.* 全班一起为老师唱'生日快乐'歌. **6** (idm 习语) **if you can't beat them join them** ⇨ BEAT[1]. **join battle (with sb)** (*fml* 文) begin fighting sb 与某人交战. **join the 'club** (said when sth bad that has already happened to oneself now happens to sb else 自己遇到过的倒霉事别人也遇到时, 可用此语表达): *You've got a parking-ticket? Well join the club!* 你收到违章停车罚款通知单了? 这真是无独有偶! **join 'forces (with sb)** come together in order to achieve a common aim 联合以达到共同的目的: *The two firms joined forces to win a major contract.* 两家公司联合起来以争得一桩大生意. **join 'hands** hold each other's hands 联手; 携手. **7** (phr v) **join in (sth/doing sth)** take part in (an activity) 参加(活动): *Can I join in (the game)?* 我参加(这个游戏)行吗? ○ *They all joined in singing the Christmas carols.* 他们一起唱圣诞颂歌. **join up** become a member of the armed forces 参军; 从军: *We both joined up in 1939.* 我们俩都是1939年入伍的.

▷ **join** *n* place or line where two things are joined 连接处; 接缝: *The two pieces were stuck together so well that you could hardly see the join.* 这两块粘合得真好, 几乎看不出接缝.

joiner /ˈdʒɔɪnə(r); ˈdʒɔɪnɚ/ *n* (*Brit*) skilled workman who makes the wooden fittings of a building, eg window frames and doors 细木工. Cf 参看 CARPENTER.

▷ **join·ery** /ˈdʒɔɪnərɪ; ˈdʒɔɪnərɪ/ *n* [U] work of a joiner 细木工的工作或制品.

joint[1] /dʒɔɪnt; dʒɔɪnt/ *n* **1** structure in the body of an animal by which bones are fitted together 关节: *ankle, knee, elbow, etc joints* 踝、膝、肘等关节 ○ *suffer from stiff joints* 患关节强直症. **2** place, line or surface at which two or more things are joined 连接处; 接缝; 接合面: *Check that the joints of the pipes are sealed properly.* 检查一下管道的接口是否封严了. **3** any of the parts into which a butcher cuts an animal's carcass; this cooked and served as meat (生的或熟的)大块肉: *a joint of beef* 一大块牛肉 ○ *carve the Sunday joint* 切开星期日吃的大块肉. **4** (*sl derog* 俚, 贬) low or shabby bar, club, etc; house or shop 下等的或破旧的酒吧、俱乐部等; 房子; 店铺. **5** (*sl* 俚) cigarette containing marijuana 含大麻的香烟. **6** (idm 习语) **case the joint** ⇨ CASE[2]. **out of joint (a)** (of bones) pushed out of position; dislocated (指骨)脱臼: *She fell and put her knee out of joint.* 她摔得膝关节脱臼了. **(b)** (*fig* 比喻) in disorder; disorganized 混乱; 紊乱: *The delays put the whole schedule out of joint.* 一再的拖延打乱了全部安排. **put sb's nose out of joint** ⇨ NOSE[1].

▷ **joint** *v* [Tn esp passive 尤用于被动语态] **1** provide (sth) with a joint or joints 给(某物)装以活节或关节: *a jointed doll, fishing-rod* 有活动关节的玩具娃娃、活动钓竿. **2** divide (a carcass) into joints or at the joints 将(屠宰后的动物)分割成大块或在关节处切开: *a jointed chicken* 切成大块的鸡.

joint[2] /dʒɔɪnt; dʒɔɪnt/ *adj* [attrib 作定语] **1** shared, held or done by two or more people together 共享的; 共有的; 共同做的: *a joint account*, ie a bank account in the name of more than one person (eg husband and wife) 联合帐户(不止一人, 如夫妇, 共有的银行户头) ○ *joint ownership, responsibility, consultation* 共同的所有权、责任、协商 ○ *a joint effort* 共同的努力. **2** sharing in an activity, a position, an achievement, etc 共同参与、持有或取得的: *joint authors, owners, winners, etc* 合著者、共同持有者、同时获胜者. ▷ **jointly** *adv*: *a jointly owned business* 共同所有的商行.

□ **joint-'stock company** = STOCK COMPANY (STOCK[1]).

joist /dʒɔɪst; dʒɔɪst/ *n* one of the long thick pieces of wood or metal that are used to support a floor or ceiling in a building 搁栅; 托梁.

joke /dʒəʊk; dʒok/ *n* **1** thing said (eg a story with a funny ending) or done to cause amusement, laughter, etc 笑话; 玩笑: *tell (sb) a joke* 给(某人)讲笑话 ○ *cracking jokes with one's friends* 跟朋友说笑话. **2** [sing] ridiculous person, thing or situation 可笑的人、事物、情形: *His attempts at cooking are a complete joke.* 他总也做不好饭, 这事成了个笑话. **3** (idm 习语) **be no 'joke; be/get beyond a 'joke** be/become a serious matter 不是闹着玩儿的事; 是[变成]正经的事: *Trying to find a job these days is no joke, I can tell you.* 我实话告诉你, 现在想找工作可不易. ○ *All your teasing of poor Michael is getting beyond a joke.* 你拿可怜的迈克尔打趣可要出圈儿了. **have a joke with sb** share the pleasure of laughing at sth with sb 与某人一起以某事取笑: *He's someone I have an occasional chat and joke with.* 我偶尔跟他闲聊, 一起说笑话. **the joke's on sb** (*infml* 口) sb who tried to make another person look foolish now looks ridiculous instead 原想要弄别人, 自己反倒成为笑料. **make a joke about/of sb/sth** speak lightly or amusingly about sb/sth 拿某人[某事]开玩笑. **play a joke/prank/trick on sb** trick sb, in order to make him appear ridiculous 戏弄某人. **see the 'joke** understand why sth said or done is amusing 理解其中的可笑之处: *I'm sorry but I can't see the joke.* 很抱歉, 我看不出来有什么可笑的. **take a 'joke** accept playful remarks or tricks with good humour 经得起玩笑话: *Can't you take a joke?* 跟你开个玩笑你都受不了吗?

▷ **joke** *v* **1** [I, Ipr] **~ (with sb) (about sth)** tell jokes (to sb) (about sth); talk in a light-hearted, frivolous way (以某事)(与某人)开玩笑; 说笑话儿: *I was only joking.* 我不过是说着玩儿的. ○ *For Pat to lose his job is nothing to joke about*, ie is a serious matter. 对帕特来说失业可不是闹着玩儿的. **2** (idm 习语) **joking a'part** speaking seriously 严肃地说; 认真地说: *Joking apart, you ought to smoke fewer cigarettes, you know.* 说正经的, 你应该少吸点儿烟了, 知道吗? **you must be/have got to be 'joking** (used to express mocking disbelief 用以嘲笑不可信的事): *'Jackie's passed her driving test.' 'You must be joking — she can't even steer straight!'* '杰基的驾驶测验及格了.' '你一定是开玩笑——她连方向盘还握不正呢!'

jokey *adj* joking; amusing or ridiculous 开玩笑的; 逗笑的; 可笑的.

jok·ingly *adv* in a joking manner 开玩笑地; 戏谑地.

joker /ˈdʒəʊkə(r); ˈdʒokɚ/ *n* **1** (*infml* 口) person who is fond of making jokes; foolish irresponsible person 爱开玩笑的人; 愚蠢而不负责任的人: *Some joker's been playing around with my car aerial!* 哪个爱胡闹的人摆弄我汽车上的天线了! **2** (*infml* 口) person who is not treated seriously 不受重视的人: *I don't want that joker in my sales team.* 我们销售部门不想要那个傢伙. **3** extra playing-card used in certain card-games (某些纸牌戏中的)百搭.

jolly /ˈdʒɒlɪ; ˈdʒɑlɪ/ *adj* (**-ier**, **-iest**) **1** happy and cheerful 愉快的; 快乐的: *a jolly person, manner, laugh* 愉快的人、态度、笑声. **2** (*dated infml* 旧, 口) lively and very pleasant; delightful or enjoyable; merry 活泼愉快的; 令人高兴的; 欢乐的: *a jolly party, song, time* 欢乐的聚会、歌曲、时候. **3** cheerful because slightly drunk 因微醉而酣畅的: *feel/look jolly* 感到[看来]微醉的畅快. **4** (idm 习语) **ˌjolly 'hockey sticks** (*Brit catchphrase* 警语) (used to suggest the cheerful athletic style of life associated with (esp private) girls' schools 用以指(尤为私立)女子学校中愉快健康的生活方式).

▷ **jol·li·fica·tion** /ˌdʒɒlɪfɪˈkeɪʃn; ˌdʒɑləfəˈkeʃən/ *n* [U, C] (*dated* 旧) merry-making; festivity 作乐; 欢乐; 欢宴.

jol·lity /ˈdʒɒlətɪ; ˈdʒɑlətɪ/ *n* [U] (*dated* 旧) state of being jolly 愉快; 欢乐.

jolly *adv* (*Brit infml* 口) **1** very 非常; 很: *She's a jolly good teacher.* 她是个非常好的老师. ○ *He can cook, and he does it jolly well.* 他会做饭, 并且做得特别好. **2** (idm 习语) **'jolly well** (used to emphasize a statement 用以强调所说的事) certainly 无疑地; 肯定地: *'Will you come back for me?' 'No — if you don't come now, you can jolly well walk home.'* '你回来接我吗?' '不——你现在要是不走, 一定得步行回家.'

jolly *v* (*pt, pp* **jollied**) (phr v) **jolly sb along** (*infml* 口) keep sb in a good/friendly mood so that he will help, work, etc 哄着某人使其帮忙、工作等: *You'll have to*

jolly him along a bit, but he'll do a good job. 得哄着他点儿, 他才好好干. **jolly sth up** make sth bright and pleasant to look at; cheer sth up 使某物看上去鲜艳夺目; 使某物有生气: *This room needs jollying up — how about yellow and red wallpaper?* 这间屋子需要弄得明快些——来点儿黄色和红色的壁纸怎么样?
□ **the ˌJolly ˈRoger** the black flag of a pirate ship (with skull and cross-bones) 海盗船的黑旗(骷髅旗).

jolly-boat /ˈdʒɒlɪ bəʊt; ˋdʒɑlɪbot/ *n* type of ship's boat 大船携带的小艇.

jolt /dʒəʊlt; dʒolt/ *v* **1** [I, Ipr, Ip, Tn, Tn·pr, Tn·p] (cause sb/sth to) move with sudden jerky movements (使某人[某物])颠簸着移动: *The old bus jolted along (a rough track).* 旧公共汽车(沿凹凸不平的小路)颠簸而行. **2** (phr v) **jolt sb into/out of sth** make sb act by giving him a sudden shock 使某人受到震惊而采取行动: *He was jolted out of his lethargy and into action when he realized he had only a short time to finish the article.* 他意识到须在很短时间就得把文章写完, 立即振作精神写起来.
▷ **jolt** *n* (esp *sing* 尤作单数) **1** sudden bump or shake; jerk 震动; 摇晃; 颠簸: *stop with a jolt* 停止时震动了一下. **2** (*fig* 比喻) surprise; shock 惊奇; 震惊: *The news of the accident gave her an unpleasant jolt/quite a jolt.* 她听到出事的消息吃了一惊[大吃一惊].
jolty *adj* jolting 震动的; 摇晃的; 颠簸的.

Joneses /ˈdʒəʊnzɪz; ˋdʒonzɪz/ *n* [pl] (idm 习语) **keep up with the Joneses** ⇨KEEP[1] 15.

jon·quil /ˈdʒɒŋkwɪl; ˋdʒɑŋkwɪl/ *n* type of narcissus with white or yellow sweet-smelling flowers 长寿花; 黄水仙.

josh /dʒɒʃ; dʒɑʃ/ *v* (*US infml* 口) **1** [I] joke 开玩笑; 说笑话儿. **2** [Tn] tease (sb) 戏弄; 逗弄(某人).

joss-stick /ˈdʒɒstɪk; ˋdʒɑsˌstɪk/ *n* thin stick that burns slowly and produces a smell of incense (点燃用的)香.

jostle /ˈdʒɒsl; ˋdʒɑsl/ *v* [I, Ipr, Tn] **1 ~ (against sb)** push roughly against (sb), usu in a crowd 推、挤(某人)(通常于人群中): *The youths jostled (against) an old lady on the pavement.* 那些青年人在人行道上推推搡搡挤着了一个老太太. **2 ~ (with sb) (for sth)** compete with (other people) in a forceful manner in order to gain sth 与(他人)争夺某物; 争抢: *advertisers jostling (with each other) for the public's attention* 竞相吸引公众注意力的广告客户.

jot[1] /dʒɒt; dʒɑt/ *v* (**-tt-**) (phr v) **jot sth down** make a quick, usu short, written note of sth 匆匆记下(通常为简短的)笔记: *I'll just jot down their phone number before I forget it.* 我得把他们的电话号码赶快记下来, 以免待一会儿忘记.
▷ **jot·ter** *n* notebook or pad for short written notes 记事本; 笔记本.
jot·tings *n* [pl] short written notes 简短的笔记; 便条.

jot[2] /dʒɒt; dʒɑt/ *n* [sing] (usu with a negative 通常与否定词连用) very small amount 极少量: *I don't care a jot for their feelings.* 我一点都不理会他们的感受. ○ *There's not a jot of truth in his story.* 他讲的一句实话都没有.

joule /dʒuːl; dʒul/ *n* (*abbr* 缩写 **J**) (*physics* 物) unit of energy or work 焦耳(能量或功的单位).

J

journal /ˈdʒɜːnl; ˋdʒɝnl/ *n* **1** newspaper or periodical, esp one that is serious and deals with a specialized subject 报纸; 定期刊物(尤指涉及某一学科的): *a medical, a scientific, an educational, etc journal* 医学、科学、教育等杂志 ○ *a trade journal* 贸易杂志 ○ *The Wall Street Journal* 《华尔街日报》○ *The Architects' Journal* 《建筑师杂志》○ *subscribe to a journal* 订阅报纸. **2** daily record of news, events, business transactions, etc 日记; 日志; 流水帐: *He kept a journal of his wanderings across Asia.* 他记自己漫游亚洲的日记.
▷ **journ·al·ese** /ˌdʒɜːnəˈliːz; ˌdʒɝnlˋiz/ *n* [U] (*derog* 贬) style of language thought to be typical of newspapers, containing many clichés 新闻文体(多陈辞套语的). Cf 参看 OFFICIALESE (OFFICIAL).
journ·al·ism /ˈdʒɜːnəlɪzəm; ˋdʒɝnlˌɪzəm/ *n* [U] work of collecting, writing, editing and publishing material in newspapers and magazines or on television and radio 新闻业; 新闻工作: *a career in journalism* 新闻工作的职业.
journ·al·ist /-nəlɪst; -nlɪst/ *n* person whose profession is journalism 新闻工作者; 新闻记者; 报人; (报纸杂志的)撰稿人: *He's a journalist on the 'Daily Telegraph'.* 他是《每日电讯报》的记者. Cf 参看 REPORTER (REPORT[1]).
journ·al·istic /ˌdʒɜːnəˈlɪstɪk; ˌdʒɝnlˋɪstɪk/ *adj* [attrib 作定语] of journalism; characteristic of journalism 新闻事业的; 新闻工作特有的.

jour·ney /ˈdʒɜːnɪ; ˋdʒɝnɪ/ *n* (*pl* **~s**) (**a**) (distance covered in) travelling, usu by land, from one place to another, often far away 行走, 行驶, 旅行(通常指经陆路); 旅程; 路程: *Did you have a good journey?* 你一路上顺利吗? ○ *go on a long train journey* 乘火车出远门 ○ *break one's journey*, ie interrupt it by stopping briefly at a place 途中在某地作短暂停留 ○ *the journey from Edinburgh to London* 由爱丁堡到伦敦的路程 ○ (*fig* 比喻) *our great journey through life* 我们一生的漫长道路. (**b**) time taken in going from one place to another 从一地到另一地所用的时间: *It's a day's journey by car.* 乘汽车得用一天的时间.
▷ **jour·ney** *v* [Ipr, Ip] go on a journey; travel 行走; 行驶; 旅行; 游历: *journeying overland across North America* 横越北美大陆.

NOTE ON USAGE 用法: **Journey** may indicate a long distance or a short one travelled regularly ☆ **journey** 可指经常走过的或长或短的距离: *'How long is your journey to work?'* '你上班要走多长的路?' *'Only about 15 minutes.'* '也就走15分钟左右.' A **voyage** is a long journey by sea or in space. ☆ **voyage** 是经海路或空间的长途行程. The word **travels** [pl] suggests a fairly long period of travelling from place to place, especially abroad, for pleasure or interest. ☆ **travels**(复数)一词指时间稍长的各处旅行, 尤指出国旅游. It is often used with a possessive adjective 这一词常与所有格的形容词连用: *She's gone off on her travels again.* 她又去旅游了. **Travel** is an uncountable noun indicating the action of travelling ☆ **travel** 是指行走、行驶或旅行的不可数名词: *Travel broadens the mind.* 旅行能使人见多识广. A **tour** is a (short or long) journey for pleasure, spent visiting several places ☆ **tour** 是为游玩而到几个地方观光的(长途或短途)旅行: *They're going on a world tour.* 他们正在环球旅行. A **trip** and (more formal) an **excursion** are short journeys and visits from and returning to a particular place. ☆ **trip** 和(较文雅的) **excursion** 是指短期的旅程和观光, 从某地出发再回到该地. **Excursion** suggests a group of people travelling together ☆ **excursion** 是指一群人一起出行: *During our holiday in Venice we went on a few trips/excursions to places near by.* 我们在威尼斯度假时曾到附近的几个地方观光过.

jour·ney·man /ˈdʒɜːnɪmən; ˋdʒɝnɪmən/ *n* (*pl* **-men** /-mən; -mən/) **1** trained worker who works for an employer 熟练工人: [attrib 作定语] *a journeyman printer* 熟练的印刷工人. **2** reliable and competent but not outstanding worker 可靠能干但不出色的工人: [attrib 作定语] *a journeyman artist* 匠气的艺术家.

joust /dʒaʊst; dʒaust/ *v* [I] (of knights in medieval times) fight on horseback with lances (指中世纪的骑士)骑着马用长矛打斗.

Jove /dʒəʊv; dʒov/ *n* (idm 习语) **by Jove** (*dated infml* 旧, 口) (used to express surprise or to emphasize a statement 用以表示惊奇或加强语气): *By Jove, I think you're right!* 啊, 我想是你对了!

jo·vial /ˈdʒəʊvɪəl; ˋdʒovɪəl/ *adj* very cheerful and good-humoured; merry 愉快的; 快乐的: *a friendly jovial fellow* 和蔼而快乐的人 ○ *in a jovial mood* 以愉快的心情. ▷ **jo·vi·al·ity** /ˌdʒəʊvɪˈælətɪ; ˌdʒovɪˋælətɪ/ *n* [U]. **jo·vi·ally** /-ɪəlɪ; -ɪəlɪ/ *adv*.

jowl /dʒaʊl; dʒaul/ *n* **1** (usu *pl* 通常作复数) jaw; lower part of the face 颌; 下颌; 脸的下部: *a man with heavy jowls/a heavy-jowled man*, ie one with heavy jaws, with a fold or folds of flesh hanging from the chin 有双下巴的人. **2** (idm 习语) **cheek by jowl** ⇨ CHEEK.

joy /dʒɔɪ; dʒɔɪ/ *n* **1** [U] feeling of great happiness 快乐; 愉快; 喜悦: *the sheer joy of seeing you again after all these years* 别后多年重见到你之不胜欣喜 ○ *overcome with (a deep sense of) joy* 喜不自胜 ○ *to dance, jump, shout, etc for joy*, ie because of feeling great joy 高兴得跳起舞来、蹦蹦跳跳、喊叫起来等. **2** [C] person or thing that makes one feel very happy 令人极快乐的人或事物: *He is a great joy to listen to.* 他这个人, 听他讲话就是极大的乐趣. ○ *one of the simple joys of life* 人生中的一件平凡乐事. **3** (idm 习语) **full of the joys of spring** ⇨

FULL. **(get/have) no joy (from sb)** (obtain) no success or satisfaction 未(获得)成功或满足: *They complained about the bad service, but got no joy from the manager.* 他们反映服务质量差, 但经理并未理会. **sb's pride and joy** ⇨ PRIDE.

▷ **joy·ful** /-fl; -fəl/ *adj* filled with, showing or causing joy 充满欢乐的; 显示快乐的; 令人高兴的: *joyful celebrations* 欢乐的庆祝活动 ○ *on this joyful occasion* 在这愉快的时刻. **joy·fully** /-fəlɪ; -fəlɪ/ *adv*. **joy·ful·ness** *n* [U].

joy·less *adj* without joy; gloomy or miserable 不快乐的; 忧郁的; 悲伤的: *a joyless marriage, childhood, etc* 没有乐趣的婚姻、童年等. **joy·lessly** *adv*. **joy·less·ness** *n* [U].

joy·ous /ˈdʒɔɪəs; ˋdʒɔɪəs/ *adj* (*fml* 文) filled with, showing or causing joy 充满欢乐的; 显示快乐的; 令人高兴的: *a joyous sense of freedom* 令人快乐的无拘无束的感觉. **joy·ously** *adv*. **joy·ous·ness** *n* [U].

□ ˈ**joy-ride** *n* (*infml* 口) car ride taken for fun and excitement, usu without the owner's permission 开车兜风(通常指未得车主允许): *teenagers going for joy-rides round town* 开着弄来的汽车在城里兜风的年轻人. ˈ**joy-rider** *n*. ˈ**joy-riding** *n* [U].

joy·stick /ˈdʒɔɪstɪk; ˋdʒɔɪˌstɪk/ *n* control-lever on an aircraft, a computer, etc (飞行器、计算机等的)操纵杆.

JP /ˌdʒeɪ ˈpi:; ˌdʒe ˋpi/ *abbr* 缩写 = (*law* 律) Justice of the Peace: *Clive Small JP* 克莱夫·斯莫尔治安官.

Jr *abbr* 缩写 = JNR.

ju·bil·ant /ˈdʒu:bɪlənt; ˋdʒubḷənt/ *adj* (*fml* 文) ~ **(about/at/over sth)** showing great happiness, esp because of a success 欢欣的, 欣喜的(尤指由于成功): *Liverpool were in a jubilant mood after their cup victory.* 利物浦队夺得优胜杯后喜气洋洋.

▷ **ju·bil·antly** *adv*.

ju·bila·tion /ˌdʒu:bɪˈleɪʃn; ˌdʒubḷˋeʃən/ *n* [U] great happiness, esp because of a success 欢欣, 欣喜(尤指因成功引起的): *express great jubilation* 表示极大的喜悦.

ju·bilee /ˈdʒu:bɪli:; ˋdʒubəˌli/ *n* (celebration of a) special anniversary of an event 周年纪念(的庆祝). Cf 参看 DIAMOND JUBILEE (DIAMOND), GOLDEN JUBILEE (GOLDEN), SILVER JUBILEE (SILVER).

Ju·da·ism /ˈdʒu:deɪɪzəm; *US* -dɪɪzəm; ˋdʒudɪˌɪzəm/ *n* [U] religion of the Jewish people; their culture 犹太教; 犹太人的文化.

▷ **Ju·daic** /dʒu:ˈdeɪɪk; dʒuˋdeˑɪk/ *adj* [attrib 作定语] of Jews and Judaism 犹太人的; 犹太教的. ⇨Usage at CHRISTIAN 用法见 CHRISTIAN.

Ju·das /ˈdʒu:dəs; ˋdʒudəs/ *n* person who betrays a friend; traitor 出卖朋友的人; 叛徒: *You Judas!* 你这个叛徒!

jud·der /ˈdʒʌdə(r); ˋdʒʌdɚ/ *v* [I, Ipr, Ip] shake violently 猛烈地震动: *The plane juddered to a halt*, ie shook violently and then stopped. 飞机猛烈地震动后停住了.

▷ **jud·der** *n* [sing] violent shaking 猛烈的震动: *The engine gave a sudden judder.* 发动机猛然一震.

judge[1] /dʒʌdʒ; dʒʌdʒ/ *n* **1** public officer with authority to decide cases in a lawcourt 审判官; 法官: *a High Court judge* 高等法院的法官 ○ *The case came before Judge Cooper last week.* 该案上周呈交库珀法官审理. ○ *The judge found him guilty and sentenced him to five years*, ie in gaol. 法官判决他有罪, 入狱五年. Cf 参看 MAGISTRATE. **2** person who decides who has won a competition, contest, etc 裁判员; 仲裁人; 评判员: *a panel of judges at the flower show* 花卉展览的评判小组 ○ (in the rules of many competitions) *The judges' decision is final*, ie it cannot be changed or challenged. 裁判的决定即是最终决定(不容更改或不得提出异议). **3** person qualified and able to give an opinion on the value or merits of sth 鉴赏家; 鉴定家: *a good judge of art, wine, character* 善于鉴别艺术、酒、人的个性的人 ○ *I thought that the third violinist was the best player — not that I'm any judge*, ie I do not know much about the subject. 我认为第三小提琴手演奏得最好——虽然我并不是行家. **4** (idm 习语) **sober as a judge** ⇨ SOBER.

judge[2] /dʒʌdʒ; dʒʌdʒ/ *v* **1** [I, Ipr, Tn, Tn·pr, Tf no passive 不用于被动语态, Tw no passive 不用于被动语态, Cn·a, Cn·t] **~ (sb/sth) by/from sth** form an opinion about (sb/sth); estimate (the value, amount, etc of sth); consider 判断(某人[某事物]); 断定(某事物的价值、数量等); 认为: *As far as I can judge, they are all to blame.* 据我判断, 他们都有责任. ○ *to judge by appearances* 从外貌来看 ○ *Judging from previous experience, he will be late.* 根据以往的经验来看, 他得迟到. ○ *It is difficult to judge the full extent of the damage.* 很难断定损失有多大. ○ *The performance was good, when judged by their usual standards.* 按他们平时的水平衡量, 这次演出不错. ○ *He judged that it was time to open the proceedings.* 他认为是开始的时候了. ○ *I find it hard to judge how the election will go*, ie who will win. 我觉得很难说谁会在选举中获胜. ○ *The committee judged it advisable to postpone the meeting.* 委员会认为会议应该延期举行. ○ *I judged him to be about 50.* 我看他有50岁. **2** [I, Tn] (**a**) decide (a case) in a lawcourt; make a decision about (sb) in a lawcourt; try[1](3a) 审理(案件); 判处(某人); 审判: *judge fairly, harshly, leniently, etc* 判得公正、严厉、宽大等 ○ *judge a murder case* 审理谋杀案. (**b**) speak critically and harshly about (sb) 批评, 抨击(某人): *You're no better than they are: who are you to judge other people?* 你不比他们强, 凭什么指责别人? **3** [Tn] decide the result or winner in (a competition) 评判, 裁判(竞赛): *The flower show was judged by the local MP.* 花卉展览由当地的下议院议员担任评判.

judge·ment (also, esp in legal use, **judg·ment** 也作 **judgment**, 尤用于法律条文) /ˈdʒʌdʒmənt; ˋdʒʌdʒmənt/ *n* **1** [C] **~ (of/about sth)** opinion about sth 意见; 看法: *make an unfair judgement of sb's character* 对某人的品格做出不公正的评语 ○ *My judgement is that/In my judgement the plan is ill-conceived.* 我的意见是[据我看来]该计划考虑不周. **2** [C, U] decision of a lawcourt or judge; verdict (法庭或法官的)判决; 裁决: *The judgement was given in favour of the accused*, ie the accused was declared not guilty. 判决为被告无罪. ○ *The court has still to pass judgement* (ie give a decision) *in this case.* 法庭对此案仍需做出判决. **3** (**a**) [U] ability to come to sensible conclusions and make wise decisions; good sense; discernment 决断力; 判断力; 见识; 眼力: *He lacks sound judgement.* 他缺乏准确的判断力. ○ *display/exercise/show excellent judgement* 显示出[运用/表现出]卓越的决断力. (**b**) [U, C] action or process of judging 判断: *errors of judgement* 判断的错误. **4** [sing] **a ~ (on sb)** misfortune considered to be a punishment from God for doing sth wrong 报应; 天谴: *This failure is a judgement on you for being so lazy.* 这次失败是你懒惰的报应. **5** (idm 习语) **against one's better judgement** ⇨ BETTER[1]. **an error of judgement** ⇨ ERROR. **reserve judgement** ⇨ RESERVE[1]. **sit in judgement** ⇨ SIT.

□ ˈ**Judgement Day** (also **the Day of** ˈ**Judgement**, **the Last** ˈ**Judgement**) the day at the end of the world when God will judge everyone who has ever lived 最后审判日; 世界末日.

ju·dic·ature /ˈdʒu:dɪkətʃə(r); ˋdʒudɪkətʃɚ/ *n* (*law* 律) **1** [U] administration of justice 司法. **2** [CGp] group of judges; judiciary 法官(总称).

ju·di·cial /dʒu:ˈdɪʃl; dʒuˋdɪʃəl/ *adj* [attrib 作定语] **1** of or by a court of law; of a judge or of judgement 法庭的; 司法的; 法官的; 审判的: *a judicial inquiry, review, system* 法庭的审讯、复审、司法制度 ○ *the judicial process* 审判的程序 ○ *take judicial proceedings against sb*, ie bring a case against him in court 提起诉讼控告某人. **2** able to judge things wisely; critical; impartial 善于判断的; 有判断力的; 明断的; 公正的: *a judicial mind* 公正的心. ▷ **ju·di·ci·ally** /-ʃəlɪ; -ʃəlɪ/ *adv*.

□ **ju**ˌ**dicial** ˈ**murder** (*law* 律) sentence of death that is legal but considered unjust 虽合法但被认为不公正的死刑判决.

juˌ**dicial sepa**ˈ**ration** (*law* 律) order that forbids a man and wife to live together but does not end the marriage 经裁定的夫妇分居(夫妻不得同居但不结束婚姻关系).

ju·di·ciary /dʒu:ˈdɪʃərɪ; *US* -ʃɪerɪ; dʒuˋdɪʃɪˌɛrɪ/ *n* [CGp] judges of a country collectively (一国的)法官(总称).

ju·di·cious /dʒu:ˈdɪʃəs; dʒuˋdɪʃəs/ *adj* showing or having good sense 有见识的; 明智的: *a judicious choice, decision, remark* 明智的选择、决定、言语. ▷ **ju·di·ciously** *adv*. **ju·di·cious·ness** *n* [U].

judo /ˈdʒu:dəʊ; ˋdʒudo/ *n* [U] sport of wrestling and self-defence between two people who try to throw each other to the ground 柔道.

J

jug[1] /dʒʌg; dʒʌg/ *n* **1** [C] (*Brit*) (*US* **pitcher**) (**a**) deep vessel, with a handle and a lip, for holding and pouring liquids (有柄有嘴盛液体用的)大罐, 壶: *pour milk into/from a jug* 将牛奶倒入罐中[从罐中倒出] ○ *a milk/coffee/water jug* 牛奶罐[咖啡壶/水罐]. (**b**) amount of liquid contained in this 一罐或一壶液体(之量): *spill a whole jug of juice* 洒了整整一罐汁液. **2** [U] (*sl* 俚) prison 监狱: *three months in jug* 坐三个月牢.

▷ **jug·ful** /-fʊl; -fʊl/ *n* amount of liquid contained in a jug 一罐或一壶液体(之量).

jug[2] /dʒʌg; dʒʌg/ *v* (**-gg-**) [Tn usu passive 通常用于被动语态] stew (hare) in a covered dish 罐焖(野兔肉): *jugged hare* 用罐焖的野兔肉.

jug·ger·naut /ˈdʒʌgənɔ:t; ˋdʒʌgɚ,nɔt/ *n* **1** (*Brit esp derog* 尤作贬义) very large articulated lorry 重型铰接卡车: *juggernauts roaring through our country villages* 隆隆驶过我们村庄的重型铰接卡车. **2** large, powerful and destructive force or institution 强大的破坏力; 有毁灭力量的机构: *the juggernaut of bureaucracy* 官僚作风的严重危害.

juggle /ˈdʒʌgl; ˋdʒʌgl/ *v* **1** [I, Ipr, Tn] **~ (with sth)** throw (a number of objects, usu balls) up into the air, catch them and throw them into the air again and again, keeping one or more in the air at the same time 耍把戏; 玩杂耍; 连续抛接(若干球等): *When did you learn to juggle?* 你什么时候学的杂耍? ○ *to juggle (with) plates, balls, hoops, etc* 用碟子、球、环等耍把戏. **2** [Ipr, Tn] **~ with sth** change the arrangement of sth constantly in order to achieve a satisfactory result or to deceive people 不断改变某事的安排(以得到满意的结果或以骗人): *juggling with one's timetable to fit in the extra classes* 反复修改自己的时间表以便插入额外课程 ○ *The government has been juggling (with) the figures to hide the latest rise in unemployment.* 政府为隐瞒最近失业率上升而一再更改数字.

▷ **jug·gler** /ˈdʒʌglə(r); ˋdʒʌglɚ/ *n* person who juggles (1) 耍把戏的人. ⇨illus 见插图.

J

jug·ular /ˈdʒʌgjʊlə(r); ˋdʒʌgjəlɚ/ *adj* of the neck or throat 颈部的; 喉部的.

▷ **jug·ular** *n* **1** (also **jugular ˈvein**) any of several veins in the neck that return blood from the head to the heart 颈静脉. **2** (idm 习语) **go for the ˈjugular** (*infml* 口) make a fierce destructive attack on the weakest point in an opponent's argument 抨击对方的致命弱点.

juice /dʒu:s; dʒus/ *n* **1** [U, C] (**a**) liquid obtained from a fruit; drink made from this 果汁; 果汁饮料: *squeeze some more juice from a lemon* 从柠檬中多榨些汁 ○ *a carton of fresh orange, pineapple, grapefruit, etc juice* 一纸盒新鲜的橙汁、菠萝汁、葡萄柚汁 ○ *One tomato juice and one soup, please.* 请来一份蕃茄汁和一份汤. (**b**) liquid that comes from a piece of meat when it is cooked (烹肉时出的)肉汁: *Wrapping aluminium foil round a joint allows the meat to cook in its own juice/juices.* 用铝箔把肉包住使之在原汁中烹制. **2** [C usu *pl* 通常作复数] liquid in the stomach or another part of the body that helps sb to digest food 胃液; 消化液: *gastric/digestive juices* 胃[消化]液. **3** [U] (*infml* 口) electric current 电流: *turn on the juice* 接通电流. **4** [U] (*infml* 口) petrol 汽油: *We ran out of juice on the motorway.* 我们在高速公路上行驶时汽油用完了. **5** (idm 习语) **stew in one's own juice** ⇨ STEW.

juicy /ˈdʒu:sɪ; ˋdʒusɪ/ *adj* (**-ier, -iest**) **1** containing a lot of juice and being enjoyable to eat; succulent 多汁又好吃的; 味道好的: *fresh juicy oranges* 新鲜多汁的橙子. **2** (*infml* 口) interesting (esp because scandalous) 有趣味的(尤指丑事): *juicy gossip, stories, scenes, etc* 有趣的流言、故事、情景等 ○ *Tell me all the juicy details!* 把有趣的细节都讲给我听! **3** (*infml* 口) producing a lot of money; profitable 赚钱的; 获利的: *a nice juicy contract* 有钱可赚的合同. ▷ **juici·ness** *n* [U].

ju-jitsu /dʒu:ˈdʒɪtsu:; dʒuˋdʒɪtsu/ *n* [U] Japanese art of self-defence from which judo was developed 柔术(柔道由此发展而来).

ju-ju /ˈdʒu:dʒu:; ˋdʒudʒu/ *n* (**a**) [C] W African charm believed to have magic power; fetish (非洲西部的)符咒, 神物. (**b**) [U] its magic power 符咒或神物的魔力.

ju·jube /ˈdʒu:dʒu:b; ˋdʒudʒub/ *n* small flavoured jelly-like sweet 软糖.

juke-box /ˈdʒu:kbɒks; ˋdʒuk,bɑks/ *n* large record-player in a café, bar, etc that automatically plays chosen records when a coin is inserted 自动点唱机(小餐馆、酒吧等的投币选唱机).

Jul *abbr* 缩写 = July: *21 Jul 1965* 1965年7月21日.

ju·lep /ˈdʒu:lɪp; ˋdʒulɪp/ *n* [C, U] (*US*) alcoholic drink made from spirit (usu whisky), sugar, mint and ice 含酒(通常为威士忌)、糖、薄荷及冰的饮料: *mint julep* 薄荷酒清凉饮料.

Ju·lian cal·en·dar /ˌdʒu:lɪən ˈkælɪndə(r); ˌdʒuljən ˋkæləndɚ/ calendar introduced by Julius Caesar in Rome in 46 BC 儒略历(公元前46年凯撒倡用的). Cf 参看 GREGORIAN CALENDAR (GREGORIAN). ⇨App 5 见附录5.

July /dʒu:ˈlaɪ; dʒuˋlaɪ/ *n* [U, C] (*abbr* 缩写 **Jul**) the seventh month of the year, next after June 七月.

For the uses of *July* see the examples at *April.* 关于July的用法见April词条中的示例.

jumble /ˈdʒʌmbl; ˋdʒʌmbl/ *v* [usu passive 通常用于被动语态: Tn, Tn·p] **~ sth (up)** mix (things) in a confused way 将(东西)胡乱混在一起: *Toys, books, shoes and clothes were jumbled (up) on the floor.* 玩具、书、鞋、衣服都杂乱地堆在地上. ○ (*fig* 比喻) *Details of the accident were all jumbled up in his mind.* 该事故的详情在他头脑中已混在一起.

▷ **jumble** *n* **1** [sing] **~ (of sth)** confused or untidy group of things; muddle 杂乱的一堆东西; 一团糟: *a jumble of books and papers on the table* 桌子上凌乱的一堆书和报纸. **2** [U] (*Brit*) mixed collection of old unwanted goods for a jumble sale 待义卖的旧杂物.

□ **ˈjumble sale** (*Brit*) (*US* **ˈrummage sale**) sale of a mixed collection of old unwanted goods in order to raise money, usu for a charity 旧杂物义卖(通常为慈善筹款): *hold a jumble sale in aid of hospital funds* 为医院筹措基金举行旧物义卖.

jumbo /ˈdʒʌmbəʊ; ˋdʒʌmbo/ *adj* [attrib 作定语] (*infml* 口) unusually large; enormous 特大的; 极大的: *a jumbo (-sized) packet of washing-powder* 特大(型)包装的洗衣粉.

▷ **jumbo** *n* (*pl* **~s**) (also **ˌjumbo ˈjet**) very large jet aircraft that can carry several hundred passengers 珍宝喷气客机(大型喷气式客机).

jump[1] /dʒʌmp; dʒʌmp/ *n* **1** [C] act of jumping 跳; 跃; 跳跃: *a parachute jump* 跳伞 ○ *a superb jump* 出色的跳跃. **2** [C] obstacle to be jumped over (需跳过的)障碍: *The horse fell at the last jump.* 那马在跳最后一个障碍时跌倒了. ○ *The water-jump is the most difficult part of the race.* 跨跃水沟是赛马中最困难的一项. **3** [C] **~ (in sth)** sudden rise in amount, price or value (数额、价格或价值的)突增, 突升, 暴涨: *The company's results show a huge jump in profits.* 公司的结算显示利润大增. **4** [C] sudden change to a different condition or set of circumstances; leap (情况或环境的)突然改变, 飞跃: *the country's great jump forward to a new technological era* 该国向新技术时代的大飞跃. **5 the jumps** [pl] (*infml* 口) state of extreme nervousness with uncontrollable movements of the body (神经性)全身颤抖: *get/have the jumps* 混身颤抖. **6** (idm 习语) **be for the high jump** ⇨ HIGH JUMP (HIGH[1]). **get the jump on sb** (*infml* 口) gain an advantage over sb 得到超越某人的优势. **give sb a ˈjump** (*infml* 口) shock or surprise sb so that he makes a sudden movement 吓某人一跳: *Oh, you did* *give me a jump!* 啊, 你可真吓了我一跳! **keep, etc one jump ahead (of sb)** remain one stage ahead (of a rival) 保持领先于(对手的)地位. **take a running jump** ⇨ RUNNING.

▷ **jumpy** *adj* (**-ier, -iest**) (*infml* 口) nervous; anxious 紧张的; 焦虑的. **jump·ily** *adv*. **jumpi·ness** *n* [U].

jump[2] /dʒʌmp; dʒʌmp/ *v* **1** [I, Ipr, Ip, In/pr] move quickly off the ground, etc, esp up into the air, by using the force of the legs and feet 跳; 跳起; 跃起: *to jump into the air, out of a window, over the wall, off a roof, onto the ground, etc* 跳起来、跳出窗户、跳过墙、跳下屋顶、跳到地上 ○ *The children were jumping up and down*, eg because they were very excited. 孩子们兴奋得跳来跳去. ○ *She can jump 2.2 metres.* 她能跳2.2米. **2** [Ipr, Ip] move quickly and suddenly 迅速而突然行动: *He jumped to his feet/jumped up* (ie stood up quickly and suddenly) *as the boss came in.* 老板一进来他立刻站了起来. ○ *'Jump in* (ie get in quickly),*' he called from the car.* '快上车,' 他在汽车里喊道. **3** [Tn] pass over (sth) by jumping; clear 跳过(某物); 跃过: *The horses jumped all the fences.* 马跳过了所有的篱笆. **4** [I] move suddenly with a jerk because of excitement, surprise, shock, etc; start (因兴奋、吃惊等)跳动, 惊跳: *The loud bang made me jump.* 砰的一声巨响吓了我一跳. ○ *Her heart jumped when she heard the news.* 她听到那消息心突突直跳. ⇨ Usage 见所附用法. **5** [I, Ipr, Ip] (of a device) move suddenly and unexpectedly, esp out of its correct position (指机械)突然地, 意外地运动(尤指离开正常位置): *a typewriter that jumps*, ie omitting letters 跳字的(漏掉字母的)打字机 ○ *The needle jumps on this record.* 唱针在这张唱片上跳针. **6** [Ipr] **~ from sth to sth** change suddenly from discussing one subject to another subject 突然改变话题: *I couldn't understand his lecture because he kept jumping from one topic to the next.* 我听不懂他的演讲, 他总是从一项内容跳到另一项内容. **7** [Ipr, It, Tn] **~ from sth to sth** pass over sth to a further point; omit or skip 跳过; 跃过; 隔过; 略过: *The film suddenly jumped from the events of 1920 to those of 1930.* 那电影从1920年的事突然跳到1930年的事. ○ *jump several steps in an argument* 在论证中跳过了几步. **8** [I, In/pr] **~ (by) sth** rise suddenly by a very large amount 突升; 暴涨; 猛增: *Prices jumped (by) 60% last year.* 物价去年暴涨60%. **9** [Tn] (*infml* 口) attack (sb) suddenly 突然攻击(某人): *The gang jumped an old woman in the subway.* 一伙歹徒在地下人行道突然袭击一老妇人. **10** [Tn] (*infml* 口 *usu US*) travel illegally on (a train) 违章搭乘(火车): *jump a freight train* 违章搭乘运货火车. **11** (idm 习语) **climb/jump on the bandwagon** ⇨ BANDWAGON (BAND). **go (and) jump in the/a 'lake** (usu in the imperative 通常用于祈使句) (*dated infml* 旧, 口) go away 走开; 滚开. **jump 'bail** fail to appear for a trial after being released on bail 弃保潜逃. **jump down sb's 'throat** (*infml* 口) speak to sb in an angry, critical way 怒斥; 斥责. **jump for 'joy** show one's delight at sth by excited movements 以兴奋的动作对某事表示高兴: *The children are jumping for joy at the thought of an extra day's holiday.* 孩子们想到多一天假日, 高兴得直跳. **jump the 'gun (a)** start a race before the starting-gun has been fired 抢跑. **(b)** do sth too soon, before the proper time 抢先做某事: *They jumped the gun by building the garage before permission had been given.* 他们未得许可就抢先盖了汽车房. **jump the 'lights** ignore and pass a red traffic-light 闯红灯. **jump out of one's 'skin** be extremely surprised 非常吃惊; 大吃一惊: *The shock of seeing her again made me nearly jump out of my skin.* 我又见到了她, 真让我大吃一惊. **jump the 'queue** (*Brit*) **(a)** go to the front of a queue of people without waiting for one's proper turn 未等轮到而抢先; 加塞儿. **(b)** obtain sth unfairly without waiting for one's proper turn 未等轮到而提前获得某事物. **jump the 'rails/'track** (of a train, etc) leave the rails suddenly (指火车等)出轨. **jump 'ship** leave the ship on which one is serving, without having obtained permission 擅自离船弃职. **jump to con'clusions** come to a decision about sb/sth too quickly, before one has thought about all the facts (未经全面考虑)匆匆对某人[某事]作出结论: *I know I was standing near the till when you came back into the shop, but don't jump to conclusions.* 我明白, 你回到商店时我确实是站在收款抽屉旁边, 但且不要忙着下结论. **jump 'to it** (usu in the imperative 通常用于祈使句) (*infml* 口) hurry up 赶快: *The bus will be leaving in five minutes, so jump to it!* 公共汽车还有五分钟就开了, 快点儿吧! **wait for the cat to jump/to see which way the cat jumps** ⇨ WAIT[1]. **12** (phr v) **jump at sth** seize (an opportunity, a chance, etc) eagerly 迫不及待地抓住(机会、机遇等): *If they offered me a job in the USA, I'd jump at the chance.* 假若他们给我一个职位在美国工作, 我一定赶紧抓住机会不放. **jump on sb** (*infml* 口) criticize or challenge sb sharply 严厉地批评或质问: *My maths teacher really used to jump on us when we got our answers wrong.* 我们过去一算错答案, 数学老师就把我们狠训一顿.

□ **'jumped-up** *adj* [attrib 作定语] (*Brit infml derog* 口, 贬) thinking of oneself as more important than one really is; upstart 自视过高的; 自负的; 暴富的; 暴发的: *that new jumped-up boss of ours* 我们那个自命不凡的新老板.

jumping-'off place (also **jumping-'off point**) place from where a journey, plan, campaign, etc is begun or launched (旅程、计划、运动等的)起点.

'jump-jet *n* jet aircraft that can take off and land vertically 垂直起降喷气机.

'jump-lead *n* (usu *pl* 通常作复数) one of two cables used for carrying electric current from one car battery to another one that has no power in it 跨接电缆(用以从一汽车电池向另一无电的汽车电池输电).

'jump-off *n* (in show-jumping) extra round held to decide the winner when two or more horses have the same score (骑马越障碍表演)加赛决胜.

'jump-start *v* [Tn] start (a car) by pushing or rolling it and then engaging the gears instead of using the starter motor 助推起动(汽车)(不使用起动器). **'jump-start** *n*.

'jump suit one-piece garment of trousers and jacket or shirt 连衫裤.

NOTE ON USAGE 用法: **Leap** and **spring** suggest a more energetic movement than **jump.** ☆ **leap** 和 **spring** 表示的动作比 **jump** 更加有力. **Spring** usually indicates a deliberate movement forward ☆ **spring** 通常指有意识的向前的动作: *The cat sprang forward and caught the mouse.* 猫向前一跳, 捉住了老鼠. We can **leap** and **jump** in any direction ☆ **leap** 和 **jump** 可指向任何方向的动作: *jump/leap into the car, onto the platform, to one's feet, up the stairs* 跳上汽车、跳到平台上、一跃而起、跳上台阶 ○ *jump/leap up, down, forwards, back, etc* 跳上、跳下、向前跳、向后跳. We also **jump** in surprise ☆ **jump** 也指吃惊时的动作: *The sudden noise made me jump.* 突然一声响, 吓了我一跳. **Bounce** indicates repeated movement up and down, often while jumping on a springy surface ☆ **bounce** 指反复的上下运动, 常指接触面有弹性: *bounce on a bed/trampoline.* 在床[蹦床]上跳跃.

jumper /'dʒʌmpə(r); 'dʒʌmpɚ/ *n* **1** (*Brit*) = JERSEY 1. **2** (*US*) pinafore 无袖连衣裙. **3** person, animal or insect that jumps 跳跃的人、鸟兽或昆虫.

Jun *abbr* 缩写 = **1** June: *12 Jun 1803* 1803年6月12日. **2** = JNR.

J

junc·tion /'dʒʌŋkʃn; 'dʒʌŋkʃən/ *n* **1** [C] place where roads or railway lines meet 公路或铁路的交叉点; 交叉路口: *a pub near the junction of London Road and Chaucer Avenue* 靠近伦敦路与乔叟大街交叉口的酒馆 ○ *Join the M1 at Junction 11.* 在11号交叉路口与1号高速公路会合. ○ *The accident happened at one of the country's busiest railway junctions.* 事故发生在该国一个极繁忙的铁路交叉点处. **2** [C, U] (*fml* 文) (instance of) joining or being joined 连接; 会合: *effect a junction of two armies* 两军会师.

□ **'junction box** box containing a connection between electric circuits 接线盒.

junc·ture /'dʒʌŋktʃə(r); 'dʒʌŋktʃɚ/ *n* (idm 习语) **at this juncture** (*fml* 文) at a particular, esp important, stage in a series of events 在此时刻; 在这一关头: *It is very difficult at this juncture to predict the company's future.* 此时很难预料公司的前景.

June /dʒu:n; dʒun/ *n* [U, C] (*abbr* 缩写 **Jun**) the sixth month of the year, next after May 六月.

For the uses of *June* see the examples at *April.* 关于

June 的用法见 April 词条中的示例.

jungle /ˈdʒʌŋgl; ˋdʒʌŋgl/ *n* **1** [U, C] area of land, usu in a tropical country, that is covered with a thick growth of trees and tangled plants 丛林地带(通常指热带国家的): *There's not much jungle 100 miles inland.* 向内地100英里丛林较少. ○ *The new road was hacked out of the jungle.* 这条新路是在丛林地带辟出的. ○ *the dense jungles of Africa and South America* 非洲和南美洲的茂密丛林 ○ [attrib 作定语] *jungle warfare*, ie war fought in the jungle, where surprise attacks by small groups are difficult to anticipate or avoid 丛林战. **2** [sing] confused, disordered and complicated mass of things 混乱而复杂的大量事物: *a jungle of welfare regulations* 纷繁的福利条例. **3** [C] place of intense or confusing struggle 发生激烈或混乱斗争的地方: *the blackboard jungle*, ie school(s) where pupils are very disruptive and hostile to their teachers 学生不守纪律并敌视教师的学校 ○ *the concrete jungle*, ie a typical modern city with a dense mass of ugly high-rise concrete buildings and in which life is bewildering and sometimes violent 高楼林立、乌烟瘴气、时有暴力事件的现代城市. **4** (idm 习语) **the law of the jungle** ⇨ LAW.

▷ **jungly** /ˈdʒʌŋglɪ; ˋdʒʌŋglɪ/ *adj* (*infml* 口) of, like or from the jungle or its inhabitants (似)丛林地带的; 丛林地带居民的.

□ ˌ**jungle** ˈ**fever** type of severe malarial fever 丛林热(恶性疟疾).

ju·nior /ˈdʒuːnɪə(r); ˋdʒunjɚ/ *adj* **1 ~ (to sb)** lower in rank or standing (than sb) (较某人)地位或身份低的: *a junior clerk in an office* 办公室的下级职员 ○ *He is several years junior to Mrs Cooper.* 他比库珀太太小几岁. **2 Junior** (*abbrs* 缩写 **Jnr**, **Jr**, **Jun**) (*esp US*) (used after a name to refer to a son who has the same name as his father or to the younger of two boys having the same name in a school, university, etc 父子同名时, 用于儿子姓名之后, 两学生同姓时, 用于年幼者之名后, 以示区别): *Sammy Davies, Jnr* 小萨米·戴维斯. Cf 参看 MINOR 2. **3** (*Brit*) of or intended for children from the ages of 7 to 11 (7至11岁)儿童的: *junior school* 小学. Cf 参看 SENIOR.

▷ **ju·nior** *n* **1** person who holds a low rank in a profession; person with an unimportant job (一职业中)地位较低者; 从事次要工作的人: *the office junior* 办公室的一般职员. **2** [sing] (used with *his, her, your,* etc 与 his、her、your 等连用) person who is a specified number of years younger than sb else 比某人小若干岁: *He is three years her junior/her junior by three years.* 他比她小三岁. **3** (*Brit*) child who goes to junior school 小学生: *The juniors' Christmas party is on Tuesday.* 小学生的圣诞节联欢会于星期二举行. **4** (*US*) student in his third year of a four-year course at college or high school (四年制的大学或中学的)三年级学生. **5** (*US infml* 口) way of addressing a son in a family 家庭中称呼儿子的用语: *Come here, Junior!* 到这儿来, 小儿子!

ju·ni·per /ˈdʒuːnɪpə(r); ˋdʒunəpɚ/ *n* evergreen bush with purple berries which are used in medicine and as a flavouring in gin 桧, 刺柏, 杜松(常绿灌木, 生有紫红色浆果供药用及杜松子酒调味之用).

junk[1] /dʒʌŋk; dʒʌŋk/ *n* [U] **1** (*infml* 口) things that are considered useless or of little value 无用的或无价值的东西: *all that junk in the boot of the car* 汽车行李箱中的所有废旧杂物 ○ *You read too much junk*, ie low-quality books. 你看低水平的书看得太多了. **2** old or unwanted things that are sold cheaply 廉价出售的废旧杂物: *pick up some interesting junk* 买些有趣的旧货 ○ [attrib 作定语] *a junk shop* 旧货店. **3** (*sl* 俚) narcotic drug; heroin 麻醉药; 海洛因.

□ ˈ**junk food** (*infml derog* 口, 贬) food (eg potato crisps) eaten as a snack and usu thought to be not good for one's health 通常认为不利健康的小吃(如炸马铃薯片).

junk[2] /dʒʌŋk; dʒʌŋk/ *n* flat-bottomed Chinese sailing-ship 中国帆船.

jun·ket /ˈdʒʌŋkɪt; ˋdʒʌŋkɪt/ *n* **1** [C, U] (dish of) sweet custard-like pudding made of milk curdled with rennet, and often sweetened and flavoured (一份)凝乳食品(用凝乳制成, 常加糖和香料). **2** [C] (*infml derog* 口, 贬 *esp US*) trip made esp for pleasure by a government official and paid for with government money 政府官员用公费的旅游. **3** social gathering for a feast; picnic 宴会; 野餐.

▷ **jun·ket** *v* [I] make merry; feast 作乐; 尽情吃喝. **jun·ket·ing** *n* **1** [U] (*infml derog* 口, 贬 *esp US*) party or celebration for visiting government officials, paid for with government money (用公款为来访的政府官员举行的)招待会. **2** [C, U] (period of) feasting or merry-making 举行宴会; 作乐.

junkie /ˈdʒʌŋkɪ; ˋdʒʌŋkɪ/ *n* (*sl* 俚) drug addict, esp one addicted to heroin 有毒瘾者; (尤指)有海洛因瘾者.

Ju·no·esque /ˌdʒuːnəʊˈesk; ˌdʒunoˋɛsk/ *adj* (of a woman) having a graceful dignified beauty (like the Roman goddess Juno) (指女子)有优雅高贵之美的(似罗马女神朱诺的).

junta /ˈdʒʌntə; *US* ˈhʊntə; ˋhʊntə/ *n* [CGp] (*esp derog* 尤作贬义) group, esp of military officers, who rule a country after taking power by force in a coup d'état 在政变中以武力夺取政权并统治国家的(尤指军官的)集团.

Ju·piter /ˈdʒuːpɪtə(r); ˋdʒupətɚ/ *n* (*astronomy* 天) the largest planet of the solar system, fifth in order from the sun 木星.

jur·id·ical /dʒʊəˈrɪdɪkl; dʒʊˋrɪdɪkl/ *adj* of law or legal proceedings 法律的; 诉讼程序的.

jur·is·dic·tion /ˌdʒʊərɪsˈdɪkʃn; ˌdʒʊrɪsˋdɪkʃən/ *n* [U] (**a**) authority to carry out justice and to interpret and apply laws; right to exercise legal authority 司法; 司法权; 审判权; 裁判权: *The court has no jurisdiction over foreign diplomats living in this country.* 法院对驻本国的外交官无裁判权. (**b**) limits within which legal authority may be exercised 管辖权限: *to come within/fall outside sb's jurisdiction* 在某人管辖权限之内[外].

jur·is·pru·dence /ˌdʒʊərɪsˈpruːdns; ˌdʒʊrɪsˋprudṇs/ *n* [U] science or philosophy of law 法学; 法理学.

jur·ist /ˈdʒʊərɪst; ˋdʒʊrɪst/ *n* expert in law 法学家; 法理学家.

juror /ˈdʒʊərə(r); ˋdʒʊrɚ/ *n* member of a jury 陪审团之一员; 陪审员; 评判员.

jury /ˈdʒʊərɪ; ˋdʒʊrɪ/ *n* [CGp] **1** group of people in a lawcourt who have been chosen to listen to the facts in a case and to decide whether the accused person is guilty or not guilty 陪审团: *Seven men and five women sat on* (ie were members of) *the jury.* 陪审团由七男五女组成. ○ *The jury returned a verdict of* (ie reached a decision that the accused was) *not guilty.* 陪审团做出被告无罪的裁决. ○ *The jury is/are still out*, ie Members of the jury are still thinking about their decision. 陪审团仍在进行审议. ○ *trial by jury* 由陪审团审理. **2** group of people chosen to decide the winner or winners in a competition (比赛的)评判委员会: *The jury is/are about to announce the winners.* 评委会即将宣布优胜者.

□ ˈ**jury-box** *n* enclosure where a jury sits in a court 陪审团席.

juryman /ˈdʒʊərɪmən; ˋdʒʊrɪmən/ *n* (*fem* 阴性作 **jurywoman** /ˈdʒʊərɪwʊmən; ˋdʒʊrɪˌwʊmən/) member of a jury 陪审员.

just[1] /dʒʌst; dʒʌst/ *adj* **1** acting or being in accordance with what is morally right and proper; fair 公道的; 公正的; 公平的: *a just and honourable ruler* 公正而正直的统治者 ○ *a just decision, law, solution, society* 公正的判决、法律、结论、社会 ○ *a just* (ie legally right) *sentence/verdict* 合法的判决[裁决] ○ *be just in one's dealings with sb* 公平地对待某人. **2** reasonable; well-founded 合理的; 有充分根据的: *a just complaint* 有根据的申诉 ○ *just demands* 合理的要求 ○ *criticized without just cause* 受到无端批评. **3** deserved; right 理所当然的; 正确的: *a just reward/punishment* 应有的报偿[惩罚] ○ *get one's just deserts* 得到应得的赏罚.

▷ **the just** *n* [pl *v*] **1** just people 正直的人们. **2** (idm 习语) **sleep the sleep of the just** ⇨ SLEEP[2].

justly *adv*: *to act justly* 行事公道 ○ *You can be justly proud of your achievement.* 你有理由为自己的成就而自豪.

just·ness *n* [U].

just[2] /dʒʌst; dʒʌst/ *adv* **1** exactly 正好; 恰好. (**a**) (before *ns* and *n* phrases 用于名词和名词词组前): *It's just two o'clock.* 现在的时间是两点正. ○ *This hammer is just the thing I need.* 这正是我要的锤子. ○ *It's just my size.* 这正是我的尺码. ○ *Just my luck!* 我的运气就是这么坏! (**b**) (before *adjs, advs* and prepositional phrases 用于形容

词、副词和介词词组前): *just right* 正对 ○ *just here/there* 就在这里[那里] ○ *just on target* 正中目标. (**c**) (before clauses 用于从句前): *just what I wanted* 正是我所要的 ○ *just where I expected it to be* 恰在我料到的地方. **2 ~ as** (**a**) exactly as; the same as 恰如; 如同: *It's just as I thought.* 恰如我所料. (**b**) at the same moment as 正当; 其时: *just as I arrived* 恰在我到达时. (**c**) (before an *adj/adv* followed by *as* 后接形容词[副词]加as) no less (than); equally 不少(于); 同样地: *just as beautiful as her sister* 与她姐姐一样漂亮 ○ *You can get there just as cheaply by air as by train.* 你坐飞机到那里同坐火车一样便宜. **3** (esp after *only* 尤用于only之后) (**a**) barely; scarcely; narrowly 仅仅; 几乎不; 勉强地: *I can (only) just reach the shelf, if I stand on tiptoe.* 我踮着脚才刚能够着架子. ○ *She (only) just caught the train with one minute to spare.* 她差一点儿没赶上那趟火车. ○ *just manage to pass the entrance exam* 入学考试勉强及格 ○ *just miss a target, fail a test, reach the top* 稍稍偏离目标、测验只差一点儿就及格、勉强达到顶端. (**b**) (with perfect tenses; in US English with the simple past tense 用于完成时态; 在美式英语中用于一般过去时态) very recently; in the immediate past 刚刚; 刚才: *I have (only) just seen John.* 我刚才见到约翰了. ○ *When you arrived he had (only) just left*, ie He left immediately before you arrived. 你来时他刚刚走. ○ *By the time you arrive, he will have just finished.* 等你来到时他刚好能做完. ○ *He has just been speaking.* 他刚才一直在说话. ○ (*US*) *I just saw him (a moment ago).* 我(几分钟之前)刚看见他. **4** at this/that moment; now; immediately 此[那]时; 现在; 即刻. (**a**) (esp with the present and past continuous tenses 尤用于现在进行时态和过去进行时态): *Please wait: I am just finishing a letter.* 请稍候, 我马上就写完信. ○ *I was just having lunch when Bill rang.* 比尔来电话时我正在吃午饭. ○ *Just/I'm just coming!* 立刻[我立刻]就来! ○ *I'm just off*, ie I'm leaving now. 我现在就走. (**b**) **~ about/going to do sth** (referring to the immediate future 表示即将): *I was just about to tell you when you interrupted.* 我正要告诉你, 你把话打断了. ○ *The clock is just going to strike noon.* 钟即将于中午时敲响. **5** (**a**) simply 仅; 只管: *Why not just wait and see what happens?* 何不静观其结果呢? ○ *You ˈcould just ask me for ˈhelp*, ie instead of making a great fuss, giving a long explanation, etc. 你不妨径直让我帮忙(无须大费周折, 多做解释). (**b**) (used, esp with the imperative, to cut short a possible argument or delay or to appeal for attention or understanding 用以避免争论或耽搁或请求注意或理解, 尤用于祈使句): *Just listen to what I'm saying!* 先听我说! ○ *Just try to understand!* 请你能理解这件事! ○ *Just let me say something!* 让我说两句吧! ○ *Just look at this!* 看看这个吧! ○ *Just listen to him* (ie and you will see how clever, funny, stupid, unusual, etc he is)*!* 听听他的(你就知道他多聪明、逗笑、愚蠢、特别等)! **6 ~ (for sth /to do sth)** only; simply 仅; 只是: *There is just one way of saving him.* 只有一个办法能救他. ○ *I waited an hour just to see you*, ie solely for that purpose. 我等了一小时就是为了见你. ○ *just for fun, a laugh, a joke, etc* 仅仅是闹着玩儿、逗笑、开玩笑等. **7** (*infml* 口) really; truly; emphatically 真正地; 实在; 的确: *The weather is just marvellous!* 天气真好! ○ *It's just a miracle that he survived the accident!* 他死里逃生实在是奇迹! ○ *'He's rather pompous.' 'Isn't he just?*(ie He certainly is!)*'* '他有点儿傲气.' '可不是吗!' **8** (idm 习语) **it is just as ˈwell (that...)** it is a good thing 也是好事; 倒也不错: *It's just as well that we didn't go out in this rain.* 我们下雨天没出去倒也是好事. **it is/would be just as well (to do sth)** it is advisable 是明智的: *It would be just as well to lock the door when you go out.* 出去的时候最好还是锁上门. **just about** (*infml* 口) (**a**) almost; very nearly 几乎; 几近; 近乎: *I've met just about everyone.* 所有的人我几乎都见到了. ○ *That's just about the limit!* ie That makes the situation almost unbearable. 这差不多到头儿了(已几乎忍无可忍). (**b**) approximately 大约; 大概: *He should be arriving just about now.* 他现在大约该到了. **(not) just ˈany** (not) simply at random (不)随意地; (不)无目的地: *You can't ask just anybody to the party.* 你不能随便把什么人都请来参加聚会. **just as one/it ˈis** without any special decoration or alteration 不特意装饰或改变; 保持原样: *The trousers are rather long, but I'll take them just as they are.* 这条裤子有点儿长; 但我还是要了吧. ○ *Tell her to come to the party (dressed) just as she is.* 告诉她就像现在这样(穿着)来参加聚会就行. **ˌjust in ˈcase** as a precaution 以防万一: *The sun is shining, but I'll take an umbrella just in case.* 现在是晴天, 但我还是带上雨伞以防万一. **ˌjust like ˈthat** suddenly, without warning or explanation 突然; 冷不防地; 莫名其妙地: *He walked out on his wife just like that!* 他突然遗弃了妻子. **ˌjust ˈnow** (**a**) at this very moment 现在; 此时; 即刻: *Come and see me later, but not just now.* 以后再来找我, 现在别来. (**b**) during this present period 目前; 现阶段: *Business is good just now.* 目前生意不错. (**c**) only a short time ago 刚才; 刚刚: *I saw him just now.* 我刚才看见他了. **ˌjust on** (*infml* 口) (esp with numbers 尤与数字连用) exactly; only just 正好; 恰好; 刚好: *It's ˌjust on ˌsix oˈclock.* 现在正好六点钟. ○ *She's ˌjust on ˌninety years ˈold.* 她整九十岁. **ˌjust the ˈsame** (**a**) identical 同样的; 完全相同的: *These two pictures are just the same (as one another).* 这两幅画(彼此)完全相同. (**b**) nevertheless 仍然; 还是: *The sun's out, but I'll take a raincoat just the same.* 尽管是晴天, 但我还是要带上雨衣. **ˌjust ˈso** (**a**) (*fml* 文 *esp Brit*) quite true 正是: *'Your name is Smythe, is it?' 'Just so.'* '你姓史密斯, 是吧?' '正是.' (**b**) performed or arranged with precision 有条理的; 井然: *She cannot bear an untidy desk. Everything must be just so.* 她就怕书桌上凌乱.样样东西都必须井然有序. **just such a sth** sth exactly like this 与此完全相像的某事物: *It was on just such a day (as this) that we left for France.* 我们动身去法国的那天就跟这天一样. **(it's/that's) ˌjust too ˈbad** (*infml* 口) (often used to show lack of sympathy 常用以表示不甚同情) the situation cannot be helped; one must simply manage as best one can 情况无可奈何, 只好尽力而为: *'I've left my purse at home.' 'That's just too bad, I'm afraid!'* '我把钱包忘在家里了.' '我看那可没办法了!' **one might just as well be/do sth** one would not benefit from being or doing otherwise 这样也好: *The weather was so bad on holiday we might just as well have stayed at home.* 假日的天气很坏, 我们呆在家里也不错. **not just ˈyet** not at this present moment but probably quite soon 并非现在, 但可能不久: *'Are you ready?' 'Not just yet.'* '你准备好了吗?' '还没有, 但很快就好.'

just·ice /ˈdʒʌstɪs; ˈdʒʌstɪs/ *n* **1** [U] (**a**) right and fair behaviour or treatment 公平; 公正; 正义: *laws based on the principles of justice* 以公正为原则的法律 ○ *efforts to achieve complete social justice* 为达到社会的完全公道而做的努力. (**b**) quality of being reasonable or fair 合理; 公道: *He demanded, with some justice, that he should be given an opportunity to express his views.* 他要求给他一次机会表达自己的观点, 这也不无道理. **2** [U] the law and its administration 法律制裁; 司法; 审判: *a court of justice* 法庭 ○ *a miscarriage of justice*, ie a wrong legal decision 误判. **3 Justice** [C] (used as a title of a High Court Judge 用作高等法院法官的头衔): *Mr Justice Smith* 法官史密斯先生. **4** [C] (*US*) judge of a lawcourt 法官. **5** (idm 习语) **bring sb to ˈjustice** arrest, try and sentence (a criminal) 使(犯人)归案受审. **ˌdo oneself ˈjustice** behave in a way that is worthy of one's abilities 发挥自己的能力: *He didn't do himself justice in the exams*, ie did not perform as well as he was capable of doing. 他在考试中没有发挥出自己的能力. **do justice to sb/sth** (**a**) recognize the true value of sb/sth; treat sb/sth fairly 承认某人[某事物]的价值; 公平对待某人[某事物]: *To do her justice, we must admit that she did deserve to win.* 说句公道话, 我们得承认她应该获胜. ○ *The photograph does not do full justice to* (ie does not truly reproduce) *the rich colours of the gardens.* 这张照片没有真实地反映出花园的丰富色彩. (**b**) deal with sb/sth adequately 尽心处理或对待某人[某事物]: *Since we'd already eaten, we couldn't do justice to her cooking*, ie could not eat all the food she had cooked. 我们已经吃过饭了, 所以吃不下她做的食物了.

□ **ˌJustice of the ˈPeace** (*abbr* 缩写 **JP**) person who judges less serious cases in a local lawcourt; magistrate (地方法院审理一般案件的)治安官, 治安法官.

jus·tify /ˈdʒʌstɪfaɪ; ˈdʒʌstəˌfaɪ/ *v* (*pt, pp* **-fied**) **1** [Tn, Tg, Tsg] show that (sb/sth) is right, reasonable or just 表明或证明(某人[某事])是正当的、有理的或公正的: *Such action can be justified on the grounds of greater efficiency.* 以提高功效为依据可以证明采取这种措施是

正确的. ○ *You shouldn't attempt to justify yourself.* 你不应想方设法证明自己有理. ○ *You can't justify neglecting your wife and children.* 你不关心妻子儿女是说不过去的. ○ *They found it hard to justify their son's giving up a secure well-paid job.* 他们难以理解儿子竟放弃了收入颇丰的稳定工作. **2** [Tn, Tg, Tsg] be a good reason for (sth) 为(某事)的正当理由: *Improved productivity justifies an increase in wages.* 提高了生产力理应增加工资. ○ *Tiredness cannot possibly justify your treating staff this way.* 你不能以疲劳为理由就这样对待职工. **3** [Tn] arrange (lines of type) so that the margins are even 调整(各行铅字等的位置)使版面四周空白均匀: *a justified text* 四周空白均匀的版面. **4** (idm 习语) **the end justifies the means** ⇨ END[1].

▷ **jus·ti·fi·able** /ˌdʒʌstɪˈfaɪəbl, *also* ˈdʒʌstɪfaɪəbl; ˈdʒʌstəˌfaɪəbl/ *adj* that can be justified 可证明为正当的; 有理由的: *a justifiable explanation, action, use* 合理的解释、行为、用法 ○ *justifiable homicide*, eg killing in self-defence 正当杀人(如出于自卫). **jus·ti·fi·ably** /-əblɪ; -əblɪ/ *adv*: *justifiably cautious, indignant, proud, etc* 有理由谨慎的、愤怒的、骄傲的等.

jus·ti·fica·tion /ˌdʒʌstɪfɪˈkeɪʃn; ˌdʒʌstəfəˈkeʃən/ *n* **1** [U, C] **~ (for sth/doing sth)** acceptable reason (for doing sth) (做某事的)正当理由: *I can see no justification for dividing the company into smaller units.* 我认为没有理由把公司划分成小单位. ○ *He was getting angry — and with some justification.* 他生气了——事出有因. ⇨Usage at REASON[1] 用法见 REASON[1]. **2** [U] arrangement of lines of type so that the margins are even. 齐行, 整版(为使版面四周空白均匀而对铅字等位置的调整). **3** (idm 习语) **in justification (for/of sb/sth)** as a defence (of sb/sth) 作为对(某人[某事]的)辩解: *I suppose that, in justification, he could always claim he had a family to support.* 我想他反正会以养家为理由来进行辩解.

jus·ti·fied *adj* **1 ~ (in doing sth)** having good reasons for doing sth (做某事)有正当理由的: *As the goods were damaged, she felt fully justified in asking for her money back.* 因商品损坏, 她认为有充分理由要求退款. **2** for which there is a good reason 事出有因的: *justified criticism, suspicion, anger* 事出有因的批评、怀疑、愤怒.

jut /dʒʌt; dʒʌt/ *v* **(-tt-)** (phr v) **jut out** stand out (from sth); be out of line (with the surrounding surface); stick out 突出; 伸出: *a balcony that juts out (over the garden)* 突出(于花园之上)的阳台 ○ *a headland that juts out into the sea* 伸入海中的岬 ○ *His chin juts out rather a lot.* 他的下巴向外突出.

jute /dʒuːt; dʒut/ *n* [U] fibre from the outer skin of certain tropical plants, used for making sacking, rope, etc 黄麻纤维: *the jute mills of Bangladesh* 孟加拉国的黄麻纤维工厂.

ju·ven·ile /ˈdʒuːvənaɪl; ˈdʒuvənaɪl/ *n* **1** (*fml or law* 文或律) young person who is not yet adult 未成年者; 少年. **2** actor or actress who plays such a part 扮演少年的演员: [attrib 作定语] *play the juvenile lead* 扮演少年主角.

▷ **ju·ven·ile** *adj* **1** [attrib 作定语] (*fml or law* 文或律) of, characteristic of or suitable for young people who are not yet adults 未成年的; 少年的; 少年特有的; 适于少年的: *juvenile crime* 少年犯罪 ○ *juvenile offenders* 少年犯 ○ *juvenile books* 少年读物. **2** (*derog* 贬) immature and foolish; childish 幼稚无知的; 孩子气的: *a juvenile sense of humour* 孩子气的幽默感 ○ *Stop being so juvenile!* 别再那么孩子气了!

□ ˌ**juvenile** ˈ**court** court that tries young people who are not yet adults 少年法庭.

ˌ**juvenile de**ˈ**linquent** young person not yet an adult, who is guilty of a crime, eg vandalism 少年犯. ˌ**juvenile de**ˈ**linquency** criminal or antisocial behaviour by juvenile delinquents 少年犯罪.

jux·ta·pose /ˌdʒʌkstəˈpəʊz; ˌdʒʌkstəˈpoz/ *v* [Tn] (*fml* 文) place (people or things) side by side or very close together, esp to show a contrast 将(人或事物)并列或并置(尤指为显示差别): *juxtapose the classical style of architecture with the modern* 将古典的与现代的建筑风格并列对照. ▷ **jux·ta·posi·tion** /ˌdʒʌkstəpəˈzɪʃn; ˌdʒʌkstəpəˈzɪʃən/ *n* [U]: *the juxtaposition of (different) ideas, civilizations, traditions* (不同的)思想、文化、传统的对比.

K k

K, k /keɪ; ke/ *n* (*pl* **K's, k's** /keɪz; kez/) the eleventh letter of the English alphabet 英语字母表的第十一个字母: *'King' begins with (a) K/'K'* king字以 k 字母开始.

K /keɪ; ke/ *abbr* 缩写 = **1** kelvin(s). **2** (*infml* 口) one thousand (Greek *kilo-*) 一千(源自希腊文*kilo-*): *She earns 12K* (ie £12 000) *a year.* 她一年挣12 000英镑.

kaf·fir /ˈkæfə(r); ˋkæfɚ/ *n* (*S African* ⚠ *offensive* 南非, 讳, 蔑) black African person 非洲黑人.

kaf·tan = CAFTAN.

Kaiser /ˈkaɪzə(r); ˋkaɪzɚ/ *n* title of the German and Austro-Hungarian emperors until 1918 (1918年以前的)德国和奥匈帝国皇帝的称号.

kale (also **kail**) /keɪl; kel/ *n* [U] type of cabbage with curly leaves 羽衣甘蓝.

kal·eido·scope /kəˈlaɪdəskəʊp; kəˈlaɪdə,skop/ *n* (**a**) toy consisting of a tube containing small loose pieces of coloured glass, etc and mirrors which reflect these to form changing patterns when the tube is turned 万花筒. (**b**) (usu *sing* 通常作单数) (*fig* 比喻) constantly and quickly changing pattern 千变万化; 瞬息万变: *His paintings are a kaleidoscope of gorgeous colours.* 他的油画色彩斑斓, 变化万千. ○ *The bazaar was a kaleidoscope of strange sights and impressions.* 集市的景象光怪陆离, 纷然杂陈. ▷ **kal·eido·scopic** /kə,laɪdəˈskɒpɪk; kə,laɪdəˈskɑpɪk/ *adj.* **kal·eido·scop·ic·ally** /-klɪ; -klɪ/ *adv.*

ka·mi·kaze /ˌkæmɪˈkɑːzɪ; ,kɑmɪˋkɑzɪ/ *n* (in World War II) (pilot of a) Japanese aircraft deliberately crashed on enemy ships, etc (第二次世界大战中日本的)神风飞机, 神风飞机飞行员(与敌舰等同归于尽的自杀飞机或驾驶员): [attrib 作定语] *a kamikaze attack* 神风飞机的攻击 ○ (*fig* 比喻) *kamikaze* (ie suicidal) *tactics* 同归于尽的战术.

kangaroo 袋鼠

kan·garoo /ˌkæŋgəˈruː; ,kæŋgəˋru/ *n* (*pl* **~s**) Australian animal that jumps along on its strong hind legs, the female carrying its young in a pouch on the front of its body 袋鼠(产于澳洲). ⇨illus 见插图.

□ ˌ**kangaroo ˈcourt** illegal court formed by a group of prisoners, striking workers, etc to settle disputes among themselves 私设的公堂(囚犯、罢工工人等为解决内部纠纷而设的).

ka·olin /ˈkeɪəlɪn; ˋkeəlɪn/ *n* [U] (also **china ˈclay**) fine white clay used in making porcelain and in medicine 高岭土; 瓷土.

ka·pok /ˈkeɪpɒk; ˋkepɑk/ *n* [U] substance like cotton wool, used for stuffing cushions, soft toys, etc 木棉.

ka·put /kəˈpʊt; kəˋpʊt/ *adj* [pred 作表语] (*sl* 俚) broken; ruined; not working properly 完蛋了; 失败了; 坏了: *The car's kaput — we'll have to walk.* 汽车坏了——我们只好步行.

karat (*US*) = CARAT 2.

kar·ate /kəˈrɑːtɪ; kəˋrɑtɪ/ *n* [U] Japanese system of unarmed combat in which the hands, feet, etc are used as weapons 空手道(日本式徒手武术): [attrib 作定语] *a karate chop*, ie a blow with the side of the hand 空手道的掌侧劈.

karma /ˈkɑːmə; ˋkɑrmə/ *n* [U] (**a**) (in Buddhism and Hinduism) sum of a person's actions in one of his successive lives, believed to decide his fate in the next (佛教和印度教的)业(音译'羯磨', 意为个人行为的总和可决定其来世的命运). (**b**) (*esp joc* 尤作戏谑语) destiny; fate 命运; 宿缘: *It's my karma always to fall in love with brunettes.* 我爱上的总是深褐色头发、浅黑色皮肤的白种女子, 这是我的缘分.

kart /kɑːt; kɑrt/ *n* = GO-KART.

kayak /ˈkaɪæk; ˋkaɪæk/ *n.* ⇨illus at CANOE 见CANOE插图. (**a**) Eskimo canoe made of light wood covered with sealskins 海豹皮船(爱斯基摩人制的单人小舟). (**b**) small covered canoe resembling this (类似海豹皮船的)小艇.

ka·zoo /kəˈzuː; kəˋzu/ *n* (*pl* **~s**) toy musical instrument that gives a buzzing sound when sb blows through it while humming 一种玩具笛.

KB /ˌkeɪ ˈbiː; ,ke ˋbi/ *abbr* 缩写 = (*Brit law* 律) King's Bench. Cf 参看 QB.

KBE /ˌkeɪ biː ˈiː; ,ke bi ˋi/ *abbr* 缩写 = (*Brit*) Knight Commander (of the Order) of the British Empire (第二等的)大英帝国最高勋爵; 英帝国爵级司令勋章: *be made a KBE* 受封(第二等的)大英帝国最高勋爵位 ○ *Sir John Brown KBE* 约翰·布朗(第二等的)大英帝国最高勋爵士. Cf 参看 CBE, DBE, MBE.

KC /ˌkeɪ ˈsiː; ,ke ˋsi/ *abbr* 缩写 = (*Brit law* 律) King's Counsel. Cf 参看 QC.

ke·bab /kɪˈbæb; kəˋbæb/ *n* (often *pl* 常作复数) small pieces of meat and vegetables cooked and (often) served on a skewer 烤肉串: *lamb kebabs* 烤羊肉串 ○ *shish kebab* 烤肉串.

ked·geree /ˈkedʒəriː, ˌkedʒəˈriː; ˋkɛdʒə,ri, ,kɛdʒəˋri/ *n* [U, C] cooked dish of rice and fish, with hard-boiled eggs and sometimes onions, all mixed together 鱼蛋烩饭(有时伴有洋葱).

keel /kiːl; kil/ *n* **1** timber or steel structure along the bottom of a ship, on which the framework is built up (船的)龙骨: *lay down a keel*, ie start building a ship 安龙骨(动工造船). **2** (idm 习语) **on an even keel** ⇨ EVEN[1].

▷ **keel** *v* (phr v) **keel over** **1** (of a ship) capsize (指船)倾覆, 翻倒. **2** (*infml* 口) fall over; collapse 倒下; 倒塌: *After a couple of drinks he just keeled over on the floor.* 他喝了两杯酒后就跌倒在地了. ○ *The structure had keeled over in the high winds.* 那座建筑物让大风给刮倒了.

keen[1] /kiːn; kin/ *adj* (**-er, -est**) **1 ~ (to do sth/that...)** eager; enthusiastic 热切的; 热情的; 热心的: *a keen swimmer* 喜好游泳的人 ○ *I'm not keen to go again.* 我不太想再去了. ○ *She's keen that we should go.* 她热情地叫我们去. **2** (of feelings, etc) intense; strong; deep (指感情等)热烈的, 强烈的, 深刻的: *a keen desire, interest, sense of loss* 强烈的愿望、兴趣、失落感. **3** (of the senses) highly developed (指感觉)灵敏的, 敏锐的: *Dogs have a keen sense of smell.* 狗的嗅觉很灵敏. **4** (of the mind) quick to understand (指头脑)敏捷的, 精明的: *a keen wit, intelligence* 敏捷的头脑、很强的理解力. **5** [esp attrib 尤作定语] (of the points and cutting edges of knives, etc) sharp (指刀等的尖和刃)锋利的, 快的: *a keen blade, edge* 锋利的刀片、刀刃. **6** (of a wind) bitterly cold (指风)刺骨的, 凛冽的. **7** (*Brit*) (of prices) low; very competitive (指价格)低廉的, 竞争力强的. **8** (idm 习语) **(as) ˌkeen as ˈmustard** (*infml* 口) extremely eager or enthusiastic 极热心的; 极热情的. **keen on sth/sb** (*infml* 口) (**a**) interested in sth 热衷于某事物: *keen on (playing) tennis* 很喜欢(打)网球. (**b**) fond of sb/sth 喜爱某人[某事物]: *He seemed mad keen on* (ie very interested in) *my sister.* 他发疯似的爱着我妹妹. ○ *I'm not too keen on jazz.* 我不太喜欢爵士乐. (**c**) enthusiastic about sth 对某事物满腔热情: *She's not very* *keen on the idea.* 她对那主张不很感兴趣. ○ *Mrs Hill is keen on Tom's marrying Susan.* 希尔太太很希望汤姆能和苏珊结婚. ▷ **keenly** *adv.* **keen·ness** *n* [U].

keen[2] /ki:n; kin/ *v* [I] (usu in the continuous tenses 通常用于进行时态) lament a dead person by wailing 为死者恸哭、哀号: *keening over her murdered son* 恸哭她那被谋害的儿子.

▷ **keen** *n* Irish funeral song accompanied by wailing 爱尔兰哀歌(边哭边唱).

keep[1] /ki:p; kip/ *v* (*pt, pp* **kept** /kept; kɛpt/) **1** (**a**) [La, Ipr, Ip] continue to be in the specified condition or position; remain or stay 继续处于某状态或地位; 留下; 保留: *She has the ability to keep calm in an emergency.* 她有处变不惊的本事. ○ *Please keep quiet — I'm trying to get some work done.* 请安静——我要处理一些工作. ○ *You ought to keep indoors with that heavy cold.* 你患重感冒应该留在屋里. ○ *The notice said 'Keep off* (ie Do not walk on) *the grass'.* 布告牌上写着'勿践草地'. ○ *Keep back! The building could collapse at any moment.* 别靠近! 那建筑物随时可能倒塌. (**b**) [Ip] **~ (on) doing sth** continue doing sth; do sth repeatedly or frequently 继续做某事物; 重复做某事物: *keep eating, laughing, smiling, walking* 一直在吃、笑、微笑、走 ○ *Keep (on) talking amongst yourselves, I'll be back in a minute.* 你们继续谈, 我一会儿就回来. ○ *How can I trust you if you keep lying to me?* 你要是一直欺骗我, 我怎么能相信你呢? ○ *I do wish you wouldn't keep interrupting me!* 希望你别老来打扰我! ○ *My shoe laces keep (on) coming undone.* 我的鞋带总是松开. ○ *Keep going* (ie Do not stop) *until you reach a large roundabout.* 继续走就走到一个宽阔的环状交叉路口了. ○ *This is exhausting work, but I manage to keep going somehow.* 这个工作很费力气, 但是我尽量设法做下去. (**c**) [Ipr, Ip] continue to move in the specified direction 继续朝某方向前进: *Traffic in Britain keeps to the left,* ie drives on the left-hand side of the road. 在英国, 车辆靠左行驶. ○ *Keep straight on until you get to the church.* 一直朝前走就走到教堂了. ○ *The sign says 'Keep Left', so I don't think we can turn right here.* 路标上写着'靠左行', 我想不能从这儿向右拐. **2** [Tn·pr, Tn·p, Cn·a, Cn·g] cause sb/sth to remain in the specified condition or position 使某人[某事物]保持某状态或某地位: *If your hands are cold, keep them in your pockets.* 要是手冷, 就揣在口袋里. ○ *Extra work kept him (late) at the office.* 他因有额外的工作, (很晚)仍留在办公室里. ○ *Don't keep us in suspense any longer — what happens at the end of the story?* 别再让我们蒙在鼓里了, 结局究竟怎么样? ○ *keep sb amused, cheerful, happy, etc* 使某人一直高兴、快乐、幸福等 ○ *These gloves will keep your hands warm.* 这种手套保暖好. ○ *Give the baby her bottle; that'll keep her quiet for a while.* 把瓶子给孩子, 那就能让她安静一会儿. ○ *He's in a coma and is being kept alive by a life-support machine.* 他处于昏迷状态, 靠生命维持器活着. ○ *I'm sorry to keep you waiting.* 对不起, 让您久等了. ○ *Add some more coal to keep the fire going.* 再添些煤, 别让火灭了. **3** [Tn] detain or delay (sb) 留住或耽搁(某人): *You're an hour late; what kept you?* 你晚了一小时, 是什么事给耽误了? Cf 参看 KEEP SB FROM STH/DOING STH. **4** [Tn] (**a**) continue to have (sth); retain 保有, 留下(某物): *You can keep that book I lent you; I don't want it back.* 我借给你的那本书你可以留下, 不用还我. ○ *Here's a five-pound note — you can keep the change.* 这是五镑的钞票——零钱不用找了. (**b**) [Tn, Tn·pr, Dn·n] **~ sth (for sb)** look after sth (for sb); retain sth (为某人)照顾某事物; 保留某事物: *Could you keep my place in the queue (for me)*(ie prevent anybody else from taking it)? 我排在队里的位置可以给我留着吗? ○ *Please keep me a place in the queue.* 排队时请给我占个位置. (**c**) [Tn, Tn·pr] have (sth) in a particular place; store 在某处存放(某物); 贮藏: *Where do you keep the cutlery?* 你的餐具在哪里? ○ *We haven't enough shelves to keep all our books on.* 我们的书架不够用, 放不下这么多书. ○ *Always keep your driving licence in a safe place.* 驾驶执照一定要妥善保管. (**d**) [Tn] retain (sth) for future use or reference 保留(某物)(以备日后之需): *These trousers are so worn they're hardly worth keeping.* 这条裤子磨损得很厉害, 不必再留着了. ○ *Let's not eat all the sandwiches now — we can keep some for later.* 咱们别把三明治都吃光——可以留些过后再吃. ○ *I keep all her letters.* 我保留着她全部的信. **5** [Tn] own and manage (a shop, restaurant, etc) 经营, 开设(商店、饭馆等): *Her father kept a grocer's shop for a number of years.* 她父亲开了几年杂货店. ○ *He plans to keep a pub when he retires.* 他打算退休后开酒馆. **6** [Tn] own and look after (animals) for one's use or enjoyment (为自用或消遣)饲养(动物): *keep bees, goats, hens, etc* 饲养蜂、羊、鸡等. **7** [Tn] have (sth) regularly on sale or in stock 经销、销售或储存(某物): *'Do you sell Turkish cigarettes?' 'I'm sorry, we don't keep them.'* '你们卖土耳其香烟吗?' '对不起, 我们不卖那种香烟.' **8** [Tn] not reveal (a secret) 保守(秘密): *Can you keep a secret?* ie If I tell you one, can I be sure that you will not tell it to sb else? 我想告诉你一件事, 你能保密吗? **9** [I] (of food) remain in good condition (指食物)保持不坏: *Do finish off the fish pie; it won't keep.* 鱼馅糕饼留不住, 都吃了吧. ○ (*fig* 比喻) *The news will keep,* ie can be told later rather than immediately. 这消息可容后宣布. **10** [I] (used with an *adv*, or in questions after *how* 与副词连用或用于疑问句中的how之后) be in the specified state of health 处于某种健康状况: *'How are you keeping?' 'I'm keeping well, thanks.'* '你身体好吗?' '很好, 谢谢.' **11** [Tn] (**a**) make written entries in (sth) 在(某物)上作书面记载: *She kept a diary for over twenty years.* 她写日记已二十多年. (**b**) write down (sth) as a record 记录(某事): *keeping an account/a record of what one spends each week* 记录每周的开支. **12** [Tn] provide what is necessary for (sb); support (sb) financially 供给(某人)必需品; 经济上支持(某人): *He scarcely earns enough to keep himself and his family.* 他挣的钱难以维持全家人的生活. **13** (**a**) [Tn] guard or protect (sth) 守卫或把守(某物): *keep goal,* ie in football 守球门(足球的) ○ *keep wicket,* ie in cricket 守三柱门(板球的). Cf 参看 GOALKEEPER (GOAL), WICKET-KEEPER (WICKET). (**b**) [Tn, Tn·pr] **~ sb (from sth)** (*fml* 文) protect sb (from sth) 保护或保佑某人: *May the Lord bless you and keep you,* ie used in prayers in the Christian Church 愿上帝祝福你、保佑你(用于基督教会的祈祷) ○ *She prayed to God to keep her son from harm.* 她祈祷上帝保佑儿子平安. **14** [Tn] be faithful to (sth); respect or observe 忠于(某事物); 尊重; 遵守: *keep an appointment, the law, a promise, a treaty* 遵守约会、法律、诺言、条约. **15** (idm 习语) ˌ**keep it ˈup** maintain a high standard of achievement 保持优秀成绩: *Excellent work, Cripps — keep it up!* 克里普斯, 你干得真好——要保持下去! ˌ**keep up with the ˈJoneses** /ˈdʒəʊnzɪz; ˋdʒonzɪz/ (*infml often derog* 口, 常作贬义) try to maintain the same social and material standards as one's neighbours 要在地位和物质方面比得上周围的人. (For other idioms containing **keep**, see entries for *ns, adjs,* etc 与**keep**搭配的其他习语见有关名词、形容词等的词条, 如 **keep house** ⇨ HOUSE[1]; **keep the ball rolling** ⇨ BALL[1].)

16 (phr v) **keep (sb) at sth** (cause sb to) continue to work at sth (使某人)继续做某事: *Come on, keep 'at it, you've nearly finished!* 加油, 别松劲, 你眼看就完成了! ○ *The teacher kept us at our 'work all morning.* 老师让我们做了一上午的功课.

keep (sb/sth) away (from sb/sth) (cause sb/sth) not to go near sb/sth (使某人[某事物])不靠近某人[某事物]: *Police warned bystanders to keep away from the blazing building.* 警察告诫围观者, 不要靠近燃烧着的建筑物. ○ *Her illness kept her away from* (ie caused her to be absent from) *work for several weeks.* 她因病数周未上班.

keep sth back (**a**) prevent sth from moving; restrain sth 使某事物不能移动; 阻止某事物: *Millions of gallons of water are kept back by the dam.* 这个堤坝拦住了滔滔的洪水. ○ *She was unable to keep back her tears.* 她无法忍住泪水. (**b**) not pay sth to sb 不将某物付给某人: *A certain percentage of your salary is kept back by your employer as an insurance payment.* 雇主扣下你部分薪金作保险金用. **keep sth ˈback (from sb)** refuse to tell sb sth; hold sth back 拒不将某事告诉某人; 隐瞒某事物: *I'm sure she's keeping something back (from us).* 我肯定她(向我们)隐瞒着什么. **keep (sb) ˈback (from sb/sth)** (cause sb to) remain at a distance from sb/sth (使某人)与某人[某事物]保持距离: *Keep well back from the road.* 离马路远些. ○ *Barricades were erected to keep* *back the crowds.* 设置了障碍以隔开人群. **keep 'down** not show where one is; not stand up 隐蔽; 不站立: *Keep down! You mustn't let anybody see you.* 蹲下! 一定不要让人看见你. **keep sb 'down** repress or oppress (a people, nation, etc) 压制或镇压(人民、国民等): *The people have been kept down for years by a brutal régime.* 人民多年遭受野蛮制度压迫. **keep sth 'down (a)** not raise (a part of the body) 不抬起(身体某部分): *Keep your head down!* 不要抬头! **(b)** retain sth in the stomach 吞下某物; 不吐出来: *The medicine was so horrid I couldn't keep it down*, ie I was sick. 这药这么难吃, 我咽不下去. **(c)** cause sth to remain at a low level; not increase sth 使某事物处于低水平; 压抑某事物: *keep down wages, prices, the cost of living, etc* 保持低工资、低价格、低生活费等 ○ *Keep your voices down; your mother's trying to get some sleep.* 小点声, 你妈妈要睡觉了. **(d)** not allow sth to multiply or grow 不使某物滋生或生长: *use chemicals to keep pests down* 用化学药品消灭害虫.

keep oneself/sb from sth/doing sth prevent oneself/sb from doing sth 使自己[某人]不能做某事物: *The church bells keep me from sleeping.* 教堂的钟声吵得我睡不着觉. ○ *I hope I'm not keeping you from your work.* 希望我没有妨碍你的工作. **keep (oneself) from doing sth** prevent oneself from doing sth; stop (oneself) doing sth 克制自己不做某事: *She could hardly keep (herself) from laughing.* 她忍不住大笑起来. ○ *I just managed to keep myself from falling.* 我差一点跌倒. **keep sth from sb** not tell sb sth 不将某事告诉某人: *I think we ought to keep the truth from him until he's better.* 我想等他好些再把实情告诉他. ○ *They don't keep anything from each other.* 他们之间无话不谈.

keep sb 'in detain (a child) after normal school hours as a punishment 罚(小学生)课后留校: *She was kept in for an hour for talking in class.* 她因上课说话被罚留校一小时. **keep sth in** not express (an emotion); restrain sth 不表露(情感); 控制某事物: *He could scarcely keep in his indignation.* 他愤怒得难以自持. **keep oneself/sb in sth** give or allow oneself/sb a regular supply of sth 使自己[某人]经常有某事物: *She earns enough to keep herself and all the family in good clothes.* 她的收入能让全家经常有好衣服穿. **keep in with sb** (*infml* 口) continue to be friendly with sb, esp in order to gain some advantage 保持与某人亲近(尤指为得到好处): *Have you noticed how he tries to keep in with the boss?* 你注意到他多巴结老板了吗?

keep 'off (of rain, snow, etc) not begin (指雨、雪等)未下: *The fête will go ahead provided the rain keeps off.* 要是不下雨, 义卖会就照常进行. **keep off (sb/sth)** not approach, touch, etc sb/sth 不接近或不接触某人[某事物]. **keep off sth (a)** not eat, drink or smoke sth 不吃、不喝或不吸食某物: *keep off cigarettes, drugs, drink, fatty foods* 不抽烟、不吸毒、不喝酒、不吃多油脂的食物. **(b)** not mention (the specified subject); avoid 不提(某话题); 避免: *Please keep off (the subject of) politics while my father's here.* 有我父亲在场, 请别谈政治. **keep sb/sth off (sb/sth)** cause sb/sth not to approach, touch, etc sb/sth 使某人[某事物]不接近或不接触某人[某事物]: *They lit a fire to keep wild animals off.* 他们燃起篝火防止野兽接近. ○ *Keep your hands off* (ie Do not touch) *me!* 别碰我!

keep 'on continue one's journey 继续行进: *Keep on past the church; the stadium is about half a mile further on.* 一直向前走过了教堂, 约莫半英里就是体育场. **keep on (doing sth)** continue (doing sth) 继续(做某事): *The rain kept on all night.* 雨彻夜不停. ○ *She kept on working although she was tired.* 她虽疲劳但仍继续工作. **keep sb 'on** continue to employ sb 继续雇用某人: *He's incompetent and not worth keeping on.* 他庸碌无能, 不值得留用. **keep sth on (a)** continue to wear sth 继续穿戴某物: *You don't need to keep your hat on indoors.* 在室内不必戴着帽子了. **(b)** continue to rent or be the owner of (a house, flat, etc) 继续租用或领有(房屋、寓所等): *We're planning to keep the cottage on over the summer.* 我们打算夏天继续租那座别墅. **keep 'on (at sb) (about sb/sth)** continue talking (to sb) in an irritating way (about sb/sth) (向某人)唠叨: *He does keep on so!* 他就是这样爱唠叨! ○ *I will mend the lamp — just don't keep on at me about it!* 我一定修这个灯——别再跟我唠叨这件事了!

keep 'out (of sth) not enter (a place); remain outside 不进入(某处); 留在外边: *The sign said 'Ministry of Defence — Danger — Keep Out!'* 牌子上写着, '国防部重地——闲人免进!' **keep sb/sth out (of sth)** prevent sb/sth from entering (a place) 不让某人[某物]进入(某处): *Keep that dog out of my study!* 别让那条狗进我的书房! ○ *She wore a hat to keep the sun out of her eyes.* 她戴着帽子遮阳, 保护眼睛. **keep (sb) out of sth** not expose oneself/sb to sth; (cause sb to) avoid sth 遮掩自己[某人]; (使某人)避开某事物: *Do keep out of the rain if you haven't a coat.* 没带雨衣那就避一下雨. ○ *That child seems incapable of keeping out of* (ie not getting into) *mischief.* 那个孩子不调皮捣蛋简直就受不了. ○ *Keep the children out of harm's way if you take them to the match.* 带孩子看比赛, 要注意他们的安全.

keep to sth (a) not wander from or leave (a path, road, etc) 不偏离, 不离开(道路等): *Keep to the track — the moor is very boggy around here.* 不要偏离车道——这一带沼泽地多. ○ (*fig* 比喻) *keep to the point/subject* 别扯远了[不要离题]. **(b)** follow or observe (a plan, schedule, etc) 遵循, 遵守(计划、时刻表等): *Things will only work out if we all keep to the plan.* 只有大家执行计划, 事情才能成功. **(c)** remain faithful to (a promise, etc) 忠于, 信守(诺言等): *keep to an agreement, an undertaking* 信守协定、承诺. **(d)** remain in and not leave (the specified place or position) 留在, 不离开(某地或某位置): *She's old and infirm and has to keep to the house.* 她因年老体弱而足不出户. **(e)** (used esp in the imperative when rebuking sb 尤用于祈使语气以指责某人) not express (a comment, view, etc) 不必说出(意见、看法等): *Keep your opinions to yourself in future!* 你有意见留着自己用吧! **keep (oneself) to oneself** avoid meeting people socially; not concern oneself with other people's affairs 不与人交往; 不管别人的事: *Nobody knows much about him; he keeps himself (very much) to himself.* 谁都不太了解他, 因为他很少与人来往. **keep sth to one'self** not tell other people about sth 不把某事告诉别人: *I'd be grateful if you kept this information to yourself.* 这事你若能保密则不胜感激.

keep sb 'under oppress sb 压迫某人: *The local population is kept under by a brutal army of mercenaries.* 当地居民备受野蛮雇佣军的欺压. **keep sth under** control or suppress sth 控制或压制某事物: *Firemen managed to keep the fire under.* 消防队员尽力控制了火势.

keep 'up (of rain, snow, good weather, etc) continue without stopping (指雨、雪、好天气等)持续不停: *Let's hope the sunny weather keeps up for Saturday's tennis match.* 但愿星期六网球比赛时还是这样的好天气. **keep sb up** prevent sb from going to bed 使某人不能去睡觉: *I do hope we're not keeping you up.* 我希望我们没有耽误你睡觉. **keep sth up (a)** prevent sth from falling down 使某物不落下: *wear a belt to keep one's trousers up* 系着腰带以系住裤子. **(b)** cause sth to remain at a high level 使某事物处于高水平: *The high cost of raw materials is keeping prices up.* 原料费用昂贵使得产品价格居高不下. **(c)** not allow (one's spirits, strength, etc) to decline; maintain 不让(精力等)衰退; 维持; 保持: *They sang songs to keep their morale up.* 他们唱着歌以保持高昂的士气. **(d)** continue sth at the same (usu high) level 继续使某事物保持同样的(通常指高的)水平: *The enemy kept up their bombardment day and night.* 敌军一直日夜不停地狂轰滥炸. ○ *We're having difficulty keeping up our mortgage payments.* 我们难以继续支付分期偿还的抵押贷款. ○ *You're all doing a splendid job; keep up the good work!* 你们干得都很出色, 要坚持下去! **(e)** continue to practise or observe sth 照旧做某事物或遵守某事: *keep up old customs, traditions, etc* 沿袭古老的风俗、传统等 ○ *Do you still keep up your Spanish?* 你仍在学西班牙语吗? **(f)** maintain (a house, garden, etc) in good condition by spending money or energy on it 保养, 维修(房屋、花园等): *The house is becoming too expensive for them to keep up.* 他们的房子维修费用贵得越来越修不起了. Cf 参看 UPKEEP. **keep 'up (with sb/sth)** move or progress at the same rate (as sb/sth) 跟上(某人[某事物]); (与某人[某事物])同步前进: *Slow down — I can't keep up (with you)!* 慢点, 我跟不上(你)了! ○ *I can't keep up with all the* *changes in computer technology.* 计算机技术的各种改进有些我已跟不上了. **keep up (with sth)** rise at the same rate (as sth) 以(某事物的)同样速率上升: *Workers' incomes are not keeping up with inflation.* 工人的收入赶不上通货膨胀. **keep up with sb** continue to be in contact with sb 保持与某人的联系: *How many of your old school friends do you keep up with?* 你和中学时的老同学保持联系的有多少? **keep up with sth** inform oneself or learn about (the news, current events, etc) 知悉(消息); 跟上(形势): *She likes to keep up with the latest fashions.* 她喜欢穿戴入时.

□ ˌ**kept** ˈ**woman** (*dated or joc* 旧或谑) woman who is provided with money and a home by a man with whom she is having a sexual relationship (受供养的)姘妇.

keep² /kiːp; kip/ *n* **1** [U] (cost of providing) food and other necessities of life 食物等生活必需品; 生活费: *It's time you got a job and started paying for your keep!* 你该找份工作, 负担自己的生活费了! ○ (*fig* 比喻) *Does that old car still earn its keep?* ie Is it useful enough to be worth the cost of keeping it? 那辆旧汽车还值得维修吗? **2** [C] strongly built tower of an ancient castle 古代城堡中的强固主楼. **3** (idm 习语) **for** ˈ**keeps** (*infml* 口) permanently; for ever 永远地; 永久地: *Can I have it for keeps or do you want it back?* 我可以永久保留它呢还是要我还给你?

keeper /ˈkiːpə(r); ˈkipɚ/ *n* **1** person who looks after animals in a zoo or a collection of items in a museum (动物园的)饲养员; (博物馆的)保管人. **2** (esp in compounds 尤用以构成复合词) person who is in charge of or looks after sth 负责或照料某事物的人: *a* ˈ*lighthouse-keeper* ○ *a* ˈ*gamekeeper* ○ *a* ˈ*shopkeeper.* **3** (*infml* 口)(**a**) = GOALKEEPER (GOAL). (**b**) = WICKET-KEEPER (WICKET). **4** (idm 习语) **finders keepers** ⇨ FINDER (FIND¹).

keep·ing /ˈkiːpɪŋ; ˈkipɪŋ/ *n* (idm 习语) **for safe keeping** ⇨ SAFE¹. **in sb's keeping** in sb's care or custody 在某人处保管; 受某人监护: *I'll leave the keys in your keeping.* 我把钥匙交你保管. **in/out of keeping (with sth)** in/not in conformity or harmony 一致[不一致]; 协调[不协调]: *a development wholly in keeping with what we expected* 与我们预期完全相符的发展 ○ *That tie is not quite in keeping.* 那条领带不十分协调. **in safe keeping** ⇨ SAFE¹.

keep·sake /ˈkiːpseɪk; ˈkipˌsek/ *n* gift, usu small and often not very costly, that is kept in memory of the giver or previous owner 纪念品: *My aunt gave me one of her brooches as a keepsake.* 我的姑母把她的一只胸针送给我作纪念.

keg /keg; kɛg/ *n* small barrel, usu containing less than 10 British or 30 US gallons of liquid 小桶(通常容量不足10英加仑或30美加仑). ⇨illus at BARREL 见 BARREL 插图.

□ **keg beer** (*Brit*) beer served from kegs, using gas pressure 小桶啤酒(用气压压出).

kelp /kelp; kɛlp/ *n* [U] type of large brown seaweed 大型褐藻.

kel·vin /ˈkelvɪn; ˈkɛlvɪn/ *n* (*abbr* 缩写 **K**) unit (equal to the Celsius degree) of an international scale of temperature (the **Kelvin scale**) with 0° at absolute zero (–273.15°C) 开(开尔文温标的计量单位, 其零度为绝对零度, 等于–273.15°C). ⇨App 11 见附录11.

ken¹ /ken; kɛn/ *n* (idm 习语) **beyond/outside one's ken** not within one's range of knowledge 超出某人知识范围: *The workings of the Stock Exchange are beyond most people's ken.* 证券交易所的运作情况大多数人都不了解.

K

ken² /ken; kɛn/ *v* (**-nn-**, *pt* **kenned** or **kent**, *pp* **kenned**) [Tn, Tf, Tw] (*Scot* 苏格兰) know 知道.

ken·nel /ˈkenl; ˈkɛnḷ/ *n* **1** [C] shelter for a pet dog 狗窝; 狗房: *Rover lives in a kennel in the back garden.* 小狗罗弗的窝在后花园. **2** [C] shelter for a pack of hounds 一群猎犬的窝棚. **3 kennels** [sing or pl *v*] place where dogs are bred, cared for, etc 养狗场: *We put the dog into kennels when we go on holiday.* 我们去度假时把狗送到养狗场寄养.

▷ **ken·nel** *v* (**-ll-**; *US also* **-l-**) [Tn] put or keep (a dog) in a kennel or kennels 将(狗)关进狗窝或送到养狗场: *She kennels her dog in the yard.* 她把狗关进院子的狗窝里.

kepi /ˈkeɪpɪ; ˈkepɪ/ *n* type of French military cap with a horizontal peak 法国军帽.

kept *pt, pp of* KEEP¹.

kerb (also *esp US* **curb**) /kɜːb; kɝb/ *n* stone or concrete edge of a pavement at the side of a road (镶石的)路缘, 路边: *Stop at the kerb and look both ways before crossing (the road).* 先站在路边看清左右再过马路.

□ ˈ**kerb-crawling** *n* [U] driving slowly along trying to persuade sb on the pavement to enter one's car, esp for sexual purposes 开车沿路边缓慢行驶(尤指为性关系勾引人): *be arrested for kerb-crawling* 因沿路边慢驶勾引人而被拘捕.

ˈ**kerb drill** set of rules for crossing the road safely 过马路的安全规则.

ˈ**kerbstone** *n* block of stone or concrete forming part of a kerb 路缘石; 路边石.

ker·chief /ˈkɜːtʃɪf; ˈkɝtʃɪf/ *n* (*arch* 古) **1** square piece of cloth worn on the head or round the neck, esp by women 方头巾, 方围巾(尤指女用的). **2** handkerchief 手绢.

ker·fuffle /kəˈfʌfl; kɚˈfʌfl/ *n* [U] (*Brit infml* 口) fuss; noise; excitement 混乱; 吵闹; 闹哄: *What's all the kerfuffle (about)?* 这乱哄哄的是怎么回事?

ker·nel /ˈkɜːnl; ˈkɝnḷ/ *n* **1** soft and usu edible part inside a nut or fruit stone (坚果或核果的)仁(通常可食). ⇨illus at NUT 见 NUT 插图. **2** part of a grain or seed within the hard outer shell (谷物去壳后的)粒, 子. **3** (*fig* 比喻) central or essential part (of a subject, plan, problem, etc) 核心; 要点; 中心: *the kernel of her argument* 她的论据的核心.

ker·os·ene (also **ker·os·ine**) /ˈkerəsiːn; ˈkɛrəˌsin/ *n* [U] (*esp US*) = PARAFFIN 1: [attrib 作定语] *a kerosene lamp* 煤油灯.

kes·trel /ˈkestrəl; ˈkɛstrəl/ *n* type of small falcon 红隼. ⇨illus at App 1 见附录1插图, page iv.

ketch /ketʃ; kɛtʃ/ *n* small sailing-boat with two masts 双桅小帆船.

ketchup /ˈketʃəp; ˈkɛtʃəp/ (also *esp US* **cat·sup** /ˈkætsəp; ˈkætsəp/) *n* [U] thick sauce made from tomatoes, vinegar, etc and used cold as a seasoning 番茄酱.

kettle /ˈketl; ˈkɛtḷ/ *n* **1** container with a spout, lid and handle, used for boiling water (烧水用的)壶: *boil (water in) the kettle and make some tea* 烧壶水沏茶. **2** (idm 习语) **a different kettle of fish** ⇨ DIFFERENT. **a** ˈ**fine,** ˈ**pretty, etc kettle of fish** messy, unpleasant or confusing situation 一团糟; 不愉快的事; 尴尬的局面. **the pot calling the kettle black** ⇨ POT¹.

ket·tle·drum /ˈketldrʌm; ˈkɛtḷˌdrʌm/ *n* large brass or copper bowl-shaped drum with skin stretched over the top, that can be tuned to an exact pitch 定音鼓. ⇨illus at App 1 见附录1插图, page xi.

key 钥匙

key¹ /kiː; ki/ *n* **1** [C] metal instrument shaped so that it will move the bolt of a lock (and so lock or unlock sth) 钥匙: *turn the key in the lock* 转动锁孔中的钥匙 ○ *the car keys* 汽车钥匙 ○ *the key to the front door* 前门的钥匙 ○ *have a duplicate key cut,* ie made 配钥匙. ⇨illus 见插图. **2** [C] similar instrument for grasping and turning sth, eg for winding a clock 类似钥匙的器具(如上钟表发条用的): *Where's the key for turning off the radiator?* 关散热器的开关在哪里? **3** [C] (**a**) (*music* 音) set of related notes, based on a particular note, and forming the basis of (part of) a piece of music 调: *a sonata in the key of E flat major/A minor* 一首降E大调[A小调]奏鸣曲 ○ *This piece changes key many times.* 这首曲子有多处变调. (**b**) (*fig* 比喻) general tone or style of sth (事

物的)基调, 调子, 调门儿: *Her speech was all in the same key*, ie monotonous. 她的演说自始至终是一个调子(单调乏味). **4** [C] any of the set of levers that are pressed by the fingers to operate a typewriter, piano, etc (打字机、钢琴等的)键. ⇨illus at App 1 见附录1插图, pages x, xi. **5** [C] **(a)** set of answers to exercises or problems 题解; 答案: *a book of language tests, complete with key* 附答案的语言测验试题集. **(b)** explanation of the symbols used in a coded message or on a map, diagram, etc (地图、图表等上的)略语表, 符号表, 凡例, 图例. **6** [C usu *sing* 通常作单数] **~ (to sth)** thing that provides access, control or understanding 关键; 要诀: *Diet and exercise are the key (to good health).* 吃规定食物、做运动是(身体健康的)关键. ○ *The key to the whole affair was his jealousy.* 整个事情的症结是因为他忌妒. **7** [sing] roughness given to a surface so that plaster or paint will stick to it (助灰浆或颜料附着的)粗糙表面: *Gently sand the plastic to provide a key for the paint.* 用砂纸在塑料上轻轻打磨出粗糙面以便涂颜料. **8** [C] (*botany* 植) winged fruit of some trees, eg the ash and elm 翅果(如梣、榆等树的果实). ⇨illus at App 1 见附录1插图, page i. **9** (idm 习语) **under lock and key** ⇨ LOCK[2].

▷ **key** *adj* [attrib 作定语] very important or essential 极重要的; 关键性的: *a key figure in the dispute* 争论中的关键人物 ○ *a key industry, speech, position* 重要的工业、讲话、位置.

□ ˈ**keyboard** *n* set of keys (KEY[1] 4) on a typewriter, piano, etc (打字机、钢琴等的)键盘. ⇨illus at COMPUTER 见COMPUTER插图. — *v* **1** [I] operate a keyboard (eg for setting printing type) 用键盘操纵(如排字). **2** [Tn] enter (data) in a computer by means of a keyboard 用键盘将(数据)输入计算机. ˈ**keyboarder** *n* person who operates a keyboard 操作键盘的人.

ˈ**keyhole** *n* hole through which a key is put into a lock 锁孔; 钥匙孔.

ˈ**key money** payment illegally demanded from a new tenant of a house or flat before he is allowed to move in 钥匙费(向新房客非法索取的费用).

ˈ**keynote** *n* **1** central theme of a speech, book, etc (演说、书等的)要旨, 主题: *Unemployment has been the keynote of the conference.* 会议的主题是失业问题. ○ [attrib 作定语] *a keynote speech*, ie one setting the tone for or introducing the theme of a meeting, etc 定基调的演说. **2** (*music* 音) note on which a musical key is based 主音.

ˈ**key-pad** *n* small keyboard of numbered buttons used instead of a dial on a telephone, for selecting a channel, etc on a television set, or for entering data in a computer 按钮式电话机键盘; 电视频道选择键盘; 计算机袖珍键盘.

ˈ**key-ring** *n* ring on which keys are kept 钥匙圈. ⇨illus 见插图.

ˈ**key signature** (*music* 音) sharps and flats shown on a piece of music indicating the key in which it is written 调号. ⇨illus at MUSIC 见MUSIC插图.

ˈ**keystone** *n* **1** (*architecture* 建) central stone at the top of an arch locking the others into position 拱顶石. **2** (usu *sing* 通常作单数) (*fig* 比喻) most important part of a plan, an argument, etc on which all the other parts depend (计划、论据等的)基础, 主旨: *Belief in a life after death is the keystone of her religious faith.* 她的宗教信仰的基础是相信死后有来生. Cf 参看 CORNER-STONE (CORNER[1]).

key[2] /kiː; ki/ *v* **1** [Tn, Tn·p] **~ sth (in)** (*computing* 计) type in (data) using a keyboard 用键盘输入(数据): *I've keyed this sentence (in) three times, and it's still wrong!* 我把这个句子输入了三次, 可是仍然不对! **2** [Tn] roughen (a surface) so that plaster or paint will stick to it 将(表面)弄粗糙(以便附着灰浆或颜料). **3** (phr v) **key sth to sth (a)** make sth similar to sth else 使某事物与他事物相似: *She keyed her mood to that of the other guests.* 她控制住情绪使之与其他客人一致. **(b)** make sth suitable for sth else 使某事物与他事物相适应: *The farm was keyed to the needs of the local people.* 农场按当地人的需要作了调整. **key sb up** (usu passive 通常用于被动语态) make sb excited, nervous or tense 使某人激动或紧张: *The manager warned us not to get too keyed up before the big match.* 领队告诫我们在大赛之前不要太激动.

key[3] (also **cay**) /kiː; ki/ *n* low island or reef, esp in the W Indies and off the coast of Florida 低岛, 暗礁, 珊瑚礁(尤指西印度群岛和美国佛罗里达州海岸处).

KG /ˌkeɪ ˈdʒiː; ˌke ˋdʒi/ *abbr* 缩写 = (*Brit*) Knight (of the Order) of the Garter 嘉德勋爵士; 英格兰最高爵级勋章: *be made a KG* 被封为嘉德勋爵士 ○ *Sir Thomas Bell KG* 托马斯·贝尔嘉德勋爵士.

kg *abbr* 缩写 = kilogram(s): *10 kg* 10公斤.

KGB /ˌkeɪ dʒiː ˈbiː; ˌke dʒi ˋbi/ *abbr* 缩写 = USSR Intelligence Agency since 1953 (former Russian *Komitet Gosudarstvennoi Bezopasnosti*) 克格勃(建于1953年, 前苏联国家安全委员会的略称): *a KGB agent* 克格勃特工人员 ○ *dealing with the KGB* 与克格勃打交道.

khaki /ˈkɑːkɪ; ˋkɑkɪ/ *n* [U], *adj* (cloth of a) dull brownish-yellow colour, used esp for military uniforms 土黄色(的), 卡其布(的)(尤指用做军服的).

kHz *abbr* 缩写 = kilohertz. Cf 参看 Hz.

kib·butz /kɪˈbʊts; kɪˋbʊts/ *n* (*pl* **kib·butzim** /kɪbʊˈtsiːm; kɪbʊˋtsim/) communal farm or settlement in Israel 基布兹(以色列的合作农场或居民点).

▷ **kib·butz·nik** /-nɪk; -nɪk/ *n* member of a kibbutz 基布兹成员.

kick[1] /kɪk; kɪk/ *v* **1 (a)** [Tn, Tn·pr] hit (sb/sth) with the foot 踢(某人[某物]): *Mummy, Peter kicked me (on the leg)!* 妈妈, 彼得踢我(腿)! **(b)** [Tn, Tn·pr, Tn·p] move (sth) by doing this 踢动(某物): *He kicked the ball into the river.* 他把球踢进河里了. ○ *Can we kick the ball around for a while?* 我们可以在这一带踢一会儿球吗? **(c)** [Tn·pr] make (sth) by kicking 踢成(某物): *He kicked a hole in the fence.* 他在篱笆上踹了个洞. **(d)** [I, Ip] move the foot or feet in a jerky violent way 猛烈地蹬、踩: *The child was screaming and kicking.* 那孩子边喊叫边踩脚. ○ *Be careful of that horse — it often kicks.* 小心那匹马——它常尥蹶子. ○ (*fig* 比喻) *She kicks out when she's angry.* 她发起怒来暴跳如雷. **2** [Tn] **~ oneself** be very annoyed with oneself because one has done sth stupid, missed an opportunity, etc (因干蠢事、坐失良机等)懊悔, 内疚, 自责: *When I discovered I'd come for the appointment on the wrong day, I could have kicked myself.* 我来赴约发现把日期弄错了, 感到非常懊恼. **3** [Tn] (esp in Rugby football) score (a goal or conversion) by kicking the ball (尤指英式橄榄球)踢球(射门)得分: *That's the twentieth goal he's kicked this season.* 这是他本赛季踢进的第二十个球. **4** [I] (of a gun) jerk backwards when fired (指枪炮)反冲, 后坐. **5** (idm 习语) **alive and kicking** ⇨ ALIVE. **hit/kick a man when he's down** ⇨ MAN. ˌ**kick against the** ˈ**pricks** hurt oneself by useless resistance or protest 作无谓的抵抗而自身受损; 自讨苦吃. ˌ**kick the** ˈ**bucket** (*sl* 俚) die 死; 蹬腿儿. ˈ**kick the habit** (*infml* 口) give up an addiction 戒除某嗜好: *Doctors should try to persuade smokers to kick the habit.* 医生应说服吸烟者戒烟. ˌ**kick one's** ˈ**heels** have nothing to do while waiting for sth 无聊地等待某事物: *She had to kick her heels for hours because the train was so late.* 火车晚点, 她无聊地等了几小时. ˌ**kick over the** ˈ**traces** (of a person) refuse to accept discipline or control (from parents, etc) (指人)拒不接受(父母等的)管束, 控制. **kick up/raise a dust** ⇨ DUST[1]. ˌ**kick up a** ˈ**fuss,** ˈ**row, shindy, stink, etc** (*infml* 口) cause a disturbance, esp by protesting about sth 闹事, 骚动(尤指抗议某事). ˌ**kick up one's** ˈ**heels** (*infml* 口) enjoy oneself enthusiastically 尽情享乐; 乐得手舞足蹈. ˌ**kick sb up**ˈ**stairs** (*infml* 口) get rid of sb by promoting him to a position that seems more important but in fact is less so 使某人明升暗降. **5** (phr v) **kick against sth** protest about or resist sth 反对或反抗某事物: *It's no use kicking against the rules.* 反对这些规定是徒劳的. **kick around** (*infml* 口) be present, alive or in existence 活着; 健在; 存在: *I've been kicking around Europe since I saw you last.* 你我分别以来, 我一直在欧洲各地生活. ○ *My shirt is kicking around on the floor somewhere.* 我的衬衫在地板上的什么地方. ○ *an idea which has been kicking around for some considerable time* 酝酿已久的意见. **kick sth around/round** (*infml* 口) discuss (plans, ideas, etc) informally 随便商谈, 非正式地讨论(计划、想法等): *We'll kick some ideas around and make a decision tomorrow.* 我们先酝酿一下, 明天再作决定. **kick sth in** break sth inwards by kicking 向内踢某物: *kick in a door*

从外面把门踢开 ○ *kick sb's teeth in* 踢掉某人的牙. **kick ˈoff** start a football match (by kicking the ball) (足球)开球: *United kicked off and scored almost immediately.* 联队开球后旋即得分. **kick (sth) off** begin (a meeting, etc) 开始(会议等): *I'll ask Tessa to kick off (the discussion).* 我叫特萨开始(讨论). **kick sth off** remove sth by kicking 踢掉某物: *kick off one's slippers, shoes, etc* 踢脱拖鞋、鞋等. **kick sb out (of sth)** (*infml* 口) expel sb or send him away by force 驱逐某人; 用武力逼走某人: *They kicked him out (of the club) for fighting.* 他因为斗殴被开除(出俱乐部).

▷ **kicker** *n* person who kicks 踢或踹的人.

□ ˈ**kick-off** *n* start of a football match (足球比赛的)开球.

kick² /kɪk; kɪk/ *n* **1** [C] act of kicking 踢; 踹: *give sb a kick up the backside* 踢某人屁股一脚 ○ *If the door won't open, give it a kick.* 门要是打不开就踹一下. **2** [C] (*infml* 口) thrill; feeling of pleasure 兴奋; 快感; 快乐: *I get a big kick from motor racing.* 我觉得汽车比赛很刺激. ○ *She gets her kicks from windsurfing and skiing.* 她从帆板运动和滑雪中得到极大乐趣. ○ *do sth (just) for kicks* (仅)为取乐而做某事. **3** [C] (*infml* 口) (usu temporary) interest or activity (通常为一时的)兴趣, 喜好, 活动: *(be on) a health-food kick* 一时喜好起保健食品. **4** [U, sing] (*infml* 口) strength; effectiveness 精力; 气力; 效力: *He has no kick left in him.* 他已精疲力竭. ○ *This drink has (quite) a kick (to it)*, ie is strong. 这酒(很)有劲儿. **5** (idm 习语) **a kick in the teeth** (*infml* 口) unpleasant and often unexpected action 讨厌的、且常为未料到的行动: *The Government's decision is a real kick in the teeth for the unions.* 政府的决定是对工会的重大打击.

□ ˈ**kick-start** *v* [Tn] start (a motor cycle, etc) by pushing down a lever with one's foot 用脚启动(摩托车等). **kick-start** (also ˈ**kick-starter**) *n* this lever (摩托车等的)脚踏起动器.

kick·back /ˈkɪkbæk; ˈkɪk,bæk/ *n* (*infml* 口) money paid to sb who has helped one to make a profit, often illegally 回扣, 酬金(常指不合法的).

kid¹ /kɪd; kɪd/ *n* **1** (**a**) [C] (*infml* 口) child or young person 小孩; 年轻人: *How are your wife and kids?* 夫人和孩子们都好吗? ○ *Half the kids round here are unemployed.* 这里的年轻人有一半失业. (**b**) [attrib 作定语] (*infml* 口 *esp US*) younger 较年幼的: *his kid sister/brother* 他的妹妹[弟弟]. **2** (**a**) [C] young goat 小山羊. ⇨illus at GOAT 见GOAT插图. (**b**) [U] leather made from its skin 小山羊皮革: *a bag made of kid* 小山羊皮手提包 ○ [attrib 作定语] *a pair of kid gloves* 一副小山羊皮手套. **3** (idm 习语) **handle, treat, etc sb with kid ˈgloves** deal with sb very gently or tactfully 以温和的或圆通的手段对待某人.

▷ **kiddy** (also **kiddie**) *n* (*infml* 口) child 小孩儿.

□ ˈ**kid-glove** *adj* [attrib 作定语] gentle; tactful 温柔的; 圆通的: *Kid-glove methods haven't worked — it's time to get tough.* 既然软的办法不行——那就来硬的.

kid² /kɪd; kɪd/ *v* (**-dd-**) **1** [I, Tn] (*infml* 口) deceive (sb), esp playfully; tease 欺骗(某人); (尤指)戏弄; 取笑: *You're kidding!* 你这是开玩笑! ○ *Don't kid yourself — it won't be easy.* 别欺骗自己——这事不容易. **2** (idm 习语) ˌ**no ˈkidding** (*infml* 口) (used to express surprise at what has been said 用于对听说的事表示惊异): (*ironic* 反语) *'It's raining.' 'No kidding! I wondered why I was getting wet!'* '下着雨呢.' '难怪! 我刚才还纳闷怎么身上有点湿呢!'

K

kid·nap /ˈkɪdnæp; ˈkɪdnæp/ *v* (**-pp-**; *US* **-p-**) [Tn] steal (sb) away by force and illegally, esp in order to obtain money or other (esp political) demands 诱拐, 绑架, 劫持(某人): *Two businessmen have been kidnapped by terrorists.* 有两个商人让恐怖分子绑架了.

▷ **kid·nap** *n* [attrib 作定语]: *a kidnap attempt, plot, victim* 绑架的企图、阴谋、事主.

kid·nap·per *n*: *The kidnappers have demanded £1 million for his safe release.* 绑架的歹徒索要100万英镑赎金才放他.

kid·nap·ping *n* [C, U] (act of) stealing sb away in this way 诱拐; 绑架; 劫持: *The kidnapping occurred in broad daylight.* 在光天化日之下竟发生绑架事件.

kid·ney /ˈkɪdnɪ; ˈkɪdnɪ/ *n* (*pl* **~s**) **1** [C] either of a pair of organs in the body that remove waste products from the blood and produce urine 肾; 肾脏. **2** [U, C] kidney(s) of certain animals used as food (用作食物的)腰子: *two kilos of lamb's kidney* 两公斤羊腰子 ○ [attrib 作定语] *steak and kidney pie* 牛肉腰子馅饼.

□ ˈ**kidney bean** (plant producing a) reddish-brown kidney-shaped bean 菜豆.

ˈ**kidney machine** (*medical* 医) machine that does the work of kidneys which have become diseased 人工肾; 血液透析器: *put a patient on a kidney machine* 给病人装置人工肾.

kill /kɪl; kɪl/ *v* **1** [I, Tn, Tn·pr] cause death or cause the death of (sb/sth) 致死; 杀死, 扼杀(某人[某事物]): *Careless driving kills!* 开车大意危及生命! ○ *Cancer kills thousands of people every year.* 每年有数以千计的人死于癌症. ○ *The guard was killed with a high-powered rifle.* 那卫兵被杀伤力大的火枪击毙了. ○ (*fig infml* 比喻, 口) *My mother will kill me* (ie be very angry with me) *when she finds out where I've been.* 我母亲要是知道我到过那地方非把我宰了不可(一定大怒). **2** [Tn] (*infml* 口) (usu in the continuous tenses 通常用于进行时态) cause pain to (sb) 使(某人)疼痛, 痛苦: *My feet are killing me.* 我的脚疼极了. **3** [Tn] (**a**) (esp in football) stop (a ball) suddenly and completely with one's foot (尤指足球)停(球). (**b**) (esp in tennis) hit (a ball) so that it cannot be returned (尤指网球)扣(球). **4** [Tn] bring (sth) to an end 终止, 结束, 了结(某事物): *kill sb's affection, interest, appetite* 使某人失去好感、兴趣、胃口 ○ *the goal that killed Brazil's chances of winning* 决定巴西队败局的一分. **5** [Tn, Cn·a] (*infml* 口) cause (sth) to fail or be rejected 使(某事物)失败, 遭拒绝: *kill a project, a proposal, an idea, etc (stone dead)* 使一计划、建议、想法等不能实现 ○ *The play was killed by bad reviews.* 那出戏被贬斥的评论扼杀了. **6** [Tn] (*infml* 口) switch or turn off 关掉: *kill a light, the radio, a car engine* 关掉灯、收音机、汽车发动机. **7** [Tn] make (one colour) appear ineffective by contrast with another 抵消(某一色彩)的效果: *The bright red of the curtains kills the brown of the carpet.* 这些鲜红色窗帘显得棕色地毯黯然失色. **8** (idm 习语) **be dressed to kill** ⇨ DRESS². **curiosity killed the cat** ⇨ CURIOSITY. **have time to kill** ⇨ TIME¹. ˌ**kill the fatted ˈcalf** (*fml or joc saying* 文或谑, 谚) joyfully celebrate sb's return or arrival 欢宴或欢庆某人的归来或到达. ˌ**kill the ˌgoose that ˌlays the ˌgolden ˈeggs** (*saying* 谚) destroy (through greed or carelessness) sth that would have produced continuous profit in the future 杀鸡取卵; 自绝财源. **kill oneself (doing sth/to do sth)** (*infml* 口) try too hard 过分努力: *The party's at eight, but don't kill yourself getting here/to get here on time.* 八点钟聚会, 但是不必勉强赶时间来. ˌ**kill or ˈcure** [esp attrib 尤作定语] (likely to) be either completely successful or a total failure 不是全胜就是大败: *a kill-or-cure approach to the problem* 对问题采取非胜即败的态度 ○ *The tough new measures on drug abuse are likely to be a case of kill or cure.* 禁毒新措施很强硬, 大有成败取决于此之势. **kill ˈtime; kill two, a few, etc hours** spend time as pleasantly as possible but unprofitably, esp while waiting for sth 消磨时间(尤指等待时): *My flight was delayed, so I killed time/killed two hours reading a book.* 我那趟班机误点了, 我只好看书消磨时间[打发了两小时]. **kill ˌtwo ˌbirds with ˌone ˈstone** achieve two aims with a single action or simultaneously 一石二鸟; 一箭双雕; 一举两得. ˌ**kill sb with ˈkindness** harm sb by being excessively or mistakenly kind 溺爱某人反而使其受损. **9** (phr v) **kill sb/sth off** destroy or get rid of sb/sth 杀死某人; 破坏某事物; 除掉某人[某事物]: *kill off weeds, insects, rats* 灭除杂草、害虫、老鼠 ○ *He killed off all his political opponents.* 他把政敌排除一空. ○ (*fig* 比喻) *The author kills off her hero in Chapter 7.* 作者把她的主人翁安排在第七章中死去.

▷ **kill** *n* **1** act of killing 杀死: *The lion made only one kill that day.* 那天狮子只捕杀了一个猎物. **2** (usu *sing* 通常作单数) animal(s) killed 被杀死的动物: *The hunters brought their kill back to camp.* 猎人把猎物带回营地. **3** (idm 习语) **go/move in for the ˈkill** prepare to finish off an opponent 准备干掉或打倒对手. **(be) ˌin at the ˈkill** (be) present at the climax of a struggle, etc 斗争等最激烈时在场: *She wants to be in at the kill when his business finally collapses.* 她想在他的公司最终倒台时亲

临现场.

killer *n* person, animal or thing that kills 杀生的人、动物或事物: *Police are hunting her killer.* 警方正在追捕杀害她的凶手. ○ *Heroin is a killer.* 海洛因是致命的毒品. ○ [attrib 作定语] *a killer disease* 致命的疾病 ○ *Sharks have the killer instinct.* 鲨鱼有嗜杀的本性.

□ ˈ**killjoy** *n* (*derog* 贬) person who spoils the enjoyment of others 使人扫兴的人.

kill·ing /ˈkɪlɪŋ; ˋkɪlɪŋ/ *n* (idm 习语) ˌ**make a** ˈ**killing** have a great financial success 大走财运; 鸿运亨通: *She's made a killing on the stock market.* 她在股票市场上大发了一笔财.

▷ **kill·ing** *adj* (*infml* 口) **1** exhausting 使人筋疲力尽的: *walk at a killing pace* 拼命赶路. **2** very amusing 极为有趣的; 滑稽可笑的: *a killing joke* 极为有趣的笑话. **kill·ingly** *adv* (*infml* 口) extremely 非常地; 极端地: *a killingly funny film* 非常有趣的影片.

kiln /kɪln; kɪln/ *n* oven for baking pottery or bricks, drying hops or wood, burning lime, etc 窑.

kilo /ˈkiːləʊ; ˋkilo/ *n* (*pl* **~s**) kilogram.

kilo- *comb form* 构词成分 thousand 千: *kilogram* ○ *kilometre.* ⇨App 11 见附录 11.

kilo·cycle /ˈkɪləsaɪkl; ˋkɪləˌsaɪkl̩/ *n* (*dated* 旧) = KILOHERTZ.

kilo·gram (also **kilo·gramme**) /ˈkɪləgræm; ˋkɪləˌgræm/ *n* (*abbr* 缩写 **kg**) basic unit of mass in the SI system; 1000 grams 千克; 公斤. ⇨App 5, 11 见附录 5、11.

kilo·hertz /ˈkɪləhɜːts; ˋkɪloˌhɝts/ *n* (*pl* unchanged 复数不变) (*abbr* 缩写 **kHz**) (also **kilocycle**) unit of frequency of electromagnetic waves; 1000 hertz 千赫(频率单位, 等于 1000 赫兹).

kilo·metre (*US* **-meter**) /ˈkɪləmiːtə(r), kɪˈlɒmɪtə(r); ˋkɪləˌmitɚ/ *n* (*abbr* 缩写 **km**) metric unit of length; 1000 metres. 公里, 千米(公制长度单位, 等于 1000 米). ⇨App 4,5 见附录 4、5.

kilo·watt /ˈkɪləwɒt; ˋkɪləˌwɑt/ *n* (*abbrs* 缩写 **kW, kw**) unit of electrical power; 1000 watts 千瓦(电的功率单位, 等于 1000 瓦特).

kilt /kɪlt; kɪlt/ *n* (**a**) pleated knee-length skirt of tartan wool, worn by men as part of Scottish national costume (苏格兰男子穿的)短褶裙(羊毛织成长及膝盖, 为苏格兰民族服装的一部分). ⇨illus at BAGPIPES 见 BAGPIPES 插图. (**b**) similar skirt worn by women or children (妇女或儿童穿的类似上述的)短褶裙.

▷ **kilted** *adj* wearing a kilt 穿着短褶裙的.

ki·mono /kɪˈməʊnəʊ; *US* -nə; kəˋmonə/ *n* (*pl* **~s**) (**a**) long loose Japanese robe with wide sleeves, worn with a sash 和服(日式长袍). (**b**) dressing-gown resembling this (和服式)晨服.

kin /kɪn; kɪn/ *n* **1** [pl *v*] (*dated or fml* 旧或文) one's family and relatives 家人和亲戚: *All his kin were at the wedding.* 他的家人和亲戚都参加了婚礼. ○ *He's my kin,* ie related to me. 他是我的亲戚. ○ *We are near kin,* ie closely related. 我们是近亲. Cf 参看 KINDRED 2. **2** (idm 习语) **kith and kin** ⇨ KITH. **no kin to sb** not related to sb 与某人无亲属关系. Cf 参看 NEXT OF KIN (NEXT[1]).

□ **kinsfolk** /ˈkɪnzfəʊk; ˋkɪnzˌfok/ *n* [pl *v*] = KIN.

ˈ**kinship** *n* [U] **1** blood relationship 血缘关系; 亲属关系: *claim kinship with sb* 声称与某人有血缘关系. **2** (*fig* 比喻) close sympathy or similarity of character 深切的同情; 性格的相似: *Even after meeting only once, they felt a kinship.* 他们虽然只见了一面, 但已是一见如故了.

kinsman /ˈkɪnzmən; ˋkɪnzmən/ *n* (*pl* **-men**/-mən; -mən/) (*fml* 文) male relative 男亲属.

ˈ**kinswoman** *n* (*pl* **-women**) (*fml* 文) female relative 女亲属.

kind[1] /kaɪnd; kaɪnd/ *adj* friendly and thoughtful to others 亲切的; 和蔼的; 友好的; 仁慈的; 慈爱的: *Would you be kind enough to/be so kind as to help me?* 请你帮帮我的忙好吗? ○ *a kind man, gesture, face, thought* 友好的人、姿势、面容、想法 ○ *She always has a kind word for* (ie stops to speak kindly to) *everyone.* 她跟谁都能和蔼地谈谈话.

▷ **kindly** *adv* **1** in a kind manner 亲切地; 和蔼地; 友好地; 仁慈地; 慈爱地: *treat sb kindly* 善待某人 ○ *He spoke kindly to them.* 他和蔼地和他们谈话. **2** (used when making polite requests or ironically when ordering sb to do sth 用作请求时的礼貌用语或把命令说成请求的反语) please 请: *Would you kindly hold this for a moment?* 请您帮着拿一会儿这个东西. ○ *Kindly leave me alone!* 劳您驾别打扰我! **3** (idm 习语) **take kindly to sb/sth** (usu in negative sentences 通常用于否定句) be pleased by sth; accept sb/sth willingly 喜欢某事物; 欣然接受或接纳某人[某事物]: *She didn't take (at all) kindly to being called plump.* 她(一点都)不喜欢人家说她丰满. ○ *I don't think he takes kindly to foreign tourists.* 我认为他不喜欢外国游客.

kind·ness *n* **1** [U] quality of being kind 亲切; 和蔼; 仁慈; 好意: *She always shows kindness to children and animals.* 她对孩子和动物总是很温柔. ○ *He did it entirely out of kindness, not for the money.* 他做那件事纯粹是出于好意, 并非为钱. **2** [C] kind act 好心的表现或行为: *I can never repay her many kindnesses to me.* 我无法回报她对我的许多帮助. **3** (idm 习语) **do/show sb a** ˈ**kindness** do sth kind for sb 好心地为某人做某事物. **kill sb with kindness** ⇨ KILL. **the milk of human kindness** ⇨ MILK[1].

□ ˌ**kind-**ˈ**hearted** *adj* having a kind nature; sympathetic 好心的; 善良的; 同情的.

kind[2] /kaɪnd; kaɪnd/ *n* **1** [C] group having similar characteristics; sort; type; variety 种类: *fruit of various kinds/various kinds of fruit* 各种水果 ○ *Do you want all the same kind, or a mixture?* 您都要同一种的还是要什锦的? ○ *Don't trust him: I know his kind,* ie what sort of person he is. 别相信他, 这种人我了解. ○ *She's not the kind (of woman/person) to lie.* 她不是那种爱撒谎的(女)人. **2** [U] nature; character 本质; 性质: *They differ in size but not in kind.* 这些东西的区别只是大小不同而实质一样. **3** (idm 习语) **in kind** (**a**) (of payment) in goods or natural produce, not in money (指偿付)以实物偿付: *When he had no money, the farmer sometimes used to pay me in kind,* eg with a sack of potatoes. 那个农民没有现款时, 有时候给我些东西抵帐(如给一袋土豆). (**b**) (*fig* 比喻) with something similar 以同样方式: *repay insults in kind,* ie by being insulting in return 受到侮辱后以同样方式侮辱对方. **a kind of** (*infml* 口) (used to express uncertainty 用以表示不确): *I had a kind of* (ie a vague) *feeling this might happen.* 我隐约感到这事可能发生. ○ *He's a kind of unofficial adviser, but I'm not sure exactly what he does.* 他像个非官方的顾问, 但说不好他究竟是干什么的. **kind of** (*infml* 口) slightly; to some extent 稍微; 有点儿; 有几分: *I'm not sure why, but I feel kind of sorry for him.* 不知为什么, 我有点为他惋惜. ○ *'Is she interested?' 'Well, kind of.'* '她感兴趣吗?' '嗯, 有点儿.' **nothing of the** ˈ**kind/sort** not at all like it 一点都不像; 毫无类似处: *People had told me she was very pleasant but she's nothing of the kind.* 人家告诉我她很可爱, 可是她根本不是那样. **of a kind** (**a**) very similar 很相似的; 同一类的: *They look alike, talk alike, even think alike — they're two of a kind/they're very much of a kind.* 他们长得很像、说话很像、连想法都很像——他们俩完全是一个类型. (**b**) (*derog* 贬) of an inferior kind 低劣的; 差劲的: *The town offers entertainments of a kind, but nothing like what you'll find in the city.* 镇上有些所谓的娱乐, 但与城里的截然不同. **something of the kind** something like what has been said 类似所说的某事: *Did you say they're moving? I'd heard something of the kind myself.* 是你说他们要搬家吗? 我也听到过这样的话.

NOTE ON USAGE 用法: **1** After **kind of/sort of** it is usual to have a singular noun 在 **kind of/sort of** 之后通常有个单数名词: *What kind of/sort of tree is that?* 那是什么树? ○ *There are many different kinds of/sorts of snake in South America.* 南美洲有很多种蛇. Informally, it is possible to use a plural noun thus 口语中可以用复数名词: *I have met all kinds of/sorts of salesmen, tourists, etc.* 我见过各种各样的售货员、游客等. In more formal usage the plural noun can be put in front 在比较庄重的用语中, 复数名词可放在前面: *People of that kind/sort never apologize.* 那种人从来不向人道歉. ○ *Snakes of many kinds/sorts are found in South America.* 南美洲有很多种蛇. **2 Kind of/sort of** are also used informally to indicate that somebody or something is not genuine or of good quality, or to suggest vagueness 口语中 **kind of/sort of** 还可指某人或某事物的情况不是真的或不那么好, 或表示说不准: *I had a kind of/sort of holiday in the summer but I couldn't really relax.* 我算是放了暑假了, 但却未能真正休息. ○ *He gave a kind of/sort of smile* *and left the room.* 他像是笑了一下就离开了房间. **3** **Kind of** and **sort of** are used in very informal English as adverbs. ☆ **kind of** 和 **sort of** 在极通俗的口语中可用作副词. They mean 'to some extent' 这两个词组的意思都是'在某种程度上': *She kind of/sort of likes him.* 她有点儿喜欢他.

kind·er·gar·ten /ˈkɪndəɡɑːtn; ˈkɪndɚˌɡɑrtn/ *n* school for very young children; nursery school 幼儿园.

kindle /ˈkɪndl; ˈkɪndl/ *v* **1** [I, Tn] (cause sth to) catch fire (使某物)燃烧, 着火: *This wood is too wet to kindle.* 这木头潮得点不着. ○ *The sparks kindled the dry grass.* 有些火星把干草给引着了. **2** (*fig* 比喻) **(a)** [Tn] arouse or stimulate (feelings, etc) 激起(感情等): *kindle hopes, interest, anger* 激起希望、兴趣、怒火. **(b)** [I, Ipr] ~ **(with sth)** become bright; shine or glow 发亮; 放光; 明亮起来: *Her eyes kindled with excitement.* 她兴奋得双目炯炯发光.

▷ **kind·ling** /ˈkɪndlɪŋ; ˈkɪndlɪŋ/ *n* [U] small dry pieces of wood, etc for lighting fires 引火物(小块的干柴等).

kindly[1] /ˈkaɪndlɪ; ˈkaɪndlɪ/ *adj* [usu attrib 通常作定语] (**-ier, -iest**) kind or friendly in character, manner or appearance 亲切的; 和蔼的; 友好的; 仁慈的; 慈爱的: *a kindly man, voice, smile* 慈祥的人、声音、微笑 ○ *give sb some kindly advice* 给某人以友好的劝告. ▷ **kind·li·ness** *n* [U].

kindly[2] ⇨ KIND[1].

kin·dred /ˈkɪndrɪd; ˈkɪndrɪd/ *n* (*fml* 文) **1** [U] family relationship 亲属关系: *claim kindred with sb* 声称与某人有亲属关系. **2** [pl *v*] one's family and relatives 家人和亲戚: *Most of his kindred still live in Ireland.* 他的亲戚大部分仍住在爱尔兰. Cf 参看 KIN 1.

▷ **kin·dred** *adj* [attrib 作定语] (*fml* 文) **1** having a common source; related 同宗的; 同源的; 有关的: *kindred families* 同宗亲属 ○ *English and Dutch are kindred languages.* 英语和荷兰语是同源的语言. **2** similar 类似的; 相似的: *hunting and shooting and kindred activities* 打猎、射击之类的活动. **3** (idm 习语) **a kindred ˈspirit** person whose tastes, feelings, etc are similar to one's own 意气相投的人: *We immediately realized that we were kindred spirits.* 我们马上发觉彼此志同道合.

kin·etic /kɪˈnetɪk; kɪˈnɛtɪk/ *adj* [esp attrib 尤作定语] of or produced by movement 运动的; 运动引起的: *kinetic energy*, ie that generated by a moving body 动能.

▷ **kin·etic·ally** /-klɪ; -klɪ/ *adv*.

kin·et·ics *n* [sing *v*] science of the relations between the movement of bodies and the forces acting on them 动力学.

□ **kiˌnetic ˈart** art (esp sculpture) that depends for its effect on the movement of some of its parts, eg in air currents 动态艺术, (尤指)动态雕塑(藉活动部件在气流等中的运动造成动感效果的).

king /kɪŋ; kɪŋ/ *n* **1** (title of the) male ruler of an independent state, usu inheriting the position by right of birth 君主; 国王; 国王的称号: *the King of Denmark* 丹麦国王 ○ *King Edward VII* 爱德华七世 ○ *be made/crowned king* 被立为[加冕为]国王. Cf 参看 QUEEN. **2** person, animal or thing regarded as best or most important in some way 重要的人、动物或事物; 大王: *To his fans, Elvis will always be 'the King'.* 埃尔维斯的歌迷永远称他为歌王. ○ *the king of beasts/of the jungle*, ie the lion 百兽[丛林]之王(狮子) ○ *Barolo is the king of Italian red wines.* 巴罗洛是意大利红葡萄酒之王. **3** [attrib 作定语] largest variety of a species 同类中之最大型的: *king cobra, penguin, prawn, etc* 眼镜王蛇、王企鹅、宽沟对虾等. **4** **(a)** (in chess) the most important piece (国际象棋的)王. ⇨illus at CHESS 见CHESS插图. **(b)** (in draughts) piece that has been crowned on reaching the opponent's side of the board (国际跳棋的)王棋(抵对方底线升为王的棋子). **(c)** (in playing-cards) any of four cards with the picture of a king on (纸牌中的)K: *the king of spades* 黑桃K. **5** (idm 习语) **the King's/Queen's English** ⇨ ENGLISH. **a ˌking's ˈransom** very large amount of money 重金; 巨款: *That painting must be worth a king's ransom.* 那幅画一定价值连城. **turn King's/Queen's evidence** ⇨ EVIDENCE. **the uncrowned king/queen** ⇨ UNCROWNED.

▷ **kingly** *adj* of, like or suitable for a king; regal (似)国王的; 适于国王的; 威严的. **king·li·ness** *n* [U].

king·ship /-ʃɪp; -ʃɪp/ *n* [U] condition of being, or official position of, a king 国王身分; 王位; 王权.

□ **ˈkingmaker** *n* person who controls appointments to positions of high (esp political) authority 操纵任命(尤指政界)要职的人.

ˈkingpin *n* **1** (*engineering* 工) vertical bolt used as a pivot 主销; 主螺栓. **2** (*fig* 比喻) essential person or thing 主要的人或事物: *He's the kingpin of the whole team.* 他是全队的主力.

ˈking-size (also **-sized**) *adj* [esp attrib 尤作定语] larger than normal; extra large 比正常大的; 特大的: *a king-size bed, cigarette, hamburger* 特大的床、香烟、汉堡包 ○ *king-sized portions* 特大份.

King's/Queen's ˈBench (*abbrs* 缩写 **KB, QB**) (*Brit law* 律) division of the High Court of Justice (高等法院中的)王座法庭.

King's/Queen's ˈCounsel (*abbrs* 缩写 **KC, QC**) (*Brit law* 律) barrister appointed to act for the government 御用律师.

king·cup /ˈkɪŋkʌp; ˈkɪŋˌkʌp/ *n* large variety of buttercup; marsh marigold 鳞茎毛茛; 驴蹄草.

king·dom /ˈkɪŋdəm; ˈkɪŋdəm/ *n* **1** country or state ruled by a king or queen 王国: *the United Kingdom* 英国. **2** any one of the three divisions of the natural world 界(大自然的三大类别): *the animal, plant/vegetable and mineral kingdoms* 动物、植物、矿物三界. **3** (*fig* 比喻) area belonging to or associated with a particular thing or person 领域: *the kingdom of the imagination* 想像的领域 ○ *the kingdom under the waves*, ie the sea 大海. **4** (idm 习语) **till/until kingdom ˈcome** (*infml* 口) for ever 永久; 永远: *Don't mention politics or we'll be here till kingdom come.* 咱们别谈政治吧, 否则一谈就没个完. **to kingdom ˈcome** (*infml* 口) into the life after death 去天国: *gone to kingdom come*, ie dead 上天国了(死了) ○ *The bomb exploded and blew them all to kingdom come.* 炸弹把他们炸得都上天堂了.

king·fisher /ˈkɪŋfɪʃə(r); ˈkɪŋˌfɪʃɚ/ *n* small brightly-coloured bird that dives to catch fish in rivers, etc 翠鸟, 鱼狗(羽毛鲜艳、能在河湖上潜水捕鱼的小鸟). ⇨illus at App 1 见附录1插图, page v.

kink /kɪŋk; kɪŋk/ *n* **1** sharp twist in sth that is normally straight, eg a wire, rope, pipe, hair, etc 扭结(如铁丝、绳索、管子、毛发等). **2** (*fig usu derog* 比喻, 通常作贬义) mental or moral peculiarity 乖僻; 奇想: *He's got a few kinks in his personality, if you ask me.* 我认为他的个性有些怪僻.

▷ **kink** *v* [I, Tn, Tn·pr] (cause sth to) form kinks (使某物)扭结: *Keep the wire stretched tight — don't let it kink.* 把铁丝拉紧, 别让它扭成结.

kinky *adj* (*infml derog* 口, 贬) bizarre or abnormal, esp in sexual behaviour 变态的, 不正常的(尤指性行为): *There's lots of straight sex in the film, but nothing kinky.* 那部影片里有不少性行为镜头, 但是没有变态的. **kin·ki·ness** *n* [U].

kins·folk, kins·man, kins·woman ⇨ KIN.

ki·osk /ˈkiːɒsk; kɪˈɑsk/ *n* **1** small open structure where newspapers, refreshments, etc are sold (出售报纸、饮料等的)小摊棚, 售货亭. **2** (*dated* 旧 *Brit*) public telephone box or booth 公用电话亭.

kip /kɪp; kɪp/ *n* [C usu *sing*, U 作可数名词时通常作单数, 亦作不可数名词] (*Brit sl* 俚) sleep 睡觉: *have a kip* 睡一觉 ○ *get some kip* 睡会儿觉.

▷ **kip** *v* **(-pp-)** [I, Ipr, Ip] (*Brit sl* 俚) lie down to sleep 躺下睡觉: *Could I kip here tonight?* 今晚我可以在这儿睡吗? ○ *kip down (on the floor)* (在地板上)躺下睡觉 ○ *kip out in a field* 在田地里露宿.

kip·per /ˈkɪpə(r); ˈkɪpɚ/ *n* salted herring, split open and dried or smoked 腌晒或熏制的鲱鱼.

kirk /kɜːk; kɝk/ *n* (*Scot* 苏格兰) church 教堂: *go to (the) kirk* 上教堂去.

kirsch /kɪəʃ; kɪɚʃ/ *n* [U] colourless liqueur made from cherries (无色的)樱桃酒.

kis·met /ˈkɪzmet, ˈkɪs-; ˈkɪzmɛt, ˈkɪs-/ *n* [U] (*rhet* 修辞) destiny; fate 命运; 天命.

kiss /kɪs; kɪs/ *v* [I, Tn, Tn·pr] **1** touch (sb/sth) with the lips to show affection or as a greeting 吻(某人[某物]): *They kissed passionately when she arrived.* 她一来到, 他们就热烈亲吻. ○ *kiss the children goodnight* 吻孩子向他

K

们道晚安 ○ *She kissed him on the lips.* 她吻了吻他的双唇. **2** (idm 习语) **kiss sth goodbye/kiss goodbye to sth** (*sl* 俚) accept the loss or failure of sth as certain 承认某事物的损失或失败已成定局: *You can kiss goodbye to a holiday this year — we've no money!* 今年你别指望度假了 —— 咱们没钱! **3** (phr v) **kiss sth away** remove sth with kisses 吻掉某物: *Let mummy kiss your tears away*, ie help you to stop crying by kissing you. 让妈妈吻去你的眼泪.

▷ **kiss** *n* **1** touch or caress given with the lips 吻: *give sb a kiss* 给某人一吻. **2** (idm 习语) **blow a kiss** ⇨ BLOW[1]. **the kiss of 'death** (*infml esp joc* 口, 尤作戏谑语) apparently favourable action that makes failure certain 貌似有利却导致失败的行动: *one of those polite lukewarm reviews that are the kiss of death for a commercial film* 措辞温和有礼而其实是扼杀一营利影片的评论.

kiss·able *adj* (*approv* 褒) inviting kisses 诱人亲吻的: *kissable lips* 撩人欲吻的唇 ○ *Darling, you look so kissable tonight.* 亲爱的, 你今晚美得诱人欲吻.

kisser *n* (*sl* 俚) mouth 嘴: *a punch in the kisser* 在嘴上的重击.

□ **the kiss of 'life** mouth-to-mouth method of restoring breathing to save the life of sb injured or rescued from drowning 口对口的人工呼吸: (*fig* 比喻) *the Government's £2 million kiss of life for the ailing cotton industry* 政府为挽救气息奄奄的棉纺工业的 200 万英镑应急款.

kit /kɪt; kɪt/ *n* **1** [U] clothing and personal equipment of a soldier, etc or a traveller (士兵等或旅行者的)衣物和装备: *They marched twenty miles in full kit.* 他们带着全副装备行军二十英里. **2** [C, U] equipment needed for a particular (esp sporting) activity, situation or trade 为某种活动(尤指运动)、场合或行业用的成套用品: *a 'tool-kit* 一套工具 ○ *a first-'aid kit* 一套急救用品 ○ *a re'pair kit* 一套修理工具 ○ *'shaving kit* 刮脸用具 ○ *'riding-kit* 骑马装备 ○ *'tennis kit* 网球用具 ○ *'sports kit* 运动用品. **3** [C] set of parts sold together to be assembled by the purchaser 配套元件(供购买者装配的): *a kit to build a model railway locomotive* 一套火车头模型拼具 ○ [attrib 作定语] *furniture in kit form* 组合家具.

▷ **kit** *v* (**-tt-**) (phr v) **kit sb out/up (with sth)** equip sb 给某人装备: *Kit this man out with everything he needs.* 他需要什么就给他什么装备. ○ *He was all kitted out to go skiing.* 他已整装待发要去滑雪了.

□ **'kitbag** *n* long canvas bag in which soldiers, etc carry their kit 背包; 背袋; 行李袋.

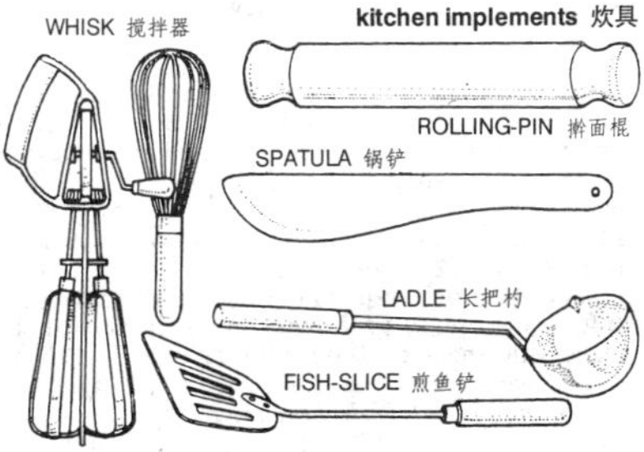

kitchen implements 炊具

kit·chen /'kɪtʃɪn; 'kɪtʃɪn/ *n* **1** room or building in which meals are cooked or prepared 厨房: [attrib 作定语] *the kitchen table* 厨房用桌 ○ *kitchen units*, ie cupboards, etc forming part of a fitted kitchen 厨房设备(如厨柜等). **2** (idm 习语) **everything but the kitchen 'sink** (*infml joc* 口, 谑) every possible (movable) object 所有(能移动的)物品: *We always seem to take everything but the kitchen sink when we go on holiday.* 我们度假时好像总把一切能带的东西都带着.

▷ **kit·chen·ette** /ˌkɪtʃɪ'net; ˌkɪtʃɪn'ɛt/ *n* small room or part of a room used as a kitchen, eg in a flat 小厨房; 房间里辟作厨事用的一角.

□ **ˌkitchen 'garden** garden or part of a garden where fruit and vegetables are grown 家庭菜园; 花园中辟作种水果蔬菜的一角.

ˌkitchen sink 'drama type of British drama that attempts to show realistic working-class family life (英国)工人阶级生活剧.

kite /kaɪt; kaɪt/ *n* **1** toy consisting of a light framework covered with paper, cloth, etc that is flown in the wind at the end of a long string 风筝. **2** bird of prey of the hawk family 鸢. **3** (idm 习语) **fly a kite** ⇨ FLY[2]. **fly a/one's kite** ⇨ FLY[2].

□ **'kite-flying** *n* [U] **1** (sport of) flying kites in the wind 放风筝(的运动). **2** (*infml* 口) testing public reaction to sth by starting a rumour about it 放风声以试探舆论反应.

Kite·mark /'kaɪtmɑ:k; 'kaɪtˌmɑrk/ *n* (*Brit*) official mark, in the form of a kite, on goods approved by the British Standards Institution 风筝标记(用在英国标准协会认可的商品上, 形似风筝).

kith /kɪθ; kɪθ/ *n* (idm 习语) **kith and kin** friends and relations 亲友.

kitsch /kɪtʃ; kɪtʃ/ *n* [U] (*derog* 贬) (**a**) cheap and showy vulgarity or pretentiousness in art, design, etc (艺术、设计等的)俗气、矫饰等: *That new lamp they've bought is pure kitsch.* 他们新买的那盏灯真俗气. (**b**) art, design, etc of this type 俗气的艺术、设计等.

kit·ten /'kɪtn; 'kɪtn̩/ *n* **1** young cat 小猫. **2** (idm 习语) **have 'kittens** (*Brit infml* 口) be very anxious, tense, etc 焦虑; 烦躁: *My mum'll have kittens if I'm not home by midnight.* 要是半夜我还不回家, 我妈妈一定很着急.

▷ **kit·ten·ish** *adj* playful like a kitten 小猫般淘气的; 顽皮的.

kitty[1] /'kɪtɪ; 'kɪtɪ/ *n* **1** (in some card-games) pool of money to be played for (某些牌戏中的)全部赌注. **2** (*infml* 口) any form of money for joint use, eg the savings of a club 共同的资金(如俱乐部的储金): *We each put £2 in the kitty, and then sent John to buy food for everybody.* 我们每人凑 2 英镑, 让约翰去给大家买吃的.

kitty[2] /'kɪtɪ; 'kɪtɪ/ *n* (*infml* 口) (used by or to young children 儿语) cat or kitten 小猫.

kiwi 几维

kiwi /'ki:wi:; 'kiwɪ/ *n* **1** New Zealand bird that cannot fly, with a long bill, short wings and no tail 几维(产于新西兰的鸟, 喙长、翼短、无尾、不能飞). **2 Kiwi** (*infml* 口) New Zealander, esp a soldier or member of a national sports team 新西兰人(尤指士兵或国家运动员).

□ **'kiwi fruit** small oval fruit with thin brown skin, soft green flesh and black seeds 猕猴桃.

KKK /ˌkeɪ keɪ 'keɪ; ˌke ke 'ke/ *abbr* 缩写 = (*US*) Ku-Klux-Klan 三K党.

klaxon /'klæksn; 'klæksən/ *n* (*propr* 专利名) powerful electric warning horn or siren 高音电喇叭或警报器.

Kleenex /'kli:neks; 'kliˌnɛks/ *n* [U, C] (*pl* unchanged or **~es** 复数或不变或作 **kleenexes**) (*propr* 专利名) (sheet of) soft paper tissue, used as a handkerchief, etc 纸巾: *a packet of Kleenex* 一包纸巾.

klep·to·mania /ˌkleptə'meɪnɪə; ˌklɛptə'menɪə/ *n* [U] illness that causes an uncontrollable desire to steal things, often with no wish to possess the things stolen 偷窃狂; 盗窃癖.

▷ **klep·to·man·iac** /-nɪæk; -nɪæk/ *n* person suffering from kleptomania 患偷窃狂者; 有盗窃癖者. — *adj* [attrib 作定语]: *kleptomaniac tendencies* 患偷窃狂的; 有盗窃癖的.

K

km *abbr* 缩写 = (*pl* unchanged or **kms** 复数或不变或作 **kms**) kilometre(s): *a 10 km walk* 步行10公里的路程 ○ *distance to beach 2 kms* 距海滨2公里.

kn *abbr* 缩写 = (*nautical* 海) knot(s): *35 kn* 35节.

knack /næk; næk/ *n* [sing] **1** skill at performing some special task; ability 技巧; 诀窍: *Making an omelette is easy once you've got the knack (of it).* 一旦你掌握了煎蛋饼的技巧, 做起来就很容易了. ○ *There's a knack in/to locking this door which takes a while to master.* 锁这门要有窍门, 得用些时间才能学会. ○ *I used to be able to skate quite well, but I've lost the knack.* 我从前滑冰滑得很不错, 可现在没有这本事了. **2 ~ of doing sth** (often annoying) habit of doing sth (常招人厌烦的)毛病, 习惯: *My car has a knack of breaking down just when I need it most.* 我的汽车总是在我最需要的时候抛锚.

knacker[1] /ˈnækə(r); ˈnækɚ/ *n* **1** person who buys and slaughters useless horses to sell the meat and hides 购买并屠杀无用的马的人(为卖马肉和皮). **2** person who buys and breaks up old buildings, etc to sell the materials in them 收买并拆除旧建筑物等以售其材料的人.

□ ˈ**knacker's yard** knacker's place of business 上述两种人做生意的场所.

knacker[2] /ˈnækə(r); ˈnækɚ/ *v* [Tn] (*Brit sl* 俚) exhaust (sb); wear out 使(某人)筋疲力尽: *All this hard work is knackering me.* 所有这些艰巨的工作把我累得筋疲力尽.

▷ **knackered** *adj* [esp pred 尤作表语] (*Brit sl* 俚) exhausted; worn out 筋疲力尽: *I'm completely knackered — I ran all the way!* 我累坏了——我是跑着来的!

knap·sack /ˈnæpsæk; ˈnæpˌsæk/ *n* (*dated* 旧) = RUCKSACK.

knave /neɪv; nev/ *n* **1** (*fml* 文) = JACK[1] 4: *the knave of hearts* 红桃杰克. **2** (*arch* 古) dishonest man; man without honour 不诚实的人; 不名誉的人.

▷ **knavery** /ˈneɪvərɪ; ˈnevərɪ/ *n* [U] (*arch* 古) dishonesty; trickery 不诚实; 欺诈.

knav·ish /ˈneɪvɪʃ; ˈnevɪʃ/ *adj* (*arch* 古) deceitful 欺诈的. **knav·ishly** *adv*.

knead /ni:d; nid/ *v* **1** [Tn, Tn·pr] press and stretch (bread dough, wet clay, etc) with the hands to form a firm smooth paste 揉, 捏(面团、湿黏土等): *Knead the dough (into a ball)* 把面团揉成球形. **2** [Tn] massage (muscles, etc) firmly to relieve tension or pain 按摩, 揉捏(肌肉等).

knee /ni:; ni/ *n* **1** (**a**) joint between the thigh and lower part of the human leg; corresponding joint in animals 膝; 膝盖. ⇨illus at HUMAN 见HUMAN插图. (**b**) upper surface of a sitting person's thigh (人坐着时)大腿的朝上的面: *sit on my knee* 坐在我的腿上 ○ *You'll have to eat your dinner off your knees, I'm afraid!* 对不起, 这顿饭你只好把餐具放在腿上吃了! **2** part of a garment covering the knee (裤子等的)膝部: *These trousers are torn at the knee.* 这裤子的膝部破了. **3** (idm 习语) **be/go (down) on one's ˈknees** kneel or be kneeling (down), esp when praying or to show that one accepts defeat 跪下, 跪着(尤指祈祷或屈服时). **the bee's knees** ⇨ BEE[1]. **bring sb to his ˈknees** force sb to submit 迫使某人屈服: (*fig* 比喻) *The country was almost brought to its knees by the long strike.* 因长期罢工, 国家已濒临崩溃的边缘. **on bended knee** ⇨ BEND[1]. **weak at the knees** ⇨ WEAK.

▷ **knee** *v* (*pt, pp* **kneed**) [Tn, Tn·pr, Cn·a] strike or push with the knee 用膝盖顶或撞: *knee sb (in the groin)* 用膝盖顶某人(的阴部) ○ *knee the door open* 用膝盖把门撞开.

□ ˈ**knee-breeches** *n* [pl] breeches reaching to or just below the knee (及膝或刚过膝的)短裤.

ˈ**kneecap** *n* small bone covering the front of the knee joint 髌骨; 膝盖骨. ⇨illus at SKELETON 见SKELETON插图. — *v* (**-pp-**) [Tn] (of terrorist groups) lame (sb) by breaking the kneecaps, esp by shooting at them (指恐怖集团)击碎(某人)的膝盖骨(尤指枪击). ˈ**kneecapping** *n* [C, U] (instance of) this practice 击碎膝盖骨.

ˌ**knee-ˈdeep** *adj* **1** deep enough to reach the knees 深及膝的: *the snow was knee-deep in places.* 有些地方雪深及膝. **2 ~ in sth** (*fig* 比喻) deeply involved in or very busy with sth 深陷其中; 忙于某事: *be knee-deep in trouble, work* 烦恼、工作缠身. — *adv*: *He went knee-deep in the icy water.* 他在及膝深的冰冷的水中跋涉.

ˌ**knee-ˈhigh** *adj* **1** high enough to reach the knees 及膝高的: ˌ*knee-high* ˈ*grass* 及膝高的草. **2** (idm 习语) **knee-high to a ˈgrasshopper** (*joc* 谑) still just a very small child 还是很小的孩子: *I've known him since he was knee-high to a grasshopper.* 他很小的时候我就认识他了.

ˈ**knee-jerk** *n* **1** involuntary jerk of the leg when a tendon below the knee is struck 膝反射. **2** [attrib 作定语] (*fig derog* 比喻, 贬) done or produced automatically and without thought 自动的; 不经思考而做的: *a knee-jerk reaction to the mention of politics* 一提政治就不加思索做出的反应.

ˈ**knee-length** *adj* long enough to reach the knee 长及膝部的: *a knee-length skirt* 长及膝部的裙子.

ˈ**knees-up** *n* (*Brit infml* 口) lively party, usu with dancing 活跃的集会(通常有跳舞项目).

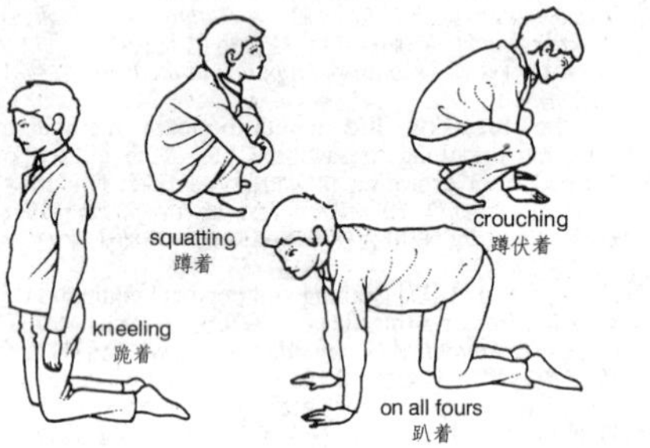

kneel /ni:l; nil/ *v* (*pt, pp* **knelt** /nelt; nɛlt/ or *esp US* **kneeled**) ⇨Usage at DREAM 用法见DREAM. [I, Ipr, Ip] **~ (down)** go down on one or both knees; rest on the knee(s) 单膝或双膝跪下; 屈膝: *She knelt in prayer.* 她跪下祈祷. ○ *kneel down (on the grass) to examine a flower* (在草地上)跪下细看一朵花.

knell /nel; nɛl/ *n* (usu *sing* 通常作单数) **1** sound of a bell rung slowly after a death or at a funeral 丧钟声. **2** (*fig rhet* 比喻, 修辞) sign that sth has ended for ever 某事物结束的征兆: *It sounded the (death-)knell of all her hopes.* 那事听起来就像是给她的一切希望敲起了丧钟.

knew *pt* of KNOW.

knick·er·bock·ers /ˈnɪkəbɒkəz; ˈnɪkɚˌbɑkɚz/ (*US* **knickers** /ˈnɪkəz; ˈnɪkæz/) *n* [pl] (esp formerly) loose wide breeches gathered just below the knee (尤指旧时)灯笼裤.

knick·ers /ˈnɪkəz; ˈnɪkɚz/ *n* [pl] **1** (*Brit*) woman's or girl's underpants (女用)内裤: *a pair of knickers* 一条女用内裤. **2** (*US*) = KNICKERBOCKERS. **3** (idm 习语) **get one's ˈknickers in a twist** (*Brit sl* 俚) become angry, confused, nervous, etc; react to sth more strongly than is necessary 恼火、困惑、紧张等; 对某事物反应过激.

knick-knack (also **nick-nack**) /ˈnɪk næk; ˈnɪkˌnæk/ *n* (esp *pl* 尤作复数) (*sometimes derog* 有时作贬义) small ornamental article, usu of little value 小饰物; 小玩意儿.

knife /naɪf; naɪf/ *n* (*pl* **knives** /naɪvz; naɪvz/) **1** sharp blade with a handle, used for cutting or as a weapon 刀: *a* ˈ*table-knife* 餐刀 ○ *a* ˈ*carving-knife* 切熟肉的刀 ○ *a* ˈ*paper-knife* 裁纸刀 ○ *He'd been stabbed four times with a kitchen knife.* 有人用菜刀捅了他四刀. **2** cutting blade in a machine or tool (机器或工具的)刀. **3** (idm 习语) **you could ˌcut it with a ˈknife** (*infml* 口) it was very obvious or heavy 很明显; 很突出; 浓重: *His accent is so thick you could cut it with a knife — I can hardly understand a word he says.* 他的口音很重——我简直一个字都听不懂. **get one's knife into sb/have one's knife in sb** try to harm sb spitefully (not usu physically) 欲加害某人(通常指非肉体的伤害). **like a knife through butter** easily; without meeting any resistance or difficulty 容易; 遇不到抵抗或困难: *The power saw sliced the logs like a knife through butter.* 电锯轻而易举就把原木锯成薄板了. ○ *His strong voice cut through the hum of conversation like a knife through butter.* 他那宏亮

K

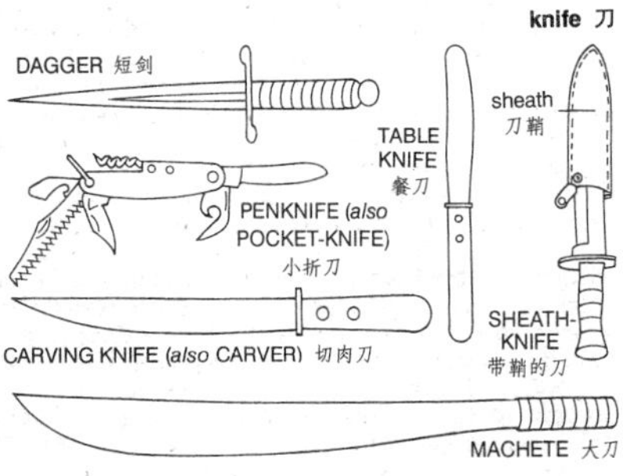

有力的声音一下子压倒了嗡嗡的谈话声. **under the ˈknife** (*dated or joc* 旧或谑) having surgery 在动手术.

▷ **knife** *v* [Tn, Tn·pr] cut or stab (sb) with a knife 用刀切割或刺(某人): *The victim had been knifed (in the chest).* 受害人(于胸部)中刀.

□ **ˈknife-edge** *n* (usu *sing* 通常作单数) **1** cutting edge of the blade of a knife 刀刃. **2** (idm 习语) **on a knife-edge** (**a**) (of a person) nervous (about the outcome of sth) (指人)(对某事物的结果)十分焦虑: *He's on a knife-edge about his exam results.* 他对考试成绩十分担心. (**b**) (of a situation, etc) at a critical point (指情况等)处于紧要关头: *The success of the project is still very much on a knife-edge.* 这一项目的成败目前仍处于关键时刻.

knight /naɪt; naɪt/ *n* **1** (*abbr* 缩写 **Kt**) man to whom the sovereign has given a rank of honour, lower than that of baronet, having the title 'Sir' used before the first name, with or without the surname 爵士(低于准男爵的等级, 其名前冠以 Sir, 带不带姓均可): *Sir James Hill (Kt)* 詹姆斯·希尔爵士 ○ *Good morning, Sir James.* 早上好, 詹姆斯爵士. **2** (in the Middle Ages) man raised to honourable military rank, serving as a heavily armed horseman (中古时代的)骑士. **3** (*abbr* 缩写 **Kt**) chess piece, usu shaped like a horse's head (国际象棋的)马. ⇨illus at CHESS 见 CHESS 插图.

▷ **knight** *v* [esp passive 尤用于被动语态: Tn, Tn·pr] make (sb) a knight 封(某人)为爵士: *He was knighted in the last Honours List (for services to industry).* 他对工业界有贡献被封为爵士, 列入最新受勋者名册.

knight·hood /-hʊd; -hʊd/ *n* **1** [C] title and rank of a knight 爵士或骑士的称号和身分: *The Queen conferred a knighthood on him.* 女王授予他爵士称号. **2** [U] rank, character or dignity of a knight 爵士或骑士的身分、品德或尊严: *Knighthood was an ideal in medieval Europe.* 在中世纪的欧洲, 骑士品德是一种风范.

knightly *adj* [usu attrib 通常作定语] (*fml* 文) of or like a knight; chivalrous (似)骑士或爵士的; 侠义的: *knightly qualities, virtues, etc* 骑士的气概、美德等.

□ ˌ**knight ˈerrant** (*pl* **knights errant**) medieval knight who wandered in search of adventure (中世纪的)游侠骑士.

knit /nɪt; nɪt/ *v* (**-tt-**, *pt*, *pp* **knitted**; in sense 3, usu 用于下述第三义时通常作 **knit**) **1** [I, Tn; Dn·n, Dn·pr] **~ sth (for sb)** make (a garment or fabric) by forming wool, silk, etc yarn into connecting loops, either by hand (using long needles) or on a machine 编织, 针织(衣物等): *Do you know how to knit?* 你会织毛活儿吗? ○ *She knitted her son a sweater.* 她给儿子织了一件毛衣. **2** [I, Tn] (in knitting instructions) make a plain (ie not a purl) stitch (编织法中)织(平针): *knit one, purl one* 织一正针、一反针. **3** [I, Ip, Tn, Tn·p] **~ (sth) (together)** (cause sth to) join or grow firmly together (使某物)连接或牢固地长在一起: *The broken bones have knit (together) well.* 断骨已愈合良好. ○ *a well-knit frame*, ie a compact sturdy body 结实的体格 ○ (*fig* 比喻) *a closely-knit argument* 严密的论据 ○ (*fig* 比喻) *The two groups are knit together by common interests.* 这两集团因有共同利益而联合在一起. **4** (idm 习语) **knit one's ˈbrow(s)** frown 皱眉.

▷ **knit·ter** *n* person who knits 编织者.

knit·ting *n* [U] material that is being knitted 编织物: *Oh dear, I've left my knitting on the bus!* 哎呀, 我把毛活儿落在公共汽车上了! **ˈknitting-machine** *n* machine that knits 编织机; 针织机. **ˈknitting-needle** *n* long thin pointed rod used esp in pairs for knitting by hand 织针; (尤指)编结针.

□ **ˈknitwear** *n* [U] knitted garments 针织衣服: [attrib 作定语] *a knitwear factory* 针织厂.

knob /nɒb; nɑb/ *n* **1** (**a**) round handle (of a door, drawer, etc) (门、抽屉等的)圆形拉手. (**b**) round control button (for adjusting a radio, TV, etc) (收音机、电视机等的)旋钮. **2** round lump on the surface of sth, eg a tree trunk 结节, 瘤, 疙瘩(如树干上的). **3** small lump (of butter, coal, etc) (黄油、煤等的)小块. **4** (idm 习语) **with knobs on** (*Brit sl* 俚) (used to indicate the return of an insult, or emphatic agreement 用以表示反唇相讥或强调同意): *'You're a selfish pig!' 'And the same to you, with knobs on!'* '自私鬼!' '你才是呢, 你是双料的!'

knobbly /ˈnɒblɪ; ˈnɑblɪ/ *adj* having many small hard lumps on 多结节的; 多疙瘩的: *knobbly knees* 长着很多结节的膝盖.

knock[1] /nɒk; nɑk/ *n* **1** (sound of a) sharp blow 短促的敲或打(的声音): *Did I hear a knock at the door?* 是有人敲门吗? ○ *If you're not up by eight o'clock I'll give you a knock*, ie wake you by knocking at your door. 要是八点钟你还不起床, 我就来敲你的门. ○ *She fell off her bike and got a nasty knock.* 她从自行车上摔下来, 摔得很重. ○ *In football you have to get used to hard knocks.* 踢足球就得经得起碰撞. **2** (in an engine) sound of knocking (KNOCK[2] 2) (发动机的)爆震声: *What's that knock I can hear?* 我听到发动机有爆震声是怎么回事啊? **3** (*infml* 口) (in cricket) innings (板球的)一局: *That was a good knock: 86 not out.* 那局真漂亮, 打了86分还未出局. **4** (idm 习语) **take a ˈknock** (*infml* 口) suffer a financial or an emotional blow 蒙受经济或感情上的打击: *She took a bad knock when her husband died.* 她丈夫一死她受到沉重的打击.

knock[2] /nɒk; nɑk/ *v* **1** [Tn, Tn·pr] strike (sth) with a sharp blow 敲, 打(某物): *Mind you don't knock your head (on this low beam).* 小心, 别(让这根低梁)撞着头. **2** [I, Ipr] make a noise by striking sth 敲击某物出声: *knock three times (at the door, on the window, etc)* 敲三下(门、窗等). ⇨Usage at BANG[1] 用法见 BANG[1]. **3** (**a**) [Cn·a, Cn·g] cause (sb/sth) to be in a certain state or position by striking (him/it) 将(某人[某物])击成某状态: *The fall knocked me senseless.* 那一跤摔得我失去了知觉. ○ *He knocked me flat with one punch.* 他一拳把我击倒了. ○ *He knocked my drink flying.* 他打翻了我的饮料. (**b**) [Tn·pr] make (sth) by striking 敲击成某物: *knock a hole in the wall* 在墙上凿个洞. **4** [I] (of a faulty petrol engine) make a tapping or thumping noise (指有故障的汽油发动机)发出爆震声. **5** [Tn] (*infml* 口) say critical or insulting things about (sb/sth) 批评, 数落, 非难(某人[某事物]): *The newspapers are too fond of knocking the England team.* 报纸专门爱挖苦英格兰队. ○ *He's always knocking the way I do things.* 他总是挑剔我做得不对. **6** (idm 习语) **beat/knock the daylights out of sb** ⇨ DAYLIGHTS. **beat/knock hell out of sb/sth** ⇨ HELL. **get/knock sb/sth into shape** ⇨ SHAPE[1]. **hit/knock sb for six** ⇨ HIT[1]. **knock sb's ˈblock/ˈhead off** (*sl* 俚) (used esp when threatening sb 尤用于威胁某人) strike sb in anger 狠打某人: *Call me that again and I'll knock your block off!* 你再那么叫我, 我就揍你! **knock the bottom out of sth** cause sth to collapse 使某事物垮台: *It knocked the bottom out of the coffee market*, ie caused the price of coffee to fall sharply. 这一来咖啡的市场价格暴跌. ○ *She knocked the bottom out of our argument.* 她把我们的论点驳得体无完肤. **knock your/their ˈheads together** (*infml* 口) force people to stop quarrelling and behave sensibly 强力使人不再争吵而恢复理智: *I often feel that politicians should have their heads knocked together, like naughty children* 我时常觉得应该像教训淘气孩子那样让政治家停止争吵. **knock sb/sth into a cocked ˈhat** defeat or outclass sb/sth 挫败或超过某人[某事物]: *A true professional could knock my efforts into a cocked hat.* 遇上真正行家我的工作就相形见绌了. **knock it ˈoff** (*sl*

俚) (esp imperative 尤用于祈使句) stop a noise, an argument, etc 别吵了、别争了: *Knock it off, kids, I'm trying to sleep!* 孩子们, 别闹了, 我要睡觉了! **knock sb off his 'pedestal/perch** (*infml* 口) defeat sb; show that sb is no longer best at sth 击败某人; 显示某人不再首屈一指. **knock sb 'sideways** (*infml* 口) defeat sb; astonish sb 击败某人; 使某人惊讶. **knock 'spots off sb/sth** (*infml* 口) be much better than sb/sth 远胜于某人[某事物]: *In learning foreign languages, the girls knock spots off the boys every time.* 学习外语女孩总是比男孩强. **knock the stuffing out of sb** (*infml* 口) make sb feeble, weak or demoralized 使某人衰弱或泄气: *His failure in the exam has knocked all the stuffing out of him.* 他考试未及格便一蹶不振. **knock them in the 'aisles** (*infml* 口) (of a theatre performance, etc) be very successful with the audience (指戏剧演出等)大受观众欢迎. **you could have knocked me down with a 'feather** (*infml* 口) (used esp as an exclamation 尤用作感叹语) I was amazed 我很惊奇.

7 (phr v) **knock about (...)** (*infml* 口) lead an unsettled life, travelling and living in various places 漫游; 流浪: *spend a few years knocking about (in) Europe* 在欧洲各地游历了几年. **knock about with sb/together** (*infml* 口) be often in sb's/each other's company 经常和某人作伴[互相在一起]. **knock sb/sth about** (*infml* 口) hit sb/sth repeatedly; treat sb/sth roughly 反复打击或粗暴对待某人[某事物]: *She gets knocked about by her husband.* 她常受丈夫虐待. ○ *The car's been knocked about a bit, but it still goes.* 汽车虽然受到多次碰撞, 但仍能开.

knock sth back (*infml* 口) drink sth quickly 很快喝掉某物: *knock back a pint of beer* 很快喝完一品脱啤酒.

knock sb down strike sb to the ground or the floor 将某人击倒或撞倒在地上: *She was knocked down by a bus.* 她被公共汽车撞倒了. ○ *He knocked his opponent down three times in the first round.* 在第一回合中他把对手击倒了三次. **knock sth down** demolish sth 拆除某物: *These old houses are going to be knocked down.* 这些旧房子将予拆除. **knock sth down (to sb)** (*infml* 口) (at an auction sale) sell sth (to a bidder) (拍卖时)卖出某物(给出价人): *The painting was knocked down (to an American dealer) for £5 000.* 那幅画拍卖时以5 000英镑售出(给一个美国商人). **knock sth/sb down** (force sb to) reduce (a price or charge) (迫使某人)减(价或费用): *I managed to knock his price/him down (from £500 to £450).* 我设法压了他的价(从500英镑减到450英镑).

knock sth in; knock sth into sth make sth enter sth by striking it 将某物打进另一物: *knock in a few nails* 钉进几颗钉子.

knock off (sth) (*infml* 口) stop doing sth (esp work) 停止做某事(尤指工作): *What time do you knock off (work)?* 你什么时候下班? **knock sb off** (*sl* 俚) murder sb 谋杀某人. **knock sth off** (**a**) deduct sth from a price or charge 减价; 杀价: *It cost me £10 but I'll knock off 20% as it's no longer new.* 那是我花10英镑买的, 因为已经旧了我减价20%. (**b**) (*infml* 口) complete sth quickly 迅速完成某事物: *knock off two whole chapters in an hour* 一小时就完成整整两章. (**c**) (*sl* 俚) steal (from) sth 偷盗某物; 抢劫某物: *knock off some watches from a shop* 从商店偷走几块手表 ○ *knock off a bank* 抢劫银行. **knock sth off (sth)** remove sth by striking it 打掉某物: *knock sb's glass off the table* 把某人的玻璃杯从桌上碰掉.

K

knock (sth) on (in Rugby football) illegally knock (the ball) forward with the hands (英式橄榄球)违例用手向前击(球): *He accidentally knocked on (the pass from Jones).* 他非故意犯规, 用手向前击了(从琼斯传来的)球.

knock sb out (**a**) (in boxing) strike (an opponent) so that he cannot rise or continue in a specified time and so loses the fight (拳击)击倒(对手)(获胜). (**b**) make sb unconscious by means of a blow, alcoholic drink, etc 击昏或灌醉某人: *Don't drink too much of this — it'll knock you out!* 这种酒别喝太多——喝多了就醉了! (**c**) (*infml* 口) overwhelm or astonish sb 使某人经受不了或极为震惊: *The film just knocked me out — it's the best thing I've ever seen.* 这电影好得不得了——是我看过的最好的一部. **knock sb/oneself out** make sb/oneself exhausted, ill, etc 使某人[自己]筋疲力尽、病倒等: *She's knocking herself out with all that work.* 她做的工作把她累得筋疲力尽. **knock sb out (of sth)** eliminate sb (from a competition) by defeating him 淘汰某人: *France knocked Belgium out (of the European Cup).* 法国队将比利时队淘汰(出欧洲杯足球赛)了. **knock sth out (on sth)** empty (a tobacco pipe) by knocking it (against sth) 磕净(烟斗).

knock sb/sth over upset sb/sth by striking him/it 撞倒某人[某物]: *You've knocked over my drink!* 你把我的饮料打翻了!

knock sth together make or complete sth quickly and often not very well 匆匆做完某事物: *knock bookshelves together from old planks* 用旧木板匆匆钉成书架 ○ *knock a few scenes together to make a play* 草草将几个场面拼凑成一出话剧.

knock up (in tennis, badminton, etc) practise hitting the ball before the start of a match (网球、羽毛球等)赛前练球. **knock sb up** (**a**) (*Brit infml* 口) awaken sb by knocking on his door, etc (敲门、窗等)叫醒某人: *Would you please knock me up at 7 o'clock?* 请7点钟敲门把我叫醒行吗? (**b**) (△ *sl* 讳, 俚 *esp US*) make (a woman) pregnant 使(女子)怀孕. **knock sth up** (**a**) prepare or make sth quickly and without much planning 匆匆准备或做某事物: *Even though they weren't expecting us, they managed to knock up a marvellous meal.* 他们虽然没想到我们要来, 但还是设法匆匆做好一顿丰盛的饭. (**b**) (in cricket) score (runs) (板球)得(分): *knock up a quick fifty* 击球后速跑得50分.

□ **'knockabout** *adj* (esp of a theatrical performance) rough and boisterous in a funny way; slapstick (尤指戏剧演出)粗俗滑稽的, 打闹的: *knockabout humour/comedy/farce* 胡闹的幽默[喜剧/闹剧].

'knock-down *adj* [attrib 作定语] (**a**) (of prices) very low (指价格)低廉的. (**b**) (of furniture) easy to dismantle and reassemble (指家具)易于拆装的.

ˌknock-'kneed *adj* having legs abnormally curved so that the knees touch when standing or walking 膝外翻的.

ˌknock-'on *n* (in Rugby football) act of knocking the ball on (英式橄榄球)违例用手向前击球. **ˌknock-'on effect** indirect result of an action 间接结果: *The closure of the car factory had a knock-on effect on the tyre manufacturers.* 汽车厂关闭后, 轮胎制造商受到间接的影响.

'knock-out *n* **1** blow that knocks a boxer out 将对方击倒而获胜的一击: *He has won most of his fights by knock-outs.* 他在拳赛中多以击倒对方获胜. ○ [attrib 作定语] *a knock-out punch* 将对手击倒的一拳. **2** [attrib 作定语] (of a drug) causing sleep or unconsciousness (指药)引起昏迷的: *knock-out drops/pills* 麻醉滴剂[丸剂]. **3** competition in which the loser of each successive round is eliminated 淘汰赛: [attrib 作定语] *a knock-out tournament* 淘汰赛. **4** (*infml* 口) outstandingly impressive person or thing 引人注目的人或物: *She's an absolute knock-out*, ie very beautiful. 她漂亮极了. ○ [attrib 作定语] *a knock-out idea* 绝妙的主意.

'knock-up *n* [sing] (in tennis, badminton, etc) period of practice before a match (网球、羽毛球等的)赛前练球: *have a quick knock-up* 用很短的时间练球.

knocker /ˈnɒkə(r); ˈnɑkɚ/ *n* **1** [C] hinged metal hammer attached to a door, used for knocking by sb outside who wants the door to be opened 门环. ⇨illus at App 1 见附录1插图, page vi. **2** [C] (*infml* 口) person who constantly criticizes 一味批评的人; 吹毛求疵的人. **3 knockers** [pl] (△ *Brit sl sexist* 讳, 俚, 性别偏见) woman's breasts 女子的乳房: *a nice pair of knockers* 一对漂亮的乳房.

knoll /nəʊl; nol/ *n* small round hill or mound 小圆丘; 小土墩.

knot[1] /nɒt; nɑt/ *n* **1** fastening made by tying a piece or pieces of string, rope, etc (绳索等的)结: *make a knot at the end of the rope* 在绳头上打个结 ○ *tie the two ropes together with a secure knot* 打个结实的结把这两条绳系在一起. ⇨illus 见插图. **2** ornament or decoration made of ribbon, etc twisted and tied (用丝带等打成的)装饰性花结. **3** tangle; twistedpiece 扭结; 纠结: *comb a knot out of one's hair* 梳个发髻. **4** hard round spot in timber where a branch used to join the trunk or another

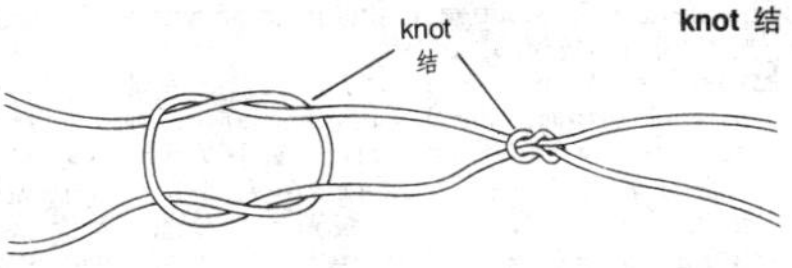

knot 结

branch (木材上的)结节, 节瘤. ⇨illus at GRAIN 见GRAIN插图. **5** small gathering (of people or things) (人或物的)小群, 小簇: *a knot of people arguing outside the pub* 在酒店外争论着的一小群人. **6** (idm 习语) **cut the Gordian knot** ⇨ GORDIAN KNOT. **tie sb/oneself in knots** ⇨ TIE[2]. **tie the knot** ⇨ TIE[2].

▷ **knot** *v* **(-tt-)** **1** [I, Tn, Tn·p] (cause sth to) form knots (使某物)打结, 缠结: *My hair knots easily.* 我的头发爱打结. ○ *knot two ropes together* 把两条绳子系在一起. **2** [Tn] fasten (sth) with a knot or knots 打结系牢(某物): *knot one's tie loosely* 打个很松的领结. **3** (idm 习语) **get 'knotted** (*Brit sl* 俚) (used to express contempt, annoyance, etc 用以表示轻蔑、恼怒等): *If he asks you for money again just tell him to get knotted.* 要是他再向你要钱, 干脆叫他滚.

knotty *adj* **(-ier, -iest)** **1** (of timber) full of knots (指木材)多结节的, 多节瘤的. **2** puzzling; difficult 棘手的; 困难的: *a knotty problem, question, etc* 难以解决的疑难、问题等.

□ **'knot-hole** *n* hole in a piece of timber where a knot[1](4) has fallen out (木材上的)节孔(节结脱落形成的空洞).

knot[2] /nɒt; nαt/ *n* (usu *pl* 通常作复数) (*nautical* 海) **1** unit of speed (one nautical mile per hour) used by ships and aircraft 节(速度单位, 为每小时一海里, 用以测船和飞行器的航速). ⇨App 5 见附录5. **2** (idm 习语) **at a rate of knots** ⇨ RATE.

know /nəʊ; no/ *v* (*pt* **knew** /nju:; *US* nu:; nu/, *pp* **known** /nəʊn; non/) **1** **(a)** [I, Tn, Tf, Tw, Tt, Cn·t] have (sth) in one's mind or memory as a result of experience or learning or information 知道, 懂得, 了解(某事物): *I'm not guessing — I know!* 我不是猜想——我知道! ○ *She doesn't know your address.* 她不知道你的地址. ○ *Every child knows (that) two and two make four.* 孩子都知道二加二等于四. ○ *I knew where he was hiding.* 我知道他躲在什么地方. ○ *Do you know who Napoleon was?* 你知道拿破仑是谁吗? ○ *Does he know to come here* (ie that he should come here) *first?* 他知道要先到这里来吗? ○ *We knew her to be honest.* 我们知道她很诚实. **(b)** [Tnt, Tni] (only in the past and perfect tenses 只用于过去时态和完成时态) have seen, heard, etc 见过、听过等: *I've never known it (to) snow in July before.* 我从未听说过有七月下雪的事. ○ *He's sometimes been known to sit there all day.* 有时能见到他整天坐在那里. **2** [Tf] feel certain 确知; 确信: *I know (that) it's here somewhere — it must be!* 我肯定是在这里的什么地方——没错! **3** **(a)** [Tn] be acquainted with (sb) 认识(某人): *Do you know Bob Hill?* ie Have you met him, talked with him, etc? 你认识鲍勃·希尔吗? ○ *I know him by sight, but not to talk to,* ie I have seen him but never spoken to him. 我见过他, 但没跟他说过话. ○ *We've known each other since we were children.* 我们从小就认识. **(b)** [Tn, Cn·n/a] **~ sth (as sth)** be familiar with (a place) 熟悉(某地): *I know Paris better than Rome.* 我对巴黎比对罗马熟悉. ○ *I know London as the place where I spent my childhood.* 我熟悉伦敦, 那是我度过童年的地方. **4** [Cn·n/a often passive 常用于被动语态] **~ sb/sth as sth** regard sb/sth as (being) sth 认定某人[某事物]为某事物: *It's known as the most dangerous part of the city.* 那地方都知道是市内最危险的地段. ○ *We know John Smith as a fine lawyer and a good friend.* 我们认为约翰·史密斯是一位很好的律师和朋友. **5** [Cn·n/a usu passive 通常用于被动语态] **~ sb/sth as sth** call, nickname or label sb/sth as sth 将某人[某事物]称为、起绰号叫作或标明为某事物: *a heavyweight boxer known as 'The Greatest'* 一名被称为'大力士'的重量级拳击手 ○ *This area is known as the 'Cornish Riviera'.* 这地区称为'康沃尔郡度假胜地'. **6** [Tn, Tn·pr] **~ sb/sth (from sb/sth)** be able to distinguish (one person or thing) from another; recognize 能区分, 辨别, 认出(人或物): *She knows a bargain when she sees one.* 她有辨别便宜货的能力. ○ *know right from wrong* 分辨是非 ○ *I met so many people at the party that I wouldn't know half of them again.* 我在聚会上见到很多人, 再见到连一半也未必能认出. **7** [Tn, Tw] understand and be able to use (a language, skill, etc) 会, 掌握(某语言、技巧等): *know Japanese* 会日语 ○ *know how to swim* 会游泳. **8** [Tn] have personal experience of (sth) 有(某事物)的亲身经历或体验: *a man who has known both poverty and riches* 经历过贫富生活的男子. **9** (idm 习语) **be,fore one ,knows where one 'is** very quickly or suddenly 迅速地; 突然地: *We were whisked off in a taxi before we knew where we were.* 我们还未明白是在哪里, 就被计程车载走了. **be known to sb** be familiar to sb 为某人所熟知: *He's known to the police,* ie has a criminal record. 警方很熟悉他(曾犯案). **better the devil you know** ⇨ BETTER[2]. **for all one knows** considering how little one knows 据自己所知; 说不定: *For all I know he could be dead.* 说不定他已经死了. **for reasons/some reason best known to oneself** ⇨ REASON. **God/goodness/Heaven knows** **(a)** I don't know 我不知道: *God knows what's happened to them.* 谁知道他们怎么了. **(b)** certainly; emphatically 确实; 的确: *She ought to succeed; goodness knows she tries hard enough.* 她应能成功, 她确实够努力的. **have/know all the answers** (*infml esp derog* 口, 尤作贬义) (seem to) be cleverer and better-informed than other people (好像)什么都知道; 比别人精明. **have/know sth off pat** ⇨ PAT[1]. **know sth as well as 'I/'you do** understand sth perfectly well 对某事物很清楚: *You know as well as I do that you're being unreasonable.* 你很清楚你不讲理. **know sth 'backwards** (*infml* 口) be thoroughly familiar with sth 极熟悉某事物: *You've read that book so many times you must know it backwards by now!* 那本书你读了很多遍, 现在一定能倒背如流了! **know 'best** know what should be done, etc better than other people 最知就里; 最在行: *The doctor told you to stay in bed, and he knows best.* 医生叫你卧床休息, 他最清楚. **know better (than that/than to do sth)** be wise or sensible (enough not to do it) 明白事理而不至于(做某事): *You ought to know better (than to trust her).* 你应当明白(她这人不能相信). **know sb by sight** recognize who sb is without knowing him as a personal friend 面熟. **know 'different/'otherwise** (*infml* 口) have information or evidence to the contrary 知道相反的情况; 有证据表明情况相反: *He says he was at the cinema, but I know different.* 他说他那时在看电影, 可是我知道不是那么回事. **know how many beans make five** be shrewd and sensible in practical matters 精明; 在行. **know sth inside 'out/like the back of one's 'hand** (*infml* 口) be thoroughly familiar with a place, subject, etc 了如指掌; 了解透彻: *He's a taxi driver, so he knows London like the back of his hand.* 他是计程车司机, 对伦敦市的街道了如指掌. **know no 'bounds** (*fml* 文) be very great or too great 无限: *When she heard the news her fury knew no bounds.* 她听到这个消息, 顿时怒不可遏. **know one's 'onions/'stuff** (*infml* 口) be good at one's work, etc 了解本行; 精通业务. **know one's own 'mind** know what one wants or intends 有自己的想法; 有决断. **know the 'score** (*infml* 口) understand the true state of affairs 知道事情真相; 深通世故. **know a thing or two (about sb/sth)** (*infml* 口) know a lot (about sb/sth) (对某人[某事物])很了解: *She's been married five times, so she should know a thing or two about men.* 她已结过五次婚, 对男人应有所了解了. **know sb through and 'through** understand sb perfectly 完全了解某人. **know one's way around** be familiar with a place, subject, procedure, etc; be capable and well-informed 熟悉某处、某事、手续等; 有阅历; 了解情况. **know what it is/what it's like (to be/do sth)** have personal experience (of being/doing sth) 有做某事物的经历: *Many famous people have known what it is to be poor.* 很多名人都领略过贫穷是什么滋味. **know what one's 'talking about** (*infml* 口) speak from experience 作经验谈. **know what's 'what** (*infml* 口) understand the important facts, rules of behaviour, etc in a particular situation 内行; 精明; 有头脑: *You're old enough now to know what's what.* 你已经不小了, 应该知道好歹了. **know which side one's 'bread is buttered** (*infml saying* 口, 谚) know where one's interests lie or what will be to one's advantage 知道自己利益所在; 善于为个人打算. **let sb 'know** inform sb about sth 让某人知道某事物: *I don't know if I can come yet, but I'll let you know tomorrow.* 我说不上是否能来, 可是我明天能告诉你. **make oneself known to sb** introduce oneself to sb 向某人作自我介绍: *There's our host; you'd better make yourself known to him.* 那位是我们的主人, 你最好向他自我介绍一下. **not know any 'better** not behave well, through lack of experience, bad upbringing, etc (因无教养或无经验)表现不好: *Don't blame the children for their bad manners — they don't know any better.* 不要责怪孩子们没规矩——他们还不懂. **not know one's ˌarse from one's 'elbow** (⚠ *sl derog* 讳, 俚, 贬) be totally ignorant, stupid or inefficient 一窍不通; 愚蠢; 无能. **not know the first thing about sb/sth/doing sth** know nothing at all about sb/sth/doing sth 对某人[某事物]一无所知: *I'm afraid I don't know the first thing about gardening.* 很遗憾, 我对园艺一无所知. **not know sb from 'Adam** (*infml* 口) not know at all who sb is 完全不认识某人. **not know what 'hit one** (**a**) be suddenly injured or killed 突遭伤害; 突受杀害: *The bus was moving so fast she never knew what hit her.* 公共汽车开得很快, 突然把她撞了. (**b**) (*infml fig* 口, 比喻) be amazed or confused 大为惊奇; 迷惑不解: *The first time I heard their music I didn't know what had hit me.* 我初次听他们的音乐时大为惊奇. **not know where/which way to look** (*infml* 口) be embarrassed, awkwardly self-conscious, etc 尴尬; 难堪; 难为情: *When he started undressing in public I didn't know where to look.* 他在大庭广众之下脱衣服, 我感到很难为情. **not want to know** ⇨ WANT[1]. **old enough to know better** ⇨ OLD. **show sb/know/learn the ropes** ⇨ ROPE. **see/know better days** ⇨ BETTER[1]. **tell/know A and B apart** ⇨ APART. **that's what I'd like to know** ⇨ LIKE[2]. **there's no 'knowing** it's difficult or impossible to know 难以逆料; 无法知道: *There's absolutely no knowing how he'll react.* 他怎样反应很难逆料. **(well) what do you 'know (about 'that)?** (*infml* 口 *esp US*) (used to express surprise on hearing news, etc 用以表示听到消息等时感到惊讶) **you know** (*infml* 口) (**a**) (used when reminding sb of sth 用以提醒某人): *Guess who I've just seen? Marcia! You know — Jim's ex-wife!* 你猜刚才我看见谁了? 玛西娅! 你知道吗, 就是吉姆的前妻呀! (**b**) (used as an almost meaningless expression when the speaker is thinking what to say next 用于说话时思索中作口头语, 无甚意义): *'I was feeling a bit bored, you know, and so...'* '我当时有点厌烦了, 你知道吗, 所以...' **you know something/what?** (*infml* 口) (used to introduce an item of news, expression of opinion, etc 用以提到一项新消息、表达看法等): *You know something? Cathy and Tim are engaged.* 你听说了吗? 卡西和蒂姆订婚了. **you never know** you cannot be certain 很难说; 事难逆料: *'It's sure to rain tomorrow.' 'Oh, you never know, it could be a lovely day.'* '明天准下雨.' '哦, 很难说, 也可能是个好天.' ○ *You should keep those old jam jars — you never know when you might need them.* 这些旧果酱瓶子应当留一留, 说不定什么时候会用得着. **10** (phr v) **know about sth** have knowledge of sth; be aware of sth 了解或知道某事物: *Not much is known about his background.* 他的背景所知不多. ○ *Do you know about Jack getting arrested?* 你知道杰克遭逮捕了吗? **know of sb/sth** have information about or experience of sb/sth 知道某人[某事物]的情况: *'Isn't tomorrow a holiday?' 'Not that I know of* (ie Not as far as I am aware).' '明天是假日吧?' '据我所知不是.' ○ *Do you know of any way to stop a person snoring?* 你知道有什么方法可以制止打呼噜吗? ○ *I don't know him personally, though I know 'of him.* 我并不认识他, 但我听说过他.

K

▷ **know** *n* (idm 习语) **in the 'know** (*infml* 口) (of a person) having information not possessed by others; well informed (指人)知情的, 消息灵通的.

□ **'know-all** *n* (*infml derog* 口, 贬) person who behaves as if he knows everything 自以为无所不知的人: *one of those young know-alls fresh from university* 大学刚毕业的一个小小的万事通.

'know-how *n* [U] (*infml* 口) practical (contrasted with theoretical) knowledge or skill in an activity 实践知识或技术; 本事; 技能.

know·ing /ˈnəʊɪŋ; ˈnoɪŋ/ *adj* [usu attrib 通常作定语] **1** showing or suggesting that one has information which is secret or not known to others (对别人不知道的秘密)知悉的, 心照不宣的: *a knowing look, glance, expression, etc* 显出了解内情的样子、眼光、表情等. **2** shrewd; cunning 世故的; 狡猾的: *She's a bit too knowing for me to feel relaxed with her.* 她很有点世故, 和她相处我觉得不自在.

▷ **know·ingly** *adv* **1** intentionally 故意地; 蓄意地: *It appears that what I said was untrue, but I did not knowingly lie to you.* 看来我说错了, 但是我并非故意向你撒谎. **2** in a knowing(1) manner 知悉地; 心照不宣地: *He winked at her knowingly.* 他会心地向她眨了眨眼.

know·ledge /ˈnɒlɪdʒ; ˈnɑlɪdʒ/ *n* **1** [U] understanding 了解; 理解: *A baby has no knowledge of good and evil.* 小孩儿不解善恶. **2** [U, sing] all that a person knows; familiarity gained by experience 个人的知识; 见闻: *I have only (a) limited knowledge of computers.* 我的计算机知识很有限. ○ *My knowledge of French is poor.* 我不太懂法语. **3** [U] everything that is known; organized body of information 学问; 学识; 知识: *all branches of knowledge* 各门学问 ○ *the sum of human knowledge on this subject* 人类对这一学科的知识总和. **4** (idm 习语) **be common/public knowledge** be known by everyone in a community or group 人所共知: *It's pointless trying to keep your friendship secret — it's common knowledge already.* 你们无谓将友情保密——其实已尽人皆知了. **come to sb's 'knowledge** (*fml* 文) become known by sb 被某人知悉: *It has come to our knowledge that you have been cheating the company.* 据我们了解你一直欺骗公司. **to one's 'knowledge** (**a**) as far as one knows 据自己所知: *To my knowledge, she has never been late before.* 据我所知, 她从未迟到过. (**b**) as one knows to be true 确知属实: *That is impossible, because to my (certain) knowledge he was in France at the time.* 那不可能, 因为我(确实)知道那时他在法国. **to the best of one's belief/knowledge** ⇨ BEST[3]. **with/without sb's 'knowledge** having/not having informed sb 告知[未告知]某人: *He sold the car without his wife's knowledge.* 他瞒着妻子把汽车卖了.

▷ **know·ledge·able** /-əbl; -əbl̩/ *adj* **~ (about sth)** well-informed 消息灵通的; 在行的: *She's very knowledgeable about art.* 她对艺术十分在行. **know·ledge·ably** /-əblɪ; -əblɪ/ *adv*: *speak knowledgeably on the subject* 对这学科谈得头头是道.

knuckle /ˈnʌkl; ˈnʌkl̩/ *n* **1** bone at the finger-joint 指节; 指关节: *graze/skin one's knuckles* 擦破指关节. ⇨ illus at HAND 见 HAND 插图. **2** (of animals) knee-joint, or the part joining the leg to the foot, esp as a joint of meat (指动物)膝关节, 踝; (尤指食用的)肘: *pig's knuckles* 猪肘. **3** (idm 习语) **a rap on/over the knuckles** ⇨ RAP[1]. **near the 'knuckle** (*infml* 口) on the borderline of indecency and therefore likely to offend 近乎下流; 猥亵: *Some of his jokes are a bit too near the knuckle for my taste.* 我觉得他有的笑话已近乎淫亵了.

▷ **knuckle** *v* (phr v) **knuckle down (to sth)** (*infml* 口) begin to work seriously (at sth) 开始认真工作: *If you want to pass that exam, you'll have to knuckle down (to some hard work).* 你要想考试及格, 就得开始下功夫(苦干)了. **knuckle under** (*infml* 口) accept or admit defeat; surrender 屈服; 认输; 投降.

□ **'knuckleduster** *n* (*US* **brass 'knuckles**) metal cover worn over the knuckles to increase the injury caused by a blow with the fist 戴在指关节上的金属套(打人时加重损伤).

'knucklehead *n* (*infml derog* 口, 贬) fool 笨蛋; 傻瓜.

KO /ˌkeɪ ˈəʊ; ˌke ˈo/ *abbr* 缩写 = (*infml* 口) knock-out (esp in boxing) 击倒(尤为拳击用语): *He was KO'd* (ie knocked out) *in the second round.* 他在第二回合中被击倒.

ko·ala /kəʊˈɑːlə; koˈɑlə/ *n* (also **koala bear**) Australian tree-climbing mammal with thick grey fur, large ears and no tail 树袋熊(产于澳洲的树栖哺乳动物, 毛密、色灰、耳大、无尾).

kobo /ˈkɒbəʊ; ˈkobo/ *n* (*pl* unchanged 复数不变) unit of

money in Nigeria; 100th part of a naira 考包(尼日利亚辅币名, 100考包＝1奈拉).

kohl /kəʊl; kol/ *n* [U] cosmetic powder used in the East to darken the eyelids 眼睑粉(东方妇女的化妆品).

kohl·rabi /ˌkəʊl'rɑ:bɪ; 'kol,rɑbɪ/ *n* [C, U] cabbage with an edible turnip-shaped stem 球茎甘蓝(可供食用).

kola = COLA.

kook /ku:k; kuk/ *n* (*US derog sl* 贬, 俚) peculiar, eccentric or crazy person 怪人; 狂人. ▷ **kooky** *adj*.

koo·ka·burra /'kʊkəbʌrə; 'kukə,bʌrə/ *n* (also **laughing jackass**) Australian giant kingfisher 笑翠鸟(产于澳洲).

kop·eck (also **kopek**) = COPECK.

koppie (also **kopje**) /'kɒpɪ; 'kɑpɪ/ *n* (in S Africa) small hill (南非的)小山.

Ko·ran /kə'rɑ:n; *US* -'ræn; kə'ræn/ *n* **the Koran** [sing] sacred book of the Muslims, written in Arabic, containing the revelations of the Prophet Muhammad 《古兰经》, 《可兰经》(伊斯兰教经典). ▷ **Kor·anic** /kə'rænɪk; kə'rænɪk/ *adj*.

kosher /'kəʊʃə(r); 'koʃɚ/ *adj* **1** (of food, food shops, etc) fulfilling the requirements of Jewish dietary law (指食物、饮食店等)合礼的(符合犹太教规戒律的): *a kosher butcher's, restaurant, meal* 合礼的肉店、餐馆、饭食. **2** (*infml* 口) genuine or legitimate 真正的; 合法的: *the real kosher article, not just any old rubbish* 真正的正品, 并不是什么旧的破烂货 ○ *something not quite kosher about the way he made his money* 他的钱来路不大正.

kou·miss = KUMIS.

kow·tow /ˌkaʊ'taʊ; kaʊ'taʊ/ *v* [I, Ipr] **~ (to sb/sth)** be submissive, humble or respectful (to sb/sth) (向某人[某事物])叩头, 磕头, 臣服: *a refusal to kowtow (to the government's wishes on this issue)* 拒绝屈从(于政府对这一问题的意旨).

kph /ˌkeɪ pi: 'eɪtʃ; ˌke pi 'etʃ/ *abbr* 缩写 = kilometres per hour 千米/小时; 公里/小时. Cf 参看 MPH.

kraal /krɑ:l; *US* krɔ:l; krɑl/ *n* (in S Africa 用于南非) **1** village of huts enclosed by a fence 用栅栏围起来的茅舍村庄. **2** enclosure for cattle, sheep, etc 家畜栏.

krem·lin /'kremlɪn; 'krɛmlɪn/ *n* **1** [C] citadel within a Russian town (俄国的)城堡. **2 the Kremlin (a)** [Gp] government of the former USSR 前苏联政府. **(b)** [sing] the citadel of Moscow 克里姆林宫.

krill /krɪl; krɪl/ *n* [pl *v*] mass of tiny shellfish eaten by whales (鲸鱼吞食的)磷虾群.

kris /kri:s; kris/ *n* Malay or Indonesian dagger (马来亚或印度尼西亚的)波形刃短剑.

krona /'krəʊnə; 'kronə/ *n* **1** (*pl* **-nor** /-nə(r); -nɔr/) unit of money in Sweden 克朗(瑞典的货币单位). **2** (*pl* **-nur** /-nə(r); -nɔr/) unit of money in Iceland 克朗(冰岛的货币单位).

krone /'krəʊnə; 'kronɛ/ *n* (*pl* **-ner** /-nə(r); -nɔr/) unit of money in Denmark and Norway 克朗(丹麦和挪威的货币单位).

kru·ger·rand /'kru:gərænd; 'krugə,rænd/ *n* South African gold coin weighing one ounce 克鲁格金币(南非金币重一盎司).

krypton /'krɪptɒn; 'krɪp,tɑn/ *n* [U] chemical element, an inert colourless and odourless gas 氪. ⇨App 10 见附录10.

Kt *abbr* 缩写 = Knight: *Sir James Bailey Kt* 詹姆斯·贝利爵士.

ku·dos /'kju:dɒs; *US* 'ku:-; 'kudɑs/ *n* [U] (*infml* 口) honour and glory; credit[1](2) 荣誉; 光荣; 赞誉: *She did most of the work but all the kudos went to him.* 工作大部分是她做的, 可是荣誉都归他了.

Ku-Klux-Klan /ˌku: klʌks 'klæn; ˌku ˌklʌks 'klæn/ *n* [Gp] (*abbr* 缩写 **KKK**) secret racialist organization of white Protestant men in the (esp southern) United States 三K党(美国的, 尤指其南部的白人基督教徒的种族主义秘密组织).

kukri /'kʊkrɪ; 'kukrɪ/ *n* type of curved knife used by Gurkhas (廓尔喀人用的)弯刀.

kumis (also **kumiss, koumiss**) /'ku:mɪs; 'kumɪs/ *n* [U] drink made from fermented mare's milk by certain Central Asian peoples 乳酒(中亚某些民族用马乳酿制的酒).

küm·mel /'kʊməl; 'kɪml̩/ *n* [U] sweet liqueur flavoured with cumin and caraway seeds (用莳萝和葛缕子调味的)烈性甜酒.

kum·quat /'kʌmkwɒt; 'kʌmkwɑt/ *n* plum-sized fruit similar to an orange 金橘.

kung fu /ˌkʊŋ 'fu:, *also* 'kʌŋ; ˌkuŋ'fu/ *n* [U] Chinese form of unarmed combat similar to karate (中国武术中的)徒手功夫.

kvass /kvæs; kvæs/ *n* [U] type of weak beer made in Russia 克瓦斯淡啤酒(俄罗斯制).

kW (also **kw**) *abbr* 缩写 = kilowatt(s): *a 2 kW electric heater* 功率2千瓦的电热器.

kwashi·or·kor /kwæʃɪ'ɔ:kɔ:(r); ˌkwɑʃɪ'ɔrkɔr/ *n* [U] severe tropical disease of children whose diet does not contain enough protein 夸希奥科, 蛋白质营养不良(热带严重儿科病).

kwela /'kweɪlə; 'kwelə/ *n* [U] kind of S African jazz music 南非的一种爵士乐.

ky·bosh (also **ki·bosh**) /'kaɪbɒʃ; 'kaɪbɑʃ/ *n* (idm 习语) **put the kybosh on sb/sth** (*sl* 俚) prevent sb/sth from continuing; stop sb/sth 止住某人[某事物]; 使某人[某事物]停止: *When he broke his leg it put the kybosh on his holiday.* 他摔坏了腿, 度假只好中止.

L l

L, l /el; ɛl/ (*pl* **L's, l's** /elz; ɛlz/) *n* the twelfth letter of the English alphabet 英语字母表的第十二个字母: *'London' begins with (an) L/'L'.* London一字以L字母开始.

L *abbr* 缩写 = **1** Lake: *L Windermere*, eg on a map 温德米尔湖(如标于地图上的字样). **2** /el; ɛl/ (*Brit*) (on a motor vehicle) learner-driver (机动车辆上的标志). Cf 参看 L-PLATE. **3** (esp on clothing, etc) large (size) (尤作衣物上尺码的标志). **4** (*Brit politics* 政) Liberal (party). Cf 参看 LIB. **5** lira: *L6 000* 6 000里拉. **6** (esp on electric plugs) live (connection) (尤作电器插头上的标志).

L (also **l**) *symb* (符号) Roman numeral for 50 (罗马数字)50.

l *abbr* 缩写 = **1** left. Cf 参看 R 2. **2** (*pl* **ll**) line: *p* (ie page) *2, l 19* 第2页第19行 ○ *verse 6, ll 8-10* 第6节第8-10行. **3** litre(s).

la = LAH.

LA /ˌel ˈeɪ; ˌɛl ˋe/ *abbr* 缩写 = Los Angeles (California) 洛杉矶(加利福尼亚州).

laa·ger /ˈlɑːgə(r); ˋlɑgɚ/ *n* (*S African* 南非) **1** (formerly) camp inside a circle of wagons (旧时)大车围成的营地. **2** (*fig* 比喻) defensive position 防御阵地: *retreat into the laager* 退至防御阵地.

lab /læb; læb/ *n* (*infml* 口) laboratory 实验室: *I'll meet you outside the science lab.* 我在科学实验室外面见你. ○ [attrib 作定语] *a lab coat*, ie one worn to protect clothes in a laboratory 实验室用罩衫.

Lab /læb; læb/ *abbr* 缩写 = (*Brit politics* 政) Labour (party): *Tom Green (Lab)* 汤姆·格林(工党党员).

la·bel /ˈleɪbl; ˋlebḷ/ *n* **1** piece of paper, cloth, metal, etc on or beside an object and describing its nature, name, owner, destination, etc 标签; 标记: *put a label on a piece of clothing, a specimen, one's luggage* 在衣物、样品、自己的行李上加标记 ○ *I read the information on the label before deciding which jam to buy.* 我先看果酱标签上的说明再决定买哪种. **2** (*fig* 比喻) descriptive word or phrase applied to a person, group, etc (用以描述人、组织等的)称号, 外号, 绰号: *hang, stick, slap, etc a label on sb/sth* 给某人[某事物]加称号、取别名、起外号 ○ *A reviewer called her first novel 'super-romantic' and the label has stuck.* 有个评论家把她的处女作称为'超级浪漫小说', 这个美称就叫开了.

▷ **la·bel** *v* (**-ll-**; *US* **-l-**) **1** [Tn] put a label or labels on (sth) 给(某事物)加标签或标记: *a machine for labelling wine bottles* 给酒瓶加标签的机器. **2** [Tn, Cn·n, Cn·n/a] **~ sb/sth as sth** (*fig* 比喻) describe or classify sb/sth 描述某人[某事物]; 将某人[某事物]归类: *His work is difficult to label accurately.* 他的工作很难准确归类. ○ *She is usually labelled (as) an Impressionist.* 人们通常把她称为印象派艺术家.

la·bia /ˈleɪbɪə; ˋlebɪə/ *n* [pl] lip-shaped folds of the female genitals 阴唇.

la·bial /ˈleɪbɪəl; ˋlebɪəl/ *adj* **1** of the lips 唇的. **2** (*phonetics* 语音) made with the lips 唇音的: *labial sounds*, eg /m, p, v/ 唇音(如/m/、/p/、/v/).

▷ **la·bial** *n* (*phonetics* 语音) sound made with the lips 唇音.

la·bi·ate /ˈleɪbɪeɪt; ˋlebɪˌet/ *n, adj* (*botany* 植) (plant) with a corolla or calyx divided into two parts that look like lips 唇形科的(植物).

la·bor·at·ory /ləˈbɒrətrɪ; *US* ˈlæbrətɔːrɪ; ˋlæbrəˌtorɪ/ *n* room or building used for (esp scientific) research, experiments, testing, etc 实验室.

la·bori·ous /ləˈbɔːrɪəs; ləˋbɔrɪəs/ *adj* **1** (of work, etc) needing much effort (指工作等)艰苦的, 费力的: *a laborious task* 艰苦的工作. **2** showing signs of great effort; not fluent or natural 吃力的; 不流畅的; 不自然的: *a laborious style of writing* 艰涩的文体. Cf 参看 LABOURED (LABOUR[2]). ▷ **la·bori·ously** *adv.* **la·bori·ous·ness** *n* [U].

la·bour[1] (*US* **la·bor**) /ˈleɪbə(r); ˋlebɚ/ *n* **1** [U] physical or mental work (体力或脑力)劳动: *manual labour* 手工劳动 ○ *Workers are paid for their labour.* 工作的人按劳获得报酬. **2** [C usu *pl* 通常作复数] task; piece of work 任务; 工作: *tired after one's labours* 工作后感到疲劳. ⇨Usage at WORK[1] 用法见 WORK[1]. **3** [U] workers as a group or class, esp as contrasted with capital, management, etc 劳动阶级; 劳工: *skilled/unskilled labour* 熟练工人[非熟练工人] ○ [attrib 作定语] *labour relations*, ie between workers and employers 劳资关系 ○ *labour leaders*, ie trade union leaders 工会领导人. **4** [U, sing] contractions of the womb during the process of childbirth (分娩时的)阵痛, 阵痛期: *begin, go into, be in labour* 开始、进入、处于阵痛期 ○ *She had a difficult labour.* 她难产. ○ [attrib 作定语] *a labour ward*, ie a set of rooms in a hospital for childbirth 产房. **5 Labour** (*abbr* 缩写 **Lab**) (*Brit politics* 政) [Gp] the Labour Party 工党: [attrib 作定语] *the Labour vote* 工党选票 ○ *Labour supporters* 工党拥护者. **6** (idm 习语) **a ˌlabour of ˈHercules** task needing great strength or effort 极艰巨的工作. **a ˌlabour of ˈlove** task done out of enthusiasm or devotion, not from necessity or for profit 为爱好而做的工作.

□ **ˈlabor union** (*US*) = TRADE UNION (TRADE).

ˈlabour camp prison camp with physical labour as a punishment 劳动营; 劳改营.

ˈLabour Day (*US* **Labor Day**) public holiday in honour of workers (1 May; in US the first Monday in September) 劳动节(五月一日); 劳工节(在美国为九月的第一个星期一).

ˈLabour Exchange (*dated* 旧 *Brit*) = JOBCENTRE (JOB).

ˌlabour-inˈtensive *adj* (of an industrial process, etc) needing to employ many people (指工业生产方法等)劳动密集型的. Cf 参看 THE CAPITAL-INTENSIVE (CAPITAL[2]).

the ˈLabour Party (*Brit politics* 政) one of the major political parties in Britain, representing esp the interests of workers 工党(英国主要政党之一, 主要代表工人利益). Cf 参看 THE CONSERVATIVE PARTY (CONSERVATIVE), THE LIBERAL DEMOCRATS (LIBERAL).

ˈlabour-saving *adj* [usu attrib 通常作定语] designed to reduce the amount of work or effort needed to do sth 省力的; 节省劳力的: *labour-saving devices*, eg a lawn-mower, a washing-machine 节省劳力的机械(如刈草机、洗衣机).

la·bour[2] (*US* **la·bor**) /ˈleɪbə(r); ˋlebɚ/ *v* **1** [I, Ipr, Ip, It] work or try hard 劳动; 工作; 努力: *labour on/at a task* 努力做某项工作 ○ *I've been labouring (away) over a hot stove all morning.* 我一上午都在热炉前忙个不停. ○ *He laboured to finish the job on time.* 他努力按时完成了任务. **2** (**a**) [I, Ipr, It] do sth only with difficulty and effort 吃力地做某事物: *The old man laboured up the hillside.* 老人吃力地登山. ○ *The ship laboured through the rough seas.* 船在波涛汹涌的海上挣扎前行. ○ *labouring to breathe* 吃力地呼吸. (**b**) [I] (of an engine) work slowly and with difficulty (指发动机)工作缓慢而费力: *You should change gear — the engine's starting to labour.* 你该换挡了——发动机有些吃不住劲了. **3** (idm 习语) **ˈlabour the point** continue to repeat or explain sth that has already been said and understood 一再重复或解释已经说过的或已为人明白的事情: *Your argument was clear to us from the start — there's no need to labour the point.* 你的论点一开头我们就清楚了——没必要一再重复. **4** (phr v) **labour under sth** (*fml* 文) (**a**) suffer because of (a disadvantage or difficulty) 因(不利或困难)而苦恼; 苦于: *people labouring under the handicaps of ignorance and superstition* 为愚昧和迷信所苦的人们. (**b**) be deceived or misled by sth 被某事物蒙蔽或误导: *He labours under the delusion that he's a fine actor.* 他有个错觉, 以为自己是个好演员.

▷ **la·boured** (*US* **la·bored**) *adj* **1** slow and difficult 缓慢而困难的: *laboured breathing* 艰难的呼吸. **2** showing signs of too much effort; not natural or spontaneous 吃力的; 不流畅的; 不自然的: *a laboured style of writing* 矫

揉造作的文体. Cf 参看 LABORIOUS 2.

la·bourer (*US* **la·borer**) /ˈleɪbərə(r); ˋlebərɚ/ *n* person who does heavy unskilled work 劳工; 工人: *a farm labourer* 农场工人.

la·burnum /ləˈbɜːnəm; ləˋbɝnəm/ *n* [C, U] small ornamental tree with hanging clusters of yellow flowers 金链花(观赏植物, 株小, 总状花序下垂, 呈黄色).

laby·rinth /ˈlæbərɪnθ; ˋlæbəˌrɪnθ/ *n* complicated network of winding passages, paths, etc through which it is difficult to find one's way 迷宫: *The old building was a labyrinth of dark corridors.* 那古老建筑是一座长廊纵横光线昏暗的迷宫. ○ (*fig* 比喻) *go through a real labyrinth of procedures to get a residence permit* 为获得居住许可证履行繁琐的手续. Cf 参看 MAZE. ▷ **laby·rinth·ine** /ˌlæbəˈrɪnθaɪn; *US* -θɪn; ˌlæbəˋrɪnθɪn/ *adj*.

lace 透孔织物

lace /leɪs; les/ *n* **1** [U] delicate fabric with an ornamental openwork design of threads 透孔织品; 网眼花边: *a wedding dress made of lace* 透孔婚纱礼服 ○ [attrib 作定语] *lace curtains* 网眼纱帘. ⇨illus 见插图. **2** [C] string or cord threaded through holes or hooks in shoes, etc to pull and hold two edges together 鞋带; 系带: *a pair of ˈshoe-laces* 一副鞋带 ○ *a broken lace* 一条断的带子. ⇨ illus at SHOE 见 SHOE 插图.

▷ **lace** *v* **1** [I, Ip, Tn, Tn·p] **~ (sth) (up)** fasten (sth) with laces 用系带系牢(某物): *a blouse that laces (up) at the front* 前襟系带的女衬衫 ○ *lace (up) one's shoes* 系鞋带. **2** [Tn, Tn·pr] **~ sth (with sth)** flavour or strengthen (a drink) with a small amount of spirits 在(饮料)中加入少量烈性酒: *a glass of milk laced with rum* 一杯掺了朗姆酒的奶 ○ *My drink has been laced.* 我的饮料中已加过酒了. **3** (phr v) **lace into sb** (*infml* 口) attack sb physically or with words 打、攻击或抨击某人.

□ ˈ**lace-ups** *n* [pl] shoes that are fastened with laces 系带的鞋: *She has to wear lace-ups at school.* 她上学得穿系带的鞋.

la·cer·ate /ˈlæsəreɪt; ˋlæsəˌret/ *v* [Tn] **1** injure (flesh) by tearing 撕伤(肌肉): *The sharp stones lacerated his feet.* 尖石把他的脚划伤了. **2** (*fig fml* 比喻, 文) hurt (the feelings) 伤害(感情).

▷ **la·cera·tion** /ˌlæsəˈreɪʃn; ˌlæsəˋreʃən/ *n* (**a**) [U] tearing of the flesh (肌肉的)撕裂, 划破. (**b**) [C] injury caused by this 破口; 裂伤: *facial lacerations* 脸部撕裂的伤口.

lach·rymal /ˈlækrɪml; ˋlækrəml̩/ *adj* [attrib 作定语] (*anatomy* 解) producing or concerned with tears or weeping 生泪的; 眼泪的; 哭泣的: *lachrymal glands, ducts, etc* 泪腺、泪管.

lach·rym·ose /ˈlækrɪməʊs; ˋlækrəˌmos/ *adj* (*fml* 文) in the habit of weeping; tearful; mournful 爱哭的; 含泪的; 哀痛的: *a lachrymose disposition* 生性爱哭.

lack /læk; læk/ *v* **1** [Tn no passive 不用于被动语态] be without (sth); have less than enough of 没有(某事物); 缺乏; 缺少; 不足: *lack creativity, self-discipline, courage* 缺乏创造性、自制力、勇气 ○ *They lacked the money to send him to university.* 他们没钱送他上大学. ○ *What he lacks in experience he makes up for in enthusiasm.* 他热心工作以弥补其经验的不足. **2** [Ipr no passive 不用于被动语态] **~ for sth** (*fml* 文) need sth 需要某事物: *They lacked for nothing,* ie had everything they wanted. 他们无所需求(已应有尽有). **3** (idm 习语) **be ˈlacking** not be available when needed 不敷所需: *Money for the project is still lacking.* 进行这个项目的钱还没有着落. **be lacking in sth** not have enough of sth 不足; 不够: *be lacking in warmth, courage, strength* 缺乏温暖、勇气、力气 ○ *The film was lacking in pace.* 这部影片不紧凑. **have/lack the courage of one's convictions** ⇨ COURAGE.

▷ **lack** *n* [U, sing] absence or shortage (of sth that is needed) (所需事物的)缺乏, 短缺: *a lack of care, money, water* 缺乏关心、金钱、水 ○ *The project had to be abandoned for* (ie because of) *lack of funds.* 工程因资金匮乏只得放弃.

□ ˈ**lack-lustre** *adj* dull; uninspiring; lifeless 无光泽的; 死气沉沉的; 无生气的: *lack-lustre eyes* 暗无光泽的眼睛 ○ *They gave a lack-lustre performance.* 他们的演出死气沉沉.

lacka·dais·ical /ˌlækəˈdeɪzɪkl; ˌlækəˋdezɪkl̩/ *adj* lacking vigour and determination; unenthusiastic 无精打采的; 无决断的; 不热心的: *a lackadaisical approach to his studies* 他在学习方面的懒散态度. ▷ **lacka·dais·ic·ally** /-klɪ; -klɪ/ *adv*.

lackey /ˈlækɪ; ˋlækɪ/ *n* **1** (formerly) footman or manservant, usu in special uniform (旧时)听差, 男仆(通常穿制服). **2** (*fig derog* 比喻, 贬) person who acts or is treated like a servant 卑躬屈膝的人; 被待如奴仆的人: *The singer was surrounded by the usual crowd of lackeys and hangers-on.* 那个歌手让那帮总是溜须拍马、前呼后拥的人给围住了.

lac·onic /ləˈkɒnɪk; ləˋkɑnɪk/ *adj* using few words; terse 简洁的; 简明的: *a laconic person, remark, style* 说话简洁的人、言简意赅的话、简练质朴的文体. ▷ **lac·on·ic·ally** /-klɪ; -klɪ/ *adv*: *'Too bad,' she replied laconically.* '那可没办法,'她回答得很干脆.

lac·quer /ˈlækə(r); ˋlækɚ/ *n* [U] **1** varnish used on metal or wood to give a hard glossy surface 漆. **2** (*becoming dated* 渐旧) liquid sprayed on the hair to keep it in place 喷发胶(使头发定型的喷剂).

▷ **lac·quer** *v* [Tn] coat (sth) with lacquer 给(某物)涂漆; 给(头发)喷喷发胶: *a lacquered table* 上过漆的桌子 ○ *lacquered hair* 喷过发胶的头发.

la·crosse /ləˈkrɒs; *US* -ˈkrɔːs; ləˋkrɔs/ *n* [U] game like hockey, played by two teams of 10 players each who use rackets to catch, carry and throw the ball 兜网球(类似曲棍球的游戏, 由两队各10人参赛, 以带网兜的球棒接球、带球、传球).

lacta·tion /lækˈteɪʃn; lækˋteʃən/ *n* [U] (*medical or biology* 医或生) **1** production of milk in the breasts of women or the udders of female animals 泌乳. **2** time during which this happens 泌乳期.

lactic /ˈlæktɪk; ˋlæktɪk/ *adj* [esp attrib 尤作定语] of or from milk 乳的; 来自乳汁的.

□ ˌ**lactic** ˈ**acid** (*chemistry* 化) acid that forms in sour milk 乳酸.

lact·ose /ˈlæktəʊs, -əʊz; ˋlæktos, -oz/ *n* [U] (*chemistry* 化) form of sugar found in milk and used in some baby foods 乳糖.

la·cuna /ləˈkjuːnə; ləˋkjunə/ *n* (*pl* **-nae** /-niː; -ni/ or **~s**) (*fml* 文) section missing from a book, an argument, etc; gap (书籍、论据等中的)脱漏, 阙文, 缺漏, 空白: *a lacuna in the manuscript* 原稿中的脱漏.

lacy /ˈleɪsɪ; ˋlesɪ/ *adj* (**-ier**, **-iest**) of or like lace 透孔织物的; 网眼状的; 系带的: *the lacy pattern of a spider's web* 蜘蛛网的形状.

lad /læd; læd/ *n* **1** boy; young man 男孩儿; 男青年; 小伙子: *The town's changed a lot since I was a lad.* 从我幼时至今, 这小城市已有了很大变化. **2** (*infml* 口) (esp in N England 尤用于英格兰北部) fellow; chap 伙伴; 傢伙: *The lads at the office have sent you a get-well card.* 办公室的哥儿们给你寄慰问卡来了. **3** (*Brit infml approv* 口, 褒) lively, daring or reckless man (used esp in the expressions shown) 活泼、大胆或鲁莽的男子(尤用于以下示例): *He's quite a lad/a bit of a lad.* 他可是个莽撞傢伙.

lad·der /ˈlædə(r); ˋlædɚ/ *n* **1** structure for climbing up and down sth, consisting of two upright lengths of wood, metal or rope joined to each other by crossbars (*rungs*) used as steps 梯子. ⇨illus 见插图. **2** (*US* **run**) fault in a stocking, etc where some stitches have come undone, causing a vertical ladder-like flaw (长统袜等的)梯形裂缝, 抽丝. **3** (*fig* 比喻) series of stages by which a person may advance in his career, etc (事业等发迹、进身、晋升等的)阶梯, 途径, 门路: *climbing the ladder of success* 攀登成功的阶梯 ○ *He is still on the bottom rung of the political ladder.* 他尚处于政治阶梯的最低一级.

▷ **lad·der** *v* (**a**) [I] (of stockings, etc) develop a ladder(2) (指长统袜等)出现梯形裂缝, 抽丝: *Have you any tights*

L

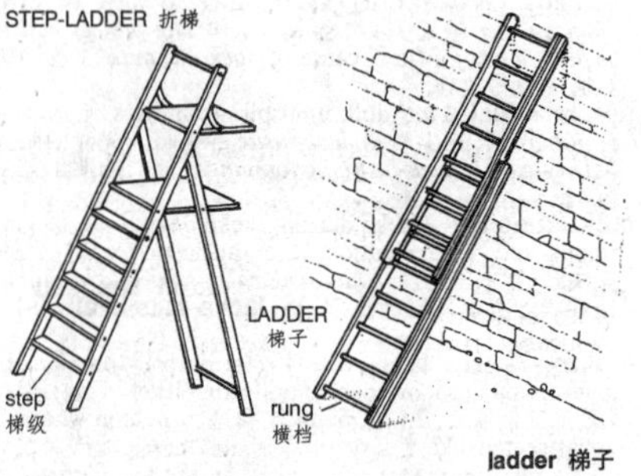

ladder 梯子

that won't ladder? 有没有不易抽丝的裤袜? (**b**) [Tn] cause (stockings, etc) to develop a ladder 使(长统袜等)出现梯形裂缝, 抽丝: *She laddered her new tights climbing the fence.* 她爬越篱笆时把她的新裤袜给勾得抽了丝.

lad·die /ˈlædɪ; ˋlædɪ/ *n* (*infml esp Scot* 口, 尤用于苏格兰) boy; young man 男孩儿; 男青年; 小伙子. Cf 参看 LASS.

laden /ˈleɪdn; ˋledn̩/ *adj* [usu pred 通常作表语] **1** ~ **(with sth)** loaded or weighted 装满的; 满载的: *trees laden with apples* 果实满枝的苹果树 ○ *a lorry laden with supplies* 满载供应品的卡车 ○ *shoppers with their baskets fully laden* 篮子装得满满的那些买东西的人. **2** ~ **with sth** (*fig* 比喻) (of a person) troubled or burdened with sth (指人)因某事而苦恼的, 负担沉重的: *laden with guilt, grief, remorse, etc* 负咎沉重的、被悲哀压抑着的、无限懊恼的.

la-di-da /ˌlɑːdɪˈdɑː; ˌlɑdɪˋdɑ/ *adj* (*infml usu derog* 口, 通常作贬义) having an affected manner or pronunciation; pretentious 做作的; 拿腔拿调的; 装模作样的: *I can't stand her or her la-di-da friends.* 我受不了她或她那些惺惺作态的朋友.

ladle /ˈleɪdl; ˋledl̩/ *n* long-handled cup-shaped spoon for serving or transferring liquids 长把勺: *a 'soup ladle* 长柄汤勺. ⇨illus at KITCHEN 见 KITCHEN 插图.

▷ **ladle** *v* **1** [Tn, Tn·pr, Tn·p] ~ **sth (out)** serve (food) with a ladle or in large quantities (用勺)舀或盛很多(食物): *She ladled cream over her pudding.* 她在布丁上浇了一大勺奶油. ○ *ladling out the stew* 把炖菜舀出来. **2** (phr v) **ladle sth out** (*infml* 口) distribute sth (too) lavishly (过分)慷慨地施予某物: *He isn't one to ladle out praise, so when he says 'Good', he means it.* 他可不轻易夸奖人, 所以他要是说'好', 他一定认为真好.

lady /ˈleɪdɪ; ˋledɪ/ *n* **1** [C] woman of good manners and dignified behaviour 举止文雅的女子; 淑女: *She's a real lady — never loses her temper.* 她是个有教养的女子——从来不发脾气. Cf 参看 GENTLEMAN. **2** [C] (esp formerly) woman of good family and social position (尤指旧时)出身高贵有地位的女子: *She was a lady by birth.* 她出身高贵. **3** [C] (esp in polite use) woman (尤作礼貌用语)女士, 夫人, 小姐: *Ask that lady to help you.* 请那位小姐帮你忙吧. ○ *The lady at the tourist office told me it opened at 1 pm.* 旅行社的那位小姐告诉我下午一点开门. ○ *the old lady next door* 隔壁那位老太太 ○ *the 'tea-lady* 女勤杂工 ○ [attrib 作定语] *a lady doctor* 女医师. **4** [C] (*US infml* 口) (used as a term of address 用作称呼) woman 女士; 太太; 夫人; 小姐: *Hey lady — you can't park there!* 嘿, 小姐——那儿不能停车! **5 Lady** (**a**) (esp in the UK) title used with the surname of the wives of some nobles (尤指在英国)夫人(某些贵族妻子的尊称, 用时带姓): *Lady (Randolph) Churchill* (伦道夫·)邱吉尔夫人. (**b**) (esp in the UK) title used with the first name of the daughters of some nobles (尤指在英国)小姐(某些贵族女儿的尊称, 用时带名): *Lady Philippa (Stewart)* 菲利帕(·斯图尔特)小姐. (**c**) part of an official title of respect 官衔敬称的一部分: *Lady 'Mayoress* (女)市长阁下 ○ *Lady 'President* (女)总统阁下. **6 Ladies** [sing *v*](*Brit*) women's public lavatory 女厕所: *Is there a Ladies near here?* 附近有女厕所吗? **7** (idm 习语) **the ˌlady of the ˈhouse** woman with authority in a household 女主人; 主妇: *Might I speak to the lady of the house?* 我可以和府上女主人说句话吗? **one's young lady/young man** ⇨ YOUNG.

□ **ˈLady Chapel** chapel in a large church, dedicated to the Virgin Mary (大教堂中的)圣母堂.

ˈLady Day the Feast of the Annunciation, 25 March 圣母领报节(3月25日).

ˌlady-in-ˈwaiting *n* (*pl* **ladies-in-waiting**) lady attending a queen or princess (伺候女王或公主的)宫女.

ˈlady-killer *n* (*infml often derog* 口, 常作贬义) man with the reputation of being very popular and successful with women 使女子倾心的男子.

ˈladylike *adj* (*approv* 褒) like or suitable for a lady; polite; dignified; delicate 淑女的; 适合淑女身分的; 端庄的; 文雅的: *ladylike behaviour, speech* 淑女般高雅的举止、谈吐 ○ *She drank her wine with small ladylike sips.* 她文雅地一小口一小口喝着葡萄酒.

ˈladyship (also **Ladyship**) *n* title used in speaking to or about a titled lady 夫人, 小姐(称呼或提及有头衔的女子时用作尊称): *their ladyships* 夫人 ○ *If your ladyship will step this way, please.* 小姐, 请这边走. ○ (*ironic or joc* 反语或谑) *Watch out, Jill — her ladyship is in one of her moods!* 吉尔, 小心为妙——小姐大人可有点不高兴了!

ˈlady's man (also **ladies' man**) man who is fond of the company of women 好与女子相处的男子.

1 POLITE ADDRESS **Ladies** and **gentlemen** are used as the plural forms of **sir** and **madam**. 称谓敬辞: **ladies** 和 **gentlemen** 用作 **sir** 和 **madam** 的复数.

OCCASION 使用场合	SINGULAR 单数	PLURAL 复数
giving a public speech 演讲时		**Ladies and gentlemen**, I would like to thank ...
in a shop 在商店中	Yes, **sir**/**madam**, will there be anything else?	Good morning, **ladies**/**gentlemen**, can I help you?
writing formal letters 公文书信	Dear **Sir**/**Madam**, Thank you for your ...	**Gentlemen**, (very formal 极郑重) Dear **Sirs**, ..(less formal 较郑重) (There is no plural form of **madam** * **madam** 无复数)

2 REFERRING TO PEOPLE **Lady** and **gentleman** are used instead of **woman** and **man** to show politeness. 间接敬称: 要用 **lady** 和 **gentleman**, 不要用 **woman** 和 **man**.

with the person present 所指的人在场时	Mr Smith, this **lady**/**gentleman** wishes to make a complaint.
describing behaviour 形容行为时	He's very **gentlemanly**. She's very **ladylike**.
approving behaviour 称赞行为时	He's/She's a real **gentleman**/**lady**.
referring to public toilets 称公共厕所	the **Gents** (*US* the **men's room**) the **Ladies** (*US* the **ladies' room**) Where's the **Gents**, please? Where's the **Ladies**, please?

lady·bird /ˈleɪdɪbɜːd; ˋledɪˌbɝd/ (*US* **lady·bug** /ˈleɪdɪˈbʌg; ˋledɪˌbʌg/) *n* small flying beetle, reddish-brown or yellow with black spots 瓢虫.

lag[1] /læg; læg/ *v* **(-gg-)** [I, Ipr, Ip] ~ **(behind sb/sth)**; ~ **(behind)** go too slow; fail to keep pace with others 走得极慢; 落后: *The small boy soon became tired and lagged far behind (the rest of the walkers).* 那小男孩儿不

L

久就走不动了, 远远落在(其他人的)后面. ○ (*fig* 比喻) *Prices are rising sharply, while incomes are lagging far behind.* 物价飞涨而收入却远远落后.

▷ **lag** (also ˈ**time-lag**) *n* period of time separating two events, esp an action and its effect; delay (两事件之间的)时间间隔; (尤指行动与效果之间的)时间差, 迟缓, 延搁: *a lag of several seconds between the lightning and the thunder* 闪电与打雷先后相差的几秒钟.

lag[2] /læg; læg/ *v* (**-gg-**) [Tn, Tn·pr] **~ sth (with sth)** cover (pipes, boilers, etc) with insulating material to prevent freezing of water or loss of heat 给(管道、锅炉等)包扎或安装绝缘材料(以防冻或保温).

▷ **lag·ging** *n* [U] material used for this 绝缘材料.

la·ger /ˈlɑːɡə(r); ˈlɑɡɚ/ *n* **1** [U] type of light pale beer 贮藏啤酒. **2** [C] glass or bottle of this 一杯或一瓶贮藏啤酒.

lag·gard /ˈlæɡəd; ˈlæɡɚd/ *n* person who lags behind 迟到者; 落后者: *He's no laggard when it comes to asking for more money*, ie He is very quick to do this. 到多要钱时他可不甘后人.

la·goon /ləˈɡuːn; ləˈɡun/ *n* **1** salt-water lake separated from the open sea by sandbanks or coral reefs 泻湖. **2** (*US or Austral or NZ* 美或澳或新西兰) small shallow freshwater lake near a larger lake or river (大湖或江河附近的)小而浅的淡水湖.

lah (also **la**) /lɑː; lɑ/ *n* (*music* 音) sixth note in the sol-fa scale 全音阶唱名的第六音.

laid *pt, pp* of LAY[1].

laid-back/ˌleɪd ˈbæk; ˈledˈbæk/ *adj* (*infml* 口) (of a person or his behaviour) calm and relaxed (指人或人的行为)安详的, 轻松的: *She always seems so laid-back.* 她总是显得那么优哉游哉. *a ˌlaid-back ˈstyle, ˈmanner, etc* 闲适的风格、举止等.

lain *pp* of LIE[2].

lair /leə(r); lɛr/ *n* **1** sheltered place where a wild animal regularly sleeps or rests; den (野兽的)巢穴, 窝. **2** (*fig* 比喻) person's hiding place (人的)藏身处: *The kidnappers' lair was an old farm in the hills.* 绑架者的藏身处是山里的一座旧农场.

laird /leəd; lɛrd/ *n* (*Scot* 苏格兰) landowner 地主.

laisser-faire (also **laissez-faire**) /ˌleɪseɪ ˈfeə(r); ˌleseˈfɛr/ *n* [U] (*French* 法) policy of freedom from government control, esp for private commercial interests 自由放任政策(尤指政府不干涉私人商业利益者): [attrib 作定语] *a ˌlaisser-faire eˈconomy* 自由放任的经济.

la·ity /ˈleɪətɪ; ˈleətɪ/ *n* **the laity** [Gp] **1** all the members of a Church who are not ordained clergymen; laymen (别于教会神职人员的)普通信徒. Cf 参看 CLERGY. **2** people outside a particular profession (contrasted with those inside it) 门外汉; 外行.

lake[1] /leɪk; lek/ *n* **1** large area of water surrounded by land 湖: *We sail on the lake in summer.* 夏天我们在湖上泛舟. ○ *Lake Victoria* 维多利亚湖 ○ *the Great Lakes* 五大湖. **2** (idm 习语) **jump in the/a lake** ⇨ JUMP 2.

□ **the ˈLake District** (also **the Lakes**) region of lakes and mountains in NW England 湖区(位于英格兰西北部). ⇨illus at App 1 见附录1插图, pages xiv, xv.

ˈ**Lake Poets** English romantic poets, esp Wordsworth, Coleridge and Southey, who lived in the Lake District 湖畔诗人(英国浪漫主义诗人, 尤指住在湖区的华兹华斯、柯尔律治和骚塞).

lake[2] /leɪk; lek/ *n* (also ˌ**crimson ˈlake**) [U] dark red colouring material 深红色颜料.

lakh /læk, lɑːk; læk, lɑk/ *n* (in India and Pakistan) one hundred thousand (印度和巴基斯坦的)十万: *50 lakhs of rupees* 500 万卢比.

lam[1] /læm; læm/ *v* (**-mm-**) (*sl* 俚) **1** [Tn] hit (sb/sth) hard; thrash 狠打(某人[某物]); 鞭打. **2** (phr v) **lam into sb** attack sb, physically or verbally 打、攻击或抨击某人: *My father really lammed into me for damaging his car.* 因为我把父亲的汽车弄坏了, 他把我狠狠打了一顿.

lam[2] /læm; læm/ *n* (*US sl* 俚) **1** sudden escape 突然逃走. **2** (idm 习语) **on the lam** escaping or hiding, esp from the police 在逃, 逃匿(尤指逃避警方追缉).

lama /ˈlɑːmə; ˈlɑmə/ *n* Buddhist priest or monk in Tibet or Mongolia 喇嘛(中国西藏或蒙古的佛教僧侣).

▷ **la·mas·ery** /ˈlɑːməsərɪ; *US* -serɪ; ˈlɑməˌserɪ/ *n* building or group of buildings where lamas live together; monastery 喇嘛寺院.

lamb /læm; læm/ *n* **1** (**a**) [C] young sheep 羔羊; 小羊. ⇨illus at SHEEP 见 SHEEP 插图. Cf 参看 EWE. (**b**) [U] its flesh as food 小羊肉; 羔羊肉: *a leg of lamb* 羔羊腿肉 ○ [attrib 作定语] *lamb chops* 小羊排. Cf 参看 MUTTON. **2** (*infml* 口) gentle or dear person 温顺的人; 亲爱的人. **3** (idm 习语) **one may/might as well be hanged/hung for a sheep as a lamb** ⇨ HANG[1]. **like a lamb (to the slaughter)** without resisting or protesting 不加反抗; 驯服地: *She surprised us all on her first day of school by going off like a lamb.* 我们感到惊奇的是开学第一天她就乖乖地上学去了. **mutton dressed as lamb** ⇨ MUTTON.

▷ **lamb** *v* [I] **1** (of a ewe) give birth to lambs (指母羊)产羔羊: *lambing ewes* 产羔羊的母羊. **2** (of a farmer) tend ewes doing this (指农民)照料母羊产羔: *the lambing season*, ie when lambs are born 产羔羊的季节.

□ ˈ**lambskin** *n* **1** [C] skin of a lamb with its wool on (used to make coats, gloves, etc) 羔羊皮毛(用以制外套、手套等). **2** [U] leather made from this 羔羊皮革.

ˈ**lamb's-wool** *n* [U] soft fine fluffy wool from lambs, used for making knitted clothes 羔羊毛纱: *a scarf made of lamb's-wool* 细羊毛围巾 ○ [attrib 作定语] *a lamb's-wool cardigan* 细羊毛对襟毛衣.

lam·baste /læmˈbeɪst; læmˈbest/ *v* [Tn] (*infml* 口) **1** hit (sb) hard and repeatedly; thrash 不断地狠打(某人); 鞭打. **2** reprimand (sb) severely 严厉斥责(某人).

lam·bent /ˈlæmbənt; ˈlæmbənt/ *adj* [esp attrib 尤作定语] **1** (of a flame) moving over a surface with soft flickering radiance (指火焰)轻轻摇曳的, 闪烁的. **2** (of the eyes, sky, etc) shining or glowing softly (指眼睛、天空等)微微发光的. **3** (of humour, style, etc) witty in a brilliant but gentle way (指幽默、风格等)诙谐的. ▷ **lam·bency** /-ənsɪ; -ənsɪ/ *n* [U].

lame /leɪm; lem/ *adj* **1** unable to walk normally because of an injury or defect 瘸的; 跛的: *The accident made him lame in the left leg.* 出事后他的左腿瘸了. ○ *Halfway through the race the horse went lame.* 那匹马赛跑中途跛了腿. **2** (of an excuse or argument) weak and unconvincing (指借口或论据)蹩脚的, 软弱无力的, 无说服力的. **3** (idm 习语) **help a lame dog over a stile** ⇨ HELP[1]. **a ˌlame ˈduck** (**a**) person, organization or thing that is in difficulties and unable to manage without help 处于困境无法自理的人、组织或事物: *The government should not waste money supporting lame ducks.* 政府不应浪费资金去扶持那些无望的企业. (**b**) (*esp US*) elected official in his final period of office (任期将满的)官员: [attrib 作定语] *a ˌlame duck ˈPresident* 即将卸任的总统.

▷ **lame** *v* [Tn] make (a person or an animal) lame; disable 使(人或动物)跛, 瘸; 使残废: *lamed in a riding accident* 骑马摔瘸了腿.

lamely *adv*.

lame·ness *n* [U].

lamé /ˈlɑːmeɪ; *US* lɑːˈmeɪ; lɑˈme/ *n* [U] fabric in which gold or silver thread is interwoven with silk, wool or cotton (丝、毛、棉与金线或银线的)交织锦缎: [attrib 作定语] *a silver lamé evening gown* 银光缎女装晚礼服.

la·ment /ləˈment; ləˈmɛnt/ *v* (**a**) [I, Ipr, Tn] **~ (for/over sb/sth)** feel or express great sorrow or regret for (sb/sth) 为(某人[某事物])感到悲痛; 哀悼; 痛惜: *lament loudly* 哀嚎 ○ *lament (for) a dead friend* 哀悼亡友 ○ *lament (over) one's misfortunes* 悲叹自己的不幸 ○ *lament the passing of old ways* 浩叹古风的沉沦. (**b**) [I, Tn] complain (about sth) 抱怨(某事): *She's always lamenting the lack of sports facilities in town.* 她总是抱怨伦敦缺少体育设施.

▷ **la·ment** *n* **1** strong expression of grief 悲恸. **2** song or poem expressing grief; dirge 挽歌; 哀诗: *a funeral lament* 挽歌.

lam·ent·able /ˈlæməntəbl; ˈlæməntəbl̩/ *adj* regrettable; deplorable 惋惜的; 可悲的: *a lamentable loss of life, lack of foresight* 令人悲叹的生命损失、缺乏远见. ˈ**lam·ent·ably** /-əblɪ; -əblɪ/ *adv*.

lam·enta·tion /ˌlæmenˈteɪʃn; ˌlæmənˈteʃən/ *n* **1** [U] lamenting 悲痛; 哀悼; 痛惜; 抱怨: *Much lamentation followed the death of the old king.* 老国王晏驾, 人们悲恸不已. **2** [C] expression of grief; lament 悲叹; 挽歌; 哀诗.

la·mented *adj* (*rhet or joc* 修辞或谑) mourned for; regretted 悲叹的；痛惜的: *the much lamented pound note* 那张令人痛惜的一镑的钞票 ○ *our late lamented friend* 令我们惋惜的故友.

lam·in·ate /ˈlæmɪneɪt; ˋlæmə,net/ *v* [Tn] **1** make (material) by bonding thin layers together (将薄片砌合在一起)制成(材料): *laminated plastic* 层积塑材. **2** beat or roll (metal) into thin sheets 将(金属)锻压成薄片.

▷ **lam·in·ate** /ˈlæmɪnət; ˋlæmɪn,et/ *n* [U] laminated material 层压材料.

lamp /læmp; læmp/ *n* **1** device for giving light, either by the use of electricity or (esp formerly) by burning gas or oil 电灯; (尤指旧时的)煤气灯, 油灯: *a street, table, bicycle lamp* 街灯、台灯、自行车车灯. **2** electrical device producing radiation (for medical, etc purposes) 发出热射线的电器装置(供医疗等用者): *an infra-red/ultraviolet lamp* 红外线[紫外线]灯.

□ ˈ**lampblack** *n* [U] black colouring matter made from soot 灯黑(从煤烟中制取, 作颜料用).

ˈ**lamplight** *n* [U] light from a lamp 灯光.

ˈ**lamplighter** *n* (formerly) person whose job was to light and extinguish gas street lamps (旧时)(专事点熄路灯的)灯夫.

ˈ**lamp-post** *n* tall post supporting a street lamp 路灯柱. ⇨illus at App 1 见附录1插图, page vi.

ˈ**lampshade** *n* cover (made of glass, cloth, etc) placed over a lamp to soften or screen its light 灯罩.

lam·poon /læmˈpuːn; læmˋpun/ *n* piece of writing that attacks and ridicules a person, a book, an institution, etc 讽刺文章.

▷ **lam·poon** *v* [Tn] publicly ridicule (sb/sth) in a lampoon, etc 用作品等讽刺或嘲笑(某人[某事物]): *His cartoons mercilessly lampooned the leading politicians of the day.* 他的讽刺漫画无情地挖苦了当今的政界要人.

lam·prey /ˈlæmprɪ; ˋlæmprɪ/ *n* eel-like water animal with a round sucking mouth which it uses to attach itself to other creatures 七鳃鳗(亦称八目鳗).

lance[1] /lɑːns; *US* læns; læns/ *n* **1** weapon used for catching fish, etc with a long wooden shaft and a pointed steel head 鱼叉. **2** (formerly) similar weapon used by mounted knights, cavalry, etc (旧时)骑士、骑兵等的长矛.

▷ **lan·cer** *n* soldier of a cavalry regiment formerly armed with lances 枪骑兵(旧时执矛).

□ ˌ**lance-ˈcorporal** *n* (in the British army or US Marines) non-commissioned officer of the lowest rank (英国陆军或美国海军陆战队中的)一等兵. ⇨App 9 见附录9.

lance[2] /lɑːns; *US* læns; læns/ *v* [Tn] prick or cut open (sth) with a lancet (用外科手术刀)刺或切开(某物): *lance an abscess, a boil, a swelling, etc* 切开脓肿、疖子、肿胀处等.

lan·cet /ˈlɑːnsɪt; *US* ˈlæn-; ˋlænsɪt/ *n* **1** (*medical* 医) sharp pointed two-edged surgical instrument used for opening abscesses, etc 柳叶刀(外科手术用的). **2** (*architecture* 建) tall narrow pointed arch or window 尖拱; 尖窗.

land[1] /lænd; lænd/ *n* **1** [U] solid part of the earth's surface (contrasted with sea or water) 陆地; 大地: *travel over land* 陆路旅行 ○ *be on, reach, come to land* 在陆地上、抵达陆地、到陆地上 ○ *The journey to the far side of the island is quicker by land than by sea*, ie by car, train, etc than by boat. 走陆路至海岛的另一端比从海路走快捷. ○ *On land the turtle is ungainly, but in the water it is very agile.* 龟在陆地上行动笨拙, 在水里则很灵活. **2** [U] expanse of country 地域: *The land west of the mountains stretched as far as the eye could see.* 群山以西的地域一望无际. **3** [U] (**a**) ground or soil of the same type (同一类型的)地带: *rich, stony, forest land* 肥沃、多岩、森林地带. (**b**) ground or soil as used for a particular purpose (作某种用途的)地, 土地: *farming land* 农业用地 ○ *arable land* 可耕地 ○ *The city suffers from a shortage of building land*, ie land on which to build houses. 该市极缺乏建筑用地. **4 the land** [U] (**a**) ground or soil used for farming 田地; 耕地: *working the land* 种地. (**b**) rural areas as contrasted with cities and towns 农村; 农业地区: *Many farmers are leaving the land to work in industry.* 很多农民离开农村转事工业劳动. **5** (**a**) [U] property in the form of land 地产; 田产: *How far does your land extend?* 你的地产远至何处? ○ *a house with a hundred acres of land adjoining it* 方圆带有一百英亩土地的住宅 ○ *land for sale* 地皮出让. (**b**) **lands** [pl] estates 私有土地. **6** [C] (*rhet* 修辞) country, state or nation 国家: *my native land* 我的祖国 ○ *the finest orchestra in the land* 国家最优秀的管弦乐队 ○ (*fig* 比喻) *the land of dreams* 梦乡. ⇨Usage at COUNTRY 用法见COUNTRY. **7** (idm 习语) **in the ˌland of the ˈliving** (*joc* 谑) alive 在世; 活着. **the ˌland of ˈNod** (*joc* 谑) sleep 睡乡. **the lie of the land** ⇨ LIE[2]. **live off/on the fat of the land** ⇨ LIVE[2]. **live off the land** ⇨ LIVE[2]. **make ˈland** (*nautical* 海) see or reach the shore 看到陆地; 抵达海岸. **(be/go) on the ˈland** work as a farmer 种庄稼; 务农: *He left his office job to try to make a living on the land.* 他辞去了办公室的工作, 改以务农为生. **the promised land** ⇨ PROMISE[2]. **see, etc how the ˈland lies** learn what the situation is, how matters stand, etc 了解情况; 知悉现状等: *We'd better find out how the land lies before taking any action.* 我们最好把情况弄清楚再采取行动. **spy out the land** ⇨ SPY *v*.

▷ **landed** *adj* [attrib 作定语] owning much land 有大量土地的: *the landed classes/gentry* 地主阶级[有大量土地的绅士].

land·less *adj* not owning land 没有土地的.

□ ˈ**land-agent** *n* (*esp Brit*) person employed to manage an estate 地产管理人.

ˈ**land-breeze** *n* light wind blowing from the land towards the sea, usu after sunset 陆风(通常为日落后从陆地吹向海面的轻风).

ˈ**landfall** *n* (**a**) first sight of or approach to land after a journey by sea (航海中)初见或接近陆地: *We made a landfall at dusk after three weeks at sea.* 在海上航行三周后的一个黄昏, 我们看到了陆地. (**b**) land sighted or reached 望见或抵达的陆地: *Our next landfall should be Jamaica.* 我们下一靠岸处应是牙买加.

ˈ**land-form** *n* (*geology* 地质) natural feature of the surface of the earth 地貌.

ˈ**landholder** *n* owner or (esp) tenant of land 土地所有者; (尤指)土地租赁者.

ˈ**land-locked** *adj* almost or entirely surrounded by land 几乎或完全为陆地包围的; 陆围的; 内陆的: *a land-locked harbour, bay, inlet, etc* 内陆港、海湾、小水湾等 ○ *Switzerland is completely land-locked.* 瑞士完全是个内陆国.

ˈ**landlubber** *n* (*derog or joc* 贬或谑) person who is not accustomed to ships or to being at sea 不习惯坐船或航海的人.

ˈ**landmark** *n* **1** object, etc easily seen and recognized from a distance (自远处易辨识的)陆标, 地标: *The Empire State Building is a famous landmark on the New York skyline.* 帝国大厦是纽约高楼大厦中著名的地面标志物. **2** (*fig* 比喻) event, discovery, invention, etc that marks an important stage or turning-point 里程碑; 分水岭: *a landmark in the history of modern art* 现代艺术史上的里程碑 ○ [attrib 作定语] *a landmark decision, victory, speech* 划时代的决定、胜利、演说.

ˈ**land mass** large area of land 地块; 陆块: *several small islands separated from the main land mass by a deep channel* 与大陆之间有一条很深的水道相隔的几个小岛.

ˈ**land-mine** *n* explosive charge laid in or on the ground, detonated by vehicles, etc passing over it 地雷.

ˈ**land office** (*US*) office that records sales of public land 土地管理局. **land-office business** (*US infml* 口) fast and active business 生意兴隆.

ˈ**landowner** *n* person who owns (esp a large area of) land 地主; (尤指大片的)土地所有者: *one of the biggest single landowners* (ie individual people owning the most land) *in England* 英格兰最大的个体土地所有者.

ˈ**Land-rover** *n* (*propr* 专利名) strongly-built motor vehicle designed for use over rough ground or farm land 越野车(供在崎岖路面或农田上行驶的机动车).

ˈ**landslide** *n* **1** (also ˈ**landslip**) sliding of a mass of earth, rock, etc down the side of a mountain, cliff, etc (山坡、崖壁等的)崩塌, 滑坡. **2** (*fig* 比喻) overwhelming majority of votes for one side in an election 选举中一方选票占的压倒性多数: *Opinion*

L

polls forecast a Conservative landslide. 民意测验预示保守党有获得压倒性多数票的可能. ○ [attrib 作定语] *a landslide victory* 获压倒性多数票的胜利.

ˈ**landsman** /-mən; -mən/ *n* (*pl* **-men** /-mən; -mən/) person who is not a sailor 陆上工作的人(以别于海员).

ˈ**landward** /ˈlændwəd; ˈlændwɚd/ *adj* towards the land 朝陆地的; 向岸的: *on the landward side of the island* 岛的向陆一侧.

ˈ**landwards** *adv* going or facing towards the land 朝陆地; 向岸.

land[2] /lænd; lænd/ *v* **1** [I, Ipr, Tn, Tn·pr] **~ (sb/sth) (at...)** (cause sb/sth to) go on land from a ship; disembark (使某人[某物])登岸, 下船: *We landed at Dover.* 我们在多佛上岸. ○ *Troops have been landed at several points.* 部队已在几个地点登陆. **2** (**a**) [Tn, Tn·pr] bring (an aircraft) down to the ground, etc 使(飞行器)着陆等: *The pilot managed to land the damaged plane safely.* 飞行员设法让受到破坏的飞机安全着陆. (**b**) [I, Ipr] come down in this way 着陆: *We shall be landing (at Gatwick airport) shortly — please fasten your seat-belts.* 我们马上就要(在盖特威克机场)着陆——请大家系好座位上的安全带. **3** [I, Ipr] reach the ground after a jump or fall 跳落或跌落地面: *Try to catch the ball before it lands.* 要把球接住, 不要让它落地. ○ *He fell down the stairs, landing in a heap at the bottom.* 他从楼梯上摔下来, 直跌到楼梯底部滚成一团. **4** [Tn] bring (a fish) to land 将(鱼)拉上岸: *Fewer herring than usual have been landed this year.* 今年鲱鱼捕获量比往年少. **5** [Tn] (*infml* 口) succeed in obtaining (sth), esp against strong competition 获得(某物)(尤指经激烈竞争): *land a good job, a big contract, the prize* 获得一份好工作、大项目的合同、奖. **6** [Tn] (*sl* 俚) strike (a blow) 打(一记): *unable to land any good punches in the early rounds* 在最初的几个回合里未能击出好拳. **7** (idm 习语) **fall/land on one's feet** ⇨ FOOT[1]. **land sb one** (*sl* 俚) hit or punch sb 揍某人: *She landed him one in the eye.* 她一拳打在他的眼睛上. **8** (phr v) **land sb/oneself in sth** (*infml* 口) get sb/oneself into difficulties, etc 使某人[自己]陷入困境等: *This is a fine mess you've landed us in!* 这是你给我们惹的一大堆麻烦! ○ *He's really landed himself in it this time.* 这一回他可是自讨苦吃了. **land up (in...)** (*infml* 口) reach a final position or situation 最终到达某处或达到某状况: *Her hat flew off and landed up in the river.* 她的帽子让风刮跑落到河里了. ○ *You'll land up in prison at this rate*, ie if you continue to act in this way. 你一个劲儿这样做, 早晚得入狱. **land up doing sth** (*infml* 口) do sth in the end, esp reluctantly 终于做某事(尤指勉强地): *They landed up not only having to apologize but also offering to pay.* 他们最后不但同意道歉, 而且还要付款. ○ *Why is it that I always land up cleaning the bath?* 为什么总是该我来洗刷浴缸? **land sb with sth/sb** (*infml* 口) give sb (a task or burden) to deal with 要某人处理(某事)或承担(重责): *I found myself landed with three extra guests for dinner.* 我到时候才知道我得多招待三个客人吃饭. ○ *Don't try and land me with your responsibilities!* 你休想把你的责任推到我身上!

land·ing /ˈlændɪŋ; ˈlændɪŋ/ *n* **1** act of coming or bringing to land 登陆; 着陆: *during the Queen's landing from the Royal Yacht* 在女王从皇家游艇上下来时 ○ *Because of engine trouble the plane had to make an emergency landing*, ie come to land suddenly to avoid further danger or damage. 由于发动机出现故障, 飞机不得不紧急着陆. ○ *She slipped and fell, but had a soft landing on some cushions.* 她滑倒了, 好在是跌在一些垫子上了. **2** (also ˈ**landing-place**) place where people and goods may be landed from a boat or ship (船只)卸货处, 登陆处: *There is no safe landing on that coast.* 那一带海岸没有安全的登陆处. ○ *a convenient landing-place in a nearby sheltered cove* 附近避风雨的小海湾里一个便于卸货的地方. **3** level area at the top of a flight of stairs, or between one flight and another 楼梯平台: *Your room opens off the top landing.* 你的房门朝向顶层楼梯平台. ⇨illus at STAIR 见 STAIR 插图.

□ ˈ**landing-craft** *n* flat-bottomed naval craft designed for putting ashore troops and equipment 登陆艇.

ˈ**landing-field** (also ˈ**landing-strip**) *n* = AIRSTRIP (AIR).

ˈ**landing-gear** *n* [U] = UNDERCARRIAGE.

ˈ**landing-net** *n* (in angling) long-handled net used for landing a fish caught on a hook (垂钓术)抄网.

ˈ**landing-stage** *n* (usu floating) platform on which people and goods are landed from a boat 码头; (通常指)浮动码头, 栈桥.

land·lady /ˈlændleɪdɪ; ˈlænd,ledɪ/ *n* **1** woman who lets rooms, etc to tenants 女房东. **2** woman who keeps a public house or a boarding-house (酒店或寄宿舍的)女店主, 女主人. Cf 参看 LANDLORD.

land·lord /ˈlændlɔ:d; ˈlænd,lɔrd/ *n* **1** person who lets land, a house, a room, etc to a tenant 地主; 房东. **2** person who keeps a public house or a boarding-house (酒店或寄宿舍的)店主, 主人: *It's a nice pub, except for the landlord.* 酒店挺不错, 可是那店主却不怎么样. Cf 参看 LANDLADY. ⇨Usage at TENANT 用法见 TENANT.

land·scape /ˈlændskeɪp; ˈlændskep/ *n* **1** [C] scenery of an area of land (陆上)风景, 景色: *a bleak urban landscape* 单调的市区景色 ○ *Mountains dominate the Welsh landscape.* 重峦叠嶂构成威尔士的主要景色. **2** (**a**) [C] picture showing a view of the countryside 野外风景画: *an exhibition of landscapes by local artists* 本地画家的野外风景画展. (**b**) [U] this type of art 风景绘画. Cf 参看 PORTRAIT 1. **3** (idm 习语) **a blot on the landscape** ⇨ BLOT[1].

▷ **land·scape** *v* [Tn] improve the appearance of (a garden, park, etc) by means of landscape gardening 用园林艺术美化(花园、公园等).

□ ˌ**landscape** ˈ**gardening** laying out a garden, etc in a way that imitates natural scenery 造园术; 园林艺术.

lane /leɪn; len/ *n* **1** narrow country road or track, usu between hedges or banks 乡间小路(通常两边有树篱或斜坡). **2** (esp in place names) narrow street or alley between buildings (尤用作路名)小巷, 胡同: ˌ*Drury* ˈ*Lane* 德鲁里巷. ⇨Usage at ROAD 用法见 ROAD. **3** strip of road marked out for a single line of traffic (有标志的)单行车道: *the inside/near side lane* 内车道 ○ *the outside/off side lane* 外车道 ○ *the slow/fast/overtaking lane of a motorway* 高速公路上的慢行[快行/超车]车道. **4** route intended for or regularly used by ships or aircraft (船或飞机预定或定期的)航道, 航路, 航线: ˈ*shipping lanes* 大洋航线 ○ ˈ*ocean lanes* 远洋航线. **5** marked strip of track, water, etc for a competitor in a race (比赛用的有标志的)跑道, 泳道: *The world champion is in lane four.* 那个世界冠军在第四跑道. ⇨ Usage at PATH 用法见 PATH.

lan·guage /ˈlæŋgwɪdʒ; ˈlæŋgwɪdʒ/ *n* **1** [U] system of sounds, words, patterns, etc used by humans to communicate thoughts and feelings 语言: *the origins of language* 语言的起源 ○ [attrib 作定语] *the development of language skills in young children* 儿童语言技能的形成. **2** [C] form of language used by a particular group, nation, etc (集团、国家等的)集团语, 地方语, 部落语, 某国语: *the Bantu group of languages* 班图语系 ○ *one's native language* 母语 ○ *a second, a foreign, an acquired language* 第二语言、外国语言、后天学得的语言. **3** [U] manner of expressing oneself 表达方式: *His language was uncompromising: he told them their work must improve or they would be fired.* 他的话说一不二; 他告诉他们必须改进工作, 否则就予解雇. ○ *bad/strong/foul language*, ie words considered improper, eg those marked ⚠ in this dictionary 坏话, 骂人话, 下流话(粗鄙的词语, 如在本词典中标示 ⚠ 者) ○ *everyday language*, ie not specialized or technical 普通语言(非专门或技术用语). **4** [U] words, phrases, etc used by a particular group of people 术语; 行话: *the language of science, drug users, the courtroom* 科学术语、嗜毒者切口、法庭用语 ○ *medical language* 医学用语. **5** [C, U] system of signs, symbols, gestures, etc used for conveying information 传达信息的手势、符号、姿势等: *Music has been called the universal language.* 人们称音乐为世界的语言. ○ *the language of flowers* 用花表达的信息 ○ *body, sign language* 身势语、手势语 ○ *This theory can only be expressed in mathematical language.* 这个理论只能用数学语言来表达. **6** [C, U] (*computing* 计) system of coded instructions used in programming 语言: *BASIC is the language most programmers learn first.* BASIC是大多数程序编制者首先学习的语言. **7** (idm 习语) **speak the same language** ⇨ SPEAK.

□ ˈ**language laboratory** room equipped with a

special tape-recording system for language learning 语言实验室.

lan·guid /ˈlæŋgwɪd; ˋlæŋgwɪd/ *adj* lacking vigour or energy; slow-moving 不活泼的; 无精打采的; 迟缓的: *languid movements* 懒洋洋的动作 ○ *speak with a languid drawl* 慢吞吞拉着长调说话. ▷ **lan·guidly** *adv*.

lan·guish /ˈlæŋgwɪʃ; ˋlæŋgwɪʃ/ *v* [I] (*fml* 文) **1** lack or lose vitality 缺乏活力; 失去活力: *Since the war the industry has gradually languished.* 开战以来, 这一工业的生产每况愈下. ○ *The children soon began to languish in the heat.* 孩子们很快就热得懒洋洋的了. **2 ~ (for sb/sth)** be or become weak and miserable because of unfulfilled longings; pine[2](1) (因求之不得)变得衰弱而难过: *languish for love, company, sympathy* 渴望得到爱、相伴、同情而憔悴. **3 ~ (in/under sth)** live wretchedly 受苦; 受煎熬: *He languished in poverty for years.* 他多年挣扎在贫困之中. ○ *languishing under foreign domination* 在外国统治下受煎熬.

▷ **lan·guish·ing** *adj* (of looks, etc) trying to win sympathy or affection (指表情等)可望同情的, 含情脉脉的: *a languishing sigh* 博人同情的叹息.

lan·guor /ˈlæŋgə(r); ˋlæŋgɚ/ *n* **1** [U] tiredness or laziness of mind and body; listlessness 倦怠; 慵困; 无精打采. **2** [sing] feeling of dreamy peacefulness 恬静; 平静: *music that induces a delightful languor* 使人心旷神怡的音乐. **3** [U] oppressive stillness (of the air, etc) (空气等的)沉闷: *the hazy languor of a summer's afternoon* 夏日午后那种令人迷离恍惚的沉闷. ▷ **lan·guor·ous** /ˈlæŋgərəs; ˋlæŋgərəs/ *adj*. **lan·guor·ously** *adv*.

lank /læŋk; læŋk/ *adj* **1** (of hair) straight and limp (指毛发)平直的, 柔软的. **2** (of a person) tall and thin (指人)瘦长的.

lanky /ˈlæŋkɪ; ˋlæŋkɪ/ *adj* **(-ier, -iest)** (of a person) ungracefully tall and thin (指人)细长难看的, 又高又瘦的: *a lanky teenager* 瘦长的少年. ▷ **lanki·ness** *n* [U].

lan·olin (also **lan·oline**) /ˈlænəlɪn; ˋlænəlɪn/ *n* [U] fat extracted from sheep's wool and used in making skin creams 羊毛脂(用以制护肤霜).

lan·tern /ˈlæntən; ˋlæntɚn/ *n* **1** (usu portable) light for use outdoors in a transparent case that protects it from the wind, etc (通常指手提的)灯笼; 提灯. **2** (*architecture* 建) structure with windows or openings to admit light or air at the top of a dome or room 天窗; 屋顶气窗.

□ ˈ**lantern jaws** long thin jaws that give the face a hollow look 瘦削而外翘的下巴(使脸部显得凹陷). ˌ**lantern-ˈjawed** *adj*.

lan·than·ide /ˈlænθənaɪd; ˋlænθəˌnaɪd/ *n* (*chemistry* 化) any of the 15 elements in the lanthanide series, with atomic numbers from 57 (lanthanum) to 71 (lutetium) 镧系元素中之任何一种(从原子序数为57的镧到71的镥).

lan·thanum /ˈlænθənəm; ˋlænθəˌnəm/ *n* [U] (*chemistry* 化) silver-white metallic element, used in certain alloys and in glass-making 镧. ⇨App 10 见附录10.

lan·yard /ˈlænjəd; ˋlænjɚd/ *n* **1** cord worn round the neck to hold a knife, whistle, etc (套在脖子上以悬小刀或哨子等的)项带, 颈带. **2** (*nautical* 海) short rope or line attached to sth to secure it 系带, 短绳, 短索.

lap[1] /læp; læp/ *n* **1** area formed by the upper part of a seated person's thighs (人坐着时)大腿的上方: *Come and sit on Grandpa's lap!* 来, 坐在爷爷的腿上! ○ *She had fallen asleep with an open book in her lap.* 她睡着了, 腿上还摊开着一本书. **2** part of a dress, etc covering this 连衣裙等盖住大腿的部分: *She gathered the fallen apples and carried them in her lap.* 她捡起掉落的苹果, 用衣服下摆兜着. **3** (idm 习语) **drop/dump sth in sb's lap** (*infml* 口) make sth the responsibility of sb else 将某事推给他人负责: *You've got to deal with this — don't try and dump it in my lap.* 这事你得去处理 —— 别想往我身上推. **in the lap of the ˈgods** (of future events) uncertain (指未来的事)难以预料. **in the lap of ˈluxury** in conditions of great luxury 在奢侈的环境里.

□ ˈ**lap-dog** *n* small pampered pet dog 娇养的小狗.

lap[2] /læp; læp/ *v* **(-pp-)** **1** [Tn·pr] **~ A round B/~ B in A** wrap or fold (cloth, etc) round sth 用(布等)包扎或包裹某物: *lap a bandage round the wrist/the wrist in a bandage* 用绷带包扎手腕[将手腕用绷带包扎住]. **2** [I, Tn] (cause sth to) overlap (使某物)重叠: *Each row of tiles laps the one below.* 每一排瓦都搭在下面的一排上. **3** [Tn] be one or more laps ahead of (another competitor) in a race (在跑道上)比(另一竞赛者)领先一圈或数圈: *She's lapped all the other runners.* 她领先于所有赛跑者至少一圈.

▷ **lap** *n* **1** part that overlaps or amount by which it overlaps 重叠部分; 重叠的量或程度. **2** single circuit of a track or racecourse 跑道的一圈: *The leading car crashed midway through the tenth lap.* 领先的那辆赛车在第十圈的中途撞毁了. ○ *do a lap of honour*, ie make a ceremonial circuit of a race-track, etc after winning a contest (比赛胜利者)绕场一周. **3** one section of a journey 一段旅程: *The next lap of our trip takes us into the mountains.* 下一段行程我们就要进山区了. **4** (idm 习语) **the last lap** ⇨ LAST[1].

lap[3] /læp; læp/ *v* **(-pp-)** **1** [Tn, Tn·p] **~ sth (up)** (esp of animals) drink sth by taking it up with the tongue (尤指动物)舔着喝某物: *a dog noisily lapping water* 舔着喝水发出啧啧声的狗. **2** [I, Ipr] (of water) make gentle splashing sounds (指水)发出轻轻的拍打声: *waves lapping on a beach, against the side of a boat, etc* 轻拍海滩、船舷等的波浪. **3** (phr v) **lap sth up** (*infml* 口) receive (praise, news, good fortune, etc) eagerly, uncritically or greedily (热切地、不加区别地或贪婪地)接受(夸奖、新情况、好运气等): *He tells her all those lies and she just laps them up.* 他对她说的是一派谎言, 可她却全部接受. ○ *The film got terrible reviews but the public are lapping it up*, ie going to see it in great numbers. 影片尽管受到猛烈的批评, 但公众却趋之若鹜. ○ *lap up sunshine, knowledge, company* 热切地渴望阳光、知识、伴侣. ▷ **lap·ping** *n* [U]: *the gentle lapping of the waves* 波浪轻柔的拍打.

lapel /ləˈpel; ləˋpɛl/ *n* front part of the collar of a coat or jacket that is folded back over the chest (大衣或夹克的)翻领: *What is that badge on your lapel?* 你翻领上的是什么徽章? ⇨illus at JACKET 见JACKET插图.

lap·id·ary /ˈlæpɪdərɪ; *US* -derɪ; ˋlæpəˌdɛrɪ/ *adj* (*fml* 文) **1** [attrib 作定语] of gems or stones, esp of their cutting, polishing or engraving 宝石的; 玉石的; (尤指)宝石或玉石切割、琢磨或雕刻的. **2** (*approv* 褒) dignified and concise 优雅简洁的: *a lapidary inscription, proverb, speech, etc* 精确的铭文、谚语、演讲等.

▷ **lap·id·ary** *n* person who cuts, polishes, sets or engraves gems 宝石匠.

lapis lazuli /ˌlæpɪs ˈlæzjʊlɪ; *US* ˈlæzəlɪ; ˋlæpɪsˋlæzjəˌlaɪ/ *n* **(a)** [U, C] bright-blue semi-precious stone 天青石; 青金石. **(b)** [U] colour of this 天蓝色: [attrib 作定语] *a sea of ˌlapis lazuli ˈblue* 天蓝色的大海.

lapse /læps; læps/ *n* **1** small error, esp one caused by forgetfulness or inattention 小错; (尤指)记错, 疏忽: *A brief lapse in the final set cost her the match.* 她在最后一盘稍有失误而致比赛失败. ○ *It was a superb performance, despite occasional lapses of intonation.* 演出非常成功, 唯偶有音调失误. **2 ~ (from sth) (into sth)** fall or departure from correct or usual standards; backsliding 堕落; 失足: *Wives were expected to forgive their husbands' lapses*, ie forgive them when they were unfaithful. 希望做妻子的原谅丈夫一时行为失检(不忠). ○ *The debate was marred by a brief lapse into unpleasant name-calling.* 因出现几句谩骂, 辩论会不欢而散. ○ *a lapse from grace*, ie becoming out of favour 失宠. **3** passing of a period of time (时间的)流逝, 过去: *after a lapse of six months* 相隔六个月之后. **4** (*law* 律) ending of a right, etc because of disuse (权利等的)失效, 中止, 结束, 消失(因不行使所致).

▷ **lapse** *v* **1** [I, Ipr] **~ (from sth) (into sth)** fail to maintain one's position or standard 未能保持自己的立场或标准: *lapse back into bad habits* 重又沾染坏习惯 ○ *a lapsed Catholic* 叛教的天主教徒. **2** [Ipr] **~ into sth** sink or pass gradually into sth 陷入或进入某状态: *She lapsed into a coma.* 她逐渐陷入昏迷状态. **3** [I] (*law* 律) (of rights and privileges) be lost or invalid because not used, claimed or renewed (指权利、特权)(因未行使、无要求或未延期)丧失, 失效: *He didn't get any compensation because his insurance policy had lapsed.* 他因保险单失效未得任何补偿.

□ ˈ**lapse rate** rate at which the temperature of the air falls in relation to its height above the earth 温度垂直递减率.

L

lap·wing /ˈlæpwɪŋ; ˋlæp,wɪŋ/ (also **peewit, pewit**) *n* type of small black and white wading bird 麦鸡.

lar·ceny /ˈlɑːsənɪ; ˋlɑrsn̩ɪ/ *n* [C, U] (*law* 律) (instance of) theft of personal goods 盗窃; 盗窃罪. ▷ **lar·cen·ous** /ˈlɑːsənəs; ˋlɑrsn̩əs/ *adj*.

larch /lɑːtʃ; lɑrtʃ/ *n* (**a**) [C] tall deciduous tree of the pine family, with small cones and needle-like leaves 落叶松. ➪illus at App 1 见附录1插图, page i. (**b**) [U] its wood 落叶松木.

lard /lɑːd; lɑrd/ *n* [U] white greasy substance made from the melted fat of pigs and used in cooking 荤油.

▷ **lard** *v* **1** [Tn] prepare (meat) for roasting by putting strips of bacon in or on it 加腌肉片烤(肉): *Lean meat can be larded to keep it moist in the oven.* 瘦肉上可加咸肉片烤制以保持水分. **2** [Tn·pr] **~ sth with sth** (*often derog* 常作贬义) embellish (speech or writing) with sth 在(说话或写作)中夹杂某内容: *a lecture larded with obscure quotations* 夹杂着晦涩引文的讲演.

larder /ˈlɑːdə(r); ˋlɑrdɚ/ *n* (esp formerly) cupboard or small room used for storing food (尤指旧时)食橱, 食物贮藏室. Cf 参看 PANTRY.

large /lɑːdʒ; lɑrdʒ/ *adj* (**-r, -st**) **1** of considerable size, extent or capacity (大小、程度或容量)大的: *A large family needs a large house.* 大家庭需要大的房子. ○ *She inherited a large fortune.* 她继承了一大笔财产. ○ *He has a large appetite*, ie eats a lot. 他胃口很大. ○ (*euph* 婉) *a large* (ie fat) *lady* 胖女人. **2** wide in range, scope or scale; broad (范围或规模)大的, 广的: *an official with large powers* 权力很大的官员 ○ *take the large view* 持豁达的观点 ○ *a book dealing with large themes* 涉及广泛内容的书 ○ *large and small farmers* 大农场主和小农. ➪ Usage at BIG 用法见 BIG. **3** (idm 习语) **(as) large as ˈlife** (*joc* 谑) seen or appearing in person, with no possibility of error or doubt 本人; 本身: *And there she was as large as life!* 那就是她本人! **bulk large** ➪ BULK *v*. **by and ˈlarge** taking everything into consideration 大体上; 一般而论; 总的来说: *By and large, the company's been pretty good to me.* 总的来说, 公司对我一直很好. **larger than ˈlife** exaggerated in size, so as to seem more impressive (为感人)夸大的: [attrib 作定语] *The hero appears as a larger-than-life character.* 男主角的表现是高于生活的. **writ large** ➪ WRIT.

▷ **large** *n* (idm 习语) **at ˈlarge** (**a**) (of a criminal, animal, etc) free; not confined (指罪犯、动物等)自由的, 未关管的, 未缚住的: *The escaped prisoner is still at large.* 越狱犯依然在逃. (**b**) at full length; thoroughly and in great detail 详细地; 充分地; 透彻地: *The question is discussed at large in my report.* 我在报告中对该问题作了详细的探讨. (**c**) (used after a *n* 用于名词后) as a whole; in general 整个地; 一般地; 总地: *the opinion of students, voters, society, etc at large* 学生、选民、社会等总的意见.

largely *adv* to a great extent; chiefly 在很大程度上; 主要地: *His success was largely due to luck.* 他的成功主要靠运气.

large·ness *n* [U].

lar·gish *adj* fairly large 相当大的.

□ ˈ**large-scale** *adj* [esp attrib 尤作定语] **1** extensive 大规模的: *a large-scale police search* 警方的大规模搜查. **2** (of a map, model, etc) drawn or made to a large scale so that many details can be shown (指地图、模型等)大比例尺的.

lar·gess (also **lar·gesse**) /lɑːˈdʒes; ˋlɑrdʒɪs/ *n* [U] **1** generous giving of money or gifts, esp to sb of lower rank or status 慷慨的赠与; (尤指)赏赐. **2** money or gifts given in this way 赏金; 赠物.

largo /ˈlɑːɡəʊ; ˋlɑrɡo/ *n* (*pl* **~s**), *adv* (*music* 音) (piece or movement) played in slow and solemn time 缓慢的乐曲或乐章; 广板; 缓慢地: *The second movement is a largo.* 第二乐章是广板乐章.

la·riat /ˈlærɪət; ˋlærɪət/ *n* (*esp US*) length of rope for catching or tethering a horse; lasso (套马或拴马用的)系绳, 套索.

lark[1] /lɑːk; lɑrk/ *n* **1** any of several small songbirds, esp the skylark 百灵科鸣禽; (尤指)云雀. **2** (idm 习语) **be/get ˌup with the ˈlark** get up early in the morning 早起.

lark[2] /lɑːk; lɑrk/ *n* (usu *sing* 通常作单数) (*infml* 口) **1** bit of adventurous fun 戏谑; 玩笑: *The boys didn't mean any harm — they were only having a lark.* 那些男孩子无意作恶——他们不过在闹着玩罢了. ○ *They stole the car for a lark, but now they're in trouble.* 他们偷了汽车原以为好玩, 现在可惹祸了. ○ *What a lark!* ie How amusing! 真有趣! **2** (*Brit ironic* 反语) (esp) unpleasant or irritating type of activity (尤指)不愉快的或令人恼怒的活动: *I don't much like this queuing lark.* 我可不太喜欢排队的事.

▷ **lark** *v* [I, Ip] **~ (about/around)** behave playfully or irresponsibly 胡闹; 行为不负责任: *Stop larking about and get on with your work.* 别到处胡闹了, 干活儿去吧.

lark·spur /ˈlɑːkspɜː(r); ˋlɑrk,spɝ/ *n* tall garden plant with blue, pink or white flowers 燕草(株高的园艺植物, 开蓝色、粉红色或白色花).

larva /ˈlɑːvə; ˋlɑrvə/ *n* (*pl* **lar·vae** /ˈlɑːviː; ˋlɑrvi/) insect in the first stage of its life, after coming out of the egg 幼虫: *A caterpillar is the larva of a butterfly.* 毛虫是蝴蝶的幼体. ➪illus at BUTTERFLY 见 BUTTERFLY 插图. ▷ **lar·val** /ˈlɑːvl; ˋlɑrvl̩/ *adj* [attrib 作定语]: *in a larval state* 幼虫的状态.

lar·ynx /ˈlærɪŋks; ˋlærɪŋks/ *n* (*pl* **larynges** /læˈrɪndʒiːz; ləˋrɪndʒiz/) (*anatomy* 解) (also ˈ**voice-box**) boxlike space at the top of the windpipe, containing the vocal cords which produce the voice 喉. ➪illus at THROAT 见 THROAT 插图.

▷ **lar·yn·gitis** /ˌlærɪnˈdʒaɪtɪs; ˌlærɪnˋdʒaɪtɪs/ *n* [U] (*medical* 医) inflammation of the larynx 喉炎.

la·sagne (also **la·sagna**) /ləˈzænjə; ləˋzɑnjə/ *n* [U] (**a**) pasta made in broad flat strips 宽面(宽而扁的干面条). (**b**) dish made from layers of this with meat sauce, tomatoes and cheese, baked in the oven 卤汁宽面(加肉汁、蕃茄和干酪烹制的).

Las·car /ˈlæskə(r); ˋlæskɚ/ *n* seaman from the E Indies 东印度水手.

las·ci·vi·ous /ləˈsɪvɪəs; ləˋsɪvɪəs/ *adj* feeling, expressing or causing sexual desire 好色的; 猥亵的; 挑动情欲的. ▷ **las·ci·vi·ously** *adv*. **las·ci·vi·ous·ness** *n* [U].

laser /ˈleɪzə(r); ˋlezɚ/ *n* device that generates an intense and highly controlled beam of light 激光器: [attrib 作定语] *laser beams, radiation, physics* 激光束、激光辐射、激光物理学 ○ *a laser-guided missile* 激光制导导弹.

lash[1] /læʃ; læʃ/ *n* **1** [C] flexible part of a whip 鞭子的皮条部分. **2** [C] blow given with or as with a whip, etc 鞭打; 抽打; 鞭挞: (*fig* 比喻) *feel the lash of sb's tongue*, ie be spoken to harshly or cruelly by sb 领教某人利口如刀的厉害. **3 the lash** [sing] (formerly) punishment by flogging (旧时)笞刑: *sailors sentenced to the lash* 被处笞刑的水手. **4** [C] = EYELASH (EYE[1]).

lash[2] /læʃ; læʃ/ *v* **1** [Ipr, Ip, Tn, Tn·pr] strike (sb/sth) with or as with a whip 鞭打, 抽打(某人[某物]): *rain lashing (down) on the roof, against the windows, etc* 猛烈敲打着屋顶、窗户等的雨点 ○ *waves lashing the shore* 拍打海岸的波浪 ○ *lashed the horses with a stick* 用棍棒打马 ○ (*fig* 比喻) *politicians regularly lashed* (ie strongly criticized) *in the popular press* 经常遭广大新闻界抨击的政客. **2** [Tn, Tn·pr, Tn·p] move (a limb, etc) like a whip 摆动(肢体等): *a tiger lashing its tail angrily to and fro/from side to side* 愤怒地摆动着尾巴的老虎. **3** [Tn, Tn·pr] **~ sb (into sth)** rouse or incite sb 激励或煽动某人: *a speech cleverly designed to lash the audience into a frenzy* 巧妙策划煽动众怒的演说. **4** [Tn·pr, Tn·p] **~ A to B/A and B together** fasten things together securely with ropes, etc (用绳索等)将物品捆在一起. **5** (phr v) **lash sth down** tie sth securely in position with ropes, etc (用绳索等)将某物系牢: *lash down the cargo on the deck* 把甲板上的货物缚牢. **lash out (at/against sb/sth)** make a sudden violent attack with blows or words 突然猛击; 猛烈抨击: *The horse lashed out with its back legs.* 那匹马尥蹶子了. ○ *He lashed out at the opposition's policies.* 他猛烈抨击反对派的政策. **lash out (on sth)** (*infml* 口) spend money freely or extravagantly 花钱大手大脚: *Let's lash out and have champagne.* 咱们挥霍一下, 喝香槟吧. ○ *This is no time to lash out on a new stereo.* 现在不是奢侈花钱买新立体音响的时候.

lash·ing /ˈlæʃɪŋ; ˋlæʃɪŋ/ *n* **1** [C] whipping or beating 鞭打; 击打: *He gave the poor donkey a terrible lashing.* 他狠命地抽打那头可怜的驴. **2** [C] rope, etc used to fasten things together or in position 捆绑用的绳索等.

3 lashings [pl] **~s (of sth)** *(Brit infml 口)* a lot 大量: *lashings of cream on one's fruit salad* 自己那份水果色拉上大量的奶油.

lass /læs; læs/ (also **lassie** /ˈlæsɪ; ˈlæsɪ/) *n* (esp in Scotland and N England) girl; young woman (尤用于苏格兰和英格兰北部)女孩儿, 少女, 姑娘. Cf 参看 LADDIE.

lassi·tude /ˈlæsɪtju:d; *US* -tu:d; ˈlæsəˌtud/ *n* [U] *(fml* 文) tiredness of mind or body 厌倦; 疲乏.

lasso /læˈsu:; læˈsu/ *n* (*pl* **~s** or **~es**) long rope with a noose at one end, used for catching horses and cattle (套捕马、牛等用的一头有活结的)套索.
▷ **lasso** *v* [Tn] catch (esp an animal) using a lasso 用套索捕捉(尤指动物): *lassoing wild horses* 用套索捕捉野马.

last[1] /lɑ:st; *US* læst; læst/ *adj* **1** coming after all others in time or order 最后的; 末尾的: *December is the last month of the year.* 十二月是一年的最后一个月份. ○ *the last Sunday in June* 六月的最后一个星期日 ○ *the last time I saw her* 我上次看见她的时候 ○ *the last two/the two last people to arrive* 最后到达的两个人. Cf 参看 FIRST[1] 1. **2** [attrib 作定语] latest; most recent (指过去) 最近的, 上一个的; 刚过去的: *last night, week, month, summer, year, etc* 昨晚、上周、上月、刚过去的夏季、去年 ○ *last Tuesday/on Tuesday last* 刚过去的星期二 ○ *in/for/during the last fortnight, few weeks, two decades, etc* 在过去的两周、几星期、二十年等 ○ *I thought her last book was one of her best.* 我认为她最近出版的那本书是她的最佳著作之一. ⇨Usage at LATE[1] 用法见 LATE[1]. **3** [esp attrib 尤作定语] only remaining; final 唯一剩下的; 最终的: *This is our last bottle of wine.* 这是我们最后的一瓶葡萄酒了. ○ *He knew this was his last hope of winning.* 他知道这是他获胜的唯一希望了. ○ *I wouldn't marry you if you were the last person on earth.* 即使世上就剩下你一个人, 我也不会和你结婚. **4** least likely or suitable 最不可能的; 最不适合的: *the last thing I'd expect him to do* 我最不希望他做的事 ○ *She's the last person to trust with a secret.* 她是最不可能保密的人. **5** (idm 习语) **at one's last ˈgasp** making one's final effort or attempt before exhaustion or death 垂死挣扎; 最后拼搏: *The team were at their last gasp when the whistle went.* 球队正作最后拼搏, 这时哨声响了. **be on one's/its last ˈlegs** be weak or in poor condition 危殆; 糟糕: *My car's on its last legs — it keeps breaking down.* 我的汽车快不行了——总出毛病. **the day, week, month, etc before last** the day, etc immediately before the most recent one; two days, etc ago 两天、两星期、两月等之前: *I haven't seen him since the Christmas before last.* 前年圣诞节过后我一直没见过他. **draw one's first/last breath** ⇨ DRAW[2]. **every last/single ˈone, etc** every person or thing (in a group) included (一群人或物中的)每一个, 全部: *We spent every last penny we had on the house.* 我们的钱全部用在房子上了. **famous last words** ⇨ FAMOUS. **first/last/next but one, two, three, etc** ⇨ FIRST[1]. **first/last thing** ⇨ THING. **have the last ˈlaugh** triumph over one's rivals, critics, etc in the end (对竞争者、批评者等)取得最后胜利. **have, etc the last ˈword** make, etc the final and decisive contribution to an argument, a dispute, etc (辩论等中)作最后一次发言, 最终决定, 最后裁决, 定论等: *We can all make suggestions, but the manager has the last word.* 我们谁都可以提建议, 但经理最后说了算. **in the last/final analysis** ⇨ ANALYSIS. **in the last reˈsort; (as) a/one's last reˈsort** (person or thing one turns to) when everything else has failed 最后手段; 最后的凭借: *In the last resort we can always walk home.* 大不了我们走回家就是了. ○ *I've tried everyone else and now you're my last resort.* 别人我都试过了, 现在就看你的了. **one's last/dying breath** ⇨ BREATH. **the ˌlast ˈditch** the last effort one can make to ensure one's safety, avoid defeat, etc (为确保安全或避免失败等所能做的)最后拼搏: [attrib 作定语] *a ˌlast-ditch ˈstand* 背水一战的立场. **the last ˈminute/ˈmoment** the latest possible time before an important event, etc (重大事件等前的)最后一刻: *change one's plans at the last minute* 事到临头改变计划 ○ *We always leave our packing to/till the last moment.* 我们总是到临行前才收拾行李. ○ [attrib 作定语] *a last-minute dash for the train* 为赶火车的奔忙. **the last ˈlap** final stage of a journey, contest, project, etc (旅行、比赛、工程等)最后阶段: *We're on the last lap, so don't slacken!* 我们已处最后阶段, 可不要松劲啊! **the last/final straw** ⇨ STRAW. **the last ˈword (in sth)** most recent, fashionable, advanced, etc thing 最新、最时髦、最先进等的事物: *Ten years ago this dress was considered the last word in elegance.* 十年前这种连衣裙还算是最高雅的款式呢. **the last ˈword (on sth)** definitive statement, account, etc 权威性的言论、说法等: *a book which may fairly claim to be the last word on the subject* 堪称该课题权威性的书. **say/be one's last ˈword (on sth)** give/be one's final opinion or decision 做出[成为]决定: *I've said my last word — take it or leave it.* 我的意见已经说过了——听不听请便. ○ *I hope that's not your last word on the subject.* 我希望这不是你对该问题的最后决定. **to a man/to the last man** ⇨ MAN. **a week last Monday, etc** ⇨ WEEK.
▷ **last** *n* **1 the ~ (of sb/sth)** (*pl* unchanged 复数不变) person or thing that is last or mentioned last 最后的或最后提到的人或事物: *These are the last of our apples.* 我们就剩下这些苹果了. ○ *We invited Bill, Tom and Sue — the last being Bill's sister.* 我们请了比尔、汤姆和休——最后提到的这位是比尔的妹妹. **2** (idm 习语) **at (long) ˈlast** after (much) delay, effort, etc; in the end 经过(种种)延误、努力等; 终于: *At last we were home!* 我们终于到家了! ○ *At long last a compromise was agreed on.* 通过互让最终达成折衷协议. **breathe one's last** ⇨ BREATHE. **from first to last** ⇨ FIRST[3]. **hear/see the last of sb/sth** (a) hear/see sb/sth for the last time 最后一次听到[见到]某人[某事物]: *That was the last I ever saw of her.* 那是我最后一次见到她. (b) not have to deal with or think about sb/sth again 不必再与某人[某事物]打交道; 不必再考虑某人[某事物]: *It would be a mistake to assume we've heard the last of this issue.* 别以为我们不再过问这事. **to/till the ˈlast** consistently, until the last possible moment (esp death) 坚持到底, 直到最后一刻(尤指直到死): *He died protesting his innocence to the last.* 他至死都坚称自己无罪.

lastly *adv* in the last place; finally 最后一点; 最后: *Lastly, we're going to visit Athens, and fly home from there.* 最后我们将访问雅典, 然后从那儿乘飞机回国.

□ **the Last ˈJudgement** = JUDGEMENT DAY (JUDGEMENT).

ˈlast name surname 姓.

the last ˈpost military bugle-call sounded at sunset, military funerals, etc (军队的)熄灯号, 葬礼号.

the last ˈrites religious ceremony for a person near death 为临终者举行的宗教仪式: *administer the last rites to sb* 为某人行临终圣礼.

the Last ˈSupper (*religion* 宗) meal eaten by Christ and his disciples on the day before the Crucifixion (耶稣被钉在十字架前夕与门徒共进的)最后晚餐.

EXPRESSING TIME 时间表示法

When referring to days, weeks, etc in the past, present and future the following expressions are used, speaking from a point of view in the present. 从现在的角度论及过去的、现在的、将来的日子、星期等, 用下列词语表示.

	PAST 过去	PRESENT 现在	FUTURE 将来
morning 上午 afternoon 下午 evening 晚上	yesterday morning, etc 昨天早晨…	this morning, etc 今天早上…	tomorrow morning, etc 明天上午…
night 夜晚	last night 昨夜	tonight 今夜	tomorrow night 明天夜里
day 日	yesterday 昨天	today 今天	tomorrow 明天
week 星期	last week 上星期	this week 本星期	next week 下星期
month 月	last month 上月	this month 本月	next month 下月
year 年	last year 去年	this year 今年	next year 明年

last[2] /lɑ:st; *US* læst; læst/ *adv* **1** after all others 在最后: *He came last in the race.* 他赛跑落得了最后. ○ *This* *country ranks last in industrial output.* 这个国家的工业生产排名最后. Cf 参看 FIRST[2]. **2** on the occasion before the present time; most recently 最近一次; 上次: *I saw him last/last saw him in New York two years ago.* 我上次见到他是两年前在纽约. ○ *They last defeated England in 1972.* 他们最近一次战胜英格兰队是在1972年. **3** (idm 习语) **first and last** ⇨ FIRST[2]. **he who laughs last laughs longest** ⇨ LAUGH. ˌ**last but not ˈleast** (used before the final item in a list 列举时用于最后一项之前) last but no less important(ly) than the others 最后的但同样重要的: *And last but not least there is the question of adequate funding.* 最后同样重要的是要有足够的资金的问题. ˌ**last ˈin, ˌfirst ˈout** those most recently employed, included, etc will be the first to be dismissed, excluded, etc if such action should become necessary 后来者先走(必要时首先解雇、排除新来者): *The firm will apply the principle of 'last in, first out'.* 公司将实行'后来者先走'的原则.

last[3] /lɑːst; US læst; læst/ *v* **1** [I, In/pr] **~ (for) sth** continue for a period of time; endure 延续; 持续; 维持; 持久: *The pyramids were really built to last.* 建造金字塔为的是要与日月齐光. ○ *How long do you think this fine weather will last?* 你看这样的好天气能持续多久? ○ *She won't last long in that job — it's too tough.* 她做那件工作坚持不了多久——那工作太困难. ○ *The war lasted (for) five years.* 战争持续了五年. **2** [I, Ip, In/pr] **~ (out); ~ (for) sth** be adequate or enough 足够维持: *Will the petrol last (out) till we reach London?* 我们的汽油够开到伦敦的吗? ○ *enough food to last (us) three days* 足够我们维持三天的食物. ⇨Usage at TAKE[1] 用法见TAKE[1]. **3** [no passive 不用于被动语态: Tn, Tn·p] **~ sth (out)** be strong enough to survive or endure sth 活下来; 忍受得住; 支撑得了: *He's very ill and probably won't last (out) the night,* ie will probably die before the morning. 他病得很厉害, 可能活不过今晚.

▷ **last·ing** *adj* continuing for a long time 持续很长一段时间的: *a lasting effect, interest, relationship* 持久的效力、兴趣、关系 ○ *a work of lasting significance* 有长远意义的工作.

last[4] /lɑːst; US læst; læst/ *n* **1** block of wood or metal shaped like a foot, used in making and repairing shoes 鞋楦. **2** (idm 习语) **stick to one's last** ⇨ STICK[2].

lat *abbr* 缩写 = latitude: *lat 70°N/S,* ie North/South 北[南]纬70度. Cf 参看 LONG *abbr* 缩写.

latch 撞锁

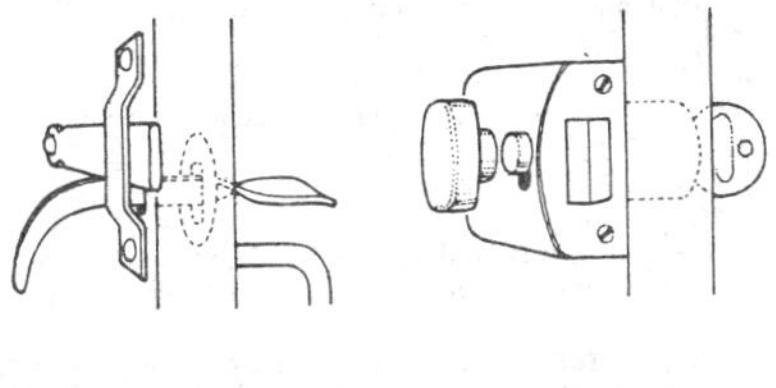

latch /lætʃ; lætʃ/ *n* **1** fastening for a gate or door, consisting of a bar that is lifted from its catch, groove, hole, etc by a lever 门闩. **2** spring lock on a door that catches when the door is closed, and that needs a key to open it from the outside 撞锁; 弹簧锁. ⇨illus 见插图. **3** (idm 习语) **on the ˈlatch** (esp of a door) closed but not locked (尤指门)关着但没上锁.

▷ **latch** *v* **1** [I, Tn] be fastened or fasten (sth) with a latch 用门闩闩牢或用弹簧锁锁住(某物): *This door won't latch properly.* 这门闩不牢. ○ *Please latch the front gate when you leave.* 走时请把大门的碰锁锁好. **2** (phr v) **latch on (to sth)** (*infml* 口) understand an idea, sth said, etc 理解某想法、说的话等: *He's a bit slow but in the end he latches on.* 他有点迟钝, 但毕竟还能理解. ○ *I haven't really latched on to what you mean — could you explain it again?* 我没有真正明白你的意思——能不能再解释一下? **latch on to sb** (*infml* 口) become sb's constant (and often unwelcome) companion 总与某人在一起(常为不受欢迎者); 纠缠住某人: *He always latches on to me when he sees me at a party.* 他在聚会上一看见我就总是缠着我.

□ ˈ**latchkey** *n* key of an outer door, esp the front door of a house or flat 钥匙. ˈ**latchkey child** (*becoming dated* 渐旧) child who has to let himself into his house or flat and look after himself, esp after returning from school, because both parents are out at work 挂钥匙的儿童(尤指因父母外出工作, 故放学回家需自行进屋的).

late[1] /leɪt; let/ *adj* (**-r, -st**) **1** [esp pred 尤作表语] after the proper or usual time 晚; 迟: *My flight was an hour late.* 我那趟航班晚了一小时. ○ *Because of the cold weather the crops are late this year.* 因天气寒冷, 今年的作物成熟得晚. ○ *It's never too late to stop smoking.* 戒烟何时都不算晚. ○ *a late marriage* 晚婚 ○ *a late riser,* ie sb who gets out of bed late in the morning 起得晚的人. Cf 参看 EARLY 2. **2** far on in the day or night, a period of time, a series, etc (日夜、时间、系列等)近末尾的, 将尽的, 末期的: *till a late hour* 直到深夜 ○ *in the late afternoon* 傍晚 ○ *in late summer* 在夏末 ○ *She married in her late twenties,* eg when she was 28. 她快30岁才结婚. ○ *the late nineteenth century* 十九世纪末叶 ○ *a late Victorian house* 维多利亚晚期的房子 ○ *Beethoven's late quartets,* ie the last ones he wrote 贝多芬最后创作的四重奏乐曲. Cf 参看 EARLY 1. **3** [attrib 作定语] (esp in the superlative 尤用于最高级) recent 最新的; 最近的: *the latest news* 最新消息 ○ *There were several clashes before this latest incident.* 在这次事件发生之前已有过几次冲突. ○ *the latest craze, fashion, vogue, etc* 最新时尚、式样、样式等 ○ *her latest novel* 她最近出版的小说 ○ (*fml* 文) *during the late political unrest* 在最近这次政治动乱时期. **4** [attrib 作定语] (**a**) no longer alive 已故的: *her late husband* 已故丈夫. (**b**) no longer holding a certain position; former 已卸任的; 前任的: *The late prime minister attended the ceremony.* 前任首相出席了典礼. **5** (idm 习语) **at the ˈlatest** no later than 至迟; 最晚: *Passengers should check in one hour before their flight time at the latest.* 乘客至迟应在班机起飞前一小时办理登机手续. **an early/late night** ⇨ NIGHT. **it's ˌnever too ˌlate to ˈmend** (*saying* 谚) it is always possible to improve one's character, habits, etc 改过不嫌晚. **of ˈlate** lately; recently 最近以来; 近来.

▷ **lat·ish** /ˈleɪtɪʃ; ˈletɪʃ/ *adj, adv* fairly late 稍迟(的); 稍后(的).

□ ˈ**latecomer** *n* person who arrives late 迟到者; 后来人: *Latecomers will not be admitted until the interval.* 迟到者在休息时间方可入场.

NOTE ON USAGE 用法: **The last** may indicate the final item in a sequence, after which there are no more ☆ **the last** 可指一系列事物中最后一个: *The last bus leaves at 11.15 pm.* 末班公共汽车晚上11时15分开出. ○ *That was the last novel he wrote before he died.* 那是他生前写的最后一部小说. It may also refer to the item before the one being discussed ☆ **the last** 也可指正在谈及的事物之前的一个: *I much prefer this job to my last one/the last one I had.* 这份工作比我原先那份工作好得多. ○ *The last time we met you had a beard.* 上次我们见面, 你还留着胡子呢. **The latest** means 'the most recent' ☆ **the latest** 意为'最近的': *She always dressed in the latest fashion.* 她总是穿最新款的时装. ○ *His latest novel is a great success.* 他最近出版的小说十分成功. **The latter** refers to the second of two items already mentioned and is rather more formal ☆ **the latter** 指已提及的两个事物中的第二个, 多用于书面语中: *One can travel there by ship or plane. Most people choose the latter.* 乘船或乘飞机去均可, 人们多取后者.

late[2] /leɪt; let/ *adv* **1** after the proper or usual time 晚; 迟: *get up, go to bed, arrive home late* 很晚才起床、睡觉、到家 ○ *I sat* (ie stayed) *up late last night.* 昨晚我一直呆到深夜. ○ *She married late.* 她结婚晚. Cf 参看 EARLY 2. **2** far on in a period of time 接近末期: *It happened late last century — in 1895, to be exact.* 事情发生在上个世纪末——准确地说, 在1895年. ○ *As late as the 1950s tuberculosis was still a threat.* 直到二十世纪五十年代, 结核病仍然使人不寒而栗. ○ *He became an author quite late in life,* ie when he was quite old. 他晚年才成为作家. Cf 参看 EARLY 1. **3** (idm 习语) **better**

late than never ⇨ BETTER². **ˌlate in the ˈday** later than is proper or desirable 比适当的或恰当的时间晚: *It's rather late in the day to say you're sorry — the harm's done now.* 现在才说对不起太晚了——危害已成事实. **later ˈon** at a later time or stage 后来; 以后; 其后: *a few days later on* 几天后 ○ *At first things went well, but later on we ran into trouble.* 起初事情进展得很顺利, 但后来我们遇到了困难. **sooner or later** ⇨ SOON.

lately /ˈleɪtlɪ; ˋletlɪ/ *adv* in recent times; recently 近来; 不久前: *Have you seen her lately?* 你最近见过她吗? ○ *It's only lately that she's been well enough to go out.* 她最近才好多了, 可以出去走走了. ○ *We've been doing a lot of gardening lately.* 近来我们做了很多园艺工作. ⇨Usage at RECENT 用法见 RECENT.

lat·ent /ˈleɪtnt; ˋletn̩t/ *adj* [esp attrib 尤作定语] existing but not yet active, developed or visible 潜在的; 不活跃的; 未发展的; 不明显的: *latent abilities* 潜在的才能 ○ *a latent infection* 潜伏性传染病.

▷ **la·tency** /ˈleɪtnsɪ; ˋletn̩sɪ/ *n* [U]. **latency period** (*psychology* 心) stage of personal development from the age of about five to the start of puberty (人的)性潜伏期(从四五岁至青春期间).

□ **ˌlatent ˈheat** heat lost or gained when a substance changes state (from solid to liquid, liquid to vapour, etc) without a change of temperature 潜热.

ˌlatent ˈimage (in photography) image on a film that is not visible until the film has been developed (摄影术)潜影.

ˈlatent period period between catching a disease and the appearance of symptoms (疾病的)潜伏期.

lat·eral /ˈlætərəl; ˋlætərəl/ *adj* [esp attrib 尤作定语] of, at, from or towards the side(s) 侧面的; 从侧面的; 向侧面的: *a lateral vein, artery, limb, etc* 侧静脉、侧动脉、侧肢 ○ *lateral buds, shoots, branches, etc* 侧芽、侧条、侧枝.

□ **ˌlateral ˈthinking** way of solving problems by letting the mind consider unusual and apparently illogical approaches to them 横向思维(解决问题的方法, 以异乎寻常而表面上不合逻辑的方法思考).

lat·er·ite /ˈlætəraɪt; ˋlætəˌraɪt/ *n* [U] type of red soil occurring in tropical regions and widely used there for making roads 砖红壤(热带地区广泛用以筑路的).

la·tex /ˈleɪteks; ˋleteks/ *n* [U] **1** milky fluid produced by (esp rubber) plants 胶乳; (尤指)橡浆. **2** synthetic product resembling this, used in paints, adhesives, etc 合成胶乳(用于油漆黏合剂等).

lath /lɑːθ; *US* læθ; læθ/ *n* (*pl* **~s** /lɑːðz; *US* læðz; læðz/) **1** [C] thin narrow strip of wood 木板条. **2** [U] (esp formerly) building material consisting of such strips used as a support for plaster (尤指旧时)挂瓦条, 抹灰板条: [attrib 作定语] *a lath-and-plaster wall* 板条抹灰的墙.

lathe 车床

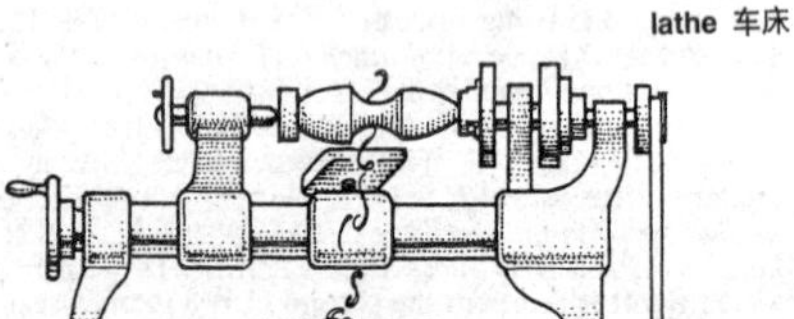

lathe /leɪð; leð/ *n* machine that shapes pieces of wood, metal, etc by holding and turning them against a fixed cutting tool 车床.

L

lather /ˈlɑːðə(r), *also* ˈlæð-; *US* ˈlæð-; ˋlæðɚ/ *n* **1** [U] white foam or froth produced by soap or detergent mixed with water (皂液或洗涤液的)泡沫: *work up a lather on one's chin*, ie before shaving 在下巴上涂皂沫(然后再刮胡子). **2** [U] frothy sweat, esp on a horse 汗沫(尤指马的). **3** (idm 习语) **be in/get into a ˈlather** (*infml* 口) **(a)** be/become excited and nervous 激动; 紧张: *She's in a lather about having to speak to such a large crowd.* 她须在这么多人面前讲话, 心情十分紧张. **(b)** be/become angry, agitated and upset 气愤; 烦乱; 烦恼: *Calm down — there's no need to get into a lather about it!* 冷静些——没有必要为这件事动肝火!

▷ **lather** *v* **1** [I, Ip] **~ (up)** form lather 起泡沫: *Soap will not lather in sea-water.* 肥皂在海水里不起泡沫. **2** [Tn] cover (sth) with lather 给(某物)涂皂沫: *lather one's chin before shaving* 刮胡子前先在下巴上涂皂沫. **3** [Tn] (*dated infml* 旧, 口) thrash (a person or an animal) 抽打(人或动物).

Latin /ˈlætɪn; *US* ˈlætn; ˋlætn̩/ *n* [U] language of ancient Rome and the official language of its empire 拉丁语.

▷ **Latin** *adj* **1** of or in Latin 拉丁语的; 用拉丁语的: *Latin poetry* 拉丁语诗歌. **2** of the countries or peoples using languages developed from Latin, eg France, Italy, Portugal, Spain 拉丁语系国家或民族的(如法兰西、意大利、葡萄牙、西班牙): *the Latin temperament, landscape* 拉丁人的气质、拉丁地区的景色. Cf 参看 ROMANCE.

Lat·in·ist *n* scholar of Latin 拉丁语学者.

□ **ˌLatin Aˈmerica** parts of Central and South America in which Spanish or Portuguese is the official language 拉丁美洲. **ˌLatin-Aˈmerican** *n, adj* (native) of these parts 拉丁美洲的; 拉丁美洲人.

the Latin ˈChurch the Roman Catholic Church 拉丁教会(即天主教会).

Latin ˈcross plain cross with the lowest arm longer than the other three 拉丁式十字架. ⇨illus at CROSS 见 CROSS 插图.

the ˈLatin Quarter area of Paris on the south bank of the Seine, traditionally frequented by students and artists 拉丁区(巴黎塞纳河南岸, 传统上为大学生及艺术家荟萃地).

lat·it·ude /ˈlætɪtjuːd; *US* -tuːd; ˋlætəˌtud/ *n* **1** (*abbr* 缩写 **lat**) [U] distance of a place north or south of the equator, measured in degrees 纬度. ⇨illus at GLOBE 见 GLOBE 插图. Cf 参看 LONGITUDE. **2 latitudes** [pl] region, esp with reference to climate 纬度地区(尤指与气候有关者): *high/low latitudes*, ie regions far from/near to the equator 高[低]纬度地区(指离赤道远近而言). **3** [U] freedom to behave and hold opinions without restriction (行动、意见的)自由: *They allow their children too much latitude, in my view; they should be stricter.* 我认为他们太纵容孩子了, 他们应当严厉一些.

▷ **lat·it·ud·inal** /ˌlætɪˈtjuːdɪnl; *US* -ˈtuːdənl; ˌlætəˋtudən̩l/ *adj* [attrib 作定语]: *latitudinal variation* 纬度的变化.

lat·it·ud·in·arian /ˌlætɪtjuːdɪˈneərɪən; *US* -ˌtuːdnˈeər-; ˌlætəˌtudn̩ˋɛrɪən/ *n, adj* (*fml* 文) (person who is) tolerant and broad-minded, esp in religious matters 宽宏大度的(人)(尤指对宗教事务).

lat·rine /ləˈtriːn; ləˋtrin/ *n* lavatory in a camp, barracks, etc, esp one made by digging a trench or hole in the earth (营地、兵营、工地等的)厕所(尤指在地面上挖坑、渠而成的).

lat·ter /ˈlætə(r); ˋlætɚ/ *adj* (*fml* 文) [attrib 作定语] near to the end of a period 后期的; 末期的: *the latter half of the year* 后半年 ○ *in the latter part of her life* 在她的后半生.

▷ **the lat·ter** *pron* the second of two things or people already mentioned (已提及的两者中之)后者: *Many support the former alternative, but personally I favour the latter (one).* 很多人都赞成前一种办法, 但我个人喜欢后一种. ⇨Usage at LATE¹ 用法见 LATE¹.

lat·terly *adv* lately; nowadays 近来; 现时. Cf 参看 FORMER.

□ **ˌlatter-ˈday** *adj* [attrib 作定语] modern; recent 近代的; 当今的: *latter-day technology* 当今的技术 ○ *They see themselves as latter-day crusading knights.* 他们把自己看成是当今改革运动的急先锋. **ˌLatter-day ˈSaints** Mormons' name for themselves 末世圣徒(摩门教徒自称).

lat·tice /ˈlætɪs; ˋlætɪs/ (also **ˈlattice-work**) *n* [U, sing] **1** framework of crossed laths or bars with spaces between, used as a screen, fence, support for climbing plants, etc 格子框架(用作屏障、篱笆、供植物攀附等的): *(a) steel lattice-work placed around dangerous machinery* 在有危险的机器周围设置的铁格栅. **2** structure or design resembling this 类似格子的结构或设计: *peering through the lattice of tall reeds* 透过高高的芦苇丛窥探.

□ **lattice 'window** window with small diamond-shaped panes set in a framework of lead strips 斜条格构窗.

laud /lɔ:d; lɔd/ *v* [Tn] (*fml or rhet* 文或修辞) praise (sb/sth); glorify 称赞(某人[某事物]); 赞美; 赞扬: *a much-lauded production* 大受赞扬的产品.

laud·able /'lɔ:dəbl; 'lɔdəbl/ *adj* (*fml* 文) deserving praise; praiseworthy 应受称赞的; 值得夸奖的: *a laudable ambition, endeavour, enterprise, etc* 值得夸赞的抱负、事业、进取心等 ○ *Her work for charity is highly laudable.* 她的慈善工作值得高度赞扬. ▷ **laud·ably** /-əblɪ; -əblɪ/ *adv*.

laud·anum /'lɔ:dənəm; 'lɔdənəm/ *n* [U] (esp formerly) opium prepared for use as a sedative (尤指旧时)鸦片酊(用作镇静剂).

laud·at·ory /'lɔ:dətərɪ; *US* -tɔ:rɪ; 'lɔdə,torɪ/ *adj* (*fml* 文) expressing or giving praise 表示称赞的; 赞赏的.

laugh /lɑ:f; *US* læf; læf/ *v* **1** [I] make the sounds and movements of the face and body that express lively amusement, joy, contempt, etc 笑; 发笑: *laugh aloud/out loud* 出声笑、大声笑 ○ *He's so funny — he always makes me laugh.* 他真滑稽——总是引得我笑. ○ *Don't laugh* (ie think me ridiculous), *but I've decided to teach myself Chinese.* 别笑话我, 我已决定自学汉语了. **2** [I] have these emotions 感到好笑: *a man who laughs in the face of danger* 面临危险而付之一笑的男子 ○ *She hasn't got much to laugh about, poor woman.* 她难得开心笑笑, 真可怜. **3** (idm 习语) **he who laughs last laughs 'longest** (*saying* 谚) (used as a warning against expressing joy or triumph too soon 用以提醒人不要过早高兴或庆幸胜利). **laugh in sb's 'face** openly show one's contempt for sb 公开表示蔑视某人. **laugh like a 'drain** (*infml* 口) laugh loudly 放声大笑. **laugh on the other side of one's face** (*infml* 口) be forced to change from joy or triumph to disappointment or regret 转喜为忧: *He'll be laughing on the other side of his face when he reads this letter.* 他看到这封信就要转喜为悲了. **laugh sb/sth out of 'court** (*infml* 口) dismiss sb/sth scornfully 对某人[某事物]藐视而不予理会: *Their allegations were simply laughed out of court.* 他们提出的指责均不屑一顾. **laugh oneself 'silly/'sick** become hysterical or ill by laughing excessively 笑得发狂或难受. **laugh till/until one 'cries** laugh so long or hard that one's eyes water 笑得流眼泪. **laugh sb/sth to scorn** (*fml* 文) mock or ridicule sb/sth 取笑或讥笑某人[某事物]. **laugh up one's 'sleeve (at sb/sth)** (*infml* 口) be secretly amused 暗笑; 窃喜: *She knew the truth all along and was laughing up her sleeve at us.* 她早就知道真相, 却一直在暗中笑话我们. **4** (phr v) **laugh at sb/sth (a)** show that one is amused by sb/sth 因某人[某事物]而发笑: *laugh at a comedian, a joke* 被喜剧演员、被笑话逗笑. **(b)** mock or ridicule sb/sth 取笑或讥笑某人[某事物]: *We all laughed at Jane when she said she believed in ghosts.* 简说她相信有鬼, 大家都笑话她. **(c)** disregard sb/sth; treat sb/sth with indifference 不在乎某人[某事物]; 对某人[某事物]不以为意: *laugh at danger* 对危险等闲视之. **laugh sth away** dismiss (an unpleasant feeling, etc) by laughing 以笑消除(不快等): *He tried without success to laugh her fears away.* 他想以笑声来驱除她的恐惧, 但无济于事. **laugh sb/sth down** silence or reject sb/sth by laughing scornfully 用轻藐的笑止住某人[某事物]的声音或驳斥某人[某事物]: *laugh down a speaker, a proposal* 用讪笑声止住演讲者的话、推翻一建议. **laugh sth off** (*infml* 口) show that one does not care about sth 一笑置之; 付之一笑: *An actor has to learn to laugh off bad reviews.* 演员需学会能对贬斥性评论一笑置之的本事. ○ *There was an embarrassing silence after her indiscreet remark but she was able to laugh it off.* 她出言不慎把大家窘得哑然无声, 她却有本事一笑置之. **laugh sb out of sth** cause sb to forget their problems, etc by making them laugh 使某人发笑以忘掉其问题等: *He could tell she was in a bad mood, and tried to laugh her out of it.* 他看出她心情不好, 想逗她笑好让她不再想烦恼的事.

▷ **laugh** *n* **1** act, sound or manner of laughing 笑; 笑声; 笑的样子: *give, let out, break into, utter, etc a (loud) laugh* (大声)笑、(大)笑起来、突然(大)笑、(朗声)一笑 ○ *a cynical, gentle, polite, hearty, etc laugh* 愤世嫉俗的、斯斯文文的、彬彬有礼的、开怀的...笑 ○ *I recognized him by his raucous, penetrating laugh.* 我听到他那沙哑而又刺耳的笑声就能认出是他. **2** (*infml* 口) amusing incident or person 引人发笑的事或人; 笑料; 笑柄: *And he didn't realize it was you? What a laugh!* 他竟没认出那是你? 真可笑! ○ (*ironic* 反语) *Her, offer to help? That's a laugh!* 她, 主动帮她忙? 简直是笑话! ○ *He's a real laugh — such fun to be with.* 他真是个活宝——跟他在一起真开心. **3** (idm 习语) **have the last laugh** ⇨ LAST[1]. **raise a laugh/smile** ⇨ RAISE.

laugh·able /-əbl; -əbl/ *adj* (*derog* 贬) causing people to laugh; ridiculous 可笑的; 荒谬的: *a laughable attempt to discredit the Government* 给政府抹黑的可笑企图. **laugh·ably** /-əblɪ; -əblɪ/ *adv*.

laugh·ing /'lɑ:fɪŋ; *US* 'læfɪŋ; 'læfɪŋ/ *adj* **1** showing amusement, happiness, etc 笑的; 带笑的: *laughing faces* 笑脸. **2** (idm 习语) **be 'laughing** (*sl* 俚) be in a satisfactory or enviable situation 满意; 满足; 令人羡慕: *It's all right for you, with a good job and a nice house — you're laughing.* 你行啊, 有份好工作又有好房子——称心如意了. **be no laughing matter** be sth serious, not to be joked about 不是开玩笑的事. **die laughing** ⇨ DIE[2].

▷ **laugh·ingly** *adv* **1** in an amused manner 笑着; 带笑地. **2** (*often derog* 常作贬义) in an amusing manner; ridiculously 引人发笑地; 可笑地: *They're fond of holding what are laughingly known as literary soirées.* 他们爱举行戏称之为文学晚会的活动.

□ **'laughing-gas** *n* [U] = NITROUS OXIDE (NITROUS).

'laughing-stock *n* (esp *sing* 尤作单数) person or thing that is ridiculed 笑柄: *His constant blunders made him the laughing-stock of the whole class.* 他总是出错, 成了全班的笑柄.

laugh·ter /'lɑ:ftə(r); *US* 'læf-; 'læftɚ/ *n* [U] act, sound or manner of laughing 笑; 笑声; 笑的样子: *roar with laughter* 放声大笑 ○ *tears of laughter* 笑出的眼泪 ○ *a house full of laughter*, ie with a happy relaxed atmosphere 充满笑声的家.

launch[1] /lɔ:ntʃ; lɔntʃ/ *v* **1** [Tn, Tn·pr] put (sth) into motion; send on its course 使(某事物)运动; 送上轨道: *launch a blow, a missile, a torpedo, a satellite* 发出一击、发射导弹、发射鱼雷、发射卫星 ○ (*fig* 比喻) *launch threats, insults, gibes, etc at sb* 威胁、侮辱、奚落...某人. **2** [Tn] cause (a ship, esp one newly built) to move into the water 使(船, 尤指新船)下水: *The Queen is to launch a new warship today.* 今天女王要主持新军舰下水仪式. ○ *The lifeboat was launched immediately to rescue the four men.* 立刻放下了救生船救那四个人. **3** [Tn, Tn·pr] put (sth/sb) into action; set going 使(某人[某事物])行动; 使开始: *launch an attack/offensive (against the enemy)* (向敌人)发起攻击[攻势] ○ *The company is launching a new model next month.* 下月公司将推出新型号产品. ○ *He's launching his son on a career in banking.* 他让儿子从事银行业. **4** (phr v) **launch (out) into sth** enter boldly or freely into (a course of action) 勇于采取(某行动); 任意进行(某活动): *He launched into a long series of excuses for his behaviour.* 他一五一十地提出很多借口为自己的行为辩解. ○ *She wants to be more than just a singer and is launching out into films*, ie starting a career as a film actress. 她不甘心只当歌手, 于是开始投身影界. **launch out at sb** attack sb, physically or verbally 攻击或抨击某人: *He suddenly launched out at me for no reason at all.* 他突然无端攻击我.

▷ **launch** *n* (esp *sing* 尤作单数) process of putting into motion a ship, spacecraft or new product (船的)下水; (航天器的)发射; (新产品的)投产或投放: *The launch of their new saloon received much media coverage.* 他们投产的新轿车广获传媒报道.

□ **'launching pad** (also **'launch pad**) base or platform from which spacecraft, etc are launched (航天器等的)发射台.

launch[2] /lɔ:ntʃ; lɔntʃ/ *n* large motor boat 大汽艇.

laun·der /'lɔ:ndə(r); 'lɔndɚ/ *v* **1** [Tn] (*fml* 文) wash and iron (clothes, etc) 洗熨(衣物等): *Send these shirts to be laundered.* 把这些衬衣送去洗熨. **2** [Tn, Tn·pr] (*fig* 比喻) transfer (money obtained from crime) to foreign banks, legitimate businesses, etc so as to disguise its source 洗(赃款)(转移到外国银行、合法公司等以掩蔽其来路): *The gang laundered the stolen money through their chain of restaurants.* 这帮匪徒通过他们的

L

连锁饭店洗赃款.
▷ **laund·ress** /ˈlɔːndrɪs; ˋlɔndrɪs/ *n* woman who earns money by laundering 洗熨女工; 洗衣妇.

laun·der·ette (also **laun·drette**) /ˌlɔːndəˈret, lɔːnˈdret; ˌlɔndəˋrɛt/ *n* business where the public may wash and dry their clothes, etc in coin-operated machines 自助洗衣店(有投币洗衣机设备).

laun·dro·mat /ˈlɔːndrəmæt; ˋlɔndrəˌmæt/ *n* (*propr* 专利名 *esp US*) launderette 自助洗衣店.

laun·dry /ˈlɔːndrɪ; ˋlɔndrɪ/ *n* **1** [C] (**a**) business where clothes, sheets, etc are laundered 洗衣店: *sent to the laundry* 送往洗衣店 ○ [attrib 作定语] *a laundry van* 洗衣店货车. (**b**) room in a house, hotel, etc where clothes, sheets, etc are laundered (家庭、旅馆等的)洗衣房. **2** [U] clothes, sheets, etc that have been or need to be laundered 洗熨好的或需洗熨的衣物: *There's not much laundry this week.* 本星期的洗熨衣物不多. ○ *Did you do the laundry today?* 你今天洗熨过衣物吗? ○ [attrib 作定语] *a laundry basket* 供盛洗熨衣物的篮子.

Laure·ate /ˈlɒrɪət; *US* ˈlɔːr-; ˋlɔrɪɪt/ *n* = POET LAUREATE (POET).

laurel /ˈlɒrəl; *US* ˈlɔːrəl; ˋlɔrəl/ *n* **1** [C] evergreen shrub with smooth glossy leaves 月桂类; 月桂树. **2** (also **laurels** [pl]) wreath of laurel leaves, used by the ancient Greeks and Romans as an emblem of victory or honour 桂冠(月桂树叶编成的花环, 古希腊人与罗马人用作胜利或荣誉的象征). **3** (idm 习语) **gain/win one's ˈlaurels** win fame or honour 赢得荣誉. **look to one's ˈlaurels** beware of losing one's position of superiority 意识到可能丧失优越的或优势的地位: *There are so many good new actors around that the older ones will soon have to look to their laurels.* 新演员人才辈出, 老演员不久就地位难保了. **rest on one's laurels** ⇨ REST[1].

lav /læv; læv/ *n* (*infml* 口) lavatory 厕所.

lava /ˈlɑːvə; ˋlɑvə/ *n* [U] **1** hot liquid rock that comes out of a volcano (火山喷出的)熔岩: *a stream of lava* 熔岩流. ⇨illus at VOLCANO 见 VOLCANO 插图. **2** type of rock formed from this when it has cooled and hardened 火山岩.

lav·at·ory /ˈlævətrɪ; *US* -tɔːrɪ; ˋlævəˌtɔrɪ/ *n* **1** (also *dated* 旧亦作 ˈ**water-closet**) device, usu consisting of a bowl connected to a drain, used for disposing of waste matter from the body 抽水马桶. **2** room, building, etc equipped with this device (有抽水马桶的)厕所. ⇨ Usage at TOILET 用法见 TOILET.

lav·en·der /ˈlævəndə(r); ˋlævəndɚ/ *n* [U] **1** (**a**) plant with sweet-smelling pale purple flowers 薰衣草(开淡紫色花, 味香). (**b**) its dried flowers and stalks used to give linen, etc a pleasant smell 干薰衣草的花及茎(用以薰香衣物等). **2** pale purple colour 淡紫色.
□ ˈ**lavender-water** *n* [U] delicate perfume made from lavender 薰衣草香水.

lav·ish /ˈlævɪʃ; ˋlævɪʃ/ *adj* **1 ~ (in/of/with sth); ~ (in doing sth)** giving or producing generously or in large quantities 慷慨的; 大方的: *He was lavish with his praise for/lavish in praising the project.* 他对那计划赞不绝口. **2** plentiful; abundant 丰富的; 大量的: *a lavish display, meal, reception* 铺张的展示、饭菜、招待.
▷ **lav·ish** *v* (phr v) **lavish sth on/upon sb/sth** give sth to sb/sth abundantly and generously 慷慨而大量地将某物给某人[某事物]: *lavish care on an only child* 对独生子女关怀备至.
lav·ishly *adv.*

law /lɔː; lɔ/ *n* **1** [C] rule established by authority or custom, regulating the behaviour of members of a community, country, etc (具体的)法, 法律, 法规, 法令: *The new law comes into force next month.* 新法规下月实施. **2** [U] (also **the law**) body of such rules (整体的)法, 法律, 法规, 法令: *respect for tribal law* 遵守部落的法规 ○ *observe/obey the law* 守法[遵法] ○ *Stealing is against the law.* 盗窃是违法的. ○ *Children not admitted — by law.* 儿童不准进入——有法律规定. ○ *I didn't know I was breaking the law*, ie doing sth illegal. 我并不知道自己已违法. ○ *be within/outside the law* 在法律许可之内[之外] ○ *She acts as if she's above the law*, ie as if the law does not apply to her. 她自以为可以凌驾法律之上. ○ *The law is on our side*, ie We are right according to the law. 我们是有法律依据的. **3** [U] such rules as a science or subject of study 法律学; 法学: *read* (ie study) *law at university* 在大学攻读法律学 ○ *He gave up law to become a writer.* 他放弃学法律而从事写作. ○ [attrib 作定语] *a law student* 法律系学生. **4** [C] rule of action or procedure, esp in the arts or a game 规则(尤指艺术或比赛中的): *the laws of perspective, harmony* 透视法、和声法 ○ *the laws of tennis* 网球规则. **5** [C] factual statement of what always happens in certain circumstances; scientific principle 规律; 法则; 定律; 原理: *the law of gravity* 引力定律 ○ *the laws of motion* 运动定律. **6 the law** [sing] (*infml* 口) the police 警方; 警察: *Watch out — here comes the law!* 注意——警察来了! **7** (idm 习语) **the arm of the law** ⇨ ARM[1]. **be a law unto oneˈself/itˈself** behave in an unconventional or unpredictable fashion 以反常规的或不可预料的方式行事: *My car's a law unto itself — I can't rely on it.* 我的汽车自行其是——靠不住了. **go to ˈlaw (against sb)** ask the lawcourts to decide about a problem, claim, etc 提起诉讼; 打官司. **have the ˈlaw on sb** (*infml* 口) report sb to the police; start legal proceedings against sb 向警方告发某人; 对某人提出起诉: *If you do that again I'll have the law on you.* 你要是再那样做, 我就报警. **law and ˈorder** situation in which the law is obeyed 法治: *a breakdown in/of law and order* 法治的衰败 ○ *establish, maintain, uphold, etc law and order* 建立、维护、坚持...法治 ○ [attrib 作定语] *a law-and-order policy* 法治方针. **the law of ˈaverages** principle according to which one believes that if one extreme occurs it will be matched by the other extreme occurring, so that a normal average is maintained 平均律. **the law of the ˈjungle** the survival or success of the strongest or the most unscrupulous 丛林法则; 弱肉强食. **lay down the ˈlaw** say with (real or assumed) authority what should be done 以(真的或假的)权威资格说话: *He's always laying down the law about gardening but he really doesn't know much about it.* 他总是对园艺工作发号施令, 其实他只是一知半解. **the letter of the law** ⇨ LETTER. **possession is nine points of the law** ⇨ POSSESSION. **take the law into one's own ˈhands** disregard the law and take independent (and usu forceful) action to correct sth believed to be wrong 无视法律而私行(通常用武力)惩治. **there's no law against sth** (*infml* 口) (doing) sth is allowed (做)某事是许可的: *I'll stay in bed as long as I like — there's no law against it.* 我在床上爱呆多久就呆多久——谁也管不着. **an unwritten law/rule** ⇨ UNWRITTEN.
▷ **law·ful** /-fl; -fəl/ *adj* **1** allowed by law; legal 合法的; 法定的: *take power by lawful means* 用合法的手段取得权力. **2** [esp attrib 尤作定语] recognized by law 法律承认的: *his lawful heir* 合法继承人. **law·fully** /-fəlɪ; -fəlɪ/ *adv.*
law·less *adj* (**a**) (of a country or area) where laws do not exist or are not enforced (指国家或地区)没有法律的, 未实施法律的. (**b**) (of people or actions) without respect for the law (指人或行为)不法的, 不遵守法律的: *a lawless mob looting and destroying shops* 洗劫和破坏商店的一群无法无天的暴民. **law·lessly** *adv.* **law·less·ness** *n* [U].
□ ˈ**law-abiding** *adj* obeying the law 遵守法律的: *law-abiding citizens* 安分守己的公民.
ˈ**law agent** (*Scot* 苏格兰) solicitor 律师.
ˈ**law-breaker** *n* person who disobeys the law; criminal 犯法的人; 罪犯.
ˈ**lawcourt** (also ˌ**court of ˈlaw**) *n* room or building in which legal cases are heard and judged 法庭; 法院. Cf 参看 COURT[1] 1.
ˈ**Law Lord** (in Britain) member of the House of Lords who is qualified to perform its legal work (英国)上议院执掌司法工作的议员.
ˈ**lawmaker** *n* person who makes laws; legislator 立法者; 立法机关成员.
ˈ**lawsuit** (also **suit**) *n* process of bringing a dispute, claim, etc before a court of law for settlement 诉讼.

lawn[1] /lɔːn; lɔn/ *n* [C, U] area of closely-cut grass in the garden of a house or a public park, or used for a game 草坪; 草地: *In summer we mow our lawn once a week.* 夏天我们一周给草坪刈草一次. ○ *The house has half an acre of lawn.* 这座房子有半英亩草坪. ○ *a ˈcroquet lawn* 槌球场. ⇨illus at App 1 见附录1插图, page vii.

□ ˈ**lawn-mower** *n* machine for cutting the grass on lawns 刈草机.

ˌ**lawn ˈtennis** (*fml* 文) = TENNIS.

lawn[2] /lɔ:n; lɔn/ *n* [U] type of fine linen used for dresses, etc 上等细麻布.

law·yer /ˈlɔ:jə(r); ˈlɔjɚ/ *n* person who is trained and qualified in legal matters, esp a solicitor 律师; (尤指)事务律师: *Don't sign anything until you've consulted a lawyer.* 未请教律师, 不要随便签字. Cf 参看 ADVOCATE *n* 2, ATTORNEY 2, BARRISTER.

lax /læks; læks/ *adj* not sufficiently strict or severe; negligent 不严格的; 不严厉的; 疏忽的: *lax security, behaviour, regulations* 不严谨的保安措施、行为、规则 ○ *He's too lax with his pupils.* 他对小学生管教太松. ▷ **lax·ity** /ˈlæksətɪ; ˈlæksətɪ/ *n* [U]. **laxly** *adv*.

lax·at·ive /ˈlæksətɪv; ˈlæksətɪv/ *n, adj* (medicine, food or drink) causing or helping the bowels to empty 缓泻的; 通便的; 泻药; 有通便作用的饮食: *If you're constipated you may need a laxative.* 便秘时可服用泻剂.

lay[1] /leɪ; le/ *v* (*pt, pp* **laid** /leɪd; led/)

▸ PLACING SOMETHING IN A CERTAIN POSITION OR ON A SURFACE 将某物置于某位置或某物表面 **1** (**a**) [Tn·pr, Tn·p, Cn·a] put (sth/sb) in a certain position or on a surface 将(某物[某人])置于某位置或某物表面: *lay the book on the table* 把书放在桌上 ○ *lay the blanket over the sleeping child* 给睡着的孩子盖毯子 ○ *lay oneself down to sleep* 躺下睡觉 ○ *He laid his hand on my shoulder.* 他把手放在我的肩上. ○ *The horse laid back its ears.* 那匹马将耳朵竖到后面. ○ *The storm laid the crops flat.* 暴风雨把庄稼刮倒了. (**b**) [Tn, Tn·pr] put (sth) in the correct position for a particular purpose (为某目的)将(某物)摆放于适当位置: *lay a carpet, cable, pipe* 铺地毯、架电缆、敷管道 ○ *lay the foundations of a house* 给房子打地基 ○ *lay the table*, ie put plates, cutlery, etc on it for a meal 摆设餐具准备吃饭 ○ *A bricklayer lays bricks to make a wall.* 砖瓦匠是砌砖垒墙的. ○ *They are laying new sewers along the road.* 他们正在沿路敷设新的排水管道. **2** [Tn, Tn·pr] **~ A (on/over B); ~ B with A** spread sth (on sth); cover or coat sth with sth (在某物上)摊开某物; 用某物覆盖或附加一层某物: *lay the paint evenly* 均匀地涂上颜料 ○ *lay straw everywhere* 四处铺上稻草 ○ *lay carpeting on the floor/lay the floor with carpeting* 铺地毯. ➪Usage at LIE[2] 用法见LIE[2].

▸ CAUSING SOMEBODY OR SOMETHING TO BE IN A CERTAIN STATE 使某人或某物处于某状态 **3** [Tn·pr] (*fml* 文) cause (sb/sth) to be in a certain state or situation 使(某人[某事物])处于某状态或情况: *lay sb under an obligation* (ie oblige sb) *to do sth* 使某人承担做某事的义务 ○ *lay new laws before parliament* 向议会提交新法令供审议. **4** [Tn] cause (sth) to settle 使(某物)沉降, 安顿: *sprinkle water to lay the dust* 洒水使尘土落下. **5** [Tn] make (sth) smooth or flat 使(某物)平顺或伏贴: *using hair cream to lay the hair sticking up at the back* 用发乳把后面竖起的头发弄服帖. **6** [Tn] (*fml* 文) cause (sth) to be less strong; allay 使(某事物)减轻, 平息, 缓解: *lay sb's fears, doubts, suspicions, etc* 消除某人的恐惧、疑虑、怀疑等.

▸ OTHER MEANINGS 其他意义 **7** [Tn, Tn·pr, Dn·n, Dn·f no passive 不用于被动语态] **~ sth (on sth)** bet (money) on sth; place (a bet) 就某事赌(钱); 压(赌注): *gamblers laying their stakes in roulette* 在轮盘赌上压赌注的赌徒 ○ *How much did you lay on that race?* 那场赛马你下了多少赌注? ○ *I'll lay you £5 that she won't come.* 我看她不来了, 我愿跟你赌5英镑. **8** [Tn esp passive 尤用于被动语态] (⚠ *sl* 讳, 俚) (of a man) have sexual intercourse with (a woman) (指男子)与(某女子)性交; 肏: *get laid* 挨肏. **9** [I, Tn] (of birds, insects, etc) produce (eggs) (指鸟、虫等)产(卵): *The hens are not laying well* (ie not producing many eggs) *at the moment.* 现在那些母鸡不爱下蛋. ○ *The cuckoo lays its eggs in other birds' nests.* 杜鹃在别的鸟巢中产卵. ○ *new-laid eggs at 90p a dozen* 90便士一打的鲜蛋. **10** (in some combinations of *lay* + *n* + *prep*/infinitive, having the same meaning as a *v* related in form to the *n* 某些lay + n + prep/infinitive的组合, 其意义与该名词形式相关的动词相同, 如 *lay the emphasis on certain points* = *emphasize certain points*): *lay stress on neatness*, ie stress it 强调整齐 ○ *Who should we lay the blame on?* ie Who should we blame? 我们该责备谁? ○ *lay (one's) plans* (ie plan) *to do sth* 计划做某事 ○ *lay a trap for* (ie prepare to trap) *sb* 将某人诱入圈套. **11** (idm 习语) **lay it ˈon (ˈthick/with a ˈtrowel)** (*infml* 口) use exaggerated praise, flattery, etc 夸大地赞扬、恭维等: *To call him a genius is laying it on a bit (too thick)!* 把他称为天才是有点过分了. (For other idioms containing **lay**, see entries for *ns, adjs*, etc 与**lay**搭配的其他习语见有关名词、形容词等的词条, 如 **lay one's hands on sb/sth** ➪ HAND[1]; **lay sth bare** ➪ BARE[1].)

12 (phr v) **lay aˈbout one (with sth)** hit out in all directions 向四周挥打: *As we approached her, she laid about her with a stick.* 我们接近她时, 她就挥棒乱打.

lay about sb/sth (with sth) attack sb/sth with words or blows 用言语或拳、棒等攻击某人[某事物]: *She laid about him, calling him a liar and a cheat.* 她攻击他, 说他说谎、是个骗子.

lay sth aside (*fml* 文) (**a**) put sth aside 把某事物放在一边: *I laid my book aside, turned off the light and went to sleep.* 我把书放在一边, 关了灯睡觉. (**b**) abandon sth; give sth up 抛弃或放弃某事物: *lay aside one's studies, one's responsibilities* 放弃学业、责任. (**c**) (also **lay sth by**) keep sth for future use; save sth 留存某物以备将来之用; 储存某物: *lay some money aside for one's old age* 积钱防老.

lay sth away (*US*) pay a deposit on sth to reserve it until full payment is made 付定钱购某物, 俟货款付齐再行交货.

lay sth down (**a**) store (wine) in a cellar, etc 将(酒)贮存于地窖等: *lay down claret* 贮存干红葡萄酒. (**b**) (begin to) build sth (开始)建造某物: *lay down a new ship, railway track* 建造新船、新铁路. (**c**) (*fml* 文) cease to perform sth; give sth up 停止行使某事物; 放弃某事物: *lay down one's office, duties* 放弃职务、中止义务. **lay sth down; lay it ˈdown that...** give sth as a rule, principle, etc; establish 制定规则、原则等: *You can't lay down hard and fast rules.* 规则不能定得太严太死. ○ *It is laid down that all applicants must sit a written exam.* 根据规定, 申请者一律需经笔试.

lay sth in provide oneself with a stock of sth 储备某物: *lay in food, coal, supplies, etc* 储存食物、煤、供应品等.

lay into sb/sth (*infml* 口) attack sb/sth violently, with words or blows 用言语或拳、棒等猛烈攻击某人[某事物]: *He really laid into her, saying she was arrogant and unfeeling.* 他痛斥她, 说她傲慢又无情.

lay ˈoff (sb) (*infml* 口) stop doing sth that irritates, annoys, etc 不再做打扰人、讨人厌等的事: *Lay off! You're messing up my hair!* 住手!你把我的头发都弄乱了! ○ *Lay off him! Can't you see he's badly hurt?* 别碰他! 你没看见他伤得很厉害吗? **lay ˈoff (sth)** (*infml* 口) stop doing or using sth harmful, etc 不再做或使用有害的事物等: *I've smoked cigarettes for years, but now I'm going to lay off (them).* 我抽烟很多年了, 现在打算戒了. ○ *You must lay off alcohol for a while.* 在一段时期内你必须禁酒. **lay sb ˈoff** dismiss (workers), usu for a short time 解雇(工人)(通常为短期): *They were laid off because of the lack of new orders.* 由于没有新的定货, 他们遭暂时解雇.

lay sth ˈon (**a**) supply (gas, water, etc) for a house, etc (给住房等)供应(煤气、水等): *We can't move in until the electricity has been laid on.* 我们得等电源接通后才能搬进去. (**b**) (*infml* 口) provide sth; arrange sth 提供某事物; 安排某事物: *lay on a party, show, trip* 组织娱乐会、展览会、出游 ○ *lay on food and drink* 提供食物和饮料 ○ *Sightseeing tours are laid on for visitors.* 已为来访者安排了观光活动.

lay sb ˈout knock sb unconscious 打昏(某人): *The boxer was laid out in the fifth round.* 那个拳击手在第五回合中被击昏在地. **lay sth ˈout** (**a**) spread sth out ready for use or to be seen easily 展开某物(为备用或易见): *beautiful jewellery laid out in the shop window* 陈列在橱窗里的漂亮珠宝 ○ *Please lay out all the clothes you want to take on holiday.* 请把你想带去度假的衣服摊开看看. (**b**) (often passive 常用于被动语态) arrange sth in a planned way 有计划地安排某事物: *lay out a town, garden* 设计城市、布置花园 ○ *a well laid out magazine* 设计得精美的杂志. (**c**) (*infml* 口) spend (money) 花

(钱): *I had to lay out a fortune on that car.* 我得为那辆汽车花上一大笔钱. (**d**) prepare (a corpse) for burial 给(尸体)作敛葬准备.

lay ˈover (*US*) stop at a place on a journey 旅途中停留: *We laid over in Arizona on the way to California.* 我们在赴加利福尼亚州途中曾在亚利桑那州停留. Cf 参看 STOP OVER (STOP[1]).

lay sb ˈup (usu passive 通常用于被动语态) cause sb to stay in bed, not be able to work, etc 使某人卧床、不能工作等: *She's laid up with a broken leg.* 她因腿伤卧床. ○ *I've been laid up with flu for a week.* 我患流感已在家休息一个星期了. **lay sth up** (**a**) save sth; store sth 保留某物; 储存某物: *lay up supplies, fuel, etc* 储备供应品、燃料等. (**b**) put (a vehicle, ship, etc) out of use 将(车、船等)搁置不用: *lay a ship up for repairs* 让船进坞修理 ○ *My car's laid up at the moment.* 我的汽车闲着没用. **lay sth up (for oneself)** ensure by what one does or fails to do that one will have trouble in the future (自)找麻烦: *You're only laying up trouble (for yourself) by not mending that roof now.* 你不趁现在修理房顶将来给自己找麻烦.

▷ **lay** *n* (⚠ *sl esp sexist* 讳, 俚, 尤含性别偏见) partner in sexual intercourse (esp a woman) 性交的对方(尤指女方): *an easy lay*, ie a person who is ready and willing to have sexual intercourse 性关系随便的人.

□ **ˈlayaway** *n* [U] (*US*) system of reserving goods by putting a deposit on them until full payment is made 预约购货法(预付定金留货, 付足供款后始予交货的制度): *She buys her Xmas presents on layaway.* 她用预约购货法购买圣诞礼物.

ˈlay-off *n* (**a**) dismissal of a worker, usu for a short time 解雇工人(通常为短期): *many lay-offs among factory workers* 工人中许多暂遭解雇的人. (**b**) period of this 暂时解雇期: *a long lay-off over the winter* 长达一冬的暂时解雇.

ˈlayout *n* way in which the parts of sth are arranged according to a plan 安排; 设计; 布局; 编排: *the layout of rooms in a building* 建筑物内房间的布局 ○ *a magazine's attractive new page layout* 某杂志醒目而新颖的版面编排.

ˈlay-over *n* (*US*) short stop on a journey 旅途中的短期停留. Cf 参看 STOPOVER (STOP[1]).

lay[2] /leɪ; le/ *adj* [attrib 作定语] **1** not belonging to the clergy 非神职的: *a lay preacher* 非神职的讲道者. **2** (**a**) not having expert knowledge of a subject 非专业的; 外行的: *lay opinion* 外行的意见 ○ *speaking as a lay person* 说外行话. (**b**) not professionally qualified, esp in law or medicine 不合职业资格的(尤指在法律或医学方面).

□ **ˈlayman** /-mən; -mən/ *n* (*pl* **-men** /-mən; -mən/) **1** person who does not have an expert knowledge of a subject 外行; 门外汉: *a book written for professionals and laymen alike* 为专业人员和外行人写的书. **2** Church member who is not a clergyman or priest 普通教徒(有别于神职人员).

lay[3] /leɪ; le/ *n* (*arch* 古) poem that was written to be sung; ballad 供吟唱的诗; 民歌; 民谣.

lay[4] *pt* of LIE[2].

lay·about /ˈleɪəbaʊt; ˈleə,baut/ *n* (*Brit infml* 口) lazy person who avoids work 懒人; 不务正业的人.

lay-by /ˈleɪ baɪ; ˈle,baɪ/ *n* (*pl* **lay-bys**) (*Brit*) (*US* **rest stop**) area at the side of a road where vehicles may stop without obstructing the flow of traffic 路侧停车处.

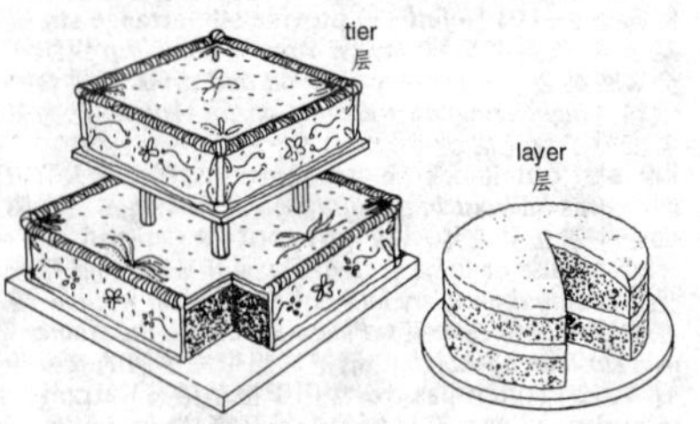

layer /ˈleɪə(r); ˈleɚ/ *n* **1** thickness of material (esp one of several) laid over a surface or forming a horizontal division 层(尤指数层中之一): *Several thin layers of clothing will keep you warmer than one thick one.* 穿几层薄的衣服总比穿一层厚的衣服暖. ○ *a layer of dust on the furniture* 家具上的一层尘土 ○ *a layer of clay in the earth* 地下的一层黏土 ○ *remove layers of old paint* 去除层层旧颜料. ⇨illus 见插图. **2** (preceded by an *adj* 用于形容词之后) hen that lays eggs 产卵鸡; 卵用鸡: *a poor, good, etc layer* 产卵少、多...的鸡. **3** (in gardening) shoot[2](1) fastened down for layering (园艺)压条.

▷ **layer** *v* [Tn] **1** arrange (sth) in layers 将某物积成层: *layer lime and garden clippings to make compost* 把石灰和修剪下的枝叶分层堆积做堆肥 ○ *layered hair*, ie cut to several differing lengths 分层削短的头发. **2** (in gardening) cause (a shoot[2](1)) to take root while still attached to the parent plant (园艺)用压条法使(嫩枝)生根.

□ **ˈlayer cake** cake consisting of layers with fillings of cream, etc between 夹层蛋糕.

lay·ette /leɪˈet; leˈɛt/ *n* set of clothes, nappies, rugs, etc for a new-born baby 新生儿全套用品(婴儿服、尿布、毯子等).

lay figure /ˌleɪ ˈfɪɡə(r); ˌleˈfɪɡɚ/ wooden figure of the human body with jointed movable limbs, used as a model by artists (艺术家用的四肢可活动的)木制人体模型.

lay·man ⇨ LAY[2].

laze /leɪz; lez/ *v* **1** [I, Ipr, Ip] **~ (about/around)** be lazy; rest; relax 懒散; 闲散; 松散: *lazing by the river all day* 整天在河边闲荡 ○ *spend the afternoon lazing around (the house)* (在家里)闲散地度过一下午. **2** (phr v) **laze sth away** spend (time) idly 懒散地打发(时光): *You can't go on lazing your life away.* 你可不能一直懒散地过一辈子.

lazy /ˈleɪzɪ; ˈlezɪ/ *adj* (**-ier, -iest**) **1** unwilling to work; doing little work 不愿工作的; 懒惰的; 懒散的: *He's not stupid, just lazy.* 他倒不笨, 就是懒. **2** showing or causing a lack of energy or activity 懒洋洋的; 无精打采的; 令人发懒的: *a lazy yawn* 懒洋洋的呵欠 ○ *a lazy summer evening* 令人发懒的夏日黄昏 ○ *We spent a lazy day at the beach.* 我们在海滩上度过了闲散的一天. ▷ **laz·ily** *adv*: *a river flowing lazily beside the meadow* 在草泽旁缓缓流着的河. **lazi·ness** *n* [U].

□ **ˈlazy-bones** *n* (*infml* 口) lazy person 懒骨头; 懒虫; 懒人.

ˌlazy ˈSusan (*US*) = DUMB WAITER (DUMB).

lb *abbr* 缩写 = (*pl* unchanged or **lbs** 复数或不变或作 **lbs**) pound (weight) (Latin *libra*) (源自拉丁文 *libra*): *apples 20p* (ie 20 pence) *per lb* 苹果每磅 20 便士 ○ *Add 2lb sugar.* 加两磅糖. Cf 参看 OZ.

lbw /ˌel biː ˈdʌbljuː; ˌɛl bi ˈdʌblju/ *abbr* 缩写 = (in cricket) leg before wicket.

LCD /ˌel siː ˈdiː; ˌɛl si ˈdi/ *abbr* 缩写 = (*electronics* 电子) liquid crystal display 液晶显示.

L/Cpl *abbr* 缩写 = Lance-Corporal: *L/Cpl (Colin) Small* (科林·)斯莫尔一等兵.

lea /liː; li/ *n* (*arch* 古) area of open grassland; meadow 草原; 草地.

LEA /ˌel iː ˈeɪ; ˌɛl i ˈe/ *abbr* 缩写 = (*Brit*) Local Education Authority 地方教育局: *an ˌLEA ˈstudy grant* 地方教育局助学金.

leach /liːtʃ; litʃ/ *v* **1** [Tn] make (liquid) percolate through soil, ore, ash, etc 使(液体)过滤. **2** [Tn·pr, Tn·p] **~ sth from sth; ~ sth out/away** remove (soluble matter) from sth by the action of a percolating fluid 滤去某物中的(可溶物质): *leach minerals from the soil* 滤去土壤中的矿物质.

lead[1] /led; lɛd/ *n* **1** [U] (*chemistry* 化) heavy soft metal of dull greyish colour, used for water pipes, in roofing, as a radiation shield, etc and which is mixed with other metals to form alloys 铅. ⇨App 10 见附录10. **2** [C, U] (thin stick of) graphite used as the part of a pencil that makes a mark 铅笔心. **3** [C] (*nautical* 海) lump of lead fastened to a cord, used for measuring the depth of water beneath a ship 测深锤. **4 leads** /ledz; lɛdz/ [pl] (**a**) strips of lead used to cover a roof (铺屋顶用的)铅皮, 长条铅板. (**b**) area of roof (esp flat) covered with these 铅皮铺的屋顶. **(c)** framework of lead strips holding glass panes, eg in a lattice window 固定玻璃的铅框(如格子窗上的). **5** (idm 习语) **swing the lead** ⇨ SWING[1].

▷ **leaded** /ˈledɪd; ˋlɛdɪd/ *adj* [usu attrib 通常作定语] covered or framed with lead 铅皮覆盖的; 铅框的: *leaded windows, glass* 铅框窗户、镶有铅框的玻璃. **ˌleaded ˈlight** small panel of leaded glass, esp coloured, forming part of a larger window 花饰铅条窗(尤指彩色的, 为大窗的一部分).

leaden /ˈledn; ˋlɛdn̩/ *adj* **1** dull, heavy or slow 沉闷的; 沉重的; 缓慢的: *the leaden atmosphere of the museum* 博物馆里那沉滞的气氛 ○ *a leaden heart* 沉重的心 ○ *moving at a leaden pace* 沉重而缓慢地移动. **2** lead-coloured; dull grey 铅灰色的; 暗灰色的: *leaden clouds promising rain* 预示有雨的铅灰色的云. **3** [attrib 作定语] (*dated* 旧) made of lead 铅制的: *leaden pipes* 铅管.

lead·ing /ˈledɪŋ; ˋlɛdɪŋ/ *n* [U] (in printing) space between lines of print (印刷术中的)行间距.

□ **ˌlead ˈpencil** stick of graphite enclosed in a wooden or metal holder, used for writing or drawing 铅笔.

ˌlead-ˈpoisoning *n* diseased condition caused by taking lead into the body 铅中毒.

lead[2] /li:d; lid/ *n* **1** [U, sing] guidance given by going first or in front; example 带领; 领头; 榜样: *He's the chief trouble-maker; the others just follow his lead.* 他是首要的捣乱分子, 其余的人只是跟着学的. **2** [sing] distance by which one competitor, etc is in front 领先的距离: *have a lead of three metres, two lengths, half a lap, etc* 领先三米、两个自首至尾的距离、半圈等 ○ *The company has built up a substantial lead in laser technology.* 该公司在激光技术方面已大大领先. **3 the lead** [sing] first place or position 首位; 最先的地位: *move/go into the lead* 进入领先地位 ○ *take (over) the lead (from sb)/lose the lead (to sb)* (从某人处)夺得领先地位; 将领导地位丧失(给某人). **4** [C] principal part in a play, etc; person who plays this part 剧中的主角; 扮演主角的演员: *play the lead in the new West End hit* 在伦敦西区群众喜闻乐见的新戏中担任主角 ○ [attrib 作定语] *the lead guitarist of the group* 队中第一吉他手. **5** [C] (in card-games) act or right of playing first (纸牌戏中)首先出牌, 首先出牌权: *Whose lead is it?* 谁先出牌? **6** [C] piece of information or evidence that might provide the solution to a problem; clue 线索: *The police are investigating an important new lead.* 警方正在调查一条重要的新线索. **7** [C] (also **leash**) strap or cord for leading or controlling a dog 系狗用的带子或绳索: *You must keep your dog on a lead in the park.* 在公园里要牵着你的狗. **8** [C] length of wire conveying electrical current from a source to a place of use 导线; 引线. **9** (idm 习语) **follow sb's example/lead** ⇨ FOLLOW. **give (sb) a ˈlead (a)** encourage others by doing sth first 带头做某事以鼓励他人: *The Church should give more of a lead on basic moral issues.* 教会应当就基本道德问题多做出些榜样. **(b)** provide a hint towards the solution of a problem 提示解决问题的线索. **take the ˈlead (in doing sth)** set an example for others to follow 为他人树立榜样.

□ **ˈlead story** (*journalism* 新闻) item of news made to appear most prominent in a newspaper or coming first in a news broadcast (报纸或新闻广播的)头条新闻.

lead[3] /li:d; lid/ *v* (*pt, pp* **led** /led; lɛd/) **1** [Tn, Tn·pr, Tn·p] **(a)** show (sb) the way, esp by going in front 给(某人)指路; (尤指)领路: *lead a guest to his room* 领客人到他自己的房间 ○ *He led the group out into the garden.* 他把那些人领出去进了花园. **(b)** guide or take (sb/sth) by holding, pulling, etc 带领(某人[某物])(扶着、牵着等): *lead a blind man across the road* 领着一盲人过马路 ○ *She grasped the reins and led the horse back.* 她抓住缰绳把马牵了回去. **2** [Tn, Tn·pr, Tn·p, Cn·t] **~ sb (to sth)** influence the actions or opinions of sb 引导某人; 影响某人的言行: *He's too easily led.* 他太容易受人左右了. ○ *What led you to this conclusion?* 你是怎样得出这个结论的? ○ *Don't be led astray* (ie tempted to do wrong) *by him.* 不要被他引入歧途. ○ *Her constant lying led me to distrust everything she said.* 她总撒谎, 我完全不相信她的话了. **3** [Ipr, Ip] be a route or means of access 通; 达: *This door leads into the garden.* 此门通往花园. **4** [Ipr] **~ to sth** have sth as its result 导致某种结果: *This misprint led to great confusion.* 这个印刷错误造成很大的混淆. ○ *Your work seems to be leading nowhere*, ie achieving nothing. 你的工作似乎不会有什么结果. **5** [Tn] have a certain kind of life (used esp with the *ns* shown) 过某种生活(尤与所示名词连用): *lead a miserable existence, a life of luxury, a double life, etc* 过悲惨的生活、豪华的生活、双重人格的生活等 ○ *decide to lead a new life* 决定过新生活. **6** [I, Ipr, Tn, Tn·pr] **~ (sb/sth) (in sth)** be in first place or ahead of (sb/sth) 处于首位或领先于(某人[某事物]): *The champion is leading by eighteen seconds.* 该冠军领先十八秒. ○ *lead the world in cancer research* 在癌症研究方面走在世界前列. **7** [I, Tn, Tn·pr] **~ (sb/sth) (into sth)** be the leader or head of (sb/sth); direct; control 为(某人[某事物])的领袖或首脑; 率领; 指挥: *I'll take part, but I won't want to lead.* 我参加, 但不想当领导. ○ *lead an army, an expedition, a strike* 领导军队、探险、罢工 ○ *lead a discussion, the singing, the proceedings* 引导讨论、指挥唱歌、主持程序 ○ *Who is to lead the party into the next election?* 谁率领该党参加下次选举? **8** [Tn] (in card games) play (sth) as one's first card (纸牌戏中)首先出(某牌): *lead trumps, the two of clubs, etc* 先出王牌、梅花2等. **9** [Ipr] **~ with sth (a)** (*journalism* 新闻) have sth as the main news item 以(某事物)作主要新闻: *We'll lead with the dock strike.* 我们把码头工人罢工当作头条新闻. **(b)** (in boxing) use (a particular punch) to begin an attack (拳击)以(某一拳法)出击: *lead with one's left/right* 以左[右]拳出击. **10** (idm 习语) **all roads lead to Rome** ⇨ ROAD. **the blind leading the blind** ⇨ BLIND[1]. **lead sb by the ˈnose** make sb do everything one wishes; control sb completely 牵着某人的鼻子走; 完全控制某人. **lead sb a (merry) ˈdance** cause sb a lot of trouble, esp by making him follow from place to place 给某人造成极大麻烦(尤指令其跟着东奔西跑). **lead a ˈdog's life** be constantly worried, troubled or miserable 过狗一般的生活(长期忧虑、痛苦或悲伤). **lead sb a ˈdog's life** make sb's life wretched 使某人生活痛苦不堪. **lead sb to the ˈaltar** (*dated or joc* 旧或谑) marry sb 与某人结婚. **lead sb to believe (that)...** cause sb to believe (sth that is false or uncertain) 使某人相信(某假事或不确之事). **lead sb up the garden ˈpath** deceive sb 欺骗某人. **lead the ˈway (to sth)** go first; show the way 先行; 带路: *Our scientists are leading the way in space research.* 我们的科学家在宇宙探索中处于领先地位. **11** (phr v) **lead (sth) off** start (sth) 开始(某事): *Her recital led off/She led off her recital with a Haydn sonata.* 她在独奏会上首先演出的是海顿的奏鸣曲. **lead sb on** (*infml* 口) persuade sb to believe or do sth by making false promises or claims 劝诱某人相信或做某事: *The salesman tried to lead me on with talk of amazing savings on heating bills.* 推销员竭力怂恿我, 说可以节省一大笔取暖费用. **lead up to sth** prepare, introduce or go before sth 于某事之先作准备、引进或进行: *the events leading up to the outbreak of war* 导致战争爆发的事件.

□ **ˈlead-in** *n* **1** introduction to a subject, etc 引子; 引言; 引论: *He told an amusing story as a lead-in to the serious part of his speech.* 他讲了一个有趣的故事作他演说中重要内容的引子. **2** wire connecting an aerial to a radio or television set (收音机或电视机天线的)引入线.

leader /ˈli:də(r); ˋlidɚ/ *n* **1** person or thing that leads 领导者; 领袖; 首领; 指挥者; 起引导作用的事物: *the leader of an expedition, a gang, the Opposition, etc* 考察队领队、团伙头目、反对党领袖等 ○ *He is well up with the leaders* (ie the leading competitors) *at the half-way stage of the race.* 比赛进行到一半时他已和最先的几名赛者并驾齐驱了. **2** (*music* 音) (*US* **ˈconcert-master**) principal first violinist of an orchestra (管弦乐队中的)首席小提琴手. **3** (*law* 律) principal counsel in a court case 居主导地位的讼务律师. **4** = LEADING ARTICLE (LEADING). **5** blank strip at the beginning of a tape, film, etc used to help when threading into a machine (磁带、胶卷等前端的)空白段. **6** (*botany* 植) long thin shoot growing from a stem or branch, esp of fruit trees, usu cut back in pruning (茎或枝上的)顶枝(尤指果树的).

▷ **lead·er·less** *adj*: *a leaderless rabble* 无领导的暴民.

lead·er·ship *n* **1** [U] being a leader 作为领导者；领导：*the responsibilities of leadership* 领导的责任 ○ [attrib 作定语] *a leadership crisis* 领导者地位的危机. **2** [U] ability to be a leader 领导能力：*qualities of leadership necessary in a team captain* 任领队的领导素质 ○ [attrib 作定语] *leadership potential* 领导潜力. **3** [CGp] group of leaders 领导人员；领导层：*calling for firm action by the union leadership* 工会领导人号召采取坚决行动.

□ ˌ**Leader of the ˈHouse** (in Britain) member of the government in the House of Commons or Lords who arranges and announces the business of the House (英国)下议院或上议院的议长.

lead·ing /ˈliːdɪŋ; ˋlidɪŋ/ *adj* [attrib 作定语] **1** most important; chief 最重要的；主要的：*one of the leading writers of her day* 她那个时代最重要的作家之一 ○ *play a leading role in sth* 在某事中起主要作用. **2** in first position(s) 首位的；前列的：*the leading runners* 跑在前面的人.

□ ˌ**leading ˈarticle** (also **leader**) (*Brit journalism* 新闻) principal newspaper article by the editor, giving opinions on events, policies, etc; editorial (报纸的)社论.

ˌ**leading ˈedge** forward edge of an aircraft's wing (飞机机翼的)前缘.

ˌ**leading ˈlady, leading man** actor taking the chief part in a play, etc (戏剧等中)演主角的演员.

ˌ**leading ˈlight** (*infml approv* 口，褒) prominent member of a group (一组织中的)重要人物：*one of the leading lights of our club* 我们俱乐部的重要人物.

ˌ**leading ˈquestion** question that is worded so as to prompt the desired answer 诱导性询问(希望按询问者的意思回答的).

ˈ**leading-rein** *n* (**a**) long rein used for leading a horse 缰绳. (**b**) (also ˈ**walking rein**) strap attached to a lightweight harness worn by a young child who has just learnt to walk 缚住学行幼儿的带子.

leaf /liːf; lif/ *n* (*pl* **leaves** /liːvz; livz/) **1** [C] one of the (usu green and flat) parts of a plant, growing from a stem or branch or directly from the root 叶子：*lettuce, cabbage, etc leaves* 莴苣、洋白菜等的叶子 ○ *sweep up the dead leaves* 扫枯叶. **2** [C] sheet of paper (esp forming two pages of a book) 叶；页；(尤指书或本中有两个印刷面的)张：*carefully turn over the leaves of the precious volume* 小心翻动珍本书的书页 ○ *a loose leaf of paper lying on the desk* 脱落在书桌上的一页纸. **3** [U] metal, esp gold or silver, in the form of very thin sheets 金属薄片；(尤指)金箔，银箔：*gold leaf* 金箔. **4** [C] hinged flap or detachable section used to extend a table-top (延长桌面的)折面或活面. **5** (idm 习语) **come into/be in ˈleaf** grow/be covered with leaves 长出[长满]叶子. **shake like a leaf** ⇨ SHAKE[1]. **take a leaf out of sb's ˈbook** copy sb; act or behave in a similar way to sb 模仿某人；行为或举止学某人. **turn over a new leaf** ⇨ NEW.

▷ **leaf** *v* (phr v) **leaf through sth** turn over the pages of (a book, etc) quickly; glance through sth 快速翻(书页等)；浏览某物：*leaf idly through a magazine while waiting* 等候时无聊地浏览杂志.

leaf·age /ˈliːfɪdʒ; ˋlifɪdʒ/ *n* [U] leaves collectively; foliage 叶子(总称).

leaf·less *adj* having no leaves 无叶的.

leafy *adj* (**-ier, -iest**) (**a**) covered in or having many leaves 多叶的；长满叶子的：*a leafy forest, branch, bush* 树叶茂密的森林、树枝、灌木. (**b**) consisting of leaves 由叶子构成的：*leafy vegetables* 叶状蔬菜. (**c**) made or caused by leaves 叶子制的；由叶子造成的：*a leafy shade* 叶子形成的荫.

□ ˈ**leaf-mould** *n* [U] soil or compost consisting mostly of decayed leaves (主要由腐叶组成的)腐叶土.

L

leaf·let /ˈliːflɪt; ˋliflɪt/ *n* **1** printed sheet of paper, usu folded and free of charge, containing information 散页印刷品；(通常指)传单：*pick up a leaflet about care of the teeth* 拿起一张宣传保护牙齿的传单. **2** (*botany* 植) small leaf 小叶.

league[1] /liːg; lig/ *n* **1** group of people or countries combined for a particular purpose 联盟；同盟：*the League of Nations* 国际联盟. **2** group of sports clubs competing against each other for a championship (参赛运动队的)联盟：*the local darts league* 地方掷镖俱乐部联盟 ○ [attrib 作定语] *the league champions* 联赛冠军 ○ *bottom of the league table* 联赛成绩名次表上的末尾. **3** (*infml* 口) class or category of excellence (好坏的)等级，范畴：*They're not in the same league.* 他们不属同一级别. ○ *I'm not in his league.* 我不是他那一类人. ○ *be out of one's league*, ie outclassed 不如与自己同类的人. **4** (idm 习语) **in league (with sb)** conspiring together; allied 共谋；联合：*He pretended not to know her but in fact they were in league (together).* 他装着不认识她，其实他们暗中勾结(在一起).

▷ **league** *v* (phr v) **league together** form a league; unite 组成联盟；联合：*We must league together against this threat.* 面对这种威胁我们必须联合起来.

league[2] /liːg; lig/ *n* (*arch* 古) former measure of distance (about 3 miles or 4.8 km) 里格(旧时长度单位，约3英里或4.8公里). ⇨App 5 见附录5.

leak /liːk; lik/ *n* **1** (**a**) hole, crack, etc through which liquid or gas may wrongly get in or out 漏洞；裂隙：*a leak in the roof*, ie allowing rain to enter 屋顶的裂隙 ○ *a leak in the gas pipe*, ie allowing gas to escape 煤气管上的裂缝 ○ *a slow leak in a bicycle tyre* 自行车内胎上的细孔. (**b**) liquid or gas that passes through this 泄出的液体或气体：*smell a gas leak* 闻出有泄出的煤气味. **2** similar escape of an electric charge, caused by faulty insulation, etc 漏电(因绝缘不良等). **3** (*fig* 比喻) accidental or deliberate disclosure of secret or confidential information 秘密或情报的泄露或透露：*the latest in a series of damaging leaks* 一系列危害性泄密事件中最新的一桩. **4** (⚠ *sl* 讳，俚) act of urination 撒尿：*have/take/go for a leak* 撒尿. **5** (idm 习语) **spring a leak** ⇨ SPRING[3].

▷ **leak** *v* **1** (**a**) [I] (of a container) allow liquid or gas to get in or out wrongly (指容器)漏：*This boat leaks like a sieve*, ie very badly. 这条船漏得像个筛子. (**b**) [I, Ipr, Ip] (of liquid or gas) get in or out in this way (指液体或气体)渗入或逸出：*The rain's leaking in.* 雨水在往里渗. ○ *Air leaked out of the balloon.* 空气自气球中逸出. ⇨ Usage at DRIP[1] 用法见DRIP[1]. **2** [Tn, Tn·pr] **~ sth (to sb)** reveal (information) 透露或泄露(情报)：*Who leaked this to the press?* 这件事是谁泄露给新闻界的? **3** (phr v) **leak out** (of information) become known (指情报)泄露，透露：*The details were supposed to be secret but somehow leaked out.* 这些细节原属秘密，可是不知怎么给泄露出去了.

leak·age /ˈliːkɪdʒ; ˋlikɪdʒ/ *n* **1** [C, U] (instance of) leaking 渗漏；泄露：*a leakage of toxic waste* 有毒废物的渗漏 ○ (*fig* 比喻) *The leakage of technological secrets is reaching alarming proportions.* 技术秘密的泄露已达到惊人的程度. **2** [C] thing that has leaked 渗漏物.

leaky *adj* having holes or cracks that leak 漏的；有漏隙的；有裂缝的：*a leaky ship, kettle, roof* 漏的船、壶、屋顶.

lean[1] /liːn; lin/ *adj* (**-er, -est**) **1** (of people and animals) without much flesh; thin and healthy (指人或动物)瘦的：*a lean athletic body* 瘦而矫健的身体. **2** (of meat) containing little or no fat (指肉)脂肪少的，无脂肪的：*lean beef* 瘦牛肉. **3** [esp attrib 尤作定语] (**a**) small in amount or quality; meagre 少量的；质量低的；贫乏的：*a lean diet, harvest* 量少的饮食、收获. (**b**) (of a period of time) not productive (指一段时间)产量低的：*lean years* 歉岁 ○ *a lean season for good films* 好影片不多的一段时期.

▷ **lean** *n* [U] lean part of meat 瘦肉：*a lot of fat but not much lean* 肥肉多瘦肉少.

lean·ness /ˈliːnnɪs; ˋlinnɪs/ *n* [U].

lean[2] /liːn; lin/ *v* (*pt, pp* **leant** /lent; lɛnt/ or **leaned** /liːnd; lind/) ⇨Usage at DREAM[2] 用法见DREAM[2]. **1** [I, Ipr, Ip] be in a sloping position; bend 倾斜；弯曲；屈身：*lean out of the window, back in one's chair, over to one side, etc* 探身窗外、仰靠椅背、俯向一侧等 ○ *Just lean forward for a moment, please.* 请稍稍向前弓一下身. **2** [Ipr] **~ against/(up)on sth** rest on sth in a sloping position for support 倚靠在某物上：*a ladder leaning against the wall* 倚着墙的梯子 ○ *The old man leant upon his stick.* 那个老先生拄着个手杖. ○ *lean on sb's arm, one's elbows, etc* 靠在某人的手臂上、支撑在两肘上. **3** [Tn·pr] **~ sth against/on sth** cause sth to rest against sth 使某物靠在另一物上：*The workmen leant their shovels against the fence and went to lunch.* 那些工人把

铁锹往篱笆上一靠就吃午饭去了. **4** (idm 习语) **bend/lean over backwards** ⇨ BACKWARDS (BACKWARD). **5** (phr v) **lean on sb** (*infml* 口 *esp US*) try to influence sb by threats 威胁或恐吓某人: *If they don't pay soon we'll have to lean on them a little.* 要是他们不马上付款, 我们就得给他们加点压力了. **lean (up)on sb/sth (for sth)** depend on sb/sth 依靠某人[某事物]: *lean upon others for guidance* 依靠别人的指导 ○ *lean on his friends' advice* (他)听信朋友们的意见. **lean towards sth** have a tendency towards sth 倾向: *He leans towards more lighthearted subjects in his later works.* 他在后期的创作中倾向于比较轻松的主题.

▷ **lean·ing** *n* tendency; inclination 倾向; 爱好: *have a leaning towards socialism/have socialist leanings* 有社会主义倾向.

□ **ˈlean-to** *n* small building or shed with its roof resting against the side of a larger building, wall or fence 披屋; 单坡棚: *They keep hens in a lean-to at the end of the garden.* 他们在园子尽头处的单坡棚里养母鸡. ○ [attrib 作定语] *a lean-to greenhouse* 单斜面温室.

leap /li:p; lip/ *v* (*pt, pp* **leapt** /lept; lɛpt/ or **leaped** /li:pt; lipt/) ⇨Usage at DREAM[2] 用法见 DREAM[2]. **1** [I, Ipr, Ip] jump vigorously 跳; 跳跃: *The cat leapt from the chair.* 猫从椅子上跳开了. ○ (*fig* 比喻) *My heart leapt for joy at the news.* 我听到这个消息心情万分激动. ○ *A frog leapt out.* 一只青蛙一跃而出. **2** [I, Ipr, Ip] move quickly in the specified direction; rush 迅速向某方向运动; 冲; 窜: *leap to the telephone, into one's car, upstairs* 冲过去抓电话、一头钻进汽车里、冲上楼去 ○ (*fig* 比喻) *They leapt to stardom with their first record.* 他们录制了第一张唱片, 一跃而入明星行列. **3** (**a**) [Tn] jump over (an obstacle) 跳过(障碍): *leap a gate, puddle, ditch, etc* 跳过大门、水洼、壕沟等. (**b**) [Tn·pr] **~ sth over sth** cause (a horse, etc) to jump over (an obstacle) 使(马等)跃过(障碍): *leap a horse over a fence* 策马跃过篱笆. ⇨Usage at JUMP[2] 用法见 JUMP[2]. **4** (idm 习语) **jump/leap to conˈclusions** ⇨ CONCLUSION. **ˌlook before you ˈleap** (*saying* 谚) consider the possible consequences before taking action 慎思而后行. **5** (phr v) **leap at sth** accept sth eagerly, without hesitation 迫不及待地接受某事物: *She leapt at the chance to go to America.* 她立刻抓住时机赴美. ○ *leap at an opportunity, offer, invitation, etc* 立刻抓住机会、接受提议、接受邀请等.

▷ **leap** *n* **1** vigorous jump 跳; 跳跃: *He crossed the garden in three leaps.* 他跳三步就跨过了花园. **2** (*fig* 比喻) rapid increase or change 激增; 骤变: *a leap in prices, oil production, the number of people out of work* 价格、石油产量、失业人数激增. **3** (idm 习语) **by/in ˌleaps and ˈbounds** very rapidly 非常迅速: *Her health is improving by leaps and bounds.* 她的健康迅速好转. **a leap/shot in the dark** ⇨ DARK[1]. **leap·ing** *adj* [attrib 作定语] moving up and down quickly and irregularly 跃动的; 跳跃的: *leaping waves, flames, etc* 翻腾的波浪、跳动的火焰.

leap-frog 跳背游戏

□ **ˈleap-frog** *n* [U] game in which each player in turn leaps with parted legs over another who is bending down 跳背游戏. — *v* (**-gg-**) [Tn] leap over (sb) in this way 跳过(某人)(作跳背游戏).

ˈleap year one year in every four years, with an extra day (29 February) 闰年.

learn /lɜ:n; lɝn/ *v* (*pt, pp* **learnt** /lɜ:nt; lɝnt/ or **learned** /lɜ:nd; lɝnd/) ⇨Usage at DREAM[2] 用法见 DREAM[2]. **1** [I, Ipr, Tn, Tn·pr, Tw, Tt] **~ (sth) (from sb/sth)** gain knowledge or skill by study, experience or being taught 学; 学习: *I can't drive yet — I'm still learning.* 我还不会开车——我仍在学. ○ *learn from one's mistakes* 从错误中学 ○ *learn a poem by heart*, ie memorize it 背熟一首诗 ○ *She learns languages with ease.* 她学语言不费劲. ○ *learn (how) to swim, to walk, to fly, etc* 学习游泳、走路、飞行等. **2** [Ipr, Tn, Tf, Tw] **~ (of/about) sth** become aware of (sth) through information or observation; realize 获悉; 得知; 认识到: *I'm sorry to learn of/about your illness.* 听说你病了, 我十分难过. ○ *I never learned his name.* 我从未听说过他的名字. ○ *learn (that) it's no use blaming other people* 认识到埋怨别人是没有用的 ○ *learn what it means to be poor* 领悟贫困的含义. **3** (idm 习语) **learn one's ˈlesson** learn what to do or not to do in future by noting the results of one's actions 汲取教训: *I'll never do that again; I've learned my lesson!* 我再也不做那种事了, 我已有了教训! **show sb/know/learn the ropes** ⇨ ROPE. **you/we live and learn** ⇨ LIVE[2].

▷ **learned** /ˈlɜ:nɪd; ˈlɝnɪd/ *adj* **1** having much knowledge acquired by study 有学问的; 博学的: *learned men* 学者 ○ *He's very learned but rather absent-minded.* 他很有学问, 可是好忘事. **2** of or for learned people 学术性的; 为学者的: *learned journals, societies, language* 学术刊物、团体、语言 ○ *the learned professions*, eg law, medicine 有学识的职业(如法律、医学) ○ (*law* 律) *my learned friend*, ie legal colleague (a term of courtesy) (法律界同行之间的敬称). **learn·edly** *adv*: *speak learnedly and at length* 讲话有学问又很详尽.

learner *n* person who is gaining knowledge or skill 学习者: *I'm still only a learner, so don't expect perfection!* 我还在学习, 别指望我十全十美! ○ *a quick/slow learner* 聪明的[迟钝的]学习者 ○ *That car's being driven by a learner*, ie a learner driver. 那辆汽车正由见习司机驾驶.

learn·ing *n* [U] knowledge obtained by study 学问; 学识; 知识: *a man of great learning* 学识渊博的人.

□ **ˌlearner ˈdriver** person who is learning to drive but has not yet passed the driving test 见习司机.

lease /li:s; lis/ *n* **1** contract by which the owner of land, a building, etc allows another person to use it for a specified time, usu in return for rent (土地、房屋等的)租约, 租契: *take out a lease on a holiday home* 租妥一所度假住宅 ○ *When does the lease expire?* 租约什么时候期满? ○ *The lease has four years left to run.* 租约还有四年到期. ○ (*esp Brit*) *have a flat on a 99-year lease* 有一套租期为99年的单元. ⇨Usage at TENANT 用法见 TENANT. **2** (idm 习语) **a new lease of life** ⇨ NEW.

▷ **lease** *v* [Tn, Tn·pr, Dn·n] **~ sth (to/from sb)** grant or obtain the use of (sth) in this way 出租; 租得: *lease a car, building, field* 租汽车、房子、土地 ○ *The firm leases an office with views over the river.* 公司租一个带临河风景的办事处.

□ **ˈleasehold** *n* **~ (of/on sth)** (*esp Brit*) holding of property by means of a lease 租赁; 租赁权; 租赁期: *have the leasehold on a house, etc* 租得一所房子等. — *adj, adv*: *a leasehold property* 租赁的房地产 ○ *own a flat leasehold* 对一套住房有租赁权. **ˈleaseholder** *n*. Cf 参看 FREEHOLD (FREE[1]).

leash /li:ʃ; liʃ/ *n* **1** = LEAD[2] 7. **2** (idm 习语) **hold sth in ˈleash** restrain sth 抑制某事物: *I managed to hold my anger in leash until she had gone.* 我压住火儿她在场时没有发作. **strain at the leash** ⇨ STRAIN[1].

least /li:st; list/ *indef det, indef pron* (used as the superlative of LITTLE[2] 用作 LITTLE[2] 的最高级) smallest in size, amount, extent, etc 最小的; 最少的; 最小; 最少. (**a**) (*det*): *He's the best teacher even though he has the least experience.* 他尽管经验最少, 但教得最好. ○ *The least worry we have is about the weather.* 我们最不担心的就是天气. ○ *If you had only the least thought for others you would not have spoken out in that way.* 你若稍为他人着想, 必不会那样说话. ⇨Usage at MUCH 用法见 MUCH. (**b**) (*pron*): *That's the least of my anxieties.* 那是我最不担心的. ○ *It's the least I can do to help.* 这是我能帮忙做的最起码的事了. ○ *She gave (the) least of all towards the wedding-present.* 她给的结婚礼物最少.

▷ **least** *adv* **1** to the smallest extent 最少; 最小: *just when we least expected it* 偏偏在我们最想不到的时候 ○ *He disliked many of his teachers and Miss Smith he liked* *(the) least.* 很多老师他都不喜欢, 最不喜欢的是那个女教师史密斯. ○ *She chose the least expensive of the hotels.* 她选了一家最便宜的旅馆. ○ *one of the least performed of Shakespeare's plays* 莎士比亚戏剧中演得最少的一出. **2** (idm 习语) **at least (a)** if nothing else is true; at any rate 反正; 无论如何: *She may be slow but at least she's reliable.* 她迟钝是迟钝, 但无论如何她很可靠. **(b)** not less than 至少: *at least 3 months, £3, 10 inches* 至少3个月、3英镑、10英寸. **ˌleast of ˈall** to an insignificant degree 最不; 尤其: *Nobody need worry, you least of all/least of all you.* 谁也不必担心, 尤其是你. ○ *Least of all would I lie to you.* 我最犯不上对你撒谎了. **ˌnot in the ˈleast** absolutely not; not at all 绝对不; 一点也不: *It doesn't matter in the least.* 那绝对不要紧. ○ *'Would you mind if I put the television on?' 'No, not in the least.'* '我开电视机影响你吗?' '一点都不影响.' **not least** especially; in particular 尤其是; 特别是: *The film caused a lot of bad feeling, not least among the workers whose lives it described.* 那影片招致许多人的反感, 尤其是工人不满其中对工人生活的描写. **last but not least** ⇨ LAST[2].

□ **ˈleastways, ˈleastwise** *advs* (*dialect or infml* 方或口) or at least 或至少: *There's no pub round here, leastways not that I know of.* 附近没有酒店, 至少据我所知没有.

leather /ˈleðə(r); ˈlɛðɚ/ *n* [U] **1** material made by tanning animal skins 皮革: *This sofa is covered in real leather.* 这沙发是真皮的. ○ [attrib 作定语] *leather shoes, gloves, belts, etc* 皮鞋、皮手套、皮带. **2** (idm 习语) **hell for leather** ⇨ HELL.

▷ **leath·er·ette** /ˌleðəˈret; ˌlɛðəˈrɛt/ *n* [U] imitation leather 人造革; 人造皮.

leath·ery /ˈleðərɪ; ˈlɛðərɪ/ *adj* as tough as leather 坚韧如皮革的: *leathery skin, meat* 粗而硬的皮肤、嚼不动的肉.

□ **ˈleather-jacket** *n* grub of the crane-fly 大蚊的幼虫.

leave[1] /liːv; liv/ *v* (*pt, pp* **left** /left; lɛft/) **1** [I, Ipr, Tn, Tn·pr] go away from (a person or place) 离开(某人或某处): *It's time for us to leave/time we left.* 我们该走了. ○ *The plane leaves Heathrow for Orly at 12.35.* 飞机于12时35分自希思罗机场起飞前往奥利. **2** [I, Tn] cease to live at (a place), belong to (a group), work for (an employer), etc 不再居于(某地)、不再归属(某团体)、不再为(某雇主)工作等: *He left England in 1964 and never returned.* 他于1964年离开英国, 一去不返. ○ *Many children leave school at 16.* 很多学生16岁就毕业了. ○ *My secretary has threatened to leave.* 我的秘书威胁说要辞职. **3** [Cn·a, Cn·g] cause or allow (sb/sth) to remain in a certain condition, place, etc 使或让(某人[某事物])处某状态、某地等: *Leave the door open, please.* 让门开着吧. ○ *Don't leave her waiting outside in the rain.* 别让她在外边雨中等着. **4** [Tn, Tn·pr] neglect or fail to take or bring (sth) 忽略或未拿或未带(某物): *I've left my gloves on the bus.* 我把手套落在公共汽车上了. **5** [Tn, Tn·pr] cause (sth) to remain as a result 使(某事物)留下而造成某结果: *Red wine leaves a stain.* 红葡萄酒能留下痕迹. ○ *The accident left a scar on her leg.* 那次事故后她的腿上留下了伤疤. **6** [Tn, Dn·n, Dn·pr] **~ sth (for sb)** hand over (sth) and then go away 留下, 交待下(某物): *Did the postman leave anything?* 邮递员什么也没有留下吗? ○ *Someone left you this note/left this note for you.* 有人给你留下这张条子. **7** [Tn, Dn·n, Dn·pr] **~ sth to sb** give sth as a legacy to sb 将某物遗赠给某人: *How much did he leave?* 他遗留下多少钱? ○ *She left you £500.* 她遗留给你500英镑. ○ *leave all one's money to charity* 把所有的钱遗赠给慈善事业. **8** [Tn·pr] entrust (sth) to another person 将(某事物)托付给他人: *You can leave the cooking to me.* 做饭的事你尽可以交给我. ○ *leave an assistant in charge of the shop/leave the shop in an assistant's charge* 留下一店员照管店铺[把店铺交付给一店员照料]. **9** [Tn, Tn·pr] **~ sth (till/until sth)** delay doing or having sth 暂时不做或不用某事物: *Let's leave the washing-up till the morning.* 餐具留到明天上午再洗吧. ○ *I like to leave the best bits till last.* 我喜欢把最好的留到最后. **10** [Tn] (*mathematics* 数) have (a certain amount) remaining 剩下(某量): *Seven from ten/Ten minus seven leaves three*, ie 10−7 = 3. 10减7得3. ○ *There are six days left before we go.* 离我们出发还剩下六天. **11** [Tn] have (sb) remaining alive 留下(某人)活在世上: *He leaves a widow and two children.* 他身后留下一个寡妇和两个孩子. **12** (idm 习语) **be left at the ˈpost** be left far behind from the start (of a contest, etc) (比赛等)一开始就被远抛在后. **keep/leave one's options open** ⇨ OPTION. **leave/let sb/sth aˈlone/ˈbe** not disturb or interfere with sb/sth 不打扰或不干预某人[某事物]: *Leave me be! Go away!* 别打扰我! 走开! ○ *I've told you to leave my things alone.* 我已经告诉过你不要动我的东西. **leave a bad/nasty ˈtaste in the mouth** (of experiences) be followed by feelings of disgust, anger or shame (指经历)留下令人厌恶、气愤或羞耻的感觉. **leave sb ˈcold** fail to move, interest or impress sb 未打动某人; 引不起某人的兴趣; 未使某人产生好感: *Her emotional appeal left him completely cold.* 她虽动情, 他却无动于衷. ○ *Jellied eels leave me cold!* 我可不喜欢吃鳗鱼冻! **leave the ˈdoor open** allow for the possibility of further discussion, negotiation, etc 门仍开着(有进一步讨论、谈判等的可能): *Although talks have broken down the door has been left open.* 谈判虽中断, 但谈判的大门却未关. **leave ˈgo/ˈhold (of sth)** release (sth) 松开(某物): *Leave go of my arm — you're hurting!* 松开我的胳膊 —— 你把我弄疼了! Cf 参看 LET SB/STH GO (LET[1]). **leave sb holding the ˈbaby** (*infml* 口) give sb unwanted responsibilities 把讨厌的事推给别人. **leave sb in the ˈlurch** (*infml* 口) abandon sb in an awkward situation 弃某人于困境. **leave/make one's, its, etc, mark** ⇨ MARK[1]. **leave it at ˈthat** (*infml* 口) say or do nothing more 就这样算了; 到此为止: *We'll never agree, so let's just leave it at that.* 我们绝不能取得一致意见, 还是到此为止吧. **leave a lot, much, something, nothing, etc to be deˈsired** be very, etc (un)satisfactory 令人极(不)满意: *Your conduct leaves a lot to be desired*, ie is extremely unsatisfactory. 你的品行极须改进. **leave the ˈroom** (*euph* 婉) go to the lavatory to relieve oneself 上厕所. **leave no stone unˈturned (to do sth)** try every possible means 千方百计; 想方设法: *They left no stone unturned in their search for the child's mother.* 他们千方百计寻找孩子的母亲. **leave sth out of acˈcount/consideˈration** fail to allow for sth; treat sth as unimportant 忽略某事; 不重视某事物. **leave sb/be/go out on a limb** ⇨ LIMB. **leave sb to his own deˈvices/to himˈself** allow or force sb to deal with problems unaided; not try to control sb 让某人独立处理问题; 不支配某人: *He leaves his staff to their own devices — as long as the work gets done he's happy.* 他让手下人自行处理 —— 只要工作能完成, 他就满意了. **leave sb/sth to the tender mercy/mercies of sb/sth** (*ironic* 反语) expose sb/sth to cruel or rough treatment by sb/sth 任某人[某事物]受他人[他事物]的粗暴对待: *Never leave a silk shirt to the tender mercies of an automatic washing-machine.* 切勿用自动洗衣机洗绸衬衫. **leave/let well alone** ⇨ WELL[3]. **leave word (with sb)** give a message (to sb) (给某人)留信息: *Please leave word with my secretary if you can't come.* 你要是不能来, 请给我的秘书留话. **13** (phr v) **leave sth aside** not consider sth; disregard 不考虑某事物; 忽视: *Leaving the expense aside, do we actually need a second car?* 费用多少不说, 且问我们真的需要再来一辆汽车吗? **leave sb/sth behind (a)** fail or forget to bring or take sb/sth 未能或忘记带某人[某物]: *Wait — don't leave me behind!* 等等 —— 别把我丢下! ○ *It won't rain: you can leave your umbrella behind.* 不会下雨, 你不必带伞了. **(b)** (*fml* 文) cause (signs of one's actions, an event, etc) to remain 留下(行为、事件等的痕迹): *a ruler who left behind a legacy of bitterness* 使后人痛苦的统治者 ○ *The storm left a trail of destruction behind.* 暴风雨过后留下满目疮痍的景象. **leave sb/sth for sb/sth** abandon sb/sth in favour of sb/sth else 抛弃某人[某事物]而追求他人[他事物]: *He left his wife for one of his students.* 他抛弃妻子去追求他的一个学生. ○ *leave advertising for a job in publishing* 离开广告业到出版界觅职. **leave ˈoff** stop 停止: *Hasn't the rain left off yet?* 雨还没停吗? **leave off sth/doing sth** (*infml* 口) stop sth/doing sth 停止某事[做某事]: *It's time to leave off work.* 是下班的时候了. ○ *I wish you'd leave off whistling like that.* 请你不要那样吹口哨了. **leave sth off** no longer wear sth 不再穿某物: *Pullovers can be left off in this warm weather.* 天气这么暖和, 可以不穿套头毛衣了. **leave sb/sth out (of sth)** not

L

include or mention; exclude; omit 不包括或不提及; 排除在外; 忽略掉: *Leave me out of this quarrel, please — I don't want to get involved.* 请别把我拉入这场争吵中——我可不想牵连进去. ○ *This word is wrongly spelt; you've left out a letter.* 这字拼错了, 你漏了一个字母. **leave sth over** postpone sth 推迟某事: *These matters will have to be left over until the next meeting.* 这些事情只好留到下次会议再讨论了.

leave[2] /li:v; liv/ *n* **1** [U] time absent from duty or work 假; 假期: *sick, shore, annual leave* 病假、离船上岸假、年假 ○ *a fortnight's leave* 两周的假期. **2** [U] **~ to do sth** (*fml* 文) (**a**) official permission to be absent from duty or work 准予做某事的假: *be given leave to visit one's mother* 获假探母. (**b**) permission 许可; 准许: *She has my leave to see him.* 她得到我的许可去看他. ⇨ Usage at HOLIDAY 用法见 HOLIDAY. **3** (idm 习语) **beg leave to do sth** ⇨ BEG. **ˌby/ˌwith your ˈleave** (*fml* 文) with your permission 承蒙俯允. **take French leave** ⇨ FRENCH. **ˌleave of ˈabsence** permission to be absent (esp from an official or a military post) 准假(尤指准予离开公职或军务者): *ask for leave of absence to attend a wedding* 请假参加婚礼. **on ˈleave** absent with permission 休假中: *He's just gone on leave.* 他刚请假走了. **take (one's) leave (of sb)** (*fml* 文) say goodbye (向某人)告别; 离别. **take ˌleave of one's ˈsenses** (*rhet or joc* 修辞或谑) go mad 发疯: *Have you all taken leave of your senses?* 你们都疯了吗? **without as/so much as a ˌby your ˈleave** (*infml* 口) without asking permission; rudely 擅自; 未经许可; 粗暴地.

□ **ˈleave-taking** *n* (*fml* 文) act of saying goodbye 告辞; 告别: *a tearful leave-taking* 洒泪而别.

-leaved (forming compound *adjs* 用以构成复合形容词) having leaves of the specified type or number 有某种类型的叶的; 有若干叶片的: *a broad-leaved plant* ○ *a three-leaved clover.*

leaven /ˈlevn; ˋlɛvən/ *n* [U] **1** substance (eg yeast) used to make dough rise before it is baked to make bread 酵母; 面肥. **2** (*fig* 比喻) quality or influence that makes people, an atmosphere, etc less serious, more lively, etc 使人、气氛等轻松、活跃等的因素: *a lively artistic community, acting as the leaven in society* 给社会增加生气的活跃的艺术团体.

▷ **leaven** *v* [Tn] **1** add leaven to (sth) 在(某物)中加酵母: *leavened bread* 发酵面包. **2** (*fig* 比喻) enliven (sth) 使(某事物)活跃.

leaves *pl* of LEAF.

leav·ings /ˈli:vɪŋz; ˋlivɪŋz/ *n* [pl] what is left, esp sth unwanted or of little value; left-overs 剩余物; 残存物: *Give our leavings* (ie unwanted food) *to the dog.* 把我们吃剩的东西喂狗吧.

lech·ery /ˈletʃərɪ; ˋlɛtʃərɪ/ *n* [C, U] (instance of) excessive interest in sexual pleasure 色欲; 淫荡.

▷ **lecher** /ˈletʃə(r); ˋlɛtʃɚ/ *n* (*derog* 贬) man who is always thinking about and looking for sexual pleasure 纵欲的人; 好色之徒.

lech·er·ous /ˈletʃərəs; ˋlɛtʃərəs/ *adj* having or showing an excessive interest in and desire for sexual pleasure 纵欲的; 好色的. **lech·er·ously** *adv*.

lec·tern /ˈlektən; ˋlɛktɚn/ *n* high sloping desk made to hold a lecturer's notes, a Bible in church, etc (台面倾斜供放讲稿的)讲台; (教堂中的)读经台. ⇨ illus at App 1 见附录1插图, page viii.

lec·ture /ˈlektʃə(r); ˋlɛktʃɚ/ *n* **1 ~ (to sb) (on sth)** talk giving information about a subject to an audience or a class, often as part of a teaching programme 演讲; 讲课: *give/deliver/read a lecture* 讲课[上课/讲学] ○ *a course of lectures on Greek philosophy* 希腊哲学系列讲演 ○ [attrib 作定语] *a lecture tour* 巡回讲演. **2** long reproach or scolding 冗长的训斥或谴责: *The policeman let me off with a lecture about speeding.* 那警察给我讲了一大顿注意车速的道理之后才让我走. ○ *give sb a lecture*, ie scold sb 训斥某人.

▷ **lec·ture** *v* **1** [I, Ipr] **~ (on sth)** give a lecture or series of lectures 作演讲; 讲课: *Professor Jones is not lecturing this term.* 琼斯教授这学期没课. ○ *He is lecturing on Russian literature.* 他正讲俄罗斯文学. **2** [Tn, Tn·pr] **~ sb (for/about sth)** scold or warn sb (about sth) (就某事)斥责或告诫某人: *Do stop lecturing me!* 别教训我了! ○ *lecture one's children for being untidy/about the virtues of tidiness* 训斥子女不讲整洁[训示子女注意整洁的美德]. **lec·turer** /ˈlektʃərə(r); ˋlɛktʃərɚ/ *n* person who gives lectures, esp at a college or university 讲师.

lec·ture·ship *n* post of lecturer (the lowest teaching grade at a British college or university) 讲师的职位.

led *pt, pp* of LEAD[3].

LED /ˌel i: ˈdi:; ˌɛl i ˋdi/ *abbr* 缩写 = (*electronics* 电子) light-emitting diode 发光二极管.

ledge /ledʒ; lɛdʒ/ *n* **1** narrow horizontal shelf coming out from a wall, cliff, etc 水平的窄长架状突出物; 壁架; 岩石架: *a window-ledge* 窗台 ○ *The climbers rested on a sheltered ledge jutting out from the cliff.* 登山者在突出于峭壁处有遮挡的岩石架上休息. ○ *a ledge for chalk beneath the blackboard* 黑板下方的粉笔槽. **2** ridge of rocks under water, esp near the shore 暗礁, 岩礁(尤指近岸的).

led·ger /ˈledʒə(r); ˋlɛdʒɚ/ *n* **1** book in which a bank, business firm, etc records its financial accounts 分类帐. **2** (*music* 音) =LEGER.

lee /li:; li/ *n* [SING] **1** part or side of sth providing shelter against the wind 背风处: *shelter in/under the lee of a hedge* 躲避在树篱的背风处. **2** [attrib 作定语] (*nautical* 海) of or on the part or side away from the wind 背风面的; 下风的: *the lee side of the ship* 船的下风舷. Cf 参看 WINDWARD (WIND[1]).

□ **ˈlee shore** (*nautical* 海) shore towards which the wind is blowing from the sea 下风岸.

leech /li:tʃ; litʃ/ *n* **1** small blood-sucking worm usu living in water and formerly used by doctors to remove blood from sick people 水蛭; 蚂蟥. **2** (*fig derog* 比喻, 贬) person who hangs about other people hoping to obtain money, food, alcohol, etc 依附于他人希望获得钱、食物、酒等的人. **3** (*arch or joc* 古或谑) doctor 医生. **4** (idm 习语) **cling/stick to sb like a ˈleech** stay very close to sb; be difficult for sb to get rid of 依附于某人; 纠缠某人不放.

leek /li:k; lik/ *n* vegetable related to the onion but with wider green leaves above a long white bulb 韭葱. ⇨ illus at ONION 见 ONION 插图.

leer /lɪə(r); lɪr/ *n* (usu *sing* 通常作单数) sly unpleasant look suggesting lust or ill will 挑逗性的或不怀好意的目光: *He has a most unpleasant leer.* 他目光猥亵, 十分讨厌.

▷ **leer** *v* [I, Ipr, Ip] **~ (at sb)** look with a leer 用挑逗性的或含敌意的目光看: *Go away; I don't enjoy being leered at.* 走开, 我讨厌让人不怀好意地看着.

leery /ˈlɪərɪ; ˋlɪrɪ/ *adj* [pred 作表语] **~ (of sb/sth)** (*infml* 口) wary; suspicious 机警; 怀疑: *I tend to be a bit leery of cut-price 'bargains'.* 我对减价商品有点戒心.

lees /li:z; liz/ *n* [pl] sediment at the bottom of a bottle of wine, etc; dregs (酒瓶等中的)沉淀物, 渣滓: *Don't shake the bottle or you will disturb the lees.* 别摇晃瓶子, 要不沉淀就都搅起来了.

lee·ward /ˈli:wəd; ˋliwɚd *or, in nautical use,* 作航海用语时读作 ˈlu:əd; ˋluɚd/ *adj, adv* on or to the side sheltered from the wind 背风(的); 下风(的); 在下风; 向下风: *sandhills on the leeward side of the island* 该岛下风处的沙丘. Cf 参看 WINDWARD (WIND[1]).

▷ **lee·ward** *n* [U] (*nautical* 海) side or direction towards which the wind blows 背风面; 下风: *steer to leeward* 驶向背风面. Cf 参看 WINDWARD *n* (WIND[1]).

lee·way /ˈli:weɪ; ˋliˌwe/ *n* [U] **1** amount of freedom to move, change, etc that is left to sb (可供某人活动、更动等的)余地: *This itinerary leaves us plenty of leeway.* 这个旅行计划给我们留有很多自由活动的余地. ○ *The parking space was big enough, but there wasn't much leeway,* ie margin for error. 停车处大是够大, 但并没有什么回旋余地. **2** sideways drift of a ship or aircraft, due to the wind (船或飞行器因风而致的)偏航, 漂移. **3** (idm 习语) **make up ˈleeway** recover lost time; get back into position 补偿失去的时间; 恢复原位: *She's been off school for a month, so she has a lot of leeway to make up.* 她一个月没上学了, 有许多课业要补上.

left[1] *pt, pp* of LEAVE[1].

□ **left-ˈluggage office** (*Brit*) (*US* **ˈbaggage room**) place (at railway stations, etc) where luggage may be temporarily deposited (火车站等的)行李寄存处.

ˈleft-overs *n* [pl] things remaining when the rest is

finished, esp food at the end of a meal; leavings 残存物; 剩余物; (尤指)残羹剩饭. ⇨Usage at REST[3] 用法见 REST[3].

left[2] /left; lɛft/ *adj, adv* **1** of, on or towards the side of the body which is towards the west when a person faces north 在左边(的); 在左侧(的); 在左面(的); 向左方(的): *Fewer people write with their left hand than with their right.* 用左手写字的人比用右手的少. ○ *Turn left here.* 由此往左. ○ [attrib 作定语] (*sport* 体) *left half, back, wing(er), etc* 左前锋、左后卫、左翼(队员)等. Cf 参看 RIGHT[5]. **2** (idm 习语) **about/left/right face** ⇨ FACE[2]. **about/left/right turn** ⇨ TURN[1]. **eyes right/left/front** ⇨ EYE[1]. **have two left 'feet** (*infml* 口) be very clumsy 非常笨拙. **,left, right and 'centre** (*infml* 口) everywhere 处处: *I've been looking for it left, right and centre — where did you find it?* 我前后左右都找遍了——你是在哪儿找到的呢? **right and left** ⇨ RIGHT[5].

▷ **left** *n* **1** [U] left side or region 左边; 左侧; 左部: *In Britain cars are driven on the left.* 在英国汽车靠左侧行驶. ○ *She was sitting immediately to my left.* 她挨着我坐在我的左边. **2** [C] (in boxing and fist-fighting) (blow given with the) left hand (拳击中)左手, 左手拳: *He knocked down his opponent with a powerful left.* 他一记有力的左手拳将对手击倒. **3 the Left** [Gp] (*politics* 政) **(a)** the left wing of a party or other group (党团的)左翼. **(b)** supporters of socialism in general (泛指)社会主义拥护者: *a history of the Left in Europe/of the European Left* 欧洲左翼政党史.

left·ist *n, adj* (*politics* 政) (supporter) of the left wing 左派的; 左派分子.

lefty (also **leftie**) *n* (*infml* 口) **1** (*derog* 贬) leftist 左派; 左派分子. **2** (*esp US*) left-handed person 左撇子.

□ **,left 'bank** bank of a river on the left side of a person facing downstream (河的)左岸(面向下游而言).

'left-hand *adj* [attrib 作定语] of or on the left 左边的; 左侧的; 在左面的: *the left-hand side of the street* 街的左侧 ○ *a left-hand drive car*, ie one with the steering wheel and other controls on the left-hand side 左侧驾驶的汽车. **,left-'handed** *adj* **1** (of a person) using the left hand more easily or usually than the right (指人)惯用左手的, 左撇子的. **2** (of a blow) delivered with the left hand (指出击)用左手的. **3** (of a tool) designed for use with the left hand (指工具)为左手使用的: *,left-handed 'scissors* 左手用的剪刀. **4** (of a screw) to be tightened by turning towards the left (指螺丝钉)向左旋的. **5** (idm 习语) **a ,left-handed 'compliment** compliment that is ambiguous in meaning and possibly ironic 暧昧的恭维(意思含混, 可能为反语). — *adv* with the left hand 用左手: *Do you always write left-handed?* 你一向用左手写字吗? **,left-'hand·ed·ness** *n* [U]. **,left-'hander** left-handed person or blow 惯用左手的人; 左撇子; 左手的一击; 左手拳.

,left 'wing (*politics* 政) supporters of a more extreme form of socialism than others in their party, group, etc 左翼; 左派: *the left wing of the Labour Party* 工党中的左翼. **,left-'wing** *adj*: *,left-wing i'deas, intel'lectuals, 'policies* 左翼思想、左翼知识分子、左倾政策. **left-'winger** *n* supporter of the left wing 左翼分子.

leg /leg; lɛg/ *n* **1** [C] one of the limbs of an animal's or person's body used for standing and walking 腿: *have long, short, straight, crooked, skinny, sturdy, bandy, shapely, etc legs* 有长、短、直、曲、皮包骨、敦实、罗圈、匀称等的腿 ○ *the powerful back legs of a frog* 青蛙强有力的后腿 ○ *the long thin legs of a spider* 蜘蛛细长的腿 ○ *a gammy* (ie lame) *leg* 跛腿. ⇨illus at HUMAN 见 HUMAN 插图. **2** [C, U] this part of an animal used as food 动物的腿(用作食物): *a leg of lamb* 羊腿 ○ *Would you like some leg or some breast* (eg of turkey)? 你要腿肉还是胸脯肉(如火鸡)? **3** [C] part of a garment covering this limb 裤腿: *The leg of my tights has torn.* 我的裤袜的裤腿破了. ○ *a trouser leg* 一条裤腿. **4** [C] one of the supports of a chair, table, etc (桌椅等的)腿: *a chair with one leg missing* 缺一条腿的椅子. **5** [C] **(a)** section of a journey 一段行程: *The last leg of our trip was the most tiring.* 我们旅行的最后一段行程最累人. **(b)** (*sport* 体) one of a series of matches between the same opponents (一连串比赛中的)一局, 一场, 一项. **6** [U] (in cricket) part of the field to the left of the wicket-keeper and behind the batsman (板球)三柱门守门员左方与击球员后方之间的场地: *long, short, square leg*, ie fieldsmen at various positions there 在此场地远离击球员的、靠近击球员的、靠近三柱门的外场员 ○ [attrib 作定语] *a leg break*, ie a ball bowled so as to move away from this side 在此场地反弹后离开此场地的球 ○ *a leg glance*, ie a stroke by batsman that sends the ball there 击球员将球击入此场地的一击 ○ *the leg stump*, ie the stump nearest this 三柱门中最靠近此场地的一柱. **7** (idm 习语) **as fast as one's legs can carry one** ⇨ FAST[1] *adv*. **be all 'legs** (*derog* 贬) have legs that are disproportionately long and thin 腿过分瘦长. **be on one's/its last legs** ⇨ LAST[1]. **be on one's 'legs** (*joc* 谑) **(a)** be standing, esp to make a speech 站着(尤指演说). **(b)** (*infml* 口) (after an illness) be well enough to walk about (病后)康复至可以走动. Cf 参看 ON ONE'S HIND LEGS (HIND[1]). **give sb a 'leg up** (*infml* 口) **(a)** help sb to mount a horse, climb a wall, etc 帮助某人上马、登墙等. **(b)** (*fig* 比喻) use money or influence to help sb 用钱或影响力帮助某人. **have hollow legs** ⇨ HOLLOW. **have, etc one's tail between one's legs** ⇨ TAIL. **,leg before 'wicket** (*abbr* 缩写 **lbw**) (in cricket) way in which a batsman may be out because of illegally obstructing, with a leg or some other part of the body, a ball that would otherwise have hit the wicket (板球中)击球员用腿或其他部位对可能击中三柱门的好球作违例阻挡而犯规出局. **not have a ,leg to 'stand on** (*infml* 口) have nothing to support one's opinion, justify one's actions, etc (论点等)站不住脚; (对行为)无合理解释等. **pull sb's leg** ⇨ PULL[2]. **shake a leg** ⇨ SHAKE[1]. **show a leg** ⇨ SHOW[2]. **stretch one's legs** ⇨ STRETCH. **talk the hind legs off a donkey** ⇨ TALK[2]. **walk one's legs off** ⇨ WALK[1]. **walk sb off his feet/legs** ⇨ WALK[1].

▷ **leg** *v* (idm 习语) **'leg it** (*infml* 口) go on foot 步行: *It's no use, the car won't start — we'll have to leg it.* 没用了, 汽车发动不起来了——我们只好走着去了.

□ **'leg-pull** *n* (*infml* 口) hoax 欺骗; 戏弄. **'leg-pulling** *n* [U].

'leg-rest *n* support for a seated person's leg (病人坐时)搁腿的凳或架.

'leg-room *n* [U] space available for a seated person's legs (坐时)腿的活动空间: *There's not much leg-room in these aircraft.* 这些飞机的坐位没有什么伸腿的空间.

'leg-warmers *n* [pl] outer coverings, usu woollen, for each leg from knee to ankle 暖腿套(通常为毛织品, 长自膝及于踝).

'leg work (*infml* 口) work involving much walking or travelling about to collect information, deliver messages, etc 跑腿活儿; 外勤: *Being a detective involves a lot of leg work.* 当侦探少不了跑腿的活儿.

leg·acy /'legəsɪ; 'lɛgəsɪ/ *n* **1** money or property left to sb in a will 遗赠产; 遗赠的财物. **2** (*fig* 比喻) thing passed to sb by predecessors or from earlier events, etc 先人或过去遗留下来的东西: *the cultural legacy of the Renaissance* 文艺复兴时期的文化遗产 ○ *His weak chest was a legacy of a childhood illness.* 他那瘦弱的胸脯是儿时患病的后遗症. Cf 参看 INHERITANCE (INHERIT).

legal /'li:gl; 'ligl/ *adj* **1** [attrib 作定语] of or based on the law 法律的; 依照法律的; 法定的: *my legal adviser/representative*, eg a solicitor 我的法律顾问[代表](如律师) ○ *seek legal advice*, ie consult a solicitor 找律师咨询 ○ *take legal action*, ie sue or prosecute 采取法律行动(提出诉讼或告发) ○ *the legal age for drinking, driving, voting, etc*, ie the minimum age for doing these things legally 喝酒、驾驶、选举等的法定年龄. **2** allowed or required by the law 法律许可的; 法律要求的; 合法的: *Should euthanasia be made legal?* 是否应将安乐死合法化? ○ (*joc* 谑) *Why shouldn't I take a holiday? It's perfectly legal.* 为什么我就不该放假? 那是完全合法的嘛.

▷ **leg·al·ism** /'li:gəlɪzəm; 'ligl,ɪzəm/ *n* [U] (*usu derog* 通常作贬义) strict adherence to or excessive respect for the law 拘泥于法律条文; 墨守法规; 条文主义. **leg·al·istic** *adj*.

leg·ally /'li:gəlɪ; 'liglɪ/ *adv*: *be legally responsible for sth* 对某事负法律责任 ○ *a legally witnessed will* 经合法签名作证的遗嘱.

□ **,legal 'aid** payment from public funds for or towards the cost of legal advice or representation 法律援助(由公共基金提供的法律服务费用).

L

ˌ**legal proˈceedings** lawsuit 法定程序; 法律诉讼: *take, begin, threaten, etc legal proceedings (against sb)* (对某人)起诉, 提起诉讼, 以起诉相威胁.

ˌ**legal ˈtender** form of money that must be accepted if offered in payment 合法货币, 法定货币(用于偿付时必须接受的货币): *The old pound note is no longer legal tender.* 旧制的英镑纸币已不是法定的货币了.

leg·al·ity /liːˈɡælətɪ; lɪˋɡælətɪ/ *n* [U] state of being legal 合法: *the legality of this action will be decided by the courts* 这一行动的合法性将由法院裁定.

leg·al·ize, -ise /ˈliːɡəlaɪz; ˋliɡlˌaɪz/ *v* [Tn] make (sth) legal 使(某事物)合法化: *Some people want to legalize the possession of cannabis.* 有些人想将私有大麻合法化.

leg·ate /ˈleɡɪt; ˋlɛɡɪt/ *n* ambassador of the Pope to a foreign country 罗马教皇的使节.

leg·atee /ˌleɡəˈtiː; ˌlɛɡəˋti/ *n* (*law* 律) person who receives a legacy 遗产继承人.

lega·tion /lɪˈɡeɪʃn; lɪˋɡeʃən/ *n* **1** [CGp] minister below the rank of ambassador, and his staff, representing his government in a foreign country 公使馆全体人员. **2** [C] this minister's official residence 公使馆.

leg·ato /ləˈɡɑːtəʊ; lɪˋɡɑto/ *adj, adv* (*music* 音) (to be played) in a smooth even manner 连奏(的).

le·gend /ˈledʒənd; ˋlɛdʒənd/ *n* **1** [C] story handed down from the past, esp one that may not be true 传奇; 传说: *the legend of Robin Hood* 罗宾汉传奇. **2** [U] such stories gathered together 民间传说; 稗史; 野史: *exploits famous in legend and song* 民间传说和歌谣中为人熟知的英雄事迹 ○ *the heroes of Greek legend* 希腊民间传说的英雄. **3** [C] (*infml* 口) famous event or person 传奇事件或人物: *Her daring work behind the enemy lines is now legend.* 她在敌后的英勇斗争业迹现在已是传奇美谈. ○ *one of the great legends of pop music, Elvis Presley* 流行摇滚乐伟大的传奇人物之一, 埃尔维斯·普雷斯利. **4** [C] (**a**) inscription on a coin or medal 硬币上的或奖章上的刻字. (**b**) (*fml* 文) words accompanying and explaining a map, picture, etc (地图、图片等的)图例, 说明, 题词. **5** (*infml* 口) person who achieves great fame while still alive (在世的)当代名人: *a legend in one's (own) lifetime* 一生为人传颂的活伟人. **6** (idm 习语) **a** ˌ**living ˈlegend** ⇨ LIVING[1].

▷ **le·gend·ary** /ˈledʒəndrɪ; *US* -derɪ; ˋlɛdʒəndˌɛrɪ/ *adj* **1** of or mentioned in legend 传奇的; 传说的; 传奇式的: *legendary heroes* 传奇英雄. **2** (*infml* 口) very well known; famous 有名的; 著名的: *a legendary recording* 著名的录音 ○ *Her patience and tact were legendary.* 她的耐心和机智是出名的.

le·ger /ˈledʒə(r); ˋlɛdʒɚ/ *n* (also ˈ**le·ger line, led·ger, led·ger line**) (*music* 音) short line added above or below the staff to take notes which are outside its range 加线. ⇨illus at MUSIC 见 MUSIC 插图.

le·ger·de·main /ˌledʒədəˈmeɪn; ˌlɛdʒɚdɪˋmen/ *n* [U] (*fml* 文) **1** skilful performance of tricks using the hands; juggling; conjuring 花招; 戏法; 障眼法. **2** cunning or deceitful way of arguing 诡辩; 狡辩.

-legged (forming compound *adjs* 用以构成复合形容词) having legs of the specified number or type 有若干条腿的; 有某类型的腿的: *a* ˌ*three-legged* ˈ*stool* ○ ˌ*bare-*ˈ*legged* ○ ˌ*long-*ˈ*legged* ○ ˌ*cross-*ˈ*legged*.

leg·gings /ˈleɡɪŋz; ˋlɛɡɪŋz/ *n* [pl] protective outer coverings for the legs 绑腿; 裹腿: *a pair of leggings* 一副绑腿.

leg·gy /ˈleɡɪ; ˋlɛɡɪ/ *adj* **1** having noticeably long legs 腿长的: *a tall leggy girl in a short dress* 穿着短连衣裙双腿修长的高个子姑娘 ○ *a leggy newborn foal* 新出生的细腿小马驹. **2** (of a plant) having a long thin stem (指植物)茎细而长的.

le·gible /ˈledʒəbl; ˋlɛdʒəbḷ/ *adj* (of print or handwriting) clear enough to be read easily (指印刷或字迹)清楚的, 易读的: *The inscription was still legible.* 铭文仍清晰可辨. Cf 参看 READABLE (READ). ▷ **le·gib·il·ity** /ˌledʒəˈbɪlətɪ; ˌlɛdʒəˋbɪlətɪ/ *n* [U]. **le·gibly** /-əblɪ; -əblɪ/ *adv*: *Please write more legibly.* 请写清楚些.

le·gion /ˈliːdʒən; ˋlidʒən/ *n* **1** (**a**) battle unit of the ancient Roman army 古罗马军团: *Caesar's legions* 凯撒军团. (**b**) special military unit, esp of volunteers serving in the army of another country 特殊军团; (尤指志愿服务于他国军队中的)外籍军团: *the French Foreign Legion* 法国军队中的外籍军团. **2** large number of people 大批的人: *This new film will please his legions of admirers.* 这部新电影将得到他的广大影迷的欢迎.

▷ **le·gion** *adj* [pred 作表语] (*rhet* 修辞) very many; numerous 极多; 大批: *Their crimes are legion.* 他们的罪行罄竹难书.

le·gion·ary /ˈliːdʒənərɪ; *US* -nerɪ; ˋlidʒənˌɛrɪ/ *n, adj* (member) of a legion(1) 古罗马军团的(成员).

le·gion·naire /ˌliːdʒəˈneə(r); ˌlidʒəˋnɛr/ *n* member of a legion, esp of the French Foreign Legion 外籍军团成员(尤指法国的外籍军团中的).

□ **legionˈnaires' disease** (*medical* 医) form of bacterial pneumonia 退伍军人协会会员病, 军团病(一种细菌性肺炎).

le·gis·late /ˈledʒɪsleɪt; ˋlɛdʒɪsˌlet/ *v* [I, Ipr] ~ **(for/ against sth)** make laws 立法; 制定法律: *It is the job of Parliament to legislate.* 立法是议会的工作. ○ *It's impossible to legislate for every contingency.* 为每一偶发事件都立法是不可能的. ○ *legislate against racial discrimination* 制定法律禁止种族歧视.

▷ **le·gis·la·tion** /ˌledʒɪsˈleɪʃn; ˌlɛdʒɪsˋleʃən/ *n* [U] (**a**) action of making laws 立法; 法律的制定: *Legislation will be difficult and take time.* 立法难且费时. (**b**) the laws made 法律; 法规: *New legislation is to be introduced to help single-parent families.* 新法规即将实施以匡助单亲家庭.

le·gis·lat·ive /ˈledʒɪslətɪv; *US* -leɪtɪv; ˋlɛdʒɪsˌletɪv/ *adj* [esp attrib 尤作定语] law-making 立法的; 制定法律的: *a legislative assembly, chamber, body, etc* 立法会议、会议厅、机关等 ○ *Legislative reform is long overdue.* 立法方面的改革早该进行.

le·gis·lator /ˈledʒɪsleɪtə(r); ˋlɛdʒɪsˌletɚ/ *n* (*fml* 文) member of a legislature 立法机关成员; 立法者.

le·gis·lat·ure /ˈledʒɪsleɪtʃə(r); ˋlɛdʒɪsˌletʃɚ/ *n* [CGp] (*fml* 文) body of people with the power to make and change laws 立法机关; 立法团体.

le·git /lɪˈdʒɪt; lɪˋdʒɪt/ *adj* (*sl* 俚) legitimate(1) 合法的: *all legit and above-board* 一切合法的和光明正大的 ○ *a legit excuse* 合法的解释.

le·git·im·ate /lɪˈdʒɪtɪmət; lɪˋdʒɪtəmɪt/ *adj* **1** in accordance with the law or rules; lawful 法定的; 依法的; 合法的: *the legitimate heir* 法定继承人 ○ *I'm not sure that his business is strictly legitimate*, ie is legal. 我说不好他的生意是否绝对合法. **2** that can be defended; reasonable 正当的; 合理的: *a legitimate argument, reason, case, etc* 合乎情理的论据、理由、例子等 ○ *Politicians are legitimate targets for satire.* 政治家理所当然是讽刺的靶子. **3** (of a child) born to parents who are legally married to each other (指孩子)婚生的, 合法婚姻所生的. Cf 参看 ILLEGITIMATE. **4** genuine 正统的: *legitimate theatre*, ie serious drama, not musicals, revues, etc 正统戏剧(非歌舞喜剧、时事讽刺剧等).

▷ **le·git·im·acy** /lɪˈdʒɪtɪməsɪ; lɪˋdʒɪtəməsɪ/ *n* [U] (*fml* 文): *question the legitimacy of his actions* 对他行为的合法性置疑.

le·git·im·ately *adv*.

le·git·im·ize, -ise /lɪˈdʒɪtɪmaɪz; lɪˋdʒɪtəˌmaɪz/ *v* (*fml* 文) [Tn] make (sth) lawful or regular 使(某事物)合法, 正当或有合法地位: *a court ruling that legitimized the position taken by the protestors* 宣布抗议者采取的立场为合法的法庭裁决.

leg·less /ˈleɡlɪs; ˋlɛɡlɪs/ *adj* **1** without legs 没有腿的. **2** [pred 作表语] (*sl* 俚) very drunk 大醉.

leg·ume /ˈleɡjuːm, lɪˈɡjuːm; ˋlɛɡjum, lɪˋɡjum/ *n* **1** type of plant that has its seeds in pods, eg the pea and bean 豆科植物. **2** edible pod or seed of this (可食的)豆荚或豆.

▷ **leg·um·in·ous** /lɪˈɡjuːmɪnəs; lɪˋɡjumɪnəs/ *adj* of this family of plants 豆科植物的.

lei /ˈleɪiː; ˋle·ɪ/ *n* (esp in Polynesian countries) garland of flowers worn around the neck (尤指波利尼西亚地区诸国人戴于颈上的)花环.

leis·ure /ˈleʒə(r); *US* ˈliːʒər; ˋliʒɚ/ *n* [U] **1** time free from work or other duties; spare time 空暇; 闲暇: *We've been working all week without a moment's leisure.* 我们整星期一直工作, 没有片刻空闲. ○ [attrib 作定语] *leisure activities*, eg sport, hobbies 康乐活动(如体育运动、业余爱好) ○ *leisure wear*, ie casual clothing 便装. **2** (idm 习语) **at leisure** (**a**) (*fml* 文) not occupied 有空; 清闲: *They're seldom at leisure.* 他们难得清闲. (**b**) without

L

hurrying 从容不迫; 不慌不忙: *I'll take the report home and read it at leisure.* 我把报告带回家去慢慢看. **at one's 'leisure** when one has free time 有空时; 方便时. **marry in haste, repent at leisure** ⇨ MARRY.

▷ **leis·ured** /ˈleʒəd; ˈliʒəd/ *adj* [attrib 作定语] having plenty of leisure 有空闲的: *the leisured classes* 有闲阶级. **leis·urely** *adj, adv* without hurry 不慌不忙(的): *walk at a leisurely pace* 步态悠闲地走 ○ *work leisurely* 从容地工作.

□ **'leisure centre** public building with facilities for sports and recreational activities 业余活动中心.

leit·motiv (also **leit·motif**) /ˈlaɪtməʊtiːf; ˈlaɪtmoˌtif/ *n* **1** (*music* 音) short, constantly repeated, theme in an opera, symphony, etc associated with a particular person, thing or idea 主导主题; 主旋律. **2** (*fig* 比喻) any recurring feature 反复出现的特征: *The leitmotiv of her speech was the need to reduce expenditure.* 她讲话中一再强调的就是需要削减开支.

lem·ming /ˈlemɪŋ; ˈlɛmɪŋ/ *n* small mouse-like rodent of the arctic regions which migrates in large numbers, often with many of the animals drowning in the sea 旅鼠(栖居极地一带的小型啮齿动物, 定期集体迁徙, 常径直入海溺亡): *a lemming-like readiness to follow their leaders into certain disaster* 像旅鼠一样盲目追随领袖赴汤蹈火.

lemon /ˈlemən; ˈlɛmən/ *n* **1** (**a**) [C, U] oval yellow fruit with acidic juice used for drinks and flavouring 柠檬. ⇨ illus at FRUIT 见 FRUIT 插图. (**b**) [C] (also **'lemon tree**) tree with glossy green leaves on which this fruit grows 柠檬树. **2** (also **ˌlemon 'yellow**) [U] pale yellow colour 柠檬黄; 淡黄色. **3** [C] (*sl* 俚) unsatisfactory or defective thing, esp a car 差的或有毛病的东西(尤指汽车).

□ **ˌlemon 'curd** (also **ˌlemon 'cheese**) thick smooth jam made from lemons, sugar, eggs and butter 柠檬酪(由柠檬、糖、鸡蛋、黄油制的果酱).

ˌlemon 'sole type of edible flatfish 柠檬鳎(可食用).

ˌlemon 'squash (*Brit*) sweet lemon-flavoured drink that is diluted with water 柠檬汁.

'lemon-squeezer *n* device for pressing the juice out of a lemon 柠檬榨汁器.

lem·on·ade /ˌleməˈneɪd; ˌlɛmənˈed/ *n* [U, C] (**a**) sweet fizzy drink 汽水. (**b**) drink made from lemon juice, sugar and water 柠檬水(柠檬汁加糖和水的饮料).

le·mur /ˈliːmə(r); ˈlimɚ/ *n* monkey-like animal of Madagascar that lives in trees and is active at night 狐猴(马达加斯加岛的树栖夜行动物).

lend /lend; lɛnd/ *v* (*pt, pp* **lent** /lent; lɛnt/) **1** [Tn, Dn·n, Dn·pr] **~ sth (to sb)** (**a**) give or allow the use of sth temporarily, on the understanding that it will be returned 借出某物; 将某物借与(某人): *Can you lend me £5? I'll pay you back tomorrow.* 可以借我5英镑吗? 我明天还你. ○ *I lent that record to John but never got it back.* 我把那张唱片借给约翰了, 可是他再也没有还给我. (**b**) provide (money) for a period of time in return for payment of interest 贷(款): *The banks are lending money at a competitive rate of interest.* 银行竞相以低利率贷款. Cf 参看 BORROW. **2** [Tn, Dn·n, Dn·pr] **~ sth (to sth)** contribute or add sth to sth 提供或增添某事物: *lend one's services* 提供服务 ○ *lend the occasion a little glamour* 给这一场合增添一点光彩 ○ *His presence lent dignity to the occasion.* 有他出席这一场合就更形庄严. ○ *A little garlic lends flavour to a sauce.* 调味汁中加点蒜, 其味益增. **3** [Tn·pr] **~ sth to sth** (*fml* 文) make an event, development, report, etc more believable, significant, etc (used esp with the *ns* shown) 使事情、发展、报道等更加可信、意义更大等(尤与所示名词连用): *lend credibility, credence, plausibility, etc to a report* 使报道增加可信度、可靠性、接近真实的程度等 ○ *This news lends some support to earlier reports of a ceasefire.* 这一消息印证了先前有关停火的报道. **4** (idm 习语) **give/lend colour to sth** ⇨ COLOUR[1]. **lend an 'ear (to sb/sth)** listen patiently and sympathetically (to sb/sth) 耐心而同情地听着(某人的话[某事物]). **lend (sb) a (helping) hand (with sth)** give (sb) help (with sth) (在某事上)帮助(某人). **lend oneself/one's name to sth** (*fml* 文) allow oneself to be associated with sth 参与某事物: *a man who would never lend himself to violence* 决不参与暴力活动的人 ○ *She lent her name to many worthy causes.* 她参与了许多有意义的事情. **5** (phr v) **lend itself to sth** be suitable for sth 适合于某事物: *a novel which lends itself well to dramatization for television* 适合于拍成电视剧的小说.

▷ **lender** *n* person who lends 出借人; 贷方. Cf 参看 BORROWER (BORROW).

length /leŋθ; lɛŋθ/ *n* **1** [U] measurement or extent from end to end 长度; 长: *a river 300 miles in length* 长300英里的河 ○ *This room is twice the length of the other, but much narrower.* 这个房间的长度是那个房间的两倍, 但窄得多. ○ *a book the length of* (ie as long as) *'War and Peace'* 像《战争与和平》篇幅那样长的书 ○ *He jogged the length of the beach.* 他沿海滩慢跑了一段距离. ⇨App 5, 11 见附录5、11. ⇨illus at DIMENSION 见 DIMENSION 插图. **2** [U] amount of time occupied by sth 某事所用的时间: *You spend a ridiculous length of time in the bath.* 你洗澡用那么长时间, 真不像话. ○ *Size of pension depends on length of service with the company.* 养老金的多少取决于为公司服务年限的长短. ○ *a speech, symphony, ceremony, etc of considerable length* 相当长的演说、交响曲、仪式等. **3** [C] extent of a thing used as a unit of measurement 作量度单位用之物的长度: *This car will turn in its own length.* 这种汽车可以在自身长度范围内掉头. ○ *The horse/boat won the race by two lengths*, ie by a distance equal to twice its own length. 那马[船]以两个自首至尾的距离领先赢得该场比赛. **4** [C] piece (of sth) (某物的)一段: *timber sold in lengths of 5, 10 or 20 metres* 圆木分别以5、10或20米三种长度规格出售 ○ *I need a length of wire or string to tie it with.* 我需要一根铁丝或绳子来捆它. ○ *a 'dress length*, ie a piece of cloth long enough to make a dress 一块连衣裙料. **5** (idm 习语) **at arm's length** ⇨ ARM[1]. **at length** (**a**) (*fml* 文) after a long time; eventually; at last 经过一段长时间之后; 终于; 最后: *At length the bus arrived, forty minutes late.* 公共汽车终于来了, 晚了四十分钟. (**b**) taking a long time; in great detail; fully 长时间地; 详尽地; 充分地: *discuss sth at some, great, excessive, etc length* 比较、极为、过分等详细地讨论某事 ○ *He went on at tedious length about his favourite hobby.* 他仍不厌其详地讲他的业余爱好. **(at) full length** ⇨ FULL. **go to any, some, great, etc 'lengths (to do sth)** be prepared to do anything, something, a lot, etc (to achieve sth) (为达到某目的)不顾一切, 不遗余力: *They went to absurd lengths to keep the affair secret.* 他们为了保密无所不用其极. ○ *There are no lengths to which an addict will not go to obtain his drug.* 瘾君子为了得到毒品什么事都做得出来. ○ *She even went to the length of driving me home.* 她甚至不嫌麻烦开车把我送回家. **keep sb at arm's length** ⇨ ARM[1]. **the length and breadth of sth** in or to all parts of sth 处处; 到处: *travel the length and breadth of the British Isles* 走遍不列颠群岛. **measure one's length** ⇨ MEASURE[1].

▷ **-length** (forming compound *adjs* 用以构成复合形容词): *a ˌknee-length 'dress* ○ *floor-length 'curtains* ○ *a feature-length 'film*, ie about two hours long.

lengthen *v* [I, Tn] (cause sth to) become longer (使某物)变长: *The days start to lengthen in March.* 三月份白昼开始变长. ○ *lengthen a skirt* 把裙子放长. Cf 参看 SHORTEN.

'length·ways (also **'length·wise, long·ways, long·wise**) *adv, adj* with the shortest sides placed together; end to end 纵长(的); 纵向(的): *The tables were laid lengthways.* 这些餐桌是纵向摆设的.

lengthy /ˈleŋθɪ; ˈlɛŋθɪ/ *adj* (**-ier, -iest**) **1** very long 很长的: *Lengthy negotiations must take place before any agreement can be reached.* 要进行多次长时间谈判才能达成协议. **2** (*derog* 贬) tiresomely long; long and boring 冗长的; 长而乏味的: *lengthy explanations, speeches, etc* 冗长的解释、讲话等. ▷ **length·ily** *adv*.

le·ni·ent /ˈliːnɪənt; ˈlinɪənt/ *adj* not severe (esp in punishing people); merciful 宽大的(尤指惩罚人); 仁慈的: *a lenient fine, law, view* 不严苛的罚款、法律、意见 ○ *I hope the judge will be lenient.* 我希望法官宽大为怀.

▷ **le·ni·ence** /-əns; -əns/ (also **le·ni·ency** /-ənsɪ; -ənsɪ/) *n* [U] being lenient 宽大; 仁慈: *a magistrate known for her leniency with first-time offenders* 因对初犯宽宏大量而知名的女法官.

le·ni·ently *adv*: *treat sb leniently* 宽待某人.

lens /lenz; lɛnz/ *n* (*pl* **~es**) **1** piece of glass or other

L

transparent material with one or more curved surfaces used to make things appear clearer, larger or smaller when viewed through it, and used in spectacles, cameras, telescopes, etc 透镜; 镜片. ⇨illus at CAMERA, GLASSES (GLASS) 见 CAMERA、GLASSES (GLASS) 插图. **2** (*anatomy* 解) transparent part of the eye, behind the pupil, that focuses light (眼球的)晶状体. ⇨illus at EYE 见 EYE 插图.

Lent /lent; lɛnt/ *n* (in the Christian religion) period from Ash Wednesday to Easter Eve, the forty weekdays observed as a time of fasting and penitence (基督教的)大斋期, 四旬斋(从大斋首日到复活节前夕为期四十天的斋戒和忏悔): *give up chocolates, smoking, meat for Lent* 在大斋期戒巧克力、烟、肉.
▷ **Lenten** /ˈlentən; ˈlɛntən/ *adj* [attrib 作定语] of Lent 大斋期的; 四旬斋的: *Lenten services* 大斋期的礼拜.

lent *pt, pp* of LEND.

len·til /ˈlentl; ˈlɛntl/ *n* **(a)** plant grown for its small bean-like seeds 小扁豆. **(b)** its seed, usu dried, prepared as food 小扁豆(常指用作食物的干豆): [attrib 作定语] *lentil soup* 小扁豆汤.

lento /ˈlentəʊ; ˈlɛnto/ *adj, adv* (*music* 音) (played or to be played slowly (指演奏)缓慢(的)).

Leo /ˈliːəʊ; ˈlio/ *n* **1** [U] the fifth sign of the zodiac, the Lion 狮子宫(黄道第五宫). **2** [C] (*pl* **~s**) person born under the influence of this sign 属狮子宫星座的人. ⇨ Usage at ZODIAC 用法见 ZODIAC. ⇨illus at ZODIAC 见 ZODIAC 插图.

le·on·ine /ˈlɪənaɪn; ˈliəˌnaɪn/ *adj* (*fml* 文) of or like a lion 狮子的; 狮子般的: *leonine dignity* 狮子般的尊严.

leo·pard /ˈlepəd; ˈlɛpɚd/ *n* large African and S Asian flesh-eating animal of the cat family with a yellowish coat and dark spots 豹. ⇨illus at CAT 见 CAT 插图.
▷ **leo·pard·ess** /ˈlepədes; ˈlɛpɚdɪs/ *n* female leopard 母豹.

leo·tard /ˈliːətɑːd; ˈliəˌtɑrd/ *n* close-fitting one-piece garment worn by acrobats, dancers, etc (杂技、舞蹈等演员穿的)紧身连衣裤.

leper /ˈlepə(r); ˈlɛpɚ/ *n* **1** person suffering from leprosy 麻风病患者. **2** (*fig* 比喻) person who is rejected and avoided by others; outcast 被排斥或摈弃的人: *His unpopular views made him a social leper.* 他因见解不受欢迎而见弃于社会.

lep·re·chaun /ˈleprəkɔːn; ˈlɛprəˌkɔn/ *n* (in Irish folklore) fairy in the shape of a little old man (爱尔兰民间传说中的)精灵(貌似矮小老人).

lep·rosy /ˈleprəsɪ; ˈlɛprəsɪ/ *n* [U] infectious disease affecting the skin and nerves, causing disfigurement and deformity 麻风病.

les·bian /ˈlezbɪən; ˈlɛzbɪən/ *n* homosexual woman 同性恋女子.
▷ **les·bian** *adj* of or concerning lesbians 女性同性恋的: *a lesbian relationship* 女性同性恋关系.
les·bian·ism *n* [U].

lèse-majesté (also **lese-majesty**) /ˌleɪzˈmæʒesteɪ; *US* ˌliːzˈmædʒɪstɪ; ˈlizˈmædʒɪstɪ/ *n* [U] (*French* 法) **1** (*law* 律) crime or offence against a sovereign or government; treason 欺君罪; 犯上罪; 反政府罪; 叛逆罪. **2** (*joc* 谑) presumptuous behaviour from a junior person 僭越行为; 犯上行为: *Firing senior staff without reference to the boss comes pretty close to lèse-majesté.* 不请示老板而解雇高级职员, 罪近欺君.

le·sion /ˈliːʒn; ˈliʒən/ *n* (*medical* 医) **1** wound; injury 损害; 损伤: *painful lesions on his arms and legs* 使他四肢疼痛的损伤. **2** harmful change in the tissue of a bodily organ, caused by injury or disease (因伤、病)身体器官组织的损伤: *a lesion of the left lung* 左肺的损伤.

less /les; lɛs/ *indef det, indef pron* **~ (sth) (than...)** (used with [U] *ns* as the comparative of LITTLE[2] 作 LITTLE[2] 的比较级, 与不可数名词连用) not as much (as...); a smaller amount (of) 较少的; 更少的. **(a)** (*det*): *less butter, sugar, time, significance* 较少的黄油、较少的糖、较少的时间、不太重要 ○ *less coffee than tea* 咖啡比茶少 ○ *I received less money than the others did.* 我比别人收到的钱少. ○ *You ought to smoke fewer cigarettes and drink less beer.* 你应当少抽烟, 少喝啤酒. ⇨Usage at MUCH 用法见 MUCH. **(b)** (*pron*): *It seems less of a threat than I'd expected.* 威胁性似比我预料的要小. ○ *There's less to do in this job than the last.* 这份工作没有上份工作量大. ○ *'You must have paid £3 000 for your car.' 'No, (it was) less.'* '你买的汽车得花 3 000 英镑吧.' '不, 没那么多.' ○ *It's not far — it'll take less than an hour to get there.* 不远——到那儿用不了一个钟头. ○ *The receptionist was less than* (ie not at all) *helpful when we arrived.* 我们到达的时候接待员什么忙也不帮. ○ *It took less than no* (ie very little) *time to write a reply.* 立即写好了回信.
▷ **less** *adv* **~ (than...)** **1** to a smaller extent; not so much (as) 较少; 更少; 少: *I read much less now than I did at school.* 我现在看书远比我上学时少. ○ *It rains less in London than in Manchester.* 伦敦的降雨量比曼彻斯特少. ○ *less colourful, expensive, hungry, intelligent, tired, etc* 色彩不太丰富的、价钱较便宜的、不太饿的、悟性较差的、不那么疲劳的 ○ *less awkwardly, enthusiastically, often* 不太笨拙地、不热情地、不常. **2** (idm 习语) **any (the) less** (used after *not* 用于 not 之后) to a smaller extent 较小; 更小; 少: *She wasn't any (the) less happy for being on her own.* 她并不因独自一人而稍有不悦. **even/much/still less** and certainly not 更不用说; 更何况: *He's too shy to ask a stranger the time, still less speak to a room full of people.* 他连向陌生人打听时间都不好意思, 更不用说向一屋子人讲话了. **less and less** at a continually decreasing rate 越来越小地; 越来越少地: *She found the job less and less attractive.* 她发觉那工作越来越缺乏吸引力. ○ *He played the piano less and less as he grew older.* 他随着年龄的增长, 弹钢琴的次数越来越少了. **the less, more, etc... the less, more etc...** ⇨ THE. **more or less** ⇨ MORE. **no less (than...)** as much as 不少于; 多达: *We won £500, no less, in a competition.* 我们在一场竞赛中赢了足足 500 英镑. ○ *We won no less than £500 in a competition.* 我们在一场比赛中赢了多达 500 英镑.
less *prep* before subtracting (sth); minus 先扣除(某量); 减除: *a monthly salary of £450, less tax and national insurance* 月薪 450 英镑, 先扣除所得税和国民保险费 ○ *send a cheque for the catalogue price, less 10% discount* 按目录价格 9 折寄一张支票.

NOTE ON USAGE 用法: **Less**, instead of **fewer**, is now commonly and increasingly used with plural nouns 与复数名词连用时, 用 **less** 而不用 **fewer** 现很常见, 且日益普遍: *There have been less accidents on this road since the speed limit was introduced.* 自从实施速度限制, 这条路上的交通事故已经少些了. However, this is still thought to be incorrect English, and careful speakers prefer **fewer** 但是, 此用法仍视为误用, 言词谨慎者愿用 **fewer**: *fewer accidents* 事故少些.

-less /-lɪs; -lɪs/ *suff* 后缀 (used widely with *ns* to form *adjs* 可与许多名词结合构成形容词) without 无; 没有: *treeless* ○ *hopeless*. ▷ **-lessly** (forming *advs* 用以构成副词): *meaninglessly*. **-lessness** (forming uncountable *ns* 用以构成不可数名词): *helplessness*.

lessee /leˈsiː; lɛsˈi/ *n* (*law* 律) person who holds a building, land, etc on a lease 承租人; 租户. Cf 参看 LESSOR. ⇨Usage at TENANT 用法见 TENANT.

lessen /ˈlesn; ˈlɛsn̩/ *v* **1** [I] become less 变少: *The pain was already lessening.* 疼痛正在减轻. **2** [Tn] reduce (sth) 减少(某事物): *lessen the impact, likelihood, risk of sth* 减少某事物的影响、可能性、冒险性.

lesser /ˈlesə(r); ˈlɛsɚ/ *adj* [attrib 作定语] **1** not as great as the other(s) 较小的; 较少的; 次要的: *one of the author's lesser works* 该作者的一部次要的著作 ○ *He's stubborn, and so is she, but to a lesser degree*, ie not as much. 他很固执, 她也是, 只是程度差些. ○ *one of the lesser lights* (ie less prominent members) *of his profession* 他那一行的一个次要人物. **2** (idm 习语) **the ˌlesser of two ˈevils** the less harmful of two bad choices 两害相权其中之轻者.

les·son /ˈlesn; ˈlɛsn̩/ *n* **1** thing to be learnt by a pupil 课; 功课; 课业: *The first lesson in driving is how to start the car.* 学驾驶汽车的第一课是启动. **2** period of time given to learning or teaching 一节课: *My yoga lesson begins in five minutes.* 我五分钟后上瑜伽课. ○ *She gives piano lessons.* 她教授钢琴课. **3 ~ (to sb)** experience from which one can learn; example 经验; 教训; 榜样: *Let this be a lesson to you never to play with matches!* 把这件事当作你的教训, 再也不要玩火柴了! ○ *His* *courage is a lesson to us all.* 他很有勇气，是我们大家的榜样。○ *We are still absorbing the lessons of this disaster.* 我们从这场灾难中仍不断汲取教训。 **4** (*religion* 宗) passage from the Bible read aloud during a church service (教堂礼拜中诵读的)圣经选段: *The first lesson is taken from St John's Gospel.* 第一段圣经选自《约翰福音》。**5** (idm 习语) **learn one's lesson** ⇨ LEARN.

lessor /ˈlesɔː(r); ˈlɛsɔr/ *n* (*law* 律) person who lets a property on lease 出租人. Cf 参看 LESSEE. ⇨Usage at TENANT 用法见 TENANT.

lest /lest; lɛst/ *conj* (*fml* 文) **1** for fear that; in order that...not 唯恐; 以免; 为不使: *He ran away lest he (should/might) be seen.* 他怕人家看见他而跑开了. ○ *Lest anyone should think it strange, let me assure you that it is quite true.* 我向你们保证那是真事，以免有人觉得奇怪。 **2** (used after *fear, be afraid, be anxious,* etc 用于 fear、be afraid、be anxious 等之后): *She was afraid lest he might drown.* 她担心他会淹死.

let[1] /let; lɛt/ *v* (**-tt-**, *pt, pp* **let**) **1** [Cn·i no passive 不用于被动语态] (often with the infinitive omitted when the context is clear 连用的动词不定式在上下文清楚时常省略) allow (sb/sth) to 允许, 让(某人[某事物])...: *Don't let your child play with matches.* 别让孩子玩火柴. ○ *My father's only just had his operation and they won't let me see him yet.* 我父亲刚动过手术，医生还不允许我去看他. ○ *She asked me if she could leave but I wouldn't let her (leave).* 她问我她是否可以走，可我不让她走. **2** [Tn·pr, Tn·p] allow (sb/oneself/sth) to go or pass in, etc 允许(某人[自己/某事物])进入, 通过: *let sb into the house* 允许某人进屋 ○ *I'll give you a key to the flat so that you can let yourself in.* 我把房门钥匙交给你，你可以自己进去. ○ *You've let all the air out of the tyres.* 你让车胎的气都跑光了. ○ *Let her past (you).* 让她(从你身旁)过去吧. ○ *Don't let the dog out (of the room).* 别让狗跑到(房间)外面去. ○ *The roof lets water through.* 屋顶漏雨. ○ *Windows let in light and air.* 窗户可透光及通风. **3** [Cn·i no passive 不用于被动语态] (used as an imperative 用于祈使语气) (**a**) (with the first person plural to make a suggestion 与复数第一人称连用, 用以提出建议): *Let's go to the cinema.* 咱们看电影去吧. ○ *I don't think we'll succeed but let's try anyway.* 我想我们不一定能成功，但是不管怎样还是试试吧. (**b**) (in requests and commands 用于要求与命令): *Let the work be done immediately.* 工作要马上完成. ○ *Let there be no mistake about it,* ie Don't misunderstand me. 不要误解我的意思. (**c**) (used to express an assumption, eg in mathematics 用以表示假设, 如于数学中): *Let line AB be equal to line CD.* 设AB线与CD线等长. ○ *Let ABC be an angle of 90°.* 设ABC为一90°角. (**d**) (used to express defiance 用以表示违抗或蔑视): *Let them do their worst.* 让他们蛮干好啦. ○ *Let them attack: we'll defeat them anyway.* 让他们进攻吧，反正我们必胜. **4** [Tn, Tn·pr, Tn·p] **~ sth (out/off) (to sb)** allow sb to use (a house, room, etc) in return for regular payments 出租(房子、房间等): *I let (out) my spare rooms (to lodgers).* 我把多余的房间出租(给房客). ○ *They decided to let (off) the smaller flats at lower rents.* 他们决定把小单元廉价出租. **5** (idm 习语) **ˌlet sb/sth ˈbe** not disturb or interfere with sb/sth 不打扰或不干涉某人[某事物]: *Let me be, I want a rest.* 别打扰我, 我要休息. ○ *Let the poor dog be,* ie Don't tease it. 别逗那条可怜的狗吧. **let it ˈgo (at ˈthat)** say or do no more about sth 不再多说; 不再多做; 就那样吧: *I don't agree with all you say, but I'll let it go at that.* 我并不完全同意你说的话，但我不再多说了. ○ *I thought she was hinting at something but I let it go.* 我想她是有所指, 不过我没有理会. **ˌlet oneself ˈgo** (**a**) no longer restrain one's feelings, desires, etc 尽情发泄感情、放纵欲望等: *Go on, enjoy yourself, let yourself go.* 继续玩, 尽情地玩个痛快吧. (**b**) stop being careful, tidy, conscientious, etc 不再谨慎、整齐、认真等: *He has let himself go a bit since he lost his job.* 他自从失业以来变得有点邋遢了. **let sb/sth go; let go of sb/sth** release (one's hold of) sb/sth 松开或释放某人[某事物]: *let the rope go/let go of the rope* 松开绳子 ○ *Let me go!* 让我走! ○ *Will they let the hostages go?* 他们会释放人质吗? **let sb ˈhave it** (*sl* 俚) shoot, punish, etc sb 射击或惩罚某人: *Hold this bucket of water, and when he comes round the corner let him have it,* ie throw the water at him. 提着这桶水, 等他从拐角那边过来就泼他. **let me ˈsee** I'm thinking or trying to remember 让我想想: *Let me see — where did I leave my hat?* 让我想想看——我把帽子落在哪儿了? **let us ˈsay** for example 比如; 例如; 譬如: *If the price is £500, let us say, is that too much?* 价钱嘛, 比如说500英镑吧, 是不是太贵了? **to ˈlet** available for renting 待租; 出租: *Rooms to let,* eg on a sign outside a house 房间出租(如房屋外的招贴). (For other idioms containing **let**, see entries for *ns, adjs,* etc 查阅与 **let** 搭配的其他习语见有关名词、形容词等的词条, 如 **let alone** ⇨ ALONE; **let rip** ⇨ RIP.)

6 (phr v) **let sb down** fail to help sb; disappoint sb 不帮助某人; 使某人失望: *Please come and support me. Don't let me down.* 请来支持我. 可别不帮忙. ○ *This machine won't let you down,* ie is very reliable. 这部机器不会出毛病, 你尽管放心. **let sth down** (**a**) lower sth 放下; 降下: *We let the bucket down by a rope.* 我们用绳子把桶吊下去. ○ *This skirt needs letting down,* ie lengthening by lowering the hem-line. 这条裙子需要放长. (**b**) deflate sth 放掉某物的气: *let sb's tyres down* 把某人车胎的气放掉.

let sth in make (a garment, etc) narrower 将(衣物等)改窄, 改瘦: *This skirt needs letting in at the waist.* 这裙子的腰部需要改瘦. **let sb/oneself in for sth** (*infml* 口) cause sb/oneself to suffer (sth unpleasant) 使某人[自己]惹上(不愉快的事): *You're letting yourself in for trouble by buying that rusty old car.* 你买那辆生了锈的旧汽车是自找麻烦. **let sb in on/into sth** (*infml* 口) allow sb to share (a secret, etc) 让某人知道(秘密等): *Are you going to let them in on the plans?* 你是否打算让他们知道这些计划?

let sth into sth put sth into the surface of sth 将某物置入另物的表面: *window let into a wall* 嵌进墙壁的窗户.

let sb off (with sth) not punish sb (severely) 不(严厉)惩罚某人: *She was let off with a fine instead of being sent to prison.* 没让她入狱, 而是罚款了事. ○ *Don't let these criminals off lightly,* ie Punish them severely. 不要轻易放过这些罪犯. **let sb off (sth)** not compel sb to do (sth) 不强迫某人做(某事物): *We've been let off school today because our teacher is ill.* 今天学校放假, 因为我们的老师病了. **let sth off** fire sth off; explode sth 放枪炮、烟火等: *The boys were letting off fireworks.* 男孩子在放烟火.

let ˈon (about sth/that...) (to sb) (*infml* 口) reveal a secret 泄露秘密: *I'm getting married next week, but please don't let on (to anyone) (about it), will you?* 下星期我就要结婚了, 但(这事)请不要泄露(给任何人), 行吗?

let sb out release sb from sth, esp sth unpleasant 放过某人免受某事之累(尤指不愉快事): *The teacher said only Janet, George and Sue were to be punished, so that let me out.* 老师说只惩罚珍妮特、乔治和休, 因而饶了我. **let sth out** (**a**) make (a garment, etc) looser or larger 放宽, 放大(衣服等): *He's getting so fat that his trousers have to be let out round the waist.* 他越来越胖, 裤腰都得放宽了. (**b**) utter (a cry, etc) 发出(叫喊等): *She let out a scream of terror.* 她发出恐怖的叫喊. (**c**) reveal (a secret, etc) 泄露(秘密等): *Don't let it out about me losing my job, will you?* 别把我丢了工作一事泄露出去, 行吗?

let sb through allow sb to pass an exam or a test 评定某人及格: *I'm a hopeless driver, but the examiner let me through.* 我开车的技术糟透了, 但考官让我及格了.

let ˈup become less strong, intense, etc; relax one's efforts 减弱; 缓和; 减少; 减小; 放松: *Will the rain ever let up?* 雨什么时候才能小些? ○ *We mustn't let up, even though we're winning.* 我们即使快赢了也决不可松劲.

□ **ˈlet-down** *n* disappointment 失望; 沮丧: *The party was a big let-down.* 这个聚会令人大失所望.

ˈlet-up *n* reduction in strength, intensity, etc; relaxation of efforts 减弱; 缓和; 减少; 减小; 放松: *There is no sign of a let-up in the hijack crisis.* 绑架危机毫无缓和迹象.

let[2] /let; lɛt/ *n* (*Brit*) letting of property; lease 出租; 租出: *I can't get a let for my house,* ie find anyone to rent it from me. 我的房子租不出去.

▷ **let·ting** *n* (*Brit*) property that is let or to be let 出租或招租的建筑物或土地: *a furnished letting,* ie a furnished house or flat that is let 带家具的房屋出租 ○ *a holiday letting* 度假房屋出租.

NOTE ON USAGE 用法: Compare **let**, **rent** and **hire**. 试比较**let**、**rent**、**hire**这三个词. In British English these three verbs indicate a person giving permission for someone else to use something in return for money 在英式英语中这三个动词均作出租解: *X lets (out)/rents (out)/hires (out) Z to Y.* ☆ X把Z租给Y. ☆ Additionally, the user (Y) can be the subject of **rent** and **hire** 此外, 承租人Y亦可作**rent**和**hire**的主语: *Y rents/hires Z from X.* ☆ Y从X处租用Z. ☆ We usually **let (out)** accommodation, buildings or land 通常**let (out)**者为住处、建筑物或土地: *He lets (out) his house to tourists during the summer.* 他夏天把房子租给游客. ○ *The biggest factory in town is to let.* 伦敦最大厂房待租. We **rent (out)** houses, cars, etc, usually for fairly long periods of time ☆ **rent (out)** 房屋、汽车等通常为期较长: *She decided to rent out a room to get extra income.* 她为获得额外收入决定租出一个房间. ○ *I don't own my video. I rent it from a shop.* 我没有录像机, 我是从商店里租来的. We **hire (out)** a building, car, suit, etc, usually for a short period and for a particular purpose ☆ **hire (out)** 建筑物、汽车、服装等通常是为某种用途短期使用: *They hire out boats by the hour.* 他们按小时出租小船. ○ *The Labour party hired a concert hall for the election meeting.* 工党租用音乐厅作选举会场. In US English **rent (out)** is used in all the above meanings and **hire** can mean 'employ' 在美式英语中**rent (out)**用于上述各义, 而**hire**可指employ(雇用): *The company's hiring more men next week.* 该公司下周要再雇些男工. This use is less common in British English. 这种用法在英式英语中不多见.

let³ /let; lɛt/ *n* **1** (in tennis) ball which, when it is served, hits the top of the net and drops into the opponent's court (网球)(发出的)擦网球. **2** (idm 习语) **without ˌlet or ˈhindrance** (*fml or law* 文或律) unimpeded; without obstruction 毫无阻碍; 顺畅地: *Please allow the bearer of this passport to pass freely without let or hindrance.* 请予护照持有人顺利通行.

-let *suff* 后缀 (with *ns* forming *ns* 用以与名词结合构成名词) **1** little 小: *booklet* ○ *piglet*. **2** unimportant; minor 不重要; 细小; 次: *starlet*.

lethal /ˈli:θl; ˈliθəl/ *adj* **1** causing or able to cause death 致死的; 能致命的: *a lethal dose of poison* 毒药的致命剂量 ○ *lethal weapons* 致命武器. **2** damaging; harmful 破坏性的; 有害的: (*fig* 比喻) *The closure of the factory dealt a lethal blow to the town.* 那座工厂关闭是对该镇的致命打击. ○ (*joc* 谑) *This wine's pretty lethal!* ie very strong. 这酒的劲儿真要命! ▷ **leth·ally** /ˈli:θəlɪ; ˈliθəlɪ/ *adv*.

leth·argy /ˈleθədʒɪ; ˈlɛθɚdʒɪ/ *n* [U] extreme lack of energy or vitality; inactivity; apathy 无生气; 死气沉沉; 呆滞; 冷漠: *She suffers from bouts of lethargy and depression.* 她一阵阵无精打采、情绪低落. ○ *government lethargy on this issue* 政府对这一问题的软弱无力. ▷ **leth·ar·gic** /ləˈθɑ:dʒɪk; lɪˈθɑrdʒɪk/ *adj*: *Hot weather makes me lethargic.* 天气炎热我觉得委靡不振. **leth·ar·gic·ally** /-klɪ; -klɪ/ *adv*.

let's *contracted form* 缩约式 let us ⇨ LET¹ 3a.

let·ter /ˈletə(r); ˈlɛtɚ/ *n* **1** [C] written or printed sign representing a sound used in speech 字母: *'B' is the second letter of the alphabet.* B是字母表中的第二个字母. ○ *Fill in your answers in capital letters, not small letters.* 答案用大写字母填写, 不要用小写字母. **2** [C] written message addressed to a person or an organization, usu in an envelope, and sent by post 信: *Are there any letters for me?* 有我的信吗? ○ *Please inform me by letter of your plans.* 请来信把你的计划告诉我. ⇨ App 3 见附录3. **3 letters** [pl] (*dated or fml* 旧或文) literature as a profession or an academic study 文学; 文学研究: *the profession of letters* 文学家的职业 ○ *a man/woman of letters* 男[女]文学家. **4** (idm 习语) **a bread-and-butter letter** ⇨ BREAD. **a dead letter** ⇨ DEAD. **the ˌletter of the ˈlaw** the exact requirements or form of words of a law, rule, etc (as opposed to its general meaning or spirit) 法律、规则等的字面意义(与其整体意义或精神相对). **to the ˈletter** paying strict attention to every detail 严密周详地; 一丝不苟地: *carry out an order to the letter* 严格执行命令 ○ *keep to the letter of an agreement, a contract, etc* 严格遵照协议、合同等的条文办事.

▷ **let·ter·ing** /ˈletərɪŋ; ˈlɛtərɪŋ/ *n* [U] letters or words, esp with reference to their visual appearance 字母, 字(尤指其形状): *The lettering on the poster is very eye-catching.* 海报上的字体非常醒目.

□ **ˈletter-bomb** *n* terrorist explosive device disguised as a letter and sent by post 信件炸弹(恐怖分子投寄的似信件的爆炸物).

ˈletter-box *n* (**a**) (*Brit*) opening in a door, covered by a movable flap, through which letters are delivered 投信口. (**b**) (*US* **ˈmailbox**) box near or at the entrance to or inside a building, in which letters and other articles brought by the postman are placed 信箱. ⇨illus at App 1 见附录1插图, page vi. (**c**) = POST-BOX (POST³).

ˈletterhead *n* (**a**) [C] name and address of a person or an organization printed as a heading on stationery 信头(印于信笺上端的姓名或机关名称及地址). (**b**) [U] stationery printed with such a heading 印有信头的信笺.

ˌletter of ˈcredit (*finance* 财) letter from a bank authorizing the bearer to draw money from another bank 信用证.

ˈletterpress *n* [U] **1** printed text in a book, etc (as opposed to illustrations) 书中的印刷文字(以别于插图). **2** method of printing from raised type 凸版印刷.

let·tuce /ˈletɪs; ˈlɛtɪs/ *n* **1** [C] garden plant with crisp green leaves 莴苣; 生菜. **2** [U] its leaves used as food (esp in salads) 生菜叶: [attrib 作定语] *a lettuce and tomato salad* 生菜蕃茄色拉. ⇨illus at SALAD 见SALAD插图.

leu·co·cyte (*US* **leu·ko·cyte**) /ˈlu:kəsaɪt; ˈlukəˌsaɪt/ *n* (*medical* 医) white blood cell 白细胞; 白血球.

leu·co·tomy /lu:ˈkɒtəmɪ; luˈkɑtəmɪ/ *n* (*Brit*) = LOBOTOMY.

leuk·aemia (*US* **leuk·emia**) /lu:ˈki:mɪə; luˈkimɪə/ *n* [U] disease in which there is an uncontrollable increase in the numbers of white corpuscles 白血病.

levee¹ /ˈlevɪ; ˈlɛvɪ/ *n* (*arch* 古) assembly of visitors, esp at a formal reception 集体接见; (尤指正式的)招待会.

levee² /ˈlevɪ; ˈlɛvɪ/ *n* (*esp US*) embankment built to prevent a flooded river from overflowing 防洪堤: *the levees along the Mississippi* 密西西比河大堤.

level¹ /ˈlevl; ˈlɛvḷ/ *adj* **1** having a horizontal surface; flat; not sloping 水平的; 平的; 平坦的: *Find level ground for the picnic table.* 找一处平坦的地面放野餐的餐桌. ○ *Add one level* (ie not heaped) *tablespoon of sugar.* 加一平餐匙糖. **2** of the same height, standard or position on a scale 等高的; 同等标准的; 同一水准的: *The two pictures are not quite level — that one is higher than the other.* 这两幅画挂得不一般高, 这幅比那幅高. ○ *France took an early lead but Wales drew level* (ie equalized the score) *before half-time.* 法国队开始时领先, 但中场休息前威尔士队已与之拉平. **3** (of voices, looks, etc) steady (指声音, 目光等)平稳的, 坚定的: *a level stare* 逼人的凝视. **4** (idm 习语) **have a level head** be able to judge well 头脑清醒; 冷静. **ˌlevel ˈpegging** making progress at the same rate 并驾齐驱.

□ **ˌlevel-ˈcrossing** *n* (*US* **ˈgrade crossing**) place where a road and a railway cross each other at the same level (公路和铁路的)平面交叉处, 平交道口. Cf 参看 CROSSING 2.

ˌlevel-ˈheaded *adj* able to judge well; sensible; calm 头脑清醒的; 明智的; 冷静的.

level² /ˈlevl; ˈlɛvḷ/ *n* **1** [C] line or surface parallel to the horizon, esp with reference to its height 水平线; 水平面; (尤指)水平高度: *1 000 metres above sea-level* 海拔1000米 ○ *a multi-level car-park*, ie one with two or more storeys 多层停车场 ○ *The controls are at eye-level.* 控制仪表盘为视平高度. **2** [C] position on a scale of quantity, strength, value, etc (测量的)数量, 强度, 数值等: *the level of alcohol in the blood* 血液中酒精的含量 ○ *Levels of unemployment vary from region to region.* 失业情形各地不同. ○ (*fig* 比喻) *I could use threats too, but I refuse to sink to your level*, ie behave as badly as you. 我也会使用威胁手段, 但我不肯堕落到你那个地步. **3** [U] relative position in rank, class or authority (官阶、等级、权威等的)级别, 水平: *discussions at Cabinet level*, ie involving members of the Cabinet 内阁阁员的磋商 ○ *high-/low-level negotiations* 高级别[低级别]的谈判. **4** [C] (**a**) more or less flat surface, layer or area 较平坦的表面、层面或区域: *The archaeologists found gold coins* *and pottery in the lowest level of the site.* 考古学家在发掘地最下层找到一些金币和陶器. **(b) levels** [pl] (*Brit*) wide area of flat open country 平原. **5** [C] = SPIRIT-LEVEL (SPIRIT). **6** (idm 习语) **find one's/its level** ⇨ FIND[1]. **on a level (with sb/sth)** at the same level 在同等的水平上; 处于同等地位: *Technically, both players are on a level*, ie of the same standard. 双方运动员在技术方面不相上下. ○ *The water rose until it was on a level with the river banks.* 河水上涨至与堤岸相平. **on the 'level** (*infml* 口) honest(ly) 诚实(地); 真诚(地): *Are you sure this deal is on the level?* 你确信这笔交易诚实无欺吗? ○ *I'd like to help, but I can't — on the level!* 我倒是愿意帮忙, 但是无能为力 —— 说老实话!

level[3] /ˈlevl; ˋlɛvl̩/ *v* (**-ll-**; *US* **-l-**) **1** [Tn] make (sth) level, equal or uniform 使(某事物)平坦, 平等或一致: *The ground should be levelled before you plant a lawn.* 先把地平整好再植草坪. ○ *She needs to win this point to level the score.* 她要赢得这一分才能将比分扳平. ○ *level social differences* 消除社会差异. **2** [Tn esp passive 尤用于被动语态] demolish (a building, etc) 夷平, 摧毁(建筑物等): *a town levelled by an earthquake* 被地震夷为平地的城市. **3** [Tn] **~ sth (at sb)** aim (a gun, etc) 以(枪炮等)瞄准, 对准: *The hostage had a rifle levelled at his head.* 一枝步枪瞄准着人质的头. **4** (phr v) **level sth at sb** bring (a charge or an accusation) against sb 向某人提出(责难或控告): *level criticism at the council* 向理事会提出批评 ○ *accusations levelled at the directors* 对董事会提出的指责. **level sth down/up** make (surfaces, scores, incomes, etc) equal by lowering the higher/raising the lower 将(表面、分数、收入等)弄平, 拉平: *Marks at the lower end need to be levelled up.* 低分的一端分数需往上提. **level off/out** (**a**) (of an aircraft, etc or its pilot) fly horizontally after a climb or dive (指飞行器等或其驾驶员)(爬升或俯冲后)水平飞行: *level off at 20 000 feet* 飞到20 000英尺高度时转入平飞. (**b**) (*fig* 比喻) become level after rising or falling (升或跌之后)呈平稳状态: *House prices show no sign of levelling off*, ie are continuing to rise or fall. 房价没有趋向平稳的迹象(继续升或跌). ○ *Share values have levelled off after yesterday's steep rise.* 股票价格经昨天急剧上扬后已趋平稳. **level with sb** (*infml* 口) speak or deal with sb in an honest and frank way 坦诚待人.

▷ **lev·el·ler** (*US* **lev·eler**) /ˈlevələ(r); ˋlɛvl̩ɚ/ *n* person who wants to abolish social distinctions 平等主义者: (*fig* 比喻) *death, the great leveller* 死亡, 这伟大的平等主义者.

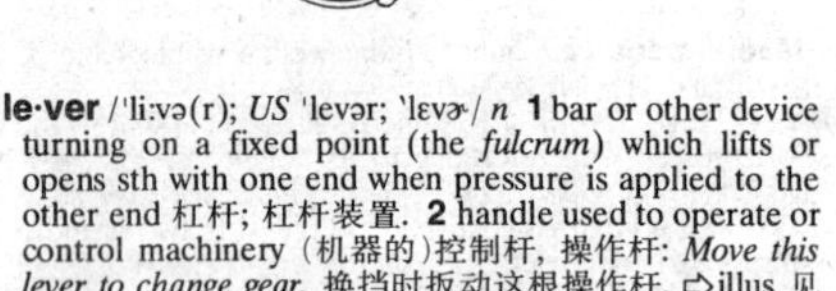

le·ver /ˈliːvə(r); *US* ˈlevər; ˋlɛvɚ/ *n* **1** bar or other device turning on a fixed point (the *fulcrum*) which lifts or opens sth with one end when pressure is applied to the other end 杠杆; 杠杆装置. **2** handle used to operate or control machinery (机器的)控制杆, 操作杆: *Move this lever to change gear.* 换挡时扳动这根操作杆. ⇨illus 见插图. **3** (*fig* 比喻) means of exerting moral pressure (施加道德压力的)手段, 方法: *This latest incident may be the lever needed to change government policy.* 最近的事件或可作为迫使政府改变其政策所需的手段.

▷ **le·ver** *v* [Tn, Tn·pr, Cn·a] move (sth) with a lever (用杠杆)撬动(某物): *They levered the rock into the hole.* 他们用杠子把大石撬进洞里. ○ *lever a crate open* 把板条箱撬开.

le·ver·age /-ərɪdʒ; -ərɪdʒ/ *n* [U] **1** action or power of a lever 杠杆作用; 杠杆的力量. **2** (*fig* 比喻) power; influence 力量; 影响: *Her wealth gives her enormous leverage in social circles.* 她有财富便于她在社会各界造成巨大影响.

lev·eret /ˈlevərɪt; ˋlɛvərɪt/ *n* young hare 幼小的野兔.

le·vi·athan /lɪˈvaɪəθn; ləˋvaɪəθən/ *n* **1** (*Bible* 圣经) sea-monster 海怪. **2** thing of enormous size and power 庞然大物.

Le·vis /ˈliːvaɪz; ˋlivaɪz/ *n* [pl] (*propr* 专利名) jeans 牛仔裤.

lev·it·ate /ˈlevɪteɪt; ˋlɛvə,tet/ *v* [I, Tn, Tn·pr] (cause sb/sth to) rise and float in the air, esp by means of supernatural powers (使某人[某物])升空飘荡(尤指藉超自然力). ▷ **lev·ita·tion** /ˌlevɪˈteɪʃn; ˌlɛvəˋteʃən/ *n* [U]: *powers of levitation* 升空飘荡之力(尤指超自然力).

lev·ity /ˈlevətɪ; ˋlɛvətɪ/ *n* [U] (*fml* 文) lack of proper seriousness or respect 轻率; 轻浮.

levy /ˈlevɪ; ˋlɛvɪ/ *v* (*pt, pp* **levied**) **1** [Tn, Tn·pr] **~ sth (on sb)** collect (a payment, etc) by authority or force; impose sth 征收, 征集(款额等); 强加某事物: *a departure tax levied on all travellers* 向所有旅客征收的离境税. **2** (phr v) **levy on sth** (*law* 律) seize sth in order to force payment of a debt 扣押某物(迫使还债): *levy on sb's property, estate, etc* 扣押某人财产、地产等.

▷ **levy** *n* **1** act of levying 征收; 扣押. **2** money, etc so obtained 征收或扣押的钱等.

lewd /ljuːd; *US* luːd; lud/ *adj* **1** treating sexual matters in a vulgar or indecent way 淫荡的; 猥亵的: *a story full of lewd innuendos* 充满淫秽影射的故事. **2** lustful 好色的: *a lewd expression, glance, gesture, etc* 显露色欲的表情、目光、姿势等. ▷ **lewdly** *adv*. **lewd·ness** *n* [U].

lex·ical /ˈleksɪkl; ˋlɛksɪkl̩/ *adj* (*linguistics* 语言) of the vocabulary of a language 词汇的: *lexical items*, ie words and phrases 词项(词或词组).

▷ **lex·ic·ally** /-klɪ; -klɪ/ *adv*.

lexis /ˈleksɪs; ˋlɛksɪs/ *n* [U] vocabulary 词汇.

lex·ico·graphy /ˌleksɪˈkɒgrəfɪ; ˌlɛksəˋkɑgrəfɪ/ *n* [U] theory and practice of compiling dictionaries 词典编纂学; 词典的编纂.

▷ **lex·ico·grapher** /ˌleksɪˈkɒgrəfə(r); ˌlɛksəˋkɑgrəfɚ/ *n* person who compiles dictionaries 词典编纂者.

lex·ico·graph·ical /ˌleksɪkəˈgræfɪkl; ˌlɛksəkoˋgræfɪkəl/ *adj*.

lex·icon /ˈleksɪkən; *US* -kɒn; ˋlɛksɪkɑn/ *n* **1** dictionary, esp of an ancient language (eg Greek or Hebrew) 词典, 字典(尤指古代语言的辞书, 如希腊语或希伯来语). **2** (*linguistics* 语言) vocabulary (contrasted with grammar) 词汇(与语法相对).

ley[1] /leɪ; le/ *n* land that is temporarily sown with grass 短期轮作的草地.

ley[2] /leɪ; le/ *n* (also **ˈley line**) supposed straight line of a prehistoric track connecting prominent features of the landscape, usu hilltops 史前地貌(通常为山顶)的假想线.

LF /ˌel ˈef; ˌɛl ˋɛf/ *abbr* 缩写 = (*radio* 无) low frequency. Cf 参看 HF.

lh *abbr* 缩写 = left hand. Cf 参看 RH.

li·ab·il·ity /ˌlaɪəˈbɪlətɪ; ˌlaɪəˋbɪlətɪ/ *n* **1** [U] **~(for sth)** state of being liable (对某事物)有责任或义务: *liability for military service* 服兵役的义务 ○ *Don't admit liability for the accident.* 不要承认对事故有责任. **2** [C] (*infml* 口) handicap 妨碍; 不利: *Because of his injury Jones was just a liability to the team.* 琼斯负了伤, 成为全队的累赘. Cf 参看 ASSET. **3 li·ab·il·it·ies** [pl] debts; financial obligations 债; 债务.

li·able /ˈlaɪəbl; ˋlaɪəbl̩/ *adj* [pred 作表语] **1 ~ (for sth)** responsible by law 负法律责任: *Is a wife liable for her husband's debts?* 妻子对丈夫的债务负法律责任吗? ○ *Be careful — if you have an accident I'll be liable.* 小心 —— 你要是出事故, 我要负责的. **2 ~ to sth** subject to sth 可能遭到某事: *a road liable to subsidence* 可能塌陷的公路 ○ *Offenders are liable to fines of up to £100.* 触犯者可予罚款达100英镑. **3 ~ to do sth** likely to do sth 有做某事物的倾向: *We're all liable to make mistakes when we're tired.* 人若疲劳谁都可能出差错.

li·aise /lɪˈeɪz; lɪˋez/ *v* [I, Ipr] **~ (with sb)**; **~ (between A and B)** (*infml* 口) act as a link or go-between 做联络人; 联络.

li·aison /lɪˈeɪzn; *US* ˈlɪəzɒn; ˋlɪə,zɑn/ *n* **1** [U] communication and co-operation between units of an organization 组织内单位间的交流与合作: *excellent liaison between our two departments* 我们两部门间出色的合作 ○ [attrib 作

定语] *a liaison officer* 联络官. **2** [C] (*often derog* 常作贬义) person who liaises 联络人; 掮客. **3** [C] (*often derog* 常作贬义) illicit sexual relationship 私通; 通奸: *a brief liaison* 短暂的姘居.

liana /lɪˈɑːnə; lɪˈɑnə/ *n* tropical climbing plant 热带藤本植物.

liar /ˈlaɪə(r); ˈlaɪɚ/ *n* person who tells lies, esp habitually 说谎者(尤指经常性的): *a good/bad liar*, ie sb who can/cannot easily deceive others by telling lies 高明的[拙劣的]撒谎者.

lib /lɪb; lɪb/ *n* [U] (*infml* 口) (in compounds 用以构成复合词) liberation 解放: *gay, women's, animal, etc lib* 同性恋、妇女、动物等的解放运动. ▷ **lib·ber** *n* (in compounds 用以构成复合词): *Is she a women's libber?* 她是妇女解放运动成员吗?

Lib /lɪb; lɪb/ *abbr* 缩写 = (*Brit politics* 政) Liberal (Party): *Joan Wells (Lib)* 琼·韦尔斯(自由党) ○ *a Lib-Lab pact*, ie between the Liberal and Labour Parties 自由党——工党协定. Cf 参看 L 4.

liba·tion /laɪˈbeɪʃn; laɪˈbeʃən/ *n* **1** (pouring out of an) offering of wine, etc to a god in former times (旧时向神的)祭酒, 奠酒. **2** (*joc* 谑) alcoholic drink 酒.

li·bel /ˈlaɪbl; ˈlaɪbl̩/ *n* **1** [C] false written or printed statement that damages sb's reputation 诽谤性文字. **2** [U] (*law* 律) act of publishing such a statement 发表诽谤性文字: *sue a newspaper for libel* 控告某报刊登诽谤性文字 ○ [attrib 作定语] *libel proceedings* 诽谤文字的诉讼. **3** [C] **~ (on sb)** (*infml* 口) thing that tends to harm the reputation of sb/sth 有损某人[某事物]名誉的事物: *That interview was an absolute libel on a honest man.* 那篇采访报道完全是对一诚实人的诽谤. Cf 参看 SLANDER.

▷ **li·bel** *v* (**-ll-**; *US* **-l-**) [Tn] harm the reputation of (sb) by publishing a false statement (发表文字等)诽谤, 中伤, 诋毁(某人的)声誉.

li·bel·lous (*US* **li·bel·ous**) /ˈlaɪbələs; ˈlaɪbl̩əs/ *adj* **1** being or containing a libel 诽谤性的; 含有诽谤性文字的: *a libellous statement* 诽谤性的说法. **2** in the habit of publishing libels 惯于发表诽谤性文字的: *a libellous magazine* 爱刊登诽谤内容的杂志.

lib·eral /ˈlɪbərəl; ˈlɪbərəl/ *adj* **1** tolerant and open-minded; free from prejudice 宽容忍耐的; 心胸宽阔的; 无偏见的: *a liberal attitude to divorce and remarriage* 对离婚和再婚看得开. **2** giving or given generously 慷慨的; 大方的: *She's very liberal with promises but much less so with money.* 她轻诺而手紧. ○ *a liberal sprinkling of sugar* 撒上厚厚的糖. **3** (of education) concerned chiefly with broadening the mind, not simply with technical or professional training (指教育)扩展心智的, 德育的(不单纯作职业或技术的训练). **4** not strict, literal or exact 不严格的; 自由的; 不讲究准确性的: *a liberal translation giving a general idea of the writer's intentions* 对作者总体意思的意译. **5 Liberal** (*politics* 政) of the Liberal Party 自由党的: *Liberal housing policy* 自由党的住房政策.

▷ **lib·eral** *n* **1** tolerant and open-minded person 宽容大度的人. **2 Liberal** (*Brit politics* 政) (*abbr* 缩写 **Lib**) member of the Liberal Party 自由党人.

lib·er·al·ism /-ɪzəm; -ˌɪzəm/ *n* [U] liberal opinions and principles 自由主义.

lib·er·ally /-rəlɪ; -rəlɪ/ *adv*: *rolls spread liberally with butter* 涂有很多黄油的面包 ○ *interpret the ruling liberally* 任意解释裁决.

□ **the ˌLiberal ˈDemocrats** (*Brit politics* 政) political party in Britain (formly called **the Liberal Party**) favouring moderate political and social reform 自由民主党(旧称自由党). Cf 参看 THE CONSERVATIVE PARTY (CONSERVATIVE), THE LABOUR PARTY (LABOUR).

lib·er·al·ity /ˌlɪbəˈrælətɪ; ˌlɪbəˈrælətɪ/ *n* [U] **1** free giving; generosity 慷慨; 大方; 大度. **2** quality of being tolerant and open-minded 宽容; 开明: *a period remarkable for its liberality* 以开明著称的时期.

lib·er·al·ize, -ise /ˈlɪbrəlaɪz; ˈlɪbərəlˌaɪz/ *v* [Tn] free (sb/sth) from political or moral restrictions 使(某人[某事物])自由化(脱离政治或道德的约束): *There is a move to liberalize literature and the Arts.* 文学与艺术有自由化的动向. ▷ **lib·er·al·iz·ation, -isation** /ˌlɪbrəlaɪˈzeɪʃn; *US* -lɪˈz-; ˌlɪbərələˈzeʃən/ *n* [U].

lib·er·ate /ˈlɪbəreɪt; ˈlɪbəˌret/ *v* [Tn, Tn·pr] **~ sb/sth (from sth)** set (sb/sth) free 解放, 释放(某人[某事物]): *liberate prisoners, an occupied country* 释放监犯、解放被占领的国家.

▷ **lib·er·ated** showing freedom from traditional ideas in social and sexual matters (在社会事务与性方面)解放的, 不受传统思想束缚的: *a liberated male, mother, lifestyle* 不受传统思想束缚的男性、母亲、生活方式.

lib·era·tion /ˌlɪbəˈreɪʃn; ˌlɪbəˈreʃən/ *n* [U]: *the liberation of Europe by Allied troops* 盟军解放欧洲 ○ *The break-up of their marriage was an enormous liberation for her.* 她离婚一事对她是一大解脱.

lib·er·ator *n*: *hailing the soldiers as liberators* 把士兵当作解放者来欢迎.

lib·er·tine /ˈlɪbətiːn; ˈlɪbɚˌtin/ *n* man who lives an irresponsible and immoral life 放荡的人; 浪子.

lib·erty /ˈlɪbətɪ; ˈlɪbɚtɪ/ *n* **1** [U] freedom from captivity, slavery, or oppressive control 自由; 自主. **2** [C, U] right or power to do as one chooses 自由权: *a liberty enjoyed by all citizens* 公民皆享的自由权 ○ *They give their children a great deal of liberty.* 他们给孩子很大自由. **3** [C esp *pl* 尤作复数] right or privilege granted by authority 当局授予的权利或特权: *liberties enjoyed by all citizens* 公民皆享的权利. **4** (idm 习语) **at liberty (to do sth)** (**a**) (of a person) free; allowed (指人)自由的, 获许可的: *You are at liberty to leave.* 你可以走. (**b**) free from restrictions or control 不受限制或支配: *You're at liberty to say what you like.* 你尽可畅所欲言. **ˌLiberty ˈHall** place or condition of complete freedom 自由自在的地方或状态: *Wear what you like for the party — it's Liberty Hall.* 参加这聚会你爱穿什么穿什么——那是逍遥宫. **set sb free/at liberty** ⇨ FREE. **take liberties (with sb/sth)** behave in a presumptuous disrespectful way 放肆: *She told him to stop taking liberties*, ie treating her with too much familiarity. 她告诉他不要太随便了(对她过分亲昵). ○ *The film takes considerable liberties with the novel on which it is based*, eg by shortening or changing it. 影片与原作颇有距离. **take the liberty of doing sth** do sth without permission 擅自或冒昧做某事物: *I took the liberty of borrowing your lawn-mower while you were away.* 你不在的时候我擅自借用了你的刈草机.

lib·id·in·ous /lɪˈbɪdɪnəs; lɪˈbɪdn̩əs/ *adj* (*fml* 文) having or showing strong sexual feelings; lustful 性欲强的; 好色的.

li·bido /lɪˈbiːdəʊ, *also* ˈlɪbɪdəʊ; lɪˈbido/ *n* (*pl* **~s**) [U, C] (*psychology* 心) emotional energy or urge, esp sexual 感情冲动; 情欲; (尤指)性欲.

Libra /ˈliːbrə; ˈlibrə/ *n* **1** [U] the seventh sign of the zodiac, the Scales 天平宫(黄道第七宫). **2** [C] person born under the influence of this sign 属天平宫星座的人. ▷ **Lib·ran** *n, adj.* ⇨Usage at ZODIAC 用法见 ZODIAC. ⇨illus at ZODIAC 见 ZODIAC 插图.

lib·rary /ˈlaɪbrərɪ; *US* -brerɪ; ˈlaɪˌbrɛrɪ/ *n* **1** (**a**) collection of books for reading or borrowing 藏书: *a public, reference, university, etc library* 公共图书馆、图书参考室、大学图书馆的藏书 ○ *He has many foreign books in his library.* 他的藏书中有许多外国书. ○ [attrib 作定语] *When is that library book due back?* ie When must it be returned to the public library? 那本公共图书什么时候到期归还? (**b**) room or building where these are kept 藏书室; 图书馆; 书库: *Let's meet outside the library.* 我们在图书馆外边见面. **2** similar collection of records, films, etc (唱片、影片等的)收藏: *a recording to add to your library* 在你收藏的录音资料中加进的一段录音 ○ *a photographic library* 摄影资料集.

▷ **lib·rar·ian** /laɪˈbreərɪən; laɪˈbrɛrɪən/ *n* person in charge of or assisting in a library 图书馆管理员; 资料收藏管理员. **lib·rar·ian·ship** *n* [U] work of being a librarian 图书馆管理(员)或资料收藏管理(员)的工作.

lib·retto /lɪˈbretəʊ; lɪˈbrɛto/ *n* (*pl* **~s** or **-retti** /-tiː; -ti/) words that are sung and spoken in an opera or musical play (歌剧或音乐剧的)剧本.

▷ **lib·ret·tist** /lɪˈbretɪst; lɪˈbrɛtɪst/ *n* author of a libretto (歌剧或音乐剧的)歌词作者.

lice *pl* of LOUSE.

li·cence (*US* **li·cense**) /ˈlaɪsns; ˈlaɪsn̩s/ *n* **1** [C] official document showing that permission has been given to own, use or do sth 执照; 许可证: *a driving licence* 驾驶执照 ○ *a licence to practise as a doctor* 医生开业执照 ○

This used to be a pub but the landlord has lost his licence, ie is no longer permitted to sell alcoholic drinks. 这铺子原是酒店，但店主已丧失营业执照(再不允许卖酒了). **2** [U] (*fml* 文) permission 准许; 许可: *Why give these people licence to enter the place at will?* 为什么允许这些人随意进入该地? **3** [U] (**a**) irresponsible use of freedom, esp to behave in an offensive way 放纵; 放任; (尤指)放肆. (**b**) freedom to rearrange or exaggerate words or images (文字或形象的)破格: *artistic/poetic licence* 艺术[诗]的破格. **4** (idm 习语) **a ˌlicence to print ˈmoney** (*infml* 口) scheme, etc that has been officially approved but is likely to be excessively costly, with little or no control over the money spent 无底洞开支(正式批准但无法控制开销的计划等).

□ **ˈlicence plate** (*US* **license plate**) *n* (*esp US*) = NUMBER-PLATE (NUMBER).

li·cense (also **li·cence**) /ˈlaɪsns; ˈlaɪsn̩s/ *v* [Tn, Cn·t] give a licence to (sb/sth) 给(某人[某事物])执照或许可证; 准许: *shops licensed to sell tobacco* 准许经销烟草的商店 ○ *licensed premises*, ie where the sale of alcoholic drinks is permitted 许可出售酒类的场所.

▷ **li·cens·ee** /ˌlaɪsənˈsiː; ˌlaɪsn̩ˈsi/ *n* person who has a licence, esp to sell alcoholic drinks 执照持有者(尤指出售酒类).

□ **ˈlicensing laws** (*Brit*) laws limiting the places and times at which alcoholic drinks may be sold 售酒法(限定酒类销售的地点与时间的法规).

li·cen·ti·ate /laɪˈsenʃɪət; laɪˈsɛnʃɪɪt/ *n* person who has a certificate showing that he is competent to practise a certain profession 持有从事某职业合格证件者: *a licentiate in dental surgery* 领有牙外科开业执照的医生.

li·cen·ti·ous /laɪˈsenʃəs; laɪˈsɛnʃəs/ *adj* (*fml* 文) disregarding the rules of behaviour, esp in sexual matters 漠视行为规范的; (尤指)放荡的, 淫乱的. ▷ **li·cen·ti·ously** *adv*. **li·cen·ti·ous·ness** *n* [U].

li·chen /ˈlaɪkən; ˈlaɪkən/ *n* [U] dry-looking plant, usu yellow, grey or green, that grows on rocks, walls, tree-trunks, etc 地衣. Cf 参看 MOSS.

lich-gate (also **lych-gate**) /ˈlɪtʃgeɪt; ˈlɪtʃˌget/ *n* roofed gateway to a churchyard 教堂墓地前有顶盖的门.

lick /lɪk; lɪk/ *v* **1** [Tn, Cn·a] pass the tongue over (sb/sth) 舔(某人[某物]): *He licked his fingers.* 他舔手指. ○ *The cat was licking its fur.* 猫在舔自己的毛. ○ *lick the back of a postage stamp*, ie to moisten the glue 舔邮票的反面(弄湿该处的胶水) ○ *He licked the spoon clean.* 他把小勺舔干净了. **2** [Tn] (of waves or flames) touch (sth) lightly (指波浪或火焰)触及某物: *flames beginning to lick the furniture* 开始燃着家具的火焰. **3** [Tn] (*sl* 俚) defeat (sb) 打败(某人). **4** (idm 习语) **lick sb's ˈboots** (*infml* 口); **lick sb's ˈarse** (⚠ *sl* 讳, 俚) be servile towards sb 舔屁股. **lick sb/sth into ˈshape** (*infml* 口) make sb/sth efficient or presentable 使某人[某事物]成器或像样: *The new recruits will be fine once they've been licked into shape.* 新兵一经训练就是好样儿的. **lick/smack one's ˈlips/ˈchops** (*infml* 口) show eager enjoyment or anticipation of sth 舔嘴唇(自喜或期待某事): *The children licked their lips as the cake was cut.* 蛋糕一切开, 孩子们就垂涎三尺了. ○ (*fig* 比喻) *She's licking her chops at the thought of spending all that money!* 她一想到能花那一大笔钱不觉心花怒放. **lick one's ˈwounds** try to restore one's strength or spirits after a defeat 自舐伤口(失败后以求恢复元气): *The disappointed losers crawled home to lick their wounds.* 输者废然而返以重整旗鼓. **5** (phr v) **lick sth from/off sth** remove sth by licking 舔掉某物: *lick blood from a cut, honey off a spoon* 舔掉伤口上的血、勺上的蜜. **lick sth up** take sth into the mouth by licking 将某物舔进嘴里: *The cat licked up its milk.* 猫把奶舔干净了.

▷ **lick** *n* **1** [C] stroke of the tongue in licking 舔: *One last lick and the milk was gone.* 剩奶最后一舔而光. ○ *a lick of ice-cream* 舔一下冰激凌. **2** [sing] slight application (of paint, etc) (颜料等的)略施: *The boat would look better with a lick of paint.* 这小船稍加颜色就好看了. **3** [sing] (*sl* 俚) speed 速度: *going at quite a, a fair old, a full, etc lick*, ie quite, fairly, extremely fast 走得很快、颇快、极快等. **4** = SALT-LICK (SALT). **5** (idm 习语) **a ˌlick and a ˈpromise** (*infml* 口) quick and careless attempt to clean or wash sth 迅速而马虎地弄干净或清洗某物.

lick·ing *n* (esp *sing* 尤作单数) (*sl* 俚) **1** defeat 打败: *give sb/get a (right) licking* (狠狠)挫败某人[遭到(惨重)失败]. **2** beating 痛打: *If your father hears about this he'll give you such a licking!* 你父亲若是知道这事非狠狠揍你一顿不可!

li·cor·ice = LIQUORICE.

lid /lɪd; lɪd/ *n* **1** hinged or removable cover for a box, pot, etc 盖子. ⇨illus at PAN 见 PAN 插图. **2** = EYELID (EYE). **3** (idm 习语) **flip one's lid** ⇨ FLIP. **put the (tin) lid on sth/things** (*infml* 口) be the final event that provokes an outburst 成为导致某事爆发的最后一件事. **take, lift, blow, etc the lid off sth** reveal unpleasant secrets concerning sth 揭露丑闻: *an article that lifts the lid off the world of professional gambling* 揭露职业赌博界内幕的文章.

▷ **lid·ded** *adj* [usu attrib 通常作定语] **1** (of a box, pot, etc) having a lid (指箱子、锅等)有盖的. **2** (of eyes) having lids of a particular type (指眼睛)有某种眼睑的: *heavily lidded eyes* 长着厚眼皮的眼睛.

lid·less *adj*.

lido /ˈliːdəʊ; ˈlido/ *n* (*pl* **~s**) public bathing beach or open air swimming-pool 海滨浴场; 露天游泳池.

lie[1] /laɪ; laɪ/ *v* (*pt, pp* **lied**, *pres p* **lying**) **1** [I, Ipr] **~ (to sb) (about sth)** make a statement one knows to be untrue 说谎: *He's lying.* 他在说谎. ○ *Don't you dare lie to me!* 你胆敢跟我撒谎! ○ *She lies about her age.* 她谎报年龄. **2** [I] give a false impression; be deceptive 给人以假象; 不可信: *The camera cannot lie.* 照相机不会造假. ○ *lying smiles* 假笑. **3** (idm 习语) **lie in one's ˈteeth/ˈthroat** (*infml* 口) lie grossly and shamelessly 扯弥天大谎; 睁着眼睛说瞎话. **lie one's way into/out of sth** get (oneself) into or out of a situation by lying 撒谎以求一逞或摆脱困境: *He's lied his way into a really plum job.* 他靠撒谎骗得一份好工作. ⇨Usage at LIE[2] 用法见 LIE[2].

▷ **lie** *n* **1** statement one knows to be untrue 谎言; 假话: *His story is nothing but a pack of lies.* 他说的纯粹是一派鬼话. Cf 参看 FIB. **2** (idm 习语) **give the lie to sth** show sth to be untrue 证明某事不实: *These figures give the lie to reports that business is declining.* 这些数字表明报告所谓业务正在滑坡的说法不实. **live a lie** ⇨ LIVE[2]. **nail a lie** ⇨ NAIL. Cf 参看 WHITE LIE (WHITE[1]).

□ **ˈlie-detector** *n* instrument that can detect changes in the pulse-rate, breathing, etc, thought to result from the stress caused by lying in response to questions 测谎器.

lie[2] /laɪ; laɪ/ *v* (*pt* **lay** /leɪ; le/, *pp* **lain** /leɪn; len/, *pres p* **lying**) **1** [Ipr] have or put one's body in a flat or resting position on a horizontal surface 躺; 平卧: *The corpse lay face down in a pool of blood.* 尸体俯卧在血泊中. ○ *lie on one's back/side/front* 仰卧[侧卧/俯卧] ○ *Don't lie in bed all morning!* 别一上午都躺在床上! ○ *a dog lying at his master's feet* 卧在主人脚旁的狗. **2** [La, Ipr] (of a thing) be at rest on a surface (指物)平放: *The letter lay open on his desk.* 那信摊开在他的书桌上. ⇨Usage 见所附用法. **3** [La, Ipr] be, remain or be kept in a certain state 在、留在或保持在某种状态: *snow lying thick on the ground* 地面上厚厚的雪 ○ *These machines have lain idle since the factory closed.* 这些机器自工厂关闭以来一直闲置着. ○ *I'd rather use my money than leave it lying in the bank.* 我宁可把钱花了也不想存在银行里. **4** [Ipr] be spread out to view; extend 展现; 伸展: *The valley lay at our feet.* 峡谷展现在我们的脚下. ○ (*fig* 比喻) *You're still young — your whole life lies before you!* 你还年轻——整个人生还长着呢! **5** [Ipr] be situated 位于: *The town lies on the coast.* 该城位于海边. ○ *a ship lying at anchor, at its moorings, alongside, etc* 锚泊的、系泊的、横泊的船. **6** [Ipr] (of abstract things) exist or be found (指抽象事物)存在, 在于: *I only wish it lay within my power to* (ie that I could) *help you.* 我但愿能够帮助你. ○ *The cure for stress lies in learning to relax.* 消除紧张的方法在于学会放松. ○ *It's obvious where our interest lies*, ie which option, development, etc would be to our advantage. 我们的利益所在是明摆着的事情. **7** [I] (*law* 律) be admissible or able to be upheld 可受理或立案: *an action, appeal that will not lie* 不能受理的诉讼、上诉. **8** (idm 习语) **as/so far as in me lies** ⇨ FAR[2]. **as one makes one's bed so one must lie in it** ⇨ BED[1]. **keep/lie close** ⇨ CLOSE[1]. **let sleeping dogs lie** ⇨ SLEEP[2]. **lie at sb's ˈdoor** be attributable to sb (责

任)归于某人；某事为某人的责任：*I accept that the responsibility for this lies squarely at my door.* 我承认这事的责任完全由我承担. **lie doggo** (*infml* 口) lie without moving or making a sign 隐伏不动. **lie heavy on sth** cause sth to feel uncomfortable 使某事物感不适，不安：*The rich meal lay heavy on my stomach.* 这顿美餐塞得我的胃很胀. ○ *a crime lying heavy on one's conscience* 使良心负咎的罪行. **lie in 'state** (of a corpse) be placed on view in a public place before burial (指遗体)安葬前停放公共地点供瞻仰. **lie in 'wait (for sb)** be hidden waiting to surprise sb 隐蔽静候以出人不意：*arrested by the police who had been lying in wait* 被隐蔽埋伏的警察捕获. **lie 'low** (*infml* 口) keep quiet or hidden 不出声；隐藏：*He's been lying low ever since I asked him for the money he owes me.* 自从我催他还钱，他就不露面了. **see, etc how the land lies** ⇨ LAND[1]. **take sth lying 'down** accept an insult, etc without protest; submit meekly 甘受侮辱等；俯首屈服；逆来顺受. **time hangs/lies heavy on one's hands** ⇨ TIME[1]. **9** (phr v) **lie behind sth** be the explanation for sth 是某事的原因或理由：*What lay behind this strange outburst?* 这莫名其妙的发作究竟是为什么？**lie back** get into or be in a resting position; relax 休息；放松；松弛：*You don't have to do anything — just lie back and enjoy the journey.* 你什么也不用做——只管轻松愉快地享受旅游的乐趣. **lie down** be in or move into a horizontal position on a bed, etc in order to sleep or rest 躺着；躺下：*Go and lie down for a while.* 去躺一会儿. ○ *He lay down on the sofa and soon fell asleep.* 他躺在沙发上很快就睡着了. **lie down under sth** (*infml* 口) accept (an insult etc) without protest; submit to sth meekly 甘受(侮辱等)；逆来顺受：*We have no intention of lying down under these absurd allegations.* 对这些荒谬的指控我们是不甘受辱的. **lie 'in (a)** (*Brit*) (*US* **sleep in**) (*infml* 口) stay in bed after the normal time for getting up 睡懒觉：*It's a holiday tomorrow, so you can lie in.* 明天是假日，你可以睡懒觉了. **(b)** (*dated* 旧) stay in bed to await the birth of a child 卧床待产：*a lying-'in hospital* 待产医院. **lie over** (of problems, business, etc) await attention or action at a later date (指问题、事务等)留待以后处理：*These items can lie over till our next meeting.* 这些问题可留待我们下次开会再处理. **lie 'to** (*nautical* 海) (of a vessel) come to a stop facing the wind; be anchored or moored (指船)逆风滞航，抛锚，停泊. **lie up** stay in bed to rest during an illness 卧床休养. **lie with sb (to do sth)** (*fml* 文) be sb's duty or responsibility 是某人的义务或责任：*The decision on whether to proceed lies with the Minister.* 是否进行取决于部长. ○ *It lies with you to accept or reject the proposal.* 对该建议是接受还是拒绝由你作主.

▷ **lie** *n* **1** [sing] way or position in which sth lies 某物所处的状态或位置. **2** [C usu *sing* 通常作单数] (in golf) where the ball comes to rest after a shot (高尔夫球)被击后球停的位置：*a good, poor, etc lie* 好落位、差落位. **3** (idm 习语) **the ,lie of the 'land** (*US* **the ,lay of the 'land**) **(a)** the natural features (esp rivers, mountains, etc) of an area 地形地貌(尤指河流、山脉等). **(b)** (*infml fig* 口，比喻) assessment of the state of a situation 情势；事态：*I'll need several weeks to discover the lie of the land before I can make any decisions about the future of the business.* 我需要几周的时间了解情况后才能对公司的未来做出决定.

□ **'lie-down** *n* (usu *sing* 通常作单数) (*Brit infml* 口) a short rest, usu in bed 躺一会儿.

'lie-in *n* (usu *sing* 通常作单数) (*infml* 口 *esp Brit*) act of staying in bed longer than usual, esp in the morning 懒觉(尤指早晨起得晚)：*look forward to a nice long lie-in on Sunday* 盼着星期天好好睡个懒觉.

NOTE ON USAGE 用法：Note the difference between the intransitive verb **lie (lying, lay, lain),** meaning 'be in a resting position' 注意不及物动词**lie (lying、lay、lain)**意为'处于休息的位置'：*I was feeling ill, so I lay down on the bed for a while* 我身体不舒服，所以在床上躺一会儿 and the transitive verb **lay (laying, laid, laid),** meaning 'put on a surface' 但是及物动词**lay (laying、laid、laid)**意为'放在某个面上'：*She laid her dress on the bed to keep it neat.* 她把连衣裙放在床上以保持平整. There is another intransitive verb **lie (lying, lied, lied),** meaning 'say something untrue' 另有一不及物动词**lie (lying、lied、lied)**意为'说谎'：*He lied about his age to join the army.* 他为了参军谎报了年龄.

lied /li:t; lit/ *n* (*pl* **lieder** /'li:də(r); 'lidɚ/) (*German music* 德，音) German song for solo voice and piano, esp of the Romantic period (独唱的和钢琴独奏的)德国歌曲(尤指浪漫主义时期的).

liege /li:dʒ; lidʒ/ *n* **1** (also **'liege lord**) (in feudal times) sovereign or lord, entitled to loyal service (封建时期)君主，王侯. **2** (also **'liege·man** /-mən; -mən/) man or servant bound to give loyal service to such a sovereign or lord (君主或王侯的)臣仆.

lien /lɪən; liən/ *n* [C] (*law* 律) **~ (on/upon sth)** right to keep sb's property until a debt owed in connection with it (for repair, transport, etc) is paid 留置权，扣押权(扣押某人财产直至债务，如修理费、运输费等清偿方予放还者).

lieu /lu:; lu *or, in British use,* 英式英语读作 lju:; lɪu/ *n* (idm 习语) **in lieu (of sth)** instead 代替：*accept a cheque in lieu of cash* 接受支票替代现金.

Lieut (also **Lt**) *abbr* 缩写 = Lieutenant: *Lieut (James) Brown* (詹姆士·)布朗中尉.

lieu·ten·ant /lef'tenənt; *US* lu:'t-; lu'tɛnənt/ *n* **1** army officer next below a captain 陆军中尉. ⇨App 9 见附录9. **2** navy officer next below a lieutenant-commander 海军上尉. ⇨App 9 见附录9. **3** (in compounds) officer ranking next below the one specified (在复合词中)仅低于某一官阶的官员：*lieu,tenant-'general* 陆军中将 ○ *lieu,tenant-'governor,* ie official next below a governor-general 副总督. **4** deputy; chief assistant 副职官员；助理官员.

▷ **lieu·ten·ancy** /-ənsɪ; -ənsɪ/ *n* rank of a lieutenant 陆军中尉、海军上尉、副职官员的军衔或职位.

life /laɪf; laɪf/ *n* (*pl* **lives** /laɪvz; laɪvz/) **1** [U] ability to function and grow that distinguishes living animals and plants from dead ones and from rocks, metals, etc 生命：*the origins of life on earth* 地球上生命的起源 ○ *The motionless body showed no signs of life.* 纹丝不动的躯体显示不出有生命的迹象. **2** [U] living things 生物；活物：*Is there life on Mars?* 火星上有生物吗？○ *animal and plant life* 动植物. **3** [U] state of being alive as a human being 人生；人的生存：*The riot was brought under control without loss of life,* ie without anyone being killed. 骚乱得到控制，无人死亡. **4** [U] qualities, events and experiences that characterize existence as a human being 生活：*He does not want much from life.* 他对生活所求无多. ○ *What do you expect? That's life!* ie These things happen and must be expected and accepted. 你期待什么呢？这就是生活(这些事常有，必须想到并承受)！**5** [C] existence of an individual human being 人命；(人的)性命：*Doctors worked through the night to save the life of the injured man.* 医生彻夜工作以拯救伤者的生命. ○ *Three lives were lost* (ie Three people died) *in the accident.* 事故中三人丧生. **6 (a)** [C] period between birth and death 一生；终身；终生：*She lived her whole life in the country.* 她在农村度过一生. ○ *He spent his adult life in Canada.* 他成年时期是在加拿大度过的. **(b)** [C] period between birth and the present 有生以来：*I've lived here all my life.* 我一生都住在这里. **7** [U] **(a)** period between the present and death 从今到死；终此一生：*a friend, job, membership for life.* 终身的朋友、工作、成员资格. **(b)** (*infml* 口) (also **life sentence**) sentence of imprisonment for the rest of one's life made by a court of law 终身监禁；无期徒刑：*be given/get/do life* 被判[落得/服]无期徒刑. **8** [U] **(a)** business, pleasure and social activities of the world 事业；欢乐；社交：*As a taxi-driver you really see life.* 你开计程车，可真是见多识广了. **(b)** activity; movement 活动：*There are few signs of life here in the evenings.* 这里晚间没有什么活动的迹象. **9** [U] liveliness; interest 生命力；活力；兴趣：*Children are always so full of life.* 儿童总是那么朝气蓬勃的. ○ *Put more life into your work.* 你的工作多增加些活力吧. **10** [U, C] way of living 生活方式：*private/public life* 私人[社交]生活方面 ○ *Village life is too dull for me.* 我觉得乡村的生活方式太单调乏味了. ○ *have an easy/hard life* 过闲适[艰苦]的生活 ○ *Singing is her life,* ie the most important thing in her existence. 唱歌是她的人生大事. ○ *That's the life (for me)!* ie the best way to live. 这就是(我)最好的生活方式! ○ *He's decided to emigrate and start a new life in America.* 他决定移居美国, 开始新的生活. **11** [C] biography 传记: *He's writing a life of Newton.* 他在写牛顿的传记. **12** [U] living model 真人模特儿; 生物模型: *a portrait drawn/taken from life* 以真人作模特儿的画像 ○ [attrib 作定语] *a 'life class*, ie one in which art students draw, etc from living models 真人模特儿写生课. **13** [C] period during which sth continues to exist or function 寿命; 有效期; 存在期: *throughout the life of the present government* 现政府任期期间 ○ [attrib 作定语] *a long-life battery* 长寿电池. **14** [C] **(a)** fresh start or opportunity after a narrow escape (脱险后的)新开端, 新机会: *The batsman was given a life* (eg because a fielder missed an easy catch) *when his score was 24.* 那击球员积分到24分时获一新机会(如外场员未接住一易接的球). **(b)** (in children's games) one of a set number of chances before a player is out of the game (儿童游戏中)参加者的一次机会(若干失误则出局). **15** (idm 习语) **at one's time of life** ⇨ TIME[1]. **the bane of sb's existence/life** ⇨ BANE. **the breath of life** ⇨ BREATH. **bring sb/sth to 'life** give sb/sth vitality 给某人[某事物]以活力: *Let's invite Ted — he knows how to bring a party to life.* 我们邀请特德吧——有他到会就热闹了. **a cat-and-dog life** ⇨ CAT[1]. **the change of life** ⇨ CHANGE[2]. **come to 'life** become animated 变活泼: *You're very cool with your brother, but with your friends you really come to life.* 你对你弟弟冷冰冰的, 但跟朋友在一起倒很活跃. ○ *Sunrise — and the farm comes to life again.* 太阳一升起, 农场就又活了. **depart this life** ⇨ DEPART. **end one's days/life** ⇨ END[2]. **expectation of life** ⇨ EXPECTATION. **a fact of life** ⇨ FACT. **the facts of life** ⇨ FACT. **for dear 'life/one's 'life** (as if) in order to escape death (仿佛)逃命般, 拼命地: *Run for your life!* 拼命跑吧! **for the 'life of one** (*infml* 口) however hard one tries 无论怎样努力: *I cannot for the life of me remember her name.* 我怎么也想不起她的名字. **frighten the life out of sb** ⇨ FRIGHTEN. **full of beans/life** ⇨ FULL. **have the time of one's life** ⇨ TIME[1]. **in fear of one's life** ⇨ FEAR[1]. **in peril of one's life** ⇨ PERIL. **large as life** ⇨ LARGE. **larger than life** ⇨ LARGE. **lay down one's life (for sb/sth)** (*rhet* 修辞) sacrifice one's life 献身; 牺牲生命: *He laid down his life for the cause of freedom.* 他为自由的事业献出了生命. **lead a dog's life** ⇨ LEAD[3]. **lead sb a dog's life** ⇨ LEAD[3]. **ˌlife and 'limb** one's survival from accident or injury 幸免于难: *Fire-fighters risk life and limb every day in their work.* 消防队员的工作每天都是出生入死的. **the life and soul of sth** (*infml* 口) the most lively and amusing person present at a party, etc (聚会等中的)最活跃和最风趣的人物. **the love of sb's life** ⇨ LOVE[1]. **make (sb's) life a 'misery** cause sb to be unhappy or suffer pain in daily life 使某人日子不好过: *Having unpleasant neighbours can make one's life an absolute misery.* 邻居不好也能叫人度日如年. **make one's way in life** ⇨ WAY[2]. **a matter of life and death** ⇨ MATTER[1]. **a new lease of life** ⇨ NEW. **not on your (sweet) 'life!** (*infml* 口) certainly not 当然不. **put an end to one's life/oneself** ⇨ END[1]. **sell one's life dearly** ⇨ SELL. **spring to life** ⇨ SPRING[3]. **the staff of life** ⇨ STAFF. **take one's (own) 'life** commit suicide 自杀. **take one's life in one's hands** risk being killed 冒生命危险: *You take your life in your hands simply crossing the road these days!* 近来就连过马路也得豁出命才行! **take sb's 'life** kill sb 取某人性命. **to the 'life** exactly like the original 逼真: *draw, imitate, resemble sb to the life* 画某人画得逼真、仿某人仿得维妙维肖、酷似某人. **true to life** ⇨ TRUE. **walk of life** ⇨ WALK[2]. **a/sb's way of life** ⇨ WAY[1].

▷ **life·less** *adj* **1** never having had life 无生命的: *lifeless stones* 无生命的石头 ○ *a lifeless planet* 没有生物的行星. **2** dead 死的: *the lifeless bodies of the slaughtered animals* 宰杀后的动物尸体. **3** lacking vitality; dull 没有生气的; 沉闷的: *a lifeless performance* 死气沉沉的演出. **life·lessly** *adv.* **life·less·ness** *n* [U].

lifer /ˈlaɪfə(r); ˈlaɪfɚ/ *n* (*sl* 俚) person sentenced to life imprisonment 被判终身监禁的人.

□ **ˌlife-and-'death** (also **ˌlife-or-'death**) *adj* [attrib 作定语] serious; crucial; deciding between life and death 严重的; 关系重大的; 生死攸关的: *desert animals locked in a life-and-death struggle with the elements* 困于沙漠中与自然环境作生死搏斗的动物 ○ (*fig* 比喻) *a life-or-death attempt to reach the grand final* 为进入大决赛而作殊死拼搏的尝试.

ˌlife an'nuity (*finance* 财) annuity paid for the rest of a person's life 终身年金.

'life assurance, 'life insurance type of insurance policy providing a specified payment on the death of the holder 人寿保险.

lifebelt (*also* lifebuoy) 救生圈　　life-jacket 救生衣

'lifebelt (also **'lifebuoy**) *n* ring of buoyant or inflatable material used to keep afloat a person who has fallen into water 救生圈.

'life-blood *n* [U] **1** blood necessary to life 生命必需的血液. **2** (*fig* 比喻) thing that gives strength and vitality 活力的来源; 元气: *Credit is the life-blood of the consumer society.* 信用是消费社会的生命线.

'lifeboat *n* **(a)** small boat carried on a ship for use if the ship has to be abandoned at sea (船上的)救生艇. **(b)** boat specially built for going to the help of people in danger in the sea along a coast (海岸的)救生船.

'life cycle (*biology* 生) series of forms into which a living thing changes as it develops 生活周期(生物发展过程的系列变形); 生活史: *the life cycle of the butterfly* 蝴蝶的生活周期.

'life expectancy **(a)** number of years that a person is likely to live, esp as statistically determined for insurance purposes 预期寿命(尤指人寿保险估计): *Women have a higher life expectancy than men.* 女人比男人的预期寿命长. **(b)** length of time sth is likely to exist or function (某事物的)预期存在的期限: *the life expectancy of the average car, the present government* 一般汽车使用的、现政府执政的预期年限.

'life-giving *adj* [esp attrib 尤作定语] that restores life or vitality 恢复生机的.

'life-guard *n* expert swimmer employed to rescue bathers in difficulty or danger (游泳场的)救生员.

'Life Guards cavalry regiment in the British army (英国陆军中的)近卫骑兵团.

ˌlife 'history (*biology* 生) record of the life cycle of an organism (生物的)生活史.

ˌlife 'interest (*law* 律) benefit (from property, etc) valid during sb's life (财产等的)终身权益.

'life-jacket *n* sleeveless jacket of buoyant or inflatable material used to keep afloat a person in danger of drowning 救生衣. ⇨illus 见插图.

'lifelike *adj* exactly like a real person or thing 栩栩如生的; 逼真的: *a lifelike statue, drawing, toy* 栩栩如生的雕像、绘画、玩具.

'lifeline *n* **1** (*nautical* 海) **(a)** line or rope for saving life such as that attached to a lifebelt, or fastened along the deck of a ship in a storm for sailors to hold on to 救生索. **(b)** line attached to a deep-sea diver (深海潜水员的)信号绳. **2** (*fig* 比喻) anything on which sb/sth depends for continued existence 生命线; 命脉: *Public transport is a lifeline for many rural communities.* 公共交通对许多农村居民来说是不可或缺的.

'lifelong *adj* [attrib 作定语] extending throughout one's life 毕生的; 终身的: *a lifelong interest, friendship, wish* 终身权益、友谊、愿望.

ˌlife 'peer peer whose title is granted only to himself, and is not inherited by his heirs (爵位不能世袭的)终身贵族.

ˈ**life-preserver** *n* (*US*) life-jacket 救生衣.
ˈ**life-raft** *n* raft (esp inflatable) for emergency use at sea 救生筏;(尤指)充气救生船.
ˈ**life-saver** *n* (**a**) (*Austral or NZ* 澳或新西兰) life-guard 救生员. (**b**) thing that restores, benefits or is of great assistance 有助恢复、有好处或大有助益的事: *The clothes-dryer was a life-saver during the wet weather.* 天气潮湿时干衣机可帮了大忙了.
ˈ**life sciences** biology and related subjects 生命科学(生物学及相关学科).
ˈ**life-size(d)** *adj* of the same size as the person or thing represented 与真人实物一样大小的: *The statue is twice life-size.* 该雕像大小为实体的两倍.
ˈ**life-span** *n* length of time that sth is likely to live, continue or function 寿命; 生命期限; 使用期; 有效期: *Some insects have a life-span of no more than a few hours.* 有些昆虫寿命只有几小时.
ˈ**life story** biography 生活史: *She told me her life story.* 她向我讲述了她的生活史.
ˈ**life-style** *n* way of life of an individual or group 生活方式: *He and his brother have quite different life-styles.* 他和他弟弟生活方式截然不同.
ˌ**life-supˈport** *adj* [attrib 作定语] (of equipment) enabling sb to live in a hostile environment (eg a spacecraft) or when natural bodily functions have failed (eg following an accident) (指设备)维持生命的; 保障生命的. ˌ**life-supˈport system** such equipment used to keep a person alive 生命维持系统; 生命保障装置.
ˈ**lifetime** *n* **1** duration of sb's life or sth's existence (人的)一生; (事物的)存在期: *a lifetime of service* 使用年限 ○ *In your lifetime you must have seen many changes.* 人的一生中一定目睹很多变革. ○ [attrib 作定语] *a lifetime subscription (to a magazine, etc)* 长期订阅(某杂志等). **2** (idm 习语) **the chance, etc of a ˈlifetime** an exceptional opportunity, etc 千载难逢的好机会等: *Book now for the holiday of a lifetime!* 为机会难再的假日现在立即预订!
ˌ**life-ˈwork** *n* (usu sing 通常作单数) (also **life's ˈwork**) activity that occupies one's whole life 毕生的工作; 终身的事业.

lift /lɪft; lɪft/ *v* **1** [Tn, Tn·pr, Tn·p] **~ sb/sth (up)** raise sb/sth to a higher level or position 将某人[某物]抬起、举起: *Lift me up, mummy — I can't see.* 妈妈, 把我抱起来——我看不见. ○ *Three men were lifted by helicopter from the burning ship.* 直升飞机把三个男人从燃烧着的船上吊起. ○ (*fig* 比喻) *This piece of luck lifted his spirits.* 这一好运振奋了他的情绪. **2** [Tn·pr] take (sth) from its resting-place in order to move it 将(某物)从原地移开: *lift a box into a lorry, out of a train, down from a shelf, etc* 把箱子抬上卡车、抬出火车、从架子上抬下来等. **3** [I] (of clouds, fog, etc) rise; disperse (指云、雾等)消失, 消散: *The mist began to lift.* 雾开始消散. ○ (*fig* 比喻) *Her heart lifted at the sight of him.* 她一看见他心里就高兴. **4** [Tn] dig up (vegetables); remove (plants) from the ground 挖掘(蔬菜); 拔去(植物): *lift potatoes, turnips, etc* 刨土豆、拔萝卜. **5** [Tn, Tn·pr] **~ sth (from sb/sth)** (*infml* 口) (**a**) steal sth 偷窃某物: *She was caught lifting make-up from the supermarket.* 她在超级市场偷窃化妆品时被捉住了. (**b**) copy (material) from another source without permission or acknowledgement 剽窃, 抄袭(资料): *Many of his ideas were lifted from other authors.* 他的很多意念都是剽窃别的作者的. **6** [Tn] remove or abolish (restrictions) 解除或撤销(限制): *lift a ban, embargo, curfew, etc* 解除禁令、封锁、戒严等. **7** [Tn, Tn·pr, Tn·p] transport (goods, livestock, people) esp by air 运送(货物、牲畜、人)(尤指空运): *fresh tomatoes lifted in from the Canary Islands* 从加那利群岛空运的新鲜番茄. **8** (idm 习语) **have one's face lifted** ⇨ FACE[1]. **lift/raise a finger/hand (to do sth)** (*infml* 口) (usu negative 通常用于否定句) give help (with sth) 帮助(做某事): *He never lifts a finger round the house,* ie never helps with the housework. 家里的事他从不帮忙. **lift/raise a hand/one's hand against sb** ⇨ HAND[1]. **lift (up) one's eyes (to sth)** (*rhet* 修辞) look up 抬眼看. **9** (phr v) **lift off** (of a rocket or spacecraft) rise from the launching site (指火箭或航天器)发射, 升空, 起飞.

▷ **lift** *n* **1** [sing] lifting; being lifted 抬; 举: *Give him a lift: he's too small to see anything.* 把他抱起来; 他人矮, 什么也看不见. **2** [C] (*Brit*) (*US* **elevator**) box-like device for moving people or goods from one floor of a building to another 电梯; 升降机: *It's on the sixth floor — let's take the lift.* 在第七层——我们乘电梯吧. **3** [C] free ride in a private vehicle 免费搭私人车; 坐他人的顺路车: *I'll give you a lift to the station.* 我用车顺便送你到车站去吧. ○ *thumb/hitch a lift*, ie hitch-hike 用拇指示意求搭便车[免费搭他人车]. **4** [U] upward pressure that air exerts on an aircraft in flight (空气作用于飞行器的)上升力. Cf 参看 DRAG[1] 2. **5** [sing] feeling of elation 鼓舞; 振奋: *Winning the scholarship gave her a tremendous lift.* 她获得奖学金后受到极大的鼓舞.

□ ˈ**lift-off** *n* vertical take-off of a rocket or spacecraft (火箭或航天器的)发射, 升空, 起飞: *We have lift-off.* 我们已发射升空.
ˈ**lift-attendant** *n* (*US* **elevator operator**) person who operates a lift(2) 电梯或升降机操纵员.

liga·ment /ˈlɪgəmənt; ˋlɪgəmənt/ *n* tough flexible tissue in a person's or an animal's body that connects bones and holds organs in position 韧带: *tear/pull a ligament* 撕裂[拉伤]韧带.

lig·at·ure /ˈlɪgətʃə(r); ˋlɪgə,tʃɚ/ *n* **1** thread, bandage, etc used for tying, esp in surgical operations (用作绑缚的)线, 绷带; (尤指外科的)结扎线, 缚线. **2** (*music* 音) smooth combination of two or more notes of different pitch, or mark indicating this; slur; tie 连音; 连结线. **3** (in printing) two or more joined letters, such as œ or ﬂ (印刷的)连字(如 œ 或 ﬂ).

light[1] /laɪt; laɪt/ *n* **1** [U] (**a**) kind of natural radiation that makes things visible 光; 光线; 光亮: *the light of the sun, a lamp, the fire, etc* 阳光、灯光、火光. (**b**) amount or quality of this 光亮的程度: *The light was beginning to fail,* ie It was getting dark. 天色渐暗. ○ *This light is too poor to read by.* 这光线太暗不能看书. ○ *the flickering light of candles* 摇曳的烛光 ○ (*fig* 比喻) *A soft light* (ie expression) *came into her eyes as she looked at him.* 她望着他, 眼中闪露出柔情. Cf 参看 DARK[1]. **2** [C] source of light, esp an electric lamp 光源; (尤指)电灯: *turn/switch the lights on/off* 开[关]灯 ○ *Far below the plane we could see the lights of London.* 从飞机上俯视远处可以看到伦敦的万家灯火. ○ *A light was still burning in his study.* 他的书房里仍有孤灯独燃. ○ *That car hasn't got its lights* (ie headlights) *on.* 那辆汽车的前灯没有打开. ○ *Keep going, the lights* (ie traffic lights) *are green.* 继续开吧, 是绿灯. **3** [C] (thing used to produce a) flame or spark 火焰; 火花; 点火物: *Have you got a light?* eg for a cigarette. 你有火儿吗? (如为点香烟). **4** [U] understanding; enlightenment 了解; 领悟; 启发: *I wrestled with the crossword clue for ages before light finally dawned,* ie I understood the solution. 那纵横字谜的提示, 我琢磨了很长时间才恍然大悟. **5** [C] (esp in compounds 尤用以构成复合词) (*architecture* 建) window or opening to admit light 采光的窗或孔: *skylight* ○ *leaded light*. **6** [U, C usu *sing* 作不可数名词或可数名词, 后者通常作单数] (*art* 美术) part of a picture shown as lighted up (图画的)亮部: *light and shade* 亮部和阴暗部. **7** (idm 习语) **according to one's ˈlights** (*fml* 文) in conformity with one's beliefs, attitudes or abilities 按照自己的信念、态度或能力: *We can't blame him: he did his best according to his lights.* 我们不能责怪他, 他已尽力而为了. **at first light** ⇨ FIRST. **be/stand in sb's ˈlight** be placed between sb and a source of light 挡住某人的光线: *Can you move? You're in my light and I can't read.* 借个光行吗? 你挡住亮我没法看书了. **the bright lights** ⇨ BRIGHT. **bring sth to ˈlight** reveal sth; make sth known 揭露或暴露某事物: *New facts have been brought to light.* 已揭露出新的情况. **by the light of nature** without special guidance or teaching 天生的; 自然而然地. **cast/shed/throw light on sth** make sth clearer 使某事物清楚些: *Recent research has shed new light on the causes of the disease.* 最近的研究结果对该病的病因已有新的了解. **come to light** be revealed; become known 显露; 为人所知: *New evidence has recently come to light.* 新证据最近才为人知. **give sb/get the green light** ⇨ GREEN[1]. **go out like a ˈlight** (*infml* 口) faint or fall asleep suddenly 突然昏厥或入睡. **hide one's light under a bushel** ⇨ HIDE[1]. **in a good, bad, favourably, etc ˈlight** (**a**) (of a picture, etc) so as to be seen well, badly, etc (指画等)看得清楚, 看不清楚:

Two pictures have been hung in a bad light. 两幅画都挂在看不清的地方. **(b)** (*fig* 比喻) well, badly, favourably, etc 好; 坏; 有利地: *Press reports make his actions appear in the worst possible light.* 新闻报道极力丑化他的举动. ○ *It is hard to view his conduct in a favourable light.* 他的行为实难恭维. **in the light of sth** (*US* **in light of sth**) in view of sth; considering sth 鉴于某事物; 考虑到某事物: *review the proposals in the light of past experience* 照老经验来评论那些建议. **jump the lights** ⇨ JUMP². **light at the end of the tunnel** success, happiness, etc after a long period of difficulty or hardship 历尽艰辛后的成功、愉快、幸福等; 苦尽甘来. **lights out** (in barracks, dormitories, etc) time when lights are (to be) turned out (军营、宿舍等的)熄灯时间: *Lights out!* 熄灯! ○ *No talking after lights out.* 熄灯后不许说话. **see the ˈlight (a)** understand or accept sth after much difficulty or doubt (几经困难或怀疑后)明白或赞同某事物. **(b)** be converted to religious belief 皈依某宗教. **see the light (of ˈday) (a)** (*rhet* 修辞) be born 降生. **(b)** (of abstract things) be conceived or made public (指抽象事物)构想出或公开: *The notion of a Channel Tunnel first saw the light of day more than a century ago.* 海峡隧道的构想在一百多年前就已提出. **set light to sth** cause sth to start burning 引火烧某物. **strike a light** ⇨ STRIKE². **sweetness and light** ⇨ SWEETNESS (SWEET¹).

▷ **light** *adj*. Cf 参看 DARK². **1** full of light; not in darkness 光线充足的; 明亮的: *a light airy room* 明亮通风的房间 ○ *In spring the evenings start to get lighter.* 春天天渐渐黑得晚了. **2** pale 淡色的; 浅色的: *Light colours suit you best.* 你最适于穿浅色衣服. ○ *light-green eyes* 淡绿色的眼睛. **ˈlight-coloured** *adj*: *I prefer light-coloured fabrics.* 我比较喜欢浅色的织物.

□ **ˈlight bulb** = BULB².

ˈlighthouse *n* tower or other structure containing a beacon light to warn or guide ships 灯塔.

ˈlight meter = EXPOSURE METER (EXPOSURE).

ˈlight pen (*computing* 计) (also **wand**) photoelectric device, shaped like a pen, that can communicate with a computer either by making marks on the screen of a visual display unit or by reading the pattern of a bar code 光笔(人机通信光电装置, 呈笔形, 可用以在屏幕上作记号或读条形码).

ˈlightship *n* moored or anchored ship with a beacon light, serving the same purpose as a lighthouse 灯塔船(系泊或碇泊的起灯塔作用的船).

ˈlight-year *n* **1** (*astronomy* 天) distance that light travels in one year (about 6 million million miles) 光年. **2 light-years** [pl] (*infml fig* 口, 比喻) a very long time 极长的时期: *Genuine racial equality still seems light-years away.* 真正的种族平等似乎仍遥遥无期.

light² /laɪt; laɪt/ *v* (*pt, pp* **lit** /lɪt; lɪt/ or **lighted**) (*Lighted* is used esp as an attributive *adj*, as in *a lighted candle*, but Cf *He lit the candle* and *The candles were lit*. lighted 一字尤用作定语形容词, 如在 lighted candle'点着的蜡烛'词组中, 试比较 He lit the candle'他点着了蜡烛'和 The candles were lit'蜡烛都点着了'.) **1** [I, Tn, Tn·pr] (cause sth to) begin burning (使某物)开始燃烧: *This wood is so damp it won't light.* 这木头湿, 点不着. ○ *light a cigarette* 点香烟 ○ *Let's light a fire in the living-room tonight.* 今晚我们在起居室生火吧. **2** [Tn] turn on (an electric lamp, etc) 开(电灯等): *Light the torch — I can't see the path.* 打开电筒吧——我看不见道儿. **3** [Tn, Tn·pr] provide (sth) with light 给(某物)提供光源: *These streets are very poorly lit.* 这些街道的照明很差. ○ *Nowadays, houses are mostly lit by electricity.* 现在房屋大多用电照明. **4** [Tn·pr] guide (sb) with a light 用光引导(某人): *a candle to light your way* 为你照路的蜡烛. **5** (phr v) **light (sth) up** (*infml* 口) begin to smoke (a cigarette, etc) 点上(烟等)吸起来: *light up a pipe* 点上烟斗. **light up (with sth)** (of a person's face, etc) become bright or animated (指人的脸等)放光彩, 容光焕发: *Her eyes lit up with joy.* 她因喜悦而目光炯炯. **light sth up (a)** illuminate sth 照亮某物: *a castle lit up with floodlights* 泛光灯照亮的城堡 ○ *flashes of lightning lit up the sky* 照亮天空的道道闪电. **(b)** make (a person's face, etc) bright or animated 使(人的脸等)放光彩, 容光焕发: *A rare smile lit up his stern features.* 他那难得一见的微笑在他死板的脸上平添一些生气.

▷ **ˈlight·ing** *n* [U] **1** equipment for providing light for a room, building, etc 照明设备: *street lighting* 街道照明设备. **2** the light itself 光; 光线: *Subtle lighting helps people relax.* 光线暗淡有助于人们松弛精神. **ˌlighting-ˈup time** time when road vehicle lights must be turned on (路上车辆的)开灯时间.

□ **lit up** /ˈlɪt ˈʌp; ˌlɪtˈʌp/ (*sl* 俚) drunk 醉.

light³ /laɪt; laɪt/ *adj* **(-er, -est) 1** easy to lift or move; not heavy 轻的; 不重的: *He's lost a lot of weight: he's three kilos lighter than he used to be.* 他体重减了很多, 比以前轻了三公斤. ○ *Carry this bag — it's the lightest.* 拿这个袋子吧——这个最轻. **2** [esp attrib 尤作定语] of less than average weight (比平均重量)轻的: *This coat is light but very warm.* 这件大衣很轻但非常暖和. ○ *light shoes, clothing*, ie for summer wear 轻便的鞋、衣物(夏季穿用的) ○ *The old bridge can only be used by light vehicles.* 那座旧桥只能通行轻型车辆. ○ *a light aircraft* 轻型飞机. **3** (following *ns* 用于名词之后) less than the expected weight (比预期的重量)轻的; 分量不足的: *This sack of potatoes is five kilos light.* 这袋土豆少五公斤. **4** [esp attrib 尤作定语] gentle; delicate 轻柔的; 轻巧的: *a light tap on the shoulder, a light patter of rain on the window* 在肩上轻轻的一拍、雨点在窗户上的轻柔拍打声 ○ *a light knock on the door*, ie not loud 轻轻的敲门声 ○ *be light on one's feet*, ie agile or nimble 步履轻快. **5** [esp attrib 尤作定语] **(a)** easy to carry out or perform 容易做的; 易为的: *Since her accident she can only do light work.* 她出事以后只能做轻活儿了. ○ *take a little light exercise* 做轻微的运动. **(b)** easy to understand 易懂的: *I took some light reading* (eg a thriller) *for the train journey.* 我带上一些轻松的读物乘火车时消遣. ○ *light music, comedy, entertainment*, ie not serious or difficult 轻音乐、轻喜剧、轻松的娱乐活动. **6** easy to bear; not severe 容易承受的; 不严厉的: *The company was fined £1 000, which critics said was too light.* 公司被罚1 000英镑, 论者称惩处过轻. ○ *a light attack of flu* 轻度流感. **7** not intense 不猛烈的: *The wind is very light.* 风很小. ○ *Trading on the Stock Exchange was light today.* 证券交易所今日交投平平. ○ *light showers of rain* 小阵雨. **8** [esp attrib 尤作定语] not dense 稀少的: *light traffic* 来往车辆稀少 ○ *The river was visible through a light mist.* 透过薄雾那河隐约可见. ○ *This plant will only grow in light* (ie sandy) *soil.* 这种植物在轻质土壤中才能生长. **9 (a)** (of meals) small in quantity (指饭食)少量的: *a light snack, supper, etc* 小吃、少量的晚餐. **(b)** (of food) that is easy to digest (指食物)易消化的, 清淡的: *a light pudding* 易消化的布丁 ○ *Her soufflés are always so light.* 她烤的蛋奶酥总是这么清淡. **10** [attrib 作定语] (of sleep) not deep (指睡眠)不沉的, 不熟的: *Please don't make any noise — my mother's a very light sleeper*, ie wakes easily. 请安静——我母亲睡觉睡不实. **11** [esp attrib 尤作定语] (of drinks) low in alcohol (指饮料)酒精含量低的, 淡的: *light ale* 淡味麦芽啤酒 ○ *a light white wine* 低度白葡萄酒. **12** [esp attrib 尤作定语] cheerful; free from worry 愉快的; 无忧无虑的: *with a light heart* 轻松愉快地. **13** (idm 习语) **(as) ˌlight as ˈair/as a ˈfeather** very light 很轻. **light reˈlief** words or actions that relax tension or relieve concentration 使人轻松或松弛的言语或行动: *His humour provided some welcome light relief.* 他的幽默可使人松了一口气. **make light of sth** treat sth as unimportant 对某事物等闲视之: *He made light of his injury*, ie said it was not serious. 他对自己的伤不以为意. **make light work of sth** do sth with little effort 不费力做某事: *We made light work of the tidying up.* 我们做整理工作轻而易举. **many hands make light ˈwork** ⇨ HAND¹.

▷ **light** *adv* with little luggage or possessions (used esp in the expression shown) 轻装地(尤用于以下示例): *travel light* 轻装旅行.

lightly *adv* **1** in a light manner 轻轻地; 轻巧地. **2** without serious consideration 轻率地; 不严肃地: *Marriage is not something to be undertaken lightly.* 婚姻大事不可掉以轻心. **3** (idm 习语) **get off ˈlightly/ˈcheaply** (*infml* 口) escape serious punishment or inconvenience 逃过重罚或麻烦事.

light·ness *n* [U]: *great lightness of touch*, eg when playing the piano 极轻的一触(如弹奏钢琴).

□ **ˌlight-ˈfingered** *adj* (*infml* 口) in the habit of stealing (esp small) things 惯行扒窃的; (尤指)小偷小

摸的.

ˌ**light-ˈheaded** *adj* feeling slightly faint or dizzy 眩晕的. ˌ**light-ˈheadedly** *adv*. ˌ**light-ˈheadedness** *n* [U].

ˌ**light-ˈhearted** *adj* (**a**) without cares; cheerful 无忧无虑的; 轻松愉快的. (**b**) (*derog* 贬) not serious or sensible enough; casual 漫不经心的; 随便的. ˌ**light-ˈheartedly** *adv*. ˌ**light-ˈheartedness** *n* [U].

ˌ**light-ˈheavyweight** *n* boxer weighing between 72.5 and 79.5 kg, next above middleweight 次重量级拳击手(体重为72.5和79.5公斤之间者, 在中量级之上).

ˌ**light ˈindustry** industry producing small consumer goods or components 轻工业.

ˈ**lightweight** *n, adj* **1** (boxer) weighing between 57 and 61 kg, next above featherweight 轻量级的(拳击手)(体重在57和61公斤之间, 在次轻量级之上): *the European lightweight champion* 欧洲轻量级拳击冠军. **2** (*infml* 口) (person or thing) of little influence or importance 无足轻重的(人或物): *a political lightweight* 政治上的无名之辈 ○ *a lightweight news item* 不重要的消息.

light[4] /laɪt; laɪt/ *v* (*pt, pp* **lit** /lɪt; lɪt/ or **lighted**) (phr v) **light into sb** (*sl* 俚) attack sb (physically or verbally) 打、打击或抨击某人. **light on/upon sb/sth** find sb/sth by chance 偶遇某人[某事物]: *Luckily, I lit on a secondhand copy of the book.* 真运气, 我无意中见到了那本书, 是本旧的. **light out** (*US sl* 俚) leave quickly 迅速离去: *I lit out for home.* 我马上回家了.

lighten[1] /ˈlaɪtn; ˋlaɪtn̩/ *v* [I, Tn] **1** (cause sth to) become lighter in weight (使某物)变轻: *lighten a burden, cargo, pack, etc* 使负担、货物、包装等变轻. **2** (cause sth to) be relieved of care or worry (使某事物)令人放心, 解除忧虑: *My mood gradually lightened.* 我的心情慢慢轻松起来. ○ *lighten sb's duties* 减轻某人的责任.

lighten[2] /ˈlaɪtn; ˋlaɪtn̩/ *v* **1** [Tn] make (sth) brighter 使(某物)更明亮: *These new windows have lightened the room considerably.* 这些新窗户显得房间亮多了. **2** [I] (*fig* 比喻) become brighter 变得更光明; 容光焕发: *His face lightened as she apologized.* 她向他道歉时, 他喜形于色.

lighter[1] /ˈlaɪtə(r); ˋlaɪtɚ/ *n* = CIGARETTE LIGHTER (CIGARETTE): *a ciˈgar lighter* 打火机.

lighter[2] /ˈlaɪtə(r); ˋlaɪtɚ/ *n* flat-bottomed boat used for loading and unloading ships not brought to a quay or in transporting goods for short distances 驳船. Cf 参看 PINNACE.

▷ ˈ**lighterage** /ˈlaɪtərɪdʒ; ˋlaɪtərɪdʒ/ *n* [U] (**a**) transport of goods by lighter 驳运. (**b**) charge for this 驳运费.

□ ˈ**lighterman** /-mən; -mən/ *n* (*pl* ˈ**lightermen** /-mən; -mən/) person who works on a lighter 驳船船员.

light·ning[1] /ˈlaɪtnɪŋ; ˋlaɪtnɪŋ/ *n* **1** [U] flash of brilliant light in the sky produced by natural electricity passing between clouds or from clouds to the ground, usu followed by thunder 闪电: *be struck by lightning* 遭雷电击中 ○ *a flash of lightning* 一道闪电. **2** (idm 习语) **lightning never strikes in the same place twice** (*saying* 谚) an unusual event, or one that happens by chance, is not likely to occur again in exactly the same circumstances or to the same people 偶发的事不会在同一环境或同一人身上重演. **like (greased) ˈlightning; like a streak of lightning; (as) quick as ˈlightning** very fast 很快.

□ ˈ**lightning-bug** *n* (*US*) firefly 萤火虫.

ˈ**lightning conductor** (*Brit*) (*US* **lightning rod**) metal rod or wire fixed to an exposed part of a building, etc to prevent damage by lightning 避雷针.

light·ning[2] /ˈlaɪtnɪŋ; ˋlaɪtnɪŋ/ *adj* [attrib 作定语] **1** rapid, brief or sudden 闪电般的; 快速的; 短暂的; 突然的: *Police made a lightning raid on the house.* 警方突然查抄了那座房子. **2** (idm 习语) **with lightning ˈspeed** very fast 很快.

□ **lightning ˈstrike** sudden industrial stoppage taken without warning 闪电式罢工: *a lightning strike called to protest about the dismissal of a workmate* 为抗议解雇一名工友而进行的闪电式罢工.

lights /laɪts; laɪts/ *n* [pl] lungs of sheep, pigs, etc used as food (供食用的)羊、猪等的肺.

lig·neous /ˈlɪgnɪəs; ˋlɪgnɪəs/ *adj* (of plants) woody (指植物)木的, 木质的.

lig·nite /ˈlɪgnaɪt; ˋlɪgnaɪt/ *n* [U] soft brownish coal 褐煤.

like[1] /laɪk; laɪk/ *v* **1** (**a**) [Tn, Tg, Tsg] find (sb/sth) pleasant or satisfactory; enjoy 喜欢, 喜爱(某人[某事物]): *Do you like fish?* 你喜欢鱼吗? ○ *She likes him* (ie is fond of him) *but doesn't love him.* 她喜欢他, 但并非爱他. ○ *She's never liked swimming.* 她从不爱游泳. ○ *I didn't like him/his taking all the credit.* 我讨厌他把全部功劳归于自己. (**b**) [Tt, Tnt, Cn·a] regularly choose (to do sth); prefer (to do sth) 喜好(做某事): *On Sundays I like to sleep late.* 星期天我爱睡懒觉. ○ *He likes his guests to be punctual.* 他喜欢客人守时. ○ *'How do you like your tea?' 'I like it rather weak.'* '你喝茶有什么喜好?' '我喜欢淡一些的.' **2** [Tt, Tg] (in negative sentences 用于否定句) be unwilling or reluctant to do sth 不愿做某事: *I didn't like* (ie felt reluctant) *to disturb you.* 我本不想打搅你. ○ *He doesn't like asking for help.* 他不愿意求助. **3** [Tn, Tt, Tnt] (used with *should/would/'d* to express a wish or preference at a particular time 与should/would/'d连用表示愿望或喜爱): *Would you like something to eat?* 想吃点东西吗? ○ *I'd like to think it over before deciding.* 我还是想想再决定吧. ○ *We would like you to come and visit us.* 我们希望你到我们这里来作客. ○ (*ironic* 反语) *So he thinks it's easy, does he? I'd like to see him try!* ie He would find it difficult. 那么说他认为很容易, 是吗? 我倒想让他试一试! (他就知道难了.) ⇨ Usage at WANT[1] 用法见 WANT[1]. **4** [Tn] (*infml* 口) (in negative sentences 用于否定句) (of food) suit sb's health (指食物)对某人的健康适宜: *I like lobster but it doesn't like me.* 我喜欢吃龙虾, 但吃了身体不适. **5** (idm 习语) **if you ˈlike** (used as a polite form of agreement or suggestion 作表示同意或建议的礼貌用语): *'Shall we stop now?' 'If you like.'* '我们现在停下来吧?' '听你的.' ○ *If you like, we could go out this evening.* 你要是愿意的话, 咱们今天晚上出去. **I like his ˈnerve, ˈcheek, etc** (*ironic* 反语) (used as an exclamation to complain that sb's behaviour is too impudent 作对某人行为卤莽无礼的感叹语): *'She has written to demand an apology.' 'I like her nerve!'* '她已写信要求给她道歉.' '她还真做得出来!' **I like ˈthat!** (*ironic* 反语) (used to protest that sth that has been said is untrue or unfair 用以表示对言语不实或不当的反感): *'She called you a cheat.' 'Well, I like that!'* '她说你是骗子.' '嗬, 亏她说得出口!' **like the look/sound of sb/sth** be favourably impressed by what one has seen of/heard about sb/sth 对有关某人[某事物]的所见所闻有好印象: *I like the look of your new assistant — she should do very well.* 我看你的新助手不错——她看样子很能干. ○ *I don't like the sound of that cough — oughtn't you to see a doctor?* 我觉得你的咳嗽声有问题——是不是该找医生看看? **that's what ˈI'd like to know** (*infml* 口) (used to express disbelief, suspicion, etc 用以表示不相信、怀疑等): *Where's all the money coming from? That's what I'd like to know.* 这些钱都是从哪儿来的? 真叫人纳闷儿.

▷ **like·able** (also **lik·able**) /ˈlaɪkəbl; ˋlaɪkəbl̩/ *adj* easy to like; pleasant 可爱的; 讨人喜欢的: *He's likeable enough, but a bit boring.* 他挺讨人喜欢, 就是有点无聊.

likes *n* [pl] (idm 习语) ˌ**likes and ˈdislikes** things one does and does not like 好恶; 爱憎: *He has so many likes and dislikes that it's impossible to please him.* 他好恶爱憎这么多, 要讨他欢心是不可能的.

NOTE ON USAGE 用法: Note these ways of using **Would you like?** 注意 **Would you like?** 的下列用法: **1** *'Would you like to come to dinner tomorrow?' 'Yes, thank you.'* (invitation) '您明天来吃饭好吗?' '好哇, 谢谢您.' (表示邀请). **2** *'Would you like to clear the table?' 'Okay.'* (request) '请你收拾桌子行吗?' '行.' (表示请求). Sometimes the speaker uses pattern **2** in order to make a complaint 有时用上述第2种方式表示不满: *'Would you like to turn that music down?' 'Yes, sorry.'* '请把音乐声放小些行吗?' '可以, 对不起.'

like[2] /laɪk; laɪk/ *prep* **1** similar to (sb/sth); resembling 像(某人[某事物]); 类似; 相似: *wearing a hat like mine* 戴着与我那顶一样的帽子 ○ *a house built like an Indian palace* 建造得像印度宫殿一样的宅邸 ○ *I've always wanted a garden like theirs.* 我总想有一座像他们那样的花园. ○ *I'm going to be a pop star like Michael Jackson.* 我要当像迈克尔·杰克逊那样的流行歌星. ○ *He's like his father*, ie in character or looks. 他像他的父亲. ○ *She looks a bit like the Queen.* 她长得有点像女王. ○ *That*

L

sounds like (ie I think I can hear) *the postman.* 听声音像是邮递员. **2** characteristic of (sb/sth) 有(某人[某事物])的特点: *It's just like her to tell everyone about it.* 只有她才会把那件事见谁就告诉谁. **3** in the manner of (sb/sth); to the same degree as 像(某人[某事物])一样: *chatter like monkeys* 像猴子那样吵叫 ○ *behave like children* 表现像孩子 ○ *run like the wind,* ie very fast 跑得快如风. ⇨Usage at AS 用法见 AS. **4** for example 例如; 比方: *We could look at some modern poets, like Eliot and Hughes.* 我们可以考虑一下现代诗人, 例如艾略特和休斯. ○ *Practical lessons, like woodwork and cookery, are not considered as important as maths.* 一般认为像木工和烹饪之类的实用课程不如数学重要. **5** (idm 习语) **like ˈanything** (*infml* 口) very fast, hard, much, etc 很快; 很努力; 很; 非常: *I had to run like anything to catch the bus.* 我只好拼命跑去赶公共汽车. ○ *We must work like anything to finish on time.* 我们必须全力以赴按时完成.

▷ **like** *conj* (*infml* 口) **1** in the same manner as 像…那样: *No one sings the blues like she did.* 唱布鲁斯歌谁也比不上她. ○ *Don't think you can learn grammatical rules like you learn multiplication tables.* 不能像记乘法表那样记语法规则. **2** (*esp US*) as if 仿佛; 好像: *She acts like she owns the place,* ie is very bossy. 她很霸道, 就好像那地方都是她的.

-like *suff* 后缀 (forming *adjs* 用以构成形容词) in the manner of; similar to 类似; 像: *childlike* ○ *ladylike* ○ *snake-like.*

like³ /laɪk; laɪk/ *adj* **1** having some or all of the qualities or features of; similar 相似的; 相同的: *They're not twins, but they're very like.* 他们俩虽非双胞胎, 却十分相像. ○ *Like causes tend to produce like results.* 类似的原因往往产生类似的结果. ○ *mice, rats and like creatures* 小家鼠、大老鼠之类的动物. **2** (idm 习语) **(as) ˌlike as two ˈpeas/as ˌpeas in a ˈpod** virtually identical 一模一样; 酷似.

▷ **like** *adv* (idm 习语) **(as) ˌlike as ˈnot; ˌlike eˈnough; most/very ˈlike** (*dated* 旧) (quite/very) probably 大概; 很可能: *It'll rain this afternoon, as like as not.* 今天下午很可能要下雨.

like *n* **1** [sing] person or thing that is like another 相似的人或事物: *You should only compare like with like.* 只应在同类事物中作比较. ○ *jazz, rock and the like,* ie similar kinds of music 爵士乐、摇滚乐之类的乐曲 ○ *a man whose like we shall not see again* 我们再也不想看到的那种男人 ○ *I've never seen the like of it!* ie anything so strange, etc. 我从未见过这种事! **2** (idm 习语) **the likes of sb/sth** (*infml* 口) a similar person or thing 类似的人或物: *He's a bit of a snob — won't speak to the likes of me.* 他这个人有点势利——不会和我这样的人说话.

□ **ˌlike-ˈminded** *adj* having similar tastes or opinions 情趣或想法相同的: *I have complained to my MP, and urge all ˌlike-minded ˈpeople to do the same.* 我已向议员提出不满的意见, 并努力敦促抱有共识的人采取同样行动.

-like *suff* 后缀 (used widely with *ns* to form *adjs* 可与许多名词结合构成形容词) similar to; resembling 像…的; 类似…的; …般的; …样的: *childlike* ○ *shell-like.*

likely /ˈlaɪklɪ; ˈlaɪklɪ/ *adj* **(-ier, -iest) 1 ~ (to do sth/that...)** that is expected; probable 预期的; 可能的: *the likely outcome, winner* 预料的结果、胜者 ○ *It isn't likely to rain.* 不大像要下雨. ○ *She's very likely to ring me tonight.* 她今晚很可能给我打电话. ○ *It's very likely that she'll ring me tonight.* 很可能今晚她给我打电话. **2** that seems suitable for a purpose 似适合于某用途的: *This looks a likely field for mushrooms.* 这地看来适合长蘑菇. ○ *a likely-looking candidate,* ie one expected to succeed 很可能当选的候选人. **3** (idm 习语) **a ˈlikely story** (*ironic* 反语) (used to express scorn and disbelief about what sb has said 用以表示对某人的话不屑一听和不相信): *He says he just forgot about it — a likely story!* 他说他仅仅是忘了——像煞有介事!

▷**like·li·hood** /ˈlaɪklɪhʊd; ˈlaɪklɪˌhʊd/ *n* [U] probability 可能; 可能性: *There's no likelihood of that happening.* 没有发生那种事情的可能. ○ *In all likelihood* (ie Very probably) *the meeting will be cancelled.* 会议十之八九要取消.

likely *adv* (idm 习语) **as ˌlikely as ˈnot; most/very ˈlikely** (very) probably (很)可能: *As likely as not she's forgotten all about it.* 很可能她把这事忘得一干二净. **not (bloody, etc) ˈlikely!** (*infml* 口) certainly not 决不可能; 当然不会: *Me? Join the army? Not likely!* 我? 参军? 没门儿!

liken /ˈlaɪkən; ˈlaɪkən/ *v* [Tn·pr] **~ sth to sth** (*fml* 文) show the resemblance between one thing and another 显示两事物的相像: *Life has often been likened to a journey.* 生活常常比作旅行.

like·ness /ˈlaɪknɪs; ˈlaɪknɪs/ *n* **1 (a)** [U] being alike; resemblance 相像; 相似: *I can't see much likeness between him and his father.* 我看不出他和他父亲有多少相像处. **(b)** [C usu *sing* 通常作单数] instance of this 相像; 相似: *All my children share a strong family likeness.* 我的孩子都有明显的家族特征. **2** [sing] (following an *adj* 用于形容词之后) extent to which a portrait, photograph, etc resembles the person portrayed 肖像、照片等酷似本人的程度: *That photo is a good likeness of David.* 戴维那张相片照得很像.

like·wise /ˈlaɪkwaɪz; ˈlaɪkˌwaɪz/ *adv* (*fml* 文) **1** similarly 同样地; 照样地: *I'm going to bed and you would be well advised to do likewise.* 我要睡觉了, 你最好也睡吧. **2** also 也; 亦: *The food was excellent, (and) likewise the wine.* 菜好极了, 酒也是.

lik·ing /ˈlaɪkɪŋ; ˈlaɪkɪŋ/ *n* (idm 习语) **have a liking for sth** be fond of sth 喜爱某事物: *I've always had a liking for the sea.* 我一向喜爱大海. **to sb's liking** (*fml* 文) giving sb satisfaction; pleasing sb 合某人意; 讨某人喜欢: *I trust the meal was to your liking.* 我相信那饭菜对你的胃口.

li·lac /ˈlaɪlək; ˈlaɪlək/ *n* **1 (a)** [C] shrub with sweet-smelling pale purple or white blossom 丁香: *The lilacs are in flower.* 丁香开花了. **(b)** [U] its blossom 丁香花: *a bunch of lilac* 一束丁香. **2** [U] pale purple colour 淡紫色.

▷ **li·lac** *adj* of a pale purple colour 淡紫色的.

lil·li·pu·tian /ˌlɪlɪˈpjuːʃn; ˌlɪləˈpjuʃən/ *adj* (*fml* 文) on a small scale; tiny 微型的; 极小的: *a model railway layout peopled with lilliputian figures* 带小人儿的模型铁路网.

lilo /ˈlaɪləʊ; ˈlaɪˌlo/ *n* (*pl* **~s**) (*Brit propr* 专利名) type of lightweight inflatable mattress for lying on, eg at the beach 充气垫(如于海滨供躺卧用的).

lilt /lɪlt; lɪlt/ *n* [sing] **1** rise and fall of the voice while speaking (说话时声音的)抑扬顿挫: *She has a faint Irish lilt.* 她有点爱尔兰口音. **2** regular rising and falling pattern in music, usu accompanied by a lively rhythm (音乐的)轻快旋律.

▷ **lilt·ing** *adj* having a lilt 抑扬顿挫的; 节奏欢快的.

lily /ˈlɪlɪ; ˈlɪlɪ/ *n* **1 (a)** any of various types of plant growing from a bulb, with large white or reddish flowers 百合; 百合花: *ˈwater lilies* 睡莲. **(b)** type of lily with white flowers 白百合: *daffodils and lilies flowering in the spring* 春天开花的黄水仙和白百合. **2** (idm 习语) **gild the lily** ⇨ GILD.

□ **lily-livered** /ˈlɪlɪ lɪvəd; ˈlɪlɪˈlɪvɚd/ *adj* (*dated* 旧) cowardly 胆小的; 懦弱的.

ˌlily of the ˈvalley plant with small sweet-smelling bell-shaped white flowers 铃兰.

limb /lɪm; lɪm/ *n* **1** leg, arm or wing 肢(腿、臂或翼): *I need to sit down and rest my weary limbs.* 我要坐下歇歇腿. **2** main branch of a tree 树的主枝. **3** (idm 习语) **life and limb** ⇨ LIFE. **out on a ˈlimb** (*infml* 口) isolated and vulnerable; without supporters (used esp in the expressions shown) 孤立而脆弱, 没有支持者(尤用于以下示例): *leave sb/be/go out on a limb* 弃某人于[处于/陷于]孤立无援的境地. **sound in wind and limb** ⇨ SOUND¹. **tear sb limb from limb** ⇨ TEAR².

▷ **-limbed** /lɪmd; lɪmd/ (forming compound *adjs* 用以构成复合形容词) having limbs of the kind specified 有某种肢体的: *ˌlong-ˈlimbed* ○ *ˌweary-ˈlimbed* ○ *ˌloose-ˈlimbed,* ie supple.

lim·ber /ˈlɪmbə(r); ˈlɪmbɚ/ *adj* (*dated* 旧) supple; flexible 柔软的; 灵活的.

▷ **lim·ber** *v* (phr v) **ˌlimber ˈup** exercise in preparation for sport, etc; warm up (WARM²) (运动等前)做准备活动, 活动肢体: *I always do a few easy exercises to limber up before a match.* 我在比赛前总要做些简单的准备活动.

limbo¹ /ˈlɪmbəʊ; ˈlɪmbo/ *n* (idm 习语) **in limbo** in an

L

intermediate or uncertain state; neglected 处于中间的或不定的状态; 受忽略; 被遗忘: *The project must remain in limbo until the committee makes its decision.* 该工程必须搁置, 等待委员会做决定.

limbo[2] /ˈlɪmbəʊ; ˋlɪmbo/ *n* (*pl* **~s** /-bəʊz; -boz/) West Indian dance in which the dancer bends back and passes under a bar that is gradually lowered 林波舞(西印度群岛的舞蹈, 舞者向后弯腰钻过逐渐降低的横竿).

lime[1] /laɪm; laɪm/ *n* [U] **1** (also ˈ**quicklime**) white substance (calcium oxide) obtained by heating limestone, used in making cement and mortar and as a fertilizer 石灰. **2** = BIRDLIME (BIRD).

▷ **lime** *v* [Tn] treat (fields, etc) with lime to improve the soil 给(田地等)施石灰(以改进土壤).

□ ˈ**lime-kiln** *n* kiln in which lime is produced 石灰窑.

ˈ**limestone** *n* [U] type of rock, eg chalk, composed esp of the remains of prehistoric plants and animals 石灰岩.

lime[2] /laɪm; laɪm/ (also ˈ**lime-tree, linden**) *n* tree with smooth heart-shaped leaves and fragrant yellow flowers 椴树(乔木, 叶光滑呈心形, 花黄, 有香味).

lime[3] /laɪm; laɪm/ *n* **1** [C] (tree bearing) round fruit like a lemon but smaller and more acid 酸橙树, 酸橙(比柠檬小但更酸). **2** [U] (also **lime green**) yellowish-green colour of this fruit 酸橙绿色; 淡黄绿色.

□ ˈ**lime-juice** *n* [U] juice of limes used for flavouring or as a drink 酸橙汁(用作调味或饮料).

lime·light /ˈlaɪmlaɪt; ˋlaɪm,laɪt/ *n* [U] publicity or attention 众人注意的中心: *She claims she never sought the limelight.* 她说她从不爱出风头. ○ *When I was President, I was always in the limelight — there was no privacy.* 我当总统时一直为公众瞩目 —— 谈不上私人的生活.

lim·er·ick /ˈlɪmərɪk; ˋlɪmərɪk/ *n* type of humorous poem with five lines, the first two rhyming with the last 五行幽默诗.

limey /ˈlaɪmɪ; ˋlaɪmɪ/ *n* (*pl* **~s**) (*US sl usu derog* 俚, 通常作贬义) British person, usu male 英国人; (通常指)英国佬.

limit[1] /ˈlɪmɪt; ˋlɪmɪt/ *n* [C] **1** point or line beyond which sth does not extend; boundary 限度; 极限; 界线; 界限: *within the city limits* 在该城范围内 ○ (*fig* 比喻) *He tried my patience to its limits.* 他把我逼得忍无可忍了. ○ *No fishing is allowed within a twenty-mile limit.* 二十英里范围内不准垂钓. **2** greatest amount allowed or possible 允许的或可能的最大限度; 限量: *The speed limit on this road is 70 mph.* 这条路的车速限制是每小时70英里. ○ *There's a limit to how much I'm prepared to spend.* 我准备花多少钱是有限度的. **3** (idm 习语) **(be) the limit** (*sl* 俚) as much or more than one can tolerate 所能忍受的或无法再忍受的极限: *You really are the (absolute) limit!* 你真让人忍无可忍! ˌ**off** ˈ**limits** (*US*) = OUT OF BOUNDS (BOUNDS). **the sky's the limit** ⇨ SKY. **within** ˈ**limits** in moderation; up to a point 适度地; 有限度地: *I'm willing to help, within limits.* 我愿适当予以帮助. **without** ˈ**limit** to any extent or degree 无限地; 无限制地.

▷ **lim·it·less** *adj* without limit 无限制的; 无限度的; 无界限的; 无止境的: *limitless ambition, greed, wealth* 无限度的野心、贪欲、财富.

limit[2] /ˈlɪmɪt; ˋlɪmɪt/ *v* [Tn, Tn·pr] **~ sb/sth (to sth)** set a limit or limits to sb/sth; restrict sb/sth 给某人[某事物]定界限; 限定某人[某事物]: *We must try and limit our expenditure.* 我们必须设法限制我们的开支. ○ *I shall limit myself to three aspects of the subject.* 我仅探讨这一问题的三个方面.

▷ **lim·ited** *adj* restricted; few or small 有限的; 少的; 小的: *Only a limited number of places is available.* 只有少数地方可供使用. ○ *His intelligence is rather limited.* 他的智力相当有限. ˌ**limited eˈdition** (production of only a) fixed, usu small, number of copies 限数版(印数固定、通常很少); 限数版本的出版. ˌ**limited liaˈbility company** (*abbr* 缩写 **Ltd**) business company whose members are liable for its debts only to the extent of the capital sum they have provided 有限责任公司: *Acme Interiors Ltd* 爱克米室内装饰有限公司.

lim·it·ing *adj* imposing limits; restrictive 限制的; 限制性的: *Time is the limiting factor.* 时间是限制性的因素.

lim·ita·tion /ˌlɪmɪˈteɪʃn; ˌlɪməˋteʃən/ *n* **1** [U] limiting; being limited 限制; 限定: *resist any limitation of their powers* 反对限制他们的权力. **2** [C] condition, fact or circumstance that limits 起限制作用的条件、事或环境; 局限; 限制: *impose limitations on imports, expenditure, reporting* 对进口、开销、报道加以限制. **3** [C] lack of ability 能力上的不足; 无能: *He knows his limitations*, ie knows what he can and cannot achieve. 他知道自己能力有限.

lim·ous·ine /ˈlɪməziːn, ˌlɪməˈziːn; ˋlɪmə,zin, ˌlɪməˋzin/ *n* large luxurious car, esp with a glass partition separating driver and passengers 豪华轿车(尤指有玻璃将司机座位隔开的).

limp[1] /lɪmp; lɪmp/ *adj* **1** not stiff or firm 柔软的: *a limp edition*, ie a book with a flexible binding 软皮书. **2** lacking strength or energy 无力的; 无精神的: *a limp handshake, gesture, response* 无力的握手、姿势、反应 ○ *The flowers looked limp in the heat.* 花在热天发蔫. ▷ **limply** *adv*. **limp·ness** *n* [U].

limp[2] /lɪmp; lɪmp/ *v* **1** [I, Ipr, Ip] walk unevenly, as when one foot or leg is hurt or stiff 跛行; 一拐一拐地走: *That dog must be hurt — he's limping.* 那条狗准是受了伤 —— 一拐一拐的. ○ *The injured footballer limped slowly off the field.* 受伤的足球队员跛着脚慢慢走出场地. ○ *limp about, along, away, off* 一拐一拐地到处走、前行、走开、走去 ○ (*fig* 比喻) *The third act limps badly.* 第三幕演得拖拖拉拉. ⇨Usage at SHUFFLE 用法见 SHUFFLE. **2** [Ipr] (of a ship, etc) proceed with difficulty in a specified direction, esp after an accident (指船等)困难地航行(尤指出事之后): *After the collision both vessels managed to limp into harbour.* 两船相撞之后都挣扎着驶进海港.

▷ **limp** *n* [sing] limping walk 跛行: *walk with/have a bad, slight, etc limp* 跛得厉害、有点跛.

lim·pet /ˈlɪmpɪt; ˋlɪmpɪt/ *n* small shellfish that sticks tightly to rocks 帽贝: *cling, hold on, etc (to sb/sth) like a limpet*, ie very tenaciously 紧紧依附、缠住(某人[某事物])不放.

limpid /ˈlɪmpɪd; ˋlɪmpɪd/ *adj* (of liquids, etc) clear; transparent (指液体等)清澈的, 透明的: *limpid eyes* 晶莹的眼睛. ▷ **limp·id·ity** /lɪmˈpɪdətɪ; lɪmˋpɪdətɪ/ *n* [U]. **limp·idly** *adv*.

linch·pin /ˈlɪntʃpɪn; ˋlɪntʃ,pɪn/ *n* **1** pin passed through the end of an axle to keep the wheel in position 轮辖; 制轮楔. **2** (*fig* 比喻) person or thing that is vital to an organization, plan, etc (组织、计划等中)关键性的人或事物: *Controlling wages is the linchpin of the Government's policies.* 控制工资是政府政策的关键.

linc·tus /ˈlɪŋktəs; ˋlɪŋktəs/ *n* [U] (*Brit*) syrupy medicine to soothe coughs 止咳糖浆.

lin·den /ˈlɪndən; ˋlɪndən/ *n* = LIME[2].

line[1] /laɪn; laɪn/ *n* **1** [C] **(a)** long narrow mark, either straight or curved, traced on a surface 线; 线条: *a straight line* 直线 ○ *Sign your name on the dotted line.* 请在虚线上签名. ○ *Don't park on the double yellow lines*, ie those painted at the side of a road in Britain. 不要把车停在双黄线处(在英国, 标于路边的). ○ *Draw a line from A to B.* 从A到B画一条线. **(b)** mark like a line on the skin 皮肤上的纹: *The old man's face was covered in lines and wrinkles.* 那老人的脸上布满皱纹和褶子. **2** [U] use of lines in art 艺术中线条的运用: *Line and colour are both important in portrait painting.* 线条和色彩在肖像绘画中都很重要. **3 lines** [pl] overall shape; outline 轮廓; 外形: *the graceful lines of the ship* 船的优美轮廓. **4 (a)** [C] (usu 通常作 **the line**) (in sport) mark on the ground to show the limits of a pitch, court, race-track, etc (运动的)场地线, 终点线: *first across the line*, ie in a race 第一个通过终点线 ○ *If the ball crosses the line it is out.* 球越线即为出界. **(b)** [C] boundary 界线; 边界: *cross the line* (ie border) *from Mexico into the US* 从墨西哥越过边界进入美国. **(c) the Line** [sing] the equator 赤道. **5** [C] series of connected defence posts, trenches, etc (碉堡、战壕等连成的)防线: *the front line*, ie that nearest to the enemy 前线 ○ *a safe position well behind the lines* 远离前线的一处安全阵地. **6** [C] row of people or things (人或事物的)行, 排, 列: *a line of customers queuing* 顾客排的队 ○ *lines of trees in an orchard* 果园里成行的树 ○ *a long line of low hills* 一长列小山. **7** [C usu *sing* 通常作单数] series of people following one another in time, esp generations of the same family 按时间顺序排列的人; (尤指)家族的世代, 家系: *a line of kings* 历代帝王 ○ *the Stuart line* 斯图亚特

L

家族 ○ *in the male/female line* 父系[母系] ○ *descended from King David in a direct line* 大卫王的嫡系. **8** (**a**) [C] row of words on a page of writing or in print 字行: *page 5, line 13* 第5页第13行 ○ *The last two lines* (ie of verse) *rhyme.* 诗的最后两行押韵. (**b**) [C] (*infml* 口) letter 信; 便条: *Just a short line to say thanks.* 只言片语聊表谢忱. (**c**) **lines** [pl] words spoken by a particular actor 台词: *Have you learnt your lines yet?* 你的台词背熟了吗? (**d**) **lines** [pl] (in schools) punishment in which a pupil is required to write out a specified number of lines (学校中)罚学生抄书: *The maths teacher was furious and gave me 50 lines.* 数学老师气坏了, 罚我抄书50行. **9** [C] (**a**) piece or length of thread, rope, etc used for a particular purpose 线; 索; 绳: *a 'fishing-line* 钓鱼线 ○ *Hang (out) the clothes on the line.* 把衣服晾到绳子上去. (**b**) (*esp nautical* 尤用于航海) rope 绳索; 缆索. **10** [C] (equipment providing a) telephone connection 电话线(路): *Our firm has twenty lines.* 我们公司有二十条电话线路. ○ *I'm sorry, the line is engaged.* 对不起, 占线. ○ *a bad* (eg noisy) *line* 不良的通话线路(如杂音多). **11** [C] (**a**) single track of a railway (铁路的)铁轨, 轨道, 轨线, 线路: *The train was delayed because of ice on the line.* 火车因铁轨结冰而误点. (**b**) one section of a railway system (铁路的)段, 线: *a 'branch line* 支线 ○ *the main 'line* 干线 ○ *the second stop from Oxford on the Worcester line* 在伍斯特线上自牛津开出之第二站. **12** [sing] course of action, behaviour or thought (行动、行为或思想的)方向, 路线, 方针: *Don't take that line with me.* 不要对我采取那种方式. ○ *I absolutely reject the management's line on this.* 我断然否绝经理部门处理此事的方法. ○ *She always takes a Marxist line.* 她一贯奉行马克思主义路线. **13** [sing] **~ (of sth)** direction or course 方向或路线: *the line of 'march (of an army, etc)* (军队等的)行军路线 ○ *the line of 'fire*, ie direction in which guns, etc are fired 射向. **14** [C] system of ships, buses, aircraft, etc regularly moving passengers or goods between certain places (轮船、公共汽车、飞机等的)运输公司: *a 'shipping line* 航运公司 ○ *an 'air line* 航空公司. **15 the lines** [pl] (esp in the army) row of tents, huts, etc (尤指军队中的)营地. **16 the line** [sing] (**a**) (*Brit*) (in the army) regular infantry regiments (excluding the Guards) (军队中的)战列步兵(不包括禁卫军). (**b**) (*US*) (in the army) regular regiments of all kinds (军队中的)战斗部队(包括各兵种). **17** [sing] (in the army) double row of soldiers standing side by side (军队中的)二列横队: *attack in extended line* 以展开的二列横队队形进攻. **18** [sing] (**a**) department of activity; type of business 活动的范围; 行业: *He's something in the 'banking line.* 他在银行工作. ○ *Her line is more selling than production.* 她搞销售而不搞生产. ○ *That's not (much in) my line*, ie not one of my skills or interests. 那我可不(大)在行. (**b**) type of product (产品的)类型, 种别: *This shop has a nice line in winter coats.* 这家商店的冬装大衣很好. **19** (idm 习语) **all along the 'line** (*infml* 口) in every way; at every point 全部地; 到处; 全面地: *I've trusted you all along the line and now you've let me down.* 我一直信任你, 可是现在你却让我失望. **along/on the same, etc 'lines** in the way specified 以某种方式: *Could you write another programme on the same lines?* 你能否以同样的方式再编写一个程序? ○ *The novel develops along traditional lines.* 这小说的情节按传统方式展开. **be in the firing line** ⇨ FIRE². **bring sth, come, fall, get, move, etc into 'line (with sb/sth)** (cause sth to) conform (使某事物)按规范, 一致, 符合: *He'll have to fall into line with the others.* 他早晚得和别人一致起来. **draw the line at sth/doing sth** ⇨ DRAW². **drop sb a line** ⇨ DROP². **the end of the line/road** ⇨ END¹. **get, have, etc one's 'lines crossed** (**a**) be unable to contact sb by telephone because of a technical fault (因技术故障)电话线路不通: *I can't get through — the lines must be crossed.* 我打不通电话——线路一定出故障了. (**b**) (*infml* 口) fail to communicate with or understand sb else correctly 未与某人联系好; 误解某人. **give sb/get/have a line on sth** (*infml* 口) give sb/get/have information about sth 把某事的消息告诉某人; 获取某事的消息. **hard lines** ⇨ HARD¹. **hold the 'line** keep a telephone connection open 不挂断电话: *Hold the line while I see if she's here.* 请别挂断电话, 我去看她在不在. **hook, line and sinker** ⇨ HOOK¹. **in (a) line (with sth)** so as to form a straight line with sth; level with sth else 与某物成一直线; 与某事物取平: *Place your right toe in line with your left heel.* 把右脚趾与左脚跟排在一直线上. **(stand) in/on line** (*US*) in a queue 站队; 排队. **in line for sth** likely to get sth 有可能获得某事物: *She's in line for promotion.* 她有可能获得晋升. **in the ˌline of 'duty** while doing one's duty 在执行任务时. **in line with sth** similar to sth; in accordance with sth 与某事物类似或一致: *in line with the others/with the latest research* 与其他的一致[根据最新的研究成果]. **ˌlay it on the 'line** (*infml* 口) talk frankly and openly 实话实说: *Let me lay it on the line — I think you're cheating.* 坦率地说, 我认为你在搞鬼. **(choose, follow, take, etc) the line of least re'sistance** the easiest way of doing sth 最省事的办法. **(put sth) on the 'line** (*infml* 口) at risk 冒风险: *If this goes wrong your job's on the line.* 这件事要是有个一差二错, 你就有丢饭碗的危险. **out of 'line (with sb/sth)** (**a**) not forming a straight line 不成一直线: *One of the soldiers is out of line.* 有一名士兵没站齐. (**b**) unacceptably different 出格; 越轨: *Our prices are out of line with those of our competitors.* 我们的价格和竞争者的相差悬殊. **read between the lines** ⇨ READ. **shoot a line** ⇨ SHOOT¹. **sign on the dotted line** ⇨ SIGN². **somewhere, etc along the 'line** at a certain stage during a process 过程中的某阶段: *He started off enthusiastically but at some point along the line boredom set in.* 开始时他很热情, 但干着干着就产生了厌倦情绪. **step out of line** ⇨ STEP¹. **take a firm, etc line (on/over sth)** deal with a problem or an issue in a firm, etc way 采取坚定...路线处理某事. **take a hard line** ⇨ HARD¹. **toe the line** ⇨ TOE *v*.

□ **'line-drawing** *n* drawing done with a pen, pencil, etc 线条画(用钢笔、铅笔等).

'line printer (*computing* 计) high-speed printer producing a complete line of text at a time 行式打印机.

line² /laɪn; laɪn/ *v* **1** [esp passive 尤用于被动语态: Tn, Tn·pr] mark (sth) with lines 以线条标示(某物); 画线于(某物): *lined paper*, ie with lines printed on it 印有横格的纸 ○ *a face lined with age and worry* 因经年忧虑而多皱纹的脸. **2** [Tn, Tn·pr] form a line along (sth) 沿(某物)排成行: *a road lined with trees* 树木成行的路 ○ *Crowds of people lined the route of the procession.* 人群在行进线路沿途站成一排. **3** (phr v) **line up (for sth)** (*US*) form a queue 形成一排. **line (sb) up** (cause people to) form a line (让人)站成一排: *line up the suspects/get the suspects to line up* 让嫌疑犯站成一排. **line sth up** (*infml* 口) arrange or organize sth 安排或组织某事物: *I've got rather a lot lined up* (ie I'm very busy) *this week.* 我这星期有很多事要做. ○ *He's lined up a live band for the party.* 他已为聚会安排了一个伴奏乐队.

□ **'line-out** *n* (in Rugby football) two parallel lines of opposing forwards jumping for the ball when it is thrown in from the touchline (英式橄榄球的)对阵争球.

'line-up *n* **1** line of people formed for inspection, etc (等候检查等的)一排人: *a line-up of men in an identification parade* 嫌疑犯辨认程序中的一排男子. **2** any set of people, items, etc arranged for a purpose 为某目的而安排的一批人、项目等: *Jones will be missing from the team line-up.* 球队阵容中将没有琼斯. ○ *A film completes this evening's TV line-up.* 今晚电视节目最后播映一部影片.

line³ /laɪn; laɪn/ *v* **1** [esp passive 尤用于被动语态: Tn, Tn·pr] **~ sth (with sth)** cover the inside surface of sth with a layer of different material 给某物安衬里; 做内衬: *an overcoat lined with silk* 衬有绸里儿的大衣 ○ *fur-lined gloves* 毛皮里儿的手套 ○ *Line the drawers with paper before you use them.* 抽屉用纸垫好再用. ○ *The walls of the room were lined with books.* 室内四壁摆满了书. **2** (idm 习语) **line one's (own)/sb's 'pocket(s)** (cause sb to) make a lot of money, esp by dishonest or corrupt methods (使某人)发财(尤指来路不正).

lin·eage /'lɪnɪɪdʒ; 'lɪnɪɪdʒ/ *n* [U] (*fml* 文) line of descent from an ancestor; ancestry 宗系; 世系; 血统: *trace one's lineage back many centuries* 回溯许多世纪以探求自己的宗谱 ○ *be of humble lineage* 出身寒微.

lin·eal /'lɪnɪəl; 'lɪnɪəl/ *adj* [usu attrib 通常作定语] **1** (*fml*

L

文) in the direct line of descent 直系的; 嫡系的: *a lineal heir to the title* 该头衔的直系承袭人. **2** = LINEAR. ▷ **lin·eally** /-ɪəlɪ; -ɪəlɪ/ *adv*: *lineally descended from sb* 为某人嫡系的.

lin·ea·ments /ˈlɪnɪəmənts; ˋlɪnɪəmənts/ *n* [pl] (*fml* 文) features of the face, etc (面部等的)特征, 轮廓: (*fig* 比喻) *the lineaments* (ie main factors) *of the situation* 情况的关键因素.

lin·ear /ˈlɪnɪə(r); ˋlɪnɪɚ/ *adj* **1** of or in lines 线的; 线状的: *a linear design* 线条图案. **2** of length 长度的: *linear measure*, eg metres, feet, inches 长度(如米、英尺、英寸). ⇨App 5 见附录5. ▷ **lin·ear·ity** /ˌlɪnɪˈærətɪ; ˌlɪnɪˋærətɪ/ *n* [U].

line·man (*esp US*) = LINESMAN.

linen /ˈlɪnɪn; ˋlɪnɪn/ *n* [U] **1** cloth made of flax 亚麻布: [attrib 作定语] *linen handkerchiefs* 亚麻手绢. **2** household articles (eg sheets, table-cloths, clothing) formerly made of this 日用织品(如床单、桌布、衣物等, 旧时多用亚麻制造): [attrib 作定语] *a linen cupboard* 日用织品柜. **3** (idm 习语) **wash one's dirty linen in public** ⇨ WASH[2].

liner[1] /ˈlaɪnə(r); ˋlaɪnɚ/ *n* **1** large passenger or cargo ship travelling on a regular route 班轮; 邮轮: *a transatlantic cruise liner* 横渡大西洋的邮轮. **2** = FREIGHTLINER (FREIGHT). **3** = EYE-LINER (EYE[1]).

liner[2] /ˈlaɪnə(r); ˋlaɪnɚ/ *n* removable lining 活衬里; 活动衬垫: ˈ*nappy-liners* 尿布衬巾 ○ ˈ*bin-liners*, ie plastic bags used to line a rubbish bin 垃圾塑料袋(衬在垃圾桶内的).

lines·man /ˈlaɪnzmən; ˋlaɪnzmən/ (also *esp US* **line·man** /ˈlaɪnmən; ˋlaɪnmən/) *n* (*pl* **-men** /-mən; -mən/) **1** official helping the referee in certain games, esp in deciding whether or where a ball crosses one of the lines 边线裁判员; 巡边员; 司线员. **2** person whose job is to repair and maintain electrical or telephone lines 线务员, 架线工(维修供电或电话线路者).

ling[1] /lɪŋ; lɪŋ/ *n* [U] type of heather 石楠.

ling[2] /lɪŋ; lɪŋ/ *n* sea-fish of N Europe used (usu salted) for food 鲟鳕(产于北欧, 通常腌制食用).

-ling *suff* 后缀 **1** (with *ns* forming *ns* 与名词结合构成名词) little 幼小: *duckling*. **2** (with *vs* forming *ns* 与动词结合构成名词) (*usu derog* 通常作贬义) person or thing connected with 与某事物有关的人或物: *hireling* ○ *nursling*.

linger /ˈlɪŋgə(r); ˋlɪŋgɚ/ *v* [I, Ipr, Ip] **1** stay for a long time; be unwilling to leave 逗留; 徘徊: *She lingered after the concert, hoping to meet the star.* 音乐会后她徘徊不去, 希望能一见明星. ○ *linger about/around/on* 在附近[在周围/不断]徘徊. **2** be slow; dawdle 动作迟缓; 磨蹭; 拖沓: *There's no time to linger — it'll soon be dark.* 没时间拖延了——天快黑了. ○ *linger (long) over one's meal* 慢腾腾吃饭. **3** remain in existence although becoming weaker 苟延残喘; 奄奄一息: *Though desperately ill he could linger on* (ie not die) *for months.* 他虽病入膏肓, 却尚能苟延数月. ○ *The custom still lingers (on) in some villages.* 此风俗在有些村里至今犹存. ○ *The smell of her perfume lingered in the empty house.* 空屋里仍然飘溢着她的香水味.

▷ **lin·gerer** *n* person who lingers 逗留者; 徘徊者.

lin·ger·ing *adj* [esp attrib 尤作定语] (**a**) long; protracted 逗留的; 拖延的: *a lingering illness* 缠绵的疾病 ○ *a last lingering look* 依依不舍的最后一瞥. (**b**) remaining 继续存在的: *a few lingering doubts* 萦绕脑际的几点疑问 ○ *a lingering sense of guilt* 耿耿于怀的愧疚感. **lin·ger·ingly** *adv*.

lin·gerie /ˈlænʒəri:; *US* ˌlɑ:ndʒəˈreɪ; ˌlɑndʒəˋre/ *n* [U] (in shops, etc) women's underwear (商店等用语)女内衣.

lingo /ˈlɪŋgəʊ; ˋlɪŋgo/ *n* (*pl* **~es**) (*infml joc or derog* 口, 谑或贬) **1** foreign language 外国语言: *If you live abroad it helps to know the local lingo.* 住在国外, 学一点当地的语言自有好处. **2** special words or expressions used by a particular group; jargon 行话; 术语: *Don't use all that technical lingo — try and explain in plain English.* 别尽用那种专门术语——用普通的词语解释吧.

lin·gua franca /ˌlɪŋgwə ˈfræŋkə; ˋlɪŋgwəˋfræŋkə/ language used for communicating between the people of an area in which several languages are spoken 混合语, 交际语(在使用几种语言的地区的人们进行交际的混合语言): *Swahili is the principal lingua franca in East Africa.* 东非的主要交际语是斯瓦希里语.

lin·guist /ˈlɪŋgwɪst; ˋlɪŋgwɪst/ *n* **1** person who knows several foreign languages well 通晓数国语言的人: *She's an excellent linguist.* 她精通数国语言. ○ *I'm afraid I'm no linguist*, ie I am poor at foreign languages. 我不懂外国语. **2** person who studies language(s) scientifically 语言学家.

lin·guistic /lɪŋˈgwɪstɪk; lɪŋˋgwɪstɪk/ *adj* of language or linguistics 语言的; 语言学的.

▷ **lin·guist·ics** *n* [sing *v*] scientific study of language or of particular languages 语言学. Cf 参看 PHILOLOGY.

lini·ment /ˈlɪnɪmənt; ˋlɪnəmənt/ *n* [C, U] liquid, esp one made with oil, for rubbing on the body to relieve aches or bruises 搽剂(尤指油质去痛剂).

lin·ing /ˈlaɪnɪŋ; ˋlaɪnɪŋ/ *n* **1** (**a**) [C] layer of material used to cover the inside surface of sth 衬里; 里子: *a coat with a fur lining* 毛皮里大衣. (**b**) [U] material used for this 衬料; 内衬. **2** [U] tissue covering the inner surface of an organ of the body (器官内壁的)组织, 膜: *the stomach lining* 胃黏膜. **3** (idm 习语) **every cloud has a silver lining** ⇨ CLOUD[1].

link /lɪŋk; lɪŋk/ *n* **1** one ring or loop of a chain (链的)环, 圈. **2** person or thing that connects two others 联系两者的人或事物; 关系; 联系: *Police suspect there may be a link between the two murders.* 警方怀疑这两起谋杀案可能有关联. ○ *commercial, cultural, diplomatic, etc links (between two countries)* (两国间的)商业、文化、外交等的往来. **3** (formerly) measure of length, one hundredth of a chain, equal to 7.92 inches or about 20 centimetres (旧时)令(长度单位, 一链的百分之一, 合7.92英寸或约20厘米). **4** (idm 习语) **the missing link** ⇨ MISS[3].

▷ **link** *v* **1** [Tn, Tn·pr, Tn·p] **~ A with B/~ A and B (together)**; **~ sth (up)** make or suggest a connection between people or things 将人或物连接或联系起来: *The crowd linked arms to form a barrier.* 群众臂挽着臂组成人墙. ○ *Television stations around the world are linked by satellite.* 全世界的电视台通过卫星联系一起. ○ *The newspapers have linked his name with hers*, ie implied that they are having an affair. 报纸报道把他和她的名字联系在一起(暗指他们有染). ○ *a new road to link (up) the two motorways* 连接两条高速公路的新路. **2** (phr v) **link up (with sb/sth)** form a connection 连接; 结合: *The two spacecraft will link up (with each other) in orbit.* 两艘宇宙飞船将于轨道上(互相)连接.

□ ˈ**linkman** /-mæn; -mən/ *n* (*pl* **-men** /-men; -mən/) person providing connecting links between parts of a radio or television programme or between programmes (广播或电视节目间作衔接工作的)节目主持人.

ˈ**link-up** *n* connection or joining 联系; 连接: *the first link-up of two satellites in space* 首次两卫星在太空中连接.

link·age /ˈlɪŋkɪdʒ; ˋlɪŋkɪdʒ/ *n* **1** [U, C] action or manner of linking or being linked 连接; 结合; 联系. **2** [C] device, etc that links 联动装置.

links /lɪŋks; lɪŋks/ *n* **1** = GOLF-LINKS (GOLF). **2** [pl] (*esp Scot* 尤用于苏格兰) grassy sand-hills near the sea 海边长草的沙丘.

lin·net /ˈlɪnɪt; ˋlɪnɪt/ *n* small brown songbird, common in Europe 赤胸朱顶雀(棕色小鸣禽, 常见于欧洲).

lino /ˈlaɪnəʊ; ˋlaɪno/ *n* [U] (*infml* 口) = LINOLEUM.

□ ˈ**linocut** *n* (**a**) design cut into the surface of a piece of thick linoleum as a form of art 麻胶版画. (**b**) print made from this 麻胶版画印刷品.

li·no·leum /lɪˈnəʊlɪəm; lɪˋnolɪəm/ (also *infml* 口语亦作 **lino**) *n* [U] type of tough floor-covering made of canvas coated with powdered cork and linseed oil, etc 油地毡.

lin·seed /ˈlɪnsi:d; ˋlɪn,sid/ *n* [U] seed of flax 亚麻籽.

□ ˌ**linseed** ˈ**oil** oil pressed from this, used in paint, varnish, etc 亚麻籽油.

lint /lɪnt; lɪnt/ *n* [U] **1** soft material used for dressing wounds (裹伤用的)纱布: [attrib 作定语] *a lint bandage* 绷带. **2** fluff 绒毛.

lin·tel /ˈlɪntl; ˋlɪntl/ *n* horizontal piece of wood or stone over a door or window, forming part of the frame (门或窗的)过梁, 楣. ⇨illus at App 1 见附录1插图, page vi.

lion /ˈlaɪən; ˋlaɪən/ *n* **1** large powerful flesh-eating animal of the cat family, found in Africa and parts of southern Asia 狮. ⇨illus at CAT 见CAT插图. **2**

(*becoming dated* 渐旧) brave or famous person 勇猛或有名气的人: *a literary lion*, ie a celebrated author 文学泰斗. **3** (idm 习语) **beard the lion in his den** ⇨ BEARD[2]. **the ˈlion's share (of sth)** the largest or best part of sth when it is divided 最大或最好的一份: *As usual, the lion's share of the budget is for defence.* 预算中的最大一项照例是国防费用.

▷ **li·on·ess** /-es; -ɪs/ *n* female lion 母狮.

li·on·ize, -ise /-aɪz; -ˌaɪz/ *v* [Tn] treat (sb) as a celebrity 将(某人)当作名人对待: *Marilyn wanted to be loved, not lionized.* 玛里琳要的是爱而不是崇拜.

□ **ˌlion-ˈhearted** *adj* very brave 勇猛的.

lip /lɪp; lɪp/ *n* **1** [C] either of the fleshy edges of the opening of the mouth 一片嘴唇: *the lower/upper lip* 下[上]嘴唇 ○ *kiss sb on the lips* 吻某人的嘴唇 ○ *She had a cigarette between her lips.* 她叼着一枝香烟. ○ *He put the bottle to his lips and drank deeply.* 他拿着瓶子对嘴儿大口喝. ⇨illus at HEAD 见 HEAD 插图. ⇨ Usage at BODY 用法见 BODY. **2** [C] edge of a hollow container or opening (容器或洞的)边, 口: *the lip of a cup, saucer, crater* 杯口、碟边、火山口. **3** [U] (*sl* 俚) impudence 唐突; 放肆: *Less of your lip!* ie Don't be so cheeky! 别那么放肆! **4** (idm 习语) **bite one's lip** ⇨ BITE[1]. **button one's lip** ⇨ BUTTON. **curl one's lip** ⇨ CURL[2]. **hang on sb's lips** ⇨ HANG[1]. **lick/smack one's lips/chops** ⇨ LICK. **one's lips are sealed** one will not or must not discuss or reveal sth 闭口不谈; 绝口不道: *I'd like to tell you what I know but my lips are sealed.* 我何尝不想把我知道的都告诉你, 只是有口难言. **a stiff upper lip** ⇨ STIFF. **there's many a slip 'twixt cup and lip** ⇨ SLIP[1].

▷ **-lipped** (forming compound *adjs* 用以构成复合形容词) having lips of the specified kind 有某种唇的: *thin-lipped* ○ *tight-lipped*.

□ **ˈlip-read** *v* (*pt, pp* **ˈlip-read** /-red; -rɛd/) [I, Tn] understand (what sb is saying) by watching his lip movements, not by hearing (eg because one is deaf) 唇读, 观唇辨意(如因耳聋). **ˈlip-reading** *n* [U].

ˈlipsalve *n* [C, U] ointment for sore lips 护唇油膏.

ˈlip-service *n* (idm 习语) **give/pay lip-service to sth** say that one approves of or supports sth while not doing so in practice 口惠而实不至: *He pays lip-service to feminism but his wife still does all the housework.* 他口口声声支持女权主义, 但全部家务仍然是妻子的事.

ˈlipstick *n* [C, U] (stick of) cosmetic for colouring the lips 口红; 唇膏.

li·quefy /ˈlɪkwɪfaɪ; ˋlɪkwəˌfaɪ/ *v* (*pt, pp* **-fied**) [I, Tn] (cause sth to) become liquid (使某物)液化: *liquefied wax* 液化的蜡. ▷ **li·que·fac·tion** /ˌlɪkwɪˈfækʃn; ˌlɪkwɪˋfækʃən/ *n* [U]: *the liquefaction of gases* 气体的液化.

li·ques·cent /lɪˈkwesnt; lɪˋkwɛsn̩t/ *adj* (of a gas or solid) becoming or apt to become liquid; melting (指气体或固体)液化的, 易液化的, 熔化的.

li·queur /lɪˈkjʊə(r); *US* -ˈkɜːr; lɪˋkɝ/ *n* strong (usu sweet) alcoholic spirit, drunk in small quantities esp after a meal (通常指甜的)烈性酒(尤作餐后少量饮用的): [attrib 作定语] *liqueur ˈbrandy*, ie one of special quality for drinking as a liqueur 白兰地甜酒 ○ *a liˈqueur glass*, ie a small one for liqueurs 小酒杯.

li·quid /ˈlɪkwɪd; ˋlɪkwɪd/ *n* **1** [C, U] substance that flows freely but is not a gas, eg water or oil 液体: *Air is a fluid but not a liquid, while water is both a fluid and a liquid.* 空气是流体不是液体, 水是流体也是液体. ○ *If you add too much liquid the mixture will not be thick enough.* 加入的液体太多, 混合液的浓度就不够. **2** [C] (*phonetics* 语音) either of the consonants /r/ or /l/ 流音(即/r/或/l/).

▷ **li·quid** *adj* [usu attrib 通常作定语] **1** in the form of a liquid; not gaseous or solid 液体的; 液态的; 流质的: *liquid food/nourishment*, ie easily swallowed, eg by sick people 流质食物[营养品] ○ (*joc* 谑) *a liquid lunch*, ie beer, etc rather than food 液体午餐(啤酒等). **2** clear and clean, like water 清澈的; 晶莹的: *eyes of liquid blue* 蓝莹莹的眼睛. **3** (of sounds) clear, pure and flowing (指声音)清脆的, 纯正的, 流畅的: *the liquid song of a blackbird* 黑鹂清脆的叫声. **4** (*finance* 财) easily converted into cash 易转换成现款的: *one's liquid assets* 流动资产.

□ **ˌliquid ˈgas** gas reduced to liquid form by intense cold 液化的气体.

li·quid·ate /ˈlɪkwɪdeɪt; ˋlɪkwɪˌdet/ *v* [Tn] **1** pay or settle (a debt) 清偿或结算(债务). **2** close down (a business) and divide up the proceeds to pay its debts 清算(公司)(清理资产以偿还债务). **3** get rid of (sb), esp by killing 清除(某人)(尤指杀掉): *liquidated his political opponents* 肃清政敌.

▷ **li·quida·tion** /ˌlɪkwɪˈdeɪʃn; ˌlɪkwɪˋdeʃən/ *n* [U] **1** liquidating or being liquidated 清偿; 结算; 清算; 清除. **2** (idm 习语) **ˌgo into liquiˈdation** (of a business) be closed down, esp because of bankruptcy (指公司)关闭; (尤指)倒闭, 破产.

li·quid·ator *n* person responsible for liquidating a business 公司债务清算人.

li·quid·ity /lɪˈkwɪdətɪ; lɪˋkwɪdətɪ/ *n* [U] **1** (*finance* 财) state of having assets that can easily be changed into cash 资产折现力; 资产流动性: *The company has good liquidity.* 该公司的资产流动性好. **2** state of being liquid 流动性.

li·quid·ize, -ise /ˈlɪkwɪdaɪz; ˋlɪkwəˌdaɪz/ *v* [Tn] **(a)** cause (sth) to become liquid 使(某物)变为液体. **(b)** crush (vegetables, fruit, etc) into a thick liquid 将(蔬菜、水果等)榨成汁.

▷ **li·quid·izer, -iser** (also *esp US* **blender**) *n* (usu electric) device for liquidizing food (通常指电动的)果汁机.

li·quor /ˈlɪkə(r); ˋlɪkɚ/ *n* [U] **1 (a)** (*Brit*) any alcoholic drink 酒: *under the influence of liquor*, ie drunk 已醉. **(b)** (*esp US*) any distilled alcoholic drink; spirits (蒸馏法制的)酒; 烈性酒: *hard liquor* 烈性酒 ○ *She drinks wine and beer but no liquor.* 她喝葡萄酒和啤酒, 但不喝烈性酒. **2** liquid produced by cooking food 烹调食物而出的汁.

li·quor·ice (*US* **li·cor·ice**) /ˈlɪkərɪs; ˋlɪkərɪs/ *n* **1** [U] **(a)** black substance used in medicine and as a sweet (用于制药或糖果的)甘草. **(b)** sweet made with this 甘草糖. **2** [U] plant from whose root this is obtained 欧甘草.

lira /ˈlɪərə; ˋlɪrə/ *n* (*pl* **lire** /ˈlɪərə; ˋlɪre/ or **liras**) (*abbr* 缩写 **L**) unit of money in Italy and Turkey 里拉(意大利和土耳其的货币单位).

lisle /laɪl; laɪl/ *n* [U] fine smooth cotton thread, used esp for stockings and gloves 莱尔棉线(尤用以织长袜和手套).

lisp /lɪsp; lɪsp/ *n* speech defect in which /s/ is pronounced as /θ/ and /z/ as /ð/ 咬舌(言语缺陷, 发/s/、/z/音时发成/θ/、/ð/): *speak with a lisp* 用咬舌音说话 ○ *have a bad, pronounced, slight, etc lisp* 有很重的、明显的、轻微的...咬舌音.

▷ **lisp** *v* [I, Tn] speak or say (sth) with a lisp 用咬舌音说(话). **lisp·ingly** *adv*.

lis·som (also **lis·some**) /ˈlɪsəm; ˋlɪsəm/ *adj* quick and graceful in movement; lithe (动作)轻快而优雅的; 柔软的. ▷ **lis·som·ness** *n* [U].

list[1] /lɪst; lɪst/ *n* **1** series of names, items, figures, etc written or printed 一览表; 清单: *a shopping list* 购物单 ○ *make a list of things one must do* 把要做的事列出清单 ○ *put sb/sth on the list* 将某人[某事物]列在单子上 ○ *take sb/sth off the list* 将某人[某事物]从单子上除掉. **2** (idm 习语) **on the danger list** ⇨ DANGER.

▷ **list** *v* [Tn] **(a)** make a list of (things) 将(事物)列于表上; 造表; 列单子: *list one's engagements for the week* 把一周要做的事列成表. **(b)** put (things) on a list 编(事物)的目录: *The books are listed alphabetically.* 这些书是按字母顺序编入目录的.

□ **ˌlisted ˈbuilding** (*Brit*) building officially registered as being of architectural or historical importance (and therefore protected from demolition, etc) 注册的文物保护建筑物.

ˈlist price (*commerce* 商) published or advertised price of goods (价目单上的)定价: *selling sth for less than the list price* 以低于定价的价格出售某物.

list[2] /lɪst; lɪst/ *v* [I, Ipr] (of a ship) lean over to one side (指船)倾侧: *The damaged vessel was listing badly.* 受损坏的船倾斜得很厉害. ○ *The ship lists to port.* 那船向左舷倾斜.

▷ **list** *n* [sing] listing position; tilt 倾侧; 倾斜: *develop a heavy list* 逐渐形成严重的倾侧.

lis·ten /ˈlɪsn; ˋlɪsn/ *v* **1** [I, Ipr] **~ (to sb/sth)** try to hear sb/sth; pay attention 听; 倾听: *We listened carefully but heard nothing.* 我们仔细地听, 但什么也没听见. ○ *You're not listening to what I'm saying!* 你没注意听我说

L

话! **2** [Ipr] **~ to sb/sth** allow oneself to be persuaded by (a suggestion, request, etc) 听从; 听信: *I never listen to* (ie believe) *what salesmen tell me.* 我从不听信推销员的话. **3** (idm 习语) **listen to/hear reason** ⇨ REASON. **4** (phr v) **listen (out) for sth** wait alertly in order to hear (a sound) 留神等着听(某声音): *Please listen out for the phone while I'm in the bath.* 我洗澡时请你留心听着有没有电话来. **listen 'in (to sth)** (**a**) listen to a radio broadcast 收听电台广播: *listening in to the BBC World Service* 收听英国广播公司国际新闻节目. (**b**) overhear (a conversation, etc) 偷听(谈话等): *She loves listening in to other people's gossip.* 她爱偷听别人闲谈. ○ *The criminals did not know the police were listening in*, eg by tapping their telephone. 罪犯不知道他们一直受着警方的监听(如窃听其电话).

▷ **lis·ten** *n* (usu *sing* 通常作单数) (*infml* 口) act of listening 听: *Have a listen and see if you can hear anything — I can't.* 你听有声音吗 —— 我听不见.

lis·tener *n* (**a**) person who listens 听者: *a good listener*, ie one who can be relied on to listen attentively or sympathetically 认真听的人. (**b**) person listening to a radio programme 收听电台广播的人: *Good evening to all our listeners!* 各位听众, 晚上好!

list·less /ˈlɪstlɪs; ˈlɪstlɪs/ *adj* having no energy, vitality or enthusiasm 倦怠的; 无精打采的; 冷淡的: *She was very listless after her illness.* 她病后懒洋洋的. ▷ **list·lessly** *adv*. **list·less·ness** *n* [U].

lists /lɪsts; lɪsts/ *n* [pl] **1** (formerly) area used for contests between men on horseback armed with lances (旧时)(骑马执矛比武的)竞技场地. **2** (idm 习语) **enter the lists** ⇨ ENTER.

lit *pt, pp* of LIGHT[2, 4].

lit·any /ˈlɪtənɪ; ˈlɪtnɪ/ *n* **1** (**a**) [C] series of prayers to God for use in church services, spoken by a priest with set responses by the congregation 连祷; 启应式祈祷. (**b**) **the Litany** [sing] that in the Book of Common Prayer of the Church of England (英国国教公祷书中的)连祷文. **2** [C] (*fig* 比喻) **~ (of sth)** long boring recital 枯燥冗长的述说: *a litany of complaints* 唠唠叨叨的抱怨.

lit·chi = LYCHEE.

liter (*US*) = LITRE.

lit·er·acy /ˈlɪtərəsɪ; ˈlɪtərəsɪ/ *n* [U] ability to read and write 读写能力.

lit·eral /ˈlɪtərəl; ˈlɪtərəl/ *adj* **1** [esp attrib 尤作定语] (**a**) corresponding exactly to the original 完全按照原文的: *a literal transcript of a speech* 讲话的全文抄本 ○ *a literal* (ie word-for-word) *translation* 直译(逐字翻译). Cf 参看 FREE[1] 11. (**b**) concerned with the basic or usual meaning of a word or phrase 照字面本义的: *His story is incredible in the literal sense of the word*, ie It is impossible to believe him, so he must be lying. 他说的情况令人难以置信, 是真的难以相信(他说的一定是谎话). Cf 参看 FIGURATIVE, METAPHORICAL (METAPHOR). **2** (*esp derog* 尤作贬义) unimaginative; prosaic 无想像力的; 刻板的; 平淡无奇的: *His interpretation of the music was rather too literal.* 那音乐他演奏得未免太乏味了. ○ *Don't be so literal-minded — you know what I meant!* 别那么死心眼嘛 —— 你知道我是什么意思!

▷ **lit·eral** *n* (also **literal error**) misprint 印刷错误.

lit·er·ally /ˈlɪtərəlɪ; ˈlɪtərəlɪ/ *adv* **1** in a literal manner; exactly 照原文; 精确地: *Idioms usually cannot be translated literally in another language.* 成语通常不能照字面译成另一种语言. ○ *When he said he never wanted to see you again I'm sure he didn't mean it literally.* 他说他再也不想见你了, 我肯定他言不由衷. **2** (*infml* 口) (used loosely, to intensify meaning 用以加强语气): *I was literally bored to death!* 我真的腻烦死了!

lit·eral·ness *n*.

lit·er·ary /ˈlɪtərərɪ; *US* ˈlɪtərerɪ; ˈlɪtə,rɛrɪ/ *adj* of or concerned with literature 文学的; 文学上的: *literary criticism* 文学批评 ○ *a literary agent*, ie one acting on behalf of writers 作者代理人 ○ *His style is a bit too literary* (ie formal or rhetorical) *for my taste.* 依我看他的文笔书卷气重了一点.

lit·er·ate /ˈlɪtərət; ˈlɪtərɪt/ *adj* **1** able to read and write 有读写能力的: *Though nearly twenty he was barely literate.* 他都快二十了, 还是睁眼瞎子. Cf 参看 NUMERATE. **2** cultured; well-read 有文化的; 博学的: *Every literate person should read this book.* 凡有文化的人都该一读此书.

lit·er·ati /ˌlɪtəˈrɑːtiː; ˌlɪtəˈrɑtɪ/ *n* [pl] (*fml* 文) educated and intelligent people who have learned much from literature and books 文人; 知识界.

lit·er·at·ure /ˈlɪtrətʃə(r); *US* -tʃʊər; ˈlɪtərə,tʃʊr/ *n* [U] **1** (**a**) writings that are valued as works of art, esp fiction, drama and poetry (as contrasted with technical books and journalism) 文学; 文学作品. (**b**) activity of writing or studying these 文学著述或研究: *a degree in American literature* 美国文学学位. (**c**) writings of this kind from a particular country or period (某国或某时期的)文学作品: *French literature* 法国文学 ○ *18th century (English) literature* 18世纪(英国)文学. **2** writings on a particular subject 某学科的著述或文献: *I've read all the available literature on poultry-farming.* 我把现有的家禽饲养方面的资料全都读过了. ○ *There is now an extensive literature on the use of computers in the home.* 现在有许多关于家庭计算机的使用资料. **3** (*infml* 口) pamphlets or leaflets 小册子; 传单: *Please send me any literature you have on camping holidays in Spain.* 请惠寄贵处有关在西班牙野营度假的宣传材料.

-lith *comb form* 构词成分 (forming *ns* 用以构成名词) of stone or rock 石的; 岩石的: *monolith* ○ *megalith*. ▷ **-lithic** (forming *adjs* 用以构成形容词): *palaeolithic*.

lithe /laɪð; laɪð/ *adj* (of a person, the body, etc) bending or turning easily; supple (指人、身体等)柔软的, 易弯曲的: *the lithe grace of a gymnast* 体操运动员轻盈而优美的体态.

lith·ium /ˈlɪθɪəm; ˈlɪθɪəm/ *n* [U] chemical element, a soft silver-white metal similar to sodium and used in alloys and certain fuels 锂. ⇨App 10 见附录10.

litho /ˈlaɪθəʊ; ˈlaɪθo/ *n* [U] (*infml* 口) lithography 平版印刷术.

litho·graph /ˈlɪθəgrɑːf; *US* -græf; ˈlɪθəgræf/ *n* picture, etc printed by lithography 平版印刷画等.

▷ **litho·graph** *v* [Tn] print (sth) by lithography 用平版印刷术印刷(某物).

li·tho·graphy /lɪˈθɒgrəfɪ; lɪˈθɑgrəfɪ/ (also *infml* 口语亦作 **litho** /ˈlaɪθəʊ; laɪθo/) *n* [U] process of printing from a smooth surface (eg a metal plate) treated so that ink adheres only to the design to be printed 平版印刷术: *a book printed by offset litho* 用平版胶印法印刷的书. ▷ **li·tho·graphic** /ˌlɪθəˈgræfɪk; ˌlɪθəˈgræfɪk/ *adj*.

lit·ig·ant /ˈlɪtɪgənt; ˈlɪtəgənt/ *n* (*law* 律) person involved in a lawsuit 诉讼当事人.

lit·ig·ate /ˈlɪtɪgeɪt; ˈlɪtə,get/ *v* (*law* 律) (**a**) [I] engage in a lawsuit; go to law 诉讼; 诉诸法律. (**b**) [Tn] contest (a claim, etc) in a lawsuit 在法庭上争辩(某事).

▷ **lit·iga·tion** /ˌlɪtɪˈgeɪʃn; ˌlɪtəˈgeʃən/ *n* (*law* 律) (**a**) [U] process of going to law 打官司. (**b**) [C] lawsuit 诉讼.

li·ti·gi·ous /lɪˈtɪdʒəs; lɪˈtɪdʒɪəs/ *adj* (*esp law* 尤用于法律) **1** of lawsuits 诉讼的; 关于诉讼的. **2** that can result in a lawsuit 可诉讼的. **3** (*often derog* 常作贬义) fond of going to law; disputatious 好诉讼的; 好打官司的.

lit·mus /ˈlɪtməs; ˈlɪtməs/ *n* [U] blue colouring-matter that is turned red by acid and can be turned blue again by alkali 石蕊(蓝色物质, 遇酸变红, 再遇碱则还原变蓝).

□ **ˈlitmus paper** paper stained with litmus, used to test if a solution is acid or alkaline 石蕊试纸.

li·to·tes /ˈlaɪtəʊtiːz; ˈlaɪto,tiz/ *n* [U] ironical understatement, esp using a negative to emphasize the contrary 曲言(尤指用否定的词语, 强调其反义的修辞法, 如It wasn't easy '此事不易' 意为It was very difficult '此事很难').

litre (*US* **liter**) /ˈliːtə(r); ˈlitɚ/ *n* (*abbr* 缩写 **l**) unit of capacity in the metric system, equal to about $1\frac{3}{4}$ pints, used for measuring liquids 升(液量单位, 约为$1\frac{3}{4}$品脱). ⇨App 5 见附录5.

Litt D /ˌlɪt ˈdiː; ˌlɪt ˈdi/ *abbr* 缩写 = D LITT.

lit·ter /ˈlɪtə(r); ˈlɪtɚ/ *n* **1** (**a**) [U] light rubbish (eg bits of paper, wrappings, bottles) left lying about, esp in a public place 乱扔的杂物(如纸屑、包装纸、瓶子); (尤指在公共场所乱扔的)垃圾: *Please do not leave litter.* 请勿乱扔垃圾. (**b**) [sing] state of untidiness 杂乱; 凌乱: *Her desk was covered in a litter of books and papers.* 她的书桌上都是乱七八糟的书和纸. ○ *His room was a litter of old clothes, dirty crockery and broken furniture.* 他的屋子里到处都是旧衣物、脏陶器和破家具. **2** [U] straw, etc used as bedding for animals 动物铺窝的草等. **3** [CGp] all the young born to an animal at one time (一胎所生的)小动物, 一窝: *a litter of puppies* 一窝小狗. **4** [C] (**a**) type of stretcher(1) 担架. (**b**) (formerly) couch carried on men's shoulders or by animals as a means of transport (旧时)轿, 舆.

▷ **lit·ter** *v* **1** [Tn, Tn·pr, Tn·p] **~ sth (up) (with sth)** make (a place) untidy with scattered rubbish 乱扔垃圾使(某处)凌乱: *Newspapers littered the floor.* 报纸扔了一地. ○ *He's always littering up the room with his old magazines.* 他老是乱扔旧杂志, 弄得房间凌乱不堪. **2** [Tn, Tn·p] **~ sth (down)** supply straw, etc as bedding for (an animal) 给(动物)的窝铺草等. **3** [I] (of animals) bring forth young (指动物)下崽, 产仔: *The sow's about to litter.* 这母猪要下崽儿了.

□ **'litter-bin, 'litter-basket** *ns* container for rubbish 废物箱.

'litter-lout (*Brit*) (also *esp US* **'litter-bug**) *n* (*infml derog* 口, 贬) person who leaves litter untidily in public places (在公共场所)乱扔废物的人.

little[1] /ˈlɪtl; ˈlɪtl/ *adj* [usu attrib 通常作定语] (The comparative and superlative forms, **littler** /ˈlɪtlə(r); ˈlɪtlɚ/ and **littlest** /ˈlɪtlɪst; ˈlɪtlɪst/ are rare. It is more common to use *smaller, smallest.* 此词的比较级和最高级罕用 **littler** 和 **littlest** 而常用 smaller 和 smallest.) **1** not big; small 小的: *six little puppies* 六只小狗 ○ *a little coffee-table* 小咖啡桌 ○ *a little movement of impatience* 不耐烦的小动作 ○ *a little group of tourists* 一小批游客 ○ *There's a little mark on your sleeve.* 你的袖子上有一小块污迹. ○ *a house with a little garden* 带小花园的房子 ○ *little holes to let air in* 通气的小孔. **2** (of distance or time) short (指距离或时间)短的: *It's only a little way now.* 现在没多远了. ○ *You may have to wait a little while.* 你可能得等上一小会儿. ○ *Shall we go for a little walk?* 散会儿步好吗? **3** (used usu after *nice, pretty, sweet, nasty*, etc to express the speaker's feeling of affection, pleasure, annoyance, etc 通常用于 nice、pretty、sweet、nasty 等之后表示亲切、快乐、嫌恶等): *a nice little room* 玲珑的房间 ○ *a sweet little child* 长得很甜的孩子 ○ *a funny little restaurant* 古里古怪的餐厅 ○ *What a nasty little man!* 多么讨人厌的傢伙! ○ *A (dear) little old lady helped me find my way.* 有位(可亲)可敬的老太太帮我找到路了. ○ *There's a little shop on the corner that sells bread.* 街角上有那么个卖面包的铺子. **4** not important; insignificant 不重要的; 不足道的: *a little mistake* 小错 ○ *We only had a little snack at lunchtime.* 我们午饭只吃了一点小吃. **5** young 幼小的: *I had curly hair when I was little.* 我小时候是鬈发. ○ *My little* (ie younger) *brother is 18.* 我弟弟18岁. **6** small when compared with others (相比之下)小的: *one's little finger* 小指 ○ *the little hand of the clock* 钟的短针 ○ *'Which packet would you prefer?' 'I'll take the little one.'* '你喜欢哪一包?' '我要小包.' ⇨ Usage at SMALL 用法见 SMALL. **7** (idm 习语) **big, etc oaks from little acorns grow** ⇨ OAK. **in little** (*fml* 文) on a small scale 小规模地. **a little bird told me (that...)** (*joc* 谑) I know but will not tell you how, or from whom, I know 我知道, 但我不告诉你我是怎么知道的. **twist sb round one's little finger** ⇨ TWIST.

□ **the ˌLittle ˈBear** small constellation near the north pole 小熊星座(在北极附近). Cf 参看 THE GREAT BEAR (GREAT).

the 'little people, the 'little folk small people with supernatural powers; fairies or elves 小仙子; 小精灵.

little[2] /ˈlɪtl; ˈlɪtl/ *indef det* (used with [U] *ns* 与不可数名词连用) a small amount (of sth); not enough 小量的; 不足的; 不多的: *I have very little time for reading.* 我没有多少时间看书. ○ *We had little rain all summer.* 一夏天几乎没下雨. ○ *There's little point in telling her now.* 现在告诉她已没有什么意义了. ⇨Usage at MUCH[1] 用法见 MUCH[1].

L

▷ **little** *indef pron* (used as a *n* when preceded by *the* 在 the 之后, 用作名词) a small amount 些少; 少量: *Little of the music was recognizable.* 那音乐差不多都难于辨识. ○ *I understood little of what he said.* 他说的我只听懂一点儿. ○ *We read a lot of poetry at school — I remember very little now.* 我们上学时念过不少诗 —— 现在我记得的所剩无几. ○ *The little that I have seen of his work is satisfactory.* 他的工作就我所见的那一小部分而言是令人满意的.

little *adv* **1** not much; only slightly 些少; 稍许: *He is little known as an artist.* 他是个不出名的艺术家. ○ *She left little more than an hour ago.* 她离开一个多钟头了. ○ *I slept very little last night.* 昨晚我睡得很少. ○ *Little does he know* (ie He doesn't know) *what trouble he's in.* 他对自己所处何种地步茫无所知. **2** (idm 习语) **ˌlittle by ˈlittle** making progress slowly, gradually 一点一点地; 逐渐地: *Little by little the snow disappeared.* 雪渐渐消失. ○ *His English is improving little by little.* 他的英语渐有提高. **ˌlittle or ˈnothing** hardly anything 几乎无: *She said little or nothing about her experience.* 她对自己的经历没怎么透露. **make little of sth** (**a**) = MAKE LIGHT OF STH (LIGHT[3]). (**b**) understand or read hardly anything of sth 不明白; 看不懂: *It's in Chinese — I can make little of it.* 这是中文 —— 我一点儿都不懂. Cf 参看 LESS.

little[3] /ˈlɪtl; ˈlɪtl/ **a little** *indef det* (used with [U] *ns* 与不可数名词连用) a small amount (of sth); some but not much 少量; 些微; 稍许: *a little milk, sugar, tea, etc* 少许牛奶、糖、茶等 ○ *Could you give a little more attention to spelling?* 你稍微多注意一下拼写好吗? ○ *I need a little help to move these books.* 我需要人来帮点忙搬这些书. ○ *It caused not a little* (ie a great deal of) *confusion.* 这事引起很大混乱.

▷ **a little** *indef pron* **1** a small amount of sth; some but not much 少量; 些微; 稍许. (**a**) (referring back 用以复指前文): *There was a lot of food but I only ate a little.* 食物很多, 但我只吃了一点儿. ○ *If you've got any spare milk, could you give me a little?* 你要是有多余的牛奶, 能不能给我一些? (**b**) (referring forward 用以预指后文): *I've only read a little of the book.* 这书我只读过一点儿. ○ *A little of the conversation was about politics.* 谈话中只涉及少许政治问题. **2** (idm 习语) **after/for a 'little** after/for a short distance or time 经过很短距离或时间: *After a little he got up and left.* 过了一会儿他站起来走了. ○ *We left the car and walked for a little.* 我们下了汽车走了一小段路.

a little *adv* to some extent 有些; 有几分: *She seemed a little afraid of going inside.* 她好像有点怕往里走. ○ *These shoes are a little too big for me.* 这鞋我穿着有点大. ○ *She was not a little* (ie very) *worried about the expense.* 她对那笔开支相当苦恼.

lit·toral /ˈlɪtərəl; ˈlɪtərəl/ *n, adj* (*fml* 文) (part of a country that is) along the coast 沿海岸的; 沿海地区.

lit·urgy /ˈlɪtədʒɪ; ˈlɪtɚdʒɪ/ *n* fixed form of public worship used in churches 礼拜仪式. ▷ **li·tur·gical** /lɪˈtɜ:dʒɪkl; lɪˈtɝdʒɪkl/ *adj.* **li·tur·gic·ally** /-ˈklɪ; -klɪ/ *adv.*

live[1] /laɪv; laɪv/ *adj* [usu attrib 通常作定语] **1** having life 有生命的; 活的: *live fish* 活鱼. **2** (used esp of surprising or unusual experiences, etc 尤用于指惊人的或异常的经历等) actual; not pretended 真正的; 不是假装的: *We saw a real live rattlesnake!* 我们看到一条真的响尾蛇! **3** glowing or burning 发着光的; 点燃着的: *live coals* 燃烧着的煤. **4** not yet exploded or lit; ready for use 还未爆炸或点火的; 随时可用的: *a live bomb* 未爆炸的炸弹 ○ *several rounds of live ammunition* 几发待用的炮弹 ○ *a live match* 未用过的火柴. **5** (of a wire, etc) charged with or carrying electricity (指电线等)带电的, 通着电的: *That terminal is live.* 那个接头有电. ○ *the live rail*, eg on an electric railway 带电的铁轨(如在电气铁路上). **6** of interest or importance at the present time 当前令人关切的; 当前重要的: *Pollution is still very much a live issue.* 污染现象仍然是当前的大问题. **7** (**a**) (of a broadcast) transmitted while actually happening, not recorded or edited (指广播)现场直播的, 实况转播的: *live coverage of the World Cup* 世界杯实况报道. (**b**) (of a musical performance or recording) given or made during a concert, not in a studio (指音乐演奏或录音)音乐会现场播出或录制的: *a live recording made at Covent Garden in 1962* 1962年在考文特公园的现场录音. Cf 参看 PRE-RECORD. **8** (idm 习语) **a live 'wire** lively and energetic person 活跃而精力充沛的人.

▷ **live** *adv* broadcast, played or recorded at an actual performance, etc without being edited 实地; 从现场; 以直播方式: *This show is going out live.* 这场演出正在进行实况转播.

□ **'live birth** baby born alive 出生时活着的婴儿. Cf 参看 STILLBIRTH (STILL[1]).

live[2] /lɪv; lɪv/ *v* **1** [I] (less common than *be alive* in this sense 用于本义时, 不如 be alive 通俗) have life; be alive 有生命; 活着. **2** [I, Ipr, It] remain alive 活; 生存: *live to* *be old/to a great age* 活到老[高龄] ○ *The doctors don't think he will live through the night.* 医生认为他活不过今晚了. ○ *Some trees can live for hundreds of years.* 有些树可以活数百年. ○ *How long do elephants live?* 象能活多久? ○ *live to see many changes* 活着看到很多人事的变化. **3** [I, Ipr] make one's home; reside 居住; 住: *Where do you live?* 你住在哪儿? ○ *live at home, in London, in a flat, abroad* 住在家中、伦敦、单元房、国外. **4** [Ln, I, Tn] conduct one's life in a specified way 以某种方式生活: *live and die a bachelor* 过一辈子独身生活 ○ *live honestly, happily* 活得清白、幸福 ○ *He lives well*, ie enjoys the luxuries of life. 他过得很好. ○ *live like a saint* 像圣徒般生活 ○ *live a peaceful life* 过平静的生活. **5** [I] (*fig* 比喻) (of things without life) remain in existence; survive (指无生命的事物)继续存在, 留存: *The memory will live in my heart for ever*, ie I will never forget it. 这记忆将永远留在我的心中. **6** [I] enjoy life fully 充分享受生活的乐趣: *I don't call that living.* 我认为那不叫生活. ○ *I don't want to work in an office all my life — I want to live!* 我不想一辈子坐办公室——我要享受人生的乐趣! **7** (idm 习语) **how the other half lives** ⇨ HALF[1]. **live and 'let live** (*saying* 谚) be tolerant of others so that they will be tolerant in turn 自己活, 也让别人活; 容让别人, 别人也容让你. **live be,yond/with,in one's 'means** spend more/less than one earns or can afford 入不敷出[量入为出]. **,live by one's 'wits** earn money by clever and sometimes dishonest means 靠小聪明, 有时用不诚实手段捞钱. **live from hand to mouth** ⇨ HAND[1]. **live in hope(s) (of sth)** remain hopeful 满怀希望: *live in hopes of better times to come* 生活在憧憬更好的未来中 ○ *The future looks rather gloomy, but we live in hope.* 前景似颇暗淡, 但我们仍满怀希望. **live in the 'past** behave as though circumstances, values, etc have not changed from what they were earlier 在回忆过去的环境中生活. **live in 'sin** (*dated or joc* 旧或谑) live together as if married 姘居; 同居. **live it 'up** (*infml* 口) live in a lively and extravagant way 享乐: *Now you've been left some money you can afford to live it up a bit.* 既然留有这些钱, 你就可以痛快享受一番了. **live a 'lie** suggest by one's way of living that sth untrue is true 过骗人的生活; 虚伪做人: *She lived a lie for 20 years by pretending to be his wife.* 她假扮他的妻子已经20年了. **live like 'fighting cocks** enjoy the best possible food 吃得好. **live like a 'lord** enjoy a luxurious style of living 过豪华生活. **live off/on the ,fat of the 'land** enjoy the best food, drink, lodging, entertainment, etc 锦衣玉食. **live off the 'land** use agricultural products for one's food needs 靠农产品生活. **live 'rough** live without comforts or amenities, esp out of doors 过艰苦生活; (尤指)餐风宿露: *He's a tramp and used to living rough.* 他是流浪汉, 惯于风餐雨卧. **you/we ,live and 'learn** (used to express surprise at some new or unexpected information, etc 用以表示对新事物或意外信息的惊讶). **8** (phr v) **live by doing sth** earn one's living by doing sth 靠做某事物为生. **live sth 'down** live in such a way that (a past embarrassment, scandal, crime, etc) is forgotten 以某种方式生活使(往日的难堪、丑闻、罪行等)淡忘: *Beaten by the worst team in the league? They'll never live it down!* 让联赛中最差劲的队打败了? 这是永远也忘不了的事! **live for sth** regard sth as the aim of one's life 以某事物为生活目标: *She lives for her work.* 她为工作献身. ○ *After she died he had nothing to live for.* 她去世后, 他便没有了生活目标. **live in/out** (of an employee) live on/off the premises where one works (指雇员)居住在受雇处内[外]: *They both go out to work and have a nanny living in.* 他们俩都外出工作, 雇了个保姆看家. **live on** continue to live or exist 继续生活或存在: *She lived on for many years after her husband died.* 丈夫死后她继续活了多年. ○ *Mozart is dead but his music lives on.* 莫扎特人已作古, 但他的音乐作品却万世流传. **live on sth (a)** have sth as one's food 以某物为食: *live on (a diet of) fruit and vegetables* 靠吃水果和蔬菜(的规定食谱)生活 ○ *You can't live on 200 calories a day.* 一天200大卡是维持不了生命的. **(b)** depend on sth for financial support 靠某种经济来源生活: *live on one's salary, on £8 000 a year, on charity* 靠自己的工资、年收入8 000英镑、救济金过活. **live through sth** experience sth and survive 经历某事物而幸存: *He lived through both world wars.* 他经历过两次世界大战. **live together (a)** live in the same house, etc 在一起生活. **(b)** live as if married 姘居; 同居. **live up to sth** behave in accordance with sth 依照某事物行事; 表现出符合某事物的标准: *failed to live up to his principles, his reputation, his parents' expectations* 没有遵守自己的原则、不符个人的声誉、辜负父母的期待. **live with sb** = LIVE TOGETHER. **live with sth** accept or tolerate sth 接受或容忍某现象: *You'll have to learn to live with it, I'm afraid.* 我看, 你得学会容忍这种现实.

live·able /ˈlɪvəbl; ˋlɪvəbḷ/ *adj* (of life) worth living; tolerable (指生活)有价值的, 可忍受的, 过得去的.

□ **'liveable-in** *adj* [pred 作表语] (*infml* 口) (of a house, etc) fit to live in (指房屋等)适于居住.

'liveable-with *adj* [pred 作表语] (*infml* 口) (of a person, etc) easy to live with (指人等)易于共同生活.

live·li·hood /ˈlaɪvlɪhʊd; ˋlaɪvlɪ,hʊd/ *n* (usu *sing* 通常作单数) **(a)** means of living; income 生活的手段; 生计; 收入: *earn one's livelihood by teaching* 靠教书为生 ○ *deprive sb of his livelihood* 剥夺某人的生计. **(b)** way of earning a living; occupation 谋生之道; 职业: *Farming is his sole livelihood.* 他唯一的谋生之道就是务农.

live·long /ˈlɪvlɒŋ; *US* ˈlaɪvlɔːŋ; ˋlaɪv,lɔŋ/ *adj* (idm 习语) **the livelong 'day/'night** (*dated or rhet* 旧或修辞) the whole length of the day/night 一整天[夜].

lively /ˈlaɪvlɪ; ˋlaɪvlɪ/ *adj* (**-ier, -iest**) **1** full of life and energy; high-spirited; vigorous 有生气的; 精力充沛的; 活跃的: *She's a lively child and popular with everyone.* 她是个活泼的孩子, 大家都喜欢她. ○ *The patient seems a little livelier/more lively this morning.* 那病人今晨好像精神些了. ○ *one of the liveliest parties I've been to* 我参加过的最热闹的一次聚会 ○ *a lively melody* 活泼的旋律 ○ *She has a lively interest in everything around her.* 她对周围的一切都有浓厚的兴趣. **2** vivid or striking 生动的; 醒目的: *a lively imagination* 生动的想像 ○ *a lively shade of pink* 鲜艳的粉红色调 ○ *She gave a lively account of her adventures.* 她生动叙述了自己惊险刺激的事. **3** moving vigorously or roughly 剧烈的; 狂暴的: *The sea is quite lively today.* 今天海面风浪很大. ○ *We batted on a lively pitch*, ie a cricket pitch that caused the ball to move sharply. 我们击中了对方快速投来的球. **4** (idm 习语) **,look 'lively** move, etc more quickly; show more energy 行动敏捷些; 干劲足些: *We'd better look lively if we're to finish in time.* 我们要按时完成, 动作就得快些. **make it/things lively for sb** (*esp ironic* 尤作反语) make things exciting and perhaps dangerous for sb 使某人兴奋或许担惊受怕. ▷ **live·li·ness** *n* [U].

liven /ˈlaɪvn; ˋlaɪvən/ *v* (phr v) **,liven (sb/sth) 'up** (cause sb/sth to) become lively (使某人[某事物])有生气, 活跃: *Put on some music to liven things up.* 放些音乐, 让气氛愉快起来. ○ *Do liven up a bit!* 活跃些吧!

liver[1] /ˈlɪvə(r); ˋlɪvɚ/ *n* **1** [C] large organ in the abdomen that produces bile and purifies the blood 肝脏. ⇨illus at DIGESTIVE 见 DIGESTIVE 插图. **2** [U, C] liver of certain animals, used as food (供食用的)肝: *pig's liver* 猪肝 ○ *chicken livers* 鸡肝.

▷ **liv·er·ish** (also **liv·ery**) *adj* **1** suffering from a disorder of the liver 患肝病的. **2** irritable; peevish 易怒的; 脾气坏的.

□ **'liver sausage** (also *esp US* **liverwurst** /ˈlɪvəwɜːst; ˋlɪvɚ,wɝst/) sausage containing cooked and finely chopped liver, usu eaten cold on bread 肝香肠.

liver[2] /ˈlɪvə(r); ˋlɪvɚ/ *n* person who lives in a specified way 过着某种生活的人: *a fast, quiet, loose, etc liver* 过淫乱、安静、放荡等生活的人.

liv·ery /ˈlɪvərɪ; ˋlɪvərɪ/ *n* **1** [U, C] special uniform such as that worn by male servants in a great household or by members of the London trade guilds (大户人家的男仆或伦敦同业公会的)制服: *in/out of* (ie wearing/not wearing) *livery* 穿[不穿]制服. **2** [U] (*rhet* 修辞) covering 装束: *trees in their spring livery*, ie with new leaves 披上春装的树木.

▷ **liv·er·ied** /ˈlɪvərɪd; ˋlɪvərɪd/ *adj* wearing livery 穿制服的: *a liveried chauffeur* 穿制服的汽车司机.

□ **'livery company** any of the London trade guilds with their own special uniforms (伦敦市有制服的)同业公会.

'liveryman /-mən; -mən/ *n* (*pl* **-men** /-mən; mən/) **1** member of a livery company (穿制服的)同业公会会员. **2** person who works in a livery stable (马房的)马夫.

ˈ**livery stable** stable where horses are kept for their owners in return for payment, or where horses may be hired（代客喂马或租马的）马房.

lives *pl* of LIFE.

live·stock /ˈlaɪvstɒk; ˈlaɪvˌstɑk/ *n* [U] animals kept on a farm for use or profit, eg cattle or sheep 家畜, 牲畜（如牛羊）.

livid /ˈlɪvɪd; ˈlɪvɪd/ *adj* **1** [usu attrib 通常作定语] of the colour of lead; bluish-grey 铅色的; 青灰色的: *a livid bruise* 青肿. **2** [usu pred 通常作表语] (*infml* 口) furiously angry 大怒: *livid with rage* 狂怒 ○ *He'd be livid if he found out what you're doing.* 要是他知道了你干的事, 他准得大发雷霆. ▷ **liv·idly** *adv*.

liv·ing[1] /ˈlɪvɪŋ; ˈlɪvɪŋ/ *adj* **1** alive, esp now 活的; 活着的: *all living things* 所有生物 ○ *the finest living pianist* 在世的最好的钢琴家 ○ *No man living could have done better.* 当今的人没有一个能做得更好. **2** used or practised; active 在使用的; 实施着的; 活动中的: *living languages*, ie those still spoken 现用的语言 ○ *a living hope, faith, reality* 现存的希望、仍在信奉的信仰、活生生的现实. **3** (idm 习语) **a ˌliving ˈlegend** person who has achieved great fame during his lifetime and is still alive 活着的名人. **be living proof of sth** show sth by the fact that one is alive 活证明: *He is living proof of the wonders of modern medicine.* 他是当代医学奇迹的活证明. **within/in ˌliving ˈmemory** at a time, or during the time, remembered by people still alive 在当今人的记忆中: *Wages were sixpence a week within living memory.* 周工资为六便士的年代, 人们记忆犹新. ○ *the coldest winter in living memory* 人们记忆中最寒冷的冬天.

▷ **the liv·ing** *n* [pl *v*] **1** people who are now alive 活着的人: *the living and the dead* 生者与死者. **2** (idm 习语) **in the land of the living** ⇨ LAND[1].

□ ˌ**living** ˈ**death** time of continuous misery 活地狱: *Exile was for him a living death.* 他遭流放是进了活地狱.

liv·ing[2] /ˈlɪvɪŋ; ˈlɪvɪŋ/ *n* **1** [C usu *sing* 通常作单数] (**a**) means of keeping alive or of living in a certain style; income 生存之道; 生计; 收入: *earn one's living as a journalist, by/from writing* 做记者、靠写作谋生 ○ *make a good, an adequate, a meagre, etc living* 过优裕的、小康的、贫困的…生活. (**b**) way of earning this 谋生之道: *It may not be the best job in the world, but it's a living.* 尽管这不是世界上最好的工作, 但不失为生活的出路. **2** [U] manner of life 生活方式: *Both the cost and the standard of living were lower before the war.* 战前生活费用和生活水准都比较低. ○ *understand the art of living*, ie how to live a worthwhile, satisfying life 懂得生活的艺术. **3** [C] (*religion* 宗) clergyman's position, providing his income; benefice 牧师的有俸职位; 牧师的俸金. **4** (idm 习语) **scrape a living** ⇨ SCRAPE[1].

□ ˈ**living-room** (also *esp Brit* ˈ**sitting-room**) *n* room in a private house for general use during the daytime 起居室. Cf 参看 DRAWING ROOM.

ˌ**living** ˈ**wage** lowest wage on which sb can afford a reasonable standard of living 生活工资（可维持最低生活水准者）.

lizard 蜥蜴

liz·ard /ˈlɪzəd; ˈlɪzɚd/ *n* (usu small) reptile with a rough skin, four legs and a long tail 蜥蜴.

ll *pl* of L 2.

llama /ˈlɑːmə; ˈlɑmə/ *n* S American animal with soft woolly hair, used for carrying loads 美洲驼（产于南美, 用作驮兽）.

LL B, LL D, LL M *abbrs* 缩写 = Bachelor, Doctor, Master of Laws 法学学士、博士、硕士: *have/be an LL B* 有法学学士学位[为法学学士] ○ *David Grafton LL B* 戴维·格拉夫顿法学学士.

lo /ləʊ; lo/ *interj* **1** (*arch* 古) look; see 看; 瞧. **2** (idm 习语) ˌ**lo and be**ˈ**hold** (*esp joc or ironic* 尤作戏谑语或作反语) (used to indicate surprise 用以表示惊讶): *As soon as we went out, lo and behold, it began to rain.* 我们刚一出门, 你瞧, 就下起雨来了.

load[1] /ləʊd; lod/ *n* **1** [C] thing that is being carried or to be carried, esp if heavy 负荷物, 载荷物（尤指沉重的）: *a load of sand* 运载的一批沙子. **2** [C] (esp in compounds 尤用以构成复合词) quantity that can be carried, eg by a vehicle 运载的量: *coach-loads of tourists* 一车车的游客 ○ *a boat-load of survivors* 一船生还的人. **3** [C] (**a**) amount of work that a dynamo, a motor, an engine, etc is required to do（发电机、电动机、发动机等的）负载, 负荷. (**b**) amount of electric current supplied by a dynamo or generating station（发电机或发电站的）发电量. **4** [C usu *sing* 通常作单数] (*fig* 比喻) weight of responsibility, worry, grief, etc（责任、忧虑、悲哀等的）沉重感: *a heavy load of guilt* 沉重的负疚感. **5 loads (of sth)** [pl] (*infml* 口) plenty (of sth) 大量; 许多: *loads of friends, money, time* 很多朋友、金钱、时间 ○ *'Have you got any change?' 'Loads!'* '你有零钱吗?' '有的是!' **6** (idm 习语) **be/take a ˌload/ˌweight off sb's ˈmind** ⇨ MIND[1]. **a ˌload of (old) ˈrubbish, etc** (*infml* 口) nonsense 胡说八道: *I've never heard such a load of garbage!* 这么胡说八道我还从来没听说过! **get a load of sb/sth** (*infml* 口) take notice of sb/sth 注意某人[某事物]: *Get a load of that old bloke with the funny hat!* 你瞧那戴怪帽子的傢伙!

□ ˈ**load-shedding** *n* [U] cutting off the supply of electric current on certain lines when the general demand is greater than the available supply 甩负荷（电源过载时切断某些线路的电源）.

load[2] /ləʊd; lod/ *v* **1** (**a**) [I, Ip, Tn, Tn·pr, Tn·p] **~ (up)/~ (up with sth); ~ sth/sb (down/up) (with sth); ~ sth (into/onto sth/sb)** put a load in or on (sth/sb) 装载; 使（某事物[某人]）负荷: *We're still loading.* 我们仍在装货. ○ *load a lorry (up) with bricks/load bricks onto a lorry* 把砖装进卡车里 ○ *loaded down with shopping* 拿着很多买来的东西 ○ (*fig* 比喻) *load sb with honours* 给某人许多荣誉. (**b**) [I] receive a load 接受负荷: *The boat is still loading.* 船仍在上货. **2** [Tn esp passive 尤用于被动语态] weight (sth) with lead, etc 用铅等加重（某物）: *a loaded cane, stick, etc*, ie for use as a weapon 加铅的手杖、棒等（用作武器）○ *loaded dice*, ie one weighted so as to fall in a certain way, eg with the six uppermost 灌铅色子（掷出后总以某面朝上, 如6点）. **3** (**a**) [I, Tn, Tn·pr] **~ sth (with sth)** put film into (a camera) or ammunition into (a gun) 将胶卷装入（照相机）; 将弹药装入（枪炮）: *Be careful, that gun's loaded.* 小心, 那枪是上了膛的. (**b**) [Tn, Tn·pr] **~ sth (into sth)** place (film or ammunition) thus 装（胶卷或弹药）: *load a new film into the camera* 把新胶卷装进照相机里. **4** [Tn] (*computing* 计) transfer (data or a program) from a storage medium into the memory of a computer 装入, 写入, 寄存（数据或程序）. **5** (idm 习语) **load the dice (against sb)** (usu passive 通常用于被动语态) put sb at a disadvantage 使某人处不利地位: *Having lost both his parents when he was a child he always felt that the dice were loaded against him.* 他因自小失去双亲, 总觉得处处受人欺负.

▷ **loaded** *adj* **1** carrying a load 带负载的. **2** [pred 作表语] (*sl* 俚) very rich 富有; 阔绰. **3** (idm 习语) **a ˌloaded ˈquestion** question intended to trap sb into saying sth which he does not want to say or which could harm him 有圈套的问题（诱人说出其不愿说或对其不利之事者）.

load·star = LODESTAR (LODE).

load·stone (also **lode·stone**) /ˈləʊdstəʊn; ˈlodˌston/ *n* (**a**) [U] magnetic oxide of iron 磁性氧化铁. (**b**) [C] piece of this used as a magnet 磁铁: (*fig* 比喻) *She seems to be a loadstone for people in trouble*, ie They come to her regularly for help. 对于患难中的人, 她仿佛是一块磁铁（人们常来求助）.

loaf[1] /ləʊf; lof/ *n* (*pl* **loaves** /ləʊvz; lovz/) **1** mass of bread shaped and baked in one piece 大面包: *Two brown loaves and one large white one, please.* 请拿两个黑面包和一个大的白面包. **2** (idm 习语) **half a loaf is better than none/than no bread** (*saying* 谚) having to accept less than one expects, or feels that one deserves, is better than having nothing 接受半块面包总比没有好; 聊胜于无. **use one's loaf** ⇨ USE[1].

□ ˈ**loaf sugar** sugar in small lumps or cubes 块糖; 方糖.

loaf[2] /ləʊf; lof/ *v* [I, Ipr, Ip] (*infml* 口) spend time idly 虚度光阴: *Don't stand there loafing — there's work to be done.* 别站在那儿呆着——有事要干呢. ○ *loaf around (the house all day)* (成天在家)闲混.

▷ **loafer** *n* **1** idler 虚度光阴者; 游手好闲者. **2** (*esp US*) flat shoe, similar to a moccasin, for casual wear 平底便鞋.

loam /ləʊm; lom/ *n* [U] rich soil containing clay, sand and decayed vegetable matter 壤土. ▷ **loamy** *adj*: *loamy land* 壤土地.

loan /ləʊn; lon/ *n* **1** [C] thing that is lent, esp a sum of money 借出物; (尤指)借款: *I'm only asking for a loan — I'll pay you back.* 我只要求借款——日后一定奉还. ○ *a bank loan*, ie money lent by a bank 银行贷款. **2** [U] lending or being lent (used esp as in the expressions shown) 借出(尤用于下列示例): *May I have the loan of* (ie borrow) *your bicycle?* 可以借你的自行车用用吗? ○ *Can we ask your father for the loan of his car?* 我们可以向你父亲借用他的汽车吗? ○ *It's not my book — I've got it on loan from the library.* 那不是我的书——是从图书馆借来的.

▷ **loan** *v* [Tn, Dn·n, Dn·pr] **~ sth (to sb)** (*esp US*) (*Brit fml* 文) lend sth 借出某物: *a painting graciously loaned by Her Majesty the Queen* 女王陛下惠借的画.

□ ˈ**loan-collection** *n* several works of art, etc lent by their owners for exhibition 收藏者借出供展览的一批艺术品等.

ˈ**loan-word** *n* word taken into one language from another 借词; 外来词.

loath (also **loth**) /ləʊθ; loθ/ *adj* [pred 作表语] (*fml* 文) **1 ~ to do sth** unwilling; reluctant 不愿意; 不情愿: *He seemed somewhat loath to depart.* 他似有不愿离去之意. **2** (idm 习语) ˌ**nothing** ˈ**loath** quite willing; eager 很乐意; 心甘情愿; 巴不得.

loathe /ləʊð; loð/ *v* (**a**) [Tn] feel great hatred or disgust for (sb/sth) 憎恨; 厌恶(某人[某事物]): *loathe the smell of fried fish* 厌恶煎鱼的味. (**b**) [Tn, Tg] (*infml* 口) dislike (sth) greatly 极不喜欢(某事物): *I loathe having to go to these conferences.* 我最讨厌的是得参加这些会议.

▷ **loath·ing** *n* [U] disgust 厌恶; 憎恨: *have a loathing of sth* 厌恶某事物 ○ *feel intense loathing for sb/sth* 对某人[某事物]极为反感.

loath·some /-səm; -səm/ *adj* causing one to feel disgusted or shocked; repulsive 讨厌的; 令人震惊的; 令人厌恶的: *a loathsome disease* 讨厌的疾病 ○ *What a loathsome creature he is!* 他是个多么讨厌的傢伙!

loaves *pl* of LOAF[1].

lob /lɒb; lɑb/ *v* (**-bb-**) [I, Tn, Tn·pr, Tn·p] (in tennis, cricket, etc) send or strike (a ball) in a high arc (网球、板球等)发或击高(球): *She lobbed the ball over her opponent's head to the back of the court.* 她把球挑高越过对方的头向后场落去.

▷ **lob** *n* (**a**) lobbed ball 高球. (**b**) slow underarm delivery in cricket (板球的)缓慢低手球.

lobby /ˈlɒbɪ; ˈlɑbɪ/ *n* **1** [C] porch, entrance-hall or ante-room 门厅; (入口的)厅堂; 前厅: *the lobby of a hotel, theatre, etc* 旅馆、戏院等的大厅. **2** [C] (in the House of Commons, etc) large hall open to the public and used for interviews with Members of Parliament (下议院等内之)民众接待厅. **3** [CGp] group of people who try to influence politicians, esp to support or oppose proposed legislation 游说议员的团体: *The anti-nuclear lobby is/are becoming stronger.* 向议员游说的反核群众声势渐强. **4** [C] = DIVISION LOBBY (DIVISION).

▷ **lobby** *v* (*pt, pp* **lobbied**) **1** [I, Ipr, Tn, Tn·pr] **~ (sb) (for sth)** try to persuade (a politician, etc) to support or oppose proposed legislation 游说(政治家等)支持或反对某立法议案: *lobby (MPs) for higher farm subsidies* 游说(议员)以提高农业补贴. **2** (phr v) **lobby sth through (sth)** get (a bill, etc) passed or rejected by lobbying 通过游说使(一法案等)通过或不通过: *lobby a bill through Parliament/the Senate* 运动议员使国会[参议院]通过一法案. **lob·by·ist** /-ɪst; -ɪst/ *n* person who lobbies 游说议员者.

lobe /ləʊb; lob/ *n* **1** lower soft part of the outer ear 耳垂. ⇨illus at HEAD 见 HEAD 插图. **2** rounded flattish part or projection of a body organ, esp the lungs or brain (器官的)叶; (尤指)肺叶, 脑叶.

▷ **lobed** *adj* having lobes 有耳垂的; 有(器官的)叶的.

lo·bo·tomy /ləʊˈbɒtəmɪ; loˈbɑtəmɪ/ (also *Brit* **leucotomy**) *n* (*medical* 医) [C, U] (operation involving) cutting into the brain tissue to treat severe mental disorders 脑白质切断(术); 脑叶纤维切断(术).

lob·ster /ˈlɒbstə(r); ˈlɑbstɚ/ *n* (**a**) [C] large bluish-black shellfish with eight legs and two long claws that turns scarlet when it is boiled 龙虾. ⇨illus at SHELLFISH 见 SHELLFISH 插图. (**b**) [U] its flesh as food (作食物的)龙虾肉.

□ ˈ**lobster-pot** *n* device for trapping lobsters, esp one like a basket 诱捕龙虾的装置; (尤指)捕龙虾的笼.

local /ˈləʊkl; ˈlokl/ *adj* [esp attrib 尤作定语] **1** belonging to a particular place or district 地方的; 本地的; 地区的: *Following the national news we have the local news and weather.* 国内新闻之后是本地新闻和天气报告. ○ *the local farmer, doctor, shopkeeper, etc* 当地的农民、医生、店主等 ○ *local knowledge*, ie detailed knowledge of an area that one gets esp by living there 地方知识(尤指居住当地而知其详者) ○ *She's a local girl*, ie from this area. 她是本地姑娘. ○ *a local train/bus*, ie not long-distance 本地的火车[公共汽车]. **2** (*esp medical* 尤用于医学) affecting a particular place; not general 局部的; 非全身的: *local inflammation* 局部炎症 ○ *Is the pain local?* 是局部疼痛吗?

▷ **local** *n* **1** (usu *pl* 通常作复数) inhabitant of a particular place or district 本地人; 当地人: *The locals tend to be suspicious of strangers.* 当地人对陌生人往往有戒心. **2** (*Brit infml* 口) public house, esp near one's home 当地酒店(尤指住处附近的): *pop into the local for a pint* 进附近酒店喝一品脱啤酒 ○ *Which is your local?* 你们邻近的酒店是哪一家? **3** (*US*) branch of a trade union, etc (工会等的)地方分会. **4** (*esp US*) local train or bus 地区的火车或公共汽车. **loc·ally** /-kəlɪ; -kəlɪ/ *adv*.

□ ˌ**local anaesˈthetic** (*medical* 医) anaesthetic that affects only a specific part of the body 局部麻醉.

ˌ**local auˈthority** (*Brit*) group of people responsible for the administration of local government 地方当局; 地方政权.

ˈ**local call** telephone call to a nearby place, charged at a low rate 本地电话.

ˌ**local ˈcolour** details that are typical of the place and time in which a novel, etc is set, used to make the story seem more real (文艺作品的)地方色彩, 地方特色.

ˌ**local ˈgovernment** system of administration of a district, county, etc by elected representatives of the people who live there 地方政府.

ˌ**local ˈoption** (esp in Scotland, New Zealand and the US) right of local residents to decide sth (eg whether alcohol should be sold there) by voting (尤指苏格兰、新西兰、美国)地方人民抉择权(如是否准予销售酒类).

ˈ**local time** (according to the) system of time being used in a given part of the world 当地时间; 本地时: *We reach Delhi at 1400 hours local time.* 我们于当地时间14时到达德里.

loc·ale /ləʊˈkɑːl; *US* -ˈkæl; loˈkæl/ *n* scene of events, operations, etc (事情发生的)现场, 场地: *The director is looking for a suitable locale for his new film.* 导演在为新片物色合适的拍摄场地.

loc·al·ity /ləʊˈkælətɪ; loˈkælətɪ/ *n* position of sth; place or district in which sth happens 位置; 地点; 现场: *trying to pinpoint the ship's exact locality* 设法确定轮船的确切位置 ○ *The entire locality has been affected by the new motorway.* 新建的高速公路影响了整个地区.

loc·al·ize, -ise /ˈləʊkəlaɪz; ˈloklˌaɪz/ *v* [Tn] restrict (sth) to a particular area or part; make local 使(某事物)局部化; 使具有地方色彩: *try to localize an outbreak of disease, violence, unrest* 尽力把疾病、暴力、暴乱的爆发限制在局部范围以内 ○ *a localized infection* 局部感染.

▷ **loc·al·iza·tion, -isation** /ˌləʊkəlaɪˈzeɪʃn; *US* -lɪˈz-; ˌlokləˈzeʃən/ *n* [U].

loc·ate /ləʊˈkeɪt; *US* ˈləʊkeɪt; ˈloket/ *v* **1** [Tn] discover the exact position or place of (sb/sth) 找出, 指出(某人[某事物])的准确位置或地点: *locate an electrical fault*

查明电路出故障的地方 ○ *locate a town on a map* 在地图上找出一城市的位置 ○ *I'm trying to locate Mr Smith. Do you know where he is?* 我要找史密斯先生. 你知道他在哪里吗? **2** [esp passive 尤用于被动语态: Tn, Tn·pr] establish (sth) in a place; situate 将(某物)设置在某处; 使坐落于: *A new factory is to be located on this site.* 新厂拟建于此. ○ *The information office is located in the city centre.* 咨询处设在市中心. **3** [Ipr] (*US*) settle in a place; establish oneself 定居某处; 安顿: *The company has located on the West Coast.* 公司设在西海岸.

loca·tion /ləʊˈkeɪʃn; loˈkeʃən/ *n* **1** [C] place or position 地方; 位置: *a suitable location for new houses* 适合建筑新房屋的地点. **2** [U] finding the position of sb/sth 发现、找出某人[某物]的位置或地点: *responsible for the location of the missing yacht* 负责查明失踪游艇的下落. **3** [C] (*computing* 计) basic unit of a computer's memory, able to store a single item of data 存储单元. **4** (idm 习语) **on location** (*cinema* 影) being filmed in suitable surroundings instead of in a film studio 外景拍摄.

loc cit /ˌlɒk ˈsɪt; ˌlɑk ˈsɪt/ *abbr* 缩写 = in the passage, etc already quoted (Latin *loco citato*) 在上述引文中(源自拉丁文 *loco citato*). Cf 参看 OP CIT.

loch /lɒk, lɒx; lɑk, lɑx/ *n* (*Scot* 苏格兰) (often in names 常用于地名) **1** lake 湖: *Loch Ness* 尼斯湖. **2** long narrow inlet of the sea 狭长的海湾. Cf 参看 LOUGH.

loci *pl* of LOCUS.

lock[1] /lɒk; lɑk/ *n* **1** [C] portion of hair that hangs or lies together 一绺或一缕毛发: *He kept a lock of her hair as a memento.* 他保留着她的一束头发作纪念. **2 locks** [pl] (*esp rhet or joc* 尤作修辞或作戏谑语) hair of the head 头发: *He gazed ruefully in the mirror at his greying locks.* 他凝视着镜中自己日见花白的头发, 感慨岁月不待人.

lock[2] /lɒk; lɑk/ *n* **1** [C] device for fastening a door, lid, etc, with a bolt that needs a key to work it 锁. **2** [C] section of a canal or river where the water level changes, enclosed by gates fitted with sluices so that water can be let in or out to raise or lower boats from one level to another (河流的)船闸, 水闸. **3** [C] (in wrestling) hold that keeps an opponent's arm, leg, etc from moving (摔跤中的)抱, 夹(对于对方的臂、腿等): *have sb's arm in a lock* 夹住某人的胳膊. **4** [U] condition in which parts are jammed or fixed together so that movement is impossible 塞住、卡住的状态. **5** [U] (maximum extent of the) turning of a motor vehicle's front wheels by use of the steering-wheel (机动车方向盘旋转时)前轮转向(的最大程度): *on full lock*, ie with the steering-wheel turned as far as it will go one way or the other 前轮最大限度转向(方向盘转到头) ○ *My car has a good lock*, ie can turn within a short distance. 我的汽车前轮转向很好(转弯用地小). **6** [C] mechanism for exploding the charge in a gun 枪机. **7** (idm 习语) **ˌlock, stock and ˈbarrel** including everything; completely 全部; 完全. **(keep sth/put sth/be) under ˌlock and ˈkey** locked up 锁起: *The criminals are now safely under lock and key.* 这些罪犯现在都已经牢牢关押起来.

□ **ˌlock-ˈgate** *n* gate on a canal or river lock (河流的)闸门.

ˈlockjaw *n* [U] form of tetanus in which the jaws become rigidly closed 牙关紧闭; 破伤风.

ˈlock-keeper *n* person in charge of a canal or river lock 河流的水闸管理人.

ˈlock-nut *n* extra nut screwed over another to prevent it becoming loose 防松螺母.

ˈlocksmith *n* person who makes and mends locks 锁匠.

ˈlock-stitch *n* [U] sewing-machine stitch that locks threads firmly together 连锁缝纫(针迹).

lock[3] /lɒk; lɑk/ *v* **1** (**a**) [Tn] fasten (a door, lid, etc) with a lock 锁(门、盖等): *Is the gate locked?* 大门锁了吗? (**b**) [Tn] make (a house, box, etc) secure in this way 锁住, 锁牢(房子、箱子等): *Be sure to lock your bicycle.* 自行车务必上锁. (**c**) [I] be able to be fastened or secured with a lock 能锁: *This suitcase doesn't lock*, ie has no lock or has a lock that is broken. 这衣箱不能锁(无锁或锁已坏). ⇨Usage at CLOSE[4] 用法见 CLOSE[4]. **2** [I, Ipr, Ip, Tn, Tn·pr] **~ (sth/sb) (in/into sth); ~ (sb/sth) (together)** (cause sb/sth to) become rigidly fixed; jam (使某人[某事物])卡住, 挤住: *The brakes locked, causing the car to skid.* 汽车因车轮刹住而打滑. ○ *The pieces of the puzzle lock into each other/lock together*, ie interlock. 拼图各块拼合时都卡在一起. ○ (*fig* 比喻) *two nations locked in mortal combat*, ie at war 处于殊死战斗中的两国 ○ *two lovers locked in each other's arms*, ie embracing 拥抱着的一对情侣. **3** (idm 习语) **lock, etc the stable door after the horse has bolted** ⇨ STABLE[2]. **4** (phr v) **lock sth away** store sth securely and safely 将某物妥善锁起: *lock away one's jewellery* 把珠宝锁好. **lock onto sth** (of a missile, etc) automatically find and follow (a target) (指导弹等)追踪(目标). **lock sb/oneself out (of sth)/in** prevent sb/oneself from entering or leaving by locking a door, etc (intentionally or unintentionally) (有意或无意地)将某人[自己]锁于某处不得进出: *At 9 pm the prisoners are locked in for the night.* 晚9时把犯人锁进牢房过夜. ○ *I've lost my key and I'm locked out!* 我丢了钥匙, 进不去了! ○ *lock oneself out of the house* 把自己锁在门外. **lock (sth) up** make (a house, etc) secure by locking the doors and windows 上锁(锁好门窗): *Don't forget to lock up before leaving home.* 离家之前别忘上锁. **lock sb up** put sb in prison, a mental institution, etc 将某人监禁起来或送进精神病院等. **lock sth up** (**a**) = LOCK STH AWAY. (**b**) invest (money) so that it cannot easily be converted into cash 将(资本)搁死: *All their capital is locked up in land.* 他们把全部资金都搁死在地产投资上了.

▷ **ˈlock·able** *adj* that can be locked 能锁的: *a lockable steering-wheel* 可锁的方向盘.

□ **ˈlock-out** *n* refusal by an employer to let workers enter a factory, etc until they agree to certain conditions (资方的)闭厂, 停工(除非工人答应某些条件, 否则不得进厂).

ˈlock-up *n* (**a**) place where prisoners can be kept temporarily 拘留所. (**b**) (*infml* 口) prison 监狱. (**c**) (*Brit*) (usu small) shop whose owner does not live in it (通常指小的)商店(店主不住在内). — *adj* [attrib 作定语] that can be locked up 可上锁的: *a lock-up garage* 可上锁的车库.

locker /ˈlɒkə(r); ˈlɑkɚ/ *n* **1** (**a**) small cupboard, esp one of several where clothes can be kept, eg at a swimming-pool 小橱柜(尤指供存放衣物的, 如在游泳池处): *left-ˈluggage lockers*, ie for depositing luggage in, eg at a railway station 行李寄存柜(如在火车站中的). (**b**) (*nautical* 海) box or compartment for storing clothes, ammunition, etc in a ship (船上贮藏衣物、弹药等的)箱, 室, 库. **2** (idm 习语) **be in/go to ˌDavy Jones's ˈlocker** be drowned at sea 葬身大海.

□ **ˈlocker-room** *n* (*esp US*) room at a sports club, etc for changing in, with lockers for clothes, etc (体育俱乐部等的)衣物间.

locket /ˈlɒkɪt; ˈlɑkɪt/ *n* small ornamental case, usu of gold or silver, holding a portrait, lock of hair, etc and worn on a chain round the neck 盒式项链坠(通常为金银制的, 用以藏照片、头发等).

loco[1] /ˈləʊkəʊ; ˈloko/ *n* (*pl* **~s**) (*infml* 口) locomotive engine 火车头; 机车: [attrib 作定语] *loco-spotting*, ie as a hobby 观察火车头(一种爱好).

loco[2] /ˈləʊkəʊ; ˈloko/ *adj* [pred 作表语] (*sl* 俚 *esp US*) mad 发疯.

lo·co·mo·tion /ˌləʊkəˈməʊʃn; ˌlokəˈmoʃən/ *n* [U] (*fml or joc* 文或谑) moving, or the ability to move, from place to place 运动; 移动; 运动力; 移动力.

▷ **lo·co·mot·ive** /ˈləʊkəməʊtɪv; ˌlokəˈmotɪv/ *adj* of, having or causing locomotion 移动的; 有移动力的; 产生运动的: *locomotive power* 移动力. — *n* = ENGINE 2: *electric, diesel, steam, etc locomotives* 电气、柴油、蒸汽等机车.

locum /ˈləʊkəm; ˈlokəm/ *n* (also *fml* 正规作 **ˌlocum ˈtenens** /ˈtiːnenz, ˈtenenz; ˈtinɛnz/) deputy acting for a doctor or priest in his absence (医生或牧师的)临时代理人: *When they are on holiday the work of doctors is often done by locums.* 医生度假时, 他们的工作常由代理医生负责.

locus /ˈləʊkəs; ˈlokəs/ *n* (*pl* **loci** /ˈləʊsaɪ; ˈlosaɪ/) exact place of sth 所在地; 场所.

□ **ˌlocus ˈclassicus** /ˈklæsɪkəs; ˈklæsɪkəs/ (*Latin* 拉) best known or most authoritative passage on a subject 关于某问题的最著名或最具权威性的章节.

locust /ˈləʊkəst; ˈlokəst/ *n* type of African and Asian winged insect that migrates in huge swarms which destroy all the vegetation of a district 飞蝗.

lo·cu·tion /lə'kju:ʃn; lo'kjuʃən/ *n* **1** [U] (*fml* 文) style of speech; way of using words 语言风格; 用词的方法. **2** [C] (*esp linguistics* 尤用于语言学) phrase or idiom 短语; 惯用语; 成语.

lode /ləʊd; lod/ *n* vein of metal ore 矿脉.

□ **'lodestar** (also **loadstar**) *n* **(a)** star used as a guide in navigation, esp the pole-star 用以指示航向的星; (尤指)北极星. **(b)** (*fig* 比喻) principle that guides one's behaviour and actions (行为和行动的)指导原则.

'lodestone *n* = LOADSTONE.

lodge[1] /lɒdʒ; lɑdʒ/ *n* **1** small house at the gates of a park or in the grounds of a large house, occupied by a gate-keeper or other employee (公园或大宅第中看门人的)房子; 下房. **2** country house or cabin for use in certain seasons (某季节中使用的)乡间小舍: *a 'hunting/'fishing/'skiing lodge* 打猎[钓鱼/滑雪]时用的小屋. **3** porter's room at the main entrance to a block of flats, college, factory, etc (公寓、学院、工厂等的)门房. **4** members or meeting-place of a branch of a society such as the Freemasons 会社(如共济会)支部的全体会员; 支部会员集会处. **5** beaver's or otter's lair (海狸或水獭的)巢穴. **6** N American Indian dwelling or household (北美印第安人的)住处, 住家.

lodge[2] /lɒdʒ; lɑdʒ/ *v* **1** [Tn, Tn·pr] provide (sb) with a place to sleep or live in for a time 供(某人)以临时住宿处: *The refugees are being lodged in an old army camp.* 难民暂时安置在一座旧军营里. **2** [I, Ipr] **~ (with sb/at...)** live for payment in sb's house 租住某人的房屋: *Where are you lodging?* 你在哪里寄宿? ○ *I'm lodging at Mrs Brown's (house)/with Mrs Brown.* 我在布朗太太家寄宿. **3** [Ipr, Tn·pr] **~ (sth) in sth** (cause sth to) enter and become fixed in sth (使某物)进入并固定于某处: *The bullet (was) lodged in his brain.* 子弹射入他的脑内. **4** [Tn·pr] **~ sth with sb/in sth** leave (money, etc) with sb/in sth for safety 将(钱等)交付某人保管, 寄存某处: *lodge one's valuables in the bank* 把贵重物品存放在银行里. **5** [Tn, Tn·pr] **~ sth (with sb) (against sb)** present (a statement, etc) to the proper authorities for attention 向负责部门提出(某事): *lodge a complaint with the police against one's neighbours* 向警方告邻居的状 ○ *lodge an appeal, a protest, an objection, etc* 提出上诉、抗议、反对意见等.

▷ **lodger** *n* person who pays to live in (part of) sb's house 房客; 租住者: *She makes a living by taking in lodgers.* 她靠收房客租金为生.

lodge·ment (also **lodg·ment**) /'lɒdʒmənt; 'lɑdʒmənt/ *n* (*fml* 文) **1** [U] action or process of lodging (LODGE[2] 5) 向负责部门提出: *the lodgement of a complaint* 投诉的提出. **2** [C] mass of material that collects in or blocks sth 积聚物; 堵塞物: *a lodgement of dirt in a pipe* 烟斗中积存的烟垢.

lodging /'lɒdʒɪŋ; 'lɑdʒɪŋ/ *n* **1** [U, C] temporary accommodation 临时寄宿; 借宿: *full board and lodging*, ie a room to stay in and all meals provided 一应膳宿 ○ *find a lodging for the night* 找地方借宿一夜. **2** **lodgings** [pl] room or rooms (not in a hotel) rented for living in 寄宿舍(非指旅馆中的): *It's cheaper to live in lodgings than in a hotel.* 住寄宿舍比住旅馆便宜.

□ **'lodging-house** *n* house in which lodgings are let, usu by the week 出租房间的公寓(通常按周出租).

lo·ess /'ləʊes; 'lo·ɪs/ *n* [U] layer of fine fertile light-coloured soil, found in large areas of Asia, Europe and America 黄土.

loft[1] /lɒft; *US* lɔ:ft; lɔft/ *n* **1** **(a)** room or space directly under the roof of a house, used for storing things 阁楼, 顶楼(用以存放东西): [attrib 作定语] *a loft conversion*, ie one that has been made into a room or rooms for living in (改装的)阁楼居室. **(b)** space under the roof of a stable or barn, used for storing hay, etc 厩楼(用以贮放干草等). **2** (*US*) one of the upper floors of a warehouse, etc (仓库等的)上层楼面, 楼上. **3** gallery or upper level in a church or hall (教堂或大厅内的)楼厢: *the 'organ-loft* 教堂内的风琴台.

loft[2] /lɒft; *US* lɔ:ft; lɔft/ *v* [Tn, Tn·pr] (*esp sport* 尤用于体育) hit, kick or throw (a ball) in a high arc 击、踢、掷高弧(球): *loft the ball over the goalkeeper* 踢高弧球越过守门员 ○ *a lofted drive*, eg at cricket or golf 击出高球(如板球或高尔夫球).

▷ **lofted** *adj* (of a golf-club) shaped to hit the ball high (指高尔夫球棒)击出高球用的.

lofty /'lɒftɪ; *US* 'lɔ:ftɪ; 'lɔftɪ/ *adj* (**-ier**, **-iest**) **1** [usu attrib 通常作定语] (of thoughts, aims, etc) noble; exalted (指思想、目标等)高尚的, 崇高的: *lofty sentiments* 高尚的情操. **2** (*derog* 贬) seeming to be proud and superior; haughty 高傲的; 骄傲的; 傲慢的: *in a lofty manner* 态度傲慢. **3** (*rhet* 修辞) (not used of people 不用于指人) very tall 极高的: *a lofty mountain* 高山 ○ *lofty halls* 高大的厅堂. ▷ **loft·ily** /-ɪlɪ; -ılı/ *adv*. **lofti·ness** *n* [U].

log[1] /lɒg; *US* lɔ:g; lɔg/ *n* **1** **(a)** length of tree-trunk that has fallen or been cut down 原木; 圆材: *birds nesting in a hollow log* 在空树干里搭巢的鸟. **(b)** short piece of this, esp one used as firewood 短的木材; (尤指)木柴: *Put another log on the fire.* 往炉子里再添一段木柴. **2** (idm 习语) **easy as falling off a log** ⇨ EASY[1]. **sleep like a log/top** ⇨ SLEEP.

▷ **log·ging** *n* [U] (*US*) work of cutting down forest trees for timber 伐木工作; 伐木业: [attrib 作定语] *a logging camp* 伐木营地.

□ **'log cabin** hut built of logs 原木小屋.

'log-jam *n* (*esp US*) deadlock; standstill 僵局; 停顿.

'log-rolling *n* [U] (*derog* 贬 *esp US*) practice of helping others in return for their help, as when authors review each other's books favourably 相互吹捧, 相互标榜(如作家间互相作好评).

log[2] /lɒg; *US* lɔ:g; lɔg/ *n* **1** (formerly 旧时用法) floating device pulled behind a ship to measure its speed 测速仪(拖带于船后以测船速者): *sail by the log*, ie calculate a ship's position using this 用测速仪测量船位. **2** log-book of a ship or an aircraft 航海或飞行日志.

▷ **log** *v* (**-gg-**) [Tn] **1** enter (facts) in a log-book 将(事情)记载于航行日志中. **2** achieve (a certain speed, distance, number of hours worked, etc) as recorded in a log-book or similar record 达到(某速度、里程、工作时数等)记录: *The pilot had logged over 200 hours in the air.* 这个飞行员的飞行记录在200小时以上. **3** (phr v) **log in/on** (*computing* 计) open one's on-line access to a database, etc 注册, 登记(接通数据库等作联机存取). **log off/out** (*computing* 计) end one's on-line access to a database, etc 注销(关闭数据库等结束联机存取).

□ **'log-book** *n* **1** detailed record of a ship's voyage or an aircraft's flight; any similar record 航海或飞行日志; 类似的记录. **2** motor vehicle's registration book (机动车辆的)车辆登记证.

log[3] /lɒg; *US* lɔ:g; lɔg/ *n* (*infml mathematics* 口, 数) logarithm 对数: [attrib 作定语] *log tables* 对数表.

-log *US* = -LOGUE.

lo·gan·berry /'ləʊgənbrɪ; *US* -berɪ; 'logən,bɛrɪ/ *n* large dark-red berry from a plant that is a cross[2](7) between a blackberry and a raspberry 洛根莓(为黑莓与悬钩子杂交植物, 结深红色聚合果).

log·ar·ithm /'lɒgərɪðəm; *US* 'lɔ:g-; 'lɔgə,rɪðəm/ *n* (*mathematics* 数) any of a series of numbers set out in tables which make it possible to work out problems in multiplication and division by adding and subtracting 对数. ⇨App 4 见附录4. ▷ **log·ar·ith·mic** /ˌlɒgə'rɪðmɪk; *US* ˌlɔ:g-; ˌlɔgə'rɪðmɪk/ *adj*: *a logarithmic function* 对数函数. **log·ar·ith·mic·ally** /-klɪ; -klı/ *adv*.

log·ger·heads /'lɒgəhedz; 'lɔgɚ,hɛdz/ *n* (idm 习语) **at loggerheads (with sb)** disagreeing or quarrelling 不和; 相争: *He and his wife are always at loggerheads.* 他和妻子总是不和. ○ *His father's will has set him at loggerheads with his brother*, ie caused them to quarrel. 他父亲的遗嘱导致了他与弟弟争执起来.

log·gia /'ləʊdʒə, 'lɒdʒɪə; 'lodʒə, 'lɑdʒɪə/ *n* open-sided gallery or arcade, esp one that forms part of a house and has one side open to the garden 凉廊(尤指房屋敞向花园的).

lo·gic /'lɒdʒɪk; 'lɑdʒɪk/ *n* [U] **1** science of reasoning 逻辑学; 论理学. **2** particular method or system of reasoning 推理的方法或体系. **3** chain of reasoning (regarded as good or bad) 逻辑性, 条理性(合乎逻辑或不合逻辑): *You have to accept the logic of his argument.* 应该承认他的论据中有逻辑性. **4** ability to reason correctly 正确推理的能力; 逻辑思维的能力. **5** (*computing* 计) **(a)** principles used in designing a computer (设计计算机的)逻辑. **(b)** the circuit(s) involved in this 逻辑电路.

▷ **lo·gi·cian** /ləˈdʒɪʃn; loˈdʒɪʃən/ *n* person who is skilled in logic 逻辑学家.

lo·gical /ˈlɒdʒɪkl; ˈlɑdʒɪkl/ *adj* **1** in accordance with the rules of logic; correctly reasoned 合逻辑的; 推理正确的: *a logical argument, conclusion* 合逻辑的论据、结论. **2** (of an action, event, etc) in accordance with what seems reasonable or natural (指行为、事情等)合乎情理的, 合乎常理的: *the logical outcome* 合情合理的结果 ○ *It seemed the only logical thing to do.* 看来那样做才合乎常理. **3** capable of reasoning correctly 有逻辑头脑的; 有推理能力的: *a logical mind* 善于推理的头脑.

▷ **lo·gic·al·ity** /ˌlɒdʒɪˈkælətɪ; ˌlɑdʒɪˈkælətɪ/ *n* [U] being logical 合逻辑; 合理.

lo·gic·ally /-klɪ; -klɪ/ *adv*: *argue logically* 有条理地辩论.

lo·gist·ics /ləˈdʒɪstɪks; ləˈdʒɪstɪks/ *n* [sing or pl *v*] organization of supplies and services, etc for any complex operation 后勤. ▷ **lo·gistic**, **lo·gist·ical** /ləˈdʒɪstɪkl; ləˈdʒɪstɪkəl/ *adjs*: *Organizing famine relief presents huge logistical problems.* 筹划饥馑救济工作在后勤方面困难极大. **lo·gist·ically** /-klɪ; -klɪ/ *adv*.

logo /ˈləʊgəʊ; ˈloˌgo/ *n* (*pl* **~s**) printed symbol designed for and used by a business, company, etc as its emblem, eg in advertising (企业、公司等的)专用标识, 标记, 商标(如用于广告中的).

-logue (*US* **-log**) *comb form* 构词成分 (forming *ns* 用以构成名词) talk or speech 话; 谈话: *monologue* ○ *travelogue*.

-logy *comb form* 构词成分 (forming *ns* 用以构成名词) **1** subject of study 论; 学: *mineralogy* ○ *sociology* ○ *theology* ○ *zoology*. **2** speech or writing 语言; 文字: *trilogy* ○ *phraseology* ○ *tautology*.

▷ **-logic(al)** *comb form* 构词成分 (forming *adjs* 用以构成形容词): *physiologic(al)* ○ *pathological*.

-logist *comb form* 构词成分 (forming *ns* 用以构成名词) person skilled in a subject of study 某学科学者: *biologist* ○ *geologist*.

loin /lɔɪn; lɔɪn/ *n* **1** [C] (*anatomy* 解) side and back of the body between the ribs and the hip-bone 腰; 腰部. **2** [C, U] (joint of) meat from this part of an animal (动物的)腰肉, 脊背肉: *some loin of pork* 猪脊背肉. **3 loins** [pl] (*dated* 旧) (**a**) lower part of the body on both sides below the waist and above the legs 胯. (**b**) (*euph* 婉) reproductive organs 下身. **4** (idm 习语) **gird one's loins** ⇨ GIRD.

□ ˈ**loincloth** *n* piece of cloth worn around the body at the hips, esp as the only garment worn 缠腰布(尤指仅有的蔽体物).

loiter /ˈlɔɪtə(r); ˈlɔɪtɚ/ *v* **1** [I, Ipr, Ip] **~ (about/around)** stand about idly 闲站着: *loitering at street corners* 在街头闲站着. **2** [I] go slowly, with frequent stops 慢走; 边走边停: *Don't loiter on the way home!* 不要在回家的路上闲逛! ▷ **loi·terer** *n*.

loll /lɒl; lɑl/ *v* **1** [I, Ipr, Ip] **~ (about/around)** rest, sit or stand lazily, often while leaning against sth 懒洋洋地呆着、坐着或站着(常指倚着某物): *loll around the house* 在家中呆着. **2** (phr v) **loll out** (of the tongue) hang loosely (指舌)耷拉, 下垂.

lol·li·pop /ˈlɒlɪpɒp; ˈlɑlɪˌpɑp/ *n* large (usu flat and round) boiled sweet on a small stick, held in the hand and sucked 棒棒糖.

□ ˈ**lollipop man** (*fem* 阴性作 ˈ**lollipop woman**, ˈ**lollipop lady**) (*Brit infml* 口) person who carries a circular sign marked 'Stop! Children Crossing' as a warning to traffic to stop, allowing children to cross a busy road, esp on their way to and from school 儿童过路辅导员(持圆形指示牌, 有'停车! 儿童过路'字样, 尤于上学、放学时间值勤者).

lol·lop /ˈlɒləp; ˈlɑləp/ *v* [I, Ipr, Ip] (*infml* 口 *esp Brit*) move in clumsy jumps; flop about 笨拙地跳动; 扑动: *lolloping along (the road)* (一路)蹦蹦跳跳.

lolly /ˈlɒlɪ; ˈlɑlɪ/ *n* (*Brit*) **1** [C] (*infml* 口) lollipop 棒棒糖. **2** [U] (*sl* 俚) money 钱.

lone /ləʊn; lon/ *adj* [attrib 作定语] (*usu rhet* 通常作修辞) **1** without companions; solitary 孤独的; 孤单的: *a lone figure trudging through the snow* 在雪地里独自跋涉的人. Cf 参看 ALONE 1, LONELY 3. **2** (idm 习语) **a** ˌ**lone** ˈ**wolf** person who prefers to be, work, etc alone 好孤独自处、独自工作等的人.

▷ **loner** *n* (*infml* 口) person who avoids the company of others 喜独处者; 不合群者: *She's been a loner all her life.* 她一生离群索居.

lonely /ˈləʊnlɪ; ˈlonlɪ/ *adj* **1** sad because one lacks friends or companions 孤寂的; 寂寞的: *I live all alone but I never feel lonely.* 我虽孑然一身, 但从不感孤寂. ○ *a lonely-looking child* 形单影只的孩子 ○ *Living in a big city can be* (ie make one feel) *very lonely.* 在大城市里生活还真很孤寂. ○ *Hers is a lonely life.* 她的生活很寂寞. **2** [attrib 作定语] (of places) far from inhabited places; not often visited; remote (指地方)偏僻的, 人迹罕至的; 偏远的: *Antarctica is the loneliest place on earth.* 南极是地球上最偏远的地区. **3** [attrib 作定语] without companions 孤单的; 无伴侣的: *a lonely traveller* 孤单的旅客. **4** (idm 习语) **plough a lonely furrow** ⇨ PLOUGH *v*. ⇨Usage at ALONE 用法见 ALONE. ▷ **lone·li·ness** *n* [U]: *suffer from loneliness* 备尝孤寂之苦.

□ ˌ**lonely** ˈ**hearts** people who are seeking friendship, esp with a view to marriage 征友者(尤指物色佳偶者): [attrib 作定语] *a lonely hearts column*, ie a section of a newspaper, etc containing messages from such people (报纸等的)征友专栏.

lone·some /ˈləʊnsəm; ˈlonsəm/ *adj* (*esp US*) **1** lonely 孤寂的; 寂寞的; 人迹罕至的; 偏僻的; 偏远的: *I get lonesome when you're not here.* 你不在时我颇感寂寞. ○ *a lonesome mountain village* 偏僻的山村. **2** causing loneliness 令人感到孤寂的: *a lonesome journey* 寂寞的旅途. ⇨Usage at ALONE 用法见 ALONE. **3** (idm 习语) **by/on one's** ˈ**lonesome** (*infml* 口) on one's own; alone 独自; 单独.

long[1] /lɒŋ; *US* lɔːŋ; lɔŋ/ *adj* (**-er** /-ŋgə(r); -ŋgɚ/, **-est** /-ŋgɪst; -ŋgɪst/) **1** having a great or specified extent in space (空间上)长的: *How long is the River Nile?* 尼罗河有多长? ○ *Your hair is longer than mine.* 你的头发比我的长. ○ *Is it a long way* (ie far) *to your house?* 到你家远吗? ○ *These trousers are two inches too long.* 这条裤子长出两英寸. Cf 参看 SHORT[1] 1. **2** having a great or specified duration or extent in time (时间上)长的: *He's been ill for a long time.* 他病了很长时间了. ○ *How long are the holidays?* 假期有多长? ○ *They're six weeks long.* 有六周之久. ○ *Don't be too long about it*, ie Do it soon or quickly. 时间别太长(早做或快做). ⇨Usage at LONG[3] 用法见 LONG[3]. **3** (*phonetics* 语音) (of vowel sounds) taking relatively more time to utter than the corresponding short vowel sound (指元音)长音的: *The vowel sound in 'caught' is long; in 'cot' it is short.* caught 中的元音是长元音; cot 中的是短元音. **4** seeming to be longer than it really is 似乎比实际为长的; 漫长的: *ten long years, miles, etc* 漫长的十年、十英里等. **5** (of memory) able to recall events distant in time (指记忆)能回忆久远的. **6** (idm 习语) **at the** ˈ**longest** not longer than the specified time (时间上)至多, 最长: *He's only away for short periods — a week at the longest.* 他只是短期外出──至多一周. **go** ˈ**far/go a long** ˈ**way** become very successful 很成功: *That girl will go a long way, I'm sure.* 我相信那姑娘很有前途. **go far/go a long way towards doing sth** make a considerable contribution towards sth 对某事物大有裨益: *concessions which go a long way towards satisfying his critics* 对批评他的人起缓解作用的让步 ○ *The new legislation does not go far enough towards solving the problem.* 新的法规对解决该问题并无多大帮助. **go a long way** (**a**) (of money, food, etc) last a long time (指钱、食物等)用很长时间, 经花, 经用: *She makes a little money go a long way*, ie buys many things by careful spending. 她用很少的钱能买很多东西. ○ *A little of this paint goes a long way*, ie covers a large area. 这种颜料用一点可以涂一片. (**b**) be as much as one can bear 叫人受不了: *A little of his company goes a long way*, ie One can tolerate his company for a short time only. 跟他呆上一会儿就叫人受不了. **happy as the day is long** ⇨ HAPPY. **have come a long way** have made much progress 大有进步: *We've come a long way since those early days of the project.* 这项工作开始以来我们已取得很大进展. **have a long** ˈ**arm** be able to make one's power or authority felt even at a distance 有深远的势力或影响力. **in long/short pants** ⇨ PANTS. **in the** ˈ**long run** ultimately; eventually 从长远看; 终究; 最后: *In the long run prices are bound to rise.* 从长远看, 物价肯定要涨. **in the long/**

short term ⇨ TERM. **it's as broad as it's long** ⇨ BROAD[1]. **(put on, have, wear, etc) a long 'face** sad expression 拉长脸; 哭丧着脸; 愁眉苦脸. **a long 'haul** long and difficult activity, etc 持久而艰苦的活动等: *It's been a long haul but at last this dictionary is published.* 经过千辛万苦这部词典才终于得以问世. **a 'long shot** wild guess or attempt 瞎猜; 姑妄一试. **ˌlong in the 'tooth** (*joc* 谑) rather old 年齿渐长; 颇老: *He's getting a bit long in the tooth to be playing football.* 他踢足球未免年齿过长了. **long time no 'see** (*infml* 口) (used as a greeting 用作招呼语) it's a long time since we last met 好久没见了. **not by a 'long chalk**; *Brit* **not by a 'long shot** not at all 完全不; 绝不: *We're not beaten yet, (not) by a long chalk.* 我们还没有败, 远远没败. **take a long (cool/hard) 'look at sth** consider a possibility, problem, etc carefully and at length 谨慎仔细考虑(可能性、问题等). **take the 'long view** consider events, effects, factors, etc a long time in the future, rather than the immediate situation 从长远考虑事情、效果、因素等. **to cut a long story short** to get to the point of what one is saying quickly 长话短说; 简而言之; 总之.

□ **'longboat** *n* largest boat carried on a sailing-ship (帆船所带的)大艇.

'longbow *n* bow drawn by hand, equal in length to the height of the archer and used to shoot feathered arrows 长弓; 大弓. Cf 参看 CROSSBOW.

ˌlong-'distance *adj, adv* travelling or operating between distant places 长距离(的); 长途(的): *a ˌlong-distance 'lorry driver, 'phone call, 'runner* 跑长途的卡车司机、长途电话、长途跑步者 ○ *to phone long-distance* 打长途电话.

ˌlong di'vision (*mathematics* 数) (process of) dividing one number by another with all the calculations written down 长除, 长除法(做除法运算时把每一步骤都写下来): *Can you do long division?* 你会长除法吗? ○ [attrib 作定语] *a long-division sum* 长除法运算.

'long drink drink that is large in quantity, filling a tall glass, eg beer 大杯饮料(如用高杯盛的啤酒).

'longhand *n* [U] ordinary writing (contrasted with shorthand, typing, etc) 普通书写(别于速记、打字等): *all written in longhand* 全部手写.

'long hop (in cricket) ball that pitches short and is easy to hit (板球中的)(短距触地)长反弹球(易被击中).

'long johns (*infml* 口) underpants with legs that extend to the ankles 长内裤(及于踝部): *a warm pair of long johns* 一条暖和的长内裤.

'long jump (*US* **'broad jump**) athletic contest of jumping as far forward as possible 跳远: *competing in the long jump* 比赛跳远.

ˌlong-'life *adj* (esp of dairy products) remaining usable for a long time (尤指乳制品)可长久保存的: *ˌlong-life 'milk* 长期保鲜奶.

long 'odds (in betting) very uneven odds, eg 50 to 1 (打赌中)悬殊的机会(如50比1).

'long-range *adj* [attrib 作定语] (**a**) of or for a period of time far in the future 长期的; 为长远计的: *long-range planning* 长远规划 ○ *a long-range weather forecast* 远期天气预报. (**b**) (of vehicles, missiles, etc) that can be used over great distances (指运载工具、导弹等)长距离的, 远程的, 长程的: *a long-range bomber* 远程轰炸机.

ˌlong-'sighted (also *esp US* **ˌfar-'sighted**) *adj* [usu pred 通常作表语] (**a**) only able to see clearly what is at a distance 远视: *She's long-sighted and needs glasses to read.* 她是远视眼, 看书要戴眼镜. (**b**) (*fig* 比喻) having foresight; prudent 有远见; 有远虑.

'longstop *n* (in cricket) fielder standing directly behind the wicket-keeper (板球)守门员身后的守场员, 外野手.

ˌlong 'suit 1 many playing-cards of one suit in a hand 长套(一手牌中有多张同花者): *Play the highest card in your longest suit.* 打你手中最长套的大牌. **2** (*fig* 比喻) thing at which one excels 特长; 长处: *Modesty is not his long suit.* 谦虚可不是他的长处.

'long-time *adj* [attrib 作定语] that has lasted for a long time 为时已久的; 历久的: *a long-time friendship* 老交情.

ˌlong-'term *adj* [usu attrib 通常作定语] of or for a long period of time 长期的: *a ˌlong-term com'mitment* 长期承担的责任.

long ton measure of weight, equal to 2 240 pounds 长吨(等于2 240磅).

'long wave (*abbr* 缩写 **LW**) radio wave having a wavelength of more than 1 000 metres 长波: [attrib 作定语] *a long-wave broadcast* 长波广播.

ˌlong week'end weekend that is made longer (as a holiday) by an extra day at the beginning or the end of it 长周末(前或后多加一天).

ˌlong-'winded *adj* talking or writing at tedious length 喋喋不休的; 啰嗦的: *a ˌlong-winded 'speaker, 'speech, 'style* 说话啰嗦的人、冗长的讲话、烦冗的风格. **ˌlong-'windedness** *n* [U].

long[2] /lɒŋ; *US* lɔːŋ; lɔŋ/ *n* **1** [U] long time or interval (used esp as in the expressions shown) 长时间, 长间歇(尤用于以下示例): *This won't take long.* 这要不了多久. ○ *Will you be away for long?* 你要离开很长时间吗? ○ *I hope to write to you before long.* 我希望不久就能给你写信. ⇨Usage at LONG[3] 用法见LONG[3]. **2** [C] long signal (eg in Morse code); long vowel or syllable (esp in Latin verse) 长信号(如摩尔斯电码); 长元音或长音节(尤指拉丁诗文中): *a long and two shorts* 一长两短. **3** (idm 习语) **the ˌlong and (the) 'short of it** all that need be said about it; the general effect or result of it 总的意思; 总的结果.

long[3] /lɒŋ; *US* lɔːŋ; lɔŋ/ *adv* (**-er** /-ŋgə(r); -ŋgər/, **-est** /-ŋgɪst; -ŋgɪst/) **1** for a long time 长久; 长期地: *Were you in Rome long?* 你在罗马呆的时间长吗? ○ *Stay as long as you like.* 你愿停留多久皆可. ○ *long into the next century* 下一个世纪之后很久 ○ *I shan't be long*, ie will come, go, etc soon. 我用不了很长时间(就来、就去等). **2** at a time distant from a specified point of time (used esp in the expressions shown) (距某一时间)很久地(尤用于以下示例): *long ago/before/after/since* 很久以前[之前很久/之后很久/很久以来] ○ *He died not long* (ie soon) *after (that).* (那之后)不久他就死了. ⇨Usage at RECENT 用法见RECENT. **3** (with *ns* indicating duration 与表示延续的名词连用) throughout the specified time 贯穿某时间: *all day long* 整天 ○ *I've waited for this moment my whole life long.* 我一生都在等待这个时刻. **4** (idm 习语) **as/so long as** (used as a *conj* 用作连词) (**a**) on condition that; provided that 只要; 如果: *As long as it doesn't rain we can play.* 只要不下雨, 我们就能玩. (**b**) (*US*) since; inasmuch as 既然; 由于. **be not long for this world** be likely to die soon 行将谢世; 历日无多. **no/any/much 'longer** after a certain point in time 不再; 已不: *I can't wait any/much longer.* 我不能再等了. ○ *He no longer lives here.* 他已不住在这里. **he who laughs last laughs longest** ⇨ LAUGH. **so long** (*dated infml* 旧, 口) goodbye 再见.

□ **ˌlong-drawn-'out** *adj* made to last too long; unnecessarily extended 拖得太长的; 拉得过长的: *long-drawn-out negotiations* 旷日持久的谈判.

ˌlong-'lived *adj* having a long life; lasting for a long time 长寿的; 长期的; 长久的: *My family tend to be quite long-lived.* 我家族的人大都相当长寿.

ˌlong-playing 'record (also *dated* 旧作 **ˌlong-'player**) (*abbr* 缩写 **LP**) type of gramophone record that plays for up to about 30 minutes on each side 密纹唱片, 慢转唱片(每一面能持续约30分钟的).

ˌlong-'standing *adj* [esp attrib 尤作定语] that has existed or lasted for a long time 长期存在的; 为时长久的: *ˌlong-standing 'grievances* 长期存在的不满 ○ *a ˌlong-standing ar'rangement* 长期安排.

ˌlong-'suffering *adj* patiently bearing problems, troubles, etc, esp those caused by another person 长期忍受的(对困难事、麻烦事等, 尤指他人引起的): *I pity his ˌlong-suffering 'wife.* 我可怜他那长期受苦的妻子.

NOTE ON USAGE 用法: Both **long** and **a long time** are used as adverbial expressions of time. ☆ **long** 和 **a long time** 都用作表示时间的状语. **1 Long** is not used in positive sentences unless it is modified by another adverb, eg *too, enough, ago* ☆ **long** 只在受另一副词如 too、enough、ago 修饰时才用于肯定句: *You've been sleeping too long/long enough.* 你睡得太久了[你睡的时间够长了]. ○ *She waited there (for) a long time.* 她在那里等了很长时间. **2** Both can be used in questions 这两者均可用于疑问句: *Have you been here long/a long time?* 你在这里呆了很久[很长时间]了吗? **3** In negative sentences there can be a difference in meaning. 在否定句中二者意义有别. Compare 试比较: *I haven't* *been here for a long time* (ie It is a long time since I was last here) and *I haven't been here long* (ie I arrived here only a short time ago). '我已很久没到这里来了(即离上次我来此已很长时间了)'和'我到这里没多久(即我刚到不久)'.

long⁴ /lɒŋ; *US* lɔːŋ; lɔŋ/ *v* [Ipr, It] **~ for sth/~ (for sb) to do sth** have an intense desire for sth; want sth very much (对某事物)渴望; 非常想有某事物: *The children are longing for the holidays.* 孩子们盼望放假. ○ *a (much) longed-for rest* 巴望着(已久)的休息 ○ *She longed for him to ask her to dance.* 她巴不得他邀请自己跳舞. ○ *I'm longing to see you again.* 我盼望再见到你.

▷ **long·ing** /ˈlɒŋɪŋ; *US* ˈlɔːŋɪŋ; ˈlɔŋɪŋ/ *n* [C, U] **~ (for sb/sth)** intense desire 渴望; 热望: *a longing for home* 想家 ○ *a deep sense of longing* 深深的渴望. — *adj* [attrib 作定语] having or showing longing 渴望的; 表示渴望的: *a longing look* 渴望的样子 ○ *gaze with longing eyes* 以渴望的目光注视. **long·ingly** *adv*: *speak longingly of one's native land* 不胜向往地谈自己的家乡 ○ *The children were gazing longingly at the toys in the shop window.* 孩子们眼巴巴地望着商店橱窗里的玩具.

long *abbr* 缩写 = longitude: *long 23°E/W*, ie East/West 东[西]经23°. Cf 参看 LAT.

lon·gev·ity /lɒnˈdʒevətɪ; lɑnˈdʒɛvətɪ/ *n* [U] (*fml* 文) long life 长寿; 长命: *a family noted for its longevity* 以长寿闻名的家族.

lon·git·ude /ˈlɒndʒɪtjuːd; *US* -tuːd; ˈlɑndʒəˌtud/ *n* [U] (*abbr* 缩写 **long**) distance east or west of the Greenwich meridian, measured in degrees 经度: *lines of longitude marked on a map* 标在地图上的经线. ⇨illus at GLOBE 见GLOBE 插图. Cf 参看 LATITUDE 1.

▷ **lon·git·ud·inal** /ˌlɒndʒɪˈtjuːdɪnl; *US* -ˈtuːdnl; ˌlɑndʒəˈtudṇl/ *adj* **1** of longitude 经度的. **2** of or in length; measured lengthwise 长度的; 纵的: *longitudinal stripes*, eg on a flag 纵条纹(如旗帜上的). **lon·git·ud·in·ally** /-nəlɪ; -nḷɪ/ *adv*.

long-shoreman /ˈlɒŋʃɔːmən; *US* ˈlɔːŋ-; ˈlɔŋˌʃɔrmən/ *n* (*pl* **-men** /-mən; -mən/) (*esp US*) person employed to work on shore loading and unloading ships 码头工人.

long·ways /ˈlɒŋweɪz; *US* ˈlɔːŋ-; ˈlɔŋˌwez/ (also **long·wise** /ˈlɒŋwaɪz; *US* ˈlɔːŋ-; ˈlɔŋˌwaɪz/) *adv* = LENGTHWISE (LENGTH).

loo /luː; lu/ *n* (*pl* **~s**) (*Brit infml euph* 口, 婉) lavatory 厕所: *I need to go to the loo.* 我要上厕所. ⇨Usage at TOILET 用法见 TOILET.

loo·fah (also *esp US* **luffa**) /ˈluːfə; ˈlufə/ *n* [C] rough bath sponge made from the dried pod of a type of gourd (浴用)丝瓜络.

look¹ /lʊk; lʊk/ *v* **1** [I, Ipr, Ip] **~ (at sb/sth)** turn one's eyes in a particular direction (in order to see sb/sth) 看; 瞧; 望: *If you look carefully you can just see the church from here.* 你仔细看的话, 可以从这里看到那座教堂. ○ *We looked but saw nothing.* 我们看了, 但什么也没看见. ○ *'Has the postman been yet?' 'I'll just look and see.'* '邮递员来过了吗?''我这就去看看. ○ *Look to see whether the road is clear before you cross.* 看清没车时再过马路. ○ *I was looking the other way when the goal was scored.* 进球时我正看着别处. ○ *She looked at me and smiled.* 她望着我微笑. ○ *She looked out of the window and saw the postman coming up the path.* 她向窗外望去, 看见邮递员正从小道上过来. ○ *They looked across the room at each other.* 他们在房间的两头彼此望着. ○ *She blushed and looked down at the floor.* 她脸一红随即低下头看着地板. **2** [Ipr, Tw] **~ at sth** (esp imperative 尤用于祈使句) pay attention to sth; observe sth 瞧; 看: *Look at the time! We should have been at the theatre ten minutes ago.* 瞧都什么时候了! 十分钟前我们就该到戏院了. ○ *Can't you look where you're going? You nearly knocked me over!* 看, 你这是往哪里走? 差点儿把我撞倒了! ○ *Look what Denise has given me for Christmas!* 看丹尼斯送我什么圣诞礼物了! ○ *Look who's here!* 看谁在这里呢! **3** (**a**) [La, Ln] seem to be; appear 看起来; 看上去; 像是: *look healthy, ill, pale, puzzled, sad, tired* 看上去健康、有病、苍白、困惑不解、忧伤、疲乏 ○ *That book looks interesting/That looks an interesting book.* 那本书好像很有意思[那好像是本有趣的书]. ○ *That pie looks good*, ie good to eat. 那馅饼看来很好吃. ○ *The town always looks deserted on Sunday mornings.* 星期日早晨这小镇总显得冷冷清清. ○ *'How do I look in this dress?' 'You look very nice (in it).'* '我穿这件连衣裙怎么样?''挺好看.' ○ *You made me look a complete fool!* 你叫我大出洋相了! (**b**) [Ipr] **~ (to sb) like sb/sth; ~ (to sb) as if.../as though...** (usu not in the continuous tenses 通常不用于进行时态) have the appearance of sb/sth; suggest by appearance that... 像某人[某事物]的样子; 外表像...: *It looks like salt and it is salt.* 那看着像盐, 也的确是盐. ○ *That photograph doesn't look like her at all.* 那张照片看上去一点都不像她. ○ *This looks to me like the right door.* 依我看就是这个门. ○ *It looks like rain/It looks as if it's going to rain.* 好像要下雨了. ○ *It looks like being/as if it's going to be a nice day.* 看样子是个好天. ○ *You look as if you slept badly.* 看你那样子仿佛没睡好觉. ○ *It doesn't look to me as if the Socialists will win the election.* 我看不出社会党人能在大选中获胜. ⇨Usage at FEEL¹ 用法见 FEEL¹. **4** [I, Ipr] **~ (for sb/sth)** search for or try to find sb/sth 寻找或寻求某人[某事物]: *'I can't find the papers.' 'Well, keep looking!'* '我找不到那些文件.''那就继续找!' ○ *Where have you been? We've been looking for you everywhere.* 你到哪里去了? 我们一直到处找你. ○ *Are you still looking for a job?* 你仍在找工作吗? ○ *Negotiators are looking for a peaceful settlement to the dispute.* 谈判双方正寻求和平解决争端的办法. ○ *The youths were clearly looking for* (ie were intending to start) *a fight.* 显然这些年轻人要寻衅闹事. **5** [Ipr, Ip] face in, or give a view in, a particular direction 面向; 朝向: *The house looks east.* 这房子朝东. ○ *The hotel looks towards the sea.* 该旅馆面向大海. ○ *My bedroom looks onto the garden.* 我的卧室对着花园. **6** (idm 习语) **be looking to do sth** try to do sth 想做某事物: *The government will be looking to reduce inflation by a further two per cent this year.* 政府力求今年把通货膨胀率再减低百分之二. **look ˈbad; not look ˈgood** be not right according to convention, and likely to make others have a bad opinion of one 不合常情; 失礼; 招人非议: *It looks bad not going to your own brother's wedding.* 连亲兄弟的婚礼都不参加, 这太说不过去了. **look ˈbad (for sb)** suggest probable failure, trouble or disaster; be ominous 可能失败、有麻烦或大祸临头: *He's had a severe heart attack; things are looking bad for him, I'm afraid*, ie he is probably going to die. 他心脏病严重发作, 我看情况不妙(可能会死). **look ˈgood** seem to be promising; seem to be making satisfactory progress 似有希望或有满意的进展: *This year's sales figures are looking good.* 今年的销售数字形势喜人. **look ˈhere** (used to express protest or to ask sb to pay attention or listen to sth 用以表示抗议或叫某人注意): *Now look here, it wasn't my fault that we missed the train.* 喂, 咱们误了火车可不是我的错. ○ *Look here, I'm not having you make remarks like that about my sister.* 哎, 我不许你们说我妹妹这种话. **(not) look oneˈself** (not) have one's normal (healthy) appearance 看起来(不)跟往常一样(健康): *You're not looking yourself today*, eg You look tired or ill. 今天你看上去气色不大好. **look sb ˌup and ˈdown** examine sb in a careful or contemptuous way 上下仔细地或轻蔑地打量某人: *I didn't like the way he looked me up and down before speaking to me.* 我不喜欢他在跟我说话之前那样上下打量我. **never/not look ˈback** (*infml* 口) continue to prosper or be successful 一直兴旺或顺利: *Her first novel was published three years ago and since then she hasn't looked back.* 她的第一部小说是三年前发表的, 从此一帆风顺. **to ˈlook at sb/sth** judging by the appearance of sb/sth 由外貌判断: *To look at him you'd never think he was a successful businessman.* 若看他的外貌, 谁也想不到他是个事业有成的商人. **not be much to ˈlook at** (*infml* 口) not have an attractive appearance 其貌不扬: *The house isn't much to look at but it's quite spacious inside.* 别看那房子外表不起眼, 里面相当宽敞. (For other idioms containing **look**, see entries for *ns*, *adjs*, etc 与 **look** 搭配的其他习语见有关名词、形容词等的词条, 如 **look one's age** ⇨ AGE; **look sharp** ⇨ SHARP.)

7 (phr v) **look ˈafter oneself/sb** make sure that one/sb is safe and well; take care of oneself/sb 照料、照顾或照看自己[某人]: *He needs to be properly looked after.* 他需要好好照顾. ○ *Who will look after the children while their mother is in hospital?* 孩子们的母亲住院期间谁照

顾他们呢? ○ *He's good at looking after himself/his own interests.* 他很会照顾自己[自己的利益]. **look after sth** be responsible for sth 负责某事物: *Our neighbours are looking after the garden while we are away.* 我们不在家的时候, 由邻居照料花园.

look a'head think about what is going to happen in the future 向前看; 为将来打算: *Have you looked ahead to what you'll be doing in five years' time?* 你是否想过五年后你要做些什么?

look at sth (a) examine sth, esp closely 检查某事物(尤指仔细查): *Your ankle is badly swollen; I think the doctor ought to look at it.* 你的脚腕子肿得很厉害, 我认为得请医生看看了. ○ *I haven't had time to look at* (ie read) *your essay yet.* 我还未得空仔细地读你的文章. ○ *I'm taking my car to the garage to be looked at.* 我要把汽车送到修车厂去检修. (b) think about, consider or study sth 考虑或研究某事物: *The implications of the new legislation will need to be looked at.* 新法规的含义需研究一下. ○ *The committee wouldn't even look at my proposal.* 委员会对我的提议甚至不予考虑. (c) view or regard sth 观察或看待某事物: *The Americans look at life differently from the British.* 美国人对生活的看法, 与英国人不同. ○ *Looked at from that point of view, the job becomes easy.* 从那个观点看, 这工作就容易了.

look 'back (on sth) think about (sth in) one's past 回顾自己的过去(的某事物): *look back on one's childhood, past, life* 回顾童年、过去、生活.

look down on sb/sth (*infml* 口) regard sb/sth with contempt; consider sb/sth inferior to oneself; despise sb/sth 鄙视或看不起某人[某事物]; 认为某人[某事物]不如己: *She looks down on people who've never been to university.* 她瞧不起没上过大学的人. ○ *He was looked down on because of his humble background.* 他因家世寒微而被人看不起.

look for sth hope for sth; expect sth 盼望或期待某事物: *We shall be looking for an improvement in your work this term.* 我们期待你这学期功课进步.

look forward to sth/doing sth anticipate sth with pleasure 欣然期待某事物: *look forward to one's holidays, the weekend, a trip to the theatre* 盼望放假、周末、去看戏 ○ *We're so much looking forward to seeing you again.* 我们非常盼望再见到你.

look 'in (on sb/at...) make a short visit to sb's house/a place 短时间探访某人家或到某处: *The doctor will look in again this evening.* 今晚医生再来探视. ○ *Why don't you look in (on me) next time you're in town?* 你下次进城来顺便来串门儿好吗? ○ *I may look in at the party on my way home.* 我回家时可能顺便到聚会处看看.

look into sth investigate or examine sth 调查或观察某事物: *A working party has been set up to look into the problem.* 已成立工作组调查该问题. ○ *His disappearance is being looked into by the police.* 他失踪一事警方正在调查.

look 'on be a spectator at an event or incident; watch sth without taking part in it oneself 观看某事物; 旁观: *Passers-by just looked on as a man was viciously attacked.* 有一男子遭人毒打, 路人只在一旁观看. **look on sb/sth as sb/sth** regard or consider sb/sth to be sb/sth 将某人[某事物]看作他人[他事物]: *She's looked on as the leading authority on the subject.* 她被认为是该问题的主要权威. **look on sb/sth with sth** regard sb/sth in the specified way 以某种态度看待某人[某事物]: *I look on him/his behaviour with contempt.* 我对他不屑一顾[瞧不起他的为人]. ○ *She was always looked on with distrust.* 人家对她总是不信任. ○ *How do people in general look on her?* 人们一般对她怎么看?

look 'out (used in the imperative 用于祈使句) be careful; watch out 小心; 当心: *Look out! There's a car coming.* 小心! 有辆汽车来了. **look out (for sb/sth)** be alert or watchful in order to see, find or be aware of sb/sth 警惕或留心某人[某事物]: *Will you go to the station and look out for Mr Hill?* 你到火车站去迎候希尔先生好吗? ○ *Look out for pickpockets.* 小心扒手. ○ *Police will be looking out for trouble-makers at today's match.* 今天的比赛有警察防备着捣乱分子. ○ *Do look out for spelling mistakes when you check your work.* 你检查作业时要当心拼写错误. **look sth out (for sb/sth)** search for sth and find it 寻出某物: *I must look out some bits and pieces for the church jumble sale.* 我得找些零碎东西捐给教堂作义卖.

look over sth inspect or examine sth 检阅或检查某事物: *We must look over the house before we decide to rent it.* 我们必须先查看一下这所房子再决定租不租. **look sth over** examine sth one by one or part by part 逐一或逐部分检查某事物: *Here's the mail. I've looked it over.* 这批邮件都在这儿. 我已逐一查过了.

look 'round (a) turn one's head in order to see sb/sth 转过头看某人[某物]: *She looked round when she heard the noise behind her.* 她听到身后有声响, 就回过头去看. (b) examine various options or possibilities 审察供选择的事物或可能性: *We're going to look round a bit before deciding where to buy a house.* 我们先到各处查看一下, 再决定买哪里的房子. **look round sth** visit (a place or building) as a tourist or sightseer 参观, 游览(某地或某建筑): *Shall we look round the cathedral this afternoon?* 我们今天下午参观大教堂好吗?

look through sb deliberately ignore sb whom one can see clearly 对某人故意视而不见: *She just looked straight through me.* 她对我连理都不理. **look through sth** examine or read sth quickly 快速检查某事物; 快速阅读某物: *She looked through her notes before the examination.* 考试前她匆匆看了一遍笔记. **look sth through** examine or read sth carefully; examine or read (a number of things) one by one 仔细检查, 逐一审查(某事物): *Always look your work through before handing it in.* 交作业前一定要仔细检查. ○ *He looked the proposals through before approving them.* 他逐一审查了各项建议才予以批准.

look to sb for sth; look to sb to do sth rely on or expect sb to provide sth or do sth 依赖或指望某人提供或做某事物: *We are looking to you for help.* 我们指望你的帮助. ○ *She's regularly looked to for advice.* 人家经常征求她的意见. ○ *Many people are looking to the new government to reduce unemployment.* 很多人都寄望新政府能减少失业的人. **look to sth** make sure that sth is safe or in good condition; be careful about sth 注意或留心某事物: *The country must look to its defences.* 国家必须注意其防御力量. ○ *You should look to your health.* 你应当注意健康.

look 'up (a) raise one's eyes 仰视: *She looked up (from her book) as I entered the room.* 我进屋时, 她(放下书)抬眼看了看. (b) (*infml* 口) (of business, sb's prospects, etc) become better; improve (指商业、某人的前景等)转好, 改善: *Inflation is coming down; unemployment is coming down; things are definitely looking up!* 通货膨胀正在缓解, 失业情形正在改善, 形势确实已好转. **look sb up** (*infml* 口) visit or contact sb, esp after not having seen him for a long time 看望或接触某人(尤指久别后): *Do look me up the next time you're in London.* 你下次到伦敦, 务必来找我. **look sth up** search for (a word or fact) in a dictionary or reference book (在词典或参考书中)查阅(词或资料): *If you want to know how a word is used, look the word up in the Advanced Learner's Dictionary.* 要想了解某词的用法, 查《高阶词典》. ○ *Look up the time of the next train in the timetable.* 查一下火车时刻表中下一趟车的时间. **look up to sb** admire or respect sb 赞赏或尊敬某人: *She has always looked up to her father.* 她一向崇敬父亲.

▷ **look** *interj* (used to make sb listen to sth important that one is saying 用以唤起某人注意听要说的重要事情): *Look, don't you think you're over-reacting slightly?* 喂, 你不认为你的反应有点过火吗?

looker *n* (*infml approv sexist* 口, 褒, 性别偏见) attractive girl or woman 漂亮姑娘; 美女: *She's a real looker!* 她真漂亮! **looker-on** /ˌlʊkərˈɒn; ˌlʊkɚˈɑn/ *n* (*pl* **lookers-on**) /ˌlʊkəzˈɒn; ˌlʊkɚzˈɑn/ person who watches sth but does not take part in it; spectator; onlooker 观者; 旁观者.

-looking (forming compound *adjs* 用以构成复合形容词) having the specified appearance 具有某种外观者: *a ˌstrange-looking ˈplace* ○ *She's not ˌbad-ˈlooking,* ie quite attractive. 她容貌不错.

□ **ˈlook-alike** *n* (often used after a person's name 常用于人名之后) person who has a very similar appearance to sb else 与某人极相似的人: *the Prime Minister's look-alike* 酷似首相的人 ○ [attrib 作定语] *a Marilyn Monroe look-alike contest* 模仿玛丽莲·梦露形象的比赛.

'look-in *n* (idm 习语) **(not) give sb/get/have a 'look-in** (*infml* 口) (not) give sb/have a chance to participate or succeed in sth (不)给某人[有]参加或完成某事物的机会: *She talks so much that the rest of us never get a look-in.* 她说话滔滔不绝, 我们都插不上嘴. ○ *He'd love to play for the school team but he never gets a look-in*, ie is never chosen. 他倒很愿意参加校队, 可是从未有过机会.

'looking-glass *n* (*dated* 旧) mirror 镜子.

'look-out *n* **1** [C] place from which sb watches carefully in order to see an enemy, intruder, etc 岗哨(指处所); 观察所; 瞭望台: [attrib 作定语] *a look-out tower* 瞭望塔. **2** [C] person who watches from such a place 岗哨(指人); 瞭望员: *We posted several look-outs.* 我们部署了几个岗哨. **3** (idm 习语) **be a bad, grim, poor, etc look-out (for sb/sth)** prospects are bad, etc for sb/sth 某人[某事物]的前景不妙等: *It's a bleak look-out for the coal industry as the number of pit closures increases.* 煤井关闭的数目日多, 煤炭工业前景暗淡. **be 'sb's look-out** (*infml* 口) (used to describe an action that is considered irresponsible 用以描述不负责任的行为) be sb's concern or responsibility 为某人的事或责任: *If you want to waste your money, that's your 'own look-out.* 你要乱花钱, 那是你的事. **be on the look-out for sb/sth; keep a look-out for sb/sth** = LOOK OUT FOR SB/STH.

'look-over *n* [sing] brief examination or inspection (简短的)察看或审阅: *Would you give these figures a look-over to check my calculations?* 请审阅一下这些数字, 看看我计算得对不对好吗?

'look-through *n* [sing] act of reading sth quickly 浏览; 粗略看一遍: *I gave her article a quick look-through.* 她的文章我匆匆读过一遍.

NOTE ON USAGE 用法: **1 Look (at)** means to direct one's eyes towards a particular object ☆ **look (at)** 指使视线接触某物体: *Just look at this beautiful present.* 快来看看这件漂亮的礼物吧. ○ *I looked in the cupboard but I couldn't find a clean shirt.* 我看过了衣橱里边, 但找不到干净的衬衫. **2 Gaze (at)** means to keep one's eyes turned in a particular direction for a long time. ☆ **gaze (at)** 指使视线长时间对着某方向. We can gaze at something without looking at it if our eyes are not focussed 假如视线不集中于某目标, 则虽为gaze at却并非look at: *He spent hours gazing into the distance.* 他半天一直凝视着远方. ○ *She sat gazing unhappily out of the window.* 她坐在那儿闷闷不乐地望着窗外. **3 Stare (at)** suggests a long, deliberate, fixed look. ☆ **stare (at)** 指长久的、有意的、目不转睛的看. Staring is more intense than gazing and the eyes are often wide open. stare比gaze精神集中, 常指张目注视. It can be impolite to stare at somebody ☆ stare at某人有时是不礼貌的: *I don't like being stared at.* 我不喜欢人家盯着瞧我. ○ *She stared at me in astonishment.* 她惊奇地注视着我. **4 Peer (at)** means to look very closely and suggests that it is difficult to see well ☆ **peer (at)** 指仔细看, 含很难看清之意: *We peered through the fog at the house numbers.* 我们透过雾气细看门牌号码. ○ *He peered at me through thick glasses.* 他透过厚厚的眼镜片盯看着我. **5 Gawp (at)** means to look at someone or something in a foolish way with the mouth open ☆ **gawp (at)** 指傻头傻脑地张着嘴看某人或某物: *What are you gawping at?* 你在傻盯着什么? ○ *He just sits there gawping at the television all day!* 他整天坐在那儿傻里傻气张着大嘴看电视!

look[2] /lʊk; luk/ *n* **1** [C usu *sing* 通常作单数] act of looking 看; 瞧; 望: *Have/Take a look at this letter.* 看一看这封信. **2** [C usu *sing* 通常作单数] search; inspection 查找; 察看: *I've had a good look (for it) but I can't find it anywhere.* 我好好找了一遍, 但是哪儿都找不到. **3** [C] way of looking; expression or appearance 样子; 表情; 外貌: *a look of pleasure, fear, relief, etc* 喜悦、害怕、欣慰等的神色 ○ *I knew something was wrong: everyone was giving me funny looks*, ie looking at me strangely. 我知道有点不对头, 因为人人都怪模怪样地看着我. ○ *The house has a Mediterranean look.* 这所房子有地中海一带的样子. **4** [C] fashion; style 时式; 风格: *The broad-shouldered look is in this year.* 今年流行宽肩的款式. ○ *They've given the shop a completely new look*, ie redesigned it. 他们把商店装修一新. ○ [attrib 作定语] *I like your new-look hair-style.* 我喜欢你的新发式. **5 looks** [pl] person's appearance 相貌; 仪表: *She's got her father's good looks.* 她有父亲端庄的容貌. ○ *She's starting to lose her looks*, ie become less beautiful. 她姿色逐渐衰减. **6** (idm 习语) **by/from the look of sb/sth** judging by sb's/sth's appearance, etc 据某人[某事物]的外表等判断: *Taxes are going to go up, by the look of it.* 看样子要加税了. **give sb/get a dirty look** ⇨ DIRTY[1]. **like the look/sound of sb/sth** ⇨ LIKE[1]. **take a long look at sth** ⇨ LONG[1].

loom[1] /lu:m; lum/ *n* machine for weaving cloth 织布机.

loom[2] /lu:m; lum/ *v* (**a**) [Ipr, Ip] appear in an indistinct and often threatening way 隐现(常令人生畏): *an enormous shape looming (up) in the distance, out of the darkness, through the mist, etc* 自远处、从黑暗中、透过雾霭等森森然逼临的庞然大物. (**b**) [La, I] (*fig* 比喻) appear important or threatening 显得重要或令人生畏: *The prospect of war loomed large in everyone's mind.* 战事将起的庞大阴影威慑人心. ○ *the looming threat of a strike* 非同小可的罢工威胁.

loony /'lu:nɪ; 'lunɪ/ *n, adj* (*sl* 俚) (person who is) crazy or eccentric; lunatic 疯狂的; 怪诞的; 疯子; 狂人: *He does have some pretty loony ideas.* 他的确有些颇为狂妄的想法.

□ **'loony-bin** *n* (*sl joc offensive* 俚, 谑, 蔑) mental home or hospital 疯人院.

loop 环或环形

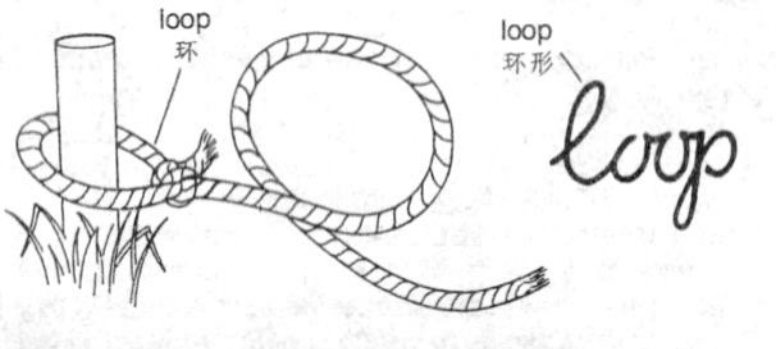

loop /lu:p; lup/ *n* **1** (**a**) shape produced by a curve crossing itself (曲线自绕所成的)环形, 圈: *a double loop like a figure eight* 像8字的双圈 ○ *handwriting with loops on many of the letters* 把很多字母都写得带圈的笔体. (**b**) any path or pattern shaped roughly like this 环形的轨迹或图案: *The plane flew round and round in wide loops.* 飞机翻着大圈一圈一圈地飞行. (**c**) length of string, wire, etc in such a shape, usu fastened at the crossing (绳、金属线等绕成的)环, 结: *a loop of ribbon to carry the package by* 包裹上供手提的缎带套. **2** complete circuit for electric current 环形线路. **3** (*computing* 计) set of instructions carried out repeatedly until some specified condition is satisfied 循环. **4** contraceptive coil 避孕环.

▷ **loop** *v* **1** [I, Tn, Tn·pr, Tn·p] form or bend (sth) into a loop or loops 使(某物)成环或圈: *strings of lanterns looping/looped between the branches of the trees* 绕树穿枝回环成串的灯笼 ○ *looped threads* 打圈的线 ○ *loop (up) a rope* 把绳子挽成圈. **2** [Tn, Tn·pr, Tn·p] fasten or join (sth) with a loop or loops 打环扣系住(某物); 缠绕: *loop the rope round the post* 把绳子缠绕在柱子上 ○ *loop the curtains back* 卷起帘子. **3** (idm 习语) **ˌloop the 'loop** (of an aircraft) fly in a complete circle vertically; (of a pilot) cause an aircraft to do this (指飞行器或驾驶员)翻圈飞行, 翻跟头飞行.

□ **'loop-line** *n* railway or telegraph line that leaves the main line and then joins it again (铁路的)会车线; (电信的)回线, 环形线路.

loop·hole /'lu:phəʊl; 'lupˌhol/ *n* **1** way of escaping a rule, the terms of a contract, etc, esp one provided by vague or careless wording (规则、合同条款等的)漏洞, 空子(尤指措辞含混或不严谨所致者): *A good lawyer can always find a loophole.* 精明的律师专会找到漏洞. **2** narrow vertical opening in the wall of a fort, etc for looking or shooting through, or to let light and air in (要塞等的)观察孔, 枪眼, 透光孔, 换气孔.

loopy /ˈlu:pɪ; ˈlupɪ/ *adj* (*sl* 俚) crazy 疯狂的: *It sounds a pretty loopy idea to me.* 那个主意我觉得有点异想天开.

loose[1] /lu:s; lus/ *adj* (**-r, -st**) **1** freed from control; not tied up 自由的; 不受束缚的; 松开的: *The cows had got out of the field and were (roaming) loose in the road.* 牛从牧场窜出, 在公路上自由自在(到处)走动. ⇨Usage 见所附用法. **2** (that can be) detached from its place; not firmly fixed (能)除下的; 不牢固的: *Be careful with that saucepan — the handle's loose.* 小心那个长把儿锅——把儿可松了. ○ *a rope hanging loose* 松垂的绳子 ○ *a loose tooth, thread, screw* 松动的牙齿、线、螺钉. **3** not fastened together; not held or contained in sth 未系在一起的; 零散的: *loose change*, ie coins carried eg in a pocket 零钱 ○ *nails sold loose by weight*, ie not in a packet 按重量零售的钉子. **4** not organized strictly 组织不严密的: *a loose confederation of states* 松散的邦联 ○ *a loose symphonic structure* 结构松散的交响乐曲. **5** not exact; vague 不精确的; 含混的: *a loose translation* 不准确的译文 ○ *loose thinking* 不严密的思想. **6** (**a**) physically slack; not tense 松弛的; 不紧张的: *loose skin* 松弛的皮肤 ○ *have loose bowels*, ie suffer from diarrhoea 腹泻. (**b**) not tight or constricting 不紧的; 未收紧的: *a loose collar* 宽松的衣领. ⇨Usage 见所附用法. **7** not compact or dense in texture 不致密的; 疏松的: *cloth with a loose weave* 织得稀疏的布 ○ *loose soil* 松土. **8** [esp attrib 尤作定语] (of talk, behaviour, etc) not sufficiently controlled (指言行等)不严谨的, 放荡的: *loose conduct* 放荡的行为 ○ *lead a loose and dissolute life* 过荒淫放荡的生活 ○ *a loose* (ie immoral) *woman* 放荡的女子. **9** (of play in a game) careless and inaccurate (指比赛中的表现)不经心的, 马虎的: *some rather loose bowling*, ie in cricket (板球中)漫不经心的投球. **10** (idm 习语) **all hell broke/was let loose** ⇨ HELL. **at a loose ˈend**; *US* also **at loose ends** having nothing to do; not knowing what to do 无事做; 不知做什么好: *Come and see us if you're at a loose end.* 闲着的时候到我们这儿来坐坐. **break ˈloose (from sb/sth)** escape confinement or restriction 挣脱束缚或限制: *The dog has broken loose*, ie got free from its chain. 那狗挣脱链子跑了. ○ *break loose from tradition* 挣脱传统的束缚. **come/work ˈloose** (of a fastening, bolt, etc) become unfastened or insecure (指扣件、闩等)松开, 不牢固. **cut ˈloose** (*infml* 口) act, speak, etc freely and without restraint (行动、说话等)自由, 无约束: *He really cut loose and told me what he thought of me.* 他单刀直入说出对我的看法. **cut sth/sb loose (from sth)** make sth/sb separate or free 使某事物[某人]分开或摆脱束缚: *cut a boat loose* 砍断缆索放船行 ○ *cut oneself loose from one's family* 摆脱家庭的束缚. **have a loose ˈtongue** be in the habit of talking too freely 说话太随便; 嘴不紧. **have a screw loose** ⇨ SCREW *n*. **let sb/sth loose** release sb/sth 释放某人[某物]: *Don't let that dog loose among the sheep.* 不要放任那条狗在羊群中乱窜. ○ *Just close your eyes and let loose your imagination.* 闭上眼睛, 海阔天空地遐想一番吧. **let sb loose on sth** allow sb to do as he likes with sth 放任某人做某事物: *I daren't let Bill loose on the garden — he'd pull up all the flowers.* 我不敢把比尔放到花园去——他会把花全都拔掉的. **play fast and ˈloose (with sb)** behave dishonestly or deceitfully 玩弄; 欺诈.

▷ **loose-** (in compounds 用以构成复合词) loosely 不受束缚地; 松开地; 不牢固地; 不严密地; 不精确地; 不紧地; 放荡地: *loose-fitting clothes*.

loosely *adv* in a loose manner 不受束缚地; 松开地; 不牢固地; 不严密地; 不精确地; 不紧地; 放荡地: *loosely speaking*, ie in general 笼统地说 ○ *loosely translated* 粗略地翻译.

loose·ness *n* [U].

□ ˈ**loose box** stall in which a horse can move about freely 可供马自由活动的马厩.

ˈ**loose covers** removable covers for chairs, etc (椅子等的)活套.

ˌ**loose-ˈleaf** *adj* [esp attrib 尤作定语] (of a note-book, etc) with pages that can be removed separately and replaced (指笔记本等)活页的.

NOTE ON USAGE 用法: The adjective **loose** has several senses. 形容词 **loose** 有几个义项. Two of these are 1 'not tied up' and 2 'not tight' 其中两项是 1 '未拴住的', 2 '不紧的': *The dogs are loose in the garden.* 狗在花园里都没拴着. ○ *a tight/loose shirt, dress, belt, etc* 紧身的[宽松的]衬衫、连衣裙、皮带等. The verb **loose** (also **unloose**) relates to the first sense and means 'set free' 动词 **loose**(及 **unloose**)与第一义有关, 意为'使不受约束': *The guard loosed the dogs when the burglar alarm went off.* 防盗警报器一响, 警卫就放出了警犬. The verb **loosen** (also **unloosen**) relates to the second sense and means 'make loose' 动词 **loosen**(及 **unloosen**)与第二义有关, 意为'使松开': *After the huge meal he loosened his belt and went to sleep.* 他饱餐一顿以后就松开腰带睡着了. Note that the verb **lose** (*pt* **lost**, *pp* **lost**) is unconnected with **loose** or **loosen**. 注意, 动词 **lose**(过去式 **lost**, 过去分词 **lost**)与 **loose** 或 **loosen** 无关.

loose[2] /lu:s; lus/ *v* **1** [Tn] release (an animal, etc) 释放(动物等): *loose the dogs* 把狗放开. **2** (phr v) **loose (sth) off (at sb/sth)** fire (a gun or missile) 放(枪); 发射(导弹): *Men were loosing off at shadows.* 士兵向黑影射击. ○ *loose off a few bullets (at the enemy)* (向敌人)射出几发枪弹. ⇨Usage at LOOSE[1] 用法见 LOOSE[1].

loose[3] /lu:s; lus/ *n* (idm 习语) **(be) on the ˈloose** enjoying oneself freely 放纵; 放荡.

loosen /ˈlu:sn; ˈlusn̩/ *v* **1** [I, Tn] become or make loose or looser 变松; 使松; 放松: *Can you loosen the lid of this jar?* 你能把这个瓶盖松开吗? ○ *This knot keeps loosening.* 这个结老松开. ○ *medicine to loosen a cough*, ie help bring up the phlegm 止咳祛痰药. ⇨Usage at LOOSE[1] 用法见 LOOSE[1]. **2** (idm 习语) **loosen/tighten the purse-strings** ⇨ PURSE[1]. **loosen sb's ˈtongue** make sb talk freely 使某人无拘束地谈话: *Wine soon loosened his tongue.* 他喝过酒话就多了. **3** (phr v) **loosen (sth) up** (cause sth to) relax (使某事物)放松: *You should loosen up (your muscles) before playing any sport.* 运动之前应先放松(肌肉). ○ *Don't be so nervous — loosen up a bit.* 别那么紧张——放松一点.

loot /lu:t; lut/ *n* [U] **1** goods (esp private property) taken from an enemy in war, or stolen by thieves 战利品, 掠夺品(尤指私人财物); 赃物. **2** (*infml* 口) money; wealth 钱; 财物.

▷ **loot** *v* (**a**) [I] carry off loot 抢劫; 劫掠: *soldiers killing and looting wherever they went* 到处屠杀劫掠的士兵. (**b**) [Tn] take (sth) as loot; take loot from (buildings, etc left unprotected, eg after a violent event) 掠夺(某物); 抢劫(建筑物等): *The mob looted many shops in the area.* 暴徒在该地抢劫了许多商店. Cf 参看 PILLAGE, PLUNDER.

looter *n*: *Looters will be shot on sight.* 打劫者格杀勿论.

lop /lɒp; lɑp/ *v* (**-pp-**) **1** [Tn] cut branches, twigs, etc off (a tree) 剪去, 砍去(树)枝等. **2** (phr v) **lop sth off/away** remove (branches, twigs, etc) from a tree, etc by cutting (从树上等)剪除, 砍掉(树枝等): *He had his arm lopped off by an electric saw.* 他让电锯给锯掉了一条胳膊.

lope /ləʊp; lop/ *v* [I, Ip] run fairly fast with long bounding strides 跳跃着大步跑: *The tiger loped off into the jungle.* 那老虎跑进丛林中去了.

▷ **lope** *n* (usu *sing* 通常作单数) long bounding step or stride 大步; 阔步: *move at a steady lope* 迈着稳健的大步行走.

lop-eared /ˌlɒp ˈɪəd; ˈlɑpˈɪrd/ *adj* having drooping ears 有垂耳的: *a ˌlop-eared ˈrabbit* 垂耳兔.

lop·sided /ˌlɒp ˈsaɪdɪd; ˈlɑpˈsaɪdɪd/ *adj* with one side lower, smaller, etc than the other; unevenly balanced 一侧比另侧低、小等的; 两侧不平衡的; 不匀称的: *a ˌlopsided ˈgrin* 歪着嘴笑.

lo·qua·cious /ləˈkweɪʃəs; loˈkweʃəs/ *adj* (*fml* 文) fond of talking; talkative 爱说话的; 多话的. ▷ **lo·qua·ciously** *adv*. **lo·qua·cious·ness**, **lo·qua·city** /ləˈkwæsətɪ; loˈkwæsətɪ/ *ns* [U].

lo·quat /ˈləʊkwɒt, ˈlɒkwæt; ˈlokwɑt/ *n* [C] (**a**) ornamental tree, common in China and Japan, having small yellow edible fruit 枇杷. (**b**) fruit of this tree 枇杷果.

lord /lɔ:d; lɔrd/ *n* **1** [C] master; male ruler 君主; 王: *our sovereign lord the king* 国王陛下. **2** [sing] (**a**) **the Lord** God; Christ 上帝; 耶稣基督. (**b**) **Our Lord** Christ 主; 耶稣基督. **3** (**a**) [C] nobleman (男性)贵族: *She married a lord.* 她嫁给了一个贵族. (**b**) **the Lords** [sing or pl *v*] (*Brit*) (members of) the House of Lords (HOUSE[1] 4)

上议院; 上议院议员: *The Lords is/are debating the issue.* 上议院正在辩论这事. **4 Lord** [C] (*Brit*) (**a**) title of certain high officials 阁下, 大人(对某些高级官员的尊称): *the Lords of the Treasury* 财政部诸大臣 ○ *the First Lord of the Admiralty* 海军大臣 ○ *the Lord Mayor of London* 伦敦市长. (**b**) title prefixed to the names of peers and barons 勋爵(用在贵族和男爵的姓名之前): *Lord Derby*, ie the title of the Earl of Derby 德比勋爵(德比伯爵的尊称). (**c**) **My Lord** respectful form of address to certain noblemen, judges and bishops 大人, 阁下(对某些贵族、法官、主教等的直接尊称). **5** (idm 习语) **drunk as a lord** ⇨ DRUNK. **good 'Lord** *interj* (expressing surprise, etc 表示惊讶等). **live like a lord** ⇨ LIVE². **one's ˌlord and 'master** (*joc* 谑) one's husband 丈夫; 夫君. **'Lord knows** nobody can say 谁也说不好; 天知道: *Lord knows where he dug up that dreadful story.* 天知道他那讨厌的故事是从哪里找来的. **year of our Lord** ⇨ YEAR.

▷ **lord** *v* (phr v) **lord it over sb** behave in a superior or domineering way to sb 对某人发威或专横: *He likes to lord it over the junior staff.* 他喜欢对下级职员逞威风.

□ **the ˌlord of the 'manor** (in the Middle Ages) master from whom men held land and to whom they owed service (中世纪时的)庄园领主.

the 'Lord's Day Sunday 主日; 星期日.

the ˌLord's 'Prayer the prayer taught by Christ to his disciples, beginning 'Our Father' 主祷文.

ˌLords 'spiritual (*Brit*) bishops and archbishops in the House of Lords 上议院中的神职议员(主教和大主教).

ˌLords 'temporal (*Brit*) noblemen in the House of Lords who inherit their titles or are given them for life 上议院中的世俗议员(世袭贵族或终身贵族).

lordly /ˈlɔːdlɪ; ˋlɔrdlɪ/ *adj* (**-ier, -iest**) **1** haughty; insolent in a superior way 傲慢的; 神气活现的: *dismiss people with a lordly gesture* 颐指气使让大家离去. **2** suitable for a lord; magnificent 贵族气派的; 堂皇的: *a lordly mansion* 堂皇的宅第. ▷ **lord·li·ness** *n* [U].

lord·ship /ˈlɔːdʃɪp; ˋlɔrdʃɪp/ *n* **1** [C] title used in speaking to or about a man of the rank of 'Lord' 大人, 阁下, 爵爷, 老爷(称呼或提到有爵位身分的人时用的敬称): *his/your lordship* 爵爷大人 ○ *their lordships* 老爷 ○ (*joc* 谑) *Would your lordship like a cup of tea?* 阁下是否用茶? **2** [U] **~ (over sb/sth)** (*dated fml* 旧, 文) authority; rule 权威; 统治.

lore /lɔː(r); lɔr/ *n* [U] knowledge and traditions about a subject or possessed by a particular group of people (某学科的或某部分人的)学问和传统: *'bird lore* 对鸟类的知识 ○ *'folklore* 民俗学 ○ *'gypsy lore* 吉卜赛人的学问和传统 ○ *'Celtic lore* 凯尔特人的传说.

lor·gnette /lɔːˈnjet; lɔrnˋjɛt/ *n* pair of eye-glasses held to the eyes on a long handle 长柄眼镜.

lorn /lɔːn; lɔrn/ *adj* (*arch or joc* 古或谑) lonely and sad 孤寂而凄凉的.

ARTICULATED LORRY
铰接车

lorry (*also esp US* **truck**)
卡车

lorry /ˈlɒrɪ; *US* ˈlɔːrɪ; ˋlɔrɪ/ *n* (*Brit*) (also *esp US* **truck**) large strong motor vehicle for transporting goods, soldiers, etc by road 卡车: *an army lorry* 军用卡车 ○ [attrib 作定语] *a lorry driver* 卡车司机. ⇨ illus 见插图.

lose /luːz; luz/ *v* (*pt, pp* **lost** /lɒst; *US* lɔːst; lɔst/) **1** [Tn] have (sth/sb) taken away from one by accident, misfortune, old age, death, etc 失去, 丧失, 损失(某事物[某人]): *lose all one's money at cards* 玩纸牌把钱输光 ○ *lose a leg in an industrial accident* 在一次工业事故中失去一条腿 ○ *lose one's hair, teeth, good looks*, ie as a result of ageing 失去头发、牙齿、美貌(如因年老) ○ *He lost both his sons* (ie They were killed) *in the war.* 他的两个儿子都在战争中死了. ○ *She's just lost her husband*, ie He has died recently. 她的丈夫刚去世. ○ *lose one's job* 失业. **2** [Tn] no longer have or maintain (esp a moral or mental quality) 不再有(尤指道德或精神的素质): *lose one's confidence, composure, etc* 失去信心、稳定的情绪等 ○ *The train was losing speed.* 火车渐渐减速. ○ *lose interest in sth/sb*, ie cease to be interested or attracted 对某事物[某人]失去兴趣 ○ *He's lost ten pounds in weight.* 他体重减了十磅. ○ *lose one's balance/equilibrium* 失去平衡[均势] ○ *She's losing colour*, ie becoming pale. 她脸色渐渐苍白了. ○ *I warn you, I'm rapidly losing patience*, ie becoming impatient. 我警告你, 我可没那么多耐性了. **3** [Tn] become unable to find 遗失; 失落: *I've lost my keys.* 我的钥匙丢了. ○ *The books seem to be lost/to have got lost.* 那些书好像不见了. ○ *She lost her husband in the crowd.* 她和她丈夫在人群中走散了. **4** [Tn] (**a**) fail to obtain or catch (sth) 得不到或未捉住(某事物): *His words were lost* (ie could not be heard) *in the applause.* 他的话让掌声淹没了. (**b**) (*infml* 口) be no longer understood by (sb) 使(某人)弄不懂: *I'm afraid you've lost me.* 对不起, 我不明白了. **5** [Tn] (*infml* 口) escape from (sb/sth); elude 逃避(某人[某事物]); 躲避: *We managed to lose our pursuers in the darkness.* 我们趁黑摆脱了追踪的人. ○ *You see that car following us? Well, lose it!* 看见那辆跟着咱们的汽车了吗? 来, 甩掉它! **6** (**a**) [I, Ipr, Tn, Tn·pr] **~ (sth) (to sb)** be defeated; fail to win (a contest, a lawsuit, an argument, etc) 输; 失败; 未赢得(竞赛、官司、辩论等): *It's only the second time the team has lost (a match) this season.* 那仅仅是本赛季该队第二次失利而已. ○ *We lost to a stronger side.* 我们输给了实力更强的一方. ○ *They won the battle but lost the war.* 他们赢了这次战斗, 但输了这场战争. ○ *lose a motion*, ie fail to carry it in a debate 动议未通过. (**b**) [Tn, Tn·pr] **~ sth (to sth/sb)** have sth taken away (by sth/sb) 丧失某事物(由某事物[某人]获得): *Railways have lost much of their business to the bus companies.* 铁路公司许多生意让汽车公司夺走了. **7** [Tn] have to give up or forfeit (sth) 被迫放弃或失去(某事物): *The Labour candidate lost his deposit*, ie did not obtain the minimum number of votes necessary in an election. 那个工党候选人失去了老本(未得到最低获选票数). ○ *lose one's no-claim bonus*, eg by making an insurance claim following an accident 失去保险金无索偿优惠(如因发生事故后曾索赔). **8** [Tn] waste (time or an opportunity) 浪费(时间或机会): *We lost twenty minutes through having to change a tyre.* 我们因为换轮胎损失了二十分钟. ○ *There's no time to lose*, ie We must hurry. 没有时间了(必须赶快). **9** (**a**) [I, Ipr, Tn, Tn·pr] **~ (sth) (on sth/by doing sth)** become poorer (as a result of sth) (由某事物导致)亏损, 变差: *We lost (a lot) on that deal.* 我们那笔生意受到(很大)损失. ○ *Poetry always loses (something) in translation.* 诗歌一经翻译总有所失. ○ *You will lose nothing by telling the truth.* 说实话并不吃亏. (**b**) [Dn·n] cause (sb) to be without or forfeit (sth) 使(某人)失去或丧失(某事物): *His carelessness lost him the job.* 他因粗心大意而丢了工作. ○ *Such behaviour will lose you everyone's sympathy.* 你这种表现大家就不会同情你了. **10** [I, Tn] (of a watch or clock) go too slowly by (an amount of time) (指钟表)慢(若干时间): *A good watch neither gains nor loses.* 好表不快也不慢. ○ *This clock loses two minutes* (ie becomes two minutes behind the correct time) *a day.* 这钟一天慢两分钟. **11** (idm 习语) **fight a losing battle** ⇨ FIGHT¹. **find/lose favour with sb/in sb's eyes** ⇨ FAVOUR¹. **find/lose one's voice/tongue** ⇨ FIND¹. **give/lose ground** ⇨ GROUND¹. **heads I win, tails you lose** ⇨ HEAD¹. **keep/lose one's balance** ⇨ BALANCE¹. **keep/lose one's cool** ⇨ COOL¹. **keep/lose count** ⇨ COUNT². **keep/lose one's temper** ⇨ TEMPER¹. **keep/lose track of sb/sth** ⇨ TRACK. **lose all 'reason** become irrational or illogical 失去理智; 不讲道理: *He lost all reason and* *started abusing his opponent.* 他蛮不讲理，大骂对手. **lose one's ˈbearings** become lost or confused 蒙头转向；不知所措；惶惑. **lose one's ˈbreath** pant for breath, eg after running hard 气喘咻咻；上气不接下气. **lose ˈcaste (with/among sb)** lose status or respect 丧失地位；为人轻视. **lose ˈcourage** become depressed or fearful; despair 丧失勇气；沮丧；害怕；绝望. **lose ˈface** be humiliated; lose credit or reputation 丢脸；受屈辱；丧失声誉. **lose one's grip (on sth)** be unable to understand or control a situation, etc 无法掌握或控制局势等：*I think the Prime Minister may be losing his grip.* 我认为首相可能控制不住局面了. **lose one's ˈhead** become confused or over-excited 昏了头；张皇失措；冲动：*Don't lose your head — keep calm!* 别惊慌失措的——沉住气! **lose ˈheart** become discouraged 泄气；灰心. **lose one's ˈheart (to sb/sth)** fall in love 爱上；钟情于. **lose one's ˈlife** be killed 丧生；遇害. **lose one's ˈmarbles** (*sl* 俚) go mad; no longer behave sensibly or rationally 发疯；丧失理智；行事无理性. **lose/waste no time in doing sth** ⇨ TIME[1]. **lose one's ˈplace** (in a book, etc) be unable to find the point at which one stopped reading (在书中等)忘记上次读到的地方. **lose one's ˈrag** (*infml* 口) express one's anger, impatience, etc in an uncontrolled way 发脾气；按捺不住. **lose one's ˈseat** (**a**) have the place where one was sitting taken by another person 座位被占. (**b**) (of a Member of Parliament) fail to be re-elected (指议员)未获连选. **lose one's ˈshirt** (*infml* 口) lose all one's money, esp as a result of gambling or speculation 输光所有的钱，赔光本钱(尤指赌博或投机)：*He lost his shirt on the horses.* 他赌马把钱输光了. **lose sight of sb/sth** (**a**) no longer be able to see sb/sth 看不见某人[某物]：*lose sight of land* 看不见陆地. (**b**) overlook sth; fail to consider sth 忽略或未考虑某事物：*We must not lose sight of the fact that...* 我们不应忽视的事实是... ○ *Our original aims have been lost sight of.* 我们原来的目标已无影无踪了. **lose the thread (of sth)** be unable to follow an argument, story, etc 失去(议论故事等的)头绪. **lose one's ˈtouch** no longer have the abilities, etc that once made one successful 丧失以前的能力等. **lose touch (with sb/sth)** no longer be in contact with sb/sth 失去和某人[某事物]的联系：*I've lost touch with all my old friends.* 我和所有的老朋友都失去了联系. ○ *Let us not lose touch with reality.* 我们不要脱离现实. **lose one's ˈway** become lost 迷路：*We lost our way in the dark.* 我们在黑暗中迷了路. **lose/take off weight** ⇨ WEIGHT. **a losing ˈbattle/ˈgame** struggle/contest in which defeat seems certain 不能获胜的争斗[比赛]：*It's a losing battle trying to persuade Henry to take more exercise.* 要说服亨利多运动纯属徒劳. **not lose sleep/lose no sleep over sth** not worry unduly about sth 不为某事物操心：*It's not worth losing sleep over.* 不值得多虑. **win/lose by a neck** ⇨ NECK. **win or lose** ⇨ WIN. **a winning/losing streak** ⇨ STREAK *n*. **win/lose the toss** ⇨ TOSS *n*. **12** (phr v) **lose oneself in sth** become totally absorbed in sth 专心致志于某事物：*I soon lost myself in the excitement of the film.* 影片中的刺激情节很快就把我吸引住了. **lose ˈout (on sth)** (*infml* 口) be unsuccessful; suffer loss 不成功；受损失：*If things go wrong I'm the one who'll lose out, not you.* 事情若有差错，受损的是我，不是你. **lose out to sb/sth** (*infml* 口) be overcome or replaced by sb/sth 被某人[某事物]战胜或取代：*Has the cinema lost out to TV?* 电影是不是让电视给取代了? ⇨Usage at LOOSE[1] 用法见 LOOSE[1].

▷ **loser** *n* person who loses or is defeated, esp habitually 受损失者，输者，失败者(尤指一贯如此者)：*a good/bad loser*, ie one who accepts defeat well/badly 输得起[输不起]的人 ○ *a born loser*, ie sb who regularly fails in life 天生的庸才.

loss /lɒs; *US* lɔːs; lɒs/ *n* **1** [U] act, instance or process of losing 丧失；遗失；损失：*loss of blood, health, prestige, money* 丧失血液、健康、威信、钱财 ○ *The loss* (ie death) *of his wife was a great blow to him.* 他妻子去世对他打击很大. ○ *without (any) loss of time* (毫)不失时 ○ *a temporary loss of power* 暂时失势 ○ *The loss of this contract would be very serious.* 未能签成这一合同关系重大. **2** [C] (**a**) person or thing lost 损失的人或物：*heat loss* 热量损失 ○ *The enemy suffered heavy losses*, ie many men killed, etc or much equipment destroyed. 敌军损失惨重. ○ *The car was so badly damaged that it had to be abandoned as a total loss.* 汽车损坏严重，只好彻底报废. (**b**) money lost in a business deal, etc (生意等的)亏损的钱：*made a loss on the deal* 这笔交易赔了钱 ○ *sell sth at a loss*, ie for less than it cost 亏本出售某物 ○ *suffer losses in the export market* 在出口市场中亏损. **3** [sing] suffering caused by losing sb/sth; disadvantage (因失去某人[某事物]而致的)损失，不利：*Her departure is a great loss to the orchestra.* 她离去是管弦乐队的一大损失. ○ *It's no loss*, ie Its loss does not matter. 那算不上损失. **4** (idm 习语) **at a ˈloss** not knowing what to do or say; perplexed or puzzled 不知如何是好；茫然；困惑：*It left him at a complete loss (for words).* 这使他完全茫然(而语塞)了. ○ *I'm at a loss what to do next.* 我不知道下一步怎么办. **cut one's ˈlosses** abandon a scheme that causes loss before one loses too much 中止某计划以免损失更大. **a dead loss** ⇨ DEAD.

□ ˌ**loss-ˈleader** *n* (*commerce* 商) article sold at a loss to attract customers to buy other goods (为招徕顾客)亏本出售的商品.

lost[1] *pt, pp* of LOSE.

lost[2] /lɒst; *US* lɔːst; lɒst/ *adj* **1** that cannot be found or recovered 失去的；丧失的；遗失的；无法恢复的：*recalling her lost youth* 回忆她失去的青春 ○ *The art of good conversation seems lost.* 高雅谈吐的艺术似已不复存在. ○ *lost tribes of Africa* 非洲消失的部落. **2** [esp pred 尤作表语] (*fig* 比喻) confused or puzzled 不知所措；困惑：*I got rather lost trying to find the station.* 我找车站找得晕头转向. ○ *We would be totally lost without your help.* 我们没有你的帮助就一筹莫展. ○ *They spoke so quickly I just got lost.* 他们说得那么快，我都糊涂了. **3** (idm 习语) ˌ**all is not ˈlost** (*saying* 谚) there is still some hope of success, recovery, etc 尚有一线(成功、恢复等的)希望. **be lost in sth** be absorbed in sth 专注于某事物：*lost in thought/wonder/admiration* 想得入神[不胜诧异/欣赏入迷]. **be lost on sb** fail to influence sb 对某人不起作用或无影响：*Our hints were not lost on him*, ie He noticed them and acted accordingly. 我们给他的暗示他已心领神会. **be lost to sth** be no longer affected or influenced by sth 不再受某事物的影响；将某事物置之度外：*When he listens to music he's lost to the world*, ie unaware of what is happening around him. 他一听音乐便把整个世界忘之脑后. **get ˈlost** (*sl* 俚) go away 滚开：*Tell him to get lost.* 叫他滚. **give sb up for ˈlost** no longer expect sb to be found alive 认为某人无生还的可能. **a lost ˈcause** project, ideal, etc that has failed or is certain to fail 已失败的或无法实现的计划、理想等. **make up for lost ˈtime** hurry, etc in order to compensate for time wasted earlier 加紧、加快等以补偿失去的时间：*He didn't have a girl-friend till he was 18, but now he's making up for lost time*, ie he has had many girl-friends since then. 他 18 岁才交女友，现在是在弥补前失了(已经交过很多女友). **there's little/no love lost between A and B** ⇨ LOVE[1].

□ ˌ**lost ˈproperty** possessions mislaid in a public place and not yet claimed by their owners 无人认领的失物：[attrib 作定语] *a* ˌ*lost-ˈproperty office* 失物招领处.

lot[1] /lɒt; lɑt/ *n* [Gp] (*infml* 口) **the ˈlot, all the ˈlot, the whole ˈlot** the whole number or amount (of sb/sth) 全体；全部；总量：*That's the lot!* 就这些! ○ *Take all the lot if you want.* 你想要就全部拿去. ○ *The whole lot was/were discovered in a field.* 那些全是在一田地发现的. ○ *I want the lot* (ie all) *of you to get out of my house.* 我要你们全滚出我家. ○ *He expects a good salary, a company car, first-class air travel — the lot.* 他想要可观的薪水、公司的汽车、头等的机票——一应俱全.

lot[2] /lɒt; lɑt/ *pron* **a lot, lots** (*infml* 口) large number or amount 大量；许多：*Have some more pie, there's lots left.* 再吃点馅儿饼吧，还多着呢. ○ *'How many do you want?' 'A lot/lots.'* '你要多少?' '要很多.'

□ **a lot of** *det* (also *infml* 口语亦作 **lots of**) a large number or amount of (sb/sth) 大量；许多：*What a lot of presents!* 多么多的礼物哇! ○ *I haven't got a lot of time.* 我时间不多了. ○ *There was lots of money in the safe.* 保险柜里有很多钱. ○ *A lot of people were queuing for the film.* 许多人排队等着看那部电影. ○ *I saw quite a lot of her* (ie I saw her quite often) *during the holidays.* 假期中我见过她很多次. ⇨Usage at MUCH[1] 用法见 MUCH[1].

lot³ /lɒt; lɑt/ *adv* (*infml* 口) **1 a lot, lots** (used with *adjs* and *advs* 与形容词和副词连用) considerably 很; 非常: *I'm feeling a lot better today.* 我今天身体好多了. ○ *I eat lots less than I used to.* 我吃得比从前少得多. **2 a lot** (used with *vs* 与动词连用) (**a**) a great amount 极; 很; 非常: *I care about you a lot.* 我对你很关心. (**b**) often 常常: *I play tennis quite a lot in the summer.* 夏天我经常打网球. Cf 参看 A FAT LOT (FAT¹ 7).

lot⁴ /lɒt; lɑt/ *n* **1 (a)** [C] item or number of items sold, esp at an auction sale (出售物品的)项目, 批(尤指拍卖物): *Lot 46: six chairs.* 第46项: 椅子六把. **(b)** [CGp] group, collection or set of people or things of the same kind (同类人或物的)组, 批, 套, 群: *Nobody in the first lot of applicants was suitable for the job.* 在第一批求职者中无人适合做那份工作. ○ *I have several lots of essays to mark this weekend.* 本周末我有几份文章要批改. ○ *This next lot of washing is the last.* 下一批是最后要洗的东西了. **2** [C] (**a**) piece of land 地皮; 土地. (**b**) (*esp US*) area used for a particular purpose (作某用途的)场地: *a 'parking lot*, ie a car-park 停车场 ○ *a vacant 'lot*, ie a building site 一块空地皮(建筑场地) ○ *a 'film lot*, ie a film studio and the land around it 电影摄影场. **3** [sing] person's fortune, destiny or share 命运; 运气: *Her lot has been a hard one.* 她命苦. ○ *I would not want to share his lot.* 我可不愿和他同甘共苦. **4** [U] method of deciding sth or selecting sb/sth by chance 抽签法; 抓阄儿法: *She was chosen by lot to represent us.* 她抽中签当我们的代表. **5** (idm 习语) **a bad egg/lot** ⇨ EGG. **cast/draw 'lots (for sth)** make a selection by lot 抽签, 抓阄儿(决定某事物): *They drew lots for the right to go first.* 他们抓阄儿决定谁先走. **fall to sb's lot to do sth** (*fml* 文) become sb's task or responsibility 成为某人的任务或责任. **throw in one's lot with sb** decide to join sb and share his fortunes 决心与某人共命运.

loth = LOATH.

lo·tion /ˈləʊʃn; ˈloʃən/ *n* [C, U] liquid medicine or cosmetic for use on the skin (外用的)药液; (化妆用的)润肤液: *soothing lotions for insect bites* 虫咬止痛药水 ○ *a bottle of cleansing lotion for the face* 一瓶洁面液.

lot·tery /ˈlɒtərɪ; ˈlɑtərɪ/ *n* **1** [C] way of raising money by selling numbered tickets and giving prizes to the holders of numbers selected at random (发行彩票)抽彩给奖(筹款法): [attrib 作定语] *a 'lottery ticket* 彩票. Cf 参看 DRAW¹ 1, RAFFLE. **2** [sing] (*fig* 比喻) thing whose success, outcome, etc is determined by luck 碰运气的事: *Some people think that marriage is a lottery.* 有些人认为婚姻是缘分.

lotto /ˈlɒtəʊ; ˈlɑto/ *n* [U] game of chance similar to bingo but with the numbers drawn by the players instead of being called 洛托(一种赌博游戏).

lo·tus /ˈləʊtəs; ˈlotəs/ *n* (*pl* **~es**) **1** type of tropical water-lily 莲: [attrib 作定语] *lotus flowers/blooms* 莲花 ○ *lotus blossom* 莲花开花期. **2** (in Greek legends) fruit that makes those who eat it lazily and dreamily contented (希腊神话中的)落柘枣(食后产生懒怠与梦幻的满足感).

□ **'lotus position** way of sitting cross-legged, used when meditating, in yoga, etc 打坐(瑜伽等盘膝端坐的姿势).

loud /laʊd; laʊd/ *adj* (**-er, -est**) **1** producing much noise; easily heard 喧闹的; 响亮的: *loud voices, screams, laughs, etc* 宏亮的嗓音、喊声、笑声等 ○ *That music's too loud; please turn it down.* 那音乐太吵人了; 请把音量调低些. **2** (*derog* 贬) (of colours, behaviour, etc) forcing people to notice them/it (指颜色、行为等)引人注目的, 刺眼的: *That dress is a bit loud* (ie gaudy), *isn't it?* 那件连衣裙有点花哨吧? ○ *His manner is too loud.* 他那样子太招摇. **3** (idm 习语) **be loud in one's praise(s) (of sb/sth)** praise sb/sth very highly 盛赞某人[某事物].

▷ **loud** *adv* (**-er, -est**) **1** (used esp with *talk, sing, laugh,* etc 尤与talk、sing、laugh等动词连用) in a loud manner 喧闹地; 响亮地: *laugh loud and long* 大笑不已 ○ *Speak louder — I can't hear you.* 大点声说 —— 我听不见. ○ *Their baby screamed loudest of all.* 他们的孩子哭叫起来声音最大. **2** (idm 习语) **actions speak louder than words** ⇨ ACTION. **for crying out loud** ⇨ CRY¹. **ˌout 'loud** aloud 出声地; 大声地: *Don't whisper; if you've got something to say, say it out loud.* 别叽咕了, 有什么要说的大声说吧.

loudly *adv*: *a dog barking loudly* 大声吠叫的狗 ○ *loudly dressed* 穿得花哨的.

loud·ness *n* [U]

loudhailer
(*US* **bullhorn**)
便携式扩音器

□ **ˌloud'hailer** *n* (*US* **bullhorn**) portable electronic device for amplifying the sound of sb's voice so that it can be heard at a great distance 便携式扩音器; 电子喇叭: *use a loudhailer to address the crowd* 用电子喇叭向人群讲话.

'loud-mouth *n* (*infml* 口) person who talks too loudly or too much, esp boastingly 大声说话的人; 多嘴的人; (尤指)爱吹牛的人. **'loud-mouthed** *adj*.

ˌloud'speaker (also **speaker**) *n* part of a radio, record-player, etc that changes electrical impulses into audible sounds 扩音器; 扬声器.

lough /lɒk, lɒx; lɑk, lɑx/ *n* (*Irish* 爱尔兰) lake or long inlet of the sea 湖; 海湾. Cf 参看 LOCH.

lounge /laʊndʒ; laʊndʒ/ *v* [I, Ipr, Ip] sit or stand in a lazy way, esp leaning against sth; loll 懒洋洋地坐或立(尤指倚靠某物): *lounge about/around (the house)* (在家里)发懒 ○ *lounging at street corners* 在街头闲荡.

▷ **lounge** *n* **1** waiting-room at an airport, etc (机场等的)等候室: *the departure lounge* 候机室. **2** public sitting-room in a hotel, club, etc (旅馆、俱乐部等的)休息室. **3** (*Brit*) sitting-room, with comfortable chairs, in a private house (私宅中有沙发等的)起居室. **4** = LOUNGE BAR.

loun·ger *n* lazy or idle person 懒惰闲散的人; 游手好闲者.

□ **'lounge bar** (*Brit*) (*US* **sa'loon bar**) smarter, and usu more expensive, bar in a pub, hotel, etc 豪华酒吧. Cf 参看 PUBLIC BAR (PUBLIC).

'lounge-suit *n* (*Brit*) man's suit with matching jacket and trousers, worn esp in offices and on more formal occasions (男子的)成套西服(尤指在办公室和较正式场合中穿的).

lour (also **lower**) /ˈlaʊə(r); laʊr/ *v* [I, Ipr] **~ (at/on sb/sth)** (**a**) look threatening; frown 作怒相; 皱眉: *louring looks* 怫然不悦的神情. (**b**) (of the sky, clouds, etc) look dark, as if threatening a storm (指天气、云等)变阴暗(似预示暴风雨).

louse /laʊs; laʊs/ *n* **1** (*pl* **lice** /laɪs; laɪs/) (**a**) small insect living on the bodies of animals and human beings, esp in dirty conditions 虱. (**b**) similar insect living on plants (靠植物生活的)小昆虫. **2** (*pl* **~s**) (*sl* 俚) contemptible person 可鄙的人.

▷ **louse** *v* (phr v) **louse sth up** (*infml* 口) spoil sth; ruin sth 搞糟或弄坏某事物: *You've really loused things up this time.* 这回你可真把事情搞糟了.

lousy /ˈlaʊzɪ; ˈlaʊzɪ/ *adj* (**-ier, -iest**) **1** infested with lice 多虱的. **2** (*infml* 口) very bad or ill 极坏的; 极不适的: *a lousy holiday* 极糟的假日 ○ *I feel lousy.* 我觉得很不舒服. **3** [pred 作表语] **~ with sth/sb** (*sl* 俚) having more than enough of sth/sb 大量; 多: *In August the place is lousy with tourists.* 八月里这地方游客多如牛毛.

lout /laʊt; laʊt/ *n* clumsy vulgar man or youth with bad manners 粗鄙的男子或青年.

▷ **lout·ish** *adj* of or like a lout (似)粗鄙之人的: *loutish behaviour* 粗鄙的行为.

louvre (also **lou·ver**) /ˈluːvə(r); ˈluvɚ/ *n* (**a**) one of a set of fixed or movable strips of wood, metal, etc arranged to let air in while keeping light or rain out (一条)百叶窗板. (**b**) set of such strips inside a supporting frame (一套)百叶窗板. ▷ **louvred** (also **lou·vered**) *adj*: *a louvred door* 百叶门.

lov·able /ˈlʌvəbl; ˋlʌvəbl/ *adj* easy to love; worthy of love 可爱的; 惹人爱的; 值得爱的: *a lovable puppy* 可爱的小狗 ○ *He's such a lovable rascal!* 他真是个讨人喜欢的小坏蛋!

love[1] /lʌv; lʌv/ *n* **1** [U] warm liking or affection; affectionate devotion 喜爱; 热爱; 钟爱: *a mother's love for her children* 母亲对其子女的爱 ○ *love of (one's) country*, ie patriotism 对祖国的热爱 ○ *She has a great love for animals.* 她酷爱动物. ○ *He shows little love towards her.* 他没怎么表现出喜爱她. **2** [U] sexual affection or passion 性爱; 恋爱; 爱情: *marry for love, not money* 为爱情而非为金钱结婚 ○ *Their love has cooled*, ie is no longer strong. 他们的爱情冷却了. **3** [U] (*religion* 宗) (in Christianity) God's benevolence towards mankind (基督教中)(上帝的)博爱, 慈爱. **4** [U, sing] strong liking for sth 酷爱某事物: *a love of learning, adventure, music* 酷爱学习、冒险、音乐. **5** [C] person who is loved; sweetheart 恋人; 情人; 爱人: *Take care, my love.* 小心, 亲爱的. ○ *one of my former loves* 我从前的一个情人 ○ (*joc* 谑) *with his lady love*, ie his girlfriend or wife 带着他的爱人(女友或妻). **6** [C] (*infml* 口) delightful person or thing 招人喜爱的人或物: *What a love her daughter is!* 她女儿多么可爱呀! ○ *Isn't this hat a perfect love?* 这顶帽子挺可爱吧? **7** [C] (*Brit infml* 口) (form of address used by a man to a woman or child (not necessarily a friend), or by a woman to a person of either sex 男人用以称呼(不一定相识的)女子或儿童; 女子用以称呼他人(男女均可)): *Mind your head, love!* 喂, 小心你的头! **8** [U] (in tennis) no score; nil (网球)零分: *love all*, ie neither player or pair has scored 零比零 ○ *The score in the game on Court One is thirty-love.* 一号球场上的比分是三十比零. **9** (idm 习语) **be in love (with sb)** feel affection and desire (for sb) 热恋着(某人): *They're very much in love (with each other).* 他们(彼此)在热恋中. ○ *I'm madly in love with her.* 我爱她爱得发狂. **be in love with sth** be very fond of sth 喜爱某事物: *a city in love with its own past* 热爱自身传统的城市 ○ *He's in love with the sound of his own voice*, ie talks too much. 他就喜欢自己的声音(太爱说话). **cupboard love** ⇨ CUPBOARD. **fall in love (with sb)** feel a sudden strong attraction for sb 突然爱上某人. **(just) for ˈlove/for the ˈlove of sth** without payment or other reward 出于爱好(不计报酬): *They're all volunteers, doing it just for the love of the thing.* 他们都是自愿的, 完全是因为喜欢做而做的. **for the ˌlove of ˈGod, etc (a)** (expressing surprise, dismay, etc 用以表示惊奇、惊慌等): *For the love of God, not another bill!* 看在上帝的分上, 别再来帐单了! **(b)** (used when urging sb to do sth 用于催促某人做某事物): *For the love of Mike let's get out of here!* 看在上帝的分上, 咱们离开这鬼地方吧! **ˌgive/ˌsend sb one's ˈlove** give/send an affectionate greeting to sb 向某人致意: *Please give your sister my love.* 请代我向令妹致意. ○ *My parents send their love.* 我父母问您好. **a labour of love** ⇨ LABOUR[1]. **the ˌlove of sb's ˈlife (a)** person's most dearly loved sweetheart 最理想的爱人: *I think I've met the love of my life.* 我认为我已找到理想的爱人了. **(b)** person's favourite possession, activity, etc 最喜爱的东西、活动等: *Sailing is the love of his life.* 帆船运动是他最喜爱的活动. **make love (to sb) (a)** have sexual intercourse 做爱; 性交: *He refused to make love before they were married.* 他决不在婚前发生性行为. **(b)** (*dated* 旧) behave amorously (towards sb), esp by being specially attentive (向某人)表示爱情; (尤指)献殷勤. **not for ˌlove or ˈmoney** not by any means 无论如何; 不管怎样: *We couldn't find a hotel room for love or money.* 我们怎么也找不到一间旅馆客房. **there's little/no ˈlove lost between A and B** they dislike each other 他们彼此厌恶: *There's never been much love lost between her and her sister.* 她和妹妹一向互相嫌恶.

▷ **love·less** *adj* without love 没有爱的: *a loveless marriage* 没有爱情的婚姻.

□ **ˈlove-affair** *n* romantic or sexual relationship between two people who are in love (两人相爱的)风流韵事, 性关系.

ˈlove-bird *n* **1** small brightly-coloured parrot that seems to show great affection for its mate 情鸟; 情侣鹦鹉. **2** (usu *pl* 通常作复数) (*infml* 口) person who is very much in love 热恋中的人: *Come along, you two love-birds!* 快点吧, 你们这一对恩爱情侣!

ˈlove-child *n* (*euph* 婉) child of unmarried parents 私生子.

love-ˈhate relationship intense emotional relationship involving feelings of both love and hate 爱恨交加的强烈感情关系.

ˈlove-letter *n* letter between two people expressing the love of one for the other 情书.

ˈlovelorn /-lɔːn; -ˌlɔrn/ *adj* unhappy because one's love is not returned 失恋的.

ˈlove-making *n* [U] sexual play between two lovers, esp including sexual intercourse 做爱; (尤指)性交.

ˈlove-match *n* marriage made because the two people are in love with each other 爱情的结合; 恋爱结婚.

ˈlove-potion (also **ˈlove-philtre**) *n* (in stories) magic drink supposed to make the person who drinks it fall in love (故事中)(饮后可产生爱情的)春药.

ˈlove-seat *n* small sofa in the shape of an S, with two seats facing in opposite directions 情人椅(供两人对坐的S形小沙发).

ˈlovesick *adj* weak or ill because of being in love 受爱情折磨而憔悴的; 害相思病的.

ˈlove-song *n* song expressing or describing love 情歌; 恋歌.

ˈlove-story *n* story or novel in which the main theme is romantic love 爱情小说; 恋爱故事.

love[2] /lʌv; lʌv/ *v* **1** [Tn] have a strong affection or deep tender feelings for (sb/sth) 爱, 热爱(某人[某事物]): *love one's parents, country, wife* 爱父母、国家、妻子 ○ *love God*, ie worship Him 崇拜上帝. **2** [Tn, Tt, Tnt, Tg, Tsg] like (sb/sth) greatly; take pleasure in 喜欢(某人[某事物]); 喜好: *She's always loved horses.* 她一向喜爱马匹. ○ *He loves his pipe*, ie smoking it. 他爱抽烟斗. ○ *Children love to play/playing.* 儿童喜欢玩耍. ○ *'Will you come?' 'I'd love to!'* '你来吗?' '我很乐意!' ○ *We'd love you to come to dinner.* 我们很愿意请你来吃饭. ○ *I love him reading to me in bed.* 我喜欢在床上听他给我读点什么. **3** (idm 习语) **ˌlove ˈme, ˌlove my ˈdog** (*saying* 谚) if one loves sb, one will or should love everyone and everything associated with him 爱吾及犬; 爱屋及乌.

lovely /ˈlʌvlɪ; ˋlʌvlɪ/ *adj* (**-ier**, **-iest**) **1** beautiful; attractive 可爱的; 美丽的; 动人的: *a lovely view, voice, woman* 可爱的景色、嗓音、女子 ○ *lovely hair, weather, music* 秀发、可爱的天气、动人的音乐. **2** (*infml* 口) enjoyable; pleasant 令人愉快的; 快乐的: *a lovely dinner, time, story* 可口的饭菜、过得愉快、有趣的故事 ○ *It's lovely and warm* (ie pleasant because warm) *in here.* 这儿的天气温暖宜人. **3** (idm 习语) **everything in the garden is lovely** ⇨ GARDEN.

▷ **love·li·ness** *n* [U].

lovely *n* (*infml* 口) pretty woman 美女: *a couple of television lovelies* 电视中的两个美女.

lover /ˈlʌvə(r); ˋlʌvɚ/ *n* **1** [C] partner (usu a man) in a sexual relationship outside marriage (婚外恋的)伴侣, 情人(通常指男性): *They say he used to be her lover.* 据说他曾是她的婚外情人. ○ *She's taken a new lover.* 她有了新的外遇情人. Cf 参看 MISTRESS 4. **2 lovers** [pl] two people who are in love or having a sexual relationship though not married 一对情侣(恋爱中的或未婚而有性关系的): *young lovers strolling in the park* 在公园漫步的年轻情侣 ○ *They met on holiday and soon became lovers.* 他们在度假时结识, 不久便成了情侣. **3** [C] (often in compounds 常用以构成复合词) person who likes or enjoys sth specified 爱好者; 热爱者: *a lover of music, horses, good wine* 爱好音乐、马匹、美酒的人 ○ *art-lovers* 艺术爱好者.

lov·ing /ˈlʌvɪŋ; ˋlʌvɪŋ/ *adj* [esp attrib 尤作定语] feeling or showing love 爱的; 表示爱意的; 亲爱的: *a loving friend* 亲爱的朋友 ○ *loving words* 体贴的话. ▷ **lov·ingly** *adv*.

□ **ˈloving-cup** *n* large wine-cup passed from person to person at a banquet, etc, so that everyone may drink from it 爱杯(宴席上供轮流饮酒的大杯).

ˌloving-ˈkindness *n* [U] (*arch* 古) tender consideration or care 慈爱; 爱护.

low[1] /ləʊ; lo/ *adj* (**-er**, **-est**) **1** not high or tall; not extending far upwards 低的; 矮的: *a low wall, ceiling, tree* 矮的墙、天花板、树 ○ *a low range of hills* 低矮的冈峦 ○ *flying at a low altitude* 在低空飞行 ○ *The sun is low* *in the sky.* 太阳很低. ○ *a low brow,* ie with hair-line and eyebrows close together 低前额(发线与眼眉靠得近者) ○ *a dress low in the neck/a low-necked dress,* ie one leaving the upper part of the breasts and much of the shoulders bare 领口低的连衣裙(袒胸露臂的). **2** below the usual or normal level, amount, intensity, etc 低于通常或正常水平、数量、强度等的: *low wages, taxes, prices, etc* 低的工资、税率、价格等 ○ *low temperature* 低温 ○ *low pressure,* eg of the atmosphere, of gas or water piped to houses, of blood 低压(如气压、煤气或自来水压、血压) ○ *low cloud* 低云 ○ *The surrounding land is low* (ie not far above sea-level) *and marshy.* 周围的地低洼而多沼泽. ○ *a low-density housing estate,* ie one with comparatively few houses in the space available 低密度的住宅区(房屋较少) ○ *The reservoir was very low after the long drought.* 久旱之后水库的水位很低了. **3** ranking below others in importance or quality (在重要性或质量上)低于或劣于其他的: *upper and lower classes of society* 社会的上下阶层 ○ *of low birth* 出身低贱的 ○ *low forms of life,* ie creatures having a relatively simple structure 低等的生物 ○ *low-grade fuel* 低级燃料. **4** vulgar or coarse 鄙俗的; 粗俗的: *low manners, tastes, etc* 粗俗的举止、低级趣味 ○ *He keeps low company.* 他结交庸俗的朋友. ○ *low comedy,* ie a crude form of farce 低级的喜剧 ○ *low cunning,* ie immoral and selfish cleverness 下流的诡计. **5** (of sound or a voice) not high in pitch; deep (指声音)不尖的, 深沉的: *A man's voice is usually lower than a woman's.* 男子的嗓音通常比女子的低. **6** not loud 小声的; 低沉的: *a low rumble of thunder* 低沉的隆隆雷声 ○ *Keep your voice low.* 要小声说话. **7** lacking in vigour; feeble or depressed 无生气的; 衰弱的; 情绪低的: *in a low state of health* 身体虚弱 ○ *feel low/in low spirits/low-spirited* 觉得情绪低落. **8** (of a gear) allowing a slower speed of a vehicle in relation to its engine speed (指变速器)低挡的: *You'll need to change into a lower gear when going up this hill.* 上这座山时得换低挡. **9** (idm 习语) **at a low ˈebb** in a poor state; worse than usual 处于低潮; 情况不佳; 比平时差: *Her spirits were at a very low ebb,* ie She was very depressed. 她的情绪极度低落. **be/run ˈlow (on sth)** (of supplies) be/become almost exhausted; have almost exhausted the supplies (of sth) (指供应品)几乎耗尽: *The petrol's running low.* 汽油快用完了. ○ *We're (running) low on petrol.* 我们的汽油不多了. **a high/low profile** ⇨ PROFILE. **lay sb/sth ˈlow (a)** bring sb/sth into a flat or horizontal position 使某人[某物]倒下或平卧: *He laid his opponent low with a single punch.* 他一拳就把对手打倒在地. **(b)** weaken or destroy 使衰弱或毁灭: *The whole family was laid low by/with* (ie was ill and in bed with) *flu.* 全家都因流感病倒在床上.

▷ **ˈlow·er·most** *adj* lowest 最低的; 最下的.

low·ness *n* [U].

□ **ˌLow ˈChurch** section of the Church of England that gives little importance to ritual and the authority of bishops and priests 低教会派(英国国教的一支, 不注重仪式及主教、牧师的权威地位): *My family is Low Church.* 我家属低教会派. **ˌLow-ˈChurchman** *n* member or supporter of this 低教会派成员.

ˌlow-ˈclass *adj* of poor quality or low social class 低级的; 低等的; 质量低劣的; 社会地位卑下的: *ˌlow-class ˈmerchandise* 低级的商品.

ˌlower ˈcase (in printing) small letters, not capitals (印刷)小楷字母, 小写字体: [attrib 作定语] *ˌlower-case ˈlettering* 小写体字.

ˌLower ˈChamber (also **ˌLower ˈHouse**) larger, usu elected, branch of a legislative assembly (eg the House of Commons in Britain, the House of Representatives in the US) 下议院(如英国的下议院, 美国的众议院).

the ˌlower ˈdeck (in the Navy) petty officers and lower ranks (not the officers) (海军中)水兵和低级军官.

ˌlow ˈfrequency (*abbr* 缩写 **LF**) radio frequency of 30 to 300 kilohertz 低频(无线电波段中 30-300 千赫范围内的频率).

ˌlow-ˈkey (also **ˌlow-ˈkeyed**) *adj* not intense or emotional; restrained 低调的; 不强烈的; 克制的; 有节制的: *The wedding was a very ˌlow-key afˈfair.* 婚礼办得毫不招摇.

lowland /ˈləʊlənd; ˈlolənd/ *n* (usu *pl* 通常作复数) low-lying land 低地. **ˈlowlander** /-ləndə(r); -ləndɚ/ *n* **(a)** person who lives in a lowland area 低地人. **(b)** (also **ˈLowlander**) native of the Scottish Lowlands 苏格兰低地人.

ˌlow-level ˈlanguage computer language using instructions that correspond closely to the operations which the computer will perform 低级语言(近于计算机作业指令的).

ˌlow-ˈpitched *adj* (of sounds) low in pitch[3](3a) (指声音)低调的, 轻的, 低沉的: *a ˌlow-pitched ˈvoice* 低沉的嗓音.

ˈlow season time of year when fewest visitors come to a resort, etc (旅游胜地等的)淡季.

ˌlow ˈtide (also **ˌlow ˈwater**) **(a)** tide when at its lowest level 低潮; 低水位. **(b)** time when this occurs 低潮期; 低水位期. **ˌlow-ˈwater mark (a)** lowest point reached by the water at low tide 低潮线; 低水位线. **(b)** (*fig* 比喻) lowest or worst point 最低点; 最坏程度: *the low-water mark of the company's fortunes* 公司业绩的最低点.

low[2] /ləʊ; lo/ *adv* **(-er, -est) 1** in, at or to a low level or position 在或向低的水平或位置: *aim, shoot, throw, etc low* 向低处瞄准、射击、投掷等 ○ *bow low to the Queen* 向女王深深鞠躬 ○ *play low,* ie play a card with a low value 打出低点数的牌 ○ *The simplest way to succeed in business is to buy low* (ie at low prices) *and sell high.* 做生意成功最简单的途径就是贱买贵卖. **2** not at a high pitch; quietly 低调地; 低声地; 悄声地: *I can't sing as low as that.* 我唱不了那么低的调. ○ *Speak lower or she'll hear you!* 低点声说, 要不她就听见了! **3** (idm 习语) **lie low** ⇨ LIE[2]. **be brought ˈlow** be reduced in health, wealth or position (健康、财富或地位等的)下降, 恶化: *Many rich families were brought low by the financial crisis.* 很多富户都因那次金融危机而家道中落. **high and low** ⇨ HIGH[3]. **stoop so low** ⇨ STOOP.

□ **ˌlow-ˈborn** *adj* of humble birth 出身低微的: *a ˌlow-born ˈleader* 出身卑贱的领袖.

ˌlow-ˈlying *adj* near to the ground or to sea-level 接近地面或海平面的; 低洼的: *fog in ˌlow-lying ˈareas* 低洼地区的雾.

ˌlow-ˈpaid *adj* paid low wages 工资低的: *They are among the ˌlowest-paid (ˌworkers) in the ˈcountry.* 他们在该国是属于低工资的(工作人员).

ˌlow-ˈrise *adj* [attrib 作定语] (of a building) having few storeys (指建筑物)低的, 层数少的: *ˌlow-rise deˈvelopments* 低矮的新建住宅区.

low[3] /ləʊ; lo/ *n* **1** low level or figure 低水平; 低数目: *The (value of the) pound has fallen to a new low against the dollar,* ie is worth less in exchange for dollars than ever before. 英镑兑换美元的比值已跌到新的低点. **2** area of low barometric pressure 低气压区: *another low moving in from the Atlantic* 从大西洋来的另一个低气压区.

low[4] /ləʊ; lo/ *n* deep sound made by cattle 牛叫声; 哞.

▷ **low** *v* [I] make this sound; moo 作牛叫声; 发哞声.

low·brow /ˈləʊbraʊ; ˈloˌbraʊ/ *adj* (*esp derog* 尤作贬义) not cultured or intellectual 无文化修养的; 无知识的; 智力低的: *a lowbrow programme, discussion, person* 粗俗的节目、议论、人.

▷ **low·brow** *n* lowbrow person 无文化修养的人. Cf 参看 HIGHBROW, MIDDLE-BROW (MIDDLE).

low-down /ˈləʊdaʊn; ˈloˈdaʊn/ *adj* [attrib 作定语] (*infml* 口) dishonourable; underhand 卑鄙的; 不名誉的; 偷偷摸摸的: *That was a pretty low-down trick to play!* 玩弄那套伎俩真可耻!

▷ **low-down** *n* (idm 习语) **give sb/get the low-down (on sb/sth)** (*infml* 口) tell sb/be told the true facts (about sb/sth) 告诉某人[获悉](有关某人[某事物]的)真相: *Give me the low-down on her divorce.* 把她离婚的实情告诉我吧.

lower[1] /ˈləʊə(r); ˈloɚ/ *v* **1** [Tn, Tn·pr] **(a)** let or bring (sb/sth) down 让, 使(某人[某事物])降低, 降下: *lower supplies to the stranded men,* eg from a helicopter 把给受困者的救济品放下去(如从直升飞机上) ○ *lower the sails, a flag, a window* 落帆、降旗、放下窗 ○ *He lowered his gun slowly.* 他慢慢把枪放下. ○ *lower one's eyes (to the ground),* ie look down 垂下眼睛(看地面) ○ (*infml* 口) *He lowered* (ie drank) *four pints of beer in an hour.* 他一小时喝下四品脱啤酒. **(b)** make less high 使减低; 放低: *lower the roof of a house* 把房子的屋顶改低 ○

lower (the height of) the ceiling 把天花板(的高度)降低. **2** [I, Ipr, Tn, Tn·pr] (cause sth to) become less in amount or quantity (使某事物)减少: *Stocks generally lowered in value.* 股票普遍下跌. ○ *lower one's voice to a whisper* 把声音降到耳语那么低 ○ *A poor diet lowers one's resistance to illness.* 饮食不佳会减低对疾病的抵抗力. **3** [Tn, Tn·pr] **~ oneself (by doing sth)** (*infml* 口) reduce one's dignity or self-respect 降低身分或自尊: *Don't lower yourself by asking 'him for help.* 不要向他求助以免降低身分. ○ *Speak to her? I'd never lower myself.* 跟她说话? 我可不自贬人格. **4** (idm 习语) **raise/lower one's sights** ⇨ SIGHT¹. **5** (phr v) **lower (sth) away** (*nautical* 海) lower (a boat, sail, etc) 放下(小船); 降下(船帆).

lower² = LOUR.

lowly /ˈləʊlɪ; ˋlolɪ/ *adj* (**-ier, -iest**) (*dated* 旧) of humble rank or condition 地位低的; 卑微的. ▷ **low·li·ness** *n* [U].

loyal /ˈlɔɪəl; ˋlɔɪəl/ *adj* **~ (to sb/sth)** true and faithful 忠诚的; 忠贞的: *remain loyal to one's principles* 信守自己的原则 ○ *a loyal supporter of the Labour Party* 工党的忠实拥护者.

▷ **loy·al·ist** *n* person who is loyal, esp to the established ruler or government during a revolt 忠诚分子(尤指在叛乱中忠于原统治者或政府者): [attrib 作定语] *loyalist troops* 忠于政府的部队.

loy·ally /ˈlɔɪəlɪ; ˋlɔɪəlɪ/ *adv*.

loy·alty /ˈlɔɪəltɪ; ˋlɔɪəltɪ/ *n* (**a**) [U] being true and faithful; loyal behaviour 忠诚; 忠诚行为: *swear an oath of loyalty to the King* 向国王宣誓效忠 ○ *Can I count on your loyalty?* 你对我的忠诚能让我信得过吗? (**b**) [C often *pl* 常作复数] bond that makes a person faithful to sb/sth 向某人[某事物]效忠的义务或约束: *We all have a loyalty to the company.* 我们对公司都有效忠的义务. ○ *a case of divided loyalties*, ie of being loyal to two different and often conflicting causes, etc 两面效忠(对常为对立双方皆效忠).

loz·enge /ˈlɒzɪndʒ; ˋlɑzɪndʒ/ *n* **1** four-sided figure in the shape of a diamond 菱形; 菱形物. **2** small tablet of flavoured sugar, esp one containing medicine, which is dissolved in the mouth 糖锭; (尤指口含的)锭剂: *a throat lozenge*, ie for a sore throat 润喉片.

LP /ˌel ˈpiː; ˌɛl ˋpi/ *abbr* 缩写 = long-playing (record): *a collection of LPs* 一批密纹唱片. Cf 参看 EP, SINGLE *n* 5.

L-plate /ˈel pleɪt; ˋɛl plet/ *n* (in Britain) sign with a large red letter L, fixed to a motor vehicle that is being driven by a learner-driver (英国)L字牌(机动车所附红色L字牌, 以示该车为见习驾驶员驾驶者). Cf 参看 L *abbr* 缩写 2.

LSD /ˌel es ˈdiː; ˌɛl ɛs ˋdi/ *abbr* 缩写 = **1** (also *sl* 俚语作 **acid**) lysergic acid diethylamide, a powerful drug that produces hallucinations 麦角酰二乙基酰胺(一种迷幻药). **2** (also **£sd**) (*dated Brit infml* 旧, 口) (in former British currency) pounds, shillings and pence (Latin *librae, solidi, denarii*); money (旧时英国货币)镑, 先令, 便士(源自拉丁文 *librae*、*solidi*、*denarii*); 钱: *I'm rather short of LSD — can you lend me some?* 我缺点儿钱, 你能借给我一些吗?

LST /ˌel es ˈtiː; ˌɛl ɛs ˋti/ *abbr* 缩写 = (*US*) Local Standard Time 地方标准时.

Lt *abbr* 缩写 = Lieutenant: *Lt-Cdr/-Col/-Gen/-Gov* 海军少校[陆军或海军陆战队中校/陆军或海军陆战队中将/副总督].

LTA /ˌel tiː ˈeɪ; ˌɛl ti ˋe/ *abbr* 缩写 = (*Brit*) Lawn Tennis Association 草地网球协会.

Ltd *abbr* 缩写 = (*Brit*) Limited (ie 'limited liability company', now used only by private companies): *Canning Bros Ltd* 坎宁·布罗斯有限公司 ○ *Pearce and Co Ltd* 皮尔斯股分有限公司. Cf 参看 INC, PLC.

lub·ber /ˈlʌbə(r); ˋlʌbɚ/ *n* (*dated* 旧) big clumsy stupid boy or man 高大而蠢笨的男子. ▷ **lub·berly** *adj*.

lub·ric·ate /ˈluːbrɪkeɪt; ˋlubrɪˌket/ *v* [Tn] put oil or grease on or in (machinery, etc) so that it moves easily 给(机械等)加润滑油: *lubricate the wheels, bearings, hinges, etc* 给轮子、轴承、合叶等加润滑油 ○ (*fig* 比喻) *My throat needs lubricating*, ie with a drink. 我需要润润嗓子了.

▷ **lub·ric·ant** /ˈluːbrɪkənt; ˋlubrɪkənt/ *n* [U, C] substance that lubricates 润滑剂.

lub·rica·tion /ˌluːbrɪˈkeɪʃn; ˌlubrɪˋkeʃən/ *n* [C, U] (action of) lubricating or being lubricated 加润滑油; 润滑.

lub·ri·cious /luːˈbrɪʃəs; luˋbrɪʃəs/ *adj* (*fml* 文) showing an unpleasant enjoyment of sexual matters; lewd 淫荡的; 猥亵的; 下流的.

lu·cerne /luːˈsɜːn; luˋsɝn/ *n* (*US* **alfalfa**) plant similar to clover, used for feeding animals 苜蓿.

lu·cid /ˈluːsɪd; ˋlusɪd/ *adj* **1** clearly expressed; easy to understand 表达清楚的; 易懂的: *a lucid explanation* 明白的解释 ○ *His style is very lucid.* 他的文体很明畅. **2** clear in one's mind; sane 头脑清晰的; 清醒的: *lucid intervals*, ie periods of sanity during mental illness 清醒期(精神病发作的间歇期). ▷ **lu·cid·ity** /luːˈsɪdətɪ; luˋsɪdətɪ/ *n* [U]. **lu·cidly** *adv*: *lucidly explained* 解释得清楚.

luck /lʌk; lʌk/ *n* [U] **1** chance, esp thought of as a force that brings good or bad fortune 运气; 造化: *have good, poor, hard* (ie bad), *little, bad, etc luck* 运气好、不好、背、欠佳、坏等. **2** good fortune 好运; 幸运: *I hope this charm will bring you luck.* 希望这个符咒会给你带来好运. ○ *I always carry one for luck.* 为讨吉利我老是带着一个. ○ *I had the luck to find him at home.* 我真幸运, 找他时他正在家. ○ *Any luck with* (ie Did you manage to get) *the job?* 找工作的事运气好吗? ○ *Our luck has run out*, ie has ended. 我们的运气到头了. **3** (idm 习语) **as (good/ill) luck would have it** fortunately/unfortunately 幸而[不幸]; 碰巧[不巧]. **(what) bad, rotten, etc 'luck!** (used to show sympathy 用以表示同情). **be bad/hard 'luck (on sb)** be unfortunate 不幸; 倒霉: *It was very hard luck (on you) to get ill on your holiday.* (你)假期得病真倒霉. **be ˌdown on one's 'luck** (*infml* 口) have a period of misfortune 倒霉的时候; 背运之时. **beginner's luck** ⇨ BEGINNER (BEGIN). **be in/out of 'luck** be fortunate/unfortunate 走运[不走运]. **better luck next time** ⇨ BETTER¹. **the devil's own luck** ⇨ DEVIL¹. **ˌgood 'luck (to sb)** may sb be fortunate and successful 祝某人好运和顺利: *Good luck in your exams!* 祝你考得好! **ˌjust one's 'luck** (indicating that sth unfortunate or inconvenient has happened to one, as usual 用以表示运气总是那么坏): *It was just my luck to go to the play on the day the star was ill.* 我总是这么倒霉, 去看戏那天偏巧明星病了. **one's 'luck is in** one is lucky 走运; 交好运. **the luck of the draw** the way in which chance decides what some people become, do, get, etc and others not 一个人一个命(有的人有运气, 有的人没有运气). **the luck of the game** the element of luck, as opposed to skill, that operates in a game, an activity, etc 手气(支配游戏、活动等的运气, 并非技巧). **ˌno such 'luck** unfortunately not 没有那份儿运气. **push one's luck** ⇨ PUSH². **take pot luck** ⇨ POT¹. **ˌtough 'luck** (**a**) (used to show sympathy 用以表示同情). (**b**) (*ironic* 反语) (used to show that one does not really care about sb's misfortune 用以表示对某人的不幸并不真正关心). **try one's luck/fortune** ⇨ TRY¹. **worse luck** ⇨ WORSE.

▷ **luck** *v* (phr v) **luck out** (*US infml* 口) be lucky or successful 走运; 交好运; 侥幸成功.

luck·less *adj* unlucky 运气不好的; 不幸的.

lucky /ˈlʌkɪ; ˋlʌkɪ/ *adj* (**-ier, -iest**) **1** having, bringing or resulting from good luck 幸运的; 有好运的; 带来好运的: *You're very lucky to be alive after that accident.* 你大难不死可真幸运. ○ *It's lucky she's still here.* 她还在这里, 真是万幸. ○ *a lucky charm* 吉符 ○ *Seven is my lucky number.* 七是我的幸运数字. ○ *a lucky guess* 侥幸猜中 ○ *a lucky break*, ie a piece of good fortune 一次好运 ○ *It's my, your, etc lucky day*, ie one on which I am, you are, etc having good fortune. 这一天是我的、你的…幸运日子. **2** (idm 习语) **strike lucky** ⇨ STRIKE². **thank one's lucky stars** ⇨ THANK. **you'll be lucky; you should be so lucky** (*ironic catchphrase* 反语, 警语) what you expect, wish for, etc is very unlikely to happen 你有那份儿运气. ▷ **luck·ily** /ˈlʌkɪlɪ; ˋlʌkɪlɪ/ *adv*: *I arrived late but luckily the meeting had been delayed.* 我迟到了, 幸而会议推迟了.

□ **ˌlucky 'dip** (*Brit*) barrel, etc containing small prizes of various values which people pick out at random for a payment, hoping to get sth that is worth more than they have paid 幸运袋, 摸彩袋(袋中装有价值不等的奖品,

付钱即可摸取).

luc·rat·ive /ˈlu:krətɪv; ˋlukrətɪv/ *adj* producing much money; profitable 赚钱的; 可获利的: *a lucrative business* 赚钱的买卖. ▷ **luc·rat·ively** *adv*. **luc·rat·ive·ness** *n* [U].

lucre /ˈlu:kə(r); ˋlukɚ/ *n* [U] **1** (*derog* 贬) profit or money-making, as a motive for doing sth 利益; 利润; 赚钱: *the lure of lucre* 利益的诱惑. **2** (idm 习语) **filthy lucre** ⇨ FILTHY.

Lud·dite /ˈlʌdaɪt; ˋlʌdaɪt/ *n, adj* (*derog* 贬) (person) opposed to change or improvement in working methods, machines, etc in industry 在工业中反对改进操作方法、改进机器等的(人).

lu·dic·rous /ˈlu:dɪkrəs; ˋludɪkrəs/ *adj* causing laughter; ridiculous; absurd 可笑的; 荒唐的; 愚蠢的: *a ludicrous idea* 荒谬的想法. ▷ **lu·dic·rously** *adv*: *His trousers were ludicrously short.* 他的裤子短得可笑. **lu·dic·rous·ness** *n* [U].

ludo /ˈlu:dəʊ; ˋludo/ *n* [U] simple game played with dice and counters on a special board 卢多(在特制板上用色子及筹码玩的简单游戏).

luff /lʌf; lʌf/ *v* [I, Tn] (*nautical* 海) steer (a sailing boat or ship) so that its front moves nearer to the direction from which the wind is blowing 转动(船)使船首抢风航行.

luffa = LOOFAH.

lug[1] /lʌg; lʌg/ *v* **(-gg-)** [Tn, Tn·pr, Tn·p] drag or carry (sth) with great effort 用力拉或拖(某物): *lugging a heavy suitcase up the stairs* 拖着沉重的衣箱上楼 ○ (*fig infml* 比喻, 口) *She had to lug the kids around/about/along all day.* 她得整天带着孩子. ⇨Usage at CARRY 用法见CARRY.

lug[2] /lʌg; lʌg/ *n* **1** projecting part of an object, by which it may be carried or fixed in place 把柄; 把手. **2** (also **ˈlug-hole**) (*Brit sl* 俚) ear 耳朵.

luge /lu:ʒ; luʒ/ *n* small toboggan for one person 单人雪橇.

luggage 行李

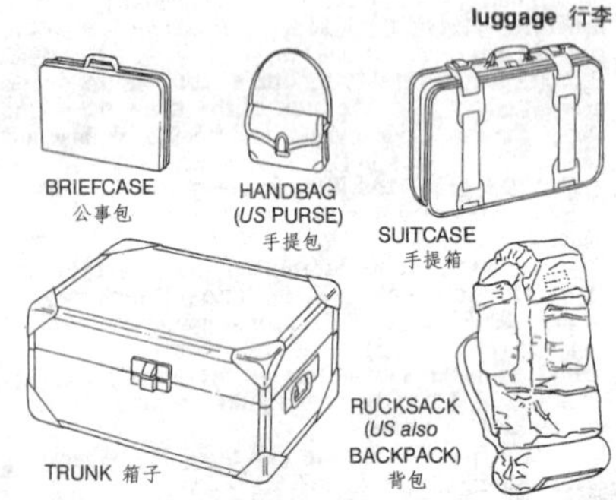

lug·gage /ˈlʌgɪdʒ; ˋlʌgɪdʒ/ (*US* **baggage**) *n* [U] bags, suitcases, etc containing sb's belongings and taken on a journey 行李: *six pieces of luggage* 六件行李 ○ *clear one's luggage through customs* 把行李交海关查验通过 ○ *Have you any hand-luggage?* 你有手提的行李吗? ⇨ illus 见插图.

□ **ˈluggage-rack** *n* **(a)** shelf for luggage above the seats in a railway carriage, coach, etc (火车或长途汽车等的)行李架. **(b)** = ROOF-RACK (ROOF).

ˈluggage-van *n* (*US* **baggage car**) carriage for passengers' luggage on a railway train (火车的)行李车.

lug·ger /ˈlʌgə(r); ˋlʌgɚ/ *n* (*nautical* 海) small ship with one or more four-cornered sails (有四角纵帆的)小帆船.

lu·gu·bri·ous /ləˈgu:brɪəs; luˋgubrɪəs/ *adj* dismal; mournful 阴郁的; 悲哀的: *Why are you looking so lugubrious?* 你怎么看上去这样忧郁? ▷ **lu·gu·bri·ously** *adv*. **lu·gu·bri·ous·ness** *n* [U].

lug·worm /ˈlʌgwɜ:m; ˋlʌg,wɝm/ *n* large worm living in the sand on the sea-shore, used as bait by fishermen 沙蠋(用作钓饵).

luke·warm /ˌlu:kˈwɔ:m; ˋlukˋwɔrm/ *adj* **1** (of liquids) only slightly warm; tepid (指液体)不冷不热的, 微温的: *Heat the milk until it is just lukewarm.* 把奶热一下, 温温就行. **2 ~ (about sb/sth)** (*fig* 比喻) not eager or enthusiastic 不热烈的; 冷淡的: *get a ˌlukewarm reˈception* 受冷漠的接待 ○ *Her love had grown lukewarm.* 她的爱情已淡薄.

lull /lʌl; lʌl/ *v* **1** [Tn, Tn·pr] **(a) ~ sb/sth (to sth)** make (a person or an animal) quiet or less active; soothe sb/sth 使(人或动物)安静, 活动减弱; 抚慰某人; 缓和某事物: *lull a baby to sleep*, ie by rocking it or singing to it 哄孩子睡觉. **(b) ~ sb/sth (into sth)** calm (sb, sb's fears, etc), esp by deception 使(某人)镇静, 消除(某人的恐惧感等)(尤指藉哄骗): *lull his suspicions* 哄他释疑 ○ *lulled us into a false sense of security* 哄骗我们使我们以为很安全. **2** [I] (of a storm or noise) become quiet; lessen (指风暴或噪音)平息, 停息, 减弱: *By dawn the wind had lulled.* 到黎明时风已停了.

▷ **lull** *n* (usu *sing* 通常作单数) interval of quiet or inactivity 间歇; 稍息; 稍止: *a lull before the storm, in the conversation, during the battle* 暴风雨前、谈话中、战斗期间的沉寂.

lul·laby /ˈlʌləbaɪ; ˋlʌlə,baɪ/ *n* soft gentle song sung to make a child go to sleep 催眠曲.

lum·bago /lʌmˈbeɪgəʊ; lʌmˋbego/ *n* [U] pain in the muscles of the lower part of the back, caused by rheumatism 腰痛(风湿所致的).

lum·bar /ˈlʌmbə(r); ˋlʌmbɚ/ *adj* [usu attrib 通常作定语] of the lower part of the back 腰的; 腰部的: *lumbar pains* 腰痛 ○ *the lumbar regions* 腰部.

□ **ˈlumbar puncture** (*medical* 医) removing fluid from the base of the spine by means of a hollow needle 腰椎穿刺.

lum·ber[1] /ˈlʌmbə(r); ˋlʌmbɚ/ *n* [U] **1** (*esp Brit*) unwanted pieces of furniture, etc that are stored away or take up space (无用的)旧家具等. **2** (*esp US*) = TIMBER 1.

▷ **lum·ber** *v* **1 (a)** [esp passive 尤用于被动语态: Tn, Tn·pr] **~ sb (with sb/sth)** give as a burden or an inconvenience to sb 给某人负担或不便: *He got lumbered with the job of finding accommodation for the whole team.* 他有个苦差事, 是要为全队物色食宿的处所. ○ *It looks as though we're going to be lumbered with Uncle Bill for the whole weekend.* 看来我们整个周末都得陪着比尔大叔了. **(b)** [esp passive 尤用于被动语态: Tn, Tn·pr, Tn·p] **~ sth (up) (with sth)** fill up (space) inconveniently 零乱堆满(空间): *a room lumbered up with junk* 堆满了无用之物的房间 ○ *a mind lumbered with useless facts* 充满无用资料的头脑. **2** [I, Tn] (*esp US*) cut and prepare (timber) for use 伐木制材.

□ **ˈlumberjack** (also **ˈlumberman** /-mən; -mən/) *n* (esp in the US and Canada) man whose job is felling trees or cutting or transporting timber (尤指美国和加拿大的)伐木工人、木材加工或运输工人.

ˈlumber-jacket *n* hip-length jacket fastening up to the neck, usu of thick checked material 夹克(通常为厚格子呢的).

ˈlumber-room *n* (*esp Brit*) room in which lumber[1](1) is kept 堆放无用家具的房间.

lum·ber[2] /ˈlʌmbə(r); ˋlʌmbɚ/ *v* [Ipr, Ip] move in a heavy clumsy way 笨重地移动: *elephants lumbering along, past, by, etc* 缓慢地走着的象群 ○ *Look where you're going, you lumbering great oaf!* 看着点道儿, 你这个马大哈!

lu·min·ary /ˈlu:mɪnərɪ; *US* -nerɪ; ˋlumə,nerɪ/ *n* **1** person who inspires or influences others 鼓舞或影响他人的人; 名人; 杰出人物: *leading/lesser luminaries* 大[小]有名气的人. **2** (*fml* 文) heavenly body that gives light, esp the sun or the moon 发光的天体; (尤指)日, 月.

lu·min·ous /ˈlu:mɪnəs; ˋlumənəs/ *adj* **1** giving out light; bright 发光的; 光亮的: *luminous paint*, ie paint that glows in the dark, used on watches, clocks, etc 发光涂料(在暗中可见, 用于钟表等). **2** (*fig* 比喻) easily understood; clear 易懂的; 清楚的: *a luminous speaker, explanation* 语意明晰的演说者、解释.

▷ **lu·min·os·ity** /ˌlu:mɪˈnɒsətɪ; ˌluməˋnɑsətɪ/ *n* [U] quality of being luminous 发光; 光辉.

lu·min·ously *adv*.
lumme (also **lummy**) /ˈlʌmɪ; ˈlʌmɪ/ *interj* (*dated Brit sl* 旧, 俚) (expressing surprise 用以表示惊讶).
lump[1] /lʌmp; lʌmp/ *n* **1** hard or compact mass, usu without a regular shape 堆, 块, 团(通常无定形): *a lump of clay* 一团黏土 ○ *a sugar lump* 一块方糖 ○ *break a piece of coal into small lumps* 把一块煤砸成小块 ○ *How many lumps* (ie of sugar) *do you take in your tea?* 你喝茶加几块方糖? **2** swelling, bump or bruise 肿; 隆起; 挫伤: *a nasty lump on her neck* 她颈上的大肿块. **3** (*infml* 口) heavy, clumsy or stupid person 大块头; 粗大笨拙的人; 傻大个儿: *Do hurry up, you great lump!* 快点, 你这笨蛋! **4** (idm 习语) **have, etc a lump in one's/the throat** feel pressure in the throat as a result of strong emotion caused by love, sadness, etc 喉咙哽住, 哽咽(因激动所致).
▷ **lump** *v* **1** [Tn, Tn·pr, Tn·p] **~ sb/sth (together)** put or consider people or things together; treat people or things as alike or under the same heading 将人或物归并一起或合并考虑; 将人或物同等对待或分类: *We've lumped all the advanced students into a single class.* 我们把程度高的学生都编在一个班里. ○ *Can we lump all these items together as 'incidental expenses'?* 我们可否把这些项目都归在'杂费'项内? **2** [I] form lumps 结块: *Stir the sauce to prevent it lumping.* 把沙司搅拌一下以免结块.
lump·ish /-ɪʃ; -ɪʃ/ *adj* (of a person) heavy; clumsy; stupid (指人)粗大的, 笨拙的, 愚蠢的.
lumpy *adj* (**-ier**, **-iest**) full of lumps; covered in lumps 多块状物的; 多隆起物的: *lumpy gravy* 有颗粒的肉汁 ○ *a lumpy mattress* 有疙瘩的褥垫.
□ **lump ˈsugar** sugar in the form of small lumps or cubes 方糖.
ˈ**lump sum** one payment for a number of separate items; one sum paid all at once rather than in several smaller amounts 一次总付的钱.
lump[2] /lʌmp; lʌmp/ *v* (idm 习语) ˈ**lump it** (*infml* 口) reluctantly accept sth unpleasant or unwanted 勉强地接受讨厌的或不想要的事物: *If you don't like the decision you'll just have to lump it.* 你不喜欢那决定, 也只好勉为其难了.
lun·acy /ˈluːnəsɪ; ˈlunəsɪ/ *n* [U] **1** unsoundness of mind; insanity; madness 精神错乱; 精神失常; 疯狂. **2** very foolish behaviour 极愚蠢的行为: *It's sheer lunacy driving in this weather.* 天气这么坏还开车, 简直是疯了. **3** [C usu *pl* 通常作复数] mad or foolish act 疯狂的或愚蠢的行动.
lunar /ˈluːnə(r); ˈlunɚ/ *adj* [usu attrib 通常作定语] of the moon 月球的; 月亮的: *lunar rocks* 月岩 ○ *a lunar eclipse* 月蚀.
□ **lunar ˈmodule** (also **lunar exˈcursion module**) part of a spacecraft circling the moon that can be detached to make a journey to the moon's surface and back 登月舱.
ˌ**lunar ˈmonth** average time between one new moon and the next (about 29½ days) 朔望月; 阴历月. ⇨App 5 见附录5. Cf 参看 CALENDAR MONTH (CALENDAR).
lun·atic /ˈluːnətɪk; ˈlunəˌtɪk/ *n* **1** (*dated* 旧) insane person 精神失常者; 疯子. **2** wildly foolish person 极愚蠢的人: *You're driving on the wrong side of the road, you lunatic!* 你现在是逆行开车, 你这个蠢材!
▷ **lun·atic** *adj* **1** (*dated* 旧) insane 精神失常的; 疯的. **2** wildly foolish 极愚蠢的: *a lunatic proposal* 极愚蠢的建议. **3** (idm 习语) **the ˌlunatic ˈfringe** (*derog* 贬) those members of a political or some other group whose views are regarded as wildly extreme or eccentric 极端分子: *The lunatic fringe is/are ignored by most members of the party.* 绝大部分党员对极端分子不予理睬.
□ ˈ**lunatic asylum** (*dated* 旧) home for the mentally ill; mental hospital 疯人院; 精神病院.
lunch /lʌntʃ; lʌntʃ/ *n* [C, U] **1** meal taken in the middle of the day 午餐; 午饭; 中饭: *We serve hot and cold lunches.* 我处供应冷热午餐. ○ *He's gone to/for lunch.* 他吃午饭去了. ○ [attrib 作定语] *a one-hour lunch break* 一小时的午餐时间. **2** (*US*) light meal taken at any time 便餐; 小吃: *We'll have a lunch after the show.* 散了电影, 咱们去吃便餐吧. ⇨Usage at DINNER 用法见 DINNER.
▷ **lunch** *v* **1** [I, Ipr, Ip] eat lunch 吃午饭; 进午餐: *Where do you usually lunch?* 您平时在哪儿吃午饭? ○ *We lunched (out) on cold meat and salad.* 我们午饭(在外面)吃的是凉肉和色拉. **2** [Tn] entertain (sb) to lunch 请(某人)吃午饭.
□ ˈ**lunch-room** *n* (*esp US*) place where light meals are served or eaten 快餐店; 小吃店.
ˈ**lunch-time** *n* [C, U] time around the middle of the day when lunch is normally eaten 午餐时间.
lunch·eon /ˈlʌntʃən; ˈlʌntʃən/ *n* [C, U] (*fml* 文) lunch 午餐; 午宴.
□ ˈ**luncheon meat** tinned cooked meat made from pork, ham, etc and usu eaten cold (罐头)午餐肉.
ˈ**luncheon voucher** (*abbr* 缩写 **LV**) (*Brit*) (*US* ˈ**meal ticket**) ticket, given to an employee as part of his pay, that can be exchanged for food at certain restaurants 就餐券(作为工资的一部分发给雇员, 可在某些餐馆用餐).
lung /lʌŋ; lʌŋ/ *n* either of the two breathing-organs in the chest of man and other animals 肺: [attrib 作定语] *lung cancer* 肺癌 ○ *a singer with good lungs*, ie a powerful voice 中气足的歌手. ⇨illus at RESPIRE 见 RESPIRE 插图.
□ ˈ**lung-power** *n* [U] ability to shout, sing, etc strongly 发声力; 中气.
lunge /lʌndʒ; lʌndʒ/ *n* sudden forward movement of the body (eg when trying to attack sb); thrust (身体的)前冲(如攻击某人时的); 刺; 戳.
▷ **lunge** *v* [I, Ipr, Ip] make a lunge 前冲; 刺; 戳: *He lunged wildly at his opponent.* 他疯狂地扑向对手. ○ *She lunged out with a knife.* 她持刀猛冲过去. ⇨illus at FENCING 见 FENCING 插图.
lu·pin (*US* **lu·pine**) /ˈluːpɪn; ˈlupɪn/ *n* garden plant with tall spikes of flowers, bearing seeds in pods 羽扇豆.
lurch[1] /lɜːtʃ; lɝtʃ/ *n* (idm 习语) **leave sb in the lurch** ⇨ LEAVE[1].
lurch[2] /lɜːtʃ; lɝtʃ/ *n* **1** [C] sudden lean or roll to one side 突然倾斜; 倾侧: *The ship gave a lurch to starboard.* 船突然向右侧倾斜. **2** [sing] unsteady swaying movement; stagger 摇晃; 蹒跚.
▷ **lurch** *v* [I, Ipr, Ip] lean or roll suddenly; stagger 跌跌撞撞; 蹒跚: *a drunken man lurching along the street* 沿街踉跄而行的醉汉.
lure /lʊə(r); lʊr/ *n* **1** (**a**) thing that attracts or invites 诱惑物: *She used all her lures to attract his attention.* 她使尽浑身解数以吸引他的注意. (**b**) (usu *sing* 通常作单数) power of attracting 诱惑力; 吸引力; 魅力: *the lure of adventure* 探险的吸引力. **2** (**a**) bait or decoy used to attract wild animals (引诱动物的)饵. (**b**) device used to make a trained hawk return to its trainer or master 唤回猎鹰的装置.
▷ **lure** *v* [Tn, Tn·pr, Tn·p] attract or tempt (a person or an animal) 吸引, 诱惑(人或动物): *lure sb into a trap* 引诱某人上圈套 ○ *Greed lured him on.* 他受了贪心的诱惑.
lurid /ˈlʊərɪd; ˈlʊrɪd/ *adj* **1** having bright glaring colours or combinations of colour 光彩耀眼的; 斑烂的: *a lurid sky, sunset* 火红的天空、夕照 ○ *the lurid glow of the blazing warehouse* 燃烧的仓库上耀眼的火光. **2** violent and shocking; sensational 暴烈而惊人的; 耸人听闻的: *the lurid details of the murder* 凶杀案耸人听闻的细节 ○ *a lurid tale* 骇人的故事. ▷ **lur·idly** *adv*. **lur·id·ness** *n* [U].
lurk /lɜːk; lɝk/ *v* [Ipr, Ip] **1** (**a**) be or stay hidden, esp when waiting to attack 埋伏; 潜伏: *a suspicious-looking man lurking in the shadows* 潜伏在暗处的一个形迹可疑的人. (**b**) wait near a place trying not to attract attention 隐藏; 隐匿: *He's usually lurking somewhere near the bar.* 他通常出没在酒吧附近. **2** (*fig* 比喻) linger (esp in the mind) without being clearly shown 潜藏(尤指心中): *a lurking suspicion* 潜藏于心的怀疑. ⇨ Usage at PROWL 用法见 PROWL.
lus·cious /ˈlʌʃəs; ˈlʌʃəs/ *adj* **1** rich and sweet in taste or smell 味道或气味香甜的: *the luscious taste of ripe peaches* 熟桃的香甜味. **2** (of art, music, etc) very rich and suggesting sensual pleasures (指艺术、音乐等)华丽的, 引起快感的: *the luscious tones of the horns* 铜管乐器悦耳的声调. **3** sensually attractive; voluptuous 肉感的; 性感的; 勾起情欲的: *a luscious blonde* 性感的金发女郎. ▷ **lus·ciously** *adv*. **lus·cious·ness** *n* [U].
lush[1] /lʌʃ; lʌʃ/ *adj* **1** growing thickly and strongly; luxuriant 繁密的; 茂盛的: *lush pastures, vegetation, etc*

茂盛的牧场、草木等. **2** (*fig* 比喻) luxurious 豪华的: *lush carpets* 华美的地毯.

lush[2] /lʌʃ; lʌʃ/ *n* (*US sl* 俚) person who is often drunk 酒鬼; 经常醉醺醺的人.

lust /lʌst; lʌst/ *n* (*often derog* 常作贬义) **1** [C, U] **~ (for sb)** strong sexual desire 强烈的性欲: *curb one's lust* 抑制情欲 ○ *gratify one's lusts* 满足情欲. **2** [C, U] **~ (for/of sth)** intense desire for sth or enjoyment of sth 对某事物的强烈欲望; 物欲; 爱好: *a lust for power, gold, adventure* 对权力、黄金、冒险的强烈欲望 ○ *filled with the lust of battle* 渴望战斗的.

▷ **lust** *v* [Ipr] **~ after/for sb/sth** (*often derog* 常作贬义) feel a strong desire for sb/sth 对某人[某事物]有强烈的欲望: *lust after women* 贪恋女色 ○ *He lusted for revenge.* 他渴望复仇.

lust·ful /-fl; -fəl/ *adj* (*often derog* 常作贬义) filled with lust 好色的; 充满情欲的; 贪婪的: *lustful glances* 色迷迷的目光. **lust·fully** /-fəlɪ; -fəlɪ/ *adv*.

lustre (*US* **luster**) /ˈlʌstə(r); ˋlʌstɚ/ *n* [U] **1** soft brightness of a smooth or shining surface; sheen (光滑表面的)柔和光泽, 光彩: *the deep lustre of pearls* 珍珠浑厚的光泽. **2** (*fig* 比喻) glory; distinction 光荣; 出色: *brave deeds adding lustre to one's name* 使自己扬名增光的英勇业绩.

▷ **lus·trous** /ˈlʌstrəs; ˋlʌstrəs/ *adj* having lustre 有光泽的; 光辉的: *lustrous eyes, hair* 有光泽的眼睛、头发. **lust·rously** *adv*.

lusty /ˈlʌstɪ; ˋlʌstɪ/ *adj* healthy, vigorous and full of vitality 健康的; 精力充沛的; 充满活力的: *lusty youngsters at play* 玩耍中的生气勃勃的儿童 ○ *give a lusty cheer* 高声欢呼. ▷ **lust·ily** /-ɪlɪ; -əlɪ/ *adv*: *sing lustily* 起劲地唱.

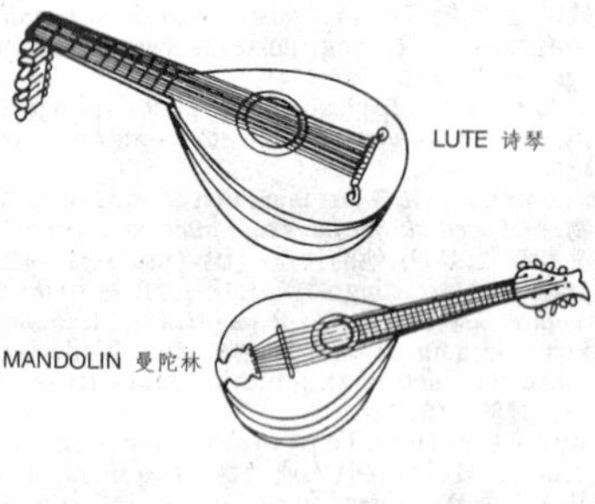

LUTE 诗琴

MANDOLIN 曼陀林

lute[1] /lu:t; lut/ *n* stringed musical instrument with a pear-shaped body, used mainly from the 14th to the 18th centuries and played by plucking with the fingers 诗琴(主要在14-18世纪使用的梨形拨弦乐器).

lute[2] /lu:t; lut/ *n* [U] type of clay or cement used for filling holes, sealing joints, etc 封泥(封堵洞穴接缝等的黏土或水泥).

▷ **lute** *v* [Tn] treat (sth) with lute[2] 用封泥封(某物).

lut·en·ist (also **lut·an·ist**) /ˈlu:tənɪst; ˋlutnɪst/ *n* person who plays the lute[1] 诗琴弹奏者.

Luth·eran /ˈlu:θərən; ˋluθərən/ *n, adj* (member) of the Protestant Church named after Martin Luther (1483-1546) 路德(1483-1546)会教友; 路德教的.

lux·uri·ant /lʌgˈʒʊərɪənt; lʌgˋʒʊrɪənt/ *adj* growing thickly and strongly; lush 繁密的; 茂盛的: *luxuriant tropical vegetation* 葱郁的热带植物 ○ (*fig* 比喻) *the poem's luxuriant imagery* 诗中的丰富意象. Cf 参看 LUXURIOUS.

▷ **lux·uri·ance** /-əns; -əns/ *n* [U] luxuriant growth 丰富; 茂盛.

lux·uri·antly *adv*.

lux·uri·ate /lʌgˈʒʊərɪeɪt; lʌgˋʒʊrɪˌet/ *v* [Ipr] **~ in sth** take great pleasure in sth; enjoy sth as a luxury 纵情享乐; 享受某事物: *a cat luxuriating in the warm sunshine* 在温暖阳光下很舒适的猫 ○ *luxuriate in a hot bath* 在热浴缸里优哉游哉.

lux·uri·ous /lʌgˈʒʊərɪəs; lʌgˋʒʊrɪəs/ *adj* **1** supplied with luxuries; very comfortable 奢侈的; 极舒适的: *live in luxurious surroundings* 生活在奢侈的环境中 ○ *This car is our most luxurious model.* 这种汽车是我们最豪华的型号了. **2** [usu attrib 通常作定语] fond of luxury; self-indulgent 爱好奢侈的; 放纵的: *luxurious habits* 奢侈的习惯. Cf 参看 LUXURIANT. ▷ **lux·uri·ously** *adv*.

lux·ury /ˈlʌkʃərɪ; ˋlʌkʃərɪ/ *n* **1** [U] (regular use and enjoyment of) the best and most expensive food and drink, clothes, surroundings, etc 豪华; 奢华; 奢侈: *live in luxury* 生活奢侈 ○ *lead/live a life of luxury* 过奢侈的生活 ○ [attrib 作定语] *a luxury hotel, flat, liner* 豪华旅馆、公寓、邮轮. **2** [C] thing that is expensive and enjoyable, but not essential 奢侈品: *caviar, champagne and other luxuries* 鱼子酱、香槟以及其他奢侈品 ○ *We can't afford many luxuries.* 很多的奢侈品我们都买不起. **3** (idm 习语) **in the lap of luxury** ⇨ LAP[1].

LV /ˌel ˈvi:; ˌɛl ˋvi/ *abbr* 缩写 = (*Brit*) luncheon voucher.

LW *abbr* 缩写 = (*radio* 无) long wave.

-ly /-lɪ; -lɪ/ *suff* 后缀 **1** (used fairly widely with *ns* to form *adjs* 可与很多名词结合构成形容词) having the qualities of 具有某性质的: *cowardly* ○ *scholarly*. **2** (with *ns* forming *adjs* and *advs* 与名词结合构成形容词和副词) occurring at intervals of 每隔某时间发生: *hourly* ○ *daily*. **3** (used widely with *adjs* to form *advs* 可与大量形容词结合构成副词) in the specified manner 以某方式: *happily* ○ *stupidly*.

ly·cée /ˈli:seɪ; *US* li:ˈseɪ; ˌliˋse/ *n* (*French* 法) state secondary school in France 法国公立中学.

ly·chee (also **lit·chi**) /ˌlaɪˈtʃi:, ˈlaɪtʃi:; ˋlaɪtʃi/ *n* (**a**) fruit with a sweetish white pulp and a single seed in a thin brown shell 荔枝. (**b**) tree (originally from China) that bears this 荔枝树.

lych-gate = LICH-GATE.

lye /laɪ; laɪ/ *n* [U] alkaline solution, esp one obtained by passing water through wood ashes and used for washing things 碱液(尤指从木灰中滤出, 供洗涤用的).

ly·ing *pres p of* LIE[1], LIE[2].

lymph /lɪmf; lɪmf/ *n* [U] **1** (*anatomy* 解) colourless fluid from the tissues or organs of the body, containing white blood-cells 淋巴. **2** (*medical* 医) this fluid taken from cows and used in vaccination against smallpox 痘苗.

▷ **lymph·atic** /lɪmˈfætɪk; lɪmˋfætɪk/ *adj* **1** (*anatomy* 解) of or carrying lymph 淋巴的; 输送淋巴的: *the lymphatic vessels*, ie those that carry lymph from the tissues with any waste matter 淋巴管. **2** (*fml* 文) (of people) slow in thought and action; sluggish (指人)迟钝的, 萎顿的.

lynch /lɪntʃ; lɪntʃ/ *v* [Tn] put to death or punish violently (sb believed to be guilty of a crime) without a lawful trial 用私刑处死或严惩(被认为有罪的人): *innocent men lynched by the angry mob* 被狂怒的暴民以私刑杀害的无辜男子.

□ **ˈlynch law** procedure followed when sb is lynched 私刑.

lynx /lɪŋks; lɪŋks/ *n* wild animal of the cat family with spotted fur and a short tail, noted for its keen sight 猞猁.

□ **ˌlynx-ˈeyed** *adj* having keen eyesight 目光锐利的.

lyre /ˈlaɪə(r); laɪr/ *n* ancient musical instrument with strings fixed in a U-shaped frame, played by plucking with the fingers 里拉琴(古代拨弦乐器, 琴弦固定在U型框架内).

□ **ˈlyre-bird** *n* Australian bird, the male having a long tail shaped like a lyre when spread out 琴鸟(产于澳洲).

lyric /ˈlɪrɪk; ˋlɪrɪk/ *adj* **1** (of poetry) expressing direct personal feelings (指诗)抒情的. **2** of or composed for singing 吟唱的; 供吟唱的.

▷ **lyric** *n* **1** lyric poem 抒情诗. **2** (esp *pl* 尤作复数) words of a song, eg in a musical play 歌词(如在歌舞喜剧中的): [attrib 作定语] *a fine lyric-writer/writer of lyrics* 优秀的抒情歌词作家.

lyr·ical /ˈlɪrɪkl; ˋlɪrɪkl/ *adj* **1** = LYRIC. **2** eagerly enthusiastic 极热情的; 狂热的: *She started to become/wax lyrical about health food.* 她对保健食品极为讲究了.

▷ **lyr·ic·ally** /-klɪ; -klɪ/ *adv*.

lyri·cism /ˈlɪrɪsɪzəm; ˋlɪrəˌsɪzəm/ *n* **1** [U] quality of being lyric, esp in poetry 抒情性; (尤指诗歌的)抒情风格. **2** [C] expression of strong emotion or enthusiasm 感情冲动; 热情奔放.

lyri·cist /ˈlɪrɪsɪst; ˋlɪrəsɪst/ *n* person who writes the words of (esp popular) songs (尤指流行歌曲的)歌词作者.

M m

M, m /em; ɛm/ *n* (*pl* **M's, m's** /emz; ɛmz/) the thirteenth letter of the English alphabet 英语字母表的第十三个字母: *'Moscow' starts with (an) M/'M'.* Moscow 一字以M字母开头.

M *abbr* 缩写 = **1** (also **med**) (esp on clothing, etc 尤作衣物等的标记) medium (size). **2** (also **m**) Roman numeral for 1 000 (Latin *mille*) 罗马数字, 表示1 000(源自拉丁文*mille*). **3** /em; ɛm/ (*Brit*) motorway: *heavy traffic on the M25* 第25号高速公路上繁忙的交通.

m *abbr* 缩写 = **1** (esp on forms 尤用于表格中) male (sex). **2** (esp on forms 尤用于表格中) married (status). **3** (also **masc**) (*grammar*) masculine (gender). **4** (**a**) metre(s): *run in the 5 000m*, ie a race over that distance 参加5 000米长跑. (**b**) (*radio* 无) metres: *800m long wave* 长波800米. **5** million(s): *population 10m* 人口1000万.

ma /mɑ:; mɑ/ *n* (*infml* 口) (usu used to address sb 通常用作称呼语) mother 妈; 妈妈: *I'm going now, ma.* 我要走了, 妈妈. ○ *He always does what his ma tells him to.* 他总是很听妈妈的话.

MA /ˌem ˈeɪ; ˌɛm ˈe/ (*US* **AM**) Master of Arts 文科硕士: *have/be an MA in Modern Languages* 有现代语言硕士学位[为现代语言硕士] ○ *Marion Bell MA (London)* 马里恩·贝尔文科硕士(伦敦大学).

ma'am /mæm *or, rarely,* 罕读作 mɑ:m; mæm, mɑm/ *n* [sing] **1** (used to address the Queen, a noblewoman, a female superior officer in the army, etc 用于对女王、贵妇人、高级女军官等的尊称) madam 夫人; 女士. **2** (*US*) (used as a polite form of address to a woman 用作对女子的尊称): *Can I help you, ma'am?* 小姐, 您有什么事?

mac[1] (also **mack**) /mæk; mæk/ *n* (*Brit infml* 口) = MACKINTOSH.

mac[2] /mæk; mæk/ *n* [sing] (*US infml* 口) (used to address a man whose name one does not know 用以称呼不知姓名的男子): *Hey, mac! What do you think you're doing?* 喂, 老兄! 你搞什么名堂呢?

ma·cabre /məˈkɑ:brə; məˈkɑbrə/ *adj* connected with death, and thus causing fear; gruesome (与死亡有关)引起恐惧的, 可怕的, 可怖的: *a macabre ghost story* 令人毛骨悚然的鬼怪故事.

mac·adam /məˈkædəm; məˈkædəm/ *n* [U] road surface made of layers of compressed broken stones 碎石路面: [attrib 作定语] *a macadam road* 碎石路. Cf 参看 TARMAC.

▷ **mac·ad·am·ize, -ise** /-aɪz; -aɪz/ *v* [Tn] make or cover (a road) with macadam 用碎石铺或筑(路): *macadamized roads* 碎石路.

ma·car·oni /ˌmækəˈrəʊnɪ; ˌmækəˈronɪ/ *n* [U] long hard tubes of pasta, often chopped into short pieces and boiled in water before eating 通心粉; 通心面.

□ ˌ**macaroni** ˈ**cheese** dish of macaroni with a cheese sauce 干酪通心面.

ma·car·oon /ˌmækəˈru:n; ˌmækəˈrun/ *n* small flat cake or biscuit made of sugar, egg-white and crushed almonds or coconut 蛋白杏仁饼; 蛋白椰子饼.

ma·caw /məˈkɔ:; məˈkɔ/ *n* type of large long-tailed tropical American parrot 鹁鸮(热带美洲产的长尾大鹦鹉); 琉璃金刚鹦鹉.

mace[1] /meɪs; mes/ *n* **1** large heavy club formerly used as a weapon, usu having a head with metal spikes (旧时用作武器的)狼牙棒, 钉头锤. **2** staff or rod, usu ornamented, carried or displayed as a sign of the authority of an official, eg a mayor 权杖(通常有装饰, 为官员如市长所携带或作显示权威之用).

□ ˈ**mace-bearer** *n* person who carries an official mace 持权杖者.

mace[2] /meɪs; mes/ *n* [U] dried outer covering of nutmegs, used for flavouring foods 肉豆蔻干皮(用作食物香料).

ma·cer·ate /ˈmæsəreɪt; ˈmæsəˌret/ *v* [I, Tn] (*fml* 文) (cause sth to) become soft or break up by soaking (使某物)浸软, 浸开. ▷ **ma·cera·tion** /ˌmæsəˈreɪʃn; ˌmæsəˈreʃən/ *n* [U].

Mach /mɑ:k, mæk; mɑk/ *n* [U] (followed by a number 后接数词) ratio of the speed of sth (esp an aircraft) to the speed of sound 马赫: *an aircraft flying at Mach two*, ie twice the speed of sound 以两倍于音速飞行的飞机.

ma·chete /məˈtʃetɪ; *US* -ˈʃetɪ; məˈʃɛtɪ/ *n* broad heavy knife used as a cutting tool and as a weapon, esp in Latin America and the West Indies (用作刀具和武器的)大刀; (尤指拉丁美洲和西印度群岛人用的)大砍刀. ⇨illus at KNIFE 见KNIFE插图.

ma·chi·avel·lian /ˌmækɪəˈvelɪən; ˌmækɪəˈvɛlɪən/ *adj* (also **Machiavellian**) cunning and deceitful in gaining what one wants; showing such cunning or deceit 狡猾欺诈的; 不择手段的: *a machiavellian person, scheme, plot* 狡猾的人、计划、阴谋.

mach·ina·tion /ˌmækɪˈneɪʃn; ˌmækəˈneʃən/ *n* (**a**) [C usu *pl* 通常作复数] evil plot or scheme 诡计; 阴谋: *attempts to counter their machinations* 为反击他们的阴谋而进行的努力. (**b**) [U] plotting 密谋; 谋划.

ma·chine /məˈʃi:n; məˈʃin/ *n* **1** [C] (often in compounds 常用以构成复合词) apparatus with several moving parts, designed to perform a particular task, and driven by electricity, steam, gas, etc, or by human power 机器; 机械: *The scrap merchant has a machine which crushes cars.* 那个废品商有个压碎汽车的机器. ○ *a* ˈ*sewing-machine,* ˈ*washing-machine, etc* 缝纫机、洗衣机等 ○ *office machines*, eg computers, word processors, photocopiers, etc 办公用机器(如计算机、文字处理机、影印机等) ○ *Machines have replaced human labour in many industries.* 在很多工业中, 机器已取代了人力操作. ⇨Usage 见所附用法. **2** [C] (*fig* 比喻) person who acts automatically, without thinking 机械般行动而不动脑筋的人: *Years of doing the same dull job can turn you into a machine.* 成年地做一种单调工作, 能把活人也做成机器人. **3** [CGp] group of people that control (part of) an organization, etc (部分)控制某组织等的一伙人: *the (political) party machine* (政)党的核心组织 ○ *The public relations machine covered up the firm's heavy losses.* 公共关系部掩饰了该商行的严重亏损. **4** (idm 习语) **a cog in the machine** ⇨ COG.

▷ **ma·chine** *v* [Tn] **1** cut, shape, polish, etc (sth) with a machine 用机器切割、制作或磨光(某物): *The edge of the disc had been machined flat/smooth.* 圆盘的边缘已用机器磨平[光]. **2** make (clothes) using a sewing-machine 用缝纫机缝制(衣服): *I have to machine the hem.* 我需用缝纫机缝边.

ma·chinery /məˈʃi:nərɪ; məˈʃinərɪ/ *n* [U] **1** (**a**) moving parts (of a machine) (机器的)转动部分: *the machinery of a clock* 钟的转动部分. (**b**) machines collectively or in general (泛指)机器, 机械: *Much new machinery has been installed.* 已安装了许多新机器. **2** ~ (**of sth/for doing sth**) organization or structure (of sth/for doing sth) 组织; 机构: *reform the machinery of government* 改革政府机构 ○ *We have no machinery for dealing with complaints.* 我们没有处理群众投诉的部门. ○ *All this will be processed by the Home Office machinery.* 这些事都要由内政部处理.

ma·chin·ist /məˈʃi:nɪst; məˈʃinɪst/ *n* **1** person who operates a machine, esp a sewing-machine 操作机器的工人; (尤指)缝纫机工. **2** person who makes, repairs or operates machine tools 机械工; 机械师.

□ **maˈchine code** (also **maˈchine language**) (*computing* 计) binary code in which instructions are written that a computer can understand and act on 机器语言.

maˈchine-gun *n* gun that fires bullets continuously while the trigger is pressed 机关枪; 机枪: *operate, set up a machine-gun* 开机枪、架起机枪 ○ [attrib 作定语] *accurate machine-gun fire* 机枪的准确火力. ⇨illus at GUN 见GUN插图. — *v* (**-nn-**) [Tn] shoot (sb) with a machine-gun 用机枪射击(某人): *They machine-gunned* *the advancing troops.* 他们用机枪扫射进攻的敌军.

ma,chine-'made *adj* made by machine 机器制造的. Cf 参看 HAND-MADE (HAND[1]).

ma,chine-'readable *adj* (*computing* 计) (of data) in a form that a computer can understand (指资料)计算机可读的: *convert a book into machine-readable form* 把一部书变换成计算机可读的形式.

ma'chine tool tool for cutting or shaping materials, driven by a machine 工作母机; 机床.

NOTE ON USAGE 用法: Compare **machine, tool,** etc. 试比较 **machine**、**tool** 等词. A **machine** consists of moving parts powered by electricity, etc and is designed for a specific job. ☆ **machine** 是由电力等驱动的机器, 是为做某种工作而设计的. An (**electrical**) **appliance** is a machine used in the house, such as a washing-machine or dishwasher. ☆ **(electrical) appliance** 是家用电器, 如洗衣机或洗碟机. An **apparatus** is a system of connected machines, wires, etc ☆ **apparatus** 是相联结的机器、导线等系统: *the apparatus for lighting the stage* 舞台照明设备. A **tool** is an object held in the hand, often used by people in their jobs, eg a hammer, drill or spanner. ☆ **tool** 是手持工具, 常为干活儿的人用的, 如锤子、钻或扳子. An **instrument** is a tool designed for a technical task, eg a surgeon's knife. ☆ **instrument** 是为技术工作设计的工具, 如手术刀. It may have some moving parts and be used in a technical operation, eg a microscope or meter. ☆ **instrument** 可能有某些运转部件并用于技术操作, 如显微镜或仪表. An **implement** is a tool generally used outdoors, especially in gardening or farming, eg a plough, rake or spade. ☆ **implement** 是通常用于户外的工具, 尤指园艺或农作中用的, 如犁、耙或锹. **Device** and **gadget** are more general terms. ☆ **device** 和 **gadget** 词义较笼统. **Device** is often used implying approval of a useful machine or instrument ☆ **device** 常含褒义, 指某机器或工具很有用处: *a labour-saving device* 省力的器具 ○ *a clever device for locking windows* 锁窗的灵巧装置. **Gadget** is more informal and can suggest disapproval ☆ **gadget** 较为通俗, 可含贬义: *Their kitchen is full of the latest gadgets.* 他们的厨房尽是最新式的器具. ○ *All these modern gadgets are more trouble than they're worth.* 所有这些现代化的装置都是花钱买麻烦的玩意儿.

mach·ismo /mə'tʃɪzməʊ, *also* mə'kɪzməʊ; mə'tʃizmo, mə'kɪzmo/ *n* [U] (*esp derog* 尤作贬义) exaggerated or aggressive pride in being male (夸大的或盛气凌人的)男子气概.

macho /'mætʃəʊ; 'mætʃo/ *adj* (*infml esp derog* 口, 尤作贬义) aggressively masculine 大男子气概的: *He thinks it's macho to drink a lot and get into fights.* 他认为酗酒斗殴就是男子气概.

mack·erel /'mækrəl; 'mækrəl/ *n* (*pl* unchanged 复数不变) **1** striped fish that lives in the sea and is eaten as food 鲭: *a good catch of mackerel* 捕获的大量鲭鱼. **2** (idm 习语) **a sprat to catch a mackerel** ⇨ SPRAT.

□ **,mackerel 'sky** sky covered with strips of fleecy cloud, similar to the stripes on a mackerel's back 鱼鳞天(布满卷毛云的天空, 状似鲭鱼背部条纹状鳞片).

mack·in·tosh /'mækɪntɒʃ; 'mækɪn,taʃ/ (also **mac**, **mack** /mæk; mæk/) *n* (*Brit*) coat made of rainproof material 雨衣.

macro- *comb form* 构词成分 large; large-scale 大的; 大规模的: *macrobiotic* ○ *macroeconomic(s)*. Cf 参看 MICRO-, MINI-.

mac·ro·bi·otics /,mækrəʊbaɪ'ɒtɪks; ,mækrobaɪ'ɑtɪks/ *n* [sing *v*] science of diets that consist of whole grains and vegetables grown without chemical treatment 益寿饮食学(对全谷及未经化学处理的蔬菜之饮食的研究). ▷ **mac·ro·bi·otic** *adj* [esp attrib 尤作定语]: *macrobiotic food* 益寿食品.

mac·ro·cosm /'mækrəʊkɒzəm; 'mækrə,kɑzəm/ *n* **1 the macrocosm** [sing] the universe 宇宙; 宏观世界. **2** [C] any large complete structure containing smaller structures (任何含有较小结构的)大而完整的结构. Cf 参看 MICROCOSM.

M

mad /mæd; mæd/ *adj* (**-dder, -ddest**) **1** (**a**) mentally ill; insane 疯的; (患)精神病的; 精神错乱的: *a mad person, act* 精神失常的人、行为 ○ *be/go mad* 发疯 ○ *drive/send sb mad* 把某人逼疯. (**b**) (*infml esp derog* 口, 尤作贬义) very foolish; crazy 极愚蠢的; 疯狂的: *What a mad thing to do!* 多愚蠢的事啊! ○ *You must be mad to drive so fast!* 你开得这样快, 简直疯了! ○ *He's quite mad: he goes round in very odd clothes.* 他真是疯了, 竟穿着稀奇古怪的衣服到处逛. **2** (*infml* 口) (**a**) **~ about/on sth/sb** very interested in sth/sb; enthusiastic about sth/sb 对某事物[某人]极感兴趣或很入迷: *mad on football, pop music, etc* 对足球、流行歌曲等着迷 ○ *He's mad about her*, ie likes/loves her very much. 他爱她爱得如醉如痴. (**b**) (following *ns* 用于名词之后) very keen on (sth/sb) 极喜爱(某事物[某人]): *be cricket mad, photography mad, pop music mad, etc* 酷爱板球、摄影、流行音乐等 ○ *a crowd of football-mad little boys* 一群迷恋足球运动的小男孩儿. **3 ~ (with sth)** (*infml* 口) very excited; wild; frenzied 非常激动的; 狂暴的; 狂乱的: *a mad dash, rush, etc* 乱冲、狂奔 ○ *mad with pain* 极疼痛 ○ *The crowd is mad with excitement!* 群众激动万分! **4** (*infml* 口) **~ (at/with sb)** angry; furious 愤怒的; 狂怒的: *His obstinacy drives me mad!* 他顽固不化把我气得火冒三丈! ○ *She was mad at/with him for losing the match.* 她对他输了这场比赛极为恼怒. ○ *mad at/with the dog for eating her shoe* (她)因狗咬她的鞋而发怒. ○ *Don't get mad (about the broken window).* 别(为窗户坏了)大动肝火. **5** (of a dog) suffering from rabies (指狗)患狂犬病的. **6** (idm 习语) **hopping mad** ⇨ HOP[1]. **like 'mad** (*infml* 口) very much, quickly, etc 非常、极快地等: *smoke, run, work, etc like mad* 拼命地吸烟、跑、工作等. **(as) mad as a 'hatter/a March 'hare** (*infml* 口) completely insane 像三月里(交尾期)野兔般疯狂. **mad 'keen (on sb/sth)** (*infml* 口) very interested (in sb/sth) or enthusiastic (about sb/sth) (对某人[某事物])极感兴趣或很入迷: *She's mad keen on hockey/on Arthur Higgins.* 她极喜爱曲棍球[阿瑟·希金斯]. **stark raving/staring mad** ⇨ STARK.

▷ **madly** *adv* **1** in an insane manner 疯狂地: *madly bent on further conquests* 疯狂地决心进一步征服. **2** (*infml* 口) extremely 极端地; 极其: *madly excited, jealous, etc* 极其激动、嫉妒等 ○ *She's madly in love with him.* 她如醉如痴地爱着他.

mad·ness *n* [U] **1** state of being insane; insane behaviour 疯狂; 精神错乱; 精神失常: *His madness cannot be cured.* 他的疯病无法医治. **2** extreme foolishness 极端的愚蠢: *It is madness to climb in such bad weather.* 天气这么坏还去爬山, 真是愚不可及. **3** (idm 习语) **method in one's madness** ⇨ METHOD. **midsummer madness** ⇨ MIDSUMMER.

□ **'madhouse** *n* **1** (*infml derog* 口, 贬) place where there is much confusion or noise 极为混乱或嘈杂之处: *This classroom is a madhouse: be quiet!* 这教室乱哄哄的, 安静点儿! **2** (*dated* 旧) mental hospital 精神病院; 疯人院.

'madman /-mən; -,mən/, **'madwoman** *ns* person who is insane 疯子; 狂人.

madam /'mædəm; 'mædəm/ *n* **1** (also **Madam**) [sing] (*fml* 文) (polite form of address to a woman, whether married or unmarried, usu sb one does not know personally 对女子的敬称, 对已婚未婚者均可使用, 通常用于不相识者): *Can I help you, madam?* 小姐, 您有什么事? ○ *Dear Madam*, ie used like *Dear Sir* in a letter 敬启者(用于信中, 如同 Dear Sir) ○ *Madam Chairman, may I be allowed to speak?* 主席先生, 我可以发言吗? Cf 参看 MISS[2] 2. **2** [C] (*infml derog* 口, 贬) girl or young woman who likes to get her own way 自行其是的年轻女子: *She's a real little madam!* 她可真是个我行我素的小姐! **3** [C esp *sing* 尤作单数] woman who is in charge of a brothel 鸨母.

Ma·dame /mə'dɑːm; *US* mə'dæm; mə'dæm/ *n* (*abbr* 缩写 **Mme**) (*pl* **Mes·dames** /meɪ'dɑːm; me'dɑm/) (*abbr* 缩写 **Mmes**) (French title given to an older, esp married or widowed, woman or to an older woman who is not British or American 法语中对非英美年长妇女(尤指已婚或孀居者)的尊称): *Madame Lee from Hong Kong* 香港的李夫人.

mad·cap *adj* [attrib 作定语], *n* (typical of a) person who acts recklessly or impulsively 鲁莽的人; 爱冲动的人: *some madcap adventure* 某种鲁莽的冒险 ○ *a complete madcap* 十分鲁莽的人.

mad·den /'mædn; 'mædn̩/ *v* [Tn] make (sb) mad(4);

irritate; annoy 使(某人)疯狂; 激怒; 使恼火: *It maddens me that she was chosen instead of me!* 选中了她而没选中我, 真把人气死!

▷ **mad·den·ing** /ˈmædnɪŋ; ˋmædnɪŋ/ *adj* annoying; irritating 激怒人的; 使人恼火的: *maddening delays* 恼人的延误 ○ *Her laziness is quite maddening.* 她很懒惰, 真气人. **mad·den·ingly** *adv*: *maddeningly unhelpful, stupid, inefficient, etc* 无用、愚蠢、效率低…得令人恼火.

mad·der /ˈmædə(r); ˋmædɚ/ *n* [U] (red dye obtained from the root of a) climbing plant with yellowish flowers 茜草; 茜草染料.

made *pt, pp* of MAKE¹.

Ma·deira /məˈdɪərə; məˋdɪrə/ *n* [U, C] white dessert wine from the island of Madeira 马德拉岛白葡萄酒.

□ **Maˈdeira cake** type of sponge-cake 马德拉蛋糕.

Ma·donna /məˈdɒnə; məˋdɑnə/ *n* **1 the Madonna** [sing] the Virgin Mary, mother of Jesus Christ 圣母马利亚(耶稣基督的母亲). **2** (usu 通常作 **madonna**) [C] statue or picture of the Virgin Mary 圣母马利亚的雕像或画像: *There was a madonna on the altar.* 祭坛上有一座圣母马利亚的雕像.

mad·rigal /ˈmædrɪgl; ˋmædrɪgl̩/ *n* (esp 16-century) song for several voices, usu without instrumental accompaniment, on the themes of love and/or nature (尤指16世纪的)牧歌(以爱情和大自然为主题, 通常无乐器伴奏的多声部歌曲).

mael·strom /ˈmeɪlstrɒm; ˋmelstrəm/ *n* (usu *sing* 通常作单数) **1** great whirlpool 大漩涡. **2** (*fig* 比喻) state of violent confusion 大动乱: *the maelstrom of war* 大战乱 ○ *She was drawn into a maelstrom of revolutionary events.* 她被卷入革命事件的洪流中.

maes·tro /ˈmaɪstrəʊ; ˋmaɪstro/ *n* (*pl* **~s** or **maes·tri** /ˈmaɪstrɪ; ˋmaɪstrɪ/) (with a capital letter when followed by a name 后接名字时其首字母需大写) (title given to a) master in the arts, esp a great musical composer, conductor or teacher (艺术)大师(尤用以称作曲家、指挥家或音乐教师): *Maestro Giulini* 指挥家朱利尼大师 ○ *the maestri of the seventeenth century* 十七世纪的音乐大师.

Mafia /ˈmæfɪə; *US* mɑ:f-; ˋmɑfɪə/ *n* [CGp] **1 the Mafia** (**a**) secret organization of criminals in Sicily 黑手党(西西里岛的秘密犯罪组织). (**b**) similar organization active esp in Italy and the USA 类似黑手党的犯罪组织(尤指在意大利和美国活动的): [attrib 作定语] *a Mafia boss, gang, killing, plot* 黑社会的首领、匪帮、谋杀、阴谋. **2 mafia** (*derog or joc* 贬或谑) group of people who (are thought to) exert great influence secretly (被认为)秘密施加巨大影响的一伙人: *The town hall mafia will prevent this plan going through.* 市政厅的幕后操纵集团将阻挠这一计划.

▷ **Ma·fi·oso** /ˌmæfɪˈəʊsəʊ; ˌmæfɪˋoso/ *n* (*pl* **Mafiosi** /-si:; -si/) member of the Mafia 黑手党党徒.

ma·ga·zine¹ /ˌmægəˈzi:n; *US* ˈmægəzi:n; ˋmægəzin/ *n* (*infml abbr* 口语缩写作 **mag**) (/mæg; mæg/) paper-covered periodical, usu weekly or monthly, with articles, stories, etc, by various writers 杂志; 期刊: *women's magazines* 妇女杂志 ○ *a literary magazine* 文学杂志 ○ [attrib 作定语] *a magazine article* 杂志上的文章.

ma·ga·zine² /ˌmægəˈzi:n; *US* ˈmægəzi:n; ˋmægəzin/ *n* **1** store for arms, ammunition, explosives, etc 武器库; 弹药库; 炸药库. **2** chamber holding the cartridges of a rifle or pistol before they are fed into the breech (枪的)弹仓, 弹盒, 弹盘. ⇨illus at GUN 见GUN插图. **3** place that holds the roll or cartridge of film in a camera (照相机内的)胶卷盒, 底片盒.

ma·genta /məˈdʒentə; məˋdʒɛntə/ *adj, n* [U] bright purplish red (dye) 洋红的; 洋红色; 洋红染料.

mag·got /ˈmægət; ˋmægət/ *n* larva or grub (esp of the bluebottle or cheese-fly), which lays its eggs in meat, cheese, etc 蛆: *People use maggots as bait when they go fishing.* 人们钓鱼时用蛆作钓饵.

▷ **mag·goty** *adj* full of maggots 生满蛆的: *maggoty cheese, meat, etc* 生蛆的干酪、肉等.

Magi /ˈmeɪdʒaɪ; ˋmedʒaɪ/ *n* [pl] **the Magi** the three wise men from the East who brought gifts to the infant Jesus (将礼物带给初生的耶稣的)东方三贤人.

ma·gic /ˈmædʒɪk; ˋmædʒɪk/ *n* [U] **1** power of apparently using supernatural forces to change the form of things or influence events; superstitious practices based on this 魔法; 巫术: *They believe that it was all done by magic.* 他们相信那都是魔法造成的. ○ *black/white magic* 诅咒[祈祷]巫术 ○ *This soap works like magic — the stains just disappear.* 这种肥皂功效神奇——污垢顿消. ○ *The paper turned green as if by magic.* 那纸像着了魔法一样, 变绿了. Cf 参看 SORCERY (SORCERER), WITCHCRAFT (WITCH). **2** (art of performing) tricks with mysterious results, done to entertain 魔术; 戏法; 幻术: *She's very good at magic; she can conjure a rabbit out of a hat.* 她很会变魔术, 能从帽子里变出兔子来. **3** (*fig approv* 比喻, 褒) (**a**) charming or enchanting quality 魔力; 魅力: *the magic of Shakespeare's poetry, of the woods in autumn* 莎士比亚诗篇的、秋天森林的魅力. (**b**) thing that has this quality 具有魅力、魔力之物: *Her piano playing is absolute magic.* 她的钢琴弹得真是出神入化.

▷ **ma·gic** *adj* **1** used in or using magic 魔法或魔术中使用的; 用魔法或魔术的: *a magic spell, word, trick, etc* 具有魔力的符咒、咒语、把戏等 ○ *the magic arts* 魔术技艺. **2** (*sl* 俚) wonderful; excellent 绝妙的; 极好的: *That music is really magic!* 那音乐真是妙不可言! ○ *We had a magic time today!* 我们今天玩得很痛快! ○ *You got the tickets? Magic!* 你弄到票了? 太棒了!

ma·gic *v* (*pt, pp* **magicked**) (phr v) **magic sth away** cause sth to disappear by magic 用魔术使某物消失: *The conjurer magicked the bird away.* 那个魔术师把鸟变没了. ○ (*fig* 比喻) *As soon as the trouble began, his bodyguards magicked him away.* 动乱刚一开始, 他的警卫就像变魔术似地把他弄走了. **magic sth from/out of sth** produce sth by magic from sth 用魔术变出某物: *She magicked a rabbit out of a hat.* 她从帽子里变出一只兔子来.

ma·gical /-kl; -kl̩/ *adj* **1** of, used in or like magic (像)魔法的; (像)魔术的; (像)魔法或魔术中使用的: *a wizard's magical hat* 男巫的魔帽. **2** (*infml* 口) charming; enchanting 迷人的; 有魅力的: *a magical view over the calm waters of the bay* 海湾里平静海水的迷人景色. **ma·gic·ally** /-klɪ; -klɪ/ *adv*.

ma·gi·cian /məˈdʒɪʃn; məˋdʒɪʃən/ *n* person who is skilled in magic(2) 魔术师; 变戏法的人. Cf 参看 CONJURER (CONJURE¹).

□ **magic ˈcarpet** (in fairy stories) carpet that is able to fly and carry people (童话故事中)能载人飞行的魔毯.

magic ˈeye (*infml* 口) photoelectric device which shows that sb/sth is present or which is used to control an electric or electronic device 电眼; 光调谐指示器; 电子射线管: *lifts opened and closed by a magic eye* 用电眼控制开关的电梯.

ma·gis·terial /ˌmædʒɪˈstɪərɪəl; ˌmædʒɪsˋtɪrɪəl/ *adj* (*fml* 文) **1** having or showing authority 有权威的; 表现出权威的: *a magisterial manner, statement, pronouncement* 权威性的态度、说法、声明. **2** of or conducted by a magistrate 地方法官的; 地方法官办的: *magisterial decisions, proceedings* 地方法官的决定、诉讼程序. ▷ **ma·gis·teri·ally** /-ɪəlɪ; -ɪəlɪ/ *adv*: *dismiss the servants magisterially* 威严地解雇仆人.

ma·gis·trate /ˈmædʒɪstreɪt; ˋmædʒɪsˌtret/ *n* official who acts as a judge in the lowest courts; Justice of the Peace 地方法官; 治安官: *The Magistrates' Courts* 地方法院 ○ *come up before the magistrate* 在地方法院出庭.

▷ **ma·gis·tracy** /ˈmædʒɪstrəsɪ; ˋmædʒɪstrəsɪ/ *n* **1** [C] position of a magistrate 地方法官或治安官的职位. **2 the magistracy** [Gp] magistrates as a group 地方法官团; 治安官团: *He's been elected to the magistracy.* 他已选进地方法官团.

magma /ˈmægmə; ˋmægmə/ *n* [U] molten rock found beneath the earth's crust 岩浆. ⇨illus at VOLCANO 见VOLCANO插图.

mag·nan·im·ous /mægˈnænɪməs; mægˋnænəməs/ *adj* having or showing great generosity (esp towards a rival, an enemy, etc) 宽宏大量的, 慷慨的(尤指对竞争者、敌人等): *a magnanimous person, gesture, gift* 大方的人、姿态、礼物 ○ *a leader who was magnanimous in victory*, ie when he won 在胜利时宽宏大度的领袖.

▷ **mag·nan·im·ity** /ˌmægnəˈnɪmətɪ; ˌmægnəˋnɪmətɪ/ *n* [U] being magnanimous 宽宏大量; 慷慨: *show great magnanimity towards an opponent* 对敌手表现出极大的宽容.

mag·nan·im·ously *adv*.

mag·nate /ˈmæɡneɪt; ˋmæɡnet/ *n* wealthy and powerful landowner or industrialist 有财有势的地主或工业家: *an industrial magnate* 工业巨头.

mag·ne·sia /mæɡˈniːʃə; mæɡˈniʃə/ *n* [U] white tasteless powder (carbonate of magnesium) used in liquid form as a medicine, and in industry 氧化镁; 镁氧.

mag·nes·ium /mæɡˈniːzɪəm; *US* mæɡˈniːʒəm; mæɡˈniʒəm/ *n* [U] (*chemistry* 化) silver-white metallic element that burns with a very bright flame and is used to make alloys and fireworks, and in flash photography 镁. ⇨App 10 见附录10.

magnet 磁铁

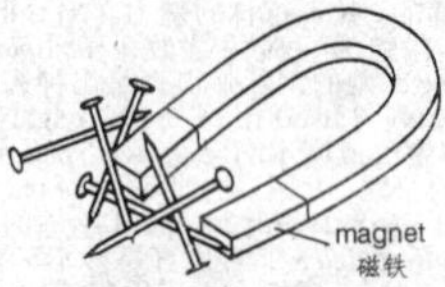

mag·net /ˈmæɡnɪt; ˋmæɡnɪt/ *n* **1** piece of iron, often in a horseshoe shape, which can attract iron, either naturally or because of an electric current passed through it, and which points roughly north and south when freely suspended 磁铁; 磁石. ⇨illus 见插图. **2** (*fig* 比喻) person or thing that has a powerful attraction 有强大吸引力的人或物: *This disco is a magnet for young people.* 这家迪斯科舞厅经常吸引大批年轻的顾客.

▷ **mag·net·ism** /ˈmæɡnɪtɪzəm; ˋmæɡnə,tɪzəm/ *n* [U] **1** (science of the) properties and effects of magnetic substances 磁性; 磁性作用; 磁学. **2** (*fig* 比喻) great personal charm and attraction 人的魅力和吸引力: *the magnetism of a great cinema performer* 一杰出电影演员的魅力.

mag·net·ize, -ise /ˈmæɡnətaɪz; ˋmæɡnə,taɪz/ *v* [Tn] **1** cause (sth) to become magnetic 使(某物)磁化, 起磁: *This screwdriver has been magnetized.* 这把改锥已经磁化了. **2** (*fig* 比喻) attract (sb) strongly, as if by magnetism 强烈吸引(某人): *She can magnetize a theatre audience.* 她能像磁石般吸引剧院观众.

mag·netic /mæɡˈnetɪk; mæɡˈnɛtɪk/ *adj* **1** with the properties of a magnet 有磁性的: *The block becomes magnetic when the current is switched on.* 通电时线圈即具磁性. **2** (*fig* 比喻) having a powerful attraction 有强大吸引力的: *a magnetic smile, personality* 极有吸引力的微笑、性格. **3** of magnetism 磁性的; 磁的: *magnetic properties, forces, etc* 磁性、磁力. ▷ **mag·net·ic·ally** /-klɪ; -klɪ/ *adv*.

□ **magnetic ˈcompass** = COMPASS[1].

magnetic ˈfield area round a magnet where a magnetic force is exerted 磁场.

magnetic ˈmine underwater mine[2](2) that explodes when a large mass of iron, eg a ship, approaches it 磁性水雷.

magnetic ˈneedle needle that points roughly north and south, used on a compass 磁针.

magnetic ˈnorth northerly direction indicated by a magnetic needle 磁北: *magnetic north pole*, ie close to the geographical North Pole but not identical with it 磁北极.

magnetic ˈtape plastic tape coated with iron oxide, used for recording sound or television pictures 磁带; 录音带; 录像带.

mag·neto /mæɡˈniːtəʊ; mæɡˈnito/ *n* (*pl* **~s**) electric apparatus that produces the sparks for the ignition of an internal combustion engine 电磁机; 永磁发电机.

Mag·ni·ficat /mæɡˈnɪfɪkæt; mæɡˈnɪfɪ,kæt/ *n* [sing] **the Magnificat** song of the Virgin Mary praising God, used in Church of England services 尊主颂(童贞女马利亚赞美上帝之歌, 用于英国国教礼拜中).

mag·ni·fi·cent /mæɡˈnɪfɪsnt; mæɡˈnɪfəsnt/ *adj* splendid; remarkable; impressive 壮丽的; 宏伟的; 壮观的: *a magnificent Renaissance palace* 文艺复兴时期的宏伟宫殿 ○ *her magnificent generosity* 她那豪爽的慷慨. ▷ **mag·ni·fi·cence** /-sns; -sns/ *n* [U]: *the magnificence of the ceremonies* 仪式的壮观. **mag·ni·fi·cently** *adv*.

M

magnify 放大

mag·nify /ˈmæɡnɪfaɪ; ˋmæɡnə,faɪ/ *v* (*pt, pp* **-fied**) **1** [Tn, Tn·pr] make (sth) appear larger, as a lens or microscope does (用放大器或显微镜)放大(某物): *bacteria magnified to 1 000 times their actual size* 比实物放大1 000 倍的的细菌. ⇨illus 见插图. **2** [Tn] (*fml* 文) exaggerate (sth) 夸大(某事物): *magnify the dangers, risks, uncertainties, etc* 夸大危险性、冒险性、易变性等. **3** [Tn] (*arch* 古) give praise to (God) 赞美(上帝): *My soul doth magnify the Lord.* 我的心赞美上主的伟大.

▷ **mag·ni·fier** /-faɪə(r); -,faɪɚ/ *n* device, etc that magnifies 放大器; 放大装置; 放大镜.

mag·ni·fica·tion /,mæɡnɪfɪˈkeɪʃn; ,mæɡnəfəˋkeʃən/ *n* **1** [U] (power of) magnifying 放大; 放大能力: *a lens with excellent magnification* 放大能力极佳的透镜. **2** [C] amount of increase in apparent size 放大率; 放大倍数: *This object has been photographed at a magnification of* × *3*, ie three times actual size. 此物体拍照时已放大了三倍.

□ ˈ**magnifying glass** hand-held lens used for magnifying objects 放大镜. ⇨illus 见插图.

mag·ni·lo·quent /mæɡˈnɪləkwənt; mæɡˈnɪləkwənt/ *adj* (*fml* 文) (**a**) (of words, speech) pompous-sounding (指言词、讲话)夸张的, 夸大的. (**b**) (of a person) using pompous-sounding words (指人)使用夸张的言词的. ▷ **mag·ni·lo·quence** /-əns; -əns/ *n* [U]. **mag·ni·lo·quently** *adv*.

mag·ni·tude /ˈmæɡnɪtjuːd; *US* -tuːd; ˋmæɡnə,tud/ *n* [U] **1** (*fml* 文) (usu large) size (通常指大的)量, 大小: *The magnitude of the epidemic was frightening.* 这种流行病传播范围之广令人惊惶不安. **2** (degree of) importance 重要; 重要性; 重要程度: *You don't appreciate the magnitude of her achievement.* 你没有认识到她这一成就的重大意义. ○ *a discovery of the first magnitude*, ie a most important discovery 一项极重要的发现. **3** (*astronomy* 天) degree of brightness of a star 星等(表示星体亮度的等级): *a star of the first, second, etc magnitude* 一等星、二等星.

mag·no·lia /mæɡˈnəʊlɪə; mæɡˋnolɪə/ *n* tree with large sweet-smelling wax-like flowers, usu white or pink 木兰.

mag·num /ˈmæɡnəm; ˋmæɡnəm/ *n* (bottle containing) 1.5 litres of wine or spirits 1.5 升的酒(瓶): *a magnum of champagne* 1.5升的香槟.

mag·num opus /,mæɡnəm ˈəʊpəs; ˋmæɡnəm ˋopəs/ (*Latin* 拉) work of art or literature regarded as its author's greatest (某艺术家或文学家的)最伟大的作品, 杰作, 巨著.

mag·pie /ˈmæɡpaɪ; ˋmæɡ,paɪ/ *n* **1** noisy black-and-white bird that is attracted by, and often takes away, small bright objects 喜鹊. ⇨illus at App 1 见附录1插图, page iv. **2** (*fig derog* 比喻, 贬) (**a**) person who collects or hoards things 爱收集或贮藏东西的人. (**b**) person who chatters a lot 爱饶舌的人.

Mag·yar /ˈmæɡjɑː(r); ˋmæɡjɑr/ *n, adj* (member or language) of the main ethnic group in Hungary 马札尔人(的); 马札尔语(的).

ma·ha·raja (also **ma·ha·rajah**) /,mɑːhəˈrɑːdʒə; ,mɑhəˋrɑdʒə/ *n* (title of an) Indian prince (印度的)土邦主, 王公(的称号).

▷ **ma·ha·rani** (also **ma·ha·ra·nee**) /,mɑːhəˈrɑːniː; ,mɑhəˋrani/ *n* wife of a maharaja; queen or princess with a position like that of a maharaja (印度的)土邦主之妻, 女土邦主.

ma·ha·rishi /,mɑːhəˈrɪʃiː; *US* məˈhɑːrəʃiː; məˋhɑrəʃi/ *n* Hindu wise man (印度的)智者, 圣贤.

ma·hatma /mə'hɑːtmə, mə'hætmə; mə'hɑtmə, mə'hætmə/ *n* (in India) title given to a person regarded with great reverence because of his wisdom and holiness (印度的)伟人, 圣贤(用作尊称): *Mahatma Gandhi* 圣雄甘地.

mahl·stick = MAULSTICK.

ma·hog·any /mə'hɒgənɪ; mə'hɑgənɪ/ *n* **1** [C, U] (tropical tree with) hard reddish-brown wood used esp for making furniture 桃花心木(树)(热带产之坚硬红木, 尤用以制家具): *I'm going to use mahogany to make the book-case.* 我打算用桃花心木做书橱. ○ *This table is mahogany.* 这张桌子是桃花心木的. ○ [attrib 作定语] *a mahogany chair, desk, etc* 桃花心木的椅子、书桌等. **2** [U] reddish-brown colour 红褐色: *with skin tanned to a deep mahogany* 皮肤晒成深红褐色.

▷ **ma·hog·any** *adj* of a reddish-brown colour 红褐色的: *mahogany skin* 红褐色的皮肤.

maid /meɪd; med/ *n* **1** (often in compounds 常用以构成复合词) woman servant 女仆; 侍女: *We have a maid to do the housework.* 我们有个女仆干家务活儿. ○ *a 'dairy-maid, 'housemaid, 'nursemaid, etc* 奶场女工、女仆、保姆. **2** (*arch* 古) young unmarried woman; girl 未婚的年轻女子; 姑娘: *love between a man and a maid* 一男子与一年轻姑娘的爱情.

□ **ˌmaid of 'honour** (**a**) principal bridesmaid 首席女傧相. (**b**) unmarried woman attending a queen or princess (女王、王后或公主的)未婚侍女.

'maidservant *n* (*dated* 旧) maid(1) 女仆; 侍女. Cf 参看 MANSERVANT (MAN).

maiden /'meɪdn; 'medn̩/ *n* **1** (*arch* 古) girl or unmarried woman 少女; 姑娘; 未婚女子. **2** (also **ˌmaiden 'over**) (in cricket) over[3] in which no runs are scored (板球)未得分的一轮投球.

▷ **'maid·en·hood** /-hʊd; -ˌhud/ *n* [U] (*fml* 文) (**a**) state of being a maiden; virginity 处女身分; 童贞. (**b**) period when one is a maiden 少女时期.

maid·enly *adj* (*approv* 褒) gentle and modest; of or like a maiden 文雅的; 温顺的; (似)少女的: *her maidenly shyness* 她那少女的腼腆.

□ **maiden 'aunt** unmarried aunt (未婚的)姑, 姨.

'maidenhair *n* [U] type of fern with fine stalks and delicate fronds 掌叶铁线蕨.

'maidenhead /-hed; -ˌhɛd/ *n* (*arch* 古) **1** [C] hymen 处女膜. **2** [U] virginity 童贞.

'maiden name woman's family name before her marriage (女子的)娘家的姓.

maiden 'speech first speech in Parliament by a Member of Parliament (议员在议会中的)首次演说.

maiden 'voyage ship's first voyage (船的)首航, 处女航.

mail[1] /meɪl; mel/ *n* **1** [U] official system of collecting, transporting and delivering letters and parcels 邮政; 邮政系统; 邮政制度: *send a letter by airmail* 寄一封航空信 ○ *The letter is in the mail.* 信在邮寄途中. ○ [attrib 作定语] *the mail van, service, train* 邮政汽车、服务、列车 ○ *the 'mail-coach*, ie horse-drawn coach formerly used for carrying letters, etc (旧时)邮政马车. **2** (**a**) [U] letters, parcels, etc sent by post 信件; 邮包; 邮件: *Post office workers sort the mail.* 邮局工作人员分拣邮件. ○ *There isn't much mail today.* 今天邮件不多. ○ *The office mail is opened in the morning.* 公务信件在早晨开启. (**b**) [C] letters, parcels, etc delivered or collected at one time 一次发送或收取的邮件: *I want this letter to catch the afternoon mail.* 我想让这封信赶得及能随下午收取的邮件走. ○ *Is there another mail in the afternoon?* 下午还另有一批邮件吗? Cf 参看 POST[3].

▷ **mail** *v* [Tn, Dn·n, Dn·pr] **~ sth (to sb)** (*esp US*) send sth (to sb) by post (给某人)寄某物: *Mail me a new form, please.* 请给我寄一张新表格. ○ *I'll mail it to you tomorrow.* 我明天把它寄给你. Cf 参看 POST[4].

mailer *n* (*US*) (usu small) container or envelope in which sth is sent by post (通常为小的)邮寄物品的容器或封套.

□ **'mail-bag** *n* strong sack in which letters, parcels, etc are carried 邮袋.

'mailbox *n* (*US*) **1** = LETTER-BOX (LETTER). **2** = POST-BOX (POST[3]).

'mailing list list of names and addresses of persons to whom advertising material, etc is to be sent regularly 邮寄名单: *Please add my name to your mailing list.* 请把我的名字加入你们的邮寄名单中.

'mailman /-mæn; -ˌmæn/ *n* (*pl* **-men** /-mən; -mən/) (*US*) = POSTMAN (POST[3]).

'mail order system of buying and selling goods by post 邮购制度: *buy sth by mail order* 以邮购方式购买某物 ○ [attrib 作定语] *a mail-order business*, ie one dealing in mail-order goods 邮购商行 ○ *a mail-order catalogue*, ie one which lists mail-order goods and their prices 邮购商品价目表.

'mailshot *n* (**a**) piece of advertising material sent to potential customers by post (寄给潜在客户的)广告材料. (**b**) act of sending these 给潜在客户邮寄广告材料.

mail[2] /meɪl; mel/ *n* [U] body armour made of metal rings or plates linked together 铠甲: *a coat of mail* 一件铠甲.

▷ **mailed** *adj* (idm 习语) **the mailed fist** (*dated or rhet* 旧或修辞) (the threat of) armed force 武力; 武力威胁.

maim /meɪm; mem/ *v* [Tn usu passive 通常用于被动语态] wound or injure (sb) so that part of the body cannot be used 使(某人)残废: *He was maimed in a First World War battle.* 他在第一次世界大战的一場战斗中受伤致残.

main[1] /meɪn; men/ *adj* [attrib 作定语] (no comparative or superlative forms 无比较级或最高级形式) **1** most important; chief; principal 最重要的; 主要的; 首要的: *the main thing to remember* 要记住的主要东西 ○ *the main street of a town* 市内的主要街道 ○ *Be careful crossing that main road.* 过那条大路时要小心. ○ *the main meal of the day* 一天的正餐 ○ *the main course (of a meal)* (一餐的)主菜 ○ *My main concern is the welfare of the children.* 我最关心的是儿童的福利. **2** (idm 习语) **have an eye for/on/to the main chance** ⇨ EYE[1]. **in the 'main** for the most part; on the whole 大体上; 大致上: *These businessmen are in the main honest.* 这些商人大都很诚实.

▷ **mainly** *adv* chiefly; primarily 主要地; 首要地: *You are mainly to blame.* 主要应当责备你. ○ *The people in the streets were mainly tourists.* 街上的人大多是游客.

□ **main 'clause** (*grammar*) clause(1) that can stand on its own to make a sentence 主句.

'main deck upper deck of a ship 主甲板.

main 'drag (*infml* 口 *esp US*) main street of a town or city (城镇的)主要街道, 大街.

'mainframe *n* (also **mainframe com'puter**) large powerful computer with an extensive memory (计算机的)主机. Cf 参看 MICROCOMPUTER, MINICOMPUTER.

'mainland /-lænd; -ˌlænd/ *n* [sing] large mass of land forming a country, continent, etc without its islands 大陆.

ˌmain 'line principal railway line between two places (铁路的)干线, 主线: *the main line from London to Coventry* 从伦敦到考文垂的铁路干线 ○ [attrib 作定语] *a ˌmain-line 'train, 'station* 铁路干线列车、车站.

'mainline *v* [Ipr, Tn, Tn·pr] **~ sth (into sth)** (*sl* 俚) inject (a drug) into a large vein for stimulation, often because of addiction 将(毒品)注入大静脉(常因犯瘾): *be mainlining on hard drugs* 注射硬性毒品 ○ *She mainlined heroin (into a vein in her arm).* 她(向臂静脉中)注射海洛因.

'mainmast *n* principal mast of a sailing ship 主桅.

'mainsail /'meɪnsl, 'meɪnseɪl; 'mensl̩, 'menˌsel/ *n* principal sail on a sailing-ship, usu attached to the mainmast (主桅上的)主帆. ⇨illus at YACHT 见 YACHT 插图.

'mainspring *n* **1** principal spring of a clock or watch (钟表的)主发条. **2** (*fml fig* 文, 比喻) chief motive or reason (for sth) (某事的)主要动机或原因: *Her jealousy is the mainspring of the novel's plot.* 这部小说情节中贯穿了她的忌妒之心.

'mainstay /-steɪ; -ˌste/ *n* **1** rope from the top of the mainmast to the base of the foremast 主桅支索. **2** (*fig* 比喻) chief support(er) 主要的依靠; 支柱: *He is the mainstay of our theatre group.* 他是我们剧组的台柱.

'mainstream *n* [sing] **1** dominant trend, tendency, etc 主要倾向、趋势等; 主流: *the mainstream of political thought* 政治思潮的主流 ○ [attrib 作定语] *mainstream politics* 主流政治学. **2** style of jazz that is neither traditional nor modern 主流派爵士乐(介乎传统与现代之间者): [attrib 作定语] *a mainstream band, player* 主流派爵士乐乐队、演奏者.

main² /meɪn; men/ *n* **1** [C] (**a**) principal pipe bringing water or gas, or principal cable carrying electric current, from the source of supply into a building (自来水、煤气等的)总管道; (电流的)干线: *a burst water main* 爆裂的自来水总管道 ○ *The gas main exploded and set fire to the house.* 煤气总管爆炸引起房子失火. (**b**) principal sewer to which pipes from a building are connected (与建筑物下水道相连的)污水总管道. **2** [sing] (*arch or rhet* 古或修辞) open sea 大海: *ships on the main* 大海中的船只 ○ *the Spanish Main* 加勒比海. **3 the mains** [sing or pl *v*] source of water, gas or electricity supply to a building or area (供应一建筑物或地方的)水源, 煤气源, 电源: *My new house is not yet connected to the mains.* 我的新房子还没接上水、电、煤气呢. ○ *The electricity supply has been cut off/disconnected at the mains.* 电力供应已在电源处截断. ○ [attrib 作定语] *mains gas/water/electricity*, ie (supplied) from the mains 由煤气源[水源/电源]处供应的煤气[水/电] ○ *a mains/battery shaver*, ie one which can be operated either from a mains electricity supply or by batteries 交流电[电池]两用剃刀.

main³ /meɪn; men/ *n* (idm 习语) **with might and main** ⇨ MIGHT².

main·brace /ˈmeɪnbreɪs; ˈmen,bres/ *n* (idm 习语) **splice the main brace** ⇨ SPLICE.

main·tain /meɪnˈteɪn; menˈten/ *v* **1** [Tn, Tn·pr] **~ sth (with sth)** cause sth to continue; keep sth in existence at the same level, standard, etc 保持或维持某事物: *maintain friendly relations, contacts, etc (with sb)* (与某人)保持友好关系、接触等 ○ *enough food to maintain one's strength* 足以维持体力的食物 ○ *maintain law and order* 维持法治 ○ *maintain prices*, ie prevent them falling 维持住物价(防止跌落) ○ *maintain one's rights* 保留自己的权利 ○ *Maintain your speed at 60 mph.* 你要保持每小时60英里的速度. ○ *The improvement in his health is being maintained.* 他的健康状况仍在继续好转. **2** [Tn] support (sb) financially 在财务上支持(某人); 赡养; 扶养: *earn enough to maintain a family in comfort* 挣的钱足以维持一家人过舒适的生活 ○ *This school is maintained by a charity.* 该校由一慈善机构资助. ○ *She maintains two sons at university.* 她供两个儿子上大学. **3** [Tn] keep (sth) in good condition or working order 保养, 维修(某物): *maintain the roads, a house, a car, etc* 保养道路、房子、汽车等 ○ *Engineers maintain the turbines.* 机修工维修涡轮机. ○ *a well-maintained house* 保养良好的房子. **4** [Tn, Tf] assert (sth) as true 断言(某事)属实; 坚持: *maintain one's innocence* 坚持自己无辜 ○ *maintain that one is innocent of a charge* 对某项指控坚称无罪.

main·ten·ance /ˈmeɪntənəns; ˈmentənəns/ *n* [U] **1** maintaining or being maintained 保持; 维持; 赡养; 保养; 维修; 坚持: *the maintenance of good relations between countries* 保持国与国之间的友好关系 ○ *price maintenance* 保持价格不变 ○ *money for the maintenance of one's family* 养家的钱 ○ *He's taking classes in car maintenance.* 他正在上汽车维修课. ○ [attrib 作定语] *a maintenance man, gang, van* 维修工人、队、车. **2** (*law* 律) money that one is legally required to pay to support sb (根据法律须付的)赡养费, 扶养费: *He has to pay maintenance to his ex-wife.* 他必须负担前妻的生活费用. Cf 参看 ALIMONY.

□ **ˈmaintenance order** (*law* 律) order to pay maintenance(2) 赡养令; 扶养令.

mais·on·ette (also **mais·on·nette**) /ˌmeɪzəˈnet; ˌmezəˈnɛt/ *n* **1** self-contained dwelling on two floors, part of a larger building or block 占有两层楼的公寓. **2** (*dated* 旧) small house 小房子.

maize /meɪz; mez/ *n* [U] tall cereal plant bearing yellow grain on large ears 玉蜀黍; 玉米. Cf 参看 CORN ON THE COB (CORN¹), SWEETCORN (SWEET¹).

Maj *abbr* 缩写 = Major: *Maj (James) Williams* (詹姆斯·)威廉斯少校 ○ *Maj-Gen* (ie Major-General) *(Tom) Phillips* (汤姆·)菲利普斯少将.

ma·jestic /məˈdʒestɪk; məˈdʒɛstɪk/ *adj* having or showing majesty; stately; grand 威严的; 壮丽的; 高贵的; 宏伟的: *majestic views, scenery, etc* 壮丽的景色、风景等 ○ *The great ship looked majestic in her new colours.* 这艘巨轮着上新漆显得很雄伟. ▷ **ma·jest·ic·ally** /-klɪ; -klɪ/ *adv*: *She strode majestically through the palace.* 她威严地大步在宫殿中走过.

M

maj·esty /ˈmædʒəstɪ; ˈmædʒəstɪ/ *n* **1** [U] (**a**) impressive dignity and stateliness; grandeur, as of a king or queen 庄严; 威严; (如国王的)尊严: *all the majesty of royal ceremonies* 皇家仪典的富丽堂皇 ○ (*fig* 比喻) *the majesty of the mountain scenery* 高山景色的雄伟. (**b**) royal power 王权. **2 Majesty** [C] (used with a preceding *possess det* to address or speak of a royal person or royal people 冠以所有格限定词, 用以称呼或提及王室人员): *Very well, Your Majesty.* 是的, 陛下. ○ *at His/Her Majesty's command* 奉国王[女王]陛下谕旨 ○ *Their Majesties have arrived.* 国王与王后陛下已驾到.

ma·jor¹ /ˈmeɪdʒə(r); ˈmedʒɚ/ *adj* **1** [usu attrib 通常作定语] (more) important; great(er) (较)重要的; (较)大的; 主要的: *a major road* 干路 ○ *the major portion* 较大的部分 ○ *a major operation*, ie a surgical operation that could be dangerous to a person's life 大手术(可能危及生命者) ○ *a major suit*, ie (in cards, esp bridge) either spades or hearts (纸牌, 尤指桥牌的)高花色牌(黑桃或红桃) ○ *We have encountered major problems.* 我们遇到大问题了. ○ *She has written a major novel*, ie one of high quality and great importance. 她写了一部高质量的小说. Cf 参看 MINOR. **2** (*Brit dated or joc* 旧或谑) (in private schools) first or older of two brothers or boys with the same surname (esp in the same school) (私立学校中)(兄弟俩或同姓男生中)年长的, 大的: *Smith major* 大史密斯. Cf 参看 MINOR, SENIOR. **3** (*music* 音) (of a key or scale) having two full tones between the first and third notes (指调或音阶)大调的, 大音阶的: *the major key* 大调 ○ *a major scale* 大音阶 ○ *the key of C major, E flat major, etc* C大调、降E大调. Cf 参看 MINOR.

▷ **ma·jor** *v* [Ipr] **~ in sth** (*US*) specialize in a certain subject (at college or university) 主修(大专院校的)科目: *She majored in maths and physics (at university).* 她(在大学)主修数学和物理.

ma·jor *n* **1** [sing] (*music* 音) major key 大调: *shift from major to minor* 由大调转到小调. **2** [C] (*US*) (**a**) principal subject or course of a student at college or university (大专院校学生的)主修科目, 主修课程, 专业: *Her major is French.* 她的主修科目是法语. (**b**) student studying such a subject 某专业的学生: *She's a French major.* 她是法语专业的学生. **3 majors** [pl] (also **major ˈleagues**) (*US sport* 体) senior and most important leagues, esp in baseball and ice hockey 高级联赛协会(尤指棒球及冰上曲棍球的): [attrib 作定语] *major league baseball* 高级联赛协会棒球赛.

□ **major ˈpremise** the first, more general statement of a syllogism (逻辑学三段论法的)大前提.

ma·jor² /ˈmeɪdʒə(r); ˈmedʒɚ/ *n* army officer ranking between a captain and a lieutenant-colonel 陆军少校. ⇨App 9 见附录9.

□ **ˌmajor-ˈgeneral** *n* army officer ranking between a brigadier and a lieutenant-general 陆军少将. ⇨App 9 见附录9.

ma·jor·ity /məˈdʒɒrətɪ; *US* -ˈdʒɔːr-; məˈdʒɔrətɪ/ *n* **1** [Gp] the greater number or part; most 大多数; 大半; 大多: *A/The majority of people seem to prefer TV to radio.* 大部分人似乎喜欢看电视而不喜欢听收音机. ○ *The majority was/were in favour of the proposal.* 多数人赞成这个建议. ○ [attrib 作定语] *majority opinion, rule* 多数人的意见、多数裁定原则. Cf 参看 MINORITY. **2** [C] **~ (over sb)** (**a**) number by which votes for one side exceed those for the other side 超过对方的票数: *She was elected by a majority of 3 749.* 她以超过对方3 749票当选. ○ *They had a large majority over the other party at the last election.* 在上次选举中他们以悬殊的票数击败了对方. ○ *The government does not have an overall majority*, ie a majority over all other parties together. 政府没有获得(超过各党派票数的)总合多数票. (**b**) (*US*) number by which votes for one candidate exceed those for all other candidates together 多数票(一候选人的选票超过其他候选人票数的总和). Cf 参看 PLURALITY 3. **3** [sing] legal age of full adulthood 成年的法定年龄: *The age of majority is eighteen.* 成年的法定年龄是18岁. ○ *She reaches her majority next month.* 她下个月就到成年年龄了. **4** (idm 习语) **be in the/a majority** form the greater part/the larger number 构成大部分[大多数]: *Among the members of the committee those who favour the proposed changes are in the majority.* 委员中赞成提出修改意见的占大多数. **the silent majority** ⇨

SILENT.

□ maˌjority ˈverdict (*law* 律) verdict of the majority of a jury (陪审团)多数的裁决.

make[1] /meɪk; mek/ *v* (*pt*, *pp* **made** /meɪd; med/)

▸ CONSTRUCTING OR CREATING 建造或创造 **1** (**a**) [Tn, Tn·pr, Dn·n, Dn·pr] **~ sth (from/(out) of sth); ~ sth (for sb)** construct, create or prepare sth by combining materials or putting parts together (用材料或零件)做、制作、制造、建造或创造某物: *make a car, a dress, a cake* 制造汽车、做连衣裙、做蛋糕 ○ *make bread, cement, wine* 做面包、制水泥、酿葡萄酒 ○ *make* (ie manufacture) *paper* 造纸 ○ *God made man.* 上帝创造了人类. ○ *She makes her own clothes.* 她的衣服都是她自己做的. ○ *Wine is made from grapes.* 葡萄酒是用葡萄酿制的. ○ *'What is your bracelet made of?' 'It's made of gold.'* '你的镯子是什么材料做的?' '是金的.' ○ *I made myself a cup of tea.* 我自己沏了一杯茶. ○ *She made coffee for all of us.* 她给我们大家煮了咖啡. ○ *This car wasn't made* (ie is not big enough) *to carry eight people.* 这辆汽车不是坐八个人的. (**b**) [Tn·pr esp passive 尤用于被动语态] **~ sth into sth** put (materials or parts) together to produce sth 将(材料或零件)做成或制成某物: *Glass is made into bottles.* 玻璃可制成瓶子. (**c**) [Tn] arrange (a bed) so that it is ready for use 铺(床): *Please make your beds before breakfast.* 请在早饭前把床铺好. **2** [Tn, Tn·pr] cause (sth) to appear by breaking, tearing, removing material or striking (藉打破、撕破、移去材料或敲击)使(某物)出现, 形成: *The stone made a dent in the roof of my car.* 我的汽车顶让石头砸了个坑. ○ *The holes in the cloth were made by moths.* 布上的洞是虫子蛀的. **3** [Tn] create (sth); establish 制定(某事物); 规定: *These regulations were made to protect children.* 这些规则是为保护儿童而制定的. ○ *Who made this ridiculous rule?* 这条荒唐的规则是谁定的? **4** [Tn] write, compose or prepare (sth) 写, 创作, 准备(某事物): *make one's will* 立遗嘱 ○ *make a treaty with sb* 与某人签订协议 ○ *She has made* (ie directed) *several films.* 她已导演了几部影片. ○ *I'll ask my solicitor to make a deed of transfer.* 我要找律师拟一份让据书.

▸ CAUSING TO BECOME, DO OR APPEAR 使变为..., 做...或显得... **5** [Tn] cause (sth) 产生, 引起(某事物): *make a noise, disturbance, mess* 产生噪音、骚乱、混乱 ○ *She's always making trouble (for her friends).* 她总(给朋友)惹麻烦. **6** [Cn·a] cause (sb/sth) to be or become 使(某人[某事物])成为, 变为, 变成, 变得: *The news made her happy.* 这消息使她很高兴. ○ *She made clear her objections/made it clear that she objected to the proposal.* 她明确表示反对此提案. ○ *His actions made him universally respected.* 他的行为使他受到普遍尊敬. ○ *Can you make yourself understood in English?* 你能用英语把意思表达清楚吗? ○ *The full story was never made public.* 详情从未公之于众. ○ *She couldn't make herself/her voice heard above the noise of the traffic.* 来往车辆噪声很大, 她无法让别人听到她的声音. **7** [Cn·i] (**a**) force or compel (sb) to do sth 强迫, 迫使(某人)做某事物: *They made me repeat/I was made to repeat the story.* 他们逼我又把那事讲了一遍. ○ *She must be made to comply with the rules.* 必须强迫她遵守这些规则. ○ *He never tidies his room and his mother never tries to make him (do it).* 他从不整理自己的房间, 而他母亲也从未想逼他(整理). ⇨Usage at CAUSE 用法见 CAUSE. (**b**) cause (sb/sth) to do sth 使(某人[某事物])做某事物: *Onions make your eyes water.* 洋葱能刺激眼睛流泪. ○ *Her jokes made us all laugh.* 她说的笑话把我们都逗乐了. ○ *I couldn't make my car start this morning.* 今天早晨我的汽车发动不起来了. ○ *What makes you say that?* 是什么原因让你说出那种话来? ○ *I rang the doorbell several times but couldn't make anyone hear.* 我摁了几次门铃, 但没人应. ○ *Nothing will make me change my mind.* 无论什么事都不能使我改变主意. **8** [Cn·a, Cn·n, Cn·i] represent (sb/sth) as being or doing sth 使(某人[某事物])表现出某状况: *You've made my nose too big,* eg in a drawing or painting. 你把我的鼻子画得太大了. ○ *The novelist makes his heroine commit suicide at the end of the book.* 那小说作者在书的结尾让他的女主人公自杀了. **9** [Cn·n] elect (sb); appoint 选举(某人); 指派: *make sb king, an earl, a peer, etc* 拥戴某人当国王、封某人为伯爵、封某人为贵族 ○ *He was made spokesman by the committee.* 委员会派他当发言人. ○ *She made him her assistant.* 她委派他作自己的助手. **10** [Tn·pr, Cn·n] **~ sth of sb/sth** cause sb/sth to be or become sth 使某人[某事物]处于某状况或变成某事物: *We'll make a footballer of him yet,* ie turn him into a good footballer despite the fact that he is not a good one now. 我们还是要把他造就成优秀的足球运动员(虽然他现在还不是). ○ *This isn't very important — I don't want to make an issue of it.* 这并不十分重要 —— 我不想使其成为争论之点. ○ *Don't make a habit of it/Don't make it a habit.* 不要养成那样的习惯. ○ *She made it her business* (ie special task) *to find out who was responsible.* 她非要弄清是谁的责任不可.

▸ BEING OR BECOMING SOMETHING 成为...或变为... **11** [Ln] be or become (sth) through development; turn out to be 演变成(某事物); 结果是: *If you train hard, you'll make a good footballer.* 你要刻苦训练就能成为优秀的足球运动员. ○ *He'll never make an actor.* 他决当不成演员. ○ *She would have made an excellent teacher.* 她本可以成为杰出的教师. **12** [Ln] serve or function as (sth); constitute 用作(某事物); 起(某事物)的作用; 组成; 构成: *That will make a good ending to the book.* 那就成了这本书很好的结尾. ○ *This hall would make an excellent theatre.* 这座大厅可当作极好的剧院. **13** [Ln] add up to (sth); equal; amount to; constitute 合计等于(某数); 总计; 构成: *5 and 7 make 12.* 5加7等于12. ○ *A hundred pence make one pound.* 一百便士为一镑. ○ *How many members make a quorum?* 起码的法定人数是多少? ○ *His thrillers make enthralling reading.* 他的惊险小说引人入胜. ○ *The play makes a splendid evening's entertainment.* 这出剧是极好的晚间消遣. **14** [Ln] count as (sth) 算做(某事物): *That makes the tenth time he's failed his driving test!* 他驾驶测验不及格, 这次算第十次了!

▸ GAINING OR WINNING 获得或赢得 **15** [Tn] earn (sth); gain; acquire 赚得(某事物); 获得; 取得: *She makes £15 000 a year.* 她一年挣15 000英镑. ○ *make a profit/loss* 盈利[亏损] ○ *He made a fortune on the stock market.* 他在股票交易中发了财. ○ *How much do you stand to make?* 你决计要赚多少钱? **16** [Tn] (in cricket) score (sth) (在板球中)得(若干)分: *England made 235 for 5.* 英格兰队5名击球手共得235分. ○ *Botham made a century.* 博瑟姆得了一百分. **17** (in card games, esp bridge 用于牌戏, 尤于桥牌中) (**a**) [Tn] win a trick with (a particular card) 打(某张牌)赢一墩: *She made her ten of hearts.* 她打出红桃十赢了一墩. (**b**) [Tn] win (a trick) or fulfil (a contract) 赢(一墩); 完成(一定约墩数的约定). (**c**) [I, Tn] shuffle (the cards) 洗(牌): *It's my turn to make.* 该我洗牌了. **18** [Tn] (*sl sexist* 俚, 性别偏见) succeed in having sex with (a woman) 与(某女子)性交: *The guy doesn't make the girl until the last chapter.* 直到最后一章那个男子才和那个姑娘发生了性关系.

▸ OTHER MEANINGS 其他意义 **19** [no passive 不用于被动语态: Cn·a, Cn·n, Cn·t] calculate or estimate (sth) to be (sth) 计算, 估计(某事物): *What time do you make it?/What do you make the time?* 你说现在几点了? ○ *How large do you make the audience?* 你估计听众有多少? ○ *I make the total (to be) about £50.* 我看总数大约50英镑. ○ *I make the distance about 70 miles.* 我估计那段距离约有70英里. **20** [Tn no passive 不用于被动语态] (**a**) travel over (a distance) 走过(一段距离): *We've made 100 miles today.* 我们今天已走了100英里. (**b**) reach or maintain (a speed) 达到, 保持(某速度): *Can your car make a hundred miles per hour?* 你的汽车一小时能开一百英里吗? (**c**) manage to reach (a place) 设法到达(某处): *D'you think we'll make Oxford by midday?* 我们中午能到牛津吗? ○ *The train leaves in five minutes — we'll never make it,* ie reach the station in time to catch it. 火车再有五分钟就开了 —— 我们绝对赶不上了. ○ *I'm sorry I couldn't make your party last night.* 很抱歉, 昨晚我没能参加你们的聚会. ○ *Her new novel has made* (ie sold enough copies to be in) *the best-seller lists.* 她的新小说已列入畅销书目了. ○ *She'll never make* (ie win a place in) *the team.* 她绝对进不了那个运动队. ○ *He made* (ie reached the rank of) *sergeant in six months.* 他六个月后就当上了中士. ○ *The* *story made* (ie appeared on) *the front page of the national newspapers.* 这件事刊登在全国各报的第一版上. **21** [Tn, Dn·n] put (sth) forward; propose; offer 提出(某事); 提议; 提供: *Has she made you an offer* (ie said how much money she would pay you) *for your car?* 她说过她愿出多少钱买你的汽车吗? ○ *make a proposal* 提出建议 ○ *The employers made a new offer* (ie of a rise in wages) *to the work-force.* 雇主向工人提出增加工资的新建议. ○ *I made him a bid for the antique table.* 我向他出了个价, 要买那张古董桌子. **22** [Tn] cause or ensure the success of (sth) 促成, 确保(某事): *A good wine can make a meal.* 有了好酒饭就香. ○ *It was the beautiful weather that really made the holiday.* 是好天气成全了假日之美. **23** [It] behave as if one is about to do sth 表现出要做某事物的样子: *He made as if to strike her.* 他做出要打她的架势. ○ *She made to go but he told her to stay.* 她好像要走, 但他叫她留下. **24** eat or have (a meal) 吃(饭); 进(餐): *We make a good breakfast before leaving.* 我们动身前好好吃顿早饭. ○ *She made a hasty lunch.* 她匆匆吃了午饭. **25** (Often used in a pattern with a *n*, in which *make* and the *n* have the same meaning as a *v* similar in spelling to the *n* 常用于与名词连用的句型中, 其中 make 和名词之组合与该名词相应之动词同义, 如 *make a decision,* 即 decide; *make a guess (at sth),* 即 guess (at sth); for other expressions of this kind, see entries for *ns* 查阅类似词组见有关名词词条) **26** (idm 习语) **make do with sth; make (sth) ˈdo** manage with sth that is not really adequate or satisfactory 用某事物勉强应付; 将就; 凑合: *We were in a hurry so we had to make do with a quick snack.* 我们时间很紧, 只好胡乱吃了顿小吃. ○ *There isn't much of it but you'll have to make (it) do.* 东西不多, 你只好将就了. **make ˈgood** become rich and successful 变富; 获得成功: *a local boy made good*, eg as a businessman 一个发迹的本地男子. **make sth good (a)** pay for, replace or repair sth that has been lost or damaged 赔偿、替换或修理损坏之物: *She promised to make good the loss.* 她答应赔偿损失. ○ *make good the damage* 修复损坏之物 ○ *The plaster will have to be made good before you paint it.* 要先重新抹好灰泥再刷浆. **(b)** carry sth out; fulfil sth 履行某事; 实现某事: *make good a promise, threat, etc* 履行诺言、进行威胁. **ˈmake it** (*infml* 口) be successful in one's career 事业上获得成功: *He's never really made it as an actor.* 他当演员从未有所成就. **make the most of sth/sb/oneself** profit as much as one can from sth/sb/oneself 从某事物[某人/自己]处获取尽可能多的好处: *make the most of one's chances, opportunities, talents, etc* 充分利用时机、机会、才能等 ○ *It's my first holiday for two years so I'm going to make the most of it.* 这是我两年来的第一个假日, 所以要好好利用一下. ○ *She really tries to make the most of herself*, eg by dressing well. 她确实想尽量发挥自己的优势(如穿着漂亮). **make much of sth/sb (a)** (in negative sentences and questions 用于否定句和疑问句) understand sth 理解某事物: *I couldn't make much of his speech — it was all in Russian.* 他的演讲我大部分都听不懂——全是用俄语讲的. **(b)** treat sth/sb as very important; stress or emphasize sth 非常重视某事物[某人]; 强调某事物: *He always makes much of his humble origins.* 他总强调自己出身卑微. ○ *She was always made much of by her adoring friends.* 她的朋友总是那么崇拜她. **make nothing of sth** easily achieve sth that appears to be difficult; treat sth as trifling 轻易做好貌似困难之事; 对某事物满不在乎. **make or break sb/sth** be crucial in making sb/sth either a success or a failure 为某人[某事物]成败的关键: *The council's decision will make or break the local theatre.* 政务委员会将要决定当地剧院的命运. ○ [attrib 作定语] *It's make-or-break time for the local theatre.* 这是当地剧院存亡攸关的时刻. (For other idioms containing **make**, see entries for *ns, adjs*, etc 查阅与 **make** 搭配的其他习语, 见有关名词、形容词等的词条, 如 **make love** ⇨ LOVE[1]; **make merry** ⇨ MERRY.)

27 (phr v) **make after sb/sth** chase or pursue sb/sth 追逐或追捕某人[某事物]: *The policeman made after the burglar.* 警察追捕那窃贼.

M

make at sb move towards sb (as if) to attack him 逼近某人(似)欲袭击: *His attacker made at him with a knife.* 那人持刀袭击他.

make aˈway with oneself commit suicide 自杀. **make away with sth** = MAKE OFF WITH STH.

make for sb/sth move in the direction of sb/sth; head for sb/sth 朝某人[某物]的方向移动: *The ship made for the open sea.* 轮船驶向公海. ○ *It's getting late; we'd better turn and make for home.* 天晚了, 我们最好折回家吧. ○ *When the interval came everyone made for the bar.* 幕间休息时, 大家都涌向酒吧. ○ *I turned and ran when I saw the bull making for* (ie charging towards) *me.* 我看见那头牛向我冲来, 我赶紧转身跑开了. **make for sth** help to make sth possible; contribute to sth 有助于做某事物; 有利于某事物: *The large print makes for easier reading.* 大号字体容易阅读. ○ *Constant arguing doesn't make for a happy marriage.* 经常争吵不利于维系和美的婚姻. **be ˈmade for sb/each other** be well suited to sb/each other 完全适合某人[彼此完全适应]: *Ann and Robert seem (to be) made for each other.* 安和罗伯特真似天生的一对.

make sb/sth into sb/sth change or convert sb/sth into sb/sth 将某人[某事物]改变成或转变成某人[某事物]: *We're making our attic into an extra bedroom.* 我们正在把阁楼改装成一间额外的卧室. ○ *The local cinema has been made into a bingo hall.* 当地的电影院已改建成宾戈游戏厅了.

make sth of sb/sth understand the meaning or nature of sb/sth to be sth 理解某人[某事物]的意义或性质: *What do you make of it all?* 你明白那都是什么意思吗? ○ *What are we to make of her behaviour?* 她的表现我们应该怎样看? ○ *What do you make of* (ie think of) *the new manager?* 你认为这位新经理怎么样? ○ *I can make nothing of this scribble.* 我一点也看不懂这种潦草的字.

make ˈoff (*infml* 口) hurry or rush away, esp in order to escape 匆匆离开; (尤指)逃走: *The thieves made off in a stolen car.* 小偷乘偷来的汽车溜掉了. **make off with sth** (*infml* 口) steal sth and hurry away with it 携偷得之物逃跑: *Two boys made off with our cases while we weren't looking.* 有两个男孩子趁我们不备, 偷了我们的箱子就跑了.

make ˈout (*infml* 口) (usu in questions after *how* 通常用于 how 之后的问句) manage; survive; fare 设法应付; 活下来; 过活: *How did he make out while his wife was away?* 他妻子不在家时他是怎么生活的? ○ *How are you making out with Mary?* ie How is your relationship with her developing? 你与玛丽的关系怎样了? **make sb ˈout** understand (sb's character) 了解(某人的性格): *What a strange person she is! I can't make her out at all.* 她这个人真怪! 我根本无法了解她. **make sb/sth out** manage to see sb/sth or read sth 辨认出某人[某物]: *I could just make out a figure in the darkness.* 我隐约看见黑暗中有个人影. ○ *The dim outline of a house could be made out.* 有一所房子的模糊轮廓依稀可辨. ○ *Can you make out what that sign says?* 你看得见牌子上写的是什么吗? **make sth out** write out sth; complete sth 写出或填写某内容: *make out a cheque for £10* 开出一张10英镑的支票 ○ *Applications must be made out in triplicate.* 申请书必须填写一式三份. ○ *The doctor made me out a prescription.* 医生给我开了一个处方. **make sth out; make out if/whether...** understand sth 理解某事物: *I can't make out what she wants.* 我不明白她想要什么. ○ *How do you make that out?* ie How did you reach that conclusion? 你怎么得出那个结论的? ○ *I can't make out if she enjoys her job or not.* 我不知道她是否喜欢她的工作. **make out that...; make oneself/sb/sth out to be...** claim; assert; maintain 声称; 断言; 坚持: *He made out that he had been robbed.* 他声称他遭到抢劫. ○ *She's not as rich as people make out/as people make her out to be.* 她并不像人们说的那么富有. ○ *He makes himself out to be cleverer than he really is.* 他把自己说得比实际聪明.

make sb/sth over (into sth) change or convert sb/sth 改变或转变某人[某事物]: *The basement has been made over into a workshop.* 地下室已改建成工作间了. **make sth over (to sb/sth)** transfer the ownership of sth 转移某事物的所有权: *The estate was made over to the eldest son.* 地产的所有权已转给长子. ○ *He has made over the whole property to the National Trust.* 他已把全部房地产转交给全国名胜古迹托管协会.

make ˈup; make oneself/sb up put powder, lipstick, greasepaint, etc on the face, etc to make it more

attractive or to prepare it for an appearance in the theatre, on television, etc 为自己[某人]化妆: *She spent an hour making (herself) up before the party.* 她在聚会前化妆用了一个小时. ○ *She's always very heavily made up*, ie She puts a lot of make-up on her face. 她总是浓妆艳抹的. **make sth up** (**a**) form, compose or constitute sth 形成、构成或组成某物: *Animal bodies are made up of cells.* 动物的身体是由细胞组成的. ○ *What are the qualities that make up her character?* 形成她性格的特质是什么? ○ *These arguments make up the case for the defence.* 这些论据是有利于被告的理由. ○ *Society is made up of people of widely differing abilities.* 社会是由能力迥异的人组成的. (**b**) put sth together from several different things 将几种东西放在一起: *make up a bundle of old clothes for a jumble sale* 把旧衣物捆起准备义卖 ○ *She made up a basket of food for the picnic.* 她为野餐装好一篮子食物. (**c**) prepare (a medicine) by mixing different ingredients together 配(药): *The pharmacist made up the prescription.* 药剂师按处方配了药. (**d**) fashion (material) into a garment 将(布料)制成衣服: *Can you make up this dress length for me?* 你能用这块衣料给我做一件连衣裙吗? (**e**) prepare (a bed) for use; set up (a temporary bed) 铺(床); 支起(临时床): *We made up the bed in the spare room for our guest.* 我们在空着的房间里给客人铺好床. ○ *They made up a bed for me on the sofa.* 他们给我在沙发上铺好被褥当作床. (**f**) add fuel to (a fire) 给(火)添燃料: *The fire needs making up*, ie needs to have more coal put on it. 这火该添点煤了. (**g**) (esp passive 尤用于被动语态) put a hard surface on (a road) to make it suitable for motor vehicles 铺(路). (**h**) arrange (type, illustrations, etc) in columns or pages for printing 编排(版面); 拼(版). (**i**) invent sth, esp in order to deceive sb 捏造、虚构某事(尤指为欺骗某人): *make up an excuse* 编造借口 ○ *I couldn't remember a story to tell the children, so I made one up as I went along.* 我想不出有什么故事可给孩子讲了, 只好现编现讲. ○ *Stop making things up!* 不要胡编了! (**j**) complete sth 补足或补齐某事物: *We still need £100 to make up the sum required.* 我们还需要100英镑才能达到所需的数目. ○ *We have ten players, so we need one more to make up a team.* 我们已有十名运动员, 尚需一名才能凑成一个队. (**k**) replace sth 代替、取代、替换或赔还某事物: *Our losses will have to be made up with more loans.* 我们需增加贷款以赔补亏损. ○ *You must make up the time you wasted this afternoon by working late tonight.* 你今晚得熬夜来补回下午浪费的时间. **make up for sth** compensate for sth 补偿、赔偿、弥补或抵消某事物: *Hard work can make up for a lack of intelligence.* 勤能补拙. ○ *Nothing can make up for the loss* (ie death) *of a child.* 孩子的死亡是无可弥补的损失. ○ *The beautiful autumn made up for the wet summer.* 美丽的秋季抵消了多雨的夏季这一缺憾. **make up (to sb) for sth** compensate sb for the trouble or suffering one has caused him (因给某人带来麻烦或苦难)酬谢或报答某人: *How can I make up for the way I've treated you?* 我这样待你, 真不知怎样才能向你赔罪. **make up to sb** (*infml* 口) be pleasant to sb in order to win favours 讨好或巴结某人: *He's always making up to the boss.* 他总是巴结老板. **make it up to sb** (*infml* 口) compensate sb for sth he has missed or suffered or for money he has spent 补偿某人的损失、遭受的不幸或花费的钱财: *Thanks for buying my ticket — I'll make it up to you later.* 感谢你给我买了票 —— 我稍后再还给你钱. **make (it) 'up (with sb)** end a quarrel or dispute with sb 与某人和解或和好: *Why don't you two kiss and make up?* 你们俩接个吻, 言归于好吧! ○ *Has he made it up with her yet/ Have they made it up yet?* 他跟她[他们]和好了吗?
make with sth (*US sl* 俚) (esp imperative 尤用于祈使句) produce or supply sth quickly 迅速拿出或提供某物: *Make with the beers, buster!* 伙计, 拿啤酒来! **make it with sb** (*sl* 俚) succeed in having sex with sb 与某人性交: *Terry made it with Sharon on the back seat of his car.* 特里在他的汽车后排座位上和沙伦发生关系了.
□ **'make-believe** *n* [U] (**a**) pretending or imagining things; fantasizing 假装; 想像; 幻想: *indulge in make-believe* 沉溺于幻想中. (**b**) things thus imagined 想像之物: *live in a world of make-believe* 生活在幻想的世界中 ○ [attrib 作定语] *a make-believe world* 想像的世界.
'make-up *n* **1** [U] cosmetics such as powder, lipstick, etc used by a woman to make herself more attractive, or by an actor 化妆品; 化装用品: *She never wears make-up.* 她从来不搽化妆品. ○ *Her make-up is smudged.* 她搽的化妆品已蹭污了. **2** [sing] (**a**) combination of qualities that form a person's character or temperament 性格; 气质: *Jealousy is not part of his make-up.* 他的品性中没有忌妒. (**b**) combination of things, people, etc that form sth; composition of sth (事物、人等的)组合; 构成: *There are plans to change the make-up of the committee*, ie to replace some of the people who work on it. 有计划要改变委员会的人员组成. **3** [C usu *sing* 通常作单数] arrangement of type, illustrations, etc on a printed page 排版; 拼版.

make[2] /meɪk; mek/ *n* **~ (of sth)** **1** [U] way a thing is made 制造(法): *a coat of excellent make* 做工精致的大衣. **2** [C] origin of manufacture; brand 产品出处; 牌子: *cars of all makes* 各种牌子的汽车 ○ *What make of radio is it?* 这是什么牌子的收音机? **3** (idm 习语) **on the 'make** (*infml derog* 口, 贬) (**a**) trying to gain an advantage or profit for oneself 追求利益. (**b**) trying to win favour with sb for sexual pleasure 为肉欲追求异性.

maker /ˈmeɪkə(r); ˋmekɚ/ *n* **1 the/our Maker** [sing] the Creator; God 造物主; 上帝. **2** [C] (esp in compounds 尤用以构成复合词) person who makes sth 制作者; 制造者: *a 'dressmaker* ○ *a 'cabinet-maker.* **3** (idm 习语) **meet one's Maker** ⇨ MEET[1].

make·shift /ˈmeɪkʃɪft; ˋmek,ʃɪft/ *n, adj* (thing that is) used temporarily until sth better is available (临时的)代用品; 权宜的; 临时凑合的: *use an empty crate as a makeshift (table)* 把一个空木箱当作临时的桌子.

make·weight /ˈmeɪkweɪt; ˋmek,wet/ *n* **1** small quantity added to get the weight required (补足所需重量的)小的量. **2** (*fig* 比喻) thing or person, usu of little value, that supplies a deficiency, fills a gap, etc (作填补空缺用的)不重要的人或物.

mak·ing /ˈmeɪkɪŋ; ˋmekɪŋ/ *n* (idm 习语) **be the making of sb** make sb succeed or develop well 使某人成功或顺利: *These two years of hard work will be the making of him.* 这两年的艰苦工作能把他造就成材. **have the makings of sth** have the qualities needed to become sth 有条件成为某事物: *She has the makings of a good lawyer.* 她具备当个好律师的素质. **in the 'making** in the course of being made, formed or developed 在制造、形成或发展的过程中: *This first novel is the work of a writer in the making*, ie not yet an expert writer. 这第一本小说是作者正在成长锻炼中的作品. ○ *This model was two years in the making*, ie took two years to make. 这一型号的产品是用了两年时间制成的.

mal- *comb form* 构词成分 bad(ly); not; incorrect(ly) 坏; 不; 错误: *maladjusted* ○ *maladministration* ○ *malfunction.*

mal·ach·ite /ˈmæləkaɪt; ˋmælə,kaɪt/ *n* [U] green mineral that can be polished and used for ornaments, decoration, etc 孔雀石.

mal·ad·jus·ted /ˌmæləˈdʒʌstɪd; ˌmæləˋdʒʌstɪd/ *adj* (of a person) unable for psychological reasons to behave acceptably or deal satisfactorily with other people (指人)心理失调的: *a school for maladjusted children* 为心理失调儿童开设的学校.
▷ **mal·ad·just·ment** /ˌmæləˈdʒʌstmənt; ˌmæləˋdʒʌstmənt/ *n* [U] state of being maladjusted 心理失调.

mal·ad·min·is·tra·tion /ˌmælədˌmɪnɪˈstreɪʃn; ˌmæləd-ˌmɪnəˋstreʃən/ *n* [U] (*fml* 文) poor or dishonest management (of public affairs, business dealings, etc) (公共事务、生意等的)处理不善, 舞弊.

mal·ad·roit /ˌmæləˈdrɔɪt; ˌmæləˋdrɔɪt/ *adj* [usu pred 通常作表语] (*fml* 文) not clever or skilful; clumsy; bungling 不聪明; 不熟练; 笨拙; 粗劣: *His handling of the negotiations was maladroit.* 他的谈判技巧十分拙劣. Cf 参看 ADROIT. ▷ **mal·ad·roitly** *adv.* **mal·ad·roit·ness** *n* [U].

mal·ady /ˈmælədɪ; ˋmælədɪ/ *n* (*fml usu fig* 文, 通常作比喻) disease; illness 疾病; 病: *Violent crime is only one of the maladies afflicting modern society.* 暴力犯罪仅是为害现代社会的弊病之一.

mal·aise /mæˈleɪz; mæˋlez/ *n* [U, sing] (*fml* 文) (**a**) general feeling of illness, without clear signs of a particular disease 微恙; 不适. (**b**) feeling of uneasiness whose exact cause cannot be explained 莫名的不安:

M

You can see signs of (a creeping) malaise in our office. 在我们办公室里可以看到有某种(令人不寒而栗的)不安迹象. ○ *a deeply-felt malaise among the working classes* 在工人阶级中可深深体会到的不安.

mal·aprop·ism /ˈmæləprɒpɪzəm; ˋmæləprɑp,ɪzəm/ *n* comical confusion of a word with another, similar-sounding, word which has a quite different meaning, eg *'an ingenuous* (for *ingenious*) *machine for peeling potatoes'* 音近词的滑稽误用: 例如'心直的(原意为"精致的")土豆削皮机'.

mal·aria /məˈleərɪə; məˋlɛrɪə/ *n* [U] fever produced when germs are introduced into the blood by a bite from certain mosquitoes 疟疾: *a bad attack of malaria* 严重的疟疾 ○ [attrib 作定语] *a malaria sufferer* 疟疾病人.

▷ **mal·arial** /-ɪəl; -ɪəl/ *adj* (**a**) of malaria 疟疾的: *malarial symptoms* 疟疾症状. (**b**) having malaria 患疟疾的: *a malarial patient* 疟疾病人.

mal·con·tent /ˈmælkəntent; ˋmælkən,tɛnt/ *n*, *adj* (person who is) discontented and rebellious 不满者; 反叛者; 不满的; 反叛的: *All the trouble is being caused by a handful of malcontents.* 这些是非都是由一小撮不满分子搬弄的.

the male reproductive system 男性生殖系统

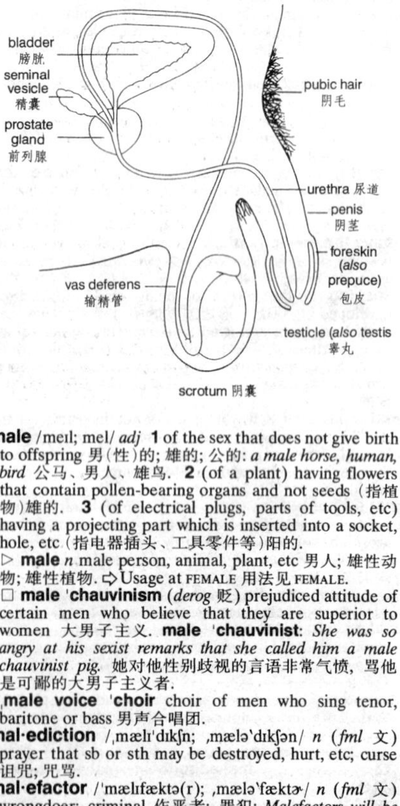

male /meɪl; mel/ *adj* **1** of the sex that does not give birth to offspring 男(性)的; 雄的; 公的: *a male horse, human, bird* 公马、男人、雄鸟. **2** (of a plant) having flowers that contain pollen-bearing organs and not seeds (指植物)雄的. **3** (of electrical plugs, parts of tools, etc) having a projecting part which is inserted into a socket, hole, etc (指电器插头、工具零件等)阳的.

▷ **male** *n* male person, animal, plant, etc 男人; 雄性动物; 雄性植物. ⇨Usage at FEMALE 用法见 FEMALE.

□ **male ˈchauvinism** (*derog* 贬) prejudiced attitude of certain men who believe that they are superior to women 大男子主义. **male ˈchauvinist**: *She was so angry at his sexist remarks that she called him a male chauvinist pig.* 她对他性别歧视的言语非常气愤, 骂他是可鄙的大男子主义者.

ˌ**male voice ˈchoir** choir of men who sing tenor, baritone or bass 男声合唱团.

mal·ediction /ˌmælɪˈdɪkʃn; ˌmæləˋdɪkʃən/ *n* (*fml* 文) prayer that sb or sth may be destroyed, hurt, etc; curse 诅咒; 咒骂.

mal·efactor /ˈmælɪfæktə(r); ˌmæləˋfæktɚ/ *n* (*fml* 文) wrongdoer; criminal 作恶者; 罪犯: *Malefactors will be pursued and punished.* 作恶的人要予以究治.

mal·efi·cent /məˈlefɪsnt; məˋlɛfəsn̩t/ *adj* (*fml* 文) causing or doing evil 作恶的; 犯罪的. ▷ **mal·efi·cence** /-sns; -sn̩s/ *n* [U].

mal·evol·ent /məˈlevələnt; məˋlɛvələnt/ *adj* ~ (**to/towards sb**) [usu attrib 通常作定语] wishing to do evil or cause harm to others; spiteful 恶意的; 恶毒的; 怀恨的: *a malevolent person, look, smile* 恶毒的人、神色、微笑.

▷ **mal·evol·ence** /-əns; -əns/ *n* [U] desire to do evil or cause harm to others; ill-will 恶意; 敌意; 怨恨. **mal·evol·ently** *adv*.

mal·forma·tion /ˌmælfɔːˈmeɪʃn; ˌmælfɔrˋmeʃən/ *n* **1** [U] state of being badly formed or shaped 畸形; 变形: *This treatment could result in malformation of the arms.* 这种处理方法能造成上肢畸形. **2** [C] badly formed part, esp of the body; deformity 畸形部位(尤指身体的): *a malformation of the spine* 脊椎的畸形.

▷ **mal·formed** /ˌmælˈfɔːmd; mælˋfɔrmd/ *adj* badly formed or shaped 畸形的; 变形的.

mal·func·tion /ˌmælˈfʌŋkʃn; mælˋfʌŋkʃən/ *v* [I] (*fml* 文) (of a machine) fail to work normally or properly (指机器)运转不正常, 发生故障, 失灵: *The computer malfunctioned and printed out the wrong data.* 计算机出了故障, 印出的资料不正确.

▷ **mal·func·tion** *n* [C, U] (*fml* 文) failure of this kind 故障; 失灵: *a major malfunction* 严重故障 ○ *several instances of malfunction* 几起故障.

mal·ice /ˈmælɪs; ˋmælɪs/ *n* [U] **1** ~ (**towards sb**) desire to harm others 敌意; 恶意; 怨恨: *She certainly bears you no malice.* 她对你肯定没有恶意. ○ *harbour no malice towards sb* 对某人不怀恨 ○ *a look of pure malice* 充满敌意的目光 ○ *She did it out of malice.* 她是出于恶意而那样做的. **2** (idm 习语) **with ˌmalice aˈforethought** (*law* 律) with the conscious intention to commit a crime 蓄意犯罪.

▷ **ma·li·cious** /məˈlɪʃəs; məˋlɪʃəs/ *adj* intended to harm others 恶意的; 恶毒的; 蓄意的: *(a) malicious gossip* 恶意的闲话 ○ *a malicious act, smile, comment* 恶毒的行为、微笑、评论. **ma·li·ciously** *adv*. **ma·li·cious·ness** *n* [U] malicious nature (of sth) 恶毒; 恶意: *the sheer maliciousness of the gossip* 这种流言蜚语所含的纯粹的恶意.

ma·lign /məˈlaɪn; məˋlaɪn/ *v* [Tn] say unpleasant or untrue things about (sb) 诽谤, 中伤, 诬蔑(某人): *malign an innocent person* 诋毁一个清白的人.

▷ **ma·lign** *adj* (*fml* 文) harmful 有害的; 恶意的: *a malign influence, intention, effect* 有害的影响、意图、效果. Cf 参看 BENIGN.

ma·lig·nity /məˈlɪgnətɪ; məˋlɪgnətɪ/ *n* [U].

ma·lig·nant /məˈlɪgnənt; məˋlɪgnənt/ *adj* **1** (of people or their actions) feeling or showing great desire to harm others; malevolent (指人或人的行为)恶毒的, 恶意的: *a malignant slander, attack, thrust* 恶意的诽谤、攻击、抨击. **2** (**a**) (of a tumour) growing uncontrollably, and likely to prove fatal (指肿瘤)恶性的, 致命的: *The growth is not malignant.* 这个瘤不是恶性的. (**b**) (of diseases) harmful to life (指疾病)恶性的, 致命的.

▷ **ma·lig·nancy** /-nənsɪ; -nənsɪ/ *n* **1** [U] state of being malignant 恶毒; 恶意; 恶性. **2** [C] malignant tumour 恶性肿瘤.

ma·lig·nantly *adv*.

ma·lin·ger /məˈlɪŋgə(r); məˋlɪŋgɚ/ *v* [I] (*derog* 贬) (usu in the continuous tenses 通常用于进行时态) pretend to be ill in order to avoid work or duty 装病(以逃避工作或责任); 诈病.

▷ **ma·lin·gerer** *n* (*derog* 贬) person who malingers (为逃避工作或责任)装病的人.

mall /mæl, mɔːl; mɔl/ *n* (*esp US*) street or covered area with rows of shops, closed to traffic 商店街, (非露天的)商店区(车辆禁止入内): *a shopping mall* 购物大街.

mal·lard /ˈmælɑːd; *US* ˈmælərd; ˋmælɚd/ *n* (*pl* unchanged 复数不变) type of common wild duck 绿头鸭(野鸭).

mal·le·able /ˈmælɪəbl; ˋmælɪəbl̩/ *adj* **1** (of metals) that can be beaten or pressed into different shapes easily (指金属)可锻的, 有延展性的. **2** (*fig* 比喻) (of a person, his ideas, etc) easily influenced or changed (指人、主意等)易受影响的, 易变的: *The young are more malleable than the old.* 年轻人比老年人容易受影响. ▷ **mal·le·ab·il·ity** /ˌmælɪəˈbɪlətɪ; ˌmælɪəˋbɪlətɪ/ *n* [U].

mal·let /ˈmælɪt; ˋmælɪt/ *n* **1** hammer with a wooden head, eg for striking the handle of a chisel 木槌(如用于敲击凿子把柄者). ⇨illus at CHISEL 见 CHISEL 插图. **2** long-handled hammer with a wooden head, used for striking the ball in croquet or polo (槌球中的)长柄木槌; (马球中的)击球棍.

M

mal·low /ˈmæləʊ; ˋmælo/ *n* plant with hairy stems and leaves and pink, purple or white flowers 锦葵.

malm·sey /ˈmɑːmzɪ; ˋmɑmzɪ/ *n* [U] strong sweet wine from Greece, Spain, Madeira, etc (产自希腊、西班牙、马德拉岛等地的)浓烈的甜葡萄酒.

mal·nour·ished /ˌmælˈnʌrɪʃt; *US* -ˈnɜː-; mælˋnɝɪʃt/ *adj* suffering from malnutrition 营养不良的. Cf 参看 UNDERNOURISHED.

mal·nu·tri·tion /ˌmælnjuːˈtrɪʃn; *US* -nuː-; ˌmælnuˋtrɪʃən/ *n* [U] condition resulting from a lack of (the right type of) food 营养不良: *children suffering from severe malnutrition* 严重营养不良的儿童.

mal·od·or·ous /ˌmælˈəʊdərəs; mælˋodərəs/ *adj* (*fml* 文) smelling unpleasant 恶臭的: *malodorous drains, ditches, bogs, etc* 臭气熏天的排水沟、沟渠、沼泽等.

mal·prac·tice /ˌmælˈpræktɪs; mælˋpræktɪs/ *n* (*law* 律) (**a**) [U] careless, illegal or unethical behaviour by sb in a professional or official position 玩忽职守; 营私舞弊; 渎职: *lawyers, doctors, etc sued for malpractice* 因渎职而受到控告的律师、医生等. (**b**) [C] instance of this 玩忽职守; 营私舞弊; 渎职: *Various malpractices by police officers were brought to light by the enquiry.* 警察的各种不法行为经调查已揭露出来.

malt /mɔːlt; mɔlt/ *n* **1** [U] grain (usu barley) that has been soaked in water and allowed to germinate and then dried, used for making beer, whisky, etc 麦芽(谷芽, 通常指大麦芽): [attrib 作定语] *malt liquors* 麦芽酒 ○ *malt whisky* 麦芽威士忌. **2** [C] variety of malt whisky 麦芽威士忌: *an excellent 12-year-old malt* 陈化12年的优质麦芽威士忌.

▷ **malt** *v* (**a**) [Tn] make (grain) into malt 使(谷物)成为麦芽. (**b**) [I] (of grain) become malt (指谷物)成为麦芽.

□ **malted ˈmilk** drink made from malt and dried milk 以麦芽和奶粉制成的饮料; 麦乳精.

Malt·ese /ˌmɔːlˈtiːz; mɔlˋtiz/ *adj, n* (*pl* unchanged 复数不变) (language or native) of Malta 马耳他的; 马耳他语; 马耳他人.

□ ˌ**Maltese ˈcross** cross with the arms of equal length, each of which tapers towards the centre 马耳他十字. ⇨ illus at CROSS 见 CROSS 插图.

mal·treat /ˌmælˈtriːt; mælˋtrit/ *v* [Tn] (*fml* 文) treat (a person or an animal) with violence or cruelty; mistreat 残暴对待(人或动物); 虐待.

▷ **mal·treat·ment** *n* [U] maltreating or being maltreated 虐待: *the man's maltreatment of his dog* 那男子对他的狗的虐待 ○ *the dog's maltreatment by his owner* 那狗受其主人的虐待.

mama /məˈmɑː; ˋmɑmə/ *n* (*dated Brit infml* 旧, 口) mother 妈妈.

mamba /ˈmæmbə; ˋmɑmbə/ *n* black or green poisonous African snake 曼巴(非洲黑色或绿色毒蛇).

mamma /ˈmɑːmə; ˋmɑmə/ *n* (*US infml* 口) mother 妈妈.

mam·mal /ˈmæml; ˋmæml̩/ *n* any of the class of animals that give birth to live offspring and feed their young on milk from the breast 哺乳动物. ▷ **mam·ma·lian** /mæˈmeɪlɪən; mæˋmelɪən/ *adj*.

mam·mary /ˈmæmərɪ; ˋmæmərɪ/ *adj* [attrib 作定语] (*biology* 生) of the breasts 乳房的: *the mammary gland*, ie the one which produces milk 乳腺.

mam·mon (also **Mammon**) /ˈmæmən; ˋmæmən/ *n* [sing] (*usu derog* 通常作贬义) god of wealth, regarded as evil or immoral 财富之神(视为邪恶的或不道德的): *those who worship mammon*, ie greedy people who value money (too) highly 那些视财如命的贪婪的人.

mam·moth /ˈmæməθ; ˋmæməθ/ *n* large hairy type of elephant, now extinct 猛犸.

▷ **mam·moth** *adj* [attrib 作定语] immense; huge 庞大的; 巨大的: *a mammoth project, corporation, undertaking* 庞大的工程、公司、企业.

mammy /ˈmæmɪ; ˋmæmɪ/ *n* (*US*) **1** (word for *mother* used by children 妈妈(儿语)) **2** (*dated now offensive* 旧, 今作轻蔑语) black nursemaid for white children 照看白人小孩的黑人保姆.

man[1] /mæn; mæn/ *n* (*pl* **men** /men; mɛn/) **1** [C] adult male human being 男人; 成年男子: *clothes for men* 男人的服装. **2** [C] human being of either sex; person 人(男女均可): *All men must die.* 人皆有一死. ○ *Growing old is something a man has to accept.* 逐渐衰老是任何人都得承认的事实. **3** [sing] (without *the* or *a* 不加 the 或 a) the human race; mankind 人类: *Man is mortal.* 人终有一死. ○ *the origin of man* 人类的起源 ○ *medieval man*, ie all people in the Middle Ages 中世纪的人类. ⇨Usage 见所附用法. **4** [C] husband, male lover, boy-friend, etc 丈夫; 男情人; 男朋友: *Her man's been sent overseas by his employers.* 她的丈夫已被雇主派到海外. ○ *be made man and wife*, ie be married 结成夫妻. **5** [C usu *pl* 通常作复数] male person under the authority of sb else (男性的)下属: *officers and men in the army, navy, etc* 陆军、海军等的官兵 ○ *The manager gave the men* (ie the workers) *their instructions.* 经理给雇员下达了指示. **6** [sing] (*fml* 文) manservant; valet 男仆; 贴身男仆: *My man will drive you home.* 我的仆人将开车送你回家. **7** [C] (*fml* 文) present or former member of a named university (与校名连用)大学生, 大学校友: *a Cambridge man* 剑桥大学学生 ○ *a Yale man* 耶鲁大学学生. **8** [sing] (*infml* 口) (used as a form of address, usu in a lively or an impatient way 用作称呼, 通常含轻松或不耐烦的语气): *Hey, man, are you coming?* 嘿, 老兄, 你来吗? ○ *Be quiet, man!* 老弟, 安静点! **9** [C] male person with the qualities of courage, toughness, etc often associated with men 男子汉; 大丈夫: *Be a man!* ie Be brave. 要做个大丈夫(拿出勇气来)! ○ *They acquitted themselves like men.* 他们表现得像男子汉. **10** [C] piece used in games such as chess, draughts, etc (国际象棋、国际跳棋等的)棋子: *capture all sb's men* 吃掉某人所有的棋子. **11** (idm 习语) **an angry young man** ⇨ ANGRY. **as good, etc as the next man** ⇨ NEXT[1]. **as one man** acting unanimously; with everyone agreeing 一齐; 一致: *The staff speak as one man on this issue.* 在这个问题上全体职员意见一致. **be sb's man** be the person required or ideally suited for a task 正是所需要的人: *If you need a driver, I'm your man.* 你要是需要司机, 我当最合适. ○ *If you want a good music teacher, he's your man.* 你们要是缺个好的音乐教师, 他就是最理想的人选. **be man enough (to do sth)** be brave enough 有足够勇气: *You're not man enough to fight me!* 你没有那个胆量跟我打! **be one's own ˈman** be able to arrange and decide things independently 能独立自主; 能作主: *He's his own man, but he doesn't ignore advice.* 他虽然自有主张, 但并不轻视别人的意见. **be twice the man/woman** ⇨ TWICE. **the child is father of the man** ⇨ CHILD. **dead men's shoes** ⇨ DEAD. **dead men tell no tales** ⇨ DEAD. **a dirty old man** ⇨ DIRTY. ˌ**every man for himˈself (and the devil take the hindmost)** (*saying* 谚) everyone must look after his own interests, safety, etc 人各为己: *In business, it's every man for himself.* 在商言商, 人各为己. ˌ**every man ˈjack** (*rhet esp derog* 修辞, 尤作贬义) every single person 人人; 每个人: *Every man jack of them ran off and left me!* 他们一个个都跑了, 把我撇下了! **the grand old man** ⇨ GRAND. **hit/kick a man when he's down** continue to attack or injure sb who is already defeated 继续打击或伤害已失败的人; 落井下石. **the inner man** ⇨ INNER. **make a ˈman (out) of sb** turn a young man into an adult 使某人长大成人: *The army will make a man of him.* 军队将把他锻炼成人. **a** ˌ**man about ˈtown** man who spends much time at fashionable parties, clubs, theatres, etc 经常出没游乐场所的男人; 花花公子. ˌ**man and ˈboy** from boyhood onwards (指男子)从小到大: *He has worked for the firm, man and boy, for thirty years.* 他从小至今已为该商行干了三十年. **the** ˌ**man in the ˈstreet; the** ˌ**man on the** ˌ**Clapham ˈomnibus** (*Brit*) the average ordinary person of either sex 普通人, 一般人(男女均可): *The man in the street is opposed to this idea.* 老百姓反对这种想法. **a** ˌ**man of ˈGod** (*fml or rhet* 文或修辞) clergyman 神职人员. **a man/woman of parts** ⇨ PART[1]. **the** ˌ**man of the ˈmatch** man who gives the best performance in a particular game of cricket, football, etc (在板球、足球等运动某场比赛中的)最佳运动员: *be voted man of the match* 被选为最佳运动员. **a** ˌ**man of ˈstraw** (*rhet* 修辞) (**a**) person of apparent, but not real, power 貌似有力的人物. (**b**) imaginary or very weak person presented as an opponent 想像的敌手; 很弱的对手. **a man/woman of his/her word** ⇨ WORD. **a man/woman of the world** ⇨ WORLD. ˌ**man to ˈman** frankly; openly 诚

恳地; 公开地: *Let's talk man to man.* 咱们推心置腹地谈谈吧. ○ [attrib 作定语] *a ˌman-to-man ˈtalk* 坦诚的交谈. **a marked man** ⇨ MARK². **the odd man/one out** ⇨ ODD. **the poor man's sb/sth** ⇨ POOR. **sort out the men from the boys** ⇨ SORT². **time and tide wait for no man** ⇨ TIME¹. **to a ˈman; to the last ˈman** all, without exception 所有人; 毫无例外地: *To a man, they answered 'Yes'.* 他们都一致回答'是'. ○ *They were killed, to the last man, in a futile attack.* 因一次进攻失败, 他们全部被杀, 无一幸免. **one's young lady/young man** ⇨ YOUNG.

▷ **man** *interj* (*infml* 口 *esp US*) (used to express surprise, admiration, etc 用以表示惊奇、赞美等): *Man! that's huge!* 好傢伙! 那么大呀!

-man (forming compound *ns* 用以构成复合名词) **1 (a)** (with *ns* 与名词结合) person who lives in 在…生活的人: *countryman.* **(b)** (with *adjs* and *ns* 与形容词和名词结合) native of …的当地人: *Irishman.* **2** (with *ns* 与名词结合) man concerned with 与…有关的人: *ˈbusinessman* ○ *doorman* ○ *ˈpostman.* Cf 参看 -WOMAN (WOMAN). ⇨ Usage at CHAIR 用法见 CHAIR.

-manship (forming uncountable *ns* 用以构成不可数名词) skill or quality of 有…技巧或性质: *craftsmanship* ○ *sportsmanship.* Cf 参看 -SHIP.

□ **ˌman-at-ˈarms** *n* (*pl* **ˌmen-at-ˈarms**) (in the Middle Ages) mounted soldier with heavy armour and weapons (中世纪的)重骑兵.

ˈman-eater *n* lion, tiger, etc that attacks men 攻击人的狮、虎等: (*fig joc* 比喻, 谑) *My sister's a real man-eater!* 我姐姐真是个母老虎! **ˈman-eating** *adj* [attrib 作定语]: *a man-eating lion, tiger, etc* 吃人的狮子、老虎等.

man ˈFriday male general assistant in an office, etc (办公室等的)男勤杂工.

ˈmanhole *n* hole in a street fitted with a lid, through which sb can enter a sewer, etc to inspect it 人孔, 检修孔(街道上设置的有盖洞口, 人可进入检修下水道等): [attrib 作定语] *manhole cover* 人孔盖.

ˈman-hour *n* work done by one person in one hour 工时: *The builder reckons 15 man-hours for the job.* 建筑者估计这个活儿需要15个工时.

ˈman-hunt *n* large-scale search for a (male or female) criminal, etc (对男或女罪犯等的)大搜捕: *Police have launched a man-hunt for the bullion robbers.* 警方已大举搜捕抢劫金条的罪犯.

ˌman of ˈletters, ˌwoman of ˈletters person who does literary work, eg as a writer or critic 文学工作者.

ˌman-ˈmade *adj* not naturally made; artificial 人工的; 人造的: *ˌman-made ˈfibres, ˈchemicals* 人造纤维、化学制品.

ˌman-of-ˈwar *n* (*pl* **ˌmen-of-ˈwar**) armed sailing-ship of a country's navy 帆式军舰.

ˈmanservant *n* (*pl* **menservants**) male servant 男仆. Cf 参看 MAIDSERVANT (MAID).

ˈman-size (also **ˈman-sized**) *adj* of a size suitable for a man; large (大小)适合男人的; 大型的; 大号的: *a man-size(d) handkerchief, beefsteak, portion* 大号的手帕、大块的牛排、一大份.

ˈmanslaughter *n* [U] crime of killing a person unlawfully but not intentionally 非预谋杀人罪; 过失杀人: *commit manslaughter* 犯了过失杀人罪. Cf 参看 HOMICIDE 1, MURDER 1.

ˈmantrap *n* trap with large jaws formerly used for catching poachers, trespassers, etc 捕人陷阱(旧时用以捕捉偷猎者、入侵私地者等).

NOTE ON USAGE 用法: **Man** can be used, in a similar way to **mankind**, to mean 'all men and women'. ☆ **man** 的用法可与 **mankind** 相同, 指不分男女所有的人. Many people consider this biased against women and avoid it by using **humanity, the human race** (singular) or **humans, human beings, people** (plural). 许多人认为这种用法是对女性的歧视而加以避免, 改用 **humanity**、**the human race**(单数)或 **humans**、**human beings**、**people**(复数).

M

man² /mæn; mæn/ *v* **(-nn-)** [Tn, Tn·pr] **~ sth (with sb)** supply sth (with men or, sometimes, women) for service or to operate something 给某事物提供(男性或有时为女性)服务人员或操作人员: *man the boat with a replacement crew* 给船提供替换船员 ○ *a warship manned by experienced officers* 配备有经验的军官的军舰 ○ *Barbara will man the telephone switchboard till we get back.* 我们回来前由巴巴拉管理电话总机.

man·acle /ˈmænəkl; ˋmænəkl/ *n* (usu *pl* 通常作复数) one of a pair of chains or metal bands for binding the hands or feet; fetter 手铐; 脚镣; 束缚.

▷ **man·acle** *v* [Tn] bind (sb/sth) with manacles 给(某人[某物])上镣铐或加束缚.

man·age /ˈmænɪdʒ; ˋmænɪdʒ/ *v* **1 (a)** [Tn] be in charge of (sth); run 负责(某事物); 管理; 经营: *manage a shop, business, factory, etc* 管理商店、企业、工厂等 ○ *manage a department, project* 负责一部门、工程 ○ *Jones manages the finances here.* 琼斯主管这里的财务. **(b)** keep (a child, an animal, etc) in order; control 管理(小孩、动物等); 控制; 驾驭; 照管: *manage a difficult horse* 驾驭一匹不驯服的马 ○ *Can you manage children well?* 你能管好孩子吗? ○ *He's good at managing his money*, ie at controlling how much he spends. 他善于理财. **2 (a)** [I, Ipr, Tn, Tt] **~ (on sth); ~ (without sb/sth)** succeed in doing (sth); cope (with sth) 做成(某事); 应付(某事): *I just can't manage* (ie live) *on £50 a week.* 我可没办法靠每星期50英镑维持生活. ○ *I can't borrow the money so I'll have to manage without.* 我借不到这笔钱, 只好将就了. ○ *I shan't be able to manage (the job) (without help).* (没有帮助)我将无法应付(这项工作). ○ *In spite of these insults, she managed not to get angry.* 她尽管受到这些侮辱, 还是忍着没发火. ○ *I just about managed to get up the stairs.* 我总算挣扎着上了楼. **(b)** [Tn] (used often with *can, could* 常与can、could连用) succeed in producing, achieving or doing (sth) 产生, 达到, 做成(某事物): *I haven't been learning French for long, so I can only manage* (ie speak) *a few words.* 我学法语的时间还不长, 所以我只能凑合着说几句. ○ *Even a schoolboy could manage* (ie write) *a better story than that.* 连小学生写的故事都比那个好. ○ *I couldn't manage* (ie eat) *another thing, I'm afraid.* 我看我再也吃不下了. ○ *Despite his disappointment, he managed a smile*, ie succeeded in smiling. 他尽管很失望, 还是强颜为笑. ○ *Can you manage lunch* (ie come to lunch) *on Tuesday?* 你星期二能来吃午饭吗?

▷ **man·age·able** *adj* that can be managed; easily controlled 能处理的; 易管理的; 易控制的: *a business of manageable size* 在规模方面便于管理的企业.

□ **ˌmanaging diˈrector** person who controls the business operations of a company 总经理.

man·age·ment /ˈmænɪdʒmənt; ˋmænɪdʒmənt/ *n* **1** [U] control and organization (of a business, etc) (企业等的)管理, 经营: *The failure was caused by bad management.* 这种挫折是经营不善所致. ○ [attrib 作定语] *a management course, consultant* 管理课程、顾问. **2** [CGp] all those who control a business, enterprise, etc (公司、企业等的)主管人员, 管理部门, 资方: *Management/The management is/are considering closing the factory.* 主管部门正在考虑把工厂关闭. ○ *joint consultation between workers and management* 劳方与资方间的协商 ○ *The business is under new management.* 该公司正由新的管理人员领导. ○ [attrib 作定语] *a top management job* 高层管理工作. **3** [U] skill in dealing with people 与人交往的技巧; 手腕: *She gets them to accept these changes by tactful management.* 她以圆滑的手腕说服他们接受这些变动.

man·ager /ˈmænɪdʒə(r); ˋmænɪdʒɚ/ *n* **1 (a)** person controlling a business, etc 经理; 管理人: *a shop, cinema, hotel, etc manager* 商店、影院、旅店等的经理 ○ *departmental managers* 部门管理人员. **(b)** person dealing with the business affairs of an entertainer, a sportsman, etc (演员、运动员等的)经理人, 经纪人. **(c)** person who controls a sports team (运动队的)经理: *the England football manager* 英格兰足球队经理. **2** (usu preceded by an *adj* 通常前面有形容词) person who controls people, a household, money, etc in the way specified 以某种方式管理人、家庭、钱财等的人: *She's not a very good manager — she always spends more money than she earns.* 她不大会理财——总是入不敷出.

▷**man·ager·ess** /ˌmænɪdʒəˈres; ˋmænɪdʒərɪs/ *n* woman who is in charge of a business, esp a shop, restaurant, hotel, etc 女经理, 女管理人(尤指商店、饭店、旅馆等的).

ma·na·ger·ial /ˌmænəˈdʒɪərɪəl; ˌmænəˈdʒɪrɪəl/ *adj* of managers or management 经理的; 管理的; 经营的: *a managerial job, meeting, decision* 管理工作、管理会议、经理的决定 ○ *managerial skills, expertise, etc* 经营管理的技巧、专门知识等.

man·darin /ˈmændərɪn; ˈmændərɪn/ *n* **1 Mandarin** [U] official standard spoken language of China (中国的)官话(普通话的旧称). **2** [C] (formerly) high-ranking government official in China (旧时)中国政府的高级官吏. **3** [C] high-ranking official who behaves and writes in a remote and difficult way 态度冷淡文字艰涩的高级官吏: *Whitehall mandarins*, ie top British civil servants 英国政府中因循守旧的官僚 ○ [attrib 作定语] *pages and pages of mandarin prose* 长篇累牍的晦涩文章. **4** [C] (also ˌ**mandarin ˈorange**) type of small orange with loose skin 橘子. **5** [C] (also ˌ**mandarin ˈduck**) small (originally Chinese) duck with brightly coloured feathers 鸳鸯(原产中国).

man·date /ˈmændeɪt; ˈmændet/ *n* (usu *sing* 通常作单数) **1 ~ (to do sth)** (**a**) authority given to a party, trade union, etc by the people who support it (党派、工会等的拥护者对所在组织的)授权: *Our election victory has given us a mandate to reform the economy.* 我们选举中获胜, 这就使我们有权进行经济改革. ○ *We have a mandate from the union membership to proceed with strike action.* 我们获得工会会员同意, 继续罢工. (**b**) order (given to sb to do sth); mission 命令; 训令; 使命: *The government gave the police a mandate to reduce crime.* 政府命令警方进一步打击犯罪活动. **2** (formerly) power given to a country to administer a territory (旧时)(授予某国对某地的)委托统治权.
▷ **man·date** *v* **1** [Tn esp passive 尤用于被动语态] put (a territory) under a mandate(2) 将(某地)委托某国管理: *the mandated territories* 托管地. **2** (**a**) [Dn·t] give (sb) the power (to do sth) by mandate(2) 授权(某人)根据委托统治权(做某事): *Britain was mandated to govern the former colony of German East Africa.* 英国受权代管德国在东非的前殖民地. (**b**) [Tn esp passive 尤用于被动语态] order (sb) to do sth 命令(某人)做某事.

man·dat·ory /ˈmændətərɪ; *US* -tɔːrɪ; ˈmændəˌtorɪ/ *adj* (*fml* 文) required by law; compulsory 依法的; 法定的; 强制性的: *a mandatory payment* 强迫支付 ○ *Attendance is mandatory at all meetings.* 所有会议皆不得缺席.

mand·ible /ˈmændɪbl; ˈmændəbl̩/ *n* (*anatomy* 解) **1** jaw, esp the lower jaw of mammals and fishes 颌; (尤指哺乳动物和鱼的)下颌. ⇨illus at SKELETON 见 SKELETON 插图. **2** upper or lower part of a bird's beak 鸟喙的上部或下部. **3** (in insects, etc) either half of the upper pair of jaws, used for biting and seizing (昆虫等的)大颚.

man·do·lin /ˈmændəlɪn, ˌmændəˈlɪn; ˈmændl̩ˌɪn/ *n* musical instrument with 6 or 8 metal strings arranged in pairs, and a rounded back 曼陀林. ⇨illus at LUTE 见 LUTE 插图.

man·drag·ora /mænˈdrægərə; mænˈdrægərə/ (also **man·drake** /ˈmændreɪk; ˈmændrek/) *n* [U] poisonous plant used to make drugs, esp ones which make people sleep 曼德拉草(有毒, 用作麻醉、催眠药).

man·drill /ˈmændrɪl; ˈmændrɪl/ *n* large W African baboon 山魈(产于西非).

mane /meɪn; men/ *n* **1** long hair on the neck of a horse, lion, etc (马等的)鬃; (狮等的)鬣. ⇨illus at HORSE 见 HORSE 插图. **2** (*joc* 谑) person's long hair (人的)长发: *a young man with a thick mane hanging over his shoulders* 留着披肩厚发的年轻男子.

man·euver (*US*) = MANOEUVRE.

man·ful /ˈmænfl; ˈmænfəl/ *adj* brave; determined 有大丈夫气概的; 勇敢的; 坚决的: *manful resistance, defence, etc* 勇敢的反抗、防卫等. ▷ **man·fully** /-fəlɪ; -fəlɪ/ *adv*: *He strove manfully to overcome his speech defect.* 他无所畏惧地努力克服自己的言语缺陷.

man·gan·ese /ˈmæŋɡəniːz; ˈmæŋɡəˌniz/ *n* [U] (*chemistry* 化) hard brittle light-grey metallic element used in making steel, glass, etc 锰 ⇨App 10 见附录10.

mange /meɪndʒ; mendʒ/ *n* [U] skin disease of hairy animals, caused by a parasite 兽疥癣.
▷ **mangy** /ˈmeɪndʒɪ; ˈmendʒɪ/ *adj* (**-ier, -iest**) **1** suffering from mange (指兽)患疥癣的: *a mangy dog* 患疥癣的狗. **2** (*fig* 比喻) shabby and becoming worn and threadbare 褴褛的; 破旧的: *a mangy old chair, blanket, etc* 破旧的椅子、毯子等.

mangel-wurzel /ˈmæŋɡl wɜːzl; ˈmæŋɡlˈwɝzl̩/ *n* type of large root vegetable used as cattle food (作牛饲料用的)甜菜.

man·ger /ˈmeɪndʒə(r); ˈmendʒɚ/ *n* **1** long open box or trough from which horses or cattle can feed (牛、马的)食槽. **2** (idm 习语) **a dog in the manger** ⇨ DOG[1].

mangle[1] /ˈmæŋɡl; ˈmæŋɡl̩/ *v* [Tn esp passive 尤用于被动语态] **1** damage (sth) greatly, (almost) beyond recognition; mutilate 严重损伤(某事物); 使面目全非; 使残缺不全: *the badly mangled bodies of those killed by the explosion* 炸得残缺不全的尸体. **2** (*fig* 比喻) (of a writer, an actor, etc) badly spoil (a piece of work, performance, etc) (指作家、演员等)弄糟(作品、演出等): *a mangled translation* 严重的误译 ○ *The symphony was dreadfully mangled.* 那首交响乐曲给糟塌得不成样子.

mangle 轧干机

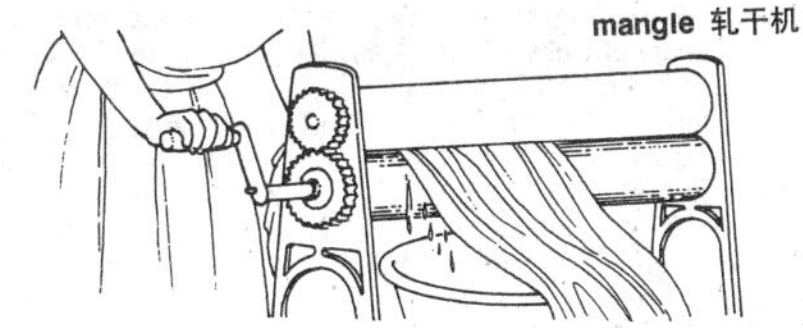

mangle[2] /ˈmæŋɡl; ˈmæŋɡl̩/ *n* machine with rollers used (esp formerly) for squeezing water from or smoothing clothes, etc that have been washed; wringer (衣服)轧干机, 碾压机(尤指旧时用滚筒轧挤者).
▷ **mangle** *v* [Tn] put (clothes, etc) through a mangle 用碾压机碾压(衣服等).

mango /ˈmæŋɡəʊ; ˈmæŋɡo/ *n* (*pl* **~es** or **~s**) (**a**) pear-shaped fruit with flesh which is yellow when ripe 芒果: [attrib 作定语] *mango chutney*, ie chutney made with green, unripe mangoes (用未成熟的绿芒果制成的)芒果酱. (**b**) tropical tree bearing these 芒果树.

man·grove /ˈmæŋɡrəʊv; ˈmæŋɡrov/ *n* tropical tree that grows in swamps and sends roots down from its branches 红树属植物(生于沼泽地, 树枝有下垂须根人土繁殖).

mangy ⇨ MANGE.

man·handle /ˈmænˌhændl; ˈmænˌhændl̩/ *v* **1** [Tn, Tn·pr] move (sth) by physical strength 用人力移动(某物): *We manhandled the piano up the stairs.* 我们已把钢琴搬上楼. **2** [Tn] treat (sb) roughly 粗暴对待(某人): *The drunk had been manhandled by a gang of youths.* 那醉汉遭受一群年轻人欺负.

man·hood /ˈmænhʊd; ˈmænhʊd/ *n* [U] **1** state of being a man (男子的)成年, 成人: *reach manhood* 达到成年. **2** qualities of a man, eg courage, virility, etc 男子的气质(如勇气、活力等): *have doubts about one's manhood* 对自己的男子气概有怀疑. **3** all the men collectively, esp of a country 男子的总称(尤指一国的): *Our nation's manhood died on the battlefield.* 我国的男儿已战死疆场.

mania /ˈmeɪnɪə; ˈmenɪə/ *n* **1** [U] (*medical* 医) mental disorder marked by extreme excitement or violence 躁狂; 狂. **2** [C] **~ (for sth)** (*infml* 口) extreme or abnormal enthusiasm 狂热; 癖好: *have a mania for sweets, for collecting things* 有嗜糖果、搜集东西的癖好.
▷ **ma·niac** /ˈmeɪnɪæk; ˈmenɪˌæk/ *n* **1** mad person 躁狂者; 疯子; 狂人. **2** (*derog or joc* 贬或谑) (**a**) person with an extreme liking (for sth) 极端喜爱某事物的人: *She's a football maniac.* 她是个足球迷. (**b**) wild or foolish person 粗野的或愚蠢的人: *That maniac drives far too fast.* 那个疯子开车开得太快了. **ma·ni·acal** /məˈnaɪəkl; məˈnaɪəkl̩/ *adj* (*fml* 文) **1** violently mad 躁狂的; 疯狂的: *maniacal behaviour* 疯狂的行为 ○ *a maniacal expression on his face* 他脸上躁狂的表情. **2** (*derog or joc* 贬或谑) extremely enthusiastic 狂热的: *He's maniacal about sex.* 他性欲旺盛. **ma·ni·ac·ally** /məˈnaɪəklɪ; məˈnaɪəklɪ/ *adv*.

-mania *comb form* 构词成分 (forming *ns* 用以构成名词) madness or abnormal behaviour of a particular type 某种疯狂的或不正常的行为: *kleptomania* ○ *nymphomania*.

M

▷ **-maniac** (forming *ns* and *adjs* 用以构成名词和形容词) (person) affected with a mania of a particular type 患某种躁狂症的(人): *dipsomaniac* ○ *pyromaniac*.

manic /ˈmænɪk; ˋmænɪk/ *adj* (of a person, his moods, etc) changing quickly and often between extremes of depression and cheerfulness (指人、心态等)躁狂的, 喜怒无常的, 狂热的.

□ ˌ**manic-deˈpressive** *n* (*medical* 医) person who is manic 躁狂抑郁症患者.

mani·cure /ˈmænɪkjʊə(r); ˋmænɪˌkjʊr/ *n* [C, U] (a) treatment for the hands and finger-nails 修剪指甲: *have a manicure once a week* 一星期修剪一次指甲 ○ *do a course in manicure* 上指甲修剪课. Cf 参看 PEDICURE.

▷ **mani·cure** *v* [Tn] give such treatment to (sb/sb's hands) 给(某人[某人的手])修剪指甲: *beautifully manicured nails* 修剪得很漂亮的指甲.

mani·cur·ist /-kjʊərɪst; -kjʊrɪst/ *n* person who practises manicure as a profession 指甲修剪师.

mani·fest[1] /ˈmænɪfest; ˋmænəˌfɛst/ *adj* **~ (to sb)** (*fml* 文) clear and obvious 明白的; 明显的: *a manifest truth, lie, difference* 明显的事实、谎言、区别 ○ *sth that is manifest to all of us* 我们大家都很清楚的事情.

▷ **mani·fest** *v* [Tn] (*fml* 文) **1** show (sth) clearly; demonstrate 清楚地表明, 显示(某事物); 证明: *manifest the truth of a statement* 证明某说法属实 ○ *manifest fear, hatred, etc* 显示恐惧、憎恨等 ○ *She manifested little interest in her studies.* 她对学习显得没有什么兴趣. **2 ~ itself/themselves** show itself/themselves; appear 显露; 出现: *The symptoms manifested themselves ten days later.* 十天后出现了症状. ○ *Has the ghost manifested itself recently?* 那鬼魂最近出现过吗? **ma·ni·festa·tion** /ˌmænɪfeˈsteɪʃn; ˌmænəfɛsˋteʃən/ *n* (*fml* 文) **1** [U] showing clearly; manifesting 显示; 表明; 证明. **2** [C usu *pl* 通常作复数] action or statement that shows sth clearly 清楚表明某事的言行: *This riot is only one manifestation of people's discontent.* 这骚乱仅仅是人们不满的一种表露而已. **3** [C] appearance of a ghost, spirit, etc (鬼魂等的)显灵: *She claims to have seen manifestations of dead people in the haunted house.* 她说她在那闹鬼的房子里看见了死人显灵.

mani·festly *adv*: *The statement is manifestly false.* 这种说法明显不确.

mani·fest[2] /ˈmænɪfest; ˋmænəˌfɛst/ *n* list of cargo, passengers, etc on a ship, an aircraft, etc (船、飞机等的)货单, 乘客名单: *the passenger manifest of a ship* 轮船乘客名单.

ma·ni·festo /ˌmænɪˈfestəʊ; ˌmænəˋfɛsto/ *n* (*pl* **~s** or **~es**) (publication containing a) public declaration by a political party, ruler, etc of principles and policy (政党、统治者等关于原则、政策的)宣言, 声明: *an election manifesto* 竞选声明 ○ *publish/issue a manifesto* 发表宣言.

mani·fold /ˈmænɪfəʊld; ˋmænəˌfold/ *adj* (*fml* 文) of many types; many and various 多种的; 繁多的; 各种各样的: *a person with manifold interests* 兴趣广泛的人 ○ *a versatile machine with manifold uses* 有多种用途的机器.

▷ **mani·fold** *n* pipe or chamber with several openings that connect with other parts, eg for taking gases into or out of cylinders in an internal combustion engine 歧管; 多支管: *the exhaust manifold* 排气歧管.

man·ikin /ˈmænɪkɪn; ˋmænəkɪn/ *n* (*dated* 旧) abnormally small man; dwarf 矮子; 侏儒.

Ma·nila (also **Ma·nilla**) /məˈnɪlə; məˋnɪlə/ *n* [U] **1** (also **Manila ˈhemp**) plant fibre used for making ropes, mats, etc 马尼拉麻, 蕉麻(用以制绳、垫等). **2 manila** (also **manila ˈpaper**) strong brown wrapping-paper made from Manila hemp 马尼拉纸: [attrib 作定语] *manila envelopes* 马尼拉纸信封.

ma·nioc /ˈmænɪɒk; ˋmænɪˌɑk/ *n* [U] cassava 木薯.

ma·nip·ulate /məˈnɪpjʊleɪt; məˋnɪpjəˌlet/ *v* [Tn] **1** control or handle (sth) with skill 熟练控制或操纵(某事物): *manipulate the gears and levers of a machine* 熟练操纵机器的排挡和变速杆 ○ *Primitive man quickly learned how to manipulate tools.* 原始人很快学会了使用工具. **2** control or influence (sb) cleverly or by unfair means (巧妙地或不正当地)控制, 操纵, 影响(某人): *a clever politician who knows how to manipulate public opinion* 善于操纵舆论的聪明的政治家 ○ *She uses her charm to manipulate people.* 她利用其魅力左右他人.

M

▷ **ma·nip·ula·tion** /məˌnɪpjʊˈleɪʃn; məˌnɪpjʊˋleʃən/ *n* [C, U] (act of) manipulating or being manipulated 操作; 操纵; 控制: *His clever manipulation of the stock markets makes him lots of money.* 他在股票交易中买卖精明, 赚了很多钱.

ma·nip·ulat·ive /məˈnɪpjʊlətɪv; *US* -leɪtɪv; məˋnɪpjəˌletɪv/ *adj* (*esp derog* 尤作贬义) tending to manipulate(2) (对他人)控制的, 操纵的: *manipulative skill, power, ability, etc* 左右别人的伎俩、力量、能力等.

ma·nip·ulator /məˈnɪpjʊleɪtə(r); məˋnɪpjuˌletɚ/ *n* (*esp derog* 尤作贬义) person who manipulates(2) 控制或操纵他人者: *an unscrupulous manipulator* 用不道德的手段操纵别人的人.

man·kind *n* [U] **1** /ˌmænˈkaɪnd; mænˋkaɪnd/ the human race 人类: *an invention that benefits mankind* 造福人类的发明. ⇨Usage at MAN[1] 用法见 MAN[1]. **2** /ˈmænkaɪnd; ˋmænˌkaɪnd/ men collectively (contrasted with *womankind*) 男子(总称, 与 womankind 相对).

man-like /ˈmænlaɪk; ˋmænˌlaɪk/ *adj* like a man in appearance, characteristics, etc (外表、特征等)像男子的, 像人的: *a man-like creature about four feet tall* 约四英尺高样子像人的动物.

manly /ˈmænlɪ; ˋmænlɪ/ *adj* (**-ier, -iest**) **1** (**a**) (*approv* 褒) (of a man) having the qualities or appearance expected of a man (指男子)有男子气质或外表的: *I've always thought he looked very manly in his uniform.* 我一向认为他穿着制服很威武. (**b**) (*derog* 贬) (of a woman) having the qualities or appearance more appropriate to a man; mannish (指女子)气质或外表男性化的. **2** (*approv* 褒) (of things) suitable for a man (指事物)适合男子的: *manly clothes* 男子的服装 ○ *a manly pose* 男子的姿势. ▷ **man·li·ness** *n* [U].

manna /ˈmænə; ˋmænə/ *n* [U] **1** (in the Bible) food provided by God for the Israelites during their forty years in the desert (圣经中的)吗哪(以色列人在旷野四十年中神赐的粮食). **2** (idm 习语) **like manna (from ˈheaven)** as an unexpected and beneficial gift 意外的好事; 天赐之物: *I needed that money so desperately, it was like manna from heaven when it arrived!* 我正急需那笔钱, 所以收到时宛如天赐!

man·ne·quin /ˈmænɪkɪn; ˋmænəkɪn/ *n* **1** (*dated* 旧) woman employed to display new styles of clothes by wearing them; fashion model 女时装模特儿. **2** life-size dummy of a human body, used by tailors when making clothes, or by shops for displaying them (真人大小的)人体模型(裁缝或服装陈列用的).

man·ner /ˈmænə(r); ˋmænɚ/ *n* **1** [sing] (*fml* 文) way in which a thing is done or happens 方式; 方法: *the manner in which he died* 他死的方式 ○ *the manner of his death*, ie the way he died 他死亡的方式 ○ *I don't object to what she says, but I strongly disapprove of her manner of saying it.* 我不反对她说的话, 但她说这话的方式我很反感. ○ *Do it in a businesslike manner.* 要郑重其事做这件事. ○ *He objected in a forceful manner.* 他表示坚决反对. **2** [sing] person's way of behaving towards others 态度: *He has an aggressive manner.* 他的态度咄咄逼人. ○ *I don't like her manner — she's very hostile.* 我不喜欢她的态度——待人如仇敌. **3 manners** [pl] (**a**) social behaviour 礼貌; 规矩: *good/bad manners* 有[没有]礼貌 ○ *It's bad manners to stare at people.* 瞪着眼睛看人是不礼貌的. ○ *He has no manners at all*, ie behaves very badly. 他毫无礼貌. ○ *Aren't you forgetting your manners* (ie being rude)? 你是不是没礼貌了? (**b**) habits and customs 习惯; 风俗: *eighteenth-century aristocratic manners* 十八世纪贵族的风俗习惯. **4** [sing] (*fml or rhet* 文或修辞) kind (of person or thing); sort (人或物的)种类: *What manner of man is he?* 他是哪种人? **5** (idm 习语) **all manner of sb/sth** (*fml* 文) every kind of sb/sth 各种各样的: *All manner of vehicles were used.* 使用了各种车辆. **bedside manner** ⇨ BEDSIDE (BED[1]). **a comedy of manners** ⇨ COMEDY. **in a manner of speaking** to some extent; if regarded in a certain way 不妨说; 可以说; 在某种意义上说: *His success is in a manner of speaking our success, too.* 他的成功也可以说是我们的成功. **in the manner of sb** in the style of literature or art typical of sb 以某人的文艺风格: *a painting in the manner of Raphael* 拉斐尔风格的画. **not by ˈany manner of means/by ˈno manner of means** (used for emphasis 用以加强语气) not at all 一

点都不; 绝不: *She hasn't won yet, (not) by any manner of means.* 她还未获胜, 远未获胜. **(as/as if) to the manner 'born** as if one has long experience of doing sth 生来就惯于做某事: *She isn't a practised public speaker, but she faced her audience as (if) to the manner born.* 她虽无演讲经验, 但(似乎)生来并不怯场.

▷ **man·nered** *adj* having an unnatural style of speaking, writing, etc; affected (语言、文字等)不自然的, 矫揉造作的: *Her prose is far too mannered and self-conscious.* 她的散文过于矫揉造作.

-man·nered (forming compound *adjs* 用以构成复合形容词) having manners of the specified type 有某种态度或举止的: *ˌill-/ˌwell-/ˌrough-'mannered* 无礼貌的[有礼貌的/粗鲁的].

man·ner·ism /'mænərɪzəm; 'mænəˌrɪzəm/ *n* **1** [C] peculiar habit of behaviour, speech, etc (行为、言语等的)特殊习惯: *an eccentric with many odd mannerisms* 言谈举止有很多怪癖的人. **2** [U] (*derog* 贬) excessive use of a distinctive style in art or literature (艺术或文学中)过分的独特风格: *painting that is not free of mannerism* 未摆脱某种风格约束的绘画.

man·nish /'mænɪʃ; 'mænɪʃ/ *adj* (*derog* 贬) **1** (of a woman) looking, sounding or behaving like a man (指女子)(样子、声音或举止)像男子的. **2** (of things) more suitable for a man than for a woman (指事物)适合男子的, 不适合女子的: *a mannish jacket, voice, walk* 男式外衣、像男子的声音、男子般的步态. ▷ **man·nishly** *adv*. **man·nish·ness** *n* [U].

man·oeuvre (*US* **man·euver**) /mə'nu:və(r); mə'nuvɚ/ *n* **1** (*military* 军) **(a)** [C] planned and controlled movement of armed forces (军队的)调遣, 调动: *a flanking manoeuvre*, ie round the sides of an enemy army 侧翼包抄. **(b)** **manoeuvres** [pl] large-scale exercises by troops or ships (部队或舰队的)大规模演习: *The army is on* (ie taking part in) *manoeuvres in the desert.* 军队正在进行沙漠作战演习. **2** [C] **(a)** movement performed with care and skill 谨慎而熟练的动作: *A rapid manoeuvre by the driver prevented an accident.* 司机动作迅速而熟练因此避免了一场事故. **(b)** (*usu fig* 通常作比喻) (esp deceptively) skilful plan or movement (尤指欺骗的)巧计, 花招: *This was a crafty manoeuvre to outwit his pursuers.* 这是一个高招, 他以此骗倒了追逐他的人. ○ *These shameful manoeuvres were aimed at securing his election.* 这种可耻的伎俩都是为了能让他当选.

▷ **man·oeuvre** (*US* **man·euver**) *v* **1 (a)** [I, Ipr, Tn, Tn·pr] (cause sth to) move about by using skill and care 谨慎地运用技巧(使某物)移动, 运动: *Cyclists were manoeuvring on the practice track.* 自行车运动员在练习用的车道上练习技巧. ○ *The yachts were manoeuvring for position*, ie moving around to get good positions (eg in a race). 那些快艇灵巧地竞相争夺有利位置(如在比赛中). ○ *his skill in manoeuvring a motorcycle* 他驾驶摩托车的熟练技巧○ *The driver manoeuvred (the car) into the garage, over to the side of the road.* 司机把汽车开进车房、开到路边. **(b)** [Tn, Tn·pr, Tn·p] (*fig* 比喻) guide (sb/sth) skilfully and craftily (in a specified direction) 熟练而巧妙地引导(某人[某事物]): *She manoeuvred her friends into positions of power*, ie used her influence, etc to put them there. 她(运用自己的影响力等)把她的朋友都安插到有权的职位上. ○ *manoeuvre the conversation round to money* 巧妙地把话题引到金钱问题上. **2** [I] (*military* 军) perform manoeuvres(1b) 演习: *The fleet is manoeuvring in the Baltic.* 该舰队正在波罗的海演习.

man·oeuv·rable (*US* **man·euv·er·able**) /-vrəbl; -vərəbl/ *adj* that can be manoeuvred (easily) 可(便于)移动的; 可引导的; 可用于演习的: *a highly manoeuvrable aircraft, motorboat, etc* 极为灵巧的飞机、摩托船等. **man·oeuv·rab·il·ity** (*US* **-neu·ver-**) /məˌnu:vrə'bɪlətɪ; məˌnuvərə'bɪlətɪ/ *n* [U].

mano·meter /mə'nɒmɪtə(r); mə'nɑmətɚ/ *n* instrument for measuring pressure in gases and liquids (流体的)压力计, 压力表.

manor /'mænə(r); 'mænɚ/ *n* **1** (formerly) unit of land under the feudal system, part of which was used by the lord of the manor (LORD), the rest being farmed by tenants (旧时)(封建贵族的)采地, 采邑, 领地(部分自用, 部分租给佃户). **2 (a)** (also **'manor-house**) large country house surrounded by an estate 庄园大宅第. **(b)** this estate 庄园. **3** (*Brit sl* 俚) (used esp by policemen 尤为警察用语) area for which a particular police station is responsible 管区(某警察局负责的地段).

▷ **man·orial** /mə'nɔ:rɪəl; mə'nɔrɪəl/ *adj* of a manor (1, 2) 采地的; 采邑的; 领地的; 庄园的.

man·power /'mænpaʊə(r); 'mænˌpaʊɚ/ *n* [U] **1** number of people working or available for work 劳动力: *There's not enough qualified manpower to staff all the hospitals.* 缺乏足够的合格人员充实各医院. ○ [attrib 作定语] *a manpower shortage* 缺乏劳动力. **2** power supplied by human physical effort 人力; 体力: *a treadmill driven by manpower rather than water-power* 人力驱动而非水力驱动的踏车.

man·qué /'mɒŋkeɪ; mɑn'ke/ *adj* (*French* 法) (following *ns* 用于名词之后) (of a person) who could have followed the career mentioned, but who failed or lacked the opportunity to do so (指人)(所提生涯、职业等)未能实现的, 未成功的, 壮志未酬的: *a teacher, an actor, a writer, etc manqué* 从未当成教师、演员、作家等.

man·sard /'mænsɑ:d; 'mænsɑrd/ *n* (also ˌ**mansard 'roof**) roof with a double slope, the lower part being steeper than the upper part 复折式屋顶(下部比上部陡).

manse /mæns; mæns/ *n* church minister's house, esp in Scotland 牧师住宅(尤指于苏格兰).

man·sion /'mænʃn; 'mænʃən/ *n* **1** [C] large and stately house 宅第; 公馆. **2 Mansions** [pl] (used in proper names for a block of flats 用于公寓楼的专有名称中): *49 Victoria Mansions, Grove Road, London* 伦敦格罗夫街维多利亚大厦49号.

man·slaugh·ter ⇨ MAN[1].

man·tel /'mæntl; 'mæntl̩/ *n* (*dated* 旧) = mantelpiece.

man·tel·piece /'mæntlpi:s; 'mæntl̩ˌpis/ (also '**chimney-piece**) *n* shelf above a fireplace 壁炉台: *A clock and two vases stood on the mantelpiece.* 壁炉台上摆着一个座钟和两个花瓶.

man·tilla /mæn'tɪlə; mæn'tɪlə/ *n* lace veil or scarf worn (esp by Spanish women) to cover the hair and shoulders 有花边的头纱或披肩(尤指西班牙女子用的).

man·tis /'mæntɪs; 'mæntɪs/ *n* (also ˌ**praying 'mantis**) insect like a grasshopper, which holds its front legs together as if in prayer 螳螂.

mantle /'mæntl; 'mæntl/ *n* **1** [C] **(a)** loose sleeveless cloak 披风; 斗篷. **(b)** (*fig* 比喻) covering 覆盖物: *hills with a mantle of snow* 覆盖着一层雪的山. **2** [sing] **the ~ of sth** (*rhet* 修辞) the responsibilites of an important job, etc (重要工作等的)责任, 职分: *assume/take on/inherit the mantle of supreme power* 担任[担当/继承]最高权力的重任. **3** [C] lace-like cover round the flame of a gas lamp that becomes very bright when heated (煤气灯的)白炽纱罩. **4** [sing] (*geology* 地质) part of the Earth below the crust and surrounding the core 地幔.

▷ **mantle** *v* (*fig* 比喻) [Tn] cover (sth) as if with a mantle 覆盖(某物): *an ivy-mantled wall* 爬满长春藤的墙 ○ *Snow mantled the hills.* 雪覆盖着山.

man·ual /'mænjʊəl; 'mænjʊəl/ *adj* of, done with or controlled by the hands 手的; 手工的; 手制的; 手控的: *Making small models requires manual skill.* 制作小模型要手巧. ○ *manual labour* 体力劳动 ○ *a manual gear-box*, ie one operated by the hand with a gear-lever, not automatically 手动变速箱. Cf 参看 MECHANICAL 1.

▷ **man·ual** *n* **1** book containing information or practical instructions (on a given subject) 手册; 指南: *a training manual* 训练手册 ○ *A workshop manual gives diagrams and instructions for repairing your car.* 维修手册可向您提供修理汽车所需的图表和说明. Cf 参看 HANDBOOK (HAND[1]). **2** keyboard of an organ, played with the hands (风琴的)键盘: *a two-manual organ* 双键盘风琴.

manu·ally /-jʊəlɪ; -jʊəlɪ/ *adv*: *manually operated* 手工操作的.

man·u·fac·ture /ˌmænjʊ'fæktʃə(r); ˌmænjə'fæktʃɚ/ *v* [Tn] **1** make (goods) on a large scale using machinery 用机器大量制造(货物): *manufacture shoes, cement, cookers* 制造鞋、水泥、炉具 ○ *manufacturing industry*, eg in contrast with industries which do not make products 制造工业. **2** (*usu derog* 通常作贬义) invent (evidence, an excuse, etc) 假造, 虚构, 捏造(证据、借口等): *She manufactured a false story to hide the facts.* 她编

造瞎话以掩盖事实.

▷ **man·u·fac·ture** *n* **1** [U] activity of manufacturing 制造; 编造: *firms engaged in the manufacture of plastics* 从事制造塑料的公司 ○ *goods of foreign manufacture,* ie made abroad 外国产品. **2 manufactures** [pl] manufactured goods or articles 制造品; 产品.

man·u·fac·turer *n* person or firm that manufactures things 制造商; 工厂主; 制造厂: *Send these faulty goods back to the manufacturer.* 把这些次货退还给厂家. ○ *a clothing, a car, an electronics, etc manufacturer* 服装、汽车、电子产品等制造厂.

ma·nu·mit /ˌmænjʊˈmɪt; ˌmænjəˈmɪt/ *v* (**-tt-**) (*fml* 文) (formerly) free (a slave) (旧时)解放(奴隶). ▷ **ma·nu·mis·sion** /ˌmænjʊˈmɪʃn; ˌmænjəˈmɪʃən/ *n* [U].

ma·nure /məˈnjʊə(r); məˈnjʊr/ *n* [U] animal dung or other material, natural or artificial, spread over or mixed with soil to make it fertile 肥料; 粪肥: *dig manure into the soil* 在土壤中施肥. Cf 参看 FERTILIZER (FERTILIZE).

▷ **ma·nure** *v* [Tn] put manure on or in (soil) 往(地)里施肥.

ma·nu·script /ˈmænjʊskrɪpt; ˈmænjəˌskrɪpt/ *n* (*abbr* 缩写 **MS**) **1** thing written by hand, not typed or printed 手稿: [attrib 作定语] *a manuscript copy of a typed letter* 一份打字信的手稿. **2** author's work when written or typed (ie not yet a printed book) (作家手写或打字的)原稿, 草稿(即尚未印刷成书者): *submit a manuscript to an editor* 把原稿交给编辑. **3** (idm 习语) **in ˈmanuscript** not yet printed 未付印的: *Her poems are still in manuscript.* 她的诗尚未付印.

Manx /mæŋks; mæŋks/ *adj* of the Isle of Man, its people or its language 马恩岛的; 马恩岛人的; 马恩语的.

▷ **Manx** *n* [U] language of the Isle of Man 马恩语.

□ **Manx ˈcat** breed of cat with no tail 马恩猫(一种无尾猫).

ˈManxman /-mən; -mən/, **ˈManxwoman** *ns* native of the Isle of Man 马恩岛人.

many /ˈmenɪ; ˈmɛnɪ/ *indef det, indef pron* (used with *pl ns* or *vs* 与复数名词或动词连用) **1** a large number of people or things 大量的人或事物. **(a)** (*det*): *Many people agree with nationalization.* 很多人都赞成国有化. ○ *I didn't see many houses under £50 000.* 我很少见到5万英镑以下的房子. ○ *Were there many pictures by British artists?* 英国画家的作品多吗? ○ *How many children have you got?* 你有几个孩子? ○ *There are too many mistakes in this essay.* 这篇文章错误太多. ○ *I don't need many more.* 我需要的不多了. **(b)** (*pron*): *Many of the students were from Japan.* 许多学生都是日本人. ○ *I have some classical records but not very many.* 我有一些古典音乐唱片, 但是不太多. ○ *Did you know many of them?* 他们中很多人你都认识吗? ○ *How many do you want?* 你要多少? ○ *I wouldn't have offered to water the plants if I'd known there were so many.* 早知道有这么多花草需要浇水, 我就不自告奋勇了. ○ *He made ten mistakes in as many* (ie ten) *lines.* 他在十行里就有十个错. ⇨Usage at MUCH[1] 用法见MUCH[1]. **2 many a** a large number of 许多 (used with a *sing n* + *sing v* 与单数名词+单数动词连用): *Many a strong man has weakened before such a challenge.* 很多坚强的人面对这种困难都动摇了. ○ *Many a famous pop star has been ruined by drugs.* 很多著名的流行音乐歌星都因使用毒品而毁了自己. ○ *I've been to the top of the Eiffel Tower many a time.* 我曾多次登上埃菲尔铁塔的塔顶. ○ (*saying* 谚) *Many a true word is spoken in jest.* 笑谈之中有真话. **3** (idm 习语) **be ˌone, etc too ˈmany (for sth)** be one, etc more than the correct or needed number 比正确的或所需的数目多…个: *There are six of us — two too many for a game of whist.* 我们有六个人——要打惠斯特牌就多了两个人. **a good/great many** very many 许多; 很多. **have had ˌone too ˈmany** (*infml* 口) be slightly drunk 有一点醉. **many's the sb/sth who/that…** there are many people/things that… 有很多的…人[事物]: *Many's the promise that has been broken.* 违反诺言的事经常有. (Cf 参看 *Many a promise has been broken.*) ○ *Many's the time that I heard him use those words.* 有很多次我听到他使用那些词语. (Cf 参看 *I heard him use those words many a time.*)

M

▷ **the many** *n* most people; the masses or majority 多数人; 群众: *a government which improves conditions for the many* 致力于改善群众生活条件的政府. Cf 参看 THE FEW (FEW[1]).

□ **ˌmany-ˈsided** *adj* having many sides 多边的: (*fig* 比喻) *We are faced with a ˌmany-sided ˈproblem.* 我们面临着一个涉及多方面的问题.

Maori /ˈmaʊrɪ; ˈmaʊrɪ/ *n* **1** [C] member of the aboriginal race of New Zealand 毛利人(新西兰的土著). **2** [U] language of this race 毛利语.

▷ **Maori** *adj* of this race or its language 毛利人的; 毛利语的: *Maori dress, customs, words* 毛利人的服装、风俗、词语.

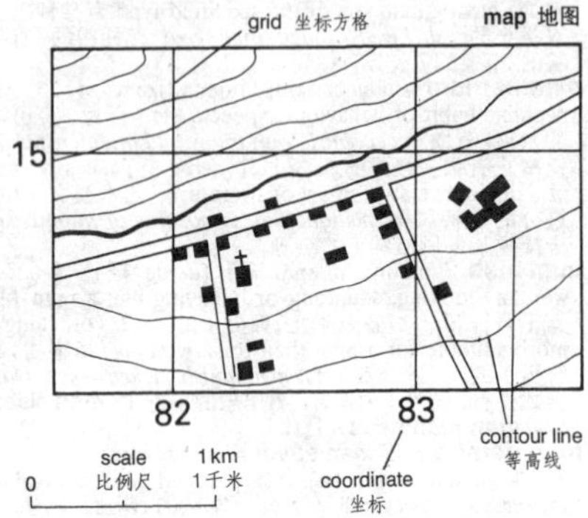

map /mæp; mæp/ *n* **1 (a)** representation on paper, etc of the earth's surface or part of it, showing countries, rivers, mountains, oceans, roads, etc 地图: *a map of France* 法国地图 ○ *find a place on the map* 在地图上寻找一个地点 ○ *a street map of London* 伦敦街道图 ○ *I'll draw you a map of how to get to my house.* 我给你画一张到我家的路线图. ⇨illus 见插图. **(b)** similar plan showing the position of the stars, etc in the sky 天体图(标示星辰等在天空的位置): *a map of the heavens* 天体图. Cf 参看 CHART, PLAN 2. **2** (idm 习语) **put sb/sth on the ˈmap** make sb/sth famous or important 使某人[某事物]出名或有重要性: *Her performance in that play really put her on the map as a comedy actress.* 她在那出剧中当喜剧演员而一举成名. **wipe sth off the map** ⇨ WIPE.

▷ **map** *v* (**-pp-**) [Tn] **1** make a map of (an area, etc); show on a map 绘制(一地区等的)地图; 用地图表示: *an unexplored country that hasn't yet been mapped* 地图上没有标示的、未经勘察的地带. **2** (phr v) **map sth out (a)** plan or arrange sth 筹划或安排某事: *He's already mapped out his whole future career.* 他对自己未来的事业有了周详的计划. **(b)** present sth in detail 详细提出某事: *She mapped out her ideas on the new project.* 她详细提出了对新项目的意见.

□ **ˈmap-reader** *n* person who follows a route on a map 依地图行进的人: *a good, poor, etc map-reader* 善于、不善于…利用地图的人 ○ *You drive and I'll be (the) map-reader.* 你开车, 我来察看地图.

maple /ˈmeɪpl; ˈmepl̩/ *n* **(a)** [C] (also **ˈmaple tree**) one of various types of tree of the northern hemisphere, grown for timber and ornament 槭树(俗称枫树). **(b)** [U] its hard wood, sometimes used for furniture 槭木: [attrib 作定语] *a maple desk* 槭木书桌.

□ **maple ˈsugar, maple ˈsyrup** sugar/syrup obtained from the sap of one kind of maple 槭糖; 槭糖浆.

ma·quis /ˈmæki:; *US* mɑ:ˈki:; ˌmɑˈki/ *n* **the maquis** (also **the Maquis**) [Gp] the secret army of French patriots who fought in France against the Germans in World War II (第二次世界大战时的)法国抗德游击队.

mar /mɑ:(r); mɑr/ *v* (**-rr-**) [Tn] **1** damage (sth); spoil 损坏(某事物); 毁损: *a mistake that could mar his career* 能毁掉他前程的错误 ○ *Nothing happened to mar the old man's happiness.* 那老人的幸福没有受到任何事情的破坏. **2** (idm 习语) **make or mar sb/sth** make sb/sth a success or a failure 使某人[某事物]成功或失败: *His handling of the crisis could make or mar his career.* 他对这一危机的处理可能决定他事业的成败.

Mar *abbr* 缩写 = March: *10 Mar 1941* 1941年3月10日.

mara·bou /ˈmærəbu:; ˋmærəˏbu/ *n* **1** [C] large W African stork 秃鹳(产于西非). **2** [U] its soft feathers used as trimming, eg for a hat 秃鹳的细软羽毛(用作帽饰等).

ma·ras·chino /ˌmærəˈski:nəʊ; ˌmærəˈskino/ *n* (*pl* **~s** /-nəʊz; -noz/) **1** [U] sweet liqueur made from a small black cherry 黑樱桃酒. **2** [C] (also ˌ**maraschino** ˈ**cherry**) cherry soaked in this liqueur, used in drinks, puddings, etc (黑樱桃酒浸泡的)樱桃(用以配制饮料、布丁等).

mara·thon /ˈmærəθən; *US* -θɒn; ˋmærəˏθɑn/ *n* **1** (also **Marathon**) long-distance running race (of about 42 km or 26 miles) 马拉松赛跑(约42公里或26英里): *I've never run a marathon.* 我从未参加过马拉松赛跑. ○ *She won the gold medal in the women's marathon at this year's Olympic Games.* 她在今年奥运会女子马拉松赛跑中赢得金牌. **2** (*fig* 比喻) long-lasting event which is hard to endure 拖时长久令人难以忍受的事情: *My job interview was a real marathon.* 我那次求职面试简直是马拉松式的长谈. ○ [attrib 作定语] *a marathon session, exam, etc* 马拉松式的会议、考试等.

ma·raud·ing /məˈrɔ:dɪŋ; məˋrɔdɪŋ/ *adj* [attrib 作定语] (of soldiers, armies, etc) going about searching for things to steal, people to attack, etc (指士兵、军队等)到处抢劫的, 劫掠的: *The countryside was overrun by marauding bands.* 郊野到处都有散兵游勇, 四出打劫.

▷ **ma·rauder** /məˈrɔ:də(r); məˋrɔdɚ/ *n* person or animal that does this 参与劫掠的人或动物.

marble /ˈmɑ:bl; ˋmɑrbḷ/ *n* **1** [U] type of hard limestone used, when cut and polished, for building and sculpture 大理石: *a slab of unpolished marble* 未经打磨的大理石板 ○ *These steps are made of marble.* 这些台阶是大理石的. ○ [attrib 作定语] *a marble statue, tomb, etc* 大理石的雕像、墓等. **2 marbles** [pl] collection of marble sculptures; works of art in marble 大理石雕刻品; 大理石艺术品. **3** (**a**) [C] small ball of glass, clay, etc used by children in games (儿童玩的)玻璃弹球, 泥弹球. (**b**) **marbles** [pl] game played with these 弹球游戏: *Let's have a game of marbles.* 咱们玩儿弹球游戏吧. **4** (idm 习语) **lose one's marbles** ⇨ LOSE.

▷ **marble** *adj* [attrib 作定语] (*fig* 比喻) like marble 像大理石的: *marble* (ie smooth and white) *skin* 大理石般光洁的皮肤 ○ *a marble* (ie cold and unfeeling) *heart* 铁石心肠.

marbled /ˈmɑ:bld; ˋmɑrbḷd/ *adj* having a pattern of streaks in different colours, resembling marble 有大理石般色彩纹理的: *a book with marbled covers* 有大理石花纹封面的书.

marb·ling /ˈmɑ:blɪŋ; ˋmɑrblɪŋ/ *n* [U] (technique of producing a) marbled pattern on paper 纸上的大理石花纹图案(制作技术).

mar·cas·ite /ˈmɑ:kəsaɪt; ˋmɑrkəˏsaɪt/ *n* [C, U] (piece of a) type of crystallized mineral, used as jewellery 白铁矿, 白铁矿石(用作饰物): [attrib 作定语] *a marcasite ring,* ie a ring with a marcasite set into it 白铁矿石戒指.

March /mɑ:tʃ; mɑrtʃ/ *n* **1** [U, C] (*abbr* 缩写 **Mar**) the third month of the year, next after February 三月. **2** (idm 习语) **mad as a March hare** ⇨ MAD.

For the uses of *March* see the examples at *April.* 关于March的用法见April词条中的示例.

march[1] /mɑ:tʃ; mɑrtʃ/ *v* **1** (**a**) [I, Ipr, Ip] walk as soldiers do, with regular steps of equal length 齐步走; 行进; 前进: *Quick march!* ie a military command to start marching 快步走! ○ *Demonstrators marched through the streets.* 示威者在街道中行进. ○ *They marched in and took over the town.* 他们进占了这一市镇. ○ *march by, past, in, out, off, away, etc* 走经、走过、开进、出发、离开、开走 ○ *The army has marched thirty miles today.* 部队今天已行军三十英里. (**b**) [I, Ipr, Ip] walk purposefully and determinedly (含有某目的和决心)走: *She marched in and demanded an apology.* 她毅然地走进来要求向她道歉. (**c**) [Tn·pr, Tn·p] cause (sb) to march 使(某人)行进: *march the troops up and down* 让部队来回练习走步 ○ *They marched the prisoner away.* 他们令监犯齐步走. ○ *She was marched into a cell.* 她被押进一间囚室. **2** (idm 习语) **get one's marching orders; give sb his/her marching orders** (*infml or joc* 口或谑) be told/tell sb to go; be dismissed/dismiss sb 被通知[告诉某人]离去; 被解雇[解雇某人]: *She was totally unreliable, so she got/was given her marching orders.* 她完全不可靠, 所以给解雇了. **3** (phr v) **march past (sb)** (of troops) march ceremonially past (an honoured guest, a high-ranking officer, etc), eg in a parade (指部队)作分列式在(贵宾、首长等)面前经过(如受检阅). ▷ **marcher** *n*: *freedom marchers* 争取自由的示威者 ○ *civil-rights marchers* 争取民权的游行者.

□ ˈ**march past** action of marching past sb ceremonially 分列式行进: *a march past by the light infantry* 轻步兵分列式行进.

march[2] /mɑ:tʃ; mɑrtʃ/ *n* **1** (**a**) [C] action of marching 行军; 行进: *a long, an arduous, etc march* 长途行军、艰难的行进 ○ *a ten-mile march* 十英里行军. (**b**) [sing] progress when marching; advance 前进; 进军: *their steady march towards the enemy* 他们稳步向敌人进逼 ○ *the line of march,* ie route followed by troops when marching (部队的)进军路线. **2** [C] procession from one place to another by many people, esp as a protest 游行; (尤指)示威游行: *a peace march* 为争取和平的游行 ○ *an anti-nuclear (weapons) march* 反核(武器)游行. Cf 参看 DEMONSTRATION 3. **3** [C] piece of music written for marching to 进行曲: *military marches* 军队进行曲 ○ *a dead march,* ie a slow one for a funeral 葬礼进行曲 ○ [attrib 作定语] *a march tune* 进行曲调 ○ *in march tempo* 以进行曲速度. **4** [sing] **the ~ of sth** the steady development or onward movement of sth 稳定的发展或前进: *the march of progress/events/time* 进步的过程[事件的发展/时间的推移]. **5** (idm 习语) **on the march** marching 行进; 行军: *The enemy are on the march at last.* 敌人终于出动了. **steal a march** ⇨ STEAL.

marches /ˈmɑ:tʃɪz; ˋmɑrtʃɪz/ *n* [pl] historical borders, esp between England and Scotland or England and Wales 历史上遗留下的边界, 边境(尤指英格兰与苏格兰或英格兰与威尔士的接界地区).

mar·chion·ess /ˌmɑ:ʃəˈnes; ˌmɑrʃəˋnɛs/ *n* (**a**) wife or widow of a marquis 侯爵夫人; 侯爵遗孀. (**b**) woman holding the same rank as a marquis 女侯爵.

Mardi Gras /ˌmɑ:dɪ ˈgrɑ:; ˋmɑrdɪˋgrɑ/ carnival held in some countries to celebrate the last day (Shrove Tuesday) or days before Lent 大斋期的前一日或前几日的节日.

mare[1] /meə(r); mɛr/ *n* **1** female horse or donkey 母马; 母驴. Cf 参看 FILLY, FOAL, STALLION. **2** (idm 习语) **a** ˈ**mare's nest** discovery that seems interesting but turns out to be false or worthless (以为有意思的却原来是虚假的或无价值的)发现. **on Shank's pony/mare** ⇨ SHANK.

mare[2] /ˈmɑ:rɪ; ˋmɑrɪ/ *n* (*pl* **maria** /ˈmɑ:rɪə; ˋmɑrɪə/) (*astronomy* 天) large flat dark area on the moon or Mars, once thought to be a sea 月球或火星表面的大片平坦的黑暗区(一度被认为是海).

mar·gar·ine /ˌmɑ:dʒəˈri:n; *US* ˈmɑ:rdʒərɪn; ˋmɑrdʒəˏrɪn/ (also *Brit infml* 英式口语作 **marge** /mɑ:dʒ; mɑrdʒ/) *n* [U] food like butter, made from animal or vegetable fats 人造黄油.

mar·gin /ˈmɑ:dʒɪn; ˋmɑrdʒɪn/ *n* **1** (**a**) blank space round the written or printed matter on a page (书写品或印刷品纸页上的)空白边缘, 页边空白: *wide/narrow margins* 宽的[窄的]页边 ○ *notes written in the margin* 写在页边上的注解. (**b**) edge or border 边; 缘; 边沿: *the margin of a lake, pool, pond, etc* 湖、水池、池塘等的边. **2** (**a**) amount of space, time, votes, etc by which sth is won 胜方在时空、票数等方面的领先幅度; 差数; 差额; 差距: *a wide margin between the winner and the loser,* eg a big difference in points scored 胜败双方比分的巨大差数 ○ *He beat the other runners by a margin of ten seconds/by a wide margin.* 他以领先十秒[很大差距]战胜了其他赛跑者. ○ *She won the seat by a margin of ten votes.* 她以十票优势赢得席位. (**b**) amount of space, time, etc which is allowed for success or safety 为成功或安全而应有的时空等的量; 余地: *Leave a good safety margin between your car and the next.* 要在你的汽车和另一辆车之间留出一段足够的安全距离. **3** (*commerce* 商) difference between cost price and selling price 成本与售价间的差额; 赢利; 利润: *a business operating on tight* (ie small) *(profit) margins* 赚头小的生意.

▷ **mar·ginal** /-nl; -nḷ/ *adj* **1** [attrib 作定语] of or in a margin(1a) (纸页)空白边缘(上)的, 页边空白(上)的: *marginal notes, marks, etc* 页边的注解、标记等.

2 small; slight 小的; 少的; 轻微的: *There's only a marginal difference between the two estimates.* 这两种估计差别很小. **3** insignificant 微不足道的; 不重要的: *This once important social group is becoming more and more marginal (to the way the country is run).* 这个一度十分重要的社会集团(对治理该国的影响)越来越无足轻重了. **4** (of land) not fertile enough for profitable farming except when prices of farm products are high (指土地)贫瘠的(非至农产品价格上涨时不值得利用的). **5** (*politics* 政 *esp Brit*) that is won by only a small majority of votes 仅以微弱多数票获胜的: *a marginal seat/constituency* 边缘席位[选区]. — *n* seat or constituency of this type 边缘席位或选区: *a Labour marginal* 工党的边缘席位.

mar·gin·ally /-nəlɪ; -nlɪ/ *adv* slightly 稍微地: *a marginally bigger area* 略大一些的面积.

mar·guer·ite /ˌmɑːgəˈriːt; ˌmɑrgəˈrit/ *n* any of various types of daisy, esp the ox-eye daisy with white petals round a yellow centre 茼蒿菊; 雏菊; (尤指)牛眼菊.

mari·gold /ˈmærɪgəʊld; ˈmærəˌgold/ *n* any of various types of garden plant with orange or yellow flowers 金盏花; 金盏菊; 万寿菊.

ma·ri·juana (also **ma·ri·huana**) /ˌmærjʊˈɑːnə; ˌmærəˈwɑnə/ *n* [U] dried leaves and flowers of Indian hemp, usu smoked as a drug 大麻; 大麻叶和花; 大麻烟. Cf 参看 CANNABIS, HASHISH.

ma·rimba /məˈrɪmbə; məˈrɪmbə/ *n* musical instrument like a xylophone 马林巴琴.

ma·rina /məˈriːnə; məˈrinə/ *n* harbour (often with leisure facilities, hotels, etc) built for yachts and pleasure-boats 游艇停泊港(常有娱乐设施、旅馆等).

mar·in·ade /ˌmærɪˈneɪd; ˌmærəˈned/ *n* [C, U] sauce of wine, herbs, etc in which fish or meat is soaked before it is cooked; fish or meat soaked in this (用酒、香料等调制的)腌泡汁; 腌泡过的鱼或肉: *a marinade of pork and lamb* 腌泡过的猪肉和羊肉.

▷ **mar·in·ade** (also **mar·in·ate** /ˈmærɪneɪt; ˈmærəˌnet/) *v* [Tn, Tn·pr] **~ sth (in sth)** soak (food) in a marinade 腌泡(食物): *marinated pork* 腌泡过的猪肉 ○ *Marinate the veal in white wine for two hours.* 把小牛肉用白葡萄酒浸泡两小时.

ma·rine[1] /məˈriːn; məˈrin/ *adj* **1** of, near, found in or produced by the sea 海的; 近海的; 海中的; 海产的: *a marine creature, plant, etc* 海产的生物、植物等 ○ *a marine painter*, ie an artist who paints seascapes 海景画家 ○ *a marine biologist*, ie a scientist who studies life in the sea 海洋生物学家. **2** of ships, sea-trade, the navy, etc 船只的; 海运的; 海军的: *marine insurance*, ie insurance of ships and cargo 海上保险 ○ *marine stores*, ie materials and supplies for ships 船用物品.

ma·rine[2] /məˈriːn; məˈrin/ *n* **1 (a)** [C] member of a body of soldiers trained to fight on land or sea 海军陆战队士兵. **(b) the Marines** [pl] body of such soldiers belonging to the forces of a country 海军陆战队. ⇨App 9 见附录9. **2** (idm 习语) **tell that to the marines** ⇨ TELL.

mar·iner /ˈmærɪnə(r); ˈmærənɚ/ *n* (*dated or fml* 旧或文) sailor 水手: *a master mariner* 商船船长.

ma·ri·on·ette /ˌmærɪəˈnet; ˌmærɪəˈnɛt/ *n* jointed puppet moved by strings 牵线木偶. ⇨illus at PUPPET 见 PUPPET 插图.

mar·ital /ˈmærɪtl; ˈmærətl/ *adj* [attrib 作定语] of a husband or wife; of marriage 夫的; 妻的; 婚姻的: *marital vows*, ie to be faithful, etc 婚誓 ○ *marital problems, disagreements, disharmony, etc* 婚姻的问题、不和睦、不和谐等.

□ **marital status** (*fml* 文) whether one is married, single or divorced 婚姻状况(已婚、单身或离婚).

mari·time /ˈmærɪtaɪm; ˈmærəˌtaɪm/ *adj* **1** of the sea, sailing or shipping 海的; 海上的; 航海的; 海事的: *maritime law* 海事法 ○ *the great maritime powers*, ie countries with powerful navies 海上强国. **2** situated or found near the sea 沿海的; 近海的: *the maritime provinces of Canada* 加拿大的沿海省份.

M

mar·joram /ˈmɑːdʒərəm; ˈmɑrdʒərəm/ *n* [U] sweet-smelling herb used as a seasoning in cooking 墨角兰(草本植物, 芳香, 用作烹饪调料).

mark[1] /mɑːk; mɑrk/ *n* **1 (a)** stain, spot, line, etc, esp one that spoils the appearance of sth 痕迹; 污点; 斑: *black marks on white trousers* 白裤子上的黑色污迹 ○ *Who made these dirty marks on my new book?* 谁把我的新书弄上了这些污迹? **(b)** noticeable spot or area on the body by which a person or animal may be recognized (人或动物身上可供识别用的)特征, 胎记: *a horse with a white mark on its head* 头上有白斑的马 ○ *This scar is her main distinguishing mark.* 这块疮疤是她主要的识别记号. Cf 参看 BIRTHMARK (BIRTH). **2 (a)** written or printed symbol; figure, line, etc made as a sign or an indication of sth (书写的或印刷的)符号; (图、线等的)记号: *ˌpunctuˈation marks* 标点符号 ○ *Put a mark in the margin to show the omission.* 在页边作个记号表示有遗漏. ○ *White marks painted on the trees show the route.* 树上涂有白色符号用以表示行进路线. **(b)** symbol on sth to show its origin, ownership or quality (表示来源、属有关系或品质的)标签, 标记: *ˈlaundry marks*, ie showing which laundry items have been sent to 洗衣房记号(表示已送到洗衣房的衣物标记) ○ *cattle branded with a distinctive mark*, ie of ownership 烙有物主标记的牛. Cf 参看 TRADE MARK (TRADE[1]). **3** visible trace; sign or indication (of a quality, feeling, etc) (性质、感情等的)痕迹, 迹象: *marks of suffering, old age* 痛苦、年老的表征 ○ *Please accept this gift as a mark of our respect.* 请接受我们这份薄礼, 聊表敬意. **4** number or letter, eg B+, used as an assessment of sb's work or conduct 评定某人的工作或操行用的数字或字母符号(如B+): *get a good/poor mark in maths* 数学获得良[劣] ○ *give sb high/low marks (for sth)* 给某人高[低]分 ○ *She got 80 marks out of 100 for geography.* 她的地理得了80分. **5** cross made on a document instead of a signature by an illiterate person (文盲在文件上当作签名的)十字画押: *put/make one's mark (on sth)* (在某物上)写十字(画押). **6 Mark** (followed by a number 后接数字) model or type (of a machine, vehicle, etc) (表示机器、车辆等的)型, 式: *the Jaguar XJ6, Mark II* 豹牌XJ6, II型轿车 ○ *a Mark IV Cortina* (福特)科天娜IV型轿车. **7** (*fml* 文) thing aimed at; target 目标; 目的; 鹄的: *The arrow reached its mark and the bird fell dead.* 那枝箭射中鹄的, 那只鸟坠地而死. **8** (in sport) line from which a race starts; point from which a bowler, jumper, etc begins his run (体育)起跑线, 起点: *be quick/slow off the mark* 起跑快[慢]. **9** (idm 习语) **be/fall wide of the mark** ⇨ WIDE. **an easy mark** ⇨ EASY[1]. **full marks** ⇨ FULL. **give sb full marks** ⇨ FULL. **ˌhit/ˌmiss the ˈmark** succeed/fail in an attempt to do sth 做成[未做成]某事物; 达到[未达到]目标. **leave/make one's, its, etc mark (on sth/sb)** leave a lasting (good or bad) impression 留下持久的(好或坏)印象: *War has left its mark on the country.* 战争给该国留下了不可磨灭的痕迹. ○ *Two unhappy marriages have left their mark on her.* 两次婚姻不幸给她留下了极坏的印象. **ˌmake one's ˈmark** become famous, successful, etc 出名; 成功: *an actor who has made his mark in films* 在电影界已崭露头角的演员. **not be/feel (quite) ˌup to the ˈmark** not feel as well, lively, etc as usual 不如平时身体好、有精神等: *I've got flu, so I'm not quite up to the mark.* 我得了流感, 所以有点不舒服. **on your ˈmarks, (get) ˈset, ˈgo!** (words said by the official starter of an athletics race 径赛发令员的号令语). **overshoot the mark** ⇨ OVERSHOOT. **overstep the mark** ⇨ OVERSTEP. **ˈup to the ˈmark** equal to the required standard 达到要求的标准: *Her school work isn't quite up to the mark.* 她的功课不大符合要求.

mark[2] /mɑːk; mɑrk/ *v* **1** [Tn, Tn·pr] **~ A (with B); ~ B on A** make (a mark or marks) on sth 在某物上做(记号): *mark one's name on one's clothes/mark one's clothes with one's name* 在自己的衣服上标上自己的名字 ○ *The route has been marked so that it is easy to follow.* 这条路线已标有记号, 很容易跟着走. ○ *Prices are marked on the goods.* 商品上都标有价目. ○ *a face marked* (ie scarred) *by smallpox* 出过天花的麻子脸. **2** [Tn] indicate or denote (sth) 表示, 指明(某事物): *This cross marks the spot where she died.* 这个十字符号标明她死去的地点. ○ *His death marked the end of an era.* 他的死标志着一个时代的结束. ○ *There will be ceremonies to mark* (ie celebrate) *the Queen's birthday.* 庆祝女王生日将要举行典礼. **3** [Tn] give marks (MARK[1] 4) to (pupils' work, etc) 给(学生作业等)批分数, 评成绩: *mark examination papers* 评阅试卷 ○ *I have twenty essays to mark tonight.* 今晚我有二十篇文章要评分数. **4** [Cn·a] show (sth) by putting a mark, eg a tick by sb's name 作记号表示(某事物)(如在某人姓名旁打勾号): *mark sb absent/present* 标出某人缺席[出席] ○ *Why have you marked the sentence wrong?* 你为什么把那句话标为病句呢? **5** [Tn, Cn·n/a] **~ sth (as sth)** be a distinguishing feature of (sth) 为(某事物)的特征: *a style marked by precision and wit* 以精巧为特征的文体 ○ *These are qualities which mark the film as quite exceptional.* 这些特点标志着那部影片与众不同. **6** [Tn, Tw] (*fml* 文) pay attention to (sth); note carefully 注意(某事物); 留心: *You mark/Mark my words,* ie You will find that what I say is correct. 留心听我说的话(你以后就明白我说得对). ○ *Mark carefully how it is done.* 仔细注意这是怎么做的. **7** [Tn] (*sport* 体) stay close to (an opposing player) so that he cannot play easily 钉住(对手): *Our defence had him closely marked throughout the first half.* 我们的后卫在整个上半场都把他钉得死死的. **8** (idm 习语) **a marked 'man** man whose conduct, etc has caused him to be disliked and selected for punishment, etc 因行为等令人不悦而遭惩罚等的人: *By breaking the rule of absolute secrecy, he became a marked man.* 他因违犯绝密条例, 成了处罚对象. **mark 'time (a)** march without moving forward 原地踏步. **(b)** (*fig* 比喻) pass one's time doing sth routine until one can do sth more interesting, etc 等待时机: *I'm just marking time in this job; I'm hoping to become an actor.* 我做这份工作是骑马找马; 我很希望当演员. **mark you** nevertheless; all the same; however 尽管如此; 反正; 可是; 然而: *She hasn't had much success yet. Mark you, she does try hard.* 她还没做出什么成绩来. 但她确实很努力. **9** (phr v) **mark sb down** reduce the marks given to sb in an examination, etc 给某人考试成绩等减分: *She was marked down because her answers were too short.* 她回答得太简短, 给减了分. **mark sth down** reduce the price of sth 减某物的价: *All goods have been marked down by 15%.* 所有货物一律八五折. **mark sth off** separate sth by marking a boundary 标明界限以隔开某物: *We have marked the playing area off with a white line.* 我们已用白线画出运动场地. **mark sb out for sth** (esp passive 尤用于被动语态) choose sb to receive sth special 选择某人接受某事物: *a woman marked out for early promotion* 被选定尽早晋升的女子 ○ *He was marked out for special training.* 他被指定接受特殊训练. **mark sth out** draw lines to show the boundaries of sth 画线标出某物的界限: *mark out a tennis court, car-park, etc* 画出网球场、停车场等的界限. **mark sb up** increase the marks given to sb in an examination 给某人考试成绩加分: *If we mark him up a tiny bit, he'll just get through.* 我们只要给他稍加点分, 他就能勉强及格. **mark sth up (a)** add a percentage to the cost/wholesale price of sth in calculating the selling/retail price 给成本[批发]价格加一百分比(以计算销售[零售]价格): *Whisky is marked up by 150%.* 威士忌在成本价上增加150%. **(b)** increase the price of sth 提高某物的价格: *Cars have been marked up recently.* 最近汽车已涨价.

▷ **marked** /mɑːkt; mɑrkt/ *adj* clear; noticeable; easily seen 清楚的; 明显的; 易见的: *a marked difference, similarity, improvement, etc* 显著的差异、相似、改进等 ○ *a woman of marked intelligence* 聪明过人的女子. **mark·edly** /'mɑːkɪdlɪ; 'mɑrkɪdlɪ/ *adv* (*fml* 文) in a marked manner; noticeably 清楚地; 显著地: *He was markedly more pleasant than before.* 他比以前和气多了.

marker *n* **1 (a)** person or tool that makes marks 作标记的人或工具: [attrib 作定语] *a 'marker pen* 标记笔. **(b)** person who keeps the score in certain games (某些比赛中的)记分员. **(c)** examiner 主考人. **2** flag, post, etc, that marks a position (指示位置的)旗、杆等: [attrib 作定语] *a 'marker buoy* 标志浮标.

mark·ing *n* (usu *pl* 通常作复数) pattern of marks, esp the colours of skin, fur or feathers 斑点, 花纹(尤指皮肤、毛皮或羽毛的颜色): *a dog with white markings on its chest* 胸部有白斑的狗.

□ **'mark-down** *n* (usu *sing* 通常作单数) reduction in price 减价; 削价: *a mark-down of 20%* 减价 20%.

'marking-ink *n* [U, C] indelible ink used for marking names on clothes, etc 不退色墨水(用以在衣物等上作标记的).

'mark-up *n* (usu *sing* 通常作单数) **1** percentage of wholesale/cost price added when calculating the retail/selling price of sth (在计算某物的零售[销售]价格时, 对批发[成本]价格的)加价百分比: *The mark-up on food in a restaurant is usually at least 100%.* 餐馆食物的成本加价率通常至少是100%. **2** increase in price 涨价; 加价: *a 10% mark-up on cigarettes after the Budget* 财政预算公布后香烟加价一成.

mark[3] /mɑːk; mɑrk/ *n* unit of money in Germany 马克(德国货币单位): *a ten-mark note* 一张十马克纸币.

mar·ket[1] /'mɑːkɪt; 'mɑrkɪt/ *n* **1** [C] gathering of people for buying and selling goods; place where they meet 集市; 市场: *She went to (the) market to sell what she had made.* 她赶集去出售自制品. ○ *The next market is on the 15th.* 下一次集市是15号. ○ *There is a covered market in the town centre.* 市中心有个有遮盖的市场. ○ [attrib 作定语] *a market stall, trader, day* 集市货摊、集市交易者、集日. **2** [C] the state of trade (in a particular type of goods) as shown by prices or the rate at which things are bought and sold 某种货物的交易情况; 行情: *a dull/lively market (in coffee)* 呆滞的[活跃的](咖啡)交易现象 ○ *a rising/falling market (in shares)*, ie in which prices are rising/falling 上涨的[下跌的](股票)行情 ○ *The (gold) market is steady*, ie Prices are not changing much. (黄金)行情稳定. **3** [sing, U] **~ (for sth)** demand 需求: *a good/poor market for motor cars* 良好的[呆滞的]汽车销路 ○ *There's not much (of a) market for these goods.* 这些货物的需求量不大. **4** [C] area, country, section of the population, etc to which goods may be sold 行销地区; 市场: *We must find new (foreign) markets for our products.* 我们必须为产品找到新的(国外)推销市场. ○ *This clothing sells well to the teenage market.* 这种衣服在青少年中间很畅销. **5 the market** [sing] buyers and sellers 买者与卖者; 市场: *The market determines what goods are made.* 有人买、有人卖就能决定做出什么货物. ○ *This product did not appeal to the German market.* 这种产品不受德国市场的欢迎. **6** (idm 习语) **come onto the 'market** be offered for sale 上市; 在市场上出售: *This house only came onto the market yesterday.* 这所房子是昨天才投放到市场出售的. **a drug on the market** ⇨ DRUG. **flood the market** ⇨ FLOOD[1]. **in the market for sth** (*infml* 口) interested in buying sth 有意买某物: *I'm not in the market for a big, expensive car.* 我无意购买大型高价汽车. **on the 'market** offered for sale; on sale 待售; 出售; 上市: *These computers are not yet on the market.* 这些计算机还未上市. ○ *put a car, house, etc on the market* 出售汽车、房子等. **play the 'market** (*infml* 口) buy and sell stocks and shares to make a profit 买卖证券和股票牟利. **price oneself/sth out of the market** ⇨ PRICE *v*.

□ **'market-day** *n* day on which a market is regularly held 交易日; 集日: *Thursday is market-day in Wetherford.* 在韦瑟福特星期四是集日.

,market 'garden (*Brit*) (*US* **'truck farm**) farm where vegetables are grown for sale in markets 蔬菜农场. **,market 'gardener** person who owns or works in a market garden 蔬菜农场的场主或工人. **,market 'gardening** [U].

'market hall large roofed area where a market is held 有遮盖的市场.

'market-place *n* **1** (also **,market-'square**) [C] open space in a town where a market is held 集市; 市场. **2 the market-place** [sing] commercial buying and selling 商业(买卖)活动: *Companies must be able to compete in the market-place.* 公司一定要在商品交易中有竞争力.

,market 'price price for which sth is or can be sold when publicly offered for sale 市场价格; 市价; 时价.

,market re'search study of why and what people buy, to make the sale of goods more successful 市场调查.

,market 'share proportion that one company, etc has of the total volume of trading in one kind of goods or services 市场占有率(一公司等的某种货物或服务项目在市场中所占的比例): *Thomsons have a 48% market share.* 汤姆森公司有48%的市场占有率.

'market town town where a market is held regularly (定期举行集市贸易的)集镇.

'market value price at which sth would be sold if offered publicly 市场价值; 市价: *offer a car at £500 below (its) market value* 以低于市场价格500英镑出售一辆汽车.

mar·ket[2] /'mɑːkɪt; 'mɑrkɪt/ *v* **(a)** [Tn] sell (sth) in a market 在市场上出售(某物): *market vegetables, fruit, etc* 在市场上卖蔬菜、水果等. (**b**) [Tn, Dn·pr] **~ sth (to sb)** offer sth for sale, esp by advertising, etc 推销某物(尤指借助广告宣传): *We need somebody to market our products (to retailers, in Germany, etc).* 我们需要有人为我们(向零售商、在德国等)推销产品.

▷ **mar·ket·able** *adj* that can be sold; suitable to be sold 可卖的; 适合在市场出售的: *a highly marketable new product* 应可畅销的新产品. **mar·ket·abil·ity** /ˌmɑːkɪtəˈbɪlətɪ; ˌmɑrkɪtəˈbɪlətɪ/ *n* [U].

mar·ket·eer /ˌmɑːkɪˈtɪə(r); ˌmɑrkɪˈtɪr/ *n* (usu in compounds 通常用以构成复合词): *black marketeers* 做黑市交易者.

mar·ket·ing *n* [U] (**a**) theory and practice of commercial selling 销售学; 市场推广. (**b**) division of a company which markets its products (公司的)销售部门, 市场推广部: *Do you work in marketing?* 你在市场推广部工作吗? ○ [attrib 作定语] *the marketing department* 市场推广部.

marks·man /ˈmɑːksmən; ˈmɑrksmən/ *n* (*pl* **-men** /-mən; -mən/) person skilled in accurate shooting 善射者; 神射手.

▷ **marks·man·ship** *n* [U] skill in shooting 射击术.

marl /mɑːl; mɑrl/ *n* [U] soil consisting of clay and lime, used as a fertilizer 泥灰(用作肥料).

mar·lin /ˈmɑːlɪn; ˈmɑrlɪn/ *n* (*pl* unchanged 复数不变) type of large sea fish with a long nose, similar to the swordfish 枪鱼.

mar·ma·lade /ˈmɑːməleɪd; ˈmɑrmlˌed/ *n* [U] type of jam made from citrus fruit, esp oranges 酸果酱; (尤指)橙子酱.

mar·mor·eal /mɑːˈmɔːrɪəl; mɑrˈmɔrɪəl/ *adj* (*fml* 文) of or like marble (似)大理石的: *marmoreal* (ie white and smooth) *skin* 洁白而光滑的皮肤.

mar·mo·set /ˈmɑːməzet; ˈmɑrməˌzɛt/ *n* type of small tropical American monkey with a bushy tail 狨(中南美洲所产尾巴蓬松的小猴).

mar·mot /ˈmɑːmət; ˈmɑrmət/ *n* type of small burrowing animal of the squirrel family 旱獭.

ma·roon[1] /məˈruːn; məˈrun/ *adj, n* [U] (of a) brownish red 褐红色(的): *a maroon jacket* 褐红色的外衣.

ma·roon[2] /məˈruːn; məˈrun/ *v* [Tn usu passive 通常用于被动语态] abandon (sb) in a place from which he cannot escape, eg a desert island 将(某人)放逐到无法逃脱的地方(如荒岛): *sailors marooned on a remote island* 放逐到偏远荒岛上的水手 ○ (*fig* 比喻) *Without a car, she was marooned at home for days.* 她没有了汽车, 多日困在家里.

ma·roon[3] /məˈruːn; məˈrun/ *n* small rocket that makes a loud bang, used as a warning signal 报警鞭炮(用作警报信号).

marque /mɑːk; mɑrk/ *n* (*fml approv* 文, 褒) (famous or particularly good) make or brand of product, esp of a car (著名的或极好的)牌子, 商标(尤指汽车): *the Mercedes marque* 奔驰(又译平治)牌.

mar·quee /mɑːˈkiː; mɑrˈki/ *n* **1** large tent used for garden parties, flower shows, circuses, etc 大帐篷(游园会、花展、马戏表演等用的). **2** (*esp US*) canopy over the entrance to a theatre, cinema, hotel, etc (戏院、电影院、旅馆等入口处的)遮檐.

mar·quetry /ˈmɑːkɪtrɪ; ˈmɑrkətrɪ/ *n* [U] pattern of pieces of wood, ivory, etc set into the surface of furniture as decoration (木料、象牙等作装饰家具的)镶嵌细工.

mar·quis (also **mar·quess**) /ˈmɑːkwɪs; ˈmɑrkwɪs/ *n* **1** (in the UK) nobleman next in rank above an earl and below a duke (英国的)侯爵(高于 earl 而低于 duke). **2** (in other countries) nobleman next in rank above a count (其他国家的)侯爵(高于 count). Cf 参看 MARCHIONESS.

mar·ram /ˈmærəm; ˈmærəm/ *n* [U] (also ˈ**marram grass**) type of coarse grass that grows esp in sand dunes 滨草.

mar·riage /ˈmærɪdʒ; ˈmærɪdʒ/ *n* **1** [U, C] legal union between a man and a woman as husband and wife; state of being married 结婚; 婚姻: *an offer of marriage* 求婚 ○ *After ten years of marriage, they are divorcing.* 他们结婚十年了, 现在正闹离婚. ○ [attrib 作定语] *a marriage feast, settlement* 婚宴、结婚授产契约 ○ *Her first marriage ended after five years.* 她的第一次婚姻维持了五年. **2** [C] ceremony at which a couple are married; wedding 婚礼: *Her second marriage was held/took place in St John's Church.* 她的第二次婚礼是在圣约翰教堂举行的. ○ *a marriage in a registry office* 在结婚登记处举行的婚礼. **3** (idm 习语) **give sb in ˈmarriage (to sb)** (*fml* 文) offer (usu one's daughter) as a wife 把某人(通常指女儿)嫁出去. **take sb in ˈmarriage** (*fml* 文) marry sb 嫁或娶某人.

▷ **mar·riage·able** *adj* (*fml* 文) old enough to marry; suitable for marriage 达到结婚年龄的; 适合结婚的: *a woman of marriageable age* 到达适婚年龄的女子. **mar·riage·abil·ity** /ˌmærɪdʒəˈbɪlətɪ; ˌmærɪdʒəˈbɪlətɪ/ *n* [U].

□ ˈ**marriage certificate** legal document which shows that two people are married 结婚证书.

ˌ**marriage** ˈ**guidance** advice given by qualified people on the problems of married couples 婚姻指导: [attrib 作定语] *a marriage guidance counsellor* 婚姻指导顾问.

ˈ**marriage licence** licence permitting a legal ceremony of marriage 结婚许可证.

ˈ**marriage lines** (*Brit infml* 口) marriage certificate 结婚证书.

ˌ**marriage of con**ˈ**venience** marriage made not for love, but for the personal benefit of one or both partners 权宜婚姻(因利害关系而非为爱情的结合).

mar·ried /ˈmærɪd; ˈmærɪd/ *adj* **1** (**a**) **~ (to sb)** having a husband or wife; united in marriage 结婚的; 已婚的: *a married man, woman, couple, etc* 已婚男子、已婚女子、一对夫妻 ○ *They like being married.* 他们愿意结成夫妻. ○ *be/get married (to sb)* (与某人)结婚 ○ *He's married to a famous writer.* 他娶了一位名作家. (**b**) [attrib 作定语] of marriage; marital 婚姻的: *married life, bliss* 婚姻生活、美满. **2** [pred 作表语] **~ to sth** (*fig* 比喻) dedicated to sth 专心于某事物: *married to one's work* 专心致志于工作.

mar·row[1] /ˈmærəʊ; ˈmæro/ *n* **1** [U] soft fatty substance that fills the hollow parts of human and animal bones 髓; 骨髓. **2** [U] (*fig* 比喻) essential part; inner meaning 精华; 精髓: *the marrow of his statement* 他所说的要点. **3** (idm 习语) **to the ˈmarrow** right through 彻骨; 透彻: *I felt frozen to the marrow.* 我觉得寒冷刺骨. ○ *She was shocked to the marrow by his actions.* 他的行为把她吓得目瞪口呆.

□ ˈ**marrowbone** *n* bone containing edible marrow (烹饪用)含髓的骨: [attrib 作定语] *marrowbone jelly* 含髓的骨的冻.

mar·row[2] /ˈmærəʊ; ˈmæro/ *n* [C, U] (also *Brit* ˈ**vegetable marrow**, *US* **marrow** ˈ**squash**) (**a**) [C] vegetable of the gourd family, with white flesh and green skin 西葫芦. (**b**) [U] its flesh used as food 西葫芦(用作食物). ⇨ illus 见插图.

mar·row·fat /ˈmærəʊfæt; ˈmæroˌfæt/ *n* (also **marrowfat** ˈ**pea**) type of large pea 一种大豌豆.

marry /ˈmærɪ; ˈmærɪ/ *v* (*pt, pp* **married**) **1** [I, Tn] take (sb) as a husband or wife 与(某人)结婚; 嫁或娶(某人): *They married (when they were) young.* 他们年轻就结了婚. ○ *She didn't marry until she was over fifty.* 她直到五十多岁才结婚. ○ *He married again six months after the divorce.* 他离婚后半年就又结婚了. ○ *Jane is going to marry John.* 简就要嫁给约翰了. **2** [Tn] (of a clergyman or civil official, etc) join (a couple) in marriage at a ceremony (指牧师或官员等)为(双方)主持婚礼: *Which priest is going to marry them?* 哪位牧师来为他们主持婚礼? ○ *They were married by her* (ie the bride's) *father, who's a bishop.* 新娘的父亲是主教, 为他们主持了婚礼. **3** [I, Ipr, Tn, Tn·p] **~ (sth) with sth** (*fig* 比喻) combine (sth) successfully with sth else 使(某事物)与另事物结合: *training that marries well with*

M

the needs of the job 密切结合工作需要的训练 ○ *She marries wit and/with scholarship in her writing.* 她的写作中融合了智慧和学识. 4 (idm 习语) ˌ**marry in ˈhaste, reˌpent at ˈleisure** (*saying* 谚) if one gets married too hurriedly one may regret it for a long time 结婚匆匆, 后悔无穷. **marry money** (*infml* 口) marry a rich person 和有钱人结婚. 6 (phr v) **marry into sth** become a part of (a family, etc) by marrying 因结婚而成为(某家庭等)的成员: *He married into the French aristocracy.* 他因婚姻关系跻身于法国贵族. **marry sb off** get rid of (a daughter) by finding a husband for her 将(女儿)嫁出. **marry up** (*infml* 口) (of parts) join up or assemble correctly; match[3] (指若干部分)配合, 匹配, 结合: *The two halves of the structure didn't marry up.* 该结构的两部分未配合好. ○ (*fig* 比喻) *The two versions of the story don't quite marry up.* 那件事的两种说法不大一致.

Mars /mɑːz; mɑrz/ *n* (*astronomy* 天) the planet fourth in order from the sun, next to the Earth 火星.

Mar·sala /mɑːˈsɑːlə; mɑrˋsɑlə/ *n* [U] light sweet Sicilian dessert wine 马尔萨拉葡萄酒(产于西西里岛马尔萨拉镇).

marsh /mɑːʃ; mɑrʃ/ *n* [C, U] (area of) low-lying wet land 沼泽(地带); 湿地: *miles and miles of marsh* 连绵无数英里的沼泽 ○ *We had to cross the marshes.* 我们须穿越沼泽地.

▷ **marshy** *adj* (**-ier, -iest**) of, like or containing a marsh (似)沼泽的; 有沼泽的: *marshy ground, fields, countryside, etc* 沼泽地、湿软的田地、有沼泽的农村.

□ ˈ**marsh gas** = METHANE.

mar·shal[1] /ˈmɑːʃl; ˋmɑrʃəl/ *n* 1 (usu in compounds 通常用以构成复合词) officer of high rank 高级军官: ˌ*Field-ˈMarshal*, ie in the Army 陆军元帅 ○ ˌ*Air-ˈMarshal*, ie in the Air Force 空军中将. ⇨App 9 见附录9. 2 official responsible for arranging or controlling crowds at certain public events, eg motor races, ceremonies, etc (负责某些公众活动, 如汽车赛、仪式等的)总指挥, 司仪, 典礼官. 3 (*US*) (**a**) officer with duties similar to a sheriff's 执法官; 保安官. (**b**) head of a police or fire department 警察局长; 消防局长.

mar·shal[2] /ˈmɑːʃl; ˋmɑrʃəl/ *v* (**-ll-**; *US* **-l-**) 1 [Tn, Tn·pr] arrange (sb/sth) in proper order; gather 安排(某人); 整理(某事物); 集结: *marshal troops, forces, crowds, etc* 集结部队、武装力量、人群等 ○ *The children were marshalled into straight lines.* 让孩子们排成直行. ○ (*fig* 比喻) *marshal one's facts, thoughts, etc* 整理自己的资料、思绪等. 2 (phr v) **marshal sb into, out of, past, etc sth** lead or guide (people) ceremoniously in the specified direction 按礼仪引导(人们): *marshal people into the presence of the Queen* 引领大家觐见女王 ○ *marshal them in/out* 带领他们进[出].

□ ˈ**marshalling yard** railway yard in which goods trains, etc are assembled (铁路的)调车场.

marsh·mal·low /ˌmɑːʃˈmæləʊ; ˋmɑrʃˌmælo/ *n* [C, U] soft sweet made from sugar and gelatine 果汁软糖.

mar·sup·ial /mɑːˈsuːpɪəl; mɑrˋsupɪəl/ *n, adj* (animal) of the class of mammals which includes the kangaroo, the female of which has a pouch on its body to hold its young 有袋总目的(动物); 有袋动物(袋鼠等).

mart /mɑːt; mɑrt/ *n* (*dated* 旧) 1 market 集市; 市场: *A model railway mart will be held on Friday.* 铁路模型展销会将于星期五举行. 2 centre of trade 贸易中心: *London is an international mart for stocks and shares.* 伦敦是个国际证券与股票的交易中心.

mar·ten /ˈmɑːtɪn; *US* -tn; ˋmɑrtn̩/ *n* 1 [C] small animal of the weasel family 貂. 2 [U] its fur 貂皮.

mar·tial /ˈmɑːʃl; ˋmɑrʃəl/ *adj* (*fml* 文) of or associated with war 战争的; 军事的: *martial music* 军乐.

□ **martial ˈarts** fighting sports such as judo and karate 武术(如柔道、空手道).

martial ˈlaw military rule imposed on a country temporarily, eg during a rebellion 军事管制; 戒严令: *declare/impose martial law* 宣布[实行]军事管制.

Mar·tian /ˈmɑːʃn; ˋmɑrʃən/ *n, adj* (supposed inhabitant) of the planet Mars (假想的)火星人; 火星的.

mar·tin /ˈmɑːtɪn; *US* -tn; ˋmɑrtn̩/ *n* bird of the swallow family 圣马丁鸟(燕科). Cf 参看 HOUSE-MARTIN (HOUSE[1]).

mar·tinet /ˌmɑːtɪˈnet; *US* -tnˈet; ˌmɑrtn̩ˋɛt/ *n* (*usu derog* 通常作贬义) person who imposes strict discipline and demands obedience to orders 严格执行纪律并主张服从命令的人.

Mar·tini (also **martini**) /mɑːˈtiːnɪ; mɑrˋtinɪ/ *n* [C, U] (*propr* 专利名) (cocktail made of) a mixture of gin and vermouth 马丁尼酒(由杜松子酒和苦艾酒混合成的鸡尾酒): *mix two martinis* 调两杯马丁尼酒.

mar·tyr /ˈmɑːtə(r); ˋmɑrtɚ/ *n* 1 person who is killed or made to suffer greatly because of his (esp religious) beliefs 烈士; (尤指)殉道者: *the early Christian martyrs* 早期的基督教殉道者 ○ *She died a martyr in the cause of progress*, ie died trying to achieve progress. 她为进步事业而牺牲. 2 (*usu derog* 通常作贬义) person who suffers or makes sacrifices, or pretends to do so, in order to be admired or pitied 为博得赞赏或同情而受苦、自我牺牲的人: *He always acts the martyr when he has to do the housework.* 他一做家务事就装成舍生取义的样子. ○ *Don't make such a martyr of yourself!* 你不必为博得赞赏而自我牺牲! 3 ~ **to sth** (*infml* 口) constant sufferer from sth 长期受某物之苦: *She's a martyr to rheumatism.* 她长期受风湿病的折磨.

▷ **mar·tyr** *v* [Tn usu passive 通常用于被动语态] kill (sb) or make (sb) suffer as a martyr 使(某人)殉难; 处死(某人)使之成殉道者: *He was martyred by the Romans.* 他被罗马人处死而成为殉道者.

mar·tyr·dom /ˈmɑːtədəm; ˋmɑrtɚdəm/ *n* [U, C] martyr's suffering or death 受苦; 受难; 殉难: *suffer martyrdom at the stake*, ie by burning 遭火刑处死.

mar·vel /ˈmɑːvl; ˋmɑrvl̩/ *n* 1 [C] wonderful or miraculous thing; thing causing (pleased) astonishment 奇异的事物; 令人惊喜的事物: *the marvels of modern science* 现代科学的奇迹 ○ *It's a marvel that he escaped unhurt.* 他竟能安然逃脱, 真不可思议. 2 [C esp *sing* 尤作单数] ~ (**of sth**) person or thing that is surprisingly good, pleasing, etc 出奇地好的、令人愉快的人或事物: *She works so hard in spite of her illness: she's a marvel!* 她带病努力工作, 真是难能可贵! ○ *He's a marvel of patience.* 他的耐心令人赞叹. ○ *Your room is a marvel of neatness and order.* 你的房间整洁得出奇. 3 **marvels** [pl] wonderful results (used esp with the *vs* shown) 奇妙的结果(尤与所示动词连用): *The doctor's treatment has worked marvels: the patient has recovered completely.* 该医生妙手回春, 病人已完全康复. ○ *perform/do marvels at the kitchen stove* 烹调出美味佳肴.

▷ **mar·vel** *v* (**-ll-**; *US* **-l-**) [Ipr, Tf] ~ **at sth** (*fml* 文) be very surprised (and often admiring) 大为惊讶(常含赞叹之意): *marvel at sb's boldness* 赞佩某人勇敢 ○ *I marvelled at the maturity of such a young child/at the beauty of the landscape.* 小小年纪如此成熟[风景之美]使我赞叹不已. ○ *I marvel that she agreed to do something so dangerous.* 我大为惊异的是, 她竟同意做如此危险的事.

mar·vel·lous (*US* **mar·vel·ous**) /ˈmɑːvələs; ˋmɑrvl̩əs/ *adj* 1 (*infml* 口) very good; excellent 极好的; 绝妙的: *a marvellous writer, car, dog* 极好的作家、汽车、狗. 2 astonishing; wonderful 不可思议的; 惊奇的; 奇妙的: *It's marvellous how he's managed to climb that far.* 他怎能爬得那么远, 真不可思议. **mar·vel·lously** (*US* **mar·vel·ously**) *adv*.

Marx·ism /ˈmɑːksɪzəm; ˋmɑrksɪzəm/ *n* [U] political and economic theory of Karl Marx (1818-83), stating that class struggle is the force behind historical change and that capitalism will inevitably be replaced by socialism and a classless society 马克思主义: *Communism is based on Marxism.* 共产主义理论是以马克思主义为基础的.

▷ **Marx·ist** /ˈmɑːksɪst; ˋmɑrksɪst/ *n* supporter of Marxism 马克思主义者. — *adj* characterized by, supporting or relating to Marxism 马克思主义的: *have Marxist views* 有马克思主义观点 ○ *a Marxist government, party, etc* 马克思主义的政府、政党等.

□ **Marxism-Leninism** /-ˈlenɪnɪzəm; -ˋlɛnɪˌnɪzəm/ *n* [U] Marxism as developed by Lenin 马克思列宁主义. **Marxist-Leninist** *n, adj*.

mar·zi·pan /ˈmɑːzɪpæn, ˌmɑːzɪˈpæn; ˋmɑrzəˌpæn/ *n* [U] thick paste of ground almonds, sugar, etc used to make sweets, decorate cakes, etc 杏仁蛋白糊(用来做糖果、装饰糕点等).

masc *abbr* 缩写 = masculine. Cf 参看 FEM.

mas·cara /mæˈskɑːrə; *US* -ˈskærə; mæsˋkærə/ *n* [U] cosmetic substance for darkening the eyelashes 染睫毛膏: *apply the mascara thickly* 浓施睫毛膏.

M

mas·cot /ˈmæskət, -skɒt; ˋmæskət, -skɑt/ *n* person, animal or thing thought to bring good luck 吉祥的人、动物或东西(认为能带来好运者): *The regimental mascot is a goat.* 这个团的吉祥物是山羊. ○ *His little son is the mascot for the local football team.* 他的小儿子是当地足球队的吉祥人物.

mas·cu·line /ˈmæskjʊlɪn; ˋmæskjəlɪn/ *adj* **1** having the qualities or appearance thought to be typical of men 有男子特质或外观的; 男子气的: *masculine looks, attitudes* 男子汉的容貌、姿态 ○ *She looks rather masculine in that suit.* 她穿着那套衣服看上去有些男性化. **2** (*grammar*) referring to the male gender 阳性的: *'He' and 'him' are masculine pronouns.* he 和 him 都是阳性代词.

▷ **mas·cu·line** *n* (*grammar*) **1** [C] a masculine(2) word or word form 阳性词; 阳性形式. **2 the masculine** [sing] the class of these 阳性: *a French adjective in the masculine* 法语的阳性形容词.

mas·cu·lin·ity /ˌmæskjʊˈlɪnətɪ; ˌmæskjəˋlɪnətɪ/ *n* [U] quality of being masculine 男性; 阳性. ⇨Usage at FEMALE 用法见FEMALE.

maser /ˈmeɪzə(r); ˋmezɚ/ *n* device for producing or amplifying microwaves 微波激射器.

mash /mæʃ; mæʃ/ *n* **1** [U] grain, bran, etc cooked in water until soft, used as food for animals (由谷物、糠、麸等煮成的)饲料. **2** (**a**) [U, C] any substance made by crushing sth into a soft mass 糊状物: *a mash of wet paper and paste* 湿纸和糨糊的混合物. (**b**) [U] (*infml* 口) boiled potatoes crushed into a soft mass 土豆泥: *bangers* (ie sausages) *and mash* 香肠和土豆泥. **3** [C, U] mixture of malt and hot water used in brewing beer (酿啤酒用的)麦芽浆.

▷ **mash** *v* [Tn, Tn·pr, Tn·p] **~ sth (up)** beat or crush sth into a mash 将某物捣成糊状: *mashed potatoes, turnips, etc* 土豆泥、萝卜泥 ○ *Mash the fruit up (with a fork) so that the baby can eat it.* (用叉子)把水果戳烂孩子就能吃了. **masher** *n* cooking utensil for mashing potatoes, etc 捣碎器(用以捣碎马铃薯等的炊具).

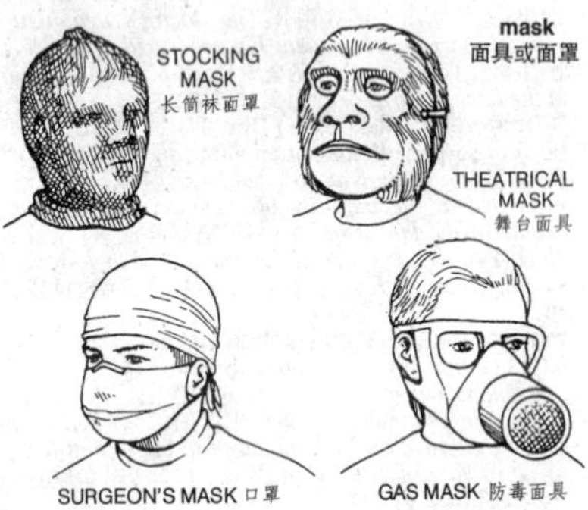

mask[1] /mɑːsk; *US* mæsk; mæsk/ *n* **1** covering for the face, or part of it, worn as a disguise 面具; 面罩: *a bank robber wearing a stocking mask* 戴着长筒袜面罩抢劫银行的匪徒. **2** (**a**) likeness of a face carved in wood, ivory, etc, or made of papier mâché, plastic, card, etc (木、象牙等的)面部雕像; (制型纸、塑料、厚纸等制的)假面具: *a child wearing a gorilla mask* 戴着猩猩面具的孩子 ○ *an actor wearing the mask of tragedy*, eg in Greek drama 戴悲剧人物面具的演员(如演希腊戏剧). (**b**) likeness of a face made by taking a mould in wax 蜡塑面部模型: *a death mask*, ie such a mould taken when a person is dead 死者蜡塑面部模型(取自死者面部者). **3** = GAS MASK. ⇨illus 见插图. **4** pad of sterile material worn over the mouth and nose, eg by doctors and nurses during a surgical operation, to protect against infection 口罩. ⇨illus 见插图. **5** (usu *sing* 通常作单数) (*fml fig* 文, 比喻) thing that hides the truth; pretence 用作掩盖的事物; 掩饰; 伪装: *Her sociable manner is really a mask for a very shy nature.* 她那好交际的作风, 实际上是她腼腆天性的伪装. ○ *He conceals his worries behind a mask of nonchalance.* 他装作若无其事, 借以掩饰内心的不安.

mask[2] /mɑːsk; *US* mæsk; mæsk/ *v* [Tn] **1** cover (the face) with a mask; cover the face of (sb) with a mask 用面具遮住(脸); 用面罩遮掩(某人)的脸: *The thief masked his face with a stocking.* 那贼套上长筒袜遮住脸. ○ *a masked robber, woman, etc* 戴面具的劫匪、女子等. **2** (*fig* 比喻) conceal (sth); disguise 掩盖(某事物); 伪装: *mask one's fear by a show of confidence* 装出有信心的样子来掩饰内心的恐惧 ○ *This perfume won't mask the unpleasant smell.* 这种香水遮不住那股难闻的气味.

□ ˌ**masked** ˈ**ball** ie formal dance at which masks are worn to disguise the guests 化装舞会.

ˈ**masking tape** adhesive tape used when painting sth to cover up the parts that one does not want to get paint on 遮蔽胶带(绘画或上漆时用以遮盖不需着色部分用的): *He put masking tape round the edges of the glass while he painted the window frame.* 他给窗框上漆时, 用遮蔽胶带把玻璃边缘贴住.

mas·och·ism /ˈmæsəkɪzəm; ˋmæzəˌkɪzəm/ *n* [U] getting (esp sexual) pleasure from one's own pain or humiliation 受虐狂; (尤指)性受虐狂. Cf 参看 SADISM. ▷ **mas·och·ist** /-kɪst; -kɪst/ *n*. **mas·och·istic** /ˌmæsəˈkɪstɪk; ˌmæsəˋkɪstɪk/ *adj*.

ma·son /ˈmeɪsn; ˋmesn̩/ *n* **1** person who builds in or works with stone 石工; 砖石工; 泥瓦匠. **2 Mason** Freemason 共济会会员.

▷ **ma·sonic** (also **Masonic**) /məˈsɒnɪk; məˋsɑnɪk/ *adj* of freemasons 共济会会员的: *masonic ritual* 共济会仪式.

ma·sonry /ˈmeɪsənrɪ; ˋmesn̩rɪ/ *n* [U] **1** that part of a building that is made of stone and mortar; stonework 砖石建筑; 泥瓦砖石结构: *crumbling masonry* 日渐崩坏的砖石结构. **2 Masonry** Freemasonry 共济会成员(总称).

masque /mɑːsk; *US* mæsk; mæsk/ *n* (**a**) [C] verse drama, often with music and dancing, popular in England in the 16th and 17th centuries 假面剧(16-17 世纪英国流行的一种诗剧, 常伴以音乐与舞蹈). (**b**) [U] this theatrical form 假面剧: *the study of Elizabethan masque* 对伊丽莎白时代假面剧的研究.

mas·quer·ade /ˌmɑːskəˈreɪd; *US* ˌmæsk-; ˌmæskəˋred/ *n* **1** false show; pretence 假装; 伪装: *Her sorrow is just a masquerade.* 她难过的样子纯粹是假装的. **2** formal dance at which masks and other disguises are worn 化装舞会.

▷ **mas·quer·ade** *v* [I, Ipr] **~ (as sth)** pretend to be sth one is not; disguise oneself as sth or sb else 伪装为某事物; 乔装为某物或某人: *masquerade as a policeman* 假扮成警察 ○ *The prince masqueraded as a peasant.* 那王子乔装为农夫. **mas·quer·ader** *n*.

Mass (also **mass**) /mæs; mæs/ *n* **1** [C, U] celebration of Christ's Last Supper, esp in the Roman Catholic Church 弥撒: *go to Mass* 望弥撒 ○ *hear Mass* 听弥撒 ○ *High Mass*, ie with incense, music and much ceremony 大弥撒(包括烧香、奏乐和许多仪式) ○ *The priest says two Masses each day.* 那神甫每天作两次弥撒. **2** [C] musical setting for this 弥撒曲: *Beethoven's Mass in D* 贝多芬的D大调弥撒曲.

mass /mæs; mæs/ *n* **1** [C] **~ (of sth)** (**a**) quantity of matter without a regular shape 团; 块; 堆: *There were masses of dark clouds in the sky.* 天上有朵朵乌云. ○ *The flowers made a mass of colour against the stone wall.* 以石墙衬托着的花朵五彩缤纷. ○ *A mass of snow and rock broke away and fell on the climbers.* 一堆积雪和岩石突然崩落到登山者的身上. (**b**) large number 大量; 大批; 众多: *a mass of spectators* 大批观众 ○ *She elbowed her way through the masses of tourists.* 她用胳膊肘开路从游客中挤了过去. ○ (*infml* 口) *I got masses of cards on my birthday.* 我生日的那天收到了很多贺卡. **2** [attrib 作定语] involving/of a large number of people 群众的; 人数极多的: *mass education* 群众教育 ○ *a mass meeting, walk-out, audience* 群众大会、大批退席、广大听众 ○ *mass murder/a mass murderer* 大屠杀[大屠杀的刽子手]. **3** [U] (*physics* 物) quantity of matter in a body, measured by its resistance to acceleration by a force (ie its *inertia*) (物体的)质量(即其惯性的大小). ⇨ App 11 见附录11. **4 the masses** [pl] ordinary working-class people, esp as seen by political leaders or thinkers 劳动者阶层(尤指政治领导人或思想家所指的劳动群众): *a* revolutionary who urged the masses to overthrow the government 鼓动群众推翻政府的革命者. **5** [sing] **the ~ of** the majority of (people) 大多数的(人): *The mass of workers do not want this strike.* 大多数工人不愿举行这次罢工. **6** (idm 习语) **be a mass of sth** be full of or covered with sth 充满; 布满: *The garden was a mass of colour.* 花园里的景色五彩缤纷. ○ *His face was a mass of bruises after the fight.* 他打完架后脸上青一块紫一块的. **in the 'mass** (*fml* 文) as a whole 总体上; 总的说来: *She says she doesn't like children in the mass.* 她说从总体上讲她不喜欢孩子.

▷ **mass** *v* [I, Ipr, Tn, Tn·pr] assemble/gather (sb/sth) into a mass 集结, 集合(某人[某物]): *clouds massing on the horizon* 地平线处积聚的云彩 ○ *The general massed his troops for a final attack.* 该将军把部队集结起来发动最后的攻击. ○ *the massed pipes and bands of several regiments* 从几个团集合起来的管乐器和管乐队.

□ **,mass communi'cations, ,mass 'media** means, such as newspapers, TV and radio, of communicating with very large numbers of people 大众传播工具, 大众传播媒介(如报刊、电视、无线电).

,mass hy'steria hysteria that affects many people at the same time 群众性的歇斯底里症.

,mass-pro'duce *v* [Tn] manufacture (identical articles) in very large quantities by mechanical processes (机械化)大量生产(某种物品): *mass-produced cars, fridges, etc* 大量生产的汽车、冰箱等. **,mass pro'duction** manufacturing in this way 大量生产.

mas·sacre /ˈmæsəkə(r); ˋmæsəkɚ/ *n* **1** cruel killing of a large number (of people or animals) 大屠杀: *the massacre of thousands of people for their religious beliefs* 因宗教信仰原因而对千万人的大屠杀. **2** (*infml* 口) defeat (of a team) by a large number of points, etc (运动队的)惨败: *The game was a 10-0 massacre.* 比赛结果是10-0惨败.

▷ **mas·sacre** *v* [Tn] **1** kill large numbers of (people or animals) 大量屠杀(人或动物). **2** (*infml* 口) defeat (a team) by a large number of points, etc 以悬殊比分等战胜(某运动队): *We were massacred in the final.* 我们在决赛中惨败.

mas·sage /ˈmæsɑːʒ; *US* məˈsɑːʒ; məˋsɑʒ/ *n* [C, U] (act of) rubbing and pressing the body, usu with the hands, to relieve or prevent stiffness or pain in muscles, joints, etc 按摩; 推拿: *give sb a relaxing massage* 给某人作放松按摩 ○ *The doctor recommended massage for my back pain.* 医生建议我作按摩医治背痛.

▷ **mas·sage** *v* [Tn] give massage to (sb, sb's muscles, etc) 给(某人、某人的肌肉等)作按摩.

mas·seur /mæˈsɜː(r); mæˋsɝ/ (*fem* 阴性作 **mas·seuse** /mæˈsɜːz; mæˋsɝz/) *ns* person who practises massage as a profession 按摩师.

mas·sif /mæˈsiːf; mæˋsif/ *n* compact group of mountain peaks 山峦.

mas·sive /ˈmæsɪv; ˋmæsɪv/ *adj* **1** (**a**) large, heavy and solid 大而重的; 巨大的: *a massive monument, rock, etc* 巨大的纪念碑、大石. (**b**) (of the features of a person or animal) heavy-looking (指人或动物的面貌)粗大的: *The gorilla had a massive forehead.* 猩猩的前额很大. **2** substantial; very large 可观的; 巨大的; 大量的: *a massive increase, crowd* 巨大的增长、大批的群众 ○ *She drank a massive amount of alcohol.* 她喝了大量的烈性酒. ○ *He suffered a massive* (ie very severe) *heart attack.* 他患了严重的心脏病. ▷ **mas·sively** *adv.* **mas·sive·ness** *n* [U].

mast[1] /mɑːst; *US* mæst; mæst/ *n* **1** upright post of wood or metal used to support a ship's sails 船桅; 樯. ➪illus at YACHT 见 YACHT 插图. **2** tall pole, eg for a flag 长杆(如旗杆). **3** tall steel structure for the aerials of a radio or TV transmitter (电视或无线电发射机的)天线塔. **4** (idm 习语) **at half-mast** ➪ HALF. **before the 'mast** (*dated or rhet* 旧或修辞) serving as an ordinary seaman 当二等水兵: *He spent ten years before the mast.* 他当了十年的海员. **nail one's colours to the mast** ➪ NAIL *v*.

▷ **-masted** (forming compound *adjs* 用以构成复合形容词) having the specified number or type of mast(s) 有若干船桅的; 有某类型船桅的: *a two-/three-masted ship* ○ *a tall-masted yacht.*

□ **'mast-head** *n* **1** highest part of a mast, often used as a look-out post 桅顶, 桅头(常用作瞭望台). **2** display title of a newspaper, etc at the top of the front page 报头, 刊头(报纸等首页上方刊载名称的部分).

mast[2] /mɑːst; *US* mæst; mæst/ *n* [U] fruit of forest trees, eg the beech, oak, etc, used as food for pigs 山毛榉、橡树等的果实(用作猪饲料).

mast·ec·tomy /mæˈstektəmɪ; mæsˋtɛktəmɪ/ *n* (*medical* 医) surgical removal of a woman's breast (女子的)乳房切除术.

mas·ter[1] /ˈmɑːstə(r); *US* ˈmæs-; ˋmæstɚ/ *n* **1** man who has others working for him or under him; employer 主人; 雇主: *master and servant* 主人和仆人 ○ *The slaves feared their master.* 奴隶惧怕奴隶主. Cf 参看 MISTRESS[1]. **2** [attrib 作定语] skilled workman or one who has his own business 熟练技工; 能手; 独立经营者: *a master carpenter, builder, etc* 手艺高的木工、独立经营的营造商. **3** male head of a household 男户主: *the master of the house* 这家的男主人. **4** captain of a merchant ship 商船的船长: *obtain a master's certificate/ticket*, ie licence that gives the holder the right to be a ship's captain 获得商船的船长证书 ○ *the master of HMS Britain* 皇家海军不列颠号舰长 ○ [attrib 作定语] *a master mariner* 商船船长. **5** male owner of a dog, horse, etc 狗、马等的男主人: *That dog is devoted to his master.* 那条狗忠于主人. **6** (**a**) (*esp Brit*) male schoolteacher (中小学的)男教师: *the 'French master*, ie person who teaches French 法语教师 ○ *'schoolmaster* 教师. (**b**) (esp in compounds 尤用以构成复合词) teacher of other subjects taught outside school (教授校外科目的)教师: *a 'dancing-master* 舞蹈教师 ○ *'riding-master* 骑术教练. **7 Master** holder of the second university degree 硕士: *She's a Master of Arts/Sciences.* 她有文学[理学]硕士学位. ○ *a Master of Engineering* 工程科硕士. **8 Master** (used as a title for boys too young to be called Mr 用以对年龄小不便称作先生的男孩的尊称): *Master Charles Smith* 查尔斯·史密斯少爷. **9 Master** title of the heads of certain colleges 某些学院院长的尊称: *the Master of Balliol College, Oxford* 牛津大学巴利奥尔学院院长. **10** great artist 艺术大师: *a painting by a Dutch master* 荷兰大师的画. **11** (**a**) **~ of sth** (*fml* 文) person who has control of sth 能控制某种事物的人: *He is master of the situation.* 他能控制这种局面. ○ *be master of a subject*, ie know it thoroughly 为精通某科目的行家 ○ *He has made himself master of the language*, ie He speaks it very well. 他精通该语言. ○ *You cannot be the master of* (ie decide) *your own fate.* 你无法决定自己的命运. ○ (*dated* 旧) *He is the master of a large fortune*, ie can use it as he wishes. 他能随意处置一大笔财产. (**b**) person who is superior 占优势者: *We shall see which of us is master*, eg which of us will win (a fight, competition, etc). 看咱们谁赢吧. ○ *He has met his master*, ie has been overcome, defeated, etc. 他遇到了克星. **12** film, tape, etc from which copies are made (可供复制的)原版影片、磁带等: *Take the master and make 20 copies by tomorrow.* 用这原版磁带明天复制出20盘来. ○ [attrib 作定语] *the master tape, film, copy, etc* 原版的磁带、影片、拷贝等. **13** [attrib 作定语] (**a**) commanding; superior; excellent 指挥的; 高超的; 优秀的: *This painting is the work of a master hand*, ie a superior and skilful artist. 这画出自名家之手. (**b**) overall; complete 总体的; 完整的: *a master plan of the building* 建筑的总体规划. (**c**) main; principal 主要的; 首要的: *the master bedroom* 主卧室 ○ *the master cylinder* 主汽缸. **14** (idm 习语) **master in one's own 'house** person who can manage his own affairs without interference 自己作主; 自己说了算. **one's lord and master** ➪ LORD. **(be) one's own 'master/'mistress** (be) free and independent 独立自主: *She likes being her own mistress, and not having to work for someone else.* 她喜欢独立自主, 不必为别人工作. **serve two masters** ➪ SERVE.

□ **'master class** lesson, esp in music, given by a famous expert to highly skilled students 名家、专家给优秀生教授的课(尤指音乐课).

'master-key *n* (also **'pass key**) key made to open many different locks, each also opened by a separate key 万能钥匙.

'mastermind *n* person who is unusually intelligent, esp one who plans the work of others 极具才智者; (尤指)决策者: *the mastermind behind the project* 该工程的幕后策划人. — *v* [Tn] plan and/or direct (a scheme, etc) 策

M

划，操纵（一阴谋等）：*mastermind a campaign, robbery, project* 策划一运动、抢劫、项目 ○ *A major criminal masterminded the huge fraud.* 一要犯策划了这个大诈骗案.

ˌ**Master of ˈCeremonies** (*abbr* 缩写 **MC**) person in charge of certain social occasions, who introduces guests, etc 司仪；典礼官.

ˈ**masterpiece** *n* task done with great skill, esp an artist's greatest work 杰作；（尤指）名著.

ˈ**Master's degree** (also ˈ**Master's**) higher degree between a Bachelor of Arts, etc and a Doctor of Philosophy 硕士学位.

ˌ**master ˈsergeant** (*US*) senior non-commissioned officer in the army, air force, or marines（陆军或海军陆战队的）二级军士长；（空军的）三级军士长. ⇨App 9 见附录 9.

ˈ**master-stroke** *n* very skilful act which ensures success 高招；绝招：*Settling the dispute needed a diplomatic master-stroke.* 要解决这一争端需有高明的手腕.

mas·ter[2] /ˈmɑːstə(r); *US* ˈmæs-; ˈmæstɚ/ *v* [Tn] **1** gain control of (sth); overcome (sth) 控制，制服（某事物）：*master one's temper, feelings, etc* 控制住脾气、感情等. **2** gain considerable knowledge of or skill in (sth) 掌握，精通（某事物）：*master a foreign language* 掌握一门外语 ○ *She has fully mastered the technique.* 她已完全掌握了这种技术. ○ *He has mastered the saxophone.* 他已精通萨克管的演奏.

mas·ter·ful /ˈmɑːstəfl; *US* ˈmæs-; ˈmæstɚfəl/ *adj* able to control others; dominating 能控制别人的；专横的：*a masterful person, character, tone* 专横的人、性格、语调 ○ *speak in a masterful manner* 用独行其是的态度说话.
▷ **mas·ter·fully** /-fəlɪ; -fəlɪ/ *adv*.

masterly /ˈmɑːstəlɪ; *US* ˈmæs-; ˈmæstɚlɪ/ *adj* (*approv* 褒) very skilful 熟练的；巧妙的：*their masterly handling of a difficult situation* 他们对困难局面的巧妙处理.

mas·tery /ˈmɑːstərɪ; ˈmæstərɪ/ *n* [U] **1 ~ (of sth)** (complete) knowledge; great skill 精通；熟练：*demonstrate a mastery of Arabic* 显示对阿拉伯语的精通 ○ *She showed complete mastery in her handling of the discussion.* 她处理这种辩论表现得应付裕如. **2 ~ (over sb/sth)** control 控制：*Which side will get the mastery?* 哪一方将获得控制权？○ *gain mastery (over an opponent)* 占上风（超越对手）.

mas·tic /ˈmæstɪk; ˈmæstɪk/ *n* [U] **1** gum or resin from the bark of certain trees, used in making varnish 乳香树脂. **2** type of pliable cement used for waterproofing joints in window-frames, roofs, etc 胶合铺料，胶粘水泥（作窗框、屋顶等填缝防水用的）.

mas·tic·ate /ˈmæstɪkeɪt; ˈmæstəˌket/ *v* [I, Tn] (*fml* 文) chew (food) 咀嚼（食物）. ▷ **mas·tica·tion** /ˌmæstɪˈkeɪʃn; ˌmæstəˈkeʃən/ *n* [U].

mas·tiff /ˈmæstɪf; ˈmæstɪf/ *n* type of large strong dog with drooping ears, often used as a watchdog 大驯犬.

mast·itis /mæˈstaɪtɪs; mæsˈtaɪtɪs/ *n* [U] (*medical* 医) inflammation, usu with swelling, of the breast or udder 乳腺炎；乳房炎.

mas·to·don /ˈmæstədɒn; ˈmæstəˌdɑn/ *n* large animal like an elephant, now extinct 乳齿象（似象之巨兽，现已绝种）.

mas·toid /ˈmæstɔɪd; ˈmæstɔɪd/ *n* part of a bone behind the ear（耳后的）乳突.
▷ **mast·oid·itis** /ˌmæstɔɪˈdaɪtɪs; ˌmæstɔɪdˈaɪtɪs/ *n* [U] inflammation of the mastoid 乳突炎.

mas·turb·ate /ˈmæstəbeɪt; ˈmæstɚˌbet/ *v* [I, Tn] give (oneself/sb) sexual pleasure by stimulating the genitals, esp by hand（刺激生殖器）给（自己[某人]）性快感；（尤指）手淫. ▷ **mas·turba·tion** /ˌmæstəˈbeɪʃn; ˌmæstɚˈbeʃən/ *n* [U]. **mas·turb·at·ory** /ˌmæstəˈbeɪtərɪ; *US* -bəˈtɔːrɪ; ˈmæstɚbəˌtɔrɪ/ *adj* [usu attrib 通常作定语]: *masturbatory fantasies* 手淫幻想.

mat[1] /mæt; mæt/ *n* **1 (a)** piece of material, made of straw, rushes, fibre, etc, used to cover part of a floor 席；垫：*a ˈdoormat* 门口蹭鞋垫. **(b)** thick pad, usu of foam, rubber, etc, used in gymnastics or wrestling for competitors to land on（用于体操或摔跤运动的）厚垫子. **2** small piece of material placed under a hot dish, or a glass, vase, etc to protect the surface underneath（用以垫热碟、杯子、花瓶等的）小垫：*a cork ˈtable-mat* 软木碗盘垫 ○ *a beer mat* 啤酒杯垫. **3** mass of things tangled thickly together 一丛；一团；一簇：*a mat of weeds, hair, threads* 一团杂草、毛发、线.
▷ **mat** *v* (**-tt-**) [I, Tn esp passive 尤用于被动语态] (cause sth to) become thickly tangled or knotted（使某物）缠结：*matted hair* 缠结在一起的毛发.

mat[2] = MATT.

mat·ador /ˈmætədɔː(r); ˈmætəˌdɔr/ *n* bullfighter whose task is to fight and kill the bull 斗牛士.

match[1] /mætʃ; mætʃ/ *n* short piece of wood or pasteboard with a head made of material that bursts into flame when rubbed against a rough or specially prepared surface 火柴：*strike a match* 划火柴 ○ *a box of matches* 一盒火柴 ○ *put a match to sth*, ie set it alight 用火柴点着某物.
□ ˈ**matchbox** *n* box for holding matches 火柴盒.
ˈ**matchstick** *n* stem of a match 火柴梗；火柴棍；火柴杆：*two thin legs, like matchsticks* 两条瘦得像火柴棍儿似的腿.
ˈ**matchwood** *n* [U] **1** wood suitable for making matches 适于做火柴杆的木材. **2** splinters or small pieces of wood 碎木；细木片：*a boat smashed to matchwood*, ie completely broken up 撞得粉碎的船.

match[2] /mætʃ; mætʃ/ *n* **1** [C] game in which individuals or teams compete against each other; contest 比赛；竞赛：*a ˈfootball, ˈwrestling, etc match* 足球、摔跤等比赛 ○ *a ˈboxing match of twenty rounds* 二十回合的一场拳击赛. ⇨Usage at SPORT 用法见 SPORT. **2** [sing] **~ for sb; sb's ~** person equal to sb else in skill, strength, etc 在技巧、力量等方面与某人相匹敌者；对手：*He's no match for her (in tennis).*（在网球上）他不是她的对手. ○ *She's his match* (ie as good as or better than him) *when it comes to chess.* 若下国际象棋的话，她与他棋逢对手. **3** [C] marriage 婚姻；匹配：*She made a good match when she married him.* 她嫁给了他，成就了美满姻缘. **4** [sing] **(a) ~ (for sb/sth)** person or thing combining well with another 相匹配的人或物：*The new curtains are a perfect match for the carpet.* 新窗帘配那地毯非常谐调. **(b) ~ (of sb/sth)** person or thing similar or identical to another 相似的或相像的人或物：*I've found a vase that's an exact match of the one we already have.* 我找到一只花瓶，和我们已有的那只一模一样. **5** (idm 习语) **find/meet one's match (in sb)** meet sb who has as much skill, determination, etc as oneself, and perhaps more 遇到不比自己差的对手：*He thought he could beat anyone at tennis, but he's met his match in her.* 他以为他打网球所向无敌，但遇到她却是旗鼓相当. **a good, bad, etc match** (*dated* 旧) person considered as a suitable, unsuitable, etc husband or wife 被视为相称、不相称等的配偶：*The young heiress was a good match.* 那个继承了大笔财产的年轻女子是理想的伴侣. **the man of the match** ⇨ MAN. **a slanging match** ⇨ SLANG *v*.
▷ **match·less** *adj* unequalled 无比的；无双的；无敌的：*matchless beauty, skill, etc* 无比的美丽、技巧等.
□ ˈ**matchmaker** *n* person who likes trying to arrange marriages for others 媒人. ˈ**matchmaking** *n* [U].
ˌ**match ˈpoint** final point needed to win a match, eg in tennis 比赛中取胜所需的最后一分（如在网球赛中）.

match[3] /mætʃ; mætʃ/ *v* **1** [I, Tn] **(a)** combine well with (sth), esp in colour 与（某物）相配（尤指颜色）：*The curtains and the carpets match perfectly.* 窗帘和地毯十分谐调. ○ *These curtains won't match your carpet.* 这窗帘和你那块地毯不相配. ○ (*fig* 比喻) *a well-matched couple* 很匹配的一对. **(b)** be like or correspond to (sth else) 与（某事物）相似、相称、相符合或相一致：*a brown dress and gloves to match* 一件棕色的连衣裙和相配的手套. **2** [Tn] find sth that is like or corresponds to (sth else) 找到与（某物）相似或相称的东西：*Can you match this wallpaper?* 你能找到和这种壁纸相配的吗？**3** [Tn] **(a)** be equal to (sb) 与（某人）相匹敌：*No one can match her at chess.* 下国际象棋谁也比不上她. ○ *The two players are well-matched*, ie roughly equal in ability. 这两人技艺不相上下. **(b)** find (sb/sth) equal to sb/sth else 认为（某人[某事物]）能与他人[他事物]相等或相当：*Can you match that story?* ie Can you tell one that is equally good, amusing, etc? 你能讲个与之相当的故事吗？ **4** [Tn·pr] **~ sb/sth with sb/sth** find sb/sth that fits or corresponds to sb/sth else 找到能与某人[某事物]相配合或相适应的人[事物]：*We try to match* *the applicants with appropriate vacancies.* 我们尽量给这些申请者找到合适的空缺. **5** (phr v) **match sth/sb against/with sth/sb** cause sth/sb to compete with sth/sb else 使某事物[某人]和他事物[他人]竞争或较量: *I'm ready to match my strength against yours.* 我已经准备好与你较量力气. ○ *Match your skill against the experts in this quiz.* 在这一测验中你与专家较量一下技巧吧. **match up** be in agreement; tally 一致; 符合: *The two statements don't match up.* 这两种说法不相符. **match sth up (with sth)** fit sth (to sth else) to form a complete whole 将某物(与另物)拼凑成一整体: *matching up the torn pieces of the photograph* 把撕碎的照片拼起来. **match up to sb/sth** be as good as or equal to sb/sth 与某人[某事物]同样好或相当: *The film didn't match up to my expectations.* 这影片没有我想的那么好.

mate[1] /meɪt; met/ *n* **1 (a)** (*infml* 口) (male) friend, companion or fellow-worker (男的)朋友, 伙伴, 同事: *He's an old mate of mine.* 他是我的老伙伴. ○ *I'm off for a drink with my mates.* 我要和同事出去喝一杯. **(b)** (*Brit sl* 俚) (used as a form of address to a man 用作对男子的称呼): *Where are you off to, mate?* 老兄, 你上哪儿去? **(c)** (in compounds 用以构成复合词) person participating in the same named activity, organization, etc or sharing the same accommodation 参与同一活动、组织等或同享食宿的人: *my room-mate/flat-mate* 与我同住一室[一单元]的人 ○ *her team-mates, class-mates, playmates* 她的队友、同学、伙伴. **2** (in job names 用于工作名称中) assistant of a skilled workman 熟练工的助手: *a plumber's mate* 铅管工的助手. **3** (in the merchant navy) ship's officer below the rank of captain (商船中)级别低于船长的职员: *the chief mate*, ie ranking just below the captain 大副 ○ *the first/second/third mate* 大[二/三]副. **4 (a)** either of a pair of birds or animals 一对鸟或兽之一: *The blackbird sat on the nest waiting for the return of her mate.* 黑鹂在巢中等候其雄鸟归来. **(b)** (*infml* 口) husband or wife 丈夫; 妻子.

mate[2] /meɪt; met/ *v* [I, Ipr, Tn, Tn·pr] **~ (sth) (with sth)** (of birds or animals) (cause to) come together to have sexual intercourse and produce young (指鸟或兽)(使)交配: *Pandas rarely mate (with each other) in captivity.* 猫熊在豢养环境中很少(彼此)交配. ○ *Our bitch should produce a fine litter. We mated her with John's dog.* 我们那条母狗应能生一窝很好的小狗. 我们让约翰的狗给她配了种. ▷ **mat·ing** *n* [U]: [attrib 作定语] *the mating season*, ie time when birds, etc mate 交配季节.

mate[3] /meɪt; met/ *n* = CHECKMATE.

ma·ter·ial[1] /mə'tɪərɪəl; mə'tɪrɪəl/ *n* **1** [C, U] substance or things from which sth else is or can be made; thing with which sth is done 材料; 原料: *raw materials for industry*, eg iron ore, oil, etc 工业原料 ○ *building materials*, eg bricks, timber, sand 建筑材料 ○ *writing materials*, eg pens, paper, ink 用于书写的材料(如钢笔、纸、墨水) ○ *We use high-quality raw material for our goods.* 我们的产品是用优质原料制造的. ○ (*fig* 比喻) *He is not officer material*, ie will not become a good officer. 他不是当官的材料(不会成为好官). **2** [U, C] fabric; cloth 织物; 布料: *enough material to make two dresses* 够做两件连衣裙的料子 ○ *tough cotton material* 结实的棉布 ○ *We sell the best materials.* 我们出售优质布料. **3** [U] facts, information, etc to be used in writing a book, as evidence, etc (写书等用的)事实, 资料: *She's collecting material for a newspaper article.* 她正在搜集素材在报纸上发表文章.

ma·ter·ial[2] /mə'tɪərɪəl; mə'tɪrɪəl/ *adj* **1** [attrib 作定语] composed of or connected with physical substance rather than the mind or spirit 物质的; 由物质构成的: *the material world* 物质世界. **2** [attrib 作定语] of bodily comfort; of physical needs 肉体舒适的; 身体需要的: *our material needs*, eg food and drink 我们身体的需要(如饮食) ○ *You think too much of material comforts.* 你对肉体的享受考虑得太多了. Cf 参看 SPIRITUAL 1. **3 ~ (to sth)** (*esp law* 尤用于法律) important; essential; relevant 重要的; 必不可少的; 有关系的: *material evidence* 重要证据 ○ *The witness held back material facts*, ie ones that might influence a decision. 证人隐瞒了重要事实. ○ *Is this point material to your argument?* 这一点对你的论点很重要吗?

▷ **ma·teri·ally** /-ɪəlɪ; -ɪəlɪ/ *adv* in a significant way; essentially 大大地; 实质性地; 重大地: *This isn't materially different from the old system.* 这和旧制度并无很大不同.

ma·teri·al·ism /mə'tɪərɪəlɪzəm; mə'tɪrɪəl,ɪzəm/ *n* [U] **1** (*usu derog* 通常作贬义) obsession with material possessions, bodily comforts, etc while neglecting spiritual values 物质享乐主义(迷恋于占有财富、肉体享受等, 而轻视精神价值): *the rampant materialism of modern society* 现代社会中蔓延成风的物质享乐主义. **2** (*philosophy* 哲) theory or belief that only material things exist 唯物主义; 唯物论.

▷ **ma·teri·al·ist** /mə'tɪərɪəlɪst; mə'tɪrɪəlɪst/ *n* **1** person excessively interested in material things 物质享乐主义者. **2** believer in materialism(2) 唯物主义者; 唯物论者. **ma·teri·al·istic** /mə,tɪərɪə'lɪstɪk; mə,tɪrɪəl'ɪstɪk/ *adj* of materialism 物质享乐主义的; 唯物主义的; 唯物论的: *a materialistic person, theory, society* 一味追求物质享乐的人、唯物主义的理论、物质至上的社会. **ma·teri·al·ist·ic·ally** /-klɪ; -klɪ/ *adv*.

ma·teri·al·ize, -ise /mə'tɪərɪəlaɪz; mə'tɪrɪəl,aɪz/ *v* [I] **1** become a reality; happen 成为现实; 实现; 发生: *Our plans did not materialize.* 我们的计划未能实现. ○ *The threatened strike never materialized.* 扬言要举行罢工, 却从未付诸行动. **2** take bodily form; become visible; appear 具体化; 实体化; 呈现; 出现: *He claimed that he could make ghosts materialize.* 他声称他可以使鬼魂现身. ○ (*infml* 口) *He failed to materialize*, ie did not come. 他并没有来. ▷ **ma·teri·al·iza·tion, -isation** /mə,tɪərɪəlaɪ'zeɪʃn; *US* -lɪ'z-; mə,tɪrɪəlɪ'zeʃən/ *n* [U].

ma·ter·nal /mə'tɜ:nl; mə'tɝnl/ *adj* **1** of or like a mother (似)母亲的: *maternal affection, feelings, duties, etc* 母亲的爱、感情、责任等 ○ *She feels very maternal towards him.* 她对他充满母爱. **2** [attrib 作定语] related through the mother's side of the family 母系的; 母亲方面的: *my maternal grandfather, aunt, etc* 我的外祖父、姨母等. Cf 参看 PATERNAL. ▷ **ma·ter·nally** /-nəlɪ; -nlɪ/ *adv*.

ma·ter·nity /mə'tɜ:nətɪ; mə'tɝnətɪ/ *n* [U] motherhood 母性; 为母之道: [attrib 作定语] *a maternity dress*, ie one for a pregnant woman 孕妇服装 ○ *a maternity ward, hospital, etc*, ie for women who have just given birth 产科病房、医院等.

ma·tey /'meɪtɪ; 'metɪ/ *adj* **~ (with sb)** (*infml* 口) sociable; familiar; friendly 亲近的; 亲热的; 友好的: *Don't get too matey with him — he's a rogue.* 别和他太亲近了——他是个无赖.

math·em·at·ics /,mæθə'mætɪks; ,mæθə'mætɪks/ *n* [sing or pl *v*] (also *Brit infml* 英式口语作 **maths** /mæθs; mæθs/ [sing or pl *v*]; *US* **math** /mæθ; mæθ/ [sing *v*]) science of numbers, quantity and space, of which eg arithmetic, algebra, trigonometry and geometry are branches 数学: *His mathematics are weak*, ie He is not very good at doing calculations, etc. 他数学不好. ○ *Maths is her strongest subject.* 数学是她最强的科目. ○ *I don't understand the mathematics* (eg the complicated calculations) *here.* 我不明白这里复杂的数学运算.

▷ **math·em·at·ical** /,mæθə'mætɪkl; ,mæθə'mætɪkl/ *adj* of mathematics 数学的: *a mathematical calculation, formula, etc* 数学运算、公式等. **math·em·at·ic·ally** /-klɪ; -klɪ/ *adv*: *She's not mathematically inclined*, ie not interested in mathematics. 她对数学不感兴趣.

math·em·at·ician /,mæθəmə'tɪʃn; ,mæθəmə'tɪʃən/ *n* expert in mathematics 数学家.

mat·inée (*US* also **mat·inee**) /'mætneɪ; *US* ,mætn'eɪ; ,mætn'e/ *n* afternoon performance at a cinema or theatre (电影院或剧院的)下午场: [attrib 作定语] *a matinée idol*, ie an actor greatly admired by women 极受女子赞赏的男演员.

mat·ins (also **mat·tins**) /'mætɪnz; *US* 'mætnz; 'mætnz/ *n* [sing or pl *v*] service of morning prayer, esp in the Church of England 晨祷(尤指英国国教的). Cf 参看 VESPERS.

matri- *comb form* 构词成分 of a mother 母亲的: *matricide* ○ *matriarch*. Cf 参看 PATRI-.

mat·ri·arch /'meɪtrɪɑ:k; 'metrɪ,ɑrk/ *n* female head of a family or tribe 女家长; 女族长. Cf 参看 PATRIARCH.

▷ **mat·ri·archal** /,meɪtrɪ'ɑ:kl; ,metrɪ'ɑrkl/ *adj*: *a matriarchal society, tribe, etc* 母系的社会、部落等. **mat·ri·archy** /'meɪtrɪɑ:kɪ; 'metrɪ,ɑrkɪ/ *n* type of society

M

in which women are the heads of families, own property and have most of the authority 母系社会; 母权制.

mat·ri·ces *pl* of MATRIX.

mat·ri·cide /ˈmætrɪsaɪd; ˋmætrəˏsaɪd/ *n* **1** [C, U] (act of) killing one's own mother 弑母. **2** [C] person who does this 弑母者. Cf 参看 PATRICIDE.

ma·tric·ulate /məˈtrɪkjʊleɪt; məˋtrɪkjəˏlet/ *v* [I, Tn] be admitted or admit (sb) as a student to a university 被录取入大学; 录取(某人)入大学.

▷ **ma·tric·ula·tion** /məˌtrɪkjʊˈleɪʃn; məˏtrɪkjəˋleʃən/ *n* [C, U] (instance of) matriculating or being matriculated 注册; 准予注册入学.

mat·ri·mony /ˈmætrɪmənɪ; *US* -məʊnɪ; ˋmætrəˏmonɪ/ *n* [U] (*fml* 文) state of being married; marriage 婚姻生活; 婚姻: *unite a couple in holy matrimony* 使双方正式结婚.

▷ **mat·ri·mo·nial** /ˌmætrɪˈməʊnɪəl; ˏmætrəˋmonɪəl/ *adj* [usu attrib 通常作定语] of matrimony 婚姻生活的; 婚姻的: *a matrimonial dispute, problem, etc* 婚姻生活中的争吵、婚姻问题.

$$\begin{pmatrix} 3 & 12 & 8 \\ 4 & 8 & 13 \\ 12 & 9 & 3 \end{pmatrix}$$

matrix 矩阵

mat·rix /ˈmeɪtrɪks; ˋmetrɪks/ *n* (*pl* **matrices** /ˈmeɪtrɪsiːz; ˋmetrɪˏsiz/ or **~es**) **1** mould into which molten metal, liquid, etc is poured to form shapes for eg printer's type, gramophone records, etc 铸模, 模型(如字模、唱片原模等). **2** mass of rock, etc in which minerals, etc are found in the ground 母岩; 脉石; 基岩. **3** place where sth begins or develops 某物产生或成长之处; 发源地; 基质; 母体: *bacteria growing in a matrix of nutrients* 生长在培养基中的细菌. **4** (*mathematics* 数) arrangement of numbers, symbols, etc in a grid, treated as a single quantity in mathematical operations 矩阵. ⇨illus 见插图. **5** (*computing* 计) group of circuit elements arranged to look like a lattice or grid 矩阵.

□ ˈ**matrix printer** (*computing* 计) printer that forms the letter, number, etc to be printed from an arrangement of tiny dots 矩阵式打印机.

mat·ron /ˈmeɪtrən; ˋmetrən/ *n* **1** woman who manages the domestic affairs of a school, etc 女舍监; 女总管. **2** (formerly) woman in charge of the nurses in a hospital (now called a *senior nursing officer*) (旧时)护士长(现称 senior nursing officer). **3** middle-aged or elderly married woman, esp one with a dignified appearance (已婚的)中老年妇女(尤指仪表庄重者).

▷ **mat·ronly** *adj* like or suitable for a matron(3); sedate 似中老年妇女的; 适于中老年妇女的; 庄重的: *a matronly manner* 像老夫人的仪态.

□ ˌ**matron of** ˈ**honour** (*esp US*) married woman acting as a bride's attendant at a wedding (已婚的)女傧相, 伴娘.

matt, mat (*US* also **matte**) /mæt; mæt/ *adj* (of surfaces, eg paper, photographs) not shiny or glossy; dull (指纸张、相片等)无光泽的, 粗面的: *Will this paint give a gloss or a matt finish?* 这种颜料有无光泽? Cf 参看 GLOSS[1] 1.

mat·ter[1] /ˈmætə(r); ˋmætɚ/ *n* **1** [C] (**a**) affair, topic or situation being considered 事情; 问题; 情况: *the heart/core/crux/root of the matter* 问题的中心[核心/要点/根源] ○ *the matter in hand, under discussion, etc* 手头上的、讨论中的…事 ○ *a matter I know little about* 我几乎不知道的事 ○ ˈ*money matters* 钱财问题 ○ *I don't discuss private matters with my colleagues.* 我不和同事谈私事. ○ *We have several important matters to deal with at our next meeting.* 下次会议我们有几件重要的事情要处理. ○ (*ironic* 反语) *There's the small matter of the money you owe me.* 有件小事, 你还欠我钱呢. (**b**) **~ of sth (to sb)** situation, problem or result that arouses the specified emotion 引起某种情感的情况、问题或结果: *matters of growing public concern* 公众日益关切的事情 ○ *This discussion is on a matter of considerable interest to me.* 这次讨论的是对我很有关系的事. **2** [U] (**a**) physical substance in general (contrasted with mind or spirit) 物质(与精神相对): *inert matter* 无生命的物质 ○ *to study the properties of matter* 研究物质的特性. ○ *The universe is composed of matter.* 宇宙是由物质组成的. (**b**) substance, material or things of a specified kind (某类的)材料, 物品, 东西: *decaying vegetable matter* 腐烂的植物 ○ *waste matter*, eg human excreta 废物(如人体排泄物) ○ *reading matter*, ie books, newspapers, etc 读物 ○ *printed matter*, ie forms, leaflets, etc 印刷品. **3** [U] (*fml* 文) ideas or topic of a book, speech, etc (contrasted with its language or style) (书、讲话等的)思想, 主题(以别于其语言或文体). **4** [U] discharge from the body; pus 身体排泄物; 脓. **5** (idm 习语) **as a matter of fact** (used for emphasis 用以加强语气) in reality; to tell the truth 事实上; 说真的; 其实: *I'm going there tomorrow, as a matter of fact.* 说实话, 明天我要去那里. **be no laughing matter** ⇨ LAUGHING. **for** ˈ**that matter** (used to indicate that a second category, topic, etc is as relevant as the first 用以指出所说的两件事物中, 后说的与先说的性质一样): *Don't talk like that to your mother, or to anyone else for that matter.* 不要跟你母亲那样说话, 其实跟谁也不要那样. **in the matter of sth** (*dated fml* 旧, 文) concerning sth 关于某事物: *I want to speak to her in the matter of my salary.* 我想跟她谈谈我的薪水问题. **it's all, only, etc a matter of** ˈ**time (before…)** this consequence is inevitable though it may not happen immediately 尽管不见得马上发生, 但一定会发生; 只是迟早的事: *It's simply a matter of time before the rebels are crushed.* 把这些叛乱分子镇压下去只是迟早的事. **let the matter** ˈ**drop**/ˈ**rest** stop mentioning sth or trying to change it 不再提起或不再更动某事物: *She reluctantly agreed to let the matter drop.* 她勉强同意这事到此为止. **make matters** ˈ**worse** make an already difficult situation more difficult 将困难情况弄得更糟: *Her attempts to calm them down only made matters worse.* 她设法使他们平静下来, 不想却适得其反. **(as) a matter of** ˈ**course** (as) a regular habit or usual procedure (作为)理所当然的事; (按照)常规: *I check my in-tray every morning as a matter of course.* 我照例每天早晨查看收文盘. **(be) the matter (with sb/sth)** (*infml* 口) the reason for unhappiness, pain, problems, etc (used esp in the expressions shown) (不幸、痛苦、问题等的)原因, 理由(尤用于以下示例): *What's the matter with him?* 他怎么了? ○ *Is anything the matter?* 怎么了? ○ *There's nothing the matter with it.* 这没有问题. **a matter of** ˈ**hours,** ˈ**minutes,** ˈ**days, etc; a matter of** ˈ**pounds,** ˈ**feet,** ˈ**ounces, etc** (**a**) not more than 不多于; 至多: *I'll be back in a matter of hours.* 用不了几小时我就回来. ○ *It's a matter of a few more miles, that's all.* 最多再有几英里, 也不过如此. (**b**) not less than 不少于; 至少: *It may be a matter of months before it's ready.* 要准备好可能得数月时间. ○ *You realize it'll be a matter of days* (ie two days or more) *before we get news?* 你明白吗, 我们至少得两三天后才能得到消息? **a** ˌ**matter of** ˌ**life and** ˈ**death** issue that is crucial to survival, success, etc 生死攸关的事情; 成败关键: *Of course this must have priority — it's a matter of life and death.* 当然这一点必须优先考虑——这是成败的关键. **a matter of o**ˈ**pinion** issue on which there is disagreement 看法不同的问题: *'She's a fine singer.' 'That's a matter of opinion.'* '她是个好歌手.' '见仁见智吧.' **(be) a matter of sth/doing sth** situation, question or issue that depends on sth else 取决于某事的情况、问题或事情: *Dealing with these problems is all a matter of experience.* 处理这些问题全凭经验. ○ *Success in business is simply a matter of knowing when to take a chance.* 商业上的成功就在于把握时机. **mind over matter** ⇨ MIND[1]. **no matter; be/make no matter (to sb) (that/whether…)** be of no importance (to sb) (对某人)无关紧要: *'I can't do it.' 'No matter, I'll do it myself.'* '我做不了.' '没关系, 我自己干吧.' ○ *It's no matter to me whether you arrive early or late.* 你来早来晚我都无所谓. **no matter who, what, where, etc** whoever, whatever, wherever, etc 无论谁、什么、何处等: *Don't open the door, no matter who comes.* 不管谁来都别开门. ○ *Don't trust him, no matter what he says.* 无论他说什么, 都别相信. **not mince matters/words** ⇨ MINCE. **take matters into one's own hands** take

M

action oneself rather than waiting for others to act 亲自采取行动; 主动处理.

□ ˌ**matter-of-ˈfact** *adj* showing no emotion or imagination 据实的; 不动感情的; 不加想像的: *She told us the news in a very ˌmatter-of-fact ˈway.* 她把那消息平铺直叙地告诉了我们.

mat·ter[2] /ˈmætə(r); ˋmætɚ/ *v* [I, Ipr] **~ (to sb)** (used esp in negative sentences and questions; in sentences containing *what, who, where, if,* etc, usu with *it* as the subject 尤用于否定句和疑问句; 句中含 what、who、where、if 等词, 通常以 it 作主语) be important 关系重大; 要紧: *What does it matter (whether he comes or goes)?* (他来也好去也好,)那有什么关系? ○ *Some things matter more than others.* 有些事情更重要. ○ *Does it matter if we're a bit late?* 我们晚到一会儿有关系吗? ○ *It doesn't matter to me what you do.* 你做什么我都无所谓.

mat·ting /ˈmætɪŋ; ˋmætɪŋ/ *n* [U] rough woven material used for making mats or for packing goods (用以制席、垫或货物包装衬垫的)粗糙编织物: *floors covered with coconut-matting* 铺着椰衣垫的地板.

mat·tins = MATINS.

mat·tock /ˈmætək; ˋmætək/ *n* heavy tool with a long handle and a metal head, one end of which is sharp and the other blunt, used for breaking up soil, cutting roots, etc 鹤嘴锄.

mat·tress /ˈmætrɪs; ˋmætrɪs/ *n* fabric case filled with soft or springy material (eg wool, hair, feathers, foam rubber, etc) and used for sleeping on 床垫. ⇨illus at App 1 见附录1插图, page xvi.

ma·ture[1] /məˈtjʊə(r); *US* -ˈtʊər; məˋtʊr/ *adj* **1** (**a**) fully grown or developed mentally or physically; having achieved one's full potential 充分发育的; (智力或体力)成熟的; 已具备全部潜力的: *a mature person, oak, starling* 成熟的人、橡树、椋鸟 ○ *a house with a mature garden,* ie one where the plants, trees, etc are fully grown and well established 有花木繁茂的花园的住宅 ○ *He's not mature enough to be given too much responsibility.* 他还不成熟, 不宜给他重任. (**b**) (of wine or cheese) having reached a stage where its flavour has fully developed (指葡萄酒或干酪)成熟的. **2** (of thought, intentions, etc) careful and thorough (指想法、意图等)深思熟虑的: *after mature consideration* 经过审慎考虑. **3** (*commerce* 商) (of insurance policies, etc) due for payment (指保险单等)到期该付款的.

▷ **ma·turely** *adv*.

ma·tur·ity /məˈtjʊərətɪ; *US* -ˈtʊə-; məˋtʊrətɪ/ *n* [U] state of being mature 成熟; 到期: *reach maturity* 到达成熟期.

ma·ture[2] /məˈtjʊə(r); *US* -ˈtʊər; məˋtʊr/ *v* **1** [I, Tn] (cause sb/sth to) become mature (使某人[某事物])成熟: *Her character matured during these years.* 这些年里她的品性已趋成熟. ○ *cheese/wine that matures slowly* 熟得慢的奶酪[葡萄酒] ○ *My plan gradually matured.* 我的计划逐渐酝酿成熟. ○ *Experience has matured him greatly.* 他经历这些事之后已经成熟多了. **2** [I] (*commerce* 商) (of insurance policies, etc) become due (指保险单等)到期.

▷ **mat·ura·tion** /ˌmætʃʊˈreɪʃn; ˌmætʃʊˋreʃən/ *n* [U, C] process of becoming or being made mature 成熟; 到期: *a slow maturation* 缓慢的成熟.

maud·lin /ˈmɔːdlɪn; ˋmɔdlɪn/ *adj* foolishly or tearfully sentimental or self-pitying, esp when drunk 伤感的, 落泪的, 自怜的(尤指酒后).

maul /mɔːl; mɔl/ *v* **1** [Tn, Tn·p] **~ sb/sth (about)** handle sb/sth roughly or brutally 粗野地对待某人[某物]: (*fig* 比喻) *Her novel has been badly mauled by the critics.* 她的小说横遭评论家抨击. **2** [Tn] injure (a person or an animal) by tearing his or its flesh 伤害(人或动物)(撕裂其皮肉): *He died after being mauled by a tiger.* 他被老虎咬死了.

maul·stick /ˈmɔːlstɪk; ˋmɔlˌstɪk/ (also **mahl·stick** /ˈmɑːlstɪk; ˋmɑlˌstɪk/) *n* stick held by a painter in one hand to support the other hand, which holds the brush 支腕杖(绘画时用一手持之以支撑握画笔之手).

maun·der /ˈmɔːndə(r); ˋmɔndɚ/ *v* [I, Ip] **1 ~ (on)** talk in a rambling way 唠叨; 胡说: *The drunk sat there maundering (on) about his troubles.* 那醉鬼坐在那里唠叨着自己的烦恼事. **2 ~ (about)** move around listlessly or idly 闲荡; 徘徊: *Don't just maunder about: do some work!* 别光闲荡了, 做点正经事吧!

Maundy Thurs·day /ˌmɔːndɪ ˈθɜːzdɪ; ˋmɔndɪˋθɝzdɪ/ the Thursday before Easter 濯足节; 圣星期四.

mau·so·leum /ˌmɔːsəˈliːəm; ˌmɔsəˋliəm/ *n* large, finely built tomb (大而精致的)陵墓.

mauve /məʊv; mov/ *adj, n* (of a) pale purple colour 淡紫色(的).

mav·er·ick /ˈmævərɪk; ˋmævrɪk/ *n* **1** (*US*) unbranded calf 未打烙印的小牛. **2** person with independent or unorthodox views 持独立见解者; 持异议者: *Politically, she's a bit of a maverick.* 在政治方面, 她有点自行其是.

maw /mɔː; mɔ/ *n* (*fml* 文) animal's stomach or throat (动物的)胃, 咽喉: (*fig* 比喻) *swallowed up in the maw of battle* 在一场战役中被吞噬.

mawk·ish /ˈmɔːkɪʃ; ˋmɔkɪʃ/ *adj* sentimental in a feeble or sickly way 多愁善感的; 伤感的. ▷ **mawk·ishly** *adv*. **mawk·ish·ness** *n* [U].

max /mæks; mæks/ *abbr* 缩写 = maximum: *temperature 60° max* 最高温度60°. Cf 参看 MIN 1.

maxim /ˈmæksɪm; ˋmæksɪm/ *n* saying that expresses a general truth or rule of conduct, eg 'Waste not, want not' 箴言, 格言(如不浪费, 不穷困).

max·im·ize, -ise /ˈmæksɪmaɪz; ˋmæksəˌmaɪz/ *v* [Tn] **1** increase (sth) as much as possible 使(某事物)增至最大限度: *We must maximize profits.* 我们必须尽量增加利润. **2** make the best use of (sth) 最大限度利用(某事物): *maximize one's opportunities* 充分利用机会. Cf 参看 MINIMIZE. ▷ **max·im·iza·tion, -isation** /ˌmæksɪmaɪˈzeɪʃn; *US* -mɪˈz-; ˌmæksəmɪˋzeʃən/ *n* [U].

max·imum /ˈmæksɪməm; ˋmæksəməm/ *n* (*pl* **maxima** /ˈmæksɪmə; ˋmæksəmə/) (*abbr* 缩写 **max**) greatest amount, size, intensity, etc possible or recorded 最大的量、体积、强度等: *obtain 81 marks out of a maximum of 100* 满分为100分而获得81分 ○ *The July maximum* (ie the highest temperature recorded in July) *was 30°C.* 七月份的最高温度是30°C. ○ *This hall holds a maximum of seventy people.* 这厅最多能容纳七十人. Cf 参看 MINIMUM.

▷ **max·imal** /ˈmæksɪml; ˋmæksəməl/ *adj* [usu attrib 通常作定语] as great as can be achieved 能达到的最大的: *She obtained maximal benefit from the course.* 她从该课程中获益极大.

max·imum *adj* [attrib 作定语] as high, great, intense, etc as possible 最高的; 最大的; 最强的: *the maximum temperature, voltage, volume* 最高温度、最高电压、最大体积 ○ *The maximum load for this lorry is one ton.* 这辆卡车最大载重量是一吨.

May /meɪ; me/ *n* [U, C] the fifth month of the year, next after April 五月: *the first of May* 五月一日 ○ *go on holiday in May* 五月去度假.

For the uses of *May* see the examples at *April.* 关于 May 的用法见 April 词条中的示例.

□ ˈ**May Day** 1st of May, celebrated as a spring festival and, in some countries, as a day for socialist and labour demonstrations 五朔节; 劳动节. Cf 参看 MAYDAY.

ˈ**May-beetle,** ˈ**May-bug** *ns* = COCKCHAFER.

ˈ**mayfly** *n* short-lived insect that appears in May 蜉蝣.

ˈ**maypole** *n* decorated pole around which people dance on May Day 五月柱.

may[1] /meɪ; me/ *modal v* (*neg* 否定式 **may not**, *rare contracted form* 罕, 缩约式 **mayn't** /meɪnt; ment/; *pt* **might** /maɪt; maɪt/, *neg* 否定式 **might not**, *rare contracted form* 罕, 缩约式 **mightn't** /ˈmaɪtnt; ˋmaɪtn̩t/) **1** (indicating permission 用以表示允许、许可): *You may come if you wish.* 你要来就来吧. ○ *May I come in?* 我可以进来吗? ○ *Passengers may cross by the footbridge.* 乘客可使用步行桥. ⇨Usage 1 见所附用法第1项. **2** (indicating possibility 用以表示可能): *This coat may be Peter's.* 这件大衣可能是彼得的. ○ *That may or may not be true.* 那可能是实情, 也可能不是. ○ *He may have* (ie Perhaps he has) *missed his train.* 他可能没赶上火车. ○ *This medicine may cure your cough.* 这药也许能治你的咳嗽. ⇨Usage 2 见所附用法第2项. **3** (indicating purpose 用以表示目的): *I'll write today so that he may know when to expect us.* 我今天就写信好让他知道我们什么时候到. ⇨Usage 3 见所附用法第3项. **4** (*dated* 旧) (asking for information 用于询问情况): *Well, who may ˈyou be?* 喂, 你是谁呀? ○ *How old may ˈshe be?* 她有多大年纪了? ⇨Usage 4 见所附用法第4项. **5** (used

M

to express wishes and hopes 用以表示愿望和希望): *May you both be very happy!* 祝你们俩幸福! ○ *Long may she live to enjoy her good fortune!* 愿她长寿幸福!

NOTE ON USAGE 用法: **1** PERMISSION (**can**[2], **could**[1], **may**[1], **might**[1]) 许可(**can**[2]、**could**[1]、**may**[1]、**might**[1]) (**a**) British speakers normally use **can** to give or request permission 英国人一般用**can**字来表示准许或请求许可: *You can come if you want to.* 你想来就可以来. ○ *Can I come too?* 我也可以来吗? **Could** is more polite but is only used in questions 用**could**一词更客气些, 但只用于疑问句中: *'Could I use your telephone?' 'Yes, of course.'* '我可以借用你的电话吗?' '当然可以.' **May** is formal ☆ **may**是较郑重的词: *You may come if you wish.* 你愿意来就可以来. However, US speakers often use **may** where British English has **can** 但是美国人常用**may**, 英国人多用**can**: *May I sit down?* 我可以坐下吗? Both British and US speakers use **could** or **might** to suggest doubt, shyness, etc 英美两国的人都用**could**或**might**来表示怀疑、羞怯等: *Might I suggest another time?* 我可以建议另找个时间吗? ○ *Could I arrange a meeting with the director?* 我可以约见负责人吗? (**b**) In indirect questions, **can** becomes **could** and **may** becomes **might** 在间接问句中, 要把**can**改成**could**, 把**may**改成**might**: *John asked if he could/might come too.* 约翰问, 他是否也可以来. **2** POSSIBILITY (**can**[2], **could**[1], **may**[1], **might**[1]) 可能性(**can**[2]、**could**[1]、**may**[1]、**might**[1]) (**a**) **Could** or **might** express more doubt or hesitation than **may** ☆ **could**或**might**比**may**更含怀疑或犹豫之意: *That may be our taxi now!* 那辆可能就是我们的计程车了. ○ *That could/might be our taxi (but I doubt it).* 那辆有可能是我们的计程车(但我有所怀疑). (**b**) In questions and negative sentences **can** replaces **may**. 在疑问句和否定句中, 用**can**代替**may**. ☆ Compare 试比较: *It may be Bill's.* 那可能是比尔的. ○ *Can it be Bill's? It can't be Bill's.* 那可能是比尔的吗? 不可能是比尔的. (**c**) **Could have**, **may have** or **might have** are used to show the possibility of something having happened in the past ☆ **could have**、**may have**或**might have**用以表示过去发生过某事的可能性: *She could have forgotten to tell him.* 她可能忘记告诉他了. ○ *He may have lost his way.* 他可能迷路了. ○ *He might just possibly have lost his keys.* 他有可能把钥匙丢了. **3** PURPOSE (**may**[1], **would**[1]) 目的(**may**[1]、**would**[1]) (**a**) **May** can be used after *so that, in order that,* to express present purpose ☆ **may**可用于so that、in order that之后, 表示现在的目的: *I'll write so that he may know when to expect us.* 我要写信好让他知道我们什么时候到. (**b**) to indicate a purpose in the past, **might** or **would** are used 要表示过去目的, 则用**might**或**would**: *I wrote so that he might/would know when to expect us.* 我写信好让他知道我们什么时候到. ○ *He died so that others might/would live.* 他为别人能够活着而牺牲了自己. **4** ASKING FOR INFORMATION (**may**[1], **might**[1]) 询问情况(**may**[1]、**might**[1]) (**a**) **May** (rather dated) and **might** are used to request information in an uncertain or a superior way ☆ **may**(较陈旧)和**might**用以询问情况, 含无把握或高傲的语气: *Well, and who may/might 'you be?* 那么, 你是谁呢? (**b**) In indirect questions, only **might** is used 在间接问句中, 只用**might**: *Bill asked who 'she might be.* 比尔问她是谁.

may[2] /meɪ; me/ *n* [U] hawthorn blossom 山楂花.

maybe /ˈmeɪbiː; ˈmebi/ *adv* **1** perhaps; possibly 也许; 可能; 大概: *Maybe he'll come, maybe he won't.* 他也许来, 也许不来. ○ *'Is that true?' 'Maybe, I'm not sure.'* '是真的吗?' '可能, 我说不准.' **2** (idm 习语) **as soon as maybe** ⇨ SOON.

may·day (also **Mayday**) /ˈmeɪdeɪ; ˈmeˌde/ *n* (*radio* 无) international distress signal, used by ships and aircraft (船和飞行器用的)国际无线电求救信号: [attrib 作定语] *a mayday call/signal* 求救呼叫[信号]. Cf 参看 SOS.

may·hem /ˈmeɪhem; ˈmehɛm/ *n* [U] **1** violent disorder or confusion; havoc 大混乱; 大破坏: *There was absolute mayhem when the cow got into the village hall.* 那牛闯进村会议厅, 造成一片混乱. **2** (*dated* 旧 *or US*) crime of maiming a person 伤人致残罪; 严重伤害罪: *commit mayhem* 犯严重伤害罪.

mayn't /ˈmeɪənt; ment/ *contracted form* 缩约式 may not ⇨ MAY[2].

may·on·naise /ˌmeɪəˈneɪz; *US* ˈmeɪəneɪz; ˌmeəˈnez/ *n* [U] (**a**) thick creamy sauce made with egg-yolks, oil and vinegar, used esp on cold foods, eg salads 蛋黄酱(尤用于调制凉菜, 如色拉). (**b**) dish made with this 美乃滋(用蛋黄酱调制的冷盘): *Egg mayonnaise is made with mayonnaise and hard-boiled eggs.* 鸡蛋美乃滋是用蛋黄酱和煮老的鸡蛋做成的.

mayor /meə(r); *US* ˈmeɪər; ˈmeɚ/ *n* head of the council of a city or borough, usu elected yearly 市长.

▷ **may·oral** /ˈmeərəl; *US* ˈmeɪə-; ˈmeərəl/ *adj* [attrib 作定语] of a mayor or mayoress 市长的: *mayoral robes, duties* 市长的礼服、责任.

may·or·alty /ˈmeərəltɪ; *US* ˈmeɪər-; ˈmeərəltɪ/ *n* (period of) office of a mayor 市长职位; 市长任期.

may·or·ess /meəˈres; *US* ˈmeɪərəs; ˈmeərəs/ *n* **1** (also ˌ**lady** ˈ**mayor**) woman holding the office of mayor 女市长. **2** mayor's wife or other woman helping a mayor or mayoress(1) to perform mayoral duties 市长夫人; 市长女助理.

maze 迷宫

maze /meɪz; mez/ *n* (usu *sing* 通常作单数) **1** network of paths or hedges designed as a puzzle in which one must find one's way 迷宫; 迷魂阵: *We got lost in Hampton Court maze.* 我们在汉普顿科特迷宫里迷了路. ⇨ illus 见插图: (*fig* 比喻) *A maze of narrow alleys leads down to the sea.* 迂回曲折的小径通往海边. **2** confused collection or complicated mass (of facts, etc) (事情等的)错综, 复杂: *finding one's way through the maze of rules and regulations* 在纷繁的规则和条例中寻找出路. Cf 参看 LABYRINTH.

ma·zurka /məˈzɜːkə; məˈzɝkə/ *n* (piece of music for a) lively Polish dance for four or eight couples 马祖卡舞(轻快的波兰舞, 供四对或八对舞者共舞); 马祖卡舞曲.

MB /ˌem ˈbiː; ˌɛm ˈbi/ *abbr* 缩写 = Bachelor of Medicine 医学士: *have/be an MB* 有医学士学位[为医学士] ○ *Philip Watt MB, ChB* 菲利普·瓦特医学士·外科学士.

MBA /ˌem biː ˈeɪ; ˌɛm bi ˈe/ *abbr* 缩写 = Master of Business Administration 工商管理学硕士: *have/be an MBA* 有工商管理学硕士学位[为工商管理学硕士] ○ *Marion Strachan MBA* 马里恩·斯特罗恩工商管理学硕士.

MBE /ˌem biː ˈiː; ˌɛm bi ˈi/ *abbr* 缩写 = (*Brit*) Member (of the Order) of the British Empire (第五等的)大英帝国最高勋爵; 英帝国员佐勋章: *be made an MBE* 受封(第五等的)大英帝国最高勋爵位 ○ *William Godfrey MBE* (第五等的)大英帝国最高勋爵士威廉·戈弗雷. Cf 参看 CBE, DBE, KBE.

MC /ˌem ˈsiː; ˌɛm ˈsi/ *abbr* 缩写 = **1** master of ceremonies. Cf 参看 EMCEE. **2** (*US*) Member of Congress 国会议员: *Senator Karl B Kaufman (MC)* 卡尔·B·考夫曼参议员. **3** (*Brit*) Military Cross 军功十字勋章: *be awarded the/an MC for bravery* 因勇敢而获军功十字勋章.

MCC /ˌem siː ˈsiː; ˌɛm si ˈsi/ *abbr* 缩写 = (*Brit*) Marylebone Cricket Club (the governing body of English cricket) 玛丽勒本板球俱乐部(英国板球运动权威组织).

Mc·Car·thy·ism /məˈkɑːθɪɪzəm; məˈkɑrθɪɪzm̩/ *n* [U] **1** (after US Senator J R McCarthy) policy of accusing people, esp in Government departments, of being Communists in order to remove them from their positions 麦卡锡主义. **2** any similar policy of pursuing people with Communist or unorthodox views; witch-hunt（对持共产主义观点者或持异见者的）政治迫害.

Mc·Coy ⇨ THE REAL McCOY (REAL[1]).

MCP /ˌem siː ˈpiː; ˌɛm si ˋpi/ *abbr* 缩写 = (*infml* 口) male chauvinist pig 可鄙的大男子主义者.

MD /ˌem ˈdiː; ˌɛm ˋdi/ *abbr* 缩写 = **1** Doctor of Medicine (Latin *Medicinae Doctor*) 医学博士(源自拉丁文*Medicinae Doctor*): *be an MD* 为医学博士 ○ *D. W. Walker MD* D.W. 沃克医学博士. **2** (*infml* 口) Managing Director: *the MD's office* 总经理办公室. **3** mentally deficient 心理不健全的.

MDT /ˌem diː ˈtiː; ˌɛm di ˋti/ *abbr* 缩写 = (*US*) Mountain Daylight Time 山区夏令时间. Cf 参看 MST.

me[1] /miː; mi/ ⇨Detailed Guide 6.2 见词条使用详细说明6.2. *pers pron* 人称代词 (used as the object of a *v* or of a *prep*; also used independently or after *be* 用作动词或介词的宾语, 也可独立使用或用于动词be之后) person who is the speaker or writer 我: *Don't hit me.* 别打我. ○ *Give it to me.* 给我. ○ *Hello, it's me.* 喂, 是我呀. ○ *'Who's there?' 'Only me.'* ‘谁在那儿?’‘只有我.’ Cf 参看 I[2].

me[2] /miː; mi/ *n* (*music* 音) = MI.

mead[1] /miːd; mid/ *n* [U] alcoholic drink made from fermented honey and water 蜂蜜酒.

mead[2] /miːd; mid/ *n* (*arch* 古) meadow 草地.

meadow /ˈmedəʊ; ˋmɛdo/ *n* [C, U] (area or field of) grassland, esp used for growing hay; (area of) low, often boggy, land near a river 草地; (尤指)牧场; (河边的)低洼地: *cattle grazing in the meadows* 在牧场上吃草的牛群 ○ *20 acres of meadow* 20英亩草地.

□ ˈ**meadow lark** type of N American songbird 草地鹨(北美产).

meagre (*US* **meager**) /ˈmiːgə(r); ˋmigɚ/ *adj* **1** small in quantity and poor in quality 少量的; 劣质的; 贫乏的; 不足的: *a meagre meal of bread and cheese* 只有面包和奶酪的一餐 ○ *her meagre contribution to our funds* 她给我们基金的微薄捐款 ○ *Our appeal for help met with a meagre response.* 我们求助的呼吁反应冷淡. **2** thin; lacking in flesh 瘦的; 皮包骨的: *the meagre faces of the starving children* 饥饿的儿童的瘦削的脸. ▷ **meagrely** *adv*. **meagre·ness** *n* [U].

meal[1] /miːl; mil/ *n* **1** occasion when food is eaten 餐; 饭食: *be present at all family meals* 每顿饭都在家里吃 ○ *breakfast, the first meal of the day* 早饭, 一天的第一顿饭. **2** food eaten on such an occasion 一餐所吃的食物: *a meal of fish and chips* 鱼和炸土豆条的一顿饭 ○ *eat a big meal*, ie a lot of food for one meal 饱餐一顿. **3** (idm 习语) **make a ˈmeal of sth** (*infml* 口) give sth more attention, effort, etc than it deserves or needs 对某事做得太过分: *She always makes such a meal of it — I could do it in half the time!* 她总是过于认真——要让我做, 一半时间就够了! **a square meal** ⇨ SQUARE[1].

□ ˌ**meals-on-ˈwheels** *n* [pl] (*Brit*) service, usu provided by a women's voluntary organization, by which meals are taken by car to old or sick people in their own homes 送饭到户服务(通常为妇女自愿组织为老弱病残者提供的服务).

ˈ**meal-ticket** *n* **1** (*US*) = LUNCHEON VOUCHER (LUNCHEON). **2** (*infml fig* 口, 比喻) person, position, etc that provides a basic income 供给基本收入的人、职位等: *His rich wife is his meal ticket.* 他靠他有钱的太太生活.

ˈ**mealtime** *n* time at which a meal is usu eaten 进餐时间.

meal[2] /miːl; mil/ *n* [U] (often in compounds 常用以构成复合词) coarsely ground grain 粗碾的谷物: ˈ*oatmeal*.

▷ **mealy** *adj* (**-ier**, **-iest**) **1** of, like, containing or covered with meal 粗粉的; 粗粉状的; 含粉的; 撒有粗粉的. **2** (of boiled potatoes) dry and powdery (指煮过的马铃薯)粉状的.

mealie /ˈmiːlɪ; ˋmilɪ/ *n* (*S African* 南非) **1 mealies** [pl] maize 玉米; 玉蜀黍. **2** [C] ear of maize 玉米穗.

mealy-mouthed /ˌmiːlɪˈmaʊðd; ˋmilɪˋmaʊðd/ *adj* (*derog* 贬) not willing to speak plainly 不愿直言的; 说话拐弯抹角的: *Don't be so mealy-mouthed, say what you mean!* 别这么绕弯子了, 有话直说吧!

mean[1] /miːn; min/ *v* (*pt, pp* **meant** /ment; mɛnt/) **1** [Tn, Tn·pr, Tf] **~ sth (to sb)** (intend to) convey sth; signify sth 意指某事; 意思是: *A dictionary tells you what words mean.* 词典是解释词义的工具书. ○ *What does this sentence mean?* 这句子是什么意思? ○ *These symbols mean nothing to me.* 这些符号我完全不明白是什么意思. ○ *The flashing lights mean that the road is blocked.* 那闪动的灯光表示此路不通. **2** [Tn, Tf, Tg, Tsg] (be likely to) result in (sth); be a sign (that); involve (很可能)造成, 导致(某结果); 是某事物的征兆; 意味; 包含: *Spending too much now will mean a shortage of cash next year.* 现在花钱过头, 来年就要缺钱. ○ *The sudden thaw means that spring is here.* 一朝解冻, 便是春天来到. ○ *This new order will mean (us) working overtime.* 这一新定单意味着(我们)得加班加点. **3** (**a**) [Tn, Tn·pr, Tf no passive 不用于被动语态, Tt, Tnt, Cn·n/a, Dn·n, Dn·pr] **~ sth for sb**; **~ sth (as sth)**; **~ sth (to sb)** have sth as a purpose; intend sth 怀有某目的; 打算; 意欲: *What does she mean by cancelling her performance?* ie Why has she done it? 她取消自己的演出是什么意思? ○ *He means what he says*, ie is not joking, exaggerating, etc. 他说话是当真的. ○ *Don't laugh! I mean it!* ie I am serious. 别笑! 我真是这个意思! ○ *He means (to cause) trouble.* 他存心捣乱. ○ *She meant this gift for you.* 她这礼物是送给你的. ○ *I never meant that you should come alone.* 我没打算要你单独来. ○ *She means to succeed.* 她立意求成. ○ *I'm sorry I hurt you: I didn't mean to.* 对不起, 我弄伤了你; 我不是故意的. ○ *I wasn't serious. I meant it as a joke.* 我并非有意. 我是想开个玩笑而已. ○ *I didn't mean you to read the letter.* 我没有要你看这封信的意思. ○ *You're meant to* (ie You are supposed to) *pay before you come in.* 你要交钱才能进来. ○ *I mean you no harm.* 我并无伤害你的意思. ○ *He means no harm to anyone.* 他无意伤害任何人. (**b**) [Tn, Tf no passive 不用于被动语态] intend to say (sth) on a particular occasion 在某场合下想说(某事); 意思是: *What did he mean by that remark?* 他那样说是什么意思? ○ *Do you mean Miss Anne Smith or Miss Mary Smith?* 你指的是安·史密斯小姐还是玛丽·史密斯小姐? ○ *Did he mean (that) he was dissatisfied with our service?* 他的意思是不满意我们的服务吗? **4** [Tn·pr esp passive 尤用于被动语态, Tn·t] **~ sb for sth** intend or destine sb to be or do sth 打算或注定要某人成为或做某事物: *I was never meant for the army*, ie did not have the qualities needed to become a soldier. 我根本就不是当兵的材料. ○ *She was never meant to be a teacher.* 她根本不是当教师的料子. ○ *His father meant him to be an engineer.* 他父亲打算让他当工程师. **5** [Tn·pr no passive 不用于被动语态] **~ sth to sb** be of value or importance to sb 对某人有价值或重要: *Your friendship means a great deal to me.* 你和我的友谊对我意义重大. ○ *£20 means a lot* (ie seems to be a lot of money) *to a poor person.* 20英镑对于穷人是个大数目. ○ *Money means nothing to him.* 金钱对他来说是无所谓的. ○ *You don't know how much you mean to me*, ie how much I like you. 你不知道我多么喜欢你. **6** (idm 习语) **mean ˈbusiness** (*infml* 口) be serious in one's intentions 是认真的: *He means business: he really will shoot us if we try to escape.* 他不是说着玩的; 我们要是逃, 他真会开枪. **mean ˈmischief** intend to do sth wrong or harmful 有意弄坏或加害. ˈ**mean well** (*derog* 贬) have good intentions, though perhaps not the will or ability to carry them out 怀有善意; 出于好心: *He's hopelessly inefficient, but I suppose he means well.* 他低能得无以复加, 然而却是出于好心. **mean well by sb** have kindly intentions towards sb 对某人抱善意.

mean[2] /miːn; min/ *adj* (**-er**, **-est**) **1 ~ (with sth)** ungenerous; selfish (esp with money) 吝啬的; 自私的(尤指金钱方面): *be very mean with money* 对钱十分吝啬 ○ *She's too mean to make a donation.* 她很小气, 不肯捐款. **2 ~ (to sb)** (of people or their behaviour) unworthy; unkind (指人或人的行为)卑鄙的, 不善良的: *That was a mean trick!* 那是卑鄙的伎俩! ○ *It was mean of you to eat all the food.* 你把东西全吃光了, 你可太坏了. ○ *Don't be so mean to your little brother!* 别对你弟弟那么刻薄! ○ *I feel rather mean for not helping more.* 我未能多帮忙, 十分抱歉. **3** (*esp US*) nasty; vicious 刻毒的; 邪恶的: *A rattlesnake is a really mean creature.* 响尾蛇是很凶的动物. ○ *He looks like a mean character.* 他看上去不似善类. **4** poor in appearance, quality, etc; shabby-looking 难看的; 劣质的; 简陋的; 破旧的: *the mean little houses where the poorest people live* 最穷苦的人赖以栖身的破败小屋. **5** (esp of the understanding or abilities) inferior (尤指理解力或能力)低劣的, 平庸的: *This should be clear even to the meanest intelligence.* 就是对智

力最差的人来说，这也应当是很清楚的. **6** (*dated* 旧) of humble birth or low social rank 出身微贱的; 社会地位低下的: *The meanest labourer has the same rights as the richest employer.* 最贫贱的劳动者享有和最富的雇主同样的权利. **7** (*infml approv* 口，褒) very skilful, effective, etc 熟练的; 有效的; 出色的: *a mean golfer, chess-player, etc* 出色的高尔夫球手、国际象棋选手等 ○ *a new tennis champion with a mean service* 发球刁钻的新网球冠军. **8** (idm 习语) **no mean sth** (*approv* 褒) a very good or great performer or performance 出色的或了不起的表演者或表现: *She's no mean player.* 她是个中高手. ○ *That was no mean achievement.* 那是巨大的成就.

▷ **meanie** (also **meany**) /ˈmiːnɪ; ˋminɪ/ *n* (*joc* 谑) ungenerous person 吝啬的人: *Give me some more, you meanie!* 再给我点儿, 你这吝啬鬼!

meanly *adv*.

mean·ness *n* [U].

mean[3] /miːn; min/ *n* **1** condition, quality, course of action, etc that is halfway between two extremes 中间; 中庸: *You must find a mean between frankness and rudeness.* 你要在坦诚与唐突之间取其中. **2** (*mathematics* 数) (**a**) midway point, quantity, etc between two extremes; average 中数; 平均数; 平均值: *The mean of 13, 5 and 27 is found by adding them together and dividing by 3.* 13、5和27的平均数可将三数相加再除以3求得. (**b**) term between the first and the last of a series 比例中项: *In 1:3 :: 3:9, the mean is 3.* 在1:3 :: 3:9中, 比例中项是3. **3** (idm 习语) **the happy/golden mean** moderate course of action 中庸之道.

▷ **mean** *adj* [attrib 作定语] midway between two extremes; average 中间的; 平均的: *the mean annual temperature* 年平均温度.

me·an·der /mɪˈændə(r); mɪˋændɚ/ *v* **1** [I] (of a river, etc) follow a winding course, flowing slowly (指河流等)蜿蜒缓慢流动. **2** [I, Ipr, Ip] (**a**) (of a person) wander aimlesssly (指人)漫步, 闲逛, 徘徊: *meander through the park* 从公园的一端漫步到另一端 ○ *meander around/along* 闲逛[信步]. (**b**) (*fig* 比喻) (of conversation) proceed in an aimless way; ramble (指谈话)漫谈, 闲聊: *The discussion meandered (on) for hours.* 讨论会漫无边际地进行了几小时.

▷ **me·an·der·ingly** /mɪˈændrɪŋlɪ; mɪˋændrɪŋlɪ/ *adv*.

me·an·der·ings /mɪˈændrɪŋz; mɪˋændrɪŋz/ *n* [pl] winding course; aimless wandering 迂回曲折的进程; 漫步; 闲逛; 徘徊.

mean·ing /ˈmiːnɪŋ; ˋminɪŋ/ *n* **1** [U, C] what is conveyed or signified; sense 意思; 意义; 含义: *You can't say that these sounds have no meaning.* 不能说这些声音全无意义. ○ *a word with many distinct meanings* 有许多含义的词 ○ *signals with certain fixed meanings* 代表某些固定意义的信号. **2** [U] purpose; significance 目的; 重要性: *My life seems to have lost all meaning.* 我的生活似乎已毫无目标. ○ *a glance full of meaning* 意味深长的一瞥.

▷ **mean·ing** *adj* full of meaning; significant 意味深长的; 有意义的: *a meaning look, gesture, etc* 意味深长的神态、姿势等.

mean·ing·ful /-fl; -fl̩/ *adj* full of purpose; significant 有目的的; 有用意的; 有意义的: *a meaningful relationship, discussion, look* 有用意的关系、讨论、表情. **mean·ing·fully** /-fəlɪ; -fl̩ɪ/ *adv*.

mean·ing·less *adj* without sense or motive 无意义的; 无动机的: *meaningless chatter* 无聊的闲扯 ○ *meaningless violence* 无意义的暴力行为.

means[1] /miːnz; minz/ *n* [sing or pl *v*] **1** action by which a result is brought about; method(s) 手段; 方法: *use illegal means to get a passport* 用非法手段获取护照 ○ *This money wasn't earned by honest means.* 这笔钱来路不正. ○ *There is no means of finding out what happened.* 无法搞清楚发生了什么事情. ○ *All possible means have been tried.* 一切办法都试过了. **2** (idm 习语) **by ˈall means** (*fml* 文) yes, of course; certainly 当然可以: *'Can I see it?' 'By all means.'* '我可以看看吗?' '当然可以.' **by fair means or foul** ⇨ FAIR[1]. **by means of sth** (*fml* 文) by using sth; with the help of sth 用某办法; 借助于某事物: *lift the load by means of a crane* 用起重机把重物吊起. **by no manner of means** ⇨ MANNER. **by ˈno means; not by ˈany means** (*esp fml* 尤作文雅语) not at all 绝不; 一点都不: *She is by no means poor: in fact, she's quite rich.* 她可不穷, 其实她很阔. **the end justifies the means** ⇨ END[1]. **a ˌmeans to an ˈend** thing or action not important in itself but as a way of achieving sth 用以达到目的的方法、事物或行动(其本身并不重要): *He regarded his marriage merely as a means to an end: he just wanted his wife's wealth.* 他仅把结婚当作达到目的的手段, 他只是想要妻子的财产. **ways and means** ⇨ WAY[1].

means[2] /miːnz; minz/ *n* [pl] **1** money; wealth; resources 金钱; 财富; 财源: *a man of means*, ie a wealthy man 富有的男子 ○ *She lacks the means to support a large family.* 她无钱养活一个大家庭. ○ *A person of your means can afford it.* 像你这样有钱的人才买得起. **2** (idm 习语) **live beyond/within one's means** ⇨ LIVE[2].

□ **ˈmeans test** official inquiry into a person's wealth or income before support is given from public funds (eg unemployment benefit) 个人经济状况调查(以确定是否给予补助, 如失业救济).

meant *pt, pp* of MEAN[1].

mean·time /ˈmiːntaɪm; ˋminˌtaɪm/ *adv* meanwhile 其间; 同时: *I continued working. Meantime, he went out shopping.* 我继续工作. 这期间他出去买东西.

▷ **mean·time** *n* (idm 习语) **in the ˈmeantime** meanwhile 在此期间; 与此同时: *The next programme starts in five minutes: in the meantime, here's some music.* 下一节目五分钟后开始, 现在先播放些音乐.

mean·while /ˈmiːnwaɪl; *US* -hwaɪl; ˋminˌhwaɪl/ *adv* in the time between two events; at the same time 其间; 同时: *She's due to arrive on Thursday. Meanwhile, what do we do?* 她预定星期四到达. 这期间我们做什么呢? ○ *I went to college. Meanwhile, all my friends got well-paid jobs.* 我上大学去了. 那时我的朋友全都找到了收入不错的工作.

measles /ˈmiːzlz; ˋmizl̩z/ *n* [sing *v*] infectious disease, esp of children, with a fever and small red spots that cover the whole body 麻疹. Cf 参看 GERMAN MEASLES (GERMAN).

measly /ˈmiːzlɪ; ˋmizlɪ/ *adj* (*infml derog* 口, 贬) ridiculously small in size, amount or value (大小、数量或价值)微不足道的: *He gave us measly little portions of cake.* 他给了我们少得可怜的一点蛋糕. ○ *What a measly birthday present!* 多么小气的生日礼物哇!

meas·ure[1] /ˈmeʒə(r); ˋmɛʒɚ/ *v* **1** (**a**) [I, Ip, Tn, Tn·pr, Tn·p] **~ (sth) (up)** find the size, length, volume, etc of (sth) by comparing it with a standard unit 量度; 测量(某物): *Can you measure accurately with this ruler?* 用这把尺子能量得准吗? ○ *First measure (it) up, then cut the timber to the correct length.* 先把尺寸量好, 再把木材锯成所需长短. ○ *measure the width of a door, the level of an electric current, the speed of a car* 测量门的宽度、电平、汽车速度 ○ *The tailor measured me (up) for a suit*, ie measured my chest, arms, legs, etc. 裁缝给我量尺寸做衣服. (**b**) [Tn] (*fig* 比喻) assess (sth); gauge 估计, 估量(某事物); 衡量; 判定: *It's hard to measure his ability when we haven't seen his work.* 没有见过他的作品, 很难估计他的能力. **2** [In/pr] be (a certain size, length, volume, etc) 为(某体积、长度、容积等): *The room measures 10 metres across.* 这房间宽10米. **3** [Tn] carefully consider (sth) 仔细考虑(某事物): *He's a man who measures his words.* 他是个用词很讲究的人. ○ *She failed to measure the effect of her actions on her family.* 她未虑及其行为对家庭的影响. **4** [Tn·pr] **~ sth against/with sth/sb** test sth through competition, conflict, etc (通过竞争、冲突等)考验某事物, 较量: *measure one's strength against sb else* 跟别人比力气 ○ *You have to measure your determination with that of other people.* 你得与其他人较量一下决心了. **5** (idm 习语) **measure one's ˈlength** (*joc* 谑) fall flat on the ground 扑跌在地上. **measure one's strength (with/against sb)** compete with sb to see who is the stronger 与某人比强弱. **6** (phr v) **measure sth off** mark out a length or lengths of sth 量出某物若干长度: *She measured off two metres of cloth.* 她量出两米的布. **measure sth out** give a measured quantity of sth 给予某量的某物: *measure out a dose of medicine* 量出一剂药. **measure up (to sth)** reach the standard required or expected 达到或符合某标准: *The discussions didn't measure up (to my expectations).* 这些讨论有负(我的)期望.

▷ **meas·ur·able** /ˈmeʒərəbl; ˋmɛʒərəbl̩/ *adj* **1** that can be measured 可量度的；可测量的；可衡量的. **2** noticeable; significant 明显的；重大的：*There's been a measureable improvement in his work.* 他的工作已有很大改进. **meas·ur·ably** /-əblɪ; -əblɪ/ *adv*.

meas·ured *adj* **1** (of language) carefully considered (指语言)仔细斟酌的，慎重的：*measured words* 斟酌过的词语. **2** slow and with a regular rhythm 缓慢而有节奏的：*with a measured tread* 以缓慢而匀称的步伐 ○ *with measured steps* 以整齐的步子.

meas·ure·less *adj* that cannot be measured; limitless 无法测量的；无可估量的；无限的.

meas·ure·ment *n* **1** [U] measuring 量度；测量；衡量：*the metric system of measurement* 公制度量衡. **2** [C] width, length, etc found by measuring (量得的)宽度、长度等：*What is your waist measurement?* 你的腰围是多少? ○ *The measurements of the room are 20 feet by 15 feet.* 这房间的面积是20英尺乘15英尺. ○ *The width measurement is 80 cm.* 宽为80厘米.

□ ˈ**measuring-tape** *n* = TAPE-MEASURE (TAPE).

meas·ure[2] /ˈmeʒə(r); ˈmɛʒɚ/ *n* **1** (**a**) [U, C] standard or system used in stating the size, quantity or degree of sth 计量制；量度法：*liquid measure* 液量 ○ *dry measure* 干量 ○ *Which measure of weight do pharmacists use?* 药剂师用哪一种计量制? ⇨App 5 见附录5. (**b**) [C] unit used in such a standard or system 计量单位：*The metre is a measure of length.* 米是长度单位. **2** [C] standard quantity of sth 标准量：*a measure of grain*, eg a bushel 一标准量的谷物(如一蒲式耳) ○ *a measure of whisky*, ie in England usu $\frac{1}{6}$ gill, in Scotland usu $\frac{1}{5}$ 一标准量的威士忌酒(在英格兰通常为$\frac{1}{6}$吉耳，在苏格兰通常为$\frac{1}{5}$吉耳). **3** [C] instrument such as a rod, tape or container marked with standard units, used for testing length, volume, etc 量具；量器：*The barman uses a small silver measure for brandy.* 酒吧服务员用银质小量器量白兰地酒. **4** [sing] **~ of sth** way of assessing sth (估价、判断事物的)尺度，标准：*His resignation is a measure of how angry he is.* 从他辞职一事可见其气愤的程度. ○ *Words cannot always give the measure of one's feelings*, ie show how strong they are. 言语往往不尽能表达自己的情感. **5** [sing] **~ of sth** degree of sth; some (事物的)程度，地步：*She achieved a measure of success with her first book.* 她的第一部书就获得了一定程度的成功. **6** [C usu *pl* 通常作复数] action taken to achieve a purpose 措施；步骤；办法：*measures against crime* 打击犯罪活动的措施 ○ *safety measures* 安全措施 ○ *The authorities took measures to prevent tax fraud.* 当局已采取措施防止偷税漏税. ○ *The government has suggested measures* (ie proposed laws) *to reduce crime.* 政府已提出遏止犯罪活动的法令. **7** [U] (*dated* 旧) verse-rhythm; metre; tempo of a piece of music 诗的韵律；音乐的拍节. **8** (idm 习语) **beyond** ˈ**measure** (*fml* 文) very great(ly) 非常地；极其：*Her joy was beyond measure.* 她无比喜悦. ○ *He fascinates me beyond measure.* 他使我神魂颠倒. **for good** ˈ**measure** as an extra amount of sth or as an additional item 额外的量；外加的项目；饶头：*The pianist gave a long and varied recital, with a couple of encores for good measure.* 那钢琴家的独奏演出会时间长、节目多，还加奏了两支曲子. **get/take the measure of sb** assess sb's character or abilities 估计某人的性格或能力：*It took the tennis champion a few games to get the measure of his opponent.* 那网球冠军打了几局才摸清对手的实力. **give full/short** ˈ**measure** give exactly/less than the correct amount 给足[少]分量：*I'm sure the shopkeeper gave me short measure when she weighed out the potatoes.* 我肯定那店老板给我称土豆时克扣了分量. ˌ**half** ˈ**measure** policy that lacks thoroughness 折衷的办法：*This job must be done properly — I want no half measures.* 这工作必须按规矩做——我不允许做得马马虎虎. **in great, large, some, etc** ˈ**measure** (*fml* 文) to a great, some, etc extent or degree 在很大的、某种的…程度上：*His failure is in great/large measure due to lack of confidence.* 他的失败在很大程度上是由于缺乏信心. ○ *Her success is in no small measure the result of luck.* 她的成功有不小的因素是靠运气. **make sth to** ˈ**measure** make (a garment) after taking individual measurements 定做(衣服)：*Do you make suits to measure?* 你定做西装吗? ○ *a made-to-measure suit* 量尺寸定做的西服.

meat /miːt; mit/ *n* **1** [U, C] flesh of animals, esp mammals rather than fish or birds, used as food (食用的)肉(尤指哺乳动物的肉)：*meat-eating animals* 吃肉动物 ○ *fresh meat*, ie from a recently killed animal 鲜肉 ○ *frozen meat*, ie meat frozen to keep it in good condition 冻肉 ○ *cooked meats* 熟肉 ○ [attrib 作定语] *a meat pie* 肉饼 ○ *a joint/slice of meat* 一大块[一片]肉 ○ (*joc* 谑) *a skinny boy without much meat on him* 瘦得皮包骨的男孩儿. **2** [U] chief or important part (of sth) (某物之)主要或重要部分：*This chapter contains the meat of the writer's argument.* 这一章包含着作者论证的主要部分. **3** [U] (*arch* 古) food in general (泛指)食物：*meat and* ˈ*drink* 饮食. **4** (idm 习语) **meat and** ˈ**drink to sb** a source of great enjoyment to sb; what sb lives for 快乐的源泉；生活的目的：*Scandal and gossip are meat and drink to him.* 各种丑闻和流言蜚语是他最感兴趣的事.

▷ **meaty** *adj* (**-ier**, **-iest**) **1** (**a**) like meat 似肉的：*a meaty smell, taste, etc* 似肉的气味、味道等. (**b**) full of meat 多肉的：*a meaty pork chop* 肉多的猪排骨 ○ *a meaty steak pie* 多肉的馅饼. **2** (*fig* 比喻) important; significant 重要的；有意义的：*a meaty book, discussion* 很有意义的书、讨论.

□ ˈ**meatball** *n* small ball of minced meat or sausage-meat 肉丸.

Mecca /ˈmekə; ˈmɛkə/ *n* **1** city in Saudi Arabia, birthplace of Muhammad and the spiritual centre of Islam 麦加(沙特阿拉伯城市，穆罕默德诞生地，伊斯兰教圣地). **2** (also **mecca**) place that very many people wish to visit, esp people with a shared interest 许多人想参观的地方(尤指有共同爱好的人)：*This exhibition is a mecca for stamp collectors.* 这个展览会是集邮者都想去的地方. ○ *Stratford-on-Avon, the Mecca of tourists in Britain* 埃文河畔斯特拉特福，英国的观光胜地.

mech·anic /mɪˈkænɪk; məˈkænɪk/ *n* worker skilled in using or repairing machines or tools 技工；机修工：*a* ˈ*car mechanic* 汽车修理工.

mech·an·ical /mɪˈkænɪkl; məˈkænɪkḷ/ *adj* **1** of, connected with, produced by or operated by a machine or machines 机械的；用机械的；机械制造的：*I have little mechanical knowledge*, ie I know little about machines. 我对机械一窍不通. ○ *mechanical power, transport, engineering* 机械力、运输、工程学 ○ *a mechanical device, toy, etc* 机械装置、玩具等. Cf 参看 MANUAL. **2** (**a**) (of people) acting (as if) without thinking, in a machine-like way (指人)机械似的，呆板的，无思想的：*She was quite mechanical and unthinking in the way she ironed the shirts.* 她熨衬衣时样子呆板，不动脑筋. (**b**) (of actions) done (as if) without thought; automatic (指行为)无意识的，机械的，自动的：*a mechanical movement, gesture, response, etc* 机械的动作、姿势、回答等.

▷ **mech·an·ic·ally** /-klɪ; -klɪ/ *adv* in a mechanical way 机械地；呆板地；无意识地：*mechanically-operated equipment* 机械操作的设备 ○ *He performed the movements very mechanically.* 他的动作非常呆板.

mech·an·ics /mɪˈkænɪks; məˈkænɪks/ *n* **1** [sing *v*] science of motion and force; science of machinery 力学；机械学：*a course in mechanics* 力学课程. **2 the mechanics** [pl] (**a**) working parts (of sth) (某物的)机件，工作部件：*The mechanics of the pump are very old.* 那泵的机件很陈旧了. (**b**) (*fig* 比喻) processes by which sth is done or operates (制做的或操作的)过程，手法，技巧：*The mechanics of staging a play are very complicated.* 排演话剧的过程很复杂.

mech·an·ism /ˈmekənɪzəm; ˈmɛkəˌnɪzəm/ *n* **1** working parts of a machine, etc 机械装置：*a delicate watch mechanism* 精细的手表机件 ○ *the firing mechanism of a rifle* 步枪的击发装置. **2** parts of an organism or system which work together (机体或装置的)结构，构造：*the mechanisms of the body* 身体的结构. **3** method or procedure for getting things done 手法；技巧；程序：*There are no mechanisms for transferring funds from one department to another.* 基金无法从一部门转移至另一部门.

mech·an·istic /ˌmekəˈnɪstɪk; ˌmɛkəˈnɪstɪk/ *adj* of the theory that all things in the universe are the result of physical and chemical processes 机械论的：*a mechanistic explanation of the origin of life* 对生命起源的机械论解释.

mech·an·ize, -ise /ˈmekənaɪz; ˈmɛkəˌnaɪz/ *v* [I, Tn]

change (a process, factory, etc) so that it is run by machines rather than people, etc 使(过程、工厂等)机械化: *We are mechanizing rapidly.* 我们正在迅速机械化. ○ *mechanize a factory, procedure* 使工厂、程序机械化 ○ *highly mechanized industrial processes* 高度机械化的工业生产过程 ○ *mechanized forces* 机械化部队 ○ *a mechanized army unit*, ie equipped with tanks, armoured cars, etc, rather than eg horses 机械化部队.
▷ **mech·an·iza·tion, -isation** /ˌmekənaɪˈzeɪʃn; *US* -nɪˈz-; ˌmɛkənəˈzeʃən/ *n* [U].

MEd /ˌem ˈed; ˌɛm ˈɛd/ *abbr* 缩写 = Master of Education 教育学硕士: *have/be an MEd* 有教育学硕士学位[为教育学硕士] ○ *Janet White MEd* 珍妮特·怀特教育学硕士.

med *abbr* 缩写 = M *abbr* 1 M缩写第1义.

medal /ˈmedl; ˈmɛdl̩/ *n* flat piece of metal, usu shaped like a coin and stamped with words and a design, which commemorates an event etc, or is awarded to sb for bravery, sporting achievement, etc 纪念章; 奖章; 奖牌; 勋章: *present/award medals for long service* 因长期服务授予奖章 ○ *win a silver medal for shooting* 赢得射击银牌.
▷ **med·al·list** (*US* **med·al·ist**) /ˈmedəlɪst; ˈmɛdlɪst/ *n* person who has been awarded a medal, eg for sporting achievement 奖牌获得者: *an Olympic gold medallist* 奥林匹克金牌获得者.

med·al·lion /mɪˈdæliən; məˈdæljən/ *n* (**a**) large medal 大纪念章; 大奖章; 大奖牌; 大勋章. (**b**) thing similar in shape, eg a piece of jewellery, design on a carpet, cut of meat, etc 类似大纪念章的东西(如珠宝上的装饰、地毯上的花样、切下的肉等): *medallions of veal* 切成大片的小牛肉.

meddle /ˈmedl; ˈmɛdl̩/ *v* [I, Ipr] (*derog* 贬) (**a**) **~ (in sth)** interfere (in sth that is not one's concern) 干预; 干涉; 管闲事: *You're always meddling.* 你老是多管闲事. ○ *Don't meddle in my affairs.* 别干预我的事. (**b**) **~ (with sth)** handle sth that one ought not to, or about which one has no specialized knowledge 乱动, 瞎弄(不应动的或不懂的事物): *Who's been meddling with my papers?* 谁翻乱了我的文件? ○ *Don't meddle with the electrical wiring: you're not an electrician.* 别瞎动电线线路, 你又不是电工.
▷ **med·dler** *n* person who meddles 干预者; 管闲事的人; 瞎摆弄的人.
med·dle·some /-səm; -səm/ *adj* (*fml* 文) fond of or in the habit of meddling 好干预的; 爱管闲事的; 好瞎摆弄的: *Get rid of that meddlesome fool!* 让那个爱管闲事的傢伙走开!

me·dia /ˈmiːdɪə; ˈmidɪə/ *n* **the media** [pl] means of mass communication, eg TV, radio, newspapers 大众传播工具, 大众传播媒介(如电视、电台、报纸): *a book that is often mentioned in the media* 大众传播媒介常提到的书 ○ *The media are to blame for starting the rumours.* 出现这些谣言, 大众宣传工具难辞其咎. ○ [attrib 作定语] *a media personality* 新闻人物 ○ *good media coverage of the event* 对该事件及时而全面的新闻报道. ⇨Usage at DATA 用法见 DATA.

me·di·aeval = MEDIEVAL.

medial /ˈmiːdɪəl; ˈmidɪəl/ *adj* (*fml* 文) **1** situated in the middle 中间的; 中央的; 居中的: *occupy a medial position* 居中间位置. **2** of average size (大小)适中的, 普通的, 一般的. ▷ **me·di·ally** /-ɪəlɪ; -ɪəlɪ/ *adv*.

me·dian /ˈmiːdɪən; ˈmidɪən/ *adj* (*mathematics* 数) situated in or passing through the middle 在中间的; 通过中点的: *a median point, line, value* 中点、中线、中值.
▷ **me·dian** *n* (*mathematics* 数) middle or average point, line, number, etc 中点; 中线; 中数.

me·di·ate /ˈmiːdɪeɪt; ˈmidɪˌet/ *v* **1** [I, Ipr] **~ (between sb and sb)** act as a peacemaker or go-between for two or more people, groups, etc who disagree 调停; 调解; 斡旋: *mediate in an industrial dispute* 调解一劳资纠纷 ○ *mediate between two countries which are at war* 在两交战国间斡旋. **2** [Tn] bring about (sth) by doing this 居间促成(某事): *mediate a peace, settlement, etc* 居间促成和平、某事的解决等.
▷ **me·di·ation** /ˌmiːdɪˈeɪʃn; ˌmidɪˈeʃən/ *n* [U]: *All offers of mediation were rejected.* 所有调解的建议均遭拒绝.
me·di·ator *n* person, organization, etc that mediates 调解人; 调停人; 斡旋者; 仲裁组织.

M

medic /ˈmedɪk; ˈmɛdɪk/ *n* (*infml* 口) medical student or doctor 医学院学生; 医生.

med·ical /ˈmedɪkl; ˈmɛdɪkl/ *adj* **1** of the art of medicine; of curing disease 医学的; 医术的; 医疗的: *a medical student, school* 医学院学生、医学院 ○ *medical skill, treatment, etc* 医疗技术、治疗 ○ *a medical examination*, ie to discover sb's state of health 体格检查 ○ *a medical practitioner*, ie a doctor 医生 ○ *a medical certificate*, ie one that states whether one is healthy or not 健康证书. **2** of treatment (of disease) that does not involve surgery 内科的: *The hospital has a medical ward and a surgical ward.* 这医院有内科病房和外科病房.
▷ **med·ical** *n* (*infml* 口) thorough physical examination (eg before joining the army) 全面体格检查: *have a medical* 作全面体格检查.
med·ic·ally /-klɪ; -klɪ/ *adv*: *medically sound* 体格健康.
□ **medical orderly** = ORDERLY[2].

me·dic·ament /məˈdɪkəmənt; məˈdɪkəmənt/ *n* (*fml* 文) substance used in or on the body to cure illness 药物; 药剂.

Medi·care /ˈmedɪkeə(r); ˈmɛdɪˌkɛr/ *n* [U] US government scheme providing medical care, esp for old people (美国的)医疗保障方案(尤为老人而设者).

med·ic·ated /ˈmedɪkeɪtɪd; ˈmɛdɪˌketɪd/ *adj* containing a medicinal substance 含药物的; 药制的: *medicated shampoo, soap, gauze, etc* 药制洗发剂、药皂、药制纱布.
▷ **med·ica·tion** /ˌmedɪˈkeɪʃn; ˌmɛdɪˈkeʃən/ *n* **1** [U] adding or giving of medicinal substances 敷药; 施药; 药物治疗: *need, prescribe, administer medication* 需要、医嘱、施行药物治疗. **2** [C] medicinal substance; medicine 药物; 药: *What is the best medication for this condition?* 这种病用什么药最好?

me·di·cinal /məˈdɪsɪnl; məˈdɪsn̩l/ *adj* having healing properties; (used for) healing 有药性的; (用作)治疗的: *medicinal herbs* 药草 ○ *a medicinal preparation* 药剂 ○ *used for medicinal purposes* 用于医治的.

me·di·cine /ˈmedsn; *US* ˈmedɪsn; ˈmɛdəsn̩/ *n* **1** [U] (art and science of the) prevention and cure of disease, esp by drugs, diet, etc, but sometimes including surgery also 医术; 医学: *study medicine at the university* 在大学学医 ○ *practise medicine* 行医 ○ *a Doctor of Medicine* 医学博士 ○ *ethical problems in medicine* 医学中的道德问题. **2** [C, U] (type of) substance, esp one taken through the mouth, used in curing disease 药; (尤指)内服药: *Has nurse given you your medicine?* 护士给你服过药了吗? ○ *Don't take too much medicine.* 药不要吃得太多. ○ *cough medicine(s)* 咳嗽药. **3** (idm 习语) **some, a little, a taste, etc of one's own ˈmedicine** the same bad treatment one has given to others 受到报应: *The smaller boys badly wanted to give the bully a dose of his own medicine.* 那些小男孩儿巴不得让那欺负人的坏蛋也尝点苦头. **take one's ˈmedicine (like a ˈman)** (*esp joc* 尤作戏谑语) submit to punishment, sth unpleasant, etc (without complaining) 认罚, 忍受不快的事物(无怨言): *He really hates shopping but he goes anyway, and takes his medicine like a man.* 他实在讨厌买东西, 但还是硬着头皮去了.
□ **ˈmedicine chest** chest or box containing medicines, bandages, etc 药箱.
ˈmedicine-man *n* = WITCH-DOCTOR (WITCH).

med·ico /ˈmedɪkəʊ; ˈmɛdɪˌko/ *n* (*pl* **~s**) (*infml* 口) medical student or doctor 医学院学生; 医生.

me·di·eval (also **me·di·aeval**) /ˌmedɪˈiːvl; *US* ˌmiːd-, *also* mɪˈdiːvl; ˌmidɪˈivl/ *adj* of the Middle Ages, about AD 1100-1400 中古的, 中世纪的(约公元1100-1400年): *medieval history, literature, etc* 中世纪的历史、文学等 ○ *The conditions were positively medieval*, ie very primitive. 条件十分简陋.

me·di·ocre /ˌmiːdɪˈəʊkə(r), *also* ˌmed-; ˈmidɪˌokɚ/ *adj* not very good; second-rate 不太好的; 平庸的; 第二流的: *His films are mediocre.* 他的电影平庸无奇. ○ *a mediocre actor, display, meal* 第二流的演员、表演、饭食.
▷ **me·di·oc·rity** /ˌmiːdɪˈɒkrətɪ, *also* ˌmed-; ˌmidɪˈɑkrətɪ/ *n* **1** [U] quality of being mediocre 平庸; 第二流: *His plays are distinguished only by their stunning mediocrity.* 他的戏剧与众不同之处就是平凡得出奇. **2** [C] person who is mediocre in ability, personal qualities, etc 平庸的人: *a government of mediocrities* 庸才政府.

med·it·ate /ˈmedɪteɪt; ˋmɛdə,tet/ *v* **1** [I, Ipr] **~ (on/upon sth)** think deeply, esp about spiritual matters 深思, 沉思, 冥想(尤指精神方面的问题): *I meditate in order to relax.* 我沉思冥想借以松弛精神. ○ *meditate on the sufferings of Christ* 默想基督的苦难. **2** [Tn, Tg] (*fml* 文) plan (sth) in one's mind; consider 内心策划(某事); 考虑: *meditate revenge, mischief, etc* 策划复仇、恶作剧等 ○ *She is meditating leaving home.* 她考虑要离开家.
▷ **me·di·ta·tion** /ˌmedɪˈteɪʃn; ˌmɛdəˈteʃən/ *n* **1** [U] deep thought, esp about spiritual matters 深思, 沉思, 冥想(尤指精神方面的问题): *religious meditation* 宗教的默念. ○ *Meditation is practised by some Eastern religions.* 东方某些宗教行默念之道. **2** [C usu *pl* 通常作复数] **~ (on sth)** (usu written) expression of deep thought (通常为书面的)沉思录: *meditations on the causes of society's evils* 社会罪恶因由思考录.
med·it·at·ive /ˈmedɪtətɪv; *US* -teɪt-; ˋmɛdə,tetɪv/ *adj* of meditation; engrossed in thought 深思的; 沉思的; 冥想的; 耽于思考的: *a meditative mood* 沉思的心境 ○ *You're very meditative today.* 你今天思考得很深沉. **med·it·at·ively** *adv*.

Me·di·ter·ran·ean /ˌmedɪtəˈreɪnɪən; ˌmɛdətəˋrenɪən/ *adj* [attrib 作定语] of or similar to the Mediterranean Sea or the countries, etc bordering it (似)地中海的; (似)地中海沿岸国家的: *a Mediterranean(-type) climate* 地中海(型)的气候.

me·dium /ˈmiːdɪəm; ˋmidɪəm/ *n* (*pl* **~s** or **media** /ˈmiːdɪə; ˋmidɪə/) **1** (*pl* usu 复数通常作 **media**) means by which sth is expressed or communicated (表达或传播的)媒介, 方法, 手段: *Commercial television is an effective medium for advertising.* 商业电视是有效的广告宣传工具. ○ *She chose the medium of print* (eg published a book) *to make her ideas known.* 她选择出版手段来表达思想. ○ *The artist chose the medium of oil* (ie used oil paints) *for the portrait.* 那画家选用油彩画肖像. ○ *In this country English is the medium of instruction*, ie all subjects are taught in English. 该国用英语教学. **2** (*pl* **mediums**) something that is in the middle between two extremes 中间物; 两极端间的居中者: *find the medium between severity and leniency* 在宽严之间找一居中的尺度. **3** (*pl usu* 复数通常作 **media**) substance or surroundings in which sth exists or moves or is transmitted (某物赖以生存或活动或传播的)介质, 环境: *bacteria growing in a sugar medium* 在糖基中生长的细菌 ○ *Sound travels through the medium of air.* 声音可通过空气介质传播. **4** (*pl* **mediums**) person who claims to be able to communicate with the spirits of the dead 通灵的人; 灵媒; 关亡人. ⇨Usage at DATA 用法见DATA. **5** (idm 习语) **a/the happy medium** ⇨ HAPPY.
▷ **me·dium** *adj* [usu attrib 通常作定语] in the middle between two amounts, extremes, etc; average 中间的; 中等的; 平均的: *a man of medium height* 中等身材的男子 ○ *a medium-sized firm* 中等规模的商行 ○ *clothes to be washed at medium temperature* 需以适中温度洗涤的衣服.
□ ˈ**medium wave** (*abbr* 缩写 **MW**) (*radio* 无) radio wave with a length of between 100 and 1 000 metres 中波(100至1 000米之间): [attrib 作定语] *a medium-wave station, broadcast, etc* 中波电台、广播等.

med·lar /ˈmedlə(r); ˋmɛdlɚ/ *n* (**a**) fruit like a small brown apple, eaten when it begins to decay 欧楂果(褐色的小果实, 宜于果实初腐时食用). (**b**) tree on which this grows 欧楂树.

med·ley /ˈmedlɪ; ˋmɛdlɪ/ *n* **1** piece of music made up of passages from other musical works 杂曲; 混成曲. **2** mixture of people or things of different kinds 混杂的人群或事物: *the medley of races in Hawaii* 夏威夷各种族的大杂烩.

meek /miːk; mik/ *adj* (**-er, -est**) humble and obedient; submissive 温顺的; 驯服的: *She's as meek as a lamb.* 她像羔羊般温顺. ▷ **meekly** *adv*: *He meekly did everything he was told to.* 他事事惟命是听. **meek·ness** *n* [U].

meer·schaum /ˈmɪəʃəm; ˋmɪrʃəm/ *n* (also ˌ**meerschaum** ˈ**pipe**) tobacco pipe with a bowl made of a type of white clay 海泡石烟斗.

meet[1] /miːt; mit/ *v* (*pt, pp* **met** /met; mɛt/) **1** (**a**) [I, Ip, Tn] come face to face with (sb); come together 遇见, 碰见(某人); 相遇; 相逢: *Goodbye till we meet again.* 再见. ○ *We write regularly but seldom meet (up)*, ie see each other. 我们常写信, 但很少见面. ○ *We met (each other) quite by chance.* 我们(彼此)相遇纯属偶然. ○ *I met her in the street.* 我在街上遇见了她. ○ (*fig* 比喻) *A terrible scene met their eyes as they entered the room.* 他们一进屋, 迎面所见是一幅可怕的景象. (**b**) [I] come together formally for discussion, etc 开会: *The Cabinet meets regularly.* 内阁定期开会. ○ *The Debating Society meets on Fridays.* 辩论社团每星期五举行例会. (**c**) [Tn no passive 不用于被动语态] (*fig* 比喻) experience (sth unpleasant); encounter 经历(不愉快的事); 遭遇: *meet disaster, one's death, etc* 遇难、死亡 ○ *meet a problem, difficulty, etc* 遇到问题、困难等. **2** [I, Tn no passive 不用于被动语态] make the acquaintance of (sb); be introduced to (sb) 结识(某人); 被引见或介绍给(某人): *I know Mrs Hill by sight, but we've never met.* 我见希尔夫人面熟, 但并不相识. ○ *He's an interesting man, would you like to meet him?* 他这个人很有趣, 你想跟他认识吗? *Meet my wife Susan*, ie as an informal style of introduction. 这是我妻子苏珊. ○ *Pleased to meet you.* 认识你很高兴. **3** [Tn] go to a place and await the arrival of (a person, train, etc) 接(人、火车等): *Will you meet me at the station?* 你到车站接我吗? ○ *I'll meet your bus.* 我到汽车站接你. ○ *The hotel bus meets all the trains.* 旅馆的汽车在火车站迎接各班车的旅客. **4** [I, Tn no passive 不用于被动语态] come together with (sb) as opponent(s) in a contest, etc 与(某人)比赛, 竞赛, 交锋: *The champion and the challenger meet next week.* 下星期冠军将迎战挑战者. ○ *City met United in the final last year, and City won.* 去年决赛中, 市队与联队交锋, 市队获胜. **5** [I, Tn] come into contact with (sth); touch; join 接触(某事物); 联结: *Their hands met.* 他们的手相触. ○ *His hand met hers.* 他的手碰到了她的手. ○ *The vertical line meets the horizontal one here.* 垂直线与水平线在此相交. ○ *These trousers won't meet* (ie fasten) *round my waist any more!* 这裤子瘦得腰都系不上了! **6** [Tn] fulfil (a demand, etc); satisfy 满足(要求等); 符合: *meet sb's wishes, conditions, needs, etc* 满足某人的愿望、条件、需要等 ○ *Can we meet all their objections?* 他们提出的反对意见我们都能圆满解决吗? **7** [Tn] pay (sth) 支付, 偿付(某费用): *meet all the expenses, bills, etc* 偿付全部开支、帐单等 ○ *The cost will be met by the company.* 费用由公司支付. **8** (idm 习语) **find/meet one's match** ⇨ MATCH[2]. **make ends meet** ⇨ END[1]. **meet the** ˈ**case** be adequate or satisfactory 适当; 令人满意: *This proposal of yours hardly meets the case.* 你的这项提议不甚恰当. **meet sb's** ˈ**eye** look into sb's eyes 与某人目光相遇: *She was afraid to meet my eye.* 她怕与我目光相遇. **meet the** ˈ**eye**/ˈ**ear** be seen/heard 被看见[听见]: *All sorts of strange sounds met the ear.* 听见了各种奇怪的声音. **meet sb half-**ˈ**way** make a compromise with sb 与某人妥协: *If you can drop your price a little, I'll meet you half-way.* 你要是能减点价, 我就愿意再让一步. **meet one's** ˈ**Maker** (*esp joc* 尤作戏谑语) die 死; 见上帝: *Poor Fred: he's gone to meet his Maker.* 可怜的弗雷德, 他已经去见上帝了. ˌ**meet one's Water**ˈ**loo** lose a decisive contest (在比赛中)惨败. **there is more in/to sb/sth than meets the eye** sb/sth is more complex, interesting, etc than one might at first think 某人[某事物]比原想的复杂、有趣等. **9** (phr v) **meet up (with sb)** meet (sb), esp by chance 偶遇(某人): *I met up with him/We met up at the supermarket.* 我们在超级市场偶然相遇. **meet with sb** (*US*) meet sb, esp for discussion 与某人会晤(尤指为商议事): *The President met with senior White House aides at breakfast.* 早餐时总统会见了白宫的高级助手. **meet with sth** encounter sth; experience sth 遇到某事物; 经历某事物: *meet with obstacles, difficulties, misfortune* 遇到障碍、困难、不幸 ○ *She met/was met with much hostility, criticism, kindness, etc.* 她受到敌视、批评、善待等.

meet[2] /miːt; mit/ *n* **1** (*esp Brit*) gathering of riders and hounds at a fixed place for fox-hunting (骑马的猎人与猎犬在出发猎狐前的)集合. **2** (*esp US*) sporting contest where many competitors gather 运动会: *an ath*ˈ*letics meet* 体育运动会 ○ *a* ˈ*track,* ˈ*swimming meet* 田径、游泳运动会. Cf 参看 MEETING 3.

meet[3] /miːt; mit/ *adj* [pred 作表语] (*arch* 古) suitable; appropriate 适合; 适当; 恰当.

meet·ing /ˈmiːtɪŋ; ˋmitɪŋ/ *n* **1** coming together of people, esp for discussion 聚会; (尤指)开会: *We've had* *three meetings, and still we haven't reached agreement.* 我们已经开过三次会了，还未取得一致意见. ○ *The meeting between the two families was a joyful one.* 这两家人的聚会十分愉快. **2** (**a**) assembly of people for a particular purpose 集会；会议: *hold, conduct a meeting* 召开、主持会议 ○ *a* ˈ*prayer meeting* 祈祷会 ○ *a political meeting* 政治集会 ○ *a staff meeting* 全体工作人员会议. (**b**) the people gathered together in this way 与会者: *Miss Smith will now address the meeting.* 史密斯小姐现在向大会致词. **3** gathering of people for a sporting contest 运动会: *a* ˈ*race-meeting* 赛马大会 ○ *an ath*ˈ*letics meeting* 体育运动会. Cf 参看 MEET². **4** (idm 习语) **a meeting of** ˈ**minds** close understanding between people, esp as soon as they meet for the first time 彼此深刻理解(尤指初会即意见一致).

□ ˈ**meeting-house** *n* building for meetings, esp those held by Quakers 聚会所(尤指基督教公谊会的).

ˈ**meeting-place** *n* place arranged for a meeting 聚会处；相会处；会场.

mega- *comb form* 构词成分 **1** million 百万: ˈ*megabyte* ○ ˈ*megacycle* ○ ˈ*megawatt*. **2** very large or great 巨大: ˈ*megaphone* ○ *a* ˈ*megastar*, ie a very famous person from films, etc 巨星(电影等的大明星). ⇨App 11 见附录11.

mega·death /ˈmeɡədeθ; ˋmɛɡə,dɛθ/ *n* death of one million people in nuclear war 核战争中一百万人的死亡.

mega·hertz /ˈmeɡəhɜ:ts; ˋmɛɡə,hɝts/ (also **mega·cycle** /ˈmeɡəsaɪkl; ˋmɛɡə,saɪkl̩/) *n* (*abbr* 缩写 **MHz**) one million hertz 兆赫.

mega·lith /ˈmeɡəlɪθ; ˋmɛɡə,lɪθ/ *n* large stone, esp one erected as (part of) a monument in ancient times 巨石(尤指古代作纪念碑用的).

▷ **mega·lithic** /ˌmeɡəˈlɪθɪk; ˌmɛɡəˋlɪθɪk/ *adj* **1** made of megaliths 用巨石建造的: *a megalithic circle, tomb, etc* 巨石建造的圆形石林、石墓等. **2** (of a period of the past, etc) marked by the use of megaliths (指古时)以使用巨石为特征的: *the megalithic era* 使用巨石的时代.

me·ga·lo·mania /ˌmeɡələˈmeɪnɪə; ˌmɛɡələˋmenɪə/ *n* [U] form of madness in which a person has an exaggerated view of his own importance, power, etc 夸大狂；妄自尊大: *The dictator was suffering from megalomania.* 那独裁者患有夸大狂.

▷ **me·ga·lo·ma·niac** /-nɪæk; -nɪ,æk/ *n* (*medical or fig* 医或比喻) person suffering from megalomania 患夸大狂的人.

me·ga·phone /ˈmeɡəfəʊn; ˋmɛɡə,fon/ *n* funnel-shaped device for speaking through, that allows the voice to be heard at a distance 扩音器；传声筒；喇叭筒.

mega·ton /ˈmeɡətʌn; ˋmɛɡə,tʌn/ *n* explosive force equal to one million tons of TNT 百万吨级(相当于一百万吨黄色炸药的威力): [attrib 作定语] *a one-megaton bomb* 百万吨级炸弹.

mei·osis /maɪˈəʊsɪs; maɪˋosɪs/ *n* (*pl* **meioses** /maɪˈəʊsi:z; maɪˋosis/) **1** [C] (*biology* 生) process in which a cell divides into two new cells, each of these having half a set of chromosomes 减数分裂. **2** [U] = LITOTES.

mel·an·choly /ˈmelənkɒlɪ; ˋmɛlən,kɑlɪ/ *n* [U] (tendency towards) deep sadness which lasts for some time; depression 忧郁；抑郁.

▷ **mel·an·cho·lia** /ˌmelənˈkəʊlɪə; ˌmɛlənˋkolɪə/ *n* [U] (*medical* 医) mental disease marked by melancholy 忧郁症.

mel·an·cholic /ˌmelənˈkɒlɪk; ˌmɛlənˋkɑlɪk/ *adj* (having a tendency to be) melancholy 忧郁的；抑郁的: *have a melancholic nature* 有忧郁的性情.

mel·an·choly *adj* (**a**) very sad; depressed 悲哀的；沮丧的: *a melancholy mood, person* 悲伤的心情、人. (**b**) causing sadness 使人忧郁的: *melancholy news* 令人悲伤的消息 ○ *A funeral is a melancholy occasion.* 葬仪是令人悲哀的场合.

mélange /ˈmeɪlɑ:nʒ; *US* meɪˈlɑ:nʒ; meˋlɑnʒ/ *n* (*French* 法) mixture; medley 混合物；混杂的人群或事物.

mel·anin /ˈmelənɪn; ˋmɛlənɪn/ *n* (*biology* 生) dark pigment found in the skin, hair, etc of humans and animals (人和动物的皮肤、毛发等上的)黑(色)素.

mêlée /ˈmeleɪ; *US* meɪˈleɪ; meˋle/ *n* (*French* 法) confused struggle; confused crowd of people 混战；乱斗；混乱的群众: *There was a scuffle and I lost my hat in the mêlée.* 因发生一场斗殴，我的帽子也在混乱中丢失了.

mel·li·flu·ous /meˈlɪflʊəs; məˋlɪflʊəs/ (also **mel·li·fluent** /meˈlɪflʊənt; məˋlɪflʊənt/) *adj* (of a voice, speech, music, etc) sweet-sounding; (almost) musical (指嗓音、说话、音乐等)甜美的，动听的: *speak in mellifluous tones* 用悦耳的声调说话. ▷ **mel·li·fluence** /-flʊəns; -flʊəns/ *n* [U]. **mel·li·flu·ously, mel·li·flu·ently** *advs*.

mel·low /ˈmeləʊ; ˋmɛlo/ *adj* (**-er, -est**) **1** (**a**) fully ripe in flavour or taste 熟透的；芳醇的: *mellow wine, fruit, etc* 香醇的酒、熟透的水果. (**b**) soft, pure and rich in colour or sound (颜色或声音)柔和的，丰富的: *the mellow colours of the dawn sky* 黎明时天空斑斓的色彩 ○ *the mellow tones of a violin* 小提琴柔曼的乐音. **2** (more) wise and sympathetic through age or experience (than previously) (因年龄或阅历而较前更)成熟的，老练的: *a mellow attitude to life* 对生活的成熟看法. **3** (*infml* 口) genial, cheerful, etc, esp as a result of being slightly drunk 欢乐的，欢快的(尤因有酒意): *I'd had two glasses of wine and I was feeling mellow.* 我喝了两杯葡萄酒，顿觉心旷神怡.

▷ **mel·low** *v* [I, Tn] (cause sb/sth to) become mellow (使某人[某事物])成熟: *Wine mellows with age.* 酒陈则味醇. ○ *Age has mellowed his attitude to some things.* 他随着年龄的增加，对某些事情的看法已日趋成熟.

mel·lowly *adv*.

mel·low·ness *n* [U].

me·lo·drama /ˈmelədrɑ:mə; ˋmɛlə,drɑmə/ *n* [U, C] **1** drama full of sensational events and exaggerated characters, often with a happy ending 情节剧(情节耸人听闻，人物表现夸张，结局多皆大欢喜): *I love Victorian melodrama(s).* 我喜爱维多利亚时代的情节剧. **2** (*fig* 比喻) events, behaviour, language, etc resembling (a) drama of this kind 情节剧式的事件、行为、语言等: *all the melodrama of a major murder trial* 一重大谋杀案审判中的情节剧式的场面 ○ *We really don't need all this ridiculous melodrama!* 别跟我们来这套荒唐的情节剧表演!

▷ **me·lo·dra·matic** /ˌmelədrəˈmætɪk; ˌmɛlədrəˋmætɪk/ *adj* of, like or suitable for (a) melodrama (似)情节剧的；适于情节剧的: *a melodramatic outburst of temper* 突如其来的大发雷霆. **me·lo·dra·mat·ic·ally** /-klɪ; -klɪ/ *adv*.

mel·ody /ˈmelədɪ; ˋmɛlədɪ/ *n* **1** [C] arrangement of words put to music; song or tune 曲调；歌曲: *old Irish melodies* 古老的爱尔兰歌曲. **2** [C] main part within a piece of harmonized music, usu more distinctly heard than the rest; theme 主调；旋律；主旋律: *The melody is next taken up by the flutes.* 这主调接着由笛子合奏. **3** [U] arrangement of musical notes in an expressive order; tunefulness 美妙的音乐；优美的音调: *There's not much melody in this piece, is there?* 这首音乐不太悦耳吧?

▷ **me·lodic** /mɪˈlɒdɪk; məˋlɑdɪk/ *adj* of melody; melodious 曲调的；旋律的；音调优美的.

me·lodi·ous /mɪˈləʊdɪəs; məˋlodɪəs/ *adj* of or producing pleasant music; tuneful 声调优美的；产生美妙音乐的；悦耳的: *a melodious cello* 悦耳的大提琴 ○ *the melodious notes of a thrush* 婉转的鸫鸣. **me·lodi·ously** *adv*. **me·lodi·ous·ness** *n* [U].

melon /ˈmelən; ˋmɛlən/ *n*. ⇨illus at FRUIT 见 FRUIT 插图. (**a**) [C] large juicy round fruit of various types of plant that trail along the ground 瓜. (**b**) [U] flesh of this fruit, used as food 瓜肉: *Would you like some melon?* 你要吃点瓜吗?

melt /melt; mɛlt/ *v* **1** [I, Tn] (cause sth to) become liquid through heating (使某物)融化: *The ice melted when the sun shone on it.* 太阳照到冰上，冰就融化了. ○ *The hot sun soon melted the ice.* 炎热的太阳很快就把冰融化了. ○ *It is easy to melt butter.* 黄油很容易化. **2** (**a**) [I] (*fig* 比喻) (of food) become soft; dissolve (指食物)变软；溶解: *a sweet that melts on the tongue* 在舌上溶化的糖果 ○ *This cake melts in the mouth!* 这种蛋糕到嘴里就软了! (**b**) [I, Tn] (of a solid in a liquid) dissolve; cause (a solid) to dissolve (指液体中的固体物)溶解；使(固体物)溶解: *Sugar melts in hot tea.* 糖放在热茶中就化了. ○ *The hot coffee melts the sugar.* 热咖啡能把糖溶化了. ⇨Usage at WATER¹ 用法见 WATER¹. **3** [I, Ipr, Tn] (*fig* 比喻) (cause sb, sb's feelings, etc to) soften because of pity, love, etc (使某人、感情等)(因怜爱等)软化: *Her anger melted*, ie disappeared. 她的怒气消了. ○ *His* heart melted with pity. 他因怜悯而心软了. ○ She melted into tears. 她心酸而落泪. ○ Pity melted her heart. 怜悯之情使她心软了. **4** (idm 习语) **butter wouldn't melt in sb's mouth** ⇨ BUTTER. **5** (phr v) **melt (sth) away** (cause sth to) disappear by melting or dissolving (使某物)融化或溶解而消失: *The sun has melted the snow away.* 太阳把雪融化掉了. ○ (*fig* 比喻) *The crowd melted away when the storm broke.* 暴风雨一来, 人群就散了. ○ *All his support melted away when he really needed it.* 在他真正需要支持时, 却得不到一丝半点. **melt sth down** melt (a metal object) to be used again as raw material 重新熔化(金属物); 回炉: *Many of the gold ornaments were melted down to be made into coins.* 很多黄金饰物回炉后铸成了金币. **melt into sth** (**a**) change by gradual degrees into sth else 逐渐改变成另物: *One colour melted into another*, eg in the sky at sunset. 一种颜色逐渐变成了另一种颜色(如日落时的天空景色). (**b**) slowly disappear into sth 缓慢消失于某物中: *He melted into the thick fog.* 他慢慢消失在浓雾中. ○ *The ship melted into the darkness.* 轮船逐渐隐没在黑暗中.

▷ **melt·ing** *adj* [usu attrib 通常作定语] (*fig* 比喻) causing feelings of love, pity, etc; tender 产生爱怜等感情的; 柔情的: *a melting voice, mood, etc* 令人感伤的声音、情绪等.

□ ˈ**meltdown** *n* melting of the overheated core of a nuclear reactor, causing the escape of radioactivity 核反应堆核心遇热之熔毁(导致核辐射泄漏).

ˈ**melting-point** *n* temperature at which a solid melts 熔点: *Lead has a lower melting-point than iron.* 铅的熔点比铁低.

ˈ**melting-pot** *n* **1** (usu *sing* 通常作单数) place where large numbers of immigrants from many different countries live together 大量多国移民聚居的地方: *New York is a vast melting-pot of different nationalities.* 纽约是不同国籍的人的聚居地. **2 be in/go into the** ˈ**melting-pot** be likely to change/be in the process of changing 要起变化[在改变中]: *All our previous ideas are now in the melting-pot; our jobs are bound to change radically.* 我们从前的一切观念都正在改变, 我们的工作肯定要有很大变动.

mem·ber /ˈmembə(r); ˋmɛmbɚ/ *n* **1** person belonging to a group, society, etc (社团等的)成员, 会员: *Every member of her family came to the wedding.* 她家的人都来参加婚礼了. ○ *an active, an honorary, a founding, etc member of the club* 俱乐部的积极分子、荣誉会员、发起人等. **2** part of a larger structure 大结构的部分: *a steel supporting member* 钢支架部分 ○ *a cross-member*, ie diagonally or horizontally positioned 横构件. **3** (*fml* 文) (**a**) part of a human or animal body; limb 人或动物身体的一部分; 肢体: *lose a vital member, such as an arm* 失去一重要肢体, 如胳膊. (**b**) (*euph* 婉) male sexual organ; penis 男性生殖器; 阴茎. **4 Member** Member of Parliament 议员: *the Member for Leeds North-East* 利兹市东北区议员.

▷ **mem·ber·ship** *n* **1** [U] state of being a member of a group, society, etc (社团等的)会员身分, 资格: *apply for membership of the association* 申请加入该协会. **2** [Gp] (number of) members 会员(总称); 会员人数: *The membership numbers 800.* 会员共有800名. ○ *The membership is/are very annoyed at your suggestion.* 会员们对你的建议甚为恼火. ○ *a club with a large membership* 有众多会员的俱乐部.

□ ˌ**Member of** ˈ**Parliament** (*abbr* 缩写 **MP**) elected representative in the House of Commons (下议院的)国会议员.

mem·brane /ˈmembreɪn; ˋmɛmbren/ *n* [C, U] (piece of) thin pliable skin-like tissue connecting, covering or lining parts of an animal or a vegetable body (动、植物的)膜, 薄膜: *rupture a membrane* 使薄膜破裂.

▷ **mem·bran·ous** /ˈmembrənəs; ˋmɛmbrənəs/ *adj* of or like a membrane 膜的; 膜状的.

me·mento /mɪˈmentəʊ; mɪˋmɛnto/ *n* (*pl* ~**s** or ~**es**) thing given, bought, etc and kept as a reminder (of a person, a place or an event) 纪念品: *a little gift as a memento of a visit* 作为访问纪念的小礼品.

memo /ˈmeməʊ; ˋmɛmo/ *n* (*pl* ~**s**) (*infml* 口) memorandum(1b) 备忘录: *an inter-office memo* 办公室间的内部备忘录 ○ [attrib 作定语] *a memo pad* 备忘录便笺.

mem·oir /ˈmemwɑː(r); ˋmɛmwɑr/ *n* **1** [C] written record of (esp important) events, usu based on personal knowledge 事件(尤指大事)的记录(通常据个人所知): *She wrote a memoir of her stay in France.* 她写了一篇旅法记事录. **2 memoirs** [pl] person's written account of his life and experiences (个人生活与经历的)回忆录; 自传: *the memoirs of a retired politician* 一个退休政治家的回忆录.

mem·or·able /ˈmemərəbl; ˋmɛmərəbl̩/ *adj* deserving to be remembered; easily remembered 值得纪念的; 容易记住的: *a memorable experience, concert, trip* 难忘的经历、音乐会、旅行 ○ *memorable verses by Keats* 济慈的值得背诵的诗句. ▷ **mem·or·ably** /-əblɪ; -əblɪ/ *adv*.

mem·or·andum /ˌmeməˈrændəm; ˌmɛməˋrændəm/ *n* (*pl* **-da** /-də; -də/ or ~**s**) **1** (**a**) note made for future use, esp to help oneself remember sth (备忘的)记录; 备忘录: *write a memorandum about sth* 记下某事备忘. (**b**) ~ **(to sb)** informal written business communication 非正式的商业文件: *circulate a memorandum to all sales personnel* 给全体销售人员传阅的商业简报. **2** (*law* 律) record of an agreement that has been reached but not yet formally drawn up and signed (已达成但尚未拟就及签字的)协议记录; 意向书.

me·mor·ial /məˈmɔːrɪəl; məˋmɔrɪəl/ *n* ~ **(to sb/sth)** monument, plaque, ceremony, etc that reminds people of an event or a person 纪念碑; 纪念章; 纪念仪式: *erect a war memorial* 竖立战争纪念碑 ○ *This statue is a memorial to a great statesman.* 这尊雕像是纪念一位伟大的政治家的. ○ *The church service was a memorial to the disaster victims.* 该礼拜仪式是为了悼念这场灾难中的受害者. ○ [attrib 作定语] *a memorial tablet, plaque, service* 纪念牌匾、纪念章、纪念仪式.

□ **Me**ˈ**morial Day** holiday, usu at the end of May, observed in the US to commemorate troops who died in war (美国)阵亡将士纪念日(通常为五月底).

mem·or·ize, -ise /ˈmeməraɪz; ˋmɛməˌraɪz/ *v* [Tn] put (sth) into one's memory; learn (sth) well enough to remember it exactly 记住(某事物); 记忆(某事物)(能确切复述): *She can memorize facts very quickly.* 她能很快记住许多资料. ○ *An actor must be able to memorize his lines.* 演员须善于熟记台词.

mem·ory /ˈmemərɪ; ˋmɛmərɪ/ *n* **1** (**a**) [U] power of the mind by which facts can be remembered 记忆力: *devices which aid memory* 增强记忆力的装置. (**b**) [C] individual person's power to remember (个人的)记忆力, 记性: *He has a good/poor memory (for dates)*, ie remembers (them) easily/with difficulty. 他(对日期)的记忆力好[差]. ○ *speak from memory*, ie without referring to notes, etc 凭记忆说 ○ *commit sth to memory*, ie memorize it 记住某事 ○ *paint from memory*, ie without a model, photograph, etc 凭印象画 ○ *I'm afraid the fact slipped my memory*, ie I forgot it. 很抱歉, 此事我记不得了. **2** [U] period over which people's memory extends; recollection 记忆所及的时期; 能回忆到的范围: *This hasn't happened before within memory.* 据记忆, 此事以前未发生过. **3** [C] thing, event, etc that is remembered 记忆的事物、事件等: *happy memories of childhood* 对童年愉快的回忆. **4** [U] what is remembered about sb after his death 对死者的记忆: *His memory will always remain with us*, ie We will always remember him. 他永远留在我们的记忆中. **5** [C] (*computing* 计) part of a computer where information is stored 存储器. **6** (idm 习语) **have a memory/mind like a sieve** ⇨ SIEVE. **if memory serves** if I remember correctly 如记忆无误. **in memory of sb/to the memory of sb** serving to remind people of sb, esp as a tribute 作为对某人的纪念; 纪念某人: *He founded the charity in memory of his late wife.* 他兴办那项慈善事业以纪念他已故的妻子. **jog sb's memory** ⇨ JOG. **refresh one's/sb's memory** ⇨ REFRESH. **to the best of my memory** ⇨ BEST[3]. **within/in living memory** ⇨ LIVING[1].

mem·sahib /ˈmemsɑːb; ˋmɛmˌsɑɪb/ *n* (used formerly in India to address or refer to a European woman 旧时印度人称呼欧洲女子的用语) madam; lady 小姐; 夫人; 太太.

men *pl* of MAN[1].

men·ace /ˈmenəs; ˋmɛnəs/ *n* **1** [U] threatening quality, tone, feeling, etc 威胁; 恐吓: *in a speech filled with* menace 在充满恫吓言词的演说中 ○ *a film that creates an atmosphere of menace* 一部营造威吓气氛的影片. **2** [sing] **(a)** **~ (to sb/sth)** person or thing that threatens 进行威胁的人或事物: *These weapons are a menace (to world peace).* 这些武器就是(对世界和平的)威胁. **(b)** (*infml or joc* 口或谑) person or thing that is a nuisance, a danger, etc 讨厌的、危险的…人或事物: *That woman is a menace! Keep her away from this machine!* 那个女人真讨厌! 别让她靠近这部机器! ○ *That low beam is a menace! I keep hitting my head on it.* 那条低梁真危险! 老磕我的头.

▷ **men·ace** *v* [Tn, Tn·pr] **~ sb/sth (with sth)** threaten sb/sth; endanger sb/sth 威胁、恐吓、危及某人[某事物]: *countries menaced by/with war* 受战争威胁的国家 ○ *Your vicious dog is menacing my cat!* 你那条恶狗对我家的猫太凶了! **men·acingly** *adv* in a threatening manner 威胁地; 恐吓地.

mén·age /meɪˈnɑːʒ; meˈnɑʒ/ *n* (*fml* 文) household 家庭; 家务; 家政.

□ **ménage à trois** /ˌmeɪnɑːʒ ɑː ˈtrwɑː; menɑʒ ɑ ˈtrwɑ/ (*French* 法) household consisting of a husband, a wife and the lover of one of them 三角家庭(夫妇与其一之情人三人同居).

me·na·gerie /mɪˈnædʒərɪ; məˈnædʒərɪ/ *n* collection of wild animals in captivity, esp in a travelling circus or for exhibition (笼中的)野兽(尤指马戏团的或作展览的).

mend /mend; mɛnd/ *v* **1** **(a)** [Tn] return (sth broken, worn out or torn) to good condition or working order; repair 修理, 修补(某物): *mend shoes, a watch, a broken toy* 修理鞋、表、破玩具. Cf 参看 FIX[1] 4. **(b)** [Tn] make (sth) better; improve 改良(某事物); 改善: *Mend your manners!* ie Don't be so rude! 要讲礼貌! ○ *That won't mend matters*, ie improve the situation. 那于事无补. **2** [I] return to health; heal 恢复健康; 痊愈: *The injury is mending slowly.* 这伤口在慢慢愈合. **3** (idm 习语) **it's ˌnever too ˌlate to ˈmend** (*saying* 谚) one can always improve one's habits, etc 改过不嫌迟. **least said, soonest mended** ⇨ SAY. **mend one's ˈways** improve one's habits, way of living, etc 培养好习惯; 改进生活方式: *There's no sign of him mending his ways.* 看不出他有改进生活方式的迹象.

▷ **mend** *n* **1** damaged or torn part of sth (esp clothing, etc) that has been mended 修补过的地方; (尤指衣物的)补丁: *The mends were almost invisible.* 修补过的地方几乎看不出来. **2** (idm 习语) **on the ˈmend** (*infml* 口) getting better after an illness, injury, etc 在康复中: *She's been very unwell, but she's on the mend now.* 她原来病得很重, 现在正在康复.

mender *n* (usu in compounds 通常用以构成复合词) person who mends sth 修理者; 修补者: *a ˈroad-mender* 修路工人 ○ *a ˈwatch-mender* 钟表匠.

mend·ing *n* [U] **1** work of repairing (esp clothes) 修补; 补缀: *do the mending* 做修补工作. **2** clothes, etc to be mended 待补的衣物: *a pile of mending* 一摞待补的衣物.

men·dacious /menˈdeɪʃəs; mɛnˈdeʃəs/ *adj* (*fml* 文) untruthful; lying 虚假的; 撒谎的: *a mendacious story, report, etc* 虚构的故事、报告等.

▷ **men·daciously** *adv*.

men·da·city /menˈdæsətɪ; mɛnˈdæsətɪ/ *n* (*fml* 文) **1** [U] untruthfulness 虚假. **2** [C] untrue statement; lie 谎言; 假话.

Men·del·ian /menˈdiːlɪən; mɛnˈdilɪən/ *adj* of the genetic theory of the biologist Mendel /ˈmendl; ˈmɛndl/, 1822-1884 孟德尔(1822-1884年)遗传学说的.

men·dic·ant /ˈmendɪkənt; ˈmɛndɪkənt/ *n, adj* (*fml* 文) (person) getting a living by begging 乞丐; 行乞的: *mendicant friars* 托钵僧.

men·folk /ˈmenfəʊk; ˈmɛnˌfok/ *n* [pl] (*infml* 口) men, esp the men of a family considered together 男人们(尤指家中的男性成员): *The menfolk have all gone out fishing.* 男人都出去打鱼了. Cf 参看 WOMENFOLK.

me·nial /ˈmiːnɪəl; ˈminɪəl/ *adj* (*usu derog* 通常作贬义) (of work) suitable to be done by servants; unskilled (指工作)适合仆人做的; 非技术性的: *a menial task, job, etc* 非技术性的任务、工作等 ○ *menial chores like dusting and washing up* 擦桌子、洗碗这类仆人做的杂务.

▷ **me·nial** *n* (*fml usu derog* 文, 通常作贬义) servant 仆人; 下人.

men·in·gitis /ˌmenɪnˈdʒaɪtɪs; ˌmɛnɪnˈdʒaɪtɪs/ *n* [U] inflammation of the membranes enclosing the brain and spinal cord 脑脊膜炎.

men·is·cus /məˈnɪskəs; məˈnɪskəs/ *n* (*pl* **-ci** /-ˈnɪsaɪ; -ˈnɪsaɪ/ or **-cuses** /-kəsəz; -kəsəz/) (*physics* 物) curved upper surface of a liquid in a tube (液柱的)弯月形面.

meno·pause /ˈmenəpɔːz; ˈmɛnəˌpɔz/ *n* **the menopause** [sing] time when a woman ceases to menstruate, usu around the age of 50 经绝期(女性更年期, 通常在50岁左右): *reach the menopause* 到达更年期.

▷ **meno·pausal** /ˌmenəˈpɔːzl; ˈmɛnəˌpɔzl/ *adj* **(a)** of the menopause 经绝期的. **(b)** experiencing the menopause 处于经绝期的.

men·ses /ˈmensiːz; ˈmɛnsiz/ *n* **the menses** [pl] (*fml or medical* 文或医) monthly flow of blood, etc from the lining of the uterus 月经.

men·stru·ate /ˈmenstrʊeɪt; ˈmɛnstrʊˌet/ *v* [I] discharge blood, etc from the uterus, usu once a month 行经; 月经来潮.

▷ **men·strual** /ˈmenstrʊəl; ˈmɛnstrʊəl/ *adj* of the menses or menstruation 月经的; 行经期的: *menstrual pain* 月经痛.

men·stru·ation /ˌmenstrʊˈeɪʃn; ˌmɛnstrʊˈeʃən/ *n* [U] process or time of menstruating 行经; 月经来潮; 行经期.

men·sura·tion /ˌmensjʊˈreɪʃn; ˌmɛnsjʊˈreʃən/ *n* [U] (*dated or fml* 旧或文) **(a)** mathematical rules for finding length, area and volume (长度、面积、体积的)测定法. **(b)** process of measuring 测量.

-ment *suff* 后缀 (with *vs* forming *ns* 与动词结合构成名词) result or means of …的结果或手段: *development* ○ *government*. ▷ **-mental** (forming *adjs* 用以构成形容词). **-mentally** (forming *advs* 用以构成副词).

men·tal /ˈmentl; ˈmɛntl/ *adj* **1** of, in or to the mind 精神的; 心理的; 智力的: *an enormous mental effort* 巨大的精神力量 ○ *a mental process, illness, deficiency* 心理过程、精神病、智力缺陷 ○ *This experience caused him much mental suffering.* 这一经历给他的精神造成极大痛苦. ○ *mental cruelty* 精神虐待 ○ *make a mental note of sth*, ie fix sth in one's mind to be remembered later 把某事记在脑子里. **2** (*infml derog* 口, 贬) mad 疯的: *You must be mental to drive so fast!* 你开得这么快, 疯啦!

▷ **men·tally** /ˈmentəlɪ; ˈmɛntlɪ/ *adv* in the mind; with regard to the mind 精神上; 心理上; 智力上: *mentally alert, aware, active, etc* 精神上警惕的、警觉的、活跃的等 ○ *mentally deficient/defective*, ie medically subnormal in the power of the brain 智力缺陷的 ○ *mentally deranged*, ie mad 精神错乱的.

□ **ˈmental age** level of sb's intellectual ability, expressed in terms of the average ability for a certain age 智力年龄; 心理年龄: *She is sixteen years old but has a mental age of five.* 她十六岁, 而智力年龄是五岁.

ˌmental aˈrithmetic calculation(s) done in the mind, without writing down figures or using a calculator, etc 心算.

ˈmental home, **ˈmental hospital** home/hospital for mental patients 精神病院.

ˈmental patient person suffering from mental illness 精神病人.

men·tal·ity /menˈtælətɪ; mɛnˈtælətɪ/ *n* **1** [C] characteristic attitude of mind; way of thinking 心态; 精神状态; 思想方法: *He has many years' experience of the criminal mentality.* 他研究犯罪心理有多年经验. **2** [U] (*fml* 文) intellectual ability 智力; 智能: *a woman of poor mentality* 智力低下的女子.

men·thol /ˈmenθɒl; ˈmɛnθɑl/ *n* [U] solid white substance obtained from oil of peppermint, used to relieve pain and as a flavouring, eg in cigarettes or toothpaste 薄荷醇; 薄荷樟脑: [attrib 作定语] *menthol cigarettes* 薄荷香烟.

▷ **men·thol·ated** /ˈmenθəleɪtɪd; ˈmɛnθəˌletɪd/ *adj* containing menthol 含有薄荷醇的.

men·tion /ˈmenʃn; ˈmɛnʃən/ *v* [Tn, Tf, Tw, Tg, Cn·n/a, Dn·pr, Dpr·f, Dpr·w] **~ sth/sb (as sth)**; **~ sth/sb (to sb)** **1** write or speak about sth/sb briefly; say the name of sth/sb; refer to sth/sb 写到、说到或提到某事物[某人]: *Did she mention it (to the police)?* 她(向警察)提过吗? ○ *Did I hear my name mentioned?* ie Was somebody talking about me? 有人提起过我吗? ○ *He* *mentioned (to John) that he had seen you.* 他(跟约翰)说他见过你. ○ *Did she mention when she would arrive?* 她说过她什么时候到吗? ○ *Whenever I mention playing football, he says he's too busy.* 我一跟他提踢足球的事,他就说太忙. ○ *They mentioned you as a good source of information.* 他们说你消息灵通. **2** (idm 习语) **don't ˈmention it** (used to indicate that thanks, an apology, etc are not necessary 用以表示不必道谢、道歉等): *'You are so kind!' 'Don't mention it.'* '谢谢!' '不用谢.' **mentioned in dispatches** mentioned by name in the official report of a battle, etc because of one's bravery (因勇敢)在战报中受到表扬. **not to mention** (*infml* 口) as well as 更不用说; 更不必说: *He has a big house and an expensive car, not to mention a villa in France.* 他有一所大房子和一辆昂贵汽车,且不说在法国还有一座别墅了.

▷ **men·tion** *n* **1** [U] reference to sb/sth (in speech or writing) (口头或书面)提及某人[某事物]: *He made no mention of your request.* 他没有提到你的要求. ○ *There was no mention of her contribution.* 没提到她的贡献. **2** [C] (*infml* 口) act of mentioning; brief reference 提及; 简述: *Did the concert get a mention in the paper?* 报纸上报道这次音乐会了吗?

-men·tioned (forming compound *adjs* 用以构成复合形容词) referred to in the specified place 于某处提及的: *aˌbove-/beˌlow-ˈmentioned*, ie mentioned before/after the current passage in a book, an article, etc 上述的[下述的].

mentor /ˈmentɔ:(r); ˈmɛntɚ/ *n* experienced and trusted adviser of an inexperienced person (无经验之人的)有经验可信赖的顾问.

menu /ˈmenju:; ˈmɛnju/ *n* **1** list of dishes available at a restaurant or to be served at a meal 菜单: *What's on the menu tonight?* 今晚的菜单上有什么菜? ○ *Fish has been taken off the menu.* 菜单上已把鱼取消了. **2** (*computing* 计) list of options from which a user can choose, displayed on a computer screen (荧光屏上显示的)项目单, 选择单.

MEP /ˌem i: ˈpi:; ˌɛm i ˈpi/ *abbr* 缩写 = Member of the European Parliament 欧洲议会议员.

meph·is·toph·elean /ˌmefɪstəˈfi:lɪən; ˌmɛfɪstəˈfilɪən/ *adj* (*fml* 文) **1** of or like Mephistopheles /ˌmefɪˈstɒfəli:z; ˌmɛfəˈstɑfəˌliz/ (the devil in a German legend) (德国传说中的)魔鬼的. **2** devilish; evil 魔鬼般的; 邪恶的: *a mephistophelean plan, trick, etc* 阴险的计划、诡计等 ○ *mephistophelean cunning* 魔鬼般的奸诈.

mer·cant·ile /ˈmɜ:kəntaɪl; *US* -ti:l, -tɪl; ˈmɝkəntɪl/ *adj* of trade and commerce; of merchants 贸易的; 商业的; 商人的.

□ **ˌmercantile maˈrine** = merchant navy.

Mer·cator's pro·jec·tion /məˌkeɪtəz prəˈdʒekʃn; mɝˈketɚz prəˈdʒɛkʃən/ method of drawing maps of the world in which the globe is represented on a flat grid of squares formed by lines of latitude and longitude, making areas far from the equator exaggerated in size 墨卡托投影.

mer·cen·ary /ˈmɜ:sɪnərɪ; *US* -nerɪ; ˈmɝsṇˌɛrɪ/ *adj* interested only in making money, etc; done from this motive 只为金钱的; 图利的: *a mercenary act, motive, etc* 只为图利的行为、动机等 ○ *His actions are entirely mercenary.* 他的行为完全是为了钱.

▷ **mer·cen·ary** *n* soldier hired to fight in a foreign army (受雇于外国的)雇佣兵.

mer·cer·ize, -ise /ˈmɜ:səraɪz; ˈmɝsəˌraɪz/ *v* [Tn esp passive 尤用于被动语态] treat (cotton thread) so that it becomes stronger and glossy like silk 将(棉纱)作丝光处理: *mercerized cotton* 丝光棉.

mer·chand·ise /ˈmɜ:tʃəndaɪz; ˈmɝtʃənˌdaɪz/ *n* [U] goods bought and sold; goods for sale 商品; 货品: *the merchandise on display in the shop window* 店铺橱窗中陈列的商品.

▷ **mer·chand·ise** *v* [Tn] buy and sell (goods); promote sales of (goods) 买卖(商品); 推销(商品): *The fabrics are merchandised through a network of dealers.* 通过经销网点销售纺织品. ○ *We merchandise our furniture by advertising in newspapers.* 我们在报上登广告推销家具. **mer·chand·ising** *n* [U].

mer·chant /ˈmɜ:tʃənt; ˈmɝtʃənt/ *n* **1** (**a**) wholesale trader, esp one who trades with foreign countries 批发商; (尤指)外贸批发商: *an ˌimport-ˈexport merchant* 进出口批发商. (**b**) (in compounds 用以构成复合词) trader in the goods stated 经营某货物的商人: *a ˈcoal-merchant* 煤商 ○ *a ˈwine-merchant* 酒商. ⇨Usage at DEALER 用法见 DEALER. **2** (*derog sl* 贬, 俚) person who is fond of a specified activity, etc (某活动等的)爱好者: *a ˈspeed merchant*, ie sb who likes to drive (too) fast 好开快车的人.

□ **ˌmerchant ˈbank** bank that specializes in (often large) commercial loans and finance for industry 商业银行.

ˌmerchant maˈrine, ˌmerchant ˈnavy the merchant ships and seamen of a country collectively (一国的)商船及船员(总称).

ˌmerchant ˈseaman sailor in the merchant navy 商船船员.

ˌmerchant ˈship, ˌmerchant ˈshipping ship(s) used for transporting goods 商船.

mer·ci·ful ⇨ MERCY.

mer·cur·ial /mɜ:ˈkjʊrɪəl; mɝˈkjʊrɪəl/ *adj* **1** (**a**) (of people or their moods, etc) often changing (指人或情绪等)多变的, 无常的: *a mercurial temperament* 喜怒无常的性情. (**b**) lively; quick-witted 活泼的; 机智的: *She has a mercurial turn of conversation.* 她谈话善转话锋. **2** (*fml or medical* 文或医) of, like, containing or caused by mercury 汞的; (像)水银的; 含水银的; 水银引起的: *a mercurial ointment, compound, etc* 含汞药膏、汞化合物 ○ *mercurial poisoning* 汞中毒.

Mer·cury /ˈmɜ:kjʊrɪ; ˈmɝkjərɪ/ *n* (*astronomy* 天) the planet nearest to the sun 水星.

mer·cury /ˈmɜ:kjʊrɪ; ˈmɝkjərɪ/ *n* [U] (also **quicksilver**) chemical element, a heavy silver-coloured metal usu found in liquid form, used in thermometers and barometers 汞; 水银. ⇨App 10 见附录 10.

mercy /ˈmɜ:sɪ; ˈmɝsɪ/ *n* **1** [U] kindness, forgiveness, restraint, etc shown to sb one has the right or power to punish 仁慈; 宽恕; 宽容: *They showed mercy to their enemies.* 他们对敌人很仁慈. ○ *We were given no/little mercy.* 我们没有得到宽恕. ○ *He threw himself on my mercy*, ie begged me to show mercy. 他求我宽恕他. ○ *a tyrant without mercy* 无情的暴君. **2** [C usu *sing* 通常作单数] (*infml* 口) event to be grateful for; piece of good luck 恩惠; 幸运: *It's a mercy she wasn't hurt in the accident.* 她在事故中未受伤, 真幸运. ○ *His death was a mercy*, eg He was in such pain that it was best that he died. 他的死是一种解脱(与其痛苦不如一死). **3** (idm 习语) **at the mercy of sb/sth** in the power of sb/sth; under the control of sb/sth 任由某人[某事物]摆布或控制: *The ship was at the mercy of the storm*, ie out of control or helpless. 那只船在暴风雨中失去控制. **be grateful/thankful for small mercies** ⇨ SMALL. **an errand of mercy** ⇨ ERRAND. **leave sb/sth to the mercy/mercies of sb/sth** ⇨ LEAVE[1]. **throw oneself on sb's mercy** (*fml* 文) beg sb to treat one kindly or leniently 恳求某人善待或宽恕.

▷ **mer·ci·ful** /-fl; -fəl/ *adj* ~ **(to/towards sb)** having, showing or feeling mercy 仁慈的; 宽恕的; 宽容的: *She was merciful to the prisoners.* 她对犯人很仁慈. ○ *a merciful gesture, action, etc* 宽厚的表示、行为等. **mer·ci·fully** /-fəlɪ; -fəlɪ/ *adv* **1** in a merciful way 仁慈地; 宽恕地; 宽容地: *treat sb mercifully* 仁慈地对待某人. **2** (*infml* 口) fortunately 幸运地; 幸而: *The play was very bad, but mercifully it was also short!* 那剧糟透了, 幸好还不算长!

mer·ci·less *adj* ~ **(to/towards sb)** showing no mercy; pitiless 不仁慈的; 不宽恕的; 无怜悯心的: *a merciless killer, beating* 残忍的杀手、殴打 ○ *This judge is merciless towards anyone found guilty of murder.* 这位法官对罪名成立的谋杀犯概不留情. **mer·ci·lessly** *adv*.

mercy *interj* (*dated* 旧) (used to express surprise or (pretended) terror 用以表示惊讶或(故作的)惊恐): *Mercy (on us)! What a noise!* 天哪! 多吵闹哇!

□ **ˈmercy killing** (*infml* 口) euthanasia 安乐死.

mere[1] /mɪə(r); mɪr/ *adj* [attrib 作定语] (no comparative form 无比较级) **1** nothing more than; no better or more important than 仅仅的; 只不过; 不超过: *She's a mere child.* 她只不过是个孩子. ○ *He's not a mere boxer: he's world champion.* 他不是一般拳击手, 而是世界冠军. ○ *Mere words* (ie Words without acts) *won't help.* 光

说(不做)无济于事. **2** (idm 习语) **the merest sth** the smallest or most unimportant thing 最微小的或最不重要的事: *The merest noise is enough to wake him.* 一丁点儿声音就足以把他吵醒.

▷ **merely** *adv* only; simply 仅; 只; 不过: *I merely asked his name.* 我只问了他的名字. ○ *I meant it merely as a joke.* 我原意只不过是开个玩笑.

mere[2] /mɪə(r); mɪr/ *n* (*esp* in place names 尤用于地名) pond; small lake 池塘; 小湖.

mere·tri·cious /ˌmerɪˈtrɪʃəs; ˌmɛrəˈtrɪʃəs/ *adj* apparently attractive but in fact valueless 虚有其表的; 华丽而无价值的: *a meretricious style, book, argument* 华而不实的文体、言之无物的书、迂阔之论. ▷ **mere·tri·ciously** *adv*. **mere·tri·cious·ness** *n* [U].

merge /mɜːdʒ; mɝdʒ/ *v* **1** [I, Ipr, Ip, Tn, Tn·pr, Tn·p] **~ (with/into sth)**; **~ (together)**; **~ A with B/~ A and B (together)** (*esp commerce* 尤用于商业) (cause two things to) come together and combine (使两事物)合并: *The two marching columns moved closer and finally merged (together).* 行进中的两路纵队越走越近, 终于合成一路. ○ *Where does this stream merge into the Rhine?* 这条小河在什么地方和莱茵河合流? ○ *The bank merged with its major rival.* 该银行与其主要对手合并了. ○ *We can merge our two small businesses (together) into one larger one.* 我们可以把我们那两个小企业合并成一个大企业. **2** [I, Ipr] **~ (into sth)** fade or change gradually (into sth else) 逐渐消失或变成(另一种事物): *One end is blue, one end is red, and the colours merge in the middle.* 一端为蓝色, 一端为红色; 这两种颜色在中间混为一色. ○ *Twilight merged into total darkness.* 暮色四合, 渐而一片漆黑.

▷ **mer·ger** /ˈmɜːdʒə(r); ˈmɝdʒɚ/ *n* [C, U] (act of) joining together (esp two commercial companies) 合并, 归并(尤指两公司): *a merger between two breweries* 两家酿酒厂的合并 ○ *The two companies are considering merger as a possibility.* 这两家公司在考虑合并的可能性. ○ [attrib 作定语] *merger discussions* 有关合并事宜的商议.

me·ri·dian /məˈrɪdɪən; məˈrɪdɪən/ *n* **1** imaginary circle round the earth, passing through (a given place and) the North and South Poles 子午线; 经线: *the Greenwich meridian*, ie longitude 0°, which passes through the North and South Poles and Greenwich, England 格林威治子午线. **2** highest point reached by the sun or other star, as viewed from a given point on the earth's surface 从地面观测太阳或其他星球到达的最高点.

me·ri·diem ⇨ ANTE MERIDIEM, POST MERIDIEM.

me·ri·di·onal /məˈrɪdɪənl; məˈrɪdɪənl̩/ *adj* of the south (esp the south of Europe) 南方的; (尤指)南欧的.

mer·ingue /məˈræŋ; məˈræŋ/ *n* **(a)** [U] mixture of whites of egg and sugar baked until crisp and used as a covering over sweet pies, tarts, etc (蛋白与糖混合烤成的)酥皮, 饼皮. **(b)** [C] small cake made of this 蛋白酥皮小饼.

me·rino /məˈriːnəʊ; məˈrino/ *n* (*pl* **~s**) **1** [C] (also **merino sheep**) breed of sheep with long fine wool 美利奴绵羊. **2** [U] **(a)** yarn or cloth made from this wool 美利奴精纺毛纱或羊毛织物. **(b)** similar soft wool and cotton material 柔软的毛棉混纺料.

merit /ˈmerɪt; ˈmɛrɪt/ *n* **1** [U] quality of deserving praise or reward; worth; excellence 值得称赞或奖励的品质; 价值; 长处; 优点: *a man/woman of merit* 值得称赞的男子[女子] ○ *There's no merit in giving away what you don't really want.* 把自己不需要的东西送给别人, 这算不上善举. ○ *I don't think there's much merit in the plan.* 我认为该计划没什么价值. ○ *She was awarded a certificate of merit for her piano-playing.* 她获钢琴演奏优秀奖状. ○ [attrib 作定语] *a merit award* 优秀奖. **2** [C usu *pl* 通常作复数] fact, action, quality, etc that deserves praise or reward 值得称赞或奖励的事情、行为、品质等: *The merits of the scheme are quite obvious.* 该计划的可取之处是相当明显的. ○ *consider, judge, etc sb/sth on his/its (own) merits*, ie according to his/its own qualities, worth, etc, regardless of one's personal feelings 根据某人[某事物](本身)的品质、价值等来考虑、判断...某人[某事物].

▷ **merit** *v* [Tn] (*fml* 文) be worthy of (sth); deserve 应获得(某事物); 值得: *merit reward, praise, punishment, etc* 应获得奖励、称赞、处罚等 ○ *I think the suggestion merits consideration.* 我认为这个建议值得考虑.

mer·ito·cracy /ˌmerɪˈtɒkrəsɪ; ˌmɛrɪˈtɑkrəsɪ/ *n* (*politics* 政) **1** **(a)** [U] system of government by people of high achievement 英才管理(制度). **(b)** [CGp] such people in a society (社会的)英才, 精英, 贤能. **2** [C] country with such a system of government 英才管理的国家: *Is Britain a meritocracy?* 英国是英才管理的国家吗?

mer·it·ori·ous /ˌmerɪˈtɔːrɪəs; ˌmɛrəˈtɔrɪəs/ *adj* (*fml* 文) deserving praise or reward 值得称赞或奖励的; 有功绩的: *a prize for meritorious conduct* 优秀行为奖. ▷ **mer·it·ori·ously** *adv*.

mer·lin /ˈmɜːlɪn; ˈmɝlɪn/ *n* type of small falcon 灰背隼.

mer·maid /ˈmɜːmeɪd; ˈmɝˌmed/ *n* mythical creature having the body of a woman, but a fish's tail instead of legs (传说中的)美人鱼.

▷ **mer·man** /ˈmɜːmæn; ˈmɝˌmæn/ *n* (*pl* **-men** /-men; -mɛn/) male mermaid (传说中的)雄性人鱼.

merry /ˈmerɪ; ˈmɛrɪ/ *adj* (**-ier, -iest**) **1** (*dated* 旧) happy and cheerful; full of joy and gaiety 高兴的; 愉快的; 兴高采烈的: *a merry laugh, party, group* 愉快的笑声、聚会、团体 ○ *wish sb a merry Christmas* 祝某人圣诞快乐. **2** (*infml* 口) slightly drunk 微醉的: *We were already merry after only two glasses of wine.* 我们只喝了两杯葡萄酒就已有醉意了. **3** (*arch* 古) pleasant 令人愉快的; 令人快乐的: *the merry month of May* 美好的五月 ○ *Merry England* 可爱的英格兰. **4** (idm 习语) **make ˈmerry** (*dated* 旧) sing, laugh, feast, etc; celebrate 欢宴作乐; 庆祝; 行乐.

▷ **mer·rily** /ˈmerəlɪ; ˈmɛrəlɪ/ *adv*.

mer·ri·ment /ˈmerɪmənt; ˈmɛrɪmənt/ *n* [U] (*fml* 文) gaiety, laughter, celebration, etc 欢乐; 欢笑; 庆祝; 行乐.

□ **ˈmerry-go-round** *n* (*Brit*) (*US* **carousel** /ˌkærəˈsel; ˌkærəˈsɛl/) = ROUNDABOUT 2.

ˈmerry-maker *n* (*dated* 旧) person who celebrates (sth) 寻欢作乐者; 行乐者; 狂欢者. **ˈmerry-making** *n* [U].

mesa /ˈmeɪsə; ˈmesə/ *n* (*US*) flat-topped hill with steep sides, common in south-western USA 平顶山(常见于美国西南部地区).

més·al·li·ance /ˌmeɪˈzælɪɑːns; meˈzælɪəns/ *n* (*French derog* 法, 贬) marriage with sb of a lower social position 与地位低的人结婚.

mes·cal·ine (also **mes·calin**) /ˈmeskəlɪn; ˈmɛskəlɪn/ *n* [U] hallucinatory drug obtained from a type of cactus 仙人球毒碱.

Mes·dames *pl* of MADAME.

Mes·dem·ois·elles *pl* of MADEMOISELLE.

mesh /meʃ; mɛʃ/ *n* **1** **(a)** [C, U] (piece of) material made of a network of wire, thread, etc 网状物: *(a) wire mesh on the front of the chicken coop* 鸡笼正面的铁丝网 ○ *stockings made of fine silk mesh* 细网眼长丝袜. **(b)** [C] any of the spaces in such material 网眼; 筛孔: *a net with half-inch meshes/with a half-inch mesh* 有半英寸网孔的网. **2** [C esp *pl* 尤作复数] network, esp for trapping sth 网状结构; (尤指捕捉某物的)网: *a fish tangled in the mesh(es) of the net* 卡在网眼上的一条鱼 ○ (*fig* 比喻) *entangled in the meshes/a mesh of political intrigue* 陷入政治阴谋的罗网. **3** (idm 习语) **in mesh** (of the teeth of gears) engaged; interlocked (指齿轮的齿)相啮合.

▷ **mesh** *v* [I, Ipr] **~ (with sth)** **(a)** (of toothed gears) engage; interlock (with others) (指齿轮)啮合: *The cogs don't quite mesh.* 这些轮齿啮合不严. **(b)** (*fig* 比喻) harmonize; be compatible; fit in 协调; 相配; 配合; 适应: *Our future plans must mesh with existing practices.* 我们未来的计划必须与当前的实践相合.

mes·mer·ism /ˈmezmərɪzəm; ˈmɛzməˌrɪzəm/ *n* [U] (*dated* 旧) hypnotism 催眠; 催眠术.

▷ **mes·meric** /mezˈmerɪk; mɛzˈmɛrɪk/ *adj* hypnotic 催眠的; 催眠术的.

mes·mer·ist /ˈmezmərɪst; ˈmɛzməˌrɪst/ *n* hypnotist 施催眠术者.

mes·mer·ize, -ise /ˈmezməraɪz; ˈmɛzməˌraɪz/ *v* [Tn esp passive 尤用于被动语态] hold the attention of (sb) completely 吸引住(某人): *an audience mesmerized by her voice* 被她的声音迷住的听众.

mess[1] /mes; mɛs/ *n* **1** [C usu *sing* 通常作单数] dirty or untidy state 脏或乱的状态: *This kitchen's a mess!* 这厨房太脏了! ○ *The children have made an awful mess in the* lounge. 孩子们把起居室弄得凌乱不堪. ○ *The spilt milk made a terrible mess on the carpet.* 牛奶洒在地毯上弄得一塌糊涂. **2** [U] (*infml euph* 口, 婉) excrement of a dog, cat, etc (狗、猫等的)粪便: *Who will clean up the cat's mess in the bedroom?* 谁去清除卧室里的猫屎? **3** [sing] difficult or confused state or situation; disorder 困难或紊乱的状态或局面; 杂乱: *My life's (in) a real mess!* 我的生活真是狼狈! ○ *You've made a mess of the job*, ie done it very badly. 你把工作搞得一团糟. ○ (*ironic* 反语) *A nice/fine mess you've made of that!* 你把那件事弄得真够瞧的! **4** [sing] person/people who is/are untidy or dirty 不整洁的人: *Get cleaned up! You're a mess!/You two are a mess!* 收拾一下吧! 你多邋遢呀! [你们俩可真邋遢!]

▷ **mess** *v* (*infml* 口) **1** [Tn] (*US*) put (sth) into an untidy, etc state 把(某事物)弄乱, 弄脏, 弄糟: *Don't mess your hair!* 别把你的头发弄乱! **2** (phr v) **mess about/around** (**a**) behave in a foolish or boisterous way 胡闹; 瞎闹: *Stop messing about and come and help!* 别闹了, 过来帮帮忙吧! (**b**) work in pleasant, casual, disorganized way; potter 轻松随意地工作; 逍遥自在地做事或闲荡: *I love just messing about in the garden*. 我就是喜欢在花园里瞎转. **mess sb about/around; mess about/around with sb** treat sb inconsiderately 轻率地对待某人: *Be nicer to him. You shouldn't mess around with him like that.* 对他好些, 你不该对他那么随便. ○ *Stop messing me about! Tell me if I've got the job or not!* 别不把我当一回事! 告诉我, 这工作给没给我! **mess sth about/around; mess about/around with sth** handle sth roughly or incompetently; make a muddle of sth 处理某事物草率或无能; 搞乱某事物: *Don't mess the files around, I've just put them in order.* 别把档案弄乱了, 我刚整理好. ○ *Somebody's been messing about with the radio and now it doesn't work.* 有人瞎摆弄收音机了, 现在不响了. **mess sth up** (**a**) make sth untidy, disordered or dirty 把某物弄乱或弄脏: *Don't mess up my hair: I've just combed it.* 别把我的头发弄乱, 我刚梳好. ○ *Who messed up my clean kitchen?* 谁把我干净的厨房弄得这么脏? (**b**) do sth incompetently; bungle sth 弄糟某事物; 胡乱做某事物: *I was asked to organize the trip, but I messed it up.* 大家要我组织这次旅游, 可是我把事情搞糟了. **mess with sb/sth** (*infml* 口) interfere with sb/sth 干预某人[某事]: *Don't mess with her: she's got a violent temper.* 别干预她的事, 她脾气很暴.

messy *adj* (**-ier, -iest**) **1** in a state of disorder; dirty 凌乱的; 脏的: *a messy kitchen* 脏乱的厨房. **2** causing dirt or disorder 造成脏的或乱的状态的: *a messy job* 把环境弄脏乱的工作.

mess² /mes; mɛs/ *n* **1** [CGp] group of people who take meals together and share living quarters, esp in the armed forces 共膳宿的集体(尤指军队的): *The mess has ordered some new furniture.* 该宿舍的人订购了一些新家具. **2** (*US* also ˈ**mess hall**) building in which these meals are taken (共膳宿者的)食堂: *the officers'/sergeants' mess* 军官[士官]食堂.

▷ **mess** *v* [Ipr, Ip] **~ (in) with sb; ~ (in) together** eat meals 共餐: *He messed with me/We messed together when we were in the Navy.* 我们在海军时, 他和我共餐[我们共餐].

mess·age /ˈmesɪdʒ; ˋmɛsɪdʒ/ *n* **1** [C] information, news, request, etc sent to sb in writing, speech, by radio, etc (以书面、口头、无线电等形式向某人传送的)信息、消息、要求等: *We've had a message (to say) that your father is ill.* 我们得到消息说你父亲病了. ○ *The ship sent a radio message asking for help.* 那船发出了无线电求救信号. **2** [sing] statement (said to be) of political, moral or social significance made by a prophet, writer, book, etc (先知、作家、书等所作的政治、道德、社会方面的)预言, 启示, 教训: *a film with a message* 有寓意的影片 ○ *the prophet's message to the world* 先知告诫世人的预言. **3** (idm 习语) **get the** ˈ**message** (*sl* 俚) understand (what sb is hinting at, trying to say, etc) 明白, 理解, 领悟, 知悉(某人的暗示等): *She said it was getting late: I got the message, and left.* 她说时间不早了; 我心领神会, 于是告辞.

mes·sen·ger /ˈmesɪndʒə(r); ˋmɛsn̩dʒɚ/ *n* person carrying a message 送信者; 报信者; 通信员.

Mes·siah /mɪˈsaɪə; məˋsaɪə/ *n* **1** (also **messiah**) [C] person expected to come and save the world (人们盼望来拯救世界的)救星: *He believes in every new political messiah.* 他对政治上每个新救星都深信不疑. **2 the Messiah** [sing] (*religion* 宗) (**a**) Jesus Christ regarded as this saviour 耶稣基督(救世主). (**b**) similar person expected by the Jews 弥赛亚(犹太人期待的救世主).

Mes·sieurs *pl* of MONSIEUR.

Messrs /ˈmesəz; ˋmɛsɚz/ *abbr* 缩写 (used as the *pl* of *Mr* (French *Messieurs*) before a list of men's names, eg *Messrs Smith, Brown and Robinson,* and before names of business firms, eg *Messrs T Brown and Co* 用作 Mr 的复数(源自法文*Messieurs*), 置于一系列男子姓名之前, 如史密斯、布朗、鲁滨逊诸位先生, 或置于公司名之前, 如T·布朗公司各位先生).

messy ⇨ MESS[1].

Met[1] /met; mɛt/ *adj* [attrib 作定语] (*Brit infml* 口) meteorological 气象学的; 气象的: *the* ˈ*Met Office* 气象局 ○ *the latest Met report*, ie weather report from the Meteorological Office 最新气象报告.

Met[2] /met; mɛt/ **the Met** *n* [Gp] (*Brit infml* 口) = the Metropolitan Police.

met *pt, pp* of MEET[1].

meta- *comb form* 构词成分 **1** above; beyond; behind 在上; 在外; 在后: *metalanguage* ○ *metacarpal* ○ *metaphysics*. **2** of change 有关变化或改变的: *metabolism* ○ *metamorphosis*.

meta·bol·ism /məˈtæbəlɪzəm; məˋtæbl̩ɪzəm/ *n* [U] (*biology* 生) chemical process by which food is built up into living matter in an organism or by which living matter is broken down into simpler substances 新陈代谢.

▷ **meta·bolic** /ˌmetəˈbɒlɪk; ˌmɛtəˋbɑlɪk/ *adj* of metabolism 新陈代谢的: *a metabolic process, rate, etc* 新陈代谢的过程、速度等.

meta·bol·ize, -ise /məˈtæbəlaɪz; məˋtæbəlˌaɪz/ *v* [Tn] (*biology* 生) break down (food) chemically for use in the body 将(食物)分解(用于身体新陈代谢): *Our bodies constantly metabolize the food we eat.* 我们吃的食物在体内不停分解产生代谢变化.

meta·carpus /ˌmetəˈkɑːpəs; ˌmɛtəˋkɑrpəs/ *n* (*anatomy* 解) point of the hand containing the five bones between the wrist and the fingers 掌.

▷ **meta·carpal** *adj*, *n* (*anatomy* 解) (of a) bone between the wrist and the fingers 掌骨(的). ⇨illus at SKELETON 见SKELETON 插图.

metal /ˈmetl; ˋmɛtl̩/ *n* **1** [C, U] any of a class of mineral substances such as tin, iron, gold, copper, etc, which are usu opaque and good conductors of heat and electricity, or any alloy of these 金属: *Various metals are used to make the parts of this machine.* 这部机器的零件是用多种金属制造的. ○ *There isn't much metal in the bodywork of this new car; it's mainly plastic.* 这辆新汽车的车身没用多少金属材料, 大部分是塑料的. ○ [attrib 作定语] *a metal support, fitting, container* 金属的支架、配件、容器. **2** = ROAD METAL (ROAD). **3 metals** [pl] railway-lines 钢轨; 铁轨: *These locomotives ran on Great Western Railway metals until 1940.* 这些火车头在1940年以前一直在大西部铁路线上运行.

▷ **metal** *v* (**-ll-**; *US* **-l-**) [Tn esp passive 尤用于被动语态] (*dated* 旧) make or repair (a road) with broken stone 用碎石铺设或修补(道路): *This rough track will soon be a metalled road.* 这条坑坑洼洼的路不久就要铺上碎石了.

me·tal·lic /mɪˈtælɪk; məˋtælɪk/ *adj* [esp attrib 尤作定语] of or like metal (似)金属的: *a metallic plate, sheet, etc* 金属板、片等 ○ *metallic paint*, ie looking like metal 有金属光泽的涂料 ○ *metallic sounds, clicks, etc*, eg made (as if) by metal objects struck together 金属撞击(般)的声音、咔嗒声等.

□ ˈ**metalwork** *n* [U] artistic or skilled work done using metal 金属工艺品; 金工制品. ˈ**metalworker** *n*.

meta·lan·guage /ˈmetəlæŋgwɪdʒ; ˋmɛtəˌlæŋgwɪdʒ/ *n* [C, U] language or set of symbols used in talking about or describing another language, etc 元语言, 纯理语言(用以讲述或描述另一语言等的语言或一套符号).

me·tal·lurgy /mɪˈtælədʒɪ; *US* ˈmetəlɜːrdʒɪ; ˋmɛtl̩ˌɝdʒɪ/ *n* [U] science of the properties of metals, their uses, methods of obtaining them from their ores, etc 冶金学.

▷ **me·tal·lur·gical** /ˌmetəˈlɜːdʒɪkl; ˌmɛtl̩ˋɝdʒɪkl̩/ *adj* of metallurgy 冶金学的; 冶金的.

me·tal·lur·gist /mɪˈtælədʒɪst; *US* ˈmetələ:rdʒɪst; ˈmɛtl-ˌɝdʒɪst/ *n* expert in metallurgy 冶金学家.

meta·morph·ose /ˌmetəˈmɔ:fəʊz; ˌmɛtəˈmɔrfoz/ *v* [I, Ipr, Tn, Tn·pr] **~ (sb/sth) (into sth)** (*fml* 文) (cause sb/sth to) change in form or nature (使某人[某物])变形, 变质: *A larva metamorphoses into a chrysalis and then into a butterfly.* 幼虫变为蛹, 然后再变成蝴蝶. ○ *The magician metamorphosed the frog into a prince.* 魔术师把青蛙变成了王子.

▷ **meta·morph·osis** /ˌmetəˈmɔ:fəsɪs; ˌmɛtəˈmɔrfəsɪs/ *n* (*pl* **-oses** /-əsi:z; -əˌsiz/) (*fml* 文) change of form or nature, eg by natural growth or development 变形; 变态; 变质: *the metamorphosis of a larva into a butterfly* 从幼虫变成蝴蝶的过程 ○ (*fig* 比喻) *the social metamorphosis that has occurred in China* 中国发生的社会变化.

meta·phor /ˈmetəfə(r); ˈmɛtəfɚ/ *n* [C, U] (example of the) use of a word or phrase to indicate sth different from (though related in some way to) the literal meaning, as in 'I'll make him *eat* his words' or 'She has a heart *of stone*' 隐喻(如I'll make him *eat* his words或She has a heart *of stone*): *striking originality in her use of metaphor* 她在运用隐喻方面的独创性. Cf 参看 SIMILE.

▷ **meta·phor·ical** /ˌmetəˈfɒrɪkl; *US* -ˈfɔ:r-; ˌmɛtəˈfɔrɪkl/ *adj* of or like a metaphor; containing metaphors 隐喻的: *a metaphorical expression, phrase, etc* 隐喻的说法、短语等. Cf 参看 FIGURATIVE, LITERAL 1a.

meta·phor·ic·ally /-klɪ; -klɪ/ *adv*. Cf 参看 MIXED METAPHOR (MIXED).

meta·physics /ˌmetəˈfɪzɪks; ˌmɛtəˈfɪzɪks/ *n* [sing *v*] **1** branch of philosophy dealing with the nature of existence, truth and knowledge 形而上学; 玄学. **2** (*esp derog* 尤作贬义) speculative philosophy; any type of abstract talk, writing, etc 思辨哲学; 抽象的言语、文字等.

▷ **meta·physical** /ˌmetəˈfɪzɪkl; ˌmɛtəˈfɪzɪkl/ *adj* **1** of metaphysics 形而上学的. **2** (of poetry) using complex imagery (applied esp to certain 17th-century poets) (指诗)玄学派的(尤用以指17世纪某些诗人).

meta·tarsus /ˌmetəˈtɑ:səs; ˌmɛtəˈtɑrsəs/ *n* (*pl* **-tarsi** /-tɑ:saɪ; -tɑrsaɪ/) (*anatomy* 解) part of the foot containing the five bones between the ankle and the toes 蹠. ▷ **meta·tarsal** *adj*. ⇨illus at SKELETON 见SKELETON 插图.

mete /mi:t; mit/ *v* (phr v) **mete sth out (to sb)** (*fml* 文) give or administer (punishment, rewards, etc) 给予, 加以(惩罚、奖励等): *The judge meted out severe penalties.* 法官对犯人予以严惩. ○ *Justice was meted out to the offenders.* 犯人均已绳之以法.

met·eor /ˈmi:tɪɔ:(r); ˈmitɪɚ/ *n* small mass of matter that enters the earth's atmosphere from outer space, making a bright streak across the night sky as it is burnt up 流星. Cf 参看 SHOOTING STAR (SHOOT[1]).

▷ **met·eoric** /ˌmi:tɪˈɒrɪk; *US* -ˈɔ:r-; ˌmitɪˈɔrɪk/ *adj* **1** of meteors 流星的. **2** (*fig* 比喻) (of a career, etc) rapidly successful (指事业等)迅速成功的: *a meteoric rise to fame* 迅速成名. **met·eor·ic·ally** *adv*.

met·eor·ite /ˈmi:tɪəraɪt; ˈmitɪərˌaɪt/ *n* piece of rock or metal that has reached the earth's surface from outer space 陨星; 陨石; 陨铁.

met·eoro·logy /ˌmi:tɪəˈrɒlədʒɪ; ˌmitɪəˈrɑlədʒɪ/ *n* [U] scientific study of the earth's atmosphere and its changes, used esp for forecasting weather 气象学.

▷ **met·eoro·lo·gical** /ˌmi:tɪərəˈlɒdʒɪkl; *US* ˌmi:tɪɔ:r-; ˌmitɪɔrəˈlɑdʒɪkl/ *adj* of meteorology 气象学的; 气象的: *a meteorological chart, forecast, etc* 气象图、气象预报 ○ *weather forecasts from the Central Meteorological Office* 中央气象局发布的天气预报.

met·eoro·lo·gist /ˌmi:tɪəˈrɒlədʒɪst; ˌmitɪəˈrɑlədʒɪst/ *n* expert in meteorology 气象学家.

meter[1] /ˈmi:tə(r); ˈmitɚ/ *n* (esp in compounds 尤用以构成复合词) device that measures the volume of gas, water, etc passing through it, time passing, electrical current, distance, etc 仪; 表; 计: *an ˌelecˈtricity meter* 电表 ○ *a ˈgas meter* 煤气表 ○ *a ˈwater meter* 水表 ○ *an exˈposure meter*, ie for measuring how long a photographic film should be exposed (照相用的)曝光表 ○ *a ˈparking-meter*, ie one into which coins are put to pay for parking a car for a certain period of time 汽车停放收费表 ○ *fares mounting up on the meter*, ie of a taxi-cab 按计程仪计量的车费.

▷ **meter** *v* [Tn] measure (sth) with a meter 用仪表测量(某物): *meter sb's consumption of gas* 计量某人的煤气用量.

meter[2] (*US*) = METRE.

-meter *comb form* 构词成分 (forming *n*s 用以构成名词) **1** device for measuring (sth) 测量(某物)的仪表, 计: *thermometer* ○ *voltameter*. **2** poetic metre with a given number of feet[1](6) (诗的)音步: *pentameter* ○ *hexameter*.

methad·one /ˈmeθədəʊn; ˈmɛθəˌdon/ *n* [U] drug used as a substitute in treating heroin addiction and as a pain-killer 美沙酮, 美散痛(用以治疗海洛英瘾和用作镇痛剂).

meth·ane /ˈmi:θeɪn; ˈmɛθen/ *n* [U] (also **marsh gas**) odourless, colourless, inflammable gas that occurs in coalmines and in marshes 甲烷; 沼气. Cf 参看 FIREDAMP (FIRE[1]).

method /ˈmeθəd; ˈmɛθəd/ *n* **1** [C] way (of doing sth) 方法; 办法: *modern methods of teaching arithmetic* 现代教算术的方法 ○ *various methods of payment*, eg cash, cheques, credit card 各种付款办法(如现款、支票、信用卡). **2** [U] orderly arrangement, habits, etc 秩序; 条理; 规律: *We must get some method into our office filing.* 我们必须把公文归档工作弄出些条理来. ○ *He's a man of accuracy and strict method.* 他是个精细而严谨的人. **3** (idm 习语) **(have, etc) method in one's madness** behaviour that is not as irrational, strange, etc as it seems 貌似疯狂而实有理智的行为.

▷ **meth·od·ical** /mɪˈθɒdɪkl; məˈθɑdɪkl/ *adj* (**a**) done in an orderly, logical way 按秩序做的; 有条理的: *methodical work, study, etc* 有条不紊的工作、学习等. (**b**) (of a person) doing things in an orderly or systematic way (指人)做事有条理的: *a methodical worker, organizer, etc* 办事有条不紊的工作者、组织者等. **meth·od·ic·ally** /-klɪ; -klɪ/ *adv*.

meth·odo·logy /ˌmeθəˈdɒlədʒɪ; ˌmɛθədˈɑlədʒɪ/ *n* **1** [C] set of methods used (in doing sth) 一套方法: *a methodology for statistical analysis* 统计分析法. **2** [U] science or study of methods 方法学; 方法论. **meth·odo·lo·gical** /ˌmeθədəˈlɒdʒɪkl; ˌmɛθədəˈlɑdʒɪkl/ *adj*. **meth·odo·lo·gic·ally** /-klɪ; -klɪ/ *adv*.

Meth·od·ism /ˈmeθədɪzəm; ˈmɛθədˌɪzəm/ *n* [U] Protestant religious denomination that originated in the teachings of John Wesley /ˈwezlɪ; ˈwɛzlɪ/, 1703-1791 循道宗, 循道公会(创始人约翰·卫斯理1703-1791).

▷ **Meth·od·ist** /ˈmeθədist; ˈmɛθədɪst/ *n*, *adj* (member) of this denomination 循道宗信徒; 循道宗的. Cf 参看 WESLEYAN.

meths /meθs; mɛθs/ *n* [U] (*infml* 口 *esp Brit*) = methylated spirits.

methyl al·co·hol /ˌmeθɪl ˈælkəhɒl, *also* ˌmi:θaɪl; ˌmɛθəl ˈælkəˌhɔl/ (also ˈ**wood spirit**) type of alcohol present in many organic compounds 甲醇.

methyl·ated spirits /ˌmeθəleɪtɪd ˈspɪrɪts; ˌmɛθəˌletɪd ˈspɪrɪts/ type of alcohol (made unfit for drinking) used as a fuel for lighting and heating 甲基化酒精(不适于饮用, 仅作燃料).

me·ticu·lous /mɪˈtɪkjʊləs; məˈtɪkjələs/ *adj* **~ (in sth/doing sth)** giving or showing great precision and care; very attentive to detail 极精细的; 极注意细节的: *a meticulous worker, researcher, etc* 一丝不苟的工作者、研究者等 ○ *meticulous work* 精细的工作 ○ *She is meticulous in her presentation of facts.* 她介绍事实十分详细. ▷ **me·ticu·lously** *adv*. **me·ticu·lous·ness** *n* [U].

mé·tier /ˈmetɪeɪ; mɛˈtje/ *n* (*French* 法) profession, trade or main area of activity, expertise, etc 职业; 行业; 专业: *Don't ask me how to make an omelette; cooking isn't my métier.* 可别问我怎么摊鸡蛋, 烹饪不是我的专长.

metre[1] (*US* **meter**) /ˈmi:tə(r); ˈmitɚ/ *n* (*abbr* 缩写 **m**) unit of length in the metric system, equal to 39.37 inches 米, 公尺(公制长度单位, 等于39.37英寸). ⇨App 4, 5, 11 见附录4、5、11.

metre[2] (*US* **meter**) /ˈmi:tə(r); ˈmitɚ/ *n* (**a**) [U] verse rhythm 诗韵. (**b**) [C] particular form of this; fixed arrangement of accented and unaccented syllables 格律: *a metre with six beats to a line* 六音步格.

M

-metre (*US* **-meter**) *comb form* 构词成分 (used in *ns* expressing a given fraction or multiple of a metre[1] 用于表示米的分数或倍数的名词中): *centimetre* ○ *millimetre* ○ *kilometre*.

met·ric /ˈmetrɪk; ˋmɛtrɪk/ *adj* **1** of or based on the metre[1] (公制长度单位)米的, 以米为基础的: *metric measurement, dimensions, scale, etc* 以米为单位的量度、维数度、刻度等. **2** made, measured, etc according to the metric system 公制的; 十进制的; 米制的: *These screws are metric*, ie have been measured in fractions of a metre. 这些螺钉是公制的. ○ *The petrol pumps have gone metric*, ie measure petrol in litres. 汽油加油泵已采用公制了. **3** = METRICAL.

▷ **met·ric·ate** /ˈmetrɪkeɪt; ˋmɛtrɪˌket/ *v* [Tn] convert (sth) to the metric system 将(某物)改为公制: *The UK metricated its currency in 1971.* 英国于1971年将货币改为十进制. **met·rica·tion** /ˌmetrɪˈkeɪʃn; ˌmɛtrɪˋkeʃən/ *n* [U]: *metrication of the currency* 十进币制.

□ **the ˈmetric system** the decimal measuring system, using the metre, the kilogram and the litre as basic units 公制; 十进制; 米制.

ˌ**metric ˈton** 1 000 kilograms; tonne 吨, 公吨(等于1 000公斤).

met·rical /ˈmetrɪkl; ˋmɛtrɪkḷ/ (also **metric**) *adj* of or composed in verse, not prose 韵律的; 有韵律的; 诗体的: *a metrical translation of the Iliad* 《伊利亚特》故事的诗体翻译.

Metro /ˈmetrəʊ; ˋmɛtro/ *n* **the Metro** underground railway system, esp in Paris 地下铁路(尤指巴黎的): [attrib 作定语] *a Metro station, sign, train* 地下铁路的车站、标志、列车. Cf 参看 TUBE, UNDERGROUND.

met·ro·nome /ˈmetrənəʊm; ˋmɛtrəˌnom/ *n* (*music* 音) device, usu with an inverted pendulum that can move back and forward at various speeds, which is used by a musician to mark time 节拍器.

met·ro·polis /məˈtrɒpəlɪs; məˋtrɑplɪs/ *n* (*pl* **-lises**) chief city of a region or country; capital 大城市; 首都; 首府: *a great metropolis like Tokyo* 像东京一样的大城市 ○ *working in the metropolis*, ie, for British people, in London 在大城市工作(对英国人来说, 在伦敦).

▷ **met·ro·pol·itan** /ˌmetrəˈpɒlɪtən; ˌmɛtrəˋpɑlətn̩/ *adj* of or in a large or capital city 大城市的; 首都的; 首府的: *the population of metropolitan New York*, ie not including its suburbs 纽约市的人口(不包括郊区). — *n* **1** person who lives in a metropolis 大城市人. **2** **Metropolitan** (also **metropolitan ˈbishop**) bishop (usu an archbishop) having authority over the bishops in his province 都主教; 大主教.

□ **Metropolitan ˈFrance** France itself, not including its colonies, etc 法国本土(不包括其殖民地等).

the Metropolitan Poˈlice (also **the Met**) the London police force 伦敦警队.

mettle /ˈmetl; ˋmɛtl/ *n* [U] **1** quality of endurance or courage, esp in people or horses 忍耐力, 勇气(尤指人或马的): *a man of mettle* 有勇气的人 ○ *test sb's mettle* 考验某人的耐力 ○ *She showed her mettle by winning in spite of her handicap.* 那匹雌马尽管增加了负重而仍能获胜, 可见很有耐力. **2** (idm 习语) **be on one's ˈmettle; put sb on his ˈmettle** be encouraged or forced to do one's best; encourage or force sb to do his best 奋发; 激励某人尽最大努力: *You'll be on your mettle during the training period.* 你要在训练期间尽最大努力. ○ *The next race will put him on his mettle.* 下次赛跑他就要全力以赴了.

▷ **met·tle·some** /-səm; -səm/ *adj* (*approv* 褒) (usu of horses, etc) high-spirited; courageous (通常指马等)精力充沛的, 勇猛的.

mew /mjuː; mju/ *n* cry characteristic of a (usu young) cat or a seabird 猫(通常指小猫)或海鸟的叫声: *We heard the mew of a cat.* 我们听到猫叫声.

▷ **mew** *v* [I] make this sound 作猫或海鸟叫; 咪咪叫; 喵喵叫.

mews /mjuːz; mjuz/ *n* (*pl* unchanged 复数不变) (*usu Brit*) square or street of stables, converted into garages or flats, etc 马厩大院; 一排马厩; 由马厩改建的车房或公寓: *live in a Chelsea mews* 住在切尔西由马厩改建的公寓里 ○ [attrib 作定语] *a mews flat* 由马厩改建成的公寓.

mez·zan·ine /ˈmezəniːn; ˋmɛzəˌnin/ *n* **1** floor between the ground floor and the first floor of a building, often in the form of a balcony 夹楼层(介于一楼与二楼之间, 通常为阳台式): [attrib 作定语] *a mezzanine floor, department, etc* 夹层楼面、在夹楼层上的部门. **2** (*US*) (first few rows of the) lowest balcony in a theatre (戏院的)最低层楼厅(前座). Cf 参看 DRESS CIRCLE (DRESS[1]).

mezzo /ˈmetsəʊ; mɛtso/ *adv* (*music* 音) moderately; half 适度; 半: *mezzo forte*, ie moderately loud(ly) 中强 ○ *mezzo piano*, ie moderately quiet(ly) 中弱.

▷ **mezzo** *n* (*infml* 口) mezzo-soprano 女中音.

□ ˌ**mezzo-soˈprano** *n* **1** (**a**) voice between soprano and contralto 女中音. (**b**) singer with such a voice 女中音歌手. **2** part in a piece of music for such a voice 乐曲中的女中音部.

mez·zo·tint /ˈmetsəʊtɪnt; ˋmɛtsəˌtɪnt/ *n* [C, U] (print produced by a) method of printing from a metal plate, parts of which are roughened to give darker areas, and parts of which are smoothed to give lighter areas 金属版印刷术; 金属版印刷品.

MF /ˌem ˈef; ˌɛm ˋɛf/ *abbr* 缩写 = (*radio* 无) medium frequency 中频.

mg *abbr* 缩写 = milligram(s): *100 mg* 100毫克.

Mgr *abbr* 缩写 = Monsignor.

MHz *abbr* 缩写 = megahertz.

mi (also **me**) /miː; mi/ *n* (*music* 音) third note in the sol-fa scale 视唱音阶的第三音.

mi *abbr* 缩写 (*US*) = ML 1.

MI5 /ˌem aɪ ˈfaɪv; ˌɛm aɪ ˋfaɪv/ *abbr* 缩写 = (*Brit*) (former name for the) National Security Division of Military Intelligence (旧名)英国安全局(陆军情报局5处).

MI6 /ˌem aɪ ˈsɪks; ˌɛm aɪ ˋsɪks/ *abbr* 缩写 = (*Brit*) (former name for the) espionage department of Military Intelligence (旧名)英国秘密情报局(陆军情报局6处).

mi·aow /miːˈaʊ; mɪˋaʊ/ *n* cry characteristic of a cat 喵(猫叫声).

▷ **mi·aow** *v* [I] make this cry 作猫叫声; 作喵喵声.

mi·asma /mɪˈæzmə; mɪˋæzmə/ *n* (esp *sing* 尤作单数) (*fml* 文) **1** unhealthy or unpleasant mist, etc 瘴气: *A miasma rose from the marsh.* 沼泽地里冒出了瘴气. **2** (*fig* 比喻) bad atmosphere or influence 坏的气氛或影响: *a miasma of despair* 绝望的气氛.

mica /ˈmaɪkə; ˋmaɪkə/ *n* [U] transparent mineral easily divided into thin layers, used as an electrical insulator, etc 云母.

mice *pl* of MOUSE.

Mich·ael·mas /ˈmɪklməs; ˋmɪkḷməs/ *n* the festival of St Michael, 29 September 米迦勒节(9月29日).

□ ˌ**Michaelmas ˈdaisy** perennial plant that flowers in autumn, with blue, white, pink or purple flowers 紫菀.

mick /mɪk; mɪk/ *n* (*usu offensive* 通常作轻蔑语) Irishman 爱尔兰人.

mickey /ˈmɪkɪ; ˋmɪkɪ/ *n* (idm 习语) **take the mickey (out of sb)** (*infml* 口) ridicule or tease sb 取笑或戏弄某人: *Stop taking the mickey (out of poor Susan)!* 别取笑(可怜的苏珊)了!

micro /ˈmaɪkrəʊ; ˋmaɪkro/ *n* (*pl* **~s**) (*infml* 口) microcomputer 微型计算机.

micro- *comb form* 构词成分 **1** very small 微; 微小: *microchip* ○ *microfiche*. **2** one millionth part of 百万分之一: *microgram*, ie one millionth of a gram 微克(百万分之一克). ⇨App 11 见附录11. Cf 参看 MACRO-, MINI-.

mi·crobe /ˈmaɪkrəʊb; ˋmaɪkrob/ *n* tiny organism that can only be seen under a microscope, esp one that causes disease or fermentation 微生物; (尤指)病菌, 酵母菌. Cf 参看 VIRUS.

mi·cro·bio·logy /ˌmaɪkrəʊbaɪˈɒlədʒɪ; ˌmaɪkrobaɪˋɑlədʒɪ/ *n* [U] study of micro-organisms 微生物学.

▷ **mi·cro·bio·lo·gist** /-lədʒɪst; -lədʒɪst/ *n* expert in microbiology 微生物学家.

mi·cro·chip /ˈmaɪkrəʊtʃɪp; ˋmaɪkrotʃɪp/ (also **chip**) *n* very small piece of silicon or similar material carrying a complex electrical circuit 微晶片(微型集成电路片).

mi·cro·com·puter /ˌmaɪkrəʊkəmˈpjuːtə(r); ˌmaɪkrokəmˋpjutɚ/ *n* small domestic or business computer in which the central processor is a microprocessor 微型计算机. Cf 参看 MAINFRAME (MAIN[1]), MINICOMPUTER.

mi·cro·cosm /ˈmaɪkrəʊkɒzəm; ˋmaɪkrəˌkɑzəm/ *n* **1** thing or being regarded as representing the universe, or

M

mankind, on a small scale; miniature representation (of a system, etc) 小天地; 小宇宙; 微观世界; 缩影: *Man is a microcosm of the whole of mankind.* 人是全人类的缩影. ○ *This town is a microcosm of our world.* 这个市镇是我们这个世界的缩影. Cf 参看 MACROCOSM. **2** (idm 习语) **in microcosm** in miniature; on a small scale 以缩影的形式; 小规模: *This small island contains the whole of nature in microcosm.* 这个小岛包含着小而完整的自然界.

mi·cro·dot /ˈmaɪkrəʊdɒt; ˋmaɪkrodɑt/ *n* photograph, usu of secret documents, etc, reduced to the size of a dot 微粒照片(缩小至颗粒大小的照片, 通常为密件).

micro-electronics /ˌmaɪkrəʊˌɪlekˈtrɒnɪks; ˌmaɪkroɪˌlɛkˋtrɑnɪks/ *n* [sing *v*] design, manufacture and use of electrical devices with very small components 微电子学.

mi·cro·fiche /ˈmaɪkrəʊfiːʃ; ˋmaɪkrofiʃ/ *n* [C, U] sheet of microfilm 缩微软片: *documents stored on microfiche* 存储在缩微软片上的文件.

mi·cro·film /ˈmaɪkrəʊfɪlm; ˋmaɪkrəˌfɪlm/ *n* [C, U] (piece of) film on which extremely small photographs are stored, esp of documents, printed matter, etc 缩微胶卷(用以保存文件、印刷材料等): *scientific papers on microfilm* 在缩微胶卷上的科学文件.

▷ **mi·cro·film** *v* [Tn] photograph (sth) using such film 用缩微胶卷拍摄(某物): *microfilm secret papers, bank accounts, etc* 用缩微胶卷拍摄秘密文件、银行帐目等.

mi·cro·form /ˈmaɪkrəʊfɔːm; ˋmaɪkroˌfɔrm/ *n* [U] any or all of the forms in which documents, etc are reproduced in miniature, eg microfiche, microfilm, etc 缩微版本; 缩微资料.

mi·cro·light /ˈmaɪkrəʊlaɪt; ˋmaɪkroˌlaɪt/ *n* type of very light miniature aircraft 微型飞机.

mi·cro·meter /maɪˈkrɒmɪtə(r); maɪˋkrɑmətɚ/ *n* device for measuring very small objects, angles or distances 测微计; 千分尺.

mi·cron /ˈmaɪkrɒn; ˋmaɪkrɑn/ *n* one millionth of a metre; micrometre 微米(一百万分之一米).

micro-organism /ˌmaɪkrəʊˈɔːgənɪzəm; ˌmaɪkroˋɔrgənˌɪzəm/ *n* organism so small that it can be seen only under a microscope 微生物.

mi·cro·phone /ˈmaɪkrəfəʊn; ˋmaɪkrəˌfon/ *n* instrument that changes sound waves into electrical current (used in recording or broadcasting speech, music, etc) 微音器; 传声器; 麦克风; 话筒.

mi·cro·pro·ces·sor /ˈmaɪkrəʊprəʊsesə(r); ˋmaɪkroˋprosɛsɚ/ *n* (*computing* 计) central data processing unit of a computer, contained on one or more microchips 微处理机.

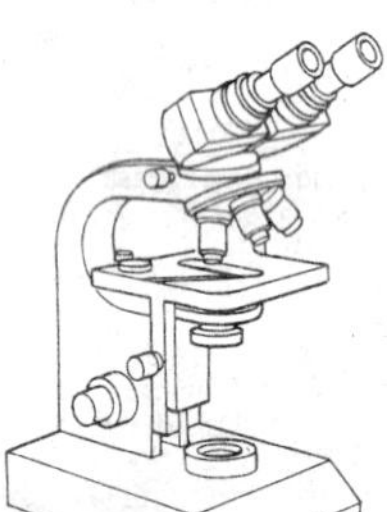

microscope 显微镜

mi·cro·scope /ˈmaɪkrəskəʊp; ˋmaɪkrəˌskop/ *n* instrument with lenses for making very small objects appear larger 显微镜: *examine bacteria under a microscope* 用显微镜检查细菌 ○ (*fig* 比喻) *put politicians under the microscope*, ie examine them closely 用显微镜观察政治家. ⇨illus 见插图.

▷ **mi·cro·scopic** /ˌmaɪkrəˈskɒpɪk; ˌmaɪkrəˋskɑpɪk/, **mi·cro·scopical** /-kl; -kḷ/ *adjs* **1** too small to be seen without the help of a microscope 用显微镜方可见的; 极微小的: *a microscopic creature, particle* 微生物、微粒 ○ *of microscopic size* 用显微镜才能看见大小的. **2** of or using a microscope 显微镜的; 用显微镜的: *microscopic examination of traces of blood* 用显微镜作血迹检查. **mi·cro·scop·ic·ally** /-klɪ; -klɪ/ *adv*.

mi·cro·wave /ˈmaɪkrəweɪv; ˋmaɪkrəˌwev/ *n* **1** very short electromagnetic wave used esp in radio and radar, and also in cooking 微波. **2** (also ˌ**microwave ˈoven**) type of oven that cooks food very quickly using microwaves 微波炉: [attrib 作定语] *microwave cookery* 微波烹饪术.

mid /mɪd; mɪd/ *adj* [attrib 作定语] the middle of 中间的; 中央的; 中部的: *from mid July to mid August* 从七月中到八月中 ○ *in mid winter* 仲冬 ○ *a collision in mid Channel/in mid air* 在英吉利海峡中部[在半空中]相撞.

mid- *comb form* 构词成分 in the middle of 在中间; 在中央; 在中部: *mid-morning coffee* ○ *a mid-air collision* ○ *midsummer/midwinter*.

□ **the ˌMidˈwest** *n* [sing] (also **the ˌMiddle ˈWest**) loosely, the northern central part of the USA, from the Great Lakes to the Ohio River, Kansas and Missouri (美国的)中西部.

mid·day /ˌmɪdˈdeɪ; ˋmɪdˌde/ *n* [U] middle of the day; noon 正午; 中午: *finish work at midday* 于正午完成任务 ○ [attrib 作定语] *the ˌmidday ˈmeal*, ie lunch 午餐.

mid·den /ˈmɪdn; ˋmɪdṇ/ *n* heap of dung or rubbish 粪堆; 垃圾堆.

middle /ˈmɪdl; ˋmɪdḷ/ *n* **1 the middle** [sing] point, position or part which is at an equal distance from two or more points, etc; point between the beginning and the end 中点; 中间; 中央; 中部: *the middle of the room* 房间的中央 ○ *in the middle of the century* 在这世纪的中叶 ○ *in the very middle of the night* 子夜时分 ○ *a pain in the middle of his back* 他背部中央的疼痛 ○ *They were in the middle of dinner* (ie were having dinner) *when I called.* 我给他们打电话时, 他们正在吃饭. ○ *I was right in the middle of reading it* (ie was busy reading it) *when she phoned.* 她打电话来时, 我正念到半截. **2** [C] (*infml* 口) waist 腰: *seize sb round the/his middle* 拦腰抱住某人 ○ *fifty inches round the middle* 腰围五十英寸. **3** (idm 习语) **the middle of ˈnowhere** (*infml* 口) somewhere very remote or isolated 偏远的某地: *She lives on a small farm in the middle of nowhere.* 她住在一个偏僻的小农场上. **pig in the middle** ⇨ PIG.

▷ **middle** *adj* [attrib 作定语] **1** (occupying a position) in the middle 在中间的; 居中的: *the middle house of the three* 三所房子的居中者 ○ *He wears a ring on his middle finger.* 他中指上戴着指环. **2** (idm 习语) **(take/follow) a middle ˈcourse** (make) a compromise between two extreme courses of action (取)中间路线; (行)中庸之道.

□ ˌ**middle ˈage** period between youth and old age 中年. ˌ**middle-ˈaged** /-eɪdʒd; -ˋedʒd/ *adj* of middle age 中年的: *a ˌmiddle-aged ˈman* 中年男子. ˌ**middle-age(d) ˈspread** (*infml* 口) stoutness of the stomach that tends to come with middle age 中年发福.

the ˌMiddle ˈAges (in European history) period from about AD 1100 to about AD 1400 (欧洲史上的)中世纪(约自公元1100年至1400年).

ˈ**middle-brow** *n*, *adj* [usu attrib 通常作定语] (*esp derog* 尤作贬义) (person who is) only moderately intellectual 平庸之辈; 才智平凡的: *middle-brow writers, books, music, interests* 平凡的作家、书籍、音乐、情趣. Cf 参看 HIGHBROW, LOWBROW.

ˌ**middle ˈC** (*music* 音) note C situated near the middle of the piano keyboard 中央C(音).

ˌ**middle ˈclass** social class between the lower/working and upper classes, including professional and business people 中产阶级: [attrib 作定语] *a ˌmiddle-class ˈneighbourhood* 中产阶级居住区.

ˌ**middle-ˈdistance** *adj* [attrib 作定语] **(a)** (in athletics) of a running race which is between a sprint and a long-distance race in length, eg 800 or 1500 metres (田径赛的)中距离的(如800米或1500米). **(b)** of a runner who takes part in such races 中距离参赛者的.

the ˌmiddle ˈdistance that part of a landscape scene, painting, etc that is between the foreground and the background (前景与背景之间的)中景.

ˌ**middle ˈear** cavity of the central part of the ear, behind the eardrum 中耳: *an infection of the middle ear* 中耳炎. ⇨illus at EAR 见EAR插图.

the ˌMiddle ˈEast loosely, an area comprising Egypt, Iran and the countries between them 中东.

ˌ**middle ˈfinger** longest finger 中指. ⇨illus at HAND 见HAND 插图.

ˈ**middleman** /-mæn; -mæn/ *n* (*pl* **-men** /-men; -mɛn/) **1** trader who passes goods from the producer to the final buyer 经销商: *She wants to buy direct from the manufacturer and cut out the middleman.* 她想避开分销商直接自厂家买进货物. **2** intermediary; go-between 中间人; 信使; 调解人; 媒人: *He acted as a middleman in discussions between the two companies.* 他在两公司的谈判中作中间人.

ˌ**middle ˈname** **1** second of two given names, eg *Bernard* in *George Bernard Shaw* 某些人的名字与姓之间的另一名字(如George Bernard Shaw中的Bernard). **2** (idm 习语) **be sb's middle ˈname** (*infml* 口) be sb's chief characteristic 为某人的主要特点: *Charm is her middle name.* 她突出之点就是很有风韵.

ˌ**middle-of-the-ˈroad** *adj* (of people, policies, etc) moderate; avoiding extremes (指人、政策等)走中间路线的, 不走极端的: *Her political beliefs are very middle-of-the-road.* 她的政治信条是持中间立场. ○ *a middle-of-the-road taste in music* 在音乐方面的大众趣味.

ˈ**middle school** (*esp Brit*) school for children aged between 9 and 13 years 中间学校(为9至13岁儿童而设的).

ˈ**middleweight** *n* boxer weighing between 71 and 75 kg, next above welterweight 中量级拳击运动员.

the Middle West = THE MIDWEST (MID-).

mid·dling /ˈmɪdlɪŋ; ˋmɪdlɪŋ/ *adj* **1** of medium size, quality, etc (大小、质量等方面)中等的, 普通的: *a man of middling height* 中等身材的男子 ○ *'Is it big or small?' 'Middling.'* '那个东西是大的还是小的?' '是中等的.' **2** [pred 作表语] in fairly good health 身体尚好: *He says he's only (feeling) middling today.* 他说他今天(身体)还算好. **3** (idm 习语) **fair to middling** ⇨ FAIR.

mid·field /ˌmɪdˈfiːld; ˋmɪdˌfild/ *n* middle part of a football, etc pitch; part of a pitch equally distant from the two goals (足球场等的)中场: [attrib 作定语] *a midfield player* 中场队员. ⇨illus at ASSOCIATION FOOTBALL (ASSOCIATION) 见 ASSOCIATION FOOTBALL (ASSOCIATION) 插图.

midge /mɪdʒ; mɪdʒ/ *n* small winged insect like a gnat 摇蚊.

mid·get /ˈmɪdʒɪt; ˋmɪdʒɪt/ *n* extremely small person 矮人; 侏儒. ▷ **mid·get** *adj* [attrib 作定语] very small 极小的: *a midget submarine* 小型潜艇.

mid·land /ˈmɪdlənd; ˋmɪdlənd/ *adj* [attrib 作定语] of the middle part of the country (一国的)中部, 中部地区: *the midland region, economy, accent* 中部地区、中部地区的经济、中部地区的口音.

▷ **the Mid·lands** *n* [sing or pl *v*] central inland counties of England 英格兰中部地区: [attrib 作定语] *a Midlands firm* 英格兰中部地区的商行. ⇨illus at App 1 见附录1插图, pages xiv, xv.

mid·night /ˈmɪdnaɪt; ˋmɪdˌnaɪt/ *n* [U] **1** 12 o'clock at night 午夜; 子夜; 半夜12点钟: *at/before/after midnight* 在午夜时分[前/后] ○ [attrib 作定语] *a midnight visit*, ie one made around midnight 半夜时的访问. **2** (idm 习语) **burn the midnight oil** ⇨ BURN[2].

□ **the midnight ˈsun** sun seen at midnight in summer near the North and South Poles (南北极地夏季所见的)子夜太阳.

mid·riff /ˈmɪdrɪf; ˋmɪdrɪf/ *n* **1** middle part of the human body, between the waist and the chest; belly 腹部; 肚子: *a punch in the midriff* 对腹部的一拳. **2** (*anatomy* 解) diaphragm 膈.

mid·ship·man /ˈmɪdʃɪpmən; ˋmɪdˌʃɪpmən/ *n* (*pl* **-men** /-mən; -mən/) **1** (*Brit*) rank below that of sub-lieutenant in the Royal Navy 海军准少尉. **2** (*US*) student training to be an officer in the US Navy 海军学校学员. ⇨App 9 见附录9.

mid·ships /ˈmɪdʃɪps; ˋmɪdˌʃɪps/ *adv* = AMIDSHIPS.

midst /mɪdst; mɪdst/ *n* (used after a *prep* 用于介词之后) middle part 中部; 中央; 中间: *in the midst of the crowd* 在人群中间 ○ *A fox darted out of the midst of the thicket.* 一只狐狸从灌木丛中窜了出来. ○ *There is a thief in our/your/their midst*, ie among or with us, you, etc. 我们[你们/他们]中间有个小偷.

mid·stream /ˌmɪdˈstriːm; ˋmɪdˌstrim/ *n* [U] **1** part of a stream, river, etc half-way between its banks 中流: *There's a fast current in midstream.* 中流的水很急. **2** (idm 习语) **change/swap horses in midstream** ⇨ HORSE. **in midstream** in the middle of an action, etc 在进行中: *The speaker stopped in midstream, coughed, then started up again.* 演讲人中途停下来咳嗽, 然后又继续讲.

mid·sum·mer /ˌmɪdˈsʌmə(r); ˋmɪdˈsʌmɚ/ *n* [U] **1** the middle of summer, around 21 June 仲夏(6月21日前后): [attrib 作定语] *a ˌmidsummer('s) ˈday* 仲夏日. **2** (idm 习语) ˌ**midsummer ˈmadness** very great madness or foolishness 极度的疯狂或愚蠢.

□ ˌ**Midsummer's ˈDay** 24 June 施洗约翰节(6月24日).

mid·way /ˌmɪdˈweɪ; ˋmɪdˌwe/ *adj, adv* ~ **(between sth and sth)** (situated) in the middle; half-way 居中(的); 中途(的): *The two villages are a mile apart, and my house lies midway between them.* 两村相距一英里, 我家在中间.

mid·week /ˌmɪdˈwiːk; ˋmɪdˈwik/ *n* [U] middle of the week, ie Tuesday, Wednesday and Thursday, but esp Wednesday 一星期的中间日子(即星期二、三、四); (尤指)星期三: *Midweek is a good time to travel to avoid the crowds.* 星期三是避开人群去旅行的最佳时间. ○ [attrib 作定语] *a ˌmidweek ˈholiday, ˈmeeting* 安排在一星期中间日子的假日、会议.

▷ **mid·week** *adv* in the middle of the week 在一星期的中间日子: *meet, travel, call, etc midweek* 在一星期的中间日子会面、旅行、通电话等.

mid·wife /ˈmɪdwaɪf; ˋmɪdˌwaɪf/ *n* (*pl* **midwives** /-waɪvz; -ˌwaɪvz/) person, esp a woman, trained to assist women in childbirth 助产士; 接生员; 产婆.

▷ **mid·wif·ery** /ˈmɪdwɪfərɪ; *US* -waɪf-; ˋmɪdˌwaɪfərɪ/ *n* [U] profession and work of a midwife 助产士的职业; 助产学; 助产; 接生: *a course in midwifery* 助产学课程.

mid·win·ter /ˌmɪdˈwɪntə(r); ˋmɪdˈwɪntɚ/ *n* [U] the middle of winter, around 21 December 仲冬(12月21日前后): [attrib 作定语] *a ˌmidwinter('s) ˈnight* 仲冬之夜.

mien /miːn; min/ *n* [sing] (*fml or rhet* 文或修辞) person's appearance or bearing, esp as an indication of mood, etc 仪表; 态度; 风采; 样子; 神态: *with a sorrowful mien* 带着悲伤的神情 ○ *a man of proud mien* 骄矜的男子 ○ *the severity of his/their mien* 他[他们]那严肃的神态.

miffed /mɪft; mɪft/ *adj* (*sl* 俚) (slightly) annoyed (稍)恼怒的, 生气的: *She was (a bit) miffed that he'd forgotten her name.* 他把她的名字忘了, 她(有点)生气了. ○ *a miffed expression* 不痛快的样子.

might[1] /maɪt; maɪt/ *modal v* (*neg* 否定式 **might not**, *contracted form* 缩约式 **mightn't** /ˈmaɪtnt; ˋmaɪtnt/) **1** (indicating permission 用以表示许可): *Might I make a suggestion?* 我可以提个建议吗? ○ *If I might just put in a word here....* 容我在此略置一词.... ⇨Usage 1 at MAY[1] 见MAY[1]所附用法第1项. **2** (indicating possibility 表示可能): *He ˈmight get here in time, but I can't be sure.* 他可能及时来到这里, 不过我不能肯定. ○ *This ointment might help to clear up your rash.* 这种药膏也许能消除你的皮疹. ○ *The pills might have cured him, if only he'd taken them regularly.* 他要是按时服用这些药丸, 本来是可能治得好的. ⇨Usage 2 at MAY[1] 见MAY[1]所附用法第2项. **3** (asking for information 用于问讯情况): *And who might ˈshe be?* 那么她能是哪一位呢? ○ *How long might ˈthat take?* 那要多长时间? ⇨Usage 4 at MAY[1] 见MAY[1]所附用法第4项. **4** (used to make polite requests or appeals 用于婉转的请求或吁请): *You might just* (ie Please) *call in at the supermarket for me.* 请顺便为我去一趟超级市场吧. ○ *I think you might at least offer to help!* 我认为你至少可以主动帮帮忙吧! ⇨Usage at WOULD 用法见WOULD.

might[2] *pt of* MAY[1].

might[3] /maɪt; maɪt/ *n* [U] **1** great strength or power 力气; 力量; 威力; 权力: *I pushed the rock with all my might.* 我用全力推那块大石. ○ *We fear the military might of the enemy.* 我们惧怕敌人强大的军事力量. **2** (idm 习语) ˌ**might is ˈright** (*saying* 谚) having the power to do sth gives one the right to do it 强权就是公理. **with ˌmight and ˈmain** (*rhet* 修辞) with all one's physical strength 竭尽全力.

mighty /ˈmaɪtɪ; ˋmaɪtɪ/ *adj* (**-ier, -iest**) **1** (*esp fml* 尤作郑重语) powerful; strong 强大的; 有力的: *a mighty* army, nation, ruler 强大的军队、国家、统治者 ○ (*infml* 口) *She gave him a mighty thump.* 她狠狠地揍了他一下. **2** great and imposing 伟大的; 威严的; 雄伟的: *mighty mountain peaks* 巍峨的山峰 ○ *the mighty ocean* 浩瀚的大海. **3** (idm 习语) **high and mighty** ⇨ HIGH[1]. **the pen is mightier than the sword** ⇨ PEN[1].

▷ **mighty** *adv* (*infml* 口 *esp US*) very 极; 很: *mighty good, clever, etc* 极好、极聪明 ○ *He's mighty pleased with himself.* 他洋洋得意.

migh·tily /-ɪlɪ; -ɪlɪ/ *adv* **1** (*fml* 文) powerfully; forcefully 强烈地; 有力地: *He struck it mightily with his sword.* 他用剑猛刺. **2** very 极; 很: *mightily pleased, relieved, etc* 极为高兴、宽慰等.

mi·graine /ˈmi:greɪn; *US* ˈmaɪgreɪn; ˋmaɪgren/ *n* [U, C] severe recurring type of headache, usu on one side of the head or face, often accompanied by nausea and disturbance of the eyesight 偏头痛.

mi·grate /maɪˈgreɪt; *US* ˈmaɪgreɪt; ˋmaɪgret/ (also **trans·mi·grate**) *v* [I, Ipr] **~ (from...) (to...)** **1** move from one place to go to live or work in another 迁居; 移居; 迁徙. **2** (of animals, etc) go from one place to another with the seasons, esp to spend the winter in a warmer place (指动物等)迁徙(尤指到暖处过冬): *These birds migrate to North Africa in winter.* 这些鸟冬天迁徙到北非.

▷ **mi·grant** /ˈmaɪgrənt; ˋmaɪgrənt/ *n, adj* [attrib 作定语] (of a) person or animal who migrates 迁徙的人或动物; 迁徙的; 移居的: *migrant workers*, ie those who travel to another region or country to work 流动工人 ○ *migrant seabirds* 迁徙的海鸟.

mi·gra·tion /maɪˈgreɪʃn; maɪˋgreʃən/ *n* **(a)** (also **trans·mi·gra·tion**) [C, U] (action of) migrating 迁居; 移居; 迁徙. **(b)** [C] number of migrating people, animals, etc 迁徙的人、动物等的数量: *a huge migration of people into Europe* 大量涌至欧洲的移民.

mi·grat·ory /ˈmaɪgrətrɪ, maɪˈgreɪtərɪ; *US* ˈmaɪgrətɔ:rɪ; ˋmaɪgrə,torɪ/ *adj* having or of the habit of migrating 有迁徙习惯的: *migratory birds* 候鸟 ○ *the migratory instinct* 迁徙的本能.

mi·kado /mɪˈkɑ:dəʊ; məˋkɑdo/ *n* (*pl* **~s**) (name formerly used outside Japan for the) Emperor of Japan (旧时日本国外所称之)日本天皇.

mike /maɪk; maɪk/ *n* (*infml* 口) = microphone.

mil·age = MILEAGE.

milch /mɪltʃ; mɪltʃ/ *adj* [attrib 作定语] (*dated* 旧) (of domestic mammals, esp cows) giving or kept for milk (指家畜, 尤指母牛)产乳的, 为产奶而饲养的: *a milch cow, goat, etc* 奶牛、奶羊.

mild /maɪld; maɪld/ *adj* **(-er, -est)** **1** **(a)** (of a person or his manner) gentle; soft (指人或人的态度)温和的, 温柔的, 和善的: *He's the mildest man you could wish to meet.* 他是最温和的人了. ○ *She's a very mild-mannered person.* 她是个很和善的人. ○ *He gave a mild answer, in spite of his annoyance.* 他尽管已恼火, 但回答得还是很和蔼. **(b)** not severe or harsh 不严厉的; 不严酷的: *mild weather, a mild climate, etc*, ie not cold 温和的天气、气候等 ○ *a mild punishment* 轻微的惩罚 ○ *the mild action of the soap* 这种肥皂的柔和的特性. **2** (of a flavour) not strong or bitter (指味道)淡的, 不强烈的: *mild cheese* 淡味奶酪 ○ *a mild cigar, curry* 淡味的雪茄烟、咖喱.

▷ **mild** *n* [U] (also **mild ale**) (*Brit*) type of beer not strongly flavoured with hops 淡味麦芽啤酒: *two pints of mild* 两品脱淡味麦芽啤酒.

mildly *adv* **1** in a gentle manner 温和地; 温柔地; 和善地: *She spoke mildly to us.* 她很和蔼地向我们讲话. **2** (idm 习语) **to put it ˈmildly** without exaggerating; using understatement 不夸张; 说得婉转些: *At 6'4", she's tall, to put it mildly*, ie She's extremely tall. 她6英尺4英寸, 比较高, 说这话留有余地(她高极了).

mild·ness *n* [U].

□ ˌ**mild ˈsteel** tough malleable type of steel with a low percentage of carbon 软钢; 低碳钢.

mil·dew /ˈmɪldju:; *US* -du:; ˋmɪl,du/ *n* [U] tiny fungus forming a (usu white) coating on plants, leather, food, etc in warm and damp conditions 霉; 霉菌: *roses ruined by mildew* 霉烂的玫瑰.

▷ **mil·dew** *v* [I, Tn esp passive 尤用于被动语态] (cause sth to) be affected by mildew (使某物)发霉: *mildewed canvas, leaves, fruit* 发霉的帆布、叶子、水果.

M

mile /maɪl; maɪl/ *n* **1** [C] unit of distance equal to 1.6 km 英里(等于1.6公里): *For miles and miles there's nothing but desert.* 绵延数英里除了沙漠别无他物. ○ *a 39-mile journey* 39英里的行程. ⇨App 4,5 见附录4、5. Cf 参看 NAUTICAL MILE (NAUTICAL). **2** [C esp *pl* 尤作复数] (*infml* 口) a great amount or distance; much 大量; 大距离; 很多: *She's feeling miles* (ie very much) *better today.* 她今天身体好多了. ○ *He's miles older than she is.* 他年纪比她大得多. ○ *There's no one within miles/a mile of her* (ie No one can rival her) *as a tennis-player.* 她打网球远无敌手. ○ *You missed the target by a mile/by miles.* 你远未中的. **3** (esp 尤作 **the mile**) [sing] race over one mile 一英里赛跑: *Who's running in the mile?* 谁参加一英里赛跑? ○ *He can run a four-minute mile*, ie run a mile in four minutes or less. 他能参加四分钟一英里赛(四分钟内跑一英里). ○ [attrib 作定语] *the world mile record* 一英里赛跑世界记录. **4** (idm 习语) ˌ**miles from ˈanywhere/ˈnowhere** in a remote or isolated place, position, etc 偏远的或孤立的地方、位置等. **a miss is as good as a mile** ⇨ MISS[1]. **run a mile (from sb/sth)** be anxious or careful to avoid sb/sth 竭力或小心躲避某人[某事物]: *I'd sooner run a mile than be interviewed on television.* 要让我接受电视采访, 我可要跑得远远的. **see/tell sth a ˈmile off** (*infml* 口) see/tell sth very easily 显而易见; 极易识别: *He's lying: you can see that a mile off.* 他在撒谎, 你一听就知道. **stand/stick out a ˈmile** be very striking or noticeable 极醒目; 极显眼: *Her honesty sticks out a mile.* 她很诚实, 这是有目共睹的. ○ *It stands out a mile that she's telling the truth.* 她说的是实情, 这是明摆着的事.

□ ˈ**milestone** *n* **1** stone put at the side of a road showing distances in miles 里程碑. **2** (*fig* 比喻) very important stage or event 重大阶段或事件; 转折点: *This victory was a milestone in our country's history.* 这一胜利是我国历史的转捩点.

mile·age (also **mi·lage**) /ˈmaɪlɪdʒ; ˋmaɪlɪdʒ/ *n* **1** [C, U] distance travelled, measured in miles 英里数: *a used car with a low/high mileage*, ie one that has not/has been driven many miles 行驶里数少[多]的旧汽车. **2** [U] (also ˈ**mileage allowance**) allowance paid for the expenses of travelling by (one's own) car (自用)汽车里数津贴: *Have you claimed your mileage?* 你申请汽车里数津贴了吗? **3** [U] (*fig infml* 比喻, 口) (amount of) benefit or advantage 利润; 好处: *He doesn't think there's any mileage in that type of advertising.* 他认为做那种广告毫无效益.

miler /ˈmaɪlə(r); ˋmaɪlɚ/ *n* (*infml* 口) person or horse specializing in races of one mile 擅长一英里赛跑的运动员或马: *He's our best miler.* 他是我们最优秀的一英里赛跑健将.

mi·lieu /ˈmi:ljɜ:; *US* ˌmi:ˈljɜ:; miˋljø/ *n* (*pl* **~s** or **~x** /-z; -z/) (usu *sing* 通常作单数) social surroundings; environment 社会环境; 环境: *Coming from another milieu, she found life as an actor's wife very strange at first.* 她嫁给一个演员后, 与自己原来的生活环境大不相同, 初时觉得这种生活十分陌生.

mil·it·ant /ˈmɪlɪtənt; ˋmɪlətənt/ *adj* using force or strong pressure, or supporting their use, to achieve one's aims 用武力或高压的; 好战的: *The strikers were in a militant mood*, ie ready to take strong action. 罢工者群情激奋(随时准备采取激烈行动).

▷ **mil·it·ancy** /-ənsɪ; -ənsɪ/ *n* [U].

mil·it·ant *n* militant person, esp in trade unionism or politics 好斗的人; (尤指工会主义或政治上的)好斗分子, 激进分子.

mil·it·ar·ism /ˈmɪlɪtərɪzəm; ˋmɪlətə,rɪzəm/ *n* [U] (*usu derog* 通常作贬义) believing in or depending on military strength and methods, esp as a government policy 黩武主义; (尤指)军国主义.

▷ **mil·it·ar·ist** /ˈmɪlɪtərɪst; ˋmɪlətərɪst/ *n* person who supports militarism 穷兵黩武者; 军国主义者.

mil·it·ar·istic /ˌmɪlɪtəˈrɪstɪk; ˌmɪlətəˋrɪstɪk/ *adj.*

mil·it·ar·ize, -ise /ˈmɪlɪtəraɪz; ˋmɪlətə,raɪz/ *v* [Tn esp passive 尤用于被动语态] use (esp land) for military purposes 将(尤指土地)改作军用: *a militarized zone* 军事区.

mil·it·ary /ˈmɪlɪtrɪ; *US* -terɪ; ˋmɪlə,tɛrɪ/ *adj* [usu attrib 通常作定语] of or for soldiers or an army; of or for (all the) armed forces 军人的; 军队的; 陆军的; 军事的; 军

用的: *military training, discipline, etc* 军事训练、纪律等 ○ *in full military uniform* 全副军人装束 ○ *be called up for, do military service*, ie go to be trained or serve as a soldier, etc for a fixed period of time 应征受军训、服兵役 ○ *the military police* 宪兵队.

▷ **the mil·it·ary** *n* [sing or pl *v*] soldiers or the army; the armed forces (as distinct from police or civilians) 军人; 军队; 武装力量(以区别于警察或平民): *The military were called in to deal with the riot.* 已将军队调来镇压暴乱.

mil·it·ate /ˈmɪlɪteɪt; ˋmɪləˌtet/ *v* [Ipr] **~ against sth** (*fml* 文) (of evidence, facts, etc) have great force or influence to prevent sth (指证据、事实等)有巨大作用或影响(以防止某事物): *Many factors militated against the success of our plan.* 有很多因素妨碍了我们实现计划.

mi·li·tia /mɪˈlɪʃə; məˋlɪʃə/ *n* [CGp] force of civilians who are trained as soldiers and reinforce the regular army in the internal defence of the country in an emergency 民兵队伍; 国民自卫队.

□ **mi·li·tia·man** /-mən; -mən/ *n* (*pl* **-men**) member of a militia 民兵; 国民自卫队队员.

milk[1] /mɪlk; mɪlk/ *n* [U] **1** white liquid produced by female mammals as food for their young, esp that of cows, goats, etc drunk by human beings and made into butter and cheese 奶; 乳; (尤指)牛奶, 羊奶: *milk fresh from the cow* 鲜牛奶 ○ *skimmed milk* 脱脂牛乳 ○ *dried/powdered milk* 奶粉 ○ [attrib 作定语] *milk products*, eg butter, cheese, yoghurt 乳制品 ○ *a milk bottle* 牛奶瓶. **2** milk-like juice of some plants and trees, eg that found inside a coconut (某些植物的乳状)汁液(如椰子汁). **3** milk-like preparation made from herbs, drugs, etc 乳状制剂. **4** (idm 习语) **cry over spilt milk** ⇨ CRY[1]. ˌ**milk and ˈwater** (*derog* 贬) feeble or sentimental talk, ideas, etc 无益的或伤感的话、想法等: *His speech was nothing but milk and water.* 他的讲话平淡无奇毫无意义. ○ [attrib 作定语] *I found it a disappointing thriller — very milk-and-water stuff.* 我认为这部惊险小说令人失望——简直味同嚼蜡. **the milk of human ˈkindness** the kindness that should be natural to human beings 人类的善良天性.

□ ˈ**milk bar** (*esp Brit*) bar for the sale of non-alcoholic drinks (esp those made from milk), ice-cream, etc 出售非酒类饮料的柜台或商店; (尤指)奶制品店.

ˌ**milk ˈchocolate** chocolate (for eating) made with milk and usu sold in wrapped bars 牛奶巧克力: *Do you prefer milk chocolate or plain (chocolate)?* 你喜欢牛奶巧克力还是纯巧克力?

ˈ**milk churn** (*Brit*) large tall metal container, fitted with a lid, for carrying milk (金属的)有盖的牛奶桶. ⇨illus at BARREL 见 BARREL 插图.

ˈ**milk-float** *n* (*Brit*) light low vehicle, usu electrically-powered, used for delivering milk to people's houses 送奶车(通常为电动的).

ˈ**milk-loaf** *n* (*pl* **-loaves**) (*Brit*) sweet-tasting white bread made with milk 牛奶甜面包.

ˈ**milkmaid** *n* woman who milks cows and works in a dairy 挤奶女工.

ˈ**milkman** /-mən; -mən/ *n* (*pl* **-men**) man who goes from house to house delivering and selling milk 送牛奶的人.

ˌ**milk ˈpudding** (*esp Brit*) rice, sago, tapioca, etc baked in milk in a dish 牛奶布丁.

ˈ**milk round** milkman's route from house to house and from street to street 挨街挨户送奶的路线: *go on/do a milk round* 挨街挨户送一趟牛奶.

ˈ**milk run** (*fig infml* 比喻, 口) regular and uneventful journey providing a service 例行差事: *I do the milk run every day taking the children to school.* 我每天照例送孩子上学.

ˌ**milk ˈshake** drink made of milk and flavouring (sometimes ice-cream) mixed or shaken until frothy 奶昔(牛奶与香料, 有时为冰激凌, 混合或搅打至起泡的饮料).

ˈ**milk-tooth** *n* (*pl* **-teeth**) (also *esp US* **baby tooth**) any of the first (temporary) teeth in young mammals 乳齿; 奶牙.

ˈ**milkweed** *n* any of various wild plants with a milky juice 有乳状汁液的野生植物.

ˌ**milk-ˈwhite** *adj* of a white colour like milk 乳白色的: *The prince rode a* ˌ*milk-white* ˈ*horse.* 那王子骑着乳白色的马.

milk[2] /mɪlk; mɪlk/ *v* **1** [I, Tn] draw milk from (a cow, goat, etc) 挤(牛、羊等的)奶: *The farmer hasn't finished milking.* 那农夫还未挤完奶. **2** [I] yield milk 产奶: *The cows are milking well*, ie giving large quantities of milk. 那些牛产奶很多. **3** [Tn, Tn·pr] **~ A (of B)/~ B (from A)** (**a**) draw (juice) from (a plant or tree) 抽取(植物)的汁液: *milk a tree of its sap* 取树的汁液 ○ *milk the sap from a tree* 从树中取汁液. (**b**) draw (venom) from (a snake) 取(蛇)的毒液. **4** [Tn, Tn·pr] **~ sb/sth (of sth); ~ sth (out of/from sb/sth)** (*fig* 比喻) extract (money, information, etc) dishonestly from (a person or an institution) 从(某人或某机构处)骗取(钱财、情报等): *milking the Welfare State (of money, resources, etc)* 骗取福利国家(的钱、资源等) ○ *His illegal deals were steadily milking the profits from the business.* 他在搞非法交易不断榨取公司的利润. **5** (idm 习语) **milk/suck sb/sth dry** ⇨ DRY[1].

▷ **milker** *n* **1** person who milks an animal (从动物身上)挤奶的人. **2** animal that gives milk 产乳动物: *That cow is a good milker.* 那头母牛产奶多.

□ ˈ**milking-machine** *n* apparatus for milking cows mechanically 挤奶机.

milk·sop /ˈmɪlksɒp; ˋmɪlkˌsɑp/ *n* (*derog* 贬) man or boy who is weak and timid 懦弱而胆怯的男子.

milky /ˈmɪlkɪ; ˋmɪlkɪ/ *adj* (**-ier, -iest**) **1** of or like milk (似)乳的: *a milky white skin* 乳白色的皮肤. **2** mixed with or made of milk 含乳的; 乳制的: *milky tea, coffee, etc* 奶茶、牛奶咖啡 ○ *I like a hot milky drink at bedtime.* 我喜欢睡前喝杯热奶饮料. **3** (of a jewel or a liquid) not clear; cloudy (指珠宝或液体)乳白色的, 白而混浊的: *Opals are milky gems.* 蛋白石是乳白色的宝石. ▷ **milki·ness** *n* [U].

□ **the** ˌ**Milky** ˈ**Way** = THE GALAXY (GALAXY 2).

mill[1] /mɪl; mɪl/ *n* **1** (building fitted with) machinery or apparatus for grinding grain into flour 磨粉机; 磨粉厂; 磨坊: *a* ˈ*water-mill* 水磨 ○ *a* ˈ*windmill* 风车. **2** machine for grinding or crushing a solid substance into powder 磨碎机; 粉碎机; 碾磨机: *a* ˈ*coffee-mill* 咖啡研磨机 ○ *a* ˈ*pepper-mill* 胡椒研磨器. **3** (building fitted with) machinery for processing materials of certain kinds 材料加工机; 工厂; 工场: *a* ˈ*cotton-mill* 纱厂 ○ *a* ˈ*paper-mill* 造纸厂 ○ *a* ˈ*steel-mill* 轧钢厂 ○ *a* ˈ*saw-mill*, ie for timber 锯木厂. ⇨Usage at FACTORY 用法见 FACTORY. **4** (idm 习语) **grist to the/one's** ˈ**mill** ⇨ GRIST. **put sb/go through the** ˈ**mill** (cause sb to) undergo hard training or an unpleasant experience (使某人)经受严格训练或磨炼, 历尽艰辛. Cf 参看 RUN-OF-THE-MILL (RUN[2]).

□ ˈ**mill-dam** *n* dam built across a stream to make water available for a mill 磨坊水坝.

ˈ**mill-hand** *n* factory worker 工人.

ˈ**mill-pond** *n* still water held by a mill-dam to flow to a mill 磨坊贮水池: *The sea was as calm as a mill-pond.* 海面静如池水.

ˈ**mill-race** *n* current of water that turns a mill-wheel 转动磨坊水轮的水流.

ˈ**millstone** *n* **1** either of a pair of flat circular stones between which grain is ground 磨石; 磨盘. **2** (idm 习语) **a millstone round one's/sb's** ˈ**neck** heavy burden or responsibility 沉重的负担或责任: *My debts were like a millstone round my neck.* 我欠的债像是在脖子上套着个磨盘.

ˈ**mill-wheel** *n* wheel used to drive a water-mill (带动水磨的)水轮.

ˈ**millwright** *n* man who designs, builds and repairs water-mills and windmills 设计、建造和修理水磨和风车的人.

mill[2] /mɪl; mɪl/ *v* [Tn esp passive 尤用于被动语态] **1** (**a**) grind or crush (sth) in a mill 用磨研磨或碾碎(某物): *The grain was coarsely milled.* 谷物粗磨过了. (**b**) produce (sth) in a mill 碾磨出(某物): *milled flour* 磨出的面粉. **2** produce regular markings on the edge of (a coin) 在(硬币)上轧花边: *English pound coins have milled edges.* 英镑的硬币轧有花边. **3** cut or shape (metal) with a rotating tool 铣(金属). **4** (phr v) **mill about/around** (of people or animals) move round and round in a confused mass (指人或动物)绕圈子, 乱转:

Groups of fans were milling about in the streets after the match. 比赛过后入迷的观众成群结队在街上乱转.

mill·board /ˈmɪlbɔːd; ˋmɪlˌbɔrd/ *n* [C, U] (piece of) strong pasteboard used in bookbinding 装订书籍用的厚纸板.

mil·len·ar·ian /ˌmɪlɪˈneərɪən; ˌmɪləˋnɛrɪən/ *n* person who believes that the millennium(3) will come 相信太平盛世会来临的人.

mil·len·nium /mɪˈlenɪəm; məˋlɛnɪəm/ *n* (*pl* **-nia** /-nɪə; -nɪə/ or **~s**) **1** [C] period of 1 000 years 一千年: *the first millennium AD* 公元第一千年. **2 the millennium** [sing] (*religion* 宗) the 1000-year reign of Christ on earth prophesied in the Bible 千禧年, 千年王国(《圣经》中预言的基督复临治理世界的一千年). **3 the millennium** [sing] future time of great happiness and prosperity for everyone (未来的)太平盛世, 黄金时代.

▷ **mil·len·nial** *adj*.

mil·le·pede (also **millipede**) /ˈmɪlɪpiːd; ˋmɪləˌpid/ *n* small worm-like creature resembling a centipede, but with two pairs of legs on each segment of its body 马陆; 千足虫.

miller /ˈmɪlə(r); ˋmɪlɚ/ *n* person who owns or runs a mill for grinding corn, esp a windmill or a water-mill 磨粉厂厂主, 磨坊主(尤指用风车或水磨者).

mil·let /ˈmɪlɪt; ˋmɪlɪt/ *n* [U] (**a**) type of cereal plant growing 3 to 4 feet high and producing a large crop of small seeds 黍类; 小米. (**b**) these seeds used as food 黍类; 小米.

milli- *comb form* 构词成分 (in the metric system) one thousandth part of (公制的)千分之一: ˈ*milligram* ○ ˈ*millimetre*. ⇨App 11 见附录11.

mil·liard /ˈmɪlɪɑːd; ˋmɪljɚd/ *n* (*Brit*) one thousand million(s), 1 000 000 000 十亿. Cf 参看 BILLION.

mil·li·bar /ˈmɪlɪbɑː(r); ˋmɪlɪˌbɑr/ *n* unit of atmospheric pressure equal to one thousandth of a bar⁴ 毫巴(大气压力单位, 等于千分之一巴).

mil·liner /ˈmɪlɪnə(r); ˋmɪlənɚ/ *n* person who makes or sells (trimmings for) women's hats 女帽(及其饰物)商.

▷ **mil·lin·ery** /-nərɪ; *US* -nerɪ; -ˌnɛrɪ/ *n* [U] (business of making or selling) (trimmings for) women's hats 女帽(及其饰物)业; 女帽饰物; 女帽: [attrib 作定语] *the millinery department*, eg in a large store 女帽部(如大商店中的).

mil·lion /ˈmɪljən; ˋmɪljən/ *pron, det* (after *a* or *one*, used to indicate quantity; no *pl* form 用于a或one之后, 表示数量; 无复数形式) 1 000 000; one thousand thousand 一百万. ⇨App 4 见附录4.

▷ **mil·lion** *n* **1** (*sing* after *a* or *one*, but often *pl* 在a或one之后作单数; 但常作复数看待) the number 1 000 000 100万; 兆: *She made her first million* (eg pounds or dollars) *before she was thirty.* 她不到三十岁就挣到了一百万. **2** (idm 习语) **one, etc in a ˈmillion** person or thing of rare or exceptional quality 极稀有的人或事物; 百里挑一的人或物: *She's a wife in a million.* 她是个百里挑一的妻子. ○ *We haven't a chance in a million* (ie We have almost no chance) *of winning.* 我们胜利的机会微乎其微.

mil·lion- (in compounds 用以构成复合词) having a million of the thing specified 有一百万之数的: *a million-dollar law-suit*, ie one costing one million dollars or more 耗费百万元的诉讼案.

mil·lionth *pron, det* 1 000 000th 第一百万的. — *n* one of one million equal parts of sth 百万分之一.

For the uses of *million* and *millionth* see examples at *hundred* and *hundredth*. 关于million和millionth的用法见hundred和hundredth词条中的示例.

mil·lion·aire /ˌmɪljəˈneə(r); ˌmɪljənˋɛr/ (*fem* 阴性作 **mil·lion·air·ess** /ˌmɪljəˈneəres; ˌmɪljənˋɛrɪs/) *n* person who has a million pounds, dollars, etc; very rich person 百万富翁; 大富翁.

mil·li·pede = MILLEPEDE.

mi·lo·meter (also **mile·om·eter**) /maɪˈlɒmɪtə(r); maɪˋlɑmɪtɚ/ *n* (*US* **odo·meter**) instrument in a vehicle or on a bicycle for measuring the number of miles travelled (车辆上的英里数)计程器.

mi·lord /mɪˈlɔːd; mɪˋlɔrd/ *n* (French word formerly used for an) English lord or wealthy Englishman (法语词, 旧用法)英国士绅, 富有的英国人.

milt /mɪlt; mɪlt/ *n* [U] (also **soft roe**) fish sperm (鱼的)精液.

mime /maɪm; maɪm/ *n* (**a**) [U] (in the theatre, etc) use of only facial expressions and gestures to tell a story 哑剧: *a play acted entirely in mime* 完全以哑剧形式演出的话剧 ○ [attrib 作定语] *a mime artist* 哑剧艺术家. (**b**) [C] performance using this 哑剧表演.

▷ **mime** *v* **1** [I] act using mime 用哑剧式动作表演: *mime to a recording of a song*, ie pretend that one is singing the words 配合录音模拟唱歌. **2** [Tn] express (sth) by mime 用哑剧动作表现(某事物): *He mimed the part of a drunken man.* 他以哑剧形式表演醉汉.

mi·meo·graph /ˈmɪmɪəgrɑːf; *US* -græf; ˋmɪmɪəˌgræf/ *n* (*dated* 旧) apparatus for making copies of written or typed material from a stencil 油印机.

▷ **mi·meo·graph** *v* [Tn] copy (sth) with a mimeograph 用油印机印刷(某物).

mi·metic /mɪˈmetɪk; mɪˋmɛtɪk/ *adj* (fond) of imitating or mimicking (好)模仿的; (好)戏弄性模仿的: *mimetic skills*, eg of some birds 模仿的技巧(如鸟的模仿力).

mimic /ˈmɪmɪk; ˋmɪmɪk/ *v* (*pt, pp* **mimicked**) [Tn] **1** copy the appearance or manner of (sb/sth) in a mocking or amusing way 戏弄性模仿(某人[某事物]): *Tom mimicked his uncle's voice and gestures perfectly.* 汤姆把他叔叔的声音和姿态模仿得惟妙惟肖. **2** (of things) resemble (sth) closely (指物)极似(某物): *wood painted to mimic marble* 漆成酷似大理石的木头.

▷ **mimic** *n* person, animal, etc clever at mimicking others 善于模仿的人、动物等: *This parrot is an amazing mimic.* 这只鹦鹉很会学舌, 逗人喜爱.

mimic *adj* [attrib 作定语] imitated or pretended 模拟的; 假装的: *mimic warfare*, eg in peacetime manoeuvres 模拟的战争 ○ *mimic colouring*, eg of animals, birds and insects, etc whose colours blend with their natural surroundings 拟色(如动物等的颜色, 与自然环境一致).

mim·icry *n* [U] mimicking (戏弄性的)模仿; 极似: *protective mimicry*, ie resemblance of animals, birds, insects, etc to the colours and patterns of their natural surroundings, as a means of hiding from their enemies 保护性拟态(动物等模拟自然环境的颜色和形态以隐蔽防敌).

mi·mosa /mɪˈməʊzə; *US* -məʊsə; mɪˋmosə/ *n* (**a**) [U, C] type of tropical tree or shrub with clusters of small, ball-shaped, sweet-smelling, yellow flowers 含羞草属植物. (**b**) [U] these flowers 含羞草花: *a bunch, spray, etc of mimosa* 一束、一小枝等含羞草花.

min *abbr* 缩写 = **1** minimum: *temperature 50° min* 最低温度50度. Cf 参看 MAX. **2** minute(s): *fastest time 6 mins* 最快6分钟. Cf 参看HR.

min·aret /ˌmɪnəˈret; ˌmɪnəˋrɛt/ *n* tall slender spire forming part of a mosque, with a balcony from which people are called to prayer by a muezzin (伊斯兰教的)宣礼塔.

min·at·ory /ˈmɪnətərɪ; *US* -tɔːrɪ; ˋmɪnəˌtorɪ/ *adj* (*fml* 文) threatening 威胁性的; 恐吓性的: *minatory actions, gestures, etc* 恫吓的行为、姿势等.

mince /mɪns; mɪns/ *v* **1** [Tn] chop or cut (esp meat) into very small pieces in a machine with revolving blades 用绞肉机绞(尤指肉). **2** [I, Ipr, Ip] (*usu derog* 通常作贬义) walk or speak in an affected manner, trying to appear delicate or refined 装腔作势地走或说: *She minced into the room wearing very high heels.* 她穿着很高的高跟鞋, 扭扭捏捏地走进房间. **3** (idm 习语) **not ˈmince matters; not mince (one's) ˈwords** speak plainly or bluntly, esp when condemning sb/sth 直言不讳(尤在指责某人[某事物]时): *I didn't mince matters: I said he was an idiot.* 我不讳言, 我说过他是白痴. ○ *I won't mince words (with you): I think your plan is stupid.* 我不(跟你)兜圈子, 我认为你的计划是胡闹.

▷ **mince** *n* [U] (*esp Brit*) (*US* **hamburger**) minced meat 绞碎的肉; 肉末: *a pound of mince* 一磅绞肉.

mincer *n* device for mincing food, esp meat 食物绞碎机; (尤指)绞肉机.

min·cing *adj* (*usu derog* 通常作贬义) affected 做作的; 装腔作势的: *take small, mincing steps* 迈着做作的小碎步. **min·cingly** *adv*.

□ ˌ**mince** ˈ**pie** small round pie containing mincemeat and eaten esp at Christmas 百果馅饼(尤指圣诞节日吃的).

mince·meat /ˈmɪnsmi:t; ˈmɪnsˌmit/ *n* [U] **1** mixture of currants, raisins, sugar, candied peel, apples, suet, etc used esp as a filling for a mince pie 百果馅(由加仑子干、葡萄干、糖、蜜饯果皮、苹果、牛羊油等混合而成). **2** (idm 习语) **make mincemeat of sb/sth** (*infml* 口) defeat sb/sth completely in a fight or an argument 彻底击败或驳倒某人[某事物]: *The Prime Minister made mincemeat of his opponent's arguments.* 首相把对方反对他的论点驳得体无完肤.

mind[1] /maɪnd; maɪnd/ *n* **1** [U] ability to be aware of things and to think and feel 感知、思维和感觉的能力; 心智: *have the right qualities of mind for the job* 有做该项工作的头脑 ○ *have complete peace of mind* 心态十分平静. **2** [C] **(a)** ability to reason; intellectual powers 推理的能力; 悟性; 智力: *have a brilliant, logical, simple, etc mind* 头脑聪明、逻辑性强、简单等. **(b)** person who uses his reasoning or intellectual powers well 有心力智慧的人: *He is one of the greatest minds of the age.* 他是当代最有才智的人. **3** [C] person's thoughts or attention 人的思想或注意力; 心思: *Are you quite clear in your own mind what you ought to do?* 你自己是否清楚该做什么? ○ *Don't let your mind wander!* 别走神儿! **4** [C] ability to remember; memory 记忆力; 记性: *I can't think where I've left my umbrella; my mind's a complete blank!* 我想不起来把伞丢在哪儿了, 一点印象都没有! **5** [U, C] normal condition of one's mental faculties; sanity 正常的神志或理智; 健全的心态: *be sound in mind and body* 身心健康 ○ *He's 94 and his mind is going*, ie he is becoming senile. 他已94岁, 神志日衰. **6** (idm 习语) **absence of mind** ⇨ ABSENCE. **at the back of one's mind** ⇨ BACK[1]. **be in one's right mind** ⇨ RIGHT[1]. **be in two ˈminds about sth/doing sth** feel doubtful about or hesitate over sth 对某事物三心二意或犹豫不决: *I was in two minds about leaving London: my friends were there, but the job abroad was a good one.* 我对是否离开伦敦一事拿不定主意; 伦敦有我的朋友, 但是国外那份工作非常好. **be/take a load/weight off sb's mind** cause one/sb great relief 使自己[某人]如释重负: *Paying my mortgage was an enormous weight off my mind!* 我还了抵押借款, 如释重负! **be of one ˈmind (about sb/sth)** agree or have the same opinion (about sb/sth) (对某人[某事物])意见一致, 有同样看法. **be on one's ˈmind; have sth on one's ˈmind** (cause sb to) worry about sth (使某人)为某事物担忧: *My deputy has resigned, so I've got a lot on my mind just now.* 我的副手辞职了, 所以现在有许多事要我操心. **be ˌout of one's ˈmind** (*infml* 口) be crazy or mad 发狂; 发疯: *You must be out of your mind if you think I'm going to lend you £50!* 你以为我会借给你50英镑, 你准是疯了! **bear in mind that...** ⇨ BEAR[2]. **bear/keep sb/sth in ˈmind** remember sb/sth 记住某人[某事物]: *We have no vacancies now, but we'll certainly bear your application in mind.* 我们目前没有空缺, 但是我们一定记住你申请的事. **bend one's mind to sth** ⇨ BEND[1]. **blow one's/sb's mind** ⇨ BLOW[1]. **boggle sb's/the mind** ⇨ BOGGLE. **bring/call sb/sth to mind** recall sb/sth to one's memory 想起某人[某事物]: *I know her face but I can't call her name to mind.* 我认得她, 但想不起她的名字了. **cast one's mind back** ⇨ CAST[1]. **change one's/sb's mind** ⇨ CHANGE[1]. **close one's mind to sth** ⇨ CLOSE[4]. **come/spring to ˈmind** present itself to one's thoughts 出现于某人的脑海中: *'Have you any suggestions?' 'Nothing immediately springs to mind.'* '你有什么建议?''一下子想不起什么来.' **concentrate one's/the mind** ⇨ CONCENTRATE. **cross one's mind** ⇨ CROSS[2]. **ease sb's conscience/mind** ⇨ EASE[2]. **frame of mind** ⇨ FRAME[1]. **give one's mind to sth** concentrate on or direct all one's attention to sth 全神贯注于某事物. **give sb a piece of one's mind** ⇨ PIECE[1]. **go out of/slip one's ˈmind** be forgotten 忘记; 想不起. **have, etc an enquiring, etc turn of mind** ⇨ TURN[2]. **have a memory/mind like a sieve** ⇨ SIEVE. **have a mind of one's ˈown** be capable of forming opinions, making decisions, etc independently 有主见; 能自作决定. **have a (good) mind to do sth** (*infml* 口) have a (strong) desire to do sth 有(强烈)愿望做某事物: *I'd a good mind to smack him for being so rude!* 他这样粗野, 我真想揍他! **have half a mind to do sth** (*infml* 口) feel a moderate desire to do sth 有点想做某事物. **have/keep an open mind** ⇨ OPEN[1]. **have it in mind to do sth** (*fml* 文) intend to do sth 想做某事物: *I have it in mind to ask her advice when I see her.* 我打算见到她时征求她的意见. **have sb/sth in mind (for sth)** be considering sb/sth as suitable (for sth) 考虑某人[某事物]适合(于某事物): *Who do you have in mind for the job?* 你考虑谁做这工作合适? **in one's mind's ˈeye** in one's imagination; in one's memory 在想像中; 在记忆中: *In my mind's eye, I can still see the house where I was born.* 我对出生时的那所房子仍记忆犹新. **keep one's mind on sth** continue to pay attention to sth; not be distracted from sth 继续专心于某事物; 不因某事物分散注意力: *Keep your mind on the job!* 专心做你的工作! **know one's own mind** ⇨ KNOW. **make up one's ˈmind** come to a decision 作出决定; 拿定主意: *I've made up my mind to be a doctor.* 我决心当医生. ○ *Have you made your mind up where to go for your holiday?* 你已决定到什么地方去度假了吗? **make up one's mind to (doing) sth** (*fml* 文) come to accept sth that cannot be changed, etc 接受无法变更的事实: *As we can't afford a bigger house we must make up our minds to staying here.* 既然我们住不起大房子, 我们就得安心住在这儿. **a meeting of minds** ⇨ MEETING. **the mind/imagination boggles** ⇨ BOGGLE. **ˌmind over ˈmatter** mental powers regarded as being stronger than those of the body or physical objects 精神胜物质: *Keeping to a strict diet is a question of mind over matter.* 坚持某一规定饮食, 是毅力能否战胜物质诱惑的问题. **of the same mind** ⇨ SAME[1]. **of unsound mind** ⇨ UNSOUND. **open one's heart/mind to sb** ⇨ OPEN[2]. **out of sight, out of mind** ⇨ SIGHT[1]. **pissed out of one's head/mind** ⇨ PISS. **poison A's mind against B** ⇨ POISON. **presence of mind** ⇨ PRESENCE. **prey on sb's mind** ⇨ PREY *v*. **put sb in mind of sb/sth** cause sb to think of or remember sb/sth 使某人想到或想起某人[某事物]: *Her way of speaking put me in mind of her mother.* 她说话的样子使我想起了她的母亲. **put/set one's/sb's ˈmind at ease/rest** cause or enable one/sb to stop worrying 使自己[某人]放心. **put/set/turn one's mind to sth** give all one's attention to (achieving) sth 专心于某事物: *You could be a very good writer if you set your ˈmind to it.* 你只要专心, 很可能成为优秀作家. **speak one's mind** ⇨ SPEAK. **stick in one's mind** ⇨ STICK[2]. **take one's/sb's mind off sth** help one/sb not to think or worry about sth 使自己[某人]不再思考或担忧某事物: *Hard work always takes your mind off domestic problems.* 工作一劳累就使人不再想着家庭问题了. **time out of mind** ⇨ TIME[1]. **to ˈmy mind** according to my way of thinking; in my opinion 照我的想法; 我认为: *To ˈmy mind, it's all a lot of nonsense!* 照我看, 这全是胡说! **turn sth over in one's ˈmind** consider or think carefully about sth for some time 仔细考虑或反复思考某事物.

□ **ˈmind-bending** *adj* (*infml* 口) strongly influencing the mind 强烈影响心绪的; 令人费精神的: *a mind-bending problem* 令人费解的问题.

ˈmind-blowing *adj* (*infml* 口) (of drugs or extraordinary sights, experiences, etc) causing mental excitement, ecstasy, hallucinations, etc (指毒品、异常的景象、经历等)令人兴奋的, 令人感到美妙的, 致幻的.

ˈmind-boggling *adj* (*infml* 口) alarming; extraordinary or astonishing 惊人的; 不寻常的; 令人惊异的: *Distances in space are quite mind-boggling.* 宇宙之大令人吃惊. Cf 参看 BOGGLE SB'S MIND (BOGGLE).

ˈmind-reader *n* person who claims to know what another person is thinking 自称了解他人思想活动的人. **ˈmind-reading** *n* [U].

mind[2] /maɪnd; maɪnd/ *v* **1** [Tn] take care of or attend to (sb/sth) 照看, 留心(某人[某事物]): *mind the baby* 照料婴儿 ○ *Mind my bike while I go into the shop, please.* 请帮我照看一下自行车, 我到商店里去. ○ *Could you mind the phone* (ie answer it if it rings) *for five minutes?* 你能替我守着五分钟电话吗? **2** [I, Ipr, Tn, Tf, Tw no passive 不用于被动语态, Tg, Tsg] **~ about sth/doing sth** (esp in questions, negative and conditional sentences and in affirmative sentences that answer a question 尤用于疑问句、否定句、条件句及用作回答问话的肯定句) feel annoyance or discomfort at (sth); object to (sth) 对(某事物)介意; 反对(某事物): *Did she mind* *(about) not getting the job?* 她没得到那份工作是不是很失意? ○ *Do you mind the noise?* 这声音影响你吗? ○ *I wouldn't mind* (ie I would very much like) *a drink.* 我很乐意喝他一杯. ○ *She minded very much that he had not come.* 他没有来, 她为此十分不悦. ○ *I don't mind how cold it is.* 我不在乎有多么冷. ○ *Do you mind if I smoke?* 我抽烟你介意吗? ○ *Would you mind helping me?* ie Would you please help me? 请帮帮我的忙好吗? ○ *Do you mind my closing the window?* 我关上窗户行吗? **3** [no passive 不用于被动语态: Tn, Tw] pay attention to or care about (sth) 注意, 关心(某事物): *There's no need to mind the expense if you're not paying!* 又不是你花钱, 管他开销有多大呢! ○ *Don't mind me! I promise not to disturb you.* 别管我! 我答应不打扰你. ○ *I mind what people think about me.* 我很注意人们对我的看法. ○ *I mind whether you like me or not.* 你是否喜欢我, 我很重视这件事. **4** [I, Tn, Tf, Tw] be careful about (sb/sth) 留心, 留神(某人[某事物]): *Mind* (ie Don't trip over) *that step!* 小心那个台阶! ○ *Mind your head!* eg Be careful not to hit it on the low doorway. 当心别磕着头! (如别碰到低矮的门框.) ○ *Mind the dog!* ie It may be fierce. 留神那条狗! (可能很凶.) ○ *This knife is sharp. Mind you don't cut yourself!* 这刀子很快. 小心别拉着! ○ *Mind you come home before 11 o'clock.* 记住, 十一点钟以前回家. ○ *Mind where you put those glasses!* 把那些杯子放在哪儿, 要看着点! **5** (idm 习语) **ˌdo you ˈmind?** (*ironic* 反语) please stop that 请别这样做: *'Do you mind?' she said, as he pushed into the queue in front of her.* 他挤到她前面来排队时, 她说: '请不要挤进来, 好吗?' **I don't mind if I ˈdo** (*infml ironic* 口, 反语) (used when accepting esp a drink gratefully 用于欣然接受, 尤指饮料): *'Will you have a drink?' 'I don't mind if I do* (ie Yes, please).' '你要喝点吗?' '那可太好了.' **ˌmind one's ˌown ˈbusiness** (esp imperative 尤用于祈使句) not interfere in other people's affairs 注意你自己的事; 少管闲事. **ˌmind one's ˌp's and ˈq's** be careful and polite about what one says or does 要讲礼貌. **mind/watch one's step** ⇨ STEP². **ˌmind ˈyou; mind** (used as an *interj* 用作感叹语) please note 请注意: *They're getting divorced, I hear — mind you, I'm not surprised.* 听说他们正闹离婚呢 —— 告诉你吧, 一点都不奇怪. **ˌnever ˈmind** don't worry 不必担心: *'Did you miss the bus? Never mind, there'll be another one in five minutes.* '你没赶上公共汽车吗? 不要紧, 五分钟后就来一辆.' **never mind (doing) sth** stop, or don't start, doing sth 别做某事了: *ˌNever mind ˌsaying you're ˈsorry, who's going to pay for the damage you've done?* 别说对不起了, 你损坏的东西谁来赔? **ˌnever you ˈmind** (*infml* 口) don't ask (because you will not be told) 不要问(因为不会告诉你): *Never you mind how I found out — it's true, isn't it?* 你就别问我是怎么知道的了 —— 反正是事实, 对吧? **6** (phr v) **ˌmind ˈout** (*infml* 口) (esp imperative 尤用于祈使句) allow sb to pass 让某人通过: *Mind out (of the way) — you're blocking the passage.* 让让(路) —— 你挡道了. **mind out (for sb/sth)** beware (of danger, etc) 注意, 留心(危险等): *Mind out for the traffic when you cross the road.* 过马路要注意来往车辆.

▷ **minder** *n* (esp in compounds 尤用以构成复合词) person whose duty it is to attend to sth 看守人; 守护人; 照料者: *a maˈchine-minder* 看管机器的人 ○ *a ˈchild-minder* 照看孩子的人.

minded /ˈmaɪndɪd; ˋmaɪndɪd/ *adj* **1** [pred 作表语] **~ (to do sth)** (*fml* 文) disposed or inclined (to do sth) 想要, 准备, 有意(做某事物): *He could do it if he were so minded.* 他要是想做的话, 他就能做. **2** (forming compound *adjs* or following *advs* 构成复合形容词或用于副词之后) having the kind of mind specified 有某种心智或头脑的: *a ˌstrong-minded, ˌnarrow-minded, ˌfeeble-minded, ˌhigh-minded, etc ˈperson* 意志坚强的、心胸狭窄的、意志薄弱的、思想高尚的…人 ○ *I appeal to all ˌlike-minded ˈpeople to support me.* 我请求有这类想法的人都来支持我. ○ *be comˌmercially, poˌlitically, ˌtechnically, etc ˈminded* 有商业、政治、技术等头脑. **3** (with *ns* forming compound *adjs* 与名词结合构成复合形容词) conscious of the value or importance of the thing specified 认识某事物的价值或重要性的: *She has become very ˈfood-minded since her holiday in France.* 她自法国度假回来, 对食物就很讲究了.

mind·ful /ˈmaɪndfl; ˋmaɪndfəl/ *adj* [pred 作表语] **~ of sb/sth** (*fml* 文) giving thought and care or attention to sb/sth 留意、关心或注意到某人[某事物]: *mindful of one's family, one's duties, one's reputation, the need for discretion* 顾及家庭的、留意职责的、关心声誉的、小心谨慎的.

mind·less /ˈmaɪndlɪs; ˋmaɪndlɪs/ *adj* **1** not requiring intelligence 不需要智慧的: *mindless drudgery* 不必用脑筋的苦活儿. **2** (*derog* 贬) lacking in intelligence; thoughtless 没头脑的; 没思想的; 愚蠢的: *mindless vandals* 愚昧的破坏公物的人. **3** [pred 作表语] **~ of sb/sth** (*fml* 文) not thinking of sb/sth; heedless of sb/sth 不顾及或不注意某人[某事物]: *mindless of personal risk* 没考虑个人所冒的风险. ▷ **mind·lessly** *adv.* **mind·less·ness** *n* [U].

mine¹ /maɪn; maɪn/ *possess pron* of or belonging to me 我的: *I think that book is mine.* 那本书是我的. ○ *He's a friend of mine*, ie one of my friends. 他是我的朋友. Cf 参看 MY.

mine² /maɪn; maɪn/ *n* **1** excavation (with shafts, galleries, etc) made in the earth for extracting coal, mineral ores, precious stones, etc 矿井; 巷道; 矿: *a ˈcoal-mine* 煤矿 ○ *a ˈgold-mine* 金矿 ○ *The inspector went down the mine.* 监察员已下到矿井里了. ○ [attrib 作定语] *a ˈmine worker* 矿工. Cf 参看 QUARRY². **2 (a)** tunnel for a charge of high explosive to destroy eg enemy fortifications 地雷坑道(如用以炸毁敌军工事的). **(b)** container filled with explosive, placed in or on the ground, and designed to explode when sth strikes it or passes near it, or after a fixed time, to destroy eg enemy troops, vehicles, etc 地雷. **(c)** such a container placed in water to damage or destroy eg enemy ships 水雷: *magnetic, acoustic, etc mines* 磁性的、声引信的…水雷 ○ *lay mines* 布雷 ○ *clear the coastal waters of mines* 清除沿岸水域的水雷 ○ [attrib 作定语] *mine warfare* 地雷战. Cf 参看 DEPTH CHARGE (DEPTH). **3** (idm 习语) **a mine of information (about/on sb/sth)** rich or abundant source of knowledge 知识的宝库; 信息的源泉: *My grandmother is a mine of information about our family's history.* 我的祖母是我们家史的资料库.

□ **ˈmine-detector** *n* electromagnetic device for finding explosive mines 探雷器.

ˈminefield *n* **1** area of land or sea where explosive mines have been laid 布雷区. **2** (*fig* 比喻) area presenting many unseen difficulties 有许多潜在困难的地区: *International law is a minefield for anyone not familiar with its complexity.* 国际法这一领域, 不熟悉其复杂性则寸步难行.

ˈminelayer *n* ship or aircraft used for laying explosive mines at sea 布雷舰艇或飞机. **ˈminelaying** *n* [U].

ˈminesweeper *n* naval vessel used for detecting and clearing explosive mines 扫雷艇. **ˈminesweeping** *n* [U].

ˈmineworker *n* person who works in a mine²(1) 矿工.

mine³ /maɪn; maɪn/ *v* **1 (a)** [I, Ipr] **~ (for sth)** dig in the ground (for coal, ores, precious stones, etc) 采掘(煤、矿物、宝石等); 开矿; 采矿: *mining for gold, diamonds, etc* 开采黄金、金刚石等. **(b)** [Tn, Tn·pr] **~ A (for B)/~ B (from A)** extract (coal, etc) from (the earth) by digging 采掘(煤等): *mine the earth for iron ore* 开采铁矿石 ○ *Gold is mined from deep under ground.* 黄金是从地下深处开采出来的. **2** [Tn] make tunnels in the earth under (sth); undermine 在(某物)下面挖掘坑道; 挖地道: *mine enemy trenches, forts, etc* 在敌军的战壕、堡垒等下面挖地道. **3** [Tn] **(a)** lay explosive mines in (sth) 在(某处)埋地雷或布水雷: *mine the entrance to a harbour* 在进港处布水雷. **(b)** destroy (sth) by means of explosive mines 用地雷或水雷炸毁(某物): *The cruiser was mined, and sank in five minutes.* 该巡洋舰触雷, 于五分钟后沉没.

miner /ˈmaɪnə(r); ˋmaɪnɚ/ *n* person who works in a mine underground 矿工: *ˈcoal-miners* 煤矿工人.

min·eral /ˈmɪnərəl; ˋmɪnərəl/ *n* **1** [C, U] substance that is not vegetable or animal, esp one with a constant chemical composition which is found naturally in the earth 矿物: *substances classified as mineral(s)* 列为矿物的物质 ○ [attrib 作定语] *mineral salts* 岩盐 ○ *the mineral kingdom* 矿物界. Cf 参看 ANIMAL, VEGETABLE. **2** [C, U] any substance got from the earth by mining, esp a metal ore 采自地下的任何物质; (尤指)金属矿石: *Coal and*

M

iron are minerals. 煤和铁都是矿物. ○ [attrib 作定语] *mineral deposits, resources, wealth, etc.* 矿藏、矿物资源、矿物财富. **3** [C usu *pl* 通常作复数] (*Brit*) (**a**) = MINERAL WATER. (**b**) (*US* **soda**) non-alcoholic canned or bottled drink containing flavouring and soda-water (罐装或瓶装的)矿泉水: *Soft drinks and minerals sold here.* 此处出售软饮料和矿泉水.

□ ˈ**mineral oil** **1** (*Brit*) any oil of mineral origin, esp petroleum 矿物油; (尤指)石油. **2** (*US*) liquid paraffin 液体石蜡.

ˈ**mineral water** water that naturally contains dissolved mineral salts or gases, and is drunk for its medicinal value 矿泉水.

min·er·al·ogy /ˌmɪnəˈrælədʒɪ; ˌmɪnəˋælədʒɪ/ *n* [U] scientific study of minerals 矿物学.

▷ **min·era·lo·gical** /ˌmɪnərəˈlɒdʒɪkl; ˌmɪnərəˋlɑdʒɪkl̩/ *adj* of or concerning mineralogy 矿物学的.

min·er·al·ogist /ˌmɪnəˈrælədʒɪst; ˌmɪnəˋælədʒɪst/ *n* student of or expert in mineralogy 矿物学研究者; 矿物学家.

min·es·trone /ˌmɪnɪˈstrəʊnɪ; ˌmɪnəˋstronɪ/ *n* [U] thick rich meat soup (of Italian origin) containing chopped mixed vegetables and pasta or rice (源于意大利的)含蔬菜和意大利粉或大米的浓汁肉汤.

mingle /ˈmɪŋgl; ˋmɪŋgl̩/ *v* **1** (**a**) [I, Ipr, Ip] **~ with sth/~ (together)** form a mixture with sth; combine 与某物混合; 结合: *The waters of the two rivers mingled (together) to form one river.* 两条河汇合成一条. (**b**) [Tn, Tn·pr, Tn·p] **~ A with B/~ A and B (together)** mix one thing with another; combine things together 将一物与另一物混合; 将事物结合一起: *truth mingled with falsehood* 搀杂虚假成分的事实 ○ *The priest mingled the water with the wine.* 牧师在水中兑上酒. ○ *He mingled the water and wine (together).* 他把水和酒混在一起了. **2** [I, Ipr, Ip] **~ with sb/sth; ~ (together)** go about among sb/sth; associate with sb/sth 混进某些人[某事物]中; 与某人[某事物]交往或联系: *Security men mingled with the crowd.* 保安人员混杂在人群中.

mingy /ˈmɪndʒɪ; ˋmɪndʒɪ/ *adj* (**-ier, -iest**) (*Brit infml* 口) mean; ungenerous; stingy 小气的; 不慷慨的; 吝啬的: *He's so mingy with his money.* 他对钱十分吝啬. ○ *This restaurant serves very mingy portions.* 这家餐厅的饮食分量很少.

mini /ˈmɪnɪ; ˋmɪnɪ/ *n* (*pl* **~s**) (*infml* 口) **1 Mini** (*propr* 专利名) type of small car 小型汽车. **2** miniskirt 超短裙.

mini- *comb form* 构词成分 of small size, length, etc; miniature (体积、长度等)小的, 短的: ˈ*minibus* ○ ˈ*minicab* ○ ˈ*miniskirt* ○ ˈ*minigolf*. Cf 参看 MACRO-, MICRO-.

mini·ature /ˈmɪnətʃə(r); *US* ˈmɪnɪətʃʊər; ˋmɪnɪətʃɚ/ *n* **1** (**a**) [C] very small detailed painting, usu of a person 微型画; (通常指)微型人像画. (**b**) [U] art of painting in this way 微型绘画术: [attrib 作定语] *a miniature artist*, ie one who specializes in this type of art 微型画画家. **2** [C] very small copy or model of sth 微型复制品; 微小模型: *a detailed miniature of the Titanic* 提坦号邮轮的精细小模型 ○ [attrib 作定语] *miniature dogs*, ie very small breeds 小种狗 ○ *miniature bottles of brandy, etc* 小瓶白兰地等 ○ *a miniature railway*, ie a small model one on which people may ride for short distances 小铁路(供人短距离使用的模型). **3** (idm 习语) **in miniature** on a very small scale 小型; 小规模; 小比例: *copy sth in miniature* 缩小复制某物 ○ *She is just like her mother in miniature.* 她简直是她母亲的缩影.

▷ **mini·atur·ist** /ˈmɪnɪtʃərɪst; ˋmɪnɪtʃərɪst/ *n* painter of miniatures 微型画画家.

mini·bus /ˈmɪnɪbʌs; ˋmɪnɪˌbʌs/ *n* (*esp Brit*) small vehicle like a bus with seats for only a few people 小型公共汽车: *hire a self-drive minibus* 租一辆自己驾驶的小型公共汽车.

mini·cab /ˈmɪnɪkæb; ˋmɪnɪˌkæb/ *n* (*Brit*) car like a taxi but available only if ordered in advance (需提前租订的)小型计程车.

mini·com·puter /ˌmɪnɪkəmˈpju:tə(r); ˌmɪnɪkəmˋpjutɚ/ *n* comparatively cheap computer that is small in size and storage capacity 小型计算机. Cf 参看 MAINFRAME (MAIN[1]), MICROCOMPUTER.

minim /ˈmɪnɪm; ˋmɪnɪm/ *n* **1** (*Brit*) (*US* **half note**) (*music* 音) note with half the time-value of a semibreve 二分音符; 半音符. ⇨ illus at MUSIC 见 MUSIC 插图. **2** unit of liquid measure equal to one sixtieth of a dram (about one drop) 量滴(液量单位, 等于 $\frac{1}{60}$ 打兰, 约为一滴之量).

min·imal /ˈmɪnɪməl; ˋmɪnɪml̩/ *adj* smallest in amount or degree (量或程度)最小的, 最低的: *We stayed with friends, so our expenses were minimal.* 我们住在朋友家, 所以我们的花费很小. ▷ **min·im·ally** *adv*.

min·im·ize, -ise /ˈmɪnɪmaɪz; ˋmɪnəˌmaɪz/ *v* [Tn] **1** reduce (sth) to the smallest amount or degree 使(某事物)减至最小量或最低程度: *To minimize the risk of burglary, install a good alarm system.* 安装可靠的报警设备以减低被盗的风险. **2** estimate (sth) at the smallest possible amount; reduce the true value or importance of (sth) 对(某事物)作最低估计; 贬低(某事物)的价值或重要性: *He minimized the value of her contribution to his research so that he got all the praise.* 他极力贬低她在那项研究中的贡献, 从而独获全部奖励. Cf 参看 MAXIMIZE.

min·imum /ˈmɪnɪməm; ˋmɪnəməm/ *n* (*pl* **minima** /-mə; -mə/) [C usu *sing* 通常作单数] **1** least or smallest amount, degree, etc possible (可能的)最小量; 最低限度: *a minimum of work, effort, etc* 最低限度的工作、努力等 ○ *keep/reduce sth to the (absolute) minimum* 将某事物保持在[减少至](绝对的)最低限度 ○ *Repairing your car will cost a minimum of £100*, ie at least £100. 修理你的汽车最低限度要100英镑. **2** (*abbr* 缩写 **min**) least or smallest amount, degree, etc allowed or recorded (许可的或记录到的)最小量, 最低限度: *The class needs a minimum of 6 pupils to continue.* 这个班最低限度要有6个学生才可以继续办. ○ *Temperatures will reach a minimum of 50°F.* 温度最低将达到50°F. Cf 参看 MAXIMUM.

▷ **min·imum** *adj* that is a minimum 最小的; 最少的; 最低限度的: *20p is the minimum fare on buses.* 公共汽车票价起码是20便士.

□ ˌ**minimum** ˈ**lending rate** (*finance* 财) lowest rate of interest at which the central bank lends money at any particular time (中央银行某时期贷款的)最低利率.

ˌ**minimum ther**ˈ**mometer** thermometer that automatically records the lowest temperature within a particular period (自动记录某时期最低温度的)最低温度计.

ˌ**minimum** ˈ**wage** lowest wage that an employer is allowed, by law or a union agreement, to pay (法定的或工会认可的)最低工资: *earn the minimum wage* 挣最低工资.

min·ing /ˈmaɪnɪŋ; ˋmaɪnɪŋ/ *n* [U] (often in compounds 常用以构成复合词) process of getting coal, ores, precious stones, etc from mines 采矿: ˈ*tin-mining* 采锡矿 ○ *open-cast mining*, ie getting coal, etc that is near the surface, using mechanical shovels, etc 露天开采 ○ [attrib 作定语] *the* ˈ*mining industry* 采矿业 ○ *a* ˈ*mining engineer* 采矿工程师.

min·ion /ˈmɪnɪən; ˋmɪnjən/ *n* (esp *pl* 尤作复数) (*derog or joc* 贬或谑) subordinate or assistant, esp one who tries to win favour by obeying a superior slavishly 下属; 助手; (尤指)唯命是从的奴仆: *the dictator and his minions* 独裁者及其奴才 ○ *Can you send one of your minions to collect this file?* 你能不能派个助手来取这份档案?

min·is·ter[1] /ˈmɪnɪstə(r); ˋmɪnɪstɚ/ *n* **1** (*US* **secretary**) person at the head of a government department or a main branch of one (and often a member of the Cabinet) 部长; 大臣(常为内阁阁员): *the Minister of Education* 教育部长 ○ *a minister of state for finance* 财政部的国务大臣 ○ *the Prime Minister* 首相. **2** person, usu of lower rank than an ambassador, representing his government in a foreign country 公使; 外交使节. **3** Christian clergyman, esp in the Presbyterian and some Nonconformist churches (基督教的)牧师(尤指长老会和某些不信奉国教派的): *a minister of religion* 牧师. Cf 参看 PRIEST, VICAR.

□ ˌ**Minister of** ˈ**State** (*Brit*) departmental senior minister between a departmental head and a junior minister 国务大臣.

min·is·ter[2] /ˈmɪnɪstə(r); ˋmɪnɪstɚ/ *v* **1** [Ipr] **~ to sb/sth** (*fml* 文) give active help or service to sb/sth 辅助或伺候某人; 为某人[某事物]服务: *nurses ministering to (the needs of) the sick and wounded* 照料伤病患者(需要的)护士. **2** (idm 习语) **a ministering** ˈ**angel** person (esp a woman) who helps or serves others with tenderness

M

and care 热心帮助或照顾别人的人(尤指女子).

min·is·ter·ial /ˌmɪnɪˈstɪərɪəl; ˌmɪnəsˈtɪrɪəl/ *adj* **1** of a minister, his position, duties, etc 部长的; 大臣的; 部长或大臣的地位或职责的; 公使的; 公使的地位或职责的; 牧师的; 牧师的地位或职责的: *hold ministerial office/rank* 主持部里的工作[具有部长的级别] ○ *a decision taken at ministerial level* 部长级的决定. **2** of or for a government ministry (or the Cabinet) (政府的)部的, 为部的; 内阁的; 为内阁的: *the ministerial benches* 执政党阁员的席位. ▷ **min·is·teri·ally** /-ɪəlɪ; -ɪəlɪ/ *adv.*

min·is·trant /ˈmɪnɪstrənt; ˈmɪnɪstrənt/ *adj* [attrib 作定语] (*fml* 文) giving help or service, esp in religious ceremonies 提供帮助或服务的(尤指于宗教仪式中).

▷ **min·is·trant** *n* (*fml* 文) supporter or helper; attendant 帮助者; 服侍者.

min·is·tra·tion /ˌmɪnɪˈstreɪʃn; ˌmɪnəˈstreʃən/ *n* (*fml* 文) **(a)** [U] helping or serving, eg at a religious ceremony 帮助, 服务(如于宗教仪式中): *the ministration of the sacraments* 行圣事. **(b)** [C usu *pl* 通常作复数] instance of this 帮助; 服务; 行宗教仪式: *The ministrations* (ie care and nursing) *of my wife restored me to health.* 我妻子护理我使我恢复了健康.

min·is·try /ˈmɪnɪstrɪ; ˈmɪnɪstrɪ/ *n* **1** (*US* **department**) [C] (buildings containing a) government department (政府的)部, 部的办公楼: *the ˈAir Ministry* 航空部 ○ *the ˌMinistry of Deˈfence* 国防部. **2 (a) the ministry** [Gp] the ministers of (esp the Protestant) religion as a body (全体)牧师(尤指新教的): *His parents intended him for the ministry,* ie wanted him to become a minister. 他父母有意让他当牧师. **(b)** [C usu *sing* 通常作单数] duties or (period of) service of a minister of religion 牧师的职责; 牧师的服务(期限): *enter/go into/take up the ministry,* ie train to become a minister of religion 做[从事/担任]牧师工作.

mink /mɪŋk; mɪŋk/ *n* **1** [C] small stoat-like animal of the weasel family 貂. **2 (a)** [U] its valuable thick brown fur 貂皮: [attrib 作定语] *a mink stole, coat* 貂皮披肩、大衣. **(b)** [C] coat made from this fur 貂皮大衣: *wearing her new mink* 穿着她的新貂皮大衣.

min·now /ˈmɪnəʊ; ˈmɪno/ *n* (*pl* unchanged or **~s** 复数或不变或作 **minnows**) any of several types of very small freshwater fish of the carp family 米诺鱼(鲤科淡水小鱼的总称).

mi·nor /ˈmaɪnə(r); ˈmaɪnɚ/ *adj* **1** [usu attrib 通常作定语] smaller, less serious, less important, etc 较小的; 程度轻的; 次要的: *a minor road,* eg in the country 辅助道路(如郊野的) ○ *minor repairs, alterations, etc* 小规模的修理、修改等 ○ *a minor operation,* ie one that does not risk the patient's life 小手术 ○ *minor injuries, burns, fractures, etc* 轻度损伤、灼伤、骨折等 ○ *a minor part/role in a play* 剧中的次要角色 ○ *minor poets* 不重要的诗人. Cf 参看 MAJOR. **2** (*Brit dated or joc* 旧或谑) (in private schools) second or younger of two brothers or boys with the same surname (esp in the same school) (私立学校中)(兄弟俩或同姓男生中)年幼的, 小的: *Smith minor* 小史密斯. Cf 参看 MAJOR, JUNIOR 2. **3** (*music* 音) of or based on a scale that has a semitone above its second note 小调的; 小音阶的: *a minor third,* ie an interval of three semitones 小三度(含三个半音的音程) ○ *a song in a minor key,* ie one based on a minor scale 小调歌曲 ○ *a symphony in C minor* C小调交响曲. Cf 参看 MAJOR.

▷ **mi·nor** *n* **1** (*law* 律) person under the age of full legal responsibility (18 in the UK) 未成年人(在英国为18岁以下). **2** (*US*) subsidiary subject or course of a student at college or university (大学中)副修科目.

mi·nor *v* [Ipr] **~ in sth** (*US*) (of a student) study sth as a subsidiary subject (指学生)副修某科.

□ **minor ˈplanet** asteroid 小行星.

minor ˈsuit (in card-games, esp bridge) diamonds or clubs (纸牌, 尤指桥牌的)低花色牌(方块或梅花).

mi·nor·ity /maɪˈnɒrətɪ; *US* -ˈnɔːr-; maɪˈnɔrətɪ/ *n* **1 (a)** [CGp] (usu *sing* 通常作单数) smaller number or part (esp of people voting or of votes cast) 少数(尤指投票者或票数): *Only a minority of British households do/does not have a car.* 英国只有少数家庭没有汽车. ○ *A small minority voted against the motion.* 投票反对该动议的人占少数. ○ [attrib 作定语] *a minority vote, opinion, point of view, etc,* ie one cast, held, etc by a smaller number of people 少数人的票、意见、观点等. **(b)** [C] small group in a community, nation, etc, differing from others in race, religion, language, etc (一社区、国家等, 其中种族、宗教, 语言等异于他人的)小团体, 少数: *the rights of ethnic minorities* 少数民族的权利 ○ [attrib 作定语] *belong to a minority group* 属于少数人团体的 ○ *minority rights* 少数派的权利. Cf 参看 MAJORITY. **2** [U] (*law* 律) state or period of being a minor 未成年: *be in one's minority,* eg under 18 in the UK 尚未成年(如在英国为18岁以下). **3** (idm 习语) **be in a/the minority** be in the smaller of esp two voting groups 是少数派(尤指在投票的两部分人中): *We're in the minority,* ie More people are against us than with us. 我们是少数派. ○ *I'm in a minority of one,* ie No one agrees with me. 我是唯一的少数派.

□ **miˌnority ˈgovernment** government that has fewer seats in a legislative assembly than the total number held by the opposition parties 在立法议会占少数席位的党派组成的政府.

min·ster /ˈmɪnstə(r); ˈmɪnstɚ/ *n* (*Brit*) large or important church, esp one that once belonged to a monastery 大教堂(尤指隐修院的): *York Minster* 约克大教堂.

min·strel /ˈmɪnstrəl; ˈmɪnstrəl/ *n* **1** (in the Middle Ages) travelling composer, player and singer of songs and ballads (中世纪的)游方诗歌演唱者. **2** (usu *pl* 通常作复数) one of a company of public entertainers with blackened faces, etc performing supposedly Negro songs and music (由白人扮演黑人的)音乐歌唱团演员: [attrib 作定语] *a minstrel show* 由白人扮演黑人的音乐演唱会.

▷ **min·strelsy** /ˈmɪnstrəlsɪ; ˈmɪnstrəlsɪ/ *n* [U] art, songs, etc of minstrels (MINSTREL 1) 游方诗歌演唱者的技艺、诗歌等.

mint[1] /mɪnt; mɪnt/ *n* **1** [U] any of various types of aromatic herb whose leaves are used for flavouring food, drinks, toothpaste, chewing-gum, etc 薄荷: *a sprig of mint,* eg in a cocktail 一小枝薄荷(如放于鸡尾酒中的) ○ [attrib 作定语] *mint ˈsauce,* ie mint leaves chopped up in vinegar and sugar, usu eaten with roast lamb 薄荷沙司(用薄荷叶末加糖和醋制成, 通常用以佐食烤小羊肉). **2** [U, C] = PEPPERMINT: *Do you like mints?* 你喜欢薄荷吗? ▷ **minty** /ˈmɪntɪ; ˈmɪntɪ/ *adj.*

mint[2] /mɪnt; mɪnt/ *n* **1** [C] place where coins are made, usu under State authority 铸币厂: *coins fresh from the mint* 刚出厂的硬币 ○ *the Royal Mint,* ie that of the UK, in Wales 皇家铸币厂(在威尔士). **2** [sing] (*infml* 口) very large amount of money 巨款: *She made an absolute mint (of money) in the fashion trade.* 她在时装业上赚了一大笔(钱). **3** (idm 习语) **in mint condition** (as if) new; unsoiled; perfect 簇新的; 无污损的; 完美的: *coins, banknotes, postage stamps, books, etc in mint condition* 崭新的硬币、纸币、邮票、书等.

▷ **mint** *v* [Tn] **1** make (a coin) by stamping metal 铸造(硬币): *newly-minted £1 coins* 新造的1英镑硬币. **2** (*fig* 比喻) invent (a word, phrase, etc) 创造(词、词组等): *I've just minted a new word!* 我刚造了一个新词!

min·uet /ˌmɪnjʊˈet; ˌmɪnjʊˈɛt/ *n* (piece of music for a) slow graceful dance in triple time 小步舞(一种缓慢优美的三拍舞蹈); 小步舞曲.

minus /ˈmaɪnəs; ˈmaɪnəs/ *prep* **1** (*mathematics* 数) with the deduction of; less 减; 减去: *Seven minus three equals four (7 — 3 = 4).* 七减三等于四. **2** below zero 零下: *a temperature of minus ten degrees centigrade (-10°C)* 零下十摄氏度的温度(-10°C). **3** (*infml* 口) without or lacking; deprived of 无; 缺少; 减少: *He came back from the war minus a leg.* 他打仗回来, 少了一条腿. ○ *I'm minus my car today,* eg because it's being repaired. 今天我没汽车了(如正在修理). Cf 参看 PLUS.

▷ **minus** *adj* **1** (*mathematics* 数) negative 负的: *a minus quantity,* ie a quantity less than zero (eg $-2x^2$) 负量(小于零, 如$-2x^2$). **2** [pred 作表语] (of marks or grades) of a standard slightly lower than the one stated (指分数或等级)略低于某标准: *I got B minus (B-) in the test.* 我测验得个B-.

minus *n* **1** (also **minus sign**) the mathematical symbol — 减号, 负号(—). ⇨App 4 见附录4. **2** (*infml* 口) disadvantage or drawback 不利; 不足; 缺点: *Let's consider the pluses and minuses of moving house.* 咱们考虑一下搬家的利弊吧. Cf 参看 PLUS.

min·us·cule /ˈmɪnəskjuːl; mɪˈnʌskjul/ *adj* very small; tiny 极小的; 微小的.

min·ute[1] /ˈmɪnɪt; ˋmɪnɪt/ *n* **1** (**a**) [C] one sixtieth part of an hour, equal to 60 seconds 分(一小时的六十分之一, 等于60秒): *It's ten minutes to/past six.* 现在是差十分六点[六点过十分]. ○ *I arrived a couple of minutes early/late.* 我早[晚]到了两三分钟. ○ *My house is ten minutes (away) from* (ie It takes ten minutes to drive, walk, etc from it to) *the shops.* 从我家到商业区(相去)有十分钟的路程. ○ *We caught the bus with only minutes to spare.* 我们只差几分钟就赶不上公共汽车了. ⇨App 5 见附录5. (**b**) [sing] very short time; moment 片刻; 瞬间; 一会儿: *It only takes a minute to make a salad.* 做色拉用不了多少时间. ○ *Will you wait for me? I shan't be a minute.* 等等我行吗? 我马上就好. (**c**) [sing] exact point of time; instant 此时此刻; 立刻: *Stop it this minute!* ie immediately 立即停止! ○ *At that very minute, Tom opened the door.* 就在那时候, 汤姆打开了门. **2** [C] one sixtieth part of a degree, used in measuring angles 分(量度弧或角的单位, 六十分之一度): *37 degrees 30 minutes (37°30')* 37度30分(37° 30'). **3** [C] official note that records a decision or comment, or gives authority for sth to be done 正式记录; 备忘录: *make a minute of sth* 记录某事物. **4 minutes** [pl] brief summary or record of what is said and decided at a meeting, esp of a society or committee 会议记录: *We read (through) the minutes of the last meeting.* 我们(从头到尾)把上次会议记录看了一遍. ○ *Who will take* (ie make notes for) *the minutes?* 谁做记录? **5** (idm 习语) **(at) any minute/moment (now)** (*infml* 口) very shortly or soon 随时; 马上: *The leading cyclist will be coming round that corner any minute now!* 为首的那个自行车手很快就要从那个转角处绕过来! **in a ˈminute** very soon 马上; 立刻: *Our guests will be here in a minute!* 我们的客人马上就到! **ˌjust a ˈminute** (*infml* 口) wait for a short time (usu while the speaker says or does sth) 稍等片刻(通常说话人此时在说或做某事): *Just a minute! Let me put your tie straight.* 请等等! 我帮你正正领带. **the last minute/moment** ⇨ LAST[1] **ˌnot for a/one ˈminute/ˈmoment** (*infml* 口) not at all 一点儿也不; 从不; 根本不: *I never suspected for a minute that you were married.* 我万万没想到你已经结婚了. **the minute/moment (that)...** as soon as... 一...就...: *I want to see him the minute (that) he arrives.* 他一来到我就要见他. **there's one born every minute** ⇨ BORN. **to the ˈminute** exactly 准时: *The train arrived at 9.05 to the minute.* 火车在9时零5分准时到达. **ˌup to the ˈminute** (*infml* 口) (**a**) fashionable 最新的; 时髦的: *Her clothes are always right up to the minute.* 她的衣着总是很入时. ○ [attrib 作定语] *an ˌup-to-the-ˈminute look, dress, style, etc* 时新的样式、连衣裙、款式等. (**b**) having the latest information 有最新消息的: [attrib 作定语] *an ˌup-to-the-minute ˈnews bulletin, summary, etc* 有最新消息的简报、总结等.

▷ **min·ute** *v* [Tn] make a note of (sth) in an official memorandum; record (sth) in the minutes (MINUTE[1] 4) 将(某事)载入备忘录或会议记录: *minute an action point, comment, etc* 记录一行动要点、评语等 ○ *Your suggestion will be minuted.* 你的建议将记录在案.

□ **ˈminute-book** *n* book in which minutes (MINUTE[1] 4) are written 会议记录本.

ˈminute-gun *n* gun fired at intervals of a minute, eg at a funeral 分炮(每一分钟放一次, 如致哀礼炮).

ˈminute-hand *n* hand on a watch or clock indicating the minutes (钟表的)分针.

ˈminute-man *n* (*pl* **-men**) (*US*) (formerly) militiaman or armed civilian ready to fight immediately if required (旧时)随时应召的民兵.

ˌminute ˈsteak thin piece of (usu beef) steak that can be cooked very quickly (速熟的)薄肉排(通常指牛排).

mi·nute[2] /maɪˈnjuːt; *US* -ˈnuːt; maɪˈnut/ *adj* (**-r, -st**) **1** very small in size or amount 极小的; 极少的: *minute particles of gold dust* 金沙中的微粒 ○ *water containing minute quantities of lead* 含有微量铅的水. **2** very detailed; accurate or precise 极详细的; 准确的; 精确的: *a minute description, inquiry, examination, inspection, etc* 详细的描述、调查、检查、视察等 ○ *The detective studied the fingerprints in the minutest detail.* 那侦探仔仔细细地研究了各个指纹. ▷ **mi·nutely** *adv.* **mi·nute·ness** *n* [U].

mi·nu·tiae /maɪˈnjuːʃiiː; *US* mɪˈnuːʃiː; mɪˈnuʃɪˌi/ *n* [pl] very small or unimportant details 微小的或不重要的细节: *I won't discuss the minutiae of the contract now.* 我现在不商谈合同的细节.

minx /mɪŋks; mɪŋks/ *n* (*derog or joc* 贬或谑) cunning, cheeky or mischievous girl 狡滑的、放肆的或顽皮的女孩儿: *She can be a proper litlle minx when she wants to get her own way!* 她有时为所欲为, 要发起坏来可真是个十足的小坏蛋!

mir·acle /ˈmɪrəkl; ˋmɪrəkḷ/ *n* **1** [C] good or welcome act or event which does not follow the known laws of nature and is therefore thought to be caused by some supernatural power 奇迹: *perform/work/accomplish miracles* 创造[产生/完成]奇迹 ○ *Her life was saved by a miracle.* 她性命得救全靠奇迹. ○ *The doctors said her recovery was a miracle.* 医生说她的康复是个奇迹. **2** [sing] (*infml fig* 口, 比喻) remarkable or unexpected event 惊人的或意外的奇事: *It's a miracle you weren't killed in that car crash!* 你在那次汽车撞车事故中大难不死, 真不可思议! ○ *It'll be a miracle if he ever gives up smoking!* 他要是真戒了烟, 那才怪呢! ○ [attrib 作定语] *a miracle cure, drug, etc* 有奇效的疗法、药物等. **3** [C] **~ of sth** remarkable example or specimen of sth 非凡的事例: *miracles of ingenuity, craftsmanship, etc* 了不起的智巧、手艺等 ○ *The compact disc is a miracle of modern technology.* 激光唱片是当代技术的奇葩. **4** (idm 习语) **do/work miracles/wonders (for/with sb/sth)** (*infml* 口) be remarkably successful in achieving positive results (for/with sb/sth) (对某人[某事物])有奇效, 极成功: *This tonic will work miracles for your depression.* 这种补药对治疗你的忧郁症十分有效. ○ *He can do miracles with a few kitchen leftovers*, eg by making them into a tasty meal. 他能用厨房里几样剩饭菜做出一顿美餐.

▷ **mi·ra·cu·lous** /mɪˈrækjʊləs; məˋrækjələs/ *adj* **1** like a miracle; contrary to the laws of nature 奇迹般的; 超自然的: *make a miraculous recovery* 奇迹般地康复. **2** (*infml* 口) remarkable or unexpected 神奇的; 不可思议的: *It's miraculous how much weight you've lost!* 你体重减轻了这么多, 真了不起! **mi·ra·cu·lously** *adv.*

□ **ˈmiracle play** medieval drama based on events in the Bible or the lives of Christian saints 神迹剧(中世纪戏剧, 取材自《圣经》或圣徒的故事). Cf 参看 MYSTERY PLAY (MYSTERY).

mir·age /ˈmɪrɑːʒ, mɪˈrɑːʒ; məˋrɑʒ/ *n* **1** optical illusion caused by hot air conditions, esp that of a sheet of water seeming to appear in the desert or on a hot road 海市蜃楼. **2** (*fig* 比喻) any illusion or hope that cannot be fulfilled 不能实现的希望; 幻想; 妄想.

mire /ˈmaɪə(r); maɪr/ *n* [U] **1** swampy ground or bog; soft deep mud 沼地; 泥潭; 泥浆; 淤泥: *sink into/get stuck in the mire* 陷入泥坑. **2** (idm 习语) **drag sb/sb's name through the mire/mud** ⇨ DRAG.

▷ **miry** /ˈmaɪərɪ; ˋmaɪrɪ/ *adj* swampy or boggy; muddy 沼泽的; 泥泞的.

mir·ror /ˈmɪrə(r); ˋmɪrɚ/ *n* **1** (often in compounds 常用以构成复合词) polished surface, usu of coated glass or of metal, that reflects images 镜子: *a ˈdriving-mirror*, eg in a car, to enable the driver to see what is behind 驾驶用反光镜(供驾驶者观看车后情况者) ○ *a ˈhand mirror*, ie a small one, esp as used by women 手镜(尤指女子用的小镜) ○ *She glanced at herself in the mirror.* 她照了一下镜子. ⇨illus at App 1 见附录1插图, page xvi. **2** (*fig* 比喻) thing that reflects or gives a likeness of sth 反映某事物的东西: *Pepys's 'Diary' is a mirror of/holds up a mirror to the times he lived in.* 佩皮斯的《日记》是他生活的那个时代的真实反映.

▷ **mir·ror** *v* [Tn] reflect (sth) as in a mirror 反射, 映照(某事物): *The trees were mirrored in the still water of the lake.* 静静的湖水映出岸上的树木. ○ (*fig* 比喻) *a novel that mirrors modern society* 反映现代社会的小说.

□ **ˌmirror ˈimage** reflection or copy of sth with the right and left sides of the original reversed 镜像, 反像(与原像左右相反).

mirth /mɜːθ; mɝθ/ *n* [U] (*fml* 文) merriment or happiness; laughter 欢乐; 快乐; 欢笑: *Her funny costume caused much mirth among the guests.* 她那滑稽的服装引得客人哄堂大笑. ▷ **mirth·ful** /-fl; -fəl/ *adj.* **mirth·less**

M

adj: *a mirthless laugh*, ie showing that one is not really amused 苦笑.

mis- *pref* 前缀 (with *vs* and *ns* 与动词和名词结合) bad; wrong; not 坏; 错; 不; 没; 无: *misdirect* ○ *misconduct* ○ *mistrust*.

mis·ad·ven·ture /ˌmɪsədˈventʃə(r); ˌmɪsədˋvɛntʃɚ/ *n* **1** [C, U] (*fml* 文) (piece of) bad luck; misfortune 不幸; 恶运; 灾祸; 不幸事件: *Their holiday was ruined by a whole series of misadventures.* 一连串的不幸事故把他们的假日全毁了. **2** [U] (*law* 律) accidental cause of death not involving crime or negligence 意外死亡: *death by misadventure* 意外致死.

mis·al·li·ance /ˌmɪsəˈlaɪəns; ˌmɪsəˋlaɪəns/ *n* unsuitable alliance, esp marriage with sb of a lower social class 不匹配的结合(尤指嫁娶地位较低的人): *make a misalliance* 作俯就的联姻.

mis·an·throp·ist /mɪˈsænθrəpɪst; mɪsˋænθrəpɪst/ (also **mis·an·thrope** /ˈmɪsənθrəʊp; ˋmɪsən,θrop/) *n* person who hates mankind and avoids human society 憎恶人类者; 避免与人交往者. Cf 参看 PHILANTHROPIST (PHILANTHROPY).

▷ **mis·an·thropic** /ˌmɪsənˈθrɒpɪk; ˌmɪsənˋθrɑpɪk/ *adj* hating or distrusting mankind or human society 憎恶人类的; 不信任世人的; 厌恶与人交往的.

mis·an·thropy /mɪˈsænθrəpɪ; mɪsˋænθrəpɪ/ *n* [U] hatred or distrust of mankind 对人类的憎恶或不信任.

mis·apply /ˌmɪsəˈplaɪ; ˌmɪsəˋplaɪ/ *v* (*pt, pp* **-lied**) [Tn] (*fml* 文) use (esp public funds) wrongly 误用, 滥用(尤指公款): *misapplied* (ie wasted) *efforts, talents* 浪费的精力、才干.

▷ **mis·ap·plica·tion** /ˌmɪsæplɪˈkeɪʃn; ˌmɪsæpləˋkeʃən/ *n* [U, C] wrong or unjust use of sth 误用; 滥用.

mis·ap·pre·hend /ˌmɪsæprɪˈhend; ˌmɪsæprɪˋhɛnd/ *v* [Tn] (*fml* 文) understand (words or a person) wrongly 误解(词语); 误会(某人)的意思.

▷ **mis·ap·pre·hen·sion** /ˌmɪsæprɪˈhenʃn; ˌmɪsæprɪˋhɛnʃən/ *n* (idm 习语) **under a misappreˈhension** not understanding correctly 在误解的情况下: *I thought you wanted to see me but I was clearly under a complete misapprehension.* 我以为你想见我, 显然完全是我误解了.

mis·ap·pro·pri·ate /ˌmɪsəˈprəʊprɪeɪt; ˌmɪsəˋproprɪ,et/ *v* [Tn] take (sb else's money) wrongly, esp for one's own use 误用, 滥用, 盗用(他人的钱财): *The treasurer misappropriated the society's funds.* 那会计盗用了协会的基金. ▷ **mis·ap·pro·pri·ation** /ˌmɪsəˌprəʊprɪˈeɪʃn; ˌmɪsə,proprɪˋeʃən/ *n* [U].

mis·be·got·ten /ˌmɪsbɪˈgɒtn; ˌmɪsbɪˋgɑtn/ *adj* [usu attrib 通常作定语] **1** badly planned; ill-advised 计划得不好的; 考虑不周的: *ˌmisbegotten ˈschemes, iˈdeas, ˈnotions, etc* 拙劣的计划、想法、主意等. **2** (**a**) (*dated* 旧) illegitimate; bastard 不合法的; 私生的. (**b**) (of a person) contemptible (指人)可鄙的.

mis·be·have /ˌmɪsbɪˈheɪv; ˌmɪsbɪˋhev/ *v* [I, Tn] **~ (oneself)** behave badly or improperly 行为不端; 举止不当. ▷ **mis·be·ha·viour** (*US* **mis·be·ha·vior**) /ˌmɪsbɪˈheɪvɪə(r); ˌmɪsbɪˋhevjɚ/ *n* [U].

misc *abbr* 缩写 = miscellaneous.

mis·cal·cu·late /ˌmɪsˈkælkjʊleɪt; mɪsˋkælkjə,let/ *v* [I, Tn, Tw] calculate (amounts, distances, measurements, etc) wrongly 误算(数量、距离、量度数等): *There's too much meat. I must have miscalculated the amount/how much I needed.* 肉多了. 准是我算错需要的量了. ▷ **mis·cal·cu·la·tion** /ˌmɪskælkjʊˈleɪʃn; ˌmɪskælkjəˋleʃən/ *n* [C, U]: *I made a slight miscalculation.* 我的计算有点错误.

mis·car·riage /ˌmɪsˈkærɪdʒ, ˈmɪskærɪdʒ; mɪsˋkærɪdʒ/ *n* **1** (**a**) [U] spontaneous, premature loss of a foetus from the womb 流产; 小产. (**b**) [C] instance of this 流产; 小产: *have/suffer a miscarriage* 流产. Cf 参看 ABORTION 1. **2** (**a**) [U, C] (*commerce* 商) (instance of) failure to arrive at, or deliver goods to, the right destination (货物的)误送, 误投, 误交: *miscarriage of goods, freight, letters, etc* 商品、货物、信件等的误送. (**b**) [U, C] failure of a plan, etc (计划等的)失败: *the miscarriage of one's hopes, schemes, etc* 希望、规划等的落空.

□ **miscarriage of ˈjustice** (*law* 律) failure of a court to administer justice properly 审判不公; 误审; 误判: *Sending an innocent man to prison is a clear miscarriage of justice.* 把无辜的人投入监狱显然是审判不公.

mis·carry /ˌmɪsˈkærɪ; mɪsˋkærɪ/ *v* (*pt, pp* **-ried**) [I] **1** (of a pregnant woman) have a miscarriage (指孕妇)流产, 小产. **2** (of plans, etc) fail; have a result different from what was hoped for (指计划等)失败, 未达预期结果. **3** (of goods, letters, etc) fail to reach the right destination (指货物、信件等)误送, 误投, 误交.

mis·cast /ˌmɪsˈkɑːst; *US* -ˈkæst; mɪsˋkæst/ *v* (*pt, pp* **miscast**) **1** [usu passive 通常用于被动语态: Tn, Cn·n/a] **~ sb (as sb/sth)** give (an actor, etc) a role for which he is not suitable 使(演员等)扮演不适合的角色: *The young actor was badly miscast as Lear/in the role of Lear.* 那个年轻演员扮演李尔王, 这一角色安排很不合适. **2** [Tn usu passive 通常用于被动语态] allocate the parts in (a play, etc) unsuitably 分派(戏剧等)的角色不当: *The film was thoroughly miscast.* 这部电影的角色分配完全失当.

mis·ce·gena·tion /ˌmɪsɪdʒɪˈneɪʃn; ˌmɪsɪdʒəˋneʃən/ *n* [U] mixture of races; production of offspring by two people of different (esp white and non-white) races 人种混杂; 异族(尤指白人与非白人)结合生育子女.

mis·cel·lan·eous /ˌmɪsəˈleɪnɪəs; ˌmɪslˋenɪəs/ *adj* [usu attrib 通常作定语] **1** of various kinds 各种各样的; 不同种类的: *miscellaneous items, goods, expenses* 杂项、杂货、杂费. **2** of mixed composition or character 不同成分的; 性质混杂的: *a miscellaneous collection, assortment, selection, etc* 多种多样的搜集、混杂、精选等 ○ *Milton's miscellaneous prose works*, eg essays, tracts, etc 弥尔顿散文集锦.

mis·cel·lany /mɪˈselənɪ; *US* ˈmɪsəleɪnɪ; ˋmɪsl̩,enɪ/ *n* **~ (of sth)** **1** varied collection of items 杂集: *The show was a miscellany of song and dance.* 那场演出是又有歌曲又有舞蹈的混合表演. **2** book containing a collection of writings, esp by different authors about different subjects 文集; (尤指不同作家不同作品的)杂集, 文选集.

mis·chance /ˌmɪsˈtʃɑːns; *US* -ˈtʃæns; mɪsˋtʃæns/ *n* [C, U] (*fml* 文) (piece of) bad luck 不幸; 坏运气: *a series of mischances* 一连串的不幸 ○ *I lost your file by pure mischance.* 我把你的文件弄没了, 纯粹是碰上的倒霉事.

mis·chief /ˈmɪstʃɪf; ˋmɪstʃɪf/ *n* **1** [U] behaviour (esp of children) that is annoying or does slight damage, but is not malicious (used esp as in the expressions shown) 恶作剧, 捣蛋, 顽皮, 淘气(尤用于以下示例): *act out of mischief* 调皮的举动 ○ *Those girls are fond of mischief*, ie of playing tricks, etc. 那些女孩儿爱淘气. ○ *Tell the children to keep out of mischief.* 告诉那些孩子别胡闹. ○ *He's up to* (ie planning) *some mischief again!* 他又在琢磨使坏呢! ○ *She's always getting into mischief.* 她总是要搞点恶作剧. **2** [C] person who is fond of mischief 调皮捣蛋的人: *Where have you hidden my book, you little mischief?* 你这个小淘气, 把我的书藏到哪里去了? **3** [U] tendency to tease or annoy playfully 淘气; 顽皮: *There was mischief in her eyes.* 她眼中流露出调皮的神情. ○ *The kittens were full of mischief.* 这些小猫很顽皮. **4** [U] moral harm or injury, esp caused by a person 道德上的损害或伤害(尤指人为的): *His malicious gossip caused much mischief until the truth became known.* 他散布流言蜚语危害很大, 事后才真相大白. **5** (idm 习语) **ˌdo sb/oneself a ˈmischief** (*infml or joc* 口或谑) hurt sb/oneself physically (肉体上)伤害某人[自己]: *You could do yourself a mischief on that barbed-wire fence!* 别碰那道铁丝网, 能钩伤你的! **make ˈmischief** do or say sth to upset, annoy or provoke others 说出气人的或招惹人的话; 做出这种事: *Don't let her make mischief between you — she's only jealous.* 别让她在你们之间挑拨 —— 她就是太忌妒了. **mean mischief** ⇨ MEAN[1].

□ **ˈmischief-maker** *n* person who deliberately causes trouble or discord 惹是非者; 制造不和者. **ˈmischief-making** *n* [U].

mis·chiev·ous /ˈmɪstʃɪvəs; ˋmɪstʃɪvəs/ *adj* **1** (of a person) filled with, fond of or engaged in mischief (指人)顽皮的, 爱胡闹的, 淘气的: *He's as mischievous as a monkey!* 他像猴子那么顽皮! **2** (of behaviour) showing a spirit of mischief (指行为)恶作剧的, 捣乱的: *a mischievous look, smile, trick* 调皮的样子、微笑、花招. **3** (*fml* 文) (of a thing) causing harm or damage (指事物)造成伤害或破坏的: *a mischievous letter,* *rumour* 恶意中伤的信、谣言. ▷ **mis·chiev·ously** *adv*. **mis·chiev·ous·ness** *n* [U].

mis·cible /ˈmɪsəbl; ˈmɪsəbl̩/ *adj* **~ (with sth)** (*fml* 文) (of liquids) that can be mixed (指液体)可混和的: *Oil and water are not miscible.* 油和水不能混和.

mis·con·ceive /ˌmɪskənˈsiːv; ˌmɪskənˈsiv/ *v* [Tn esp passive 尤用于被动语态] (*fml* 文) have a wrong idea or understanding of (sth) 对(某事)有错误观念; 误解(某事): *The housing needs of our inner cities have been misconceived from the start.* 我们旧城区的住房需求一开始就受到误解. ▷ **mis·con·cep·tion** /ˌmɪskənˈsepʃn; ˌmɪskənˈsɛpʃən/ *n* [U, C]: *dispel misconceptions* 消除误解 ○ *It is a popular misconception* (ie Many people wrongly believe) *that all Scotsmen are mean.* 很多人误以为苏格兰人都很小气. Cf 参看 PRECONCEPTION.

mis·con·duct /ˌmɪsˈkɒndʌkt; mɪsˈkɑndʌkt/ *n* [U] (*fml* 文) **1** (*esp law* 尤用于法律) improper behaviour, esp of a sexual or professional kind 不端行为(尤指性关系或职业方面): *guilty of grave/serious misconduct* 有重大的[严重的]行为不端罪 ○ *She sued for divorce on the grounds of her husband's alleged misconduct with his secretary.* 她以其夫与秘书有染为由提起离婚诉讼. **2** bad management; professional negligence 管理或处理不善; 疏忽职守: *misconduct of the company's affairs* 对公司事务管理不善.

▷ **mis·con·duct** /ˌmɪskənˈdʌkt; ˌmɪskənˈdʌkt/ *v* (*fml* 文) **1** [Tn, Tn·pr] **~ oneself (with sb)** behave improperly, esp with a member of the opposite sex 行为不检(尤指与异性). **2** [Tn] manage (sth) badly 管理或处理(某事物)不当.

mis·con·struc·tion /ˌmɪskənˈstrʌkʃn; ˌmɪskənˈstrʌkʃən/ *n* [C, U] (*fml* 文) (instance of) false or inaccurate interpretation or understanding 曲解; 误解: *What you say is open to misconstruction*, ie could easily be misunderstood. 你的话易遭曲解. ○ *It is possible to place/put a misconstruction on these words*, ie assume them to mean what they do not. 这些词语有可能引起误解.

mis·con·strue /ˌmɪskənˈstruː; ˌmɪskənˈstru/ *v* [Tn, Tw] (*fml* 文) get a wrong idea of or misinterpret (sb's words, acts, etc) 误解, 误会(某人的话、行为等): *You have completely misconstrued me/my words/what I said.* 你完全误解了我[我的话/我的意思]了.

mis·count /ˌmɪsˈkaʊnt; mɪsˈkaʊnt/ *v* [I, Tn] count (sth) wrongly 算错, 数错(某物): *We've got too many chairs — I must have miscounted.* 我们的椅子太多了 —— 一定是我算错了.

▷ **mis·count** /ˈmɪskaʊnt; ˈmɪsˌkaʊnt/ *n* wrong count, esp of votes at an election 计算错误; (尤指选票的)误计, 数错, 算错.

mis·cre·ant /ˈmɪskrɪənt; ˈmɪskrɪənt/ *n* (*dated* 旧) villain; wrongdoer 歹徒; 恶棍; 坏人.

mis·date /ˌmɪsˈdeɪt; mɪsˈdet/ *v* [Tn] **1** give a wrong date to (an event, etc) 将(事情等)日期弄错. **2** write a wrong date on (a letter, cheque, etc) 在(信、支票等)上写错日期.

mis·deal /ˌmɪsˈdiːl; mɪsˈdil/ *v* (*pt, pp* **misdealt** /-ˈdelt; -ˈdɛlt/) [I, Tn] deal (playing-cards) wrongly 发错(纸牌).

▷ **mis·deal** *n* error in dealing cards; hand of cards wrongly dealt 发牌错误; 发错的牌: *I've got 14 cards; it's a misdeal!* 我得了14张牌, 发错了!

mis·deed /ˌmɪsˈdiːd; mɪsˈdid/ *n* (usu *pl* 通常作复数) (*fml* 文) wicked act; crime 恶行; 罪行: *punished for one's many misdeeds* 因多行不义受惩罚.

mis·de·mean·our (*US* **mis·de·meanor**) /ˌmɪsdɪˈmiːnə(r); ˌmɪsdɪˈminɚ/ *n* **1** (*infml or joc* 口或谑) minor wrongdoing; misdeed 程度轻的恶行; 罪行: *petty misdemeanours* 越轨. **2** (*law* 律) (formerly, in Britain) punishable offence less serious than a felony (旧时, 英国)轻罪, 小罪.

mis·dir·ect /ˌmɪsdɪˈrekt, -daɪˈrekt; ˌmɪsdəˈrɛkt, -daɪˈrɛkt/ *v* **1** [Tn, Tn·pr] **~ sb/sth (to sth)** instruct sb to go or send sth to the wrong place 给某人指错方向; 将某物送错地方: *misdirect sb to the bus station instead of the coach station* 错将公共汽车站当作长途汽车站指示给某人 ○ *The letter was misdirected to our old address.* 那信误投到我们原来的地址了. **2** [Tn esp passive 尤用于被动语态] use (sth) in a wrong or pointless way 误用, 滥用(某物): *misdirected energies, abilities, etc* 使用不当的精力、能力等 ○ *misdirected* (ie undeserved) *criticism, sarcasm, etc* 不应受到的批评、讽刺等 ○ *Your talents are misdirected — study music, not maths!* 你的才能没有发挥出来 —— 应该学音乐, 不应该学数学! **3** [Tn] (*law* 律) (of a judge in a lawcourt) give (the jury) wrong information on a point of law (指法官)给(陪审团)错误的指示. ▷ **mis·dir·ec·tion** /ˌmɪsdɪˈrekʃn, -daɪˈrek-; ˌmɪsdəˈrɛkʃən, -daɪˈrɛk-/ *n* [U].

mis·do·ing /ˌmɪsˈduːɪŋ; mɪsˈduɪŋ/ *n* (usu *pl* 通常作复数) (*fml* 文) wicked act; misdeed 恶行; 罪行.

mise-en-scène /ˌmiːz ɒn ˈseɪn; ˌmizɑnˈsen/ *n* [sing] (*French* 法) **1** (arrangement of) scenery, furniture, etc of a play on a stage; dramatic setting 舞台的布景、道具等; 舞台布置. **2** (*fig* 比喻) general surroundings of an event 事件的背景或环境: *the magnificent mise-en-scène of the Royal Wedding* 皇族婚礼的豪华场面.

miser /ˈmaɪzə(r); ˈmaɪzɚ/ *n* person who loves wealth for its own sake and spends as little as possible 守财奴; 吝啬鬼: (*infml fig* 口, 比喻) *Why don't you buy me a drink for a change, you old miser!* 你就不能也请我喝一杯, 你这老财迷!

▷ **miserly** *adj* (*derog* 贬) **1** like a miser; mean or selfish 似守财奴的; 吝啬的; 自私的: *miserly habits* 吝啬的习性. **2** barely adequate; meagre 贫乏的; 不足的: *a miserly allowance, share, portion, etc* 少得可怜的津贴、一份、一部分等. **miser·li·ness** *n* [U].

mis·er·able /ˈmɪzrəbl; ˈmɪzrəbl̩/ *adj* **1** very unhappy or uncomfortable; wretched 悲惨的; 难受的; 不幸的; 可怜的: *miserable from cold and hunger* 饥寒交迫 ○ *Refugees everywhere lead miserable lives.* 各地难民过着凄惨的生活. ○ *He makes her life miserable*, eg by his cruelty, selfishness, etc. 他使她的生活十分痛苦. ○ *Don't look so miserable!* 别这么愁眉苦脸的! **2** causing unhappiness or discomfort; unpleasant 造成不幸或痛苦的; 令人不快的: *miserable* (eg cold and wet) *weather* 令人难受的天气 ○ *a miserable afternoon* 使人不快的下午 ○ *live in miserable conditions* 在困苦的环境中生活. **3** poor in quality or quantity; too small or meagre 低劣的; 贫乏的; 小得或少得可怜的: *What a miserable meal that was!* 那顿饭真差劲! ○ *How can I keep a family on such a miserable wage?* 我怎么能靠这么可怜的工资养家? **4** [attrib 作定语] mean; contemptible 卑鄙的; 可耻的: *What a miserable old devil Scrooge was!* 斯克鲁奇是多么可恶的吝啬鬼呀! ○ *The plan was a miserable failure.* 那计划遭到狼狈不堪的失败. **5** (idm 习语) **miserable/ugly as sin** ⇨ SIN. ▷ **mis·er·ably** /-əblɪ; -əblɪ/ *adv*: *die miserably* 悲惨地死去 ○ *a miserably wet day* 令人不快的雨天 ○ *be miserably poor* 穷得可怜 ○ *We failed miserably to agree.* 我们不幸未能达成一致意见.

mis·ery /ˈmɪzərɪ; ˈmɪzərɪ/ *n* **1** [U] great suffering or discomfort (of mind or body) (精神或肉体的)痛苦, 难受: *suffer the misery of toothache* 受牙痛之苦 ○ *living in misery and want*, ie in wretched conditions and poverty 在穷困中生活 ○ *lead a life of misery* 过悲惨的生活. **2** [C usu *pl* 通常作复数] painful happening; great misfortune 痛苦的事; 大不幸: *the miseries of unemployment* 失业的痛苦. **3** [C] (*Brit infml* 口) person who is always miserable and complaining 总发牢骚不痛快的人: *It's no fun being with you, you old misery!* 你老发牢骚, 跟你在一起真没意思! **4** (idm 习语) **make sb's life a misery** ⇨ LIFE. **put sb out of his 'misery (a)** end sb's sufferings by killing him 杀死某人以结束其痛苦; 让某人一死百了. **(b)** (*joc* 谑) end sb's anxiety or suspense 使某人不再担忧或疑虑: *Put me out of my misery — tell me if I've passed or not!* 你就别让我受罪了 —— 告诉我我及格不及格! **put an animal, bird, etc out of its 'misery** end the suffering of an animal, etc by killing it 杀死某动物以结束其痛苦.

mis·fire /ˌmɪsˈfaɪə(r); mɪsˈfaɪr/ *v* **1** [I] (of a gun, rocket, etc) fail to go off correctly (指枪炮、火箭等)误发, 走火, 不发火, 射不出. **2** [I, Ipr] (of an engine, etc) fail to start or function properly (指发动机等)不能正常发动或工作: *The engine is misfiring badly on one cylinder.* 发动机有一个汽缸严重失灵. **3** [I] (*fig infml* 比喻, 口) fail to have the desired effect 未得到预期的结果; 未能奏效: *The joke misfired completely.* 这个笑话讲得完全不成功. Cf 参看 BACKFIRE (BACK[3]). ▷ **mis·fire** *n*.

mis·fit /ˈmɪsfɪt; ˈmɪsˌfɪt/ *n* **1** person not well suited to his work or his surroundings 不适应工作或环境的人: *a* *social misfit* 与社会格格不入的人 ○ *He always felt a bit of a misfit in the business world.* 他总觉得自己在商业界有些不适应. **2** article of clothing which does not fit well 不合身的衣着.

mis·for·tune /ˌmɪsˈfɔːtʃuːn; mɪsˋfɔrtʃən/ *n* **1** [U] bad luck 不幸; 厄运: *suffer great misfortune* 遭到极大不幸 ○ *companions in misfortune* 难友 ○ *Misfortune struck early in the voyage.* 起航之后即遭不测. ○ *They had the misfortune to be hit by a violent storm.* 他们不幸遇上了猛烈的风暴. **2** [C] instance of this; unfortunate condition, accident or event 不幸事故; 灾难; 灾祸: *She bore her misfortunes bravely.* 她勇敢地忍受着苦难.

mis·giv·ing /ˌmɪsˈgɪvɪŋ; mɪsˋgɪvɪŋ/ *n* [U, C esp *pl* 作不可数名词或可数名词, 后者尤作复数] (*fml* 文) (feeling of) doubt, worry, suspicion or distrust 疑虑; 担忧; 顾虑: *a heart/mind full of misgiving(s)* 心中疑虑丛生 ○ *I have serious misgivings about taking the job.* 我对是否接受那份工作顾虑重重.

mis·gov·ern /ˌmɪsˈgʌvn; mɪsˋgʌvɚn/ *v* [Tn] govern (a country, etc) badly or unjustly 治理(国家等)不当. ▷ **mis·gov·ern·ment** *n* [U].

mis·guided /ˌmɪsˈgaɪdɪd; mɪsˋgaɪdɪd/ *adj* [usu attrib 通常作定语] (*fml* 文) **1** (led by sb/sth to be) mistaken in one's opinions, thoughts, etc 受意见、想法等错误引导的: *His untidy clothes give one a misguided impression of him.* 他衣冠不整往往给人一种假象. **2** wrong or foolish in one's actions (because of bad judgement) (因判断力差)举措失当的或愚蠢的: *misguided zeal, energy, ability, etc* 未用于正途的热情、精力、能力等 ○ *The thief made a misguided attempt to rob a policewoman.* 那个贼不识好歹竟要抢劫一个女警察. ▷ **mis·guidedly** *adv*.

mis·handle /ˌmɪsˈhændl; mɪsˋhændl/ *v* [Tn] **1** handle or treat (sb/sth) roughly 粗暴处理或对待(某人[某物]); 虐待: *damage* (eg to a parcel) *caused by mishandling* 胡乱处理造成的损坏(如对包裹) ○ *A sensitive child should not be mishandled.* 对敏感的儿童不应粗暴. **2** (*fig* 比喻) deal with (sth) wrongly or inefficiently 处理(某事)不当或不力: *mishandle a situation, an affair, a business deal, etc* 处理一局势、事务、生意等不力 ○ *He mishandled the meeting badly and lost the vote.* 他没有主持好会议, 结果落选.

mis·hap /ˈmɪshæp; ˋmɪsˌhæp/ *n* (**a**) [C] unlucky accident (usu not serious) 不幸事故(通常不严重): *arrive home after many mishaps* 历经种种不幸后回到家中 ○ *We had a slight mishap with the car*, eg a puncture. 我们的汽车出了点小事儿(如轮胎扎破). (**b**) [U] bad luck 坏运气; 不幸: *Our journey ended without (further) mishap.* 我们的旅程(后来)一路平安.

mis·hear /ˌmɪsˈhɪə(r); ˌmɪsˋhɪr/ *v* (*pt, pp* **misheard** /-ˈhɜːd; -ˋhɝd/) [Tn, Tw] hear (sb/sth) incorrectly 听错(某人)的话; 听错(某事): *Was she asking for a lift? I must have misheard her/what she was saying.* 她是要求搭便车吗? 我一定是听错[她的话]了.

mis·hit /ˌmɪsˈhɪt; ˌmɪsˋhɪt/ *v* (**-tt-**, *pt, pp* **mishit**) [Tn] (in cricket, golf, etc) hit (the ball) badly or in a faulty way (板球、高尔夫球等)击(球)不佳或犯规.

▷ **mis·hit** /ˈmɪshɪt; ˋmɪsˌhɪt/ *n* bad or faulty hit 不佳的或犯规的一击.

mish·mash /ˈmɪʃmæʃ; ˋmɪʃˌmæʃ/ *n* [sing] **~ (of sth)** (*infml derog* 口, 贬) confused mixture 杂乱的一堆; 混杂: *not a proper plan, just a mishmash of vague ideas* 不是像样的计划, 仅是一些含混的想法.

mis·in·form /ˌmɪsɪnˈfɔːm; ˌmɪsɪnˋfɔrm/ *v* [esp passive 尤用于被动语态: Tn, Tn·pr] **~ sb (about sth)** (*fml* 文) give wrong information to sb; mislead sb intentionally or unintentionally 向某人提供错误信息; 有意或无意地错误引导某人: *I regret to say you have been misinformed (about that).* 很遗憾, (关于那事)你听到的情况不确. ▷ **mis·in·forma·tion** /ˌmɪsɪnfəˈmeɪʃn; ˌmɪsɪnfɚˋmeʃən/ *n* [U]. Cf 参看 DISINFORMATION.

mis·in·ter·pret /ˌmɪsɪnˈtɜːprɪt; ˌmɪsɪnˋtɝprɪt/ *v* [Tn, Tw] interpret (sb/sth) wrongly; make a wrong inference from (sth) 误解(某人[某事]); 误译; 误以为: *misinterpret sb's remarks/what sb says* 误解某人的话[某人的意思] ○ *He misinterpreted her silence as indicating agreement.* 他误以为她的沉默就是同意. ▷ **mis·in·ter·preta·tion** /ˌmɪsɪntɜːprɪˈteɪʃn; ˌmɪsɪnˌtɝprɪˋteʃən/ *n* [U, C]: *comments, actions, views, etc open to misinterpretation*, ie likely to be misinterpreted 易引起误解的评论、行为、观点等.

M

mis·judge /ˌmɪsˈdʒʌdʒ; mɪsˋdʒʌdʒ/ *v* [Tn, Tw] **1** form a wrong opinion of (sb/sth) 形成对(某人[某事物])的错误概念: *I'm sorry I misjudged you/your motives.* 对不起, 我误会你[你的动机]了. **2** estimate (eg time, distance, quantity) wrongly 错误估计(如时间、距离、数量): *I misjudged how wide the stream was and fell in.* 我对小河的宽度估计错误, 结果掉进河里了. ▷ **mis·judge·ment** (also **mis·judg·ment**) *n* [U, C].

mis·lay /ˌmɪsˈleɪ; mɪsˋle/ *v* (*pt, pp* **mislaid** /-ˈleɪd; -ˋled/) [Tn] (*often euph* 常作委婉语) put (sth) where it cannot easily be found; lose (sth), usu for a short time only 将(某物)放错地方(难以找到); 遗失(某物)(尤指一时): *I seem to have mislaid my passport — have you seen it?* 我好像把护照放在什么地方找不到了 —— 你看见了吗?

mis·lead /ˌmɪsˈliːd; mɪsˋlid/ *v* (*pt, pp* **misled** /-ˈled; -ˋlɛd/) **1** [Tn, Tn·pr] **~ sb (about/as to sth)** cause sb to have a wrong idea or impression about sb/sth 使某人对他人[某事物]产生错误想法或印象: *You misled me as to your intentions.* 你误使我对你的意图信以为真. **2** [Tn esp passive 尤用于被动语态] (**a**) lead or guide (sb) in the wrong direction 给(某人)领错路, 引错方向: *We were misled by the guide.* 向导给我们引错了路. (**b**) (*fig* 比喻) lead or guide (sb) into wrong behaviour or beliefs 将(某人)引入歧途: *misled by bad companions* 被损友带坏. **3** (phr v) **mislead sb into doing sth** cause sb to do sth by deceiving him 骗某人做某事: *He misled me into thinking he was rich.* 他使我误以为他很有钱.

▷ **mis·lead·ing** *adj* giving wrong ideas, etc; deceptive 使人误解的; 欺骗的: *misleading comments, advertisements, instructions* 使人产生误解的评论、广告、指令. **mis·lead·ingly** *adv*.

mis·man·age /ˌmɪsˈmænɪdʒ; mɪsˋmænɪdʒ/ *v* [Tn] manage (sth) badly or wrongly 处理或管理(某事物)不善或失当: *mismanage one's business affairs, finances, accounts, etc* 管理商务、财务、帐目不当 ○ *The company had been mismanaged for years.* 那公司多年经营不善. ▷ **mis·man·age·ment** *n* [U].

mis·match /ˌmɪsˈmætʃ; ˌmɪsˋmætʃ/ *v* [Tn usu passive 通常用于被动语态] match (people or things) wrongly or unsuitably 将(人或物)配合错, 配合不当: *mismatching colours* 不协调的颜色 ○ *The two players were badly mismatched*, eg one was much better than the other. 这两个选手实力悬殊.

▷ **mis·match** /ˈmɪsmætʃ; ˋmɪsˌmætʃ/ *n* act or result of mismatching 配错; 不相匹配; 不协调; 配合不当: *Their marriage was a mismatch — they had little in common.* 他们的婚姻不般配 —— 两人几无共同之处.

mis·name /ˌmɪsˈneɪm; mɪsˋnem/ *v* [Tn usu passive 通常用于被动语态] call (sb/sth) by a wrong or an unsuitable name 叫错, 误称(某人[某事物]); 给(某人[某事物])取错名; 姓或名不当: *That tall man is misnamed Mr Short!* 那个高个儿男子偏偏姓Short(矮小之意)!

mis·nomer /ˌmɪsˈnəʊmə(r); mɪsˋnomɚ/ *n* wrong use of a name, word or description 错用名称; 用词错误; 描述失当: *'First-class hotel' was a complete misnomer for the tumbledown farmhouse we stayed in.* 把我们住的那个摇摇欲坠的村舍称作'一流旅馆', 纯粹是乱用词语.

miso·gyn·ist /mɪˈsɒdʒɪnɪst; mɪˋsɑdʒənɪst/ *n* person who hates women 厌恶女人的人. ▷ **miso·gyny** *n* [U].

mis·place /ˌmɪsˈpleɪs; mɪsˋples/ *v* (*fml* 文) [Tn esp passive 尤用于被动语态] **1** put (sth) in the wrong place 将(某物)放错地方: *I've misplaced my glasses — they're not in my bag.* 我把眼镜放错地方了 —— 没在我的包里. **2** give (love, affection, etc) wrongly or unwisely 错误地或愚昧地付出(爱情、情感等): *misplaced admiration, trust, confidence, etc* 不应有的崇拜、信任、信心等. **3** use (words or actions) unsuitably 用词或行事不当: *If you think deafness is funny, you've got a very misplaced sense of humour.* 假若认为耳聋有趣, 这种幽默感十分不当.

mis·print /ˌmɪsˈprɪnt; mɪsˋprɪnt/ *v* [Tn, Tn·pr] **~ sth (as sth)** make an error in printing sth 印错或错印某物: *They misprinted John as Jhon.* 他们把John印成Jhon了.

▷ **mis·print** /ˈmɪsprɪnt; ˋmɪsˌprɪnt/ *n* error in printing 印刷错误: *Jhon is a misprint for John.* Jhon是John一字的印刷错误.

mis·pro·nounce /ˌmɪsprəˈnaʊns; ˌmɪsprəˋnaʊns/ *v* [Tn, Tn·pr] **~ sth (as sth)** pronounce (words or letters) wrongly 念错(字或字母); 发错(字或字母)的音: *She mispronounced 'ship' as 'sheep'.* 她把ship(船)念成sheep(羊)了. ▷ **mis·pro·nun·ci·ation** /ˌmɪsprəˌnʌnsɪˈeɪʃn; ˌmɪsprəˌnʌnsɪˈeʃən/ *n* [U, C].

mis·quote /ˌmɪsˈkwəʊt; mɪsˈkwot/ *v* [Tn, Tw] quote (sth written or spoken) wrongly, either intentionally or unintentionally (有意或无意地)错误引证(书面或口头的资料): *misquote a price, figure, etc* 引证价格、数字等有误 ○ *He is frequently misquoted in the press.* 新闻界常常错误地引证他的话. ○ *You misquoted me/what I said.* 你引用的不是我的原话. ▷ **mis·quo·ta·tion** /ˌmɪskwəʊˈteɪʃn; ˌmɪskwoˈteʃən/ *n* [C, U]: *misquotations from Shakespeare* 引述莎士比亚作品而出现的错误.

mis·read /ˌmɪsˈri:d; mɪsˈrid/ *v* (*pt, pp* **misread** /-ˈred; -ˈrɛd/) **1** [Tn, Tn·pr, Tw] **~ sth (as sth)** read sth wrongly 读错, 看错(某文字材料): *I misread the instructions/what the instructions said.* 我把说明书看错了. ○ *He misread 'the last train' as 'the fast train'.* 他把'末班车'误读成'快车'了. **2** [Tn] interpret (sb/sth) wrongly 误解(某人[某事]): *His tactlessness showed that he had completely misread the situation.* 他不能随机应变, 这表明他对情势完全误解了. ▷ **mis·read·ing** *n* [C, U]: *a misreading of the gas meter* 看错煤气表的数字.

mis·rep·res·ent /ˌmɪsˌreprɪˈzent; ˌmɪsrɛprɪˈzɛnt/ *v* [esp passive 尤用于被动语态: Tn, Tn·pr] **~ sb/sth (as sb/sth)** represent (sb/sth) wrongly; give a false account of sb/sth 表述(某人[某事物])失实; 歪曲(某人[某事物]): *She was misrepresented in the press as (being) a militant.* 新闻界把她歪曲为激进分子. ▷ **mis·rep·res·enta·tion** /ˌmɪsˌreprɪzenˈteɪʃn; ˌmɪsrɛprɪzɛnˈteʃən/ *n* [C, U]: *a gross misrepresentation of the facts* 对事实的严重歪曲.

mis·rule /ˌmɪsˈru:l; mɪsˈrul/ *n* [U] bad government; disorder or confusion 施政恶劣; 混乱; 无政府状态: *The country suffered years of misrule under a weak king.* 该国因国王懦弱而长期混乱不治.

miss¹ /mɪs; mɪs/ *n* **1** failure to hit, catch or reach sth aimed at 未击中; 未抓住; 未达到目标: *score ten hits and one miss* 共计击中十次, 未击中一次 ○ *The ball's gone right past him — that was a bad miss,* ie one he ought to have stopped, caught, etc. 那球就在他旁边经过——这一失误太不应该. **2** (idm 习语) **give sb/sth a 'miss** (*infml* 口) (**a**) omit sb/sth 略去、省掉或排除某人[某事物]: *I think I'll give the fish course a miss.* 我就不要鱼那道菜了吧. (**b**) not do sth, not go somewhere, not see sb, etc as one is in the habit of doing (与往常相反)不做某事、不去某处、不见某人等: *give yoga, the cinema, my boy-friend a miss tonight* 今晚权且不练瑜伽、不看电影、不见男朋友. **a ˌmiss is as ˌgood as a 'mile** (*saying* 谚) (**a**) an escape by a narrow margin (from danger, defeat, etc) is just as successful as an escape by a wide margin 九死一生总是生. (**b**) a failure by a narrow margin (to achieve success, etc) is just as disappointing as a failure by a wide margin 功败垂成终是败. **a near miss** ⇨ NEAR¹.

miss² /mɪs; mɪs/ *n* **1 Miss** (**a**) (title used with the name of an unmarried woman or kept by a married woman eg for professional reasons 用作未婚女子姓名之前的称谓语或已婚女子(如因职业关系)持有的称谓语): *Miss (Gloria) Kelly* (格洛丽亚·)凯利小姐 ○ *the Miss Hills* 希尔家的小姐们 ○ (*fml* 文) *the Misses Hill* 希尔家的小姐们. Cf 参看 MRS, MS. (**b**) (title given to the winner of a beauty contest in the specified country, town, etc 选美会上优胜者的头衔): *Miss England* 英格兰小姐 ○ *Miss Brighton* 布赖顿小姐 ○ *the Miss World contest* 世界小姐选美比赛. **2 Miss** (**a**) (used as a polite form of address to a young woman, eg by taxi-drivers, hotel staff, etc 用作对年轻女子的尊称(如为计程车司机、旅馆服务员等所使用)): *I'll take your luggage to your room, Miss.* 小姐, 我把您的行李送到您的房间去. Cf 参看 MADAM. (**b**) (used as a form of address by schoolchildren to a woman teacher 小学生对女教师的称呼): *Good morning, Miss!* 老师, 您早! Cf 参看 SIR 1. **3** (*joc or derog* 谑或贬) young girl or schoolgirl; young unmarried woman 年轻女子; 女学生; 年轻未婚女子: *She's a saucy little miss!* 她是个黄毛丫头!

miss³ /mɪs; mɪs/ *v* **1** [I, Tn, Tg] fail to hit, catch, reach, etc (sth aimed at) 未击中, 未抓住, 未达到(目标): *He shot at the bird but missed.* 他打鸟未打中. ○ *miss the target, mark, goal, etc* 未射中靶子、目标、球门等 ○ *The goalkeeper just missed (stopping) the ball.* 守门员只差一点儿就能把球接住了. ○ *miss one's footing,* ie slip or stumble, eg while climbing 失足(如攀登时打滑或跌倒) ○ *The plane missed the runway by several yards.* 飞机偏离跑道几码远. **2** [Tn, Tw] fail to see, hear, understand, etc (sb/sth) 未看见(某人[某事物]); 未听见(某人[某事物])的声音; 未明白(某人[某事物])的意思: *The house is on the corner; you can't miss it.* 那房子就在拐角处; 你不会找不到的. ○ *I'm sorry, I missed that/what you said.* 对不起, 我没听见那件事[你说的话]. ○ *He missed the point of my joke.* 他没有听懂我讲的笑话. **3** [Tn, Tg] fail to be present at (sth); arrive too late for (sth) 未出席, 未赶上(某事物): *miss a meeting, a class, an appointment, etc* 未参加会议、未上课、未赴约 ○ *He missed the 9.30 train.* 他没赶上9点30分的火车. ○ *We only missed (seeing) each other by five minutes.* 我们只因五分钟之差而未能见面. **4** [Tn, Tg] fail to take advantage of (sth) 未能利用(某事物): *miss the chance/opportunity of doing sth* 失掉或错过做某事的时机[机会] ○ *Don't miss our bargain offers!* 本店大减价, 勿失良机! **5** (**a**) [Tn] notice the absence or loss of (sb/sth) 发现(某人[某事物])不在或遗失: *When did you first miss your purse?* 你什么时候发现丢了钱包的? ○ *He's so rich that he wouldn't miss £100.* 他很有钱, 丢了100英镑也不在意. ○ *We seem to be missing two chairs.* 我们好像少了两把椅子. (**b**) [Tn, Tg, Tsg] feel regret at the absence or loss of (sb/sth) 因(某人[某事物])不在或遗失而感到惋惜: *Old Smith won't be missed,* eg when he is away, retires, dies, etc. 谁也不会因老史密斯不在而感到遗憾. ○ *I miss you bringing me cups of tea in the mornings!* 我常怀念早晨你给我送茶的情景! **6** [Tn, Tg] avoid or escape (sth) 避免, 躲避(某事物): *If you go early you'll miss the traffic.* 你早些走就能避开交通拥挤时间. ○ *We only just missed having a nasty accident.* 我们险些出了严重事故. **7** [I] (of an engine) misfire (指发动机)发动不起来. **8** (idm 习语) **hit/miss the mark** ⇨ MARK¹. **ˌmiss the 'boat/'bus** (*infml* 口) be too slow to take an opportunity 错过机会: *If we don't offer a good price for the house now, we'll probably miss the boat altogether,* ie It will be sold to someone else. 这所房子, 现在我们不给个高价, 可能就要失去机会了(可能要卖给别人了). **not 'miss much; not miss a 'trick** (*infml* 口) be very aware or alert 非常机警或警觉: *Jill will find out your secret — she never misses a trick!* 吉尔会发现你的秘密的——她很警觉! **(be) too good to 'miss** (be) too attractive or profitable to reject 很吸引人或很有利而无法拒绝或放弃: *The offer of a year abroad with all expenses paid seemed too good to miss.* 免付一切费用出国一年的优待未免太诱人了, 实在难以放弃. **9** (phr v) **miss sb/sth out** not include sb/sth 不包括某人[某事物]: *I'll miss out the sweet course,* ie not take it at a meal. 我不吃那道甜食了. ○ *We'll miss out* (eg not sing) *the last two verses.* 最后两句歌词我们不唱了. ○ *The printers have missed out a whole line here.* 排版工人在这里漏掉了一整行. **miss 'out (on sth)** (*infml* 口) lose an opportunity to benefit from sth or enjoy oneself 失去获得利益或获得乐趣的机会: *If I don't go to the party, I shall feel I'm missing out.* 我要是不去参加聚会一定觉得损失很大.

▷ **miss·ing** *adj* **1** (**a**) that cannot be found or that is not in its usual place; lost 找不到的; 不在原处的; 失去的: *The book had two pages missing/two missing pages.* 那本书缺两页. ○ *The hammer is missing from my tool-box.* 我的工具箱里少了一把锤子. (**b**) not present 不在场的: *He's always missing when there's work to be done.* 一到干活儿的时候, 他就不见了. **2** that cannot be found; absent from home 失踪的; 不在家的: *a police file on missing persons* 警方为失踪者立的档案 ○ *The child had been missing for a week.* 孩子下落不明已有一周了. **3** (of a soldier, etc) neither present after a battle nor known to have been killed (指士兵等)(战斗后)下落不明的: *Two planes were reported (as) missing.* 据报有两架飞机失踪. **4** (idm 习语) **a/the ˌmissing 'link** (**a**) thing needed to complete a series or solve a puzzle (为完成一系列事物或解决一难题)所缺的一环. (**b**) type of animal thought to have existed between the apes and early man 设想在类人猿和早期人类之间的过渡动物.

the missing *n* [pl *v*]: *Captain Jones is among the*

missing. 失踪者中有琼斯上尉.

mis·sal /ˈmɪsl; ˋmɪsḷ/ *n* book containing the prayers, etc for Mass throughout the year in the Roman Catholic Church (天主教的)弥撒书.

mis·shapen /ˌmɪsˈʃeɪpən; mɪsˋʃepən/ *adj* (esp of the body or a limb) badly shaped; deformed (尤指身躯或肢体)畸形的.

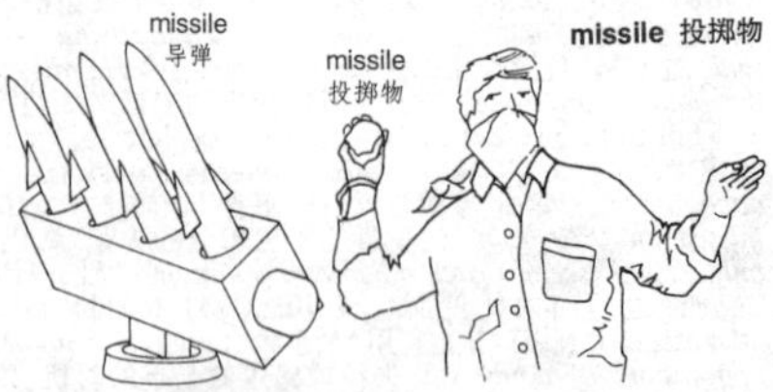

missile 投掷物

mis·sile /ˈmɪsaɪl; *US* ˈmɪsl; ˋmɪsḷ/ *n* **1** object or weapon that is thrown or fired at a target 可抛掷或发射之物或武器: *Missiles thrown at the police included stones and bottles.* 向警察投掷的东西有石块和瓶子. **2** (esp explosive) weapon directed at a target by remote control or automatically 导弹; 飞弹: *ballistic, guided, nuclear, etc missiles* 弹道、制导、核...导弹 ○ [attrib 作定语] *missile bases, sites, launching pads, etc* 导弹基地、发射场、发射台等. ⇨illus 见插图.

mis·sion /ˈmɪʃn; ˋmɪʃən/ *n* **1** (work done by a) group of people sent abroad, esp on political or commercial business 派往国外(尤指从事政治的或商务的)团体(的任务); (外交)使命团; (商业)代表团: *a British trade mission to China* 英国派往中国的商务代表团 ○ *go/come/send sb on a mission of inquiry* 去[来/派某人]执行调查任务 ○ *The delegation completed its mission successfully.* 代表团圆满地完成了任务. **2** (**a**) (work done by a) group of religious teachers sent to convert people (被派作传教活动的)布道团; 传教; 布道: *a Catholic, Methodist, etc mission in Africa* 天主教、循道宗信徒等在非洲的传教活动. (**b**) building or settlement where the work of such a mission is done, esp among poor people 布道的处所(尤指贫民居住区的): *The doctor works at the mission.* 那医生在贫民教区工作. ○ [attrib 作定语] *a mission station, school, hospital, etc* 布道所、教会学校、教会医院等. **3** (**a**) particular task or duty undertaken by an individual or a group (个人或集团担负的)特殊任务, 使命: *a top-secret mission* 绝密使命 ○ *My mission in life is to help poor people.* 我的天职是帮助穷人. (**b**) such a task or duty performed by an individual or a unit of the armed forces (部队个人或单位的)特别任务, 使命: *The squadron flew a reconnaissance mission.* 该空军中队执行一侦察任务. ○ [attrib 作定语] *mission control, headquarters, etc* 特别任务指挥中心、总指挥部等.

mis·sion·ary /ˈmɪʃənrɪ; *US* -nerɪ; ˋmɪʃənˌɛrɪ/ *n* person sent to preach usu the Christian religion, esp among people who are ignorant of it 传教士: *Catholic, Anglican, etc missionaries* 天主教、圣公会等传教士 ○ [attrib 作定语] *speak with missionary zeal*, ie great enthusiasm and commitment 以传教士般的热心讲话.

mis·sis = MISSUS.

mis·sive /ˈmɪsɪv; ˋmɪsɪv/ *n* (*fml or joc* 文或谑) letter, esp a long or official one 信件; (尤指)长信, 公函.

mis·spell /ˌmɪsˈspel; mɪsˋspɛl/ *v* (*pt, pp* **misspelled** or **misspelt** /-ˈspelt; -ˋspɛlt/) [Tn] spell (sth) wrongly 拼写错(某字). ⇨Usage at DREAM[2] 用法见 DREAM[2]. ▷ **mis·spell·ing** *n* [U, C].

mis·spend /ˌmɪsˈspend; mɪsˋspɛnd/ *v* (*pt, pp* **misspent** /-ˈspent; -ˋspɛnt/) [Tn esp passive 尤用于被动语态, Tn·pr] **~ sth (on sb/sth)** spend or use (money, time, etc) wrongly, foolishly or wastefully 滥用, 浪费, 虚掷(金钱、光阴等): *ˌmisspent ˈenergy, ˈtalent, enˈthusiasm, etc* 浪费精力、才能、热情等 ○ *a ˌmisspent ˈyouth*, ie one wasted on foolish pleasures 虚度的青春.

mis·state /ˌmɪsˈsteɪt; mɪsˋstet/ *v* [Tn] (*fml* 文) state (facts, etc) wrongly 错误地叙述(事实等): *Be careful not to misstate your case.* 小心别把你的情况讲错了. ▷ **mis·state·ment** *n*: *I wish to correct my earlier misstatement.* 我想更正我先前的不实之词.

mis·sus (also **mis·sis**) /ˈmɪsɪz; ˋmɪsəz/ *n* **1** (*infml or joc* 口或谑) (used esp by uneducated speakers; with *the, my, your, his* 未受过教育的人尤多用; 并与 the、my、your、his 连用) wife 妻子; 老婆: *How's the missus* (ie your wife)? 你老婆好吗? ○ *My missis hates me smoking indoors.* 我老婆讨厌我在屋里抽烟. **2** (*sl* 俚) (used as a form of address to a woman 用作对女子的称呼): *Are these your kids, missis?* 太太, 这些孩子是你的吗?

missy /ˈmɪsɪ; ˋmɪsɪ/ *n* (*dated infml* 旧, 口) (used as a polite or affectionate form of address to a young girl 用作对少女客气的或亲昵的称呼): *Well, missy, what do you want?* 喂, 小姐, 你要什么?

mist /mɪst; mɪst/ *n* **1** (**a**) [U, C] cloud of minute drops of water vapour hanging just above the ground, less thick than fog but still difficult to see through 薄雾; 雾霭; 雾气: *hills hidden/shrouded in mist* 雾霭笼罩着的小山 ○ *early morning mists in autumn* 秋日清晨的薄雾 ○ [attrib 作定语] *mist patches on the motorway* 高速公路上阵阵的雾. (**b**) [C usu *pl* 通常作复数] (*fig* 比喻) thing that is difficult to penetrate 难以透彻了解的事物: *dispel the mists of ignorance* 驱散愚昧的迷雾 ○ *lost in the mists of time* 湮没在时间的迷雾中. ⇨Usage at FOG 用法见 FOG. **2** [U] water vapour condensed on a cold surface, eg a window, mirror, etc making it look cloudy (凝结于物体表面的)水蒸气, 水汽, 水雾. **3** [sing] dimness or blurring of the sight 视线模糊不清: *She saw his face through a mist of tears.* 她泪眼朦胧地望着他的脸. **4** [U] fine spray of liquid, eg from an aerosol 液体细雾(如喷雾器喷出的): *A mist of perfume hung in the air.* 空气中飘溢着香水的雾气.

▷ **mist** *v* **1** [I, Tn] (cause sth to) be covered with mist or as if with mist (使某物)蒙上薄雾, 似被薄雾笼罩: *His eyes (were) misted with tears.* 他泪眼模糊了. ○ *mist the plants*, ie with an aerosol of water 给植物喷水. **2** (phr v) ˌ**mist ˈover** become covered with mist 蒙上薄雾: *The scene misted over.* 薄雾遮住了风景. ○ *When I drink tea, my glasses mist over.* 我喝茶时眼镜蒙上了一层水汽. ○ *His eyes misted over.* 他的眼睛模糊了. **mist (sth) up** cover or become covered by a film of water vapour 蒙上一层水蒸气: *Our breath is misting up the car windows.* 我们呼出的气渐渐给汽车的窗户上蒙上一层水蒸气.

misty *adj* (**-ier, -iest**) **1** full of or covered with mist 充满雾气的; 薄雾笼罩的: *a misty morning* 薄雾笼罩的早晨 ○ *misty weather* 雾天 ○ *a misty view* 雾景. **2** (*fig* 比喻) not clear; blurred or indistinct 不清楚的; 朦胧的; 模糊的: *a misty photograph* 一张模糊的照片. **mist·ily** *adv*. **mis·ti·ness** *n* [U].

mis·take[1] /mɪˈsteɪk; məˋstek/ *n* **1** wrong idea or opinion; misconception 错误的想法或见解; 误解; 误会: *You can't arrest me! There must be some mistake!* 你们不能逮捕我! 一定是弄错了! **2** thing done incorrectly through ignorance or wrong judgement; error 错误; 过失; 失策: *spelling mistakes* 拼写错误 ○ *learn by one's mistakes* 从错误中汲取教训 ○ *The waiter made a mistake over the bill.* 服务员把帐算错了. ○ *It was a big mistake to leave my umbrella at home.* 我把雨伞留在家里失算得很. **3** (idm 习语) **by miˈstake** as a result of carelessness, forgetfulness, etc; in error 错误地(因粗心、遗忘等所致): *I took your bag instead of mine by mistake.* 我错拿了你的手提包, 还以为是我的呢. **and ˌno miˈstake** (*infml* 口) without any doubt 毫无疑问; 的确: *It's hot today and no mistake!* 今天确实很热! ˌ**make no miˈstake (about sth)** (*infml* 口) do not be misled into thinking otherwise 别误会; 别误解: *Susan seems very quiet, but make no mistake (about it), she has a terrible temper!* 苏珊样子很文静, 可别产生误会, 她脾气坏极了!

NOTE ON USAGE 用法: **Mistake, error, blunder, fault** and **defect** all refer to something done incorrectly or improperly. ☆ **mistake**、**error**、**blunder**、**fault**、**defect** 都用以指没有做对或做得不妥的事物. **Mistake** is the most general, used of everyday situations ☆ **mistake** 词义最笼统, 可用于日常各种情况: *Your essay is full of mistakes.* 你的文章错误很多. ○ *It was a mistake to go there on holiday.* 跑到那儿度假真是失策.

Error is more formal ☆ **error** 较文: *an error in your calculations* 你计算中出现的错误 ○ *a technical error* 技术性错误. A **blunder** is a careless mistake, often unnecessary or resulting from misjudgement ☆ **blunder** 是粗心的错误, 常为不该有的或出于判断错误: *I made a terrible blunder in introducing her to my husband.* 我把她介绍给我的丈夫是犯了一个极大的错误. **Fault** emphasizes a person's responsibility for a mistake ☆ **fault** 侧重于造成错误的个人责任: *The child broke the window, but it was his parents' fault for letting him play football indoors.* 孩子把窗户打破了, 但是让他在屋里踢足球是他父母的过错. **Fault** can also indicate an imperfection in a person or thing ☆ **fault** 还可指人或物的缺点: *He has many faults, but vanity is not one of them.* 他有很多缺点, 但并没有虚荣心. ○ *an electrical fault* 电路的故障. A **defect** is more serious ☆ **defect** 指更为严重的缺陷: *The new car had to be withdrawn from the market because of a mechanical defect.* 那种新汽车因有机械缺陷只好撤出市场.

mis·take[2] /mɪˈsteɪk; məˋstek/ *v* (*pt* **mistook** /mɪˈstʊk; məsˋtʊk/, *pp* **mistaken** /mɪsˈteɪkən; məˋstekən/) **1** [Tn, Tw] be wrong or get a wrong idea about (sb/sth) 弄错、误解或误会(某人)或(某事物)的意思: *I must have mistaken your meaning/what you meant.* 我一定误会了你的意思. ○ *Don't mistake me, I mean what I say.* 别误解我的意思, 我说的就是这个意思. ○ *We've mistaken the house*, ie come to the wrong house. 我们找错门了. **2** [Tn·pr] **~ sb/sth for sb/sth** wrongly suppose that sb/sth is sb/sth else 误将某人[某事物]认作他人[他事物]: *mistake a toadstool for a mushroom* 误把毒菌当作蘑菇 ○ *She is often mistaken for her twin sister.* 她常被误认为是她的孪生妹妹. **3** (idm 习语) **there's no mistaking sb/sth** there is no possibility of being wrong about sb/sth 决不可能搞错某人[某事物]: *There's no mistaking what ought to be done.* 该做的事十分清楚.

▷ **mis·taken** *adj* **1** [usu pred 通常作表语] **~ (about sb/sth)** wrong in opinion 见解错误: *If I'm not mistaken, that's the man we saw on the bus.* 要是我没认错人的话, 我们在公共汽车上看见的就是那个男子. ○ *You're completely mistaken.* 你全错了. **2** wrongly judged; not correct 判断上错误的; 不正确的: *a case of mistaken identity* 认错人的事 ○ *mistaken ideas, views, etc* 错误的想法、见解等 ○ *I helped him in the mistaken belief that he needed me.* 我误以为他需要我所以去帮助他了. **3** applied unwisely 应用不当的; 行事不智的: *mistaken kindness, zeal, etc* 枉费的好心、热情等. **mis·tak·enly** *adv*.

mis·ter /ˈmɪstə(r); ˋmɪstɚ/ *n* **1** (full form, rarely used in writing, of the abbreviation *Mr* ☆ Mr之本字, 很少用于书写中). Cf 参看 MR. **2** (*sl* 俚) (used as a form of address to a man, esp by children, tradespeople, etc 用作对男子的称呼, 尤为儿童、商人等多用): *Please mister, can I have my ball back?* 先生, 请把球还给我行吗? ○ *Now listen to me, mister!* 先生, 请听我说!

mis·time /ˌmɪsˈtaɪm; mɪsˋtaɪm/ *v* [Tn esp passive 尤用于被动语态] say or do (sth) at a wrong or an unsuitable time 说或做(某事)非当其时, 不合时宜: *a mistimed remark, comment, etc* 不合时宜的话、评论等 ○ *a mistimed shot*, eg in golf 不适时的一击(如在打高尔夫球中) ○ *The government's intervention was badly mistimed.* 政府干涉得太不是时候了.

mis·tle·toe /ˈmɪsltəʊ; ˋmɪslˌto/ *n* [U] evergreen plant with small white berries that grows as a parasite esp on apple trees and is hung indoors as a Christmas decoration 槲寄生(常青植物, 尤寄生于苹果树, 结白色小浆果, 用作圣诞节室内悬挂的饰物): *the tradition of kissing under the mistletoe* 在槲寄生树下接吻的传统.

mis·took *pt* of MISTAKE.

mis·tral /ˈmɪstrəl, mɪˈstrɑːl; ˋmɪstrəl, mɪsˋtrɑl/ *n* **the mistral** [sing] strong cold dry N or NW wind that blows in S France, usu in winter 密史脱拉风(冬季法国南部的一种干冷而强劲的北风或西北风).

mis·trans·late /ˌmɪstrænsˈleɪt; ˌmɪstrænsˋlet/ *v* [I, Tn] translate (eg words) wrongly 误译; 译错(如词语). ▷ **mis·trans·la·tion** /-ˈleɪʃn; -ˋleʃən/ *n* [U, C].

mis·treat /ˌmɪsˈtriːt; ˌmɪsˋtrit/ *v* [Tn esp passive 尤用于被动语态] treat (sb/sth) badly or unkindly 虐待(某人); 糟蹋(某事物): *I hate to see books being mistreated.* 我看见人家糟蹋书籍就感到讨厌. ▷ **mis·treat·ment** *n* [U].

mis·tress /ˈmɪstrɪs; ˋmɪstrɪs/ *n* **1** woman in a position of authority or control 有权位的女子; 女主人: *mistress of the situation* 控制局面的女人 ○ *She wants to be mistress of her own affairs*, ie organize her own life. 她的事情她要自己作主. ○ (*dated* 旧) *Is the mistress of the house in?* (ie the female head of the household) 女主人在家吗? ○ (*fig* 比喻) *Venice was called the 'Mistress of the Adriatic'.* 威尼斯曾别称'亚得里亚海的门户'. Cf 参看 MASTER[1] 1. **2** female owner of a dog or other animal (狗的或其他动物的)女主人. **3** (*esp Brit*) female school teacher (中小学的)女教师: *the 'French mistress*, ie teacher of French (but not necessarily a Frenchwoman) 法语(女)教师(不一定是法国人) ○ *We've got a new 'games mistress* (ie one in charge of sport) *this year.* 今年我校新来了个女的体育教师. **4** woman having an illicit but regular sexual relationship, esp with a married man 情妇: *have/keep a mistress* 有情妇. Cf 参看 LOVER 1. **5** (*arch* 古) woman loved and courted by a man; sweetheart (女)情人, 爱人: *O mistress mine!* 噢, 我的爱人! **6** (idm 习语) **be one's own master/mistress** ⇨ MASTER[1].

mis·trial /ˌmɪsˈtraɪəl; mɪsˋtraɪəl/ *n* (*law* 律) **1** trial that is invalid because of some error in the proceedings (因诉讼程序有误的)无效审判. **2** (*US*) trial in which the jury cannot agree on a verdict (因陪审团意见有分歧的)未决审判.

mis·trust /ˌmɪsˈtrʌst; mɪsˋtrʌst/ *v* [Tn] **1** feel no confidence in (sb/sth) 不相信, 不信任(某人[某事物]): *mistrust one's own judgement* 不相信自己的判断. **2** be suspicious of (sb/sth) 怀疑(某人[某事物]): *mistrust sb's motives* 怀疑某人的动机.

▷ **mis·trust** *n* [U, sing] **(a) ~ (of sb/sth)** **1** lack of confidence in sb/sth 不相信; 不信任. **2** suspicion of sb/sth 怀疑: *She has a deep mistrust of anything new or strange.* 她对任何新奇事物皆十分怀疑. **mis·trust·ful** /-fl; -fl/ *adj* **~ (of sb/sth)**: *be mistrustful of one's ability to make the right decision* 怀疑自己能否作出正确决断. **mis·trust·fully** /-fəlɪ; -fəlɪ/ *adv*.

misty ⇨ MIST.

mis·un·der·stand /ˌmɪsˌʌndəˈstænd; ˌmɪsʌndɚˋstænd/ *v* (*pt, pp* **-stood** /-ˈstʊd; -ˋstʊd/) [Tn, Tw] interpret (instructions, messages, etc) incorrectly; form a wrong opinion of (sb/sth) 误会, 误解(指令、信息等); 对(某人[某事物])看法有误: *Don't misunderstand me/what I'm trying to say.* 别误解我[我要说的话]. ○ *She had always felt misunderstood*, ie that people did not appreciate her. 她总觉得别人对她有看法.

▷ **mis·un·der·stand·ing** *n* **1** [U, C] failure to understand rightly or correctly 误会; 误解: *There must be some misunderstanding!* 一定有误会了! **2** [C] minor disagreement or quarrel 不和; 争执: *clear up* (eg by discussion) *a misunderstanding between colleagues* 排解同事间的纷争 ○ *We had a slight misunderstanding over the time.* 我们在时间方面意见稍有分歧.

mis·use /ˌmɪsˈjuːz; mɪsˋjuz/ *v* [Tn esp passive 尤用于被动语态] **1** use (sth) in the wrong way or for the wrong purpose 误用, 滥用(某事物): *misuse a word, expression, etc* 误用一词、词组等 ○ *misuse public funds* 滥用公共基金. **2** treat (sb/sth) badly 虐待, 苛待(某人); 糟蹋(某事物): *He felt misused by the company.* 他觉得受到公司苛待. Cf 参看 ABUSE.

▷ **mis·use** /ˌmɪsˈjuːs; mɪsˋjus/ *n* [C, U] (instance of) wrong or incorrect use 误用; 滥用: *the misuse of power, authority, etc* 滥用权力、滥施权威.

mite[1] /maɪt; maɪt/ *n* **1** [C usu *sing* 通常作单数] very small or modest contribution or offering 菲薄的贡献或捐助: *offer a mite of comfort to sb* 给某人一点儿安慰 ○ *give one's mite to a good cause* 对一事业竭尽绵薄. **2** [C] small child or animal (usu when treated as an object of sympathy) 小孩儿, 小动物(通常为寄予同情的对象): *Poor little mite!* 可怜的小家伙!

▷ **a mite** *adv* (*infml* 口) a little; somewhat 一点儿: *This curry is a mite too hot for me!* 这咖喱我觉得有点儿太辣了!

mite[2] /maɪt; maɪt/ *n* small spider-like creature that may be found in food, and may carry disease 螨(可于食物中发现的似蜘蛛的小虫, 能传播疾病): *'cheese-mites* 干酪虫.

mit·ig·ate /ˈmɪtɪɡeɪt; ˋmɪtə,ɡet/ *v* [Tn] (*fml* 文) make (sth) less severe, violent or painful; moderate 使(某事物)减轻, 和缓; 节制: *mitigate sb's suffering, anger, anxiety, etc* 使某人少受苦、息怒、稍安等 ○ *mitigate the severity of a punishment, sentence, etc* 减轻惩罚、刑期等 ○ *mitigate the effects of inflation*, eg by making credit easily obtainable 和缓通货膨胀的影响.

▷ **mit·ig·at·ing** *adj* [attrib 作定语] reducing the severity, violence or pain of sth; moderating 减轻的; 和缓的; 节制的: *mitigating circumstances*, ie those that partially excuse a mistake, crime, etc (可使错误、罪行等)减轻的情节 ○ *the mitigating effect of pain-killing drugs* 镇痛药物的缓解作用.

mit·iga·tion /ˌmɪtɪˈɡeɪʃn; ˌmɪtəˋɡeʃən/ *n* [U]: *say sth in mitigation of sb's faults, crimes, etc*, ie to make them seem less serious 为减轻某人的过失、罪行等说情.

mitre (*US* **mi·ter**) /ˈmaɪtə(r); ˋmaɪtɚ/ *n* **1** tall pointed head-dress worn by bishops and abbots on ceremonial occasions as a symbol of their office 主教冠(主教和男修道院院长行典礼时所戴, 为职位的象征). **2** (also ˈ**mitre-joint**) corner joint esp of two pieces of wood with their ends evenly tapered so that together they form a right angle 斜接口, 斜榫(尤指两木相接成直角的).

▷ **mitre** (*US* **mi·ter**) *v* [Tn esp passive 尤用于被动语态] join (esp two pieces of wood) with a mitre-joint 斜接(尤指两木): *mitred corners* 斜接角.

mitt /mɪt; mɪt/ *n* **1** = MITTEN. **2** (in baseball) large padded leather glove worn by the catcher 棒球手套. **3** (*infml* 口) boxing-glove 拳击手套. **4** (usu *pl* 通常作复数) (*sl* 俚) hand; fist 手; 拳: *Take your mitts off me!* 别碰我!

mit·ten /ˈmɪtn; ˋmɪtn̩/ *n* **1** (also **mitt**) type of glove covering four fingers together and the thumb separately 连指手套(四指相连与拇指分开者). ⇨illus at GLOVE 见GLOVE 插图. **2** covering for the back and palm of the hand only, leaving most of the thumb and fingers bare 露指手套.

mix[1] /mɪks; mɪks/ *v* **1** [Tn, Tn·p, Dn·n, Dn·pr] **~ sth (up) (for sb/sth)** make or prepare sth by putting substances, etc together so that they are no longer distinct 混合或搀和某物: *mix cement, mortar, etc* 和水泥、灰浆等 ○ *mix cocktails, drinks, etc* 兑鸡尾酒、饮料等 ○ *He mixed his guests a salad.* 他给客人拌色拉. ○ *She mixed a cheese sauce for the fish.* 她调吃鱼用的奶酪沙司. ○ *The chemist mixed (up) some medicine for me.* 药剂师给我配了些药. **2 (a)** [I, Ipr, Ip] **~ with sth/~ (together)** be able to be combined; make a suitable combination 能相混合; 结合适当: *Oil and water don't mix.* 油和水不能混合. ○ *Oil won't mix with water.* 油不能和水混合. ○ *Pink and blue mix well together.* 粉色和蓝色在一起很协调. **(b)** [Tn, Tn·pr, Tn·p] **~ A with B/~ A and B (together)** combine one thing with another; blend things together 使一物与另一物混合; 拌和; 搀和: *mix the sugar with the flour* 把糖与面粉和在一起 ○ (*fig* 比喻) *Don't try to mix business with pleasure.* 不要把正事和娱乐混在一起. ○ *Don't mix your drinks* (ie have different ones in close succession) *at parties!* 在宴会上别接连喝不同种类的酒! ○ *If you mix red and yellow, you get orange.* 把红色和黄色混在一起就是橙色. ○ *Many women successfully mix marriage and a career.* 很多妇女都能做到婚姻、事业两不误. ○ *Many races are mixed together in Brazil.* 在巴西, 有多种民族杂居在一起. **3** [I, Ipr] **~ (with sb/sth)** (of people) come or be together socially (指人)相处, 交往: *He finds it hard to mix at parties.* 他感到很难在聚会上与人攀谈. ○ *In my job, I mix with all sorts of people.* 我在工作中常和各种人打交道. **4** (idm 习语) **be/get mixed ˈup in sth** (*infml* 口) be/become involved in or connected with sth 和某事物有牵连或有关联: *I don't want to be mixed up in the affair.* 我不想牵连到这件事情中去. **be/get mixed ˈup with sb** (*infml* 口) be/become associated with sb (esp sb disreputable) 与某人(尤指名誉不佳者)来往, 厮混: *Don't get mixed up with him — he's a crook!* 别跟他厮混——他是个无赖! **mix it (with sb)**; *US* **mix it up (with sb)** (*sl* 俚) start a quarrel or a fight 吵嘴; 打架: *Don't try mixing it with me — I've got a gun!* 别想跟我打架——我可有枪! **5** (phr v) **mix sth in** (esp in cooking) combine one ingredient with another (尤指烹饪时)和入, 搀进: *Mix the eggs in slowly.* 把鸡蛋慢慢搀入其中. ○ *Mix in the butter when melted.* 黄油化了再搀进去. **mix sth into sth (a)** add (another ingredient) to sth and combine the two 将(另一成分)加进某物中混匀: *mix the yeast into the flour* 往面粉里加酵母后和匀. **(b)** make sth by blending (one or more ingredients) 混合(某成分)做某物: *mix the flour and water into a smooth paste* 把水和面和成光滑的面团. **mix sb up (about/over sth)** cause sb to become confused 把某人弄糊涂: *Now you've mixed me up completely!* 你可把我完全弄糊涂了! **mix sb/sth up (with sb/sth)** confuse sb/sth with sb/sth else; be unable to distinguish between (people or things) 混淆某人[某事物]与他人[他事物]; 分辨不出(两人或两事物): *You're always mixing me up with my twin sister!* 你老是把我和我的孪生妹妹弄混了! ○ *I got the tickets mixed up and gave you mine.* 我把票混在一起了, 结果把我的给你了.

□ ˈ**mix-up** *n* (*infml* 口) confused situation; misunderstanding 混乱; 杂乱; 误会; 误解: *There's been an awful mix-up over the dates!* 日期问题乱得无以复加!

mix[2] /mɪks; mɪks/ *n* **1** [C usu *sing* 通常作单数] mixture or combination of things or people (事物或人的)混合, 结合: *a good social, racial, etc mix*, eg in a group of students 由不同社会阶层、种族组成的和睦群体. **2** [C, U] mixture of ingredients sold for making kinds of food, etc (供出售的)食物混合配料: *a packet of ˈcake mix* 一包蛋糕混合料.

mixed /mɪkst; mɪkst/ *adj* **1** composed of different qualities or elements 由不同质量或成分组成的; 混合的: *The critics gave the new play a mixed reception*, ie one of criticism and praise. 评论家对那出新剧的评价褒贬不一. ○ *The weather has been very mixed recently.* 近来天气好坏无常. **2** of different shapes, flavours, etc 不同形状的; 不同味道的: *a tin of mixed biscuits, sweets, etc* 一盒什锦饼干、糖果等. **3** having or showing various races or social classes 不同种族或阶级混合的: *live in a mixed society* 生活在种族混杂的社会中 ○ *people of mixed blood* 混血的人. **4** for members of both sexes 男女混合的: *a mixed school* 男女生混合学校 ○ *mixed changing rooms*, eg at a sports centre 男女合用更衣室(如在运动中心的). **5** (idm 习语) **have ˌmixed ˈfeelings (about sb/sth)** react to sb/sth with confused or conflicting feelings, eg joy and sorrow 对某人[某事物]产生纷扰的或矛盾的感情(如悲喜交集).

□ ˌ**mixed ˈbag** (*infml* 口) assortment of things or people, esp of varying quality (物或人的)混合体(尤指好坏不等的): *The competition entries were a very mixed bag.* 参赛者是错落不齐的大杂烩.

ˌ**mixed ˈblessing** thing that has advantages and also disadvantages 有利亦有弊的事物.

ˌ**mixed ˈdoubles** game (esp of tennis) in which a man and a woman are partners on each side 男女混合双打(尤指网球赛).

ˌ**mixed ˈfarming** farming of both crops and livestock (耕种与畜牧兼营的)混合务农.

ˌ**mixed ˈgrill** dish of various grilled meats, often with tomatoes and mushrooms 烤什锦, 什锦烤肉(常伴有蕃茄和蘑菇).

ˌ**mixed ˈmarriage** marriage between people of different races or religions (异族或异教的)通婚.

ˌ**mixed ˈmetaphor** combination of two or more metaphors that do not fit together and therefore produce a ludicrous effect, eg *The hand that rocks the cradle has kicked the bucket* 混杂隐喻(至少两个隐喻的合用, 因不通而产生滑稽效果, 如将 the hand that rocks the cradle (rules the world) 和 kick the bucket 合用).

ˌ**mixed-ˈup** *adj* (*infml* 口) mentally or emotionally confused; not well-adjusted socially 头脑或情绪紊乱的; 不很适应人际关系的: *She feels very mixed-up about life since her divorce.* 她离婚后觉得生活十分迷惘. ○ ˌ*mixed-up* ˈ*kids who take drugs* 服用毒品的迷茫孩子.

mixer /ˈmɪksə(r); ˋmɪksɚ/ *n* **1** (esp electrical) device for mixing things (尤指电动的)搅拌机: *a ceˈment-mixer* 水泥搅拌机 ○ *a ˈfood-mixer* 食物搅拌器. **2** (*infml* 口) person able or unable (as specified) to mix easily with others, eg at parties 善于或不善于交际的人: *be a good/bad mixer* 是个易于[难于]交际的人. **3** drink that can be mixed with another, eg to make cocktails 可作调配用的饮料(如用以调配鸡尾酒的): *use fruit juice as a mixer*

用果汁作配料. **4** (**a**) (in films and TV) person or device that combines shots onto one length of film or video-tape (电影和电视的)剪接师, 剪接器. (**b**) (in sound recording) person or device that combines sounds onto one tape 录音师; 混录调音机.

mix·ture /ˈmɪkstʃə(r); ˈmɪkstʃɚ/ *n* **1** [U] mixing or being mixed 混合; 混合状态. **2** [C] thing made by mixing 混合之物: *a ˈcough mixture*, ie containing several medicines 复方咳嗽药 ○ *The city was a mixture of old and new buildings.* 该市是新旧建筑物的混合体. **3** [sing] (*chemistry* 化) combination of two or more substances which do not alter their composition 混合物: *Air is a mixture, not a compound, of gases.* 空气是多种气体的混合物, 不是化合物. Cf 参看 COMPOUND[1] 1, ELEMENT 3.

miz·zen (also **mizen**) /ˈmɪzn; ˈmɪzn̩/ *n* (*nautical* 海) **1** = MIZZEN-MAST. **2** (also ˈ**mizzen-sail**) lowest square fore-and-aft sail set on the mizzen-mast 后桅纵帆.

□ ˈ**mizzen-mast** *n* third mast from the bow on a sailing-ship with three or more masts; mast nearest the stern on smaller ships 第三桅(三桅或多桅船上最近船尾的桅); 后桅.

Mk *abbr* 缩写 = **1** mark (currency): *Mk 300* 300马克. **2** (on cars) mark (ie model or type) (汽车上的)牌子(即型号): *Ford Granada Ghia Mk II* 福特牌格拉纳达·吉亚II型汽车.

ml *abbr* 缩写 = (*pl* unchanged or **mls** 复数或不变或作 **mls**) **1** (*US* **mi**) mile(s): *distance to village 3mls* 距村3英里. **2** millilitre(s): *25ml* 25毫升.

MLitt /ˌem ˈlɪt; ˌɛmˈlɪt/ *abbr* 缩写 = Master of Letters (Latin *Magister Litterarum*) (源自拉丁文 *Magister Litterarum*): *have/be an MLitt in philosophy* 有文学硕士学位[为文学硕士] ○ *Debra Kahn MLitt* 黛布拉·卡恩文学硕士.

mm *abbr* 缩写 = (*pl* unchanged or **mms** 复数或不变或作 **mms**) millimetre(s): *rainfall 6mm* 雨量6毫米 ○ *a 35mm camera* 35毫米照相机.

mne·monic /nɪˈmɒnɪk; niˈmɑnɪk/ *adj* of or designed to help the memory 记忆的; 帮助记忆的: *mnemonic verses*, eg for remembering spelling or grammar rules, etc 帮助记忆的歌诀 ○ *The verb patterns are shown in this dictionary by mnemonic codes.* 动词模式在本词典中用易于记忆的符号标示.

▷ **mne·monic** *n* **1** [C] word, verse, etc designed to help the memory 帮助记忆的词、诗句等. **2 mne·mon·ics** [usu sing *v* 通常与单数动词连用] art of or system for improving the memory 记忆术; 增进记忆的方法.

mo /məʊ; mo/ *n* (*pl* **mos**) (*Brit infml* 口) short period of time; moment 一会儿: *Half a mo* (ie Wait a little), *I'm not quite ready.* 等一下, 我还没完全准备好.

MO /ˌem ˈəʊ; ˌɛmˈo/ *abbr* 缩写 = **1** Medical Officer. **2** money order.

mo *abbr* 缩写 (*US*) = MTH.

moan /məʊn; mon/ *n* **1** (**a**) [C] long low mournful sound, usu expressing regret, pain or suffering 呻吟声; 呜咽声: *the moans of the wounded* 受伤者的呻吟. (**b**) [sing] similar sound as made by eg the wind 似呻吟的声音(如风声). **2** [C] (*infml* 口) grumble or complaint 牢骚; 怨声: *We had a good moan about the weather.* 我们对天气着实抱怨了一番.

▷ **moan** *v* **1** (**a**) [I, Ip, Tn] utter moans or say (sth) with moans 呻吟; 呻吟着说(某事): *He was moaning (away) all night long.* 他整夜不断呻吟. ○ *'Where's the doctor?' he moaned.* '医生在哪儿啊?'他呻吟着问. (**b**) [I, Ipr] make a moaning sound 发出呻吟的声音: *The wind was moaning through the trees.* 风穿林木声萧萧. **2** [I, Ipr, Ip] ~ (**about sth**) (*infml* 口) grumble or complain 抱怨; 发牢骚: *moaning and groaning (away)* 怨声不已 ○ *He's always moaning (on) about how poor he is.* 他总是抱怨穷.

moat /məʊt; mot/ *n* deep wide ditch filled with water, dug round a castle, etc as a defence (城堡等的)壕沟; 城壕; 护城河. ⇨ illus at CASTLE 见 CASTLE 插图.

▷ **moated** *adj* having a moat 有城壕的: *a moated manor house* 有护城河的领主邸宅.

mob /mɒb; mɑb/ *n* **1** [CGp] large disorderly crowd, esp one that has gathered to attack or cause mischief 无秩序的民众; (尤指)暴民: *The fans rushed onto the pitch in an excited mob.* 球迷群情激昂, 一窝蜂涌进球场. ○ [attrib 作定语] *mob law/rule*, ie that imposed or enforced by a mob 暴民的法律[统治] ○ *mob oratory*, ie speech-making that appeals to the emotions of the masses, not to their intellect 煽动群众的演讲. **2 the mob** [sing] (*derog* 贬) the masses or the common people 民众. **3** [C esp *sing* 尤作单数] (*sl* 俚) gang of criminals 犯罪集团; 匪帮: *Whose mob is he with?* 他是哪个匪帮的人?

▷ **mob** *v* (**-bb-**) [Tn esp passive 尤用于被动语态] crowd round (sb) noisily in great numbers, either to attack or admire 聚众包围(某人)(为攻击或赞赏): *The pop singer was mobbed by teenagers.* 那个唱流行歌曲的歌手被一群青少年团团围住.

mob-cap /ˈmɒb kæp; ˈmɑbˌkæp/ *n* large round cotton cap covering the whole of the hair, worn indoors by women in the 18th century (18世纪室内用的)女帽.

mo·bile /ˈməʊbaɪl; *US* -bl, *also* -biːl; ˈmobl̩, ˈmobil/ *adj* **1** (**a**) that can move or be moved easily and quickly from place to place 易于快速移动的: *mobile troops, artillery, etc* 机动部队、炮兵等 ○ *a mobile library*, ie one inside a vehicle 流动图书馆. (**b**) (of people) able to change class, occupation or place of residence easily (指人)易改变阶层、职业或住址的, 流动的: *a mobile work-force* 流动劳力. Cf 参看 STATIONARY. **2** (of a face, its features, etc) changing shape or expression easily and often (指脸、五官等)易变和常变其形状或表情的. **3** [pred 作表语] (*infml* 口) having transport, esp a car 有交通工具(尤指汽车): *Can you give me a lift if you're mobile?* 你要是有车, 捎我一程行吗?

▷ **mo·bile** *n* ornamental hanging structure of metal, plastic, cardboard, etc, whose parts move freely in currents of air 风动饰物(用金属、塑料、纸板等组成的悬挂饰物, 其部件可随风而动).

mo·bil·ity /məʊˈbɪlətɪ; moˈbɪlətɪ/ *n* [U] being mobile 移动性; 流动性; 机动性; 可动性.

□ ˌ**mobile** ˈ**home** large caravan that can be towed by a vehicle but is normally parked in one place and used as a home (可用车拖拉的)活动住房.

mo·bil·ize, -ise /ˈməʊbɪlaɪz; ˈmoblˌaɪz/ *v* **1** [I, Tn] (cause sb/sth to) become ready for service or action, esp in war (使某人[某事物])准备行动; (尤指战时)动员, 调动: *The troops received orders to mobilize.* 部队接到动员令. **2** [Tn] organize or assemble (resources, etc) for a particular purpose (为某目的)组织, 集合(资源等): *They are mobilizing their supporters to vote at the election.* 他们动员其支持者去投票.

▷ **mo·bil·iza·tion, -isation** /ˌməʊbɪlaɪˈzeɪʃn; *US* -lɪˈz-; ˌmoblə̩ˈzeʃən/ *n* [U] mobilizing or being mobilized 动员: [attrib 作定语] *mobilization orders* 动员令.

mob·ster /ˈmɒbstə(r); ˈmɑbstɚ/ *n* member of a gang of criminals; gangster 犯罪集团成员; 匪徒; 歹徒.

moc·casin /ˈmɒkəsɪn; ˈmɑkəsn̩/ *n* flat-soled shoe made from soft leather, as originally worn by N American Indians 软皮平底鞋(原为北美印第安人穿的).

mocha /ˈmɒkə; *US* ˈməʊkə; ˈmokə/ *n* [U] **1** type of strong fine-quality coffee, originally shipped from the Arabian port of Mocha 穆哈咖啡(自阿拉伯穆哈港输出的优质咖啡). **2** flavouring made by mixing this and chocolate 穆哈咖啡与巧克力制成的调味料: [attrib 作定语] *mocha ice-cream* 穆哈冰激凌.

mock[1] /mɒk; mɑk/ *v* **1** [I, Ipr, Tn] ~ (**at sb/sth**) make fun of (sb/sth), esp by mimicking him/it contemptuously; ridicule 取笑(某人[某事物]); (尤指以模仿)嘲弄, 愚弄: *a mocking smile, voice, laugh* 嘲弄的微笑、声音、大笑 ○ *mock (at) sb's fears, efforts, attempts* 嘲笑某人的恐惧、努力、尝试 ○ *It is wrong to mock cripples.* 模仿瘸子走路来取笑是不对的. **2** [Tn] (*fml esp fig* 文, 尤作比喻) defy (sb/sth) contemptuously 蔑视, 抗拒(某人[某事物]): *The heavy steel doors mocked our attempts to open them.* 沉重的铁门嘲笑我们不自量力, 无法打开.

▷ **mock** *n* (idm 习语) **make (a) ˈmock of sb/sth** make sb/sth seem foolish; ridicule sb/sth 嘲弄或嘲笑某人[某事物].

mocker *n* **1** person who mocks 嘲弄者; 嘲笑者. **2** (idm 习语) **put the ˈmockers on sb** (*sl* 俚) bring bad luck to sb 使某人倒霉.

mock·ingly *adv*.

□ ˈ**mocking-bird** *n* type of American bird of the thrush family that mimics the calls of other birds 嘲鸫(产于美洲, 能模仿其他鸟鸣叫).

ˈ**mock-up** *n* **1** full-scale experimental model or replica, eg of a machine, made for testing, etc (用作试验等的)实体模型, 实物复制品(如机器等). **2** arrangement of text, pictures, etc of sth to be printed (印刷文字、图片等的)版面安排: *do a mock-up of a book cover* 安排书的封面版面.

mock² /mɒk; mɑk/ *adj* [attrib 作定语] (**a**) not real; substitute 非真实的; 模拟的: *a mock battle, exam*, eg for training or practice 模拟战争、考试. (**b**) not genuine; counterfeit 假的; 假装的; 仿制的: ˌ*mock* ˈ*modesty*, ie pretence of being modest 假谦虚 ○ ˌ*mock-he*ˈ*roic style*, ie making fun of the heroic style in art or literature (艺术或文学中)戏仿英雄体的风格.

□**mock** ˌ**turtle** ˈ**soup** soup made from calf's head or other meat to resemble turtle soup (用小牛头等肉做的)仿甲鱼汤.

mock·ery /ˈmɒkərɪ; ˈmɑkərɪ/ *n* **1** [U] action of mocking sb/sth; scorn or ridicule 嘲弄; 嘲笑; 讥笑: *He replied with a note of mockery in his voice.* 他带着嘲笑的声调回答. **2** [C] **~ (of sth)** completely inadequate or ridiculous action or representation (of sth); travesty 拙劣可笑的模仿或歪曲: *The performance was an utter mockery.* 这演出纯粹是拙劣的模仿. ○ *The trial was a mockery of justice.* 这一审判是对正义的歪曲. **3** [sing] person or thing that is mocked; occasion when this happens 嘲弄的对象或场合; 笑柄. **4** (idm 习语) **make a mockery of sth** make sth appear foolish or worthless 使某事物显得荒谬或无价值: *The unfair and hasty decision of the court made a mockery of the trial.* 法院匆促做出的不公正裁决使这次审判形同儿戏.

mod /mɒd; mɑd/ *n* (also **Mod**) (*Brit*) member of a group of young people, prominent in Britain in the 1960's, who liked to wear neat and fashionable clothes and to ride motor-scooters 摩德派成员(20世纪60年代英国的一类年轻人, 穿着整齐时髦, 常骑小型摩托车). Cf 参看 ROCKER (ROCK²).

MOD /ˌem əʊ ˈdiː; ˌɛm o ˈdi/ *abbr* 缩写 = (*Brit*) Ministry of Defence.

modal /ˈməʊdl; ˈmodl̩/ *n* (also **modal verb**, **modal auˈxiliary**, **modal auˈxiliary verb**) (*grammar*) verb that is used with another verb (not a modal) to express possibility, permission, obligation, etc 情态动词: *'Can', 'may', 'might', 'must' and 'should' are all modals.* can、may、might、must、should 都是情态动词.

▷ **modal** *adj* [usu attrib 通常作定语] **1** (*grammar*) of a modal 情态动词的. **2** relating to mode or manner, in contrast to substance 形式的, 形态的, 方式的(与实质相对).

mod cons /ˌmɒd ˈkɒnz; ˌmɑdˈkɑnz/ (*Brit infml approv* 口, 褒) (used esp by advertisers of houses 尤作售房广告用语) modern installations in a house (eg hot water, electricity, heating, telephone) that make the house easier and more comfortable to live in 现代化生活设备(如热水、电、供暖、电话): *a house with all mod cons* 现代化生活设备一应俱全的住房.

mode /məʊd; mod/ *n* **1 ~ (of sth)** (*fml* 文) way or manner in which sth is done 方式; 方法: *a mode of life, living, operation, thought, transport* 生活模式、生活方式、操作方法、思想方法、交通工具类型 ○ *The level of formality determines the precise mode of expression.* 不同的礼节程度决定所需的确切表达方式. **2** (usu *sing* 通常作单数) style or fashion in clothes, art, drama, etc (衣着、艺术、戏剧等的)样式, 形式, 风格: *the latest mode* 最新款式. **3** any of several arrangements of musical notes, eg the major or minor scale system in modern music (近代音乐的)调式(如大调式、小调式). **4** arrangement or setting of equipment to perform a certain task (设备中的)操作安排, 状态, 模式, 模: *a spacecraft in re-*ˈ*entry mode* 处于重返大气层运行中的航天器 ○ *a tape-recorder in* ˈ*play-back/re*ˈ*cording mode* 处于重放[录音]工作状态的录音机.

model¹ /ˈmɒdl; ˈmɑdl/ *n* **1** (**a**) representation of sth, usu smaller than the original 模型(通常小于原物): *a model of the proposed new airport* 拟建的新机场模型 ○ *construct a scale model of the Eiffel Tower* 建造埃菲尔铁塔的比例模型 ○ [attrib 作定语] *a model train, aeroplane, car, etc* 模型火车、飞机、汽车等. ⇨illus 见插图. (**b**) design of sth that is made so that it can be copied in another material (供用他种材料做复制品的)模型: *a clay/wax model for a statue*, eg to be copied in stone or metal 塑像的泥质[蜡质]模型(如供用石或金属做复制品). **2** particular design or type of product (产品的某种)设计, 型号: *All this year's new models are displayed at the motor show.* 汽车展览会上展出了今年所有的新型号. ○ *This is the most popular model in our whole range.* 这是我们所有产品中最受欢迎的型号. **3** simplified description of a system used in explanations, calculations, etc (供讲解、计算等的)模型: *a model of a molecule* 分子模型 ○ *a statistical/mathematical/economical model*, eg used to forecast future trends 统计学[数学/经济学]模型(如用以预测趋势的). **4** system used as a basis for a copy; pattern 模式: *The nation's constitution provided a model that other countries followed.* 该国的宪法提供了他国效法的模式. **5 ~ (of sth)** (*approv* 褒) person or thing regarded as excellent of his/its kind and worth imitating (值得仿效的)优秀的人或物; 模范: *a model of tact, fairness, accuracy, etc* 圆通、公正、准确等的范例 ○ [attrib 作定语] *a model pupil, husband, teacher, etc* 模范学生、丈夫、教师等 ○ *model behaviour* 模范行为 ○ *a model farm, prison, etc*, ie one that has been specially designed to be very efficient 模范农场、监狱等. **6** (**a**) person employed to pose for an artist, photographer, etc (艺术家、摄影家等用的)模特儿. (**b**) person employed to display clothes, hats, etc to possible buyers, by wearing them 时装模特儿: *She is one of the country's top models.* 她是全国的顶尖模特儿. ○ *a male* ˈ*model* 男模特儿 ○ *a* ˈ*fashion model* 时装模特儿. **7** (copy of a) garment, hat, etc fashioned by a well-known designer and shown in public 著名服装设计师设计并展览的衣、帽等或其复制品: *see, buy, wear, etc the latest Paris models* 参观、购买、穿着...最新巴黎时装.

model 模型

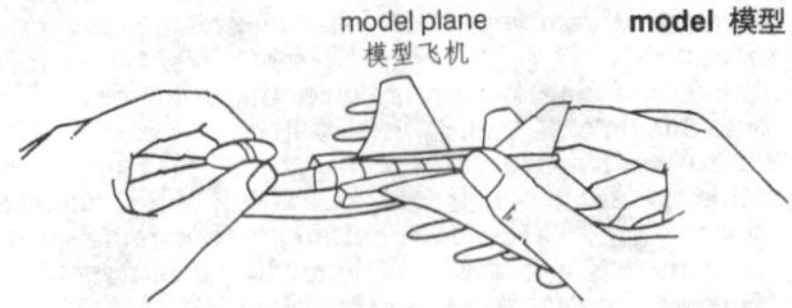

model² /ˈmɒdl; ˈmɑdl/ *v* (**-ll-**; *US* **-l-**) **1** [Tn·pr] **~ oneself/sth on sb/sth** take sb/sth as an example for one's action, plans, etc 以某人[某事物]作榜样; 仿效: *She models herself on her favourite novelist.* 她以最喜爱的小说家为榜样. ○ *The design of the building is modelled on classical Greek forms.* 那建筑物的设计是模仿希腊的古典形式. **2** [I, Tn] work as a model¹(6); display (clothes, hats, etc) by wearing them 当模特儿; (亲身穿戴)展示(衣帽等): *She earns a living by modelling (dresses, swim-suits, etc).* 她当(时装、泳装等)模特儿为生. **3** [I, Tn] make a model of (sth) in clay, wax, etc; shape (clay, wax, etc) to form sth 用泥、蜡等做(某物)的模型; 用(泥、蜡等)塑造某物: *modelling (in) plasticine* 用橡皮泥塑造.

▷ **mod·eller** (*US* **mod·eler**) *n* person who practises modelling 制造模型者: *a railway modeller* 铁路模型制作者.

mod·el·ling (*US* **mod·el·ing**) *n* [U] **1** art of making models (MODEL¹ 1a); way in which this is done 模型制造(术): *clay modelling* 黏土模型制造法 ○ *by skilful modelling* 用熟练的模型制造技术. **2** working as a model¹(6) 当模特儿: *She did some modelling as a student to earn a bit of money.* 她上学时当过模特儿赚些钱.

mo·dem /ˈməʊdem; ˈmoˌdɛm/ *n* device linking a computer system and eg a telephone line so that data can be transmitted at high speeds from one computer to another 调制解调器(计算机系统与例如电话线的联接装置, 可使资料高速传至另一计算机).

mod·er·ate¹ /ˈmɒdərət; ˈmɑdərət/ *adj* **1** average in amount, intensity, quality, etc; not extreme (量、强度、质等)中等的, 适度的: *moderate price increases* 适度的涨价 ○ *travelling at a moderate speed* 中速行驶的 ○ *a moderate-sized bathroom* 中等大小的浴室 ○ *a moderate performance*, ie neither very good nor very bad 不好不坏的演出 ○ *a moderate sea*, ie neither calm nor rough 中

浪 ○ *a moderate breeze*, ie a wind of medium strength 和风. **2** of or having (usu political) opinions that are not extreme 见解(通常指政治方面)不极端的, 不偏激的, 温和的: *a man with moderate views* 意见温和的人 ○ *moderate policies* 稳健的政策. **3** keeping or kept within limits that are not excessive 有节制的; 不过分的: *a moderate drinker* 饮酒有节制的人 ○ *moderate wage demands* 适度的工资要求.

▷ **mod·er·ate** /ˈmɒdərət; ˋmɑdərɪt/ *n* person with moderate opinions, esp in politics 持温和意见的人(尤指政见).

mod·er·ately *adv* to a moderate extent; not very; quite 适度地; 不过分地: *a moderately good performance* 很不错的演出 ○ *a moderately expensive house* 价钱稍高的房子 ○ *She only did moderately well in the exam.* 她考试成绩尚可.

mod·er·ate² /ˈmɒdəreɪt; ˋmɑdə,ret/ *v* [I, Tn] (cause sth/sb to) become less violent, extreme or intense (使某人)节制, 克制; (使某事物)和缓, 减轻: *The wind has moderated, making sailing safer.* 风势已减弱, 做帆船运动较为安全了. ○ *He must learn to moderate his temper.* 他得改改脾气了. ○ *exercise a moderating* (ie controlling, restraining) *influence on sb* 对某人施加约束性影响.

mod·era·tion /ˌmɒdəˈreɪʃn; ˌmɑdəˋreʃən/ *n* **1** [U] quality of being moderate; freedom from excess; restraint 温和; 适度; 节制: *They showed a remarkable degree of moderation in not quarrelling publicly on television.* 他们表现得极为克制, 未在电视上公开吵起来. **2** (idm 习语) **in mode'ration** (of smoking, drinking alcohol, etc) in a moderate manner; not excessively (指吸烟、饮酒等)适度地, 不过分: *Whisky can be good for you if taken in moderation.* 威士忌酒如饮用适度是有益的.

mod·er·ator /ˈmɒdəreɪtə(r); ˋmɑdə,retɚ/ *n* **1** person who arbitrates in a dispute; mediator 仲裁人; 调解人. **2** person who makes sure that the same standards are used by different examiners when marking an examination 评分监督(统一各主考人评分标准者). **3** Presbyterian minister presiding over a church court 长老会教会法庭上的主持者. **4** (*physics* 物) substance in which neutrons are slowed down in a nuclear reactor 减速剂, 慢化剂(核反应堆中使中子减速的物质).

mod·ern /ˈmɒdn; ˋmɑdɚn/ *adj* **1** [attrib 作定语] of the present or recent times; contemporary 现代的; 近代的: *Unemployment is one of the major problems of modern times.* 失业问题是现代的主要问题. ○ *in the modern world/age* 在当今世界[时代] ○ *modern history*, eg of Europe from about 1475 onwards 近代史(如自1475年起之欧洲史). **2** (*esp approv* 尤作褒义) using or having the newest methods, equipment, buildings, etc; up to date (方法、设备、建筑等)新式的, 时髦的, 最新的: *modern marketing techniques* 最新市场推广技巧 ○ *one of the most modern shopping centres in the country* 全国最先进的购物中心. **3** [attrib 作定语] of a contemporary style of art, fashion, etc, esp one that is experimental and not traditional (艺术、时装等)当代风格的, 现代派的: *modern dance* 现代派舞蹈. ⇨Usage at NEW 用法见NEW.

▷ **mod·ern** *n* (*dated or fml* 旧或文) person living in modern times 现代人.

mod·ern·ity /məˈdɜːnətɪ; məˋdɝnətɪ/ *n* [U] being modern 现代性.

□ ˌ**modern** ˈ**language** (*esp Brit*) language that is spoken or written now, esp a European language such as French, German or Spanish 现代语言(尤指欧洲语言, 如法语、德语或西班牙语): *study modern languages at university* 在大学学习现代语言.

mod·ern·ism /ˈmɒdənɪzəm; ˋmɑdɚn,ɪzəm/ *n* [U] modern ideas or methods in contrast to traditional ones, esp in art or religion (有别于传统的)现代思潮或方法; (尤指艺术或宗教的)现代主义.

▷ **mod·ern·ist** /ˈmɒdənɪst; ˋmɑdɚnɪst/ *n* believer in or supporter of modernism 拥护现代思潮者; 现代主义者. — *adj* [attrib 作定语] of or associated with modernism 现代思潮的; 现代方法的; 现代主义的. **mod·ern·istic** /ˌmɒdəˈnɪstɪk; ˌmɑdɚˋnɪstɪk/ *adj* noticeably modern; showing modernism (显然)现代化的; 显示现代思潮或现代主义的: *modernistic furniture designs* 现代家具图样.

mod·ern·ize, -ise /ˈmɒdənaɪz; ˋmɑdɚn,aɪz/ *v* **1** [Tn] make (sth) suitable for modern needs or habits; bring up to date 使(某事物)现代化: *modernize a transport system, a factory, farming methods* 使运输系统、工厂、耕作方法现代化 ○ *a fully modernized shop* 十分现代化的商店. **2** [I] adopt modern ways or views 采用现代方法或观点; 现代化: *If the industry doesn't modernize it will not survive.* 该制造业若不现代化就不能继续存在.

▷ **mod·ern·iza·tion, -isation** /ˌmɒdənaɪˈzeɪʃn; *US* -nɪˈz-; ˌmɑdɚnəˋzeʃən/ *n* [U]: *the modernization of the telephone system* 电话设备的现代化 ○ [attrib 作定语] *embark on a major modernization programme* 实施重大的现代化计划.

mod·est /ˈmɒdɪst; ˋmɑdɪst/ *adj* **1** (**a**) not large in amount, size, etc; moderate (数量、体积等)不大的, 适度的, 中等的: *live on a modest income* 靠不高的收入生活 ○ *make very modest demands* 提出非常适度的要求 ○ *a modest improvement, success* 一定程度的改善、成功. (**b**) not showy or splendid in appearance; not expensive 不浮夸的; 朴素的; 不豪华的: *live in a modest little house* 住在朴素的小房子里. **2** (**a**) **~ (about sth)** (*approv* 褒) having or showing a not too high opinion of one's abilities, qualities, etc; not vain or boastful 谦逊的; 不虚夸的; 质朴的: *be modest about one's achievements* 对自己的成就很谦逊. (**b**) rather shy; not putting oneself forward; bashful 羞怯的; 不突出自己的; 腼腆的: *Might I make a modest suggestion?* 我可以提个小小的建议吗? **3** (esp of women or their appearance or behaviour) having or showing respect for conventional ideas of decency and purity (尤指女子或其容貌或行为)端庄的, 高雅的, 正派的, 纯洁的: *a modest dress, blouse, neckline, etc*, ie one that is not sexually provocative 样子庄重的连衣裙、女衬衫、领口等.

▷ **mod·estly** *adv*.

mod·esty /ˈmɒdɪstɪ; ˋmɑdəstɪ/ *n* [U] (*esp approv* 尤作褒义) state of being modest 适度; 朴实; 谦恭; 羞怯; 庄重: *speak with genuine modesty/without (a trace of) false modesty* 真正谦虚地[(绝)不故作谦虚地]讲话 ○ *I'd like to tell you all about my success but modesty forbids.* 我并非不愿将成绩一一相告, 只是君子不自肖其功.

mod·icum /ˈmɒdɪkəm; ˋmɑdɪkəm/ *n* [sing] **~ (of sth)** small or moderate amount of sth 少量; 适量: *achieve success with a modicum of effort* 稍微努力就获得成功 ○ *Anyone with even a modicum of intelligence would have realized that!* 稍有头脑的人都能认识到那点!

mod·ify /ˈmɒdɪfaɪ; ˋmɑdə,faɪ/ *v* (*pt, pp* **-fied**) [Tn] **1** change (sth) slightly, esp to make it less extreme or to improve it 稍改(某事物); (尤指)使缓和, 使改善, 使改进: *The union has been forced to modify its position.* 工会被迫稍稍改变立场. ○ *The policy was agreed by the committee, but only in a modified form.* 那政策惟经修改后始获委员会同意. ○ *The heating system has recently been modified to make it more efficient.* 最近供暖设备已稍加改动以提高效率. ⇨Usage at CHANGE¹ 用法见CHANGE¹. **2** (*grammar*) (esp of an *adj* or *adv*) limit the sense of (another word) (尤指形容词或副词)修饰, 限定(另一词)的意义: *In 'the black cat' the adjective 'black' modifies the noun 'cat'.* 在'黑猫'这一词组中, 形容词'黑'修饰名词'猫'.

▷ **mo·di·fica·tion** /ˌmɒdɪfɪˈkeɪʃn; ˌmɑdəfəˋkeʃən/ *n* (**a**) [U] modifying or being modified 修改; 缓和; 改善; 修饰; 限定: *The design of the spacecraft is undergoing extensive modification.* 航天器的设计正大加修改. (**b**) [C] instance of this; change or alteration 修改; 缓和; 改善; 修饰; 限定: *The plan was approved, with some minor modifications.* 那计划已批准, 仅作了些许更动.

modi·fier /-faɪə(r); -,faɪɚ/ *n* (*grammar*) word or phrase that modifies (MODIFY 2) another word or phrase 修饰语.

mod·ish /ˈməʊdɪʃ; ˋmodɪʃ/ *adj* (*sometimes derog* 有时作贬义) fashionable 流行的; 时髦的. ▷ **mod·ishly** *adv*.

modu·late /ˈmɒdjʊleɪt; *US* -dʒʊ-; ˋmɑdʒə,let/ *v* **1** [Tn] vary the strength, volume or pitch of (one's voice) 改变(嗓音)的强弱、大小、高低: *the actor's clearly modulated tones* 那演员显然改变了的声调. **2** [I, Ipr] **~ (from sth) (to sth)** change from one musical key to another 变调; 转调: *music that modulates frequently* 频繁变调的乐曲 ○ *to modulate from C major to A minor* 从C大调变至A小调. **3** [Tn] (*fml* 文) adjust or moderate (sth)

M

调节, 调整(某事物). **4** [Tn] vary the amplitude, phase or frequency of (a radio wave) so as to convey a particular signal 调制(无线电波). ▷ **modu·la·tion** /ˌmɒdjʊˈleɪʃn; US -dʒʊˈl-; ˌmɑdʒəˈleʃən/ *n* [C, U].

mod·ule /ˈmɒdju:l; US -dʒu:l; ˈmɑdʒul/ *n* **1** (**a**) any one of a set of standardized parts or units that are made separately and are joined together to construct a building or piece of furniture (标准尺寸的)建筑部件, 家具组件. (**b**) unit, esp of a computer or computer program, that has a particular function 单位; 单元; (尤指计算机或计算机程序的)模件, 组件, 模块: *a software module* 软件元. **2** (*aerospace* 航空) independent self-contained unit of a spacecraft (航天器中独立的)舱: *a service module* 服务舱 ○ *the command module*, ie for the astronaut in command 指挥舱 ○ *a lunar module*, ie used to land on the moon 登月舱. **3** any one of several independent units or options that make up a course of study, esp at a college or university (组成一门课程的)独立单元, 选修部分(尤指大专院校的).
▷ **modu·lar** /ˈmɒdjʊlə(r); US -dʒʊ-; ˈmɑdʒulɚ/ *adj* **1** using a module or modules as the basis of design or construction 以标准化的部件或单元为基础设计或建造的; 标准化的; 组件化的; 模块化的: *modular components* 标准元件 ○ *modular furniture* 标准化组合家具. **2** (of a course of study) composed of a number of separate units from which students may select a certain number (指课程)由独立单元组成的, 分单元的(其单元可由学生选修).

modus op·er·andi /ˌməʊdəs ˌɒpəˈrændi:; ˈmodəsˌɑpəˈrændaɪ/ (*Latin* 拉) (**a**) person's method of dealing with a task (个人的)做法, 工作方法. (**b**) way in which a thing operates 操作法.

modus vi·vendi /ˌməʊdəs vɪˈvendi:; ˈmodəsvɪˈvɛndaɪ/ (*Latin* 拉) **1** temporary practical arrangement by which people who are opposed or quarrelling can continue to live or work together while waiting for their dispute to be settled (争持期间的)暂时解决办法: *We managed to achieve a kind of modus vivendi.* 我们设法达成了某种临时的妥协. **2** way of living or coping 生活方式; 处理方法.

mog·gie (also **moggy**) /ˈmɒgɪ; ˈmɑgɪ/ (also **mog** /mɒg; mɑg/) *n* (*Brit infml esp joc* 口, 尤作戏谑语) cat 猫.

mo·gul /ˈməʊgl; ˈmogʌl/ *n* very rich, important or influential person 富有的、重要的或有势力的人; 巨子: *Hollywood moguls* 好莱坞大亨 ○ *a television mogul* 电视界泰斗.

MOH /ˌem əʊ ˈeɪtʃ; ˌɛm o ˈetʃ/ *abbr* 缩写 = (*Brit*) Medical Officer of Health (eg a doctor in charge of public health in a particular area) 保健检查官.

mo·hair /ˈməʊheə(r); ˈmoˌhɛr/ *n* [U] (cloth or thread made from the) fine silky hair of the Angora goat 安哥拉山羊毛; 马海毛; 安哥拉羊毛线; 马海毛织物; 马海毛呢: [attrib 作定语] *a mohair sweater* 马海毛毛衣.

Mo·ham·medan = MUHAMMADAN (MUHAMMAD).

moi·ety /ˈmɔɪətɪ; ˈmɔɪətɪ/ *n* (usu *sing*通常作单数) **~ (of sth)** (*fml or law* 文或律) either of two parts into which sth is divided; half 一半; 二分之一.

moist /mɔɪst; mɔɪst/ *adj* slightly wet 潮湿的; 湿润的: *moist eyes, lips, etc* 湿润的眼睛、嘴唇等 ○ *a rich moist fruit-cake* 味浓松软的水果蛋糕 ○ *Water the plant regularly to keep the soil moist.* 按时给植物浇水以保持土壤湿润.
▷ **moisten** /ˈmɔɪsn; ˈmɔɪsn̩/ *v* [I, Tn] (cause sth to) become moist (使某物)潮湿, 湿润: *His eyes moistened (with tears).* 他的眼睛(给泪水)润湿了. ○ *She moistened her lips with her tongue.* 她舔湿了嘴唇. ○ *Moisten the cloth slightly before applying the lotion.* 先把布稍弄潮湿再使用此溶液.

mois·ture /ˈmɔɪstʃə(r); ˈmɔɪstʃɚ/ *n* [U] (thin layer of) tiny drops of water on a surface, in the air, etc 潮湿; 湿气; 水气: *The rubber seal is designed to keep out all the moisture.* 橡胶的密封垫是用以隔绝湿气的. ○ *Humidity is a measure of moisture in the atmosphere.* 湿度是空气内含水分多少的量度.
▷ **mois·tur·ize, -ise** /ˈmɔɪstʃəraɪz; ˈmɔɪstʃəˌraɪz/ *v* [Tn] make (the skin) less dry by the use of certain cosmetics (施化妆品)使(皮肤)滋润: *moisturizing cream for the face and hands* 搽脸和手的润肤霜. **mois·tur·izer, -iser** *n* [C, U] cream used for moisturizing the skin 润肤霜.

moke /məʊk; mok/ *n* (*Brit infml esp joc* 口, 尤作戏谑语) donkey 驴.

molar /ˈməʊlə(r); ˈmolɚ/ *n* any of the teeth at the back of the jaw used for grinding and chewing food 磨牙; 臼齿: *upper/lower/front/back molars* 上[下/前/后]磨牙. ⇨illus at TOOTH 见 TOOTH 插图.
▷ **molar** *adj* of such teeth 磨牙的; 臼齿的: *molar cavities* 磨牙龋洞.

mo·lasses /məˈlæsɪz; məˈlæsɪz/ *n* [U] **1** thick dark syrup drained from raw sugar during the refining process 糖蜜. **2** (*US*) treacle 糖浆.

mold (*US*) = MOULD.

molder (*US*) = MOULDER.

mold·ing (*US*) = MOULDING.

moldy (*US*) = MOULDY (MOULD^3).

mole^1 /məʊl; mol/ *n* small permanent dark spot on the human skin 痣; 色素痣. Cf 参看 FRECKLE.

mole^2 /məʊl; mol/ *n* **1** small dark-grey fur-covered animal with tiny eyes, living in tunnels which it makes underground 鼹. ⇨illus at App 1 见附录1插图, page iii. **2** (*infml* 口) person who works within an organization and secretly passes confidential information to another organization or country (将本组织的秘密情报暗中传给另一组织或国家的)内奸: *The authorities believe there is a mole at the Treasury.* 当局认为财政部里有内奸. Cf 参看 SPY.
□ ˈ**molehill** *n* **1** small pile of earth thrown up by a mole^2(1) when it is digging underground 鼹丘. **2** (idm 习语) **make a mountain out of a molehill** ⇨ MOUNTAIN.
ˈ**moleskin** *n* [U] **1** fur of a mole 鼹鼠皮. **2** type of strong cotton cloth that looks like this, used for making clothes 厚毛头斜纹棉布: [attrib 作定语] *moleskin trousers* 厚毛头斜纹棉布裤.

mole^3 /məʊl; mol/ *n* stone wall built from the shore into the sea as a breakwater or causeway 防波堤.

mo·lecule /ˈmɒlɪkju:l; ˈmɑləˌkjul/ *n* smallest unit (usu consisting of a group of atoms) into which a substance can be divided without a change in its chemical nature 分子: *A molecule of water consists of two atoms of hydrogen and one atom of oxygen.* 水分子含有两个氢原子和一个氧原子.
▷ **mo·lecu·lar** /məˈlekjʊlə(r); məˈlɛkjəlɚ/ *adj* [attrib 作定语] of or relating to molecules 分子的: *molecular structure, weight, mass, etc* 分子结构、量、质量等 ○ *molecular biology* 分子生物学.

mo·lest /məˈlest; məˈlɛst/ *v* [Tn] (**a**) trouble or annoy (sb) in a hostile way or in a way that causes injury 骚扰, 招惹, 伤害(某人): *an old man molested and robbed by a gang of youths* 受到一帮年轻人骚扰和抢劫的老人. (**b**) attack or annoy (usu a woman or child) sexually; interfere with 对(通常为妇女或儿童)作性骚扰; 调戏; 搅扰: *He was found guilty of molesting a young girl.* 他被判猥亵少女罪. ▷ **mo·les·ta·tion** /ˌməʊleˈsteɪʃn; ˌmolɛsˈteʃən/ *n* [U]. **mo·les·ter** /məˈlestə(r); məˈlɛstɚ/ *n*: *a child molester* 对儿童进行性骚扰者.

moll /mɒl; mɑl/ *n* (*sl* 俚) woman companion of a gangster 歹徒的女伙伴或情妇.

mol·lify /ˈmɒlɪfaɪ; ˈmɑləˌfaɪ/ *v* (*pt, pp* **-fied**) [Tn] lessen the anger of (sb); make calmer; soothe 使(某人)息怒; 使平静; 抚慰: *He tried to find ways of mollifying her.* 他想方设法安慰她. ▷ **mol·li·fica·tion** /ˌmɒlɪfɪˈkeɪʃn; ˌmɑləfəˈkeʃən/ *n* [U].

mol·lusc (*US* also **mol·lusk**) /ˈmɒləsk; ˈmɑləsk/ *n* any of the class of animals, including oysters, mussels, snails and slugs, that have a soft body, no backbone, and usu a hard shell 软体动物(包括牡蛎、贻贝、蜗牛、蛞蝓等).

mol·ly·coddle /ˈmɒlɪkɒdl; ˈmɑlɪˌkɑdl/ *v* [Tn] (*derog* 贬) treat (sb) with too much kindness and protection; pamper 娇宠, 溺爱, 纵容(某人): *He doesn't believe that children should be mollycoddled.* 他认为不应溺爱儿童.

Mol·otov cock·tail /ˌmɒlətɒf ˈkɒkteɪl; ˌmɑlətɔf ˈkɑkˌtel/ type of simple bomb that consists of a bottle filled with petrol and stuffed with a rag which is lit 瓶装汽油弹.

molt (*US*) = MOULT.

mol·ten /ˈməʊltən; ˈmoltn̩/ *adj* [usu attrib 通常作定语] melted or made liquid by heating to a very high temperature 熔化的; 熔融的: *molten rock, steel, lava* 熔化的岩石、钢水、岩浆.

molto /ˈmɒltəʊ; *US* ˈməʊltəʊ; ˈmolto/ *adv* (*music* 音) very 甚; 极: *molto adagio*, ie very slowly 极慢.

mol·yb·denum /məˈlɪbdənəm; məˈlɪbdənəm/ *n* [U] chemical element, a silvery-white hard metal used in alloys for making high-speed tools 钼. ⇨App 10 见附录 10.

mom /mɒm; mɑm/ *n* (*US infml* 口) =MUM².

mo·ment /ˈməʊmənt; ˈmomənt/ *n* **1** [C] very brief period of time 瞬间; 片刻: *He thought for a moment and then spoke.* 他想了片刻, 然后说. ○ *It was all over in a few moments.* 不一会儿就都完了. ○ *Can you wait a moment or two, please?* 请等一下, 好吗? ○ *She answered without a moment's hesitation.* 她毫不迟疑立即回答. ○ *One moment please*, ie Please wait a short time. 请稍候. ○ *I shall only be a moment.* 我一会儿就回来. ○ *I'll be back in a moment*, ie very soon. 我这就回来. ○ *Extra police arrived not a moment too soon*, ie It was almost too late when they arrived. 增援的警察赶到时未免太迟了. **2** [sing] exact point in time 就在那时; 当时: *At that (very) moment, the phone rang.* 就在那时电话铃响了. ○ *the moment of birth* 出生时刻 ○ *'Could you go to the post office for me, please?' 'I've only this moment come in'*, ie I came in a very short time ago. '你可以替我去趟邮局吗?' '我才刚进来嘛.' **3** [C] time for doing something; occasion 做某事的时刻; 时机: *This is a suitable moment to ask for the afternoon off.* 这是请下午假的最好时机. ○ *wait for the right moment* 等候恰当的时机 ○ *in moments of great happiness* 在非常快活的时刻. **4** [C usu *sing* 通常作单数] (*physics* 物) tendency to cause movement, esp rotation about a point (力)矩: *the moment of a force* 力矩. **5** (idm 习语) **any minute/moment** ⇨ MINUTE¹. **at the ˈmoment** at the present time; now, considered as a shorter or longer period 此刻, 现在, 目前(可指较短或较长的时间): *The number is engaged at the moment. Try again in five minutes.* 这个号现在占线. 五分钟后再试试吧. ○ *He's unemployed at the moment and has been for over six months.* 他目前失业, 已经有半年多了. **for the ˈmoment/ˈpresent** temporarily; for now 暂时; 目前: *We're happy living in a flat for the moment but we may want to move to a house soon.* 目前我们住单元房很满意, 不过不久我们也许想住个独门独院的房子. **have one's/its ˈmoments** (*infml* 口) have short times that are more interesting than the ordinary usual times 有快乐的时候: *My job is not a very glamorous one but it does have its moments.* 我的工作虽不算十分吸引人, 但也自有其乐趣所在. **in the heat of the moment** ⇨ HEAT¹. **in a ˈmoment** very soon 一会儿; 立刻; 马上: *I'll come in a moment.* 我一会儿就来. **the last minute/moment** ⇨ LAST¹. **the man, woman, boy, girl, etc of the ˈmoment** person that is highly praised, most popular or most important at present 当前备受称赞、红极一时或最重要的人物. **the minute/moment (that...)** ⇨ MINUTE¹. **the ˌmoment of ˈtruth** point at which the reality of the condition of sb/sth has to be faced and an important decision has to be made 重要关头; 决定性时刻. **not for a/one minute/moment** ⇨ MINUTE¹. **of ˈmoment** (*fml* 文) of importance 重要的; 关系重大的: *This is a matter of great/some/little/no small moment.* 此事关系重大[不无关系/关系不大/非同小可]. **on the spur of the moment** ⇨ SPUR. **the psychological moment** ⇨ PSYCHOLOGICAL (PSYCHOLOGY). **a weak moment** ⇨ WEAK.

mo·ment·ary /ˈməʊməntrɪ; *US* -terɪ; ˈmomənˌtɛrɪ/ *adj* lasting for a very short time 短暂的; 瞬间的; 片刻的: *a momentary pause, interruption, success* 暂短的停顿、中断、成功.

▷ **mo·ment·ar·ily** /ˈməʊməntrəlɪ; *US* ˌməʊmənˈterəlɪ; ˌmomənˈtɛrəlɪ/ *adv* **1** for a very short time 短暂地; 瞬间地; 片刻地: *He shuddered momentarily.* 他哆嗦了一下. **2** (*esp US*) very soon; immediately 立即; 即刻: *The doctor will see you momentarily.* 医生马上就来看你.

mo·ment·ous /məˈmentəs, məʊˈm-; məˈmɛntəs, moˈm-/ *adj* very important; serious 极重要的; 严重的: *a momentous decision, occasion, event* 重要的决定、场合、事件 ○ *momentous changes* 重大的变化.

mo·mentum /məˈmentəm, məʊˈm-; məˈmɛntəm, moˈm-/ *n* [U] **1** force that increases the rate of development of a process; impetus 动力; 冲力; 势头: *The movement to change the union's constitution is slowly gathering momentum.* 修改工会宪章的运动正慢慢加强. **2** (*physics* 物) quantity of motion of a moving object, measured as its mass multiplied by its velocity 动量: *The sledge gained momentum as it ran down the hill.* 雪橇从山上下冲时动量越来越大.

momma /ˈmɒmə; ˈmʌmə/ (also **mommy** /ˈmɒmɪ; ˈmʌmɪ/) *n* (*US infml* 口) =MUMMY².

Mon *abbr* 缩写 = Monday: *Mon 21 June* 6月21日星期一.

mon·arch /ˈmɒnək; ˈmɑnɚk/ *n* supreme ruler; king, queen, emperor or empress 最高统治者; 国王; 女王; 皇帝; 女皇: *the reigning monarch* 在位的君主.

▷ **mon·archic** /məˈnɑːkɪk; məˈnɑrkɪk/, **mon·arch·ical** /məˈnɑːkɪkl; məˈnɑrkɪkḷ/ *adjs* [attrib 作定语] of a monarch or monarchy 君主的; 君主政体的; 君主制度的: *the system of monarchical government* 君主政体.

mon·arch·ist /ˈmɒnəkɪst; ˈmɑnɚkɪst/ *n* person who believes that a country should be ruled by a monarch 君主主义者. **mon·arch·ism** /-kɪzəm; -ˌkɪzəm/ *n* [U].

mon·archy /ˈmɒnəkɪ; ˈmɑnɚkɪ/ *n* **1** (usu 通常作 **the monarchy**) [sing] system of government by a monarch 君主政体; 君主制: *plans to abolish the monarchy* 废除君主政体的计划. **2** [C] state governed by such a system 君主国: *The United Kingdom is a constitutional monarchy.* 英国是君主立宪国. Cf 参看 REPUBLIC.

mon·as·tery /ˈmɒnəstrɪ; *US* -terɪ; ˈmɑnəsˌtɛrɪ/ *n* building in which monks live as a community 隐修院. Cf 参看 CONVENT, NUNNERY (NUN).

mon·astic /məˈnæstɪk; məˈnæstɪk/ *adj* **1** of or relating to monks or monasteries 修士的; 隐修院的: *a monastic community* 隐修院修士集体. **2** like life in a monastery; simple and quiet 隐修院式生活的; 简朴而清静的: *lead a monastic life* 过隐居的生活.

▷ **mon·asti·cism** /məˈnæstɪsɪzəm; məˈnæstəˌsɪzəm/ *n* [U] way of life of monks in monasteries 隐修院修士的生活方式.

mon·aural /ˌmɒnˈɔːrəl; mɑnˈɔrəl/ *adj* ⇨ MONOPHONIC.

Mon·day /ˈmʌndɪ; ˈmʌndɪ/ *n* [C, U] (*abbr* 缩写 **Mon**) the second day of the week, next after Sunday 星期一: *He was born on a Monday.* 他是星期一出生的. ○ *They met on the Monday and were married on the Friday*, ie on those days in a particular week. 他们星期一相遇, 星期五就结婚了. ○ *last/next Monday* 上[下]星期一 ○ *the Monday before last* 上上星期一 ○ *'What's today?' 'It's Monday'.* '今天星期几?' '星期一.' ○ *We'll meet on Monday.* 我们星期一见面. ○ (*Brit infml or US* 英式英语口语或美式英语) *We'll meet Monday*, ie on the day before next Tuesday. 我们下星期一见面. ○ *'When did they meet?' '(On) Monday* (ie On the day before last Tuesday).' 他们是什么时候见的面?' '上星期一.' ○ *I work Monday(s) to Friday(s).* 我星期一至星期五工作. ○ *(On) Monday(s)* (ie Every Monday) *I do the shopping.* 每星期一我都去买东西. ○ *I always do the shopping on a Monday.* 我总是在星期一买东西. ○ [attrib 作定语] *Monday morning/afternoon/evening* 星期一上午[下午/晚上].

mon·et·ary /ˈmʌnɪtrɪ; *US* -terɪ; ˈmʌnəˌtɛrɪ/ *adj* [attrib 作定语] of money or currency 钱的; 货币的: *the government's monetary policy* 政府的货币政策 ○ *the international monetary system* 国际货币制度 ○ *The monetary unit of Japan is the yen.* 日本的货币单位是元.

▷ **mon·et·ar·ism** /-tərɪzəm; -təˌrɪzəm/ *n* [U] policy of controlling the amount of money available as the chief method of stabilizing a country's economy 货币主义(以控制货币供给量作为稳定国家经济的主要方法的政策). **mon·et·ar·ist** /-tərɪst; -tərɪst/ *n* person favouring monetarism 货币主义者. — *adj* of or relating to monetarism 货币主义的: *monetarist policies* 货币主义政策.

money /ˈmʌnɪ; ˈmʌnɪ/ *n* (*pl* in sense 3 **moneys** or **monies** 用于下述第3义时复数作 **moneys** 或 **monies**) **1** [U] means of payment, esp coins and banknotes, given and accepted in buying and selling 钱; 金钱; 货币: *have money in one's pocket* 口袋里有钱 ○ *earn, borrow, save, etc a lot of money* 挣、借、节省...很多钱 ○ *How much money is there in my (bank) account?* 我的(银行)户头里有多少钱? ○ *change English money into French money/francs* 把英国钱换成法国钱[法郎]. ⇨App 4 见附录 4. **2** [U] wealth; (total value of) sb's property 财富; 某人的财产(总值): *inherit money from sb* 从某人处继承财

产 ○ *lose all one's money* 失掉个人的全部家当 ○ *marry sb for his money*, ie for the sake of wealth and possessions that he has or will inherit later 为获得财产而嫁给某人. **3 moneys** or **monies** [*pl*] (*arch or law* 古或律) sum of money 金额: *to collect all monies due* 收集到期的全部金额. **4** (idm 习语) **be in the 'money** (*infml* 口) have a lot of money to spend; be rich 有钱; 富有. **coin it/money** ⇨ COIN. **easy money** ⇨ EASY[1]. **even chances/odds/money** ⇨ EVEN[1]. **a fool and his money are soon parted** ⇨ FOOL[1]. **for 'my money** (*infml* 口) in my opinion 据我看: *For my money, Ann's idea is better than Mary's.* 我认为安的主意比玛丽的好. **get one's 'money's-worth** get the full value in goods or services for the money one has spent 花得上算. **good 'money** a lot of money; money that is hard-earned and not to be wasted 大笔的钱; 来之不易的钱: *earn, pay, cost good money* 赚、付、值很多钱. **have 'money to burn** have so much money that one can spend it freely 有的是钱. **a licence to print money** ⇨ LICENCE. **'made of money** (*infml* 口) very wealthy 极有钱: *I'm not made of money, you know!* 你知道我又不是财神爷! **make 'money** make a profit; earn a lot of money 赚钱; 发财. **make money ,hand over 'fist** make big profits from business, etc 发大财; 赚大钱. **marry money** ⇨ MARRY. **money burns a hole in sb's pocket** sb is eager to spend money or spends it quickly or extravagantly 有钱就想花; 大手大脚. **money for 'jam/old 'rope** (*infml* 口) money or profit earned from a task that requires very little effort 容易赚的钱; 便宜买卖. **money talks** (*saying* 谚) if one is wealthy it enables one to get special treatment, influence people, promote one's own interests, etc 有钱就灵. **not for love or money** ⇨ LOVE[1]. **put money into sth** invest money in (an enterprise, etc) 投资于(某企业等): *put money into stocks and shares, the Channel tunnel project, property* 投资于债券与股票、海峡隧道工程、房地产. **put one's money on sb/sth** (**a**) place a bet that (a horse, dog, etc) will win a race 在参赛的(马、狗等)上下赌注. (**b**) confidently expect sb/sth to succeed 确信某人[某事]会成功: *I'll put my money on him.* 我确信他能成功. **put one's money where one's 'mouth is** (*infml* 口) show one's support in a practical way, not just by one's words 以实际行动支持, 并非说空话. **a run for one's money** ⇨ RUN[1]. **see the colour of sb's money** ⇨ COLOUR[1]. **there's money in sth** profit can be obtained from sth (某事物)有利可图. **throw one's money about** (*infml* 口) spend one's money recklessly and ostentatiously 大肆挥霍. **you pays your money and you takes your choice** ⇨ PAY[2].

▷ **moneyed** /ˈmʌnɪd; ˋmʌnɪd/ *adj* (*dated* 旧) having a lot of money; wealthy 有钱的; 富有的: *the moneyed classes* 有钱阶级.

money·less *adj* having no money 无钱的.

□ **'money-back guarantee** guarantee to return the money paid if the buyer is not satisfied 退款保证(顾客不满意, 保证退款).

'money-bags *n* (*pl* unchanged 复数不变) (*infml esp derog* 口, 尤作贬义) rich person 有钱人.

'money-box *n* small closed box with a slot in the top, into which coins are put as a method of saving money 扑满; 存钱罐.

'money-changer *n* person whose business is to change money of one country for that of another, usu at the official rate 外币兑换商(通常指按官价兑换的).

'money-grubber *n* person who greedily wants to gain money, usu by dishonest methods 敛财者(通常指用不正当手段). **'money-grubbing** *adj*.

'money-lender *n* person whose business is to lend money, usu at a high rate of interest 放款者; (通常指)放债者.

'money-maker *n* **1** person who works to gain a lot of money 赚大钱的人. **2** (*infml usu approv* 口, 通常作褒义) product or business investment that produces a large profit 赚钱的产品或投资. **'money-making** *adj*: *a money-making plan* 有利可图的计划.

M

'money-market *n* place of operation of dealers in short-term loans 短期贷款市场.

'money order official document for payment of a specified sum of money, issued by a bank or Post Office 汇票; 汇款单.

'money-spinner *n* (*infml* 口 *usu Brit*) thing that earns a lot of money 赚大钱的东西: *Her new book is a real money-spinner.* 她的新书真是棵摇钱树.

the 'money supply total amount of money that exists in the economy of a country at a particular time (一定时期内全国流通的)货币供应量: *control, reduce, increase, etc the money supply* 控制、减少、增加...货币供应量.

mon·ger /ˈmʌŋgə(r); ˋmʌŋgɚ/ *n* (only in compounds 仅用以构成复合词) **1** trader or dealer 贩子: *fishmonger* ○ *ironmonger*, ie sb who sells hardware. **2** (*derog* 贬) person who makes something unpleasant widely known 传播坏事的人: *a gossip monger* ○ *a scandalmonger* ○ *a warmonger*.

mon·gol /ˈmɒŋgəl; ˋmɑŋgəl/ *n* (*usu offensive* 通常作轻蔑语) person suffering from Down's syndrome 患有唐氏综合征的人; 先天愚型患者. ▷ **mon·gol·ism** /-ɪzəm; -ɪzəm/ *n* [U] (*usu offensive* 通常作轻蔑语) =DOWN'S SYNDROME.

mongoose 獴

mon·goose /ˈmɒŋgu:s; ˋmɑŋgus/ *n* (*pl* ~**s** /-sɪz; -sɪz/) small furry tropical mammal that kills snakes, birds, rats, etc 獴.

mon·grel /ˈmʌŋgrəl; ˋmʌŋgrəl/ *n* **1** dog of mixed breed 杂种狗. **2** any plant or animal of mixed origin 杂交的动植物: [attrib 作定语] *a mongrel breed* 杂种 ○ *of mongrel stock* 混种的.

mon·itor /ˈmɒnɪtə(r); ˋmɑnətɚ/ *n* **1** device used to observe, record or test sth 监听器; 监视器; 监测器: *a heart monitor* 心脏监测器 ○ *a monitor for radioactivity* 放射量探测器. **2** person who listens to and reports on foreign radio broadcasts and signals 监听外国广播者. **3** (**a**) TV screen used in a studio to check or choose the broadcast picture (电视台选播用的)监视屏. (**b**) (*computing* 计) screen or other device used for checking the progress and operation of a computer system 监控荧光屏或装置. ⇨illus at COMPUTER 见 COMPUTER 插图. **4** (*fem* 阴性作 **mon·it·ress** /ˈmɒnɪtrɪs; ˋmɑnətrɪs/) pupil with special duties in a school 任某职责的学生: *the homework monitor* 家庭作业检查员. **5** any of various large lizards of Africa, Asia or Australia 巨蜥(产于非洲、亚洲、澳洲).

▷ **mon·itor** *v* [Tn] **1** make continuous observation of (sth); record or test the operation of (sth) 持续观察(某事物); 记录或测试(某物)的运作: *monitor sb's performance/progress* 监督某人的表现[进步] ○ *monitor a patient's pulse* 监测病人的脉搏. **2** listen to and report on (foreign radio broadcasts and signals) 监听(外国无线电广播和信号).

monk /mʌŋk; mʌŋk/ *n* member of a religious community of men who live apart from the rest of society and who have made solemn promises, esp not to marry and not to have any possessions 修士、僧侣(尤指誓言不结婚、不要财产者). Cf 参看 FRIAR, NUN.

▷ **monk·ish** *adj* of or like monks (似)修士的, 僧侣的.

mon·key /ˈmʌŋkɪ; ˋmʌŋkɪ/ *n* **1** member of the group of animals most similar to humans in appearance, esp a type of small long-tailed tree-climbing animal 猴; 猿. ⇨ illus 见插图. **2** (*infml* 口) lively mischievous child 顽皮的儿童: *Come here at once, you little monkey!* 马上过来, 你这个小捣蛋! **3** (*sl* 俚) £500 or $500 500英镑; 500元.

▷ **mon·key** *v* (phr v) **monkey about/around** (*infml* 口) behave in a foolish mischievous way 调皮; 捣蛋: *Stop monkeying about!* 别调皮了! **monkey about/around with sth** (*infml* 口) play or interfere with sth in a careless way 胡摆弄某物或干扰某事: *monkey about with a fire extinguisher* 乱摆弄灭火器.

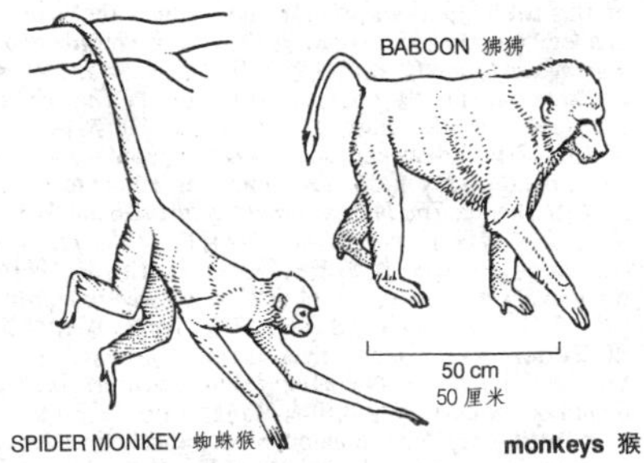

monkeys 猴

□ ˈ**monkey business** mischievous or dishonest activity or behaviour 胡闹; 骗人的把戏; 恶作剧: *There's been some monkey business going on here!* 有人在这里搞鬼!

ˈ**monkey-nut** *n* peanut 花生.

ˈ**monkey-puzzle** *n* (also ˈ**monkey-puzzle tree**) evergreen tree with narrow stiff sharp leaves and interlaced branches 猴谜树(常绿植物, 叶尖而硬, 树枝缠结).

ˈ**monkey-wrench** *n* spanner with a jaw that can be adjusted to hold things of different widths 活动扳手; 活扳子.

mono /ˈmɒnəʊ; ˈmɑno/ *adj* (*infml* 口) =MONOPHONIC.

▷ **mono** *n* [U] (*infml* 口) monophonic sound or reproduction 单声道录放音或复制: *a recording in mono* 单声道录音. Cf 参看 STEREO.

mon(o)- *comb form* 构词成分 one; single 单; 一: *monogamy* ○ *monomania* ○ *monorail*.

mono·chrome /ˈmɒnəkrəʊm; ˈmɑnəˌkrom/ *adj* **1** having or using images in black, white and shades of grey; black and white 黑白的: *a monochrome photograph, print, drawing, etc* 黑白照片、印刷品、图画等 ○ *monochrome television* 黑白电视. **2** having or using varying shades of one colour 单色的.

▷ **mono·chrome** *n* (**a**) [U] monochrome reproduction 单色复制(品): *painting in monochrome* 用单色复制的画. (**b**) [C] monochrome painting, photograph, etc 单色的画、照片等.

mon·ocle /ˈmɒnəkl; ˈmɑnəkl/ *n* single glass lens for one eye, kept in position by the muscles round the eye 单眼镜.

mono·co·ty·ledon /ˌmɒnəˌkɒtɪˈliːdən; ˌmɑnəˌkɑtḷˈidṇ/ *n* (*botany* 植) flowering plant that has one leaf at the embryonic stage 单子叶植物.

mono·gamy /məˈnɒgəmɪ; məˈnɑgəmɪ/ *n* [U] practice or custom of being married to only one person at a time 一夫一妻(制). Cf 参看 POLYGAMY. ▷ **mono·gam·ous** /məˈnɒgəməs; məˈnɑgəməs/ *adj*

monogram
字母组合图案

mono·gram /ˈmɒnəgræm; ˈmɑnəˌgræm/ *n* two or more letters(esp a person's initials) combined in one design and marked on handkerchiefs, notepaper, etc 字母组合图案(用至少两个字母, 尤指姓名首字母, 组成的图案, 用于手帕、信笺等上). ▷ **monogrammed** *adj*: *a monogrammed shirt* 有字母组合图案的衬衫. ⇨ illus 见插图.

mono·graph /ˈmɒnəgrɑːf; *US* -græf; ˈmɑnəˌgræf/ *n* detailed scholarly study of one subject 专题研究; 专论; 专文.

mono·lin·gual /ˌmɒnəˈlɪŋgwəl; ˌmɑnəˈlɪŋgwəl/ *adj* using only one language 只用一种语言的: *a monolingual dictionary* 单语词典. Cf 参看 BILINGUAL, MULTILINGUAL.

mono·lith /ˈmɒnəlɪθ; ˈmɑnḷˌɪθ/ *n* large single upright block of stone, usu shaped into a pillar or monument 单块巨石(通常用作柱体或纪念碑).

▷ **mono·lithic** /ˌmɒnəˈlɪθɪk; ˌmɑnḷˈɪθɪk/ *adj* **1** consisting of one or more monoliths 单块巨石的; 整石料的; 由巨石块料组成的: *a monolithic monument* 整块巨石纪念碑. **2** single, massive and unchangeable 庞大而坚如磐石的: *the monolithic structure of the state* 国家坚如磐石的庞大结构.

mono·logue (*US* also **mono·log**) /ˈmɒnəlɒg; *US* -lɔːg; ˈmɑnḷˌɔg/ *n* **1** [C] long speech by one person in a conversation, which prevents other people from talking; soliloquy 长篇谈话(使别人无从插话); 自言自语. **2** [C, U] (**a**) long speech in a play, film, etc spoken by one actor, esp when alone; soliloquy (戏剧、电影等中的)独白; 自言自语. (**b**) dramatic story, esp in verse, recited or performed by one person 独角戏(尤指诗体的).

mono·ma·nia /ˌmɒnəʊˈmeɪnɪə; ˌmɑnəˈmenɪə/ *n* [U] state of mind in which a person is obsessed with one idea or subject 单狂; 偏狂.

▷ **mono·ma·niac** /ˌmɒnəʊˈmeɪnɪæk; ˌmɑnəˈmenɪˌæk/ *n* sufferer from monomania 单狂者; 偏狂者.

mono·phonic /ˌmɒnəˈfɒnɪk; ˌmɑnəˈfɑnɪk/ *adj* (also *infml* 口语作 **mono**) (of sound reproduction) using only one channel of transmission (指声音的复制)单声道的: *a monophonic recording* 单声道录音. Cf 参看 STEREOPHONIC.

mon·oph·thong /ˈmɒnəfθɒŋ; ˈmɑnəfˌθɔŋ/ *n* simple or pure vowel sound, in which the speech organs remain in the same position as the sound is pronounced 单元音. Cf 参看 DIPHTHONG.

mono·plane /ˈmɒnəpleɪn; ˈmɑnəˌplen/ *n* aeroplane with only one set of wings 单翼机. Cf 参看 BIPLANE.

mono·pol·ize, -ise /məˈnɒpəlaɪz; məˈnɑpḷˌaɪz/ *v* [Tn] have a very large share of (sth), so preventing others from sharing it; dominate 独占(某事物)的绝大部分; 垄断: *monopolize a conversation* 垄断谈话 ○ *trying to monopolize the supply of oil* 企图垄断石油供应 ○ (*fig* 比喻) *Don't monopolize our special guest — there are others who would like to talk to her.* 别把持着我们的贵宾——别人还想跟她谈话呢. ▷ **mono·pol·iza·tion, -isation** /məˌnɒpəlaɪˈzeɪʃn; *US* -lɪˈz-; məˌnɑpḷəˈzeʃən/ *n* [U].

mono·poly /məˈnɒpəlɪ; məˈnɑplɪ/ *n* **1** (**a**) sole right to supply or trade in some commodity or service 专卖(权); 专利(权): *gain/hold/secure a monopoly* 获得[持有/得到]专利权. (**b**) commodity or service controlled in this way 专卖品; 专营服务: *In some countries tobacco is a government monopoly.* 在有些国家烟草是政府的专卖品. **2** sole possession or control of sth 独占; 控制: *A good education should not be the monopoly of the rich.* 良好的教育不应是富人独享的事. ○ *You can't have a complete monopoly of the car — I need to use it occasionally.* 你不能一人独霸这辆汽车——我偶尔也要用.

▷ **mono·pol·ist** /-lɪst; -lɪst/ *n* person who has a monopoly 有专卖或专利权的人; 专卖或专营者. **mono·pol·istic** /məˌnɒpəˈlɪstɪk; məˌnɑpəˈlɪstɪk/ *adj*.

mono·rail /ˈmɒnəʊreɪl; ˈmɑnəˌrel/ *n* [U, C] railway system in which trains travel along a track consisting of a single rail, usu placed high above the ground 单轨, 单轨铁路(通常指高架的).

mono·so·dium glut·am·ate /ˌmɒnəʊˌsəʊdɪəm ˈgluːtəmeɪt; ˌmɑnəˌsodɪəm ˈglutəˌmet/ white chemical compound that is added to foods, usu meat, to make their flavour stronger 谷胺酸钠; 味精.

mono·syl·lable /ˈmɒnəsɪləbl; ˈmɑnəˌsɪləbl/ *n* word with only one syllable, eg *it, and, no* 单音节词(如it、and、no): *speak in monosyllables*, eg when not wanting to talk to sb 用单音节词说话(如不想和某人说话时). Cf 参看 DISYLLABLE.

▷ **mono·syl·labic** /ˌmɒnəsɪˈlæbɪk; ˌmɑnəsɪˈlæbɪk/ *adj* **1** having only one syllable 单音节的: *a monosyllabic word* 单音节的词. **2** made up of words of only one syllable 由单音节词组成的: *monosyllabic answers*, eg saying only 'Yes' or 'No' when not wanting to give sb any information 单音节词的回答(如不愿提供信息, 只答yes或no). **mono·syl·labic·ally** /-klɪ; -klɪ/ *adv*. **M**

mono·the·ism /ˈmɒnəʊθiːɪzəm; ˈmɑnəθiˌɪzəm/ *n* [U]

belief that there is only one God 一神论; 一神教. Cf 参看 POLYTHEISM.

▷ **mono·the·ist** /ˈmɒnəʊθiːɪst; ˈmɑnəθiɪst/ *n* believer in monotheism 一神论者; 信一神教者.

mono·the·istic /ˌmɒnəʊθiːˈɪstɪk; ˌmɑnəθiˈɪstɪk/ *adj.*

mono·tone /ˈmɒnətəʊn; ˈmɑnəˌton/ *n* [sing] **1** (sound in a) way of speaking in which the pitch of the voice remains level and unchanging 单调(的声音): *to speak in a monotone* 用单调的声音说话. **2** lack of variety, as in a style of writing (文体的)单调, 无变化.

▷ **mono·tone** *adj* [attrib 作定语] without changing the pitch of the voice or the shade of colour (声音或色彩)单调的, 无变化的: *monotone concrete buildings* 单调的混凝土建筑.

mono·ton·ous /məˈnɒtənəs; məˈnɑtn̩əs/ *adj* not changing and therefore uninteresting; boring or tedious 单调乏味的; 使人厌倦的; 无聊的: *a monotonous voice*, ie one with little change of pitch 单调的声音 ○ *monotonous work* 单调乏味的工作. ▷ **mono·ton·ously** *adv*.

mono·tony /məˈnɒtənɪ; məˈnɑtnɪ/ *n* [U] state of being monotonous; lack of variety that causes weariness and boredom 单调乏味; 无聊: *relieve the monotony of everyday life* 缓解日常生活的单调状况.

mon·ox·ide /mɒˈnɒksaɪd; mɑnˈɑksaɪd/ *n* [U, C] chemical compound whose molecules contain one atom of oxygen combined with one or more other atoms 一氧化物: *carbon monoxide* 一氧化碳.

Mon·sieur /məˈsjɜː(r); məˈsjɝ/ *n* (*abbr* 缩写 **M**) (*pl* **Messieurs** /meɪˈsjɜː(r); meˈsjɝ/) (*French* 法) (title used before the name of a man to refer to him, or used alone as a formal and polite term of address 对男子的称谓, 用于姓名前; 若单独使用时较庄重、客气) Mr; sir 先生: *M Hercule Poirot* 赫尔克里·波瓦先生 ○ *Yes, monsieur.* 是, 先生.

Mon·signor /mɒnˈsiːnjə(r); mɑnˈsinjɚ/ *n* (*abbr* 缩写 **Mgr**) (title of a) high-ranking priest in the Roman Catholic Church 阁下(对天主教高级教士的尊称).

mon·soon /ˌmɒnˈsuːn; mɑnˈsun/ *n* **1** seasonal wind in S Asia, esp in the Indian Ocean, blowing from SW from April to October and from NE from October to April (南亚的)季风(尤指印度洋上四月至十月的西南风和十月至四月的东北风). **2** very rainy season that comes with the SW monsoon (西南季风带来的)雨季.

mon·ster /ˈmɒnstə(r); ˈmɑnstɚ/ *n* **1** (**a**) large, ugly and frightening creature, esp an imaginary one 巨大、丑陋、可怕的怪物(尤指想像的): *A hideous monster attacked the helpless villagers.* 有个丑恶的怪物袭击了手无寸铁的村民. ○ *prehistoric monsters* 史前怪物 ○ *Do you believe in the Loch Ness monster?* 你相信内斯湖有水怪吗? (**b**) (usu ugly) animal or plant that is abnormal in form (通常指难看的)畸形的动植物. **2** cruel or evil person 残忍的人; 恶人: *Let go of me, you vicious monster!* 放开我, 你这可恶的傢伙! **3** thing that is extremely large 极大的东西: [attrib 作定语] *monster high-rise blocks of flats* 庞大的高层公寓大楼.

mon·strous /ˈmɒnstrəs; ˈmɑnstrəs/ *adj* **1** shocking, unjust or absurd; outrageous 令人震惊的; 不公正的; 荒谬的; 凶暴的: *a monstrous lie* 厚颜无耻的谎言 ○ *monstrous crimes* 骇人听闻的罪行 ○ *It's absolutely monstrous to pay men more than women for the same job.* 男女同工而报酬男多于女, 简直太不像话了. **2** like a monster in appearance; ugly and frightening 似怪物的; 丑恶而可怕的: *the monstrous form of a fire-breathing dragon* 喷火巨龙可怕的形状. **3** extremely large; gigantic 极大的; 巨大的.

▷ **mon·stros·ity** /mɒnˈstrɒsətɪ; mɑnˈstrɑsətɪ/ *n* thing that is large and very ugly 巨大而丑陋的东西: *That new multi-storey car-park is an utter monstrosity!* 那座新建的多层停车场难看极了!

mon·strously *adv*

mont·age /ˈmɒntɑːʒ; *US* mɒnˈtɑːʒ; mɑnˈtɑʒ/ *n* **1** (**a**) [C] picture, film or piece of music or writing made up of many separate items put together, esp in an interesting combination 蒙太奇(由许多部分组合而成的画面、影片、音乐或文字). (**b**) [U] process of making such a picture, film, etc 蒙太奇手法. **2** [U] choosing, cutting and joining of different pieces of film to indicate a passage of time, change of place, etc 蒙太奇(对影片不同镜头的剪辑, 借以表现时间推移、地点转换等).

month /mʌnθ; mʌnθ/ *n* **1** (also ˌ**calendar ˈmonth**) any of the twelve periods of time into which the year is divided, eg May and June 月份; 月: *We're going on holiday next month.* 我们准备下月去度假. ○ *She earns £1 000 a month.* 她一个月挣1 000英镑. ○ *The rent is £300 per calendar month.* 租金每历月300英镑. **2** period of time between a day in one month and the corresponding day in the next month, eg 3 June to 3 July 一个月的时间: *The baby is three months old.* 孩子三个月大了. ○ *several months later* 数月后 ○ *the first few months of marriage* 结婚最初数月 ○ [attrib 作定语] *a six-month contract* 六个月的合同 ○ *a seven-month-old baby* 七个月大的孩子. **3** (idm 习语) **for/in a ˌmonth of ˈSundays** (esp in negative sentences 尤用于否定句) for a very long time 很长时间: *I've not seen her for/in a month of Sundays.* 我很久没有见到她了.

▷ **monthly** *adj* **1** done, happening, published, etc once a month or every month 每月的; 每月一次的: *a monthly meeting, visit, magazine* 每月一次的例会、访问、刊物. **2** payable, valid or calculated for one month 按月支付的; 有效期为一个月的; 按月计算的: *a monthly season ticket* 月票 ○ *a monthly income of £800* 800英镑的月收入. — *adv* every month; once a month 每月; 按月; 一月一次地: *to be paid monthly* 每月得到一次付款. — *n* **1** magazine published once a month 月刊: *a literary monthly* 文学月刊. **2** season-ticket valid for a month 月票: *A monthly is more economical than 4 weeklies.* 一张月票比四张周票上算.

monu·ment /ˈmɒnjʊmənt; ˈmɑnjəmənt/ *n* **1** building, column, statue, etc built to remind people of a famous person or event 纪念馆; 纪念碑; 纪念像; 纪念物: *a monument erected to soldiers killed in the war* 阵亡将士纪念碑. **2** building, etc that is preserved because of its historical importance to a country (对国家有重要性的)历史遗迹: *an ancient monument* 一处古迹. **3 ~ to sth** notable thing that stands as a lasting reminder of sb's deeds, achievements, etc (对某人业绩、成就等的)永久性纪念物: *This whole city is a monument to his skill as a planner and administrator.* 这整座城市经他亲自设计并管理, 正是对他的才能的纪念.

mo·nu·mental /ˌmɒnjʊˈmentl; ˌmɑnjəˈmɛntl̩/ *adj* **1** [attrib 作定语] of, related to or serving as a monument 纪念物的; 用作纪念的: *a monumental inscription*, ie inscribed on a monument 碑铭 ○ *monumental brasses, sculptures, figures, etc* 有纪念意义的黄铜纪念牌、雕塑物、塑像等. **2** [attrib 作定语] (of buildings, sculptures, etc) very large and impressive (指建筑物、雕塑等)巨大而了不起的: *a monumental arch, column, façade, etc* 雄伟的拱形牌坊、纪念柱、外观等. **3** [usu attrib 通常作定语] (of a literary or musical work) large and of lasting value (指文学或音乐作品)伟大而不朽的: *a monumental production* 伟大不朽的作品. **4** [usu attrib 通常作定语] exceptionally great 极大的: *a monumental achievement, success, blunder, failure, etc* 极大的成就、成功、错误、失败等 ○ *What monumental ignorance!* 真是无知之极!

▷ **mo·nu·ment·ally** /-təlɪ; -tl̩ɪ/ *adv* extremely 极度地; 极端地: *monumentally boring, stupid, successful* 极为烦人的、愚蠢的、成功的.

□ ˌ**monumental ˈmason** maker of tombstones, etc 墓碑匠.

moo /muː; mu/ *n* long deep sound made by a cow 牛叫声.

▷ **moo** *v* [I] make this sound 作牛叫声.

□ ˈ**moo-cow** *n* (used by or to young children 儿语) cow 牛.

mooch /muːtʃ; mutʃ/ *v* **1** [Tn, Tn·pr] **~ sth (off/from sb)** (*US infml* 口) get sth by asking; cadge sth 乞讨某物: *mooch money off sb* 向某人讨钱. **2** (phr v) **mooch about/around (...)** (*infml* 口) wander aimlessly around (a place) 漫步; 闲逛: *mooching around the house with nothing to do* 在房子周围无事闲逛.

mood[1] /muːd; mud/ *n* **1** state of one's feelings or mind at a particular time 心境; 情绪: *She's in a good mood* (ie happy) *today.* 她今天心情很好. ○ *He's always in a bad mood* (ie irritable and angry) *on Mondays.* 他每星期一情绪都很坏. ○ *His mood suddenly changed and he became calm.* 他的情绪突然一变, 冷静了下来. **2** fit of bad temper; depression 发脾气; 情绪低落: *He's in a mood/in one of his moods today.* 他今天闹情绪了.

M

3 (usu *sing* 通常作单数) way a group or community feels about sth; atmosphere (人群或社会对某事物的)心态, 气氛: *The film captured* (ie described very well) *the mood of quiet confidence at the hospital.* 影片捕捉到了医院里沉着而自信的气氛. **4** (idm 习语) **(be) in the mood for (doing) sth/to do sth** feeling like doing sth; inclined to do sth 有做某事物的心思或兴致: *I'm not in the mood to disagree with you.* 我没有心思跟你争论. **(be) in no mood for (doing) sth/to do sth** not feeling like doing sth; not inclined to sth 没有做某事物的心思或兴致: *He's in no mood for (telling) jokes/to tell jokes.* 他没心情说笑话.

▷ **moody** *adj* (**-ier, -iest**) **1** having moods that change quickly 喜怒无常的: *moody and unpredictable* 喜怒无常而又不可捉摸的. **2** bad-tempered; gloomy or sullen 脾气坏的; 闷闷不乐的. **mood·ily** /-ɪlɪ; -əlɪ/ *adv.* **moodi·ness** *n* [U].

mood[2] /muːd; mud/ *n* (*grammar*) any of the three sets of verb forms that show whether what is said or written is considered certain, possible, doubtful, necessary, desirable, etc 式, 语气(以动词形式表现的三种语法特征, 可表示确实、可能、怀疑、必要、愿望等语气): *the indicative/imperative/subjunctive mood* 陈述[祈使/虚拟]语气.

moon[1] /muːn; mun/ *n* **1** [sing] (**a**) (usu 通常作 **the moon**) the natural body that moves round the earth once every 28 days and shines at night by light reflected from the sun 月球: *explore the surface of the moon* 探察月球的表面 ○ [attrib 作定语] *a moon landing* 登月. (**b**) this body as it appears in the sky at a particular time 月亮: *There's no moon tonight*, ie No moon can be seen. 今天晚上没有月亮. ○ *a crescent moon* 弦月 ○ *a new moon* 新月 ○ *a full moon* 满月. **2** [C] body that moves round a planet other than the earth (地球以外的)行星的卫星: *How many moons does Jupiter have?* 木星有多少卫星? **3** (idm 习语) **many 'moons ago** a long time ago 很久以前: *All that happened many moons ago.* 那一切都发生在很久以前. **once in a blue moon** ⇨ ONCE. **over the 'moon** (*infml* 口) absolutely delighted; ecstatic 非常快乐; 狂喜: *The whole team were over the moon at winning the competition.* 全队都为赢得这场比赛而欣喜若狂. **promise the earth/moon** ⇨ PROMISE[2].

▷ **moon·less** *adj* without a visible moon 没有月亮的: *a dark, moonless sky/night* 黑暗的、没有月亮的天空[夜晚].

□ **'moonbeam** *n* ray of moonlight (一道)月光.

'moon-face *n* round face like a moon when seen as a complete circle 圆脸.

'moonlight *n* [U] light of the moon 月光: *a walk by moonlight/in the moonlight* 月光下的漫步. — *v* (*pt, pp* **-lighted**) [I] (*infml* 口) have a second job, esp at night, in addition to one's regular one during the day 兼职(尤指夜晚的). **'moonlighting** *n* [U]. — *adj* [attrib 作定语] **1** lit by the moon; moonlit 有月光的: *a moonlight night* 月夜. **2** (idm 习语) **do a moonlight 'flit** (*Brit infml* 口) leave a place quickly, secretly and at night to avoid paying one's debts, rent, etc 夜间潜逃(为躲债、逃避交租金等).

'moonlit *adj* lit by the moon 有月光的: *a moonlit night* 月夜.

'moonshine *n* [U] **1** foolish talk, ideas, etc; nonsense 空谈; 妄想; 废话. **2** (*US*) whisky or other spirits illegally distilled 非法酿造的威士忌或其他烈性酒.

'moon-shot *n* launch of a spacecraft to the moon 向月球发射宇宙飞船.

'moonstone *n* semi-precious stone with a pearly appearance used in making jewellery 月长石.

'moonstruck *adj* slightly mad; unbalanced in the mind; wild and wandering in the mind (supposedly as a result of the moon's influence) 轻度狂乱的, 心态失衡的, 迷乱的(据说因月亮影响所致).

moon[2] /muːn; mun/ *v* **1** [I, Ip] **~ (about/around)** (*infml* 口) wander about aimlessly or listlessly 闲逛; 无精打采地徘徊: *Stop mooning and get on with some work!* 别闲逛了, 干点正事吧! ○ *She spent the whole summer mooning about at home.* 她一夏天都在家中混日子. **2** (phr v) **moon over sb** (*infml* 口) spend one's time dreamily thinking about sb one loves 如梦如痴地想念所爱的人.

▷ **moony** *adj* foolishly dreamy 如梦如痴的: *a moony person, look* 精神恍惚的人、样子.

moor[1] /mɔː(r); *US* muər; mur/ *n* (often *pl* 常作复数) open uncultivated high area of land, esp one covered with heather 漠泽, 高沼, 荒野, 旷野(尤指石南丛生者): *go for a walk on the moor/the moors* 到野外散步 ○ *the Yorkshire moors* 约克郡的漠泽 ○ *a grouse moor*, ie where grouse are reared for shooting in sport 松鸡狩猎场.

□ **'moorhen** *n* small water-hen 泽鸡; 水鸡.

'moorland /-lənd; -ˌlənd/ *n* [U, C usu *pl* 作不可数名词或可数名词, 后者通常作复数] land that consists of moor 高沼地: [attrib 作定语] *moorland regions* 高沼地带.

moor[2] /mɔː(r); *US* muər; mur/ *v* [I, Tn, Tn·pr] **~ sth (to sth)** attach (a boat, ship, etc) to a fixed object or the land with a rope or an anchor, etc 使(船等)停泊: *We moored alongside the quay.* 我们靠码头停泊. ○ *The boat was moored to (a post on) the river bank.* 船系泊到河岸(的一根桩子)上.

▷ **moor·ing** /ˈmɔːrɪŋ; *US* ˈmuərɪŋ; ˈmurɪŋ/ *n* **1 moorings** [pl] ropes, anchors, chains, etc by which a ship, boat, etc is moored 系泊设备(绳、锚、链等): *Let go your moorings!* 起锚吧! **2** [C usu *pl* 通常作复数] place where a ship, boat, etc is moored 停泊处: *private moorings* 私人停泊处 ○ [attrib 作定语] *mooring ropes* 系缆.

Moor /muə(r); mur/ *n* (**a**) member of a Muslim people living in NW Africa 摩尔人(居于非洲西北部的穆斯林民族). (**b**) one of the Muslim Arabs who invaded Spain in the 8th century 8世纪入侵西班牙的阿拉伯穆斯林.

▷ **Moor·ish** /ˈmuərɪʃ; ˈmurɪʃ/ *adj* of the Moors and their culture 摩尔人的; 摩尔人文化的.

moose /muːs; mus/ *n* (*pl* unchanged 复数不变) (*US*) = ELK.

moot /muːt; mut/ *adj* (idm 习语) **a moot 'point/'question** matter about which there is uncertainty 悬而未决的事: *It's a moot point whether men or women are better drivers.* 男女司机孰优孰劣尚有争论.

▷ **moot** *v* [Tn usu passive 通常用于被动语态] (*fml* 文) raise (a matter) for discussion; propose 提出(一事)供讨论: *The question was first mooted many years ago.* 这个问题是许多年前就提出的.

mop 拖把

mop /mɒp; mɑp/ *n* **1** (**a**) tool consisting of a bundle of thick strings or a piece of sponge fastened to a long handle, used for cleaning floors 拖把; 墩布. (**b**) similar tool with a short handle, used for various purposes, eg cleaning dishes 短柄拖把状用具(如洗碗刷): *a dish mop* 洗碗刷. **2** mass of thick (usu untidy) hair 蓬松的(通常指蓬乱的)头发: *a mop of curly red hair* 鬈曲而蓬乱的红头发.

▷ **mop** *v* (**-pp-**) **1** [Tn] clean (sth) with a mop 用拖把擦洗(某物): *mop the floor* 擦地板. **2** (**a**) [Tn] wipe (the face), esp with a handkerchief, to remove sweat, tears, etc 擦(脸)(尤指用手帕擦去汗、泪等): *mop one's brow (with a handkerchief)* (用手帕)擦前额. (**b**) [I, Ipr, Tn, Tn·pr] **~ (sth) with sth; ~ sth (from sth)** wipe (a liquid) from a surface using an absorbent cloth 用吸水的布擦掉(液体): *keep mopping (with a towel)* 继续(用毛巾)擦 ○ *mop tears (from one's face) (with a handkerchief)* (用手帕)擦去(脸上的)泪水. **3** (phr v) **mop sth/sb up** (**a**) remove (spilt or unwanted liquid) by wiping it with an absorbent cloth, a mop, etc (用吸水的布、拖把等)擦去(泼洒的或不想要的液体): *She mopped up the pools of water on the bathroom floor.* 她擦

去浴室地面上一滩滩的水. ○ (*Brit*) *mop up* (ie soak up, absorb) *one's gravy with a piece of bread* 用面包吸干肉汁. (**b**) complete (the final parts of a task); deal with (the final members of a group) 结束, 完成(一任务的最后部分); 对付, 处理(一批中的最后几个): *mop up the last few bits of work* 完成最后的几件工作. (**c**) capture or kill (the remaining small groups of people who continue to fight an army) 扫荡(残敌); 肃清(残余分子): *mop up isolated pockets* (ie small areas) *of resistance* 扫荡几处孤立顽抗的小片地区 ○ *engaged in mopping-up operations* 进行扫荡.

mope /məʊp; mop/ *v* **1** [I] feel very unhappy and pity oneself 抑郁不乐; 顾影自怜: *Stop moping!* 别那么垂头丧气的! **2** (phr v) **mope about/around (...)** wander about (a place) in an unhappy or listless mood 闷闷不乐地或无精打采地徘徊: *He's been moping around (the house) all day.* 他整天都在(房子)周围瞎转悠.

▷ **mope** *n* **1** [C] person who mopes 闷闷不乐的人. **2** [sing] act of moping 抑郁不乐; 顾影自怜: *have a bit of a mope* 有些闷闷不乐.

mo·ped /ˈməʊped; ˈmopɛd/ *n* motor cycle with pedals and a petrol engine of low power 摩托自行车. ⇨illus at MOTOR CYCLE (MOTOR) 见 MOTOR CYCLE (MOTOR) 插图.

mo·quette /mɒˈket; *US* məʊ-; moˈkɛt/ *n* [U] thick velvety fabric used for carpets and furniture covers 家具绒头织物; 机织绒面毯: [attrib 作定语] *a moquette sofa* 绒面沙发.

mo·raine /mɒˈreɪn, məˈreɪn; moˈren/ *n* mass of earth, stones, etc carried along and deposited by a glacier 冰碛(由冰河夹带而淤积的泥土、砂石等).

moral[1] /ˈmɒrəl; *US* ˈmɔːrəl; ˈmɔrəl/ *adj* **1** [attrib 作定语] concerning principles of right and wrong behaviour; ethical 道德的; 伦理的: *the decline of moral standards* 道德标准的下降 ○ *a moral question, problem, judgement, dilemma, etc* 有关道德的议题、问题、判断、困惑等 ○ *moral philosophy* 伦理学 ○ *challenge sth on moral grounds* 就某事的道德依据质疑 ○ *strong moral fibre,* ie the courage to face opposition bravely when doing what is right 坚强的道德观念. **2** [attrib 作定语] based on people's sense of what is right and just, not on legal rights and obligations 道德上的; 道义上的: *a moral law, duty, obligation, etc* 道德律、道义上的责任、道义上的义务 ○ *show moral courage* 表现出道德上的勇气. **3** following standards of right behaviour; good or virtuous 有道德的; 品行端正的: *lead a moral life* 过着规规矩矩的生活 ○ *a very moral person* 品行端正的人. **4** [attrib 作定语] able to understand the differences between right and wrong 能分辨是非的: *Human beings are moral individuals.* 人是有辨别是非能力的. **5** teaching or illustrating good behaviour 道德教育的; 有教育意义的: *a moral story, tale, poem, etc* 有教育意义的事迹、故事、诗等.

▷ **mor·ally** /-rəlɪ; -rəlɪ/ *adv* **1** in a moral manner 有道德地: *to behave morally* 行为端正. **2** with respect to standards of right and wrong 道德上: *morally wrong, unacceptable, reprehensible, etc* 道德上错误的、不以为然的、应受谴责的 ○ *hold sb morally responsible* 认为某人须负道义上的责任.

□ ˌ**moral** ˈ**certainty** thing that is so probable that there is little room for doubt 确定无疑的事.

ˌ**moral** ˈ**support** expression of sympathy or encouragement, rather than practical or financial help 道义上的支持; 精神上的援助: *give sb moral support* 给某人道义上的支持.

ˌ**moral** ˈ**victory** defeat that is in some ways as satisfying as a victory, eg when the principles that one is fighting for are shown to be right 精神上的胜利.

moral[2] /ˈmɒrəl; *US* ˈmɔːrəl; ˈmɔrəl/ *n* **1** [C] practical lesson that a story, an event or an experience teaches (故事的)寓意; (事情或经历所含的)教训, 教益: *The moral of this story is 'Better late than never'.* 这个故事的寓意是'迟做总比不做好'. **2 morals** [pl] standards of behaviour; principles of right and wrong 行为的标准; 是非的原则; 道德; 伦理: *question sb's morals* 对某人的品行提出异议 ○ *the corruption of public morals* 社会风气的败坏 ○ *a person of loose morals,* ie one who has had many casual sexual partners 行为放荡的人(多风流韵事者).

M

mor·ale /məˈrɑːl; *US* -ˈræl; məˈræl/ *n* [U] state of confidence, enthusiasm, determination, etc of a person or group at a particular time 士气; 精神状态: *affect/raise/boost/lower/undermine sb's morale* 影响[提高/鼓舞/降低/损害]某人的士气 ○ *The news is good for (the team's) morale.* 这消息对提高(全队的)士气大有好处.

mor·al·ist /ˈmɒrəlɪst; *US* ˈmɔːr-; ˈmɔrəlɪst/ *n* (*often derog* 常作贬义) person who expresses or teaches moral principles, esp one who tells people how they should behave 道德说教者; 卫道士.

mor·al·istic /ˌmɒrəˈlɪstɪk; *US* ˌmɔːr-; ˌmɔrəˈlɪstɪk/ *adj* (*usu derog* 通常作贬义) having or showing definite but narrow beliefs and judgements about right and wrong actions 是非观念狭隘的; 道德说教的: *a moralistic attitude* 说教的态度.

mor·al·ity /məˈrælətɪ; məˈrælətɪ/ *n* **1** [U] principles of good behaviour 美德; 道德; 道义; 伦理: *matters of public/private morality* 公共的[个人的]道德问题 ○ *Have standards of morality improved?* 道德标准是否已有所改进? **2** [U] (degree of) conforming to moral principles; goodness or rightness 道德原则; 道德性; 道义性; 正当性: *discuss the morality of abortion* 讨论堕胎的道德性. **3** particular system of morals 道德体系: *Muslim, Hindu, Christian, etc morality* 伊斯兰教的、印度教的、基督教的道德规范.

□ **moˈrality play** form of drama, popular in the 15th and 16th centuries, in which good behaviour is taught and where the characters represent good and bad qualities 道德剧(流行于15-16世纪, 以代表善与恶的角色寓意感化的戏剧).

mor·al·ize, -ise /ˈmɒrəlaɪz; *US* ˈmɔːr-; ˈmɔrəlˌaɪz/ *v* [I, Ipr] **~ (about/on sth)** (*esp derog* 尤作贬义) talk or write (usu critically) about right and wrong behaviour, esp in a self-righteous way 训导, 说教(尤指自以为是): *He's always moralizing about the behaviour of young people.* 他总是就年轻人的行为进行说教.

mor·ass /məˈræs; məˈræs/ *n* (usu *sing* 通常作单数) **1** stretch of low soft wet land; marsh 沼泽. **2 ~ (of sth)** (*fig* 比喻) thing that confuses people or prevents progress 困扰人或阻碍进步的事物; 困境: *a morass of confusion, doubt, despair, etc* 困惑、怀疑、绝望等的境地 ○ *be caught up in, bogged down in, floundering in a morass of bureaucratic procedures* 掉进、陷入、挣扎在官僚主义繁文缛节的泥淖中.

mo·ra·tor·ium /ˌmɒrəˈtɔːrɪəm; *US* ˌmɔːr-; ˌmɔrəˈtɔrɪəm/ *n* (*pl* **~s**) **1 ~ (on sth)** temporary stopping of an activity, esp by official agreement 暂停, 中止(尤指经官方同意者): *declare a moratorium on arms sales* 宣布暂停出售武器. **2** legal authorization to delay payment of a debt 延期偿付权.

mor·bid /ˈmɔːbɪd; ˈmɔrbɪd/ *adj* **1** (of sb's mind or ideas) having or showing an interest in gloomy or unpleasant things, esp disease or death (指人的心思或观念)病态的, 忧郁的(尤指只想到疾病、死亡等不快事物者): *a morbid imagination* 病态的想像 ○ *'He might even die.' 'Don't be so morbid.'* '他甚至有可能死.' '别净往坏处想.' **2** (*medical* 医) diseased 疾病的: *a morbid growth,* eg a cancer or tumour 肿瘤. ▷ **mor·bid·ity** /mɔːˈbɪdətɪ; mɔrˈbɪdətɪ/ *n* [U]. **mor·bidly** *adv.*

mord·ant /ˈmɔːdnt; ˈmɔrdn̩t/ *adj* (*fml* 文) very sarcastic; biting 讽刺的; 尖酸的: *mordant criticism/humour/wit* 尖刻的批评、幽默、妙语.

more /mɔː(r); mɔr/ *indef det, indef pron* **~ (sth) (than...)** **1** a greater or additional number or amount (of) 更大的; 更多的. (**a**) (*det*): *more people, cars, money, imagination* 更多的人、汽车、钱、想像物 ○ *more accuracy than originality* 准确性多, 创造性少 ○ *more food than could be eaten at one time* 一次吃不完的食物 ○ *Would you like some more coffee?* 你再来点咖啡吗? ○ *There are two more students here than yesterday.* 今天比昨天多两个学生. ○ *I know many more people who'd like to come.* 我知道还有很多人想来. (**b**) (*pron*): *Thank you, I couldn't possibly eat any more.* 谢谢你, 我真的再也吃不下了. ○ *Is there much more of this film?* 这部电影还很长吗? ○ *What more can I say* (ie in addition to what has already been said)? 我还能再说什么? ○ *We need a few more.* 我们还需要一些. ○ *I'll take three more.* 我再要三个. ○ *room for no more than three cars* 只能容下三辆汽车的空间 ○ *I hope we'll see more of you,* ie see you more often. 我希望我们能多和你见面. ⇨ Usage at MUCH[1] 用法见 MUCH[1]. **2** an increasing number or amount (of sb/

sth) 不断增长的数量: *She spends more and more time alone in her room.* 她独自呆在房间里的时间越来越多了. ○ *He's always hungry — he seems to want more and more to eat.* 他总饿 —— 好像越来越能吃了.

▷ **more** *adv* **1** (used to form the comparative of *adjs* and *advs* with two or more syllables 与至少有两个音节的形容词或副词构成比较级): *more expensive, intelligent, generous, frightened, anxiously* 更昂贵、聪明、慷慨、惊慌、担心 ○ *She read the letter more carefully the second time.* 她第二次看信时更仔细了. **2** to a greater extent 更加; 更甚: *I like her more than her husband.* 我喜欢她甚于她的丈夫. ○ *Try and concentrate more on your work.* 你做事精神要再集中些. ○ *This costs more than that.* 这个比那个贵. ○ *Please repeat it once more,* ie one more time. 请再重复一遍. ○ *It had more the appearance of a deliberate crime than an accident.* 那很像是蓄意的罪行, 而不象是意外的事故. **3** (idm 习语) **ˌmore and ˈmore** increasingly 越来越; 越发: *I am becoming more and more irritated by his selfish behaviour.* 我对他那种自私的行为愈加恼火起来. ○ *He speaks more and more openly about his problem.* 他越来越公开地谈他的问题. **ˌmore or ˈless** (**a**) almost 差不多; 几乎: *I've more or less finished reading the book.* 我差不多已经把这本书看完了. (**b**) approximately 大致; 大约; 或多或少: *It took more or less a whole day to paint the ceiling.* 粉刷天花板用了将近一整天的时间. ○ *I can earn £20 a night, more or less, as a waiter.* 我当服务员一晚上能挣20英镑左右. **more than happy, glad, willing etc (to do sth)** very happy, glad, etc (to do sth) 非常乐意(做某事): *I'm more than happy to take you there in my car.* 我非常愿意用汽车把你送去. **no more** (**a**) neither 也不: *He couldn't lift the table and no more could I.* 他抬不动那张桌子, 我也抬不动. (**b**) not more 和…一样不; 和…都不; 不超过: *You're no more capable of speaking Chinese than I am.* 你我都不会说汉语. ○ *It's no more than a mile to the shops.* 离商业区不过一英里. **what is ˈmore** in addition; more importantly 而且; 此外; 还有; 更有甚者: *They are going to get married, and what's more they are setting up in business together.* 他们就要结婚了, 而且还要一起做生意呢. ○ *He's dirty, and what's more he smells.* 他很脏, 身上还有味儿呢.

more·over /mɔːˈrəʊvə(r); mɔrˈovɚ/ *adv* (used to introduce sth new that adds to or supports the previous statement 用以引入新内容以补充或支持前言) further; besides; in addition 再说; 此外; 而且: *They knew the painting was a forgery. Moreover, they knew who had painted it.* 他们知道那幅画是赝品. 而且还知道是谁仿画的.

mores /ˈmɔːreɪz; ˈmoriz/ *n* [pl] (*fml* 文) customs or conventions considered typical of or essential to a group or communtiy 传统; 习俗: *social mores* 社会习俗.

mor·gan·atic /ˌmɔːɡəˈnætɪk; ˌmɔrɡəˈnætɪk/ *adj* (of a marriage) between a man of high rank (eg a prince) and a woman of lower rank who keeps her lower status, the children having no claim to the property, titles, etc of their father (指婚姻)贵贱联姻的(地位高的子弟, 如王子, 娶地位低的女子, 女方须保持其平民身分, 子女亦不得继承父亲的财产或头衔). ▷ **mor·gan·at·ic·ally** /-klɪ; -klɪ/ *adv*.

morgue /mɔːɡ; mɔrɡ/ *n* building in which dead bodies are kept before being buried or cremated; mortuary 停尸房; 陈尸所.

mori·bund /ˈmɒrɪbʌnd; *US* ˈmɔːr-; ˈmɔrəˌbʌnd/ *adj* (*fml* 文) at the point of death; about to come to an end 垂死的; 行将消亡的: *a moribund civilization, industry, custom* 日趋消亡的文明、工业、习惯.

Mor·mon /ˈmɔːmən; ˈmɔrmən/ *n, adj* (member) of a religious group founded in the USA in 1830, officially called 'The Church of Jesus Christ of Latter-day Saints' 摩门教徒, 摩门教派的, 摩门教徒的(1830年创立于美国的宗教, 正式名称为'耶稣基督后期圣徒教会') ▷ **Mor·mon·ism** /-ɪzəm; -ˌɪzəm/ *n* [U].

morn /mɔːn; mɔrn/ *n* (*usu sing* 通常作单数) (*arch* 古) (esp in poetry) morning (尤用于诗中)早晨.

morn·ing /ˈmɔːnɪŋ; ˈmɔrnɪŋ/ *n* [C, U] **1** (**a**) early part of the day between dawn and noon or before the midday meal 上午; 早晨; 早上: *They left for Spain early this morning.* 他们今天早晨去西班牙了. ○ *The taxi came at 8 o'clock the next morning.* 计程车第二天早上8点钟来到. ○ *The discussion group meets in the mornings.* 参加讨论的人都在上午开会. ○ *(on) one fine summer morning* (在)夏天的一个早晨 ○ *They stayed till Monday morning.* 他们住到星期一上午. ○ *I'll see him tomorrow morning.* 我明天上午见他. ○ *He swims every morning.* 他每天早晨游泳. ○ *on the morning of the wedding* 在举行婚礼的那天早晨 ○ *I've been painting the room all morning.* 我一上午都在粉刷房间. ○ *She works hard from morning to night.* 她从早到晚辛勤工作. ○ [attrib 作定语] *an early morning run* 清晨的跑步 ○ *the fresh morning air* 早晨清新的空气 ○ *read the morning papers* 读晨报 ○ *Morning coffee is now being served.* 现在供应早晨的咖啡. (**b**) period from midnight to noon 半夜至正午的时间: *He died in the early hours of Sunday morning.* 他于星期日凌晨逝世. **2** (idm 习语) **good ˈmorning** (used as a polite greeting or reply to a greeting when people first see each other in the morning and sometimes also when people leave in the morning 用作上午初次见面时的相互问候语, 有时亦用作上午分别时的告别语): *Good morning, Rosalind/Miss Dixon.* 罗莎琳德[狄克逊小姐]你好. (In informal use the greeting *Good morning* is often shortened to just *Morning* 口语中Good morning常略作Morning). **in the ˈmorning** (**a**) during the morning of the next day 第二天上午: *I'll ring her up in the morning.* 我明天上午给她打电话. (**b**) between midnight and noon, not in the afternoon or evening 半夜至中午前的时间: *The accident must have happened at about 11 o'clock in the morning.* 事故必是发生在上午11时左右. **the morning ˈafter (the night beˈfore)** (*infml* 口) the effects of drinking too much alcohol the previous evening; hangover 宿醉.

▷ **morn·ings** *adv* (*esp US*) in the morning; every morning 上午; 每天上午: *I only work mornings.* 我只在上午工作.

□ **ˌmorning-ˈafter pill** pill taken by a woman some hours after sexual intercourse to prevent conception 房事后几小时内口服的女用避孕药.

ˈmorning coat long black or grey tailcoat with the front part cut away, worn as part of morning dress 常燕尾服(男子日间穿的黑色或灰色礼服).

ˈmorning dress clothes worn by a man on very formal occasions, eg a wedding, including a morning coat, (usu striped) grey trousers and a top hat 常礼服(男子在婚礼等极隆重场合穿用者, 包括常燕尾服、通常为有条纹的灰色长裤和高顶礼帽).

ˌmorning ˈglory climbing plant with trumpet-shaped flowers that usu close in the afternoons 牵牛花.

ˌMorning ˈPrayer service in the Church of England for morning worship (英国国教的)晨祷.

ˈmorning sickness feeling of sickness in the morning during the first few months of pregnancy 害喜; 孕妇晨吐.

the ˌmorning ˈstar bright planet, esp Venus, seen in the east before sunrise 晨星; (尤指)金星.

NOTE ON USAGE 用法: Usually the preposition **in** is used with **morning/afternoon/evening,** on their own and in combination with other time expressions 介词 **in** 通常与 **morning/afternoon/evening** 等词连用, 也与含这些词的时间词组连用: *in the morning/afternoon/evening* 在上午[下午/晚上] ○ *at 3 o'clock in the afternoon* 下午三点 ○ *on the 4th of September in the morning* 在9月4日上午. **In** is also used with the adjectives **early** and **late** ☆ **in** 也与形容词 **early** 和 **late** 连用: *in the early/late morning* 清晨[近午时分]. With other adjectives and in certain other expressions **on** is used 与其他形容词及某些词组连用时需用 **on**: *on a cool morning in spring* 春天的一个凉爽的早晨 ○ *on Monday afternoon* 在星期一下午 ○ *on the previous/following evening* 在头天[第二天]晚上 ○ *on the morning of the 4th of September* 在9月4日的上午. No preposition is used in combination with **tomorrow/this/yesterday afternoon** 在 **tomorrow/this/yesterday afternoon** 这种形式的词组之前不用任何介词: *We arrived yesterday afternoon.* 我们昨天下午到的. ○ *They'll leave this evening.* 他们今天晚上离开. ○ *I'll start work again tomorrow morning.* 我明天早晨重新开始工作. See also usage note at TIME[1]. 另见TIME[1]用法说明.

mo·rocco /məˈrɒkəʊ; məˈrɑko/ *n* [U] fine soft leather made from goatskins, or an imitation of this, used for making shoes and covers for books 摩洛哥羊皮革, 仿摩洛哥羊皮革(用以制鞋和封面).

moron /ˈmɔːrɒn; ˈmɔrɑn/ *n* **1** (*infml derog* 口, 贬) very stupid person 傻瓜; 笨蛋: *He's an absolute moron!* 他纯粹是个傻子! ○ *They're a load of morons.* 他们是一群笨蛋. **2** adult with the intelligence of an average child of 8-12 years 鲁钝者(智力仅及8-12岁儿童的成年人).
▷ **mor·onic** /məˈrɒnɪk; məˈrɑnɪk/ *adj* (*infml derog* 口, 贬) (behaving) like a moron 似鲁钝者的: *a moronic laugh* 傻笑.

mor·ose /məˈrəʊs; məˈros/ *adj* very unhappy, bad-tempered and silent; sullen 闷闷不乐的; 脾气坏的; 抑郁的: *a morose person, manner, expression* 闷闷不乐的人、样子、表情. ▷ **mor·osely** *adv*. **mor·ose·ness** *n* [U].

morph·eme /ˈmɔːfiːm; ˈmɔrfim/ *n* (*linguistics* 语言) smallest meaningful unit into which a word can be divided 词素: *'Run-s' contains two morphemes and 'un-like-ly' contains three.* run-s 含有两个词素, un-like-ly 含有三个词素.

mor·phia /ˈmɔːfɪə; ˈmɔrfɪə/ *n* [U] (*dated* 旧) = MORPHINE.

mor·phine /ˈmɔːfiːn; ˈmɔrfin/ *n* [U] drug made from opium, used for relieving pain 吗啡.

mor·pho·logy /mɔːˈfɒlədʒɪ; mɔrˈfɑlədʒɪ/ *n* [U] **1** (*biology* 生) scientific study of the form and structure of animals and plants 形态学. **2** (*linguistics* 语言) study of the morphemes of a language and how they are combined to make words 形态学. Cf 参看 GRAMMAR 1, SYNTAX. ▷ **mor·pho·lo·gical** /ˌmɔːfəˈlɒdʒɪkl; ˌmɔrfəˈlɑdʒɪkəl/ *adj*.

mor·ris dance /ˈmɒrɪs dɑːns; *US* ˈmɔːrɪs dæns; ˈmɔrɪs ˌdæns/ old English folk-dance traditionally performed by men wearing special costumes, with ribbons, bells and sticks 莫里斯舞(英国民间传统的男子舞蹈). ▷ **mor·ris dan·cer**.

mor·row /ˈmɒrəʊ; *US* ˈmɔːr-; ˈmɔro/ *n* **1 the morrow** [sing] (*dated or rhet* 旧或修辞) the next day after the present or after any given day 翌日; 次日; 第二天: *on the morrow* 于翌日 ○ *They wondered what the morrow had in store for them.* 他们想知道明天等待他们的是什么. **2** (idm 习语) **good ˈmorrow** (*arch* 古) (used as a greeting 用作问候语).

Morse /mɔːs; mɔrs/ *n* [U] (also ˌ**Morse ˈcode**) system of sending messages, using dots and dashes or short and long sounds or flashes of light to represent letters of the alphabet and numbers 莫尔斯电码: *send a message in Morse* 用莫尔斯电码发送一信息.

mor·sel /ˈmɔːsl; ˈmɔrsl̩/ *n* ~ **(of sth)** small amount or piece of sth, esp food 少量, 一小块(尤指食物): *a tasty/dainty/choice morsel of food* 一点美味的[可口的/精选的]食物 ○ *not have a morsel of common sense* 毫无常识.

mor·tal /ˈmɔːtl; ˈmɔrtl̩/ *adj* **1** that must die; that cannot live for ever 终有一死的; 不能永生的: *All human beings are mortal.* 人总有一死. ○ *Here lie the mortal remains of George Chapman*, eg as an inscription on a tombstone. 乔治·查普曼的遗体葬于此处(如墓碑上的志文). **2** causing death; fatal 致死的; 致命的: *a mortal wound, injury, etc* 致命的伤、伤害等 ○ (*fig* 比喻) *The collapse of the business was a mortal blow* (ie a great emotional shock) *to him and his family.* 公司倒闭是对他及其家庭的致命打击. **3** [attrib 作定语] lasting until death; marked by great hatred; deadly 终生的; 有深仇大恨的; 不共戴天的: *mortal enemies* 不共戴天的敌人 ○ *locked in mortal combat*, ie a fight that is only ended by the death of one of the fighters 进行殊死的斗争. **4** [attrib 作定语] extreme or intense 极大的; 极度的: *live in mortal fear, terror, danger, etc* 生活在极度的恐惧、恐怖、危险等中. **5** [attrib 作定语] (*dated infml* 旧, 口) (used to emphasize what follows and to show annoyance 用以加强后一词的语气, 表示恼怒): *They stole every mortal thing in the house.* 他们把屋里所有的东西都通通偷光了.
▷ **mor·tal** *n* human being 人: (*joc* 谑) *They're so grand these days that they probably don't talk to ordinary mortals like us any more.* 他们这些日子神气活现, 大概不再和我们这样的普通人说话了.
mor·tally /-təlɪ; -tl̩ɪ/ *adv* **1** resulting in death 致命地: *mortally wounded* 受致命伤. **2** greatly; intensely 极; 很; 非常: *mortally afraid* 害怕得要命.
□ ˌ**mortal ˈsin** (in the Roman Catholic Church) sin that causes the loss of God's grace and leads to damnation unless it is confessed and forgiven (天主教中)弥天大罪.

mor·tal·ity /mɔːˈtælətɪ; mɔrˈtælətɪ/ *n* [U] **1** state of being mortal 不免一死. **2** (also **morˈtality rate**) number of deaths in a specified period of time 死亡率: *Infant mortality* (ie The rate at which babies die) *was 20 deaths per thousand live births in 1986.* 1986年的婴儿死亡率为生育成活率的千分之二十. **3** large number of deaths caused by a disease, disaster, etc (疾病、灾难等造成的)大量死亡.
□ **morˈtality table** (esp in insurance) table showing how long people at various ages may normally be expected to live (尤指保险业的)死亡率表.

mor·tar[1] /ˈmɔːtə(r); ˈmɔrtɚ/ *n* [U] mixture of lime or cement, sand and water, used to hold bricks, stones, etc together in building 砂浆; 灰浆.
▷ **mor·tar** *v* [Tn] join (bricks, etc) with mortar 用砂浆砌合(砖等).

mor·tar[2] /ˈmɔːtə(r); ˈmɔrtɚ/ *n* **1** short cannon that fires shells at a high angle 迫击炮: [attrib 作定语] *under mortar fire/attack*, ie being fired at by a mortar or mortars 在迫击炮火[攻击]之下. **2** strong bowl in which substances are crushed and ground with a pestle 臼; 研钵. ⇨ illus at PESTLE 见 PESTLE 插图.

mortar-board /ˈmɔːtə bɔːd; ˈmɔrtɚˌbɔrd/ *n* (usu black) cap with a stiff square top, worn by certain university students and teachers on formal occasions (通常为黑色的)方顶帽, 学位帽(某些大学师生在隆重场合戴的).

mort·gage /ˈmɔːgɪdʒ; ˈmɔrgɪdʒ/ *n* **(a)** agreement in which money is lent by a building society, bank, etc for buying a house or other property, the property being the security 抵押; 抵押契据: *apply for/take out a mortgage* 申请[办妥]抵押事宜 ○ *It's difficult to get a mortgage on an old house.* 以旧房作抵押很难获准. ○ [attrib 作定语] *a mortgage agreement/deed* 抵押协议[契约]. **(b)** sum of money lent in this way 押款: *We've got a mortgage of £40 000.* 我们得到40 000英镑的抵押借款. ○ [attrib 作定语] *monthly mortgage payments*, ie money to repay the sum borrowed and the interest on it 按月偿还抵押借款本息的钱.
▷ **mort·gage** *v* [Tn, Tn·pr, Dn·pr] ~ **sth (to sb) (for sth)** give sb the legal right to take possession of (a house or some other property) as a security for payment of money lent 抵押(房产等): *He mortgaged his house in order to start a business*, ie borrowed money with his house as a security. 他用房产押款创业. ○ *The house is mortgaged (to the bank) (for £30 000).* 这所房子已经(以30 000英镑)(向银行)作了抵押. **mort·ga·gee** /ˌmɔːgɪˈdʒiː; ˌmɔrgɪˈdʒi/ *n* person or firm that lends money in mortgage agreements 承受抵押者. **mort·ga·ger** /ˈmɔːgɪdʒə(r); ˈmɔrgɪdʒɚ/ (also, in legal use 用于法律条文, 亦作 **mort·ga·gor** /ˌmɔːgɪˈdʒɔː(r); ˈmɔrgɪdʒɔr/) *n* person who borrows money in a mortgage agreement 抵押者.

mor·ti·cian /mɔːˈtɪʃn; mɔrˈtɪʃən/ *n* (*US*) = UNDERTAKER.

mor·tify /ˈmɔːtɪfaɪ; ˈmɔrtəˌfaɪ/ *v* (*pt, pp* **-fied**) **1** [Tn usu passive 通常用于被动语态] cause (sb) to be very ashamed or embarrassed 使(某人)深感羞辱或难堪: *He was/felt mortified.* 他深感羞愧. ○ *a mortifying failure, defeat, mistake, etc* 使人丢脸的失败、挫折、错误等. **2** [Tn] (*fml or joc* 文或谑) control (human desires or needs) by discipline or self-denial 约束, 克制(欲望或需要): *mortify the flesh*, ie one's body 克制肉欲. ▷ **mor·ti·fica·tion** /ˌmɔːtɪfɪˈkeɪʃn; ˌmɔrtəfəˈkeʃən/ *n* [U]: *To his mortification, he was criticized by the managing director in front of all his junior colleagues.* 他在全体下级同事面前受到总经理的批评, 感到很难堪.

mor·tise (also **mor·tice**) /ˈmɔːtɪs; ˈmɔrtɪs/ *n* (usu rectangular) hole cut in a piece of wood, etc to receive the end of another piece so that the two are held together (通常为矩形的)卯眼, 榫眼, 榫孔. Cf 参看 TENON.
▷ **mor·tise** (also **mor·tice**) *v* **1** [Tn·pr, Tn·p] ~ **A to/into B; ~ A and B together** join or fasten things with a mortise 用卯眼接合: *The cross-piece is mortised into the upright post.* 横梁和立柱是用榫眼接合一起的.

M

2 [Tn] cut a mortise in (sth) 在(某物上)开榫眼.

□ 'mortise lock lock that is fitted inside a hole cut into the edge of a door, not one that is screwed onto the surface (嵌入门里的)暗锁.

mor·tu·ary /ˈmɔːtʃəri; *US* ˈmɔːtʃueri; ˋmɔrtʃu,ɛri/ *n* room or building (eg part of a hospital) in which dead bodies are kept before being buried or cremated 停尸房, 太平间(如医院中的). ▷ **mor·tu·ary** *adj* [attrib 作定语] (*fml* 文) of death or burial 死的; 埋葬的: *mortuary rites* 葬礼.

mo·saic /məʊˈzeɪɪk; moˋze·ɪk/ *n* **1** [C, U] picture or pattern made by placing together small pieces of glass, stone, etc of different colours 马赛克(用不同颜色的小块玻璃, 石子等材料拼凑, 镶嵌成的图画或图案): *ancient Greek mosaics* 古希腊的马赛克 ○ *a design in mosaic* 马赛克图案 ○ [attrib 作定语] *a mosaic design, pavement, ceiling* 马赛克的图案、地面、天花板. **2** [C usu *sing* 通常作单数] **~ (of sth)** design or pattern made up of many different individual items; patchwork 镶嵌画; 镶嵌图案: *a rich mosaic of meadows, rivers and woods* 由草地、河流和林木组成的五光十色的镶嵌画.

Mo·saic /məʊˈzeɪɪk; moˋze·ɪk/ *adj* [usu attrib 通常作定语] of or associated with Moses 摩西的: *Mosaic law* 摩西的律法.

mos·elle /məʊˈzel; moˋzɛl/ *n* [C, U] (type of) dry white wine from the valley of the river Moselle in Germany 摩泽尔白葡萄酒(产自德国摩泽尔河流域).

mo·sey /ˈməʊzi; ˋmozɪ/ *v* [Ipr, Ip] (*US infml* 口) walk aimlessly (in the specified direction); amble 漫步; 溜达: *I'd best be moseying along*, ie leaving. 我最好还是走吧. ○ *Why don't you mosey round to my place?* 你溜达着到我这儿来好吗?

Mos·lem =MUSLIM.

mosque /mɒsk; mɑsk/ *n* building in which Muslims worship 清真寺.

mos·quito /məsˈkiːtəʊ, *also, in British use,* 英式英语读作 mɒs-; məˋskito/ *n* (*pl* **~es**) small flying insect (esp the type that spreads malaria) the female of which sucks the blood of people and animals 蚊; (尤指)疟蚊.

□ **mos'quito-net** *n* net hung over a bed, etc to keep mosquitoes away 蚊帐.

moss /mɒs; *US* mɔːs; mɔs/ *n* **1** [U, C] very small green or yellow flowerless plant growing in thick masses on damp surfaces or trees or stones 藓; 苔: *moss-covered rocks, walls* 长满青苔的岩石、墙. Cf 参看 LICHEN. **2** (idm 习语) **a rolling stone gathers no moss** ⇨ ROLL[2].

▷ **mossy** *adj* **1** covered with moss 长满青苔的: *mossy bark* 长满表苔的树皮. **2** like moss 似苔的: *mossy green* 像苔藓的绿色.

□ **'moss-grown** *adj* covered with moss 长满青苔的.

moss·back /ˈmɒsbæk; *US* ˈmɔːs-; ˋmɔs,bæk/ *n* (*US infml* 口) old-fashioned person with very conservative ideas 守旧的人.

most[1] /məʊst; most/ *indef det, indef pron* (used as the superlative of MANY, MUCH[2] 用作MANY、MUCH[2]的最高级) **1** greatest in number, amount or extent 最大的; 最多的. **(a)** (*det*): *Who do you think will get (the) most votes?* 你认为谁会得票最多? ○ *Peter made the most mistakes of all the class.* 彼得的错误是全班最多的. ○ *When we toured Italy we spent most time in Rome.* 我们到意大利旅行时, 在罗马花的时间最多. ○ *Most racial discrimination is based on ignorance.* 种族歧视的产生大都出于无知. **(b)** (*pron*): *We all had some of the cake; I probably ate (the) most*, ie more than the others ate. 我们都吃了一些蛋糕, 我可能吃得最多. ○ *Harry got 6 points, Susan got 8 points but Alison got most.* 哈里得了6分, 苏珊得了8分, 但艾莉森得分最多. ○ *The person with the most to lose is the director.* 损失最大的是主任. ⇨Usage at MUCH[1] 用法见MUCH[1]. **2** more than half of sb/sth; the majority of sb/sth 大部分的; 大半的; 大多数的. **(a)** (*det*): *Most European countries are democracies.* 大多数欧洲国家都是民主国家. ○ *Most classical music sends me to sleep.* 古典音乐我大多听着听着就睡着了. ○ *The new tax laws affect most people.* 新税则影响到大多数人. ○ *I like most vegetables.* 大多数的蔬菜我都喜欢. **(b)** (*pron*): *It rained for most of the summer.* 夏天大部分时间都下雨. ○ *As most of you know, I've decided to resign.* 你们多数人都已经知道, 我决定辞职了. ○ *There are hundreds of verbs in English and most are regular.* 英语动词数以千计, 大多数都是规则动词. ○ *He has a lot of free time — he spends most of it in the garden.* 他空闲时间很多 —— 大都消磨在花园里了. **3** (idm 习语) **'at (the) most** as a maximum; not more than 至多; 最多; 顶多; 不超过: *At (the) most I might earn £250 a night.* 一晚上我至多可挣250英镑. ○ *There were 50 people there, at the very most.* 那里满打满算有50人.

▷ **mostly** *adv* almost all; generally 几乎全部; 大多; 多半; 大体: (*infml* 口) *The drink was mostly lemonade.* 当时的饮料主要是汽水. ○ *We're mostly out on Sundays.* 我们星期日多半不在家.

most[2] /məʊst; most/ *adv* **1 (a)** (used to form the superlative of *adjs* and *advs* of two or more syllables 用以构成双音节或多音节形容词和副词的最高级): *most boring, beautiful, impressive, etc* 最乏味的、美丽的、令人钦佩的 ○ *The person who gave most generously to the scheme has been blind from birth.* 赞助这一项目最慷慨的是个先天盲人. ○ *It was the most exciting holiday I've ever had.* 那是我经历过的最使人兴奋的假日. **(b)** to the greatest extent 最: *What did you most enjoy?* 你最欣赏的是什么? ○ *She helped me (the) most when my parents died.* 我父母死时她给我的帮助最多. ○ *I saw her most* (ie most often) *when we were at university.* 我们上大学的时候, 我常常见到她. **2 (a)** very 很; 极; 非常: *We heard a most interesting talk about Japan.* 我们听了一个关于日本的最有趣的谈话. ○ *I received a most unusual present from my aunt.* 我收到姨母给我的一件极不寻常的礼物. ○ *It was most kind of you to take me to the airport.* 多谢你把我送到了飞机场. ○ *He spoke most bitterly of his experiences in prison.* 他十分痛苦地讲述了他在监狱中的经历. **(b)** absolutely 绝对地: *'Can we expect to see you at church?' 'Most certainly.'* '我们可以在教堂见你吗?' '太可以了.' **3** (*infml* 口 *esp US*) almost 几乎: *I go to the shop most every day.* 我差不多每天都去商店.

-most *suff* 后缀 (with *preps* and *adjs* of position forming *adjs* 与表示位置的介词和形容词构成形容词): *inmost* ○ *topmost* ○ *uppermost*.

MOT /ˌem əʊ ˈtiː; ˌɛm o ˋti/ *abbr* 缩写 = (*Brit*) **(a)** Ministry of Transport 运输部. **(b)** (also **MOT test**) (*infml* 口) compulsory annual test of cars, etc over a certain age 汽车年检(对超过规定年限的机动车所作的年度检验): *She took her car in for its MOT.* 她把汽车开去作年检了. ○ *Has your car been MOT'd/had its MOT?* 你的汽车作过年检吗?

mote /məʊt; mot/ *n* **1** small particle, usu of dust; speck 微粒; (通常指)尘埃. **2** (idm 习语) **the mote in sb's 'eye** (*dated* 旧) the minor fault that sb has committed, when compared with one's own much greater fault (与自己的大错相比)某人的小错、小毛病或小缺点.

mo·tel /məʊˈtel; moˋtɛl/ *n* hotel for motorists, with space for parking cars near the rooms 汽车旅馆(为驾车旅客提供停车场者).

mo·tet /məʊˈtet; moˋtɛt/ *n* short piece of church music, usu for voices only 经文歌(通常无伴奏). Cf 参看 ANTHEM.

moth /mɒθ; *US* mɔːθ; mɔθ/ *n* **1** insect like a butterfly but less brightly coloured, flying mainly at night and attracted to bright lights 蛾. **2** (also **clothes moth**) small similar insect that breeds in cloth, fur, etc, its young feeding on the cloth and making holes in it 衣蛾.

□ **'mothball** *n* **1** small ball made of a strong-smelling substance, used for keeping moths away from stored clothes 卫生球; 樟脑丸. **2** (idm 习语) **in 'mothballs** stored and not used for a long time 封存不用: *old aircraft kept in mothballs* 封存的旧飞机.

'moth-eaten *adj* **1** eaten, damaged or destroyed by moths 虫蛀的; 蛀坏的: *moth-eaten old clothes* 蛀坏的旧衣物. **2** (*infml derog* 口, 贬) **(a)** looking very old; shabby or worn out 破旧的; 破烂的: *moth-eaten armchairs* 破旧的单座沙发. **(b)** old-fashioned; out of date 陈旧的; 过时的: *moth-eaten ideas* 陈腐的想法.

'mothproof *adj* (of clothes) treated chemically against damage by moths (指衣物)防蛀的, 不蛀的. — *v* [Tn] make (clothes) mothproof 对(衣物)作防虫处理.

mother /ˈmʌðə(r); ˋmʌðɚ/ *n* **1** female parent of a child or animal 母亲; 妈妈: *My mother died when I was 6.* 我6岁时母亲去世了. ○ *the relationship between mother and* *baby* 母婴之间的关系 ○ *How are you, Mother?* 妈妈, 您好吗? ○ *an expectant* (ie a pregnant) *mother* 孕妇 ○ [attrib 作定语] *Look how the mother chimpanzee cares for her young.* 瞧, 母黑猩猩多爱护小仔儿啊. ⇨App 8 见附录 8. **2** (way of addressing the) head of a female religious community 女子宗教团体的主持人或对其之称呼: *Pray for me, Mother.* 教母, 请为我祈祷吧. **3** (way of addressing an old woman) (对年长妇女的称呼)大妈, 大娘. **4** (idm 习语) **necessity is the mother of invention** ⇨ NECESSITY. **old enough to be sb's father/mother** ⇨ OLD.

▷ **mother** *v* [Tn] **1** care for (sb/sth) as a mother does; rear 像母亲般关怀或照管(某人[某事物]); 养育: *piglets mothered by a sow* 由一母猪照料的猪崽. **2** treat (sb) with too much protection or care 溺爱(某人); 对(某人)过分爱护: *He likes being mothered by his landlady.* 他喜欢女房东无微不至地照顾他.

ˈ**Mothering Sunday** (also ˈ**Mother's Day**) the fourth Sunday in Lent, when mothers traditionally receive gifts and cards from their children 母亲节.

moth·er·hood /-hʊd; -ˌhʊd/ *n* [U] state of being a mother 母亲身分: *She finds motherhood very rewarding.* 她认为做母亲得偿所愿.

moth·er·less *adj* having no mother 无母亲的.

moth·er·like *adj* in the manner of a mother 像母亲的: *a motherlike smile, embrace* 慈母般的微笑、拥抱.

moth·erly *adj* having or showing the kind and tender qualities of a mother 母亲的; 母性的; 母爱的: *motherly love, affection, care, etc* 母亲的爱、疼爱、关怀等 ○ *a motherly kiss* 慈母的吻. **moth·er·li·ness** *n* [U].

□ ˈ**mother country** (*fml* 文) **1** one's native country 祖国. **2** country in relation to its colonies (殖民地的)母国.

ˈ**mother-in-law** *n* (*pl* **mothers-in-law**) mother of one's wife or husband 岳母; 婆婆. ⇨App 8 见附录 8.

ˈ**motherland** /-lænd; -ˌlænd/ *n* one's native country 祖国.

ˌ**Mother** ˈ**Nature** (*often joc* 常作戏谑语) nature considered as a force that affects the world and human beings 大自然(视为影响万物的力量): *Leave the cure to Mother Nature. She knows best.* 要想痊愈就听其自然吧. 老天爷最有办法.

ˌ**mother-of-**ˈ**pearl** *n* [U] (also **nacre**) hard smooth shiny rainbow-coloured substance that forms the lining of some shells (eg oysters, mussels) and is used for making buttons, ornaments, etc 珠母层; 珍珠母: [attrib 作定语] *a mother-of-pearl ear-ring, necklace, brooch, etc* 珠母耳环、项链、饰针等.

ˈ**mother's boy** (*infml derog* 口, 贬) boy or man, esp one considered emotionally weak, whose character and behaviour are influenced too much by the protection of his mother (因性格和行为受母亲溺爱的影响)感情脆弱的男性儿童或成人.

ˈ**Mother's Day** = MOTHERING SUNDAY.

ˈ**mother ship** ship from which smaller ships get supplies 母船, 母舰(可供给小船补给的).

ˌ**Mother Su**ˈ**perior** head of a convent 女隐修院院长.

ˌ**mother-to-**ˈ**be** *n* (*pl* **mothers-to-be**) woman who is pregnant 孕妇.

ˈ**mother tongue** language that one first learned to speak as a child; one's native language 母语; 本国语; 本族语.

mo·tif /məʊˈtiːf; moˈtif/ *n* **1** decorative design or pattern 装饰的图案或式样: *an eagle motif on the curtains* 帷幕上的鹰的图案. **2** theme or idea that is repeated and developed in a work of music or literature (音乐的)乐旨, 动机; (文学的)主题.

mo·tion /ˈməʊʃn; ˈmoʃən/ *n* **1** [U] (manner of) moving 运动; 移动; 动态: *the swaying motion of the ship* 船的左右摇摆 ○ *The object is no longer in motion*, ie has stopped moving. 该物体已不处于运动状态. **2** [C] particular movement; way of moving part of the body; gesture 动作; 身体某部分的运动方式; 姿态: *with a sudden, single, upward, downward, etc motion of the hand* 手的突然的、单一的、向上的、向下的…一动. **3** [C] formal proposal to be discussed and voted on at a meeting 动议; 提议: *propose, put forward, reject, etc a motion* 提、提出、否决…一动议 ○ *The motion was adopted/carried by a majority of six votes.* 该动议以六票的多数获采纳[通过]. **4** [C] (*fml* 文) (**a**) act of emptying the bowels 大便: *regular motions* 按时大便. (**b**) waste matter emptied from the bowels; faeces 粪便: *solid motions* 成形粪便. **5** (idm 习语) **go through the motions (of doing sth)** (*infml* 口) pretend to do sth; do sth but without sincerity or serious intention 装出做某事物的样子; 敷衍: *He went through the motions of welcoming her friends but then quickly left the room.* 他虚应故事欢迎一下她的朋友, 转眼就离开了房间. **put/set sth in** ˈ**motion** cause sth to start moving or operating 使某物开始运动或运转: *set machinery in motion* 开动机器 ○ (*fig* 比喻) *put the new campaign in motion* 开展新的运动. Cf 参看 SLOW MOTION (SLOW[1]).

▷ **mo·tion** *v* **1** [Ipr, Dn·t no passive 不用于被动语态, Dpr·t] **~ to sb** indicate to sb by a gesture 以姿势向某人示意: *He motioned to the waiter.* 他向侍者示意. ○ *He motioned (to) me to sit down.* 他示意我坐下. **2** [Tn·pr, Tn·p] direct (sb) in the specified direction by a gesture 用姿势给(某人)指示方向: *motion sb to a chair, away, in, etc* 示意某人就座、离开、进入等.

mo·tion·less *adj* not moving; still 不动的; 静止的: *standing motionless* 站着不动.

□ ˌ**motion** ˈ**picture** (*esp US*) cinema film 电影.

mo·tiv·ate /ˈməʊtɪveɪt; ˈmotəˌvet/ *v* **1** [Tn usu passive 通常用于被动语态] be the reason for (sb's action); cause (sb) to act in a particular way; inspire 作为(某人行为)的动机; 使(某人)以某方式行事: *be motivated by greed, fear, love, etc* 受贪欲、恐惧、爱等驱使. **2** [Tn, Cn·t] stimulate the interest of (sb); cause to want to do sth 激发(某人)的兴趣; 使欲做某事物: *a teacher who can motivate her pupils (to work harder)* 善于诱导学生(努力学习)的教师. ▷ **mo·tiv·ated** *adj*: *a politically motivated murder* 出于政治动机的谋杀 ○ *be highly motivated*, ie very keen to do sth 有高度积极性(非常热衷于做某事物). **mo·tiva·tion** /ˌməʊtɪˈveɪʃn; ˌmotəˈveʃən/ *n* [C, U]: *the basic financial motivations for the decision* 做出该决定的基本上在财务方面的考虑 ○ *They lack the motivation to study.* 他们缺乏学习的积极性.

mo·tive /ˈməʊtɪv; ˈmotɪv/ *n* **~ (for sth)** that which causes sb to act in a particular way; reason 动机; 原因: *The police could not find a motive for the murder.* 警方未能找出谋杀者的动机. ○ *question sb's motives* 对某人的动机提出疑问 ○ *the profit motive*, ie the desire to make a profit 图利的动机. ⇨Usage at REASON[1] 用法见 REASON[1].

▷ **mo·tive** *adj* [attrib 作定语] causing movement or action 产生运动的; 起动的; 发动的: *motive force/power*, eg electricity, to operate machinery 动力.

mo·tive·less *adj*: *an apparently motiveless crime* 显然无动机的犯罪行为.

mot·ley /ˈmɒtlɪ; ˈmɑtlɪ/ *adj* **1** (*derog* 贬) of many different types of people or things 混杂的; 形形色色的: *wearing a motley collection of old clothes* 穿着各式各样的旧衣服 ○ *a motley crowd/crew*, ie a group of many different types of people 成分混杂的人群[一帮人]. **2** [attrib 作定语] of various colours 杂色的; 不同颜色的: *a motley coat*, eg one worn by a jester in former times 杂色花衣(如旧时小丑穿的).

▷ **mot·ley** *n* [U] (formerly) clothes worn by a jester (旧时)(小丑穿的)杂色花衣: *put on/wear the motley*, ie dress as or play the part of a jester 穿杂色花衣(穿得像小丑或扮演小丑).

mo·tor /ˈməʊtə(r); ˈmotɚ/ *n* **1** (**a**) device that changes (usu electric) power into movement, used to make machines work 发动机; 马达: *an electric motor* 电动机. (**b**) device that changes fuel (eg petrol) into energy to provide power for a vehicle, boat, etc 内燃机: *an outboard motor*, ie one attached to the back of a small boat 船外发动机(装于小船尾部者). **2** (*Brit dated or joc* 旧或谑) car 汽车.

▷ **mo·tor** *adj* [attrib 作定语] **1** having or driven by a motor (1) 有发动机的; 由发动机驱动的: *motor vehicles* 机动车辆 ○ *a motor mower* 机动刈草机. **2** of or for vehicles driven by a motor 机动车辆的; 为机动车辆的: *motor racing* 汽车比赛 ○ *motor insurance* 汽车保险 ○ *the motor trade* 汽车业 ○ *the Motor Show* 汽车展览 ○ *a motor mechanic* 汽车机械工. **3** giving or producing motion 产生运动的: *motor nerves*, ie those that carry impulses from the brain to the muscles 运动神经.

mo·tor *v* [I, Ipr, Ip] (*dated* 旧 *Brit*) travel by car 乘汽

车: *They spent a pleasant afternoon motoring through the countryside.* 他们一下午都在郊野开着汽车，十分愉快.

mo·tor·ing /ˈməʊtərɪŋ; ˋmotərɪŋ/ *n* [U] driving in a car 开汽车: [attrib 作定语] *a motoring offence* 汽车驾驶违章.

mo·tor·ist /ˈməʊtərɪst; ˋmotərɪst/ *n* person who drives a car 开汽车的人. Cf 参看 PEDESTRIAN.

mo·tor·ize, -ise /ˈməʊtəraɪz; ˋmotəˌraɪz/ *v* [Tn usu passive 通常用于被动语态] **1** equip (sth) with a motor 给(某物)装发动机: *motorized vehicles* 机动车辆. **2** equip (troops, etc) with motor vehicles 给(部队等)装备机动车辆: *motorized infantry* 摩托化步兵.

□ **ˈmotor bike** (*infml* 口) = MOTOR CYCLE.

ˈmotor boat (usu small) fast boat driven by an engine (通常指小的)摩托船.

motorcade /ˈməʊtəkeɪd; ˋmotəˌked/ *n* procession of motor vehicles, often with important people travelling in them 汽车长列(其中常有要人).

ˈmotor car (*Brit fml* 文) = CAR 1.

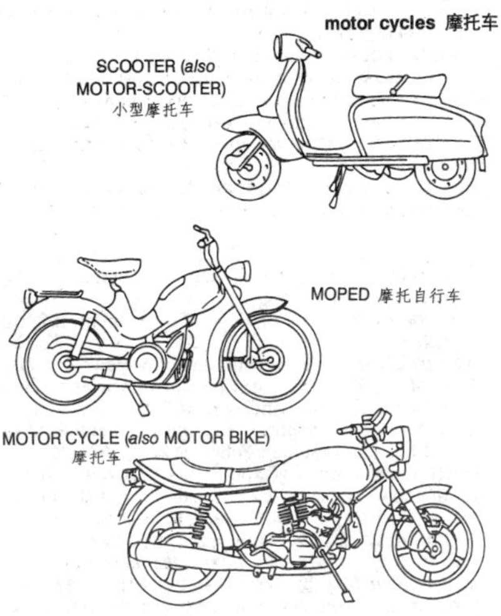

ˈmotor cycle (also *infml* 口语作 **ˈmotor bike**) road vehicle with two wheels, driven by an engine, with one seat for the driver and usu with space for a passenger behind the driver 摩托车. **ˈmotor-cyclist** *n* rider of a motor cycle 骑摩托车的人.

ˈmotor-scooter = SCOOTER 1.

ˈmotorway *n* (*Brit*) (*abbr* 缩写 **M**) (*US* **exˈpressway**) wide road specially built for fast-moving traffic, with a restricted number of places for entry and exit and separate carriageways for vehicles travelling in opposite directions 高速公路: *join/leave a motorway* 开上[开离]高速公路 ○ *You're not allowed to stop on motorways.* 高速公路上不得停车. ○ [attrib 作定语] *a motorway service station* 高速公路汽车加油站. ⇨Usage at ROAD 用法见 ROAD.

mot·tled /ˈmɒtld; ˋmɑtḷd/ *adj* marked with patches of different colours without a regular pattern 杂色的; 斑驳的: *the mottled skin of a snake* 蛇身上有花纹的皮.

motto /ˈmɒtəʊ; ˋmɑto/ *n* (*pl* **~es**) **1** short sentence or phrase chosen and used as a guide or rule of behaviour or as an expression of the aims or ideals of a family, a country, an institution, etc 箴言; 格言; 座右铭: *My motto is: 'Live each day as it comes.'* 我的座右铭是: '有一天过一天.' ○ *What's your school motto?* 你们校训是什么? **2** (*esp Brit*) witty remark or riddle or short saying printed on a piece of paper, esp inside a Christmas cracker 隽语、谜语或谚语的纸签(尤指圣诞节彩包爆竹中的).

mould[1] (*US* **mold**) /məʊld; mold/ *n* **1** (**a**) hollow container with a particular shape, into which a soft or

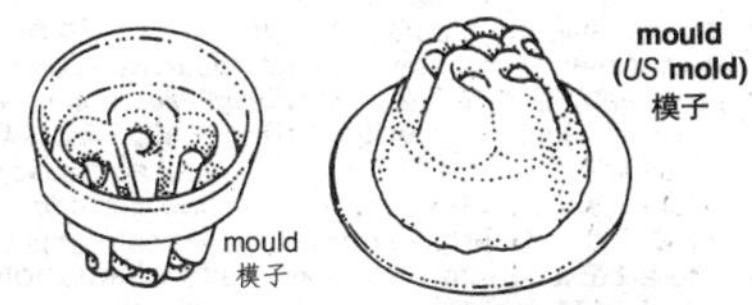

liquid substance (eg jelly or molten metal) is poured to set or cool into that shape 模子; 铸模; 铸型: *a jelly mould in the shape of a racing car* 赛车形果冻模子. ⇨ illus 见插图. (**b**) jelly, pudding, etc made in such a container 用模子塑出的果冻、布丁等. **2** (usu *sing* 通常作单数) particular type of (a person's) character 性格; 气质: *He doesn't fit (into) the traditional mould of a university professor.* 他没有大学教授那种传统的气质. ○ *They are all cast in the same/a similar mould,* ie They all have similar attitudes and ways of behaving. 他们都是一个模子铸出的(态度和行为一模一样).

▷ **mould** *v* **1** [Tn, Tn·pr] (**a**) **~ sth (into sth)** shape (a soft substance) into a particular form or object 使(软材料)成形: *mould plastic (into drain-pipes)* 用塑料模压(成排水管). (**b**) **~ sth (from/out of/in sth)** make sth by shaping it 塑造某物: *mould a head out of/in clay* 用黏土塑造头像. **2** [Tn, Tn·pr] **~ sb/sth (into sb/sth)** guide or control the development of sb/sth; shape or influence sb/sth 指导或控制某人[某事物]的发展; 塑造或影响某人[某事物]: *mould sb's character* 塑造某人的性格 ○ *Television moulds public opinion.* 电视能影响舆论. ○ *mould a child into a mature adult* 把孩子造就为成熟的成年人. **3** [Ipr, Tn·pr] **~ (sth) to/round sth** (cause sth to) fit tightly round the shape of (an object) (使某物)与(某物体)的外形吻合: *Her wet clothes moulded round her body.* 她的湿衣服紧贴在身上.

mould[2] (*US* **mold**) /məʊld; mold/ *n* [U, C] fine furry growth of fungi that forms on old food or on objects left in moist warm air 霉; 霉菌.

▷ **mouldy** (*US* **moldy**) *adj* **1** covered with mould; smelling of mould 发霉的; 发霉味的: *mouldy cheese* 发霉的乳酪. **2** (*infml derog* 口, 贬) old and decaying; fusty 陈腐的; 古旧的; 过时的: *Let's get rid of this mouldy old furniture.* 咱们把这件老掉牙的旧家具扔掉吧. **3** (*Brit infml* 口) unpleasant because dull, mean or miserable 乏味的; 小气的; 卑劣的; 令人沮丧的: *We had a mouldy holiday — it rained every day.* 我们假日过得无聊极了——每天都下雨. ○ *They've given us a pretty mouldy pay increase this year.* 我们今年的加薪少得可怜.

mould[3] (*US* **mold**) /məʊld; mold/ *n* [U] soft fine loose earth, esp from decayed vegetable matter 细而松软的土壤(尤指因含腐殖质): *leaf mould,* ie from decayed leaves and twigs that have fallen off trees 腐殖质土.

moulder (*US* **molder**) /ˈməʊldə(r); ˋmoldə/ *v* [I, Ip] **~ (away)** crumble to dust; decay slowly 崩塌; 碎裂; 腐烂: *the mouldering ruins of an old castle* 古堡逐渐坍塌的遗迹.

mould·ing (*US* **mold·ing**) /ˈməʊldɪŋ; ˋmoldɪŋ/ *n* **1** [U] action of shaping; way in which sth is shaped 模制; 压模; 模塑; 造型法: (*fig* 比喻) *the moulding of young people's characters* 对年轻人性格的塑造. **2** [C] (*architecture* 建) line of ornamental plaster, carved woodwork, etc typically along the top of sth, eg a wall 线脚.

moult (*US* **molt**) /məʊlt; molt/ *v* [I] (**a**) (of birds) lose feathers before a new growth (指鸟类)换羽. (**b**) (of dogs, cats, etc) lose hair (指狗、猫等)脱毛: *a dog that moults all over the house* 那条狗, 脱的毛满屋都是.

▷ **moult** *n* [C, U] process or time of moulting 换羽; 脱毛; 换羽期; 脱毛期.

mound /maʊnd; maʊnd/ *n* **1** mass of piled-up earth; small hill 小丘; 土墩; 小土岗. **2** pile or heap; quantity of things to do 堆; 垛; 要做的一堆事: *a mound of mashed potato* 一堆捣烂的土豆泥 ○ *a mound of washing and ironing* 一堆要洗熨的衣物.

mount[1] /maʊnt; maʊnt/ *n* (*arch*, except in place names, usu written *Mt* 古词, 但仍可用于地名, 通常略作 Mt) mountain; hill 山; 峰: *Mt Etna, Everest, etc* 埃特纳火山、埃佛勒斯峰(即珠穆朗玛峰) ○ *the Mount of Olives* 橄榄

山 ○ *St Michael's Mount* 圣迈克尔山.

mount² /maʊnt; maʊnt/ *v* **1** [I, Ipr, Tn] **~ (to sth)** go up; ascend 登上: *The climbers mounted higher and higher.* 攀登者越爬越高. ○ *a staircase that mounts to the top of a building* 通往楼顶的楼梯 ○ *A blush mounted to the child's face,* ie The blood spread to the child's cheeks. 孩子的双颊泛出红晕. ○ *mount the stairs* 上楼梯. **2** [I, Tn, Tn·pr] **~ sb (on sth)** get onto or put (sb) onto a horse, etc for riding; provide (sb) with a horse for riding 骑上马; 使(某人)骑上马; 为(某人)备马: *He quickly mounted (his horse) and rode away.* 他迅速上马疾驰而去. ○ *He mounted the boy on the horse.* 他把孩子抱上马. ○ *The policemen were mounted on* (ie rode) *black horses.* 那些警察骑着黑色的马. **3** [I, Ipr, Ip] **~ (up) (to sth)** increase in amount or intensity (量或强度)增加, 上升: *The death toll mounted (to 100).* 死亡人数上升(至100). ○ *Concern is mounting over the fate of the lost expedition.* 对失踪探险队命运的担心与时俱增. ○ *bills, debts, expenses, etc that mount up* 日益增多的帐单、债务、费用等. **4** [Tn, Tn·pr] **~ sth (on/onto/in sth)** put sth into place on a support; fix sth in position for use, display or study 将某物置于架上; 将某物固定住(以备使用、展示或研究): *mount a collection of stamps onto card/in an album* 把搜集的邮票安放到卡片纸上[集邮册中] ○ *mount specimens on slides* 把标本固定到载片上 ○ *a brooch of diamonds mounted in silver* 镶于银托上的钻石胸针. **5** [Tn, Tn·pr] **~ sth (in sth)** set sth up; organize sth; begin sth 发起; 组织或开始某事: *mount an exhibition, a production, a display, etc* 举办展览、开始生产、筹备陈列 ○ *mount a protest, a demonstration, an attack, an offensive, etc* 发起抗议、示威、攻击、攻势等 ○ *The pop concert was mounted in a sports stadium.* 流行歌曲演唱会是在体育场举行的. **6** [Tn, Tn·pr] **~ sb (on/around sth)** place sb on guard 派某人站岗: *mount sentries on a wall, round a palace, etc* 在墙上、宫殿周围等设置警卫. **7** [I, Tn] (esp of large male animals, eg bulls) get up on (a female) in order to copulate (尤指大型雄性动物, 如公牛)趴到(雌性动物)身上交配. **8** (idm 习语) **mount guard (at/over sb/sth)** act as a guard or sentinel 做警卫; 站岗: *soldiers mounting guard at/over the palace* 在宫殿做警卫的士兵. **mount the 'throne** become king, queen, etc 即王位.

▷ **mount** *n* thing on which a person or thing is mounted (eg a card for a picture, a glass slide for a specimen, a horse for riding, etc) 承载物(如镜框的衬纸板、标本载片、乘坐的马等).

mounted *adj* provided with a mount 配有承载物的; 安装好的: *a mounted photograph,* ie fixed on a card 经裱褙的照片 ○ *mounted policemen,* ie on horses 骑警.

mount·ing *adj* increasing 逐渐增加的: *mounting tension* 不断加剧的紧张状况.

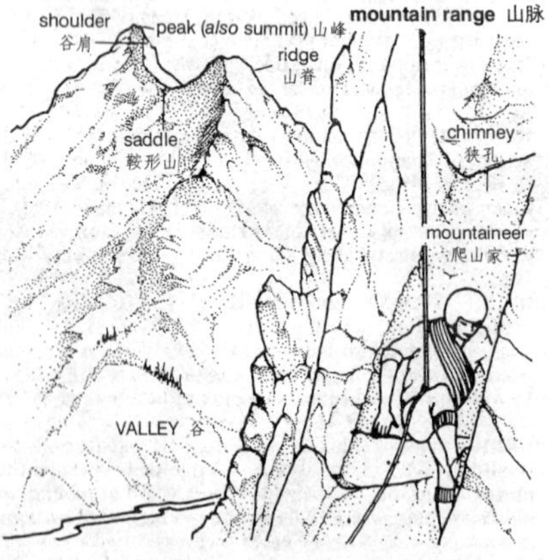

M

moun·tain /ˈmaʊntɪn; *US* -ntn; ˋmaʊntn̩/ *n* **1** [C] mass of very high rock going up to a peak 山; 山岳: *Everest is the highest mountain in the world.* 埃佛勒斯(即珠穆朗玛)峰是世界上最高的山. ○ [attrib 作定语] *mountain peaks, paths, streams, etc* 山峰、山道、山溪 ○ *the refreshing mountain air* 山中清新的空气. **2** [sing] **~ of sth** (*fig* 比喻) (**a**) large heap or pile, esp of work needing attention 大量, 大堆(尤指需处理的工作): *a mountain of paperwork, unanswered letters, correspondence, washing and ironing, etc* 大批书面作业、未复函件、信件、洗熨的衣物等. (**b**) large overwhelming amount (of difficulties) 大量, 重重(的困难): *a mountain of debts, complaints, queries* 大量的欠债、投诉、询问. **3** [C usu *sing* 通常作单数] large surplus stock 大量的积压或过剩: *the butter mountain,* ie large unsold amount of butter in the EEC 黄油过剩(欧洲经济共同体大量积压的黄油). **4** (idm 习语) **make a ˌmountain out of a ˈmolehill** (*derog* 贬) make a trivial matter seem important 小题大做.

▷ **moun·tain·eer** /ˌmaʊntɪˈnɪə(r); *US* -ntnˈɪər; ˌmaʊntn̩ˋɪr/ *n* person who is skilled at climbing mountains 爬山家. **moun·tain·eer·ing** /ˌmaʊntɪˈnɪərɪŋ; *US* -ntnˈɪə-; ˌmaʊntn̩ˋɪrɪŋ/ *n* [U] climbing mountains (as a sport) 登山(运动): [attrib 作定语] *a mountaineering expedition* 登山探险.

moun·tain·ous /ˈmaʊntɪnəs; *US* -ntənəs; ˋmaʊntn̩əs/ *adj* **1** having many mountains 多山的: *mountainous country* 山国. **2** huge; rising like mountains 巨大的; 高耸如山的: *mountainous waves* 排山巨浪.

□ ˌ**mountain ˈash** type of tree with scarlet berries; rowan 欧洲花楸.

ˌ**mountain ˈchain**, ˌ**mountain ˈrange** row or series of mountains more or less in a straight line 山脉. ⇨illus 见插图.

ˌ**mountain ˈlion** = PUMA.

ˈ**mountain sickness** illness caused by thin air on high mountains 高山病.

ˈ**mountainside** *n* side or slope of a mountain 山腹; 山腰; 山坡.

moun·te·bank /ˈmaʊntɪbæŋk; ˋmaʊntəˌbæŋk/ *n* (*dated or rhet derog* 旧或修辞, 贬) person who tries to cheat others by clever talk; swindler 江湖骗子.

Mountie /ˈmaʊntɪ; ˋmaʊntɪ/ *n* (*infml* 口) member of the Royal Canadian Mounted Police 加拿大皇家骑警.

mourn /mɔːn; mɔrn/ *v* [I, Ipr, Tn] **~ (for/over sb/sth)** feel or show sorrow or regret for the loss of sb/sth 因丧失某人[某事物]而悲痛或表示哀悼: *She mourned (for/over) her dead child for many years.* 她孩子死了多年, 她仍哀伤不已. ○ *We all mourn the destruction of a well-loved building.* 我们都为毁掉心爱的建筑物而痛惜.

▷ **mourner** *n* person who mourns, esp one who attends a funeral as a friend or relative of the dead person 哀悼者(尤指参加葬礼的亲友).

mourn·ful /-fl; -fəl/ *adj* (*often derog* 常作贬义) sad; sorrowful 悲哀的; 令人悲痛的: *a mournful look on her face* 她脸上的悲哀神情 ○ *I wish you'd stop playing that mournful music.* 你别奏那种哀乐了吧. **mourn·fully** /-fəlɪ; -fəlɪ/ *adv*. **mourn·ful·ness** *n* [U].

mourn·ing *n* [U] black or dark clothes worn as a (conventional) sign of grief at sb's death 丧服(黑色或深色的): *When grandmother died they went into* (ie started to wear) *mourning.* 祖母逝世时他们开始服丧. ○ *She was in mourning for a month.* 她服丧一个月.

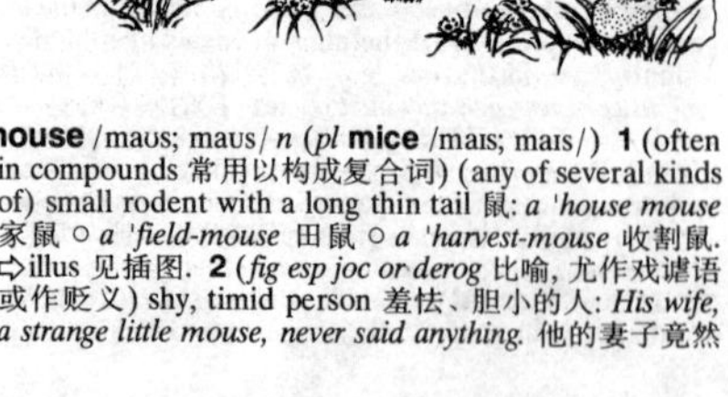

mouse /maʊs; maʊs/ *n* (*pl* **mice** /maɪs; maɪs/) **1** (often in compounds 常用以构成复合词) (any of several kinds of) small rodent with a long thin tail 鼠: *a 'house mouse* 家鼠 ○ *a 'field-mouse* 田鼠 ○ *a 'harvest-mouse* 收割鼠. ⇨illus 见插图. **2** (*fig esp joc or derog* 比喻, 尤作戏谑语或作贬义) shy, timid person 羞怯、胆小的人: *His wife, a strange little mouse, never said anything.* 他的妻子竟然

胆小如鼠, 一句话都没说. ○ *Are you a man or a mouse* (ie brave or cowardly)? 你是男子汉还是胆小鬼? **3** (*computing* 计) small hand-held device that is moved across a desk-top, etc to produce a corresponding movement of the cursor, with buttons for entering commands 鼠标; 滑鼠. ⇨illus at COMPUTER 见COMPUTER 插图. **4** (idm 习语) **play cat and mouse/a cat-and-mouse game with sb** ⇨ CAT[1]. **quiet as a mouse** ⇨ QUIET.

▷ **mouser** /ˈmaʊsə(r), ˈmaʊzə(r); ˈmaʊzər/ *n* cat that hunts for or catches mice 善捕鼠的猫.

mousy /ˈmaʊsɪ; ˈmaʊsɪ/ *adj* (**-ier**, **-iest**) (*derog* 贬) **1** (esp of hair) dull brown (尤指毛发)灰褐色的. **2** (of people) timid; shy (指人)胆小的, 羞怯的.

□ ˈ**mousetrap** *n* trap for catching mice 捕鼠器. ˌ**mousetrap** ˈ**cheese** (*joc* 谑) cheese of poor quality or taste, not good to eat 劣质奶酪.

mous·saka /muːˈsɑːkə; muˈsɑkə/ *n* [U] Greek dish made of minced meat and vegetables (usu including aubergine and tomato), cooked in the oven 希腊式肉末烧茄子.

mousse /muːs; mus/ *n* [U, C] **1** cold dish made of cream, egg-whites, etc mixed lightly and flavoured with sth sweet (fruit or chocolate) or sth savoury (fish or meat) 奶油冻: *a/some banana, strawberry, raspberry, etc mousse* 一份[一些]香蕉、草莓、悬钩子...奶油冻 ○ *salmon mousse* 鲑鱼奶油冻. **2** thick creamy liquid put on the hair to shape it or improve its condition 护发定型乳剂: *styling/conditioning mousse* 固发定型[护发]乳剂.

mous·tache /məˈstɑːʃ; məˈstæʃ/ (*US* **mus·tache** /ˈmʌstæʃ; ˈmʌstæʃ/) *n* **1** [C] hair allowed to grow on the upper lip 髭. ⇨illus at HEAD 见HEAD 插图. Cf 参看 BEARD[1] a, WHISKER 1. **2 moustaches** [pl] long moustache 长髭.

mouth[1] /maʊθ; maʊθ/ *n* (*pl* **~s** /maʊðz; maʊðz/) **1** [C] opening through which animals take in food; space behind this containing the teeth, tongue, etc 嘴; 口: *'Open your mouth a little wider,' said the dentist.* '把嘴张大点,' 牙科医生说. ○ *Don't talk with your mouth full.* 嘴里有东西时不要说话. ○ (*fig* 比喻) *Every time I open my mouth* (ie speak) *he contradicts me.* 我一说话他就反对. ○ (*derog* 贬) *She's got a big mouth*, ie talks a lot and (esp) reveals secrets. 她嘴不稳(话多, 尤指泄密). ⇨ illus at HEAD 见HEAD 插图. **2** [U] (*infml derog* 口, 贬) **(a)** meaningless or ineffectual talk 空话; 无聊的话: *He's all mouth and no action.* 他这人光说不干. **(b)** impudent talk; rudeness 无礼的话; 粗鲁: *I don't want any mouth from you!* 你别给我多嘴! **3** [C] place where sth (eg a bag, bottle, tunnel, etc) opens 开口处(如袋口、瓶口、隧道口等): *inside/in/at the mouth of a cave* 在洞口内[里/旁]. **4** [C] place where a river enters the sea 河口. **5** [C] person requiring to be fed (需要供养的)人: *She's got five mouths to feed*, eg children. 她得养活五口人. **6** (idm 习语) **born with a silver spoon in one's mouth** ⇨ BORN. **butter wouldn't melt in sb's mouth** ⇨ BUTTER. **by word of mouth** ⇨ WORD. **down in the mouth** dejected; depressed 沮丧; 情绪低落. **from the horse's mouth** ⇨ HORSE. **keep one's** ˈ**mouth shut** (*infml* 口) not reveal a secret, esp of dishonest or criminal activity 一声不吭, 保持缄默(尤指对坏事或罪行): *He'd better keep his mouth shut, or else...!* 他最好保持沉默, 否则...! **leave a bad/nasty taste in the mouth** ⇨ LEAVE[1]. **live from hand to mouth** ⇨ LIVE[2]. **look a gift horse in the mouth** ⇨ GIFT. **out of the mouths of babes and** ˈ**sucklings** (*saying* 谚) children often speak wisely 黄口小儿的话也常有道理. **put one's money where one's mouth is** ⇨ MONEY. **put words into sb's mouth** ⇨ WORD. **shoot one's mouth off** ⇨ SHOOT[1]. **shut one's mouth/face** ⇨ SHUT. **shut sb's mouth** ⇨ SHUT. **take the bread out of sb's mouth** ⇨ BREAD. **take the words out of sb's mouth** ⇨ WORD.

▷ **-mouthed** /maʊðd; maʊðd/ (forming compound *adjs* 用以构成复合形容词) **1** having the specified type of mouth 有某种嘴的: *small-mouthed, wide-mouthed, open-mouthed, etc* 小嘴的、大嘴的、张着嘴的等. **2** (*usu derog* 通常作贬义) having the specified way of speaking 有某种说话方式的: *loud-mouthed, foul-mouthed, etc* 大嗓门的、说脏话的等.

mouth·ful /-fʊl; -ˌfʊl/ *n* **1** [C] as much as can easily be put into the mouth at one time 一口(的量): *eat a few mouthfuls of food* 吃几口食物 ○ *swallow sth in a/one mouthful* 一口吞下某物. **2** [sing] (*infml joc* 口, 谑) word or phrase that is too long or difficult to pronounce 长或拗口的词语: *Timothy Thistlethwaite? That's a bit of a mouthful!* 蒂莫西·西斯尔思韦特? 真有点绕嘴!

□ ˈ**mouth-organ** *n* (also **harmonica**) small musical instrument played by passing it along the lips while blowing or sucking air 口琴.

ˈ**mouthpiece** *n* **1** part of a musical instrument, pipe, telephone, etc that is placed at or between the lips (乐器的)吹口; (烟斗的)咬嘴; (电话的)送话口. ⇨illus at App 1 见附录1插图, page x. **2** (*usu derog* 通常作贬义) person, newspaper, etc that expresses the opinions of others 代言人; 喉舌: *a newspaper which is merely the mouthpiece of the Tory party* 仅为英国保守党喉舌的报纸.

ˌ**mouth-to-**ˈ**mouth** *adj* [usu attrib 通常作定语] done by placing one's mouth over a dying (esp drowning) person's mouth and breathing into the lungs 口对口人工呼吸(尤指对溺水者): *mouth-to-mouth resuscitation* 口对口复苏法.

ˈ**mouthwash** *n* [U] liquid for cleaning the mouth 漱口药.

ˈ**mouthwatering** *adj* (*approv* 褒) that makes one want to eat; extremely delicious 令人垂涎的; 诱人食欲的; 美味的: *the mouthwatering smell of freshly baked bread* 新烤的面包诱人的气味.

mouth[2] /maʊð; maʊð/ *v* **1** [I, Tn] speak or say (sth) with movement of the jaw but no sound 嘴动而不出声地说(某事): *silently mouthing curses* 嘴动而不出声地咒骂. **2** [Tn] (*derog* 贬) say (sth) insincerely or without understanding 言不由衷或不知所云地说: *mouthing the usual platitudes about the need for more compassion* 言不由衷地说些需要更加同情之类的老一套话.

mov·able /ˈmuːvəbl; ˈmuvəbl/ *adj* **1** that can be moved 可动的; 活动的: *a machine with a movable arm for picking up objects* 有活动臂可提起物体的机器. **2** (*law* 律) (of property) that can be taken from place to place (eg furniture, as opposed to buildings or land, called *real property*) (指财产)动产的. **3** varying in date from year to year (指日期)逐年不同的, 不固定的: *Christmas is fixed, but Easter is a movable feast.* 圣诞节的日期是固定的, 但复活节的日期却因年而异.

▷ **mov·ables** *n* [pl] (*esp law* 尤用于法律) personal property; articles that can be removed from a house 个人的财产; 动产. Cf 参看 FITTING[2] 2, FIXTURE 1.

move[1] /muːv; muv/ *n* **1** change of place or position 地点或位置的变动: *She sat in the corner, watching my every move.* 她坐在角落里注视着我的一举一动. ○ *'One false move and you're dead!' he said, pointing a gun at me.* '你乱动一下, 就要你的命!' 他用枪对准我说. **2 ~ (from...) (to/into...)** action or process of changing the place where one lives, works, etc 迁移; 迁居; 变动: *a move from the town into the country* 从市区到乡间的迁移 ○ *a move to a new job/office* 转至新的工作[办公室] ○ *The move took six hours with a team of three men.* 搬迁用了三个人六小时. **3** **(a)** act of changing the position of a piece in chess or other board game (下棋的)步, 着: *Do you know all the possible moves in chess?* 国际象棋的各种走法你都会吗? **(b)** player's turn to do this (轮到的)一步, 一着: *Whose move is it?* 该谁走了? **4 ~ (towards sth/to do sth)** action (to be) done to achieve a purpose 步骤; 行动: *We've tried peaceful persuasion; what's our next move?* 我们已经试过了平心静气的说服方法, 下一步怎么办呢? ○ *The government's announcement is seen as a move towards settling the strike.* 政府的通告已视为迈向解决罢工问题的一步. ○ *In a move to restrict imports, the government raised custom duties.* 政府在限制进口的措施中提高了关税. **5** (idm 习语) **a false move** ⇨ FALSE. **get a** ˈ**move on** (*infml* 口) hurry up 赶快; 加紧. **make a** ˈ**move** **(a)** set off on a journey; leave 出发; 起程; 动身: *It's getting dark; we'd better make a move.* 天越来越黑了, 我们最好动身吧. **(b)** take action 采取行动: *We're waiting to see what our competitors do before we make a move.* 我们先等着看看竞争对手怎么办再说. **on the** ˈ**move** moving

在移动中: *The army is on the move.* 军队在移动. ○ *Don't jump off a train when it's on the move.* 火车未停稳时万勿跳下.

move[2] /mu:v; muv/ *v* **1** [I, Ipr, Ip, Tn, Tn·pr, Tn·p] **~ (sb/sth) (about/around)** (cause sb/sth to) be in motion, or change position or place (使某人[某物])移动, 改变位置: *Don't move; stay perfectly still.* 别动, 在原地一点儿都别动. ○ *The leaves were moving in the breeze.* 树叶在微风中摆动. ○ *I could hear someone moving (about/around) in the room above.* 我听见楼上有人(来回)走动. ○ *move one's head, arm, leg, etc* 移动头部、胳膊、腿等 ○ *move a chair nearer to the fire* 把椅子挪近火炉 ○ *Has someone moved my book? I left it on this desk.* 有人动过我的书了吗? 我原来放在这张书桌上的. ○ *She is too ill to be moved.* 她病得很厉害, 经不住转移. ○ (*fig* 比喻) *That car was really moving!* ie travelling fast. 那辆汽车真快! **2** [I, Ipr, Ip] **~ (from...) (to...)** change residence 搬家; 迁居: *We're moving to Scotland.* 我们要搬到苏格兰去. ○ *The new neighbours moved in yesterday.* 新邻居是昨天搬来的. ○ *He couldn't pay his rent, so he had to move out.* 他付不起房租, 所以得搬走. **3** [I, Ip] **~ (ahead/on)** make progress 进步; 有进展: *work which moves (ahead) steadily, quickly, etc* 稳步、快速等(向前)推进的工作 ○ *Time moves (on)* (ie passes) *slowly.* 时光慢慢流逝. ○ *Share prices moved ahead* (ie rose) *today.* 股票价格今日上扬. ○ *Things are not moving as fast as we hoped.* 事情的进展不像我们希望的那么快. **4** [I, Tn] (in chess and other board games) change the position of (a piece) (棋戏中)下, 走: *It's your turn to move.* 该轮到你下了. **5** [Tn, Tn·pr] **~ sb (to sth)** cause sb to have very powerful feelings, esp of sadness 使某人十分感动(尤指感伤): *The story of their sufferings moved us deeply.* 他们的苦难深深打动了我们. ○ *move sb to laughter, tears, etc* 引得某人发笑、流泪等. **6** [Tn, Cn·t] cause or prompt (sb) (to do or not do sth) 驱使, 激励或鼓动(某人)(做或不做某事): *He works as the spirit moves him*, ie when he feels the desire to do so. 他有精神上的鼓舞而工作. ○ *It was so odd that I was moved to ask her where she got it.* 那东西十分希罕, 我禁不住问她是从哪里弄来的. **7** [Tn, Tf] propose (sth) formally for discussion and decision (at a meeting) (在会上)提议(某事); 动议: *The MP moved an amendment to the Bill.* 那位下院议员动议修订该法案. ○ *Mr Chairman, I move that the matter be discussed after lunch.* 主席先生, 我建议此事午饭后再讨论. **8** [I, Tn] (cause or persuade sb/sth to) change one's attitude (促使或说服某人[某事物])改变态度: *The government won't move on this issue.* 政府决不改变对这一问题的态度. ○ *She's made up her mind and nothing can move her.* 她主意已定, 无法改变. **9** [I] take action; do sth 采取行动; 做某事: *Unless the employers move quickly, there will be a strike.* 雇主若不尽快采取措施, 就要引起一场罢工. ○ *The government has moved to dispel the rumours.* 政府已进行辟谣. **10** [I, Tn] (*medical or fml* 医或文) (of the bowels) be emptied; (of people) empty (the bowels) (指肠)通便; (指人)排便. **11** (idm 习语) **get 'moving** begin, leave, etc quickly 迅速开始、离去等: *It's late; we'd better get moving.* 天晚了, 咱们快走吧. **get sth 'moving** cause sth to make vigorous progress 使某事大有进展; 推动某事物: *A new director in this department will really get things moving.* 此部门的新主任能把工作开展起来. **go/move in for the kill** ⇨ KILL *n*. **move the 'goal-posts** (*Brit infml* 口) change the accepted conditions within which a particular matter is being discussed or a particular action taken 改变原已认可的条件. **move heaven and 'earth** do everything one possibly can in order to achieve sth 全力以赴; 竭尽全力. **move 'house** move one's furniture, goods, etc to another place to live in 搬家. **12** (phr v) **move across/along/down/over/up** move further in the direction indicated so as to make space for others 向所示方向移动以腾出空间: *'Move along, please,' said the bus conductor.* '请往里走走,'公共汽车售票员说. ○ *Move over so I can get into bed.* 躺过去一点儿我好上床. **move for sth** (*US esp law* 尤用于法律) request sth formally 正式要求某事: *Your honour, I move for an adjournment.* 法官阁下, 我请求休会. **move in sth** live, be active, pass one's time, etc in a particular social group 在某社交集体中生活、活动、消遣等: *move in high society* 活跃于上层社会 ○ *She only moves in the best circles.* 她只在精英圈子中活动. **move in on sb/sth** converge on sb/sth, esp in a menacing way 向某人[某事物]逼近, 进逼: *The police moved in on the (house occupied by the) terrorists.* 警察向恐怖分子(占据的房子)进逼. **move off** (esp of a vehicle) start a journey; leave (尤指车辆)起程, 出发, 离开: *The signal was given, and the procession moved off.* 信号发出后车队随即出发. **move on** (**a**) continue one's journey 继续行进: *It's time we moved on.* 我们该继续赶路了. (**b**) move to another place; stop loitering (eg when ordered by the police) 走开, 别停留, 不要逗留(如作警方用语). **move sb on** (of police) order sb to move away from the scene of an accident, etc (指警方)命令某人离开事故等现场.

▷ **mover** /ˈmu:və(r); ˋmuvɚ/ *n* **1** person who moves 行动者: *She's a lovely mover*, ie moves (eg dances) elegantly. 她动作优美. **2** person who formally makes a proposal 提议人.

mov·ing *adj* **1** [attrib 作定语] that which moves 移动的; 活动的: *a moving staircase* 自动扶梯 ○ *a mechanism with no moving parts* 没有活动部件的机械装置 ○ *a moving picture*, ie cinema film 电影片. **2** causing one to have deep feelings, esp of sadness or sympathy 感人的; 动人的; (尤指)令人感伤或同情的: *a moving story, film, tragedy, etc* 感人的故事、影片、悲剧等 ○ *His speech was very moving.* 他的讲话非常感人. **mov·ingly** *adv*.

move·ment /ˈmu:vmənt; ˋmuvmənt/ *n* **1** (**a**) [U, C] moving or being moved 移动; 运动; 活动: *the movement of his chest as he breathes* 他呼吸时胸部的起伏 ○ *lie still without (making) any movement* 静卧不动 ○ *Loose clothing gives you greater freedom of movement.* 穿宽松的衣服就能活动自如. ○ *I detected a slight movement in the undergrowth.* 我发现灌木丛中有些动静. (**b**) [U] action; activity 动作; 活动: *a play, novel, etc that lacks movement* 情节呆滞的戏剧、小说等. **2** [C] act of changing position, esp as a military manoeuvre 移动; (尤指)军事调动: *Troop movements can be observed from space by a satellite.* 借助卫星可观察到部队的调动. **3 movements** [pl] actions, journeys, etc over a period of time (esp as observed and/or recorded by sb else) 某时期的活动、行踪等(尤指受到监视或记录的): *The police have been keeping a close watch on the suspects' movements.* 警方一直严密监视着可疑分子的活动. **4** [sing] **~ (away from/towards sth)** trend (in society) (社会中的)动向, 趋向, 倾向: *the movement towards greater freedom in fashion styles* 时装款式向更开放方面发展的趋势. **5** [U, C] **~ (in sth)** change in amount (esp the rise or fall of prices in a stock market) 变动; (尤指股票市场价格的)涨落: *not much movement in oil shares* 石油股价无大波动. **6** [CGp, C] **~ (to do sth)** (group of people with a) shared set of aims or principles (具有共同目标或原则的)团体; (此种团体开展的)运动: *the aims, members, etc of the Labour Movement* 工人运动的目标、成员等 ○ *poets of the Romantic movement* 浪漫派诗人 ○ *founding a movement to promote women's rights* 创建女权运动. **7** [C] (*music* 音) any of the main divisions in a long musical work 乐章: *a symphony in four movements* 一首四乐章的交响曲. **8** [C] moving parts in a mechanism, esp those in a clock or watch which turn the hands (活动的)机件; (尤指钟表的)机心. **9** [C] (*medical or fml* 医或文) emptying of the bowels 通便.

movie /ˈmu:vɪ; ˋmuvɪ/ *n* (*esp US*) **1** [C] cinema film 电影: *go to (see) a movie* 去看电影 ○ [attrib 作定语] *a movie producer* 电影制片人 ○ *movie stars* 电影明星. **2 the movies** [pl] (**a**) (also **movie house, movie theater**) the cinema 电影院: *go to the movies* 去看电影. (**b**) the film industry 电影界; 电影业: *She is in/works in the movies.* 她在电影界工作.

▷ **'movie-goer** *n* (*esp US*) person who (regularly) goes to the cinema (常)看电影的人.

mow /məʊ; mo/ *v* (*pt* **mowed**, *pp* **mown** /məʊn; mon/ or **mowed**) **1** [I, Tn] cut (grass, etc) using a machine with blades, or a scythe (用机器或镰刀)刈, 割(草等): *mow the lawn* 刈草坪 ○ *mow a field*, ie cut the crops or vegetation in it 收割(地里的庄稼或蔬菜) ○ *the smell of new-mown hay* 新割牧草的气味. **2** (phr v) **mow sb down** kill (people) in large numbers, as if by making a sweeping movement 大量杀死(人); 扫灭; 撂倒: *soldiers mown down by machine-gun fire* 被机枪撂倒的士兵 ○

M

The lorry's brakes failed, and it mowed down several people in the bus queue. 卡车的闸失灵了，撞倒了几个排队等公共汽车的人.

▷ **mower** *n* (esp in compounds 尤用以构成复合词) machine or person that mows 刈草机；割草人：*a 'lawn-mower* 草坪刈草机 ○ *an electric mower* 电动刈草机 ○ *mowers and reapers* 刈草者和收割者.

MP /ˌem ˈpiː; ˌɛm ˋpi/ *abbr* 缩写 = **1** (*esp Brit*) Member of Parliament (esp in the House of Commons) 议员(尤指下院的)：*Annie Hill MP* 下院议员安妮·希尔 ○ *become an MP* 成为下院议员. **2** military police(man) 宪兵.

mpg /ˌem piː ˈdʒiː; ˌɛm pi ˋdʒi/ *abbr* 缩写 = miles per gallon 英里/加仑(每加仑所行英里数)：*This car does 40 mpg*, ie of petrol. 这汽车每加仑汽油能走40英里.

mph /ˌem piː ˈeɪtʃ; ˌɛm pi ˋetʃ/ *abbr* 缩写 = miles per hour 英里/小时(每小时英里数)：*a 70 mph speed limit* 每小时70英里的速度限制 ○ *driving at a steady 35 mph* 以每小时35英里的稳定车速驾驶. Cf 参看 KPH.

MPhil /ˌem ˈfɪl; ˌɛm ˋfɪl/ *abbr* 缩写 = Master of Philosophy 哲学硕士；(某学科的)硕士：*have/be an MPhil in English* 有英语硕士学位[为英语硕士] ○ *Mary Karlinski MPhil* 玛丽·卡琳斯基哲学硕士.

Mr /ˈmɪstə(r); ˋmɪstɚ/ *abbr* 缩写 = **1** title that comes before the (first name and the) surname of a man; Mister 先生(冠于男子姓或姓名前的称呼)：*Mr (John) Brown* (约翰·)布朗先生 ○ *Mr and Mrs Brown* 布朗先生及其夫人. **2** (*fml* 文) title for certain men in official positions 某些男子职务的称呼：*Mr Chairman* 主席先生 ○ (*esp US*) *Mr President* 总统先生.

MRBM /ˌem ɑː biː ˈem; ˌɛm ɑr bi ˋɛm/ *abbr* 缩写 = medium-range ballistic missile 中程弹道导弹. Cf 参看 ICBM, IRBM.

MRC /ˌem ɑː ˈsiː; ˌɛm ɑr ˋsi/ *abbr* 缩写 = (*Brit*) Medical Research Council 医学研究委员会：*an MRC-funded project* 医学研究委员会资助的项目.

Mrs /ˈmɪsɪz; ˋmɪsɪz/ *abbr* 缩写 = title that comes before the (first name and the) surname of a married woman 夫人(冠于已婚女子姓或姓名前的称呼)：*Mrs (Jane) Brown* (简·)布朗夫人 ○ (*fml sexist* 文, 性别偏见) *Mrs John Brown* 约翰·布朗太太. Cf 参看 MISS², MISTER.

MS *abbr* 缩写 = (*pl* **MSS**) manuscript.

Ms /mɪz; mɪz/ *abbr* 缩写 = title that comes before the (first name and the) surname of a woman whether married or unmarried 女士(冠于已婚或未婚女子姓或姓名前的称呼)：*Ms (Mary) Green* (玛丽·)格林女士. Cf 参看 MISS², MISTER.

MSc /ˌem es ˈsiː; ˌɛm ɛs ˋsi/ *abbr* 缩写 = Master of Science 理科硕士：*have/be an MSc in Chemistry* 有化学硕士学位[为化学硕士] ○ *Wendy O'Connor MSc* 温迪·奥康瑙尔理科硕士.

MST /ˌem es ˈtiː; ˌɛm ɛs ˋti/ *abbr* 缩写 = (*US*) Mountain Standard Time 山区标准时间. Cf 参看 MDT.

Mt *abbr* 缩写 = Mount: *Mt Kenya*, eg on a map 肯尼亚山(如地图上的标记).

mth *abbr* 缩写 = (*US* **mo**) (*pl* **mths**; *US* **mos**) month: *6 mths old* 6个月大的.

much¹ /mʌtʃ; mʌtʃ/ *indef det, indef pron* (used with [U] *ns*; esp with negative and interrogative *vs* or after *as, how, so, too* 与不可数名词连用，尤与否定式和疑问式动词连用或用于as、how、so、too之后) **1** a large amount or quantity (of sth) 多的；大量的. **(a)** (*det*): *I haven't got much money.* 我的钱不多. ○ *There's never very much news on Sundays.* 星期日从来就没有多少新闻. ○ *Did you have much difficulty finding the house?* 你找到这所房子很困难吗? ○ *How much* (ie What volume of) *petrol do you need?* 你需要多少汽油? ○ *Take as much time as you like.* 你愿意用多长时间都可以. ○ *There was so much traffic that we were stationary for half an hour.* 来往车辆很多，我们在路上耽搁了半小时. ○ *I have much pleasure in introducing our speaker.* 我能给大家介绍我们的演讲人，感到非常高兴. ○ *After much applause the audience went home.* 热烈掌声过后，观众都回家去了. **(b)** (*pron*): *He sat at his desk all morning but he didn't write much.* 他一上午都坐在书桌前却并未写多少东西. ○ *'Is there any mail?' 'Not (very) much.'* '有邮件吗?' '不(太)多.' ○ *She never eats much for breakfast.* 她早点从不多吃. ○ *Did the President say much to you?* 总统跟你说得多吗? ○ *How much is it?* ie What is its price? 多少钱? ○ *Eat as much as you can.* 尽量吃吧. ○ *He drank (far) too much last night.* 昨天晚上他喝得(也)太多了. ○ *You'll find you have much to learn in your new job.* 你会发现在新的工作中有很多可学的. ○ *I lay awake much of the night.* 我昨夜大部分时间都醒着. ○ *We have much to be thankful for.* 有很多事情值得我们庆幸. **2** (idm 习语) **not much of a** not a good (sth) 不太好的：*He's not much of a cricketer.* 他算不上好板球手. ○ *I'm not much of a correspondent*, ie I rarely write letters. 我不爱写信. **'this much** what I am about to say 我要说的是：*I will say this much for him — he never leaves a piece of work unfinished.* 关于他我要说的是——他工作未做完决不罢休. ○ *This much is certain, you will never walk again.* 有一点是肯定的，你再也不能行走了. **(with) not/without so much as** ⇨ so¹.

▷ **much·ness** *n* (idm 习语) ˌ**much of a 'muchness** very similar; almost alike 极相像；几乎相同：*It's hard to choose between the two candidates: they're both much of a muchness.* 很难在这两个候选人中作选择；他们俩不分上下.

EXPRESSING QUANTITY 数量表示法

	uncountable nouns 不可数名词	countable nouns 可数名词
positive statements 肯定式	lots of money 好多钱 (*less fml* 较通俗)	lots of coins 好多硬币 (*less fml* 较通俗)
	a lot of money 很多钱	a lot of coins 很多硬币
	much money 许多钱 (*more fml* 较文)	many coins 许多硬币 (*more fml* 较文)
negative statements 否定式	not much money 不多的钱	not many coins 不多的硬币
	little money 没多少钱 (*more fml* 较文)	few coins 没多少硬币 (*more fml* 较文)
questions 疑问式	How much money? 多少钱?	How many coins? 多少硬币?

1 Notice the difference between **little/few** and **a little/a few**. 注意 **little/few** 和 **a little/a few** 这两组词的区别. If we say, *'I have little money and few interests'*, we sound disappointed and negative. 若说：'I have little money and few interests(我没有什么钱，也没有什么爱好)'，言犹怅然若失，含否定义. If we say, *'I have a little money and a few interests'*, we sound more positive. 若说：'I have a little money and a few interests(我有点儿钱，也有些爱好)'，则含肯定义. Compare 试比较：He's lived here a long time but has few friends (他在这儿住了很长时间，可是没什么朋友)和He's lived here a short time but already has a few friends (他在这儿住得时间很短，可是已经有些朋友了).

2 **A lot of** can also be used in questions ☆ **a lot of** 亦可用于疑问句：*Have we got a lot of time/cards left?* (我们剩下的时间[卡片]多不多?) It suggests that the speaker knows that there is/are some left and wants to know whether the amount/number is big or small. 这句话的含义是发问者知道有些剩余，还想知道剩余的数量是多是少.

3 The comparative and superlative forms of **much, many,** and **a lot of** are **more** and **(the) most**. ☆ **much**、**many**、**a lot of** 的比较级是 **more**，最高级是 **(the) most**. For **little** the comparative and superlative forms are **less** and **(the) least** and for **few** they are **fewer** and **(the) fewest**. ☆ **little** 的比较级是 **less**，最高级是 **(the) least**；**few** 的比较级是 **fewer**，最高级是 **(the) fewest**.

much² /mʌtʃ; mʌtʃ/ *adv* to a great extent or degree 很；非常；在很大程度上. **1** (often used with negative *vs* 常与否定式动词连用)：*She didn't enjoy the film (very) much.* 她不大欣赏那部电影. ○ *He isn't in the office (very) much*, ie often. 他不常在办公室. ○ *I would very* much like you to come to dinner next week. 我非常欢迎你下星期来吃饭. ○ It doesn't much matter what you wear. 你穿什么衣服没有多大关系. ○ Much to her surprise he came back next day. 她颇感惊奇的是他第二天就回来了. **2** (**a**) (with past participles used adjectivally and *afraid*, *alive*, *aware*, etc 与作形容词的过去分词以及afraid、alive、aware等连用): *I was very much frightened by the report.* 这报告使我惊骇不已. ○ *He was (very) much surprised to find us there.* 他见我们在那里感到十分惊奇. ○ *I'm very much aware of the lack of food supplies.* 我深知食物贮备不足. (**b**) (used with comparatives and superlatives 与比较级和最高级连用): *much slower, bigger, heavier, etc* 慢、大、重等得多 ○ *much harder, faster, louder, etc* 困难、快、响亮等得多 ○ *much more expensive* 远为昂贵 ○ *much more confidently* 更大有信心 ○ *She's much better today.* 她今天好多了. ○ *That was much the best meal I've ever tasted.* 那是我尝过的最好的一餐了. ○ *My favourite is usually much the most expensive.* 我最喜爱的通常是最贵的. ○ *I would never willingly go anywhere by boat, much less go on a cruise.* 我到哪儿去从来都不愿意坐船, 更不用说为了兜风了. ⇨ Usage at VERY 用法见VERY. **3** (idm 习语) **as much** the same; equal(ly) 同样地; 同等程度地: *Please help me get this job — you know I would do as much for you.* 请帮我谋得这份工作 —— 你知道我为你也能这样做. ○ *That is as much as saying I am a liar.* 那无异于说我撒谎. ○ *I thought/said/knew as much.* ie My thoughts/statements/beliefs are confirmed. 我就是这样想[说/认为]的. **as much as sb can do** the maximum that sb can do 尽量; 尽最大努力: *I won't have a pudding — it was as much as I could do to finish the very large first course.* 我不要布丁了 —— 我能把第一道大菜吃完就已经很不容易了. **much as** although 尽管; 虽然: *Much as I would like to stay, I really must go home.* 我倒是很愿意呆在这儿, 可确实得回家了. ˌ**much the ˈsame** in about the same condition 情况大致相同: *The patient is much the same this morning.* 今晨病人情况几无变化. **not much good at sth** (*infml* 口) not very good at (doing) sth 不太善于(做)某事物: *I'm not much good at tennis.* 我打网球打得不太好. **not so much sth as sth** ⇨ SO[1].

mu·cil·age /ˈmjuːsɪlɪdʒ; ˋmjuslɪdʒ/ *n* [U] thick sticky fluid produced by plants, esp seaweed (植物的)黏液(尤指海草的).

▷ **mu·cil·agin·ous** /ˈmjuːsɪˌlædʒɪnəs; ˌmjuslˈædʒənəs/ *adj* **1** producing mucilage 分泌黏液的. **2** (*fml* 文) (of liquid) (unpleasantly) thick and sticky (指液体)(厌恶状)黏稠的.

muck /mʌk; mʌk/ *n* **1** [U] excrement of farm animals, esp as used for fertilizing; manure (牲畜的)粪便; (尤指)粪肥: *spreading muck on the fields* 往地里施粪肥 ○ [attrib 作定语] *a ˈmuck heap* 粪肥堆. **2** [U] (*infml* 口 *esp Brit*) dirt; filth; anything disgusting 污秽; 脏物; 令人讨厌之物: *Don't come in here with your boots all covered in muck.* 你别穿着脏靴子进来. ○ *Do you call that food? I'm not eating that muck!* 那也能叫做食物吗? 我可不吃那行子! ○ (*fig* 比喻) *You shouldn't believe all the muck and scandal you read in the Sunday papers.* 千万别尽信在星期日报纸上看到的秽迹丑闻. ○ *I don't want my name dragged through the muck*, ie mentioned contemptuously, in connection with scandal. 我可不想把我的名字扯进丑事中去. **3** (idm 习语) **common as dirt/muck** ⇨ COMMON[1]. **in a ˈmuck** (*Brit infml* 口) in an untidy state 乱七八糟; 凌乱不堪: *You can't leave your room in a muck like that.* 你不能把房间弄得那么乱七八糟的. **make a muck of sth** (*infml* 口) (**a**) make sth dirty 弄脏某物. (**b**) do sth badly; spoil sth; bungle sth 弄坏、弄糟或弄乱某事物: *I made a real muck of that exam.* 那次考试我可考糟了.

▷ **muck** *v* (phr v) **muck about/around** (*Brit infml* 口) behave in an aimless and silly way; waste time in useless activity 鬼混; 混日子; 虚掷光阴: *Stop mucking about and finish your work!* 别胡混了, 把工作做完吧! **muck in** (*Brit infml* 口) share tasks or accommodation equally 同工作; 同吃住: *Let's all muck in together, and we'll soon finish the job.* 咱们一起干吧, 很快就能做完. ○ *The officers had to muck in with their men.* 军官须与士兵同住. **muck (sth) out** clean out (stables, etc) by removing excrement 打扫, 清扫(马厩等). **muck sth up** (*infml* 口 *esp Brit*) (**a**) make sth dirty 弄脏某物: *muck up one's clothes* 弄脏衣服. (**b**) do sth badly; spoil sth; bungle sth 弄坏、弄糟或弄乱某事物: *I really mucked up my chances by doing badly in the interview.* 我真把机会耽误了, 面试考砸了.

mucky *adj* (**-ier, -iest**) **1** dirty 脏的: *My hands are all mucky.* 我的手全弄脏了. **2** obscene; rude 下流的; 粗野的: *telling those mucky stories of his* 讲他那些下流的故事.

□ ˈ**muck-raker** *n* (*derog* 贬) person who tries to find out bad things that people have done and spread scandal about them 搜集并张扬丑闻的人. ˈ**muck-raking** *n* [U] (*derog* 贬) activity of a muck-raker 搜集并张扬丑闻的活动.

ˈ**muck-up** *n* (usu *sing* 通常作单数) (*infml* 口 *esp Brit*) act of bungling or spoiling sth; mess 弄乱或弄糟某事物; 一团糟: *make a complete muck-up of sth* 把某事物弄得一团糟.

mu·cous /ˈmjuːkəs; ˋmjukəs/ *adj* of, like or covered with mucus (像)黏液的; (覆)有黏液的.

□ ˌ**mucous ˈmembrane** (*anatomy* 解) moist skin that lines the nose, mouth and certain internal organs 黏膜.

mu·cus /ˈmjuːkəs; ˋmjukəs/ *n* [U] sticky slimy substance produced by the mucous membrane; any similar slimy substance (黏膜分泌的)黏液; 类似黏液的物质: *a nose blocked with mucus* 黏液堵塞的鼻子 ○ *a trail of mucus left by a snail or slug* 蜗牛或蛞蝓留下的黏液痕迹.

mud /mʌd; mʌd/ *n* [U] **1** soft wet earth 泥; 烂泥; 淤泥: *rain that turns dust into mud* 化尘为泥的雨 ○ *My shoes were covered/plastered in/with mud.* 我的鞋沾满了泥. ○ *The armies got bogged down in the thick squelching mud.* 军队都陷入泥沼中, 行进时烂泥扑哧作声. **2** (idm 习语) **clear as mud** ⇨ CLEAR[1]. **drag sb/sb's name through the mire/mud** ⇨ DRAG[2]. **fling, sling, throw, etc ˈmud (at sb)** try to damage sb's reputation (by slander, libel, etc) 企图败坏某人的名声(藉造谣、诽谤等). ˌ**mud ˈsticks** (*saying* 谚) people tend to believe and remember bad or slanderous things said about sb 恶事如泥沾身洗不清. **sb's name is mud** ⇨ NAME[1].

▷ **muddy** *adj* (**-ier, -iest**) **1** full of or covered in mud 泥泞的; (覆)有泥的: *muddy roads, shoes* 泥泞的路、沾满泥的鞋. **2** (**a**) (of liquids or colours) coloured by or like mud; not clear; thick like mud (指液体或颜色)泥土色的, 泥土般的, 混浊的, 稠如泥浆的: *a muddy stream* 混浊的河 ○ *muddy water* 泥水 ○ *muddy coffee* 土褐色的咖啡 ○ *clothes of a muddy* (ie brownish) *green* 土绿色的衣物. (**b**) (*fig derog* 比喻, 贬) not clear; confused 模糊不清的; 混乱的: *muddy thinking* 紊乱的思绪. **mud·di·ness** *n* [U].

muddy *v* (*pt, pp* **muddied**) **1** [Tn] make (sb/sth) muddy 使(某人)沾上泥; 使(某物)泥泞、有泥、呈泥土色或混浊: *muddy one's face, clothes* 弄得脸上、衣服上有泥. **2** (idm 习语) **muddy the ˈwaters** (*derog* 贬) make a situation confused and unclear 把水搅浑; 弄乱情况.

□ ˈ**mud-bath** *n* bath in mud believed to have health-giving qualities (eg in treating rheumatism) 泥浴(如用以治疗风湿病): (*fig* 比喻) *the pitch was a mud-bath after the heavy rain* 大雨过后球场成了泥潭.

ˈ**mud-flat** *n* (often *pl* 常作复数) (stretch of) muddy land covered by the sea at high tide (涨潮时海水没过的)泥滩.

ˈ**mudguard** *n* curved cover over a wheel (of a bicycle, etc) (自行车等的)挡泥板. ⇨illus at App 1 见附录1插图, page xiii.

ˌ**mud ˈhut** simple hut made of mud that has dried and hardened 泥屋; 土坯房.

ˈ**mud pack** paste applied thickly to the face, for improving the health and appearance of the skin (贴于脸上作治疗或美容用的)泥膏.

ˈ**mud-slinging** *n* [U] (*derog* 贬) trying to damage sb's reputation by saying bad things about him 诽谤; 中伤: *There's too much mud-slinging by irresponsible journalists.* 不负责任的新闻工作者肆意诽谤的事太多了.

muddle /ˈmʌdl; ˋmʌdl/ *v* **1** [Tn, Tn·p] (**a**) **~ sth (up)** put sth into disorder; mix sth up 将某事物弄乱或混在一起: *The cleaner had muddled my papers, and I couldn't find the one I wanted.* 清洁工把我的文件弄乱了, 我找

不到我要的那份了. ○ *My papers were all muddled up together.* 我的文件全混在一起了. **(b) ~ sb (up)** confuse sb mentally 使某人糊涂: *Stop talking, or you'll muddle me (up) completely.* 别说了, 要不你把我全搞糊涂了. **(c) ~ sb/sth (up)** be confused about two or more things, people, etc and therefore make mistakes in arrangements 将事物与事物或人与人弄混淆(因而产生错误): *I muddled (up) the dates and arrived three days late.* 我把日期弄乱了, 所以迟到了三天. **2** [Tn·pr, Tn·p] **~ A (up) with B; ~ A and B (up)** fail to distinguish two people or things 分辨不出两人或两事物: *You must be muddling me up with my twin brother.* 你一定是把我看成我的孪生兄弟了. **3** (phr v) **muddle along** (*derog* 贬) live one's life in a foolish or helpless way, with no clear purpose or plan 混日子: *We muddle along from day to day.* 我们一天天地混日子. **muddle through** (*often joc* 常作戏谑语) achieve one's aims even though one does not act efficiently, have the proper equipment, etc 胡乱应付过去: *I expect we shall muddle through somehow!* 我看我们总能应付过去!

▷ **muddle** *n* **~ (about/over sth)** **1** [C] state of untidiness or confusion 凌乱; 杂乱; 紊乱: *Your room's in a real muddle.* 你的房间真是乱七八糟. ○ *There was a muddle over our hotel accommodation.* 我们旅馆的食宿安排十分混乱. **2** [sing] mental confusion 糊涂; 困惑: *The old lady gets in(to) a muddle trying to work the video.* 那老太太想开录像机, 但是越搞越糊涂.

muddled *adj* confused 糊涂的; 混乱的: *muddled thinking* 紊乱的思绪.

mud·dling *adj* confusing 令人迷惑的; 令人糊涂的: *These government forms are very muddling.* 政府的这些表格真费解.

□ ˌ**muddle-ˈheaded** *adj* lacking clearness of thought; confused 头脑不清的; 糊涂的; 混乱的: *muddle-headed people, ideas, arguments* 糊涂的人、思想、论据. ˌ**muddle-ˈheadedness** *n* [U].

muesli /ˈmju:zlɪ; ˋmjuzlɪ/ *n* [U] breakfast food that is a mixture of uncooked cereal, nuts, dried fruit, etc 由生的谷物、坚果、干果等混合制成的早餐食品.

mu·ez·zin /mu:ˈezɪn; *US* mju:-; mjuˋɛzɪn/ *n* man who calls out the hours of prayer for Muslims, usu from the minaret of a mosque 宣礼员(通常自清真寺的宣礼塔上呼唤穆斯林到时做礼拜的人).

muff[1] /mʌf; mʌf/ *n* hollow roll of fur or other warm material used to keep the hands warm in cold weather 皮手筒; 手笼.

muff[2] /mʌf; mʌf/ *v* [Tn] (*infml derog* 口, 贬) fail to catch or seize (sth); miss; bungle 未抓住(某事物); 错过; 弄糟: *The fielder muffed an easy catch.* 外野手把一个很好接的球接漏了. ○ *She had a wonderful opportunity, but she muffed it.* 她有一个绝好的机会, 但是她错过了.

muf·fin /ˈmʌfɪn; ˋmʌfɪn/ *n* **1** (*Brit*) (*US* ˌ**English ˈmuffin**) small flat round bun, usu toasted and eaten hot with butter 小松饼(通常加黄油烤热吃). **2** (*US*) small sweet bread roll or cake, often eaten with butter 甜的小面包卷或小饼(常加黄油).

muffle /ˈmʌfl; ˋmʌfl/ *v* **1** [Tn, Tn·pr, Tn·p] **~ sb/sth (up) (in sth)** wrap or cover sb/sth for warmth or protection 包裹或覆盖某人[某物](为保暖或保护): *He walked out into the snow, heavily muffled (up) in a thick scarf and warm overcoat.* 他雪天出门, 裹着厚厚的围巾, 穿着暖和的大衣. **2** [Tn, Tn·pr] **~ sth (with sth)** make the sound of sth (eg a bell or a drum) quieter by wrapping it, covering it in cloth, etc 包住(如铃或鼓)(使声音低沉): *muffle the oars of a boat*, ie wrap the blades to stop them splashing noisily 包住船桨(包住桨叶以减低溅水声).

▷ **muf·fled** *adj* (of sounds) heard indistinctly, because an obstacle is in the way (指声音)听不清的(因有物体相隔): *muffled voices coming from the next room* 隔壁房间传来含糊的说话声.

muf·fler /ˈmʌflə(r); ˋmʌflɚ/ *n* **1** (*dated* 旧) scarf or other cloth worn round the neck for warmth 围巾; 领巾. **2** (*US*) =SILENCER.

mufti /ˈmʌftɪ; ˋmʌftɪ/ *n* [U] ordinary clothes worn by people (eg soldiers) who normally wear uniform in their job (常穿制服的人, 如士兵, 所穿的)便服: *Soldiers wear mufti on leave, not uniform.* 士兵度假时穿便服, 不穿制服. ○ *officers in mufti* 穿便服的军官.

mug[1] /mʌg; mʌg/ *n* **1 (a)** (usu straight-sided, fairly large) drinking vessel of china, metal or plastic with a handle, for use without a saucer 缸子(圆筒形有柄大杯): *a coffee mug* 咖啡缸子. **(b)** its contents 一缸子之物: *a mug of coffee* 一缸子咖啡. ⇨illus at CUP 见 CUP 插图. **2** (*sl derog or joc* 俚, 贬或谑) face 脸: *What an ugly mug!* 多难看的脸!

▷ ˈ**mug·ful** /-fʊl; -fʊl/ *n* amount (of tea, coffee, etc) contained in a mug 一缸子的(茶、咖啡等的)量: *drink two mugfuls* 喝两缸子.

mug[2] /mʌg; mʌg/ *n* (*infml* 口) **1** person who is easily deceived 易受骗的人; 傻瓜. **2** (idm 习语) **a ˈmug's game** (*derog* 贬 *esp Brit*) activity unlikely to be successful or profitable 不易成功的事; 无利可图的事: *Trying to sell overcoats in midsummer is a real mug's game.* 大夏天推销大衣真是白费力气.

mug[3] /mʌg; mʌg/ *v* (**-gg-**) (phr v) **mug sth up** (*Brit infml* 口) (try to) learn sth, usu in a short time for a special purpose (eg an exam) 突击式学习: *mugging up the Highway Code before a driving test* 驾驶测验前突击背公路法规.

mug[4] /mʌg; mʌg/ *v* (**-gg-**) [Tn] (*infml* 口) attack and rob (sb) violently out of doors (户外)行凶抢劫(某人): *an old lady mugged by a gang of youths in the park* 在公园里遭一帮年轻人行凶抢劫的老太太.

▷ **mug·ger** *n* person who does this 行凶抢劫者.

mug·ging *n* [C, U] such an attack or attacks 行凶抢劫: *several reported muggings* 报道的几起行凶抢劫案.

mug·gins /ˈmʌgɪnz; ˋmʌgɪnz/ *n* [sing] (*Brit infml joc* 口, 谑) fool 傻瓜; 笨蛋: *Don't do that, you silly muggins!* 别干那事, 你这笨蛋! ○ *Muggins here locked his keys in the car!* 这笨蛋把自己的钥匙锁在汽车里了!

muggy /ˈmʌgɪ; ˋmʌgɪ/ *adj* (**-ier, -iest**) (of weather) oppressively warm and damp (指天气)闷热而潮湿的, 闷人的: *a muggy August day* 闷热的八月天. ▷ **mug·gi·ness** *n* [U].

Mu·ham·mad /məˈhæmɪd; muˋhæməd/ *n* the prophet and founder of Islam 穆罕默德(伊斯兰教的先知和创始人).

▷ **Mu·ham·madan** (also **Mu·ham·medan, Moham·medan**) /-ən; -ən/ *adj, n* (of or being a) Muslim 伊斯兰教信徒(的); 穆斯林(的). **Muh·am·mad·an·ism** (also **Muh·am·med·an·ism, Moh·am·med·an·ism**) /məˈhæmɪdənɪzəm; muˋhæməd-ən,ɪzəm/ *n* [U] Islam (the preferred name) 伊斯兰教(用Islam一词为佳). ⇨Usage at CHRISTIAN 用法见 CHRISTIAN.

mu·latto /mju:ˈlætəʊ; *US* məˈl-; məˋlæto/ *n* (*pl* **~s** or *esp US* **~es**) person who has one black parent and one white (黑人与白人所生的)黑白混血儿.

mul·berry /ˈmʌlbrɪ; *US* ˈmʌlberɪ; ˋmʌl,bɛrɪ/ *n* **(a)** tree with broad, dark-green leaves on which silkworms feed 桑树. **(b)** its purple or white fruit 桑椹: [attrib 作定语] *mulberry juice* 桑椹汁.

mulch /mʌltʃ; mʌltʃ/ *n* protective covering (eg of straw, rotting leaves, or plastic sheeting) spread over the roots of trees and bushes, to retain moisture, kill weeds, etc 护根(用以保持水分、消灭杂草等的覆盖物, 如稻草、腐叶或塑料膜).

▷ **mulch** *v* [Tn] cover (plant roots or the ground round them) with a mulch 用护根覆盖(植物根部或其周围地面).

mule[1] /mju:l; mjul/ *n* **1** animal that is the offspring of a donkey and a horse, used for carrying loads and noted for its stubbornness 骡; 骡子. **2** (*fig infml* 比喻, 口) stubborn person 顽固的人. **3** (idm 习语) **(as)** ˌ**obstinate/**ˌ**stubborn as a ˈmule** very obstinate or stubborn 非常执拗或顽固.

▷ **mu·leteer** /ˌmju:ləˈtɪə(r); ˌmjuləˋtɪr/ *n* (*dated* 旧) person who leads mules 赶骡子的人.

mul·ish *adj* stubborn; obstinate 顽固的; 执拗的. **mul·ishly** *adv.* **mul·ish·ness** *n* [U].

mule[2] /mju:l; mjul/ *n* slipper that is open around the heel 拖鞋.

mull[1] /mʌl; mʌl/ *v* [Tn] make (wine, beer, etc) into a hot drink with sugar, spices, etc 将(葡萄酒、啤酒等)制成热饮(加糖、香料等): *mulled claret* 热的红葡萄酒.

mull[2] /mʌl; mʌl/ *n* (*Scot* 苏格兰) (esp in place-names) long piece of land sticking out into the sea (尤用于地名

M

中)岬,海角: *the Mull of Kintyre* 金泰尔角.

mull[3] /mʌl; mʌl/ *v* (phr v) **mull sth over** think about or consider sth long and carefully 思索或思考某事物: *I haven't decided yet; I'm mulling it over in my mind.* 我还没有决定,一直在仔细考虑.

mul·lah /ˈmʌlə; ˋmʌlə/ *n* Muslim teacher of theology and sacred law (伊斯兰教神学和圣律的)教师.

mul·let /ˈmʌlɪt; ˋmʌlɪt/ *n* (*pl* unchanged 复数不变) any of several types of seafish used as food, esp *red mullet* and *grey mullet* 鲻科鱼(尤指鲱鲤和鲻鱼).

mul·li·ga·tawny /ˌmʌlɪɡəˈtɔːnɪ; ˌmʌlɪɡəˋtɔnɪ/ *n* [U] thick, highly seasoned soup with curry powder in it 浓咖喱汤.

mul·lion /ˈmʌlɪən; ˋmʌljən/ *n* vertical (stone, wood or metal) division between two parts of a window, esp in a large old building (窗扇间的)直棂, 竖框, 中挺. ⇨illus at App 1 见附录1插图, page viii.

▷ **mul·lioned** /ˈmʌlɪənd; ˋmʌljənd/ *adj* having mullions 有直棂的.

multi- *comb form* 构词成分 having many of 有很多…的: *multicoloured* 多色的 ○ *a ˌmultimillioˈnaire*, ie a person having more than two million pounds, dollars, etc (有二百万镑、元等以上的)百万富翁 ○ *a ˌmultiracial comˈmunity, soˈciety, ˈcountry, etc*, ie with many different races 多种族社区、社会、国家等 ○ *a ˌmulti-storey ˈcar park*, ie consisting of a building with several floors 多层停车场.

mul·ti·fari·ous /ˌmʌltɪˈfeərɪəs; ˌmʌltəˋfɛrɪəs/ *adj* (*fml* 文) of many different kinds; having great variety 多种的; 各式各样的: *the multifarious life-forms that can be found in a coral reef* 珊瑚礁上可见的各种各样的生命形式 ○ *the multifarious rules and regulations of the bureaucracy* 官僚主义的种种规章制度.

mul·ti·lat·eral /ˌmʌltɪˈlætərəl; ˌmʌltɪˋlætərəl/ *adj* involving two or more participants 多方面的; 多边的: *a ˌmultilateral aˈgreement* 多边协议 ○ *ˌmultilateral nuclear disˈarmament*, ie involving all or most countries which have nuclear weapons 多国核裁军. Cf 参看BILATERAL, UNILATERAL.

mul·ti·lin·gual /ˌmʌltɪˈlɪŋɡwəl; ˌmʌltɪˋlɪŋɡwəl/ *adj* **1** speaking or using many languages 使用多种语言的: *India is a ˌmultilingual ˈcountry.* 印度是使用多语种的国家. **2** written or printed in many languages 用多种文字书写或印刷的: *a ˈmultilingual ˈdictionary, ˈphrasebook, eˈdition, etc* 多语词典、短语集、版本等 ○ *electrical goods sold with ˌmultilingual ˈoperating instructions* 带多语使用说明的电气商品. Cf 参看 BILINGUAL, MONOLINGUAL.

mul·ti·na·tional /ˌmʌltɪˈnæʃnəl; ˌmʌltɪˋnæʃənl/ *adj* involving many countries 多国的: *a multinational organization, operation, agreement* 多国组织、行动、协议.

▷ **mul·ti·na·tional** *n* (usu very large) company that does business in many different countries 跨国公司: *Some people believe that the multinationals have too much power.* 有人认为跨国公司的权力太大了.

mul·tiple /ˈmʌltɪpl; ˋmʌltəpl/ *adj* [attrib 作定语] having or involving many individuals, items or types 有多种、多项或多类型的: *a multiple crash on a motorway*, ie one involving many vehicles 公路上的连环撞车事故 ○ *person with multiple injuries*, ie with many cuts, broken bones, etc 受多种伤的人(多处割伤、骨折等).

▷ **mul·tiple** *n* **1** (*mathematics* 数) quantity which contains another quantity an exact number of times 倍数: *14, 21 and 28 are multiples of 7.* 14、21、28都是7的倍数. ○ *30 is a common multiple of 2, 3, 5, 6, 10 and 15.* 30是2、3、5、6、10、15的公倍数. ○ *least/lowest common multiple*, ie smallest quantity that contains two or more given quantities exactly (usu shortened to *LCM*, eg *The LCM of 4, 5, 6, 10 and 12 is 60*) 最小公倍数(略作LCM, 如4、5、6、10、12的最小公倍数是60). **2** (also ˌ**multiple** ˈ**store**) (*esp Brit*) shop with many branches throughout a country 连锁商店.

□ ˌ**multiple-**ˈ**choice** *adj* (of examination questions) showing several possible answers from which the correct one must be chosen (指试题)多项(答案供)选择的.

ˌ**multiple scle**ˈ**rosis** (*abbr* 缩写 **MS**) disease of the nervous system causing gradual paralysis 多发性硬化(症).

mul·ti·plex /ˈmʌltɪpleks; ˋmʌltəˌplɛks/ *adj* [usu attrib 通常作定语] (*fml* 文) having many parts or forms; consisting of many (usu complex) elements 有很多部分的; 多种形式的; 多种(通常为复杂)成分组成的.

mul·ti·plica·tion /ˌmʌltɪplɪˈkeɪʃn; ˌmʌltəpləˋkeʃən/ *n* **1** [U] multiplying or being multiplied 增多; 增加; 乘; 繁殖: *children learning to do multiplication and division* 学习乘除法的儿童 ○ *an organism that grows by the multiplication of its cells* 因细胞繁殖而生长的有机体 ○ [attrib 作定语] *the multiplication sign/symbol* x 乘号x. **2** [C] instance of this 乘法: *2 × 3 is an easy multiplication.* 2×3是简单的乘法.

□ ˌ**multiplic**ˈ**ation table** list showing the results when a number is multiplied by a set of other numbers (esp 1 to 12) in turn 乘法表.

mul·ti·pli·city /ˌmʌltɪˈplɪsətɪ; ˌmʌltəˋplɪsətɪ/ *n* [sing] ~ **of sth** large number or great variety of things 多; 多样; 多样性: *a computer with a multiplicity of* (ie many) *uses* 多用途计算机.

mul·ti·ply /ˈmʌltɪplaɪ; ˋmʌltəplaɪ/ *v* (*pt, pp* **-lied**) **1** [I, Tn, Tn·pr, Tn·p] **~ A by B/~ A and B (together)** add a number to itself a particular number of times 乘: *children learning to multiply and divide* 学习乘法和除法的儿童 ○ *2 and 3 multiply to make 6*, ie 2 × 3 = 2 + 2 + 2 = 6. 2和3相乘得6. ○ *2 multiplied by 4 makes 8*, ie 2 × 4 = 8. 2乘以4得8. ○ *One can make 12 by multiplying 2 and 6 (together) or 4 and 3 (together)*, ie 12 = 2 × 6 or 4 × 3. 以2、6或4、3相乘可得12. **2** [I, Tn] increase (sth) in number or quantity 增多, 增加(某事物): *Our problems have multiplied since last year.* 自去年以来我们的问题增多了. ○ *Buy lots of raffle tickets and multiply your chances of success.* 多买彩票, 增加你中奖的机会. **3** [I, Tn] (*biology* 生) (cause sb/sth to) produce large numbers of offspring by procreation, fertilization, etc (使某人[某物])繁殖, 增殖: *Rabbits multiply rapidly.* 兔子繁殖得很快. ○ *It is possible to multiply bacteria and other living organisms in the laboratory.* 在实验室能够繁殖细菌和其他生物.

mul·ti·tude /ˈmʌltɪtjuːd; *US* -tuːd; ˋmʌltəˌtud/ *n* (*fml* 文) **1** [C] **~ (of sb/sth)** extremely large number of people or things (esp of people gathered or moving about in one area) 多数, 大批(尤指在一处集结或移动的人群): *A large multitude had assembled to hear him preach.* 一大群人聚集起来听他布道. ○ *Vast multitudes of birds visit this lake in spring.* 春天有大批的鸟飞临此湖. ○ *just one of a multitude of problems, reasons, etc* 仅就大量问题、理由等中的一个. **2 the multitude** [Gp] (*sometimes derog* 有时作贬义) ordinary people; the masses 群众; 大众; 群氓: *special qualities which mark her out from the multitude* 令她超群出众的特殊品质 ○ *demagogues who appeal to the multitude* 迎合民心的煽动家. **3** (idm 习语) **cover/hide a multitude of sins** (*often joc* 常作戏谑语) conceal a (usu unpleasant) reality 掩盖(通常为不快的)实情: *The description 'produce of more than one country' can cover a multitude of sins.* '多国产物'之说尽可遮人耳目了.

▷ **mul·ti·tud·in·ous** /ˌmʌltɪˈtjuːdɪnəs; *US* -tuːdɪnəs; ˌmʌltəˋtudn̩əs/ *adj* (*fml* 文) extremely large in number 众多的; 大量的: *multitudinous crowds, problems, debts* 大批的人群、问题、债务.

mum[1] /mʌm; mʌm/ *adj* (*Brit infml* 口) **1** silent 沉默的: *keep mum*, ie say nothing 保持沉默. **2** (idm 习语) ˌ**mum's the** ˈ**word** (*Brit infml* 口) (used when asking sb to keep a secret 用以要某人保密) say nothing about this 别说出去.

mum[2] /mʌm; mʌm/ (*US* usu 美式英语通常作 **mom** /mɒm; mɑm/) *n* (*infml* 口) mother 妈; 妈妈: *This is my mum.* 这是我妈妈. ○ *Hello, mum!* 妈, 你好!

mumble /ˈmʌmbl; ˋmʌmbl/ *v* [I, Ipr, Tn, Tf, Dn·pr] **~ (about sth); ~ sth (to sb)** speak or say sth unclearly and usu quietly, so that people cannot hear what is said 含糊地说某事; 叽咕; 咕哝: *He always mumbles when he's embarrassed.* 他感到难为情时说话就含糊不清了. ○ *What are you mumbling about? I can't understand a word!* 你叽里咕噜说什么呀? 我一句也听不懂! ○ *He mumbled something to me which I didn't quite catch.* 他对我叽咕了几句话, 可我没太听清楚. ○ *She mumbled that she didn't want to get up yet.* 她咕哝着说还不想起床.

▷ **mumble** *n* [sing] speech that is not heard clearly; noise like this 含糊的话或声音; 咕哝: *a mumble of* *voices, conversation, etc* 喃喃人语声、谈话声等 ○ *an incoherent, indistinct, distant, etc mumble* 不连贯的、分辨不清的、远处的...低语声.

mum·bler /ˈmʌmblə(r); ˋmʌmblɚ/ *n*.

mumbo-jumbo /ˌmʌmbəʊ ˈdʒʌmbəʊ; ˋmʌmboˋdʒʌmbo/ *n* [U] (*infml derog* 口, 贬) **1** complicated but meaningless ritual 繁琐而无意义的仪式; 繁文缛节: *go through the mumbo-jumbo of joining a secret society* 参加秘密社团要履行复杂繁琐的仪式. **2** meaningless or unnecessarily complicated language 无意义的或过于艰涩的语言: *These government forms are full of such mumbo-jumbo, I can't understand them at all.* 政府的这些表格中净是些晦涩的词, 我一点都看不懂.

mum·mer /ˈmʌmə(r); ˋmʌmɚ/ *n* actor in an old form of drama without words 哑剧演员.

▷ **mum·ming** /ˈmʌmɪŋ; ˋmʌmɪŋ/ *n* [U] performance of such drama 哑剧表演.

mum·mify /ˈmʌmɪfaɪ; ˋmʌmɪˌfaɪ/ *v* (*pt, pp* **-fied**) [Tn] preserve (a corpse) by treating it with special oils and wrapping it in cloth 将(尸体)制成木乃伊: *a mummified body* 制成木乃伊的尸体. Cf 参看 EMBALM.

▷ **mum·mi·fica·tion** /ˌmʌmɪfɪˈkeɪʃn; ˌmʌmɪfəˋkeʃən/ *n* [U] this method of preservation 木乃伊化.

mummy[1] /ˈmʌmɪ; ˋmʌmɪ/ *n* body of a human being or animal that has been mummified for burial 木乃伊; 干尸: *an Egyptian mummy* 埃及木乃伊.

mummy[2] /ˈmʌmɪ; ˋmʌmɪ/ (*US* usu 美式英语通常作 **mommy** /ˈmɒmɪ; ˋmɑmɪ/) *n* (*infml* 口) (used mainly by young children 多用作儿语) mother 妈妈.

mumps /mʌmps; mʌmps/ *n* [sing *v*] disease with painful swellings in the neck, caught esp by children 腮腺炎.

munch /mʌntʃ; mʌntʃ/ *v* [I, Ipr, Tn] **~ (at/on sth)** chew (sth) with much movement of the jaw 用力咀嚼(某物); 大嚼: *munch (at/on) an apple* 用力嚼苹果.

mun·dane /mʌnˈdeɪn; ˋmʌnden/ *adj* (*often derog* 常作贬义) ordinary and typically unexciting 平凡的; 平淡的: *I lead a pretty mundane life; nothing interesting ever happens to me.* 我生活平凡, 从无趣事. ○ *a mundane book, film, etc* 平淡无奇的书、影片等.

mu·ni·cipal /mjuːˈnɪsɪpl; mjuˋnɪsəpl/ *adj* [usu attrib 通常作定语] of a town or city with its own local government 市的; 市政的: *municipal buildings*, eg town hall, public library 市属建筑物(如市政厅、公共图书馆) ○ *municipal affairs, elections*, ie of the local council and its members 地方事务、选举 ○ *the municipal transport system, rubbish dump* 市交通系统、垃圾场.

▷ **mu·ni·cip·al·ity** /mjuːˌnɪsɪˈpælətɪ; ˌmjunɪsəˋpælətɪ/ *n* town, city or district with its own local government; governing body of such a town, etc 自治市; 自治区; 自治市或区的政府当局.

mu·ni·fi·cent /mjuːˈnɪfɪsnt; mjuˋnɪfəsn̩t/ *adj* (*fml* 文) extremely generous; (of sth given) large in amount or splendid in quality 极慷慨的; (指礼赠)丰厚的, 精美的: *a munificent giver, gift* 慷慨的施主、馈赠.

▷ **mu·ni·fi·cence** /-sns; -sn̩s/ *n* [U] (*fml* 文) great generosity 慷慨; (礼物的)丰厚: *overwhelmed by their munificence* 深受他们慷慨精神感动.

mu·ni·fi·cently *adv*.

mu·ni·ments /ˈmjuːnɪmənts; ˋmjunəmənts/ *n* [pl] (*law* 律) documents kept as evidence of rights or privileges (证明权利或特权的)契据, 证书.

mu·ni·tions /mjuːˈnɪʃnz; mjuˋnɪʃənz/ *n* [pl] military supplies, esp guns, shells, bombs, etc 军需品; (尤指)军火: *The war was lost because of a shortage of munitions.* 因军火不足而战败. ○ [attrib 作定语] *a munitions worker, factory* 生产军需品的工人、兵工厂.

▷ **mu·ni·tion** *v* [Tn, Tn·pr] **~ sth (with sth)** provide sth with munitions 给某部门提供军火: *munitioning the fleet (with fresh supplies of shells)* 给舰队补给(炮弹).

mural /ˈmjʊərəl; ˋmjʊrəl/ *n* (usu large) painting done on a wall (通常指大型的)壁画.

▷ **mural** *adj* of or on a wall 墙壁的; 在墙上的: *mural art, decoration, etc* 壁画艺术、墙上装饰.

mur·der /ˈmɜːdə(r); ˋmɝdɚ/ *n* **1** (**a**) [U] unlawful killing of a human being intentionally 谋杀; 谋杀案: *commit murder* 进行谋杀 ○ *be guilty of murder* 犯谋杀罪 ○ *the murder of a six-year-old child* 杀害一六岁儿童的案件 ○ [attrib 作定语] *Her latest book's a murder mystery.* 她的新书写的是凶杀疑案. (**b**) [C] instance of this 谋杀; 谋杀案: *six murders in one week* 一周之内的六起凶杀案. Cf 参看 HOMICIDE 1, MANSLAUGHTER (MAN[1]). **2** [U] (*derog* 贬) sacrifice of large numbers of people (esp in war) 杀戮(尤指战时): *10 000 men died in one battle: it was sheer murder.* 一次战斗死亡10 000人, 这纯粹是大屠杀. **3** [U] (*fig infml* 比喻, 口) (**a**) very difficult or frustrating experience 极艰难或令人沮丧的经历: *It's murder trying to find a parking place for the car.* 找个停车的地方比登天还难. (**b**) **~ (on sth)** thing that causes great harm or discomfort (to sth) (对某事物)造成极大伤害或不便的事物: *This hot weather's murder on my feet.* 这种炎热的天气苦了我的脚. **4** (idm 习语) ˌ**get away with** ˈ**murder** (*infml esp joc* 口, 尤作戏谑语) succeed in ignoring rules, ordinary standards, etc without being punished, corrected, etc 违章犯规等而未被惩罚、纠正等: *His latest book is rubbish. He seems to think that because he's a famous author he can get away with murder!* 他的近作粗制滥造. 他似乎自以为是名作家便可免遭物议! ˌ**murder will** ˈ**out** (*saying* 谚) a crime such as murder cannot be hidden 谋杀案终究要败露; 纸里包不住火. **scream, etc blue murder** ⇨ BLUE[1].

▷ **mur·der** *v* **1** [I, Tn, Tn·pr] **~ sb (with sth)** kill (sb) unlawfully and intentionally 谋杀某人: *He murdered his wife with a knife.* 他用刀杀害了妻子. **2** [Tn] (*fig infml* 比喻, 口) spoil (sth) by lack of skill or knowledge (因无技巧或知识)糟蹋(某事物): *murder a piece of music*, ie play it very badly 糟蹋一首乐曲(演奏恶劣) ○ *murder the English language*, ie speak or write in a way that shows ignorance of correct usage 糟蹋英语(罔顾读写规则). **mur·derer** /ˈmɜːdərə(r); ˋmɝdərɚ/ *n* person guilty of murder 谋杀犯; 凶手: *a mass murderer*, ie one who has killed many people 杀人魔王. **mur·der·ess** /ˈmɜːdərɪs; ˋmɝdərɪs/ *n* female murderer 女谋杀犯; 女凶手.

mur·der·ous /ˈmɜːdərəs; ˋmɝdərəs/ *adj* **1** intending or likely to murder 蓄意谋杀的; 杀人的; 凶残的: *a murderous villain, look, attack* 穷凶极恶的暴徒、样子、袭击 ○ *a murderous-looking knife* 凶光闪闪的刀. **2** (*infml* 口) very severe or unpleasant 极厉害的; 极讨厌的; 要命的: *I couldn't withstand the murderous heat.* 热得要命, 我受不了. **mur·der·ously** *adv*.

murk /mɜːk; mɝk/ *n* [U] darkness; gloom 黑暗; 昏暗: *peering through the murk* 自黑暗中窥视.

▷ **murky** *adj* (**-ier, -iest**) **1** unpleasantly dark; gloomy 阴暗的; 昏暗的: *a murky night, with no moon* 昏暗无月的夜 ○ *The light was too murky to continue playing.* 光线太暗不能再玩要了. ○ *London's streets, murky with November fog.* 伦敦的街道, 在十一月的雾中模糊不清. **2** (of water) dirty; unclear (指水)脏的, 混浊的: *She threw it into the river's murky depths.* 她把它扔进了混浊的河水深处. **3** (*fig derog or joc* 比喻, 贬或谑) (of people's actions or character) not known but suspected of being immoral or dishonest (指人的行为或性格)可疑的, 不可告人的: *She had a decidedly murky past.* 她的历史背景令人捉摸不透. **murk·ily** /-ɪlɪ; -əlɪ/ *adv*.

murmur /ˈmɜːmə(r); ˋmɝmɚ/ *n* **1** low continuous indistinct sound 低沉、持续而不清的声音: *the murmur of bees in the garden* 花园中蜜蜂的嗡嗡声 ○ *the distant murmur of the sea, of a brook, of traffic, etc* 远处海浪的澎湃声、溪水的潺潺声、车辆的隆隆声. **2** quietly spoken word(s) 低语声: *a murmur of conversation, of voices from the next room, etc* 喃喃的谈话声、隔壁的人语声等. **3** quiet expression of feeling 低声的情感表述: *There were murmurs of discontent from the work-force.* 工人不满, 颇有微词. **4** (*medical* 医) faint blowing sound in the chest, usu a sign of disease or damage in the heart 心区杂音(通常为心脏疾患或损伤的症状). **5** (idm 习语) **with**ˌ**out a** ˈ**murmur** without complaining 不抱怨; 无怨言: *He paid the extra cost without a murmur.* 他付了额外的费用而毫无怨言.

▷ **murmur** *v* **1** [I] make a murmur 发连续而低沉的声音: *The wind murmured in the trees.* 风在林中低鸣 ○ *a murmuring brook* 流水淙淙的小溪. **2** [Ipr, Tn, Tf] **~ about sth** say (sth) in a low voice 低声说(某事): *He was delirious, murmuring about his childhood.* 他精神恍惚, 低声叨念着童年往事. ○ *murmuring words of love into her ear* 向她喃喃耳语, 倾诉爱慕之意 ○ *He murmured that he wanted to sleep.* 他咕哝着说他想睡觉. **3** [Ipr] **~ against sb/sth** complain about sb/sth quietly, not openly 私下低声抱怨某人[某事物]: *For*

M

some years the people had been murmuring against the government. 几年来人们一直在私下议论政府.

mur·mur·ous /ˈmɜːmərəs; ˋmɝmərəs/ *adj* (*esp rhet* 尤作修辞) consisting of a low continuous indistinct sound 发出持续细声的: *the murmurous hum of bees* 蜜蜂的嗡嗡声.

mus·cat /ˈmʌskæt; ˋmʌsˏkæt/ *n* type of grape used for eating and making wine 麝香葡萄.

mus·ca·tel /ˌmʌskəˈtel; ˏmʌskəˋtɛl/ *n* [C, U] raisin or wine made from muscat grapes 麝香葡萄干; 麝香葡萄酒.

muscle 肌肉

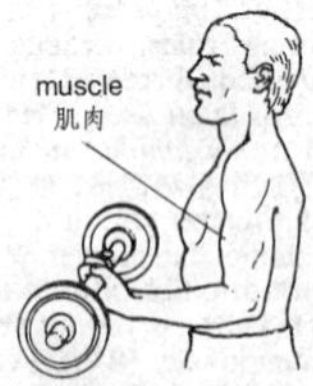

muscle /ˈmʌsl; ˋmʌsl̩/ *n* **1** (**a**) [C] length of stretchable tissue in an animal body that is attached at each end to bone and can be tightened or relaxed to produce movement 肌肉: *arm, leg, face, etc muscles* 胳膊、大腿、面部等的肌肉 ○ *strain/tear/pull a muscle* 扭伤[撕裂/拉伤]肌肉 ○ *exercises to develop the muscles* 做运动以锻炼肌肉 ○ *Don't move a muscle!* ie Stay completely still. 呆着别动! (**b**) [U] such tissue 肌肉组织: *The heart is made of muscle.* 心脏是肌肉组织. ○ [attrib 作定语] *muscle fibres* 肌肉纤维. **2** [U] muscular power 肌肉的力量: *have plenty of muscle but no brains* 肌肉发达, 头脑简单. **3** [U] (*fig* 比喻) power to make others do as one wishes (操纵他人的)力量: *political, industrial, etc muscle* 政治的、工业的...力量 ○ *a trade union with plenty of muscle* 强大的工会. **4** (idm 习语) **flex one's muscles** ⇨ FLEX.

▷ **muscle** *v* (phr v) **muscle in (on sb/sth)** (*infml derog* 口, 贬) join in sth when one has no right to do so, for one's own advantage 强行挤入某事物以分享利益: *I wrote the book, and now she's trying to muscle in on its success by saying she gave me the ideas.* 书是我写的, 现在她却要分享其成, 硬说是她给我的构思.

□ ˈ**muscle-bound** *adj* having large stiff muscles as the result of excessive exercise (因锻炼过度)肌肉粗而硬的.

ˈ**muscleman** /-mæn; -ˏmæn/ *n* (*pl* **-men** /-men; -mɛn/) (*infml sometimes derog* 口, 有时作贬义) man with large muscles and (often) great strength 肌肉发达而有力的男子.

mus·cu·lar /ˈmʌskjʊlə(r); ˋmʌskjələ/ *adj* **1** of the muscles 肌肉的: *muscular effort, contraction* 肌肉的力量、收缩 ○ *muscular tissue* 肌肉组织. **2** having large strong muscles 肌肉发达的: *his powerful muscular arms* 他那肌肉发达而有力的双臂. ▷ **mus·cu·lar·ity** /ˌmʌskjʊˈlærətɪ; ˏmʌskjəˋlærətɪ/ *n* [U].

□ ˌ**muscular** ˈ**dystrophy** long-lasting illness in which the muscles become gradually weaker 因营养障碍造成的肌肉萎缩.

muse[1] /mjuːz; mjuz/ *n* **1 the Muses** [pl] (in Greek or Roman myth) the nine goddesses, daughters of Zeus or Jupiter, who protected and encouraged poetry, music, dancing, history and other branches of art and literature (希腊或罗马神话中的)缪斯(九位女神, 均为宙斯或朱庇特之女, 专管诗歌、音乐、舞蹈、历史及其他文艺科目). **2** [C] (*rhet* 修辞) spirit that inspires a creative artist, esp a poet 艺术家(尤指诗人)的创作灵感: *His muse had deserted him, and he could no longer write.* 他已无灵感, 不能再写作了.

muse[2] /mjuːz; mjuz/ *v* **1** [I, Ipr] **~ (about/over/on/upon sth)** think in a deep or concentrated way, ignoring what is happening around one 沉思; 冥想: *sit musing on the events of the day, memories of the past, etc* 坐着默默反省日间的事、缅怀往事. **2** [Tn] say (sth) to oneself in a thoughtful way 沉思自语说(某事): *'I wonder if I shall ever see them again,' he mused.* '我不知道是否还能再见到他们,' 他沉思自问.

mu·seum /mjuːˈzɪəm; mjuˋzɪəm/ *n* building in which objects of artistic, cultural, historical or scientific importance and interest are displayed 博物馆: *a museum of natural history* 自然历史博物馆 ○ *an anthropological museum* 人类学博物馆.

□ **muˈseum piece 1** fine specimen suitable for a museum 适于博物馆陈列的精品. **2** (*joc derog* 谑, 贬) out-of-date or obsolete thing or person 过时的物或人; 老古董: *This old radio of yours is a bit of a museum piece; it's about time you got a new one!* 你这个旧收音机该进博物馆了, 早就该买个新的了!

mush /mʌʃ; mʌʃ/ *n* **1** [U, sing] (*usu derog* 通常作贬义) soft thick mixture or mass 软而稠的混合物或块; 糊状物: *The vegetables had been boiled to a mush, and were quite uneatable.* 菜煮烂了, 都没法吃了. **2** [U] (*US*) boiled corn meal 玉米粥. **3** [U] (*infml derog* 口, 贬) (speech or writing full of) weak sentimentality 脆弱的感情; 感伤; 伤感的言语或文字: *I've never read such a load of mush!* 我从来没有读过如此哀思绵绵的作品!

▷ **mushy** *adj* **1** like mush 糊状的. **2** (*infml derog* 口, 贬) weakly sentimental 多愁善感的; 感情脆弱的: *a mushy film, book, etc* 沉郁伤感的影片、小说等.

mush·room /ˈmʌʃrʊm, -ruːm; ˋmʌʃrum, -rum/ *n* fast-growing fungus with a round flattish head and a stalk, of which some kinds can be eaten 蕈; 菇; 蘑菇: *grilled/fried mushrooms* 烤[炸]蘑菇 ○ *a button mushroom*, ie a small one with a round head like a button 钮粒蘑菇 ○ [attrib 作定语] *mushroom soup* 蘑菇汤. ⇨illus at FUNGUS 见 FUNGUS 插图. Cf 参看 TOADSTOOL.

▷ **mush·room** *v* [I] **1** (usu 通常作 **go mushrooming**) gather mushrooms (in a field or wood) (在地里或林子里)采集蘑菇. **2** (*sometimes derog* 有时作贬义) spread or increase in number rapidly 迅速扩散或增加: *new blocks of flats and offices mushrooming all over the city* 在全市各处如雨后春笋般出现的新公寓楼和办公楼.

□ ˌ**mushroom** ˈ**cloud** cloud (shaped like a mushroom) that forms after a nuclear explosion (核爆炸后形成的)蘑菇云.

music /ˈmjuːzɪk; ˋmjuzɪk/ *n* [U] **1** (**a**) art of arranging the sounds of voice(s) or instrument(s) or both in a pleasing sequence or combination 音乐: *study music* 研习音乐 ○ [attrib 作定语] *a music lesson, teacher* 音乐课、教师. (**b**) compositions made by doing this 音乐作品; 乐曲: *Mozart's music* 莫扎特的乐曲 ○ *play a piece of music* 演奏一首乐曲 ○ [attrib 作定语] *a music lover* 热爱音乐的人. (**c**) (book, sheets of paper, etc containing) written or printed signs representing such compositions 乐谱: *I'd left my music at home.* 我把乐谱落在家里了. ○ *read music* 识乐谱. **2** (idm 习语) **face the music** ⇨ FACE[2]. **music to one's ˈears** information that pleases one very much 佳音; 好消息: *The news of his resignation was music to my ears.* 听说他辞职, 我高兴极了. **put/set sth to ˈmusic** write music to go with words (eg of a poem) so that they can be sung 为(如诗)谱曲.

□ ˈ**music box** (*US*) = MUSICAL BOX (MUSICAL).

ˈ**music centre** equipment combining a radio, record player and tape recorder 组合音响(收音机、电唱机、磁带录放机合为一体者).

ˈ**music-hall** *n* (**a**) [C] (esp in the late 19th and early 20th centuries) theatre used for variety entertainment (eg songs, acrobatic performances, juggling) (尤指19世纪末20世纪初的)歌舞杂耍戏院. (**b**) [U] the entertainment itself 歌舞杂耍: [attrib 作定语] *music-hall songs, entertainers, etc* 歌舞杂耍戏院的歌唱、表演者等.

ˈ**music-stand** *n* light (usu folding) framework for holding sheets of printed music 乐谱架.

ˈ**music-stool** *n* seat without a back (usu adjustable in height) used when playing a piano 琴凳(通常为可调节高度的).

mu·sical /ˈmjuːzɪkl; ˋmjuzɪkl/ *adj* **1** [usu attrib 通常作定语] of or for music 音乐的; 用于音乐的: *a musical entertainment* 音乐表演 ○ *musical instruments*, ie for producing music, eg piano, violin, flute, horn 乐器 ○ *musical talent* 音乐天才 ○ *She has no formal musical qualifications.* 她没有正式的音乐方面资历. ○ *a musical society*, ie for people to listen to music or perform music

musical notation 音乐符号

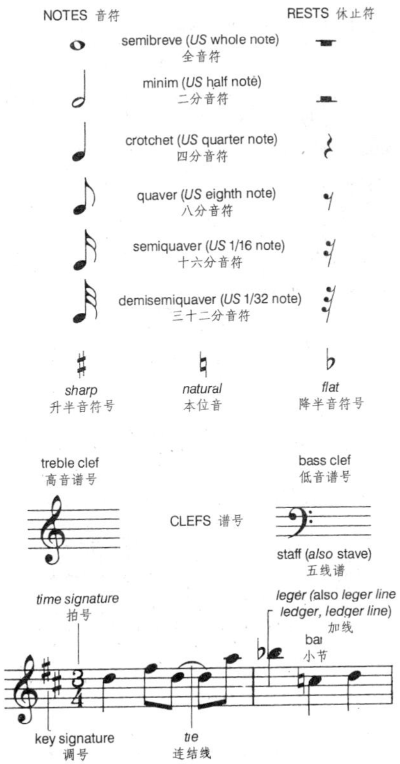

together 音乐社团. **2** fond of or skilled in music 喜爱或精于音乐的: *She's very musical.* 她非常喜爱音乐. **3** melodious; pleasant to listen to 音调优美的; 悦耳的: *He has quite a musical voice.* 他的声音非常动听.

▷ **mu·sical** *n* (also ˌ**musical** ˈ**comedy**) light, amusing play or film with songs and usu dancing 音乐喜剧: *Rogers and Hammerstein's musical 'South Pacific'.* 罗杰斯和哈默斯坦的音乐喜剧'南太平洋'.

mu·sic·ally /-klɪ; -klɪ/ **1** in or of music 在音乐方面: *musically gifted, talented, ignorant* 音乐方面有禀赋的、有天才的、无知的. **2** in a way that is pleasing to listen to 动听地; 悦耳地: *play, sing, speak, etc musically* 演奏、歌唱、说话等动听.

□ ˈ**musical box** (also ˈ**music box**) box with a mechanical device that produces a tune when the box is opened 八音盒.

ˌ**musical** ˈ**chairs** **1** game in which players go round a row of chairs (one fewer than the number of players) until the music stops, when the one who finds no chair to sit on has to leave the game 抢椅子游戏(参加者随乐声绕椅子行走, 椅数比人数少一, 音乐停时抢椅而坐, 无座者淘汰). **2** (*fig often derog* 比喻, 常作贬义) situation in which people frequently take turns to have sth, esp a job 靠轮流才获得某事物的情形(尤指获得工作): *He had come out on top in the game of musical chairs by which senior posts seemed to be filled.* 已经轮到他获得高级职位了, 这种职位似乎是要轮候的.

mu·si·cian /mjuːˈzɪʃn; mjuˈzɪʃən/ *n* person who makes music by playing or conducting 音乐家: *She is a fine musician.* 她是位优秀的音乐家.

▷ **mu·si·cian·ship** *n* [U] art and skill in (performing) music 音乐(演奏)艺术和技巧: *the pianist's sensitive musicianship* 钢琴家细腻的音乐技艺.

mu·si·co·logy /ˌmjuːzɪˈkɒlədʒɪ; ˌmjuzɪˈkɑlədʒɪ/ *n* [U] academic study of music 音乐学. ▷ **mu·si·co·lo·gical** /ˌmjuːzɪkəˈlɒdʒɪkl; ˌmjuzɪkəˈlɑdʒɪkəl/ *adj.* **mu·si·co·lo·gist** /ˌmjuːzɪˈkɒlədʒɪst; ˌmjuzɪˈkɑlədʒɪst/ *n.*

musk /mʌsk; mʌsk/ *n* [U] **1** strong-smelling substance produced in glands by the male musk-deer, used in the manufacture of perfume 麝香. **2** any of several plants with a similar smell 麝香植物.

▷ **musky** *adj* (**-ier, -iest**) (smelling) like musk 像麝香(味)的: *a musky odour* 麝香气味.

□ ˈ**musk-deer** *n* small hornless deer of Central Asia 麝, 香獐子(产于中亚).

ˈ**musk-melon** *n* sweet juicy type of melon 甜瓜; 香瓜.

ˈ**musk-rat** (also ˈ**musquash**) *n* large rat-like water animal of N America, valuable for its fur 麝鼠(产于北美, 毛皮珍贵).

ˈ**musk-rose** *n* rambling rose with large, sweet-smelling flowers 麝香蔷薇.

mus·ket /ˈmʌskɪt; ˈmʌskɪt/ *n* long-barrelled firearm used by soldiers from the 16th to the 19th centuries (now replaced by the rifle) 滑膛枪(16世纪至19世纪士兵所用的).

▷ **mus·ket·eer** /ˌmʌskɪˈtɪə(r); ˌmʌskəˈtɪr/ *n* soldier armed with a musket 装备滑膛枪的士兵.

mus·ketry /ˈmʌskɪtrɪ; ˈmʌskɪtrɪ/ *n* [U] (*dated* 旧) (science of or instruction in) shooting with rifles 滑膛枪射击术: *learn skill in musketry* 学习滑膛枪射击技术.

Mus·lim /ˈmʊzlɪm; *US* ˈmʌzləm; ˈmʌzləm/ (also **Mos·lem** /ˈmɒzləm ˈmɑzləm/) *n* person whose religion is Islam; follower of Muhammad 穆斯林; 伊斯兰教信徒.

▷ **Mus·lim** (also **Mos·lem**) *adj* of Muslims and Islam 穆斯林的; 伊斯兰教信徒的: *Muslim historians, holidays, leaders* 穆斯林史学家、节日、领袖. ⇨Usage at CHRISTIAN 用法见CHRISTIAN.

mus·lin /ˈmʌzlɪn; ˈmʌzlɪn/ *n* [U] thin fine cotton cloth, used for dresses, curtains, etc 平纹细布(用作衣物、窗帘等).

mus·quash /ˈmʌskwɒʃ; ˈmʌskwɑʃ/ *n* [U, C] (**a**) = MUSK-RAT (MUSK). (**b**) fur of the musk-rat 麝鼠毛皮: [attrib 作定语] *a musquash coat* 麝鼠皮大衣.

muss /mʌs; mʌs/ *v* [Tn, Tn·p] **~ sth (up)** (*infml* 口) (*esp US*) put sth into disorder 把某物弄乱; 搞乱某物: *Don't muss (up) my hair!* 别弄乱我的头发!

mus·sel /ˈmʌsl; ˈmʌsl̩/ *n* any of several types of edible shellfish with a black shell in two parts 贻贝; 壳菜; 淡菜. ⇨illus at SHELLFISH 见SHELLFISH插图.

must[1] /məst; məst, *strong form* 强读式 mʌst; mʌst/ *modal v* (*neg* 否定式 **must not**, *contracted form* 缩约式 **mustn't** /ˈmʌsnt; ˈmʌsn̩t/) **1** (**a**) (indicating obligation 表示必要): *I must go to the bank to get some money.* 我得到银行去取些钱. ○ *When you enter the building you must show the guard your pass.* 进入大楼时须向警卫出示通行证. ○ *Cars must not park in front of the entrance.* 入口处不得停放汽车. ○ *You mustn't open the oven door before the cake is ready.* 饼未熟不得打开烤箱的门. ○ *We mustn't be late, must we?* 我们不能迟到, 是吧? ○ *'Must you go so soon?' 'Yes, I must.'* '你一定得这么早就走吗?''是的, 必须这么早.' ⇨Usage 1 见所附用法第1项. (**b**) (indicating advice or recommendation 表示劝告或建议): *We must see what the authorities have to say.* 我们应该看看当局怎么说. ○ *I must ask you not to do that again.* 我得劝你不要再做那种事情了. ⇨Usage 2 见所附用法第2项. **2** (drawing a logical conclusion 做出逻辑推断): *You must be hungry after your long walk.* 你走了那么长的路, 一定饿了吧. ○ *She must be having a lot of problems with the language.* 她在语言上一定有很多困难. ○ *You must be Mr Smith — I was told to expect you.* 你准是史密斯先生吧——我是按吩咐来接你的. ○ *They must be twins.* 他们一定是双胞胎. ○ *He must have known* (ie Surely he knew) *what she wanted.* 他当时肯定知道她需要什么. ○ *We must have read the same report.* 咱们看的一定是同一份报道. ⇨Usage 3 见所附用法第3项. **3** (indicating insistence 表示坚持): *You ˈmust put your name down for the team.* 你必须报名参加该队. ○ *You simply ˈmust read this book — it's so funny.* 你一定得看看这本书——太有趣了. ○ *ˈMust you make so much noise?* 你就非得弄出这么大声吗?

M

▷ **must** *n* (*infml* 口) thing that must be done, seen, heard, etc 必须做、看、听等的事: *His new novel is a must for all lovers of crime fiction.* 他的新小说是罪案小说爱好者必须一读的.

NOTE ON USAGE 用法: **1** OBLIGATION (**must**, **need**[1,2], **have to**, **ought to**, **should**[1]) 义务或责任 (**must**、**need**[1, 2]、**have to**、**ought to**、**should**) (**a**) **Must** is used to show that the speaker orders or expects something to be done ☆ **must** 用以表示说话者命令或期待做成某事: *The children must be back by 4 o'clock.* 孩子必须4点钟以前回来. ○ *I must go now*, ie I feel obliged to go. 我现在得走了, 即我觉得有此必要. **Need to** (informal **have to**) is used when somebody else is giving orders or controlling events ☆ **need to** (通俗用词为 **have to**) 用于他人发出指令或操纵的情况下: *You need to/have to pass a special exam to get into the school.* 你要上那所学校得通过一次特别的考试. ○ *I have to go now*, ie something (or somebody else) requires it. 我现在得走了, 即某事或某人要求我如此. **Ought to** and **should** indicate that the speaker is giving an order, but suggest that he or she is not sure it will be obeyed ☆ **ought to** 和 **should** 表示说话者发出指令, 但暗含对方是否听从并无把握之意: *She really ought to/should be leaving now.* 她现在可真该走了. ○ *You ought to/should apologize* (though I'm not sure you will). 你应该道歉(虽然我不知道你是否这样做). (**b**) **Mustn't** (and **oughtn't to**, **shouldn't**) are used when the speaker wants somebody *not* to do something ☆ **mustn't** (和 **oughtn't to**、**shouldn't**) 用于说话者要某人不做某事: *You mustn't leave the gate open.* 你不要敞着大门. ○ *You oughtn't to/shouldn't neglect the garden.* 你不要不管花园. **Needn't** and **don't have to** mean that there is a lack of obligation to do something ☆ **needn't** 和 **don't have to** 意指没有做某事的义务或责任: *You needn't/don't have to arrive early.* (Cf *You mustn't arrive early.*) 你不必早来. (参看: 你不要早来.) (**c**) In indirect commands, **had to** replaces **must** 在间接指令中用 **had to** 取代 **must**: *Mother said that the children had to be back by 4 o'clock.* (Cf *Mary said he ought to/should apologize.*) 母亲说了孩子4点以前必须回来. (参看: 玛丽说他应该道歉.) **2** ADVICE (**must**, **have got to**, **ought to**, **should**[1]) 劝告或建议 (**must**、**have got to**、**ought to**、**should**[1]) (**a**) **Must** (informal **have got to**) is used to advise or recommend ☆ **must** (通俗用词为 **have got to**) 用以提出劝告或建议: *You simply must see that film.* 你可得看看这部电影. ○ *You've got to take life more seriously.* 你对待生活要严肃一些. **Ought to** and **should** suggest that the speaker is less confident the advice will be taken ☆ **ought to** 和 **should** 含有说话者对劝告之是否接受更无把握之意: *You really ought to/should do something about that cough!* 你咳嗽那么厉害, 真得治一治了! (**b**) To advise somebody not to do something, **mustn't**, **oughtn't to** and **shouldn't** are used 劝某人不做某事时, 用 **mustn't**、**oughtn't to**、**shouldn't**: *You mustn't/oughtn't to/shouldn't miss this opportunity.* 你不可[不该/不应]错过这个机会. (**c**) In indirect speech, the same rules apply as for OBLIGATION. 在间接引用语中, 前述用于表示义务或责任的规则也适用于此. **3** DRAWING CONCLUSIONS (**must**, **have to**, **ought to**, **should**[1]) 作结论 (**must**、**have to**、**ought to**、**should**[1]) (**a**) **Must** and **have to** (informal) are used when drawing a conclusion about which there is no doubt ☆ **must** 和 **have to** (较通俗) 用于毫无怀疑的结论: *He must be/has to be the wanted man: he's exactly like his picture.* 他一定是受通缉的那个男子: 他和照片上的人一模一样. **Ought to** and **should** indicate that the speaker is being more tentative ☆ **ought to** 和 **should** 表示说话者有较大的试探性: *He ought to/should be here in time — he started early enough.* 他该[应]按时到这里—— 他出发得够早的. (**b**) To show that a conclusion cannot be drawn, **can't** is used 表示无法定论则用 **can't**: *He can't be the wanted man.* 他不会是那个被通缉的男子. ○ *He can't (surely) get here in time.* 他(肯定)不能及时赶到这里. (**c**) **Must have**, **ought to have** and **should have** are used to draw a conclusion from some past event ☆ **must have**、**ought to have**、**should have** 用以对某件过去的事情作结论: *She must have received the parcel: I sent it by registered post.* 她一定已经收到包裹了, 我是用挂号寄的.

must[2] /mʌst; mʌst/ *n* [U] grape-juice before fermentation has changed it into wine (未发酵成酒的)葡萄汁.

mus·tache (*US*) = MOUSTACHE.

mus·tachio /məˈstɑːʃɪəʊ; *US* -stæʃ-; məˈstæʃo/ *n* (*pl* **~s**) large (usu long-haired) moustache 大的(通常为长的)髭.

mus·tang /ˈmʌstæŋ; ˋmʌstæŋ/ *n* small wild or half-wild horse of the N American plains (北美平原产)小野马, 半野马.

mus·tard /ˈmʌstəd; ˋmʌstɚd/ *n* **1** [U] plant with yellow flowers and (black or white) sharp-tasting seeds in long thin pods 芥. **2** (**a**) [U] (also ˈ**mustard powder**) these seeds ground into powder 芥末. (**b**) [U, C] these seeds or this powder mixed into a strong-flavoured sauce with (esp) vinegar and served with savoury food 芥子酱: [attrib 作定语] *a mustard pot/jar/spoon* 芥末瓶[罐/勺]. **3** [U] darkish yellow colour (like the sauce made from the seeds of the mustard plant) 芥末黄; 深黄色: [attrib 作定语] *a mustard (yellow) sweater* 芥末黄(深黄色)毛衣. **4** (idm 习语) **keen as mustard** ⇨ KEEN[1].

□ ˈ**mustard gas** kind of liquid poison with vapour that burns the skin (used in World War I) 芥子气(糜烂皮肤的毒气, 曾用于第一次世界大战中).

mus·ter /ˈmʌstə(r); ˋmʌstɚ/ *n* **1** assembly or gathering of people or things, esp for review or inspection (人或物的)集合, 集中(尤指为检查的): *a muster of troops* 集合的部队. **2** (idm 习语) **pass muster** ⇨ PASS[2].

▷ **mus·ter** *v* **1** [I, Tn] come or bring (people) together, esp for a military parade (人员)集合, 召集(人员)(尤指为军事检阅): *The troops mustered (on the square).* 部队已(在广场上)集合. ○ *He mustered all the troops.* 他召集了所有的部队. **2** [Tn, Tn·p] **~ sth (up)** gain sth by collecting it from other people or by drawing it from within oneself; summon sth up (自他人处)搜集某事物; (自本身)激发, 激起: *muster public support for sth* 征集公众对某事物的支持 ○ *I couldn't muster up much enthusiasm for it.* 我对这件事鼓不起劲来.

musty /ˈmʌstɪ; ˋmʌstɪ/ *adj* (**-ier**, **-iest**) **1** smelling or tasting stale, mouldy and damp 有陈腐、发霉和潮湿味的: *musty old books* 发霉的旧书 ○ *a musty room full of damp* 弥漫着潮湿气味的房间 ○ *The wine tastes musty.* 这酒有霉味了. **2** (*fig derog* 比喻, 贬) out-of-date; obsolete 过时的; 陈腐的: *the same musty old ideas presented as if they were new* 提出貌似新颖的老一套陈旧想法. ▷ **mus·ti·ness** /ˈmʌstɪnɪs; ˋmʌstɪnɪs/ *n* [U].

mut·able /ˈmjuːtəbl; ˋmjutəbl/ *adj* (*rhet* 修辞) liable to change; likely to change 可变的; 易变的; 不定的. ▷ **mut·ab·il·ity** /ˌmjuːtəˈbɪlətɪ; ˌmjutəˋbɪlətɪ/ *n* [U].

mut·ant /ˈmjuːtənt; ˋmjutənt/ *n* **1** (*biology* 生) living thing that differs basically from its parents as a result of genetic change; mutation(c) 突变体; 突变型. **2** (*infml* 口) (esp in science fiction) living thing that is deformed or disfigured as a result of genetic change (尤指科幻小说中的)(因基因变异而致的)畸形怪物.

▷ **mut·ant** *adj* differing as a result of genetic change 因基因变异而不同的; 变种的; 变异的: *a mutant gene* 突变基因 ○ *a mutant strain of a virus* 病毒突变株.

muta·tion /mjuːˈteɪʃn; mjuˋteʃən/ *n* (**a**) [U] change; alteration 变化; 转变; 突变; 变异: (*biology* 生) *mutation of cells* 细胞的突变 ○ (*linguistics* 语言) *mutation of sounds* 语音的变化 ○ *vowel mutation* 元音变化. (**b**) [C] instance of this 变化; 转变; 突变; 变异: *mutations in plants caused by radiation* 放射线引起的植物变异. (**c**) [C] new organism resulting from such a change; mutant (1) 变种; 突变体; 突变型.

▷ **mut·ate** /mjuːˈteɪt; *US* ˈmjuːteɪt; ˋmjuˌtet/ *v* [I, Ipr, Tn] **~ (into sth)** (cause sth to) undergo mutation (使某物)变化, 转变, 突变, 变异: *cells that mutate/are mutated* 变异的细胞 ○ *organisms that mutate into new forms* 变成新种的生物.

mu·ta·tis mut·andis /muːˌtɑːtɪs muːˈtændɪs; mjuˋtetɪs mjuˋtændɪs/ (*Latin* 拉) with appropriate changes (when comparing cases) (根据情况)作适当变动: *What I have said about the army also applies, mutatis mutandis, to the navy.* 我谈到的陆军方面, 如作适当变动, 也适用于海军.

mute /mju:t; mjut/ *adj* **1** silent; making no sound 沉默的; 无声的: *stare in mute amazement, admiration, astonishment, etc* 因惊奇、钦佩、惊讶等而目瞪口呆 ○ *remain mute* 保持沉默. **2** (*dated* 旧) (of people) unable to speak; dumb (指人)不能说话的, 哑的: *mute from birth* 生来就哑的. **3** (of a letter in a written word) not pronounced when spoken (指字中字母)不发音的: *The 'b' in 'dumb' is mute.* 在 dumb 一字中 b 不发音.

▷ **mute** *n* **1** (**a**) piece of metal, plastic, etc used to soften the sounds produced from a stringed instrument 弱音器(使弦乐器发声柔和的金属、塑料等附件). (**b**) pad placed in the opening of a wind instrument to change the quality of the sounds produced 弱音器(改变管乐器音质用的管口塞头). ⇨illus at App 1 见附录1插图, page x. **2** (*dated* 旧) dumb person 哑巴.

mute *v* [Tn esp passive 尤用于被动语态] make the sound of (esp a musical instrument) quieter or softer, esp with a mute 使声音(尤指乐器声)减弱, 柔和(尤指用弱音器): *The strings are muted throughout the closing bars of the symphony.* 该交响曲结束部分各节中的弦乐全为弱化音. **muted** *adj* **1** (of sounds) quiet and often indistinct (指声音)弱化的, (常指)微弱不清的: *They spoke in muted voices.* 他们轻声说话. **2** not openly or vigorously expressed 非公开或非强烈表达的; 暗中的: *muted excitement* 内心的激动 ○ *muted criticism* 温和的批评. **3** (of musical instruments) fitted with a mute (指乐器)装有弱音器的: *muted strings* 装有弱音器的琴弦. **4** (of colours) not bright; subdued (指颜色)不耀眼的, 柔和的: *muted greens and blues* 各种柔和的绿色和蓝色. **mutely** *adv* silently; dumbly 沉默地; 哑然. **mute·ness** *n* [U].

mu·til·ate /ˈmju:tɪleɪt; ˋmjutḷ,et/ *v* [Tn] injure, damage or disfigure (sb/sth) by breaking, tearing or cutting off a necessary part (折断、撕去、割掉某部分)使(某人[某事物])损伤, 残缺, 外形损毁: *The invaders cut off their prisoners' arms and legs and threw their mutilated bodies into the ditch.* 侵略者把俘虏的四肢砍掉, 然后把残缺不全的躯体扔进沟里. ○ *A madman mutilated the painting by cutting holes in it.* 有个疯子破坏了那幅画, 在上面捅了许多窟窿. ○ (*fig* 比喻) *The editor mutilated my text by removing whole paragraphs from it.* 那编辑把我的文稿整段整段删掉, 弄得面目全非.

▷ **mu·tila·tion** /ˌmju:tɪˈleɪʃn; ˌmjutḷˋeʃən/ *n* (**a**) [U] mutilating or being mutilated (除掉某组成部分之类的)损伤, 残缺, 外形损毁: *Thousands suffered death or mutilation as a result of the bomb attacks.* 这场空袭造成数千人死的死伤的伤. (**b**) [C] injury, damage or loss caused by this (因除掉某组成部分而造成的)损伤, 残缺, 外形损毁.

mu·tin·ous /ˈmju:tɪnəs; ˋmjutṇəs/ *adj* guilty of mutiny; refusing to obey; rebellious 反叛的; 抗命的; 造反的: *mutinous sailors, workers, children, etc* 叛变的水兵、反抗的工人、不听话的孩子 ○ *mutinous behaviour* 反叛行为. ▷ **mu·tin·ously** *adv*.

mu·tiny /ˈmju:tɪnɪ; ˋmjutṇɪ/ *n* [C, U] rebellion against lawful authority, esp by soldiers or sailors 叛乱; (尤指军人或水手的)哗变, 兵变: *The crew tried to seize control of the ship, and were shot for mutiny.* 船员夺船未遂, 均以叛乱罪被枪决. ○ *If the manager hadn't accepted some of the team's demands he could have had a mutiny on his hands.* 领队要不是答应了队员的部分要求, 他可能已众叛亲离了.

▷ **mu·tin·eer** /ˌmju:tɪˈnɪə(r); ˌmjutṇˋɪr/ *n* person guilty of mutiny 反叛者; 叛兵.

mu·tiny *v* [I, Ipr] **~ (against sb/sth)** be guilty of mutiny; revolt (against sb/sth) 反叛, 叛变(某人[某事物]): *a crew that mutinies (against its captain, against bad living conditions)* (因反抗船长、抗议生活条件恶劣而)哗变的船员.

mutt /mʌt; mʌt/ *n* **1** (*infml* 口) foolish, incompetent and awkward person 愚蠢、无能而笨拙的人: *You silly big mutt!* 你这大笨蛋! **2** (*derog* 贬) mongrel dog 杂种狗: *What an ugly mutt!* 多难看的杂种狗哇!

mut·ter /ˈmʌtə(r); ˋmʌtɚ/ *v* **1** [I, Ipr, Tn, Tn·pr, Tf, Dn·pr] **~ (sth) (to sb) (about sth)** speak or say (sth) in a low voice that is hard to hear 低语; 咕哝(某事): *Don't mutter! I can't hear you.* 别叽叽咕咕的! 我听不见. ○ *Sarah was muttering away to herself as she did the washing-up.* 萨拉一边洗碗碟一边独自咕哝个没完. ○ *He muttered something (to the salesgirl) (about losing his wallet).* 他低声(向女售货员)述说着(他的钱包丢了). **2** [I, Ipr] **~ (about/against/at sb/sth)** complain or grumble privately or in a way that is not openly expressed (私下)埋怨, 发牢骚, 讲怪话: *For some time people had been muttering about the way she ran the department.* 人们对她的管理方式私下抱怨已有时日. **3** [I] (of thunder) be heard distantly; rumble (指雷)自远处发低沉声, 隆隆作响.

▷ **mut·ter** *n* (usu *sing* 通常作单数) indistinct utterance or sound 含糊低语声; 含混不清的声音.

mut·terer /ˈmʌtərə(r); ˋmʌtɚrɚ/ *n* person who mutters 喃喃低语者.

mut·ter·ing /ˈmʌtərɪŋ; ˋmʌtərɪŋ/ *n* [U] (also **mut·ter·ings** [pl]) complaints that are privately or not openly expressed 私下的抱怨.

mut·ton /ˈmʌtn; ˋmʌtṇ/ *n* **1** [U] meat from a fully grown sheep 羊肉: *a leg/shoulder of mutton* 羊腿[羊肩]肉 ○ *roast, boiled, stewed mutton* 烧、清炖、焖羊肉 ○ [attrib 作定语] *mutton stew* 焖羊肉 ○ *a mutton chop*, ie a piece of rib of mutton 羊排. Cf 参看 LAMB 2. **2** (idm 习语) **dead as mutton** ⇨ DEAD. **mutton dressed (up) as ˈlamb** (*infml derog* 口, 贬) older person dressed in a style suitable for a younger person 作年轻打扮的老年人; 老来俏.

□ **ˈmutton-head** *n* (*infml derog* 口, 贬) stupid person 笨蛋; 傻瓜.

mu·tual /ˈmju:tʃʊəl; ˋmjutʃʊəl/ *adj* **1** (of a feeling or an action) felt or done by each towards the other (指感想或行为)相互的, 彼此的: *mutual affection, suspicion, etc*, ie A is fond/suspicious of B, and B is fond/suspicious of A 彼此间的爱、猜疑等 ○ *mutual aid, assistance, etc* 相互的援助、帮助等. **2** [attrib 作定语] (of people) having the same specified relationship to each other (指人)有相同关系的: *We are mutual friends, enemies, etc.* 我们彼此是朋友、敌人等. **3** [attrib 作定语] (*infml* 口) shared by two or more people (人与人之间)共同的, 共有的, 共享的: *our mutual friend, Smith*, ie Smith, a friend of both of us 我们两人共同的朋友史密斯. **4** (idm 习语) **a mutual admiration society** (*derog* 贬) situation in which two or more people praise or openly admire each other 互相吹捧. ▷ **mu·tu·ally** /-ʊəlɪ; -ʊəlɪ/ *adv*: *The two assertions are mutually exclusive*, ie cannot both be true. 这两种说法相互排斥.

□ **ˌmutual ˈfunds** (*US*) = UNIT TRUSTS (UNIT).

ˌmutual inˈsurance company one in which some or all of the profits are divided among the policy-holders 相互保险公司(部分或全部利润由投保人分享者).

Muzak /ˈmju:zæk; ˋmjuzæk/ *n* [U] (*propr often derog* 专利名, 常作贬义) continuous recorded light music often played in shops, restaurants, factories, etc 常在商店、餐馆、工厂等处连续播放的轻音乐.

muzzle /ˈmʌzl; ˋmʌzḷ/ *n* **1** (**a**) nose and mouth of an animal (eg a dog or fox) (动物, 如狗、狐等的)鼻口部分. (**b**) guard of straps or wires placed over this part of an animal's head to prevent it biting, etc (防动物咬人等的)口套. **2** open end of a firearm, out of which the bullets, etc come 枪口; 炮口: *a ˌmuzzle-loading ˈgun* 前膛装填的枪炮. Cf 参看 BREECH.

▷ **muzzle** *v* [Tn esp passive 尤用于被动语态] **1** put a muzzle on (a dog, etc) 给(狗等)戴口套: *Such a fierce animal ought to be muzzled.* 这动物太凶, 应该给它戴上口套. **2** (*fig derog* 比喻, 贬) prevent (a person, society, newspaper, etc) from expressing opinions freely 禁止(某人、社团、报纸等)自由发表意见: *accuse the government of muzzling the press, freedom of speech, etc* 谴责政府箝制新闻、言论自由等.

□ **ˈmuzzle velocity** speed of a bullet, shell, etc as it leaves the muzzle of a firearm (枪弹、炮弹等离开枪炮口时的)初速.

muzzy /ˈmʌzɪ; ˋmʌzɪ/ *adj* (**-ier, -iest**) **1** unable to think clearly; confused 迷糊的; 糊涂的: *After a couple of whiskies my head felt all muzzy.* 我喝了两杯威士忌, 就昏头昏脑的了. **2** blurred 模糊不清. ▷ **muz·zily** *adv*. **muz·zi·ness** *n* [U].

MV /ˌem ˈvi:; ˌɛm ˋvi/ *abbr* 缩写 = motor vessel 内燃机船.

MW *abbr* 缩写 = (*radio* 无) medium wave.

my /maɪ; maɪ/ *possess det* **1** of or belonging to the speaker or writer 我的: *Where's my hat?* 我的帽子在哪里? ○ *My feet are cold.* 我脚冷. ○ *He always forgets my birthday.* 他老是忘记我的生日. **2** (used before a *n* or an *adj* as a form of address 于名词或形容词前作称呼用): *my dear, darling, love, etc* 我亲爱的、我的宝贝、我亲爱的 ○ *my dear fellow, chap, man, girl, woman, etc* 亲爱的朋友、小伙子、老兄、姑娘、妻子等 ○ *Come along, my boy.* 快点, 老兄. **3** (used in exclamations 用于感叹语): *My goodness, what a surprise!* 我的天哪, 真想不到! ○ *My God, look at the time!* 啊呀, 都什么时候啦! Cf 参看 MINE[1].

my·co·logy /maɪˈkɒlədʒɪ; maɪˋkɑlədʒɪ/ *n* [U] science or study of fungi 真菌学.

my·el·itis /ˌmaɪəˈlaɪtɪs; ˌmaɪəˋlaɪtɪs/ *n* [U] (*medical* 医) inflammation of the spinal cord 脊髓炎.

mynah (also **myna, mina**) /ˈmaɪnə; ˋmaɪnə/ *n* any of several types of starling of SE Asia, known for their ability to copy human speech 鹩哥, 家八哥, 八哥(产于东南亚, 能模仿人说话).

my·opia /maɪˈəʊpɪə; maɪˋopɪə/ *n* [U] **1** (*medical* 医) short-sightedness 近视. **2** (*derog* 贬) inability to look into the future 缺乏远见; 目光短浅: *ministers charged with myopia* 受指责缺乏远见的大臣.

▷ **my·opic** /maɪˈɒpɪk; maɪˋɑpɪk/ *adj* **1** (*medical* 医) short-sighted 近视的: *myopic eyes, vision, etc* 近视眼、近视. **2** (*fig derog* 比喻, 贬) showing inability to look ahead into the future 缺乏远见的; 目光短浅的: *a myopic outlook, attitude, etc* 缺乏远见的看法、态度等 ○ *a government with myopic policies* 缺乏深谋远虑的政府. **my·op·ic·ally** /-klɪ; -klɪ/ *adv*.

myriad /ˈmɪrɪəd; ˋmɪrɪəd/ *n* extremely large number 无数; 极大数量: *Each galaxy contains myriads of stars.* 每一星系都有无数的恒星.

▷ **myriad** *adj* [attrib 作定语] uncountably many 无数的: *a butterfly's wing, with its myriad tiny scales* 带有无数细小鳞片的蝴蝶翅膀.

myr·midon /ˈmɜːmɪdən; *US* -dɒn; ˋmɝməˌdɑn/ *n* (*derog or joc* 贬或谑) person who carries out orders without question 盲目执行命令的人: *myrmidons of the law*, eg bailiffs 法律的奴仆(如法警).

myrrh /mɜː(r); mɝ/ *n* [U] sweet-smelling, bitter-tasting type of gum or resin obtained from shrubs and used for making incense and perfumes 没药.

myrtle /ˈmɜːtl; ˋmɝtl̩/ *n* [U] any of several types of evergreen shrub with shiny leaves and sweet-smelling white flowers 香桃木, 番樱桃, 爱神木(桃金娘科常绿灌木).

my·self /maɪˈself; maɪˋsɛlf/ *reflex, emph pron* 反身、强调代词 (only taking the main stress in sentences when used emphatically 仅用以加强语气时方读重音) **1** (*reflex* 反身) (used when the speaker or writer is also the person affected by an action 用于动作及于说话者或写作者本人时): *I ˌcut myself with a ˈknife.* 我用刀把自己拉伤了. **2** (*emph* 强调) (used to emphasize the speaker or writer 用以强调说话者或写作者本人): *I my'self will present the prizes.* 我亲自来发奖. ○ *I said so my'self only last week.* 我自己在上星期还这样说过. **3** (idm 习语) **(all) by my'self** (**a**) alone 独自. (**b**) without help 独自地; 独力地: *I finished the crossword (all) by myself.* 我自己(一个人)做出的纵横填字字谜.

mys·ter·ious /mɪˈstɪərɪəs; mɪsˋtɪrɪəs/ *adj* **1** full of mystery; hard to understand or explain 神秘的; 不可思议的; 难解的: *a mysterious event, crime, etc* 神秘的事件、罪行等 ○ *a mysterious letter, parcel, etc*, ie whose contents or sender are unknown 神秘的信件、包裹等(内容或寄件人不明). **2** keeping or liking to keep things secret 保密的; 好故弄玄虚的: *He was being very mysterious, and wouldn't tell me what he was up to.* 他神秘莫测, 不告诉我他想干什么. ○ *She gave me a mysterious look*, ie suggesting secret knowledge. 她向我使个神秘的眼色(意谓知道秘密). ▷ **mys·ter·iously** *adv*: *The main witness had mysteriously disappeared.* 主要见证人神秘地失踪了. ○ *Mysteriously, there was no answer when I rang.* 真怪, 我按了铃, 但没人应. **mys·ter·ious·ness** *n* [U].

mys·tery /ˈmɪstrɪ; ˋmɪstərɪ/ *n* **1** [C] (**a**) thing of which the cause or origin is hidden or impossible to explain 神秘的事物; 不可解释的事物; 秘密: *the mystery/mysteries of life* 生命的奥秘 ○ *a crime that is an unsolved mystery* 一宗未破的神秘罪案 ○ *It's a mystery to me why they didn't choose him.* 他们为什么不选择他我觉得是个谜. ○ [attrib 作定语] *a mystery guest, visitor, tour*, ie kept secret until a certain moment 神秘的客人、来访者、旅行(不到时候不公开). (**b**) (*infml* 口) person about whom not much is known or can be found out 来历不明或难探究竟的人: *He's a bit of a mystery!* 他这人有点来历不明! **2** [U] condition of being secret or obscure 秘密; 神秘: *His past is shrouded in mystery*, ie one cannot find out the truth about it. 他的过去使人捉摸不透. **3** [U] practice of or fondness for making things secret; secrecy 卖弄玄虚; 故作神秘; 奥秘: *You're full of mystery tonight; what's going on?* 你今天晚上很神秘, 搞的什么名堂? ○ [attrib 作定语] *a 'mystery man/woman* 神秘的男子[女子]. **4** [C] religious truth or belief that is beyond human understanding (宗教的)真谛, 信仰, 奥秘: *the mystery of the Incarnation, of the Eucharist, etc* 神灵化身、圣餐等的玄理. **5 mysteries** [pl] secret religious ceremonies (of the ancient Greeks, Romans, etc) (古希腊、罗马等的)秘密宗教仪式: (*fig* 比喻) *initiating the new recruit into the mysteries* (ie customs and practices) *of army life* 带领新兵熟悉军队生活中的规矩. **6** [C] story or play about a puzzling crime 神秘罪案的故事或戏剧: *a murder mystery* 凶杀奇案 ○ [attrib 作定语] *a mystery thriller* 惊险悬疑作品.

□ **'mystery play** medieval drama containing stories from the life of Jesus 神秘剧(中世纪描写耶稣生平的戏剧). Cf 参看 MIRACLE PLAY (MIRACLE).

mystic /ˈmɪstɪk; ˋmɪstɪk/ (also **mys·tical** /ˈmɪstɪkl; ˋmɪstəkl̩/) *adj* **1** of hidden meaning or spiritual power, esp in religion 神秘的; 玄理的; 不可思议的; (尤指宗教方面)秘教的: *mystic rites and ceremonies* 神秘的仪式. **2** of or based on mysticism 神秘主义的: *the world's mystic religions* 世界上的神秘主义宗教 ○ *the mystical writings of St John of the Cross* 十字架的圣约翰的奥秘神学著述. **3** causing feelings of awe and wonder 引起敬畏和惊奇的: *mystic beauty* 惊人的美丽 ○ *For me, standing before the temple door as the sun rose was a mystical experience.* 旭日东升, 我站在神殿门前, 体验到油然而生的敬畏之情.

▷ **mystic** *n* person who tries to be united with God and, through that, to reach truths beyond human understanding 神秘主义者(寻求神人交融借以获得人类不解之真理者).

mys·tic·ally /-klɪ; -klɪ/ *adv*.

mys·ti·cism /ˈmɪstɪsɪzəm; ˋmɪstəˌsɪzəm/ *n* [U] belief or experiences of a mystic; teaching and belief that knowledge of God and of real truth may be reached through meditation or spiritual insight, independently of reason and the senses 神秘主义者的信仰和体验; 神秘主义(相信不用理性和感官而藉默想与心灵内省即可认识上帝与真理的学说): *Christian mysticism* 基督教的神秘主义 ○ *A strain of mysticism runs through his poetry.* 他的诗作中贯穿着神秘主义的情调.

mys·tify /ˈmɪstɪfaɪ; ˋmɪstəˌfaɪ/ *v* (*pt, pp* **-fied**) [Tn] make (sb) confused through lack of understanding; puzzle; bewilder 使(某人)困惑不解; 使迷惑: *I'm mystified; I just can't see how he did it.* 我大惑不解, 就是不明白他是怎么做到的. ○ *her mystifying disappearance* 她神秘的失踪.

▷ **mys·ti·fica·tion** /ˌmɪstɪfɪˈkeɪʃn; ˌmɪstəfəˋkeʃən/ *n* [U] **1** mystifying or being mystified 迷惑; 困惑. **2** (*derog* 贬) deliberately making sth mysterious or hard to understand, so as to prevent people finding out about it 神秘化; 故弄玄虚.

mys·tique /mɪˈstiːk; mɪsˋtik/ *n* [sing] quality of sth which is not fully known about or understood but is seen to be admirable or special 神秘性: *the mystique of the British monarchy* 英国君主体制的神秘色彩 ○ *a simple, straightforward textbook that helps to dispel some of the mystique surrounding computers* 有助于消除关于计算机的某些神秘观念的简明教科书 ○ *There is a certain mystique about eating oysters.* 人们对吃牡蛎有某种神秘感.

myth /mɪθ; mɪθ/ *n* **1** [C] story that originated in ancient times, esp one dealing with ideas or beliefs about the early history of a race, or giving explanations of natural events, such as the seasons 神话(尤指有关一民族早期历史的观念或信仰的, 或解释如季节等自然现象的):

the Creation myth 创世的神话 ○ *ancient Greek myths* 古希腊神话. **2** [U] such stories collectively 神话(总称): *famous in myth and legend* 神话和传奇中著名的. **3** [C] thing, person, etc that is imaginary, fictitious or impossible 想像的、虚构或不可能存在的事物、人等: *the myth of racial superiority, of human perfectibility* 种族优越的、人类完美的神话 ○ *The rich uncle of whom he boasts is only a myth.* 他吹嘘的那个有钱的叔叔只是个乌有翁.

▷ **myth·ical** /ˈmɪθɪkl; ˋmɪθɪkl̩/ *adj* **1** existing (only) in myth (只)存在于神话中的: *mythical heroes* 神话中的英雄. **2** imaginary; fictitious 想像的; 虚构的: *mythical wealth* 假想的财富 ○ *that mythical 'rich uncle' of whom he boasts* 他吹嘘的那个虚构的'阔叔叔'.

mytho·logy /mɪˈθɒlədʒɪ; mɪˋθɑlədʒɪ/ *n* **1** [U] study or science of myths 神话学. **2** [U] myths collectively 神话(总称): *Greek mythology* 希腊神话. **3** [C] body or collection of myths 神话集: *the mythologies of primitive races* 原始民族神话集.

▷ **mytho·lo·gical** /ˌmɪθəˈlɒdʒɪkl; ˌmɪθəˋlɑdʒɪkl̩/ *adj* of or in mythology or myths 神话(中)的; 神话学(中)的: *mythological literature* 神话文学 ○ *Pluto, the mythological king of the underworld* 普卢托, 神话中的冥王.

mytho·lo·gist /mɪˈθɒlədʒɪst; mɪˋθɑlədʒɪst/ *n* person who studies myths 神话学研究者.

myx·oma·tosis /ˌmɪksəməˈtəʊsɪs; ˌmɪksəməˋtosɪs/ *n* [U] fatal infectious disease of rabbits 多发性黏液瘤病, 黏液瘤变性(兔瘟).

M

N n

N, n /en; ɛn/ *n* (*pl* **N's, n's** /enz; ɛnz/) the fourteenth letter of the English alphabet 英语字母表的第十四个字母: *'Nicholas' begins with (an) N/'N'.* Nicholas 一字以 N 字母开始.

N *abbr* 缩写 = **1** (*US* also **No**) north(ern): *N Yorkshire* 北约克郡 ○ *London N14 6BS*, ie as a postal code 伦敦 N14 6BS(邮政编码). **2** (esp on electric plugs) neutral (connection) (尤用于电器插头上)不带电的(接线).

n *abbr* 缩写 = **1** (esp on forms) name (尤用于表格栏目中). **2** (*grammar*) neuter (gender).

NAACP /ˌen eɪ eɪ siː ˈpiː; ˌɛn e ˌe si ˈpi/ *abbr* 缩写 = (*US*) National Association for the Advancement of Colored People 全国有色人种协进会.

NAAFI /ˈnæfɪ; ˈnæfɪ/ *abbr* 缩写 = (*Brit*) Navy, Army and Air Force Institutes (providing canteens, shops, etc for British servicemen in England and abroad) 海陆空军小卖店经营机构. Cf 参看 PX.

nab /næb; næb/ *v* (**-bb-**) [Tn] (*Brit infml* 口) catch (sb) doing wrong; seize 逮住, 捉住(某人); 抓住: *He was nabbed (by the police) for speeding.* 他超速行车被(警察)逮住了.

na·celle /næˈsel; nəˈsɛl/ *n* outer casing for an aircraft engine (飞行器的)发动机舱.

nacre /ˈneɪkə(r); ˈnekɚ/ *n* [U] = MOTHER-OF-PEARL (MOTHER).

na·dir /ˈneɪdɪə(r); *US* ˈneɪdər; ˈnedɚ/ *n* **1** point in the heavens directly beneath an observer 天底. Cf 参看 ZENITH. **2** (*fig* 比喻) lowest point; time of greatest depression, despair, etc 最低点; 最压抑、消沉等的时刻: *This failure was the nadir of her career.* 这次失败是她事业上的低谷.

naff /næf; næf/ *adj* (*Brit sl* 俚) lacking taste or style; worthless; unfashionable 无滋味的; 无风格的; 无价值的; 不时髦的: *That suit's pretty naff.* 那套西装不像样子.

nag[1] /næg; næg/ *n* (*infml often derog* 口, 常作贬义) horse 马: *It's a waste of money betting on that old nag!* 把赌金压在那匹老马上就是白扔钱!

nag[2] /næg; næg/ *v* (**-gg-**) **1** [I, Ipr, Tn] **~ at sb** scold or criticize (sb) continuously 不断挑剔或批评(某人): *He nagged (at) her all day long.* 他一天到晚地说她. **2** [Tn] worry or hurt (sb) persistently 不断烦扰或伤害(某人): *a nagging pain* 令人心烦的疼痛 ○ *The problem had been nagging me for weeks.* 那问题把我困扰了几个星期.

naiad /ˈnaɪæd; ˈnaɪæd/ *n* (*pl* **~s** or **~es** /ˈnaɪədiːz; ˈnaɪəˌdiz/) (in Greek mythology) water-nymph (希腊神话中的)水神.

nail /neɪl; nel/ *n* **1** layer of horny substance over the outer tip of a finger or toe 指甲; 趾甲: *'finger-nails* 手指甲 ○ *a 'toe-nail* 脚趾甲 ○ *cut one's nails* 剪指甲. ⇨illus at HAND 见 HAND 插图. **2** small thin piece of metal with a sharp point at one end and a (usu) flat head at the other, hammered into articles to hold them together, or into a wall, etc for use as a peg to hang things on 钉子. ⇨illus at HAMMER 见 HAMMER 插图. **3** (idm 习语) **a nail in sb's/sth's 'coffin** thing that hastens or ensures sb's death, or the end, failure, etc of sb/sth 加速某人死亡或使某人必死的事物; 某人[某事物]的结局、失败等: *The long and costly strike proved to be the last nail in the company's coffin.* 长期罢工损失巨大致使该公司一蹶不振. **fight, etc tooth and nail** ⇨ TOOTH. **hard as nails** ⇨ HARD. **hit the nail on the head** ⇨ HIT[1]. **on the nail** (*infml* 口) (of payment) without delay (指付款)立即: *I want cash on the nail.* 我要立即支付的现金. **(as) tough as 'nails** ⇨ TOUGH.

▷ **nail** *v* **1** [Tn] (*infml* 口) catch or arrest (sb) 抓住或逮捕(某人): *Have the police nailed the man who did it?* 警方逮着做案的人了吗? ○ *She finally nailed me in the corridor.* 她最后在走廊里把我抓住了. **2** [Tn] (*infml* 口) reveal (sth) to be untrue 显示(某事物)不属实: *I've finally nailed the myth of his infallibility*, ie shown that he can make mistakes. 我终于揭穿了他'一贯正确'的神话(表明他也会犯错误). **3** (idm 习语) **nail one's colours to the 'mast** declare openly and firmly what one believes, whom one supports, etc (公开而坚决地)表明自己相信的事、支持的人等; 旗帜鲜明. **nail a lie (to the counter)** prove that a statement is untrue 证明说法不属实; 揭穿谎言. **4** (phr v) **nail sth down** **(a)** make (a carpet, lid, etc) secure with nails 将(地毯、盖子等)用钉子钉牢. **(b)** define sth precisely 确定某事物. **nail sb down (to sth)** make sb say precisely what he believes or wants to do 使某人明确地说出其相信的事或要做的事物: *She says she'll come, but I can't nail her down to a specific time.* 她说她来, 我却无法让她说出确切的时间. **nail sth on; nail sth on/onto/to sth** fasten sth to sth with nails 将某物用钉子钉在某物上: *nail a lid on (the crate)* 把盖子钉在(板条箱)上 ○ *nail a sign to the wall* 在墙上钉一标志. **nail sth up** **(a)** fasten sth with nails so that it hangs from a wall, post, etc 将某物用钉子钉牢使之悬挂于墙、柱等上. **(b)** make (a door, window, etc) secure with nails so that it cannot easily be opened 将(门窗等)用钉子钉牢使之不易开启.

□ **'nail-brush** *n* small brush with stiff bristles for cleaning the finger-nails 指甲刷. ⇨illus at BRUSH 见 BRUSH 插图.

'nail-file *n* small flat file for shaping the finger-nails 指甲锉.

'nail-scissors *n* [pl] small scissors for trimming the finger-nails and toe-nails 指甲剪: *a pair of nail-scissors* 一把指甲剪.

'nail varnish (also **varnish**) (*Brit*) (*US* **'nail polish**) varnish for giving a shiny tint to the finger-nails and toe-nails 指甲油.

naira /ˈnaɪrə; ˈnaɪrə/ *n* (*pl* unchanged 复数不变) unit of Nigerian money, 100 kobos 奈拉(尼日利亚货币单位, 合 100 考包).

naive (also **naïve**) /naɪˈiːv; nɑˈiv/ *adj* **1** natural and innocent in speech and behaviour; unaffected (言行)自然而天真的, 不做作的. **2** (*esp derog* 尤作贬义) **(a)** too ready to believe what one is told; credulous (对他人的话)过于相信的, 轻信的: *You weren't so naive as to believe him, were you?* 你没有轻易相信他, 是吧? **(b)** showing lack of experience, wisdom or judgement 显得缺少经验、智慧或判断力的: *a naive person, remark* 幼稚的人、言语.

▷ **naively** (also **naïvely**) *adv.*

naiv·ety (also **naïv·ety** /naɪˈiːvtɪ; nɑˈivtɪ/, **naïv·eté** /naɪˈiːvteɪ; nɑˈivte/) *n* **1** [U] quality of being naive 天真. **2** [C] naive remark, action, etc 天真的言语、举动等.

naked /ˈneɪkɪd; ˈnekɪd/ *adj* **1** **(a)** without clothes on 裸体的: *a naked body* 裸体 ○ *as naked as the day he was born* 像他出生时那样赤裸的. **(b)** [usu attrib 通常作定语] without the usual covering 没有通常的遮盖物的: *a naked sword*, ie one without its sheath 无鞘的剑 ○ *fight with naked fists*, ie without boxing-gloves 赤手拳击(不戴拳击手套) ○ *naked trees*, ie without leaves 光秃秃的树(无树叶) ○ *a naked light*, eg an electric bulb without a lampshade 无灯罩的电灯. **2** (*fig* 比喻) not disguised 无隐蔽的; 无掩饰的: *the naked truth* 赤裸裸的事实. **3** (idm 习语) **the naked 'eye** eyesight without the use of a telescope, a microscope, etc 肉眼: *Microbes are too small to be seen by the naked eye.* 微生物很小, 肉眼看不见. ▷ **nakedly** *adv.* **naked·ness** *n* [U].

namby-pamby /ˌnæmbɪ ˈpæmbɪ; ˈnæmbɪˈpæmbɪ/ *adj* (*derog* 贬) (of people or their talk) foolishly sentimental (指人或谈话)多愁善感的, 忧天忧地的.

▷ **namby-pamby** *n* such a person 多愁善感的人: *Don't be such a namby-pamby!* 别那么千愁万虑的!

name[1] /neɪm; nem/ *n* **1** [C] word or words by which a person, an animal, a place or a thing is known and spoken to or of 名字; 名称: *My name is Peter.* 我名叫彼得. ○ *What is the name of the town where you live?* 你住的那个城市叫什么名字? **2** **(a)** [sing] reputation; fame 名誉; 名声: *a shop with a (good, bad, etc) name for reliability* 信誉(好、不好等)的商店. **(b)** [attrib 作定语]

(*esp US*) having a well-known name or an established reputation 有名的; 名声卓著的: *a name brand of soap* 名牌肥皂 ○ *a big-name company* 大名鼎鼎的公司. **3** [C] famous person 著名的人物; 名人: *the great names of history* 历史上的伟人 ○ *All the big names in the pop music world were at the party.* 流行音乐界的头面人物都参加了聚会. **4** (idm 习语) **answer to the name of sth** ⇨ ANSWER². **be sb's middle name** ⇨ MIDDLE. **by name** having or using a name or names 名为; 名叫: *A strange man, Fred by name, came to see me.* 有个名叫弗雷德的陌生人来找我. ○ *The teacher knows all his students by name.* 这位老师叫得出所有学生的名字. ○ *I only know her by name*, ie from hearing others speak of her, not personally. 我只知道她的名字(只听说过, 并不认识). **by/of the name of** named 称做; 叫做: *He goes by the name of Henry.* 他名叫亨利. ○ *Someone of the name of Henry wants to see you.* 有个叫亨利的要见您. **call sb names** ⇨ CALL². **drag sb/sb's name through the mire/mud** ⇨ DRAG². **drop names** ⇨ DROP². **enter one's name/put one's name down (for sth)** apply to enter (a school, college, course, etc) 报名上(学、课等). **give a dog a bad name** ⇨ DOG¹. **give one's name to sth** invent or originate sth which then becomes known by one's own name 以自己的名字命名某发明创造: *He gave his name to a well-known brand of frozen food.* 他以自己的名字命名的冷冻食品成了名牌. **a household name/word** ⇨ HOUSEHOLD. **in the name of sb/sth** (**a**) on behalf of sb/sth 代表某人[某事物]: *I greet you in the name of the President.* 我代表总统前来迎接您. (**b**) by the authority of sth 凭借某事物的权威: *I arrest you in the name of the law.* 我依法逮捕你. (**c**) calling sb/sth to witness 以某人[某事物]为证: *In God's name, what are you doing?* 苍天在上, 你究竟在干什么? (**d**) for the sake of sth 为某事物的缘故: *They did it all in the name of friendship.* 他们完全是出于友谊而那样做. **in name only** not in reality 表面上; 名义上: *He is leader in name only: his deputy has effectively taken over.* 他不过是个应名儿领导, 他的副手实际上已取而代之. **lend one's name to sth** ⇨ LEND. **make a ˈname for oneself/make one's ˈname** become well known 成名; 出名: *She first made a name for herself as an actress.* 她最初是以当演员而成名的. **sb's name is mud** sb is disliked or (often temporarily) unpopular because of sth he has done 某人因所做某事而不受欢迎或(常为一时)不得人心. **name names** ⇨ NAME². **the name of the ˈgame** the main purpose or most important aspect of an activity 一项活动的主要目的或最重要的方面: *Hard work is the name of the game if you want to succeed in business.* 要想生意兴隆, 关键就是苦干. **a name to conjure with** name of a person, group, company, etc that is respected and influential 受尊敬而有影响的人、团体、公司等的名字. **not have sth to one's ˈname** not possess even a small amount of (esp money) 一点儿(尤指钱)都没有; 一文不名: *She hasn't a penny to her name*, ie is very poor. 她已一文不名(极穷). **put a name to sb/sth** know or remember what sb/sth is called 知道或记住某人[某事物]的名称: *I've heard that tune before but I can't put a name to it.* 我以前听过那曲调, 但说不出名字了. **take sb's name in vain** use a name, esp God's, disrespectfully 滥用(尤指上帝的)名字; 亵渎上帝之名. **under the name (of) sth** using sth as a name instead of one's real name 用某某作名字(不用自己的真名): *He writes under the name of Nimrod.* 他用尼姆罗德这个名字写作.

□ **ˈname-day** *n* feast day of the saint whose name one was given at christening 圣名日(以某圣徒名命名者的纪念日).

ˈname-dropping *n* [U] practice of casually mentioning the names of famous people one knows or pretends one knows in order to impress others 随便提起自己认识的或假装认识的名人以引人瞩目的做法. **ˈname-drop** *v* (**-pp-**) [I] talk in this way 以上述方式谈话.

ˈname-part *n* title-role in a play, etc (戏剧等中的)与剧名相同的角色: *He's got the name-part in 'Hamlet'.* 他获演《哈姆雷特》一剧中哈姆雷特这一角色.

ˈname-plate *n* plaque on or near the door of a room, building, etc, showing the name of the occupant 姓名牌(挂在房间、建筑物等门上的牌子).

ˈnamesake *n* person or thing having the same name as another 同姓、同名或同姓名的人; 同名的事物: *She's my namesake but we're not related.* 她与我同姓, 但我们不是亲戚.

ˈname-tape *n* small tape with the owner's name on it, sewn into clothing 名字标签(缝在衣服里标明所有者姓名的布条).

NOTE ON USAGE 用法: Your **first name** (*US* often **given name**) is, in English-speaking countries, the name given to you by your parents at birth. 在说英语的国家中**first name**(美语常作**given name**)是名字, 是出生时父母给取的. The name common to your family is your **family name** or, more usually, **surname.** 姓是**family name**, 多作**surname.** ☆ In Christian countries **Christian name** is often used for **first name.** 在基督教国家中, 常以教名(**Christian name**)为名(**first name**). ☆ **Forename**, also meaning **first name,** is formal and is often found on documents, application forms, etc. ☆ **forename**也是**first name**, 但用法较庄重, 常见于文件、申请表格等中.

name² /neɪm; nem/ *v* **1** [Tn, Tn·pr, Cn·n] **~ sb/sth (after sb)**; *US* **~ sb/sth (for sb)** give a name to sb/sth 给某人[某事物]取名; 命名: *The child was named after its father*, ie given its father's first name. 那个孩子是按他父亲的名字取的名. ○ *Tasmania was named after its discoverer, A. J. Tasman.* 塔斯曼尼亚岛是以其发现者塔斯曼的名字命名的. ○ *They named their child John.* 他们给孩子取名叫约翰. **2** [Tn] give the name(s) of (sb/sth); identify 说出(某人[某事物])的名字; 识别: *Can you name all the plants in this garden?* 你能说出这花园里所有植物的名字吗? ○ *Police have named a man they would like to question.* 警方已查出他们要审讯的男子. **3** [Tn] state (sth) precisely; specify 确定(某事物); 指定: *We have named a date for the party.* 我们已定好聚会的日期. ○ *Name your price*, ie Say what price you want to charge. 你开价吧(说出你想要的价钱). ○ *The young couple have named the day*, ie chosen the day on which they will get married. 这对年轻人已定下婚期. **4** [Tn, Tn·pr, Cn·n/a] **~ sb (for sth)**; **~ sb as sth** nominate sb for, or appoint sb to, a position 提名某人或指定某人任一职务: *Ms X has been named for the directorship/named as the new director.* 某女士已被提名任董事职务[任命为新董事]. **5** (idm 习语) **name ˈnames** give the name of a person or people being criticized, accused, praised, etc 指出受批评、受指责、受称赞等人的名字: *He said someone had lied but wouldn't name names.* 他说有人说谎, 但他不愿指名道姓. **to name but a ˈfew** giving only these as examples 仅以这些为例: *Lots of our friends are coming: Anne, Ken and George, to name but a few.* 我们的好多朋友都来: 如安妮、肯、乔治等. **you ˈname it** (*infml* 口) every thing, place, etc you can name or think of 能说出或想到的任何东西、地方等: *She can make anything: chairs, tables, cupboards — you name it.* 她什么都会做: 椅子、桌子、柜橱——你说出什么她都会做.

name·less /ˈneɪmlɪs; ˈnemlɪs/ *adj* **1** (**a**) [esp attrib 尤作定语] having no name or no known name; anonymous 无名的; 不知名的; 匿名的: *a nameless grave* 无名墓 ○ *a nameless 13th century poet* 13世纪的一个不知名的诗人 ○ *the nameless thousands who built the pyramids* 建筑金字塔的成千上万不知姓名的人. (**b**) not mentioned by name 未提及姓名的; 不道出姓名的: *He had received information from a nameless source in the government.* 他从政府中一未透露姓名者那里得到了消息. ○ *a well-known public figure, who shall be/remain nameless*, ie whose name I will not mention 一位知名人士, 姑隐其姓名. **2** [esp attrib 尤作定语] (**a**) (esp of emotions) not easy to describe (尤指情感)不可名状的, 难以形容的: *a nameless longing, fear, etc* 不可名状的渴望、恐惧等. (**b**) too terrible to describe; unmentionable (糟糕得)难以形容的; 难以启齿的: *the nameless horrors of the prison camp* 战俘营中难以形容的恐怖.

namely /ˈneɪmlɪ; ˈnemlɪ/ *adv* that is to say; specifically 即; 就是: *Only one boy was absent, namely Harry.* 只有一个男孩儿缺席, 就是哈里. ⇨Usage at VIZ 用法见 VIZ.

nanny /ˈnænɪ; ˈnænɪ/ *n* (*Brit*) **1** child's nurse (儿童的)保姆. **2** (*infml* 口) grandmother 奶奶; 姥姥.

nanny-goat /ˈnænɪ gəʊt; ˈnænɪˌgot/ *n* female goat 母山

N

羊. ⇨illus at GOAT 见GOAT 插图. Cf 参看 BILLY-GOAT.

nap[1] /næp; næp/ *n* short sleep, esp during the day 小睡, 打盹(尤指在白天): *have/take a quick nap after lunch* 午饭后小睡片刻.

▷ **nap** *v* (**-pp-**) [I] **1** have a short sleep 睡一小觉; 打个盹. **2** (idm 习语) **catch sb napping** ⇨ CATCH[1].

nap[2] /næp; næp/ *n* [U] short fibres on the surface of cloth, felt, etc, usu smoothed and brushed in one direction (布、呢子等表面上的)绒毛: *with/against the nap*, ie in the same direction as/the opposite direction to that of the nap 顺着[戗着]绒毛. Cf 参看 PILE[4].

nap[3] /næp; næp/ *n* (*Brit*) type of card-game 纳普牌(一种纸牌游戏).

nap·alm /ˈneɪpɑːm; ˋneˌpɑm/ *n* [U] petrol in jellied form, used in making fire-bombs 凝固汽油(用以制造燃烧弹).

nape /neɪp; nep/ *n* (usu *sing* 通常作单数) back part of the neck 项(颈的后部): *He kissed her on the nape of her neck.* 他亲吻她的颈背. ⇨illus at HEAD 见 HEAD 插图.

naph·tha /ˈnæfθə; ˋnæfθə/ *n* [U] type of inflammable oil obtained from coal tar and petrol 石油精; 石脑油.

▷ **naph·thal·ene** /-liːn; -ˌlin/ *n* [U] strong-smelling substance obtained from coal tar and petrol, used in making dyes and mothballs 萘.

nap·kin /ˈnæpkɪn; ˋnæpkɪn/ *n* **1** (also ˈ**table napkin**) piece of cloth or paper used at meals for protecting one's clothes and wiping one's lips and fingers (布的或纸的)餐巾. **2** (*Brit fml* 文) = NAPPY.

nappy /ˈnæpɪ; ˋnæpɪ/ *n* (*Brit infml* 口) (also *fml* 文作 **napkin**) (*US* **diaper**) piece of towelling cloth or similar soft padding folded round a baby's bottom and between its legs to absorb or hold its urine and excreta 尿布: *a disposable nappy*, ie one that is made to be thrown away after being used once 一次性尿布(用后即弃的).

nar·ciss·ism /ˈnɑːsɪsɪzəm; nɑrˋsɪsˌɪzəm/ *n* [U] (*psychology* 心) abnormal and excessive love or admiration for oneself 自恋; 自我陶醉. ▷ **nar·ciss·istic** /ˌnɑːsɪˈsɪstɪk; nɑrsɪˋsɪstɪk/ *adj*.

nar·cissus /nɑːˈsɪsəs; nɑrˋsɪsəs/ *n* (*pl* ~**es** /nɑːˈsɪsəsɪz; nɑrˋsɪsəsɪz/ or **-cissi** /nɑːˈsɪsaɪ; nɑrˋsɪˌsaɪ/) any of several types of spring flowering bulbs, including the daffodil 水仙属; 水仙.

nar·cotic /nɑːˈkɒtɪk; nɑrˋkɑtɪk/ *n* **1** substance causing sleep or (sometimes extreme) drowsiness 催眠的或麻醉的物质: *The juice of this fruit is a mild narcotic.* 这种果汁有轻度催眠作用. **2** (often *pl* 常作复数) drug that affects the mind 麻醉剂; 毒品: *Narcotics are a major threat to health.* 毒品是危害健康的大敌. ○ [attrib 作定语] *a narcotics agent*, ie one investigating the illegal trade in narcotics 毒品探员.

▷ **nar·cotic** *adj* of or having the effect of a narcotic 麻醉的; 催眠的: *a narcotic effect, substance* 麻醉的作用、物质.

nark[1] /nɑːk; nɑrk/ *n* (*Brit sl* 俚) police informer or spy (警方的)眼线, 密探.

nark[2] /nɑːk; nɑrk/ *v* [Tn usu passive 通常用于被动语态] (*Brit sl* 俚) annoy 苦恼: *feeling narked about being ignored* 受到忽视而感到苦恼.

nar·rate /nəˈreɪt; *US* ˈnæreɪt; ˋnæret/ *v* [Tn] tell (a story); give a written or spoken account of 讲(故事); 描写或叙述: *narrate one's adventures* 叙述奇遇 ○ *The story is narrated by its hero.* 这故事是由主人公自己讲的.

▷ **nar·ra·tion** /nəˈreɪʃn; næˋreʃən/ *n* **1** [U] activity of telling a story, etc 讲述; 叙述. **2** [C] story; account of events 故事; (事情的)叙述.

nar·rator *n* person who narrates 讲述者; 叙述者.

nar·rat·ive /ˈnærətɪv; ˋnærətɪv/ *n* **1** [C] spoken or written account of events; story 叙事; 故事: *a gripping narrative about the war* 扣人心弦的战况报道. **2** [U] (**a**) story-telling 讲述; 叙述; 叙事体: *a master of narrative* 擅长叙述的人. (**b**) narrated parts of a book, etc 书等中的叙述部分: *The novel contains more narrative than dialogue.* 这部小说里的叙述比对话多.

▷ **nar·rat·ive** *adj* [attrib 作定语] of, or in the form of, story-telling 叙述的; 叙事体的: *narrative literature*, ie stories and novels 叙事文学(故事和小说) ○ *narrative poems* 叙事诗 ○ *a writer of great narrative power*, ie able to describe events vividly 擅长叙事的作家.

nar·row /ˈnærəʊ; ˋnæro/ *adj* (**-er**, **-est**) **1** of small width compared with length 窄的: *a narrow bridge, path, ledge* 窄的桥、路、檐 ○ *The road was too narrow for cars to pass.* 路很窄, 汽车过不去. Cf 参看 BROAD[1] 1, THIN 1, WIDE 1. **2** of limited range or variety; small or restricted (范围或种类)有限的, 小的, 受限制的: *a narrow circle of friends* 交游不广 ○ *the narrow confines of small-town life* 小镇生活的狭小天地. **3** [usu attrib 通常作定语] with only a small margin; barely achieved 勉强的; 几乎未成的: *a narrow escape from death* 九死一生 ○ *elected by a narrow majority*, eg when voting is 67 to 64 以微弱多数当选(如以67票对64票) ○ *The favourite had a narrow lead over* (ie was not far ahead of) *the rest.* 那匹热门马稍稍领先. **4** limited in outlook; having little sympathy for the ideas, etc of others 偏狭的; 狭隘的; 度量小的: *He has a very narrow mind.* 他度量很小. ○ *She takes a rather narrow view of the subject.* 她对这一问题有些偏见. **5** strict; exact 严格的; 精确的: *What does the word mean in its narrowest sense?* 这个词的最狭义的意思是什么? **6** (idm 习语) **a narrow ˈsqueak** situation in which one barely avoids failure or escapes danger 险遭失败或危险的情况. **the straight and narrow** ⇨ STRAIGHT[1].

▷ **nar·row** *v* [I, Tn] (cause sth to) become narrower (使某物)变窄: *The road narrows here.* 路到这里变窄了. ○ *Her eyes narrowed* (ie She partly closed them) *menacingly.* 她威胁地眯起眼睛. ○ *The gap between the two parties has narrowed considerably.* 双方的隔阂已明显缩小. ○ *In order to widen the road they had to narrow the pavement.* 为了拓宽道路只好将人行道弄窄.

nar·rowly *adv* **1** only just; by only a small margin 仅仅; 勉强地: *We won narrowly.* 我们仅是险胜. ○ *He narrowly escaped drowning.* 他差点儿淹死. **2** closely; carefully 严密地; 仔细地; 小心地: *observe someone narrowly* 密切注意某人.

nar·row·ness *n* [U].

nar·rows *n* [pl] **1** narrow strait or channel connecting two larger bodies of water 海峡; 江峡. **2** narrow place in a river or pass 河流的狭窄处; 隘路.

□ ˌ**narrow-ˈminded** /ˈmaɪndɪd; ˋmaɪndɪd/ *adj* not ready to listen to or tolerate the views of others 心胸狭窄的; 狭隘的; 度量小的: *a narrow-minded bigot* 狭隘偏执的人. ˌ**narrow-ˈmindedly** *adv*. ˌ**narrow-ˈmindedness** *n* [U].

nar·whal /ˈnɑːwəl; ˋnɑrhwəl/ *n* Arctic animal like a whale, the male of which has a long spiral tusk 独角鲸.

NASA /ˈnæsə; ˋnæsə/ *abbr* 缩写 = (*US*) National Aeronautics and Space Administration 国家航空航天局; 美国航空及太空总署.

nasal /ˈneɪzl; ˋnezl̩/ *adj* of, for or in the nose 鼻的; 为鼻的; 在鼻中的: *nasal sounds*, eg /m, n, ŋ/ 鼻音(如/m/、/n/、/ŋ/) ○ *a nasal spray*, ie one sprayed into the nose to make breathing easier 鼻喷雾剂 ○ *a nasal voice*, ie one which produces sounds through both the nose and the mouth 鼻音.

▷ **nasal** *n* nasal sound 鼻音.

nas·al·ize, -ise /ˈneɪzəlaɪz; ˋnezl̩ˌaɪz/ *v* [Tn] make (a sound) with the air stream, or part of it, passing through the nose 使(声音)鼻音化; 将(声音)发成鼻音.

nas·ally /ˈneɪzəlɪ; ˋnezəlɪ/ *adv*.

nas·cent /ˈnæsnt; ˋnæsn̩t/ *adj* (*fml* 文) beginning to exist; not yet well developed 新生的; 初生的; 尚未成熟的; 尚不发达的: *a nascent industry, talent, suspicion* 新兴的工业、新人才、新发现的疑点.

nas·tur·tium /nəˈstɜːʃəm; *US* næ-; næˋstɝʃəm/ *n* garden plant with red, orange or yellow flowers and round flat leaves 旱金莲.

nasty /ˈnɑːstɪ; *US* ˈnæ-; ˋnæstɪ/ *adj* (**-ier**, **-iest**) **1** unpleasant; disgusting 令人不愉快的; 令人厌恶的: *a nasty smell, taste, sight* 令人厌恶的气味、味道、情景 ○ *I don't like the colour they've chosen for their new carpet — it looks really nasty.* 我不喜欢他们挑的那块新地毯的颜色——看着真让人恶心. Cf 参看 NICE. **2** (**a**) unkind; spiteful 不善良的; 恶意的: *What a nasty man!* 这个恶人! ○ *Don't be nasty to your little brother.* 别跟你小弟弟动坏心眼儿. ○ *She has a nasty temper.* 她脾气不好. (**b**) morally bad 道德败坏的: *a person with a nasty mind* 思想肮脏的人 ○ *nasty stories* 下流故事. **3** (**a**) dangerous; threatening 危险的; 威胁的: *The weather is too nasty for sailing.* 这种天气作帆船运动太危险. ○ *He had a nasty* *look in his eye.* 他眼露凶光. ○ *This is a nasty corner,* ie is dangerous for cars going fast. 这个街角对疾驰的汽车来说非常危险. (**b**) painful; severe 疼痛的; 严重的: *a nasty cut, wound, etc* 严重的割伤、伤口等 ○ *She had a nasty skiing accident.* 她滑雪时出了严重事故. ○ *The news gave me a nasty shock.* 我得知那一消息大为震惊. **4** (idm 习语) **leave a bad/nasty taste in the mouth** ⇨ LEAVE[1]. **a nasty piece of work** (*infml* 口) unpleasant or untrustworthy person 讨厌的或不可靠的人. ▷ **nas·tily** *adv.* **nas·ti·ness** *n* [U].

na·tion /ˈneɪʃn; ˋneʃən/ *n* large community of people, usu sharing a common history, language, etc, and living in a particular territory under one government 国民; 民族; 国家: *the nations of Western Europe* 西欧国家 ○ *the United Nations Organization* 联合国组织. ⇨Usage at COUNTRY 用法见 COUNTRY.

□ ˌ**nation-ˈwide** *adj, adv* over the whole of a nation 遍及全国(的); 全国性(的): *a ˌnation-wide ˈsurvey, camˈpaign, etc* 全国性的调查、活动等 ○ *Police are looking for him nation-wide.* 警方正在全国各地寻找他.

na·tional /ˈnæʃnəl; ˋnæʃənl/ *adj* [usu attrib 通常作定语] **1** of a nation; common to or characteristic of a whole nation 国民的; 民族的; 国家的; 全国共有的或特有的: *a national treasure, institution, campaign, trait* 国宝、国家机构、全民的活动、民族特性 ○ *national and local newspapers* 全国和地方报纸 ○ *the British national character* 英国的国民特性 ○ *national opposition* (ie that expressed by all the citizens) *to government policy* 全国人民对政府政策的反对 ○ *national and international issues*, ie those that concern only one's own nation and those that concern many nations 国内和国际的问题. **2** owned, controlled or financially supported by the State 国有的; 国立的; 国营的: *a national theatre* 国家剧院.

▷ **na·tional** *n* citizen of a particular nation (某国的)公民: *He's a French national working in Italy.* 他是在意大利工作的法国人.

na·tion·ally /ˈnæʃnəlɪ; ˋnæʃənlɪ/ *adv.*

□ ˌ**national ˈanthem** song or hymn adopted by a nation, used to express loyalty and patriotism, esp on ceremonial occasions 国歌.

ˌ**national asˈsistance** (*Brit*) (formerly) money given by the government to people in need through illness, old age, etc (now called *supplementary benefit*) (旧时)(政府给病人、老年人等的)救济金, 补助金(现称为supplementary benefit).

the ˌ**National ˈDebt** the total amount of money owed by a country to those who have lent it money 国债; 公债.

ˌ**National ˈGuard** (*US*) state militia that can be called into active service by the state or federal government 国民警卫队.

ˌ**National ˈHealth Service** (*abbr* 缩写 **NHS**) (in Britain) public service providing medical care, paid for by taxation (英国)国民保健署: *I got my hearing aid on the National Health (Service).* 我的助听器是国民保健署资助的.

ˌ**National Inˈsurance** (*abbr* 缩写 **NI**) (*Brit*) system of compulsory payments made by employees and employers to provide State assistance to people who are ill, unemployed, retired, etc 国民保险制度.

ˌ**national ˈpark** area of countryside whose natural beauty is maintained by the State for the public to enjoy 国家公园.

ˌ**national ˈservice** period of compulsory service in the armed forces 义务兵役: *do one's national service* 服兵役.

ˌ**National ˈTrust** (in Britain) society founded in 1895 to preserve places of natural beauty or historic interest (英国)全国名胜古迹托管协会(创立于1895年).

na·tion·al·ism /ˈnæʃnəlɪzəm; ˋnæʃənl͵ɪzəm/ *n* [U] **1** devotion to one's own nation; patriotic feelings, principles or efforts 爱国心; 国家主义; 民族主义. **2** movement favouring political independence in a country that is controlled by another or is part of another (受他国管辖的国家里的)政治独立运动.

▷ **na·tion·al·ist** /ˈnæʃnəlɪst; ˋnæʃənlɪst/ *n* supporter of nationalism(2) 政治独立运动的拥护者: *Scottish nationalists*, ie those who want Scotland to have more self-government 苏格兰自治论者 ○ [attrib 作定语] *nationalist sympathies* 对政治独立运动的同情.

na·tion·al·istic /ˌnæʃnəˈlɪstɪk; ͵næʃənlˋɪstɪk/ *adj* strongly favouring nationalism 国家主义的; 民族主义的: *nationalistic fervour during the World Cup* 世界杯足球赛期间的国家主义狂热.

na·tion·al·ity /ˌnæʃəˈnælətɪ; ͵næʃənˋælətɪ/ *n* **1** [U, C] membership of a particular nation 国籍: *What is your nationality?* 你是哪国人? ○ *He has French nationality.* 他是法国籍. ○ *There were diplomats of all nationalities in Geneva.* 日内瓦有世界各国的外交官. **2** [C] ethnic group forming part of a political nation (构成国家一部分的)民族群体: *the two main nationalities of former Czechoslovakia* 前捷克斯洛伐克的两大民族.

na·tion·al·ize, -ise /ˈnæʃnəlaɪz; ˋnæʃənl͵aɪz/ *v* [Tn] **1** transfer (sth) from private to public ownership 将(某物)归为公有; 公有化: *nationalize the railways, the coal-mines, the steel industry, etc* 把铁路、煤矿、钢铁工业等归为公有 ○ *a nationalized industry* 公有化的工业. Cf 参看 DENATIONALIZE, PRIVATIZE. **2** make (sb) a national 使(某人)归化为一国的公民: *nationalized Poles and Greeks in the USA* 已成为美国公民的波兰人和希腊人.

▷ **na·tion·al·iza·tion, -isation** /ˌnæʃnəlaɪˈzeɪʃn; *US* -lɪˈz-; ͵næʃənlɪˋzeʃən/ *n* [U] nationalizing or being nationalized 国有化: *the nationalization of the railways* 铁路的国有化.

nat·ive /ˈneɪtɪv; ˋnetɪv/ *n* **1** (**a**) person born in a place, country, etc, and associated with it by birth 当地人; 本国人: *a native of London, Wales, India, Kenya* 伦敦、威尔士、印度、肯尼亚的本地人. (**b**) local inhabitant 当地居民: *When we're on holiday in Greece, we live like the natives.* 我们在希腊度假时, 就像当地人那样生活. **2** (*esp offensive* 尤作轻蔑语) local inhabitant as distinguished from immigrants, visitors, etc, when the race to which he belongs is regarded as less civilized 土著; 土人: *The white people here don't mix socially with the natives.* 这里的白种人不与土人交往. ○ *the first meeting between Captain Cook and the natives* (ie the aboriginal inhabitants) *of Australia* 库克上校与澳洲土著的初次会面. **3** animal or plant that lives or grows naturally in a certain area 天然生长于某地的动物或植物: *The kangaroo is a native of Australia.* 袋鼠是产于澳洲的动物.

▷ **nat·ive** *adj* **1** associated with the place and circumstances of one's birth 出生地的; 与出生地有关的: *one's native land, city, etc* 故土、故里 ○ *Her native language/tongue is German.* 她的母语是德语. **2** of natives(1a) 当地人的: *native customs, rituals, etc* 当地人的风俗、礼仪等. **3** (of qualities) belonging to a person's basic personality or character, not acquired by education, training, etc (指品质)与生俱来的, 天赋的, 天生的: *He has a great deal of native intelligence, ability, charm, etc.* 他天生聪明、能力强、有魅力等等. **4** **~ to...** (of plants, animals, etc) originating in a place (指动植物等)原产于某地的: *plants native to America*, eg tobacco, potatoes 原产于美洲的植物(如烟草、马铃薯) ○ *The tiger is native to India.* 这种虎原产于印度. **5** (idm 习语) **go ˈnative** (*esp joc* 尤作戏谑语) (of an immigrant, a visitor, etc) adopt the customs of the local people and abandon those of one's own (指移民、访客等)接受当地人的(而放弃自己的)风俗习惯, 同化: *He's emigrated to the USA and gone completely native.* 他已移居美国, 完全成了美国人.

□ ˌ**native ˈspeaker** person who has spoken (a particular language) since birth, rather than learning it later 生来就说某种语言的人: *a native speaker of French, Italian, etc* 生来就说法语、意大利语等的人 ○ *Her English accent is so good, you would think she was a native speaker.* 她的英语口音很纯正, 谁都以为她生来就说英语.

na·tiv·ity /nəˈtɪvətɪ; nəˋtɪvətɪ/ *n* **1 the Nativity** [sing] the birth of Jesus Christ 耶稣基督的诞生. **2 Nativity** [C] painting of the birth of Christ 基督诞生图.

□ **naˈtivity play** play about the birth of Christ 基督诞生剧.

NATO (also **Nato**) /ˈneɪtəʊ; ˋneto/ *abbr* 缩写 = North Atlantic Treaty Organization (an alliance of several European countries, USA, Canada and Iceland agreeing to give each other military help if necessary) 北大西洋公约组织. Cf 参看 SEATO.

nat·ter /ˈnætə(r); ˋnætɚ/ *v* [I, Ipr, Ip] **~ (on) (about**

N

sth) (*Brit infml* 口) talk informally and aimlessly; chatter 闲聊; 喋喋不休: *He nattered (on) about his work.* 他唠叨自己的工作.

▷ **nat·ter** *n* [sing] (*Brit infml* 口) informal conversation 随便的交谈: *have a quick natter* 匆匆地交谈.

natty /ˈnætɪ; ˋnætɪ/ *adj* (**-ier, -iest**) (*infml* 口) **1** (*often derog* 常作贬义) smart and tidy; neat 神气而整齐的; 齐整的: *natty new uniforms for policewomen* 给女警察穿的神气笔挺的新制服. **2** well thought out; clever 考虑周到的; 聪明的; 机敏的: *a natty little machine* 设计小巧的机器 ○ *a natty solution to a problem* 对一问题妥善的解决办法. ▷ **nat·tily** *adv* (*often derog* 常作贬义): *nattily dressed* 穿得神气而整齐.

nat·ural /ˈnætʃrəl; ˋnætʃrəl/ *adj* **1** [attrib 作定语] of, concerned with or produced by nature(1), not by human beings 自然的; 与自然有关的; 自然产生的; 天然的: *natural phenomena, forces, etc*, eg thunderstorms, earthquakes, gravity 自然现象、力量等 ○ *the natural world*, ie of trees, rivers, animals and birds 自然界 ○ *animals living in their natural state*, ie in the wild 生活于自然环境中的动物 ○ *a country's natural resources*, ie its coal, oil, forests, etc 国家的自然资源 ○ *land in its natural state*, ie not used for industry, farming, etc 天然状态的土地(未用于工业、耕种等). **2** of or in agreement with the character or personality of a living thing 与(生物的)特性或本性一致的; 本能的: *natural charm, ability, etc* 天赋的魅力、能力等 ○ *She has the natural grace of a born dancer.* 她生来具有舞蹈家的优雅风度. ○ *It is natural for a bird to fly.* 鸟天生就会飞. **3** [attrib 作定语] (of people) born with a certain skill, ability, etc (指人)(某种技能、能力等)生来就有的: *He's a natural orator*, ie is very good at making speeches. 他是天生的演说家(很善于演讲). ○ *She's a natural linguist*, ie learns languages easily. 她有语言天赋(学习语言毫不费力). **4** as (might be) expected; normal 意料之中的; 正常的: *die a natural death/of natural causes*, ie not by violence, etc, but normally, of old age 自然死亡(非暴力等所致, 而是寿终) ○ *It's only natural that she should be upset by the insult.* 她因受侮辱而生气, 那是很自然的. **5** not exaggerated or self-conscious; straightforward 不夸张的; 不做作的; 坦率的: *natural behaviour, manners, speech, etc* 不做作的行为、举止、讲话等 ○ *It is difficult to be natural when one is tense.* 人在紧张的时候很难泰然自若. **6** (*music* 音) (used after the name of the note 用于音符名称之后) (of notes) neither sharp nor flat (指音符)本位音的: *B natural* B本位音. ⇨ illus at MUSIC 见 MUSIC 插图, Cf 参看 FLAT[4] 2, SHARP *n*. **7** (**a**) (of a son or daughter) related by blood (指子女)有血统关系的, 亲生的: *He's not our natural son — we adopted him when he was three.* 他不是我们的亲儿子——他三岁时我们领养的. (**b**) illegitimate 私生的: *her natural child* 她的私生子. **8** based on human reason alone 仅基于人的理性的: *natural justice* 天赋的正义感 ○ *natural religion*, ie not based on divine revelation 自然宗教(并非基于神的启示).

▷ **nat·ural** *n* **1** (*music* 音) (**a**) musical note that is neither sharp nor flat 本位音: *There are two naturals in this chord.* 这一和弦中有两个本位音. (**b**) the sign (♮) placed before a note in printed music to show that it is neither sharp nor flat (乐谱上的)本位记号. **2** ~ **(for sth)** person considered ideally suited for a role, a job, an activity, etc (对某角色、职业、活动等)适合的人: *He's a natural for the role of Lear.* 他是李尔王这一角色的理想人选. ○ *She didn't have to learn how to run: she's a natural.* 她不用学跑步技巧, 她天生就擅跑.

nat·ural·ness *n* [U] state or quality of being natural 自然状态; 自然性.

□ ˌ**natural** ˈ**childbirth** method of childbirth in which the mother is given no anaesthetic and does breathing and relaxation exercises 自然分娩法.

ˌ**natural** ˈ**gas** gas found in the earth's crust, not manufactured 天然气.

ˌ**natural** ˈ**history** study of plants and animals 动植物学; 博物学: *the natural history of the Gobi desert* 戈壁沙漠的动植物学 ○ [attrib 作定语] *a natural history programme on TV* 电视播放的博物学节目.

ˌ**natural** ˈ**law** rules for behaviour considered to be basic to human nature 自然法.

ˌ**natural phi**ˈ**losophy** (*dated* 旧) science of physics, or physics and dynamics 自然哲学; 物理学; 物理学和力学.

ˌ**natural se**ˈ**lection** evolutionary theory that animals survive or become extinct according to their ability to adapt themselves to their environment 自然选择; 天择.

nat·ur·al·ism /ˈnætʃrəlɪzəm; ˋnætʃrəlˌɪzəm/ *n* [U] **1** style of art and literature in which there is faithful representation of real life (文艺的)自然主义. **2** (*philosophy* 哲) theory that rejects the supernatural and claims that natural causes and laws explain everything 自然主义. ▷ **nat·ur·al·istic** /ˌnætʃrəˈlɪstɪk; ˌnætʃrəlˈɪstɪk/ *adj*: *a naturalistic style, writer, painter* 自然主义的风格、作家、画家.

nat·ur·al·ist /ˈnætʃrəlɪst; ˋnætʃrəlɪst/ *n* person who studies animals, plants, birds and other living things 博物学家.

nat·ur·al·ize, -ise /ˈnætʃrəlaɪz; ˋnætʃrəlˌaɪz/ *v* [Tn usu passive 通常用于被动语态] ~ **sb/sth (in...)** **1** make (sb from another country) a citizen (of the specified country) 使(外国人)入籍, 归化: *a naturalized American who was born in Poland* 出生于波兰而入美国籍的人 ○ *She's a German who was naturalized in Canada.* 她是入了加拿大籍的德国人. **2** adopt (a foreign word, expression, etc) into a language 引进(外国词语等): *English sporting terms have been naturalized in many languages.* 英语的运动术语已被多种语言采用. **3** introduce (a plant or an animal) into a country where it is not native 引进(动植物).

▷ **nat·ur·al·iza·tion, -isation** /ˌnætʃrəlaɪˈzeɪʃn; *US* -lɪˈz-; ˌnætʃrəlɪˋzeʃən/ *n* [U] naturalizing or being naturalized 归化; 入籍; 引进: [attrib 作定语] *naturalization papers*, ie documents that prove that a person has been made a citizen of a country 归化证书.

nat·ur·ally /ˈnætʃrəlɪ; ˋnætʃrəlɪ/ *adv* **1** by nature(4a) 天生地: *a naturally gifted actor* 天才的演员 ○ *She's naturally musical.* 她天生喜爱音乐. **2** of course; as might be expected 当然; 必然: *'Did you answer her letter?' 'Naturally!'* '你给她回信了吗?' '当然了!' ○ *Naturally, as a beginner I'm not a very good driver yet.* 我初学开车, 当然开不好了. **3** without artificial help, special treatment, etc 天然; 非人为地: *Her hair curls naturally.* 她天生鬈发. ○ *Plants grow naturally in such a good climate.* 在这么好的气候条件下, 植物可以自然生长. **4** without exaggeration; unselfconsciously 不夸张地; 不做作地: *She speaks and behaves naturally.* 她言谈举止很自然. ○ *Try to act naturally, even if you're tense.* 即使紧张也不要做作. **5** easily; instinctively 容易地; 本能地: *He's such a good athlete that most sports come naturally to him.* 他擅长运动, 多数运动项目对他来说都轻而易举.

na·ture /ˈneɪtʃə(r); ˋnetʃɚ/ *n* **1** [U] the whole universe and every created, not man-made, thing 宇宙和(非人造的)万物; 自然界; 大自然: *the wonders of nature* 大自然的奥妙 ○ *This phenomenon is unique in (the whole of) nature.* 这种现象在(整个)自然界是罕见的. ○ [attrib 作定语] *nature worship* 自然崇拜. **2** [U] simple life of man before he became civilized (文明前的)简朴生活: *He wants to give away all his modern possessions and return to nature.* 他要舍弃一切时髦的东西而归真返璞. **3** [U] (esp 尤作 **Nature**) force(s) controlling the events of the physical world 大自然的力量: *Man is engaged in a constant struggle with Nature.* 人类与大自然进行不懈的斗争. ○ *Miracles are contrary to nature.* 奇迹是与大自然的力量相对的. **4** (**a**) [C, U] typical qualities and characteristics of a person or an animal (人或动物的)本性, 天性: *It's his nature* (ie It's his natural reaction) *to be kind to people.* 他为人厚道. ○ *There is no cruelty in her nature.* 她心地善良. ○ *Cats and dogs have quite different natures — dogs like company, cats are independent.* 猫和狗的习性迥异——狗喜欢有伴, 猫爱独来独往. ○ *She is proud by nature.* 她生性傲慢. (**b**) [sing] qualities of a material or non-material thing 性质: *Chemists study the nature of gases.* 有的化学家研究气体的性质. ○ *He knows nothing of the nature of my work.* 他一点也不了解我的工作性质. **5** [sing] sort; kind 种类; 类别: *Things of that nature do not interest me.* 我对那种事物不感兴趣. **6** (idm 习语) **against** ˈ**nature** unnatural; immoral 违反自然的; 不合情理的; 不道德的. **one's better feelings/nature** ⇨ BETTER[1]. **a call of nature** ⇨ CALL[1]. **in the nature of sth** similar to/like sth; a type of sth 与某事物相似[类似]; 某事物之类: *His speech was in the nature* *of an apology.* 他讲的话就算是道歉. **in a state of nature** ⇨ STATE[1]. **second 'nature (to sb)** what seems natural or instinctive, but has been learned 第二种天性(学得的近于天生的或本能的事物): *After a while, driving becomes second nature to you.* 过不多久, 开车的动作就像本能的反应一样了.

▷ **-natured** (forming compound *adjs* 用以构成复合形容词) having qualities or characteristics of the specified kind 具有某种本性或性格的: *ˌgood-'natured* ○ *pleasant-natured.*

□ **'nature study** (in school) study of plants, animals, insects, etc (学校的)自然课.

'nature trail path through woods or countryside, along which interesting plants, animals, etc can be seen 穿过树林或郊野的小路(沿途可见有趣的动植物等).

na·tur·ism /ˈneɪtʃərɪzəm; ˋnetʃərɪzəm/ *n* [U] = NUDISM.
▷ **na·tur·ist** /ˈneɪtʃərɪst; ˋnetʃərɪst/ *n* = NUDIST.

na·turo·path /ˈneɪtʃrəpæθ; ˋnetʃərəˌpæθ/ *n* person who treats illness by suggesting changes of diet, exercise, etc and without using medicines 自然疗法家(通过改变饮食、锻炼等而不用药物治病者). ▷ **na·turo·pathic** /ˌneɪtʃrəˈpæθɪk; ˌnetʃərəˋpæθɪk/ *adj.* **na·turo·pathic·ally** /-klɪ; -kəlɪ/ *adv.* **na·turo·pathy** /ˌneɪtʃəˈrɒpəθɪ; ˌnetʃəˋrɑpəθɪ/ *n* [U].

naught = NOUGHT 2.

naughty /ˈnɔːtɪ; ˋnɔtɪ/ *adj* (**-ier**, **-iest**) **1** (*infml* 口) (used by adults when talking to or about children 成年人与儿童说话或谈论儿童时用) disobedient; bad; causing trouble 不听话的; 坏的; 惹麻烦的: *He's a terribly naughty child.* 他是个调皮捣蛋的孩子. ○ *You were naughty to pull the cat's tail.* 你揪猫尾巴, 太淘气了. **2** shocking or intended to shock people through mild indecency (用隐晦的低级言行)刺激人的: *a naughty joke, story, etc* 低级的笑话、故事等. ▷ **naugh·tily** *adv.* **naugh·ti·ness** *n* [U].

nausea /ˈnɔːsɪə; *US* ˈnɔːʒə; ˋnɔʒə/ *n* [U] feeling of sickness or disgust 作呕; 恶心: *overcome by nausea after eating raw meat* 吃生肉以后恶心得难受 ○ *filled with nausea at the sight of cruelty to animals* 看到虐待动物而极为厌恶.

▷ **naus·eate** /ˈnɔːsɪeɪt; *US* ˈnɔːz-; ˋnɔzɪˌet/ *v* [Tn] make (sb) feel nausea 使(某人)感到恶心: *The idea of eating raw shellfish nauseates me.* 我一想到吃生贝就恶心. **naus·eat·ing** *adj*: *nauseating food* 令人作呕的食物 ○ *a nauseating person* 令人厌恶的人 ○ *The smell is quite nauseating.* 这气味真叫人恶心. **naus·eat·ingly** *adv.*

naus·eous /ˈnɔːsɪəs; *US* ˈnɔːʃəs; ˋnɔʃəs/ *adj* **1** causing nausea; disgusting 令人作呕的; 令人厌恶的. **2** (*esp US*) feeling nausea or disgust 感到恶心或厌恶的: *She felt/was nauseous during the sea crossing.* 她渡海时觉得恶心.

naut·ical /ˈnɔːtɪkl; ˋnɔtɪkl/ *adj* of ships, sailors or navigation 船舶的; 海员的; 航海的: *nautical terms,* ie used by sailors 航海术语 ○ *A nautical almanac gives information about the sun, moon, tides, etc.* 航海年历中有日、月、潮汐等的资料.

□ **ˌnautical 'mile** (also **sea mile**) measure of distance at sea, about 6 080 ft (1 852 metres) 海里(约6 080英尺或1 852米). ⇨App 5 见附录5.

naut·ilus /ˈnɔːtɪləs; *US* ˈnɔːtələs; ˋnɔtḷəs/ *n* (*pl* **~es**) small sea animal that has a spiral-shaped shell, the female's being very thin 鹦鹉螺.

naval /ˈneɪvl; ˋnevḷ/ *adj* of a navy; of warships 海军的; 军舰的: *a naval officer, uniform, battle* 海军军官、海军制服、海战 ○ *a naval power,* ie a country with a strong navy 海军强国.

nave /neɪv; nev/ *n* long central part of a church, where the congregation(1) sits 中堂(教堂的正厅). ⇨illus at App 1 见附录1插图, page viii.

na·vel /ˈneɪvl; ˋnevḷ/ *n* (in humans) small hollow in the middle of the belly where the umbilical cord was attached at birth 肚脐. ⇨illus at HUMAN 见HUMAN插图.

□ **ˌnavel 'orange** large orange with a navel-like formation at the top 脐橙.

nav·ig·able /ˈnævɪgəbl; ˋnævəgəbl/ *adj* **1** (of seas, rivers, etc) suitable for ships, boats, etc to sail on (指海洋、江河等)适于行船的, 可通航的: *The Rhine is navigable from Strasbourg to the sea.* 莱茵河从斯特拉斯堡入海这一段可以通航. **2** (of ships, etc) that can be steered and sailed (指船等)可驾驶的, 可航行的: *not in a navigable condition* 不能航行. ▷ **nav·ig·ab·il·ity** /ˌnævɪgəˈbɪlətɪ; ˌnævəgəˋbɪlətɪ/ *n* [U].

nav·ig·ate /ˈnævɪgeɪt; ˋnævəˌget/ *v* **1** [I] find the position and plot the course of a ship, an aircraft, a car, etc, using maps and instruments (利用地图和仪器)测定(船、飞行器、汽车等的)位置和路线; 导航; 领航: *Which officer in the ship navigates?* 舰上哪个军官引航? ○ *I'll drive the car: you navigate,* ie tell me which way to go. 我来开车, 你指路. **2** [Tn, Tn·pr] steer (a ship); pilot (an aircraft) 驾驶(船舶、飞行器等): *navigate the tanker round the Cape* 驾驶油轮绕过好望角 ○ (*fig* 比喻) *navigate a Bill through Parliament* 使一法案在国会通过. **3** [Tn] (**a**) sail along, over or through (a sea, river, etc) 在(海、河等)上航行; 横渡(海、河等): *Who first navigated the Atlantic?* 是谁首先横渡大西洋的? ○ *the first woman to navigate the Amazon alone* 第一个独自在亚马孙河上航行的女子. (**b**) (*fig* 比喻) find one's way through, over, etc (sth) 设法穿越: *I don't like having to navigate London's crowded streets.* 我不愿意在伦敦拥挤的街道上穿行.

▷ **nav·iga·tion** /ˌnævɪˈgeɪʃn; ˌnævəˋgeʃən/ *n* [U] **1** action of navigating 航海; 航空; 驾驶. **2** art or science of navigating 航行学; 航海术; 航空术: *an expert in navigation* 航行学专家. **3** movement of ships over water or aircraft through the air 航行: *There has been an increase in navigation through the canal,* ie More ships use it. 通过该运河的船只已经增加了.

nav·ig·ator *n* **1** person who navigates 导航者; 领航员; 驾驶员; 司机的引路人. **2** early explorer travelling by ship 早期的航海探险者: *the 16th-century Spanish and Portuguese navigators* 16世纪西班牙和葡萄牙的航海家.

navvy /ˈnævɪ; ˋnævɪ/ *n* (*Brit*) unskilled manual labourer who works on a building site, etc (工地等的)无技术的工人.

navy /ˈneɪvɪ; ˋnevɪ/ **1** *n* (**a**) [C] country's force of ships and their crews 海军: *naval exercises involving six navies* 有六国海军参加的海军演习. (**b**) **the navy, the Navy** [Gp] warships of a specific country with their crews and the organization that administers them 海军部队: *join the navy,* ie of one's own country 参加海军 ○ *an officer/sailor in the Royal Navy* 皇家海军军官[水兵] ○ *The navy is/are introducing a new class of warship this year.* 海军今年要装备新一级的军舰. ⇨App 9 见附录9. **2** [U] = NAVY BLUE.

□ **ˌnavy 'blue** (also **navy**) dark blue as used for naval uniforms 海军蓝; 深蓝色: *Where's my navy (blue) suit?* 我那套海军蓝的西装在哪儿?

nay /neɪ; ne/ *adv* (*dated or rhet* 旧或修辞) **1** and more than that; and indeed 不止于此; 而且的确: *I suspect, nay, I am certain, that he is wrong.* 我怀疑, 何止怀疑, 我肯定他错了. **2** (*arch* 古) no 无; 否. Cf 参看 YEA.

Nazi /ˈnɑːtsɪ; ˋnɑtsɪ/ *n, adj* (member) of the German National Socialist Party founded by Hitler (希特勒创建的)德国国家社会党的(党员); 纳粹党的(党员): *the rise of the Nazis* 纳粹党的崛起 ○ *a Nazi meeting, newspaper* 纳粹的集会、报纸.

▷ **Naz·ism** /ˈnɑːtsɪzəm; ˋnɑtsˌɪzəm/ *n* ideology of the Nazis, including belief in German racial superiority 纳粹主义.

NB (also **nb**) /ˌen ˈbiː; ˌɛn ˋbi/ *abbr* 缩写 = (used before a written note 用于书面注意事项前) take special notice of; note well (Latin *nota bene*) 注意, 留心(源自拉丁文 *nota bene*).

NBC /ˌen biː ˈsiː; ˌɛn bi ˋsi/ *abbr* 缩写 = (*US*) National Broadcasting Company 全国广播公司: *heard it on NBC* 从美国全国广播公司电台听到的.

NCO /ˌen siː ˈəʊ; ˌɛn si ˋo/ *abbr* 缩写 = (*Brit*) non-commissioned officer 军士.

NE *abbr* 缩写 = North-East(ern): *NE Kent* 肯特郡东北部.

Ne·an·der·thal /niːˈændətɑːl; nɪˋændɚˌtɑl/ *adj* of an extinct type of man living in Europe in the Stone Age (石器时代生活于欧洲, 现已绝种的)尼安德特人的: *Neanderthal man* 尼安德特人 ○ *Neanderthal culture, artefacts, etc* 尼安德特文化、手工制品等.

neap /niːp; nip/ (also **'neap-tide**) *n* tide when there is least difference between high and low water 小潮. Cf 参看 SPRING-TIDE (SPRING[1]).

N

Nea·pol·itan /nɪəˈpɒlɪtən; ˌniəˈpɑlətn̩/ **1** *n, adj* (inhabitant) of Naples 那不勒斯的; 那不勒斯人. **2 neapolitan** *adj* (of ice cream) in layers of different colours and flavours (指冰激凌)多味的(各层颜色、味道不同的).

near[1] /nɪə(r); nɪr/ *adj* (**-er** /ˈnɪərə(r); ˈnɪrɚ/ **-est** /ˈnɪərɪst; ˈnɪrɪst/) **~ (to sb/sth) 1** [usu pred except *nearest* 通常作表语, 仅 nearest 例外] within a short distance or time from sb/sth; not far (from sb/sth) 与某人[某事物]距离或时间近; (距某人[某事物])不远: *His flat's very near.* 他的公寓就在附近. ○ *Where's the nearest bus-stop?* 最近的公共汽车站在哪儿? ○ *The supermarket is very near (to) the station.* 超级市场离车站很近. ○ *We hope to move to the country in the near future,* ie very soon. 我们希望最近搬到乡村去住. ○ *4.15 is too near to the time of departure.* 4点15分离分别的时间太近了. **2** closely related 关系近的; 关系密切的: *a near relation/relative* 血统关系近的人 ○ *The nearest member of my family still alive is a rather distant cousin.* 我家在世的近亲是我的远房堂兄. **3** [pred except *nearest* 作表语, 仅 nearest 例外] similar 近似; 相似: *We don't have that colour in stock — this is the nearest.* 我们的现货中没有那种颜色 —— 这是最近似的. ○ *This copy is nearer the original than the others I've seen.* 这个副本比我见到的其他副本更接近原件. ⇨Usage at NEXT[1] 用法见 NEXT[1]. **4** = NEARSIDE. **5** (idm 习语) **close/dear/near to sb's heart** ⇨ HEART. **a close/near thing** ⇨ THING. **close/near to home** ⇨ HOME[1]. **one's ˌnearest and ˈdearest** (*joc* 谑) one's close family 亲人: *I always spend Christmas with my nearest and dearest.* 我总是和亲人一起过圣诞节. **or ˌnear(est) ˈoffer** (*abbr* 缩写 **ono**) or an amount that is less than the specified price but more than other offers 或略低于此价; 可还价: *I'll accept £350 for the car, or nearest offer.* 我的汽车卖350英镑, 可还价. **a ˌnear ˈmiss (a)** bomb, shot, etc that lands near the target but not quite on it 炸弹、炮弹等接近目标, 但未命中. **(b)** situation where one just avoids, or escapes from, some mishap 幸免: *Luckily the van ahead of us skidded off the road on our left, but it was a very near miss.* 我们前面的客货车滑出我们左边的路, 侥幸没撞上.

▷ **near** *v* [I, Tn] come closer to (sth) in space or time; approach (在空间或时间上)更接近(某事物); 接近; 靠近: *The day is nearing when we'll have to decide.* 我们必须做出决定的日子即将来临. ○ *The job is at last nearing completion.* 这项工作终于快要完成了. ○ *The ship was nearing land.* 船已接近陆地. ○ *The old man was nearing his end.* 那老人大限已到.

near·ness *n* [U].

□ **the ˌnear ˈdistance** part of a scene between the foreground and the background 近景: *You can see the river in the near distance and the mountains beyond.* 从这里可以看到近处的河及远处的山.

the ˌNear ˈEast = THE MIDDLE EAST (MIDDLE).

ˈnearside (also **near**) *adj* [attrib 作定语] (*Brit*) (of a part of a vehicle, a road or an animal) on the left-hand side (指车辆、道路或动物的部分)左边的: *the nearside front wheel, door, lane of traffic, etc* 左前轮、左边的门、左边的车道 ○ *the near foreleg of a horse* 马的左前腿 ○ *He didn't see the car approaching on his nearside.* 他没有看见左边来的汽车. Cf 参看 OFFSIDE[2].

ˌnear-ˈsighted *adj* only able to see clearly things that are close to one's eyes; short-sighted 近视的: *I'm very near-sighted without my glasses on.* 我要是不戴眼镜十分近视. **ˌnear-ˈsightedness** *n* [U]

NOTE ON USAGE 用法: Compare **near**, **nearby** and **near by**. 试比较 **near**、**nearby**、**near by**. ☆ Only **near** has a comparative and superlative form and can relate to time as well as space. 只有 **near** 有比较级和最高级形式, 且可指时间和空间. **1** Both **near** and **nearby** are adjectives. ☆ **near** 和 **nearby** 都是形容词. **Nearby**, not **near**, is used attributively when space, not time, is referred to 若指空间, 非时间, 要用 **nearby** 修饰, 不可用 **near**: *the near future* 不久的将来 ○ *Those shops are nearer/the nearest.* 那些商店离得更近[最近]. ○ *a nearby village* 附近的村子. **2** Both **near** and **near by** can be used adverbially. ☆ **near** 和 **near by** 都可用作状语. **Near by** sometimes modifies the whole sentence ☆ **near by** 有时可修饰整个句子: *Do you live near/near by?* 你住在附近吗? ○ *My exams are getting nearer.* 我不久就要考试了. ○ *Near by, the cars could be heard speeding past on the motorway.* 在附近可以听到汽车从高速公路上疾驶而过的声音. **3 Near (to)** is a preposition ☆ **near (to)** 是介词: *Is there a cinema near here?* 附近有电影院吗?

near[2] /nɪə(r); nɪr/ *prep* **1** with only a short distance or time between (距离或时间)接近, 靠近: *Bradford is near Leeds.* 布拉福靠近利兹. ○ *Don't sit near the door.* 别坐在门口儿. ○ *My birthday is very near Christmas.* 我的生日离圣诞节很近. **2** (idm 习语) **be, come, etc near to sth/doing sth** almost experience, reach or do sth 几乎; 差点儿: *I came near to screaming.* 我险些喊叫起来. ○ *She was near to tears,* ie almost crying. 她差点儿就哭了. ○ *He felt near to death.* 他觉得快要死了.

▷ **near** *adv* **1** at a short distance away; near by 在近处; 在附近: *We found some shops quite near.* 我们发现附近有几个商店. ○ *Are you all sitting near enough to see the screen?* 你们都坐得离屏幕够近吗? **2** (idm 习语) **as near as** as accurately as 达到...的准确程度: *There were about 500 people there, as near as I could judge.* 那里有500人, 依我看有这么多. **as ˌnear as ˈdammit; as ˌnear as ˌmakes no ˈdifference** (*infml* 口) an amount, a measurement, etc that is not significantly more or less 相差无几: *It's going to cost £200 or as near as dammit.* 这要花200英镑上下. ○ *It's 500 miles from here, or as near as makes no difference.* 离这儿有500英里, 差也差不多. **far and near/wide** ⇨ FAR[2]. **not anywhere/nowhere ˈnear** certainly not; far from 绝无; 肯定不; 离得远; 差得远: *The hall was nowhere near full.* 那大厅远未满座. ○ *I've nowhere near enough for the fare.* 我的钱肯定不够买车票的. ○ *There wasn't anywhere near enough to eat and drink.* 离吃饱喝足还远呢. ○ *It's nowhere near the colour I'm looking for.* 这种颜色跟我找的那种差远了. **so ˌnear and ˌyet so ˈfar** (used to comment on an attempt that was nearly successful but failed finally 用以评论几近成功却终于失败的尝试) 功亏一篑.

near- (forming compound *adjs* 用以构成复合形容词) almost 几乎; 近于: *near-ˈperfect* ○ *near-ˈvertical* ○ *a near-featureless ˈlandscape.*

□ **ˈnearby** *adj* [attrib 作定语] near in position; not far away 位置近的; 不远的: *a nearby church, river, town* 近处的教堂、河流、小镇.

near ˈby *adv* at a short distance from sb/sth 在附近: *They live near by.* 他们住在附近. ○ *The beach is quite near by.* 海滨离得很近. ⇨Usage at NEAR[1] 用法见 NEAR[1].

nearly /ˈnɪəlɪ; ˈnɪrlɪ/ *adv* **1** not completely; almost; very close to 不完全地; 几乎; 很接近地: *nearly empty, full, finished, etc* 近于空的、满的、结束等 ○ *It's nearly one o'clock.* 将近一点钟了. ○ *It's nearly time to leave.* 差不多是该走的时候了. ○ *We're nearly there.* 我们离那儿很近了. ○ *There's nearly £1 000 here.* 这儿差不多有1 000英镑. ○ *She nearly won first prize.* 她几乎得到头奖. **2** (idm 习语) **not nearly** far from; much less than 相差很远; 远远少于: *There isn't nearly enough time to learn all these words.* 要把这些新词都学会了, 时间远远不够. ○ *We aren't nearly ready for the inspection.* 对检查一事, 我们还远未准备好. **pretty much/nearly/well** ⇨ PRETTY. ⇨Usage at ALMOST 用法见 ALMOST.

neat /ni:t; nit/ *adj* **1 (a)** (of things) arranged in an orderly way; done carefully; tidy (指事物)安排有序的, 细心完成的, 整齐的: *a neat cupboard, room, row of books, garden* 整齐的柜橱、房间、一排书、花园 ○ *neat work, writing, etc* 精心的作品、写得匀整的字. **(b)** (of people) liking to keep order and do things carefully; tidy (指人)喜欢整齐的, 细心的, 齐整的: *a neat worker, dresser, etc* 利落的工人、衣着整齐的人. **2 (a)** (of clothes) simple and elegant (指衣服)朴素而雅致的: *a neat uniform, dress, etc* 朴素的制服、雅致的连衣裙. **(b)** having a pleasing shape or appearance 形状或外貌悦目的: *She has a neat figure.* 她身材匀称. **3** economical with time and effort; skilful; efficient 省时省力的; 熟练的; 效率高的: *a neat way of doing the job* 做事的简捷方法 ○ *a neat solution to the problem* 对该问题妥善的解决 ○ *He gave a neat summary of the financial situation.* 他对财务状况做了简要的概括. **4** (*infml* 口 *esp US*) fine; splendid 好的; 绝妙的: *a neat movie, idea, car* 好的电影、主意、汽车. **5** (*US* usu 美式英语通常作 **straight**) (of spirits or wines) unmixed with water; undiluted (指酒类)不搀水的, 不稀释的, 纯的: *a neat whisky, vodka, etc* 纯威士忌、伏特加等 ○ *drink one's whisky neat* 喝纯威士忌. ▷ **neatly** *adv*. **neat·ness** *n* [U].

neb·ula /ˈnebjʊlə; ˋnɛbjələ/ *n* (*pl* **~e** /-liː; -ˌli/ or **~s**) light or dark patch in the night sky caused by a cluster of very distant stars or a cloud of dust or gas 星云: *the Crab nebula* 巨蟹座星云.

▷ **neb·ular** /-lə(r); -lɚ/ *adj* of nebulas 星云的.

neb·ulous /ˈnebjʊləs; ˋnɛbjələs/ *adj* **1** cloudlike; hazy 似云的; 云状的; 模糊的. **2** (*fig* 比喻) vague; unclear 含糊的; 模糊的; 不清晰的; 不明白的: *nebulous ideas, plans, concepts, etc* 模糊的思想、计划、概念等.

ne·ces·sar·ily /ˌnesəˈserəlɪ *or, in British use,* 英式英语读作 ˈnesəsərəlɪ; ˋnɛsəˌsɛrəlɪ/ *adv* as an inevitable result 必然; 必定: *Big men aren't necessarily strong men.* 高大的人不一定强壮.

ne·ces·sary /ˈnesəsərɪ; *US* -serɪ; ˋnɛsəˌsɛrɪ/ *adj* **1** essential for a purpose; that cannot be done without or avoided 必须的; 必需的; 必不可少的; 不可避免的: *I haven't got the necessary tools.* 我没有必需的工具. ○ *Is it necessary for us to meet/necessary that we meet?* 我们非见面不可吗? ○ *She hasn't the experience necessary for the job.* 她没有做那事所需要的经验. ○ *Sleep is necessary to/for one's health.* 睡眠对健康是必不可少的. **2** that must be; inevitable 必然的; 必定的; 无可避免的: *If a = b, and b = c, then the necessary conclusion is that a = c.* 设 a = b, b = c, 则结论必定是 a = c. ○ *the necessary consequences* 必然的结果. **3** (idm 习语) **a ˌnecessary ˈevil** thing that is undesirable and possibly harmful but must be accepted for practical reasons (按照实际情况)不得不认可的不合意甚至有害的事物: *The loss of jobs is regarded by some as a necessary evil in the fight against inflation.* 有些人认为要遏止通货膨胀就难免有人得失业.

▷ **ne·ces·sar·ies** *n* [pl] things needed for living 生活必需品: *the little necessaries of life* 一点儿生活必需品.

ne·ces·sit·ate /nɪˈsesɪteɪt; nəˋsɛsəˌtet/ *v* [Tn, Tg, Tsg] (*fml* 文) make (sth) necessary 使(某事物)成为必要: *It's an unpopular measure, but the situation necessitates it.* 这是不得人心的办法, 但形势需要这样做. ○ *Your proposal will necessitate borrowing more money.* 依你的建议, 就必须增加借款.

ne·ces·sit·ous /nɪˈsesɪtəs; nəˋsɛsətəs/ *adj* (*fml* 文) poor; needy 贫穷的; 贫困的: *in necessitous circumstances*, ie in poverty 处于贫困的境地.

ne·ces·sity /nɪˈsesətɪ; nəˋsɛsətɪ/ *n* **1** [U] **~ (for sth/to do sth)** circumstances that force one to do sth; state of being necessary; need 迫使人做某事的情况; 必要性; 需要: *He felt a great necessity to talk about his problems.* 他觉得很有必要谈谈自己的问题. ○ *She was driven by necessity to steal food for her starving children.* 环境逼得她为挨饿的儿女偷窃食物. ○ *We will always come in cases of extreme necessity*, ie if we are very much needed. 遇到紧急关头我们一定来. ○ *There's no necessity (for you) to write to your mother every single day.* (你)不必每天都给你母亲写信. ○ *We must all bow to necessity*, ie accept what is inevitable. 对无可奈何的事, 我们都得听之任之. **2** [C] necessary thing 必需品: *Food, clothing and shelter are all basic necessities of life.* 衣、食、住所是生活的基本必需品. **3** [sing] natural law that is seen as governing human action (控制人类活动的)自然规律: *Is it a logical necessity that higher wages will lead to higher prices?* 工资一高物价就高, 这是不是合乎逻辑的必然规律? **4** (idm 习语) **make a virtue of necessity** ⇨ VIRTUE. **neˌcessity is the ˌmother of inˈvention** (*saying* 谚) the need for sth forces people to find a way of getting it 需要是发明之母. **of neˈcessity** necessarily; unavoidably; inevitably 必要地; 不可避免地.

neck /nek; nɛk/ *n* **1** [C] (**a**) part of the body that connects the head to the shoulders 颈; 脖子: *wrap a scarf round one's neck* 在脖子上围条围巾 ○ *She fell and broke her neck.* 她摔断了脖子. ○ *Giraffes have very long necks.* 长颈鹿的脖子很长. ⇨illus at HEAD 见 HEAD 插图. (**b**) part of a garment round this 领口: *a V-neck sweater* V字领套头毛衣 ○ *My shirt is rather tight in the neck.* 我的衬衫领子太紧. ⇨illus 见插图. **2** [U, C] flesh of an animal's neck as food (作食物的)动物的颈肉: *buy some neck of lamb* 买点儿羊颈肉. **3** [C] narrow part of sth,

N

necks 领口

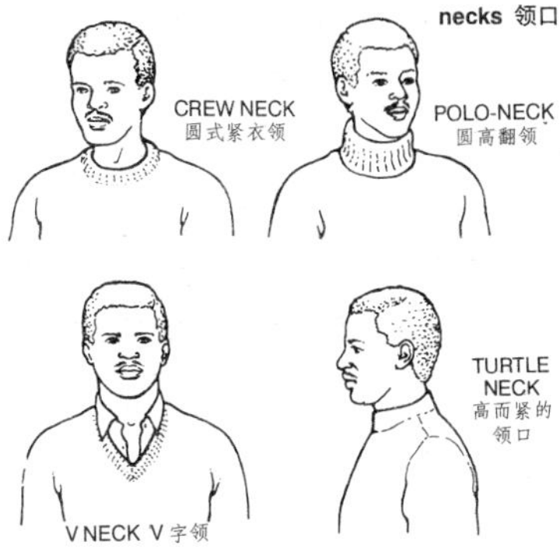

like a neck in shape or position 物体的狭窄部分(形状或部位像颈的): *the neck of a bottle/violin* 瓶子[小提琴]的颈部 ○ *a neck of land*, eg an isthmus 陆地的狭窄地带(如地峡). ⇨illus at App 1 见附录1插图, page xi. **4** (idm 习语) **break one's ˈneck (doing sth/to do sth)** (*infml* 口) work especially hard at sth 拼命做某事: *I'm not going to break my neck to finish my essay today — my teacher doesn't want it until next week.* 我今天不想玩儿命写完那篇文章——老师下星期才要呢. **breathe down sb's neck** ⇨ BREATHE. **ˌget it in the ˈneck** (*infml* 口) be severely scolded or punished for sth 因某事而受到严厉叱责或处罚: *You'll get it in the neck if you're caught stealing.* 要是发现你偷东西, 就要严厉处罚你. **a millstone round one's neck** ⇨ MILLSTONE (MILL[1]). **ˌneck and ˈcrop** completely 完全地; 全部地: *His shot beat the goalkeeper neck and crop.* 守门员根本挡不住他射门. **ˌneck and ˈneck (with sb/sth)** (in horse-racing or in a contest, struggle, etc) with neither one nor the other having an advantage or lead; level (在赛马或竞赛、斗争等中)双方势均力敌或无一领先, 平局, 平手: *The two contestants are neck and neck with 20 points each.* 比赛双方各得20分, 打成平局. **ˌneck of the ˈwoods** (*infml* 口) area; neighbourhood 地区; 附近: *What are you doing in this neck of the woods?* 你在这块儿干什么呢? **ˌneck or ˈnothing** taking great risks 冒很大危险; 拼命: *She drove neck or nothing to get there on time.* 她拼命开车以准时赶到那里. **a pain in the neck** ⇨ PAIN. **risk/save one's ˈneck** risk/save one's life; risk/avoid great misfortune 拼着[保住]性命; 可能遭遇[避免]不幸: *He saved his own neck by fleeing the country.* 他逃出国才得以活命. **stick one's neck out** ⇨ STICK[2]. **(be) up to one's neck in sth** very deeply involved in sth 深深陷入某事物中: *Even as a young man he was up to his neck in crime.* 他年轻时即已恶贯满盈. **win/lose by a ˈneck** (in horse-racing, etc) win/lose by a small margin (赛马等中的)稍胜[负], 小赢[输]. **wring sb's neck** ⇨ WRING.

▷ **neck** *v* [I] (*infml* 口) (of couples) hug and kiss each other intimately (指恋人)拥抱互吻: *The two of them were necking on a park bench.* 他们俩在公园的长凳上拥抱亲吻.

□ **ˈneckband** *n* narrow strip of material round the neck of a garment (衣服的)领圈.

neckerchief /ˈnekətʃɪf; ˋnɛkɚtʃɪf/ *n* scarf or piece of cloth worn round the neck 围巾; 领巾.

necklace /ˈneklɪs; ˋnɛklɪs/ *n* ornament of pearls, beads, etc worn round the neck 项链.

necklet /ˈneklɪt; ˋnɛklɪt/ *n* ornament or fur worn round the neck 颈饰; 毛皮围巾.

ˈneckline *n* outline of the edge of (esp) a woman's garment at or below the neck (尤指女装的)领口, 开领: *a dress with a high/low/plunging neckline* 高领[低领/深V字领]的连衣裙.

ˈnecktie *n* (*dated* 旧 *or US*) = TIE[1] 1.

ˈneckwear *n* [U] (in shops 商店用语) ties, scarves, etc 颈部服饰(领带、围巾、头巾、披肩等).

necr(o)- *comb form* 构词成分 of death or the dead 死

N

亡的；亡者的：*necromancer* ○ *necropolis*.

nec·ro·mancy /ˈnekrəʊmænsɪ; ˋnɛkrə,mænsɪ/ *n* [U] art or practice of communicating by magic with the dead in order to learn about the future 通灵(术)(与亡魂相通以占卜未来的巫术).

▷ **nec·ro·man·cer** /-sə(r); -sɚ/ *n* person who practises necromancy 通灵巫师.

nec·ro·polis /nɪˈkrɒpəlɪs; nɪˋkrɑpəlɪs/ *n* (*pl* **~es** /-lɪsɪz; -lɪsɪz/) cemetery, esp a large ancient one 墓地；公墓；(尤指)大片古塚.

nec·tar /ˈnektə(r); ˋnɛktɚ/ *n* [U] **1** sweet liquid produced by flowers and collected by bees for making honey 花蜜. **2** (in Greek and Roman mythology) the drink of the gods (希腊和罗马神话中的)神的饮品：(*fig* 比喻) *On a hot summer day a long cool drink is like nectar.* 在炎热的夏天喝一通冷饮如获琼浆玉液. Cf 参看 AMBROSIA.

nec·tar·ine /ˈnektərɪn; ˋnɛktə,rin/ *n* type of peach with a thin smooth skin and firm flesh 油桃.

NEDC /ˌen iː diː ˈsiː; ,ɛn i di ˋsi/ (also *infml* 口语作 **Neddy** /ˈnedɪ; ˋnɛdɪ/) *abbr* 缩写 = (*Brit*) National Economic Development Council 国家经济发展委员会.

née /neɪ; ne/ *adj* (used after the name of a married woman and before her father's family name 用于已婚妇女姓名之后，娘家姓氏之前) having had the maiden name; born with the name 娘家姓…的；本姓…的：*(Mrs) Jane Smith, née Brown* 娘家姓布朗的简·史密斯(夫人).

need[1] /niːd; nid/ *modal v* (*neg* 否定式 **need not**, *contracted form* 缩约式 **needn't** /ˈniːdnt; ˋnidn̩t/) (used only in negative sentences and questions, after *if* and *whether* or with *hardly, scarcely, no one*, etc 仅用于否定句及疑问句，或用于if及whether之后或与hardly、scarcely、no one等连用) **1** (indicating obligation 表示必要)：*You needn't finish that work today.* 你今天不必把那项工作做完. ○ *'Need you go yet?' 'No, I needn't.'* '你一定得去吗？''我不必去.' ○ *He wondered whether they need send a deposit.* 他不知道他们是否得交定金. ○ *If she wants anything, she need only ask.* 她想要什么，只需说一声就行. ○ *I need hardly tell you* (ie You must already know) *that the work is dangerous.* 无须我说你也知道那工作有危险. ○ *Nobody need be afraid of catching the disease.* 谁都不用害怕能得这种病. ⇨Usage 1 at MUST 见MUST所附用法第1项. **2** (used with *have* + a past participle to indicate that actions in the past were or may have been unnecessary 与have＋过去分词连用，表示曾做的事无必要)：*You needn't have hurried.* 你当时实在不必那么匆忙. ○ *She needn't have come in person — a letter would have been enough.* 她本不必亲自来——写封信来就足可以了. ○ *Need you have paid so much?* 你当时真须要付那么多钱吗？○ *Need they have sold the farm?* 他们那时非得把农场卖掉吗？

need[2] /niːd; nid/ *v* **1** [Tn, Tt, Tg] require (sth/sb); want; lack 需要(某事物[某人])；要；缺乏：*That dog needs a bath.* 那狗该洗澡了. ○ *Do you need any help?* 你需要帮助吗？○ *Don't go — I may need you.* 别走——我也许用得着你. ○ *I need to consult a dictionary.* 我需要查字典. ○ *This plant needs to be watered twice a week.* 这种花一星期要浇两次. ○ *The garden doesn't need watering — it rained last night.* 花园不用浇水了——昨夜刚下过雨. ○ (*ironic* 反语) *What that child needs* (ie deserves) *is a good spanking.* 那孩子欠揍. **2** [Tt] (indicating obligation 用以表示有义务或责任)：*She needs to have access to our files.* 她需要用我们的文件. ○ *What do you need to take with you on holiday?* 你去度假得带什么东西？○ *I didn't need to go to the bank — I borrowed some money from Mary.* 我不必去银行——我找玛丽借了点儿钱. ○ *I didn't need to go out but I wanted a breath of fresh air.* 我不一定要出去，只想吸些新鲜空气. ○ *A dog needs to be taken out for a walk every day.* 狗得每天带出去遛. ○ *Will we need to show our passports?* 我们要出示护照吗？⇨ Usage 1 at MUST 见MUST所附用法第1项.

need[3] /niːd; nid/ *n* **1** [sing, U] **~ (for sth); ~ (for sb) to do sth** circumstances in which sth is lacking, or necessary, or which require sth to be done; necessity 缺乏；必须；需要：*There's a great need for a new book on the subject.* 非常需要有一本这方面的新书. ○ *I feel a need to talk to you about it.* 我觉得有必要跟你谈谈那件事. ○ *There's no need for you to start yet.* 你现在还不必动身. **2 needs** [pl] basic necessities or requirements 基本的必需品；基本需要：*supply a baby's needs* 提供幼儿的必需品 ○ *I don't live in luxury but I have enough to satisfy my needs.* 我生活不奢侈，但能满足基本需要. ○ *Will £20 be enough for your immediate needs?* 20英镑能否够你急需之用？**3** [U] poverty; misfortune; adversity 贫穷；不幸；逆境：*He helped me in my hour of need.* 他在我困难时帮助过我. **4** (idm 习语) **a friend in need** ⇨ FRIEND. **if need be** if necessary 如果需要的话：*There's always the food in the freezer if need be.* 需要食物的话，冰箱里就有. ○ *If need be, I can do extra work at the weekend.* 必要时我可以在周末加班. **ˌyour need is ˌgreater than ˈmine** (*saying* 谚) we both want this but you must have it because you need it more than I do 你比我更需要(所以我让给你).

▷ **need·ful** /-fl; -fəl/ *adj* **1** necessary 需要的；必要的：*promise to do what is needful* 答应做必须做的事. **2** (idm 习语) **do the ˈneedful** do what is required, esp by providing money for sth 做必须做的事(尤指为某事物提供金钱). **need·fully** /-fəlɪ; -fəlɪ/ *adv*.

need·less *adj* **1** without need; unnecessary 无需要的；不必要的：*needless work, trouble, worry* 不必要的工作、麻烦、烦恼. **2** (idm 习语) **ˌneedless to ˈsay** as you already know or would expect 不用说：*Needless to say, I survived.* 不用说，我得救了. ○ *Needless to say, he kept his promise.* 不用说，他实践了诺言. **need·lessly** *adv*.

needs *adv* (*arch or rhet* 古或修辞) (used only with *must*, often indicating sarcasm 只与must连用，常含讥讽之意) **1** of necessity; from a sense of personal obligation 必要地；偏要；偏偏；非得：*He must needs break a leg just before we go on holiday*, ie It was a foolish action causing great inconvenience. 我们正要去度假，他却偏偏摔断了腿. **2** (idm 习语) **ˌneeds ˌmust when the ˌdevil ˈdrives** (*saying* 谚) one is sometimes forced by circumstances to do what one does not want to do 情势所迫，只得去做.

needy *adj* without the things that are needed for life, ie food and shelter; very poor 缺乏生活必需品(即食物、住所)的；贫穷的：*a needy family* 贫穷的家庭 ○ *help the poor and needy* 帮助贫穷的人.

needle /ˈniːdl; ˋnidl̩/ *n* **1** [C] small thin piece of polished steel with a point at one end and a hole for thread at the other, used in sewing 针；缝衣针. **2** [C] long thin piece of plastic, metal, polished wood, etc without a hole but with a pointed end (for knitting) or a hook (for crocheting) 编织针；钩针：*ˈknitting needles* 织针 ○ *a ˈcrochet needle* 钩针. **3** [C] thin (usu metal) pointer on a dial, eg of a compass, meter, etc 指针(如指南针、仪表等的针). **4** [C] **(a)** pointed hollow end of a syringe used for giving injections (注射器的)针头. ⇨illus at INJECTION 见INJECTION插图. **(b)** (*US infml* 口) injection 注射；打针：*She was given a needle for whooping cough.* 她因患百日咳打了一针. **5** [C] thing like a needle(1) in shape, appearance or use, eg the thin pointed leaf of a pine tree, a pointed rock or peak, an obelisk, etc 针状物(如松树的针叶、尖的岩石或山峰、方尖石碑等). ⇨ illus at App 1 见附录1插图, page i. **6** [C] stylus used in playing gramophone records (唱机的)唱针. **7** [U] (*infml* 口) anger or hostility, esp in situations of rivalry 愤怒，敌意(尤指在竞争中)：*A certain amount of needle has crept into* (ie gradually appeared in) *this game.* 比赛中逐渐出现了一些敌对情绪. ○ [attrib 作定语] *a needle match/game*, ie one in which there is particularly fierce rivalry between the two sides 双方都怀有强烈敌意的比赛. **8** (idm 习语) **give sb/get the ˈneedle** (*sl* 俚) (cause sb to) become annoyed (使某人)恼怒；刺激(某人). **look for a needle in a ˈhaystack** (*saying* 谚) look for one thing among many others, without hope of finding it 草堆里寻针；海底捞针：*Searching for one man in this big city is like looking for a needle in a haystack.* 在这座大城市里寻找一个人犹如大海捞针. **sharp as a needle** ⇨ SHARP. Cf 参看 PINS AND NEEDLES (PIN[1]).

▷ **needle** *v* [Tn] (*infml* 口) provoke or annoy (sb), esp with words 激怒或烦扰(某人)(尤指用言语)：*Stop needling him or he might hit you.* 别再拿话激他了，不然他会揍你.

□ **ˈneedlecraft** *n* [U] skill in sewing or embroidery 缝纫或刺绣的技巧.

ˈneedlewoman *n* (*pl* **-women**) woman who sews (usu

skilfully); seamstress 善缝纫的女子; 擅长女红的女子; 女裁缝: *a good, poor, etc needlewoman* 针线活儿好、不好…的女子.

ˈneedlework *n* [U] sewing or embroidery 缝纫; 刺绣.

needy /ˈni:dɪ; ˋnidɪ/ *adj* **(-ier, -iest)** lacking the necessities of life; very poor 缺乏生活必需品的; 贫穷的: *a needy family* 贫穷的家庭 ○ *food for the poor and needy* 穷人的食物.

ne'er /neə(r); nɛr/ *adv* (*arch* 古) never 永不; 决不; 从未.

ne'er-do-well /ˈneə du: wel; ˋnɛrdu,wɛl/ *n* useless, lazy or irresponsible person 无用的人; 懒惰的人; 不负责任的人: [attrib 作定语] *How is that ne'er-do-well brother of yours?* 你那不成材的弟弟现在怎么样了?

ne·fari·ous /nɪˈfeərɪəs; nɪˋfɛrɪəs/ *adj* (*fml* 文) wicked; unlawful 邪恶的; 不法的: *nefarious deeds, activities, etc* 不法的行为、活动等. ▷ **ne·fari·ously** *adv*. **ne·fari·ous·ness** *n* [U].

neg *abbr* 缩写 = negative.

neg·ate /nɪˈgeɪt; nɪˋget/ *v* [Tn] (*fml* 文) **1** deny or disprove the existence of (sb/sth) 否定或否认(某人[某事物])的存在: *How can you negate God?* 你怎么能否定上帝的存在? **2** cancel the effect of (sth); nullify 消除(某事物)的作用; 使无效: *These facts negate your theory.* 这些事实否定了你的理论.

▷ **nega·tion** /nɪˈgeɪʃn; nɪˋgeʃən/ *n* (*fml* 文) **1** [U] action of denying 否定; 否认; 无效: *Shaking the head is a sign of negation.* 摇头表示否认. **2** [C] denial 否定; 否认: *This theory is a negation of all traditional beliefs.* 这理论否定了一切传统信念.

neg·at·ive /ˈnegətɪv; ˋnɛgətɪv/ *adj* **1** (of words, sentences, etc) expressing denial or refusal; indicating 'no' or 'not' (指词、句等)表示否定或拒绝的: *a negative sentence, question, adverb* 否定句、否定疑问句、有否定含义的副词 ○ *give sb a negative answer* 给某人以否定的答复 ○ *a negative decision on an application* 对申请的否决. Cf 参看 AFFIRMATIVE. **2** lacking in definite, constructive or helpful qualities or characteristics 消极的; 败事的; 无助益的: *He has a very negative attitude to his work*, ie is not interested in trying to do it well or properly. 他的工作态度很消极. ○ *negative criticism*, ie that does not suggest how the thing criticized could be improved 消极的批评(未对所批评的事物提出改进意见的) ○ *a negative definition*, ie one that defines a word, etc by saying what it does not mean 反面定义(通过说明一词不是某意思来给该词下定义者) ○ *The results of her pregnancy test were negative*, ie showed that she was not pregnant. 她的妊娠试验结果呈阴性. **3** (*mathematics* 数) (of a quantity) less than zero; (of a number) that has to be subtracted from other numbers or from zero (指值或数)负的. **4** containing or producing the type of electric charge carried by electrons (电)阴极的, 负极的: *the negative terminal of a battery*, ie the one through which current enters from an external circuit 电池的负极. **5** (of a photograph) with the light areas of the actual object(s) or scene appearing as dark, and the dark areas as light (指摄影)底片的. Cf 参看 POSITIVE.

▷ **neg·at·ive** *n* **1** word or statement that expresses or means denial or refusal 否定词; 否定语: *'No', 'not' and 'neither' are negatives.* no、not、neither 都是否定词. **2** developed photographic film, etc on which the light and dark areas of the actual object(s) or scene are reversed and from which positive pictures can be made (摄影等的)底片, 负片. **3** (idm 习语) **in the ˈnegative** (*fml* 文) (of a sentence, etc) containing a negative word; expressing denial, refusal, etc (指句子等)含有否定词的, 表示否定或拒绝等的, 否定的: *She answered in the negative*, ie said 'no'. 她做出否定的回答.

neg·at·ive *v* [Tn] (*fml* 文) **1** refuse to approve or grant (sth); veto 否定, 否认(某事); 否决: *negative a request, an application, etc* 否决一要求、申请等. **2** prove (sth) to be untrue; disprove 证明(某事物)不实; 驳斥; 反驳. **3** neutralize (an effect) 抵消(一作用).

neg·at·ively *adv*.

neg·lect /nɪˈglekt; nɪˋglɛkt/ *v* **1** [Tn] give no or not enough care or attention to (sb/sth) 疏忽, 忽略(某人[某事物]): *neglect one's studies, children, health* 忽视自己的学习、孩子、健康. **2** [no passive 不用于被动语态: Tt, Tg] fail or forget to do sth, esp carelessly; leave undone (what one ought to do) 未做或忘记做某事(尤指因粗心); 疏漏, 未做完(该做的事): *He neglected to write and say 'Thank you'.* 他因疏忽而未写信道谢. ○ *Don't neglect writing to your mother.* 别忘了给你母亲写信.

▷ **neg·lect** *n* [U] neglecting or being neglected 疏忽; 忽略; 疏漏: *She was severely criticized for neglect of duty.* 她因玩忽职守而受到严厉批评. ○ *The car shows signs of neglect.* 这汽车看样子疏于保养. ○ *The garden was in a state of total neglect.* 那花园完全无人整理.

neg·lected *adj* showing a lack of care or attention 不经心的; 不注意的: *a neglected appearance* 未加修饰的外貌 ○ *The house looks very neglected.* 那房子看来严重失修.

neg·lect·ful /-fl; -fəl/ *adj* **~ (of sth/sb)** in the habit of neglecting things or people 疏忽的; 忽视的; 不留心的: *neglectful of one's appearance, responsibilities, family* 不关注自己的外表、责任、家庭. **neg·lect·fully** /-fəlɪ; -fəlɪ/ *adv*. **neg·lect·ful·ness** *n* [U].

nég·ligé (also **neg·ligee**) /ˈneglɪʒeɪ; *US* ,neglɪˈʒeɪ; ,nɛglɪˋʒe/ *n* woman's light flimsy dressing-gown 轻而薄的女晨衣.

neg·li·gence /ˈneglɪdʒəns; ˋnɛglədʒəns/ *n* [U] lack of proper care or attention; carelessness 疏忽; 忽视; 不留心; 粗心大意: *The accident was due to her negligence.* 这次事故是因她疏忽所致. ○ (*law* 律) *accused of criminal negligence*, ie that can be punished by law 被控犯疏忽罪.

neg·li·gent /ˈneglɪdʒənt; ˋnɛglədʒənt/ *adj* not giving proper attention or care to sth; careless 忽视的; 疏忽的; 粗心大意的: *She was negligent in her work.* 她对工作粗心大意. ○ *He was negligent of his duties.* 他玩忽职守. ▷ **neg·li·gently** *adv*.

neg·li·gible /ˈneglɪdʒəbl; ˋnɛglədʒəbl̩/ *adj* of little importance or size; not worth considering 不重要的; 很小的; 不值得考虑的: *a negligible amount, error, effect* 微不足道的数量、错误、作用 ○ *Losses in trade this year were negligible.* 今年的交易损失无足轻重.

ne·go·ti·able /nɪˈgəʊʃɪəbl; nɪˋgoʃɪəbl̩/ *adj* **1** that can be settled by discussion 可经商讨解决的; 可经谈判处理的: *The salary is negotiable.* 工资问题可商议解决. **2** (of a cheque, bond, etc) that can be exchanged for cash or passed to another person instead of cash (指支票、债券等)可兑换现金的, 可转让的: *negotiable securities* 可转让的证券. **3** (of rivers, roads, etc) that can be crossed, passed along or over, etc (指河流、道路等)可穿越的, 可通行的: *The mountain track is negotiable, but only with difficulty.* 山上的小路可以通行, 只是难走.

ne·go·ti·ate /nɪˈgəʊʃɪeɪt; nɪˋgoʃɪ,et/ *v* **1** (**a**) [I, Ipr] **~ (with sb)** try to reach agreement by discussion 商议; 谈判; 协商: *We've decided to negotiate with the employers about our wage claim.* 我们决定就工资问题与雇主谈判. (**b**) [Tn, Tn·pr] **~ sth (with sb)** arrange or settle sth in this way 通过商议、谈判等处理或解决某事; 商订; 洽谈: *negotiate a sale, loan, treaty* 商订销售事宜、贷款、条约 ○ *a negotiated settlement* 经谈判的解决方法. **2** [Tn] get or give money for (cheques, bonds, etc) 兑现, 转让(支票、债券等). **3** [Tn] get over or past (an obstacle, etc) successfully 超越, 越过(障碍等): *The climber had to negotiate a steep rock face.* 那攀登者得攀越一陡峭岩石. ○ *The horse negotiated* (ie jumped over) *the fence with ease.* 那马轻易跳过了栅栏. **4** (idm 习语) **the neˈgotiating table** formal meeting to discuss wages, conditions, etc 谈判桌(商讨工资、条件等的会议): *Both sides still refuse to come to the negotiating table.* 双方仍拒绝谈判.

▷ **ne·go·ti·ator** *n* person who negotiates 商议者; 谈判者.

ne·go·ti·ation /nɪ,gəʊʃɪˈeɪʃn; nɪ,goʃɪˋeʃən/ *n* [U, C often *pl* 作不可数名词或可数名词, 后者常作复数] discussion aimed at reaching an agreement; negotiating 商议; 谈判; 让与; 流通: *be in negotiation with sb* 与某人商议 ○ *The price is a matter of/for negotiation.* 价格是可以商议的. ○ *Negotiation of the sale took a long time.* 有关销售的谈判用了很长时间. ○ *enter into/open/carry on/resume negotiations with sb* 与某人着手[展开/进行/恢复]谈判 ○ *A settlement was reached after lengthy negotiations.* 经过长时间的谈判而达成协议.

Ne·gress /ˈni:gres; ˋnigrɪs/ *n* (*sometimes offensive* 有时作轻蔑语) Negro woman or girl 黑人女子; 黑妞儿.

N

Ne·gro /ˈniːgrəʊ; ˋnigro/ *n* (*pl* **~es** /-rəʊz; -roz/) (*sometimes offensive* 有时作轻蔑语) member of the black-skinned race of mankind that originated in Africa 黑种人; 黑人.

Ne·groid /ˈniːgrɔɪd; ˋnigrɔɪd/ *adj* having the physical characteristics that are typical of Negroes 黑种人特有的; 黑人的: *a Negroid face, nose, etc* 有黑人特征的脸型、鼻子等.
▷ **Ne·groid** *n* Negroid person 有黑人特征的人; 黑人.

neigh /neɪ; ne/ *n* long high-pitched cry of a horse 马的嘶叫声.
▷ **neigh** *v* [I] make this cry (马)嘶叫.

neigh·bour (*US* **neigh·bor**) /ˈneɪbə(r); ˋnebɚ/ *n* **1** (**a**) person living next to or near another 邻人; 邻居: *Turn your radio down, or you'll wake the neighbours.* 把收音机的声音调小些, 不然会把邻居吵醒. ○ *We're next-door neighbours*, ie Our houses are side by side. 我们是隔壁邻居. ○ *They are close neighbours of ours*, ie live not far from us. 他们是我们的近邻. (**b**) person, thing or country that is next to or near another 邻近的人或物; 邻国: *We were neighbours* (ie sat side by side) *at dinner.* 我们用餐时坐在一起. ○ *When the big tree fell, it brought down two of its smaller neighbours*, ie two smaller trees near it. 那棵大树一倒把附近的两棵小树也弄倒了. ○ *Britain's nearest neighbour is France.* 英国最接近的邻国是法国. **2** fellow human being 世人: *Love your neighbour.* 要爱世人. ○ *be a good neighbour*, ie treat others kindly 善待他人.
▷ **neigh·bour** (*US* **-bor**) *v* [Ipr] **~ on sth** be next or near to sth (与某物)相邻; 邻近(某物): *The garden neighbours on a golf-course.* 那花园与高尔夫球场相邻.
neigh·bour·ing (*US* **-boring**) /ˈneɪbərɪŋ; ˋnebərɪŋ/ *adj* [attrib 作定语] situated or living next or near to sb/sth 相邻的; 邻近的: *the neighbouring country, town, village, etc* 邻国、邻近的城市、邻近的村庄 ○ *neighbouring families* 邻家.
neigh·bour·hood (*US* **-borhood**) /ˈneɪbəhʊd; ˋnebɚ,hʊd/ *n* **1** [CGp] (people living in a) district; area near a particular place 地区; 某地区的人; 与某处邻近的地区: *She is liked by the whole neighbourhood.* 邻近的人都喜爱她. ○ *We live in a rather rich neighbourhood.* 我们住在很富裕的住宅区. ○ *There's some beautiful scenery in our neighbourhood.* 我们附近有几处景色很美. ○ *We want to live in the neighbourhood of London.* 我们想住在伦敦附近. **2** (idm 习语) **in the neighbourhood of** approximately 大约: *a sum in the neighbourhood of £500* 大约500英镑的一笔款.
neigh·bourly (*US* **-borly**) *adj* kind and friendly, as neighbours should be (如邻居般)和睦友好的. **neigh·bour·li·ness** (*US* **-bor·li·ness**) *n* [U].

nei·ther /ˈnaɪðə(r), ˈniːðə(r); ˋniðɚ/ *indef det, indef pron* not one nor the other of two (二者)都不. (**a**) (*det*): *Neither boy is to blame.* 两个男孩子都不应责怪. ○ *Neither answer is correct.* 两个答案都不对. ○ *I saw neither Mr nor Mrs Smith at church.* 我在教堂里既没看见史密斯先生也没看见他太太. ○ *Neither one of us could understand German.* 我们俩没一个懂德语的. ○ *In neither case was a decision reached.* 对这两种情况都未做出决定. (**b**) (*pron*): *I chose neither of them.* 这两个我都不要. ○ *'Which is your car?' 'Neither, mine's being repaired.'* '哪辆汽车是你的?''这两辆都不是, 我的正在修理.'
▷ **neither** *adv* **1** not either 也不 (used before a *modal v* or *aux v* placed in front of its subject 用于主语前面的情态动词或助动词之前): *He doesn't like Beethoven and neither do I.* 他不喜欢贝多芬的作品, 我也不喜欢. ○ *I haven't been to New York before and neither has my sister.* 我以前没去过纽约, 我妹妹也没去过. ○ *'Did you see it?' 'No.' 'Neither did I.'* '你看见那个了吗?''没看见.''我也没看见.' **2 neither ... nor** not ... and not 既不…也不: *He neither knows nor cares what happened.* 他对发生的事情不闻不问. ○ *The hotel is neither spacious nor comfortable.* 这旅馆既不宽敞也不舒服.

nelly /ˈnelɪ; ˋnɛlɪ/ *n* (idm 习语) ˌ**not on your** ˈ**nelly** (*Brit sl* 俚) certainly not 决不.

nem con /ˌnem ˈkɒn; ˌnɛm ˋkɑn/ *abbr* 缩写 = without any objection being raised; unanimously (Latin *nemine contradicente*) 无异议地, 全体一致地 (源自拉丁文 *nemine contradicente*): *The resolution was carried nem con.* 决议案获一致通过.

nem·esis /ˈneməsɪs; ˋnɛməsɪs/ *n* (*pl* **-eses** /-əsiːz; -ə,siz/) (usu *sing* 通常作单数) (*fml* 文) deserved and unavoidable punishment for wrongdoing 报应; 罪有应得的惩罚: *to meet one's nemesis* 遭报应.

neo- *comb form* 构词成分 new; modern; in a later form 新的; 新近的; 现代的; 新式的: *neolithic* ○ *neoclassical.*

neo·clas·sical /ˌniːəʊˈklæsɪkl; ˌnioˋklæsɪkəl/ *adj* of or in a style of art, literature or music that is based on or influenced by the classical style (在文艺或音乐风格方面)新古典主义的.

neo-colonialism /ˌniːəʊ kəˈləʊnɪəlɪzəm; ˌniokəˋlonɪə-ˌlɪzəm/ *n* [U] use of economic or political pressure by powerful countries to obtain or keep influence over other countries, esp former colonies 新殖民主义.

neo·lithic /ˌniːəˈlɪθɪk; ˌniəˋlɪθɪk/ *adj* of the later part of the Stone Age 新石器时代的: *neolithic man* 新石器时代的人 ○ *neolithic tools* 新石器时代的工具.

neo·lo·gism /niːˈɒlədʒɪzəm; niˋɑlə,dʒɪzəm/ *n* **1** [C] newly-invented word 新创造的词; 新词. **2** [U] creating or using new words 新词的创造或使用: *an author with a fondness for neologism* 爱造新词的作者.

neon /ˈniːɒn; ˋniɑn/ *n* [U] chemical element, a colourless inert gas much used in illuminated signs because it glows with a bright light when an electric current is passed through it 氖: [attrib 作定语] *a neon lamp/light/sign* 霓虹灯[霓虹灯光/霓虹灯广告]. ⇨App 10 见附录10.

neo·phyte /ˈniːəfaɪt; ˋniə,faɪt/ *n* (*fml* 文) **1** person recently converted to some belief or religion 新近改变信仰或皈依某宗教的人. **2** beginner learning a new skill 初学者.

nephew /ˈnevjuː, ˈnefjuː; ˋnɛfju/ *n* son of one's brother or sister, or son of one's brother-in-law or sister-in-law 侄子; 外甥. ⇨App 8 见附录8. Cf 参看 NIECE.

neph·ritis /nɪˈfraɪtɪs; nɪˋfraɪtɪs/ *n* [U] inflammation of the kidneys 肾炎.

nep·ot·ism /ˈnepətɪzəm; ˋnɛpə,tɪzəm/ *n* [U] practice among people with power or influence of favouring their own relatives, esp by giving them jobs 优厚亲属的作风(尤指为其安排工作); 裙带关系.

Nep·tune /ˈneptjuːn; *US* -tuːn; ˋnɛptun/ *n* (*astronomy* 天) the planet eighth in order from the sun, one of the furthest in the solar system 海王星.

nerve /nɜːv; nɝv/ *n* **1** [C] fibre or bundle of fibres carrying impulses of sensation or of movement between the brain and all parts of the body 神经: *pain caused by a trapped nerve* 压迫神经产生的疼痛. ⇨illus at TOOTH 见TOOTH插图. **2 nerves** [pl] (*infml* 口) condition in which one is very nervous, irritable, worried, etc; nervousness 神经过敏; 神经紧张; 神经质: *suffer from nerves*, ie be easily upset, worried, etc 患神经过敏 ○ *She doesn't know what nerves are*, ie is never worried, upset, etc by events. 她根本就不知道什么是神经紧张(遇事从不着急、烦恼等). ○ *He has nerves of steel*, ie a very calm temperament in times of stress, danger, etc. 他沉得住气. **3** (**a**) [U] boldness; courage 胆量; 勇气: *lose/regain one's nerve* 失去[恢复]勇气 ○ *a first-class skier with a lot of nerve* 勇敢的滑雪健将 ○ *It takes nerve to be a racing driver.* 当赛车手要有胆量. ○ *Rock-climbing is a test of nerve and skill.* 攀岩运动能考验人的勇气和技巧. ○ *I wouldn't have the nerve to try anything so dangerous.* 我可不敢做那么危险的事. (**b**) [sing] (*derog infml* 贬, 口) impudence (used esp as in the expressions shown) 厚脸皮, 放肆(尤用于以下示例): *What a nerve! She just walked off with my radio!* 脸皮真厚! 她一声不吭把我的收音机拿走了! ○ *He's got a nerve, going to work dressed like that.* 他胆子可真大, 竟敢穿着那样的衣服去上班. ○ *She had the nerve to say I was cheating.* 她竟敢说我作弊, 太放肆了. **4** [C] (*botany* 植) rib of a leaf 叶脉. **5** (idm 习语) **a bundle of nerves** ⇨ BUNDLE. **get on sb's** ˈ**nerves** (*infml* 口) irritate or annoy sb 刺激或烦扰某人: *Stop whistling! It's/You're getting on my nerves!* 别吹口哨了! 扰得我心烦! **hit/touch a (raw)** ˈ**nerve** refer to a subject that causes sb pain, anger, etc 提及使某人痛苦、气愤等的事: *You hit a raw nerve when you mentioned his first wife.* 你曾提到他的前妻刺到了他的痛处. **strain every nerve** ⇨ STRAIN[1]. **a war of nerves** ⇨ WAR.
▷ **nerve** *v* [Tn·pr, Cn·t] **~ sb/oneself for sth** give sb/oneself the courage, strength or determination to do sth

使某人[自己]有勇气、力量或决心做某事: *Her support helped nerve us for the fight.* 她给予的支持使我们有勇气去拼搏. ○ *I nerved myself to face my accusers.* 我下决心迎击指责我的人.

nerve·less *adj* lacking strength; unable to move 无力的; 不能活动的: *The knife fell from her nerveless fingers.* 刀子从她那无力的手中落下. **nerve·lessly** *adv*.

□ ˈ**nerve-cell** *n* cell that carries impulses in nerve tissue 神经细胞.

ˈ**nerve-centre** *n* **1** group of closely connected nerve-cells 神经中枢. **2** (*fig* 比喻) place from which a large factory, organization, project, etc is controlled and instructions sent out 控制中心: *the nerve-centre of an election campaign* 竞选控制中心.

ˈ**nerve-racking** *adj* causing great mental strain 造成精神紧张的; 使人心烦的: *a nerve-racking wait for exam results* 对考试成绩心神不安的等待.

nerv·ous /ˈnɜːvəs; ˋnɝvəs/ *adj* **1** of the nerves (NERVE 1) 神经的: *a nervous disorder* 神经失常 ○ *the nervous system of the human body* 人体的神经系统. **2** ~ **(of sth/doing sth)** fearful; timid 害怕的; 胆怯的; 胆小的: *a frail, nervous little person* 脆弱、胆小的可怜人 ○ *I'm nervous of (being in) large crowds.* 我在大庭广众之下感到胆怯. ○ *Are you nervous in the dark?* 你在黑暗处觉得害怕吗? ○ *She gave a nervous laugh.* 她胆怯地一笑. **3** tense; excited; unstable 神经紧张的; 神经过敏的; 神经质的: *full of nervous energy* 精力充沛 ○ *a nervous style of writing*,刚劲的笔力. ▷ **nerv·ously** *adv*: *smile, fidget, whisper nervously* 神经质地微笑、烦躁、低语. **nerv·ous·ness** *n* [U].

□ ˌ**nervous** ˈ**breakdown** (time of) mental illness that causes depression, tiredness and general physical weakness 神经衰弱.

ˈ**nervous system** system of nerves throughout the body of a person or an animal 神经系统.

nervy /ˈnɜːvɪ; ˋnɝvɪ/ *adj* (**-ier, -iest**) (*infml* 口) **1** (*Brit*) excitable; uneasy; jumpy 易激动的; 烦躁不安的; 神经紧张的. **2** (*US*) impudent; cheeky 厚脸皮的; 无耻的.

-ness /-nɪs; -nɪs/ *suff* 后缀 (with *adjs* forming uncountable *ns* 与形容词结合构成不可数名词) quality, state or character of ... 的性质、状态或特点: *dryness* ○ *silliness*.

nest /nest; nɛst/ *n* **1** (**a**) place or structure chosen or made by a bird for laying its eggs and sheltering its young (鸟的)窝, 巢: *sparrows building a nest of straw and twigs* 用干草和树枝筑窝的麻雀. (**b**) place where certain other creatures live, or produce and keep their young (其他一些生物的)窝, 巢, 穴: *an ants' nest* 蚁穴 ○ *a wasps' nest* 黄蜂巢. **2** snug, comfortable or sheltered place 安乐、舒适或隐蔽之处; 安乐窝: *make oneself a nest of cushions* 用垫子给自己做个安乐窝. **3** secret or protected place, esp for criminals and their activities 藏匿处; 庇护所(尤指供罪犯用的): *a nest of thieves* 贼窟 ○ *a nest of vice, crime, etc* 罪恶等的渊薮. **4** group or set of similar things of different sizes made to fit inside each other (大小不等, 可以套放在一起的)一组或一套相似物件: *a nest of boxes/tables/bowls* 一套盒子[桌子/盆]. **5** site where guns, etc are placed (枪炮的)掩体: *a machine-gun nest* 机关枪掩体. **6** (idm 习语) **feather one's nest** ⇨ FEATHER². **foul one's nest** ⇨ FOUL². **a hornet's nest** ⇨ HORNET. **a mare's nest** ⇨ MARE¹.

▷ **nest** *v* [I] **1** make and use a nest 做窝; 筑巢: *nesting robins* 正在筑巢的鸲鸟 ○ *Swallows are nesting in the garage.* 燕子正在汽车房做窝. **2** (usu 通常作 **go nesting**) search for the nests of wild birds and take the eggs 寻鸟窝(寻找野鸟的窝掏鸟蛋).

□ ˈ**nest-egg** *n* sum of money saved for future use 存储备用的钱; 储备金: *a tidy little nest-egg of £5 000* 5 000 英镑的一小笔储金.

nestle /ˈnesl; ˋnɛsl/ *v* **1** [Ipr, Ip] settle comfortably and warmly in a soft place (在柔软的地方)安顿下来(舒适而温暖): *nestle (down) among the cushions* 在一堆垫子里舒服地呆着 ○ *nestle into bed* 躺在暖和的床上. **2** [Ipr] lie in a half-hidden or sheltered position 处于半隐蔽或遮掩处: *The egg nestled in the long grass.* 蛋隐藏在高草中. ○ *The village nestled at the foot of the hill.* 那村庄位于山脚下. **3** [Tn] hold (sb/sth) snugly, as if in a nest; cradle 容纳(某人[某物])(使之温暖、舒适, 如在巢中); 抱; 怀抱: *She nestled the baby in her arms.* 她把孩子抱在怀里. ○ *The cat lay nestled in the cushions.* 猫舒舒服服地卧在一堆垫子中. **4** [Tn·pr] ~ **sth against, on, etc sth** push (one's head, shoulder, etc) lovingly against, etc sth 使(头、肩等)依偎、紧挨某物: *She nestled her head on his shoulder.* 她将头依偎在他的肩上. **5** (phr v) **nestle up (against/to sb/sth)** settle oneself against sb/sth comfortably 使自己舒服地倚着、靠着某人[某物]: *The child nestled up to its mother and fell asleep.* 孩子倚着母亲舒服地睡了. ○ *The dog nestled up against the warm radiator.* 狗倚着暖烘烘的散热器.

nest·ling /ˈnestlɪŋ; ˋnɛstlɪŋ/ *n* bird that is too young to leave the nest 雏鸟.

net¹ /net; nɛt/ *n* **1** (**a**) [U] loose open material made of string, thread, wire, etc knotted or woven together 网眼织物: *a large piece of net* 一张大网 ○ [attrib 作定语] *net curtains* 网眼帘布 ○ *a wire-net fence* 铁丝网栅栏. (**b**) [C] piece of this used for a particular purpose, eg catching fish, holding hair in place, etc (有某种用途的)网(如捕鱼、罩头发等): *ˈfishing-nets* 鱼网 ○ *a ˈtennis net* 网球网 ○ *a ˈhair-net* 发网 ○ *a mosˈquito net* 蚊帐 ○ *kick/hit the ball into the net*, eg in football, hockey, etc 踢[击]球入网(如足球、曲棍球等). **2** [C] (*esp fig* 尤作比喻) trap or snare 陷阱; 罗网: *caught in a net of crime* 落入罪恶的陷阱 ○ *The wanted man has so far escaped the police net.* 那个遭通缉的人至今仍未落入警方的罗网. **3** (**a**) **the nets** [pl] (in cricket) one or more wickets set up inside a net or nets for practice (板球)有网围住的练球场: *have an hour in the nets* 在板球练球场练习一小时. (**b**) [sing] period of practice in these 在有网围住的板球练球场练习: *The players had a short net before the game.* 板球运动员于比赛前在练球场练了练球. **4** [C] network (esp of communications) 网络; (尤指)通讯网. **5** (idm 习语) **cast one's net wide** ⇨ CAST¹. **spread one's net** ⇨ SPREAD.

▷ **net** *v* (**-tt-**) **1** [Tn, Dn·n, Dn·pr] ~ **sth/sb (for sb)** catch or obtain sth/sb with or as if with a net (似)以网捕捉某物[某人]: *They netted a good haul of fish.* 他们捕了满满一网鱼. ○ *The deal netted (him) a handsome profit.* 这笔交易(他)捞到可观利润. **2** [Tn] cover (eg fruit trees) with a net or nets (以网)罩住(例如果树): *If you don't net your peas the birds will eat them.* 若不用网把豌豆罩上, 鸟就要来吃了. **3** [Tn] (*sport* 体) kick, hit, etc (a ball) into the goal net 将(球)踢、击等入球门网.

□ ˈ**netball** *n* [U] team game in which a ball has to be thrown so that it falls through a high horizontal ring with a net hanging from it 无挡板篮球.

ˈ**network** *n* **1** complex system of roads, etc crossing each other 网状系统: *a network of roads, railways, canals, etc* 公路网、铁路网、运河网. **2** (**a**) closely linked group of people, companies, etc 联络网: *a spy network* 间谍网 ○ *a network of shops all over the country* 遍及全国的商店网 ○ *a communications network*, eg for radio and TV, using satellites 通讯网(如利用人造卫星的无线电及电视通讯网). (**b**) group of broadcasting stations that link up to broadcast the same programmes at the same time 联播网(同时播送同一节目的一组广播电台): *the three big US television networks* 美国的三大电视网. **3** (idm 习语) **the old-boy network** ⇨ OLD.

net² (also **nett**) /net; nɛt/ *adj* **1** ~ **(of sth)** remaining when nothing more is to be taken away 净的; 纯的: *a net price*, ie one from which a discount has been deducted 实价 ○ *net profit*, ie one that remains when working expenses have been deducted 纯利 ○ *net weight*, ie that of the contents only, excluding the weight of the wrappings, the container, etc 净重 ○ *What do you earn, net of tax* (ie after tax has been paid)? 你完税后净得多少? Cf 参看 GROSS² 4. **2** [attrib 作定语] (of an effect, etc) final, after all the major factors have been considered (指结果等)最后的, 最终的: *The net result of the long police investigation is that the identity of the killer is still a complete mystery.* 警方经长时间调查, 结果凶手的身分仍全然不知.

▷ **net** *v* (**-tt-**) [Tn] gain (sth) as a net profit 净得, 净赚(某利润等): *net a profit, sum, etc* 净得利润、金额等 ○ *She netted £5 from the sale.* 她从出售中净赚 5 英镑.

nether /ˈneðə(r); ˋnɛðɚ/ *adj* (*arch or joc* 古或谑) lower 下面的: *the nether regions/world*, ie the world of the dead, hell 阴间[地狱] ○ *nether garments*, ie trousers 下身儿(裤子). ▷ **neth·er·most** /-məʊst; -ˌmost/ *adj*.

net·ting /ˈnetɪŋ; ˋnɛtɪŋ/ *n* [U] string, wire, etc knotted or

N

woven into a net 网: *five yards of wire netting* 五码金属网 ○ *windows screened with netting* 装有纱窗的窗户.

nettle /ˈnetl; ˋnɛtl̩/ *n* **1** common wild plant with hairs on its leaves that sting and redden the skin when touched 荨麻. **2** (idm 习语) **grasp the nettle** ⇨ GRASP.

▷ **nettle** *v* [Tn] make (sb) angry; annoy; irritate 使(某人)发怒; 惹恼; 刺激: *My remarks clearly nettled her.* 我的言语显然激怒了她.

□ ˈ**nettle-rash** *n* [U] condition caused by an allergy, producing red patches on the skin like nettle stings 荨麻疹.

net·work ⇨ NET[1].

neural /ˈnjʊərəl; ˋnjʊrəl/ *adj* (*anatomy* 解) of the nerves 神经的.

neur·al·gia /njʊəˈrældʒə; *US* nʊ-; nʊˋrældʒə/ *n* [U] (*medical* 医) intermittent sharp pain felt along a nerve, usu in the head or face 神经痛(尤指头部或颜面).

▷ **neur·al·gic** /njʊəˈrældʒɪk; nʊˋrældʒɪk/ *adj* (*medical* 医) of neuralgia 神经痛的: *neuralgic pain* 神经疼痛.

neur·as·thenia /ˌnjʊərəsˈθiːnɪə; *US* ˌnʊr-; ˌnʊrəsˋθinɪə/ *n* [U] (*medical* 医) weak condition of the nerves, causing tiredness, worry, dizziness, etc 神经衰弱.

▷ **neur·as·thenic** /-ˈθenɪk; -ˋθɛnɪk/ *adj* (*medical* 医) of or suffering from neurasthenia (患)神经衰弱的. — *n* (*medical* 医) person suffering from neurasthenia 神经衰弱者.

neur·itis /njʊəˈraɪtɪs; *US* nʊ-; nʊˋraɪtɪs/ *n* [U] (*medical* 医) inflammation of a nerve or nerves 神经炎.

neur(o)- *comb form* 构词成分 of nerves or the nervous system 神经的; 神经系统的: *neuralgia* ○ *neuritis* ○ *neurosis*.

neuro·logy /njʊəˈrɒlədʒɪ; *US* nʊ-; nʊˋrɑlədʒɪ/ *n* [U] scientific study of nerves and their diseases 神经学; 神经病学.

▷ **neuro·lo·gical** /ˌnjʊərəˈlɒdʒɪkl; *US* ˌnʊ-; ˌnʊrəˋlɑdʒɪkəl/ *adj*: *neurological research* 神经病学的研究.

neuro·lo·gist /njʊəˈrɒlədʒɪst; *US* nʊ-; nʊˋrɑlədʒɪst/ *n* expert in neurology 神经学家; 神经病学家.

neur·osis /njʊəˈrəʊsɪs; *US* nʊ-; nʊˋrosɪs/ *n* (*pl* **-oses** /-əʊsiːz; -osiz/) (*medical* 医) mental illness that causes depression or abnormal behaviour, often with physical symptoms but with no sign of disease 神经症; 神经官能症.

neur·otic /njʊəˈrɒtɪk; *US* nʊ-; nʊˋrɑtɪk/ *adj* caused by or suffering from neurosis; abnormally anxious or obsessive 神经症的; 神经官能症的; 异常焦虑的; 有强迫观念的: *neurotic worries, outbursts, letters* 神经症引起的焦虑、神经官能症的发作、反映出异常焦虑情绪的信件 ○ (*infml* 口) *She's neurotic about switching lights off at home to save electricity.* 她为省电把家里的灯都关了, 真是精神病.

▷ **neur·otic** *n* neurotic person 神经症患者.

neur·ot·ic·ally /-klɪ; -klɪ/ *adv*.

neu·ter /ˈnjuːtə(r); *US* ˈnuː-; ˋnutɚ/ *adj* **1** (*grammar*) (of a word) neither masculine nor feminine in gender (指词)中性的: *a neuter noun* 中性名词. **2** (of plants) having neither male nor female parts (指植物)无性的. **3** (of insects) sexually undeveloped; sterile (指昆虫)性机能未发育的, 不能生育的.

▷ **neu·ter** *n* **1** neuter noun or gender 中性名词; 中性. **2** (**a**) sexually undeveloped insect 性机能未发育的昆虫. (**b**) castrated animal 已阉割的动物: *My cat is a neuter.* 我的猫是阉过的.

neu·ter *v* [Tn] castrate (an animal) 阉割(动物): *a neutered tom-cat* 去势的猫.

neut·ral /ˈnjuːtrəl; *US* ˈnuː-; ˋnutrəl/ *adj* **1** (**a**) not supporting or helping either side in a dispute, contest, war, etc; impartial 中立的; 不偏不倚的; 公平的: *a neutral country, judge, assessment* 中立国、公正的法官、公正的评价 ○ *be/remain neutral* 保持中立. (**b**) of a country that remains neutral in war 中立国的: *neutral territory, ships, etc* 中立国的领土、船只等. **2** (**a**) having no distinct or positive qualities 无明显特性的: *He is rather a neutral character*, ie has no obvious virtues or faults. 他品性平平. (**b**) (of colours) not strong or vivid, eg grey or fawn (指颜色)不鲜艳的(如灰色或浅黄褐色): *A neutral tie can be worn with a shirt of any colour.* 暗灰色的领带配什么颜色的衬衣都行. **3** (of a gear) in which the engine is not connected with the parts driven by it (指汽车的排挡)空挡的: *leave a car in neutral gear* 让汽车排挡置于空挡位置 ○ *Put the gear lever in the neutral position.* 把变速杆推到空挡的位置. **4** (*chemistry* 化) neither acid nor alkaline 中性的.

▷ **neut·ral** *n* **1** [C] person, country, etc that is neutral 中立的人、国家等. **2** [U] neutral(3) position of the gears 空挡位置: *slip (the gears) into neutral* 把(排挡)推到空挡位置 ○ *The car's in neutral.* 那汽车在空挡位置.

neut·ral·ity /njuːˈtrælətɪ; *US* nuː-; nuˋtrælətɪ/ *n* [U] state of being neutral, esp in war 中性; (尤指战时的)中立: *armed neutrality*, ie readiness to fight if attacked, while remaining neutral until this happens 武装中立(保持中立, 但如遭攻击可立即应战).

neut·ral·ize, -ise *v* [Tn] **1** take away the effect or special quality of (sth) by using sth with the opposite effect or quality 使(某物)无效; 中和: *neutralize a poison, an acid* 解毒、把酸中和. **2** make (a region, country, etc) neutral by agreement; keep free or exclude from fighting (通过协议)使(某地区、国家等)中立; 不使参战: *a neutralized zone* 通过协议保持中立的地区.

neut·ral·iza·tion, -isation /ˌnjuːtrəlaɪˈzeɪʃn; *US* -lɪˈz-; ˌnjutrələˋzeʃən/ *n* [U].

neu·trally /-rəlɪ; -rəlɪ/ *adv*.

neut·ron /ˈnjuːtrɒn; *US* ˈnuː-; ˋnutrɑn/ *n* particle carrying no electric charge, with about the same mass as a proton, and forming part of the nucleus of an atom 中子. Cf 参看 ELECTRON, PROTON.

□ ˈ**neutron bomb** bomb that kills people by intense radiation, but does little damage to buildings, etc 中子弹.

never /ˈnevə(r); ˋnɛvɚ/ *adv* **1** at no time; on no occasion; not ever 从未; 未曾; 永不: *She never goes to the cinema.* 她向来不看电影. ○ *He has never been abroad.* 他从未出过国. ○ *I will never agree to their demands.* 我决不同意他们的要求. ○ *I'm tired of your never-ending complaints.* 我听腻了你那没完没了的抱怨. ○ *'Would you do that?' 'Never.'* '你会做出那种事吗?' '永远不会.' ○ *Never in all my life have I heard such nonsense!* 我这辈子从没听过这种废话! ○ *I shall never (ever) stay at that hotel again.* 我再也不住那家旅馆了. ○ *Such a display has never been seen before/never before been seen.* 这种展览前所未见. **2** (used for emphasis 用于加强语气) not (used esp as in the expressions shown) 不(尤用于以下示例): *That will never do*, ie is completely unacceptable. 那绝对不行. ○ *He never so much as smiled*, ie didn't smile even once. 他从来就没笑过. ○ *You never did!* ie Surely you didn't! 你肯定没做过! ○ *Never fear!* ie Don't be afraid! 别害怕! **3** (idm 习语) **on the ˌnever-ˈnever** (*sl joc* 俚, 谑) on the hire-purchase system 以分期付款的方式: *buy sth on the never-never* 以分期付款的方式购买某物. **well, I never (did)!** (expressing surprise, disapproval, etc 表示惊讶、不赞成等): *Well, I never! Fancy getting married and not telling us!* 嗬, 好傢伙! 想偷偷结婚不告诉我们!

▷ **never** *interj* (*infml* 口) surely not 当然不: *'I got the job.' 'Never!'* '我得到那份工作了.' '绝不可能!'

nev·er·more /ˌnevəˈmɔː(r); ˌnɛvɚˋmɔr/ *adv* (*arch* 古) never again; at no future time 永不再; 再不.

nev·er·the·less /ˌnevəðəˈles; ˌnɛvɚðəˋlɛs/ *adv, conj* (*fml* 文) in spite of this; however; still 虽然如此; 然而; 依然: *Though very intelligent, she is nevertheless rather modest.* 她很聪明, 倒也很谦虚. ○ *There was no news; nevertheless we went on hoping.* 尽管毫无消息, 我们仍抱着希望. ○ *He is often rude to me, but I like him nevertheless.* 他时常对我粗鲁无礼, 但我还很喜欢他.

new /njuː; *US* nuː; nu/ *adj* (**-er, -est**) **1** not existing before; seen, introduced, made, invented, etc recently or for the first time 新的: *a new school, idea, film, novel, invention, car* 新的学校、想法、影片、小说、发明、汽车 ○ *new clothes, furniture* 新的衣服、家具 ○ *new potatoes*, ie ones dug from the soil early in the season 新下来的土豆 ○ *new* (ie freshly baked) *bread* 刚出炉的面包 ○ *the newest* (ie latest) *fashions* 最新款式. ⇨Usage 见所附用法. **2** (**a**) **~ (to sb)** already existing but not seen, experienced, etc before; unfamiliar to sb 未见过的; 未经历过的; 生疏的: *learn new words in a foreign language* 学习外国语的生词 ○ *a new* (ie recently discovered) *star* 新发现的一颗星 ○ *As a beginner, everything is very new to him.* 他刚起步, 对一切都很生

疏. (**b**) **~ (to sth)** not yet accustomed to sth; unfamiliar with sth 尚未习惯的; 不熟悉的: *I am new to this town.* 我不熟悉此城. ○ *They are still new to the work.* 他们对这工作还不习惯. ○ *You're new here, aren't you?* 你对这里不熟悉, 是吧? **3** changed from the previous one(s); different 转换的; 不同的: *a new job, teacher, home* 新的工作、老师、家 ○ *make new friends* 交新朋友. **4** (usu with *the* 通常与 the 连用) modern; of the latest type 现代的; 最新型的: *the new poor/rich*, ie those recently made poor/rich by social changes, etc 新形成的穷人[富人] ○ *the new conformism among the young* 年轻人中新兴起的循规蹈矩风气. **5** [usu attrib 通常作定语] (**a**) just beginning 刚开始的: *a new day* 新的一天 ○ *a new era in the history of our country* 我国历史上的一个新时代. (**b**) beginning again; renewed 重新的; 更新的: *start a new life* 开始新生活 ○ *This government offers new hope to the people.* 本届政府给人民带来新的希望. (**c**) refreshed in mind or body (脑力或体力)已恢复的: *I feel (like) a new man.* 我觉得精力又充沛了. **6** (idm 习语) **brave new world** ⇨ BRAVE. **break fresh/new ground** ⇨ GROUND[1]. **clean as a new pin** ⇨ CLEAN[1]. **fresh/new blood** ⇨ BLOOD[1]. **(as) good as ˈnew** in as good a condition as when new 完好如新: *I'll just sew up that tear, and the coat will be as good as new.* 我把大衣的破处缝好, 就会完好如新了. **a new ˈbroom (sweeps clean)** (*saying* 谚) a person newly appointed to a responsible position (starts to change and improve things energetically, in a way that is sometimes resented by others) 新扫帚(扫得净); 新官上任(三把火). **a new deal** programme of political, social and economic reform 政治、社会和经济改革的计划. **a ˌnew lease of ˈlife**; *US* **a ˌnew lease on ˈlife** chance to live longer or with greater vigour, satisfaction, etc 延年益寿; 活得更带劲、更惬意等: *Since recovering from her operation, she's had a new lease of life.* 她手术复元以后活得更有劲了. ○ (*fig* 比喻) *A bit of oil and some paint could give that old bike a new lease of life.* 给那辆旧自行车上点儿油和漆, 就能多骑些日子. **ring out the old year and ring in the new** ⇨ RING[2]. **teach an old dog new tricks** ⇨ TEACH. **turn over a new ˈleaf** change one's way of life to become a better, more responsible person 重新做人; 改恶从善: *The thief was determined to turn over a new leaf once he was released from prison.* 那盗贼下决心, 一旦获释便重新做人.

▷ **new-** (forming compound *adjs* 用以构成复合形容词) recently 新近的: *a new-born baby* ○ *new-laid eggs* ○ *new-mown hay* ○ *new-found faith.*

newly *adv* (usu before a past participle 通常用于过去分词之前) **1** recently 新近地: *a newly married couple* 新婚夫妇 ○ *a newly formed group* 新组成的小组. **2** in a new different way 以新方式: *newly arranged furniture* 以新方式陈设的家具. ˈ**newly-wed** *n* (usu *pl* 通常作复数) person who has recently married 新婚的人: *the young newly-weds* 年轻的新婚夫妇.

new·ness *n* [U].

□ ˈ**newcomer** *n* person who has recently arrived in a place 新来的人.

ˈ**newfangled** *adj* [usu attrib 通常作定语] (*usu derog* 通常作贬义) (of ideas or things) modern or fashionable in a way that many dislike or refuse to accept (指观念或事物)新潮的, 时髦的(很多人不喜欢或不赞成): *I don't like all these newfangled gadgets.* 这些新潮玩意儿我不都喜欢. ○ *You and your newfangled notions!* 又来了, 又是你那些时髦儿货色!

new ˈmoon (**a**) the moon when it is seen as a thin crescent 新月. (**b**) time when this is so 新月出现时: *after the next new moon* 下次新月出现后. Cf 参看 FULL MOON (FULL).

the New ˈTestament the second part of the Bible, concerned with the teachings of Christ and his earliest followers (《圣经》中的)《新约全书》.

ˈ**new town** (*Brit*) town planned and built all at once with the help of government funds 新市镇(政府资助整体规划建设的).

the New ˈWorld North and South America 新大陆, 新世界(南北美洲). Cf 参看 THE OLD WORLD (OLD).

new ˈyear the first few days of January 新年: *I'll see you in the new year.* 新年期间我去看你. ○ *Happy New Year!* 新年快乐! **New Year's ˈDay** (*US* **New Year's**) 1 January 元旦; 1月1日. **New Year's ˈEve** 31 December 除夕; 12月31日.

NOTE ON USAGE 用法: Compare **recent, current, contemporary, modern** and **new.** 试比较 **recent**、**current**、**contemporary**、**modern**、**new** 这几个词. **1 Recent** and **current** have the most restricted and neutral meanings. ☆ **recent** 和 **current** 的词义最狭窄也最无褒贬分别. **Recent** describes events that occurred a short time ago, but which may now have finished, or things which no longer exist ☆ **recent** 指不久前发生的事, 可能现已结束, 也可指不复存在的事物: *Recent problems have been solved.* 最近的问题已经解决. ○ *She's spent all her recent pay rise.* 她把新增加的工资都花光了. **Current** suggests a situation that exists today but which may be temporary ☆ **current** 意为目前存在的情况, 可能是暂时的: *The factory cannot maintain current levels of production.* 该工厂不能保持目前的生产水平. ○ *How long will she keep her current job?* 她现在这份工作能维持多久? **2 Modern, contemporary** and **new** often indicate a positive quality of being up-to-date, especially in style ☆ **modern**、**contemporary**、**new** 常指符合时代潮流的好的特性, 尤指式样或风格: *contemporary/modern dance, music, art, etc* 当代的[现代的]舞蹈、音乐、艺术等. **Modern** can refer to a longer period up to the present ☆ **modern** 可指直至当前的一段较长时期: *Modern English*, ie since 1500 现代英语, 即自1500年使用至今者. **Contemporary** need not relate to the present ☆ **contemporary** 不一定与现今有关: *Shakespeare's plays tell us a lot about contemporary life*, ie the life of the 16th century. 莎士比亚的戏剧向我们介绍了当时生活的许多情况(即16世纪的生活). **New** can also mean 'original' ☆ **new** 还有'创新'的意思: *a completely new type of computer* 全新型计算机. Note that **actual** cannot be used to mean **contemporary** or **current.** 注意, 不能用 **actual** 表示 **contemporary** 或 **current** 的意思. It means 'real' 该词的含义是'真实的': *I need the actual figures, not an estimate.* 我需要确实的数字, 不要估计的. ○ *His actual age was 45, not 40 as he had stated on his form.* 他的实际年龄是45岁, 并非他填在表格上的40岁.

newel /ˈnjuːəl; *US* ˈnuːəl; ˈnuəl/ *n* **1** central pillar of a winding staircase (螺旋式楼梯的)中心柱. **2** (also ˈ**newel post**) post supporting the handrail of a stair at the top or bottom of a staircase (楼梯顶部或底部的)端柱.

news /njuːz; *US* nuːz; nuz/ *n* **1** (**a**) [U] new or fresh information; report(s) of recent events 消息; 新闻; 新闻报道: *What's the latest news?* 有什么最新消息? ○ *Have you heard the news? Mary has got a job!* 你听说了吗? 玛丽找到工作了! ○ *I want to hear all your news.* 我想听听你的新鲜事. ○ *items/pieces/bits of news* 几项新闻 ○ *It's news to me*, ie I haven't heard about it before. 这事我头一次听说. ○ *She is always in the news*, ie Her doings are regularly reported in the newspapers, on TV, etc. 她一向是新闻人物(报纸、电视等经常报道她的事). ○ *The news that the enemy were near alarmed everybody.* 敌军迫近的消息搅得人心惶惶. ○ *Have you any news of* (ie Have you heard anything about) *where she is staying?* 你有她现在何处的消息吗? ○ [attrib 作定语] *a news item, report, broadcast, bulletin, etc* 新闻项目、报道、广播、简报等 ○ *the news media*, ie newspapers, TV, radio, etc 新闻媒介(报纸、电视、无线电等). (**b**) **the news** [sing *v*] regular broadcast of the latest news on the radio and TV (无线电及电视的)定时新闻广播: *Here is the news*, eg said by a newsreader at the start of a broadcast. 现在报告新闻. ○ *The news lasts half an hour.* 新闻节目播送半小时. **2** [U] person, thing, event, etc that is (interesting enough to be) reported as news (可当作新闻内容的)人, 物, 事: *When a man bites a dog, that's news!* 人要是咬了狗, 那才是新闻! ○ *Pop stars are always news.* 唱流行歌曲的歌星什么时候都是新闻人物. **3** (idm 习语) **break the ˈnews (to sb)** be the first to tell sb about sth, esp sth exciting or unwelcome 最先(向某人)道出实情(尤指令人惊异或不悦的事). ˌ**no news is ˈgood news** (*saying* 谚) if there were bad news we would hear it, so since we have heard nothing we can assume that all is well 没有消息就是好消息.

N

▷ **newsy** *adj* (**-ier**, **-iest**) (*infml* 口) full of (usu not very serious) news 新闻多的(通常指不重要的新闻): *a newsy letter* 有很多消息的信 ○ *a bright, newsy magazine* 内容活泼的、新闻很多的杂志.

□ ˈ**newsagent** *n* (*Brit*) (*US* ˈ**newsdealer**) shopkeeper who sells newspapers, magazines, etc 报刊经销人.

ˈ**news agency** agency that gathers news and sells it to newspapers, TV, radio, etc 通讯社.

ˈ**newscast** *n* broadcast news report 新闻广播. ˈ**newscaster** (also ˈ**news-reader**) *n* person who reads the news on TV, radio, etc (电视、无线电等的)新闻播音员.

ˈ**newsdealer** *n* (*US*) = NEWSAGENT.

ˈ**news flash** (also **flash**) short item of important news broadcast on radio or television, sometimes interrupting another programme (无线电、电视播送的)要闻简报(有时需中断其他节目而播出).

ˈ**news-letter** *n* informal printed report giving information and regularly sent to members of a club, society, etc (定期发送给俱乐部、社团等成员的)简讯.

ˈ**newsmonger** *n* (*usu derog* 通常作贬义) person who gossips 爱说闲话的人.

newspaper /ˈnjuːspeɪpə(r); *US* ˈnuːz-; ˈnuzˌpepɚ/ *n* **1** [C] printed publication, issued usu daily or weekly with news, advertisements, articles on various subjects, etc 报. **2** [U] paper on which newspapers are printed 报纸: *a parcel wrapped in newspaper* 用报纸裹着的小包.

ˈ**newsprint** *n* [U] paper used for printing newspapers on 白报纸; 新闻纸.

ˈ**news-reader** *n* = NEWSCASTER.

ˈ**newsreel** *n* short film of recent events, with a commentary 新闻影片.

ˈ**news-room** *n* room at a newspaper office or radio or TV station where news is received and prepared for printing or broadcasting (报馆、电台或电视台的)新闻编辑室.

ˈ**news-sheet** *n* simple type of newspaper, with few pages 单张报纸.

ˈ**news-stand** *n* = BOOKSTALL (BOOK[1]).

ˈ**news-vendor** *n* person selling newspapers 卖报者; 报贩.

ˈ**newsworthy** *adj* interesting or important enough to be reported as news 值得报道的; 有新闻价值的: *a newsworthy story, scandal, etc* 值得报道的事、丑闻等.

newt /njuːt; *US* nuːt; nut/ *n* **1** small lizard-like animal that can live in water or on land 蝾螈. **2** (idm 习语) **pissed as a newt** ⇨ PISSED (PISS).

New·ton·ian /njuːˈtəʊnɪən; *US* nuː-; nuˈtonɪən/ *adj* [attrib 作定语] of the theories of the English scientist Sir Isaac Newton (1642-1727) 牛顿学说的: *Newtonian physics* 牛顿物理学.

next[1] /nekst; nɛkst/ *adj* [attrib 作定语] **~ (to sb/sth)**; **~ (to do sth/that...)** **1** (usu with *the* 通常与the连用) coming immediately after (sb/sth) in order, space or time (在顺序、空间或时间上)紧随(某人[某事物])之后的; 其次的; 下一个的; 邻近的: *the next name on the list* 名单上的下一个名字 ○ *How far is it to the next* (ie nearest) *petrol station?* 最近的加油站离此地多远? ○ *The next train to Manchester is at 10.00.* 下一班去曼彻斯特的火车是10点整. ○ *The very next time I saw her she was working in London.* 就在那次之后我又见到她时, 她正在伦敦工作. ○ *The next person to speak* (ie who speaks) *will be punished.* 再有人说话就要受罚. ○ *The next six months will be the hardest.* 以后的半年最困难. ○ *I felt a sharp pain in my head and the next thing I knew was waking up in hospital.* 我觉得头部一阵剧痛, 等明白过来才知道自己是在医院里. **2** (used without *the* before eg *Monday, week, winter, year* to indicate the one immediately following 在Monday、week、winter、year等词之前不用the, 表示随之而来者): *Next Thursday is 12 April.* 即将到来的星期四是4月12日. ○ *I'm going skiing next winter.* 我打算在即将到来的冬天去滑雪. ⇨ Usage at LAST[1] 用法见LAST[1]. **3** (idm 习语) **better luck next time** ⇨ BETTER[1]. **first/last/next but one, two, three, etc** ⇨ FIRST[1]. **as good, well, far, much, etc as the** ˈ**next man** as good, well, etc as the average person 与一般人一样好等等: *I can enjoy a joke as well as the next man, but this is going too far.* 我跟别人一样喜欢开玩笑, 但这个玩笑太离谱了. **the next world** state that one is believed to pass into after death 来世; 来生; 下辈子.

▷ **the next** *n* [sing] person or thing that is next 下一个人或事物: *The first episode was good — now we have to wait a week for the next.* 头一集很好——下一集还得等一个星期.

□ ˌ**next** ˈ**door** in or into the next house or room 隔壁: *She lives next door.* 她住在隔壁. ○ *The manager's office is just next door.* 经理办公室就在隔壁. ○ [attrib 作定语] *our* ˌ*next-door* ˈ*neighbours* 我们隔壁的邻居. **next door to** in the house or flat next to (sb/sth) 与(某人[某物])相邻: *Next door to us there's a couple from the USA.* 我们隔壁住着来自美国的一对夫妇. ○ (*fig* 比喻) *Such ideas are next door to* (ie close to) *madness.* 这种主意迹近疯狂.

ˌ**next of** ˈ**kin** (*fml* 文) (with *sing* or *pl v* 与单数或复数动词连用) closest living relative(s) (在世的)最近的亲属: *Her next of kin have been informed.* 已通知她最近的亲属了. ○ *Who is your next of kin?* 谁是你的健在的最近的亲属?

next to *prep* **1** in or into a position immediately to one side of (sb/sth); beside 在紧接着(某人[某物])的一侧; 在...的旁边: *Peter sat next to Paul on the sofa.* 彼得挨着保罗坐在沙发上. **2** in the position after (sb/sth); following 在(某人[某物])的后面; 跟在...之后: *Next to skiing her favourite sport was ice-hockey.* 她最喜爱的运动是滑雪, 其次是冰球. ○ *Birmingham is the largest city in Britain next to London.* 在英国伯明翰是仅次于伦敦的大城市. **3** almost 几乎; 近于: *Papering the ceiling proved next to impossible without a ladder.* 要裱糊天花板没有梯子可以说是办不到. ○ *I got it for next to nothing in a jumble sale.* 这是我在旧货拍卖场简直没花钱买到的. ○ *My horse came next to last* (ie last but one) *in the race.* 我的那匹马在比赛中得了倒数第二名.

NOTE ON USAGE 用法: Compare **nearest** and **next**. 试比较**nearest**和**next**这两个词. **(The) next** indicates 'the following' in a sequence of events or places 在涉及事情或地方的顺序时, **(the) next**指'下一个': *When is your next appointment?* 你下一次的预约时间是什么时候? ○ *Turn left at the next traffic lights.* 在下一个交通信号灯处向左拐. **(The) nearest** means 'the closest' (of several) in time or place ☆ **(the) nearest**是指在时间或地方方面(几个之中)'最接近的一个': *'When can I have my birthday party?' 'On the Saturday nearest to it.'* '我的生日庆祝会能在哪天举行?''在离你生日最近的那个星期六吧.' ○ *Where's the nearest supermarket?* 离这里最近的超级市场在哪儿? Notice the difference between the prepositions **nearest (to)** and **next (to)** 注意介词**nearest (to)**和**next (to)**的区别: *Janet's sitting nearest (to) the window (of all the children).* 珍妮特(在所有的孩子中)坐得离窗户最近. ○ *Sarah's sitting next to the window (beside it).* 萨拉坐在窗户旁边.

next[2] /nekst; nɛkst/ *adv* **1** after this or that; then 在这之后; 在那之后; 然后; 后来: *Who's next on the list?* 名单上的下一个是谁? ○ *What did you do next?* 然后你做了什么? ○ *Next we visited Tokyo.* 后来我们游览了东京. ○ *What comes next* (ie follows)? 接下来是什么? **2** taking the following place in order 其次: *The next oldest building is the church.* 第二古老的建筑物是那个教堂. **3** (used after question words to express surprise 用于疑问词之后表示惊讶): *You're learning to be a parachutist! Whatever next!* 你竟然学跳伞! 还想怎么着!

□ ˌ**next-**ˈ**best** *adj* to be preferred if one's first choice is not available 退而求其次的; 仅次于首选的: *The next-best solution is to abandon the project altogether.* 仅次于最佳的解决方法是放弃全部计划. ○ *Borrowing tapes from the library would be the next-best thing.* 从资料库借磁带是退而求其次的办法. ○ *That's the best idea. Bill's is next-best.* 那是最好的主意. 比尔的主意次之.

nexus /ˈneksəs; ˈnɛksəs/ *n* (*pl* **~es** /-səsɪz; -səsɪz/) (*fml* 文) connected group or series; bond or connection 相关联的群体或系列; 联结; 连系: *Shared ambition is the vital nexus between them.* 共同的志向是把他们联结在一起的重要纽带.

NHS /ˌen eɪtʃ ˈes; ˌɛn etʃ ˈɛs/ *abbr* 缩写 = (*Brit*) National Health Service 国民保健署: *I got my hearing-aid on the NHS.* 我的助听器是国民保健署资助的.

NI *abbr* 缩写 = **1** (*Brit*) National Insurance 国民保险制

度: *NI deductions*, eg on a pay slip 国民保险扣除额(如工资单所列的). **2** Northern Ireland 北爱尔兰.

ni·acin /ˈnaɪəsɪn; ˋnaɪəsɪn/ *n* [U] vitamin found in meat, yeast and some cereals 烟碱酸(肉类、酵母和某些谷物中的维生素).

nib /nɪb; nɪb/ *n* metal point of a pen 钢笔尖.

nibble /ˈnɪbl; ˋnɪbl/ *v* **1** (**a**) [I, Ipr, Tn, Tn·p] **~ (at sth)** take tiny bites of sth 小口咬某物; 轻咬: *fish nibbling (at) the bait* 轻咬鱼饵的鱼 ○ *She nibbled his ears playfully.* 她轻轻咬他的耳朵玩. ○ *Mice have nibbled all the cheese away.* 老鼠一点一点地把干酪都啃光了. (**b**) [I] eat small amounts 吃少量东西: *No nibbling between meals!* 不要在两顿饭之间吃零食! **2** (phr v) **nibble at sth** show cautious interest in (an offer, etc) 对(好意、提议等)审慎地表示有意接受: *He nibbled at my idea, but would not make a definite decision.* 他对我的想法颇感兴趣, 但不做出决定.

▷ **nibble** *n* (**a**) act of nibbling 小口的咬; 轻咬: *I felt a nibble on the end of my line.* 我觉得有鱼轻轻地咬钩. (**b**) small amount of food 少量的食物: *Drinks and nibbles will be served.* 将有饮品小吃招待.

nibs /nɪbz; nɪbz/ *n* (idm 习语) **his nibs** (*Brit infml joc* 口, 谑) (used as a mock title by others when talking about a man (esp one in authority) who thinks he is more important than he really is 谈论自命不凡者时, 用作戏称, 尤用于主事人): *Please tell his nibs that we'd like his help with the washing-up!* 请转告那位大人, 我们想请他帮助刷锅洗碗!

nice /naɪs; naɪs/ *adj* (**-r**, **-st**) **1** (**a**) pleasant; agreeable 好的; 令人愉快的; 宜人的: *a nice person, smile, taste, remark* 令人愉快的人、微笑、味道、言语 ○ *a nice day* 美好的一天 ○ *nice weather* 好天气 ○ *a nice little girl* 可爱的姑娘 ○ *That tastes nice!* 味道挺好! ○ *We had a nice time at the beach.* 我们在海滨时开心极了. ○ *It's not nice to pick your nose.* 挖鼻孔很不雅观. (**b**) **~ (to sb)** kind; friendly 亲切的; 友好的: *Try to be nice to my father when he visits.* 我父亲到这里来时尽量对他好些. Cf 参看 NASTY. **2** (*ironic* 反语) bad; unpleasant 坏的; 令人不愉快的: *This is a nice mess you've got us into!* 你把我们弄到了这种地步! ○ *That's a nice thing to say!* 这种好话能说得出口! **3** needing precision and care; fine; subtle 需精确和慎重的; 细微的; 微妙的: *a nice distinction* 细微的区别 ○ *a nice point of law*, ie one that may be difficult to decide 法律上难以决定之处 ○ *nice* (ie very slight) *shades of meaning* 意义的细微差别. **4** (**a**) hard to please; having refined tastes 难以取悦的; 讲究的: *too nice in one's dress* 衣着过分讲究. (**b**) (usu in negative expressions 通常用于否定用语) respectable; scrupulous 体面的; 高尚的; 谨慎的; 细致的: *She's not too nice in her business methods.* 她的经营方法不敢恭维. **5** (idm 习语) **nice and** (used before *adjs* 用于形容词之前) (*infml approv* 口, 褒) agreeably 宜人地: *nice and warm by the fire* 在火边暖烘烘的 ○ *nice and cool in the woods* 森林里凉爽宜人. **good/nice work** ⇨ WORK[1]. **nice work if you can get it** (*saying* 谚) (used to express envy of what sb has been lucky or clever enough to get or do 因某人幸运或聪明而得到或得以做某事物, 用此语表达羡慕或忌妒之意).

▷ **nicely** *adv* **1** in a pleasant manner 愉快地; 美好地; 亲切地: *nicely dressed, done, said* 穿得、做得、说得很像样子. **2** (*infml* 口) very well; all right 很好; 相宜: *That will suit me nicely.* 那对我很合适. ○ *The patient is doing nicely*, ie is making good progress. 那病人好得很快.

nice·ness *n* [U].

ni·cety /ˈnaɪsətɪ; ˋnaɪsətɪ/ *n* **1** [U] accuracy; precision 准确; 精确: *nicety of judgement* 判断的准确 ○ *a point of great nicety*, ie one that requires very careful and detailed thought 需要仔细考虑之处. **2** [C usu *pl* 通常作复数] subtle distinction or detail 细微的区别; 微小的细节: *I can't go into all the niceties of meaning.* 我无法详述意义上的细微区别. ○ *observe the social niceties*, ie of polite behaviour, etc 遵守社交礼节. **3** (idm 习语) **to a nicety** exactly right 正确地; 恰好地: *You judged the distance to a nicety.* 你对那段距离的判断十分精确.

niche /nɪtʃ, niːʃ; nɪtʃ/ *n* **1** shallow recess, esp in a wall (浅的)凹处; (尤指)壁龛: *a niche with a shelf* 有格架的壁龛. ⇨illus 见插图. **2** (*fig* 比喻) suitable or comfortable position, place, job, etc 适合的或舒适的位置、地方、职业等: *I don't think he's yet found his niche in life*, ie the occupation that gives him most satisfaction and happiness. 我认为他还没找到生活的归宿.

niche 壁龛

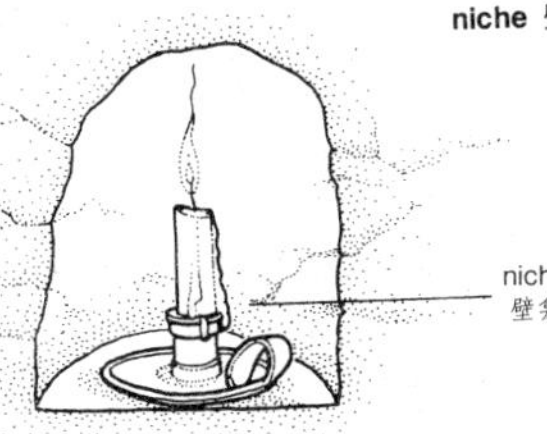

nick[1] /nɪk; nɪk/ *n* **1** small cut or notch 小切口; 刻痕; 缺口: *Make a nick in the cloth with the scissors.* 用剪子在布料上剪个缺口. **2** (idm 习语) **in good, bad, etc ˈnick** (*Brit sl* 俚) in good, etc condition or health 情况或身体好、坏等: *She's in pretty good nick for a 70-year-old.* 对70岁的人来说, 她身体很好. ○ *The car's in poor nick.* 那辆汽车的情况糟透了. **in the ˌnick of ˈtime** only just in time; at the last moment 刚来得及; 在最后时刻: *You got here in the nick of time — the train's just leaving.* 你来得真是时候 —— 火车正要开.

▷ **nick** *v* [Tn] make a nick in (sth) 在(某物)上切口, 刻痕: *nick one's chin when shaving* 刮胡子时将下巴割破.

nick[2] /nɪk; nɪk/ *n* **the nick** [sing] (*Brit sl* 俚) prison or police station 监狱; 警察分局; 派出所: *She spent a year in the nick.* 她在班房里蹲了一年. ○ *The burglar was taken to the local nick.* 窃贼已带到警察分局.

▷ **nick** *v* [Tn, Tn·p] (*Brit sl* 俚) **1 ~ sb (for sth)** arrest sb 逮捕某人: *He was nicked for stealing.* 他因偷窃而被捕. **2 ~ sth (from sb/sth)** steal sth 偷窃某物: *He nicked £5 (from his friend).* 他偷了(朋友)5英镑.

nickel /ˈnɪkl; ˋnɪkl/ *n* **1** [U] chemical element, a hard silver-white metal often used in alloys 镍: *nickel-plated* 镀镍的. ⇨App 10 见附录10. **2** [C] coin of the US or Canada, worth 5 cents (美国或加拿大的)5分镍币. ⇨App 4 见附录4.

▷ **nickel** *v* (**-ll-**; *US* **-l-**) [Tn] coat (sth) with nickel 将(某物)镀镍.

□ **nickel silver** alloy of nickel, zinc and copper 德银(镍锌铜的合金).

nick-nack = KNICK-KNACK.

nick·name /ˈnɪkneɪm; ˋnɪkˌnem/ *n* familiar or humorous name given to a person instead of or as well as his real name, often a short form of the real name, or a reference to the person's character, etc 爱称; 绰号; 诨名; 外号: *Harold's nickname was Harry.* 哈罗德的昵称是哈里. ○ *As he was always cheerful he had the nickname 'Smiler'.* 他总是快快乐乐的, 因而得了个外号叫'乐乐'.

▷ **nick·name** *v* [Tn, Cn·n esp passive 尤用于被动语态] give a nickname to (sb) 给(某人)起绰号: *He was nicknamed Shorty because he was so tall!* 因为他很高, 就给他起个外号叫'矮子'.

nic·ot·ine /ˈnɪkətiːn; ˋnɪkəˌtin/ *n* [U] poisonous oily substance found in tobacco 尼古丁: *nicotine-stained fingers* 被尼古丁熏黄的手指 ○ [attrib 作定语] *cigarettes with a low nicotine content* 尼古丁含量低的香烟.

niece /niːs; nis/ *n* daughter of one's brother or sister, or daughter of one's brother-in-law or sister-in-law 侄女; 甥女. ⇨App 8 见附录8. Cf 参看 NEPHEW.

niff /nɪf; nɪf/ *n* (*Brit sl* 俚) smell; stink 难闻的气味; 恶臭: *What a niff!* 太臭了!

▷ **niffy** *adj* (*Brit sl* 俚) having an unpleasant smell; smelly 有臭味的; 发臭的: *That meat's a bit niffy.* 那肉有点儿臭了.

nifty /ˈnɪftɪ; ˋnɪftɪ/ *adj* (**-ier**, **-iest**) (*infml* 口) **1** (**a**) clever; skilful 聪明的; 伶俐的; 有技巧的; 熟练的: *a footballer's nifty footwork* 足球运动员熟练的脚下功夫. (**b**) efficient; useful; handy 有效的; 有用的; 便利的: *a nifty little gadget for peeling potatoes* 削土豆皮的小巧的工具. **2** smart; stylish 漂亮的; 时髦的: *wearing a nifty new outfit* 穿着时髦的新衣服.

nig·gard /ˈnɪgəd; ˋnɪgɚd/ *n* mean stingy person 小气鬼; 吝啬鬼.

N

▷ **nig·gardly** *adj* **1** mean; stingy 小气的; 吝啬的: *a niggardly old miser* 吝啬的守财奴. **2** (of a gift, etc) having little value (指礼物等)无价值的, 小气的: *a niggardly contribution to the fund* 小气的捐助. **nig·gard·li·ness** *n* [U].

nig·ger /ˈnɪgə(r); ˋnɪgɚ/ *n* (⚠ *derog offensive* 讳, 贬, 蔑) black person; negro 黑人; 黑鬼.

niggle /ˈnɪgl; ˋnɪgḷ/ *v* **1** [I, Ipr] **~ (about/over sth)** give too much time and attention to unimportant details; criticize in a petty way 过分为琐事费时及操心; 挑剔: *Stop niggling about every penny we spend.* 别再为我们花的每个小钱费心思了. **2** [Tn] irritate (sb) in a minor way; annoy 惹(某人)不痛快; 惹恼: *His untidiness constantly niggled her.* 他邋邋遢遢总惹她讨厌.

▷ **nig·gling** /ˈnɪglɪŋ; ˋnɪglɪŋ/ *adj* **1** too unimportant to give time or attention to; trifling 不值得费时或操心的; 无关紧要的; 琐碎的: *Don't waste time on niggling details.* 不要为琐事浪费时间. **2** annoying in a minor but persistent way 令人烦恼的, 讨厌的(事不大但不断): *a niggling pain* 烦人的疼痛 ○ *niggling criticism* 恼人的批评.

nigh /naɪ; naɪ/ *adv, prep* **(-er, -est)** (*arch* 古) near (to) 接近(于); 靠近: *The end of the world is nigh!* 世界末日就要到了! Cf 参看 WELLNIGH.

night /naɪt; naɪt/ *n* [C, U] **1** time of darkness between sunset and sunrise 夜; 夜里; 夜间; 夜晚; 晚上: *in/during the night* 在夜里 ○ *on Sunday night* 在星期日晚上 ○ *on the night of Friday 13 June* 在6月13日星期五夜晚 ○ *a late-night show at the cinema*, ie one given much later than the other shows 深夜场电影 ○ *Night fell*, ie It became dark. 天黑了. ○ *He stayed three nights at the hotel*, ie slept there for three nights. 他在旅馆住了三夜. ○ *Can you stay the night/stay over night* (ie spend the night here)? 你能在这里过夜吗? **2** evening on which a specified activity takes place 进行某项活动的夜晚: *the first night of a play* 戏剧的首演夜场 ○ *the last night of the Proms* 逍遥音乐会的告别夜场. **3** (idm 习语) **all night (long)** throughout the whole night 整夜; 通宵; 彻夜. **all right on the night** ⇨ RIGHT[1]. **at night** when night comes; during the night 夜里; 夜间; 晚上: *These animals only come out at night.* 这些动物仅在夜间才出来. ○ *10 o'clock at night*, ie 10 pm 晚上10点钟. **by day/night** ⇨ DAY: *travelling by night* 夜行. **an early/a late ˈnight** night when one goes to bed earlier/later than usual 比平时睡得早[晚]的夜晚: *You've been having too many late nights recently.* 你近来晚睡的次数太多了. **have a good/bad ˈnight** sleep well/badly during the night (夜里)睡得好[不好]. **in the/at dead of night** ⇨ DEAD. **like a thief in the night** ⇨ THIEF. **the livelong day/night** ⇨ LIVELONG. **make a ˈnight of it** spend much of the night in celebrating, eg at a party 痛快地玩一晚上(如参加聚会). **ˌnight after ˈnight** for many nights in succession 一夜又一夜; 连着几夜. **ˌnight and ˈday/ˌday and ˈnight** continuously; all the time 夜以继日; 日以继夜: *machines kept running night and day* 日夜不停运转着的机器. **a night ˈout** evening spent enjoying oneself away from home 出外玩乐的一个晚上: *I enjoy an occasional night out at the theatre.* 我偶尔晚上出去看看戏. **ships that pass in the night** ⇨ SHIP[1]. **in the still of the night** ⇨ STILL[1] *n*. **spend the night with sb** ⇨ SPEND. **things that go bump in the night** ⇨ THING. **turn ˌnight into ˈday** do at night what is usually done during the day 以夜作昼; 昼夜颠倒.

▷ **nightie** (also **nighty**) *n* (*infml* 口) = NIGHT-DRESS.

nightly *adj, adv* (happening, done, etc) at night or every night 夜间或每夜(发生、做等)(的): *nightly performances* 夜间演出 ○ *a film show twice nightly* 每晚放映两次的电影 ○ *appearing nightly at the local theatre* 每晚在地区剧院登台演出.

nights *adv* (*esp US*) in the night-time repeatedly 夜夜: *I can't sleep nights.* 我夜里经常失眠. ○ *He works nights.* 他总在夜间工作.

□ **ˈnight-bird** *n* **1** bird (eg an owl) that is active at night 夜间活动的鸟(如猫头鹰). **2** (*fig infml* 比喻, 口) person who is most active at night 夜间活动的人.

night-ˈblindness *n* [U] inability to see properly in the dark or in dim light 夜盲.

ˈnightcap *n* **1** (formerly) soft cap worn in bed (旧时)睡帽. **2** (usu alcoholic) drink taken before going to bed 睡前的饮料(通常指酒).

ˈnight-club *n* club open until late at night for drinking, dancing, entertainment, etc 夜总会.

ˈnight-dress (also *infml* 口语作 **nightie, nighty**) *n* long loose garment worn by a woman or child in bed (女子或儿童的)长睡衣, 睡袍.

ˈnightfall *n* [U] time when darkness comes; dusk 傍晚; 黄昏: *We hope to be back by nightfall.* 我们希望傍晚时能回来.

ˈnight-gown *n* = NIGHT-DRESS.

ˈnightjar *n* night-bird with a long tail, like a swift's, and with a harsh cry 欧夜鹰.

ˈnight-life *n* [U] entertainments available at night in a particular town, area, etc 夜生活: *There's not much night-life in this small town.* 这个小镇里没有什么夜生活.

ˈnight-light *n* small candle or bulb that is kept burning in a bedroom at night 通宵灯(卧室中彻夜不熄的小蜡烛或电灯).

ˈnight-line *n* fishing line left in a lake, river, etc to catch fish at night 夜钓丝(夜间留在湖、河等中的钓丝).

ˈnight-long *adj, adv* throughout the night 通宵(的); 彻夜(的).

ˈnightmare *n* **1** frightening dream 恶梦; 梦魇: *I have nightmares about falling off a cliff.* 我作恶梦梦见从悬崖上摔下来了. **2** (*infml* 口) very frightening or unpleasant experience 非常可怕的或不愉快的经历: *Driving during the blizzard was a nightmare.* 在暴风雪中开车真吓人. **nightmarish** /ˈnaɪtmeərɪʃ; ˋnaɪtˌmɛrɪʃ/ *adj*.

ˈnight porter hotel porter on duty during the night (旅馆的)夜班服务员.

ˈnight safe safe in the outside wall of a bank where money, etc can be deposited when the bank is closed 夜间保险箱(装于银行外墙内的保险箱, 客户可在银行下班后将金钱等存放其中).

ˈnight-school school where lessons are given in the evening for those who cannot attend classes during the day 夜校.

ˈnight shift (**a**) [CGp] group of workers at work during the night 夜班工作人员; 夜班班组: *The night shift come/comes off at dawn.* 夜班工作人员天亮时下班. (**b**) [C] time when these workers work 夜班: *be on the night shift* 上夜班. Cf 参看 DAY SHIFT (DAY).

ˈnight-shirt *n* boy's or man's long shirt for sleeping in (男用)睡衣.

ˈnight-soil *n* [U] (*euph* 婉) human excrement removed from latrines, etc at night (夜间从粪坑中清除的)粪便.

ˈnightstick *n* (*US*) policeman's truncheon 警棍.

ˈnight-time *n* time of darkness 夜间; 夜里: *in the night-time* 在夜间 ○ *at night-time* 在夜里.

ˌnight-ˈwatch *n* (person or group of people keeping) watch at night 守夜; 守夜者. **ˌnight-ˈwatchman** /-mən; -mən/ *n* (*pl* **-men**) man employed to guard a closed building (eg a factory) at night (受雇守卫建筑物, 如工厂的)守夜者.

NOTE ON USAGE 用法: Compare **at night, by night, in the night, during the night, on a (...) night (...)**. 试比较 **at night**、**by night**、**in the night**、**during the night**、**on a (...) night (...)** 等词组. **At night** is used of something habitually happening during the hours of darkness ☆ **at night** 用以表示惯常在夜间发生的事: *Nocturnal animals such as bats and owls only come out at night.* 夜行动物, 如蝙蝠和猫头鹰只在夜里才出来. ○ *I don't like driving at night.* 我不喜欢在夜间开车. **By night** can cover the meanings of **at night.** ☆ **by night** 包括 **at night** 的意思. It is used especially when the conditions or circumstances of an action are being emphasized 但 **by night** 尤用以强调某活动的条件或环境: *The enemy attacked by night,* ie under cover of darkness. 敌人趁夜袭击(即有夜色作掩蔽). **In the night** usually refers to the night immediately past ☆ **in the night** 通常指刚刚过去的那个夜晚: *I'm exhausted. The baby woke up three times in the night.* 我累坏了. 孩子夜里醒了三次. **During the night** can also be used in this sense 这一含义也可用 **during the night** 来表示: *Everything was quiet during the night.* 昨夜万籁俱寂. **On** is used when the night in question is further defined 对 **night** 有所限定时, 要用 **on**: *on a night in May* 五月的一

N

个夜晚 ○ *on a cold winter's night* 严冬的一个夜晚. For further information on prepositions of time, see the note on usage at TIME[1]. 欲进一步了解时间介词, 参看 TIME[1] 所附用法.

night·in·gale /ˈnaɪtɪŋgeɪl; *US* -tŋg-; ˈnaɪtn̩,gel/ *n* small reddish-brown bird of the thrush family, the male of which sings tunefully by night as well as by day 歌鸲; 夜莺.

night·shade /ˈnaɪt-ʃeɪd; ˈnaɪt,ʃed/ *n* [U, C] any of several types of wild plant with poisonous berries 茄类植物: *deadly nightshade* 颠茄.

ni·hil·ism /ˈnaɪɪlɪzəm, ˈnɪhɪl-; ˈnaɪəl,ɪzəm, ˈnɪhəl-/ *n* [U] **1** total rejection of all religious and moral beliefs (否认一切宗教信仰和道德观念的)虚无主义. **2** belief that nothing really exists (否认一切存在的)虚无主义.
▷ **ni·hil·ist** /-ɪst; -ɪst/ *n* believer in nihilism 虚无主义者. **ni·hil·istic** /ˌnaɪɪˈlɪstɪk, ˌnɪhɪˈl-; ˌnaɪəˈlɪstɪk, ˌnɪhəˈl-/ *adj* of nihilism 虚无主义的.

nil /nɪl; nɪl/ *n* [U] nothing, esp as the score in games 无; (尤作比赛中的)零分: *Our team won the game three nil/three goals to nil*, ie 3-0. 我们队以三比零获胜. ➪Usage at NOUGHT 用法见 NOUGHT.

nimble /ˈnɪmbl; ˈnɪmbl̩/ *adj* (**-r** /ˈnɪmblə(r); ˈnɪmblɚ/, **-st** /ˈnɪmblɪst; ˈnɪmblɪst/) **1** able to move quickly and neatly; agile 迅速的; 敏捷的; 灵敏的; 灵活的: *as nimble as a goat* 像山羊一样敏捷 ○ *sewing with nimble fingers* 以灵活的手指缝纫. **2** (*fig* 比喻) (of the mind) able to think quickly; sharp (指头脑)聪敏的, 敏锐的: *a lad with nimble wits* 机敏的男孩儿. ▷ **nimble·ness** *n* [U]. **nimbly** /ˈnɪmblɪ; ˈnɪmblɪ/ *adv*.

nim·bus /ˈnɪmbəs; ˈnɪmbəs/ *n* (*pl* **~es** /-bəsɪz; -bəsɪz/ or **-bi** /-baɪ; -baɪ/) **1** (in paintings, etc) bright circle shown round or over the head of a saint; halo (画等中的)(圣者头部四周或上方的)光环, 光轮. **2** rain cloud 雨云.

nin·com·poop /ˈnɪŋkəmpu:p; ˈnɪŋkəm,pup/ *n* (*infml* 口) foolish person 傻瓜; 笨蛋.

nine /naɪn; naɪn/ *pron, det* **1** 9; one more than eight 9, 九(个). ➪App 4 见附录 4. **2** (idm 习语) ˌ**nine to** ˈ**five** normal working hours in an office, etc 九时至五时(办公室等的正常工作时间): *I work nine to five.* 我上九点至五点的班. ○ [attrib 作定语] *a nine-to-five job* 九点上班五点下班的工作.
▷ **nine** *n* **1** the number 9 ☆ 9; 九. **2** (idm 习语) **dressed up to the nines** ➪ DRESS[2].
nine- (in compounds 用以构成复合词) having nine of the thing specified 有九个…的: *a nine-hole golf-course*.
ninth /naɪnθ; naɪnθ/ *pron, det* 9th; next after eighth 第9, 第九(个). — *n* one of nine equal parts of sth 九分之一. **ninthly** *adv*.
For the uses of *nine* and *ninth* see the examples at *five* and *fifth*. 关于 nine 和 ninth 的用法见 five 和 fifth 词条中的示例.

nine·pin /ˈnaɪnpɪn; ˈnaɪn,pɪn/ *n* **1 ninepins** [sing *v*] game in which a ball is rolled along the floor at nine bottle-shaped blocks of wood in order to knock them down 九柱地滚球(沿地面滚球撞击九根瓶状木柱的游戏). Cf 参看 SKITTLE, TENPIN BOWLING. **2** [C] any of these blocks of wood (九柱地滚球的)瓶状木柱. **3** (idm 习语) ˌ**go down like** ˈ**ninepins** fall or be knocked over, etc in great numbers (大量地)倒下, 打翻: *There's a lot of flu about — people are going down* (ie catching the disease) *like ninepins.* 流感正在蔓延 —— 传染的人越来越多.

nine·teen /ˌnaɪnˈti:n; naɪnˈtin/ *pron, det* 19; one more than eighteen 19, 十九(个). ➪App 4 见附录 4.
▷ **nine·teen** *n* the number 19 ☆ 19; 十九.
nine·teenth /ˌnaɪnˈti:nθ; naɪnˈtinθ/ *pron, det* 19th; next after eighteenth 第19, 第十九(个). — *n* one of nineteen equal parts of sth 十九分之一.
For the uses of *nineteen* and *nineteenth* see the examples at *five* and *fifth*. 关于 nineteen 和 nineteenth 的用法见 five 和 fifth 词条中的示例.

ninety /ˈnaɪntɪ; ˈnaɪntɪ/ *pron, det* 90; one more than eighty-nine 90, 九十(个). ➪App 4 见附录 4.
▷ **nineti·eth** /ˈnaɪntɪəθ; ˈnaɪntɪəθ/ *pron, det* 90th; next after eighty-ninth 第90, 第九十(个). — *n* one of ninety equal parts of sth 九十分之一.
ninety *n* **1** the number 90 ☆ 90; 九十. **2 the nineties** [pl] numbers, years or temperature from 90 to 99 从90到99的数目、年数或温度. **3** (idm 习语) **in one's nineties** between the ages of 90 and 100 在90岁到100岁之间. **ninety-nine times out of a hundred** almost always 几乎总是; 十之八九.
For the uses of *ninety* and *ninetieth* see the examples at *five* and *fifth*. 关于 ninety 和 ninetieth 的用法见 five 和 fifth 词条中的示例.

ninny /ˈnɪnɪ; ˈnɪnɪ/ *n* (*infml* 口) foolish person 傻瓜; 笨蛋: *Don't be such a ninny!* 别这么傻里傻气的!

nip /nɪp; nɪp/ *v* (**-pp-**) **1** (**a**) [Tn] press (sth) hard (eg between the finger and thumb, or the teeth, or with the claws as a crab does); pinch 捏住, 咬住, 夹住, 掐住(某物): *A crab nipped my toe while I was paddling.* 我蹚水时脚趾让螃蟹给夹了. ○ *She nipped her finger in the door*, ie between the door and the doorpost. 她的手指给门夹了. ○ *The dog nipped me in the leg.* 那狗咬了我的腿. (**b**) [I, Ipr] **~ (at sth)** take small bites with the front teeth (用前牙)啃: *That dog nips!* 那狗一点儿点儿地啃. ○ *The dog was nipping at her ankles.* 那狗咬着她的脚腕子了. **2** [Tn] (of frost, cold wind, etc) stop the growth of (plants); damage (指霜、寒风等)伤害(植物), 摧残: *The icy breeze nipped the young blooms.* 寒风摧残了初绽的花朵. **3** [Ipr, Ip] (*infml* 口) move quickly; hurry 快速行动; 赶快行动: *Where did she nip off to?* 她急急忙忙到哪儿去了? ○ *He nipped in* (ie got in quickly) *just in front of me.* 他赶在我前面进来. ○ *I'll nip on ahead and open the door.* 我要赶到前面去开门. ○ *She has nipped out to the bank.* 她急忙去银行了. ➪Usage at WHIZ 用法见 WHIZ. **4** (idm 习语) ˌ**nip and** ˈ**tuck** a situation in which sth is narrowly avoided, or where there is close competition 极难避免的情况; 势均力敌: *The two runners contested the race closely — it was nip and tuck all the way.* 那两个赛跑选手竞争激烈 —— 在赛程中一直不相上下. **nip sth in the bud** stop or destroy sth at an early stage in its development 将某事物阻止或消灭于萌芽中: *She wanted to be an actress, but her father soon nipped that idea in the bud.* 她想当演员, 但她父亲一知道这个想法就阻止住了. **5** (phr v) **nip sth in** (in sewing) reduce the width of sth (缝纫)将某物改瘦: *nip the waist in* 把腰身改瘦 ○ *nip in the sides of a dress*, eg by altering the seams 把连衣裙的两侧改瘦. **nip sth off (sth)** remove sth by nipping 掐掉某物: *nip the shoots off (a plant)* 掐掉花木的幼芽.
▷ **nip** *n* **1** sharp pinch or bite 捏; 箝; 夹; 咬: *The dog gave me a nasty nip on the leg.* 那狗在我腿上狠咬了一口. ○ *a cold nip in the air*, ie a feeling of frost 刺骨的寒气. **2** (*infml* 口) small drink, esp of spirits 少量(尤指烈酒): *a nip of brandy* 少量的白兰地.

nip·per /ˈnɪpə(r); ˈnɪpɚ/ *n* **1** [C usu *pl* 通常作复数] claw of a crab, lobster, etc (蟹、龙虾等的)螯. **2 nippers** [pl] (*infml* 口) any tool for gripping or cutting, eg pincers 夹或剪的工具(如镊子): *a pair of nippers* 一把钳子. **3** [C] (*Brit infml* 口) small child 小孩儿: *a mother with two young nippers* 带着两个子女的妇女 ○ *He's a cheeky little nipper.* 他是个小赖皮.

nipple /ˈnɪpl; ˈnɪpl̩/ *n* **1** (**a**) small projection on the breast through which a baby sucks its mother's milk (女子的)乳头, 奶头. (**b**) similar projection on the chest of a human male (男子的)乳头. Cf 参看 TEAT. ➪illus at HUMAN 见 HUMAN 插图. **2** = TEAT. **3** thing shaped like a nipple 似乳头之物: ˈ*grease nipples*, ie for squirting grease into machinery 油脂喷嘴.

nippy /ˈnɪpɪ; ˈnɪpɪ/ *adj* (**-ier, -iest**) (*infml* 口) **1** nimble; quick 敏捷的; 快的: *a nippy little car* 速度快的小汽车. **2** cold; chilly 冷的; 寒冷的: *It's jolly nippy today, isn't it?* 今天可够冷的, 是吧?

nir·vana /nɪəˈvɑ:nə; nɪrˈvɑnə/ *n* [U] (in Buddhism and Hinduism) state of perfect bliss in which the individual becomes absorbed into the supreme spirit (佛教和印度教的)涅槃.

Nis·sen hut /ˈnɪsn hʌt; ˈnɪsn̩,hʌt/ tunnel-shaped hut made of curved sheets of corrugated iron covering a concrete floor 尼森式简易房屋.

nit /nɪt; nɪt/ *n* **1** (egg of a) louse or other parasitic insect 虱或其他寄生虫(的卵). **2** (*infml* 口 *esp Brit*) = NITWIT.
□ ˈ**nit-picking** *adj, n* [U] (*derog* 贬) finding fault in a petty way 挑剔(的); 刻薄(的): *nit-picking criticism* 刻薄的批评.

N

ni·trate /ˈnaɪtreɪt; ˈnaɪtret/ *n* [U, C] salt formed by the chemical reaction of nitric acid with an alkali, esp *potassium nitrate* or *sodium nitrate*, used as fertilizers 硝酸盐; (尤指作肥料用的)硝酸钾, 硝酸钠: *soil enriched with nitrates* 施硝酸盐肥料的土壤.

nitre (*US* **ni·ter**) /ˈnaɪtə(r); ˈnaɪtɚ/ *n* [U] potassium or sodium nitrate; saltpetre 硝酸钾; 硝酸钠; 硝石.

ni·tric /ˈnaɪtrɪk; ˈnaɪtrɪk/ *adj* of or containing nitrogen 氮的; 含氮的.

□ **nitric acid** clear colourless powerful acid that corrodes and destroys most substances 硝酸.

ni·tro·gen /ˈnaɪtrədʒən; ˈnaɪtrədʒən/ *n* [U] chemical element, a gas without colour, taste or smell that forms about four-fifths of the atmosphere 氮. ⇨App 10 见附录10. ▷ **ni·tro·gen·ous** /naɪˈtrɒdʒɪnəs; naɪˈtrɑdʒənəs/ *adj*.

nitro-glycerine (also *esp US* **-glycerin**) /ˌnaɪtrəʊˈglɪsəriːn; *US* -rɪn; ˌnaɪtrəˈglɪsərɪn/ *n* [U] powerful explosive made by adding glycerine to a mixture of nitric acid and sulphuric acid 硝化甘油; 甘油三硝酸酯.

ni·trous /ˈnaɪtrəs; ˈnaɪtrəs/ *adj* of or like nitre 硝石的; 似硝石的.

□ ˌ**nitrous ˈoxide** (also **laughing-gas**) gas sometimes used as an anaesthetic, esp by dentists 氧化亚氮, 笑气(有时用作麻醉剂, 尤用于牙科).

nitty-gritty /ˌnɪtɪ ˈgrɪtɪ; ˌnɪtɪˈgrɪtɪ/ *n* **the nitty-gritty** [sing] (*infml* 口) the basic facts or realities of a matter 基本事实; 实情: *Let's get down to (discussing) the nitty-gritty.* 咱们着手探讨实际情况吧.

nit·wit /ˈnɪtwɪt; ˈnɪtˌwɪt/ (also **nit**) *n* (*infml* 口) stupid or foolish person 笨蛋; 傻瓜: *Why did you do that, you nitwit?* 你这傻瓜, 为什么做那种事?

▷ **nit·wit·ted** /ˌnɪtˈwɪtɪd; ˌnɪtˈwɪtɪd/ *adj* (*infml* 口) stupid; foolish 蠢的; 笨的; 傻的.

nix /nɪks; nɪks/ *n* [U] (*sl* 俚) nothing 没有; 无: *It cost me absolutely nix.* 我一分钱没花.

no /nəʊ; no/ *neg det* **1** (used with *pl* [C] *ns*, *sing* [C] *ns* or [U] *ns* 与可数名词的单数、复数或不可数名词连用) not any; not one; not a 没有; 无: *No words can express my grief.* 我的忧伤无法用语言表达. ○ *No student is to leave the room.* 学生不得离开这个房间. ○ *I have no time at all to write to you.* 我根本没时间给你写信. ○ *No two people think alike.* 没有两个人的想法是一样的. **2** (used to indicate that sth is not allowed 用以表示某事被禁止): *No smoking.* 禁止吸烟. ○ *No dogs in the restaurant.* 不得携狗进入饭店. **3** (used to express the exact opposite of what is said 用以表示与所说的事截然相反): *It was no easy part to play*, ie It was very difficult. 那可不容易. ○ *She was wearing no ordinary hat*, ie Her hat was very unusual. 她戴的那顶帽子可不一般. ○ *She's no fool*, ie She is intelligent. 她可不是傻子.

▷ **no** *interj* (used to give a negative reply 用作否定的答复): *'Is it raining?' 'No, it isn't.'* '现在下雨吗?' '没下.' ○ *'Haven't you finished?' 'No, not yet.'* '你做完了吗?' '还没有.' ○ *'Are you still a student?' 'No, I've got a job now.'* '你还是学生吗?' '不是, 我现已经工作了.'

no *neg adv* (used before comparative *adjs* and *advs* 用于形容词和副词的比较级之前) not 不: *It's no worse than the last exercise.* 这并不比上次的练习糟. ○ *This book is no more expensive than that one.* 这本书并不比那本贵. ○ *If you're no better by tomorrow I'll call the doctor.* 你明天若再不好, 我就请大夫.

noes /nəʊz; noz/ *n* [pl] total number of people voting 'no' in a formal debate (在正式的辩论中)投反对票者的总人数: *The noes have it*, ie Those voting 'no' are in the majority. 投反对票者占多数.

□ ˌ**no-ˈball** *n* unlawfully bowled ball in cricket (板球)投球犯规. — *v* [Tn usu passive 通常用于被动语态] (of an umpire) declare (a bowler) to have bowled such a ball (指裁判员)宣布(投球手)投球犯规.

ˌ**no-claims ˈbonus** sum deducted from the money paid annually, esp by a motorist, for insurance after a year when no claims are made 无索偿优惠(自每年投保金额中扣除的, 尤指对机动车主的).

ˌ**no-ˈgo area** area to which entry is forbidden to certain people or groups 禁区(禁止某些人或团体进入的地区). Cf 参看 NO GO (GO[1]).

ˈ**no man's land** (in war) ground between the fronts of two opposing armies (战争时两军阵前的)无人地带.

ˈ**no one** = NOBODY.

no-ˈshow *n* (*infml* 口) person who has a ticket for a journey by air, rail or sea but does not use it 有飞机票、火车票或船票而不使用的人.

No *abbr* 缩写 = **1** (*US*) North(ern). **2** (also **no**) (*pl* **Nos, nos**) (*US symb* 美式符号为 #) number 号码: *No 10 (Downing Street)*, ie the official residence of the British Prime Minister (唐宁街)10号(英国首相府) ○ *room no 145*, eg in a hotel 145号房间(如旅馆中的).

nob /nɒb; nɑb/ *n* (*sl derog* 俚, 贬 *esp Brit*) upper-class, important or high-ranking person 上流社会人物; 要人; 地位高的人: *He acts as if he's one of the nobs.* 他装得像个大人物似的.

nobble /ˈnɒbl; ˈnɑbl/ *v* (*Brit sl* 俚) [Tn] **1** tamper with (a racehorse) so that it is less likely to win a race 对(参赛的马)做手脚(使之不易获胜). **2** influence or get the favour of (sb), esp by unfair or illegal means 影响(某人), 受到(某人)的偏袒(尤指用不公平的或非法的手段): *nobble* (eg bribe) *the judge before a trial* 在审判前贿赂法官. **3** get (sth) dishonestly or by devious means 以不正当的手段取得(某事物). **4** catch (a criminal) 逮捕(罪犯).

No·bel Prize /nəʊˌbel ˈpraɪz; ˈnoˌbɛl ˈpraɪz/ each of six international prizes awarded each year for outstanding achievements in the fields of science, literature and the promotion of world peace 诺贝尔奖: *the winner of this year's Nobel Prize for chemistry* 诺贝尔化学奖今年的获奖者.

no·bil·ity /nəʊˈbɪlətɪ; noˈbɪlətɪ/ *n* **1** [U] quality of being noble in mind, character, birth or rank 高尚的思想或品格; 高贵的出身或地位: *Her nobility of character made her much admired.* 她的高尚品格令人钦佩. **2 the nobility** [Gp] people of noble birth or rank 贵族: *a member of the British nobility* 英国贵族的一员 ○ *marry into the nobility* 与贵族成员结婚. Cf 参看 ARISTOCRACY.

noble /ˈnəʊbl; ˈnobl/ *adj* (**-r** /ˈnəʊblə(r); ˈnoblɚ/, **-st** /ˈnəʊblɪst; ˈnoblɪst/) **1** belonging to the aristocracy by birth or rank 贵族的; 贵族出身的; 贵族阶层的: *a family of noble descent* 世袭的贵族家庭. **2** having or showing an excellent character; not petty or mean 高尚的; 高贵的; 崇高的: *a noble leader, mind, gesture* 伟大的领袖、高尚的思想、高雅的姿态 ○ *noble sentiments* 高尚的情操 ○ *It was noble of you to accept a lower salary to help the company.* 你为了帮助公司而接受低工资真是难能可贵. **3** impressive in size, appearance, etc; splendid (大小、外貌等)给人深刻印象的; 卓越的; 非凡的: *a noble building, horse* 宏伟的建筑、骏马 ○ *a woman with a noble bearing* 举止高雅的女子.

▷ **noble** *n* person of noble birth or rank 贵族的成员.

nobly /ˈnəʊblɪ; ˈnoblɪ/ *adv* in a noble manner; splendidly 高尚地; 高贵地; 华贵地: *nobly born* 出身高贵 ○ *thoughts nobly expressed* 表现崇高的思想.

□ ˈ**nobleman** /-mən; -mən/ (*pl* **-men**), ˈ**noblewoman** (*pl* **-women**) *ns* person of noble birth or rank; peer or peeress 出身高贵的人; 贵族阶层的人; 贵族的成员. Cf 参看 ARISTOCRAT.

no·blesse ob·lige /nəʊˌbles əˈbliːʒ; noˈblɛs əˈbliʒ/ (*French saying* 法, 谚) people with high rank, privilege, etc must accept the responsibilities that go with their position 位高则任重.

no·body /ˈnəʊbədɪ; ˈnobədɪ/ (also **no one** /ˈnəʊwʌn; ˈnoˌwʌn/) *neg pron* not anybody; no person 没有人; 无人: *Nobody came to see me.* 没人来看我. ○ *When I arrived there was nobody there.* 我到的时候那里没人. ○ *He found that nobody could speak English.* 他发觉没人会说英语. ○ *Nobody remembered to sign their names.* 谁也没记着应当签名. ⇨Usage at SOMEBODY 用法见 SOMEBODY.

▷ **no·body** *n* unimportant person 不重要的人; 小人物: *He was just a nobody before he met her.* 他认识她之前只是个小人物. ○ *Your friends are all just a bunch of nobodies.* 你的朋友都不过是无名之辈.

noc·turnal /nɒkˈtɜːnl; nɑkˈtɝnl/ *adj* **1** of or in the night; done or happening in the night 夜间的; 在夜间的; 在夜间做的; 在夜间发生的: *a nocturnal visit, trip, etc* 夜访、夜行. **2** (of creatures) active during the night (指生物)夜间活动的: *nocturnal birds*, eg owls 夜间活动的鸟(如猫头鹰). ▷ **noc·turn·ally** *adv*.

noc·turne /ˈnɒktɜːn; ˈnɑktɝn/ *n* **1** soft dreamy piece of music 夜曲；梦幻曲. **2** painting of a night scene（画的）夜景.

nod /nɒd; nɑd/ *v* (**-dd-**) **1** [I, Ipr, Tn] **~ (to/at sb)** move (the head) down and then up again quickly to show agreement, or as a greeting or command 点头: *The teacher nodded in agreement.* 老师同意地点点头. ○ *I asked her if she wanted to come and she nodded.* 我问她是否想来，她点了点头. ○ *She nodded (to me) as she passed.* 她从我身边走过时向我点头致意. ○ *Why are you nodding (your head) if you disagree?* 你若不同意为什么要点头呢? **2** [Tn, Dn·n, Dn·pr, Dpr·t] **~ sth (to sb)** indicate sth by nodding 点头示意: *She nodded her approval.* 她点头表示赞成. ○ *He nodded me a welcome/nodded a welcome to me.* 他对我点点头表示欢迎. ○ *He nodded to me to leave the room.* 他向我点头示意让我离开房间. **3** [I] let one's head fall forward when drowsy or asleep 垂着头打瞌睡；打盹: *The old lady sat nodding by the fire.* 那老太太坐在火炉旁打瞌睡. **4** [I] (of flowers, etc) bend downwards and sway（指花等）垂下并摇摆: *nodding pansies* 摇摆着的三色堇. **5** [I] make a mistake because of lack of alertness or attention（因不机警或不留心）犯错误. **6** (idm 习语) **have a nodding acquaintance with sb/sth** know sb/sth slightly 与某人有点头之交；对某事物略知一二: *I have no more than a nodding acquaintance with her novels.* 我对她写的小说不甚了解. **Homer (sometimes) nods** (*saying* 谚) even the best, greatest, etc people occasionally make mistakes 荷马也有打盹的时候(最杰出、最伟大的人偶尔也犯错误)；智者千虑，必有一失. **7** (phr v) **nod off** (*infml* 口) fall asleep 睡着: *I often nod off for a little while after lunch.* 我在午饭后常睡一小觉.

▷ **nod** *n* **1** act of nodding the head 点头: *She gave me a nod as she passed.* 她走过时朝我点一下头. **2** (idm 习语) **the Land of Nod** ⇨ LAND[1]. **a nod is as good as a wink (to a blind horse)** (*saying* 谚) a hint, suggestion, etc can be understood without being explicitly stated 暗示已足，不必明言. **on the 'nod** (*infml* 口) (**a**) (*Brit*) with formal assent and without discussion 未经讨论而正式表示赞成: *The proposal went through* (ie was approved) *on the nod.* 提议未经讨论而通过. (**b**) (*esp Brit*) on credit 赊购: *buy sth on the nod* 赊购某物.

noddle /ˈnɒdl; ˈnɑdl/ *n* (*infml* 口) head 头；脑袋.

node /nəʊd; nod/ *n* **1** (*botany* 植) (**a**) knob on a root or branch（根或枝上的）瘤，节. (**b**) point on the stem of a plant where a leaf or bud grows out 茎节(长叶或发芽的部位). **2** hard swelling, eg on a joint in the human body 硬结(如生于人体关节处的). **3** (*physics* 物) point or line in a vibrating body that remains still（物理）波节(振动体的静止点或线). **4** (*mathematics* 数) point at which a curve crosses itself（数学）结点(曲线本身的交点)；叉点. ▷ **nodal** /ˈnəʊdl; ˈnodl/ *adj.*

nod·ule /ˈnɒdjuːl; *US* ˈnɒdʒuːl; ˈnɑdʒul/ *n* small rounded lump or swelling 小圆块；小瘤.

▷ **nodu·lar** /-lə(r); -lɚ/, **nodu·lated** /-leɪtɪd; -letɪd/ *adjs* having nodules 有小圆块的；有瘤块的.

Noel /nəʊˈel; noˈɛl/ *n* (esp in carols) Christmas（尤用于圣诞颂歌中）圣诞节.

nog·gin /ˈnɒgɪn; ˈnɑgɪn/ *n* **1** small measure of alcoholic drink, usu $\frac{1}{4}$ pint（酒的）少量(通常为$\frac{1}{4}$品脱). **2** (*infml* 口) head 头；脑袋.

no·how /ˈnəʊhaʊ; ˈno,haʊ/ *adv* (*dialect or infml* 方或口) in no way; not at all 决不；毫不: *We couldn't fix it nohow.* 我们怎么也不能把它固定住.

noise /nɔɪz; nɔɪz/ *n* **1** [C, U] sound, esp when it is loud, unpleasant, confused or unwanted 声音；响声；(尤指)噪声，噪音，杂音: *the noise of jet aircraft* 喷气飞机发出的噪声 ○ *I heard a rattling noise.* 我听见格登格登的响声. ○ *What's that noise?* 那是什么响? ○ *Who's making those strange noises?* 谁弄出的那种怪声? ○ *Don't make so much noise.* 别那么吵闹. **2 noises** [pl] conventional remarks (used esp as in the expressions shown) 应酬话（尤用于下列示例）: *She made polite noises about my work.* 她对我的工作情况说了些客套话. ○ *He made all the right noises.* 他说了许多得体的应酬话. **3** (idm 习语) **a big noise** ⇨ BIG. **make a noise (about sth)** talk or complain loudly 高声谈论或抱怨: *She made a lot of noise about the poor food.* 她高声抱怨食物太差.

▷ **noise** *v* (phr v) **noise sth abroad** (*dated or fml* 旧或文) make sth publicly known 张扬某事: *It is being noised abroad that he has been arrested.* 他被捕的事已满城风雨.

noise·less *adj* making little or no noise 无声的；静的: *with noiseless footsteps* 以无声的脚步. **noise·lessly** *adv.* **noise·less·ness** *n* [U].

noi·some /ˈnɔɪsəm; ˈnɔɪsəm/ *adj* (*fml* 文) offensive; disgusting; stinking 令人不快的；令人讨厌的；有臭味的: *a noisome sight, smell, etc* 令人讨厌的情景、气味等.

noisy /ˈnɔɪzɪ; ˈnɔɪzɪ/ *adj* (**-ier, -iest**) **1** making or accompanied by a lot of noise 吵闹的；发出噪声的: *noisy children* 吵闹的孩子们 ○ *noisy games* 伴有喧闹声的游戏 ○ *Don't be so noisy! Jim's asleep.* 别那么吵! 吉姆睡觉呢. **2** full of noise 喧闹的；嘈杂的: *a noisy classroom, playground, etc* 乱哄哄的教室、操场等 ○ *I can't work in here — it's far too noisy.* 我无法在这里工作——太吵了. ▷ **nois·ily** /-ɪlɪ; -ɪlɪ/ *adv.* **noisi·ness** *n* [U].

no·mad /ˈnəʊmæd; ˈnomæd/ *n* **1** member of a tribe that wanders from place to place looking for pasture for its animals and having no fixed home 游牧部落的人. **2** (*fig* 比喻) wanderer 流浪者.

▷ **no·madic** /nəʊˈmædɪk; noˈmædɪk/ *adj* of nomads; wandering 游牧的；流浪的: *a nomadic existence, society* 游牧的生活方式、社会.

nom de plume /ˌnɒm də ˈpluːm; ˈnɑmdə,plum/ *n* (*pl* **noms de plume** /ˌnɒm də ˈpluːm; nɑmdə,plum/) (*French* 法) = PSEUDONYM.

no·men·cla·ture /nəˈmenklətʃə(r); *US* ˈnəʊmənkleɪtʃər; ˈnomən,kletʃɚ/ *n* (*fml* 文) (**a**) [C, U] system of naming, esp in a particular branch of science 命名法(尤指某学科的): *botanical nomenclature* 植物命名法 ○ *the nomenclature of chemistry* 化学术语命名法. (**b**) [U] names used in such a system（依命名法采用的）名称，学名.

nom·inal /ˈnɒmɪnl; ˈnɑmənḷ/ *adj* **1** existing, etc in name only; not real or actual 名义上的；不实际的；不真实的: *the nominal ruler of the country* 名义上的国家统治者 ○ *the nominal value of the shares* 股分的面值 ○ *She is only the nominal chairman: the real work is done by somebody else.* 她只是名义上的主席，实际工作是别人做的. **2** (of a sum of money, etc) very small, but paid because some payment is necessary（指一笔钱等）很少的，象征性的: *a nominal rent*, ie one very much below the actual value of the property 象征性租金(远低于实际租金) ○ *She charged only a nominal fee for her work.* 她为所做工作只收取象征性费用. **3** (*grammar*) of a noun or nouns 名词的. ▷ **nom·in·ally** /-nəlɪ; -nḷɪ/ *adv.*

nom·in·ate /ˈnɒmɪneɪt; ˈnɑmə,net/ *v* **1** [Tn, Tn·pr, Cn·n/a, Cn·t] **~ sb (for/as sth)** formally propose that sb should be chosen for a position, office, task, etc 提名某人(为某职位、职务、任务等的候选人): (*infml* 口) *I nominate Tom to make the tea.* 我建议汤姆去沏茶. ○ *She has been nominated (as candidate) for the Presidency.* 她已被提名为总统(候选人). **2** [Tn, Tn·pr, Cn·n/a] **~ sb (to/as sth)** appoint sb to an office 任命某人(任某职)；指定；指派: *be nominated to a committee* 被任命为委员会委员 ○ *The board nominated her as the new director.* 董事会指定她为新董事. **3** [Tn, Cn·n/a] **~ sth (as sth)** formally decide on (a date or place) for an event, meeting, etc 确定(某事、会议等的日期或地点): *1 December has been nominated as the day of the election.* 已指定12月1日为选举日.

nom·ina·tion /ˌnɒmɪˈneɪʃn; ˌnɑməˈneʃən/ *n* (**a**) [U] nominating or being nominated 提名；任命. (**b**) [C] instance of this 提名；任命: *How many nominations have there been* (ie How many people have been nominated) *so far?* 到现在已提名多少人了?

nom·in·at·ive /ˈnɒmɪnətɪv; ˈnɑmənətɪv/ *n* special form of a noun, a pronoun or an adjective used (in some inflected languages) when it is the subject, or is in agreement with the subject, of a verb 主格: *Is this noun in the nominative?* 这个名词是主格形式的吗?

▷ **nom·in·at·ive** *adj* of or in the nominative 主格的: *'I', 'we', 'she' and 'they' are all nominative pronouns.* I、we、she、they 都是主格形式的代词.

nom·inee /ˌnɒmɪˈniː; ˌnɑməˈni/ *n* person who is nominated for an office, a position, etc 被提名的候选人；被任命的人.

non- *pref* 前缀 (used widely with *ns*, *adjs* and *advs* 可与

N

许多名词、形容词、副词连用) not 不; 非; 无: *nonsense* ○ *non-fiction* ○ *non-alcoholic* ○ *non-profit-making* ○ *non-committally.* ⇨Usage at UN- 用法见 UN-.

non·age /ˈnəʊnɪdʒ; ˋnonɪdʒ/ *n* [U] (*fml* 文) state of being under full legal age; minority(2) 未成年.

nona·gen·ar·ian /ˌnɒnədʒɪˈneərɪən; ˌnɑnədʒəˋnɛrɪən/ *n, adj* (person who is) of any age from 90 to 99 90至99岁的(人).

non-aggression /ˌnɒn əˈgreʃn; ˌnɑnəˋgrɛʃən/ *n* [U, esp attrib 尤作定语] not attacking; not starting a war, etc 不攻击; 不发动战争; 不侵略: *a non-aggression pact/treaty* 互不侵犯协定[条约].

non-aligned /ˌnɒn əˈlaɪnd; ˌnɑnəˋlaɪnd/ *adj* (of a state) not allied to or supporting any major country or group of countries (指国家)不结盟的: *the non-aligned movement, nations* 不结盟运动、国家.

▷ **non-align·ment** /ˌnɒn əˈlaɪnmənt; ˌnɑnəˋlaɪnmənt/ *n* [U] principle or practice of being non-aligned 不结盟原则; 不结盟.

nonce /nɒns; nɑns/ *n* (idm 习语) **for the nonce** (*dated or rhet* 旧或修辞) (**a**) for this one occasion only 只限于这一场合. (**b**) for the time being 目前; 暂时.

□ ˈ**nonce-word** *n* word invented for one particular occasion 临时词语(为某场合而杜撰的).

non·chal·ant /ˈnɒnʃələnt; ˋnɑnʃələnt/ *adj* not feeling or showing interest or enthusiasm; calm and casual 不感兴趣的; 不热心的; 不激动的; 漠不关心的: *She defeated all her rivals for the job with nonchalant ease.* 她从容不迫地击败求职的所有竞争者. ▷ **non·chal·ance** /-ləns; -ləns/ *n* [U]: *Beneath his apparent nonchalance he is as nervous and excited as the rest of us.* 他外表上冷静, 实际上跟我们一样紧张不安. **non·chal·antly** *adv*.

non-combatant /ˌnɒn ˈkɒmbətənt; ˌnɑnˋkɑmbətənt/ *n* person (esp in the armed forces, eg a doctor or chaplain) not involved in the fighting in a war 非战斗人员(尤指军中, 如军医或牧师).

non-commissioned /ˌnɒn kəˈmɪʃənd; ˌnɑnkəˋmɪʃənd/ *adj* not having a commission(5) in the armed services 无军官衔委任状的: *non-commissioned officers,* eg sergeants or corporals 军士(如中士或下士).

non-committal /ˌnɒn kəˈmɪtl; ˌnɑnkəˋmɪtl/ *adj* not showing what one thinks, which side one supports, etc; not committing oneself (思想、立场等)不表明的, 不表态的, 不作承诺的: *a non-committal attitude, reply, letter* 观点不明确的态度、答复、信 ○ *She was very non-committal about my suggestion.* 她对我的建议不置可否. Cf 参看 COMMIT 4. ▷ **non-com·mit·tally** *adv*.

non-compliance /ˌnɒn kəmˈplaɪəns; ˌnɑnkəmˋplaɪəns/ *n* [U] refusal to comply (with an order, a rule, etc) (对命令、规章等的)不服从.

non compos mentis /ˌnɒn ˌkɒmpəs ˈmentɪs; ˋnɑnˌkɑmpəsˋmɛntɪs/ *adj* [pred 作表语] (*Latin* 拉) **1** (*law* 律) not legally responsible because of insanity (因精神失常)不负法律责任. **2** (*infml* 口) not able to think clearly 头脑不清醒; 糊涂: *I had had a few beers and was completely non compos mentis.* 我喝了些啤酒就头昏脑胀了.

non-conductor /ˌnɒn kənˈdʌktə(r); ˌnɑnkənˋdʌktɚ/ *n* substance that does not conduct heat or electricity 非导体; 绝缘体.

non·con·form·ist /ˌnɒnkənˈfɔːmɪst; ˌnɑnkənˋfɔrmɪst/ *n, adj* **1** (person) who does not conform to normal social conventions 不遵循社会常规的(人). **2 Nonconformist** (member) of a (usu Protestant) sect that does not conform to the beliefs and practices of the Church of England 不信奉国教(通常为新教)派的(教徒). Cf 参看 DISSENTER (DISSENT[2]).

▷ **non·con·form·ity** *n* [U] **1** (also **non·con·form·ism**) failure to conform to normal social conventions 不遵循社会常规. **2** (also **non·con·form·ism**) beliefs and practices of Nonconformist sects 不信奉国教派的教义; 不信奉国教. **3** lack of correspondence between things 不一致; 不符合.

non-contributory /ˌnɒn kənˈtrɪbjʊtrɪ; *US* -tɔːrɪ; ˌnɑnkənˋtrɪbjuˌtɔrɪ/ *adj* not involving the payment of contributions 不必摊付公积金的: *a non-contributory pension scheme* 雇员不必摊付公积金的养老金制度.

non·des·cript /ˈnɒndɪskrɪpt; ˋnɑndɪˌskrɪpt/ *n, adj* (person or thing) without a distinctive character and so not easily classified 无明显特征而不易分类的(人或事物): *He's such a nondescript you'd never notice him in a crowd.* 他没有什么特征, 在人群里决显不出他来. ○ *a nondescript landscape, face, voice* 无特点的风景、面孔、嗓音 ○ *nondescript clothes* 难以归类的衣服.

none /nʌn; nʌn/ *indef pron* **1** (**a**) **~ (of sb/sth)** (referring back to a plural *n* or *pron* 用以复指前文的复数名词或代词) not one; not any 一个也没有; 毫无: *We had three cats once — none (of them) is/are alive now.* 我们曾有三只猫 —— 现在一个活的也没有了. (**b**) **~ of sb/sth** (referring forward to a plural *n* or *pron* 用以预指后文的复数名词或代词) not one; not any 一个也没有; 毫无: *None of the guests wants/want to stay.* 客人中没有一个想留下不走的. (Cf 参看 *They none of them want to stay.*) ○ *None of them has/have come back yet* 他们谁也没回来. **2** (**a**) **~ (of sb/sth)** (referring back to a [U] *n* or *pron* 用以复指前文的不可数名词或代词) not any 毫无: *I wanted some string but there was none in the house.* 我需要一些绳子, 但家里一根也没有. ○ *'Is there any bread left?' 'No, none at all.'* '还有面包吗?' '一点儿也没有了.' (**b**) **~ of sb/sth** (referring forward to a [U] *n* or *pron* 用以预指后文的不可数名词或代词) not any 毫无: *None of this money is mine.* 这笔钱没有一点是我的. ○ *I want none of your cheek!* ie Stop being cheeky! 别那么厚脸皮! ○ *I'll have none of* (ie I do not wish to take part in) *your wild ideas.* 我可不想参与你那异想天开的计划. **3** (*fml* 文) (with comparatives and *than* 与比较级和 than 连用) nobody 无人; 没有一个人: *He is aware, none better than he, that...* 谁也没有他更清楚地知道... ○ *The choir sang sweetly, and none more so than the Welsh boy.* 唱诗班唱得很悦耳, 尤其是没人比得上那个威尔士男孩儿. **4** (idm 习语) ˈ**none but** only 仅; 只: *None but the best is good enough for my child.* 只有最好的才配得上我的孩子. ○ (*saying* 谚) *None but the brave deserves the fair.* 只有勇士才配得到美人. **none ˈother than** (used for emphasis 用以加强语气): *The new arrival was none other than the President.* 刚到达的不是别人, 正是总统.

▷ **none** *adv* **1** (used with *the* and a comparative 与 the 和比较级连用) not at all 毫不; 毫无: *After hearing her talk on computers I'm afraid I'm none the wiser.* 我听了她关于计算机的讲话之后似乎毫无收获. ○ *He's none the worse for falling into the river.* 他跌进河里但什么事也没有. **2** (used with *too* and *adjs* or *advs* 与 too 和形容词或副词连用) not very 不很; 不太: *The salary they pay me is none too high.* 他们付给我的薪水不太高.

□ ˌ**none the ˈless** nevertheless 尽管如此; 依然; 然而: *It's not cheap but I think we should buy it none the less.* 这个虽然不便宜, 但我觉得我们还是应该买.

non·ent·ity /nɒˈnentətɪ; nɑnˋɛntətɪ/ *n* **1** (*derog* 贬) person without any special qualities or achievements; unimportant person 无专长或成就的人; 庸人; 不重要的人: *How could such a nonentity become chairman of the company?* 这样的庸才怎么能当公司的董事长? **2** thing that does not exist or exists only in the imagination 不存在的事物; 想像中的事物.

none·such (also **non·such**) /ˈnʌnsʌtʃ; ˋnʌnˌsʌtʃ/ *n* [sing] (*fml* 文) person or thing that is better than all others 出类拔萃的人或物; 精英; 精品. Cf 参看 NONPAREIL.

non-event /nɒnɪˈvent; ˌnɑnɪˋvɛnt/ *n* (*infml* 口) event that is expected to be interesting, etc, but is in fact a disappointment 扫兴的事: *The party was a non-event; hardly anyone came!* 那聚会真扫兴, 几乎没什么人来!

non-existent /nɒnɪgˈzɪstənt; ˌnɑnɪgˋzɪstənt/ *adj* not present or existing in a particular place (在某地)没有的, 不存在的: *Bread was practically non-existent.* 实际上没有面包. ○ *a non-existent danger, threat, enemy* 不存在的危险、威胁、敌人.

non-fiction /ˌnɒnˈfɪkʃn; ˌnɑnˋfɪkʃən/ *n* [U] prose writings that deal with facts (as distinct from novels, stories, etc which deal with unreal people and events) (记实性的)散文文学(有别于小说、故事等非真人真事者): *I prefer non-fiction to fiction.* 我喜欢散文类的作品, 不喜欢小说类的. ○ [attrib 作定语] *the non-fiction shelves in the library* 图书馆中放散文类书籍的书架. Cf 参看 FICTION 1.

non-flammable /ˌnɒnˈflæməbl; ˌnɑnˋflæməbḷ/ *adj* (in official use 法定用语) (of clothes, materials, etc) not catching fire easily (指衣物、材料等)不易燃的. ⇨ Usage at INVALUABLE 用法见 INVALUABLE.

non-interference /ˌnɒnɪntəˈfɪərəns; ˌnɑnɪntəˈfɪrəns/ (also **non-intervention** /ˌnɒnɪntəˈvenʃn; ˌnɑnɪntəˈvɛnʃən/) *n* [U] principle or practice of not becoming involved in the disputes of others, esp in international affairs 不干涉(尤指国际事务): *a strict policy of non-interference in the internal affairs of other countries* 不干涉他国内政的坚定政策.

non-iron /ˌnɒnˈaɪən; *US* -ˈaɪərn; nɑnˈaɪən/ *adj* drying without creases after washing, without needing to be ironed (洗后)免熨的: *a non-iron ˈfabric, ˈshirt, ˈblouse, etc* 免熨的织物、男衬衫、女衬衫等.

non-observance /ˌnɒnəbˈzɜːvəns; ˌnɑnəbˈzɝvəns/ *n* [U] (*fml* 文) failure to keep or observe (a rule, custom, etc) 不遵从, 违反(规则、习俗等): *accused of non-observance of the test-ban agreement* 被控违反禁止核试验协定.

no-nonsense /ˌnəʊˈnɒnsns; *US* -sens; ˌnoˈnɑnsɛns/ *adj* [attrib 作定语] straightforward, sensible and serious 合情合理而坦率认真的: *Let's have a clear no-nonsense agreement to start work as soon as possible.* 让我们达成切实可行的协议以尽快开始工作. ○ *She has a firm, no-nonsense attitude towards her staff.* 她对下属的态度严肃而认真.

non·par·eil /ˌnɒnpəˈreɪl; *US* -ˈrel; ˌnɑnpəˈrɛl/ *n* [sing], *adj* [attrib 作定语] (*fml* 文) (person or thing) without an equal or rival 无双的, 无匹的(人或物). Cf 参看 NONESUCH.

non-payment /ˌnɒnˈpeɪmənt; ˌnɑnˈpemənt/ *n* [U] (*fml* 文) failure to pay (a debt, fine, etc) 未偿付(债务); 不支付(罚款等): *He was taken to court for non-payment of rent.* 他因不付租金而遭控告.

non·plus /ˌnɒnˈplʌs; nɑnˈplʌs/ *v* (**-ss-**; *US* **-s-**) [Tn esp passive 尤用于被动语态] surprise or puzzle (sb) greatly 使(某人)惊讶或困惑: *I was completely nonplussed by his sudden appearance.* 他突然出现使我大吃一惊.

non-proliferation /ˌnɒnprəlɪfəˈreɪʃn; ˌnɑnproˈlɪfəˈreʃən/ *n* [U, esp attrib 尤作定语] limitation of the number and spread (esp of nuclear and chemical weapons) 不增加和不扩散(尤指核武器和化学武器): *a non-proliferation treaty aimed at stopping the spread of nuclear weapons* 旨在制止核武器扩散的防止核扩散条约.

non-resident /ˌnɒnˈrezɪdənt; ˌnɑnˈrɛzədənt/ *adj* (*fml* 文) **1** not living in a place 不住在某地的: *This block of flats has a non-resident caretaker.* 这座公寓的管理员不在公寓里住. **2** (also **non-residential** /ˌnɒnrezɪˈdenʃl; ˌnɑnˈrɛzəˈdɛnʃəl/) (of a job) not requiring the holder to live on the premises (指工作)不要求任职者住在工作地点的: *a non-resident(ial) post* 不必在工作地点住宿的职位.

▷ **non-resident** *n* person not staying at a hotel, etc 不住在旅馆等中的人: *The bar is open to non-residents.* 酒吧对外营业.

non·sense /ˈnɒnsns; *US* -sens; ˈnɑnsɛns/ *n* **1** [U] meaningless words 无意义的词语: *jumble up the words in a sentence to produce nonsense* 打乱句子的词序而失去意义 ○ *This so-called translation is pure nonsense.* 这种所谓的翻译纯粹一窍不通. **2** (**a**) [U, sing] foolish talk, ideas, etc 胡说; 废话; 荒唐念头; 糊涂想法: *You're talking nonsense!* 你胡说八道! ○ *'I won't go.' 'Nonsense! You must go!'* '我不去.' '胡说! 你必须去!' ○ *This discovery makes (a) nonsense of* (ie clearly disproves) *previous theories.* 这一发现证明了过去的理论不能成立. (**b**) [U] foolish or unacceptable behaviour 愚蠢的行为; 胡闹: *Stop that nonsense, children, and get into bed!* 别胡闹了, 孩子们, 都睡觉去! ○ *He won't stand any nonsense from the staff.* 他决不容忍员工胡作非为. **3** (idm 习语) **stuff and nonsense** ⇨ STUFF[1].

▷ **non·sens·ical** /nɒnˈsensɪkl; nɑnˈsɛnsɪkl/ *adj* not making sense; absurd 无意义的; 不合理的; 荒谬的: *a nonsensical sentence, remark, suggestion, etc* 荒谬的句子、言词、建议等. **non·sens·ic·ally** /-klɪ; -klɪ/ *adv*.

non sequitur /ˌnɒn ˈsekwɪtə(r); nɑnˈsɛkwɪtə/ *n* (*Latin* 拉) statement that does not follow logically from the previous statement(s) or argument(s) 不根据前提的推理: *This non sequitur invalidates his argument.* 他不根据前提推理因而论证无效.

non-skid /ˌnɒnˈskɪd; ˌnɑnˈskɪd/ *adj* (of tyres) designed to prevent or reduce the risk of skidding (指轮胎)防滑的.

non-smoker /ˌnɒnˈsməʊkə(r); nɑnˈsmokə/ *n* **1** person who does not smoke tobacco 不吸烟的人. **2** compartment in a train, etc where smoking is forbidden (火车等的)禁烟车厢. ▷ ˌ**non-ˈsmoking** *adj*: *a non-smoking section in the cinema* 电影院的禁烟区.

non-starter /ˌnɒnˈstɑːtə(r); ˌnɑnˈstɑrtə/ *n* **1** horse that is entered for a race but does not run in it 虽参赛但未上场跑的马: *Number 18 in the 2.30 at Lingfield is a non-starter.* 在灵菲尔德2时30分一场赛马中, 第18号马不出赛. Cf 参看 STARTER 1. **2** (*fig infml* 比喻, 口) thing or person that has no chance of success 无成功机会的事或人: *Your proposal is absurd; it's an absolute non-starter.* 你的建议不合理, 绝对行不通.

non-stick /ˌnɒnˈstɪk; nɑnˈstɪk/ *adj* (of a pan, surface, etc) coated with a substance that prevents food sticking to it during cooking (指锅、物体表面等)不粘食物的: *It's very difficult to make pancakes without a ˌnon-stick ˈfrying-pan.* 没有那种不粘锅底的铛就烙不好饼.

non-stop /ˌnɒnˈstɒp; ˌnɑnˈstɑp/ *adj, adv* (**a**) (of a train, journey, etc) without any stops (指火车、旅行等)中途不停(的), 直达(的): *a non-stop flight to Tokyo* 直达东京的航线 ○ *fly non-stop from New York to Paris* 从纽约直飞巴黎. (**b**) (done) without ceasing 不停地(做)(的): *ˌnon-stop ˈtalk, ˈwork, etc* 不停的谈话、工作等 ○ *He chattered non-stop all the way.* 他一路上不停地闲聊.

non·such = NONESUCH.

non-U /ˌnɒnˈjuː; ˌnɑnˈju/ *adj* (*Brit infml* 口) (of language, behaviour or dress) not upper-class (指谈吐、举止或装束)非上流社会的: *a ˌnon-U ˈaccent* 非上流社会的口音 ○ *ˌnon-U ˈspeech, voˈcabulary, ˈmanners* 非上流社会的言谈、词汇、举止. Cf 参看 U.

non-union /ˌnɒnˈjuːnɪən; ˌnɑnˈjunjən/ *adj* [usu attrib 通常作定语] **1** not belonging to a trade union 不属于工会的: *Non-union labour was used to end the strike.* 雇用了没参加工会的工人以结束罢工行动. **2** (of a business, company, etc) not having trade-union members (指企业、公司等)没有工会会员的: *a ˌnon-union ˈfactory, ˈindustry, etc* 没有工会会员的工厂、工业等.

non-violence /ˌnɒnˈvaɪələns; nɑnˈvaɪələns/ *n* [U] policy of not using force to bring about political or social change 非暴力政策. ▷ **non-violent** /-lənt; -lənt/ *adj*: *a non-violent protest, rally, demonstration, etc* 非暴力的抗议、集会、示威等.

non-white /ˌnɒnˈwaɪt; nɑnˈhwaɪt/ *n, adj* (person) not belonging to the white-skinned races 非白种的(人): *These policies will affect non-whites especially.* 这些政策对非白种人的影响特别大.

noodle[1] /ˈnuːdl; ˈnudl/ *n* (usu *pl* 通常作复数) long thin strip made of flour-and-water or flour-and-egg paste and used in soups, with sauces, etc 面条: *Chinese food is often served with rice or noodles.* 中餐常有米饭或面条. ○ [attrib 作定语] *chicken noodle soup* 鸡汤面. Cf 参看 PASTA.

noodle[2] /nuːdl; ˈnudl/ *n* (*dated infml* 旧, 口) fool 傻子; 傻瓜.

nook /nʊk; nʊk/ *n* **1** sheltered quiet place or corner 隐蔽而安静的地方或角落: *a shady nook in the garden* 花园中阴凉幽静的角落. **2** (idm 习语) **every ˌnook and ˈcranny** (*infml* 口) every part of a place; everywhere 某地方的各处; 到处: *I've searched every nook and cranny but I still can't find the keys.* 我找遍所有的地方也没找到钥匙.

noon /nuːn; nun/ *n* [sing] (*fml* 文) (used without *a* or *the* 不用冠词a或the) 12 o'clock in the middle of the day; midday 正午; 中午: *They arrived at noon.* 他们是中午到的. ○ *My lecture's at twelve noon.* 我的课在中午十二点. ○ *She stayed until noon.* 她呆到中午才走. ○ *He has been working since noon.* 他从中午就开始工作了. ○ [attrib 作定语] *the noon bell*, ie bell rung at noon 正午的钟声.

□ ˈ**noonday** /-deɪ; -ˌde/ ˈ**noontide** /-taɪd; -ˌtaɪd/ *ns* [sing] (*dated or rhet* 旧或修辞) midday 中午: [attrib 作定语] *the noonday sun* 中午的太阳.

noose /nuːs; nus/ *n* **1** loop in one end of a rope, with a knot that allows the loop to be tightened as the other end of the rope is pulled 索套; 活结; 活套: *He's facing the hangman's noose*, ie waiting to be hanged. 他面临绞刑. ⇨illus 见插图. **2** (idm 习语) **put one's head in the noose** ⇨ HEAD[1].

N

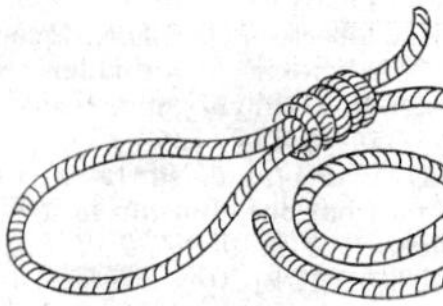
noose 索套

nope /nəʊp; nop/ *interj* (*sl* 俚) no! 不!

nor /nɔ:(r); nɔr/ *conj, adv* **1** (used after *neither* or *not* 用于neither或not之后) and not 也不; 也没: *He has neither talent nor the desire to learn.* 他既无天分也不想学习. ○ *Not a leaf nor an insect stirred.* 不单是树叶, 连个虫子都不动. **2** (*fml* 文) (used with *aux vs* and *modal vs*, with the subject following the *v* 与助动词和情态动词连用, 句中主语与动词倒置) and... not... either ... 也不: *He can't see, nor could he hear until a month ago.* 他现在看不见, 一个月之前他还听不见. ○ *She isn't rich; nor do I imagine that she ever will be.* 她现在不富, 我看她将来也富不了. ○ *It won't arrive today. Nor tomorrow.* 今天到不了. 明天也不会到. ○ *Nor am I aware that anyone else knows the secret.* 我也不知道别人谁还能知道这个秘密. Cf 参看 NEITHER.

nor'- ⇨ NORTH.

Nordic /ˈnɔ:dɪk; ˈnɔrdɪk/ *adj* **1** of the countries of Scandinavia 斯堪的纳维亚国家的. **2** of the European racial type that is tall, with blue eyes and blond hair 北欧人的, 有北欧人特征的(身材高大、蓝眼、金发): *Nordic features, peoples* 有北欧人特征的相貌、民族.

norm /nɔ:m; nɔrm/ *n* **1** (usu with *the* when *sing* 作单数时通常与the连用) standard or pattern that is typical (of a group, etc) 标准; 规范: *Criminal behaviour seems to be the norm in this neighbourhood.* 犯罪行为似乎是这一带的正常现象. ○ *You must adapt to the norms of the society you live in.* 在社会中生活就要遵循社会行为准则. **2** [C] (in some industries) amount of work expected or required in a working day (在某些工业中)每一工作日的标准工作量: *fulfil one's norm* 完成自己一日的标准工作量 ○ *There's a production norm below which each worker must not fall.* 每个工人的产量都不得低于生产指标.

nor·mal /ˈnɔ:ml; ˈnɔrml/ *adj* **1** in accordance with what is typical, usual or regular 正常的; 常态的; 正规的: *the normal time, place, method, position* 通常的时间、地点、方法、位置 ○ *normal behaviour, thinking, views* 正确的行为、思想、观点 ○ *in the normal course of events* 在事情的一般发展过程中 ○ *the normal temperature of the human body* 人体的正常温度 ○ *Weeping is a normal response to pain.* 哭泣是痛苦的正常反应. **2** free from mental or emotional disorder 心理正常的; 精神健全的: *People who commit crimes like that aren't normal.* 犯这种罪的人心理都不正常. Cf 参看 ABNORMAL.

▷ **nor·mal** *n* [U] usual state, level, standard, etc 常态; 正常; 标准: *Her temperature is above/below normal.* 她的体温高于[低于]正常标准. ○ *Things have returned to normal.* 事情已恢复常态.

nor·mal·ity /nɔ:ˈmælətɪ; nɔrˈmælətɪ/ (also *esp US* **nor·malcy** /ˈnɔ:mlsɪ; ˈnɔrmḷsɪ/) *n* [U] state of being normal 常态; 正常.

nor·mal·ize, -ise /ˈnɔ:məlaɪz; ˈnɔrmḷ,aɪz/ *v* **1** [I, Tn] (cause sth to) become normally friendly again after a period of dispute (使某事)正常, 正常化: *Relations between our two countries have normalized.* 我们两国的关系已恢复正常. ○ *Our relationship has been normalized.* 我们的关系正常了. **2** [Tn] make (sth) regular in pattern or as expected 使(某事物)合标准、合规格或要求: *The editors have normalized the author's rather unusual spelling.* 编辑已将作者不太规范的拼写改正过来. **nor·mal·iza·tion, -isation** /ˌnɔ:məlaɪˈzeɪʃn; *US* -lɪˈz-; ˌnɔrmḷəˈzeʃən/ *n* [U].

norm·ally /ˈnɔ:məlɪ; ˈnɔrmḷɪ/ *adv*.

Nor·man /ˈnɔ:mən; ˈnɔrmən/ *adj* **1** (*architecture* 建) of the style introduced into England in the 11th century by invaders from Normandy in France (**Normans**) 诺曼式的(11世纪法国诺曼底人侵者引进英国的风格): *a Norman arch, cathedral, etc* 诺曼式拱顶、大教堂等. **2** of the Normans 诺曼人的: *the Norman Conquest*, ie the invasion of England by Normans in the 11th century 诺曼征服(诺曼人于11世纪人侵英格兰).

norm·at·ive /ˈnɔ:mətɪv; ˈnɔrmətɪv/ *adj* (*fml* 文) describing or setting standards or rules of language, behaviour, etc, which should be followed (语言、行为等)标准的, 规范的: *A normative grammar of a language describes how its authors think the language should be spoken or written.* 规范语法阐述的是该派语法学家认为的某语言的口语或书面语的标准形式.

Norse /nɔ:s; nɔrs/ *n* [U] (also **Old Norse**) language of ancient Scandinavia, esp Norway 古代斯堪的纳维亚语; (尤指)古代挪威语.

▷ **Norse** *adj* [esp attrib 尤作定语] of ancient Scandinavia, esp Norway 古代斯堪的纳维亚的; (尤指)古代挪威的: *Norse myths and legends* 古代斯堪的纳维亚神话和传奇.

north /nɔ:θ; nɔrθ/ *n* [sing] (*abbr* 缩写 **N**) **1** (esp with *the* 尤与the连用) one of the four main points of the compass, lying to the left of a person facing the sunrise 北; 北方: *cold winds from the north* 寒冷的北风 ○ *He lives to the north of here.* 他住在这里以北的地方. ○ *Do you know which way is north?* 你知道哪边是北方吗? Cf 参看 EAST, SOUTH, WEST. **2 the north, the North** part of any country, etc that lies further in this direction than other parts 北部: *the North of England* 英格兰北部 ○ *The north is less expensive to live in than the south.* 北方的生活费用比南方低.

▷ **north** *adj* [attrib 作定语] (**a**) of, in or towards the north 北方的; 在北方的; 向北的; 朝北的: *the North Star*, ie the pole-star 北极星 ○ *the North Pole* 北极 ○ *the north wall*, ie the one facing north 北墙(朝北的墙). (**b**) coming from the north 来自北方的: *a north wind*, ie blowing from the north 北风 ○ *a north light*, ie from the north 从北面来的光线.

north *adv* to or towards the north 在北方; 向北方: *sail, drive, walk, etc north* 向北航行、行驶、走等.

north·erly /ˈnɔ:ðəlɪ; ˈnɔrðəlɪ/ *adj* **1** (of winds) from the north (指风)从北面来的. **2** to, towards or in the north 到、向或在北方的: *travel in a northerly direction* 向北走. — *n* northerly wind 北风: *Cold northerlies will bring rain to Scotland this week.* 寒冷的北风本星期将给苏格兰带来雨水.

north·wards /ˈnɔ:θwədz; ˈnɔrθwədz/ (also **north·ward**) *adv* towards the north 向北方. ⇨Usage at FORWARD[2] 用法见 FORWARD[2].

□ ˈ**northbound** travelling or leading in a northerly direction 北行的; 向北方的: *northbound traffic* 北行车辆 ○ *the northbound carriageway of the M6* 通向北方的6号车道.

the ˈNorth Country the northern part of England 英格兰的北部. ˌ**North-ˈcountryman** /-mən; -mən/ *n* native of the North of England 英格兰北部的人.

ˌ**north-ˈeast** (sometimes, esp nautical, **nor'-east** /ˌnɔ:rˈi:st; nɔrˈist/ 有时作 **nor'-east**, 尤于航海用语中) *n* [sing], *adj, adv* (*abbr* 缩写 **NE**) (region, direction, etc) midway between north and east (地区、方向等)东北.

ˌ**northˈeaster** *n* strong wind, storm, etc from the north-east 东北大风; 东北风暴. ˌ**north-ˈeasterly** *adj* (of direction) towards the north-east; (of wind) blowing from the north-east (指方向)向东北的; (指风)从东北吹来的. — *n* such a wind 东北风. ˌ**north-ˈeastern** /-ˈi:stən; -ˈistən/ *adj* of, from or situated in the north-east 东北的; 来自东北的; 在东北的. ˌ**north-ˈeastwards** /-ˈi:stwədz; -ˈistwədz/ (also ˌ**north-ˈeastward**) *adv* towards the north-east 向东北.

the ˌNorth ˈPole the northernmost point of the Earth 北极.

ˌ**north-ˈwest** (sometimes, esp nautical, **nor'-west** /ˌnɔ:ˈwest; nɔrˈwɛst/ 有时作 **nor'-west**, 尤于航海用语中) *n* [sing], *adj, adv* (*abbr* 缩写 **NW**) (region, direction, etc) midway between north and west (地区、方向等)西北.

ˌ**northˈwester** *n* strong wind, storm, etc from the north-west 西北大风; 西北风暴. ˌ**north-ˈwesterly** *adj* (of direction) towards the north-west; (of wind) blowing from the north-west (指方向)向西北的; (指风)从西北吹来的. — *n* such a wind 西北风. ˌ**north-ˈwestern** /-ˈwestən; -ˈwɛstən/ *adj* of, from or situated in the north-west 西北的; 来自西北的; 在西北的. ˌ**north-ˈwestwards** /-ˈwestwədz; -ˈwɛstwədz/ (also ˌ**north-ˈwestward**) *adv* towards the north-west 向西北.

north·ern /ˈnɔːðən; ˋnɔrðɚn/ *adj* [usu attrib 通常作定语] of or in the north 北方的; 在北方的: *the northern region, frontier, climate* 北方的地区、边界、气候 ○ *the northern hemisphere* 北半球.

▷ **north·erner** /ˈnɔːðənə(r); ˋnɔrðɚnɚ/ *n* person born or living in the northern part of a country 北方人.

north·ern·most /-məʊst; -ˌmost/ *adj* [usu attrib 通常作定语] lying farthest to the north 最北的; 极北的.

□ **the ˌnorthern ˈlights** ⇨ AURORA 1.

Nos (also **nos**) *abbr* 缩写 = numbers.

nose[1] /nəʊz; noz/ *n* **1** [C] part of the face above the mouth, used for breathing and smelling 鼻子: *give sb a punch on the nose* 打某人鼻子一拳. ⇨illus at HEAD 见HEAD 插图. ⇨Usage at BODY 用法见 BODY. **2** [C] thing like a nose in shape or position, eg the front of an aircraft body, the front of a car, etc (形状或位置)似鼻子的东西(如飞机的机首、汽车的前端等): *He brought the aircraft's nose up and made a perfect landing.* 他拉起机头, 平稳地降落下来. ⇨illus at AIRCRAFT 见 AIRCRAFT 插图. **3** [sing] **(a)** sense of smell 嗅觉: *a dog with a good nose* 嗅觉灵敏的狗. **(b)** **~ for sth** (*infml* 口) an ability to detect or find sth 探查或发现某事物的能力: *a reporter with a nose for news, scandal, etc* 善于搜寻新闻、丑闻等的记者. **4** (idm 习语) **be no skin off one's nose** ⇨ SKIN. **blow one's nose** ⇨ BLOW[1]. **by a nose** by a very small margin 以少许之差: *The horse won by a nose.* 那匹马以微弱优势险胜. ○ *The candidate lost the election by a nose.* 那候选人以微弱之差竞选失败. **ˌcut off one's ˌnose to ˌspite one's ˈface** (*infml* 口) hurt oneself in trying to take revenge on sb else 想报复别人而害了自己: *If you refuse her help because you're angry with her, you're cutting off your nose to spite your face.* 你要是因为跟她赌气而拒绝她的帮助, 那你是自讨苦吃. **follow one's nose** ⇨ FOLLOW. **get up sb's ˈnose** (*sl* 俚) annoy sb 惹恼某人; 使人生厌: *Her cheeky remarks really get up my nose!* 她那些不要脸的话真惹我生气! **have one's nose in sth** (*infml* 口) read sth very attentively 专心地阅读某物: *Peter's always got his nose in a book.* 彼得总是专心地看书. **keep one's ˈnose clean** (*infml* 口) avoid doing anything unacceptable, illegal, etc 不做讨厌、违法等的事: *If you keep your nose clean, the boss might promote you.* 你若是规规矩矩的, 老板就可能提拔你. **keep one's/sb's nose to the ˈgrindstone** (*infml* 口) keep oneself/sb working hard 使自己[某人]努力工作. **lead sb by the nose** ⇨ LEAD[3]. **look down one's ˈnose at sb/sth** (*infml* 口) treat sb/sth with contempt 轻视、蔑视某人[某事物]: *I gave the dog some lovely steak, and he just looked down his nose at it!* 我给狗一些挺好的肉排, 可它却看不上. **on the ˈnose** (*esp US sl* 俚) precisely; exactly 正好; 恰好; 准确: *You've hit it* (ie described or understood it) *on the nose!* 你描述得恰到好处. **pay through the nose** ⇨ PAY[2]. **plain as the nose on one's face** ⇨ PLAIN[1]. **poke/stick one's nose into sth** (*infml* 口) interfere in sth although it is not one's concern 干预、插手与己无关的事; 管闲事: *Don't go poking your nose into other people's business!* 少管闲事! **put sb's ˈnose out of joint** (*infml* 口) embarrass, offend or annoy sb 使某人难堪; 冒犯或惹恼某人: *He's so conceited that when she refused his invitation, it really put his nose out of joint.* 他很自负, 她没接受他的邀请可把他的鼻子气歪了. **rub sb's nose in it** ⇨ RUB[2]. **thumb one's nose at sb/sth** ⇨ THUMB *v*. **turn one's ˈnose up at sth** (*infml* 口) treat sth with contempt 轻视、蔑视某事物; 看不起; 看不上: *She turned her nose up at my small donation.* 她嫌我捐赠微薄而嗤之以鼻. **(right) under sb's (very) ˈnose** (*infml* 口) **(a)** directly in front of sb 就在某人面前: *I put the bill right under his nose so that he couldn't miss it.* 我把帐单就放在他眼前, 他不会看不见的. **(b)** in sb's presence, usu without him noticing anything 当着某人面(通常未被其察觉); 在某人眼皮下、鼻子尖底下: *They were having an affair under my very nose, and I didn't even realize!* 他们就在我眼皮底下勾搭上了, 而我竟没看出来! **with one's nose in the ˈair** (*infml* 口) very haughtily; in a very superior way 非常傲慢; 自高自大: *She walked past us with her nose in the air.* 她从我们身旁走过, 神气得鼻孔朝天.

▷ **-nosed** (forming compound *adjs* 用以构成复合形容词) having a nose of the specified kind 有某种鼻子的: *red-nosed* ○ *long-nosed*.

□ ˈ**nosebag** (*US* ˈ**feedbag**) *n* bag containing food for a horse, fastened to its head (挂在马头上的)饲料袋.

ˈ**nosebleed** *n* bleeding from the nose 鼻出血.

ˈ**nose-cone** *n* cone-shaped front end of a rocket, guided missile, etc (火箭、导弹等的)头锥, 前锥体.

ˈ**nosedive** *n* **1** sharp vertical descent by an aircraft, etc, with the nose pointing towards the earth (飞行器等的)俯冲: *go into a sudden nosedive* 突然俯冲. **2** (*fig* 比喻) sudden plunge or drop 突降; 暴跌: *Prices have taken a nosedive.* 价格已暴跌. — *v* [I] **1** (of an aircraft, etc) descend vertically with the nose pointing towards the earth (指飞行器等)俯冲. **2** (*fig* 比喻) fall sharply 急降; 暴跌: *Demand for oil has nosedived.* 对石油的需求已骤减.

ˈ**nose-flute** *n* musical instrument blown with the nose, used in parts of Asia 鼻笛(用鼻子吹的乐器, 用于亚洲的部分地区).

ˈ**nosering** *n* ring fixed in the nose of a bull, etc, for leading it (牛等的)鼻环(供人牵引的).

ˈ**nose-wheel** *n* front landing-wheel under the nose of an aircraft (飞行器机首下的)前轮, 鼻轮.

nose[2] /nəʊz; noz/ *v* **1** [Ipr, Tn·pr] (cause sth to) go forward slowly (使某物)缓慢前行: *The car nosed carefully round the corner.* 汽车缓慢地拐过街角. ○ *The plane nosed into the hangar.* 飞机缓缓地进入机库. ○ *He nosed the car into the garage.* 他把汽车慢慢地开入车房. ○ *The ship nosed its way slowly through the ice.* 那艘船缓慢地破冰前进. **2** (phr v) **nose about/around; nose into sth** (*infml* 口) pry into or search sth 打听或探索某事: *a reporter nosing around for news* 四处探听消息的记者 ○ *Don't nose into/nose about in other people's affairs.* 不要打听别人的事. **nose sth out** (*infml* 口) **(a)** discover sth by smelling 闻出、嗅到某物: *The dog nosed out a rat.* 那只狗闻到了老鼠的气味. **(b)** (*fig* 比喻) discover sth by searching 寻找出某事物: *That man can nose out a news story anywhere.* 那个人在任何地方都能搜寻出新闻.

nosegay /ˈnəʊzgeɪ; ˋnozˌge/ *n* small bunch of (usu sweet-smelling) flowers 花束(通常指香的).

nosey (also **nosy**) /ˈnəʊzɪ; ˋnozɪ/ *adj* (**-ier**, **-iest**) (*infml often derog* 口, 常作贬义) over-curious; rudely inquisitive 过分好奇的; 爱管闲事的: *I've always found her unbearably nosey.* 我发觉她总爱管闲事真让人受不了. ▷ **nos·ily** *adv*. **nosi·ness** *n* [U].

□ ˌ**Nosey** ˈ**Parker** *n* (*Brit infml derog* 口, 贬) over-inquisitive person; busybody 爱打听别人事情的人; 好管闲事的人: *I caught that Nosey Parker reading my diary.* 那个好事的傢伙偷看我的日记, 让我给抓个正着.

nosh /nɒʃ; nɑʃ/ *n* (*sl esp Brit or Austral* 俚, 尤用于英国或澳大利亚) **1** [U] food 食物: *There was lots of nosh at the party.* 聚会上有很多吃的东西. **2** [sing] (quick) meal, snack, etc (快)餐; 小吃; 点心: *We'll have a (quick) nosh, then start out.* 我们先吃些快餐再出门儿.

▷ **nosh** *v* (*sl* 俚 *esp Brit*) [I] eat 吃.

□ ˈ**nosh-up** *n* (*sl* 俚 *esp Brit*) meal, esp a large one 饭; (尤指)大餐: *We had a great nosh-up at Bill's wedding.* 我们在比尔的婚礼上大吃了一顿.

nos·tal·gia /nɒˈstældʒə; nɑˈstældʒə/ *n* [U] sentimental longing for things that are past 对往事的怀恋; 怀旧.

▷ **nos·tal·gic** /nɒˈstældʒɪk; nɑˈstældʒɪk/ *adj* of, feeling or causing nostalgia 对往事怀恋的; 怀旧的; 感到或引起对往事怀恋的: *I get very nostalgic when I watch these old musicals on TV.* 我从电视中看到这些旧音乐影片, 怀旧之情油然而生. ○ *a nostalgic song, poem, etc* 令人怀念往事的歌曲、诗等. **nos·tal·gic·ally** /-klɪ; -klɪ/ *adv*.

nos·tril /ˈnɒstrəl; ˋnɑstrəl/ *n* either of the two external openings in the nose through which the breath passes 鼻孔. ⇨illus at HEAD 见 HEAD 插图.

nos·trum /ˈnɒstrəm; ˋnɑstrəm/ *n* (*fml derog* 文, 贬) **1** medicine falsely recommended as effective; quack remedy 江湖药; 骗人的疗法. **2** over-simple measure put forward as a solution to political or social problems (解决政治或社会问题的)绝招, 妙计: *Some nostrum peddled as a cure for unemployment.* 鼓吹可解决失业问题的妙策.

not /nɒt; nɑt/ *adv* **1** **(a)** (used with *aux vs* and *modal vs* to form the negative; often contracted to *-n't* /nt; n̩t/ in speech and informal writing 与助动词和情态动词连用

构成否定式；在口语或语体文中常略作 -n't): *She did not see him.* 她没见他. ○ *You may not be chosen.* 可能挑不上你. ○ *They aren't here.* 他们没在这儿. ○ *I mustn't forget.* 我决不能忘记. ○ *Wouldn't you like to go home?* 你不愿意回家吗? (**b**) (used with non-finite *vs* to form the negative 与非限定动词连用构成否定式): *He warned me not to be late.* 他提醒我别迟到. ○ *The difficulty was in not laughing out loud.* 难就难在没笑出声来. **2** (**a**) (used after *believe, expect, hope, trust,* etc instead of a clause beginning with *that* and containing a negative *v* 用于believe、expect、hope、trust等动词之后，代替that引导的否定从句): *'Will it rain?' 'I hope not* (ie that it will not rain).' '这种天会下雨吗?''我希望别下雨.' ○ *'Does he know?' 'I believe not.'* '他知道吗?''我认为他不知道.' ○ *'Can I come in?' 'I'm afraid not.'* '我可以进来吗?''很抱歉，不可以.' (**b**) (used to indicate the negative alternative after questions with *Are you, Can he, Shall we,* etc 用于含有Are you、Can he、Shall we等的疑问句之后，构成选择疑问句): *Is she ready or not?* 她准备好了没有? ○ *Can you mend it or not?* 你能不能修理它? ○ *I don't know if/whether he's telling the truth or not.* 我不知道他说的是否是实话. **3** (**a**) (used to reply in the negative to part or all of a question 用于对疑问句做部分的或全部的否定回答): *'Are you hungry?' 'Not hungry, just very tired.'* '你饿吗?''不饿，只是很累.' ○ *'Would you like some more?' 'Not for me, thank you.'* '你再要点儿吗?''别给我了，谢谢.' ○ *'Do you go in the sea every day?' 'Not in the winter.'* '你每天都下海吗?''冬天不下海.' (**b**) (used to deny the significance of the following word or phrase 用以否定紧跟其后的词或短语的意义): *It was not greed but ambition that drove him to crime.* 驱使他犯罪的并非贪婪而是野心. ○ *Not all the students have read the book.* 不是所有的学生都读过那本书. ○ *'Who will do the washing-up?' 'Not me.'* '谁管刷锅洗碗?''我不管.' (**c**) (used to show that the opposite of the following word or phrase is intended 用以表示与紧跟其后的词或短语相反的意思): *a town that is not a million miles from here,* ie very close 距此地并非十万八千里的一座城市(很近) ○ *She argued, and not without reason* (ie reasonably), *that no one could afford to pay.* 她辩称没人能付得起钱，这也不无道理. ○ *We plan to meet again in the not too distant future,* ie quite soon. 我们打算不久以后再次见面. **4** (idm 习语) **not only ... (but) also** (used to emphasize the addition of sb/sth 用以强调递进关系的某人[某事物]): *Not only the grandparents were there but also the aunts, uncles and cousins.* 不光是祖父母，连姑母、叔父及其子女也在那里. ○ *He not only writes his own plays, he also acts in them.* 他不仅是自编剧本，还饰演其中的角色. **ˈnot that** though one is not suggesting that 并不是说: *She hasn't written to me yet — not that she ever said she would.* 她还没给我来信——倒不是她说过要给我写信.

not·able /ˈnəʊtəbl; ˈnotəbl/ *adj* deserving to be noticed; remarkable 值得注意的；显著的；著名的: *a notable success, event, discovery* 令人瞩目的成功、事件、发现 ○ *a notable artist, writer, etc* 著名的艺术家、作家等.

▷ **not·able** *n* famous or important person 名人；要人.

not·ab·il·ity /ˌnəʊtəˈbɪlətɪ; ˌnotəˈbɪlətɪ/ *n* [C] famous or important person 名人；要人.

not·ably /ˈnəʊtəblɪ; ˈnotəblɪ/ *adv* noticeably; remarkably 显而易见地；明显地；显著地: *notably successful* 显著地成功.

not·ary /ˈnəʊtərɪ; ˈnotərɪ/ *n* (also ˌ**notary** ˈ**public**) person with official authority to witness the signing of legal documents and perform certain other legal functions 公证人.

nota·tion /nəʊˈteɪʃn; noˈteʃən/ *n* **1** [C] system of signs, symbols, etc used to represent numbers, amounts, musical notes, etc (代表数字、数量等的)一套符号；(音乐的)乐谱，记谱法: *develop a new and simpler notation* 形成一套新的、更简单的符号. **2** [U] representing of numbers, etc by such signs, symbols, etc (有系统的)符号，数字，音符: *musical notation* 音乐符号 ○ *scientific notation* 科学符号.

notch /nɒtʃ; nɑtʃ/ *n* **1 ~ (in/on sth)** V-shaped cut in an edge or surface (边缘或表面上的)V型切口，刻痕: *cut/make a notch in a stick* 在棍上刻一V型痕记. ⇨illus at GROOVE 见GROOVE插图. **2** level or grade of excellence 水平；等级: *Acting and direction are several notches up on the standards we are used to.* 表演和导演水平远在我们熟知的标准之上. **3** (*US*) narrow mountain pass 山间小径；隘路.

▷ **notch** *v* [Tn] **1** make a notch or notches in (sth) 在(某物)上刻V形痕. **2** (phr v) **notch sth up** (*infml* 口) score sth; achieve sth 获得某分数；完成某事: *notch up a win, record, etc* 获胜、创纪录 ○ *With this performance, she has notched up her third championship title.* 她因这一成绩而获得第三个冠军称号.

note[1] /nəʊt; not/ *n* **1** [C] short written record (of facts, etc) to aid the memory 笔记；摘记: *make a note (of sth)* 做(某事的)摘记 ○ *She lectured without notes.* 她讲演不用演稿. ○ *He sat taking notes of everything that was said.* 他坐在那里把说的每件事都记录下来. **2** [C] (**a**) short letter 短信；短简: *a note of thanks* 谢函 ○ *He wrote me a note asking if I would come.* 他给我写了个便条，问我是否能来. (**b**) official diplomatic letter 照会；通牒: *an exchange of notes between governments* 两国政府互致照会. **3** [C] short comment on or explanation of a word or passage in a book, etc 评注；注释: *a new edition of 'Hamlet', with copious notes* 新版《哈姆雷特》，附详细注释 ○ *See the editor's comments, page 259, note 3.* 见编者按语，第259页之注释3. Cf 参看 FOOTNOTE (FOOT[1]). **4** [C] (also ˈ**banknote**, *US* usu 美式英语通常作 **bill**) piece of paper money issued by a bank 纸币: *a £5 note* 5英镑的纸币 ○ *Do you want the money in notes or coins?* 你要纸币要硬币? **5** [C] (**a**) single sound of a certain pitch and duration, made by a musical instrument, voice, etc (乐器、嗓子等发出的)单音，鸣声，音调，调: *the first few notes of a tune* 曲子的头几个音 ○ (*arch* 古) *the blackbird's merry note,* ie song 黑鹂轻快的鸣声. (**b**) sign used to represent such a sound in a manuscript or in printed music (乐谱上的)音符: *Quavers, crotchets and minims are three of the different lengths of note in written music.* 八分音符、四分音符和二分音符在乐谱上是不同长度的三个音符. ⇨illus at MUSIC 见MUSIC插图. (**c**) any one of the keys of a piano, organ, etc (钢琴、风琴等的)键: *the black notes and the white notes* 黑键和白键. **6** [sing] **~ (of sth)** a quality (of sth); hint or suggestion (of sth) (某事物的)特征；(某事的)暗示，含义，表示: *There was a note of self-satisfaction in his speech.* 他的言谈中流露着自满的口气. ○ *The book ended on an optimistic note.* 该书的结尾寓意乐观. **7** [U] notice; attention 注意: *worthy of note* 值得注意 ○ *Take note of what he says,* ie pay attention to it. 要注意他说的话. **8** (idm 习语) **compare notes** ⇨ COMPARE. **of ˈnote** that is important, distinguished, well-known, etc 重要的；非凡的；著名的: *a singer, writer, etc of some note* 有些名气的歌唱家、作家等 ○ *Nothing of particular note happened.* 没发生特别值得注意的事. **make a mental note (of sth/to do sth)** ⇨ MENTAL. **hit/strike the right/wrong note** ⇨ HIT[1]. **strike/sound a ˈnote (of sth)** express feelings, views, etc of the stated kind 表示某种感情、观点等: *She sounded a note of warning in her speech.* 她在讲话中表示要引起警惕. ○ *The article struck a pessimistic note; it suggested there would be no improvement.* 那篇文章不甚乐观，暗示将无改进. **strike/sound a false note** ⇨ FALSE.

▷ **note·let** /ˈnəʊtlɪt; ˈnotlɪt/ *n* sheet of paper, often decorated, for writing short letters on 便笺.

□ ˈ**notebook** *n* small book for writing notes (NOTE 1) in 笔记本；记事本.

ˈ**notecase** *n* wallet for banknotes 钱夹；钱包.

ˈ**notepad** *n* block of sheets of paper for taking notes (NOTE 1) on 便条本.

ˈ**notepaper** *n* [U] paper for writing letters on 信纸；信笺.

note[2] /nəʊt; not/ *v* **1** [Tn, Tf, Tw] (*esp fml* 尤作文雅语) notice (sth); observe 注意(某事物)；观察: *Please note my words.* 请注意我的话. ○ *She noted (that) his hands were dirty.* 她看到他的手很脏. ○ *Note how I do it, then copy me.* 注意看我是怎么做的，然后照我的样子做. **2** (phr v) **note sth down** record sth in writing; write sth down 记录某事；将某事记下: *The policeman noted down every word she said.* 警察把她说的每句话都记了下来.

▷ **noted** *adj* **~ (for/as sth)** well-known; famous 闻名的；著名的: *a noted pianist* 著名的钢琴家 ○ *a town noted for its fine buildings, as a health resort* 以精美的建

筑物、疗养地而闻名的城镇.

□ ˈ**noteworthy** *adj* deserving to be noted; remarkable 值得注意的; 显著的: *a noteworthy performance by a young soloist* 青年独奏演员的出色表演.

no·thing /ˈnʌθɪŋ; ˋnʌθɪŋ/ *neg pron* **1** not anything; no single thing 没什么; 没什么东西; 无物; 一个也没有: *Nothing gives me more pleasure than listening to Mozart.* 再没有比听莫扎特的乐曲更让我高兴的事了. ○ *There's nothing interesting in the newspaper.* 报纸上没什么有趣的新闻. ○ *I've had nothing to eat since lunchtime.* 从午饭时间到现在我什么都没吃. ○ *There's nothing you can do to help.* 你帮不上忙. ○ *He's five foot nothing*, ie exactly five feet tall. 他整整五英尺高. ○ *It used to cost nothing to visit a museum.* 过去参观博物馆是不收分文的. ○ *What's the matter? Nothing serious, I hope.* 怎么了? 我希望没什么大不了的事. ○ *There is nothing as refreshing as lemon tea.* 什么都不如柠檬茶那样提神. ○ *I had nothing stronger than orange juice to drink.* 我只喝了橙汁, 没喝酒. ⇨Usage at NOUGHT 用法见 NOUGHT. **2** (idm 习语) **be nothing to sb** be a person for whom sb has no feelings 对某人来说无所谓的人: *'What is she to you?' 'She's nothing to me.'* ʻ她在你心目中如何?ʼʻ她对我来说无所谓.ʼ **for ˈnothing (a)** without payment; free 不要钱; 免费: *Children under 5 can travel for nothing.* 5 岁以下儿童可免付旅费. ○ *We could have got in for nothing — nobody was collecting tickets.* 我们本可以不买票就进去 —— 根本没人收票. **(b)** with no reward or result; to no purpose 无酬劳; 无结果; 徒劳: *All that preparation was for nothing because the visit was cancelled.* 因为访问取消了, 一切准备工作都白费了. **have nothing on sb** (*infml* 口) **(a)** not be as clever, capable, etc as sb 不如某人聪明、有能力等; 比不上某人: *Sherlock Holmes has nothing on you — you're a real detective.* 福尔摩斯也没有你本事大 —— 你是真的侦探. **(b)** (of the police) have no information that could lead to sb's arrest (指警方)没有逮捕某人的罪证: *They've got nothing on me — I've got an alibi.* 他们没抓我的罪证 —— 我有不在现场的证据. **have nothing to ˈdo with sb/sth** not concern oneself with sb/sth; avoid sb/sth 自己与某人[某事]无关; 避开某人[某事]: *He's a thief and a liar; I'd have nothing to do with him, if I were you.* 他又偷东西又说谎; 我要是你的话, 就不跟他来往. ˈ**nothing but** only 仅仅; 只不过; 只: *Nothing but a miracle can save her now.* 现在只有出现奇迹她才能得救. ○ *I want nothing but the best for my children.* 我要把最好的给我的孩子. **nothing if not** (*infml* 口) extremely; very 极; 非常; 很: *The holiday was nothing if not varied.* 假日活动极其丰富多彩. **nothing less than** completely; totally 完全; 全部: *His negligence was nothing less than criminal.* 他的粗心大意无异于犯罪. **nothing like** (*infml* 口) **(a)** not at all like 丝毫不像; 完全不像: *It looks nothing like a horse.* 这完全看不出像马. **(b)** absolutely not 绝对不: *Her cooking is nothing like as good as yours.* 她做饭的手艺绝比不上你. **nothing more than** only 仅仅; 只不过: *It was nothing more than a shower.* 只不过下了场阵雨. ˌ**nothing ˈmuch** not a great amount (of sth); nothing of great value or importance 非大量(的某物); 少量; 价值不大; 不重要: *There's nothing much in the post.* 邮件中没什么要紧的东西. ○ *I got up late and did nothing much all day.* 我起晚了, 一整天也没做什么事. **(there's) nothing ˈto it** (it's) very simple (这)非常简单: *I did the crossword in half an hour — there was nothing to it.* 我用了半小时就把纵横字谜填好了 —— 容易极了. **there is/was nothing (else) ˈfor it (but to do sth)** there is no other action to take (except the one specified) (除去指出的办法外)别无他法: *There was nothing else for it but to resign.* 除了辞职别无他法.

▷ **no·thing·ness** *n* [U] state of not being; state of being nothing 不存在; 无; 空: *pass into nothingness* 化为乌有.

no·tice /ˈnəʊtɪs; ˋnotɪs/ *n* **1** [C] (sheet of paper, etc giving) written or printed news or information, usu displayed publicly 布告; 公告; 告示; 启事: *put up a notice* 张贴布告 ○ *notices of births, deaths and marriages in the newspapers* 报上登的出生喜报、讣告、结婚启事. **2** [U] **(a)** warning (of what will happen) 通知; 预告; 警告: *receive two months' notice to leave (a house, job, etc)* 收到两个月后搬家、解雇等的通知 ○ *at short notice*, ie with little warning, little time for preparation, etc 在短时间内(突如其来、无充分准备时间等) ○ *leave at (only) ten days' notice*, ie with a warning given only ten days beforehand (仅)提前十天通知离去 ○ *You must give notice* (ie tell people beforehand) *of changes in the arrangements.* 你要改变计划必须事先通知大家. ○ *The bar is closed until further notice.* 酒吧现已歇业, 开业时间另行通知. **(b)** formal letter, etc stating that sb is to leave a job at a specified time 辞职书; 辞职报告; 辞呈: *He handed in his notice* (ie left his job) *last week.* 他上星期递了辞呈. ○ *He gave her a month's notice*, ie told her that she had to leave her job in a month's time. 他通知她一个月内离职. ○ *leave without notice*, ie without giving the agreed amount of warning 擅自离去(未履行应预先通知之约). **3** [C] short review of a book, play, etc in a newspaper, etc (报刊上对书、戏剧等的)短评, 评介: *The play received good notices.* 那个剧受到好评. **4** (idm 习语) **be beneath one's notice** (*fml* 文) be sth one should ignore 不为某人理会; 不值一顾: *He regarded all these administrative details as beneath his notice.* 他认为行政管理上的这些琐事都不值一顾. **bring sth to sb's ˈnotice** (*fml* 文) tell sb about sth, show sb sth, etc 将某事知会某人; 使某人注意某事物: *It was Susan who brought the problem to our notice.* 是苏珊提醒我们注意那个问题的. **come to sb's notice** (*fml* 文) be seen, heard, etc by sb 被某人看到、听到等: *It has come to my notice that you have been stealing.* 我察觉到了你经常偷窃. **escape notice** ⇨ ESCAPE[1]. **sit up and take notice** ⇨ SIT. **take no ˈnotice/not take any notice (of sb/sth)** pay no attention (to sb/sth) 不注意(某人[某事物]); 不理会: *Take no notice/Don't take any notice (of what he says)!* 别理会(他的话)!

▷ **no·tice** *v* **1** [I, Tn, Tf, Tw, Tng, Tni] become aware of (sb/sth); observe 注意到(某人[某事物]); 留心; 看到: *Didn't you notice? He has dyed his hair.* 你没注意? 他染头发了. ○ *Sorry, I didn't notice you.* 对不起, 我没看见你. ○ *I noticed (that) he left early.* 我注意到他走得很早. ○ *I noticed how she did it.* 我看见她怎么做了. ○ *Did you notice him coming in/come in?* 你看见他进来了吗? **2** [Tn esp passive 尤用于被动语态] pay attention to (sb) 注意(某人): *a young actor trying desperately to be noticed by the critics* 极力想引起评论家注意的青年演员 ○ *She just wants to be noticed, that's why she dresses so strangely.* 她就是想引人注意才穿得那么稀奇古怪的.

no·tice·able /-əbl; -əbḷ/ *adj* easily seen or noticed 易见的; 明显的; 显著的: *There's been a noticeable improvement in her handwriting.* 她的书法有了明显的进步. **no·tice·ably** /-əblɪ; -əblɪ/ *adv*.

□ ˈ**notice-board** *n* (*US* ˈ**bulletin board**) board for notices (NOTICE[1]) to be pinned on 布告牌.

no·tify /ˈnəʊtɪfaɪ; ˋnotəˌfaɪ/ *v* (*pt, pp* **-fied**) [Tn, Tn·pr, Dn·pr, Dn·f] **~ sb (of sth); ~ sth to sb** (*fml* 文) inform sb (of sth); report sth to sb 通知某人(某事); 将某事报告某人: *Have the authorities been notified (of this)?* 当局是否已得知(此事)? ○ *notify the police (of a loss)/notify a loss to the police* 向警方报(失窃)案 ○ *He notified us that he was going to leave.* 他通知我们说他要辞职.

▷ **no·ti·fi·able** /ˈnəʊtɪfaɪəbl; ˋnotəˌfaɪəbḷ/ *adj* [esp attrib 尤作定语] (of diseases) which must by law be reported to the public health authorities because they are so dangerous (指疾病)(因危险)依法须报告卫生当局的: *Typhoid is an example of a notifiable disease.* 伤寒是必须报告卫生当局的病例.

no·ti·fica·tion /ˌnəʊtɪfɪˈkeɪʃn; ˌnotəfəˋkeʃən/ *n* [C, U] (*fml* 文) (act of) notifying (a birth, death, case of infectious disease, etc) (对出生、死亡、传染病例等的)通知, 报告: *There have been no more notifications of cholera cases in the last week.* 上星期已没有霍乱病例的报告.

no·tion /ˈnəʊʃn; ˋnoʃən/ *n* **1** [C] **~ (that...)** **(a)** idea or belief; concept 观念; 信念; 概念: *a system based on the notions of personal equality and liberty* 基于人的平等、自由等观念的制度. **(b)** idea or belief that is odd, vague or possibly incorrect (奇怪的、模糊的或可能不正确的)观念, 想法, 信念: *I had a notion that she originally came from Poland.* 我有个想法认为她的原籍是波兰. ○ *Your head is full of silly notions.* 你满脑子都是糊涂思想. ○ *He has a notion that I'm cheating him.* 他以为我欺骗他. **2** [sing] **~ (of sth)** (used esp after *no, any, some* 尤用于

N

no、any、some 之后) understanding 懂得; 明白; 理解; 了解: *Do you have the slightest notion of what this means?* 你能明白一点儿这是什么意思吗? ○ *She has no notion of the difficulty of this problem.* 她不了解这个问题的难处. **3 notions** [pl] (*US*) small items used for sewing, eg pins, buttons, reels of thread, etc (缝纫用的)零碎东西(如针、纽扣、线轴等); 针头线脑.

▷ **no·tional** /-ʃənl; -ʃənḷ/ *adj* assumed to be actual or real for a particular purpose; based on guesses or estimates 假定的; 猜测的; 想像的; 估计的: *My calculation is based on notional figures, since the actual figures are not yet available.* 因尚无实际数字, 我是根据估计的数字计算的.

no·tori·ous /nəʊˈtɔːrɪəs; noˈtorɪəs/ *adj* **~ (for/as sth)** (*derog* 贬) well-known for some bad quality, deed, etc 臭名昭著的; 声名狼藉的: *a notorious criminal, area, bend in the road* 天怒人怨的罪犯、地区、急转弯 ○ *She's notorious for her wild behaviour.* 她因行为野蛮而知名. ○ *He was notorious as a gambler and rake.* 他是声名狼藉的赌徒、浪荡子.

▷ **no·tori·ety** /ˌnəʊtəˈraɪətɪ; ˌnotəˈraɪətɪ/ *n* [U] (*derog* 贬) fame for being bad in some way 恶名; 臭名: *achieve a certain notoriety* 落得恶名 ○ *His crimes earned him considerable notoriety.* 他因犯罪而声名狼藉.

no·tori·ously *adv*.

not·with·stand·ing /ˌnɒtwɪθˈstændɪŋ; ˌnɑtwɪθˈstændɪŋ/ *prep* (*fml* 文) (can also follow the *n* to which it refers 亦可用于其所指名词之后) without being affected by (sth); in spite of 尽管; 虽然: *Notwithstanding a steady decline in numbers, the school has had a very successful year.* 尽管学生人数持续减少, 但该校这一年仍很成功. ○ *Language difficulties notwithstanding, he soon grew to love the country and its people.* 虽然言语不通, 他还是很快就爱上了这个国家及该国人民.

▷ **not·with·stand·ing** *adv* (*fml* 文) in spite of this; however; nevertheless 尽管如此; 然而; 仍然: *Many people told her not to try, but she went ahead notwithstanding.* 很多人劝她不要尝试, 她仍立意去做了.

nou·gat /ˈnuːgɑː, *also* ˈnʌgət; *US* ˈnuːgət; ˈnugət/ *n* [U] type of hard sweet made with nuts, sugar or honey, and egg-white 牛轧糖(用果仁、糖或蜂蜜及蛋白制的硬糖).

nought /nɔːt; nɒt/ *n* **1** the figure 0 零; 0: *write three noughts on the blackboard* 在黑板上写三个0 ○ *nought point one (0.1)* 零点一(0.1). ⇨App 4 见附录4. **2** (also **naught**) (*arch* 古) nothing 无; 无物: *His crime has gained him naught.* 他既犯了罪又一无所获.

□ ˌ**noughts and** ˈ**crosses** (*US* ˌ**tick-tack-**ˈ**toe**) game played by writing 0s and Xs on a grid of nine squares, attempting to complete a row of three 0s or three Xs 圈叉游戏(在井字形九格中各画0或X, 先将三个连成一行者胜).

NOTE ON USAGE 用法: The figure **0** has several different names in British English. 在英式英语中**0**这一数字有几个名称. **1** In speaking about temperature and in the language of science **zero** is used 说到温度时以及在科学术语中用**zero**: *The temperature rarely falls below zero here.* 这里的温度很少降到0度以下. **2 Nought** is commonly used when referring to the figure 0 as part of a number ☆ **nought**一般用作数字中的0: *A million is 1 followed by six noughts (1 000 000).* 一百万是1后面有六个0(1 000 000). **3** When reading a telephone or bank account number (ie when the number does not represent a quantity) we say the letter **'O'** /əʊ; o/ 读电话号码或银行帐号(即该数字不表示量)时, 将0读作字母**O**的名称: *The account number is 0-two-0-four-three-eight-one (0204381).* 该帐号是/əʊ-tuː: -əʊ-fɔː: -θriː-eɪt-wʌn; o-tu-o-fɔr-θri-et-wʌn/ (0204381). ○ *Their phone number is four-seven-double 0-five (47005).* 他们的电话号码是/fɔː-ˈsevn-ˈdʌbl əʊ-faɪv; fɔr-ˈsɛvn̩-ˈdʌbl̩o-faɪv/ (47005). **4** In reporting the score in a team game we use **nil** or **nothing** 说分队比赛项目的比分时, 用**nil**或**nothing**表示0: *The final score was three nil/nothing (3-0).* 最后比分是三比零(3-0). ○ *Wales won 28-nil.* 威尔士队以28比0获胜. In US English **zero** is commonly used in all these cases. 在上述情况下, 美式英语一概用**zero**表示0.

noun /naʊn; naʊn/ *n* (*grammar*) word which can be the subject or object of a verb or the object of a preposition; word marked *n* in this dictionary 名词. Cf 参看 COMMON NOUN (COMMON[1]), PROPER NAME (PROPER).

□ ˈ**noun phrase** (*grammar*) phrase whose function in a sentence is equivalent to that of a noun, and which usu contains a noun or pronoun as its main part 名词词组; 名词短语.

nour·ish /ˈnʌrɪʃ; ˈnʌrɪʃ/ *v* [Tn] **1** keep (a person, an animal or a plant) alive and well with food 养, 滋养(人、动物、植物): *Most plants are nourished by water drawn up through their roots.* 多数植物是靠着根吸收水分来维持生命的. ○ *well-nourished/undernourished children* 营养好的[不足的]儿童. **2** (*fml fig* 文, 比喻) maintain or increase (a feeling, etc) 保持, 增长(情绪等): *nourish feelings of hatred* 怀恨 ○ *nourish hopes of a release from captivity* 抱有囚禁获释的希望.

▷ **nour·ish·ing** *adj*: *nourishing food* 滋养的食物.

nour·ish·ment *n* [U] food 食物: *obtain nourishment from the soil* 从泥土中获取食物.

nous /naʊs; naʊs/ *n* [U] (*Brit infml approv* 口, 褒) common sense; resourcefulness 常识; 机智: *None of them had the nous to shut the door when the fire broke out.* 他们谁也不懂得失火时要关上门.

nou·veau riche /ˌnuːvəʊ ˈriːʃ; nuvoˈriʃ/ *n* (*pl* **nouveaux riches** /ˌnuːvəʊ ˈriːʃ; nuvoˈriʃ/) (usu *pl* 通常作复数) (*derog* 贬) person who has recently, and often suddenly, become rich, esp one who displays his wealth ostentatiously 暴发户.

Nov *abbr* 缩写 = November: *21 Nov 1983* 1983年11月21日.

nova /ˈnəʊvə; ˈnovə/ *n* (*pl* **~s** or **-vae** /-viː; -vi/) (*astronomy* 天) star that suddenly becomes much brighter for a short period 新星(在短时期内亮度突然增大者). Cf 参看 SUPERNOVA.

novel[1] /ˈnɒvl; ˈnɑvḷ/ *adj* (*esp approv* 尤作褒义) new and strange; of a kind not known before 新奇的; 新颖的; 新的: *a novel idea, fashion, design, experience* 新的观念、风尚、设计、经验.

novel[2] /ˈnɒvl; ˈnɑvḷ/ *n* book-length story in prose about either imaginary or historical characters (长篇)小说: *the novels of Jane Austen* 奥斯汀的小说 ○ *historical novels* 历史小说.

▷ **nov·el·ette** /ˌnɒvəˈlet; ˌnɑvḷˈɛt/ *n* short novel, often of inferior quality 中篇小说(常指质量低劣的).

nov·el·ist /ˈnɒvəlɪst; ˈnɑvḷɪst/ *n* writer of novels 小说家.

nov·elty /ˈnɒvltɪ; ˈnɑvltɪ/ *n* **1** [U] quality of being novel; newness; strangeness 新奇; 新颖; 奇异: *The novelty of his surroundings soon wore off*, ie He grew accustomed to them. 他对环境的新鲜感很快就消失了. ○ [attrib 作定语] *There's a certain novelty value in this approach.* 这种方法含有某种创新的意义. **2** [C] previously unknown thing, experience, etc; new or strange thing or person 新鲜的事物、经验等; 新奇的事物或人: *A British businessman who can speak a foreign language is still something of a novelty.* 能说某种外国语的英国商人仍可算是新奇人物. **3** [C] small toy, ornament, etc of low value (廉价的)小玩具、小装饰品等: *a chocolate egg with a plastic novelty inside* 内藏塑料小玩意儿的蛋形巧克力.

No·vem·ber /nəʊˈvembə(r); noˈvɛmbɚ/ *n* [U, C] (*abbr* 缩写 **Nov**) the eleventh month of the year, next after October 十一月.

For the uses of *November* see the examples at *April.* 关于November的用法见April词条中的示例.

nov·ice /ˈnɒvɪs; ˈnɑvɪs/ *n* **1** person who is new and inexperienced in a job, situation, etc; beginner 新手; 生手; 初学者: *She's a complete novice as a reporter.* 她初任记者, 完全是个生手. ○ [attrib 作定语] *a novice writer, salesman, cook, etc* 新的作家、售货员、厨师等. **2** person who is to become a monk or a nun but has not yet taken the final vows 见习修士或修女. Cf 参看 POSTULANT.

▷ **no·vi·ci·ate** (also **no·vi·ti·ate**) /nəˈvɪʃɪət; nəˈvɪʃɪɪt/ *n* period or state of being a novice(2) 修士或修女的见习期.

now /naʊ; naʊ/ *adv* **1 (a)** at the present time 现在; 目前: *Where are you living now?* 你现在住在哪里? ○ *It is now possible to put a man on the moon.* 目前已能将人送到月球上. ○ *Now* (eg After all these interruptions) *I can get on with my work.* 现在我可以继续工作了(如受多次

打扰之后). ○ *Now is the best time to visit the gardens.* 现在是最适合逛花园的时候. **(b)** immediately; at once 马上; 立刻: *Start writing now.* 立刻开始写. ○ *You've got to ask her. It's now or never.* 你得去问她. 马上就去否则就没机会了. **(c)** (used after a *prep* 用于介词之后) the present time 现在: *I never realized I loved you until now.* 我至今才意识到我爱你. ○ *He should have arrived by now.* 此时他本该到了. Cf 参看 THEN. **2** (used by the speaker, without reference to time, to continue a narrative, request, warning, etc 说话者用以表示继续进行叙述、请求、警告等, 不表示时间): *Now the next thing he did was to light a cigarette.* 然后他点了一枝烟. ○ *Now be quiet for a few moments and listen to this.* 请安静一会儿, 注意听着. ○ *No cheating, now.* 不许作弊. **3** (idm 习语) **(every) now and again/then** at irregular intervals; occasionally 时而; 偶尔; 有时: *I like to go to the opera now and then.* 我喜欢偶尔去看歌剧. ○ *Every now and again she went upstairs to see if he was still asleep.* 她时而到楼上看看他是否还在睡着. **ˌnow, ˈnow; ˈnow then** (used before expressing disapproval or admonishment 用于表示不赞成或劝慰的话语之前): *Now, now, stop quarrelling.* 行了, 行了, 别再吵了. ○ *Now then, that's enough noise.* 可以啦, 别再闹了. ○ *Now, now, cheer up and forget about it.* 好啦, 好啦, 振作起来, 别再想它了. **now...now/then** at one time...at another time 时而...时而...: *Her moods kept changing — now happy, now filled with despair.* 她的情绪多变 —— 时而高兴, 时而感到绝望. **ˈnow then (a)** ⇨ NOW, NOW. **(b)** (used to introduce a statement that makes a suggestion or invites a response 用以引出要说的话, 以提出建议或征询回应): *Now then, why don't you volunteer?* 那你为什么不自告奋勇呢? ○ *Now then, are there any comments on this report?* 喂, 对这个报告有什么意见吗? **(c)** (used to fill a pause when one is thinking what to do or say next 考虑下一步要做的事或要说的话时, 用以填补暂时的停顿): *I must say I enjoyed that. Now then, what's next?* 我的确很喜欢这个. 那么, 下一个呢? **now for sb/sth** (used when turning to a fresh task or subject 用以转折, 以提出新任务或新话题): *Now for a spot of gardening.* 现在来弄弄花草. ○ *And now for some travel news.* 下面报告旅游新闻.

▷ **now** *conj* **~ (that)...** because of the fact (that)... 由于...; 既然...: *Now (that) you mention it, I do remember the incident.* 经你一提, 我想起那件事了. ○ *Now you've passed your test you can drive on your own.* 你驾驶考试既已合格, 就可以独自开车了.

now·adays /ˈnaʊədeɪz; ˈnaʊəˌdez/ *adv* at the present time (in contrast with the past) 时下, 现今(与过去相对): *Nowadays, children often prefer watching TV to reading.* 如今, 儿童常爱看电视而不爱看书.

no·where /ˈnəʊweə(r); *US* -hweər; ˈnoˌhwɛr/ *adv* **1** not anywhere 无处: *'Where are you going at the weekend?' 'Nowhere special* (ie Not to any special place).' '你打算到哪儿去度周末?' '无处可去.' ○ *He was getting nowhere* (ie making no progress) *with his homework until his sister helped him.* 他在姐姐的帮助之下作业才有些进步. ○ *£20 goes nowhere* (ie does not buy much) *when you're feeding a family these days.* 如今要养家的话, 20 英镑到不了哪儿(买不了多少东西). ○ *One of the horses I backed came second; the rest were/came nowhere*, ie were not among the first three to finish the race. 我下赌注的几匹马中有一匹跑第二; 其余的没上名(没进前三名). **2** (idm 习语) **in the middle of nowhere** ⇨ MIDDLE. **nowhere near** ⇨ NEAR[2]. **ˌnowhere to be ˈfound/ˈseen** impossible for anyone to find or see 任何人都找不到或看不见: *The children were nowhere to be seen.* 孩子们都没影儿了. ○ *The money was nowhere to be found.* 哪儿也找不到那笔钱.

nox·ious /ˈnɒkʃəs; ˈnɑkʃəs/ *adj* (*fml* 文) harmful; poisonous 有害的; 有毒的: *noxious fumes, gases, etc* 有毒的烟雾、气体等. ▷ **nox·iously** *adv*. **nox·ious·ness** *n* [U].

nozzle /ˈnɒzl; ˈnɑzl̩/ *n* spout or end-piece of a pipe, etc through which a stream of air or liquid is directed (管子等的)喷嘴, 管嘴.

nr *abbr* 缩写 = near (eg in the address of a small village 如用于小村庄的地址中): *Warpsgrove, nr Chalgrove, Oxfordshire* 牛津郡查尔格罗夫附近沃普斯格罗夫.

NSB /ˌen es ˈbiː; ˌɛn ɛs ˈbi/ *abbr* 缩写 = (*Brit*) National Savings Bank (operated by the Post Office) 国家储蓄银行.

NSPCC /ˌen es ˌpiː siː ˈsiː; ˌɛn ɛs ˌpi si ˈsi/ *abbr* 缩写 = (*Brit*) National Society for the Prevention of Cruelty to Children 全国防止虐待儿童协会.

NT *abbr* 缩写 = (*Brit*) **1** National Trust (land), eg on a map 国立托拉斯(土地)(如地图上的标记). **2** New Testament (of the Bible) (《圣经》的)《新约全书》. Cf 参看 OT.

nth /enθ; ɛnθ/ *adj* (*infml* 口) **1** [attrib 作定语] latest or last in a long series (一系列中的)最新的, 最后的: *You're the nth person to ask me that*, ie Many others have asked me the same thing. 你是又一个问我这件事的人(已有很多人问过这件事了). ○ *For the nth time, you can't go!* 再说最后一次, 你不能去! **2** (idm 习语) **to the ˌnth deˈgree** in a very extreme way 到极点; 极度; 极端: *He's methodical to the nth degree.* 他做事有条不紊算是到家了.

Nth *abbr* 缩写 = North: *Nth Pole*, eg on a map 北极(如地图上的标记).

nu·ance /ˈnjuːɑːns; *US* ˈnuː-; ˈnuɑns/ *n* subtle difference in meaning, colour, feeling, etc (意义、颜色、感觉等的)细微差异: *be able to react to nuances of meaning* 能够对意义上的细微差异做出反应.

nub /nʌb; nʌb/ *n* [sing] **the ~ of sth** central or essential point of a problem, matter, etc (问题、事情等的)中心, 要点: *The nub of the problem is our poor export performance.* 问题的关键是我们出口贸易方面太差.

nu·bile /ˈnjuːbaɪl; *US* ˈnuːbl; ˈnubl̩/ *adj* (of girls or young women 指姑娘或少女) **1** old enough to marry 到结婚年龄的. **2** sexually attractive 性感的: *a photograph of a nubile young woman* 妙龄女郎的艳照.

nuc·lear /ˈnjuːklɪə(r); *US* ˈnuː-; ˈnuklɪɚ/ *adj* [usu attrib 通常作定语] **1** of a nucleus, esp of an atom 核的; (尤指)原子核的: *a nuclear particle* 核微粒 ○ *nuclear physics* 核物理学. **2** using or producing nuclear energy 使用或生产核能的: *a nuclear missile, power-station, reactor* 核导弹、电站、反应堆 ○ *nuclear-powered submarines* 核动力潜艇.

□ **ˌnuclear disˈarmament** removal or dismantling of nuclear weapons 核裁军.

ˌnuclear ˈenergy (also **ˌnuclear ˈpower**) extremely powerful form of energy produced by the splitting of the nuclei of atoms 核动力.

ˌnuclear ˈfamily (*sociology* 社) the family considered as mother, father and children only, and not including any less close relations 核心家庭, 小家庭(仅由父母和子女组成, 不包括关系较远的亲属).

ˌnuclear-ˈfree *adj* [esp attrib 尤作定语] (of an area, etc) not having or allowing any nuclear weapons or materials (指地区等)无核的: *They have declared their country a ˌnuclear-free ˈzone.* 他们宣布本国为无核区.

ˌnuclear ˈwar war waged with weapons using nuclear energy as their explosive force 核战争.

ˌnuclear ˈwinter period without light, heat or growth which would follow a nuclear war 核冬天(核战争带来的无光、无热或无生长物的时期).

nuc·leic acid /njuːˌkliːɪk ˈæsɪd; *US* nuː-; nuˈkliɪk ˈæsɪd/ either of two acids (DNA and RNA) occurring in all living cells 核酸.

nuc·leus /ˈnjuːklɪəs; *US* ˈnuː-; ˈnuklɪəs/ *n* (*pl* **nuclei** /-klɪaɪ; -klɪˌaɪ/) **1** central part, around which other parts are grouped or collected 中心; 核心: *The fortress was the nucleus of the ancient city.* 这城堡是这座古城的中心. ○ *These paintings will form the nucleus of a new collection*, ie Others will be added to them. 这些画将构成新的收藏品的主要部分(还将增加其他收藏品). **2 (a)** (*physics* 物) central part of an atom, consisting of protons and neutrons 核, 原子核(包括质子和中子). **(b)** (*biology* 生) central part of a living cell 细胞核.

nude /njuːd; *US* nuːd; nud/ *adj* (esp of a human figure in art) naked (尤指艺术人像)裸体的: *the nude torso* 裸露的躯干.

▷ **nude** *n* **1** naked human figure, esp in painting, photography, etc 裸体人像(尤指绘画、摄影等). **2** (idm 习语) **in the ˈnude** having no clothes on; naked 未穿衣的; 裸露的: *swimming in the nude* 裸体游泳.

nud·ism /-ɪzəm; -ɪzəm/ (also **naturism**) *n* [U] practice of not wearing clothes, esp for health reasons 裸体主义(尤指因于健康有益).

nud·ist /-ɪst; -ɪst/ (also **naturist**) *n* person who practises nudism 裸体主义者.

nud·ity /ˈnju:dətɪ; *US* ˈnu:-; ˈnudətɪ/ *n* [U] nakedness 裸体; 裸露: *Some people regard nudity as offensive.* 有些人认为裸体有伤风化.

□ ˈ**nudist camp** (also ˈ**nudist colony**) place where nudists can live and move about naked 天体营(裸体主义者可以裸体生活及活动的场所).

nudge /nʌdʒ; nʌdʒ/ *v* [Tn] **1** touch or push (sb) with one's elbow to draw his attention to sth 以肘碰或推(某人)(使其注意某事物): *I nudged her and pointed to the man across the street.* 我用肘碰了她一下并指了指街对面的那个男的. **2** push (sb/sth) gently or gradually 轻推或渐渐触到(某人[某物]): *The horse nudged my pocket with its nose.* 马用鼻子轻轻地拱我的衣袋. ○ *He accidentally nudged the gatepost with the front of the car.* 他一不留神汽车的头部碰上了门柱.

▷ **nudge** *n* push given in this way (此种)轻碰或轻推: *She gave me a nudge in the ribs.* 她以肘轻触我肋部一下.

NOTE ON USAGE 用法: **Nudge, prod, poke, jab** and **stab** indicate the action of pushing a hard or sharp object (eg a finger or stick) into a person or thing and are shown here in increasing order of force or violence. ☆ **nudge**、**prod**、**poke**、**jab**、**stab** 等动词表示的动作是以坚硬或尖锐的物体(如手指或棍棒)触及人或物,其力量大小或猛烈程度按由弱到强的顺序排列如下. **Nudge** = push or touch gently, especially with one's elbow, in order to catch somebody's attention ☆ **nudge** 是轻推或轻触, 尤指用肘部, 为使某人注意: *She nudged him with her elbow.* 她用肘轻触了他一下. **Prod (at)** = push, especially with a finger or stick, in order, for example, to make something move ☆ **prod (at)** 是推, 尤指用手指或棍棒, 如为使物体移动: *He prodded at the pig with his walking-stick.* 他用手杖推那口猪. The three remaining verbs can be used in two constructions 余下的三个动词可用于以下两种结构: **poke/jab/stab** somebody or something with a sharp object OR **poke/jab/stab** a sharp object into somebody or something. **Poke (at)** = push sharply ☆ **poke (at)** 是戳或捅: *He poked (at) the fire with a stick.* 他用棍拨火. He poked *a stick into the fire.* 他把棍子插进火里. **Jab (at)** = strike forcefully and roughly with a sharp object ☆ **jab (at)** 是用锋利的物体猛刺或乱戳: *The vet jabbed (at) the dog with a needle/jabbed a needle into the dog.* 兽医给狗扎针. **Stab** = strike forcefully into somebody or something with a pointed object, especially a knife, in order to wound ☆ **stab** 是用尖锐的物体用力刺入某人或某物,尤指用刀刺伤: *The killer stabbed him with a knife/stabbed a knife into him.* 凶手用刀刺他.

nu·gat·ory /ˈnju:gətərɪ; *US* ˈnu:gətɔ:rɪ; ˈnugəˌtorɪ/ *adj* (*fml* 文) worthless; pointless; not valid 无价值的; 无意义的; 无效的: *a nugatory idea, argument, proposal, etc* 无意义的想法、争论、建议等.

nug·get /ˈnʌgɪt; ˈnʌgɪt/ *n* **1** lump of (esp valuable) metal, eg gold, found in the earth (尤指贵重的)金属块(如天然金块). **2** (*fig* 比喻) small thing that is regarded as valuable (有价值的)小东西: *a book full of nuggets of useful information* 有很多有用的零碎资料的书.

nuis·ance /ˈnju:sns; *US* ˈnu:-; ˈnusn̩s/ *n* thing, person or behaviour that is troublesome or annoying 令人讨厌的事物、人、行为: *You are a confounded nuisance. Stop pestering me.* 你这个可恶的东西. 别再缠着我了. ○ *The noise was so loud that it was a nuisance to the neighbours.* 那声音大得让邻居讨厌.

null /nʌl; nʌl/ *adj* (idm 习语) **null and void** (*law* 律) having no legal force; not valid 无法律约束力的; 无效的: *This contract is null and void.* 此合同无效.

▷ **nul·lify** /ˈnʌlɪfaɪ; ˈnʌləˌfaɪ/ *v* (*pt, pp* **-fied**) [Tn] **1** make (an agreement, etc) lose its legal force 使(协议等)失去法律约束力. **2** make (sth) ineffective; counteract 使(某事物)无效; 抵消: *How can we nullify the enemy's propaganda?* 怎样才能抵消敌人的宣传?

nul·li·fica·tion /ˌnʌlɪfɪˈkeɪʃn; ˌnʌləfəˈkeʃən/ *n* [U].

null·ity /ˈnʌlətɪ; ˈnʌlətɪ/ *n* [U] lack of legal force; lack of validity 无法律约束力; 无效: *the nullity of a marriage* 婚姻无效 ○ [attrib 作定语] *a nullity suit*, ie legal action that asks for a marriage to be declared null and void 要求宣判婚姻无效的诉讼.

numb /nʌm; nʌm/ *adj* without the power to feel or move 失去感觉的; 麻木的: *fingers numb with cold* 冻僵了的手指 ○ (*fig* 比喻) *The shock left me numb.* 我惊呆了. ○ *She was numb with terror.* 她吓得不能动了.

▷ **numb** *v* [Tn esp passive 尤用于被动语态] **1** make (sb/sth) numb 使(某人[某物])失去感觉, 麻木: *Her fingers were numbed by the cold.* 她的手指冻僵了. ○ *His leg was numbed by the intense pain.* 他的腿因剧痛而麻木. **2** (*fig* 比喻) make (sb) emotionally incapable of thinking or acting 使(某人)麻木不仁: *She was completely numbed by the shock of her father's death.* 她父亲去世造成的打击使她目瞪神呆.

numb·ly *adv*.

numb·ness *n* [U].

num·ber /ˈnʌmbə(r); ˈnʌmbɚ/ *n* **1** [C] symbol or word indicating a quantity of units; numeral 号码; 数字; 数目: *3, 13, 33 and 103 are numbers.* 3、13、33、103 等都是数字. ○ *Three and thirteen are also numbers.* 三和十三也是数字. ○ *My telephone number is 622998.* 我的电话号码是 622998. ○ *What's the number of your car?* 你的汽车多少号儿? ⇨App 4 见附录 4, Cf 参看 CARDINAL NUMBER (CARDINAL[1]), ORDINAL NUMBER (ORDINAL). **2** (*sing* or *pl* in form; always with *pl v* when the subject is preceded by an *adj* 可用单数或复数形式; 主语前有形容词时, 动词一定用复数) quantity or amount 数量; 数额: *A large number of people have applied.* 很多人都已申请. ○ *Considerable numbers of* (ie very many) *animals have died.* 有大量动物死亡. ○ *The enemy won by force of numbers*, ie because there were so many of them. 敌人以人多获胜. ○ *A number of* (ie some) *problems have arisen.* 已经出现了一些问题. ○ *A large number of books have been stolen from the library.* 图书馆遗失了很多书. ○ *The number of books stolen from the library is large.* 图书馆遗失的书很多. ○ *We were fifteen in number*, ie there were fifteen of us. 我们共计十五个人. **3** [sing] (*fml* 文) group; collection 组; 集体: *one of our number*, ie one of us 我们中的一员 ○ *among their number*, ie among them 在他们之中. **4** [C] (*abbrs* 缩写 **No, no**; *US symb* 美式的符号为 #) (used before a figure to indicate the place of sth in a series 用于数字前表示某物在某一系列中的位置): *Room number 145 is on the third floor of the hotel.* 145 号房间在旅馆的四楼. ○ *He's living at No 4*, ie house number four. 他住在 4 号. ○ *No 10 (Downing Street) is the official residence of the British Prime Minister.* (唐宁街)10 号是英国首相府. **5** [C] issue of a periodical, newspaper, etc (期刊、报纸等的)一期: *the current number of 'Punch'* 最近一期的《庞奇》杂志 ○ *back numbers* (ie earlier issues) *of 'Nature'* 过期的《自然》杂志. **6** [C] (*music* 音) song, dance, etc, esp in a theatrical performance 一首歌, 一段舞蹈(尤指在剧场演出的): *sing a slow, romantic number* 唱缓慢的浪漫的歌曲. **7** [U] (*grammar*) variation in the form of nouns and verbs to show whether one or more than one thing or person is being spoken of (名词和动词的)数(表示所叙述的事物或人是一个或是不止一个): *'Men' is plural in number.* men 是复数形式. ○ *The subject of a sentence and its verb must agree in number.* 句子的主语和动词的数必须一致. **8** [sing] (preceded by an *adj* or *adjs* 用于形容词之后) (*sl* 俚) item (eg a dress, car, etc) that is admired 喜爱的物品(如连衣裙、汽车等): *She was wearing a snappy little red number.* 她身着一款时髦的红色连衣裙. ○ *That new Fiat is a fast little number.* 那辆新的菲亚特是速度很快的汽车. **9 numbers** [pl] (*infml* 口) arithmetic 算术; 计算: *He's not good at numbers.* 他的算术不怎么样. **10** (idm 习语) **by** ˈ**numbers** following a sequence of instructions identified by numbers 根据数字顺序的指示: *drill movement by numbers* 按口令的操练动作 ○ *painting by numbers* 按数字顺序着色. **a cushy number** ⇨ CUSHY. **have got sb's** ˈ**number** (*sl* 俚) know what sb is really like, what his intentions really are, etc 了解某人的真面目、动机等; 知道某人的底: *She pretends to be friendly but I've got her number; she just likes to know everything.* 她装得挺亲热, 可我了解她的底; 她就是什么事都爱打听. **in round figures/numbers** ⇨ ROUND[1]. **sb's** ˈ**number is up** (*sl* 俚) the time has come when sb will die, be ruined, etc 某人的死期、劫数等已到: *When the wheel came off the car I thought my number was up!* 汽车轮一脱落, 我就想我算完了. **number** ˈ**one** (*infml*

口) (**a**) oneself 自己: *You can depend on it that she'll always look after number one.* 她总是关心自身的利益, 对这一点可以打包票. (**b**) the most important (person or thing) 最重要的(人或事物); 头号的: *This company is number one in the oil business.* 这家公司在石油业中首屈一指. ○ [attrib 作定语] *the number one problem, project, etc* 最重要的问题、计划等. **sb's opposite number** ⇨ OPPOSITE. **there's safety in numbers** ⇨ SAFETY. **times without number** ⇨ TIME[1]. **weight of numbers** ⇨ WEIGHT.

▷ **num·ber** *v* **1** [Tn, Tn·pr] give a number to (sth) 给(某事物)编号: *The doors were numbered 2, 4, 6 and 8.* 这些门编为2、4、6、8号. ○ *We'll number them from one to ten.* 我们将给这些东西编为一至十号. **2** [In/pr] amount to (sth); add up to 计有; 总共: *We numbered 20* (ie There were 20 of us) *in all.* 我们共计20人. **3** (idm 习语) **sb's/sth's days are numbered** ⇨ DAY. **4** (phr v) **number sb/sth among sth** include sb/sth in a particular group 将某人[某事物]包括于某群体内: *I number her among my closest friends.* 我把她归为挚友之列. ○ *I number that crash among the most frightening experiences of my life.* 我认为那次事故是我一生中最可怕的遭遇. **number off** (*military* 军) call out one's number in a sequence 报数: *The soldiers numbered off, starting from the right-hand man.* 士兵从右至左报数.

num·ber·less *adj* (*fml* 文) too many to be counted; innumerable 多得数不清的; 无数的: *numberless stars, bacteria, grains of sand* 无数的星星、细菌、沙粒. ⇨ Usage at INVALUABLE 用法见 INVALUABLE.

□ ˈ**number-plate** (also *esp US* **licence plate, license plate**) *n* plate on a motor vehicle bearing its registration number (车辆的)牌照. ⇨illus at App 1 见附录1插图, page xii.

nu·meral /ˈnjuːmərəl; *US* ˈnuː-; ˋnumərəl/ *n* word or figure representing a number 数字. Cf 参看 ARABIC NUMERALS (ARABIC), ROMAN NUMERALS (ROMAN). ⇨App 4 见附录4.

nu·mer·ate /ˈnjuːmərət; *US* ˈnuː-; ˋnumərɪt/ *adj* having a good basic knowledge of arithmetic or mathematics in general 识数的; 有数学基本功的: *the importance of making children numerate* 使儿童打下良好的数学基础的重要性. Cf 参看 LITERATE 1. ▷ **nu·mer·acy** /ˈnjuːmərəsɪ; *US* ˈnuː-; ˋnumərəsɪ/ *n* [U].

nu·mera·tion /ˌnjuːməˈreɪʃn; *US* ˌnuː-; ˌnuməˋreʃən/ *n* [U] (*mathematics* 数) **1** method or process of numbering 计算; 计算法; 运算过程. **2** expression in words of numbers written in figures 命数法; 读数法.

nu·mer·ator /ˈnjuːməreɪtə(r); *US* ˈnuː-; ˋnumə,retɚ/ *n* number above the line in a vulgar fraction, eg 3 in $\frac{3}{4}$ (分数中的)分子(如$\frac{3}{4}$中的3). Cf 参看 DENOMINATOR.

nu·mer·ical /njuːˈmerɪkl; *US* nuː-; nuˋmɛrɪkl/ *adj* of, expressed in or representing numbers 数字的; 以数字表示的; 表示数字的: *in numerical order* 按数字顺序 ○ *numerical symbols* 表示数字的符号.

▷ **nu·mer·ic·ally** /-klɪ; -klɪ/ *adv* in terms of numbers 在数量上: *The enemy were numerically superior*, ie There were more of them. 敌人在数量上占优势.

nu·mer·ous /ˈnjuːmərəs; *US* ˈnuː-; ˋnumərəs/ *adj* (*fml* 文) very many 很多: *her numerous friends* 她的许多朋友 ○ *on numerous occasions* 无数次.

nu·min·ous /ˈnjuːmɪnəs; *US* ˈnuː-; ˋnumənəs/ *adj* (*religion* 宗) inspiring awe; divine 令人敬畏的; 神圣的.

nu·mis·matics /ˌnjuːmɪzˈmætɪks; *US* ˌnuː-; ˌnumɪzˋmætɪks/ *n* [sing *v*] study of coins, coinage and medals 钱币学; 奖章的研究.

▷ **nu·mis·mat·ist** /njuːˈmɪzmətɪst; *US* nuː-; nuˋmɪzmətɪst/ *n* expert in numismatics; collector of coins and medals 钱币学家; 钱币及奖章收藏家.

num·skull (also **numb·skull**) /ˈnʌmskʌl; ˋnʌm,skʌl/ *n* (*infml derog* 口, 贬) stupid person 笨蛋; 傻瓜.

nun /nʌn; nʌn/ *n* woman living in a convent, usu after taking religious vows 修女; 尼姑. Cf 参看 MONK.

▷ **nun·nery** /ˈnʌnərɪ; ˋnʌnərɪ/ *n* house where an order of nuns lives; convent 女修道院; 尼姑庵. Cf 参看 MONASTERY.

nun·cio /ˈnʌnsɪəʊ; ˋnʌnʃɪ,o/ *n* (*pl* **~s**) Pope's ambassador or representative in a foreign country 罗马教皇的驻外使节.

nup·tial /ˈnʌpʃl; ˋnʌpʃəl/ *adj* [attrib 作定语] (*fml or joc* 文或谑) of marriage or of a wedding 婚姻的; 婚礼的: *the nuptial ceremony* 婚礼 ○ *nuptial bliss* 婚姻美满.

▷ **nup·tials** *n* [pl] (*fml or joc* 文或谑) wedding 结婚; 婚礼: *the day of his nuptials* 他结婚的日子.

nurse[1] /nɜːs; nɝs/ *n* **1** person, usu female, trained to help a doctor to look after the sick or injured 护士: *Red Cross nurses* 红十字会护士 ○ *Male nurses are often employed in hospitals for the mentally ill.* 精神病院常雇用男护士护理精神病人. ○ *a psychiatric nurse*, ie one who works in a mental hospital 精神病院的护士. **2** (also ˈ**nurse·maid**) woman or girl employed to look after babies or small children 保育员; 保姆; 照顾小孩的女用人. Cf 参看 NANNY 1. **3** (also ˈ**wet nurse**) woman employed to breast-feed a baby who is not her own 奶妈; 奶母.

nurse[2] /nɜːs; nɝs/ *v* **1** [I, Tn] take care of (the sick or injured); look after (sb) 看护, 护理(病人或受伤者); 照顾(某人): *My mother's been nursing for 40 years.* 我母亲40年来一直做护理工作. ○ *She nurses her aged mother.* 她照顾年迈的母亲. **2** [I, Tn] be breast-fed; breast-feed (sb) 以人乳哺养; 给(某人)喂奶, 哺乳: *The baby was nursing/being nursed at its mother's breast.* 那个孩子正在吃母亲的奶. **3** [Tn] hold (sb/sth) carefully and lovingly (小心、疼爱地)抱, 持(某人[某物]): *nurse a child, puppy* 疼爱地搂着小孩、小狗 ○ *nurse a fragile vase in one's arms* 小心地抱着易碎的花瓶. **4** (**a**) [Tn, Tn·p] give special care to (sth); help to develop 特别照料(某事物); 培养: *nurse young plants (along)* 培育幼苗 ○ *nurse a project* 协助一计划 ○ *nurse a constituency*, ie visit it often, etc in order to gain or retain votes 笼络选区的选民(时常访问等以争取选票) ○ *nurse a cold*, ie stay warm, stay in bed, etc in order to cure it quickly 调治伤风(保暖、卧床等以便早日痊愈). (**b**) [Tn] think a lot about (sth); foster (sth) in the mind 思考(某事); 心存, 心怀(某事): *nurse feelings of revenge, hopes of promotion, etc* 心存报复、晋升的希望等 ○ *nurse a grievance* 心怀不满.

▷ **nurs·ing** *n* [U] art or practice of looking after the sick or injured 护理: *train for (a career in) nursing* 进行护理(职业)培训 ○ [attrib 作定语] *the nursing profession* 护理的职业 ○ *nursing skills* 护理技能.

□ ˈ**nursing-home** *n* small, usu privately owned, hospital 小型(通常为私立的)医院.

ˌ**nursing** ˈ**mother** woman breast-feeding her baby 用自己的乳汁哺育子女的女子.

nursery /ˈnɜːsərɪ; ˋnɝsərɪ/ *n* **1** place where young children are cared for, usu while their parents are at work, etc 托儿所; 保育院; 育儿室: *a day nursery* 日间托儿所. Cf 参看 CRÊCHE. **2** room in a (usu large) house for the special use of children 幼儿室: *We've turned the smallest bedroom into a nursery for our new baby.* 我们已将最小的那间卧室改成新生婴儿的幼儿室. **3** (often *pl* though referring to a single place 常作复数表示单一处所) place where young plants and trees are grown for transplanting later and usu for sale 苗圃; 育苗场: *I'm going to the nursery/nurseries in Hampton to buy some plants.* 我准备到汉普敦的苗圃去买些花草.

□ ˈ**nurseryman** /-mən; -mən/ *n* (*pl* **-men**) man who works in a plant nursery 花圃工; 苗木培育工.

ˈ**nursery nurse** nurse trained to look after small children 保育员.

ˈ**nursery rhyme** (usu traditional) poem or song for children (通常为传统的)儿歌, 童谣.

ˈ**nursery school** school for children aged from 2 or 3 to 5 幼儿园. Cf 参看 PLAYGROUP (PLAY[1]).

ˈ**nursery slope** slope suitable for inexperienced skiers, ie not steep 适合初学滑雪者的坡地.

ˈ**nursery stakes** race for two-year-old horses 两岁口的马参加的比赛.

nur·ture /ˈnɜːtʃə(r); ˋnɝtʃɚ/ *v* [Tn] **1** care for and educate (a child) 养育, 教养, 教育(儿童): *children nurtured by loving parents* 受慈爱的双亲养育的孩子. **2** (**a**) encourage the growth of (sth); nourish 培育, 培养(某物); 滋养: *nurture delicate plants* 培育幼嫩的植物. (**b**) (*fig* 比喻) help the development of (sth); support 扶植(某物); 支持: *We want to nurture the new project, not destroy it.* 我们要支持这个新工程, 不要破坏它.

▷ **nur·ture** *n* [U] care; encouragement; support 照顾; 鼓励; 支持: *the nurture of a delicate child, plant* 对纤弱的孩子、植物的照料 ○ *the nurture of new talent* 对新人

才的扶植.

nut /nʌt; nʌt/ *n* **1** [C] (often in compounds 常用以构成复合词) fruit consisting of a hard shell with a kernel inside it that can be eaten 坚果: *chocolate with fruit and nuts* 果料巧克力 ○ *a Brazil-nut* 巴西果 ○ *a hazelnut* 榛子. ⇨illus at App 1 见附录1插图, page i. ⇨illus 见插图. **2** [C] small (usu six-sided) piece of metal with a hole through the centre, used for screwing onto a bolt to secure it 螺母; 螺帽. ⇨illus at BOLT 见 BOLT 插图. **3** [C] (*sl* 俚) head (of a person) (人的)头: *He cracked his nut on the ceiling.* 他的头让天花板碰破了. **4 nuts** [pl] small lumps of coal 小煤块. **5 nuts** [pl] (⚠ *sl* 讳, 俚 *esp US*) testicles 睾丸: *kick sb in the nuts* 踢某人的睾丸. **6** [C] (*sl derog* 俚, 贬) (**a**) (*Brit* also **nutter**) foolish, eccentric or mad person 傻子; 怪人; 疯子: *He drives like a nut — he'll kill himself one day.* 他开汽车像个疯子——不定哪天就得撞死. (**b**) (preceded by a *n* 用于名词之后) person very interested in sth; fanatic 迷恋于某事物的人; 入迷的人; 迷: *a movie, fitness, health, soccer nut* 影迷、健美迷、健康迷、足球迷. **7** (idm 习语) **do one's ˈnut** (*Brit sl* 俚) be very angry 发怒; 气炸: *She'll do her nut when she sees the broken window.* 她要是看见窗户破了准得气炸了. **for ˈnuts/ˈpeanuts** (*Brit sl derog* 俚, 贬) (used with a negative 与否定词连用) at all 根本; 全然; 一点都: *He can't play football for nuts!* 他对踢足球一点儿不摸门儿. **a hard/tough ˈnut (to crack)** (*infml* 口) (**a**) difficult problem or situation (to deal with) 难以应付的问题或情况: *The final exam was a tough nut.* 毕业考试不好对付. (**b**) person who is difficult to persuade, influence, etc 难以说服、影响等的人: *She's a tough nut to crack; I don't think she'll give us permission.* 她这个人不好说话, 我想她不会答应我们的. **the ˌnuts and ˈbolts** (*infml* 口) basic practical details 基本要点: *dealing with the nuts and bolts of the project* 处理该计划的基本要点. **ˌoff one's ˈnut** (*sl* 俚) mad 疯狂的: *You must be off your nut!* 你准是疯了!

nut 坚果

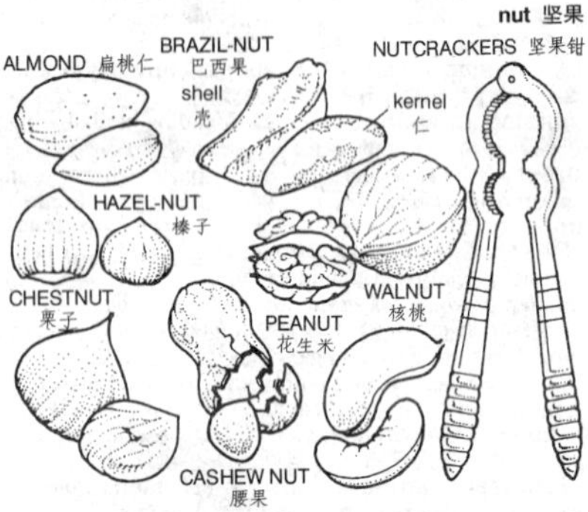

▷ **nutty** *adj* (**-ier, -iest**) **1** tasting of or containing nuts 坚果味的; 含果仁的: *a nutty flavour* 坚果的味道 ○ *nutty cake, chocolate, etc* 果仁蛋糕、巧克力等. **2** (*sl* 俚) crazy; eccentric 发狂的; 古怪的: *I love her nutty behaviour!* 我倒喜欢她那股疯劲儿! **3** (idm 习语) **(as) nutty as a ˈfruitcake** (*sl* 俚) very crazy or eccentric 极疯狂的; 极古怪的.

□ **ˌnut-ˈbrown** *adj* (eg of ale) having the dark rich brown colour of ripe hazelnuts (如麦芽啤酒)深棕色的, 栗色的.

ˈnut-case *n* (*sl* 俚) mad or eccentric person 疯狂的或古怪的人.

ˈnutcrackers *n* [pl] pincers for cracking open the shells of nuts 坚果钳. ⇨illus 见插图.

ˈnut-house *n* (*sl offensive* 俚, 蔑) mental hospital 疯人院.

ˈnutshell /-ʃel; -ʃɛl/ *n* **1** hard covering around the kernel of a nut 坚果的外壳. **2** (idm 习语) **(put sth) in a nutshell** (say sth) in very few words 用很少的言语(说明某事物): *To put it in a nutshell, we're bankrupt.* 简断截说, 我们破产了.

nut·meg /ˈnʌtmeg; ˈnʌtmɛg/ *n* **1** [C] hard fragrant seed of an E Indian tree 肉豆蔻. **2** [U] this seed grated to powder, used as a flavouring in food 肉豆蔻末(用作食物中的香料).

nu·tri·ent /ˈnjuːtrɪənt; *US* ˈnuː-; ˈnutrɪənt/ *n, adj* (*fml* 文) (substance) serving as or providing nourishment, esp for plants or animals 营养的, 滋养的(物质): *Plants draw minerals and other nutrients from the soil.* 植物从泥土中吸收矿物质和其他养料.

nu·tri·ment /ˈnjuːtrɪmənt; *US* ˈnuː-; ˈnutrəmənt/ *n* [C, U] (*fml* 文) nourishing food 营养品; 食物: *essential nutriments for a growing child* 儿童成长中必需的营养品.

nu·tri·tion /njuːˈtrɪʃn; *US* nuː-; nuˈtrɪʃən/ *n* [U] **1** (process of giving and receiving) nourishment; food 营养; 滋养; 食物: *adequate nutrition of the body* 身体需要的充足的营养 ○ *This food provides all the nutrition your dog needs.* 本食品含有狗所必需的一切营养. **2** the study of human diet 营养学: *a number of books on nutrition* 若干本营养学的书.

▷ **nu·tri·tional** /-ʃənl; -ʃənəl/ *adj*: *the nutritional value of a food* 某种食物的营养价值. **nu·tri·tion·ally** /-ʃənəlɪ; -ʃənəlɪ/ *adv*.

nu·tri·tion·ist /-ʃənɪst; -ʃənɪst/ *n* expert in nutrition 营养学家.

nu·tri·tious /njuːˈtrɪʃəs; *US* nuː-; nuˈtrɪʃəs/ *adj* (*fml* 文) of (high) value as food; nourishing 有营养价值的; 营养价值高的; 滋养的: *a nutritious meal, snack, etc* 有营养的饭菜、小吃等.

nu·trit·ive /ˈnjuːtrətɪv; *US* ˈnuː-; ˈnutrətɪv/ *adj* (*fml* 文) **1** serving as food 用作食物的; 有营养的: *a nutritive substance* 营养物. **2** of nutrition(1) 营养的: *the nutritive process* 营养作用.

nuts /nʌts; nʌts/ *adj* [pred 作表语] (*sl* 俚) **1** crazy; insane 疯狂; 发疯. **2 ~ about sth; ~ about/on sth** very much in love with sb; very enthusiastic about sth 热恋某人; 迷恋某事物: *She's beautiful. I'm nuts about her.* 她很漂亮. 我爱她爱得着了迷. ○ *He's nuts about/on cars.* 他迷上汽车了.

nut·ter /ˈnʌtə(r); ˈnʌtə˞/ *n* (*Brit infml* 口) = NUT 6.

nuzzle /ˈnʌzl; ˈnʌzl/ *v* **1** [Tn] press or rub (sb/sth) gently with the nose 以鼻子轻触或轻擦(某人[某物]): *The horse nuzzled my shoulder* 马用鼻子蹭我的肩膀. **2** (phr v) **nuzzle up to sb/sth; nuzzle (up) against sb/sth** press close to sb/sth, esp by pushing gently with the head or nose 紧挨, 紧贴某人[某物](尤指用头或鼻子轻拱): *The dog nuzzled up to/against me on the sofa.* 狗在沙发上依偎着我.

NW *abbr* 缩写 = North-West(ern): *NW Australia* 澳大利亚的西北部 ○ *London NW6 2PS*, ie as a postal code 伦敦NW6 2PS.

NY *abbr* 缩写 = New York 纽约.

NYC *abbr* 缩写 = New York City 纽约市.

ny·lon /ˈnaɪlɒn; ˈnaɪlɑn/ *n* **1** [U] very strong man-made fibre used for hosiery, rope, brushes, etc 尼龙: *This dress is 80% nylon.* 这件连衣裙的料子含80%尼龙. ○ [attrib 作定语] *nylon tights, blouses, etc* 尼龙裤袜、女衬衫等. **2 nylons** [pl] women's stockings 女长袜: *a pair of nylons* 一双女长袜.

nymph /nɪmf; nɪmf/ *n* **1** (in Greek and Roman mythology) minor goddess living in rivers, trees, hills, etc (希腊与罗马神话)(居住在河里、林中、山上等的)小仙女. **2** (esp in poetry 尤用于诗中) young woman, esp a beautiful one 少女; (尤指)妙龄美女. Cf 参看 SYLPH. **3** young insect (eg a young dragonfly) that has a similar form to the adult (与成虫形状相似的)昆虫的幼虫(如蜻蜓的幼虫).

nymphet /nɪmˈfet; nɪmˈfɛt/ *n* (*infml or joc* 口或谑) young girl regarded as sexually desirable 性感的少女.

nym·pho /ˈnɪmfəʊ; ˈnɪmfo/ *n* (*pl* **~s**) (*infml often derog sexist* 口, 常作贬义, 性别偏见) nymphomaniac 患色情狂的女子.

nym·pho·mania /ˌnɪmfəˈmeɪnɪə; ˌnɪmfəˈmenɪə/ *n* [U] excessive and uncontrollable sexual desire in women (女性的)色情狂.

▷ **nym·pho·ma·niac** /-ˈmeɪnɪæk; -ˈmenɪæk/ *n, adj* (*often derog* 常作贬义) (woman) suffering from nymphomania 患色情狂的(女子).

NZ *abbr* 缩写 = New Zealand 新西兰.

O o

O, o /əʊ; o/ *n* (*pl* **O's, o's** /əʊz; oz/) **1** the fifteenth letter of the English alphabet 英语字母表的第十五个字母: *There are two O's in Oxford.* 在Oxford一词中有两个O. **2** O-shaped sign or mark O形符号或记号: *The child's mouth formed a big O in surprise.* 那孩子惊奇得张着嘴像个大O字. **3** (in saying telephone, etc numbers aloud) zero; nought (说电话等号码时的)0, 零: *'My number is six o double three'*, ie 6033. '我的号码是6033.' ○ *'He's in room one o two'*, ie 102. '他在102号房间.' ⇨Usage at NOUGHT 用法见 NOUGHT.

O, oh /əʊ; o/ *interj* **1** cry of surprise, fear, pain, sudden pleasure, etc 啊, 哎呀, 哎哟, 噢(表示惊讶、恐惧、痛苦、突然的欣喜等): *Oh look!* 瞧哇! **2** expression used when addressing a person, thing, etc (用以称呼人或事物等)(汉语用于词语后)啊, 呀, 哇, 哪: *O God our help in ages past* 上帝呀, 自古以来帮助我们的主 ○ *O Zeus!* 宙斯啊!

o' /ə; ə/ *prep* (used esp in certain compound phrases 尤用以构成复合词组) of: *3 o'clock* ○ *man-o'-war* ○ *will-o'-the-wisp*.

oaf /əʊf; of/ *n* (*pl* **~s**) stupid, clumsy and awkward person (usu male) 傻瓜, 笨蛋(通常指男性): *Why did she marry that great oaf?* 她怎么会嫁给那个大笨蛋了呢?

▷ **oaf·ish** *adj* like an oaf; roughly behaved 蠢笨的; 笨拙的; 粗鲁的: *oafish behaviour* 愚蠢的行为.

oak /əʊk; ok/ *n* **1** (**a**) (also ˈ**oak-tree**) [C] type of tree with tough hard wood, common in many parts of the world 栎树; 橡树; 柞树: *a forest of oaks* 栎树林 ○ [attrib 作定语] *an oak forest* 栎树林. ⇨illus at App 1 见附录1插图, page i. (**b**) [U] wood of this tree 栎木; 橡木; 柞木: *The table is (of) solid oak.* 这桌子是纯粹栎木的. ○ [attrib 作定语] *oak panels* 栎木板 ○ *an oak table* 栎木桌. **2 the Oaks** [sing *v*] name of a horse-race run at Epsom, near London, every year 欧克斯赛(在伦敦附近的埃普瑟姆一年一度的赛马会). **3** (idm 习语) **big/tall/great/large oaks from little ˈacorns grow** (*saying* 谚) great things may come from small or modest beginnings 大橡树生自小橡实; 合抱之木, 生于毫末; 大事恒自小事始.

▷ **oaken** /ˈəʊkən; ˈokən/ *adj* [attrib 作定语] (*dated fml* 旧, 文) made of oak 栎木制的; 橡木制的.

□ ˈ**oak-apple** *n* growth on an oak leaf or stem, caused by an insect 栎瘿; 栎五倍子. Cf 参看 GALL[3].

OAP /ˌəʊ eɪ ˈpi:; ˌo e ˈpi/ *abbr* 缩写 = (*Brit infml* 口) old-age pensioner 领养老金的人.

oar /ɔ:(r); ɔr/ *n* **1** long pole with a flat blade, pulled by hand in order to drive a boat through the water 桨. ⇨ illus at ROW 见 ROW 插图. **2** (idm 习语) **put/shove/stick one's ˈoar in; put/shove/stick in one's ˈoar** (*infml* 口) give an opinion, some advice, etc without being asked; interfere 干涉; 干预: *I know how to mend a fuse and I don't need you shoving your oar in!* 我知道怎么弄保险丝, 用不着你管!

□ ˈ**oarlock** *n* (*US*) = ROWLOCK.

oarsman /ˈɔ:zmən; ˈɔrzmən/ *n* (*pl* **-men**), ˈ**oarswoman** *n* (*pl* **-women**) person who rows a boat; rower 划桨人.

OAS /ˌəʊ eɪ ˈes; ˌo e ˈɛs/ *abbr* 缩写 = (*US*) Organization of American States 美洲国家组织.

oasis /əʊˈeɪsɪs; oˈesɪs/ *n* (*pl* **oases** /-si:z; -siz/) **1** fertile place, with water and trees, in a desert (沙漠中的)绿洲. **2** (*fig* 比喻) experience, place, etc which is pleasant in the middle of sth unpleasant, dull, etc (在枯燥、厌恶等事物中)使人感到愉快的事、地方等: *The study was an oasis of calm in a noisy household.* 在喧闹的家中, 书房可谓宁静之一隅.

oast /əʊst; ost/ *n* kiln for drying hops 忽布(啤酒花)烘干窑.

□ ˈ**oasthouse** *n* building containing an oast 忽布烘干房.

oath /əʊθ; oθ/ *n* (*pl* **~s** /əʊðz; oðz/) **1** (words used in making a) solemn promise to do sth or solemn declaration that sth is true (usu appealing to God, etc as a witness) 誓言; 誓词; 誓约; 宣誓: *There is a standard form of oath used in lawcourts.* 法庭中使用的誓词有固定的格式. **2** casual or improper use of the name of God, etc to express anger, surprise, etc; swear-word (表示愤怒、惊奇等的)咒骂, 诅咒语: *He hurled a few oaths at his wife and walked out, slamming the door.* 他咒骂了妻子几句, 砰的一声关上门就走了. **3** (idm 习语) **be on/under ˈoath** (*law* 律) have sworn to tell the truth in a court of law 在法庭上宣过誓要说实话: *The judge reminded the witness that she was still under oath.* 法官提醒证人, 她发过誓要说实话. **on my ˈoath** (*dated* 旧) (used to emphasize that one is telling the truth 用以强调本人所言属实): *I didn't tell anyone, on my oath.* 我保证我没有告诉过任何人. **put/place sb on/under ˈoath** (*law* 律) require sb to swear an oath 要求某人宣誓: *The witnesses were placed under oath.* 要求证人宣誓. **swear/take an ˈoath** (*esp law* 尤用于法律) promise solemnly to tell the truth, give one's loyalty, etc 发誓, 宣誓, 立誓(说实话、效忠等): *Before giving evidence the witness had to take an oath.* 证人作证前要先宣誓. ○ *Government employees swear an oath not to reveal official secrets.* 政府雇员宣誓不泄露官方机密.

oats /əʊts; ots/ *n* **1** [pl, sometimes sing *v* 有时用单数动词] (grain from a) type of cereal plant grown in cool climates as food 燕麦: *Give the horse some oats.* 给马喂些燕麦. ○ *fields of ripe barley and oats* 成熟的大麦和燕麦田 ○ *Oats is a crop grown widely in Europe.* 燕麦是欧洲广泛种植的作物. **2** [sing or pl *v*] oatmeal porridge 燕麦粥: *Is/Are porridge oats on the breakfast menu?* 早餐的食谱上有燕麦粥吗? **3** (idm 习语) **feel one's oats** ⇨ FEEL[1]. **be getting one's ˈoats** (*infml* 口) have sex regularly 有正常的性生活. **(be) off one's ˈoats** (*infml* 口) (be) lacking appetite for food 胃口不好: *He's been a bit off his oats since his illness.* 他生病以来胃口就不大好. **sow one's wild oats** ⇨ SOW[2].

□ ˈ**oatcake** *n* [U, C] (esp in Scotland and N England) thin flat cake made of oatmeal (尤指苏格兰和英格兰北部的)燕麦饼: *oatcake served with butter and cheese* 带黄油和干酪的燕麦饼.

ˈ**oatmeal** *n* [U] meal made from crushed oats, used in porridge, oatcakes, etc 燕麦片(用以煮粥、做燕麦饼等).

OAU /ˌəʊ eɪ ˈju:; ˌo e ˈju/ *abbr* 缩写 = Organization of African Unity 非洲统一组织.

ob *abbr* 缩写 = died (Latin *obiit*) 死(源自拉丁文 *obiit*). Cf 参看 D 2.

ob·bli·gato /ˌɒblɪˈgɑ:təʊ; ˌɑblɪˈgɑto/ *n* (*pl* **~s** or **-ti** /-ti:; -ti/) (*music* 音) accompanying part forming an essential part of a composition 助奏; 助唱: *with piano obbligato* 钢琴助奏.

▷ **ob·bli·gato** *adj* to be included in a performance (演奏或演唱中)不可缺的, 必需的.

ob·dur·ate /ˈɒbdjʊərət; *US* -dər-; ˈɑbdərɪt/ *adj* (*fml* 文) impossible to change; stubborn 固执的; 执拗的: *an obdurate refusal* 坚决的拒绝 ○ *He remained obdurate, refusing to alter his decision.* 他依然固执己见, 拒不改变决定. ▷ **ob·dur·acy** /ˈɒbdjʊərəsɪ; *US* -dər-; ˈɑbdərəsɪ/ *n* [U]. **ob·dur·ately** *adv*: *obdurately refusing to go* 坚决不去.

OBE /ˌəʊ bi: ˈi:; ˌo bi ˈi/ *abbr* 缩写 = (*Brit*) Officer (of the Order) of the British Empire (第四等的)大英帝国最高勋爵; 英帝国官佐勋章: *be (made) an OBE* 受封(第四等的)大英帝国最高勋爵位 ○ *Matthew Silkin OBE* (第四等的)大英帝国最高勋爵士马修·西尔金.

obedi·ent /əˈbi:dɪənt; əˈbidɪənt/ *adj* **1** doing what one is told to do; willing to obey 服从的; 顺从的; 听话的: *obedient children* 听话的孩子 ○ *His dog is very obedient.* 他的狗很顺从. Cf 参看 DISOBEDIENT. **2** (idm 习语) **your obedient ˈservant** (*dated fml* 旧, 文) (used as a very formal ending to an official letter, before the signature 用作公函的结尾套语, 置于签名之前).

▷ **obedi·ence** /-əns; -əns/ *n* [U] action of obeying; being obedient 服从; 顺从; 听话: *The commanding officer expected unquestioning obedience from his men.* 指挥官要下属绝对服从.

obedi·ently *adv*: *He whistled, and the dog came obediently.* 他一吹口哨, 那狗就乖乖地来了.

obeis·ance /əʊˈbeɪsns; oˈbesn̩s/ *n* (*dated fml* 旧, 文) **1** deep bow (of respect or obedience) 深深的鞠躬(表示尊敬或服从). **2** (idm 习语) **do/pay/make obeisance to sb** show respectful obedience or submission to sb 表示尊从或屈服于某人: *He made obeisance to the king.* 他向国王表示臣服.

ob·el·isk /ˈɒbəlɪsk; ˋɑbl̩,ɪsk/ *n* tall pointed stone pillar with four sides, set up as a monument or landmark 方尖碑(用作纪念碑或地标).

obese /əʊˈbi:s; oˋbis/ *adj* (*fml or medical* 文或医) (of people) very fat (指人)过度肥胖的: *Obese patients are advised to change their diet.* 建议肥胖病人改变饮食. ⇨ Usage at FAT[1] 用法见 FAT[1].

▷ **obes·ity** /əʊˈbi:sətɪ; oˈbisətɪ/ *n* [U] being obese 过度肥胖: *Obesity is a problem for many people in western countries.* 西方国家很多人都有过度肥胖的问题.

obey /əˈbeɪ; əˋbe/ *v* [I, Tn] do what one is told or obliged to do by (sb); carry out (a command) 服从; 顺从; 执行(命令): *Soldiers are trained to obey without question.* 士兵已训练得绝对服从命令. ○ *obey orders* 服从命令 ○ *obey the law* 遵守法律.

ob·fus·cate /ˈɒbfəskeɪt; ˋɑbfəs,ket/ *v* [Tn] (*fml* 文) (deliberately) make (sth) confused or difficult to understand (故意)使(某事物)混乱或艰涩难懂: *The writer often obfuscates the real issues with petty details.* 那作家常以细枝末节来混淆实质问题.

ob·iter dictum /ˌɒbɪtə ˈdɪktəm; ˋɑbɪtɚˋdɪktəm/ *n* (*pl* **dicta** /ˈdɪktə; ˋdɪktə/) (*Latin law or fml* 拉, 律或文) incidental remark or statement not essential to the main argument 附带意见; 附言.

ob·itu·ary /əˈbɪtʃʊərɪ; *US* -tʃʊerɪ; əˋbɪtʃʊ,ɛrɪ/ (*infml* 口语作 **obit**) *n* printed notice (eg in a newspaper) of a person's death, often with a short account of his life and achievements 讣闻; 讣告: [attrib 作定语] *obituary notices* 讣闻 ○ *He writes obits for the local newspaper.* 他为当地报纸撰写讣文.

ob·ject[1] /ˈɒbdʒɪkt; ˋɑbdʒɪkt/ *n* **1** solid thing that can be seen and touched 可见到及可触摸的实物; 物体: *glass, wooden and plastic objects* 玻璃、木质和塑料的物体 ○ *There were several objects on the floor of the room.* 房间的地板上有几样东西. **2** ~ **of sth** person or thing to which sth is done or some feeling or thought is directed 对象, 客体(行为、感觉或思想所及的人或物): *an object of attention, pity, admiration, etc* 注意、怜悯、欣赏等的对象 ○ *This church is the main object of his interest.* 他最感兴趣的是这座教堂. ○ *The sole object of all the child's affection was a soft toy.* 那孩子最心爱的东西是个柔软的玩具. **3** thing aimed at; intention; purpose 目标; 意向; 目的: *with the object of going into business* 有打入工商业的意向 ○ *with no object in life* 无生活目标 ○ *fail/succeed in one's object* 在追求个人目的方面失败[成功] ○ *His one object in life is to earn as much money as possible.* 他生活的目标就是尽可能多挣钱. **4** (*infml* 口 *esp Brit*) person or thing of strange appearance, esp if ridiculous 怪模怪样的人或物(尤指可笑者): *What an object you look in that old hat!* 你戴着那顶帽子, 样子可真怪! **5** (*grammar*) noun, noun phrase or noun clause which refers to a person, thing, etc affected by the action of a verb, or which depends on a preposition, eg in *He took the money* and *He took what he wanted, 'the money'* and *'what he wanted'* are direct objects; in *I gave him the money, 'him'* is an indirect object; and in *I received the money from her, 'her'* is a prepositional object 宾语(受动词影响的或受介词限制的人或事物, 由名词、名词词组或名词从句充任, 如在 He took the money 和 He took what he wanted 两句中, the money 和 what he wanted 是直接宾语; 在 I gave him the money 句中, him 是间接宾语; 在 I received the money from her 句中, her 是介词宾语). Cf 参看 SUBJECT[1] 4. **6** (idm 习语) **expense, money, etc no 'object** expense, etc is not important, not a limiting factor, etc 费用、钱等并不重要、不是限制因素等: *He always travels first class — expense is no object.* 他出门总是用头等票——费用不成问题.

□ **object glass, object lens** = OBJECTIVE 2.

ˈ**object lesson** practical illustration of some principle, often given or used as a warning 实际教训: *Let this accident be an object lesson in the dangers of drinking and driving.* 这一事故可以作为醉酒驾驶危害的实际教训.

ob·ject[2] /əbˈdʒekt; əbˋdʒɛkt/ *v* **1** [I, Ipr] ~ **(to sb/sth)** say that one is not in favour (of sb/sth); protest 不赞成(某人[某事]); 反对; 抗议: *She wanted to cut down the hedge, but her neighbour objected.* 她想把树篱剪低些, 可是邻居不同意. ○ *I object to such treatment /to being treated like this.* 对这种待遇[受到这样的待遇]我表示抗议. ○ *I object to the plan on the grounds that it is too expensive.* 我反对该项计划, 理由是花费太大. **2** [Tn, Tf] give (sth) as a reason for opposing sb/sth 以(某事物)为理由反对某人[某事物]: *I objected that he was too young for the job.* 我反对的理由是因为他太年轻, 不适合做那件工作. ○ *'But he's too young,' I objected.* ˋ但是他太年轻了,ˊ我表示了反对意见.

▷ **ob·jector** *n* person who objects 反对者; 抗议者: *objectors to the plans for a new motorway* 反对修筑新高速公路计划的人 ○ *conscientious objectors* 拒服兵役者(因觉不合道义).

ob·jec·tion /əbˈdʒekʃn; əbˋdʒɛkʃən/ *n* **1** [C, U] ~ **(to sth/doing sth)** (expression of a) feeling of dislike, disapproval or opposition 厌恶; 不赞成; 反对; 异议: *raise/lodge/voice an objection* 提出异议 ○ *He has a strong objection to getting up so early.* 他十分反感这么早起床. ○ *I'd like to come too, if you've no objection.* 你要不反对的话, 我也愿意来. ○ *Objections to the plan will be listened to sympathetically.* 欢迎对该计划提出反对意见. **2** [C] ~ **(to/against sb/sth)** reason for objecting 反对的理由: *My main objection to the plan is that it would be too expensive.* 我反对该计划的主要理由是代价太高.

▷ **ob·jec·tion·able** /-ʃənəbl; -ʃənəbl̩/ *adj* causing opposition or disapproval; unpleasant 引起反对的; 令人反感的; 令人不快的: *an objectionable smell* 难闻的气味 ○ *objectionable remarks* 令人反感的言语 ○ *His drunken behaviour was extremely objectionable.* 他醉后的举动极为讨厌. ○ *I find him most objectionable.* 我对他十分厌恶. **ob·jec·tion·ably** /-ʃənəblɪ; -ʃənəblɪ/ *adv*.

ob·ject·ive /əbˈdʒektɪv; əbˋdʒɛktɪv/ *adj* **1** not influenced by personal feelings or opinions; unbiased; fair 客观的; 不受个人的感情或意见影响的; 无偏见的: *an objective report, account, assessment, etc* 客观的报道、叙述、评估等 ○ *A jury's decision in a court case must be absolutely objective.* 陪审团裁定案件必须绝无偏见. ○ *It's hard for nurses to be objective about their patients, if they become too emotionally involved with them.* 护士对病人太动感情就难以客观地处理问题. ○ *He finds it difficult to remain objective where his son is concerned.* 他觉得事关自己的儿子就很难保持客观态度了. **2** (*philosophy* 哲) having existence outside the mind; real 客观存在的; 真实的. Cf 参看 SUBJECTIVE. **3** (*grammar*) of the object[1](5) 宾语的: *the objective case*, ie (in Latin and other inflected languages) the form of a word used when it is the object of a verb or a preposition 宾格(词的一种形式, 在拉丁语和其他屈折语中作动词或介词的宾语).

▷ **ob·ject·ive** *n* **1** (**a**) thing aimed at or wished for; purpose 目标; 目的: *Her principal objective was international fame as a scientist.* 她的主要目标是当个有国际声誉的科学家. ○ *Everest is the climber's next objective.* 埃佛勒斯峰(即珠穆朗玛峰)是这个登山者的下一个目标. ○ *Let justice be our objective.* 让正义作我们奋斗的目标吧. (**b**) (in war) position that soldiers are aiming to capture (战争中要夺取的)军事目标: *All our objectives were gained.* 我们要夺取的军事目标均已拿下. **2** (also ˈ**object glass**, ˈ**object lens**) lens of a microscope or telescope closest to the object being viewed (显微镜或望远镜的)物镜.

ob·ject·ively *adv* in an objective(1) manner; impartially 客观地; 无偏见地: *see/view/judge things objectively* 客观地看[观察/判断]事物.

ob·jec·tiv·ity /ˌɒbdʒekˈtɪvətɪ; ˌɑbdʒɛkˋtɪvətɪ/ *n* state of being objective(1); ability to free oneself from personal prejudice; impartiality 客观(性); 无偏见: *The judge had a reputation for complete objectivity.* 那法官素以大公无私著称.

ob·jet d'art /ˌɒbʒeɪ ˈdɑ:; ˌɔbˌʒeˋdɑr/ *n* (*pl* **objets d'art**

ˌɒbʒeɪ ˈdɑː; ˌɔbˌʒeˋdɑr) (*French* 法) small decorative or artistic object 小饰物; 小艺术品: *a house full of antique furniture and objets d'art* 摆满古老家具和小艺术品的房子.

ob·late /ˈɒbleɪt; ˋɑblet/ *adj* (*geometry* 几) (of a sphere) flattened at the top and bottom (指球面)扁圆的, 横椭圆的: *The earth is an oblate sphere.* 地球是一扁圆球体.

ob·lig·ate /ˈɒblɪgeɪt; ˋɑbləˌget/ *v* [Cn·t usu passive 通常用于被动语态] (*fml* 文) compel (sb) legally or morally (to do sth) (在法律上或道义上)强迫(某人)(做某事): *He felt obligated to help.* 他觉得有责任予以帮助. ○ *We were obligated to attend the opening ceremony.* 我们有必要参加开幕式.

ob·liga·tion /ˌɒblɪˈgeɪʃn; ˌɑbləˋgeʃən/ *n* **1** [C] law, moral pressure, promise, etc that forces one to do sth (法律、道义、承诺等的)义务, 职责, 责任: *the obligations of conscience* 良心上的责任 ○ *the obligations imposed by parenthood* 为人父母者的义务 ○ *repay/fulfil an obligation*, eg by returning hospitality that one has received 报恩[尽义务](如还人情). **2** [C, U] being forced or required to do sth (被迫或被要求做某事的)责任, 义务: *We attended the party more out of a sense of obligation than anything else.* 我们参加那个聚会是迫于人情, 而并无别的原因. **3** (idm 习语) **be under an/no obligation (to sb/to do sth)** (not) be compelled by law, etc; (not) have a moral duty (没)有义务; (没)有道义责任: *You're under no obligation to pay for goods which you did not order.* 没有订购的货物就无须付款. ○ *She's under an obligation to him because he lent her money.* 因为他把钱借给她了, 所以她有偿还他的义务. **place/put sb under an/no obliˈgation (to sb/to do sth)** (not) compel sb by law, etc (to do sth); (not) make sb indebted or grateful (to sb) (不)使某人有义务(做某事物); (不)使某人欠(某人的)人情或受(某人的)恩惠: *Damaging the goods puts you under an obligation to buy them.* 你损坏了这些商品, 你就得都买下来. ○ *His kindness places us under an obligation to him.* 他待我们很好, 我们觉得欠着他一份人情.

ob·lig·at·ory /əˈblɪgətrɪ; *US* -tɔːrɪ; əˋblɪgəˌtɔrɪ/ *adj* (*fml* 文) required by rule, law or custom; compulsory (按规则、法律或习俗)必须的, 强制的: *Attendance at school is obligatory.* 上学是强制性的. ○ *It is obligatory to remove your shoes before entering.* 入室必须脱鞋.

ob·lige /əˈblaɪdʒ; əˋblaɪdʒ/ *v* **1** [Cn·t usu passive 通常用于被动语态] compel or require (sb) by law, agreement or moral pressure to do sth (按法律、协议或道义)强迫或要求(某人)做某事物: *The law obliges parents to send their children to school.* 法律上要求父母送子女入学. ○ *They were obliged to sell their house in order to pay their debts.* 他们被迫卖房还债. ○ *You are not obliged to answer these questions, but it would make our task easier.* 这些问题并非非答不可, 但答问对我们大有助益. **2** [I, Tn, Tn·pr] **~ sb (with sth/by doing sth)** (*fml* 文) do sth for sb as a favour or small service 为某人效劳; 帮忙: *We'd be happy to oblige.* 我们乐于效劳. ○ *Could you oblige me with* (ie lend or give me) *five pounds until the weekend?* 能借我5英镑吗, 周末还你? ○ *Could you oblige us with a song* (ie perform a song for us)? 给我们唱支歌好吗? ○ *Please oblige me by closing the door.* 劳驾, 替我把门关上.

▷ **obliged** *adj* **1** [pred 作表语] **~ (to sb) (for sth/doing sth)** grateful (to sb) for performing some service 受恩惠而感激(某人): *I'm much obliged to you for helping us.* 非常感激你帮助了我们. **2** (idm 习语) **much oˈbliged** thank you 多谢: *'Much obliged,' he said as I opened the door for him.* 我给他开门时他说了一声'多谢'.

ob·li·ging *adj* willing to help 愿意帮助的: *obliging neighbours* 乐于助人的邻居 ○ *You'll find him most obliging.* 你能了解到他很愿意帮助人. **ob·li·gingly** *adv*.

ob·lique /əˈbliːk; əˋblik/ *adj* **1** not horizontal or vertical; sloping; slanting 斜的; 倾斜的; 歪斜的: *an oblique line* 斜线. **2** [usu attrib 通常作定语] (*fig* 比喻) not going straight to the point; indirect 拐弯抹角的; 间接的: *He made oblique references to her lack of experience.* 他拐弯抹角地说她缺乏经验.

▷ **ob·lique** *n* (also **oblique stroke, slash**) mark (/) used in maths or punctuation to separate numbers, words, etc 用于数学或分隔数字、文字等的符号(/), 如 *4/5 people, male/female, 25/7/1949*.

ob·liquely *adv*.

ob·li·quity /əˈblɪkwətɪ; əˋblɪkwətɪ/ (also **ob·lique·ness**) [C, U] (instance of the) state of being oblique 倾斜; 歪斜; 间接.

□ **oblique ˈangle** any angle that is not a right angle (ie not 90°); acute or obtuse angle 斜角(非90°的角, 即锐角或钝角).

ob·lit·er·ate /əˈblɪtəreɪt; əˋblɪtəˌret/ *v* [Tn] (*fml* 文) **1** remove all signs of (sth); rub or blot out 除去(某物)的痕迹; 涂去; 擦掉: *obliterate all fingerprints* 擦去全部指印 ○ (*fig* 比喻) *She tried to obliterate all memory of her father.* 她想忘却对父亲的一切记忆. ○ *The view was obliterated by the fog.* 景色被浓雾遮住了. **2** destroy (sth) completely 彻底破坏或毁灭(某事物): *The entire village was obliterated by the tornado.* 整个村庄被龙卷风摧毁了. ▷ **ob·lit·era·tion** /əˌblɪtəˈreɪʃn; əˌblɪtəˋreʃən/ *n* [U].

ob·li·vion /əˈblɪvɪən; əˋblɪvɪən/ *n* [U] **1** state of forgetting; state of being unaware or unconscious 遗忘; 忘却; 无感觉; 无知觉: *Alcoholics often suffer from periods of oblivion.* 饮酒过度的人常阵阵失去记忆力. ○ *The pain made him long for oblivion.* 他疼得恨不得能失去知觉才好. **2** state of being forgotten 被遗忘; 被忘却: *His work fell/sank into oblivion after his death.* 他死后, 他的作品便被淡忘了.

ob·li·vi·ous /əˈblɪvɪəs; əˋblɪvɪəs/ *adj* [usu pred 通常作表语] **~ of/to sth** unaware of or not noticing sth; having no memory of sth 未觉察; 不注意; 忘记: *oblivious of one's surroundings* 不注意周围事物 ○ *oblivious to what was happening* 对发生的事情无记忆 ○ *oblivious to danger* 未觉察到危险. ▷ **ob·li·vi·ous·ness** *n* [U].

ob·long /ˈɒblɒŋ; *US* -lɔːŋ; ˋɑblɔŋ/ *n, adj* (figure) with four straight sides and angles of 90°, longer than it is wide 长方形; 长方形的: *an oblong table* 长方桌 ○ *an oblong bar of chocolate* 长方形的巧克力.

ob·lo·quy /ˈɒbləkwɪ; ˋɑbləkwɪ/ *n* [U] (*fml* 文) public shame or disgrace; abuse; discredit 公开的羞辱; 辱骂; 败坏名誉.

ob·nox·ious /əbˈnɒkʃəs; əbˋnɑkʃəs/ *adj* very unpleasant; nasty; offensive 极不愉快的; 讨厌的; 可憎的: *obnoxious behaviour* 讨厌的品行 ○ *He is the most obnoxious man I know.* 他是我认识的最可憎的人. ▷ **ob·nox·iously** *adv*: *obnoxiously drunk* 醉得令人讨厌. **ob·nox·ious·ness** *n* [U].

oboe /ˈəʊbəʊ; ˋobo/ *n* (*music* 音) woodwind instrument of treble pitch, played through a double reed 双簧管. ⇨ illus at App 1 见附录1插图, page x.

▷ **obo·ist** /-ɪst; -ɪst/ *n* person who plays the oboe 双簧管吹奏者.

ob·scene /əbˈsiːn; əbˋsin/ *adj* (of words, thoughts, books, pictures, etc) indecent, esp sexually; disgusting and offensive; likely to corrupt (指词语、思想、书画等)下流的, (尤指)淫秽的, 猥亵的, 可憎的, 伤风败俗的: *obscene phone calls* 下流的电话 ○ *obscene suggestions, gestures, etc* 猥亵的暗示、姿势等 ○ *obscene literature, language, etc* 淫秽的文学、语言等.

▷ **ob·scenely** *adv*.

ob·scen·ity /əbˈsenətɪ; əbˋsɛnətɪ/ *n* **1** [U] being obscene 淫秽; 猥亵; 下流: *laws against obscenity on the television* 禁止在电视上出现有伤风化事物的法令. **2** [C] obscene word or act 淫秽的词语或行为: *He shouted obscenities at the woman.* 他用下流话大骂那女子.

ob·scure /əbˈskjʊə(r); əbˋskjʊr/ *adj* **1** not easily or clearly seen or understood; indistinct; hidden 不易看清的; 费解的; 不分明的; 隐藏的: *an obscure corner of the garden* 花园里偏僻的一角 ○ *Is the meaning still obscure to you?* 你觉得意思仍然不清楚吗? ○ *His real motive for the crime remains obscure.* 他犯罪的真正动机仍不清楚. **2** not well-known 不著名的: *an obscure poet* 名不见经传的诗人 ○ *an obscure village in the country* 在乡下的一个不出名的村子.

▷ **ob·scure** *v* [Tn] make (sth) obscure(1); hide (sb/sth) from view 使(某事物)不分明; 遮掩(某人[某事物]): *The moon was obscured by clouds.* 月亮被云遮住了. ○ *Mist obscured the view.* 薄雾笼罩着周围的景色. ○ *The main theme of the book is obscured by frequent digressions.* 该书文字枝蔓, 主题不明.

ob·scurely *adv*.

ob·scur·ity /əbˈskjʊərətɪ; əbˈskjʊrətɪ/ *n* **1** [U] state of being obscure 不明; 费解; 隐晦; 无闻: *content to live in obscurity* 安于默默无闻的生活. **2** [C] (*fml* 文) thing that is obscure or indistinct 晦涩或不明的事物: *a philosophical essay full of obscurities* 充满晦涩文字的哲学文章.

ob·sequies /ˈɒbsɪkwɪz; ˈɑbsɪkwɪz/ *n* [pl] (*fml* 文) funeral ceremonies 葬礼.

ob·sequi·ous /əbˈsiːkwɪəs; əbˈsikwɪəs/ *adj* (*derog* 贬) **~ (to sb)** too willing to obey or serve; too respectful (esp in the hope of getting a reward or favour from sb) 逢迎的; 巴结的; 卑躬的: *an obsequious shop owner* 善于讨好顾客的店主 ○ *a worker who is obsequious to the boss* 对老板卑躬屈膝的人. ▷ **ob·sequi·ously** *adv*: *obsequiously flattering* 阿谀奉承. **ob·sequi·ous·ness** *n* [U].

ob·serv·able /əbˈzɜːvəbl; əbˈzɝvəbl/ *adj* [usu attrib 通常作定语] that can be seen or noticed 看得见的; 觉察得到的: *an observable lack of enthusiasm* 觉察到缺乏热情 ○ *an observable improvement* 看得出的改进.

ob·serv·ance /əbˈzɜːvəns; əbˈzɝvəns/ *n* **1** [U] **~ (of sth)** keeping or observing (OBSERVE 2b) a law, custom, festival, holiday, etc (法律、习俗等的)遵守, 奉行; (节日等的)纪念: *the observance of school rules* 对校规的遵守 ○ *the observance of New Year's Day as a public holiday* 把元旦当作公众节日的习俗. **2** [C] (*fml* 文) act performed as part of a religious or traditional ceremony 宗教仪式; 传统庆典: *religious observances* 宗教仪式.

ob·serv·ant /əbˈzɜːvənt; əbˈzɝvənt/ *adj* **1** quick at noticing things 善于观察的; 机警的; 注意的: *An observant shop assistant had remembered exactly what the man was wearing.* 有个机警的店员准确记得那个男子的穿着. ○ *Journalists are trained to be observant.* 新闻记者都要训练成有敏锐观察力的人. **2** (*fml* 文) careful to observe (2a) laws, customs, traditions, etc (对法律、习俗、传统等)谨慎遵守的: *observant of the rules* 遵守规则. ▷ **ob·serv·antly** *adv*.

ob·ser·va·tion /ˌɒbzəˈveɪʃn; ˌɑbzɚˈveʃən/ *n* **1** [U] action of observing; (state of) being observed 观察; 注意: *observation of an animal's behaviour* 观察动物的习性 ○ *observation of a patient* 观察病人 ○ *We escaped observation*, ie were not seen. 我们避开了人们的注意. **2** [U] ability to observe things 观察力: *powers of observation* 观察力 ○ *A scientist's observation should be very good.* 科学家的观察力应该很敏锐. **3** [C] remark or comment 言语; 评论: *She made one or two observations about the weather.* 她说了一两句关于天气的话. **4 ob·ser·va·tions** [pl] (*fml* 文) (recording of) collected information 观察资料; 观察记录; 观察报告: *He's just published his observations on British bird life.* 他刚发表了英国鸟类生活观察报告. **5** (idm 习语) **be under obserˈvation** be carefully and closely watched 受严密监视: *He was under observation by the police.* 他受到警方严密监视. **keep sb under obserˈvation** watch sb carefully (esp a suspected criminal or a hospital patient) 严密监视或细心观察某人(尤指嫌疑犯或医院病人): *The patient is seriously ill and is being kept under continuous observation.* 病人病情严重, 现接受持续观察. **take an obserˈvation** observe the position of the sun or another heavenly body in order to find one's exact geographical position 测天(观测太阳或另一天体的位置以确定自己的确切位置).

□ **obserˈvation car** special railway carriage in a train, with wide windows for watching the scenery (列车中的)观赏车厢(车窗宽大供观赏风景者).

obserˈvation post position from which the enemy's movements can be watched 观察所; 观察哨; 瞭望哨: *an observation post in a border fortress* 边界要塞上的观察所.

ob·ser·vat·ory /əbˈzɜːvətrɪ; *US* -tɔːrɪ; əbˈzɝvəˌtɔrɪ/ *n* building from which the stars, the weather, etc can be observed by scientists 天文台; 气象台; 观象台.

ob·serve /əbˈzɜːv; əbˈzɝv/ *v* **1** [I, Tn, Tf, Tw, Tnt only passive 只用于被动语态, Tng, Tni] see and notice (sb/sth); watch carefully 看到, 注意到(某人[某事物]); 观察; 监视: *He observes keenly, but says little.* 他观察敏锐, 但是很少说话. ○ *observe the behaviour of birds* 观察鸟类的行为 ○ *She observed that he'd left but made no comment.* 她看见他离去, 但未置一词. ○ *They observed how the tiny wings were fitted to the body.* 他们观看了微型翼的安装情况. ○ *The woman was observed to follow him closely.* 有人看到那女子紧跟着他. ○ *The police observed the man entering/enter the bank.* 警方监视着那男子进入银行的情况. **2** [Tn] (*fml* 文) **(a)** obey (rules, laws, etc) 遵守, 奉行(规则、法令等): *observe the speed limit* 遵守速度限制规定 ○ *observe the laws of the land* 遵守该国法律. **(b)** celebrate (festivals, birthdays, anniversaries, etc) 庆祝, 过(节日、生日、周年等): *Do they observe Christmas Day in that country?* 那个国家的人过圣诞节吗? **3** [Tn, Tf] (*fml* 文) say by way of comment; remark 评说; 评论: *He observed that it would probably rain.* 他说很可能下雨. ○ *'It may rain,' he observed.* '可能要下雨,' 他说.

▷ **ob·ser·ver** *n* **1** person who observes 观察者; 遵守者; 评论者: *an observer of nature* 自然界的观察家 ○ *a poor observer of speed restrictions* 不遵守速度限制的人. **2** person who attends a conference, lesson, etc to listen and watch but not to take part (会议、课堂等的)观察员, 旁听者: *an observer at a summit conference* 高峰会议上的观察员 ○ *send sb along as an observer* 派某人作观察员.

ob·sess /əbˈses; əbˈsɛs/ *v* [Tn usu passive 通常用于被动语态] fill the mind of (sb) continually 使(某人)牵挂、惦念、着迷或困扰: *The fear of death obsessed her throughout her old age.* 她晚年一直受着死亡恐惧的困扰. ○ *obsessed by/with the fear of unemployment* 老是害怕失业 ○ *She was obsessed with the idea that she was being watched.* 她总觉得受人监视而心神不宁.

▷ **ob·ses·sion** /əbˈseʃn; əbˈsɛʃən/ *n* **~ (with/about sth/sb)** **1** [U] state of being obsessed 牵挂; 惦念; 着迷; 困扰: *His obsession with computers began six months ago.* 他半年前就迷上了计算机了. **2** [C] thing or person that obsesses; fixed idea that fills the mind 萦绕于心的事物或人; 强迫观念: *He has many obsessions.* 他有许多事耿耿于怀. **ob·ses·sional** /əbˈseʃənl; əbˈsɛʃənl/ *adj* (*derog* 贬) of, having or causing obsession(s) 困扰于心的; 着迷的; 引起执着想法的: *obsessional thoughts* 令人困扰的想法 ○ *an obsessional character* 执拗的性格.

ob·sess·ive /əbˈsesɪv; əbˈsɛsɪv/ *adj* (*derog* 贬) of or having an obsession 萦绕于心的; 有执着想法的: *an obsessive concern for neatness* 好整洁癖 ○ *She's obsessive about punctuality.* 她对守时十分固执. — *n* (*medical* 医) person who has an obsession or obsessions 强迫(观念)症患者: *hysterics and obsessives* 癔病患者与强迫观念症患者 ○ *The psychiatrist has done a lot of work with obsessives.* 该精神病学家对强迫症患者做了大量工作. **ob·sess·ively** *adv* in an obsessive manner 着迷地; 着魔似地; 念念不忘地: *obsessively concerned with her appearance* 对她的外貌念念在心.

ob·sol·es·cent /ˌɒbsəˈlesnt; ˌɑbsəˈlɛsnt/ *adj* becoming out of date; going out of use 即将过时的; 逐步废弃或淘汰的: *obsolescent technology* 行将过时的技术 ○ *Electronic equipment quickly becomes obsolescent.* 电子设备淘汰得很快.

▷ **ob·sol·es·cence** /-ˈlesns; -ˈlɛsns/ *n* [U] being obsolescent 过时; 废弃; 淘汰: *a product with built-in/planned obsolescence*, ie deliberately designed by the manufacturer not to last long, so that consumers are encouraged to buy again 内设[计划]淘汰的产品(制造商故意设计成不耐久者, 以期消费者再购买).

ob·sol·ete /ˈɒbsəliːt; ˈɑbsəˌlit/ *adj* no longer used; out of date 不再使用的; 过时的: *obsolete words found in old texts* 在旧文本中发现的不再使用的词语 ○ *The horse-drawn plough is now obsolete in most European countries.* 马拉的犁现在在欧洲多数国家均已不再使用.

ob·stacle /ˈɒbstəkl; ˈɑbstəkl/ *n* (*usu fig* 通常作比喻) thing in the way that either stops progress or makes it difficult 障碍; 妨害物: *obstacles on the race-course* 赛马跑道上设置的障碍物 ○ *obstacles to world peace* 世界和平的障碍 ○ *Not being able to pass his mathematics exam proved an obstacle to his career.* 他数学考试不及格是他前途上的一大障碍.

□ **ˈobstacle race** race in which the runners have to climb over, under, through, etc various natural or artificial obstacles, such as hedges, ditches, tyres, etc 障碍赛跑.

ob·stet·rics /əbˈstetrɪks; əbˈstɛtrɪks/ *n* [sing *v*] (*medical* 医) branch of medicine and surgery concerned with childbirth 产科学: *gynaecology and obstetrics* 妇产科 ○ *She specializes in obstetrics.* 她是产科专家.

▷ **ob·stet·ric** /əbˈstetrɪk; əbˋstɛtrɪk/ (also **ob·stet·rical** /-ɪkl; -kḷ/) of obstetrics 产科的: *the obstetric ward* 产科病房 ○ *obstetrical complications* 产科并发症.

ob·stet·ri·cian /ˌɒbstəˈtrɪʃn; ˌɑbstɛˋtrɪʃən/ *n* doctor who specializes in obstetrics 产科医生: *Her obstetrician could not be present at the birth.* 产科医生不能前来为她接生.

ob·stin·acy /ˈɒbstənəsɪ; ˋɑbstənəsɪ/ *n* [U] being obstinate; stubbornness 固执; 倔强; 顽固: *His obstinacy was irritating.* 他那顽固劲真气人. ○ *Sheer obstinacy prevented her from apologizing.* 她固执得就是不道歉.

ob·stin·ate /ˈɒbstənət; ˋɑbstənɪt/ *adj* **1** refusing to change one's opinion or chosen course of action; stubborn 固执的; 倔强的; 顽固的: *The obstinate old man refused to go to hospital.* 那个顽固老头就是不肯进医院. ○ *There's a very obstinate streak in that child,* ie Some of his behaviour is very obstinate. 那孩子有的方面非常倔强. **2** not easily overcome or removed 难克服的; 不易去除的: *obstinate resistance* 顽强的抵抗 ○ *an obstinate rash on his face* 他脸上的顽疹 ○ *an obstinate stain on the carpet* 地毯上除不掉的污斑. **3** (idm 习语) **obstinate/stubborn as a mule** ⇨ MULE[1]. ▷ **ob·stin·ately** *adv*.

ob·strep·er·ous /əbˈstrepərəs; əbˋstrɛpərəs/ *adj* (*fml* 文) noisy and uncontrolled; unruly 喧闹失控的; 不守秩序的: *obstreperous behaviour, children* 难以管束的行为、儿童 ○ *He becomes obstreperous when he's had a few drinks.* 他喝了些酒就爱撒酒疯. ▷ **ob·strep·er·ously** *adv*: *obstreperously drunk* 醉得疯疯癫癫的. **ob·strep·er·ous·ness** *n* [U].

ob·struct /əbˈstrʌkt; əbˋstrʌkt/ *v* **(a)** [Tn, Tn·pr] **~ sth (with sth)** be or get in the way of (sb/sth); block (a road, passage, etc) 阻碍, 阻挡(某人[某事物]); 遮断, 阻塞(道路、通道等): *Tall trees obstructed his view of the road.* 有大树遮挡着, 他看不见道路. ○ *He was charged with obstructing the highway.* 他因阻碍公路交通而受控告. **(b)** [Tn] deliberately prevent (sb/sth) from making progress; put difficulties in the way of (sb/sth) (故意)妨碍(某人[某事物]); 在(某人[某事物])的途中设置障碍: *obstruct the police in the course of their duty* 妨碍警方执行任务 ○ *obstruct a player on the football field* 在足球场上阻挡球员 ○ *obstruct the passage of a bill through Parliament,* ie try to prevent a law being passed 阻碍议会通过某法案.

ob·struc·tion /əbˈstrʌkʃn; əbˋstrʌkʃən/ *n* **1** [U] action of obstructing; being obstructed 阻碍; 障碍; 妨碍: *obstruction of the factory gates* 工厂大门的障碍 ○ *a policy of obstruction* 阻遏政策. **2** [C] thing that obstructs; obstacle 障碍物; 阻塞物: *an operation to remove an obstruction in the throat, intestine, stomach, etc* 去除咽喉、肠、胃等梗阻的手术 ○ *obstructions on the road,* eg fallen trees 公路上的障碍物(如倒下的树木) ○ *Your car is causing an obstruction,* ie getting in the way of others. 你的汽车挡道了. **3** [C, U] (*sport* 体) (act of) unfairly stopping the movement of a player in the other team 违例阻挡: *commit an obstruction* 违例阻挡犯规 ○ *be found guilty of obstruction* 被判违例阻挡犯规.

▷ **ob·struc·tion·ism** /-ʃənɪzəm; -ʃən,ɪzəm/ *n* [U] (*fml* 文) deliberate and systematic obstruction of plans, legislation, etc (对计划、立法等的)阻挠: *The government were defeated by the obstructionism of their opponents.* 政府受到反对派阻挠而挫败.

ob·struc·tion·ist /-ɪst; -ɪst/ *n* (*fml* 文) person who uses or favours obstructionism 进行或主张阻挠的人: *a political obstructionist* 政治上的阻挠者 ○ *an obstructionist policy* 阻挠者的政策.

ob·struct·ive /əbˈstrʌktɪv; əbˋstrʌktɪv/ *adj* obstructing or likely or intended to obstruct 阻碍的; 妨碍的; 阻挠的: *deliberately obstructive* 故意妨碍的 ○ *a policy obstructive to our plans* 阻挠我们计划的政策. ▷ **ob·struct·ively** *adv*.

ob·tain /əbˈteɪn; əbˋten/ *v* **1** [Tn, Dn·pr] **~ sth (for sb)** get sth; come to own or possess sth (by buying, borrowing, taking, etc) 取得某物; (经买、借、拿等)获得, 得到某物: *Where can I obtain a copy of her latest book?* 在哪里能买到她最新出版的书? ○ *He always manages to obtain what he wants.* 他总是有办法得到他想要的东西. ○ *I obtained this record for you with difficulty.* 我好不容易为你弄到了这张唱片. **2** [I] (*fml* 文) (of rules, customs, etc) be in use; exist (指规则、风俗等)通行, 流行: *The practice still obtains in some areas of England.* 这种做法在英格兰一些地区仍很流行.

▷ **ob·tain·able** *adj* that can be obtained 能得到的; 可获得的: *no longer obtainable* 再也得不到的 ○ *Are his records still obtainable?* 他的唱片还能买到吗?

ob·trude /əbˈtru:d; əbˋtrud/ *v* [I, Ipr, Tn, Tn·pr] **~ (oneself/sth) (on/upon sb/sth)** (*fml* 文) force (oneself, one's opinions, ideas, etc) upon sb/sth, esp when unwanted 强使(自己、自己的意见、想法等)加入某人处[某事物中]; 闯入: *I've no wish to obtrude, but...* 我无意多管闲事, 但是... ○ *obtrude on sb's grief* 硬要过问某人的伤心事 ○ *He persisted in obtruding himself despite our efforts to get rid of him.* 尽管我们设法避开他, 他还是硬要插进来.

▷ **ob·tru·sion** /əbˈtru:ʒn; əbˋtruʒən/ *n* **1** [U] (*fml* 文) action of obtruding 强行加入; 闯入: *the obtrusion of unwelcome guests* 不速之客的闯入. **2** [C] thing that obtrudes 强加的事物: *unwelcome obtrusions* 强加的令人不快的事物.

ob·trus·ive /əbˈtru:sɪv; əbˋtrusɪv/ *adj* very noticeable or obvious; inclined to obtrude 显著的; 突出的; 强加的; 闯入的: *I find the music in the bar very obtrusive.* 我觉得酒吧里的音乐太吵人了. ○ *Try to wear a colour that is less obtrusive.* 尽量穿得颜色别太显眼. **ob·trus·ively** *adv*. **ob·trus·ive·ness** *n* [U].

ob·tuse /əbˈtju:s; *US* -ˈtu:s; əbˋtus/ *adj* (*fml derog* 文, 贬) slow to understand; stupid 迟钝的; 愚笨的: *He's being deliberately obtuse.* 他装糊涂. ○ *She cannot possibly be so obtuse.* 她不可能如此迟钝. ▷ **ob·tusely** *adv*. **ob·tuse·ness** *n* [U].

□ **obtuse ˈangle** (*geometry* 几) angle between 90° and 180° 钝角(90°-180°之间者). ⇨illus at ANGLE 见 ANGLE 插图.

ob·verse /ˈɒbvɜ:s; ˋɑbvɝs/ *n* (*fml* 文) **1** face, side, or part of a thing that is most noticeable or intended to be seen or shown 正面; 前面; 主要的一面: [attrib 作定语] *the obverse side* 正面. **2** side of a coin or medal that has the head or main design on it (货币或奖章的)正面: *The head of the Queen appears on the obverse of British coins.* 英国硬币的正面有女王的头像. Cf 参看 REVERSE[2] 2. **3** counterpart; opposite 对应部分; 对立面: *The obverse of love is hate.* 与爱相对的是恨.

ob·vi·ate /ˈɒbvɪeɪt; ˋɑbvɪ,et/ *v* [Tn] (*fml* 文) remove (sth); get rid of 排除, 消除(某事物): *obviate dangers, difficulties, etc* 排除危险、困难等 ○ *The new road obviates the need to drive through the town.* 有了新路, 车辆不必再穿行市区了.

ob·vi·ous /ˈɒbvɪəs; ˋɑbvɪəs/ *adj* easily seen, recognized or understood; clear 显然的; 明显的; 明白的; 清楚的: *His nervousness was obvious right from the start.* 他从一开始就显然十分紧张. ○ *It was obvious to everyone that the child had been badly treated.* 大家都清楚那孩子受过虐待. ○ *Spending less money is the obvious answer to his financial problems.* 他经济困难, 明摆着的出路是少花钱.

▷ **ob·vi·ously** *adv* as can be clearly seen; plainly 显然; 明白地: *Obviously, she needs help.* 她显然需要帮助. ○ *He was obviously drunk.* 他显然是醉了. ⇨Usage at HOPEFUL 用法见 HOPEFUL.

ob·vi·ous·ness *n* [U]: *The obviousness of the lie was embarrassing.* 那是明摆着的谎话, 真叫人难为情.

oc·ar·ina /ˌɒkəˈri:nə; ˌɑkəˋrinə/ *n* small high-pitched musical instrument, shaped like an egg, with holes for the fingertips, played by blowing and made of clay, metal or plastic 埙, 洋埙(高音小笛, 形如卵, 用陶土、金属或塑料制成).

oc·ca·sion /əˈkeɪʒn; əˋkeʒən/ *n* **1** [C] particular time (at which an event takes place) (事情发生的)时刻, 时候, 场合: *on this/that occasion* 此时[彼时] ○ *on the present/last occasion* 在这次[上次] ○ *on one occasion,* ie once 有一次 ○ *on rare occasions* 偶尔 ○ *I've met him on several occasions.* 我见过他几次. **2** [sing] **~ (for sth)** suitable or right time (for sth); opportunity 时机; 机会: *This is not an occasion for laughter.* 这不是笑的时候. ○ *I'll buy one if the occasion arises,* ie if I get the chance. 有机会我就买一个. ○ *He used the occasion to express all his old grievances against the chairman.* 他利用那机会表达了对主席积压已久的怨气. **3** [U] (*fml* 文) reason; need 原因; 理由; 需要: *I've had no occasion to visit him recently.* 我最近无需去看他. ○ *You have no*

O

occasion to be angry. 你没有理由生气. ○ *She's not had much occasion to speak French.* 她没有多少说法语的需要. **4** [C] special event or celebration 特殊的事件或庆典: *The wedding was quite an occasion.* 该婚礼是一盛会. **5** [C] (*fml* 文) immediate but incidental or subordinate cause (of sth) (偶然的或次要的)直接事因, 近因: *The real cause of the riot was unclear, but the occasion was the arrest of two men.* 骚乱的真正原因不明, 但起因是由于逮捕了两名男子. **6** (idm 习语) **on ocˈcasion** (*fml* 文) now and then; whenever there is need 不时; 必要时. **on the occasion of sth** (*fml* 文) at the time of (a certain event) 在(某事件)的时候: *on the occasion of his daughter's wedding* 在他女儿的婚礼上. **(have) a sense of ocˈcasion** (have a) natural feeling for what is right or fitting for a particular event, etc (有)场合意识或应景观念: *He wore his shabbiest clothes to the party: he has no sense of occasion!* 他穿着最寒酸的衣服去参加聚会, 毫无场合意识!

▷ **oc·ca·sion** *v* [Tn, Dn·n, Dn·pr] **~ sth (to sb)** (*fml* 文) be the cause of sth 引起或招致某事物; 为某事物的原因: *What occasioned such an angry response?* 何故引起如此愤怒的反应? ○ *Stephen's behaviour occasioned his parents much anxiety.* 斯蒂芬的行为使其父母十分担心.

NOTE ON USAGE 用法: **Occasion, opportunity** and **chance** all indicate a time when it is possible to do something. ☆ **occasion**、**opportunity**、**chance** 都表示有可能做某事的时候. **Occasion** suggests that the time is socially suitable for the activity ☆ **occasion** 指社交上从事某活动的合适时机: *A wedding is an occasion for celebration.* 婚礼是欢庆的时刻. ○ *I'll speak to him if the occasion arises.* 有机会我跟他说说. **Opportunity** and **chance** suggest that the necessary physical circumstances for doing something are present ☆ **opportunity** 和 **chance** 指有做某事所必需的实际环境: *I took the opportunity of visiting my aunt while I was in Birmingham.* 我利用在伯明翰的机会探望了我的姨母. ○ *I hope you get a chance to relax.* 希望你有机会松弛一下. **Chance** can also indicate a degree of probability ☆ **chance** 还可以指可能性的程度: *What are your chances of being promoted?* 你晋升的可能性如何? **Occasion** may refer to the particular time when something happens ☆ **occasion** 可指某事发生的时刻: *I've met her on several occasions recently.* 我最近见到过她好几次.

oc·ca·sional /əˈkeɪʒənl; əˈkeʒənl/ *adj* [usu attrib 通常作定语] **1** happening, coming, done, etc from time to time; not regular 偶然的; 偶尔的; 非定时的: *He pays me occasional visits.* 他偶尔来看看我. ○ *There will be occasional showers during the day.* 白天将偶有阵雨. ○ *I drink an occasional cup of coffee; but usually I take tea.* 我偶尔喝杯咖啡, 但平常都喝茶. ○ *He reads the occasional book, but mostly just magazines.* 他偶尔也看书, 但大多只看杂志. **2** (*fml* 文) used, meant, written, etc for a special event 应时的; 应景的; 为某场合的: *occasional verses*, eg written to celebrate an anniversary 应景诗 ○ *occasional music for a royal wedding* 皇家婚礼上的应制音乐.

▷ **oc·ca·sion·ally** /-nəlɪ; -nəlɪ/ *adv* now and then; at times 偶然地; 不时地; 有时: *He visits me occasionally.* 他偶尔来看我.

□ **ocˈcasional table** small table for use as required 备用小桌: *The coffee cups were placed on an antique occasional table.* 咖啡杯放在一张古色古香的备用小桌上.

Oc·ci·dent /ˈɒksɪdənt; ˈɑksədənt/ *n* **the Occident** [sing] (*fml* 文) the countries of the West, ie Europe and America 西方国家. Cf 参看 ORIENT[1].

▷ **Oc·ci·dental** /ˌɒksɪˈdentl; ˌɑksəˈdɛntl/ *n* (*fml* 文) person from the Occident 西方人; 西洋人.

oc·ci·dental *adj* of or from the Occident 西方的; 西洋的.

oc·cult /ɒˈkʌlt; *US* əˈkʌlt; əˈkʌlt/ *adj* (**a**) only for those with special knowledge or powers; hidden, secret 玄奥的; 神秘的; 隐秘的; 秘密的: *occult practices* 神秘的习俗. (**b**) involving supernatural or magical powers 超自然的; 有魔力的: *occult arts*, eg witchcraft 秘术(如魔法).

▷ **the occult** *n* supernatural practices, ceremonies, powers, etc 神秘学(超自然的习俗、仪式、力量等): *He's interested in the occult.* 他对神秘学很感兴趣.

oc·cult·ist *n* (*fml* 文) person involved in or believing in the occult 神秘学者; 术士.

oc·cu·pant /ˈɒkjʊpənt; ˈɑkjəpənt/ *n* person who occupies a house, room or position, or who possesses and occupies land (房屋的)居住者; (职位的)占据者; (土地的)占有者: *The previous occupants had left the house in a terrible mess.* 前房客走后房里凌乱不堪. ○ *the next occupant of the post* 该职位的下一任.

▷ **oc·cu·pancy** /-pənsɪ; -pənsɪ/ *n* **1** [U] action or fact of occupying a house, land, etc (房屋、土地等)占有, 占领, 占用, 占据: *a change of occupancy* 占有权的更换 ○ *sole occupancy of the house* 这所房子的唯一占有权. **2** [C] period of occupying a house, etc as an owner or a tenant (房子等的)占有期, 占用期: *an occupancy of six months* 六个月的占有期 ○ *During her occupancy the garden was transformed.* 在她居住期间花园改观了.

oc·cu·pa·tion /ˌɒkjʊˈpeɪʃn; ˌɑkjəˈpeʃən/ *n* **1** [U] (**a**) action of occupying; state of being occupied (OCCUPY 1) 居住; 占据: *the occupation of a house by a family* 某家庭在某房子中的居住. (**b**) taking and keeping possession 占领; 领有: *a country under enemy occupation* 被敌人占领的国家 ○ *an army of occupation* 占领军. **2** [C] period of time during which a house, country, etc is occupied (OCCUPY 1,2) 居住期; 占据期; 占有期; 占领期: *their four-year occupation of the farm, that country* 他们对该农场四年的占用期、对该国四年的占领期. **3** [C] (**a**) (*fml* 文) job; employment 工作; 职业: *'What's your occupation?' 'I'm a dancer.'* '你的职业是什么?' '我是跳舞的.' ○ *Please state your name, age and occupation.* 请说明姓名、年龄和职业. (**b**) activity that occupies a person's (esp spare) time; pastime 占据某人时间的活动; (尤指)业余活动; 消遣: *She has many occupations including gardening and wine-making.* 她有许多消遣, 包括园艺和酿酒. ○ *His favourite occupation is reading.* 他的业余爱好是看书. ⇨Usage at TRADE[1] 用法见 TRADE[1]. **4** [U, C] action of occupying a building, factory, etc as part of a political or other demonstration (对建筑物、工厂等的)占领, 占据(作为政治等示威行动).

▷ **oc·cu·pa·tional** /-ʃənl; -ʃənl/ *adj* [usu attrib 通常作定语] of, caused by or connected with a person's job 职业的; 职业造成的: *an occupational advice service* 职业咨询服务. **occupational diˈsease** disease connected with a particular job 职业病: *Skin disorders are common occupational diseases among factory workers.* 皮肤病是工人中常见的职业病. **occupational ˈhazard** risk or danger connected with a particular job 职业性危害: *Explosions, though infrequent, are an occupational hazard for coal-miners.* 矿井爆炸虽然不常发生, 但却是煤矿工人职业中的危险. **occupational ˈtherapy** way of treating people with certain physical or mental illnesses by giving them creative or productive work to do 职业疗法(给患者创造性或生产性工作以治疗其身心某些疾病的方法). **occupational ˈtherapist** specialist in this 职业疗法专家.

oc·cu·pier /ˈɒkjʊpaɪə(r); ˈɑkjəˌpaɪɚ/ *n* person who has (esp temporary) possession of land or a building; occupant (土地或建筑物的, 尤指临时的)占有者, 占用者, 居住人: *The letter was addressed to the occupier of the house.* 这封信是寄给房子的居住人的.

oc·cupy /ˈɒkjʊpaɪ; ˈɑkjəˌpaɪ/ *v* (*pt, pp* **-pied**) **1** [Tn] live in or have possession of (a house, land, etc) 占用, 占有(房屋、土地等): *They occupy the house next door.* 他们住在隔壁. ○ *The family have occupied the farm for many years.* 这一家在农场已居住多年. **2** [Tn] take possession of and establish troops in (a country, position, etc) (军事)占领(国家、阵地等): *The army occupied the enemy's capital.* 军队占领了敌国首都. **3** [Tn] take up or fill (time, space, sb's mind, etc) 占据, 充满(时间、空间、某人的头脑等): *The speeches occupied three hours.* 发言共占去三小时. ○ *A bed occupied the corner of the room.* 一张床占去了房间的一角. ○ *Her time is fully occupied with her three children.* 她的时间全部用在她的三个孩子身上了. ○ *Many problems occupied his mind.* 他脑子里装着许多问题. **4** [Tn, Tn·pr] **~ oneself (in doing sth/with sth)** fill one's time or keep oneself busy (doing sth/with sth) 忙着(做某事物); 忙(于某事物): *How* *does he occupy himself now he's retired?* 他既已退休，那如何打发日子呢？ ○ *The child occupied himself in playing his flute.* 那孩子只顾着吹笛子. **5** [Tn] hold or fill (an official position) 担任(某职); 居(某地位): *My sister occupies an important position in the Department of the Environment.* 我姐姐在环境部担任要职. **6** [Tn] place oneself in (a building, etc) as a political or other demonstration (作政治等方面示威)占领, 占据(某建筑物等): *The terrorists have occupied the Embassy.* 恐怖分子占领了大使馆. ○ *The striking office workers have occupied the whole building.* 罢工的办公室人员占据了整座建筑物.

▷ **oc·cu·pied** *adj* [pred 作表语] **1** in use; filled 在使用中; 已占用; 不空闲: *This table is already occupied.* 这桌位已经有主儿了. ⇨Usage at EMPTY[1] 用法见 EMPTY[1]. **2** ~ **(in doing sth/with sth)** involved or busy 无暇; 忙碌: *She's occupied at the moment; she cannot speak to you.* 她这会儿很忙，无法和你谈话. ○ *He's fully occupied in looking after/with three small children.* 他忙于照料三个小孩儿.

oc·cur /əˈkɜː(r); əˈkɝ/ *v* **(-rr-)** **1** (**a**) [I] come into being as an event or a process; happen 发生: *When did the accident occur?* 事故是什么时候发生的? ○ *Death occurred about midnight, the doctor says.* 医生说大约是在半夜死的. (**b**) [I, Ipr] (*fml* 文) exist; be found 存在; 被发现: *Misprints occur on every page.* 每页都有印刷错误. ○ *The disease occurs most frequently in rural areas.* 那疾病多见于农村地区. ⇨Usage at HAPPEN 用法见 HAPPEN. **2** [Ipr] **~ to sb** come into (a person's mind) 想到; 想起: *An idea has occurred to me.* 我有主意了. ○ *Did it ever occur to you that...?* ie Did you ever think that...? 你可曾想到...? ○ *It never occurred to her to ask anyone.* 她从未想到问问他人.

oc·cur·rence /əˈkʌrəns; əˈkʌrəns/ *n* **1** [C] event; incident; happening 事件; 事情; 发生的事: *Robbery is now an everyday occurrence.* 抢劫的事现在每天都有. ○ *an unfortunate occurrence* 不幸事件. **2** [U] (*fml* 文) fact, frequency, etc of sth happening 事情发生的事实或频率: *He's studying the occurrence of accidents on this piece of road,* ie how often, etc they take place. 他在研究这段路上发生事故的情形. **3** (idm 习语) **be of frequent, rare, common, etc ocˈcurrence** (*fml* 文) happen or take place frequently, rarely, etc 经常、很少...发生: *Riots are of frequent occurrence in this province.* 这个省经常发生骚乱.

NOTE ON USAGE 用法: Compare **event, occurrence** and **incident.** 试比较 **event**、**occurrence**、**incident** 三词. Occurrence is the most neutral and does not indicate a particular type of happening ☆ **occurrence** 为中性词, 并不特指某类型的事: *Divorce has become an everyday occurrence.* 离婚已成为每天都有的事了. An **event** is often a happening of importance ☆ **event** 常指重大事件: *Their wedding will be quite an event,* ie a large number of people will attend. 他们的婚礼将是件大事(即将有许多人参加). ○ *The events of 1968 changed Western society.* 1968年的事件改变了西方社会. An **incident** is usually of less importance, often occurring in a narrative ☆ **incident** 通常指不太重要的事情, 经常出现于叙述中: *You don't have to write down every little incident in your life.* 你不必把生活中每一件事都记录下来. It can also refer to a conflict or disagreement, often involving violence 这个词还可指冲突或不和, 常涉及暴力行动: *The kidnapping caused an international incident.* 这一绑架事件引起了国际纠纷.

ocean /ˈəʊʃn; ˈoʃən/ *n* **1** [U] mass of salt water that covers most of the earth's surface 洋; 海洋; 大海: [attrib 作定语] *an ocean voyage* 海洋航行 ○ *the ocean waves* 海浪. **2 Ocean** [C] one of the main areas into which this is divided (地球上划分出的)洋: *the Atlantic/Pacific/Indian/Arctic/Antarctic Ocean* 大西洋[太平洋/印度洋/北冰洋/南冰洋]. **3** (idm 习语) **a drop in the bucket/ocean** ⇨ DROP[1]. **oceans of sth** (*infml* 口) very many or much; lots of sth 很多; 大量: *oceans of food and drink* 大量的食物和饮料 ○ *Don't worry — we've got oceans of time.* 别担心——我们有的是时间.

▷ **oceanic** /ˌəʊʃɪˈænɪk; ˌoʃɪˈænɪk/ *adj* [usu attrib 通常作定语] (*fml* 文) of, like or found in the ocean (似)海洋的; 见于海洋的: *an oceanic survey* 海洋调查 ○ *oceanic plant life* 海洋植物.

oceano·graphy /ˌəʊʃəˈnɒgrəfɪ; ˌoʃəˈnɑgrəfɪ/ *n* [U] scientific study of the oceans 海洋学. **oceano·grapher** *n* specialist in this 海洋学家.

□ **ˈocean-going** *adj* (of ships) made for crossing the sea, not for coastal or river journeys (指船)远洋的, 越洋的.

ocean ˈlane one of the routes regularly used by ships 远洋航线; 远洋航路: *The ocean lanes are always busy.* 远洋航路总是很繁忙.

ocelot /ˈəʊsɪlɒt; US ˈɒsələt; ˈɑsəˌlət/ *n* type of Central and S American wild cat, similar to a leopard 小豹猫(产于中南美).

ochre (*US* also **ocher**) /ˈəʊkə(r); ˈokɚ/ *n* [U] **1** (any of various types of) light yellow or red earth used for making colourings, eg in paints 赭石(用作颜料). **2** light yellowish-brown colour 赭色; 暗棕色; 土黄色; 红褐色: *He painted the walls ochre.* 他把墙壁涂成赭色了.

o'clock /əˈklɒk; əˈklɑk/ *adv* (used with the numbers 1 to 12 when stating the time, to specify an hour 说钟点时与1至12数字连用): *He left between five and six o'clock.* 他在五点与六点之间离开的. ○ *go to bed at/after/before eleven o'clock* 十一点[之后/之前]睡觉.

Oct *abbr* 缩写 = October: *6 Oct 1931* 1931年10月6日.

oct (also 8vo) *abbr* 缩写 = octavo.

oc·ta·gon /ˈɒktəgən; US -gɒn; ˈɑktəˌgɑn/ *n* (*geometry* 几) flat figure with eight sides and eight angles 八边形; 八角形.

▷ **oc·ta·gonal** /ɒkˈtægənl; ɑkˈtægənl̩/ *adj* having eight sides 八边形的; 八角形的: *an octagonal coin, table, building* 八角形硬币、桌子、建筑物 ○ *The room is octagonal.* 这个房间是八角形的.

oct·ane /ˈɒkteɪn; ˈɑkten/ *n* hydrocarbon compound present in petrol and used as a measure of its quality and efficiency 辛烷.

□ **ˈoctane number** (also **ˈoctane rating**) measure of the efficiency and quality of a petrol in comparison with those of a fuel taken as standard (the highest number indicating the highest quality) 辛烷值.

oct·ave /ˈɒktɪv; ˈɑktɪv/ *n* **1** (*music* 音) (**a**) note that is six whole tones above or below a given note 第八音. (**b**) space between two such notes 八度: *These notes are an octave apart.* 这些音相距八度. (**c**) note and its octave played together 八度和音: *The child's hands are too small to stretch to an octave on the piano.* 这孩子的手太小, 按不到钢琴上八度和音的键. (**d**) note and its octave with the six notes in between 八度音程(包括两个八度音之间的六个音). Cf 参看 SCALE[2] 6. **2** (also **octet**) (in poetry) first eight lines of a sonnet; verse of eight lines (诗)十四行诗的前八行, 八行诗.

oc·tavo /ɒkˈteɪvəʊ; ɑkˈtevo/ *n* (*pl* **~s**) (*abbrs* 缩写 **oct, 8vo**) (size of a) book or page produced by folding a piece of paper of standard size three times to give eight sheets 八开; 八开的纸; 八开本的书.

octet (also **octette**) /ɒkˈtet; ɑkˈtɛt/ *n* **1** (piece of music for) eight singers or players 八重唱; 八重奏; 八重演唱或演奏者: *an octet by a modern composer* 现代作曲家创作的八重奏乐曲 ○ *a jazz octet* 爵士乐八重奏. **2** = OCTAVE 2.

oct(o)- *comb form* 构词成分 having or made up of eight of sth (有)八(个): *octagon* ○ *octogenarian* ○ *octopus*.

Oc·to·ber /ɒkˈtəʊbə(r); ɑkˈtobɚ/ *n* [U, C] (*abbr* 缩写 **Oct**) the tenth month of the year, next after September 十月.

For the uses of *October* see the examples at *April.* 关于October的用法见April词条中的示例.

oc·to·gen·arian /ˌɒktədʒɪˈneərɪən; ˌɑktədʒəˈnɛrɪən/ *n* person between 80 and 89 years of age 八旬老人(80至89岁之间): *She is very active for an octogenarian.* 她已经是八旬老人了, 还很精神.

oc·to·pus /ˈɒktəpəs; ˈɑktəpəs/ *n* (*pl* **~es**) sea-animal with a soft body and eight long arms with suckers on them 章鱼: *Have you ever tasted octopus?* 你吃过章鱼吗? Cf 参看 SQUID.

ocu·lar /ˈɒkjʊlə(r); ˈɑkjəlɚ/ *adj* [esp attrib 尤作定语] (*fml* 文) **1** of, for, by, the eyes 眼睛的; 适于眼睛的; 用眼睛的: *ocular defects* 视力缺陷. **2** that can be seen;

visual 可见的；视觉的：*ocular proof/demonstration* 可见到的证实.

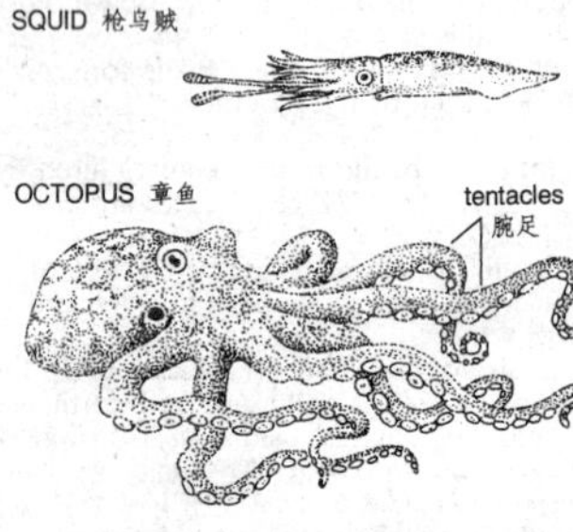

ocu·list /ˈɒkjʊlɪst; ˈɑkjəlɪst/ *n* specialist in treating diseases and defects of the eye 眼科医生.

odd /ɒd; ɑd/ *adj* (**-er, -est**) **1** strange; unusual; peculiar 奇怪的；不寻常的；古怪的：*What an odd man!* 多古怪的男人哪！○ *How odd!* 多奇怪呀！○ *She wears rather odd clothes.* 她穿的衣服很怪. ○ *She gets odder as she grows older.* 她越老越古怪. **2** (no comparative or superlative 无比较级或最高级) (of numbers) that cannot be divided by two; not even (指数目)奇数的：*1, 3, 5 and 7 are odd numbers.* 1、3、5、7是奇数. **3** [usu attrib 通常作定语] (no comparative or superlative 无比较级或最高级) (**a**) of one of a pair, set, series, etc when the other(s) is/are missing 单的(指一双、一套、一组…中的单个)：*an odd shoe/sock/glove* 单只的鞋[袜子/手套] ○ *two odd volumes of an encyclopedia* 百科全书中的两个单本 ○ *You're wearing odd socks*, ie two that do not form a pair. 你穿的两只袜子不是一双. (**b**) left over; extra; surplus 剩余的；多余的；多出的：*She made a cushion out of odd bits of material.* 她用碎布头做了个靠垫. **4** (no comparative or superlative; usu placed directly after a number 无比较级或最高级, 通常直接置于数字之后) a little more than 稍多于：*five hundred odd*, ie slightly more than 500 五百多 ○ *thirty-odd* (ie between 30 and 40) *years later* 三十多年后 ○ *twelve pounds odd*, ie £12 and some pence extra 十二英镑多. **5** [attrib 作定语] (no comparative or superlative 无比较级或最高级) not regular or fixed; occasional 不规则的；非固定的；临时的：*weed the garden at odd times/moments*, ie at various irregular moments 用零星时间给花园除草 ○ *I take the odd bit of exercise, but nothing regular.* 我偶尔稍微锻炼一下，但无规律. ○ *The landscape was bare except for the odd cactus.* 那片地上除了偶见的仙人掌以外，什么都没有. ○ *Do you have an odd minute* (ie a little spare time) *to help me with this?* 你有空儿帮我做这件事吗？ **6** (idm 习语) **an odd/a queer fish** ⇨ FISH[1]. **the/an odd man/one ˈout** (**a**) person or thing left over when the others have been put into pairs or groups 配对或分组时多出的人或物：*There's always an odd one out when I sort out my socks.* 我给袜子配对时，总是有单只的剩下. ○ *That boy is always the odd man out when the children are divided into teams.* 孩子分组时，那男孩总是单个儿. (**b**) person or thing that is different from the others 与众不同的人或物：*Banana, grape, apple, daisy — which of these is the odd one out?* 香蕉、葡萄、苹果、雏菊——这几样东西哪一样与众不同？(**c**) (*infml* 口) person who cannot fit easily into the society, community, etc of which he is a member 与集体不融洽的人；不合群者：*At school she always felt the odd one out.* 她上学时总觉得和大家格格不入. ○ *His formal clothes made him the odd one out in the club.* 他衣冠楚楚，在俱乐部中如鹤立鸡群.

▷ **oddly** *adv* in a strange or peculiar manner 奇怪地；古怪地：*behave oddly* 行为怪异 ○ *be oddly dressed* 衣着奇特 ○ *She looked at him very oddly.* 她怪模怪样地看着他. ○ *Oddly enough, we were just talking about the same thing.* 说也奇怪，我们刚谈的正是这件事.

odd·ness *n* [U] quality of being odd(1); strangeness 奇怪；古怪；怪异；与众不同：*the oddness of her appearance* 她的怪模怪样 ○ *His oddness frightened her.* 他那古怪的样子把她吓了一跳.

□ ˈ**oddball** *n* (*infml* 口) strange or eccentric person 古怪的人：*The new boss is a bit of an oddball.* 新老板有点古怪.

ˌ**odd ˈjobs** small jobs of various types, usu done for other people 零工；零活儿：*He did odd jobs around the house during his holiday.* 假日中他在家做些零活儿. ○ *The man does odd jobs in my father's garden.* 那人在我父亲的花园里打零工. **odd ˈjob man** /mæn; mæn/ person paid to do such jobs 打短工者；做散工者.

ˈ**odd-looking** *adj* of strange or unusual appearance 外观奇特的；样子异常的：*an odd-looking house* 样子奇特的房子 ○ *She's rather odd-looking.* 她的样子很怪.

odd·ity /ˈɒdɪtɪ; ˈɑdətɪ/ *n* **1** [U] (also **oddness**) quality of being odd(1); strangeness 奇特；古怪；奇怪：*I was puzzled by the oddity of her behaviour.* 她行为古怪我感到莫名其妙. **2** [C] unusual act, event, person or thing 异常的行为、事情、人或东西：*a grammatical oddity* 语法上的怪异 ○ *He's something of an oddity in the neighbourhood*, ie unusual in some ways. 左邻右舍的人觉得他有些古怪.

odd·ment /ˈɒdmənt; ˈɑdmənt/ *n* (usu *pl* 通常作复数) piece left over or remaining; remnant 剩余物；零头：*a chair sold as an oddment at the end of the sale* 减价销售最后，作为剩余货物售出的椅子 ○ *a patchwork quilt made out of oddments* 用布头拼成的被. Cf 参看 ODDS AND ENDS (ODDS).

odds /ɒdz; ɑdz/ *n* [pl] **1** probability or chance (that a certain thing will or will not happen) 可能性；机会：*The odds are in your favour* (ie You are likely to succeed) *because you have more experience.* 你经验丰富，成功的机会居多. ○ *The odds are against him*, ie He's unlikely to succeed. 他可能失败. ○ *The odds are that* (ie It is probable that) *she'll win.* 可能她赢. **2** difference in strength, numbers, etc (in favour of one person, team, etc); inequalities 差异，不平等(力量、数目等有利于某一方)：*a victory against overwhelming odds* 以弱胜强 ○ *They were fighting against heavy odds*, ie a much stronger enemy. 他们在抗击强敌. **3** (in betting) difference in amount between the money bet on a horse, etc and the money that will be paid if it is successful (赌博的)投注赔率：*The horse was running at odds of ten to one.* 那匹马参赛赔率是十比一. ○ *The odds are five to one on that horse.* 那匹马的赔率是五比一. ○ *I bet three pounds on a horse running at twenty to one and won sixty pounds!* 我用三镑压在赔率为二十比一的马上，结果赢了六十镑！ **4** (idm 习语) **against (all) the ˈodds** despite strong opposition or disadvantages 尽管极为不利或遭强烈反对：*Against all the odds she achieved her dream of becoming a ballerina.* 她冲破重重困难，实现了当芭蕾舞演员的梦想. **be at odds (with sb) (over/on sth)** be disagreeing or quarrelling (with sb) (about sth) (与某人)(在某事上)不和，争吵：*They're constantly at odds with each other.* 他们常互相争吵. ○ *He's always at odds with his father over politics.* 在政治上他总和父亲意见不一. **even chances/odds/money** ⇨ EVEN[1]. **give/receive ˈodds** (*sport* 体) give/receive an advantage at the beginning of a game (eg golf) to make it more difficult for the stronger player to win (比赛开始时强弱双方之间)让步[接受让步]. **have the cards/odds stacked against one** ⇨ STACK *v*. **it makes no ˈodds** it will not affect matters; it is of no consequence 无关紧要；没关系：*It makes no odds to me whether you go or stay.* 你是去是留与我无关. **lay (sb) odds (of)** offer (sb) odds(3) (of) 向(某人)以(某赔率)打赌：*I'll lay odds of three to one that he gets the job.* 我以三比一的赔率打赌，他能得到那份工作. ˌ**odds and ˈends**; (*Brit infml* 口) ˌ**odds and ˈsods** small articles; bits and pieces of various sorts, usu without much value 零星杂物；琐碎物品：*He's moved most of his stuff; there are just a few odds and ends left.* 他把大部分东西都搬走了，只留下一些零星杂物. Cf 参看 ODDMENT. **over the ˈodds** (*Brit infml* 口) more than is expected, necessary, etc 比预期的或必要的为多：*The firm pays over the odds for working in unpopular areas.* 在条件差的地区工作，公司多给酬金. ○ *We offered over the odds for the house to make sure we got it.* 我们为有把握得到那所房子就多出了价. **what's the ˈodds?** (*infml* 口) what does it matter?; it's not important 那有什么关系?; 那无所谓: *He's left her? What's the odds? He was never at home anyhow.* 他离开她了? 那算得了什么? 他反正从来都不在家里.

□ **ˌodds-ˈon** *adj* better than even (chance); likely (to win) (可能性)较大的; 很可能(获胜)的: *It's odds-on that he'll be late.* 他多半得迟到. ○ *That horse is the ˌodds-on ˈfavourite.* 那匹马很有希望获胜.

ode /əʊd; od/ *n* (usu long) poem expressing noble feeling, often written to a person or thing, or celebrating some special event (通常为长篇的)颂诗: *Keats's 'Ode to Autumn'* 济慈的《秋颂》.

odi·ous /ˈəʊdɪəs; ˈodɪəs/ *adj* (*fml* 文) **1** disgusting; hateful 可憎的; 可恨的: *What an odious man!* 多可恨的男子! ○ *I find his flattery odious.* 我觉得他的谀词十分讨厌. **2** (idm 习语) **comparisons are odious** ⇨ COMPARISON. ▷ **odi·ous·ness** *n* [U].

odium /ˈəʊdɪəm; ˈodɪəm/ *n* [U] (*fml* 文) general or widespread hatred or disgust felt towards a person or his actions 憎恨; 厌恶: *behaviour that exposed him to odium* 他那招人憎恶的行为 ○ *He incurred the odium of everyone by sacking the old caretaker.* 他因解雇老管理员而激起公愤.

odo·meter /ɒˈdɒmɪtə(r), əʊˈ-; oˈdɑmətɚ/ *n* (*US*) = MILOMETER.

odor·ous /ˈəʊdərəs; ˈodərəs/ *adj* (*dated fml* 旧, 文) having a (pleasant or unpleasant) smell 有(香的或臭的)气味的.

odour (*US* **odor**) /ˈəʊdə(r); ˈodɚ/ *n* (*fml* 文) **1** [C] (pleasant or unpleasant) smell (香的或臭的)气味: *the delicious odour of freshly-made coffee* 新煮的咖啡的香味 ○ *the unpleasant odour of over-ripe cheese* 干酪过熟的臭味 ○ *emit, give off a pungent odour* 发出辛辣的气味 ○ (*fig* 比喻) *An odour of corruption hangs about him.* 他浑身散发着腐化堕落的气味. **2** (idm 习语) **be in good/bad ˈodour (with sb)** be well/badly thought of (by sb); have a good/bad reputation (with sb) 受[不受](某人)欢迎; 声誉好[坏]: *I'm in rather bad odour with my boss at the moment.* 现在老板对我很反感.

▷ **odour·less** *adj* without a smell 无气味的: *an odourless liquid* 无气味的液体 ○ *Our new product will keep your bathroom clean and odourless.* 我厂新产品能保持您的浴室洁净无味.

odys·sey /ˈɒdɪsɪ; ˈɑdəsɪ/ *n* long adventurous journey 长途的冒险行程: (*fig* 比喻) *a spiritual odyssey* 精神上的长征.

OECD /ˌəʊ iː siː ˈdiː; ˌo i si ˈdi/ *abbr* 缩写 = Organization for Economic Co-operation and Development 经济合作与发展组织.

oecu·men·ical = ECUMENICAL.

Oed·ipus com·plex /ˈiːdɪpəs kɒmpleks; *US* ˈed-; ˈɛdəpəs ˈkɑmplɛks/ (*psychology* 心) unconscious sexual desire of a child for the parent of the opposite sex (esp of a boy for his mother), and jealousy of the other parent 俄狄浦斯情结(儿童对异性生身亲长的性欲望, 对同性生身亲长的忌妒); (女)恋父情结; (尤指)(子)恋母情结.

o'er /ɔː(r); ɔr/ *adv, prep* (*arch* 古) over: *o'er valleys and hills* 越过溪谷与山丘.

oe·so·phagus (also *esp US* **e·so·phagus**) /ɪˈsɒfəgəs; ɪˈsɑfəgəs/ *n* (*pl* **~es** or **-gi** /dʒaɪ; ˌdʒaɪ/) (*medical* 医) tube through which food, etc passes from the mouth to the stomach; gullet 食道; 食管: *cancer of the oesophagus* 食道癌. ⇨illus at DIGESTIVE, THROAT 见 DIGESTIVE、THROAT 插图.

oes·tro·gen /ˈiːstrədʒən; ˈɛstrədʒən/ (also *esp US* **es·tro·gen** /ˈes-; ˈɛs-/) *n* [U, C] any of a group of female sex hormones, produced by the ovaries, which develop and maintain the characteristic features of the female body, eg large breasts, and prepare the body for pregnancy 雌激素: *an oestrogen deficiency* 雌激素缺乏. Cf 参看 PROGESTERONE.

of /əv; əv *strong form* 强读式 ɒv; ɑv/ *prep* **1** belonging to (sb/sth) 属于(某人[某事物]). **(a)** (followed by a *possess pron* or by a *n*, usu with *'s* 后接物主代词或名词, 通常带's): *a friend of mine* 我的朋友 ○ *an acquaintance of my wife's* 我妻子认识的人 ○ *that house of yours in the country* 你在乡下的那所房子. **(b)** (followed by a *n* referring to an inanimate object 后接表示无生命物体的名词): *the handle of the umbrella* 伞的把 ○ *the lid of the box* 箱子的盖. **(c)** (after a *n* referring to sb's rights or duties 用于表示某人的权利或责任的名词之后): *the role of the teacher* 教师的职责 ○ *the rights of man* 人的权利 ○ *the privileges of the élite* 上层人物的特权 ○ *the responsibilities of a nurse* 护士的责任. **2** originating from (a background) or living in (a place) 出身于(某背景); 居住于(某地): *a woman of royal descent* 出身皇族的女子 ○ *a man of humble origin* 出身卑贱的男子 ○ *the miners of Wales* 威尔士的矿工 ○ *the inhabitants of the area* 该地区的居民. **3** created by (esp referring to sb's works as a whole) 由(某人)创作的(尤指其全部作品): *the works of Shakespeare* 莎士比亚的著作 (Cf 参看 *Shakespeare's comedies*) ○ *the paintings of Picasso* 毕加索的画 ○ *the poems of John Lennon* 约翰·伦农的诗. **4** **(a)** concerning or depicting (sb/sth) 关于, 描绘(某人[某事物]): *stories of crime and adventure* 犯罪与冒险的故事 ○ *a photograph of my dog* 我的狗的照片 ○ *a picture of the Queen* 女王的像 ○ *a map of Ireland* 爱尔兰的地图. **(b)** about (sb/sth) 关于(某人[某事物]): *I've never heard of such places.* 我从未听说过这些地方. ○ *He told us of his travels.* 他给我们讲了他的旅行见闻. **5** (indicating the material used to make sth 表示制作某物的材料): *a dress of silk* 丝的连衣裙 ○ *shirts made of cotton* 棉布制的衬衫 ○ *a house (built) of stone* 石(筑的)房子. Cf 参看 FROM 8. **6** (used to show a special grammatical relationship 用以表示某种语法关系) **(a)** (introducing the object of the action expressed by the preceding *n* 引入前一名词所示行为的客体): *a lover of* (ie sb who loves) *classical music* 爱好古典音乐的人 ○ *fear of the dark* 怕黑 ○ *any hope of being elected* 当选的希望 ○ *the forging of a banknote* 伪造钞票. **(b)** (introducing the subject of the action expressed by the preceding *n* 引入前一名词所示行为的主体): *the support of the voters*, ie the voters supporting sb 选民的支持 ○ *the feelings of a rape victim towards her attacker* 遭强奸的受害人对暴徒的愤怒 ○ *the love of a mother for her child* 母亲对其孩子的爱 ○ *the beliefs of religious groups* 宗教团体的信仰. **7** **(a)** (indicating what is measured, counted or contained 表示数量或内容): *a pint of milk* 一品脱奶 ○ *2 kilos of potatoes* 2公斤土豆 ○ *a sheet of paper* 一张纸 ○ *a loaf of bread* 一个面包 ○ *a box of matches* 一盒火柴 ○ *a bottle of lemonade* 一瓶汽水 ○ *a bag of groceries* 一袋食品杂货. **(b)** (showing the relationship between part and the whole of sth 表示某物的部分和整体的关系): *a member of the football team* 足球队一队员 ○ *for six months of the year* 全年的六个月. **(c)** (used after *some, many, a few*, etc and between a numeral or superlative *adj* and a *pron* or *det* 用于some、many、a few等之后以及数词或最高级形容词与代词或限定词之间): *some of his friends* 他的一些朋友 ○ *a few of my records* 我的几张唱片 ○ *not much of the food* 不多的食物 ○ *six of them* 他们中的六个人 ○ *five of the team* 球队中的五个人 ○ *the last of the girls* 这些姑娘中的最后一人 ○ *the most expensive of the presents* 那些礼物中的最贵重者 ○ *the richest of all her friends* 她的朋友中最有钱的. **8** **(a)** (used in expressions showing distance in space or time 用于表示时空距离的词组中): *a village 5 miles north of Leeds* 利兹以北5英里的一个村庄 ○ *within 100 yards of the station* 该站100码以内 ○ *Within a year of their divorce he had remarried.* 他离婚不到一年就又结婚了. ○ (*US*) *a quarter of eleven*, ie 10.45 am or pm 差一刻十一点. **(b)** (used in dates 用于日期): *the twenty-second of July* 七月二十二日 ○ *the first of May* 五月一日. **9** so that sb no longer has or suffers from (sth) 因而某人不再有(某事物): *rob sb of sth* 抢某人的某物 ○ *deprived of his mother's protection* 被剥夺了母亲对他的保护 ○ *relieved of responsibility* 解除了责任 ○ *cure sb of drug-addiction* 医好某人的毒瘾. **10** (indicating a cause 表示原因): *die of pneumonia* 死于肺炎 ○ *ashamed of one's behaviour* 对自己的行为感到羞耻 ○ *proud of being captain* 因当队长而骄傲. **11** (introducing a phrase in apposition 引入同位语): *the city of Dublin* 都柏林市 ○ *the issue of housing* 住房问题 ○ *on the subject of education* 论教育 ○ *at the age of 16* 在16岁那年. **12** (introducing a phrase that describes a preceding *n* 引入名词的后置修饰语): *a coat of many colours* 一件彩色大衣 (Cf 参看 *a multi-coloured coat*) ○ *a girl of ten* 10岁的女孩儿 (Cf 参看 *a ten-year-old girl*) ○ *a woman of genius*

O

有天才的女子 ○ *a child of strange appearance* 外貌奇特的孩子 ○ *an item of value* 一件值钱的物品 ○ *products of foreign origin* 外国的产品. **13** (used between *ns*, the first describing the second 用于两名词之间, 前者修饰后者): *He's got the devil of a temper.* 他脾气极坏. ○ *Where's that fool of a receptionist?* 那个笨蛋接待员在什么地方? ○ *He's a fine figure of a man.* 他是个体型好看的男子. **14** in relation to (sth); concerning (sth) 涉及, 有关(某事物): *the result of the debate* 辩论的结果 ○ *the time of departure* 起程的时刻 ○ *the topic of conversation* 谈话的题目 ○ *a dictionary of English* 英语词典 ○ *the Professor of Mathematics* 数学教授 ○ *his chance of winning* 他赢的机会 ○ *sure of one's facts* 确信自己的论据. **15** chosen from (others of a kind); contrasted with 从(同类中)择出; 与...成对照: *I'm surprised that you of all people think that.* 我奇怪, 在所有人当中只有你想着那件事. ○ *A flat tyre today of all days — what bad luck!* 偏偏今天车胎瘪了——真倒霉! **16** (used to show who is being described by *It is/was + adj* 用在it is/was+形容词的句型里, 表示描述的对象): *It was kind of you to offer.* 谢谢你的好意. ○ *It's wrong of your boss to suggest it.* 你们老板那样提是不对的. **17** (*dated* 旧) frequently happening at (a specified time) 经常在(某时刻)发生: *They used to visit me of a Sunday*, ie on Sundays. 从前他们每星期日都来看我. ○ *Often, of an evening* (ie in the evening), *we'd hear the sirens.* 我们常常在傍晚听到警报声.

off[1] /ɒf; US ɔ:f; ɔf/ *adj* **1** [attrib 作定语] = OFF-SIDE[2]. **2** [pred 作表语] **~ (with sb)** (esp after *rather, very, slightly*, etc 尤用于rather、very、slightly等之后); (*infml* 口) impolite or unfriendly (towards sb) (对某人)不礼貌, 不友好: *She sounded rather off on the phone.* 她在电话中说话不太客气. ○ *He was a bit off with me this morning.* 他今天早晨对我有些冷淡. **3** [pred 作表语] (of food) no longer fresh (指食物)不新鲜: *This fish has gone/is off*, ie can no longer be eaten. 这条鱼已经不新鲜了. ○ *The milk smells/tastes decidedly off.* 牛奶闻起来[尝起来]完全变味了.

□ **'off chance** slight possibility 微小的可能性: *There is still an off chance that the weather will improve.* 天气转好尚有一线希望. ○ *He came on the off chance of finding me at home.* 他来找我时是想到我或许有可能正在家中.

off[2] /ɒf; US ɔ:f; ɔf/ *adv part* (For special uses with many *vs*, eg *go off, turn sth off, clear off*, see the *v* entries. 可与许多动词连用, 如go off、turn sth off、clear off, 其释义见各动词词条.) **1** (**a**) at or to a point distant in space; away 距, 离, 到(远至某处); 离开: *The town is still five miles off.* 那小城尚在五英里以外. ○ *We are some way off*, eg our destination. 我们有一段距离(如距目的地). ○ *He ran off with the money.* 他携款潜逃了. ○ *Be off/Off with you!* ie Go away! 走开[滚开]! (**b**) at a point distant in time; away 距, 离, 到(远至某时); 离开: *The holidays are not so far off.* 假期已经不那么远了. **2** (indicating removal or separation, esp from the human body 表示除掉或分离(尤指离开身体)): *He's had his beard shaved off.* 他把胡子剃掉了. ○ *What beautiful curls — why do you want to have them (cut) off?* 你那鬈发多漂亮啊——为什么要剪掉呢? ○ *take one's hat, coat, tie, etc off* 摘帽、脱大衣、解领带 (Cf 参看 *have (got) one's hat, coat, tie, etc on*) ○ *Don't leave the toothpaste with the top off.* 牙膏用后别忘了盖上盖. Cf 参看 ON[1] 3. **3** starting a journey or race 出发; 起跑: *She's off to London tomorrow.* 她明天出发上伦敦. ○ *I must be off soon.* 我很快就得走了. ○ *We're off/Off we go!* 我们出发喽! ○ *They're off*, ie The race has begun. 他们已经起跑了. **4** (*infml* 口) (of sth arranged or planned) not going to happen; cancelled (指已安排或计划的事)不发生, 取消: *The wedding/engagement is off.* 婚礼[婚约]取消了. ○ *The miner's strike is off.* 矿工的罢工取消了. Cf 参看 ON[1] 8. **5** (**a**) disconnected at the mains; not being supplied (自供应的来源处)断开, 不供应: *The water/gas/electricity is off.* 水[煤气/电]停了. (**b**) (of appliances) not being used (指电器)关掉, 不用: *The TV, radio, light, etc is off.* 电视、收音机、电灯等已关掉. ○ *Make sure the central heating is off.* 集中供暖设备一定要关掉. Cf 参看 ON[1] 4. (**c**) (of an item on a menu) no longer available or being served (指菜谱上某菜肴)不再供应: *The steak pie is off today.* 今日牛肉饼停止供应. ○ *Soup's off — we've only got fruit juice.* 汤已售完——现只供应果汁. **6** away from work or duty 不工作; 不上班; 不值班: *I think I'll take the afternoon off*, ie not do my usual work, etc. 我想下午歇班. ○ *She's off today.* 她今天休息. ○ *The manager gave the staff the day off.* 经理放员工一天假. ○ *I've got three days off next week.* 下星期我有三天假. **7** reduced in price; cheaper 减价; 削价; 折扣: *All shirts have 10% off.* 衬衫一律九折. ○ *Shoes are on sale with £5 off.* 各类鞋减价5英镑出售. ○ *buy a calendar at 50% off* 以半价买一日历. **8** (in the theatre) behind or at the sides of the stage; not on the stage (剧院中)在台后或台侧, 不在台上: *noises/voices off* 幕后发出嘈杂声[人声]. **9** (idm 习语) **be off for sth** (*infml* 口) have supplies of sth 有需要的某物: *How are you off for cash?* ie How much have you got? 你有多少现款? Cf 参看 WELL OFF (WELL[3]), BADLY OFF (BAD[1]). **ˌoff and ˈon/ˌon and ˈoff** from time to time; now and again 断断续续地; 不时: *It rained on and off all day.* 整天断断续续地下着雨.

▷ **off** *n* [sing] **1 the off** start of a race 起跑: *They're ready for the off.* 他们已准备好起跑. **2 the off** (in cricket) that half of the field towards which a batsman is facing when waiting to receive a ball (板球)击球员面对着的半边场地: *play the ball to the off* 击球员把球击到他面对着的半边场地 ○ [attrib 作定语] *the off stump*, ie the stump on this side 三柱门中在此场地的一柱. Cf 参看 LEG.

□ **off of** *prep* (*US*) = OFF[3].

off[3] /ɒf; US ɔ:f; ɔf/ *prep* (For special uses with many *vs*, eg *get off sth, take (sth) off sth*, see the *v* entries. 可与许多动词连用, 如get off sth、take (sth) off sth, 其释义见各动词词条.) **1** down or away from (a position on sth) 从(某物的位置)上落下或离开: *fall off a ladder, tree, horse, wall* 从梯子上、树上、马上、墙上跌下 ○ *The rain ran off the roof.* 雨水自屋顶流下. ○ *The ball rolled off the table.* 球自桌上滚落. ○ *Keep off the grass.* 勿践踏草地. ○ *Cut another slice off the loaf.* 再切下一片面包. ○ *Take a packet off the shelf.* 从架子上取下一包. ○ *They were only 100 metres off the summit when the accident happened.* 事故发生时他们离峰顶只有100米远. ○ (*fig* 比喻) *We're getting right off the subject.* 我们正在偏离主题. ○ *Scientists are still a long way off (finding) a cure.* 科学家还远未找到解决办法. **2** (esp of a road or street) accessible from (sth) (尤指道路)可由(某处)进入的: *a narrow lane off the main road* 可由公路进入的乡间小路 ○ *another bathroom off the main bedroom* 可从大卧室进入的另一浴室. **3** at some distance from (sth) 距(某处)某距离: *a big house off the high street* 离大街不远的一所大房子 ○ *an island off the coast of Cornwall* 康沃尔海岸附近的一个岛 ○ *The ship sank off Cape Horn.* 轮船在合恩角外沉没了. **4** (*infml* 口) not wishing or needing to take (sth) 不想用, 不需要(某事物): *I was off* (ie did not enjoy eating) *my food for a week.* 我已经有一个星期不想吃东西了. ○ *He's finally off* (ie is no longer addicted to) *drugs.* 他终于戒了毒了.

off(-) /ɒf; US ɔ:f; ɔf/ *pref* 前缀 (used widely to form *ns, adjs, vs* and *advs* 可用以构成许多名词、形容词、动词和副词) not on; away or at a distance from 不在...上; 离...; 距...某距离: *off-print* ○ *off-stage* ○ *off-shore* ○ *off-key* ○ *off-load*.

of·fal /ˈɒfl; US ˈɔ:fl; ˈɔfl/ *n* [U] internal parts of an animal (eg heart, kidneys, liver, brains, etc) used as food; once considered to be less valuable than its flesh (食用的)动物内脏, 下水: *Offal is now thought to be very nutritious.* 现在认为下水很有营养.

off-beat /ˌɒfˈbi:t; US ˌɔ:f-; ˌɔfˈbit/ *adj* (*infml* 口) unusual; unconventional 不寻常的; 非传统的: *ˌoff-beat ˈhumour* 别饶风趣的幽默 ○ *an off-beat TV comedy* 别具一格的电视喜剧 ○ *Her style of dress is definitely off-beat.* 她的服装确实与众不同.

off-cut /ˈɒfkʌt; US ˈɔ:f-; ˈɔfˌkʌt/ *n* piece of wood, paper, etc remaining after the main piece has been cut; remnant 下脚料: *She bought some timber off-cuts to build kitchen shelves.* 她买了一些木材下脚料做厨房用架子.

off-day /ˈɒfdeɪ; US ˈɔ:f-; ˈɔfde/ *n* (*infml* 口) day when one does things badly, is unlucky, clumsy, etc 不顺利、倒霉、不顺心...的一天: *Monday is always an off-day for me.* 对我来说星期一总是诸事不宜.

of·fence (*US* **of·fense**) /əˈfens; əˈfɛns/ *n* **1** [C] **~**

(against sth) breaking of a rule or law; illegal act; crime 犯规；犯法；违法行为；罪行：*commit an offence* 犯过错 ○ *an offence against society, humanity, the state, etc* 违反社会、人性、国家等的罪行 ○ *a capital offence*, ie one punishable by death 死罪 ○ *sexual offences* 性犯罪 ○ *be charged with a serious offence* 被控犯重罪 ○ *Because it was his first offence* (ie the first crime of which he'd been found guilty), *the punishment wasn't too severe.* 他因属初犯而获从轻惩处. **2** [U] **~ (to sb/sth)** (act or cause of) upsetting or annoying (sb); insult 使(某人)不悦，恼怒(的行为或原因)；冒犯：*I'm sorry; I intended no offence when I said that.* 对不起，我说那事并无恶意. ○ *I'm sure he didn't mean to cause offence (to you).* 我肯定他并非有意得罪你. ○ *The anti-British propaganda gave* (ie caused) *much offence.* 反英宣传触犯了众怒. **3** [C] **~ (to sb/sth)** (*fml* 文) thing that causes displeasure, annoyance or anger 使人不悦、讨厌或生气的事物：*The new shopping centre is an offence to the eye*, ie unpleasant to look at. 新购物中心很不顺眼. **4** [U] (*fml* 文) attack 攻击：*weapons of offence rather than defence* 攻击型的而不是防御型的武器. **5** (idm 习语) **no ofˈfence (to sb)** (used to explain that one does/did not intend to upset or annoy sb 用以解释自己无意冒犯或触怒某人)：*I'm moving out — no offence to you or the people who live here, but I just don't like the atmosphere.* 我要搬出去了——请你或住在这里的人不要见怪，我只不过是不喜欢这里的空气罢了. **take ofˈfence (at sth)** feel hurt, upset or offended (by sth) 觉得受到(某事物的)伤害、烦扰或招惹：*She's quick to take offence*, ie easily offended. 她动不动就生气.

of·fend /əˈfend; əˈfɛnd/ *v* **1** (**a**) [Tn esp passive 尤用于被动语态] cause (sb) to feel upset or angry; hurt the feelings of 触怒，冒犯(某人)；伤(某人)的感情：*She was offended at/by his sexist remarks.* 他那些性别歧视的话把她惹恼了. ○ *She may be offended if you don't reply to her invitation.* 她请你，你要是不回个信儿就可能把她得罪了. (**b**) [Tn] cause displeasure or annoyance to (sb/sth) 使(某人)不快，恼怒；使(某物)不适：*sounds that offend the ear* 刺耳的声音 ○ *an ugly building that offends the eye* 一座难看的建筑物. **2** [Ipr] **~ against sb/sth** (*fml* 文) do wrong to sb/sth; commit an offence against sb/sth 触犯、冒犯或得罪某人；触犯、侵犯或违犯某事物：*offend against humanity* 违反人性 ○ *His conduct offended against the rules of decent behaviour.* 他的行为已经离格儿了.

▷ **of·fender** *n* (**a**) person who offends, esp by breaking a law 冒犯者；犯规者；(尤指)犯法者，犯罪者，犯人：*an offender against society* 为害社会的人. (**b**) person found guilty of a crime 罪犯；有罪者：*a persistent offender* 惯犯. Cf 参看 FIRST OFFENDER (FIRST[1]).

of·fense /əˈfens; əˈfɛns/ *n* **1** [Gp, U] (*US sport* 体) attacking team or section; method of attack 攻方；进攻的方法：*Their team had a poor offense.* 他们队进攻不力. ○ *They deserved to lose; their offense was badly planned.* 他们也该输，进攻全无章法. Cf 参看 DEFENCE 3. **2** [C, U] (*US*) = OFFENCE.

of·fens·ive /əˈfensɪv; əˈfɛnsɪv/ *adj* **1** upsetting or annoying; insulting 烦扰人的；使人恼怒的；冒犯的；得罪人的：*offensive remarks, language, behaviour* 无礼的言语、语言、行为 ○ *I find your attitude most offensive.* 我觉得你十分失态. Cf 参看 INOFFENSIVE. **2** disgusting; repulsive 讨厌的；使人反感的：*an offensive smell* 难闻的气味 ○ *She finds tobacco smoke offensive.* 她对烟草的烟很反感. **3** (*fml* 文) used for, or connected with, attack; aggressive 用于进攻的；与进攻有关的；侵犯的：*offensive weapons* 进攻性武器 ○ *an offensive style of play in rugby* 橄榄球赛的进攻型风格. Cf 参看 DEFENSIVE.

▷ **of·fens·ive** *n* **1** aggressive action, campaign or attitude; attack 进攻的行动；进攻；攻势；攻击：*The new general immediately launched an offensive against the enemy.* 新任命的将军立即向敌人发起攻击. ○ (*fig* 比喻) *The company has launched a strong marketing offensive to try to increase sales.* 公司已发动争取市场的强大攻势以期增加销售量. **2** (idm 习语) **be on the offensive** be making an attack; act aggressively 采取攻势；主动出击：(*fig* 比喻) *He's always expecting criticism of his work, so he's always on the offensive.* 他料到自己的作品总归要受到批判，所以总是以攻为守. ○ *It's difficult to make friends with her; she's constantly on the offensive.* 跟她交朋友十分困难；她这个人口角尖酸、咄咄逼人. **go on/take the ofˈfensive** begin to attack 开始攻击：*In meetings she always takes the offensive before she can be criticized.* 在会上，她不等别人批评她而总是先发制人.

of·fens·ively *adv*: *offensively loud music* 喧闹已极的音乐 ○ *offensively ugly buildings* 丑陋不堪的建筑物.

of·fens·ive·ness *n* [U].

of·fer /ˈɒfə(r); *US* ˈɔːf-; ˈɔfɚ/ *v* **1** [Tn, Tn·pr, Dn·n, Dn·pr] **~ sth (to sb) (for sth)** put forward sth (to sb) to be considered and accepted or refused; present (向某人)提出某事物供考虑、接受或拒绝；提供：*The company has offered a high salary.* 公司已提出高薪相聘. ○ *She offered a reward for the return of her lost bracelet.* 她为寻回遗失的手镯提出以酬金答谢. ○ *I've been offered a job in Japan.* 日本有份工作要聘请我去做. ○ *He offered her a cigarette.* 他敬她一枝烟. ○ *We offered him the house for £35 000.* 这所房子我们向他索价35 000英镑. ○ *He offered £30 000 for the house.* 他还价30 000英镑买这所房子. **2** [I, Tn, Tt, Dn·n, Dn·pr] **~ sth (to sb)** show or express the willingness or intention to do, give, etc sth 表示愿意或有意做、给...某事物：*I don't think they need help, but I think I should offer anyway.* 我认为他们无须帮助，不过我想我应有所表示. ○ *They offered no resistance.* 他们没有抵抗. ○ *We offered to leave.* 我们表示要走了. ○ *We offered him a lift, but he didn't accept.* 我们建议他搭我们的车，但他没有接受. ○ *The company offered the job to someone else.* 公司把这工作给别人了. **3** [I] (*fml* 文) occur; arise 发生；出现；呈现：*Take the first opportunity that offers*, ie that there is. 有机会切勿放过. **4** [Tn] (*fml* 文) give opportunity for (sth); provide 为(某事物)提供机会；给予：*The job offers prospects of promotion.* 这份工作有晋升的机会. ○ *The trees offered welcome shade from the sun.* 这些树凉儿十分宜人. **5** [Tn, Tn·p, Dn·n, Dn·pr] **~ sth/sb (up) (to sb) (for sth)** (*fml* 文) present or give sth/sb, usu to God or a god and esp as a sacrifice 奉献，(通常指向上帝或其他神)祭献(某事物[某人])(尤指作为牺牲)：*She offered (up) a prayer to God for her husband's safe return.* 她向上帝祷告保佑她丈夫平安回来. ○ *A calf was offered up as a sacrifice to the goddess.* 向女神祭献了一头牺牲小牛. **6** (idm 习语) **ˈoffer itself/themselves** (*fml* 文) be present; happen 有；出现；发生：*Ask her about it when a suitable moment offers itself.* 这个问题你在适当的时候问问她吧. **offer (sb) one's ˈhand** (*fml* 文) hold out one's hand (in order to shake hands with sb) 伸出手(为和某人握手)：*He came towards me, smiled and offered his hand.* 他向我走来，微笑着伸出手来和我握手. **offer one's hand (in ˈmarriage)** (*fml* 文) propose marriage to a woman 向女子求婚.

▷ **of·fer** *n* **1** [C] **~ (to sb/to do sth)** statement offering to do or give sth to sb (为某人做某事物或给某人某事物的)提议，建议：*an offer of help from the community* 社区提出的帮助建议 ○ *your kind offer to help* 你愿意帮忙的好意 ○ *an offer of marriage* (ie proposal) *to the youngest sister* 向最小的妹妹的求婚. **2** [C] **~ (for sth)** amount offered 提供考虑的数量；出价：*a firm offer*, ie one which was genuinely meant and not likely to be withdrawn 实盘 ○ *I've had an offer of £1 200 for the car.* 有人向我出价1 200英镑买这辆汽车. ○ *They made an offer which I couldn't refuse.* 他们出的价我十分满意. **3** (idm 习语) **be open to (an) offer/offers** ⇨ OPEN[1]. **on ˈoffer** for sale at a reduced price 削价出售：*Baked beans are on offer this week at the local supermarket.* 当地超级市场本周烘豆罐头大减价. **or nearest offer** ⇨ NEAR[1]. **under ˈoffer** (*Brit*) (of a building for sale) having a prospective buyer who has made an offer (指待售房屋)已有人出价要买：*The office block is under offer.* 办公大楼已有人出价购买.

of·fer·ing /ˈɒfərɪŋ; *US* ˈɔːf-; ˈɔfərɪŋ/ *n* **1** [U] action of presenting sth (to be accepted or refused) 提供，给予(以备对方接受或拒绝)：*the offering of bribes* 行贿 ○ *the offering of financial assistance* 提供财务帮助. **2** [C] (*fml* 文) thing offered, esp as a gift or contribution 提供之物；(尤指)礼物，奉献物：*a church offering* 给教堂的捐献 ○ *He gave her a box of chocolates as a peace offering*, ie in the hope of restoring peace after an argument, etc. 他送她一盒巧克力以示和解之意.

of·fer·tory /ˈɒfətrɪ; *US* -tɔːrɪ; ˈɔfɚˌtɔrɪ/ *n* [C] (*fml* 文)

money collected during or at the end of a religious service（礼拜时的）献金: [attrib 作定语] *Money should be put in the offertory box.* 献金应放进奉献箱里.

off·hand /ˌɒfˈhænd; *US* ˌɔːf-; ˈɔfˈhænd/ *adj* (of behaviour, speech, etc) too casual; abrupt（指行为、言语等）过于随便的, 唐突的: *He was rather offhand with me.* 他对我未免太随便了. ○ *I don't like his offhand manner.* 我不喜欢他那粗鲁的态度.

▷ **off·hand** *adv* without previous thought 未假思索地; 不经考虑地: *I can't say offhand how much money I earn.* 我一下子说不上来我挣多少钱. ○ *Offhand I can't quote you an exact price.* 我无法立即给你报个准价.

off·handed *adj*: *an ˌoffhanded ˈattitude* 过于随便的态度. **off-handedly** *adv*.

of·fice /ˈɒfɪs; *US* ˈɔːf-; ˈɔfɪs/ *n* **1** [C] (**a**) [C often *pl* 常作复数] room(s) or building used as a place of business, esp for clerical or administrative work 办公室; 办公楼: *our London offices* 我们在伦敦的办事处 ○ *Our office is in the centre of the town.* 我们的办公楼在市中心. ○ [attrib 作定语] *an ˈoffice job* 办公室的工作 ○ *ˈoffice equipment*, ie stationery, typewriters, etc 办公设备 ○ *ˈoffice workers* 办公室工作人员. (**b**) (usu small) room in which a particular person works（通常指小的）办公室, 事务所, 办事处: *a lawyer's office* 律师事务所 ○ *the school secretary's office* 学校秘书办公室 ○ *The editors have to share an office.* 编辑须合用一间办公室. (**c**) (*US*) doctor's surgery 诊所: *the pediatrician's office* 小儿科诊所. **2** [C] (often in compounds 常用以构成复合词) room or building used for a particular purpose (esp to provide a service) 有特定用途的房间或建筑物(尤指服务性的): *the lost ˈproperty office* 失物招领处 ○ *a ˈticket office at a station* 火车站售票处 ○ *the local ˈtax office* 地方税务所. **3 Office** [sing] (esp in compounds 尤用以构成复合词) (buildings of a) government department, including the staff, their work and duties（政府部门的）部, 局, 厅(的建筑物): *the ˈForeign Office* 外交部 ○ *the ˈHome Office* 内政部. **4** [C, U] (work and duties connected with a) (public) position of trust and authority, esp as (part of) the government 公职; 官职; 公务: *He has held the office of chairman for many years.* 他当主席已经很多年了. ○ *seek/accept/leave/resign office as a cabinet minister* 谋求[接受/放弃/辞退]内阁阁员的职务 ○ *the office of mayor* 市长职位 ○ *His political party has been out of office* (ie has not formed a government) *for many years.* 他们政党已在野多年. ○ *Which political party is in office in your country?* 贵国是哪一个政党执政? **5 Office** [sing] (*religion* 宗) authorized form of Christian worship（基督教徒的）仪式, 祷告: *Divine ˈOffice*, ie daily service in the Roman Catholic church 日课(天主教的每日礼拜) ○ *the Office for the dead* 为死者举行的宗教仪式. **6** (idm 习语) **ˌlay down ˈoffice** (*fml* 文) resign a position of authority 辞职. **through sb's good ˈoffices** (*fml* 文) with sb's kind help 承某人的好意协助.

□ **ˈoffice-block** *n* (usu large) building containing offices (OFFICE 1b), usu belonging to more than one company 办公大楼(通常为数公司合用的): *ugly concrete office-blocks* 丑陋的混凝土办公楼群 ○ *The bank and the building society are in the same office-block.* 银行和房屋建筑协会在同一座办公大楼里.

ˈoffice boy (*fem* 阴性作 **ˈoffice girl**) young person employed to do less important duties in an office 办公室的年轻工友: *The office boy will deliver the package.* 工友将把这个包送去.

ˈoffice holder (also **ˈoffice bearer**) person who holds an office 公务员; 官员: *All the office bearers have to be elected.* 这些官员均需选举产生.

ˈoffice hours hours during which business is regularly conducted 办公时间: *Office hours vary from company to company and country to country.* 因公司、国家不同, 办公时间也有所不同.

of·ficer /ˈɒfɪsə(r); *US* ˈɔːf-; ˈɔfəsɚ/ *n* **1** person appointed to command others in the army, navy, air force, etc 军官: *All the officers and ratings were invited.* 全体海军官兵都受到邀请. ○ *Both commissioned and non-commissioned officers attended.* 有军衔的和无军衔的军官都出席了. **2** (often in compounds 常用以构成复合词) person with a position of authority or trust, eg in the government or a society（政府的）官员;（会社的）高级职员: *executive and clerical officers*, eg in the Civil Service 行政的主管人员和办事员 ○ *a customs officer* 海关官员 ○ *officers of state*, ie ministers in the government 政府部长 ○ *the Medical Officer of Health* 卫生官员 ○ *We had to vote to appoint all three officers: President, Secretary and Treasurer.* 我们要用投票方式决定三大任命: 会长、秘书、财务主管. **3** (**a**) = POLICE OFFICER (POLICE). (**b**) (used as a form of address to a policeman or policewoman 警察（用作对男女警察的称呼）): *'Yes, officer, I saw the man approach the girl.'* '是的, 警察先生, 我看见那男子向那姑娘走去.'

of·fi·cial /əˈfɪʃl; əˈfɪʃəl/ *adj* **1** of or concerning a position of authority or trust 公务的; 公职的; 职权的: *official responsibilities, powers, records* 公务、职权、公认的记录 ○ *in his official capacity as mayor* 以其市长的官方身分. **2** said, done, etc with authority; recognized by authority 官方的; 正式的; 官方认可的: *an official announcement, statement, decision, etc* 官方公告、声明、决定等 ○ *the official biography of the princess* 官方发表的公主传记 ○ *The news is almost certainly true although it is not official.* 尽管消息是非官方的, 但是几乎确凿无疑. **3** for, suitable for or characteristic of persons holding office (4); formal 为公职人员的; 适合官员的; 有官员特点的: *an official reception, dinner, etc* 官式的接待、宴会等 ○ *written in an official style* 以官式文体写的.

▷ **of·fi·cial** *n* person who holds a public office (eg in national or local government) 官员: *government officials* 政府官员 ○ *the officials of a political party* 政党官员.

of·fi·cial·dom /-dəm; -dəm/ *n* (*fml often derog* 文, 常作贬义) **1** [Gp] officials as a group 官员(总称): *Officialdom will no doubt decide our future.* 当官的无疑将决定我们的未来. **2** [U] the ways of doing the business of bureaucracy 官僚作风; 官场: *We suffer from too much officialdom.* 我们深受官僚作风之害.

of·fi·cial·ese /əˌfɪʃəˈliːz; əˌfɪʃəˈliz/ *n* [U] (*derog* 贬) language characteristic of official documents (and thought to be too formal or complicated) 公文体的文字: *the incomprehensible officialese of income tax documents* 所得税公文上的晦涩文字. Cf 参看 JOURNALESE (JOURNAL).

of·fi·cially /əˈfɪʃəlɪ; əˈfɪʃəlɪ/ *adv* **1** in an official manner; formally 公务或公职上; 正式地: *I've been officially invited to the wedding.* 我正式获得邀请去参加婚礼. ○ *We already know who's got the job but we haven't yet been informed officially.* 我们已经知道是谁得到这份工作了, 但是尚未得到正式通知. **2** as announced publicly (esp by officials) though not necessarily true in fact 据称(尤指官员所称, 但未必属实): *Officially, the director is in a meeting, though actually he's playing golf.* 据说主任正在开会, 可他实际上正打高尔夫球呢.

of·fi·ci·ate /əˈfɪʃɪeɪt; əˈfɪʃɪˌet/ *v* [I, Ipr] **~ (at sth)** perform the duties of an office(4) or position 执行职务; 主持: *The Reverend Mr Smith will officiate at the wedding*, ie perform the marriage ceremony. 史密斯牧师将主持婚礼.

of·fi·cious /əˈfɪʃəs; əˈfɪʃəs/ *adj* too ready or willing to give orders, offer advice or help, or use one's authority; bossy and interfering 爱发号施令的; 好管闲事的; 好用权威的: *We were tired of being pushed around by officious civil servants.* 我们厌烦那些官老爷把我们支来支去. ▷ **of·fi·ciously** *adv*. **of·fi·cious·ness** *n* [U].

off·ing /ˈɒfɪŋ; *US* ˈɔːf-; ˈɔfɪŋ/ *n* (idm 习语) **in the offing** (*infml* 口) likely to appear or happen soon; not far away 即将来临; 将发生; 不远: *The smell of cooking told them there was a meal in the offing.* 他们闻到做菜的味儿, 知道眼看要吃饭了.

off-key /ˌɒf ˈkiː; *US* ˌɔːf; ˈɔfˈki/ *adj, adv* out of tune 走调(的); 不和谐(的): *sing off-key* 唱走了调 ○ (*fig* 比喻) *Some of his remarks were rather off-key*, ie not fitting or suitable. 他的话有些是走了板儿了.

off-licence /ˈɒf laɪsns; ˈɔfˌlaɪsn̩s/ *n* (*Brit*) (**a**) (*US* **ˈpackage store**) shop or part of a public house where alcoholic drinks are sold to be taken away 持有准许外卖酒类执照的酒店或柜台. (**b**) licence for this 准许外卖酒类的执照.

off-line /ˌɒf ˈlaɪn; *US* ˌɔːf; ˌɔfˈlaɪn/ *adj* (*computing* 计) (using equipment) that is not controlled by a central processor 脱机的; 线外的; 使用脱机设备的: *an ˌoff-line ˈprocess* 脱机处理. Cf 参看 ON-LINE.

off-load /ˌɒf ˈləʊd; *US* ˌɔːf; ˌɔfˈlod/ *v* **1** [Tn] unload (sth)

卸(某物): *off-load sacks of coal from a lorry* 从卡车上卸下一袋袋的煤. **2** [Tn·pr] **~ sb/sth on/onto sb** (*infml* 口) get rid of (sb/sth unpleasant or unwelcome) by passing him/it to sb else 转移或转嫁至他人以摆脱或推卸(某人[某事物]): *We'll be able to come if we can off-load the children onto my sister.* 要是我妹妹肯替我们照管孩子, 我们就能来.

off-peak /ˌɒf ˈpiːk; *US* ˌɔːf; ˈɔfˈpik/ *adj* [attrib 作定语] in or used at a time that is less popular or less busy (and therefore usu cheaper) 非高峰期的, 非最繁忙时的(因而通常较便宜): ˌ*off-peak elecˈtricity* 非高峰期的电力 ○ ˌ*off-peak ˈholiday prices* 非高峰假日价格. Cf 参看 PEAK[1] 4.

off·print /ˈɒfprɪnt; *US* ˈɔːf-; ˈɔfˌprɪnt/ *n* separate printed copy of an article that is part of a larger publication (书刊中选文的)单行本.

off-putting /ˌɒf ˈpʊtɪŋ; *US* ˌɔːf; ˈɔfˌpʊtɪŋ/ *adj* (*infml* 口 *esp Brit*) unpleasant; disturbing; disconcerting 令人厌恶的; 令人烦恼的; 令人尴尬的: *His rough manners were rather off-putting.* 他举止粗鲁很使人难堪.

off-season /ˈɒf siːzn; *US* ˈɔːf; ˈɔfˌsizn/ *n* [sing] (in business and tourism) least active time of the year; period when there are few orders or visitors (指商业和旅游业)淡季: *Hotel workers wait until the off-season to take their holidays.* 旅馆工作人员等到淡季再休假.

off·set[1] /ˈɒfset; *US* ˈɔːf-; ɔfˈsɛt/ *v* (**-tt-**; *pt, pp* **offset**) [Tn, Tn·pr] **~ sth (by sth/doing sth)** compensate for sth; balance sth 补偿或抵消某事物: *He put up his prices to offset the increased cost of materials.* 他提高了售价以补偿材料成本的增加. ○ *Higher mortgage rates are partly offset by increased tax allowances.* 抵押款高了, 其中一部分可因免税额增加而相抵消.

off·set[2] /ˈɒfset; *US* ˈɔːf-; ˈɔfˌsɛt/ *n* (also **offset process**) method of printing in which the ink is transferred from a metal plate to a rubber surface and then onto paper 胶印法.

off·shoot /ˈɒfʃuːt; *US* ˈɔːf-; ˈɔfˌʃut/ *n* stem or branch growing from a main stem 枝子; 枝条; 枝杈: *remove offshoots from a plant* 修剪植物的枝桠 ○ (*fig* 比喻) *the offshoot of a wealthy family* 富家的旁系.

off·shore /ˌɒfˈʃɔː(r); *US* ˌɔːf-; ˈɔfˈʃɔr/ *adj* [usu attrib 通常作定语] **1** at sea not far from the land 近海的: *an* ˌ*offshore ˈoil rig,* ˈ*island,* ˈ*anchorage* 近海的石油钻塔、岛、锚地 ○ ˌ*offshore ˈfishing* 近海捕鱼. **2** (of winds) blowing from the land towards the sea (指风)向海的, 离岸的: ˌ*offshore ˈbreezes* 离岸微风.

off·side[1] /ˌɒfˈsaɪd; *US* ˌɔːf-; ˈɔfˈsaɪd/ *adj, adv* (*sport* 体) **1** (of a player in football, hockey, etc) in a position where the ball may not be legally played, between the ball and the opponents' goal 越位的; 越位: *The forwards are all offside.* 前锋都越位了. **2** of or about such a position 越位的: *be in an* ˌ*offside poˈsition* 处于越位位置 ○ *the* ˌ*offside ˈrule* 越位规则. Cf 参看 ONSIDE.

off·side[2] /ˌɒfˈsaɪd; *US* ˌɔːf-; ˈɔfˈsaɪd/ (also **off**) *adj* [attrib 作定语] (*Brit*) (of a vehicle, a road or an animal) on the right-hand side (指车辆、道路或动物)在右侧的, 在右边的: *the rear* ˌ*offside ˈtyre* 右后轮胎 ○ *the off front wheel of a car* 汽车的右前轮. Cf 参看 NEARSIDE (NEAR[1]).

off·spring /ˈɒfsprɪŋ; *US* ˈɔːf-; ˈɔfˌsprɪŋ/ *n* (*pl* unchanged 复数不变) (*fml* 文) (**a**) child or children of a particular person or couple (某人或某夫妇的)孩子, 子女: *She's the offspring of a scientist and a musician.* 她是一位科学家和一位音乐家的女儿. ○ *Their offspring are all very clever.* 他们的子女都很聪明. (**b**) young of an animal 崽儿: *How many offspring does a cat usually have?* 一只猫通常能产多少小猫?

off-stage /ˌɒf ˈsteɪdʒ; *US* ˌɔːf; ˈɔfˈstedʒ/ *adj, adv* not on the stage; not visible to the audience 不在舞台上(的); 幕后(的): *an* ˌ*off-stage ˈscream* 幕后的喊叫声 ○ *At this point in the play, most of the actors are off-stage.* 戏演至此, 多数演员都已退出舞台.

off-street /ˈɒf striːt; *US* ˈɔːf; ˈɔfˈstrit/ *adj* [attrib 作定语] not on the public road 不在道路上的: *off-street parking only* 只准在路面以外停车.

off-white /ˌɒf ˈwaɪt; *US* ˌɔːf ˈhwaɪt; ˈɔfˈhwaɪt/ *n, adj* not pure white, but with a very pale grey or yellow tinge 灰白色(的); 米色(的): *paint a room off-white* 把房间涂成米色 ○ ˌ*off-white ˈpaint* 米色涂料.

oft /ɒft; *US* ɔːft; ɔft/ *adv* (*arch* 古) (esp in compounds 尤用以构成复合词) often 常: *an oft-told tale* 常讲的故事 ○ *an oft-repeated warning* 常重复的警告.

□ ˈ**oft-times** *adv* (*arch* 古) often 常; 屡.

of·ten /ˈɒfn, *also* ˈɒftən; *US* ˈɔːfn; ˈɔfən/ *adv* **1** many times; at short intervals; frequently 常常; 经常; 时常: *We often go there.* 我们常去那儿. ○ *We have often been there.* 我们常在那里. ○ *We've been there quite often.* 我们经常在那里. ○ *It very often rains here in April.* 这儿四月份常下雨. ○ *He writes to me often.* 他经常给我写信. ○ *How often* (ie At what intervals) *do the buses run?* 公共汽车隔多长时间一班? **2** in many instances 在很多情况下: *These types of dog often have eye problems.* 这种狗的眼睛很多都有毛病. ○ *Old houses are often damp.* 旧房大都潮湿. **3** (idm 习语) **as often as** each time that; as many times as 每次; 每当: *As often as I tried to phone him the line was engaged.* 每次我给他打电话都占线. **as** ˌ**often as** ˈ**not; more** ˌ**often than** ˈ**not** very frequently 往往; 大抵: *When it's foggy the trains are late more often than not.* 雾大时火车往往误点. ˌ**every so** ˈ**often** occasionally; from time to time 偶尔; 有时; 不时. **once too often** ⇨ ONCE.

ogle /ˈəʊgl; ˈogḷ/ *v* [I, Ipr, Tn] **~ at sb** (*derog* 贬) look or stare at (esp a woman) in a way that suggests sexual interest 色迷迷地看(尤指看女子): *Most women dislike being ogled (at).* 多数女子都讨厌让人色迷迷地盯着.

ogre /ˈəʊgə(r); ˈogɚ/ *n* (*fem* 阴性作 **og·ress** /ˈəʊgres; ˈogrɛs/) **1** (in legends and fairy stories) cruel and frightening giant who eats people (传说和童话中的)吃人巨妖. **2** (*fig* 比喻) very frightening person 极可怕的人: *My boss is a real ogre.* 我的老板是个十足的恶魔.

▷ **og·rish** /ˈəʊgərɪʃ; ˈogərɪʃ/ *adj* of or like an ogre (似)吃人巨妖的; 极可怕的.

oh /əʊ; o/ *interj* **1** (expressing surprise, fear, joy, etc 表示惊奇、恐惧、快乐等): *Oh look!* 啊, 瞧哇! ○ *Oh, how horrible!* 哎呀, 多可怕呀! **2** (used for emphasis or to attract sb's attention 用以加强语气或引人注意): *Oh yes I will.* 啊, 我当然愿意. ○ *Oh Pam, can you come over here for a minute?* 喂, 帕姆, 你能来一下吗?

ohm /əʊm; om/ *n* unit of electrical resistance 欧姆(电阻单位).

OHMS /ˌəʊ eɪtʃ em ˈes; ˌo etʃ ɛm ˈɛs/ *abbr* 缩写 = (*Brit*) (esp on official forms, envelopes, etc) On Her/His Majesty's Service (尤作公文、信封等的标记)为女王[英王]陛下效劳.

oho /əʊˈhəʊ; oˈho/ *interj* (expressing surprise or triumph 表示惊奇或胜利).

-oid *suff* 后缀 (with *adjs* and *ns* 与形容词和名词结合) resembling; similar to 像…的; 似…的: *humanoid* ○ *rhomboid.*

oil /ɔɪl; ɔɪl/ *n* **1** [U] any of various thick slippery liquids that do not mix with water and (usu) burn easily, obtained from animals, plants, minerals, etc 油: ˈ*coconut,* ˈ*sunflower,* ˈ*vegetable, etc oil* 椰子、葵花籽、菜籽…油 ○ ˌ*olive ˈoil* 橄榄油 ○ ˈ*cooking oil* 食用油 ○ ˌ*cod-liver ˈoil* 鱼肝油 ○ ˈ*salad oil* 色拉油. **2** [U] (**a**) petroleum found in rock underground 石油: *drilling for oil in the desert* 在沙漠中钻探石油. (**b**) (often in compounds 常用以构成复合词) form of petroleum used as fuel, as a lubricant, etc (用作燃料、润滑剂等的)油: *an* ˈ*oil-heater/-lamp/-stove* 油加热器[灯/炉] ○ *Put some oil in the car.* 给汽车加润滑油. **3** [C] (*infml* 口) picture painted in oil-colours 油画. **4 oils** [pl] paints made by mixing colouring matter in oil 油画颜料: *paint in oils* 画油画. **5** (idm 习语) **burn the midnight oil** ⇨ BURN[2]. **pour oil on the flames** ⇨ POUR. **pour oil on troubled waters** ⇨ POUR. **strike lucky/oil/gold** ⇨ STRIKE[2].

▷ **oil** *v* [Tn] **1** put oil on or into (sth) (eg to make part of a machine run smoothly); lubricate 给(某物)加润滑油; 用油润滑: *oil a lock, one's bicycle, a stiff hinge* 给锁、自己的自行车、不灵活的合叶上油. **2** (idm 习语) **oil the** ˈ**wheels** make things go smoothly by behaving tactfully or craftily 用圆滑手段使事情顺利进行. **oiled** *adj* = WELL-OILED (WELL[3]).

□ ˈ**oil-bearing** *adj* (of areas of rock underground) containing mineral oil (指地下岩层)含矿物油的.

ˈ**oilcake** *n* [U] cattle food made from seeds after the oil has been pressed out 油渣饼(作家畜饲料).

ˈ**oilcan** *n* can (usu with a nozzle) containing oil, used for oiling machinery 加油壶; (通常指)长嘴油壶.

'oilcloth *n* [U] cotton material treated with oil to make it waterproof and used as a covering for shelves, tables, etc 油布.

'oil-colour (also **'oil-paint**) *n* [C, U] = OILS (OIL 4).

'oilfield *n* area where oil is found in the ground or under the sea 油田: *North Sea oilfields* 北海油田.

ˌoil-'fired *adj* (of a boiler, furnace, etc) burning oil as fuel (指锅炉、高炉等)燃油的: *ˌoil-fired central 'heating* 燃油集中供热设备.

'oil-painting *n* **1** [U] art of painting using oil-colours 油画艺术: *She enjoys oil-painting.* 她喜欢画油画. **2** [C] picture painted in oil-colours 油画. **3** (idm 习语) **be no 'oil-painting** (*infml joc* 口, 谑) be a plain or ugly person 其貌不扬的或丑陋的人.

'oil-palm *n* tropical palm-tree yielding oil 油棕.

oil rig 石油钻塔

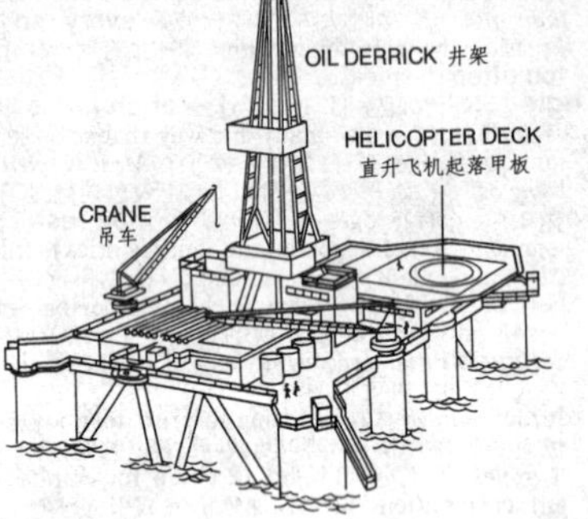

'oil rig structure and equipment for drilling oil (eg in the sea-bed) 石油钻塔, 钻油设备(如用于海底的). Cf 参看 DERRICK.

'oilskin *n* (**a**) [C, U] (coat, etc made of) cloth treated with oil to make it waterproof 防水油布; 防水衣. (**b**) **oilskins** [pl] suit of clothes made of this material 防水衣裤: *Sailors wear oilskins in stormy weather.* 水手遇到暴风雨天气都穿着防水服.

'oil slick = SLICK.

'oil-tanker *n* large ship with tanks for carrying oil (esp petroleum) 油轮.

'oil well hole drilled into the ground or sea bed to obtain petroleum 油井.

oily /'ɔɪlɪ; 'ɔɪlɪ/ *adj* (**-ier, -iest**) **1** of or like oil (似)油的: *an oily liquid* 油状液体. **2** covered or soaked with oil; containing much oil 涂有油的; 浸透油的; 含油多的: *oily fingers* 沾有油的手指 ○ *an oily skin* 油性皮肤 ○ *an oily old pair of jeans* 一条沾满油污的旧牛仔裤 ○ *oily food* 油腻的食物. **3** (*derog* 贬) trying too hard to win favour by flattery; fawning 过于奉承的; 油滑的; 谄媚的: *I don't like oily shop assistants.* 我不喜欢过分殷勤的店员. ▷ **oili·ness** *n.*

oint·ment /'ɔɪntmənt; 'ɔɪntmənt/ *n* [C, U] **1** smooth greasy paste rubbed on the skin to heal injuries or roughness, or as a cosmetic 软膏; 油膏. Cf 参看 SALVE 1. **2** (idm 习语) **a/the fly in the ointment** ⇨ FLY[1].

okapi /əʊ'kɑːpɪ; o'kɑpɪ/ *n* animal of Central Africa, similar to a giraffe but with a shorter neck and a striped body 獾㹢狓 (产于中非, 类似长颈鹿, 但颈短身有条斑).

okay (also **OK**) /ˌəʊ'keɪ; 'o'ke/ *adj, adv* (*infml* 口) all right; satisfactory or satisfactorily 好; 不错: *I hope the children are okay.* 希望孩子们都好. ○ *I think I did OK in the exam.* 我认为我考得不错. ○ *We'll go to the cinema tomorrow, OK?* ie is that agreed? 咱们明天去看电影好吗?

▷ **okay** (also **OK**) *interj* (*infml* 口) all right; yes 好的; 是; 行: *'Will you help me?' 'OK, I will'.* '你来帮帮我好吗?' '好, 我来帮你.' ○ *Okay children, we'll clear up the room now.* 好啦, 孩子们, 咱们现在打扫房间吧.

okay (also **OK**) *v* [Tn] (*infml* 口) agree to (sth); approve of 同意(某事); 认可: *He okayed/OK'd my idea.* 他同意我的主意.

okay (also **OK**) *n* (*infml* 口) agreement; permission 同意; 允许: *Have they given you their okay?* 他们准许你了吗? ○ *We've got the OK from the council at last.* 我们终于获得了委员会的同意. Cf 参看 A-OK (A[1]).

okra /'əʊkrə; 'okrə/ *n* [U] (tropical plant with) green seed pods eaten as a vegetable 秋葵(荚)(可作蔬菜).

old /əʊld; old/ *adj* (**-er, -est**) ⇨Usage at ELDER[1] 用法见 ELDER[1]. **1** (with a period of time or with *how* 与表示一段时间的词或how连用) of (a particular) age (某)年龄的: *He's forty years old.* 他四十岁了. ○ *At fifteen years old he left school.* 他十五岁时中学毕业了. ○ *How old are you?* 你多大岁数了? ○ *A seven-year-old* (ie A child who is seven years of age) *should be able to read.* 七岁的儿童应当识字了. **2** having lived a long time; advanced in age; no longer young 老的; 年老的: *Old people cannot be so active as young people.* 老年人无法像年轻人那样活跃. ○ *He's too old for you to marry.* 他比你大得多, 你不宜嫁给他. ○ *What will she do when she is/gets/grows old?* 她年老时要做什么呢? **3** (**a**) having been in existence or use for a long time (存在或使用)很久的, 陈旧的: *old customs, beliefs, habits, etc* 一贯的风俗、信仰、习惯等 ○ *old clothes, cars, houses* 旧衣物、汽车、房子 ○ *This carpet's getting rather old now.* 这块地毯现在很旧了. (**b**) [attrib 作定语] belonging to past times; not recent or modern 古老的; 古代的; 旧时的: *old religious practices* 古老的宗教活动 ○ *Things were different in the 'old days.* 在过去情况就不同了. **4** [attrib 作定语] known for a long time; familiar 早已认识的; 熟悉的: *an old friend of mine*, ie one I've known for a long time, but not necessarily old in years 我的老朋友(不一定年纪大) ○ *We're old rivals*, ie We've been rivals for a long time. 我们是老对手了. **5** former; previous (but not necessarily old in years) 以前的, 从前的(不一定年代久远): *in my old job* 在我以前的那份工作中 ○ *at my old school* 在我从前的学校里 ○ *I prefer the chair in its old place.* 我觉得这把椅子还是放在老地方好. ○ *We had a larger garden at our old house.* 我们以前住的房子花园大. ⇨Usage 见所附用法. **6** [attrib 作定语] (*infml or joc* 口或谑) (used as a term of affection or intimacy 用作表示亲昵或亲密关系的用语): *Dear old John!* 亲爱的约翰! ○ *Good old Angela!* 可爱的安杰拉! ○ *You're a funny old thing!* 你真是个活宝! **7** [attrib 作定语] (*infml* 口) (used for emphasis 用以加强语气): *Any old thing* (ie Anything whatever) *will do.* 什么东西都行. **8** (*fml* 文) having much experience or practice 有经验的; 老练的: *old in diplomacy* 擅长外交事务的 ○ *an old trooper* 老练的装甲兵. **9** (idm 习语) **'any old how** (*infml* 口) carelessly; untidily 随便地; 胡乱地: *The books were scattered round the room any old how.* 屋里到处乱放着书. **a chip off the old block** ⇨ CHIP[1]. **a dirty old man** ⇨ DIRTY[1]. **for old times' 'sake** because of tender or sentimental memories of one's past 看在旧日情分上. **the 'good/'bad old days** an earlier period of time (in one's life or in history) seen as better/worse than the present 过去的好[坏]日子: *The friends met occasionally to chat about the good old days at school.* 朋友偶尔相聚畅谈上学时的大好时光. **the grand old man** ⇨ GRAND. **have/give sb a high old time** ⇨ HIGH. **money for jam/old rope** ⇨ MONEY. **no fool like an old fool** ⇨ FOOL[1]. **of 'old** of, in or since former times 从前的; 过去; 自古以来: *in days of old* 在古时 ○ *We know him of old*, ie have known him for a long time and so know him well. 我们老早就认识他. **(as) old as the 'hills** very old; ancient 很老的; 古老的: *This dress is as old as the hills.* 这件连衣裙算是老古董了. **ˌold beyond one's 'years** more mature or wise than is usual or expected for one's age 超常的成熟或聪明. **old 'boy, 'chap, 'man, etc** (*dated infml* 旧, 口) (used esp by older men of the middle and upper classes as a familiar form of address when talking to another man 尤作中上阶层年长男子称呼另一男子的用语): *'Excuse me, old man, can I borrow your newspaper?'* 老兄, 请问能借你的报纸看看吗? **(be) old enough to be sb's 'father/'mother** (be) significantly older than sb 比某人年龄大很多: *You can't marry him! He's old enough to be your father!* 你可不能嫁给他! 他那岁数都能当你父亲了! **(be) old enough to know 'better** (be) old enough to act in a more sensible way than one did 已经长大该懂好歹了: *Have you been drawing on the walls? I thought you were old enough to know better.* 墙上是你画的吧？我还以为你都懂事了呢. **old 'hat** (*infml derog* 口, 贬) not new or original; old-fashioned 不新; 非独创的; 老式的: *His ideas are all terribly old hat.* 他的想法都老掉牙了. **(have) an ˌold head on young 'shoulders** (be) a more mature person than is expected for one's age 少年老成. **an old 'trout** (*infml* 口) bad-tempered or unpleasant old person, esp a woman 脾气坏的或讨人厌的老人(尤指女人). **an old 'wives' tale** old and usu foolish idea or belief 陈腐的且多为愚蠢的想法或观念. **one of the 'old school** old-fashioned or conservative person 老派人物; 保守人物. **pay/settle an old 'score** have one's revenge for a wrong done to one in the past 算旧帐; 报仇. **rake over old ashes** ⇨ RAKE[1]. **ring out the old year and ring in the new** ⇨ RING[2]. **the same old story** ⇨ SAME[1]. **teach an old dog new tricks** ⇨ TEACH. **tough as old boots** ⇨ TOUGH. **young and old** ⇨ YOUNG.

▷ **the old** *n* [pl *v*] old people 老人(总称): *The old feel the cold weather more than the young.* 老年人比年轻人怕冷.

oldie *n* (*infml* 口) old person or thing 老人; 陈旧之物: *This record is a real oldie.* 这张唱片真是老古董了.

old·ish *adj* rather old 颇老的; 颇旧的.

□ ˌ**old 'age** the later part of life; state of being old 晚年; 老年: *Old age can bring many problems.* 人老了有时麻烦事就多了. ˌ**old-age 'pension** pension paid by the State to people above a certain age 养老金. ˌ**old-age 'pensioner** (*abbr* 缩写 **OAP**) (also **pensioner, senior citizen**) person who receives such a pension 领取养老金的人.

'old boy (*fem* 阴性作 **'old girl**) **1** former pupil of a particular school 校友: *an old boys' reunion* 男校友聚会. **2 old 'boy, old 'girl** (*infml* 口) old person 老人: *the old 'girl who lives next door* 住在隔壁的老太太. **3** (idm 习语) **the old-boy network** the tendency among old boys, esp of British private schools, to help each other in later life (男的)老同学关系网.

the 'old country one's country of birth (esp when one has left it to live elsewhere) 故国; 祖国.

Old English = ANGLO-SAXON 3.

ˌ**old-'fashioned** *adj* (*often derog* 常作贬义) **1** out of date 过时的; 老式的: *ˌold-fashioned 'clothes, 'styles* 老式的衣物、式样. **2** believing in old ways, ideas, customs, etc 守旧的; 保守的: *My aunt is very old-fashioned.* 我的姑姑非常守旧. ○ *She gave me an ˌold-fashioned 'look*, ie one expressing disapproval. 她用古板的眼光看着我(表示不以为然). — *n* (*US*) type of cocktail made with whisky 以威士忌调成的鸡尾酒.

old fogey (*US* **old fogy**) /ˌəʊld ˈfəʊɡɪ; ˌold ˋfoɡɪ/ person (esp a man) with old-fashioned ideas which he is unwilling to change 老顽固, 守旧的人(尤指男子).

old 'folks' home (*infml* 口) type of hospital in which old people live and are cared for 养老院: *His mother is in an old folks' home.* 他母亲住在养老院里.

old girl ⇨ OLD BOY.

Old 'Glory (*US*) the American flag 美国国旗.

the old 'guard original or conservative members of a group (集团的)元老派, 保守派.

Old 'Harry (also **Old 'Nick, Old 'Scratch**) (*dated infml joc* 旧, 口, 谑) the devil 撒旦; 魔王.

old 'lady (*infml* 口) one's mother or wife 母亲; 妻子.

old 'lag (*infml* 口) person who has been in prison many times 多次入狱的人.

old 'maid (*infml derog* 口, 贬) unmarried woman who is thought to be too old for marriage 老小姐; 老处女. **old-'maidish** *adj* (*derog* 贬) fussy; prim 大惊小怪的; 矜持的.

old 'man (*infml* 口) one's father or husband or employer, etc 父亲; 丈夫; 老板: *How's your old man* (eg your husband) *these days?* 你丈夫近来好吗?

old man's 'beard type of wild flowering plant with grey fluffy hairs around the seeds 铁线莲.

old 'master (picture painted by an) important painter of the past (esp the 13th-17th centuries in Europe) 大画家, 大画家的画(尤指13-17世纪欧洲的).

old 'school school one attended as a boy or girl (中小学的)母校. **old school 'tie** (*esp Brit*) **1** tie worn by former pupils of a particular school (某中学的)校友领带. **2** (*fig* 比喻) symbol of excessive or sentimental loyalty to traditional values, ideas, etc (对传统价值观、思想等极度忠诚的)守旧标志.

old 'stager (*infml* 口) person with long experience in a particular activity 有经验的人; 老手.

old 'sweat (*Brit infml* 口) person (esp a soldier) with many years' experience 经验丰富的人; (尤指)老兵.

the Old 'Testament first of the two main divisions of the Bible, telling the history of the Jews and their beliefs (《圣经》中的)《旧约全书》.

'old-time *adj* belonging to or typical of former times 从前的; 古老的: *old-time dancing* 古老的舞蹈. **old-'timer** *n* person who has lived in a place or been associated with a club, job, etc for a long time 老居民; 老前辈; 老手.

old 'woman (*infml* 口) **1** one's wife or mother 妻子或母亲. **2** (*derog* 贬) fussy or timid man 大惊小怪的或胆怯的男子. **old-'womanish** *adj* (*derog* 贬) (esp of a man) fussy or timid (尤指男子)大惊小怪的; 胆怯的, 婆婆妈妈的.

'old-world *adj* belonging to past times; not modern 古时的; 旧式的: *a cottage with old-world charm* 古色古香的村舍.

the Old 'World Europe, Asia and Africa 旧世界(欧洲、亚洲和非洲). Cf 参看 THE NEW WORLD (NEW).

NOTE ON USAGE 用法: Compare **old, aged, elderly, ancient** and **antique.** 试比较**old**、**aged**、**elderly**、**ancient**、**antique**. ☆ **Old** has the widest use and can be applied to people, animals and things. ☆ **old** 使用最广, 可用于人、动物和事物. It usually indicates that somebody or something has lived or existed for a long time 这个词通常指生活或存在已久的人或事物: *an old woman, dog, church* 老的妇人、狗、教堂. It may describe a person who has been known for a long time but is not necessarily old in years 也可用以指早已认识的人, 但不一定年老: *She's an old friend of ours.* 她是我们的老朋友. **Old** can also mean 'former' or 'previous' ☆ **old** 还可表示'先前的'或'早先的': *I was much happier in my old job.* 我做我原先的那份工作要带劲得多. **Aged** is more formal than **old** and is used of very old people who have possibly become physically weak. ☆ **aged** 比 **old** 文些, 用以指年老的人, 可能身体亦衰弱. If one wishes to be polite and respectful, one can describe old people as **elderly.** 若想客气些、尊敬些, 可用 **elderly** 来形容老人. **Ancient** and **antique** are usually only applied to things. ☆ **ancient** 和 **antique** 通常仅用于事物. We call **ancient** something that existed a long time ago ☆ **ancient** 用以形容经历了久远年代的事物: *an ancient civilization* 古老的文明 ○ *ancient history, customs, etc* 古代的历史、习俗等. **Antique** describes an object which has survived from the past and is therefore valuable today ☆ **antique** 用以形容古代留传下来的器物, 因而如今十分宝贵: *antique furniture, silver, etc* 古董家具、银币等.

olden /ˈəʊldən; ˋoldn̩/ *adj* [attrib 作定语] (*arch* 古) of a past age 往昔的; 古时的: *in olden times/days* 曩时[日].

old·ster /ˈəʊldstə(r); ˋoldstɚ/ *n* (*infml joc* 口, 谑) old person 老人.

olea·gin·ous /ˌəʊlɪˈædʒɪnəs; ˌolɪˋædʒənəs/ *adj* (*fml* 文) like oil or producing oil; oily; fatty 似油的; 产油的; 油质的; 肥的: *oleaginous seeds* 多油的种子.

olean·der /ˌəʊlɪˈændə(r); ˌolɪˋændɚ/ *n* [C, U] evergreen Mediterranean shrub with red, white or pink flowers and tough leaves 夹竹桃.

O level /ˈəʊ levl; ˋo ˌlɛvl/ (*infml* 口) = ORDINARY LEVEL (ORDINARY). Cf 参看 A LEVEL.

ol·fact·ory /ɒlˈfæktərɪ; ɑlˋfæktərɪ/ *adj* (*fml* 文) of or concerned with the sense of smell 嗅觉的: *the olfactory nerves/organs* 嗅觉神经[器官].

ol·ig·archy /ˈɒlɪɡɑːkɪ; ˋɑlɪˌɡɑrkɪ/ *n* (*politics* 政) **1 (a)** [U] form of government in which a small group of people hold all the power 寡头政治; 寡头统治. **(b)** [C] these people as a group 寡头统治集团. **2** [C] country governed by an oligarchy 寡头统治的国家.

▷ **ol·ig·arch** /ˈɒlɪɡɑːk; ˋɑlɪˌɡɑrk/ *n* member of an

oligarchy(1) 寡头政治家; 寡头统治集团成员.

ol·ive /ˈɒlɪv; ˋɑlɪv/ *n* **1** (**a**) [C] small bitter oval fruit, green when unripe and black when ripe, used for food and for oil 橄榄: *stuffed olives* 有填充料的橄榄 ○ *put olives in a salad* 在色拉中加入橄榄. (**b**) (also ˈ**olive-tree**) [C] evergreen tree on which this fruit grows 橄榄树: *a grove of olives* 橄榄树园. **2** (also **olive-green**) [U] yellowish-green colour of an unripe olive 橄榄色.

▷ **ol·ive** *adj* **1** yellowish-green 橄榄色的: *olive paint* 橄榄色颜料. **2** (of the complexion) yellowish-brown (指面色)黄褐色的: *an olive skin* 黄褐色的皮肤.

□ ˈ**olive-branch** *n* **1** emblem of peace 橄榄枝(和平的象征). **2** (*fig* 比喻) thing said or done to show that one wishes to make peace with sb 与某人和解的言行: *After years of quarrelling we at last sent our cousins a Christmas card as an olive-branch.* 我们与堂兄弟多年不和, 最后我们送给他们一张圣诞卡, 算是化干戈为玉帛.

ˌ**olive ˈoil** oil extracted from olives 橄榄油.

Olym·piad /əˈlɪmpɪæd; əˋlɪmpɪˌæd/ *n* **1** celebration of the modern Olympic Games (现代的)奥林匹克运动会: *The 21st Olympiad took place in Montreal.* 第21届奥林匹克运动会是在蒙特利尔举行的. **2** period of four years between celebrations of the Olympic Games 两届奥林匹克运动会之间的四年期间.

Olym·pian /əˈlɪmpɪən; əˋlɪmpɪən/ *adj* (*fml* 文) (of manners, etc) majestic; superior; god-like (指举止等)威严的, 高傲的, 似神的: *Even when those around her panic she always maintains an Olympian calm.* 即使周围的人都惊惶不已, 她也总是保持着超然的镇静.

Olym·pic /əˈlɪmpɪk; əˋlɪmpɪk/ *adj* [attrib 作定语] of or connected with the Olympic Games 奥林匹克运动会的: *an Olympic athlete* 奥林匹克运动员 ○ *She has broken the Olympic 5 000 metres record.* 她打破了奥林匹克运动会5 000米长跑纪录.

□ **the Olympic ˈGames** **1** the sports contests held at Olympia in Greece in ancient times (在古希腊奥林匹亚举行的)奥林匹克运动会. **2** (also **the Olympics**) the international athletic competitions held in modern times every four years in a different country (现代)奥林匹克运动会, 奥运会.

OM /ˌəʊ ˈem; ˌo ˋɛm/ *abbr* 缩写 = (*Brit*) (member of the) Order of Merit 功绩勋章(获得者): *be awarded the OM* 被授予功绩勋章 ○ *John Field OM* 功绩勋章获得者约翰·菲尔德.

om·buds·man /ˈɒmbʊdzmən, *also* -mæn; ˋɑmbudzmən, -ˌmæn/ *n* (*pl* **ombudsmen** /-mən; -mən/) official appointed by a government to investigate and report on complaints made by citizens against public authorities 巡视官(调查公民对政府提出陈诉的特派员).

omega /ˈəʊmɪgə; *US* əʊˈmegə; oˋmɛgə/ *n* **1** the last letter of the Greek alphabet (Ω, ω) 希腊字母表的最后一个字母(Ω, ω). **2** (idm 习语) **Alpha and Omega** ⇨ ALPHA.

om·elette (also **om·elet**) /ˈɒmlɪt; ˋɑmlɪt/ *n* **1** eggs beaten together and fried, often with cheese, herbs, vegetables, etc or with a sweet filling 煎蛋(常加入干酪、作料、蔬菜等); 煎蛋卷(有甜馅): *a cheese and mushroom omelette* 干酪蘑菇煎蛋卷. **2** (idm 习语) **(one can't) make an omelette without breaking eggs** (*saying* 谚) (one can't) achieve a desired aim without some loss or damage 不打破鸡蛋就做不成煎蛋卷; 不破不立.

omen /ˈəʊmen; ˋomɪn/ *n* [C, U] **~ (of sth)** (event regarded as a) sign that sth good or bad will happen in the future 预兆; 征兆: *a good/bad omen* 好[坏]兆头 ○ *an omen of victory* 胜利的预兆 ○ *a bird of ill omen* 不祥的鸟.

om·in·ous /ˈɒmɪnəs; ˋɑmənəs/ *adj* suggesting that sth bad is about to happen; threatening 不祥的; 不吉的; 险恶的: *an ominous silence* 不祥的静寂 ○ *Those black clouds are/look a bit ominous.* 乌云压顶, 来势不妙.

omis·sion /əˈmɪʃn; əˋmɪʃən/ *n* **1** [U] action of omitting or leaving out sb/sth 忽略; 疏忽; 省略; 删除; 遗漏; 排除: *The play was shortened by the omission of two scenes.* 该剧经删去两场而缩短了. ○ *His omission from the team is rather surprising.* 队里没有他, 令人惊奇. ○ (*fml* 文) *sins of omission*, ie not doing things that should be done 疏忽罪. **2** [C] thing that is omitted 省略、删除、遗漏或排除之事物: *This list of names has a few omissions.* 这名单有若干缺漏.

omit /əˈmɪt; əˋmɪt/ *v* (**-tt-**) **1** [Tt, Tg] fail or neglect to do sth; leave sth not done 未做某事物; 忘记做某事物; 不做某事物; 忽略; 疏忽: *omit to do/doing a piece of work* 未做一件工作. **2** [Tn] not include (sth); leave out 未包括, 不包括(某事物); 省略; 删除; 遗漏; 排除: *This chapter may be omitted.* 这一章可以删除.

omni- *comb form* 构词成分 all or everywhere 全; 总; 遍及: *omnipotence* ○ *omniscience* ○ *omnivorous*.

om·ni·bus /ˈɒmnɪbəs; ˋɑmnəbəs/ *n* (*pl* **~es**) **1** (*dated fml* 旧, 文) (esp in names) bus (尤用于名称中)公共汽车. **2** large book containing a number of books or stories, eg by the same author 汇编; 选集: *an omnibus volume/edition* 选本[选集] ○ *a George Orwell omnibus* 乔治·奥威尔选集. **3** (idm 习语) **the man on the Clapham omnibus** ⇨ MAN.

om·ni·po·tent /ɒmˈnɪpətənt; ɑmˋnɪpətənt/ *adj* (*fml* 文) having unlimited or very great power 有无限权力的; 全能的: *the omnipotent officials, bureaucrats, state police, etc* 有极大权力的官员、官僚、州警察等. ▷ **om·ni·po·tence** /-təns; -təns/ *n* [U]: *the omnipotence of God* 上帝的全能.

om·ni·pres·ent /ˌɒmnɪˈpreznt; ˌɑmnɪˋprɛznt/ *adj* (*fml* 文) present everywhere 无处不在的; 普遍存在的: *the omnipresent squalor, dread* 普遍存在的污秽、恐惧.

om·ni·sci·ent /ɒmˈnɪsɪənt; ɑmˋnɪʃənt/ *adj* (*fml* 文) knowing everything 无所不知的; 全知的: *Christians believe that God is omniscient.* 基督教徒相信上帝是无所不知的. ▷ **om·ni·sci·ence** /-sɪəns; -ʃəns/ *n* [U].

om·ni·vor·ous /ɒmˈnɪvərəs; ɑmˋnɪvərəs/ *adj* (*fml* 文) **1** (of animals) eating both plants and animal flesh (指动物)杂食的: *the omnivorous domestic pig* 杂食的驯养猪. **2** (*fig* 比喻) reading all types of books, etc; watching all types of TV programmes, etc 各种书、电视节目等都看的: *an omnivorous reader* 读书无类的人.

on[1] /ɒn; ɑn/ *adv part* (For special uses with many *vs*, eg *hang on, go on, take sth on*, see the *v* entries. 可与许多动词连用, 如hang on、go on、take sth on, 其释义见各动词词条.) **1** (indicating continued activity, progress or state 表示继续的活动、进展或状态): *She talked on for two hours without stopping.* 她不停地讲了两个钟头. ○ *He can work on without a break.* 他能不停地工作. ○ *If you like a good story, read on.* 好的小说要是喜欢就一直看下去. ○ *They wanted the band to play on.* 他们要乐队接着演奏下去. ○ *The war still went on*, ie didn't end. 战争仍在进行. ○ *He slept on through all the noise.* 他在一片嘈杂声中仍睡他的觉. **2** (indicating movement forward or progress in space or time 表示在空间或时间中的移动前进或进展): *run, walk, hurry, etc on to the bus-stop* 跑、走、赶着去公共汽车站 ○ *Please send my letter on to my new address.* 请把我的信送往新址. ○ *from that day on*, ie from then until now 从那天起 ○ *On with the show* (ie Let it begin/continue)! 节目开始[继续进行]吧! **3** (**a**) (of clothes) in position on sb's body; being worn (指衣物)穿上, 戴上, 穿着, 戴着: *Put your coat on.* 穿上你的大衣. ○ *Why hasn't she got her glasses on?* 她怎么没戴眼镜呢? ○ *Your hat's not on straight.* 你的帽子没戴正. (**b**) in the correct position above or forming part of sth 在某物上; 构成某物的一部分: *Make sure the lid is on.* 盖子要盖上. ○ *Leave it with the cover on.* 就让它带着套子吧. ○ *The skirt is finished — I'm now going to sew a pocket on.* 裙子做好了——我现在再缝上个口袋. Cf 参看 OFF[2] 2. **4** (**a**) (esp of electrical apparatus, etc or power supplies) in action or use; being operated (尤指电器等或电源)在接通或使用中: *The lights were all on.* 灯都开着. ○ *The TV is always on in their house.* 他们家电视老开着. ○ *Someone has left the tap on*, ie The water is running. 有人忘了关水龙头了. ○ *I can smell gas — is the oven on?* 我闻到煤气味了——烤箱开着呢吧? ○ *leave the handbrake on* 手闸要拉上. (**b**) available or connected 可用的; 接通的: *We were without electricity for three hours but it's on again now.* 我们的电停了三小时, 现在又有了. ○ *Is the water on?* 自来水接通了吗? Cf 参看 OFF[2] 5. **5** (of a performance, play, etc) in progress (指演出、戏剧等)在进行中: *The film was already on when we arrived.* 我们到时, 电影已经开演了. ○ *The strike has been on now for six weeks.* 罢工至今已进行六个星期了. **6** planned to take place in the future 按计划将发生: *Is the match on at 2 pm or 3 pm?* 比赛是下午2时还是3时开始? ○ *The postal strike is still on*, ie has not been cancelled. 邮政工人罢工仍要举行. Cf 参看 OFF^2 4. **7** (of programmes, films, entertainments, etc) that can be seen; showing; being performed (指节目、电影、娱乐等)在上演, 在放映, 在演出: *Look in the TV guide to see what's on.* 看看电视节目表上有什么节目? ○ *What's on at the cinema tonight?* 今晚电影院演什么? ○ *There's a good play on at the local theatre.* 本地剧院正在上演一出好剧. ○ *What time is the news on?* 新闻节目什么时候开始? **8** arranged to take place; happening 安排; 事情; 活动: *Have we got anything* (ie any engagements, plans, etc) *on for this evening?* 今天晚上我们有什么安排吗? **9** (**a**) (of a performer) on the stage; performing (指演员)在台上, 在演出: *I'm on in five minutes.* 我五分钟后就要上场. ○ *What time is the group on?* 这一组什么时候演出? Cf 参看 OFF^2 8. (**b**) (of a worker) on duty; working (指工作人员)在班上, 值班, 工作: *The night nurse is/goes on at 7pm.* 晚班护士7点钟上班. Cf 参看 OFF^2 6. **10** in or into a vehicle; inside 进入车辆里; 在里面: *The coach-driver waited until everybody was on.* 大轿车司机等着大家都上了车. ○ *Four people got on.* 四个人上了车. **11** with the specified part in front or at the point of contact 以某部分在前面或在接触点上: *enter the harbour broadside on* 船侧向前进港 ○ *crash head on with a car* 迎头与汽车相撞 ○ *place it end on with the others* 将末端与其他的相连接. **12** (idm 习语) **be 'on** (*infml* 口) be practical, right or acceptable 行得通的; 对头的; 认可的: *That just isn't on.* 那样不行. ○ *You're on/not on!* ie I accept/don't accept the proposition, bet, etc. 我接受[不接受]! (指你的建议、赌注等). **be on (for sth)** (*infml* 口) take part (in sth) 参加(某事): *Are you on for this game?* 这场有你参加吗? **be/go/keep on about sth** (*infml derog* 口, 贬) talk in a boring, tedious or complaining way about sth 唠叨; 抱怨: *What's he on about now?* 他在絮叨什么? **be/go/keep on at sb (to do sth)** (*infml derog* 口, 贬) nag or pester sb (to do sth) 责怪或纠缠某人(做某事): *He was on at me again to lend him money.* 他又来缠着我借钱了. Cf 参看 BE ONTO SB (ONTO). **later on** ⇨ LATE. **on and off** ⇨ OFF^2. **ˌon and 'on** without stopping; continuously 不停地; 不断地: *He kept moaning on and on.* 他呻吟不已.

□ **on to** *prep* = ONTO.

on^2 /ɒn; ɑn/ *prep* (For special uses in many idioms, eg *have pity on sb*, and phrasal verbs, eg *pin sth on sb*, see the *n* and *v* entries. 在许多习语如 have pity on sb 中, 及短语动词如 pin sth on sb 中, 有特定用法, 其释义见各名词及动词词条.) **1** (also **upon**) (**a**) (in or into a position) covering, touching or forming part of (a surface) (在某位置中或进入某位置中)覆盖, 接触(某表面)或形成其一部分: *a picture on the wall* 墙上的画 ○ *a drawing on the blackboard* 黑板上画的图 ○ *dirty marks on the ceiling* 天花板上的污斑 ○ *Leave the glasses on the table.* 杯子就在桌上放着吧. ○ *sit on the grass* 坐在草地上 ○ *leaves floating on the water* 浮在水面上的叶子 ○ *the diagram on Page 5* 第5页上的图表 (Cf 参看 *in the next chapter, paragraph*) ○ *stick a stamp on an envelope* 往信封上贴邮票 ○ *a carpet on the floor* 地板上的地毯 ○ *hit sb on the head* 击某人的头部 ○ *travel on the continent* 在大陆上旅行 (Cf 参看 *a country in Europe*). (**b**) supported by or attached to (sb/sth) 由(某人[某事物])支撑; 依附于(某人[某物]): *a roof on a house* 房顶 ○ *stand on one foot* 单脚站立 ○ *a spot on one's chin* 下巴上的斑点 ○ *a blister on one's foot* 脚上的泡 ○ *a ring on one's finger* 手指上的戒指 ○ *lean on me/my arm* 靠着我[我的胳膊] ○ *a flag on a pole* 旗杆上的旗 ○ *a coat on a hook* 衣钩上的大衣 ○ *hanging on a string* 在绳子上挂着 ○ *a hat on one's head* 头上的帽子 ○ *sit on a chair* 坐在椅子上 ○ (*fig* 比喻) *have sth on one's mind* 有心事. **2** in or into (a large public vehicle) 在(大型交通工具)中或进入其中: *on the plane from London to New York* 在从伦敦飞往纽约的飞机上 ○ *have lunch on the train* 在火车上用午餐 ○ *travel on the bus, the tube, the coach, etc* 乘坐公共汽车、地铁、长途汽车等 (Cf 参看 *travel by bus, etc; sitting in the bus, etc*). **3** (used esp with *pers prons* 尤与人称代词连用) being carried by (sb); in the possession of 身上带着; 有: *Have you got any money on you?* 你带着钱呢吗? ○ *The burglar was caught with the stolen goods still on him.* 窃贼被捕时人赃并获. **4** (**a**) (indicating a time when sth happens; in US English often with *on* omitted 表示事情发生的时间; 在美式英语中on常予省略): *on Sunday(s)* 在星期日 ○ *on May the first* 在五月一日 ○ *on the evening of May the first* 在五月一日晚上 (Cf 参看 *in the evening*) ○ *on this occasion* 在这一次 ○ *on a sunny day in August* 在八月中一个晴朗的日子 ○ *on your birthday, New Year's day, Christmas day, etc* 在你的生日、新年、圣诞节等. Cf 参看 IN^2 3, AT 2. ⇨Usage at TIME^1 用法见 TIME^1. (**b**) (also **upon**) at or immediately after the time or occasion of 就在某时或某场合(之后): *On my arrival home/On arriving home I discovered the burglary.* 我一到家就发现家中被盗. ○ *On (my) asking for information I was told I must wait.* 我一打听, 说我得等着. ○ *on the death of his parents* 在他父母去世时 ○ *on the unexpected news of his accident* 在获悉他发生事故这一意外的消息后. **5** about; concerning 关于; 论及: *speak, write, lecture, etc on Shakespeare* 有关莎士比亚的演讲、写作、讲授等 ○ *a lesson on philosophy* 一堂哲学课 ○ *an essay on political economy* 政治经济学方面的文章 ○ *a programme on twentieth-century musicians* 二十世纪音乐家的节目. ⇨ Usage at ABOUT^3 用法见 ABOUT^3. **6** (indicating membership of a group or an organization 表示为某集团或某组织的成员): *on the committee, staff, jury, panel* 在委员会、全体职员、陪审团、评判小组中 ○ *Which/Whose side are you on?* ie Which of two or more opposing views do you support? 你站在哪[谁]一边(支持哪种意见)? **7** regularly consuming (sth) 按时消耗或用掉(某物): *Most cars run on petrol.* 多数汽车用汽油驱动. ○ *The doctor put me on these tablets.* 医生让我服用这些药片. ○ *live on bread and water* 靠面包和水生活 ○ *on* (ie addicted to) *heroin* 有海洛因瘾. **8** (indicating direction) towards (指示方向)朝, 向: *marching on the capital* 向首都进发 ○ *turn one's back on sb* 把背朝向某人 ○ *pull/draw a knife on sb*, ie to attack him 拔出[抽出]刀攻击某人 ○ *creep up on sb* 悄悄地向某人爬去 ○ *On the left you can see the palace.* 往左你可以看到那座宫殿. **9** (also **upon**) near; close to (a place or time) 接近, 靠近(某地点或时间): *a town on the coast* 沿海的市镇 ○ *a house on the main road* 公路旁的房子 ○ *a village on the border* 边界附近的村子 ○ *Just on* (ie Almost exactly) *a year ago I moved to London.* 就在一年以前我搬到了伦敦. ○ *boats moored on both sides of the river* 在河的两边停泊着的船 ○ *hedges on either side of the road* 道路两侧的树篱. **10** (also **upon**) (indicating a basis, ground or reason for sth) as a result of; because of (表示为某事物的基础、根据或理由)由于, 因为: *a story based on fact* 以事实为依据的故事 ○ *have sth on good authority* 对某事物有可靠根据 ○ *On your advice I applied for the job.* 我听从你的建议申请了这份工作. ○ *arrested on a charge of theft* 因盗窃被捕 ○ *You have it on my word*, ie I promise you it will happen, etc. 相信我的话, 那事肯定会发生. **11** supported financially by (sb/sth) 财务上依靠(某人[某事物]): *live on a pension, one's savings, a student grant, etc* 靠养老金、积蓄、助学金等生活 ○ *be on a low wage* 依靠很低的工资 ○ *feed a family on £20 a week* 靠每周20英镑养家 ○ *an operation on the National Health Service* 靠国民保健署资助进行的手术 ○ (*infml* 口) *Drinks are on me*, ie I will pay for them. 饮料钱归我付. **12** by means of (sth); using 借助于, 靠, 用(某事物): *play a tune on the recorder* 用竖笛吹奏一曲 ○ *broadcast on the TV/radio* 在电视台上[电台上]播放 ○ *speak on the telephone* 在电话中说. **13** (also **upon**) (indicating an increase, esp of cost) 表示加上(尤指费用): *a tax on tobacco* 烟草税 ○ *charge interest on the loan* 要为借款付息 ○ *a strain on our resources* 我们资源上的负担. **14** (indicating an activity, a purpose or a state 表示活动、目的或状态): *on business/holiday* 办公[度假] ○ *go on an errand* 出差 ○ *on loan for a week* 暂借一星期 ○ *on special offer* 特别优惠. **15** in addition to (sth); following 除(某事物)之外; 接连: *suffer disaster on disaster* 一再遭受灾祸 ○ *receive insult on insult* 屡受侮辱.

once /wʌns; wʌns/ *adv* **1** on one occasion only; (for) one time 仅仅一次; (作为)一次: *I've only been there once.* 我只去过那里一次. ○ *He cleans the car once a week, a fortnight, etc*, ie every week, every fortnight, etc. 他一星期、半月等擦一次车. ○ *She goes to see her parents in Wales once every six months.* 她每半年回威尔士看父母一次. **2** (**a**) at some (indefinite) time in the past 一度;

曾经: *I once met your mother.* 我曾经见过你的母亲. ○ *He once lived in Zambia.* 他一度住在赞比亚. (**b**) formerly 从前; 过去; 往日: *This book was once famous, but nobody reads it today.* 这本书从前很出名, 现在没人看了. **3** (in negative sentences or questions 用于否定句或疑问句) ever; at all; even for one time 根本; 即使一次: *He never once/He didn't once offer to help.* 他从未[根本没]主动提出帮忙. ○ *Did she once show any sympathy?* 她表示过同情吗? **4** (idm 习语) **ˌall at ˈonce** suddenly 突然: *All at once the door opened.* 门突然打开了. ○ *All at once she lost her temper.* 她突然大发雷霆. **at ˈonce** (**a**) immediately; without delay 立刻; 马上; 立即: *Come here at once!* 立刻到这里来! ○ *I'm leaving for Rome almost at once.* 我马上就要去罗马. (**b**) at the same time 同时: *Don't all speak at once!* 不要大家一齐说! ○ *I can't do two things at once.* 我无法同时做两件事. ○ *The film is at once humorous and moving.* 这部电影既幽默又动人. **(just) for ˈonce; just this ˈonce** on this occasion only, as an exception 仅此一次; 作为例外: *Just for once he arrived on time.* 只有这次他是按时到了. ○ *Be pleasant to each other — just this once.* 彼此要和睦些 —— 就只为这一次吧. **get/give sb/sth the ˈonce-over** (*infml* 口) get/give sb/sth a quick inspection or examination 粗略检查或察看某人[某事物]: *Before buying the car he gave it the once-over.* 他买那辆车前曾草草看了一下. ○ *She felt his parents were giving her the once-over.* 她感到他父母打量着她. **once ˈagain; once ˈmore** one more time as before 再一次: *I'll tell you how to do it once again.* 我再告诉你一次怎么做. ○ *Amanda is home from college once again.* 阿曼达又从学校回到家中. **ˌonce and for ˈall** now and for the last (and only) time 这一次且为最后一次: *I'm warning you once and for all.* 我给你最后一次警告. ○ *He's travelled a lot but he's now come back to Britain once and for all.* 他游历了许多地方, 现在落叶归根又回到了英国. **ˌonce ˈbitten, ˌtwice ˈshy** (*saying* 谚) after an unpleasant experience one is careful to avoid sth similar 一次被咬, 下次胆小; 一次上当, 下次小心: *She certainly won't marry again — once bitten, twice shy.* 她肯定不再结婚了 —— 所谓一朝被蛇咬, 十年怕井绳. **ˌonce in a blue ˈmoon** (*infml* 口) very rarely or never 极少; 从不: *I see her once in a blue moon.* 我难得看到她. **(every) ˌonce in a ˈwhile** occasionally 偶尔; 间或: *Once in a while we go to a restaurant — but usually we eat at home.* 我们偶尔下馆子 —— 但一般都在家吃. **once ˈmore** (**a**) one more time; again 再一次; 又一次: *Let's sing it once more.* 咱们再唱一次吧. (**b**) = ONCE AGAIN. **ˌonce or ˈtwice** a few times 一两次: *I don't know the place well, I've only been there once or twice.* 我对那地方不大熟悉, 只去过一两次. **ˌonce too ˈoften** once more than is sensible or safe 这一次却未能倖免: *He had driven home drunk once too often — this time he got stopped by the police.* 他多次醉酒开车回家, 上得山多终遇虎 —— 这回让警察截住了. **ˌonce upon a ˈtime** (used as the beginning of a fairy-tale 用于童话开头) at some indefinite time in the past 从前; 古时候: *Once upon a time there was a beautiful princess...* 从前有个美丽的公主.... **you're only young once** ⇨ ONLY[2].

▷ **once** *conj* as soon as; when 一旦; 一...就...: *Once you understand this rule, you'll have no further difficulty.* 一旦明白了这条规则, 就再也没有困难了. ○ *How would we cope once the money had gone?* 钱一用完, 我们怎么办?

the once *n* [sing] (*infml* 口) the one time; on one occasion 这一次; 一次: *She's only done it the once so don't be too angry.* 她只做了这一次, 不要太生气.

on·com·ing /ˈɒnkʌmɪŋ; ˋɑnˌkʌmɪŋ/ *adj* [attrib 作定语] advancing; approaching 即将来临的; 接近的: *oncoming traffic* 迎面驶来的车辆.

▷ **on·com·ing** *n* [U] (*fml* 文) approach 来临; 接近: *the oncoming of winter* 冬天的来临.

one[1] /wʌn; wʌn/ *pron, det* **1** 1; one less than two; a single 1, 一(个); 单个: *I've got two brothers and one sister.* 我有两个弟弟和一个妹妹. ○ *There's only one piece of cake left.* 只剩下一块饼了. ○ *Book One, Chapter One*, ie the first chapter of the first book 第一册, 第一章 ○ *One of my friends lives in Brighton.* 我有个朋友住在布赖顿. ○ *One of the girls brought her sister.* 那些姑娘有一个把妹妹带来了. **2** (**a**) (esp of periods of time) a particular but unspecified (尤指时间的段)某一(但非特指某时间): *one day/morning/afternoon/evening/night last week* 上星期的一天[一个上午/一个下午/一个晚上/一夜] ○ *One day* (ie At an indefinite time in the future) *you'll be glad she left you.* 有朝一日你就庆幸她离开了你. ○ *One morning in June...* 六月的一个早晨.... (**b**) (used for emphasis and always stressed 用以加强语气, 必须重读) a particular (person or thing) 某(人或物): *The ˈone way to succeed is to work hard and live a healthy life.* 成功的唯一途径是勤奋及过健康的生活. ○ *No ˈone of you could lift that piano*, ie Two or more of you would be needed. 你们一个人谁也抬不动那架钢琴. **3** (*usu fml* 通常作文雅语) (used with somebody's name to show that the speaker does not know the person 用于姓名之前表示说话者不知其人) a certain(5) 某; 某个; 某位: *One Tim Smith* (Cf 参看 *A Mr Smith*) *called to see you but you were out.* 有个叫蒂姆·史密斯的来过电话找你, 你不在. ○ *The author of the anonymous article turned out to be one Stanley Carter.* 那篇匿名文章的作者原来是个叫作斯坦利·卡特的人. **4** (used with *the other, another* or *other(s)* to show a contrast 与the other、another或other(s)连用表示对比、对照或区别): *The two girls are so alike that strangers find it difficult to tell (the) one from the other.* 那两个女孩儿像极了, 外人难以分清她们谁是谁. ○ *I see you add the egg before the milk. That's ˈone way of doing it*, ie suggesting there are other and possibly better ways. 我看见你先加鸡蛋后放牛奶. 这是一种做法(言外之意, 可能有别的、更好的做法). ○ *I'm sorry I can't help you. For one thing* (ie As a first reason) *I'm in a hurry, and for another I have a bad back.* 对不起, 我帮不了忙. 一来我有急事, 二来我后背有毛病. **5** the same 同一: *They all went off in one direction.* 他们都往同一方向走了. ○ *After the union meeting the workers were all of one mind*, ie all had the same opinion. 工会开过会后, 工人们都心齐了(获得共识). **6** (*infml* 口 *esp US*) (used instead of *a* or *an* to emphasize the *n* or phrase that follows it 代替a或an以强调其后的名词或词组): *That's one handsome guy.* 那是个漂亮的小伙子. ○ *It was one hell of a match*, ie a very good and exciting match. 那场比赛精彩极了. **7** (idm 习语) **be all one to sb** ⇨ ALL[3]. **be at ˈone (with sb/sth)** be in agreement (with sb/sth) (与某人[某事物])相同, 一致: *I'm at one with you/We are at one on this subject*, ie Our opinions are the same. 在这个问题上我和你[我们]意见一致. **get one over sb/sth** (*infml* 口) gain an advantage over sb/sth 胜于或优于某人[某事物]: *They got one over us in the end by deciding to speak in German.* 他们决定说德语, 终于略胜我们一筹. **get sth in ˈone** (*infml* 口) immediately be able to give an explanation, solve a problem, etc 马上能作出解释、解决问题等: *'We have to attract younger customers.' 'Exactly, you've got it in one!'* '我们得设法吸引年轻顾客.' '太对了, 你真是一语中的!' **I, you, etc/sb for ˈone** certainly I, you, etc/sb 我[你/某人]就是: *I for one have no doubt that he's lying.* 起码我就深信不疑他撒谎. ○ *Lots of people would like to come — your mother for one.* 很多人都愿意来 —— 你母亲就是其中之一. **(ˌall) in ˈone** combined 合在一起: *He's President, Treasurer and Secretary in one.* 他身兼会长、司库和秘书三职. ○ [attrib 作定语] *the ˌall-in-one first-ˈaid kit for everyday use* 日用综合急救包. **ˌone after aˈnother/the ˈother** first one person or thing, and then another, and then another up to any number or amount 一个接一个; 相继; 陆续. **ˌone and ˈall** (*dated infml* 旧, 口) everyone 人人; 每人; 大家: *A Happy New Year to one and all!* 祝大家新年快乐! **ˌone and ˈonly** (used for emphasis 用以加强语气) only; sole 唯一的; 仅有的: *You have always been my one and only true love.* 你一向是我唯一的真正的爱人. ○ *Here he is — the one and only Frank Sinatra!* 这就是他 —— 独一无二的弗兰克·西纳特拉! **ˌone and the ˈsame** (used for emphasis 用以加强语气) the same 同一个; 完全一样; 完全一回事: *One and the same idea occurred to each of them.* 他们都产生同样的想法. **ˈone by ˈone** individually in order 一个一个地; 逐一: *go through the items on a list one by one* 逐个处理单子上的项目. **ˌone or ˈtwo** a few 几个; 一两个: *One or two people can't come.* 有一两个人不能来. **one ˈup (on/over sb)** having an advantage over sb; one step ahead of sb 略胜某人一筹; 领先某人一步: *Your experience as a sales assistant puts you one up on the*

other candidates. 你当过推销员，这一经历就比其他申请人强.
For the uses of *one* see the examples at *five*. 关于one的用法见five词条中的示例.

▷ **one** *n* **1** the number 1 ☆ 1; 一. **2** (idm 习语) **number one** ⇨ NUMBER.

one- (in compounds 用以构成复合词) having one of the thing specified 有一…的: *a one-act play* 独幕剧 ○ *a one-piece swimsuit* 一件式泳装 ○ *a one-parent family* 单亲家庭.

□ ˌ**one-armed** ˈ**bandit** = FRUIT MACHINE (FRUIT).

ˌ**one-**ˈ**horse** *adj* [attrib 作定语] **1** using a single horse 用一匹马的: *a* ˌ*one-horse* ˈ*cart* 一匹马拉的车. **2** (*fig joc* 比喻, 谑) badly equipped; small and uninteresting 装备差的; 小而乏味的: *a* ˌ*one-horse* ˈ*town*, ie a quiet town without much business, entertainment, etc 冷清的小镇.

ˌ**one-**ˈ**liner** *n* (*infml* 口) short joke or remark in a play, comedy programme, etc (戏剧、喜剧节目等的)短小的笑话或妙语: *deliver some good one-liners* 讲几句俏皮话.

ˌ**one-man** ˈ**band** musician, usu in the street, playing two or three instruments at the same time 单人乐队(通常在街上一人同时演奏两三种乐器者): (*fig* 比喻) *I run the business as a one-man band — just me and no one else.* 我是单干户——只有我一人, 没有别人.

ˌ**one-man** ˈ**show** **1** public performance by one person of dramatic or musical items normally requiring more performers 单人演出(通常应有合演者的戏剧或音乐节目). **2** person doing by himself things that are usually done by several people 做通常需几人做的事情的人.

ˌ**one-night** ˈ**stand** **1** single performance in one place of a play, concert, etc as part of a tour of different places (戏剧、音乐会等巡回表演时)在某地的一次演出. **2** (*infml* 口) (person involved in a) (usu) sexual relationship that lasts for a very short time, usu a single night (通常指)短暂的性关系(通常指一夜); 有这种行为的人: *I was hoping for a lasting affair, not just a one-night stand.* 我希望的是长久恩爱, 而不是一夜露水之欢.

ˌ**one-**ˈ**off** *n*, *adj* (thing) made or happening only once 一次性的; 一次性的事物: *Her novel was just a one-off — she never wrote anything as good as that again.* 她的小说是她绝无仅有的作品——后来她再也没写出那样好的东西.

ˌ**one** ˈ**p** (also **1p**) (*Brit*) (coin worth) one new penny (新币)一便士, 一便士硬币: [attrib 作定语] *Two one p stamps, please.* 劳驾, 买两张一便士的邮票.

ˌ**one-**ˈ**sided** *adj* **1** (esp of ideas, opinions, etc) unfair; prejudiced (尤指思想、意见等)不公正的, 偏颇的: *a* ˌ*one-sided* ˈ*argument* 片面的论点 ○ *His attitude towards the unemployed is very one-sided.* 他对于失业者的态度很不公正. **2** (esp in sport, etc) with opposing players of unequal abilities (尤指体育运动等)彼此实力悬殊的: *It was a very one-sided game: our team won easily.* 那场比赛双方水平悬殊: 我队轻易获胜. ˌ**one-**ˈ**sidedly** *adv*. ˌ**one-**ˈ**sidedness** *n* [U].

ˈ**one-time** *adj* [attrib 作定语] former 过去的; 从前的: *a* ˌ*one-time poli*ˈ*tician* 昔日的政治家.

ˌ**one-to-**ˈ**one** *adj*, *adv* with one member of one group corresponding to one of another 一对一(的); 一比一(的): *a* ˌ*one-to-one* ˈ*ratio between teachers and pupils* 师生比例一比一 ○ *teaching one-to-one* 一对一地教授.

ˌ**one-track** ˈ**mind** mind that can think only of a single subject, interest, etc 只能想着一件事的头脑: *He's got a one-track mind — all he ever thinks about is sex!* 他只有一个心思——想的都是性事!

ˌ**one-**ˈ**upmanship** *n* (*infml* 口) [U] art of getting (and keeping) the advantage over other people 能超越别人的本事.

ˌ**one-**ˈ**way** *adv*, *adj* [attrib 作定语] (allowing movement) in one direction only 单行(的); 单程(的): *I'll go by boat one way.* 我单程坐船去. ○ ˌ*one-way* ˈ*traffic* 单行车辆 ○ *a* ˌ*one-way* ˈ*street* 单行道 ○ *a* ˌ*one-way* (ie not a return) ˈ*ticket* 单程票.

one[2] /wʌn; wʌn/ *indef pron* **1** (used as the object of a *v* or *prep* to avoid *a* and the repetition of a *n* 用作动词或介词的宾语以免重复a与名词): *I forgot to bring a pen. Can you lend me one?* 我忘带钢笔了. 你借我一枝行吗? (Cf 参看 *I can't find the pen I was given. Have you seen it?*) ○ *I haven't got any stamps. Could you give me one?* 我没有邮票. 你能给我一枚吗? ○ *There have been a lot of accidents in the fog. I read about one this morning.* 这大雾天已发生了很多事故. 今天上午我就看到其中一宗的报道. **2 ~ of** (used with a *pl n* preceded by a *det*, eg *the*, *my*, *your*, *these*, etc to indicate a member of a class or group 与带有限定词如the、my、your、these等的复数名词连用, 指一类或一组中的一个): *Mr Smith is not one of my customers.* 史密斯先生不是我的主顾. ○ *She's knitting a jumper for one of her grandchildren.* 她正在给一个孙儿织套头毛衣. ○ *He's staying with one of his friends.* 他现住在一个朋友家里. (Cf 参看 *a friend of his*) ○ *We think of you as one* (ie a member) *of the family.* 我们把你当成家里人.

▷ **one** *n* (never taking main stress 不重读) **1** (used after *this*, *that*, *which* or as a 'prop-word' after an *adj* which cannot stand alone 用于this、that、which之后, 或用于不能独立使用的形容词之后作'代词'): *I prefer* ˈ*that one.* 我喜欢那个. ○ *Which ones have you read?* 你读过的是哪些? ○ *Your plan is a* ˈ*good one.* 你的计划很好. ○ *I need a* ˈ*bigger one.* 我需要一个大的. ○ *Those shoes are too small. We must buy some* ˈ*new ones.* 那些鞋太小了, 我们得买几双新的. ○ *The chance was too good a one to* ˈ*miss.* 那机会真好, 不容错过. ○ *Her new car goes faster than her* ˈ*old one.* 她的新汽车比旧的那辆跑得快. **2** (used with a group of words that identify the person(s) or thing(s) being considered 与修饰所指的人或事物的词组连用): *Our hotel is the one nearest the beach.* 我们的旅馆是离海滩最近的一家. ○ *The boy who threw the stone is the one with curly hair.* 扔石头的那个男孩子是鬈发的. ○ *Students who do well in examinations are the ones who ask questions in class.* 考试成绩好的都是上课爱提问的学生. **3** (idm 习语) **a one** (*infml* 口 *esp Brit*) (used to show amused surprise at sb's behaviour 用以表示对某人行为感到有趣得出奇): *You asked your teacher how old she was? You are a one!* 是你问老师她有多少岁的吗? 可真有你的! ○ *He is a one, your son. Never out of trouble!* 你的儿子真是个活宝. 没有一会儿不惹麻烦的! **the one about sb/sth** the joke about sb/sth 关于某人[某事物]的笑话: *Do you know/Have you heard the one about the bald policeman?* 你知道[听说过]那个秃头警察的笑话吗?

NOTE ON USAGE 用法: In formal speech or writing the use of the nouns **one/ones** in senses 1 and 2 is avoided in the following cases 在正式的演说或文章中作1与2义的名词**one/ones**应避免用于下列情形: **1** After a possessive (eg *your*, *Mary's*), unless it is followed by an adjective 在表示属有关系的词(如your、Mary's)之后, 除非这类词后有形容词: *This is my car and that's my husband's.* 这是我的汽车, 那辆是我丈夫的. ○ (with adjective) *My cheap camera takes better pictures than his expensive one.* (与形容词连用)我的廉价照相机比他昂贵的照相机拍出的照片好. **2** When two adjectives indicate a contrast 在两个形容词表示对比时: *compare British and/with American universities* (*compare British universities with American ones* is less formal) 试比较英国和美国的大学(compare British universities with American ones是较通俗的说法). **3** After *these* and *those* 在these和those之后: *Do you prefer these designs or those* (more formal than *those ones*)? 你喜欢这些图样还是那些图样(比those ones来得文些)? **One/Ones** may be used after *which*, even in formal speech, to distinguish singular from plural 即使在正式的演说中**one/ones**亦可用于which之后以区分单复数: *Here are the designs. Which one(s) do you prefer?* ie You can choose one or several of them. 这就是那些图样. 你喜欢哪一个[些]? (即你可以从中选择一个或几个.)

one[3] /wʌn; wʌn/ *n* (used, esp *pl*, after an *adj*, to refer to a person or people not previously specified 用于形容词之后, 尤其是复数ones, 指前文中未曾限定的人): *It's time the* ˌ*little ones were in* ˈ*bed.* 小家伙们该睡觉了. ○ *pray to the* ˌ*Holy One* (ie God) *for for*ˈ*giveness* 祈求上帝宽恕.

▷ **one** *pron* (*fml* 文) **1** someone 某人: *He worked like one possessed*, ie someone possessed by a spirit. 他干活儿像着了魔似的. ○ *She was never one to gossip*, ie who would gossip. 她可不说人闲话. ○ *He's not one who is easily frightened.* 他不是动不动就害怕的人. ○ *John is* *one who must certainly be invited.* 约翰当然是必须邀请的. **2** (idm 习语) **(be) one for (doing) sth** (be) a person who is good at, spends a lot of time on or enjoys doing sth 善于、爱好或热衷于(做)某事物的人: *She's a great one for (solving) puzzles.* 她是解谜能手.

□ ˌ**one aˈnother** each of two or more reciprocally; each other 互相; 彼此: *We help one another with the extra work in the summer.* 我们互相帮助做夏季的额外工作. ○ *listening to one another's records* 交换听彼此的唱片.

one⁴ /wʌn; wʌn/ *pers pron* (*fml* 文) (used as the subject or object of a *v*, or after a *prep* to refer to people generally, including the speaker or writer 用作动词的主语或宾语, 或用在介词之后泛指人们, 包括说话者或写作者在内): *In these circumstances one prefers to be alone.* 在这种情况下谁都愿意独处. ○ *A little delay will give one time to prepare.* 只要稍稍推迟些就有时间作准备了. ○ *One must be sure of one's facts before making a public accusation.* 要先掌握实据才可公开指责. ○ (*US*) *One does not like to have his word doubted.* 谁都不愿意别人怀疑自己的话.

on·er·ous /ˈɒnərəs; ˋɑnərəs/ *adj* (*fml* 文) needing effort; burdensome 艰巨的; 繁重的: *onerous duties* 繁重的职务 ○ *This is the most onerous task I have ever undertaken.* 这是我承担过的最艰巨的任务.

one·self /wʌnˈself; wʌnˋself/ *reflex, emph pron* 反身、强调代词 (only taking the main stress in sentences when used emphatically 只在加强语气时于句中作重读) **1** (*reflex* 反身) (used when people in general cause and are also affected by an action 用于主体的动作反及自身时): *one's ability to wash and ˈdress oneself* 洗澡和穿衣的能力. **2** (*emph* 强调) (used to emphasize *one* 用以强调 one): *One could easily arrange it all oneˈself.* 谁都能自己安排好. **3** (idm 习语) **(all) by oneˈself** (**a**) alone 单独; 独自. (**b**) without help 靠自己; 无他人帮助.

on·go·ing /ˈɒngəʊɪŋ; ˋɑnˌgoɪŋ/ *adj* [esp attrib 尤作定语] continuing to exist or progress 继续存在的; 进行中的: *an ongoing debate* 持续的辩论 ○ *an ongoing programme of research* 正在进行的研究计划.

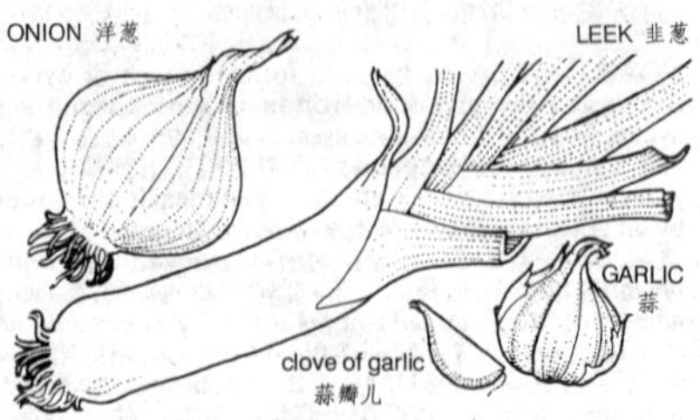

on·ion /ˈʌnɪən; ˋʌnjən/ *n* **1** (**a**) [C] type of vegetable plant with a round bulb that has a strong smell and flavour, used in cooking 洋葱; 葱头: *Spanish onions* 西班牙葱 ○ *a crop of onions* 洋葱的收获 ○ *spring onions* 春葱. (**b**) [C, U] this plant as food 洋葱, 葱头(食物): *chop onions to make a sauce* 剁洋葱作沙司 ○ *too much onion in the salad* 色拉中洋葱太多 ○ [attrib 作定语] *French onion soup* 法式洋葱汤. **2** (idm 习语) **know one's onions/stuff** ⇨ KNOW.

on-line /ˌɒnˈlaɪn; ˌɑnˋlaɪn/ *adj* (*computing* 计) (of a device) connected to and controlled by a computer 联机的; 联线的: *an ˌon-line ˈticket booking system* 联机订票系统 ○ *We've been on-line* (ie have had on-line equipment) *for about a year now.* 我们安装联机设备约有一年了.

on·looker /ˈɒnlʊkə(r); ˋɑnˌlʊkɚ/ *n* person who watches sth happening (without taking part); spectator 旁观者: *By the time the ambulance had arrived, a crowd of onlookers had gathered.* 救护车赶到时, 围观的人已经很多了.

only¹ /ˈəʊnlɪ; ˋonlɪ/ *adj* [attrib 作定语] **1** with no other(s) of the same group, style, etc existing or present; sole 唯一的; 仅有的: *She was the only person able to do it.* 她是唯一能做那事的人. ○ *His only answer was a grunt.* 他只咕哝了一声算是回答了. ○ *This is the only painting in this style that we have.* 这种风格的画我们仅有这一幅. ○ *We were the only people there.* 只有我们在那里. **2** (*infml* 口) most worth considering; best 最值得考虑的; 最好的: *She's the only woman for the job.* 她是最适合做这一工作的人. ○ *She says Italy is the only place to go for a holiday.* 她说意大利是度假的最佳去处. **3** (idm 习语) **one and only** ⇨ ONE¹. **an only ˈchild** child having no brothers or sisters 独生子女: *My mother was an only child.* 我母亲是独生女. ○ *Only children are sometimes spoilt.* 独生子女有时被宠坏了.

only² /ˈəʊnlɪ; ˋonlɪ/ *adv* **1** (modifies a word or phrase and is placed close to it in written or formal spoken style; in informal speech, stress may show which word, etc is modified, so that *only* may have various positions 可修饰一词或词组, 在书面语或正式演说体中 only 的位置应接近所修饰的词语; 在口语中因可用重音表明所修饰的词语, 故 only 的位置不拘) and no one or nothing else; solely 只; 仅; 仅仅: *I only saw ˈMary*, ie I saw Mary and no one else. 我只看见玛丽了(没看见其他人). ○ (*fml* 文) *I saw only Mary.* 我仅见到玛丽. ○ *I only ˈsaw Mary*, ie I saw her but I didn't speak to her. 我只是看见玛丽了(但没有跟她说话). ○ *Only ˈmembers may use the bar.* 只有会员才可使用这酒吧. ○ *Only ˈfive people were hurt in the accident; the rest were uninjured.* 事故中仅五人受伤, 其余皆无恙. ○ *He only lives just round the ˈcorner.* 他就住在附近. ○ *We only waited a few ˈminutes but it seemed like hours.* 我们只等了几分钟, 但觉得像几小时. ○ *Women only*, eg on a sign or poster 女子专用 ○ *We can only guess* (ie We cannot be certain about) *what happened.* 我们只能猜测发生了什么事. **2** (idm 习语) **for X's eyes only** ⇨ EYE¹. **if only** ⇨ IF. **not only ... but also** both ... and 不但 ... 而且 ...: *He not only read the book, but also remembered what he read.* 他不仅读过这本书, 还记得内容. **only have eyes for sb/have eyes only for sb** ⇨ EYE. **only ˈjust** (**a**) not long ago/before 刚刚: *We've only just arrived.* 我们刚到. ○ *I've only just moved to London.* 我刚刚搬到伦敦. (**b**) almost not; scarcely 差一点没; 几乎不: *He only just caught the train.* 他差点没赶上火车. ○ *I've enough milk for the coffee — but only just.* 我的牛奶够喝咖啡用的——刚刚够. **only to do sth** (used to indicate sth that happens immediately afterwards, esp sth that causes surprise, disappointment, relief, etc 用以指随即发生的事, 尤指使人惊讶、失望、放心等的事) 反而; 却: *I arrived at the shop only to find I'd left all my money at home.* 我到商店却发现钱全落在家了. **only too** (with an *adj* or *pp* 与形容词或过去分词连用) very 很; 非常; 十分: *I shall be only too pleased to get home.* 我要回到家里就非常高兴. ○ *That's only too true, I'm afraid*, ie really true, and not untrue as the speaker might have hoped or wanted. 我看这是真事(说话者但愿并非真事). **you're only young ˈonce** (*saying* 谚) let young people have what enjoyment and freedom they can get, because they will have to work and worry later in their lives 青春只一度: *Enjoy the disco — you're only young once.* 尽情跳起迪斯科——须知青春只一度.

only³ /ˈəʊnlɪ; ˋonlɪ/ *conj* (*infml* 口) (**a**) except that; but 只是; 但是; 可是: *I'd love to come, only I have to work.* 我倒是很愿意来, 但是我还得工作呢. ○ *This book's very good, only it's rather expensive.* 这书很好, 只是太贵了点. ○ *He's always making promises, only he never keeps them.* 他总是许愿, 不过从不兑现. (**b**) were it not for the fact that 要不然; 要不是: *He would probably do well in the examination only he gets very nervous.* 他要不是考试很紧张, 成绩可能不错.

ono /ˌəʊ en ˈəʊ; ˌo ɛn ˋo/ *abbr* 缩写 = (*Brit*) (esp in classified advertisements) or near offer (尤指分类广告中)或略低于此价, 可还价: *lady's bike £25 ono*, ie the seller might accept £20 坤车 25 英镑, 可还价.

ono·ma·to·poeia /ˌɒnəˌmætəˈpɪə; ˌɑnəˌmætəˋpiə/ *n* [U] combination of sounds in a word that imitates or suggests what the word refers to eg *hiss, cuckoo, thud* 拟声; 象声词(如 hiss、cuckoo、thud). ▷ **ono·ma·to·poeic** /-ˈpiːɪk; -ˋpiɪk/ *adj*: *'Sizzle' and 'hush' are onomatopoeic words.* sizzle 和 hush 是象声词.

on·rush /ˈɒnrʌʃ; ˋɑnˌrʌʃ/ *n* [sing] (*fml* 文) strong forward rush or flow 猛冲; 急流: *an onrush of water* 水的奔流 ○ *the onrush of powerful feelings* 强烈感情的抒发.

on·set /ˈɒnset; ˋɑnˌsɛt/ *n* [sing] vigorous beginning (esp of sth unpleasant) (爆发性的)开始(尤指不愉快的事): *the onset of winter* 冬天的突然降临 ○ *the onset of glandular fever* 腺热病的发作.

on·shore /ˈɒnʃɔ:(r); ˋɑnˌʃɔr/ *adj* [usu attrib 通常作定语], *adv* **(a)** (of wind) blowing from the sea towards the land (指风)向岸(的), 向陆(的): *an onshore breeze* 向岸微风. **(b)** on or near the shore 在岸上(的); 近岸(的): *an onshore development* 近海的开发.

on·side /ˌɒnˈsaɪd; ˌɑnˋsaɪd/ *adj* [usu pred 通常作表语], *adv* (*sport* 体) (of a player in football, hockey, etc) in a position where the ball may legally be played (ie behind the ball or with the necessary number of opponents between the player and the goal) (指足球、曲棍球等运动中的球员)不越位, 非越位: *He was definitely onside when he scored that goal.* 他射门得分时, 显然并未越位. ○ *The referee declared him onside.* 裁判宣布他没有越位. Cf 参看 OFFSIDE[1].

on·slaught /ˈɒnslɔ:t; ˋɑnˌslɔt/ *n* ~ **(on sb/sth)** fierce attack 猛攻: *They survived an onslaught by tribesmen.* 他们承受住了部落人发起的一次猛攻. ○ (*fig* 比喻) *an onslaught on government housing policies* 对政府住房政策的猛烈抨击.

on-stage /ˌɒnˈsteɪdʒ; ˌɑnˋstedʒ/ *adj, adv* on the stage, visible to the audience 在舞台上(的): *three actors on-stage* 在台上的三个演员 ○ *She walked slowly on-stage.* 她在台上慢慢地走着.

onto (also **on to**) /ˈɒntə; ˋɑntə, *before vowels and finally* 于元音前及末尾处读作 ˈɒntu:; ˋɑntu/ *prep* **1** moving to a position on (a surface) 移到(某物表面)上: *move the books onto the second shelf* 把书挪到第二格 ○ *step out of the train onto the platform* 从火车上下到月台上 ○ *Water was dripping onto the floor.* 水正滴到地板上. ○ *The crowd ran onto the pitch.* 群众都跑到球场上去了. ○ *The child climbed up onto his father's shoulders.* 孩子爬到他爸爸的肩膀上了. Cf 参看 OFF[3] 1. **2** (phr v) **be onto sb (a)** (*infml* 口) pursue sb in order to find out about his illegal activities 追查某人的违法活动: *The police are onto him about the stolen paintings.* 警方正在追查他与被盗画的事. **(b)** be talking to sb in order to inform him of sth or persuade him to do sth 与某人谈话告知某事或劝其做某事物: *Have you been onto the solicitor yet?* 你跟律师谈过了吗? ○ *My mother's been onto me for ages about the mess in my room.* 我母亲早就怪我把自己的房间搞得乌七八糟. Cf 参看 GET ONTO SB (GET). **be onto sth** have some information or evidence that could lead to an important discovery 有潜在重大发现的信息或证据: *When did you realize you were onto something really big?* 你什么时候知道你已掌握了重大线索?

on·to·logy /ɒnˈtɒlədʒɪ; ɑnˋtɑlədʒɪ/ *n* [U] (*philosophy* 哲) branch of metaphysics that deals with the nature of existence 本体论; 实体论. ▷ **on·to·lo·gical** /ˌɒntəˈlɒdʒɪkl; ˌɑntəˋlɑdʒɪkəl/ *adj*: *ontological speculation* 本体论的演绎.

onus /ˈəʊnəs; ˋonəs/ *n* **the onus** [sing] (*fml* 文) duty or responsibility (for doing sth); burden 职责; 责任; 负担: *the onus of bringing up five children* 抚养五个孩子的责任 ○ *The onus of proof rests/lies with you*, ie You must prove what you say. 证明你所言属实的责任在你.

on·ward /ˈɒnwəd; ˋɑnwɚd/ *adj* [attrib 作定语] (*esp fml* 较文) directed or moving forward 向前的; 前进的: *an onward march, movement, etc* 前进、前移 ○ *the onward march of time* 时间的流逝. ▷ **on·ward** (also **on·wards** /ˈɒnwədz; ˋɑnwɚdz/) *adv*: *The shop is open from lunchtime onwards.* 该店午后开始营业. ○ *move steadily onwards* 稳定前移. ⇨Usage at FORWARD[2] 用法见 FORWARD[2].

onyx /ˈɒnɪks; ˋɑnɪks/ *n* [U] stone like marble that has different coloured layers in it, used for ornaments, etc 缟玛瑙: [attrib 作定语] *an onyx paperweight* 缟玛瑙镇纸.

oodles /ˈu:dlz; ˋudl̩z/ *n* [pl] ~ **(of sth)** (*infml* 口) great amounts (of sth); lots (of sth) 大量; 很多: *oodles of hot water* 大量的热水 ○ *oodles of money* 很多钱.

oomph /ʊmf; ʊmf/ *n* (*infml* 口) energy; enthusiasm; sex-appeal 精力; 热情; 性感: *Marilyn Monroe had lots of oomph.* 玛丽莲·梦露十分性感.

ooze /u:z; uz/ *v* **1** [Ipr, Ip] ~ **from/out of sth**; ~ **out/away** (of thick liquids) come or flow out slowly (指浓稠液体)慢慢流出: *All the toothpaste had oozed out.* 牙膏全都慢慢流了出来. ○ *Black oil was oozing out of the engine.* 发动机渗出了黑油. ○ *Blood was still oozing from the wound.* 伤口仍在渗血. ○ (*fig* 比喻) *Their courage was oozing away.* 他们的勇气慢慢消失. **2** [Ipr, Tn] ~ **(with sth)** allow (sth) to come out in this way 使(某物)慢慢流出: *toast oozing with butter* 渗着黄油的烤面包片 ○ *The wound was oozing pus.* 伤口在流脓. ○ (*fig* 比喻) *She was simply oozing (with) charm.* 她浑身散发着魅力. ○ *They oozed confidence*, ie showed it freely. 他们充满了信心. ⇨Usage at DRIP[1] 用法见 DRIP[1].

▷ **ooze** /u:z; uz/ *n* **1** [U] soft liquid mud, esp at the bottom of a river, lake, pond, etc 泥浆, 软泥(尤指河、湖、塘…底的). **2** [sing] (*fml* 文) slow flow 缓慢的流动: *the ooze of pus from a wound* 脓自伤口之渗出.

op /ɒp; ɑp/ *n* (*infml* 口) = OPERATION 3.

op (also **Op**) *abbr* 缩写 = opus: *Beethoven's Piano Sonata No 30 in E major, Op 109* 贝多芬E大调第30号钢琴奏鸣曲, 作品第109号.

opa·city /əʊˈpæsətɪ; oˋpæsətɪ/ (also **opaqueness**) *n* [U] quality of being opaque 不透明性: *the opacity of frosted glass* 磨砂玻璃的不透明性.

opal /ˈəʊpl; ˋopl̩/ *n* bluish-white or milky-white semi-precious stone, often used in jewellery, in which changes of colour are seen 蛋白石: *a bracelet made of opals* 蛋白石手镯 ○ [attrib 作定语] *an opal ring* 蛋白石戒指.

▷ **opal·es·cent** /ˌəʊpəˈlesnt; ˌopl̩ˋɛsn̩t/ *adj* (*fml* 文) changing colour like an opal; iridescent 色彩变幻的; 似彩虹的: *an opalescent silky material* 色彩变幻的丝织物.

opaque /əʊˈpeɪk; oˋpek/ *adj* **1** not allowing light to pass through; not transparent 不透明的; 不透光的: *opaque glass* 不透明的玻璃 ○ *an opaque lens* 不透光的镜片. **2** (of a statement, piece of writing, etc) not clear; difficult to understand (指言语、写作等)不清晰的, 难懂的, 意义不明的: *I felt his report was deliberately opaque.* 我觉得他的报告故意含糊其辞. ▷ **opaquely** *adv*. **opaque·ness** (also **opacity**) *n* [U]: *the opaqueness of her reasoning* 她推理上的含混.

op art /ˈɒp ɑ:t; ˋɑp ɑrt/ (also **optical art**) form of modern abstract art using geometrical patterns that produce optical illusions 光效应艺术(利用几何图形产生视幻觉的抽象艺术).

op cit /ˌɒp ˈsɪt; ˌɑp ˋsɪt/ *abbr* 缩写 = in the work already quoted (Latin *opere citato*) 在前面所引的书中(源自拉丁文 *opere citato*). Cf 参看 LOC CIT.

OPEC /ˈəʊpek; ˋoˌpɛk/ *abbr* 缩写 = Organization of Petroleum Exporting Countries 石油输出国组织.

open[1] /ˈəʊpən; ˋopən/ *adj* **1** allowing things or people to go or be taken in, out or through; not closed 开着的: *leave the door open* 让门开着 ○ *The door burst open and the children rushed in.* 门突然撞开了, 孩子们闯了进来. ○ *sleep in a room with the windows open* 在窗户敞开的屋里睡觉 ○ *with both eyes open* 睁着双眼 ○ *The dog escaped through the open gate.* 那狗穿过敞着的大门逃走了. **2** [usu attrib 通常作定语] not enclosed, fenced in or blocked 敞开的; 未围起的; 未堵塞的; 开阔的; 空旷的: *He prefers open fires to stoves or radiators.* 他喜欢用明火取暖, 不喜欢炉子或暖气. ○ *open country*, ie without forests, buildings, etc 空旷的郊野 ○ *open fields* 田野 ○ *an open stretch of moor* 一片空旷的沼泽 ○ *crack open a nut* 弄开坚果 ○ *break open a safe* 破开保险柜. **3** [usu pred 通常作表语] ready for business; admitting customers or visitors 营业; 办公; (顾客或观众等)可进入: *The banks aren't open yet.* 银行尚未开始营业. ○ *The shop isn't open on Sundays.* 这个商店星期日休息. ○ *Doors open (eg of a theatre) at 7.00 pm.* 下午7时开门(如剧院). ○ *Is the new school open yet?* 那所新校开学了吗? ○ *She declared the festival open.* 她宣布庆祝会开始. ○ *He kept two bank accounts open.* 他有两个银行户头可用. **4 (a)** spread out; unfolded 伸开的; 展开的; 开放的: *The flowers are all open now.* 现在花儿都开了. ○ *The book lay open on the table.* 那本书在桌上摊开放着. **(b)** not fastened; undone 未系住的; 解开的; 松开的: *an open shirt* 没系钮扣的衬衫 ○ *a blouse open at the neck* 敞领口的女衬衫 ○ *His coat was open.* 他的大衣敞开着. **5** [attrib 作定语] not covered in or over 没覆盖的; 没遮掩的; 裸露着的: *an open car*, ie one with no roof or with a roof that is folded back 敞篷汽车 ○ *an open wound*, ie one in which the skin is broken or damaged 开放性创伤

○ *He has open sores all over his arms.* 他的胳膊上长着烂疮. ○ *an open drain/sewer* 排水[污水]明沟. **6 ~ (to sb/sth)** that anyone can enter, visit, etc; public 公开的; 任何人都可以(进入、参观等)的; 公共的: *an open competition, championship, scholarship* 公开的比赛、冠军赛、奖学金 ○ *This garden is open to the public.* 这座花园向公众开放. ○ *She was tried in open court*, ie with the public being freely admitted to hear the trial. 她受法庭公开审讯. **7 (a)** not kept hidden or secret; known to all 不隐秘的; 不保密的; 众所周知的: *an open quarrel, scandal, etc* 公开的争吵、丑闻等 ○ *the lovers' open display of affection* 情人的坦诚示爱. **(b)** willing to talk; honest; frank 愿意谈话的; 诚实的; 坦率的: *an open character* 直爽的性格 ○ *He was quite open about his reasons for leaving.* 他毫不隐瞒自己离去的原因. **8** not finally decided or settled 未做最后决定的; 尚未解决的: *Let's leave the matter open.* 这件事先悬着吧. ○ *Is the job/vacancy/position still open* (ie available, unfilled)? 那工作[空缺/位置]还接受申请吗? **9** [usu attrib 通常作定语] (of cloth, etc) with wide spaces between the threads (指布等)稀疏的, 稀松的: *an open texture/weave* 稀松织法. **10** (idm 习语) **be an open 'secret** be known to many people, though not publicly or officially acknowledged 已是公开的秘密: *Their love affair is an open secret.* 他们的风流韵事是公开的秘密. **be/lay oneself (wide) open to sth** behave so that one is likely to receive (esp) criticism, etc 使自己易受(尤指)批评等: *Don't lay yourself open to attack.* 不要让自己轻易受人攻击. ○ *You're laying yourself wide open to accusations of dishonesty.* 你这样做就是让人指责你不诚实. **be ˌopen to 'offer/'offers** be willing to consider a price to be offered by a buyer 欢迎开价: *We haven't decided on a price but we're open to offers.* 价钱未定, 欢迎顾主开价. **have/keep an open 'mind (about/on sth)** be willing to listen to or accept new ideas, consider other people's suggestions, etc 愿听取、接受或考虑别人的意见、想法等: *I'm not convinced your idea will work, but I'll keep an open mind for the moment.* 我还没想通是否你的意见可行, 不过我先考虑一下. **in the open 'air** not inside a house or building; outside 在户外; 在露天: *picnics in the open air* 露天野餐 ○ *sleeping in the open air* 露宿. **keep one's 'ears/'eyes open** be alert and quick to hear or notice things 留心听[看]; 密切注意. **keep an eye open/out** ⇨ EYE[1]. **keep one's eyes open/peeled/skinned** ⇨ EYE[1]. **keep open 'house** offer hospitality to visitors at all times 好客; 随时接待来宾. **keep/leave one's options open** ⇨ OPTION. **keep a weather eye open** ⇨ WEATHER[1]. **leave the door open** ⇨ LEAVE[1]. **an open 'book** person who is easily understood and very frank 直爽而容易了解的人: *His mind is an open book.* 他胸无城府. **open 'Sesame** (magic words used in one of the Arabian Nights stories to cause a door to open《天方夜谭》故事中用以叫开门的咒语). **an open sesame (to sth)** an easier way of gaining sth that is usu difficult to obtain 可得到(通常指难以得到的)某事物的捷径或窍门: *Being the boss's daughter is not an open sesame to every well-paid job in the firm.* 作为老板的女儿并不是获得本公司任何优薪职位的包票. **open to sb** possible for or available to sb …可供某人取舍; 某人可有…: *It seems to me that there are only two options open to her.* 我觉得她只有两种选择. **open to sth** willing to receive sth 乐于接受某事物: *open to suggestions* 乐于听取建议 ○ *open to conviction*, ie willing to be persuaded about sth 愿听取有说服力的不同意见. **throw sth open (to sb)** make sth available to everybody 使大家可接触或获得某事物: *throw the debate open to the audience* 让听众参予辩论 ○ *throw one's house open to the public* 敞开家门接待公众. **wide open** ⇨ WIDE. **with one's eyes open** ⇨ EYE[1]. **with open 'arms** with great affection or enthusiasm 热烈地; 热情地: *He welcomed us with open arms.* 他热情地欢迎我们.

▷ **the open** *n* [sing] **1** open space or country; the open air 户外; 野外; 露天: *The children love playing out in the open.* 孩子们喜欢在户外玩耍. Cf 参看 IN THE OPEN AIR. **2** (idm 习语) **bring sth/be/come (out) in(to) the 'open** make (esp secret plans, ideas, etc) known publicly; be/become known publicly 公开(尤指秘密计划、想法等); 人人皆知: *Now the scandal is out in the open, the President will have a lot of questions to answer.* 由于丑事已公开, 总统有许多问题要答复.

openly *adv* without secrecy; honestly; publicly 公然地; 坦率地; 公开地: *discuss a subject openly* 坦率讨论某题目 ○ *go somewhere openly*, ie where one might be expected to go secretly 公开到某处.

open·ness *n* [U] honesty; frankness 真诚; 坦率: *They were surprised by her openness when talking about her private life.* 她谈起私生活时非常坦率, 大家都很吃惊.

□ **ˌopen-'air** *adj* [attrib 作定语] (taking place) in the open air; outside 露天的; 户外的: *an ˌopen-air 'swimming-pool* 室外游泳池 ○ *an ˌopen-air 'party* 露天聚会.

ˌopen-and-'shut *adj* completely straightforward and obvious 显然的; 明显的: *As far as I can see the whole matter is open-and-shut.* 我看整件事是一清二楚. ○ *He's obviously guilty — it's an open-and-shut case.* 他显然有罪——此案昭然若揭.

'opencast *adj* [usu attrib 通常作定语] (of mines or mining) at or from a level near the earth's surface (指矿或采矿)露天开采的: *opencast coal-mining* 露天采煤. Cf 参看 DEEP-MINED (DEEP[2]).

ˌopen 'cheque one that may be cashed at the bank on which it is drawn; cheque that is not crossed (CROSS[2] 4) 普通支票; 非划线支票.

'open day day when the public may visit a place normally closed to them 开放日(接待公众参观之日, 平时该处不对外开放): *an open day at the village school* 该乡村学校的开放日.

ˌopen-'ended *adj* without any limits, restrictions or aims set in advance 无限制的; 无预期目标的: *an ˌopen-ended 'contract* 敞口合同 ○ *an ˌopen-ended di'scussion* 自由讨论.

ˌopen-'eyed *adj* **(a)** with open eyes, as in surprise 睁大眼睛的(表示惊讶): *open-eyed in terror* 吓得目瞪口呆. **(b)** watchful; alert 警觉的; 机警的; 警惕的.

ˌopen-'handed *adj* giving freely; generous 慷慨的; 大方的. **ˌopen-'handedly** *adv*. **ˌopen-'handedness** *n* [U].

ˌopen-'hearted *adj* sincere; kind 真诚的; 善良的.

ˌopen-heart 'surgery (*medical* 医) surgical operation on the heart while blood is kept flowing by machine 体外循环心脏手术.

ˌopen 'letter letter, usu of protest or comment, addressed to a person or group, but intended to be made public, esp by being printed in a newspaper 公开信: *The students wrote an open letter to the Minister of Education.* 学生们给教育部长写了一封公开信.

ˌopen-'minded *adj* willing to consider new ideas; unprejudiced 愿接受新思想的; 无偏见的: *He wished his parents were more open-minded on political issues.* 他希望父母在政治问题上开通一些.

ˌopen-'mouthed /-maʊðd; -'maʊðd/ showing great surprise, etc 目瞪口呆的; 吃惊的: *The child stared open-mouthed at the huge cake.* 那孩子惊奇地瞪着大蛋糕.

ˌopen-'plan *adj* (of a building) with few interior walls (指建筑物)开敞布置的: *the lack of privacy in an ˌopen-plan 'office* 在开敞布置的办公室里私人环境之不足.

ˌopen 'prison prison with fewer restrictions than usual on prisoners' movements, etc 开放式监狱(对犯人行动限制较少者).

ˌopen 'question matter on which different views are possible; question that is not yet decided or answered 可自由发表意见的问题; 尚未解决的问题: *How many people will lose their jobs is an open question.* 有多少人将要失业, 这一问题尚无定论.

ˌopen 'sandwich slice of bread with meat, cheese, etc on top 单片三明治(一片面包上有肉、干酪等): *a Danish open sandwich* 丹麦式单片三明治.

the ˌopen 'sea area of sea that is not closed in by land 外海; 公海: *Sail in and out of the bays — not on the open sea.* 在港湾内外航行——不在公海上.

the 'open season period of the year when certain fish and animals may be legally killed or hunted for sport (渔猎)开放季节: *October to February is the open season for pheasants in Britain.* 在英国十月至二月是猎雉的开放季节.

the ˌOpen Uni'versity (*Brit*) university whose students study chiefly from home through correspondence and special TV and radio programmes 开放大学(学生通过

函授和电视及电台节目学习).

ˌ**open** ˈ**verdict** jury's verdict that does not specify what action or crime caused a person's death 存疑裁决(陪审团对死因不详案的裁决).

ˌ**open** ˈ**vowel** (*phonetics* 语音) vowel made with the tongue lowered considerably from the roof of the mouth, eg /ɑː/, /ɒ/ 开元音(发音时舌位较低)如/ɑː/、/ɒ/.

ˈ**open-work** *n* [U] pattern (in metal, lace, etc) with spaces between threads or strips (金属, 饰边等)透雕细工, 网状细工: [attrib 作定语] *open-work lace* 网眼饰边 ○ *open-work wrought iron* 透雕细工锻铁.

open[2] /ˈəʊpən; ˈopən/ *v* **1 (a)** [I, Ip] become open; be opened 开; 打开; 张开: *Does the window open inwards or outwards?* 这窗户是朝里开的还是朝外开的? **(b)** [Tn, Tn·pr] cause (sth) to be open; unfasten 打开(某物); 使松开: *Open your coat.* 你宽宽大衣吧. ○ *open a box, parcel, envelope, etc* 打开箱子、包裹、信封等 ○ *She opened the door for me to come in/to let me in.* 她开门让我进去. ○ *open the window a crack/fraction/bit/little*, ie open it slightly 把窗户稍稍打开. **2** [Tn, Tn·pr] cut or make a passage through or opening in (sth) 穿过(某物)开辟通道; 在(某物)上开孔: *open a mine, well, tunnel, etc* 开矿、打井、凿隧道 ○ *open a new road through a forest* 开辟一条穿过森林的新路. **3** [I, Ipr, Tn, Tn·p] ~ **(sth) (out)** (cause sth to) spread out; unfold (使某物)展开, 铺开, 张开: *The flowers are opening (out).* 花都开了. ○ *open a book, a newspaper, etc* 打开书、报等 ○ *open (out) a map on the table* 在桌上摊开地图 ○ *Open your hand — I know you're hiding something.* 你把手张开——我知道你手里藏着东西呢. **4 (a)** [Tn] start (sth) 开始(某事物): *open an account*, eg at a bank 开户头 ○ *open a meeting, a debate, etc* 开会、开辩论会. **(b)** [I, Tn] (cause sth to) be ready for business, admit users or visitors, etc (使某事物)开张, 营业, 开放: *Another supermarket opened last week.* 上星期又有一家超级市场开张了. ○ *Banks don't open on Sundays.* 银行星期日不办公. ○ *open a business, new shop, hospital, etc* 开公司、新商店、医院等. **(c)** [Tn] ceremonially declare (a building, etc) to be open 在仪式上宣布(某建筑物等)开始使用: *open a garden fête* 在仪式上宣布游园义卖会开始 ○ *The Queen opens Parliament.* 女王宣布议会开会. **5** (idm 习语) **the heavens opened** ⇨ HEAVEN. **open one's/sb's eyes (to sth)** make one/sb realize sth that surprises one/him 使自己[某人]了解到意想不到的事物; 长见识: *Foreign travel opened his eyes to poverty for the first time.* 他一到外国才初次见识到什么是贫穷. **open** ˈ**fire (at/on sb/sth)** start shooting 开火: *He ordered his men to open fire.* 他命令士兵开火. **open the floodgates (of sth)** release a great force of emotion, destruction, rebellion, etc previously held under control 打开闸门(释放出感情、破坏、反叛等的能量). **open one's** ˈ**heart**/ˈ**mind to sb** express or discuss one's feelings or ideas freely 开诚相见; 倾心吐胆. **6** (phr v) **open into/onto sth** give access to sth; lead to sth; allow one to reach sth 通向某处: *This door opens onto the garden.* 这道门通往花园. ○ *The two rooms open into one another.* 这两个房间有门相通. **open out (a)** become wider; become visible 打开; 张开; 展现; 显示: *The road opened out into a dual carriageway.* 这条路已扩展成了复式车行道. ○ *The view opened out in front of us as the fog cleared.* 雾一消散景色就呈现在我们眼前了. **(b)** develop (in personality, etc) (个性等)形成, 发展: *She opened out a lot while she was staying with us.* 她与我们相处期间个性已强多了. **open up** (*infml* 口) talk freely and openly 畅谈: *After a few drinks he began to open up a bit.* 他喝了几杯酒话就多起来了. **open (sth) up**; **(a)** (cause sth to) open (使某物)打开, 张开: *Coughing like that might open up your wound.* 你那样咳嗽会把伤口震开的. **(b)** (cause sth to) be available for development, production, etc (使某物)供开发, 生产: *New mines are opening up.* 新矿正在开发. ○ *open up undeveloped land, new territory, etc* 开发未开发的地区等 ○ *His stories opened up new worlds of the imagination.* 他的小说开拓了想像力新天地. **(c)** (cause sth to) begin business (使某事物)开业, 开张: *open up a new restaurant* 开一家新餐厅 ○ *He never opens up shop on a Sunday.* 星期日他的商店从不营业. **open sth up** unwrap, undo sth; unlock (a room, door, etc) 解开、拆开某物; 打开(房间、门等): *open up a package* 打开包裹 ○ *open up the boot of a car* 开开汽车的行李箱 ○ *open up an unused room* 打开未用过的房间 ○ *'Open up!'* (ie 'Unlock the door!') *shouted the police officer.* '开门!'警察喊道. **open (sth) with sth** start with sth 以某事物开始: *The story opens with a murder.* 这故事以一件谋杀案开始. ○ *He opened the conference with a speech.* 会议首先由他致词.

▷ **opener** /ˈəʊpnə(r); ˈopənɚ/ *n* (usu in compounds 通常用以构成复合词) **1** person or (esp) thing that opens 开启的人或(尤指)工具: *a* ˈ*tin-opener* ○ *a* ˈ*bottle-opener*. **2** (idm 习语) **for** ˈ**openers** (*US infml* 口) for a start; as a beginning 作为开始: *For openers we'll get rid of this old furniture.* 我们首先要把这些旧家具搬走.

open·ing /ˈəʊpnɪŋ; ˈopənɪŋ/ *n* **1** [C] way in or out; open space; gap (进出的)通路; 开口; 孔; 洞: *an opening in a hedge, fence, etc* 树篱、篱笆等上的豁口 ○ *an opening in the clouds* 云中的缝隙. **2** [C esp *sing* 尤作单数] beginning 开始; 开端: *the opening of a book, speech, film, etc* 书、演说、影片等的开头. **3** [sing] process of becoming or making open 开; 张开: *the opening of a flower* 花的开放 ○ *the opening of a new library* 新图书馆的开幕. **4** [C] ceremony to celebrate (a public building, etc) being ready for use 庆祝(公共建筑物等)开始使用的仪式: *Many attended the opening of the new sports centre.* 很多人参加了新体育中心的开始使用典礼. **5** [C] **(a)** position (in a business or firm) which is open or vacant (公司等的)空缺: *an opening in an advertising agency* 广告公司的空缺 ○ *There are few openings in publishing for new graduates.* 出版业中几乎没有给新毕业生的空缺. **(b)** good opportunity to do or talk about sth; favourable conditions 良机; 有利的环境: *excellent openings for trade* 做生意的大好机会 ○ *The last speaker gave me the opening I was waiting for.* 最后的发言者给了我等待已久的讲话机会.

▷ **open·ing** *adj* [attrib 作定语] first 首先的; 第一个的; 开头的: *his opening remarks* 他的开场白 ○ *the opening scene of a film* 电影开始的镜头.

□ ˌ**opening** ˈ**night** night on which a new play/film is performed/shown to the public for the first time and to which critics are invited (戏剧或电影的)首次夜场或晚场(邀请评论界人士参加): *The princess attended the opening night of the opera.* 公主观看了那歌剧首次演出的夜场.

ˈ**opening-time** *n* time at which public houses open and begin to serve drinks (酒店的)开始营业时间.

op·era /ˈɒprə; ˈɑpərə/ *n* **1** [C] play in which words are sung to a musical accompaniment 歌剧(剧本): *an opera by Wagner* 瓦格纳的歌剧 ○ *Verdi's later operas* 威尔地的后期歌剧. **2** [U] dramatic works of this kind as entertainment, an art form, etc (演出的)歌剧作品; 歌剧艺术: *We're very fond of opera.* 我们很喜爱歌剧. ○ *sing in comic opera* 演唱喜歌剧 ○ *grand* (ie serious) *opera* 大歌剧 ○ *light* (ie not serious) *opera* 轻歌剧 ○ *tickets for the opera* 歌剧票 ○ [attrib 作定语] *the opera season* 歌剧演出季节. **3** [C] company performing opera 歌剧团: *The Vienna State Opera* 维也纳国家歌剧院.

▷ **op·er·atic** /ˌɒpəˈrætɪk; ˌɑpəˈrætɪk/ *adj* of or for an opera 歌剧的; 适于歌剧的: *operatic music, singers, scores, arias* 歌剧音乐、演员、总谱、咏叹调. **op·er·at·ic·ally** /-klɪ; -klɪ/ *adv*.

□ ˈ**opera-glasses** *n* [pl] small binoculars for use in the theatre (观剧用的)小型双筒望远镜.

ˈ**opera-house** *n* theatre for performances of operas 歌剧院.

op·er·ate /ˈɒpəreɪt; ˈɑpəˌret/ *v* **1 (a)** [I] (*fml* 文) work; be in action 工作; 运转: *This machine operates night and day.* 这台机器日夜运转. ○ *The lift was not operating properly.* 电梯有些失灵了. **(b)** [Tn] cause (a machine, etc) to work; control 开动(机器等); 操纵; 操作: *operate machinery* 操纵机器 ○ *He operates the lift.* 他是开电梯的. ○ *The kettle is operated by electricity.* 这水壶是电热的. **2** [I, Ipr, It] have or produce an effect; be in action 有效; 起作用; 发生影响: *The system operates in five countries.* 有五个国家实施这种体制. ○ *The new law operates to our advantage.* 新法规对我们有利. ○ *Several causes operated to bring about the war.* 那场战争的起因有几个. **3** [Ipr, Tn] ~ **(from sth)** do business; manage or direct (sth) 经营; 管理或掌管(某事物): *The company* *operates from offices in London.* 那公司由设在伦敦的办事处管理. ○ *They operate three factories and a huge warehouse.* 他们管着三家工厂和一个大仓库. **4** [I, Ipr] **~ (on sb) (for sth)** perform a surgical operation 动手术: *The doctors decided to operate (on her) immediately.* 医生决定马上(给她)动手术. **5** [I, Ipr] (of soldiers, the police, etc) carry out raids, patrols, etc (指士兵、警方等)出击、巡逻等: *bombers operating from bases in the North* 从北方各空军基地起飞的轰炸机 ○ *Police speed traps are operating on this motorway.* 这条高速公路上有超速监测器.

▷ **op·er·able** /ˈɒpərəbl; ˈɑpərəbl/ *adj* that can be treated by means of an operation 可动手术的: *operable diseases of the chest* 可用手术治疗的胸部疾病 ○ *The tumour is operable.* 这肿瘤可动手术割除.

□ ˈ**operating system** controlling computer program that organizes the running of a number of other programs at the same time 操作系统.

ˈ**operating-table** *n* table on which surgical operations are performed 手术台: *The patient died on the operating table.* 病人死在手术台上了.

ˈ**operating-theatre** *n* (also ˈ**theatre**, *esp US* ˈ**operating room**) room in a hospital used for surgical operations 手术室.

op·era·tion /ˌɒpəˈreɪʃn; ˌɑpəˈreʃən/ *n* **1** [U] way in which sth works; working 运转; 操作; 工作: *I can use a word processor but I don't understand its operation.* 我能使用文字处理机, 但不了解其运转机制. **2** [C] activity, often involving several people and/or spread over a period of time 行动: *mount a rescue operation* 发起营救行动 ○ *at each stage of the massive police operation* 在警方大规模行动的每一阶段上 ○ *The entire operation will take about five days.* 整个行动约需时五日. **3** (also **op**) [C] **~ (on sb) (for sth); ~ (to do sth)** (*medical* 医) action performed by a surgeon on any part of the body, to treat or remove by cutting a diseased or an injured part 手术: *undergo an operation for appendicitis* 接受阑尾切除手术 ○ *perform an operation to amputate his leg* 把他的一条腿截除 ○ *a liver transplant operation* 肝脏移植手术. **4** [C] business company 公司: *a huge multinational electronics operation* 一家大规模的跨国电子公司. **5** (**a**) [C usu *pl* 通常作复数] (also **ops**) movement of ships, troops, aircraft, etc in war or during training (作战或训练中的)军事行动, 作战行动: *the officer in charge of operations* 军事行动指挥官. (**b**) **Operation** [sing] (used as part of a code name for military campaigns 用作军事行动代号的一部分): *Operation Overlord* 领主行动. (**c**) [C usu *pl* 通常作复数] planned campaign in industry, business, etc (工商业等的)有计划的业务活动: *involved in building, banking, business operations* 经营建筑业、银行业、商业 ○ *operations research*, ie study of business operations to improve efficiency in industry 运筹学. **6** [C] (*mathematics* 数) addition, multiplication, subtraction, division, etc 运算. **7** (idm 习语) **be in operation; bring sth/come into operation** (cause sth to) be/become effective (使某事物)生效, 起作用: *When does the plan come into operation?* 这项计划什么时候实施? ○ *Is this rule in operation yet?* 这条规则生效了吗?

▷ **op·era·tional** /-ʃənl; -ʃənl/ *adj* (*fml* 文) **1** of, for or used in operations 操作的; 行动的; 手术的; 公司的; 军事行动的; 交易上的; 运算上的: *early operational problems* 行动初期的问题 ○ *operational costs/expenditure*, ie money needed for operating (machines, etc) 操作成本[费用]. **2** ready for use; ready to act 即可使用的; 即可行动的: *The telephone is fully operational again.* 电话又完全可以使用了. ○ *The squadron is not yet operational.* 飞行中队尚未能马上行动.

□ **opeˈrations room** room from which military operations are controlled 作战指挥室.

op·er·at·ive /ˈɒpərətɪv; *US* -reɪt-; ˈɑpəˌretɪv/ *adj* (*fml* 文) **1** [usu pred 通常作表语] operating; effective; in use 操作; 有效; 使用中: *This law becomes operative on 12 May.* 此法令自5月12日起生效. ○ *The station will be operative again in January.* 该车站将于一月份恢复使用. ○ *The oil rig is now fully operative.* 石油钻塔现全面开工. **2** (idm 习语) **the operative word** the most significant word (in a phrase, etc that has just been used) (刚用过的)最重要的词, 最关键的词: *The boss is hopping mad about it — and 'mad' is the operative word.* 老板对此事暴跳如雷——'暴跳如雷'这个成语在句中最重要.

▷ **op·er·at·ive** *n* (*fml* 文) **1** worker, esp a manual one 工作者; (尤指)体力劳动者, 工人: *factory operatives* 工厂工人. **2** secret agent; spy 特务; 间谍: *undercover operatives* 密探.

op·er·ator /ˈɒpəreɪtə(r); ˈɑpəˌretɚ/ *n* **1** person who operates equipment, a machine, etc (设备、机器等的)操作者: *a lift operator* 电梯操作员 ○ *a computer operator* 计算机操作员. **2** person who operates a telephone switchboard at the exchange 电话接线员: *Dial 100 for the operator.* 拨100找接线员. **3** person who operates or owns a business or an industry (esp a private one) 经营者(尤指私人工商业的): *a private operator in civil aviation* 私营民航企业家 ○ *Our holiday was cancelled when the travel operator went bankrupt.* 旅行社破产了, 我们度假的事取消了. **4** (*infml esp derog* 口, 尤作贬义) person acting in the specified (esp cunning) way 有某种(尤指狡滑的)行为的人: *He's a smooth/slick/shrewd/clever operator.* 他是个圆滑的[狡滑的/精明的/聪明的]人.

op·er·etta /ˌɒpəˈretə; ˌɑpəˈrɛtə/ *n* short light musical comedy 轻歌剧.

oph·thal·mic /ɒfˈθælmɪk; ɑfˈθælmɪk/ *adj* (*medical* 医) of or for the eye (为)眼睛的: *ophthalmic surgery* 眼外科.

□ **ophˌthalmic opˈtician** = OPTICIAN 2.

oph·thal·mo·logy /ˌɒfθælˈmɒlədʒɪ; ˌɑfθælˈmɑlədʒɪ/ *n* [U] (*medical* 医) scientific study of the eye and its diseases 眼科学.

▷ **oph·thal·mo·lo·gist** /-lədʒɪst; -lədʒɪst/ *n* person specializing in ophthalmology 眼科学家; 眼科医生: *the ophthalmologist at our local eye clinic* 我们地方眼科诊所的眼科医生.

oph·thal·mo·scope /ɒfˈθælməskəʊp; ɑfˈθælməˌskop/ *n* (*medical* 医) instrument for examining the eye closely, having a mirror with a hole in the centre 检眼镜; 眼底镜.

opi·ate /ˈəʊpɪət; ˈopɪˌet/ *n* (*fml* 文) drug containing opium, used to relieve pain or to help sb sleep 鸦片制剂; 麻醉剂: *become addicted to opiates* 对鸦片制剂上瘾 ○ (*fig derog* 比喻, 贬) *the opiate of all-day television* 终日对电视的沉迷.

opin·ion /əˈpɪnjən; əˈpɪnjən/ *n* **1** [C] **~ (of/about sb/sth)** belief or judgement (about sb/sth) not necessarily based on fact or knowledge 意见; 看法; 主张: *political opinions* 政见 ○ *What's your opinion of the new President?* 你对新总统有什么看法? ○ *The chairman's opinion should be sought.* 应该征求主席的意见. ○ *He was asked to give his honest opinion.* 已请他直言不讳发表意见. **2** [U] beliefs or views of a group; what people in general feel 集体的意见或看法; 舆论: *Opinion is shifting in favour of the new scheme.* 舆论正逐渐转向支持新计划. ○ *The project seems excellent, but local opinion is against it.* 该项目极佳, 但地方舆论却表示反对. **3** [C] professional estimate or advice 专业性的评估或意见: *get a lawyer's opinion on the question* 请教律师对这问题的意见 ○ *You'd better get a second opinion before you let that man take out all your teeth.* 先别让那个人把你的牙都拔掉, 最好再征求一下别人的意见. **4** (idm 习语) **be of the opinion that...** (*fml* 文) believe or think that... 主张...; 认为...: *I'm of the opinion that he is right.* 我认为他对. **one's considered opinion** ⇨ CONSIDER. **have a good, bad, high, low, etc opinion of sb/sth** think well, badly, etc of sb/sth 对某人[某事物]有好感、恶感、高的或低的评价等: *The boss has a very high opinion of her.* 老板很器重她. ○ *She has a rather poor opinion of your written work.* 她认为你的书面作业不太好. **in my, your, etc opinion** it is my, your, etc view or feeling that 按照我的、你的...看法: *In my opinion and in the opinion of most people, it is a very sound investment.* 照我的和大多数人的看法, 这是很可靠的投资. **a matter of opinion** ⇨ MATTER[1].

▷ **opin·ion·ated** /-eɪtɪd; -etɪd/ (also ˌ**self-oˈpinionated**) *adj* (*derog* 贬) holding very strong views which one is not willing to change 固执己见的; 武断的: *a self-opinionated young fool* 固执而愚蠢的年轻人 ○ *He is the most opinionated man I know.* 他是我所认识的最固执己见的人.

□ **o'pinion poll** = POLL[1] 2.

opium /ˈəʊpɪəm; ˈopɪəm/ *n* [U] drug made from poppy seeds, used to relieve pain or to help sb sleep 鸦片: *opium smuggling* 鸦片走私.

opos·sum /əˈpɒsəm; əˈpɑsəm/ (*US* also **possum** /ˈpɒsəm; ˈpɑsəm/) *n* type of small American or Australian animal that lives in trees and carries its young in a pouch 负鼠(产于美洲或澳洲).

opp *abbr* 缩写 = opposite.

op·pon·ent /əˈpəʊnənt; əˈponənt/ *n* (**a**) **~ (at/in sth)** person who is against another person in a fight, a struggle, a game or an argument 对手; 敌手; (争论的)对方: *our opponents in Saturday's game* 我们星期六的比赛对手 ○ *a political opponent* 政敌 ○ *Her opponent left the tennis court in tears.* 她的对手含泪离开了网球场. (**b**) **~ (of sth)** person who is against sth and tries to change or destroy it 反对者: *a fierce opponent of nuclear arms* 强烈反对核武器的人 ○ *opponents of abortion* 反对堕胎的人.

op·por·tune /ˈɒpətjuːn; *US* -tuːn; ˌɑpɚˈtun/ *adj* (*fml* 文) **1** (of time) suitable or favourable for a purpose (指时间)合适的, 恰好的, 适宜的: *arrive at an opportune moment* 来得正好. **2** (of an action or event) done or coming at the right time (指行动或事情)适时的, 及时的: *an opportune remark, statement, intervention, etc* 合时宜的言词、言语、干预等 ○ *Your arrival was most opportune.* 你来得真是时候. ▷ **op·por·tune·ly** *adv*.

op·por·tun·ism /ˌɒpəˈtjuːnɪzəm; *US* -ˈtuːn-; ˌɑpɚˈtunɪzəm/ *n* [U] (*esp derog* 尤作贬义) looking for and using opportunities to gain an advantage for oneself, without considering if this is fair or right 机会主义: *political opportunism* 政治上的机会主义 ○ *a record of shameless opportunism* 空前无耻的机会主义历史.

▷ **op·por·tun·ist** /-ɪst; -ɪst/ *n* (*esp derog* 尤作贬义) person who acts like this 机会主义者: *There were many opportunists and few men of principle.* 机会主义者多, 坚持原则的人绝无仅有.

op·por·tun·ity /ˌɒpəˈtjuːnətɪ; *US* -ˈtuːn-; ˌɑpɚˈtunətɪ/ *n* [C, U] **1 ~ (for/of doing sth); ~ (to do sth)** favourable time, occasion or set of circumstances 良机; 机会: *have/get/find/create an opportunity* 有[得到/找到/创造]机会 ○ *have few opportunities of meeting interesting people* 难得遇上有趣的人 ○ *have no/little/not much opportunity for hearing good music* 没有[很少有/不大有]机会听到好的音乐 ○ *a great, golden, marvellous, etc opportunity to travel* 旅游的大好、极好、绝妙等时机 ○ *I had no opportunity to discuss it with her.* 我没有机会和她谈这件事. ○ *Don't miss this opportunity: it may never come again.* 良机莫失, 失不再来. ⇨Usage at OCCASION 用法见OCCASION. **2** (idm 习语) **take the opportunity to do sth/of doing sth** recognize and use a good or suitable time to do sth 趁机; 藉此机会: *Let me take this opportunity to say a few words.* 请让我趁此机会讲几句话. ○ *We took the opportunity of visiting the palace.* 我们趁便参观了皇宫.

op·pose /əˈpəʊz; əˈpoz/ *v* **1** [Tn] (**a**) express strong disapproval of or disagreement with (sth/sb), esp with the aim of preventing or changing a course of action 反对(某事[某人]); (尤指)反抗, 抵制: *oppose the building of a motorway* 反对修筑高速公路 ○ *oppose a scheme* 反对某计划 ○ *oppose the Government* 反政府 ○ *He opposed the proposal to build a new hall.* 他反对修建新礼堂的建议. (**b**) (*fml* 文) compete against (sb) 对抗(某人); 与(某人)较量: *Who is opposing you in the match?* 你和谁比赛? **2** [Tn·pr] **~ sth to/against sth** (*fml* 文) present sth as a contrast or opposite to sth else 使某事物与另一事物对照或对抗: *Do not oppose your will against mine.* 不要用你的意愿和我的抗衡.

▷ **op·posed** *adj* **1 ~ to sth** strongly against sth 强烈反对某事物: *She seems very much opposed to your going abroad.* 她好像很反对你出国. **2** (idm 习语) **as opposed to** in contrast to 与…对照; 与…对比: *I am here on business as opposed to a holiday.* 我在这里是办公事而不是度假.

op·pos·ite /ˈɒpəzɪt; ˈɑpəzɪt/ *adj* **1** [usu attrib 通常作定语] **~ (to sb/sth)** having a position on the other side (of sb/sth); facing 另一侧的; 相对着的: *on the opposite page* 对面一页上 ○ *In England you must drive on the opposite side of the road to the rest of Europe.* 在英国路上开车, 要与欧洲其他国家方向相反. ○ *John and Mary sat at opposite ends of the table (to each other).* 约翰和玛丽(面对面地)坐在桌子两端. ○ *This is Number 6, so Number 13 must be on the opposite side of the street.* 这是6号, 那么13号一定在街的对面. **2** (used after the *n* 用于名词之后) facing the speaker or a specified person or thing 面对着的; 对面的: *I asked the man opposite if he would open the door.* 我问对面的人他愿意不愿意开门. ○ *I could see smoke coming out of the windows of the house opposite.* 我看见有烟从对面房子的窗户冒出来. ○ *Can you see where the grammar books are? The dictionaries are on the shelf directly opposite.* 你看见语法书在哪儿呢吗? 词典都在正对着的书架上. **3** [attrib 作定语] entirely different; contrary 完全不同的; 相反的: *travelling in opposite directions* 朝相反的方向行进 ○ *contact with the opposite sex*, ie of men with women or women with men 与异性接触 ○ *The opposite approach is to use a bilingual dictionary.* 另一种方法截然不同就是使用双语词典.

▷ **op·pos·ite** *adv*: *There's a couple with a dog who live opposite.* 对面住着一对夫妇养着一条狗. ○ *The woman sitting opposite is a detective.* 坐在对面的那个女子是侦探.

op·pos·ite *prep* **~ (to) sb/sth 1** on the other side of a specific area from (sb/sth); facing (sb/sth) 在(某人[某物])另侧; 面对(某人[某物]): *I sat opposite to him during the meal.* 吃饭的时候我坐在他的对面. ○ *The bank is opposite the supermarket.* 银行在超级市场对面. ○ *Put the wardrobe in the corner opposite the door.* 把衣柜放在对着门的那个角落里. **2** (of actors) taking a part in a play, film, etc as the partner of (sb) (指演员)与(某人)配戏, 合演: *She had always dreamed of appearing opposite Olivier.* 她一直梦想着能与奥利维尔配戏.

op·pos·ite *n* **~ (of sth)** word or thing that is as different as possible (from sth) 反义词; 对立的事物: *Hot and cold are opposites.* 热和冷是一对反义词. ○ *Light is the opposite of heavy.* 轻是重的反义词. ○ *I thought she would be small and pretty but she's completely the opposite.* 我以为她娇小而漂亮, 结果完全相反.

□ **one's ˌopposite ˈnumber** person with a similar job or position to one's own in another group or organization (在另一部门或组织中工作或职位)与自己相当的人: *talks with her opposite number in the White House* 和与她职位相当的白宫官员的会谈.

op·posi·tion /ˌɒpəˈzɪʃn; ˌɑpəˈzɪʃən/ *n* **1** [U] **~ (to sb/sth)** state or action of opposing (sb/sth); resistance 反对; 敌对; 相反; 相对; 抵抗; 对抗: *violent opposition to the new committee* 对新委员会的强烈反对 ○ *There's not much opposition to the scheme.* 反对该规划的意见不太多. ○ *Her proposal met with strong opposition.* 她的建议遭到强烈反对. ○ *The army came up against fierce opposition in every town.* 军队在各个城镇都遇到顽强抵抗. **2** [Gp] people who oppose (sb); competitors; rivals 反对派; 竞争者; 对手; 敌手: *The opposition have a strong defence.* 对方防卫力量很强. ○ *Before setting up in business, she wanted to get to know the opposition.* 她开业之前想了解一下竞争者的情形. **3 the Opposition** [Gp] (*politics* 政 *esp Brit*) (MPs of the) political party or parties opposing the Government 反对党; 反对党议员: *It is an effective Opposition.* 这是一个能起作用的反对党. ○ *the leader of the Opposition* 反对党领袖 ○ [attrib 作定语] *the Opposition benches*, ie seats where MPs of the Opposition sit in Parliament 反对党议席 ○ [attrib 作定语] *Opposition MPs are few in number.* 反对党议员人数很少. **4** (idm 习语) **in opposition (to sb/sth)** (**a**) opposing 相对; 面对: *We found ourselves in opposition to several colleagues on this issue.* 我们在这一问题上与几个同事意见相左. (**b**) forming the Opposition 形成反对党: *The Conservative party was in opposition for the first time in years.* 多年以来保守党第一次处于反对党的地位.

op·press /əˈpres; əˈprɛs/ *v* [Tn esp passive 尤用于被动语态] **1** rule or treat (sb) with continual injustice or cruelty 压迫, 压制(某人): *The people are oppressed by the military government.* 人民受军政府的压迫. ○ *Women are often oppressed by men.* 女人经常受男人压迫. **2** make (sb) feel worried, uncomfortable or unhappy 使(某人)担心、烦恼或不幸: *oppressed with anxiety, worry, poverty, etc* 因焦虑、忧虑、贫穷等而烦恼 ○ *The heat* *oppressed him and made him ill.* 他热得病了.

▷ **op·pressed** *adj* unjustly or cruelly treated 受压迫的; 受压制的: *an oppressed people, group, class, etc* 被压迫的人民、团体、阶级等. **the op·pressed** *n* [pl *v*] oppressed people 被压迫的人民: *the oppressed of the world* 世界上被压迫的人民.

op·pres·sion /əˈpreʃn; əˈprɛʃən/ *n* [U] oppressing or being oppressed 压迫; 压制: *a tyrant's oppression of his people* 暴君对人民的压迫 ○ *a history of oppression* 一部压迫史 ○ *victims of oppression* 受迫害者.

op·press·ive /əˈpresɪv; əˈprɛsɪv/ *adj* **1** unjust; cruel 不正义的; 暴虐的: *oppressive laws, rules, measures, etc* 不公正的法规、规则、措施等. **2** hard to bear; causing distress 难以忍受的; 令人苦恼的: *oppressive weather* 令人难受的天气 ○ *The heat in the tropics can be oppressive.* 热带气候热得难受. **op·press·ively** *adv*: *oppressively hot* 热得难受.

op·pressor *n* person or group that oppresses; cruel or unjust ruler 压迫人的人或集团; 暴虐的统治者; 暴君: *suffer at the hands of an oppressor* 在暴君的统治下受苦.

op·probri·ous /əˈprəʊbrɪəs; əˋprobrɪəs/ *adj* (*fml* 文) (of words, etc) showing scorn or reproach; abusive (指词语等)表示轻蔑的, 申斥的, 辱骂的: *opprobrious language, remarks, deeds* 辱骂的语言、言语、行为.

▷ **op·probri·ously** *adv* (*fml* 文).

op·pro·brium /-brɪəm; -brɪəm/ *n* [U] (*fml* 文) public disgrace and shame 羞辱; 耻辱; 不名誉: *excite/incur opprobrium* 招致羞辱.

ops /ɒps; ɑps/ *n* [pl] (*infml* 口) = OPERATIONS (OPERATION 5a).

opt /ɒpt; ɑpt/ *v* **1** [Tt] decide to do sth; choose 决定做某事物; 选择: *He opted to go to Paris rather than London* 他决定去巴黎, 不去伦敦. **2** (phr v) **opt for sth** decide on sth; choose sth 决定某事物; 选择某事物: *Fewer students are opting for science courses nowadays.* 现在选修理科的学生少了. ⇨Usage at CHOOSE 用法见 CHOOSE. **opt out (of sth)** choose not to take part (in sth) 决定不参加(某事): *I think I'll opt out of this game.* 我不想参加这场比赛.

op·tic /ˈɒptɪk; ˋɑptɪk/ *adj* [esp attrib 尤作定语] (*fml* 文) of or concerned with the eye or the sense of sight 眼睛的; 视觉的: *the optic nerve*, ie from the eye to the brain 视神经.

▷ **op·tics** *n* [sing *v*] scientific study of sight and of light in relation to it 光学.

op·tical /ˈɒptɪkl; ˋɑptɪkḷ/ *adj* [esp attrib 尤作定语] **1** of the sense of sight 视觉的; 视力的: *optical effects and sound effects* 视觉效果与声音效果. **2** for looking through; to help the eyes 供视力透过的; 有助于眼睛的: *optical instruments*, eg microscopes and telescopes 光学仪器(如显微镜和望远镜). ▷ **op·tic·ally** /-klɪ; -klɪ/ *adv*.

□ ˌ**optical ˈart** = OP ART.

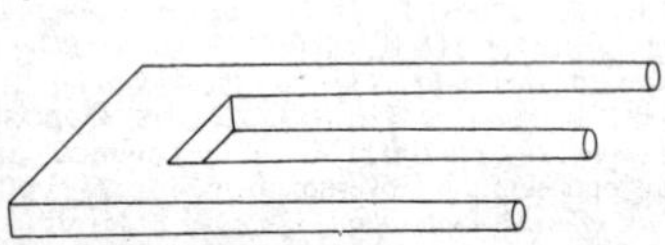

Are there two prongs or three?
是两根还是三根?

optical illusion 视错觉

ˌ**optical ilˈlusion** thing by which the eye is deceived 视错觉; 光错视; 光幻视: *A mirage is an optical illusion.* 海市蜃楼是一种视错觉. ○ *I thought I saw a ghost but it was just an optical illusion.* 我以为我看见鬼了, 其实只是一种幻觉.

op·ti·cian /ɒpˈtɪʃn; ɑpˈtɪʃən/ *n* **1** person who makes and sells optical instruments, esp contact lenses and glasses (兼营制造与销售的)光学仪器商; (尤指)眼镜商. **2** (also **ophˌthalmic opˈtician**) person qualified to examine the eyes and prescribe glasses, etc as well as issue them (兼配制眼镜的)验光师: *The optician said I needed new glasses.* 验光师说我需要配新眼镜. ○ *I've just been to the optician's*, ie the optician's practice. 我刚去眼镜店验过光.

op·tim·ism /ˈɒptɪmɪzəm; ˋɑptəˌmɪzəm/ *n* [U] tendency to expect the best in all things; confidence in success; belief that good will triumph over evil in the end 乐观; 乐观主义: *He was still full of optimism for the future despite his many problems.* 他尽管有许多问题, 但对未来仍十分乐观. ○ *There was a feeling of optimism in the country when the new government was elected.* 经选举产生新政府, 举国上下对前景十分乐观. Cf 参看 PESSIMISM.

▷ **op·tim·ist** /-mɪst; -mɪst/ *n* person who is always hopeful and expects the best in all things 乐观的人; 乐观主义者: *He's such an optimist that he's sure he'll soon find a job.* 他很乐观, 认为自己一定很快就能找到工作. Cf 参看 PESSIMIST (PESSIMISM).

op·tim·istic /ˌɒptɪˈmɪstɪk; ˌɑptəˈmɪstɪk/ *adj* **~ (about sth)** expecting the best; confident 乐观的; 有信心的: *an optimistic view of events* 对事情的乐观看法 ○ *She's not optimistic about the outcome.* 她对结果不很乐观. **op·tim·ist·ic·ally** /-klɪ; -klɪ/ *adv*.

op·timum /ˈɒptɪməm; ˋɑptəməm/ (also **op·timal** /ˈɒptɪməl; ˋɑptəməl/) *adj* [attrib 作定语] (*fml* 文) best or most favourable 最佳的; 最适宜的; 最有利的: *the optimum temperature for the growth of plants* 植物生长的最佳温度 ○ *enjoy optimum economic conditions* 处于最佳经济状况.

op·tion /ˈɒpʃn; ˋɑpʃən/ *n* **1** [U] power or freedom of choosing; choice 选择权; 选择自由; 选择: *have little option*, ie not much choice 没有多少选择的余地 ○ *I haven't much option in the matter*, ie I cannot choose. 在这件事情上我无可选择. ○ *I have little option but to go*, ie I have to go. 我别无选择只好走. ○ *He did it because he had no other option*, ie no other choice. 他这样做是因为他没有其他办法. ○ *He was given one month's imprisonment without the option* (ie alternative) *of a fine.* 他被判监禁一个月, 不得以罚款相抵. **2** [C] thing that is or may be chosen; choice 可供选择的事物; 选择: *Make a list of the various options.* 列出可供选择的项目. ○ *There weren't many options open to him*, ie there was little choice available. 他没有什么选择余地. **3** [C] **~ (on sth)** (*commerce* 商) right to buy or sell sth at a certain price within a certain time (按其价格在规定期限内买或卖某物的)选择权: *an option on a package holiday* 包价旅游选择权 ○ *have an option on a piece of land* 有买卖一地皮的选择权 ○ *We have a 12-day option on the house.* 我们是否购买那所房子有12天的选择权. **4** (idm 习语) **keep/leave one's ˈoptions open** avoid making a decision now, so that one still has a choice later 暂不作决定; 留有选择余地: *Don't take the job now — keep your options open until you leave university.* 先别接受这份工作 —— 暂时保留选择权, 到离开这所大学再说.

▷ **op·tional** /-ʃənl; -ʃənḷ/ *adj* that may be chosen or not, as one wishes; not compulsory 可选择的; 随意的; 非强迫的: *optional subjects at school* 学校的选修课 ○ *Formal dress is optional.* 是否穿礼服自便. ○ *The cassette player is an optional extra in this make of car*, ie It will cost extra if one chooses to have it. 这种型号汽车如需盒式磁带唱机费用另计.

opu·lent /ˈɒpjʊlənt; ˋɑpjələnt/ *adj* (*fml* 文) **1** having or showing signs of great wealth 富裕的; 富有的; 阔气的: *opulent furnishings* 华丽的陈设 ○ *an opulent suburb* 富裕的市郊 ○ *opulent tastes in cars* 对汽车豪华装饰的讲究. **2** abundant 丰富的; 大量的: *opulent vegetation* 茂盛的草木. ▷ **opu·lence** /-ləns; -ləns/ *n* [U]. **opu·lently** *adv*: *opulently furnished rooms* 陈设豪华的房间.

opus /ˈəʊpəs; ˋopəs/ *n* (*pl* **opera** /ˈɒpərə; ˋɑpərə/) **1** musical composition numbered as one of a composer's works (WORK[1] 5b) (usu in order of publication) 编号的音乐作品(通常以出版的先后为序): *Beethoven's opus 112* 贝多芬第112号作品. **2** (*fml* 文) work of art, esp on a large scale 艺术作品; (尤指)巨著, 大作.

or /ɔ:(r); ɔr/ *conj* **1** (introducing an alternative 表示选择关系) (用于陈述句中)或, 或者; (用于疑问句中)还是: *Answer yes or no.* 回答是或者不是. ○ *Is it green or blue?* 是绿的还是蓝的? ○ *Are you coming or not?* 你来不来? ○ *Is the baby a boy or a girl?* 是男孩儿还是女孩儿? Cf 参看 EITHER...OR (EITHER). **2** (introducing all but the first of a series of alternatives 表示除首项事物外的选择关系) (用于陈述句中)或, 或者; (用于疑问句中)还是: *I'd like it to be black, (or) white or grey.* 那个东西我喜欢黑

的、(或)白的或灰的. ○ *Will you have tea, (or) coffee or lemonade?* 你喝茶、(还是)咖啡还是汽水? **3** if not; otherwise 否则; 要不然: *Turn the heat down or your cake will burn.* 把热度调低吧, 要不蛋糕就要煳了. Cf 参看 OR ELSE. **4** (after a negative 用于否定词之后) and neither 也不: *He can't read or write.* 他不会看书也不会写字. ○ *They never dance or sing.* 他们从不跳舞, 也不唱歌. Cf 参看 NEITHER...NOR. **5** (**a**) (introducing a word or phrase that explains, or means the same as, another 表示一词语对另一词语的解释关系或为其同义词语) 即, 亦即: *an increase of 50p, or 10 shillings in old money* 增加50便士, 合旧币10先令 ○ *a kilo, or two pounds* 一公斤, 亦即两磅 ○ *geology, or the science of the earth's crust* 地质学, 即研究地壳的科学. (**b**) (introducing an afterthought 表示事后想到而添加的关系): *He was obviously lying — or was he?* 他显然在撒谎——是不是呢? ○ *I need a new coat — or do I?* 我需要一件新大衣了——需要不需要呢? **6** (idm 习语) **either...or** ⇨ EITHER. **or 'else** (**a**) otherwise; because if not; or(3) 否则; 要不然: *Hurry up or ˌelse you'll be 'late.* 快点吧, 要不就迟到了. ○ *You must go to work or ˌelse you'll lose your 'job.* 你得去上班了, 要不然就要失去这份工作了. (**b**) (*infml* 口) (used as a threat) or something bad will happen (用以表示威胁)否则后果不妙: *Pay up or else!* 快付钱, 要是不付! ○ *You'd better give me that book — or else!* 你最好把那本书给我——不给的话! **or rather** (used when making a statement more accurate or correct 说得更确切些或加以更正): *We stayed at my friend's house, or rather at my friend's parents' house.* 我们住在我朋友家里, 说得确切些是在我朋友的父母家. ○ *He is my cousin — or rather my 'father's cousin.* 他是我表亲——我是说是我父亲的表亲. **or so** (suggesting vagueness or uncertainty about quantity 表示含糊的或不确定的量): *There were 'twenty or so*, ie about twenty. 大约有二十个. ○ *We stayed for an 'hour or so.* 我们停留了一小时左右. **or somebody/something/somewhere; somebody/something/somewhere or other** (*infml* 口) (expressing uncertainty or vagueness about a person, thing or place 表示人、物或地点的不确定的或含糊的情形): *He's a bank manager or something.* 他是银行经理这类的人. ○ *I put it in the cupboard or somewhere.* 我把它放在柜橱之类的地方了. ○ *'Who told you?' 'Oh, somebody or other, I've forgotten who.'* '谁告诉你的?' '啊, 有个人, 我忘了是谁了.' ○ *It's somewhere or other in the kitchen.* 就在厨房的什么地方. **or two** (after a singular *n* 用于单数名词之后) or more; about 或更多; 大约: *After a 'minute or two we saw him.* 一两分钟后我们看见他了. ○ *I haven't seen him for a 'year or two.* 我有一两年没见他了. **whether...or; whether or not** ⇨ WHETHER.

-or *suff* 后缀 (with *vs* forming *ns* 与动词结合构成名词) person or thing that does 施动的人或事物: *actor* ○ *governor* ○ *resistor*. Cf 参看 -EE, -ER.

or·acle /'ɒrəkl; US 'ɔːr-; 'ɔrəkḷ/ *n* **1** (**a**) (in ancient Greece) holy place where the gods could be asked about the future (古希腊的)神示所: *the oracle at Delphi* 在德尔斐的神示所. (**b**) the answer given (which was often ambiguous or obscure) 神谕(常含糊费解). (**c**) priest(ess) giving the answers 传达神谕的(女)祭司: *consult the oracle* 请示神谕. **2** (*fig* 比喻) person considered able to give reliable advice 能提供可靠意见的人: *My sister's the oracle on beauty matters.* 我妹妹是美容方面的大行家.

▷ **orac·ular** /ə'rækjʊlə(r); ə'rækjələr/ *adj* (*fml or joc* 文或谑) of or like an oracle; with hidden meaning (似)神谕的; 有隐意的: *oracular utterances from the headmaster* 校长的金口玉言.

oral /'ɔːrəl; 'ɔrəl/ *adj* **1** not written; spoken 口头的; 口述的: *an oral examination* 口试 ○ *stories passed on by oral tradition*, ie from one generation to the next without being written down 口头流传的故事. **2** of, by or for the mouth 口的; 用口的; 口用的: *oral hygiene* 口腔卫生 ○ *oral contraceptives* 口服避孕药.

▷ **oral** *n* oral examination 口试: *He failed the oral.* 他口试不及格.

or·ally /'ɔːrəlɪ; 'ɔrəlɪ/ *adv* **1** through the spoken word 经口述: *Tribal lore and custom have been passed down orally.* 部落的知识和风俗口耳相传保存下来. **2** of, by or for the mouth 口中; 用口; 适用于口: *orally administered drugs* 口服药 ○ *not to be taken orally*, eg of medicines, not to be swallowed 不可口服.

or·ange /'ɒrɪndʒ; US 'ɔːr-; 'ɔrɪndʒ/ *n* **1** [C] round thick-skinned juicy edible fruit that is a reddish-yellow colour when ripe 柑橘; 橙: *oranges, lemons and other citrus fruits* 橙子、柠檬和其他柑橘属水果 ○ [attrib 作定语] *orange juice* 橙子汁. ⇨illus at FRUIT 见 FRUIT 插图. **2** [C] (usu 通常作 **orange tree**) evergreen tree on which this fruit grows 柑橘树: *an orange grove* 柑橘园. **3** [U] reddish-yellow colour of this fruit 橘红色; 橙黄色: *a pale shade of orange* 淡橘红色. ⇨illus at SPECTRUM 见 SPECTRUM 插图. **4** [U, C] (glass of a) drink made from oranges (一杯)柑橘饮料: *Would you like some orange?* 你要橘子水吗? ○ *A fresh orange, please*, ie real orange juice as opposed to orangeade or orange squash. 请来一杯鲜橙汁. ○ *I'd like a gin and orange please.* 请来一杯橙汁杜松子酒.

▷ **or·ange** *adj* of the colour orange 橘红色的; 橙黄色的: *an orange hat* 橘红色的帽子 ○ *an orange light* 橙黄色的光.

or·ange·ade /ˌɒrɪndʒ'eɪd; US ˌɔːr-; ˌɔrɪndʒ'ed/ *n* [C, U] (glass of a) fizzy orange-flavoured soft drink (一杯)橙子汽水.

□ **'orange-blossom** *n* white sweet-scented flower of the orange tree 橙花: *Orange-blossom is associated with weddings.* 看到橙花可以使人联想到婚礼.

ˌorange 'squash (*Brit*) still, orange-flavoured soft drink made from juice or syrup diluted with water 橙子水.

orang-utan /ɔːˌræŋuː'tæn; US əˌræŋə'tæn; ə'ræŋəˌtæn/ (also **orang-outang** /-uː'tæŋ; -əˌtæŋ/, **orang-outan**) *n* large ape with long arms found in Borneo and Sumatra 猩猩(产于婆罗州和苏门答腊). ⇨illus at APE 见 APE 插图.

ora·tion /ɔː'reɪʃn; ɔ'reʃən/ *n* (*fml* 文) formal speech made on a public occasion, esp as part of a ceremony 演讲, 演说(尤指作为仪式的一部分): *a funeral oration* 悼词.

or·ator /'ɒrətə(r); US 'ɔːr-; 'ɔrətər/ *n* (*fml* 文) (**a**) person who makes formal speeches in public 演说者. (**b**) person who is good at public speaking 演说家: *a fine political orator* 优秀的政治演说家.

▷ **ora·tor·ical** /ˌɒrə'tɒrɪkl; US ˌɔːrə'tɔːr-; ˌɔrə'tɔrɪkḷ/ *adj* (*fml sometimes derog* 文, 有时作贬义) of speech-making or orators 演说的; 演说家的; 高谈阔论的: *oratorical phrases, gestures, etc* 演说家的辞令、姿势等 ○ *an oratorical contest* 演讲比赛.

ora·torio /ˌɒrə'tɔːrɪəʊ; US ˌɔːr-; ˌɔrə'tɔrɪo/ *n* (*pl* **~s**) musical composition for solo voices, chorus and orchestra, usu with a Biblical theme (通常以《圣经》内容为主题的)清唱剧, 神剧: *Handel's oratorios* 韩德尔的清唱剧. Cf 参看 CANTATA.

ora·tory[1] /'ɒrətrɪ; US 'ɔːrətɔːrɪ; 'ɔrəˌtorɪ/ *n* small chapel for private prayer or worship 私人礼拜堂.

ora·tory[2] /'ɒrətrɪ; US 'ɔːrətɔːrɪ; 'ɔrəˌtorɪ/ *n* [U] (art of) public speaking, esp when used skilfully to affect an audience 演讲; (尤指)雄辩的演说, 演讲术, 雄辩术: *His oratory soon had the crowd booing his opponents.* 他能言善辩, 很快就鼓动起人群向他的对手们大喝倒彩. ○ *Some politicians are famous for their powers of oratory.* 有些政治家以辩才著称.

orb /ɔːb; ɔrb/ *n* **1** (*fml or arch* 文或古) globe, esp the sun, the moon or one of the planets 球体; 星球; 天体; (尤指)日, 月, 行星: *an orb of golden light* 发金光的星球. **2** jewelled ball with a cross on top carried by a king or queen as part of ceremonial dress 王权宝球(球顶饰有十字架, 为国王礼服的一部分).

or·bit /'ɔːbɪt; 'ɔrbɪt/ *n* **1** (**a**) path followed by a planet, star, moon, etc round another body (天体运行的)轨道: *the earth's orbit round the sun* 地球绕行太阳的轨道. (**b**) path of a man-made object, eg a satellite or space-craft, round a planet, star, etc (人造物体如卫星、航天器等飞行的)轨道: *The spacecraft is in orbit* (ie moving in orbit) *round the moon.* 该航天器在绕月球轨道上飞行. ○ *How many satellites have been put into orbit round the earth?* 有多少颗人造卫星已送入绕地球轨道? **2** area of power or influence; scope 势力范围: *Marketing does not come within the orbit of his department.* 市场推销业务不归他这一部门管.

▷ **or·bit** *v* [I, Tn] move in orbit round (sth) 在绕(某

物)的轨道上运行; 环绕轨道运行: *orbit in space* 在太空中沿轨道运行 ○ *How many spacecraft have orbited the moon?* 有多少航天器绕月球轨道运行?

or·bital /ˈɔːbɪtl; ˈɔrbɪtl/ *adj* of an orbit (星体的或人造飞行物体的)轨道的; 势力范围的: *a spacecraft's orbital distance from the earth* 航天器的远地轨道距离 ○ *an orbital motorway,* ie round the outside of a city 外环高速公路. — *n* road passing round the outside of a city (城市的)外环路: *Take the London orbital.* 走伦敦外环路.

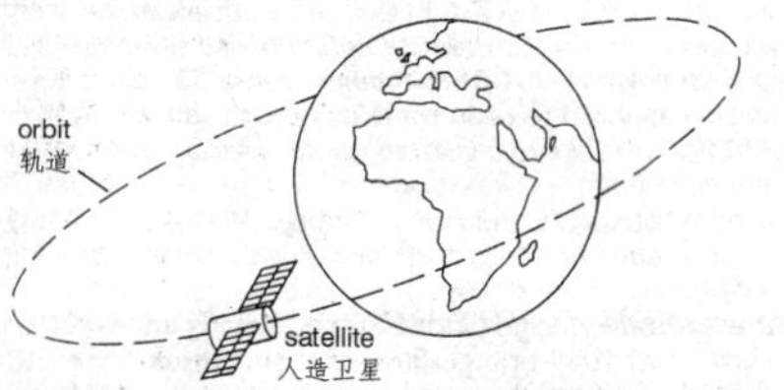

orch *abbr* 缩写 = orchestra(1); orchestrated (by).

orch·ard /ˈɔːtʃəd; ˈɔrtʃɚd/ *n* (usu enclosed) piece of land in which fruit trees are grown (通常指围起来的)果园: *apple orchards* 苹果园.

or·ches·tra /ˈɔːkɪstrə; ˋɔrkɪstrə/ *n* [CGp] (usu large) group of people playing various musical instruments together (通常为大型的)管弦乐队: *a dance, string, symphony orchestra* 舞蹈乐队、弦乐队、交响乐团 ○ *She plays the flute in an orchestra.* 她在管弦乐队中吹奏笛子. ○ *He conducts the London Symphony Orchestra.* 他指挥伦敦交响乐团. Cf 参看 BAND 3.

▷ **or·ches·tral** /ɔːˈkestrəl; ɔrˋkɛstrəl/ *adj* [usu attrib 通常作定语] of, for or by an orchestra 管弦乐队的; 为管弦乐队的; 管弦乐队演奏的: *orchestral instruments, music, performances* 管弦乐队的乐器、音乐、演出 ○ *an orchestral concert* 管弦乐演奏会.

□ **ˈorchestra pit** = PIT[1] 7.

ˈorchestra stalls (*US* **orchestra**) front seats on the floor of a theatre (剧场的)正厅前座.

or·ches·trate /ˈɔːkɪstreɪt; ˋɔrkɪsˌtret/ *v* [Tn] **1** arrange (a piece of music) for an orchestra to play 将(一音乐作品)编成管弦乐曲: *a set of piano pieces orchestrated by the composer* 由作曲家谱写成管弦乐的一套钢琴曲. **2** carefully (and sometimes unfairly) arrange (sth) in order to bring about a desired result 精心安排(某事物)(有时指手段不正当): *The demonstration was carefully orchestrated to attract maximum publicity.* 该示威经过精心策划以尽量吸引公众注意. ▷ **or·ches·tra·tion** /ˌɔːkɪˈstreɪʃn; ˌɔrkɪsˋtreʃən/ *n* [C, U].

orchid /ˈɔːkɪd; ˋɔrkɪd/ (also **orchis** /ˈɔːkɪs; ˋɔrkɪs/) *n* **1** plant, usu with flowers of unusual shapes and brilliant colours, having one petal larger than the other two 兰科植物: *Many kinds of wild orchid are becoming rare.* 很多种野生兰越来越罕见了. **2** one of these flowers (usu expensive to buy) 兰花: *She wore a single orchid on her evening dress.* 她在晚礼服上缀着一朵兰花.

or·dain /ɔːˈdeɪn; ɔrˋden/ *v* **1** [Tn, Cn·n] make (sb) a priest or minister 任命(某人)为司铎、神父或牧师: *He was ordained priest last year.* 去年授予他司铎一职. **2** [Tn, Tf] (*fml* 文) (of God, law, authority, fate, etc) order or command; decide in advance (指上帝、法律、权威、命运等)命令, 规定, 注定: *Fate had ordained that he should die in poverty.* 命中注定他得死于贫困. ⇨ Usage at DECREE 用法见 DECREE.

or·deal /ɔːˈdiːl, ˈɔːdiːl; ɔrˋdil, ˋɔrdil/ *n* difficult or painful experience (esp one that tests a person's character or powers of endurance) 苦难经历; (尤指对品格、耐力的)严峻考验: *the ordeal of divorce* 离婚的痛苦 ○ *The hostages went through a dreadful ordeal.* 个个人质都经历了可怕的折磨.

or·der[1] /ˈɔːdə(r); ˋɔrdɚ/ *n* **1** [U] way in which people or things are placed or arranged in relation to one another 次序; 顺序: *names in alphabetical order* 按字母顺序排列的名字 ○ *events in chronological order,* ie according to times, dates, etc 按时间先后排列的事件 ○ *arranged in order of size, merit, importance, etc,* ie according to size, etc 按大小、功绩、重要性等排列的. **2** condition in which everything is carefully and neatly arranged 整齐; 有条理: *put/leave/set one's affairs, papers, accounts in order* 把个人的事务、文件、帐目整理得井井有条 ○ *Get your ideas into some kind of order before beginning to write.* 把思绪理清再写. Cf 参看 DISORDER. **3** [U] (condition brought about by) obedience to laws, rules, authority 治安; 秩序; 规矩: *Some teachers find it difficult to keep order in their classes/to keep their classes in order.* 有些教师觉得课堂秩序很难维持. ○ *The police must try to restore order.* 警方必须努力恢复治安. Cf 参看 DISORDER. **4** [C] **~ (for sb to do sth); ~ (that...)** command or instruction given by sb in authority 命令; 指挥; 指示: *Soldiers must obey orders.* 军人必须服从命令. ○ *He gave orders for the work to be started/that the work should be started immediately.* 他发出指示要立即开始工作. ○ *My orders prevent me from doing that,* ie I have been instructed not to do it. 我接到指示不可做此事. **5** [C] **~ (for sth)** **(a)** request to make or supply (goods) 定购; 定单; 定货: *fill an order,* ie supply the goods asked for 交付定货 ○ *He gave his order to the waiter.* 他把他点的东西告诉服务员了. ○ *We've received an order for two tons of coal.* 我们已收到两吨煤的定单. **(b)** goods supplied 交付的货: *A delivery van has brought the grocery order.* 送货车已把定购的杂货送来了. ○ *Your order has arrived.* 您的货已到. **6** [C] written instruction that allows the holder to be paid money or to do sth 汇票; 授权凭证: *a ˈbanker's/ˈpostal order,* ie an order to a bank/post office to pay money 银行[邮政]汇票 ○ *obtain a court order to allow a divorced man to visit his children* 获得法院授权书以使某离婚男子可探视子女. **7** [U] system of rules or procedures (at public or committee meetings, or in Parliament, lawcourts, etc) (会议、国会、法庭等的)规则, 规程, 程序, 秩序: *rules of order* 议事规程 ○ *speak to order,* ie according to rules laid down by the meeting 按会议规定的程序发言 ○ *the order of business* 议程 ○ *(on) a point of order,* ie (on) a question of procedure (在)程序问题(上) ○ *I wish to raise a point of order.* 我想提个议程的问题. **8** **(a)** [C] (*fml* 文) (arrangement of) groups, classes, etc in society (in relation to one another) 集团; 阶级; 阶层: *The social order of ants is very interesting.* 蚂蚁的社会结构非常有趣. **(b)** [C esp *pl* 尤作复数] (*derog or joc* 贬或谑) members of such a group, class, etc 集团、阶级、阶层等的成员: *the lower orders* 下层社会. **9** [CGp] (*biology* 生) group of related animals or plants below a class(7) and above a family(4) 目: *the order of primates* 灵长目 ○ *The rose and the bean families belong to the same order.* 蔷薇科和豆科同属一目. Cf 参看 PHYLUM, GENUS 1, SPECIES 1. **10** **(a)** [CGp] group of people appointed to a special class as an honour or reward (荣誉的)勋位: *The Order of the Garter is an ancient order of chivalry.* 嘉德勋位是古老的骑士勋位. **(b)** [C] badge, sign, etc worn by members of such a group 勋章: *wear all one's orders and medals* 佩带全部的勋章和奖章. **11** [CGp] group of people who have been ordained as clergymen (神职的)级别: *the Order of Priests/Deacons/Bishops* 牧师[执事/主教]级别. **12** [CGp] group of people, esp monks, living under religious rules 宗教团体; (尤指)修道会: *the monastic orders* 修士会 ○ *the Order of Dominican Friars* 多明我会. **13** [C] style of ancient Greek or Roman architecture characterized by the type of column used (古希腊或罗马建筑的)柱型, 柱式: *the five classical orders of architecture* 建筑学上的五种古典柱式 ○ *the Doric order* 多利斯柱式. **14** [U] (*fml* 文) kind; sort 种类: *skills of the highest order* 最高技巧. **15** [sing] **~ of sth** exact form of a religious service 宗教礼仪: *the order of service as laid down in the Prayer Book* 祈祷书上规定的礼仪. **16** (idm 习语) **be in/take (holy) ˈorders** be/become a priest 是[成为]司铎. **be under orders (to do sth)** have been instructed or commanded (to do sth) 受命(做某事物): *I'm under strict orders not to let any strangers in.* 我奉命严禁外人入内. **by order of sb/sth** according to directions given by a person in authority 奉某人之命; 按某人的指示: *by order of the Governor* 奉总督之命 ○ *by order of the court* 依据法庭指令. **call sb/sth to order** ⇨ CALL[2]. **get one's/give sb his marching orders** ⇨ MARCH[1]. **in apple-pie order** ⇨ APPLE. **in running/working order** (esp of machines) working well, smoothly, etc (尤指机器)运转良好、正常等: *This lift is hardly ever in working order.* 这个电梯从来就不大好用. ○ *The engine has been tuned and is now in perfect working order.* 发动机已经调好, 现在运转状况极佳. **in 'order** as it should be; able to be used 妥当的; 能用的: *Is your passport in order* (ie still valid)*?* 你的护照仍然有效吗? **in order (to do sth)** (*fml* 文) according to the rules, etc of a meeting, etc 根据会议等的规定等: *It is not in order to interrupt.* 打断别人发言是违反会议规则的. ○ *Is it in order to speak now?* 按规定现在可以发言吗? **in order that** (*fml* 文) with the intention that; so that 目的在于; 为了; 以便: *He left early in order that he should/would/might arrive on time.* 他早早动身好按时到达. **in order to do sth** with the purpose or intention of doing sth 目的在于做某事物: *She arrived early in order to get a good seat.* 她到得很早, 图的是得个好座位. **in/into reverse order** ⇨ REVERSE. **in short order** ⇨ SHORT 1. **law and order** ⇨ LAW. **of/in the order of sth** (*fml* 文) about (the same quality, quantity or number as) 大约(同样的质量、数量或数目): *Her salary is of the order of £150 a week.* 她的薪金约为每周150英镑. **on 'order** requested but not yet received 定购中的; 定制中的: *I've got two books on order at the bookshop.* 我在书店订购了两本书. **the ˌorder of the 'day** programme of business to be discussed in Parliament, or at a formal meeting (议会的或其他正式会议的)议程: (*fig joc* 比喻, 谑) *Good behaviour must be the order of the day when the school inspector comes.* 督学一来, 品行良好问题必在议事之列. **Order! Order!** (used to call attention to the fact that a person is not observing the usual rules or procedures at a debate, meeting, etc 用以提请与会者注意遵守规则的用语). **an ˌorder to 'view** written authority from an estate agent to look over a house, etc with the idea of buying it 看房许可证(房地产经纪人签发给有意买房者的). **ˌout of 'order (a)** (of a machine, etc) not working properly (指机器等)工作不正常, 出故障: *The phone is out of order.* 电话坏了. **(b)** (*fml* 文) not allowed by the rules of a formal meeting, etc 违反会议规则: *His objection was ruled to be out of order.* 他提出的异议被裁定为有违会议规则. **the pecking order** ⇨ PECK. **a point of order** ⇨ POINT[1]. **put/set one's (own) house in order** ⇨ HOUSE. **take orders from sb** do as sb instructs 受命于某人; 按某人之命做: *She said she wouldn't take orders from a junior clerk.* 她说她不能听低级职员的指挥. **a tall order** ⇨ TALL. **(made) to order** (made) according to a customer's special requirements 按顾客要求(做): *This company will tailor a suit to order.* 这家公司可定制套服. **under the orders of sb** commanded or instructed by sb 受某人的指挥; 在某人的指令下: *serve under the orders of a new general* 在新将军麾下. **under starter's orders** ⇨ STARTER.

□ **'order-book** *n* book in which a business records orders from customers 定货簿: *have a full order-book* 记满定货项目的定货簿.

'order-form *n* printed form to be filled in by a customer ordering goods 定货单: *It will speed up delivery if you complete the official order-form.* 填妥定单便于尽早送货.

'order-paper *n* written or printed programme of business for a committee, Parliament, etc on a particular day 议事日程表.

or·der[2] /ˈɔːdə(r); ˋɔrdɚ/ *v* **1** [Tn, Tn·pr, Tf, Dn·t] give an order[1](4) to (sb); command 命令(某人); 吩咐; 指令: *The chairman ordered silence.* 主席要大家安静. ○ *The doctor ordered me to (stay in) bed.* 医生吩咐我卧床. ○ *The boy was ordered out of the room.* 那男孩受指示离开房间. ○ *The judge ordered that the prisoner should be remanded.* 法官命令将犯人还押候审. ○ *We ordered him to leave immediately.* 我们要他立即离开. **2** [Tn, Tn·pr, Dn·n, Dn·pr] **~ sth (for sb)** request sb to supply or make (goods, etc) 定购; 定做; 预定: *I've ordered a new carpet (from the shop).* 我已(向商店)定购了一块新地毯. ○ *We don't have the book in stock but we can order it.* 这书我们没有存货, 但是可以预订. ○ *He ordered himself three shirts.* 他定做了三件衬衫. ○ *She ordered a garden chair for her husband.* 她为丈夫定做了一把庭院用椅. **3** [I, Tn, Tn·pr, Dn·n, Dn·pr] **~ sth (for sb)** request sb to bring (food, drink, etc) in a hotel, restaurant, etc (在旅馆、饭店等)叫(饭菜、饮料等): *We haven't ordered yet.* 我们还没点菜呢. ○ *I've ordered a steak.* 我要了一份牛排. ○ *She ordered lunch for* (ie to be served at) *1.30.* 她定了午餐, 在1时30分开饭. ○ *He ordered himself a pint of beer.* 他要了一品脱啤酒. ○ *I've ordered you egg and chips/egg and chips for you.* 我给你要了鸡蛋和炸土豆条. **4** [Tn] (*fml* 文) put (sth) in order; arrange; direct 整理(某事物); 布置; 指示: *He ordered his life according to strict rules.* 他把生活安排得十分刻板. ○ *I must have time to order my thoughts.* 我得找时间整理一下想法. **5** (phr v) **order sb about/around** keep on telling sb to do things 不断驱使某人做事; 把某人差来遣去: *Even as a boy he was always ordering his friends about.* 他从小就老爱支使朋友. **order sb off** (*sport* 体) order sb to leave a sports field, usu for breaking a rule 罚某人退场; 勒令某人退出比赛: *The referee ordered Johnson off in the second half for kicking another player.* 在下半场约翰逊踢人犯规, 裁判罚他退场. **order sb out** order (police or troops) to parade, esp to control civil unrest, etc 下令出动(军警)(尤指为平息暴乱等): *The government ordered the police out to restore order in the streets.* 政府派警方出动恢复治安.

▷ **or·dered** /ˈɔːdəd; ˋɔrdɚd/ *adj* arranged (esp well-arranged) 有安排的; (尤指)安排好的: *an ordered life* 井井有条的生活 ○ *a badly ordered existence* 杂乱无章的生活.

NOTE ON USAGE 用法: Compare **tell, order, instruct, direct, command.** 试比较 **tell**、**order**、**instruct**、**direct**、**command**这五个词. **Tell** is the most generally used verb. It is not very strong and is the word used in everyday situations ☆ **tell**是用得最广的动词, 语气不太强, 是日常生活用词: *I keep telling him to cut his hair but he takes no notice.* 我再三告诉他理理发去, 可他就是不听. ○ *Do what you're told.* 叫你做什么就做什么. ○ *They've been told to finish the job by tomorrow.* 已吩咐他们明天完工. **Order** is stronger and is used of people in authority who expect to be obeyed ☆ **order**语气较强, 为有权威者用以指令别人服从: *The policeman ordered the motorist to stop.* 警察指示让那开车的人停车. **Instruct** and **direct** suggest the giving of a precise description of necessary action. ☆ **instruct**和**direct**意为对需采取的行动有准确说明. They are used in impersonal and official situations 这两个词均用于客观的及公事的场合: *I have been instructed by the company to offer you a refund.* 公司让我给您退款. ○ *The judge directed the defendant to answer.* 法官责令被告回答. **Command** is mainly used in military situations ☆ **command**主要用于军事场合: *The officer commanded his men to open fire.* 军官命令士兵开火.

or·derly[1] /ˈɔːdəlɪ; ˋɔrdɚlɪ/ *adj* **1** well-arranged; in good order; tidy 安排好的; 有秩序的; 有顺序的; 有条理的; 整齐的: *an orderly room, desk, etc* 整洁的房间、书桌等 ○ (*fig* 比喻) *an orderly mind* 有条理的头脑. **2** well-behaved; peaceful 品行良好的; 守秩序的: *an orderly football crowd* 守秩序的足球观众. ▷ **or·der·li·ness** /ˈɔːdəlɪnɪs; ˋɔrdɚlɪnɪs/ *n* [U].

or·derly[2] /ˈɔːdəlɪ; ˋɔrdɚlɪ/ *n* **1** (also **medical orderly**) attendant in a hospital, usu without special training, who does unskilled jobs (医院的)勤杂工. **2** army officer's attendant 勤务兵.

or·dinal /ˈɔːdɪnl; *US* -dənl; ˋɔrdn̩əl/ *adj* (of a number) showing order or position in a series (指数字)序数的. ▷ **or·dinal** *n* (also **ˌordinal 'number**): *'First', 'second' and 'third' are ordinals.* 第一、第二、第三都是序数词. ⇨App 4 见附录4. Cf 参看 CARDINAL[1].

or·din·ance /ˈɔːdɪnəns; ˋɔrdn̩əns/ *n* [C, U] (*fml* 文) order, rule or law made by a government or an authority 法令; 法规; 条例: *the ordinances of the City Council* 市议会的法令 ○ *by ordinance of the mayor* 奉市长指令.

or·din·ary /ˈɔːdənrɪ; *US* ˈɔːrdənerɪ; ˋɔrdnˌɛrɪ/ *adj* **1** normal; usual 平常的; 正常的; 通常的; 普通的: *an ordinary sort of day* 平常的一天 ○ *in the ordinary course of events* 按照事情的正常发展 ○ *ordinary people like you and me* 你我之类的老百姓 ○ *We were dressed up for the party but she was still in her ordinary clothes.* 我们都盛装赴会, 而她却依然日常装束. ○ (*derog* 贬) *a very ordinary meal*, ie nothing special 很平常的饭菜. Cf 参看

EXTRAORDINARY. **2** (idm 习语) **in the ˈordinary way** if the circumstances were usual 如果情况如常; 就通常情况而言: *In the ordinary way he would have come with us, but he's not feeling well.* 在一般情况下他都和我们一起来，只是他现在身体不太好. **out of the ˈordinary** unusual; exceptional 不正常的; 例外的; 特殊的: *Her new house is certainly out of the ordinary.* 她的新居真是不同凡响. ○ *His behaviour is nothing out of the ordinary,* ie not unusual. 他举止没有任何反常之处.

O

▷ **or·din·ar·ily** /ˈɔːdənrəlɪ; *US* ˌɔːrdnˈerəlɪ; ˌɔrdnˋɛrəlɪ/ *adv* **1** in an ordinary way 平常地; 正常地; 通常地; 普通地: *behave quite ordinarily* 表现得很平常. **2** as a general rule; usually 一般地; 如常地; 照例地: *Ordinarily, I find this job easy, but today I'm having problems.* 平时我认为这工作很容易, 岂知今日却有了问题.

□ **ˈordinary level** (also **O level**) (formerly in British education) examination of basic standard in the General Certificate of Education (旧时英国普通教育文凭的)普通级考试.

ˌ**ordinary** ˈ**seaman** sailor of the lowest rank on a ship 二等水兵. ⇨App 9 见附录 9.

or·dina·tion /ˌɔːdɪˈneɪʃn; *US* -dnˈeɪʃn; ˌɔrdnˋeʃən/ *n* (**a**) [U] ceremony of ordaining (a priest or minister) (司铎、神父或牧师等的)任命仪式. (**b**) [C] example of this 授圣职礼.

ord·nance /ˈɔːdnəns; ˋɔrdnəns/ *n* [U] **1** military supplies and materials 军需品和军用器材. **2** government service dealing with these 军械署.

□ ˌ**Ordnance** ˈ**Survey** (*Brit*) (government department that prepares) accurate and detailed maps of Great Britain (英国的)全国地形测量(局): [attrib 作定语] *an Ordnance Survey map* 英国全国地形测量局绘制的地图.

ord·ure /ˈɔːdjʊə(r); *US* -dʒər; ˋɔrdʒɚ/ *n* [U] (*fml or euph* 文或婉) excrement; dung; filth 排泄物; 粪; 污物.

ore /ɔː(r); ɔr/ *n* [U, C] rock, earth, mineral, etc from which metal can be obtained 矿石: *iron ore* 铁矿石 ○ *an area rich in ores* 矿产丰富的地区.

or·gan[1] /ˈɔːgən; ˋɔrgən/ *n* **1** part of an animal body or plant serving a particular purpose 器官: *the organs of speech*, ie the tongue, teeth, lips, etc 发音器官 ○ *The eye is the organ of sight.* 眼睛是视觉器官. ○ *the reproductive organs* 生殖器官 ○ *The surgeon removed the infected organ.* 医生切除了受感染的器官. **2** (*fml* 文) (official) organization that serves a special purpose; means of getting work done (官方的)机关, 机构: *Parliament is the chief organ of government.* 议会是政府的主要机关. **3** (*fml* 文) means for communicating the views of a particular group or party (集团或党派的)宣传工具, 机关报刊, 新闻媒介: *organs of public opinion*, ie newspapers, TV, radio, etc 舆论工具 ○ *This paper is the official organ of the Labour Party.* 这份报纸是工党的官方喉舌.

or·gan[2] /ˈɔːgən; ˋɔrgən/ *n* **1** (*US* also **ˈpipe-organ**) large musical instrument from which sounds are produced by air forced through pipes, played by keys pressed with the fingers and pedals pressed with the feet 风琴; 管风琴: *He plays the organ in church.* 他在教堂弹奏风琴. ○ [attrib 作定语] *organ music* 风琴曲. **2** any similar type of instrument without pipes 类似风琴的(无管的)乐器: *an electric organ* 电风琴 ○ *a mouth-organ* 口琴. Cf 参看 HARMONIUM.

▷ **or·gan·ist** *n* person who plays an organ 风琴演奏者; 风琴手: *a church organist* 教堂中的风琴手.

□ **ˈorgan-grinder** *n* person who plays a barrel organ 手摇风琴手.

ˈorgan-loft *n* gallery (in some churches, etc) where the organ is placed (教堂等中的)风琴台.

or·gan·die (*US* also **or·gan·dy**) /ɔːˈgændɪ; *US* ˈɔːrgəndɪ; ˋɔrgəndɪ/ *n* [U] type of fine, slightly stiff cotton material 奥甘迪; 蝉翼纱: *a blouse made of white organdie* 用白色奥甘迪制的女衬衫 ○ [attrib 作定语] *an organdie dress* 蝉翼纱连衣裙.

or·ganic /ɔːˈgænɪk; ɔrˋgænɪk/ *adj* **1** (*fml* 文) of or affecting an organ or organs of the body 器官的; 器质性的: *The illness is organic in origin.* 该病起初是器质性疾患. ○ *organic diseases, disorders, etc* 器官疾病、器官功能紊乱. **2** [esp attrib 尤作定语] of, found in, or formed by living things 生物的; 有机体的; 有机物的: *organic substances, compounds, matter, etc* 有机物质、有机化合物、有机物 ○ *rich organic soil* 肥沃的有机质土壤. Cf 参看 INORGANIC. **3** [esp attrib 尤作定语] (of food, farming methods, etc) produced or practised without artificial fertilizers or pesticides (指食物、耕作法等)施用有机肥料或有机农药的: *organic vegetables* 施有机肥料的蔬菜 ○ *organic horticulture* 有机物施用园艺学. **4** (*fml* 文) made of related parts; arranged as a system 有机的; 建制的; 有组织的; 有系统的: *an organic part of our business* 我公司的一个组成部分. ▷ **or·gan·ic·ally** /-klɪ; -klɪ/ *adv*: *The doctor said there was nothing organically wrong with me.* 医生说我没有器质性的毛病. ○ *organically grown tomatoes* 用有机肥料培植的蕃茄.

□ **orˌganic ˈchemistry** chemistry of carbon compounds 有机化学. Cf 参看 INORGANIC CHEMISTRY (INORGANIC).

or·gan·ism /ˈɔːgənɪzəm; ˋɔrgənˌɪzəm/ *n* **1** (**a**) (usu small) living being with parts that work together (通常指微小的)生物, 有机体: *study the minute organisms in water* 研究水中的微生物. (**b**) individual plant or animal 生物体. **2** (*fml* 文) system made up of parts which are dependent on each other 有机体系; 有机组织: *The business is a large, complicated organism.* 该企业是一个大而复杂的组织.

or·gan·iza·tion, -isa·tion /ˌɔːgənaɪˈzeɪʃn; *US* -nɪˈz-; ˌɔrgənəˋzeʃən/ *n* **1** [U] (**a**) activity of organizing 组织的活动: *He's involved in the organization of a new club.* 他参与了新俱乐部的组织工作. (**b**) condition or state of being organized 组织性; 系统性; 条理性: *She is brilliant but her work lacks organization.* 她很有才华, 但工作缺乏条理. **2** [C] organized group of people; system 组织; 机构; 系统: *all the local leisure organizations* 所有的地方康乐组织 ○ *The human body has a very complex organization.* 人体是个非常复杂的机体. ▷ **or·gan·iza·tional, -isational** /-ʃənl; -ʃənl/ *adj* [esp attrib 尤作定语]: *excellent organizational skills* 高超的组织艺术.

or·gan·ize, -ise /ˈɔːgənaɪz; ˋɔrgənˌaɪz/ *v* **1** [Tn, Tn·pr] **~ sb/sth (into sth)** put sb/sth into working order; arrange (parts, people) into an efficient system 组织某人[某事物]; 将(部件、人)编入组织或系统: *organize a political party, a government, a club, an army, etc* 组织政党、政府、俱乐部、军队等 ○ *She loves to organize people.* 她喜欢做组织工作. ○ *She organized the class into four groups.* 她把全班分成四组. **2** [Tn] make arrangements or preparations for (sth) 为(某事物)作安排或准备: *organize a picnic* 筹备野餐活动 ○ *organize a protest meeting* 组织抗议集会 ○ *They organized an expedition to Everest.* 他们组织了埃佛勒斯峰(即珠穆朗玛峰)之行. ⇨Usage at ARRANGE 用法见 ARRANGE. **3** [Tn, Tn·pr] **~ sb (into sth)** form (workers) into a trade union, etc 组织(工人)成立工会等: *organize the work force* 把工人组织起来 ○ *organize peasant farmers into a co-operative* 把农民组织起来成立合作社.

▷ **or·gan·ized, -ised** *adj* **1** ordered; orderly; efficient 有组织的; 有秩序的; 效率高的: *a highly organized person* 很有条理的人 ○ *a well-organized office* 工作效率高的办事处. **2** arranged or prepared 有组织的; 安排的; 有准备的: *a badly organized event* 组织得不好的事情 ○ *organized crime* 有组织的犯罪活动. **3** (of workers) in a trade union (指工人)在工会的: *organized labour* 工会工人.

or·gan·izer, -iser *n* person who organizes sth 组织者: *The organizer of the event, function, party, etc* 事件、宴会、聚会等的组织者.

or·gasm /ˈɔːgæzəm; ˋɔrgæzəm/ *n* climax of sexual excitement 性高潮: *failure to achieve (an) orgasm* 未达到性高潮.

or·gi·astic /ˌɔːdʒɪˈæstɪk; ˌɔrdʒɪˋæstɪk/ *adj* (*fml* 文) of or like an orgy; frenzied 狂欢的; 纵欲的; 狂乱的: *orgiastic revels* 狂欢活动.

orgy /ˈɔːdʒɪ; ˋɔrdʒɪ/ *n* **1** (*often derog* 常作贬义) wild party, usu with a lot of drinking and/or sexual activity 狂欢(通常伴有纵酒、淫乐的行为): *a drunken orgy* 纵酒狂欢. **2 ~(of sth)** (*infml* 口) great indulgence in one or more activity 放纵: *an orgy of killing and destruction* 大肆杀戮和破坏 ○ *an orgy of spending before Christmas* 圣诞节前的大笔花费.

oriel /ˈɔːrɪəl; ˋɔrɪəl/ *n* (also ˌ**oriel** ˈ**window**) window projecting from the upper storey of a house, etc 凸肚窗.

ori·ent[1] /ˈɔːrɪənt; ˋɔrɪənt/ *n* **the Orient** [sing] (*fml or rhet* 文或修辞) countries of the (Far) East (eg Japan,

China) 东方国家(如日本、中国): *perfumes and spices from the Orient* 东方的香水和香料. Cf 参看 OCCIDENT.

ori·ent[2] /ˈɔːrɪent; ˋɔrɪ,ɛnt/ *v* (*esp US*) = ORIENTATE.

ori·ental /ˌɔːrɪˈentl; ,ɔrɪˋɛntḷ/ *adj* of or from the Orient 东方国家的; 来自东方国家的: *oriental art* 东方艺术 ○ *a department of oriental studies* 东方问题研究部.

▷ **Ori·ental** *n* (sometimes offensive 有时作轻蔑语) person from the Orient, esp Japan or China 东方人; (尤指)日本人, 中国人.

ori·ent·al·ist /-təlɪst; -tḷɪst/ *n* person who studies the language, arts, etc of oriental countries 研究东方国家语言、艺术等的人; 东方学学者.

ori·ent·ate /ˈɔːrɪənteɪt; ˋɔrɪɛn,tet/ (also *esp US* **orient** /ˈɔːrɪent; ˋɔrɪ,ɛnt/) *v* **1** [Tn esp passive 尤用于被动语态, Tn·pr] **~ sb/sth (towards sb/sth)** (**a**) direct the interest of sb (to sth) 对某人的兴趣(朝向某事物)进行引导: *Try to orientate your students towards the science subjects.* 把学生的兴趣尽力引导到理科方面. ○ *Our firm is orientated towards the export side of the business.* 我公司业务已转向出口方面. (**b**) direct or aim sth (at sb); specially design sth (for sb) 使某物朝向或瞄准(某人); (为某人)专门设计某物: *The course was orientated towards foreign students.* 该课程是专为外国学生开的. **2** [Tn] **~ oneself** (**a**) find out how one stands in relation to points of the compass, one's surroundings, etc 确定自己的方位: *The mountaineers found it difficult to orientate themselves in the fog.* 登山的人在浓雾中难以确定自己的方位. (**b**) make oneself familiar with (a new situation) 使自己熟悉(新情况): *It took him some time to orientate himself in his new school.* 他花了一些时间才了解了新学校的情况.

▷ **ori·enta·tion** /ˌɔːrɪənˈteɪʃn; ,ɔrɪɛnˋteʃən/ *n* [U] activity of orientating oneself; state of being orientated 熟悉情况; 认识环境; 确定方位: *the orientation of new employees* 新雇员对环境的了解.

-orientated (forming compound *adjs* 用以构成复合形容词) directed towards 朝某方向的: *a ˈsports-orientated course* 以体育为宗旨的课程.

ori·ent·eer·ing /ˌɔːrɪənˈtɪərɪŋ; ,ɔrɪənˋtɪrɪŋ/ *n* [U] sport of finding one's way across country on foot using a map and compass 越野识途比赛(靠地图和罗盘徒步寻找目的地): *He has taken up orienteering.* 他参加过越野识途赛.

ori·fice /ˈɒrɪfɪs; ˋɑrəfɪs/ *n* (*fml* 文) outer opening in the body, etc (身体等的)外孔, 外口: *the nasal orifices*, ie nostrils 鼻孔 ○ *at the dark orifice of the cave* 在黑暗的洞口.

ori·gin /ˈɒrɪdʒɪn; ˋɑrədʒɪn/ *n* **1** [C, U] starting-point; source 起点; 开端; 来源: *the origins of life on earth* 地球上生命的起源 ○ *words of Latin origin* 拉丁语源的词 ○ *The origins of the custom are unknown.* 该风俗起源不详. **2** [C esp *pl* 尤作复数] person's parentage, background, etc 血统; 背景; 出身: *He never forgot his humble origins.* 他从未忘记过自己出身卑微.

ori·ginal /əˈrɪdʒənl; əˋrɪdʒənḷ/ *adj* **1** [attrib 作定语] existing from the beginning; first or earliest 原始的; 最初的; 原先的; 最早的: *The Indians were the original inhabitants of North America.* 印第安人是北美最早的居民. ○ *I prefer your original plan to this one.* 我认为你原来的计划比这个好. **2** (*usu approv* 通常作褒义) (**a**) newly created or formed; fresh 新创的; 新颖的; 创新的: *an original idea* 创见 ○ *His designs are highly original.* 他的设计独树一帜. (**b**) able to produce new ideas; creative 有创见的; 创造性的: *an original thinker, writer, painter, etc* 有创见的思想家、作家、画家等 ○ *an original mind* 有创造力的头脑. **3** painted, written, etc by the artist; not copied 创作的; 非抄袭的; 非模仿的: *The original manuscript has been lost; this is a copy.* 原稿已失, 这是副本.

▷ **ori·ginal** *n* **1 the original** [C] the earliest form of sth (from which copies can be made) 原作; 原稿; 原型; 原物: *This painting is a copy; the original is in Madrid.* 这幅画是复制品, 原作在马德里. ○ *This is a translation; the original is in French.* 这是译文, 原文是法文的. **2 the original** [sing] language in which sth was first written 原文(最初写作时所用的文字): *read Homer in the original*, ie in ancient Greek 读荷马的(古希腊文)原作. **3** (*infml esp joc* 口, 尤作戏谑语) person who thinks, behaves, dresses, etc unusually; eccentric person (思考、行为、衣着等)与众不同的人, 古怪的人: *Her Aunt Effie is certainly an original.* 她的姨妈埃菲真是个怪人.

ori·gin·al·ity /əˌrɪdʒəˈnæləti; ə,rɪdʒəˋnæləti/ *n* [U] state or quality of being original(2) 创新; 独创性; 创造力; 独特: *Her designs have great originality.* 她的设计十分新颖. ○ *The work lacks originality*, ie is copied or imitated. 那作品缺乏创造性.

ori·gin·ally /-nəlɪ; -nḷɪ/ *adv* **1** in an original(2) way 独创地; 独特地: *speak, think, write, etc originally* 说得、想得、写得…富有创见. **2** from or in the beginning 最初; 起先; 本来: *The school was originally quite small.* 这所学校原先很小.

□ **oˌriginal ˈsin** (*religion* 宗) (in Christianity) condition of wickedness thought to be present in everybody since Adam and Eve first sinned in the garden of Eden (基督教义中的)原罪(人与生俱来的罪, 始于亚当夏娃在伊甸园中犯的罪).

ori·gin·ate /əˈrɪdʒɪneɪt; əˋrɪdʒə,net/ *v* (*fml* 文) **1** [Ipr] **~ in sth; ~ from/with sb** have sth/sb as a cause or beginning 始自某事物[某人]; 起因; 发端: *The quarrel originated in rivalry between the two families.* 这次争吵是两家不和引起的. ○ *The style of architecture originated from/with the ancient Greeks.* 这种建筑风格起源于古希腊. **2** [Tn] be the creator or author of (sth) 创作, 发明(某事物): *originate a new style of dancing* 创作一种新的舞步 ○ *Who originated the concept of stereo sound?* 立体声是谁设想出来的?

▷ **ori·gin·ator** *n* person who originates sth 创始者; 创作者; 发明人.

ori·ole /ˈɔːrɪəʊl; ˋɔrɪ,ol/ *n* **1** (also ˌ**golden** ˈ**oriole**) type of European bird with black and yellow feathers 黄鹂. **2** similar type of N American bird of which the male has black and yellow feathers (北美)金莺.

or·molu /ˈɔːməluː; ˋɔrmə,lu/ *n* [U, C] (article made of or decorated with) gilded bronze or a gold-coloured alloy of copper, zinc and tin 金色铜(铜、锌、锡的合金); 金色铜物件: [attrib 作定语] *an ormolu clock* 金色铜的时钟.

or·na·ment /ˈɔːnəmənt; ˋɔrnəmənt/ *n* **1** [U] (*fml* 文) decoration; adornment 装饰; 点缀: *The palace was rich in ornament.* 宫廷装饰琳琅满目. ○ *The clock is simply for ornament, it doesn't actually work.* 那时钟纯粹是为了装饰, 其实不能走. **2** [C] thing designed to add beauty to sth, but usu without practical use 装饰物; 点缀品; 摆设: *a shelf crowded with ornaments*, ie vases, pieces of china, etc 摆满装饰物的架子(花瓶、瓷器等) ○ *I've just dropped one of your china ornaments.* 我刚才把你的一件瓷器的摆设给弄掉了. **3** (*dated fml* 旧, 文) person, act, quality, etc that adds beauty, charm, etc 增添美感、魅力等的人、行为、品质等: *He is an ornament to his profession.* 他为同业增了光.

▷ **or·na·ment** /ˈɔːnəment; ˋɔrnə,mɛnt/ [esp passive 尤用于被动语态: Tn, Tn·pr] **~ sth (with sth)** add ornament to sth; decorate sth 装饰、点缀或美化某物: *a dress ornamented with lace* 带花边的连衣裙 ○ *a Christmas tree ornamented with tinsel* 饰有金银箔的圣诞树.

or·na·mental /ˌɔːnəˈmentl; ,ɔrnəˋmɛntḷ/ *adj* of or for ornament 装饰的; 为装饰的: *Ornamental copper pans hung on the wall.* 墙上挂着装饰性的铜盘.

or·na·menta·tion /ˌɔːnəmenˈteɪʃn; ,ɔrnəmɛnˋteʃən/ *n* [U] that which ornaments; decoration 装饰物; 装饰: *a church with no ornamentation* 没有装饰的教堂.

or·nate /ɔːˈneɪt; ɔrˋnet/ *adj* (*often derog* 常作贬义) (**a**) richly decorated 装饰华丽的: *ornate carvings in a church* 教堂中华丽的雕刻饰物 ○ *That style of architecture is too ornate for my taste.* 那种建筑风格太华丽了, 不对我的口味. (**b**) (of prose, verse, etc) using complicated language and figures of speech; not simple in style or vocabulary (指散文、韵文等)词藻华丽的, 词句繁复的: *ornate descriptions* 堆砌词藻的描述 ○ *an ornate style* 雕章琢句的风格. ▷ **or·nately** *adv*. **or·nate·ness** *n* [U].

or·ni·tho·logy /ˌɔːnɪˈθɒlədʒɪ; ,ɔrnəˋθɑlədʒɪ/ *n* [U] scientific study of birds 鸟类学.

▷ **or·ni·tho·lo·gical** /ˌɔːnɪθəˈlɒdʒɪkl; ,ɔrnɪθəˋlɑdʒɪkḷ/ *adj* [esp attrib 尤作定语]: *an ornithological survey* 鸟类考察.

or·ni·tho·lo·gist /ˌɔːnɪˈθɒlədʒɪst; ,ɔrnɪˋθɑlədʒɪst/ *n* expert in ornithology 鸟类学家.

oro·tund /ˈɒrəʊtʌnd; ˈɑrə,tʌnd/ *adj* (*fml sometimes joc* 文, 有时作戏谑语) **1** (of the voice) dignified; grand (指嗓音)洪亮的, 高亢的: *the orotund tones of the priest* 牧师朗朗的语调. **2** boastful; pompous 夸张的; 夸大的; 浮夸的.

orphan /ˈɔːfn; ˈɔrfən/ *n* person (esp a child) whose parents are dead 父母双亡的人; (尤指)孤儿: *He has been an orphan since he was five.* 他五岁时即沦为孤儿. ○ [attrib 作定语] *an orphan nephew* 双亲亡故的侄儿.

▷ **orphan** *v* [Tn usu passive 通常用于被动语态] make (a child) an orphan 使(儿童)沦为孤儿: *She was orphaned in the war.* 她在战争中沦为孤儿.

orph·an·age /ˈɔːfənɪdʒ; ˈɔrfənɪdʒ/ *n* home for children who are orphans 孤儿院.

orris-root /ˈɒrɪsruːt; *US* ˈɔːr-; ˈɔrɪs,rut/ *n* sweet-smelling root of certain types of iris plant, dried and used in perfumes and medicines 鸢尾根(用作香料或药材).

orth(o)- *comb form* 构词成分 correct; standard 正确; 正统; 标准: *orthography* ○ *orthopaedic*.

or·tho·dont·ics /ˌɔːθəˈdɒntɪks; ˌɔrθəˈdɑntɪks/ *n* [sing *v*] (*medical* 医) (branch of dentistry that deals with) preventing and correcting irregularities in the position of the teeth and jaws 正牙(学).

▷ **or·tho·dontic** *adj* of orthodontics 正牙(学)的: *orthodontic surgery* 正牙外科.

or·tho·dont·ist /-ˈdɒntɪst; -ˈdɑntɪst/ *n* specialist in orthodontics 正牙医师; 正牙学家.

or·tho·dox /ˈɔːθədɒks; ˈɔrθə,dɑks/ *adj* **1** (having beliefs, opinions, etc that are) generally accepted or approved 持普遍赞同的信仰、见解等的; 规范的; 公认的; 普遍赞同的: *orthodox behaviour* 合乎传统的行为 ○ *Her ideas are very orthodox.* 她的思想非常合乎规范. Cf 参看 HETERODOX, UNORTHODOX. **2** (*esp religion* 尤用于宗教) following the older, more traditional, practices strictly 正统的; 传统的; 循规蹈矩的: *orthodox Jews* 正统的犹太教徒.

▷ **or·tho·doxy** /ˈɔːθədɒksɪ; ˈɔrθə,dɑksɪ/ *n* **1** [U] state of being orthodox or holding orthodox beliefs 规范性; 正统性; 持传统信仰. **2** [C esp *pl* 尤作复数] (*fml* 文) orthodox belief, character, practice, etc 正统; 正统的信仰、特性、做法等: *a firm supporter of Catholic orthodoxies* 坚决拥护天主教正统观念的人.

□ **the ˈOrthodox Church** (also **The Eastern ˈOrthodox Church**) branch of the Christian church, found esp in eastern Europe and Greece, which recognizes the Patriarch of Constantinople (ie Istanbul) as its head bishop 正教; 正教会; 东正教会.

or·tho·graphy /ɔːˈθɒgrəfɪ; ɔrˈθɑgrəfɪ/ *n* [U] (*fml* 文) **1** (study or system of) spelling 正字; 正字法; 拼字法: *In dictionaries, words are listed according to their orthography.* 在词典中, 词是按照字母拼写顺序排列的. **2** correct or conventional spelling 正确的或传统的拼写形式. ▷ **or·tho·graphic** (also **or·tho·graph·ical**) /ˌɔːθəˈgræfɪk, -fɪkl; ˌɔrθəˈgræfɪk, -fɪkḷ/ *adj*. **or·tho·graph·ic·ally** /-kəlɪ; -kəlɪ/ *adv*.

or·tho·paed·ics (also **or·tho·ped·ics**) /ˌɔːθəˈpiːdɪks; ˌɔrθəˈpidɪks/ *n* [sing *v*] (*medical* 医) (branch of surgery that deals with) correction of bone deformities and diseases 矫形(外科学): [attrib 作定语] *the orthopaedics department in the hospital* 医院中的矫形外科.

▷ **or·tho·paedic** (also **or·tho·pedic**) /ˌɔːθəˈpiːdɪk; ˌɔrθəˈpidɪk/ *adj* of or concerning orthopaedics 矫形的: *orthopaedic surgery on his spine* 为他的脊椎骨做的矫形外科手术.

or·tho·paed·ist (also **or·tho·ped·ist**) /-ˈpiːdɪst; -ˈpidɪst/ *n* specialist in orthopaedics 矫形外科医生.

or·to·lan /ˈɔːtələn; ˈɔrtələn/ *n* [U, C] (meat of a) small wild European bird eaten as a delicacy 圃鹀(欧洲产); 圃鹀肉(可食).

-ory *suff* 后缀 (with *vs* and *ns* forming *adjs* 与动词和名词结合构成形容词): *inhibitory* ○ *congratulatory*.

oryx /ˈɒrɪks; *US* ˈɔːr-; ˈɔrɪks/ *n* large African antelope with long straight horns (非洲)大羚羊.

OS /ˌəʊ ˈes; ˌo ˈɛs/ *abbr* 缩写 = **1** ordinary seaman. **2** (*Brit*) Ordnance Survey: *an OS map* 英国全国地形测量局绘制的地图. **3** (esp on clothing, etc) outsize (尤指衣物等上之标志)超大号.

Os·car /ˈɒskə(r); ˈɔskɚ/ *n* (statuette presented as an) annual award in the US for excellence in cinema directing, acting, composing, etc 奥斯卡金像(奖)(在美国为优秀电影导演、演员、编剧等颁发的年奖): *be nominated for/win an Oscar* 被提名候选[获得]奥斯卡金像奖 ○ *He received an Oscar for his performance.* 他获得奥斯卡金像奖. ○ *This film is the winner of four Oscars.* 这部影片获得四项奥斯卡金像奖. Cf 参看 ACADEMY AWARD (ACADEMY).

os·cil·late /ˈɒsɪleɪt; ˈɑsḷ,et/ *v* **1** [I, Tn] (cause sth to) move repeatedly and regularly from one position to another and back again (使某物)摆动: *A pendulum oscillates.* 摆锤能摆动. **2** [I, Ipr] **~ (between sth and sth)** (*fml fig* 文, 比喻) keep moving backwards and forwards between extremes of feeling, behaviour, opinion, etc; waver (感情、行为、想法等)波动, 动摇, 犹豫: *He oscillates between political extremes.* 他的政治观点在两个极端之间摇摆不定. ○ *Manic depressives oscillate between depression and elation.* 躁狂抑郁症患者抑郁与躁狂交替发作. Cf 参看 VACILLATE. **3** [I] (*physics* 物) (of electrical current, radio waves, etc) change in strength or direction at regular intervals (指电流、无线电波等)振荡, 振动.

▷ **os·cil·la·tion** /ˌɒsɪˈleɪʃn; ˌɑsḷˈeʃən/ *n* (*fml* 文) **1** [U] action of oscillating or being oscillated 摆动; 动摇; 振荡: *the oscillation of the compass needle* 罗盘指针的摆动 ○ *the oscillation of radio waves* 无线电波的振荡. **2** [C] single swing or movement of a thing or person that is oscillating (物或人的)一次摆动, 动摇: *Her oscillations in mood are maddening.* 她喜怒无常能把人气疯.

os·cil·lator /-tə(r); -tɚ/ *n* (*physics* 物) instrument for producing electrical oscillations 振荡器.

os·cil·lo·graph /əˈsɪləgrɑːf; *US* -græf; əˈsɪlə,græf/ *n* (*physics* 物) instrument for recording electrical oscillations 示波器; 示波仪.

os·cil·lo·scope /əˈsɪləskəʊp; əˈsɪlə,skop/ *n* (*physics* 物) instrument that shows variations in electrical current as a wavy line on the screen of a cathode ray tube 示波管; 示波器.

os·ier /ˈəʊzɪə(r); *US* ˈəʊʒər; ˈoʒɚ/ *n* type of willow tree, the twigs of which are used to make baskets 杞柳(柳条可编筐篮): [attrib 作定语] *an osier basket* 柳条筐.

os·mosis /ɒzˈməʊsɪs; ɑzˈmosɪs/ *n* [U] **1** (*biology or chemistry* 生或化) gradual passing of a liquid through a porous partition 渗透: *Blood can be cleaned by osmosis if the kidneys have failed.* 若肾功能衰退, 可通过渗透作用使血液净化. **2** gradual, and often hardly noticeable, acceptance of ideas, etc (思想、观念等)潜移默化: *Children seem to learn about computers by osmosis.* 儿童似乎不知不觉地就了解了计算机. ▷ **os·motic** /ɒzˈmɒtɪk; ɑzˈmɑtɪk/ *adj*.

os·prey /ˈɒspreɪ; ˈɑsprɪ/ *n* (type of) large fish-eating bird with a dark back and whitish head 鹗.

os·se·ous /ˈɒsɪəs; ˈɑsɪəs/ *adj* (*fml* 文) of bone; having bones; bony 骨的; 有骨的; 多骨的.

os·sify /ˈɒsɪfaɪ; ˈɑsə,faɪ/ *v* (*pt, pp* **-fied**) [I, Tn esp passive 尤用于被动语态] (*fml* 文) **1** (cause sth to) become hard like bone; change into bone (使某物)骨化; 变成骨. **2** (*fml derog* 文, 贬) (cause sth to) become rigid and unable to change (使某事物)僵化, 不能更动: *Beliefs have ossified into rigid dogma.* 信仰已僵化为不可更动的教条.

▷ **os·si·fica·tion** /ˌɒsɪfɪˈkeɪʃn; ˌɑsəfəˈkeʃən/ *n* [U] (*fml* 文) process or action of ossifying 骨化; 僵化: *the ossification of traditional practices* 习俗的僵化.

os·tens·ible /ɒˈstensəbl; ɑsˈtɛnsəbḷ/ *adj* [attrib 作定语] stated (as a reason, etc) though perhaps not true; apparent 声称(为理由等)的; 表面的: *The ostensible reason for his absence was illness, but everyone knew he'd gone to a football match.* 他称病缺席, 但谁都知道他去看足球赛了. ▷ **os·tens·ibly** /-əblɪ; -əblɪ/ *adv*: *Ostensibly he was on a business trip, but he spent most of the time on the beach.* 表面上他是因公外出, 实际上大部分的时间都是在海滨.

os·ten·ta·tion /ˌɒstenˈteɪʃn; ˌɑstɛnˈteʃən/ *n* [U] (*derog* 贬) exaggerated display (of wealth, knowledge, skill, etc) intended to impress people or make them envious (对财富、知识、技巧等的)夸耀, 炫示, 夸示, 卖弄: *the vulgar ostentation of the newly rich* 暴发户庸俗的摆阔 ○ *Their daughter's wedding reception was sheer ostentation.* 他们女儿大办婚事纯然是为了炫耀.

os·ten·ta·tious /ˌɒstenˈteɪʃəs; ˌɑstɛnˈteʃəs/ *adj* (*derog* 贬) showing or liking ostentation 夸耀的; 炫示的; 夸示的; 卖弄的: *ostentatious jewellery* 招眼的珠宝 ○ *dress in a very ostentatious manner* 穿着非常显眼. ▷ **os·ten·ta·tiously** *adv*: *ostentatiously dressed* 衣着引人注目.

oste(o)- *comb form* 构词成分 of or concerning bone or the bones 骨的: *osteopath* ○ *osteo-arthritis*.

osteo-arthritis /ˌɒstɪəʊɑːˈθraɪtɪs; ˌɑstɪoɑrˈθraɪtɪs/ *n* [U] (*medical* 医) painful disease of the joints of the body that causes inflammation and stiffness 骨关节炎.

os·teo·pathy /ˌɒstɪˈɒpəθɪ; ˌɑstɪˈɑpəθɪ/ *n* [U] (*medical* 医) treatment of certain diseases by manipulation of the bones and muscles 按骨术; 整骨术.
▷ **os·teo·path** /ˈɒstɪəpæθ; ˈɑstɪəˌpæθ/ *n* person who practices osteopathy 按骨医士; 整骨医士: *An osteopath has been treating her injured back.* 整骨医士正给她治疗受伤的背部.

ost·ler /ˈɒslə(r); ˈɑslɚ/ *n* (formerly) man looking after horses at an inn; stableman (旧时)客栈的马夫.

os·tra·cize, -ise /ˈɒstrəsaɪz; ˈɑstrəˌsaɪz/ *v* [Tn] (*fml* 文) exclude (sb) from a group, club, etc; refuse to meet, talk to, etc 将(某人)排除出某团体、俱乐部等; 拒绝会晤、交谈等: *He was ostracized by his colleagues for refusing to support the strike.* 他因不支持罢工而受同事排斥.
▷ **os·tra·cism** /-sɪzəm; -ˌsɪzəm/ *n* [U] (*fml* 文) action of ostracizing; state of being ostracized (对人的)排除, 排斥, 不理睬: *suffer ostracism* 受排斥.

ostrich 鸵鸟

os·trich /ˈɒstrɪtʃ; ˈɔstrɪtʃ/ *n* **1** very large African bird with a long neck, unable to fly, but fast-running 鸵鸟: [attrib 作定语] *Her dress was trimmed with ostrich feathers.* 她的衣边饰有鸵鸟的羽毛. ○ *an ostrich-egg* 鸵鸟蛋. **2** (*infml fig* 口, 比喻) person who refuses to face unpleasant realities 不正视不利现实的人: *He's such an ostrich — he doesn't want to know about his wife's love affairs.* 他真是自己骗自己 —— 对妻子有外遇不闻不问.

OT *abbr* 缩写 = Old Testament. Cf 参看 NT 2.

other /ˈʌðə(r); ˈʌðɚ/ *indef det* **1** (person or thing) additional to that or those previously mentioned or implied 其他的, 另外的, 别的(人或事物): *Mr Smith and Mrs Jones and three other teachers were there.* 史密斯先生和琼斯太太以及另外三位老师都在那儿. ○ *Other people may disagree but I feel the whole thing has gone far enough.* 尽管别人不同意, 但我觉得整个事情已经够可以的了. ○ *She's engaged to Peter but she often goes out with other men.* 她已经和彼得订了婚, 但她还常跟其他男子约会. ○ *Did you see any other films?* 你看过别的电影吗? ○ *Not now, some other time* (ie at an unspecified time in the future), *perhaps.* 现在不行, 改天再说吧. Cf 参看 ANOTHER. **2** (used after *the*, *my*, *your*, *his*, etc with a singular *n* 用于 the、my、your、his 等之后与一单数名词连用) the second of two (两个中的)另一个: *Hold the bottle and pull the cork out with the other hand.* 握住瓶子, 用另一只手拔瓶塞. ○ *Those trousers are dirty — you'd better wear your other pair.* 这条裤子脏了 —— 你最好穿另一条. ○ *You may continue on the other side of the paper.* 可在纸的背面接着写. **3** (used after *the* or a possessive with a plural *n* 用于 the 或物主代词之后与一复数名词连用) the remaining (people or things) in a group 其余的, 剩下的(人或事物): *The other students in my class are from Italy.* 我班其余同学都是意大利人. ○ *Mary is older than me but my other sisters are younger.* 玛丽比我大, 其余都是我的妹妹. ○ *I haven't read 'Cymbeline' but I've read all the other plays by Shakespeare/all Shakespeare's other plays.* 莎士比亚的剧作除了《辛白林》, 别的我都读过了. **4** (idm 习语) **every other** ⇨ EVERY. **none other than** ⇨ NONE. **one after the other** ⇨ ONE[1]. **the other ˈday, ˈmorning, ˈweek, ˈmonth, etc** recently 不久前的一天、一个上午、一个星期、一个月等: *I saw him in town the other day.* 我最近有一天在伦敦见过他. **somebody/something/somewhere or other** ⇨ OR. **this, that and the other** ⇨ THIS.
▷ **other** *adj* [attrib 作定语] **~...than...** (*fml* 文) different (people, things, etc) from... (人、物等)不同于...: *You will have time to visit other places than those on the itinerary.* 你能有时间参观计划行程之外的一些地方. ○ *Other women than Sally would have said nothing.* 除了萨莉, 别的女子就都什么也不说了.
others *pron* **1** people or things that are additional to or different from those already mentioned or implied 其他的、另外的或别的人或事物: *Some people came by car, others came on foot.* 有些人是坐汽车来的, 其他人是走着来的. ○ *These shoes don't fit — haven't you got any others?* 这双鞋不合脚 —— 还有别的鞋吗? ○ *We must help others less fortunate than ourselves.* 我们要帮助那些不那么幸运的人. **2** (used after *the* or a *possess det* 用于 the 或一表示所属关系的限定词之后) the remaining persons or things in a group 其余的或剩下的人或事物: *I went swimming while the others played tennis.* 我去游泳, 其余的人都打网球去了. ○ *I can't do the fourth and fifth questions but I've done all the others.* 第四题和第五题我不会, 但是剩下的我都答了. ○ *She was the only person who replied to the invitation — none of the others bothered.* 她是唯一对邀请做了回应的人 —— 其余的人谁也没理会.
□ **other than** *prep* (esp after a negative 尤用于否定词之后) **1** except 除了(表示所说的不包括在内): *He never speaks to me other than to ask for something.* 他除了向我要东西, 从不跟我说话. ○ *She has no close friends other than him.* 她除了他以外没有好朋友. **2** different(ly) from; not 不同于; 而不: *I have never known him behave other than selfishly.* 我只知道他一向自私自利. ○ *She seldom appears other than happy.* 她很少有不高兴的时候.
other-worldly /ˌʌðəˈwɜːldlɪ; ˈʌðɚˈwɝldlɪ/ *adj* concerned with or thinking about spiritual (rather than mundane) matters 专心于心灵问题的; 超脱世俗的.

oth·er·wise /ˈʌðəwaɪz; ˈʌðɚˌwaɪz/ *adv* **1** (*fml* 文) in another or a different way 用别的方法; 不同地: *You obviously think otherwise.* 显然你的想法不同. ○ *He should have been working, but he was otherwise engaged,* ie doing something else. 他应该在工作, 可他却干别的事. **2** in other or different respects; apart from that 在其他方面; 除此以外: *The rent is high, (but) otherwise the house is fine.* 租金贵是贵, (但)房子倒很好.
▷ **oth·er·wise** *conj* if conditions were different; if not 不然; 否则: *Put the cap back on the bottle, otherwise the juice will spill.* 把瓶盖儿盖好, 要不汁液就洒出来了. ○ *We must run, otherwise we'll be too late.* 我们得跑着去, 要不就太晚了. ○ *Do as you're told, otherwise you'll be in trouble.* 叫你怎么做就怎么做, 否则有麻烦.
oth·er·wise *adj* [pred 作表语] in a different state; not as supposed 不这样; 并非如此: *The truth is quite otherwise.* 实情大有出入.

oti·ose /ˈəʊtɪəʊs; *US* ˈəʊʃɪəʊs; ˈoʃɪˌos/ *adj* (*fml* 文) (of language, ideas, etc) serving no useful purpose; unnecessary (指语言、想法等)无用的, 多余的: *long, otiose passages of description* 冗长而多余的描写段落.

ot·ter /ˈɒtə(r); ˈɑtɚ/ *n* **(a)** [C] small fish-eating river animal with four webbed feet, a flat tail and thick brown fur 水獭. ⇨illus at App 1 见附录1插图, page iii. **(b)** [U] its fur 水獭毛皮: [attrib 作定语] *a jacket made of otter skins* 水獭皮甲克.

ot·to·man /ˈɒtəmən; ˈɑtəmən/ *n* long cushioned seat without a back or arms, often used as a box for storing things (eg sheets and blankets) (有垫的)长凳(常兼作放床单、毯子之物的箱子).

OU /ˌəʊ ˈjuː; ˌo ˈju/ *abbr* 缩写 = (*Brit*) Open University 开放大学: *an OU degree in maths* 开放大学数学学位.

ou·bli·ette /ˌuːblɪˈet; ˌublɪˈɛt/ *n* (esp formerly) secret dungeon or underground prison with an entrance only by a trapdoor in the roof (尤指旧时)地下密牢(出入口在顶部).

ouch /aʊtʃ; aʊtʃ/ *interj* (expressing sudden pain 表示突然疼痛): *Ouch! That hurts!* 哎哟! 疼!

ought to /ˈɔ:t tə; ˈɔt tə *before vowels and finally* 于元音前及末尾处读作 ˈɔ:t tu:; ˈɔt tu/ *modal v* (*neg* 否定式 **ought not to**; *contracted form* 缩约式 **oughtn't to** /ˈɔ:tnt; ˈɔtn̩t/) **1** (**a**) (indicating obligation 表示责任或义务): *We ought to start at once.* 我们应当马上动身. ○ *You ought to say you're sorry.* 你应该说声对不起. ○ *Such things ought not to be allowed.* 这类事不该容许. ○ *They oughtn't to let their dog run on the road.* 他们不该把狗放出来满街跑. ○ *'Ought I to write to say thank you?' 'Yes, I think you ought (to).'* '我应该写封感谢信吗?' '对, 我看应该写.' ○ *She ought to have been more careful.* 她本该小心些. ⇨Usage 1 at MUST 见 MUST 所附用法第1项. (**b**) (indicating advice or recommendation 表示劝告或推荐): *You ought to improve your English before going to work in America.* 你应该把英语学好些再去美国工作. ○ *There ought to be more buses during the rush hour.* 高峰期间应该多开几趟公共汽车. ○ *You ought to see her new film.* 你应当看看她新拍的电影. ○ *She ought to have been a teacher*, ie She would probably have been a good one. 她本该当教师(很可能是个好教师). ⇨Usage 2 at MUST 见 MUST 所附用法第2项. **2** (drawing a tentative conclusion 作推测性的结论): *If he started at nine, he ought to be here by now.* 要是他九点出发, 现在该到这儿了. ○ *That ought to be enough food for all of us.* 那些该够我们大家吃的了. ○ *Look at the sky — it ought to be a fine afternoon.* 看看天——下午一定很晴朗. ⇨Usage 3 at MUST 见 MUST 所附用法第3项.

Ouija /ˈwi:dʒə; ˈwidʒə/ (also ˈ**Ouija-board**) *n* (*propr* 专利名) board marked with letters of the alphabet and other signs, used in seances to receive messages said to come from the dead 灵应牌(上有字母等符号, 用于降神会中接收亡魂传来的信息).

ounce /aʊns; aʊns/ *n* **1** [C] (*abbr* 缩写 **oz**) unit of weight, one sixteenth of a pound, equal to 28.35 grams 盎司($\frac{1}{16}$磅, 等于28.35克). ⇨App 5 见附录5. **2** [sing] **~ of sth** (*infml* 口) (used esp with neg *vs* 尤与动词否定式连用) very small quantity of sth; any 少量; 一点: *She hasn't an ounce of common sense.* 她一点儿常识也没有. ○ *There's not an ounce of truth in his story.* 他说的没有一点儿是真的.

our /ɑ:(r), ˈaʊə(r); ɑr, aʊr/ *possess det* **1** of or belonging to us 我们的: *Our youngest child is six.* 我们最小的孩子六岁. ○ *Our main export is rice.* 我们主要的出口货是大米. ○ *Has anybody seen our two dogs?* 谁看见我们家那两只狗了吗? ○ *They want us to show some of our colour slides.* 他们想看看我们的彩色幻灯片. **2 Our** (used to refer to or address God, etc 用以直接或间接称呼上帝等): *Our Father*, ie God 天父(上帝) ○ *Our Lady*, ie the Virgin Mary 圣母马利亚.

▷ **ours** /ɑ:z, ˈaʊəz; ɑrz, aʊrz/ *possess pron* of or belonging to us 我们的: *Their house is similar to ours, but ours has a bigger garden.* 他们的房子和我们的差不多, 只是我们的花园大些. ○ *Your photos are lovely — do you want to see some of ours?* 你们的照片很漂亮——想看看我们的吗?

our·selves /ɑ:ˈselvz, aʊəˈselvz; ɑrˈsɛlvz, aʊrˈsɛlvz/ *reflex, emph pron* 反身、强调代词 (only taking the main stress in sentences when used emphatically 只在强调时重读) **1** (*reflex* 反身) (used when I and another or others, or I and you, cause and are affected by an action 用于复数第一人称施动而自身受该行动触及时): *We try and ˌkeep ourselves inˈformed about current trends.* 我们设法随时了解形势的发展. ○ *Let's ˈsign ourˈselves 'Your affectionate students'.* 咱们签上'爱戴您的学生'吧. ○ *We'd like to see it for ourselves.* 我们想亲眼看看. **2** (*emph* 强调) (used to emphasize *we* or *us* 用以强调we或us): *We've often thought of going there ourˈselves.* 我们常想亲自到那里去. **3** (idm 习语) **by ourˈselves** (**a**) alone 我们单独地. (**b**) without help 靠我们自己; 我们独自地.

-ous *suff* 后缀 (with *ns* forming *adjs* 与名词结合构成形容词) having the qualities or character of 具有…性质或特征的: *poisonous* ○ *mountainous* ○ *glorious*. ▷ **-ously** (forming *advs* 用以构成副词): *grievously*. **-ousness** (forming uncountable *ns* 用以构成不可数名词): *spaciousness*.

oust /aʊst; aʊst/ *v* [Tn, Tn·pr] **~ sb (from sth)** (*fml* 文) remove sb (from a position, job, etc) sometimes in order to take his place 免某人(职); 罢黜; 剥夺; 取代: *oust a rival from office* 把竞争者从其职位上挤走 ○ *He was ousted from his position as chairman.* 他的主席职位被罢免了.

out /aʊt; aʊt/ *adv part* (For special uses with many *vs*, eg *pick sth out, put sb out*, see the *v* entries. 可与许多动词连用, 如pick sth out、put sb out, 其释义见各动词词条.) **1** away from or not inside a place 离开某地; 不在里面: *go out for some fresh air* 出去呼吸新鲜空气 ○ *get up and walk out* 起来到外面去 ○ *open the door and run out into the garden* 开门出去跑进花园 ○ *open a bag and take sth out* 打开袋子取出某物 ○ *find one's way out* 寻找出路 ○ *lock sb out* 把某人锁在外面 ○ *She shook the bag and some coins fell out.* 她抖了抖手提包, 掉出了几枚硬币. ○ *Out you go!* ie Go out! 滚出去! Cf 参看 IN[1] 1. **2** (**a**) not at home or at a place of work 不在家; 不在工作地点: *I phoned Sally but she was out.* 我给萨莉打电话, 可是她不在. ○ *The manager is out at the moment.* 现在经理不在. ○ *Let's go out this evening/have an evening out*, eg go to the cinema, a restaurant, the theatre, a disco, etc. 咱们今天晚上出去吧[玩一个晚上吧]. (**b**) (of a book, record, etc) not in the library (指书、唱片等)不在图书馆或资料库, 借出: *The book you wanted is out.* 你要的书已借出. Cf 参看 IN[1] 3. **3** (indicating distance away from land, one's country, a town, etc 表示远离陆地、祖国、城镇等): *The boats are all out at sea.* 船都已出海. ○ *She's out in Australia at the moment.* 现在她远在澳大利亚. ○ *He lives right out in the country.* 他住在偏远的乡间. ○ *The ship was four days out from Lisbon*, ie had left Lisbon four days earlier. 轮船四日前已驶离里斯本. **4** (indicating that sth is no longer hidden 表示某事物已暴露, 不再隐蔽): *The secret is out*, ie revealed or discovered. 那秘密已泄露了. ○ *The flowers are out*, ie open. 花开了. ○ *The sun is out*, ie not behind a cloud. 太阳出来了 ○ *Her new book is out*, ie published. 她的新书出版了. ○ *There's a warrant out* (ie issued) *against him.* 对他的逮捕令已发出. ○ *Out with it!* ie Say what you know. 说出来呀! **5** (used with superlative *adjs* 与形容词的最高级连用) in existence; among known examples 存在着; 在已知者中: *It's the best game out.* 这是上策. **6** not in power, in office or in a position 无权力; 不在其位: *The Labour party went out in 1980.* 工党于1980年下野. Cf 参看 IN[1] 10. **7** not fashionable 不再流行; 不时兴: *Flared trousers are out this year.* 今年喇叭裤不时兴了. Cf 参看 IN[1] 8. **8** unconscious 失去知觉; 无知觉: *He's been out (cold) for ten minutes.* 他昏迷已有十分钟. **9** (of a tide) away from the shore; low (指潮汐)落潮, 退潮: *We couldn't swim — the tide was too far out.* 我们不能游泳了——潮水退得太远了. Cf 参看 IN[1] 6. **10** on strike 在罢工中: *The dockers in Liverpool are out.* 利物浦的码头工人罢工了. **11** (*infml* 口) not possible or desirable 不可能; 不可取: *Swimming in the sea is out until the weather gets warmer.* 在海里游泳还不是时候, 等天暖些再游. **12** (of fire, lights, burning materials, etc) extinguished; not burning (指火、灯、燃烧物等)熄灭: *The fire, gas, candle, etc is out.* 火、煤气、蜡烛等熄灭了. ○ *The fire has gone/burnt out.* 火灭了. (Cf 参看 *The fire is still in.*) ○ *All the lights were out in the streets.* 街上的灯光都熄灭了. ○ *Put that cigarette out!* 把香烟熄灭! ○ *The wind blew the candles out.* 风把蜡烛吹灭了. **13** to the end; completely 到尽头; 到底; 全部; 彻底: *hear sb out* 听某人说完 ○ *work out a problem* 解决一难题 ○ *Supplies are running out*, ie becoming low. 供应品快用完了. ○ *fight it out*, ie settle a dispute by fighting 武力解决争端 ○ *I'm tired out*, ie exhausted. 我筋疲力尽了. ○ *before the week is out*, ie finished 不出这一星期. **14** clearly and loudly; without hesitation 清晰而响亮地; 毫不犹豫地: *call/cry/shout out* 大声叫[嚷/喊] ○ *the need to speak out about sth* 就某事物大胆发表意见的必要 ○ *say sth out loud* 大声说某事 ○ *tell sb sth right/straight out* 直截了当告诉某人某事物. **15** (indicating a mistake) more or less than the correct amount (表示误差)有差错, 或多或少: *be out in one's calculations, reckoning, etc* 自己的计算、估计等稍有误差 ○ *We're ten pounds out in our accounts.* 我们的帐算错了十镑. ○ *Your guess was a* *long way out*, ie completely wrong. 你猜得差得太远了. ○ *My watch is five minutes out*, ie showing a time five minutes earlier or later than the correct time. 我的手表差了五分钟. **16** (*sport* 体) (**a**) (in cricket, baseball, etc) no longer batting, having been dismissed (板球、棒球等中)出局, 退场: *The captain was out for three*, ie after having made only 3 runs in cricket. 队长仅跑垒三次后出局. ○ *Kent were all out for 137.* 肯特队共得137分. (**b**) (in tennis, badminton, etc) (of a ball, etc) having landed outside the line (网球、羽毛球等)(指球)出界, 界外: *He lost the point because the ball was out.* 他丢了那分是因为球出界了. Cf 参看 IN[1] 10. **17** (idm 习语) **all out** ⇨ ALL. **be out for sth** be trying to get or eager to obtain sth 企求; 力图获得某事物: *I'm not out for compliments.* 我并不是想要得到称赞. ○ *He's out for your blood*, ie seeking to attack you. 他要打你. **be out to do sth** be trying, aiming or hoping to do sth 力求、旨在或希望做某事物: *I'm not out to change the world.* 我并不想要改革世界. ○ *The company is out to capture the Canadian market.* 该公司希望占据加拿大市场. **ˌout and aˈbout** able to get up, go outdoors, etc after being in bed through illness, injury, etc (病、伤等卧床后)能下床, 能到户外: *It's good to see old Mr Jenkins out and about again.* 看见詹金斯老先生又能起床出来走动了, 可真高兴. **ˌout and aˈway** (with superlatives 与形容词的最高级连用) by far 远远地: *She was out and away the most intelligent student in the class.* 她是班上最最聪明的学生.

▷ **out** *n* **1** (*US*) (in baseball) act, fact or instance of being out(16a) (棒球中)出局. **2** (idm 习语) **the ins and outs** ⇨ IN[3].

□ **ˌout-and-ˈout** *adj* [attrib 作定语] thorough; complete 彻底的; 完全的: *an ˌout-and-out ˈcrook, proˈfessional* 十足的无赖、内行人.

ˈout-tray *n* tray for holding letters, etc that have been dealt with and are ready to be dispatched 发文盘.

out- *pref* 前缀 **1** (with *vs* and *ns* forming transitive *vs* 与动词和名词结合构成及物动词) to a greater extent; surpassing 极大地; 超过: *outlive* ○ *outgrow* ○ *outnumber* ○ *outwit*. **2** (with *ns* 与名词结合) separate; isolated 独立的; 孤立的: *outhouse* ○ *outpost*. **3** (with *vs* forming *ns, adjs* and *advs* 与动词结合构成名词、形容词和副词): *outburst* ○ *outgoing* ○ *outspokenly*.

out·back /ˈaʊtbæk; ˋaʊtbæk/ *n* [sing] (esp in Australia) remote inland area where few people live (尤指澳大利亚的)内地: *lost in the outback* 在内地迷失.

out·bid /ˌaʊtˈbɪd; aʊtˋbɪd/ *v* (**-dd-**; *pt, pp* **outbid**) offer more money than (another person at an auction, etc); bid higher than 出价高于(拍卖场的另一人): *She outbid me for the vase.* 那个花瓶她出价比我高.

out·board motor /ˌaʊtbɔːd ˈməʊtə(r); ˌautbɔrd ˋmotɚ/ removable engine that is attached to the outside of the back (*stern*) of a boat (装在船尾外可拆卸的)船外发动机. ⇨illus at DINGHY 见 DINGHY 插图.

out·break /ˈaʊtbreɪk; ˋaʊtˌbrek/ *n* sudden appearance or start (esp of disease or violence) 爆发, 突然发生, 发作(尤指疾病或暴力行为): *an outbreak of typhoid, hostilities, rioting* 伤寒的发作、战争的爆发、暴乱的发生.

out·build·ing /ˈaʊtbɪldɪŋ; ˋaʊtˌbɪldɪŋ/ *n* building, eg a shed or stable, separate from the main building (与主建筑物分开的)附属建筑物(如棚或厩): *a large farmhouse with useful outbuildings* 带有实用附属建筑物的大型农舍. Cf 参看 OUTHOUSE.

out·burst /ˈaʊtbɜːst; ˋaʊtˌbɝst/ *n* (**a**) bursting out; explosion 爆发; 爆炸: *an outburst of steam from the pressure-cooker* 从压力锅中喷发出来的一股蒸汽. (**b**) sudden violent expression, esp of strong emotion 迸发, 发作(尤指感情的): *an outburst of laughter, anger, etc* 一阵大笑、勃然大怒 ○ *outbursts of vandalism* 对公物的大破坏.

out·cast /ˈaʊtkɑːst; *US* -kæst; ˋaʊtˌkæst/ *n, adj* ~ **(from...)** (person) driven away from home, friends, society, etc; homeless and friendless (person) 被(家庭、朋友、社会等)抛弃的(人); 既无家又无亲友的(人): *be treated as an outcast* 遭到被人赶出似的对待.

out·caste /ˈaʊtkɑːst; *US* -kæst; ˋaʊtˌkæst/ *n, adj* (esp in India) (person) expelled from or not belonging to a fixed social class or caste (尤指印度的)被驱逐出或不属于某阶级或种姓的(人), 贱民.

out·class /ˌaʊtˈklɑːs; *US* -ˈklæs; aʊtˋklæs/ *v* [Tn esp passive 尤用于被动语态] be much better than (sb/sth); surpass 大大优于, 超过(某人[某事物]): *I was outclassed from the start of the race.* 比赛一开始我就大大落后. ○ *In design and quality of manufacture they were outclassed by the Italians.* 在产品设计和质量上, 意大利人大大超过了他们.

out·come /ˈaʊtkʌm; ˋaʊtˌkʌm/ *n* (usu *sing* 通常作单数) effect or result (of an event, circumstances, etc) 结果; 效果: *What was the outcome of your meeting?* 你们会晤的结果如何?

out·crop /ˈaʊtkrɒp; ˋaʊtˌkrɑp/ *n* (*geology* 地质) part of a layer (of rock, etc) that can be seen above the surface of the ground (岩层等的)露头(露出地表的部分).

out·cry /ˈaʊtkraɪ; ˋaʊtˌkraɪ/ *n* (esp *sing* 尤作单数) ~ **(about/against sth)** strong public protest 公开的强烈抗议: *There was a public outcry about the building of a new airport.* 公众强烈反对修建新机场.

out·dated /ˌaʊtˈdeɪtɪd; aʊtˋdetɪd/ *adj* (made) out of date (by the passing of time); old-fashioned 过时的; 老式的: *ˌoutdated ˈclothing* 老式衣物 ○ *Her ideas on education are rather outdated now.* 她的教育思想现在看来很陈腐.

out·dis·tance /aʊtˈdɪstəns; aʊtˋdɪstəns/ *v* [Tn] move faster than (another person or animal) and leave him/it behind 超越(人或动物); 将(人或动物)抛在后面: *The favourite soon outdistanced the other horses in the race.* 那匹热门马很快就跑到最前面去了. ○ *His wife has outdistanced* (ie has been promoted more often than) *him in her career.* 他的妻子在事业上比他进展快.

outdo /ˌaʊtˈduː; aʊtˋdu/ *v* (*3rd pers sing pres t* **-does** /-ˈdʌz; -ˋdʌz/, *pt* **-did** /-ˈdɪd; -ˋdɪd/, *pp* **-done** /-ˈdʌn; -ˋdʌn/) [Tn] do more or better than (sb) 比(某人)做得多或做得好; 超过; 胜过: *determined to outdo her brother at work and games* 决心在工作和体育活动中胜过她的哥哥 ○ *Not to be outdone* (ie Not wanting to let sb else do better) *she tried again.* 她很好强, 又试了一次.

out·door /ˈaʊtdɔː(r); ˋaʊtˌdɔr/ *adj* [attrib 作定语] **1** of, used in, done in or existing in the open air (ie outside a building or house) 户外的; 户外用的; 露天的: *outdoor activities* 户外活动 ○ *outdoor clothing* 户外穿的衣服 ○ *outdoor sports* 户外运动. Cf 参看 INDOOR. **2** fond of activities done in the open air 喜欢户外活动的: *He's not really an outdoor type.* 他算不上是喜爱户外活动的人.

out·doors /ˌaʊtˈdɔːz; aʊtˋdɔrz/ *adv* in the open air; outside; out of doors 在露天; 在外面; 在户外: *It's cold outdoors.* 外面很冷. ○ *In hot countries you can sleep outdoors.* 在天气热的国家可以露天睡觉. ○ *Farm workers spend most of their time outdoors.* 农民大部分时间都在户外. Cf 参看 INDOORS.

▷ **out·doors** *n* (idm 习语) **the ˌgreat outˈdoors** the open air, esp away from towns and cities 露天; (尤指)郊外, 旷野: *I couldn't live in London, I enjoy the great outdoors too much.* 我住不了伦敦, 我酷爱郊外的环境.

outer /ˈaʊtə(r); ˋaʊtɚ/ *adj* [attrib 作定语] (**a**) of or for the outside 外面的; 外部的; 为外边的: *the outer layer of wallpaper* 壁纸的外层 ○ *outer garments* 外衣 ○ *the outer walls of a house* 房子的外墙. (**b**) farther from the inside or centre 远离内部或中心的: *the outer hall* 外厅 ○ *the outer suburbs of the city* 城市的远郊. Cf 参看 INNER.

▷ **out·er·most** /ˈaʊtəməʊst; ˋaʊtɚˌmost/ *adj* farthest from the inside or centre; most remote 最外面的; 远离中心的: *the outermost planet from the sun* 离太阳最远的行星 ○ *the outermost districts of the city* 城市的偏远地区.

□ **ˌouter ˈspace** = SPACE 5: *journeys to outer space* 太空旅行.

out·face /ˌaʊtˈfeɪs; aʊtˋfes/ *v* [Tn] make (sb) feel uncomfortable or embarrassed by staring at him boldly 将(某人)盯得侷促不安: *outface one's opponent without flinching* 直视对手而无惧色.

out·fall /ˈaʊtfɔːl; ˋaʊtˌfɔl/ *n* place where water falls or flows out (of a lake, river, etc); outlet (湖、河等的)出水口.

out·field /ˈaʊtfiːld; ˋaʊtˌfild/ *n* **1 the outfield** (in cricket and baseball) part of the field furthest from the batsmen or batter (板球和棒球的)外场, 外野. **2** [Gp] players in this part of the field as a group 外场手, 外野手(总称): [attrib 作定语] *Their outfield play is weak.* 他们的外场手截击力不强. Cf 参看 INFIELD.

▷ **out·fielder** *n* player in the outfield 外场手; 外野手.

out·fight /ˌaʊtˈfaɪt; aʊtˋfaɪt/ *v* (*pt, pp* **outfought** /-ˈfɔːt; -ˋfɔt/) [Tn] fight better than (an opponent) in battle or in a sports match (在战斗或比赛中)比(对手)出色; 赛过; 胜过: *We were outmanoeuvred and outfought throughout the winter campaign.* 我们在整个冬季战役中始终不如对手.

out·fit /'aʊtfɪt; 'aʊt,fɪt/ *n* **1** [C] all the equipment or articles needed for a particular purpose; kit 全套装备; 全套工具; 全部用品: *a complete car repair outfit* 修理汽车用的整套工具. **2** [C] set of clothes worn together (esp for a particular occasion or purpose) 一套衣服(尤指用于某场合的): *a white tennis outfit* 一套白色网球装 ○ *She bought a new outfit for her daughter's wedding.* 她为女儿买了一套婚礼新装. **3** [CGp] (*infml* 口) group of people working together; organization (协同工作的)集体, 组织: *a small publishing outfit* 小型出版单位.

▷ **out·fit·ter** *n* supplier of equipment or of men's or children's clothes (设备、男服或童服的)供应商, 商店: *He bought a jacket at the gentleman's outfitters.* 他在那间男服店买了一件夹克. ○ *They are the official school outfitters.* 他们是指定的校服供应商.

out·flank /,aʊt'flæŋk; aʊt'flæŋk/ *v* [Tn] (*fml* 文) (**a**) pass round the side of (an enemy force) 包围(敌人)的侧翼: *an outflanking movement* 侧翼包围的调动. (**b**) gain an advantage over (sb) esp by taking an unexpected action 胜过(某人); (尤指)出奇制胜: *He was totally outflanked in the debate.* 他在那场辩论中一败涂地.

out·flow /'aʊtfləʊ; 'aʊt,flo/ *n* [C usu *sing* 通常作单数] **~ (from sth)** flowing out; amount that flows out 流出; 外流; 流出量: *a steady outflow from the tank* 从箱中不断的流出 ○ *an illegal outflow of currency* 货币的非法外流.

out·fox /,aʊt'fɒks; aʊt'fɑks/ *v* [Tn] (*infml* 口) gain an advantage over (sb) by being more cunning; outwit 智胜(某人); 比(某人)精明: *He always outfoxes his opponents at chess.* 他下国际象棋总是胜人一筹.

out·go·ing /'aʊtgəʊɪŋ; 'aʊt,goɪŋ/ *adj* **1** [attrib 作定语] (**a**) going out; leaving 外出的; 离开的: *an outgoing ship, tide* 离岸的船、退落的潮水 ○ *the outgoing tenant*, ie the one who is leaving the house 即将迁出的房客. (**b**) leaving office, a political post, etc 将离任、离职等的: *the outgoing government* 即行交班的政府 ○ *the outgoing president* 将卸任的总统. **2** friendly and sociable 友好而好交际的; 外向的: *She's very outgoing.* 她很外向. ○ *an outgoing personality* 外向的个性 ○ *He's never been an outgoing type.* 他可不是那种好交际的人.

out·go·ings /'aʊtgəʊɪŋz; 'aʊt,goɪŋz/ *n* [pl] amount of money spent; expenditure 支出; 开支: *monthly outgoings on rent and food* 每月的食宿花消.

out·grow /,aʊt'grəʊ; aʊt'gro/ *v* (*pt* **outgrew** /-'gru:; -'gru/, *pp* **outgrown** /-'grəʊn; -'gron/) [Tn] **1** grow too big for (esp one's clothes) 长大而穿不下(尤指原有的衣服). **2** grow faster or taller than (another person) 长得比(某人)快或高: *He's already outgrown his older brother.* 他已长得比哥哥还高. **3** leave (sth) behind or grow weary of (sth) as one grows older; grow out of 年长而不再要(某事物); 长大而厌倦(某事物): *outgrow bad habits, childish interests, etc* 年长而放弃坏习惯、儿时的兴趣等 ○ *He has outgrown his passion for pop music.* 他已长大不再热衷于流行音乐了. **4** (idm 习语) **outgrow one's 'strength** grow too quickly (during childhood) so that one easily becomes weak or ill (儿童时期)生长过快而体弱或易病.

out·growth /'aʊtgrəʊθ; 'aʊt,groθ/ *n* (*fml* 文) **1** natural development or result 自然的发展或结果: *The manufacture of this material is an outgrowth of the space industry.* 这种材料的生产是航天工业发展的结果. **2** that which grows out of another thing (某物上的)生长物: *an outgrowth on a beech tree* 山毛榉上的瘤 ○ *an outgrowth of hair from the nostrils* 鼻孔的毛.

out·house /'aʊthaʊs; 'aʊt,haʊs/ *n* **1** small building (eg a shed or stable) outside the main building (在主建筑物外面的)附属建筑物(如棚或厩): *She did her washing in one of the outhouses.* 她在户外的一间小屋里洗衣服. Cf 参看 OUTBUILDING. **2** (*US*) outside lavatory (enclosed, but separate from the main building) 户外厕所.

out·ing /'aʊtɪŋ; 'aʊtɪŋ/ *n* short pleasure trip; excursion 短途旅行; 远足: *go on an outing* 去远足 ○ *an outing to the seaside* 到海滨游玩 ○ *the firm's annual outing to the theatre* 公司一年一度的外出观剧活动.

out·land·ish /aʊt'lændɪʃ; aʊt'lændɪʃ/ *adj* (*esp derog* 尤作贬义) looking or sounding strange (样子或声音)怪异的, 奇特的: *outlandish clothes, behaviour* 奇装异服、怪异行为 ○ *Her views on children are rather outlandish.* 她对儿童的看法很奇怪. ▷ **out·land·ishly** *adv*. **out·land·ish·ness** *n* [U].

out·last /,aʊt'lɑ:st; *US* -'læst; aʊt'læst/ *v* [Tn] last or live longer than (sth/sb) 比(某物)耐久; 比(某人[某物])命长: *This clock has outlasted several owners.* 这座时钟的寿命比它的几个主人的寿命都长. ○ *The political system will outlast most of us.* 我们大多数人将看不到这一政治制度的消亡. Cf 参看 OUTLIVE.

out·law /'aʊtlɔ:; 'aʊt,lɔ/ *n* (esp formerly) person who has broken the law and is hiding to avoid being caught (尤指旧时)犯法后躲藏起来的人: *Bands of outlaws lived in the forest.* 成群的歹徒犯法后栖身于树林中.

▷ **out·law** *v* [Tn] **1** (formerly) make or declare (sb) an outlaw (旧时)使(某人)或宣布(某人)成为犯法后躲藏起来的人. **2** declare (sth) to be illegal 宣布(某事物)非法: *outlaw certain addictive drugs* 宣布某些致瘾药物为禁品.

out·lay /'aʊtleɪ; 'aʊt,le/ *n* **~ (on sth)** (**a**) [U] spending, esp to help future developments in a business, etc 花费, 开支(尤指有助于公司等进一步发展的): *There was very little outlay on new machinery.* 添置新机器的开支微乎其微. (**b**) [sing] sum spent in this way (作上述用途的)费用, 款项: *a considerable outlay on basic research* 发展基础研究的一大笔费用.

out·let /'aʊtlet; 'aʊt,lɛt/ *n* **1 ~ (for sth)** way out (for water, steam, etc) (水蒸气等的)出口, 出路, 排放孔: *an outlet for water* 排水孔 ○ *the outlet of a lake* 湖的出水口 ○ [attrib 作定语] *an outlet valve* 排气阀. **2 ~ (for sth)** (*fig* 比喻) means of releasing (energy, strong feelings, etc) (精力、强烈情感等的)发泄的出路: *Children need an outlet for their energy.* 儿童的精力需要发泄出来. ○ *He needs an outlet for all that pent-up anger.* 他那积愤需要有机会倾吐. **3** (*commerce* 商) shop, etc that sells goods made by a particular company 经销店: *This cosmetics firm has 34 outlets in Britain.* 这家化妆品公司在英国有34个经销店.

out·line /'aʊtlaɪn; 'aʊt,laɪn/ *n* **1** line(s) showing the shape or outer edge (of sth) 轮廓; 外形: *She could see only the outline(s) of the trees in the dim light.* 朦胧中她只看见树木的轮廓. ○ [attrib 作定语] *He drew an outline map of Italy.* 他画了一张意大利的略图. **2** statement of the main facts or points 要点; 大纲; 纲要: *an outline for an essay, a lecture, etc* 文章、讲演等的要点 ○ *an outline of European History*, eg as the title of a book which summarizes the most important historical events, etc 欧洲历史纲要. **3** (idm 习语) **in 'outline** giving only the main points 扼要地: *describe a plan in (broad) outline* 概述一计划.

▷ **out·line** *v* [Tn] **1** draw or mark the outer edge of (sth) 画出或标出(某物)的轮廓、外形: *He outlined the triangle in red.* 他用红笔画出三角形. **2** give a short general description of (sth) 概述(某事物): *We outlined our main objections to the proposal.* 我们扼要地说明了反对该建议的意见.

out·live /,aʊt'lɪv; aʊt'lɪv/ *v* [Tn] live longer than (sb) 比(某人)活得久: *He outlived his wife by three years.* 他比妻子多活了三年. ○ (*fig* 比喻) *When he retired he felt that he had outlived his usefulness*, ie was no longer useful. 他退休时方觉得自己年老无用了. Cf 参看 OUTLAST.

out·look /'aʊtlʊk; 'aʊt,lʊk/ *n* **1 ~ (onto/over sth)** view on which one looks out 景色; 景致: *The house has a pleasant outlook over the valley.* 从这所房子可以看到山谷景色优美. **2 ~ (on sth)** person's way of looking at life, etc; mental attitude (对生活等的)看法, 观点, 态度: *a narrow outlook on life* 狭隘的人生观 ○ *a tolerant, forgiving, pessimistic, etc outlook* 宽容的、宽恕的、悲观的…态度. **3 ~ (for sth)** what seems likely to happen; future prospects 展望; 前景: *a bright outlook for trade* 商业的光明展望 ○ *a bleak outlook for the unemployed* 失业者惨淡的前景 ○ *further outlook, dry and sunny*, eg as a weather forecast 天气预测, 干燥而晴朗.

out·ly·ing /'aʊtlaɪɪŋ; 'aʊt,laɪɪŋ/ *adj* [attrib 作定语] far from a centre or a city; remote 远离中心的; 远离城市的; 偏远的: *outlying regions* 边远地区 ○ *outlying villages, with poor communications* 与外界联系不便的偏僻村落.

out·man·oeuvre (*US* **out·ma·neu·ver**) /ˌaʊtməˈnuːvə(r); ˌaʊtməˋnuvɚ/ *v* [Tn] do better than (an opponent, etc) by acting more skilfully and cleverly 比(对手等)技高一着, 智胜一筹: *He was completely outmanoeuvred in his campaign to win the support of other ministers.* 他为赢得其他大臣的支持而竭尽全力, 却因失算而彻底受挫.

out·moded /ˌaʊtˈməʊdɪd; aʊtˋmodɪd/ *adj* (*often derog* 常作贬义) no longer fashionable 过时的; 不流行的: *outmoded ideas, styles, views, etc* 陈旧的观念、款式、看法等.

out·num·ber /ˌaʊtˈnʌmbə(r); aʊtˋnʌmbɚ/ *v* [Tn esp passive 尤用于被动语态] be more in number than (sb) 在数量上超过(某人): *The demonstrators were outnumbered by the police.* 示威者没有警方的人数多. ○ *We were outnumbered two to one by the enemy*, ie There were twice as many of them. 我们的人数只及敌人的一半.

out of /ˈaʊt əv; ˋaʊtəv/ *prep* **1** (situated) at a distance from (a place seen as an enclosed area or volume); not in (位于)离(某处)一段距离; 不在内; 在外: *Mr Green is out of town this week.* 格林先生本星期不在伦敦. ○ *Fish can survive for only a short time out of water.* 鱼离开水后活得时间很短. Cf 参看 IN[2] 1. **2** (moving) away from (a place seen as an enclosed area or volume) 离开(某处); 从里面出来: *jump out of bed* 跳下床 ○ *go out of the shop* 走出商店 ○ *fly out of the cage* 飞出笼子. **3** (indicating motive or cause 表示动机或原因): *do sth out of mischief, spite, malice, etc* 出于恶作剧、怨恨、恶意等而做某事 ○ *help sb out of pity, kindness, generosity, etc* 出于怜悯、好意、慷慨等帮助某人 ○ *ask out of curiosity* 因好奇而问. **4** from among (a number) 从(若干)中: *Choose one out of the six.* 从六个里挑一个. ○ *To give you only one example out of several....* 从几个例子中仅给你举出一例.... **5** by using (sth); from 用, 以(某事物): *The hut was made out of pieces of wood.* 这小屋是用木板建造的. ○ *She made a skirt out of the material I gave her.* 她用我给她的料子做了一条裙子. Cf 参看 FROM 8, OF 5. **6** lacking (sth); without 缺乏(某物); 无: *I'm beginning to feel out of patience.* 我觉得有些不耐烦了. ○ *He's been out of work for six months.* 他已失业六个月了. ○ *be out of* (ie have no) *flour, sugar, tea, etc* 没有面粉、糖、茶叶等. **7** not in the condition specified by the following *n* 不处于 out of 后之名词所示的情况: *These books are out of order.* 这些书都乱了. ○ *He's still in hospital but out of danger.* 他仍在住院, 但已脱离了危险. (See *n* entries for similar examples. 类似示例见有关名词词条.) **8** having (sth) as its origin or source; from 以(某事物)为起源或来源; 从: *a scene out of a play by Pinter* 品特的剧作中的一场 ○ *copy a recipe out of a book* 从书上抄下一份菜谱 ○ *drink beer out of the can* 持罐装啤酒对嘴儿喝 ○ *pay for a new car out of one's savings* 拿储蓄的钱买新汽车. **9** (indicating the loss of sth, esp as a result of dishonesty 表示失去某事物, 尤指被骗): *cheat sb out of his money* 骗走某人的钱 (See *v* entries for similar examples. 类似示例见有关动词词条.) **10** at a specified distance from (sth) 在离(某地)某距离处: *The ship sank 10 miles out of Stockholm.* 船在离斯德哥尔摩10英里处沉没了. **11** not concerned with (sth); not involved in 与(某事物)无关; 不牵连在内: *It's a dishonest scheme and I'm glad to be out of it.* 那是个骗局, 我幸而置身事外. ○ *Brown is out of the England team.* 布朗与英格兰球队无关. **12** (idm 习语) ˈ**out of it** (*infml* 口) sad because excluded from a group of people or a community 因被排斥在某集体之外而难过: *We've only just moved here so we still feel a bit out of it.* 我们刚刚搬到这里, 和别人不熟感到仍有些冷清. ○ *She looks rather out of it — perhaps she doesn't speak English.* 她看上去像是局外人——大概是她不会说英语的缘故吧.

out-patient /ˈaʊtpeɪʃnt; ˋaʊtˌpeʃənt/ *n* person who goes to a hospital for treatment, but does not stay there 门诊病人: *If you do not require surgery you can be treated as an out-patient.* 不必动手术的可在门诊就医. ○ [attrib 作定语] *the out-patient department* 门诊部.

out·play /ˌaʊtˈpleɪ; aʊtˋple/ *v* [Tn esp passive 尤用于被动语态] play much better than (an opponent) 远胜, 大败(对手): *The English team were totally outplayed by the Brazilians.* 英国队被巴西队打得一败涂地.

out·point /ˌaʊtˈpɔɪnt; aʊtˋpɔɪnt/ *v* [Tn esp passive 尤用于被动语态] (in boxing, etc) defeat (sb) by scoring more points (拳击等中)以得分多而胜(某人): *He was outpointed by the champion.* 他以点数输给了冠军.

out·post /ˈaʊtpəʊst; ˋaʊtˌpost/ *n* **1** (group of soldiers at an) observation point some distance away from the main army 前哨(站). **2** any distant settlement 偏远居民区: *a missionary outpost in the jungle* 丛林区传教居民点 ○ (*joc* 谑) *You'd better get petrol here — where we're going is the last outpost of civilization.* 你最好在这儿加足汽油——咱们要去的算是人类文明的边缘地区.

out·pour·ing /ˈaʊtpɔːrɪŋ; ˋaʊtˌpɔrɪŋ/ *n* (usu *pl* 通常作复数) uncontrolled expression of strong feeling (强烈感情的)流露, 洋溢: *outpourings of the heart* 倾吐衷曲 ○ *an outpouring of frenzied grief* 悲愤的倾吐 ○ *the outpourings of a madman* 疯子的癫狂发作.

out·put /ˈaʊtpʊt; ˋaʊtˌpʊt/ *n* [sing] **1** quantity of goods, etc produced (by a machine, worker, etc) (机器、工人等的)产量: *The average output of the factory is 20 cars a day.* 该工厂的平均产量是每天20辆汽车. ○ *We must increase our output to meet demand.* 我们必须提高产量以满足需求. ○ *the literary output of the year*, ie all the books, etc published in a year 一年的出版物数量. **2** power, energy, etc produced (by a generator, etc) (发电机等的)输出功率: *an output of 100 watts* 功率100瓦. **3** (*computing* 计) information produced from a computer (信息的)输出. Cf 参看 INPUT 3.

▷ **out·put** *v* (**-tt-**; *pt*, *pp* **output** or **outputted**) [Tn] (*computing* 计) supply (information, results, etc) 输出(信息、结果等). Cf 参看 INPUT *v*.

□ ˈ**output device** machine by which information is received from a computer 输出设备.

out·rage /ˈaʊtreɪdʒ; ˋaʊtˌredʒ/ *n* (*derog* 贬) **1** [C, U] (act of) great violence or cruelty 暴虐; 残忍; 暴行: *outrages committed by armed mobs* 武装暴民的肆虐 ○ *never safe from outrage* 永受暴行威胁. **2** [C] act or event that shocks or angers the public 骇人事件; 激起民愤的行为或事情: *'The building of the new shopping centre is an outrage,' she protested.* '修建新购物中心是践踏民意,' 她抗议道. **3** [U] strong resentment or anger 义愤; 愤慨: *When he heard the news he reacted with a sense of outrage.* 他得悉此事义愤填膺. ○ *He leapt up and down in sheer outrage.* 他气得暴跳如雷.

▷ **out·rage** *v* [Tn esp passive 尤用于被动语态] shock or offend (sb); upset greatly 震骇或触犯(某人); 大大激怒(某人): *outrage public opinion* 违反民意 ○ *They were outraged by the announcement of massive price increases.* 物价大幅上涨的消息一公布, 他们气愤填膺.

out·ra·geous /aʊtˈreɪdʒəs; aʊtˋredʒəs/ *adj* **1** very offensive or immoral; shocking 蛮横无礼的; 无道德的; 骇人的: *His treatment of his wife is outrageous.* 他待妻子十分蛮横. ○ *The price is outrageous*, ie much too high. 价钱高得吓人. **2** very unusual and unconventional 不寻常的; 不依惯例的: *outrageous hats at Ascot* 阿斯科特赛马会上千奇百怪的帽子 ○ *outrageous remarks designed to shock listeners* 故意耸人听闻的言论. ▷ **out·ra·geously** *adv*: *outrageously expensive clothes* 极昂贵的衣物 ○ *outrageously pornographic magazines* 露骨的色情杂志.

out·rank /ˌaʊtˈræŋk; aʊtˋræŋk/ *v* [Tn] (*fml* 文) be of higher rank than (sb) 级别高于(某人): *Colonel Jones outranks everyone here.* 琼斯上校比这里所有人的级别都高.

outré /ˈuːtreɪ; *US* uːˈtreɪ; uˋtre/ *adj* (*French derog or joc* 法, 贬或谑) (esp of behaviour, ideas, tastes, etc) not conventional; very unusual or peculiar; eccentric (尤指行为、思想、情趣等)非传统的, 异常的, 奇特的, 古怪的: *an outré style of dress* 奇装异服 ○ *She likes to shock people with her outré remarks.* 她爱出语惊人.

out·rider /ˈaʊtraɪdə(r); ˋaʊtˌraɪdɚ/ *n* person on a motor cycle (or, esp formerly, on horseback) escorting the vehicle of an important person (重要人物乘坐车辆的)摩托车警卫(或尤指旧时的骑马护卫): *The President's car was flanked by motor-cycle outriders.* 总统的汽车由摩托车警卫护行.

out·rigger /ˈaʊtrɪgə(r); ˋaʊtˌrɪgɚ/ *n* **1** structure projecting over the side of a boat or ship, eg for the rowlocks in a racing boat or to give stability to a canoe 舷外撑架. **2** boat fitted with one of these structures 有舷外撑架的船.

out·right /ˈaʊtraɪt; ˋaʊtˌraɪt/ *adv* **1** openly and honestly, with nothing held back 坦率地; 率直地; 诚实地; 无保留

地: *I told him outright what I thought of his behaviour.* 我把我对他所作所为的看法直率地告诉了他. **2** not gradually; instantly 一下子; 立即: *be killed outright by a single gunshot* 一枪击毙 ○ *buy a house outright*, ie not by instalments 以一次付款方式买房. **3** clearly and completely 完全彻底地: *He won outright.* 他赢得干脆.

▷ **out·right** *adj* [attrib 作定语] **1** without any doubt or reservation 毫无疑义的; 毫无保留的: *an outright denial, refusal, etc* 矢口否认、断然拒绝. **2** clear; unmistakable 清楚的; 无疑的: *She was the outright winner.* 毫无疑问她是优胜者.

O

out·ri·val /ˌaʊtˈraɪvl; autˈraɪvḷ/ *v* (**-ll-**; *US also* **-l-**) [Tn] (*fml* 文) be or do better than (sb) in competition with him (竞争中)胜过(某人): *She outrivals him at all board games.* 她下什么棋都比他强.

out·run /ˌaʊtˈrʌn; autˈrʌn/ *v* (*pt* **outran** /-ˈræn; -ˈræn/, *pp* **outrun**) [Tn] run faster or better than (sb/sth) 比(某人[某物])跑得快, 善跑: *The favourite easily outran the other horses in the field.* 那匹热门马一下子就把其他的马甩在了后边. ○ (*fig* 比喻) *His ambition outran his ability*, ie He was ambitious to do more than he was able. 他志大才疏.

out·sell /ˌaʊtˈsel; autˈsɛl/ *v* (*pt, pp* **outsold** /-ˈsəʊld; -ˈsold/) [Tn] **1** sell more (quickly) than (sb) 比(某人)销售得快或多: *The Japanese can outsell any competitor in the market.* 日本人比谁都会搞市场推销. **2** be sold in greater quantities than (sth) 销售数量大于(某物): *This model outsells all others on the market.* 这种型号在市场上较其他型号畅销.

out·set /ˈaʊtset; ˈautˌsɛt/ *n* (idm 习语) **at/from the outset (of sth)** at/from the beginning (of sth) 开端; 开始: *At the outset of her career she was full of optimism but not now.* 她事业伊始十分乐观, 但现在已今非昔比了. ○ *From the outset it was clear that he was guilty.* 一开始就很清楚: 他有罪.

out·shine /ˌaʊtˈʃaɪn; autˈʃaɪn/ *v* (*pt, pp* **outshone** /-ˈʃɒn; -ˈʃon/) [Tn] (*usu fig* 通常作比喻) shine more brightly than (sb/sth) 比(某人[某事物])光亮, 出色, 优异: *The young girl violinist outshone* (ie was much better than) *all the other competitors.* 那年轻姑娘演奏小提琴使所有的竞争者相形见绌.

out·side[1] /ˌaʊtˈsaɪd; ˈautˈsaɪd/ *n* **1** [C usu *sing* 通常作单数] outer side or surface 外面; 外部: *The outside of the house needs painting.* 房子的外部需要粉刷. ○ *a fruit with a prickly outside* 外皮多刺的水果 ○ *Lower the window and open the door from the outside.* 落下窗户, 从外面打开门. ○ *Make sure the contents are clearly labelled on the outside.* 外面的标签一定要注明里面的内容. ○ (*fig* 比喻) *She seems calm on the outside but I know how worried she really is.* 她表面很镇静, 但我知道她实际上很不安. **2** [sing] area that is close to but not part of the specified building, etc 与某建筑物等接近的地方: *walk round the outside of the building* 在楼房周围散步 ○ *I only saw it from the outside.* 我只是从外面看见那个东西了. Cf 参看 INSIDE[1]. **3** (idm 习语) **at the outside** estimated or calculated as the highest possible figure; at the most 至多; 充其量: *room for 75 people at the outside* 至多能容75人的地方 ○ *With tips I can earn £150 a week, at the very outside.* 连小费在内我每星期最多能挣150英镑. **on the outside** (of motorists, motor vehicles, etc) using the lane that is nearest to the middle of the road or motorway (指机动车辆或驾驶员)使用外侧行车道: *overtake sb on the outside* 使用外侧行车道超越某人.

▷ **out·side** /ˈaʊtsaɪd; ˈautˈsaɪd/ *adj* [attrib 作定语] **1** of, on or facing the outer side 外部的; 在外面的; 对着外面的: *outside repairs, measurements, appearance* 外部的修理、外部的量度、外观 ○ *a house with only two outside walls* 只有两面外墙的房子. **2** (**a**) not in the main building; not internal 不在主建筑物内的; 外面的: *an outside toilet* 户外厕所. (**b**) not included in or connected with a group, an organization, etc 集团外的; 组织外的; 外界的; 局外的: *We'll need outside help before we can finish.* 我们需要外界援助才能完成. ○ *We may have to use an outside firm of consultants.* 我们可能得请教外面的咨询公司. ○ *She has a lot of outside interests*, ie not connected with her job or main subject of study. 她有许多业余爱好. **3** (of choice, possibility, etc) very small (指选择余地、可能性等)非常小的: *an outside chance of winning the game* 微乎其微的获胜可能. **4** greatest possible or probable 可能性最大的; 最可能的: *My outside price is £100 000.* 我出的价最高是100 000英镑. ○ *150 is an outside estimate.* 150是最高的估计.

□ ˌ**outside** ˈ**broadcast** programme filmed or recorded in a place other than the main studio 实况广播(不在主播音室内摄制或录制的节目).

ˌ**outside** ˈ**lane** section of a road or motorway nearest the middle, where traffic moves fastest 外侧行车道.

ˌ**outside** ˈ**left**, ˌ**outside** ˈ**right** player (in football, etc) in the forward line who is furthest to the left/right of the centre-forward (足球等中的)左[右]翼, 左[右]边锋.

ˌ**outside** ˈ**line** connection by telephone to a place that is outside the building or organization (电话)外线.

out·side[2] /ˌaʊtˈsaɪd; autˈsaɪd/ (also *esp US* **out·side of**) *prep* **1** on or to a place on the outside of (sth) 在或向(某物)的外面: *You can park your car outside our house.* 你可以把汽车停在我们房子外面. ○ *Don't go outside the school playground.* 不要到学校运动场以外的地方去. Cf 参看 INSIDE[2]. **2** not within the range or scope of (sth) 超出(某事物)的范围: *The matter is outside my area of responsibility.* 此事超出我的责任范围. ○ *I'm not concerned with what you do outside working hours.* 我不管你工作时间以外做什么事. **3** except for (sb); other than 除了(某人)(表示所说的不包括在内): *Outside her brothers and sisters she has no real friends.* 她除了兄弟姐妹以外没有真正的朋友.

▷ **out·side** *adv* **1** on or to the outside 在外面; 向外面: *Please wait outside.* 请在外面等候. ○ *The house is painted green outside.* 这房子外面刷成了绿色. ○ *The children are playing outside.* 孩子们在外面玩儿呢. ○ *Don't go outside — it's too cold.* 不要到外面去——天气太冷. **2** in the open air; not enclosed 在户外; 露天: *It's warmer outside than in this room.* 外面比这间屋子里暖和. ○ *The car wouldn't start after standing outside all week.* 汽车在露天停放了一个星期, 已经发动不起来了.

out·sider /ˌaʊtˈsaɪdə(r); autˈsaɪdɚ/ *n* **1** person who is not (or is not accepted as) a member of a society, group, etc 外人; 局外人; 组织之外的人: *Although she's lived there for ten years, the villagers still treat her as an outsider.* 她虽然在那儿住了十年, 村里人仍视她如外人. ○ *Women feel like outsiders in that club.* 女子在那个俱乐部里感觉是外人. **2** competitor thought to have little chance of winning a race or contest 不大可能获胜的竞争者: *That horse is a complete outsider; I wouldn't waste your money on it.* 那匹马绝无获胜可能, 我要是你可不把钱压在它身上. ○ *Amazingly, the job went to a rank outsider.* 真怪, 那工作竟然交给了一个万万想不到的人.

out·size /ˈaʊtsaɪz; ˈautˌsaɪz/ *adj* [usu attrib 通常作定语] (*sometimes derog* 有时作贬义) (of clothing or people) larger than the standard sizes (指衣物或人)大于标准大小的, 特大的: *outsize dresses for larger ladies* 适合特大体型女士的特号连衣裙 ○ *She's not really outsize — just well-built.* 她不算真正的特大体型——只是魁梧罢了.

out·skirts /ˈaʊtskɜːts; ˈautˌskɝts/ *n* [pl] outlying districts (esp of a city or large town); outer areas 外围地区; (尤指)市郊: *They live on the outskirts* (ie in an outlying district) *of Paris.* 他们住在巴黎市郊.

out·smart /ˌaʊtˈsmɑːt; autˈsmɑrt/ *v* [Tn] be cleverer or more cunning than (sb); outwit 比(某人)精明, 狡猾; 智胜(某人): *We outsmarted them and got there first by taking a shorter route.* 我们比他们机灵, 抄近道先到了.

out·spoken /ˌaʊtˈspəʊkən; autˈspokən/ *adj* **~ (in sth/doing sth)** saying openly exactly what one thinks; frank 直言的; 坦率的: *an outspoken critic of the government* 直言批评政府的人 ○ *be outspoken in one's remarks* 直言不讳. ▷ **out·spokenly** *adv*: *outspokenly critical* 坦率批评的. **out·spoken·ness** *n* [U].

out·spread /ˌaʊtˈspred; ˈautˌsprɛd/ *adj* spread or stretched out 展开的; 伸展的; 张开的: *She ran towards him with ˌoutspread ˈarms/with ˌarms outˈspread.* 她伸开双臂朝他奔去.

out·stand·ing /ˌaʊtˈstændɪŋ; ˈautˈstændɪŋ/ *adj* **1** exceptionally good; excellent 杰出的; 优秀的: *an outstanding student, piece of work, performance* 优秀的学生、作品、表演. **2** [usu attrib 通常作定语] in a position to be easily noticed; conspicuous 地位显著的; 为人瞩目

的; 突出的: *the outstanding features of the landscape* 景色的显著特点 ○ *an outstanding landmark* 突出的地面标志. **3** (of payment, work, problems, etc) not yet paid, done, resolved, etc (指报酬、工作、问题等)未偿付的, 未完成的, 未解决的: *outstanding debts* 未偿清的债务 ○ *A good deal of work is still outstanding.* 不少工作尚未完成.

▷ **out·stand·ing·ly** *adv* exceptionally 非常: *outstandingly good* 非常好的 ○ *play outstandingly (well)* 演得非常好.

out·sta·tion /ˈaʊtsteɪʃn; ˋaʊt,steʃən/ *n* remote station(1); outpost 设在边远地区的分站; 前哨站.

out·stay /ˌaʊtˈsteɪ; aʊtˋste/ *v* [Tn] **1** stay longer than (sb) 比(某人)停留的时间长: *outstay all the other guests* 停留的时间比其他客人长久. **2** (idm 习语) **outstay/overstay one's welcome** ⇨ WELCOME.

out·stretched /ˌaʊtˈstretʃt; aʊtˋstrɛtʃt/ *adj* (with limbs) stretched or spread out as far as possible (四肢)伸开的, 展开的: *He lay outstretched on the grass.* 他手脚摊开躺在草地上. ○ *with ˌarms outˈstretched/with ˌoutstretched ˈarms* 张开双臂.

out·strip /ˌaʊtˈstrɪp; aʊtˋstrɪp/ *v* (**-pp-**) [Tn] **1** run faster than (sb in a race) and leave him behind (赛跑中)超越(某人): *We soon outstripped the slower runners.* 我们很快就超过那些跑得慢的人. **2** become larger, more important, etc than (sb/sth) 胜过, 超过(某人[某事物]): *Demand is outstripping current production.* 现在需求逐渐超过了生产能力.

out·vote /ˌaʊtˈvəʊt; aʊtˋvot/ *v* [Tn esp passive 尤用于被动语态] defeat (sb) by a majority of votes; win more votes than 以多数票击败(某人); 得票多于: *Richard and David tried to get the question put on the agenda but they were heavily outvoted.* 理查德和戴维极力想把问题列入议程, 但遭多数票否决.

out·ward /ˈaʊtwəd; ˋaʊtwɚd/ *adj* [attrib 作定语] **1** (of a journey) going out or away from (a place that one is going to return to) (指旅行)外出的, 出外的: *He got lost on the outward journey.* 他外出旅行不知所终. **2** of or on the outside 外面的; 在外面的: *the outward appearance of things* 东西的外表 ○ *To (all) outward appearances* (ie As far as one can judge from the outside) *the child seems very happy.* 这孩子从外表看似乎很高兴. **3** in, or relating to, one's expressions or actions (in contrast to one's mental state or emotions) 表情或行动中的, 言行表露的(与心态和内心感受相对): *She gives no outward sign of the sadness she must feel.* 她一定很难过, 但毫不形之于色. ○ *An outward show of confidence concealed his nervousness.* 他表现出很有信心的样子以掩盖内心的紧张.

▷ **out·wardly** *adv* on the surface; apparently 表面上; 外表上: *Though badly frightened, she appeared outwardly calm.* 她虽然非常害怕, 但表面上还是显得很镇静.

out·wards /-wədz; -wɚdz/ (Brit) (also *esp US* **out·ward**) *adv.* ⇨Usage at FORWARD². 用法见FORWARD². **1** towards the outside 向外: *The two ends of the wire must be bent outward(s).* 铁丝的两端须向外弯. ○ *Her feet turn outwards.* 她双足外翻. **2** away from home or from the point from which one started 离家; 离出发地: *a train travelling outwards from London* 从伦敦向外开行的火车. **outward ˈbound** going away from home, etc 离开家、国等: *The ship is outward bound.* 那船是开往外地的. ○ [attrib 作定语] *the outward bound train* 开往外地的火车. **Outward ˈBound Movement** scheme designed to provide adventure training outdoors for young people (培养年轻人冒险精神的)户外训练活动: [attrib 作定语] *an Outward Bound (Movement) School* 户外训练(活动)学校.

out·weigh /ˌaʊtˈweɪ; aʊtˋwe/ *v* [Tn] be greater in weight, value or importance than (sth) 在重量、价值或重要性上超过(某事物): *This outweighs all other considerations.* 这一点是首要考虑的. ○ *The advantages far outweigh the disadvantages.* 利远大于弊.

out·wit /ˌaʊtˈwɪt; aʊtˋwɪt/ *v* (**-tt-**) [Tn] win or defeat (sb) by being cleverer or more cunning than him 以智胜过, 以计击败(某人): *Two prisoners outwitted their guards and got away.* 有两个囚犯设计欺骗了警卫而逃走了.

out·work /ˈaʊtwɜːk; ˋaʊt,wɝk/ *n* [U] sewing, assembly work, etc supplied by a factory or shop to an individual to be done at home 外包活(工厂或商店供给个人在家做的): *do outwork for a clothing factory* 为一制衣厂做外包活.

▷ **out·worker** *n* person who does outwork 外包工: *Outworkers in the clothing industry are usually badly paid.* 服装业中的外包工通常工酬非薄.

out·worn /ˌaʊtˈwɔːn; ˋaʊtˋwɔrn/ *adj* [usu attrib 通常作定语] no longer useful; outdated; old-fashioned 不能再用的; 过时的; 旧式的: *outworn practices in industry* 工业中过时的做法 ○ *outworn scientific theories* 落伍的科学理论.

ou·zel /ˈuːzl; ˋuzl̩/ *n* any of various types of small songbird of the thrush family 黑鸫: *a ring ouzel* 环颈鸫.

ouzo /ˈuːzəʊ; ˋuzo/ *n* [U] Greek alcoholic drink flavoured with aniseed, usu drunk with water 茴香烈酒(希腊产, 通常搀水饮用).

ova /ˈəʊvə; ˋovə/ *pl* of OVUM.

oval /ˈəʊvl; ˋovl̩/ *n, adj* (flat shape or outline that is) shaped like an egg 卵形的; 椭圆形(的): *The playing-field is a large oval.* 球场很大, 呈椭圆形. ○ *an oval brooch* 椭圆形胸针 ○ *an oval-shaped face* 鸭蛋脸 ○ *The mirror is oval.* 镜子是椭圆的.

ovary /ˈəʊvərɪ; ˋovərɪ/ *n* **1** either of the two organs in female animals that produce egg-cells (*ova*) 卵巢: *an operation to remove diseased ovaries* 卵巢切除手术. ⇨ illus at FEMALE 见FEMALE插图. Cf 参看 OVUM. **2** (*botany* 植) part of a plant that produces seeds 子房.

▷ **ovarian** /əʊˈveərɪən; oˋvɛrɪən/ *adj* [attrib 作定语] of the ovary 卵巢的; 子房的: *an ovarian cyst* 卵巢囊肿.

ova·tion /əʊˈveɪʃn; oˋveʃən/ *n* great applause or cheering expressing welcome or approval 热烈鼓掌或欢呼: *She received an enthusiastic ovation from the audience.* 她获得观众热烈的欢迎. ○ *The speaker was given a standing ovation*, ie The audience stood to clap, etc. 听众起立向演讲人热烈鼓掌欢呼.

oven /ˈʌvn; ˋʌvən/ *n* **1** enclosed box-like space (usu part of a cooker) in which things are cooked or heated 烤炉; 烤箱: *Bread is baked in an oven.* 面包是在烤炉里烤制的. ○ *a gas oven* 煤气烤箱 ○ *a microwave oven* 微波炉 ○ [attrib 作定语] *You've left the oven door open.* 你没把烤箱的门关上. Cf 参看 STOVE 1. **2** (idm 习语) **have a bun in the oven** ⇨ BUN. **like an ˈoven** very hot 非常热: *Open the window, it's like an oven in here!* 打开窗户吧, 这里热得像火炉!

□ **ˌoven-ˈready** *adj* prepared and ready for cooking 已加工即可入炉烤制的: *ˌoven-ready ˈchickens* 已加工即可烤制的鸡.

ovenware /ˈʌvnweə(r); ˋʌvən,wɛr/ *n* [U] heatproof dishes that can be used for cooking food in an oven (烤箱用)耐热盘碟: [attrib 作定语] *ovenware pottery* 耐热陶器.

over¹ /ˈəʊvə(r); ˋovɚ/ *adv part* (For special uses with many *vs*, eg *give over*, see the relevant *v* entries. 可与许多动词连用, 如give over, 其释义见各动词词条.) **1** (**a**) outwards and downwards from an upright position 从直立位置向外和向下: *Don't knock that vase over.* 别把那个花瓶碰倒. ○ *He fell over on the ice.* 他摔倒在冰上. ○ *I wobbled uncertainly for a couple of paces, then over I went.* 我踉跄了几步就跌倒了. ○ *The wind must have blown it over.* 一定是风把它吹掉了. (**b**) from one side to another side 从一边到另一边: *Turn the patient over onto his front.* 把病人翻过去让他俯卧. ○ *Turn over the page.* 把这页翻过去. ○ *The car skidded off the road and rolled over and over down the slope.* 汽车滑出路面, 打着滚翻下坡去. ○ *After ten minutes, turn the meat over*, ie to cook the other side. 烹调十分钟后把肉翻个个儿. (**c**) across (a street, an open space, etc) 穿过, 横过(街道、开阔地等): *Take these letters over to the post office.* 把这些信送到对面邮局去. ○ *Let me row you over to the other side of the lake.* 我把你划到湖对岸去吧. ○ *He has gone over to/is over in France.* 他到法国去了. ○ *Let's ask some friends over*, ie to our home. 咱们请几个朋友来吧. ○ *Put the tray over there.* 把托盘放到那边去. **2** (*esp US*) again 再; 又: *He repeated it several times over* (ie again and again) *until he could remember it.* 他重复了几遍直到记住为止. ○ *We did the house over* (ie redecorated it) *and bought new furniture.* 我们把房子重新布置一番并买了新家具. **3** left unused; remaining 剩余; 余下: *If there's any food (left) over, put it in the fridge.* 食物要是剩下就放进冰箱里. ○ *I'll have just £10 over when I've paid all my debts.* 要是我把债还清了, 我就只剩下10英

锈了. ○ *7 into 30 goes 4 with 2 over.* 用7除30得4余2. **4** in addition; more 加上; …多: *children of fourteen and over* 十四岁和十四岁以上的少年 ○ *10 metres and a bit over* 10米多一点. Cf 参看 UNDER 4. **5** ended 结束; 完结: *Their relationship is over.* 他们的关系已经吹了. ○ *By the time we arrived the meeting was over.* 我们到达时, 会议已结束了. ○ *'It's all over with him* (ie He is going to die),*' the doctor said gently.* '他不行了,'医生轻声地说. **6** (**a**) (indicating transfer or change from one person, group, place, etc to another 表示转移或更换): *He's gone over to the enemy,* ie joined them. 他已投敌. ○ *Please change the plates over,* ie exchange their positions. 请把盘子调一下. (**b**) (used when communicating by radio 用于无线电通话): *Message received. Over,* ie It is your turn to speak. 信息收到. 完毕. (该你说了.) **7** so as to cover (sb/sth) entirely 全部遮盖(某人[某物]): *paint sth over* 把某物全部涂上颜料 ○ *The lake is completely frozen over.* 湖面全部封冻. ○ *Cover her over with a blanket.* 给她盖好毯子. **8** (idm 习语) **(all) over a'gain** a second time (from the beginning) (从头)再一次: *He did the work so badly that I had to do it all over again myself.* 他干的太差劲了, 我只好亲自重做. **over against sth** (*fml* 文) in contrast with sth 与某事物对比: *the benefits of private education over against state education* 私人办学比起国家教育的好处. **ˌover and ˌover (a'gain)** many times; repeatedly 一再; 多次; 反复: *I've warned you over and over (again) not to do that.* 我已多次告诫过你不要做那件事. ○ *Say the words over and over to yourself.* 把这些话自己重复几遍吧.

over[2] /ˈəʊvə(r); ˋovɚ/ *prep* (For special uses with many *vs*, eg *argue over sth, get over sth, fall over sth,* see the *v* entries. 可与许多动词连用, 如argue over sth、get over sth、fall over sth, 其释义见各动词词条.) **1** (not replaceable by *above* in this sense 此义不可用above替换) resting on the surface of and partly or completely covering (sb/sth) 附于(某人[某物])之上并将之部分或全部遮住: *Spread a cloth over the table.* 在桌子上铺上桌布. ○ *She put a rug over the sleeping child.* 她给睡着的孩子盖上了毯子. ○ *He put his hand over her mouth to stop her screaming.* 他伸手捂住她的嘴, 不让她叫喊. ⇨ Usage at ABOVE[2] 用法见ABOVE[2] **2** in or to a position higher than but not touching (sb/sth) 在或向(某人[某物])的上方但不接触: *They held a large umbrella over her.* 他们给她打着一把大伞. ○ *The sky was a clear blue over our heads.* 我们头顶上是蔚蓝的天空. ○ *The balcony juts out over the street.* 那个阳台伸出于街道上方. ○ *There was a lamp (hanging) over the table.* 桌子上方悬(挂)着一盏灯. Cf 参看 ABOVE[2] 1a, UNDER. ⇨ Usage at ABOVE[2] 用法见ABOVE[2] **3** (**a**) from one side of (sth) to the other; across 从(某物)的一边到另一边; 横越: *a bridge over the river* 桥横跨河面 ○ *run over the grass* 跑过草地 ○ *escape over the frontier* 逃出边界 ○ *look over the hedge* 隔着树篱看. (**b**) on the far or opposite side of (sth) 在(某物)的远端或对面: *He lives over the road.* 他住在马路对过. ○ *Who lives in that house over the way* (ie on the other side of the road or street)? 谁住在路对面那所房子里? ○ *Over the river is private land.* 河的那边是私人的土地. ○ (*fig* 比喻) *We're over* (ie We have completed) *the most difficult stage of the journey.* 我们已渡过旅程中最困难的阶段. (**c**) so as to cross (sth) and be on the other side 越过(某物)到另一边: *climb over a wall* 爬过一堵墙 ○ *jump over the stream* 跳过小溪 ○ *go over the mountain* 翻过那座山. **4** (esp with *all* 尤与all连用) in or across every part or most parts of (sth/a place) 遍及(某物[某地])各处或大部分: *Snow is falling (all) over the country.* 全国各地都在下雪. ○ *He's famous all over the world.* 他名闻全世界. ○ *He sprinkled sugar over his cereal.* 他在麦片粥里撒上了糖. **5** more than (a specified time, amount, cost, etc) 多于, 超过(某时间、数量、价钱等): *over 3 million copies sold* 售出300万份以上 ○ *She stayed in Lagos (for) over a month.* 她在拉各斯逗留了一个多月. ○ *She's over two metres tall.* 她身高两米多. ○ *The river is over fifty kilometres long.* 这条河长五十多公里. ○ *He's over fifty.* 他五十开外了. Cf 参看 UNDER 4. ⇨ Usage at ABOVE[2] 用法见ABOVE[2] **6** (indicating control, command, authority, superiority, etc 表示控制、掌握、权威、优越等): *He ruled over a great empire.* 他统治着一个大帝国. ○ *She has only the director over her.* 她的职位之上只有主任了. ○ *He has little control over his emotions.* 他控制不住自己的感情. Cf 参看 UNDER 5, BELOW. **7** (**a**) (indicating the passing of time 表示时间流逝) while doing, having, eating, etc (sth); during 在…期间: *discuss it over lunch* 吃午饭时商议此事 ○ *He went to sleep over his work.* 他干着干着活儿就睡着了. ○ *We had a pleasant chat over a cup of tea.* 我们一边喝茶一边愉快地聊天. ○ *Over the next few days they got to know the town well.* 在随后的几天里他们就一定熟悉那个城市了. (**b**) throughout (a period); during 贯穿(一时间段); 在…期间: *stay in Wales over* (ie until after) *Christmas and the New Year* 在威尔士度过圣诞和新年. **8** because of or concerning (sth) 因为, 关于(某事物): *an argument over money* 因钱而起的争执 ○ *a disagreement over the best way to proceed* 对于用哪种方式进行最好而产生的分歧. **9** transmitted by (sth) 通过(某事物)传送: *We heard it over the radio.* 我们从无线电广播中听到了这件事. ○ *She wouldn't tell me over* (ie when speaking on) *the phone.* 她不愿在电话里告诉我. **10** (idm 习语) **ˌover and aˈbove** besides; in addition to 此外; 另外: *The waiters get good tips over and above their wages.* 服务员除工资外还有不少小费.

over[3] /ˈəʊvə(r); ˋovɚ/ *n* (in cricket) series of six balls bowled in succession from one end of the wicket by the same bowler (板球中)一个投球手一次连续投出的六个球: *dismiss two batsmen in the same over* 在一次连续投球中淘汰两名击球手.

over- *pref* 前缀 **1** (with *ns* forming *ns, vs, adjs* and *advs* 与名词结合构成名词、动词、形容词和副词) above; outside; across 在上; 在外; 越过: *overcoat* ○ *overhang* ○ *overall* ○ *overhead.* Cf 参看 SUPER-. **2** (used widely with *vs, ns, adjs* and *advs* 与许多动词、名词、形容词和副词连用) to excess; too much 过度; 过多: *overeat* ○ *overwork* ○ *overtime* ○ *over-rich* ○ *over-aggressively.* Cf 参看 HYPER-.

over·act /ˌəʊvərˈækt; ˋovɚˋækt/ *v* [I, Tn] (*derog* 贬) act[2] (2a) (one's part) in an exaggerated way; overplay 表演(角色)夸张; 演得过火: *Amateur actors often overact.* 业余演员往往表演过火. ○ *He overacts the part of the loving husband.* 他扮演一个体贴的丈夫的角色, 演得肉麻. Cf 参看 UNDERACT.

over·all[1] /ˌəʊvərˈɔːl; ˋovɚˌɔl/ *adj* [attrib 作定语] (**a**) including everything; total 包括一切的; 全部的; 总计的: *the overall measurements of a room* 一个房间的总面积 ○ *the overall cost of the carpet including sales tax and fitting* 地毯的总值, 包括营业税及附件在内. (**b**) taking everything into account; general 全面考虑的; 总的: *There's been an overall improvement recently.* 近来各方面都有所改进.

▷ **over·all** *adv* **1** including everything 一切包括在内; 总共: *How much will it cost overall?* 一共多少钱? **2** on the whole; generally 大致上; 大体上; 总体上: *Overall it's been a good match.* 总的来说, 那场比赛很好.

over·all[2] /ˈəʊvərɔːl; ˋovɚˌɔl/ *n* **1** [C] (*Brit*) loose-fitting coat worn over other clothing to protect it from dirt, etc 长罩衣: *The shop assistant was wearing a white overall.* 那店员穿着白色长罩衣. ⇨illus at APRON 见APRON插图. **2 overalls** (*Brit*) (*US* **coveralls** /ˈkʌvərɔːlz; ˋkʌvəˌrɔlz/) [pl] loose-fitting one-piece garment made of heavy material and covering the body and legs, usu worn over other clothing by workmen, etc to protect them from dirt, etc 工装裤: *The carpenter was wearing a pair of blue overalls.* 那木匠穿着蓝色的工装裤. Cf 参看 BOILER SUIT (BOILER).

over·arm /ˈəʊvərɑːm; ˋovɚˌɑrm/ *adj, adv* (of bowling in cricket) with the arm swung over the shoulder (板球中投球时)挥臂过肩(的): *an overarm bowler* 投球时挥臂过肩的投球手 ○ *bowl overarm* 挥臂过肩投球. Cf 参看 UNDERARM.

over·awe /ˌəʊvərˈɔː; ˌovɚˋɔ/ *v* [Tn usu passive 通常用于被动语态] cause (sb) to feel a great deal of fear and respect 使(某人)大感敬畏: *overawed into submission by senior colleagues* 被高职同事慑服 ○ *He was overawed by rather grand surroundings.* 周围景象十分壮丽, 他为之惊叹不已.

over·bal·ance /ˌəʊvəˈbæləns; ˌovɚˋbæləns/ *v* [I, Tn] (cause sb/sth to) lose balance and fall over (使某人[某物])失去平衡而倒下: *He overbalanced and fell into the water.* 他失去平衡跌入水中. ○ *If you stand up you'll overbalance the canoe.* 要是站起来, 能把独木舟弄翻.

over·bear·ing /ˌəuvəˈbeərɪŋ; ˌovɚˈbɛrɪŋ/ *adj* (*derog* 贬) forcing others to do what one wants (without caring about their feelings); domineering 专横的; 跋扈的; 横行霸道的: *an overbearing manner* 专横的态度. ▷ **over·bear·ingly** *adv*: *overbearingly proud* 盛气凌人.

over·bid /ˌəuvəˈbɪd; ˌovɚˈbɪd/ *v* (**-tt-**; *pt, pp* **overbid**) **1** [Tn] offer more money than (sb) at an auction; outbid (拍卖时)出价高于(某人); 出高价压倒(他人). **2** [I, Tn] (in the game of bridge) make a higher bid than (one's partner) or than one's cards are worth (桥牌中)叫牌压过(对方)或超过自己的实力. Cf 参看 UNDERBID. ▷ **over·bid** /ˈəuvəbɪd; ˈovɚˌbɪd/ *n* act of overbidding 高于别人的出价; (桥牌中压过对方或超过自己实力的)叫牌.

over·blown /ˌəuvəˈbləun; ˌovɚˈblon/ *adj* **1** (of flowers) past their best; too fully open (指花)盛期已过的, 开得过盛的: ˌ*overblown* ˈ*roses* 盛极而衰的玫瑰 ○ (*fig* 比喻) ˌ*overblown* ˈ*beauty* 迟暮美人. **2** (*fml* 文) overdone; pretentious 做得过分的; 做作的: *an overblown style of writing* 华而不实的文体.

over·board /ˈəuvəbɔːd; ˈovɚˌbord/ *adv* **1** over the side of a ship or boat into the water 越过船舷进入水中: *fall, jump, be washed overboard* 经船舷跌入、跳入、被冲入水中. **2** (idm 习语) **go overboard (about sb/sth)** (*infml often derog* 口, 常作贬义) be very or too enthusiastic (about sth/sb) (对某事物[某人])极感兴趣或过分感兴趣: *He goes overboard about every young woman he meets.* 他对年轻的女子见一个爱一个. **throw sth/sb overboard** abandon sth; get rid of or stop supporting sb 抛弃某事物; 除掉或不再支持某人: *After heavily losing the election the party threw their leader overboard.* 该党惨败落选后罢免了党魁.

over·book /ˌəuvəˈbuk; ˌovɚˈbuk/ *v* [Tn esp passive 尤用于被动语态] make reservations for too many passengers or visitors for (an aircraft flight, a hotel, etc) 使(航班、旅馆等)订位超员: *The flight was heavily overbooked.* 该班机订位已超员.

over·bur·den /ˌəuvəˈbɜːdn; ˈovɚˈbɝdn̩/ *v* [usu passive 通常用于被动语态: Tn, Tn·pr] **~ sb (with sth)** load sb with too much weight, work, worry, etc 使某人负担过重: *overburdened with committee meetings* 因委员会会议繁多而不胜重负 ○ *overburdened with guilt, remorse, debt* 罪过深重、追悔无及、负债累累.

over·cap·it·al·ize, -ise /ˌəuvəˈkæpɪtəlaɪz; ˈovɚˈkæpətl̩ˌaɪz/ *v* [Tn] fix or estimate the money supply of (a company, business, etc) too high 将(公司、企业等)的资本定得或估价过高. ▷ **over·cap·it·al·iza·tion, -isation** /ˌəuvəˌkæpɪtəlaɪˈzeɪʃn; *US* -lɪˈz; ˈovɚˌkæpətlɪˈzeʃən/ *n* [U].

over·cast /ˌəuvəˈkɑːst; *US* -ˈkæst; ˌovɚˈkæst/ *adj* (of the sky) covered with cloud (指天空)阴的, 多云的: *a dark, overcast day* 阴暗的一天 ○ *It's a bit overcast — it might rain.* 天有点阴——可能有雨. ○ (*fig* 比喻) *a gloomy, overcast* (ie unhappy) *expression on his face* 他愁眉苦脸.

over·charge /ˌəuvəˈtʃɑːdʒ; ˈovɚˈtʃɑrdʒ/ *v* **1** [I, Ipr, Tn, Tn·pr, Dn·n] **~ (sb) (for sth)** charge (sb) too high a price (for sth) (为某事物)(向某人)索价或索费过高: *That grocer never overcharges.* 那杂货商从不多要价. ○ *We were overcharged for the eggs.* 我们的鸡蛋买贵了. ○ *They overcharged me (by) £1 for the shopping.* 我买东西他们多要了我1英镑. Cf 参看 UNDERCHARGE. **2** fill or load (sth) too full or too heavily 将(某物)装得过满或过重: *overcharge an electric circuit* 使电路超负荷 ○ (*fig* 比喻) *a poem overcharged with emotion* 感情过于丰富的诗.

over·coat /ˈəuvəkəut; ˈovɚˌkot/ *n* (also *dated* 旧作 ˈ**topcoat**) long warm coat worn over other clothes (when going outdoors in cold weather) 大衣: *He wore a hat, gloves and an overcoat.* 他戴着帽子、手套, 还穿着大衣.

over·come /ˌəuvəˈkʌm; ˌovɚˈkʌm/ *v* (*pt* **overcame** /-ˈkeɪm; -ˈkem/, *pp* **overcome**) **1** [Tn] succeed in a struggle against (sth); defeat 战胜, 克服(某事物): *overcome a bad habit* 改掉坏习惯 ○ *He overcame a strong temptation to run away.* 他抵制了要逃跑的强烈诱惑. **2** [I] (*fml* 文) be victorious; triumph 得胜; 获胜: *We shall overcome!* 我们一定胜利! **3** [Tn usu passive 通常用于被动语态] make (sb) weak or ill; cause (sb) to become faint or lose control 使(某人)软弱或不适; 使(某人)昏厥或失去控制力: *be overcome by gas fumes* 被煤气熏倒 ○ *be overcome by/with grief, anger, despair, etc* 因悲哀、气恼、绝望等而不能自持. **4** [Tn] find a way of dealing with or solving (a problem, etc) 找到处理或解决(问题等)的办法: *We'll overcome that difficulty when we get to it.* 那种困难到时候我们自有办法解决.

over-compensate /ˌəuvəˈkɒmpenseɪt; ˌovɚˈkɑmpɛnˌset/ *v* [I, Ipr] **~ (for sth)** try to correct (an error, a weakness, etc) but go too far (in the opposite direction) 矫枉过正; 为纠正(错误、偏差等)做得过分: *He had over-compensated for the effect of the wind, and taken the aircraft off course.* 他矫正风力的影响超过了限度使飞机偏离了航线. ○ *Working mothers often over-compensate for their absences from home by spoiling their children.* 有工作的妇女无法在家中照顾子女, 往往因此而矫枉过正反倒惯坏了孩子. ▷ **over-compensation** /ˌəuvəˌkɒmpenˈseɪʃn; ˌovɚˌkɑmpɛnˈseʃən/ *n* [U].

over·crop /ˌəuvəˈkrɒp; ˌovɚˈkrɑp/ *v* (**-pp-**) [Tn] take too many crops from (farmland) so that it loses fertility 过度使用(耕地)而使之贫瘠.

over·crowded /ˌəuvəˈkraudɪd; ˌovɚˈkraudɪd/ *adj* with too many people in (a place); crowded too much 过度拥挤的: *Shops are very overcrowded before Christmas.* 商店在圣诞节前非常拥挤. ○ ˌ*overcrowded* ˈ*buses,* ˈ*trains, etc* 拥挤不堪的公共汽车、火车等. ▷ **over·crowd·ing** /ˌəuvəˈkraudɪŋ; ˌovɚˈkraudɪŋ/ *n* [U] state of having too many people in one place 拥挤: *the serious overcrowding in the poorer areas of the city* 城市贫困区的严重拥挤状况.

overdo /ˌəuvəˈduː; ˈovɚˈdu/ *v* (*pt* **overdid** /-ˈdɪd; -ˈdɪd/, *pp* **overdone** /-ˈdʌn; -ˈdʌn/) [Tn] **1** do, perform or express (sth) too fully or for too long; exaggerate 将(某事物)做得、表现得或表达得过火: *She rather overdid the sympathy*, ie was so sympathetic that she did not seem sincere. 她同情得有些过分了(显得缺乏诚意). **2** overact (sth) 将(某事物)演得过火: *The comic scenes in the play were overdone.* 这剧的滑稽场面太夸张了. **3** use too much of (sth) 过多使用(某事物); 滥用: *Don't overdo the garlic in the food — not everyone likes it.* 蒜别放太多——不是人人都喜欢的. ○ *I think they've rather overdone the red in this room,* ie used too much red paint, wallpaper, etc. 我认为他们把这房间弄得太红了. **4** cook (sth) for too long 把(某物)煮得过久: *The fish was overdone and very dry.* 鱼烧得过火了, 太干了. **5** (idm 习语) **overˈdo it/things** (**a**) work, study, exercise, etc too hard 工作、学习、运动等过分努力: *He's been overdoing things recently.* 近来他做事过分努力. ○ *You must stop overdoing it — you'll make yourself ill.* 不要过劳了——你要生病的. (**b**) behave in an exaggerated way (in order to achieve one's aim) (为达到目的)做得过分: *He was trying to be helpful, but he rather overdid it.* 他想尽力帮忙, 但做得有些过分了.

over·dose /ˈəuvədəus; ˈovɚˌdos/ *n* too great an amount (of a drug) taken at one time (药物一次使用的)过量: *take a massive overdose of sleeping tablets* 服用过量的安眠药 ○ *die of a heroin overdose* 死于使用过量海洛因 ○ (*fig* 比喻) *I've had rather an overdose of T. V. this week,* ie watched too much. 这个星期我看电视看得太多了. ▷ **over·dose** *v* **1** /ˌəuvəˈdəus; ˈovɚˈdos/ [Tn, Tn·pr] **~ sb (with sth)** give sb an overdose (of sth) 给某人(药物的)过量: *He's been overdosing himself.* 他用药一直过量. ○ *She overdosed the old woman with pain-killers.* 她给那老太太使用过量的止痛药. **2** /ˈəuvədəus; ˈovɚˌdos/ [I, Ipr] **~ (on sth)** take an overdose (of sth) 使用(药物的)过量: *He overdosed (on sleeping-pills) and died.* 他服用安眠药过量致死.

over·draft /ˈəuvədrɑːft; *US* -dræft; ˈovɚˌdræft/ *n* amount of money by which a bank account is overdrawn 透支; 透支额: *He has a huge overdraft to pay off.* 他有一大笔透支要偿还. ○ *I took out an overdraft to pay for my new car.* 我用透支来付新汽车的钱. ○ [attrib 作定语] *an overdraft arrangement* 透支安排.

over·draw /ˌəuvəˈdrɔː; ˈovɚˈdrɔ/ *v* (*pt* **overdrew** /-ˈdruː; -ˈdru/, *pp* **overdrawn** /-ˈdrɔːn; -ˈdrɔn/) **1** [I, Tn] draw more money from (a bank account) than the amount that is in it 从(银行帐户)透支. **2** [Tn] give an exaggerated account of (sth) 夸张(某事物): *The characters in this novel are overdrawn,* ie not true to life. 这部小说人物都太夸张了.

▷ **over·drawn** /ˌəʊvəˈdrɔːn; ˋovɚˋdrɔn/ *adj* **(a)** [pred 作表语] (of a person) having an overdraft（指人）有透支: *I am overdrawn by £500.* 我透支了500英镑. **(b)** (of an account) with more money drawn out than paid or left in（指帐户）透支的: *a heavily overdrawn account* 巨额透支的帐户.

over·dress /ˌəʊvəˈdres; ˋovɚˋdrɛs/ *v* [I, Tn usu passive 通常用于被动语态] (*usu derog* 通常作贬义) dress (oneself or another person) more formally, richly, etc than is suitable for the occasion 过分打扮(自己或某人)(不适于某场合): *I feel rather overdressed in this suit — everyone else is wearing jeans!* 我觉得穿这身西服太讲究了——别人全都穿牛仔裤!

over·drive /ˈəʊvədraɪv; ˋovɚˌdraɪv/ *n* **1** [U] mechanism providing an extra gear above the normal top gear in a vehicle（车辆中的）加速传动装置, 加速挡. **2** (idm 习语) **go into ˈoverdrive** use the overdrive mechanism 使用加速挡: (*fig* 比喻) *She always goes into overdrive* (ie starts working very hard) *before the holidays.* 她总是在放假前特别努力.

over·due /ˌəʊvəˈdjuː; *US* -ˈduː; ˋovɚˋdu/ *adj* [usu pred 通常作表语] not paid, completed, arrived, etc by the due or expected time（到期或到时）未付款, 未完成, 未到达: *These bills are overdue*, ie should have been paid before now. 这些帐单已逾期未付. ○ *The baby is two weeks overdue*, ie still not born two weeks after the expected date of birth. 那胎儿已超过预产期两个星期了. ○ *The train is overdue*, ie late. 火车误点了.

over·eat /ˌəʊvərˈiːt; ˋovɚˋit/ *v* (*pt* **overate** /-ˈet; -ˋet/, *pp* **overeaten** /-ˈiːtn; -ˋitn̩/) [I] eat more than one needs or more than is healthy 吃得过多: *I overate at the party last night and got violent indigestion.* 昨日晚宴我吃多了, 严重消化不良. ○ *Obese people find it difficult to stop overeating.* 胖人觉得一吃就过量, 难以控制.

over·es·tim·ate /ˌəʊvərˈestɪmeɪt; ˋovɚˋɛstəˌmet/ *v* [Tn] estimate (sth) to be bigger, higher, better, etc than it is 过高估计(某事物): *I overestimated the amount of milk we'd need for the weekend.* 我过高估计了我们周末的用奶量. ○ *I overestimated his abilities — he's finding the job very difficult.* 我过高估计了他的能力——现在他觉得工作非常困难. Cf 参看 UNDERESTIMATE.

over·ex·pose /ˌəʊvərɪkˈspəʊz; ˋovərɪkˋspoz/ *v* [Tn esp passive 尤用于被动语态] expose (a film, etc) for too long or in too bright a light（胶片等）曝光过度. Cf 参看 UNDEREXPOSE. ▷ **over·ex·pos·ure** *n* [U].

over·flow /ˌəʊvəˈfləʊ; ˌovɚˋflo/ *v* **1** [I, Tn] flow over the edges or limits of (sth) 从(某物)中溢出: *Your bath is overflowing.* 你澡盆里的水都溢出来了. ○ *The river overflowed (its banks).* 河水泛滥(溢过堤岸)了. ⇨illus at OVERLAP 见OVERLAP插图. **2** [I, Ipr, Tn] **~ (into sth)** spread beyond the limits of (a room, etc) 扩展到(房间等)的范围以外: *The meeting overflowed into the streets.* 与会者太多, 会场扩大到街上了. ○ *The audience easily overflowed the small theatre.* 这小剧院很快就已经盛不下观众了. **3** [Ipr] **~ with sth** be more than filled with sth; be very full of sth 充满或洋溢某事物: *overflowing with happiness, kindness, gratitude, etc* 充满幸福、善意、感激等 ○ *a heart overflowing with love* 充满爱的心.

▷ **over·flow** /ˈəʊvəfləʊ; ˋovɚˌflo/ *n* **1** [U] **(a)** flowing over of liquid 溢出: *stop the overflow from the cistern* 止住水使之不再从水箱溢出. **(b)** that which overflows 溢出物: *Put a bowl underneath to catch the overflow.* 把盆放在下面接住溢出物. ○ [attrib 作定语] *an overflow canal* 泛滥的运河. **2** [U, sing] something that is too much for the space available 容纳不下的人或事物: *a large overflow of population from the cities* 从城市外流的大批人 ○ *find a smaller hall for the overflow from the main meeting* 找个小礼堂容纳主会场盛不下的人. **3** [C] (also ˈ**overflow pipe**) outlet that allows excess liquid to escape 溢流管: *The overflow from the bath is blocked.* 浴盆的溢流管堵塞了.

over·fly /ˌəʊvəˈflaɪ; ˌovɚˋflaɪ/ *v* (*pt* **overflew** /-ˈfluː; -ˋflu/, *pp* **overflown** /-ˈfləʊn; -ˋflon/) [Tn] fly over (a city, country, etc) 飞越, 飞过(一城市、国家等): *The journey back took longer than normal, because the plane could not overfly the war zone.* 回程用的时间比平时长, 因为飞机不能飞越战区.

over·grown /ˌəʊvəˈgrəʊn; ˋovɚˋgron/ *adj* **1** [usu attrib 通常作定语] having grown too large or too fast 长得太大或太快的: *That man behaves like an ˌovergrown ˈchild.* 那男子一举一动像个大孩子. **2** [pred 作表语] **~ (with sth)** covered with (plants, weeds, etc that have grown too thickly in an uncontrolled way)（野草等）蔓生: *walls overgrown with ivy* 爬满长春藤的墙 ○ *The garden's completely overgrown (with nettles).* 花园里长满了(荨麻科)植物.

over·growth /ˈəʊvəgrəʊθ; ˋovɚˌgroθ/ *n* **1** [U, C] plants, weeds, etc growing in an uncontrolled way 滋蔓生长物: *an overgrowth of nettles* 蔓生的荨麻. **2** /ˌəʊvəˈgrəʊθ; ˋovɚˌgroθ/ [U] growth that is too fast or too much 生长太快; 生长过度: *Overgrowth is common in adolescents.* 青少年成长过快是普遍现象.

over·hang /ˌəʊvəˈhæŋ; ˌovɚˋhæŋ/ *v* (*pt, pp* **overhung** /-ˈhʌŋ; -ˋhʌŋ/) [I, Tn] hang over or stand out over (sth) like a shelf 悬于或突出于(某物)之上: *The ledge overhangs by several feet.* 壁架凌空伸出几英尺. ○ *The cliff overhangs the beach.* 悬崖俯临着海滩.

▷ **over·hang** /ˈəʊvəhæŋ; ˋovɚˌhæŋ/ *n* part that overhangs 悬垂的部分: *a bird's nest under the overhang of the roof* 房檐下的鸟巢.

over·haul /ˌəʊvəˈhɔːl; ˌovɚˋhɔl/ *v* [Tn] **1** examine (sth) carefully and thoroughly and make any necessary repairs 彻底检修(某物): *have the engine of a car overhauled* 检修汽车的发动机 ○ (*fig* 比喻) *The language syllabus needs to be completely overhauled.* 那个语言教学大纲需全面修订. **2** catch up with and overtake (sth) 追上并超过(某事物): *The fast cruiser soon overhauled the old cargo boat.* 快速巡逻艇迅即赶上那艘旧货船.

▷ **over·haul** /ˈəʊvəhɔːl; ˋovɚˌhɔl/ *n* thorough examination followed by any necessary repairs 彻底检修; 大修: *I've taken my typewriter in for an overhaul.* 我已把打字机拿去彻底检修了. ○ *The engine is due for an overhaul.* 那台发动机该大修了. ○ (*infml joc* 口, 谑) *I'm going to the doctor for my annual overhaul*, ie physical examination. 我要到医生那里作年度身体检查.

over·head /ˈəʊvəhed; ˋovɚˌhɛd/ *adj* **1** raised above the ground; above one's head 离地面的; 头顶上的; 上空的: *overhead wires, cables, etc* 架空线、缆等 ○ *an overhead railway*, ie built on a level higher than the street 高架铁路. **2** of or relating to overheads（企业的）经费的: *overhead expenses, charges, etc* 经费的开支、应付款项等.

▷ **over·head** /ˌəʊvəˈhed; ˋovɚˋhɛd/ *adv* above one's head; in the sky 在头顶上; 在空中: *the stars overhead* 天上的星星 ○ *birds flying overhead* 空中的飞鸟.

over·heads /ˈəʊvəhedz; ˋovɚˋhɛdz/ *n* [pl] regular expenses involved in running a business, eg rent, light, heating, salaries（企业等的）经费(如房租、电费、取暖费、薪金): *Heavy overheads reduced his profits.* 经费开销大因而减少了他的利润. ○ *If you move to a smaller office you will reduce your overheads.* 搬到小一些的办公室可以节省开支.

over·hear /ˌəʊvəˈhɪə(r); ˌovɚˋhɪr/ *v* (*pt, pp* **overheard** /-ˈhɜːd; -ˋhɝd/) [Tn, Tng, Tni] hear (sb, a conversation, etc) without the knowledge of the speaker(s); hear by chance 偷听到(某人说话、谈话等); 无意中听到: *I overheard their argument/them.* 我偷听到他们争论[他们说话]. ○ *I overheard them quarrelling.* 我无意中听到他们吵架. ○ *I overheard him say/saying he was going to France.* 我偶然听到他说他要到法国去.

over·joyed /ˌəʊvəˈdʒɔɪd; ˋovɚˋdʒɔɪd/ *adj* [usu pred 通常作表语] **~ (at sth/to do sth)** filled with great happiness 极欣喜; 极高兴: *He'll be overjoyed at your news.* 他一定对你的消息大喜过望. ○ *She was overjoyed to hear about the arrival of the baby.* 她听说婴儿出生而欣喜若狂.

over·kill /ˈəʊvəkɪl; ˋovɚˌkɪl/ *n* [U] (*usu fig* 通常作比喻) much greater amount than is needed to defeat sb/sth or achieve sth（为战胜某人[某事物]或达到某目的之）过火行动: *It was surely overkill to screen three interviews on the same subject in one evening.* 一晚放映三个同一主题的访问记实, 真是小题大做.

over·land /ˈəʊvəlænd; ˋovɚˌlænd/ *adj* across the land; by land (not by sea or air) 横越陆地的; 经由陆路的(非航海或航空): *an overland route, journey, etc* 陆上的路线、旅行等. ▷ **over·land** *adv*: *travel overland* 陆上旅行.

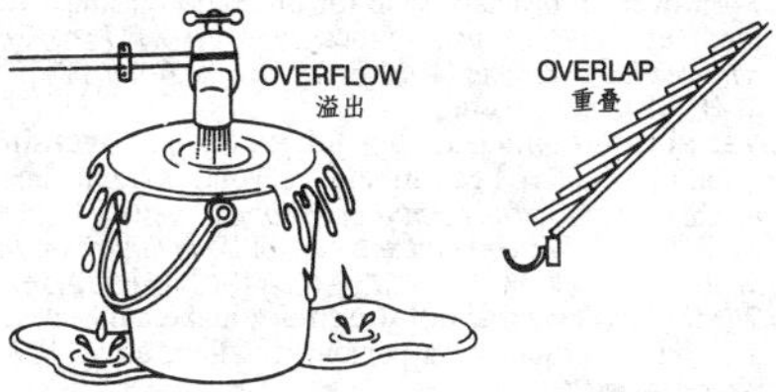

over·lap /ˌəʊvəˈlæp; ˌovɚˋlæp/ *v* (**-pp-**) [I, Tn] **1** partly cover (sth) by extending over its edge (与某物)部分重叠: *a boat made of overlapping boards* 用鱼鳞板材造的船 ○ *The tiles on the roof overlap one another.* 房上的瓦是一块搭着一块的. **2** (*fig* 比喻) partly coincide (with sth) 部分(和某事物)巧合、一致: *Our visits to the town overlapped.* 我们彼此都恰巧到那小城观光. ○ *His duties and mine overlap*, ie cover part of the same area of interest. 他的职责和我的有部分重叠.

▷ **over·lap** /ˈəʊvəlæp; ˋovɚˌlæp/ *n* **1** [C] overlapping part or amount 重叠的部分或程度: *an overlap of 50 cm* 50厘米的重叠部分 ○ *a large overlap* 大部分重合. **2** [U] fact or process of overlapping 重叠; 重合; 重复: *There is no question of overlap between the two courses.* 这两门课程之间不存在重叠的问题. ⇨illus 见插图.

over·lay /ˌəʊvəˈleɪ; ˌovɚˋle/ *v* (*pt, pp* **overlaid** /-ˈleɪd; -ˋled/) [usu passive 通常用于被动语态: Tn, Tn·pr] **~ sth (with sth)** put a thin layer over the surface of (sth) 在(某物)表面上铺一薄层: *wood overlaid with gold* 敷金箔的木 ○ *He overlaid the walls with hessian.* 他在墙上贴了一层麻布.

▷ **over·lay** /ˈəʊvəleɪ; ˋovɚˌle/ *n* thing laid over sth 覆盖物: *a table covered with a copper overlay* 包铜桌子.

over·leaf /ˌəʊvəˈliːf; ˋovɚˋlif/ *adv* on the other side of the page (of a book, etc) 在(书等的)某页的另一面、后面、背面或下一页: *see picture overleaf*, ie as an instruction to the reader 见次页图.

over·load /ˌəʊvəˈləʊd; ˌovɚˋlod/ *v* [esp passive 尤用于被动语态: Tn, Tn·pr] **~ sth (with sth)** **1** put too great a load on or into (sth) 使(某物)装载过重: *The donkey was so overloaded, it could hardly climb the hill.* 那驴负载过重, 几乎爬不过岗. **2** put too great an electric charge into (a circuit, etc) 使(电路等)超负荷: *The lights fused because the system was overloaded with electrical appliances.* 电灯灭了, 因线路上用电器超负荷把保险丝烧断了.

over·look /ˌəʊvəˈlʊk; ˌovɚˋlʊk/ *v* [Tn] **1** have or give a view of (a place) from above 俯瞰, 俯视(某处): *My room overlooks the sea.* 从我的房间可眺望大海. ○ *We overlook the church from our house.* 我们可从家中俯瞰教堂. ○ *Our garden is overlooked by our neighbours' windows*, ie They can see into our garden from their windows. 从邻居的窗户可看到我家的花园. **2** (**a**) fail to see or notice (sth); miss 未看到, 未注意到(某事物): *He overlooked a spelling error on the first page.* 他没有看出第一页中有个拼写错误. (**b**) take no (official) notice of (sb/sth); ignore 忽视, 忽略(某人[某事物]); 不理会: *He was overlooked* (ie He was not considered for the job) *when they set about choosing a new manager.* 选任新经理时没有考虑他. ○ *We can afford to overlook minor offences.* 我们可以不计较小过. ○ *She overlooked his rudeness and tried to pretend nothing had happened.* 她没有理会他的粗鲁举动, 竭力装作若无其事的样子.

over·lord /ˈəʊvəlɔːd; ˋovɚˌlɔrd/ *n* (formerly) nobleman on whose land people of lower rank worked (旧时的)领主, 大地主: *a feudal overlord* 封建领主 ○ *The peasants owed service and obedience to their overlord.* 农民不得不俯首贴耳为地主效劳.

overly /ˈəʊvəlɪ; ˋovɚlɪ/ *adv* (*fml esp Scot or US* 文, 尤用于苏格兰或美国) (before an *adj* or a *v* 用于形容词或动词之前) too; excessively 太; 过度: *overly cautious* 过于谨慎 ○ *I am not overly impressed by his work.* 我认为他的作品不太出色. Cf 参看 OVER-.

over·manned /ˌəʊvəˈmænd; ˌovɚˋmænd/ *adj* (of a factory, etc) having more workers than are needed to do the work that needs to be done (指工厂等)人手过多的, 人浮于事的: *Management decided the office was overmanned and sacked three junior typists.* 管理部门认为办公室人浮于事, 于是裁去了三名级别低的打字员. Cf 参看 OVERSTAFFED, UNDERMANNED. ▷ **over·man·ning** /ˌəʊvəˈmænɪŋ; ˌovɚˋmænɪŋ/ *n* [U]: *Overmanning can be a serious problem in industry.* 工业中人员超编可产生严重问题.

over·mas·ter·ing /ˌəʊvəˈmɑːstərɪŋ; *US* -ˈmæs-; ˌovɚˋmæstərɪŋ/ *adj* [esp attrib 尤作定语] (*fml or rhet* 文或修辞) overpowering; overwhelming 压倒; 征服: *an overmastering passion*, ie one that is difficult to control 难以抑制的热情.

over-much /ˌəʊvəˈmʌtʃ; ˋovɚˋmʌtʃ/ *adj, adv* (*fml* 文) (esp with a negative *v* 尤与动词否定式连用) too much; very much 太多(的); 过多(的); 过度(的): *His book did not display ˌover-much ˈtalent.* 他写的这本书没有什么文采. ○ *I do not like her over-much.* 我不太喜欢她.

over·night /ˌəʊvəˈnaɪt; ˋovɚˋnaɪt/ *adv* **1** during or for the night 在晚上; 在夜里: *stay overnight at a friend's house*, ie sleep there for the night 在朋友家过夜. **2** (*infml* 口) suddenly or very quickly 突然; 很快: *She became a celebrity overnight.* 她一下子成了名人了.

▷ **over·night** /ˈəʊvənaɪt; ˋovɚˋnaɪt/ *adj* [attrib 作定语] **1** during or for the night 晚上的; 夜里的: *an overnight journey* 夜间旅行 ○ *an overnight bag* 装过夜用品的旅行袋 ○ *an overnight stop in Rome* 在罗马停留一夜. **2** (*infml* 口) suddenly; very quickly 突然的; 很快的: *an overnight success* 突然间的成功.

over·pass /ˈəʊvəpɑːs; *US* -pæs; ˋovɚˌpæs/ *n* (*esp US*) (*Brit* also **flyover** /ˈflaɪəʊvə(r); ˋflaɪˌovɚ/) bridge that carries a road over a motorway 立体交叉桥; 立交桥. Cf 参看 UNDERPASS.

over·pay /ˌəʊvəˈpeɪ; ˋovɚˋpe/ *v* (*pt, pp* **overpaid** /-ˈpeɪd; -ˋped/) [Tn, Tn·pr] **~ sb (for sth)** pay sb too much or too highly 付给某人太多或太高: *They don't exactly overpay their work-force.* 他们给工人的报酬并非过高. ○ *I think he's overpaid for the little he does.* 我认为他干得很少而所得过多. Cf 参看 UNDERPAY.

over·play /ˌəʊvəˈpleɪ; ˌovɚˋple/ *v* **1** [Tn] give too much importance to (sth) 过分重视(某事物): *overplay certain factors* 过分看重某些因素 ○ *You must not overplay his part in the negotiations.* 你不可过高估计他在谈判中的作用. Cf 参看 UNDERPLAY. **2** (idm 习语) **overplay one's ˈhand** take too great or too many risks (by overestimating one's own strength) (因过高估计自己的力量)冒风险: *The union is in danger of overplaying its hand in the current dispute.* 工会在目前纠纷中高估自己实力有失败之虞.

over·power /ˌəʊvəˈpaʊə(r); ˌovɚˋpaʊɚ/ *v* [Tn] be too strong or powerful for (sb); defeat (sb) by greater strength or numbers 强得使(某人)承受不住; 以力量或数量胜(某人): *The burglars were easily overpowered by the police.* 警方轻而易举制服了窃贼. ○ *He was overpowered by the heat.* 他热得受不了了.

▷ **over·powering** /ˌəʊvəˈpaʊərɪŋ; ˌovɚˋpaʊərɪŋ/ *adj* too strong; very powerful 太强的; 力量极大的: *find the smell overpowering* 觉得气味难忍 ○ *overpowering grief* 难以承受的悲伤.

over·print /ˌəʊvəˈprɪnt; ˌovɚˋprɪnt/ *v* (**a**) [Tn, Tn·pr] **~ sth (with sth)** print additional matter on (an already printed surface, eg a postage stamp) 在(印刷品, 如邮票)上加印: *overprint stamps with a new price* 在邮票上加印新值. (**b**) [I, Ipr, Tn, Tn·pr] **~ (sth) (on sth)** print (additional matter) in this way 加印; 加盖: *Additional material is overprinted in red.* 附加材料是用红色加印上的. ○ *overprint a grid on a map* 在地图上加印座标格.

▷ **over·print** /ˈəʊvəprɪnt; ˋovɚˌprɪnt/ *n* (*fml* 文) thing overprinted 加印的图文.

over·rate /ˌəʊvəˈreɪt; ˋovɚˋret/ *v* [Tn esp passive 尤用于被动语态] have too high an opinion of (sb/sth); put too high a value on 对(某人[某事物])评价过高: *I think I overrated him; he can't handle a senior job.* 我看我对他估计过高了, 他胜任不了高职位的工作. ○ *He overrated his abilities as a salesman.* 他对自己当推销员的能力评价过高. Cf 参看 UNDERRATE.

▷ **over·rated** *adj* (*derog* 贬) having too high a value placed on it 评价过高的: *I think his work is extremely overrated.* 我认为对他的工作评价实在太高了. ○ *an overrated film* 评价过高的影片.

O

over·reach /ˌəʊvəˈriːtʃ; ˌovɚˈritʃ/ *v* [Tn no passive 不用于被动语态] **~ oneself** (*esp derog* 尤作贬义) fail by trying to achieve more than is possible 做不可能做到的事而失败: *Don't apply for that job: you're in danger of overreaching yourself.* 不要申请那份工作, 以免有不自量力之嫌.

over-react /ˌəʊvərɪˈækt; ˌovɚrɪˈækt/ *v* [I, Ipr] **~ (to sth)** react too strongly or too intensely to difficulty, danger, etc (对困难、危险等)反应过火或过激: *She tends to over-react when things go wrong.* 事情一有差错她往往反应过激. ○ *He over-reacted to the bad news.* 他对那则坏消息反应过于强烈. ▷ **over-reaction** /-ˈækʃn; -ˈækʃən/ *n* [U, C]: *The stock-market panic was simply over-reaction to the news from Tokyo.* 股市上那场惊惶纯粹是对东京消息的过敏反应.

over·ride /ˌəʊvəˈraɪd; ˌovɚˈraɪd/ *v* (*pt* **overrode** /-ˈrəʊd; -ˈrod/, *pp* **overridden** /-ˈrɪdn; -ˈrɪdn̩/) [Tn] **1** disregard or set aside (sb's opinions, etc) 不顾, 不理会(某人意见等): *override sb's views, decisions, wishes, etc* 无视某人的看法、决定、愿望等 ○ *They overrode my protest and continued with the meeting.* 他们不顾我的抗议仍继续开会. **2** be more important than (sth) 比(某事物)更重要: *Considerations of safety override all other concerns.* 对安全的考虑压倒一切.

▷ **over·rid·ing** /ˌəʊvəˈraɪdɪŋ; ˌovɚˈraɪdɪŋ/ *adj* [usu attrib 通常作定语] more important than any other considerations 首要的: *It is of overriding importance to finish the project this week.* 最重要的是本星期要完成这一项目.

over·rule /ˌəʊvəˈruːl; ˌovɚˈrul/ *v* [Tn] decide against (something already decided, etc) by exercising one's higher authority 否决, 驳回(某决定): *overrule a claim, objection, etc* 驳回某项要求、异议等 ○ *The judge overruled the previous decision.* 法官宣布撤销原判. ○ *We were overruled by the majority.* 我们的意见被多数人否决了.

over·run /ˌəʊvəˈrʌn; ˌovɚˈrʌn/ *v* (*pt* **overran** /-ˈræn; -ˈræn/, *pp* **overrun**) **1** [Tn esp passive 尤用于被动语态] spread over and occupy (a place) in great numbers 扩展并占领(一地): *a country overrun by enemy troops* 被敌军占领的国家 ○ *a warehouse overrun by rats* 老鼠肆虐的货栈. **2** [I, Tn] continue beyond or exceed (a time allowed, etc) 超过, 超越(时限等): *The lecturer overran by ten minutes.* 演讲人超过规定时间十分钟. ○ *The news programme overran the allotted time.* 新闻节目超出了规定的时间.

over·seas /ˌəʊvəˈsiːz; ˈovɚˈsiz/ *adj* (at, to, from, etc places or countries) across the sea; foreign (在、向、来自等)海外的, 国外的: *ˌoverseas ˈtrade* 海外贸易 ○ *an ˌoverseas ˈbroadcast* 对外广播 ○ *overseas students in Britain* 在英国的外国留学生.

▷ **over·seas** *adv* across the sea; abroad 到海外; 在国外: *go, live, travel, etc overseas* 到海外去、生活、旅行等.

over·see /ˌəʊvəˈsiː; ˌovɚˈsi/ *v* (*pt* **oversaw** /-ˈsɔː; -ˈsɔ/, *pp* **overseen** /-ˈsiːn; -ˈsin/) [Tn] watch over and control (sb/sth); supervise 监督, 监视(某人[某事物]): *You must employ someone to oversee the project.* 你得雇个人监督这一工程.

▷ **over·seer** /ˈəʊvəsɪə(r); ˈovɚˌsɪr/ *n* person whose job is to take charge of work and see that it is properly done 监工; 监督者: *the production overseer* 生产监督 ○ *The overseer was explaining the job to young trainees.* 监工向年轻的实习工讲解工作情况.

over-sexed /ˌəʊvəˈsekst; ˌovɚˈsɛkst/ *adj* having greater sexual desire than is usual; obsessed by sex 性欲比通常旺盛的; 耽于性事的. Cf 参看 UNDER-SEXED.

over·shadow /ˌəʊvəˈʃædəʊ; ˌovɚˈʃædo/ *v* [Tn] **1** cause (sth) to be shaded or to have little light 使(某物)被遮暗; 使阴暗: *a village overshadowed by mountains* 被山影笼罩的村庄 ○ *Large oak trees overshadow the garden.* 高大的栎树把花园遮得很暗. **2** (*fig* 比喻) cause (sth) to be unhappy or less happy 使(某事物)令人不快或减少乐趣: *His recent death overshadowed the family gathering.* 他最近去世了, 这给家庭聚会蒙上了阴影. **3** (*fig* 比喻) cause (sb) to seem less important or noticeable 使(某人)相形见绌或黯然失色: *Despite her professional success, she was always overshadowed by her husband.* 尽管她事业有成, 但和丈夫相比总觉逊色.

over·shoe /ˈəʊvəʃuː; ˈovɚˌʃu/ *n* rubber or plastic shoe worn over an ordinary shoe for protection against wet, mud, etc 套鞋: *a pair of overshoes* 一双套鞋 ○ *She removed her overshoes at the front door.* 她在前门脱下了套鞋. Cf 参看 GALOSHES.

over·shoot /ˌəʊvəˈʃuːt; ˌovɚˈʃut/ *v* (*pt, pp* **overshot** /-ˈʃɒt; -ˈʃɑt/) [Tn] **1** go further or beyond (a point aimed at) 超过(目标): *The aircraft overshot the runway.* 飞机冲出了跑道. ○ *We overshot the exit for Manchester on the motorway.* 我们错过了通往曼彻斯特的高速公路路口. **2** (idm 习语) **overshoot the ˈmark** make a mistake as a result of misjudging a person, situation, etc 对某人、情况等判断错误.

over·sight /ˈəʊvəsaɪt; ˈovɚˌsaɪt/ *n* (**a**) [U] unintentional failure to notice sth 疏忽; 失察: *Many errors are caused by oversight.* 有很多错误都是因疏忽造成的. (**b**) [C] example of this 疏忽; 失察: *Through an unfortunate oversight your letter was left unanswered.* 因不慎疏忽未能给你复信.

over-simplify /ˌəʊvəˈsɪmplɪfaɪ; ˌovɚˈsɪmpləˌfaɪ/ *v* (*pt, pp* **-fied** /-faɪd; -faɪd/) [I, Tn esp passive 尤用于被动语态] state or explain (a problem, fact, etc) too simply for the truth to be told 叙述或说明(一问题、事实等)过于简单: *an over-simplified analysis of the problems we face* 对我们面临的问题所做的简单化的分析 ○ *an over-simplified interpretation of the reasons for the child's behaviour* 对这个孩子表现出这种行为的原因做出的过于简单化的解释.

▷ **over-simplification** /ˌəʊvəˌsɪmplɪfɪˈkeɪʃn; ˌovɚˌsɪmpləfəˈkeʃən/ *n* [C, U] (instance of) over-simplifying 过于简单的叙述或说明.

over·sleep /ˌəʊvəˈsliːp; ˈovɚˈslip/ *v* (*pt, pp* **overslept** /-ˈslept; -ˈslɛpt/) [I] sleep longer or later than one intended 睡得太久; 睡过头: *I'm afraid I overslept and missed my usual bus.* 很遗憾我睡过头了, 误了我通常坐的那班公共汽车.

over·spill /ˈəʊvəspɪl; ˈovɚˌspɪl/ *n* [U] (*esp Brit*) people from the overcrowded parts of a city, etc who are provided with housing, usu of a better standard, in the surrounding areas 迁出市区的过剩人口(通常为他们提供附近较好的住房): *build new houses for London's overspill* 为伦敦市过剩人口建新居 ○ [attrib 作定语] *an overspill housing development* 城市过剩人口住房开发.

over·staffed /ˌəʊvəˈstɑːft; *US* -ˈstæft; ˌovɚˈstæft/ *adj* (of an office, etc) having more members of staff than are needed for the work to be done (指办公室等)超编的, 人浮于事的: *No wonder the firm makes a loss; the office is terribly overstaffed.* 难怪公司亏损, 办公室严重超编. Cf 参看 OVERMANNED, UNDERSTAFFED.

over·state /ˌəʊvəˈsteɪt; ˈovɚˈstet/ *v* [Tn] express or state (sth) too strongly; exaggerate 夸大(某事); 言过其实: *Don't overstate your case or no one will believe you.* 不要夸大自己的情况, 要不没人相信你的话. ○ *The problems have been greatly overstated.* 问题过于夸大了.

▷ **over·state·ment** /ˈəʊvəsteɪtmənt; ˈovɚˈstetmənt/ *n* **1** [U] action of overstating; exaggeration 夸大; 言过其实. **2** [C] exaggerated statement 夸张的叙述: *a wild overstatement of the facts* 对事实过分夸张的叙述.

over·stay /ˌəʊvəˈsteɪ; ˈovɚˈste/ *v* **1** [Tn] stay longer than (a period of time) 呆得超过(某期限): *We've already overstayed our visit to Aunt Sophie.* 我们看望索菲姨妈逗留的时间太长了. **2** (idm 习语) **outstay/overstay one's welcome** ⇨ WELCOME.

over·step /ˌəʊvəˈstep; ˌovɚˈstɛp/ *v* (**-pp-**) [Tn] **1** go beyond (what is normal or permitted) 超越(正常或容许的范围): *overstep one's authority* 越权. ○ *overstep the bounds of modesty* 谦逊过头. **2** (idm 习语) **overstep the ˈmark** do or say more than one should or more than is wise or acceptable; go too far 做得或说得过分; 超出限度: *It's surely overstepping the mark to behave so rudely to your guests.* 你对客人如此粗鲁真太离谱了.

over·stock /ˌəʊvəˈstɒk; ˌovɚˈstɑk/ *v* [Tn, Tn·pr] **~ sth (with sth)** supply sth with too large a stock 向某处供给过多的存货: a shop overstocked with *out-of-date furniture* 存有过多过时家具的商店 ○ *overstock a farm with cattle*, ie with more cattle than there is food or space for 使农场的牛存栏过多(饲料或空间不足).

over·strung *adj* **1** /ˌəʊvəˈstrʌŋ; ˈovɚˈstrʌŋ/ (of a person) too sensitive and nervous; easily excited(指人)太敏感而紧张的, 易激动的 : *She was tense and* *overstrung before the performance.* 她在演出前过于紧张. **2** /ˈəʊvəstrʌŋ; ˈovɚˈstrʌŋ/ (of a piano) with strings in sets crossing each other at an oblique angle (指钢琴)琴弦斜向交叉的.

over-subscribe /ˌəʊvəsəbˈskraɪb; ˈovɚsəbˈskraɪb/ *v* [Tn esp passive 尤用于被动语态] (*esp finance* 尤用于财政、金融) apply for more of (an issue of shares, tickets, etc) than are available 认购, 订购(股票、票等)超过供应量: *Tickets for this concert have been over-subscribed.* 这个音乐会门票预订已超额. ○ *The flight has been over-subscribed; there are no seats.* 该航班订票已逾限额, 没有座位了.

overt /ˈəʊvɜːt; *US* əʊˈvɜːrt; oˈvɝt/ *adj* [usu attrib 通常作定语] (*fml* 文) done or shown openly or publicly; not secret or hidden 公开的; 不隐秘的: *overt hostility* 公开的敌意. Cf 参看 COVERT. ▷ **overtly** *adv* (*fml* 文): *overtly critical of his work* 公开批评他的作品.

over·take /ˌəʊvəˈteɪk; ˌovɚˈtek/ *v* (*pt* **overtook** /-ˈtʊk; -ˈtʊk/ *pp* **overtaken** /-ˈteɪkən; -ˈtekən/) **1** [I, Tn] come level with and pass (esp a moving person or vehicle) 追上, 超越(尤指运动着的人或车): *It's dangerous to overtake on a bend.* 在转弯处超车十分危险. ○ *overtake other cars on the road* 在路上超越其他汽车 ○ (*fig* 比喻) *Supply will soon overtake demand*, ie There will soon be more of sth than is needed. 供很快就要过于求. ○ *Italy's economy has overtaken that of its nearest competitors.* 意大利的经济已超过其最接近的几个竞争者. **2** [Tn esp passive 尤用于被动语态] (of unpleasant events) come to (sb/sth) suddenly and unexpectedly(指不愉快的事情)突然降临(某人[某事物]): *be overtaken by/with fear, surprise, etc* 不胜恐惧、惊奇等 ○ *be overtaken by events*, ie by circumstances changing so rapidly that plans, etc become out of date 受意外事情影响(情况剧变以致计划过时等) ○ *Disaster overtook the project.* 工程为突发灾难所阻. ○ *On his way home he was overtaken by a storm.* 他在回家的路上遭遇暴风雨.

over·tax /ˌəʊvəˈtæks; ˈovɚˈtæks/ *v* [Tn] **1** (*fml* 文) put too great a strain on (sb/sth)使(某人[某事物])负担过重、受过重压力: *overtax one's strength* 用力过度 ○ *overtax sb's patience* 使某人失去耐性. **2** make (sb) pay too much tax; tax too heavily 对(某人)课税过重: *If you have been overtaxed you will get a tax rebate*, ie money will be paid back to you. 若被课税过重, 可得到退还的税款.

over·throw /ˌəʊvəˈθrəʊ; ˌovɚˈθro/ *v* (*pt* **overthrew** /-ˈθruː; -ˈθru/, *pp* **overthrown** /-ˈθrəʊn; -ˈθron/) [Tn] cause the downfall or defeat of (sb/sth); put an end to 推翻, 打倒(某人[某事物]); 使终止或结束: *The rebels tried to overthrow the government.* 叛乱者企图推翻政府.

over·throw /ˈəʊvəθrəʊ; ˈovɚˌθro/ *n* **1** [C usu *sing* 通常作单数] act of overthrowing; defeat推翻; 打倒; 终止; 结束: *the overthrow of the monarchy* 君主政体的覆灭 ○ *the attempted overthrow of the tyrant* 推翻暴君的尝试. **2** [C] (in cricket) throw of the ball by a fielder which goes too far, esp when this results in an extra score for the batsman (板球中)守场员掷球过远(尤指导致击球员得分者).

over·time /ˈəʊvətaɪm; ˈovɚˌtaɪm/ *n* [U] *adv* (time spent at work) after the usual working hours 加班; 加班时间; 在加班时间内; 超时地: *working overtime* 加班工作 ○ *be paid extra for overtime* 因加班获额外付酬 ○ [attrib 作定语] *overtime payments* 加班费 ○ *be on overtime*, ie working overtime 加班工作.

over·tone /ˈəʊvətəʊn; ˈovɚˌton/ *n* (usu *pl* 通常作复数) something suggested or implied in addition to what is actually stated; hint 暗示; 含义; 弦外之音: *overtones of despair in a letter* 信中字里行间的绝望之意 ○ *threatening overtones in his comments* 他在评论中的威胁意味. Cf 参看 UNDERTONE.

over·ture /ˈəʊvətjʊə(r); ˈovɚˌtʃʊr/ *n* **1** [C usu *pl* 通常作复数] **~ (to sb)** (*fml* 文) friendly approach, proposal or offer made (to sb) with the aim of starting discussions (向某人做出的)友好表示、姿态或提议: *overtures of peace to the enemy* 向敌方提议和谈 ○ *make overtures of friendship to the new neighbours* 对新邻居表示友好. **2** [C] piece of music written as an introduction to an opera, a ballet, a musical play, etc (歌剧、芭蕾舞、音乐剧等的)序曲, 前奏曲: *The audience must be in their seats before the overture.* 观众务必于序曲演奏前入座.

over·turn /ˌəʊvəˈtɜːn; ˌovɚˈtɝn/ *v* **1** [I, Tn] (cause sb/sth to) turn over or upside-down; upset (使某人[某物])翻转, 颠倒, 倾覆, 翻倒: *The boat overturned.* 船翻了. ○ *He overturned the boat.* 他把船弄翻了. ○ (*fig* 比喻) *The Labour candidate overturned the previous Conservative majority of 4 000.* 工党候选人击败了保守党人前次多获4 000票的优势而获胜. ○ (*fig* 比喻) *The House of Lords overturned* (ie reversed) *the decision by the House of Commons.* 上议院撤销了下议院的决定. **2** [Tn] cause the downfall of (esp a government); overthrow 使垮台(尤指政府); 推翻: *overturn the military regime* 推翻军政权.

over·view /ˈəʊvəvjuː; ˈovɚˌvju/ *n* (*fml* 文) short general description (without unnecessary details); survey综览; 概观; 概述: *an overview of the company's plans for the next year* 公司下年度计划概述.

over·ween·ing /ˌəʊvəˈwiːnɪŋ; ˈovɚˈwinɪŋ/ *adj* [attrib 作定语] (*fml* 文) showing too much self-confidence or conceit 过于自信的; 自负的; 傲慢的: *overweening ambition, vanity, pride etc* 自负的雄心、虚荣、骄傲等.

over·weight /ˌəʊvəˈweɪt; ˈovɚˈwet/ *adj* **1** heavier than is usual or allowed 超重的; 过重的: *If your luggage is overweight you'll have to pay extra.* 行李超重需额外付费. ○ *Your suitcase is five kilograms overweight.* 你的衣箱超重五公斤. **2** (of people) too heavy; fat (指人)体重超常的, 肥胖的: *an ˌoverweight ˈchild* 过胖的孩子 ○ *I'm overweight by 2kg according to my doctor.* 据医生说, 我超重2公斤. ○ *He's very overweight.* 他很胖. Cf 参看 UNDERWEIGHT. ⇨Usage at FAT[1] 用法见 FAT[1].

▷ **over·weighted** /ˌəʊvəˈweɪtɪd; ˈovɚˈwetɪd/ *adj* **~ (with sth)** (*fml* 文) carrying too much (of sth) 超载的; 载物太多的: *overweighted with packages* 因包裹过重而超载的 ○ (*fig* 比喻) *Her lecture was overweighted with quotations.* 她的演讲引文太多.

over·whelm /ˌəʊvəˈwelm; *US* -ˈhwelm; ˌovɚˈhwɛlm/ *v* [Tn usu passive 通常用于被动语态] (**a**) cover (sth/sb) completely by flowing over or pouring down on it/him; submerge suddenly (以浇或灌的方式)淹没(某物[某人]); 使突然没入或浸入: *overwhelmed by a flood* 被洪水淹没的 ○ *A great mass of water overwhelmed the village.* 大水淹没了村庄. ○ (*fig* 比喻) *be overwhelmed with grief, sorrow, despair, etc* 陷入悲哀、悲痛、绝望等之中 ○ (*fig* 比喻) *Overwhelmed with gratitude, he fell to his knees.* 他感激万分, 跪倒地上. (**b**) overpower (sb/sth), esp by force of numbers; defeat 压倒, 制服(某人[某事物])(尤指以数量胜); 击败: *be overwhelmed by the enemy/by superior forces* 被敌军[优势兵力]击溃.

▷**over·whelm·ing** *adj* [usu attrib 通常作定语] too great to resist or overcome; very great 压倒一切的; 势不可挡的; 无法抗拒的; 巨大的: *an overwhelming urge to smoke* 不可遏止的吸烟冲动 ○ *an overwhelming victory* 极大的胜利 ○ *the overwhelming majority of people*, ie the majority by a great number 压倒性多数. **over·whelm·ingly** *adv*: *overwhelmingly successful, generous* 极为成功、慷慨.

over·work /ˌəʊvəˈwɜːk; ˈovɚˈwɝk/ *v* **1** [I, Tn] (cause a person or an animal to) work too hard or too long (使人或动物)工作过劳或时间过长: *You'll become ill if you continue to overwork.* 你这样劳累下去就要病了. ○ *overwork a horse* 使马疲劳过度. **2** [Tn esp passive 尤用于被动语态] use (a word, etc) too much (and so weaken its importance or effectiveness) 滥用(词等)(因而削弱词义的力量): *an overworked phrase, metaphor, expression, etc* 因使用频繁而失去原有力量的短语、比喻、固定词组等 ○ *'Situation' is a word that is greatly overworked.* '情况'一词因使用过多而失去了准确性.

▷ **over·work** /ˈəʊvəwɜːk; ˈovɚˈwɝk/ *n* [U] working too hard or too long 工作过劳或时间过长: *ill through overwork* 积劳成疾 ○ *stress caused by overwork* 工作过累造成的紧张.

over·wrought /ˌəʊvəˈrɔːt; ˈovɚˈrɔt/ *adj* in a state of nervous excitement, anxiety, etc; tense and upset 神经紧张的; 忧虑的; 烦恼的: *She was in a very overwrought state after the accident.* 事故发生后她精神十分紧张. ○ *She didn't mean to offend you; she was overwrought.* 她无意得罪你, 她是情绪不好.

ovi·duct /ˈəʊvɪdʌkt; ˈovɪˌdʌkt/ *n* = FALLOPIAN TUBE.

ovi·par·ous /əʊˈvɪpərəs; oˈvɪpərəs/ *adj* (*biology* 生) (of fish, birds, reptiles, etc) producing eggs that hatch outside the body (指鱼、鸟、爬虫等)卵生的.

ovoid /ˈəʊvɔɪd/ *adj, n* (*fml* 文) egg-shaped (object)卵形的; 卵形物: *large ovoid pebbles* 大鹅卵石.

ovu·late /ˈɒvjʊleɪt; ˋɑvjə,let/ *v* [I] (*medical or biology* 医或生) produce or discharge an ovum from an ovary 排卵; 产卵: *Women who do not ovulate regularly have difficulty in becoming pregnant.* 妇女排卵期不正常就不易受孕. ▷ **ovu·la·tion** /ˌɒvjʊˈleɪʃn; ˌɑvjəˋleʃən/ *n* [U]: *She is taking a drug to stimulate ovulation.* 她现正服药使排卵正常.

ovum /ˈəʊvəm; ˋovəm/ *n* (*pl* **ova** /ˈəʊvə; ˋovə/) (*biology* 生) female egg-cell capable of developing into a new individual when fertilized by male sperm 卵; 卵子; 卵细胞. ⇨illus at FEMALE 见 FEMALE 插图. Cf 参看 OVARY.

owe /əʊ; o/ *v* **1** (**a**) [Ipr, Tn, Tn·pr, Dn·n Dn·pr] ~ (sb) for sth; **~ sth (to sb) (for sth)** be in debt to (sb) (for goods, etc) 欠(某人)债(因货物等): *He still owes (us) for the goods he received last month.* 他上月收到货物, 现在还欠着(我们)款呢. ○ *He owes (his father) £50.* 他欠(他父亲)50英镑. ○ *He owes £50 to his father.* 他欠他父亲50英镑. (**b**) [Dn·pr] **~ sth to sb/sth** recognize sb/sth as the cause or source of sth; be indebted to sb/sth for sth 将某事物归因、归源或归功于某人[某事物]: *He owes his success more to luck than to ability.* 他认为他的成功是靠运气而不是因为自己有能力. ○ *We owe this discovery to Newton.* 我们的这一发现归功于牛顿. **2** [Dn·n, Dn·pr] **~ sth to sb** (**a**) be under an obligation to sb; give sth as a duty to sb 对某人有义务; 对某人尽责: *owe loyalty to a political party, one's union, the company, etc* 对某政党、联盟、公司等效忠. (**b**) feel gratitude (to sb) in return for a service, favour, etc (对某人)感激, 感恩: *I owe my teachers and parents a great deal.* 我深深感激师长与父母. ○ *I owe a lot to my wife and children.* 我很感激我的妻子和孩子. **3** (idm 习语) **the world owes one a living** ⇨WORLD.

ow·ing /ˈəʊɪŋ; ˋoɪŋ/ *adj* [pred 作表语] (esp of money that has been earned, lent or promised) not yet paid (尤指挣的、借的或允诺的钱)未付, 欠着: *£5 is still owing.* 仍欠5英镑.

□ **owing to** *prep* because of or on account of (sth) 由于; 因为: *Owing to the rain, the match was cancelled.* 比赛因雨取消了. ⇨Usage at DUE[1] 用法见 DUE[1].

owl /aʊl; aul/ *n* **1** bird of prey that flies at night and feeds on small animals, eg mice, and is traditionally regarded as a symbol of wisdom 鸮, 猫头鹰(传统上认为是聪明的象征). **2** (idm 习语) **wise as an owl** ⇨ WISE.

▷ **ow·let** /ˈaʊlɪt; ˋaulɪt/ *n* young owl 幼鸮; 小猫头鹰.

owl·ish *adj* of or like an owl; (trying to look) solemn and wise (似)猫头鹰的; (装得)严肃而聪明的: *Her new glasses make her look rather owlish.* 她戴着新眼镜看上去很文气. **owl·ishly** *adv*: *owlishly earnest* 严肃认真的.

own[1] /əʊn; on/ *det, pron* **1** (used after possessives to emphasize the idea of personal possession or the individual character of sth 用于所有格后, 强调某事物的个人所有或私人性质) belonging to oneself, itself, ourselves, etc 属于自己的: *I saw it with my own eyes*, ie I didn't hear about it from someone else. 那是我亲眼所见. ○ *It was her own idea.* 那是她自己的想法. ○ *This is my own house/This house is my own*, ie not rented, etc. 这是我的房子[这房子是我的]. ○ *Use your own pen; I need mine.* 用你自己的钢笔吧, 我的笔我还要用呢. ○ *Our children have grown up and have children of their own.* 我们的孩子都大了, 而且也有了自己的孩子了. ○ *I wish I had my (very) own room*, ie didn't have to share one, borrow one, etc. 但愿我有自己的房间. ○ *Your day off is your own*, ie You can spend it as you wish. 你的假日是你自己的(可以自由支配). ○ *For reasons of his own* (ie particular reasons that perhaps only he knew about), *he refused to join the club.* 他因个人原因拒不参加那个俱乐部. **2** (used to indicate the idea of personal activity) done or produced by and for oneself (用以表示个人活动的概念)自己做的, 为自己的: *She makes all her own clothes.* 她的衣服都是自己做的. ○ *I can cook my own meals.* 我能做自己的饭. ○ *It's unwise to try to be your own lawyer.* 自己给自己当律师是不明智的. **3** (idm 习语) **come into one's own** receive the credit, recognition, fame, etc one deserves获得应有的荣誉、承认、名声等: *This car really comes into its own on rough ground.* 这辆汽车在颠簸的路上才真正显示出它独特的性能. ○ *She really comes into her own when someone is ill.* 有人生病时才真正看出她的为人. **hold one's ˈown (against sb/sth) (in sth)** (**a**) maintain one's position against attack, etc; not be defeated坚守立场(抵抗攻击等); 不被击败: *She can certainly hold her own against anybody in an argument.* 她在辩论中决不会输给任何人. (**b**) not lose strength 支撑得住: *The patient is holding her own although she is still very ill.* 她虽然病重, 却仍在支撑着. **of one's ˈown** belonging to oneself and no one else 属于自己的: *He'd like a car of his own.* 他喜欢有辆自己的汽车. ○ *Children need toys of their own.* 儿童需要有自己的玩具. **(all) on one's ˈown** (**a**) alone 独自: *I'm all on my own today.* 今天我是独自一人. ○ *She lives on her own.* 她独自过日子. (**b**) without help or supervision; alone 独力地; 单独地: *He can be left to work on his own.* 工作可交给他一个人去做. ○ *Although her father is in the firm she got the job on her own.* 尽管她父亲在公司里, 但她那份工作却是靠自己得到的. (**c**) (*infml* 口) excellent; exceptional 出色的; 非凡的; 卓越的: *When it comes to craftsmanship, Sally is on her own*, ie is better than anyone. 说到手艺, 萨莉是独一无二的. ⇨Usage at ALONE 用法见 ALONE. **get/have one's ˈown back (on sb)** (*infml* 口) have one's revenge 报复: *After the fight the defeated boxer swore he'd get his own back (on his rival).* 那场拳赛后败北者发誓要(向对手)报仇雪恨.

□ ˌ**own ˈbrand** class of goods in a shop marked with the name of the shop or store instead of that of the manufacturer 本店商标货物(以自己店名代替厂家商标者): [attrib 作定语] *Own brand goods are often cheaper.* 有本店商标的货物往往比较便宜.

ˌ**own ˈgoal** goal scored by a member of a team against his own side 本队队员射入己方的球(对方得分).

own[2] /əʊn; on/ *v* **1** [Tn] have (sth) as one's property; possess有(某事物)(作为自己的财富); 领有: *This house is mine; I own it.* 这房子是我的, 归我所有. ○ *She owns a car but rarely drives it.* 她有一辆汽车, 但很少开. ○ *Who owns this land?* 这块土地是谁的? **2** [Ipr, Tn, Tf, Cn·a, Cn·n] **~ (to sth/doing sth)** (*dated* 旧) recognize or admit (that sth is true or that one is responsible for sth); confess 确认, 承认(某事属实或属自己所为): *own to having told a lie* 承认撒了谎 ○ *Finally she owned the truth of what he had said.* 她终于承认他所说的属实. ○ *They own that the claim is justified.* 他们确认那要求是正当的. ○ *He owned himself defeated.* 他承认自己失败了. **3** (phr v) **own up (to sth)** (*infml* 口) admit or confess that one is to blame (for sth) (就某事)承认有错, 坦白: *Nobody owned up to the theft.* 这件偷窃事没有人承认是自己干的. ○ *Eventually she owned up.* 她终于认错了.

owner /ˈəʊnə(r); ˋonɚ/ *n* person who owns sth 物主; 某物的所有者: *the owner of a black Mercedes* 一辆黑色奔驰(亦称平治)牌汽车车主 ○ *the dog's owner* 狗的主人 ○ *Who's the owner of this house?* 谁是这房子的房主?

▷ **own·er·less** *adj* having no owner or no known owner 无主的: *ownerless dogs* 无主的狗 ○ *wrecked ownerless cars* 毁坏的无主的汽车.

own·er·ship *n* [U] state of being an owner; (right of) possession 物主的身分; 所有权: *The ownership of the land is disputed.* 那土地的所有权有争议. ○ *Ownership of property involves great expense.* 有房地产就要有很大开销. ○ *The restaurant is under new ownership.* 那餐馆已易新主.

□ ˌ**owner-ˈdriver** *n* person who owns the car he drives 自己开车的车主.

ˌ**owner-ˈoccupied** *adj* (of a house, etc) lived in by the owner (not rented to sb else) (指房子等)主人自住的: *Most of the houses in this street are owner-occupied.* 这条街上多数房子都是自用的. ˌ**owner-ˈoccupier** *n* person who owns the house he lives in 住自己房子的房主.

ox /ɒks; ɑks/ *n* (*pl* **oxen** /ˈɒksn; ˋɑksn̩/) **1** fully grown bullock used (esp formerly) for pulling carts, farm machinery, etc or for food (去势的)大公牛(尤指旧时供役使或食用的). Cf 参看 BULL, STEER[2]. **2** (esp *pl* 尤作复数) (*dated* 旧) any domestic cow or bull (饲养的)牛(母牛或未阉割的公牛). Cf 参看 CATTLE.

□ ˈ**oxtail** *n* tail of an ox, used for making soup, etc 牛尾(用以做汤等): [attrib 作定语] *oxtail soup* 牛尾汤.

Ox·bridge /ˈɒksbrɪdʒ; ˋɑks,brɪdʒ/ *n* (*sometimes derog* 有时作贬义) (invented name for) Oxford and/or Cambridge (contrasted with newer British universities) (创造的名词)牛津剑桥(牛津大学和[或]剑桥大学, 以别于英国其他大学): *You don't have to go to Oxbridge to receive a good university education.* 不上牛津剑桥也可获得良好的大学教育. Cf 参看 REDBRICK (RED).

ox-eye /ˈɒksaɪ; ˋɑksˌaɪ/ *n* (**a**) any of several types of flowering plants 牛眼菊属植物. (**b**) flower of one of these 牛眼菊: [attrib 作定语] *a vase of ox-eye daisies* 一花瓶春白菊.

Oxfam /ˈɒksfæm; ˋɑksˌfæm/ *abbr* 缩写 = Oxford Committee for Famine Relief 牛津饥荒救济委员会(也译乐施会): *a concert in aid of Oxfam* 赞助牛津饥救会的音乐会.

ox·ide /ˈɒksaɪd; ˋɑksaɪd/ *n* [C, U] (*chemistry* 化) compound of oxygen and one other substance 氧化物: *iron oxide* 氧化铁 ○ *oxide of tin* 氧化锡.

▷ **ox·ida·tion** /ˌɒksɪˈdeɪʃn; ˌɑksəˋdeʃən/ (also **ox·id·iza·tion, -isation** /ˌɒksɪdaɪˈzeɪʃn; *US* -dɪˈz-; ˌɑksədɪˋzeʃən/) *n* action or process of oxidizing 氧化.

ox·id·ize, -ise /ˈɒksɪdaɪz; ˋɑksəˌdaɪz/ *v* [I, Tn] (**a**) (cause sth to) combine with oxygen (使某物)氧化. Cf 参看 REDUCE 6. (**b**) (cause sth to) become rusty (使某物)生锈.

Oxon /ˈɒksn; ˋɑksɑn/ *abbr* 缩写 = **1** (esp in addresses) Oxfordshire (Latin *Oxonia*) (尤用于地址中)牛津郡(源自拉丁文 *Oxonia*). **2** (esp in degree titles) of Oxford University (Latin *Oxoniensis*) (尤用于学衔中)牛津大学的(源自拉丁文 *Oxoniensis*): *Alice Tolley MA (Oxon)* 艾丽斯·托利(牛津大学)文学硕士. Cf 参看 CANTAB.

oxy-acetylene /ˌɒksɪəˈsetəliːn; ˌɑksɪəˋsɛtl̩ˌin/ *adj, n* (of or using) a mixture of oxygen and acetylene gas (esp for cutting or welding metal)氧(乙)炔的; 用氧(乙)炔的; 氧(乙)炔: *oxy-acetylene torches, blowpipes, equipment*, ie devices burning oxy-acetylene 氧炔焊炬、吹管、设备 ○ *oxy-acetylene welding*, ie joining metal by means of a hot flame of oxy-acetylene 氧炔焊接.

oxy·gen /ˈɒksɪdʒən; ˋɑksədʒən/ *n* [U] chemical element, a gas without colour, taste or smell, present in the air and necessary for all forms of life on earth氧; 氧气: *There was a shortage of oxygen at the top of the mountain.* 该山顶上缺氧. ○ *She died from lack of oxygen.* 她缺氧致死. ⇨App 10 见附录10.

▷ **oxy·gen·ate** /-eɪt; -ˌet/ (also **oxy·genize, -ise** /-aɪz; -ˌaɪz/) *v* [Tn] supply, treat or mix (sth) with oxygen 供(某物)氧; 用氧处理(某物); 使(某物)与氧混合.

□ ˈ**oxygen mask** mask placed over the nose and mouth through which a person can breathe oxygen, eg in an aircraft or hospital 氧气面具; 氧气罩: *Oxygen masks are used in aircraft only in emergencies.* 飞机上的氧气面具只用于紧急情况.

ˈ**oxygen tent** small tent or canopy placed over the head and shoulders of a sick person who needs an extra supply of oxygen 氧幕; 氧气帐: *They placed the child in an oxygen tent when he had difficulty in breathing.* 那孩子呼吸困难时, 他们把他放进氧幕里.

oyez /əʊˈjez; ˋojɛz/ (also **oyes** /əʊˈjes; ˋojɛs/) *interj* (cry meaning 'listen' shouted three times (esp formerly) by a town crier or by an official in a lawcourt to demand silence and attention '肃静'的喊声(连喊三次), (尤指旧时)街头公告员或法庭中的官员的呼喊).

oys·ter /ˈɔɪstə(r); ˋɔɪstɚ/ *n* **1** shellfish (used as food and usu eaten uncooked) some types of which produce pearls inside their shells 牡蛎, 蠔(常生吃): *fresh oysters* 新鲜牡蛎 ○ [attrib 作定语] *oyster stew* 炖牡蛎. ⇨illus at SHELLFISH 见SHELLFISH 插图. **2** (idm 习语) **the world is one's/sb's oyster** ⇨ WORLD.

□ ˈ**oyster bed** place on the bottom of the sea where oysters breed or are bred for food or for producing pearls 牡蛎养殖场.

ˈ**oyster-catcher** *n* type of black and white wading sea-bird which catches and eats oysters 蛎鹬.

oz *abbr* 缩写 = (*pl* unchanged or **ozs** 复数或不变或作 **ozs**) ounce (Italian *onza*)盎司(源自意大利文 *onza*): *Add 4oz sugar.* 加4盎司糖. Cf 参看 LB.

ozone /ˈəʊzəʊn; ˋozon/ *n* [U] (**a**) form of oxygen with a sharp and refreshing smell 臭氧. (**b**) (*infml* 口) pure refreshing air as at the seaside (海边等的)清新空气: *Just breathe in that ozone!* 吸吸那种新鲜空气吧!

□ ˈ**ozone layer** layer of ozone high above the earth's surface that helps to protect the earth from harmful ultraviolet rays from the sun 臭氧层.

P p

P, p /piː; pi/ *n* (*pl* **P's, p's** /piːz; piz/) **1** the sixteenth letter of the English alphabet 英语字母表的第十六个字母: *'Philip' begins with (a) P/'P'.* Philip 一字以P字母开始. **2** (idm 习语) **mind one's p's and q's** ⇨ MIND[2].

P *abbr* 缩写 = (on a road sign) parking (area) (路标所示)停车(区).

p *abbr* 缩写 = **1** (*pl* **pp**) page: *see p 94* 见第94页 ○ *pp 63-97* ☆ 63至97页. **2** /piː; pi/ (*Brit infml* 口) (decimal) penny or pence (十进制的)便士: *a 12p stamp* 一张12便士的邮票. Cf 参看 D 1. **3** (*music* 音) softly; quietly (Italian *piano*) 柔和地, 轻轻地(源自意大利文*piano*). Cf 参看 F 3.

pa /pɑː; pɑ/ *n* (*infml* 口) father 爸; 爸爸.

PA /ˌpiː ˈeɪ; ˌpi ˈe/ *abbr* 缩写 = **1** (*infml* 口) personal assistant 私人助理: *She works as PA to the managing director.* 她给总经理作私人助理. **2** Press Association 新闻协会. **3** public address (system) 广播(系统); 播音(系统): *I heard it on the PA.* 我从广播里听到的.

pa *abbr* 缩写 = per year (Latin *per annum*) 每年(源自拉丁文*per annum*): *salary £12 000 pa* 年薪12 000英镑.

pace[1] /peɪs; pes/ *n* **1** [C] (length of a) single step in walking or running (走或跑的)一步, 一步的距离: *only a few paces away* 仅数步之外 ○ *She took two paces forward/She advanced two paces.* 她向前走了两步. **2** [sing] **(a)** speed, esp of walking or running 速度(尤指走或跑的): *at a good, fast, slow, walking, etc pace* 以很快的、快的、慢的、步行的...速度 ○ *quicken one's pace* 加速步伐 ○ *She slowed down her pace so I could keep up with her.* 她放慢脚步好让我跟上她. ○ (*fig* 比喻) *He gave up his job in advertising because he couldn't stand the pace,* ie found the pressure of work too great. 他放弃了做广告的工作, 因为工作节奏太快, 他受不了. **(b)** [U] rate of progress or development, esp of an activity 进步或发展的速度; (尤指)活动的速度: *the pace of change in the electronics industry* 电子工业的发展速度 ○ *This novel lacks pace,* ie Its plot develops too slowly. 这部小说的节奏太慢. **3** (idm 习语) **at a snail's pace** ⇨ SNAIL. **force the pace** ⇨ FORCE[2]. **keep pace (with sb/sth)** move forward, develop or increase at the same rate (as sb/sth) (与某人[某事物])并驾齐驱, 齐头并进: *He was so unfit he couldn't keep pace (with us).* 他身体很不好, 跟不上(我们). ○ *It's important for a firm to keep pace with changes in the market.* 对一个公司来说, 能跟上市场的发展是很重要的. ○ *Are wages keeping pace with inflation?* 工资的增长跟得上通货膨胀的速度吗? **put sb/sth through his/its 'paces** test the ability or quality of sb/sth 考验、试验某人[某事物]的能力或质量: *The new recruits were put through their paces.* 新兵正接受考验. ○ *put a new car through its paces* 试验新汽车的性能. **ˌset the 'pace** run, walk, etc at a (usu fast) speed which others try to follow 定速度(使他人跟从): (*fig* 比喻) *This company is setting the pace* (ie is the most successful) *in the home computer market.* 这家公司在国内计算机市场上是先行者.

□ **'pacemaker** *n* **(a)** (also **'pace-setter**) runner, rider or driver in a race who moves at a (usu fast) speed which others try to follow (速度赛中)定速度者(使其他参赛者跟从): (*fig* 比喻) *That firm was the pace-setter in car design for many years,* ie introduced new ideas which were copied by others. 那家公司在汽车设计上多年来一直领先. **(b)** electronic device placed on the heart to make weak or irregular heartbeats stronger or more regular (心脏)起搏器.

pace[2] /peɪs; pes/ *v* **1** **(a)** [Ipr, Ip] walk with slow or regular steps 缓慢而行; 以规律的步伐行走; 踱: *He paced up and down (the platform), waiting for the train.* 他(在月台上)踱来踱去等候火车. **(b)** [Tn] walk backwards and forwards across (sth) in this way 来回或前后缓慢而有规律地走动; 来回踱步: *The prisoner paced the floor of his cell.* 那犯人在牢房里来回地走着. **2** [Tn] set a speed for (a runner, rider, etc in a race) (为速度赛的参赛者)定速度. **3** (phr v) **pace sth off/out** measure sth by taking regular steps across it 以步数测量某物: *She paced out the length of the room.* 她用步子测量了房间的长度.

pace[3] /ˈpeɪsiː; ˈpesɪ/ *prep* (*Latin* 拉) with respect to (a specified person) who does not or may not agree 请(可能与自己意见不同的人)原谅.

pa·chy·derm /ˈpækɪdɜːm; ˈpækəˌdɝm/ *n* any of various types of thick-skinned, four-footed animal, eg an elephant or a rhinoceros 厚皮兽(如象或犀牛).

pa·ci·fic /pəˈsɪfɪk; pəˈsɪfɪk/ *adj* (*fml* 文) making or loving peace; peaceful 和解的; 求和的; 爱和平的; 和平的. ▷ **pa·ci·fic·ally** /-klɪ; -klɪ/ *adv*.

pa·ci·fism /ˈpæsɪfɪzəm; ˈpæsəˌfɪzəm/ *n* [U] belief that all war is morally wrong and that disputes should be settled by peaceful means 和平主义; 反战主义.

▷ **pa·ci·fist** /-ɪst; -ɪst/ *n* person who believes in pacifism (and who therefore refuses to fight in a war) 和平主义者; 反战主义者. Cf 参看 CONSCIENTIOUS OBJECTOR (CONSCIENTIOUS).

pa·cify /ˈpæsɪfaɪ; ˈpæsəˌfaɪ/ *v* (*pt, pp* **-fied**) [Tn] **1** calm or soothe the anger or distress of (sb) 使(某人)安静, 息怒; 抚慰: *He tried to pacify his creditors by repaying part of the money.* 他为安抚债权人偿还了部分借款. **2** establish peace in (an area, a country, etc where there is war) 在(有战争的地区、国家等)实现和平.

▷ **pa·ci·fica·tion** /ˌpæsɪfɪˈkeɪʃn; ˌpæsəfəˈkeʃən/ *n* [U] pacifying or being pacified 平定; 平息; 安抚; 绥靖: *the pacification of the rebel states* 对发动叛乱的州的平定.

pa·ci·fier *n* (*US*) = DUMMY 3.

pack[1] /pæk; pæk/ *n* **1** [C] **(a)** number of things wrapped or tied together for carrying, esp on the back 包, 包裹(尤指背负的): *The tramp carried his belongings in a pack on his back.* 那个流浪者把所有的东西捆成一包背在背上. **(b)** bag, usu of canvas or leather, fitted with straps for carrying on the back 背包. Cf 参看 BACKPACK, HAVERSACK, RUCKSACK. **2** [C] small paper or cardboard container in which goods are packed for selling; packet 小纸盒; 小硬纸板箱; 小纸包: *a six-pack of beer,* ie six cans of beer wrapped and sold together 半打装啤酒 ○ (*esp US*) *a pack of cigarettes* 一包香烟. ⇨Usage at PACKET 用法见PACKET. **3** [CGp] **(a)** group of wild animals that hunt together (野兽的)一群: *Wolves hunt in packs.* 狼总是成群猎食. **(b)** group of dogs kept for hunting, esp with horses (猎狗的)一群(尤指骑马狩猎用者): *a pack of hounds* 一群猎狗. **(c)** organized group of Cub Scouts or Brownies (童子军的)一队: *a 'Brownie pack* 一队女童子军. **(d)** the forwards of a Rugby football team (一支橄榄球队的)全体前锋. **4** [CGp] **~ (of sb/sth)** (*derog* 贬) number of people or things (used esp in the expressions shown) (指人、物的)一帮, 一伙, 一堆(尤用于以下示例): *a pack of fools/thieves* 一伙傻瓜[小偷] ○ *a pack of lies* 一派谎言. **5** [C] (*US* **deck**) complete set of 52 playing-cards (纸牌的)一副(为52张). **6** [C] (only in compounds 仅用以构成复合词) thing placed on a part of the body for a period of time, such as a layer of cream or paste for cleansing the skin of the face or a bag of ice for soothing a burn 一时敷于身体之物(如润面霜、冰袋): *a 'face-pack* ○ *an 'ice-pack.*

□ **'pack-animal** *n* animal used for carrying things, eg a horse, mule or camel 力畜, 役畜(如马、骡、骆驼).

'pack-ice *n* [U] large mass of ice floating in the sea, formed from smaller pieces which have frozen together 海上的大堆浮冰.

'pack-saddle *n* saddle with straps for holding packs 驮鞍.

'packthread *n* [U] strong thread for sewing or tying up packs (缝包或打包用的)捆扎线, 粗线, 打包绳.

pack[2] /pæk; pæk/ *v* **1** **(a)** [I, Tn, Tn·pr] **~ A (in/into B); ~ B (with A)** put sth into a container for transport or storing; fill (a container, esp a suitcase) with sth 将某物装入(箱、盒等)(尤指装入衣箱): *Have you packed* *(your suitcase) yet?* 你装好(衣箱)了吗? ○ *Don't forget to pack your toothbrush!* 别忘了把牙刷放到箱子里去! ○ *All these books need to be packed (into boxes).* 这些书都要打点(装箱). ○ *pack clothes into a trunk/pack a trunk with clothes* 把衣物装进箱子里 ○ *He takes a packed lunch* (ie sandwiches, etc packed into a box or some other container) *to work every day.* 他每天带(盒装)午饭上班. (**b**) [I, Ipr] **~ (into sth)** be able to be put into a container for transport or storing 能被包装(便于装运): *This dress packs easily.* 这件连衣裙易于装箱. ○ *These clothes won't all pack into one suitcase.* 这些衣物一个箱子装不下. **2** [Tn, Tn·pr] **~ sth (in sth)** cover or protect sth with (esp soft) material pressed tightly on, in or round it 用材料(尤指软物)充填、衬垫或包裹某物(以覆盖或保护): *pack china in newspaper* 用报纸包裹瓷器 ○ *glass packed in straw* 用稻草包垫的玻璃. **3** [Tn] prepare and put (meat, fish, etc) in tins in order to preserve it 把(肉、鱼等)装罐保存; 做(鱼、肉等)罐头. **4** [esp passive 尤用于被动语态: Tn, Tn·pr] **~ sth (with sth/sb)** fill, cram or crowd sth (with sth/sb) (事物)塞满、充满某处; (人)挤满某处: *Chanting fans packed the stadium/The stadium was packed with chanting fans.* 热情的观众挤满了体育场, 不停地喊叫着有节奏的口号. ○ *The show played to packed houses*, ie large audiences. 那节目演出时场场爆满. ○ *This book is packed with useful information.* 这本书里有很多有用的资料. ○ *an action-packed film, novel, etc* 充满刺激动作的影片、小说等 ○ *The restaurant was packed*, ie crowded with people. 饭馆里挤满了人. **5** [I, Tn] (of snow, ice, etc) (cause sth to) form a hard compact mass (指冰、雪等)(使之)形成硬块: *The snow had packed against the wall.* 墙根的雪形成了硬块. ○ *The wind packed the snow against the wall.* 风把雪吹到墙边堆积起来. **6** [Tn] (*US infml* 口) carry (sth); be equipped with (sth) 携带(某物); 装备有(某物): *pack a gun* 带着枪. **7** [Tn] (*derog* 贬) choose (the members of a committee, etc) so that they are likely to decide in one's favour 挑选(委员等)使之偏袒自己. **8** (idm 习语) **ˌpack one's ˈbags** (prepare to) leave (准备)离开: *After their row she packed her bags and left.* 他们争吵后, 她收拾好提包就走了. ○ *He was told to pack his bags.* 已经告诉他让他走人. **ˌpack a (hard, etc) ˈpunch** (*infml* 口) (**a**) (of a boxer) be capable of delivering a powerful blow (指拳击手)能发出重击. (**b**) (*fig* 比喻) have a very powerful effect 极有效力: *Those cocktails pack quite a punch!* 那些鸡尾酒劲儿可真大! **send sb packing** ⇨ SEND.

9 (phr v) **pack sth away** put sth into a box, cupboard, etc because it is not needed 将某物放入盒、箱等中收起: *She packed away the deck-chairs for the winter.* 冬天她把折叠躺椅收了起来.

pack (sb/sth) in; pack (sb/sth) into sth (cause sb/sth to) crowd or press together into a limited space (使某人[某物])挤进, 紧挤入(一有限空间): *All six of us packed into the tiny car.* 我们六个人全挤进那辆小型汽车里. ○ *That show has been packing them in for months*, ie attracting large audiences. 那个表演一直吸引着大批观众, 经月不减. **ˌpack it ˈin** (*infml* 口) (esp imperative 尤用于祈使语气) stop doing or saying sth that angers or annoys sb else 不再做令人讨厌的事; 不再说令人生气的话: *I'm sick of your complaining — just pack it in, will you?* 你老发牢骚我都烦死了 —— 别说了, 行不行? **pack sth in** (*infml* 口) give sth up; abandon sth 放弃或抛弃某事物: *She's packed in her job.* 她已辞掉了她的工作. ○ *Smoking's bad for you; you ought to pack it in.* 吸烟对你很不好, 应该戒掉. **pack sth in; pack sth in/into sth** do (a lot of things) in a limited time 在有限的时间里做(大量的事): *She managed to pack a lot of sightseeing into three days.* 她三天中设法观光了许多地方.

pack sb off (to...) send sb away, esp quickly and decisively 打发某人(尤指迅速而果断地): *She packed the children off to bed.* 她把孩子全打发去睡觉了. ○ *We were packed off to stay in the country.* 都把我们送到乡下去了.

pack sth out (esp passive 尤用于被动语态) completely fill (a theatre, cinema, etc) with people 人挤满(电影院、剧院等): *Opera houses were packed out whenever she was singing.* 她一演唱剧院就满座.

pack up (*infml* 口) (**a**) stop doing sth; give up or abandon sth 不再做某事; 放弃某事物: *Business is terrible — I might as well pack up.* 生意很不好做 —— 我还是关门算了. (**b**) (of a machine, engine, etc) stop working or operating; break down (指机器、发动机等)不工作或不运转, 出毛病, 有故障: *My car has packed up.* 我的汽车坏了. **pack (sth) up** put (one's possessions) into cases, etc before leaving a place 将(东西)装箱打包离开某地: *He packed up his things and left.* 他把东西装进箱子里就动身了.

▷ **packer** *n* person, company or machine that packs goods, esp food 包装工人, 包装公司, 包装机(尤指包装食品的).

pack·age /ˈpækɪdʒ; ˋpækɪdʒ/ *n* **1** (**a**) object or objects wrapped in paper or packed in a box; parcel 用纸包裹或用箱、盒所盛之物; 包裹: *The postman brought me a large package.* 邮递员给我送来了一个大包裹. (**b**) box, etc in which things are packed 盒、箱等包装用物. **2** (*US*) = PACKET. ⇨Usage at PACKET 用法见 PACKET. **3** (also ˈ**package deal**) set of proposals offered or accepted as a whole 整批交易; 一揽子交易: *Ministers are trying to put together a package that will end the dispute.* 大臣们力图搞个一揽子交易结束这场争论.

▷ **pack·age** *v* [Tn] make (sth) into or put (sth) in a package, eg for selling 将(某物)包装(如为出售): *Their products are always attractively packaged.* 他们的产品总是包装得非常精美. **pack·aging** *n* [U] (design and manufacture of) materials for packing goods 包装材料; 包装材料的设计与生产. ⇨Usage at PACKET 用法见 PACKET.

□ ˈ**package store** (*US*) = OFF-LICENCE.

ˈ**package holiday**, ˈ**package tour** holiday/tour organized by a travel agent, for which one pays a fixed price that includes the cost of transport, accommodation, etc 一切由旅行社代办而费用固定的假日旅游.

packet /ˈpækɪt; ˋpækɪt/ *n* **1** [C] (**a**) (*US* usu 美式英语通常作 **pack·age**) small paper or cardboard container in which goods are packed for selling (包装商品的)小包, 小盒, 小袋: *a packet of biscuits, cigarettes, tea, etc* 一小包饼干、香烟、茶叶等. (**b**) small package or parcel 用小包、小箱、小盒所盛之物; 小包裹. **2** [sing] (*infml* 口) large amount of money (used esp in the expressions shown) 大笔款项(尤用于以下示例): *make* (ie earn) *a packet* 挣一大笔钱 ○ *cost (sb) a packet* 花(某人)一大笔钱. **3** [C] (also ˈ**packet-boat**) boat that carries mail and passengers on a fixed short route (短途)定期邮船, 班轮. **4** (idm 习语) **cop a packet** ⇨ COP[2].

NOTE ON USAGE 用法: Some things in shops are sold in **packets** (*US* **pack**) 商店中某些商品以 **packet** (小包装)形式出售(美式英语用 **pack**): *a packet of sweets, crisps, cigarettes* 小包的糖果、炸土豆片、香烟 ○ *a six-pack of beer* 半打装啤酒. Note that *a packet/pack of cigarettes* contains some cigarettes but *a cigarette packet/pack* may be empty. 注意 a packet/pack of cigarettes (一盒香烟)有一定数量的香烟, 而 a cigarette packet/pack (一个香烟盒)可能是空的. A **parcel** (*US* also **package**) is something wrapped, often in brown paper, so that it can be sent by post. ☆ **parcel** (美式英语亦作 **package**)指包起来(常指用牛皮纸包裹)邮寄的物品: *The postman rang the bell because he had a parcel/package to deliver.* 邮递员按门铃叫门投递包裹. A **package** in British English is usually carried and not sent. 英式英语中 **package** 通常指携带的而不是寄送的包裹. **Packaging** is the material used to wrap and protect products sold in shops or sent through the post. ☆ **packaging** 是指商店售出商品或邮递物品的包装材料.

pack·ing /ˈpækɪŋ; ˋpækɪŋ/ *n* [U] **1** process of packing goods (货物)包装, 包装法. **2** material used for packing (esp fragile objects) 包装材料; (尤指)包装易碎物品的材料: *pay extra for postage and packing*, ie when ordering goods by post 另付邮费和包装费.

□ ˈ**packing-case** *n* wooden box or case used for storing or transporting goods 装货木箱.

pact /pækt; pækt/ *n* agreement (between people, groups, countries, etc); treaty (人、团体、国家等间的)契约, 协议, 条约, 公约: *They made a pact not to tell anyone.* 他们

P

约定好绝不告诉任何人. ○ *a non-aggression pact* 互不侵犯条约.

pad[1] /pæd; pæd/ *n* **1** thick piece of soft material used to protect sth from rubbing, jarring or blows, to improve the shape or increase the size of sth, or to absorb liquid 垫料; 垫块: *put a pad of cotton wool and gauze over a wound* 在伤口上敷脱脂棉和纱布 ○ *ˈshoulder pads*, ie to give shape to a jacket or dress 垫肩(衣服的). **2** (usu *pl* 通常作复数) piece of flexible padded material worn in certain sports (esp cricket) to protect the legs and ankles (在某些运动中保护胫和踝的)护垫(尤指板球运动用的): *ˈshin pads*, ie worn by footballers, etc to protect the shins 护腿(足球运动员的). ⇨illus at CRICKET 见 CRICKET 插图. **3** number of sheets of writing-paper or drawing-paper fastened together at one edge 便笺本; 拍纸簿: *a ˈwriting pad* 拍纸簿. **4** = ˈINK-PAD. **5** soft fleshy under-part of the foot of certain animals, eg dogs, foxes (某些动物的)肉趾(如狗、狐的). **6** flat surface from which spacecraft are launched or helicopters take off 航天器发射台; 直升飞机升降处: *a ˈlaunching pad* 发射台. **7** (*sl* 俚) place where sb lives 住处: *Come back to my pad.* 回到我的住处.

pad[2] /pæd; pæd/ *v* **(-dd-)** **1** [Tn esp passive 尤用于被动语态] fill or cover (sth) with soft material, esp in order to protect it or give it a particular shape or increase its size 用软物填塞、覆盖、垫或衬(某物): *a padded envelope*, ie for sending fragile objects in 有垫料夹层的封套(用以邮寄易碎物品) ○ *a jacket with padded shoulders* 带垫肩的外衣 ○ *a padded bra*, ie one worn to make the breasts appear larger 带衬垫的乳罩. **2** (phr v) **pad sth out** (**a**) put soft material into (a garment) in order to give it a particular shape 给(衣服)衬软物使成形: *pad out the shoulders of a jacket to make them look square* 给外衣衬上垫肩显得挺括. (**b**) make (a book, an essay, a speech, etc) longer by adding unnecessary material (用空话)拉长, 充斥(书、文章、讲话等): *I padded out my answer with plenty of quotations.* 我用了大量引文把答案拉长.

▷ **pad·ding** *n* [U] **1** soft material used to pad things (软的)垫料, 衬料. **2** unnecessary material in a book, an essay, a speech, etc (书、文章、讲话等的)凑篇幅的材料: *There's a lot of padding in this novel.* 这部小说有大量空洞无物的内容.

□ ˌ**padded** ˈ**cell** room in a mental hospital that has soft walls to prevent violent patients from injuring themselves 软墙病房; (墙上装有衬垫以防精神病人自伤的)软垫小室.

pad[3] /pæd; pæd/ *v* **(-dd-)** (phr v) **pad about, along, around, etc** walk in the specified direction with a soft steady sound of steps 放轻脚步走: *The dog padded along next to its owner.* 那狗跟在主人身旁轻轻地走着. ○ *pad about the house in one's slippers* 穿着拖鞋在家中轻轻走来走去.

paddle[1] /ˈpædl; ˋpædl/ *n* **1** [C] short oar with a broad blade at one end or both ends, used to move a canoe through the water 短桨, 双叶桨(划独木舟的). ⇨illus at CANOE 见 CANOE 插图. **2** [sing] act or period of paddling (PADDLE 1) 划桨; 荡桨. **3** [C] instrument shaped like a paddle, esp one used for beating, mixing or stirring food 桨形工具(尤指用于击打、混合或搅拌食物的).

▷ **paddle** *v* [Ipr, Ip, Tn, Tn·pr, Tn·p] **1** (**a**) move (a canoe) through the water using a paddle 用桨划(独木舟): *We paddled (the canoe) slowly upstream.* 我们慢慢地划着(独木舟)逆流而上. (**b**) row (a boat) with light easy strokes 轻轻地划(船); 荡桨. **2** (idm 习语) ˌ**paddle one's** ˌ**own** ˈ**canoe** (*infml* 口) depend on oneself and no one else; be independent 自力更生; 独立自主.

□ ˈ**paddle-boat** *n* boat moved by a paddle-wheel 明轮船.

ˈ**paddle-steamer** *n* steam vessel moved by paddle-wheels 明轮汽船.

ˈ**paddle-wheel** *n* wheel with boards round its rim which make a boat move forwards by pressing against the water as the wheel revolves 明轮; 桨轮.

paddle[2] /ˈpædl; ˋpædl/ *v* **1** [I, Ipr, Ip] walk with bare feet in shallow water 蹚水; 涉水: *paddling (about) at the water's edge* 在水边蹚水玩. Cf 参看 WADE. **2** [Tn] move (one's feet or hands) gently in water 用(脚或手)轻轻划水或拨水: *paddle one's toes in the water* 用脚趾撩水玩.

▷ **paddle** *n* [sing] act or period of paddling 蹚水; 涉水.

□ ˈ**paddling pool** (*US* ˈ**wading pool**) shallow pool in which children may paddle (供儿童嬉水的)浅水池.

pad·dock /ˈpædək; ˋpædək/ *n* **1** small field where horses are kept or exercised (放牧和驯马用的)小围场. **2** enclosure at a racecourse or race-track where horses or racing-cars are brought together and paraded before a race (准备参赛的马或车的)检阅场.

paddy[1] /ˈpædɪ; ˋpædɪ/ *n* **1** (also ˈ**paddy-field**) [C] field where rice is grown 稻田. **2** [U] rice that is still growing or in the husk 稻; 稻谷.

paddy[2] /ˈpædɪ; ˋpædɪ/ *n* (*Brit infml* 口) fit of anger or temper 大怒; 发脾气: *There's no need to get into such a paddy.* 不必这么大动肝火.

Paddy /ˈpædɪ; ˋpædɪ/ *n* (*infml offensive* 口, 蔑) Irish person 爱尔兰人.

pad·lock /ˈpædlɒk; ˋpædˌlɑk/ *n* detachable lock with a U-shaped bar or chain that fastens through the loop of a staple or ring 挂锁; 扣锁. ⇨illus at CHAIN 见 CHAIN 插图.

▷ **pad·lock** *v* [Tn, Tn·pr] fasten (sth) with a padlock 用挂锁锁(某物): *The gate was padlocked.* 大门用挂锁锁着. ○ *She padlocked her bike to the railings.* 她用挂锁把自行车和栏杆锁在一起.

padre /ˈpɑ:dreɪ; ˋpɑdrɪ/ *n* (*infml* 口) (used esp as a form of address 尤用作称呼语) **1** clergyman in the armed forces 随军牧师: *Good morning, padre!* 牧师, 早上好! Cf 参看 CHAPLAIN. **2** (*Brit*) priest or parson 神父; 牧师.

paean (*US* **pean**) /ˈpi:ən; ˋpiən/ *n* (*fml* 文) song of praise or triumph 赞歌; 凯歌: *a paean of praise* 赞歌.

paed·er·asty = PEDERASTY.

pae·di·at·rics (*US* **pe·di·at·rics**) /ˌpi:dɪˈætrɪks; ˌpidɪˋætrɪks/ *n* [sing *v*] branch of medicine concerned with children and their illnesses 儿科学.

▷ **pae·di·at·ric** (*US* **pe·di·at·ric**) *adj* relating to paediatrics 儿科学的: *a paediatric ward*, ie for sick children 儿科病房.

pae·di·at·ri·cian (*US* **pe·di-**) /ˌpi:dɪəˈtrɪʃn; ˌpidɪəˋtrɪʃən/ *n* doctor who specializes in paediatrics 儿科医师; 儿科学家.

paed(o)- (*US* **ped(o)-**) *comb form* 构词成分 child or children 儿童: *paediatrics*.

pae·do·philia (*US* **pedo-**) /ˌpi:dəˈfɪlɪə; ˌpidəˋfɪlɪə/ *n* [U] condition of being sexually attracted to children 恋童癖.

pa·ella /paɪˈelə; pɑˋɛlə/ *n* [U] Spanish dish of rice, chicken, seafood, vegetables, etc cooked and served in a large shallow pan 西班牙什锦饭(有米、鸡肉、海味、菜蔬等).

pa·gan /ˈpeɪgən; ˋpegən/ *n* **1** person who is not a believer in any of the world's chief religions, esp one who is neither a Christian, a Jew nor a Moslem 异教徒(尤指非基督教、犹太教或回教教徒). **2** (formerly) person who did not believe in Christianity; heathen (旧时)非基督教徒, 异教徒. Cf 参看 ATHEIST (ATHEISM).

▷ **pa·gan** *adj* of or relating to pagans 异教徒的; 无宗教信仰者的: *pagan worship of the sun* 异教徒对太阳的崇拜.

pa·gan·ism /-ɪzəm; -ɪzəm/ *n* [U] beliefs and practices of pagans 异教信仰.

page[1] /peɪdʒ; pedʒ/ *n* **1** (**a**) (*abbr* 缩写 **p**) one side of a sheet of paper in a book, magazine, etc (书、杂志等的)页: *read a few pages of a book* 看几页书 ○ *You'll find the quotation on page 35.* 引文见第35页. (**b**) this sheet of paper itself (纸的)张: *Several pages have been torn out of the book.* 书中有几页撕掉了. **2** episode or period of history that might be written about in a book 可写入书中的历史事件或时期: *a glorious page of English history* 英国历史上光荣的一页.

▷ **page** *v* [Tn] number the pages of (sth) 标明(某物)的页数.

page[2] /peɪdʒ; pedʒ/ (also ˈ**page-boy**) *n* (**a**) (*US* ˈ**bellboy**) boy or young man, usu in uniform, employed in a hotel or club to carry luggage, open doors for people, etc (旅馆或俱乐部雇用的、通常为穿制服的)年轻男侍. (**b**) boy attendant of a person of rank or a bride 年轻的男侍从或傧相.

▷ **page** *v* [Tn] call the name of (sb) over a loudspeaker (eg in an airport) in order to give him a message (用扩音喇叭)呼叫(某人).

pa·geant /ˈpædʒənt; ˋpædʒənt/ *n* **1** public entertainment consisting of a procession of people in costume, or an outdoor performance of scenes from history 盛装的游行; 露天演出的历史剧: (*fig* 比喻) *the pageant of history*, ie history as a succession of colourful events 丰富多彩的历史. **2** brilliant display or spectacle 壮丽的场面; 伟观.

▷ **pa·geantry** /ˈpædʒəntrɪ; ˋpædʒəntrɪ/ *n* [U] spectacular display 壮丽的展示; 盛况: *all the pageantry of a coronation* 加冕盛典.

pa·gin·ate /ˈpædʒɪneɪt; ˋpædʒə͵net/ *v* [Tn] number the pages of (a book, etc) 标明(书等)的页码.

▷ **pa·gina·tion** /͵pædʒɪˈneɪʃn; ͵pædʒəˋneʃən/ *n* [U] (figures used in) numbering the pages of a book, etc 标记页数(的数字); 页码.

pagoda 塔

pa·goda /pəˈɡəʊdə; pəˋɡodə/ *n* religious building in India and E Asia, usu a tall tower with several storeys each of which has its own overhanging roof (印度和东亚的)塔, 宝塔.

paid *pt, pp* of PAY[2].

pail /peɪl; pel/ *n* (**a**) bucket 桶: *a pail of water* 一桶水. (**b**) amount contained in this 一桶的量.

▷ **pail·ful** /ˈpeɪlfʊl; ˋpel͵fʊl/ *n* amount a pail contains 一桶的量.

paill·asse = PALLIASSE.

pain /peɪn; pen/ *n* **1** (**a**) [U] physical suffering or discomfort caused by injury or disease (肉体上的)疼, 痛, 疼痛: *be in (great) pain* (剧)痛 ○ *feel some, no, not much, a lot of, etc pain* 感到有些、不、不很、非常...疼 ○ *a cry of pain* 疼痛的叫喊 ○ *scream with pain* 疼得尖叫 ○ *suffer from acute back pain* 患剧烈的背痛 ○ *Her back causes/gives her a lot of pain.* 她背痛得厉害. (**b**) [C] feeling of suffering or discomfort in a particular part of the body 身体某部分的疼痛或不适: *have a pain in one's back, chest, shoulder, etc* 背痛、胸痛、肩痛 ○ *stomach pains* 胃痛. (**c**) [U] mental suffering or distress (精神上的)痛苦, 苦痛: *His harsh words caused her much pain.* 他说话很刺耳, 她听了很不舒服. ○ *the pain of separation* 分离的苦痛. **2** [C] (*infml* 口) annoying or boring person or thing 令人厌烦的人或事物: *She's been complaining again — she's a real pain!* 她又发牢骚了——真烦人! ○ *We've missed the last bus — what a pain!* 我们没赶上末班公共汽车——真倒霉! **3** (idm 习语) **a pain in the neck** (*infml* 口) annoying or boring person or thing; pain (2) 令人厌烦的人或事物. **on/under pain/penalty of sth** (*fml* 文) with the risk of incurring a particular punishment 违则受某种惩罚: *Prisoners were forbidden to approach the fence under pain of death.* 犯人严禁接近围栏, 违者格杀勿论.

▷ **pain** *v* [Tn no passive 不用于被动语态] cause pain to (sb) 使(某人)痛苦: *My foot is still paining me.* 我的脚还痛. ○ *It pains me to have to tell you that...* 我以沉痛的心情告诉你.... **pained** *adj* showing pain or distress 显示痛苦的或难过的: *a pained look, expression, glance, etc* 痛苦的样子、表情、目光等.

pain·ful /-fl; -fəl/ *adj* **1** causing or suffering pain 令人疼痛的; 痛苦的; 疼的: *a painful blow on the shoulder* 肩上挨的一击很疼 ○ *Her shoulder is still painful.* 她的肩还很痛. **2** causing distress or embarrassment 令人痛苦的; 令人难堪的: *a painful experience, memory* 痛苦的经历、记忆 ○ *His incompetence was painful to witness.* 他很无能, 让人看着难受. ○ *It was my painful duty to tell him he was dying.* 要我把他即将去世的事告诉他, 这使我十分为难. ○ *Her performance was painful*, ie very bad. 她的表演拙劣得令人难堪. **3** difficult or tedious 困难的; 麻烦的; 费事的: *the painful process of stripping the paint off the wall* 剥除墙壁漆皮的麻烦事. **pain·fully** /-fəlɪ; -fəlɪ/ *adv*: *Her thumb is painfully swollen.* 她的大拇指肿痛难忍. ○ *become painfully aware of sth* 意识到某事而感到痛苦. **pain·ful·ness** *n* [U].

pain·less *adj* not causing pain or distress 无痛的; 不引起痛苦的: *a painless injection* 无痛注射. **pain·lessly** *adv*. **pain·less·ness** *n* [U].

□ ˈ**pain-killer** *n* drug that reduces pain 止痛药: *She's on (ie taking) pain-killers.* 她在服用止痛药.

pains /peɪnz; penz/ *n* [pl] (idm 习语) **be at pains to do sth** take great care or make a particular effort to do sth 费尽苦心, 努力做某事: *She was at pains to stress the benefits of the scheme.* 她极力强调该计划的好处. ○ *He was at great pains to deny the rumour of redundancies.* 他煞费苦心平息裁员的谣言. **be a fool for one's pains** ⇨ FOOL[1]. **for one's pains** as a response to one's efforts or trouble 作为辛劳的报酬; 费尽苦心的结果: *She looked after her sick mother for 10 years and all she got for her pains was ingratitude*, ie she received no thanks for her efforts. 她母亲生病, 她照顾了十年, 到头来却是费力不讨好. **spare no pains doing/to do sth** ⇨ SPARE[2]. **take (great) pains (with/over/to do sth)** take great care or make a careful effort to do sth 小心谨慎地做某事: *She takes great pains with her work.* 她工作兢兢业业. ○ *Great pains have been taken to ensure the safety of passengers.* 为确保乘客安全而不遗余力.

□ **painstaking** /ˈpeɪnzteɪkɪŋ; ˋpenz͵tekɪŋ/ *adj* done with, requiring or taking great care or trouble 极小心的; 辛勤的; 辛苦的: *a painstaking job, investigation* 艰苦的工作、调查 ○ *painstaking accuracy* 高度的精确性 ○ *a painstaking student, worker, etc* 勤奋的学生、工人等. **painstakingly** *adv*.

paint[1] /peɪnt; pent/ *n* **1** (**a**) [U] substance applied to a surface in liquid form to give it colour 涂料: *red, green, yellow, etc paint* 红的、绿的、黄的等涂料 ○ *give the door two coats of paint*, ie put two layers of paint on it 给门油两层漆 ○ *wet paint*, eg written on a notice to warn people not to touch it 油漆未干 ○ [attrib 作定语] *paint marks* 带颜色的记号. (**b**) [U] layer of dried paint on a surface (已干燥的)涂层, 漆层. **2 paints** [pl] (set of) tubes or blocks of paint (一套)管装或块状的颜料: *The artist brought his paints with him.* 那画家自带颜料. ○ *a set of oil-paints* 一套油画颜料. **3** [U] (*usu derog* 通常作贬义) cosmetics for applying to the face 化妆品: *She wears far too much paint.* 她化妆太浓.

□ ˈ**paintbox** *n* box containing a set of paints 颜料盒.

ˈ**paintbrush** *n* brush used for applying paint 画笔; 漆刷.

ˈ**paintwork** *n* [U] painted surface or surfaces 已涂颜料或油漆的表面: *The paintwork is in good condition.* 漆面良好. ○ *A stone hit the car and damaged the paintwork.* 有个石子击到汽车上, 打坏了漆面.

paint[2] /peɪnt; pent/ *v* **1** [Tn, Cn·a] put paint onto (sth)

在(某物)上涂颜料或油漆: *paint a door, wall, room* 给门、墙、房间上漆 ○ *paint a house blue* 把房子刷成蓝色. **2** [I, Ipr, Tn] make (a picture) using paints; portray or represent (sb/sth) in paint 用颜料绘画; 画像; 画(某人[某事物]): *She paints well.* 她善于绘画. ○ *paint in oils/water-colours* 画油画[水彩画] ○ *paint a picture, a portrait, a still life, etc* 画图画、肖像画、静物画等 ○ *paint flowers, a girl, a landscape* 画花卉、女孩、风景 ○ (*fig* 比喻) *In her latest novel she paints a vivid picture of life in Victorian England.* 她在最新的一部小说里生动描绘了维多利亚时代的英国生活. **3** [Tn, Cn·a] (*often derog* 常作贬义) put powder, lipstick, etc onto (the face, etc) 涂或搽(脂粉、口红等): *She spends hours painting her face.* 她一化妆就是几个小时. ○ *paint one's nails red* 把指甲涂成红的. **4** (idm 习语) **not as black as it/one is painted** ⇨ BLACK[1]. **paint the 'town red** (*infml* 口) go out and enjoy a lively, boisterous time in bars, night-clubs, etc 到酒吧、夜总会等处寻欢作乐. **5** (phr v) **paint sth in** add sth to a picture using paint 在画上添画某物. **paint sth out** cover (a part of a painting) by putting paint on top of it 用涂料覆盖或涂掉(部分画面). **paint over sth** cover sth with paint 用涂料覆盖某物: *We'll have to paint over the dirty marks on the wall.* 我们得用涂料把墙壁上的污斑遮盖住.

painter[1] /ˈpeɪntə(r); ˋpentɚ/ *n* **1** person whose job is painting buildings, walls, etc 粉刷工; 油漆工: *He is a painter and decorator.* 他是油漆装饰工. **2** artist who paints pictures 画家: *a famous painter* 名画家.

painter[2] /ˈpeɪntə(r); ˋpentɚ/ *n* rope fastened to the front of a boat, used for tying it to a quay, ship, etc 艇首缆; 系艇索.

paint·ing /ˈpeɪntɪŋ; ˋpentɪŋ/ *n* **1** [U] action or skill of painting sth 涂色; 上油漆; 粉刷; 油漆技巧; 绘画. **2** [C] picture that has been painted 图画: *a painting by Rembrandt* 伦勃朗的画 ○ *famous paintings* 名画.

pair /peə(r); pɛr/ *n* **1** [C] two things of the same kind, usu used together 两件一起使用的同类东西: *a pair of gloves, shoes, socks, ear-rings* 一副手套、一双鞋、一双袜子、一对耳环 ○ *a huge pair of eyes* 一双大眼睛. **2** [C] object consisting of two parts joined together 由两部分组成的单件物品: *a pair of spectacles, tights, scissors, compasses* 一副眼镜、一双裤袜、一把剪子、一个圆规 ○ *My spectacles are broken — I'll need to buy another pair.* 我的眼镜坏了——我要再买一副. ○ *These trousers cost £30 a pair.* 这种裤子30英镑一条. **3** [pl *v*] two people closely connected or doing sth together 关系密切的或共做某事的两人: *the happy pair*, ie the newly married couple 燕尔新婚的一对 ○ (*infml* 口) *You've behaved very badly, the pair of you!* 你们表现得糟极了, 你们俩! **4** [CGp] one male and one female animal of the same species that mate with each other 雌雄一对的动物: *a pair of swans nesting by the river* 栖息河边的一对天鹅. **5** [C] two horses harnessed together to pull a carriage, etc 套在同一马车上的两匹马: *a coach and pair* 双驾马车. **6** [C] (either of) two Members of Parliament of opposing parties who agree that neither will vote in a division, so that neither need attend 议会中相约放弃投票权的对立两党的两名议员或其中一方. **7** (idm 习语) **in 'pairs** two at a time; in twos 一次两个; 两个一组: *Cuff-links are only sold in pairs.* 袖扣论对卖. **show a clean pair of heels** ⇨ SHOW[2]. ▷ **pair** *v* **1** [esp passive 尤用于被动语态: Tn, Tn·pr] **~ A with B** arrange (people or things) in a pair or pairs 使(人或物)成对或成双: *I've been paired with Bob* (ie Bob and I will play together as partners) *in the next round of the competition.* 下一轮比赛我和鲍勃搭档. **2** [I] (of animals) mate (指动物)交配, 交尾. **3** [esp passive 尤用于被动语态: Tn, Tn·pr] **~ with sb; ~ A with B** (in Parliament) (cause sb to) form a pair(6) (在议会中)(使敌对两党各一议员)相约放弃投票权. **4** (phr v) **pair (sb/sth) off (with sb)** (cause to) form a pair or pairs (使)成对, 成双: *The students had all paired off by the end of term.* 到学期末学生都已成双结对的了. ○ *Her parents tried to pair her off with a rich neighbour.* 她的父母想让她和一个有钱的邻居结婚. **pair up (with sb)** form a pair or pairs in order to work, play a game, etc together (为工作、比赛等)结成对或搭档.

Pais·ley /ˈpeɪzlɪ; ˋpezlɪ/ *adj* having a detailed pattern of curved petal-shaped figures 佩斯利涡旋纹图案的: *a Paisley tie, dressing-gown, etc* 佩斯利涡旋花纹领带、晨衣等.

pa·ja·mas (*esp US*) = PYJAMAS.

pal /pæl; pæl/ *n* (*infml* 口) **1** friend 朋友: *We've been pals for years.* 我们是多年的朋友. **2** (*sometimes ironic* 有时作反语) (used as a form of address 用作称呼语) man; fellow 老兄; 老弟; 兄弟: *Now look here, pal, you're asking for trouble!* 我说, 兄弟, 你是自找麻烦哪!

▷ **pal** *v* (**-ll-**) (phr v) **pal up (with sb)** (*infml* 口) become friendly (with sb) (与某人)结交, 为友.

pally /ˈpælɪ; ˋpælɪ/ *adj* **~ (with sb)** (*infml* 口) friendly 友好的: *She's become very pally with the boss/They've become very pally (with each other).* 她和老板关系非常好了[他们(彼此)非常要好了].

pal·ace /ˈpælɪs; ˋpælɪs/ *n* **1** official home of a sovereign, an archbishop or a bishop 宫殿; 皇宫; (大主教的)宅第: *Buckingham Palace* 白金汉宫 ○ *The palace* (ie A spokesman for the king, queen, etc) *has just issued a statement.* 王宫发言人刚宣布了一项声明. ○ [attrib 作定语] *a palace spokesman* 王宫发言人. **2** any large splendid house 豪华住宅: *Compared to ours their house is a palace.* 他们的房子和我们的相比简直太豪华了.

□ **ˌpalace revoˈlution** overthrow of a monarch, president, etc by people in positions of power working closely with him 宫廷革命.

palae(o)- (also *esp US* **pale(o)-**) *comb form* 构词成分 of ancient times; very old 古代的; 非常古老的: *palaeolithic* ○ *palaeontology*.

pal·aeo·graphy /ˌpælɪˈɒgrəfɪ; ˌpelɪˋɑgrəfɪ/ (also *esp US* **pal·eo·graphy** /ˌpeɪl-; ˌpel-/) *n* [U] study of ancient writing and documents 古文学; 古文书学. ▷ **pal·aeo·grapher** (also *esp US* **pal·eo-**) /-grəfə(r); -grəfɚ/ *n*. **pal·aeo·graphic** /ˌpælɪəʊˈgræfɪk; ˌpelɪəˋgræfɪk/ (also *esp US* **pal·eo-** /ˌpeɪl-; ˌpel-/) *adj*.

pal·aeo·lithic /ˌpælɪəʊˈlɪθɪk; ˌpelɪəˋlɪθɪk/ (also *esp US* **pal·eo-** /ˌpeɪl-; ˋpel-/) *adj* of or relating to the early part of the Stone Age 旧石器时代的.

pal·ae·on·to·logy /ˌpælɪɒnˈtɒlədʒɪ; ˌpelɪɑnˋtɑlədʒɪ/ (also *esp US* **pal·eon-** /ˌpeɪl-; ˌpel-/) *n* [U] study of fossils as a guide to the history of life on earth 古生物学. ▷ **pal·ae·on·to·lo·gist** (also *esp US* **pal·eon-**) /-ədʒɪst; -ədʒɪst/ *n*.

pal·at·able /ˈpælətəbl; ˋpælətəbḷ/ *adj* (**a**) pleasant to taste 可口的; 美味的. (**b**) (*fig* 比喻) pleasant or acceptable to the mind 合意的; 认可的; 认同的: *The truth is not always very palatable.* 事实真相并非尽如人意. ▷ **pal·at·ably** /-blɪ; -blɪ/ *adv*.

pal·atal /ˈpælətl *or, rarely,* 罕读作 pəˈleɪtl; ˋpælətḷ/ *adj* **1** of the palate 腭的. **2** (*phonetics* 语音) (of a speech sound) made by placing the tongue against or near the palate (usu the hard palate) (指语音)腭音的.

▷ **pal·atal** *n* (*phonetics* 语音) palatal speech sound (eg /j, ʒ, ʃ, dʒ/) 腭音(如/j/、/ʒ/、/ʃ/、/dʒ/).

pal·ate /ˈpælət; ˋpælɪt/ *n* **1** roof of the mouth 腭: *the hard/soft palate*, ie its front/back part 硬腭[软腭]. ⇨ illus at THROAT 见THROAT插图. **2** (usu *sing* 通常作单数) sense of taste; ability to distinguish one taste from another 味觉; 品味的能力: *a refined palate* 精于品味 ○ *have a good palate for fine wine* 善于品尝好酒.

pa·la·tial /pəˈleɪʃl; pəˋleʃəl/ *adj* (**a**) like a palace 像宫殿的. (**b**) extremely large or splendid 极大的; 富丽的: *a palatial dining room, hotel, residence* 富丽堂皇的餐厅、旅馆、居所.

pa·lat·in·ate /pəˈlætɪnət; *US* -tənət; pəˋlætṇɪt/ *n* area (formerly) ruled over by an earl or a count having some of the privileges of a sovereign 巴拉丁领地(旧时指欧洲享有特权的伯爵的领地).

pa·la·ver /pəˈlɑːvə(r); *US*-ˈlæv-; pəˋlævɚ/ *n* [U, sing] **1** (*infml derog* 口, 贬) fuss or bother, often with a lot of talking 忙乱, 烦恼, 麻烦(常指交涉): *What a palaver there was about paying the bill!* 付帐的事真费口舌呀! **2** (*often joc* 常作戏谑语) discussion 商量; 商议.

pale[1] /peɪl; pel/ *adj* (**-r, -est**) **1** (of a person, his face, etc) having little colour; having less colour than usual (指人、面色等)苍白的, 气色不如平时的: *She has a pale complexion.* 她面色苍白. ○ *Are you feeling all right? You look rather pale.* 你身体好吗? 你气色不太好. ○ *He went/turned deathly pale at the news.* 他得知这一消息后, 吓得面如土色. ○ *pale with anger, fear, shock, etc* 气得、

吓得、震惊得…脸色发白. **2** (**a**) (of colours) not bright or vivid (指颜色)浅的, 淡的, 暗淡的: *pale blue eyes* 淡蓝色的眼睛 ○ *a pale sky* 灰蒙蒙的天空. (**b**) (of light) dim; faint (指光)微弱的, 暗淡的: *the pale light of dawn* 晨曦的微光.

▷ **pale** *v* **1** [I, Ipr] **~ (with sth) (at sth)** become pale 变苍白: *She paled with shock at the news.* 她听到那消息大惊失色. **2** (phr v) **pale before, beside, etc sth** become less important in comparison with sth 相形见绌; 相形失色: *Her beauty pales beside her mother's.* 她的美貌和她母亲相比就逊色了. ○ *Their other problems paled into insignificance beside this latest catastrophe.* 最近发生这一灾祸后, 他们其他的问题都显得无关重要了.

palely /ˈpeɪllɪ; ˋpellɪ/ *adv*.

pale·ness *n* [U].

□ ˈ**pale-face** *n* (*derog* 贬) (said to have been used by N American Indians 据说为北美印第安人用语) white man 白脸(白种人).

pale[2] /peɪl; pel/ *n* **1** (**a**) pointed piece of wood forming part of a fence; stake (围栏的)尖木条. (**b**) fence or boundary 篱笆; 栅栏; 界限. **2** (idm 习语) **be**ˌ**yond the** ˈ**pale** considered unacceptable or unreasonable by people in general 越轨的; 社会不容的: *Those remarks he made were quite beyond the pale.* 他说的那些话太出圈了.

pale(o)- ⇨ PALAE(O)-.

pal·ette /ˈpælət; ˋpælɪt/ *n* thin board on which an artist mixes colours when painting, with a hole for the thumb to hold it by 调色板.

□ ˈ**palette-knife** *n* (**a**) thin flexible knife used by artists for mixing (and sometimes spreading) oil-paints 调色刀; 画刀. (**b**) knife with a long flexible round-ended blade used for spreading and smoothing soft substances in cooking 软铲(摊平软食物的炊具).

pal·imp·sest /ˈpælɪmpsest; ˋpælɪmpˌsɛst/ *n* (usu old) manuscript from which the original writing has been removed in order to create space for new writing (通常指旧的)手稿(已除去原文以供书写新内容).

pal·in·drome /ˈpælɪndrəʊm; ˋpælɪnˌdrom/ *n* word or phrase that reads the same backwards as forwards, eg *madam* or *nurses run* 回文(正读反读皆同的词或词组, 如madam或nurses run).

pal·ing /ˈpeɪlɪŋ; ˋpelɪŋ/ *n* fence made of pales (PALE[2] 1a) 栅栏; 木栅.

pal·is·ade /ˌpælɪˈseɪd; ˌpæləˋsed/ *n* **1** [C] strong fence made of pointed wooden stakes or iron poles, esp one used to defend a building 尖木栅, 铁栅栏(尤指护围建筑物的). **2 palisades** [pl] (*US*) line of steep high cliffs, esp along a river 峭壁(尤指河边的).

▷ **pal·is·ade** *v* [Tn] enclose (sth) with a palisade, esp in order to defend it 设栅栏护卫(某物).

pal·ish /ˈpeɪlɪʃ; ˋpelɪʃ/ *adj* rather pale 稍苍白的.

pall[1] /pɔːl; pɔl/ *v* [I, Ipr] **~ (on sb)** become uninteresting or boring by being experienced too often (因过多或过久)生厌, 感到乏味, 厌烦: *The pleasures of sunbathing began to pall (on us) after a week on the beach.* 我们在沙滩待了一周之后, 对日光浴已兴致大减.

pall[2] /pɔːl; pɔl/ *n* **1** cloth spread over a coffin 柩衣; 墓布; 棺罩. **2** (*fig* 比喻) dark or heavy covering (used esp as in the expression shown) 深色的或厚重的覆盖物(尤用于以下示例): *A pall of smoke hung over the town.* 市镇上空笼罩着烟幕.

□ ˈ**pallbearer** *n* one of a group of people who walk beside or carry the coffin at a funeral (出殡时)护柩者, 抬棺者.

pal·let[1] /ˈpælɪt; ˋpælɪt/ *n* large wooden or metal tray or platform for carrying goods, esp one that can be raised using a fork-lift truck (木或金属的)托盘或平台; (尤指可用铲运车叉起的)货板. ⇨illus at BOX 见BOX插图.

pal·let[2] /ˈpælɪt; ˋpælɪt/ *n* **1** mattress filled with straw 草荐; 草垫. **2** hard narrow bed 窄小的硬床.

pal·li·asse (also **paill·asse**) /ˈpælɪæs; *US* ˌpælɪˈæs; ˌpælˋjæs/ *n* mattress filled with straw; pallet 草荐; 草垫.

pal·li·ate /ˈpælɪeɪt; ˋpælɪˌet/ *v* [Tn] (*fml* 文) **1** make (esp a pain or disease) less severe or unpleasant, without removing its cause; alleviate 减轻, 缓和(尤指疼痛或疾病). **2** make (a crime, an offence, etc) seem less serious; excuse or extenuate 减轻, 掩饰(罪行、过失等); 为(罪行、过失等)辩解.

▷ **pal·li·ation** /ˌpælɪˈeɪʃn; ˌpælɪˋeʃən/ *n* [U] palliating or being palliated 减轻; 缓和; 掩饰; 辩解.

pal·li·at·ive /ˈpælɪətɪv; ˋpælɪˌetɪv/ *n, adj* **1** (medicine) that reduces pain without removing its cause 减轻的; 缓和的; 姑息剂; 治标剂: *Aspirin is a palliative (drug).* 阿斯匹林是一种缓解剂. **2** (thing) that reduces the harmful effects of sth without removing its cause 缓和物; 减轻的; 缓和的: *Security checks are only a palliative (measure) in the fight against terrorism.* 安全检查仅是反恐怖主义的一种消极措施.

pal·lid /ˈpælɪd; ˋpælɪd/ *adj* (of a person, his face, etc) pale, esp because of illness (指人、面色等)苍白的(尤指因病): *a pallid complexion* 苍白的面色 ○ *You look a bit pallid — do you feel all right?* 你脸色有点苍白——你没事儿吧? ▷ **pal·lidly** *adv*. **pal·lid·ness** *n* [U].

pal·lor /ˈpælə(r); ˋpælɚ/ *n* [U] (esp unhealthy) paleness of the face (尤指不健康所致的)脸色苍白: *Her cheeks have a sickly pallor.* 她面色苍白带有病容.

pally ⇨ PAL.

palm[1] /pɑːm; pɑm/ *n* **1** (**a**) inner surface of the hand between the wrist and the fingers 掌; 手掌; 掌心; 手心: *sweaty palms* 有汗的手掌 ○ *read sb's palm*, ie tell sb's fortune by looking at the lines on his palm 看某人的手相 ○ *He held the mouse in the palm of his hand.* 他把那老鼠放在手心上. ⇨illus at HAND 见HAND插图. (**b**) part of a glove that covers this (手套的)掌部: *gloves with leather palms* 掌部为皮革的手套. **2** (idm 习语) **cross sb's palm with silver** ⇨ CROSS[2]. **grease sb's palm** ⇨ GREASE *v*. **have sb in the** ˌ**palm of one's** ˈ**hand** have complete power or control over sb 完全掌握某人; 完全控制某人. **have an itching palm** ⇨ ITCH *v*.

▷ **palm** *v* **1** [Tn] hide (a coin, card, etc) in the hand when performing a conjuring trick (变戏法时)将(硬币、纸牌等)藏于手中. **2** [Tn, Tn·pr] hit (a ball) with the palm of the hand 用手掌击(球): *The goalkeeper just managed to palm the ball over the crossbar.* 守门员用手掌勉强把球挡过球门横木. **3** (phr v) **palm sb off (with sth)** (*infml* 口) dishonestly persuade sb to accept sth 诓骗某人接受某事物: *He tried to palm me off with some excuse about the bus being late.* 他托词公共汽车晚点骗我原谅他. **palm sb/sth off (on sb)** (*infml* 口) get rid of (an unwanted person or thing) by persuading sb else to accept him/it 将(自己不想要的人或物)劝说别人接受: *They palmed their unwelcome guests off on the neighbours.* 他们花言巧语哄得邻居同意, 便把不喜欢的客人打发到他们那里去了.

palm-trees 棕榈树

palm[2] /pɑːm; pɑm/ *n* **1** (also ˈ**palm-tree**) any of several types of tree growing in warm or tropical climates, with no branches and a mass of large wide leaves at the top 棕榈树: *a* ˈ*date palm* 枣椰树 ○ *a* ˈ*coconut palm* 椰子树 ○ [attrib 作定语] *palm fronds* 棕榈叶. ⇨illus 见插图. **2** leaf of such a tree as a symbol of victory or success (象征胜利的)棕榈叶: *the victor's palm* 胜利者的棕榈叶.

▷ **palmy** *adj* (**-ier, -iest**) **1** full of palm trees 多棕榈的; 棕榈树成林的. **2** [esp attrib 尤作定语] flourishing; prosperous 繁荣的; 兴盛的: *in my palmy days* 在我春风得意时.

□ ˈ**palm-oil** *n* [U] oil obtained from the nuts of various types of palm 棕榈油.

ˌ**Palm** ˈ**Sunday** the Sunday before Easter 棕枝主日(即复活节前的星期日).

pal·metto /pæl'metəʊ; pæl'mɛto/ *n* (*pl* **~s**) type of small palm-tree with fan-shaped leaves 矮棕榈.

palm·ist /'pɑːmɪst; 'pɑmɪst/ *n* person who claims to be able to interpret sb's character or tell sb's future by looking at the lines on the palm of his hand 看手相者.
▷ **palm·istry** /'pɑːmɪstrɪ; 'pɑmɪstrɪ/ *n* [U] (skill of) doing this 手相术.

palp·able /'pælpəbl; 'pælpəbḷ/ *adj* **1** that can be felt or touched 可触知的; 摸得出的. **2** (*fml* 文) clear to the mind; obvious 明显的; 明白的: *a palpable lie, error* 明显的谎言、错误. ▷ **palp·ably** /-əblɪ; -əblɪ/ *adv*.

palp·ate /'pælpeɪt; 'pælpet/ *v* [Tn] (*medical* 医) examine (sth) by feeling with the hands, esp as part of a medical examination 触摸检查(某物); (尤指)触诊. ▷ **palpa·tion** /pæl'peɪʃn; pæl'peʃən/ *n* [U].

pal·pit·ate /'pælpɪteɪt; 'pælpə,tet/ *v* **1** [I] (of the heart) beat rapidly (指心脏)急速跳动. **2** [I, Ipr] **~ (with sth)** (of a person or a part of his body) tremble or quiver because of fear, excitement, etc (指人或身体某部分)颤抖, 颤动(因恐惧、激动等): *palpitating with terror* 吓得发抖.
▷ **pal·pita·tion** /ˌpælpɪ'teɪʃn; ˌpælpə'teʃən/ *n* **1** [U] act of palpitating 心悸; 颤动. **2 palpitations** [pl] (period of) rapid beating of the heart 心悸(期): *I get palpitations if I run too fast.* 我跑得太快时就心悸. ○ (*fig* 比喻) *The thought of flying gives me palpitations*, ie makes me very nervous. 一想到飞行我心情就紧张.

palsy /'pɔːlzɪ; 'pɔlzɪ/ *n* [U] paralysis, esp with trembling of the limbs 麻痹, 瘫痪(尤指伴有四肢颤动者): *cerebral palsy* 大脑性麻痹.
▷ **pal·sied** /'pɔːlzɪd; 'pɔlzɪd/ *adj* affected with palsy 麻痹的; 瘫痪的.

pal·try /'pɔːltrɪ; 'pɔltrɪ/ *adj* (**-ier, -iest**) **1** very small; unimportant 微小的; 不重要的: *a paltry amount, sum, etc* 微不足道的数量、金额等. **2** worthless; contemptible 无价值的; 可鄙的: *a paltry excuse* 可鄙的借口.

pam·pas /'pæmpəs; *US* -əz; 'pæmpəz/ *n* **the pampas** [pl] extensive grassy treeless plains in S America 南美无树木的大草原. Cf 参看 PRAIRIE, SAVANNAH, STEPPE, VELD.
□ **'pampas-grass** *n* [U] type of tall ornamental grass with a silver-white feathery flower 蒲苇.

pam·per /'pæmpə(r); 'pæmpɚ/ *v* [Tn] (*often derog* 常作贬义) treat (a person or an animal) with too much kindness or indulgence; spoil 纵容(某人或动物); 宠; 娇养: *the pampered children of the rich* 有钱人家娇生惯养的子女 ○ *pamper oneself after a hard day at work* 劳累工作一日之后放纵自己.

pamph·let /'pæmflɪt; 'pæmflɪt/ *n* small book with a paper cover, usu containing information on a subject of public interest or expressing a political opinion 小册子(通常指有关时事或政治见解的).
▷ **pamph·let·eer** /ˌpæmflə'tɪə(r); ˌpæmflɪ'tɪr/ *n* person who writes pamphlets (上述的)小册子作者.

pans 锅类

pan[1] /pæn; pæn/ *n* (often in compounds 常用以构成复合词) **1** (**a**) wide flat (usu metal) container, with a handle or handles, used for cooking food in 锅; (通常为金属的)盘状器皿: *a 'frying-pan* 煎锅 ○ *a saucepan* 长柄炖锅 ○ *pots and pans* 锅壶盆罐. ⇨illus 见插图. (**b**) amount contained in this 一锅之量: *a pan of hot fat* 一锅热脂油. **2** any of various types of bowl-shaped containers 盆状器皿: *a lavatory pan*, ie its porcelain bowl 瓷便池 ○ *a 'bedpan* 床上便盆 ○ *a 'dustpan* 簸箕. **3** either of the dishes on a pair of scales (天平的)秤盘. ⇨illus at SCALE 见SCALE插图. **4** metal dish in which gravel is washed to separate it from gold or other valuable minerals (淘沙金等的)淘盘. **5** = SALT-PAN (SALT). **6** = HARD-PAN (HARD). **7** small cavity for gunpowder in the lock of an old type of gun (旧式枪上的)火药池. **8** (idm 习语) **a flash in the pan** ⇨ FLASH[1].
▷ **pan** *v* (**-nn-**) **1** [I, Ipr] **~ (for sth)** wash gravel in a pan in order to find gold or other valuable minerals 用淘盘淘: *prospectors panning for gold* 淘金的人. **2** [Tn] (*infml* 口) criticize (sth) severely 严厉批评(某事): *The film was panned by the critics.* 影片受到评论家的严厉批评. **3** (phr v) **pan sth off/out** wash (gravel) in a pan, to separate gold or other valuable minerals from it 用淘盘淘洗(含金或贵重矿物的砂砾). **pan out** (**a**) (of gravel, a river, an area, etc) yield gold or other valuable minerals (指砂砾、河流、地区等)产金或其他贵重矿物. (**b**) (*infml* 口) (of events or circumstances) develop; turn out (指事情或环境)发展, 结果: *It depends how things pan out.* 那得看事情结果怎样了.
□ **'pan-fish** *n* (*pl* unchanged 复数不变) (*US*) fish, usu caught for one's own use, that can be fried whole in a pan 可整条放入锅中煎的鱼(通常指自钓的).

pan[2] /pæn; pæn/ *v* (**-nn-**) (*cinema or broadcasting* 影或播) (**a**) [Tn, Tn·pr] move (a camera) to the right or left to follow a moving object or to show a wide view (为拍摄动景或全景)向右或向左移动(摄影机). (**b**) [I, Ipr] (of a camera, etc) move in this way (指摄影机等)移动拍摄: *The shot panned slowly across the room.* 镜头慢慢移动拍摄房间全景.

pan- *comb form* 构词成分 of or relating to all or the whole of 全的; 总的; 泛的: *panchromatic* ○ *pan-African* ○ *pantheism*.

pana·cea /ˌpænə'sɪə; ˌpænə'sɪə/ *n* **~ (for sth)** remedy for all diseases or troubles 治百病的药; 万灵药: *There's no single panacea for the country's economic ills.* 国家经济弊病百出, 并无万灵药可以医治.

pan·ache /pæ'næʃ; *US* pə-; pə'næʃ/ *n* [U] confident stylish manner 神气十足; 炫耀自负: *She dresses with great panache.* 她穿着十分浮华.

pan·ama /'pænəmɑː; 'pænə,mɑ/ *n* (also ˌ**panama** '**hat**) hat made of fine woven straw-like material 巴拿马草帽. ⇨illus at HAT 见HAT插图.

pa·na·tella /ˌpænə'telə; ˌpænə'tɛlə/ *n* long thin cigar 细长的雪茄烟.

pan·cake /'pæŋkeɪk; 'pæŋ,kek/ *n* **1** [C] thin cake of batter fried on both sides and (usu) eaten hot, sometimes rolled up with a filling 烙饼; 薄饼. **2** [U] make-up for the face consisting of powder pressed into a flat solid cake (化妆品的)粉饼. **3** (idm 习语) **flat as a pancake** ⇨ FLAT[2].
□ **'Pancake Day** Shrove Tuesday, when pancakes are traditionally eaten 薄饼日(忏悔节前一日, 按传统吃薄饼). ˌ**pancake 'landing** landing (usu made in an emergency) in which an aircraft descends vertically in a level position (飞机的)平坠着陆(通常为紧急降落).

pan·chro·matic /ˌpænkrəʊ'mætɪk; ˌpænkro'mætɪk/ *adj* (of photographic film) sensitive to all colours and able to reproduce them accurately (指摄影胶片)全色的.

pan·creas /'pæŋkrɪəs; 'pæŋkrɪəs/ *n* gland near the stomach that produces substances which help in the digestion of food 胰; 胰腺. ⇨illus at DIGESTIVE 见DIGESTIVE插图.
▷ **pan·cre·atic** /ˌpæŋkrɪ'ætɪk; ˌpæŋkrɪ'ætɪk/ *adj* of or relating to the pancreas 胰脏的; 胰腺的: ˌ*pancreatic* '*juice* 胰液.

panda /'pændə; 'pændə/ *n* **1** (also ˌ**giant** '**panda**) large rare bear-like black and white animal living in the mountains of SW China 大猫熊, 大熊猫(产于中国西南山区). **2** Indian animal like a raccoon, with brown fur and a long bushy tail 小猫熊, 小熊猫(产于印度, 似浣熊, 毛棕色, 尾长蓬松).
□ **'panda car** (*Brit*) police patrol car 警察巡逻车.

pan·demic /pæn'demɪk; pæn`dɛmɪk/ *n, adj* disease occurring over a whole country or the whole world 全国或全世界流行的(疾病). Cf 参看 ENDEMIC, EPIDEMIC.

pan·de·mon·ium /ˌpændɪ'məʊnɪəm; ˌpændɪ`monɪəm/ *n* [U] wild and noisy disorder or confusion 大混乱; 喧闹: *There was pandemonium when the news was announced.* 消息宣布后一片混乱. ○ *Pandemonium reigned in the classroom until the teacher arrived.* 教师来到之前教室里乱哄哄的.

pan·der /'pændə(r); `pændɚ/ *v* (phr v) **pander to sth/sb** (*derog* 贬) try to satisfy (a vulgar, weak or immoral desire, or sb having this); gratify sth/sb 迎合(他人的低级趣味或淫欲); 纵容某人; 迁就某事物: *newspapers pandering to the public love of scandal* 迎合公众喜好而报道丑闻的报纸. ▷ **pan·der** *n* = PIMP.

P and O /ˌpi: ən 'əʊ; ˌpi ən `o/ *abbr* 缩写 = Peninsular and Oriental (Steamship Company) (英国)半岛暨东方轮船公司: *the P and O line* 半岛暨东方轮船公司航线.

p and p /ˌpi: ən 'pi:; ˌpi ən `pi/ *abbr* 缩写 = (*Brit commerce* 商) (price of) postage and packing 邮资与包装费: *price £28.95 including p and p* ☆ 28.95 英镑, 包括邮资与包装费.

pane /peɪn; pen/ *n* single sheet of glass in a window 窗户上的单块玻璃: *a pane of glass* 一块窗玻璃 ○ *a 'window-pane* 一块窗玻璃. ⇨ illus at App 1 见附录1插图, page vi.

pan·egyric /ˌpænɪ'dʒɪrɪk; ˌpænə`dʒɪrɪk/ *n* (*fml* 文) speech or piece of writing praising sb/sth 颂词; 颂文.

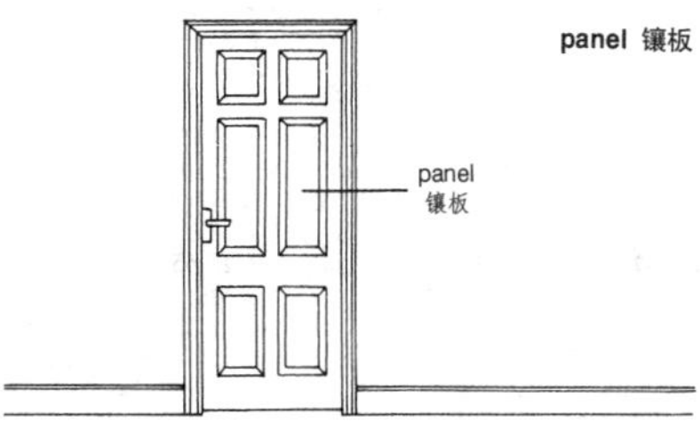

panel 镶板

panel /'pænl; `pænḷ/ *n* **1** [C] separate, usu rectangular, part of the surface of a door, wall, ceiling, etc, usu raised above or sunk below the surrounding area (门、墙、天花板等的)镶板, 嵌板(通常为矩形, 高出或低于周围部分): *a ceiling with carved panels* 带刻花镶板的天花板. ⇨ illus 见插图. **2** [C] piece of metal forming a section of the bodywork of a vehicle (车身的)金属板. **3** [C] strip of material inserted into a garment (衣服上的)镶条, 饰片, 嵌料. **4** [C] vertical board on which the controls and instruments of an aircraft, a car, etc are mounted (飞行器、汽车等的)控制面板, 仪表板: *an 'instrument panel* 仪表板 ○ *a con'trol panel* 控制板. **5** [CGp] group of people chosen to take part in a quiz, discussion, etc with an audience (esp of listeners to a radio or TV programme) (广播、电视中)与观众或听众一起进行智力竞赛、讨论等的一组人: *a panel of experts* 专家小组 ○ [attrib 作定语] *a 'panel game* 小组智力竞赛节目. **6 (a)** [C] list of people chosen to serve on a jury 陪审团成员名单. **(b)** [CGp] jury 陪审团. **7** [C] (*Brit*) list of doctors who treat patients in a certain area as part of the National Health Service 国民保健署医生名单.

▷ **panel** *v* (**-ll-**; *US* **-l-**) [Tn esp passive 尤用于被动语态] cover or decorate (sth) with panels (用镶板)镶嵌(某物); (用饰条)镶饰(衣服): *a panelled room, ceiling, wall, etc* 有镶板的房间、天花板、墙壁等. **pan·el·ling** (*US* **pan·el·ing**) *n* [U] **1** series of panels, eg on a wall 镶板细工; 镶板饰面: *a room with fine oak panelling* 带栎木细工镶板的房间. **2** wood used for making panels 镶板木料.

pan·el·list (*US* **pan·el·ist**) /'pænəlɪst; `pænḷɪst/ *n* member of a panel(5) (电台、电视台的)智力竞赛、专题讨论等的参加者.

□ **'panel-beater** *n* person whose job is removing dents from the bodywork of motor vehicles with a hammer 汽车板金工.

'panel truck (*US*) small enclosed van for delivering goods, etc 小型货车.

pang /pæŋ; pæŋ/ *n* (usu *pl* 通常作复数) **(a)** sudden sharp feeling of pain 突然的剧痛: *pangs of hunger/hunger pangs* 饥饿引起的胃疼. **(b)** feeling of painful emotion 悲痛: *pangs of jealousy, remorse, guilt, conscience, etc* 一阵阵忌妒、悔恨、负疚、自责等的痛苦.

pan·handle /'pænhændl; `pænˌhændḷ/ *n* (*US*) narrow piece of land projecting from a larger area (从一大片地向外伸出的)狭长地带.

▷ **pan·handle** *v* [I, Tn] (*infml* 口) beg for money from (sb) in the street 在街上行乞; 向(路人)乞讨.

panic /'pænɪk; `pænɪk/ *n* [C, U] **1 (a)** sudden irrational feeling of great fear 恐慌; 惊惶: *be in a (state of) panic (about sth)* (对某事)惊惶失措 ○ *I got into a panic when I found the door was locked.* 我发觉门锁上了, 十分惊慌. ○ *The thought of flying fills me with panic.* 我一想到飞行便吓得战战兢兢. ○ [attrib 作定语] *a panic decision*, ie one resulting from panic 慌乱中作出的决定. **(b)** fear that spreads quickly through a group of people (迅速传开的)大恐慌: *There was (an) immediate panic when the alarm sounded.* 警报响起时立刻引起一片恐慌. ○ *The collapse of the bank caused (a) panic on the Stock Exchange*, ie the value of shares fell quickly. 那银行倒闭, 证券市场上惶恐万状. **2** (idm 习语) **'panic stations** (*infml* 口) state of alarm or panic 惶惶不安; 惊慌: *It was panic stations when the police arrived to search the building.* 警方来搜查大楼时, 大家都很惊慌.

▷ **panic** *v* (**-ck-**) [I, Tn] **1** (cause a person or an animal to) be affected with panic (使人或动物)受惊: *Don't panic!* 别慌! ○ *The gunfire panicked the horses.* 枪声惊吓了马. **2** (phr v) **panic sb into doing sth** (often passive 常用于被动语态) make sb do (sth unwise or hasty) because of panic 使某人(因惊惶)仓促做(蠢事): *The banks were panicked into selling sterling.* 银行因恐慌而抛售英国货币.

pan·icky /'pænɪkɪ; `pænɪkɪ/ *adj* (*infml* 口) affected or caused by panic 受惊吓的; 由惊慌引起的: *Don't get panicky!* 不要惊慌! ○ *a panicky reaction, feeling, etc* 惊慌的反应、感觉等.

□ **'panic-stricken** *adj* in a state of panic; terrified 惊慌失措的; 万分恐慌的: *You look panic-stricken!* 看你惊惶失措的样子!

pan·jan·drum /pæn'dʒændrəm; pæn`dʒændrəm/ *n* (*joc* 谑) pompous self-important person 自命不凡的人.

pan·nier /'pænɪə(r); `pænɪɚ/ *n* **1** one of a pair of bags on either side of the back wheel of a bicycle or motor cycle (挂在自行车或摩托车后轮两侧的)挂篮, 挂包. **2** one of a pair of baskets carried on either side of its back by a horse or donkey (挂在马或驴两侧的)驮篮.

pan·ni·kin /'pænɪkɪn; `pænəkɪn/ *n* (*Brit*) **(a)** small metal cup 小金属杯. **(b)** its contents 小杯中之物.

pan·oply /'pænəplɪ; `pænəplɪ/ *n* (*fml* 文) **1** complete or splendid display of sth (某物的)全部的或华丽的展示; 气派; 盛况. **2** (formerly) complete suit of armour (旧时的)全副甲胄.

▷ **pan·op·lied** /'pænəplɪd; `pænəplɪd/ *adj* (*fml* 文) having a panoply 华丽的; 盛装的; 披挂甲胄的.

pan·or·ama /ˌpænə'rɑ:mə; *US* -'ræmə; ˌpænə`ræmə/ *n* **1 (a)** view of a wide area 全景: *From the summit there is a superb panorama of the Alps.* 从峰巅俯瞰, 阿尔卑斯山壮丽的景色尽收眼底. **(b)** picture or photograph of this 全景画; 全景照片. **2** view of a constantly changing scene or series of events (不断变化的)一连串景象或事情: *The book presents a panorama of British history since the Middle Ages.* 该书概述了中世纪以来的英国历史. ▷ **pan·or·amic** /ˌpænə'ræmɪk; ˌpænə`ræmɪk/ *adj*: *a panoramic view from the top of the tower* 自塔顶俯瞰的全景.

pan-pipes /'pæn paɪps; `pænˌpaɪps/ *n* [pl] musical instrument made of a series of reeds or pipes fixed together and played by blowing across the open ends 排箫; 潘神箫.

pansy /'pænzɪ; `pænzɪ/ *n* **1** garden plant with a short stem and broad flat brightly-coloured petals 三色堇. ⇨ illus at App 1 见附录1插图, page ii. **2** (*infml derog* 口, 贬) effeminate man; homosexual 女性化的男子; 同性恋男子.

P

pan-pipes 排箫

pant /pænt; pænt/ *v* [I, Ipr] **1** breathe with short quick breaths 喘; 喘息; 气喘: *He was panting heavily as he ran.* 他气喘吁吁地跑着. **2** (phr v) **pant along, down, etc** walk or run in the specified direction while panting 气喘吁吁地走或跑: *The dog panted along (the road) beside me.* 那狗一路跟在我身旁边喘边跑. **pant for sth** (used only in the continuous tenses 只用于进行时态) (**a**) show by one's rapid breathing that one needs to drink, catch one's breath, etc 呼吸急促显示渴、喘不过气来等: *panting for breath, a cool drink* 喘不过气来、喘着要冷饮. (**b**) have or show a strong desire for sth 渴望某事物: *panting for revenge* 渴望复仇 ○ *He was panting with desire for her.* 他拼命地追求她. **pant sth out** say sth with difficulty, while panting 气喘吁吁地说出某事: *He panted out the message.* 他上气不接下气地说出此事.

▷ **pant** *n* short quick breath 喘; 喘息; 气喘: *breathe in short pants* 气喘吁吁.

pant·ingly *adv*.

pan·ta·loon /ˌpæntəˈluːn; ˌpæntḷˈun/ *n* **1 pantaloons** [pl] (*US*; *Brit joc* 谑) trousers 裤子. **2** (also **Pantaloon**) (in pantomime) foolish old man on whom the dame plays tricks (童话剧中的)傻老头(常遭滑稽老太婆捉弄).

pan·tech·nicon /pænˈteknɪkən; pænˋtɛknɪkən/ *n* (*Brit*) large van used for moving furniture from one house to another 家具搬运车.

pan·the·ism /ˈpænθiɪzəm; ˋpænθiˌɪzəm/ *n* [U] **1** belief that God is everything and everything is God 泛神论. **2** belief in and worship of all gods 泛神信仰和崇拜.

▷ **pan·the·ist** /-θiɪst; -θiɪst/ *n* believer in pantheism 泛神论者.

pan·the·istic /ˌpænθiˈɪstɪk; ˌpænθiˋɪstɪk/ *adj* of, like or relating to pantheism (似)泛神论的; 关于泛神论的.

pan·theon /ˈpænθiən; *US* -θiɒn; ˋpænθiˌɑn/ *n* **1** (esp in ancient Greece and Rome) temple dedicated to all the gods (尤指古希腊和罗马的)万神庙. **2** all the gods of a nation or people (一国或一民族信奉的)众神: *the ancient Egyptian pantheon* 古埃及众神. **3** building in which the famous dead of a nation are buried or have memorials 先贤祠; 伟人祠.

pan·ther /ˈpænθə(r); ˋpænθɚ/ *n* **1** leopard, esp a black one 豹; (尤指)黑豹: *a black panther* 黑豹. **2** (*US*) puma 美洲狮.

pant·ies /ˈpæntɪz; ˋpæntɪz/ *n* [pl] (*infml* 口) short close-fitting knickers worn by women (女用)紧身短衬裤.

pan·ti·hose (also **pan·ty·hose**) /ˈpæntɪhəʊz; ˋpæntɪˌhoz/ *n* [pl *v*] (*US*) = TIGHTS.

pan·tile /ˈpæntaɪl; ˋpænˌtaɪl/ *n* curved roof-tile 波形瓦: [attrib 作定语] *a pantile roof* 波形瓦屋顶.

pant(o)- *comb form* 构词成分 all; universal 全部; 所有; 每: *pantograph* ○ *pantomime*.

panto /ˈpæntəʊ; ˋpænto/ *n* (*pl* **pantos** /ˈpæntəʊz; ˋpæntoz/) (*infml* 口) = PANTOMIME 1.

panto·graph /ˈpæntəgrɑːf; *US* -græf; ˋpæntəˌgræf/ *n* **1** instrument used to draw an exact copy of a plan, map, etc on any scale 缩放仪; 比例绘图仪. **2** device for carrying an electric current from overhead wires to a train (电气列车顶上的)导电弓架.

pan·to·mime /ˈpæntəmaɪm; ˋpæntəˌmaɪm/ *n* **1** (**a**) [C] type of play with music, dancing and clowning, based on a traditional story or fairy-tale and usu performed at Christmas 童话剧(通常于圣诞节期间演出): *Let's take the children to the pantomime!* 咱们带孩子去看童话剧吧! ○ [attrib 作定语] *a pantomime dame, horse* 童话剧中的滑稽老太婆、马. (**b**) [U] plays of this type 童话剧(总称): *She's acted in a lot of pantomime.* 她演过很多童话剧. **2** [U] expressive movements of the face and body used to tell a story (讲故事时)面部和身体的表意动作.

pan·try /ˈpæntrɪ; ˋpæntrɪ/ *n* **1** small room in a house where food is kept; larder 食品储藏室或柜. **2** (in a hotel, ship, large house, etc) room where glass, silver, table-linen, etc are kept (旅馆、轮船、大宅第等的)餐具室.

pants /pænts; pænts/ *n* [pl] **1** (**a**) (*Brit*) men's underpants; women's or children's knickers (贴身的)裤衩(男用的、女用的或儿童用的): *a clean pair of pants* 一条干净的短内裤. (**b**) (*esp US*) trousers 长裤; 裤子. **2** (idm 习语) **bore, scare, etc the ˈpants off sb** (*infml* 口) bore, scare sb extremely 使某人厌烦透顶、吓得要死等. **by the seat of one's pants** ⇨ SEAT[1]. **catch sb with his pants/trousers down** ⇨ CATCH[1]. **have ants in one's pants** ⇨ ANT. **in long/short pants** (*US*) grown-up/not grown-up 成年[未成年]: *I've known him since he was in short pants.* 我从他小时候就认识他. **wear the pants/trousers** ⇨ WEAR[2].

pap /pæp; pæp/ *n* [U] **1** soft or semi-liquid food suitable for babies or invalids (幼儿或病人的)软食, 半流质食物. **2** undemanding, trivial or worthless reading-matter 浅显的、无聊的或无价值的读物: *How can you bear to read such pap!* 这样无聊的读物你怎能看得下去!

papa /pəˈpɑː; *US* ˈpɑːpə; ˋpɑpə/ *n* (*dated infml* 旧, 口) (esp used by children 尤作儿语) father 爸爸. Cf 参看 POP[2], POPPA.

pap·acy /ˈpeɪpəsɪ; ˋpepəsɪ/ *n* **1 the Papacy** [sing] position or authority of the Pope 教皇的职位或权力. **2** (**a**) [U] system of government of the Roman Catholic Church by popes 罗马教廷. (**b**) [C] period of time when a pope is in office 教皇的任期: *during the papacy of John Paul II* 约翰·保罗二世在位期间.

▷ **papal** /ˈpeɪpl; ˋpepl/ *adj* of the Pope or the Papacy 教皇的; 教皇的职位或权力的; 罗马教廷的; 教皇任期的: *papal authority* 教皇的权力.

pa·paw (also **paw·paw**) /pəˈpɔː; *US* ˈpɔːpɔː; ˋpɔpɔ/ *n* **1** (**a**) (also **pa·paya** /pəˈpaɪə; pəˋpaɪə/) [C] tropical American tree similar to a palm tree 番木瓜树(似棕榈的热带美洲树). (**b**) [C, U] its edible oblong orange-coloured fruit 木瓜. **2** (**a**) [C] small N American evergreen tree 北美产矮小的常绿树. (**b**) [C, U] its small fleshy edible fruit 上述树结的可食小果.

pa·per /ˈpeɪpə(r); ˋpepɚ/ *n* **1** (often in compounds 常用以构成复合词) [U] substance made in thin sheets from wood pulp or rags and used for writing, printing or drawing on, or for wrapping and packing things 纸: *a piece/sheet of paper* 一张纸 ○ *ˈwriting paper* 书写用纸 ○ *ˈtissue paper* 薄棉纸 ○ [attrib 作定语] *a paper bag, handkerchief, towel, etc* 纸袋、纸巾、纸面巾等. **2** [C] newspaper 报纸: *Where's today's paper?* 今天的报纸在哪儿? ○ *a daily, an evening, a Sunday paper* 日报、晚报、星期日报. **3** [C, U] wallpaper 壁纸; 墙纸: *a pretty striped paper for the bedroom* 卧室用的精美的条纹壁纸. **4 papers** [pl] (**a**) official documents, esp showing sb's identity, nationality, etc 文件(尤指身分、国籍等证明材料): *Immigration officials will ask to see your papers.* 移民局的官员将要求你出示证件. (**b**) pieces of paper which have been written on 写有字的纸: *His desk is always covered with papers.* 他的办公桌上老是堆满写着字的纸. **5** [C] (**a**) set of examination questions on a particular subject 试卷(试题): *The geography paper was difficult.* 地理试题很难. ○ *The French paper was set by our form teacher.* 法语试卷是我们的班主任出的. (**b**) written answers to examination questions 试卷(答卷): *She spent the evening marking examination papers.* 她一晚上都在批试卷. **6** article or essay, esp one read to an audience of academics or specialists 文章; (尤指)论文: *He read a paper at a medical conference on the results of his research.* 他在医学会议上宣读了他的研究论文. **7** (idm 习语) **on paper** (**a**) in writing 以书面形式: *Could you put a few ideas down on paper?* 把你的一些想法写出来可以吗? (**b**) when judged from written or printed evidence; in theory 据书面材料; 在理论上; 从道理上说: *It's a fine scheme on paper, but will it work in practice?* 那计划不错, 不过实践上是否可行? ○ *She looks good on paper*, ie has good qualifications. 她看来资历很好. **a ˌpaper ˈtiger** person or thing that is less powerful or threatening than he/it seems or claims to be 纸老虎(外强中干的人或事物). **put pen to paper** ⇨ PEN.

▷ **pa·per** *v* **1** [Tn] put wallpaper on (the walls of a room) 用壁纸裱糊(墙壁): *We're papering the bathroom.* 我们正给浴室贴壁纸. **2** (idm 习语) **paper over the cracks (in sth)** hide a disagreement, fault or difficulty, esp quickly or imperfectly 隐瞒或掩饰分歧、错误或困难(尤指仓促或有漏洞): *Critics of government policy argue that the new measures introduced to fight crime are simply papering over the cracks.* 批评政府政策的人指责反犯罪活动新措施, 认为纯粹是为掩盖过错而制定的. **3** (phr v) **paper sth over** (**a**) cover sth with wall paper 用壁纸覆盖某物: *We papered over the stains on the wall.* 我们贴上壁纸盖住了墙上的污斑. (**b**) hide (a disagreement, fault or difficulty), esp quickly or imperfectly 隐瞒或掩饰(分歧、错误或困难)(尤指仓促或有漏洞).

pa·pery /ˈpeɪpərɪ; ˋpepərɪ/ *adj* like paper in texture (质地)像纸的: *wrinkled, papery skin* 像皱纹纸似的皮肤.

□ ˈ**paperback** *n* [C, U] book bound in a flexible paper cover 简装书; 平装书: *a cheap paperback* 廉价简装书 ○ *When is the novel coming out in paperback?* 那部小说的平装本什么时候出版? ○ [attrib 作定语] *a paperback book, edition* 平装的书、版本. Cf 参看 HARDBACK (HARD[1]).

ˈ**paper-boy** (*fem* 阴性作 ˈ**paper-girl**) *n* boy/girl who delivers newspapers to people's houses 送报的男孩[女孩].

ˈ**paper-chase** *n* cross-country run in which the leader drops a trail of pieces of paper for the other runners to follow 追纸游戏(领头者作越野跑, 沿途撒纸屑供他人循踪追逐).

ˈ**paper-clip** *n* piece of bent wire or plastic used for holding sheets of paper together 回形针.

ˈ**paper-knife** *n* knife used for cutting the pages of books, opening envelopes, etc 裁纸刀.

ˈ**paper-mill** *n* factory where paper is made 造纸厂.

ˌ**paper** ˈ**money** money in the form of banknotes 纸币.

ˈ**paperweight** *n* small heavy object placed on top of loose papers to keep them in place 镇纸.

ˈ**paperwork** *n* [U] written work in an office, such as filling in forms, writing letters and reports, etc 文书工作: *She's good at paperwork.* 她善做文书工作.

pa·pier mâché /ˌpæpɪeɪ ˈmæʃeɪ; *US* ˌpeɪpər məˈʃeɪ; ˋpepəməˋʃe/ (*French* 法) moulded paper pulp used for making boxes, trays, ornaments, etc 制型纸浆(用以制纸盒、纸盘、纸装饰物等的).

pap·ist /ˈpeɪpɪst; ˋpepɪst/ *n* (*derog* 贬) (used esp by Protestants 尤为新教徒用语) Roman Catholic 天主教徒.

pa·poose /pəˈpuːs; *US* pæˈpuːs; pæˋpus/ *n* **1** type of bag fixed to a frame, used for carrying a young baby on the back (背负幼儿用的)有框架的背袋. **2** N American Indian baby 北美印第安人的幼儿.

pap·rika /ˈpæprɪkə; *US* pəˈpriːkə; pəˋprikə/ *n* (**a**) [C] type of sweet pepper 一种甜辣椒. (**b**) [U] red powder made from this and used as a spice 辣椒粉.

pa·pyrus /pəˈpaɪərəs; pəˋpaɪrəs/ *n* **1** [U] tall reed-like water-plant with thick fibrous stems used by the Ancient Egyptians to make paper 纸莎草(古埃及人用以制纸的). **2** [U] this paper 纸莎草纸. **3** [C] (*pl* **pa·pyri** /pəˈpaɪriː; pəˋpaɪraɪ/) manuscript written on this paper (纸莎草纸上的)文献, 手稿.

par /pɑː(r); pɑr/ *n* **1** [sing] (also **par value**) price that is printed on stocks and shares; face value (证券与股票的)票面价值, 面值: *sell shares above/at/below par* 以高于[等于/低于]面值的价格出售股票. **2** [sing] (also **par of exchange**) recognized value of one country's currency in terms of another's 汇兑平价; 外汇牌价. **3** [sing] (in golf) number of strokes considered necessary for a first-class player to complete a hole or course (高尔夫球的)(一洞或一场球的)标准杆数: *Par for the course is 72.* 该球场规定的标准杆数是 72. ○ *She went round the course in three below* (ie three strokes less than) *par.* 她用比标准杆数少三杆打完该场. Cf 参看 BIRDIE 2, BOGEY 1, EAGLE 2. **4** (idm 习语) **below** ˈ**par** (*infml* 口) less well, alert, etc than usual 一般水平以下; 不大好: *I'm feeling a bit below par today.* 我今天不大舒服. **be** ˌ**par for the** ˈ**course** (*infml* 口) be what one would expect to happen or expect sb to do 不出所料; 料到某人要做某事: *She was an hour late, was she? That's about par for the course for her.* 她晚了一个钟头了吧? 她就是这样. **on a par with sb/sth** equal in importance, quality, etc to sb/sth 与某人[某事物]同等重要、同水平等: *As a writer she was on a par with the great novelists.* 她是与伟大小说家齐名的作家. **up to** ˈ**par** (*infml* 口) as good/well as usual 达到平常的高水平: *I didn't think her performance was up to par.* 我认为她表现得不及平时.

par (also **para** /ˈpærə; ˋpærə/) *abbr* 缩写 = paragraph: *see par 19* 见第19段 ○ *paras 39-42*, eg in a contract 第39至第42段.

para-[1] *pref* 前缀 (forming *ns* 用以构成名词) **1** beside; near 旁; 侧; 近: *parameter* ○ *paramilitary*. **2** beyond 外; 超: *parapsychology* ○ *paranormal*.

para-[2] *comb form* 构词成分 protecting from 保护; 防护: *parachute* ○ *parasol*.

par·able /ˈpærəbl; ˋpærəbḷ/ *n* (esp in the Bible) story told to illustrate a moral or spiritual truth (尤指《圣经》中)寓言故事: *Jesus taught in parables.* 耶稣以寓言讲道. ○ *the parable of the prodigal son* 浪子回头的故事.

para·bola /pəˈræbələ; pəˋræbələ/ *n* (*geometry* 几) plane curve formed by cutting a cone on a plane parallel to its side 抛物线. ⇨illus at HYPERBOLA 见 HYPERBOLA 插图.

para·bolic /ˌpærəˈbɒlɪk; ˌpærəˋbɑlɪk/ *adj* **1** of or expressed in a parable 寓言的; 以寓言故事表达的. **2** of or like a parabola (似)抛物线的.

para·chute /ˈpærəʃuːt; ˋpærəˌʃut/ *n* device for making people or objects fall slowly and safely when dropped from an aeroplane, consisting of an umbrella-shaped canopy attached to a harness 降落伞: *land by parachute* 跳伞着陆 ○ [attrib 作定语] *a parachute jump/drop* 跳伞[空投].

▷ **para·chute** *v* [I, Ipr, Tn, Tn·pr] (cause sb/sth to) drop by parachute from an aircraft (使某人)跳伞; 用降落伞空投(某物): *She enjoys parachuting.* 她喜爱跳伞运动. ○ *We parachuted into enemy territory.* 我们跳伞空降到敌占区. ○ *Supplies were parachuted into the earthquake zone.* 救援物资已空投到地震区.

para·chut·ist /-ɪst; -ɪst/ *n* person who drops from an aircraft using a parachute 跳伞者.

par·ade /pəˈreɪd; pəˋred/ *n* [C] **1** formal gathering of troops for inspection, a roll-call, etc (部队的)检阅、点名等: *a drill parade* 阅兵训练 ○ *ceremonial parades* 阅兵式. **2** = PARADE-GROUND. **3** procession of people or things (人的)游行, 行进; (物的)展示: *a parade of players before a football match* 足球赛前队员列队出场 ○ *a fashion parade*, ie one in which models display new clothes to an audience 时装表演. **4** (esp in names) public promenade or street of shops (尤指用于名称中的)广场, 商业街: *He lives in North Parade.* 他住在伦敦北街. **5** (idm 习语) **make a parade of sth** (*esp derog* 尤作贬义) display sth in order to impress people 炫示; 卖弄: *He's always making a parade of his knowledge.* 他老爱炫耀知识. **on parade** taking part in a parade; being paraded 接受检阅; 参加游行; 展示: *The regiment is on parade.* 该团正接受检阅. ○ *A number of new hats were on parade at the wedding.* 在婚礼上见到有些人戴着新式的帽子.

▷ **par·ade** *v* **1** [I, Tn] (cause sb to) gather together for inspection, a roll-call, etc (使某些人)集合接受检阅、点名等: *The colonel paraded his troops.* 上校检阅自己的部队. **2** [I, Ipr, Ip] march or walk in a procession or in order to display sth 游行; 列队行进; 为展示某事物而行进或行走: *The strikers paraded through the city centre.* 罢工者游行通过市中心. ○ *She paraded up and down in her new hat.* 她戴着新帽子在人前走来走去. **3** [Tn] display (sth); show (sth) off 展示, 炫耀(某事物): *She was parading her new fur coat yesterday*, ie wearing it to show it off to others. 昨天她向人炫耀她那件新的毛皮大衣.

□ **paˈrade-ground** *n* place where soldiers gather for inspection, a roll-call, etc 阅兵场.

para·digm /ˈpærədaɪm; ˋpærəˌdaɪm/ *n* **1** set of all the different forms of a word (一词的)词形变化表: *verb paradigms* 动词的词形变化表. **2** type of sth; pattern; model 范例; 样式; 模范: *a paradigm for others to copy* 供他人效法的范例. ▷ **para·dig·matic** /ˌpærədɪgˈmætɪk;

ˌpærədɪgˈmætɪk/ *adj*.

para·dise /ˈpærədaɪs; ˋpærəˌdaɪs/ *n* **1** [sing, without *a* or *the* 不用冠词 a 或 the] heaven 天堂; 天国. **2** (**a**) [C] ideal or perfect place 理想的或完美的地方; 乐园; 乐土: *This island is a paradise for bird-watchers.* 这个岛是鸟类观察者的理想去处. (**b**) [U] state of perfect happiness 完美快乐的境界; 至福; 极乐: *Being alone is his idea of paradise.* 他认为一人独处最美. **3** **Paradise** [sing, without *a* or *the* 不用冠词 a 或 the] (in the Bible) the Garden of Eden, where Adam and Eve lived in a state of innocence. (《圣经》中的)伊甸园. **4** (idm 习语) **a fool's paradise** ⇨ FOOL[1].

▷ **para·disa·ical** /ˌpærədɪˈzaɪəkl; ˌpærədɪˋseɪkḷ/ *adj* of or like (a) paradise (似)天堂的, 极乐的, 乐园的.

para·dox /ˈpærədɒks; ˋpærəˌdɑks/ *n* **1** (**a**) [C] statement that seems to be absurd or contradictory but is or may be true 似非而是的隽语; 看似矛盾而实际(或可能)正确的说法: *'More haste, less speed' is a well-known paradox.* '欲速不达'是人所熟知的隽语. (**b**) [U] use of this in talking or writing 用于语言文字中的上述隽语或说法: *Paradox and irony are characteristics of her style.* 她善于运用似非而是的隽语和反语. **2** [C] person, thing or situation displaying contradictory features 有矛盾特点的人、事物或情况: *It is a paradox that such a rich country should have so many poor people living in it.* 如此富足的国家竟有如此多的穷人, 这是个矛盾的现实.

▷ **para·dox·ical** /ˌpærəˈdɒksɪkl; ˌpærəˋdɑksɪkl/ *adj*. **para·dox·ic·ally** /-klɪ; -klɪ/ *adv*.

par·af·fin /ˈpærəfɪn; ˋpærəfɪn/ *n* [U] **1** (also ˈ**paraffin oil**) (*Brit*) (*US* ˈ**coal oil, kerosene**) oil obtained from petroleum, coal, etc and used as a fuel in heaters and lamps and as a solvent 煤油: [attrib 作定语] *a paraffin lamp, stove* 煤油灯、炉. **2** (also ˈ**paraffin wax**) wax-like substance obtained from petroleum, used esp for making candles 石蜡.

par·agon /ˈpærəgən; *US* -gɒn; ˋpærəˌgɑn/ *n* (**a**) ~ **of sth** person who is a perfect example of a quality (used esp in the expression shown) 有某品质的典范人物(尤用于以下示例): *a paragon of virtue* 美德的典范. (**b**) completely perfect person 完人: *I make no claim to be a paragon.* 我绝不认为自己是完人.

para·graph /ˈpærəgrɑːf; *US* -græf; ˋpærəˌgræf/ *n* **1** distinct section of a written or printed text, usu consisting of several sentences dealing with a single theme and starting on a new (usu indented) line 段落: *begin a new paragraph* 开始一个新段落. **2** (also ˈ**paragraph mark**) sign (¶) used to show where a new paragraph is to begin or as a reference mark 段落号¶(表示新段落开始处). **3** short report in a newspaper (报纸上的)短篇报道: *There's a paragraph on the accident in the local paper.* 当地报纸对该事故有一短篇报道.

▷ **para·graph** *v* [Tn] divide (sth) into paragraphs 将(某篇文字)分成段落.

para·keet /ˈpærəkiːt; ˋpærəˌkit/ *n* any of various types of small long-tailed parrot 长尾鹦鹉.

par·al·lel /ˈpærəlel; ˋpærəˌlɛl/ *adj* **1** (**a**) (of two or more lines) having the same distance between each other at every point (指至少两条线)平行的: *parallel lines* 平行线. ⇨illus at CONVERGE 见 CONVERGE 插图. (**b**) [pred 作表语] ~ **to/with sth** (of a line) having this relationship with another one (指一条线)与另一条线平行: *The road runs parallel with the railway.* 该公路与铁路平行. ○ *The road and the railway are parallel to each other.* 该公路与铁路相互平行. **2** exactly corresponding; similar 相对应的; 相同的; 类似的: *a parallel case, career, development* 相同的事例、职业、发展.

▷ **par·al·lel** *n* **1** [C] (also ˌ**parallel** ˈ**line**) line that is parallel to another 平行线. **2** (also ˌ**parallel of** ˈ**latitude**) [C] imaginary line on the earth's surface, or a corresponding line on a map, parallel to and passing through all points the same distance north or south of the equator (地球或地图的)纬线, 纬度圈: *the 49th parallel* 第49纬度线. **3** [C, U] person, situation, event, etc that is exactly similar to another 极相似的人、情况、事情等: *a career without parallel in modern times* 当代无匹的业绩. **4** [C] (**a**) comparison (used esp in the expression shown) 对比, 比较(尤用于以下示例): *draw a parallel between A and B* 把A和B相比较. (**b**) similarity 相似处: *I see parallels between the two cases.* 我看这两种情况有相似处. **5** (idm 习语) **in parallel** (of an electric current) having the negative terminals attached to one conductor and the positive ones to another (指电流)并联. Cf 参看 SERIES 2.

par·al·lel *v* [Tn esp passive 尤用于被动语态] **1** be equal to (sth); match (sth) 与(某事物)相当, 相匹敌: *His performance has never been paralleled.* 他的表演举世无匹. **2** be comparable or similar to (sth) 可与(某事物)相比; 与(某事物)相似: *Her experiences parallel mine in many instances.* 她的经历多与我的相似.

par·al·lel·ism /-ɪzəm; -ˌɪzəm/ *n* [U] state of being parallel; similarity 平行; 相同; 相似; 类似; 对应: *Don't exaggerate the parallelism between the two cases.* 不要夸大那两件事的相似性.

□ ˌ**parallel** ˈ**bars** pair of bars on posts, used for gymnastic exercises 双杠.

par·al·lelo·gram /ˌpærəˈleləgræm; ˌpærəˋlɛləˌgræm/ *n* (*geometry* 几) four-sided plane figure with its opposite sides parellel to each other 平行四边形. ⇨illus at QUADRILATERAL 见 QUADRILATERAL 插图.

para·lyse (*US* **para·lyze**) /ˈpærəlaɪz; ˋpærəˌlaɪz/ *v* **1** [Tn] affect (sb) with paralysis 使(某人)瘫痪或麻痹: *The accident left her paralyzed from the waist down.* 事故后她腰部以下瘫痪了. ○ *She is paralysed in both legs.* 她两腿麻痹. **2** [Tn·pr esp passive 尤用于被动语态] ~ **sb** (**with sth**) prevent sb from moving or acting normally 使某人不能正常活动: *be paralysed with fear, horror, shock, etc* 恐惧、恐怖、惊骇…得不知所措.

para·lysis /pəˈræləsɪs; pəˋræləsɪs/ *n* (*pl* **-ses** /-siːz; -ˌsiz/) **1** [C, U] loss of feeling in or control of a part of the body, caused by a disease of or an injury to the nerves 麻痹; 瘫痪: *suffer from paralysis of the right leg* 右腿麻痹 ○ *The paralysis affects his right leg and he can only walk with difficulty.* 他右腿瘫痪步履维艰. **2** [U] (*fig* 比喻) total inability to move, act, operate, etc (活动、运行等)瘫痪: *the complete paralysis of industry caused by the electricians' strike* 电气工人罢工造成的工业完全瘫痪.

para·lytic /ˌpærəˈlɪtɪk; ˌpærəˋlɪtɪk/ *adj* **1** suffering from paralysis(1) 患麻痹的; 瘫痪的. **2** (*Brit infml* 口) very drunk 烂醉如泥的: *She was/got completely paralytic last night.* 她昨天晚上喝得酩酊大醉.

▷ **para·lytic** *n* person suffering from paralysis 麻痹症患者; 瘫痪病人.

para·med·ical /ˌpærəˈmedɪkl; ˌpærəˋmɛdɪkḷ/ *adj* (of services) supporting and supplementing the work of doctors (指服务)辅助医务的, 护理的.

para·meter /pəˈræmɪtə(r); pəˋræmətɚ/ *n* **1** (*mathematics* 数) quantity that does not vary in a particular case but does vary in other cases 参量; 参数. **2** characteristic or feature, esp one that can be measured or quantified 特点, 特性(尤指可以衡量或计量的). **3** (usu *pl* 通常作复数) limiting factor or characteristic; limit (限定性的)因素, 特性; 界限: *We have to work within the parameters of time and budget.* 我们工作受时间和财力所限.

para·mil·it·ary /ˌpærəˈmɪlɪtrɪ; *US* -terɪ; ˌpærəˋmɪlɪˌtɛrɪ/ *adj* (relating or belonging to a military force that is) organized like but not part of the official armed forces 准军事的; 辅助军事的: *a paramilitary organization* 准军事组织 ○ *paramilitary activity* 辅助性军事行动.

▷ **para·mil·it·ary** *n* member of a paramilitary group or organization 准军事部队或组织的成员.

para·mount /ˈpærəmaʊnt; ˋpærəˌmaʊnt/ *adj* (*fml* 文) having the greatest importance or significance; supreme 最重要的; 最重大的; 至上的: *This matter is of paramount importance.* 此事至关重大. ○ *The reduction of unemployment should be paramount in the government's economic policy.* 降低失业率应是政府经济政策的头等大事.

▷ **para·mountcy** /-tsɪ; -tsɪ/ *n* [U] (*fml* 文) (state of) being paramount 至关重要; 至关重大; 至上.

para·noia /ˌpærəˈnɔɪə; ˌpærəˋnɔɪə/ *n* [U] **1** mental illness in which a person is obsessed by mistaken beliefs, esp that he is being badly treated by others or that he is somebody very important 偏执狂; 妄想狂. **2** (*infml* 口) abnormal tendency to suspect and mistrust other people 多疑. ▷ **para·noiac** /ˌpærəˈnɔɪæk; ˌpærəˋnɔɪæk/ *n, adj* = PARANOID.

para·noid /ˈpærənɔɪd; ˋpærəˌnɔɪd/ (also **para·noiac**) *adj* of, like, suffering from or showing paranoia (似)

(患)有偏执狂或妄想狂的; 多疑的: *paranoid fears* 偏执恐惧症 ○ *paranoid schizophrenia* 妄想型精神分裂症 ○ *She's getting paranoid about what other people think of her.* 她越来越怀疑别人对自己有什么看法. ○ *I don't think she likes me — or am I just being paranoid?* 我认为她不喜欢我 —— 难道只是我多心吗?

▷ **para·noid** *n* paranoid person (似)(患)有偏执狂或妄想狂的人; 多疑的人.

para·nor·mal /ˌpærəˈnɔːml; ˌpærəˈnɔrməl/ *adj* unable to be explained scientifically or rationally 超常的(无法用科学或常理解释的): *paranormal phenomena* 超常现象.

para·pet /ˈpærəpɪt, -pet; ˈpærəpɪt, -ˌpɛt/ *n* **1** low protective wall along the edge of a balcony, bridge, roof, etc 矮护墙; 女(儿)墙. **2** (in war) protective bank of earth, stones, etc along the front edge of a trench 胸墙.

para·pher·na·lia /ˌpærəfəˈneɪlɪə; ˌpærəfəˈneljə/ *n* [U] numerous small articles or personal belongings, esp the equipment needed for a hobby or sport 零星物品, 个人随身物品(尤指业余爱好或体育活动所需的): *skiing, climbing, jogging, etc paraphernalia* 滑雪、登山、慢跑等用的随身物品. ⇨Usage at DATA 用法见 DATA.

para·phrase /ˈpærəfreɪz; ˈpærəˌfrez/ *n* re-wording of a piece of writing, statement, etc, esp in order to make it easier to understand (对一段文字等的)释义, 意译(尤指为易于理解): *a paraphrase of the sonnet* 该十四行诗的意译.

▷ **para·phrase** *v* [Tn] express the meaning of (a piece of writing, statement, etc) in different words, esp in order to make it easier to understand 将(一段文字等)释义或意译(尤指为易于理解): *paraphrase a speech in colloquial English* 用通俗英语意译一篇讲稿.

para·ple·gia /ˌpærəˈpliːdʒə; ˌpærəˈplidʒə/ *n* [U] paralysis of the legs and part or all of the trunk(2) 截瘫; 下身麻痹.

▷ **para·ple·gic** /ˌpærəˈpliːdʒɪk; ˌpærəˈplidʒɪk/ *n, adj* (person) suffering from paraplegia 患截瘫或下身麻痹的(人): *She's (a) paraplegic.* 她下身麻痹. ○ [attrib 作定语] *ˌparaplegic ˈsports*, ie of or for paraplegics 截瘫患者体育运动会.

para·quat /ˈpærəkwɒt; ˈpærəˌkwɑt/ *n* [U] (*propr* 专利名) extremely poisonous weed-killer 百草枯, 对草快(除草剂, 极毒).

para·site /ˈpærəsaɪt; ˈpærəˌsaɪt/ *n* **1** animal (eg a flea, louse) or plant (eg mistletoe) that lives on or in another and gets its food from it 寄生物(如寄生虫或寄生植物). **2** (*derog* 贬) person who lives off others and gives nothing in return 靠他人为生的人: *live as a parasite on society* 像寄生虫似的靠社会为生.

▷ **para·sitic** /ˌpærəˈsɪtɪk; ˌpærəˈsɪtɪk/, **para·sit·ical** /ˌpærəˈsɪtɪkl; ˌpærəˈsɪtɪkl̩/ *adjs* (**a**) living as a parasite; like a parasite 寄生的; 似寄生物的; 靠他人为生的: *a parasitic plant, worm* 寄生的植物、蠕形动物 ○ (*fig* 比喻) *He lives a parasitic existence, borrowing money from his friends.* 他靠向友人借贷过寄生生活. (**b**) caused by a parasite 寄生物引起的: *a parasitic disease* 寄生性病害. **para·sit·ic·ally** /-klɪ; -klɪ/ *adv*.

para·sol /ˈpærəsɒl; *US* -sɔːl; ˈpærəˌsɔl/ *n* light umbrella used to give shade from the sun 阳伞. Cf 参看 SUNSHADE (SUN). ⇨illus at App 1 见附录1插图, page vii.

para·troops /ˈpærətruːps; ˈpærəˌtrups/ *n* [pl] soldiers trained to drop from an aircraft by parachute 伞兵部队.

▷ **para·trooper** /ˈpærətruːpə(r); ˈpærəˌtrupɚ/ *n* one of these soldiers 伞兵.

para·ty·phoid /ˌpærəˈtaɪfɔɪd; ˌpærəˈtaɪfɔɪd/ *n* [U] type of fever similar to typhoid, but less dangerous 副伤寒.

par·boil /ˈpɑːbɔɪl; ˈpɑrˌbɔɪl/ *v* [Tn] boil (food) until it is partly cooked 将(食物)煮到半熟: *Potatoes can be parboiled before roasting.* 土豆可先煮至半熟再烤.

par·cel /ˈpɑːsl; ˈpɑrsl̩/ *n* **1** (*US* also **package**) thing or things wrapped up for carrying or sending by post 包裹: *The postman has brought a parcel for you.* 邮递员给你送来了一个包裹. ○ *She was carrying a parcel of books under her arm.* 她胳膊下夹着一包书. ⇨Usage at PACKET 用法见 PACKET. **2** piece of land, esp on an estate (used esp in the expression shown) 一块地(尤指产业之一部分)(尤用于以下示例): *a parcel of land* 属产业上的一片地. **3** (idm 习语) **part and parcel of sth** ⇨ PART[1].

▷ **par·cel** *v* (**-ll-**; *US* **-l-**) (phr v) **parcel sth out** divide sth into parts or portions 将某物分成若干部分: *He parcelled out the land into small plots.* 他把那片土地分成小块. **parcel sth up** make sth into a parcel; wrap sth up 将某物打包; 包起某物: *She parcelled up the books.* 她把书包了起来.

□ ˈ**parcel bomb** bomb wrapped up to look like a normal parcel and sent by post 邮包炸弹.

ˈ**parcel post** system of sending parcels by post 包裹邮递: *send sth (by) parcel post* 用包裹邮寄某物.

parch /pɑːtʃ; pɑrtʃ/ *v* [Tn esp passive 尤用于被动语态] **1** make (sth) very dry and hot 使(某物)极干极热: *earth parched by the sun* 被太阳晒得干热的土地 ○ *the parched deserts of N Africa* 北非干热的沙漠 ○ *parched lips*, eg of a person with a fever 干裂的嘴唇(如发烧病人的). **2** make (sb) very thirsty 使(某人)极渴: *Give me a drink — I'm parched.* 给我点喝的 —— 我渴死了.

parch·ment /ˈpɑːtʃmənt; ˈpɑrtʃmənt/ *n* **1** (**a**) [U] heavy paper-like material made from the skin of sheep or goats and used for writing on 羊皮纸. (**b**) [C] piece of this material which has been written on 羊皮纸文稿. **2** [U] type of paper similar to parchment 仿羊皮纸.

par·don[1] /ˈpɑːdn; ˈpɑrdn̩/ *n* **1** [U] **~ (for sth)** forgiveness 原谅; 宽恕: *ask/seek sb's pardon for sth* 就某事请求某人原谅. **2** [C] (**a**) cancellation of a punishment incurred for a crime 赦免: *He was granted a pardon after new evidence had proved his innocence.* 有新证据证明他无辜, 因而他获得赦免. (**b**) document on which this is written 赦免令; 赦免状. **3** (idm 习语) **beg sb's pardon** ⇨ BEG. **I beg your pardon** ⇨ BEG.

par·don[2] /ˈpɑːdn; ˈpɑrdn̩/ *v* **1** [Tn, Tn·pr, Tsg] **~ sb (for sth/doing sth)** (*esp fml* 尤作郑重语) forgive or excuse sb for (sth) 就(某事)宽恕或原谅某人: *He begged her to pardon him (for his rudeness).* 他求她原谅他(无礼). ○ *pardon an offence, a fault, etc* 宽恕罪过、错误等 ○ *Pardon me (for) asking/Pardon my asking, but isn't that my hat you're wearing?* 对不起冒昧问一下, 您戴的是不是我的帽子? **2** (idm 习语) **excuse/pardon my French** ⇨ FRENCH.

▷ **par·don** *interj* (*US* also ˌ**pardon** ˈ**me**) (used to ask sb to repeat sth because one didn't hear it 用以请求某人重复所说). ⇨Usage at EXCUSE[2] 用法见 EXCUSE[2].

par·don·able /ˈpɑːdnəbl; ˈpɑrdnəbl̩/ *adj* that can be forgiven or excused 可宽恕的; 可原谅的: *a pardonable error* 可原谅的错误. **par·don·ably** /-əblɪ; -əblɪ/ *adv* (*fml* 文) understandably 可理解地; 可谅解地: *She is pardonably proud of her wonderful cooking.* 她对自己出色的烹调技术感到骄傲, 是可以理解的.

par·doner *n* (in the Middle Ages) person who was allowed to sell papal indulgences (INDULGENCE 4b) (中世纪时)获准出售天主教赎罪券的人.

pare /peə(r); pɛr/ *v* [Tn] **1** trim (sth) by cutting away the edges 修剪(某物)边缘: *pare one's finger-nails* 修剪指甲. **2** cut away the skin or outer covering from (sth); peel 剥或削(某物)的皮: *pare an apple* 削苹果. **3** (phr v) **pare sth down** reduce sth considerably 大量削减某物: *We have pared down our expenses to a bare minimum.* 我们已最大限度地削减了开支. **pare sth off (sth)** remove (skin, peel, etc) from sth in thin strips 一条条地剥去或削掉(外皮): *She pared off the thick peel with a sharp knife.* 她用一把锋利的刀削去厚厚的果皮. ⇨ Usage at CLIP[2] 用法见 CLIP[2].

▷ **par·ings** /ˈpeərɪŋz; ˈpɛrɪŋz/ *n* [pl] pieces that have been pared off 修剪、剥或削下之物: *ˈnail parings* 剪下的指甲.

par·ent /ˈpeərənt; ˈpɛrənt/ *n* **1** (usu *pl* 通常作复数) father or mother 父或母: *May I introduce you to my parents* (ie my father and mother)? 我把你介绍给我的父母行吗? ○ *Denise and Martin have recently become parents.* 丹尼斯和马丁最近当爸爸妈妈了. ○ *Do you get on with your parents?* 你和父母合得来吗? ○ *the duties of a parent* 为人父母者的责任. ⇨App 8 见附录8. **2** animal or plant from which others are produced (动植物的)亲代, 亲本, 父本, 母本: [attrib 作定语] *the parent bird, tree* 亲代的鸟、树.

▷ **par·ent·age** /-ɪdʒ; -ɪdʒ/ *n* [U] descent from parents; origin; ancestry 父母的身分; 家世; 世系; 出身: *a person of unknown parentage*, ie having parents whose identity

P

is not known 家世不明的人 ○ *of humble parentage* 出身卑贱.

par·ental /pə'rentl; pə'rɛntḷ/ *adj* [usu attrib 通常作定语] of or relating to a parent or parents 父的; 母的; 父母的: *parental affection, love, support, etc* 父母的疼爱、爱、养育等 ○ *children lacking parental care* 缺乏父母关怀的儿童. **par·entally** /pə'rentəlɪ; pə'rɛntlɪ/ *adv*.

par·ent·hood /'peərənthʊd; 'pɛrənt,hʊd/ *n* [U] (state of) being a parent 做父母的身分: *the responsibilities of parenthood* 父母的责任.

□ ˌ**parent 'company** commercial company that owns or controls one or more other companies 母公司; 总公司.

ˌ**parent-'teacher association** (*abbr* 缩写 **PTA**) organization of teachers and schoolchildren's parents, formed to improve relations and understanding between them 家长教师联谊会.

P

par·en·thesis /pə'renθəsɪs; pə'rɛnθəsɪs/ *n* (*pl* **-eses** /-əsi:z; -ə,siz/) **1** [C] additional word, phrase or sentence inserted into a passage which would be complete without it, and usu separated from it by brackets, dashes or commas 插入成分, 插入词语, 插入句(通常置于括号内或以破折号或逗号隔开). **2** [C usu *pl* 通常作复数] either of a pair of round brackets (like these) used to enclose an additional word, phrase, etc (圆)括号(一边或一对). ⇨App 3 见附录3. **3 in parenthesis** enclosed between parentheses 在(圆)括号里: *The statistics were given in parenthesis.* 统计数字在括号里. ○ (*fig* 比喻) *Let me add, in parenthesis,* ..., ie as an aside ... 让我加一句题外话....

▷ **par·en·thetic** /ˌpærən'θetɪk; ˌpærən'θɛtɪk/, **par·en·thet·ical** /-ɪkl; -ɪkḷ/ *adjs* of, relating to or inserted as a parenthesis (有关)插入词语的, 括号的, 括号里的: *parenthetical remarks* 插入的词语. **par·en·thet·ic·ally** /-klɪ; -klɪ/ *adv*.

par ex·cel·lence /ˌpɑ:r 'eksəlɑ:ns; *US* ˌeksə'lɑ:ns; pɑr 'ɛksə,lɑns/ *adv* (*French* 法) (used after a *n* 用于名词后) more than all others of its kind; to the highest degree 出众地; 超群地; 最高级: *He is the elder statesman par excellence.* 他是最优秀的年长的国务活动家. ○ *the fashionable quarter par excellence* 上流社会高级住宅区.

pa·ri·ah /pə'raɪə, 'pærɪə; pə'raɪə, 'pærɪə/ *n* **1** social outcast 社会的遗弃者; 贱民: *be treated as a pariah* 被待作贱民. **2** (in India) person of no caste or of very low caste (印度的)贱民, 帕利亚(洁净种姓以外的社会阶层的人).

pa·ri·etal /pə'raɪətl; pə'raɪətḷ/ *adj* (*anatomy* 解) of either of the bones (**parietal bones**) forming part of the sides and top of the skull 颅腔壁的; 顶骨的.

par·ish /'pærɪʃ; 'pærɪʃ/ *n* **1** [C] area within a diocese, having its own church and clergyman 牧区: *He is vicar of a large rural parish.* 他是农村一大牧区的牧师. ○ [attrib 作定语] *a parish church* 牧区教堂 ○ *a parish priest* 牧区牧师 ○ *parish boundaries* 牧区范围. **2** (also **civil 'parish**) [C] (in England) area within a county, having its own local government (英国)郡以下的行政区. Cf 参看 BOROUGH 1. **3** [CGp] people living in a parish, esp those who attend church regularly 牧区的居民; (尤指)牧区内按时上教堂的教徒: *The parish objected to some of the vicar's reforms.* 牧区教徒反对牧师的某些改革措施. **4** (idm 习语) ˌ**parish 'pump** [attrib 作定语] of or relating to local affairs 地方事务的; 区域性的: *parish-pump affairs, politics, gossip* 区域性的事务、政治、流言蜚语.

▷ **pa·rish·ioner** /pə'rɪʃənə(r); pə'rɪʃənɚ/ *n* inhabitant of a parish, esp one who attends church regularly 牧区居民; (尤指)牧区内按时上教堂的教徒.

□ ˌ**parish 'clerk** official with various duties in connection with a parish church 牧区执事.

ˌ**parish 'council** administrative body in a parish(1) 牧区管理委员会.

ˌ**parish 'register** book recording the christenings, marriages and burials that have taken place at the parish church 牧区记事录(记载牧区居民的洗礼、婚丧等事).

Pa·ris·ian /pə'rɪzɪən; *US* -ɪʒn; pə'rɪʒən/ *adj* of or relating to Paris 巴黎的; 关于巴黎的.

▷ **Pa·ris·ian** *n* native or inhabitant of Paris 巴黎人; 巴黎居民.

par·ity /'pærətɪ; 'pærətɪ/ *n* [U] (*fml* 文) **1** state of being equal; equality 同等; 相等; 平等: *parity of status, pay, treatment* 地位、工资、待遇的平等 ○ *Primary school teachers are demanding parity with* (ie as much pay as) *those in secondary schools.* 小学教师要求与中学教师同酬. **2** (*finance* 财) equivalence of one currency in another; being at par 平价; 价值对等: *The two currencies have now reached parity,* ie are at par. 这两种货币现已达到同等价值.

□ ˌ**parity of ex'change** official rate of currency exchange agreed by governments 平价汇率.

park[1] /pɑ:k; pɑrk/ *n* **1** public garden or recreation ground in a town 公园: *The children have gone to play in the park.* 孩子们到公园玩耍去了. **2** enclosed area of grassland, usu planted with trees, attached to a large country house (乡间巨宅的)庭园, (通常指)园林. **3** (*US*) sports ground or playing-field 运动或游戏场地. **4** (in compounds 用以构成复合词) (large) area of land used for recreation by the public 公共游乐场地: *a ˌnational 'park* 国家公园 ○ *a sa'fari park* 野生动物园 ○ *an a'musement park* 游乐场.

□ '**parkland** /-lænd; -lænd/ *n* [U] open grassland with clumps of trees 有树丛的开阔草地: *The house stands in 500 acres of rolling parkland.* 那所房子周围有500英亩起伏不平的草地.

'**parkway** *n* (*US*) wide road with trees, shrubs, etc along the sides and/or the central strip 林阴大道.

park[2] /pɑ:k; pɑrk/ *v* **1** [I, Ipr, Tn, Tn·pr] stop and leave (a vehicle) in a place for a time 停放(车): *Where can we park (the car)?* 我们在哪儿可以停(车)啊? ○ *You can't park in this street.* 这条街不准停车. ○ *You are/Your car is very badly parked.* 你的汽车停放得很不好. **2** [Tn, Tn·pr] (*infml* 口) **(a)** leave (sb/sth) in a place for a time (暂时)留下(某人); 寄存(某物): *Park your luggage here while you buy a ticket.* 你去买票, 行李就先放在这儿吧. **(b) ~ oneself** sit down 坐下: *Park yourself in that chair while I make you a cup of tea.* 你坐在那张椅子上, 我给你沏茶去.

parka /'pɑ:kə; 'pɑrkə/ *n* **1** jacket made from skin and with a hood, worn by Eskimos (爱斯基摩人穿的)带风帽的皮外套. **2** jacket or coat shaped like this and worn by mountaineers, etc (登山者穿的类似上述式样的)外套, 大衣, 皮猴儿.

par·kin /'pɑ:kɪn; 'pɑrkɪn/ *n* [U] type of cake made with ginger, oatmeal and treacle 麦片糖姜饼.

park·ing /'pɑ:kɪŋ; 'pɑrkɪŋ/ *n* [U] **(a)** stopping a motor vehicle at a place and leaving it there for a time 机动车停放: *There is no parking between 9 am and 6 pm.* 上午9时至下午6时禁止停放机动车辆. ○ [attrib 作定语] *a parking fine,* ie one incurred for parking illegally 违章停车罚款. **(b)** space or area for leaving vehicles 停车场: *Is there any parking near the theatre?* 剧院附近有停车场吗?

□ '**parking-lot** *n* (*US*) = CAR-PARK (CAR).

'**parking-meter** *n* meter into which one inserts coins to pay for parking a car beside it for a certain time 停车计时收费器.

'**parking-ticket** *n* notice of a fine imposed for parking illegally 违章停车罚款通知单: *I got a parking-ticket today!* 今天我接到一张违章停车罚款通知单!

Par·kin·son's dis·ease /'pɑ:kɪnsnz dɪzi:z; 'pɑrkɪnsənz dɪ,ziz/ (also **Par·kin·son·ism** /'pɑ:kɪnsənɪzəm; ˌpɑrkɪnsən,ɪzm/ *n* [U]) chronic disease of the nervous system causing tremors and weakness of the muscles 帕金森(氏)病; 震颤性麻痹.

Par·kin·son's law /'pɑ:kɪnsnz lɔ:; ˌpɑrkɪnsənz 'lɔ/ (*joc* 谑) idea that work will always take as long as the time available for it 帕金森定律(只要时间许可, 工作总得拖拉到最后).

parky /'pɑ:kɪ; 'pɑrkɪ/ *adj* [usu pred 通常作表语] (*Brit dialect infml* 方, 口) (of the air, weather, etc) cold; chilly (指空气、天气等)冷, 寒冷.

par·lance /'pɑ:ləns; 'pɑrləns/ *n* [U] (*fml* 文) particular way of speaking or use of words; phraseology 说法; 用语; 措辞; 术语: *in common parlance* 用普通的说法 ○ *in legal parlance* 用法律术语.

par·ley /'pɑ:lɪ; 'pɑrlɪ/ *n* (*pl* **~s**) (esp formerly) meeting between enemies or opponents to discuss terms for peace, etc (尤指旧时)敌对双方的和谈: *arrange/hold a parley with sb* 安排和某人讲和.

▷ **par·ley** *v* [I, Ipr] **~ (with sb)** have a parley 与某人谈判.

par·lia·ment /ˈpɑːləmənt; ˋpɑrləmənt/ *n* **1** [CGp] assembly that makes the laws of a country 议会; 国会: *the French, Spanish, etc parliament* 法国、西班牙等的议会. **2 Parliament** chief law-making assembly of the United Kingdom, consisting of the House of Commons, the House of Lords and the sovereign 英国国会(包括下议院、上议院和英王): *the ˌHouses of ˈParliament* 国会两院 ○ *a ˌMember of ˈParliament* 国会议员 ○ *The issue was debated in Parliament.* 这问题在国会中辩论过. ○ *get into* (ie be elected a Member of) *Parliament* 被选为议员 ○ *adjourn, dissolve (a) Parliament* 国会休会、解散国会 ○ *the State Opening of Parliament*, ie the ceremony in which the sovereign opens a new session of Parliament (君主参加的新的一届)国会会议开幕式. **3** [C] Parliament as it exists during the period of time between one General Election and the next 两次大选之间的一届议会或国会: *The government is unlikely to get the bill through within (the lifetime of) this Parliament.* 政府不大可能在本届国会(会期)内通过该项法案. **4** [C] building where a parliament meets 议会或国会的大厦.

▷ **par·lia·ment·arian** /ˌpɑːləmənˈteərɪən; ˌpɑrləmɛnˋtɛrɪən/ *n* person who is skilled at debating in parliament 议会中的雄辩家: *one of our most eminent parliamentarians* 我国议会中数一数二的雄辩家.

par·lia·ment·ary /ˌpɑːləˈmentrɪ; ˌpɑrləˋmɛntərɪ/ *adj* **1** [usu attrib 通常作定语] of or relating to parliament 国会的; 议会的; 关于议会或国会的: *parliamentary debates* 议会辩论 ○ *parliamentary procedure* 议会程序 ○ *a parliamentary recess* 国会休会期. **2** (of behaviour, language, etc) polite enough and suitable for parliament (指举止、语言等)符合议会礼节的.

par·lour (*US* **par·lor**) /ˈpɑːlə(r); ˋpɑrlɚ/ *n* **1** (formerly) sitting-room in a private house, esp one where people may receive visitors or talk privately (旧时)起居室, 客厅, 会客室. **2** (in compounds 用以构成复合词) (*esp US*) shop providing certain goods or services (出售商品或提供服务的)店, 馆: *a ˈbeauty/an ice-ˈcream/a ˈfuneral parlor* 美容院、冷食店、殡仪馆.

□ **ˈparlour car** = PULLMAN.

ˈparlour game game played in the home, eg a word-game 家中玩的游戏(如填字游戏).

par·lous /ˈpɑːləs; ˋpɑrləs/ *adj* (*fml or rhet* 文或修辞) full of danger or uncertainty; dangerous; very bad 充满危险或不定因素的; 危险的; 恶劣的: *the parlous state of international relations* 国际关系危机四伏 ○ *English tennis is in a parlous condition.* 英国网球运动不堪设想.

Par·mesan /ˈpɑːmɪzæn; *US* ˌpɑːrmɪˈzæn; ˌpɑrməˋzæn/ *n* [U] (also ˌ**Parmesan ˈcheese**) type of hard cheese made in Italy, usu grated and served on pasta dishes 帕尔马干酪(意大利产的硬干酪, 通常磨碎佐面食用).

pa·ro·chial /pəˈrəʊkɪəl; pəˋrokɪəl/ *adj* **1** [usu attrib 通常作定语] (*fml* 文) of or relating to a church parish 牧区的; 关于牧区的: *parochial matters* 牧区事务. **2** (*derog* 贬) showing interest in a limited area only; narrow 偏狭的; 狭隘的: *a parochial person, attitude, event* 心胸狭隘的人、偏狭的态度、地方事件 ○ *He is rather too parochial in his outlook.* 他的眼界未免过于狭隘了. ▷ **pa·ro·chi·al·ism** /-ɪzəm; -ˌɪzm/ *n* [U] **pa·ro·chi·ally** /-kɪəlɪ; -kɪəlɪ/ *adv*.

par·ody /ˈpærədɪ; ˋpærədɪ/ *n* **1** [C, U] **~ (of sth)** (piece of) speech, writing or music that imitates the style of an author, composer, etc in an amusing and often exaggerated way; comic imitation 诙谐模仿的言语、文字或音乐(作品): *a parody of a Shakespearian sonnet, an operatic aria, a well-known politician* 对莎士比亚十四行诗、歌剧咏叹调、著名政治家演说的滑稽模仿 ○ *She has a gift for parody.* 她有模仿他人风格的天才. **2** [C] thing that is done so badly that it seems to be an intentional mockery of what it should be; travesty 做得极糟的事物(迹近荒谬); 拙劣的模仿: *The trial was a parody of justice.* 那场审判是对正义的嘲弄.

▷ **par·od·ist** /-ɪst; -ɪst/ *n* person who writes parodies 滑稽模仿作品作者: *a gifted parodist* 有才华的滑稽模仿作品作者.

par·ody *v* (*pt, pp* **-died**) [Tn] make a parody(1) of (sb/sth); imitate comically 滑稽地模仿(某人[某事物]): *parody an author, a style, a poem* 滑稽地模仿一作家、一种风格、一首诗.

pa·role /pəˈrəʊl; pəˋrol/ *n* **1** [C, U] promise made by a prisoner that he will not try to escape if released for a limited time, or commit another crime if released before the end of his sentence (used esp in the expressions shown) (为获假释而作刑满前不逃跑或不犯罪的)誓言(尤用于以下示例): *be on parole*, ie have been released after making this promise 宣誓后获假释 ○ *let sb out/release sb on parole* 让某人宣誓后出狱[获假释] ○ *break (one's) parole*, ie commit a crime after being released from prison or fail to return to prison at the specified time 违誓(假释期间犯新罪或逾期不返监狱). **2** [sing] release of a prisoner after he has made this promise of good behaviour 假释: *He's hoping to get parole.* 他希望获得假释.

▷ **pa·role** *v* [Tn] release (a prisoner) on parole 准许(犯人)宣誓后获假释.

par·ox·ysm /ˈpærəksɪzəm; ˋpærəksˌɪzəm/ *n* sudden attack or outburst (of anger, laughter, pain, etc) (愤怒、大笑、疼痛等的)发作: *He went into a paroxysm of rage*, ie became very angry. 他勃然大怒. ○ *paroxysms of coughing, giggling, etc* 一阵咳嗽、傻笑等.

par·quet /ˈpɑːkeɪ; *US* pɑːrˈkeɪ; pɑrˋke/ *n* [U] flooring made of wooden blocks arranged in a pattern 拼花地板: [attrib 作定语] *a parquet floor* 拼花地板.

parr /pɑː(r); pɑr/ *n* (*pl* unchanged or **~s** 复数或不变或作 **parrs**) young salmon 幼鲑.

par·ri·cide /ˈpærɪsaɪd; ˋpærəˌsaɪd/ *n* **1** [C, U] (act of) killing one's father or a close relative 杀父或杀近亲(的行为). **2** [C] person guilty of this 杀父者; 杀近亲者. Cf 参看 PATRICIDE. ▷ **par·ri·cidal** /ˌpærɪˈsaɪdl; ˌpærəˋsaɪdḷ/ *adj*.

parrot 鹦鹉

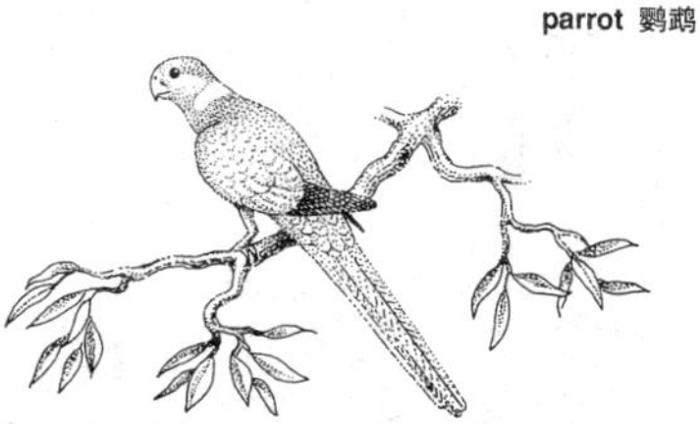

par·rot /ˈpærət; ˋpærət/ *n* **1** any of various types of tropical bird with hooked beaks and brightly-coloured feathers, some of which can be trained to imitate human speech 鹦鹉. ⇨illus 见插图. **2** (*esp derog* 尤作贬义) person who repeats sb else's words or imitates his actions without thinking 盲目重复他人的话或模仿他人行为的人. **3** (idm 习语) **sick as a parrot** ⇨ SICK.

▷ **par·rot** *v* [Tn] repeat (the words or actions of sb else) without thinking 盲目重复(某人的话); 盲目模仿(某人的行为).

□ **ˈparrot-fashion** *adv* (*derog* 贬) without thinking about or understanding the meaning of sth 鹦鹉学舌般地: *learn/repeat sth parrot-fashion* 机械地学习[重复]某事物.

parry /ˈpærɪ; ˋpærɪ/ *v* (*pt, pp* **parried**) [Tn] **1** turn aside or ward off (a blow or an attack) by using one's own weapon or one's hand to block it (用手中武器或徒手)格开, 挡开(打击). ⇨illus at FENCING 见 FENCING 插图. **2** (*fig* 比喻) avoid having to answer (sth) 对(某事)避而不答, 支吾搪塞: *parry an awkward question* 回避一令人尴尬的问题.

▷ **parry** *n* act of parrying, esp in fencing and boxing 挡开, 闪避(尤指击剑和拳击中).

parse /pɑːz; *US* pɑːrs; pɑrs/ *v* [Tn] (*grammar*) **1** describe the grammatical form and function of (a word), giving its part of speech, case[1](8), etc 对(一词)作语法分析. **2** divide (a sentence) into parts and describe them grammatically 对(句子)作语法分析.

Par·see /ˌpɑːˈsiː; pɑrˋsi/ *n* member of a religious sect in India whose ancestors originally came from Persia; believer in Zoroastrianism 琐罗亚斯德教教徒(祖先来自波斯的印度教派).

par·si·mony /ˈpɑːsɪmənɪ; US -məʊnɪ; ˋpɑrsəˌmonɪ/ n [U] (fml 文) excessive carefulness in spending money or using resources; meanness 吝啬; 小气; 过分节俭.
▷ **par·si·mo·ni·ous** /ˌpɑːsɪˈməʊnɪəs; ˌpɑrsəˋmonɪəs/ adj (fml 文) very careful in spending money or using resources; mean 吝啬的; 小气的; 非常节俭的: *a parsimonious old man* 非常节俭的老头. **par·si·mo·ni·ously** adv. **par·si·mo·ni·ous·ness** n [U] = PARSIMONY.

pars·ley /ˈpɑːslɪ; ˋpɑrslɪ/ n [U] herb with crinkled green leaves used for flavouring and decorating food 欧芹: [attrib 作定语] *parsley sauce* 欧芹沙司.

pars·nip /ˈpɑːsnɪp; ˋpɑrsnɪp/ n (**a**) [C] plant with a long, pale yellow, edible root 欧洲防风(根长, 淡黄色, 可食). ⇨illus at TURNIP 见 TURNIP 插图. (**b**) [C, U] this root cooked as a vegetable 欧洲防风根: [attrib 作定语] *parsnip soup* 欧洲防风根汤.

P

par·son /ˈpɑːsn; ˋpɑrsn̩/ n **1** (in the Church of England) parish priest; vicar or rector (英国国教的)牧区牧师, 牧区教堂牧师. **2** (infml 口) any Protestant clergyman 新教教士.
▷ **par·son·age** /-ɪdʒ; -ɪdʒ/ n parson's house; vicarage or rectory 牧区牧师住宅; 牧区教堂牧师的住所.
□ **parson's ˈnose** (US **pope's ˈnose**) (infml 口) piece of flesh at the tail end of a cooked bird, esp a chicken (烹调过的禽类的)屁股肉(尤指鸡的).

part[1] /pɑːt; pɑrt/ n (often without *a* when singular 用作单数时, 常不用冠词 a) **1** [C] **~ (of sth)** some but not all of a thing or number of things 部分: *We spent (a) part of our holiday in France.* 我们假期一段时间是在法国度过的. ○ *The early part of her life was spent in Paris.* 她早年住在巴黎. ○ *She had a miserable holiday — she was ill for part of the time.* 她假日过得很不痛快——因为病了一段时间. ○ *The film is good in parts.* 这部影片有些部分还不错. ○ *Parts of the book are interesting.* 这部书有些地方写得很有趣. ○ *We've done the difficult part of the job.* 我们已把工作中的困难部分做完了. ○ *The police only recovered part of the stolen money.* 警方只追回了部分赃款. ○ *Part of the building was destroyed in the fire.* 建筑物有一部分已烧毁. **2** [C] **~ (of sth)** (**a**) distinct portion of a human or animal body or of a plant (人或动植物可区分的)部分: *the parts of the body* 身体各部 ○ *Which part of your leg hurts?* 你腿上哪儿痛? (**b**) (usu essential) piece or component of a machine or structure (机器或结构的)部件, (通常指)组成部分: *lose one of the parts of the lawn-mower* 丢失刈草机上的一个零件 ○ *the working parts of a machine* 机器的操作部件 ○ *spare parts* 备件. (**c**) area or region of a country, town, etc (国家、市镇等的)地区, 区域: *Which parts of France have you visited?* 你去过法国哪些地方? ○ *Which part of London do you come from?* 你是伦敦什么地方的人? ○ *Do come and visit us if you're ever in our part of the world.* 什么时候到我们这一带来, 一定来和我们见见面. (**d**) member of sth 成员: *We'd like you to feel you're part of the family.* 希望你能感到像一家人一样. ○ *work as part of a team* 作为小组中一员进行工作. **3** [C] division of a book, broadcast serial, etc, esp as much as is published or broadcast at one time (书、广播连续节目等)部, 集(尤指长短适合于一次出版或播出者): *a TV serial in 10 parts*, ie instalments 十集电视连续剧 ○ *an encyclopaedia published in 25 weekly parts* 每周出一次, 分 25 个星期出齐的一套百科全书 ○ *Henry IV, Part II* 《亨利四世·第二部分》. **4** [C] each of several equal portions of a whole (整体的若干等份中的)一部分: *a sixtieth part of a minute* 一分钟的六十分之一 ○ *She divided the cake into three parts.* 她把饼分成三份. **5** [C usu *sing* 通常作单数] **~ (in sth)** person's share in an activity; role (活动中的)个人部分, 作用, 本分: *Everyone must do his part.* 大家都要做好分内的事. ○ *He had no part in the decision.* 他并未参予那一决定. ○ *I want no part in this sordid business.* 我不想和这一肮脏勾当有任何瓜葛. **6** [C] (**a**) role played by an actor in a play, film, etc (戏剧、电影等中的)人物, 角色: *He took/played the part of Hamlet.* 他去哈姆雷特这个角色. ○ *He was very good in the part.* 这个角色他扮演得十分出色. ○ (fig 比喻) *He's always acting/playing a part*, ie pretending to be what he is not. 他老是装模作样. (**b**) words spoken by an actor playing a particular role 角色的台词: *Have you learnt your part yet?* 你的台词背熟了吗? **7** [C] (music 音) melody or other line of music given to a particular voice or instrument 部; 声部; 段: *sing in three parts* 三部合唱 ○ *the piano, violin, cello, etc part* 钢琴、小提琴、大提琴等部. **8 parts** [pl] region or area 地区; 地域: *She's not from these parts.* 她不是这一带的人. ○ *He's just arrived back from foreign parts.* 他刚从国外归来. **9** [C] (US) =PARTING 2. **10** (idm 习语) **the best part of sth** most of sth (esp a period of time) (某事物的)绝大部分(尤指一段时间): *I spent the best part of an hour trying to find my car keys.* 我花了近一个小时找汽车钥匙. ○ *You must have drunk the best part of a bottle of wine last night.* 你昨天晚上喝了准有一瓶葡萄酒. **the better part of sth** more than half of sth (某事物的)大半, 多半: *We've lived here for the better part of a year.* 我们在这里住了多半年了. **discretion is the better part of valour** ⇨ DISCRETION. **for the ˈmost part** on the whole; usually; mostly 整体上; 通常; 多半: *Japanese TV sets are, for the most part, of excellent quality.* 日本电视机大多质量优良. **for ˈmy part** as far as I am concerned 就我来说: *For my part, I don't mind where we eat.* 对我来说, 到哪儿吃饭都无所谓. **the greater part of sth** ⇨ GREAT. **in ˈpart** to a certain extent; partly 在某种程度上; 部分地: *His success was due in part to luck.* 他成功的部分原因是运气好. **look the part** wear clothes or have an appearance suitable for a job, role, position, etc 在什么场合就有什么扮相: *At her wedding the new princess certainly looked the part.* 王妃在婚礼上还挺是那么回事. **a man/woman of (many) ˈparts** person with many skills or talents 多面手; 多才多艺的人. **on the part of sb/on sb's part** made or done by sb 由某人做出: *It was an error on my part.* 那是我的过失. ○ *The agreement has been kept on my part but not on his*, ie by me but not by him. 我一直遵守协议, 但他并不遵守. **part and parcel of sth** an essential part of sth 主要部分; 重要部分: *Keeping the accounts is part and parcel of my job.* 我的工作主要是记帐. **play a part (in sth)** (**a**) be involved in an activity 参加某活动: *She plays an active part in local politics.* 她积极参与地方政治活动. (**b**) make a contribution to sth; have a share in sth 对某事起作用、有贡献; 参与: *She played a major part in the success of the scheme.* 她对该计划的成功起了重要作用. ○ *We all have a part to play in the fight against crime.* 在与犯罪活动的斗争中人人有责. ○ *Economic factors have played a significant part in Britain's decline as a world power.* 英国在世界强国中的地位逐渐衰弱, 主要是经济因素造成的. **take sth in good ˈpart** react to sth in a good-natured way; not be offended by sth 对某事物往好处想; 不计较; 不介意: *He took the teasing in good part.* 他认为逗弄他并无恶意. **take part (in sth)** have a share or role in sth with others; be involved in sth; participate in sth 参加, 参与(某事物): *take part in a discussion, demonstration, game, fight, celebration* 参加讨论、游行、比赛、战斗、庆祝 ○ *How many countries will be taking part (in the World Cup)?* 有多少国家要参加(世界杯赛)? **take sb's ˈpart** support sb (eg in an argument) 支持某人(如在辩论中): *His mother always takes his part.* 他母亲总是站在他一边. ▷ **part** adv partly 部分地: *She is part French, part English.* 她有法国血统, 也有英国血统. ○ *The dress is part silk, part wool.* 这件连衣裙是丝毛混纺的. ○ *Her feelings were part anger, part relief.* 她既感愤怒又觉宽慰.
partly adv to some extent 在一定程度上: *She was only partly responsible for the accident.* 这次事故她只有几分责任. ○ *It was partly her fault.* 有一部分是她的错.
□ **ˌpart-exˈchange** n [U] method of buying sth in which an article (eg a car) is given as part of the payment for a more expensive one 部分抵价交易法(用旧物抵一部分价款购买较昂贵同类物品的方法, 如将旧汽车作价): *offer/take sth in part-exchange* 以部分抵价交易法出售[购买]某物.

ˌpart of ˈspeech (grammar) one of the classes into which words are divided in grammar, eg noun, adjective, verb, etc 词类(如名词、形容词、动词等).

ˌpart-ˈowner n person who shares the ownership of sth with sb else 共有者(与他人共同所有某事物者): *Tim is part-owner of the flat.* 蒂姆有该居住单位的部分产权. **ˌpart-ˈownership** n [U].

ˈpart-singing n [U] singing part-songs 多声部合唱.

ˈpart-song n song with three or more parts (PART[1] 7) 合唱曲.

ˌ**part-'time** *adj, adv* for only a part of the working day or week (一天或一星期中)部分时间工作的；兼职的：*ˌpart-time 'work/em'ployment* 兼职工作[非全职雇佣] ○ *She's looking for a ˌpart-time 'job.* 她在寻找兼职工作. ○ *ˌpart-time 'workers* 兼职工作人员 ○ *work part-'time* 兼职工作. ˌ**part-'timer** *n* part-time worker 兼职工作者. Cf 参看 FULL-TIME (FULL).

part[2] /pɑːt; pɑrt/ *v* **1** [I, Ipr, Tn, Tn·pr] **~ (from sb); ~ sb (from sb)** (cause sb to) go away or separate from sb (使某人)离开或与某人分离: *I hope we can part (as) friends*, ie leave one another with no feeling of anger or resentment, eg after a quarrel. 希望我们能像朋友般和气分手. ○ *They exchanged a final kiss before parting.* 他们最后相互亲吻而分离. ○ *She has parted from her husband/She and her husband have parted*, ie started to live apart. 她和丈夫已分居了. ○ *The children were parted from their father.* 孩子们和父亲分开了. **2** [I, Tn] (cause sb/sth to) divide or form separate parts (使某人[某物])分开，分成部分：*Her lips parted in a smile.* 她绽唇微笑. ○ *The crowd parted to let them through.* 人群分开好让他们通过. ○ *The clouds parted and the sun shone through.* 云开日出. ○ *The police parted the crowd.* 警察驱散了人群. **3** [Tn] separate (the hair of the head) along a line and comb the hair away from it 将(头发)梳成分头：*He parts his hair in the middle.* 他的头发是中分的. **4** (idm 习语) **a fool and his money are soon parted** ⇨ FOOL[1]. **part 'company (with sb/sth)** (**a**) go different ways or separate after being together 分手；各奔东西；各奔前程：*We parted company at the bus-stop.* 我们在公共汽车站分手了. ○ *He and his agent have parted company/He has parted company with his agent.* 他和他的代理人散伙了. ○ (*joc* 谑) *Her blouse had parted company with her skirt*, ie become untucked. 她的上衣从裙子里出来了. ○ (*fig* 比喻) *It is on political questions that their views part company*, ie are different. 他们在政治问题上见解不同. (**b**) disagree with sb 与某人意见不合：*I'm afraid I have to part company with you there.* 看来在这一点上我不敢苟同. **5** (phr v) **part with sth** give away or relinquish sth 放弃或出让某物：*Despite his poverty, he refused to part with the family jewels.* 他尽管贫穷，却不肯变卖家中的珠宝. ○ *He hates parting with* (ie spending) *his money.* 他很不喜欢花钱.

par·take /pɑːˈteɪk; pɑrˋtek/ *v* (*pt* **partook** /-ˈtʊk; -ˋtʊk/, *pp* **partaken** /-ˈteɪkən; -ˋtekən/) [I, Ipr] **~ (of sth)** (*fml or rhet* 文或修辞) eat or drink a part or portion of sth 吃；喝：*They invited us to partake of their simple meal.* 他们邀请我们吃便饭. ○ *Will you partake of a glass of sherry?* 你要喝杯雪利酒吗?

par·terre /pɑːˈteə(r); pɑrˋtɛr/ *n* level space in a large garden, with ornamental flower beds separated by lawns or paths (花园中的)花坛区.

par·theno·gen·esis /ˌpɑːθɪnəʊˈdʒenəsɪs; ˌpɑrθəno-ˋdʒɛnəsɪs/ *n* [U] (*biology* 生) type of reproduction in some insects and plants, in which the ovum develops without being fertilized by the male 单性生殖；孤雌生殖.

Par·thian shot /ˌpɑːθɪən ˈʃɒt; ˌpɑrθɪən ˋʃɑt/ sharp or telling remark made by sb as he leaves 临别所说的刻薄话. Cf 参看 A PARTING SHOT (PARTING).

par·tial /ˈpɑːʃl; ˋpɑrʃəl/ *adj* **1** of or forming a part; not complete 部分的；不完全的：*a partial recovery*, eg after an illness 部分复原 ○ *Our holiday was only a partial success.* 我们的假日过得只能说是差强人意. ○ *a partial eclipse of the sun* 日偏食. **2** [usu pred 通常作表语] **~ (towards sb/sth)** showing too much favour to one person or side; biased 偏心；偏向；偏袒：*The referee was accused of being partial (towards the home team).* 裁判受指责(对本地队)偏心. Cf 参看 IMPARTIAL. **3** [pred 作表语] **~ to sb/sth** having a strong liking for sb/sth 偏爱某人[某事物]的：*He's (rather) partial to a glass of brandy after dinner.* 他(很)爱饭后喝一杯白兰地.

▷ **par·ti·al·ity** /ˌpɑːʃɪˈælətɪ; ˌpɑrʃɪˋælətɪ/ *n* **1** [U] **~ (towards sb/sth)** being partial(2); bias; favouritism 偏向；偏见；偏袒：*He judged the case without partiality.* 他判决该案十分公正. **2** [C] **~ for sb/sth** liking or fondness for sb/sth 偏爱、爱好某人[某事物]：*She has a partiality for French cheese.* 她偏爱法国干酪.

par·tially /ˈpɑːʃəlɪ; ˋpɑrʃəlɪ/ *adv* **1** not completely; partly 不完全地；部分地：*He is partially paralysed.* 他身体有一部分瘫痪了. **2** in a partial(2) manner 偏心地；偏向地；偏袒地.

par·ti·cip·ate /pɑːˈtɪsɪpeɪt; pɑrˋtɪsəˌpet/ *v* [I, Ipr] **~ (in sth)** take part or become involved (in an activity) 参加，参与(某活动)：*participate in a competition, discussion, meeting* 参加竞赛、讨论、会议 ○ *She actively participates in local politics.* 她积极参与本地政治活动. ○ *How many countries will be participating (in the Olympic Games)?* 有多少国家要参加(奥林匹克运动会)?

▷ **par·ti·cip·ant** /pɑːˈtɪsɪpənt; pɑrˋtɪsəpənt/ *n* **~ (in sth)** person or group of people who participate in sth 参加者：*All the participants in the debate had an opportunity to speak.* 所有参加辩论的人都有机会发言.

par·ti·cipa·tion /pɑːˌtɪsɪˈpeɪʃn; pɑrˌtɪsəˋpeʃən/ *n* [U] **~ (in sth)** (action of) participating in sth 参加：*Union leaders called for the active participation of all members in the day of protest.* 工会领袖号召抗议那天全体会员积极参加.

par·ti·ciple /ˈpɑːtɪsɪpl; ˋpɑrtəˌsɪpl/ *n* (*grammar*) word formed from a verb, ending in *-ing* (*present participle*) or *-ed, -en*, etc (*past participle*) and used in verb phrases (eg *She is going* or *She has gone*) or as an adjective (eg *a fascinating story*) 分词：*'Hurrying' and 'hurried' are the present and past participles of 'hurry'.* hurrying 和 hurried 是 hurry 的现在分词和过去分词.

▷ **par·ti·ci·pial** /ˌpɑːtɪˈsɪpɪəl; ˌpɑrtəˋsɪpɪəl/ *adj* consisting of or being a participle 由分词组成的；分词的：*'Loving' in 'a loving mother' and 'polished' in 'polished wood' are participial adjectives.* ☆ loving mother 中的 loving 和 polished wood 中的 polished 是分词形容词.

par·ticle /ˈpɑːtɪkl; ˋpɑrtɪkl/ *n* **1** very small bit or piece (of sth) 微粒；粒子：*particles of dust/dust particles* 尘埃 ○ *He choked on a particle of food.* 他让一小粒食物噎住了. **2** smallest possible amount 极少量：*There's not a particle of truth in her story.* 她讲的没有一句实话. **3** (also **adˌverbial 'particle**) (*grammar*) word (eg *away, back, down*) used esp after a verb to show position, direction of movement, etc 副词小词(如 away、back、down, 尤用于动词后，表示位置、运动方向等)：*In 'break down' and 'tell sb off', 'down' and 'off' are adverbial particles.* 在 break down 和 tell sb off 两词组中，down 和 off 都是副词小词.

par·ti·col·oured /ˈpɑːtɪkʌləd; ˋpɑrtɪˌkʌlɚd/ (*US* **-col·ored**) *adj* having different colours in different parts 杂色的；斑驳的.

par·ticu·lar /pəˈtɪkjʊlə(r); pɚˋtɪkjəlɚ/ *adj* **1** [attrib 作定语] relating to one person or thing rather than others; individual 个别的；个人的：*in this particular case* 在此个别情况中 ○ *his particular problems* 他个人的问题 ○ *Is there any particular colour you would prefer?* 你有什么特别喜欢的颜色吗? **2** [attrib 作定语] more than usual; special; exceptional 非一般的；特别的；特殊的：*a matter of particular importance* 特别重要的事情 ○ *for no particular reason* 无特殊原因 ○ *She took particular care not to overcook the meat.* 她特别小心不把肉烹调过火. ○ *He is a particular friend of mine.* 他是我的特殊朋友. **3** **~ (about/over sth)** giving close attention to detail; difficult to please; fussy 非常讲究的；难以满足的；挑剔的；吹毛求疵的：*She's very particular about what she wears.* 她对衣着很讲究. ○ *She's a very particular person.* 她这个人很挑剔. ○ *particular about cleanliness, money matters, one's appearance* 对清洁、钱财、个人仪表很认真. **4** (idm 习语) **in par'ticular** especially or specifically 尤其；特别：*The whole meal was good but the wine in particular was excellent.* 整顿饭都很好，尤其是葡萄酒更好. ○ *'Is there anything in particular you'd like for dinner?' 'No, nothing in particular.'* '正餐你有什么特别喜欢的菜吗?' '没有，什么都行.'

▷ **par·ticu·lar** *n* (often *pl* 常作复数) piece of information; detail; fact 信息；细节；事项：*Her account is correct in every particular/all particulars.* 她的帐目笔笔无误. ○ *He gave full particulars of the stolen property.* 他详细列出全部被盗的财物. ○ *The policewoman wrote down his particulars*, ie his name, address, etc. 女警记下了他的个人资料.

par·ti·cu·lar·ity /pəˌtɪkjʊˈlærətɪ; pɚˌtɪkjəˋlærətɪ/ *n* [U] (**a**) quality of being individual or particular(1) 个别的特性；个性. (**b**) attention to detail; exactness 仔细；精细；详细；精确.

P

par·ti·cular·ize, -ise /pəˈtɪkjʊləraɪz; pɚˈtɪkjələˌraɪz/ *v* [I, Tn] name or state (sth) specially or one by one; specify (items) 逐一列举或具体说明(某事物). **par·tic·ular·iza·tion, -isation** /pəˌtɪkjʊləraɪˈzeɪʃn; pɚˌtɪkjələrəˈzeʃən/ *n* [U].

par·ticu·larly *adv* especially 尤其; 特别地; 特殊地: *I like all her novels, but her latest is particularly good.* 她的小说我都喜欢, 最新的一部尤其好. ○ *Be particularly careful when driving at night.* 晚上开车要特别小心. ○ *I particularly want to see that film.* 我特别想看那部电影.

part·ing /ˈpɑːtɪŋ; ˈpɑrtɪŋ/ *n* **1** [C, U] (act of) leaving sb; departure 离开某人; 分别; 分手: *a tearful parting* 洒泪而别 ○ [attrib 作定语] *a parting kiss* 离别一吻. **2** [C] (*US* **part**) line where the hair is combed away in different directions (头发的)分缝. ⇨illus at HAIR 见HAIR插图. **3** (idm 习语) **a/the ˌparting of the ˈways** (**a**) place where a road, etc divides into two (道路等的)一分为二的地方; 三岔路口; 丁字街. (**b**) point at which one has to decide between two courses of action 须在两者间做出抉择之点. **a ˌparting ˈshot** action or comment, esp an unfriendly or unkind one, made by a person as he departs 临别的言行(尤指不友好的或恶意的). Cf 参看 PARTHIAN SHOT.

P

par·tisan /ˌpɑːtɪˈzæn, ˈpɑːtɪzæn; *US* ˈpɑːrtɪzn; ˈpɑrtəzn̩/ *n* **1** enthusiastic and often uncritical supporter of a person, group or cause (对某人、团体或事业)热心的而常为盲目的拥护者. **2** member of an armed resistance movement in a country occupied by enemy forces 沦陷区内的武装抗敌分子; 游击队员: [attrib 作定语] *partisan warfare* 游击战.

▷ **par·tisan** *adj* uncritically supporting a person, group or cause; biased 盲从的; 帮派性强的; 偏袒的: *partisan attitudes, feelings, thinking, etc* 朋党的看法、情绪、见解等 ○ *You must listen to both points of view and try not to be partisan.* 你必须兼听双方观点, 尽量做到不偏不倚.

par·tis·an·ship /-ʃɪp; -ˌʃɪp/ *n* [U].

par·ti·tion /pɑːˈtɪʃn; pɑrˈtɪʃən/ *n* **1** (**a**) [U] action of dividing or state of being divided into parts, esp the division of one country into two or more nations 分割, 划分, 分裂(尤指国家): *the partition of India in 1947* 1947年印度的分裂. (**b**) [C] part formed in this way; section (以上述方式形成的)部分. **2** [C] structure that divides a room or space into two parts, esp a thin wall in a house 将房间或空间分成两部分的结构; (尤指房子中的)隔断, 板壁, 隔扇.

▷ **par·ti·tion** *v* **1** [Tn] divide (sth) into parts 将(某事物)分成部分; 分割: *India was partitioned in 1947.* 印度于1947年分裂. **2** (phr v) **partition sth off** separate (one area, part of a room, etc) from another with a partition (用分隔物)分隔, 隔开(某处); 打隔断: *We've partitioned off one end of the kitchen to make a breakfast room.* 我们已把厨房的一头隔开作吃早饭的房间.

par·tit·ive /ˈpɑːtɪtɪv; ˈpɑrtətɪv/ *adj* (*grammar*) (of a word or phrase) referring to or indicating a part or quantity of sth (指词或词组)表示部分的.

▷ **par·tit·ive** *n* (*grammar*) partitive word or phrase 表示部分的词或词组: *'Some' and 'any' are partitives.* some和any是表示部分的词.

part·ner /ˈpɑːtnə(r); ˈpɑrtnɚ/ *n* **1** person who takes part in an activity with another or others, esp one of several owners of a business 伙伴; 同伙; (尤指)合伙人, 股东: *She was made a partner in the firm.* 她当上了该商行的股东. ○ *a senior/junior partner in a firm of solicitors* 律师事务所中资深[资浅]的合伙人 ○ *They were partners in crime.* 他们是共犯. **2** either of two people dancing together or playing tennis, cards, etc on the same side (跳舞、打网球、玩纸牌等的)同伴, 搭档: *dancing partners* 舞伴 ○ *Take your partners for the next dance.* 现在开始下一舞曲, 请找好舞伴. ○ *be sb's partner at bridge, badminton, etc* 作某人的搭档打桥牌、羽毛球等. **3** either of two people who are married to one another or having a sexual relationship with one another 配偶; 性伴侣; 情人: *He doesn't have a regular (sexual) partner at the moment.* 他现在没有固定的(性)伴侣.

▷ **part·ner** *v* **1** [Tn] act as or be the partner of (sb) 做(某人的)同伴或搭档: *partner sb at bridge, tennis, etc* 在桥牌、网球等中做某人的搭档 ○ *partner sb in a tango* 和某人共跳探戈舞. **2** (phr v) **partner (sb) off (with sb)** (cause two people to) become partners (PARTNER 2) (使两人)配成对, 作搭档: *We (were) partnered off for the next dance.* 下一舞曲我们两人一起跳.

part·ner·ship /-ʃɪp; -ʃɪp/ *n* **~ (with sb)** (**a**) [U] state of being a partner or partners, esp in business 合伙人身分; 合股; 合伙经营: *She worked in partnership with her sister/They worked in partnership.* 她和妹妹合股经营[他们合伙经营]. ○ *He went/entered into partnership with his brother.* 他和弟弟合伙做生意. ○ *He and his brother went/entered into partnership.* 他和弟弟合伙做生意. (**b**) [C] two or more people working, playing, etc together as partners (在一起工作、游戏等的)两人, 一伙人: *a successful partnership* 配合默契的人.

par·took *pt* of PARTAKE.

part·ridge /ˈpɑːtrɪdʒ; ˈpɑrtrɪdʒ/ *n* (**a**) [C] (*pl* unchanged or **~s** 复数或不变或作 **partridges**) any of various types of game-bird with brown feathers, plump bodies and short tails 山鹑. ⇨illus at App 1 见附录1插图, page v. (**b**) [U] its flesh eaten as food 山鹑肉.

par·turi·tion /ˌpɑːtjʊˈrɪʃn; *US* -tʃʊ-; ˌpɑrtjʊˈrɪʃən/ *n* [U] (*medical* 医) process of giving birth; childbirth 分娩.

party /ˈpɑːtɪ; ˈpɑrtɪ/ *n* **1** [C] (esp in compounds 尤用以构成复合词) social gathering to which people are invited, esp in order to celebrate sth 社交集会; (尤指)庆祝会, 纪念会: *a ˈbirthday party* 生日庆祝会 ○ *a ˈdinner party* 宴会 ○ *a ˈgarden party* 游园会 ○ *I'm giving/having/holding a party next Saturday night.* 星期六我举行晚会. ○ [attrib 作定语] *a ˈparty dress* 宴会服. **2** [CGp] (used esp in compounds or attributively with *ns* 尤用以构成复合词或用以修饰名词) group of people working or travelling together (一起工作、同行的)群, 组, 团, 队: *a ˈsearch party* 搜索组 ○ *The Government set up a working party to look into the problem.* 政府成立了工作组调查那个问题. ○ *a party of schoolchildren, tourists, etc* 一群小学生、游客等. **3** [CGp] (used esp in compounds or attributively with *ns* 尤用以构成复合词或用以修饰名词) political organization with stated aims and policies that puts forward candidates in elections 党; 政党; 党派: *The main political parties in the United States are the Democrats and the Republicans.* 美国的主要政党是民主党和共和党. ○ *She's a member of the ˈCommunist Party.* 她是共产党员. ○ [attrib 作定语] *the party ˈleader, ˈpolicy, maniˈfesto* 党的领袖、政策、宣言 ○ *party ˈinterests, ˈfunds, ˈmembers* 党的利益、基金、成员 ○ *the ˈparty system*, ie government based on political parties 政党制度(即政党统治). **4** [C] (*law* 律) person or people forming one side in a legal agreement or dispute (契约或争论中的)一方, 当事人: *the guilty party*, ie the person who is to blame for sth 有罪过的一方 ○ *Is this solution acceptable to all parties concerned?* 这个解决办法有关各方是否都能接受? **5** [C] (*dated infml* 旧, 口) person 人. **6** (idm 习语) **be (a) party to sth** participate in, know about or support (an action, a plan, etc) 参与、了解或支持(某行动、计划等): *be party to an agreement, a crime, a decision* 参与协议、犯罪活动、决定 ○ *They refused to be party to any violence.* 他们拒不参加任何暴力活动.

□ ˈ**party line** telephone line shared by two or more customers who each have their own number 电话合用线; 同线电话.

ˌ**party ˈline** official policies of a political party 政党的路线: *Some MPs refused to follow/toe the party line on defence.* 有些议员拒不遵循党的防务政策.

ˌ**party ˈpolitics** political activity carried out through, by or for parties 政党政治. ˌ**party poˈlitical** of or relating to a political party or parties 政党政治的: *a party political broadcast by the Labour Party* 工党的政治广播节目.

ˌ**party ˈspirit** **1** strong liking for parties (PARTY 1) 对社交聚会的喜爱. **2** loyalty to a political party 党性.

ˌ**party-ˈwall** *n* wall that divides one property from another and is the joint responsibility of the owners of those properties 界墙; 共用墙.

par·venu /ˈpɑːvənjuː; *US* -nuː; ˈpɑrvəˌnu/ *n* (*derog* 贬) person who has suddenly risen from a low social or economic position to one of wealth or power 暴发户; 新贵.

pas·chal /ˈpæskl, *also* ˈpɑːskl; ˈpæskl/ *adj* (*religion* 宗) **1** of the Jewish Passover 逾越节的. **2** of Easter 复活节的.

pass[1] /pɑːs; *US* pæs; pæs/ *n* **1** success in an examination

及格: *get a pass in French* 法语及格 ○ *2 passes and 3 fails* 两门及格, 三门不及格. **2 (a)** paper or card giving sb permission, eg to enter, leave or be absent from a place 通行证; 许可证: *All visitors must show their passes before entering the building.* 参观者须出示许可证方可进入该建筑物. ○ *There is no admittance without a pass.* 无通行证者不得入内. **(b)** any of various types of bus ticket or train ticket, esp one allowing sb to travel regularly along a particular route over a specified period of time or to travel at a reduced fare or free of charge (公共汽车或火车的)乘车券(尤指在某期间在某固定路线上使用的或优待或免费搭乘的票据): *a monthly bus pass*, ie one that is valid for a month 公共汽车月票. **3 ~ (to sb)** (in football, hockey, Rugby, etc) act of kicking, hitting or throwing the ball to a player of one's own side (足球、曲棍球、橄榄球等中的)传球: *a long pass to the striker* 给前锋的长传. **4** (route through a) gap or low point in a range of mountains 关隘; 山口; 山道; 山路. **5** (in card-games) act of not playing a card or making a bid when it is one's turn (纸牌戏中)不出牌, 不叫牌, 弃权. **6** (esp in conjuring) movement of the hand or of sth held in the hand over or in front of sth (尤指变戏法时)用手或手中物对某物施遮眼法的动作, 手法: *The conjuror made a few passes with his hand over the hat.* 魔术师用手在帽子上方来回移动了几下. **7** (in fencing) thrust or lunge (击剑中的)戳刺, 滑刺, 滑剑. **8** (idm 习语) **bring sth to 'pass** (*fml* 文) cause sth to happen 使某事发生. **come to 'pass** (*fml* 文) actually occur as predicted, planned or hoped for 实现; 发生: *Many people would like the electoral system to be reformed but I don't believe this will ever come to pass.* 很多人都想要改革选举制度, 但我认为不可能实现. **come to such a 'pass/a pretty 'pass** reach a sad or critical state 处境不妙; 情况危急: *Things have come to a pretty pass when the children have to prepare their own meals.* 要孩子自己动手做饭, 事情就一塌糊涂了. **make a pass at sb** (*infml* 口) try to attract sb sexually 向某人调情. **sell the pass** ⇨ SELL.

□ **'passbook** *n* **(a)** book recording the amounts of money a customer pays into or takes out of an account with a bank or building society 银行存折; 房屋建筑协会借贷簿. Cf 参看 BANK-BOOK (BANK[3]). **(b)** (in S Africa) official document giving details of one's race, residence and employment, which must be carried at all times by non-Whites (南非的)有色人种身分证明书.

'pass degree (in British universities) degree awarded to a student whose work is thought to be acceptable but not of a good enough standard to qualify for honours (HONOUR[1] 6) (英国大学的)普通学士学位.

'passkey *n* **(a)** key to a door or gate given to people who have a right to enter 专用钥匙(给予有权进入某处者持有). **(b)** =MASTER-KEY (MASTER[1]).

'pass law (in S Africa) any of a group of laws restricting the movement of non-Whites and requiring them to carry identification at all times (南非的)有色人种旅行法.

'password (also **watchword**) *n* secret word or phrase used by sb to indicate to sb else (eg a sentry) that he is a friend rather than an enemy 口令: *give the password* 答口令.

pass[2] /pɑːs; *US* pæs; pæs/ *v* **1** [I, Tn] move forward or to the other side of (sb/sth) 前行, 穿行, 越过(某人[某物]): *The street was so crowded that cars were unable to pass.* 街道十分拥挤, 汽车无法通行. ○ *pass a barrier, sentry, checkpoint, etc* 通过障碍、哨卡、检查站等 ○ (*fig* 比喻) *Not a word passed her lips*, ie She said nothing. 她一言不发. **2** [I, Tn] leave (sb/sth) on one side or behind as one goes forward; go past (sb/sth) 越过, 经过(某人[某物]): *Turn right after passing the Post Office.* 过了邮局向右拐. ○ *She passed me in the street without even saying hello.* 她在街上从我身旁走过, 连招呼都不打. ○ *I pass the church on my way to work.* 我上班时经过教堂. ○ *A car passed* (ie overtook) *me at 90 mph on the motorway.* 在高速公路上有一辆汽车以每小时90英里的速度越过了我. **3** [Ipr, Ip] go or move in the specified direction 沿某方向行进或移动: *The procession passed slowly down the hill.* 队伍从山上慢慢向山下移动. ○ *We passed through Oxford on our way to London.* 我们在去伦敦的路上经过牛津. ○ *He glanced at her and then passed on*, ie continued to walk forward. 他看了她一眼, 然后继续朝前走. **4** [Tn·pr] cause sth to move in the specified direction or to be directed in a certain position 使某物沿某方向移动; 使某物移至某位置: *She passed her hand across her forehead.* 她用手抹了一下额头. ○ *pass a thread through the eye of a needle* 引线穿针 ○ *pass a rope round a post* 把绳子绕在柱子上. **5** [Tn, Tn·pr, Tn·p, Dn·n, Dn·pr] **~ sth (to sb)** give sth to sb by handing it to him 将某物递给某人: *Pass (me) the salt, please.* 请把盐递给我. ○ *They passed the photograph round*, ie from one person to the next. 他们传看照片. ○ *Pass me (over) that book.* 把书递给我. ○ *She passed the letter to Mary.* 她把信转交给玛丽了. **6** [I, Ipr, Tn, Tn·pr] **~ sth (to sb)** (in football, hockey, Rugby, etc) kick, hit or throw (the ball) to a player of one's own side (在足球、曲棍球、橄榄球中)将球传、踢、击、掷给己方队员: *He passed (the ball) to the winger.* 他传给边锋(一个球). **7** [Ipr] **~ to sb** be transferred from one person to another, esp by inheritance 传; (尤指)继承, 遗传: *On his death, the title passed to his eldest son.* 他死后, 爵位传给了长子. **8** [Ipr] **~ from sth to/into sth** change from one state or condition to another 从一种状况变成另一种状况: *Water passes from a liquid to a solid state when it freezes.* 水结冰是由液态变为固态. ○ *pass from boyhood to manhood* (他)从童年长到成年. **9 (a)** [I] (of time) go by; be spent (指时间)消逝, 过去: *Six months had passed, and we still had no news of them.* 六个月过去了, 我们仍然没有他们的消息. ○ *The holidays passed far too quickly.* 假期过得太快了. **(b)** [Tn] occupy or spend (time) 消磨, 打发, 度过(时间): *What did she do to pass the time* (ie to make the period of boredom less tedious) *while she was convalescing?* 她在康复期间做些什么来消磨时间呢? ○ *How did you pass the evening?* 你晚上是怎么过的? **10** [I] come to an end; be over 结束; 完结: *They waited for the storm to pass.* 他们等待暴风雨过去. ○ *His anger will soon pass.* 他生气一会儿就完. **11 (a)** [I, Tn] achieve the required standard in (an examination, a test, etc) 考(试)及格; 测验合格: *You'll have to work hard if you want to pass (the exam).* 要想考(试)及格就得用功. ○ *She hasn't passed her driving test yet.* 她驾驶测验没合格. **(b)** [Tn] examine (sb/sth) and declare to be satisfactory or acceptable 考核(某人[某事物])后宣布合格或通过: *The examiners passed all the candidates*, ie decided that their work was of the required standard. 主考人评定全部考生合格. **12 (a)** [Tn] approve (a bill, law, proposal, etc) by voting 表决通过(法案、法规、建议等): *Parliament passed the bill.* 议会通过了该法案. ○ *The motion was passed by 12 votes to 10.* 那动议以12票对10票通过. **(b)** [I, Tn] (esp of a bill, law, proposal, etc) be approved or accepted by (a parliament, an assembly, etc) (尤指法案、法规、建议等)被(议会、大会等)通过或批准: *The bill passed and became law.* 该法案已通过成为法规. ○ *This film will never pass the censors*, eg because it is too sexually explicit. 这部电影一定不能通过审查这一关(如因色情过于露骨). **13** [I] be allowed or tolerated 许可; 容忍; 放过: *I don't like it, but I'll let it pass*, ie will not make objections. 我不喜欢, 但就让它过去吧. ○ *His rudeness passed without comment*, ie People ignored it. 他粗鲁无礼而未受到批评. ○ *Such behaviour may pass in some circles but it will not be tolerated here.* 这种行为在某些圈子里可能行得通, 但在这里是不允许的. **14** [Tn, Tn·pr] **~ sth (on sb/sth)** pronounce or utter sth (used esp as in the expressions shown) 宣布某事(尤用于以下示例): *pass sentence (on sb found guilty of a crime)* (对罪名成立的人)宣判 ○ *pass judgement on a matter* 宣布对某事的裁决 ○ *pass a remark* 作评论. **15** [I, Ipr] **~ (between A and B)** happen; be said or done 发生; 说出或做出: *after all that has passed between them* 尽管他们之间有过这些事. **16** [Tn] go beyond the limits of (sth) (used esp in the expressions shown) 超越、超出(某事物)的限度(尤用于以下示例): *pass belief*, ie be unbelievable 难以相信 ○ *pass one's comprehension*, ie be impossible for one to understand 难以理解. **17** [I] (in card-games) not play a card or make a bid when it is one's turn (纸牌戏中)不出牌, 不叫牌, 弃权. **18** [Tn] send (sth) out from the body as or with urine or faeces 排(大小便); (随大小便)排出: *If you're passing blood you ought to see a doctor.* 要是便血, 就该找医生看看.

19 (idm 习语) **make/pass water** ⇨ WATER[1]. **,pass the 'buck (to sb)** (*infml* 口) shift the responsibility or blame for sth to sb else 将某事的责任或过失推委给别人. **pass the 'hat round** (*infml* 口) collect money, esp for a colleague who is ill or to pay for a celebration 集资, 筹款(尤指为生病的同事或搞庆祝活动). **pass 'muster** be accepted as adequate or satisfactory 被认为符合要求; 过得去. **pass the time of 'day (with sb)** greet sb and have a short conversation with him 与某人打招呼和寒暄. **ships that pass in the night** ⇨ SHIP[1].
20 (phr v) **pass as sb/sth** =PASS FOR SB/STH.

pass a'way (*euph* 婉) die 死: *His mother passed away last year.* 他母亲去年去世了.

P

pass by (sb/sth) go past 走过; 经过: *I saw the procession pass by.* 我看见队伍走过. ○ *The procession passed right by my front door.* 队伍就在我家门前经过.

pass sb/sth by (**a**) occur without affecting sb/sth 对某人[某事物]无影响或不起作用: *The whole business passed him by,* ie he was hardly aware that it was happening. 整件事情都已过去了, 他却未曾察觉到. ○ *She feels that life is passing her by,* ie that she is not profiting from or enjoying the opportunities and pleasures of life. 她觉得生活与她形同陌路(未能从生活中得到好处、机会与乐趣). (**b**) pay no attention to sb/sth; ignore or avoid sb/sth 不注意某人[某事物]; 忽视或避免接触某人[某事物]: *We cannot pass this matter by without protest.* 我们不能对此事听之任之.

pass sth down (esp passive 尤用于被动语态) pass sth from one generation to the next 将某物从一代传给下一代: *knowledge which has been passed down over the centuries* 世代相传的知识.

pass for sb/sth be accepted as sb/sth 被认为或被当作某人[某事物]: *He speaks French well enough to pass for a Frenchman.* 他法语流利得使人以为他是法国人.

pass in (to sth) be admitted (to a school, college, etc) by passing an examination 考试及格获准(入学等).

pass into sth become a part of sth 成为某事物的一部分: *Many foreign words have passed into the English language.* 有很多外来语已成为英语的一部分. ○ *His deeds have passed into legend,* ie because of their bravery, importance, etc. 他的事迹已成为人间传奇.

pass 'off (**a**) (of an event) take place and be completed (指事情)发生并完成: *The demonstration passed off without incident.* 游行自始至终未发生意外. (**b**) (of pain, the effects of a drug, etc) come to an end gradually; disappear (指疼痛、药效等)慢慢消失, 消退: *The numbness in your foot will soon pass off.* 你脚上的麻木感一会儿就会消失. **pass sb/sth off as sb/sth** represent sb/sth falsely as sb/sth 冒充某人[某物]: *She passed him off as* (ie pretended that he was) *her husband.* 她把他假充作自己的丈夫. ○ *He escaped by passing himself off as a guard.* 他冒充警卫逃走了.

pass 'on =PASS AWAY. **pass on (to sth)** move from one activity, stage, etc to another 从一活动、阶段等进入另一活动、阶段等: *Let's pass on to the next item on the agenda.* 咱们进行议事日程的下一个项目吧. **pass sth on (to sb)** hand or give sth (to sb else), esp after receiving or using it oneself 将某物传、交、给(某人)(尤指自己收到或用过后): *Pass the book on to me when you've finished with it.* 那本书你看完给我. ○ *I passed her message on to his mother.* 我把她的口信带给他母亲了. ○ *She caught my cold and passed it on to* (ie infected) *her husband.* 我感冒传染了她, 她又传给她丈夫了.

pass 'out lose consciousness; faint 失去知觉; 昏厥. **pass out (of sth)** leave (a military college) after completing a course of training 完成(军校)学业: *a passing-'out ceremony/parade,* ie for cadets who have completed their training 军校毕业典礼[阅兵式].

pass sb over not consider sb for promotion (esp when he is or thinks he is eligible) 不考虑提升某人(尤指合格者或自以为合格者): *He was passed over in favour of a younger man.* 没考虑提升他而提升了一个小伙子.

pass over sth ignore or disregard sth; avoid sth 忽略或不理会某事物; 回避某事: *They chose to pass over her rude remarks.* 他们对她的粗话不予理会. ○ *Sex is a subject he prefers to pass over,* eg because it embarrasses him. 关于性这一问题他尽量回避(如因使他尴尬).

pass through go through a town, etc, stopping there for a short time but not staying 经过市镇等(逗留但不长久): *We came to say hello as we were passing through.* 我们路经此镇, 顺便来看你. **pass through sth** experience (a period of time) 经历(一段时间): *She passed through a difficult period after her marriage failed.* 她婚姻破裂后一度十分困难.

pass sth up (*infml* 口) refuse to accept (a chance, opportunity, etc) 放弃, 放过(机会等): *Imagine passing up an offer like that!* 真想不到竟放弃这样好的条件!

□ **,passer-'by** /ˌpɑːsə ˈbaɪ; *US* ˌpæsər; ˎpæsɚˋbaɪ/ *n* (*pl* **passers-by** /ˌpɑːsəz ˈbaɪ; ˎpæsɚzˋbaɪ/) person who is going past sb/sth, esp by chance 过路人; (尤指)偶然路过的人: *Police asked passers-by if they had seen the accident happen.* 警察询问过路的人是否见到事故发生的经过.

pass·able /ˈpɑːsəbl; *US* ˈpæs-; ˋpæsəbl̩/ *adj* **1** [usu pred 通常作表语] (**a**) (of roads) clear of obstructions (esp snow) and therefore able to be driven on (指道路)可通行(尤指清除积雪后): *The mountain roads are not passable until late spring.* 山路要到春季末期才能通行. (**b**) (of a river) that can be crossed (指河流)可以横渡. **2** fairly good but not excellent; adequate 还好的; 尚可的; 过得去的: *a passable knowledge of German* 粗通德语.

▷ **pass·ably** /-əblɪ; -əblɪ/ *adv* adequately or acceptably 还好; 尚可; 过得去.

pas·sage /ˈpæsɪdʒ; ˋpæsɪdʒ/ *n* **1** [U] (**a**) process of passing 过; 经过: *the passage of time* 时间的推移. (**b**) action of going past, through or across sth 通过; 穿过; 横过: *The passage of motor vehicles is forbidden.* 机动车禁止通行. (**c**) freedom or right to go through or across sth 通行权; 通行自由: *They were denied passage through the occupied territory.* 他们被禁止穿越占领区. **2** [C usu *sing* 通常作单数] way through sth 通路; 通道: *force a passage through the crowd* 在人群中挤出一条通路. **3** [C] (cost of a ticket for a) journey from one place to another by ship or plane; voyage (乘船或飞机的)航程, 旅行, 旅费: *book one's passage to New York* 订购去纽约的票 ○ *He worked his passage to Australia,* eg paid for the journey by doing jobs on the ship he was travelling on. 他在去澳大利亚旅行的船上做工偿付船费. **4** (also **'pas·sage·way**) [C] narrow way through sth, esp with walls on both sides; corridor 通道; (尤指)走廊. **5** [C] tube-like structure in the human body, through which air, secretions, etc pass (人体内的)管道(如气管、分泌管道等): *the nasal passages* 鼻腔通道 ○ (*infml* 口) *the back passage,* ie the anus 肛门. **6** [C] short section from a book, speech, piece of music, etc quoted or considered on its own (书、讲话、音乐等的)一段, 一节: *a passage from the Bible* 《圣经》的一段经文. **7** [U] passing of a bill[1](4) by a parliament so that it becomes law (法案的)通过.

passé /ˈpæseɪ; *US* pæˈseɪ; pæˋse/ *adj* [usu pred 通常作表语] (*French* 法) (**a**) out of date; old-fashioned 过时; 陈旧; 旧式: *I'm beginning to find her novels rather passé.* 我逐渐觉得她的小说格调陈旧. (**b**) past his/her/its best 全盛期已过: *He was a fine actor but he's a bit passé now.* 他曾是优秀演员, 但现在最红时期已过.

pas·sen·ger /ˈpæsɪndʒə(r); ˋpæsn̩dʒɚ/ *n* **1** person travelling in a car, bus, train, plane, ship, etc, other than the driver, the pilot or a member of the crew 乘客: *The driver of the car was killed in the crash but both passengers escaped unhurt.* 事故中汽车司机丧生, 但两名乘客幸未受伤. ○ [attrib 作定语] *the passenger seat,* ie the seat next to the driver's seat in a motor vehicle (司机座旁的)客座 ○ *a passenger train,* ie one carrying passengers rather than goods 铁路的客车. **2** (*infml* 口 *esp Brit*) member of a team, crew, etc who does not do as much work as the others (团体中的)闲散人员: *This firm can't afford (to carry) passengers.* 这家商行养不起闲散人员.

passim /ˈpæsɪm; ˋpæsɪm/ *adv* (*Latin* 拉) (of phrases, etc) occurring throughout or at several points in a book, an article, etc (指词语等)(在某书、某文章等中出现于)各处, 到处, 多处.

pass·ing /ˈpɑːsɪŋ; *US* ˈpæs-; ˋpæsɪŋ/ *adj* **1** lasting for a short time; brief; fleeting 短暂的; 短促的; 飞逝的: *a passing thought, fancy* 闪现的念头、幻想. **2** casual; cursory 随便的; 不经意的; 粗略的: *a passing glance, reference, remark* 顺便的看一眼、一提、一说.

▷ **pass·ing** *n* [U] **1** process of going by 经过: *the*

passing of time, the years 时间、年月的流逝. **2** (*fml* 文) (**a**) end 末尾; 尽头: *the passing of the old year,* ie on New Year's Eve 除夕. (**b**) (*euph* 婉) death 去世: *They all mourned his passing.* 大家都对他的逝世表示悲痛. **3** (idm 习语) **in passing** casually; incidentally 随便地; 碰巧地; 顺便地: *mention sth in passing* 顺便提某事.

pas·sion /ˈpæʃn; ˋpæʃən/ *n* **1** (**a**) [U, C] strong feeling, eg of hate, love or anger 强烈的情感(如恨、爱、怒): *She argued with great passion.* 她争论时情绪很激动. ○ *Passions were running high at the meeting,* ie people were in an angry or emotional state. 会上群情鼎沸. (**b**) [sing] angry state; rage (used esp in the expressions shown) 愤怒, 盛怒(尤用于以下示例): *be in a passion* 在盛怒中 ○ *get/fly into a passion,* ie become very angry 勃然大怒. **2** [U] **~ (for sb)** intense, esp sexual, love 强烈的爱(尤指性爱): *His passion for her made him blind to everything else.* 他强烈地爱着她, 对其他一切都已熟视无睹. **3** [sing] (**a**) **~ for sth** strong liking or enthusiasm for sth 酷爱; 热爱: *a passion for chocolate, detective stories, tennis* 很喜欢巧克力、侦探小说、网球. (**b**) thing for which sb has a strong liking or enthusiasm 酷爱或热中的事物: *Horse-racing is her passion.* 赛马是她最喜爱的运动. ○ *Music is a passion with him.* 他酷爱音乐. **4 the Passion** [sing] (*religion* 宗) the suffering and death of Christ 耶稣的受难.

□ ˈ**passion-flower** *n* any of several types of climbing plant with brightly-coloured flowers 西番莲.

ˈ**passion-fruit** *n* [C, U] edible fruit of certain types of passion-flower 西番莲果实: [attrib 作定语] *passion-fruit ice-cream* 西番莲果冰激凌.

ˈ**passion-play** *n* play in which the Passion of Christ is re-enacted 耶稣受难复活剧.

ˌ**Passion** ˈ**Sunday** (in the Christian Church) the fifth Sunday in Lent (基督教的)受难主日(大斋期中的第五个星期日).

ˈ**Passion Week** (in the Christian Church) the week between Passion Sunday and Palm Sunday (基督教的)受难周(从受难主日到棕枝主日的一周).

pas·sion·ate /ˈpæʃənət; ˋpæʃənɪt/ *adj* **1** (**a**) caused by or showing intense sexual love 出于或表现强烈性爱的: *a passionate kiss, lover, relationship* 热恋的吻、情人、关系. (**b**) caused by or showing strong feelings 出于或表现强烈感情的: *a passionate plea for mercy* 恳切的求情 ○ *her passionate support for our cause* 她对我们事业的热情支持 ○ *a passionate defender of civil liberties* 公民自由权利的积极捍卫者. **2** dominated or easily affected by strong feelings 受强烈感情支配的; 易受强烈感情影响的: *a passionate nature, temperament, woman* 易动感情的天性、脾气、女子.

▷ **pas·sion·ately** *adv* (**a**) in a passionate(1a) way (指性爱)强烈地: *He loved her passionately.* 他热烈地爱着她. (**b**) (used before *adjs* 用于形容词之前) intensely; very 非常; 极度地: *She is passionately fond of tennis.* 她热爱网球. ○ *He is passionately opposed to racial discrimination.* 他极端反对种族歧视.

pass·ive /ˈpæsɪv; ˋpæsɪv/ *adj* **1** not active; submissive 被动的; 消极的: *play a passive role in a marriage* 在婚姻中扮演被动的角色 ○ *passive obedience, acceptance* 消极的服从、接受 ○ *passive smoking,* ie breathing in fumes from tobacco being smoked by others 被动吸烟(吸进他人喷出的烟). **2** showing no interest, initiative or forceful qualities 冷淡的; 不主动的: *a passive audience* 无精打采的听众 ○ *He had a passive expression on his face.* 他脸上有一种漠然的表情. **3** of the form of a verb used when the grammatical subject is affected by the action of the verb, as in *Her leg was broken* and *He was bitten by a dog* 被动的, 被动语态的(如Her leg was broken和He was bitten by a dog两句中的动词形式): *a passive sentence* 被动句. Cf 参看 ACTIVE.

▷ **pass·ive** *n* [sing] (also ˌ**passive** ˈ**voice**) (*grammar*) passive(3) form of a verb (phrase) or sentence 动词被动形式; 被动句; 被动语态: *In the sentence 'He was seen there', 'was seen' is in the passive.* 在He was seen there句中的was seen是被动形式. Cf 参看 ACTIVE VOICE (ACTIVE).

pass·ively *adv.*

pass·ive·ness (also **pas·siv·ity** /pæˈsɪvətɪ; pæˋsɪvətɪ/) *n* [U] state or quality of being passive(1,2) 消极; 被动; 无兴趣; 冷淡.

□ ˌ**passive re**ˈ**sistance** resistance to an enemy who has occupied one's country, or to a government, by refusing to co-operate or obey orders 消极抵抗.

Pass·over /ˈpɑːsəʊvə(r); *US* ˈpæs-; ˋpæsˌovɚ/ *n* Jewish religious festival commemorating the freeing of the Jews from their slavery in Egypt 逾越节(犹太教节日).

pass·port /ˈpɑːspɔːt; *US* ˈpæs-; ˋpæsˌpɔrt/ *n* **1** official document issued by the government of a particular country, identifying the holder as a citizen of that country and entitling him to travel abroad under its protection 护照: *a British passport* 英国护照. **2 ~ to sth** thing that enables one to achieve sth (获得某事物的)手段, 保障: *The only passport to success is hard work.* 通往成功的唯一途径是努力奋斗.

P

past[1] /pɑːst; *US* pæst; pæst/ *adj* **1** gone by in time 过去的; 以前的: *in past years, centuries, ages* 在过去的年月、世纪、年代里 ○ *The time for discussion is past.* 讨论的时间已经过去. ○ *in times past* 在过去. **2** gone by recently; just finished or ended 刚过去的; 刚完成的; 刚结束的: *The past month has been a difficult one for him.* 上个月他很困难. ○ *I've seen little of her in the past few weeks.* 近几周我很少见到她. **3** belonging to an earlier time 先前的; 前期的; 以往的: *past happiness* 昔日的快乐 ○ *past and present students of the college* 该学院的校友和在校学生 ○ *past achievements, failures, generations, presidents* 以前的成就、失败、世代、总统. **4** (*grammar*) (of a verb form) indicating a state or an action in the past (指动词形式)过去式的: *The past tense of 'take' is 'took'.* take的过去式是took. ○ *a past participle,* eg *passed, taken, gone* 过去分词(如passed、taken、gone).

▷ **past** *n* **1 the past** (**a**) [sing] time that has gone by 往时; 昔时; 过去: *I've been there many times in the past.* 我从前去过那儿很多次. (**b**) [sing] things that happened in an earlier time; past events 往事: *memories of the past* 对往事的记忆 ○ *look back on, remember, regret the past* 回顾、缅怀、追悔往事 ○ *We cannot change the past.* 往事无可改变. **2** [C] person's past life or career, esp one that is discreditable 过去的生活或职业经历(尤指不名誉的): *We know nothing of his past.* 我们对他的经历一无所知. ○ *She's a woman with a 'past'.* 她早年生活放荡. **3** [sing] (also **past tense**) (form of a verb) used to describe actions in the past 过去式的(动词形式): *The past of the verb 'take' is 'took'.* take的过去式是took. **4** (idm 习语) **a thing of the past** ⇨ THING. **live in the past** ⇨ LIVE[2].

□ ˌ**past** ˈ**master ~ (in/of sth)**; **~ (at sth/doing sth)** person who is very skilled or experienced in a particular activity; expert 能手; 老手; 专家: *She's a past master at the art of getting what she wants.* 她想要什么就能得到什么, 堪称一绝.

past[2] /pɑːst; *US* pæst; pæst/ *prep* **1** (**a**) (of time) later than (sth); after (指时间)晚于, 迟于, 在…之后: *half past two* 两点半 ○ *ten (minutes) past six* 六点十分 ○ *There's a bus at twenty minutes past the hour,* ie at 1.20, 2.20, 3.20, etc. 每小时的第二十分钟有一班公共汽车. ○ *It was past midnight when we got home.* 我们到家时已过半夜. (**b**) older than (the specified age) 超过(某年龄): *an old man past seventy* 七十多岁的老人 ○ *She's past her thirties,* ie at least 40. 她至少四十岁了. **2** on the far side of (sth); from one side to the other of (sth/sb) 在(某物)的远端, 另一边; 经过(某处[某人]): *You can see the house past the church.* 你可以看到教堂那边的那所房子. ○ *She walked past the shop.* 她走过那家商店. ○ *He hurried past me without stopping.* 他匆忙从我身边走过, 连停都没停. **3** (**a**) beyond the limits of (sth/doing sth) 超过(某事物[做某事物])的限度: *The man is past working,* ie too old, weak, etc to work. 那男子已不能工作了(因年老、体弱等). ○ *I'm past caring* (ie I no longer care) *what he does.* 他做什么我再也不管了. ○ *It's quite past my comprehension,* ie I can't understand it. 这件事已远超出我的理解力了. (**b**) beyond the age of (sth/doing sth) 超过(某事物[做某事物])的年纪: *She's past playing with dolls.* 她已不是玩玩偶的年纪了. ○ *She's long past retirement age.* 她早已过了退休的年龄. **4** (idm 习语) ˈ**past it** (*infml* 口) too old to do what one was once capable of; too old to be used for its normal function 年龄过大而不能再做以前做的事; 过旧而不适用: *At 93 he's finally realized he's getting past it.* 他到了93岁终于意识到自己已不中用. ○ *That overcoat is looking* *decidedly past it.* 那件大衣看来是绝对旧得穿不出去了. ▷ **past** *adv part* from one side to the other of sth 经过: *walk, march, go, rush, etc past* 步行、行军、行走、奔跑等经过.

pasta /ˈpæstə; *US* ˈpɑːstə; ˈpɑstə/ *n* [U] dried paste made from flour, eggs and water and cut into various shapes, eg macaroni, spaghetti, ravioli 意大利面食(如通心粉、细面条、方形饺): [attrib 作定语] *a pasta dish*, eg lasagne 一盘面食(如宽面). Cf 参看 NOODLE.

paste[1] /peɪst; pest/ *n* **1** [sing] moist soft mixture, esp of a powdery substance and a liquid 面团: *a smooth, thin, thick, etc paste* 一块光滑的、薄的、厚的…面团 ○ *She mixed the flour and water to a paste.* 她用水和面做成面团. **2** [U] mixture of flour and water used to stick things together, esp to stick paper to a wall 糨糊. **3** [U] (esp in compounds 尤用以构成复合词) mixture of ground meat or fish for spreading on bread 肉酱; 鱼酱: *anchovy paste* 鳀鱼酱 ○ *liver paste* 肝酱. **4** [U] hard glass-like substance used to make artificial gems (制人造宝石的)铅玻璃: [attrib 作定语] *paste jewellery* 人造宝石.

P

paste[2] /peɪst; pest/ *v* **1** [I, Tn] put paste[1](2) on (sth) 在(某物)上涂糨糊. **2** [Tn·pr, Tn·p] **~ sth (on/to sth; ~ sth on (sth); ~ A and B together** stick sth to sth else with paste[1](2) 用糨糊将某物粘贴于某处: *She pasted posters onto the wall.* 她把海报贴在墙上了. ○ *paste pieces of paper together* 把纸粘在一起. **3** [Tn] (*dated infml* 旧, 口) hit or beat (sb) 打, 揍(某人). **4** (phr v) **paste sth down** fasten the cover or flap of sth with paste[1](2) 用糨糊粘住某物的盖. **paste sth in; paste sth into sth** stick (a photo, label, etc) onto a page of a book with paste[1](2) 用糨糊将(照片、标签等)贴在本子上: *She pasted the pictures into a scrapbook.* 她把图片贴在剪贴簿上. **paste sth up** (**a**) stick sth to an upright surface with paste[1](2) 用糨糊张贴某物: *paste up an advertisement, a notice, a poster, etc* 张贴广告、告示、海报等. (**b**) fasten (sheets or strips of paper with text and illustrations) onto a larger sheet of paper or board, in order to design a page for a book, magazine, etc 将(文字或图画等纸块)贴在大张纸或板上(以设计版面).
▷ **past·ing** *n* (*infml* 口) severe beating; defeat 狠揍; 打败: *give sb a pasting* 把某人狠揍一顿 ○ *Our team got/took a real pasting on Saturday.* 我们队星期六一败涂地.
□ ˈ**paste-up** *n* sheet of paper or board to which the text and illustrations for a page of a book, magazine, etc have been fastened 粘贴文字、图画等的纸或板.

paste·board /ˈpeɪstbɔːd; ˈpest,bɔrd/ *n* [U] type of thin board made by pasting thin sheets of paper together (用多层纸粘合的)纸板.

pas·tel /ˈpæstl; *US* pæˈstel; pæsˈtɛl/ *n* **1** type of crayon made from coloured chalk 彩色粉笔; 蜡笔: *She works in (ie uses) pastels.* 她用彩色粉笔作画. **2** picture drawn with this 彩色粉笔画; 蜡笔画. **3** pale delicate colour 清淡柔和的颜色: [attrib 作定语] *pastel shades/colours* 清淡柔和的色彩.

pas·tern /ˈpæstən; ˈpæstɚn/ *n* part of a horse's foot between the fetlock and the hoof (马的)系部. ⇨illus at HORSE 见 HORSE 插图.

pas·teur·ize, -ise /ˈpɑːstʃəraɪz; *US* ˈpæs-; ˈpæstə,raɪz/ *v* [Tn] heat (a liquid, esp milk) to a certain temperature and then chill it, in order to kill harmful bacteria 用巴氏杀菌法将(液体, 尤指乳)消毒.
▷ **pas·teur·iza·tion, -isation** /ˌpɑːstʃəraɪˈzeɪʃn; *US* ˌpæstʃərɪˈzeɪʃn; ˌpæstərəˈzeʃən/ *n* [U] process of pasteurizing sth 巴氏杀菌(法).

pas·tiche /pæˈstiːʃ; pæsˈtiʃ/ *n* **1** [C] literary, musical or artistic work in the style of another author, composer, etc (文学、音乐或艺术的)风格模仿作品. **2** [C] musical, literary or artistic work consisting of elements from various sources (音乐、文学或艺术的)拼凑品, 混成物, 集锦. **3** [U] art of composing pastiches 模仿艺术: *He has a gift for pastiche.* 他有模仿他人作品的天赋.

pas·tille /ˈpæstəl; *US* pæˈstiːl; pæsˈtil/ *n* small flavoured sweet for sucking, esp one containing medicine for a sore throat; lozenge (药的)锭剂, 糖锭: *throat pastilles* 喉片.

pas·time /ˈpɑːstaɪm; *US* ˈpæs-; ˈpæs,taɪm/ *n* thing done to pass the time pleasantly 消遣; 娱乐: *Photography is her favourite pastime.* 摄影是她喜爱的消遣.

pas·tor /ˈpɑːstə(r); *US* ˈpæs-; ˈpæstɚ/ *n* minister, esp of a Nonconformist church 牧师(尤指不从国教者).

pas·toral /ˈpɑːstərəl; *US* ˈpæs-; ˈpæstərəl/ *adj* **1** relating to or portraying country life, the countryside or shepherds, esp in an idealized way 乡村生活的, 田园风光的, 牧人的, 田园式的(尤指理想化描述的): *a pastoral scene, poem, painting* 田园风光、诗、画 ○ *pastoral poetry/verse* 田园诗 ○ *Beethoven's 'Pastoral' Symphony* 贝多芬的《田园交响曲》. **2** (of land) used for pasture; grassy (指土地)供放牧的, 长满草的. **3** of or relating to a clergyman or his work (esp the spiritual guidance he gives to his congregation) 牧师的, 牧师工作的(尤指对会众心灵上的指引): *pastoral care, duties, responsibilities, etc* 牧师对会众的关顾、职责、责任等.
▷ **pas·toral** *n* **1** pastoral(1) poem, picture, etc 田园诗、画等. **2** (also **pastoral ˈletter**) letter from a clergyman to his congregation, esp one from a bishop to the members of his diocese 教牧书信, (尤指)主教教书(牧师或主教给会众或神职人员的公开信); 牧函.

pas·trami /pæˈstrɑːmɪ; pəˈstrɑmɪ/ *n* [U] highly seasoned smoked beef 五香熏牛肉.

pas·try /ˈpeɪstrɪ; ˈpestrɪ/ *n* **1** [U] mixture of flour, fat and water baked in an oven and used as a base or covering for tarts, pies, etc 酥皮糕点; 油酥面团: *You eat too much pastry*, ie food made with pastry. 你吃油酥点心吃得太多了. **2** [C] item of food in which pastry is used, eg a pie or tart 酥皮糕点: *Danish pastries* 丹麦点心.
□ ˈ**pastry-cook** *n* person who makes pastry 制作酥皮糕点的人.

pas·ture /ˈpɑːstʃə(r); *US* ˈpæs-; ˈpæstʃɚ/ *n* **1** [C, U] (piece of) land covered with grass and similar plants, suitable for grazing animals 牧场; 牧地; 草原: *acres of rich pasture* 广阔富饶的牧场. **2** [U] grass, etc growing on this land 牧草.
▷ **pas·ture** *v* **1** [Tn, Tn·pr] put (animals) to graze in a pasture 放, 牧(牛、羊等): *pasture one's sheep on the village common* 在村庄的公地上放羊. **2** [I, Ipr] (of animals) graze (指牛、羊等)(在草地上)吃草.

pas·tur·age /ˈpɑːstʃərɪdʒ; *US* ˈpæs-; ˈpæstʃərɪdʒ/ *n* [U] **1** land where animals can graze 牧场. **2** right to graze animals on this land 放牧权.

pasty[1] /ˈpeɪstɪ; ˈpestɪ/ *adj* (**-ier, -iest**) **1** of or like paste 糨糊的; 糊状的: *a pasty substance* 糊状物质 ○ *mix to a pasty consistency* 混合至糊状的浓度. **2** pale and unhealthy-looking 苍白的; 不健康的: *a pasty face, complexion* 苍白的面孔、脸色.
□ ˌ**pasty-ˈfaced** *adj* having a pasty complexion 脸色苍白的: *a ˌpasty-faced ˈyouth* 脸色苍白的青年.

pasty[2] /ˈpæstɪ; ˈpæstɪ/ *n* (*Brit*) piece of pastry folded round a filling of meat, fruit, jam, etc (肉、水果、果酱等的)馅饼: *a Cornish pasty*, ie one with a filling of meat and potatoes 康沃尔馅饼(用肉和土豆做馅的).

pat[1] /pæt; pæt/ *adv* **1** at once and without hesitation 立刻而不犹豫地: *Her answer came pat.* 她回答得很干脆. **2** (idm 习语) **have/know sth off ˈpat** have memorized or know sth perfectly 对某事物记得或了解得很清楚: *He had all the answers off pat.* 他把所有答案都记得很清楚. ○ *She knows the rules off pat.* 她对规则了如指掌. **stand pat** (*esp US*) refuse to change a decision one has made, an opinion one holds, etc 坚持自己的决定、意见等.
▷ **pat** *adj* **1** exactly right; appropriate 恰好的; 适当的; 适时的. **2** (*derog* 贬) too quick; glib 过于快的; 伶牙俐齿的; 油嘴滑舌的: *It's a complex question and her answer was too pat.* 那问题很复杂, 但她的回答简直是脱口而出.

pat[2] /pæt; pæt/ *v* (**-tt-**) **1** [Tn, Tn·pr] tap (sb/sth) gently with the open hand or with a flat object (用掌或扁平之物)轻拍(某人[某物]): *pat a dog* 轻轻拍狗 ○ *pat sb's hand* 轻拍某人的手 ○ *pat a child on the head*, ie as a sign of affection 拍拍孩子的头(表示疼爱) ○ *pat a ball*, ie so that it bounces up and down 拍球. **2** [Tn·pr, Tn·p, Cn·a] put (sth) in the specified state or position by patting 将(某物)拍成某状态或拍至某处: *She patted her hair into place/shape.* 她把头发拍整齐了. ○ *She patted down a few wisps of hair.* 她拍落几绺头发. ○ *He patted his face dry (with a towel).* 他(用手巾)轻轻把脸拍干. **3** (idm 习语) **pat sb/oneself on the ˈback** congratulate sb/oneself 对某人[自己]表示庆贺、鼓励或赞扬.

▷ **pat** *n* **1** gentle tap with the open hand or with a flat object 轻拍: *She gave the child a pat on the head.* 她轻轻拍了一下那孩子的头. ○ *He gave her knee an affectionate pat/He gave her an affectionate pat on the knee.* 他深情地拍了一下她的膝盖. **2** slight sound made by tapping sth gently 轻拍某物发出的声音. **3 ~ (of sth)** small mass of sth (esp butter) that has been shaped by patting (拍成的)小团, 小块(尤指黄油): *a pat of butter* 一小块黄油. **4** (idm 习语) **a ˌpat on the ˈback (for sth/doing sth)** 鼓励; 赞扬: *give sb/get a pat on the back* 给某人[得到]鼓励 ○ *She deserves a pat on the back for all the hard work she's done.* 她辛勤努力值得赞扬.

Pat *abbr* 缩写 = patent (number) 专利(号): *Pat 1 230 884* 专利1 230 884号.

patch[1] /pætʃ; pætʃ/ *n* **1** piece of material placed over a hole or a damaged or worn place to cover or strengthen it 补丁; 补片; 补块: *a jacket with leather patches on the elbows* 肘部有皮补丁的外套 ○ *She sewed a patch onto the knee of the trousers.* 她在裤子的膝部打了个补丁. ○ *a patch on the inner tube of a tyre* 车轮内胎上的补丁. **2** pad worn over an injured eye to protect it (保护受伤的眼睛的)眼罩: *He wears a black patch over his right eye.* 他右眼上戴着黑色的眼罩. **3** part of a surface that is different in colour, texture, etc from the surrounding area (与周围颜色、材料等不同的)斑, 块: *a black dog with a white patch on its neck* 脖子上有块白斑的黑狗 ○ *a worn patch on the elbow of a sweater* 毛衣肘部的磨损处 ○ *damp patches on a wall* 墙上一块块的潮斑. **4 ~ (of sth)** small area of sth 小块; 小片: *patches of fog, ice, sunlight* 片片的雾、块块的冰、斑斑的阳光 ○ *patches of blue in a cloudy sky* 云海中露出的几块蓝天 ○ *The ground is wet in patches.* 地上湿处片片. **5** small piece of land, esp one used for growing vegetables 小块土地(尤指种菜用的): *a ˈcabbage, an ˈonion, a poˈtato, etc patch* 洋白菜、洋葱、马铃薯等菜地. **6** (*Brit infml* 口) area in which sb (esp a policeman) works or which he knows well 地区, 地段(尤指警察巡视的): *He knows every house in his patch.* 他熟悉自己管辖区中每所房子. **7** (idm 习语) **(go through, hit, strike, etc) a bad ˈpatch** (be in, reach, etc) a particularly difficult or unhappy period of time (处于、遭遇等)困难、不幸或倒霉的时期: *Their marriage has been going through a bad patch.* 他们的婚姻正处在困难时期. ○ *Our firm has just struck a bad patch.* 我公司刚遭厄运. **not be a patch on sb/sth** (*infml* 口) not be nearly as good as sb/sth 远不如某人[某事物]: *Her latest novel isn't a patch on her others.* 她这部新小说比以前所写的差得远.

□ **ˌpatch-ˈpocket** *n* pocket made by sewing a piece of material onto the outside of a garment (衣服上的)贴口袋, 贴兜.

patch[2] /pætʃ; pætʃ/ *v* **1 (a)** [Tn] cover (a hole or a worn place) with a patch 在(有洞或磨损处)打补丁: *patch a hole in a pair of trousers* 在裤子上的洞上打补丁. **(b)** [Tn, Tn·p] **~ sth (up)** mend (a garment) by covering a hole or worn place with a patch 补(衣服): *patch up an old pair of jeans* 补一条旧牛仔裤 ○ *The elbows of your jersey are worn — I'll need to patch them.* 你的套头毛衣的肘部磨坏了 — 我得给补一补. **2** [Tn] (of material) be used as a patch for (sth) (指材料)被用作(某物)的补丁、补片. **3** (phr v) **patch sth up (a)** repair sth, esp quickly or temporarily 修理某物; (尤指)迅速或临时修补: *The wrecked car was patched up and resold.* 撞坏的汽车草草修理一下就卖掉了. **(b)** settle or resolve (a quarrel, dispute, etc) 调停, 解决(纷争、争执等): *They patched up their differences.* 他们解决了彼此间的分歧.

patch·ouli /ˈpætʃʊlɪ, pəˈtʃuːlɪ; ˋpætʃʊlɪ, pəˋtʃulɪ/ *n* **1** [C] fragrant plant grown in the Far East 广藿香(产自远东). **2** [U] perfume made from this plant 广藿香水.

patch·work /ˈpætʃwɜːk; ˋpætʃ,wɝk/ *n* **1** [U] type of needlework in which small pieces of cloth with different designs are sewn together 花布拼缝物: [attrib 作定语] *a patchwork bedcover, cushion, quilt, etc* 杂拼花布床罩、垫子、棉被等. **2** [sing] thing made of various small pieces or parts 拼凑的东西: *a patchwork of fields seen from an aeroplane* 从飞机上俯瞰的块块田地.

patchy /ˈpætʃɪ; ˋpætʃɪ/ *adj* **(-ier, -iest) 1** existing in or having patches 有补丁的; 有斑或块的: *patchy fog, mist, cloud, etc* 团团的雾、霭、云等. **2** (*fig* 比喻) not of the same quality throughout; uneven 东拼西凑的; 质量不一致的; 不均匀的: *a patchy essay, novel, performance* 拼凑的文章、小说、演出 ○ *His work is rather patchy.* 他的作品瑕瑜互见. ○ *My knowledge of German is patchy,* ie not complete. 我对德语一知半解. ▷ **patch·ily** *adv.* **patchi·ness** *n* [U].

pate /peɪt; pet/ *n* (*arch or joc infml* 古或谑, 口) head or skull 头; 脑袋: *a shiny bald pate* 亮光光的秃顶.

pâté /ˈpæteɪ; *US* pɑːˈteɪ; pɑˋte/ *n* [U] rich paste made of finely minced meat or fish 肉酱; 鱼酱: *liver, duck, mackerel pâté* 肝、鸭、鲭鱼酱.

□ **pâté de foie gras** /ˌpæteɪ də fwɑː ˈgrɑː; pɑˋtedəfwɑˋgrɑ/ pâté made from the liver of a fattened goose 鹅肝酱.

pa·tel·la /pəˈtelə; pəˋtɛlə/ *n* (*pl* **-lae** /-liː; -li/) (*anatomy* 解) kneecap 髌骨; 膝盖骨. ⇨illus at SKELETON 见 SKELETON 插图.

P

pa·tent[1] /ˈpeɪtnt, *also* ˈpætnt; *US* ˈpætnt; ˋpætn̩t/ *adj* **~ (to sb)** obvious; clear; evident 显著的; 清楚的; 明显的: *a patent lie* 明显的谎言 ○ *his patent dislike of the plan* 他对该计划明显的不喜欢 ○ *a patent disregard for the truth* 公然无视事实 ○ *It was patent to anyone that she disliked the idea.* 谁都知道她不喜欢那个主意.

▷ **pa·tently** *adv* unmistakably; obviously 明白无误地; 明显地: *It was patently obvious that he was lying.* 显然他在撒谎.

pa·tent[2] /ˈpætnt, *also* ˈpeɪtnt; *US* ˈpætnt; ˋpætn̩t/ *n* **1 (a)** official document giving the holder the sole right to make, use or sell an invention and preventing others from imitating it 许可证; 特许状; 专利证书: *take out* (ie obtain) *a patent to protect an invention* 取得专利证书以保护一项发明 ○ *patent applied for*, eg marked on goods not yet protected by patent 已申请专利(如标在尚未获专利保护产品上的字样). **(b)** right granted by this 专利权. **2** invention or process that is protected by a patent 专利发明; 专利方法: *It's my patent.* 那是我的专利发明.

▷ **pa·tent** *adj* **1** [attrib 作定语] (of an invention, a product, etc) protected by or having a patent (指发明、产品等)有专利的, 受专利权保护的. **2** [attrib 作定语] made and sold by a particular firm 专利生产的; 专利经销的: *patent drugs, medicines, etc* 专利药物等 ○ (*joc* 谑) *his patent* (ie personal) *remedy for hangovers* 他私有的治宿醉偏方.

pa·tent *v* [Tn] obtain a patent for (an invention or process) 取得(某项发明或方法的)专利权.

pa·tentee /ˌpeɪtnˈtiː; *US* ˌpætn-; ˌpætn̩ˋti/ *n* person who obtains or holds a patent 专利权人.

□ **patent ˈleather** leather with a hard shiny surface, used for shoes and handbags 漆皮.

ˈpatent office government department that issues patents 专利局.

pa·ter·fa·mi·lias /ˌpeɪtəfəˈmɪlɪæs; ˋpetɚfəˋmɪlɪ,æs/ *n* (*pl* **patresfamilias** /ˌpɑːtreɪzfəˈmɪlɪæs; ˌpɑtrezfəˋmɪlɪæs/) (*fml or joc* 文或谑) head of a family; father 家长; 户主; 父亲.

pa·ter·nal /pəˈtɜːnl; pəˋtɝnl̩/ *adj* **1** of a father; fatherly 父亲的; 父亲般的: *paternal affection, authority* 父爱、父亲的威信 ○ *He has a paternal concern for your welfare*, ie like that of a father for his child. 他像慈父般关怀你. **2** related through one's father 父系的: *her paternal grandmother*, ie her father's mother 她的祖母. Cf 参看 MATERNAL. ▷ **pa·tern·ally** /-nəlɪ; -nl̩ɪ/ *adv.*

pa·ter·nal·ism /pəˈtɜːnəlɪzəm; pəˋtɝnl̩,ɪzəm/ *n* [U] policy (of governments or employers) of controlling people in a paternal way by providing them with what they need but giving them no responsibility or freedom of choice 家长式的统治、管理或作风; 家长主义. ▷ **pa·ter·nal·istic** /pəˌtɜːnəˈlɪstɪk; pə,tɝnl̩ˋɪstɪk/ *adj.* **pa·ter·nal·istic·ally** /-klɪ; -klɪ/ *adv.*

pa·tern·ity /pəˈtɜːnətɪ; pəˋtɝnətɪ/ *n* [U] **1** state of being a father; fatherhood 父亲的身分; 父亲的地位: *He denied paternity of the child*, ie denied that he was its father. 他不承认是那孩子的父亲. **2** descent from a father 父系: *a child of unknown paternity* 生父不明的孩子.

pa·ter·nos·ter /ˌpætəˈnɒstə(r); ˋpætɚˋnɑstɚ/ *n* the Lord's Prayer, esp when said in Latin 主祷文(尤指用拉丁文的).

path /pɑːθ; *US* pæθ; pæθ/ *n* (*pl* **~s** /pɑːðz; *US* pæðz; pæðz/) **1** (also **ˈpath·way**, **ˈfoot·path**) way or track made for or by people walking 小路; 小径: *Keep to the* *path or you'll lose your way.* 沿着这条小道走，否则就要迷路. ○ *The path follows the river and then goes through the woods.* 这条小径与河并排，而后穿过林子. ○ *We took the path across the fields.* 我们顺着横越田地的小路走. ⇨illus at App 1 见附录1插图, page vi. **2** line along which sb/sth moves (人或事物移动的)路线, 轨道: *the moon's path round the earth* 月亮绕地球的轨道 ○ *the path of a tornado* 龙卷风经过的路线 ○*She threw herself in the path of* (ie in front of) *an oncoming vehicle.* 她一下子朝对面来车扑去. ○ (*fig* 比喻) *She has had a difficult path through life.* 她生活中有过一段困难的历程. **3** course of action 行动步骤; 办事程序; 做法: *I strongly advised him not to take that path.* 我极力劝他不要采取那种做法. **4** (usu *sing* 通常作单数) **~ to sth** way to reach or achieve sth (达到或成就某事的)途径, 方式: *the path to success, victory, riches, power, ruin* 通往成功、胜利、富裕、权力、毁灭的道路. **5** (idm 习语) **cross sb's path** ⇨ CROSS². **lead sb up the garden path** ⇨ LEAD³. **the primrose path** ⇨ PRIMROSE. **smooth sb's path** ⇨ SMOOTH².

□ **path·finder** /ˈpɑːθfaɪndə(r); *US* ˈpæθ-; ˈpæθˌfaɪndɚ/ *n* **1** person who discovers new places or new ways of doing things 探险者; 开路人; 探索者; 开拓者. **2** pilot of an aircraft guiding other aircraft to a target which they are going to bomb 导航飞机驾驶员.

NOTE ON USAGE 用法: A **lane** is a narrow country road. ☆ **lane** 是乡间小径. A **path** or **footpath** is a way marked out for people to walk along, between houses in a town or across fields, beside rivers, etc in the country. ☆ **path** 或 **footpath** 是市镇中住宅之间或郊野中穿越田地、沿河等有标志的人行道. A **track** is a rough path in the country, often not officially marked, but made by the constant passing of people, animals or vehicles. ☆ **track** 指郊野土路, 常无正式标志, 仅为人、动物或车辆走得多而形成者. **Lane** and **track** can also refer to the separate parts of a road (**lane**) or railway (**track**) separating cars or trains passing in opposite directions or overtaking ☆ **lane** 和 **track** 还可指分开来自对面车辆或供超车用的部分路面, 公路用 **lane**, 铁路用 **track**: *a six-lane motorway* 有六条行车线的高速公路 ○ *a double-track railway line* 双轨铁路线. Runners in an athletics stadium run in individual **lanes.** 在田径运动场上赛跑的人有各自的 **lane**. ☆ The whole area they run on is called the **track.** 进行赛跑的整个地段称为 **track**.

-path ⇨ -PATHY.

path·etic /pəˈθetɪk; pəˈθɛtɪk/ *adj* **1** causing one to feel pity or sadness 招人怜悯的; 可悲的: *pathetic cries for help* 求助的哀怜呼号 ○ *the pathetic sight of starving children* 饥童悲惨可悯的样子 ○ *His tears were pathetic to witness.* 他的眼泪引起在场人的怜悯. **2** (*infml* 口) extremely inadequate; contemptible 极不足的; 可鄙的: *a pathetic attempt, performance, excuse* 极不充分的尝试、表现、借口 ○ *You're pathetic! Can't you even boil an egg?* 你可真没用! 连鸡蛋都不会煮吗? ▷ **path·et·ic·ally** /-klɪ; -klɪ/ *adv*: *pathetically thin* 瘦得怪可怜的 ○ *His answers were pathetically inadequate.* 他的回答太不充分.

□ **paˌthetic ˈfallacy** (in literature) describing inanimate objects as if they are living things with feelings (文学中)拟人谬想(将无生命物体作拟人化处理).

path(o)- *comb form* 构词成分 disease 疾病: *pathology.*

pa·tho·lo·gical /ˌpæθəˈlɒdʒɪkl; ˌpæθəˈlɑdʒɪkl/ *adj* **1** of or relating to pathology 病理学的; 与病理学有关的. **2** of or caused by a physical or mental illness 疾病的; 由疾病引起的. **3** (*infml* 口) unreasonable; irrational 无道理的; 非理智的; 病态的: *a pathological fear of spiders, obsession with death, hatred of sb* 对蜘蛛无端的恐惧、受死亡强迫观念的困扰、对某人病态的憎恨 ○ *a pathological* (ie compulsive) *liar* 病态说谎者. ▷ **pa·tho·lo·gic·ally** /-klɪ; -klɪ/ *adv*: *pathologically jealous, mean, etc* 忌妒狂的、吝啬狂的.

patho·logy /pəˈθɒlədʒɪ; pəˈθɑlədʒɪ/ *n* [U] scientific study of diseases of the body 病理学.

▷ **patho·lo·gist** /pəˈθɒlədʒɪst; pəˈθɑlədʒɪst/ *n* expert in pathology 病理学家.

pathos /ˈpeɪθɒs; ˈpeθɑs/ *n* [U] quality, esp in speech, writing, acting, etc that causes a feeling of pity or sadness 激起怜悯、悲伤的性质(尤指演讲、写作、表演等中的): *the pathos of Hamlet's death* 哈姆雷特之死使人产生的哀怜.

-pathy *comb form* 构词成分 (forming *ns* 用以构成名词) **1** method of treating disease 疗法: *homeopathy* ○ *osteopathy.* **2** feeling 感觉: *telepathy.*

▷ **-path** *comb form* 构词成分 (forming *ns* 用以构成名词) doctor using a particular method of treating disease 使用某种疗法的专门医生: *homeopath* ○ *osteopath.*

-pathic *comb form* 构词成分 (forming *adjs* 用以构成形容词): *homeopathic* ○ *telepathic.*

pa·tience /ˈpeɪʃns; ˈpeʃəns/ *n* [U] **1 ~ (with sb/sth)** ability to accept delay, annoyance or suffering without complaining 耐性; 忍耐力; 耐心: *I warn you, I'm beginning to lose (my) patience (with you),* ie become impatient. 我警告你, 我(对你)已经渐渐失去耐性了. ○ *After three hours of waiting for the train, our patience was finally exhausted.* 我们等了三个小时的火车, 最后再也没有耐性了. ○ *She has no patience with* (ie cannot tolerate) *people who are always grumbling.* 她腻烦那些总发牢骚的人. ○ (*saying* 谚) *Patience is a virtue.* 忍耐是美德. **2 ~ (for sth/to do sth)** ability to persevere with sth; perseverance 坚忍; 坚持; 毅力: *Learning to walk again after his accident required great patience.* 他出事后重新学习走路要有极大的毅力. ○ *She hasn't the patience to do embroidery.* 她没有做刺绣的常性. **3** (*Brit*) (*US* **solitaire**) type of card-game, usu for one player 一种纸牌戏(通常为单人玩的). **4** (idm 习语) **the ˌpatience of ˈJob** very great patience(1) 极大的耐性: *His behaviour would try* (ie test) *the patience of Job.* 无论耐性多大的人也无法忍受他的行为.

pa·tient¹ /ˈpeɪʃnt; ˈpeʃənt/ *adj* **~ (with sb/sth)** having or showing patience 有耐性的; 忍耐的; 容忍的: *You'll have to be patient with my mother — she's going rather deaf.* 你对我母亲得有耐心——她的耳朵越来越背了. ○ *patient research, questioning, listening* 耐心的研究、询问、听 ○ *She's a patient* (ie persevering) *worker.* 她工作很有耐心. ▷ **pa·tiently** *adv*: *wait, sit, listen patiently* 耐心地等着、坐着、听着.

pa·tient² /ˈpeɪʃnt; ˈpeʃənt/ *n* (**a**) person who is receiving medical treatment, esp in a hospital (接受治疗的)病人(尤指医院中的). (**b**) person who is registered with a doctor, dentist, etc and is treated by him when necessary (在某医生处注册的)病人(病时由此医生诊治): *I have been a patient of Dr Smith for many years.* 多年来我一生病就请史密斯医生给我看.

pat·ina /ˈpætɪnə; ˈpætɪnə/ *n* [sing] **1** green coating that forms on the surface of old bronze or copper 铜绿. **2** glossy surface on old wood (古木器上的)光泽.

patio /ˈpætɪəʊ; ˈpɑtɪˌo/ *n* (*pl* **~s** /-əʊz; -oz/) **1** paved area next to a house where people can sit, eat, etc outdoors (与房子相连有铺砌面的)露台, 平台(作户外歇息、用餐处). Cf 参看 VERANDA. **2** roofless courtyard within the walls of a Spanish or Spanish-American house (西班牙式或拉丁美洲式住宅的)院子, 天井. Cf 参看 TERRACE 3.

pa·tis·serie /pəˈtiːsərɪ; pəˈtisərɪ/ *n* **1** [C] shop selling French pastries and cakes 出售法式糕点的商店. **2** [U] pastries and cakes sold in such a shop 法式糕点.

pat·ois /ˈpætwɑː; ˈpætwɑ/ *n* (*pl* unchanged 复数不变 /-twɑːz; -twɑz/) dialect spoken by the common people of a region and differing from the standard language of the country 方言; 土语; 土话: *He speaks the local patois.* 他会说当地方言.

patri- *comb form* 构词成分 of a father 父亲的: *patricide* ○ *patriarch.* Cf 参看 MATRI-.

pat·ri·arch /ˈpeɪtrɪɑːk; ˈpetrɪˌɑrk/ *n* **1** male head of a family or tribe (男性)家长, 族长. Cf 参看 MATRIARCH. **2 Patriarch** (in the Eastern Orthodox and Roman Catholic Churches) high-ranking bishop (东正教和天主教的)牧首, 宗主教. **3** old man who is greatly respected 极受尊敬的年老男子.

▷ **pat·ri·archal** /ˌpeɪtrɪˈɑːkl; ˌpetrɪˈɑrkl/ *adj* **1** of or like a patriarch (似)(男性)家长的, 族长的, 牧首的, 宗主教的, 长者的. **2** ruled or controlled by men 由男性统治或控制的: *a patriarchal society* 父权社会.

pat·ri·arch·ate /-eɪt; -et/ *n* position or period of office of a Patriarch of the Church 牧首或宗主教的职位或任期.

pat·ri·archy /-kɪ; -kɪ/ *n* [C, U] (society, country, etc with a) patriarchal(2) system of control or government 父权制(的社会或国家).

pa·tri·cian /pəˈtrɪʃn; pəˈtrɪʃən/ *n* member of the aristocracy (esp in ancient Rome) 贵族(尤指古罗马的). Cf 参看 PLEBEIAN *n*.

▷ **pa·tri·cian** *adj* of or like a patrician; aristocratic (似)贵族的; 出身高贵的: *patrician arrogance, haughtiness, good looks* 贵族的高傲、傲慢、气派.

pat·ri·cide /ˈpætrɪsaɪd; ˋpætrɪˌsaɪd/ *n* **(a)** [C, U] (act of) killing one's own father 弑父(行为). **(b)** [C] person who does this 弑父者. Cf 参看 MATRICIDE, PARRICIDE.

pat·ri·mony /ˈpætrɪmənɪ; *US* -məʊnɪ; ˋpætrəˌmonɪ/ *n* [U] **1** property inherited from one's father or ancestors 祖传财产. **2** income or property that a church receives from endowments (得自捐赠的)教会收入或财产.

▷ **pat·ri·mo·nial** /ˌpætrɪˈməʊnɪəl; ˌpætrəˈmonɪəl/ *adj* of or relating to a patrimony 祖传财产的; 教会收入的; 教会财产的.

pat·riot /ˈpætrɪət; *US* ˈpeɪt-; ˋpetrɪət/ *n* person who loves his country, esp one who is ready to defend it against an enemy 爱国者(尤指随时为捍卫国家抵抗外敌的): *a true patriot* 真正的爱国者.

▷ **pat·ri·otic** /ˌpætrɪˈɒtɪk; *US* ˌpeɪt-; ˌpetrɪˋɑtɪk/ *adj* having or showing love of one's country 爱国的; 有爱国心的: *patriotic members of the public* 公众中的爱国分子 ○ *patriotic support, fervour* 表现爱国的支持、热情 ○ *patriotic songs* 爱国歌曲. **pat·ri·otic·ally** /-klɪ; -klɪ/ *adv*.

pat·ri·ot·ism /-ɪzəm; -ˌɪzəm/ *n* [U] love of one's country and readiness to defend it 爱国心; 爱国主义; 爱国精神.

pa·trol /pəˈtrəʊl; pəˋtrol/ *v* **(-ll-)** [I, Tn] go round (a town, an area, etc) to check that all is secure and orderly or to look for wrongdoers, an enemy or people who need help 在(某城、地带等)巡逻; 巡查: *The army regularly patrol (along) the border.* 军队按时沿边界巡逻. ○ *Police patrol the streets at night.* 警察晚间在街道上巡逻.

▷ **pa·trol** *n* **1** action of patrolling 巡逻; 巡查: *carry out a patrol* 执行巡逻任务 ○ *The army make hourly patrols of the area.* 军队在该地带每小时巡逻一次. ○ *The navy are maintaining a 24-hour air and sea patrol*, eg in order to find survivors from a ship that has sunk. 海军正在进行24小时海空巡逻(如寻找遇难船只上的幸存者). **2** person, group of people, vehicle, ship or aircraft that patrols an area 巡逻者; 巡逻队; 巡逻车; 巡逻艇; 巡逻机: *a naval, army, police patrol* 海军、陆军、警察的巡逻人员 ○ [attrib 作定语] *a police paˈtrol car* 警察巡逻车. **3** group of (usu) 6 members of a Scout troop or a Girl Guide company 童子军小队(通常为6人). **4** (idm 习语) **on patrol** patrolling a particular area 在巡逻中: *Terrorists attacked two soldiers on patrol.* 恐怖分子袭击了两名正在巡逻的士兵.

□ **paˈtrolman** /-mən; -mən/ *n* (*pl* **-men** /-mən; -mən/) **1** person employed by a motorists' organization to patrol roads and help motorists who are in difficulty (汽车协会的)公路巡查员(帮助遇到困难的司机). **2** (*US*) policeman who patrols a particular area 巡警.

paˈtrol wagon (*US*) = BLACK MARIA (BLACK¹).

pat·ron /ˈpeɪtrən; ˋpetrən/ *n* **1** person who gives money or other support to a person, cause, activity, etc 资助人; 赞助人: *a wealthy patron of the arts* 艺术方面的富有的赞助人. **2** (*fml* 文) (regular) customer of a shop, restaurant, theatre, etc (老)主顾, 顾客: *Patrons are requested to leave their bags in the cloakroom.* 顾客请将手提包留在衣帽间.

□ ˌ**patron ˈsaint** saint regarded as protecting a particular person, place, etc 守护神: *St Christopher is the patron saint of travellers.* 圣·克里斯托弗是旅行者的守护神.

pat·ron·age /ˈpætrənɪdʒ; *US* ˈpeɪt-; ˋpetrənɪdʒ/ *n* [U] **1** support and encouragement given by a patron 资助; 赞助; 支持: *patronage of the arts* 对艺术方面的赞助 ○ *Without the patronage of several large firms, the festival could not take place.* 没有几大公司的赞助, 就没有这一庆典. ○ *The theatre is under the patronage of the Arts Council.* 那剧院得到了艺术委员会的赞助. **2** (*fml* 文) customer's support for a shop, restaurant, etc; custom¹(2) 光顾; 惠顾: *We thank you for your patronage.* 谢谢您的惠顾. **3** right or power to appoint sb to or recommend sb for an important position (重要职务的)任命权, 举荐权. **4** (*dated* 旧) patronizing (PATRONIZE 1) manner 施恩的态度.

pat·ron·ize, -ise /ˈpætrənaɪz; *US* ˈpeɪt-; ˋpetrənˌaɪz/ *v* [Tn] **1** treat (sb) as an inferior; treat (sb) in a condescending way 以高人一等的态度对待(某人); 屈尊俯就对待(某人): *He resented the way she patronized him.* 她待他那种纡尊降贵的样子, 他十分愤恨. **2** (*fml* 文) be a regular customer of (a shop, etc) 作为老主顾经常去(某商店等); 经常光顾、惠顾: *The restaurant is patronized by politicians and journalists.* 这家饭馆常有政治家和记者光顾. **3** act as a patron(1) to (sb/sth); support or encourage (sb/sth) 做(某人[某事物])的赞助人; 资助、赞助或支持(某人[某事物]).

▷ **pat·ron·iz·ing, -ising** *adj* condescending 屈尊俯就的: *a patronizing person, manner, attitude, smile, tone of voice* 高人一等的人、派头、态度、笑容、腔调. **pat·ron·iz·ingly, -isingly** *adv*.

pat·ronymic /ˌpætrəˈnɪmɪk; ˌpætrəˋnɪmɪk/ *n, adj* (name) derived from the name of one's father or some other male ancestor 从父名或父系祖先之名衍生出的(名字).

patsy /ˈpætsɪ; ˋpætsɪ/ *n* (*US infml derog* 口, 贬) person who is easily cheated or fooled 易上当或易受愚弄的人.

pat·ter¹ /ˈpætə(r); ˋpætɚ/ *n* [U] rapid and often glib speech used by a comedian, conjuror or salesman (滑稽演员、变戏法者或推销员的)顺口溜: *You have to learn to resist the sales patter.* 你可得学乖点, 不要轻信推销员的那套话.

▷ **pat·ter** *v* **1** [Tn] say or repeat (prayers, etc) in a rapid mechanical way 喋喋地重复(祷告等). **2** [I] talk quickly or glibly 快速地说; 喋喋不休地说.

pat·ter² /ˈpætə(r); ˋpætɚ/ *n* **1** [sing] sound of quick light steps or taps 轻快的脚步声或拍打声: *the patter of rain on a roof* 雨点打在屋顶的啪嗒声 ○ *the patter of footsteps* 急速的脚步声. **2** (idm 习语) **the patter of tiny ˈfeet** (*joc* 谑) (used to refer to a baby that sb is going to or might be going to have 用以指即将出生的婴儿) the sound of young children in a home 家中小儿的声音: *She can't wait for the patter of tiny feet.* 她巴不得婴儿早日出生.

▷ **pat·ter** *v* **1** [I] make this sound 发出轻快的脚步声或拍打声: *rain pattering on the window panes* 雨点啪嗒啪嗒地打在窗户上. **2** (phr v) **patter along, down, etc (sth)** walk quickly in the specified direction with light footsteps 以轻快的脚步沿某方向走: *She pattered along (the corridor) in her bare feet.* 她赤着脚轻快地走过(走廊).

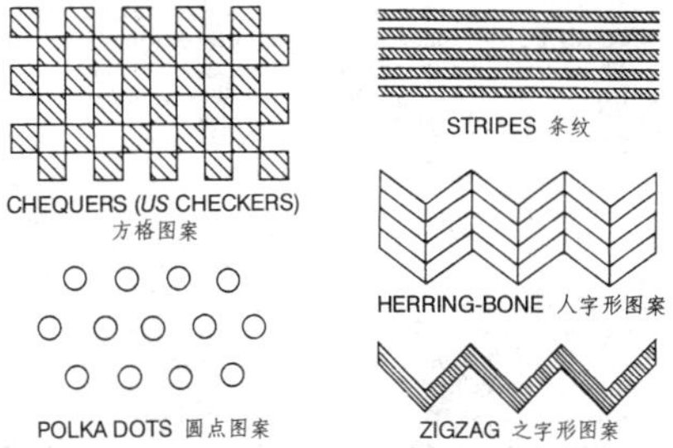

patterns 图案

pat·tern /ˈpætn; ˋpætɚn/ *n* **1** arrangement of lines, shapes, colours, etc, esp as a decorative design on clothes, carpets, wallpaper, etc 图案, 花样, 式样(尤指衣物、地毯、壁纸等的): *a checked, flowery, Paisley pattern* 格子的、花卉的、佩斯利涡旋纹的图案 ○ *What a pretty pattern!* 多漂亮的图案哪! ○ *She wore a dress with a pattern of roses on it.* 她穿着有玫瑰花图案的连衣裙. ⇨illus 见插图. **2 (a)** (often in compounds 常用以构成复合词) model, design or instructions from which sth is to be made (据以制作某物的)模型, 样式, 说明: *a knitting/sewing pattern* 编织[缝纫]样式 ○ *a paper pattern*, ie a set of pieces of paper that show the shapes of the various parts of a garment 纸样(缝制衣服用的). **(b)** piece of wood used to make a mould for casting metal（用以制造铸模的）木模，模型. **3** sample of cloth or some other material（布等的）样品: *a book of tweed patterns* 粗花呢样品簿. **4** way in which sth happens, moves, develops or is arranged 模式; 方式; 形式: *patterns of behaviour/behaviour patterns* 行为模式 ○ *the pattern of economic decline in Britain* 英国经济衰退的形式 ○ *the pattern of events which led up to the war* 导致战争的事件发展状况 ○ *These sentences all have the same grammatical pattern.* 这些句子的语法模式都相同. ○ *The murders all seem to follow a set pattern,* ie occur in a similar way. 这些谋杀案似乎都为同一手法. **5** excellent example; model 模范; 典范; 榜样: *This company's profit-sharing scheme set a pattern which others followed.* 这家公司的利润分成计划已成为各公司的样板.

P

▷ **pat·tern** *v* [Tn·pr] **~ oneself/sth on sb/sth** imitate sb/sth; model sth on sth 模仿某人[某事物]; 按某模型仿造某物: *He patterns himself upon his father.* 他模仿父亲. ○ *Her ideas are patterned on Trotsky's.* 她的思想是仿效托洛茨基的. **pat·terned** *adj* decorated with a pattern 有图案装饰的; 带花样的: *patterned china, fabric, wallpaper* 有图案的瓷器、织物、壁纸.

□ **'pattern-maker** *n* person who makes patterns in an engineering factory 制模工; 翻砂工.

'pattern-shop *n* room in a factory where patterns (PATTERN 2b) are made 制模车间.

pau·city /ˈpɔːsətɪ; ˋpɔsətɪ/ *n* [sing] **~ (of sth)** (*fml* 文) smallness of number or quantity 少量; 少许; 少数: *a paucity of evidence* 少量证据.

paunch /pɔːntʃ; pɔntʃ/ *n* fat stomach, esp a man's 大肚子（尤指男子的）: *You're getting quite a paunch,* eg from drinking a lot of beer. 你的肚子越来越大了（如因喝大量啤酒）.

▷ **paunchy** *adj* **(-ier, -iest)** having a paunch 肚子大的（尤指男子）. **paunchi·ness** *n* [U].

pau·per /ˈpɔːpə(r); ˋpɔpɚ/ *n* very poor person 贫民; 穷人: *He died a pauper.* 他死时身无分文.

▷ **pau·per·ism** /ˈpɔːpərɪzəm; ˋpɔpɚˌɪzəm/ *n* [U] state of being a pauper 贫穷; 贫困.

pause /pɔːz; pɔz/ *n* **1 ~ (in sth)** temporary stop in action or speech（行为、讲话中的）暂停, 临时中止: *a moment's pause* 短暂的停顿 ○ *He slipped out during a pause in the conversation.* 谈话中稍一停顿他就溜了出去. ○ *After a short pause, they continued walking.* 他们稍稍停了停, 然后继续走路. ○ *She spoke for an hour without a pause.* 她不停地讲了一小时. ⇨Usage at BREAK² 用法见 BREAK². **2** (*music* 音) sign (𝄐) over a note(5b) or rest²(3) to show that it should be longer than usual 延长记号𝄐（标在音符或休止符上表示该符应比通常所示为长）. **3** (idm 习语) **give pause to sb/ give sb pause** make sb hesitate before doing sth 使某人做某事前犹豫: *Weather conditions were bad enough to give pause to even the most experienced climbers.* 天气十分恶劣, 即使最有经验的登山者也犹豫不决. **a pregnant pause/silence** ⇨ PREGNANT.

▷ **pause** *v* [I, Ipr] **~ (for sth)** make a pause 中止; 暂停; 停顿: *He paused for a moment, and then continued his speech.* 他停顿了一下然后继续讲话. ○ *Let's pause for a cup of coffee.* 我们歇歇喝杯咖啡吧. ○ *speak without pausing for breath,* ie very quickly 一口气说下去.

pave /peɪv; pev/ *v* **1** [esp passive 尤用于被动语态: Tn, Tn·pr] **~ sth (with sth)** cover (a surface) with flat stones or bricks 用石或砖铺(路): *The path is paved with concrete slabs.* 这条路是用混凝土板铺成的. **2** (idm 习语) **ˌpave the ˈway (for sb/sth)** create a situation in which sth specified is possible or can happen（为某人[某事物]）创造条件, 做准备: *His economic policies paved the way for industrial expansion.* 他的经济政策为工业的扩展铺平了道路. **the road to hell is paved with good intentions** ⇨ ROAD.

□ **'paving stone** slab of stone used for paving 铺路石板.

pave·ment /ˈpeɪvmənt; ˋpevmənt/ *n* **1** [C] (*Brit*) (*US* **sidewalk**) path with a paved surface at the side of a road for people to walk on 人行道: *Don't ride your bicycle on the pavement.* 不要在人行道上骑自行车. **2** [U] (*US*) hard surface of a road, street, etc（道路等的）硬路面. **3** [C] paved area or surface 用石或砖铺的面.

□ **'pavement artist** person who draws on the pavement with coloured chalks, esp in order to be given money by passers-by 马路画家（用彩色粉笔在街上作画, 尤指向行人讨钱的）.

pa·vil·ion /pəˈvɪlɪən; pəˋvɪljən/ *n* **1** (*Brit*) building next to a sports ground, esp a cricket field, used by players and spectators（运动场旁, 尤指板球场旁供运动员和观众用的）建筑物: *a cricket pavilion* 板球队员更衣室. **2** light building used as a shelter, eg in a park 亭子, 阁（如公园中的）. **3** ornamental building used for concerts, dances, etc（音乐会、舞会等用的）装饰华美的建筑物: *the Royal Pavilion in Brighton* 布赖顿皇家剧场. **4** temporary building, esp a large tent used to display items at an exhibition（展览会陈列物品用的）临时建筑物,（尤指）大帐篷.

pav·ing /ˈpeɪvɪŋ; ˋpevɪŋ/ *n* [U] **(a)** paved surface 用石或砖铺的面. ⇨illus at App 1 见附录1插图, page vii. **(b)** material used for this（石、砖等）铺面材料.

pav·lova /ˈpævləvə; pævˋlovə/ *n* [C, U] (also **pav·lova cake**) dessert consisting of a layer of meringue topped with cream and fruit 蛋白奶油酥.

paw /pɔː; pɔ/ *n* **1** foot of an animal with claws or nails 爪子: *a dog's paw* 狗爪子. ⇨illus at App 1 见附录1插图, page iii. **2** (*infml joc or derog* 口, 谑或贬) person's hand 手: *Take your dirty little paws off me!* 别用你的小黑爪子抓着我!

▷ **paw** *v* **1** [Ipr, Tn] **~ (at) sth** (of an animal) feel or scratch sth with the paws（指动物）用爪子触或抓挠（某物）. **2** [Tn] (of a horse or bull) scrape (the ground) with a hoof（指马或牛）用蹄子刨或扒（地）. **3** [Tn] touch (sb/sth) with the hands roughly, awkwardly or in a sexually improper manner 用手胡乱地或猥亵地摸（某人[某物]）: *He can't be near a woman without pawing her.* 他一接近女人就忍不住动手动脚.

pawky /ˈpɔːkɪ; ˋpɔkɪ/ *adj* **(-ier, -iest)** (*Brit dialect* 方) drily humorous 木然幽默的. ▷ **pawk·ily** *adv*. **pawki·ness** *n* [U].

pawl /pɔːl; pɔl/ *n* **1** lever with a catch that fits between the teeth (TOOTH 2) of a ratchet to prevent slipping or movement in a particular direction（防逆转的）棘爪, 掣爪. **2** (*nautical* 海) short bar used to prevent a capstan or windlass from recoiling（防止绞盘或起锚机逆转的）掣转杆.

pawn¹ /pɔːn; pɔn/ *n* **1** one of the eight chess-men of the smallest size and value（国际象棋中的）卒. ⇨illus at CHESS 见 CHESS 插图. **2** (*fig* 比喻) person or group whose actions are controlled by others 被人利用的人: *We are mere pawns in the struggle for power.* 在权力斗争中我们只是一批小卒.

pawn² /pɔːn; pɔn/ *v* [Tn] **1** leave (an object) with a pawnbroker in exchange for money that can be repaid in order to get the object back 典当, 抵押（某物）: *He pawned his gold watch to pay the rent.* 他典当了金表用以交租. **2** (*fig* 比喻) abandon (sth) in order to gain sth 以（某事物）担保: *pawn one's honour* 以个人名誉担保.

▷ **pawn** *n* (idm 习语) **in pawn** in a state of being pawned 在抵押中; 已典当: *My watch is in pawn.* 我把表当了.

□ **'pawnbroker** *n* person licensed to lend money in exchange for articles left with him 开当铺者; 当铺老板.

'pawnshop *n* place where a pawnbroker works 当铺.

'pawn-ticket *n* receipt given by a pawnbroker for articles left with him 当票.

paw·paw = PAPAW.

pay¹ /peɪ; pe/ *n* [U] **1** money paid for regular work 工资; 薪金: *an increase in pay/a pay increase* 加薪 ○ *He doesn't like the job, but the pay is good.* 他不喜欢那工作, 但薪水很高. ○ (*infml* 口) *What's the pay like* (ie How much are you paid) *in your job?* 你挣多少钱? ○ [attrib 作定语] *pay negotiations* 工资谈判. ⇨Usage at INCOME 用法见 INCOME. **2** (idm 习语) **in the pay of sb/sth** (*derog* 贬) employed by sb/sth, esp secretly 受雇于某人[某事物]（尤指秘密工作）: *a spy in the pay of the enemy* 敌人收买的间谍.

□ **'pay-claim** *n* demand for an increase in pay made by a union for its members（工会为其会员提出的）加薪要求.

'pay-day *n* **1** day of the week or month on which wages or salaries are paid 发薪日. **2** (in the Stock Exchange) day when stock that has been transferred has to be paid for（证券交易所的）过户结帐日.

ˈ**pay dirt** (*US*) earth containing enough ore to make mining profitable (有开采价值的)矿石, 矿砂.

ˈ**payload** *n* **1** part of the load of a ship, an aircraft, etc for which payment is received, eg passengers and cargo, but not fuel 收费载重, 酬载(船舶、飞机等的收费运载量, 如乘客、货物而不包括燃料). **2** explosive power of a bomb or warhead carried in an aircraft or a missile (飞行器或导弹所携的炸弹或弹头的)炸药量. **3** equipment carried by a satellite or spacecraft 有效荷载(卫星或航天器携带的仪器设备).

ˈ**paymaster** *n* **1** official who pays troops, workers, etc 负责发薪饷的军需官; 工薪出纳员. **2** (usu *pl* 通常作复数) (*derog* 贬) person who pays another person or group to do sth for him and who therefore controls his/their actions 雇用并操纵他人的人: *The paymasters of these petty crooks are the big crime syndicates.* 操纵这帮小流氓的就是那个大犯罪集团. ˌ**Paymaster** ˈ**General** (*Brit*) minister in charge of the department of the Treasury through which payments are made (财政部)主计长.

ˈ**pay-packet** *n* envelope containing an employee's wages 薪水袋.

ˈ**pay phone** (*US* ˈ**pay station**) coin-operated telephone (投币式)公用电话.

ˈ**payroll** *n* (**a**) list of people employed by a company and the amount of money to be paid to each of them (公司员工的)薪水名册: *a firm with 500 employees on the payroll*, ie one that employs 500 people 有500名雇员的公司. (**b**) total amount of wages and salaries to be paid to the employees of a company (公司员工的)薪水总额.

ˈ**pay-slip** *n* piece of paper that gives details of an employee's pay, including deductions for tax, insurance, etc 薪水单.

pay[2] /peɪ; pe/ *v* (*pt, pp* **paid**) **1** (**a**) [I, Ipr, Tn, Tn·pr, Dn·n, Dn·pr] **~ (sb) (for sth); ~ sth (to sb) (for sth)** give (sb) money (for goods, services, etc) 付钱给(某人)(作为货物、服务等的费用): *My firm pays well*, ie pays high wages. 我公司工酬优厚. ○ *Are you paying in cash or by cheque?* 你用现款还是用支票支付? ○ *They tried to leave the restaurant without paying (for their meal).* 他们不付饭钱就要溜走. ○ *Her parents paid for her to go* (ie paid the cost of her travel) *to America.* 她去美国的旅费是父母给的. ○ *Have you paid the milkman this week?* 这星期给送奶人钱了吗? ○ *pay sb by the hour/by the job* 计时[计件]给某人付酬 ○ *How much did you pay for your house?* 你买房花了多少钱? ○ *We paid £50 000 for our house.* 我们买房花了5万英镑. ○ *You haven't paid me the money you owe me.* 你欠我的钱还没还给我呢. ○ *She paid a dealer £2 000 for that car.* 她用2千英镑从汽车行买的这辆汽车. ○ *Have you paid that money to the bank yet?* 你把那笔钱付给银行了吗? ○ *You're not paid to sit around doing nothing!* 花钱雇你来可不是让你光坐着不干活的! (**b**) [Tn, Dn·n, Dn·pr] **~ sth (to sb)** give (what is owed); hand over the amount of sth 还; 偿还; 缴付: *pay taxes, rates, rent, etc* 纳税、交地方税、缴租 ○ *pay a bill, debt, fine, subscription, etc* 付帐、还债、缴罚款、交订费 ○ *He paid the terrorist a ransom of £50000 for his kidnapped son.* 他为救出被绑架的儿子向恐怖分子交付了5万英镑的赎金. ○ *Membership fees should be paid to the club secretary.* 会费应交给俱乐部秘书. **2** (**a**) [I] (of a business, etc) be profitable (指商业等)有利可图, 有收益: *The shop closed because it didn't pay.* 该店因不赚钱而关闭. ○ *It's difficult to make sheep farming pay here.* 养羊业在这里难有收益. (**b**) [I, Tn] be advantageous or profitable to (sb) 对(某人)有利或有好处: *Crime doesn't pay.* 犯罪是得不偿失的. ○ *It would pay (you) to use an accountant.* 雇会计划得来. ○ *It pays to be honest with the taxman.* 纳税诚实不吃亏. **3** (idm 习语) **expenses paid** ⇨ EXPENSE. **give/pay lip-service to sth** ⇨ LIP-SERVICE (LIP). **he who ˌpays the ˌpiper ˌcalls the ˈtune** (*saying* 谚) the person who provides the money for sth should control how it is spent 花钱的人说话算数. **pay attention (to sb/sth)** listen carefully to sb/sth; take notice of sb/sth 仔细听某人说的话[某事物]; 注意某人[某事物]: *Pay attention when I'm talking to you!* 我跟你说话的时候, 你要留心听! ○ *pay attention to one's teacher* 注意听老师讲课. **pay sb a compliment/pay a compliment to sb** praise sb about sth 就某事物夸奖某人. **pay court to sb** (*becoming dated* 渐旧) treat (esp a woman) with great respect or admiration in order to gain favour 向(尤指女人)献殷勤; 讨好; 求爱. **pay ˈdividends** produce benefits or advantages 产生效益; 得到好处: *I suggest you take more exercise; I think you'll find it pays dividends*, ie it will make you fitter. 我建议你多运动, 多运动你就会觉得有好处. **pay heed (to sb/sth)** take careful notice of sb/sth; heed sb/sth 注意某人[某事物]: *She paid no heed to our warnings.* 她不把我们的警告放在心上. **pay sb (back) in his own/the same ˈcoin** punish sb for treating one badly, by treating him in the same way 以其人之道还治其人之身. **pay/settle an old score** ⇨ OLD. **pay the ˈpenalty (for sth/doing sth)** suffer because of wrongdoing, misfortune or an error 因过失、不幸或谬误而受苦或受害: *I'm paying the penalty for drinking too much last night; I've got a dreadful headache!* 昨晚我酒喝得太多真是自讨苦吃, 现在头疼得很厉害! **pay a/the ˈprice (for sth)** suffer a disadvantage or loss in return for sth one has gained 为所得付出代价: *Our troops recaptured the city, but they paid a heavy price for it*, ie many were killed. 我军收复了该市, 但为此付出了沉重代价. **pay one's reˈspects (to sb)** (*fml* 文) visit sb as a sign of respect for him 探望某人以示敬意; 拜访; 拜见: *Please pay my respects to your mother.* 请代我向伯母致意. ○ *Hundreds came to pay their last respects to the dead president*, eg by attending his funeral. 数以百计的人前来向总统遗体告别. **pay through the ˈnose (for sth)** (*infml* 口) pay too much or a lot of money for sth 为某事物花钱过多. **pay (a) tribute to sb/sth** express one's admiration or respect for sb/sth 对某人[某事物]表示赞赏或敬意: *His colleagues paid generous tributes to the outgoing president.* 同事们纷纷向即将卸任的总裁致敬. **pay sb/sth a visit** visit sb/sth 访问某人; 参观某处. **pay one's/its ˈway** (of a person, business, etc) support oneself/itself with money one/it has earned (指人)挣钱维持生活; (指企业)赢利维持营业. **put ˈpaid to sth** (*infml* 口) stop or destroy sth 结束或毁掉某事物: *Coming to work drunk put paid to her hopes of promotion.* 她上班总是醉醺醺的, 把晋升的希望都失去了. **rob Peter to pay Paul** ⇨ ROB. **there'll be the devil to pay** ⇨ DEVIL[1]. **there will be/was hell to pay** ⇨ HELL. **you ˌpays your ˌmoney and you ˌtakes your ˈchoice** (*infml catchphrase* 口, 警语) one should choose whatever alternative course of action, explanation etc, one wants, since any one is as good as any other 你花钱, 你挑选(谁都一样碰运气).

P

4 (phr v) **pay sb back (sth); pay sth back** return (money) to sb that one has borrowed from him 还(钱)给某人: *Have you paid (me) back the money you owe me yet?* 你向我借的钱还(给我)了吗? ○ *I'll pay you back next week.* 我下星期还给你. **pay sb back (for sth)** punish sb or get one's revenge 惩罚某人; 报复: *I'll pay him back for the trick he played on me.* 他对我使坏, 我得治治他.

pay for sth suffer or be punished for sth 为某事吃苦头或受惩罚: *The home team paid (dearly) for their defensive errors*, eg by losing the match. 主队因防守错误而(大)吃苦头(例如比赛输了). ○ *I'll make him pay for his insolence!* 他蛮横无礼, 我要让他尝尝苦头!

pay sth in; pay sth into sth put (money) into (a bank account) 将(钱)存入(银行): *pay a cheque into one's account* 把支票存入帐户.

pay off (*infml* 口) (of a risky policy, course of action, etc) bring good results; be successful; work (尤指冒风险的政策、做法等)带来好结果, 成功, 行得通: *The gamble paid off.* 赌赢了. **pay sb off** (**a**) pay the wages of sb and dismiss him from a job 付清某人工资予以解雇: *pay off the crew of a ship* 付清全体船员工资并予以解雇. (**b**) (*infml* 口) give money to sb to prevent him from doing sth; bribe sb 用钱收买某人使之不做某事; 贿赂某人. **pay sth off** pay in full (money owed for sth) 全部偿还; 偿清: *pay off one's debts, a loan, a mortgage, etc* 还清债务、贷款、抵押款等.

pay sth out (**a**) (regularly) make a large payment (of money) for sth (按时)为某事物付巨款: *I had to pay out £200 to get my car repaired!* 我得花200英镑修理汽车! ○ *We're paying out £300 a month on our mortgage.* 我们每

月要付300英镑抵押贷款. (**b**) release or pass (a length of rope, cord, etc) through the hands (自手中)放松, 放出(一段绳索等).

pay up pay in full money that is owed for sth 付清全部欠款: *I'll take you to court unless you pay up immediately.* 除非马上还清欠款, 否则我和你打官司.

▷ **pay·able** /ˈpeɪəbl; ˋpeəbl/ *adj* [pred 作表语] that must or may be paid 应付; 可付: *Instalments are payable on the last day of the month.* 分期付的款可于每月最后一日交付. ○ *The price of the goods is payable in instalments.* 货款可以分期支付.

payee /peɪˈiː; peˋi/ *n* person to whom sth is (to be) paid 受款人; 收款人.

payer *n* person who pays or who has to pay for sth 付款人; 交款人.

□ ˌ**paid-ˈup** *adj* having paid all money or subscriptions owed to a club, political party, etc (会员费、党费等)已付清的, 已缴齐的: *She's a (fully) ˌpaid-up member of the ˈparty.* 她是缴(清)了党费的党员.

ˌ**pay-as-you-ˈearn** *n* [U] (*Brit*) (*abbr* 缩写 **PAYE**) method of collecting income tax by deducting it from an employee's wages or salary 预扣所得税法(从薪金中扣除所得税的制度).

ˈ**pay-bed** *n* (*Brit*) bed in a National Health hospital for which the user has paid as a private patient (国民保健医院的)自费病床.

ˌ**paying ˈguest** person who lives in sb's house and pays for his board and lodging; lodger (私人家中的)寄膳宿者, 房客.

ˈ**pay-off** *n* (*infml* 口) **1** act or occasion of paying money (esp a bribe) to sb 付给某人钱(尤指贿赂). **2** deserved reward or punishment (应有的)报偿, 惩罚. **3** climax of a story or of a series of events (故事或事件的)高潮.

PAYE /ˌpiː eɪ waɪ ˈiː; ˌpi e waɪ ˋi/ *abbr* 缩写 = (*Brit*) (of income tax) pay-as-you-earn.

pay·ment /ˈpeɪmənt; ˋpemənt/ *n* **~ (for sth) 1** [U] paying or being paid 支付; 付款; 缴纳; 报酬: *We would be grateful for prompt payment of your account.* 如即付款无任感激. ○ *Payment of subscriptions should be made to the club secretary.* 会费应交给俱乐部秘书. **2** [C] sum of money (to be) paid 付出的或要付的款项: *The television can be paid for in ten monthly payments of £50.* 这电视机可月付50英镑10次付清. ○ *Would you accept £50 as payment (for the work)?* (这工作)给你50英镑你愿意做吗? **3** [U, sing] reward for sth 报答; 报偿: *We'd like you to accept this book in payment for your kindness.* 我们奉送此书聊表谢忱. ○ (*ironic* 反语) *Personal abuse was the only payment he got for his efforts.* 他努力所得只是一顿臭骂.

pay·ola /peɪˈəʊlə; peˋolə/ *n* (*esp US*) **1** [C] sum of money offered to sb to use his position or influence to promote the sales of a commercial product 为利用某人的地位或影响以推销商品而向其行贿的钱. **2** [U] practice of paying money in this way 上述情况的行贿.

PC /ˌpiː ˈsiː; ˌpi ˋsi/ *abbr* 缩写 = (*Brit*) **1** personal computer 个人用计算机; 个人电脑. **2** (*pl* **PCs**) police constable: *PC (Tom) Marsh* (汤姆·)马什警察. Cf 参看 WPC. **3** Privy Councillor.

pc *abbr* 缩写 = **1** (*US* **pct**) (*symb* 符号为 **%**) per cent: *20 pc* 20%. **2** /ˌpiː ˈsiː; ˌpi ˋsi/ (*infml* 口) postcard.

pd *abbr* 缩写 = paid (eg on a bill) 已付, 付讫(如帐单上的标记).

Pde *abbr* 缩写 = (in street names) parade (用作街名)街: *29 North Pde* 北街29号.

PDSA /ˌpiː diː es ˈeɪ; ˌpi di ɛs ˋe/ *abbr* 缩写 = (*Brit*) People's Dispensary for Sick Animals 人民兽医诊所.

PDT /ˌpiː diː ˈtiː; ˌpi di ˋti/ *abbr* 缩写 = (*US*) Pacific Daylight Time 太平洋夏季时间.

PE /ˌpiː ˈiː; ˌpi ˋi/ *abbr* 缩写 = physical education 体育(课): *do PE at school* 在学校上体育课 ○ *a PE lesson* 体育课. Cf 参看 PT.

pea /piː; pi/ *n* **1** (**a**) climbing plant with long green pods containing edible green seeds that are eaten as a vegetable 豌豆. (**b**) one of these seeds 豌豆(粒). **2** (idm 习语) **like as two peas/as peas in a pod** ⇨ LIKE[3].

□ ˌ**pea-ˈgreen** *adj*, *n* (having a) bright green colour like that of peas 青豆色(的); 浅绿色(的).

ˈ**pea-shooter** *n* small tube from which dried peas are shot by blowing through the tube 射豆枪.

ˌ**pea ˈsoup** soup made from dried peas 豌豆汤.

ˌ**pea-ˈsouper** *n* (*dated Brit infml* 旧, 口) very thick yellow fog 黄色浓雾.

peace /piːs; pis/ *n* **1** (**a**) [U] state of freedom from war or violence 和平; 太平: *The two communities live together in peace (with one another).* 这两个社区和平相处. ○ *After years of fighting the people longed for peace.* 经过多年的战斗, 人民渴望和平. ○ [attrib 作定语] *a peace treaty* 和平条约 ○ *peace studies, negotiations* 和平研究、和谈 ○ *the Peace Movement*, ie the movement campaigning for nuclear disarmament 和平运动(争取核裁军的). (**b**) [sing] period of this 和平时期: *a lasting peace* 持久和平 ○ *After a brief peace, fighting broke out again.* 经暂短的和平时期, 战事又起. **2** (often 常作 **Peace**) [U, sing] treaty ending a war 和约: *Peace/A Peace was signed between the two countries.* 两国签定了和约. ○ *The Peace of Versailles* 凡尔赛和约. **3** [U] (state of) calm or quiet 安静; 平静: *break/disturb the peace* 打破[搅扰]宁静 ○ *the peace of a summer evening, the countryside* 夏日傍晚的、郊野的寂静 ○ *I would work better if I had a bit of peace and quiet.* 要是再静一些我就能工作得更好了. ○ *He just wants to be left in peace*, ie not to be disturbed. 他只是希望别打扰他. ○ *peace of mind*, ie freedom from worry 心态平静 ○ *May he rest in peace*, eg carved as an inscription on sb's tombstone. 愿他安息(如刻于墓碑上的字样). **4** [U] (state of) harmony and friendship 和睦; 友好. **5** (idm 习语) **(be) at peace (with oneself/sb/sth)** in a state of friendship or harmony (with oneself/sb/sth) 让(自己)平静; 与(某人[某事物])和好、和睦: *She's never at peace with herself*, ie is always restless. 她总是静不下来. ˌ**hold one's ˈpeace/ˈtongue** (*dated* 旧) remain silent or keep quiet although one would like to say sth 保持缄默; 忍住不说. ˌ**keep the ˈpeace** (**a**) not create a disturbance in public 维持治安. (**b**) prevent people from quarrelling, fighting or creating a disturbance in public 维持秩序: *a peace-keeping force*, ie armed troops sent to a country where there is civil war, to prevent more fighting 维持和平部队. **make one's peace with sb** end a quarrel with sb, esp by apologizing 与某人和解(尤指主动道歉). **make peace** (of two people, countries, etc) agree to end a war or a quarrel (指两人、两国等)媾和, 和解.

□ ˈ**Peace Corps** (*US*) organization that sends young volunteers to work in other countries 和平队.

ˈ**peace-loving** *adj* peaceable(1); peaceful(2) 爱好和平的; 和平的; 安宁的: *a peace-loving nation, people, tribe, etc* 爱好和平的民族、人民、部落等.

ˈ**peacemaker** *n* person who persuades people or countries to make peace 调解人; 调停人.

ˈ**peace offering** present offered to show that one is willing to make peace or in order to apologize for sth 为求和解而赠送的礼物: *I bought her some flowers as a peace offering.* 我买了一些花送给她表示歉意.

ˈ**peace-pipe** *n* (also ˌ**pipe of ˈpeace**) tobacco pipe smoked by N American Indians when they have made peace with an enemy 和平烟斗(北美印第安人与敌人和解时吸用的).

ˈ**peacetime** *n* [U] period when a country is not at war 和平时期.

peace·able /ˈpiːsəbl; ˋpisəbl/ *adj* **1** not quarrelsome; wishing to live in peace with others 不争吵的; 愿与别人和睦相处的: *a peaceable temperament, person* 温和的脾气、人. **2** without fighting or disturbance; peaceful 安宁的; 和平的: *a peaceable settlement, discussion* 心平气和的解决、商讨 ○ *peaceable methods* 和平的方法. ▷ **peace·ably** /-əblɪ; -əblɪ/ *adv*: *live peaceably with one's neighbours* 与邻居和睦相处.

peace·ful /ˈpiːsfl; ˋpisfəl/ *adj* **1** not involving war or violence 不诉诸战争或暴力的; 和平的: *a peaceful demonstration, reign, period of history* 和平示威、太平盛世、历史上的和平时期 ○ *peaceful uses of atomic energy* 原子能的和平利用 ○ *peaceful co-existence*, eg of countries with opposing political systems 和平共处. **2** loving or seeking peace 爱好和平的; 寻求和平的: *peaceful nations* 爱好和平的国家 ○ *peaceful aims* 追求和平的目的. **3** quiet; calm; tranquil 安静的; 安宁的; 宁静的: *a peaceful evening, scene, death* 宁静的黄昏、静谧

的景色、安祥的死亡 ○ *peaceful sleep* 安宁的睡眠 ○ *It's so peaceful out here in the country.* 郊区这地方多么恬静.
▷ **peace·fully** /-fəlɪ; -fəlɪ/ *adv*: *die, sleep peacefully* 死、睡得安祥. **peace·ful·ness** *n* [U].

peach /pi:tʃ; pitʃ/ *n* **1** [C] round juicy fruit with downy yellowish-red skin and a rough stone 桃: *tinned peaches* 桃罐头 ○ [attrib 作定语] *a 'peach stone* 桃核. ⇨illus at FRUIT 见FRUIT 插图. **2** [C] (also **'peach tree**) tree on which this grows 桃树. **3** [U] yellowish-red colour of a peach 桃红色. **4** (*infml* 口) (**a**) [C] very attractive young woman 美人儿; 漂亮妞儿: *She's a real peach.* 她真是个美人儿. (**b**) [sing] **~ (of a sth)** thing that is exceptionally good or attractive of its kind (同类事物中)极好的或极吸引人的事物: *That was a peach of a shot!* 射得真棒!
▷ **peachy** *adj* (**-ier, -iest**) like a peach in colour or texture 像桃的; 颜色像桃的.
□ ˌ**peaches and 'cream** (*approv* 褒) having an attractive pink colour 漂亮的粉红色: *a peaches-and-cream complexion* 白里透红的面容.
ˌ**peach 'Melba** desert made with ice-cream, peaches and raspberry sauce 冰激凌、桃加悬钩子沙司的甜品.

peacock 孔雀

pea·cock /'pi:kɒk; 'piˌkɑk/ *n* **1** large male bird with long blue and green tail feathers which can be spread out like a fan 孔雀: [attrib 作定语] *peacock feathers* 孔雀羽毛. **2** (idm 习语) **proud as a peacock** ⇨ PROUD.
□ ˌ**peacock 'blue** *adj, n* (having a) bright blue-green colour 孔雀蓝(的).

pea·hen /'pi:hen; 'piˌhɛn/ *n* female of a peacock 雌孔雀.

peak[1] /pi:k; pik/ *n* **1** (**a**) pointed top, esp of a mountain 尖顶; (尤指)山峰: *The plane flew over the snow-covered peaks.* 飞机在积雪的山峰上飞过. ⇨illus at MOUNTAIN 见MOUNTAIN 插图. (**b**) the mountain itself 山: *The climbers made camp half-way up the peak.* 登山队员在半山腰扎营. **2** any shape, edge or part of sth that narrows to a point 尖顶; 尖头; 尖端: *the peak of a roof* 屋的尖顶 ○ *hair combed into a peak* 梳起尖儿的头发 ○ *widow's peak*, ie hair-style or growth that slopes back on each side from a point in the centre of the forehead 前额上的v形发尖. **3** pointed front part of a cap 帽舌. ⇨illus at HAT 见HAT 插图. **4** (**a**) point of highest intensity, value, achievement, etc (强度、价值、成就等的)最高点, 顶峰: *Traffic reaches a peak between 8 and 9 in the morning.* 早晨八九点钟是交通的高峰时刻. ○ *She's at the peak of her career.* 她正处于她事业的顶峰. (**b**) [attrib 作定语] maximum, most busy or intense, etc 最大的; 最忙的; 最紧张的: *peak periods, production, load* 高峰时期、最高产量、最高负荷 ○ *the peak hour*, ie when the greatest number of people are travelling to or from work 高峰时间(上下班交通繁忙时间) ○ *peak hours*, ie when demand for sth, eg electricity, is highest 高峰时期(如用电的) ○ *peak time*, eg when the greatest number of people are watching television 黄金时间(如看电视的) ○ *peak rate*, ie highest prices charged at the busiest periods by hotels, airlines, etc 高峰价(旅馆、班机等在最繁忙时期的收费). Cf 参看 OFF-PEAK (OFF).
▷ **peaked** *adj* having a peak 带尖顶的; 带帽舌的: *a peaked cap, roof* 带帽舌的帽子、尖的屋顶.
□ **the 'Peak District** area in Derbyshire, England where there are many peaks (PEAK 1) 皮克区(英格兰德比郡北部行政区, 该处多高峰). ⇨illus at App 1 见附录1 插图, pages xiv, xv.

peak[2] /pi:k; pik/ *v* [I] **1** reach the highest point or value 达到高峰; 达到最高值: *Toy sales peaked just before Christmas and are now decreasing.* 玩具销售额在圣诞节前夕达到最高峰, 现已逐渐下降. ○ *Demand for electricity peaks in the early evening.* 用电量最大的时候是在黄昏时. **2** (idm 习语) **peak and pine** become ill because of grief; waste away (因悲哀)憔悴, 消瘦.
▷ **peaky** (**-ier, -iest**) (also **peaked**) *adj* (*infml* 口) ill or pale 憔悴的; 苍白的: *look, feel a bit peaky* 看上去、觉得有点虚弱.

peal /pi:l; pil/ *n* **1** (**a**) loud ringing of a bell or a set of bells with different notes 响亮的铃声或钟声. (**b**) one of a number of musical patterns that can be rung on a set of bells (可用编钟演奏的)钟乐. **2** set of bells with different notes tuned to each other 编钟. **3** loud burst of sound 洪亮的响声: *a peal of thunder* 雷声隆隆 ○ *break into peals of laughter* 哈哈大笑.
▷ **peal** *v* **1** [I, Ip] **~ (out)** sound in a peal 发出响亮的声音; 发出钟乐声: *The bells pealed (out) over the countryside.* 钟声响彻郊野. **2** [Tn] cause (bells) to ring or sound loudly 使(钟或铃)声音大作: *peal the bells to celebrate victory* 让钟声齐鸣庆祝胜利.

pean (*US*) = PAEAN.

pea·nut /'pi:nʌt; 'piˌnʌt/ *n* **1** [C] (**a**) plant of the pea family bearing edible seeds in pods which ripen underground 落花生; 花生. (**b**) (also **'ground-nut**) one of these seeds 花生米; 花生仁. ⇨illus at NUT 见NUT 插图. **2 peanuts** [pl] (*sl* 俚) very small amount (esp of money) 极少的量(尤指钱): *He gets paid peanuts for doing that job.* 他那份工作报酬甚微.
□ ˌ**peanut 'butter** paste made from roasted ground peanuts, used as a food 花生酱.
ˌ**peanut 'oil** oil made from peanuts, used in cooking 花生油.

pear /peə(r); pɛr/ *n* **1** sweet juicy yellow or green fruit with a rounded shape that becomes narrower towards the stalk 梨. ⇨illus at FRUIT 见FRUIT 插图. **2** (also **'pear tree**) tree on which this grows 梨树.

pearl /pɜ:l; pɝl/ *n* **1** (**a**) small, hard, round, silvery-white or bluish-grey lustrous mass that forms inside the shells of some oysters and is of great value as a gem 珍珠: *a string of pearls* 一串珍珠 ○ [attrib 作定语] *a pearl necklace* 珍珠项链. (**b**) man-made imitation of this 人造珍珠: *cultivated pearls* 人工养殖的珍珠. **2** thing resembling a pearl in shape or colour (形状或颜色)似珍珠之物: *pearls of dew on the grass* 草上的露珠. **3** very precious or highly valued person or thing (used esp in the expressions shown) 极宝贵或极有价值的人或事物(尤用于以下示例): *a pearl among women* 女子中的杰出者 ○ *pearls of wisdom* 智慧的结晶. **4** (idm 习语) **cast pearls before swine** ⇨ CAST[1].
▷ **pearly** *adj* (**-lier, -liest**) of or like a pearl (似)珍珠的: *a pearly sheen* 珍珠的光泽 ○ (*joc* 谑) *the Pearly Gates*, ie the gates of Heaven 珍珠之门(天国的门).
pearlies *n* [pl] (*Brit*) traditional costume of some London costermongers, decorated with pearl buttons 伦敦某些小贩在节日穿的缀有珠母钮扣的传统服装.
ˌ**pearly 'king**, ˌ**pearly 'queen**, (*Brit*) costermonger/costermonger's wife wearing pearlies 穿着缀有珠母钮扣的节日服装的小贩或小贩的妻子.
□ ˌ**pearl 'barley** barley ground into small round grains 珍珠麦(磨成小圆粒的大麦).
ˌ**pearl 'button** button made from mother-of-pearl 珠母钮扣.
'pearl-diver (also **'pearl-fisher**, **pearler**) *n* person who dives or fishes for pearl-oysters 潜水采珠母贝的人.
'pearl-oyster *n* type of oyster in which pearls are found 珠母贝; 珍珠贝.

pear·main /'peəmeɪn; 'pɛrmen/ *n* any of several types of apple with a red skin and firm white flesh 一种红皮苹果.

peas·ant /'peznt; 'pɛznt/ *n* **1** (in the rural areas of some countries) farmer owning or renting a (usu small) piece of land which he cultivates himself (某些国家的)农民(自己有或租有通常为小片土地的耕作者): [attrib 作定语] *peasant farming* 农作. **2** (formerly) poor agricultural worker (旧时)贫穷的雇农. **3** (*infml derog* 口, 贬) person with rough unrefined manners 举止粗鲁的人: *He's an absolute peasant.* 他是个大老粗.

▷ **peas·antry** /ˈpezntrɪ; ˋpɛzntrɪ/ *n* [Gp] (**a**) all the peasants (of a country) (一国的)农民. (**b**) peasants as a social group or class 农民阶级.

pease-pudding /ˌpi:zˈpʊdɪŋ; ˌpizˋpʊdɪŋ/ *n* [C, U] (*esp Brit*) (dish of) split peas boiled and made into a thick creamy liquid 豌豆布丁(黏稠状餐后甜食).

peat /pi:t; pit/ *n* [U] plant material partly decomposed by the action of water, esp in marshy places (**peat bogs**) and used in horticulture or as a fuel 泥煤; 泥炭: *a bag, bale of peat* 一袋、一桶泥煤 ○ [attrib 作定语] *a peat fire*, ie one in which cut pieces of peat are burned 泥煤火.

▷ **peaty** *adj* of, like or containing peat (似)泥煤的; 含泥煤的: *peaty soil* 泥炭土.

pebble /ˈpebl; ˋpɛbl̩/ *n* **1** small stone made smooth and round by the action of water, eg in a stream or on the seashore 卵石; 砾石. **2** (idm 习语) **not the only pebble on the beach** not the only person who matters or who has to be considered 并非唯一要紧的或要考虑的人.

▷ **pebbly** *adj* covered with pebbles 多卵石的: *a pebbly beach* 遍布卵石的海滩.

□ ˈ**pebble-dash** *n* [U] (*Brit*) cement mixed with small pebbles used as a coating for the outside walls of a house (房子外墙的)灰泥卵石涂层.

pe·can /ˈpi:kən, pɪˈkæn; *US* pɪˈkɑ:n; pɪˋkɑn/ *n* **1** pinkish-brown smooth nut with an edible kernel 美洲山核桃. **2** tree on which this grows, a type of hickory from the southern USA 美洲山核桃树.

pec·ca·dillo /ˌpekəˈdɪləʊ; ˌpɛkəˋdɪlo/ *n* (*pl* **~es** or **~s** /-ləʊz; -loz/) small unimportant offence or sin 小过失; 轻罪: *guilty of some mild peccadillo* 有某种小过失.

pec·cary /ˈpekərɪ; ˋpɛkərɪ/ *n* type of wild pig-like animal found in Central and S America 西貒(中美和南美产的似野猪的动物).

peck[1] /pek; pɛk/ *v* **1** [I, Ipr, Tn] **~ (at sth)** (try to) strike (sth) with the beak 啄或鸽(某物): *Hens feed by pecking.* 母鸡啄食. ○ *birds pecking at the window* 啄玻璃窗的鸟儿 ○ *The lamb had been pecked by crows.* 那只小羊被乌鸦鸽着. ○ (*fig* 比喻) *peck at one's food*, ie (of people) eat very small pieces or eat without appetite (指人)一点一点地吃(或因无食欲而没精打采地吃). **2** [Tn, Tn·pr] get or make (sth) by striking with the beak 啄到或鸽成(某物): *peck corn* 啄粟粒 ○ *The birds pecked a hole in the sack.* 鸟儿把袋子啄出一个洞. **3** [Tn, Tn·pr] **~ sb (on sth)** (*infml* 口) kiss sb lightly and hurriedly 匆匆轻吻某人: *peck sb on the cheek* 在某人脸颊上匆匆一吻. **4** (idm 习语) **a/the ˈpecking order** (*infml* 口) system of grading that exists in a group of people, so that some are more important, powerful, etc than others 集体中重要性或势力等的强弱顺序: *Newcomers have to accept their position at the bottom of the pecking order.* 新来的人论资排辈只好屈居于最底层. **5** (phr v) **peck sth out** remove sth by pecking 啄出或鸽出某物: *Vultures had pecked out the dead sheep's eyes.* 秃鹫啄出了那只死羊的眼睛.

▷ **peck** *n* **1** (**a**) stroke made by pecking 啄; 鸽. (**b**) mark or wound made by pecking 啄痕; 鸽痕; 啄伤; 鸽伤: *The parrot gave me a sharp peck on the finger.* 鹦鹉把我的手指鸽得很疼. **2** (*infml* 口) hurried kiss 匆匆一吻: *She gave her aunt a quick peck on the cheek.* 她在姑姑的脸颊上匆匆吻了一下.

peck[2] /pek; pɛk/ *n* (formerly) measure of capacity for dry goods, esp grain, equal to 2 gallons (or approximately 9 litres) (旧时)配克(干量单位, 尤用以量谷物, 等于2加仑或相当于9升).

pecker /ˈpekə(r); ˋpɛkɚ/ *n* **1** (*US sl* 俚) penis 阴茎. **2** (idm 习语) ˌ**keep one's ˈpecker up** (*Brit infml* 口) remain cheerful, esp in spite of difficulties 保持乐观(尤指不惧所处的困难).

peck·ish /ˈpekɪʃ; ˋpɛkɪʃ/ *adj* (*infml* 口) hungry 饿的: *feel a bit peckish* 觉得有点饿.

pec·tin /ˈpektɪn; ˋpɛktɪn/ *n* [U] (*chemistry* 化) substance similar to sugar that forms in some fruit when ripe and causes jam to set 果胶.

▷ **pec·tic** /ˈpektɪk; ˋpɛktɪk/ *adj* (**a**) of or from pectin 果胶的; 得自果胶的. (**b**) producing pectin 产生果胶的.

pec·toral /ˈpektərəl; ˋpɛktərəl/ *adj* **1** of the chest or breast 胸的; 胸部的: *pectoral muscles* 胸肌 ○ *a pectoral fin* 胸鳍. **2** worn on the chest or breast 戴于胸前的: *a pectoral cross*, ie worn by a bishop 戴在胸前的十字架(主教戴的).

▷ **pec·torals** *n* [pl] (*often joc* 常作戏谑语) chest muscles 胸肌.

pecu·late /ˈpekjʊleɪt; ˋpɛkjəˌlet/ *v* [I, Tn] (*fml* 文) take (money) dishonestly, esp from public funds; embezzle 盗用(钱财); (尤指)侵吞, 挪用(公款).

▷ **pec·ula·tion** /ˌpekjʊˈleɪʃn; ˌpɛkjəˋleʃən/ *n* (**a**) [U] peculating 盗用; 侵吞; 挪用. (**b**) [C] instance of this 盗用; 侵吞; 挪用.

pe·cu·liar /pɪˈkju:lɪə(r); pɪˋkjuljɚ/ *adj* **1** (**a**) odd or strange 奇怪的; 奇异的; 罕有的: *a peculiar taste, smell, noise, etc* 怪异的口味、气味、噪音等 ○ *a peculiar feeling that one has been here before* 似曾来过这里的奇怪感觉 ○ *My keys have disappeared — it's most peculiar!* 我的钥匙不见了——这可太奇怪了! Cf 参看 FUNNY PECULIAR (FUNNY). (**b**) (of people) eccentric (指人)怪僻的, 古怪的: *He's a bit peculiar!* 他有点怪! ○ *her rather peculiar behaviour* 她那颇古怪的行为. **2** (*infml* 口) unwell 不舒服的: *I'm feeling rather peculiar — I think I'll lie down for a while.* 我觉得不太舒服——我想躺一会儿. **3** [pred 作表语] **~ to sb/sth** (**a**) belonging only to sb/sth 独有; 独特: *an accent peculiar to the north of the region* 该地北部独特的口音 ○ *a flavour peculiar to food cooked on an open fire* 明火炙烤食物独有的味道 ○ *a species of bird peculiar to Asia* 亚洲独有的鸟种. (**b**) used or practised only by sb/sth 专用的; 特有的: *customs peculiar to the 18th century* 18世纪特有的风俗习惯 ○ *slang peculiar to medical students* 医学院学生的专用俚语. **4** [attrib 作定语] special or particular 专门的; 特别的: *a matter of peculiar interest* 特别使人感兴趣的事 ○ *his own peculiar way of doing things* 他自己专门的做事方法.

▷ **pe·cu·li·ar·ity** /pɪˌkju:lɪˈærətɪ; pɪˌkjulɪˋærətɪ/ *n* **1** [U] quality of being peculiar(1a) 独特性; 特质. **2** [C] distinctive feature; characteristic 特点; 特色; 特性: *These small spiced cakes are a peculiarity of the region.* 这些别有风味的小蛋糕是该地的特产. **3** [C] odd or eccentric thing, quality, habit, etc 怪异的事物、性质、癖好等: *peculiarities of dress, behaviour, diet, etc* 衣着、行为、在饮食习惯方面...的怪癖.

pe·cu·liarly *adv* (**a**) in a peculiar(1b) manner 古怪地; 怪僻地: *behave peculiarly* 举动古怪. (**b**) more than usually; especially 异常地; 特殊地; 特别地: *a peculiarly annoying noise* 特别讨厌的噪音.

pe·cu·ni·ary /pɪˈkju:nɪərɪ; *US* -ɪerɪ; pɪˋkjunɪˌɛrɪ/ *adj* (*fml* 文) of or concerning money 金钱的; 关系钱财的: *pecuniary advantage, aid, difficulties* 钱财上的好处、帮助、困难 ○ *work without pecuniary reward* 无偿劳动.

ped·agogue (*US* **-gog**) /ˈpedəgɒg; ˋpɛdəˌgɑg/ *n* **1** (*arch or fml* 古或文) teacher 教师. **2** (*derog* 贬) strict or formal teacher 严厉的教师; 学究式教师.

▷ **ped·agogy** /ˈpedəgɒdʒɪ; ˋpɛdəˌgɑdʒɪ/ *n* [U] study or science of ways and methods of teaching 教育学; 教学法. **ped·ago·gic** /ˌpedəˈgɒdʒɪk; ˌpɛdəˋgɑdʒɪk/ (also **ped·ago·gical** /-ɪkl; -ɪkl̩/) *adj* of or concerning teaching methods 教学法的. **ped·ago·gic·ally** /-klɪ; -klɪ/ *adv*: *a pedagogically accepted method of testing students' knowledge* 符合教学法的测验学生知识的方法.

pedal[1] /ˈpedl; ˋpɛdl̩/ *n* **1** lever that drives a machine (eg a bicycle or sewing-machine) when pressed down by the foot or feet (自行车、缝纫机等的)踏板, 脚蹬子: [attrib 作定语] *a pedal cyclist* 骑自行车的人 ○ *a pedal boat*, ie one propelled by pedals 用脚踏驱动的船. ⇨illus at App 1 见附录1插图, page xiii. **2** lever or key on a musical instrument (eg a piano, a harp or an organ) operated by the foot (钢琴等的)踏板; (风琴等的)踏瓣: *the loud/soft pedal*, ie on a piano 钢琴的强音〔弱音〕踏板. ⇨illus at App 1 见附录1插图, page xi.

▷ **pedal** *v* (**-ll-**; *US also* **-l-**) **1** [I] use a pedal or pedals 踩踏板: *pedal rapidly to make the machine run smoothly* 快速踩踏板好让机器转得平稳. **2** [I, Ipr, Ip] move by pedalling; ride 踩踏板驱动行进; 骑车: *pedal fast* 踏板踏得快 ○ *pedal down the hill* 骑车下山 ○ *pedal along* 踩动踏板行进. **3** [Tn, Tn·pr] move or operate (a machine) by pedalling 踩动踏板驱动或操纵(机器): *pedal a bicycle across the field* 骑自行车越过田野.

□ ˈ**pedal bin** rubbish bin (usu in a kitchen) with a lid that opens when a pedal is pressed 踏板垃圾桶(踩踏板

开盖式, 通常用于厨房).

pedal² /ˈpi:dl; ˋpidḷ/ *adj* of or concerning the foot or feet 足的; 脚的.

ped·ant /ˈpednt; ˋpɛdṇt/ *n* (*derog* 贬) **1** person who attaches too much importance to detail or to rules, esp when learning or teaching 学究; 书呆子. **2** person who values academic knowledge and likes to display his learning 卖弄学问的人.

▷ **pe·dantic** /pɪˈdæntɪk; pɪˋdæntɪk/ *adj* of or like a pedant 学究式的; 书呆子气的; 卖弄学问的: *a pedantic insistence on the rules* 墨守成规. **pe·dant·ic·ally** /-klɪ; -klɪ/ *adv*.

ped·antry /ˈpedntrɪ; ˋpɛdṇtrɪ/ *n* (**a**) [U] too much emphasis on formal rules or detail 迂腐; 拘泥. (**b**) [U] boastful and unnecessary display of learning 卖弄学问; 炫耀知识. (**c**) [C] instance of this 迂腐; 拘泥; 卖弄学问.

peddle /ˈpedl; ˋpɛdḷ/ *v* **1** [I] go from house to house to sell goods; be a pedlar 挨家兜售; 沿街叫卖; 做小贩. **2** [Tn, Dn·pr] **~ sth (to sb)** try to sell (goods) by going from house to house or by offering them to individual people (挨家)兜售(货物): *peddle one's wares* 上门推销货物 ○ *be arrested for peddling illegal drugs* 因贩毒被捕. ⇨Usage at SELL 用法见SELL. **3** [Tn, Dn·pr] **~ sth (to sb)** offer (ideas, gossip, etc) to individual people 宣扬, 散播(主张、流言等): *peddle malicious gossip* 散播恶毒的流言蜚语 ○ *peddling his crazy plan to other party members* 向其他党员宣传他那疯狂的计划.

▷ **ped·dler** /ˈpedlə(r); ˋpɛdlɚ/ *n* **1** (*US*) = PEDLAR. **2** person who sells illegal drugs 贩毒者: *dope addicts exploited by peddlers* 受毒品贩子盘剥的那些吸毒者.

ped·er·asty (also **paed·er·asty**) /ˈpedəræstɪ; ˋpɛdə͵ræstɪ/ *n* [U] practice of a man having sexual relations with a boy (男人与男童间的)鸡奸.

▷ **ped·er·ast** /ˈpedəræst; ˋpɛdə͵ræst/ *n* man who practises pederasty 鸡奸男童的人.

pedestal 基座

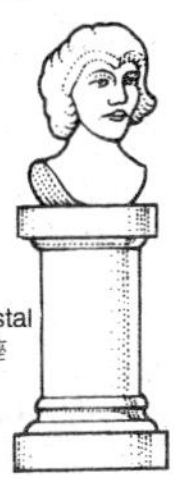

ped·es·tal /ˈpedɪstl; ˋpɛdɪstḷ/ *n* **1** base of a column 柱脚; 柱基. **2** base on which a statue or some other piece of sculpture stands (雕像等的)基座. ⇨illus 见插图. **3** (idm 习语) **knock sb off his pedestal/perch** ⇨ KNOCK². **place, etc sb on a ˈpedestal** admire sb greatly, esp without noticing his faults 崇拜某人(尤指盲目地).

□ **ˈpedestal table** table supported on a central column 独腿桌(只中间有一支柱).

ped·es·trian /pɪˈdestrɪən; pəˋdɛstrɪən/ *n* person walking in the street (contrasted with people in vehicles) 行人: *Two pedestrians and a cyclist were injured when the car skidded.* 汽车打滑时伤了两个行人和一个骑自行车的. Cf 参看 MOTORIST (MOTOR).

▷ **ped·es·trian** *adj* **1** lacking imagination or inspiration; dull 缺乏想像力或灵感的; 平淡的; 沉闷的: *a pedestrian description of events that were actually very exciting* 对极激动人心的事所作的乏味描叙 ○ *Life in the suburbs can be pretty pedestrian.* 郊区生活有时相当沉闷. **2** [attrib 作定语] of or for pedestrians 行人的; 为行人而设的: *a pedestrian walkway* 人行道.

□ **pe͵destrian ˈcrossing** (*Brit*) (*US* **crosswalk**) part of a road specially marked with studs, white lines, etc, where vehicles must stop to allow pedestrians to cross 人行横道. Cf 参看 PELICAN CROSSING (PELICAN), ZEBRA CROSSING (ZEBRA).

pe͵destrian ˈprecinct part of a town, esp a shopping area, where vehicles may not enter (禁止车辆通行的)行人区(尤指商业区).

pedi- *comb form* 构词成分 of the feet 足的; 脚的: *pedicure*.

pedi·cel /ˈpedɪsel; ˋpɛdəsḷ/ (also **pedicle** /ˈpedɪkl; ˋpɛdɪkḷ/) *n* (*biology* 生) small stalk-like structure in a plant or an animal (植物的)柄; 蒂; 花梗; (动物的)肉茎, 梗节.

pedi·cure /ˈpedɪkjʊə(r); ˋpɛdɪ͵kjur/ *n* [C, U] treatment of the feet, esp corns, bunions, etc, and care of the toe-nails, for medical or cosmetic reasons 足部治疗; 修脚. Cf 参看 MANICURE.

pedi·gree /ˈpedɪgri:; ˋpɛdə͵gri/ *n* **1** (**a**) [C] line of ancestors 世系: *proud of his long pedigree* 为其源远流长的世系而骄傲. (**b**) [U] quality of having this 门第; 出身: *people without pedigree* 非名门出身的人. **2** [C] (**a**) table or list of a person's ancestors; family tree 家谱; 系谱. (**b**) official record of the animals from which an animal has been bred 动物纯种系谱.

▷ **pedi·gree** *adj* [attrib 作定语] (of an animal) descended from a known line of (usu specially chosen) animals of the same breed; pure bred (指动物的)纯种的: [attrib 作定语] *pedigree cattle, dogs, horses, etc* 纯种的牛、狗、马等.

pedi·ment /ˈpedɪmənt; ˋpɛdəmənt/ *n* (*architecture* 建) (usu) triangular part above the entrance of a building, first used in the buildings of ancient Greece (通常为)三角楣饰(最初用于古希腊的建筑物上). ⇨illus at COLUMN 见COLUMN 插图.

ped·lar (*US* **ped·dler**) /ˈpedlə(r); ˋpɛdlɚ/ *n* (esp formerly) person who travels from place to place selling goods at fairs, etc (尤指旧时的)流动小贩.

ped(o)- (*US*) = PAED(O)-.

pe·do·meter /pɪˈdɒmɪtə(r); pɪˋdɑmətɚ/ *n* instrument that measures the distance a person walks by recording the number of steps taken 计步器; 步程计.

pee /pi:; pi/ *v* [I, Ipr] (*infml* 口) urinate 撒尿: *a dog peeing against a fence* 对着篱笆撒尿的狗.

▷ **pee** *n* (*infml* 口) (**a**) [U] urine 尿. (**b**) [sing] act of urinating 撒尿: *go for/have a quick pee* 去小便.

peek /pi:k; pik/ *v* [I, Ipr] **~ (at sth)** look quickly and often secretively (at sth) 匆匆地(常为秘密地)看(某物); 偷看; 窥视: *No peeking!* 禁止窥视! ○ *peek over the fence* 向篱笆那边瞥一眼 ○ *peek at sb's diary* 偷看某人的日记. Cf 参看 PEEP¹ 1, PEER².

▷ **peek** *n* [sing] quick (often sly) glance 匆匆的(常为诡秘的)一瞥; 偷看; 窥视: *take a peek at what was hidden in the cupboard* 偷眼看了一下柜子里藏着的东西.

peek·aboo /͵pi:kəˈbu:; ˋpikə͵bu/ (*Brit* also **peepbo** /ˈpi:pbəʊ; ˋpipbo/) *interj*, *n* [U] (exclamation used in a) game played to amuse young children, in which one hides one's face and then uncovers it 躲躲猫(把脸一隐一现逗乐小儿的游戏); 做这种游戏时发出的声音.

peel /pi:l; pil/ *v* **1** (**a**) [Tn, Dn.n, Dn.pr] **~ sth (for sb)** take the skin off (fruit, etc) 除掉(水果等)的皮: *peel a banana, an apple, a potato, etc* 剥香蕉皮、削苹果皮、刮土豆皮 ○ *Would you peel me an orange?* 给我剥个橙子行吗? (**b**) [Ip, Tn·p] **~ (sth) away/off** (cause skin, etc on a surface to) be removed (使外皮等)剥落: *peel away the outer layer* 剥掉外层 ○ *The label will peel off if you soak it in water.* 那标签用水浸湿即可脱落. (**c**) [I] have a skin or outer layer which comes off 脱皮; 外层脱落: *These oranges peel easily.* 这些橙子的皮好剥. **2** (**a**) [I, Ip] **~ (off)** (of a covering) come off in strips or flakes (指覆盖层)剥落, 脱落: *The wallpaper is peeling (off).* 壁纸正在剥落. ○ *After sunbathing, my skin began to peel.* 我作了日光浴后, 皮肤有些脱落了. ○ *The bark of plane trees peels off regularly.* 悬铃木的树皮到时候就脱落. (**b**) [I] (of a surface) lose its covering in strips or flakes (指表面)脱皮, 剥落: *My face is peeling.* 我的脸脱皮了. ○ *The walls have begun to peel.* 墙皮已开始剥落了. **3** (idm 习语) **keep one's eyes peeled/skinned** ⇨ EYE¹. **4** (phr v) **peel off** (of cars, aircraft, etc) leave a group and turn to one side (指汽车、飞行器等)离队转向一侧: *One squadron peeled off to attack enemy bombers.* 一中队战机脱离编队攻击敌轰炸机群. **peel (sth) off** (*infml* 口) remove (one's clothes), esp when one is hot or before exercise 脱掉(衣服)(尤指因热或于运动前): *peel off and dive into the sea* 脱掉衣服跳进大海 ○ *peel off one's jumper* 脱下毛衣.

▷ **peel** *n* [U] outer covering or skin of fruit, vegetables, etc (蔬菜、水果等的)皮: *lemon peel* 柠檬皮 ○ *candied* *pel*, ie peel of oranges, lemons, etc coated in sugar 蜜饯果皮. Cf 参看 RIND, SKIN 4, ZEST 3.

peeler *n* (esp in compounds 尤用以构成复合词) device for peeling (fruit, etc) (水果等的)剥皮机, 削皮器: *a po'tato peeler* 马铃薯削皮器.

peel·ings /ˈpi:lɪŋz; ˋpilɪŋz/ *n* [pl] (esp of fruit and vegetables) parts peeled off (尤指水果和蔬菜)削下或剥下的皮.

peep[1] /pi:p; pip/ *v* [I, Ipr, Ip] **1 ~ (at sth)** look quickly and slyly or cautiously (at sth) 匆匆地(且诡秘地或小心地)看(某物); 偷看; 窥视: *peep at a secret document* 偷看秘密文件 ○ *be caught peeping through the keyhole* 贴近锁眼窥视被当场抓住. Cf 参看 PEEK, PEER[2]. **2** (of light) appear through a narrow opening (指光)通过细孔透入: *daylight peeping through the curtains* 穿过窗帘的阳光. **3** appear slowly or partly 慢慢露出; 部分出现: *The moon peeped out from behind the clouds.* 月亮从云层中隐现. ○ *green shoots peeping up through the soil* 慢慢破土而出的绿芽.

▷ **peep** *n* **1** (esp *sing* 尤作单数) short quick look, esp a secret or sly one 一瞥(尤指秘密的或诡秘的); 偷看; 窥视: *have a peep through the window* 隔着窗户偷看 ○ *take a peep at the baby asleep in her cot* 悄悄地看看小床里熟睡的孩子. **2** (idm 习语) **peep of 'day** first light of day; dawn 晨曦; 破晓.

peeper *n* (usu *pl* 通常作复数) (*sl* 俚) eye 眼睛.

□ **'peep-hole** *n* small opening in a wall, door, curtain, etc through which one may peep at sth 窥孔.

ˌPeeping 'Tom (*derog* 贬) person who likes to spy on people when they do not know they are being watched; voyeur 爱偷看他人活动的人; 有窥淫癖的人.

'peep-show *n* exhibition of small pictures in a box, which are viewed through a magnifying lens placed in a small opening 西洋景; 西洋镜.

peep[2] /pi:p; pip/ *n* **1** [C] short weak high sound made by mice, young birds, etc; squeak (鼠、小鸟等的)吱吱声, 啾啾声. **2** [C] (also **peep 'peep**) (imitation of the) sound of a car's horn (模拟的)汽车的喇叭声. **3** [sing] (*infml* 口) sound made by sb, esp sth said 人声; (尤指)人语声: *I haven't heard a peep out of the children for an hour.* 有一个小时我没听见孩子们出声了.

▷ **peep** *v* [I] make a peep 作吱吱声或啾啾声; 发出(模拟的)汽车喇叭声; (指人)出声.

pee·pul = PIPAL.

peer[1] /pɪə(r); pɪr/ *n* **1** (**a**) [C] person who is equal to another in rank, status or merit (官阶、等级、地位或功绩)同等的人: *It will not be easy to find his peer.* 很不容易找到像他那样的人. ○ *be judged by one's peers* 受到与自己地位相同的人的评价. (**b**) [C usu *pl* 通常作复数] person who is the same age as another 同龄人: *He doesn't spend enough time with his peers.* 他不大与其同龄人交往. **2** [C] (in Britain) male member of one of the ranks of nobility (eg duke, marquis, earl, viscount, baron) (在英国)有爵位的男子(如公、侯、伯、子、男等贵族): *a 'life peer* 终身为贵族的男子.

▷ **peer·age** /ˈpɪərɪdʒ; ˋpɪrɪdʒ/ *n* **1** [Gp] the whole body of peers 贵族(总称): *elevate/raise sb to the peerage*, ie make sb a peer or peeress 封某人为贵族. **2** [C] rank of a peer 贵族的爵位: *inherit a peerage* 承袭贵族的爵位. **3** [C] book containing a list of the peers and details of their ancestry 贵族名册(记载所有贵族家谱的).

peer·ess /ˈpɪəres; ˋpɪrɪs/ *n* (**a**) female peer 女贵族. (**b**) wife or widow of a peer 贵族的夫人或遗孀.

peer·less *adj* superior to all others; without equal 无与匹敌的; 无双的.

□ **'peer group** group of people of approximately the same age or status 年龄或地位相近的人: *mix with one's peer group* 与自己类似的人交往.

ˌpeer of the 'realm (in Britain) hereditary peer with the right to sit in the House of Lords (在英国)可成为上议院议员的世袭贵族.

peer[2] /pɪə(r); pɪr/ *v* [I, Ipr, Ip] **~ (at sth/sb)** look closely or carefully, esp as if unable to see well 仔细看(尤指似因看不清): *peer shortsightedly* 因近视而仔细看 ○ *peer at sb over one's spectacles* 戴着眼镜认真打量某人 ○ *peer into the mist* 向雾中张望 ○ *peer out of the window/over the wall/through a gap* 凝视窗外[隔墙细看/从缝隙中窥视]. ⇨Usage at LOOK[1] 用法见 LOOK[1]. Cf 参看 PEEK, PEEP[1] 1.

peeve /pi:v; piv/ *v* [Tn] (*infml* 口) annoy (sb); put (sb) in a bad temper 惹恼(某人); 惹(某人)发脾气: *It peeves me to be ordered out of my own house.* 命令我从自己的家中出去, 真太气人了.

▷ **peeved** *adj* **~ (about sth)** (*infml* 口) annoyed 生气的; 恼怒的: *He looks very peeved about something.* 他好像对什么事很生气.

peev·ish /ˈpi:vɪʃ; ˋpivɪʃ/ *adj* easily annoyed (esp by unimportant things); irritable 易怒的(尤指对小事); 急躁的. **peev·ishly** *adv.* **peev·ish·ness** *n* [U].

pee·wit (also **pe·wit**) /ˈpi:wɪt; ˋpiwɪt/ *n* = LAPWING.

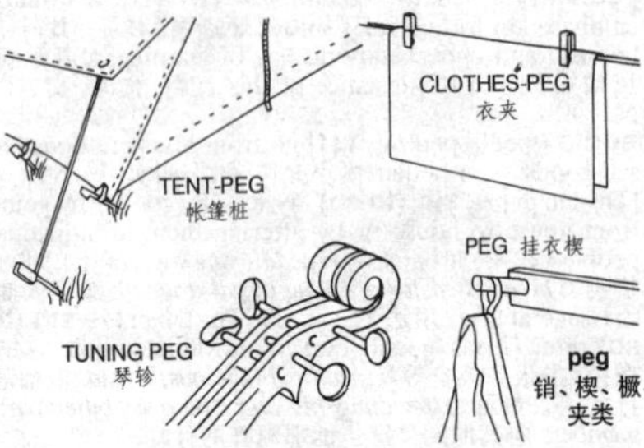

peg[1] /peg; pɛg/ *n* **1** wooden, metal or plastic pin or bolt, usu narrower at one end than the other, used to hold things together, to hang things on, to mark a position, etc (木、金属或塑料的)钉, 栓, 销, 挂钉, 短桩. **2** (**a**) pin fastened to a wall or door, on which hats and coats may be hung 挂衣帽的钩或钉: *a hat/coat peg* 挂帽钉[挂衣钩]. (**b**) (also **'tent-peg**) pin hammered into the ground to hold one of the ropes of a tent in place 系帐篷的桩. ⇨illus 见插图. (**c**) pin used to mark a position, eg on a piece of land 界桩(如在地界上的): *a surveyor's peg* 测标. **3** small wooden or metal pin or bolt used to fasten together esp pieces of wood (木或金属的)小钉, 小栓. **4** = CLOTHES-PEG (CLOTHES). **5** (also **'tuning peg**) any of several wooden screws for tightening or loosening tension in the strings of a violin, etc (提琴等上的)琴轸, 琴栓. **6** piece of wood used to seal the vent in a barrel, etc (桶等的)孔塞. **7** (also **peg-leg**) (*infml* 口) (**a**) artificial leg, usu wooden 假腿(通常为木制的). (**b**) person with an artificial leg 装有假腿的人. **8** (idm 习语) **a peg to hang sth on** reason, excuse or opportunity for (doing) sth (做)某事的理由、借口或机会: *a minor offence which provided a peg to hang their attack on* 给人以攻击口实的小过失. **off the 'peg** (of clothes) not made to measure; ready-made (指衣服)现成的: *buy a suit off the peg* 买一套成衣 ○ [attrib 作定语] *an off-the-peg suit* 一套成衣. **a square peg** ⇨ SQUARE[1]. **ˌtake sb 'down a peg (or two)** make (a proud or conceited person) more humble 煞(傲慢或自负者)的傲气、锐气或威风.

□ **'peg-board** *n* (**a**) [C, U] (type of) board with holes in, on which things may be fastened or hung with pegs or hooks for display, etc (有孔的)展览板(可供挂物或展示物品用). (**b**) [C] board with holes in, into which pegs may be inserted, esp for a game or as a toy 插孔游戏板.

peg[2] /peg; pɛg/ *v* **(-gg-)** **1** [Tn, Tn·pr, Tn·p] fasten (sth) with pegs 用钉或桩等固定(某物): *peg a tent* 用桩固定帐篷 ○ *peg the clothes (out) on the line* 把衣服用衣夹夹在晾衣绳上 ○ *peg sth in place* 用钉子将某物固定住. **2** [esp passive 尤用于被动语态: Tn, Tn·pr] **~ sth (at sth)** fix or keep (wages or prices) at a certain level 使(工资或价格)固定或维持在某水平上: *Pay increases were pegged at five per cent.* 工资增长率已限制在百分之五. **3** (idm 习语) **level pegging** ⇨ LEVEL[1]. **4** (phr v) **peg away (at sth)** (*infml* 口) work hard and persistently 坚持不懈努力工作: *He's been pegging away at his thesis for months.* 他写论文已经忙了几个月了. **peg sb down (to sth)** force or persuade sb to be specific or make a definite promise; pin sb down 迫使或说服某人表态、落实或承诺: *I pegged him down to a price for the work.* 我已经让他把那作品的价钱定妥.

peg sth down fix sth in place with pegs 用钉或桩固定某物: *have difficulty pegging the tent down in a storm* 在暴风雨中固定帐篷有困难. **peg out** (*infml* 口) die 死. **peg sth out** (**a**) mark (an area of land) with pegs 用界桩标出(地段): *peg out a claim*, ie mark out the land of which one claims ownership 用界桩标出认为是属于自己的地段. (**b**) (esp in the game of cribbage) show (a score) by putting pegs in a board (尤指在一种纸牌游戏中)用木钉插在板上记(分).

pe·jor·at·ive /pɪˈdʒɒrətɪv; US -ˈdʒɔːr- *or, rarely*, 罕读作 ˈpiːdʒərətɪv; pɪˈdʒɔrətɪv/ *adj* (*fml* 文) expressing criticism or scorn; derogatory; disparaging 贬抑的; 贬损的; 轻蔑的: *pejorative remarks, comments, words, etc* 贬抑的言语、评语、词语等. ▷ **pe·jor·at·ively** *adv*.

peke /piːk; pik/ *n* (*infml* 口) Pekinese 北京狗; 狮子狗; 哈叭狗.

Pe·kin·ese (also **Pe·king·ese**) /ˌpiːkɪˈniːz; ˌpikɪnˈiz/ *n* (*pl* unchanged or **~s** 复数或不变或作 **Pekineses**) small dog with short legs and long silky hair, originally from China 北京狗, 狮子狗, 哈叭狗(原产中国). ⇨illus at App 1 见附录1插图, page iii.

pe·koe /ˈpiːkəʊ; ˈpiko/ *n* [U] type of high-quality tea made from the young buds of the tea plant 白毫(用茶树嫩叶制的高级茶).

pe·la·gic /pəˈlædʒɪk; pəˈlædʒɪk/ *adj* (*fml* 文) (**a**) (of fishing, whaling, etc) carried out on the open sea (指捕鱼、捕鲸等)在公海进行的, 远洋的. (**b**) (of fish, etc) living near the surface of the open sea (指鱼等)栖居于海洋上层的, 浮游的.

pel·ican /ˈpelɪkən; ˈpɛlɪkən/ *n* large water-bird with a pouch under its long bill for storing food 鹈鹕; 淘河.

□ ˌ**pelican** ˈ**crossing** pedestrian crossing with traffic lights that are operated by pedestrians 交通指挥灯由行人控制的人行横道. Cf 参看 PEDESTRIAN CROSSING (PEDESTRIAN), ZEBRA CROSSING (ZEBRA).

pel·lagra /pəˈlæɡrə, -ˈleɪɡ-; pəˈlæɡrə, -ˈleɡ-/ *n* [U] (*medical* 医) disease that causes cracking of the skin and often leads to insanity 糙皮病.

pel·let /ˈpelɪt; ˈpɛlɪt/ *n* **1** small tightly-packed ball of a soft material such as bread or wet paper, made eg by rolling it between the fingers (面包或湿纸等的)小团, 小球, 小丸(如用手指捻成的): *paper pellets* 纸团. **2** small pill 小药丸. **3** small piece of shot[1](5), esp for firing from an airgun 小弹丸(尤指气枪的).

pell-mell /ˌpelˈmel; ˈpɛlˈmɛl/ *adv* **1** in a hurrying, disorderly manner; headlong 匆忙地; 杂乱地; 仓促地: *The children rushed pell-mell down the stairs.* 孩子们乱哄哄地冲下楼去. **2** in disorder; untidily 乱糟糟地; 杂乱地: *The books were scattered pell-mell over the floor.* 书本凌乱地散置在地上.

pel·lu·cid /peˈluːsɪd; pəˈlusɪd/ *adj* (*fml* 文) **1** transparent or translucent; very clear 透明的, 半透明的; 清澈的. **2** (*fig* 比喻) (of style, meaning, etc) very clear (指文体、意义等)清晰的, 清通的.

pel·met /ˈpelmɪt; ˈpɛlmɪt/ (also *esp US* **valance**) *n* strip of wood, cloth, etc placed above a window to hide a curtain rail 窗帘盒; 窗帘短帷.

pel·ota /pəˈləʊtə; pəˈlotə/ *n* [U] game played in Spain, Latin America and the Philippines, in which the players use a long basket strapped to the wrist to hit a ball against a wall 回力球(西班牙、拉丁美洲和菲律宾的一种球类运动).

pelt[1] /pelt; pɛlt/ *n* skin of an animal, esp with the fur or hair still on it 动物的皮; (尤指)毛皮: *beaver pelts* 海狸皮.

pelt[2] /pelt; pɛlt/ *v* **1** [Tn, Tn·pr] **~ sb (with sth)**; **~ sth (at sb)** throw sth at sb repeatedly in order to attack him 为攻击某人而连续投掷某物: *pelt sb with snowballs, stones, rotten tomatoes, etc* 向某人投掷雪球、石子、烂西红柿等 ○ *The crowd pelted bad eggs at the speaker.* 群众纷纷向演讲人扔臭鸡蛋. **2** [I, Ipr, Ip] **~ (down)** (of rain, etc) fall very heavily; beat down (指雨等)下得很大, 滂沱: *It was pelting with rain.* 大雨如注. ○ *The rain was pelting down.* 大雨倾盆. ○ *hail pelting on the roof* 冰雹打在屋顶上. **3** (idm 习语) **full pelt/tilt/speed** ⇨ FULL. **4** (phr v) **pelt along, down, up, etc (sth)** run very fast in the specified direction 向某方向飞跑: *pelting down the hill* 飞跑下山.

pel·vis /ˈpelvɪs; ˈpɛlvɪs/ *n* (*pl* **~es** /ˈpelvɪsɪz; ˈpɛlvɪsɪz/ or **pelves** /ˈpelviːz; ˈpɛlvɪz/) (*anatomy* 解) basin-shaped framework of bones at the lower end of the body, containing the bladder, rectum, etc 骨盆. ⇨illus at SKELETON 见 SKELETON 插图.

▷ **pel·vic** /ˈpelvɪk; ˈpɛlvɪk/ *adj* of or relating to the pelvis 骨盆的; 关于骨盆的.

pem·mican /ˈpemɪkən; ˈpɛmɪkən/ *n* [U] dried meat beaten and made into cakes (originally by N American Indians) 干肉饼(源于北美印第安人制法).

pen[1] /pen; pɛn/ *n* **1** [C] (often in compounds 常用以构成复合词) instrument for writing with ink, consisting of a pointed piece of split metal, a metal ball, etc, fixed into a metal or plastic holder (用有颜色液体书写的)笔; 钢笔; 圆珠笔: *fountain pen* 自来水笔 ○ *ball-point pen* 圆珠笔 ○ *felt-tip pen* 毡头笔. **2** [sing] writing, esp as a profession 写作(尤指职业性的): *He lives by his pen.* 他靠写作为生. **3** (idm 习语) **the** ˌ**pen is** ˌ**mightier than the** ˈ**sword** (*saying* 谚) poets, thinkers, etc, affect human affairs more than soldiers do 笔墨胜刀剑. **put** ˌ**pen to** ˈ**paper** (*fml* 文) (start to) write sth, eg a letter (开始)写(信等). **a slip of the pen/tongue** ⇨ SLIP[1].

▷ **pen** *v* (**-nn-**) [Tn] (*fml* 文) write (a letter, etc) 写(信等): *She penned a few words of thanks.* 她写了几句致谢的话.

□ ˌ**pen-and-**ˈ**ink** *adj* [esp attrib 尤作定语] drawn with a pen 用钢笔画的: *pen-and-ink drawings, sketches, illustrations, etc* 钢笔画的画、素描、插图等.

ˈ**pen-friend** (also *esp US* ˈ**pen-pal**) *n* person with whom one builds a friendship by exchanging letters, esp sb in a foreign country whom one has never met 笔友.

ˈ**penknife** (also ˈ**pocket-knife**) *n* (*pl* **-knives**) small knife with one or more blades that fold down into the handle, usu carried in the pocket 小折刀. ⇨illus at KNIFE 见 KNIFE 插图.

ˈ**pen-name** *n* name used by a writer instead of his real name; pseudonym 笔名.

ˈ**pen-pusher** *n* (*infml derog* 口, 贬) person (esp a clerk) whose job involves a lot of boring paperwork 做大量单调文书工作的人(如文员). ˈ**pen-pushing** *n* [U] (*infml derog* 口, 贬) boring paperwork 乏味的文书工作.

pen[2] /pen; pɛn/ *n* **1** small piece of land surrounded by a fence, esp for keeping cattle, sheep, poultry, etc in (牛、羊、家禽等的)圈, 围栏: *a* ˈ*sheep-pen* 羊圈. **2** bomb-proof shelter for submarines (潜艇用的)防空隐蔽坞.

▷ **pen** *v* (**-nn-**) (phr v) **pen sb/sth in/up** shut sb/sth in, or as if in, a pen 将某人[某物](宛如)关入围栏中: *pen up the chickens for the night* 把鸡关进鸡棚过夜 ○ *She feels penned in by her life as a housewife.* 她觉得做家庭主妇很受束缚.

pen[3] /pen; pɛn/ *n* (*US infml* 口) penitentiary (联邦或州的)监狱.

Pen *abbr* 缩写 = (esp on a map) Peninsula (尤指地图上的标记)半岛.

penal /ˈpiːnl; ˈpinḷ/ *adj* [esp attrib 尤作定语] **1** of, relating to or used for punishment, esp by law (有关或用作)处罚的, (尤指)刑罚的: *penal laws, reforms* 刑法、刑法改革 ○ *a* ˈ*penal colony/settlement*, ie a place where criminals are sent as a punishment 罪犯流放地 ○ *penal taxation*, ie taxation which is so heavy that it seems like a punishment 繁重的课税(重如惩罚). **2** punishable by law 应受刑罚的: *a penal offence* 刑事罪. ▷ **pen·ally** /ˈpiːnəlɪ; ˈpinḷɪ/ *adv*.

□ ˈ**penal code** system of laws relating to crime and its punishment 刑法典.

ˌ**penal** ˈ**servitude** (*Brit law* 律) (formerly) punishment in which sb is sent to prison and forced to do hard physical work (旧时)劳役刑, 劳役监禁.

pen·al·ize, -ise /ˈpiːnəlaɪz; ˈpinḷˌaɪz/ *v* **1** [Tn, Tn·pr esp passive 尤用于被动语态] **~ sb (for sth)** punish sb for breaking a rule or law, esp (in games and sports) by giving an advantage to his opponent (因犯规或违法)处罚某人; (尤指比赛中)判罚: *People who drive when they are drunk should be heavily penalized.* 对酒醉开车者应予重罚. ○ *He was penalized for a foul on the striker*, eg A free kick was awarded to the striker's team. 他因对前锋犯规而受罚(如对方球队获踢任意球). **2** [Tn] put (sb) at a disadvantage; handicap (sb) unfairly 使(某人)处不利地位; 不正当地妨碍(某人): *The new law penalizes the poorest members of society.* 新法规对社会中最贫困者不

P

利. **3** [Tn] make (sth) punishable by law 使(某事)可以刑法论处. ▷ **pen·al·iza·tion** /ˌpiːnəlaɪˈzeɪʃn; *US* -lɪˈz-; ˌpinlɪˈzeʃən/ *n* [U].

pen·alty /ˈpenltɪ; ˋpɛnltɪ/ *n* **1 ~ (for sth)** (**a**) punishment for breaking a law, rule or contract 刑罚; 处罚; 惩罚: *It is part of the contract that there is a penalty for late delivery.* 合同中有延迟交货的惩罚规定. (**b**) thing imposed as a punishment, eg imprisonment or a fine 施加的惩罚(如监禁、罚款): *the ˈdeath penalty* 死刑 ○ *It is an offence to travel without a valid ticket — penalty £100.* 无有效票证乘搭交通工具——违章罚款100英镑. ○ *The maximum penalty for this crime is 10 years' imprisonment.* 这种罪行的最高刑罚是10年监禁. **2** disadvantage, suffering or inconvenience caused by an action or a circumstance (行为或处境造成的)不利、苦恼或不便: *One of the penalties of fame is loss of privacy.* 成名的弊端之一是失去了私人活动自由. **3** (**a**) (in sports and games) disadvantage imposed on a player or team as a punishment for breaking a rule, esp (in football) a free shot at goal by the opposing team (运动和竞赛等的)处罚(尤指足球中罚任意球): *The referee awarded a penalty to the home team.* 裁判判给主队罚对方任意球. (**b**) (in football) goal scored with a penalty kick (足球)罚球得分. **4** (idm 习语) **on/under pain/penalty of sth** ⇨ PAIN. **pay the penalty** ⇨ PAY[2].

□ ˈ**penalty area** (in football) area in front of the goal within which a foul by the defenders is punished by the award of a penalty kick to the attacking team (足球)罚球区. ⇨illus at ASSOCIATION FOOTBALL (ASSOCIATION) 见 ASSOCIATION FOOTBALL (ASSOCIATION) 插图.

ˈ**penalty clause** part of a contract stating that money must be paid if sb breaks the contract 合同中违约罚款的规定.

ˈ**penalty kick** (in football) free kick at the goal awarded to the attacking team for a foul committed in the penalty area (足球)罚点球.

pen·ance /ˈpenəns; ˋpɛnəns/ *n* **1** [C, U] **~ (for sth)** punishment that one imposes on oneself to show that one is sorry for having done wrong (表示忏悔的)自我惩罚: *an act of penance* 自惩 ○ *do penance* (ie perform an act that shows one is sorry) *for one's sins* 为赎罪进行自我惩罚 ○ (*joc* 谑) *She made him do the washing-up as (a) penance for forgetting her birthday.* 因为他把她生日忘了, 所以她罚他洗碗. **2** [U] (in the Roman Catholic and Orthodox Churches) sacrament that includes confession, absolution and an act of penance imposed by the priest (天主教和东正教的)补赎圣事, 告解圣事, 修和圣事.

pence *pl* of PENNY.

pen·chant /ˈpɑːnʃɑːn; *US* ˈpentʃənt; ˋpɛntʃənt/ *n* (*French* 法) **~ for sth** liking or taste for sth 爱好; 嗜好: *She has a penchant for Indian food.* 她爱吃印度食物.

pen·cil /ˈpensl; ˋpɛnsl/ *n* **1** (**a**) [C] instrument for drawing or writing with, consisting of a thin stick of graphite or coloured chalk enclosed in a cylinder of wood or fixed in a metal case 铅笔: [attrib 作定语] *a pencil drawing* 铅笔画. (**b**) [U] writing done with a pencil 铅笔字: *Should I sign my name in pencil or ink?* 我用铅笔还是用钢笔签字? ○ *Pencil rubs out easily.* 铅笔写的容易擦掉. **2** [C] (usu in compounds 通常用以构成复合词) thing used or shaped like a pencil 用途或形状似笔之物: *an ˈeyebrow pencil*, ie a stick of cosmetic material used by women to darken the eyebrows 眉笔.

▷ **pen·cil** *v* (**-ll-**; *US* **-l-**) **1** [Tn] write, draw or mark (sth) with a pencil 用铅笔写、画或标记(某物): *She pencilled the rough outline of a house.* 她用铅笔画出房子的轮廓图. ○ *pencilled eyebrows* 描过的眉毛. **2** (phr v) **pencil sth in** write (a suggested date, arrangement, etc) provisionally in a diary 在日志中临时记下(建议的日期、安排等): *Let's pencil in 3 May for the meeting.* 我们把会议日期暂定为5月3日吧.

□ ˈ**pencil-case** *n* small bag, box, etc for holding pencils and pens 铅笔盒; 铅笔袋.

ˈ**pencil-sharpener** *n* device for sharpening pencils 削铅笔器.

pen·dant /ˈpendənt; ˋpɛndənt/ *n* **1** ornament that hangs from a chain worn round the neck (项链上的)垂饰. **2** piece of decorated glass hanging from a chandelier (枝形吊灯的)玻璃垂饰物. **3** = PENNANT.

pen·dent /ˈpendənt; ˋpɛndənt/ *adj* (*fml* 文) hanging from sth 下垂的; 悬挂着的.

pend·ing /ˈpendɪŋ; ˋpɛndɪŋ/ *adj* [pred 作表语] (*fml* 文) (**a**) waiting to be decided or settled 待决; 未决: *The lawsuit was then pending.* 那件讼案因而尚未解决. (**b**) about to happen; imminent 即将发生; 逼近: *A decision on this matter is pending.* 此事即将作出决定.

▷ **pend·ing** *prep* (*fml* 文) (**a**) while waiting for (sth); until 在等待(某事物)之际; 直至: *She was held in custody pending trial.* 她被拘留候审. (**b**) during (sth) 在(某事)期间: *pending the negotiations* 谈判期间.

pen·du·lous /ˈpendjʊləs; *US* -dʒʊləs; ˋpɛndʒələs/ *adj* (*fml* 文) hanging down loosely so as to swing from side to side 下垂的; 悬垂而摇摆不定的: *pendulous breasts* 松垂的乳房.

pendulum 摆锤

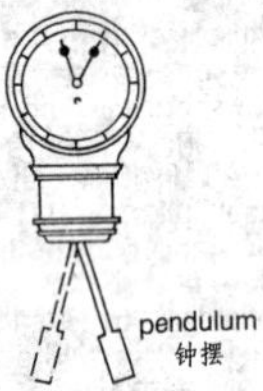

pen·du·lum /ˈpendjʊləm; *US* -dʒʊləm; ˋpɛndʒələm/ *n* **1** weight hung on a cord from a fixed point so that it can swing freely 摆; 摆锤. **2** rod with a weight at the bottom that regulates the mechanism of a clock 钟摆. ⇨illus 见插图. **3** (idm 习语) **the swing of the pendulum** ⇨ SWING[2].

pen·et·rable /ˈpenɪtrəbl; ˋpɛnətrəbl/ *adj* (*fml* 文) that can be penetrated 可被穿过的; 可被充满的; 可被看穿的; 可深刻理解的. ▷ **pen·et·rab·il·ity** /ˌpenɪtrəˈbɪlətɪ; ˌpɛnətrəˋbɪlətɪ/ *n* [U].

pen·et·rate /ˈpenɪtreɪt; ˋpɛnəˌtret/ *v* **1** [Ipr, Tn] **~ (into/through) sth** make a way into or through sth 进入或穿过某物: *Our troops have penetrated (into) enemy territory.* 我部队已深入到敌占区. ○ *The mist penetrated (into) the room.* 雾已渗入室内. ○ *The heavy rain had penetrated right through her coat.* 大雨湿透了她的大衣. ○ (*fig* 比喻) *The cat's sharp claws penetrated* (ie pierced) *my skin.* 猫的尖爪刺进了我的皮层. ○ *The party has been penetrated* (ie infiltrated) *by extremists.* 有些极端分子已打入该党. ○ *A shrill cry penetrated the silence.* 一声尖叫划破了寂静. **2** [Tn, Tn·pr esp passive 尤用于被动语态] **~ sb/sth (with sth)** fill or spread through sb/sth 充满; 遍布: *Cold horror penetrated her whole being.* 她吓得浑身发凉. **3** [Tn] see or show a way into or through (sth) 看穿或透过(某事物): *Our eyes could not penetrate the darkness.* 我们的眼睛在黑暗中看不见东西. ○ *The headlamps penetrated the fog.* 车的前灯的光射进雾中. ○ (*fig* 比喻) *We soon penetrated his disguise*, ie saw who he really was. 我们很快看穿了他的伪装. **4** [Tn] understand or discover (sth) 洞察或发现(某事物): *It was impossible to penetrate the mystery.* 那奥秘无法揭穿. ○ *He penetrated their thoughts.* 他了解他们的想法. **5** [I, Tn] be fully understood or realized (by sb) 被(他人)充分理解或领悟: *I explained the problem to him several times but it didn't seem to penetrate.* 那问题我向他解释多次, 他似无所悟. ○ *Nothing we say penetrates his thick skull!* 无论我们说什么他都不懂!

▷ **pen·et·rat·ing** *adj* **1** having or showing the ability to think and understand quickly and deeply 思想敏锐的; 有洞察力的: *a penetrating mind, question, thinker* 敏捷的头脑、尖锐的问题、有洞察力的思想家 ○ *a penetrating look, glance, stare, etc* 深明其意的目光、一瞥、注视等. **2** (of a voice or sound) loud and carrying; piercing (指声音)响亮的, 尖锐的: *a penetrating cry, shriek, yell, etc* 刺耳的哭喊、尖叫、叫喊等. **pen·et·rat·ingly** *adv*.

pen·et·ra·tion /ˌpenɪˈtreɪʃn; ˌpɛnəˋtreʃən/ *n* [U] **1** (action or process of) penetrating 进入; 穿过; 充满; 看穿; 洞察; 领悟: *our penetration of the enemy's defences* 我军对敌人防线的突破. **2** ability to think and understand quickly and deeply 洞察力; 领悟力: *the penetration of her mind/her powers of penetration* 她的悟性.

pen·et·rat·ive /ˈpenɪtrətɪv; *US* -treɪtɪv; ˋpɛnəˏtretɪv/ *adj* **1** that can penetrate 有穿透力的; 能将他物充满的; 有看穿能力的; 有洞察力的; 有领悟力的. **2** (of sb's mind, thoughts, etc) astute (指人的头脑、想法等)精明的, 敏锐的: *a penetrative analysis* 精辟的分析.

penguin 企鹅

pen·guin /ˈpeŋgwɪn; ˋpɛŋgwɪn/ *n* black and white sea-bird living in the Antarctic, with webbed feet and wings like flippers that are used for swimming 企鹅.

pe·ni·cil·lin /ˌpenɪˈsɪlɪn; ˏpɛnɪˋsɪlɪn/ *n* [U] substance obtained from mould fungi, used as an antibiotic drug to prevent or treat infections caused by bacteria 青霉素; 盘尼西林.

pen·in·sula /pəˈnɪnsjʊlə; *US* -nsələ; pəˋnɪnsələ/ *n* area of land almost surrounded by water or projecting far into the sea 半岛: *the Iberian peninsula*, ie Spain and Portugal 伊比利亚半岛(即西班牙和葡萄牙所在地).
▷ **pen·in·su·lar** /-lə(r); -lɚ/ *adj* of or like a peninsula (似)半岛的.

penis /ˈpiːnɪs; ˋpinɪs/ *n* organ with which a male animal copulates and (in mammals) urinates 阴茎. ⇨illus at MALE 见MALE插图.

pen·it·ence /ˈpenɪtəns; ˋpɛnətəns/ *n* [U] **~ (for sth)** sorrow or regret for having done sth wrong 悔过; 悔罪; 忏悔: *show penitence for one's sins* 对罪过表示忏悔.

pen·it·ent /ˈpenɪtənt; ˋpɛnətənt/ *adj* feeling or showing regret or remorse for having done sth wrong 后悔的; 悔罪的; 忏悔的: *a penitent sinner* 悔悟的罪人.
▷ **pen·it·ent** *n* (*religion* 宗) penitent person, esp one who is doing penance(2) 悔罪者; 忏悔者; (尤指)告解者.
pen·it·ently *adv*.

pen·it·en·tial /ˌpenɪˈtenʃl; ˏpɛnəˋtɛnʃəl/ *adj* of or relating to penitence or penance 忏悔的; 悔过的; 悔罪的; 苦行赎罪的. ▷ **pen·it·en·tially** /-ʃəlɪ; -ʃəlɪ/ *adv*.

pen·it·en·tiary /ˌpenɪˈtenʃərɪ; ˏpɛnəˋtɛnʃərɪ/ *n* (*US*) federal or state prison for people who have committed serious crimes (联邦或州的)监狱.
▷ **pen·it·en·tiary** *adj* (**a**) of or relating to penance 自我惩罚的; 赎罪的. (**b**) of or relating to treatment intended to reform offenders 感化的.

pen·man·ship /ˈpenmənʃɪp; ˋpɛnmənˏʃɪp/ *n* [U] skill or style in writing or in handwriting 书写的技巧或风格; 书法.

pen·nant /ˈpenənt; ˋpɛnənt/ (also **pen·dant**, **pennon**) *n* (**a**) long narrow flag tapering to a point, used on a ship for signalling or as identification (船上用作信号或识别标志的)长三角旗. ⇨illus at FLAG 见FLAG插图. (**b**) (*US*) flag of this shape used as a school banner or as the symbol of a sports championship (长三角形的)校旗, 锦标旗.

pen·ni·less /ˈpenɪlɪs; ˋpɛnɪlɪs/ *adj* having no money; very poor; destitute 一文不名的; 赤贫如洗的: *a penniless old man* 穷老头.

pen·non /ˈpenən; ˋpɛnən/ *n* **1** long narrow triangular or swallow-tailed flag, originally used by a knight on his lance 狭长三角旗, 燕尾旗(原为骑士所执长矛上的饰物). **2** = PENNANT.

penn'orth /ˈpenəθ; ˋpɛnɚθ/ *n* [sing] (*infml* 口) = PENNYWORTH (PENNY).

penny /ˈpenɪ; ˋpɛnɪ/ *n* (*pl* **pence** /pens; pɛns/ or **pennies** /ˈpenɪz; ˋpɛnɪz/) **1** (*abbr* 缩写 **p**) (since decimal coinage was introduced in 1971) British bronze coin worth one hundredth of a pound 便士(英国黄铜硬币, 自1971年实行十进位制后, 其值为一英镑的百分之一): *Potatoes are 20 pence a pound.* 土豆每磅20便士. ○ *These pencils cost 40p each.* 这些铅笔每枝40便士. **2** (*abbr* 缩写 **d**) former British bronze coin worth one twelfth of a shilling, in use until 1971 便士(为英国黄铜硬币, 1971年以前其值为一先令的十二分之一). **3** (*US infml* 口) cent 分(钱币单位). **4** (idm 习语) **be two/ten a ˈpenny** (**a**) be very cheap 非常便宜. (**b**) be numerous and easy to obtain 多而易得. **earn/turn an honest penny** ⇨ HONEST. **ˌin for a ˈpenny, ˌin for a ˈpound** (*saying* 谚) having started to do sth, it is worth spending as much time or money as is necessary to complete it 既已开始, 应该完成; 一不做, 二不休. **the ˈpenny drops** (*infml* 口 *esp Brit*) sb now understands or realizes sth that he had not understood or realized before 原来如此; 恍然大悟: *I had to explain the problem to her several times before the penny finally dropped.* 那问题我给她解释了好几次, 最后她才明白. **a ˌpenny for your ˈthoughts** (*catchphrase* 警语) (used to ask sb what he is thinking about 用以问某人在想什么). **ˌpenny ˈwise (and) ˌpound ˈfoolish** careful about spending small amounts of money but reckless about spending large sums of money 小处节约, 大处浪费. **a pretty penny** ⇨ PRETTY. **spend a penny** ⇨ SPEND. **turn up like a bad ˈpenny** (*infml* 口) (habitually) appear when one is unwelcome or unwanted (不受欢迎的或讨厌的人)又来了.
□ **ˌpenny ˈfarthing** old type of bicycle with a large front wheel and a small back wheel 旧式的前轮大后轮小的自行车.
ˈpenny-pincher (*infml* 口) mean person; miser 小气鬼; 吝啬鬼. **ˈpenny-pinching** *adj* miserly 吝啬的; 小气的. — *n* [U] miserliness 吝啬; 小气.
ˈpennyweight *n* unit of weight equal to 24 grains 本尼威特(金衡单位, 等于24格令).
ˌpenny ˈwhistle = TIN WHISTLE (TIN).
ˈpennyworth /ˈpenɪwəθ; ˋpɛnɪˏwɝθ/ (also **penn'orth**) *n* [sing] as much as can be bought for a penny 一便士之值; 值一便士之物.

peno·logy /piːˈnɒlədʒɪ; piˋnɑlədʒɪ/ *n* [U] study of crime and its punishment, and the management of prisons 刑罚学; 监狱管理学.

pen·sion[1] /ˈpenʃn; ˋpɛnʃən/ *n* [C, U] sum of money paid regularly by the State to people above a certain age and to widowed or disabled people, or by an employer to a retired employee 养老金; 抚恤金; 退休金: *an old-age ˈpension* 养老金 ○ *a retirement pension* 退休金 ○ *an army pension* 军队发放的抚恤金 ○ *draw one's pension*, eg obtain it regularly from a Post Office 领取退休金(如定期到邮局领取) ○ *live on a pension* 靠退休金生活.
▷ **pen·sion** *v* **1** [Tn] pay a pension to (sb) 发给(某人)养老金、退休金或抚恤金. **2** (phr v) **pension sb off** (often passive 常用于被动语态) allow or force sb to retire, and pay him a pension 准予或迫使某人退休并发给退休金: *He was pensioned off and replaced with a younger man.* 他被迫退休, 由一年轻人接替其职务. **pension sth off** (often passive 常用于被动语态) (*infml* 口) no longer use sth, because it is old and worn 因破旧不堪再用: *The old printing press will have to be pensioned off.* 那个旧印刷机得报销了.
pen·sion·able *adj* giving sb the right to receive a pension 可领取退休金、养老金或抚恤金的: *a pensionable job, position, post, etc* 可领取养老金的工作、职位等 ○ *She is of pensionable age.* 她已到领取养老金的年纪了.
pen·sioner /ˈpenʃənə(r); ˋpɛnʃənɚ/ *n* person who is receiving a pension (esp an old-age pension) 领退休金或抚恤金的人; (尤指)领养老金的人: *an old-age pensioner* 领养老金的人.

pen·sion[2] /ˈpɒnsɪɒn; ˋpɑnsɪˏɑn/ *n* (*French* 法) small private hotel in France and certain other European countries (法国及欧洲其他一些国家的)私人小旅店.

pens·ive /ˈpensɪv; ˋpɛnsɪv/ *adj* thinking deeply about sth, esp in a sad or serious way 沉思的; (尤指)忧虑的: *a pensive expression, look, mood* 忧虑的表情、样子、情绪 ○ *She looked pensive when she heard the news.* 她听到这消息时神情严肃. ▷ **pens·ively** *adv*. **pens·ive·ness** *n* [U].

penta- *comb form* 构词成分 having or made up of five of sth 有五个某物; 由五个某物组成: *a pentagon* ○ *the* *pentathlon*.

penta·gon /ˈpentəgən; *US* -gɒn; ˋpɛntəˌgɑn/ *n* **1** [C] geometric figure with five sides and angles 五角形; 五边形. **2 the Pentagon** (**a**) [sing] the five-sided building near Washington that is the headquarters of the US Department of Defence and the US armed forces 五角大楼(美国国防部办公处). (**b**) [Gp] the leaders of the US armed forces 美国三军首脑: *a spokesman for the Pentagon* 美国国防部发言人.
▷ **pen·ta·gonal** /penˈtægənl; pɛnˋtægənl/ *adj* having five sides 五边形的; 五角形的.

pen·ta·meter /penˈtæmɪtə(r); pɛnˋtæmətɚ/ *n* line of verse with five metrical feet 五音步诗行.

Pen·ta·teuch /ˈpentətju:k; ˋpɛntəˌtjuk/ *n* **the Pentateuch** [sing] the first five books of the Bible 摩西五经(《圣经》的首五卷).

pent·ath·lon /penˈtæθlən, -lɒn; pɛnˋtæθlən, -lɑn/ *n* athletic contest in which each competitor takes part in five events (running, riding, swimming, fencing and shooting) 五项全能运动(跑步、骑马、游泳、击剑和射击).

Pente·cost /ˈpentɪkɒst; *US* -kɔ:st; ˋpɛntɪˌkɔst/ *n* [sing] **1** Jewish harvest festival that takes place fifty days after the second day of the Passover (犹太人的)五旬节(庆祝收获的节日, 为逾越节次日起之50日). **2** (*Brit* also **Whit Sunday**) (in the Christian Church) seventh Sunday after Easter, commemorating the descent of the Holy Ghost on the apostles (基督教的)圣灵降临节(复活节后第七个星期日).
▷ **pente·costal** /ˌpentɪˈkɒstl; *US* -ˈkɔ:stl; ˌpɛntɪˋkɔstl/ *adj* **1** of or relating to Pentecost (犹太人)五旬节的; 圣灵降临节的. **2 Pentecostal** (of a religious group) emphasizing the divine gifts, esp the power to heal the sick (指教派)五旬节派的(着重神的恩赐, 尤指治病能力).

pent·house /ˈpenthaʊs; ˋpɛntˌhaʊs/ *n* **1** house or flat built on the roof of a tall building (高楼的)顶层房子: [attrib 作定语] *a luxury penthouse flat/apartment/suite* 豪华的楼顶的公寓[单元房/一套房间]. **2** sloping roof (esp for a shelter or shed) attached to the wall of a building and supported by it 庇檐, 披屋(靠墙的单坡顶).

pent up /ˌpent ˈʌp; ˋpɛntˋʌp/ *adj* (of feelings) not expressed; repressed (指感情)不流露的, 被抑制的: *feelings that have been pent up for too long* 压抑过久的感情 ○ *ˌpent-up ˈanger, eˈmotion, fruˈstration, etc* 郁结的愤懑、情感、沮丧等.

pen·ul·tim·ate /peˈnʌltɪmət; pɪˋnʌltəmɪt/ *adj* [attrib 作定语] next to and before the last one; last but one 倒数第二的: *the penultimate letter of a word* 一词的倒数第二个字母 ○ *the penultimate day of the month* 月底的前一日.

pen·um·bra /pɪˈnʌmbrə; pɪˋnʌmbrə/ *n* (*pl* **-brae** /-bri:; -bri/ or **-bras** /-brəz; -brəz/) partly shaded area around the shadow of an opaque object (esp around the total shadow of the moon or earth in an eclipse) 半阴影; (尤指日、月蚀的)半影. Cf 参看 UMBRA.

pen·uri·ous /pɪˈnjʊərɪəs; *US* -ˈnʊr-; pəˋnʊrɪəs/ *adj* (*fml* 文) **1** very poor 贫穷的. **2** mean with money; stingy 吝啬的; 小气的. ▷ **pen·uri·ously** *adv*. **pen·uri·ous·ness** *n* [U] = PENURY.

pen·ury /ˈpenjʊrɪ; ˋpɛnjərɪ/ *n* [U] (*fml* 文) extreme poverty 贫穷: *living in penury* 过着贫穷的生活 ○ *reduced to penury* 陷于贫困之中.

peon /ˈpi:ən; ˋpiən/ *n* **1** (in India, etc) person employed as a messenger (印度等国的)信差. **2** (in Latin America) farm labourer (拉丁美洲的)农场工人.

pe·ony /ˈpi:ənɪ; ˋpiənɪ/ *n* garden plant with large round pink, red or white flowers 芍药; 牡丹.

people /ˈpi:pl; ˋpipl/ *n* **1** [pl *v*] persons 人: *Were there many people at the party?* 聚会上的人多吗? ○ *Some people are very inquisitive.* 有些人好管闲事. ○ *streets crowded with people* 挤满人的街道 ○ *He meets a lot of famous people in his job.* 他在工作中常能见到许多名人. ○ *Many old people live alone.* 不少老年人都独自生活. ⇨Usage at MAN[1] 用法见MAN[1]. **2** (**a**) [C] (all the persons belonging to a) nation, race, tribe or community 民族; 种族; 部落; 人民: *the English-speaking peoples* 说英语的民族 ○ *The Spartans were a warlike people.* 斯巴达人是尚武的民族. (**b**) [pl *v*] those persons who live in a particular place or have a particular nationality 生活在某地或有某国籍的人们: *the people* (ie inhabitants) *of London* 伦敦居民 ○ *the British, French, Russian, etc people* 英国人、法国人、俄国人. ⇨Usage 见所附用法. **3 the people** [pl *v*] the citizens of a country, esp those with the right to vote 国民, 公民(尤指有选举权者): *The President no longer has the support of the people.* 总统已失去国民的支持. **4 the people** [pl *v*] ordinary persons who do not have a special rank or position in society 普通人; 平民; 民众: *the common people* 老百姓 ○ *a man of the people*, eg a politician who is popular with ordinary people 受民众欢迎的人(如受欢迎的政治家). **5** [pl *v*] subjects (of a king) or supporters (of a leader) (国王的)臣民; (领袖的)拥护者: *a king loved by his people* 受臣民爱戴的国王 ○ *His people worked hard to get him elected.* 拥护他的人都为使他当选而努力. **6** [pl *v*] (*infml* 口) person's parents or other relatives 父母或亲戚: *She's spending Christmas with her people.* 她与亲人一起过圣诞节. **7** (idm 习语) **people (who live) in glass houses shouldn't throw stones** (*saying* 谚) one should not criticize others for faults similar to one's own 住在玻璃房子里, 不要向人扔石头; 自己有错就不要批评别人.
▷ **people** *v* [esp passive 尤用于被动语态: Tn, Tn·pr] fill (a place, an area, etc) with people; populate 使(某地)住满人; 居住于: *He believes the world is peopled with idiots.* 他认为世上多白痴.

NOTE ON USAGE 用法: Compare **person, persons, people** and **peoples.** 试比较**person**、**persons**、**people**、**peoples**的用法. **1 People** is the most usual plural of **person.** ☆ **people**是**person**最通用的复数形式. **Persons** is formal and mostly used in legal language. ☆ **persons**较文, 主要作法律用语. **2** Person can also sound formal and is often avoided. ☆ **person**有时也较文, 通常避免使用. In general statements, the sentence can be made plural 在泛指时, 此词在句中可用其复数形式: *A person has the right to defend himself/People have the right to defend themselves.* 人人均有自卫权. When referring to a particular situation, we can say *I saw someone/a man/a woman riding a horse* instead of *I saw a person riding a horse.* 在特指时, 可以说'我看见有个人[男的/女的]骑着马'(英文句中可以不用person, 用someone/a man/a woman). **3** People is also a singular noun (plural **peoples**) meaning 'nation', 'tribe' or 'race' ☆ **people**作'民族'、'部落'或'种族'解时, 是单数名词(复数是**peoples**): *The Ancient Egyptians were a fascinating people.* 古埃及人是个令人神往的民族. ○ *the French-speaking peoples of the world* 世界上说法语的民族.

pep /pep; pɛp/ *n* [U] (*infml* 口) feeling of liveliness; vigour 精力; 精神; 活力: *full of pep and running around like a puppy* 生龙活虎般跑来跑去.
▷ **pep** *v* (**-pp-**) (phr v) **pep sb/sth up** make sb/sth (feel) more lively or energetic; stimulate sb/sth 使某人活跃或精力充沛; 使某事物振奋: *A walk in the fresh air will pep me up.* 我在空气新鲜的地方散步就感到精神饱满. ○ *lively music to pep up the party* 活跃聚会气氛的欢快的音乐.
□ ˈ**pep pill** pill containing a drug (usu amphetamine) that stimulates the nervous system 兴奋药丸; (通常指)安非他明.
ˈ**pep talk** talk intended to improve morale, esp by encouraging the listener(s) to work harder, try to win, etc 鼓励的话; 激励的话: *The team was given a pep talk on the morning of the big match.* 运动队在大赛当天早晨听了一次鼓舞士气的讲话.

pep·per /ˈpepə(r); ˋpɛpɚ/ *n* **1** [U] hot-tasting powder made from the dried berries of certain plants and used for flavouring food 胡椒粉: *a dash of pepper* 少许胡椒粉. **2** [C] (**a**) garden plant with large green, yellow or red hollow seed pods; capsicum 辣椒; 番椒. (**b**) one of these pods used as a vegetable 辣椒(蔬菜): *peppers stuffed with meat and rice* 肉末大米填充的辣椒.
▷ **pep·per** *v* **1** [Tn] put pepper on (food) 在(食物)上撒胡椒粉. **2** [Tn·pr] **~sb/sth with sth** hit sb/sth repeatedly with small objects 用小物体不断打击某人

[某物]: *The wall had been peppered with bullets.* 墙上有密集的子弹痕迹. ○ *a batsman peppering the field with shots* 击球手把球连续不断地击向场地 ○ (*fig* 比喻) *pepper sb with questions* 像开连珠炮般向某人提出许多问题.

pep·pery /ˈpepərɪ; ˋpɛpərɪ/ *adj* **1** tasting of or like pepper (似)胡椒味的, 辣椒味的; 辣的. **2** easily angered; hot-tempered 暴躁的; 易怒的; 性子急的: *a peppery old colonel* 脾气暴躁的老上校.

□ ˌ**pepper-and-ˈsalt** *adj* **1** (of cloth) having dark and light wools woven together to show a mixture of dark and light spots (指布料)黑白毛混纺的. **2** (of hair) white and brown together (指毛发)花白的, 灰褐色的.

ˈ**peppercorn** *n* dried berry that is ground to make pepper 胡椒粒. ˌ**peppercorn ˈrent** very low rent 极低的租金.

ˈ**pepper-mill** *n* container in which peppercorns are ground to powder for sprinkling on food (用手碾的)胡椒磨.

ˈ**pepper-pot** *n* small container with holes in the top, used for sprinkling pepper on food 胡椒瓶. Cf 参看 SALT-CELLAR (SALT).

pep·per·mint /ˈpepəmɪnt; ˋpɛpɚˌmɪnt/ *n* (**a**) [U] type of mint grown for its strong-flavoured oil which is used in sweets and in medicine 胡椒薄荷: *oil of peppermint* 胡椒薄荷油. (**b**) (also **mint**) [C] sweet flavoured with oil of peppermint 薄荷糖: *suck a peppermint* 吃薄荷糖 ○ [attrib 作定语] *peppermint creams* 薄荷奶油. Cf 参看 SPEARMINT.

pep·sin /ˈpepsɪn; ˋpɛpsɪn/ *n* [U] liquid produced in the stomach which helps food to be digested 胃蛋白酶.

▷ **pep·tic** /ˈpeptɪk; ˋpɛptɪk/ *adj* of digestion or the digestive system 消化的; 消化系统的: *a peptic ulcer*, ie one in the digestive system 消化性溃疡.

per /pə(r); pɚ; *strong form* 强读式 pɜː(r); pɝ/ *prep* (used to express rates, prices, etc 用以表示比率、价格等) for each (unit of time, length, etc) 每, 每一(时间、长度等单位): *£60 per day* 每天60英镑 ○ *£2 per person* 每人2英镑 ○ *calculated per square yard* 以每平方码计算的 ○ *45 revolutions per minute* 每分钟45转 ○ *100 miles per hour* 每小时100英里.

per·am·bul·ate /pəˈræmbjʊleɪt; pɚˋæmbjəˌlet/ *v* (*fml or rhet* 文或修辞) **1** [Tn] walk about, through or over (a place) 漫步于, 步行通过(某地): *perambulate the boundaries of his estate* 巡视他的庄园地界. **2** [I] walk around or up and down 到处走; 漫步; 散步: *perambulate after lunch* 午饭后散步. ▷ **per·am·bu·la·tion** /pəˌræmbjʊˈleɪʃn; pɚˌæmbjəˋleʃən/ *n* [C, U]: *He saw many strange things during his perambulations in the old city.* 他到那古老的城市里闲逛, 看见很多奇怪的事物.

per·am·bu·lator /pəˈræmbjʊleɪtə(r); pɚˋæmbjəˌletɚ/ *n* (*Brit fml* 文) pram (手推的四轮的)幼儿车.

per an·num /pər ˈænəm; pɚˋænəm/ *adv* for each year 每年: *earning £15 000 per annum* 每年挣15 000英镑.

per cap·ita /pə ˈkæpɪtə; pɚˋkæpɪtə/ *adv, adj* [attrib 作定语] for each person 每人(的); 人均(的): *Per capita incomes rose sharply last year.* 去岁人均收入剧增.

per·ceive /pəˈsiːv; pɚˋsiv/ *v* **1** [Tn, Tf, Tw, Tnt, Tng] (*fml* 文) become aware of (sb/sth); notice; observe 意识到, 注意到, 观察到(某人[某事物]): *I perceived a change in his behaviour/that his behaviour had changed.* 我发觉他的行为有些变化. ○ *We had already perceived how the temperature fluctuated.* 我们已注意到温度的波动情形. ○ *The patient was perceived to have difficulty in standing and walking.* 据观察所见, 病人站立和行走都有困难. **2** [Cn·n/a] **~ sth as sth** interpret sth in a certain way; view 理解或领悟某事物; 认为: *I perceived his comment as a challenge.* 我认为他的批评是对我的激励. ▷ **per·ceiv·able** *adj*.

per cent (*US* **per·cent**) /pə ˈsent; pɚˋsɛnt/ *adj, adv* in or for every hundred 每一百之中(的): *a fifty per cent* (ie 50%) *increase in price* 价格上涨百分之五十(即50%) ○ working twenty per cent harder 再多使二分劲儿.

▷ **per cent** (*US* **per·cent**) *n* [C usu *sing*, but with sing or pl *v* 通常作单数, 但可与单数或复数动词连用] one part in every hundred; percentage 百分之一; 百分比: *half a per cent*, ie 0.5% 百分之零点五(即0.5%) ○ *Over sixty per cent of families own/owns a television.* 百分之六十以上的家庭已有电视机. ○ *What per cent of the population read/reads books?* 识字的人占人口的百分之几?

per·cent·age /pəˈsentɪdʒ; pɚˋsɛntɪdʒ/ *n* **1** [C] rate, number or amount in each hundred 百分比; 百分率: *The figure is expressed as a percentage.* 那数字是以百分比表示的. ○ *The salesmen get a percentage* (ie a commission) *on everything they sell.* 这些推销员可从推销的商品上获得一定百分比的佣金. ○ [attrib 作定语] *a percentage increase in ticket prices* 票价上涨的百分比. **2** [sing or pl *v*] proportion 比例; 部分: *What percentage of his income is taxable?* 他的收入有多少需纳所得税? ○ *An increasing percentage of the population own their own homes.* 自己有房子的人占人口比例越来越大了.

per·cent·ile /pəˈsentaɪl; pɚˋsɛntaɪl/ (*US* **centile**) *n* (**a**) (in statistics) any of 99 points at which a range of data is divided to make 100 groups of equal size (统计学上的)百分位数. (**b**) any of these groups 百分位数之一: *an examination score in the 85th percentile*, ie a score higher than 85 per cent of all scores attained in an examination 第85百分位的考分(高于考试中总得分的85%的分数).

per·cept·ible /pəˈseptəbl; pɚˋsɛptəbḷ/ *adj* **~ (to sb)** (*fml* 文) **1** that can be observed with the senses 可感知的; 可觉察的: *perceptible movements, sounds, etc* 可察觉的物体运动、声响等. **2** great enough to be noticed or observed 能感觉到的; 看得出的; 可观察到的: *perceptible change, deterioration, improvement, increase, loss of colour* 看得出的变化、恶化、改善、增长、褪色. ▷ **per·cept·ib·il·ity** /pəˌseptəˈbɪlətɪ; pɚˌsɛptəˋbɪlətɪ/ *n* [U]. **per·cept·ibly** /-əblɪ; -əblɪ/ *adv*: *The patient has improved perceptibly.* 已看出病人有好转.

per·cep·tion /pəˈsepʃn; pɚˋsɛpʃən/ *n* (*fml* 文) **1** [U] ability to see, hear or understand 感知能力; 认识能力: *improve one's powers of perception* 提高认识能力. **2** [U] quality of understanding; insight 悟性; 洞察力: *His analysis of the problem showed great perception.* 他对该问题的分析显示出敏锐的洞察力. **3** [C] **~ (that...)** way of seeing or understanding sth 看法; 理解: *My perception of the matter is that...* 我对此事的看法是... ○ *his perception that conditions had not changed* 他认为情况无变化.

per·cept·ive /pəˈseptɪv; pɚˋsɛptɪv/ *adj* (*fml* 文) **1** quick to notice and understand things 观察敏锐的; 善于理解的: *The most perceptive of the three, she was the first to realize the potential danger of their situation.* 她在他们三人中最敏感, 首先意识到他们处境的潜在危险. **2** having or showing understanding or insight; discerning 有理解力的; 有洞察力的; 有识别力的: *a perceptive analysis, comment, judgement, etc* 富有见地的分析、评论、判断等. **3** [attrib 作定语] of or concerning perception 感知的; 有感知的; 有理解力的; 有洞察力的: *perceptive skills* 理解的技巧. ▷ **per·cept·ively** *adv*. **per·cept·ive·ness**, **per·cept·iv·ity** /ˌpɜːsepˈtɪvətɪ; ˌpɝsɛpˋtɪvətɪ/ *ns* [U]: *show rare perceptiveness* 显示罕有的理解力.

perch[1] /pɜːtʃ; pɝtʃ/ *n* **1** (**a**) place where a bird rests, eg a branch 鸟类的栖息处(如树枝). (**b**) bar or rod for this purpose, eg in a bird-cage or hen-roost (作此用途的)棍, 杆(如鸟笼或鸡窝中的). **2** (*infml* 口) high seat or position 高座; 高位: *He watched the game from his perch on top of the wall.* 他在墙头居高临下看比赛. **3** (also **pole**, **rod**) measure of length equal to $5\frac{1}{2}$ yds or 5.03 metres, used esp for land 杆(长度单位, 等于$5\frac{1}{2}$码或5.03米, 尤用以丈量土地). ⇨App 5 见附录5. **4** (idm 习语) **knock sb off his pedestal/perch** ⇨ KNOCK.

▷ **perch** *v* **1** [I, Ipr] **~ (on sth)** (of a bird) come to rest or stay (on a branch, etc) (指鸟)栖息, 停留(枝上等): *The birds perched on the television aerial.* 鸟停在电视天线上. **2** [I, Ipr] **~ (on sth)** (of a person) sit, esp on sth high or narrow (指人)坐着(尤指坐在高处或窄物上): *perch on high stools at the bar* 坐在酒吧的高凳上 ○ *perch dangerously on a narrow ledge* 坐在狭窄的边缘上, 十分危险 ○ *perch on the edge of one's seat* 坐在座位的边上. **3** [Tn, Tn·pr] place (sth), esp in a high or dangerous position 将(某物)置于尤指高处或危险处: *a hut perched at the edge of the cliff* 悬崖边上的小舍 ○ *perch a beret on the side of one's head* 歪戴贝雷帽 ○ *a castle perched above the river* 临河而建的城堡.

perch² /pɜːtʃ; pɝtʃ/ *n* (*pl* unchanged 复数不变) any of several types of freshwater fish with spiny fins, eaten as food 鲈.

per·chance /pəˈtʃɑːns; *US* -ˈtʃæns; pɚˈtʃæns/ *adv* (*arch* 古) **1** perhaps 也许; 可能. **2** by chance 偶然; 万一.

per·cipi·ent /pəˈsɪpɪənt; pɚˈsɪpɪənt/ *adj* (*fml* 文) **1** noticing or understanding things quickly or clearly; perceptive 感知或理解敏锐的; 观察深刻的: *a percipient onlooker* 目光敏锐的旁观者. **2** having or showing insight; discerning 有洞察力的; 有识别力的: *a percipient comment* 精辟的评论. ▷ **per·cipi·ence** /pəˈsɪpɪəns; pɚˈsɪpɪəns/ *n* [U].

per·col·ate /ˈpɜːkəleɪt; ˈpɝkəˌlet/ *v* **1** (*infml* 口语作 **perk**) (**a**) [I, Ipr, Ip] **~ (through sth)/~ (through)** (of water) pass slowly through (coffee); filter through (指水)经(咖啡)渗透, 过滤: *The coffee is percolating*, ie Boiling water is passing through ground coffee beans. 正在用过滤法煮咖啡. (**b**) [Tn, Tn·pr, Tn·p] **~ sth (through sth/through)** cause (water) to pass slowly through (coffee) 使(水)经(咖啡)过滤: *coffee made by percolating boiling water through ground coffee beans* 用过滤法煮的咖啡 ○ *I'll percolate some coffee*, ie make it by percolating. 我去用过滤法煮些咖啡. **2** (**a**) [Ipr, Ip] **~ through (sth)** (of liquid) pass slowly through (sth) (指液体)渗透过(某物): *water percolating through sand* 渗过沙层的水. (**b**) [Ipr] **~ through sth** (of an idea, a feeling, information) spread or become known gradually (指思想、感情、信息)逐渐传播或透露: *The rumour percolated through the firm.* 那谣言在公司里慢慢流传开来.

▷ **per·cola·tion** /ˌpɜːkəˈleɪʃn; ˌpɝkəˈleʃən/ *n* [C, U].

per·col·ator *n* (**a**) pot for making and serving coffee, in which boiling water is repeatedly forced up a central tube and filtered down through ground coffee 过滤式咖啡壶. (**b**) any other apparatus for percolating liquids 过滤器.

per·cus·sion /pəˈkʌʃn; pɚˈkʌʃən/ *n* **1** [U] (**a**) striking of two (usu hard) objects together 两物相撞(通常指硬物). (**b**) sound or shock that is the result of this 碰撞发出的声音或震动. **2** [U] method of playing a musical instrument by striking it with another object (打击乐器的)演奏(法), 打击. **3 the percussion** [pl *v*] (also **perˈcussion section**) (players of) percussion instruments in an orchestra (管弦乐队的)打击乐器(的演奏组). ⇨ illus at App 1 见附录1插图, page xi. **4** [U] (*medical* 医) gentle tapping of the surface of the body as part of a medical examination 叩诊.

▷ **per·cus·sion·ist** /-ʃənɪst; -ʃənɪst/ *n* person who plays percussion instruments 打击乐器演奏者.

□ **perˈcussion cap** (also **cap**) small metal or paper device containing explosive powder, which explodes when struck 发火帽; 雷管.

perˈcussion instrument musical instrument (eg drum, tambourine, xylophone) played by striking it with another object 打击乐器(如鼓、铃鼓、木琴).

per·di·tion /pəˈdɪʃn; pɚˈdɪʃən/ *n* [U] **1** (*fml religion* 文, 宗) everlasting punishment of the wicked after death (恶人死后的)永久惩罚: *damned to perdition* 万劫不复. **2** (*arch* 古) total destruction 全部毁灭.

per·eg·rina·tion /ˌperɪgrɪˈneɪʃn; ˌpɛrəgrɪˈneʃən/ *n* (*fml* 文) **1** [U] travelling 旅行. **2** [C] journey 旅程; 游历: *his peregrinations in southern Europe* 他在南欧的游历.

per·eg·rine /ˈperɪgrɪn; ˈpɛrəgrɪn/ *n* (also **per·eg·rine fal·con**) large black and white bird of prey that can be trained to hunt and catch small birds and animals 游隼; 鸭鹰.

per·emp·tory /pəˈremptərɪ; *US* ˈperəmptɔːrɪ; ˈpɛrəmpˌtorɪ/ *adj* (*fml* 文) **1** (*esp derog* 尤作贬义) (of a person, his manner, etc) insisting on immediate obedience or submission; domineering (指人、举止等)专横的, 霸道的: *His peremptory tone of voice irritated everybody.* 他那专横的口气激怒了大家. **2** (of commands) not to be disobeyed or questioned (指命令)不容抗拒的, 不容分说的, 强制的: *a peremptory dismissal, rebuke, shout* 不容分说的解雇、指责、喊叫. ▷ **per·emp·tor·ily** /-trəlɪ; *US* -tɔːrəlɪ; -tərəlɪ/ *adv*.

□ **peremptory ˈwrit** (*law* 律) document in which a defendant is ordered to appear in court 传票.

per·en·nial /pəˈrenɪəl; pəˈrɛnɪəl/ *adj* **1** lasting for a long time 长久的; 持久的: *a perennial subject of interest* 永恒的主题. **2** constantly recurring 一再的; 反复出现的: *a perennial problem* 反复出现的问题 ○ *perennial complaints* 一再的抱怨. **3** (of plants) living for more than two years (指植物)多年生的.

▷ **per·en·nial** *n* perennial plant 多年生植物: *hardy perennials*, ie plants that can normally tolerate frost 耐寒的多年生植物.

per·en·ni·ally /-nɪəlɪ; -nɪəlɪ/ *adv*.

pe·re·stroi·ka /ˌpereˈstrɔɪkə; ˌpɛrəˈstrɔɪkə/ *n* [U] (*Russian* 俄) (formaly) restructuring of the Soviet economic and political system (旧时)(苏联经济与政治体制的)改革.

per·fect¹ /ˈpɜːfɪkt; ˈpɝfɪkt/ *adj* **1** (**a**) having everything needed; complete 完备的; 完全的: *in perfect condition* 情况完好 ○ *a perfect set of teeth* 一副完整的牙齿. (**b**) without fault; excellent 完美的; 无瑕的; 优异的: *a perfect performance of the play* 该剧完美的演出 ○ *perfect weather, behaviour* 美好的天气、优秀的品行 ○ *a perfect score*, ie one in which no points have been lost; 100 per cent 满分(100分) ○ *Nobody is perfect.* 人无完人. ○ *speak perfect English* 英语说得地道. **2** the best of its kind; ideal 最佳的; 理想的: *the perfect meal* 精美的饭食 ○ *the perfect crime*, ie one in which the criminal is never discovered 不露蛛丝马迹的罪行. **3** exact; precise 准确的; 精确的: *a perfect circle, square* 正圆、正方 ○ *a perfect copy, match, fit* 精确的副本、匹配、配合 ○ *perfect accuracy, timing* 极精确、极合时机. **4 ~ for sb/sth** highly suitable for sb/sth; exactly right for sb/sth 极适合于某人[某事物]; 对某人[某事物]正合适: *perfect for each other* 最佳搭档 ○ *perfect day for a picnic* 最适合野餐的日子. **5** (*grammar*) (of verb tenses) composed of *has/have* or *had* + past participle (指动词时态)完成式的(由has/have或had + 过去分词组成): *the present and past perfect tenses*, eg 'I have eaten'/'I had eaten' 现在完成式和过去完成式(如I have eaten/I had eaten). **6** [attrib 作定语] (*infml* 口) total; absolute 全部的; 绝对的: *perfect nonsense, rubbish, etc* 纯粹胡说八道、一派胡言 ○ *a perfect fool, pest, stranger, etc* 十足的傻瓜、害人精、异乡人等 ○ *She's a perfect angel!* 她是真正的好人! **7** (idm 习语) **practice makes perfect** ⇨ PRACTICE.

▷ **per·fect** *n* **the perfect** [sing] perfect tense 完成时态: *The verb is in the perfect.* 那动词是完成式. ○ *the present/past perfect* 现在[过去]完成式.

per·fectly *adv* **1** in a perfect way 完美地; 完满地; 极佳地: *The trousers fit perfectly.* 这条裤子非常合身. **2** completely; quite 完全地; 十分: *perfectly happy, satisfied, content, etc* 十分快乐、满意、满足等 ○ *perfectly well* 极好 ○ *perfectly able to find her own way* 完全能找到她自己的出路. **3** (*infml* 口) extremely; absolutely 极; 非常; 绝对地: *a perfectly delicious cake* 非常好吃的蛋糕 ○ *perfectly awful weather* 极坏的天气 ○ *a perfectly foul headache* 剧烈的头痛.

□ ˌ**perfect ˈpitch** (also ˌ**absolute ˈpitch**) (*music* 音) ability to recognize or sing any musical note 完全音高(感), 绝对音高(感)(对任何一个乐音的识别力或演唱力): *She has perfect/absolute pitch.* 她有完全音高感.

per·fect² /pəˈfekt; pɚˈfɛkt/ *v* [Tn] make (sth) perfect or complete 使(某事物)完美、完善或完备: *She needs to perfect her Arabic before going to work in Cairo.* 她需要把阿拉伯语学好才能到开罗工作. ○ *a violinist who spent years perfecting his technique* 花了多年时间使演奏技术炉火纯青的小提琴手.

▷ **per·fect·ible** *adj* that can be perfected 可使之完美的; 可臻完善的. **per·fect·ib·il·ity** /pəˌfektəˈbɪlətɪ; pɚˌfɛktəˈbɪlətɪ/ *n* [U].

per·fec·tion /pəˈfekʃn; pɚˈfɛkʃən/ *n* **1** [U] making perfect 完美, 完善, 完备, 圆满(指过程): *They are working on the perfection of their new paint formula.* 他们正在努力研制尽善尽美的新颜料配方. **2** [U] state of being perfect; faultlessness 完美, 完善, 完备, 圆满(指状况): *Perfection is impossible to achieve in that kind of work.* 那种工作不可能做到十全十美. ○ *aim for perfection* 力求完善 ○ *bring sth to perfection* 使某事十全十美. **3** [U] highest state or quality; ideal 尽善尽美的状况或质量; 理想: *Her singing was perfection.* 她的歌唱得已是炉火纯青. **4** (idm 习语) **a counsel of perfection** ⇨ COUNSEL. **to perˈfection** exactly to the right degree; perfectly 恰到好处; 尽善尽美: *wine aged to perfection* 陈年佳酿 ○ *a dish cooked to perfection* 烹调

至恰到好处的菜.

▷ **per·fec·tion·ist** /-ʃənɪst; -ʃənɪst/ *n* **1** person who is not satisfied with anything less than perfection 完美主义者; 至善论者. **2** (*derog* 贬) person who insists on perfection in every detail even when it is not necessary 过分的完美主义者. **per·fec·tion·ism** /pəˈfekʃənɪzəm; pɚˋfekʃənɪzəm/ *n* [U].

per·fidy /ˈpɜːfɪdɪ; ˋpɝfədɪ/ *n* **~ (to/towards sb)** (*fml* 文) (**a**) [U] acting in a treacherous or disloyal way 背叛; 背信弃义; 不忠. (**b**) [C] instance of this 背叛; 背信弃义; 不忠.

▷ **per·fi·di·ous** /pəˈfɪdɪəs; pɚˋfɪdɪəs/ *adj* **~ (to/towards sb)** (*fml* 文) treacherous, deceitful or disloyal 背叛的; 背信弃义的; 不忠的: *betrayed by perfidious allies* 遭背信弃义的盟友出卖. **per·fi·di·ously** *adv*. **per·fi·di·ous·ness** *n* [U].

per·for·ate /ˈpɜːfəreɪt; ˋpɝfəˌret/ *v* [Tn] **1** make a hole or holes through (sth) 在(某物)上穿孔或打眼: *perforate the cover to let air in* 在盖子上打眼让空气进入 ○ [attrib 作定语] *a perforated ulcer* 穿孔的溃疡. **2** make a row of small holes (esp in paper) so that it will tear easily 在(尤指纸)上打齿孔(以便撕开): [attrib 作定语] *a perforated sheet of postage stamps* 有齿孔的邮票联张.

▷ **per·fora·tion** /ˌpɜːfəˈreɪʃn; ˌpɝfəˈreʃən/ *n* **1** [U] perforating or being perforated (在某物上)穿孔; (在纸等上)打齿孔. **2** [C] series of small holes made in paper, etc (纸等上的)齿孔: *tear the sheet along the perforations* 顺齿孔撕下该页.

per·force /pəˈfɔːs; pɚˋfɔrs/ *adv* (*arch or fml* 古或文) because it is necessary or inevitable 必; 必然; 必定.

per·form /pəˈfɔːm; pɚˋfɔrm/ *v* **1** [Tn] do (a piece of work, sth one is ordered to do, sth one has agreed to do) 做, 执行, 履行(某事): *perform a task, one's duty, a miracle* 执行任务、履行义务、做出奇迹 ○ *perform an operation to save his life* 动手术挽救他的生命. **2** [I, Ipr, Tn] act (a play), play (a piece of music) or do (tricks) to entertain an audience 表演(戏剧); 演奏(音乐); 表演(戏法): *They are performing his play/piano concerto tonight.* 他们今晚演出他的剧[钢琴协奏曲]. ○ *watch sb perform* 看某人表演 ○ *perform skilfully on the flute* 熟练地吹奏横笛 ○ *perform live on television* 电视实况演出 ○ *performing seals in a circus* 在马戏团里表演驯海豹. **3** [I] (with an *adv* 与副词连用) (of a machine, an invention, etc) work or function (指机器等)工作, 运转; (指发明等)运用, 使用: *How is the new car performing?* 新汽车性能如何? ○ *The new drug has performed well in tests.* 那种新药试验效果不错. **4** [Tn] act in an official way (at sth) 正式进行, 施行(某事): *perform a ceremony, rite, ritual, etc* 举行典礼、仪式等.

▷ **per·former** *n* person who performs in front of an audience 表演者; 演出者: *an accomplished performer* 有造诣的表演者.

□ **perˌforming ˈarts** drama, music, dance, etc which are performed in front of an audience 表演艺术.

per·form·ance /pəˈfɔːməns; pɚˋfɔrməns/ *n* **1** [sing] process or manner of performing 执行; 履行; 工作; 作用; 施行; 进行: *faithful in the performance of his duties* 忠于(他的)职守. **2** (**a**) [C] performing of a play at the theatre or some other entertainment (在剧院等的)演出, 表演: *the evening performance* 晚场演出 ○ *give a performance of 'Hamlet'* 演出《哈姆雷特》. (**b**) [U] **in ~** performing in a concert or other entertainment (在音乐会等的)演出, 演奏: *Come and see her in performance with the new band.* 来看她在新乐队中的演奏吧. **3** (**a**) [C] (esp outstanding) action or achievement (尤指出色的)表现, 行为, 成就: *She won a gold medal for her fine performance in the contest.* 她在竞赛中成绩优异获金牌. ○ *His performance in the test was not good enough.* 他在测验中做的不够好. (**b**) [U] ability to move quickly, operate efficiently, etc (良好的)性能, 工作情况: *The customer was impressed by the machine's performance.* 客户对机器的良好性能很满意. ○ *Performance is less important than reliability in a car.* 汽车的可靠性比其机械性能更重要. **4** [C] (*infml* 口) (**a**) ridiculous or disgraceful behaviour (可笑的或丢脸的)行为, 举动: *What a performance the child made!* 那孩子真丢人! (**b**) (esp unnecessary) fuss or trouble (尤指不必要的)忙乱, 麻烦: *He goes through the whole performance of checking the oil and water every time he drives the car.* 他每次开汽车都总是不厌其烦地把油和水整个检查一遍.

per·fume /ˈpɜːfjuːm; *US also* pərˈfjuːm; ˋpɝfjum, pɚˋfjum/ *n* [C, U] **1** fragrant or pleasant smell 香味; 芳香: *the perfume of the flowers* 花的香味 ○ *flowery perfumes* 花的香味. **2** (any of several types of) sweet-smelling liquid, often made from flowers, used esp on the body 香水: *sell perfumes and toilet-waters* 经售各种香水和化妆水 ○ *French perfume* 法国香水.

▷ **per·fume** /pəˈfjuːm; pɚˋfjum/ *v* [Tn] **1** (of flowers, etc) give a fragrant smell to (sth) (指花等)使(某物)带香味: *The roses perfumed the room.* 玫瑰花熏得室内一片香. **2** put perfume on (sb/sth) 向(某人[某物])洒香水: *perfume a handkerchief* 往手绢上洒香水.

per·fumer /pəˈfjuːmə(r); pɚˋfjumɚ/ (also **per·fumier** /pəˈfjuːmɪeɪ; pɚˋfjumɪe/) *n* person who makes and/or sells perfume 香水制造商; 售香水者.

per·fumery /pəˈfjuːmərɪ; pɚˋfjumərɪ/ *n* **1** [C] place where perfumes are made or sold 香水制造厂; 香水商店. **2** [U] process of making perfume 香水的制造.

per·func·tory /pəˈfʌŋktərɪ; pɚˋfʌŋktərɪ/ *adj* (*fml* 文) (**a**) (of an action) done as a duty or routine, without care or interest (指行为)敷衍的, 马虎的, 例行的: *a perfunctory examination, greeting, salute* 例行的考试、问候、致意. (**b**) (of a person) doing things in this way (指人)做事敷衍塞责的. ▷ **per·func·tor·ily** /-trəlɪ; -tərəlɪ/ *adv*: *check the luggage perfunctorily* 对行李作例行的检查. **per·func·tori·ness** *n* [U].

per·gola /ˈpɜːgələ; ˋpɝgələ/ *n* structure of posts for climbing plants, forming an arbour or a covered walk in a garden (花园中的)凉棚, 藤架.

per·haps /pəˈhæps, *also* præps; pɚˋhæps, præps/ *adv* it may be (that); possibly 也许; 大概; 可能: *Perhaps the weather will change this evening.* 今晚可能要变天. ○ *Perhaps it will, perhaps it won't.* 也许会, 也许不会. ○ *It is, perhaps, the best known of his works.* 大概那是他最著名的作品了. ○ *Perhaps not/so*, ie expressing half-hearted agreement with what a person says. 未必吧[也许如此]. ○ *Perhaps you would be kind enough to...*, ie a polite way of saying 'Would you...?' 是否可以请您....

peri- *pref* **1** around 周围: *periscope* ○ *periphrasis* ○ *perimeter*. **2** near 近: *perihelion* ○ *perigee*.

peri·gee /ˈperɪdʒiː; ˋperəˌdʒi/ *n* point in the orbit of the moon, a planet or a spacecraft at which it is nearest to the earth 近地点(月球、行星或航天器轨道上距地球最近的点).

peri·he·lion /ˌperɪˈhiːlɪən; ˌperɪˋhilɪən/ *n* (*pl* **-lia** /-lɪə; -lɪə/) point in the orbit of a planet, comet, etc at which it is nearest to the sun 近日点(行星、彗星等轨道上距太阳最近的点).

peril /ˈperəl; ˋperəl/ *n* **1** [U] serious danger (esp of death) 严重危险(尤指死亡的): *in great, mortal, etc peril* 在严重的、致命的...危险中. **2** [C usu *pl* 通常作复数] dangerous thing or circumstance 危险的事物或环境: *face the perils of the ocean*, ie storm, shipwreck, etc 面对海上的危险(风暴、船只失事等) ○ *These birds are able to survive the perils of the Arctic winter.* 这些鸟能在北极的严冬中生存. **3** (idm 习语) **at one's peril** (used esp when advising sb not to do sth 尤用于劝某人不做某事) with a risk of harm to oneself 冒险: *The bicycle has no brakes — you ride it at your peril.* 这辆自行车没闸——你要骑可太危险了. ○ *One ignores letters from the bank manager at one's peril.* 忽视银行经理来函, 后果堪虑. **in ˌperil of one's ˈlife** in danger of death 冒生命危险.

▷ **per·il·ous** /ˈperələs; ˋperələs/ *adj* full of risk; dangerous 多险的; 危险的: *a perilous journey across the mountains* 横越重山的艰险征途. **per·il·ously** *adv*: *perilously hot, fast, steep, etc* 热得、快得、陡得...易出危险 ○ *They were perilously close to the edge of the precipice.* 他们离悬崖边很近, 十分危险.

peri·meter /pəˈrɪmɪtə(r); pəˋrɪmətɚ/ *n* **1** (length of the) outer edge of a closed geometric shape 周; 周边; 边缘; 周长. **2** boundary of an area 周围的界限: *Guards patrolled the perimeter of the airfield.* 卫兵沿机场四周巡逻. ○ [attrib 作定语] *the perimeter fence* 周围的篱笆. Cf 参看 CIRCUMFERENCE.

period /ˈpɪərɪəd; ˋpɪrɪəd/ *n* **1** length or portion of time 一段时间; 时期: *a period of three years* 三年的时间 ○ *He has had several long periods of work abroad.* 他在国外长期工作过几次. ○ *a period of peace, recovery, uncertainty*

P

和平、恢复、不稳定时期 ○ *showers and sunny periods*, eg in a weather forecast 阵雨间晴(如在天气预报所述) ○ *The work must be completed within a two-month period.* 工作须于两月内完成. ○ *The incubation period* (ie The delay between catching a disease and the symptoms appearing) *is two weeks.* 该疾病的潜伏期为两星期. **2** (**a**) portion of time in the life of a person, nation or civilization (人、国家、文明的)时期, 时代: *a painting belonging to the artist's early period* 该画家早期的画 ○ *the period of the French Revolution* 法国大革命时期 ○ *the post-war period* 战后时期 ○ *The house is 18th century and has furniture of the period*, ie of the same century. 那房子是18世纪的, 而且还有那时代的家具. ○ *The actors wore costumes of the period*, ie of the time when the events of the play took place. 演员穿着剧中时代的服装. ○ [usu attrib 通常作定语] *period dress, furniture, etc* 某时代的服装、家具等 ○ *a period cottage*, ie not modern 某时代的村舍. (**b**) (*geology* 地质) portion of time in the development of the earth's surface 纪: *the Jurassic period* 侏罗纪. **3** (time allowed for a) lesson in school (学校的)课, 课时, 学时: *a teaching period of 45 minutes* 45分钟的一堂课 ○ *a free period* 没课的一节 ○ *three periods of geography a week* 每周三节地理课. **4** (**a**) monthly flow of blood from the womb of a woman; menstruation 月经: *have a period* 来月经 ○ [attrib 作定语] *period pains* 月经痛. (**b**) time of this 月经期. **5** (*esp US*) (**a**) = FULL STOP (FULL). (**b**) sign of punctuation (.) marking this in writing and print 句号. ⇨App 3 见附录3. (**c**) (*infml* 口) (added to the end of a statement to stress its completeness 加于一段话之后以强调完毕): *We can't pay higher wages, period*, ie that is final. 我们不能付再高的工资了, 话就说到这里. **6** (*grammar*) complete sentence, esp one having several clauses 完全句(尤指有几个分句者). **7** (*astronomy* 天) time taken to complete one revolution 周期.

□ ˈ**period piece** (*infml* 口) old-fashioned person or thing 旧式的、老式的或过时的人或事物: *The play, which once seemed so modern, has become a period piece.* 那出戏, 一度似乎相当时新, 如今已成明日黄花.

peri·odic /ˌpɪərɪˈɒdɪk; ˌpɪrɪˋɑdɪk/ *adj* occurring or appearing at (esp regular) intervals 定期的; 周期的: *periodic attacks of dizziness* 眩晕的周期性发作 ○ *a periodic review of expenditure* 对支出的定期核查.

▷ **peri·od·ical** /-kl; -kḷ/ *n*, *adj* (magazine or other publication) that is published at regular intervals, eg weekly or monthly 定期出版的; 期刊. **peri·od·ic·ally** /-klɪ; -klɪ/ *adv* at (esp regular) intervals 定期地; 周期地.

□ ˌ**periodic** ˈ**table** (*chemistry* 化) arrangement of chemical elements according to their atomic weights 周期表. ⇨App 10 见附录10.

peri·pat·etic /ˌperɪpəˈtetɪk; ˌpɛrəpəˋtɛtɪk/ *adj* **1** going from place to place 到处走的; 漫游的; 巡回的. **2** (*Brit*) (of teachers) employed at two or more schools and travelling between them (指教师)在多所学校兼课的: *Peripatetic music teachers visit the school regularly.* 兼职音乐教师定期到校授课. ▷ **peri·pat·et·ic·ally** /-klɪ; -klɪ/ *adv*.

peri·phery /pəˈrɪfərɪ; pəˋrɪfərɪ/ *n* (*fml* 文) **1** (**a**) boundary of a surface or an area 外围; 边缘. (**b**) area near this on either side 外围或边缘的地方: *industrial development on the periphery* (ie outskirts) *of the town* 郊区的工业发展. **2** (*fig* 比喻) (esp in social, political or intellectual life) position far away from the centre; the fringe (尤指社交、政治或文化生活的)外围, 边缘: *The ideas are also expressed by minor poets on the periphery of the movement.* 该运动外围一些不大出名的诗人也表达了这些观点. **3** (also **peˌripheral deˈvice**) (*computing* 计) device attached to a computer that transfers information into or out of the computer 外围设备: *display units, printers and other peripherals* 显示装置、打印机及其他外部设备.

▷ **peri·pheral** /-ərəl; -ərəl/ *adj* **1** ~ **(to sth)** of secondary or minor importance (to sth) 次要的; 不重要的: *topics peripheral to the main theme* 围绕中心议题的小题目. **2** of or on a periphery 外围的; 边缘的: *peripheral zones* 边缘地带. **peri·pher·ally** /-ərəlɪ; -ərəlɪ/ *adv*.

peri·phrasis /pəˈrɪfrəsɪs; pəˋrɪfrəsɪs/ *n* (*pl* **-ases** /-əsi:z; -əˌsiz/) (*fml* 文) **1** (**a**) [U] roundabout way of expressing sth; circumlocution 折绕; 迂说法; 婉曲. (**b**) [C] roundabout expression in speaking or writing, eg *'give expression to'* instead of *'express'* 折绕语, 婉曲修辞(如用give expression to而不用express). **2** (*grammar*) (**a**) [U] use of an auxiliary word or a syntactic pattern in place of an inflected form, eg *'It does work'* for *'It works'* or *'the word of God'* for *'God's word'* 迂说法(用助动词或句法形式而不用动词词尾变化形式, 如用It does work代替It works或用the word of God代替God's word). (**b**) [C] example of this 迂说.

▷ **peri·phrastic** /ˌperɪˈfræstɪk; ˌpɛrəˋfræstɪk/ *adj* of, expressed in or using periphrasis 迂说法的; 用迂说法表达的. **peri·phrastic·ally** /-klɪ; -klɪ/ *adv*.

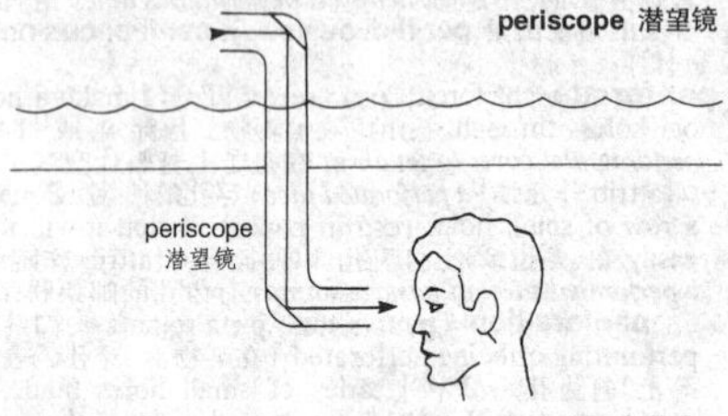

peri·scope /ˈperɪskəʊp; ˋpɛrəˌskop/ *n* apparatus with mirrors and lenses arranged in a tube so that the user has a view of the surrounding area above, eg from a submarine when it is under water 潜望镜.

▷ **peri·scopic** /ˌperɪˈskɒpɪk; ˌpɛrəˋskɑpɪk/ *adj* of or like a periscope (似)潜望镜的.

per·ish /ˈperɪʃ; ˋpɛrɪʃ/ *v* **1** [I] (*fml* 文) be destroyed; die 毁灭; 死亡: *Thousands of people perished in the earthquake.* 那次地震死者数以千计. ○ *We shall do it or perish in the attempt.* 我们将拼死一试. **2** [I, Tn] (*esp Brit*) (cause sth to) rot; (cause rubber to) lose its elasticity (使某物)腐烂; (使橡胶)失去弹性, 老化: *The seal on the bottle has perished.* 瓶子的封记已经腐烂. ○ *If any oil gets on the car tyres, it will perish them.* 汽车胎沾上油就会毁坏. **3** (idm 习语) ˌ**perish the** ˈ**thought** (*infml* 口) may it never happen 但愿别这样: *The neighbours' children want to learn to play the trumpet, perish the thought!* 邻居的孩子想学吹小号, 但愿他们别学!

▷ **per·ish·able** *adj* (esp of food) likely to decay or go bad quickly (尤指食物)易腐的, 易坏的: *Perishable food should be stored in a refrigerator.* 易腐的食物应储存在冰箱里. **per·ish·ables** *n* [pl] goods (esp food) which go bad or decay quickly, such as fish or soft fruit 易腐物品(尤指食物, 如鱼或浆果): *Perishables need to be consumed as quickly as possible.* 易腐烂的食物要尽快吃掉.

per·ished *adj* [pred 作表语] (*esp Brit*) in extreme discomfort through cold, etc (因寒冷等)极不适, 极难受: *We were perished with cold and hunger.* 我们饥寒交迫. ○ *The children were perished when they arrived home.* 孩子们到家时难受已极.

per·isher *n* (*dated Brit sl* 旧, 俚) annoying person, esp a child 讨厌鬼(尤指孩子): *Wait till I catch the little perisher!* 等着, 瞧我逮住那小淘气!

per·ish·ing *adj* (*esp Brit*) **1** extremely cold 极冷的: *I'm perishing!* 我冷得要命! ○ *It's perishing out there.* 外面冷极了. ○ *a period of perishing cold* 极冷的一段时间. **2** (*dated sl* 旧, 俚) (used to express annoyance 用以表示恼怒) damned, etc 讨厌的; 该死的: *I can't get in — I've lost the perishing key!* 我进不去——我把该死的钥匙丢了! **per·ish·ing** (also **per·ish·ingly**) *adv* (*sl* 俚 *esp Brit*) (used to emphasize sth bad 用以强调坏事) very 极; 很: *It's perishing/perishingly cold out there.* 外面冷极了. ○ *He's too perishing mean to pay his share.* 他小气极了, 连自己的那份钱也不付.

peri·style /ˈperɪstaɪl; ˋpɛrəˌstaɪl/ *n* (*architecture* 建) (**a**) row of columns around a temple, courtyard, etc (殿堂、庭院等的)周柱廊: *the imposing peristyle of the Parthenon* 帕台农神庙雄伟的柱廊. (**b**) area enclosed by this 周柱中庭.

peri·ton·itis /ˌperɪtəˈnaɪtɪs; ˌpɛrətəˋnaɪtɪs/ *n* [U] (*medical* 医) painful inflammation of the membrane that covers the inside wall of the abdomen 腹膜炎.

peri·winkle[1] /ˈperɪwɪŋkl; ˈpɛrə,wɪŋkl/ *n* any of several types of evergreen plant with trailing stems and blue or white flowers 蔓长春花: [attrib 作定语] *periwinkle blue* 蔓长春花的蓝色.

peri·winkle[2] /ˈperɪwɪŋkl; ˈpɛrə,wɪŋkl/ (also **winkle**) *n* any of several types of small edible shellfish shaped like a snail 滨螺.

per·jure /ˈpɜːdʒə(r); ˈpɝdʒɚ/ *v* [Tn] **~ oneself** (*law* 律) tell a lie (esp in a court of law) after one has sworn an oath to tell the truth 发假誓, 作伪证(尤指在法庭上): *Several witnesses at the trial were clearly prepared to perjure themselves in order to protect the accused.* 在审判时几个证人显然已准备好为袒护被告而作伪证.

▷ **per·jurer** /ˈpɜːdʒərə(r); ˈpɝdʒərɚ/ *n* (*law* 律) person who has perjured himself 发假誓者; 作伪证者.

per·jury /ˈpɜːdʒərɪ; ˈpɝdʒərɪ/ *n* (*law* 律) (**a**) [U] action of perjuring oneself 发假誓; 作伪证: *They tried to persuade her to commit perjury.* 他们竭力说服她出庭作伪证. (**b**) [C] lie told after swearing to tell the truth, esp in a court of law 假誓, 伪证(尤指在法庭上的).

perk[1] /pɜːk; pɝk/ *v* (phr v) **perk up** (*infml* 口) become more cheerful, lively or vigorous, esp after illness or depression 愉快、活跃或振作起来(尤指病后或曾消沉): *He looked depressed but perked up when his friends arrived.* 他看上去无精打采的, 但朋友一来就精神起来了. **perk sb/sth up** (*infml* 口) (**a**) make sb feel more cheerful or lively 使某人快活或活泼起来: *A holiday would perk you up.* 一放假你就快活了. (**b**) make sb look smarter 打扮某人: *He had perked himself up for the occasion.* 他为此事打扮了一番. (**c**) make (an outfit, a room, a garden, etc) look smarter, better, more vigorous, etc 使(服装、房间、花园等)美观、精神: *perk up the plants with a good watering* 给花草浇足水使之精神 ○ *You need a bright red scarf to perk up that grey suit.* 你围上一条大红围巾能显得那套灰西装更漂亮. **3** lift up (one's head or ears) 昂起(头); 竖起(耳朵): *The horse perked up its head when I shouted.* 我吆喝时那马扬起了头.

▷ **perky** *adj* (**-ier, -iest**) (*infml* 口) **1** full of energy; lively 精力充沛的; 活跃的: *He's still in hospital, but he seems quite perky.* 他虽然还住着院, 可是看上去倒挺精神. **2** (too) full of self-confidence; cheeky (太)自信的; 厚脸皮的: *That child is a bit too perky!* 那孩子有点太放肆了! **per·kily** /-ɪlɪ; -əlɪ/ *adv*. **per·ki·ness** *n* [U].

perk[2] /pɜːk; pɝk/ *n* (usu *pl* 通常作复数) (*infml* 口) (**a**) money or goods received as a right in addition to one's pay; perquisite (工资以外的)财物补贴, 额外收入, 津贴, 奖金, 小费: *His perks include a car provided by the firm.* 他的额外津贴包括公司提供的一辆汽车. (**b**) advantage or benefit of a particular job, one's position, etc (工作、职位等带来的)好处, 利益, 便利, 特权, 优待: *One of the perks is the use of the official car park.* 其中一项好处是可以使用公家的停车场.

perk[3] /pɜːk; pɝk/ *v* = PERCOLATE 1.

perm /pɜːm; pɝm/ *n* **1** (*infml* 口) = PERMANENT WAVE (PERMANENT). **2** (*infml* 口) = PERMUTATION 1.

▷ **perm** *v* [Tn] **1** give (sb's hair) a permanent wave 烫(发): *Her hair has been permed.* 她的头发烫过了. **2** make a permutation of (numbers) in a football pool (足球普尔赌博中)选定(数字组合).

per·ma·frost /ˈpɜːməfrɒst; *US* -frɔːst; ˈpɝmə,frɔst/ *n* [U] subsoil that is permanently frozen, eg in polar regions 永冻土, 永冻层(如在极地的).

per·man·ence /ˈpɜːmənəns; ˈpɝmənəns/ *n* [U] state of continuing or remaining for a long time 永久; 永恒; 恒久: *Nothing threatens the permanence of the system.* 该体系的永恒性不受任何事物的影响.

▷ **per·man·ency** /-nənsɪ; -nənsɪ/ *n* (*fml* 文) **1** [U] = PERMANENCE. **2** [C] permanent thing (esp a job) 永久性的事物(尤指工作): *Is the new post a permanency?* 这一新职位是长期的吗?

per·man·ent /ˈpɜːmənənt; ˈpɝmənənt/ *adj* (**a**) lasting or expected to last for a long time or for ever 永久的; 永恒的; 长久的; 长期的: *She is looking for permanent employment.* 她正在找固定的工作. ○ *The injury left him with a permanent limp.* 他受伤后就一直瘸了. (**b**) not likely to change 不大可能改变的: *my permanent address* 我的固定地址. Cf 参看 IMPERMANENT, TEMPORARY. ▷ **per·man·ently** *adv*.

□ ,**permanent ˈwave** (*fml* 文) (*abbr* 缩写 **perm**) (*US* **permanent**) method of styling the hair in which it is treated with chemicals and set in waves or curls that last for several months (化学)烫发.

,**permanent ˈway** (*Brit*) railway track, ballast and sleepers on which the track is laid 铁路钢轨; 铁路路基.

per·man·gan·ate /pəˈmæŋɡəneɪt; pɝˈmæŋɡə,net/ (also **po,tassium perˈmanganate**, **per,manganate of ˈpotash**) *n* [U] dark purple salt of an acid containing manganese, used as a disinfectant and antiseptic when dissolved in water 高锰酸钾.

per·meate /ˈpɜːmɪeɪt; ˈpɝmɪ,et/ *v* [Ipr, Tn] **~ (through) sth** (*fml* 文) enter sth and spread to every part 弥漫; 散布; 充满; 遍布: *Water has permeated (through) the soil.* 水已渗遍那片土壤. ○ *The smell of cooking permeates (through) the flat.* 整套房间都弥漫着做菜的气味. ○ (*fig* 比喻) *A mood of defeat permeated the whole army.* 失败的情绪感染了全军.

▷ **per·meable** /ˈpɜːmɪəbl; ˈpɝmɪəbl/ *adj* (*fml* 文) that can be permeated by fluids or gas; porous 可渗入的; 可渗透的. Cf 参看 IMPERMEABLE. **per·meab·il·ity** /,pɜːmɪəˈbɪlətɪ; ,pɝmɪəˈbɪlətɪ/ *n* [U].

per·mea·tion /,pɜːmɪˈeɪʃn; ,pɝmɪˈeʃən/ *n* [U] (*fml* 文) permeating or being permeated 弥漫; 散布; 充满; 遍布.

per·miss·ible /pəˈmɪsəbl; pɚˈmɪsəbl/ *adj* (*fml* 文) that is or may be allowed 容许的; 可准许的: *Delay is not permissible, even for a single day.* 不得延误, 即使一日亦不可. ○ *driving with more than the permissible level of alcohol in the blood* 在血液中酒精含量超过许可标准的情况下开车. ▷ **per·miss·ibly** /-əblɪ; -əblɪ/ *adv*.

per·mis·sion /pəˈmɪʃn; pɚˈmɪʃən/ *n* [U] **~ (to do sth)** act of allowing sb to do sth; consent 许可; 准许; 允许; 同意: *You have my permission to leave.* 我准你离开. ○ *She refused to give her permission.* 她拒不同意. ○ *They entered the area without permission.* 他们未经许可擅入该地. ○ *with your (kind) permission*, ie if you will allow me 如蒙俯允.

per·miss·ive /pəˈmɪsɪv; pɚˈmɪsɪv/ *adj* [usu attrib 通常作定语] (*often derog* 常作贬义) (**a**) allowing great freedom of behaviour, esp to children or in sexual matters 纵容的, 放任的(尤指对儿童或性关系): *a permissive upbringing* 放任的教养 ○ *permissive parents* 纵容子女的父母. (**b**) showing this freedom 显示纵容或放任的(尤指对儿童或性关系): *permissive attitudes, behaviour* 放任的态度、行为 ○ *the permissive society*, ie the one resulting from social changes that began in the 1960s, with eg greater freedom of sexual behaviour, lessening of censorship, etc 放任的社会(60年代社会变化的产物, 如性解放、放宽审查尺度等).

▷ **per·miss·ively** *adv*: *children who have been brought up permissively* 娇生惯养的儿童.

per·miss·ive·ness *n* [U] being permissive in outlook or behaviour (看法或行为的)纵容, 放任.

per·mit /pəˈmɪt; pɚˈmɪt/ *v* (**-tt-**) (*fml* 文) **1** [Tn, Tg, Dn·n, Dn·t] give permission for (sth); allow 允许, 许可, 容许(某事物): *Dogs are not permitted in the building.* 不得携狗进入楼内. ○ *We do not permit smoking in the office.* 在我们的办公室里不准吸烟. ○ *The prisoners were permitted two hours' exercise a day.* 允许犯人每天有两小时户外活动. ○ *Permit me to explain.* 容我解释一下. ○ *The council will not permit you to build here.* 委员会不会允许你们在这一带搞建筑. **2** [I, Tn, Cn·t] make (sth) possible 使(某事物)有可能性: *I'll come tomorrow, weather permitting*, ie if the weather doesn't prevent me. 要是天气许可, 我明天一定来. ○ *The new road system permits the free flow of traffic at all times.* 新的道路系统可使车辆在任何时候都畅通无阻. ○ *The windows permit light and air to enter.* 这些窗户采光及通风性能良好. **3** [Ipr no passive 不用于被动语态] (esp in negative sentences 尤用于否定句) **~ of sth** admit sth as possible; tolerate 认可; 容忍: *The situation does not permit of any delay.* 情势刻不容缓.

▷ **per·mit** /ˈpɜːmɪt; ˈpɝmɪt/ *n* official document that gives sb the right to do sth, esp to go somewhere 许可证; (尤指)通行证: *You cannot enter a military base without a permit.* 无通行证者不得擅入军事基地.

per·mu·ta·tion /,pɜːmjuːˈteɪʃn; ,pɝmjəˈteʃən/ *n* (*fml* 文) **1** (*esp mathematics* 尤用于数学) (**a**) [U] variation in the order of a set of things 排列; 置换. (**b**) [C] any one of these arrangements 一组排列: *The permutations of x, y and z are xyz, xzy, yxz, yzx, zxy, zyx.* x、y、z的排列是xyz、xzy、yxz、yzx、zxy、zyx. **2** (*infml* 口语作 **perm**) (*Brit*) (esp in football pools) selection of items from a group, to be arranged in a number of combinations (尤指足球普尔赌博中的)选定组合.

per·mute /pəˈmjuːt; pɚˈmjut/ *v* [Tn] vary the order or arrangement of (sth) 改变(某事物)的次序或排列.

per·ni·cious /pəˈnɪʃəs; pɚˈnɪʃəs/ *adj* (*fml* 文) **~ (to sb/sth)** having a very harmful or destructive effect (on sb/sth) 有害的; 恶性的; 破坏性的: *a pernicious influence on society* 对社会有害的影响 ○ *a pernicious campaign to blacken his character* 旨在诋毁他的人格的恶意宣传活动 ○ *Pollution of the water supply reached a level pernicious to the health of the population.* 水源污染已达到危及居民健康的程度. ▷ **per·ni·ciously** *adv*. **per·ni·cious·ness** *n* [U].

□ **per,nicious aˈnaemia** (*medical* 医) severe form of anaemia that is sometimes fatal 恶性贫血.

per·nick·ety /pəˈnɪkətɪ; pɚˈnɪkɪtɪ/ *adj* (*infml often derog* 口, 常作贬义) worrying too much about details or unimportant things; fussy 吹毛求疵的; 爱挑剔的.

per·ora·tion /ˌperəˈreɪʃn; ˌpɛroˈreʃən/ *n* (*fml* 文) **1** last part of a speech; summing up (演讲的)结尾, 总结, 结论. **2** (*often derog* 常作贬义) lengthy speech 冗长的演说: *We had to listen to a peroration on the evils of drink!* 我们得听一个关于酗酒害处的冗长报告!

per·ox·ide /pəˈrɒksaɪd; pəˈrɑksaɪd/ *n* [U] **1** any of several compounds of oxygen with another element, containing the maximum proportion of oxygen 过氧化物. **2** (also ˌ**hydrogen peˈroxide**, **pe,roxide of ˈhydrogen**) colourless liquid used as an antiseptic and to bleach hair 过氧化氢: [attrib 作定语] *a peroxide blonde*, ie a woman with hair that has been bleached with peroxide 假金发女子(头发经漂染处理的).

▷ **per·ox·ide** *v* [Tn] bleach (hair) with hydrogen peroxide 用过氧化氢漂白(头发): *peroxided curls* 漂白过的鬈发.

per·pen·dic·ular /ˌpɜːpənˈdɪkjʊlə(r); ˌpɝpənˈdɪkjəlɚ/ *adj* **1 ~ (to sth)** at an angle of 90° (to another line or surface) 成直角的; 垂直的: *a line drawn perpendicular to another* 向一线引一垂线. **2** at a right angle to the horizontal; upright 竖立的; 直立的: *the perpendicular marble columns of a Greek temple* 希腊庙宇直立的大理石柱. **3** (of a cliff, rock-face, etc) rising very steeply (指悬崖、石壁等)陡峭的, 壁立的: *The valley ended in a perpendicular rim of granite.* 那山谷的尽头是花岗石的断崖. **4** (also **Perpendicular**) (*architecture* 建) of the style of English Gothic architecture in the 14th and 15th centuries, characterized by the use of vertical lines in its decoration 垂直式的(14-15世纪英国哥特式建筑风格的).

▷ **per·pen·dic·ular** *n* **1** [C] perpendicular line 垂直线. **2** (also **the perpendicular**) [U] perpendicular position or direction 垂直; 垂直方向: *The wall is a little out of (the) perpendicular.* 那墙有点倾斜.

per·pen·dic·ular·ity /ˌpɜːpənˌdɪkjʊˈlærətɪ; ˌpɝpənˌdɪkjəˈlærətɪ/ *n* [U].

per·pen·dic·ularly *adv*.

per·pet·rate /ˈpɜːpɪtreɪt; ˈpɝpəˌtret/ *v* [Tn] (*fml or joc* 文或谑) (**a**) commit (a crime, etc) 犯(罪等): *perpetrate a dreadful outrage* 犯下暴行. (**b**) be guilty of (a blunder, an error, etc) 做(错事); 犯(过失): *Who perpetrated that dreadful extension to the front of the building?* 谁在那楼房正面加盖了那么一截讨厌的建筑物?

▷ **per·pet·rat·ion** /ˌpɜːpɪˈtreɪʃn; ˌpɝpəˈtreʃən/ *n* [U].

per·pet·rator *n* person who commits a crime or does sth considered outrageous 犯罪者; 作恶者; 犯过者: *the perpetrator of a hoax* 诈骗犯.

per·petual /pəˈpetʃʊəl; pɚˈpɛtʃʊəl/ *adj* [usu attrib 通常作定语] **1** continuing indefinitely; permanent 永久的; 永恒的: *the perpetual snow of the Arctic* 北极终年不化的积雪. **2** without interruption; continuous 不间断的; 持续的: *the perpetual noise of traffic* 不绝于耳的交通噪音. **3** (*infml* 口) frequently repeated; continual 反复的; 不断的: *He was irritated by their perpetual complaints.* 他们一再发牢骚把他惹火了. ▷ **per·petu·ally** /-tʃʊəlɪ; -tʃʊəlɪ/ *adv*.

□ **per,petual ˈmotion** [U] movement (eg of an imagined machine) that would continue for ever without getting power from an outside source 永动(不需外加能量永久运转, 如假想的机器).

per·petu·ate /pəˈpetʃʊeɪt; pɚˈpɛtʃʊˌet/ *v* [Tn] cause (sth) to continue 使(某事物)永久、永存或持续: *These measures will perpetuate the hostility between the two groups.* 采取这些措施势必使那两集团永远对立. ○ *They decided to perpetuate the memory of their leader by erecting a statue.* 他们为永远纪念那位领袖决定建一座雕像. ▷ **per·petu·ation** /pəˌpetʃʊˈeɪʃn; pɚˌpɛtʃʊˈeʃən/ *n* [U].

per·petu·ity /ˌpɜːpɪˈtjuːətɪ; *US* -ˈtuː-; ˌpɝpəˈtuətɪ/ *n* (idm 习语) **in perpetuity** (*fml* 文) for ever; permanently 永久; 永恒; 永远: *The site of the memorial is granted in perpetuity to Canada.* 纪念馆址已选定在加拿大作为永久的纪念.

per·plex /pəˈpleks; pɚˈplɛks/ *v* [Tn] make (sb) feel puzzled or confused; bewilder 使(某人)困惑、糊涂或迷惑: *The question perplexed me.* 那问题把我难住了. ○ *We were perplexed by his failure to answer the letter.* 他何以不复信, 我们大惑不解. ○ *The whole affair is very perplexing.* 整件事令人感到莫名其妙.

▷ **per·plexed** *adj* puzzled or confused 困惑的; 糊涂的: *The audience looked perplexed.* 听众看样子都没听懂. ○ *She had to explain her behaviour to her perplexed supporters.* 她要向那些不明所以的拥护者解释自己的那种行为. ○ *He gave her a perplexed look.* 他茫然地看了她一眼. **per·plex·edly** /-ɪdlɪ; -ɪdlɪ/ *adv*: *'What is this?' he asked perplexedly.* '这是什么?'他困惑地问道.

per·plex·ity /-ətɪ; -ətɪ/ *n* [U] **1** state of being perplexed; bewilderment 困惑; 混乱: *She looked at us in perplexity.* 她茫然地望着我们. **2** state of being complicated or difficult 复杂; 困难: *a problem of such perplexity that it was impossible to solve* 复杂得无法解决的问题.

per pro /ˌpɜː ˈprəʊ; ˌpɝ ˈpro/ *abbr* 缩写 = PP 2.

per·quis·ite /ˈpɜːkwɪzɪt; ˈpɝkwəzɪt/ *n* (esp pl 尤作复数) (*fml* 文) **1** (*infml* 口语作 **perk**) money or goods given or regarded as a right in addition to one's pay (工资以外的)财物补贴, 额外收入, 津贴, 奖金, 小费: *Perquisites include the use of the company car.* 福利包括可以使用公司的汽车. **2** special advantage or right enjoyed as a result of one's position (随职位而得到的)好处, 利益, 便利, 特权, 优待: *Politics in Britain used to be the perquisite of the property-owning classes.* 英国的政治以往是有产阶级的特权.

perry /ˈperɪ; ˈpɛrɪ/ *n* (**a**) [U] drink made from the fermented juice of pears 梨酒. (**b**) [C] glass of this 一杯梨酒. Cf 参看 CIDER.

pers *abbr* 缩写 = person; personal.

per se /ˌpɜː ˈseɪ; ˈpɝˈsi/ (*Latin* 拉) by or of itself; intrinsically 本身; 本质上: *The drug is not harmful per se, but is dangerous when taken with alcohol.* 该药本身并无害处, 但与酒类同服则有危险.

per·se·cute /ˈpɜːsɪkjuːt; ˈpɝsɪˌkjut/ *v* **1** [esp passive 尤用于被动语态: Tn, Tn·pr] **~ sb (for sth)** treat sb cruelly, esp because of his race, his political or religious beliefs, etc 迫害某人(尤指基于种族、政治或宗教信仰等原因): *Throughout history religious minorities have been persecuted (for their beliefs).* 纵观历史, 宗教上的少数派始终(因其信仰关系)受迫害. **2** [Tn, Tn·pr] **~ sb (with sth)** allow no peace to sb; hound sb 烦扰、困扰或骚扰某人: *Once the affair became public, he was persecuted by the press.* 事情公开后, 他便受到新闻界的纠缠.

▷ **per·se·cu·tion** /ˌpɜːsɪˈkjuːʃn; ˌpɝsɪˈkjuʃən/ *n* (**a**) [U] persecuting or being persecuted 迫害; 烦扰; 困扰; 骚扰: *his persecution of his political opponents* 他对政治反对派的迫害 ○ *They suffered persecution for their beliefs.* 他们因信仰问题受到迫害. (**b**) [C] instance of this 迫害; 烦扰; 困扰; 骚扰: *He is writing a history of the persecutions endured by his race.* 他在写一部关于其种族所受迫害的历史书. **perseˈcution complex** (also **perseˈcution mania**) (*psychology* 心) insane belief that one is being persecuted 受迫害妄想狂.

per·se·cutor *n* person who persecutes others 迫害者: *His persecutors were severely punished.* 迫害他的人受到了严厉的惩处.

per·se·vere /ˌpɜːsɪˈvɪə(r); ˌpɝsəˈvɪr/ *v* [I, Ipr] **~ (at/in/**

with sth); ~ (with sb) (*usu approv* 通常作褒义) continue trying to do sth, esp in spite of difficulty 坚持做某事(尤指不畏困难): *You'll need to persevere if you want the business to succeed.* 要想事业成功, 就得持之以恒. ○ *She persevered in her efforts to win the championship.* 她为赢得冠军而不断努力. ○ *It's difficult, but I'm going to persevere with it.* 难是难, 但我一定坚持到底. ○ *He was hopeless at French, but his teacher persevered with him.* 他怎么也学不会法语, 可是老师仍锲而不舍地帮助他.

▷ **per·se·ver·ance** /ˌpɜːsɪˈvɪərəns; ˌpɝsəˈvɪrəns/ *n* [U] continued steady effort to achieve an aim; steadfastness 坚持不懈; 不屈不挠: *After months of disappointment, his perseverance was finally rewarded.* 数月来他经历挫折而不断努力, 终于有了收获. ○ *perseverance in the face of extreme hardship* 面对极端困苦而百折不挠.

per·se·ver·ing /ˌpɜːsɪˈvɪərɪŋ; ˌpɝsəˈvɪrɪŋ/ *adj* showing perseverance 坚持的; 不屈不挠的: [attrib 作定语] *persevering efforts* 坚持不懈的努力 ○ *A few persevering climbers finally reached the top.* 少数几个攀登者坚忍不拔, 终于登上了顶峰. **per·se·ver·ingly** *adv*.

Per·sian /ˈpɜːʃn; *US* ˈpɜːrʒn; ˈpɝʒən/ *adj* of Persia (now called Iran), its people or its language 波斯(现称伊朗)的; 波斯人的; 波斯语的.

▷ **Per·sian** *n* **1** [C] inhabitant of Persia 波斯人. **2** [U] language of Persia 波斯语.

□ ˌ**Persian** ˈ**carpet** (also ˌ**Persian** ˈ**rug**) carpet of traditional design from the Near East, handmade from silk or wool 波斯地毯.

ˌ**Persian** ˈ**cat** (also **Persian**) type of pure-bred cat with long silky hair 波斯猫.

ˌ**Persian** ˈ**lamb** silky curled fur, usu black, of a type of Asian lamb, used for coats; astrakhan 波斯羔羊皮(通常为黑色).

per·si·flage /ˈpɜːsɪflɑːʒ; ˈpɝsɪˌflɑʒ/ *n* [U] (*fml* 文) light good-humoured teasing; banter 戏谑; 打趣; 玩笑.

per·sim·mon /pəˈsɪmən; pɚˈsɪmən/ *n* **1** large orange-red plum-like edible fruit 柿子. **2** any of several types of tropical tree on which this grows 柿子树.

per·sist /pəˈsɪst; pɚˈsɪst/ *v* **1** [I, Ipr] **~ (in sth/in doing sth)** continue to do sth, esp in an obstinate and determined way and in spite of opposition, argument or failure 坚持; 执意: *If you persist, you will annoy them even more.* 你若固执, 他们就更恼火了. ○ *He will persist in riding that dreadful bicycle.* 他执意要骑那辆破自行车. ○ *She persists in the belief/in believing that she is being persecuted.* 她认定自己受到了迫害. **2** [Ipr] **~ with sth** continue doing sth in spite of difficulties 不畏困难继续做某事: *They persisted with the agricultural reforms, despite opposition from the farmers.* 他们不顾农民反对, 仍继续进行农业改革. **3** [I] continue to exist 持续; 存留: *Fog will persist throughout the night.* 雾将整夜不散. ○ *Loyalty to the former king still persists in parts of the country.* 该国一些地方仍有人忠于前国王.

▷ **per·sist·ence** /-əns; -əns/ *n* [U] (**a**) being persistent 坚持不懈; 执意; 持续; 存留: *His persistence was rewarded when they finally agreed to resume discussions.* 他们终于同意继续谈判, 这是他坚持不懈的结果. (**b**) continuing existence 继续存在: *The doctor couldn't explain the persistence of the high temperature.* 医生无法解释高烧何以持久不退.

per·sist·ent /-ənt; -ənt/ *adj* **1** refusing to give up 坚持的; 不屈不挠的: *She eventually married the most persistent of her admirers.* 她终于嫁给了最执着追求她的人. **2** (**a**) continuing without interruption 持续不断的; 不间断的: [attrib 作定语] *persistent noise, rain, pain* 持续的噪音、雨水、疼痛 ○ *persistent questioning* 无休止的讯问. (**b**) occurring frequently 反复出现的; 一再发生的: [attrib 作定语] *persistent attacks of coughing* 咳嗽的频繁发作 ○ *Despite persistent denials, the rumour continued to spread.* 尽管一再否认, 谣言还是不胫而走. **per·sist·ently** *adv*.

per·son /ˈpɜːsn; ˈpɝsn̩/ *n* (*pl* 复数作 **people** /ˈpiːpl; ˈpipl̩/ or, in formal or derogatory use, 作郑重或贬抑用词时复数作 **persons**). ⇨Usage at PEOPLE 用法见 PEOPLE. **1** human being as an individual with distinct characteristics (有某种个性或特性的)人: *He's just the person we need for the job.* 他正是我们需要的做那种工作的人. ○ *Here she is — the very person we were talking about!* 就是她——我们刚刚谈到的那个人. ○ *I had a letter from the people who used to own the corner shop.* 我收到从前街角那家商店的老板寄来的一封信. **2** (*fml or derog* 文或贬) (esp known or unspecified) human being (尤指已知的或非特指的)人: *A certain person* (ie somebody that I do not wish to name) *told me everything.* 有个人把一切都告诉我了. ○ *Any person found leaving litter will be prosecuted.* 禁扔垃圾, 违者必究. ○ (*law* 律) *accused of conspiring with person or persons unknown*, eg said when charging sb in court 被控与人合谋(如于法庭控告某人所说). **3** (*grammar*) any of the three classes of personal pronouns, the first person *'I/we'* referring to the person(s) speaking, the second person *'you'* referring to the person(s) spoken to, and the third person *'he, she, it, they'* referring to the person(s) or thing(s) spoken about 人称(第一人称 I/we 指谈话者, 第二人称 you 指谈话的对象, 第三人称 he、she、it、they 指谈及的人或事物). **4** (idm 习语) **about/on one's** ˈ**person** carried about with one, eg in one's pocket 带在身上(如在口袋里): *A gun was found on his person.* 从他身上搜出一枝枪. **be no/not be any respecter of persons** ⇨ RESPECTER (RESPECT[2]). **in** ˈ**person** physically present 亲身; 亲自; 本人: *The winner will be there in person to collect the prize.* 奖金需获奖者本人领取. ○ *You may apply for tickets in person or by letter.* 需票者可亲自来申请亦可来信索取. **in the person of sb** (*fml* 文) in the form or shape of sb 即某人; 乃某人; 其人: *Help arrived in the person of his father.* 前来帮忙的是他的父亲. ○ *The firm has an important asset in the person of the director of research.* 公司有一巨大财富, 就是研究部主任这个人.

□ ˌ**person-to-**ˈ**person call** *n* (*esp US*) telephone call made via the operator to a particular person and paid for from the time that person answers the phone 叫人电话(经接线员接通, 至指定受话人答话时起计费).

per·sona /pəˈsəʊnə; pɚˈsonə/ *n* (*pl* **-nae** /-niː; -ni/) (*psychology* 心) character of a person as presented to others or as others perceive it 面具人格; 伪装人格.

□ **per**ˌ**sona** ˈ**grata** /ˈɡrɑːtə; ˈɡrɑtə/ (*Latin* 拉) person who is acceptable to others, esp a diplomat acceptable to a foreign government 受欢迎的人(尤指受驻在国政府欢迎的外交官).

ˌ**persona non** ˈ**grata** /nɒn ˈɡrɑːtə; ˌnɑnˈɡrɑtə/ (*Latin* 拉) person who is not acceptable to others, esp to a foreign government 不受欢迎的人(尤指不受外国政府欢迎的): *He was declared persona non grata and forced to leave the country.* 他被宣布为不受欢迎的人而被迫离开该国. ○ (*joc* 谑) *He forgot to buy more coffee yesterday, so he was persona non grata at breakfast this morning!* 他因昨日忘了多买些咖啡, 今晨早餐上遂成为家中众矢之的.

per·son·able /ˈpɜːsənəbl; ˈpɝsn̩əbl̩/ *adj* [esp attrib 尤作定语] having a pleasant appearance or manner 英俊的; 有风度的: *The salesman was a very personable young man.* 推销员是个风度翩翩的年轻人. ▷ **per·son·ably** /-əblɪ; -əblɪ/ *adv*.

per·son·age /ˈpɜːsənɪdʒ; ˈpɝsn̩ɪdʒ/ *n* person, esp an important or distinguished one 人; (尤指)要人, 名人: *Political and royal personages from many countries attended the funeral.* 许多国家的政界要人和皇族人士参加了葬礼.

per·sonal /ˈpɜːsənl; ˈpɝsn̩l/ *adj* **1** [attrib 作定语] of or belonging to a particular person rather than a group or an organization 个人的: *one's personal affairs, beliefs* 私事、个人信仰 ○ *a car for your personal use only* 仅供你个人用的汽车 ○ *She made a personal donation to the fund.* 她以个人名义向基金会捐款. ○ *give sth the personal touch*, ie make it individual or original 使某事物带有个人色彩. **2** not of one's public or professional life; private 私人的: *a letter marked 'Personal'* 注明'亲收'字样的信件 ○ *Please leave us alone — we have something personal to discuss.* 请让我们单独在一起——我们有点私事要谈. ○ *His personal life is a mystery to his colleagues.* 他的同事认为他的私生活是个谜. **3** [attrib 作定语] done or made by a particular person 本人所做的: *The Prime Minister made a personal appearance at the meeting.* 首相亲临会议. ○ *I shall give the matter my personal attention.* 我将亲自过问此事. **4** [attrib 作定语] done or made for a particular person 为某个人所做的: *We offer a personal service to our customers.* 我们为

顾客提供个人服务. ○ *Will you do it for me as a personal favour?* 请你帮我个人一个忙行吗? ○ *a personal account,* ie a bank or building society account in a person's name (银行或房屋建筑协会的)个人帐户. **5** critical of a person's faults 人身攻击: *The argument was becoming too personal.* 那场争论已演变成过分的人身攻击了. ○ *Try to avoid making personal comments.* 尽量避免人身攻击. **6** [attrib 作定语] of the body 人身的; 身体的: *personal cleanliness, freshness, hygiene, etc* 身体的清洁卫生、活力、卫生等.

▷ **per·son·ally** /-ənəlɪ; -n̩lɪ/ *adv* **1** not represented by another; in person 亲身; 亲自: *She presented the prizes personally.* 她亲自颁奖. ○ *The plans were personally inspected by the minister.* 这计划经部长亲自审阅过. **2** as a person 作为个人; 就个人而论: *I don't know him personally, but I've read his books.* 我对他个人并不了解, 但我看过他的书. **3** (often at the beginning of a statement, followed by a comma 常用于一句话的开始, 后有逗号) as far as I am concerned; for myself 就我来说; 就自己而言: *Personally, I don't like him at all.* 就我而言, 我一点都不喜欢他. ○ *Personally speaking/Speaking personally, I'm in favour of the scheme.* 就本人而言, 我赞成这个计划. ⇨Usage at HOPEFUL 用法见 HOPEFUL. **4** (idm 习语) **take sth ˈpersonally** be offended by sth 为某事所触怒: *I'm afraid he took your remarks personally.* 我看他对你的话很不高兴.

□ **ˌpersonal asˈsistant** (*abbr* 缩写 **PA**) secretary who assists an official or a manager 私人秘书; 私人助理.

ˈpersonal column column in a newspaper or some other periodical for private messages or short advertisements 个人启事栏; 私人广告栏.

ˌpersonal ˈpronoun (*grammar*) any of the pronouns 人称代词 *I, me, she, her, he, him, we, us, you, they, them,* etc.

ˌpersonal ˈproperty (also **ˌpersonal eˈstate**) (*law* 律) property owned by a person, except land or income from land, that passes to his heir 动产. Cf 参看 REAL ESTATE (REAL[1]).

per·son·al·ity /ˌpɜːsəˈnælətɪ; ˌpɝsn̩ˋælətɪ/ *n* **1** [C] characteristics and qualities of a person seen as a whole 人格; 个性: *a likeable personality* 讨人喜欢的个性 ○ *She has a very strong personality.* 她个性很强. ○ *influences which affect the development of a child's personality* 影响儿童性格发展的因素. **2** [U, C] distinctive, esp socially attractive, qualities 特色(尤指社交上有吸引力的素质): *We need someone with lots of personality to organize the party.* 我们需要有个人见人爱的人来组织聚会. ○ *His wife was very beautiful, but seemed to have no personality.* 他的妻子很漂亮, 但似乎没有什么特点. **3** [C] famous person, esp in the world of entertainment or sport 名人(尤指娱乐界或体育界的): *personalities from the film world* 影界名流 ○ *a television personality* 电视圈中的名人 ○ *one of the best-known personalities in the world of tennis* 网球界最著名的人物之一. **4 personalities** [pl] critical or impolite remarks about a person 人身攻击; 诽谤: *indulge in personalities,* ie make such remarks 一味进行人身攻击 ○ *Let's keep personalities out of it,* ie avoid criticizing individual people. 咱们不要进行人身攻击.

□ **persoˈnality cult** (*often derog* 常作贬义) excessive admiration of a famous person, esp a political leader (对名人的)个人崇拜(尤指对政治领袖的).

per·son·al·ize, -ise /ˈpɜːsənəlaɪz; ˋpɝsn̩lˌaɪz/ *v* **1** [Tn esp passive 尤用于被动语态] mark (sth) in order to show that it belongs to a person, esp by putting his address or initials on it 在某物上作物主标志(尤指标示物主的地址或姓名的首字母): *handkerchiefs personalized with her initials* 有她的姓名首字母的手帕 ○ [attrib 作定语] *a personalized number-plate,* ie one on a car, with personally selected letters 有个人选择字母标记的汽车号码牌. **2** [Tn] cause (sth) to become concerned with personal matters or feelings 使(某事物)针对个人、带有个人感情或个人化: *We don't want to personalize the issue.* 我们不想把问题搞得个人化了.

per·son·ify /pəˈsɒnɪfaɪ; pɚˋsɑnəˌfaɪ/ *v* (*pt, pp* **-fied**) [Tn] **1** (**a**) treat (sth) as if it were a human being 将(某事物)人格化、拟人化: *The sun and the moon are often personified in poetry.* 诗歌中常把日、月拟人化. (**b**) represent (an idea, a quality, etc) in human form; symbolize 以人的形象表现(思想、品质等); 象征: *Justice is often personified as a blindfolded woman holding a pair of scales.* 常把蒙着眼睛手持天平的女人当作正义的象征. **2** be an example in human form of a quality or characteristic, esp one possessed to an extreme degree 为某品质或特点的化身(尤指极典型的): *He personifies the worship of money.* 他是拜金的化身. ○ *He is kindness personified.* 他是善良的化身.

▷ **per·soni·fica·tion** /pəˌsɒnɪfɪˈkeɪʃn; pɚˌsɑnəfəˋkeʃən/ *n* **1** (**a**) [U] treating sth that is without life as a human being or representing it in human form 人格化; 拟人化; 象征; 化身: *The personification of evil as a devil is a feature of medieval painting.* 用魔鬼象征罪恶是中世纪绘画的特色. (**b**) [C] instance of this 人格化; 拟人化; 象征; 化身. **2** [C usu *sing* 通常作单数] **~ of sth** person who possesses a quality or characteristic to an extreme degree 极具某品质或特点的人; 典型: *He looked the personification of misery.* 他那副样子可谓是苦难的典型. ○ *She was the personification of elegance.* 她是文雅的典范.

per·son·nel /ˌpɜːsəˈnel; ˌpɝsn̩ˋɛl/ *n* **1** [pl *v*] people employed in one of the armed forces, a firm or a public office; staff 人员; 职员: *trained personnel* 培训过的职员 ○ *Army personnel are not allowed to leave the base.* 军事人员不准离开基地. ○ *Airline personnel can purchase flight tickets at reduced prices.* 航空公司的职员可以优惠价购买飞机票. ○ [attrib 作定语] *a personnel carrier,* ie a ship or an aeroplane that carries troops 运兵的船(或飞机). **2** [Gp] (also **personˈnel department**) department in a firm which deals with employees, esp with their appointment and welfare 人事部门: *Personnel is/are organizing the training of the new members of staff.* 人事部门正在组织新雇员的培训. ○ [attrib 作定语] *personˈnel manager/officer* 人事部主任[负责人].

perspective 透视图

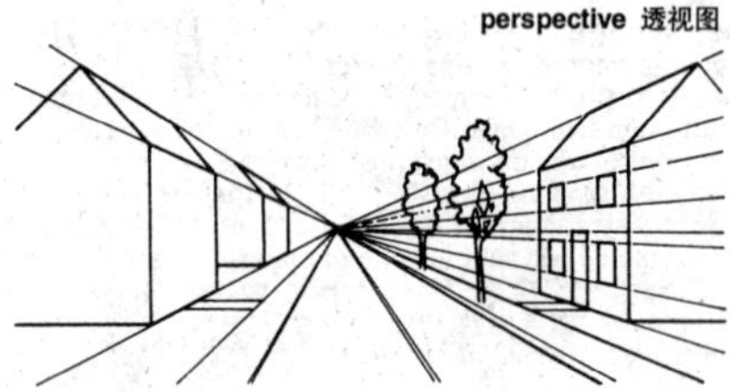

per·spect·ive /pəˈspektɪv; pɚˋspɛktɪv/ *n* **1** (**a**) [U] art of drawing solid objects on a flat surface so as to give the right impression of their height, width, depth and position in relation to each other 透视法: *She drew a row of trees receding into the distance to demonstrate the laws of perspective.* 她画了一排由近而远高度递减的树以演示透视法的规律. ○ [attrib 作定语] *a perspective drawing* 一幅透视画. (**b**) [C] drawing made this way 透视图. ⇨illus 见插图. **2** [C] view, esp one stretching into the distance 远景, 景(尤指由近而远的): *get a perspective of the whole valley* 取整个山谷的远景 ○ (*fig* 比喻) *a personal perspective of the nation's history* 国家历史之我见. **3** (idm 习语) **in/out of perspective** (**a**) showing the correct/incorrect relationship between visible objects 可见物体的位置或比例正确[不正确]; 按照[不按照]透视法: *draw the buildings in perspective* 按比例画某建筑物 ○ *That tree on the left of the picture is out of perspective.* 画中左边那棵树不合比例. (**b**) [U] in a way that does not exaggerate any aspect/that exaggerates some aspects 不夸大[夸大]; 恰当[不恰当]: *He sees things in their right perspective.* 他观察事物很正确. ○ *view/put/see sth in (its true/its proper) perspective* 从实际的[恰当的]角度观察[处置/看待]某事物 ○ *see the events in their historical perspective* 用历史的观点看待这些事件 ○ *get things badly out of perspective* 处事极为失当.

Per·spex /ˈpɜːspeks; ˋpɝˌspɛks/ *n* [U] (*propr* 专利名) strong transparent plastic material that is often used instead of glass because it does not splinter 有机玻璃(一种高强度透明塑料).

per·spic·acious /ˌpɜːspɪˈkeɪʃəs; ˌpɝspɪˋkeʃəs/ *adj* (*fml* 文) having or showing great insight or judgement;

discerning 有洞察力的；判断力强的；有识别力的：*a perspicacious analysis of the problem* 对问题的精辟分析 ○ *It was very perspicacious of you to find the cause of the trouble so quickly.* 你真是明察秋毫，问题的原因这么快就找出来了。▷ **per·spic·aciously** *adv.* **per·spi·ca·city** /ˌpɜːspɪˈkæsətɪ; ˌpɝspɪˈkæsətɪ/ *n* [U].

per·spic·uous /pəˈspɪkjʊəs; pɚˈspɪkjʊəs/ *adj* (*fml* 文) (**a**) expressed clearly 表达得清楚的. (**b**) (of a person) expressing things clearly; lucid (指人)有表达力的，表达清楚的. ▷ **per·spic·uously** *adv.* **per·spic·uous·ness**, **per·spi·cu·ity** /-ˈkjuːətɪ; -ˈkjuətɪ/ *ns* [U].

per·spire /pəˈspaɪə(r); pɚˈspaɪr/ *v* [I] (*fml* 文) give off moisture through the skin; sweat 出汗；流汗：*perspiring profusely after a game of squash* 壁球赛后大汗淋漓.

▷ **per·spira·tion** /ˌpɜːspəˈreɪʃn; ˌpɝspəˈreʃən/ *n* [U] (**a**) moisture given off by the body; sweat 汗；汗水：*drops of perspiration rolling down one's forehead* 从额头上滚落的汗珠. (**b**) process of giving off moisture through the skin 出汗；流汗：*Perspiration cools the skin in hot weather.* 天热时出汗可使皮肤降温.

per·suade /pəˈsweɪd; pɚˈswed/ *v* **1** [Tn, Tn·pr, Cn·t] **~ sb (into/out of sth)** cause sb to do sth by arguing or reasoning with him 说服或劝说某人做某事：*You try and persuade her (to come out with us).* 你去试试劝她(跟我们一起出去)吧. ○ *He is easily persuaded.* 他这人好说话. ○ *How can we persuade him into joining us?* 怎么才能说服他参加我们的活动呢? ○ *He persuaded his daughter to change her mind.* 他说服女儿改变主意. **2** [Tn esp passive 尤用于被动语态, Tn·pr esp passive 尤用于被动语态, Dn·f] **~ sb (of sth)** (*fml* 文) cause sb to believe sth; convince sb 使某人相信某事物；使某人信服：*I am not fully persuaded by the evidence.* 这证据不足以使我充分信服. ○ *We are persuaded of the justice of her case.* 我们确信对她案件的审理是公正的. ○ *How can I persuade you that I am sincere?* 怎样才能使你相信我是真心实意的呢?

per·sua·sion /pəˈsweɪʒn; pɚˈsweʒən/ *n* **1** [U] persuading or being persuaded 说服；劝说；信服：*Defeated by her powers of persuasion, I accepted.* 她的劝说很有力，我完全接受. ○ *After a lot of persuasion, he agreed to come.* 好说歹说，他才同意来. ○ *Gentle persuasion is more effective than force.* 温和的说服胜于压服. **2** [C] (group who hold a) set of (esp religious or political) beliefs 持有(尤指宗教的或政治的)信仰(的宗派)：*people of all persuasions* 持各种信仰的人们 ○ *He is not of their (religious) persuasion.* 他和他们的(宗教)信仰不同. **3** [sing] (*fml* 文) something that one believes; conviction 信念；见解：*It is my persuasion that the decision was a mistake.* 我认为那个决定是错误的.

per·suas·ive /pəˈsweɪsɪv; pɚˈswesɪv/ *adj* able to persuade; convincing 能说服人的；有说服力的；令人信服的：*a persuasive manner* 晓人以理的态度 ○ *persuasive arguments, reasons, excuses, etc* 有说服力的论据、理由、借口等. ▷ **per·suas·ively** *adv.* **per·suas·ive·ness** *n* [U]: *the persuasiveness of his argument* 他的论据的说服力.

pert /pɜːt; pɝt/ *adj* **1** (esp of a girl or young woman) not showing respect; cheeky (尤指女孩或年轻女子)无礼的，冒失的：*a pert child, reply* 无礼的孩子、回答 ○ *Don't be so pert!* 放庄重些! **2** (*esp US*) amusing; lively 好玩的；别致的；精神的：*a pert little red hat* 一顶别致的小红帽. ▷ **pertly** *adv.* **pert·ness** *n* [U].

per·tain /pəˈteɪn; pɚˈten/ *v* [Ipr] **~ to sth** (*fml* 文) (used esp in the continuous tenses 尤用于进行时态) **1** be connected with or relevant to sth 与某事物有关联：*evidence pertaining to the case* 与案件有关的证据. **2** belong to sth as a part of it 依附于或从属于某事物：(*law* 律) *the manor and the land pertaining to it* 庄园及其所属土地. **3** be appropriate to sth 符合于或适合于某事物：*the enthusiasm pertaining to youth* 青年特有的热情.

per·ti·na·cious /ˌpɜːtɪˈneɪʃəs; *US* -tnˈeɪʃəs; ˌpɝtnˈeʃəs/ *adj* (*fml* 文) holding firmly to an opinion or a course of action; determined 坚持的；固执的；坚决的：*His style of argument in meetings is not so much aggressive as pertinacious.* 他在会议上的辩论态度并非锋芒逼人而是坚持己见. ▷ **per·ti·na·ciously** *adv.* **per·ti·na·city** /ˌpɜːtɪˈnæsətɪ; *US* -tnˈæ-; ˌpɝtnˈæsətɪ/ *n* [U].

per·tin·ent /ˈpɜːtɪnənt; *US* -tənənt; ˈpɝtnənt/ *adj* **~ (to sth)** (*fml* 文) relevant (to sth); to the point 有关的；中肯的；恰当的：*pertinent comments, points, questions, etc* 中肯的意见、观点、问题等 ○ *remarks not pertinent to the matter we are discussing* 与我们正在讨论的事情不相干的话. ▷ **per·tin·ently** *adv.* **per·tin·ence** /-əns; -əns/ *n* [U].

per·turb /pəˈtɜːb; pɚˈtɝb/ *v* [Tn esp passive 尤用于被动语态] (*fml* 文) make (sb) very worried; disturb 使(某人)烦恼、不安：*perturbing rumours* 令人不安的谣言 ○ *We were perturbed to hear of his disappearance.* 我们听说他失踪了，都很不安.

▷ **per·turba·tion** /ˌpɜːtəˈbeɪʃn; ˌpɝtɚˈbeʃən/ *n* [U] (*fml* 文) state of being perturbed; anxiety 不安；烦扰；忧虑.

per·use /pəˈruːz; pəˈruz/ *v* [Tn] **1** (*fml* 文) read (sth), esp carefully or thoroughly 读(某篇文字)；(尤指)细阅，审阅：*peruse a document* 细阅一文件. **2** (*joc* 谑) read (sth) quickly and without concentrating 匆匆读或心不在焉地浏览(某篇文字)：*absent-mindedly perusing the notices on the waiting-room wall* 漫不经心地看等候室墙上的布告.

▷ **per·usal** /pəˈruːzl; pəˈruzl/ *n* [C, U] (action of) reading carefully 细读.

per·vade /pəˈveɪd; pɚˈved/ *v* [Tn] spread to and be perceived in every part of (sth) 弥漫，渗遍，遍布，充满(某处)：*The smell of baked apples pervaded the house.* 房子里弥漫着烤苹果的香味. ○ *a pervading sense of disaster* 普遍有大祸临头的感觉 ○ *Her work is pervaded by nostalgia for a past age.* 她的作品充满怀旧之情.

▷ **per·va·sion** /pəˈveɪʒn; pɚˈveʒən/ *n* [U] (*fml* 文) pervading or being pervaded 弥漫；渗透；遍布；充满.

per·vas·ive /pəˈveɪsɪv; pɚˈvesɪv/ *adj* present and perceived everywhere; pervading 无处不在的；遍布的；充斥各处的：*pervasive smell, dust, damp etc* 到处都有的气味、尘埃、湿气等 ○ *the pervasive mood of pessimism* 普遍存在的悲观情绪. ▷ **per·vas·ively** *adv.* **per·vas·ive·ness** *n* [U].

per·verse /pəˈvɜːs; pɚˈvɝs/ *adj* (*fml* 文) **1** (of a person) deliberately continuing to behave in a way that is wrong, unreasonable or unacceptable (指人)固执错误的，背理的，不合常情的：*a perverse child* 任性的孩子 ○ *You are being unnecessarily perverse.* 你无谓一意孤行. **2** [esp attrib 尤作定语] (of behaviour) stubbornly unreasonable (指行为)任性的，蛮不讲理的：*his perverse refusal to see a doctor* 他那拒不就医的固执态度 ○ *It would be perverse to take a different view.* 持异议之见未免不近情理. ○ *a perverse decision, judgement, etc*, ie one that ignores the facts or evidence 罔顾事实的决定、裁决等. **3** [esp attrib 尤作定语] (of feelings) unreasonable or excessive (指感情)不近情理的，过分的：*take a perverse pleasure in upsetting one's parents* 以忤逆父母作反常之乐 ○ *a perverse desire to shock* 故意使人吃惊的反常心理.

▷ **per·versely** *adv*: *She continued, perversely, to wear shoes that damaged her feet.* 她偏偏穿那双挤脚的鞋. **per·verse·ness, per·vers·ity** *ns* [U].

per·ver·sion /pəˈvɜːʃn; *US* -ʒn; pɚˈvɝʒən/ *n* **1** (**a**) [U] changing sth from right to wrong; perverting 变错；变坏；反常：*the perversion of innocence* 纯洁心灵的变坏 ○ *the perversion of the evidence to suit powerful interests* 因利欲熏心而颠倒是非. (**b**) [C] perverted form of sth; distortion 歪曲；颠倒；曲解：*Her account was a perversion of the truth.* 她所讲的歪曲了事实. **2** [U] (**a**) (esp of sexual feelings) being or becoming unnatural or abnormal (尤指对性的情感)反常，异常：*the perversion of normal desires* 欲望的反常. (**b**) [C] (esp sexual) taste or desire which has been perverted (尤指性的)变态心理，倒错：*the treatment of sexual perversion by psychotherapy* 用心理疗法医治性变态 ○ *His craving for publicity has become almost a perversion.* 他渴望出风头已迹近病态.

per·vert /pəˈvɜːt; pɚˈvɝt/ *v* [Tn] **1** turn (sth) away from its proper nature or use 误用，滥用(某事物)：*pervert the truth/the course of justice* 歪曲事实[妨碍司法公正] ○ *an expression whose meaning has been perverted by constant misuse* 积非成是的说法. **2** cause (a person, his mind) to turn away from what is right or natural 使(人、心理)入邪路、反常或堕落：*pervert (the mind of) a child* 把儿童(的思想)教坏 ○ *an idealist perverted by the desire for power* 被权欲引入歧途的理想主义者 ○ *Do pornographic books pervert those who read them?* 看色情

P

书刊能诱人堕落吗? ○ *a perverted desire to make others suffer* 虐待他人的反常心理.

▷ **per·vert** /ˈpɜːvɜːt; ˋpɝvɝt/ *n* (*derog* 贬) person whose (esp sexual) behaviour is considered abnormal or unacceptable 走上邪路者; 堕落者; 反常者; (尤指)性变态者, 性欲倒错者.

pe·seta /pəˈseɪtə; pəˈsetə/ *n* (**a**) unit of money in Spain; 100 centimos 比塞塔(西班牙货币单位, 等于100分). (**b**) coin of this value 一比塞塔硬币.

pesky /ˈpeskɪ; ˋpɛskɪ/ *adj* (**-ier, -iest**) (*US infml* 口) causing trouble; annoying 引起麻烦的; 恼人的: *pesky kids, mosquitoes, weeds* 讨厌的孩子、蚊子、杂草.

peso /ˈpeɪsəʊ; ˋpeso/ *n* (*pl* **~s**) unit of money in many Latin American countries and the Philippines 比索(拉丁美洲国家和菲律宾的货币单位).

pess·ary /ˈpesərɪ; ˋpɛsərɪ/ *n* (*medical* 医) **1** small tablet placed in a woman's vagina and left to dissolve (to prevent conception or to cure an infection); vaginal suppository 阴道栓(避孕或治疗炎症的). **2** device placed in a woman's vagina to prevent conception (also **diaphragm pessary**) or to support the womb 子宫帽(避孕用的); 子宫托(治疗子宫下垂的).

pess·im·ism /ˈpesɪmɪzəm; ˋpɛsə,mɪzəm/ *n* [U] **1** tendency to be gloomy and believe that the worst will happen 悲观: *His pessimism has the effect of depressing everyone.* 他的悲观情绪感染得大家情绪低落. **2** (*philosophy* 哲) belief that evil will always triumph over good 悲观主义. Cf 参看 OPTIMISM.

▷ **pess·im·ist** /-ɪst; -ɪst/ *n* person who expects the worst to happen 悲观主义者: *It's easy to sell insurance to a pessimist.* 向悲观的人推销保险很容易. Cf 参看 OPTIMIST (OPTIMISM).

pess·im·istic /ˌpesɪˈmɪstɪk; ˌpɛsəˋmɪstɪk/ *adj* **~ (about sth)** influenced by or showing pessimism 悲观的; 悲观主义的: *a pessimistic view of the world* 对世界的悲观主义看法 ○ *After the pessimistic sales forecasts, production was halved.* 在做了悲观销售预测之后, 产量降低了一半. **pess·im·ist·ic·ally** /-klɪ; -klɪ/ *adv*.

pest /pest; pɛst/ *n* **1** [C] (*infml* 口) annoying person or thing 讨厌的人; 害人虫; 坑人的事物: *That child is an absolute pest — he keeps ringing the doorbell and then running away!* 那孩子讨厌极了——老是来按门铃, 按完就跑了! **2** [C] insect or animal that destroys plants, food, etc 害虫、害兽、害鸟等有害动物: *Stores of grain are frequently attacked by pests, especially rats.* 储存的谷物经常受损坏, 尤其是老鼠为患最甚. ○ *garden pests*, eg slugs, greenfly 花园中的害虫(如蛞蝓、蚜虫). Cf 参看 VERMIN 1. **3** [C, U] (*arch* 古) = PESTILENCE.

□ ˈ**pest control** [U] destruction of pests, eg with poison, traps, etc 消灭有害动物(如用毒药、诱捕装置等).

pes·ter /ˈpestə(r); ˋpɛstɚ/ *v* [Tn, Tn·pr, Dn·t] **~ sb (for sth); ~ sb (with sth)** annoy or disturb sb, esp with frequent requests 打扰或纠缠某人(尤指不断提出要求): *He told the photographers to stop pestering him.* 他告诉照相的人别再缠着他. ○ *The horses in the meadow were being pestered by flies.* 牧场上的马不断受马蝇滋扰. ○ *Beggars pestered him for money.* 乞丐缠着向他讨钱. ○ *He pestered her with requests for help.* 他缠着她要她帮忙. ○ *They pestered her to join in the scheme.* 他们不断要求她参与那计划.

pes·ti·cide /ˈpestɪsaɪd; ˋpɛstə,saɪd/ *n* [C, U] chemical substance used to kill pests, esp insects 消灭有害动物的化学药物; (尤指)杀虫剂: *The flea-infested room had to be sprayed with a strong pesticide.* 房间里有跳蚤, 得喷强力杀虫剂. Cf 参看 INSECTICIDE (INSECT).

pes·ti·lence /ˈpestɪləns; ˋpɛstl̩əns/ (also **pest**) *n* [C, U] (*arch* 古) (any of various types of) deadly infectious disease that spreads quickly through large numbers of people, esp bubonic plague 瘟疫; (尤指)腺鼠疫.

▷ **pes·ti·lent** /-ənt; -ənt/ (also **pes·ti·len·tial** /ˌpestɪˈlenʃl; ˌpɛstl̩ˋɛnʃəl/) *adj* **1** of or like a pestilence (似)瘟疫的, 腺鼠疫的. **2** [attrib 作定语] (*infml* 口) very irritating 极讨厌的; 极恼人的; 极可恶的: *the pestilential noise of aeroplanes coming in to land* 飞机着陆的讨厌噪音 ○ *We must get rid of these pestilential flies.* 我们得把这些可恶的苍蝇消灭掉.

pestle /ˈpesl; ˋpɛsl̩/ *n* heavy round-ended tool used for crushing and grinding things to powder, esp in a special

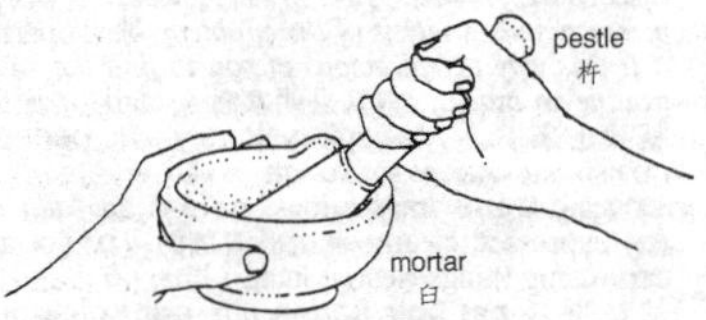

bowl (*mortar*) (捣碎或研磨用的)杵.

pet[1] /pet; pɛt/ *n* **1** tame animal or bird kept as a companion and treated with care and affection 玩赏动物; 宠物: *They have many pets, including three cats.* 他们有很多宠物, 猫就有三只. ○ [attrib 作定语] *a pet mouse, snake, lamb, etc* 作宠物的老鼠、蛇、羊羔等 ○ *pet food* 饲养宠物的食物. **2** (**a**) (*often derog* 常作贬义) (used esp in the expressions shown 尤用于以下示例) person treated as a favourite 宠儿; 宝贝: *(a/the) teacher's pet* 老师的得意门生 ○ *make a pet of sb* 宠爱某人. (**b**) thing that is given special attention by sb 某人特别关心的事物: [attrib 作定语] *a pet project, theory, cause, etc* 深受重视的工程、理论、事业等 ○ *one's pet hate/aversion* 耿耿于心的仇恨[反感]. **3** (*infml* 口) (**a**) kind or lovable person 善良的人; 讨人喜欢的人: *Their daughter is a perfect pet.* 他们的女儿很可爱. ○ *Be a pet and post this letter for me.* 做件好事, 替我把信发了吧. (**b**) (used as a term of affection, esp for a child or young woman 用作亲昵的称呼, 尤用于孩子或年轻女子): *That's kind of you, pet.* 谢谢你, 小宝贝.

▷ **pet** *v* (**-tt-**) **1** [Tn] treat (esp an animal) with affection, esp by stroking it 宠爱(尤指动物); (尤指)抚摸(动物). **2** [I] (*infml* 口) (of a man and a woman) kiss and caress each other (指男女)亲吻和爱抚: *heavy* (ie passionate) *petting* 热烈亲吻和爱抚.

□ ˈ**pet name** name used affectionately, that is different from, or a short form of, a person's real name 爱称; 昵称. ⇨App 7 见附录7.

ˈ**pet shop** shop where animals, birds etc are sold as pets 宠物商店.

pet ˈ**subject** subject that obsesses one; hobby-horse 爱讲的话题: *Once he starts talking about censorship you can't stop him — it's his pet subject.* 他一谈起新闻检查一类的事, 你就别想让他停——那是他最爱讲的话题.

pet[2] /pet; pɛt/ *n* (idm 习语) **in a** ˈ**pet** in a fit of bad temper, esp about sth trivial 发脾气, 生气(尤指为小事): *There's no need to get in a pet about it!* 没必要为这件小事发火!

petal /ˈpetl; ˋpɛtl̩/ *n* any of the delicate, coloured, leaf-like divisions of a flower 花瓣: *yellow petals with black markings* 带黑纹的黄色花瓣 ○ ˈ*rose petals* 玫瑰花瓣. ⇨illus at App 1 见附录1插图, page ii.

▷ **pet·alled** (*US* **pet·aled**) /ˈpetld; ˋpɛtl̩d/ *adj* (esp in compounds 尤用以构成复合词) having petals 有花瓣的: *a four-petalled flower* 有四瓣的花 ○ *blue-petalled flowers* 蓝瓣的花.

pe·tard /peˈtɑːd; pɪˋtɑrd/ *n* (idm 习语) **hoist with one's own petard** ⇨ HOIST.

peter /ˈpiːtə(r); ˋpitɚ/ *v* (phr v) **peter out** decrease or fade gradually before coming to an end 逐渐减少; 渐渐消失: *The path petered out deep in the forest.* 小路漫漫消失在密林深处. ○ *The story begins dramatically but the plot peters out before the end.* 这故事有些虎头蛇尾.

petit bour·geois /ˌpetɪ ˈbɔːʒwɑː; *US* -bʊərʒ-; ˌpɛtɪ ˋbʊrʒwa/ *n* (*pl* unchanged 复数不变) (*French* 法) member of the lower middle class 小资产阶级: [attrib 作定语] *petit bourgeois interests, occupations, prejudices, etc* 小资产阶级的情趣、职业、偏见等.

pe·tite /pəˈtiːt; pəˋtit/ *adj* (*approv* 褒) (of a girl or a woman) having a small and dainty physique (指女孩或妇女)娇小的.

pe·ti·tion /pəˈtɪʃn; pəˋtɪʃən/ *n* **~ (to sb)** **1** formal written request, esp one signed by many people appealing to sb in authority 请愿书: *a petition against closing the swimming-pool signed by hundreds of local residents* 数百名当地居民联合签名反对关闭游泳池的请愿书 ○ *get up a petition about sth* 就某事征集签名请愿. **2** (*law* 律) formal application made to a court (向法院呈交的)诉状. **3** (*fml* 文) earnest request, esp to

God; prayer 祈求；(尤指向上帝的)祈祷.

▷ **pe·ti·tion** *v* **1** [Dn·pr, Dn·t] **~ sb (for sth)** make a formal request to sb (for sth) (为某事)向某人祈求或请愿: *petition the government for a change in the immigration laws* 向政府请愿要求修改移民法 ○ *petition Parliament to allow shops to open on Sunday* 向国会请愿要求准许商店星期日营业. **2** [Ipr] **~ for sth** ask earnestly or humbly for sth 请求或恳求某事: (*law* 律) *petition for divorce*, ie ask a court of law to grant a divorce 请求批准离婚 ○ *petition for a retrial in the light of new evidence* 根据新证据请求重审. **pe·ti·tioner** /-ʃənə(r); -ʃənɚ/ *n* person who petitions, esp in a court of law 请愿人; (尤指)原告, 上诉人.

pet·rel /ˈpetrəl; ˋpɛtrəl/ *n* any of several types of black and white sea-bird that fly far from land 海燕. Cf 参看 STORMY PETREL (STORM).

pet·rify /ˈpetrɪfaɪ; ˋpɛtrə,faɪ/ *v* (*pt, pp* **-fied**) **1** [esp passive 尤用于被动语态: Tn, Tn·pr] **~ sb (with sth)** make sb unable to think, move, act, etc because of fear, surprise, etc 使某人惊呆或吓呆: *The idea of making a speech in public petrified him.* 一想到要在大庭广众面前讲演, 他就紧张得不知所措. ○ *I was absolutely petrified (with fear).* 我完全吓傻了. **2** [I, Tn] (cause sth to) change into stone (使某物)石化.

▷ **pet·ri·fac·tion** /ˌpetrɪˈfækʃn; ˌpɛtrəˋfækʃən/ *n* [U] petrifying or being petrified 惊呆; 吓呆; 石化.

petro- *comb form* 构词成分 **1** of petrol 石油的: *petrochemical*. **2** of rocks 岩石的: *petrology*.

pet·ro·chem·ical /ˌpetrəʊˈkemɪkl; ˌpɛtroˋkɛmɪkəl/ *n* [U, C] any of various chemical substances obtained from petroleum or natural gas 石油化学产品: [attrib 作定语] *the petrochemical industry* 石油化学工业.

pet·ro·dol·lar /ˈpetrəʊdɒlə(r); ˋpɛtro,dɑlɚ/ *n* US dollar earned by a country that exports petroleum 石油美元 (国家出口石油所得的美元).

pet·rol /ˈpetrəl; ˋpɛtrəl/ (*US* **gasoline**, **gas**) *n* [U] inflammable liquid obtained from petroleum by a refining process and used as a fuel in internal-combustion engines 汽油: *fill a car up with petrol* 给汽车的油箱灌满汽油 ○ *an increase in the price of petrol* 汽油价格的提高.

□ ˈ**petrol bomb** device (often a bottle) filled with petrol that explodes when it hits something 汽油弹(常为瓶中注入汽油者).

ˈ**petrol station** (also ˈ**filling station**, ˈ**service station**) (*US* ˈ**gas station**) place beside a road where petrol and other goods are sold to motorists 汽车加油站. Cf 参看 GARAGE 2.

ˈ**petrol tank** container for petrol in a motor vehicle (机动车的)汽油箱. ⇨illus at App 1 见附录1插图, page xii.

pet·ro·leum /pəˈtrəʊlɪəm; pəˋtrolɪəm/ *n* [U] mineral oil that forms underground and is obtained from wells sunk into the ground, from which petrol, paraffin, diesel oil, etc are obtained by processing 石油.

□ **pe**ˌ**troleum** ˈ**jelly** (*US* **petrolatum** /ˌpetrəˈleɪtəm; ˌpɛtrəˋletəm/) greasy jelly-like substance obtained from petroleum, used in ointments 矿脂; 凡士林.

pet·ro·logy /pəˈtrɒlədʒɪ; piˋtrɑlədʒɪ/ *n* [U] scientific study of rocks 岩石学.

▷ **pet·ro·lo·gist** /-dʒɪst; -dʒɪst/ *n* person who specializes in petrology 岩石学家.

pet·ti·coat /ˈpetɪkəʊt; ˋpɛtɪ,kot/ *n* woman's or girl's lightweight undergarment of dress length, worn hanging from the shoulders or the waist; slip 衬裙.

pet·ti·fog·ging /ˈpetɪfɒgɪŋ; ˋpɛtɪ,fɑgɪŋ/ *adj* (**a**) (of a person) paying too much attention to unimportant detail, esp in an argument (指人)吹毛求疵的, 挑剔的(尤指在争论中的). (**b**) unimportant; trivial 不重要的; 琐碎的: *pettifogging details, objections, etc* 无关宏旨的细节、异议等.

pet·tish /ˈpetɪʃ; ˋpɛtɪʃ/ *adj* (**a**) (of a person) childishly bad-tempered or impatient, esp about unimportant things (指人)爱发小孩脾气的, 任性的, 不耐烦的(尤指为小事). (**b**) (of a remark or act) said or done in a bad-tempered, petulant way (指言行)发脾气时说的或做的. ▷ **pet·tishly** *adv*. **pet·tish·ness** *n* [U]

petty /ˈpetɪ; ˋpɛtɪ/ *adj* (**-ier, -iest**) (*derog* 贬) **1** small or trivial; unimportant 小的; 琐碎的; 不重要的: *petty details, petty queries, regulations, troubles* 细节、小问题、琐碎的规章、小麻烦. **2** (**a**) concerned with small and unimportant matters 注重琐事的: *petty observance of the regulations* 遵守规章制度上的细节. (**b**) having or showing a small mind; mean 狭隘的; 器量小的; 小气的: *petty and childish behaviour* 小心眼和孩子气的行为 ○ *petty spite* 心胸狭窄的怨恨 ○ *a petty desire to have her revenge* 她想要报复的狭隘念头 ○ *petty about money* 金钱上很小气. ▷ **pet·tily** /ˈpetɪlɪ; ˋpɛtɪlɪ/ *adv*. **pet·ti·ness** *n* [U]: *The pettiness of their criticisms enraged him.* 他们鸡毛蒜皮地挑剔, 他十分气愤.

□ ˌ**petty** ˈ**cash** (usu small) amount of money kept in an office from or for small payments (通常指小额的)零用现金.

ˌ**petty** ˈ**larceny** theft of articles of small value 小偷小摸.

ˌ**petty** ˈ**officer** (*abbr* 缩写 **PO**) senior non-commissioned officer in the navy 海军士官. ⇨App 9 见附录9.

pet·ulant /ˈpetjʊlənt; *US* -tʃʊ-; ˋpɛtʃələnt/ *adj* unreasonably impatient or irritable 性急的; 暴躁的: *the petulant demands of spoilt children* 宠坏的孩子提出的任性要求.

▷ **pet·ulantly** *adv*. **pet·ulance** /-əns; -əns/ *n* [U]: *He tore up the manuscript in a fit of petulance.* 他一怒之下把手稿撕碎了.

pe·tu·nia /pəˈtjuːnɪə; *US* -ˈtuː-; pəˋtunjə/ *n* garden plant with funnel-shaped flowers in white, pink, purple or red 矮牵牛; 碧冬茄.

pew /pjuː; pju/ *n* **1** any of the long bench-like seats with a back and (usu) sides, placed in rows in a church for people to sit on 教堂长椅. ⇨illus at App 1 见附录1插图, page viii. **2** (*infml joc* 口, 谑) seat 座位 (used esp in the following expressions 尤用于以下示例): *Take/Grab a pew!* ie Sit down. 坐下吧!

pewit = PEEWIT.

pew·ter /ˈpjuːtə(r); ˋpjutɚ/ *n* [U] (**a**) grey metal made by mixing tin with lead, used (esp formerly) for making mugs, dishes, etc 白镴(锡、铅合金, 尤于旧时用以制缸子、碟等): [attrib 作定语] *pewter goblets, bowls, tankards, etc* 白镴高脚杯、碗、带把啤酒杯等. (**b**) objects made of this 白镴制品: *a fine collection of old pewter* 一批古白镴器皿.

pey·ote /peɪˈəʊtɪ; peˋotɪ/ *n* **1** [C] type of Mexican cactus; mescal 佩奥特掌(墨西哥仙人掌属植物). **2** [U] drug made from this which causes hallucinations; mescaline 仙人球毒碱(取自佩奥特掌的致幻药).

pfen·nig /ˈfenɪg; ˋfɛnɪg/ *n* (German coin of the value of) 100th part of a mark 芬尼(德国硬币, 为一马克的百分之一).

PG /ˌpiː ˈdʒiː; ˌpi ˋdʒi/ *abbr* 缩写 = **1** (*Brit*) (of films) parental guidance, ie containing scenes unsuitable for young children (指电影)须有家长指导观看的(有儿童不宜的镜头). **2** paying guest.

pha·go·cyte /ˈfægəsaɪt; ˋfægə,saɪt/ *n* type of white blood cell capable of protecting the body against infection because it absorbs bacteria (吞)噬细胞.

phal·anx /ˈfælæŋks; ˋfelæŋks/ *n* (*pl* **phalanges** /fəˈlændʒiːz; fəˋlændʒiz/ or **~es**) **1** (in ancient Greece) close formation, esp of infantry ready for battle (古希腊)方阵(尤指步兵作战时的). **2** number of people standing together to form a compact mass 密集队形: *a phalanx of riot police* 防暴警察的密集队伍. **3** (*anatomy* 解) any of the bones in a finger or toe 指骨; 趾骨. ⇨illus at SKELETON 见 SKELETON 插图.

phal·lus /ˈfæləs; ˋfæləs/ *n* (*pl* **-li** /-laɪ; -laɪ/ or **~es**) (esp in some religions) image of the erect penis as a symbol of the productive power of nature (尤指某些宗教的)视作生殖力象征的勃起的阴茎像.

▷ **phal·lic** /ˈfælɪk; ˋfælɪk/ *adj* of or like a phallus (似)阴茎像的: *phallic imagery, symbolism, symbols, etc* 阴茎的意象、象征、象征物等.

phant·asm /ˈfæntæzəm; ˋfæntæzəm/ *n* (*fml* 文) **1** thing seen in the imagination; illusion 幻象; 幻影; 幻觉; 幻想. **2** = PHANTOM.

▷ **phant·as·mal** /fænˈtæzməl; fænˋtæzməl/ *adj* (*fml* 文) of or like a phantasm (似)幻象的, 幻影的, 幻觉的, 幻想的: *phantasmal images, figures, etc* 幻想的形象、人物等.

phant·as·ma·goria /ˌfæntæzməˈgɒrɪə; *US* -ˈgɔːrɪə; ˌfæntæzməˋgɔrɪə/ *n* (*fml* 文) changing scene of real or imagined figures, etc, eg as seen in a dream or created as an effect in a film (真实的或想像的)变

幻情景(如梦中所见的); 幻觉效应(如电影中的).
phant·as·ma·goric /-ˈgɒrɪk; *US* -ˈgɔ:rɪk; -ˈgɔrɪk/ *adj* (*fml* 文) of or like a phantasmagoria (似)变幻情景的, 幻觉效应的.
phant·asy = FANTASY.
phantom /ˈfæntəm; ˋfæntəm/ *n* **1** (**a**) (also **phantasm**) ghostly image or figure; ghost 幽灵; 鬼魂: *the phantom of his dead father* 他亡父的幽灵 ○ [attrib 作定语] *the legend of the phantom ship* 鬼船的传说. (**b**) [esp attrib 尤作定语] (*joc* 谑) person whose actions are known about, but whose identity is (supposedly) not known 知其行为而不知其身分的人: *The phantom cake-eater has been here again!* 那神出鬼没的偷吃蛋糕的人又来过这儿了! **2** unreal or imagined thing, as seen in a dream or vision; illusion 不真实的或想像的事物; 梦幻之物; 幻觉: [attrib 作定语] *the phantom visions created by a tormented mind* 受折磨的心灵产生的幻觉 ○ *phantom pregnancy*, ie condition in which a woman wrongly believes she is pregnant and in which some of the symptoms of pregnancy may appear 精神性假妊娠.
Phar·aoh /ˈfeərəʊ; ˋfɛro/ *n* (title of the) ruler of ancient Egypt 法老(古埃及国王或其称谓).
phar·ma·ceut·ical /ˌfɑ:məˈsju:tɪkl; *US* -ˈsu:-; ˌfɑrməˋsutɪkl/ *adj* of or connected with the making and distribution of drugs and medicines 制药的; 配药的: *the pharmaceutical industry* 制药工业. ▷ **phar·ma·ceut·ics** /-ɪks; -ɪks/ *n* [sing *v*] = PHARMACY 1.
phar·ma·cist /ˈfɑ:məsɪst; ˋfɑrməsɪst/ *n* (**a**) person who has been trained to prepare medicines; pharmaceutical chemist 药剂师. (**b**) person trained in this way, whose job is to sell medicines 药商. Cf 参看 CHEMIST.
phar·ma·co·logy /ˌfɑ:məˈkɒlədʒɪ; ˌfɑrməˋkɑlədʒɪ/ *n* [U] scientific study of drugs and their use in medicine 药理学; 药物学.
▷ **phar·ma·co·lo·gical** /ˈfɑ́:məkəˈlɒdʒɪkl; ˌfɑrməkəˋlɑdʒɪkəl/ *adj* of or concerning pharmacology 药理学的; 药物学的: *pharmacological research* 药理研究.
phar·ma·co·lo·gist /-ˈkɒlədʒɪst; -ˋkɑlədʒɪst/ *n* person who specializes in pharmacology 药理学家; 药物学家.
phar·ma·co·poeia /ˌfɑ:məkəˈpi:ə; ˌfɑrməkəˋpiə/ *n* book containing a list of medicinal drugs and directions for their use, esp one officially published for use in a particular country 药典: *the British Pharmacopoeia* 英国药典.
phar·macy /ˈfɑ:məsɪ; ˋfɑrməsɪ/ *n* **1** [U] (study of the) preparation and giving out of medicines and drugs 药学; 药剂学; 制药; 配药. **2** [C] (**a**) place (eg in a hospital) where medicines are prepared and given out; dispensary 药房(如医院中的). (**b**) (*US* **drugstore**) (part of a) shop where medicines and drugs are sold; chemist's shop 药店; 药房; 医药用品商店.
pharynx /ˈfærɪŋks; ˋfærɪŋks/ *n* (*pl* **pharynges** /fəˈrɪndʒi:z; fəˋrɪnˌdʒiz/ or **~es**) (*anatomy* 解) cavity at the back of the mouth and nose, where the passages to the nose and to the mouth connect with the throat 咽. ⇨illus at THROAT 见 THROAT 插图.
▷ **pha·ryn·gitis** /ˌfærɪnˈdʒaɪtɪs; ˌfærɪnˋdʒaɪtɪs/ *n* [U] (*medical* 医) inflammation of the pharynx 咽炎.
phase /feɪz; fez/ *n* **1** [C] stage in a process of change or development 阶段; 时期: *a phase of history* 历史的一个阶段 ○ *a critical phase of an illness* 疾病的危险期 ○ *the most exciting phase of one's career* 事业上最得意的时期 ○ *The child is going through a difficult phase.* 那孩子正经历着困难的阶段. ○ (*infml* 口) *It's just a phase (she's going through)*, eg in childhood or adolescence. 就是(她正在经历的)那么一个阶段(如处于儿童时期或青春期). **2** [C] amount of the bright surface of the moon that is visible at a given time (new moon, full moon, etc) (月球的)位相, 消长盈亏(新月、满月等): *the phases of the moon* 月相. **3** (idm 习语) **in/out of phase** being/not being in the same state at the same time 同相[异相]; 同步[不同步]; 协调[不协调]: *The two sets of traffic lights were out of phase* (ie did not show the same change at the same time) *and several accidents occurred.* 那两组交通灯不同步因而发生了几起事故.
▷ **phase** *v* **1** [Tn esp passive 尤用于被动语态] plan or carry out sth in stages 按阶段计划或进行某事: *The modernization of the industry was phased over a 20-year period.* 工业现代化分20年逐步实现. ○ *a phased withdrawal of troops* 分阶段撤军. **2** (phr v) **phase sth in** introduce sth gradually or in stages 逐步或分阶段引进某事物: *The use of lead-free petrol is now being phased in.* 无铅汽油的应用现正逐步推广. **phase sth out** withdraw or discontinue sth gradually or in stages 逐步或分阶段撤出或中止某事物: *The old currency will have been phased out by 1990.* 旧币分阶段至1990年将全部禁止流通.
PhD /ˌpi: eɪtʃ ˈdi:; ˌpi etʃ ˋdi/ *abbr* 缩写 = Doctor of Philosophy 哲学博士学位; 博士学位: *have/be a PhD in History* 有历史学博士学位[为历史学博士] ○ *Bill Crofts PhD* 比尔·克罗夫茨哲学博士. Cf 参看 DPHIL.
pheas·ant /ˈfeznt; ˋfɛznt/ *n* (**a**) [C] (*pl* unchanged or **~s** 复数或不变或作 **pheasants**) any of several types of long-tailed bird that are often shot for sport and food, the male of which usu has brightly-coloured feathers 雉; 野鸡: *a brace of pheasants* 一对野鸡. ⇨illus at App 1 见附录1插图, page v. (**b**) [U] its flesh prepared as food 野鸡肉: *roast pheasant* 烧野鸡.
phe·no·bar·bit·one /ˌfi:nəʊˈbɑ:bɪtəʊn; ˌfinoˋbɑrbɪˌton/ *n* [U] medicinal drug that calms the nerves and helps one to sleep 苯巴比妥(用作镇静剂和催眠药).
phenol /ˈfi:nɒl; ˋfinol/ *n* [U] = CARBOLIC ACID.
phe·nom·enal /fəˈnɒmɪnl; fəˋnɑmənl/ *adj* **1** very remarkable; extraordinary 非凡的; 格外的; 了不起的: *the phenomenal success of the film* 影片非常成功 ○ *The rocket travels at phenomenal speed.* 火箭以惊人的速度飞行. ○ *The response to the appeal fund has been phenomenal.* 对呼吁募集基金的反应格外热烈. **2** (*fml* 文) of (the nature of) a phenomenon 现象的; 现象性质的.
▷ **phe·no·men·ally** /-nəlɪ; -nḷɪ/ *adv* (*infml* 口) to an amazing degree 惊人地: *Interest in the subject has increased phenomenally.* 人们对此事的兴趣激增.
phe·nom·enon /fəˈnɒmɪnən; *US* -nɒn; fəˋnɑməˌnɑn/ *n* (*pl* **-ena** /-ɪnə; -ənə/) **1** fact or occurrence, esp in nature or society, that can be perceived by the senses 现象: *natural, social, historical, etc phenomena* 自然的、社会的、历史的...现象 ○ *An eclipse of the moon is a rare phenomenon.* 月蚀是罕见的现象. ○ *Bankruptcy is a common phenomenon in an economic recession.* 在经济衰退时破产是常见的现象. **2** remarkable person, thing or event 非凡的人、物或事: *the phenomenon of their rapid rise to power* 他们迅速掌权的奇迹.
phew /fju:; fju/ (also **whew**) *interj* (written representation of a short soft whistling sound made by blowing out or sucking in one's breath, and used to express relief, exhaustion or amazement 呼气或吸气发出的很短的口哨声, 用以表示松口气、疲劳或惊奇): *Phew! That was a nasty moment — that car nearly hit us.* (发出口哨声)当时可真危险——那辆汽车差点撞上我们.
phial /ˈfaɪəl; ˋfaɪəl/ (also **vial**) *n* small glass container, esp one for liquid medicine or perfume 玻璃的小容器; (尤指)小药水瓶, 小香水瓶.
phil·an·der /fɪˈlændə(r); fəˋlændɚ/ *v* [I, Ipr] **~ (with sb)** (*usu derog* 通常作贬义) (of a man) amuse oneself by flirting with women (指男子)挑逗女子, 与女子调情: *He spent his time philandering with the girls in the village.* 他把时间花在和村子里的姑娘们调情上了. ▷ **phil·an·derer** /-dərə(r); -dərɚ/ *n* (*derog* 贬) man who does this 挑逗女子或与女子调情的男子: *He's a bit of a philanderer — don't take him too seriously!* 他这个人有点轻薄——别跟他太认真!
phil·an·thropy /fɪˈlænθrəpɪ; fəˋlænθrəpɪ/ *n* [U] (**a**) concern for the welfare of mankind; benevolence 博爱; 慈善; 仁慈. (**b**) charitable actions inspired by this 慈善行为; 善事.
▷ **phil·an·thropic** /ˌfɪlənˈθrɒpɪk; ˌfɪlənˋθrɑpɪk/ *adj* of or inspired by philanthropy 博爱的; 慈善的; 仁慈的: *philanthropic organizations*, eg to help poor or disabled people 慈善机构 ○ *philanthropic motives* 仁慈的动机. **phil·an·throp·ic·ally** /-klɪ; -klɪ/ *adv*.
phil·an·throp·ist /fɪˈlænθrəpɪst; fəˋlænθrəpɪst/ *n* person who helps others, esp through charitable work or donations of money 帮助他人的人; (尤指)慈善家, 捐款人: *The university was founded by a millionaire philanthropist.* 这所大学的创建人是位腰缠万贯的慈善家. Cf 参看 MISANTHROPIST.
phil·ately /fɪˈlætəlɪ; fəˋlætḷɪ/ *n* [U] (hobby of) collecting

and studying postage stamps 集邮(的爱好).
▷ **phil·atelic** /ˌfɪləˈtelɪk; ˌfɪləˈtɛlɪk/ *adj.*
phil·atel·ist /fɪˈlætəlɪst; fəˈlætl̩ɪst/ *n* **(a)** person who collects postage stamps 集邮者. **(b)** person with expert knowledge of postage stamps 邮票专家.

phil·har·monic /ˌfɪlɑːˈmɒnɪk; ˌfɪlɑrˈmɑnɪk/ *adj* (esp in names of orchestras, music societies, etc) devoted to or loving music (尤用于管弦乐队、音乐社团等名称中)爱好音乐的: *the London Philharmonic Orchestra* 伦敦爱乐管弦乐团.

phil·hel·lene /ˌfɪlˈheliːn; fɪlˈhɛlin/ *n, adj* (person) friendly to or admiring the Greeks and Greek civilization 爱希腊人及其文明的(人). ▷ **phil·hel·lenic** /ˌfɪlheˈliːnɪk; *US* -ˈlenɪk; ˌfɪlhɛˈlɛnɪk/ *adj.*

-philia *comb form* 构词成分 (forming *ns* 用以构成名词) **1** (esp abnormal) love of or fondness for (尤指不正常的)爱, 迷, 癖好. **2** inclination towards 倾向; 亲; 嗜: *haemophilia*. Cf 参看 -PHOBIA.
▷ **-phile** (also **-phil**) *comb form* 构词成分 (forming *ns* and *adjs* 用以构成名词和形容词) (person who is) fond of 爱好(者): *Anglophile* ○ *bibliophile*. Cf 参看 -PHOBE (-PHOBIA).
-philiac (forming *adjs* 用以构成形容词).

phil·ip·pic /fɪˈlɪpɪk; fɪˈlɪpɪk/ *n* (*fml* 文) speech bitterly attacking sb; invective (抨击某人的)演说; 痛斥.

phil·is·tine /ˈfɪlɪstaɪn; *US* -stiːn; ˈfɪləsˌtin/ *n* person who has no interest in or understanding of the arts, or is hostile to them; uncultured person 对艺术无兴趣或无认识的人; 讨厌艺术的人; 无教养的人: *He accused those who criticized his work of being philistines.* 他指责那些批评他的作品的人是对艺术一窍不通.
▷ **phil·is·tine** *adj* having no interest in or understanding of the arts, or being hostile to them 对艺术无兴趣的; 不懂艺术的; 讨厌艺术的: *The philistine attitude of the public resulted in the work being abandoned.* 由于公众对艺术不感兴趣, 那个作品备受冷遇.
phil·is·tin·ism /-tɪnɪzəm; -tɪnɪzəm/ *n* [U]: *the philistinism of the popular press* 为大众服务的新闻界对艺术缺乏认识.

phil(o)- *comb form* 构词成分 liking or fond of 喜好; 爱好: *philanthropy* ○ *philology*.

philo·logy /fɪˈlɒlədʒɪ; fɪˈlɑlədʒɪ/ *n* [U] science or study of the development of language or of a particular language 语文学; 语文研究. Cf 参看 LINGUISTICS (LINGUISTIC).
▷ **philo·lo·gical** /ˌfɪləˈlɒdʒɪkl; ˌfɪləˈlɑdʒɪkl/ *adj* of or concerning philology 语文学的; 语文研究的.
philo·lo·gist /fɪˈlɒlədʒɪst; fɪˈlɑlədʒɪst/ *n* expert in or student of philology 语文学家; 研究语文学的人.

philo·sopher /fɪˈlɒsəfə(r); fəˈlɑsəfɚ/ *n* **1 (a)** person who studies or teaches philosophy 研究或教授哲学的人; 哲学教师. **(b)** person who has developed a particular set of philosophical theories and beliefs 哲学家; 思想家: *the Greek philosophers* 希腊哲学家. **2 (a)** person whose mind is untroubled by passions and hardships 不受强烈感情和苦难左右的人; 豁达的人. **(b)** person whose life is governed by reason 哲人; 贤人. **(c)** (*infml* 口) person who thinks deeply about things 善于思考的人: *He's quite a philosopher.* 他很爱动脑筋.
□ **philosopher's ˈstone** imaginary substance which, it was formerly believed by alchemists, would change any metal into gold; elixir 点金石(旧时炼金术士认为能使金属变成黄金的物质).

philo·sophy /fɪˈlɒsəfɪ; fəˈlɑsəfɪ/ *n* **1 (a)** [U] search for knowledge and understanding of the nature and meaning of the universe and of human life 哲学: *moral philosophy*, ie study of the principles on which human behaviour is based; ethics 伦理学. **(b)** [C] any particular set or system of beliefs resulting from this search for knowledge 哲学体系: *the philosophy of Aristotle* 亚里士多德的哲学体系 ○ *conflicting philosophies* 互相矛盾的哲学体系. **2** [C] set of beliefs or an outlook on life that is a guiding principle for behaviour 人生哲学; 生活的信念或原则: *a man without a philosophy of life* 没有生活信念的人 ○ *Enjoy yourself today and don't worry about tomorrow — that's my philosophy!* 且享今朝乐, 莫管明朝愁——这就是我的人生哲学! **3** [U] calm quiet attitude towards life even in the face of suffering, danger, etc 即使面对困苦、危险等, 对生活仍持冷静沉着的态度; 达观: *The philosophy of the prisoners during their worst sufferings impressed even their captors.* 俘虏们在最困苦时仍处之泰然, 连捉住他们的人都深有感触.
▷ **philo·soph·ical** /ˌfɪləˈsɒfɪkl; ˌfɪləˈsɑfɪkl/, **philo·sophic** *adjs* **1** of or according to philosophy 哲学的; 根据哲学的: *philosophical principles* 哲学原则. **2** devoted to philosophy 研究哲学的: *philosophical works* 哲学著作. **3 ~ (about sth)** having or showing the calmness and courage of a philosopher(2); resigned 豁达的; 达观的; 处之泰然的: *She seemed fairly philosophical about the loss.* 她对所受损失似乎很看得开. ○ *He heard the news with a philosophical smile.* 他听到那消息后若无其事地付之一笑. **philo·soph·ic·ally** /-klɪ; -klɪ/ *adv*: *He accepted the verdict philosophically.* 他泰然自若地接受了那一裁决.
philo·soph·ize, -ise /fɪˈlɒsəfaɪz; fəˈlɑsəˌfaɪz/ *v* **1** [I] think or argue as or like a philosopher 像哲学家般思考或辩论. **2** [I, Ipr] **~ (about/on sth)** discuss or speculate 讨论; 思考: *They spend their time philosophizing about the mysteries of life.* 他们用很多时间探讨生命的奥秘.

phle·bitis /flɪˈbaɪtɪs; flɪˈbaɪtɪs/ *n* [U] inflammation of a vein 静脉炎.

phlegm /flem; flɛm/ *n* [U] **1** thick semi-liquid substance which forms in the air passages, esp when one has a cold, and which can be removed by coughing 痰. **2** (*dated or fml* 旧或文) quality of being slow to act or react, or to show feeling; calmness 迟钝; 冷漠; 冷静: *show considerable phlegm in facing the crisis* 面对危机表现得相当冷静.
▷ **phleg·matic** /flegˈmætɪk; flɛgˈmætɪk/ *adj* calm and even-tempered; showing the quality of phlegm(2) 冷静而温和的; 迟钝的; 冷漠的: *Commuting in the rush-hour requires a phlegmatic temperament.* 在上下班交通高峰期间乘坐通勤车要有安之若素的心境. **phleg·mat·ic·ally** /-klɪ; -klɪ/ *adv.*

phlox /flɒks; flɑks/ *n* [U] (*pl* unchanged or **~es** 复数或不变或作 **phloxes**) any of several types of garden plant with clusters of reddish, purple or white flowers 福禄考(园艺植物, 花簇生, 呈红色、紫色或白色).

pho·bia /ˈfəʊbɪə; ˈfobɪə/ *n* extreme or abnormal dislike or fear of sth; aversion (对某事物极端的或反常的)憎恶, 恐惧; 恐怖(症): *learning to control one's phobia about flying* 学会克服飞行的恐惧感 ○ *Dislike of snakes or spiders is a common phobia.* 害怕蛇或厌恶蜘蛛是很常见的事.

-phobia *comb form* 构词成分 (forming *ns* 用以构成名词) extreme or abnormal fear of 对...极端的或反常的恐惧; 恐怖: *claustrophobia* ○ *hydrophobia* ○ *xenophobia*. Cf 参看 -PHILIA.
▷ **-phobe** *comb form* 构词成分 (forming *ns* 用以构成名词) person who dislikes sth 憎恶某事物的人: *Anglophobe* ○ *xenophobe*.
-phobic *comb form* 构词成分 (forming *adjs* 用以构成形容词) having or showing extreme or abnormal fear of 对...极端或反常恐惧的: *claustrophobic* ○ *xenophobic*. Cf 参看 -PHILE (-PHILIA).

phoenix /ˈfiːnɪks; ˈfinɪks/ *n* mythical bird of the Arabian desert, said to live for several hundred years before burning itself and then rising born again from its ashes 长生鸟(神话中的鸟, 在阿拉伯沙漠中, 可活数百年, 然后自焚为灰而再生).

phone[1] /fəʊn; fon/ *n* **1** telephone 电话: *tell sb sth/order sth over the phone*, ie instead of writing 用电话把某事告诉某人[订购某物] ○ *The phone is ringing.* 电话铃响了. *communicating by phone* 通电话 ○ [attrib 作定语] *make a phone call* 打电话. **2** (idm 习语) **(be) on the ˈphone (a)** (be) talking on the phone 用电话交谈; 在通话: *You can't see her now — she's on the phone.* 你现在不能见她——她正在打电话. ○ *They've been on the phone for an hour.* 他们已通话一小时了. **(b)** (of a person, business, etc) having a telephone (指人或公司等)有电话: *Are you on the phone yet?* 你安电话了吗?
▷ **phone** *v* **1** [I, Ip, Tn, Tn·p] **~ (sb) (up)** telephone (sb) 给(某人)打电话: *Did anybody phone?* 有人打电话来吗? ○ *I'll phone them up now.* 我现在给他们打电话. **2** (phr v) **phone in** telephone (esp one's place of work) 打电话(尤指打至自己的工作处): *phone in sick*, ie telephone to say one is absent from work because of illness 打电话请病假.

□ 'phone book =TELEPHONE DIRECTORY (TELEPHONE). 'phone booth (also 'phone box) telephone kiosk; call-box 电话亭.

'phone-in (*Brit*) (*US* **call-in**) *n* radio or television programme in which telephoned questions and comments from listeners or viewers are broadcast (电台或电视台的)听众可来电话的直播节目(向主持人提问和作评论): [attrib 作定语] *a phone-in show* 有听众来电话的直播节目.

phone[2] /fəʊn; fon/ *n* (*linguistics* 语言) single sound (vowel or consonant) in speech 音子; 音素.

-phone *comb form* 构词成分 **1** (forming *ns* 用以构成名词) instrument using sound 使用声音的仪器: *telephone* ○ *dictaphone* ○ *xylophone*. **2** (forming *adjs* 用以构成形容词) speaking a particular language 说某种语言的: *anglophone* ○ *francophone*.

▷ **-phonic** *comb form* 构词成分 (forming *adjs* 用以构成形容词) of an instrument using sound 使用声音的仪器的: *telephonic*.

P

phon·eme /'fəʊni:m; 'fonim/ *n* (*linguistics* 语言) any one of the set of smallest distinctive speech sounds in a language that distinguish one word from another 音位; 音素: *English has 24 consonant phonemes.* 英语有24个辅音音素. ○ *In English, the 's' in 'sip' and the 'z' in 'zip' represent two different phonemes.* 英语中sip中的s和zip中的z为两个不同的音素.

▷ **phon·emic** /fə'ni:mɪk; fə'nimɪk/ *adj* of or concerning phonemes 音位的; 音素的. **phon·emic·ally** /-klɪ; -klɪ/ *adv*.

phon·em·ics *n* [sing *v*] study of the phonemes of a language 音位学.

phon·etic /fə'netɪk; fə'nɛtɪk/ *adj* (*linguistics* 语言) **1** of or concerning the sounds of human speech 语音的. **2** (of a method of writing speech sounds) using a symbol for each distinct sound or sound unit (指标音法)使用音标的: *phonetic symbols, alphabet, transcription* 音标、语音字母、标音. **3** (of spelling) corresponding closely to the sounds represented (指拼写)拼写与发音相似的: *Spanish spelling is phonetic.* 西班牙语的拼写与发音相似.

▷ **phon·et·ic·ally** /-klɪ; -klɪ/ *adv*.

phon·eti·cian /ˌfəʊnɪ'tɪʃn; ˌfonə'tɪʃən/ *n* expert in or student of phonetics 语音学家; 研究语音学的人.

phon·et·ics *n* [sing *v*] study of speech sounds and their production 语音学.

pho·ney (also **phony**) /'fəʊnɪ; 'fonɪ/ *adj* (**-ier -iest**) (*infml derog* 口, 贬) (**a**) (of a person) pretending or claiming to be what one is not (指某人)假装的, 冒充的: *There's something very phoney about him.* 他这人有些地方很假. ○ *a phoney doctor*, ie a quack doctor 冒牌医生. (**b**) (of a thing) false or faked (指事物)假的, 伪造的: *a phoney American accent* 假装的美国腔 ○ *phoney jewels, qualifications, mannerisms* 假珠宝、伪资格、矫饰的风格 ○ *some phoney excuse for the delay* 因延误而找的假借口 ○ *The story sounds phoney to me.* 我觉得这件事听起来有假.

▷ **pho·ney** (also **phony**) *n* (*pl* **~s**) phoney person or thing 冒充者; 伪造物; 赝品: *The man's a complete phoney.* 这个男子的身分是冒充的. ○ *This diamond is a phoney.* 这钻石是假的.

pho·ni·ness *n* [U].

phonic /'fɒnɪk; 'fɑnɪk/ *adj* **1** of or concerning sound 声音的. **2** of or concerning the sounds of speech 语音的.

phon(o)- *comb form* 构词成分 of sound or sounds 声的; 音的: *phonetic* ○ *phonograph*.

phono·graph /'fəʊnəgrɑ:f; *US* -græf; 'fonə,græf/ *n* (*dated* 旧) =RECORD PLAYER (RECORD).

phono·logy /fə'nɒlədʒɪ; fo'nɑlədʒɪ/ *n* [U] (*linguistics* 语言) **1** study of the system of speech sounds, esp in a particular language 音位学, 音韵学, 音系学(尤指某语言的): *a course in phonology* 音系学课程. **2** system of sounds in a particular language, esp at a particular point in its development 语音体系(尤指历时的): *the phonology of Old English* 古英语语音体系.

▷ **phono·lo·gical** /ˌfəʊnə'lɒdʒɪkl; ˌfonə'lɑdʒɪkl/ *adj*.

phono·lo·gist /fə'nɒlədʒɪst; fo'nɑlədʒɪst/ *n* expert in or student of phonology 音位学、音韵学、音系学的专家或研究者.

phooey /'fu:ɪ; 'fuɪ/ *interj* (*infml* 口) (expressing contempt, disappointment or a refusal to accept the truth of sth 表示对某事物轻视、失望或不信的叹词).

phos·gene /'fɒzdʒi:n; 'fɑsdʒin/ *n* [U] poisonous colourless gas used in chemical warfare, and in industry to make dyes, fertilizers, etc 光气; 碳酰氯.

phos·phate /'fɒsfeɪt; 'fɑsfet/ *n* (**a**) [C, U] any salt or compound of phosphoric acid 磷酸盐; 磷酸酯. (**b**) [C often *pl*, U 作可数名词时常作复数, 亦作不可数名词] any artificial fertilizer composed of or containing these 磷肥.

phos·phor·es·cence /ˌfɒsfə'resns; ˌfɑsfə'rɛsns/ *n* [U] (**a**) giving out of light without heat or with so little heat that it cannot be felt 磷光; 磷火; 鬼火. (**b**) giving out of a faint glow in the dark, eg by certain insects or sea creatures (黑暗中的)微光(如某些昆虫或海洋生物的). Cf 参看 FLUORESCENCE.

▷ **phos·phor·es·cent** /-snt; -snt/ *adj* (**a**) giving out light without heat 发磷光的. (**b**) glowing in the dark 在黑暗中发光的.

phos·phorus /'fɒsfərəs; 'fɑsfərəs/ *n* [U] (*chemistry* 化) (**a**) pale yellow waxlike poisonous substance that glows in the dark and catches fire easily 磷. (**b**) red non-poisonous form of this, used for the coating on match heads 红磷. ⇨App 10 见附录10.

▷ **phos·phoric** /fɒs'fɒrɪk; *US* -'fɔ:r; fɑs'fɔrɪk/ (also **phos·phor·ous** /'fɒsfərəs; 'fɑsfərəs/) *adj* concerning or containing phosphorus 磷的; 含磷的.

photo /'fəʊtəʊ; 'foto/ *n* (*pl* **~s** /-təʊz; -toz/) (*infml* 口) = PHOTOGRAPH.

□ ˌphoto 'finish (in horse racing) finish of a race where the leading horses are so close together that only a photograph of them passing the winning-post can show which is the winner (马赛中的)摄影定名次(参赛者到达终点时需藉照片判断名次者).

photo- *comb form* 构词成分 **1** of light 光的: *photoelectric* ○ *photosensitize* ○ *photosynthesis*. **2** of photography 摄影的; 照相的: *photocopy* ○ *photogenic*.

pho·to·cell /'fəʊtəʊsel; 'foto,sɛl/ *n* = PHOTOELECTRIC CELL (PHOTOELECTRIC).

pho·to·copy /'fəʊtəʊkɒpɪ; 'foto,kɑpɪ/ *n* photographic copy of (written, printed or graphic work) 照相复制本; 影印本. Cf 参看 XEROX, PHOTOSTAT.

▷ **pho·to·copy** *v* (*pt, pp* **-pied**) (**a**) [Tn] make a photographic copy of (written, printed or graphic work) 照相复印, 影印(文字、图表等). (**b**) [I] make photographic copies of documents, etc 照相复制; 影印: *do some photocopying* 影印.

pho·to·copier /-pɪə(r); -pɪɚ/ *n* machine for photocopying documents 照相复印机; 影印机.

pho·to·el·ec·tric /ˌfəʊtəʊɪ'lektrɪk; ˌfotoɪ'lɛktrɪk/ *adj* of or using the electrical effects produced by light 光电的.

□ ˌphotoelectric 'cell (also 'photocell, eˌlectric 'eye) electronic device that uses the effect of light to produce electric current (used eg in photographic light meters and burglar alarms) 光电管; 电眼.

pho·to·genic /ˌfəʊtəʊ'dʒenɪk; ˌfotə'dʒɛnɪk/ *adj* (**a**) being a good subject for photography 适于拍照的: *a photogenic sunset, village, kitten* 适于拍照的日落、村子、小猫. (**b**) (of a person) looking attractive in photographs (指人)上相的, 上镜的: *I'm not very photogenic.* 我这人不大上相.

pho·to·graph /'fəʊtəgrɑ:f; *US* -græf; 'fotə,græf/ (also *infml* 口语作 **photo**) *n* **1** picture formed by means of the chemical action of light on a specially prepared surface, eg film or a glass plate, and then transferred to specially prepared paper 照片; 相片: *take a photograph (of sb/sth)* 给(某人[某物])拍照. **2** (idm 习语) **take a good 'photograph** look attractive in photographs; be photogenic 照出像来好看; 上相; 上镜.

▷ **pho·to·graph** *v* **1** [Tn] take a photograph of (sb/sth) 给(某人[某物])拍照: *photograph the bride, the wedding, a flower* 给新娘、婚礼、花拍照. **2** [I] (followed by an *adv* 后接副词) appear in a certain way in photographs 在照片上显出的某种样子: *photograph well/badly* 照出来好看[不好看]. **pho·to·grapher** /fə'tɒgrəfə(r); fə'tɑgrəfɚ/ *n* person who takes photographs, esp as a job 摄影者; (尤指)摄影师: *The competition is open to both amateur and professional photographers.* 业余的和职业的摄影者均可参赛. ○ *a* newspaper photographer 报社摄影记者 ○ *one of the best photographers in the world* 世界上最优秀的摄影师之一. Cf 参看 CAMERAMAN (CAMERA).

pho·to·graphic /ˌfəʊtəˈɡræfɪk; ˌfotəˈɡræfɪk/ *adj* [usu attrib 通常作定语] **1** of, used in or produced by photography 摄影(术)的; 摄影用的; 摄制的: *photographic equipment, images, records, reproduction* 摄影设备、摄影影像、摄制的纪录、照相复制. **2** (of sb's memory) able to remember things in great detail, exactly as they were seen (指某人的记忆)记得详细准确的.

pho·to·graph·ic·ally /-klɪ; -klɪ/ *adv*.

pho·to·graphy /fəˈtɒɡrəfɪ; fəˈtɑɡrəfɪ/ *n* [U] art or process of taking photographs 摄影术; 摄影: *black and white/colour/still photography* 黑白[彩色/静物]摄影 ○ *Her hobby is photography.* 她的业余爱好是摄影. ○ *The photography in the film about arctic wildlife was superb.* 那部影片中拍摄的极地野生动物好看极了.

pho·to·litho·graphy /ˌfəʊtəʊlɪˈθɒɡrəfɪ; ˌfotolɪˈθɑɡrəfɪ/ *n* [U] process of transferring an image onto a metal plate by a photographic method, and printing from it 照相平版印刷(术).

photon /ˈfəʊtɒn; ˈfotɑn/ *n* (*physics* 物) indivisible unit of electromagnetic radiation 光子; 光量子.

pho·to·sens·it·ive /ˌfəʊtəʊˈsensətɪv; ˌfotəˈsɛnsətɪv/ *adj* reacting when exposed to light, esp by changing colour 光敏的; (尤指)感光的: *photosensitive paper* 感光纸.

▷ **pho·to·sens·it·ize, -ise** /-taɪz; -taɪz/ *v* [Tn] make (sth) photosensitive 使(某物)具感光性; 使光敏.

Pho·to·stat (also **photostat**) /ˈfəʊtəstæt; ˈfotəˌstæt/ *n* (*propr* 专利名) photocopy 照相复印件; 影印本: [attrib 作定语] *a Photostat copy* 影印件.

▷ **pho·to·stat** *v* [Tn] make a photocopy of (sth) 照相复印, 影印(文字、图表等).

pho·to·syn·thesis /ˌfəʊtəʊˈsɪnθəsɪs; ˌfotəˈsɪnθəsɪs/ *n* [U] process by which green plants convert carbon dioxide and water into food using the energy in sunlight 光合作用. Cf 参看 CHLOROPHYLL.

▷ **pho·to·syn·thes·ize, -ise** /-əsaɪz; -əˌsaɪz/ *v* [Tn] change (eg carbon dioxide or water) into food by photosynthesis 对(如二氧化碳或水)进行光合作用.

pho·to·syn·thetic /-sɪnˈθetɪk; -sɪnˈθɛtɪk/ *adj*.

phrase /freɪz; frez/ *n* **1** [C] (**a**) (*grammar*) group of words without a verb, esp one that forms part of a sentence 词组; 短语; 片语: *'The green car' and 'at half past four' are phrases.* the green car(绿色的汽车)和 at half past four(在四点半)都是词组. (**b**) group of words forming a short expression, esp an idiom or a clever, striking way of saying sth 固定词组; (尤指)习语, 成语, 警语, 隽语: *an apt, a memorable, a well-chosen, etc phrase* 恰当的、值得记住的、选用得切当的...习语 ○ *That's exactly the phrase I was looking for myself.* 这就是我一直找的那个成语. **2** [U] way of expressing oneself; style 个人的表达方式; 风格: *the poet's beauty of phrase* 该诗人表达风格之美. **3** [C] (*music* 音) short distinct passage forming part of a longer passage 乐句; 分句. **4** (idm 习语) **to coin a phrase** ⇨ COIN *v*. **turn a 'phrase** express oneself in an amusing and witty way 诙谐地表达; 作妙语. **a turn of 'phrase** way of expressing or describing sth 表达方式; 措词: *an interesting, unusual, unpleasant, etc turn of phrase* 有趣的、不寻常的、令人不快的...措词.

▷ **phrasal** /ˈfreɪzl; ˈfrezl̩/ *adj* (**a**) of or concerning a phrase 词组的; 短语的; 片语的. (**b**) in the form of a phrase 词组形式的; 短语形式的: *phrasal verbs such as 'go in for', 'fall over', 'blow up'* 短语动词, 如 go in for、fall over、blow up.

phrase *v* [Tn] **1** express (sth) in words (in the specified way) (以某种方式)措词表达(某事): *phrase one's criticism very carefully* 对批评用语字斟句酌 ○ *How shall I phrase it?* 我用什么词语表达呢? ○ *an elegantly phrased compliment* 措词优雅的赞语. **2** divide (music) into phrases, esp in performance 将(乐曲)分成乐句(尤指演奏时). **phras·ing** *n* [U] **1** (*music* 音) action or manner of dividing a line into phrases, in composing or performing 乐句划分; 分句法: *The singer was criticized for her poor phrasing.* 她演唱歌曲时乐句划分失当受到批评. **2** = PHRASEOLOGY a.

phras·eo·logy /ˌfreɪzɪˈɒlədʒɪ; ˌfrezɪˈɑlədʒɪ/ *n* [U] (**a**) choice or arrangement of words; wording 措词; 用词; 遣词. (**b**) study of fixed phrases and idioms 成语学.

□ **ˈphrase-book** *n* book listing common expressions and their equivalents in another language, esp for use by travellers in a foreign country 外语常用语手册(尤指供到国外旅游用的): *a Spanish phrase-book* 西班牙语常用语手册.

phren·etic = FRENETIC.

phreno·logy /frəˈnɒlədʒɪ; frɛˈnɑlədʒɪ/ *n* [U] (esp formerly) study of the shape of a person's skull, esp the natural bumps on it, in order to determine his character and abilities (尤指旧时)颅相学.

▷ **phreno·lo·gical** /ˌfrenəˈlɒdʒɪkl; ˌfrɛnəˈlɑdʒɪkəl/ *adj*.

phreno·lo·gist /frəˈnɒlədʒɪst; frɛˈnɑlədʒɪst/ *n* person who practises phrenology 颅相学家.

phut /fʌt; fʌt/ *adv* (idm 习语) **go ˈphut** (*infml* 口) (**a**) (esp of electrical or mechanical things) stop functioning; break down (尤指电器或机械用具)停止运转, 出故障: *The washing machine has gone phut.* 洗衣机坏了. (**b**) be ruined; collapse 毁掉; 垮掉: *The business went phut.* 公司倒闭了. ○ *Our holiday plans have gone phut.* 我们的假日计划已经吹了.

phylum /ˈfaɪləm; ˈfaɪləm/ *n* (*pl* **-la** /-lə; -lə/) (*biology* 生) major division in the animal or plant kingdom (动物或植物分类上的)门: *The mollusc phylum includes all soft-bodied animals without backbones.* 软体动物门包括所有无脊椎的软体动物. Cf 参看 CLASS 7, ORDER[1] 9, FAMILY 4, GENUS 1, SPECIES 1.

phys·ical /ˈfɪzɪkl; ˈfɪzɪkl̩/ *adj* **1** of or concerning material things (contrasted with moral or spiritual matters) 物质的(与道德的或精神的相对): *the physical world, universe, etc* 物质世界、宇宙等. **2** (**a**) of the body 身体的; 肉体的: *physical fitness, well-being, strength, etc* 健康、安康、体力 ○ *physical exercise*, eg walking, running, playing sports 体育活动 ○ *physical education*, eg athletics, gymnastics, games, etc 体育 ○ (*Brit infml* 口) *physical jerks*, ie gymnastics 体操. (**b**) bodily 身体的: *physical presence* 亲临. **3** of or according to the laws of nature 自然规律的; 按自然法则的: *It is a physical impossibility to be in two places at once.* 同时身处两地在自然法则上是不可能的. ○ *physical necessity* 自然法则的必然性. **4** [attrib 作定语] of the natural features of the material world 物质世界的自然特征的: *physical geography*, ie geography of the earth's structure 自然地理学 ○ *a physical map*, ie one showing mountains, rivers, etc 自然地理图. **5** [attrib 作定语] of or concerning physics 物理的; 物理学的: *physical chemistry*, ie use of physics in the study of chemistry 物理化学 ○ *physical science* 物理学. **6** (*infml euph* 口, 婉) using violence; treating roughly 使用暴力的; 粗暴对待的: *Are you going to co-operate or do we have to get physical?* 你是跟我们合作呢还是要我们动武?

▷ **phys·ical** *n* (*infml* 口) medical examination to see if one is fit 体格检查.

phys·ic·ally /-klɪ; -klɪ/ *adv* (**a**) bodily 身体上: *physically exhausted, fit, handicapped* 身体疲劳、健康、残疾 ○ *attack sb physically* 攻击某人身体. (**b**) according to the laws of nature 根据自然法则: *physically impossible* 按照自然法则不可能.

physi·cian /fɪˈzɪʃn; fəˈzɪʃən/ *n* doctor, esp one specializing in areas of treatment other than surgery 医生; (尤指)内科医生. Cf 参看 SURGEON.

physi·cist /ˈfɪzɪsɪst; ˈfɪzəsɪst/ *n* expert in or student of physics 物理学家; 物理学研究者.

phys·ics /ˈfɪzɪks; ˈfɪzɪks/ *n* [sing *v*] (scientific study of the) properties of matter and energy (eg heat, light, sound, magnetism, gravity) and the relationship between them 物理(学): *Physics has made enormous progress in this century.* 本世纪物理学的发展突飞猛进. ○ *nuclear physics* 原子核物理学 ○ *the laws of physics* 物理学定律 ○ [attrib 作定语] *a physics textbook* 物理学教科书 ○ *the physics of the electron* 电子物理学.

physi(o)- *comb form* 构词成分 **1** of or relating to nature or natural forces or functions 自然的; 自然力的; 自然功能的: *physiology*. **2** physical 物理的: *physiotherapy*.

physi·ognomy /ˌfɪzɪˈɒnəmɪ; *US* -ˈɒɡnəʊmɪ; ˌfɪzɪˈɑɡnəmɪ/ *n* (*fml* 文) **1** [C] (**a**) features of a person's face 相貌; 容貌. (**b**) facial type 脸型: *a typical North European physiognomy* 典型的北欧人脸型. **2** [U] art of judging a person's character from the features of his face 相面术.

3 [C] physical features of a country or area（一国或一地的）地势，地貌，地理特征.

physi·ology /ˌfɪzɪˈɒlədʒɪ; ˌfɪzɪˋɑlədʒɪ/ *n* [U] (**a**) scientific study of the normal functions of living things 生理学: *reproductive physiology* 生殖生理学. (**b**) way in which the body of a particular living thing functions 生理机能: *the physiology of the snake* 蛇的生理机能.

▷ **physio·logical** /ˌfɪzɪəˈlɒdʒɪkl; ˌfɪzɪəˋlɑdʒɪkl/ *adj* (**a**) of or concerning physiology 生理学的: *physiological research* 生理学研究. (**b**) of or concerning the bodily functions 生理的；生理机能的: *the physiological effects of space travel* 宇宙航行的生理影响.

physi·olo·gist /ˌfɪzɪˈɒlədʒɪst; ˌfɪzɪˋɑlədʒɪst/ *n* expert in or student of physiology 生理学家；生理学研究者.

physio·ther·apy /ˌfɪzɪəʊˈθerəpɪ; ˌfɪzɪoˋθɛrəpɪ/ *n* [U] treatment of disease, injury or weakness in the joints or muscles by exercises, massage and the use of light, heat, etc 物理治疗；理疗.

▷ **physio·ther·ap·ist** /-pɪst; -pɪst/ *n* (also *infml* 口语作 **physio** /ˈfɪzɪəʊ; ˋfɪzɪo/) person trained to give such treatment 理疗医生；物理治疗师.

phys·ique /fɪˈziːk; fɪˋzik/ *n* [C] general appearance and size of a person's body, esp of the muscles 体格，体形（尤指肌肉方面）: *a well-developed physique* 发育匀称的体格 ○ *build up one's physique* 长身体 ○ *a fine/poor physique* 健壮的［羸弱的］体格 ○ *He doesn't have the physique for such heavy work.* 干这样的重活他的体格不行.

pi /paɪ; paɪ/ *n* **1** the sixteenth letter of the Greek alphabet (Π, π), represented in English spelling by 'p' 希腊字母表的第十六个字母（Π，π），英语拼写中用p表示. **2** (*geometry* 几) symbol (π) representing the ratio of the circumference of a circle to its diameter (ie 3.14159) 圆周率（即3.14159）.

piano[1] /ˈpjɑːnəʊ; pɪˋɑno/ *adv, adj* (*music* 音) (*abbr* 缩写 **p**) soft(ly) 柔和（的）；弱（的）. Cf 参看 FORTE[2].

▷ **pi·an·is·simo** /pɪəˈnɪsɪməʊ; ˌpiəˋnɪsəˌmo/ *adv, adj* (*abbr* 缩写 **pp**) very soft(ly) 极弱（的）.

piano[2] /pɪˈænəʊ; pɪˋæno/ *n* (*pl* **~s** /-nəʊz; -noz/) (also *fml* 文作 **pi·ano·forte** /pɪˌænəʊˈfɔːtɪ; *US* pɪˋænəfɔːrt; pɪˋænəˌfɔrt/) large musical instrument played by pressing the black or white keys of a keyboard, thus causing small hammers to strike metal strings to produce different notes 钢琴: *play a tune on the piano* 用钢琴弹一个曲子 ○ *grand piano*, ie one with horizontal strings, esp used for concerts 大钢琴 ○ *upright piano*, ie one with vertical strings 竖式钢琴 ○ [attrib 作定语] *piano music* 钢琴曲 *a piano teacher, lesson* 钢琴教师、课 ○ *a piano-player* 钢琴演奏者 ○ *a piano-stool* 钢琴凳. ⇨illus at App 1 见附录1插图, page xi.

▷ **pi·an·ist** /ˈpɪənɪst; ˋpiənɪst/ *n* person who plays the piano 钢琴演奏者；钢琴家: *She's a good pianist.* 她钢琴弹得很好. ○ *a famous concert pianist* 著名的音乐会钢琴家.

pi·an·ola (also **Pi·an·ola**) /pɪəˈnəʊlə; ˌpɪəˋnolə/ *n* (*propr* 专利名) type of mechanical piano in which the keys are operated by air pressure 自动钢琴.

□ **piˌano-acˈcordion** *n* = ACCORDION.

pi·astre (*US* **pi·as·ter**) /pɪˈæstə(r); pɪˋæstɚ/ *n* (**a**) 100th part of the unit of money in several Middle Eastern countries 皮阿斯特（中东几国的货币单位）. (**b**) coin or banknote of this value（硬币或纸币的）一皮阿斯特.

pi·azza /pɪˈætsə; *US also* piːˈɑːzə; pɪˋæzə/ *n* public square or marketplace, esp in an Italian town; plaza 广场，市场（尤指意大利城镇中的）.

pib·roch /ˈpiːbrɒk; ˋpibrɑk/ *n* piece of music to be played on the bagpipes, consisting of a theme and variations 风笛变奏曲.

pica /ˈpaɪkə; ˋpaɪkə/ *n* **1** one of the sizes of letters used in typewriting (ten letters per inch) 英文打字机上相当于12点活字的字型（每英寸10个字母）. **2** (in printing) unit of measurement for type[2](1)（印刷）12点活字.

pic·ador /ˈpɪkədɔː(r); ˋpɪkəˌdɔr/ *n* (in bullfighting) man mounted on a horse who attacks the bull with a lance in order to make it angry and weaken it 骑马斗牛士.

pi·car·esque /ˌpɪkəˈresk; ˌpɪkəˋrɛsk/ *adj* (of a style or type of literature) dealing with the adventures of (often likeable) rogues and vagabonds（指文学的风格或体裁）以（常为讨人喜欢的）无赖和流浪汉的冒险事迹为题材的.

pic·ca·lilli /ˌpɪkəˈlɪlɪ; ˌpɪkəˋlɪlɪ/ *n* [U] yellow hot-tasting pickle made from chopped vegetables, mustard and spices 辣泡菜.

pic·ca·ninny /ˌpɪkəˈnɪnɪ; ˋpɪkəˌnɪnɪ/ *n* (⚠ *dated offensive* 讳，旧，蔑) young Negro or Aboriginal child 黑人小孩儿；澳洲土著小孩儿.

pic·colo /ˈpɪkələʊ; ˋpɪkəˌlo/ *n* (*pl* **~s**) small musical instrument like the flute but producing notes an octave higher than those of the flute 短笛. ⇨illus at App 1 见附录1插图, page x.

pick[1] /pɪk; pɪk/ *n* [sing] **1** (right of) selecting; choice 挑选；选择；选择权: *Of course I'll lend you a pen. Take your pick*, ie whichever one you choose. 我当然可以借给你钢笔用. 自己挑吧. ○ *The winner has first pick of the prizes.* 胜者有选择奖品的优先权. **2 the ~ of sth** the best (example) of sth 最佳选择（的事物）；精华: *Only the pick of the crop is good enough for us*, eg in food advertising. 本公司原料皆为精选作物（如见于食品广告）. ○ *the pick of the new season's fashions* 新款精选 ○ (*infml* 口) *the pick of the bunch*, ie the best of a number of things or people 出类拔萃者.

pick[2] /pɪk; pɪk/ *n* **1** (also **pickaxe**, *US* **pickax** /ˈpɪkæks; ˋpɪkˌæks/) large tool consisting of a curved iron bar with sharp ends fixed onto a wooden handle, used for breaking up stones, hard ground, etc 鹤嘴锄；镐. ⇨illus at AXE 见AXE插图. **2** (esp in compounds 尤用以构成复合词) instrument with a sharp point, used for the purpose specified 锄；镐: *an ˈice-pick* ○ *a ˈtoothpick.*

pick[3] /pɪk; pɪk/ *v* **1** [Tn] choose or select (sth), eg from a group of things, esp thoughtfully and carefully 挑选，选择（某物）；（尤指）精选: *You can pick whichever one you like.* 你喜欢哪个就挑哪个. ○ *Only the best players were picked to play in the match.* 选出参赛的都是最佳选手. ○ *pick one's words*, ie express oneself carefully, eg so as not to annoy sb 斟酌词句（如以免得罪人）○ *pick one's way along a muddy path*, ie walk carefully, choosing the best places to put one's feet 在泥泞的小道上走路时小心下脚. ⇨Usage at CHOOSE 用法见CHOOSE. **2** [Tn] pluck, gather or remove (flowers, vegetables, etc) from the place where they grow 采摘，采集（花、菜等）: *flowers freshly picked from the garden* 从花园中新采的花 ○ *pick lettuce, plums, spinach, strawberries, etc* 收获莴苣、梅子、菠菜、草莓等. **3** (**a**) [Tn, Cn·a] remove small pieces of matter from (sth), esp in order to clean it 从（某处）除掉小块物（尤指为弄干净）: *pick one's nose*, ie remove dried mucus from the nostrils 挖鼻孔 ○ *pick one's teeth*, ie use a small pointed piece of wood, etc to remove particles of food from one's teeth 剔牙 ○ *The dogs picked the bones clean*, ie removed all the meat from the bones. 狗把骨头啃得干干净净. (**b**) [Tn·pr] **~ sth (from/off sth)** remove sth from a surface, esp with one's fingers or a sharp instrument（从物体表面）除掉某物（尤指用手指或尖物）: *pick the tacking threads (from a garment)* 拆掉（衣服上的）绷线 ○ *pick a hair from the collar of one's coat* 捡去衣领上的一根头发 ○ *pick the toys off the floor* 拾起地板上的玩具 ○ *pick the nuts off the top of the cake* 拣去蛋糕上的果仁. (**c**) [Tn] open (a lock) without a key, eg by using a piece of bent wire or a pointed tool（用尖细之物或铁丝）拨开（锁）. **4** [Tn, Tn·pr] **~ sth (in sth)** make (a hole) in sth by pulling at it or by using one's finger-nails or a sharp instrument（用指甲或尖物）扎开，抠开（一孔）: *The child has picked a hole in his new jumper.* 孩子的新毛衣上勾了一个洞. ○ *The bird picked a hole in the ice with its beak.* 那鸟在冰上啄出了一个洞. **5** (**a**) [In] (of birds) take up (grain, etc) in the bill（指鸟）叼起，啄起（谷粒等）: *chickens picking corn* 啄食玉米的小鸡. (**b**) [Ipr] **~ at sth** eat (food) in very small amounts or without appetite 小口地吃（某物）（或吃时无食欲）: *Sparrows picked at the crumbs.* 麻雀啄食着面包屑. ○ *He never feels hungry and just picks at his food.* 他从不觉得饿，吃东西也没有胃口. **6** [Tn] = PLUCK 4: *pick a banjo* 弹班卓琴. **7** (idm 习语) **have a bone to pick with sb** ⇨ BONE. **pick and ˈchoose** make a selection from a number of things, esp in a slow, careful or fussy way 挑选；（尤指）挑挑拣拣: *I spent days picking and choosing before deciding on the wallpaper and curtains.* 我挑选壁纸和帘子用了好几天的时间. ○ *We had to find a flat in a* hurry — there was no time to pick and choose. 我们只好匆忙找套房子——没有时间挑选了. **pick sb's 'brains** ask sb questions in order to obtain information that one can use oneself 问某人问题以获取有用的信息: *I need a new French dictionary. Can I pick your brains about the best one to buy?* 我需要一部新的法语词典. 能否向您请教哪本最好? **pick a 'fight/'quarrel (with sb)** deliberately cause a fight/quarrel (with sb), eg by behaving aggressively (向某人)寻衅, 找茬儿: *He tried to pick a quarrel with me about it but I refused to discuss the matter.* 他极力想就那事找我的茬儿, 但我绝不谈论此事. ○ *It was foolish of you to pick a fight with a heavyweight boxing champion!* 你傻了, 竟敢和重量级的拳击冠军寻衅闹事! **pick holes in sth** find fault with sth 挑某事物的毛病; 找某事物的漏洞: *It was easy to pick holes in his argument.* 在他的论据里不难找到漏洞. ○ *They pick holes in everything I suggest.* 只要是我提的建议他们就挑毛病. **pick sb's 'pocket** steal money, etc from sb's pocket 扒窃. **pick/pull sb/sth to pieces** ⇨ PIECE[1]. **pick up/take up/throw down the gauntlet** ⇨ GAUNTLET[1]. **pick up the 'pieces/'threads** restore to normality or make better (a situation, one's life, etc), esp after a setback, shock, disaster, etc 恢复或改进(局面、生活状况等)(尤指于受挫、受惊、受灾等之后): *Their lives were shattered by the tragedy and they are still trying to pick up the pieces.* 他们的生活被这场悲剧摧垮了, 但他们仍尽力重新整顿. **pick up 'speed** go faster 加速: *We reached the outskirts of town and began to pick up speed.* 我们到达市郊后开始加速. **pick a 'winner** (**a**) (in horse-racing) choose correctly the horse which will win the race, esp in order to bet on it (马赛中)挑中定能跑赢的马. (**b**) make a very good choice 挑选得极好: (*ironic* 反语) *I really picked a winner with this car — it's always breaking down!* 这辆汽车我算挑着了——总出故障!

8 (phr v) **pick sb off** shoot (a person, an animal, a bird, etc, esp one of a group) after aiming carefully (有选择地)瞄准射击(人、兽、鸟等): *A sniper hidden on a roof picked off three of the soldiers on patrol.* 藏在屋顶上的狙击手击毙了三名巡逻兵.

pick on sb (**a**) choose sb (esp repeatedly) for punishment, criticism or blame 选中某人(尤指屡次)惩罚、批评或责怪: *She felt that her parents were picking on her.* 她觉得父母老是偏偏责备她. (**b**) choose sb for a task, esp an unpleasant one 选中某人做某事(尤指厌恶的事): *I was picked on to announce the bad news.* 偏偏选中我去宣布这个坏消息.

pick sb/sth out (**a**) choose sb/sth from a number of people/things 挑选出某人[某事物]: *She was picked out from thousands of applicants for the job.* 从数千申请人中挑选出她来做那份工作. ○ *He picked out the ripest peach.* 他把熟得最透的桃挑了出来. (**b**) distinguish sb/sth from surrounding people or things 分辨出某人[某事物]: *pick out sb/sb's face in a crowd* 在人群中认出某人[某人的脸] ○ *It was just possible to pick out the hut on the side of the mountain.* 那小舍座落在山边, 隐约可见. ○ *The window frames are picked out in blue against the white walls.* 蓝色的窗框衬在白墙上十分显眼. **pick sth out** (**a**) play (a piece of music), eg on the piano, esp hesitantly or by trial and error, without having written music to follow 凭记忆奏(乐曲)(如用钢琴). (**b**) discover or recognize sth after careful study 细心研究后发现或领会某事物: *pick out recurring themes in an author's work* 领会出作者作品中反复出现的主题思想 ○ *Can you pick out the operatic arias quoted in this orchestral passage?* 你能听出这段管弦乐曲里有歌剧式的咏叹调吗?

pick sth over look carefully at (vegetables, fruit, clothing, etc) in order to select the best or throw away bad ones 检查(蔬菜、水果、衣物等)以挑出最佳者或剔除劣品: *Pick over the lentils carefully in case there are any stones amongst them.* 把这些豆子里的沙粒挑出去.

pick up (**a**) become better; improve 好转; 改善: *The market always picks up in the spring.* 一到春天市场就活跃了. ○ *We're waiting until the weather picks up a bit.* 我们等到天气好些再说. ○ *The performance started badly but picked up towards the end.* 演出开始时很差劲, 但近结尾处就好多了. ○ *Her health soon picked up after a few days' rest.* 她休息了几天, 身体很快复元了. (**b**) start again; continue 重新开始; 继续: *We'll pick up where we finished yesterday.* 我们从昨天停止的地方继续进行. **pick oneself up** get to one's feet, esp after a fall 站起来(尤指跌倒后): *Pick yourself up and brush yourself down.* 自己站起来, 把衣服掸干净. **pick sb up** (**a**) give sb a lift in a car; collect sb 用汽车搭载某人或接某人: *I'll pick you up at 7 o'clock.* 7点钟我开车来接你. ○ *He picked up a hitch-hiker.* 他中途让个搭便车的人上了车. (**b**) (*infml often derog* 口, 常作贬义) make the acquaintance of sb casually 偶然结识某人: *He picked up the girl at a college disco.* 他在学校的迪斯科舞会上偶然结识了那姑娘. ○ *She's living with some man she picked up on holiday.* 她与一个在假日认识的男人同住. (**c**) rescue sb (eg from the sea) 救起某人(如从海上): *The lifeboat picked up all the survivors.* 救生船救起了全部幸存者. (**d**) (of the police, etc) stop and seize sb (eg for questioning) (指警方等)逮捕某人(如为讯问): *The police picked him up as he was trying to leave the country.* 他正要离开该国时, 警方把他捉住了. ○ *He was picked up and taken for questioning.* 他被拘捕接受审讯. (**e**) reprimand sb 责备某人: *She picked him up for using bad language.* 她指责他出言不逊. **pick sb/sth up** (**a**) take hold of and lift sb/sth 举起或抬起某人[某物]; 拿起; 拾起: *He picked up the child and put her on his shoulders.* 他抱起孩子让她骑在自己的肩膀上. ○ *I picked up your bag by mistake.* 我错拿了你的手提包. ○ *pick up a stitch*, ie in knitting 补织一针(编织中) ○ *He picked up the book from the floor.* 他从地板上把书拾起来. ○ *She picked up the telephone and dialled his number.* 她拿起电话就拨了他的号码. (**b**) see or hear sb/sth, esp by means of apparatus 见到, 听到(尤指借助仪器): *They picked up the yacht on their radar screen.* 他们在雷达屏上看到了那艘游艇. ○ *I was able to pick you up on the short wave radio.* 我能用短波收音机收听到你的信号. ○ *The equipment picked up the signal from the satellite.* 这设备收到了卫星发出的信号. **pick sth up** (**a**) learn (a foreign language, a technique, etc) by practising 通过实践学会(外语、技术等): *She soon picked up French when she went to live in France.* 她到法国居住后很快就学会了法语. ○ *The children have picked up the local accent.* 孩子都学会了当地口音了. ○ *pick up bad habits* 染上陋习. (**b**) catch (an illness) 得, 染(疾病): *pick up an infection, a cold, the flu, etc* 受传染、着凉、得流感. (**c**) buy sth, esp cheaply or luckily 买到某物(尤指价廉或运气好): *She picked up a valuable first edition at a village book sale.* 她在乡村图书展销会上买到一本珍贵的首版书. ○ *They picked up most of the furniture at auctions in country towns.* 他们大部分的家具都是在乡村镇上的拍卖处买的. (**d**) hear or learn (gossip, news, etc) 听到(闲话等); 获悉或打听到(消息等): *He picked up an interesting piece of news.* 他听到一则有趣的新闻. ○ *See if you can pick up anything about their future plans.* 你看能不能打听到他们未来计划的消息. (**e**) collect sth 取或收集某物: *I've got to pick up my coat from the cleaners.* 我得到洗染店去取大衣了. ○ *I'll pick up* (ie buy) *something for dinner on my way home.* 我在回家的路上要顺便买些东西做饭. ○ *We can pick up the tickets an hour before the play begins.* 我们可以在话剧开演前一小时去取票. (**f**) draw or derive sth 吸取或得到某物: *The trolley bus picks up current from an overhead wire.* 无轨电车的电能是通过架空线供给的. (**g**) find sth; locate sth; (re)join 发现某事物; 找到某事物; (重新)接合或会合: *pick up a trail, a scent* 发现踪迹、察出气味 ○ *pick up the track on the other side of the river* 在河对岸发现踪迹. **pick up with sb** (*often derog* 常作贬义): *She's picked up with some peculiar people.* 她勾搭上一些不三不四的人.

▷ **picker** *n* (esp in compounds 尤用以构成复合词) person or thing that picks (PICK[3] 2) 采摘者; 采集者; 采摘机; 采摘工具: *'hop-pickers* 啤酒花采集者 ○ *a mechanical 'apple-picker* 摘苹果机.

□ **pick-me-up** /ˈpɪkmiʌp; ˈpɪkmiʌp/ *n* (*infml* 口) drink taken as a tonic when one feels weak, tired, ill, etc, esp medicine or an alcoholic drink (虚弱、疲劳、生病等时饮的)提神饮料(尤指含药或酒精者).

pickpocket /ˈpɪkpɒkɪt; ˈpɪkˌpɑkɪt/ *n* person who steals money, etc from other people's pockets, esp in crowded places 扒手(尤指在人多处行窃的).

'pick-up *n* **1** (*infml derog* 口, 贬) person one has met casually, esp in a sexual context 偶然结识的人(尤指涉及性关系的). **2** part of a record-player that holds the stylus 拾音器; 唱头. **3** (also ˈ**pick-up truck**) small van or truck, open and with low sides, used by builders, farmers, etc 轻型小货车. ⇨ illus at JEEP 见 JEEP 插图.

pick-a-back /ˈpɪkəbæk; ˋpɪkə,bæk/ (also **piggyback** /ˈpɪgɪbæk; ˋpɪgɪ,bæk/) *adv* on the shoulders or back like a bundle 在背上; 在肩上: *carry a child pick-a-back* 背着孩子.

▷ **pick-a-back** (also **piggyback**) *n* ride on a person's back 骑在某人背上: *Her father gave her a pick-a-back (ride) for the last bit of the journey.* 在最后的一段路程上她父亲背着她走.

picket /ˈpɪkɪt; ˋpɪkɪt/ *n* **1** worker or group of workers stationed outside the entrance to a place of work during a strike to try to persuade others not to enter (罢工时守在工作地点门口阻拦他人上班的)纠察队员, 纠察队: *Five pickets were injured in the scuffle.* 在混战中有五名罢工纠察队员受伤. ○ [attrib 作定语] *a ˈpicket line*, ie a line of pickets, eg outside a factory 罢工纠察线. **2** small group of people on police duty or of soldiers sent out to watch the enemy 警察或士兵的警戒队. **3** pointed stake set into the ground, eg as part of a fence or to tether a horse to 尖板条(作篱笆或栓马用的): [attrib 作定语] *a picket fence* 尖板条栅栏.

▷ **picket** *v* **1** (**a**) [Tn] place pickets at (a place of work) (在工作地点)设置罢工纠察队: *picket all the company's offices* 在公司所有的办公室附近设置罢工纠察队. (**b**) [I, Tn] act as a picket at (a place of work) 担任罢工纠察员: *Some of the union members did not want to picket.* 工会的一些会员不想担任罢工纠察员. **2** [Tn] place (guards) in position 布置(警卫)警戒. **3** [Tn] enclose (a place) with stakes or make secure with a stake 用尖板条围住(某地); 用尖板条围护.

pick·ings /ˈpɪkɪŋz; ˋpɪkɪŋz/ *n* [pl] **1** profits or gains that are easily or dishonestly earned or obtained 轻易挣得的或来路不正的财物、好处、利益等: *He promised us rich pickings if we bought the shares immediately.* 他向我们保证假若我们立刻买进股票, 很容易赚大钱. **2** left over scraps of food, etc 残留的食物等.

pickle /ˈpɪkl; ˋpɪkḷ/ *n* **1** (**a**) [U] food (esp vegetables) preserved in vinegar or salt water 腌菜(尤指蔬菜): *red cabbage pickle* 红卷心菜泡菜. (**b**) [C usu *pl* 通常作复数] particular vegetable preserved in this way 泡菜: *The dish was accompanied by a variety of pickles.* 这盘菜配有什锦泡菜. ○ *cheese and pickles* 奶酪加泡菜. (**c**) [U] liquid used to preserve food in this way 泡菜水; 腌菜的汁: *leave an ox tongue in salt pickle* 把牛口条放在腌菜汁里腌制. Cf 参看 RELISH 3, SAUCE 1. **2** [C] (*Brit infml* 口) mischievous child 调皮孩子: *She's a real little pickle!* 她真是个小调皮! **3** (idm 习语) **(in) a sad, sorry, nice, pretty, etc** ˈ**pickle** (in) a difficult or unpleasant situation; (in) a mess 处境困难或不愉快; 又脏又乱.

▷ **pickle** *v* [Tn] preserve (vegetables, etc) in pickle (用腌菜汁)腌渍(蔬菜等): *pickled cabbage, onions, walnuts, etc* 腌洋白菜、洋葱、胡桃等. **pickled** *adj* (*infml* 口) drunk 醉的: *By this time, he was hopelessly pickled.* 到这时他已经烂醉如泥了.

picky /ˈpɪkɪ; ˋpɪkɪ/ *adj* (**-ier, iest**) (*infml derog* 口, 贬 *esp US*) fussy; choosy 挑剔的; 难以取悦的.

pic·nic /ˈpɪknɪk; ˋpɪknɪk/ *n* **1** (**a**) (*esp Brit*) meal eaten out of doors, esp as part of a pleasure trip 野餐(尤指旅游中的): *We'll go to the river and take a picnic with us.* 我们要到河边玩耍并带着野餐. ○ [attrib 作定语] *a picnic table, hamper, lunch* 野餐桌、食篮、盒饭. (**b**) pleasure trip that includes a picnic 带有野餐的旅游: *It's a nice day — let's go for a picnic.* 天气真好 —— 咱们去野餐游玩吧. **2** (idm 习语) **be no** ˈ**picnic** (*infml* 口) be difficult or troublesome 有困难或麻烦: *Bringing up a family when you are unemployed is no picnic.* 失了业又要养家, 这可不是玩儿的.

▷ **pic·nic** *v* (**-ck-**) [I, Ipr] take part in or have a picnic 参加野餐; 去野餐: *They were picnicking in the woods.* 他们正在林子里野餐. **pic·nicker** *n* person who picnics 野餐者: *Picnickers are requested not to leave litter behind,* eg on a notice. 野餐者不得随地丢弃垃圾(如告示牌上所示者).

pic·ric acid /ˌpɪkrɪk ˈæsɪd; ˌpɪkrɪk ˋæsɪd/ *n* [U] bitter yellow substance used in dyeing and in making explosives 苦味酸.

pic·tor·ial /pɪkˈtɔ:rɪəl; pɪkˋtɔrɪəl/ *adj* (**a**) represented in a picture or pictures 用图片、照片等表示的: *a pictorial record of the wedding* 婚礼的照片集. (**b**) having pictures; illustrated 有图片、照片等的; 用图片、照片等说明的: *a pictorial calendar, magazine, etc* 带画的日历、杂志等.

▷ **pic·tor·ial** *n* newspaper or magazine in which pictures are the most important feature 画报.

pic·tori·ally /-əlɪ; -əlɪ/ *adv*.

pic·ture /ˈpɪktʃə(r); ˋpɪktʃɚ/ *n* **1** [C] (**a**) painting, drawing, sketch, etc, esp as a work of art 绘画, 图画, 素描(尤指作为艺术作品): *His picture of cows won a prize.* 他画的牛的作品获了奖. ○ *Draw a picture of the house so we know what it looks like.* 画出房子的图来让我们看看是什么样子的. (**b**) photograph 照片; 相片: *They showed us the pictures of their wedding.* 他们给我们看结婚照片. ○ *She's taking a picture of the children.* 她正给孩子们拍照. (**c**) portrait (of sb) (某人的)肖像画: *Will you paint my picture?* 您给我画像行吗? **2** [C usu *sing* 通常作单数] beautiful object, scene, person etc 美丽的物、景、人等: *The park is a picture when the daffodils are in bloom.* 水仙花开时公园非常漂亮. ○ *The children were a picture in their pretty dresses.* 孩子们穿上漂亮的衣服好看极了. **3** [C usu *sing* 通常作单数] (**a**) account or description of sth that enables one to form a mental picture or impression of it 形象的叙述: *The book gives a good picture of everyday life in ancient Rome.* 那部书对古罗马人的日常生活描写得很生动. (**b**) this mental picture 心目中的情景: *Her careful description enabled us to form an accurate picture of what had happened.* 她描述得十分细致, 使我们对所发生的事历历如见. **4** [C] (quality of the) image on a television screen 电视图像(的清晰度): *The picture is much clearer with the new aerial.* 装上新天线后画面清晰多了. **5** (*Brit dated* 旧) (**a**) [C] cinema film 影片; 电影: *Have you seen her latest picture?* 你看过她新拍的电影吗? (**b**) **the pictures** [pl] cinema 电影院: *We don't often go to the pictures.* 我们不常到电影院看电影. **6** (idm 习语) **be/put sb in the** ˈ**picture** be/cause sb to be fully informed about sth 了解[使某人了解]实情: *Are you in the picture now?* 你现在知道怎么回事了吗? ○ *Members of Parliament insisted on being put in the picture about the government's plans.* 议员坚持要充分了解政府计划的详情. **be the picture of health, happiness, etc** look very healthy, happy, etc 看上去很健康、愉快等. **get the** ˈ**picture** (*infml* 口) understand 明白; 理解: *I get the picture — you two want to be left alone together.* 我现在明白了 —— 你们俩想单独在一起. **pretty as a picture** ⇨ PRETTY.

▷ **picture** *v* **1** [Tn, Tn·pr] **~ sth (to oneself)** form a mental image of sth; imagine sth 想像或设想某事物: *He pictured to himself what it might be like to live in Java.* 他想像要是生活在爪哇的情形. ○ *I can't picture the village without the old church.* 我无法设想村子里没有那座旧教堂像什么样子. **2** [Tn esp passive 尤用于被动语态] make a picture of (sth/sb) 画(某物[某人])的画; 给(某物[某人])拍照: *They were pictured against a background of flowers.* 他们在画中背景有很多花.

□ ˈ**picture-book** *n* book with many pictures, esp one for children 图画书(尤指为儿童阅读的).

ˈ**picture-card** *n* (in a pack of playing-cards) card with a picture on it, ie the king, queen or knave; court-card (纸牌中的)人像牌(即K、Q、J).

ˈ**picture-gallery** room or building in which paintings are exhibited 绘画陈列室; 画廊.

ˌ**picture** ˈ**postcard** postcard with a picture on one side 美术明信片.

pic·tur·esque /ˌpɪktʃəˈresk; ˏpɪktʃəˋrɛsk/ *adj* **1** forming a pretty scene; charming or quaint 美如画的; 迷人的; 奇特有趣的: *a picturesque fishing village in the bay* 风景如画的海湾渔村 ○ *a picturesque setting* 别致有趣的背景. **2** (of language) strikingly expressive; vivid (指语言)绘声绘色的, 生动的. **3** (of a person, his appearance, his manner, etc) strange or unusual; eccentric (指人、外貌、举止等)奇特的, 异常的, 古怪的: *a picturesque figure in her flowery hat and dungarees* 她戴着花帽子穿着粗蓝布工作服的怪样子. ▷ **pic·tur·esquely** *adv*. **pic·tur·esque·ness** *n* [U].

piddle /ˈpɪdl; ˋpɪdḷ/ *v* [I] (*infml* 口) urinate 撒尿.

▷ **piddle** *n* [U, C] (*infml* 口) urine 尿: *dog piddle* 狗尿 ○ *The puppy has done a piddle on the carpet.* 小狗在地毯上撒了一泡尿.

pid·dling /ˈpɪdlɪŋ; ˋpɪdlɪŋ/ *adj* [esp attrib 尤作定语] (*infml derog* 口, 贬) (**a**) unimportant; trivial 不重要的; 琐碎的: *I don't want to hear all the piddling little details!* 我不想听那些琐碎的事! (**b**) small 小的: *It's annoying to have to get authorization for spending such piddling amounts of money.* 花这么一点钱也要去请示, 真烦人.

pid·gin /ˈpɪdʒɪn; ˋpɪdʒɪn/ *n* any of several languages resulting from contact between European traders and local peoples, eg in W Africa and SE Asia, containing elements of the local language(s) and esp English, French or Dutch, and still used for internal communication 洋泾浜语: *speak in pidgin* 讲洋泾浜话 ○ [attrib 作定语] *pidgin English*, ie language derived from English and another language 洋泾浜英语. Cf 参看 CREOLE.

pie /paɪ; paɪ/ *n* [C, U] **1** (**a**) (*Brit*) meat or fruit encased in pastry and baked in a (usu deep) dish 排; 肉馅排; 果馅排: *an apple pie* 苹果排 ○ *Have some more pie.* 再吃点排吧. (**b**) (*US*) meat or fruit cooked in a pastry-lined dish, with or without a covering of pastry (有盖或无盖的)肉馅排, 果馅排. Cf 参看 FLAN, TART[2]. **2** (idm 习语) **easy as pie** ⇨ EASY[1]. **eat humble pie** ⇨ EAT. **have a finger in every pie** ⇨ FINGER. ˌ**pie in the** ˈ**sky** (*infml* 口) hoped-for or planned event that is very unlikely to happen 希望中的或计划中的事情(不大可能实现的): *Their ideas about reforming the prison system are just pie in the sky.* 他们打算改革监狱制度的想法纯粹是空中楼阁.

□ ˈ**pie chart** diagram consisting of a circle divided into sections that represent specific proportions of the whole, eg in order to show spending in various areas as part of total expenditure 圆形统计图; 饼分图. ⇨illus at CHART 见 CHART 插图.

pie·crust /ˈpaɪkrʌst; ˋpaɪˌkrʌst/ *n* [U] baked pastry covering on a pie 排的盖或皮.

ˌ**pie-**ˈ**eyed** *adj* (*infml* 口) drunk 醉的.

pie·bald /ˈpaɪbɔːld; ˋpaɪˌbɔld/ *adj* (of a horse) covered with irregularly-shaped patches of two colours, usu black and white (指马)有花斑的, (通常指)有黑白斑的. Cf 参看 SKEWBALD.

▷ **pie·bald** *n* piebald horse or pony (黑白)花斑马.

piece[1] /piːs; pis/ *n* **1** [C usu *pl* 通常作复数] (used esp after the *preps in, into, to* 尤用于介词 in、into、to 之后) (**a**) any of the parts of which sth is made 部件; 部分: *He lost one of the pieces of his model engine.* 他的火车头模型缺了一个零件. ○ *The table is made in five pieces.* 这桌子是五部分组成的. ○ *pull sth/take sth/come to pieces* 拆散某物[散成碎块] ○ *The furniture is delivered in pieces and you have to assemble it yourself.* 家具送货时是散件的, 得自己装配. (**b**) any of the portions into which sth breaks 碎片; 碎块; 断片: *The vase shattered into a thousand pieces.* 花瓶已经粉碎了. ○ *The cup lay in pieces on the floor.* 地上是那杯子的碎片. ○ *break, hack, pull, smash, tear sth to pieces* 打碎、劈碎、扯碎、砸碎、撕碎某物 ○ *The boat (was) smashed to pieces on the rocks.* 船触礁而撞碎了. **2** [C] **~ (of sth)** (**a**) amount of a substance (separated or broken from a larger piece) (从大物体上分离下来的)块, 片, 段, 截: *buy a piece of glass to fit the window frame* 买块玻璃安窗户 ○ *put a piece of wood on the fire* 向火里添块木头 ○ *get a piece of grit in one's eye* 眼里迷进一粒沙子 ○ *a piece* (ie a slice) *of bread, cake, meat, etc* 一块面包、蛋糕、肉等. (**b**) amount or area of sth, esp for a particular purpose (某物质的)块, 片, 段, 截(尤指有某用途的): *a piece of chalk*, ie for writing with 一枝粉笔 ○ *a piece of land*, ie for farming or building on 一块地(耕地或建筑用地) ○ *a piece* (ie a sheet) *of paper* 一张纸. ⇨Usage 见所附用法. **3** [C] **~ of sth** (**a**) single instance or example of sth (事情的)项, 桩, 条: *a piece of advice, information, luck, news, treachery* 一个忠告、一项信息、一件幸事、一则新闻、一宗背叛事件 ○ *a fine piece of work* 一部好作品. (**b**) single article; item 件; 个: *a piece of furniture, jewellery, luggage, porcelain* 一件家具、珠宝、行李、瓷器. **4** [C] (**a**) (esp in compounds 尤用以构成复合词) any of the parts of a set 一套中的任何一件、一部分: *a jigsaw with 1000 pieces* 有一千块板片的拼图玩具 ○ *a three-piece suite*, ie a sofa and two armchairs 三件一套的沙发(一张长沙发及两张单座沙发) ○ *a 50-piece orchestra*, ie with 50 players 50 人的管弦乐队. (**b**) any of the small objects or figures used in board games, esp in chess 棋子. **5** [C] standard length of cloth, wallpaper, etc as an item for sale (按标准长度整件出售的布、壁纸等的)匹, 卷, 条: *cloth sold by the piece* 按匹发售的布. **6** [C] **~ (of sth)** (**a**) (in art, music, etc) single work or composition (艺术品、音乐等的)幅, 篇, 首: *a piece of music, poetry, sculpture* 一支乐曲、一首诗、一件雕刻. (**b**) essay or newspaper article 文章; 报道: *Did you read her piece in today's paper?* 你看过今天报纸上她那篇文章吗? **7** [C] coin 硬币: *a ten-pence piece* 十便士硬币 ○ *a five-cent piece* 五分硬币 ○ *a piece of eight*, ie an old Spanish silver coin 一个西班牙旧时银币. **8** [C usu *sing* 通常作单数] (*infml becoming dated derog* 口, 渐旧, 贬) woman or girl 女人; 丫头: *a nice little piece* 小乖妞儿 ○ *Do you know the piece he was with last night?* 你认识昨晚和他一起的那个女人吗? **9** [C] (*dated* 旧) (esp in compounds 尤用以构成复合词) gun 枪; 炮: *a* ˈ*fowling-piece*, ie a gun for shooting wildfowl 鸟枪. **10** [sing] (*US infml* 口) distance 距离: *His house is over there a piece.* 他的房子在那边, 离这儿有一段距离. **11** (idm 习语) **a bit/piece of tail** ⇨ TAIL. **bits and pieces** ⇨ BIT[1]. **give sb a piece of one's** ˈ**mind** (*infml* 口) tell sb frankly what one thinks, esp when one disapproves of his behaviour 坦诚相告(尤指不满对方行为). **go (all) to** ˈ**pieces** (of a person) have a breakdown; lose control of oneself (指人)(精神、身体方面)崩溃, 失去自制力: *After the car accident, she seemed to go to pieces.* 撞车事故后, 她好像精神崩溃了. ○ *He went to pieces when they told him the tragic news.* 人们告诉他那悲惨的消息后, 他已六神无主了. **in one** ˈ**piece** (of a person) unharmed, esp after a dangerous experience (指人)无恙, 平安, (尤指)脱险: *They were lucky to get back in one piece.* 他们安全返回, 十分幸运. **a nasty piece of work** ⇨ NASTY. **(all) of a piece with sth** (**a**) consistent with sth 与某事物一致: *The new measures are all of a piece with the government's policy.* 新措施和政府的政策完全一致. (**b**) of the same substance or character as sth 与某物同一物质或同一性质. **pick/pull sb to** ˈ**pieces** criticize sb, esp when they are absent 批评, 痛斥某人(尤指背后). **pick/pull sth to** ˈ**pieces** argue against sth; find fault with sth 批驳某事; 吹毛求疵. **pick up the pieces/threads** ⇨ PICK[3]. ˌ**piece by** ˈ**piece** one part at a time 一块一块地: *The bridge was moved piece by piece to a new site.* 把那桥一段一段地运到了新址. **a piece/slice of the action** ⇨ ACTION. **a** ˌ**piece of** ˈ**cake** (*infml* 口) thing that is very easy 容易的事: *The exam paper was a piece of cake.* 那份试卷十分容易. ○ *Persuading him to give us the day off won't be a piece of cake.* 要说通他放我们假可不是容易事. **a piece of goods** ⇨ GOODS. **say one's piece** ⇨ SAY. **take a piece out of sb** reprimand sb severely 痛斥某人. **the villain of the piece** ⇨ VILLAIN.

□ ˈ**piece-work** *n* [U] work paid for by the amount done and not by the hours worked 计件工作. ˈ**piece-worker** *n*.

NOTE ON USAGE 用法: The word **piece** can often be replaced by a more specific word ☆ **piece** 一词常可用较具体的词替换: *a slice of bread* 一片面包 ○ *a bar of soap* 一块肥皂. Please consult the relevant entry to find the correct word for the item concerned. 查阅与物品搭配用的确切量词, 请参考有关词条.

piece[2] /piːs; pis/ *v* (phr v) **piece sth together** (**a**) assemble sth from individual pieces 拼合、凑合或组装某物: *piece together a jigsaw* 装配好线锯 ○ *piece together the torn scraps of paper in order to read what was written* 把破碎的文件拼凑起来以阅读其内容. (**b**) discover (a story, facts, etc) from separate pieces of evidence 从各种证据中发现(事情原委、事实等): *We managed to piece together the truth from several sketchy accounts.* 我们从几方面粗略的说法中设法弄清了真相.

pièce de résistance /ˌpjes də reˈzɪstɑːns; *US* -ˌrezɪˈstɑːns; pjɛsdərezisˋtɑ̃s/ *n* (*pl* **pièces de résistance** /ˌpjes də-; pjɛsdə-/) (*French* 法) (**a**) (esp of creative work) the most important or impressive item (尤指创造性的工作)主要项目, 得意之作: *The architect's pièce de*

P

résistance was the City Opera House. 这位建筑师的最得意之作是市歌剧院. (**b**) (at a meal) the most impressive (usu the main) dish[1](2) (一餐中的)主菜.

piece·meal /ˈpi:smi:l; ˋpisˌmil/ *adv* piece by piece; a part at a time 一块一块地; 一件一件地; 零碎地: *work done piecemeal* 一部分一部分做完的工作.

▷ **piece·meal** *adj* arriving, done, etc piecemeal 一块一块的; 一件一件的; 零碎的: *I've only had a piecemeal account of what happened.* 我对发生的事情只有支离破碎的了解.

pied /paɪd; paɪd/ *adj* (esp of birds) having mixed colours, esp black and white (尤指鸟)杂色的, (尤指)黑白的: *a pied wagtail* 一只黑白斑的鹡鸰.

pied-à-terre /ˌpjeɪd ɑ: ˈteə (r); ˌpjedɑˋtɛr/ *n* (*pl* **pieds-à-terre** /ˌpjeɪd ɑ:-; ˌpjedɑ-/) (*French* 法) small flat or other accommodation that one keeps for use when necessary (私人备用的)小公寓, 住所: *They own a cottage in Scotland and a house in London as well as a pied-à-terre in Paris.* 他们在苏格兰有一村舍, 在伦敦有一所房子, 在巴黎还有一套备用公寓.

pier 突堤

pier /pɪə(r); pɪr/ *n* **1** (**a**) structure of wood, iron, etc built out into the sea, a lake, etc so that boats can stop and take on or put down passengers or goods (伸入海、湖等的)码头; 突码头. Cf 参看 JETTY. (**b**) similar structure built as a promenade at a seaside resort, often with a restaurant and places of entertainment on it (供散步游乐的)突堤(常设有餐厅及娱乐场所). ⇨illus 见插图. **2** one of the pillars supporting an arch or a span of a bridge 桥墩. **3** wall between two windows or other openings 窗间壁; 户间壁; 扶壁.

pierce /pɪəs; pɪrs/ *v* **1** [Tn, Tn·pr] (**a**) (of sharp-pointed instruments) go into or through (sth) (指尖物)刺入, 刺透(某物): *The arrow pierced his shoulder.* 那枝箭刺入他的肩膀. ○ (*fig* 比喻) *Her suffering pierced their hearts,* ie moved them deeply. 她遭受的苦难使他们心如刀绞. (**b**) make a hole in or through (sth), esp with a sharp-pointed instrument 在(某物)上扎眼、穿孔: *pierce holes in leather before sewing it* 先在皮子上扎眼然后再缝 ○ *pierce the skin of cooking sausages with a fork* 用叉子在要烹调的香肠上扎孔 ○ *She had her ears pierced so that she could wear ear-rings.* 她已扎了耳朵眼好戴耳环. **2** [Tn] (of light, sound, etc) penetrate (sth) (指光、声等)透入, 进入(某处): *Her shrieks pierced the air.* 她尖锐的叫声直刺云天. ○ *The beam of the searchlight pierced the darkness.* 探照灯的光柱射入黑暗中. **3** [Ipr] ~ **through sth** force a way into sth; penetrate sth 穿入、穿过或进入某处: *Earth-moving equipment pierced through the jungle.* 推土机穿过丛林.

▷ **pier·cing** *adj* (**a**) (of voices, sounds, etc) shrill; penetrating (指声音等)尖锐的, 刺耳的: *a piercing shriek* 尖锐的叫声. (**b**) (of wind, cold, etc) bitter; penetrating (指风、寒冷等)刺骨的, 穿透的: *a piercing chill, breeze* 透心的寒冷、沁人心脾的微风. **pier·cingly** *adv*: *a piercingly cold wind* 刺骨寒风.

pier·rot /ˈpɪərəʊ; ˌpiəˋro/ *n* (*fem* 阴性作 **pier·rette** /pɪəˈret; piˋrɛt/) **1** (also **Pierrot**) character in French pantomime 法国童话剧中的角色. **2** (esp formerly) member of a group of entertainers performing esp at seaside resorts, dressed in loose white clothes and with whitened faces (尤指旧时)穿肥大的白衣涂白脸的表演者(尤指在海滨娱乐场的).

pietà /ˌpi:eˈtɑ:; pieˋtɑ/ *n* (*Italian* 意) painting or sculpture of the Virgin Mary holding the dead body of Christ on her lap 圣母怜子(圣母马利亚抱耶稣遗体于膝上的画像或雕像).

piety /ˈpaɪətɪ; ˋpaɪətɪ/ *n* (**a**) [U] devotion to God and respect for religious principles; being pious (对上帝的)虔敬, 虔诚: *filial piety,* ie respect for and obedience to a parent 孝顺. (**b**) [C] act showing this 虔敬; 虔诚.

piezo-electric /pi:ˌeɪzəʊɪˈlektrɪk; paɪˌizoɪˋlɛktrɪk/ *adj* worked by electricity which is produced by exerting pressure on certain crystals 压电的.

piffle /ˈpɪfl; ˋpɪfl/ *n* [U] (*infml derog* 口, 贬) meaningless or worthless talk; nonsense 废话; 无聊的话: *You're talking piffle!* 你胡说八道!

▷ **piff·ling** /ˈpɪflɪŋ; ˋpɪflɪŋ/ *adj* (*infml derog* 口, 贬) (**a**) trivial 琐碎的: *piffling complaints* 无谓的牢骚. (**b**) very small; worthless 极小的; 无价值的: *He got paid a piffling sum after weeks of work.* 他工作数周所得甚微.

pig 猪

pig /pɪg; pɪg/ *n* **1** (**a**) [C] domestic or wild animal with short legs, cloven hooves and a broad blunt snout 猪; 野猪. Cf 参看 BOAR, HOG 1, SOW[1], SWINE. (**b**) (also **ˈpig-meat**) [U] its flesh as meat, ie bacon, ham or pork 猪肉. **2** [C] (*infml derog* 口, 贬) (**a**) dirty, greedy, inconsiderate or ill-mannered person 肮脏的、贪婪的、不顾别人的或粗野的人: *Don't be such a pig!* 别这么贪心! ○ *You pig!* 你可真脏! ○ *Some drivers are real pigs.* 有些人开车真粗野. (**b**) difficult or unpleasant thing, task, etc 困难的或讨厌的事情: *a pig of a job, day, exam* 讨厌的工作、日子、考试. **3** (**a**) [C] oblong mass of metal (esp iron or lead) from a smelting furnace 金属锭; (尤指)铁锭, 铅锭. (**b**) [U] = PIG-IRON. **4** [C] (*dated sl* 旧, 俚) policeman (男)警察. **5** (idm 习语) **buy a pig in a poke** ⇨ BUY. **make a ˈpig of oneself** (*infml* 口) eat or drink too much 吃得或喝得过多. **make a ˈpig's ear (out) of sth** (*infml* 口) do sth badly; make a mess of it 弄糟或弄乱某事物. **pig/piggy in the ˈmiddle** person who is caught eg between two people who are fighting or arguing, and suffers because of it 夹在打架或争吵双方之间的人; 受夹板气的人. **ˌpigs might ˈfly** (*saying* 谚) (used to express disbelief 用以表示对某事不相信) miracles may happen but they are extremely unlikely 即使能有奇迹也不太可能出现: *Tom give up smoking? Yes, and pigs might fly!* 汤姆戒烟? 嘿, 能有这种事儿!

▷ **pig** *v* (**-gg-**) **1** [Tn] ~ **oneself** (*infml* 口) overeat greedily 贪食过量. **2** (idm 习语) **ˈpig it/pig toˈgether** live or behave in a dirty or untidy way 生活或行为方面邋遢.

pig·gery /ˈpɪgərɪ; ˋpɪgərɪ/ *n* (**a**) place where pigs are bred 猪圈; 养猪场. (**b**) pig-farm 养猪场. (**c**) pigsty 猪圈.

pig·gish /ˈpɪgɪʃ; ˋpɪgɪʃ/ *adj* (**a**) like a pig 像猪的. (**b**) dirty or greedy 肮脏的; 贪婪的. **pig·gishly** *adv.* **pig·gish·ness** *n* [U].

piggy /ˈpɪgɪ; ˋpɪgɪ/ *n* (*infml* 口) little pig 小猪. — *adj* (*infml* 口) piggish 像猪的; 肮脏的; 贪婪的: *He has piggy eyes!* 他的眼睛像猪的眼睛似的! **ˈpig·gy·back** *adv, n* = PICK-A-BACK. **ˈpiggy bank** money-box, usu shaped like a pig, with a slot for putting in coins 扑满, 储蓄罐(通常为猪形).

□ **ˌpigˈheaded** *adj* stubborn 顽固的; 固执的. **ˌpigˈheadedly** *adv.* **ˌpigˈheadedness** *n* [U].

ˈpig-iron *n* [U] impure form of iron from a smelting furnace 生铁.

ˈpigskin /-skɪn; -ˌskɪn/ *n* [U] (leather made from a) pig's skin 猪皮革: [attrib 作定语] *a ˌpigskin ˈbriefcase* 猪

皮公事包.

'**pigsty** /-staɪ; -staɪ/ (also **sty**) *n* **1** (*US* '**pigpen**) building in which pigs are kept 猪圈. ⇨illus 见插图. **2** (*infml* 口) very dirty or untidy place 肮脏或邋遢的地方: *He makes a pigsty of the kitchen whenever he does the cooking.* 他一做饭就把厨房弄得很脏.

'**pigswill** /-swɪl; -ˌswɪl/ *n* [U] = SWILL *n* 2.

pi·geon /ˈpɪdʒɪn; ˋpɪdʒən/ *n* **1** (**a**) [C] any of several types of wild or tame bird of the dove family 鸽子: *a 'carrier-/'homing-pigeon*, ie one trained to carry messages or to race as a sport 信鸽. ⇨illus at App 1 见附录1插图, page iv. (**b**) [U] flesh of a wild pigeon eaten as food 野鸽肉: [attrib 作定语] *pigeon pie* 鸽肉排. **2** (idm 习语) '**one's pigeon** (*infml* 口) one's responsibility or business 自己的责任或事情: *I don't care where the money comes from: that's not 'my pigeon.* 我不管钱从哪儿来, 那不是我的事. **put/set the cat among the pigeons** ⇨ CAT[1].

□ '**pigeon-breasted** *adj* (of a person) having a deformed chest with the breastbone curving outwards (指人)鸡胸的.

'**pigeon-hole** *n* any one of a set of small open boxes, esp in a desk, for keeping papers in, or fixed on a wall for messages, letters, etc (文件或信件的)分类格架. — *v* [Tn esp passive 尤用于被动语态] **1** put (papers, etc) in a pigeon-hole (and ignore or forget them) 将(文件等)放进分类架中(置之不理或搁置): *The scheme was pigeon-holed after a brief discussion.* 那计划草议后就搁置一边了. **2** classify or categorize (sth) esp in a rigid manner 将(某事物)分类、归档(尤指硬性地): *She felt her son had been pigeon-holed as a problem child.* 她认为自己的儿子硬被划入了有问题儿童之列.

'**pigeon-toed** *adj* (of a person) having toes that turn inwards (指人)足趾内翻的.

pig·let /ˈpɪglɪt; ˋpɪglɪt/ *n* young pig 小猪. ⇨illus at PIG 见 PIG 插图.

pig·ment /ˈpɪgmənt; ˋpɪgmənt/ *n* **1** [U, C] colouring matter used for making dyes, paint, etc 颜料: *pigment in powder form* 颜料粉 ○ *mix pigment with oil* 把颜料与油混合 ○ *They used only natural pigments to dye the wool.* 他们只用天然颜料染毛. **2** [U] colouring matter occurring naturally in the skin, hair, etc of living beings 色素.

▷ **pig·menta·tion** /ˌpɪgmenˈteɪʃn; ˌpɪgmənˋteʃən/ *n* [U] colouring of the skin, hair, etc by pigment 色素沉着: *The disease causes patches of pigmentation on the face.* 这种疾病能引起面部色素斑沉着.

pigmy = PYGMY.

pig·tail /ˈpɪgteɪl; ˋpɪgˌtel/ *n* plait of hair that hangs from the back of the head 辫子. ⇨illus at PLAIT 见 PLAIT 插图.

pike[1] /paɪk; paɪk/ *n* type of spear with a long wooden handle, formerly used as a weapon by soldiers on foot 矛.

□ '**pikestaff** /-stɑːf; -ˌstæf/ *n* **1** wooden handle of a pike (木制的)矛柄. **2** (idm 习语) **plain as a pikestaff** ⇨ PLAIN[1].

pike[2] /paɪk; paɪk/ *n* (*pl* unchanged 复数不变) large freshwater fish with a long narrow snout and very sharp teeth 狗鱼.

pike[3] /paɪk; paɪk/ *n* (*dialect* 方) (in N England) pointed or peaked top of a hill (在英格兰北部)尖峰, 陡峰: *Langdale Pike in the Lake District* 湖区的兰代尔峰.

pike[4] /paɪk; paɪk/ *n* = TURNPIKE.

pi·laff /pɪˈlæf; *US* -ˈlɑːf; pəˋlɑf/ (also **pilaf**, **pilau** /pɪˈlaʊ; pɪˋlaʊ/) *n* [U, C] oriental dish of steamed rice, vegetables and spices, often with meat or fish 肉饭(有蔬菜和作料的东方风味蒸饭, 常有肉或鱼).

pi·las·ter /pɪˈlæstə(r); pəˋlæstɚ/ *n* rectangular column, esp an ornamental one set into a wall and partly projecting from it 长方柱; (尤指)壁柱, 半露柱.

pilch·ard /ˈpɪltʃəd; ˋpɪltʃɚd/ *n* small sea-fish similar to a herring, eaten as food 沙丁鱼.

pile[1] /paɪl; paɪl/ *n* heavy column of wood, metal or concrete placed upright in the ground or the sea-bed as a foundation for a building, support for a bridge, etc (桥梁等的)桩.

□ '**pile-driver** *n* machine for forcing piles into the ground 打桩机.

pile[2] /paɪl; paɪl/ *n* **1** number of things lying one upon another 堆; 摞; 叠: *a pile of books, laundry, wood* 一堆书、洗的衣物、木头 ○ *The rubbish was left in a pile on the floor.* 地板上堆着垃圾. **2** (often *pl* 常作复数) ~ **of sth** (*infml* 口) a lot of sth 一大堆; 一大批; 一大团; 大量: *a pile of work to do* 要做的大量工作 ○ *The children eat piles of butter on their bread.* 孩子们吃面包爱多抹黄油. ○ *The engine seems to need piles of oil.* 这种发动机似乎需要很多油. **3** (*fml or joc* 文或谑) large impressive building or group of buildings 高大的建筑物. **4** (also '**funeral pile**) = PYRE. **5** dry battery for making electric current 干电池. **6** (also **atomic 'pile**) nuclear reactor 核反应堆. **7** (idm 习语) **make a 'pile** (*infml* 口) earn a lot of money 赚大钱; 发财: *I bet they are making a pile out of the deal.* 我肯定他们这笔生意一定赚大钱. **make one's 'pile** (*infml* 口) make enough money to live on for the rest of one's life; make one's fortune (为以后的生活)挣够钱; 发财: *He made his pile during the property boom.* 在房地产生意兴隆期间他发了大财.

pile[3] /paɪl; paɪl/ *v* **1** [Tn, Tn·pr, Tn·p] ~ **sth (up)** put (things) one on top of the other; form a pile of (things) 堆叠、堆积、堆放或堆起(东西): *pile the books into a stack* 把书堆成一摞 ○ *pile (up) the logs outside the door* 把木头码在门外 ○ *pile the books up* 把书摞起来 ○ *pile up the old furniture in the shed* 把旧家具堆放到棚子里. **2** [Tn·pr] ~ **A on(to) B**/~ **B with A** put sth on sth in a pile; load sth with sth 将某物堆在某物上; 将某物放到某处: *pile papers on the table* 把报纸堆放在桌子上 ○ *pile the table with papers* 桌子上堆着报纸 ○ *pile plenty of coal onto the fire* 往火上加很多煤 ○ *a table piled high with dishes* 桌子上高高地摞着碟子. **3** (idm 习语) **pile it 'on** (*infml* 口) exaggerate 夸张; 夸大: *It's probably not as bad as she says — she does tend to pile it on.* 大概不像她说的那么糟 — 她确实有意夸大事实. **pile on the 'agony** (*infml* 口) treat an unpleasant situation as if it was worse than it really is (and enjoy doing so) (欣欣然)夸大坏的情况: *The situation is frightful, but it's just piling on the agony to keep discussing it.* 情况很可怕, 可是还一个劲儿地议论让人觉得更可怕. **4** (phr v) **pile into sth/out of sth**; **pile in/out** enter/leave sth in a disorderly way 一窝蜂地进入[离开]某处: *The taxi arrived and we all piled in.* 计程车一到, 我们一拥而上. ○ *The children piled noisily into the bus.* 孩子们闹哄哄地挤上了公共汽车. ○ *The police were waiting for the hooligans as they piled out of the train.* 那些流氓从火车上纷纷下来, 警察早已在那儿等着他们了. **pile up** (**a**) increase in quantity; accumulate 增多; 积累: *Evidence was piling up against them.* 不利于他们的证据越来越多. ○ *Her debts are piling up and she has no money to pay them.* 她债台日高已无力偿还. (**b**) (of a number of vehicles) crash into each other, esp with each car hitting the one in front (指若干辆车)互相碰撞, (尤指)连环碰撞.

□ '**pile-up** *n* crash involving several vehicles 几辆车相撞: *The thick fog has caused several bad pile-ups on the motorway.* 因大雾弥漫, 高速公路上发生了几起严重的连环撞车事故.

pile[4] /paɪl; paɪl/ *n* [U] soft surface, eg of velvet or of certain carpets, formed from cut or uncut loops of fibre 绒面, 绒头(如织物或地毯的): *the thick pile of a luxurious bath towel* 华丽浴巾的厚绒面 ○ [attrib 作定语] *a deep pile carpet* 厚绒地毯. Cf 参看 NAP[2].

piles /paɪlz; paɪlz/ *n* [pl] = HAEMORRHOIDS.

pil·fer /ˈpɪlfə(r); ˋpɪlfɚ/ *v* [I, Ipr, Tn] ~ (**sth**) (**from sb/sth**) steal (sth, esp of small value or in small quantities) 偷窃(尤指价值低的或少量的东西); 小偷小摸: *He was caught pilfering.* 他行窃当场被抓住. ○ *She had been pilfering from the petty cash for months.* 她多月来一直从零用现金中偷钱.

▷ **pil·ferer** /ˈpɪlfərə(r); ˋpɪlfərɚ/ *n*.

pil·ferage /ˈpɪlfərɪdʒ; ˋpɪlfərɪdʒ/ *n* [U] (**a**) action of pilfering 小偷小摸. (**b**) loss caused by pilfering, esp during transport or storage of goods 被窃的损失(尤指货物在运输或贮藏中发生的): *Pilferage in the warehouse reduces profitability by about two per cent.* 仓库中的失窃使利润损失了百分之二.

pil·grim /ˈpɪlgrɪm; ˋpɪlgrəm/ *n* person who travels to a holy place as an act of religious devotion 朝圣者; 香客: *pilgrims on their way to Mecca* 赴麦加的朝圣者 ○

P

pilgrims visiting the shrine 到圣徒墓地朝圣的人.

▷ **pil·grim·age** /-ɪdʒ; -ɪdʒ/ *n* **1** [C, U] journey made as a pilgrim 朝圣之行: *go on/make a pilgrimage to Benares* 到贝拿勒斯朝圣 ○ *Santiago de Compostela was an important place of pilgrimage in the Middle Ages.* 中世纪圣地亚哥一德孔波斯特拉是朝圣的要地. **2** [C] journey made to a place associated with sb/sth one respects 到敬仰的某人[某事物]处之行: *a pilgrimage to Shakespeare's birthplace* 到莎士比亚诞生地的参谒.

□ **the Pilgrim ˈFathers** (also **the Pilgrims**) name given to the English Puritans who went to America in 1620 and founded the colony of Plymouth, Massachusetts 1620年到美洲创立麻省普里茅斯殖民地的英国清教徒.

P

pill /pɪl; pɪl/ *n* **1** [C] small ball or flat round piece of medicine made to be swallowed whole 药丸; 药片: *a vitamin pill* 维生素丸 ○ *He has to take* (ie swallow) *six pills a day until he recovers.* 他每天要服六粒药丸直到痊愈. **2 the pill** (also **the Pill**) [sing] (*infml* 口) artificial hormone in pill form taken regularly to prevent conception; oral contraceptive 口服避孕药: *be/go on the pill*, ie be/start taking contraceptive pills regularly 正[开始]按时服用避孕药 ○ *do research on the side-effects of the pill* 研究口服避孕药的副作用. **3** (idm 习语) **a bitter pill** ⇨ BITTER. **sugar/sweeten the pill** make sth unpleasant seem less unpleasant 降低某事物令人厌恶的程度.

□ **ˈpillbox** *n* **1** small round box used as a container for pills 药丸盒; 药片盒. **2** small concrete shelter for soldiers, often partly underground, from which a gun may be fired 混凝土射击掩体; 碉堡. **3** small round hat 小圆帽.

pil·lage /ˈpɪlɪdʒ; ˋpɪlɪdʒ/ *n* [U] (*fml* 文) (esp formerly) stealing or damaging of property, esp by soldiers in war (尤指旧时)掠夺, 抢劫(尤指战时士兵所为). Cf 参看 LOOT, PLUNDER.

▷ **pil·lage** *v* [I, Tn] rob (sb/sth) of goods, crops, etc with violence, as in war 掠夺, 抢劫(某人[某处]的物品、庄稼等)(如于战时): *The town was pillaged by the invading army.* 入侵的军队将该市掠夺一空. **pil·la·ger** /-ɪdʒə(r); -ɪdʒɚ/ *n* person who pillages 掠夺者; 抢劫者.

pil·lar /ˈpɪlə(r); ˋpɪlɚ/ *n* **1** (**a**) upright column of stone, wood, metal, etc used as a support or an ornament, a monument, etc 柱子; 支柱. ⇨illus at App 1 见附录1插图, page viii. (**b**) thing in the shape of this 柱形物: *a pillar of cloud, fire, smoke, etc* 云柱、火柱、烟柱. **2 ~ of sth** strong supporter of sth (某事物的)强大支持者: *a pillar of the Church, the establishment, the faith* 教会、统治集团、该信仰的拥护者 ○ *a scandal involving several pillars* (ie respected members) *of society* 涉及几个社会要人的丑闻 ○ *She was a pillar of strength to us* (ie supported us strongly) *when our situation seemed hopeless.* 在我们近乎绝望之际, 她给了我们有力的支持. **3** (idm 习语) **(go) from ˌpillar to ˈpost** (go) from one person or thing to another (esp in an unsatisfactory or upsetting way) 到处奔走; (尤指)到处碰壁: *She was driven from pillar to post and each person she spoke to was more unhelpful than the last.* 她被迫四处奔走求救于人, 但愿意帮她的人一个不如一个.

□ **ˈpillar-box** *n* (*Brit*) public post-box in the shape of a pillar about five feet high and painted bright red 邮筒, 信筒(柱形, 约五英尺高, 大红色): [attrib 作定语] *pillar-box red* 邮筒的红色.

pillory 枷

pil·lion /ˈpɪlɪən; ˋpɪljən/ *n* seat for a passenger behind the driver of a motor cycle 摩托车后座: [attrib 作定语] *pillion passenger/seat* 摩托车后座坐着的人[座位]. ▷ **pil·lion** *adv*: *ride pillion*, ie ride on the pillion 坐在摩托车后座上.

pil·lory /ˈpɪlərɪ; ˋpɪlərɪ/ *n* wooden framework with holes for the head and hands, into which wrongdoers were locked in former times, so that they could be publicly ridiculed 枷. ⇨illus 见插图.

▷ **pil·lory** *v* (*pt, pp* **-ried** /-lərɪd; -lərɪd/) [Tn] attack or ridicule (sb) in public 公开攻击或嘲笑(某人): *She was pilloried in the press for her extravagant parties.* 她的聚会十分铺张, 新闻界对她大加揶揄.

pil·low /ˈpɪləʊ; ˋpɪlo/ *n* (**a**) cushion used to support the head, esp in bed 枕头: *sit in bed propped up with pillows* 靠着枕头坐在床上. (**b**) anything on which one rests one's head when sleeping 睡觉时枕着的任何物件: *He was found asleep on a pillow of leaves and moss.* 有人看见他枕着树叶和苔藓睡着了.

▷ **pil·low** *v* [Tn] rest or support (sth) on or as if on a pillow 将(某物)放在枕头等物上; 以枕头等支撑(某物): *He pillowed his head on her lap.* 他把头枕在她的大腿上.

□ **ˈpillowcase** (also **ˈpillowslip**) *n* removable washable cover made of cotton, linen, etc for a pillow 枕套.

ˈpillow-fight *n* mock fight between children using pillows as weapons 儿童用枕头打闹的游戏.

pi·lot /ˈpaɪlət; ˋpaɪlət/ *n* **1** person who operates the controls of an aircraft (飞行器的)驾驶员; 飞行员. **2** person with special knowledge of a canal, the entrance to a harbour, etc who is licensed to guide ships through them (船舶的)领航员, 领港员. **3** person or thing acting as a guide 作向导的人或事物.

▷ **pi·lot** *adj* [attrib 作定语] done as an experiment, esp on a small scale, to test sth before it is introduced on a large scale 试验性的; 试点的: *a ˈpilot project, study, survey, etc* 试验性工程、研究、勘察等 ○ *a pilot edition of a new language course* 新语言教程的试用版 ○ *a pilot scheme to vaccinate children against German measles* 为儿童接种抗风疹疫苗的试验计划.

pi·lot *v* **1** [Tn, Tn·pr] **~ sb/sth (through sth)** (**a**) act as a pilot of sth 驾驶(飞行器); (为船)引航: *pilot a plane* 驾驶飞机 ○ *pilot a ship through the Panama Canal* 引领一船通过巴拿马运河. (**b**) guide sb/sth 带领、指引或引导某人[某事物]: *pilot sb through a crowd* 带领某人穿过人群. (**c**) (in Parliament) make sure that sth (esp a bill) is successful (在议会中)使(尤指法案)顺利通过: *pilot a bill through the House* 使法案在议会中获得通过. **2** [Tn] test (sth) by means of a pilot scheme 试行, 试用(某事物): *Schools in this area are piloting the new maths course.* 这一带的学校正试用新的数学教程.

□ **ˈpilot-boat** *n* boat that takes a pilot to a ship at sea 领航船(送领航员到轮船上的小船).

ˈpilot-fish *n* type of small fish that accompanies ships or swims together with sharks, etc 引水鱼, 舟鰤(跟随船或鲨等的小鱼).

ˈpilot-light (also **ˈpilot-burner**) *n* small flame that burns continuously, eg on a gas cooker or boiler, and lights a larger burner when the gas is turned on 引火火苗(如为引燃煤气用具的常燃火苗).

ˈPilot Officer (*Brit*) officer in the Royal Air Force below the rank of Flying Officer 英国皇家空军少尉. ⇨ App 9 见附录9.

pi·mento /pɪˈmentəʊ; pɪˋmento/ *n* (*pl* **~s**) **1** (**a**) (also **allspice**) [U] dried aromatic berries used as a spice 多香果(干后用作香料). (**b**) [C] West Indian tree on which these grow 多香果树(产自西印度). **2** (also **pimiento** /pɪˈmjentəʊ; pɪˋmjɛnto/) [C] sweet pepper; capsicum 甜辣椒; 番椒.

pimp /pɪmp; pɪmp/ *n* (**a**) (also **pander**) man who finds customers for a prostitute or a brothel (为妓女、男妓或妓院)拉皮条的男子. (**b**) man who controls prostitutes and lives on the money they earn 妓院男老板.

▷ **pimp** *v* [I, Ipr] **~ (for sb)** find customers (for a prostitute or brothel); act as a pimp (指男子为妓女、男妓或妓院)拉客, 拉皮条; 当拉皮条的.

pim·per·nel /ˈpɪmpənel; ˋpɪmpɚˌnɛl/ *n* wild plant with small, star-shaped, scarlet, blue or white flowers that close up in wet or cloudy weather 海绿(矮小野生植物, 花星形, 呈红、蓝或白色, 阴雨天闭合).

pimple /ˈpɪmpl; ˋpɪmpḷ/ *n* small raised inflamed spot on the skin 丘疹; 小脓疱; 粉刺: *a pimple on one's chin* 下巴上的小脓疱 ○ *teenage pimples* 青少年长的粉刺.

▷ **pimpled** *adj* having pimples 有丘疹、小脓疱或粉刺的: *a pimpled back* 长丘疹的背.

pimply /ˈpɪmplɪ; ˋpɪmplɪ/ *adj* **1** having pimples 有丘疹、小脓疱或粉刺的: *a pimply face* 长粉刺的脸 ○ *pimply skin* 有丘疹的皮肤. **2** (*infml derog* 口, 贬) (of a person) immature (指人)未成熟的: *I don't want to speak to some pimply youth, I want to see the manager!* 我不想和小青年说话, 我要见经理!

pin[1] /pɪn; pɪn/ *n* **1** [C] (**a**) short thin piece of stiff wire with a sharp point at one end and a round head at the other, used for fastening together pieces of cloth, paper, etc 大头针. (**b**) (esp in compounds 尤用以构成复合词) similar piece of wire with a sharp point and a decorated head, used for a special purpose 饰针: *a diamond pin* ○ *a ˈtie-pin* ○ *a ˈhat-pin.* **2** [C] (esp in compounds 尤用以构成复合词) peg of wood or metal for various special purposes 锁; 钉; 插头; 闩: *a 2-pin plug,* ie a type of electric plug ○ *a ˈdrawing-pin* ○ *a ˈhairpin* ○ *a ˈrolling-pin* ○ *ˈninepins* ○ (*US*) *a ˈclothes-pin,* ie a clothes-peg. **3** [C] (also **ˈsafety pin**) clip on a hand grenade that stops it from exploding (手榴弹上的)保险针, 保险锁. **4 pins** [pl] (*infml* 口) legs 腿. **5** (idm 习语) **clean as a new pin** ⇨ CLEAN[1]. **for two pins** with very little persuasion or provocation 只要再有一点外力或再受一点招惹: *For two pins I'd tell him what I think of him.* 再有个风吹草动, 我就把对他的看法挑明了. **hear a pin drop** ⇨ HEAR. **not care/give a ˈpin/two ˈpins (for sth)** attach no importance or value to sth 对某事物毫不重视或毫不在乎: *He doesn't give two pins for what the critics say about his work.* 他毫不在乎别人对他作品的批评. **on one's pins** (*infml* 口) when standing or walking 站立或行走时: *She's not very steady on her pins.* 她站得不太稳. ○ *be quick on one's pins* 腿脚矫健.

□ **ˈpin-ball** *n* [U] game in which small metal balls are aimed at numbered pins placed on a sloping board 弹球戏(弹出金属小球沿斜板滚入记分钉孔处的游戏): [attrib 作定语] *a pin-ball machine* 弹球机.

ˈpincushion *n* small pad used (esp by dressmakers) for sticking pins in when they are not being used 针插(尤指裁缝用的).

ˈpin-head *n* (*infml* 口) (**a**) (*derog* 贬) stupid person 傻瓜; 笨蛋. (**b**) very small thing or spot 极小的东西或斑点.

ˈpin-money *n* [U] (**a**) (esp formerly) small amount of money given to a woman or earned by her for her personal needs, esp clothes (尤指旧时)(给女子的或女子挣的)零花钱, 私房钱(尤指买衣物用的). (**b**) money saved or earned for small extra expenses 小积蓄; 少量备用钱.

ˈpinpoint *n* (**a**) sharp end of a pin 针尖. (**b**) anything that is very small or sharp 小的或尖的东西. — *v* [Tn] (**a**) find the exact position of (sth) 找出(某物)的确切位置: *pinpoint the spot on a map* 找出该处在地图上的位置. (**b**) define (sth) exactly 准确解释或确定(某事物): *pinpoint the causes of the political unrest* 确定政治动乱的原因 ○ *pinpoint the areas in most urgent need of help* 确定需要紧急帮助的地区.

ˈpinprick *n* thing that is annoying although small or unimportant 令人烦恼的小事或不重要的事.

ˌpins and ˈneedles tingling sensation in a part of the body, esp a limb, caused by the blood flowing again after being stopped by pressure 针刺感, 发麻(尤指手脚).

ˈpin-stripe *n* very narrow stripe in cloth (布上的)细条纹: [attrib 作定语] *a pin-stripe suit* 一套细条纹服装.

ˈpin-table *n* table used in pin-ball 弹球戏桌.

pin[2] /pɪn; pɪn/ *v* (**-nn-**) **1** [Tn, Tn·pr, Tn·p] **~ sth to sth; ~ sth (together)** attach sth with a pin or pins 用针、别针等固定、钉住或别住某物: *Be careful when you try on the dress — it's only pinned.* 试穿这件连衣裙要小心——只是用针别住的. ○ *a note pinned to the document* 别在文件上的便条 ○ *Pin the bills together so you don't lose them.* 把帐单别在一起以防遗失. ○ (*fig* 比喻) *They held him with his arms pinned to his side.* 他们抓住了他, 把他的胳膊按在肋部. **2** [Tn·pr] **~ sth on sb** attach or fix sth to sb 将某事物附加在某人身上: *We're pinning all our hopes on you,* ie relying on you completely. 我们把希望完全寄托在你身上了. **3** (phr v) **pin sb/sth against/under sth** make it impossible for sb to move/sth to be moved 使某人[某物]不能动: *They pinned him against the wall.* 他们把他按在墙上使他不能动弹. ○ *She was pinned under the wreckage of the car.* 撞毁的汽车把她压在下面动弹不得. ○ *The car was pinned under a fallen tree.* 汽车被倒下的树压住了. **pin sth back/down/up** fasten sth with pins in the position specified 用针或别针等将某物固定在某处: *pin up a notice on the board,* ie with drawing-pins 用图钉把通知按在布告板上. **pin sb down** (**a**) make sb unable to move, esp by holding him firmly 使某人不能动(尤指捉住或抱住): *He was pinned down by his attackers.* 袭击他的人把他按住了. (**b**) make sb be specific or declare his intentions clearly 使某人具体或确切说明意图: *She's a difficult person to pin down.* 她这人行事、说话没个准儿. **pin sb down (to sth/doing sth)** make sb agree (to sth) 使某人同意(某事): *I managed to pin him down to meeting us after work.* 我设法让他同意下班后和我们见面了. ○ *You'll find it difficult to pin him down to (naming) a price.* 到时候你就知道了很难让他说出个准价. **pin sth down** define sth exactly 明确说明或确定某事物: *There's something wrong with this colour scheme but I can't quite pin it down.* 这种颜色搭配不太合适, 可是我也说不清楚怎么不合适. **pin sth on sb** make sb seem responsible or take the blame for sth 使某人似应对某事负责; 将责任推到某人身上: *The bank manager was really to blame, though he tried to pin it on a clerk.* 真正受责备的应该是银行经理, 可是他却想把责任推到一个职员身上.

□ **ˈpin-up** *n* (*infml* 口) (**a**) picture of an attractive or famous person, eg a film star, for pinning on a wall (可钉在墙上的漂亮的或有名的人的)画像, 照片(如影星的): [attrib 作定语] *a pin-up pose* 海报中名人的姿势. (**b**) person portrayed in such a picture (可钉在墙上的)画像或照片中的人.

PIN *abbr* 缩写 = (also **PIN number**) personal identification number (issued by a bank, etc to a customer for use with a cash card) (银行等发给顾客与提款卡配合使用的)身分号码.

pin·afore /ˈpɪnəfɔ:(r); ˋpɪnə,fɔr/ *n* loose sleeveless garment worn over clothes to keep them clean; apron 连胸围裙. ⇨illus at APRON 见 APRON 插图.

□ **ˈpinafore dress** dress without sleeves or a collar, worn over a blouse or sweater 无袖或无领的连衣裙.

pince-nez /ˌpænsˈneɪ; ˋpæns,ne/ *n* (*pl* unchanged 复数不变) [sing or pl *v*] pair of spectacles with a spring that clips on the nose, instead of side-pieces which fit over the ears 夹鼻眼镜.

pincers 钳或螯

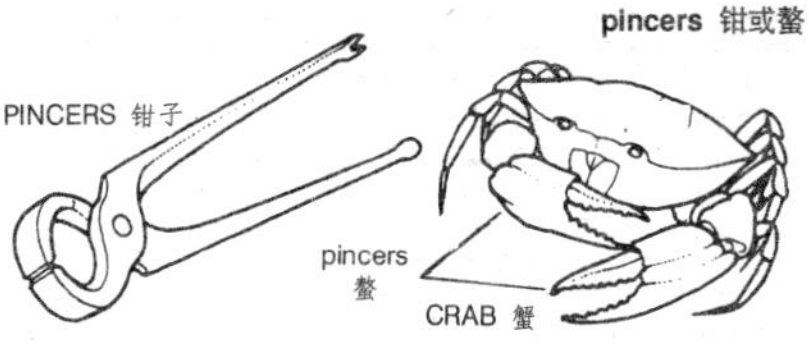

pin·cer /ˈpɪnsə(r); ˋpɪnsɚ/ *n* **1** [C] either of the pair of curved claws of certain types of shellfish, eg lobsters, crabs, etc (甲壳动物的)螯(如龙虾、蟹等的). **2 pincers** [pl] tool made of two crossed pieces of metal and used for pulling nails, etc out of wood 钳子: *a pair of pincers* 一把钳子. ⇨illus 见插图.

□ **ˈpincer movement** military attack on an enemy position by forces advancing from two sides 钳形攻势; 钳形突击.

pinch /pɪntʃ; pɪntʃ/ *v* **1** [Tn, Tn·pr] (**a**) take or hold (sth) in a tight grip between the thumb and finger 捏, 掐(某物): *He pinched the child's cheek playfully.* 他捏那孩子的脸颊玩. (**b**) hurt (sb) by holding his flesh in this way 掐, 捏, 拧(某人): *The child was crying because somebody had pinched her.* 那孩子哭了, 因为有人掐她. ○ *I was so amazed I had to pinch myself in case it was all a dream.* 我非常惊讶, 连忙掐了自己一把看是否这一切都是一场梦. (**c**) have (sth) in a tight grip between two hard things that are pressed together 夹紧(某物): *The door pinched my finger as it shut.* 关门时把我手指夹住了. **2** [I, Tn] (esp of shoes) hurt (sb) by being too tight (尤指鞋)夹痛(某人), 夹脚: *These new boots pinch (me).* (我

觉得)这双新靴子挤脚. 3 [Tn] **~ sth (from sb/sth)** (*infml* 口) take sth without the owner's permission; steal sth 擅自拿走或偷窃某物: *He's been pinching money from the cashbox.* 他一直在偷钱箱里的钱. ○ *Who's pinched my dictionary?* 谁把我的词典拿去了? 4 [Tn esp passive 尤用于被动语态] (*sl* 俚) (of the police) catch and arrest (sb) (指警察)捉住, 逮捕(某人): *He was still carrying the stolen goods when he was pinched.* 抓住他的时候他身上还带着赃物. ○ *get pinched for driving while drunk* 因醉酒开车被逮住. 5 (idm 习语) **pinch and ˈsave/ˈscrape** live in a very miserly way 省吃俭用: *Her parents pinched and scraped so that she could study singing abroad.* 她父母省吃俭用好让她出国学习声乐. Cf 参看 SCRIMP AND SAVE (SCRIMP). 6 (phr v) **pinch sth off/out** remove sth by pinching 掐掉某物: *pinch out the weak shoots on a plant* 掐掉植物上发育不良的芽 ○ *pinch off the dead flowers* 掐掉凋谢的花.

▷ **pinch** *n* 1 act of pinching; painful squeeze 捏; 掐; 拧; 夹; 挤: *She gave him a pinch (on the arm) to wake him up.* 她掐了他(胳膊)一下, 把他叫醒. 2 as much as can be held between the tips of the thumb and forefinger 能捏住或掐住的量: *a pinch of chilli powder* 一捏辣椒粉 ○ *Put another pinch of tea in the pot.* 往茶壶里再捏点茶叶. 3 (idm 习语) **at a ˈpinch** just possibly, in a case of necessity 必要时: *We can get six people round this table at a pinch.* 必要时这张桌子可以坐六个人. **feel the pinch** ⇨ FEEL[1]. **if it ˌcomes to the ˈpinch** in a case of necessity or in an emergency 必要时; 紧急时: *If it comes to the pinch, we shall have to sell the house.* 实在不行我们只好把房子卖了. **take sth with a pinch of salt** think that sth is not likely to be true; not wholly believe sth 认为某事物不大可能属实; 对某事物半信半疑.

pinched *adj* (**a**) **~ (with sth)** suffering (from sth); wretched (因某事物)受苦的, 受罪的, 痛苦的: *be pinched with cold/poverty* 受冻[穷] ○ *look pinched/have a pinched look*, ie drawn or haggard 愁眉苦脸. (**b**) [pred 作表语] **~ for sth** not having enough of sth 不足; 缺乏: *pinched for money, space, time* 金钱、空间、时间不足.

pinch·beck /ˈpɪntʃbek; ˋpɪntʃbek/ *n* [U] alloy of copper and zinc that looks like gold and is used in cheap jewellery, etc 金色铜, 铜锌合金(仿金合金, 用以制廉价首饰等).

▷ **pinch·beck** *adj* imitation; sham 仿造的; 假的.

pine[1] /paɪn; paɪn/ *n* (**a**) [C] (also ˈ**pine tree**) any of several types of evergreen tree that bear cones and have needle-shaped leaves growing in clusters 松树: [attrib 作定语] *pine-scented*, ie (esp of a deodorant, disinfectant, soap, etc) smelling of pines 有松树香味的(尤指除臭剂、消毒剂、香皂等). ⇨illus at App 1 见附录1插图, page i. (**b**) [U] its pale soft wood, used in making furniture, floors, window frames, etc 松木: [attrib 作定语] *a pine dresser* 松木碗橱.

□ ˈ**pine-cone** *n* fruit of the pine 松球; 松果.

ˈ**pine-needle** *n* leaf of the pine 松针; 松叶.

pine[2] /paɪn; paɪn/ *v* 1 [I] be very unhappy, esp because sb has died or gone away 痛苦(尤指因生离死别): *She certainly hasn't been pining while you were away!* 你不在的时候她可并不难受! 2 [Ipr, It] **~ (for sb/sth)** long for or miss sb/sth 渴望或想念某人[某事物]: *She was pining for her mother.* 她思念着母亲. ○ *They were pining to return home.* 他们渴望返回家园. 3 (idm 习语) **peak and pine** ⇨ PEAK[2]. 4 (phr v) **pine away** become ill or waste away (and die) because of grief (因悲哀)憔悴, 消瘦(而死亡): *She lost interest in living and just pined away.* 她已了无生趣, 日渐憔悴.

pin·eal /ˈpaɪnɪəl; ˋpaɪnɪəl/ *adj* shaped like a pine-cone 松球状的.

□ ˌ**pineal** ˈ**gland** cone-shaped gland in the brain 松果腺; 松果体.

pine·apple /ˈpaɪnæpl; ˋpaɪnˌæpl/ *n* (**a**) [C, U] large juicy tropical fruit with sweet yellow flesh and a prickly skin 凤梨; 菠萝: *fresh/tinned pineapple* 新鲜的[罐头的]菠萝 ○ [attrib 作定语] ˈ*pineapple juice* 菠萝汁. ⇨illus at FRUIT 见FRUIT插图. (**b**) [C] tropical plant that bears this fruit 凤梨(植物).

ping /pɪŋ; pɪŋ/ *n* short sharp ringing sound (as) of a hard object hitting a hard surface 硬物相碰发出的声音: *the ping of a spoon hitting a glass* 羹匙碰到玻璃杯的丁当声 ○ *the ping of bullets hitting the rocks* 子弹击中石头的乒乓声 ○ *There was a loud ping as the elastic broke.* 橡皮带断裂时发出砰的一声巨响.

▷ **ping** *v* 1 [I, Tn] (cause sth to) make this sound (使某物)发出撞击声: *bullets pinging overhead* 在头顶上乒乓作响的子弹 ○ *ping a knife against a glass* 用刀碰到玻璃杯发出丁当声. 2 [I] (*US*) = PINK[3].

ping-pong /ˈpɪŋpɒŋ; ˋpɪŋˌpɑŋ/ *n* [U] (*infml* 口) (also ˈ**table tennis**) game played like tennis with bats and a plastic ball on a table with a net across it 乒乓球运动: *a game of ping-pong* 乒乓球比赛 ○ [attrib 作定语] *a ping-pong champion* 乒乓球冠军.

pin·ion[1] /ˈpɪnɪən; ˋpɪnjən/ *n* (*fml* 文) 1 (**a**) outer segment of a bird's wing (鸟翼的)翼梢. (**b**) (*dated* 旧) bird's wing 鸟翼; 翅膀. 2 any of the stiff feathers which support a bird when it is flying; flight-feather 飞羽; 拨风羽.

▷ **pin·ion** *v* 1 [esp passive 尤用于被动语态: Tn, Tn·pr, Tn·p] **~ sb/sth against/to sth; ~ sth together** bind or hold (sb or sb's arms) to prevent him moving 绑住或固定住(某人或某人的胳膊): *They were pinioned against the wall by the lorry.* 那辆卡车把他们挤到墙根动弹不得. ○ *He was held with his arms pinioned together behind his back.* 他被捉住反剪着双臂. 2 [Tn] cut off the pinions from (a bird or its wing) to prevent it from flying 剪去(鸟或鸟翼)的飞羽.

pin·ion[2] /ˈpɪnɪən; ˋpɪnjən/ *n* small cog-wheel with teeth which fit into those of a larger cog-wheel 小齿轮; 副齿轮. Cf 参看 RACK[1] 3.

pink[1] /pɪŋk; pɪŋk/ *adj* 1 of a pale red colour 粉红色的; 淡红色的: *rose/salmon pink walls* 淡玫瑰红的[浅橙色的]墙壁 ○ *go/turn pink with confusion, embarrassment, etc* 因困惑、尴尬等而脸红. 2 (*infml* 口) having slightly left-wing political views 略带左翼政治观点的. Cf 参看 RED[2]. 3 (idm 习语) **be tickled pink/to death** ⇨ TICKLE.

▷ **pink** *n* 1 [U] (clothes of a) pink colour 粉红色(的衣物): *Pink is her favourite colour.* 她喜欢的颜色是粉红色. ○ *dressed in pink* 穿着粉红色的衣服. 2 [C] garden plant with sweet-smelling pink, crimson or variegated flowers 石竹. 3 (idm 习语) **in the pink (of condition/health)** extremely healthy; in perfect condition 极健康; 状况极佳: *The children all looked in the pink after their holiday.* 孩子度假后个个红光满面.

pink·ish *adj* fairly pink 略呈粉红色的: *a pinkish glow* 略带粉红色的光泽.

□ ˈ**pink-eye** *n* [U] infectious disease causing inflammation of the surface of the eye; conjunctivitis 红眼病; 传染性结膜炎.

ˌ**pink** ˈ**gin** drink of gin flavoured (and coloured slightly pink) with angostura bitters 苦味杜松子酒(含安古苦味汁, 略呈粉红色).

pink[2] /pɪŋk; pɪŋk/ *v* [Tn] 1 pierce (sth) slightly (轻轻地)刺, 扎, 戳(某物). 2 cut a zigzag or scalloped edge on (sth) 将(某物)的边剪成锯齿形或扇边形.

□ ˈ**pinking shears** (also ˈ**pinking scissors**) scissors with serrated blades used to make a zigzag edge on fabric and prevent it from fraying 齿边布样剪刀. ⇨illus at SCISSORS 见SCISSORS插图.

pink[3] /pɪŋk; pɪŋk/ (*US* **ping** /pɪŋ; pɪŋ/) *v* [I] (of a car engine) make small explosive sounds when not running properly; knock[2](4) (指汽车发动机)(运转不正常时)发响爆声, 爆震.

pinkie (also **pinky**) /ˈpɪŋkɪ; pɪŋkɪ/ *n* (*Scot or US* 苏格兰或美)the smallest finger of the human hand; the little finger (手的)小指.

pin·nace /ˈpɪnɪs; ˋpɪnɪs/ *n* small motor boat carried on a ship for taking people ashore, loading goods, etc 船载艇, 舰载艇(用以载客上岸、装运货物等). Cf 参看 LIGHTER[2].

pin·nacle /ˈpɪnəkl; ˋpɪnəkl/ *n* 1 small pointed ornament built on to a roof or buttress (屋顶或扶壁上的)小尖塔, 尖顶. ⇨illus at App 1 见附录1插图, page viii. 2 high pointed rock or mountain peak 尖锥形岩石; 山峰; 高峰. 3 (*fig* 比喻) highest point; peak 顶点; 顶峰: *the pinnacle of one's career, fame, success, etc* 事业、声誉、成功等的顶峰.

pin·nate /ˈpɪneɪt; ˋpɪnet/ *adj* (*botany* 植) (of a leaf) formed of a stem with a row of small leaves on either side (指叶)羽状的.

pinny /ˈpɪnɪ; ˋpɪnɪ/ *n* (*infml* 口) pinafore 连胸围裙: *Where's my kitchen pinny?* 我厨房用的围裙在哪儿呢?

pint /paɪnt; paɪnt/ *n* **1** (*abbr* 缩写 **pt**) (**a**) (*Brit*) unit of measure for liquids and some dry goods, ⅛ of a gallon (equal to 0.568 of a litre) 品脱(液量或某些干量的计量单位, 等于⅛加仑, 或0.568升): *a pint of beer, milk, shrimps* 一品脱啤酒、牛奶、小虾. (**b**) (*US*) similar measure (equal to 0.473 of a litre) 品脱(等于0.473升). ⇨App 5 见附录5. **2** this quantity of (esp) milk or beer 一品脱(尤指)牛奶或啤酒: *They stopped at the pub for a pint.* 他们到酒店喝了一品脱的啤酒. **3** (idm 习语) **put a quart into a pint pot** ⇨ QUART.

□ ˈ**pint-sized** *adj* (*infml* 口) very small 极小的.

pinto /ˈpɪntəʊ; ˋpɪnto/ *n* (*pl* **~s**) (*US*) horse with irregular markings of two or more colours; piebald 有花斑的马; (通常指)有黑白斑的马.

▷ **pinto** *adj* mottled 斑驳的; 杂色的: ˈ*pinto beans* 斑豆.

pi·on·eer /ˌpaɪəˈnɪə(r); ˌpaɪəˋnɪr/ *n* **1** (**a**) person who is among the first to go into an area or country to settle or work there 拓荒者; 开发者: *land cleared by the pioneers* 拓荒者开垦的土地 ○ [attrib 作定语] *pioneer wagons* 拓荒者的四轮大车. (**b**) person who goes into previously unknown regions; explorer 探险者: *pioneers in space* 探索宇宙空间的人. **2** person who is the first to study a new area of knowledge 探索新知识领域的人: *They were pioneers in the field of microsurgery.* 他们是显微外科学领域的创始人. ○ [attrib 作定语] *pioneer work* 探索新知识领域的工作. **3** any one of a group of soldiers who go into an area in advance of an army to clear paths, make roads, etc 工兵.

▷ **pi·on·eer** *v* **1** [I] act as a pioneer(1a) 当拓荒者; 当开发者. **2** [Tn] open up (a way, etc) 开辟(道路等): *pioneer a new route to the coast* 开辟通往海岸的新路线. **3** [Tn] be the first person to develop (new methods); help the early development of (sth) 倡导(新方法); 促进(某事物)的初期发展: *She pioneered the use of the drug.* 是她最先使用的这种药品.

pi·ous /ˈpaɪəs; ˋpaɪəs/ *adj* **1** having or showing a deep devotion to religion (对宗教)虔诚的. **2** (*derog* 贬) hypocritically virtuous 假虔诚的; 虚伪的: *He dismissed his critics as pious do-gooders who were afraid to face the facts.* 他把批评他的人斥之为不敢面对事实的假善人.

▷ **pi·ously** *adv*. **pi·ous·ness** *n* [U].

pip[1] /pɪp; pɪp/ *n* seed, esp of a lemon, an orange, an apple, a pear or a grape 种子(尤指柠檬、橙子、苹果、梨或葡萄的).

pip[2] /pɪp; pɪp/ *n* (idm 习语) **give sb the ˈpip** (*Brit infml* 口) give sb a feeling of annoyance, bad temper or depression 使某人恼怒、生气或沮丧: *She gives me the pip.* 她老让我生气. ○ *His disgusting jokes gave everybody the pip.* 他那些令人作呕的笑话弄得大家都不痛快.

pip[3] /pɪp; pɪp/ *n* (usu *pl* 通常作复数) short high-pitched sound used esp as a time-signal on the radio or telephone; bleep (电台报时信号的或电话中的)尖而短的声音: *Wait until you hear the pips and then put in more money,* eg when using a pay phone. 等听到嘟嘟声时再加投硬币(如使用投币电话时). ○ *The weather forecast is followed by the pips at 6 o'clock.* 天气预报之后即为6点钟报时信号.

pip[4] /pɪp; pɪp/ *n* **1** any of the spots on playing-cards, dice and dominoes (纸牌、色子、骨牌上的)点. **2** (*Brit infml* 口) star on the shoulder-strap of an army officer's uniform (军官肩章上的)星.

pip[5] /pɪp; pɪp/ *v* (**-pp-**) (*infml* 口) **1** [Tn] hit (sb) with a shot 以枪弹击中(某人): *pipped in the shoulder* 肩部中弹. **2** (idm 习语) **pip sb at the post** (esp passive 尤用于被动语态) defeat sb narrowly or at the last moment 险胜某人; 终于击败某人: *We didn't win the contract: we were pipped at the post by a firm whose price was lower.* 我们未得到那份合同的生意, 最后是让一家出价低的公司击败了我们.

pipal (also **pee·pul**) /ˈpiːpəl; ˋpipəl/ *n* large Indian fig-tree 菩提树(印度产).

pipe[1] /paɪp; paɪp/ *n* **1** [C] (esp in compounds 尤用以构成复合词) tube through which liquids or gases can flow 管子: *a* ˈ*water-pipe* ○ *a* ˈ*gas-pipe* ○ *a* ˈ*drain-pipe* ○ *the* ˈ*windpipe*, ie air-passage in the body. **2** [C] (**a**) (also **toˈbacco pipe**) narrow tube with a bowl at one end, used for smoking tobacco 烟斗: *smoke a pipe* 吸烟斗 ○ [attrib 作定语] ˈ*pipe tobacco* 烟斗丝. (**b**) (also **pipe·ful** /-fʊl; -fʊl/) amount of tobacco this can hold 一烟斗的烟丝. **3** [C] (*music* 音) (**a**) wind instrument consisting of a tube with holes that are covered and uncovered by the fingers to make musical notes 管乐器: *pipes of Pan*, ie pan-pipes 排箫. (**b**) each of the tubes from which sound is produced in an organ (管风琴的)音管. (**c**) **pipes** [pl] = BAGPIPES. **4** [C] (sound of a) whistle used by a boatswain 水手长吹的哨子(声). **5** [C] song or note of a bird 鸟鸣; 鸟鸣声. **6** [C] (contents of a) cask which can hold about 105 gallons of wine 大酒桶(约容105加仑); 一大酒桶的量. **7** (idm 习语) **put ˈthat in your pipe and smoke it** (*infml* 口) you have to accept what I have said, whether you like it or not 我说的话不管你喜欢不喜欢都得听: *I'm not giving up my holiday to suit you, so you can put that in your pipe and smoke it!* 我不打算放弃我的假日来迁就你, 你不听也得听!

□ ˈ**pipeclay** *n* [U] fine white clay used (esp formerly) for making tobacco pipes and for whitening leather, etc 白陶土(尤于旧时用以制烟斗、使皮革增白等).

ˈ**pipe-cleaner** *n* flexible piece of wire covered with soft material, for cleaning inside a tobacco pipe 烟斗通条(清除烟垢用的).

ˈ**pipe-dream** *n* hope or plan that is impossible or unworkable 不切实际的希望; 行不通的计划.

ˈ**pipeline** *n* **1** series of connected pipes, usu underground, for conveying oil, gas, etc to a distant place (长距离输送油、气等的)管道(通常指地下的). **2** (*fig* 比喻) channel of information or supply, esp direct, privileged or confidential (信息或供应的)渠道, 途径(尤指直接的、基于特权而获得的或秘密的): *a pipeline to head office, the Prime Minister, the manufacturer* 联系总部、首相、厂商的渠道. **3** (idm 习语) **in the ˈpipeline** (**a**) (of goods, orders, etc) being dealt with; on the way (指货物、定单等)在处理或运送中. (**b**) (of changes, laws, proposals, etc) being prepared or discussed; about to happen (指变化、法令、建议等)在准备、讨论或酝酿中, 即将发生: *New laws to deal with this abuse are in the pipeline.* 正在制定处理这种弊端的新法令.

pipe[2] /paɪp; paɪp/ *v* **1** [Tn, Tn·pr] convey (water, gas, etc) in pipes 用管道输送(水、煤气等): *pipe water into a house/to a farm* 用管道向住宅[农场]送水 ○ *pipe oil across the desert* 用管道穿过沙漠输油. **2** [esp passive 尤用于被动语态: Tn, Tn·pr] transmit (esp music) by wire or cable (用有线系统等)传送(尤指音乐): *Nearly all the shops have piped music*, ie recorded music played continuously. 差不多所有商店都连续播放有线广播的音乐. **3** [I, Tn] (**a**) play (a tune) on a pipe or pipes 用管乐器演奏(一曲): *He piped (a jig) so that we could dance.* 他用笛子吹奏(吉格舞曲)好让我们跳舞. (**b**) (of a bird) whistle or sing (sth) (指鸟)鸣啭或唱(某声音). (**c**) (of a person, esp a child) speak (sth) in a high voice (指人, 尤指儿童)尖声说(某事). **4** [Tn·pr, Tn·p] (*nautical* 海) (**a**) summon (sailors) by blowing a boatswain's pipe 吹水手长用的哨子召集(水手): *pipe all hands on deck* 吹哨召集所有水手到甲板上. (**b**) lead or welcome (sb) by the sound of a boatswain's pipe 用水手长的哨声引领或欢迎(某人): *pipe the captain aboard/on board* 用哨声欢迎船长登船 ○ *pipe the guests in* 用哨声迎接客人. **5** [Tn] (**a**) trim or decorate (sth) with piping(2a) 为(衣物等)绲边: *pipe a skirt, cushion, etc with blue silk* 给裙子、垫子等绲蓝绸边. (**b**) put a decoration on (a cake) with icing 在(糕点)上加奶油、巧克力等花饰: *pipe 'Happy Birthday' on a cake* 在蛋糕上加上'生日快乐'字样. **6** (phr v) **pipe down** (*infml* 口) be less noisy; stop talking 安静些; 停止谈话: *She told the children to pipe down while she was talking on the telephone.* 她告诉孩子别吵了, 她正在打电话. **pipe up** (*infml* 口) begin to sing or speak, esp suddenly and in a high-pitched voice 开始唱或说(尤指突然而声音尖).

piper /ˈpaɪpə(r); ˋpaɪpɚ/ *n* **1** person who plays on a pipe, esp the bagpipes 吹奏者; (尤指)风笛吹奏者. **2** (idm 习语) **he who pays the piper calls the tune** ⇨ PAY.

pip·ette /pɪˈpet; pɪˋpɛt/ *n* (esp in chemistry) slender tube, usu filled by sucking, used in a laboratory for transferring or measuring small quantities of liquids (尤

指用于化学实验的)吸(量)管; 移液管.

pip·ing /ˈpaɪpɪŋ; ˋpaɪpɪŋ/ *n* [U] **1** **(a)** (system of) pipes, esp for water or drains 管道, 管道系统, 管道设备(尤指给水或排水的): *The piping will need to be renewed.* 这套管子该换了. **(b)** pipe of a certain length 一段管子: *ten feet of lead piping* 十英尺长的铅管. **2** **(a)** folded strip of fabric, often enclosing a cord, used to decorate the edges or seams of a garment, cushion, etc 花饰边, 绲边(常包有绳). **(b)** cord-like lines of icing or whipped cream used to decorate a cake, etc (巧克力、奶油等的)线条(用以装饰蛋糕等). **3** (sound made by) playing a pipe[1](3a) 吹奏管乐器(的声音): *We heard their piping in the distance.* 我们听见他们在远处吹奏的笛声.

▷ **pip·ing** *adj* **1** (esp of a person's voice) high-pitched (尤指人声)尖声的, 声调高的. **2** (idm 习语) **piping ˈhot** (of liquids, food) very hot (指液体、食物)烫的: *a bowl of soup served piping hot* 滚烫的一碗汤.

pipit /ˈpɪpɪt; ˋpɪpɪt/ *n* type of small songbird resembling a lark 鹨.

pip·pin /ˈpɪpɪn; ˋpɪpɪn/ *n* type of apple that can be eaten raw 苹果.

pip-squeak /ˈpɪpskwiːk; ˋpɪpskwik/ *n* (*infml or derog* 口或贬) small, young or unimportant person, esp one who is conceited 小人, 年轻人, 不重要的人(尤指自负的).

pi·quant /ˈpiːkənt; ˋpikənt/ *adj* **1** having a pleasantly sharp taste 辛辣而开胃的: *Bland vegetables are often served with a piquant sauce.* 清淡的蔬菜常以辛辣的沙司调味. **2** pleasantly exciting and stimulating to the mind 令人兴奋的; 刺激的: *a piquant bit of gossip* 有趣的闲谈.

▷ **pi·quancy** /-ənsɪ; -ənsɪ/ *n* [U] quality or state of being piquant 辛辣; 刺激; 兴奋: *the delicate piquancy of the soup* 那汤的香辣可口.

pi·quantly *adv*.

pique /piːk; pik/ *v* [Tn esp passive 尤用于被动语态] **1** hurt the pride or self-respect of (sb); offend 伤害(某人)的自尊心; 冒犯: *She seemed rather piqued.* 她似乎很生气. ○ *He was piqued to discover that he hadn't been invited.* 他因未被邀请而觉受辱. **2** arouse (a person's interest or curiosity) 引起(兴趣); 产生(好奇心): *Her curiosity was piqued.* 她产生了好奇心.

▷ **pique** *n* [U] feeling of annoyance or hurt, usu because one's pride has been offended; resentment 恼怒, 生气(通常指自尊心受到伤害); 怨恨: *When he realized nobody was listening to him, he left the room in a fit of pique.* 他发觉谁也没听他讲话, 一气之下就走了. ○ *Out of pique they refused to accept the compromise offered.* 他们气得拒不接受对方提出的妥协建议.

pi·quet /pɪˈket; pɪˋkɛt/ *n* [U] card-game for two players, played with a pack of 32 cards 皮克牌(用32张牌二人玩的牌戏).

pi·ranha /pɪˈrɑːnjə; pɪˋrɑnjə/ *n* any of various types of small tropical American freshwater fish which attack and eat live animals 锯脂鲤, 比拉鱼(南美淡水小鱼, 能掠食活动物).

pir·ate /ˈpaɪərət; ˋpaɪrət/ *n* **1** **(a)** (esp formerly) person on a ship who attacks and robs other ships at sea (尤指旧时)海盗: [attrib 作定语] *a pirate crew, ship, flag* 海盗团伙、船、旗. **(b)** (esp formerly) ship used for this purpose (尤指旧时)海盗船. Cf 参看 CORSAIR. **2** person who copies illegally sth protected by copyright, esp in order to sell it 侵犯版权非法复印或复制者, 盗印者, 盗制者(尤指为出售): [attrib 作定语] *a pirate edition, video, tape, etc* 盗印版、盗制的录像带、盗制的录音带. **3** **(a)** (also **pirate ˈradio**) radio station that broadcasts without a licence (esp from a ship) 无执照电台(尤指从船上播音的): *interference with radio reception caused by pirates* 无执照电台造成的无线电接收干扰. **(b)** broadcaster on an illegal radio station 无执照电台的广播员.

▷ **pir·acy** /ˈpaɪərəsɪ; ˋpaɪrəsɪ/ *n* **(a)** [U] robbery by pirates (PIRATE 1a) 海盗的掠夺. **(b)** [U] illegal copying or broadcasting 非法复制或广播. **(c)** [C] instance of either of these 非法复制或广播.

pir·ate *v* [Tn] illegally use or reproduce (printed or recorded material which is protected by copyright), esp for profit 非法窃用或复制(有版权的印刷品或录制的材料)(尤指为牟利): *a pirated edition of the plays* 戏剧集的盗印本. ⇨Usage at SMUGGLE 用法见 SMUGGLE.

pir·at·ical /ˌpaɪəˈrætɪkl; paɪˋrætɪkḷ/ *adj* of or in the manner of a pirate 海盗的; 海盗式的; 盗印的; 盗制的.

pir·at·ically /-klɪ; -klɪ/ *adv*.

pi·rou·ette /ˌpɪrʊˈet; ˌpɪrʊˋɛt/ *n* rapid turn or spin made by a ballet-dancer while balanced on the point of the toe or the ball of the foot (跳芭蕾舞者的)单足旋转.

▷ **pi·rou·ette** *v* [I] perform a pirouette or pirouettes (跳芭蕾舞时)用单足旋转.

pis·cat·orial /ˌpɪskəˈtɔːrɪəl; ˌpɪskəˋtɔrɪəl/ *adj* **1** of or concerning fishing or fishermen 渔业的; 渔民的. **2** (of a person) enthusiastic about fishing (指人)爱钓鱼的.

Pis·ces /ˈpaɪsiːz; ˋpaɪsiz/ *n* **1** [pl] the twelfth sign of the zodiac, the Fishes 双鱼宫(黄道第十二宫). **2** [C] person born under the influence of this sign 属双鱼宫星座的人. ▷ **Pis·cean** *n, adj*. ⇨Usage at ZODIAC 用法见 ZODIAC. ⇨illus at ZODIAC 见 ZODIAC 插图.

piss /pɪs; pɪs/ *v* (⚠ *sl* 讳, 俚) **1** **(a)** [I] pass urine; urinate 撒尿. **(b)** [Tn] **~ oneself** make oneself wet when doing this 尿湿自己: (*fig* 比喻) *piss oneself laughing*, ie laugh uncontrollably 笑得止不住. **(c)** [Tn] pass (blood) with urine 尿(血): *piss blood* 尿血. **2** (phr v) **piss (sb) about/around** act (towards sb) in a foolish, time-wasting or deliberately unhelpful way (对某人)胡闹、浪费时间或故意捣乱: *Stop pissing about and get on with your work.* 别再胡闹了, 干你的事去吧. ○ *We were pissed around for hours before they finally gave us the right form.* 他们浪费了我们好几个小时, 最后才把那份表格给我们. **piss down** rain heavily 下大雨. **piss off** (*esp Brit*) (used esp as a command) go away (尤用作命令)滚开. **piss sb off** (esp passive 尤用于被动语态) annoy or bore sb 使某人恼怒或厌烦: *Everybody is pissed off (with all the changes of plan).* 大家(对计划的诸多变动)均感厌烦.

▷ **piss** *n* (⚠ *sl* 讳, 俚) **1** **(a)** [U] urine 尿. **(b)** [C esp *sing* 尤作单数] (act of) urination 撒尿: *go for/have a piss* 去撒尿. **2** (idm 习语) **take the ˈpiss (out of sb)** make fun (of sb) 取笑(某人).

pissed *adj* (⚠ *Brit sl* 讳, 俚) **1** drunk 醉. **2** (idm 习语) **(as) pissed as a ˈnewt** very drunk 大醉.

pis·ta·chio /pɪˈstɑːʃɪəʊ; *US* -æʃɪəʊ; pɪsˋtæʃɪˌo/ *n* (*pl* **~s**) **(a)** (also **piˈstachio nut**) nut with a green edible kernel 阿月浑子, 开心果(其仁色绿, 可吃): [attrib 作定语] *pistachio ice-cream* 开心果冰激凌. **(b)** tree on which this nut grows 阿月浑子树. **(c)** (also **pistachio ˈgreen**) colour of this kernel 开心果绿; 淡草绿色.

piste /piːst; pist/ *n* (*French* 法) track of firm snow for skiing on 滑雪道.

pis·til /ˈpɪstl; ˋpɪstḷ/ *n* female seed-producing part of a flower 雌蕊.

pis·tol /ˈpɪstl; ˋpɪstḷ/ *n* **1** type of small gun, held and fired with one hand 手枪: *an automatic pistol* 自动手枪. ⇨illus at GUN 见 GUN 插图. **2** (idm 习语) **hold a pistol to sb's head** (try to) force sb to do sth he does not want to do by using threats 胁迫某人做某事物.

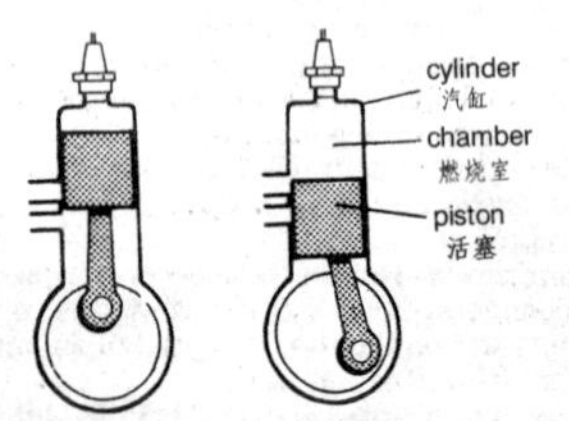

pis·ton /ˈpɪstən; ˋpɪstṇ/ *n* **1** round plate or short cylinder, usu made of metal or wood, that fits closely inside another cylinder or tube and moves up and down or backwards and forwards inside it; used eg in steam or internal combustion engines to cause other parts to move by means of a **connecting rod** (**ˈpiston-rod**) 活塞. ⇨illus 见插图. **2** sliding valve in a trumpet or other brass wind instrument (铜管乐器上的)活门.

□ **ˈpiston-engined** *adj* (of an aircraft) having engines with pistons, not jet engines (指飞机)有活塞发动机的(非喷气式的).

ˈpiston ring split metal ring that fits into a groove on the rim of a piston to make a gas-tight seal 活塞环.

pit[1] /pɪt; pɪt/ *n* **1** [C] large (usu deep) hollow or opening in the ground (地面的)大坑, (通常指)深坑. **2** [C] (esp in compounds 尤用以构成复合词) (**a**) hole in the ground, usu with steep sides, from which esp minerals are dug out 坑; (尤指)矿井: *a 'chalk-pit* 白垩取土坑 ○ *a 'gravel-pit* 采石场 ○ *a 'lime-pit* 石灰采石场. (**b**) hole in the ground made for any of various industrial purposes (作工业用途的)坑: *a 'saw-pit* 锯木坑. **3** [C] = COAL-MINE (COAL): *go down the pit*, ie work as a miner 下井(做矿工). **4** [C] natural hollow in the surface of a plant or an animal's body 动植物体的自然凹陷处; 窝; 凹: *the pit of the stomach*, ie the hollow between the ribs below the breastbone, thought to be the place where fear is felt 胸口 ○ *'armpit*, ie hollow underneath the shoulder where the arm joins the body 腋窝. **5** [C] (**a**) hollow scar left on the skin, esp after smallpox; pock-mark 皮肤上凹陷的疤痕; (尤指天花的)麻点, 痘痕. (**b**) small hollow on a surface, esp of metal or glass 物体表面的小凹陷处(尤指金属或玻璃的). **6 the pit** [sing] (*Brit*) (people sitting in) seats on the ground floor of a theatre behind the stalls 剧院正厅后座(的观众). **7** [sing] (also **'orchestra pit**) sunken part of the floor of a theatre in front of the stage, for the orchestra 乐池. ⇨illus at App 1 见附录1插图, page ix. **8** (**a**) [C] sunken area in the floor of a garage or workshop where the underneath part of a vehicle can be examined or repaired (修车处的)检修坑. (**b**) **the pits** [pl] (in motor racing) place near the race-track where cars can stop for fuel, new tyres, etc during a race (机动车赛中的)检修加油站. **9** [sing] (*US*) (esp in compounds 尤用以构成复合词) part of the floor of a commodity exchange used for a particular commodity (某些商品的)交易场所: *the 'wheat-pit* 小麦交易场. **10 the pit** [sing] (*Bible or rhet* 《圣经》或修辞) hell 地狱. **11** [C] hole dug as a trap for wild animals; pitfall (捕猎野兽用的)陷阱. **12** (idm 习语) **be the pits** (*infml* 口 *esp US*) be very bad or the worst example of sth 极坏; 最糟糕: *The comedian's performance was the pits!* 这喜剧演员的表演糟透了! ○ *The food in this restaurant is the pits!* 这家饭馆的东西难吃极了!

▷ **pit** *v* (**-tt-**) **1** [Tn, Tn·pr esp passive 尤用于被动语态] **~ sth (with sth)** make pits (PIT 5) or hollows in sth 使某物上有凹陷、有麻点: *Acid had pitted the surface of the silver.* 酸把银器的表面腐蚀了. ○ *a face pitted with smallpox* 麻子脸 ○ *The surface of the moon is pitted with craters.* 月球表面有很多环形坑. **2** (phr v) **pit sb/sth against sb/sth** test sb/sth in a struggle or competition with sb/sth 使某人[某事物]与他人[他事物]较量: *pit one's wits against the bureaucracy of the tax office* 与税务局的官僚作风斗智 ○ *pit oneself against the reigning champion* 与本届冠军较量.

□ **'pit-head** *n* entrance of a coal-mine and the offices, machinery, etc in the area around it 煤矿井口处及周围的办公室、机械设备等: [attrib 作定语] *a pit-head ballot*, ie a vote, esp about union matters, taken by miners at the pit-head (矿工的)井口投票表决(尤指关于工会事宜).

'pit pony pony used (esp formerly) underground in a mine to pull heavy loads (尤指旧时的)矿井下运输用的小马.

'pit-prop *n* prop used to support the roof of a part of a coal-mine from which coal has been removed (煤矿的)坑木, 支柱.

pit[2] /pɪt; pɪt/ *n* (*esp US*) = STONE 5.

▷ **pit** *v* [Tn] (**-tt-**) (*esp US*) remove pits from (fruit) 除去(水果)的核: *pitted olives* 去核的橄榄.

pit-a-pat /ˌpɪtəˈpæt; ˈpɪtəˌpæt/ (also **pitter-patter** /ˌpɪtəˈpætə(r); ˈpɪtɚˌpætɚ/) *adv* with the sound of quick light steps or tapping 有轻快的步伐或拍击声的; 劈劈啪啪地: *Her heart/feet went pit-a-pat.* 她的心噗噗地跳[她的脚步声劈劈啪啪的].

▷ **pit-a-pat** (also **pitter-patter**) *n* this sound 劈啪声: *the pit-a-pat of the rain on the roof* 雨点打在屋顶上的劈啪声.

pitch[1] /pɪtʃ; pɪtʃ/ *n* [U] **1** black substance made from coal tar, turpentine or petroleum which is sticky and semi-liquid when hot, and hard when cold, and is used to fill in cracks or spaces, eg between the planks of a floor or of a ship's deck, to make roofs waterproof, etc 沥青. **2** (idm 习语) **black as ink/pitch** ⇨ BLACK.

□ **ˌpitch-'black** *adj* completely black 乌黑的.

ˌpitch-'dark *adj* (**a**) with no light at all 黑暗无光的. (**b**) completely black 乌黑的. **the ˌpitch-'dark** *n* [U] state of complete darkness 黑暗: *We couldn't see our way in the pitch-dark.* 我们在黑暗中看不见路.

'pitch-pine *n* [U, C] (wood of a) type of pine-tree which gives off a lot of resin 刚松(木).

pitch[2] /pɪtʃ; pɪtʃ/ *v* **1** [Tn] erect and fix in place (a tent or camp), esp for a short time 搭(帐篷), 扎(营)(尤指临时): *They pitched camp on the moor for the night.* 他们在高沼地搭帐篷过夜. Cf 参看 STRIKE[2] 11. **2** [Tn·pr, Cn·a] (**a**) (in music) set in a certain pitch[3](3a) or key (音乐)定调: *The song is pitched too low for me.* 这歌起调太低, 我唱不了. ○ *pitch sth in a higher key* 把某乐曲的调子定高一些 ○ *a high-/low-pitched voice* 高[低]嗓音 ○ (*fig* 比喻) *pitch one's hopes high* 把希望定得很高. (**b**) (*fig* 比喻) express (sth) in a particular style or at a particular level 以某形式、风格或水平表达(某事物): *The programme was pitched at just the right level.* 大纲所定水平恰到好处. ○ *an explanation pitched at a simple level so that a child could understand it* 使用浅显的解释以便于儿童理解 ○ *pitch sth a bit high/strong*, ie exaggerate 表达某事略过甚其词. **3** [I, Ipr, Ip, Tn, Tn·pr, Tn·p] (cause sb/sth to) fall heavily, esp forwards or outwards (使某人[某物])重重倒下(尤指向前或向外): *He pitched (forward) on his head.* 他(向前)一头栽倒. ○ *The car hit the child and she pitched over backwards.* 汽车把那孩子撞了, 她重重向后倒下. ○ *The carriage overturned and the passengers (were) pitched out.* 马车翻了, 车上的人都(被)摔出来了. **4** [I, Ip] (of a ship or an aircraft) move up and down on the water or in the air (指船或飞行器)颠簸: *The ship pitched and rolled and many passengers were sick.* 那轮船颠簸摇晃, 很多乘客头晕恶心. Cf 参看 ROLL[2] 6. **5** [Tn, Tn·pr] throw (sb/sth) in the specified direction; toss 将(某人[某物])向某方向投、掷、扔或抛: *Let's pitch out the troublemakers.* 把这些捣乱分子赶出去. ○ *pitch a stone into the river* 向河中扔石头 ○ *People just pitch their rubbish over the wall.* 人们径直把垃圾扔过墙去. **6** (**a**) [I, Ipr, Ip, Tn·p] (in cricket) (cause the ball to) strike the ground near or around the wicket (板球戏中)(使投出的球)在三柱门附近触地: *The ball was pitched short.* 投的球是短球. ○ *pitch the ball up a bit* 把球投高一点. (**b**) [I, Tn] (in baseball) throw (the ball) to the batter (棒球戏中)将(球)投给击球员. **7** [Tn] (*infml* 口) tell (a story) or give (an excuse) 讲(故事); 使用(借口): *They pitched a yarn about finding the jewels.* 他们编了一个找到宝石的故事. **8** (phr v) **pitch in; pitch into sth** (*infml* 口) (**a**) start working energetically 使劲地干起来: *They all pitched in and soon finished the job.* 大家七手八脚, 工作很快就完成了. ○ *They pitched into the work immediately.* 他们立刻干了起来. (**b**) eat (sth) with a good appetite 大吃(某物): *We had prepared supper for the team and they all pitched in.* 我们给队员准备了晚餐, 他们全都大吃起来. ○ *They pitched into the meal.* 他们大吃了一顿. **pitch into sb** (*infml* 口) attack sb violently 猛烈攻击某人. **pitch in (with sth)** offer help or support 主动帮助或支持: *They pitched in with contributions of money.* 他们主动捐款支援此事.

▷ **pitched** *adj* (of a roof) sloping from a ridge; not flat (指屋顶)倾斜的, 坡的. **pitched 'battle** battle fought with troops arranged in prepared positions and using all available resources 对阵战: (*fig* 比喻) *Conservationists fought a pitched battle with developers over the future of the site.* 主张保护自然环境的人同地产开发公司就该地前途进行了针锋相对的论战. Cf 参看 SKIRMISH.

□ **ˌpitch-and-'toss** *n* [U] game of skill and chance in which coins are thrown at a particular mark 掷硬币游戏.

pitchfork /ˈpɪtʃfɔːk; ˈpɪtʃˌfɔrk/ *n* long-handled fork with sharp prongs for lifting and moving hay, etc 干草叉. — *v* **1** [Tn] lift or move (sth) (as) with a pitchfork 用干草叉(般)叉起或叉走(某物). **2** (phr v) **pitchfork sb into sth** force sb into (a position, job, etc), esp suddenly 强行使某人进入(某位置)或做(某工作)(尤指突然间): *young men pitchforked into the army* 被强征入伍的年轻人.

P

pitch[3] /pɪtʃ; pɪtʃ/ *n* **1** [C] (*sport* 体) **(a)** (in cricket) part of the ground between the wickets (板球的)球场. ⇨ illus at CRICKET 见 CRICKET 插图. **(b)** (in football, hockey, etc) area of ground marked out for a game; sports ground or field (足球、曲棍球等的)球场. ⇨illus at ASSOCIATION FOOTBALL (ASSOCIATION) 见 ASSOCIATION FOOTBALL (ASSOCIATION) 插图. **2** [C] **(a)** act or process of throwing sth; toss 投; 掷; 扔; 抛. **(b)** (in cricket) way in which the ball is bowled (板球的)投球: *a full pitch*, ie a bowled ball that does not bounce before reaching the batsman 全场球(投出的球直至击球员, 中间不落地). **(c)** (in baseball) act or manner of throwing the ball (棒球的)投球. **3** [U] **(a)** degree of highness or lowness of a musical note or a voice (音符或嗓音的)高度; 音高: *give the pitch* 定出音高 ○ *have absolute/perfect pitch*, ie the ability to recognize or reproduce the pitch of a note 有绝对[完全]音高感(对一乐音音高的识别力或演唱、演奏的能力). **(b)** quality of a sound in music 音质. **4** [sing] degree or intensity of sth 程度; 强度: *Speculation has reached such a pitch that a decision will have to be made immediately.* 这种胡乱猜测甚嚣尘上, 已经到了必须立即解决的程度了. **5** [U] **~ of sth** highest point of sth 最高点: *the pitch of perfection* 完美的顶点. **6** [U] movement of a ship up and down on the water (船的)颠簸. Cf 参看 ROLL[1] 3. **7** [U] degree of slope (esp of a roof) 倾斜度(尤指屋顶的). **8** [C] (*esp Brit*) place where a street trader usu does business or a street entertainer usu performs (街头的)商贩摊位, 艺人表演场地. **9** [C] (also **'sales pitch**) persuasive talk or arguments used by a salesman to sell things 推销员唱的高调: *a clever sales pitch* 动听的推销员高调. **10** (idm 习语) **at concert pitch** ⇨ CONCERT. **at/to fever pitch** ⇨ FEVER. **queer sb's pitch** ⇨ QUEER *v*.

pitch·blende /ˈpɪtʃblend; ˈpɪtʃˌblɛnd/ *n* [U] black shiny mineral ore which is the main source of uranium and radium 沥青铀矿.

pitcher[1] /ˈpɪtʃə(r); ˈpɪtʃɚ/ *n* **(a)** (*esp Brit*) large (usu earthenware) container for liquids, with one or two handles and a lip for pouring (单柄或双柄, 带嘴的, 通常为陶制的)大罐, 大壶. **(b)** (*US*) jug 罐.

pitcher[2] /ˈpɪtʃə(r); ˈpɪtʃɚ/ *n* (in baseball) player who throws the ball to the batter (棒球的)投手.

pit·eous /ˈpɪtɪəs; ˈpɪtɪəs/ *adj* (*fml* 文) arousing or deserving pity 值得同情的; 可怜的: *a piteous cry, sight, story* 值得同情的哭声、情景、事情 ○ *in a piteous condition* 可怜的境地. ▷ **pit·eously** *adv*. **pit·eous·ness** *n* [U].

pit·fall /ˈpɪtfɔːl; ˈpɪtˌfɔl/ *n* **1** unsuspected danger or difficulty 意想不到的危险或困难: *This text presents many pitfalls for the translator.* 这篇文字有很多潜在的难点, 译者稍一不慎就要出错. **2** = PIT[1] 11.

pith /pɪθ; pɪθ/ *n* **1** [U] **(a)** soft spongy substance that fills the stems of certain plants, eg reeds (木)髓(某些植物茎中的海绵样组织, 如芦苇的茎髓). **(b)** similar substance inside the skin of oranges, etc (柑橘等果皮肉的)类似髓的组织. **2** [sing] (*fig* 比喻) **the ~ of sth** most important or essential part of sth; essence 最重要部分; 精髓: *That was the pith of his argument.* 那就是他论据的重点.

▷ **pithy** *adj* (**-ier**, **-iest**) **1** concise and full of meaning; terse 精练的; 简洁的: *a pithy description of the event* 对事件的简明扼要的叙述 ○ *a pithy comment, remark, saying, etc* 简要的评论、话、谚语等. **2** of, like or full of pith(1) 有髓的; 似木髓的; 多髓的. **pith·ily** /-ɪlɪ; -ɪlɪ/ *adv* in a pithy(1) manner 精简地; 简洁地. **pithi·ness** *n* [U] state of being pithy(1) 精练; 简洁: *Her work is known for pithiness of style.* 她的作品以简洁著称.

□ **'pith hat** (also **'pith helmet**) hat made of dried pith(1a) worn (esp formerly) to protect the head from the sun 木髓制的遮阳帽(尤指旧时用的).

pi·ti·able /ˈpɪtɪəbl; ˈpɪtɪəbḷ/ *adj* **1** deserving or arousing pity 令人怜悯的; 可怜的: *in a pitiable state* 处境可怜 ○ *pitiable misery* 令人哀怜的不幸. **2** deserving contempt 可鄙的: *a pitiable attempt to save himself from disgrace* 他为保全面子的卑鄙做法 ○ *a pitiable lack of talent* 可鄙的无能. ▷ **pi·ti·ably** /-əblɪ; -əblɪ/ *adv*.

pi·ti·ful /ˈpɪtɪfl; ˈpɪtɪfəl/ *adj* **1** arousing pity 令人怜悯的; 可怜的: *a pitiful condition, invalid, sight* 可怜的情形、病人、情景 ○ *Their suffering was pitiful to see.* 他们受的苦让人见了感到同情. **2** deserving contempt 可鄙的: *pitiful efforts, excuses, lies* 卑劣的做法、借口、谎言 ○ *a pitiful coward* 可鄙的胆小鬼.

▷ **pi·ti·fully** /-fəlɪ; -flɪ/ *adv* **1** in a pitiful(1) manner 令人怜悯地: *pitifully injured* 伤得很惨 ○ *The child was pitifully thin.* 那孩子瘦得可怜. **2** in a pitiful(2) manner 可鄙地: *a pitifully bad performance* 可鄙的拙劣表演.

pi·ti·less /ˈpɪtɪlɪs; ˈpɪtɪlɪs/ *adj* **1** showing no pity or mercy; cruel 无怜悯心的; 无情的; 残酷的: *a pitiless killer, bandit, tyrant, etc* 残酷的杀手、匪徒、暴君等 ○ *pitiless retribution, revenge, etc* 无情的报应、复仇等. **2** (*fig* 比喻) very harsh or severe; unrelenting 严酷的; 严厉的; 冷酷的: *a scorching, pitiless sun* 灼人烈日 ○ *the pitiless winds of a Siberian winter* 西伯利亚冬天凛冽的寒风. ▷ **pi·ti·lessly** *adv*. **pi·ti·less·ness** *n* [U].

piton /ˈpiːtɒn; ˈpitɑn/ *n* (*sport* 体) metal spike or peg, with a ring at one end to hold a rope, that is hammered into a rock or a crack between rocks to support a rope or climber (登山者用的)钢锥(顶端有环可穿绳索).

Pitot tube /ˈpiːtəʊ tjuːb; *US* -tuːb; ˈpito ˌtub/ *n* (*propr* 专利名) small tube, open at one end, used in instruments that measure fluid pressure or velocity 皮托管(用以测量流体压力或速度的管).

pitta /ˈpɪtə; ˈpɪtə/ *n* [U] (also **pita**, **'pitta bread**) type of bread in flat loaves, eaten esp in Greece and the Middle East 希腊人和中东人食用的一种扁平的面包.

pit·tance /ˈpɪtns; ˈpɪtṇs/ *n* (usu *sing* 通常作单数) very small or insufficient amount of money paid or received as wages or an allowance 微薄的工资或津贴: *work all day for a mere pittance* 为菲薄的报酬整天工作 ○ *She could barely survive on the pittance she received as a widow's pension.* 她靠着极少的孤寡抚恤金仅够糊口.

pitter-patter = PIT-A-PAT.

pi·tu·it·ary /pɪˈtjuːɪtərɪ; *US* -tuːəterɪ; pɪˈtuəˌtɛrɪ/ *n* (also **pi'tuitary gland**) small gland at the base of the brain which secretes hormones that influence growth and development 垂体; 脑下垂体.

pity /ˈpɪtɪ; ˈpɪtɪ/ *n* **1** [U] **~ (for sb/sth)** feeling of sorrow caused by the suffering, troubles, etc of others 同情; 怜悯: *be full of/filled with pity for sb* 十分同情某人 ○ *be moved to pity by sb's suffering* 受某人的痛苦所感动而产生同情 ○ *do sth out of pity for sb*, ie because one feels pity for him 出于怜悯为某人做某事 ○ *feel very little pity for sb* 不太可怜某人. **2** [sing] **~ (that...)** cause for mild regret or sorrow (but not a real disaster) 遗憾的事; 可悲的事: *It's a pity the weather isn't better for our outing today.* 我们今天出去游玩天气不见好, 真遗憾. ○ *What a pity that you can't come to the theatre with us tonight.* 你今晚不能和我们一起去看戏, 真可惜. ○ *The pity (of it) is that...*, ie The regrettable thing is that... 遗憾的是.... **3** (idm 习语) **have pity on sb** show mercy towards sb 对某人表示同情或怜悯. **ˌmore's the 'pity** (*infml* 口) unfortunately 真不幸: *'Did you insure the jewels before they were stolen?' 'No, more's the pity!'* '你那些被窃的珠宝买保险了吗?''没有, 真倒霉!' **take pity on sb** help sb because one feels pity for him 出于同情或怜悯而帮助某人.

▷ **pity** *v* (*pt, pp* **pitied**) [Tn] **1** feel pity for (sb) 对(某人)感到同情或怜悯: *Pity the poor sailors at sea in this storm!* 可怜可怜在这场风暴中在海上航行的那些倒霉的水手吧! ○ *Survivors of the disaster who lost their relatives are much to be pitied.* 灾难中丧失亲人的幸存者很值得同情. **2** feel contempt for (sb) 觉得(某人)可鄙: *I pity you if you think this is an acceptable way to behave.* 你要是认为这种行为可以原谅, 那你就太可鄙了. ○ *I pity you* (ie I am threatening you) *if you can't pay me the money by tomorrow.* 你明天不把钱还给我, 我就不客气了. **pity·ing** *adj* **(a)** expressing pity 同情的; 怜悯的: *He lay helpless in the street under the pitying gaze of the bystanders.* 他孤零零地躺在路边, 旁观的人都投以怜悯的目光. **(b)** showing pity and some contempt 表示同情或怜悯并带有一些鄙夷的: *The performer received only pitying looks from his audience.* 从观众的表情看, 那表演者得到的只是同情和怜悯. **pity·ingly** *adv*.

pivot /ˈpɪvət; ˈpɪvət/ *n* **1** central point, pin or shaft on which sth turns 中心点; 支点; 枢; 枢轴. **2** (*fig* 比喻) central or most important person or thing 中心的或最重要的人或事物: *Because her job had been the pivot of her life, retirement was very difficult.* 因为她的工作一向是她生命的支柱, 所以退休后的日子很不好过. ○ *That* *is the pivot of the whole argument.* 这是整个论据的关键. ⇨illus at SCALE 见SCALE插图.

▷ **pivot** *v* **1** (**a**) [I, Ipr] **~ (on sth)** turn (as) on a pivot (似)在枢轴上转动: *The doll pivots at the waist and neck.* 那洋娃娃的腰和颈可以转动. ○ *She pivoted on her heels and swept out.* 她一转身, 匆匆走了出去. (**b**) [Tn, Tn·pr] provide (sth) with a pivot; mount on a pivot 给(某物)安枢轴; 装于枢轴上. **2** (phr v) **pivot on sth** (no passive 不用于被动语态) (of an argument, etc) depend on sth central or essential; hinge on sth (指论证等) 取决于某中心或要点, 随某事物而转移: *The whole discussion pivots on this one point.* 整个讨论内容均以此点为准.

piv·otal /-tl; -tl/ *adj* **1** of or forming a pivot 轴的; 作为旋轴的. **2** (*fig* 比喻) of great importance because other things depend on it; central (因受其他事物的依附)极重要的, 关键的, 中心的: *a pivotal decision* 重要的决策.

pixie (also **pixy**) /ˈpɪksɪ; ˋpɪksɪ/ *n* small elf or fairy (eg in children's fairy-tales) 小精灵, 小仙子(如童话中的).

pizza /ˈpi:tsə; ˋpitsə/ *n* [C, U] Italian dish consisting of a flat (usu round) piece of dough covered with tomatoes, cheese, anchovies, etc and baked in an oven 意大利饼(饼上覆蕃茄、奶酪、鳀等, 在烤箱中烘制).

piz·zi·cato /ˌpɪtsɪˈkɑ:təʊ; ˌpɪtsɪˋkɑto/ *adj, adv* (*music* 音) (played) by plucking the strings of a violin, etc instead of using the bow (提琴等)用指弹拨(的), 拨奏(的).

▷ **piz·zi·cato** *n* (*pl* **~s**) note or passage (of music) (to be) played in this way 拨奏的音符或(乐曲的)片段.

Pk *abbr* 缩写 = (esp on a map 尤用作地图上的标记) Park: *St* (ie Saint) *James' Pk* 圣·詹姆斯公园.

pkg *abbr* 缩写 = package.

pkt *abbr* 缩写 = packet: *1 pkt cigarettes* 一包香烟.

Pl *abbr* 缩写 = (esp on a map 尤用作地图上的标记) Place: *St* (ie Saint) *James' Pl* 圣·詹姆斯街.

pl *abbr* 缩写 = (*grammar*) plural.

plac·ard /ˈplækɑ:d; ˋplækɑrd/ *n* written or printed notice (designed to be) publicly displayed, eg by being fixed to a wall or carried on a stick 布告; 招贴; 海报; 标语牌; 告示牌: *The placards condemned the government's action.* 那些标语牌上写着谴责政府措施的词句. ⇨illus at FLAG 见FLAG插图.

▷ **plac·ard** *v* [Tn] **1** stick placards on (sth) 将布告、海报或标语张贴于(某处). **2** announce (sth) by using placards (用布告、海报等)公布(某事).

pla·cate /pləˈkeɪt; *US* ˈpleɪkeɪt; ˋpleket/ *v* [Tn] make (sb) less angry; soothe or pacify 安慰, 抚慰(某人); 使(某人)平静、息怒.

▷ **pla·cat·ory** /pləˈkeɪtərɪ; *US* ˈpleɪkətɔ:rɪ; ˋplekəˌtorɪ/ *adj* designed to placate or having this effect 安慰的; 抚慰的; 和解的: *placatory remarks* 安抚的话.

place[1] /pleɪs; ples/ *n* **1** [C] particular area or position in space occupied by sb/sth 地方; 场所; 所在地: *Is this the place where it happened?* 这就是事发地点吗? ○ *This place seems familiar to me — I think I've been here before.* 这地方好像很熟悉 —— 大概我从前来过这里. ○ *I can't be in two places at once.* 我分身乏术. ○ *He loves to be seen in all the right places*, ie at all the important social events. 他喜欢在所有重大的社交场合上出头露面. **2** [C] city, town, village, etc 城、镇、村等: *We saw so many places on the tour I can't remember them all.* 我们旅行到过很多地方, 我记都记不清. ○ *This town is the coldest place in Britain.* 这镇子是英国最寒冷的地方. ○ *Australia is a big place.* 澳大利亚这个地方很大. **3** [C] **~ (of sth)** (often in compounds 常用以构成复合词) building or area of land used for a particular purpose or where sth occurs (作某用途或发生某事的)建筑物或场所: *a ˈmeeting-place, ˈbirthplace, ˈhiding-place, etc* 会面地点、出生地、隐蔽所 ○ *places of amusement/entertainment*, ie theatres, cinemas, etc 娱乐场所(戏院、影院等) ○ *a place of worship*, ie a church 礼拜的场所(教堂) ○ *He can usually be contacted at his place of business/work.* 通常可在他的办公[工作]地点和他联系. ○ *a place of learning*, eg a university 做学问的地方(如大学) ○ *one's place of birth/death* 出生[死亡]之地. **4** [C] particular spot or area on a surface 物体表面的某点或某处: *a sore place on my foot* 脚的痛处 ○ *The wall was marked with damp in several places.* 那堵墙有几处潮斑. **5** [C] particular passage or point in a book, play, etc (书、戏剧等的)某段落或某点: *The audience laughed in all the right places*, eg in a play. 观众看到有趣处无不大笑不已(如在观剧时). ○ *Put a piece of paper in* (ie in your book) *to mark your place.* 在你读到的地方夹上张纸条. **6** [C] seat or position, esp one reserved for or occupied by a person, vehicle, etc 座位或位置(尤指某人、车等保留或占据的): *Come and sit here — I've kept you a place.* 到这儿来坐 —— 我给你占了一个座位. ○ *There's only one place left in the car park.* 停车场里只剩一个位置了. ○ *the place of honour at the head of the table* 餐桌上首的贵宾席 ○ *There will always be a place for you here if you decide to come back.* 只要你决定回来, 这里永远给你保留位置. ○ *Return to your places and get on with your work.* 各回各位去干自己的工作吧. ○ (*fig* 比喻) *have an assured place in history* 在历史上占有一定的地位 ○ *I went to buy a newspaper and lost my place in the queue.* 我去买了份报纸, 回来就找不到我排队中的位置了. ⇨ Usage at SPACE 用法见SPACE. **7** [sing] rank, position or role in society (used esp with the *vs* shown) (社会的)等级, 地位, 身分(尤与所示动词连用): *keep/know one's place* 保持个人的地位[知道自己的身分] ○ *forget one's place*, ie not behave according to one's social position 举止与身分不合 ○ *not be one's place* (ie one's proper role) *to give advice* 无资格进言. **8** [C] (**a**) position or office, esp as an employee 职位或职务(尤指雇员的): *She hopes to get a place in the Civil Service.* 她希望获得一份公职. (**b**) opportunity to study at a school or university (在学校)学习或研究的机会: *She was awarded a place at the Royal College of Music.* 她获得皇家音乐学院的学籍. ○ *The ballet school offers free places to children who are exceptionally talented.* 该芭蕾舞蹈学校给有特殊天赋的儿童提供免费学习的机会. (**c**) membership of a sports team 运动队员的资格或身分: *She worked hard for her place in the Olympic team.* 她为进入奥林匹克运动队而努力. **9** [C] (**a**) natural or suitable position (for sth) (某物的)自然的或恰当的位置: *Put everything away in its correct place.* 把东西放到该放的地方去. ○ (*saying* 谚) *A place for everything and everything in its place.* 物各有其位, 物各在其位. ○ *The dustbin is the only place for most of these clothes.* 这些衣服大都只配进垃圾箱. (**b**) (usu negative 通常用否定式) suitable or proper location (for sb to be) (某人的)相宜的或应在的地方: *A railway station is no place for a child to be left alone at night.* 火车站可不是让儿童在晚上独自呆的地方. ○ *City streets are no place to be if you don't like noise or crowds.* 要是怕吵、怕人多就别上街. **10** [C] (*mathematics* 数) position of a figure after a decimal point, etc (小数点后的)位: *calculated/correct to 5 decimal places/5 places of decimals*, eg 6.57132 计算[精确]到小数点后5位数(如6.57132). **11** [C usu *sing* 通常作单数] (**a**) (in a competition) position among the winning competitors (竞赛中)获胜者的名次: *He finished in third place.* 他得了第三名. (**b**) (in horse-racing) position among the first three, esp second or third (赛马的)位置(获胜的前三名, 尤指第二名或第三名): *Did you back the horse for a place or to win?* 那匹马你买的是位置还是独赢? **12** [C] (**a**) house, esp a large one in the country 房子; (尤指)乡间巨宅: *They have a flat in town as well as a place in the country.* 他们在城里有一套公寓, 在乡村还有一所房子. (**b**) (*infml* 口) home 家: *We're having the party at my place.* 我们的聚会在我家举行. **13 Place** [sing] (*esp Brit*) (**a**) (as part of a name for a short street, square etc 用于短街、广场等名称中): *Langham Place* 兰厄姆广场. (**b**) (as part of a name for a large country house 用于乡村巨宅的名称中): *Wakehurst Place* 韦克赫斯特山庄. **14** (idm 习语) **all ˈover the place** (*infml* 口) (**a**) everywhere 到处: *Firms are going bankrupt all over the place.* 各地的商行都纷纷破产了. (**b**) in an untidy state; disordered 凌乱; 紊乱; 杂乱: *The contents of the drawers were strewn all over the place.* 抽屉里的东西乱七八糟. ○ *Your hair is all over the place.* 你的头发乱蓬蓬的. **change/swap ˈplaces (with sb)** (**a**) take sb's position, seat, etc and let him take one's own 与某人交换位置、座位等: *Let's change places — you'll be able to see better from here.* 咱们换一下位置吧 —— 你从这儿看清楚些. (**b**) be in sb else's situation or circumstances 在他人的处境或环境: *I'm perfectly happy — I wouldn't change places with anyone.* 我十分愉快 —— 这种幸福我跟谁都不换. **fall, fit, slot, etc into ˈplace** (of a set of facts or series of events) begin to make sense in relationship to each other (指一系列事实或事件)开始有头绪: *It all begins to fall into place.* 一切开始明朗了. **give place to sb/sth** be replaced by sb/sth; give way to sb/sth 为某人[某事物]所取代; 让位给某人[某事物]: *Houses and factories gave place to open fields as the train gathered speed.* 火车越开越快, 把房子和工厂抛在后面进入了一片开阔的田野. **'go places** (*infml* 口) be increasingly successful, esp in one's career 不断进展(尤指在个人事业上): *two young people who are really going places* 两个事业顺利的年轻人. **have one's heart in the right place** ⇨ HEART. **in the 'first, 'second, etc place** (used eg when making points in an argument 用于如列举理由时) firstly, secondly, etc 第一点、第二点等. **in high places** ⇨ HIGH[1]. **in 'my, 'your, etc place** in my, your, etc situation or circumstances 处于我的、你的等情况、处境: *What would you do in my place?* 你要是处于我的地位, 你怎样做? ○ *In her place I'd sell the lot.* 我要是她就全部卖掉. **in 'place (a)** in the usual or proper position 在平常的或应在的地方: *She likes everything to be in place before she starts work.* 她喜欢东西都摆好再开始工作. **(b)** suitable or appropriate 合适的; 恰当的: *A little gratitude would be in place.* 应当略表谢意. **in place of sb/sth; in sb's/sth's place** instead of sb/sth 代替某人[某事物]: *The chairman was ill so his deputy spoke in his place.* 主席有病, 所以由副主席代为致词. **lay/set a 'place** put cutlery, dishes, etc for one person in position on the table 在餐桌上摆上一份一人用的餐具: *Set a place for him when you lay the table — he may come after all.* 铺桌子时给他摆上一份餐具—— 毕竟他有可能来. **lightning never strikes in the same place twice** ⇨ LIGHTNING. **lose one's place** ⇨ LOSE. **out of 'place (a)** not in the usual or a correct or suitable place 不在平常的或应在的或适当的地方. **(b)** unsuitable; improper 不适合的; 不适当的: *Her criticisms were quite out of place.* 她的批评太不相宜了. ○ *Modern furniture would be out of place in a Victorian house.* 在维多利亚时代式的房子里摆设现代家具很不谐调. **a place in the 'sun** situation of equal or shared privilege 平等的或均等的有利地位或处境: *Nations that had been oppressed for centuries were now fighting for a place in the sun.* 多少世纪以来受压迫的国家现在都在争取平等. **pride of place** ⇨ PRIDE. **put oneself in sb else's/sb's 'place** imagine oneself in sb else's situation or circumstances 设想自己处于他人的地位或处境. **put sb in his (proper) 'place** humiliate sb who has been impertinent or boastful 对无礼的或自夸的人加以羞辱: *He tried to kiss her but she quickly put him in his place.* 他想要吻她, 她顿时让他自讨没趣. **take 'place** occur; happen 发生: *When does the ceremony take place?* 仪式什么时候举行? ○ *We have never discovered what took place (between them) that night.* 我们从未发觉那天晚上(他们之间)发生了什么事情. ⇨ Usage at HAPPEN 用法见HAPPEN. **take sb's/sth's place; take the place of sb/sth** replace sb/sth 代替某人[某事物]: *She couldn't attend the meeting so her assistant took her place.* 她不能出席会议, 所以由助手替她. ○ *Nothing could take the place of the family he had lost.* 他失去了家庭, 这一损失是无法弥补的. **there's ,no place like 'home** (*saying* 谚) one's home is the best place to be 哪里也不如自己的家.

□ **'place-bet** *n* (in horse-racing) bet that a horse will be one of the first three past the winning-post (赛马的)位置赌(赌某匹马可跑得第一、第二或第三名).

'place-kick *n* (in Rugby football) kick made after the ball has been placed on the ground for that purpose (橄榄球的)定位踢(将球放在地上踢出者).

'place-mat *n* mat on a table on which a person's plates are laid (餐桌上用餐人的)餐具垫.

'place-name *n* name of a city, town, hill, etc (城、镇、山等的)地名: *an expert on the origin of place-names* 地名考源专家.

'place-setting *n* set of cutlery, dishes, etc for one person (供一人使用的)一套餐具.

place[2] /pleɪs; ples/ *v* **1** [Tn·pr, Tn·p] **(a)** put (sth) in a particular place 将(某物)置于某处: *He placed the money on the counter.* 他把钱放在柜台上. ○ *The notice is placed too high — nobody can read it.* 布告贴得太高—— 谁也没法看. **(b)** put (sth) in its proper place 将(某物)放在应放之处: *Be sure to place them correctly.* 务必把这些东西放对地方. ○ *He placed the books in order on the shelf.* 他把书按顺序摆在书架上. **2** [Tn·pr, Tn·p] put (sb) in the situation or circumstances specified (used esp as in the expressions shown) 使(某人)处于某处境或环境(尤用于以下示例): *place sb in charge/command (of sth)*, ie make him the leader 让某人负责[指挥](某事物) ○ *place sb under arrest*, ie arrest him 逮捕某人 ○ *place sb in a dilemma/difficult position/quandary*, ie make matters difficult for sb 使某人进退两难[处于困境/犹豫不决] ○ *place one's faith/trust in sb/sth* 信赖某人[相信某事物] ○ *place confidence in sb*, ie be confident that he will help, etc 对某人抱有信心 ○ *Responsibility for the negotiations was placed in his hands*, ie He was made responsible for them. 由他负责谈判事宜. **3** [Tn] identify (sb/sth) by using one's memory or past experience 凭记忆或经验辨认(某人[某事物]): *I've seen his face before but I can't place him.* 我以前见过他, 但我认不出他是谁. ○ *She has a foreign accent that I can't quite place.* 她有外国口音, 但我听不出是哪儿的口音. **4** [Tn, Tn·pr, Tn·p] make a judgement about (sb/sth) in comparison with others; class (sb/sth) 经比较评价(某人[某事物]); 将(某人[某事物])分类: *I would place her among the world's greatest sopranos.* 我认为她可以算是世界上第一流的女高音. **5** [Tn, Tn·pr] **~ sth (with sb/sth)** give (an order or a bet) to a person or firm (向某人或某公司)发(定单)或打(赌): *They have placed an order with us for three new aircraft.* 他们向我们订购了三架新飞机. ○ *Place your bets now — the race begins in half an hour!* 现在可以下赌注 —— 赛事于半小时后开始! **6** [Tn, Tn·pr] **~ sb (in sth); ~ sb (with sb/sth)** find a home, job, etc for sb 为某人找到、安排或安置(家、工作等): *The agency places about 2000 secretaries per annum.* 该代理机构每年可为约2000名秘书安排工作. ○ *They placed the orphans with foster-parents.* 他们为这些孤儿找到了养父养母. **7** [Tn, Tn·pr] invest (money), esp in order to earn interest 投(资): *The stockbroker has placed the money in industrial stock.* 证券经纪人已用那笔钱购入了工业股票. **8** [esp passive 尤用于被动语态: Tn, Cn·a] state the finishing position of runners (in a race) or contestants (in athletics) (体育竞赛中)定出(选手的)名次: *He was reponsible for placing the winners.* 他负责评定选手名次. ○ *She was placed third.* 她被定为第三名. **9** (idm 习语) **be placed (a)** (*Brit*) (in horse-racing) finish first, second or third (赛马中)得第一、第二或第三名. **(b)** (*US*) (in horse-racing) finish second (赛马中)得第二名.

▷ **place·ment** /'pleɪsmənt; 'plesmənt/ *n* [U] action of placing or state of being placed 放置; 安置; 辨认; 评价; 预订; 下赌注; 定名次: [attrib 作定语] *the placement of orphans* 对孤儿的安置 ○ *a placement agency for secretarial staff* 秘书介绍所.

pla·cebo /plə'si:bəʊ; plə'sibo/ *n* (*pl* **~s**) **1** (*medical* 医) harmless substance given as if it were medicine to calm a patient who mistakenly believes he is ill 安慰剂: [attrib 作定语] *placebo effect*, ie beneficial effect of taking a placebo 宽慰作用(服安慰剂后的). **2** thing done or said only to please or humour sb 使人宽慰的事物; 安慰话.

pla·centa /plə'sentə; plə'sɛntə/ *n* (*pl* **-tae** /-ti:; -ti/ or **~s**) (*anatomy* 解) organ lining the womb during pregnancy by which the foetus is nourished through the umbilical cord, and which is expelled after birth 胎盘. ▷ **pla·cen·tal** /-tl; -tl̩/ *adj*: *a placental mammal* 有胎盘哺乳动物.

pla·cid /'plæsɪd; 'plæsɪd/ *adj* **(a)** calm and peaceful; undisturbed 安静的; 平静的; 宁静的: *the placid waters of the lake* 平静的湖水. **(b)** (of a person, his temperament, etc) not easily excited or irritated (指人、性情等)温和的, 文静的: *a placid smile* 恬静的微笑. ▷ **pla·cidly** *adv*: *cows placidly chewing grass* 静静地吃着青草的母牛. **pla·cid·ity** /plə'sɪdətɪ; plə'sɪdətɪ/ *n* [U]: *the placidity of his temperament* 他温和的性情.

placket /'plækɪt; 'plækɪt/ *n* opening in a woman's skirt to make it easier to put on and take off (裙子的)开口.

pla·gi·ar·ize, -ise /'pleɪdʒəraɪz; 'pledʒə,raɪz/ *v* [Tn, Tn·pr] **~ sth (from sb/sth)** take (sb else's ideas, words, etc) and use them as if they were one's own 剽窃, 抄袭(他人的意念、言词等): *Whole passages of the* *work are plagiarized.* 那作品整段整段都是剽窃的. ○ *He has plagiarized most of the book from earlier studies of the period.* 他那本书大部分都是从研究那个时期的著作中剽窃的内容.

▷ **pla·gi·ar·ism** /-rɪzəm; -rɪzəm/ *n* (**a**) [U] action of plagiarizing 剽窃; 抄袭: *be accused of plagiarism* 被控剽窃. (**b**) [C] instance of this 剽窃; 抄袭.

pla·gi·ar·ist /-rɪst; -rɪst/ *n* person who plagiarizes 剽窃者; 抄袭者.

plague /pleɪg; pleg/ *n* **1** (**a**) **the plague** [sing] = BUBONIC PLAGUE (BUBONIC). (**b**) [C] any deadly infectious disease that kills many people 瘟疫: [attrib 作定语] *The incidence of cholera in the camps has reached plague proportions.* 营中霍乱流行已酿成瘟疫之灾. **2** [C] **~ of sth** large numbers of a pest that invade an area and cause annoyance or damage 侵扰一地造成破坏的大量有害动物: *a plague of flies, locusts, rats, etc* 蝇、蝗、鼠等灾害. **3** [C usu *sing* 通常作单数] (*infml* 口) cause of annoyance; nuisance 惹人烦恼的事物、人或原因: *What a plague that boy is!* 那男孩太讨厌了! **4** (idm 习语) **avoid sb/sth like the plague** ⇨ AVOID.

▷ **plague** *v* **1** [Tn, Tn·pr] **~ sb/sth (with sth)** (**a**) annoy sb, esp by repeatedly asking questions or making demands 烦扰某人(尤指一再询问或要求): *plague sb with questions, requests for money, etc* 一再询问、要钱等烦扰某人. (**b**) cause suffering or discomfort to sb 使某人受苦或难受: *She was plagued with arthritis.* 她患关节炎十分痛苦. **2** [Tn] cause trouble or difficulty to (sb/sth) 给(某人[某事物])造成麻烦或困难: *a construction schedule plagued by bad weather* 因天气恶劣受阻的工程进度.

□ **'plague-ridden** (also **'plague-stricken**) *adj* infected with a/the plague(1,2) 瘟疫流行的; 有害动物为患的.

plaice /pleɪs; ples/ *n* (*pl* unchanged 复数不变) type of flat-fish with reddish spots, eaten as food 鲽(有红斑的比目鱼, 可食).

plaid /plæd; plæd/ *n* (**a**) [C] long piece of woollen cloth, worn over the shoulders by Scottish Highlanders (苏格兰高地人用的毛呢的)长披肩. (**b**) [U] cloth (usu with a tartan pattern) used for this, and for kilts, etc (用作长披肩、男子短裙等的)毛呢, (通常为)格子呢: [attrib 作定语] *a plaid kilt* (苏格兰男子穿的)格子呢短裙. (**c**) [C] tartan pattern for cloth 布料的格子图案.

plain[1] /pleɪn; plen/ *adj* (**-er, -est**) **1** easy to see, hear or understand; clear 清楚的; 明白的; 易懂的; 清晰的: *The markings along the route are quite plain.* 路线沿途的标志都十分清楚. ○ *in plain English* 用浅近的英语 ○ *He made it plain (to us) that he did not wish to continue.* 他向我们明白表示他不想继续下去. ○ *She made her annoyance plain.* 她已怒形于色. **2** (of people or their actions, thoughts, etc) not trying to deceive; frank and direct (指人、其行为、思想等)率直的, 坦率的, 直接的: *in plain words*, ie frankly 明言 ○ *a plain answer* 直截了当的回答 ○ *the plain truth* 明显的事实 ○ *Let me be plain with you*, ie speak openly and frankly: *There will have to be some plain speaking.* 让我开诚布公跟你说吧. 得公开而明白地谈一谈. **3** (**a**) not decorated or luxurious; ordinary and simple 不矫饰的; 朴素的; 普通的; 平凡的; 简单的: *a plain but very elegant dress* 朴素而极雅致的连衣裙 ○ *plain food/cooking*, ie not spicy or rich 清淡的食物[烹调风味] ○ *plain cake*, ie without fruit, etc 纯蛋糕(无水果等配料的) ○ *plain chocolate*, ie made without adding milk 纯巧克力. (**b**) without a pattern or marking on it 没有图案或花纹的: *plain paper*, ie without lines 无格纸 ○ *plain fabric*, ie without a pattern or design 素的织物 ○ *under plain cover*, ie in an envelope without any special marking 在普通信封中(无特殊标记). **4** not beautiful or good-looking 不漂亮的; 不好看的: *a few rather plain bits of furniture* 几件很不起眼的家具 ○ *From a rather plain child she had grown into a beautiful woman.* 她从一个相貌平平的女孩成长为一个漂亮的妇人. **5** (idm 习语) **in plain 'English** bluntly or simply expressed 用直率的或简单明了的英语: *If you wanted me to go why didn't you say so in plain English instead of making vague hints?* 你想叫我走, 为什么拐弯抹角而不直说? **make oneself plain** make one's meaning clear 表达清楚: *There is no more money — do I make myself plain?* 再也没钱了——我的意思清楚吗? **(as) plain as a pikestaff/the nose on one's face** very obvious or clearly visible 一清二楚; 显然易见; 明摆着的事. **(all) ˌplain 'sailing** course of action that is simple and free from trouble 十分顺利; 一帆风顺: *Once the design problems were solved, it was all/everything was plain sailing.* 设计问题一经解决, 就容易办了.

▷ **plain** *adv* (*esp US*) (**a**) clearly 清楚地: *speak plain* 清楚地说. (**b**) absolutely; simply 绝对地; 简直: *That is just plain stupid.* 那简直是愚不可及.

plainly *adv* (**a**) clearly 清楚地: *The mountain tops are plainly visible from the village.* 自该村望去, 群山之巅清晰可见. ○ *Try to express yourself more plainly.* 尽量表达得清楚些. (**b**) obviously 显然: *That is plainly wrong.* 那显然不对. ○ *You are plainly unwilling to co-operate.* 你显然不愿合作. ○ *He was plainly unwelcome.* 他显然不受欢迎.

plain·ness *n* [U].

□ **ˌplain 'clothes** (esp of police officers) ordinary clothes, not uniform (尤指警察的)普通衣服, 便衣: *The detectives were in plain clothes.* 警探穿着便衣. **'plain-clothes** *adj* wearing plain clothes 穿便衣的: *a plain-clothes detective* 便衣侦探.

ˌplain 'dealing honesty; straightforwardness 诚实; 直率.

ˌplain 'flour flour that does not contain baking powder 不含发酵粉的普通白面. Cf 参看 SELF-RAISING FLOUR.

ˌplain-'spoken *adj* frank in speech, often to the point of rudeness; outspoken 说话坦率的(常近于粗俗的); 直言的.

plain[2] /pleɪn; plen/ *n* large area of flat land; prairie 平原: *a vast, grassy plain* 大平原、草原 ○ *the great plains of the American Midwest* 美国中西部的大平原.

▷ **plains·man** /-zmən; -zmən/ *n* (*pl* **-men**) person living in a region of plains, esp in the great plains of the US 平原居民(尤指在美国大平原上居住的人).

plain[3] /pleɪn; plen/ *n* (in knitting) simple basic stitch (编织中的)平针. Cf 参看 PURL.

plain·chant /ˈpleɪntʃɑːnt; *US* ˈpleɪntʃænt; ˈplenˌtʃænt/ (also **'plainsong** /-sɒŋ; -ˌsɔŋ/) *n* [U] medieval type of church music for a number of voices singing together, used in the Anglican and Roman Catholic Churches 素歌(中世纪的宗教合唱曲, 为圣公会及天主教所采用).

plaint /pleɪnt; plent/ *n* (*law* 律) charge made against sb in court; accusation 起诉; 诉状.

plaint·iff /ˈpleɪntɪf; ˈplentɪf/ (also **complainant**) *n* person who brings a legal action against sb 原告. Cf 参看 DEFENDANT.

plaint·ive /ˈpleɪntɪv; ˈplentɪv/ *adj* sounding sad; sorrowful (听起来)哀伤的; 悲哀的: *a plaintive cry, melody, voice, etc* 悲伤的哭泣、曲调、声音等. ▷ **plaint·ively** *adv*. **plaint·ive·ness** *n* [U].

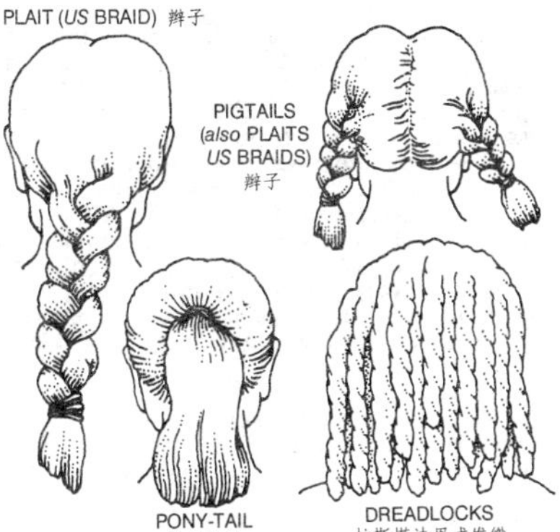

plait /plæt; plet/ (*US* **braid**) *v* [Tn] (**a**) weave or twist (three or more lengths of hair, straw, etc) under and over one another to make one rope-like length 将(发、草等)编成辫: *plait one's hair* 编辫子. (**b**) make (sth) by doing this 编(某物): *plait a basket, cord, rope* 编篮子、

绳、索.

▷ **plait** *n* form made by plaiting 编成的东西; 辫子: *wear one's hair in plaits/a plait* 把头发编成辫子. ⇨illus 见插图.

plan /plæn; plæn/ *n* **1 ~ (for sth/doing sth); ~ (to do sth)** arrangement for doing or using sth, considered or worked out in advance 计划; 规划; 方案: *make plans (for sth)* (为某事)定计划 ○ *a plan to produce energy from waste material* 利用废物作能源的计划 ○ *What are your plans for the holidays?* 你假期打算做什么? ○ *a carefully worked-out plan* 精心设计的方案 ○ *a change of plan*, ie deciding not to do what was planned 计划的变动 ○ *a development plan*, eg for an industry, a town or an area 发展规划(如工业、城镇或地区的) ○ *The best plan* (ie The best thing to do) *would be to ignore it completely.* 上策是完全不予理睬. ○ *a plan of attack/campaign*, ie a way of doing sth, esp sth difficult 攻坚[攻关]方案. **2** (**a**) detailed, large-scale diagram of part of a town, district, group of buildings, etc (城市、区、建筑群等的)详图: *a plan of the royal palace and its surroundings* 皇宫及其环境详图 ○ *a plan of the inner city* 市中心详图. (**b**) (esp *pl* 尤作复数) outline drawing (of a building or structure) showing the position and size of the various parts in relation to each other (建筑或结构的)平面图, 设计图: *draw up plans for an extension* 绘制扩建图 ○ *The architect submitted the plans for approval.* 建筑师将设计图表交付审批. ○ *The plans of the new development are on show at the Town Hall.* 镇公所大厅展出了新开发平面图. (**c**) diagram (of the parts of a machine) (机器部件的)图解, 说明图: *plans of early flying machines* 早期飞行器的说明图. Cf 参看 CHART, MAP. **3** way of arranging sth, esp when shown on a drawing; scheme 安排, 方式, 方法(尤指图示); 示意图: *a seating plan*, ie one showing where people are to sit at a table 座位示意图. **4** (idm 习语) **go according to plan** (of events, etc) take place successfully (指事情等)顺利进行, 按计划实现: *If everything goes according to plan, I shall be back before dark.* 假若一切顺利, 我天黑之前就回来.

▷ **plan** *v* **(-nn-) 1** [Tn] make a plan of or for (sth) 为(某事物)定计划或绘设计图、平面图等: *plan a garden* 设计花园 ○ *a well-planned city* 精心设计的城市 ○ *a planned economy*, ie controlled by the government 计划经济. **2** [I, Ipr] **~ (for/on/sb/sth)** make preparations (为某事物)做准备: *plan for the future, one's retirement, etc* 为将来、退休等做准备 ○ *I had planned for 20 guests, but only 10 arrived.* 我做好了招待20位客人的准备, 可是只来了10位 ○ *We hadn't planned on twins!* 我们没有生双胞胎的准备! ⇨Usage at ARRANGE 用法见ARRANGE. **3** [Tt] make plans (to do sth); intend 计划, 打算(做某事); 意欲: *When do you plan to take your holiday?* 你打算什么时候休假? ○ *We're planning to visit France this summer.* 我们正计划今年夏天到法国旅行. **4** (phr v) **plan sth out** consider sth in detail and arrange it in advance 策划、筹划或详细安排某事物: *plan out one's annual expenditure* 做出全年的开支预算 ○ *plan out a traffic system for the town* 为该镇筹划交通系统. **plan·ner** *n* (**a**) person who makes plans 设计者; 策划者. (**b**) (also ˌ**town** ˈ**planner**) person who works in or studies town planning 城市规划的工作者或研究者. **plan·ning** *n* [U] (**a**) making plans (for sth) (做某事物的)计划: *family planning*, ie using birth control to limit the number of children a couple have 计划生育. (**b**) = TOWN PLANNING (TOWN). **planning permission** (*esp Brit*) licence to build a new building or change an existing one, granted by a local authority (兴建或改建建筑物前当局授予的)建筑许可证.

plane[1] /pleɪn; plen/ *n* **1** (**a**) (*geometry* 几) surface such that a straight line joining any two points in it touches it at all points 几何平面. (**b**) any flat or level surface 平面. **2** (*fig* 比喻) level of thought, existence or development (思想、存在或发展的)水平, 水准, 程度, 阶段: *They seem to exist on a different spiritual plane.* 他们似乎生活在不同的精神境界. ○ *This species has reached a higher plane of development.* 这一种属已达到更高的发展阶段.

▷ **plane** *adj* completely flat; level 平的; 平面的: *a plane surface* 平面.

plane *v* [I, Ip] (of an aeroplane) move through the air, esp without an engine; glide (指飞机)航行, (尤指)滑行.

□ ˌ**plane ge**ˈ**ometry** geometry of two-dimensional or plane figures 平面几何学.

ˌ**plane** ˈ**sailing** method of calculating a ship's position as though the ship were on a plane surface instead of the curved surface of the earth 平面航法(将地球曲面视作平面测定船的位置).

ˈ**plane-table** *n* instrument used by surveyors for drawing plans in fieldwork, consisting of a circular table with a pivoted sighting-device 平板仪.

plane 刨子

plane[2] /pleɪn; plen/ *n* tool, consisting of a blade set in a flat surface, which makes the surface of wood smooth by shaving very thin layers from it 刨子.

▷ **plane** *v* **1** (**a**) [Tn] use a plane on (sth) 用刨子刨(某物): *plane the edge of the plank* 刨木板的边缘. (**b**) [Cn·a] make (sth) smooth, etc by using a plane 用刨刨平(某物): *plane sth smooth* 将某物刨平滑. **2** (phr v) **~ sth away/down/off** remove sth using a plane 用刨刨去某物: *plane away the irregularities on a surface* 把一物体表面上的突出物刨掉.

plane[3] /pleɪn; plen/ (also ˈ**plane-tree**) *n* any of several types of deciduous tree with spreading branches, broad leaves and thin bark that comes off in flakes 悬铃木.

plane[4] /pleɪn; plen/ *n* = AEROPLANE: *travel by plane* 乘飞机 ○ *The plane is about to land.* 飞机即行着陆. ○ [attrib 作定语] *a plane flight* 飞机的飞行.

planet /ˈplænɪt; ˈplænɪt/ *n* any of the bodies in space that move around a star (such as the sun) and are illuminated by it 行星: *The planets of our solar system are Mercury, Venus, Earth, Mars, Jupiter, Saturn, Uranus, Neptune and Pluto.* 我们太阳系的行星是水星、金星、地球、火星、木星、土星、天王星、海王星、冥王星.

▷ **plan·et·arium** /ˌplænɪˈteərɪəm; ˌplænəˈtɛrɪəm/ *n* (*pl* **~s** or **-ia** /-ɪə; -ɪə/) (building with a) device for representing the positions and movements of the planets and stars by projecting spots of light on a dome which represents the sky 天象仪; 天象馆; 天文馆.

plan·et·ary /ˈplænɪtrɪ; *US* -terɪ; ˈplænəˌtɛrɪ/ *adj* of or like a planet or planets (似)行星的: *planetary movements* 行星的运动.

plan·gent /ˈplændʒənt; ˈplændʒənt/ *adj* (*fml* 文) **1** (of sounds) throbbing loudly; reverberating (指声音)震荡的, 回响的. **2** (of sounds) expressing sadness; mournful (指声音)凄切的, 悲戚的. ▷ **plan·gency** /-dʒənsɪ; -dʒənsɪ/ *n* [U]. **plan·gently** *adv*.

plank /plæŋk; plæŋk/ *n* **1** long flat piece of sawn timber, 50-150mm thick and at least 200mm wide, used for making floors, etc 木板(厚50-150毫米, 宽至少200毫米, 用以铺地面等). **2** (*esp politics* 尤用于政治) any of the main principles of the policy or programme of a political party (政党的)政策或政纲的准则: *the main planks of their disarmament platform* 他们的裁军政纲准则. **3** (idm 习语) **thick as two planks** ⇨ THICK. **walk the plank** ⇨ WALK[1].

▷ **plank** *v* (phr v) **plank sth down** (*infml* 口) (**a**) put (sth) down heavily 重重地放下(某物): *plank down one's luggage* 重重地放下行李. (**b**) pay (money) at once 立即付(钱). Cf 参看 PLONK[1] *v*.

plank·ing *n* [U] planks used esp to make a floor; structure made of planks 板材; (尤指)地板: *Are you going to cover the planking with carpet?* 你打算在地板上铺地毯吗?

plank·ton /ˈplæŋktən; ˈplæŋktən/ *n* [U] any of the (mainly microscopic) forms of plant and animal life that drift in or float on the water of seas, rivers, lakes, etc 浮游生物.

plant[1] /plɑːnt; *US* plænt; plænt/ *n* **1** [C] (**a**) living organism that is not an animal, which grows in the earth and usu has a stem, leaves and roots 植物: *Plants need* *light and water.* 植物需要光和水. ○ [attrib 作定语] *'plant life* 植物. (**b**) any of the smaller kinds of these as distinct from shrubs or trees 花草: *garden plants* 园中的花草 ○ *a 'strawberry plant* 一株草莓 ○ *plants flowering in the window-box* 窗口花坛中开着花的花草. **2** (**a**) [U] machinery, equipment, etc used in an industrial or a manufacturing process (用于工业生产中的)机器、设备等: *The firm has made a huge investment in new plant.* 该公司投入巨资购置新设备. ○ [attrib 作定语] *'plant hire,* ie renting of machines or equipment 机器租赁. (**b**) [C] piece of machinery or equipment 机器; 设备: *The farm has its own 'power plant.* 这家农场自己有发电设备. **3** [C] (*esp US*) place where an industrial or a manufacturing process takes place; factory 工厂: *a 'chemical plant* 化工厂 ○ *a nuclear re'processing plant* 核燃料后处理工厂. ⇨ Usage at FACTORY 用法见 FACTORY. **4** [C] (*infml* 口) (**a**) thing placed deliberately so that its discovery will make an innocent person appear guilty; false or misleading evidence 栽赃物; 伪证: *He claimed that the stolen jewellery found in his house was a plant.* 他声称在他家中发现的那些失窃的珠宝是有人给他栽赃. (**b**) person who joins a group of criminals, conspirators, etc in order to spy on them for others (在犯罪、阴谋等集团中卧底的)眼线, 坐探: *They discovered that he was a police plant.* 他们发现他是警方的眼线.

plant[2] /plɑ:nt; *US* plænt; plænt/ *v* **1** (**a**) [Tn, Tn·pr] put (plants, seeds, etc) in the ground to grow 种植; 栽种: *plant flowers around the pool* 在池子周围栽花 ○ *We planted beans and peas in the garden.* 我们在花园中种菜豆和豌豆. ○ *Plant in rows two feet apart.* 每隔两英尺种一行. (**b**) [Tn, Tn·pr] **~ sth (with sth)** put bushes, trees, flowers, etc in (a garden, flower-bed, etc) 在(花园、花圃等)中栽种花草树木: *plant a garden* 在花园中种花 ○ *plant the border with spring flowers* 在边上种上春天开花的植物 ○ *mountain slopes planted with conifers* 栽有松柏的山坡. Cf 参看 sow[2]. **2** [Tn·pr] (**a**) place (sth) in position firmly or forcefully 牢固地或用力地安放(某物): *He planted his feet firmly on the ground.* 他在地上双脚站得很稳. ○ *He stood with his feet planted wide apart.* 他两脚叉开很大距离站着. (**b**) (*infml* 口) position (oneself) 使(自己)处于某一位置: *plant oneself in a chair in front of the fire* 坐到炉前的椅子上. **3** [Tn, Tn·pr] (*infml* 口) (**a**) **~ sth (on sb)** hide sth where it will be found in order to deceive sb or make an innocent person seem guilty 给某人栽赃: *plant stolen goods on sb* 把赃物栽给某人 ○ *He claimed that the weapons had been planted (on him).* 他称那些武器是别人(给他)栽的赃. (**b**) **~ sb (in sth)** cause sb to join a group secretly, esp to spy on its members 使某人秘密加入一集团; (尤指)安插眼线或坐探: *The police had planted a spy in the gang.* 警方在那团伙中安插了一名坐探. ○ *The speaker's supporters were planted in the audience and applauded loudly.* 听众中安插了演讲人的支持者; 他们使劲给他鼓掌. **4** [Tn·pr] **~ sth in sth** fix or establish (an idea, etc) in sb's mind 给某人灌输(某思想等): *Who planted that idea in your head?* 是谁给你灌输的这种思想? ○ *His strange remarks planted doubts in our minds about his sanity.* 他那些怪话使我们心中生疑, 不知他精神是否正常. **5** [Tn·pr] deliver (a blow, etc) with deliberate aim 给以(一击等): *plant a kiss on sb's cheek* 在某人的面颊上吻一下 ○ *plant a blow on the side of sb's head* 向某人头侧一击 ○ *plant a knife in sb's back* 把刀插入某人的背上. **6** (phr v) **plant (sth) out** place (plants) in the ground so that they have enough room to grow 移栽, 移植(植物): *plant out tomato seedlings* 把西红柿移栽到地里.

▷ **planter** *n* **1** person who grows crops on or manages a plantation 农场的种植者或经管者: *a 'sugar-planter, 'tea-planter, 'rubber-planter, etc* 糖料作物、茶、橡胶等的种植者. **2** machine for planting (PLANT[2] 1) 种植机. **3** (*esp US*) container in which plants are grown, esp in a house as an ornament 花盆(尤指室内的).

plan·tain[1] /'plæntɪn; 'plæntɪn/ *n* (**a**) [C, U] tropical fruit, similar to a banana but usu cooked before being eaten 大蕉(果实). (**b**) [C] tree-like plant that bears this 大蕉(植物).

plan·tain[2] /'plæntɪn; 'plæntɪn/ *n* common wild plant with broad flat leaves and small green flowers, that bears seeds which are used as food for cage-birds 车前草.

planta·tion /plæn'teɪʃn, *also, in British use,* 英式英语亦读作 plɑ:n-; plæn'teʃən/ *n* **1** large piece of land, esp in a tropical country, where tea, cotton, sugar, tobacco, etc are grown (茶、棉、甘蔗、烟草等的)大种植园, 大农场(尤指热带国家的): [attrib 作定语] *a plantation manager* 种植园经管者. **2** (**a**) area of land planted with trees 造林地: *plantations of fir and pine* 枞树及松树林地. (**b**) group of trees or plants planted together 人工林; 人工植物带.

plaque[1] /plɑ:k; *US* plæk; plæk/ *n* flat (usu round) piece of stone, metal or porcelain fixed on a wall as an ornament or a memorial (装于墙上作饰物或纪念物的石质、金属或瓷制的)饰板(通常为圆形): *A simple plaque marks the spot where the martyr died.* 有一块朴素的饰板用以纪念该烈士的殉难处.

plaque[2] /plɑ:k; *US* plæk; plæk/ *n* [U] (*medical* 医) soft substance that forms on teeth and encourages the growth of harmful bacteria 牙斑: *It is necessary to remove plaque by brushing one's teeth.* 需刷牙以去除牙斑. Cf 参看 TARTAR[1] 1.

plasma /'plæzmə; 'plæzmə/ (also **plasm** /'plæzəm; 'plæzəm/) *n* [U] (*anatomy* 解) **1** (**a**) clear yellowish liquid part of blood, in which the corpuscles float 血浆. (**b**) (*medical* 医) (also '**blood plasma**) this fluid taken from the blood and specially treated for use in blood transfusions (输血用的)血浆. **2** = PROTOPLASM. **3** (*physics* 物) type of gas containing positively and negatively charged particles in approximately equal numbers, and present in the sun and most stars 等离子体.

plas·ter /'plɑ:stə(r); *US* 'plæs-; 'plæstɚ/ *n* **1** [U] soft mixture of lime, sand, water, etc that becomes hard when dry and is used for making a smooth surface on walls and ceilings 灰泥(涂平墙壁和天花板用的): *The plaster will have to dry out before you can paint the room.* 待房间的灰泥干后才可粉刷. **2** [U] (also ˌ**plaster of 'Paris**) white paste made from gypsum that becomes very hard when dry, used for making moulds, holding broken bones in place, etc 烧石膏; 熟石膏: *She broke her ankle weeks ago and it's still in plaster.* 她的踝关节数周前骨折, 至今仍打着石膏. **3** [C, U] = STICKING PLASTER (STICK[2]).

▷ **plas·ter** *v* **1** (**a**) [Tn] cover (a wall, etc) with plaster(1) 用灰泥涂抹(墙壁等). (**b**) [Tn·pr] **~ A with B/~ B on(to) A** cover sth with sth thickly, as one puts plaster on a wall 用黏稠物涂抹某物: *hair plastered with oil* 抹油的头发 ○ *an artist who plasters the paint on the canvas* 在画布上涂颜料的画家 ○ *plaster the town with posters* 把海报贴遍市镇. **2** [Tn] cover (a wound, etc) with a plaster(2) 给(受伤处等)打石膏. **3** (phr v) **plaster sth down** make sth lie flat by putting a wet or sticky substance on it (敷湿或黏之物)使某物平贴: *plaster one's hair down* 用发蜡把头发梳平. **plas·tered** *adj* (*sl* 俚) drunk 醉的: *be/get plastered* 醉了. **plas·terer** /'plɑ:stərə(r); 'plæstərɚ/ *n* person whose job is to put plaster on walls and ceilings 粉刷匠; 泥水匠.

□ '**plasterboard** *n* [U] board made of sheets of cardboard with plaster(1) between them, used for inside walls and ceilings 灰泥板(以灰泥夹心, 作内墙壁及天花板用的).

'**plaster cast** (**a**) mould made with gauze and plaster of Paris to hold a broken or dislocated bone in place 石膏绷带(作折断或脱位之骨复位固定用者). (**b**) mould (eg for a small statue) made of plaster of Paris 石膏模型(如做小塑像的).

plas·tic /'plæstɪk; 'plæstɪk/ *n* **1** (**a**) [C usu *pl* 通常作复数] any of several chemically produced substances that can be formed into shapes when heated or made into thin threads and used in textiles 塑料: *the use of plastics in industry* 塑料在工业中的应用. (**b**) [U] substance made in this way 可塑性物质: *Many items in daily use are made out of plastic.* 有很多日常生活用品是塑料制的. ○ *Plastic is sometimes used instead of leather.* 塑料有时可以代替皮革. **2 plastics** [sing *v*] science of making plastics (PLASTIC 1a) 塑料学. **3** [U] (also **plastic money**) (*infml* 口) credit card(s) 信用卡: *'Have you got any cash or shall we use plastic?' 'Put it on the plastic.'* '你有没有现金? 还是我们用信用卡呢?' '用信用卡吧.'

▷ **plas·tic** *adj* **1** (of goods) made of plastic(1b) (指物品)塑料的: *a plastic cup, raincoat, spoon, toy, wrist-watch* 塑料杯、雨衣、羹匙、玩具、手表 ○ *fabric with a plastic coating* 塑料涂层纤维织物 ○ *a plastic bag*, ie made from very thin soft plastic material 塑料袋. **2** (of materials or substances) easily shaped or moulded (指材料或物质)可塑的: *Clay is a plastic substance.* 黏土是可塑物质. ○ (*fig* 比喻) *The mind of a young child is quite plastic.* 儿童的思想很有可塑性. **3** of the art of modelling eg clay or wax 制造模型的艺术的(如用黏土或蜡等): *the plastic arts*, ie sculpture, ceramics, etc 制造模型的艺术. **plas·ti·city** /plæˈstɪsətɪ; plæsˈtɪsətɪ/ *n* [U] state or quality of being able to be moulded or shaped 可塑性.

□ ˌ**plastic** ˈ**bomb** bomb that contains plastic explosive 塑料炸弹.

ˌ**plastic ex**ˈ**plosive** explosive material that can easily be formed into different shapes or moulded around the object it is used to destroy 塑料炸药.

ˌ**plastic** ˈ**surgery** repairing or replacing injured or damaged tissue on the surface of the body, eg after a person has been badly burned 整形外科.

plas·ti·cine (also **Plas·ti·cine**) /ˈplæstɪsiːn; ˈplæstəˌsin/ *n* [U] (*propr* 专利名 *esp Brit*) substance similar to clay but which does not harden like clay, used for modelling, esp by children 橡皮泥.

plate[1] /pleɪt; plet/ *n* **1** [C] (**a**) (often in compounds 常用以构成复合词) shallow (usu round) dish made usu of earthenware or china, from which food is served or eaten 盘子; 碟子: *a* ˈ*dinner,* ˈ*meat,* ˈ*soup, etc plate* 餐盘、肉盘、汤盘 ○ *paper/plastic* ˈ*plates*, eg at a picnic 纸[塑料]盘(如野餐用的). ⇨illus 见插图. (**b**) contents of this 一盘所盛之物: *a plate of soup, stew, etc* 一盘汤、炖肉等. (**c**) similar dish, usu made of metal or wood, used to collect money from the congregation in church (教会的)捐款盘, 奉献盘: *pass round the plate* 传递捐献盘 ○ *put £5 in the plate* 把5英镑放入捐献盘中. **2** [U] (**a**) spoons, forks, dishes, bowls, etc made of gold or silver, esp for use at meals 金的或银的餐具: *a fine piece of plate*, ie one of these articles 一件精致的贵金属餐具. (**b**) dishes, bowls, chalices, etc made of gold or silver for use in church 教会的金的或银的圣餐具: *The plate is kept in a locked cupboard.* 圣餐具放在有锁的橱里. **3** [U] (often in compounds 常用以构成复合词) metal other than silver or gold that has been covered with a thin coating of silver or gold 镀金或镀银的金属: *electroplate*, ie object(s) coated with a thin layer of metal 电镀物品 ○ *gold/silver plate* 镀金[镀银] ○ *I thought the teapot was silver, but it's only plate.* 我以为那把茶壶是银的, 原来只是电镀的. **4** [C] (**a**) thin flat sheet of metal, glass, etc (金属、玻璃等的)薄板材: *steel plates*, eg used in shipbuilding 钢板(如造船用的). (**b**) (*biology* 生) thin flat piece of horn, bone, etc (骨质、角质等的)盾片, 鳞片: *The armadillo has a protective shell of bony plates.* 犰狳有角质鳞片的护甲. **5** [C] (*geology* 地质) any of the large rigid sheets of rock that make up the earth's surface 板岩; 页岩: [attrib 作定语] *plate tectonics*, ie study of the structure and formation of the earth's surface through the movements of its plates 板块构造学. **6** [C] oblong piece of metal with sth stamped or engraved on it (印或刻有名号等的)金属牌: *a brass* ˈ*plate*, eg on the door of a doctor, solicitor, etc with his name on it 黄铜牌(如医生、律师等门上的名牌) ○ *a* ˈ*licence-/*ˈ*number-plate*, eg on a car 牌照[号码牌](如汽车上的). **7** [C] (**a**) sheet of metal, plastic, rubber, etc treated so that words or pictures can be printed from it (金属、塑料、橡胶等制的印刷用的)版, 印版. (**b**) (esp photographic) book illustration, esp one that is printed separately from the rest of the text 书籍插图(尤指照片版插页, 与正文分开印刷的): ˈ*colour plate* 彩色插图. **8** [C, U] (in photography) sheet of (esp) glass coated with a film sensitive to light (照相用的)感光底片, (尤指)玻璃感光片: ˈ*whole-/*ˈ*half-/*ˈ*quarter-plate*, ie the usual sizes 整张[半张/四分之一张]感光片. **9** (also ˈ**dental plate**, **denture**) [C] thin piece of plastic material moulded to the shape of the gums or roof of the mouth for holding artificial teeth 托牙板. **10** [C] (**a**) silver or gold cup as a prize for a horse-race (作赛马奖品的)金杯, 银杯. (**b**) the race itself (以金杯或银杯作奖品的)赛马. **11** [C] (in baseball) home base of the batting side (棒球中的)本垒. **12** (idm 习语) **hand/give sb sth on a** ˈ**plate** (*infml* 口) give sb sth or allow sb to obtain sth without any effort on his part 把某事物奉送某人; 让某人轻易获得某事物: *You can't expect promotion to be handed to you on a plate.* 晋升的事休想会给你送货上门. **on one's** ˈ**plate** to occupy one's time or energy 花个人的时间或精力: *have enough/a lot/too much on one's plate* 有够多[很多/太多]的事要做 ○ *I can't help you at the moment — I've far too much on my plate already.* 我现在无法帮助你——我自己的事已经太多了.

▷ ˈ**plate·ful** /-fʊl; -ˌfʊl/ *n* amount that a plate[1](1a) holds 一盘的量: *The child has eaten three platefuls of porridge!* 这孩子已经喝了三盘粥了!

□ ˌ**plate** ˈ**glass** very clear glass of fine quality made in thick sheets, used eg for doors, mirrors, shop windows, etc 厚玻璃板(如门、镜子、商店橱窗等用的): [attrib 作定语] *a plate-glass window* 厚玻璃板的窗户.

ˈ**plate-rack** *n* rack in which food plates are stored or left to drain after being washed 餐具架(供储放或控干餐具用的). ⇨illus at RACK 见 RACK 插图.

plate[2] /pleɪt; plet/ *v* **1** [Tn, Tn·pr esp passive 尤用于被动语态] **~ sth (with sth)** cover (another metal) with a thin layer esp of gold or silver 镀(另一金属)(尤指镀金或镀银): *a copper tray plated with silver* 镀银的铜托盘 ○ *gold-plated dishes* 镀金餐碟 ○ *silver-plated spoons* 镀银羹匙. **2** [Tn] cover (esp a ship) with metal plates 给(尤指船)覆金属板.

plat·eau /ˈplætəʊ; *US* plæˈtəʊ; plæˈto/ *n* (*pl* **~s** or **-eaux** /-təʊz; -ˈtoz/) **1** large area of fairly level land high above sea-level 高原. Cf 参看 RIDGE 2. **2** state of little or no change following a period of rapid growth or development (迅速增长或发展后的)稳定状态: *After a period of rapid inflation, prices have now reached a plateau.* 经急剧通货膨胀之后物价现已趋于平稳.

plate·layer /ˈpleɪtleɪə(r); ˈpletˌleɚ/ *n* (*Brit*) person whose job is to lay and repair railway tracks (铺设及维修钢轨的)路工.

plate·let /ˈpleɪtlɪt; ˈpletlɪt/ *n* any of the numerous tiny discs in the blood that help it to clot 血小板.

plat·form /ˈplætfɔːm; ˈplætˌfɔrm/ *n* **1** level surface raised above the surrounding ground or floor, esp one from which public speakers, performers, etc can be seen by their audience 台; 平台; (尤指)讲台, 舞台, 戏台: *the concert platform*, ie place where a pianist performs 钢琴演奏台 ○ *Your questions will be answered from the platform.* 你的问题将由台上的人作答. ○ *appear on the same platform/share a platform with sb*, ie make speeches, etc at the same public meeting 与某人在同一公众集会上发表演说. **2** (at a railway station) flat surface built next to and at a higher level than the track, where passengers get on and off trains (火车站的)站台, 月台: *Which platform does the Brighton train leave from?* 开往布赖顿市的火车在第几站台? ○ *Your train is waiting at platform 5.* 你要坐的那趟火车在第5站台. ○ *He came running along the platform just as the train was leaving.* 火车刚开就见他沿月台跑过来. **3** (*Brit*) floor area at the entrance to a bus where passengers get on and off (公共汽车供乘客上下车的)入口平台. **4** (*politics* 政) main policies and aims of a political party, esp as stated before an election; manifesto (政党的)纲领; (尤指选举前发表的)政纲; 宣言: *fight the election/come to power on a platform of economic reform* 以经济改革为政纲竞选[掌权].

plat·ing /ˈpleɪtɪŋ; ˈpletɪŋ/ *n* [U] **1** thin covering of metal, esp silver or gold, on another metal 极薄的金属(尤指

金或银)的镀层或包层: *The plating is beginning to wear off in places.* 镀层有的地方已经磨掉了. **2** layer or covering esp of metal plates 层, 外层(尤指金属板): *protected with steel plating* 用钢板防护的.

plat·inum /ˈplætɪnəm; ˋplætn̩əm/ *n* [U] (*chemistry* 化) greyish-white metallic element that does not tarnish, used to make jewellery and, esp in alloys with other metals, in industry 铂; 白金: *a sapphire in a platinum setting* 白金托镶着的蓝宝石. ⇨App 10 见附录 10.

□ ˌ**platinum** ˈ**blonde** (*infml* 口) (woman) having hair that is very fair or silvery white (but not white with age) 有浅色或银白色头发的(女子)(非因年老所致).

plat·it·ude /ˈplætɪtjuːd; *US* -tuːd; ˋplætəˌtud/ *n* [C] (*fml derog* 文, 贬) commonplace remark or statement, esp when it is said as if it were new or interesting 陈词滥调; (尤指当作新内容或津津乐道的)老调重弹: *We shall have to listen to more platitudes about the dangers of overspending.* 我们又得再听一通超支危害的陈词滥调了.

▷ **plat·it·ud·in·ous** /ˌplætɪˈtjuːdɪnəs; *US* -ˈtuːdənəs; ˌplætəˋtudn̩əs/ *adj* (*fml derog* 文, 贬) commonplace or banal 平凡的; 陈腐的; 乏味的: *platitudinous remarks* 老生常谈 ○ *The whole speech was platitudinous nonsense.* 整篇讲话都是陈谷子烂芝麻.

pla·tonic /pləˈtɒnɪk; pləˋtɑnɪk/ *adj* **1 Platonic** of or concerning the Greek philosopher Plato or his teachings 柏拉图的; 柏拉图哲学的. **2** (of love or a friendship between two people) close and deep but not sexual (指两人的爱或友谊)亲密(但无性欲)的, 纯友谊的, 柏拉图式的: *He said that his feelings for her were entirely platonic.* 他说他对她的感情完全是友谊. ○ *They'd had a close platonic relationship for more than thirty years.* 他们之间的柏拉图式的亲密关系已有三十多年了.

pla·toon /pləˈtuːn; pləˋtun/ *n* group of soldiers, a subdivision of a company, acting as a unit under the command of a lieutenant 排(军队中连的下一级).

plat·ter /ˈplætə(r); ˋplætɚ/ *n* **1** (**a**) large shallow dish for serving food, esp meat or fish 大浅盘(尤指盛肉或鱼的). (**b**) (*arch* 古 *Brit*) flat dish usu made of wood (通常为木制的)盘, 碟. **2** (*US infml* 口) gramophone record 唱片.

platy·pus /ˈplætɪpəs; ˋplætəpəs/ *n* (*pl* **~es**) (also ˌ**duck-billed** ˈ**platypus**) small Australian furred animal with a duck-like beak, webbed feet and a flat tail, that lays eggs but gives milk to its young 鸭嘴兽(产于澳洲).

plaudit /ˈplɔːdɪt; ˋplɔdɪt/ *n* (usu *pl* 通常作复数) (*fml* 文) applause, praise or some other sign of approval 鼓掌; 喝彩; 称赞: *She won plaudits for the way she presented her case.* 她妙语陈情博得众口交赞.

plaus·ible /ˈplɔːzəbl; ˋplɔzəbl̩/ *adj* **1** (of a statement, an excuse, etc) seeming to be right or reasonable; believable (指陈述、借口等)似乎正确的, 似有道理的, 可信的: *She could find no plausible explanation for its disappearance.* 她无法解释清楚何以不翼而飞. ○ *His story was/sounded perfectly plausible.* 他的话[听起来]言之成理. **2** (*derog* 贬) (of a person) skilled in producing convincing arguments, esp in order to deceive (指人)能说会道的(尤指为行骗): *a plausible trickster, rogue, liar, etc* 花言巧语的骗子、无赖、说谎大王等 ○ *She was so plausible — she would have deceived anyone.* 她鼓舌如簧——把谁都能骗倒. Cf 参看 IMPLAUSIBLE.

▷ **plaus·ib·il·ity** /ˌplɔːzəˈbɪlətɪ; ˌplɔzəˋbɪlətɪ/ *n* [U] state of being plausible 似正确或有理; 可信; 能言善辩: *the plausibility of her alibi* 她申辩不在现场言之凿凿 ○ *Beware of the plausibility of salesmen!* 要警惕推销员的花言巧语!

plaus·ibly /-əblɪ; -əblɪ/ *adv*: *The case was presented very plausibly.* 案情的申述似很可信. ○ *He argued very plausibly for its acceptance.* 他为使之认可辩解得头头是道.

play[1] /pleɪ; ple/ *n* **1** [U] activity done for amusement, esp by children; recreation 游戏, 玩耍(尤指儿童的); 娱乐: *the happy sounds of children at play* 儿童游戏时欢乐的声音 ○ *the advantages of learning through play* 寓学习于娱乐的优点 ○ *His life is all work and no play.* 他的生活是只知工作没有娱乐. **2** (*sport* 体) (**a**) [U] playing of a game 比赛; 竞赛; 运动: *There was no play/Rain stopped play yesterday.* 昨天没有[因雨停止]比赛. ○ *The tennis players need total concentration during play.* 网球运动员在比赛中需要全神贯注. (**b**) [U] manner of playing a game 比赛、竞赛或运动的表现或作风: *There was some excellent play in yesterday's match.* 昨天的比赛有些出色的表现. ○ *They were penalized for too much rough play.* 他们因在比赛中过于粗野而受罚. (**c**) [C] (*esp US*) action or manoeuvre in a game 比赛中的动作或技巧: *a good play* 漂亮的动作 ○ *a fine defensive/passing play* 精彩的防守[传递]动作. **3** [C] work (written to be) performed by actors; drama 戏剧; 剧本: *a radio play* 电台广播剧 ○ *a fine edition of Shakespeare's plays* 莎士比亚戏剧集锦 ○ *She has just written a new play.* 她刚写完一部新剧. ○ *act/take part in a play* 在一剧中[参加一剧的]演出 ○ *We are going to see the new play at the Playhouse.* 我们要到大剧院看新剧. **4** [U] (scope for) free and easy movement 自由活动(的范围): *Give the line more play*, eg in fishing. 把线放松些(如钓鱼线). ○ *a knot with too much play*, ie one that is not tight enough 松的结(系得不紧的) ○ *We need more play on the rope.* 绳子要松些. **5** [U] activity; operation; interaction 活动; 作用; 相互的影响: *the play of supernatural forces in human destiny* 超自然的力量对人类命运的影响. **6** [U] light, quick, constantly shifting movement 轻的、快的、不断转换的动作: *the play of sunlight on water* 阳光在水面上的闪烁. **7** [U] taking part in card-games, or board games, roulette, etc when playing for money; gambling 赌博: *lose £500 in one evening's play* 一晚上赌博输掉 500 英镑. **8** [sing] turn or move in cards, chess, etc (纸牌、下棋等游戏中)轮到的机会: *It's your play*, ie You are the next to make a move. 轮到你了. **9** (idm 习语) **bring sth into** ˈ**play** cause sth to have an influence 使某事物发生作用或影响: *This financial crisis has brought new factors into play.* 这次金融危机引发新的因素起了作用. **call sth into play** ⇨ CALL[2]. **child's play** ⇨ CHILD. **come into** ˈ**play** (begin to) be active or have an influence (开始)积极活动或起作用: *Personal feelings should not come into play when one has to make business decisions.* 为公事作决策不应搀杂个人情感. **fair play** ⇨ FAIR[1]. **give, etc free play/rein to sb/sth** ⇨ FREE[2]. **give sb/sth full play** ⇨ FULL. **in full play** ⇨ FULL. **in** ˈ**play** as a joke; not seriously 开玩笑地; 打趣地: *The remark was only made in play.* 那话只是说着玩的. **in/out of** ˈ**play** (*sport* 体) (of the ball in football, cricket, etc) in/not in a position where the rules allow it to be played (指足球、板球等的球)按规则处于可[不可]比赛状态中. **make a play for sb/sth** (*esp US*) perform actions that are designed to achieve a desired result 为得到意想的结果而采取行动: *She was making a big play for the leadership of the party.* 她千方百计要当党的领导. ○ *He was making a play for the prettiest girl in the college.* 他挖空心思想勾引那所学院中最漂亮的女生. **a play on** ˈ**words** pun 双关语: *The advertising slogan was a play on words.* 那条广告口号是双关语. **the state of play** ⇨ STATE[1].

▷ **play·let** /ˈpleɪlɪt; ˋplelɪt/ *n* short play[1](3) 短剧.

□ ˈ**play-act** *v* [I] make a show of feelings one does not really have; pretend 做作; 假装. ˈ**play-acting** *n* [U] (**a**) performing in a play[1](3) 演戏. (**b**) pretence, esp of feelings 假装(尤指感情的).

ˈ**playbill** *n* poster announcing the performance of a play[1](3) 戏剧海报.

ˈ**playboy** *n* rich (esp young) man who spends his time enjoying himself 寻欢作乐的男子(尤指年轻的); 花花公子.

ˌ**play-by-**ˈ**play** *n* (*US sport* 体) detailed commentary on a game, broadcast as it happens (比赛的)实况详细述评.

ˈ**playfellow** (also ˈ**playmate**) *n* companion with whom (esp) a child plays 游戏伙伴(尤指儿童的).

ˈ**playgoer** /-gəʊə(r); -ˌgoɚ/ *n* person who (often) goes to the theatre (常)看戏的人.

ˈ**playground** *n* (**a**) area of land where children play, eg as part of a school 游戏场, 运动场(如学校的操场). (**b**) (*fig* 比喻) area where people like to go on holiday 度假胜地: *The island has become a playground for the rich businessmen of the city.* 那个岛已成为城里富商的度假胜地.

ˈ**playgroup** (also ˈ**playschool**) *n* [CGp] group of children below school age who meet regularly and play together under the supervision of adults (学龄前的)幼儿学校. Cf 参看 NURSERY SCHOOL (NURSERY).

ˈ**playhouse** *n* **1** theatre 剧院. **2** (also ˈ**Wendy house**) model of a house large enough for a child to play in 游戏房(儿童可进入的模型房子).

ˈ**play-pen** *n* small portable enclosure with wooden bars or netting where a baby or small child can play 游戏围栏(供幼儿在其中玩耍的便携式围栏).

ˈ**play-room** *n* room in a house for children to play in (家庭中的)儿童游戏室.

ˈ**plaything** *n* (**a**) toy 玩具. (**b**) person treated as an unimportant object of amusement by sb else 被玩弄的人: *She seemed content with her life as a rich man's plaything.* 她似乎满足于做有钱男子的玩物.

ˈ**playtime** *n* [C, U] (period of) time for recreation and relaxation, esp in school 游戏或娱乐的时间(尤指学校中的): *The children have three playtimes during the day.* 那些学生一天有三次游戏时间. ○ *The children are outside during playtime.* 在娱乐时间学生都在室外活动.

playwright /ˈpleɪraɪt; ˈpleˌraɪt/ *n* person who writes plays; dramatist 剧作家.

play² /pleɪ; ple/ *v*.

► DOING THINGS FOR AMUSEMENT 玩耍 **1** (**a**) [I, Ipr, Ip] **~ (with sb/sth)** do things for pleasure, as children do; enjoy oneself, rather than work 玩; 玩耍; 游戏: *There's a time to work and a time to play.* 有工作的时间, 也要有娱乐的时间. ○ *play with a ball, toy, bicycle* 玩球、玩玩具、骑自行车玩 ○ *a little child playing with his friend* 和小朋友一起玩耍的小男孩 ○ *children playing for hours in the garden* 在花园里玩了几小时的儿童. (**b**) [Ipr no passive 不用于被动语态, Tn no passive 不用于被动语态, Tg] **~ (at) sth/~ (at) doing sth** (esp of children) pretend to be sth or do sth for amusement (尤指儿童)装扮, 假装: *Let's play (at) (being) pirates.* 咱们装海盗玩儿吧. ○ *The children were playing at keeping shop.* 孩子们假装开商店玩儿. **2** [Tn, Tn·pr, Dn·n no passive 不用于被动语态] **~ sth (on sb)** trick sb for amusement 开某人玩笑: *play a joke/prank/trick (on sb)* 开某人玩笑[对某人搞恶作剧/作弄某人] ○ *They played me a rotten trick.* 他们跟我开了一个很讨厌的玩笑.

► TAKING PART IN A GAME 参加比赛 **3** [I, Ipr, Tn, Tn·pr] **~ (sth) (with/against sb); ~ sb (at sth)** take part in a game; compete against sb in a game 参加比赛; 同某人比赛: *play football, cricket, chess, cards, etc* 踢足球、打板球、下国际象棋、玩纸牌 ○ *playing (darts) with one's friends* 和朋友玩(掷镖游戏) ○ *She plays (hockey) for England.* 她在英格兰队打(曲棍球). ○ *On Saturday France play(s) (Rugby) against Wales.* 星期六法国(橄榄球)队和威尔士队比赛. ○ *Have you played her (at tennis) yet?* 你同她比赛过(网球)了吗? **4** [I, Tn] gamble at or on (sth) 赌(某事物); 在(某事物)中赌博: *play at the roulette table* 赌轮盘赌 ○ *play the casinos* 在娱乐场赌博 ○ *play the stock-market*, ie buy and sell shares, etc to make money 买卖股票. **5** (**a**) [Ipr, Tn] take (a particular position) in a team (在体育队中)担任(某角色): *Who's playing in goal?* 谁做守门员? ○ *I've never played (as/at) centre-forward before.* 我以前从未当过中锋. (**b**) [Tn, Tn·pr, Cn·n/a] **~ sb (as sth)** include sb in a team 让某人加入队中比赛: *I think we should play Bill on the wing in the next match.* 我认为下一场应当让比尔任边锋. ○ *Who shall we play at/as centre-forward?* 咱们派谁当中锋? **6** (**a**) [I, Ipr, Ip, Tn, Tn·pr, Tn·p] (in sport) (try to) strike, kick, throw, etc (the ball, etc), esp in the specified manner or direction (体育运动中)击, 踢, 掷, 投(球等)(尤指以某种方式或向某方向): *She played (at the ball) and missed.* 她击球未中. ○ *In soccer, only the goal-keeper may play the ball with his hands.* 在足球运动中只有守门员可以用手触球. ○ *He played the ball onto his wicket*, ie accidentally struck it so that it hit the wicket. 他把球打进了自己的三柱门. (**b**) [Tn] (in sport) make (a stroke, etc) (体育运动中)做出(某动作): *play a fast backhand volley* 作快速反手拦击. **7** [I] (of a sports pitch, etc) be in a certain condition for playing (指体育比赛场地等)处于某条件: *a pitch that plays well, poorly, etc*, ie allows the ball to move easily, slowly, etc 好用、不好用等的场地. **8** [I, Tn] (**a**) move (a piece) in chess, etc 下, 移动(棋子等): *She played her bishop.* 她走了象. (**b**) put (a playing-card) face upwards on the table in a game of cards (纸牌游戏中)出牌: *Have you played?* 你出牌了吗? ○ *Don't play out of turn!* 别抢出牌! ○ *play one's ace, a trump, etc* 出A、王牌等.

► PRODUCING MUSIC OR SOUND 演奏或放音 **9** (**a**) [I, Ipr, Tn, Dn·n, Dn·pr] **~ (sth) (on sth); ~ sth (to sb)** perform on (a musical instrument); perform (music) 演奏(乐器或音乐): *In the distance a band was playing.* 远处一乐队在演奏. ○ *play (the violin, flute, etc) (well)* 演奏(小提琴、笛子等)(演奏得优美) ○ *play (a sonata) to an audience* 给听众演奏(一奏鸣曲) ○ *play a tune on a guitar* 用吉他弹一曲调 ○ *play sb a piece by Chopin* 给某人演奏萧邦的一首乐曲. (**b**) [I] (of music) be performed (指音乐)演奏: *I could hear music playing on the radio.* 我听到收音机里演奏着音乐. **10** (**a**) [Tn, Dn·n, Dn·pr] **~ sth (for sb)** cause (a record, record-player, etc) to produce sound 用(唱片、唱机等)播放: *Can you play (me) her latest record?* 给我放放她最新录制的唱片行吗? ○ *Play that jazz tape for me, please.* 请给我放那盘爵士乐录音带吧. (**b**) [I] (of a tape, record, etc) produce sound (指录音带、唱片等)放音: *There was a record playing in the next room.* 隔壁房间里正在放唱片.

► ACTING 表演 **11** (**a**) [Tn] act in (a drama, etc); act the role of (sb) 演(戏等); 扮演(某人)的角色: *They're playing 'Carmen' at the Coliseum.* 他们在伦敦的大剧场上演《卡门》. ○ *play (the part of) Ophelia* 扮演奥菲莉娅(的角色). (**b**) [I, Ipr] **~ (to sb)** (of a drama) be performed (指戏剧)演出, 上演: *a production of 'Hamlet' playing to enthusiastic audiences* 为热情的观众演出的《哈姆雷特》. **12** [La, Ln, Tn no passive 不用于被动语态] behave in a specified way; act as if one were (a particular type of person) 以某种方式表现; 装成(某种人): *play dead*, ie pretend to be dead in order to trick sb 装死(骗人) ○ *play the politician, diplomat, etc* 扮政治家、外交家等 ○ *play the fool*, ie act foolishly 做蠢事 ○ *play the sympathetic friend, the wronged wife, the busy tycoon, etc* 装成有同情心的朋友、受委屈的妻子、忙碌的企业家等.

► OTHER MEANINGS 其他意义 **13** (**a**) [Ipr] move quickly and lightly, esp often changing direction 快而轻地动(尤指常变换方向): *sunlight playing on/over the surface of the lake* 湖面上闪动的阳光 ○ (*fig* 比喻) *A smile played on/about her lips.* 她双唇露出一丝微笑. ○ *His mind played on the idea of going away for a holiday.* 他心里动着度假的念头. (**b**) [Tn·pr] direct (esp light or water) in a specified direction 将(尤指光或水)对准某处: *play the torch beam over the walls* 用电筒照墙的那一边 ○ *The firemen played their hoses on the burning building.* 消防队员用水龙喷射燃烧着的建筑物. ○ *They played the searchlights along the road.* 他们用探照灯照射那条路. (**c**) [I] (of fountains, etc) produce a steady stream of water (指喷泉等)持续喷水. **14** [Tn] allow (a fish) to exhaust itself by pulling against the line 让(鱼)拉钓线使之疲乏. **15** (idm 习语) **what sb is playing at** (usu expressing anger, irritation, etc 通常用以表示愤怒、烦躁等) what sb is doing 某人在搞什么名堂: *I don't know ˈwhat he thinks he's ˈplaying at.* 我不知道他在搞什么名堂. (For other idioms containing **play**, see entries for *ns, adjs*, etc 与 **play** 搭配的其他习语见有关名词、形容词等的词条, 如 **play fair** ⇨ FAIR²; **play the game** ⇨ GAME¹.)

16 (phr v) **play aˈbout/aˈround (with sb/sth)** act or handle sb/sth in a casual irresponsible way 玩弄某人; 摆弄或乱弄某物: *Stop playing around and get on with the job.* 别胡闹了, 接着做工作吧. ○ *You shouldn't play around with* (ie flirt with) *another woman's husband.* 你不应该和人家的丈夫厮混. ○ *Don't play about with my expensive tools!* 别乱摆弄我的昂贵的工具!

play aˈlong (with sb/sth) pretend to co-operate 假装与某人合作; 假意参与某事: (*infml* 口) *She was in charge, so I had to play along with her odd ideas.* 她是负责人, 对她的怪念头我只好假意听从.

ˈ**play at sth/being sth** do sth only casually, without true interest 应付事; 敷衍地做: *He's only playing at his job in the city: he's much more interested in being a racing driver.* 他对城里的工作只是敷衍而已, 一心想的是当赛

车手.
play sth 'back (to sb) allow the material recorded on a tape, etc to be heard or seen 播放(已录制的录音带、录像带等): *I rewound the cassette and played her voice back to her.* 我把录音带转回去, 把她的声音放给她听.
play sth 'down try to make sth appear less important than it is 欲使某事物显得没有实际上那么重要: *The government are trying to play down their involvement in the affair.* 政府极力淡化与该事的瓜葛.
play sb in, out, etc play music as sb enters, leaves, etc (a place) 奏乐欢迎或欢送某人: *The band played the performers onto the stage.* 乐队奏乐欢迎演员登台. **play oneself 'in** play slowly and cautiously at the beginning of a game (比赛开始时)缓慢而谨慎地进行.
play (sth) 'off (of two teams, etc that have the same number of points, have drawn in an earlier match, etc) play the deciding match (两队得分相同或打成平局等时)作决赛: *The match between the joint leaders will be played off tomorrow.* 两优胜队明天决赛. **play A off against B** cause two people or groups to oppose each other, esp for one's own advantage 挑拨离间(尤指为渔利): *She played her two rivals off against each other and got the job herself.* 她挑拨两个对手相争, 自己却获得了那份工作.
play 'on (*sport* 体) continue to play; start playing again 继续比赛; 恢复比赛: *Some of the players claimed a penalty but the referee told them to play on.* 有些队员认为应当判罚, 但裁判让他们继续比赛. **play on sth** rouse (sb's feelings, etc) for one's own purposes (为达到个人目的)激起(某人情感等): *They played on his fears of losing his job to get him to do what they wanted.* 他们利用他怕失掉工作的心理, 让他做他们想做的事. ○ *Her speech played heavily on the angry mood of her audience.* 她用演说激起听众的极大愤怒.
play sth out perform or enact sth, esp in real life 演出或现出某事物(尤指在现实生活中): *Their love affair was played out against the background of a country at war.* 他们恋爱那时国家正进行着战争.
play (sb) up (*infml* 口) cause (sb) problems, pain or difficulties 给(某人)带来麻烦、痛苦或困难: *My injured shoulder is playing (me) up today.* 我受伤的肩膀今天很疼. ○ *schoolchildren playing up their teacher*, eg by being noisy 给老师惹麻烦的小学生(如很吵闹). **play sth up** try to make sth appear more important than it is 欲使某事物显得比实际重要: *She played up her past achievements just to impress us.* 她夸耀过去的成绩就是为了让我们觉得她了不起. **play up to sb** (*infml* 口) flatter sb in order to win favour 讨好或奉承某人.
'play with oneself (*euph* 婉) masturbate 手淫. **play with sb/sth** = PLAY ABOUT/AROUND (WITH SB/STH). **play with sth** consider (an idea, etc) lightly; toy with sth 不认真地考虑(一主意等); 轻率对待某事物: *She's playing with the idea of starting her own business.* 她胡乱想着自己开业的事.
□ **'play-back** *n* [C, U] (device for) playing back recorded sound or pictures, eg on a video recorder 播放(录音或录像的装置)(如录像机的).
played 'out *adj* (*infml* 口) exhausted; finished; no longer useful 衰竭; 结束; 失去作用: *After a hard gallop, the horse was played out.* 那马跑得精疲力竭. ○ *Is this theory played out* (ie no longer worth considering)*?* 这理论过时了吗?
'play-off *n* match between two players or teams that are level, to decide the winner (两队或队员打成平局后的)决胜比赛, 延长赛, 加赛.

player /ˈpleɪə(r); ˈpleɚ/ *n* **1** person who plays a game 游戏者; 选手; 运动员: *a game for four players* 四人玩的游戏 ○ *She's an excellent 'tennis player.* 她是优秀的网球选手. ○ *Two players were injured during the match.* 有两名运动员在比赛中受伤. **2** actor 演员. **3** person who plays a musical instrument 演奏者: *a 'trumpet player* 吹奏小号的人. **4** = RECORD-PLAYER (RECORD[1]).
□ **'player-piano** *n* piano fitted with a mechanism that allows it to be played automatically 自动钢琴(有自动演奏装置的).

play·ful /ˈpleɪfl; ˈplefəl/ *adj* **1** fond of playing; full of fun 爱玩的; 爱游戏的; 有趣的: *as playful as a kitten* 像小猫一样顽皮 ○ *a playful mood* 快活的心情. **2** done in fun; not serious 闹着玩的; 取乐的: *a playful slap on the hand* 闹着玩打一下手 ○ *playful remarks* 开玩笑的话. ▷ **play·fully** /-fəlɪ; -flɪ/ *adv*. **play·ful·ness** *n* [U].

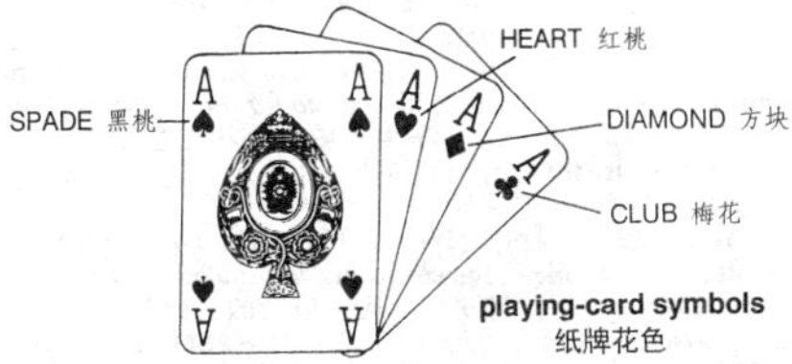

playing-card symbols 纸牌花色

P

playing-card /ˈpleɪɪŋ kɑːd; ˈpleɪŋˌkɑrd/ (also **card**) *n* any of a set of 52 oblong cards, used for various games (eg bridge, canasta, poker) 纸牌; 扑克牌: *a pack of playing-cards* 一副纸牌.

playing-field /ˈpleɪɪŋ fiːld; ˈpleɪŋˌfild/ *n* (*sport* 体) (**a**) field with special markings, used for cricket, football, hockey, etc (板球、足球、曲棍球等的)球场, 操场, 运动场. (**b**) = PLAYGROUND (PLAY[1]).

plaza /ˈplɑːzə; *US* ˈplæzə; ˈplæzə/ *n* **1** open square or market-place (esp in a Spanish town) 广场, 集市(尤指西班牙城镇中的). **2** (*esp US*) shopping centre 购物中心.

PLC (also **plc**) /ˌpiː el ˈsiː; ˌpi ɛl ˈsi/ *abbr* 缩写 = (*Brit*) Public Limited (ie limited liability) Company 股分公开有限公司: *Lloyd's Bank PLC* 劳埃德银行(亦译劳合银行). Cf 参看 INC, LTD.

plea /pliː; pli/ *n* **1** (*fml* 文) **~ (for sth)** earnest request; appeal 恳求; 请求: *a plea for forgiveness, money, more time* 恳求原谅、给予金钱、多给些时间 ○ *He was deaf to* (ie refused to listen to) *her pleas.* 他对她的请求充耳不闻. **2** (*law* 律) statement made by or for a person charged with an offence in court (法庭中被告一方的)抗辩, 答辩, 辩护: *enter a plea of guilty/not guilty* 承认有罪[不承认有罪]. **3** (idm 习语) **on the plea of sth/that...** (*fml* 文) giving sth as the reason or excuse for not doing sth or for having done sth wrong (为未做某事或做错某事而作的)辩解, 托词, 借口: *withdraw on the plea of ill health* 借口健康不佳而退出 ○ *He refused to contribute, on the plea that he couldn't afford it.* 他借口无能为力拒不捐献.

pleach /pliːtʃ; plitʃ/ *v* [Tn esp passive 尤用于被动语态] make or repair (a hedge) by weaving branches together 用枝条编筑或修理(篱笆): *pleached hedges* 用枝条编的篱笆.

plead /pliːd; plid/ *v* (*pt, pp* **pleaded**; *US* **pled** /pled; plɛd/) **1** [Ipr, It] **~ (with sb) (for sth)** make repeated urgent requests (to sb) (for sth) 再三恳求或请求(某人)(做某事): *plead for mercy* 祈求发慈悲 ○ *He pleaded with his parents for a more understanding attitude.* 他求父母多加谅解. ○ *She pleaded with him not to leave her alone.* 她恳求他不要留下她一个人. ○ *The boy pleaded to be allowed to ride on the tractor.* 那男孩请求让他坐坐拖拉机. **2** [Tn] offer (sth) as an explanation or excuse, esp for failing to do sth or for doing sth wrong 提出(理由或借口)(尤指因未做某事或做错某事): *They asked him to pay for the damage but he pleaded poverty.* 他们要他付损害赔偿金, 但他借口贫穷而不偿还. ○ *He apologized for not coming to the party, pleading pressure of work.* 他为不能到会而道歉, 推说是工作太忙. ○ *Pleading ignorance of the law won't help you if you are caught.* 假若因犯法被抓住, 借口不知是犯法亦无济于事. **3** [Ipr] **~ for/against sb** (*law* 律) (of a lawyer) speak to a lawcourt (on behalf of the plaintiff/defendant) (指律师)(在法庭上为原告[被告])提出申诉、答辩或辩护. **4** [Tn] (*law* 律) present (a case) to a court of law 向法庭陈述(案情): *They employed the best lawyer they could get to plead their case.* 他们聘请了能请到的最好的律师为他们陈述案情. **5** [Tn] (*law* 律) put (sth) forward as the basis of a case in a court of law (on behalf of sb) (代表某人)向法庭提出(某事)(作为案件的基础): *Counsel for the accused said that he intended to plead insanity*, ie that his client was insane and therefore not responsible for his actions. 被告的律师说他想提出

案发时被告精神失常这一理由，为被告不需负法律责任进行辩护. ○ *plead guilty/not guilty*, ie declare that one is guilty/not guilty of the crime one has been accused of 承认有罪[不承认有罪]. **6** [Ipr, Tn] **~ (for) sth** argue in support of sth; support (a cause) by argument 极力主张; 以辩论支持(某事业): *plead the cause of political prisoners* 声援政治犯的事业 ○ *plead for the modernization of the city's public transport* 力主城市公共交通现代化.

▷ **plead·ingly** *adv* in a begging or an imploring manner 恳求地; 乞求地.

plead·ings *n* [pl] (*law* 律) formal (usu written) statements, replies to accusations, etc made by each side in a legal action (原告的)诉状; (被告的)答辩状.

P

pleas·ant /ˈpleznt; ˋplɛzn̩t/ *adj* **(-er, -est)** **(a)** **~ (to sth)** giving pleasure to the mind, feelings or senses; enjoyable 使人愉快的; 合意的; 可喜的: *a pleasant surprise, smell, wine* 惊喜、令人舒服的气味、可口的葡萄酒 ○ *a pleasant breeze, temperature, climate* 宜人的微风、温度、气候 ○ *pleasant to the taste* 可口的. **(b)** **~ (to sb)** polite and friendly 礼貌而友好的: *a pleasant smile, voice, manner* 友好的微笑、声音、举止 ○ *make oneself pleasant to visitors* 亲切和蔼地待客 ○ *What a pleasant girl!* 多么讨人喜欢的姑娘啊! ○ *Do try to be more pleasant!* 尽量亲切友好一些! ▷ **pleas·antly** *adv*: *smile pleasantly* 亲切地微笑 ○ *We were pleasantly surprised at the profit we made.* 我们获得了利润而惊喜交加. **pleas·ant·ness** *n* [U].

pleas·antry /ˈplezntrɪ; ˋplɛzn̩trɪ/ *n* (*fml* 文) **(a)** humorous remark; joke 幽默的话; 笑话: *The children smiled politely at the visitor's pleasantries.* 孩子听了客人说的幽默话，都斯文地笑了. **(b)** polite remarks 有礼貌的话; 客气话: *After an exchange of pleasantries, the leaders started their negotiations.* 领导人互相寒暄一番，然后开始谈判.

please /pliːz; pliz/ *v* **1** [Tn] be agreeable to (sb); make (sb) happy 使(某人)满意或愉快: *It's difficult to please everybody.* 很难做到人人满意. ○ *Our main aim is to please the customers.* 我们的目的是让顾客满意. ○ *He's a very hard/difficult man to please.* 他是个很难让人讨好的人. ○ *I shall have nothing to do on holiday but please myself*, ie do as I like. 我在假日只图快乐，别的什么事都不做. **2** [I] (in subordinate clauses beginning with *as* or *what* 用于以as或what开头的从句中) (*fml* 文) **(a)** think desirable or appropriate; choose 认为满意或合适; 愿意: *You may stay as long as you please.* 你爱呆多久就呆多久. ○ *Take as many as you please.* 你要拿多少就拿多少. **(b)** want; like 想要; 喜欢: *That child behaves just as he pleases.* 那孩子想干什么就干什么. ○ *I shall do as I please.* 我喜欢怎么做就怎么做. ○ *Do what you please.* 你想做什么都行. **3** (idm 习语) **ˌif you ˈplease** **(a)** (*fml* 文) (used when making a polite request 用于客气的请求): *Come this way, if you please.* 请您这边走. **(b)** (used to express annoyance or outrage when reporting sth 用于转述某事时表示恼怒或愤恨): *And now, if you please, I've been told I'm to get nothing for my work!* 嘿，真岂有此理，听说我是白干工作毫无报酬! ○ *He says the food isn't hot enough, if you please!* 他竟然说吃的东西不够热，你听听这话! **ˌplease ˈGod** may God let it happen; if it is pleasing to God 但愿上帝让它实现; 若天意如愿: *Please God, things will start to improve soon.* 但愿事情很快开始好转. ○ *She'll get better one day, please God.* 她总有一天会好起来的，愿上帝开恩. **ˌplease yourˈself** (*ironic* 反语) do as you like; I don't care what you do 请便; 我才不在乎你做什么呢: *'I don't want to come with you today.' 'Oh, please yourself then!'* '我今天不想和你一起去.' '哦，请便吧!'

▷ **please** *interj* **1** **(a)** (used as a polite way of making a request or giving an order 用于客气的请求或吩咐): *Please come in.* 请进. ○ *Come in, please.* 请进. ○ *Two cups of tea, please.* 请来两杯茶. ○ *Tickets, please!* 请把票拿出来! ○ *Would you go now, please!* 请您现在走吧! **(b)** (used to add emphasis or urgency to a request or statement 用以加强请求或陈述的语气或迫切性): *Please don't leave me here alone!* 请别把我一个人留在这里! ○ *Please, please, don't be late!* 可千万别迟到! ○ *Please, I don't understand what I have to do!* 真是的，我不明白该做什么好! **2** (*infml* 口) (used when accepting an offer emphatically 在接受别人好意时用以加强语气) yes, please 那太好了: *'Shall I help you carry that load?' 'Please!'* '我帮你拿那个重东西好吗?' '那太好了!' **3** (idm 习语) **yes, please** (used as a polite way of accepting the offer of sth 用作接受好意时的客气话) I accept and am grateful 我接受并且感谢: *'Would you like some coffee?' 'Yes, please.'* '你要点咖啡吗?' '好的，谢谢.' ○ *'Would you like a lift into town?' 'Yes, please.'* '你愿意顺便坐我的汽车去伦敦吗?' '好哇，谢谢你.'

pleased *adj* **1** **~ (with sb/sth)** feeling or showing satisfaction or pleasure (with sb/sth) (对某人[某事物])欣喜的, 满意的, 高兴的, 愉快的: *Your mother will be very pleased with you.* 你母亲将对你十分满意. ○ *They were all very pleased with the news.* 他们听到那消息都很高兴. ○ *Are you pleased with the new flat?* 你对这套新公寓满意吗? ○ *He looks rather pleased with himself*, ie pleased with what he has done. 他看起来对自己做的事颇为得意. **2** **~ to do sth** happy to do sth 乐意做某事: *I was very pleased to be able to help.* 我能够帮上忙感到很高兴. ○ *We were pleased to hear the news.* 我们听到那消息非常高兴. ○ (*fml* 文) *The Governor is pleased to accept the invitation.* 总督欣然接受邀请. **3** (idm 习语) **(as) ˌpleased as ˈPunch** very pleased 非常快乐.

pleas·ing *adj* **~ (to sb/sth)** giving pleasure (to sb/sth); pleasant 使人愉快的; 合意的; 可爱的: *a pleasing colour scheme, singing voice* 协调的颜色、悦耳的歌喉 ○ *The news was very pleasing to us.* 那消息使我们非常愉快. ○ *sounds that are pleasing to the ear* 悦耳的声音. **pleas·ingly** *adv*: *everything pleasingly arranged for the guests* 为客人安排得称心如意的一切.

pleas·ure /ˈpleʒə(r); ˋplɛʒɚ/ *n* **1** **(a)** [U] state or feeling of being happy or satisfied 愉快; 快乐; 高兴; 满足: *a work of art that has given pleasure to millions of people* 给上百万人带来乐趣的艺术品 ○ *It gives me great pleasure to welcome our speaker.* 我很高兴去迎接我们的演讲人. ○ *Has she gone to Paris on business or for pleasure* (ie for work or for fun)*?* 她到巴黎是办公事还是游玩去了? **(b)** [C] thing that gives happiness or satisfaction 乐事; 快事: *the pleasures of living in the country* 乡居的乐趣 ○ *She has few pleasures left in life.* 她生活中已没有什么乐趣了. ○ *It's been a pleasure meeting you.* 认识你是十分高兴的事. ○ *'Thank you for doing that!' 'It's a pleasure.'* '多谢你做了那件事!' '不客气.' ○ *Remembering the past was his only pleasure.* 他唯一的乐趣是回忆往事. **2** [U] sensual enjoyment 感官的享受; 声色之乐; 肉体之乐(常指肉欲): *His life is spent in the pursuit of pleasure.* 他一生都在寻欢作乐. **3** [U] (*fml* 文) what a person wants; desire 意愿; 愿望: *We await your pleasure.* 我们听您的意思. ○ *You are free to come and go at your pleasure*, ie as you wish. 来去自由，悉听尊便. ○ *Is it your pleasure that I cancel the arrangements?* 您的意思是否要我取消这些安排? **4** (idm 习语) **have the pleasure of sth/doing sth** (used to make polite requests, issue invitations, etc 用于客气的请求、邀请等): *May I have the pleasure of this dance?* 我可以邀请您跳这个舞吗? ○ (*fml or joc* 文或谑) *Are we to have the pleasure of seeing you again?* 我们是不是有福气再见到你? **take (no/great) pleasure in sth/doing sth** enjoy/not enjoy (doing) sth 以[不以](做)某事为乐; 喜欢[不喜欢](做)某事: *She seemed to take pleasure in our suffering.* 她似乎对我们的痛苦幸灾乐祸. ○ *They take great pleasure in reminding us of our poverty.* 他们特别喜欢向我们提到我们穷. ○ *She took no pleasure in her work.* 她觉得自己的工作毫无乐趣. **with ˈpleasure** one is pleased to accept, agree, etc 愉快地接受、同意等: *'Will you join us?' 'Thank you, with pleasure.'* '你愿意和我们在一起吗?' '谢谢，非常愿意.' ○ *'May I borrow your car?' 'Yes, with pleasure.'* '我可以借用你的汽车吗?' '可以，很愿意借给你.'

▷ **pleas·ur·able** /ˈpleʒərəbl; ˋplɛʒərəbl̩/ *adj* giving pleasure; enjoyable 令人愉快的; 使人快乐的: *a pleasurable sensation* 快感 ○ *pleasurable companionship* 令人愉快的友谊. **pleas·ur·ably** /-əblɪ; -əblɪ/ *adv*.

□ **ˈpleasure-boat** *n* boat used for pleasure only 游艇.

ˈpleasure-craft *n* (*pl* unchanged 复数不变) boat used for pleasure only 游艇: *Fishing boats and pleasure-craft followed the great liner into the harbour.* 渔船和游艇跟随着大型班轮进入了港口.

ˈpleasure-ground *n* area used for public amusement or recreation 游乐场; 娱乐场.

ˈpleasure-seeking *adj* devoted to pleasure(2) 寻欢作

乐的.

pleat /pli:t; plit/ *n* pressed or stitched fold made in a piece of cloth (布料上压的或缝的)褶: *a shirt with pleats in the front* 前面有褶的衬衫.

▷ **pleat** *v* [Tn] make pleats in (sth) 在(某物)上打褶: *pleat a skirt* 在裙子上打褶 ○ *pleated curtains* 有褶的帘.

pleb /pleb; plɛb/ *n* (*infml derog* 口, 贬) **1** [C] = PLEBEIAN. **2 the plebs** [pl] the masses 群众; 百姓.

ple·beian /plɪ'bi:ən; plɪ'biən/ *adj* **1** (*fml or derog* 文或贬) of the lower social classes 下层社会的; 平民的: *of plebeian origins* 平民出身的. **2** (*derog* 贬) lacking refinement; vulgar 平庸的; 粗俗的: *plebeian tastes* 庸俗的趣味. ▷ **ple·beian** (also **pleb**) *n* (*derog* 贬) person belonging to the lower social classes (esp in ancient Rome) 下层人; (尤指古罗马时的)平民, 庶民. Cf 参看 PATRICIAN.

pleb·is·cite /'plebɪsɪt; *US* -saɪt; 'plɛbə,saɪt/ *n* (*politics* 政) (decision made by a) direct vote by all qualified citizens on an important political matter 公民投票(的表决): *A plebiscite was held to decide the fate of the country.* 举行了公民投票以决定国家的命运. ○ *The question of which state the minority group should belong to was decided by (a) plebiscite.* 该少数民族应归属哪一州的问题已由公民投票表决. Cf 参看 REFERENDUM.

plec·trum /'plektrəm; 'plɛktrəm/ *n* (*pl* **-tra** /-trə; -trə/) (*music* 音) small piece of metal, wood, plastic or bone that is attached to the finger and used for plucking the strings of certain musical instruments, eg the guitar, mandolin, etc (戴在手指上弹奏弦乐器用的)拨子, 琴拨.

pled *pt, pp* of PLEAD.

pledge /pledʒ; plɛdʒ/ *n* **1** solemn promise; vow 誓言; 誓约; 保证: *give a pledge never to reveal the secret* 保证决不泄密. **2** (**a**) thing left with a person to be kept until the giver has done sth promised, eg paid a debt 抵押品(如为还债的). (**b**) article left with a pawnbroker in exchange for sth, esp money 典当物. **3** thing given to sb as a sign of friendship, love, etc (表示友情、爱情等的)信物, 象征物: *gifts exchanged as a pledge of friendship* 交换的象征友谊的礼物. **4** (idm 习语) **in/out of pledge** left with sb until the giver has paid a debt, etc/no longer left on these conditions 在抵押中[已不在抵押中]: *put/hold sth in pledge* 以[收下]某物作抵押 ○ *take sth out of pledge* 赎回抵押的某物. **sign/take the 'pledge** (*esp joc* 尤作戏谑语) make a solemn promise never to drink alcohol 发誓戒酒. **under pledge of sth** in the state of having agreed to or promised sth 在誓约或承诺某事的约束下: *You are under pledge of secrecy.* 你已发过誓要保密.

▷ **pledge** *v* **1** (**a**) [Tn, Tn·pr, Dn·n, Dn·t] **~ sth (to sb/sth)** (*fml* 文) promise solemnly to give (support, etc); give (one's word, honour, etc) as a pledge 保证给予(支持等); 以(誓言、名誉等)作担保: *pledge allegiance* (ie loyalty) *to the king* 发誓效忠国王 ○ *pledge a donation (to a charity)* 承诺(向慈善机构)捐献 ○ *be pledged to secrecy/to keeping a secret* 誓守秘密. (**b**)[Tn, Tn·pr, Cn·t] **~ sb/oneself (to sth/to do sth)** promise solemnly that sb/one will do sth or support a cause, etc 保证某人[自己]做某事或支持某事业等: *The Government has pledged itself to send aid to the famine victims.* 政府已承诺赈济饥民. **2** [Tn] leave (sth) with sb as a pledge (2b) 典当(某物): *He's pledged* (ie pawned) *his mother's wedding ring.* 他把母亲的结婚戒指典当了. **3** [Tn] (*fml* 文) drink to the health of (sb); toast (sb) 为(某人)的健康祝酒; 向(某人)祝酒: *pledge the bride and bridegroom* 向新娘和新郎祝酒.

Pleis·to·cene /'plaɪstəsi:n; 'plaɪstə,sin/ *adj* (*geology* 地质) of the epoch in the earth's history that started about a million years ago and lasted for about 800000 years, when glaciers covered most of the northern hemisphere 更新世的.

▷ **the Pleis·to·cene** *n* the Pleistocene epoch 更新世.

plen·ary /'pli:nərɪ; 'plinərɪ/ *adj* **1** (of meetings, etc) attended by all who have the right to attend (指会议等)全体出席的: *a plenary session of the assembly* 大会的全体会议. **2** (of powers, authority, etc) without limits; absolute (指权力、权威等)无限的, 绝对的, 全权的: *assume plenary authority* 掌握绝对权威.

ple·ni·po·ten·ti·ary /,plenɪpə'tenʃərɪ; ,plɛnəpə'tɛnʃərɪ/ *n* person (esp an ambassador) with full powers to act on behalf of his government (esp in a foreign country) (代表政府的)全权代表(尤指在外国); (尤指)全权大使.

▷ **ple·ni·po·ten·ti·ary** *adj* of or like a plenipotentiary (似)全权代表的, 全权大使的: *The minister was given plenipotentiary powers in the trade negotiations.* 该部长获有全权进行贸易谈判.

plent·eous /'plentɪəs; 'plɛntɪəs/ *adj* (*fml* 文) plentiful 大量的; 丰富的. ▷ **plent·eously** *adv*.

plen·ti·ful /'plentɪfl; 'plɛntɪfəl/ *adj* in large quantities or numbers; abundant 大量的; 丰富的: *find plentiful supplies of fresh fruit and vegetables* 得到大量新鲜水果和蔬菜的供应 ○ *Eggs are plentiful at the moment.* 现在鸡蛋很多. Cf 参看 SCARCE. ▷ **plen·ti·fully** /-fəlɪ; -flɪ/ *adv*: *The visitors were plentifully supplied with food and drink.* 给来宾准备了丰富的食物和饮料.

plenty /'plentɪ; 'plɛntɪ/ *pron* **1** number or amount that is sufficient for sb or more than sb needs 充裕; 大量: *plenty of eggs, money, time* 很多的鸡蛋、金钱、时间 ○ *'Do you need more milk?' 'No thanks, there's plenty in the fridge.'* '你还要牛奶吗?' '不要, 谢谢. 冰箱里还有很多呢.' ○ *'Have we got enough plates?' 'Yes, there are plenty in the cupboard.'* '咱们的盘子够用吗?' '够, 碗橱里有很多.' ○ *They always gave us plenty to eat.* 他们总是给我们很多东西吃. **2** (idm 习语) **days, years, etc of 'plenty** (*fml or rhet* 文或修辞) time when very many necessities, esp food and money, are available 富裕(尤指食物和钱)的日子、年月: *looking back on the years of plenty* 回顾富足的年月. **in 'plenty** (*fml* 文) in a large quantity; in abundance 大量; 丰富; 充裕: *food and drink in plenty* 大量的食物和饮料. ▷ **plenty** *adv* **1** (used with *more* to indicate an excess 与 more 连用表示超过的量): *We've got plenty more (of it/them) in the shop.* 我们店里还有很多(那种货物). ○ *There's plenty more paper if you need it.* 你需要纸的话, 有的是. **2** (*infml* 口) (used with *big, long, tall,* etc followed by *enough* 与 big、long、tall 等连用, 后接 enough): *The rope was plenty long enough to reach the ground.* 绳子长可及地.

ple·on·asm /'plɪənæzəm; 'pliə,næzəm/ *n* (**a**) [U] use of more words than are necessary to express the meaning 冗笔, 赘述(的运用). (**b**) [C] instance of this 冗笔; 赘述: *'Hear with one's ears' and 'divide into four quarters' are pleonasms.* '用耳朵听' 和 '分成四个四分之一' 是赘述. Cf 参看 TAUTOLOGY. ▷ **ple·on·astic** /,plɪə'næstɪk; ,pliə'næstɪk/ *adj*.

pleth·ora /'pleθərə; 'plɛθərə/ *n* [sing] (*fml* 文) quantity greater than what is needed; over-abundance 过量; 过剩: *The report contained a plethora of detail.* 报告中细节过多.

pleur·isy /'plʊərəsɪ; 'plʊrəsɪ/ *n* [U] (*medical* 医) serious illness, with inflammation of the delicate membrane of the thorax and the lungs, causing severe pain in the chest or sides 胸膜炎.

plexus /'pleksəs; 'plɛksəs/ *n* (*pl* unchanged or **~es** 复数或不变或作 **plexuses**) (*anatomy* 解) network of fibres or vessels in the body (纤维或血管的)丛: *the solar plexus*, ie the network of nerves in the abdomen 太阳神经丛(腹腔丛).

pli·able /'plaɪəbl; 'plaɪəbl/ *adj* **1** easily bent, shaped or twisted; flexible 易弯的; 可塑的; 可扭曲的; 柔韧的: *Cane is pliable when wet.* 藤条潮湿时易弯曲. **2** (of a person or a person's mind) easily influenced (指人或思想)易受影响的: *the pliable minds of children* 儿童容易受影响的头脑. ▷ **pli·ab·il·ity** /,plaɪə'bɪlətɪ; ,plaɪə'bɪlətɪ/ *n* [U].

pli·ant /'plaɪənt; 'plaɪənt/ *adj* **1** bending easily; supple 易弯的; 柔韧的: *the pliant branches of young trees* 小树柔软的枝条. **2** adapting easily; yielding 易适应的; 顺从的. ▷ **pli·ancy** /'plaɪənsɪ; 'plaɪənsɪ/ *n* [U]. **pli·antly** *adv*.

pli·ers /'plaɪəz; 'plaɪɚz/ *n* [pl] tool with long jaws which have flat surfaces that can be brought together for holding, bending, twisting or cutting wire, etc 钳子; 老虎钳: *a pair of pliers* 一把钳子.

plight[1] /plaɪt; plaɪt/ *n* [sing] serious and difficult situation or condition 严重和困难的境况; 困境; 苦境: *the plight of the homeless* 无家可归的人的苦境 ○ *The crew were in a sorry plight by the time they reached shore.* 船员们抵达岸边时境况已十分悲惨. ○ *I was in a* *dreadful plight — I had lost my money and missed the last train home.* 我身陷困境——钱丢了，又没赶上回家的末班火车.

plight[2] /plaɪt; plaɪt/ *v* (idm 习语) **plight one's 'troth** (*arch* 古) make a promise to marry sb 订婚.

plim·soll /ˈplɪmsəl; ˋplɪmsl̩/ (also **pump**) *n* (*Brit*) (*US* **sneaker**) rubber-soled canvas sports shoe; gym-shoe 橡皮底帆布鞋: *a pair of plimsolls* 一双体操鞋.

Plim·soll line /ˈplɪmsəl laɪn; ˋplɪmsəl ˌlaɪn/ (also **'Plimsoll mark** /mɑːk; ˌmɑrk/) line marked on a ship's side to show how far it may legally go down in the water when loaded (船的)载货吃水线.

plinth /plɪnθ; plɪnθ/ *n* square block or slab on which a column or statue stands (柱或雕像的)底座, 基底. ⇨ illus at COLUMN 见COLUMN插图.

Plio·cene /ˈplaɪəʊsiːn; ˋplaɪəˌsin/ *adj* (*geology* 地质) of the last epoch of the Tertiary period in the earth's history (when many modern mammals appeared) 上新世的.

▷ **the Plio·cene** *n* the Pliocene epoch 上新世.

plod /plɒd; plɑd/ *v* (**-dd-**) **1** [I, Ipr, Ip] **~ (along/on)** walk with heavy steps or with difficulty; trudge 迈着沉重的脚步行走; 艰难地行走: *Labourers plodded home through the muddy fields.* 工人们穿过泥泞的田地吃力地走回家去. ○ (*fig* 比喻) *We plodded on through the rain for several hours.* 我们在雨中跋涉了几小时. ⇨Usage at STUMP 用法见STUMP. **2** (phr v) **plod along** move slowly (at some task) 缓慢地进行(某工作): *'How's the book?' 'Oh, I'm plodding along.'* '那本书怎么样?' '哦, 我正在磨蹭呢.' **plod away (at sth)** work steadily but slowly (and with difficulty) 持续而缓慢地(并艰难地)工作: *He plodded away all night at the accounts but didn't finish them in time.* 他彻夜不眠地清理帐目, 却未能按时完成.

▷ **plod·der** *n* (*usu derog* 通常作贬义) person who works slowly and with determination, but without inspiration 不动脑筋慢慢苦干的人. **plod·ding** *adj*. **plod·dingly** *adv*.

plonk[1] /plɒŋk; plɑŋk/ (also **plunk** /plʌŋk; plʌŋk/) *n* (usu *sing* 通常作单数) (*infml* 口) sound (as) of sth dropping heavily (似)物体沉重坠落的声音; 砰的一声: *to hear a plonk* 听到砰的一声.

▷ **plonk** *adv* (*infml* 口) with a plonk 砰的一声: *The lamp fell plonk on the table.* 台灯砰的一声倒在桌上了.

plonk *v* (phr v) **plonk sth down; plonk sth (down) on sth** (*infml* 口) drop sth or put sth down heavily or with a plonking sound 扔下某物; 重重放下某物(并发出砰的声音): *He plonked the groceries on the kitchen floor.* 他把买的食物杂货砰的一声扔到厨房的地板上了. ○ (*fig* 比喻) *We plonked ourselves (down) by the fire.* 我们猛地一下子坐在了炉火旁.

plonk[2] /plɒŋk; plɑŋk/ *n* [U] (*infml* 口 *esp Brit*) cheap wine of poor quality (劣质的)便宜的酒.

plop /plɒp; plɑp/ *n* (usu *sing* 通常作单数) sound (as) of a smooth object dropping into water without making a splash (光滑物体落入水中而不溅泼的)落水声, 扑通声: *He dropped a pebble from the bridge and waited for the plop.* 他从桥上扔下一颗卵石, 然后等着听那扑通的一声.

▷ **plop** *adv* with a plop 扑通一声: *The stone fell plop into the water.* 那石头扑通一声落入水中.

plop *v* (**-pp-**) **1** [I] make a plop 发出落水声; 发出扑通声: *Did you hear it plop?* 你听到它落入水中的声音了吗? **2** [Ipr, Ip] fall with a plop 扑通一声落下: *The jelly plopped into the dish.* 果冻噗的一声落到碟里. ○ *The fish plopped back into the river.* 那鱼扑通一声跃回河中.

plo·sive /ˈpləʊsɪv; ˋplosɪv/ *n, adj* (*phonetics* 语音) (consonant sound) made by closing the air passage and then audibly releasing the air, eg /t/ and /p/ in *top* 爆破音(的)(如top中的/t/和/p/).

plot[1] /plɒt; plɑt/ *n* small marked or measured piece of land, esp for a special purpose (有标记的或测量出的)小块土地(尤指有某用途的): *a building plot* 一块建筑用地 ○ *a vegetable plot* 一块菜地 ○ *a small plot of land* 一小块地皮.

▷ **plot** *v* (**-tt-**) **1** [Tn] (**a**) make a plan or map of (sth) 绘制(某事物)的图: *plot an escape route* 画出逃跑路线. (**b**) mark (sth) on a chart or diagram (在图表上)标绘(某物): *plot the ship's course* 标绘该船的航线. (**c**) make (a curve, etc) by connecting points on a graph (在图上连接标定的点)绘制(曲线等): *plot a temperature curve* 绘制温度曲线图. **2** [Tn, Tn·p] **~ sth (out)** divide sth into plots 将(某大片土地)分成小块.

plot[2] /plɒt; plɑt/ *n* **1** (plan or outline of the) events in the story of a play or novel (戏剧或小说的)故事情节(的构思或布局): *a neatly worked-out plot* 丝丝入扣的故事情节 ○ *The plot was too complicated for me — I couldn't follow it.* 我觉得情节太复杂——我看不明白. **2** secret plan made by several people to do sth; conspiracy (几人的)密谋, 阴谋: *a plot to overthrow the government* 推翻政府的阴谋 ○ *The plot was discovered in time.* 那阴谋已被及时揭露. **3** (idm 习语) **hatch a plot** ⇨ HATCH. **the plot 'thickens** (*catchphrase* 警语) a situation in real life, or the plot of a work of fiction, is suddenly more complicated or intriguing 现实生活中的情况或小说中的情节, 突然复杂起来或更引人注意了.

▷ **plot** *v* (**-tt-**) (**a**) [I, Ipr, Ip, It] **~ (with sb) (against sb); ~ (together)** make a secret plan (to do sth); take part in a plot 密谋(做某事); 参与阴谋: *plot with others against the State* 伙同他人阴谋反对政府 ○ *plot (together) to do sth* (一起)密谋做某事. (**b**) [Tn] plan (sth) with others 与他人谋划(某事): *They were plotting the overthrow of the government.* 他们正在策划推翻政府. **plot·ter** *n* person who plots; conspirator 密谋策划者; 搞阴谋的人.

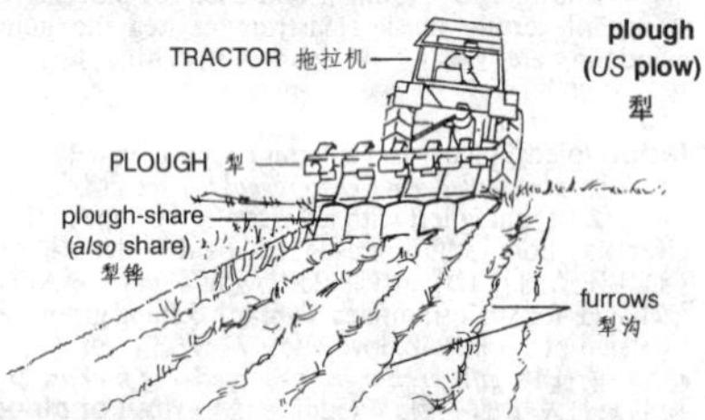

plough (*US* **plow**) /plaʊ; plaʊ/ *n* **1** (**a**) [C] implement with a curved blade, used for digging furrows in the soil, esp before seeds are planted, pulled by animals or by a tractor 犁. (**b**) (esp in compounds 尤用以构成复合词) implement resembling this 似犁的工具: *a 'snow-plough*, ie one for clearing snow from roads and railways 雪犁(清除路面或铁道积雪的). **2 the Plough** [sing] (also **Charles's Wain**) (*Brit*) (*US also* **the Big Dipper**) (*astronomy* 天) group of the seven brightest stars in the constellation of the Great Bear, visible only from the Northern hemisphere 北斗七星. **3** [U] land that has been ploughed 犁过的地; 耕地: *100 acres of plough* 100英亩耕地. **4** (idm 习语) **under the 'plough** (of land) used for growing grain and not for pasture (指土地)用于种庄稼的(非牧用的).

▷ **plough** (*US* **plow**) *v* **1** [Tn, Tn·p] **~ sth (up)** break up the surface of (land) with a plough 犁(地); 耕(地): *plough a field* 耕田 ○ *The meadow's been ploughed up.* 那片草地已用犁翻过. **2** [I, Tn] (*dated Brit sl* 旧, 俚) (cause sb to) fail (an examination) (使某人)考(试)不及格: *I ploughed my finals.* 我期末考试不及格. ○ *The examiners ploughed half the candidates.* 主考人员刷掉了一半应试者. **3** (idm 习语) **plough a lonely 'furrow** work without help or support 孤独无援地工作. **4** (phr v) **plough sth back** (**a**) put (a crop or grass) back in the soil by ploughing in order to enrich the soil 将(作物或草)犁入土中作肥料. (**b**) (*fig* 比喻) re-invest (profits) in the business that produced them 将(利润)作为资本再投资于原企业中. **plough into sth/sb** crash violently into sth/sb 猛力撞某物[某人]: *The car went out of control and ploughed into the side of a bus.* 那汽车失控拦腰撞上了一辆公共汽车. **plough (one's way) through sth** (**a**) force a way through sth 费力穿过某处: *plough one's way through the mud* 在泥泞中艰难跋涉 ○ *The ship ploughed through the waves.* 那轮船破浪前进. (**b**) make progress slowly or with difficulty through sth 缓慢或费力地在某方面取得进展: *plough through legal text books, a pile of documents, mountains of work,*

etc 吃力地钻研法律教科书、缓慢地阅读一堆文件、费力地处理堆积如山的工作.
□ ˈ**ploughman** (*US* **plow-**) /-mən; -mən/ *n* (**-men** /-mən; -mən/) man who guides a plough(1a), esp one pulled by animals 把犁人(尤指用力畜拉的犁). ˌ**ploughman's** ˈ**lunch** (*Brit*) meal of bread, cheese and pickles, often served with beer in a pub 农夫午餐(有面包、干酪、泡菜, 常有啤酒, 多在小酒店中供应).
ˈ**ploughshare** (*US* **plow-**) (also **share**) *n* broad blade of a plough(1a) 犁铧; 铧. ⇨illus 见插图.

plover /ˈplʌvə(r); ˋplʌvɚ/ *n* any of various types of long-legged short-tailed land bird that live on marshy ground near the sea 鸻(腿长、尾短, 栖于近海的沼泽地). ⇨illus at App 1 见附录1插图, page v.

ploy /plɔɪ; plɔɪ/ *n* words or actions, eg in a game, intended to win an advantage over one's opponent (克敌制胜的)策略, 手法(如在比赛中的): *It was all a ploy to distract attention from his real aims.* 那纯粹是障眼法, 用以分散人们对他真正意图的注意力.

pluck /plʌk; plʌk/ *v* **1** [Tn, Tn·pr, Tn·p] ~ **sth (off/out)** gather or remove sth by pulling; pick sth 拔除或摘除某物; 采某物: *pluck a rose from the garden* 从花园里摘一朵玫瑰花 ○ *pluck one's eyebrows*, ie use tweezers to remove unwanted hairs 拔眉毛 ○ *pluck off the dead flowers* 掐掉凋谢的花 ○ *pluck out a grey hair* 拔下一根灰白的头发. **2** [Tn] pull the feathers off (a goose, chicken, etc) in order to prepare it for cooking 拔去(鹅、鸡等)的毛(以备烹调): *Have the turkeys been plucked?* 火鸡的毛都拔了吗? **3** [Tn, Tn·pr] ~ **(at sth)** take hold of (sth) and pull it; snatch at (sth) 拉住或抓住(某物): *The child was plucking at her mother's skirt.* 那孩子揪住母亲的裙子. ○ *A stranger plucked at my sleeve as I was leaving.* 我刚要离去, 一个陌生人拽我的袖子. **4** (*US* **pick**) [Tn] sound (the strings of a musical instrument) by pulling and releasing them 弹或拨(乐器的弦): *pluck the strings of a guitar* 弹吉他的弦. **5** (idm 习语) **pluck up** ˈ**courage (to do sth)** make an effort to be brave 鼓起勇气: *I shall have to pluck up courage and speak to her about it.* 我得鼓起勇气跟她谈这件事. ○ *He can't pluck up the courage to leave home.* 他鼓不起离开家的勇气.
▷ **pluck** *n* **1** [U] (*infml* 口) courage, esp in the face of a stronger opponent or of hardship; bravery 勇气, 胆量(尤指面对强敌或困难的): *She showed a lot of pluck in dealing with the intruders.* 她对付那些闯人的歹徒表现得十分勇敢. **2** [C usu *sing* 通常作单数] short sharp pull 快而猛的拉: *feel a pluck at one's sleeve* 觉得袖子被人猛拉了一下. **3** [U] heart, liver and lungs of an animal, as food (动物的)心, 肝, 肺(作食物者). **plucky** *adj* (**-ier, -iest**) having or showing pluck; brave 勇敢的; 有胆量的. **pluck·ily** *adv*.

plug /plʌg; plʌg/ *n* **1** (**a**) piece of metal, rubber or plastic that fits tightly into a hole (eg in a barrel, wash-basin, bath, etc) 塞子(如用以塞大桶、洗脸池、浴缸等的): *Pull (out) the plug and let the water drain away.* 拔掉塞子, 把水放掉. ○ *He put plugs in his ears because the noise was too loud.* 因为太吵闹了, 他用耳塞堵住了耳朵. (**b**) (*US*) = STOPPER. **2** (**a**) device with metal pins that fit into holes in a socket to make an electrical connection 插头; 插塞: *a three-/two-pin plug* 三线[双线]插头 ○ *Put the plug in the socket.* 把插头插入插座里. ○ *I'll have to change the plug on the hair drier.* 我得更换吹风机的插头了. ⇨illus at SOCKET 见SOCKET插图. (**b**) (*infml* 口) electric socket 插座. **3** = SPARKING PLUG (SPARK). **4** (*infml* 口) piece of favourable publicity in the media for a commercial product, eg a record or book (在传播媒介中插入宣传商品的)推销广告(如宣传唱片或书的). **5** (**a**) cake or stick of pressed or twisted tobacco 板烟. (**b**) piece of this cut off for chewing 口嚼烟(切成小块的板烟). **6** (idm 习语) **pull the plug on sb/sth** ⇨ PULL².
▷ **plug** *v* (**-gg-**) **1** [Tn, Tn·p] ~ **sth (up)** fill (a hole) or stop up sth with a plug 用塞子堵(洞): *plug a leak in the barrel* 用塞子堵住大桶的漏洞. **2** [Tn] (*infml* 口) mention (sth) favourably in the media, esp repeatedly (在传播媒介中)宣传(某事物)(尤指反复地): *They've been plugging his new show on the radio.* 他们一直在电台上宣传他的新节目. **3** [Tn] (*infml* 口 *esp US*) shoot or hit (sb) 射击或打(某人). **4** (phr v) **plug away (at sth)** work hard and steadily (at sth) (对某事物)努力不懈地干: *She's been plugging away at her French lessons for months.* 她已刻苦攻读法语数月. **plug sth in** connect (sth) to the electricity supply with a plug(2a) 用插头将(某物)与电源接通: *Plug in the radio, please.* 请把收音机的插头插上. ○ *The recorder wasn't plugged in.* 录音机的插头没插上.
□ ˈ**plug-hole** *n* (*Brit*) (*US* **drain**) hole into which a plug(1) fits, esp in a basin, sink or wash-basin 排水孔(尤指洗脸池、洗物池等的).

plum /plʌm; plʌm/ *n* **1** (**a**) [C] soft round smooth-skinned fruit with sweet flesh and a flattish pointed stone 李子; 梅子. ⇨illus at FRUIT 见FRUIT插图. (**b**) [C] (also ˈ**plum tree**) tree on which this grows 李树; 梅树. **2** [U] dark reddish-purple colour 紫红色. **3** (*infml* 口) thing considered good or worth having, esp a well-paid job 好的事物; (尤指)报酬高的工作: *She's got a plum of a job.* 她得到一份高薪的工作. ○ [attrib 作定语] *a plum job* 报酬高的工作.
□ ˌ**plum** ˈ**pudding** rich boiled suet pudding with dried fruits and spices, traditionally eaten at Christmas 干果布丁(圣诞节传统食物).

plum·age /ˈplu:mɪdʒ; ˋplumɪdʒ/ *n* [U] feathers covering a bird's body 羽衣(鸟体的全部羽毛): *the brightly coloured plumage of tropical birds* 热带鸟类色彩斑斓的羽毛.

plumb /plʌm; plʌm/ *n* **1** piece of lead that is tied to a cord and used to find the depth of water or test whether a wall, etc is vertical 测深锤, 铅锤(悬挂于绳上的铅块, 用以测水深或墙等是否垂直). **2** (idm 习语) **out of** ˈ**plumb** not vertical 不垂直的.
▷ **plumb** *adv* **1** exactly 恰恰; 正: *plumb in the centre* 在正中. **2** (*US infml* 口) quite; absolutely 十分; 完全; 绝对: *He's plumb crazy.* 他真是疯了.
plumb *v* **1** [Tn] (**a**) test (sth) by using a plumb-line 用铅垂线测(某物). (**b**) (*fig* 比喻) (try to) understand (sth) thoroughly 探索, 探究(某事物): *plumb the mysteries of the universe* 探索宇宙的奥秘. **2** (idm 习语) **plumb the depths of sth** reach the lowest point of sth 到达某事物的最低点: *plumb the depths of despair* 绝望已极 ○ *a film that really plumbs the depths of bad taste* 趣味低级得真正到了极点的一部影片. **3** (phr v) **plumb sth in** attach (eg a washing-machine) to water-pipes 将(如洗衣机)与水管接通: *We've plumbed in the dishwasher.* 我们已给洗碟机接上水管了.
□ ˈ**plumb-line** *n* line with a plumb(1) attached to one end 铅垂线.

plumber /ˈplʌmə(r); ˋplʌmɚ/ *n* person whose job is to fit and repair water-pipes, water-tanks, cisterns, etc in buildings 铅管工; 管子工; 水暖工.

plumb·ing /ˈplʌmɪŋ; ˋplʌmɪŋ/ *n* [U] **1** system of water-pipes, water-tanks, cisterns, etc in a building (建筑物的)管道装置: *There is something wrong with the plumbing.* 水管设备出毛病了. **2** work of a plumber 铅管工的工作: *We employed a local man to do the plumbing.* 我们雇了一个当地人做管道装修工作.

plume /plu:m; plum/ *n* (**a**) feather, esp a large one used as a decoration 羽毛; (尤指作装饰用的)翎子. (**b**) ornament of feathers or similar material, worn in the hair or on a hat or helmet 羽毛或类似羽毛材料的饰物(装饰在头发上或帽上): *a plume of ostrich feathers* 鸵鸟羽毛的装饰. (**c**) thing that rises into the air in the shape of a feather 貌似羽毛升空之物: *a plume of smoke/steam* 一缕烟[蒸汽].
▷ **plume** *v* **1** [Tn] (of a bird) smooth (sth) with its beak; preen (指鸟)用喙整理(某物): *a bird pluming itself/its feathers/its wing* 用喙整理自己[羽毛/翅膀]的鸟. **2** [Tn, Tn·pr] ~ **oneself (on sth)** congratulate or pride oneself (on sth) (为某事)自喜, 自豪. **plumed** *adj* having or decorated with a plume or plumes 有羽毛或翎子的; 用羽毛或翎子装饰的: *a plumed hat* 有羽毛装饰的帽子.

plum·met /ˈplʌmɪt; ˋplʌmɪt/ *n* **1** (weight attached to a) plumb-line 测深锤; 铅锤; 铅垂线. **2** weight attached to a fishing-line to keep the float upright (钓丝上的)铅坠, 坠子(用以使鱼漂竖起).
▷ **plum·met** *v* [I, Ipr, Ip] fall steeply or rapidly 大坡度或快速落下: *House prices have plummeted in this area.* 此地房价大跌. ○ *Pieces of rock plummeted down the*

mountainside to the ground below. 岩石一块块顺着山的陡坡滚落到地面.

plummy /ˈplʌmɪ; ˋplʌmɪ/ *adj* (**-mier, -miest**) **1** (*infml* 口) desirable; good 合意的; 很好的: *a plummy job* 顺心的工作. **2** (*esp derog* 尤作贬义) (of a voice) affectedly upper-class; sounding as if one is speaking with sth (eg a plum) in one's mouth (指嗓音)拿腔拿调的, 像嘴里含着东西似的: *a plummy accent/voice* 拿腔捏调的口音*[嗓音]*.

plump[1] /plʌmp; plʌmp/ *adj* (**a**) (esp of an animal, a person, parts of the body) having a full rounded shape; fleshy (尤指动物、人、身体的局部)肥胖的, 丰满的: *a plump baby, chicken, face* 胖乎乎的婴儿、肥肥的小鸡、圆圆的脸蛋 ○ *a baby with plump cheeks* 双颊胖乎乎的婴儿. (**b**) (*euph* 婉) overweight; fat 过胖的: *You're getting a bit plump — you need to diet!* 你有点发胖了——得节食了! ⇨Usage at FAT[1] 用法见FAT[1].

▷ **plump** *v* (phr v) **plump (sth) out/up** (cause sth to) become rounded (使某物)变圆, 变丰满: *His cheeks are beginning to plump out/up.* 他的脸颊胖起来了. ○ *She plumped up the pillows.* 她把枕头弄得鼓鼓的.

plump·ness *n* [U].

plump[2] /plʌmp; plʌmp/ *v* (phr v) **plump (oneself/sb/sth) down** (cause sb/sth to) fall or drop suddenly and heavily (使某人[某物])突然而重重地落下: *plump down the heavy bags* 把重袋子一下子放下 ○ *plump (oneself) down in a chair* 一屁股坐到椅子上. **plump for sb/sth** choose or vote for sb/sth with confidence 有信心地选择或选举某人[某事物]: *The committee plumped for the most experienced candidate.* 委员会很有把握地选择了那个最有经验的候选人. ○ *The children plumped for a holiday by the sea.* 孩子们特别想去海边度假.

▷ **plump** *n* (usu *sing* 通常作单数) (sound made by a) sudden heavy fall 突然沉重的坠落(的声音): *The book landed with a plump on the floor.* 那书砰的一声掉在地板上.

plump *adv* with a plump 砰的一声: *fall plump into the hole* 砰的一声掉进洞里.

plun·der /ˈplʌndə(r); ˋplʌndɚ/ *v* **1** [I, Ipr, Tn, Tn·pr] ~ **(sth) (from sth)** steal (goods) from a place, esp during a time of war or civil disorder; pillage 掠夺或抢劫某地的(货物)(尤指战时或内乱时): *The conquerors advanced, killing and plundering as they went.* 征服者一路上杀人越货无所不为. ○ *The invaders plundered food and valuables from coastal towns and villages.* 侵略者在沿海城乡抢劫食物和贵重物品. **2** [Tn, Tn·pr] ~ **sth (of sth)** steal goods from (a place), esp during a time of war, etc 掠夺或抢劫(某地)的货物(尤指战时等): *plunder a palace of its treasures* 劫掠宫殿财宝 ○ *Tourists have plundered all the archaeological sites.* 游客简直是洗劫了考古场地. Cf 参看 LOOT, PILLAGE.

▷ **plun·der** *n* [U] **1** (action of) plundering 掠夺; 抢劫: *be guilty of plunder* 犯抢劫罪 ○ *goods obtained by plunder* 掠夺的财物. **2** goods that have been plundered 抢夺物; 赃物: *They loaded the carts with plunder.* 他们把掠夺来的东西装进大车里.

plun·derer /ˈplʌndərə(r); ˋplʌndərɚ/ *n* person who plunders 掠夺者; 抢劫者.

plunge /plʌndʒ; plʌndʒ/ *v* **1** [Ipr, Ip, Tn·pr, Tn·p] ~ **(sth) into sth**; ~ **(sth) in** (**a**) (cause sth to) fall into sth suddenly and with force (使某物)突然而猛力投入、穿入、进入等: *plunge (one's hand) into cold water* (把手)一下子伸进冷水中 ○ *They plunged in*, ie dived into the water. 他们跳进了水中. ○ *plunge a rod into a blocked drain to clear it* 用棍通下水道使之畅通. (**b**) (cause sth to) enter a specified state or condition (使某事物)进入或陷入某状态: *The country (was) plunged into civil war after the death of the President.* 总统死后全国陷入了内战. ○ *The news plunged us into despair.* 我们听到那消息后就陷入了绝望. ○ *events which plunged the world into war* 把世界推入战争的事件 ○ *Their extravagant life-style plunged them into debt.* 他们生活方式奢侈, 背上了很多债. **2** (**a**) [I, Ipr, Ip, Tn·pr, Tn·p] (cause sb/sth to) move suddenly forwards and/or downwards (使某人[某物])突然前移或跌落: *The horse plunged and she fell off.* 马一个前失, 把她摔了下来. ○ *Share prices plunged as a result of the gloomy economic forecast.* 该项预测展望经济前景暗淡, 因而股票价格大跌. ○ *The car plunged over the cliff.* 汽车冲下了悬崖. ○ *The sudden jolt plunged her forward.* 突然颠了一下, 她向前打了个趔趄. (**b**) [I] (of a ship) move with the bows going violently up and down in the water (指船)剧烈颠簸.

▷ **plunge** *n* **1** (**a**) [C esp *sing* 尤作单数] plunging movement, esp a steep fall (向前或向下的)冲, 投, 落; (尤指)骤降, 猛跌: *a plunge into debt, chaos* 背债、陷入混乱. (**b**) [C] act of diving or bathing in water 跳水; 游泳: *a plunge into the sea from the rocks* 从岩石上跳入海中 ○ *a refreshing plunge in the lake* 在湖中游泳焕发精神. **2** (idm 习语) **take the ˈplunge** take a bold decisive step, esp after thinking about it for some time 采取大胆果断措施(尤指曾经一番考虑): *They have finally decided to take the plunge and get married.* 他们最后毅然决定结婚.

plun·ger *n* **1** part of a mechanism that moves up and down 柱塞; 活塞. **2** (in plumbing) rubber cup fixed on a handle, used for clearing a blocked pipe by means of suction (疏通管道的)搋子.

plunk = PLONK[1].

plu·per·fect /ˌplu:ˈpɜ:fɪkt; ˌpluˋpɝfɪkt/ *adj* (also **past perfect**) (*grammar*) (of the form of the verb phrase) expressing an action completed before a particular point in the past (指动词词组形式)过去完成式的: *a pluperfect (form of a) verb phrase* 过去完成式动词词组.

▷ **plu·per·fect** *n* (also **past perfect**) such a form (in English *had* and a past participle, as in 'As he *had* not *received* my letter, he did not come') 过去完成式(在英语中had加过去分词, 如此处例句中的had加received).

plural /ˈplʊərəl; ˋplurəl/ *n* (*grammar*) form of a noun or verb which refers to more than one person or thing (名词的或动词的)复数, 复数形式: *The plural of 'child' is 'children'.* child的复数形式是children. ○ *The verb should be in the plural*, eg 'have' in 'they have'. 这个动词应用复数形式(如they have中的have). Cf 参看 SINGULAR 1.

▷ **plural** *adj* (*grammar*) **1** of or having this form 复数的; 有复数形式的: *Most plural nouns in English end in 's'.* 英语的复数名词多以s结尾. **2** of more than one 不止一个的: *a plural society*, ie one with more than one ethnic group 多元社会(由不止一个种族组成的).

plur·al·ism /ˈplʊərəlɪzəm; ˋplurəlɪzm̩/ *n* [U] **1** (**a**) existence in one society of a number of groups that belong to different races or have different political or religious beliefs 多元性(一社会中有不同民族或有不同政治或宗教信仰的群体共同生活的状态). (**b**) principle that these different groups can live together peacefully in one society 多元主义(一社会中多民族或有不同政治、宗教信仰的人和平共处的原则). **2** (*usu derog* 通常作贬义) holding of more than one office at one time, esp in the Church 兼任, 兼职(尤指神职).

▷ **plur·al·ist** /ˈplʊərəlɪst; ˋplurəlɪst/ *n* supporter of pluralism (1b) 多元主义者. **plur·al·ist** (also **plur·al·istic**) /ˌplʊərəˈlɪstɪk; ˌplurəˋlɪstɪk/ *adj*: *a pluralist society* 多元主义社会.

plur·al·ity /plʊəˈrælətɪ; pluˋrælətɪ/ *n* **1** [U] (*grammar*) state of being plural 复数; 复数形式. **2** [C] large number 大量; 多数: *a plurality of influences, interests* 极大的影响、利益. **3** [C] (*US politics* 政) majority of less than 50%; relative majority (未超过半数的)多数; 相对多数. Cf 参看 MAJORITY 2. **4** (**a**) [U] = PLURALISM 2. (**b**) [C] office held jointly with another 兼任的职务.

plus /plʌs; plʌs/ *prep* (**a**) with the addition of 加; 加上: *Two plus five is seven.* 二加五等于七. ○ *The bill was £10, plus £1 for postage.* 帐款是10英镑, 再加上1英镑邮费. (**b**) (*infml* 口) as well as 和: *We've got to fit five people plus all their luggage in the car.* 我们得在汽车里挤下五个人和全部行李. Cf 参看 MINUS.

▷ **plus** *adj* **1** more than the amount or number indicated 比所示数量多的: *The work will cost £10000 plus.* 那作品可值10 000英镑以上. **2** above zero; positive 零上的; 正的: *5 is a plus quantity.* 5是正数. ○ *The temperature is plus four degrees.* 温度零上四度.

plus *n* **1** the sign + 加号, 正号(+): *He seems to have mistaken a plus for a minus.* 他似乎把正号误作负号了. ⇨App 4 见附录4. **2** (*infml* 口) positive quality; advantage 正面因素; 好处: *Her knowledge of French is a plus in her job.* 她会法语, 这对她工作很有好处. Cf 参看 MINUS.

□ ˌ**plus-ˈfours** *n* [pl] wide loose knickerbockers, worn

esp by golfers 灯笼裤(尤指打高尔夫球时穿的): *a pair of plus-fours* 一条灯笼裤.

plush /plʌʃ; plʌʃ/ *n* [U] type of silk or cotton cloth with a surface like velvet (丝或棉的)长毛绒.
▷ **plush** *adj* **1** (also **plushy**) (*infml* 口) luxuriously smart 豪华的; 漂亮的: *a plush hotel, restaurant, etc* 豪华的旅馆、餐厅等. **2** made of plush 长毛绒的: *plush curtains* 长毛绒的帘子.

plushy /ˈplʌʃɪ; ˋplʌʃɪ/ *adj* (**-ier, -iest**) (*infml* 口) = PLUSH 1.
▷ **plushiness** *n* [U].

Pluto /ˈpluːtəʊ; ˋpluto/ *n* (*astronomy* 天) the planet ninth in order and furthest from the sun 冥王星.

plu·to·cracy /pluːˈtɒkrəsɪ; pluˋtɑkrəsɪ/ *n* **1** (**a**) [U] government by a rich and powerful class 富豪统治; 财阀统治. (**b**) [C] state governed in this way 富豪或财阀统治的国家. **2** [CGp] group or class of rich and powerful people; wealthy élite 富豪阶级; 财阀阶级.
▷ **plu·to·crat** /ˈpluːtəkræt; ˋplutə͵kræt/ *n* (*often derog* 常作贬义) person who is powerful because of his wealth 有钱有势的人.
plu·to·cratic /͵pluːtəˈkrætɪk; ͵plutəˋkrætɪk/ *adj* (**a**) of plutocracy 富豪或财阀统治的国家或阶级的. (**b**) of or like a plutocrat (似)有钱有势的人的: *plutocratic control of a media empire* 财阀势力对传播媒介的控制.

plu·to·nium /pluːˈtəʊnɪəm; pluˋtonɪəm/ *n* [U] (*chemistry* 化) artificially produced radioactive metallic element, derived from uranium and used in nuclear reactors and nuclear weapons 钚. ⇨App 10 见附录10.

ply[1] /plaɪ; plaɪ/ *n* [U] (esp in compounds 尤用以构成复合词) **1** layer of wood or thickness of cloth (木的)层; (布的)厚度: *three-ply wood* 三层胶合板. **2** strand of rope or yarn (绳或纱的)股: *three-/four-ply knitting wool* 三[四]股毛线.
□ **plywood** /ˈplaɪwʊd; ˋplaɪ͵wʊd/ *n* [U] board(s) made by gluing thin layers of wood on top of each other 胶合板: *sheets of plywood* 一张一张的胶合板 ○ [attrib 作定语] *plywood furniture* 胶合板家具.

ply[2] /plaɪ; plaɪ/ *v* (*pt, pp* **plied** /plaɪd; plaɪd/) **1** [Tn] (*fml* 文) use or wield (a tool or weapon) 使用(工具或武器): *ply one's needle*, ie work busily at one's sewing 忙于缝纫 ○ *ply the oars*, ie row a boat 划桨. **2** [I, Ipr, Tn] (of ships, buses, etc) go regularly to and fro along (a course) (指船、公共汽车等)沿(某路线)定时运行: *ply the routes between the islands* 定期在两岛间航行 ○ *ferries that ply between England and France* 往返英法间的渡轮 ○ *ships that ply (across) the South China Sea* (经)南中国海的定期班轮. **3** (idm 习语) **ply one's ˈtrade** work at a (skilled) job 从事某(熟练)工作. **ply for ˈhire** (of taxi drivers, boatmen, etc) wait in a place or move about, looking for passengers (计程车司机、船夫等)候客, 揽客, 等生意: *taxis licensed to ply for hire at the railway station* 许可在火车站候客的计程车. **4** (phr v) **ply sb with sth** (**a**) (repeatedly) give or offer sb (food and drink) (反复)给或让某人(食物或饮料): *She plied us with cakes.* 她再三让我们吃蛋糕. (**b**) repeatedly ask sb (questions) 反复问某人(问题).

PM /͵piː ˈem; ͵pi ˋɛm/ *abbr* 缩写 = (*infml* 口 *esp Brit*) Prime Minister: *an interview with the PM* 与首相会晤.

pm /͵piː ˈem; ͵pi ˋɛm/ *abbr* 缩写 = (*US* **PM**) after noon (Latin *post meridiem*) 下午, 午后(源自拉丁文*post meridiem*): *at 3 pm*, ie in the afternoon 下午3时. Cf 参看 AM *abbr* 缩写.

PMT /͵piː em ˈtiː; ͵pi ɛm ˋti/ *abbr* 缩写 = (*infml* 口) premenstrual tension.

pneu·matic /njuːˈmætɪk; *US* nuː-; nuˋmætɪk/ *adj* (**a**) filled with air 充气的: *a pneumatic tyre* 充气轮胎. (**b**) worked by compressed air 由压缩空气操作或推动的; 风动的: *a pneumatic drill* 风钻. ▷ **pneu·mat·ic·ally** /-klɪ; -klɪ/ *adv*.

pneu·mo·nia /njuːˈməʊnɪə; *US* nuː-; nuˋmonjə/ *n* [U] serious illness with inflammation of one or both lungs, causing difficulty in breathing 肺炎.

PO /͵piː ˈəʊ; ͵pi ˋo/ *abbr* 缩写 = **1** Petty Officer. **2** (also **po**) postal order. **3** Post Office: *PO Box 920*, eg in an address 邮政信箱920号.

poach[1] /pəʊtʃ; potʃ/ *v* [Tn, Tn·pr] (**a**) cook (fish, fruit, etc) by simmering it gently in a small amount of liquid (用少量水)炖, 煨(鱼、水果等): *apricots poached in syrup* 糖水煨杏. (**b**) cook (an egg without its shell) by putting it in (or in a container over) simmering water 煮(荷包蛋).
▷ **poacher** *n* pan with one or more cup-shaped containers in which eggs may be poached 荷包蛋锅(锅中有杯形煮蛋容器).

poach[2] /pəʊtʃ; potʃ/ *v* **1** [I, Ipr, Tn] **~ (for sth)** catch (game birds, animals or fish) without permission on sb else's property (进入他人地界)偷猎, 偷捕(鸟、兽或鱼): *go out poaching on a farmer's land* 到农场主土地上偷猎 ○ *Fred was caught poaching hares.* 弗雷德因偷猎野兔被捉. **2** (**a**) [Ipr] **~ on sth** be active in an area that properly belongs to sb else 在他人范围内活动: *Rival salesmen were poaching on his territory.* 这些推销员是竞争对手, 却跑到他的地盘来兜生意. ○ *By interfering in this matter you are poaching on my preserve*, ie dealing with sth that is my responsibility. 你干预此事就是在我的责任范围内越俎代庖. (**b**) [Tn] take (staff or ideas) from sb/sth, esp in an underhand way 从某人[某处]挖走(人员)或窃取(思想): *A rival firm poached our best computer programmers.* 我公司的竞争对手把我们最好的计算机程序编制员挖走了. ○ *A new political party usually poaches ideas from its rivals.* 新政党往往把敌对政党的思想攫为己有.
▷ **poacher** *n* person who poaches 偷捕动物的人; 在他人范围内活动的人; 挖走人员或窃取思想的人. Cf 参看 POACH[1].

POB /͵piː əʊ ˈbiː; ͵pi o ˋbi/ *abbr* 缩写 = Post Office Box (number) 邮政信箱(号码): *POB 63* 邮政信箱63号.

pock /pɒk; pɑk/ *n* (**a**) any of the swellings on the skin caused by certain diseases, esp smallpox 痘疱; (尤指天花的)疱疹, 脓疱. (**b**) (also ˈ**pock-mark**) hollow mark left on the skin by this 麻子(天花的疤痕).
▷ **pocked** *adj* **~ (with sth)** having holes or depressions in the surface 有洞的; 有坑的: *The moon's surface is pocked with small craters.* 月球表面有许多小型月坑.
□ ˈ**pock-marked** *adj* having marks left after (esp) smallpox 有麻子的: *The man's face was badly pock-marked.* 那个男的脸上有许多麻子.

pocket /ˈpɒkɪt; ˋpɑkɪt/ *n* **1** (**a**) small bag sewn into or onto a garment and forming part of it, for carrying things in (衣服上的)口袋, 袋子, 兜儿; 衣袋: *a coat, jacket, trouser, etc pocket* 大衣、外衣、裤子等的口袋 ○ *stand with one's hands in one's pockets* 双手插在口袋里站着 ○ [attrib 作定语] *a pocket dictionary, edition, guide, etc* ie small enough to fit in one's pocket 袖珍词典、版本、指南等. (**b**) container resembling this, eg on the inside of a car-door, suitcase, cardboard folder, etc; flap[1](1) (汽车门、衣箱、文件夹等内侧的)口袋: *You will find information about safety procedures in the pocket in front of you*, eg on an aircraft. 在您座位前方的袋子里有安全措施须知(如在飞机上). **2** (usu *sing* 通常作单数) money that one has available for spending; financial means (现成的)钱; 财力: *luxury far beyond my pocket* 远非我财力可及的奢侈品 ○ *easy/hard on the pocket*, ie easy/difficult to afford 手头充裕[拮据] ○ *The resort provides accommodation to suit every pocket.* 这个度假地提供的食宿丰俭随意. ○ *The expedition was a drain on her pocket.* 这次探险耗尽了她的钱财. **3** small isolated group or area 孤立的小的群体或范围: *Pockets of opposition/resistance to the new regime still remained.* 反对[抵制]新政权的某些势力仍然存在. ○ *pockets of unemployment in an otherwise prosperous region* 繁荣地区中个别的失业现象. **4** small cavity in the ground or in rock, containing gold or ore 矿穴; 矿囊; 矿袋: *pockets of coal* 煤矿穴. **5** = AIR POCKET (AIR[1]). **6** (*sport* 体) any of the six string pouches round a billiard-table into which balls are hit (台球的)球袋. ⇨illus at SNOOKER 见SNOOKER插图. **7** (idm 习语) **be, etc in sb's ˈpocket** be very close to or intimate with sb 与某人很亲密: *They live in each other's pockets.* 他们两人十分密切. **have sb in one's ˈpocket** have influence or power over sb 可以影响或支配某人. ͵**in/**͵**out of ˈpocket** having gained/lost money as a result of sth 因某事赚[赔]钱: *Even after paying all the expenses, we'll still be £100 in pocket.* 即使扣除所有费用, 我们仍能赚100英镑. ○ *His mistake left us all out of pocket.* 他这一错, 我们大家都跟着赔了钱. ○ [attrib 作定语] ͵*out-of-pocket exˈpenses*, ie money that one has spent (and which will be reimbursed, eg by one's employer) 已支付的开销(可报销的, 如由雇主发

还). **line one's/sb's pocket** ⇨ LINE[3]. **money burns a hole in sb's pocket** ⇨ MONEY. **pick sb's pocket** ⇨ PICK[3]. **put one's hand in one's pocket** ⇨ HAND[1]. **put one's pride in one's pocket** ⇨ PRIDE.

▷ **pocket** *v* [Tn] **1** put (sth) into one's pocket 将(某物)放入衣袋: *He pocketed the tickets.* 他把票放进衣袋里了. ○ *She quickly pocketed the note without reading it.* 她很快把通知放进口袋里, 连看都没看. **2** keep or take (sth) for oneself (esp dishonestly) 将(某物)据为己有: *She pays £2 for them, sells them for £4 and pockets the difference.* 那些东西她2英镑买入、4英镑卖出, 把赚头塞进了腰包. ○ *He was given £20 for expenses, but pocketed most of it.* 他得到20英镑的公款, 但大部分都进了自己的口袋了. **3** (eg in billiards) hit (a ball) into a pocket (6) (如在台球戏中)将(球)击入球袋. **4** (idm 习语) **pocket one's 'pride** hide or suppress one's feelings of anger or shame 隐藏或压抑愤怒或羞耻感.

pock·et·ful /-fʊl; -,fʊl/ *n* amount a pocket holds 一衣袋的量: *a pocketful of coins* 一衣袋硬币.

□ **'pocket-book** *n* **1** small notebook 小笔记本; 袖珍记事本. **2(a)** (= WALLET). **(b)** (*US*) purse or small handbag 钱包; (尤指女用)小手提包.

'pocket-knife *n* (*pl* **-knives**) = PENKNIFE (PEN[1]). ⇨ illus at KNIFE 见 KNIFE 插图.

'pocket-money *n* [U] (*Brit*) **(a)** small amount of money given to a child, esp weekly (给孩子的)零花钱(尤指每周给的). **(b)** money for small expenses 零用钱: *We've paid for our travel and accommodation, so we only need to take some pocket-money with us.* 我们已付了旅费与食宿费, 所以只需带些零用钱.

pod /pɒd; pɑd/ *n* **1** long seed-case of various plants, esp peas and beans 荚; (尤指)豆荚. **2** (idm 习语) **like as peas in a pod** ⇨ LIKE[1].

▷ **pod** *v* (**-dd-**) [Tn] take (peas, beans, etc) from their pods 剥掉(豌豆等)的荚.

podgy /'pɒdʒɪ; 'pɑdʒɪ/ *adj* (**-ier, -iest**) (*infml usu derog* 口, 通常作贬义) (of people or parts of the body) short and fat (指人或身体的部分)矮胖的, 短粗的: *podgy fingers* 短粗的手指. ⇨Usage at FAT[1] 用法见FAT[1]. ▷ **pod·gi·ness** *n* [U].

po·di·atry /pə'daɪətrɪ; pə'daɪətrɪ/ *n* [U] (*US*) = CHIROPODY. ▷ **po·di·atrist** /-trɪst; -trɪst/ *n* (*US*) = CHIROPODIST.

po·dium /'pəʊdɪəm; 'podɪəm/ *n* small platform for the conductor of an orchestra, a lecturer, etc to stand on (乐队的)指挥台; 讲台.

poem /'pəʊɪm; 'po·ɪm/ *n* piece of creative writing in verse, esp one expressing deep feelings or noble thoughts in beautiful language, written with the intention of communicating an experience 诗; 韵文; 诗体文: *write/compose poems* 写[作]诗.

poet /'pəʊɪt; 'po·ɪt/ *n* writer of poems 诗人.

▷ **po·et·ess** /-es; -ɛs/ *n* woman poet 女诗人.

□ **,Poet 'Laureate** (also **Laureate**) poet officially appointed to the Royal Household in Britain, to write poems for state occasions. 桂冠诗人(正式任命为英国王室成员, 为国家大典作诗者).

po·etic /pəʊ'etɪk; po'ɛtɪk/ *adj* **1** (*approv* 褒) like or suggesting poetry, esp in being graceful and aesthetically leasing 像诗的, 有诗意的(尤指优美的): *a poetic rendering of the piano sonata* 富有诗意的钢琴奏鸣曲演奏. **2** [attrib 作定语] = POETICAL 1: *his entire poetic output* 他的全部诗作.

▷ **po·et·ical** /-kl; -kḷ/ *adj* **1** [attrib 作定语] of or being poetry 诗的; 韵文的; 诗体文的: *the poetical works of Keats* 济慈的诗作. **2** [attrib 作定语] = POETIC 1. **po·et·ic·ally** /-klɪ; -klɪ/ *adv*.

□ **po,etic 'justice** well-deserved punishment or reward 应得的赏罚.

po,etic 'licence freedom to change the normal rules of language when writing verse (eg by reversing word order, changing meaning, etc) 诗的破格(如词序倒装、词义变更等): (*ironic* 反语) *his garden shed which, with a certain amount of poetic licence, he calls his summer-house* 他那美其名曰夏季别墅的花园棚.

po·etry /'pəʊɪtrɪ; 'po·ɪtrɪ/ *n* [U] **1** poems collectively or in general 诗(总称): *epic, lyric, dramatic, pastoral, symbolist, etc poetry* 史诗、抒情诗、戏剧诗、田园诗、象征派的诗 ○ *Dryden's poetry* 德莱顿的诗 ○ [attrib 作定语] *a poetry book* 诗集 ○ *a poetry reading* 诗歌朗诵会. Cf 参看 PROSE, VERSE. **2** (*approv* 褒) aesthetically pleasing quality 诗意; 美感: *a ballet dancer with poetry in every movement* 动作皆富诗意的芭蕾舞演员 ○ *the poetry of motion*, eg in ballet or some forms of athletics 动作的优美(如芭蕾舞或某些体育动作).

po-faced /'pəʊ feɪst; 'po,fest/ *adj* (*Brit infml derog* 口, 贬) with a too solemn or disapproving expression 一本正经的; 不以为然的.

pogo /'pəʊgəʊ; 'pogo/ *n* (*pl* **~s**) (also **'pogo stick**) pole, with bars for standing on and a spring at the bottom end, used as a toy for jumping about on 弹簧单高跷(一种跳跃游戏器具).

pog·rom /'pɒgrəm; *US* pə'grɒm; po'grɑm/ *n* organized persecution or killing of a particular group or class of people, esp because of their race or religion (有组织的)集体迫害或杀戮(尤指因种族或宗教矛盾所致的).

poign·ant /'pɔɪnjənt; 'pɔɪnjənt/ *adj* affecting one's feelings deeply, making one sad, full of pity, etc 痛切的; 伤心的; 心酸的: *poignant sorrow, regret, memories* 深沉的悲哀、痛悔、辛酸的回忆 ○ *a poignant moment* 伤心的时候.

▷ **poign·ancy** /-jənsɪ; -jənsɪ/ *n* [U] state or quality of being poignant 痛切; 伤心; 心酸.

poign·antly /-jəntlɪ; -jəntlɪ/ *adv*.

poin·set·tia /pɔɪn'setɪə; pɔɪn'sɛtɪə/ *n* tropical plant with large red leaves that form flower-like clusters, often grown indoors in pots 一品红; 猩猩木.

point[1] /pɔɪnt; pɔɪnt/ *n* **1** [C] (often in compounds 常用以构成复合词) sharp or tapered end of sth; tip (物体的)尖端; 尖儿: *the point of a pin, knife, pencil, etc* 大头针、刀子、铅笔等的尖儿 ○ *a pin-point, knife-point, pencil point, etc* 针尖儿、刀尖儿、铅笔尖儿 ○ *The stake had been sharpened to a vicious-looking point.* 木桩削得尖得吓人. ○ *the point of the jaw*, eg as the target for a punch in boxing 颌端(如拳击的攻击目标). **2** [C] (often with a capital as part of a name 常用于名称中, 首字母大写) narrow piece of land sticking out into the sea; headland or promontory 岬角; 海角: *The ship rounded the point.* 船绕过了岬角. ○ *Pagoda Point* 宝塔角. **3** [C] (*geometry* 几) thing that has position but no size, eg the place where two lines cross 点: *AB and CD intersect at (the point) P.* AB线和CD线在P点相交. **4** [C] **(a)** any dot used in writing or printing, eg as a full-stop, as a marker of decimals, etc (书写或印刷用的)点(如句号、小数点等): *Two point six (2.6) means the same as* $2\frac{6}{10}$. 二点六(2.6)即为$2\frac{6}{10}$. ○ *The first two figures after the decimal point indicate tenths and hundredths respectively.* 小数点后的头两位数分别表示十分位和百分位. ⇨App 4 见附录4. **(b)** tiny dot or mark of light or colour (光亮的或有颜色的)小点: *stars seen as points of light in a dark sky* 在黑暗的天空中点点发光的星星. **5** [C] (often in compounds 常用以构成复合词) particular place or locality 地点; 位置: *Guards had been posted at several points around the perimeter.* 在环形防线上已布置了几处岗哨. ○ *an assembly, rallying, meeting, etc point* 集会、集合、会面等的地点 ○ *a steamer service calling at Port Said, Aden and all points east*, ie all other ports further east 到塞得港、亚丁以及东部各港口的航运业务. **6** [C] particular time or instant 某一时刻或瞬间: *At one point I thought she was going to refuse, but in the end she agreed.* 当时我以为她要拒绝, 但最后她却同意了. ○ *The film started to get very violent, at which point I left.* 那部电影看着看着出现了极残暴的场面, 我立刻就走了. ○ *at the point of death*, ie about to die at any moment 在临死时. **7** [C] (often in compounds 常用以构成复合词) stage or degree of progress, increase, temperature, etc (进展、增进等的)阶段, 程度; (温度等的)度: *reach danger point*, ie reach a dangerous level 达到危险的地步 ○ *boiling/freezing/melting point* 沸[冰/熔]点. **8** [C] any of the 32 marks on the circumference of a compass 罗经点(罗盘上的32个刻度): *the cardinal points*, ie the four main points: N, E, S and W 基本方位(北、东、南、西等四个主要方位) ○ (*fig* 比喻) *Search-parties had been sent out to all points of the compass*, ie in every direction. 已向四面八方派出了搜索队. **9** [C] unit of measurement, value, scoring, etc (作测量、数值、记分等单位的)点、分等: *a point on a scale* 刻度上的一点 ○ *The pound fell several points on the Stock Market today.* 今天证券市场上英镑下跌了好几点. ○ *We need one more point to win the game.* 我们再得一分就能胜这一

局. ○ [attrib 作定语] *a points system* 点数制. ⇨App 4 见附录4. **10** [C] individual idea of sth said, done or planned; single item or detail (说法、做法或想法的)点; 项; 条: *the main points of a story, a discussion, an argument, etc* 故事、议论、争论等的要点 ○ *points of difference, similarity, agreement, disagreement, etc* 差异、相似、一致、分歧等之处 ○ *One point in favour of her plan is its cheapness.* 她的计划可取之处是花费少. ○ *explain a theory point by point*, ie explain each individual idea in it, in order 逐点阐释一理论. **11** [C] (**a**) thing said as part of a discussion 论点; 见解; 观点: *Various committee members made interesting points.* 许多委员提出了使人关注的意见. (**b**) effective argument 有力的论据: *'But she might not agree.' 'You've got a point there/That's a point* (ie I had not thought of that.)'. '可是她有可能不同意呀.' '你说得对[有道理](我没想到这一点).' **12** [C] distinctive feature or characteristic 特点; 特征: *sb's good, strong, bad, weak, etc points* 某人的优点、长处、缺点、弱点 ○ *I'm afraid tidiness is not his strong point*, ie he is untidy. 我看他这个人不大讲究整洁. **13 the point** [sing] the matter under discussion; the essential thing 谈论的事; 要点; 核心问题: *Let's stop discussing trivial details and come/get to the point.* 咱们别再谈琐碎细节了, 说正事吧. ○ *The speaker kept wandering off/away from the point.* 讲演的那个人总是走题. ○ *The point (at issue) is this....* 问题的要点是这样的.... **14** [U, sing] essential meaning, main feature (of a story, joke, remark, etc); reason; purpose; value (故事、笑话、意见等的)中心意思, 重点; 理由; 目的; 价值: *get, see, miss, understand the point of sth* 明白、了解、不明白、理解某事的中心意思 ○ *a story, remark, etc with a/some/no/little point (to it)* 有[有些/没有/没什么]重点的故事、意见等 ○ *There's not much point in complaining; they never take any notice.* 埋怨也没什么用, 人家根本不理睬. **15** [U] (*fml* 文) effectiveness; urgency 效力; 鼓动力: *speech, words, remarks, etc that have/lack point* 有[没有]分量的讲话、词语、话等. **16** [C] (often in compounds 常用以构成复合词) electrical socket, into which a plug is put 插座: *a lighting, power, cooker point* 照明、电源、电炊具插座 ○ *a 13-amp point* 13安培的插座. **17 points** [pl] (in ballet) the tips of the toes (芭蕾舞用语)足尖, 脚尖: *dancing on points* 用足尖跳舞. **18 points** [pl] (*Brit*) (*US* **switch**) set of movable rails at a place where a railway line divides into two tracks, which can be altered to allow a train to use either track (铁路上的)转辙器, 道岔: *change/switch the points* 转换道岔 ○ [attrib 作定语] *a points lever, mechanism, etc* 转辙器扳手、装置等. **19** [sing, U] (in cricket) fielder near the batsman on the off side; his position (板球中的)(击球员右侧的)防守球员, 防守位置. **20** [U] (as a compound after a number 用于数词后构成复合词) unit of measurement of type-size in printing (作活字大小单位的)点: *6-point is small and 18-point is large* 6点的活字小, 18点的活字大. **21** (idm 习语) **at the ˌpoint of a ˈsword, ˈgun, etc** by threatening sb with death or wounding by a sword, gun, etc 以死威胁某人; 用剑、枪等加害某人: *captured at the point of a sword* 在武力威胁下被捕. **beside the ˈpoint** irrelevant 离题的; 不相干的. **carry/gain one's ˈpoint** persuade people to accept one's argument 说服别人接受自己的论点. **a case in point** ⇨ CASE[1]. **the finer points** ⇨ FINE[2]. **give sb points (at sth)** offer sb advantages and still win 比赛中向某人让分而仍获胜: *He can give me points at golf*, ie He plays better than I do. 打高尔夫球他让我几分还能赢. **have one's ˈpoints** have certain good qualities 有某些优点: *I suppose wine has its points, but I prefer beer.* 葡萄酒固然有它的好处, 但我还是喜欢啤酒. **if/when it ˌcomes to the ˈpoint** if or when the moment for action or decision comes 到必须采取行动时; 到做决定时: *If it came to the point, would you sacrifice your job for your principles?* 必要时你肯为坚持原则而牺牲工作吗? **in ˌpoint of ˈfact** in reality; actually 事实上; 实际上: *He said he would pay, but in point of fact he has no money.* 他说他付钱, 可实际上他并没有钱. **labour the point** ⇨ LABOUR[2]. **make one's ˈpoint** explain fully what one is proposing 充分解释自己提出的事: *All right, you've made your point; now keep quiet and let the others say what they think.* 好啦, 你已经把话说清楚了; 那就别说了, 让别人谈谈看法. **make a point of doing sth** do sth because one considers it important or necessary 认为做某事重要或有必要: *I always make a point of checking that all the windows are shut before I go out.* 我出门前总是要检查所有的窗户, 看是否都关好了. **a moot point/question** ⇨ MOOT. **not to put too fine a point on it** ⇨ FINE[2]. **on the point of doing sth** just about to do sth 正要做某事时: *I was on the point of going to bed when you rang.* 你来电话时我正要睡觉. **on ˈpoints** (of a win in boxing) by the number of points scored without knocking out one's opponent (指拳击取胜)靠点数. **a ˌpoint of deˈparture** (**a**) place or time at which a journey begins 启程的地点或时间. (**b**) (*fig* 比喻) starting point for a discussion or enterprise (讨论或事业的)起点: *Let's take 'Das Kapital' as a point of departure for our survey of Marxism.* 咱们以《资本论》为出发点来研究一下马克思主义. **a ˌpoint of ˈhonour/ˈconscience** thing of great importance to one's honour or conscience 关系到荣誉或良心的事: *I always pay my debts punctually; it's a point of honour with me.* 我还债总是很准时, 这是我的名誉问题. **the ˌpoint of ˈno ˈreturn** (**a**) point (on a long voyage, flight, etc) at which fuel supplies, etc will not be sufficient for a return to the starting point, so that one must continue the journey in order to survive 航线临界点(长途航行中之某处, 燃料等不敷返回原地之用只得继续前进). (**b**) (*fig* 比喻) point at which one becomes committed to an action or a decision that cannot be reversed (行动或决定)已到欲罢不能的境地. **a ˌpoint of ˈorder** (in formal discussions, eg debates) matter of correct procedure according to the rules (正式讨论中, 如辩论时)(符合规定的)程序问题: *On a point of order, Mr Chairman, can associate members vote on this matter?* 主席先生, 按规定准会员对这件事可以投票吗? **a/one's ˌpoint of ˈview** attitude; opinion 态度; 观点; 看法: *This is unacceptable from my point of view.* 依我看, 这事不能同意. ○ *What's your point of view on nuclear power?* 你对核动力有什么看法? **possession is nine points of the law** ⇨ POSSESSION. **prove one's/the case/point** ⇨ PROVE. **score a point/points** ⇨ SCORE[2]. **a sore point** ⇨ SORE. **stretch a point** ⇨ STRETCH. **one's/sb's strong point/suit** ⇨ STRONG. **take sb's ˈpoint** understand and accept sb's argument 理解并接受某人的论点. **to the ˈpoint** (in a way that is) relevant and appropriate 中肯; 恰当: *remarks that were very much to the point* 切中要害的评论 ○ *His speech was short and to the point.* 他的讲话简明中肯. **to the point of sth** to a degree that can be described as sth 达到某程度: *His manner was abrupt to the point of rudeness.* 他举止唐突, 近乎粗鲁. **up to a (certain) ˈpoint** to some extent; in some degree 在某程度上: *I agree with you up to a (certain) point.* 我在某种程度上同意你的看法.

□ **ˈpoint-duty** *n* [U] (*Brit*) traffic control by a policeman standing typically in the middle of the road (警察在马路中间指挥交通的)岗位值勤.

ˈpointsman *n* (*pl* **-men**) (*Brit*) (*US* **ˈswitchman**) person in charge of railway points (铁路的)转辙工, 扳道工.

ˌpoint-to-ˈpoint *n* (*Brit*) race on horses across country from one point to another 定点越野赛马.

point[2] /pɔɪnt; pɔɪnt/ *v* **1** (**a**) [I, Ipr] **~ (at/to sb/sth)** direct people's attention at sb/sth by extending one's finger towards him/it, or by using any similar sign or indicator; show the position or direction of sb/sth 指出某人[某事物]或其位置或方向: *It's rude to point.* 指手划脚是不礼貌的. ○ *'That's the man who did it,' she said, pointing at me.* '那事就是他干的,' 她指着我说. ○ *He pointed to a tower on the distant horizon.* 他指向远处地平线上的一座塔. ○ *A compass needle points (to the) north.* 罗盘的指针永远指向北方. ○ *The clock hands pointed to twelve*, ie it was noon or midnight. 那座钟的时针、分针都对着十二(正午或午夜). (**b**) [Ipr] **~ to sth** (*fig* 比喻) suggest (the likelihood of) sth; indicate sth 暗示某事物(的可能性); 指示某事物: *I can't point to any one particular reason for it.* 那件事我找不出具体原因来. ○ *All the evidence points to his guilt.* 所有证据都表明他有罪. **2** [Tn, Tn·pr] **~ sth (at/towards sb/sth)** aim or direct sth 以某物瞄准或对着: *point one's finger (at sb/sth)* 用手指着(某人[某物]) ○ *point a gun at sb* 用枪瞄准某人 ○ *point a telescope at/towards the moon*

用望远镜对准月亮. **3** [Ipr, Ip] face or be turned in a particular direction 面对或转至某方向: *A hedgehog's spines point backwards.* 刺猬的刺毛是向后长的. **4** [Tn] give force to (sth); make more noticeable 强调, 着重(某事物); 使更显著: *a story that points a moral* 突出某寓意的故事. **5** [Tn] fill in the spaces between the bricks of (sth) with mortar or cement 用灰泥或水泥勾(某物)的砖缝: *point a wall, chimney, etc* 勾墙、烟囱等的缝. **6** [I] (of a hunting dog) take up a position with the body steady and the head indicating the direction of a hunted bird, etc (指猎狗)站定并用头指示猎物方向. **7** (idm 习语) **point the 'finger (at sb)** (*infml* 口) accuse sb openly 公开指责某人. **point the 'way (to/towards sth)** show the possibility of future development 指出发展的可能性: *Large electronics companies developed television, but Baird pointed the way with his experiments.* 大型电子工业公司研制出了电视, 但这有赖于贝尔德的实验为此指出了方向. ○ *tax reforms which point the way to a more prosperous future* 预示前景更为繁荣的税制改革. **8** (phr v) **point sth out (to sb)** direct attention to sth 使注意某事物: *point out a mistake* 指出错误 ○ *point out to sb the stupidity of his/her behaviour* 向某人指出其行为愚蠢 ○ *I must point out that further delay would be unwise.* 我必须指明再延误就要吃大亏了. **point sth up** give special emphasis to one particular aspect of sth; show sth very clearly 强调某事物的某方面; 明确显示某事物: *The recent disagreement points up the differences between the two sides.* 最近的争执清楚显示双方有分歧.

▷ **poin·ted** *adj* **1** having a sharp tip, end, etc 有尖的; 尖的: *a (sharp-)pointed instrument, tool, etc* 尖(锐)的器具、工具等 ○ *a pointed hat* 尖帽子. **2** (*fig* 比喻) directed clearly against a particular person or his behaviour 针对某人或其行为的; 直截了当的: *a pointed remark, rebuke, etc* 直言不讳的评论、指责等 ○ *She made some pointed references to his careless work.* 她明确指出他工作粗心大意. **3** (*fig* 比喻) (of wit) incisive (指头脑)敏锐的. **point·edly** *adv* in a way that indicates criticism of a particular person or that suggests one's meaning clearly 有针对性地; 尖锐地; 有用意地; 直截了当地: *She stared pointedly at me.* 她严厉地瞪着我. ○ *He looked pointedly at the door,* eg indicating that I should open it, close it, leave, etc. 他有用意地看着门(如示意我应开开、关上、离去等).

point·ing *n* [U] cement, mortar, etc put in the spaces between the bricks of a wall, etc (勾墙等砖缝用的)水泥、灰泥等填充物.

point-blank /ˌpɔɪnt ˈblæŋk; ˈpɔɪntˈblæŋk/ *adj* [attrib 作定语] **1** (of a shot) aimed or fired at very close range (指射程)近距离内瞄准的或射击的: *He shot her at point-blank range.* 他在近距离射程内射中了她. **2** (*fig* 比喻) (of sth said) direct, complete and immediate, and often rather rude (指说的话)直接的, 断然的, 直率的(常为粗鲁的): *a ˌpoint-blank reˈfusal* 断然的拒绝.

▷ **point-blank** *adv* in a point-blank manner; directly (指瞄准或射击)在近距离内; (指言语)直截了当地: *fire point-blank at sb* 在近距离内向某人射击 ○ *I asked him point-blank what he was doing there.* 我直截了当地问他在那里做什么呢. ○ *refuse point-blank to do sth* 断然拒绝做某事.

pointer /ˈpɔɪntə(r); ˈpɔɪntɚ/ *n* **1** long thin piece of metal, plastic, etc which moves to indicate figures, positions, etc on a dial, scale, etc (仪表盘、刻度等上的)指针. **2** rod or stick used to point to things on a map, blackboard, etc (作指示用的)棍、教鞭等. **3 ~ (on sth)** (*infml* 口) piece of advice 意见; 主意: *Could you give me a few pointers on how to tackle the job?* 这工作怎么做, 你能不能给我出点主意? **4 ~ (to sth)** thing that shows likely future developments (预示事物发展的)暗示, 线索: *journalists studying the minister's speech for pointers to the contents of next month's policy statement* 研究部长讲话以揣摩下月施政报告中的动向的新闻工作者. **5** large short-haired hunting dog trained to stand still with its nose pointing in the direction of hunted birds, etc which it smells (经训练可示意猎物方向的)短毛大猎犬.

poin·til·lism /ˈpɔɪntɪlɪzəm, *also* ˈpwæntiːɪzəm; ˈpɔɪntḷˌɪzəm, ˈpwæntiˌɪzəm/ *n* [U] technique of painting developed in France in the late 19th century in which the picture is built up from tiny dots of different colours which the eye sees as a blend of colour 点彩画法(19世纪末从法国发展起来的绘画方法).

▷ **poin·til·list** /-lɪst; -lɪst/ *n* person who paints in this way 点彩派画家.

point·less /ˈpɔɪntlɪs; ˈpɔɪntlɪs/ *adj* with little or no sense, aim or purpose 无意义的; 无目标的: *make a pointless remark* 说不相干的话 ○ *It is pointless to have a car if you cannot drive it!* 假若不会开汽车, 有辆汽车又有什么用呢? ▷ **point·lessly** *adv.* **point·less·ness** *n* [U]: *the pointlessness of his existence* 他生活毫无目标.

poise /pɔɪz; pɔɪz/ *v* [Ipr, Ip, Tn·pr, Tn·p] be or keep (sth) balanced or suspended 处于平衡或悬起状态; 使(某物)平衡或悬起: *The eagle poised in mid-air ready to swoop on its prey.* 那鹰在半空中盘旋准备扑向猎物. ○ *He poised the javelin in his hand before throwing it.* 他把手中标枪握稳后掷了出去.

▷ **poise** *n* [U] **1** graceful and balanced (control of) bodily position or movement (身体的优美而平衡的)姿势, 动作(的控制): *poise of the body, head, etc* 身体、头部等优美的姿势 ○ *moving with the assured poise of a ballet dancer* 带有芭蕾舞演员那种稳健姿势的动作. **2** quiet dignified self-confidence and self-control (安然的)自信, 自制: *a woman of great poise* 极稳重的女子.

poised *adj* **1** [pred 作表语] **~ (in, on, above, etc sth)** in a state of balance, stillness 平衡; 平稳: *poised on tiptoe, in mid-air, etc* 用足尖、在半空中...保持平衡 ○ *sth poised on the edge of a table,* ie likely to fall off if lightly touched 在桌子边上稍触即掉的东西. **2** [pred 作表语] **~ (in/on/above/for sth); ~ (to do sth)** (of people, animals, etc) in a state of physical tension, ready for action (指人、动物等)身体处于紧张状态, 准备行动: *poised on the edge of the swimming-pool,* ie ready to jump in 在游泳池边作出跳水的姿势 ○ (*fig* 比喻) *The Allies were poised* (ie ready) *for their invasion of Europe.* 同盟国准备随时入侵欧洲. ○ *Combined Breweries are poised to* (ie about to) *take over the British Beer Company.* 联合酿酒公司准备接管不列颠啤酒公司. **3** (*fig* 比喻) calmly self-controlled; full of poise (2) 泰然自若的; 自信的; 自制的: *a poised young lady* 文静自若的年轻女子 ○ *a poised manner* 沉着的态度.

poison /ˈpɔɪzn; ˈpɔɪzn̩/ *n* [C, U] **1** substance causing death or harm if absorbed by a living thing (animal or plant) 毒药; 毒物: *rat poison* 老鼠药 ○ *poison for killing weeds* 除草剂 ○ *commit suicide by taking poison* 服毒自杀 ○ [attrib 作定语] *poison gas,* ie esp as used to kill people in war 毒气(尤指战争中用的). **2** (*infml derog* 口, 贬) extremely unpleasant food 极糟的食物: *I'm not eating that poison!* 我可不吃那种猪食!

▷ **poison** *v* [Tn, Tn·pr] **~ sb/sth (with sth)** **1** (**a**) give poison to (a living thing); kill or harm sb/sth with poison 施毒于(某生物); 用毒药毒死或毒害某人[某物]: *His wife poisoned him with arsenic.* 他妻子用砒霜把他毒死了. ○ *Are our children being poisoned by lead in the atmosphere?* 我们的儿童是否受着空气中铅的毒害? (**b**) put poison in sth 在某物中放毒: *The chemical companies are poisoning our rivers with effluent.* 这些化学公司排出废水污染着我们的河流. **2** (**a**) injure sth morally; corrupt sth (在道德上)败坏某事物; 腐化某事物: *poison sb's mind with propaganda* 通过宣传毒害某人的思想. (**b**) fill sth with suffering, bitterness, etc; spoil or ruin sth 使某事物受苦、受难、受罪等; 破坏或毁坏某事物: *a quarrel which poisoned our friendship* 有损我们友谊的争吵 ○ *an experience that poisons sb's life* 使某人一生受害的经历. **3** (idm 习语) **poison A's mind against B** (*derog* 贬) make A dislike B by telling A bad and usu untrue things about B 对A说B的坏话(通常指不实之词). **poisoned** *adj* **1** inflamed because of an infected cut, scratch, etc (因伤口感染等)发炎的: *a poisoned hand* 发炎的手. **2** having poison applied to it 有毒的; 施过毒药的: *a poisoned arrow* 毒箭. **poisoner** /ˈpɔɪzənə(r); ˈpɔɪzənɚ/ *n* person who murders by means of poison 施毒者. **pois·on·ing** /ˈpɔɪzənɪŋ; ˈpɔɪzənɪŋ/ *n* [C, U] (act or result of) giving or taking poison 施毒; 中毒: *blood poisoning,* ie poisoning of the blood 血中毒 ○ *lead poisoning,* ie poisoning by lead 铅中毒.

pois·on·ous /ˈpɔɪzənəs; ˈpɔɪzn̩əs/ *adj* **1** (**a**) using poison as a means of attacking enemies or prey 用毒物杀敌或猎物的: *poisonous snakes, insects, etc* 毒蛇、有毒

的昆虫. (**b**) causing death or illness if taken into the body 引起中毒的: *poisonous plants, chemicals* 有毒的植物、化学物质. **2** (*fig derog* 比喻, 贬) (**a**) morally harmful 败坏道德的: *the poisonous doctrine of racial superiority* 毒害良知的种族优越论. (**b**) spiteful; malicious 恶意的; 恶毒的: *sb with a poisonous tongue*, ie who spreads malicious rumours about people 言语恶毒的人. **pois·on·ously** *adv*.

□ ˌ**poison-ˈpen letter** malicious letter sent deliberately to upset or offend the receiver 诽谤信.

poke[1] /pəʊk; pok/ *v* **1** (**a**) [Tn, Tn·pr] **~ sb/sth (with sth)** push sb/sth sharply (with a stick, one's finger, etc); jab sb/sth (用棍棒、手指等)捅、拨或戳某人[某物]: *poke sb in the ribs*, ie nudge him in a friendly way 轻触某人肋部(促其注意) ○ *poke the fire (with a poker)*, ie to make it burn more strongly 用通条捅火(使之更旺). (**b**) [Tn·pr] **~ sth in sth** make (a hole) in sth by pushing one's finger, a sharp instrument, etc through it (用手指、尖物等)在某物上扎(洞): *Poke two holes in the sack so you can see through it.* 在袋子上戳两个洞就能透过它看了. (**c**) [Ipr] **~ at sth** make repeated small pushing movements at sth 反复轻推某物: *She poked at her meal unenthusiastically.* 她无精打采地拨弄着盘中的饭菜. **2** [Tn·pr, Tn·p] put or move sth in a specified direction, with a sharp push; thrust 猛推某物; 插; 刺: *She poked her finger into the hole.* 她把手指插入那孔中. ○ *poke food through the bars of a cage* 把食物从笼子的栏杆间塞进去 ○ *poke one's head out of a window* 把头伸出窗外 ○ *Mind you don't poke her eye out with that stick!* 小心别让那杆子扎着她的眼睛! ○ *He poked his head round the door to see if she was in the room.* 他在门口探一下头, 看她是否在屋里. ⇨Usage at NUDGE 用法见 NUDGE. **3** (idm 习语) **poke ˈfun at sb/sth** (*usu derog* 通常作贬义) make fun of sb/sth; mock or ridicule sb/sth 开某人[某事物]的玩笑; 嘲弄或嘲笑某人[某事物]: *He enjoys poking fun at others.* 他好开别人的玩笑. **poke/stick one's nose into sth** ⇨ NOSE[1]. **4** (phr v) **poke about/around** (*infml* 口) search inquisitively 好奇地寻找或打听: *Why are you poking about among my papers?* 你为什么乱翻我的文件? **poke out of/through sth; poke out/through/up** be visible coming through (a hole, slit, etc); protrude (从洞、缝等中)呈现, 显露; 伸出: *a pen poking out (of sb's pocket)* (从某人口袋中)露出的钢笔 ○ *I see a finger poking through (a hole in your glove).* 我看见你的手指(从你手套的窟窿里)露出来了. ○ *A few daffodils were already poking up*, ie starting to grow. 有几棵水仙花已经开始抽芽.

▷ **poke** *n* act of poking; nudge 捅; 拨; 戳; 刺; 轻触: *give the fire a poke* 拨一拨火 ○ *give sb a poke in the ribs* 捅某人肋部一下.

poke[2] /pəʊk; pok/ *n* (idm 习语) **buy a pig in a poke** ⇨ BUY.

poker[1] /ˈpəʊkə(r); ˈpokɚ/ *n* strong metal rod or bar for moving or breaking up coal in a fire 拨火棒; 通条.

□ ˈ**poker-work** *n* [U] (**a**) art of making designs, pictures, etc on wood, leather, etc by burning the surface with a very hot tool 烙画术, 烫画术(用烙铁在木、皮革等上烙出图案等). (**b**) such designs 烙画; 烫画.

poker[2] /ˈpəʊkə(r); ˈpokɚ/ *n* [U] card-game for two or more people in which the players bet on the values of the cards they hold 扑克牌戏.

□ ˈ**poker-face** *n* (*infml* 口) face that shows no sign of what the person is thinking or feeling 无表情的面孔. ˈ**poker-faced** *adj*.

poky /ˈpəʊkɪ; ˈpokɪ/ *adj* (**-ier, -iest**) (*infml derog* 口, 贬) (of a place, house, flat, etc) small; limited in space (指地方、房子、公寓等)小的, 狭小的: *a poky little room* 狭窄的小屋. ▷ **po·ki·ness** *n* [U].

po·lar /ˈpəʊlə(r); ˈpolɚ/ *adj* [attrib 作定语] **1** of or near the North or South Pole (南、北)极的; 地极的; 近地极的: *polar ice* 地极的冰 ○ *the polar regions* 极区. **2** of (one of) the poles of a magnet 磁极的: *polar attraction* 极向引力. **3** (*fml* 文) (of opposites) complete; extreme (指相对的事物)完全相反的, 极端对立的.

▷ **po·lar·ity** /pəˈlærətɪ; pəˈlærətɪ/ *n* **1** [U, C] (in a magnet) possession or location of negative and positive poles (磁体的)极性: *the polarity of a magnet* 磁体的极性 ○ *reversed polarity/polarities* 反转极性. **2** [U] **~ (between A and B)** (*fig* 比喻) difference or separation (between people or things) in condition, views, etc (人或物之间条件、看法等的)分歧, 对立: *the growing polarity between the left and right wings of the party* 党内左右翼间日益增大的分歧.

□ ˈ**polar bear** white bear living in the north polar regions 北极熊; 白熊. ⇨illus at BEAR 见 BEAR 插图.

po·lar·ize, -ise /ˈpəʊləraɪz; ˈpoləˌraɪz/ *v* **1** [Tn] (*physics* 物) cause (light-waves, etc) to vibrate in a single direction or plane 使(光波等)偏振. **2** [Tn] give magnetic polarity to (a body) 使(物体)极化; 使有极性. **3** [I, Ipr, Tn, Tn·pr] **~ (sth/sb) (into sth)** (cause people, views, etc to) form into two groups which conflict with or are completely opposite to each other (使人、观点等)两极分化, 相冲突, 截然相反: *Public opinion has polarized on this issue.* 在这个问题上公众的意见已两极分化. ○ *an issue which has polarized public opinion* 使舆论两极分化的问题.

▷ **po·lar·iza·tion, -isation** /ˌpəʊləraɪˈzeɪʃn; *US* -rɪˈz-; ˌpolərəˈzeʃən/ *n* [C, U] act of polarizing; state of being polarized 偏振(现象); 极化(作用); 两极分化.

Po·lar·oid /ˈpəʊlərɔɪd; ˈpoləˌrɔɪd/ *n* (*propr* 专利名) **1** [U] thin transparent film put on sun-glasses, car windows, etc to lessen the brightness of sunlight (太阳眼镜、汽车窗户等上的)偏光薄膜. **2 Polaroids** [pl] sun-glasses treated with Polaroid 有偏光薄膜的太阳眼镜.

□ ˌ**Polaroid** ˈ**camera** camera that can produce photographs within seconds after the picture has been taken 拍立得(亦译宝丽莱)照相机(一次成像的).

Pole /pəʊl; pol/ *n* native or inhabitant of Poland 波兰人.

pole[1] /pəʊl; pol/ *n* **1** either of the two points at the exact top and bottom of the Earth, which are the opposite ends of the axis on which it turns 地极: *the North/South Pole* 北[南]极. ⇨illus at GLOBE 见 GLOBE 插图. **2** (*physics* 物) either of the two ends of a magnet or the terminal points of an electric battery 磁极; 电极: *the negative/positive pole* 负[正]极. **3** (*fig* 比喻) either of two opposite, conflicting or contrasting extremes 相反的、冲突的或对立的两极之一: *Our points of view are at opposite poles.* 我们的观点截然相反. **4** (idm 习语) **be ˈpoles apart** be widely separated; have nothing in common 截然相反; 南辕北辙: *The employers and the trade union leaders are still poles apart*, ie are far from reaching an agreement or a compromise. 雇主和工会领袖的意见仍相距甚远.

□ ˈ**pole-star** *n* the North Star, which is almost exactly overhead in the northern half of the world 北极星.

pole[2] /pəʊl; pol/ *n* **1** long thin rounded piece of wood or metal, used esp as a support for sth or for pushing boats, etc along 杆; 竿; 棒; 杖; 篙: *a tent, flag, telegraph, etc pole* 帐篷支柱、旗杆、电线杆 ○ *a punt, barge, ski, etc pole* 撑船的篙、滑雪杖. **2** = PERCH[1] 3. **3** (idm 习语) **up the ˈpole** (*infml* 口 *esp Brit*) (**a**) in difficulty 处于困境. (**b**) wrong; mistaken 错误的; 弄错的. (**c**) crazy; eccentric 发疯的; 古怪的.

▷ **pole** *v* [Tn·pr, Tn·p] push (a boat, etc) along by using a pole 用杆、篙、杖等撑(船等): *pole a punt up the river* 用篙撑方头平底船逆流而上.

□ ˈ**pole-vault** *n* (*sport* 体) jump over a raised bar, using a long pole which is held in the hands 撑竿跳高. ⇨illus at VAULT 见 VAULT 插图. — *v* [I] perform such a jump 作撑竿跳高. ˈ**pole-vaulter** *n*. ˈ**pole-vaulting** *n* [U].

pole-axe /ˈpəʊl æks; ˈpolˌæks/ *n* **1** (formerly) axe for use in war, with a long handle (旧时)长柄战斧. **2** long-handled axe-like tool used, esp formerly, by butchers for killing cattle by hitting them on the head 长柄屠斧(尤指旧时屠宰牲畜用的).

▷ **pole-axe** *v* [Tn] **1** strike (sb/sth) down with a pole-axe 用长柄斧砍或劈(某人[某物]): (*fig* 比喻) *The punch caught him on the jaw, and he sank down pole-axed*, ie completely knocked out. 他颌部挨了一记重拳立即瘫倒在地上. **2** (usu passive 通常用于被动语态) (*fig* 比喻) overwhelm (sb) with surprise and distress 使(某人)因惊愕、悲痛而手足无措: *We were all absolutely pole-axed by the terrible news.* 那可怕的消息传来, 我们都吓得不知所措.

pole·cat /ˈpəʊlkæt; ˈpolˌkæt/ *n* **1** small European animal of the weasel family which has dark brown fur and gives off an unpleasant smell 艾鼬. **2** (*US*) = SKUNK.

po·lemic /pəˈlemɪk; poˈlɛmɪk/ *n* (*fml* 文) **1** (**a**) [C] **~ (against/in favour of sth/sb)** speech, piece of writing, etc containing very forceful arguments (against or for sth/sb) (反对或赞成某事物[某人]的)慷慨陈词, 辩论文章: *He launched into a fierce polemic against the government's policies.* 他猛烈地抨击政府的政策. (**b**) [U] such speeches, pieces of writing, etc 慷慨陈词; 辩论文章: *engage in polemic* 进行辩论. **2 polemics** [pl] art or practice of arguing a case formally and usu forcefully 辩论法; 争辩术.

▷ **po·lem·ical** /-ɪkl; -ɪkḷ/ (also **po·lemic**) *adj* (*fml* 文) **1** [attrib 作定语] of polemics 辩论法的; 争辩术的: *polemic(al) skills* 辩论的技巧. **2** arguing a case very forcefully, often with the intention of being controversial or provocative 好辩的; 挑起争论的: *a polemic(al) article, speech, etc* 挑起争论的文章、讲话等. **po·lem·ic·ally** /-klɪ; -klɪ/ *adv*.

po·lem·ic·ist /pəˈlemɪsɪst; pəˈlɛmɪsɪst/ *n* person skilled in polemics 善于辩论的人.

po·lice /pəˈli:s; pəˈlis/ *n* **(the) police** [pl *v*] (members of an) official organization whose job is to keep public order, prevent and solve crime, etc 警方; 警察部门; 警察: *the local, state, national, etc police* 地方、州、国家等的警察部门 ○ *There were over 100 police on duty at the demonstration.* 游行期间有100多名警察值勤. ○ *The police have not made any arrests.* 警方未逮捕任何人. ○ [attrib 作定语] *a police car, enquiry, raid, report* 警车、警方的询问、警方的突击搜查、警方的报告.

▷ **po·lice** *v* [Tn] keep order in (a place) with or as if with police; control 维持(某地)的治安; 监督: *The teachers on duty are policing the school buildings during the lunch hour.* 在午饭时间, 值班教师负责维持校内秩序. ○ (*fig* 比喻) *a committee to police the new regulations,* ie make sure they are obeyed 监督实施新规章的委员会.

□ **poˌlice ˈconstable** (*abbr* 缩写 **PC**) (also **constable**) (in Britain and some other countries) policeman or policewoman of the lowest rank (英国及某些国家中的)普通警员.

poˈlice dog dog trained to track or attack suspected criminals 警犬.

poˈlice force body of police officers of a country, district or town (国家、地区、城镇全体的)警察.

poˈliceman /-mən; -mən/ *n* (*pl* **-men** /-mən; -mən/) male member of the police force (男)警察.

poˈlice-officer (also **officer**) *n* policeman or policewoman (男或女)警察.

poˈlice state (*derog* 贬) country controlled by political police, usu a totalitarian state 警察国家(通常为极权主义国家).

poˈlice station office of a local police force 警察局; 警察分局; 派出所: *The suspect was taken to the police station for questioning.* 那个嫌疑犯被带到警察局问话.

poˈlicewoman *n* (*pl* **-women**) (abbr 缩写 **PW**) female member of the police force (女)警察.

pol·icy[1] /ˈpɒləsɪ; ˈpɑləsɪ/ *n* [U, C] **~ (on sth)** plan of action, statement of ideals, etc proposed or adopted by a government, political party, business, etc (政府、政党、公司等的)方针, 政策: *according to our present policy* 据我们的现行政策 ○ *adopt fresh policies* 采取新政策 ○ *British foreign policy* 英国的外交政策 ○ *What is the Labour Party's policy on immigration?* 工党在移民问题上的政策是怎样的? ○ (*fig* 比喻) *Is honesty the best policy* (ie the best principle for people to live by)? 诚实是不是处世的最佳原则? ○ [attrib 作定语] *a policy maker* 制定政策的人.

pol·icy[2] /ˈpɒləsɪ; ˈpɑləsɪ/ *n* (written statement of the) terms of a contract of insurance 保险单: *a ˈfire-insurance policy* 火灾保险单 ○ [attrib 作定语] *a ˈpolicy document* 保险单据 ○ *a ˈpolicy holder* 投保人.

po·lio /ˈpəʊlɪəʊ; ˈpolɪo/ (also *fml* 正规作 **po·lio·my·el·itis** /ˌpəʊlɪəʊˌmaɪəˈlaɪtɪs; ˌpolɪoˌmaɪəˈlaɪtɪs/) *n* [U] infectious disease caused by a virus in which the spinal cord becomes inflamed, often resulting in paralysis 脊髓灰质炎; 小儿麻痹症: [attrib 作定语] *polio vaccine* 脊髓灰质炎疫苗 ○ *ˌanti-ˈpolio injections* 预防小儿麻痹症的注射.

Pol·ish /ˈpəʊlɪʃ; ˈpolɪʃ/ *adj* of Poland or the Poles 波兰的; 波兰人的.

▷ **Pol·ish** *n* [U] language of the Poles 波兰语: *written in Polish* 用波兰文写的.

pol·ish /ˈpɒlɪʃ; ˈpɑlɪʃ/ *v* **1** [I, Ipr, Ip, Tn, Tn·pr, Tn·p] **~ (sth) (up) (with sth)** (cause sth to) become smooth and shiny by rubbing 磨光, 擦亮(某物): *This table-top polishes up nicely.* 这个桌面能擦得很亮. ○ *polish (up) wood, furniture, shoes etc with a cloth* 用布把木器、家具、鞋等擦亮. **2** [Tn] (*fig* 比喻) improve (sth) by correcting, making small changes or adding new material 修正, 修改, 修饰(某物): *polish a speech, an article, etc* 给讲稿、文章等润色. **3** (phr v) **polish sth off** (*infml* 口) finish sth quickly 迅速做完某事: *polish off a big plateful of stew* 很快吃完一大盘炖菜 ○ *polish off the arrears of correspondence* 匆匆写完待复的信件.

▷ **pol·ish** *n* **1** (**a**) [sing] shiny surface, etc obtained by polishing (磨或擦而成的)光亮的面: *a table-top with a good polish* 打磨得很亮的桌面. (**b**) [sing] action of polishing 磨光; 擦亮; 修饰: *give the floor a thorough polish* 把地板彻底弄光亮. (**c**) [U, C] substance used for polishing 擦光剂; 上光剂: *ˈfurniture, ˈfloor, ˈshoe polish* 家具上光蜡、地板蜡、鞋油 ○ *a tin of metal polish* 一罐金属擦光剂 ○ *apply polish to sth* 给某物上光. **2** [U] (*fig* 比喻) additional quality of fineness or elegance; refinement 文雅; 高雅; 优雅; 优美: *an unsophisticated country fellow who completely lacked polish* 全无文雅气质不懂世故的乡下人 ○ *a crude performance of the symphony, quite without polish* 那首交响乐拙劣的演奏, 毫无美感. **3** (idm 习语) **spit and polish** ⇨ SPIT[1].

pol·ished *adj* **1** shiny from polishing 磨光的; 擦亮的: *polished wood* 磨光的木头. **2** refined; elegant 文雅的; 优美的: *polished manners* 优雅的风度 ○ *a polished style, performance* 优美的风格、表演.

pol·isher *n* machine for polishing 磨光机: *a floor polisher* 地板磨光机.

pol·it·buro /ˈpɒlɪtbjʊərəʊ; ˈpɑlɪtbjʊro/ *n* (*pl* **~s**) chief party decision-making committee in Communist countries (共产党国家中)党的政治局.

po·lite /pəˈlaɪt; pəˈlaɪt/ *adj* **1** having or showing that one has good manners and consideration for other people 有礼貌的; 客气的: *a polite child* 有礼貌的孩子 ○ *It wasn't very polite of you to serve yourself without asking.* 你也不问一声就自己吃起来是不太礼貌的. ○ *making a few polite remarks to keep the conversation going* 说几句客气话以免谈话冷场. **2** [attrib 作定语] (*fml* 文) (typical) of a superior class in society; refined (典型的)上流社会的; 高雅的; 有教养的: *a rude word not mentioned in polite society* 在上流社会中不说的粗话.

▷ **po·litely** *adv*.

po·lite·ness *n* (**a**) [U] quality of being polite 有礼貌; 客气: *He was noted for his politeness.* 大家都知道他很有礼貌. (**b**) [C] polite act 有礼貌的表现: *I recall his many politenesses over the years.* 我还记得他多年来很多有礼貌的事情.

pol·itic /ˈpɒlətɪk; ˈpɑləˌtɪk/ *adj* (*fml* 文) (of actions) well judged; prudent (指行为)得当的, 审慎的: *When the fight began, he thought it politic to leave.* 刚一打起来他就想到还是走为上策.

po·lit·ical /pəˈlɪtɪkl; pəˈlɪtɪkḷ/ *adj* **1** of the State; of government; of public affairs in general 政治的; 国家的; 政府的; 政权的; 行政的: *political rights, liberties, etc* 政治的权利、自由等 ○ *a political system* 政治制度. **2** of the conflict or rivalry between two or more parties 政党的; 党派的; 党派斗争的: *a political party, debate, crisis* 政党、政治论战、政治危机 ○ *political skill, know-how, opinions* 为政之术、为政之道、政见 ○ *a party political broadcast*, eg to explain government policy 党的施政广播(如阐述政府的政策) **3** (of actions) considered to be harmful to the State or government (指行为)被认为有害于国家或政府的: *a political offence, crime, etc* 政治上的违法行为、政治罪 ○ *imprisoned on political grounds* 由于政治原因而被监禁. **4** (of people) interested in or active in politics (指人)关心政治的, 政治上活跃的: *sb who is very political (in outlook)* 颇有政治头脑的人 ○ *I'm not a political animal*, ie person. 我不是搞政治的. **5** (*euph derog* 婉, 贬) concerned with power, status, etc within an organization rather than with the true merits of a case 互相倾轧的; 实际上与权位等利益有关的: *One suspects he was dismissed for political reasons.* 有人

怀疑他是由于人事上的原因而被解职的. ○ *It must have been a political decision.* 这一决定准是和互相倾轧有关. ▷ **po·lit·ic·ally** /-klɪ; -klɪ/ *adv* with regard to politics 政治上: *a politically active, astute, naïve, etc person* 政治上很活跃、很精明、很幼稚…的人 ○ *politically useful, sound, disastrous, etc ideas* 政治上有好处、没问题、祸害无穷等的意见 ○ *a politically sensitive decision* 政治上很敏感的决定.

□ **po,litical a'sylum** protection given by a state to sb who has left his own country because he opposes its government (某国给予他国之流亡人士的)政治庇护: *seek/ask for/be granted political asylum* 寻求[申请/获得]政治庇护.

po,litical ge'ography geography dealing with boundaries, communications, etc between countries 政治地理学(研究国与国之间的边界、地域交往等).

po,litical 'prisoner person who is imprisoned because he or she opposes the (system of) government 政治犯(因反对政府或其政治制度而遭关押者).

po,litical 'science (also **politics**) academic study of government and political institutions 政治学.

po·li·ti·cian /,pɒlɪ'tɪʃn; ,pɑlə'tɪʃən/ *n* **1** person actively (and usu professionally) concerned with politics 积极从事政治活动的人; (通常指职业的)政治家. **2** (*often derog* 常作贬义) person who is skilled at handling people or situations, or at getting people to do what he wants 政客; 玩弄权术者: *You need to be a bit of a politician to succeed in this company.* 要想在这家公司步步登高, 就需要耍点手腕.

po·li·ti·cize, -ise /pə'lɪtɪsaɪz; pə'lɪtə,saɪz/ *v* [I, Tn] (cause sb/sth to) become politically conscious or organized (使某人[某事物])具有政治性或政党化: *The strike has now been politicized.* 这次罢工现已带有政治色彩.

pol·it·ick·ing /'pɒlətɪkɪŋ; 'pɑlə,tɪkɪŋ/ *n* [U, C] (*often derog* 常作贬义) political activity, esp to win votes or support 政治活动(尤指拉选票或拉拢支持者): *A lot of politicking preceded the choice of the new director.* 在选新领导人之前进行了大量的拉拢活动.

pol·it·ics /'pɒlətɪks; 'pɑlə,tɪks/ *n* **1** (**a**) [sing or pl *v*] political affairs or life 政治事务; 政治生活; 政治活动: *party politics* 政党政治 ○ *local politics* 地方上的政治活动 ○ *He's thinking of going into politics*, eg trying to become a Member of Parliament. 他正打算参政(如争取当下院议员). (**b**) [pl] political views, beliefs 政治观点; 政治信仰: *What are your politics?* 你的政见如何? (**c**) [sing *v*] (*derog* 贬) rivalry between political parties 政党之间的斗争: *They're not concerned with welfare: it's all politics!* 他们并非关心福利问题, 完全是党同伐异. **2** [sing *v*] = POLITICAL SCIENCE (POLITICAL): *She's reading politics at university.* 她在大学里攻读政治学. **3** [sing *v*] (*derog* 贬) manoeuvring for power or advantage within a group or organization 权术; 勾心斗角: *office politics* 公务上的争权夺利 ○ *church politics* 教会的明争暗斗.

pol·ity /'pɒlətɪ; 'pɑlətɪ/ *n* (*fml* 文) **1** [U] form or process of government 政权形式; 政体. **2** [C] society as an organized state 国家组织; 政府.

polka /'pɒlkə; *US* 'pəʊlkə; 'polkə/ *n* (piece of music for a) lively dance of E European origin 波尔卡舞(源自东欧的一种轻快舞蹈); 波尔卡舞曲.

□ **'polka dots** regular pattern of large dots on cloth (布料上的)圆点图案: [attrib 作定语] *a polka-dot scarf* 有圆点图案的围巾. ⇨illus at PATTERN 见 PATTERN 插图.

poll[1] /pəʊl; pol/ *n* **1** (**a**) [C usu *sing* 通常作单数] voting at an election; counting of votes 选举投票; 计票: *be successful at the poll* 选举投票中获胜 ○ *The result of the poll has now been declared.* 选举结果已经公布. (**b**) [sing] number of votes cast (投的)票数: *head the poll*, ie have the largest number of votes 得票最多 ○ *a light/heavy poll*, ie voting by a small or large proportion of those entitled to vote 低[高]投票率. (**c**) **the polls** [pl] place where people vote 投票处: *The country is going to the polls* (ie is voting in an election) *tomorrow.* 明天将在全国进行选举投票. **2** [C] survey of public opinion by putting questions to a representative selection of people 民意测验: *a public opinion poll* 民意测验 ○ *the Gallup poll* 盖洛普民意测验 ○ *We're conducting a poll among school leavers.* 我们正在对中学毕业生进行民意调查.

□ **'poll-tax** *n* tax levied at the same rate on every (or every adult) person in the community 人头税.

poll[2] /pəʊl; pol/ *v* [Tn] **1** (of a candidate at an election) receive (a certain number of votes) (指候选人)获得(一定数量的选票): *Mr Hill polled over 3 000 votes.* 希尔先生获得了3 000多张选票. **2** ask (sb) his or her opinion as part of a public-opinion poll (在民意测验中)调查(某人); 对(某人)作民意调查: *Of those polled, seven out of ten said they preferred brown bread.* 那些被调查者十人中有七人说他们比较爱吃黑面包. **3** (**a**) cut off the top of the horns of (cattle) 截去(牛)的角的顶端. (**b**) = POLLARD *v*.

▷ **polling** *n* [U] (**a**) voting 投票: *heavy polling*, ie in large numbers 高的投票率. (**b**) conducting of public-opinion polls 进行民意测验. **'polling-booth, 'polling-station** *ns* place where people go to vote in an election 投票站. **'polling-day** *n* day appointed for an election 投票日.

pol·lard /'pɒləd; 'pɑlɚd/ (also **poll**) *v* [Tn esp passive 尤用于被动语态] cut off the top of (a tree) so that many new thin branches will grow, forming a dense head of leaves 截去(树)的梢(以便长出繁茂的枝叶形成树冠): *The willows need to be pollarded.* 这些柳树需截去树梢.

▷ **pol·lard** *n* pollarded tree 截去了梢的树.

pol·len /'pɒlən; 'pɑlən/ *n* [U] fine (usu yellow) powder formed in flowers, which fertilizes other flowers when carried to them by the wind, insects, etc 花粉.

□ **'pollen count** number indicating the amount of pollen in the atmosphere, used as a guide to possible attacks of hay fever, etc 花粉计数(指示空气中的花粉数量, 供预测枯草热等病症之参考).

pol·lin·ate /'pɒləneɪt; 'pɑlə,net/ *v* [Tn] make (sth) fertile with pollen 给(某物)传授花粉. ▷ **pol·lina·tion** /,pɒlə'neɪʃn; ,pɑlə'neʃən/ *n* [U].

poll·ster /'pəʊlstə(r); 'polstɚ/ *n* (*infml* 口) person who conducts public-opinion polls 民意测验者; 民意调查者.

pol·lute /pə'lu:t; pə'lut/ *v* [Tn, Tn·pr] **~ sth (with sth)** **1** make sth dirty or impure, esp by adding harmful or unpleasant substances 污染或弄脏某物或使某物含有杂质(尤指因搀入有害的或不好的物质): *rivers polluted with chemical waste from factories* 受到工厂排放的化学废料污染的河流 ○ *polluted water*, ie unfit to drink 污染的水(不宜饮用). **2** (*fig* 比喻) destroy the purity or sanctity of sth; corrupt 玷污或亵渎某事物; 败坏: *pollute the minds of the young with foul propaganda* 宣传不良事物腐蚀青年人的思想.

▷ **pol·lut·ant** /-ənt; -ənt/ *n* substance that pollutes, eg exhaust fumes from motor vehicles 污染物质(如机动车辆排出的废气): *releasing pollutants into the atmosphere* 将污染物质排放到空气里.

pol·lu·tion /pə'lu:ʃn; pə'luʃən/ *n* [U] (**a**) polluting or being polluted 污染; 弄脏; 玷污; 亵渎; 败坏: *the pollution of our beaches with oil* 石油对我们海滩的污染. (**b**) substance that pollutes 污染物质.

polo /'pəʊləʊ; 'polo/ *n* [U] game in which players on horseback try to hit the ball into a goal using long-handled hammers 马球(体育运动, 骑马用长柄槌将球击入球门).

□ **'polo neck** (style of) high round turned-over collar 圆高翻领; 圆高翻领式样: [attrib 作定语] *a ,polo-neck 'sweater* 套头高翻领毛衣. ⇨illus at NECK 见 NECK 插图.

pol·on·aise /,pɒlə'neɪz; ,pɑlə'nez/ *n* (piece of music for a) slow dance of Polish origin 波洛内兹舞(源出波兰的慢步舞); 波洛内兹舞曲.

pol·ter·geist /'pɒltəgaɪst; 'poltɚ,gaɪst/ *n* type of ghost that makes loud noises, throws objects about, etc (弄出噪声、乱扔东西等的)鬼.

poly /'pɒlɪ; 'pɑlɪ/ *n* (*pl* **~s**) (*infml* 口) = POLYTECHNIC.

poly- *comb form* 构词成分 many 多: *polygamy* ○ *polyphony* ○ *polysyllable* ○ *polygamous* ○ *polyphonic* ○ *polysyllabic*.

poly·andry /'pɒlɪændrɪ; 'pɑlɪ,ændrɪ/ *n* [U] custom of having more than one husband at the same time 一妻多夫(制).

▷ **poly·and·rous** /,pɒlɪ'ændrəs; ,pɑlɪ'ændrəs/ *adj* **1** of or practising polyandry 一妻多夫的; 实行一妻多夫制的. **2** (*botany* 植) (of plants) having many stamens (指植物)多雄蕊的.

poly·anthus /,pɒlɪ'ænθəs; ,pɑlɪ'ænθəs/ *n* [U, C] garden plant of the primrose family, with several (usu multi-coloured) flowers on one stalk 西洋樱草; 多花水仙.

poly·es·ter /,pɒlɪ'estə(r); *US* 'pɒli:estər; ,pɑlɪ'ɛstɚ/ *n*

[U, C] artificial fabric used for making clothes, etc 聚酯纤维: [attrib 作定语] *a polyester shirt* 聚酯纤维衬衫.

poly·ethyl·ene /ˌpɒlɪˈeθəliːn; ˌpɑlɪˈɛθəˌlin/ *n* [U] (*US*) = POLYTHENE.

poly·gamy /pəˈlɪɡəmɪ; pəˈlɪɡəmɪ/ *n* [U] custom of having more than one wife at the same time 一夫多妻(制). Cf 参看 MONOGAMY.

▷ **poly·gam·ist** /-ɡəmɪst; -ɡəmɪst/ man who practices this 多配偶的男子.

poly·gam·ous /pəˈlɪɡəməs; pəˈlɪɡəməs/ *adj* of or practising polygamy 一夫多妻的; 实行一夫多妻制的.

poly·glot /ˈpɒlɪɡlɒt; ˈpɑlɪˌɡlɑt/ *adj* (*fml* 文) knowing, using or written in many languages 通晓或使用多种语言的; 以多种语言写成的: *a polyglot edition* 多语种对照的版本.

P

▷ **poly·glot** *n* person who speaks many languages 操多种语言的人.

poly·gon /ˈpɒlɪɡən; *US* -ɡɒn; ˈpɑlɪˌɡɑn/ *n* (*geometry* 几) figure with many (usu five or more) straight sides 多边形, 多角形(通常指至少有五个直边). ▷ **poly·gonal** /pəˈlɪɡənl; pəˈlɪɡənḷ/ *adj*.

poly·hed·ron /ˌpɒlɪˈhiːdrən; ˌpɑlɪˈhidrən/ *n* (*pl* **~s** or **-hedra** /-ˈhiːdrə; -ˈhidrə/) solid figure with many (usu seven or more) faces 多面体(通常指至少有七面).

poly·math /ˈpɒlɪmæθ; ˈpɑləˌmæθ/ *n* (*fml approv* 文, 褒) person who knows a great deal about many different subjects 博学之士.

poly·mer /ˈpɒlɪmə(r); ˈpɑlɪmɚ/ *n* (*chemistry* 化) natural or artificial compound made up of large molecules which are themselves made from combinations of small simple molecules 聚合物; 聚合体.

poly·morph·ous /ˌpɒlɪˈmɔːfəs; ˌpɑlɪˈmɔrfəs/, **poly·morphic** /-fɪk; -fɪk/ *adjs* (*fml* 文) having or passing through many stages (of development, growth, etc) (在发展或成长中)有多种形式或形态的.

polyp /ˈpɒlɪp; ˈpɑlɪp/ *n* **1** (*biology* 生) very simple form of animal (eg a sea anemone) found in water 水螅体(如海葵): *Coral is formed by certain types of polyp.* 珊瑚是由某些水螅体构成的. **2** (*medical* 医) any of several kinds of tumour (eg in the nose) 息肉(如鼻腔中的). ▷ **polypous** /-pəs; -pəs/ *adj*.

poly·phony /pəˈlɪfənɪ; pəˈlɪfənɪ/ *n* [U] combination of several different melodic patterns to form a single piece of music; counterpoint 复音音乐; 对位法. ▷ **poly·phonic** /ˌpɒlɪˈfɒnɪk; ˌpɑlɪˈfɑnɪk/ *adj*.

poly·sty·rene /ˌpɒlɪˈstaɪriːn; ˌpɑlɪˈstaɪrin/ *n* [U] type of light firm plastic with good insulating properties, used esp for making containers 聚苯乙烯: [attrib 作定语] *a polystyrene box* 聚苯乙烯塑料盒.

poly·syl·lable /ˈpɒlɪsɪləbl; ˈpɑləˌsɪləbl/ *n* word of several (usu more than three) syllables 多音节词(通常指多于三个音节者). ▷ **poly·syl·labic** /ˌpɒlɪsɪˈlæbɪk; ˌpɑləsɪˈlæbɪk/ *adj*.

poly·tech·nic /ˌpɒlɪˈteknɪk; ˌpɑləˈtɛknɪk/ (also *infml* 口语作 **poly**) *n* (esp in Britain) college for advanced full-time and part-time education, esp in scientific and technical subjects (尤指英国的)理工学院: [attrib 作定语] *polytechnic courses, students* 理工学院的课程、学生.

poly·the·ism /ˈpɒlɪθiːɪzəm; ˈpɑləθiˌɪzəm/ *n* [U] belief in or worship of more than one god 多神信仰; 多神论; 多神崇拜. Cf 参看 MONOTHEISM. ▷ **poly·the·istic** /ˌpɒlɪθiːˈɪstɪk; ˌpɑləθiˈɪstɪk/ *adj*.

poly·thene /ˈpɒlɪθiːn; ˈpɑləθin/ *n* [U] type of plastic widely used in the form of flexible, often transparent, sheets for waterproof packaging, insulation, etc 聚乙烯: [attrib 作定语] *a polythene bag, cover* 聚乙烯塑料袋、套.

poly·un·sat·ur·ated /ˌpɒlɪʌnˈsætʃəreɪtɪd; ˌpɑlɪʌnˈsætʃəˌretɪd/ *adj* (of many vegetable and some animal fats) having a chemical structure which does not help the harmful formation of cholesterol in the blood (指许多植物脂肪和一些动物脂肪)含有多重不饱和化合物的: *Polyunsaturated margarine is very popular now.* 含有多重不饱和化合物的人造黄油现已很受欢迎. Cf 参看 SATURATED 2.

poly·ureth·ane /ˌpɒlɪˈjʊərɪθeɪn; ˌpɑlɪˈjʊrəˌθen/ *n* [U] type of plastic used in making paints 聚氨酯(用以制造油漆): [attrib 作定语] *polyurethane gloss*, ie paint that dries with a hard shiny surface 聚氨酯亮光漆.

pom /pɒm; pɑm/ *n* (*infml* 口) **1** = POMMY. **2** = POMERANIAN.

po·man·der /pəˈmændə(r); poˈmændɚ/ *n* (round container for a) ball of mixed sweet-smelling substances (eg flowers, leaves, spices, etc) used to perfume cupboards, rooms, etc 香丸(混有香味物质, 如花、叶、香料等, 用以使橱柜、房间等生香); 盛香丸的圆形容器; 香盒.

pom·egran·ate /ˈpɒmɪɡrænɪt; ˈpɑmˌɡrænɪt/ *n* (tree with a) thick-skinned round fruit which, when ripe, has a reddish centre full of large juicy seeds 石榴(树): [attrib 作定语] *pomegranate juice, seeds* 石榴汁、子.

Pom·er·anian /ˌpɒməˈreɪnɪən; ˌpɑməˈrenɪən/ (also *infml* 口语作 **pom**) *n* type of small long-haired dog 波美拉尼亚狗(一种长毛小狗).

pom·mel /ˈpɒml; ˈpɑmḷ/ *n* **1** rounded part of a saddle which sticks up at the front (马鞍的)前桥(鞍前向上突起的圆形部分); 鞍头. **2** rounded knob on the handle of a sword (剑柄上的)圆球. ▷ **pom·mel** /ˈpʌml; ˈpʌmḷ/ *v* (**-ll-**; *US* **-l-**) [Tn] = PUMMEL.

pommy /ˈpɒmɪ; ˈpɑmɪ/ *n* (*Austral or NZ infml usu derog* 澳或新西兰, 口, 通常作贬义) (also **pom**) British person 英国人.

pomp /pɒmp; pɑmp/ *n* [U] **1** (**a**) splendid display or magnificence, esp at a public event 宏伟壮观的景象(尤指群众场面); 盛况: *the pomp and ceremony of the State Opening of Parliament* 国会揭幕的盛况. (**b**) (*derog* 贬) such display seen as trivial and meaningless 不必要和无意义的铺张和排场; 虚荣; 浮华: *forsaking worldly pomp for the life of a monk* 摒弃世间的浮华而出家. **2** (idm 习语) **pomp and circumstance** magnificent and/or ceremonious display and procedure 盛大的和[或]隆重的场面和仪式.

pom-pom /ˈpɒmpɒm; ˈpɑmpɑm/ *n* small woollen ball used for decoration, eg on a hat, on the border of a piece of fabric, etc (装饰性的)绒球(如帽子上、织物边缘等处的).

pom·pous /ˈpɒmpəs; ˈpɑmpəs/ *adj* (*derog* 贬) feeling, or showing that one feels, that one is much more important than other people 自大的; 自负的; 浮夸的: *a pompous official* 自命不凡的官员 ○ *pompous language*, ie full of high-sounding words 浮夸的语言.

▷ **pom·pos·ity** /pɒmˈpɒsətɪ; pɑmˈpɑsətɪ/ *n* (**a**) [U] being pompous 自大; 自负; 浮夸. (**b**) [C] instance of this 自大; 自负; 浮夸.

pom·pously *adv*.

ponce /pɒns; pɑns/ *n* (*Brit*) **1** man who lives with a prostitute and lives on her earnings 与妓女同居并靠其养活的男子. **2** (*infml derog* 口, 贬) man who acts in a showy, esp effeminate, way 爱炫耀的男子; (尤指)女人气的男子.

▷ **ponce** *v* (phr v) **ponce about/around** (*Brit infml derog* 口, 贬) (**a**) act in a showy, esp effeminate, way 炫耀; (尤指)表现女子气. (**b**) act or behave in an ineffective or time-wasting way 游手好闲: *Stop poncing about and get that job finished.* 别闲逛了, 把那活儿干完了吧.

pon·cho /ˈpɒntʃəʊ; ˈpɑntʃo/ *n* (*pl* **~s**) type of cloak made from a large piece of cloth with a slit in the middle for the head (大块布料正中开领口的)斗篷.

pond /pɒnd; pɑnd/ *n* small area of still water, esp one used or made as a drinking place for cattle or as an ornamental garden pool 池塘(尤指供牲畜饮水或作为花园之装饰者): *a fish pond* 养鱼池 ○ [attrib 作定语] *pond life*, ie animals living in a pond 在池塘中生活的动物.

pon·der /ˈpɒndə(r); ˈpɑndɚ/ *v* [I, Ipr, Tn, Tw] **~ (on/over sth)** think about (sth) carefully and for a long time, esp in trying to reach a decision; consider (长时间地仔细)考虑(某事物)(尤指以便作出决定); 深思: *You have pondered long enough; it is time to decide.* 你考虑的时间够长的了, 该作决定了. ○ *I pondered (over) the incident, asking myself again and again how it could have happened.* 我反复思考那件事, 一再自问究竟是怎么回事. ○ *pondering on the meaning of life* 深深地思索人生的意义 ○ *I am pondering how to respond.* 我在琢磨该怎样回答.

pon·der·ous /ˈpɒndərəs; ˈpɑndərəs/ *adj* **1** slow and awkward because of great weight 笨重的: *a fat man's ponderous movements* 胖男人的笨拙动作. **2** (*derog* 贬)

(of speech, written style, etc) without vigour or inspiration; dull; laboured (指讲话、文章风格等)沉闷的, 乏味的, 艰涩的. ▷ **pon·der·ously** *adv*. **pon·der·ous·ness** *n* [U].

pone /pəʊn; pon/ *n* [U] = CORN PONE (CORN[1]).

pong /pɒŋ; pɔŋ/ *n* (*Brit infml often joc* 口, 常作戏谑语) strong, usu unpleasant, smell 强烈的(通常为难闻的)气味: *What a horrible pong!* 臭死了!

▷ **pong** *v* [I] smell strongly and usu unpleasantly 发出强烈的、通常为难闻的气味.

pongy /ˈpɒŋɪ; ˈpɔŋɪ/ *adj* (**-ier**, **-iest**): *Your feet are rather pongy!* 你的脚真臭!

pon·tiff /ˈpɒntɪf; ˈpɑntɪf/ *n* **1** (*arch* 古) bishop; chief priest; high priest 主教; 大祭司. **2 the (Supreme) Pontiff** the Pope 教皇; 教宗.

pon·ti·fical /pɒnˈtɪfɪkl; pɑnˈtɪfɪkḷ/ *adj* **1** (**a**) of the Pope 教皇的; 教宗的. (**b**) [usu attrib 通常作定语] celebrated by a bishop, cardinal, etc 由主教、红衣主教等主持的: *pontifical high mass* 由主教、红衣主教等主持的大弥撒. **2** (*derog* 贬) tending to pontificate; opinionated 独断专行的; 固执武断的.

pon·ti·fic·ate /pɒnˈtɪfɪkət; pɑnˈtɪfɪkɪt/ *n* office of a pontiff, esp of the Pope; period of this 主教或大祭司的职位或任期; (尤指)教皇的职位或任期.

▷ **pon·ti·fic·ate** /-keɪt; -ket/ *v* [I, Ipr] **~ (about/on sth)** (*derog* 贬) speak as if one were the only person who knew the facts or had the right opinions about sth 武断地或自封为权威地谈论某事物: *He sat there pontificating about the legal system although it was clear that he knew very little about it.* 他坐在那儿发表他对法制的高论, 虽然他对此一窍不通.

pon·toon[1] /pɒnˈtu:n; pɑnˈtun/ *n* any of a number of flat-bottomed boats or hollow metal structures joined together to support a temporary roadway over a river, an estuary, etc (作浮桥用的)平底船或金属空筒; 趸船: [attrib 作定语] *a pontoon bridge* 浮桥.

pon·toon[2] /pɒnˈtu:n; pɑnˈtun/ *n* (also **twenty-one**, **vingt-et-un**) (*Brit*) (*US* **ˈblackjack**) (**a**) card-game in which players try to acquire cards with a face value totalling 21 二十一点牌戏. (**b**) (in this game) score of 21 from two cards (二十一点牌戏中)两张牌的点数之和为21点.

pony /ˈpəʊnɪ; ˈponɪ/ *n* **1** small type of horse 一种矮马; 小型马. **2** (*dated Brit sl* 旧, 俚) £25 25英镑. **3** (idm 习语) **on Shanks's pony/mare** ⇨ SHANK.

□ **ˈpony-tail** *n* woman's or girl's long hair drawn back and tied at the back of the head so that it hangs like a horse's tail (女子的)马尾发型. ⇨illus at PLAIT 见PLAIT 插图.

ˈpony-trekking *n* [U] making a journey for pleasure by riding on ponies 骑小型马出游.

poodle /ˈpu:dl; ˈpudḷ/ *n* type of small dog with thick curling hair which is often cut into an elaborate pattern 鬈毛小狗(其毛常经修剪). ⇨illus at App 1 见附录1插图, page iii.

poof /pʊf; puf/ (*pl* **~s** or **pooves** /pu:vz; puvz/) *n* (also **poof·ter** /ˈpʊftə(r); ˈpuftɚ/) (*Brit sl derog* 俚, 贬) (**a**) effeminate man 女人气的男子. (**b**) male homosexual 男同性恋者.

pooh /pu:; pu/ *interj* (**a**) (used to express impatience or contempt 用以表示不耐烦或轻蔑): *Pooh! What nonsense!* 呸! 胡说! (**b**) (used to express disgust at a bad smell 用以对难闻的气味表示厌恶): *Pooh! This meat is rotten.* 嗳呀! 这肉臭啦.

pooh-pooh /ˌpu:ˈpu:; ˈpuˈpu/ *v* [Tn] (*infml* 口) treat (an idea, a suggestion, etc) with contempt; dismiss scornfully 蔑视(主意、建议等); 藐视: *They pooh-poohed our scheme for raising money.* 他们对我们的筹款方案嗤之以鼻.

pool[1] /pu:l; pul/ *n* **1** small area of still water, esp one that has formed naturally 水池, 水塘, 水坑(尤指自然形成者): *After the rainstorm, there were pools on the roads.* 暴雨过后路上有许多水洼儿. **2** shallow patch of water or other liquid lying on a surface 一滩水或其他液体: *The body was lying in a pool of blood.* 尸体躺在血泊中. **3** place in a river where the water is deep and there is not much current 河中水深甚少流动之处. **4** = SWIMMING-POOL (SWIM).

pool[2] /pu:l; pul/ *n* **1** [C] common fund of money, esp the stakes of all the players in a gambling game (集中在一起的)款额; 共同储金; (尤指)各赌博者的合计赌金. **2** [C] (**a**) common supply of funds, goods or services which are available to a group of people to be used when needed 集中使用的资金、物资、服务等: *a pool of cars used by the firm's salesmen* 公司推销人员共用的一些汽车 ○ [attrib 作定语] *a pool car* 公用汽车. (**b**) group of people available for work when required 可招之即来的一些人: *a pool of doctors available for emergency work* 为应付紧急情况而待命的一些医生 ○ *a* ˈ*typing pool*, ie a pool of typists 提供联合服务的打字人员. **3** [C] arrangement by a number of business firms to agree on prices and share profits, in order to avoid competition 联营(公司之间为避免竞争而在价格和利润上订立协议的措施). **4** [U] (*esp US*) game played with (usu) 16 coloured balls on a billiard-table, similar to snooker 普尔弹子戏(类似落袋台球的游戏, 通常用16个彩色球). **5 the pools** [pl] = FOOTBALL POOLS (FOOTBALL): *do the pools every week* 每星期都赌足球普尔 ○ *have a win on the pools* 赢得足球普尔彩金. **6** (idm 习语) **shoot pool** ⇨ SHOOT[1].

▷ **pool** *v* [Tn] put (money, resources, etc) into a common fund 向共同基金提供(金钱、资源等): *They pooled their savings and bought a house in the country.* 他们用积蓄的钱合资在乡间买了一所房子. ○ (*fig* 比喻) *If we pool our ideas, we may find a solution.* 我们集思广益就能找到解决办法.

□ **ˈpoolroom** *n* (*US*) place where pool[2](4) is played 普尔弹子球室.

poop /pu:p; pup/ *n* (**a**) stern of a ship 船尾. (**b**) (also **ˈpoop deck**) raised deck at the stern of a ship 船尾楼甲板.

pooped /pu:pt; pupt/ *adj* [pred 作表语] (also **ˌpooped ˈout**) (*infml* 口 *esp US*) very tired; exhausted 很累; 筋疲力尽.

poor /pɔ:(r); *US* pʊər; pur/ *adj* (**-er**, **-est**) **1** having very little money with which to buy one's basic needs 贫穷的; 贫困的: *She was too poor to buy clothes for her children.* 她穷得没钱给孩子买衣服. ○ *He came from a poor family.* 他出身于穷苦人家. ○ *the poorer countries of the world* 世界上的贫穷国家. **2** [pred 作表语] **~ in sth** having sth only in very small quantities; deficient in sth 缺乏某物; 某方面不足: *a country poor in minerals* 缺乏矿产的国家 ○ *soil poor in nutrients* 缺少养分的土壤. **3** (**a**) not good; inadequate, esp in contrast with what is usual or expected 不好的, 不充分的, 不足的(尤与一般的或所期望的情况相比): *We had a poor crop of raspberries this year.* 今年我们的悬钩子歉收. ○ *They received a poor return on their investment.* 他们的投资获利甚微. ○ *Attendance at the concert was very poor.* 那次音乐会的上座率极低. ○ *the party's poor performance in the election* 该党在选举中的拙劣表现. (**b**) of low quality; deficient 劣质的; 不足的: *poor food, light, soil* 劣质食品、微弱的光线、贫瘠的土壤 ○ *a poor diet* 粗劣的日常饮食 ○ *be in poor health* 健康欠佳 ○ *Her remarks were in very poor taste.* 她的话真没意思. (**c**) inferior; insignificant 差的; 无关紧要的: *Watching the event on television was a poor substitute for actually being there.* 从电视上观看那个比赛比现场观看可差远了. ○ *Getting third prize was poor consolation for all their hard work.* 他们那么努力才获得三等奖, 真有点说不过去. ○ *She came a poor second*, ie a long way behind the winner. 她得了个第二名, 成绩很差(远远落在第一名的后面). (**d**) (of a person) not good or skilled at sth (指人)在某方面不好的, 对某事物不熟练的: *a poor judge of character* 对品性判断不准 ○ *a poor loser*, ie one who shows anger at losing in games or sport 输不起的人(输了就生气的人) ○ *a poor sailor*, ie sb who gets sea-sick easily 容易晕船的人. **4** (*esp infml* 尤作口语) deserving pity or sympathy; unfortunate 值得怜悯或同情的; 可怜的; 不幸的: *The poor little puppy had been abandoned.* 那可怜的小狗被人遗弃了. ○ *Poor chap, his wife has just died.* 不幸的小伙子啊, 他刚刚死了妻子. ○ *'I've been feeling ill for two weeks.' 'Poor you!'* '两周以来我身体一直不好.' '真叫人同情!' **5** (**a**) (*derog* 贬) deserving contempt 可鄙的: *What a poor creature he is!* 他真卑鄙! ○ *his poor attempts to be witty* 他那卑劣的取巧行为. (**b**) (*esp joc or ironic* 尤作戏谑语或反语) humble 谦恭的: *in my poor opinion* 依本人拙见. **6** (idm 习语) **the poor**

man's sb/sth person or thing that is an inferior or a cheaper alternative to a well-known person, institution, food, etc 降而求其次的人或事物: *Sparkling white wine is the poor man's champagne.* 白葡萄汽酒算是廉价的香槟. **a poor relation** person or thing with less power, prestige or respect than others of the same type 较同类逊色的人或事物: *Some people may regard radio as the poor relation of broadcasting.* 有些人可能认为无线电广播在广播事业中稍逊一筹.

▷ **the poor** *n* [pl *v*] **1** people with little money or possessions 穷人: *raising money for the poor and needy* 为穷苦人筹款. **2** (idm 习语) **grind the faces of the poor** ⇨ GRIND.

□ ˈ**poor-box** *n* (esp formerly) box placed in a church, in which people may put gifts of money for the poor (尤指旧时)(教堂中募集济贫款的)慈善箱.

ˈ**Poor Law** (*Brit*) (formerly) group of laws concerned with giving help and care to poor people (旧时)济贫法.

ˌ**poor-ˈspirited** *adj* lacking courage; timid 缺乏勇气的; 胆小的.

ˌ**poor ˈwhite** (*usu derog or offensive* 通常作贬义或作轻蔑语) (esp in Southern US) member of a class of poor white-skinned people in a mainly Black community (尤指美国南方以黑人为主的社区中的)贫苦白人.

poorly /ˈpɔːlɪ; *US* ˈpʊərlɪ; ˋpʊrlɪ/ *adv* **1** in a poor(3) manner; badly 很糟地; 不充分地; 不足地: *poorly dressed* 穿得不好的 ○ *The street is poorly lit.* 街上灯光暗淡. ○ *She was poorly prepared for the examination.* 她考试准备得不充分. **2** (idm 习语) **poorly ˈoff** (*infml* 口) having very little money 贫困的; 没钱的: *The widow and children are very poorly off.* 那寡妇和孩子们一贫如洗.

▷ **poorly** *adj* [esp pred 尤作表语] (*infml* 口) not well; ill 健康欠佳; 不舒服: *The child has been poorly all week.* 那孩子整个星期都病病歪歪的. ○ *You look rather poorly to me.* 我看你好像不大舒服. ⇨Usage at SICK 用法见 SICK.

poor·ness /ˈpɔːnɪs; *US* ˈpʊərnɪs; ˋpʊrnɪs/ *n* [U] lack of a desirable quality or element; state of being poor(2) 贫乏; 不足: *the poorness of the soil* 土壤的瘠薄. Cf 参看 POVERTY.

pop[1] /pɒp; pɑp/ *n* **1** [C] short sharp explosive sound 短促清脆的爆破声: *The cork came out of the bottle with a loud pop.* 瓶塞砰的一声拔出来了. **2** [U] (*infml* 口) (esp non-alcoholic) fizzy drink (尤指不含酒精的)起泡饮料; 汽水: *a bottle of pop* 一瓶汽水. **3** (idm 习语) **in pop**; *US* **in hock** (*sl* 俚) in pawn 已典当; 在当铺里.

▷ **pop** *adv* with a pop 砰的一声: *It came out pop.* 那东西砰的一声就出来了. ○ *go pop*, ie make a pop 发出短促清脆的爆破声.

pop[2] /pɒp; pɑp/ *n* (*infml* 口) (used esp as a term of address 尤用作呼唤语) (**a**) father 爸爸. Cf 参看 PAPA, POPPA. (**b**) any older man 老大爷; 老伯伯.

pop[3] /pɒp; pɑp/ *n* [U, C usu *pl* 作不可数名词或可数名词, 后者通常作复数] (*infml* 口) modern popular style, esp in music 现代流行风格(尤指音乐的): *pop music, culture* 流行音乐、普及文化 ○ *a pop singer, song, concert* 流行歌曲歌手、流行歌曲、流行歌曲音乐会 ○ *top of the pops*, ie the most popular current recordings 最受欢迎的流行音乐录音. Cf 参看 CLASSICAL 2.

□ ˈ**pop art** style of art developed in the 1960's, based on popular culture and the mass media, using material such as advertisements, comic strips, etc 波普艺术(20 世纪60年代的一种艺术风格, 以大众文化和大众传播媒介, 如以广告、连环漫画等为基础发展而成).

ˈ**pop festival** large (usu outdoor) gathering of people to hear performances by pop musicians, sometimes lasting several days 流行音乐会演(通常为在室外举行的大型活动, 由流行音乐家表演节目, 有时持续多日).

ˈ**pop group** band and singer(s) who play pop music 表演流行音乐的乐队和歌手.

pop[4] /pɒp; pɑp/ *v* (**-pp-**) **1** [I, Ip] make a short sharp explosive sound (as when a cork comes out of a bottle) 发出短促清脆的爆破声(如拔瓶塞的声音): *Champagne corks were popping (away) throughout the celebrations.* 庆祝会上开香槟酒瓶塞的砰砰声不绝于耳. **2** [Tn] cause (sth) to burst with such a sound 使(某物)破裂, 发出短促清脆的声音: *The children were popping balloons.* 孩子们把汽球弄得劈啪作响. **3** [Tn] (*US*) dry (corn) until it bursts open and puffs up 爆(玉米): *pop maize* 爆玉米花. **4** [Ip] ~ **away/off (at sth)** (*infml* 口) fire a gun (at sth) (向某物)开枪: *They were popping away at the rabbits all afternoon.* 他们一下午都在用枪打兔子. **5** [Tn] (*dated Brit infml* 旧, 口) pawn (sth) 典当(某物). **6** (idm 习语) **pop the ˈquestion** (*infml* 口) make a proposal of marriage 求婚. **7** (phr v) **pop across, down, out etc** come or go quickly or suddenly in the direction specified (迅速或突然)来, 去: *He's just popped down the road to the shops.* 他刚才急匆匆地沿这条路去商店了. ○ *She's popped over to see her mother.* 她赶着去看她的母亲. ○ *He's only popped out for a few minutes.* 他刚出去一会儿. ○ *Where's Tom popped off to?* 汤姆一眨眼上哪里去了? **pop sth across, in, into, etc sth** put or take sth somewhere quickly or suddenly (迅速或突然)将某物放到或带到某处: *pop a letter in the post* 把信一下子投进邮筒 ○ *She popped the tart into the oven.* 她把果馅饼很快地放进烤箱里. ○ *He popped his head round the door to say goodbye.* 他从门口探进头来说了声再见. **pop in** make a brief visit 作短暂的访问; 来或去一会儿: *She often pops in for coffee.* 她常来喝杯咖啡. **pop sth in** deliver sth as one is passing 顺便带交某物: *I'll pop the books in on my way home.* 我要在回家时顺路把这些书送到. **pop off** (*infml* 口) die 死: *She said she had no intention of popping off for some time yet.* 她说她还想多活几天. **pop out (of sth)** come out suddenly 突然出来: *The rabbits popped out as soon as we opened the hutch.* 我们一打开兔箱, 兔子就突然跑出来了. ○ (*fig* 比喻) *His eyes nearly popped out of his head when he saw what he had won.* 他一看到自己赢得的东西, 顿时两眼瞪得大大的. **pop up** (*infml* 口) appear or occur, esp when not expected 出现, 发生(尤指出乎意料): *He seems to pop up in the most unlikely places.* 在他似乎绝不可能到的地方, 他往往就在那里出现.

□ ˈ**popcorn** /ˈpɒpkɔːn; ˋpɑpˌkɔrn/ *n* [U] maize that has been heated so that it bursts and forms fluffy balls (热爆的)玉米花.

ˈ**pop-eyed** *adj* (**a**) having naturally bulging eyes 眼球突出的. (**b**) with eyes wide open with surprise (因惊讶)睁大眼睛的: *She was pop-eyed with amazement.* 她惊奇得瞪着眼发愣.

ˈ**popgun** /ˈpɒpgʌn; ˋpɑpˌgʌn/ *n* child's toy gun that shoots a cork with a popping sound 玩具木塞气枪.

ˈ**pop-up** *adj* **1** (of the pages of a book) rising into a 3-dimensional form as the book is opened (指书页)打开书本时呈立体状的. **2** [attrib 作定语] (of an automatic toaster) that operates by causing the toast to move quickly upwards when it is ready (指自动的面包片加热器)面包片加热后自动弹起的.

pop *abbr* 缩写 = population: *pop 12m*, ie 12 million 人口1200万.

pope /pəʊp; pop/ *n* head of the Roman Catholic Church who is also the Bishop of Rome (天主教的)教皇, 教宗: *the election of a new pope* 新教皇的选举 ○ *Pope John Paul* 约翰·保罗教皇(亦译若望·保禄教宗).

▷ **popery** /ˈpəʊpərɪ; ˋpopərɪ/ *n* [U] (*derog* 贬) (**a**) Roman Catholicism 天主教. (**b**) papal system 教皇制度.

pop·ish /ˈpəʊpɪʃ; ˋpopɪʃ/ *adj* (*derog* 贬) (**a**) of or relating to Roman Catholicism 天主教的; 与天主教有关的: *popish forms of worship* 天主教的崇拜仪式. (**b**) of or relating to the papal system 教皇制度的; 与教皇制度有关的.

□ **pope's ˈnose** (*US infml* 口) = PARSON'S NOSE (PARSON).

pop·in·jay /ˈpɒpɪndʒeɪ; ˋpɑpɪnˌdʒe/ *n* (*dated derog* 旧, 贬) conceited person, esp a man who is vain about his clothes; fop 骄矜的人; (尤指)衣着上追求虚荣的人; 花花公子; 纨绔子弟.

pop·lar /ˈpɒplə(r); ˋpɑplɚ/ *n* (**a**) [C] any of several types of tall straight slender tree 杨树. ⇨illus at App 1 见附录1插图, page i. (**b**) [U] its soft wood 杨木.

pop·lin /ˈpɒplɪn; ˋpɑplɪn/ *n* [U] **1** type of shiny (usu) cotton cloth used esp for making skirts 府绸. **2** (formerly) type of cloth with a ribbed surface, made from silk and wool (旧时)毛葛(丝与羊毛合织的一种起棱的布料).

pop·over /ˈpɒpəʊvə(r); ˋpɑpˌovɚ/ *n* (*US*) cake in the form of a thin hollow shell made of batter 酥脆饼(由面糊烤成的一种空心薄松饼).

poppa /ˈpɒpə; ˋpɑpə/ *n* (*US infml* 口) (used esp as

a term of address 尤用作呼唤语) father 爸爸. Cf 参看 PAPA, POP[2].

pop·per /ˈpɒpə(r); ˋpɑpɚ/ *n* (*Brit infml* 口) = PRESS-STUD (PRESS[2]).

pop·pet /ˈpɒpɪt; ˋpɑpɪt/ *n* (*Brit infml* 口) (**a**) (used esp as an affectionate name for a child 尤用作对小孩的昵称) darling 宝宝; 宝贝儿: *How's my little poppet today?* 我的小乖乖今天好吗? ○ *Don't cry, poppet.* 宝宝, 别哭了. (**b**) small and dainty person 可爱的人儿: *Isn't she a poppet?* 她多可爱呀!

poppy /ˈpɒpɪ; ˋpɑpɪ/ *n* any of several types of wild or cultivated plant with showy (esp bright red) flowers, milky juice and small black seeds 罂粟: *the* ˈ*opium poppy*, ie the type from which opium is obtained 可制取鸦片的罂粟 ○ [attrib 作定语] *poppy fields* 罂粟田. ⇨ illus at App 1 见附录1插图, page ii.

pop·py·cock /ˈpɒpɪkɒk; ˋpɑpɪˌkɑk/ *n* [U] (*infml* 口) nonsense 胡扯; 废话: *He dismissed the official explanation as complete poppycock.* 他认为官方的解释是一派胡言, 不值一顾.

Pop·sicle /ˈpɒpsɪkl; ˋpɑpsɪkḷ/ *n* (*US propr* 专利名) = ICE LOLLY (ICE).

pop·ulace /ˈpɒpjʊləs; ˋpɑpjələs/ (usu 通常作 **the populace**) *n* [Gp] (*fml* 文) the general public; ordinary people 民众; 平民; 百姓; 人民大众: *He had the support of large sections of the populace.* 他获得大多数民众的支持. ○ *The populace at large is/are opposed to sudden change.* 人民群众普遍反对突然实行的变革.

pop·ular /ˈpɒpjʊlə(r); ˋpɑpjəlɚ/ *adj* **1** (**a**) liked, admired or enjoyed by many people 为众人所喜爱、赞赏或欢迎的; 流行的: *a popular politician* 深孚众望的政治家 ○ *Jeans are popular among the young.* 牛仔裤年轻人很喜爱. ○ *Jogging is a popular form of exercise.* 慢跑是一种十分普及的体育活动. (**b**) **~ with sb** liked, admired or enjoyed by sb 某人所喜爱、赞赏或欢迎的: *measures popular with the electorate* 受选民欢迎的措施 ○ (*infml* 口) *I'm not very popular with the boss* (ie He is annoyed with me) *at the moment.* 我现在不称老板的心. **2** [attrib 作定语] (*sometimes derog* 有时作贬义) suited to the taste or the education level of the general public 适应大众口味或教育水平的; 普及的; 通俗的; 庸俗的: *popular music* 流行音乐 ○ *the popular press* 通俗报刊 ○ *novels with popular appeal* 适合大众口味的小说 ○ *popular* (ie simplified) *science* 大众科学 ○ *popular* (ie low) *prices* 廉价. **3** [attrib 作定语] of or by the people 人民的; 依靠人民的: *the popular vote* 人民的投票 ○ *issues of popular concern* 人民群众关心的问题 ○ *by popular demand* 根据人民群众的要求. **4** [attrib 作定语] (of beliefs, etc) held by a large number of people (指信念等)广大民众所持有的: *a popular myth, superstition, misconception, etc* 民众的神话、迷信、错误观念等.

▷ **popu·larly** *adv* by many or most people (人们)普遍地, 广泛地; 由大多数人: *a popularly held belief* 一般人所持的看法 ○ *It is popularly believed that* ... 人们普遍认为... ○ *the European Economic Community, popularly known as the Common Market* 欧洲经济共同体, 即众所周知的共同市场.

□ ˌ**popular** ˈ**front** political party representing left-wing groups 人民阵线(代表左翼团体的政党).

popu·lar·ity /ˌpɒpjʊˈlærətɪ; ˌpɑpjəˋlærətɪ/ *n* [U] quality or state of being liked or admired by many people 受大家喜爱或赞赏的性质或状态; 普及; 流行; 通俗性; 声望: *win/gain/enjoy/command the popularity of the voters* 获得广大选民的拥戴 ○ *His popularity among working people remains as strong as ever.* 他在劳动人民中一如既往声望很高. ○ *Her books have grown in popularity recently.* 她的书近来大受欢迎.

pop·ular·ize, -ise /ˈpɒpjʊləraɪz; ˋpɑpjələˌraɪz/ *v* [Tn] **1** make (sth) generally liked 使(某事物)受大家欢迎. **2** make (sth) known or available to the general public, esp by presenting it in an easily understandable form 使(某事物)众所周知或普及(尤指以通俗易懂形式): *popularize new theories in medicine* 普及医学新理论 ○ *popularize the use of personal computers* 推广个人计算机的使用. ▷ **pop·ular·iza·tion, -isation** /ˌpɒpjʊləraɪˈzeɪʃn; *US* -rɪˈz-; ˌpɑpjələrɪˋzeʃən/ *n* [U].

popu·late /ˈpɒpjʊleɪt; ˋpɑpjəˌlet/ *v* [Tn esp passive 尤用于被动语态] (**a**) live in (an area) and form its population 居住于(某地区)(而构成其人口成分): *deserts populated by nomadic tribesmen* 游牧部落居住的沙漠地区 ○ *densely/thickly/sparsely/thinly populated regions* 人口密度大[稠密/密度小/稀疏]的地区. (**b**) move to (an area) and fill it with people 落户于, 移居于(某地区); 向(某地区)移民: *The islands were gradually populated by settlers from Europe.* 岛上逐渐迁入很多欧洲移民.

popu·la·tion /ˌpɒpjʊˈleɪʃn; ˌpɑpjəˋleʃən/ *n* **1** [CGp] (**a**) people who live in an area, a city, a country, etc (地区、城市、国家等的)全体居民: *the populations of Western European countries* 西欧各国的全体人民 ○ *The government did not have the support of the population.* 政府不得人心. (**b**) particular group or type of people or animals inhabiting an area, etc (聚居于某地区的)一群或一类的人或动物: *the working population* 全体劳动者 ○ *the immigrant population* 全体移民. (**c**) total number of these 人口; 区域内动物的总数: *What is the population of Ireland?* 爱尔兰人口有多少? ○ *a city with a population of over 10 million* 人口超过1 000万的城市. **2** [U] degree to which an area has been populated 人口密度; 动物聚居的密度: *areas of dense/sparse population* 人口稠密[稀疏]的地区.

□ **popuˌlation exˈplosion** sudden increase in population resulting from an increased birth-rate and/or a reduced death-rate 人口爆炸(由于出生率上升和[或]死亡率下降而引起的人口急剧增加).

popu·lism /ˈpɒpjʊlɪzəm; ˋpɑpjəlɪzṃ/ *n* [U] type of politics that claims to represent the interests of ordinary people 平民主义, 平民论(声言代表民众利益的政治主张).

▷ **popu·list** /-ɪst; -ɪst/ *n* supporter or representative of populism 平民主义者; 平民论者. — *adj*: *populist theories* 平民主义的理论.

popu·lous /ˈpɒpjʊləs; ˋpɑpjələs/ *adj* having a large population; densely populated 人口多的; 人口稠密的: *the populous areas near the coast* 沿海人口稠密的地区.

por·cel·ain /ˈpɔːsəlɪn; ˋpɔrsḷɪn/ *n* [U] (**a**) hard white translucent material made from china clay, used for making cups, plates, ornaments, etc 瓷: [attrib 作定语] *a porcelain figure* 瓷像. (**b**) objects made of this 瓷器: *a valuable collection of antique porcelain* 一批珍贵的古代瓷器收藏品.

porch /pɔːtʃ; pɔrtʃ/ *n* **1** covered entrance to a building, esp a church or house 门廊(尤指教堂或房子的). ⇨ illus at App 1 见附录1插图, pages vi, viii. **2** (*US*) = VERANDA.

por·cine /ˈpɔːsaɪn; ˋpɔrsaɪn/ *adj* (*fml* 文) of or like a pig (似)猪的: *her rather porcine features* 她那有点像猪的面貌.

por·cu·pine /ˈpɔːkjʊpaɪn; ˋpɔrkjəˌpaɪn/ *n* animal related to the squirrel, with a body and tail covered with long spines which it can stick out to protect itself when attacked 豪猪; 箭猪.

pore[1] /pɔː(r); pɔr/ *n* any of the tiny openings in the surface of the skin or of a leaf, through which moisture can pass (皮肤上的)毛孔; (叶子上的)气孔: *He was sweating at every pore.* 他汗流浃背.

pore[2] /pɔː(r); pɔr/ *v* (phr v) **pore over sth** study sth by looking at it or thinking about it very carefully 钻研(某事物); 审察; 审视: *She was poring over an old map of the area.* 她正在仔细查阅该地区的旧地图. ○ *The child spends hours poring over her books.* 那孩子用了几个小时仔细阅读她的那些书.

pork /pɔːk; pɔrk/ *n* [U] (usu fresh, not salted or cured) flesh of a pig eaten as food (通常指未加盐或未加工处理的新鲜的)猪肉; 鲜猪肉: *roast pork* 烤猪肉 ○ *a leg of pork* 猪腿肉 ○ [attrib 作定语] *pork sausages* 猪肉香肠. Cf 参看 BACON, GAMMON, HAM 1.

▷ **porker** *n* pig raised for food, esp a young pig fattened for killing 食用猪; (尤指育肥待宰的)小猪.

□ **pork-barrel** *n* (*US sl* 俚) government money spent on local projects in order to win votes 政府为争取选票而花费在地方项目上的款项.

ˈ**pork-butcher** *n* (*Brit*) butcher who sells pork, ham, bacon and food made from pork, eg sausages, pies, etc 出售猪肉制品的商人; 猪肉商.

ˌ**pork** ˈ**pie** pie made of pastry filled with minced pork, often eaten cold 猪肉馅饼(常冷吃). ˌ**pork-pie** ˈ**hat** hat with a flat top and a brim turned up all round 平顶卷边

圆帽.

porn /pɔːn; pɔrn/ *n* [U] (*infml* 口) = PORNOGRAPHY.

porno /ˈpɔːnəʊ; ˋpɔrno/ *adj* (*infml* 口) = PORNOGRAPHIC (PORNOGRAPHY).

por·no·graphy /pɔːˈnɒɡrəfɪ; pɔrˋnɑɡrəfɪ/ *n* [U] (**a**) describing or showing sexual acts in order to cause sexual excitement 色情描绘; 色情表演. (**b**) books, films, etc that do this 色情作品(书刊、影片等): *the trade in pornography* 色情作品的交易.

▷ **por·no·grapher** /pɔːˈnɒɡrəfə(r); pɔrˋnɑɡrəfɚ/ *n* person who produces or sells pornography 制作或贩卖色情作品的人.

por·no·graphic /ˌpɔːnəˈɡræfɪk; ˌpɔrnəˋɡræfɪk/ *adj* of or relating to pornography 色情的; 诲淫的: *pornographic films, magazines, subjects* 色情电影、刊物、题材. **por·no·graph·ic·ally** /-klɪ; -klɪ/ *adv*.

P

por·ous /ˈpɔːrəs; ˋpɔrəs/ *adj* **1** allowing liquid or air to pass through, esp slowly 能使液体或气体(尤指缓慢地)穿透的; 能渗透的: *He added sand to the soil to make it more porous.* 他往土里搀沙子以提高渗水性能. ○ *In hot weather clothes made of a porous material like cotton are best.* 热天穿棉布之类有渗透性的材料做的衣服最为适宜. Cf 参看 PERMEABLE (PERMEATE). **2** containing pores 有毛孔或气孔的.

▷ **por·ous·ness**, **por·os·ity** /pɔːˈrɒsətɪ; pɔˋrɑsətɪ/ *ns* [U] quality or state of being porous 渗透性.

por·phyry /ˈpɔːfɪrɪ; ˋpɔrfərɪ/ *n* [U] type of hard red rock which contains red and white crystals, and may be polished and made into ornaments 斑岩(色红、坚硬, 可制装饰品).

por·poise /ˈpɔːpəs; ˋpɔrpəs/ *n* sea mammal with a blunt rounded snout, similar to a dolphin or small whale 鼠海豚.

por·ridge /ˈpɒrɪdʒ; *US* ˈpɔːr-; ˋpɔrɪdʒ/ *n* **1** [U] soft food made by boiling a cereal (esp crushed oats) in water or milk (谷类加水或牛奶煮成的)粥; (尤指)麦片粥: *a bowl of porridge with milk and sugar for breakfast* 早餐吃的一碗甜奶粥. **2** (idm 习语) **do porridge** (*Brit sl* 俚) be in prison; serve a prison sentence 坐牢; 服刑.

port[1] /pɔːt; pɔrt/ *n* **1** [C, U] place where ships load and unload cargo or shelter from storms; harbour 港; 港口: *a naval/fishing port* 军[渔]港 ○ *The ship spent four days in port.* 该船在港口里停泊了四天. ○ *They reached port at last.* 他们终于抵港了. **2** [C] town or city with a harbour, esp one where ships load and unload cargo and where customs officers are stationed 港口城市(尤指船只装卸货物并设有关卡者); 港市; 口岸: *Rotterdam is a major port.* 鹿特丹是个重要的港口城市. ○ [attrib 作定语] *the port authorities* 港务局. **3** (esp in compounds 尤用以构成复合词) any place where goods or people enter or leave a country 货物或人员出入境的任何场所: *an airport* 飞机场 ○ *a port of entry* 进口港. **4** (idm 习语) **any port in a ˈstorm** (*saying esp ironic* 谚, 尤作反语) in times of trouble or difficulty one takes whatever help is available 危难之时任何解救方法均可一试; 慌不择路.

□ ˌ**port of ˈcall** **1** place where a ship stops during a voyage (途中)停靠港. **2** (*infml* 口) place where a person goes or stops, esp during a journey 前往或停留之处, 落脚处(尤指旅途中): *The visiting politician's first port of call was the new factory.* 那位政界人士到访, 第一个地点是那座新工厂.

port[2] /pɔːt; pɔrt/ *n* (*nautical* 海) **1** opening in the side of a ship where people may enter or for loading and unloading cargo (船的)舱门, 上下货口. **2** = PORTHOLE.

port[3] /pɔːt; pɔrt/ *n* [U] the side of a ship or aircraft that is on the left when one is facing forward (船或飞行器的)左舷: *put the helm to port* 把舵转向左舷 ○ *The ship was leaning over to port.* 船正向左舷倾斜. ○ [attrib 作定语] *the port side* 左舷 ○ *a port tack*, ie a course sailed with the wind blowing on the port side 左舷抢风航行. Cf 参看 STARBOARD.

port[4] /pɔːt; pɔrt/ *n* (**a**) [U] strong sweet (usu dark-red) wine made in Portugal 波尔图葡萄酒(产自葡萄牙, 性醇, 通常为深红色). (**b**) [C] glass of this 一杯波尔图葡萄酒.

port·able /ˈpɔːtəbl; ˋpɔrtəbl̩/ *adj* that can be (easily) carried; not fixed permanently in place 便携式的; 手提式的; 轻便的: *a portable radio, television set, typewriter, etc* 便携式收音机、电视机、打字机等.

▷ **port·ab·il·ity** /ˌpɔːtəˈbɪlətɪ; ˌpɔrtəˋbɪlətɪ/ *n* [U]: *I bought it for its portability, not its appearance.* 我是图其轻便才买的, 并不是因为样子好看.

port·able *n* that can be (easily) carried; not permanently in place 便携式物品; 轻便物品: *The document had been typed on a small portable.* 这份文件是用便携式打字机打的.

port·age /ˈpɔːtɪdʒ; ˋpɔrtɪdʒ/ *n* **1** [U] (cost of) carrying goods; carriage 搬运(费); 运输. **2** (*esp US*) (**a**) [U] carrying boats or goods overland between two rivers, lakes, etc, eg on a canoeing trip (两水路间的)陆运(将小船或货物从一水域经陆地运至另一水域之作业, 如乘小划子途中所需的). (**b**) [C] place where this is done (两水路间的)陆运区间.

portal /ˈpɔːtl; ˋpɔrtl̩/ *n* (often *pl* 常作复数) (*fml* 文) doorway or gateway, esp a grand and imposing one 门; 入口; (尤指)壮观的大门: *temple portals of carved stone* 寺院的石雕大门.

□ **portal ˈvein** (*anatomy* 解) vein carrying blood to the liver or to any organ other than the heart 门静脉.

port·cul·lis /ˌpɔːtˈkʌlɪs; pɔrtˋkʌlɪs/ *n* (formerly) strong heavy iron grating raised or lowered at the entrance to a castle (旧时)(城堡入口可升降的)铁闸门, 吊闸. ⇨illus at CASTLE 见 CASTLE 插图.

por·tend /pɔːˈtend; pɔrˋtɛnd/ *v* [Tn] (*fml* 文) be a sign or warning of (sth in the future); foreshadow 预示; 预兆; 预告: *His silence portends trouble.* 他沉默不语可不是好兆头.

por·tent /ˈpɔːtent; ˋpɔrtɛnt/ *n* **~ (of sth)** (*fml* 文) sign or warning of a future (often unpleasant) event; omen 预示; 预兆; (常指)凶兆: *portents of disaster* 凶兆 ○ *I see it as a portent of things to come.* 我把它看作是将要到来的事物的前兆.

▷ **por·tent·ous** /pɔːˈtentəs; pɔrˋtɛntəs/ *adj* **1** of or like a portent; ominous (似)预示的, 预兆的; 不祥的: *portentous events, signs* 不祥的事件、征兆. **2** (*derog* 贬) pompously solemn 装腔作势的; 煞有介事的. **por·tent·ously** *adv*: *'No good will come of this,' she announced portentously.* '这绝好不了,'她煞有介事地说.

porter[1] /ˈpɔːtə(r); ˋpɔrtɚ/ *n* **1** person whose job is carrying people's luggage and other loads, eg in railway stations, airports, hotels, markets, etc 搬运工, 脚夫(如于车站、机场、旅馆、市场等处的): *a hospital porter* 医院中任搬运工作的勤杂工. **2** (*US*) attendant in a sleeping-car or parlour-car on a train (铁路之卧车或特等客车上的)列车员, 服务员.

▷ **port·er·age** /ˈpɔːtərɪdʒ; ˋpɔrtərɪdʒ/ *n* [U] (**a**) carrying of luggage or goods by a porter (行李或其他物品的)搬运, 搬运工作. (**b**) cost of this 搬运费.

porter[2] /ˈpɔːtə(r); ˋpɔrtɚ/ *n* (*Brit*) (*US* **doorman**) person whose job is to be on duty at the entrance to a hotel, large building, etc (旅馆、大建筑物等的)门卫, 门房, 守门人: *The hotel porter will call a taxi for you.* 旅馆的门卫可以给你叫计程车.

□ **porter's ˈlodge** (*Brit*) **1** room at the entrance to a large building, esp a university college (大建筑物的)门房, 传达室(尤指大学之学院的). **2** house at the gates of an estate 庄园入口处的房子.

porter[3] /ˈpɔːtə(r); ˋpɔrtɚ/ *n* [U] (esp formerly) type of dark-brown bitter beer (尤指旧时的)黑啤酒.

port·er·house steak /ˌpɔːtəhaʊs ˈsteɪk; ˌpɔrtɚˌhaʊs ˋstek/ piece of top-quality beefsteak cut for grilling, etc (供炙烤等的)上等牛排.

port·fo·lio /pɔːtˈfəʊlɪəʊ; pɔrtˋfolɪˌo/ *n* (*pl* **~s**) **1** flat case (often made of leather) for carrying loose papers, documents, drawings, etc 公事包, 文件夹(常为皮制的). **2** set of investments (eg stocks and shares) owned by a person, bank, etc (个人、银行等所有的)投资组合(如债券和股票): *My stockbroker manages my portfolio for me.* 我的证券经纪人替我管理投资组合. ○ [attrib 作定语] *portfolio management* 投资组合管理. **3** position and duties of a minister of State 大臣或部长的职位或职责: *She resigned her portfolio.* 她辞去了大臣职务. ○ *Minister without portfolio*, ie (in Britain) a Cabinet Minister without responsibility for a particular department (英国)不管部大臣(有职无责者).

port·hole /ˈpɔːthəʊl; ˋpɔrtˌhol/ (also **port**) *n* window-like structure in the side of a ship or an aircraft (船或飞行器的)舷窗.

por·tico /ˈpɔːtɪkəʊ; ˋpɔrtɪ,ko/ *n* (*pl* **~es** or **~s**) roof supported by columns, esp one forming an entrance to a large building 柱廊; (尤指高大建筑物的)有柱的门廊.

por·tion /ˈpɔːʃn; ˋpɔrʃən/ *n* **1** [C] part or share into which sth is divided 部分; (分事物时的)一份: *He divided up his property and gave a portion to each of his children.* 他把财产分给子女, 每人一份. ○ *You give this portion of the ticket to the inspector and keep the other.* 把票的这一部分交给检票员, 另一部分自己留着. ○ (*dated* 旧) *a marriage portion*, ie a dowry 嫁妆. **2** [C] amount of food suitable for or served to one person (食物的)一份, 一客: *a generous portion of roast duck* 一大份烤鸭 ○ *She cut the pie into six portions.* 她把馅饼切成六份. ○ *Do you serve children's* (ie smaller) *portions?* 你们供应儿童量(小份)的餐食吗? **3** [sing] (*fml* 文) person's fate or destiny (人的)命运: *It seemed that suffering was to be his portion in life.* 他好像命中注定了要受苦受难似的.

▷ **por·tion** *v* (phr v) **portion sth out (among/between sb)** divide sth into shares (SHARE[1] 1) to give to several people 把某事物按份儿分给(若干人): *She portioned out the money equally between both children.* 她把钱均分给两个孩子. ○ *The work was portioned out fairly.* 工作分配得很公平. Cf 参看 APPORTION.

Port·land ce·ment /ˌpɔːtlənd sɪˈment; ˋpɔrtlənd səˋmɛnt/ type of cement made from chalk and clay similar in colour to Portland stone 普通水泥; 波特兰水泥.

Port·land stone /ˌpɔːtlənd ˈstəʊn; ˋpɔrtlənd ston/ type of yellowish-white limestone used for building 波特兰石(一种白中发黄的石灰石, 用于建筑).

portly /ˈpɔːtlɪ; ˋpɔrtlɪ/ *adj* (**-ier, -iest**) (esp of an older person) having a stout body; fat (尤指年长者)发福的, 胖的: *a portly old gentleman* 胖胖的老绅士 ○ *portly members of the city council* 体形丰满的市议员们. ▷ **portli·ness** *n* [U].

port·man·teau /pɔːtˈmæntəʊ; pɔrtˋmænto/ *n* (*pl* **~s** or **-teaux** /-təʊz; -toz/) (*dated* 旧) large oblong (usu leather) case for clothes that opens on a hinge into two equal parts 旅行衣箱(通常为皮制, 以合叶联接相同的两部分).

□ **portmanteau ˈword** (also **blend**) invented word that combines parts of two words and their meanings eg *motel* from *motor* and *hotel* or *brunch* from *breakfast* and *lunch* 紧缩词, 合并词(将两个词的词素合并构成一个新词, 如motel为motor和hotel的紧缩词, brunch为breakfast和lunch的紧缩词).

por·trait /ˈpɔːtreɪt, *also* -trɪt; ˋpɔrtret, -trɪt/ *n* **1** painted picture, drawing or photograph of (esp the face of) a person or an animal (人或动物的)画像, 照片; (尤指面部的)肖像: *paint sb's portrait* 给某人画像 ○ *She had her portrait painted.* 她让人给自己画了像. ⇨illus at CARICATURE 见CARICATURE插图. Cf 参看 LANDSCAPE. **2** description in words 文字描绘; 描写: *The book contains a fascinating portrait of life at the court of Henry VIII.* 该书生动地描写了亨利八世的宫廷生活.

▷ **ˈpor·trait·ist** /-ɪst; -ɪst/ *n* person who makes portraits 肖像画家; 画像者; 人像摄影师: *a skilled portraitist* 擅长画像的人.

ˈpor·trait·ure /-tʃə(r); *US* -tʃʊər; -tʃur/ *n* [U] (art of making) portraits (PORTRAIT 1) (人或动物的)画像, 照片; 画像或人像摄影的技法.

□ **ˈportrait painter** person who paints portraits; portraitist 画像者; 肖像画家.

por·tray /pɔːˈtreɪ; pɔrˋtre/ *v* [Tn, Cn·n/a] **~ sb (as sb/sth)** **1** make a picture of sb 为某人画像; 画某人的像: *She is portrayed wearing her coronation robes.* 给她画的是她穿着加冕礼服的像. ○ *a picture of the general portraying him as a Greek hero* 把这位将军画成希腊英雄的一幅画. **2** describe sb/sth in words 描述或描写某人[某事物]: *The diary portrays his family as quarrelsome and malicious.* 日记中描述了他家反宅乱的事. **3** act the part of sb or represent sth in a play, etc (在戏剧等中)扮演某人或表现某事物: *She frowned and stamped her feet to portray anger*, eg in a mime. 她又皱眉头又跺脚表示生气(如在哑剧中).

▷ **por·trayal** /pɔːˈtreɪəl; pɔrˋtreəl/ *n* **1** [U] action of portraying 画像; 描述; 描写; 扮演. **2** [C] description or representation 描摹; 表现: *a skilful portrayal of a lonely and embittered old man* 对一个孤苦伶仃的老人惟妙惟肖的描绘.

pose /pəʊz; poz/ *v* **1** (**a**) [I, Ipr] **~ (for sb)** sit or stand in a particular position in order to be painted, drawn or photographed 摆好姿势(以便画像或拍照): *He had to pose wearing a laurel wreath.* 他得摆好戴着月桂花冠的姿势. ○ *The artist asked her to pose for him.* 那位画家要求她摆好姿势以便为她画像. (**b**) [Tn] put (sb) in a particular position in order to paint, draw or photograph him 使(某人)摆好姿势(以便画像或拍照): *The artist posed his model carefully.* 那位画家仔细摆好模特儿的姿势. ○ *The subjects are well posed in these photographs.* 这些照片中的人物姿势都挺好. **2** [I] (*derog* 贬) behave in an unnatural or affected way in order to impress people 装腔作势: *Stop posing and tell us what you really think.* 别装蒜啦, 告诉我们你的真实想法吧. **3** [Ipr] **~ as sb/sth** claim or pretend to be sb/sth 自称或装成某人[某事物]: *She poses as an expert in old coins.* 她自诩为古钱币专家. ○ *The detective posed as a mourner at the victim's funeral.* 那侦探佯装成吊唁者参加了受害人的葬礼. **4** [Tn] cause (sth) to arise; create or present (followed esp by the *ns* shown) 引起(某事物); 造成, 提出(尤接下列名词): *Winter poses particular difficulties for the elderly.* 冬天给上年纪的人带来特殊的困难. ○ *Heavy traffic poses a problem in many old towns.* 交通拥挤是许多旧城镇的难题. ○ *His resignation poses the question of whether we now need a deputy leader.* 他一辞职引出了一个问题, 即我们目前是否需要有人代理领导职务.

▷ **pose** *n* **1** position in which a person poses or is posed (POSE 1b) (为画像或拍照而摆的)姿势, 姿态: *a relaxed pose for the camera* 为拍照摆成的自然的姿势 ○ *She adopted an elegant pose.* 她摆了一个优美的姿势. **2** (*derog* 贬) unnatural or affected way of behaving, intended to impress people 装腔作势的举动: *His concern for the poor is only a pose.* 他对穷人的关心只不过是做做样子罢了. **3** (idm 习语) **strike an attitude/a pose** ⇨ STRIKE[2].

poser *n* **1** (*infml* 口) awkward or difficult question or problem 棘手的或困难的问题: *That's quite a poser!* 那事真伤脑筋! **2** =POSEUR.

pos·eur /pəʊˈzɜː(r); poˋzɝ/ *n* (*fem* 阴性作 **pos·euse** /pəʊˈzɜːz; poˋzɝz/) (also **poser**) (*derog* 贬) person who behaves in an unnatural affected way in order to impress others 装腔作势的人: *Some people admired him greatly while others considered him a poseur.* 有的人对他佩服得五体投地, 而有的人则认为他装腔作势.

posh /pɒʃ; pɑʃ/ *adj* (**-er, -est**) (*infml* 口) (**a**) elegant or luxurious; smart 精美的; 豪华的; 漂亮的: *a posh car, hotel* 豪华的轿车、旅馆 ○ *a posh wedding* 隆重的婚礼 ○ *You look very posh in your new suit.* 你穿上新衣服漂亮极了. (**b**) (*sometimes derog* 有时作贬义) upper-class 上等阶层的: *a posh accent* 上等人的腔调 ○ *They live in the posh part of town.* 他们住在高等住宅区.

posit /ˈpɒzɪt; ˋpɑzɪt/ *v* [Tn] (*fml* 文) suggest or assume (sth) as a fact; postulate 断定或假定(某事物)为实; 假设.

po·si·tion /pəˈzɪʃn; pəˋzɪʃən/ *n* **1** [C] place where sb/sth is 位置; 方位: *From his position on the cliff top, he had a good view of the harbour.* 他位于悬崖顶上, 海湾看得清清楚楚. ○ *fix a ship's position*, ie by observing the sun or stars 确定船只的方位(藉观察太阳或星体) ○ *We were sitting in a draughty position near the door.* 我们坐在门边有穿堂风经过的地方. ○ *The troops stormed the enemy position*, ie where the enemy had placed soldiers and guns. 部队向敌人的阵地发起了猛攻. **2** [U] state of being advantageously placed (eg in a competition or a war) 有利的状况(如竞争中或战争中的): *Several candidates had been manoeuvring for position long before the leadership became vacant.* 领导职位尚未空缺, 几个竞争者早就在为向上爬而钩心斗角了. **3** [C, U] way in which sb/sth is placed or arranged; attitude or posture 某人[某物]所处的或被安置的方式; 姿态; 姿势: *sit/lie in a comfortable position* 舒舒服服地坐[躺]着 ○ *in an upright, a horizontal, etc position* 以垂直、水平等方式 ○ *They had to stand for hours without changing position.* 他们得一动不动地站几个小时. **4** [C] **~ (on sth)** view or opinion held by sb 看法; 观点: *The candidates had to state their position on unilateral disarmament.* 候选人须

表明他们对单方面裁军所持的立场. ○ *She has made her position very clear.* 她已明确阐述了自己的观点. **5** [C esp *sing* 尤作单数] situation or circumstances, esp when they affect one's power to act 处境, 情势(尤指影响自己的行动能力者): *Their failure to come to a decision put her in an impossible position.* 他们未能做出决定, 这使她进退无门. ○ *He was in the unenviable position of having to choose between imprisonment or exile.* 他已陷于进退维谷的地步, 不是坐牢就是流放, 必须在两者间做出抉择. ○ *What would you do in my position?* 你处在我的地位, 你怎样做呢? ○ *I am not in a position* (ie I am unable) *to help you.* 我没有能力帮助你. ○ *The economic position of the country is disastrous.* 国家的经济形势非常糟糕. **6** (**a**) [C] place or rank in relation to others (相对于他人的)地位, 等级: *a high/low position in society* 高的[低的]社会地位 ○ *'What is his position in class?' 'He's third from the top.'* '他在班上得第几名?' '第三名.' (**b**) [U] high rank or status 高的等级或地位: *people of position* 上层人士 ○ *Wealth and position were not important to her.* 财富和地位她都不放在心上. **7** [C] (*fml* 文) paid employment; job (有报酬的)职位; 工作: *a position in/with a big company* 在一家大公司中的职务 ○ *He applied for the position of assistant manager.* 他申请副经理一职. ○ *She had worked for the firm for twenty years and was in a position of trust.* 她为这家公司工作了二十年, 因而被委以重任. **8** [C] (*sport* 体) (in team games) function and/or part of the playing area assigned to a player (队际竞技活动中)某一队员的职责和[或]位置: *'What position does he play?' 'Centre-forward.'* '他在比赛中在什么位置?' '中锋.' **9** (idm 习语) **in a false position** ⇨ FALSE. **in/into position** in/into the right or proper place 在[进入]适当的位置; 在位; 就位; 到位: *The orchestra were all in position, waiting for the conductor.* 管弦乐队队员都已各就各位, 等待着指挥. ○ *The runners got into position on the starting line.* 赛跑运动员已进入起跑线上的位置. **out of poˈsition** not at the right place 不在适当的位置上: *The chairs are all out of position.* 椅子全都放得不是地方.

▷ **po·si·tion** *v* [Tn] **1** place (sth) in (a certain) position 将(某物)放在(某一)位置上: *position the aerial for the best reception* 把天线安装在接收效果最好的位置上 ○ *She positioned herself near the warm fire.* 她待在温暖的炉子的旁边. **2** find or mark the position of (sth); locate 找出或标出(某物)的位置; 定位: *They were able to position the yacht by means of radar.* 他们能够用雷达测定快艇的方位.

po·si·tional /-ʃənl; -ʃənəl/ *adj.*

pos·it·ive /ˈpɒzətɪv; ˋpɑzətɪv/ *adj* **1** with no possibility of doubt; clear and definite 无可怀疑的; 明确的; 确定的: *positive instructions, orders, rules, etc* 明确的指示、命令、规定等 ○ *We have no positive proof of her guilt.* 我们没有她犯罪的确切证据. **2** ~ (**about sth/that...**) (of a person) confidently holding an opinion; convinced (指人)有把握的, 确信的: *Are you absolutely positive that it was after midnight?* 你是否有绝对把握认为那事是在午夜以后发生的? ○ *She was quite positive about the amount of money involved.* 她对所涉及的钱数十分肯定. **3** (**a**) providing help; constructive 有助益的; 建设性的: *make positive proposals, suggestions, etc* 提出有益的建议、意见等 ○ *Try to be more positive in dealing with the problem.* 对解决该问题再积极一些. (**b**) showing confidence and optimism 自信的; 乐观的: *a positive attitude, feeling, etc* 乐观的态度、情绪等 ○ *positive thinking*, ie a determined mental attitude that helps one achieve success 必胜的思想. **4** (*infml* 口) absolute; complete 彻底的; 绝对的; 完全的: *Her behaviour was a positive outrage.* 她的行为残暴到了极点. ○ *It was a positive miracle that we arrived on time.* 我们能够及时赶到, 这简直是奇迹. **5** (of the results of a test or an experiment) indicating that a substance is present (指试验或实验的结果)表明存在某物质的, 阳性的: *a positive reaction* 阳性反应 ○ *The tests proved positive.* 试验结果呈阳性. ○ *They were hoping for a positive result from the experiment.* 他们希望从实验中获得阳性结果. **6** (*mathematics* 数) (of a quantity) greater than zero (指数量)正的: *a positive number* 正数 ○ *the positive sign* (+) 正号. **7** tending towards increase or improvement 倾向于增加或改善的: *Positive progress has been achieved during the negotiations.* 谈判取得了良好的进展. ○ *There have been positive developments in international relations.* 国际关系已逐步改善. ○ *positive discrimination*, ie deliberately favouring an underprivileged group, esp in employment policy 具有积极意义的区别对待(尤指在就业政策中所实施的偏向贫困阶层的做法). **8** containing or producing the type of electrical charge produced by rubbing glass with silk 正电的; 正极的: *a positive charge* 正电荷 ○ *the positive terminal of a battery*, ie the one through which electric current leaves the battery 电池的正极端子. **9** (of a photograph) showing light and shadows as in nature or in the object photographed, not reversed as in a negative (指照片)正片的: *a positive image* 正片影像. Cf 参看 NEGATIVE. **10** (*grammar*) (of an adjective or adverb) in the simple form, not the comparative or superlative (指形容词或副词)原级的(非比较级的或最高级的).

▷ **pos·it·ive** *n* **1** (*grammar*) positive adjective 原级形容词: *'Silly' is the positive and 'sillier' the comparative.* ☆ silly 是原级形容词, sillier 是比较级形容词. **2** positive quality or quantity 确实; 正量; 正数. **3** photograph printed from a negative plate or film (照片的)正片.

pos·it·ively *adv* (**a**) (*infml* 口) extremely; absolutely 极其; 绝对地: *He was positively furious when he saw the mess.* 他看到混乱的情况, 气得不得了. ○ *She was positively bursting to tell us the news.* 她迫不及待地要把那消息告诉我们. (**b**) with complete certainty; firmly 十分肯定地; 坚定地: *She positively assured me that it was true.* 她向我明确地保证那是事实. ○ *Are you positively convinced that he is not coming back?* 你确信他不回来了吗?

pos·it·ive·ness *n* [U].

□ ˌ**positive** ˈ**pole** (**a**) positive terminal of an electric battery; anode (电池的)正极, 阳极. (**b**) north-seeking pole of a magnet (磁体的)北极.

pos·it·iv·ism /ˈpɒzɪtɪvɪzəm; ˋpɑzətɪvˌɪzəm/ *n* [U] system of philosophy based on things that can be seen or proved rather than on speculation 实证主义, 实证论(一种哲学体系, 以可眼见或证明之事物为基础, 忽视理性的作用).

▷ **pos·it·iv·ist** /-vɪst; -vɪst/ *n* person who studies or teaches positivism 实证主义者; 实证论者.

posi·tron /ˈpɒzɪtrɒn; ˋpɑzɪˌtrɑn/ *n* (*physics* 物) minute piece of matter (*elementary particle*) that has a positive electric charge and the same mass as an electron 正电子; 阳电子. Cf 参看 ELECTRON.

posse /ˈpɒsɪ; ˋpɑsɪ/ *n* [CGp] (*esp US*) group of people who can be summoned by an officer of the law, eg a sheriff, to find a criminal, maintain order, etc 地方武装团队(可由执法官员召集以查缉罪犯、维持治安等).

pos·sess /pəˈzes; pəˋzɛs/ *v* **1** [Tn] (**a**) have (sth) as one's belongings; own 领有(某事物); 持有: *He decided to give away everything he possessed and become a monk.* 他决定放弃他所有的一切, 出家为僧. ○ *They possess property all over the world.* 他们在世界各地均拥有财产. ○ *The family possessed documents that proved their right to ownership.* 这家人持有可以证明他们享有所有权的文件. (**b**) have (sth) as a quality 具有(某品质): *Does he possess the necessary patience and tact to do the job well?* 他有做好这项工作必备的耐性和应变能力吗? **2** [Tn esp passive 尤用于被动语态, Cn·t] control or dominate (a person's mind) 控制, 支配(人的思想): *She seemed to be possessed (by the devil).* 她好像着了魔似的. ○ *She was possessed by jealousy.* 她妒火中烧. ○ *He is possessed with the idea that he is being followed.* 他老是觉得有人跟踪他. ○ *What possessed you to do that?* 是什么驱使你做出那种事的? **3** (idm 习语) **be possessed of sth** (*fml* 文) have (a quality) 具有(某品质): *She is possessed of a wonderfully calm temperament.* 她性情非常文静. **like one possessed** violently or with great energy, as if taken over by madness or a supernatural spirit 猛烈地, 拼命地(如同发疯或有妖魔附体一般): *He fought like a man possessed.* 他进行了殊死的战斗.

▷ **pos·sessor** *n* person who possesses sth 所有人; 持有某物的人: *He is at last the proud possessor of a driving-licence.* 他终于获得了驾驶执照, 这使他颇为得意.

pos·ses·sion /pəˈzeʃn; pəˋzɛʃən/ *n* **1** [U] state of possessing; ownership 领有; 持有; 具有: *fight for/win/get possession of the ball* 争球 ○ *The possession of a passport is essential for foreign travel.* 去国外旅行需持有护照. ○

On her father's death, she came into possession of a vast fortune. 她在父亲死后继承了大量财产. ○ *She has valuable information in her possession.* 她掌握了重要的信息. ○ *The house is for sale with vacant possession*, ie without tenants. 空房出售(无租户). **2** [C esp *pl* 尤作复数] thing that is possessed; property 所有物; 财产: *He lost all his possessions in the fire.* 他在火灾中损失了所有的财产. ○ *He came here without friends or possessions and made his fortune.* 他来时举目无亲、身无长物, 全凭白手起家. **3** [C] country controlled or governed by another 属地; 殖民地: *The former colonial possessions are now independent states.* 以前的许多殖民地现已成为独立的国家. **4** (idm 习语) **in possession (of sth)** (**a**) having or controlling (sth) so that others are prevented from using it 占有, 控制(某物)(致使他人无法使用): *Their opponents were in possession of the ball for most of the match.* 他们的对手在比赛的大部分时间里控制着球. (**b**) having or living in sth 占据某物; 住在某处所中: *He was caught in possession of stolen goods/with stolen goods in his possession.* 他人赃并获. ○ *While they are in possession we can't sell the house.* 他们还住着这所房子, 我们无法出售. **possession is nine points of the 'law** (*saying* 谚) a person who occupies or controls sth is in a better position to keep it than sb else whose claim to it may be greater 现实占有, 败一胜九(占有或控制某物者打起官司来总占上风). **take possession (of sth)** (*fml* 文) become the owner or occupier (of sth) 成为(某物的)所有者; 占有(某物).

pos·sess·ive /pə'zesɪv; pə'zɛsɪv/ *adj* **1 ~ (with sth/sb)** (**a**) showing a desire to own things and an unwillingness to share what one owns 显示占有欲的; 不愿与人分享的: *The child was very possessive with his toys.* 那孩子把自己的玩具把得紧紧的. (**b**) treating sb as if one owns him, demanding total attention or love (视某人为己有而欲霸占其全部精力或感情)占有欲强的: *possessive parents* 让子女唯命是从的父母 ○ *She found her boyfriend's possessive behaviour intolerable.* 她忍受不了男朋友控制她感情的行为. **2** (*grammar*) of or showing possession 表示所属关系的; 属有格的: *the possessive case* 属有格 ○ *'Anne's', 'the boy's', 'the boys'' are possessive forms.* Anne's、the boy's、the boys' 都是属有格形式. ○ *'Yours', 'his', etc are possessive pronouns.* ☆ yours、his 等是物主代词.

▷ **pos·sess·ive** *n* (*grammar*) **1** [C] possessive word or form 表示所属关系的词或词语形式: *'Ours' is a possessive.* ours是属有代词. **2 the possessive** [sing] the possessive case 属有格. Cf 参看 GENITIVE.

pos·sess·ively *adv*.

pos·sess·ive·ness *n* [U].

pos·set /'pɒsɪt; 'pɑsɪt/ *n* type of drink made with warm milk and ale or wine with spices, used formerly as a remedy for colds 牛奶酒(热牛奶加麦芽啤酒或葡萄酒以及香料而成之饮料, 旧时用以治感冒).

pos·sib·il·ity /ˌpɒsə'bɪlətɪ; ˌpɑsə'bɪlətɪ/ *n* **1** [U] **~ (of sth/doing sth); ~ (that...)** state of being possible; likelihood 可能; 可能性: *within/beyond the bounds of possibility* 在可能范围之内[之外] ○ *The possibility of breaking the world record never occurred to him.* 他从来没想到有可能打破世界记录. ○ *Is there any possibility that we'll see you this weekend?* 我们本周末能见到你吗? ○ *What is the possibility of the weather improving?* 天气有可能变好吗? **2** [C] event that may happen; prospect 可能的事; 想见中的事: *Changing jobs is one possibility.* 换换工作是有可能的事. ○ *Bankruptcy is a distinct possibility if sales don't improve.* 倘若销售情况得不到改善, 保不住要破产. ○ *She prepared for all possibilities by taking a sunhat, a raincoat and a woolly scarf.* 她带了太阳帽、雨衣和毛围巾, 一切有备无患. **3** [C esp *pl* 尤作复数] capability of being used or improved; potential 可以利用或改善的余地; 潜力: *The house is very dilapidated but it has possibilities.* 这房子已破旧不堪, 但还有可利用的价值. ○ *She saw the possibilities of the scheme from the beginning.* 她从一开始就预见到这计划可能成功.

pos·sible /'pɒsəbl; 'pɑsəbl/ *adj* **1** (**a**) that can be done 可能的; 可能做到的: *It is not humanly possible* (ie A human is not able) *to lift the weight.* 人举不起这样的重量. ○ *Come as quickly as possible*, ie as quickly as you can. 尽快来吧. (**b**) that can exist or happen 可能存在或发生的: *Frost is possible, although unlikely, at this time of year.* 在一年中的这个时候, 下霜也是可能的, 虽然可能性并不大. ○ *Are you insured against all possible risks?* 你对一切可能发生的危险都投保了吗? **2** that is reasonable or acceptable 合理的; 可以认可的: *a possible solution to the dispute*, ie one that may be accepted, although not necessarily the best 行得通的解决争端的办法(但不见得是最好的办法) ○ *There are several possible explanations.* 存在着几种合乎情理的解释.

▷ **pos·sible** *n* person who is suitable for selection, eg for a job or a sports team (工作、运动队等的)适合候选的人: *They interviewed 30 people of whom five were possibles.* 他们对30人进行了面试, 其中有五人符合候选条件. ○ *a Rugby trial between 'probables' and 'possibles'* '预备队员'和'候补队员'之间的橄榄球选拔赛.

pos·sibly /-əblɪ; -əblɪ/ *adv* **1** perhaps 大概; 也许; 或许: *'Will you be leaving next week?' 'Possibly.'* 你打算下周离开吗? '有可能.' ○ *She was possibly the greatest writer of her generation.* 她也许是她那时代最伟大的作家. **2** reasonably; conceivably 合理地; 可以想见地: *I can't possibly lend you so much money.* 我没有可能借给你这么多钱. ○ *I will come as soon as I possibly can.* 我尽可能早来. ○ *You can't possibly take all that luggage with you.* 你绝无可能把所有那些行李都带着.

pos·sum /'pɒsəm; 'pɑsəm/ *n* **1** = OPOSSUM. **2** (idm 习语) **play 'possum** (*infml* 口) pretend to be unaware of sth in order to deceive sb (as a possum pretends to be dead when being attacked) 佯装不知以欺骗人(如负鼠受袭时装死状); 装傻; 装糊涂.

post[1] /pəʊst; post/ *n* **1** [C] (esp in compounds 尤用以构成复合词) piece of metal or wood set upright in the ground to support sth, mark a position, etc (金属或木头的)柱子, 支柱, 桩, 标柱, 标杆: *'gate posts* 门柱 ○ *a 'goal post* 球门柱 ○ *a 'lamp-post*, ie supporting a street light 路灯柱 ○ *a 'signpost* 路标 ○ *'boundary posts*, ie marking a boundary 界桩 ○ *a 'bedpost*, ie any of the upright supports of a bedstead, esp a four-poster 床柱(床架的垂直支柱, 尤指四根的). **2** [sing] place where a race starts or finishes (速度竞赛的)起点或终点标志: *the 'starting/'finishing/'winning post* 起点[终点/获胜]标. **3** (idm 习语) **be left at the post** ⇨ LEAVE[1]. **deaf as a post** ⇨ DEAF. **(be) first past the post** winning in an election because one has received the most votes though not necessarily an absolute majority 以得票最多(但不一定超过半数)在选举中获胜. **from pillar to post** ⇨ PILLAR. **pip sb at the post** ⇨ PIP[5].

▷ **post** *v* **1** (**a**) [Tn, Tn·p] **~ sth (up)** display (a notice, placard, etc) in a public place 公布(告示、招贴等): *Post no bills*, eg warning that advertisements, etc must not be posted on a wall. 禁止招贴. ○ *Advertisements have been posted up everywhere announcing the new show.* 到处贴满了广告宣传这一新节目. (**b**) [esp passive 尤用于被动语态 Tn, Cn·a, Cn·n/a] **~ sb/sth (as sth)** announce sth about sb/sth by means of a poster, list, etc displayed publicly (以张贴招贴、名单等形式)公开宣布某事: *Details of the election will be posted outside the town hall.* 选举的详情将贴在市政厅外. ○ *The ship was posted (as) missing*, ie was announced as missing. 布告称该船失踪. **2** [Tn, Tn·p] **~ sth (over)** cover sth with bills, placards, etc 将告示、招贴等贴在某物上: *post a wall (over) with advertisements* 在墙上张贴广告.

post[2] /pəʊst; post/ *n* **1** position of paid employment; job (有报酬的)职位; 工作: *He was appointed to the post of general manager.* 他获任命为总经理. ○ *She was offered a post in the new government.* 她受聘在新政府中任职. ○ *She had been in the same post for 20 years.* 她担任同一职务已20年. ○ *He asked to be relieved of his post*, ie offered his resignation. 他提出辞职. **2** place where a person is on duty, esp a soldier on watch 岗位; (尤指士兵的)哨位: *The sentries are all at their posts.* 哨兵们都已各就各位. ○ *The guards were ordered not to leave their posts.* 卫兵们奉令不得离开岗位. **3** (**a**) place occupied and defended by soldiers, esp a frontier fort (部队的)驻地, 防区; (尤指)边防要塞. (**b**) soldiers occupying this 驻军. **4** (also **'trading post**) (esp formerly) settlement developed for trading, esp in a region that is undeveloped or sparsely populated (尤指旧时的)贸易站(尤指设于不发达或人口稀少之地区的).

▷ **post** *v* [Tn, Tn·pr] **1 ~ sb (to sth)** appoint sb to a job or a responsibility 派某人做某工作或担负某任务: *post an officer to a unit, the front, overseas* 把一名军官派往某单位、前线、海外 ○ *After several years in London, he was posted to the embassy in Moscow.* 他在伦敦任职几年后被派往驻莫斯科大使馆工作. **2 ~sb (at/on sth)** place (a soldier, etc) at his post²(2) 布置(士兵等)站岗: *We posted sentries (at the gates).* 我们(在大门口)设了岗哨. **posting** /-ɪŋ; -ɪŋ/ *n* (*esp Brit*) appointment to a post²(1), esp an official one 任命, 委派(尤指担任官职): *The ambassador expects that his next posting will be (to) Paris.* 那位大使预期他下次派驻巴黎.

post³ /pəʊst; post/ *n* **1** (also *esp US* **mail**) (**a**) [C, U] letters, parcels, etc; correspondence 信件、包裹等; 邮件: *There was a big post/a lot of post this morning.* 今早邮件很多. ○ *He's dealing with his post at the moment.* 他此刻正在处理信件. (**b**) [U] official transport and delivery of these 邮政; 邮递: *send sth by post* 邮寄某物 ○ *The parcel was damaged in the post.* 包裹在邮寄中损坏了. (**c**) [C] any of the regular collections (esp from a post-box) or deliveries (eg to a house) of letters, etc 信件等的定时收集(尤指自邮筒中)或投递(如入户): *catch/miss* (ie be in time/too late for) *the 2 o'clock post* 赶上[错过]两点钟的邮局收信时间 ○ *The parcel came in this morning's post*, ie by this morning's delivery. 包裹是今早邮来的. (**d**) **the post** [sing] post-box or post office 邮筒; 邮箱; 邮局: *Please take these letters to the post.* 请将这些信件投邮. (**e**) **the Post** [sing] = THE POST OFFICE. **2** [C] (**a**) (formerly) any of a number of men placed at stages along a route in order to ride to the next stage with letters, etc (旧时)驿站之间骑马传送信件等的人. (**b**) (formerly) cart, etc for carrying letters (旧时)运送信件的马车等, 驿车. **3** (idm 习语) **by return post** ⇨ RETURN².

□ ˈ**post-bag** *n* **1** (*US* ˈ**mail-bag**) bag for carrying post 邮袋. **2** (*esp Brit infml* 口) letters received by sb at a particular time 一次收取的信件: *The newspaper received a huge post-bag of complaints.* 报社一次收到了大量的投诉信件.

ˈ**post-box** (*US* ˈ**mailbox**) *n* box where letters are placed for collection 邮筒; 邮箱. Cf 参看 PILLAR-BOX (PILLAR).

ˈ**postcard** *n* card for sending messages by post without an envelope and often with a picture or photograph on one side 明信片. Cf 参看 LETTER-CARD, PICTURE POSTCARD (PICTURE).

ˈ**postcode** (also ˈ**postal code**, *US* ˈ**Zip code**) *n* group of numbers (or letters and numbers) used as part of an address so that letters can by sorted by machine 邮政编码(为一组数字或字母加数字, 用作地址之一部分, 以便机器分拣信件).

ˌ**post-ˈfree** *adv, adj* (**a**) (carried) free of charge by post or with postage already paid (邮件)免付邮资(的), 邮资已付(的): *ˌpost-free deˈlivery* 免费投递 ○ *The book will be delivered post-free.* 该书将免费寄送. (**b**) (of a price) including the charge for postage (指价格)包括邮费在内(的): *a special offer at a post-free price of £5/at £5 post-free* 5英镑免付邮资的特别优惠.

ˈ**postman** /-mən; -mən/ (*US* ˈ**mailman**) (*pl* **-men**) *n* person employed to collect and deliver letters, etc 邮递员; 邮差.

ˈ**postmark** *n* official mark stamped on letters, parcels, etc giving the place and date of posting and cancelling the postage stamps 邮戳: [attrib 作定语] *postmarked Tokyo* 盖了东京邮戳的 ○ *postmarked Friday* 盖了星期五邮戳的.

ˈ**post office** **1** building or room where postal business, eg sale of postage stamps, etc takes place 邮政局(指建筑物). **2 the ˈPost Office** (also **the Post**) public department or corporation responsible for postal services 邮政局(指部门或机构). ˈ**post-office box** (*abbr* 缩写 **PˈO box**) numbered place in a post office where letters are kept until the person or company they are for collects them 邮政信箱.

ˌ**post-ˈpaid** *adj, adv* with postage already paid 邮资已付(的).

ˈ**post-town** *n* town to which the post for a district is delivered (某一地区中)设有邮局的镇.

post⁴ /pəʊst; post/ *v* **1** (also *esp US* **mail**) (**a**) [Tn] put (a letter, etc) into a post-box or take it to a post office 投寄(信件等); 邮寄: *Could you post this letter for me?* 你替我把这封信寄出去行吗? (**b**) [Dn·n, Dn·pr] **~ sth (to sb)** send (a letter, etc) to sb 将(信等)寄给某人: *They will post me the tickets/post the tickets to me as soon as they receive my cheque.* 他们收到我的支票后就立刻把票寄给我. **2** (**a**) [Tn] (in bookkeeping) enter (an item) in a ledger (簿记)将(帐目)登入分类帐: *post export sales* 把出口销售额登入分类帐. (**b**) [Tn·p] **~ sth up** (in bookkeeping) bring (a ledger) up to date by transferring items from a day-book (簿记)把日记帐过入(分类帐): *post up a ledger* 过入分类帐. **3** [Ipr] (formerly) travel by stages, using relays of horses (旧时)骑驿马递送: *post from town to town* 骑驿马到各城镇递送. **4** (idm 习语) **keep sb posted** keep sb informed of the latest developments, news, etc 使某人不断获悉最新发展情况、消息等: *He asked them to keep him posted about the sales of his book.* 他要求他们把他著作的销售情况随时告诉他.

□ ˌ**post-ˈhaste** *adv* with great speed 火速地; 赶紧: *She went post-haste to the bank and cashed the cheque.* 她急忙赶到银行, 把支票兑换成现金.

post- *pref* 前缀 (with *ns*, *vs* and *adjs* 与名词、动词和形容词结合) after 后: *postgraduate* ○ *post-date* ○ *Post-Impressionist*. Cf 参看 ANTE-, PRE-.

post·age /ˈpəʊstɪdʒ; ˈpostɪdʒ/ *n* [U] amount charged or paid for carrying letters, etc by post 邮费; 邮资: *What is the postage on this parcel?* 寄这个包裹要多少钱? ○ *How much is the postage for an airmail letter to Canada?* 寄往加拿大的航空信要多少邮费?

□ ˈ**postage stamp** small stamp²(1) for sticking on letters, parcels, etc, showing the amount paid for postage 邮票.

postal /ˈpəʊstl; ˈpostl̩/ *adj* (**a**) of the post³(1b) 邮政的; 邮务的; 邮递的: *postal charges, workers, districts* 邮费、邮政员工、邮区. (**b**) sent by post³(1b) 邮寄的: *Postal applications must be received by 12 December.* 邮寄的申请书须于12月12日以前寄达. ○ *If you will be on holiday on election day, you may apply for a postal vote.* 倘若选举那天你在休假, 可以申请用邮寄方法投票.

□ ˈ**postal code** = POSTCODE (POST³).

ˈ**postal order** (*Brit*) (*US* ˈ**money order**) official piece of paper bought from a post office, representing a certain sum of money that can be posted to a specified person who then can exchange it for that sum 邮政汇票.

post-date /ˌpəʊstˈdeɪt; ˌpostˈdet/ *v* [Tn] **1** put a date on (a document, etc) that is later than the actual date 在(文件等)上填入比实际晚的日期: *a ˌpostdated ˈcheque*, ie one which cannot be cashed until the date specified 期票(在所示日期前不能兑现). **2** give to (an event) a date later than its actual date or the date previously given to it 将(某事)的日期确定为比实际晚的日期或比以前所称之较晚的日期. **3** be or occur at a later date than (sth) 日期较(某事物)为晚; 发生在(某事物)之日期之后. Cf 参看 ANTEDATE.

poster /ˈpəʊstə(r); ˈpostɚ/ *n* (**a**) large placard displayed in a public place 招贴; 海报: *a poster advertising the circus* 宣传马戏团的海报. (**b**) large printed picture 印成的大幅画: *Her bedroom is hung with posters.* 她的卧室里挂着一些大画片.

□ ˈ**poster paint** (also ˈ**poster colour**) type of artist's paint, in strong bright colours 广告色; 广告颜料.

poste rest·ante /ˌpəʊst ˈrestɑːnt; *US* reˈstænt; ˌpostrɛsˈtɑnt/ (*US* also **general delivery**) department in a post office where letters for a person may be sent and kept until he collects them (邮局的)邮件待领处.

pos·ter·ior /pɒˈstɪərɪə(r); pɑsˈtɪrɪɚ/ *adj* (*fml* 文) **1 ~ (to sth)** later (than sth) in time or in a series (时间或次序)在(某事物)之后的. Cf 参看 PRIOR¹. **2** (in architecture, biology, medicine) placed behind or at the back; from the back (用于建筑学、生物学、医学)后置的, 位于背面的, 自后面的: *a posterior view of the skull* 颅骨背视图. Cf 参看 ANTERIOR.

▷ **pos·ter·ior** *n* (*infml joc* 口, 谑) buttocks 屁股; 臀部: *a large posterior* 大屁股 ○ *a slap on the posterior* 打屁股.

pos·ter·ity /pɒˈsterətɪ; pɑsˈtɛrətɪ/ *n* [U] **1** following or future generations 后代; 后世: *plant trees for the benefit of posterity* 为造福后代而植树. **2** (*fml* 文) person's children, grandchildren, etc; descendants 子孙; 后裔: *recorded for posterity* 为后人而记载下来的 ○ *Posterity* *will remember him as a truly great man.* 他的子孙永远不会忘记他是真正的伟人.

pos·tern /ˈpɒstən; ˋpɑstɚn/ *n* (*arch* 古) side or back entrance, esp a concealed entrance to a castle, etc 边门; 后门; 边道; 便道; (尤指城堡等的)暗道: [attrib 作定语] *a postern door/gate* 后门.

post·gradu·ate /ˌpəʊstˈɡrædʒʊət; postˈɡrædʒʊɪt/ (*US* **graduate**) *adj* (of studies, etc) done after taking a first degree (指学习或研究等)大学毕业后所进行的.

▷ **post·gradu·ate** *n* person doing postgraduate studies 研究生. Cf 参看 GRADUATE, UNDERGRADUATE.

post·hum·ous /ˈpɒstjʊməs; *US* ˈpɒstʃəməs; ˋpɑstʃuməs/ *adj* (**a**) happening or given after death 死后发生的; 死后获得的: *posthumous fame, earnings* 死后获得的名声、收入 ○ *the posthumous award of a medal for bravery* 死后获得的勇敢勋章. (**b**) (of a literary work) published after its author's death (指著作)作者死后出版的: *Forster's posthumous novel* 福斯特身后出版的小说. (**c**) (of a child) born after its father's death (指小孩)父亲死后出生的, 遗腹的. ▷ **post·hum·ously** *adv*: *The prize was awarded posthumously.* 该奖是在获奖人死后追赠的.

pos·til·ion (also **post·til·lion**) /pɒˈstɪlɪən; pɑˋstɪljən/ *n* (formerly) person whose job was to ride on one of the horses pulling a carriage (旧时)骑在多匹马驾辕的马车之一匹马上的御者.

post·mas·ter /ˈpəʊstmɑːstə(r); *US* -mæst-; ˋpost,mæstɚ/ *n* (*fem* 阴性作 **postmis·tress** /-mɪstrɪs; -,mɪstrɪs/) person in charge of a post office 邮政局长.

□ ˌ**Postmaster** ˈ**General** person in charge of the postal system of a country 邮政大臣; 邮政部长.

post-mortem /ˌpəʊst ˈmɔːtəm; ,postˋmɔrtəm/ *n* **1** medical examination made after death in order to find the cause of death; autopsy 验尸; 尸体剖检: *A post-mortem showed that the victim had been poisoned.* 尸体检验表明受害者是被毒死的. ○ *The doctor carried out a post-mortem on the body.* 那医生对尸体进行了剖验. **2** (*infml* 口) discussion or review of an event after it has happened 事后的分析或反思: *a post-mortem on the election defeat* 对选举失败的事后剖析.

▷ **post-mortem** *adj* (**a**) made or occurring after death 死后进行的; 死后发生的: *a post-mortem examination* 尸体剖检. (**b**) (*infml* 口) occurring after an event has happened 事后发生的: *post-mortem recriminations* 事后的反责.

post·natal /ˌpəʊstˈneɪtl; ,postˋnetḷ/ *adj* (**a**) occurring in the period after childbirth 分娩后的; 产后的: ˌ*postnatal deˈpression* 产后抑郁症. (**b**) concerning a newborn child 与初生婴儿有关的: *postnatal care* 对初生婴儿的照料 ○ *a postnatal nurse, unit* 照料初生婴儿的护士、部门. Cf 参看 ANTENATAL, PRE-NATAL.

post·pone /pəˈspəʊn; posˋpon/ *v* **1** [Tn, Tn·pr, Tg] ~ **sth (to sth)** arrange sth at a later time; defer sth 使某事物延期; 推迟某事物: *The match was postponed to the following Saturday because of bad weather.* 比赛因天气不好而延期到下星期六进行. ○ *Let's postpone making a decision until we have more information.* 咱们在获取更多情报之后再做决定不迟. Cf 参看 ADVANCE 6, CANCEL 1. **2** (idm 习语) **postpone the evil ˈhour/ˈday** put off until a later time an unpleasant task, etc, that one will eventually have to do 缓做一终须做的厌恶事.

▷ **post·pone·ment** *n* (**a**) [U] act of postponing or delaying 延期; 推迟: *Rain caused the postponement of several race-meetings.* 几次赛马大会因雨延期. (**b**) [C] instance of this 延期的事: *After many difficulties and postponements, the ship was ready for launching.* 该船几经周折拖宕后, 已准备下水.

post·pran·dial /ˌpəʊstˈprændɪəl; postˈprændɪəl/ *adj* (*fml* 文) happening immediately after a meal 饭后的: *postprandial speeches* 餐后的演说 ○ (*joc* 谑) *His postprandial nap was disturbed by the arrival of the boss.* 老板一到, 惊扰了他餐后假寐.

post·script /ˈpəʊsskrɪpt; ˋposskrɪpt/ *n* ~ **(to sth)** **1** (*abbr* 缩写 **PS**) extra message added at the end of a letter after the signature (信末签名后的)附笔, 又及: *She mentioned in a postscript to her letter that the parcel had arrived.* 她在信末附笔中说包裹已寄到. **2** facts or information added to sth after it is completed 补遗; 补笔; 后话: *There was an interesting postscript to these events when her private diaries were published.* 她的日记发表后, 补充了一些有关这些事件的趣闻.

pos·tu·lant /ˈpɒstjʊlənt; *US* -tʃʊ-; ˋpɑstʃələnt/ *n* person who lives in a monastery or convent in preparation for entering a religious order 住在修道院里准备担任圣职的人. Cf 参看 NOVICE 2.

pos·tu·late /ˈpɒstjʊleɪt; *US* -tʃʊ-; ˋpɑstʃə,let/ *v* [Tn, Tf] (*fml* 文) put (sth) forward as a fact or accept (sth) as true, esp as a basis for reasoning or argument 假定, 假设(某事物)(尤指作推理或论证之出发点): *The school building programme postulates an increase in educational investment.* 修建校舍的计划是在增加教育经费的前提下拟定的. ○ *He postulated that a cure for the disease will have been found by the year 2000.* 他推断到2000年能研究出治愈该病的方法.

▷ **pos·tu·late** /ˈpɒstjʊlət; *US* -tʃʊ-; ˋpɑstʃələt/ *n* thing assumed to be true, or accepted as a basis for reasoning or calculation 假定; 假设; 公设: *the postulates of Euclidean geometry* 欧几里得几何学的公设.

pos·tu·la·tion /ˌpɒstjʊˈleɪʃn; *US* -tʃʊ-; ,pɑstʃəˋleʃən/ *n* [U, C].

pos·ture /ˈpɒstʃə(r); ˋpɑstʃɚ/ *n* **1** (**a**) [C] attitude or position of the body 姿势; 姿态: *an awkward posture* 笨拙的姿态 ○ *The artist asked his model to take a reclining posture.* 画家要求模特儿取斜倚着的姿势. (**b**) [U] way in which a person holds himself as he stands, walks or sits 坐立或行走的方式; 举止: *She has very good posture.* 她举止很优雅. ○ *Poor posture will give you backache.* 坐姿不好会使人腰背酸痛. **2** [C] way of looking at sth; attitude 看法; 态度: *The government adopted an uncompromising posture on the issue of independence.* 政府在独立这一问题上采取了毫不妥协的态度. Cf 参看 STANCE.

▷ **pos·ture** *v* **1** [I] stand, sit, etc in a self-conscious, exaggerated manner; pose 以不自然的、装模作样的方式站着、坐着等; 摆姿势: *Stop posturing in front of that mirror and listen to me!* 别对着那面镜子摆样子了, 听我的吧! **2** [Tn] put or arrange (sb) in a certain posture (1a) 摆(某人)的姿势: *posture a model* 摆模特儿的姿势.

pos·tur·ing /ˈpɒstʃərɪŋ; ˋpɑstʃərɪŋ/ *n* [U, C esp *pl* 作不可数名词或可数名词, 后者尤作复数] (**a**) standing, sitting, etc in a self-conscious, exaggerated manner 不自然的、装模作样的站姿、坐姿等; 摆出的姿势. (**b**) behaving in an insincere or artificial manner, esp expressing views one does not really hold 装模作样或故作姿态的行为; (尤指)言不由衷: *Her liberal views were soon revealed as mere posturing.* 她那些开明的观点很快地就暴露出只不过是做做样子而已. ○ *The electorate is growing tired of his posturings.* 选民对他的口是心非逐渐生厌.

post-war /ˌpəʊst ˈwɔː(r); ˋpostˋwɔr/ *adj* [esp attrib 尤作定语] existing or happening (in the period) after a war, esp World War II 战后的; (尤指)第二次世界大战之后的: *the post-war period of economic expansion* 战后经济成长时期 ○ *post-war developments in industry* 战后的工业发展.

posy /ˈpəʊzɪ; ˋpozɪ/ *n* small bunch of flowers; bouquet (小的)花束.

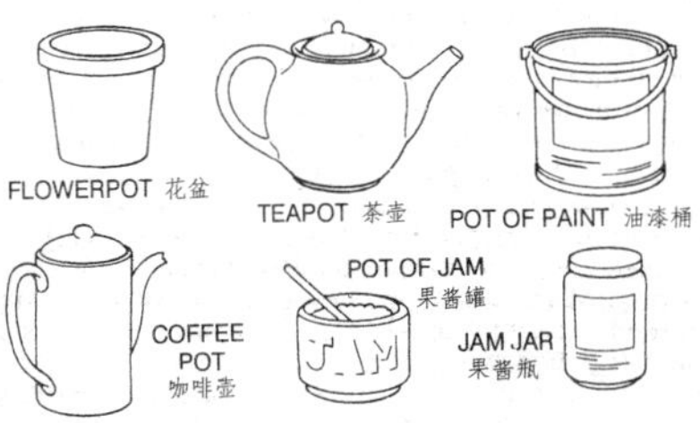

pot[1] /pɒt; pɑt/ *n* **1** [C] (**a**) round vessel made of earthenware, metal, etc for cooking things in (烹饪用的)锅: *pots and pans* 锅碗瓢盆 ○ *a chicken ready for the pot* 待下锅的鸡. (**b**) (esp in compounds 尤用以构成复合词) any of various types of vessel made for a particular purpose 作某用途的器皿: *a* ˈ*teapot* ○ *a* ˈ*coffee-pot* ○ *a* ˈ*flowerpot* ○ *a* ˈ*chamber-pot* ○ *a* ˈ*lobster-pot.* ⇨ illus 见插图. (**c**) amount contained in a pot 一锅、罐、壶等的量: *They've eaten a whole pot of jam!* 他们吃了满满一罐果酱. ○ *Bring me another pot of coffee.* 给我再来一壶咖啡. ⇨illus 见插图. **2** [C esp *pl* 尤作复数] (*infml* 口) large sum; a lot of money 大量; 大笔钱: *making pots of money* 赚大钱. **3** [C] (*sl* 俚) prize in an athletic contest, esp a silver cup (运动会的)奖品; (尤指)银杯. **4 the pot** [sing] (*esp US*) (**a**) total amount of the bets made on one hand in a card-game 纸牌戏中一局赌注的总额. (**b**) all the money pooled by a group of people for a common purpose, esp for buying food; kitty 为某一共同目的(尤指购买食品)而集体凑集的基金总数; 储金. **5** [C] = POT-BELLY a. **6** [U] (*sl* 俚) marijuana 大麻烟. **7** [C] (*Brit*) (in billiards) stroke that sends the correct ball into one of the pockets (台球)击球入袋的一击. **8** [C] = POT-SHOT. **9** (idm 习语) **go to ˈpot** (*infml* 口) be spoilt or ruined 被损坏; 被毁掉; 完蛋: *The firm is going to pot under the new management.* 公司在新人管理下就要垮台了. **keep the ˈpot boiling** (**a**) keep sth (eg a children's game) moving at a fast pace 使某事物(如儿童游戏)快速进行. (**b**) keep interest in sth alive 使对某事物的兴趣不减. **put a quart into a pint pot** ⇨ QUART. **take ˌpot ˈluck** accept whatever is available, esp food at a meal, without any choice or alternative being offered 赶上什么是什么; (尤指)有什么吃什么, 吃便饭: *You are welcome to eat with us, but you'll have to take pot luck.* 欢迎你和我们一起吃饭, 可要有什么吃什么. ○ *We seldom book hotels when travelling, we usually just take pot luck.* 我们旅游时很少预定旅馆的房间, 通常都是赶上什么算什么. **the ˌpot calling the ˈkettle black** (*saying* 谚) the accuser having the same fault as the person he is accusing 锅笑壶黑; 乌鸦笑猪黑: *She accused us of being extravagant — talk about the pot calling the kettle black!* 她指责我们铺张浪费 —— 老鸹别嫌猪黑!

□ ˈ**pot-belly** *n* (**a**) (also **pot**) large protruding belly 大肚子. (**b**) person who has this 肚子大的人. ˌ**pot-ˈbellied** *adj* (**a**) (of a person) having a pot-belly (指人)肚子大的. (**b**) (*fig* 比喻) (of a container) curving out below the middle (指容器)下部向外鼓的: *a pot-bellied stove*, ie one with a pot-bellied container in which the fuel burns 炉膛大的火炉.

ˈ**pot-boiler** *n* book, picture, etc written or painted only to earn money 仅为赚钱而创作的书、画等: *She produced regular pot-boilers while also working on her masterpiece.* 她一面不断发表为餬口的作品, 一面搞她的大作.

ˈ**pot-bound** *adj* (of a plant) having roots that fill its pot[1](1b) completely (指植物)根生满花盆的.

ˈ**pot-herb** *n* any plant whose leaves, stems or roots are used in cooking to add flavour, esp to soups and stews (调味用的)植物性香料.

ˈ**pot-hole** *n* **1** deep hole worn in rock, eg in limestone caves by water 瓯穴(石灰石洞穴等内之岩石上被水侵蚀成的深洞). **2** rough hole in a road surface made by rain and traffic (路面上因下雨和行车而形成的)坑洼. ˈ**pot-holer** *n*. ˈ**pot-holing** *n* [U] (*sport* 体) exploring pot-holes in rocks and caves 瓯穴探测.

ˈ**pot-hunter** *n* (**a**) (in shooting) person who shoots every bird or animal he sees and thinks only of profit rather than sport (射击活动)纯为牟利而非以运动为目的的行猎者. (**b**) person who takes part in a contest only for the sake of the prize 只为获奖而参加比赛的人.

ˈ**pot plant** plant grown in a flowerpot 盆栽植物.

ˈ**pot-roast** *n* piece of meat browned in a pot[1](1a) and cooked slowly with very little water 炖肉.

ˈ**pot-shot** (also **pot**) *n* (**a**) shot made without taking careful aim 胡乱射击. (**b**) (*fig* 比喻) random attempt at sth (对某事物的)随便一试.

pot[2] /pɒt; pɑt/ *v* (**-tt-**) **1** (**a**) [Tn esp passive 尤用于被动语态] plant (sth) in a flowerpot 将(植物)栽在花盆里: *a potted azalea* 盆栽的杜鹃花. (**b**) [Tn, Tn·p] **~ sth (up)** plant (cuttings or seedlings) in a pot 把(插枝或籽苗)种在花盆里: *pot up chrysanthemum cuttings* 把菊花插枝种到花盆里. **2** [Tn] (*infml* 口) put (a baby or young child) on a chamber-pot 使(幼儿)坐便盆. **3** [Tn] (in billiards) drive (a ball) into a pocket(6) (台球)击(球)入袋. **4** [Ipr] **~ at sth** shoot at sth 向某物射击: *pot at a rabbit* 向兔子射击. **5** [Tn] kill (sth) with a pot-shot 乱射(动物): *They potted dozens of rabbits.* 他们胡乱射击打死几十只兔子. **6** [Tn esp passive 尤用于被动语态] put (cooked meat or fish) in a pot in order to preserve it 将(熟的肉或鱼)装入罐内保存: *potted beef, ham, shrimps, etc* 装罐保存的牛肉、火腿、小虾等.

□ ˈ**potting-shed** *n* shed where plants are grown in pots (POT[1] 1b) before being planted outside 盆栽棚舍(植物先在此处作盆中栽培, 然后移到室外种植).

pot·able /ˈpəʊtəbl; ˈpotəbl/ *adj* (*fml* 文) fit for drinking; drinkable 适于饮用的; 可喝的.

pot·ash /ˈpɒtæʃ; ˈpɑtˌæʃ/ *n* [U] any of various salts of potassium (esp potassium carbonate) used to make fertilizers, soap and various chemicals 钾碱; (尤指)碳酸钾, 氢氧化钾.

pot·as·sium /pəˈtæsɪəm; pəˈtæsɪəm/ *n* [U] chemical element, a soft shiny silvery-white metal occurring in rocks and in the form of minerals and essential for all living things 钾. ⇨App 10 见附录10.

po·ta·tion /pəʊˈteɪʃn; poˈteʃən/ *n* (*fml or joc* 文或谑) (**a**) [U] act of drinking 喝; 饮. (**b**) [C] drink, esp an alcoholic one 饮料; (尤指)酒.

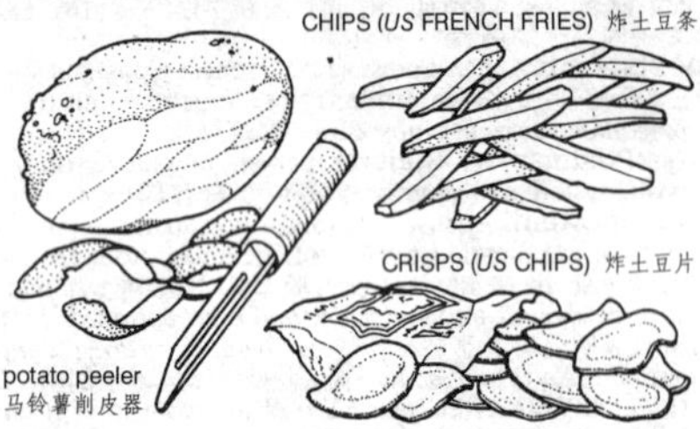

potato 马铃薯

po·tato /pəˈteɪtəʊ; pəˈteto/ *n* (*pl* **~es**) **1** (**a**) [C] plant grown for its rounded starchy tubers which are eaten cooked as a vegetable 马铃薯: *The potato is vulnerable to several pests.* 马铃薯易受几种害虫的侵害. (**b**) [C] one of these tubers 马铃薯的块茎; 土豆: *The potatoes are ready to be dug up.* 快要收获土豆了. ○ *Would you like another potato?* 你要不要再来个土豆? (**c**) [U] this served as food (熟的)马铃薯: *a dish of meat topped with mashed potato* 一盘土豆泥盖浇肉 ○ [attrib 作定语] *potato soup* 土豆汤. **2** (idm 习语) **a hot potato** ⇨ HOT.

□ **potato** ˈ**crisp** (*Brit*) (*US* **potato** ˈ**chip**) = CRISP.

ˈ**potato beetle** pest that destroys the leaves of potato plants 三带负泥虫(伤害马铃薯叶子的害虫).

po·teen /pɒˈtiːn; poˈtin/ *n* [U] (in Ireland) whisky made in an illicit still[3] (爱尔兰)私酿的威士忌酒.

po·tent /ˈpəʊtnt; ˈpotnt/ *adj* **1** (**a**) (of drugs, etc) having a strong effect (指药物等)效力大的: *a potent charm, cure, medicine* 很有效的符咒、治疗法、药物. (**b**) having great power 威力大的: *potent weapons* 威力大的武器. (**c**) strongly persuasive; convincing 说服力强的; 令人信服的: *potent arguments, reasoning, etc* 有说服力的论据、推理等. **2** (of males) capable of having sexual intercourse; not impotent (指男性)有性交能力的; 无阳痿的. ▷ **po·tency** /-nsɪ; -nsɪ/ *n* [U]. **po·tently** *adv*.

po·tent·ate /ˈpəʊtnteɪt; ˈpotnˌtet/ *n* (esp formerly) ruler with direct power over his people; autocratic monarch (尤指旧时)统治者, 君主: *the splendid court of an Eastern potentate* 东方君主的豪华宫廷.

po·ten·tial /pəˈtenʃl; pəˈtɛnʃəl/ *adj* [attrib 作定语] (**a**) that can or may come into existence; possible 可能存在或出现的; 可能的: *a potential source of conflict* 可能引起冲突的根源 ○ *a potential leader* 可能成为领导者的人 ○ *The book is arguably a potential best seller.* 该书或可成为一部畅销书. (**b**) in existence and capable of being developed or used 潜在的; 有潜力的: *potential energy, power, resources, etc* 潜力、潜能、潜在的资源 ○ *a machine with several potential uses* 具有多种潜在功能的机器.

▷ **po·ten·tial** *n* [U] **1** (**a**) **~ (for sth)** possibility of being developed or used 潜在性; 可能性: *She recognized the potential for error in the method being used.* 她意识到在所采用的方法中可能出错. ○ *He studied the German market to find the potential there for profitable investment.* 他对德国的市场进行了研究以寻求投资获利的可能性. (**b**) qualities that exist and can be developed 潜力; 潜能: *exploit/fulfil/realize one's potential* 发掘[发挥/认识]自己的潜力 ○ *She has artistic potential/potential as an artist.* 她有做艺术家的潜质. ○ *The product has even more potential in export markets.* 这种产品在出口市场上甚至会有更大的销售潜力. **2** energy of an electric charge expressed in volts; voltage 电势; 电位; 电压: *a current of high potential* 高压电.

po·ten·ti·al·ity /pəˌtenʃɪˈælətɪ; pəˌtɛnʃɪˈælətɪ/ *n* (esp *pl* 尤作复数) (*fml* 文) power or quality that exists but has not been developed 潜力; 潜在性: *a country with great potentialities* 具有很大潜力的国家.

po·ten·tially /-ʃəlɪ; -ʃəlɪ/ *adv*: *a potentially rich country*, ie one with many natural resources that could be developed 潜力大的国家(有丰富自然资源可开发者) ○ *a potentially catastrophic situation* 可能引发严重灾难的形势.

po·tion /ˈpəʊʃn; ˋpoʃən/ *n* (formerly) drink of medicine, poison or a liquid used in magic (旧时)(药物、毒物或有魔力的)饮料: *a ˈlove potion* 春药饮剂 ○ *The magician displayed his charms and potions.* 魔术师展示了咒符和有魔力的饮品.

pot-pourri /ˌpəʊˈpʊərɪ; *US* ˌpəʊpəˈriː; pɑtˋpʊrɪ/ *n* **1** [C, U] mixture of dried petals and spices used to perfume a room, cupboard, etc 干燥的花瓣及香料之混合物(用以使房间、橱柜等生香). **2** [C] musical or literary medley (音乐或文学作品的)杂集, 杂曲, 杂文集.

pot·sherd /ˈpɒt-ʃɜːd; ˋpɑtˌʃɝd/ *n* (esp in archaeology) broken piece of pottery (尤指考古学)陶器碎片. Cf 参看 SHARD.

pot·ted /ˈpɒtɪd; ˋpɑtɪd/ *adj* **1** grown or preserved in a pot 盆栽的; 罐装的. ⇨POT[1] 1,6. **2** (*often derog* 常作贬义) (of a book, etc) in a short simplified form (指书等)简写的, 节略的: *a potted history of England* 英国简史 ○ *a potted version of 'Hamlet'*《哈姆雷特》的节本 ○ (*fig* 比喻) *She gave her parents a potted version of the night's events*, ie an account that omitted anything disturbing. 她把夜间发生的事向父母粗略地讲了一遍(略去了一些令人担心的内容).

pot·ter[1] /ˈpɒtə(r); ˋpɑtɚ/ (*US* **putter** /ˈpʌtər; ˋpʌtɚ/) *v* **1** [I] work or move in a leisurely aimless way 懒散地工作; 漫无目的地走动: *He loves to potter in the garden.* 他喜欢在花园里随便走走. **2** (phr v) **potter about/around (sth)** (**a**) move from one place or thing to another in a leisurely way 游逛; 闲逛; 闲荡: *potter about the exhibition* 慢悠悠地参观展览. (**b**) work in an unhurried relaxed way, doing small or trivial tasks 磨磨蹭蹭地做琐碎的事情: *We spent the weekend pottering around (in) the house.* 我们周末做一些琐碎的家务事.

▷ **pot·terer** /ˈpɒtərə(r); ˋpɑtərɚ/ *n* (*often derog* 常作贬义) person who potters, esp one who never finishes a task 懒散的人; (尤指)磨洋工的人.

pot·ter[2] /ˈpɒtə(r); ˋpɑtɚ/ *n* person who makes earthenware pots by hand 制陶工人; 陶工.

▷ **pot·tery** /ˈpɒtərɪ; ˋpɑtərɪ/ *n* **1** [U] earthenware pots, etc made by hand 陶器: *a valuable collection of Japanese pottery* 一批珍贵的日本陶器收藏品. **2** [U] craft of making pots, esp by hand 陶器制造术(尤指手工业): *She is learning pottery.* 她在学习制陶技术. ○ [attrib 作定语] *a pottery class* 制陶技术学习班. **3** [C] place where pottery is made; potter's workshop 陶器制造厂; 陶器作坊. **4 the Potteries** [pl] district in Staffordshire, the centre of the English pottery industry 波特里斯(英国斯塔福德郡之一区, 为陶器工业中心). ⇨illus at App 1 见附录1插图, pages xiv, xv.

□ **ˌpotter's ˈwheel** horizontal revolving disc on which wet clay is shaped to make pots 陶均, 陶轮(制陶器用的转盘).

potty[1] /ˈpɒtɪ; ˋpɑtɪ/ *adj* (**-ier, -iest**) (*Brit infml* 口) **1** (**a**) (of a person or his behaviour) foolish or mad (指人或其行为)傻气的, 疯癫的: *Surely you don't expect me to take your potty suggestions seriously?* 你肯定不会指望我认真考虑你那些荒谬的建议吧? ○ *He seems to have gone/to be quite potty.* 他好像疯疯癫癫的了. ○ *That noise is driving me potty!* 那噪声要把我吵疯了! (**b**) **~ about sb/sth** extremely enthusiastic about sb/sth 对某人[某事物]着迷的: *She's potty about jazz.* 她迷上了爵士音乐. **2** (*derog* 贬) small or unimportant 微小的; 不重要的: *A person with his ambition won't stay long in a potty little firm like this.* 一个有雄心大志的人在这样一个不起眼的小公司里是待不长的.

potty[2] /ˈpɒtɪ; ˋpɑtɪ/ *n* (*infml* 口) child's chamber-pot (儿童的)便盆, 尿壶.

□ **ˈpotty-trained** *adj* (of a baby or young child) no longer needing to wear a nappy (指幼儿)不再需要裹尿布的.

pouch /paʊtʃ; paʊtʃ/ *n* **1** (esp in compounds 尤用以构成复合词) small (esp leather) bag carried in the pocket or attached to a belt (放在衣袋里或连在腰带上的)小袋(尤指皮制的): *a toˈbacco-pouch* 烟袋 ○ *an ˌammuˈnition-pouch* 子弹袋. **2** area of baggy loose skin, eg under the eyes of a sick person 皮肤的松弛下垂处(如病人眼下的). **3** (**a**) bag-like pocket of skin in which a female marsupial, eg a kangaroo, carries her young 育儿袋(袋鼠等雌性有袋动物的袋). (**b**) bag-like pocket of skin in the cheeks of some rodents, eg hamsters, in which they store and carry food 颊囊, 颊嗛(某些啮齿类动物如仓鼠等口腔内两侧的)袋囊(用以储存和携带食物).

▷ **pouch** *v* **1** [I, Tn, Tn·pr] (cause sth to) form a pouch (使某物)成为袋状: *wear a dress pouched over a belt* 穿着腰带上方蓬松的连衣裙. **2** [Tn] put (sth) into a pouch; pocket 将(某物)装入袋内: *to pouch a ball*, ie catch it, eg in cricket 接住球(如板球戏中).

pouffe (also **pouf**) /puːf; puf/ *n* **1** large thick cushion used as a seat or for resting the feet on (大而厚的)坐垫, 脚垫. **2** = POOF.

poult·erer /ˈpəʊltərə(r); ˋpoltərɚ/ *n* (*Brit*) person who sells poultry and game 贩卖家禽和野味的人.

poult·ice /ˈpəʊltɪs; ˋpoltɪs/ *n* soft heated mass spread on a cloth and put on a sore place on the body to soothe pain, reduce swelling, etc 泥罨剂; 泥敷剂; 膏药: *a kaolin, mustard, etc poultice* 高岭土、芥子末等泥罨剂.

▷ **poult·ice** *v* [Tn] put a poultice on (sth) 敷泥罨剂于(某处).

poultry /ˈpəʊltrɪ; ˋpoltrɪ/ *n* (**a**) [pl *v*] hens, ducks, geese, turkeys, etc kept for eating or for their eggs; domestic fowls 家禽: *The poultry have been fed.* 家禽已经喂过饲料了. ○ [attrib 作定语] *poultry farming* 家禽饲养业. (**b**) [U] meat of these eaten as food 家禽肉: *Poultry is expensive at this time of year.* 一年中的这个时候禽肉很贵. ○ *There's not much poultry in the shops.* 商店里禽肉不太多.

pounce /paʊns; paʊns/ *v* [I, Ipr] **~ (on sb/sth)** make a sudden attack by swooping or springing down 突然袭击; 猛扑: *We saw the tiger about to pounce (on the goat).* 我们看见老虎要(向那只山羊)扑过去. ○ *The hawk pounced on its prey and carried it off.* 那只鹰向那小动物猛扑过去把它叼走了. ○ *We hid behind the bushes, ready to pounce on the intruder.* 我们藏在灌木丛后面, 准备向来犯者发起突然袭击. ○ (*fig* 比喻) *pounce on a mistake*, ie spot it very quickly 一眼就看到错误.

▷ **pounce** *n* [sing] sudden attack by pouncing 突然的袭击; 猛扑的举动.

pound[1] /paʊnd; paʊnd/ *n* **1** [C] (**a**) (*abbr* 缩写 **lb**) standard measure of weight, 16 ounces in the avoirdupois system, equal to 0.454 kg (常衡)磅(重量单位, 合16盎司或0.454千克): *Apples are sold by the pound.* 苹果按磅出售. ○ *The luggage weighs 40 lbs.* 这行李重40磅. ○ *He's eaten a whole pound of plums!* 他吃了整整一磅李子. (**b**) standard measure of weight, 12 ounces in the troy system, equal to 0.373 kg. (金衡)磅(重量单位, 合12盎司或0.373千克). ⇨App 4, 5 见附录4、5. **2** [C] (*symb* 符号为 **£**) (**a**) (also **ˌpound ˈsterling**) unit of British money; 100 pence (英)镑(英国货币单位, 合100便士): *The ticket will cost about a pound.* 该票价约为一英镑. ○ *I've spent £5 on food today.* 今天我买食物花了5英镑. ○ [attrib 作定语] *a five-pound note*, ie a banknote for £5 一张五英镑的钞票 ○ *a pound coin*, ie a coin worth £1 一枚一英镑的硬币. ⇨App 4 见附录4. Cf 参看 STERLING *n*. (**b**) unit of money of various other countries, eg Cyprus, Egypt, Ireland, Israel and Malta

镑(其他一些国家如塞浦路斯、埃及、爱尔兰、以色列以及马尔他等的货币单位). **(c) the pound** [sing] value of the British pound on international money markets 英国货币在外汇市场上的比价: *The Government is worried about the weakness of the pound (against other currencies).* 英国政府忧虑货币(较之其他货币)疲软. **3** (idm 习语) **(have, want, demand, etc) one's pound of 'flesh** (insist on) receiving the full amount that is legally due to one even when it is morally offensive to do so (坚持)要讨回全部数额(尽管合法但不合理): *Their distress had no effect on him — he was determined to have his pound of flesh.* 他对他们的不幸无动于衷——坚持向他们讨债. **in for a penny, in for a pound** ⇨ PENNY. **penny wise pound foolish** ⇨ PENNY.

pound[2] /paʊnd; paund/ *n* **1** (formerly) enclosed area in a village where cattle, etc that had strayed were kept until their owners claimed them (旧时)乡村中收留走失的牲畜以待失主认领的围场. **2 (a)** place where stray cats and dogs are kept until their owners claim them 收留走失的猫狗以待失主认领的处所. **(b)** place where motor vehicles that have been parked illegally are kept until their owners claim them 扣押违章停放之机动车以待车主认领的处所.

pound[3] /paʊnd; paund/ *v* **1** [Tn, Tn·pr] **~ sth (to sth)** crush or beat sth with repeated heavy strokes 连续地猛撞或猛击某物: *pound crystals (to powder)* 把结晶体捣碎(成粉末) ○ *pound garlic (to a paste) in a mortar* 在臼中把大蒜舂烂(成糊状) ○ *The ship was pounded to pieces against the rocks.* 那船在岩石上撞得粉碎. **2** [Ipr, Ip, Tn] **~ (away) (at/against/on sth)** hit (sth) with repeated heavy blows or gunfire 连续地猛击或射击(某物): *the sound of feet pounding on the stairs* 楼梯上响起的沉重脚步声 ○ *Someone was pounding at the door.* 有人在砰砰地敲门. ○ *The heavy guns pounded (away at) the walls of the fort.* 重炮对着要塞外墙(不停地)轰击. ○ *Who is that pounding (on) the piano?* 是谁用那么大劲儿弹钢琴呢? **3** [I, Ipr] **~ (with sth)** (of the heart) beat heavily (指心脏)剧烈地跳动: *a heart pounding (with fear)* (因恐惧)剧烈跳动的心脏 ○ *She could feel her heart pounding painfully as she finished the race.* 她跑完赛程后感到心脏都快要跳出来了. **4** (idm 习语) **pound the 'beat** (*infml* 口) (esp of a policeman) regularly patrol an allotted district on foot (尤指警察)在辖区作例行徒步巡逻. **5** (phr v) **pound along, down, up, etc** move in the direction specified with heavy rapid steps 以沉重而快速的步伐朝某方向移动: *The horses came pounding along the track.* 马都在沿着跑道奔驰. ○ *Don't pound up the stairs!* 上楼梯脚步轻点吧!

pound·age /ˈpaʊndɪdʒ; ˋpaundɪdʒ/ *n* [U] **1** charge of a certain sum (eg 5p) per pound in value (£1) 按每英镑价值所付的费用(如5便士); 每英镑收费. **2 (a)** charge of a certain sum (eg 5p) per pound in weight (1 lb) 按每磅重量所付的费用(如5便士); 每磅收费. **(b)** charge of a certain amount (eg 3 oz) per pound in weight (1 lb) 按每磅重量之定量(如3盎司)所付的费用.

pounder /ˈpaʊndə(r); ˋpaundɚ/ *n* **1** thing that weighs a pound (1 lb) 一磅重的东西. **2** (in compounds 用以构成复合词) **(a)** thing that weighs a specified number of pounds ...磅重的东西: *a three-pounder*, eg a fish weighing 3 lb 三磅重的东西(如3磅重的一条鱼). **(b)** gun that fires a shell of the specified number of pounds 发射...磅重炮弹的炮: *an eighteen-pounder*, ie a gun that fires shells weighing 18 lb each 发射18磅重炮弹的炮.

pour /pɔ:(r); pɔr/ *v* **1 (a)** [Ipr, Ip] (of a liquid or substance that flows like liquid) flow, esp downwards, in a continuous stream (指液体或液体般流动之物)不断流动(尤指自上而下): *Blood was pouring from the wound.* 血从伤口中涌出. ○ *I knocked over the bucket and the water poured (out) all over the floor.* 我打翻了水桶, 水流了一地. ○ *Sweat was pouring down his face.* 他满头大汗. ○ *The ceiling collapsed and rubble poured into the room.* 天花板坍塌了, 碎砖破瓦掉落到了屋里. **(b)** [Tn, Tn·pr, Tn·p] cause (a liquid or substance that flows like liquid) to flow in a continuous stream 使(液体或液体般流动之物)不断流动; 倒; 灌; 注: *Although I poured it carefully, I spilt some of the oil.* 虽然我倒油时很小心, 但还是洒了一些. ○ *Pour the milk into a jug.* 把牛奶灌进壶里. ○ *Pour out the water left in the bucket.* 把桶里的剩水倒出来. ⇨illus 见插图. **(c)** [I, Ipr, Ip, Tn, Tn·pr, Tn·p, Dn·n, Dn·pr] **~ sth (for sb)** serve (esp tea or coffee) (to sb) by putting it into a cup (为某人)斟, 倒(尤指茶或咖啡): *This teapot doesn't pour well.* 这个茶壶不好倒. ○ *Shall I pour (out) (the tea)?* 我来倒(茶)好吗? ○ *I've poured two cups of coffee.* 我倒了两杯咖啡. ○ *I've poured coffee into your cup by mistake.* 我错把咖啡倒在你的杯子里了. ○ *Shall I pour you some tea?* 我给你斟点茶好吗? ○ *Let me pour you a glass of wine.* 让我给你倒杯酒吧. ○ *I've poured a glass of wine for you.* 我给你斟了一杯酒. **2** [I, Ipr, Ip] (of rain) fall heavily (指雨)倾盆而下: *It's pouring (down).* 大雨如注. ○ *She watched the rain pouring down the windows.* 她注视着顺着窗户往下流的大雨. ○ (*infml* 口) *a pouring wet day* 大雨天. **3** [Ipr, Ip, Tn·pr, Tn·p] (cause people or things to) come or go in a continuous stream (使人或事物)不断地涌来或涌现: *Commuters were pouring into the station.* 通勤者涌入车站. ○ *The fans poured out of the stadium cheering wildly.* 体育爱好者们欣喜若狂地从体育场中蜂涌而出. ○ *The shops and offices pour millions of workers into the street at this time of day.* 一天的这段时间有数以百万计的职工从工厂和办公场所涌向街头. ○ *Letters of complaint poured in (to head office).* 投诉信件源源不断地寄到(总部). **4** (idm 习语) **it never rains but it pours** ⇨ RAIN[2]. **pour oil on the 'flames** make a bad situation worse 使情况变得更糟; 火上加油. **pour oil on troubled 'waters** (try to) calm a disagreement, violent dispute, etc (试图)调解争端、平息风波等. **pour scorn on sb/sth** speak of sb/sth with contempt 以鄙夷的口气说到某人[某事物]: *She poured scorn on the suggestion that he might never return.* 她鄙弃有人暗示他一去不复返之意. **pour/throw cold water on sth** ⇨ COLD[1]. **5** (phr v) **pour (sth) out** (cause sth to) be expressed freely (and fully) (将某事物)尽情表达出来: *When he realized we knew the truth, the whole story came pouring out.* 他意识到我们已了解真相, 便把事情的原委和盘托出. ○ *She poured out her troubles to me over a cup of coffee.* 她边喝咖啡边向我倾诉她的苦恼.

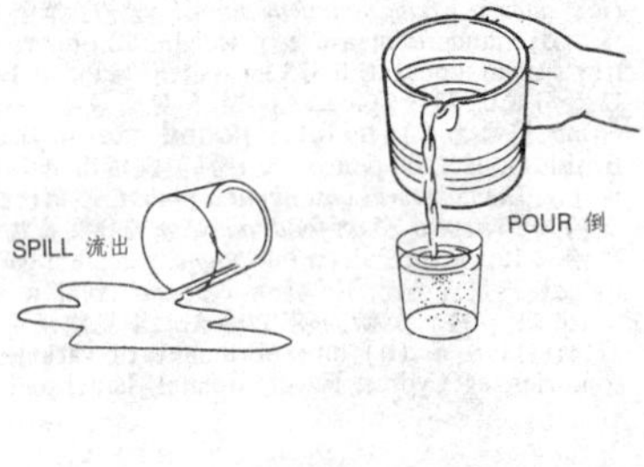

pout /paʊt; paut/ *v* **(a)** [I] push the lips or the lower lip forward, esp as a sign of annoyance or sulking 撅嘴(尤指表示烦恼或生气): *Tell that child to stop pouting!* 叫那孩子别撅着嘴撒娇! ○ *She pouted to show off her new lipstick.* 她撅着嘴炫耀她的新口红. **(b)** [Tn] push (the lips) forward in this way 撅(嘴): *pout one's lips provocatively* 挑衅地撅着嘴.

▷ **pout** *n* (esp *sing* 尤作单数) pouting expression of the face 撅嘴的面部表情.

pout·ingly *adv* with a pout; sulkily 撅着嘴地; 板着脸地; 生气地.

pov·erty /ˈpɒvətɪ; ˋpɑvɚtɪ/ *n* [U] **1** state of being poor 贫穷; 贫困: *live in poverty* 过着穷困的生活 ○ *She had been worn down by poverty and illness.* 她贫病交加, 受尽折磨. **2** existing in too small amounts; scarcity or lack 贫乏; 缺乏: *His work was criticized for its poverty of imagination.* 他的作品因缺乏想像力而受到批评. ○ *They were handicapped by (a) poverty of resources.* 他们因资源短缺处境窘迫. **3** state of being inferior; poor quality 低劣; 劣质: *the poverty of the soil* 土地的贫瘠 ○ *They were recognizable by the poverty of their dress.* 根据衣着寒酸这一点可以把他们认出来. **4** (idm 习语) **grinding poverty** ⇨ GRINDING (GRIND). Cf 参看 POORNESS.

□ **'poverty line** minimum level of income needed to buy the basic necessities of life 贫困线(购买基本的生活必需品所需之收入的最低水平): *There are still too* *many people living below the poverty line.* 生活在贫困线以下的人数仍然过多.

ˈ**poverty-stricken** *adj* affected by poverty(1); extremely poor 贫困不堪的; 极度贫穷的: *poverty-stricken families, homes, housing* 一贫如洗的家庭、缺衣乏食的家、四壁萧然的房屋.

ˈ**poverty trap** situation in which one is unable to improve one's income because one depends on state benefits that are reduced as one's earnings increase 贫困陷阱(受政府津贴者因工资增加而津贴减少, 无法改善经济状况).

POW /ˌpiː əʊ ˈdʌbljuː; ˌpi o ˈdʌblju/ *abbr* 缩写 = prisoner of war: *a POW camp* 战俘营.

pow·der /ˈpaʊdə(r); ˈpaʊdɚ/ *n* **1** (**a**) [U] (substance in the form of a) mass of fine dry particles 粉; 粉末; 粉状物质: *crush lumps of sugar to powder* 把成块的糖压成粉末 ○ *The snow was as dry as powder.* 雪干得像粉一样. (**b**) [C, U] (esp in compounds 尤用以构成复合词) substance in this form, esp one for a special use, eg as a cosmetic or medicine 粉状物质(尤指有某种用途者, 如作化妆品或药剂的): *ˈface-powder* 扑面粉 ○ *ˈtalcum powder* 爽身粉 ○ *take a powder* (ie powdered medicine) *to cure indigestion* 服用药粉以治消化不良 ○ *a special powder for cleaning fur* 一种可清洗毛皮衣服的皂粉 ○ *ˈsoap powder* 肥皂粉 ○ *ˈbaking-powder* 发酵粉. **2** [U] = GUNPOWDER (GUN). **3** (idm 习语) **keep one's ˈpowder dry** keep in a state of readiness to cope with a possible emergency 作好准备以对付可能出现的紧急情况: *The problem may not arise, but there's no harm in keeping our powder dry.* 问题不一定会发生, 但有备无患并无害处.

▷ **pow·der** *v* [Tn] put powder on (sth) 施粉于(某物): *powder one's face/nose* 在脸上[鼻子上]搽粉 ○ *powder a baby after her bath*, ie with talcum powder 给幼儿洗澡后再给她扑爽身粉 ○ *the fashion for powdered hair* 在头发上施以粉末装饰的流行发型. **pow·dered** *adj* (of a substance that is naturally liquid) dried and made into powder (指原为液体之物质)经干燥而成粉的: *The paint is sold in powdered form.* 该油漆以粉制品形式出售. ○ *powdered milk, eggs, etc* 奶粉、蛋粉.

pow·dery /ˈpaʊdərɪ; ˈpaʊdərɪ/ *adj* **1** like powder 粉状的: *a light fall of powdery snow* 细雪的轻轻飘落. **2** covered with powder 布满粉状物的: *a powdery nose* 敷粉的鼻子.

□ ˌ**powder ˈblue** (of a) pale blue 淡蓝色(的).

ˈ**powder-keg** *n* **1** small metal barrel for holding gunpowder (金属的)小型火药桶. **2** (*fig* 比喻) potentially dangerous or explosive situation 具有潜在危险的或爆炸性的情势: *Rising tensions have turned the area into a powder-keg and any incident could set off a riot.* 形势越来越紧张, 该地区已成了火药桶, 任何小事均能激起一场动乱.

ˈ**powder-magazine** *n* place where gunpowder is stored 火药库.

ˈ**powder-puff** (also **puff**) *n* soft fluffy pad used for applying face-powder 粉扑.

ˈ**powder-room** *n* (*euph* 婉) ladies' lavatory in a department store, hotel, theatre, etc (百货商店、旅馆、剧院等的)女厕所.

power /ˈpaʊə(r); ˈpaʊɚ/ *n* **1** [U] (in people) ability to do or act (人的)能力: *It is beyond/outside/not within my power* (ie I am unable or am not in a position) *to help you.* 我没有能力帮助你. ○ *I will do everything in my power to help you.* 我愿尽我的力量帮助你. **2** (**a**) [U] (also **powers** [pl]) particular faculty of the body or mind (生理上或精神上)某方面的能力: *He has lost the power of speech.* 他丧失了言语能力. ○ *The drug affects one's power(s) of concentration.* 这种药影响人精神不能集中. ○ *He had to use all his powers of persuasion.* 他只好尽力进行说服. (**b**) **powers** [pl] all the faculties of a person's body or mind 体力; 智力: *a woman of impressive intellectual powers* 智力超群的女人 ○ *His powers are failing*, ie He is becoming weak. 他的体力正在衰退. **3** [U] strength or energy behind or contained in sth 力; 力量: *There was a lot of power behind that blow.* 那一击的力量很大. ○ *The ship was helpless against the power of the storm.* 那船抵挡不住风暴的力量. ○ (*fig* 比喻) *They were defeated by the power of her oratory.* 她靠能言善辩战胜了他们. ⇨Usage at STRENGTH 用法见STRENGTH. **4** [U] (**a**) control over others 操纵力; 影响力: *the power of the law* 法律的力量 ○ *have sb in one's power*, ie be able to do what one wishes with sb 对某人具有影响力(能操纵某人) ○ *have power over sb/sb's fate* 能决定某人的命运 ○ *fall into sb's power* 落入某人的手心中 ○ *He made the mistake of underestimating the power of the press.* 他犯的错误是低估了新闻界的力量. (**b**) political control; rule 政权; 统治: *seize power*, ie in a political coup 夺取政权 ○ *This government came (in)to power at the last election.* 这一届政府是经最近大选后上台执政的. **5** [C esp *pl* 尤作复数] right possessed by or given to a person or group; authority (个人或团体所掌握或获得的)职权; 权势: *The powers of the police need to be clearly defined.* 必须对警方的权限作出明确的规定. ○ *The President has exceeded his powers*, ie has done more than he is allowed or has the right to do. 总统已逾越了自己的职权. ○ (*law* 律) *power of attorney*, ie the right to act on sb's behalf in business or financial matters 委任权(在商务或财务中代表某人之权利). **6** [C] person, group or state with great authority or influence 很有权力或影响力的人、团体或国家: *world powers*, ie countries with the most influence in international affairs 世界大国(在国际事务中最具影响力的国家) ○ *'Is the press a great power in your country?' 'Yes, it's far more important than the Church.'* '贵国的新闻界有很大的影响力吗?' '有, 新闻界比起教会来要重要得多.' ○ *The country was a great naval power in past centuries*, ie had great international influence because it had a large navy. 该国在前几个世纪是海上强国. ○ *No power on earth could force me to do it.* 谁也不能强迫我做这事. **7** [U] (**a**) energy that can be harnessed and used to do work 动力: *wind, nuclear, hydroelectric power* 风力、核动力、水电动力 ○ *We need to provide industry with power it can afford.* 我们需向工业界提供他们负担得起的电力. ○ [attrib 作定语] *the power supply* 电源. (**b**) [attrib 作定语] operated by mechanical or electrical energy 机动的; 电动的: *power brakes/steering* 动力制动器[转向装置] ○ *power tools* 电动工具. (**c**) (of an engine, etc) capacity or performance (发动机等的)功率, 性能: *a car's power of acceleration* 汽车的加速性能 ○ *the terrifying power of the huge machine* 巨型机器的巨大功率. **8** [C esp *sing* 尤作单数] (*mathematics* 数) result obtained by multiplying a number by itself a certain number of times 乘方; 幂: *the third power of 2 (= 2 × 2 × 2 = 8)* 2的三次幂(= 2 × 2 × 2 = 8) ○ *the second, third, fourth, etc power of x* $(= x^2, x^3, x^4$, *etc*) x的二次、三次、四次等幂$(= x^2、x^3、x^4$ 等) ○ *to the power of sth*, ie multiplied by itself a certain number of times 某数的自乘 ○ 4^4 *represents four to the power of four*, ie 4 × 4 × 4 × 4 = 256 4^4表示4自乘4次. **9** [U] (of a lens) capacity for magnifying (指透镜)放大率, 放大倍数: *the power of a microscope, telescope, etc* 显微镜、望远镜等的放大倍数. **10** [C] good or evil spirit 神灵; 鬼怪: *She believed in the existence of a benevolent power.* 她相信有大慈大悲的神仙. ○ *the powers of darkness*, ie the forces of evil or of the Devil 邪恶的势力. **11** (idm 习语) **the corridors of power** ⇨ CORRIDOR. **do sb a ˈpower of good** (*infml* 口) be very beneficial to sb 对某人大有好处: *Her holiday has done her a power of good.* 她度过了这一假期对她大有好处. ○ *A long cool drink would do us all a power of good!* 我们要是能喝上一大杯清凉饮料, 那多好哇! **in ˈpower** having control or authority 掌握权力: *the party in power* 执政党 ○ *The Government has been in power for two years.* 这届政府已执政两年. **more power to sb's ˈelbow** (*infml* 口) (used to express encouragement to sb doing sth 用以鼓励某人做某事): *She is campaigning for an improved bus service — more power to her elbow!* 她正在发起一项改进公共汽车运营服务的活动——祝她成功! **the (real) power behind the ˈthrone** the person who really controls an organization, a country, etc, in contrast to the person who is legally in charge (组织、国家等中)幕后实际掌握权力的人: *The President's wife was suspected of being the real power behind the throne.* 总统夫人有充当幕后掌权者之嫌. **the ˌpowers that ˈbe** (*often ironic* 常作反语) people who control an organization, a country, etc (组织、国家等之)当权者, 当权派: *He was waiting for the powers that be to decide what his next job would be.* 他在等待当权派给他分派下一工作.

▷ **powered** *adj* equipped with or operated by mechanical energy 有动力装置的; 用动力推动的: *a new aircraft* *powered by Rolls Royce engines* 一架装备有罗尔斯·罗伊斯(亦译劳斯·莱斯)发动机的新飞机 ○ *a high-powered car* 马力大的小汽车 ○ (*fig* 比喻) *rather low-powered political discussions* 显得有点没精打采的政治讨论.

□ ˈ**power-boat** *n* boat with an engine, esp a very powerful one, for racing or towing water-skiers 汽艇; 快艇.

ˈ**power cut** interruption in the supply of electricity 电力供应的中断; 停电: *the violent storms caused several power cuts* 造成几处停电的狂风暴雨.

ˈ**power-dive** *n* steep dive made by an aircraft with its engines working (飞机的)动力俯冲, 开油门俯冲. — *v* [I] (of an aircraft) make such a dive (指飞机)开油门俯冲.

P

ˈ**power house** **1** = POWER-STATION. **2** (*fig* 比喻) (**a**) very powerful group, organization, etc 强大的团体、组织等. (**b**) very strong or energetic person 身强力壮的人; 精力充沛的人.

ˈ**power-point** *n* socket on a wall, etc where electrical appliances can be plugged in to an electric circuit (墙上等处的)电源插座.

ˈ**power politics** political action or diplomacy based on the threat of using force 强权政治.

ˈ**power-station** (*US* ˈ**power plant**) *n* building where electricity is generated 发电站; 发电厂: *a coal-fired power-station* 燃煤火力发电站 ○ *a nuclear power-station* 核电站.

power·ful /ˈpaʊəfl; ˋpaʊɚfəl/ *adj* (**a**) of or having great power 强有力的; 力量大的: *a powerful blow* 有力的一击 ○ *a powerful machine, motor bike, engine, etc* 大功率的机器、摩托车、发动机等. (**b**) having a strong effect 很有效力的; 作用大的: *a powerful image, remedy, speech* 清晰的影像、特效的药品、有力的讲话 ○ *a powerful appeal to the public's sense of justice* 要求公众主持正义的强烈呼吁. (**c**) physically strong 强健的: *powerful legs* 强健的腿部 ○ *a man with a powerful physique* 身强力壮的男子. (**d**) having great control or influence 权力大的; 有势力的: *a powerful enemy, nation, ruler, trade union* 强敌、强国、强有力的统治者、有势力的工会. ▷ **power·fully** /-fəlɪ; -fəlɪ/ *adv*: *He is very powerfully built*, ie has a large strong physique. 他身强力壮.

power·less /ˈpaʊəlɪs; ˋpaʊɚlɪs/ *adj* **1** without power or strength 无权力的; 无力量的: *render sb powerless* 使某人失去权力. **2** ~ **to do sth** completely unable to do sth 对做某事无能为力的: *I am powerless to intervene in the matter.* 我对调停此事无能为力. ○ *They were powerless to resist.* 他们无力抵抗. ▷ **power·lessly** *adv*. **power·less·ness** *n* [U].

pow·wow /ˈpaʊwaʊ; ˋpaʊ,waʊ/ *n* **1** meeting or conference of N American Indians (北美印第安人的)会议. **2** (*infml* 口) meeting to discuss sth 讨论会: *hold a powwow* 举行讨论会.

▷ **pow·wow** *v* [I, Ipr] ~ **(about sth)** (*infml* 口) have a discussion (about sth) 讨论(某事物).

pox /pɒks; pɑks/ *n* **1 the pox** [sing] = SYPHILIS. **2** [U] (in compounds 用以构成复合词) disease that causes pock-marks 痘: ˈ*smallpox* ○ ˈ*chicken-pox*.

pp *abbr* 缩写 = **1** pages. **2** /ˌpiː ˈpiː; ˌpi ˋpi/ (also **per pro** /pɜː ˈprəʊ; ˌpɝ ˋpro/) (before a signature) on behalf of (Latin *per procurationem*) (签字前)代表...(源自拉丁文*per procurationem*): *pp J E Symonds*, eg signed by his secretary in his absence 代表J·E·西蒙兹(例如本人不在场而由秘书代签者). **3** (*music* 音) very softly; very quietly (Italian *pianissimo*) 极柔和, 极轻(源自意大利文*pianissimo*). Cf 参看 FF 2.

PPE /ˌpiː piː ˈiː; ˌpi pi ˋi/ *abbr* 缩写 = (*Brit*) (esp at Oxford University) philosophy, politics and economics (尤用于牛津大学)哲学、政治学和经济学: *a degree in PPE* 哲学、政治学和经济学学位.

PPS (also **pps**) /ˌpiː piː ˈes; ˌpi pi ˋɛs/ *abbr* 缩写 = (esp at the end of a letter) additional postscript (Latin *post postscriptum*) (尤用于信末)再附言(源自拉丁文*post postscriptum*). Cf 参看 PS 2.

PR /ˌpiː ˈɑː(r); ˌpi ˋɑr/ *abbr* 缩写 = **1** proportional representation. **2** (*infml* 口) public relations: *a PR exercise*, ie one that tries to create good will while not solving problems or achieving results 公关活动.

pr *abbr* 缩写 = **1** (*pl* **prs**) pair. **2** price.

prac·tic·able /ˈpræktɪkəbl; ˋpræktɪkəbl̩/ *adj* **1** that can be put into practice; workable 可以实施的; 行得通的: *a practicable scheme, solution, suggestion, etc* 切实可行的计划、解决办法、建议等. **2** (of roads, etc) fit to be used by traffic; passable (指道路等)适于车辆往来的, 可通行的: *the mountain route that is practicable only in summer* 只有在夏季才可以通行的山路. Cf 参看 IMPRACTICABLE. ▷ **prac·tic·ab·il·ity** /ˌpræktɪkəˈbɪlətɪ; ˌpræktɪkəˋbɪlətɪ/ *n* [U]. **prac·tic·ably** /-əblɪ; -əblɪ/ *adv*.

prac·tical /ˈpræktɪkl; ˋpræktɪkl/ *adj* **1** concerned with practice(1) and action rather than theory 实践的; 实际的: *practical experience, skills* 实践经验、实际技能 ○ *It's an interesting idea but there are many practical difficulties.* 这是一个很有意思的想法, 然而却存在着许多实际困难. Cf 参看 THEORETICAL 1. **2** suitable for the purpose for which it was made; useful 切合实际的; 实用的: *a practical device with many different uses* 一种多用途的实用器械 ○ *practical clothing for outdoor sports* 适于室外运动穿的衣服 ○ *Your invention is ingenious, but not very practical.* 你所发明的东西巧是巧, 但不太实用. **3** (**a**) (of a person) clever at doing and making things (指人)心灵手巧的: *She's very practical.* 她心灵手巧. ○ *He has a practical partner who organizes everything for him.* 他有个很能干的伙伴, 替他把一切弄得井井有条. (**b**) sensible and realistic 讲求实际的; 实事求是的: *We must be practical and work out the cost before we make a decision.* 我们应该实事求是地先把费用算出来, 然后再做决定. **4** that is so in effect; virtual 事实上的; 实际上的: *The owner's brother has been in practical control of the firm for years.* 业主的弟弟实际控制该商行已有多年. **5** (idm 习语) **for (all) ˈpractical purposes** as far as really matters; in reality 事实上; 实际上: *The sale was supposed to last for a week, but for all practical purposes it's over.* 减价销售原来预料要持续一周, 然而实际上现在已经结束了. Cf 参看 IMPRACTICAL.

▷ **prac·tical** *n* (*infml* 口) practical(1) examination or lesson, eg in a scientific subject 实验课考试, 实习课(如某一学科的): *a physics practical* 物理实验.

prac·tic·al·ity /ˌpræktɪˈkælətɪ; ˌpræktɪˋkælətɪ/ *n* **1** [U] quality or state of being sensible and realistic 实际性; 现实性; 实用性: *He questioned the practicality of the proposal.* 他对该项建议的可行性表示怀疑. **2 practicalities** [pl] practical(1) matters rather than ideas 实际的事务: *We need to start discussing practicalities.* 我们需要着手讨论实际问题.

prac·tic·ally /-klɪ; -klɪ/ *adv* **1** almost; virtually 几乎; 实际上: *It rained practically every day.* 几乎天天下雨. ○ *His work is practically unknown here.* 他的作品在这里实际上不为人知. **2** in a practical manner 实际地; 实事求是地: *She solved the problem very practically.* 她很实事求是地解决了这个问题.

□ ˌ**practical** ˈ**joke** trick played on sb for amusement, usu involving some physical action 恶作剧: *The children put salt in the sugar bowl as a practical joke.* 孩子们玩恶作剧把盐放进了糖罐里. ˌ**practical** ˈ**joker** person who plays practical jokes 玩恶作剧的人.

prac·tice /ˈpræktɪs; ˋpræktɪs/ *n* **1** [U] actual doing of sth; action as contrasted with theory 实践; 实际: *put a plan into practice* 实行某计划 ○ *The idea would never work in practice*, ie It seems good in theory but would be useless if carried out. 那种设想永远也实现不了. **2** (**a**) [U] regularly repeated exercise done in order to improve one's skill (经常反复的)练习: *an hour's practice every day* 每天一小时的练习 ○ *Playing the piano well requires a lot of practice.* 要弹好钢琴就得多练习. ○ [attrib 作定语] *a practice game* 练习赛. (**b**) [C] period of time spent doing this 进行练习的一段时间; 练习期间: *The players will meet for a practice in the morning.* 运动员们在早上一起训练. **3** (**a**) [U] way of doing sth that is common or habitual 惯例; 常规: *It is accepted/standard practice to pay a deposit with one's order.* 在预订时交付定金是一般的[普遍遵守的]惯例. ○ *Paying bills promptly is good financial practice.* 及时付帐是理财的好习惯. ○ *It is the practice in Britain to drive on the left.* 车辆靠左行驶是英国的制度. (**b**) [C] thing done regularly; habit or custom 惯常做的事; 习惯; 习俗: *the practice of closing shops on Sundays* 星期天店铺休业的惯例 ○ *I had coffee after dinner, as is my usual practice.* 我饭后喝咖啡, 这是我的习惯. **4** (**a**) [U] work of a doctor or lawyer (医生或律师的)工作: *a doctor working in general practice*, ie as a family doctor 全科医生(如家庭医生) ○ *She has retired from practice/is no longer in practice.* 她已退休[已不再执业]. (**b**) [C] (place of) business of a doctor or lawyer (医生或律师的)业务; 诊所; 律师事务所: *a medical/legal practice* 诊所[法律事务所] ○ *a group practice*, ie a partnership of several doctors 联合诊所(由几位医生联合执业) ○ *His practice is in the centre of the city.* 他的事务所位于市中心. ○ *She has just bought (into) a very profitable practice.* 她刚买下一个赢利很高的事务所(的股票). **5** [U] (**a**) (esp of a doctor or lawyer) practising one's profession (尤指医生或律师的)执业, 生意: *the practice of law/medicine* 律师的业务[医生的行医]. (**b**) exercising one's faith, etc 修养: *the practice of one's religion* 修道. **6** (idm 习语) **ˌin/ˌout of ˈpractice** having/not having spent time doing practice 勤于[疏于]实践或练习: *It's important to keep in practice.* 经常练习很重要. ○ *If you don't play, you'll get out of practice.* 不练习就会荒疏. **make a habit/practice of sth** ⇨ HABIT. **ˌpractice makes ˈperfect** (*saying* 谚) doing sth (eg a skill or craft) repeatedly is the only way to become very good at it 熟能生巧. **sharp practice** ⇨ SHARP.

prac·ti·cian /prækˈtɪʃn; prækˈtɪʃən/ *n* = PRACTITIONER.

prac·tise (*US* **prac·tice**) /ˈpræktɪs; ˈpræktɪs/ *v* **1** [I, Ipr, Tn, Tn·pr, Tg] **~ (sth) (on sth)** do sth repeatedly or regularly in order to improve one's skill 练习; 实习: *I haven't been practising enough.* 我练习得还不够. ○ *She's practising (a new piece) on the piano.* 她在练习弹奏(一支新曲子). ○ *I need to practise my Italian before my business trip.* 我出差以前需要练习一下意大利语. ○ *Practise throwing the ball into the net.* 练习投篮. **2** [Tn] make (sth) part of one's behaviour by doing it regularly 经常做(某事)养成习惯: *practise economy, patience, self-control, etc* 厉行节约、锻炼耐性、锻炼自制力. **3** [I, Ipr, Tn] **~ (as sth)** work as a doctor or lawyer 执业为医生或律师: *Does he still practise?* 他还在执业吗? ○ *She practised as a solicitor for many years.* 她当了许多年事务律师. ○ *practise homoeopathic medicine* 施行顺势疗法. **4** [I, Tn] do (sth) actively 积极从事(某事物): *He was a Catholic but didn't practise (his religion).* 他那时是天主教徒, 但并不实践信仰. ○ *a practising Anglican* 实践信仰的圣公会教徒. **5** (idm 习语) **ˌpractise what one ˈpreaches** do habitually oneself what one tells others to do 躬行实践; 身体力行.

▷ **prac·tised** (*US* **-ticed**) *adj* **~ (in sth)** expert, esp as a result of much practice; experienced 熟练的; 内行的; 有经验的: *He performed the job with practised skill.* 他干这工作很熟练. ○ *practised in the art of deception* 善使手腕骗人的.

prac·ti·tioner /prækˈtɪʃənə(r); prækˈtɪʃənɚ/ (also **practician**) *n* **1** person who practises a skill or an art 习艺者; 实习者. **2** person who practises a profession, esp medicine 从业者; (尤指)行医者: *a general practitioner* 全科医生.

prae·si·dium = PRESIDIUM.

prag·matic /prægˈmætɪk; prægˈmætɪk/ *adj* **1** treating things in a sensible and realistic way; concerned with practical results 务实的; 实事求是的; 注重实效的: *a politician valued for his pragmatic approach* 因讲求实际而受人尊重的政治家 ○ *a pragmatic solution to the problem* 实事求是地解决问题的方法. **2** of or concerning pragmatism(2) 实用主义的; 实用主义观点的. ▷ **prag·mat·ic·ally** /-klɪ; -klɪ/ *adv*.

prag·mat·ism /ˈprægmətɪzəm; ˈprægmə,tɪzəm/ *n* [U] (*fml* 文) **1** thinking about or treating things in a practical way 实用的观点或思想方法. **2** (in philosophy) belief that the truth or value of a theory can only be judged by its practical results (哲学)实用主义.

▷ **prag·mat·ist** /-tɪst; -tɪst/ *n* **1** person who acts in a practical way 做事从实际出发的人. **2** believer in pragmatism(2) 实用主义者.

prairie /ˈpreərɪ; ˈprɛrɪ/ *n* wide area of level grassland, esp in N America; plain[2] 大草原(尤指北美洲的). Cf 参看 PAMPAS, SAVANNAH, STEPPE, VELD.

□ **ˌprairie-ˈdog** *n* small N American burrowing animal with a bark like a dog's 草原犬鼠(产自北美洲, 穴居, 叫声似犬吠).

praise[1] /preɪz; prez/ *v* **1** [Tn, Tn·pr, Cn·n/a] **~ sb/sth (for sth); ~ sb/sth as sth** express approval or admiration for sb/sth 称赞或赞赏某人[某事物]: *The guests praised the meal.* 客人们称赞这顿饭做得好. ○ *He was obviously expecting to be praised.* 他显然想要得到表扬. ○ *He praised her for her courage.* 他赞扬她很勇敢. ○ *Critics praised the work as highly original.* 评论家们称赞该作品独树一帜. **2** [Tn] honour or glorify (God) in prayer; worship 赞美, 颂扬(上帝); 崇拜. **3** (idm 习语) **praise, etc sb to the skies** ⇨ SKY.

praise[2] /preɪz; prez/ *n* [U] **1** expression of approval or admiration; act of praising (PRAISE[1] 1)称赞; 赞美; 赞扬: *high* (ie great) *praise* 高度的赞扬 ○ *courage beyond* (ie too great for) *praise* 无与伦比的勇气 ○ *He received praise from his colleagues for winning the prize.* 他因获得该奖而受到同事们的称赞. ○ *an achievement worthy of great praise* 值得大加表扬的成绩 ○ *The leader spoke in praise of those who had died for their country.* 领导人表彰为国捐躯的人们. **2** worship (of God); glory (对上帝的)崇拜; 荣耀: *a hymn of praise* 赞美诗 ○ *Praise be (to God)*, ie Thank goodness! 谢天谢地! **3** (idm 习语) **be loud in one's praise** ⇨ LOUD. **damn sb/sth with faint praise** ⇨ DAMN[1]. **sing sb's/sth's praises** ⇨ SING.

▷ **ˈpraise·worthy** /-wɜːðɪ; -wɝðɪ/ *adj* deserving praise; commendable 值得称赞的; 值得表扬的: *a very praiseworthy achievement* 值得大大夸奖的成绩. **praise·worthily** /-ðɪlɪ; -ðəlɪ/ *adv*. **praise·wor·thi·ness** *n* [U].

pra·line /ˈprɑːliːn; ˈprɑ,lin/ *n* sweet[2](1) made by browning nuts in boiling sugar, used esp as a flavouring or filling for chocolate confectionery 果仁糖(尤用作巧克力点心的加料或夹馅).

pram /præm; præm/ *n* (*Brit*) (*US* **ˈbaby buggy, baby carriage, buggy**) four-wheeled carriage, pushed by hand, for a baby (手推的)婴儿车(有四轮).

prance /prɑːns; *US* præns; præns/ *v* **1** [I] (of a horse) move jerkily by raising the forelegs and springing forward from the hind legs (指马)腾跃. **2** (phr v) **prance about, along, around, in, out, etc** move in the specified direction in a high-spirited or arrogant way 手舞足蹈地或神气活现地朝某方向移动: *She was prancing along in her new outfit.* 她穿着全套新衣服神气活现地走着. ○ *He pranced out of the room in a fury.* 他盛怒之下大摇大摆走出了房间. ○ *They were prancing about* (ie jumping or dancing happily) *to the music.* 他们跟着音乐欢蹦乱跳.

▷ **prance** *n* [sing] prancing movement (马的)腾跃; 欢蹦乱跳; 昂首阔步.

prang /præŋ; præŋ/ *v* [Tn] (*sl* 俚 *esp Brit*) damage (a vehicle) in a crash 撞毁, 撞坏(车辆): *He's pranged his new bike.* 他把他那辆新自行车撞坏了.

▷ **prang** *n* (damage caused to a vehicle in a) crash (车辆等的)撞毁, 碰撞: *He's had a bit of a prang.* 他出了严重的撞车事故.

prank /præŋk; præŋk/ *n* playful or mischievous trick 玩笑; 恶作剧: *a childish prank* 像孩子般的胡闹 ○ *play a prank on sb* 戏弄某人.

▷ **prank·ster** /ˈpræŋkstə(r); ˈpræŋkstɚ/ *n* person who plays pranks 开玩笑者; 搞恶作剧的人.

prate /preɪt; pret/ *v* (*derog* 贬) (**a**) [I, Ip] **~ (on about sth)** talk or chatter too much (about sth) (对某事物)喋喋不休, 唠唠叨叨: *Listen to him prating on about nothing.* 听他瞎唠叨. (**b**) [I] talk (foolishly) 胡扯: *a prating idiot* 胡说八道的笨蛋.

prattle /ˈprætl; ˈprætḷ/ *v* [I, Ip] (**a**) **~ (away)** (of a child) talk in a simple way; babble (指儿童)说简单的话, 牙牙学语: *The baby is prattling (away) happily in her cot.* 那幼儿在小床上牙牙自语, 快活得很. (**b**) (*often derog* 常作贬义) **~ (on about sth)** (of an adult) talk at length, esp about unimportant things (指成人)絮絮叨叨地说; (尤指)闲聊: *prattle on about the village gossip* 闲扯些村里的事.

▷ **prattle** *n* [U] unimportant chatter; gossip 闲聊; 闲话.

prat·tler /ˈprætlə(r); ˈprætlɚ/ *n* (*often derog* 常作贬义) person who prattles (PRATTLE b) 说话絮叨的人.

prawn /prɔːn; prɔn/ *n* type of edible shellfish like a large shrimp 大虾; 对虾; 明虾: [attrib 作定语] *a ˌprawn ˈcocktail*, ie a dish of prawns served with mayonnaise 一盘浇有蛋黄酱的大虾.

pray /preɪ; pre/ *v* **1** [I, Ipr, Tn·pr, Tf, Tt] **~ (to sb) (for sb/sth); ~ sb (for sth)** offer thanks, make requests known, etc (to God) 祈祷; 祷告: *The priest prayed for the dying man.* 牧师为死者做祷告. ○ *They prayed (to God) for an end to their sufferings/for their sufferings to end.* 他们为早日结束苦难而祈祷. ○ *They prayed that she would recover.* 他们为她尽快康复而祈祷. ○ *She prayed to be forgiven/(to) God for forgiveness.* 她祈求宽恕[上帝宽恕]. **2** [Tn·pr, Dn·t] **~ sb (for sth)** (*dated fml* 旧, 文) ask sb (for sth/to do sth) as a favour; beg (为某事物)恳求某人; 乞求某人(做某事物): *We pray you for mercy/to show mercy.* 我们恳求你发慈悲. ○ *We pray you to set the prisoner free.* 我们恳求你释放这个囚犯.

P

prayer /preə(r); prɛr/ *n* **1** (**a**) [C] **~ (for sth)** solemn request to God or to an object of worship 祈祷; 祷告: *say one's prayers* 做祷告 ○ *a prayer for forgiveness, rain, success* 为获得宽恕、雨水、成功而做的祷告 ○ *He arrived, as if in answer to her prayers.* 他终于来了, 好像她祷告很灵验. (**b**) fixed form of words used for this 祈祷文: *the Lord's Prayer* 主祷文 ○ *prayers he had learnt as a child* 他儿时念过的祈祷文. **2** [U] action of praying 祈祷; 祷告: *spend time in prayer* 做祷告 ○ *Let us kneel in prayer.* 我们跪下祈祷吧. ○ *She believed in the power of prayer.* 她相信祈祷的力量. **3** (**a**) [sing] form of religious service consisting mainly of prayers (宗教的)祈祷式: *Evening/Morning Prayer* 晚[早]祷. (**b**) **prayers** [pl] informal meeting in order to pray (非正式的)祷告会: *family/morning/evening/daily prayers* 家庭的[早晨的/晚上的/每天的]祷告会.

□ ˈ**prayer-book** *n* (**a**) book containing prayers, for use in church, etc (教堂等使用的)祈祷书. (**b**) **the** ˈ**Prayer Book** (also **the** ˌ**Book of** ˌ**Common** ˈ**Prayer**) prayer-book used in Anglican services (圣公会的)祈祷书, 公祷书.

ˈ**prayer-mat** (also ˈ**prayer-rug**) *n* small carpet on which Muslims kneel when praying (穆斯林做祷告时用的)跪毯.

ˈ**prayer-meeting** *n* (esp in Protestant churches) meeting where people say personal prayers aloud to God (尤指新教教会的)祷告会.

ˈ**prayer-wheel** *n* revolving drum-shaped box inscribed with or containing prayers, used esp by Tibetan Buddhists (西藏喇嘛教徒用的刻有或带有祈祷文的)祈祷轮, 地藏车.

pre- *pref* 前缀 (used fairly widely with *vs*, *ns*, *adjs* and *advs* 与大量动词、名词、形容词、副词连用) before 在...前; 先于: *pre-cook* ○ *prefabricate* ○ *pre-medication* ○ *pre-Christian* ○ *prematurely*. Cf 参看 ANTE-, POST-.

preach /priːtʃ; pritʃ/ *v* **1** (**a**) [I, Ipr] **~ (to sb) (about/against/on sth)** give a sermon, esp in church 讲道, 布道(尤指在教堂中): *The vicar preached to the congregation for half an hour.* 那位教区牧师向会众讲道半个小时. ○ *He preaches well.* 他讲道讲得好. ○ *What did he preach about/on?* 他宣讲了什么? ○ *He preached against violence.* 他讲道中宣讲反对暴力的道理. (**b**) [Tn, Dn·pr] **~ sth (to sb)** give (a sermon) 讲(道); 布(道): *He preaches the same sermon every Christmas.* 他每逢圣诞节都宣讲同一教旨. (**c**) [Tn, Dn·pr] **~ sth (to sb)** make (a religion or teaching) known by talking about it publicly; teach (sth) 宣扬(教义或教条); 教导(某事物): *preach the Gospel/the word of God* 传布福音[上帝的道] ○ *They preached the new doctrines throughout Europe.* 他们在全欧洲宣讲这一新学说. **2** [Tn] try to persuade people to accept or support (sth); advocate 劝说人们赞成或支持(某事物); 说教; 鼓吹: *She preached economy as the best means of solving the crisis.* 她大力鼓吹节约是解决危机的关键. ○ *He was always preaching the virtues of capitalism.* 他总是宣传资本主义的长处. **3** [I, Ipr] **~ (at/to sb)** (*often derog* 常作贬义) give unwanted advice on morals, behaviour, etc, esp in a persistent, annoying manner 进行道德、操守等方面的说教(尤指唠叨、令人厌烦): *I am tired of listening to you preach (at me).* 我懒得听你(对我讲)的大道理. ○ *You are in no position to preach to me about efficiency!* 你没有资格对我大谈什么效率问题! **4** (idm 习语) **practise what one preaches** ⇨ PRACTISE. **preach to the conˈverted** speak to people in support of views that they already hold 对人们宣传他们早已持有的观点: *Telling conservationists that we need to preserve the natural heritage really is preaching to the converted!* 向自然资源保护论者宣讲需要保护自然界遗产的道理, 真是多此一举.

▷ **preacher** *n* person who preaches, esp a clergyman who preaches sermons: 说教者; 鼓吹者; (尤指)传道人, 讲道的教士 ○ *a good preacher* 善于说教的人 ○ *a preacher famous for his inspiring sermons* 以讲道能激励人心见称的传道人.

pre·amble /priːˈæmbl; ˈpriæmbl̩/ *n* [C, U] **~ (to sth)** opening statement explaining the purpose of the book, document, lecture, etc that follows (书籍、文件、讲演等的)前言, 序言, 开场白: *He launched into his statement without any preamble.* 他开门见山地发表言论.

pre-arrange /ˌpriːəˈreɪndʒ; ˌpriəˈrendʒ/ *v* [Tn] arrange (sth) in advance 预先安排(某事物): *Run to your positions when you hear the prearranged signal.* 你们听到预定的信号时, 就各就各位. ▷ **pre-arrangement** *n* [U].

preb·end /ˈprebənd; ˈprɛbənd/ *n* (*religion* 宗) income paid to a priest from the revenue of a church, esp a cathedral 牧师的薪俸.

▷ **preb·end·ary** /ˈprebəndrɪ; *US* -derɪ; ˈprɛbəndˌɛrɪ/ *n* priest who receives a prebend 受俸牧师.

pre·car·ious /prɪˈkeərɪəs; prɪˈkɛrɪəs/ *adj* **1** depending on chance; uncertain 依靠机会的; 不确定的: *She makes a rather precarious living as a novelist.* 她当小说家, 过着不太稳定的生活. **2** unsteady; unsafe 不稳固的; 不安全的: *He was unable to get down from his precarious position on the rocks.* 他无法从岩石危险的位置上下来.

▷ **pre·car·iously** *adv*: *to perch precariously* 摇摇欲坠 ○ *They lived precariously on the income from a few small investments.* 他们依靠些微投资中的收入, 过着朝不保夕的生活. **pre·car·ious·ness** *n* [U].

pre-cast /ˌpriːˈkɑːst; *US* -ˈkæst; ˈpriˈkæst/ *adj* (of concrete) made into blocks ready for use in building (指混凝土)预先浇铸的, 预制的.

pre·cau·tion /prɪˈkɔːʃn; prɪˈkɔʃən/ *n* **~ (against sth)** thing done in advance to avoid danger, prevent problems, etc 预防措施或方法: *take an umbrella just as a precaution* 带把伞, 有备无患 ○ *fire precautions/precautions against fire* 防火措施 ○ *I took the precaution of locking everything in the safe.* 我把一切东西都锁在保险箱里以防万一.

▷ **pre·cau·tion·ary** /prɪˈkɔːʃənərɪ; *US* -nerɪ; prɪˈkɔʃənˌɛrɪ/ *adj* done as a precaution; preventive 防备的; 预防的: *precautionary measures* 预防措施.

pre·cede /prɪˈsiːd; prɪˈsid/ *v* **1** [I, Tn] come or go before (sth) in time, order, rank, etc (在时间、顺序、行列等上)在(某事物)之前; 先于(某事物): *The Mayor entered, preceded by members of the council.* 市政会的委员们入场后, 市长也入场了. ○ *This point has been dealt with in the preceding paragraph.* 这一点在前面一段里已经交代过了. ○ *the days that preceded the final catastrophe* 大祸即将临头的那些日子. **2** [Tn·pr] **~ sth with sth** say sth before sth 在讲某话之前先讲某话; 在讲...前加上...: *She preceded her speech with a vote of thanks to the committee.* 她发表讲话以前先提议向全体委员表示感谢.

pre·ced·ence /ˈpresɪdəns; ˈprɛsədəns/ *n* [U] **~ (over sb/sth)** right to come before sb/sth in time, order, rank, etc (在时间、顺序、行列等上)领先于某人[某事物]的权利; 优先权: *The longest-serving officer always takes precedence.* 任职时间最长的官员事事优先. ○ *The elder son has precedence over the younger one.* 长子较之非长子享有优先权. ○ *The needs of the community must take precedence over* (ie must be met before) *individual requirements.* 公众的利益高于个人的利益. ○ *a list of the English aristocracy in order of precedence*, ie in order of social rank 按社会等级排列的英国贵族名单.

pre·ced·ent /ˈpresɪdənt; ˈprɛsədənt/ *n* (**a**) [C] earlier decision, case, event, etc that is regarded as an example or rule for what comes later 可援为先例的判决、事例、事件等: *create/establish/set a precedent (for sth)* (为某事物)开创先例 ○ *serve as a precedent for sth* 为某事物提供范例 ○ *There is no precedent for such an action.* 这种行动没有先例可循. (**b**) [U] existing precedents (used esp in the expressions shown) 先例(尤用于下列示例): *without precedent* 没有先例 ○ *break with precedent*, ie not act according to precedents 打破先例(不按先例行事).

▷ **pre·ced·en·ted** *adj* having or supported by a precedent 有先例的; 有前例可援的: *a decision not* *precedented in English law* 在英国法律中无前例可援的判决.

pre·centor /prɪˈsentə(r); prɪˈsɛntɚ/ *n* clergyman who is in charge of the music in a cathedral and (often) leads the singers (教堂歌咏班的)领唱者.

pre·cept /ˈpri:sept; ˈprisɛpt/ *n* **1** [C] rule or guide, esp for behaviour 规范; 准则; (尤指)格言, 箴言: *follow the precepts of one's religion* 遵循自己的宗教戒律 ○ *He lived by the precept 'practise what you preach'.* 他奉行'言行一致'的准则. **2** [U] moral instruction 道德箴言; 教训: *Example is better than precept.* 身教胜于言教.

▷ **pre·ceptor** /prɪˈseptə(r); prɪˈsɛptɚ/ *n* (*fml* 文) teacher 教师; 导师.

pre·ces·sion /prɪˈseʃn; prɪˈsɛʃən/ *n* [U] (also **pre,cession of the 'equinoxes**) gradual change in the angle at which the earth revolves daily, causing the equinoxes to occur slightly earlier in each successive year 岁差(地球自转角度的渐次变化, 使每年的春分点及秋分点比上年略为提前).

pre·cinct /ˈpri:sɪŋkt; ˈprisɪŋkt/ *n* **1** [C] area enclosed by definite boundaries, esp the walls of a cathedral, church or college (有界限围成的)区域; (尤指)教堂或大学墙以内的境域: *a sacred precinct* 教堂的地界范围 ○ *these hallowed precincts* 这些神圣的境域. **2** [C] (*Brit*) area in a town for specific or restricted use, esp one where vehicles may not enter 城镇中有某用途的或受限制的地区; (尤指禁止机动车通行的)行人专用区: *a shopping precinct* 购物区 ○ *a pedestrian precinct* 行人专用区. **3** [C] (*US*) subdivision of a county, city, etc (县、市等的)分区: *an election precinct* 选区 ○ *a police precinct* 警察分管区. **4 precincts** [pl] (**a**) boundaries; limits 界限; 范围: *No parking within the hospital precincts.* 医院范围内禁止停放车辆. (**b**) area around a place; environs 周围地区; 附近: *the old city and its precincts* 旧城市及其郊区 ○ *the airport and precincts* 机场及周围地区.

pre·ci·os·ity /ˌpreʃɪˈɒsətɪ; ˌprɛʃɪˈɑsətɪ/ *n* (*fml* 文) (**a**) [U] over-refinement in language and art; being precious(3) (语言和艺术的)过于讲究; 矫揉造作. (**b**) [C often *pl* 常作复数] instance of this 过于讲究.

pre·cious /ˈpreʃəs; ˈprɛʃəs/ *adj* **1** of great value (and beauty) 贵重的; 宝贵的: *the precious metals*, ie gold, silver and platinum 贵金属(金、银、白金) ○ *precious gems/stones*, ie diamonds, rubies, emeralds, etc 宝石(钻石、红宝石、绿宝石等). **2 ~ (to sb)** highly valued; dearly loved 珍贵的; 受到珍爱的: *precious moments together* 相处在一起的珍贵时刻 ○ *Each life is precious.* 生命都是非常宝贵的. ○ *a precious memento of happier times* 幸福时日的珍贵纪念品 ○ *She is very precious to him.* 她在他心中占着非常重要的地位. ○ (*infml ironic* 口, 反语) *She talks about nothing except her precious car!* 她说话离不开她那宝贝汽车! **3** (*derog* 贬) (of language, style, etc) over-refined; unnatural (指语言、风格等)过于讲究的, 矫揉造作的: *poetry full of precious images* 尽是挖空心思的意象的诗篇 ○ *a rather precious young man* 惺惺作态的年轻男子. **4** (*infml often ironic* 口, 常作反语) considerable 可观的: *A precious lot of good that will do!* 那样做大有好处!

▷ **pre·cious** *adv* (used before *little, few* 用于 little、few 之前) (*infml* 口) very 很; 非常: *Precious few people can afford prices like that.* 没有什么人出得起那个价钱. ○ *She has precious little to be cheerful about.* 她几乎毫无乐趣.

pre·cious *n* (*infml* 口) (used as an affectionate name when speaking to sb 用作表示亲昵的称呼语) dear 亲爱的: *What did you say, (my) precious?* (我)亲爱的, 你说什么呀?

pre·ciously *adv* in a precious(3) manner 过于考究地; 矫揉造作地.

pre·cious·ness *n* [U] quality of being precious(1, 2) 贵重; 宝贵; 珍贵; 珍爱.

pre·cip·ice /ˈpresɪpɪs; ˈprɛsəpɪs/ *n* very steep or vertical face of a cliff, mountain or rock 悬崖; 峭壁: (*fig* 比喻) *The country's economy was on the edge of the precipice*, ie in danger of collapsing. 该国的经济已处于崩溃的边缘.

pre·cip·it·ate /prɪˈsɪpɪteɪt; prɪˈsɪpəˌtet/ *v* **1** [Tn] (*fml* 文) cause (sth) to happen suddenly or soon(er); hasten 使(某事物)突然或迅速地发生; 加速: *events that precipitated his ruin* 突然毁了他的事件 ○ *One small error precipitated the disaster.* 一个小小的错误酿成这一灾难. **2** [Tn, Tn·pr] (*fml* 文) (**a**) throw (sb/sth) with force (as if) from a great height (似)自极高处将(某人[某物])猛然扔下; 猛摔(某人[某物]). (**b**) **~ sb/sth into sth** (*fig* 比喻) throw sb/sth suddenly (into a state or condition) 使某人[某事物]突然陷入(某种状况): *The assassination of the ambassador precipitated the country into war.* 由于大使遇刺, 该国顿时进入了战争状态. **3** (*chemistry* 化) (**a**) [I] (of a substance) separate into solid form from the liquid in which it is held (指物质)沉淀, 淀析. (**b**) [Tn] cause (a substance) to do this 使(物质)沉淀; 析出(某种物质). **4** [I, Ipr, Tn, Tn·pr esp passive 尤用于被动语态] **~ (sth) (as sth)** (cause vapour to) condense and form rain, snow etc (使水气)冷凝成为雨、雪等: *The clouds precipitate/are precipitated as snow in winter.* 在冬天云冷凝成为雪.

▷ **pre·cip·it·ate** *n* [C, U] (**a**) solid matter that has been precipitated (PRECIPITATE 3b) from a solution 沉淀物; (液体的)析出物; 冷凝物. (**b**) moisture condensed from vapour and deposited (as rain, dew, etc) (水气的)凝结物(如雨、露等).

pre·cip·it·ate /prɪˈsɪpɪtət; prɪˈsɪpəˌtɪt/ *adj* (**a**) violently hurried 急促的; 迅猛的: *a precipitate dash* 猛冲. (**b**) (of an action) done without care or thought; rash[2] (指行动)鲁莽的, 未经考虑的, 仓促的: *his precipitate action in selling the property* 他变卖财产的草率行为. (**c**) (of a person) acting without care or thought; impulsive (指人)鲁莽的, 仓促行事的, 感情用事的. **pre·cip·it·ately** *adv*.

pre·cip·ita·tion /prɪˌsɪpɪˈteɪʃn; prɪˌsɪpəˈteʃən/ *n* **1** [U] (*fml* 文) violent haste 迅急; 匆促; 仓促; 鲁莽: *to act with precipitation* 仓促行事. **2** [U] separation of a solid substance from the liquid in which it is held 沉淀; 淀析. **3** (**a**) [C] fall of rain, sleet, snow or hail (雨、雨夹雪、雪、雹子等的)降落: *a heavy precipitation* 一场大雨(或雨夹雪、雪、雹子). (**b**) [U] amount of rain, etc that falls in an area 某地区降雨等的量: *the annual precipitation of the region* 该地区的年降雨量.

pre·cip·it·ous /prɪˈsɪpɪtəs; prɪˈsɪpətəs/ *adj* (*fml* 文) dangerously high or steep 险峻的; 陡峭的: *From a precipitous height we looked at the town spread out below.* 我们从险峻的高处眺望铺展在下面的城镇. ○ *a precipitous path down the mountainside* 沿山腰而下的一条陡峭的小路 ○ *a precipitous climb to the peak* 向着陡峭山顶的攀登. ▷ **pre·cip·it·ously** *adv*: *perched precipitously on the edge of the cliff* 位于峭壁上的.

pré·cis /ˈpreɪsi:; *US* preɪˈsi:; preˈsi/ *n* [U, C] (*pl* unchanged 复数不变 /-i:z; -iz/) restatement in shortened form of the main points or ideas of a speech or written text; summary (演说或文章的)摘要, 大意, 梗概, 大纲.

▷ **pré·cis** *v* [Tn] make a précis of (sth) 作(某事)的摘要; 写(某事)的大纲: *précising a scientific report* 给一份科学报告写摘要.

pre·cise /prɪˈsaɪs; prɪˈsaɪs/ *adj* **1** stated clearly and accurately 叙述清楚而准确的: *precise details, instructions, measurements* 准确的细节、明确的指示、精确的尺寸 ○ *a precise record of events* 对事件的准确的记载. **2** [attrib 作定语] exact; particular 精确的; 独特的: *at that precise moment* 恰在那时 ○ *It was found at the precise spot where she had left it.* 那东西正好在她遗落的那个地点找到了. **3** (of a person, his mind, etc) taking care to be exact and accurate, esp about minor details (指人、思想等)精细的, (尤指)一丝不苟的: *a precise mind, worker* 一丝不苟的头脑、工作者 ○ *100, or 99.8 to be precise* 100, 或准确说来是 99.8 ○ (*often derog* 常作贬义) *a man with a very prim and precise* (ie too careful or fussy) *manner* 一个锱铢必较的男子.

▷ **pre·cisely** *adv* **1** (**a**) exactly; just 精确地; 恰好: *at 2 o'clock precisely* 正好在两点钟 ○ *I can't remember precisely what happened.* 我记不准所发生的事情了. ○ *That is precisely what I mean.* 那正是我的意思. ○ *The two accounts are precisely the same.* 这两种说法如出一辙. (**b**) in a precise(2) manner; carefully 精确地; 细心地: *He enunciated the words very precisely.* 他吐字非常清楚. **2** (used to express agreement with a statement and often to suggest that it states the obvious 用以表示同意并常含有当然如此之意) you are right; quite so 对; 的确如此: *'But if the delivery is late, we will lose the order!' 'Precisely.'* '可要是不能如期交货, 我们就要失去这笔生意!' '的确如此.'

P

P

pre·cise·ness *n* [U] **1** quality of being precise (1) 准确; 精确; 明确. **2** = PRECISION 1.

pre·ci·sion /prɪˈsɪʒn; prɪˈsɪʒən/ *n* [U] **1** (also **preciseness**) exactness and clarity; quality of being precise(1) 准确(性); 明确(性); 精确(性): *Your report lacks precision.* 你的报告不够准确. ○ *Aim for more precision in your style.* 写东西时要力求准确. **2** accuracy 精密(度): *clockwork precision* 无比精确 ○ *The diagram had been copied with great precision.* 该图表的复制件极精确. ○ [attrib 作定语] *precision timing* 恰到好处的时机 ○ *precision instruments/tools,* ie those designed for very accurate work, measurements, etc 精密仪器[工具].

pre·clude /prɪˈklu:d; prɪˈklud/ *v* [Tn, Tn·pr, Tsg] **~ sb from doing sth** (*fml* 文) prevent (sth, or sb doing sth); make (sth) impossible 妨碍(某事物), 阻止(某人做某事); 使(某事物)行不通: *That sale precludes further development on this site.* 卖出以后妨碍了这一地点的进一步发展. ○ *Their move does not preclude others from investing.* 他们这一行动并不影响其他人进行投资. ○ *These conditions preclude our taking part in the negotiations.* 这些条件使我们无法参加谈判. ▷ **pre·clu·sion** /prɪˈklu:ʒn; prɪˈkluʒən/ *n* [U].

pre·co·cious /prɪˈkəʊʃəs; prɪˈkoʃəs/ *adj* (**a**) (of a child) having developed certain abilities at an earlier age than usual (指儿童)在某方面早熟的, 较早具备某种能力的, 超常的: *a precocious child who could play the piano at the age of three* 三岁就能弹奏钢琴的早慧儿童. (**b**) (of behaviour, ability, etc) showing this development (指行为、能力等)较早显出的, 超常的: *a precocious talent for mimicry* 超常的模仿才能 ○ *He shows a precocious interest in the opposite sex.* 他年纪轻轻就表现出对异性的兴趣. (**c**) (*derog* 贬) (of a child) behaving in a manner more suited to an older person (指儿童)老气的: *That child is far too precocious!* 那孩子过于老成! ▷ **pre·co·ciously** *adv.* **pre·co·cious·ness, pre·co·city** /prɪˈkɒsətɪ; prɪˈkɑsətɪ/ *ns* [U] being precocious (指儿童)早熟, 早慧, 老气.

pre·cog·ni·tion /ˌpri:kɒɡˈnɪʃn; ˌprikɑɡˈnɪʃən/ *n* [U] (*fml or psychology* 文或心) knowledge of sth before it occurs 早知; 预知; 预见.

pre·con·ceived /ˌpri:kənˈsi:vd; ˌprikənˈsivd/ *adj* [attrib 作定语] (of an idea, opinion, etc) formed in advance and not based on knowledge or experience (指思想、观点等)事先形成的: *Tourists forget their preconceived ideas as soon as they visit our country.* 游客访问了我国之后立刻消除了他们的先入之见.

pre·con·cep·tion /ˌpri:kənˈsepʃn; ˌprikənˈsɛpʃən/ *n* **~ (about sb/sth)** opinion or idea formed in advance and not based on experience or knowledge 事先形成的观点或思想; 先入之见: *Common preconceptions about life in this district are increasingly being challenged.* 原先普遍存在着对那一地区生活的成见越来越站不住脚了. Cf 参看 MISCONCEPTION (MISCONCEIVE).

pre-condition /ˌpri:kənˈdɪʃn; ˌprikənˈdɪʃən/ *n* = PREREQUISITE.

pre·cursor /ˌpri:ˈkɜ:sə(r); prɪˈkɝsɚ/ *n* (*fml* 文) **~ (of sth)** **1** person or thing that comes before sth; forerunner 先驱; 先行者; 先兆; 前兆: *small disturbances that were precursors of the revolution to come* 预示革命将爆发的小规模动乱. **2** machine or invention that is later developed further (机器或发明物的)初期形式: *The first telephone was the precursor of modern communications networks.* 最早出现的电话是现代通讯网的雏型.

pred·ator /ˈpredətə(r); ˈprɛdətɚ/ *n* **1** animal that kills and eats other animals 捕食其他动物的动物; 食肉动物: *predators of the African grasslands* 非洲草原的食肉动物. **2** (*derog or joc* 贬或谑) person who exploits others, esp financially or sexually 奴役他人者(尤指在财务或性关系方面): *He denounced all landlords and money-lenders as evil predators.* 他痛斥所有地主和放债者都是罪恶的剥削者.

pred·at·ory /ˈpredətrɪ; *US* -tɔ:rɪ; ˈprɛdəˌtɔrɪ/ *adj* **1** (of animals) (living by) killing other animals for food (指动物)捕食其他动物的, 食肉的: *predatory birds* 捕食动物的鸟 ○ *The domesticated cat retains its predatory instincts.* 猫依然保持着捕食动物的天性. **2** (**a**) (for the purpose of) plundering 掠夺的; 以掠夺为目的的: *predatory groups of bandits* 抢劫财物的匪帮 ○ *a predatory attack* 掠夺性的攻击. (**b**) (*derog or joc* 贬或谑) (of a person) wishing to exploit others for financial or sexual reasons (指人)(在财务或性关系方面)企图奴役他人的: *predatory advances, attentions, etc* 好色者的勾引、殷勤等 ○ *We were pestered by predatory salesmen.* 贪心的商人敲了我们竹杠.

pre·de·cease /ˌpri:dɪˈsi:s; ˌpridɪˈsis/ *v* [Tn] (*law* 律) die before (sb) 死于(某人)之前: *He left all his money to his wife without thinking that she might predecease him.* 他把全部金钱都交给了妻子, 而没有考虑到妻子可能死得比他早.

pre·de·ces·sor /ˈpri:dɪsesə(r); *US* ˈpredə-; ˌprɛdɪˈsɛsɚ/ *n* **1** person who held an office or position before sb else (职务或职位的)前任者: *The decision was made by my predecessor.* 那一决定是我的前任作出的. **2** thing that has been followed or replaced by sth else 被接继或被取代的事物: *Will the new plan be any more acceptable than its predecessors?* 新计划比原先的计划更能令人满意吗? Cf 参看 SUCCESSOR.

pre·des·tina·tion /ˌpri:destɪˈneɪʃn; ˌpridɛstəˈneʃən/ *n* [U] **1** (**a**) theory or belief that everything that happens has been predetermined by God and that man cannot change it 宿命论. (**b**) destiny that cannot be changed; fate 命运; 造化. **2** doctrine or belief that God has decreed in advance that certain souls will be saved and others will not 得救预定论(认为上帝已预先选定某些灵魂得救, 余者受咒诅).

pre·des·tine /ˌpri:ˈdestɪn; prɪˈdɛstɪn/ *v* [esp passive 尤用于被动语态: Tn, Cn·t] (*fml* 文) decide or determine sth (as if) by fate (仿佛)命中注定某事物: *It seemed that his failure was predestined.* 他的失败似乎是命中注定的. ○ *She was obviously predestined to succeed.* 她显然注定了能成功. ○ *They both felt that they were predestined to spend their lives together.* 他们俩都觉得他们注定了要在一起生活一辈子.

pre·de·ter·mine /ˌpri:dɪˈtɜ:mɪn; ˌpridɪˈtɝmɪn/ *v* (*fml* 文) [Tn esp passive 尤用于被动语态] decide or fix (sth) in advance; prearrange 预先决定或确定(某事物); 事先安排: *predetermined behaviour, strategies, responses* 既定的行为、策略、答复 ○ *A person's health is often genetically predetermined.* 人的体质通常是由遗传决定的. ▷ **pre·de·ter·mina·tion** /ˌpri:dɪˌtɜ:mɪˈneɪʃn; ˌpridɪˌtɝməˈneʃən/ *n* [U].

pre·dica·ment /prɪˈdɪkəmənt; prɪˈdɪkəmənt/ *n* difficult or unpleasant situation, esp one in which sb is uncertain what to do (困难的或为难的)处境, 窘况(尤指不知所措者): *Your refusal puts me in an awkward predicament.* 你一拒绝让我感到十分为难. ○ *A loan of money would help me out of my predicament.* 只需一笔贷款就能帮我摆脱困境.

pre·dic·ate[1] /ˈpredɪkət; ˈprɛdɪkət/ *n* (*grammar*) part of a statement that says sth about the subject, eg 'is short' in 'Life is short' 谓语(话中对主语进行陈述的部分, 如 Life is short 中的 is short). Cf 参看 SUBJECT[1] 4.

pre·dic·ate[2] /ˈpredɪkeɪt; ˈprɛdɪˌket/ *v* (*fml* 文) **1** [Tn, Tf, Tnt] declare or assert that (sth) is the case 宣称或断言(某事物): *predicate a motive to be good* 断言某动机是好的 ○ *predicate that the market collapse was caused by weakness of the dollar* 声称市场价格暴跌是由于美元疲弱而引起的. **2** [Tn·pr esp passive 尤用于被动语态] **~ sth on sth** base sth on sth; make sth necessary as a consequence of sth 使某事物依据于另事物; 使某必需的事物成为另事物的结果: *The project was predicated on the assumption that the economy was expanding.* 这一计划是以经济发展的设想为依据的.

pre·dic·at·ive /prɪˈdɪkətɪv; *US* ˈpredɪkeɪtɪv; ˈprɛdɪˌketɪv/ *adj* (*grammar*) (of an adjective or a noun) coming after a verb such as *be, become, get, seem, look* (指形容词或名词)用作表语的(即用在诸如be、become、get、seem、look 等动词后面的). Cf 参看 ATTRIBUTIVE. ▷ **pre·dic·at·ively** *adv.*

□ **predicative 'adjective** adjective used only after *be,* etc, eg 'asleep' as in 'She is asleep' 表语形容词(即只能用在be等之后的形容词, 如 She is asleep 中的 asleep).

pre·dict /prɪˈdɪkt; prɪˈdɪkt/ *v* [Tn, Tf, Tw] say in advance that (sth) will happen; forecast 预言(某事物)将发生; 预报; 预告: *The earthquake had been predicted several months before.* 这次地震早在几个月以前就发布了预报. ○ *She predicted that the improvement would continue.* 她预测情况将继续好转. ○ *It is impossible to predict who will win.* 要预测出谁将获胜是不可能的.

▷ **pre·dict·able** /-əbl; -əbḷ/ *adj* (**a**) that can be predicted 可预言的; 可预报的: *predictable behaviour, results, weather* 可预料的行为、结果、天气. (**b**) (*often derog* 常作贬义) (of a person) behaving in a way that can be predicted (指人)举动可以料到的: *I knew you'd say that — you're so predictable!* 我早就知道你会这样说——果不其然! ○ *Opposition to the proposal came from predictable quarters.* 对这项提案的反对意见来自那些早经料到会持反对态度的人. **pre·dict·ab·il·ity** /prɪˌdɪktəˈbɪlətɪ; prɪˌdɪktəˋbɪlətɪ/ *n* [U]. **pre·dict·ably** *adv*.

pre·dic·tion /prɪˈdɪkʃn; prɪˋdɪkʃən/ *n* **1** [U] (action of) predicting 预言; 预报; 预告. **2** [C] forecast or prophesy 预言; 预报; 预告: *Do you take seriously his prediction of a government defeat?* 他预料政府要受挫, 你认为这话靠得住吗?

pre·dictor *n* person, instrument, etc that predicts 进行预测或预报的人、仪器等; 预言者; 预测器.

pre·di·gest /ˌpriːdaɪˈdʒest; ˌpridaɪˋdʒɛst/ *v* [Tn esp passive 尤用于被动语态] treat (food) so that it is easy to digest 预先处理(食物)(以易于消化): *special predigested food for babies* 经特殊处理而易于消化的幼儿食品 ○ (*fig* 比喻) *predigested reading matter* 经过简写的阅读材料.

pre·di·lec·tion /ˌpriːdɪˈlekʃn; *US* ˌpredlˈek-; ˌprɛdḷˋɛkʃən/ *n* (*fml* 文) **~ (for sth)** special liking (for sth); preference (对某事物的)特殊爱好, 偏爱: *a predilection for Japanese food* 对日本食物的偏爱.

pre·dis·pose /ˌpriːdɪˈspəʊz; ˌpridɪsˋpoz/ *v* (*fml* 文) **1** [Tn·pr esp passive 尤用于被动语态, Tnt] **~ sb to/towards sth** influence sb (in a specified way) in advance 事先(在某方面)影响某人: *His early training predisposed him to a life of adventure.* 他早年所受的教养使他热衷于冒险活动. ○ *be predisposed in sb's favour*, ie be inclined to favour him 偏向某人(因事先受到影响). **2** [Tn·pr esp passive 尤用于被动语态] **~ sb to sth** cause sb to be liable to sth 使某人倾向于某事物; 使某人易患某病: *The inhabitants are predisposed to rheumatism by the damp climate.* 因气候潮湿, 居民易患风湿症.

pre·dis·posi·tion /ˌpriːdɪspəˈzɪʃn; ˌpridɪspəˋzɪʃən/ *n* [U, C] **~ (to/towards sth); ~ (to do sth)** state of mind or body that makes sb liable to act in a certain way or to suffer from a certain disease 性向; 癖性; 易患某病之身心素质: *a predisposition towards melancholia* 易患忧郁症的精神倾向 ○ *a predisposition to rheumatism* 易患风湿症的体质 ○ *a predisposition to criticize others* 喜欢挑人毛病的癖性.

pre·dom·in·ant /prɪˈdɒmɪnənt; prɪˋdɑmənənt/ *adj* **1** having more power or influence than others 有势力的; 占优势的: *Which country is the predominant member of the alliance?* 哪个国家在联盟中居于支配地位? ○ *The Socialists were predominant in the last Parliament.* 在上届国会中社会党人占优势. **2** most noticeable; prevailing 极其显著的; 盛行的: *Her predominant characteristic is honesty.* 她最为突出的特点是诚实.

▷ **pre·dom·in·ance** /-əns; -əns/ *n* **1** [U, sing] **~ (of sth)** state of being greater in strength, numbers, etc (力量、数量等的)优势: *the predominance of blue in the colour scheme* 在色彩设计中以蓝色为主 ○ *There is a predominance of men in the club.* 该俱乐部男人居多. **2** [U] **~ (over sb/sth)** state of being more powerful or influential (than sb/sth) 主导或支配(他人[他事物])的地位: *The policy is designed to prevent the predominance of one group over another.* 该政策旨在防止一些人压制另一些人. **pre·dom·in·antly** *adv* for the most part; mainly 大多; 主要地: *a predominantly English-speaking population* 以操英语者为主的居民.

pre·dom·in·ate /prɪˈdɒmɪneɪt; prɪˋdɑməˌnet/ *v* **1** [I, Ipr] **~ (over sb/sth)** have control, power or influence (over sb/sth) 支配, 统治, 左右(某人[某事物]): *A small group has begun to predominate in policy-making.* 一小撮人在制定政策中已开始起主导作用. **2** [I] be superior in numbers, strength, etc (在数量、力量等上)占优势: *a colour scheme in which red predominates* 以红色为主的色彩设计 ○ *Oak-trees predominate in this forest.* 这片森林以橡树居多.

pre-eminent /ˌpriːˈemɪnənt; prɪˋɛmənənt/ *adj* superior to all others; outstanding 超群的; 杰出的: *a scientist pre-eminent in his field* 在其领域中出类拔萃的科学家.

▷ **pre-eminence** /-əns; -əns/ *n* [U]: *awards for those who achieve pre-eminence in public life* 给予在社会生活中有突出表现者的奖励. **pre-eminently** *adv*.

pre-empt /ˌpriːˈempt; prɪˋɛmpt/ *v* **1** [Tn] obtain (sth) by acting in advance of others 抢先取得(某物); 预先占有(某物). **2** [Tn] (*US*) occupy (public land) in order to have the right to buy it before others (为获得优先购买权而)占有(公地). **3** [Tn] prevent (sth) by taking action in advance; forestall 抢先采取行动以阻止(某事物); 先发制人: *The workers took control of the factory in order to pre-empt its sale by the owners.* 工人们先发制人接管了工厂以阻止厂主将工厂出售. **4** [I] (in bridge) make a high opening bid despite having poor cards, in order to prevent further bidding (桥牌中)先发制人叫牌(尽管牌不好也仍叫得很高以阻止对方叫牌).

▷ **pre-emption** /ˌpriːˈempʃn; prɪˋɛmpʃən/ *n* [U] **1** (*fml* 文) (**a**) purchase by one person, group, etc before others have the chance to buy 优先购买. (**b**) right to do this 优先购买权. **2** obtaining or preventing (sth) by acting in advance 抢先行动以占有或阻止(某事物).

pre-emptive /-tɪv; -tɪv/ *adj* of or concerning pre-emption 优先购买的; 预先采取行动的: *a pre-emptive right to buy* 优先购买权 ○ *pre-emptive purchase* 优先购买 ○ *a pre-emptive attack/strike*, ie one designed to forestall a likely enemy attack 先发制人的攻击[打击] ○ *a pre-emptive bid*, ie (in bridge) one made to prevent further bidding 先发制人的叫牌(用以阻止对方叫牌).

preen /priːn; prin/ *v* [Tn] **1** (of a bird) clean or smooth (its feathers or itself) with its beak (指鸟)用喙整理(羽毛). **2 ~ oneself** (*often derog* 常作贬义) (**a**) (of a person) make oneself look tidy by combing one's hair, etc (指人)(以梳头等动作)打扮自己: *preen oneself in front of the mirror* 对着镜子梳妆打扮. (**b**) congratulate oneself; be pleased with oneself 自我欣赏; 沾沾自喜.

pre-exist /ˌpriːɪɡˈzɪst; ˌprɪɪɡˋzɪst/ *v* [I] (**a**) exist beforehand 先存; 先在. (**b**) live a life before this life 生存于前世.

▷ **pre-existence** /-əns; -əns/ *n* [U] earlier form of existence, esp that of the soul before it enters the body 先存(尤指灵魂在进入肉体前的存在); 前世.

pre-existent /-ənt; -ənt/ *adj* existing previously, esp in an earlier life 先存的; (尤指)前世的.

pre·fab /ˈpriːfæb; *US* ˌpriːˈfæb; ˌpriˋfæb/ *n* (*infml* 口) prefabricated house 预制房屋.

pre·fab·ric·ate /ˌpriːˈfæbrɪkeɪt; priˋfæbrəˌket/ *v* [Tn] manufacture (a building, ship, etc) in sections that can be assembled later on a building site, in a shipyard, etc (以预制构件)组装(建筑物、船舶等): *prefabricated kitchens, houses, schools, etc* 由预制构件组装的厨房、房屋、校舍等. ▷ **pre·fab·rica·tion** /ˌpriːfæbrɪˈkeɪʃn; ˌpriˌfæbrɪˋkeʃən/ *n* [U].

pre·face /ˈprefɪs; ˋprɛfɪs/ *n* **1** introductory statement at the beginning of a book, esp one that explains the author's aims 序言; 前言. Cf 参看 FOREWORD, INTRODUCTION 2. **2** preliminary part of a speech 开场白; 引语.

▷ **pre·face** *v* [Tn·pr] **1 ~ sth with sth** provide sth with a preface(1) 给某书作序: *He prefaced the diaries with a short account of how they were discovered.* 他给这本日记写了序言, 简述日记发现的经过. **2 ~ sth with sth/by doing sth** begin or introduce (a speech, etc) 开始(讲话等); 作(讲话等的)开场白: *She prefaced her talk with an apology/by apologizing for being late.* 她先为迟到表示歉意, 然后开始讲话.

pre·fat·ory /ˈprefətrɪ; *US* -tɔːrɪ; ˋprɛfəˌtɔrɪ/ *adj* acting as a preface; introductory 作为开场白的; 作为开端的: *after a few prefatory remarks, comments, etc* 在几句开场白之后.

pre·fect /ˈpriːfekt; ˋprifɛkt/ *n* **1** (*esp Brit*) any of a group of older pupils in a school who have authority over younger pupils and certain responsibilities for discipline, etc 学生长(中学的校级负有管理或维持纪律等责任的年长的学生). **2** (also **Prefect**) (**a**) (title of the) chief administrative officer of an area in certain countries, eg France and Japan 某些国家中的地区最高行政长官(如法国的省长和日本的县长)或其官衔. (**b**) head of the Paris police 巴黎警察局的局长.

▷ **pre·fec·ture** /ˈpriːfektjʊə(r); *US* -tʃər; ˋprifɛktʃɚ/ *n* **1** area administrated by a prefect (2) in certain countries, eg France and Japan 某些国家中最高地方官管辖的行政区(如法国的省和日本的县). **2** (in France) prefect's official place of work or residence (法国的)省长或巴黎

警察局长的官署或官邸. **3** position or period of office of a prefect 法国的省长、日本的县长等地区最高行政长官或巴黎警察局长的职位或任期. **pre·fec·tural** /priːˈfektʃərəl; prɪˈfɛktʃərəl/ *adj* of a prefect(2) 最高地方官的; 巴黎警察局长的: *the prefectural offices* 省长等最高地方官的官府.

pre·fer /prɪˈfɜː(r); prɪˈfɝ/ *v* **(-rr-)** **1** [Tn, Tn·pr, Tf, Tt, Tnt, Tg, Cn·a] **~ sth (to sth)** choose sth rather than sth else; like sth better 选择某事物(而不选择他事物); 更喜欢某事物: *There's coffee or tea. Which would you prefer?* 有咖啡或茶. 你喜欢哪样? ○ *I prefer walking to cycling.* 我愿意步行, 不愿意骑自行车. ○ (*fml* 文) *I should prefer that/prefer it if you did not go there alone.* 我倒希望你不要一个人去那里. ○ *She prefers to be alone.* 她宁愿独自一人. ○ *Their father prefers them to be home early.* 他们的父亲希望他们早点儿回家. ○ *I prefer walking alone.* 我比较喜欢一个人溜达. ○ *I prefer my coffee black.* 我爱喝不加奶的咖啡. **2** (idm 习语) **prefer a ˈcharge/ˈcharges (against sb)** (*law* 律) make an accusation (against sb) for consideration in a lawcourt (对某人)提出控告: *prefer a charge against a motorist* 对一个驾驶机动车的人提出控告 ○ *We haven't enough evidence to prefer charges.* 我们没有进行起诉的充分证据.

▷ **pre·fer·able** /ˈprefrəbl; ˈprɛfrəbl/ *adj* (not used with *more* 不可与 more 连用) **~ (to sth/doing sth)** to be preferred (to sth); more desirable or suitable (对某事物来说)更可取的, 更称心的, 更适宜的: *Cold food would be preferable in this heat.* 在这样的热天吃冷食更好. ○ *He finds country life preferable to living in the city.* 他感到在乡村生活比在城市生活要好些. ○ *Anything was preferable to that dreadful din in the house.* 这屋子里乱七八糟的声音叫人难受得无以复加. **pre·fer·ably** /ˈprefrəblɪ; ˈprɛfrəblɪ/ *adv* rather than anything, anywhere, etc else (较之其他任何事物、处所等)更可取: *She wanted a cake, preferably one with chocolate icing.* 她想吃蛋糕, 最好是有巧克力糖衣的. ○ *They want to buy a new house, near the sea preferably.* 他们要购买一所新房子, 最好在海边.

pref·er·ence /ˈprefrəns; ˈprɛfrəns/ *n* **1** (**a**) [U, sing] **~ (for sth)** liking for sth (more than sth else) (与他物相较之)喜爱; 偏爱: *There is milk and cream — do you have a preference?* 有牛奶也有奶油 —— 你喜欢哪样? ○ *It's entirely a matter of preference.* 这完全是个见仁见智的问题. ○ *She has a preference for blue.* 她特别喜欢蓝色. (**b**) [C] thing that is liked better or best 偏爱的事物; 特别爱好的事物: *What are your preferences?* 你最喜欢什么? **2** [U] **~ (to/towards sb)** favour shown to one person, group, etc rather than another 优待; 优惠; 优先权: *Employees who have worked here for many years will be given preference over newcomers.* 与新来乍到者不同, 对那些工作多年的雇员将予以优待. ○ *She tried not to show preference in her treatment of the children in her care.* 她对待她所照顾的孩子尽可能不厚此薄彼. **3** (idm 习语) **in preference to sb/sth** rather than sb/sth 而不取某人[某事物]: *She chose to learn the violin in preference to the piano.* 她愿学小提琴而不学钢琴.

□ **ˈpreference shares, ˈpreference stock** (*US* **ˈpreferred shares/stock**) (*finance* 财) shares/stock on which a firm must pay the dividend before distributing profits to holders of ordinary shares 优先股(可比普通股之持有者优先分得股息).

pref·er·en·tial /ˌprefəˈrenʃl; ˌprɛfəˈrɛnʃəl/ *adj* **1** of, giving, receiving or showing preference(2) 优先的; 给予优先的; 得到优先的; 优待的: *preferential import duties, tariffs, etc,* ie favouring a particular group, country, etc 特惠关税(优待某团体、国家等). **2** (idm 习语) **give sb/get preferential ˈtreatment** treat sb/be treated more favourably than sb else 偏向某人[得到优待]: *Nobody gets preferential treatment in this office!* 本办事处无论对谁均一视同仁! ▷ **pref·er·en·tially** /-ʃəlɪ; -ʃəlɪ/ *adv*: *be treated preferentially* 得到优先.

pref·er·ment /prɪˈfɜːmənt; prɪˈfɝmənt/ *n* [C, U] (*fml* 文) promotion to a higher position or rank 晋升: *His preferment pleased his many admirers.* 他获晋升, 喜欢他的许多人都感到高兴. ○ *He was hoping for preferment.* 他希望获得提升.

pre·fig·ure /ˌpriːˈfɪgə(r); *US* -gjər; priˈfɪgjɚ/ *v* (*fml* 文) **1** [Tn] represent beforehand (sth that will happen in the future); foreshadow 预示(某事物将发生); 预兆: *worrying events that may prefigure a period of economic recession* 可能显示要出现一段经济衰退时期的令人担心的情况. **2** [Tn, Tf, Tw] picture (sth) to oneself beforehand; imagine 设想(某事物); 想像.

pre·fix /ˈpriːfɪks; ˈpriˌfɪks/ *n* **1** (abbreviated as *pref* in this dictionary 本词典中略为 pref) word or syllable (eg *co-, ex-, non-, pre-, re-*) placed in front of a word to add to or change the meaning of that word, eg *un-* in *unhappy* 前缀(置于单词之前, 以增加或改变其意义的词或音节, 如 co-、ex-、non-、pre-、re-, 又如 unhappy 中的 un-). **2** word (eg *Dr, Mrs,* etc) placed before a person's name as a title (人名前的)称谓(如 Dr、Mrs 等). Cf 参看 SUFFIX.

▷ **pre·fix** /ˌpriːˈfɪks; priˈfɪks/ *v* [Tn, Tn·pr] **~ sth (to sth)** **1** add sth at the beginning or as an introduction 将某事物加在前面: *The official prefixed an explanatory note to the list of statistics.* 那官员在统计表前加了一段说明文字. **2** add sth as a prefix (to a word, name, etc) (在单词上)加前缀; (在人名前)加称谓.

preg·nant /ˈpregnənt; ˈprɛgnənt/ *adj* **1** (of a woman or female animal) having a baby or young animal developing in the womb (指妇女或雌性动物)怀孕的, 妊娠的: *She was six months pregnant,* ie had been pregnant for six months. 她那时已怀有六个月的身孕. ○ *She is/got pregnant by another man.* 是另一个男子使她怀孕的. **2 ~ with sth** (**a**) full of sth 充满着某事物的; 富于某事物的: *pregnant with joy, meaning, possibilities* 洋溢着喜悦之情的、富有意义的、具有各种可能性的. (**b**) likely to cause sth 可能产生某事物的: *pregnant with consequences, danger* 可能产生重大影响的、造成危险的. **3** (idm 习语) **a pregnant ˈpause/ˈsilence** pause/silence full of unexpressed meaning or significance 耐人寻味的或意味深长的停顿[沉默]: *There was a pregnant pause before she answered my question.* 她耐人寻味地停顿了一下才回答我的问题. ○ *His only reaction was a pregnant silence.* 他唯一的反应是一阵意味深长的沉默.

▷ **preg·nancy** /-nənsɪ; -nənsɪ/ *n* (**a**) [U] state or period of being pregnant(1) 怀孕; 孕期; 妊娠期: *discomfort caused by pregnancy* 因怀孕而引起的不适 ○ *These drugs should not be taken during pregnancy.* 这些药物在孕期内不得服用. ○ [attrib 作定语] *a pregnancy test* 妊娠试验. (**b**) [C] instance of being pregnant(1) 怀孕: *She's had three pregnancies in four years.* 她在四年中怀孕三次.

pre-heat /ˌpriːˈhiːt; priˈhit/ *v* [Tn esp passive 尤用于被动语态] heat (sth) beforehand (esp an oven to a specified temperature before putting food in it to cook) 预热(某物, 尤指烤箱, 待达到一定温度后将食物放入进行烹调): *Cook the pie for 20 minutes in a pre-heated oven.* 在经过预热的烤箱里烘烤馅饼 20 分钟.

pre·hens·ile /ˌpriːˈhensaɪl; *US* -sl; prɪˈhɛnsl/ *adj* (of an animal's foot or tail) able to grasp and hold things (指动物的足或尾)能抓物的, 能缠绕东西的: *the monkey's prehensile tail* 猴子那能缠住东西的尾巴 ○ *the prehensile claws of an eagle* 老鹰那能抓住东西的爪.

pre·his·toric /ˌpriːhɪˈstɒrɪk; *US* -tɔːrɪk; ˌprihɪsˈtɔrɪk/ *adj* of or concerning the time before recorded history 史前的: *prehistoric man, monuments, cave paintings* 史前的人类、遗迹、洞穴壁画 ○ (*joc or derog* 谑或贬) *His ideas on the education of girls are positively prehistoric,* ie extremely old-fashioned. 他在女子教育问题上所持的观点是老掉牙的.

pre·his·tory /ˌpriːˈhɪstrɪ; priˈhɪstrɪ/ *n* **1** [U] (study of the) period before recorded history 史前; 史前学: *European, Mexican, Aboriginal prehistory* 欧洲、墨西哥、澳洲土著居民的史前史. **2** [sing] earliest stages of the development of sth 某事物的最早发展阶段: *the prehistory of Western art* 西方艺术的肇端.

pre·judge /ˌpriːˈdʒʌdʒ; priˈdʒʌdʒ/ *v* [Tn] **1** make a judgement about (a person or case) before a proper inquiry has been held 对(人或事)未经详察而预作判断: *prejudge a matter, issue, client* 未充分了解情况而判断某事、问题、当事人. **2** form an opinion about (sb/sth) without having the necessary information (在缺乏了解的情况下)形成对(某人[某事物])的看法: *He felt he had been prejudged by his colleagues.* 他觉得同事们对他怀有成见. ▷ **pre·judge·ment** *n* [U, C].

pre·ju·dice /ˈpredʒʊdɪs; ˈprɛdʒədɪs/ *n* **1** (**a**) [U] opinion, or like or dislike of sb/sth, that is not founded on experience or reason 偏见；成见：*colour/racial prejudice*, ie prejudice felt or shown against members of other races 种族偏见 ○ *Her friendliness soon overcame the prejudice of her stepchildren.* 她很热情，因而丈夫前妻的孩子很快就消除了对她的偏见。○ *The selectors were accused of showing prejudice in failing to include him in the team.* 有人指责遴选者怀有成见才未吸收他加入该队。(**b**) [C] **~ (against/in favour of sb/sth)** instance of this 偏见；成见：*In order to succeed here you will need to overcome your prejudices.* 你需要消除偏见，才能在这里获得成功。○ *She has a prejudice against modern music.* 她对现代音乐怀有偏见。○ *The anthology reveals a prejudice in favour of lyric poets.* 这部选集显示出对抒情诗人有所偏爱。 **2** (idm 习语) **to the prejudice of sth** (*esp law* 尤用于法律) with the result that sb's interests are harmed 损及某人的利益：*to the prejudice of sb's rights* 有损于某人的权利 ○ *The newspaper reported his remarks, to the prejudice of his chances of being elected.* 该报报道了他说的话，这可能对他参加竞选产生不利影响。 **without 'prejudice (to sth)** (*law* 律) without having an effect on an existing right or claim 无损于现有的权益：*The firm agreed to pay compensation without prejudice*, ie without admitting liability. 公司在未承认负有责任的情况下同意付给赔偿金。○ *The offer was accepted without prejudice to the current pay negotiations.* 该提议获得接纳，但对目前正在进行的工资谈判并无影响。

▷ **pre·ju·dice** *v* **1** [Tn, Tn·pr] **~ sb (against/in favour of sb/sth)** cause sb to have a prejudice; influence sb 使某人抱偏见；影响某人：*The judge told the jury that they must not allow their feelings to prejudice them.* 法官对陪审团说他们不应该感情用事。○ *Newspaper gossip had prejudiced her against him.* 报上那些不三不四的文章使她对他抱有偏见。○ *Her charm prejudiced the judges in her favour.* 她姿色迷人，因而评委都偏向她。 **2** [Tn] cause harm to (a case, claim, etc); weaken 使(事情、权益等)受到损害；削弱：*He prejudiced his claim by demanding too much compensation.* 他索赔过高反而使他的要求无法实现。○ *Lack of self-discipline prejudiced her chances of success.* 她缺乏自制力对她获得成功有所影响。

pre·ju·diced *adj* (*usu derog* 通常作贬义) having or showing prejudice 有偏见的；有成见的；偏颇的；偏心的：*Try not to be prejudiced in your judgements.* 你作判断时要尽量做到不存偏见。○ *She regarded her critics as ignorant and prejudiced.* 她认为那些批评她的人既无知又存有偏见。○ *Since I am his mother, my opinion of him is naturally a prejudiced one.* 因为我是他的母亲，对他的看法自然是带有偏向的。

pre·ju·di·cial /ˌpredʒʊˈdɪʃl; ˌprɛdʒəˈdɪʃəl/ *adj* **~ (to sth)** (*fml* 文) causing harm (to a person's rights, interests, etc) (对某人的权利、利益等)造成损害的：*developments prejudicial to the company's future* 对公司的未来有不利影响的一些新情况.

prel·acy /ˈpreləsɪ; ˈprɛləsɪ/ *n* **1** [C] office, rank or see of a prelate 高级教士的职务、级别或地位. **2 the prelacy** [Gp] the whole body of prelates 主教或高级教士(总称)；主教或高级教士团.

prel·ate /ˈprelət; ˈprɛlət/ *n* high-ranking clergyman, eg a bishop or an archbishop 高级教士(如主教或大主教).

pre·lim /ˈpriːlɪm; ˈpriˌlɪm/ *n* (*infml* 口) **1** [C usu *pl* 通常作复数] preliminary examination 初试；预考. **2 prelims** [pl] pages of a book (with the title, contents, etc) that come before the text 正文前的书页(包括书名、目录等).

pre·lim·in·ary /prɪˈlɪmɪnərɪ; *US* -nerɪ; prɪˈlɪməˌnɛrɪ/ *adj* **~ (to sth)** coming before a more important action or event; preparatory (作为某一重要行动或事情的)开端的；预备性的：*after a few preliminary remarks* 在几句开场白之后 ○ *preliminary inquiries, experiments, negotiations* 初步的调查、实验、谈判 ○ (*sport* 体) *a preliminary contest, heat, round, etc*, ie held before a main contest in order to eliminate weaker players or teams 预赛、初赛、选拔赛 ○ *All this is preliminary to the main election struggle.* 这一切都只是进行大选较量的预选活动.

▷ **pre·lim·in·ary** *n* (usu *pl* 通常作复数) preliminary action, event, measure, etc 初步的行动、事件、措施等：*the necessary preliminaries to a peace conference*, eg the discussions about agenda and procedures 为召开和平会议而举行的必要的筹备会.

pre·lude /ˈpreljuːd; ˈprɛljud/ *n* **1 ~ (to sth)** (**a**) action or event that happens before another larger or more important one and forms an introduction to it (行动或事件的)序幕，前奏：*His frequent depressions were the prelude to a complete mental breakdown.* 他经常抑郁寡欢，后来精神完全崩溃了。○ *The bankruptcy of several small firms was the prelude to general economic collapse.* 几家小商行倒闭了，随之而来的是经济大萧条。○ *I'm afraid that these troubles are just a prelude*, ie to worse ones. 我看这些为难事只是个引子(大问题在后面). (**b**) introductory part of a poem, etc (诗等的)序：*The lines form a prelude to his long narrative poem.* 这几行诗是他那长篇叙事诗的序诗. **2** (*music* 音) (**a**) introductory movement coming before a fugue or forming the first part of a suite 前奏曲. (**b**) short piece of music of a similar type 类似上述乐曲之小段.

pre·mar·ital /ˌpriːˈmærɪtl; priˈmærətl̩/ *adj* happening before marriage 婚前的：*premarital sex, affairs, etc* 婚前的性行为、风流韵事等.

pre·ma·ture /ˈpremətjʊə(r); *US* ˌpriːməˈtʊər; ˌpriməˈtʊr/ *adj* **1** (**a**) happening before the proper or expected time 提前的；过早的；未到期的：*premature baldness, senility* 早秃、早衰 ○ *A fire in the gallery caused the premature closing of the exhibition.* 在美术陈列室里发生的火灾迫使展览会提前结束. (**b**) (of a baby, its birth, etc) born or occurring at least three weeks before the expected time (指婴儿、其出生等)早产的(比预产期至少提前三周)：*the special care of premature babies* 对早产婴儿的特别护理 ○ *The baby was five weeks premature.* 这个婴儿是提早五周生下来的. **2 ~ (in doing sth)** (*derog* 贬) acting or done too soon; hasty 赶做的；仓促的：*a premature conclusion, decision, judgement, etc* 草率作出的结论、决定、判决等 ○ *Let's not be premature in closing this case*, eg in a police investigation. 咱们先别急于结案(如刑事调查). ▷ **pre·ma·turely** *adv*: *born prematurely* 早产的 ○ *prematurely bald, grey, wrinkled, etc* 早秃的、早白的、过早起皱纹的.

pre·med·it·ate /ˌpriːˈmedɪteɪt; prɪˈmɛdəˌtet/ *v* [Tn esp passive 尤用于被动语态] plan (sth) in advance 预先计划(某事物)；预谋：*a premeditated attack, murder, insult, etc* 有预谋的攻击、凶杀、冒犯行为等 ○ *We needed to know whether the crime had been premeditated.* 我们需要知道的是这一犯罪行为是否经过事先策划. ▷ **pre·med·ita·tion** /ˌpriːmedɪˈteɪʃn; ˌprimɛdəˈteʃən/ *n* [U].

pre·men·strual ten·sion /ˌpriːˌmenstrʊəl ˈtenʃn; priˈmɛnstrʊəl ˈtɛnʃən/ (*abbr* 缩写 **PMT**) mental and physiological upset caused by hormonal changes occurring before menstruation 月经之前的紧张.

prem·ier /ˈpremɪə(r); *US* ˈpriːmɪər; ˈprimɪɚ/ *adj* [attrib 作定语] first in importance, position, etc (重要性、位置等方面)第一的，首位的：*Britain's premier exporter of drilling equipment* 英国全国最大钻机出口商 ○ *The company has achieved a premier position in the electronics field.* 该公司执电子行业之牛耳.

▷ **prem·ier** *n* head of a government; prime minister 首相；(政府)总理. **prem·ier·ship** [U] position or period of office of a premier 首相或总理的职位或任期：*during her premiership* 在她担任首相期间 ○ *He was offered the premiership.* 他被任命为总理.

premi·ère /ˈpremɪeə(r); *US* prɪˈmɪər; prɪˈmɪr/ *n* first public performance of (a production of) a play or showing of a film; first night (戏剧或电影的)首次公演，首次公演之夜场.

▷ **premi·ère** *v* [Tn esp passive 尤用于被动语态] perform (a play) or show (a film) to the public for the first time 首次公演(戏剧或电影)：*The film was premièred at the Cannes festival.* 该影片是在戛纳电影节上首次放映的.

pre·mise (also **pre·miss**) /ˈpremɪs; ˈprɛmɪs/ *n* **1** statement or idea on which reasoning is based; hypothesis (推理所依据的)前提；假定：*Advice to investors was based on the premise that interest rates would continue to fall.* 给予投资者的建议是以利率将继续下降这一点为前提的. **2** (in logic) each of the first two parts (*major premise* and *minor premise*) of a forward argument (逻辑学中的)(大小)前提：*If the major premise is 'Boys like fruit' and the minor premise is*

'You are a boy', then the conclusion is 'Therefore you like fruit'. 设若大前提为'男孩儿爱吃水果', 小前提为'你是男孩儿', 则结论为'所以你爱吃水果'. Cf 参看 SYLLOGISM.

pre·mises /ˈpremɪsɪz; ˈprɛmɪsɪz/ *n* [pl] **1** house or other buildings with its outbuildings, land, etc (包括附属建筑、土地等在内的)房屋或其他建筑物: *business premises*, ie building(s), esp offices, where a business is carried on 事务所 ○ *The firm is looking for larger premises.* 该公司正在寻找较大的经营场址. ○ *He was asked to leave the premises immediately.* 人家要他立刻离开该建筑物. **2** (*law* 律) details of property, names of people, etc specified in the first part of a legal agreement 契据之缘起部分(记述财产之详情、当事人姓名等). **3** (idm 习语) **off the ˈpremises** outside the boundary of the premises(1) 在建筑物范围以外: *see sb off the premises*, ie take a visitor, etc to the exit 把某人送出大门(送客). **on the ˈpremises** in the building (s), etc 在建筑物等内: *There is always a manager on the premises.* 事务所里总有一名主管人员. ○ *Alcohol may not be consumed on the premises.* 场内不准饮酒.

pre·mium /ˈpriːmɪəm; ˈprimɪəm/ *n* **1** amount or instalment (to be) regularly paid for an insurance policy 保险费: *Your first premium is now due.* 你的第一期保险费现已到期. **2** additional payment, eg one added to wages or interest payments; bonus 额外费用; 津贴; 奖金; 花红: *A premium of 2 per cent is paid on long-term investments.* 对投资期限较长者可获百分之二的奖励. ○ *You have to pay a premium for express delivery.* 你得支付特快投递的补加费用. ○ [attrib 作定语] *Premium rents are charged in the city centre.* 市中心要收取额外的租金. **3** (idm 习语) **at a ˈpremium** (**a**) (*finance* 财) (of stocks and shares) above the normal or usual value (指公债和股票)超过正常或市面的价值; 溢价: *Shares are selling at a premium.* 股票溢价出售. (**b**) rare or difficult to obtain, and therefore more expensive or more highly valued than usual 因稀少或难得而较之一般昂贵或宝贵: *Space is at a premium in this building.* 在这个建筑物里场地面积十分昂贵. ○ *Honesty is at a premium in this profession, I'm afraid!* 依我看, 干这一行诚实的人实在难得! **put a premium on sb/sth** (**a**) make (sb/sth) seem important 使(某人[某事物])受到重视: *The high risk of infection puts a premium on the use of sterile needles.* 由于受感染的风险很大, 无菌注射针的使用受到了重视. (**b**) attach special value or importance to sb/sth 高度评价某人[某事物]: *The examiners put a premium on rational argument.* 评委们对以理服人的论据给以高度评价.

□ ˈ**Premium Bond** (*Brit*) government savings bond that pays no interest[1](7) but offers instead the chance of winning money as a prize in a monthly draw[1](1b) 有奖储蓄公债(以每月进行抽奖代替付息).

pre·moni·tion /ˌpriːməˈnɪʃn, ˌprem-; ˌprimə'nɪʃən, ˌprɛm-/ *n* ~ (**of sth/that...**) feeling that sth unpleasant is going to happen (不祥的)预感: *a premonition of disaster* 大祸临头的预感 ○ *My premonition was right.* 我的预感应验了. ○ *As we approached the house, I had a premonition that something terrible had happened.* 我们走近这所房子时, 我预感到出事了.

▷ **pre·mon·it·ory** /prɪˈmɒnɪtərɪ; US -tɔːrɪ; prɪˈmɑnəˌtɔrɪ/ *adj* (*fml* 文) giving a warning 给予警告的: *premonitory signs* 警告的信号.

pre-natal /ˌpriːˈneɪtl; priˈnetl/ *adj* (*esp US*) of or occurring in the period before (giving) birth; antenatal 出生前的; 产前的; 孕期的: ˌ*pre-natal ˈcheck-ups, ˈclasses, ˈexercises* 产前检查、孕期卫生课程、孕期体操. Cf 参看 POSTNATAL.

pre·oc·cu·pa·tion /ˌpriːɒkjʊˈpeɪʃn; priˌɑkjəˈpeʃən/ *n* **1** [U] (**a**) state of being preoccupied; absent-mindedness 占据思想; 心不在焉. (**b**) ~ (**with sth**) state of constantly thinking or worrying about sth; obsession 全神贯注; 苦思苦想; 缠在心头; 如痴如迷: *She found his preoccupation with money irritating.* 她发觉他心里只有钱, 感到很生气. **2** [C] thing that a person thinks about all the time 心里总想着的事物; 耿耿于怀的事物: *His main preoccupation at that time was getting enough to eat.* 他那时盘算的是如何填饱肚子. ○ *A pension is not usually one of the preoccupations of an eighteen year-old!* 一个十八岁的人通常是不会老惦着养老金的!

pre·oc·cupy /priːˈɒkjʊpaɪ; priˈɑkjəˌpaɪ/ *v* (*pt, pp* **-pied**) [Tn] engage (sb or his mind, thoughts, etc) so that he cannot think of other things; obsess 占据(某人)思想; 使(某人)心无二用; 迷住: *Something seems to be preoccupying her at the moment.* 她此刻好若有所思. ○ *Health worries preoccupied him for the whole holiday.* 整个假期里他一直为健康状况而担忧.

▷ **pre·oc·cu·pied** *adj* inattentive because one is thinking of or worrying about sth else 心不在焉的; 心事重重的: *She seemed preoccupied all the time I was talking to her.* 我跟她讲话时她始终显得心事重重. ○ *He answered me in a rather preoccupied manner.* 他心不在焉地回答我.

pre-ordain /ˌpriːɔːˈdeɪn; ˌpriɔrˈden/ *v* [esp passive 尤用于被动语态: Tn, Tf] decide or determine (sth) beforehand 预先决定或确定(某事物); 注定: *Fate had pre-ordained their meeting/that they should meet.* 他们的相逢是命中注定的. ○ *Her success in life seemed pre-ordained.* 她似一生注定功成德立.

prep /prep; prɛp/ *n* (*infml* 口) **1** [C, U] (*Brit*) (esp in private boarding schools 尤用于私立寄宿学校) (**a**) school work (to be) done after lessons; homework 课外作业; 家庭作业. (**b**) time when this is (to be) done 做课外作业的时间: *He felt ill during prep.* 他在做课外作业时觉得身体不舒服. **2** (*US*) student in a preparatory school 预科学校的学生.

□ ˈ**prep school** = PREPARATORY SCHOOL (PREPARATORY).

pre-package /ˌpriːˈpækɪdʒ; priˈpækɪdʒ/ (also **pre-pack** /ˌpriːˈpæk; priˈpæk/) *v* [Tn esp passive 尤用于被动语态] put (goods) into packs ready for sale before distribution to shops 预先包装(货物)(再批发到商店): *pre-packaged fruit* 预先包装的水果.

pre·para·tion /ˌprepəˈreɪʃn; ˌprɛpəˈreʃən/ *n* **1** [U] preparing or being prepared 预备; 准备: *You can't pass an exam without preparation.* 不准备就考不及格. ○ *The preparation of the meals is your job.* 做饭是你分内之事. ○ [attrib 作定语] *Food preparation areas must be kept clean.* 制作食物的场所应保持清洁. **2** [C usu *pl* 通常作复数] ~ (**for sth/to do sth**) thing done to prepare for sth 准备工作; 准备措施: *The country is making preparations for war/to go to war.* 该国正进行备战[准备打仗]. ○ *Was your education a good preparation for your career?* 你所受的教育是否为你的事业打下了良好的基础? **3** [C] substance that has been specially prepared for use as a cosmetic, medicine, etc 适合于某一用途如化妆、医药等的)配制品: *a pharmaceutical preparation* 药剂 ○ *a preparation for hiding/to hide skin blemishes* 肤斑遮盖霜. **4** [C, U] (*Brit*) = PREP 1. **5** (idm 习语) **in preparation (for sth)** being prepared (for sth) (为某事物)作好准备: *The advertising campaign is still in preparation.* 广告宣传攻势仍在准备中. ○ *They've sold their house and car in preparation for leaving the country.* 他们卖掉了房子和汽车准备出国.

pre·par·at·ory /prɪˈpærətrɪ; US -tɔːrɪ; prɪˈpærəˌtɔrɪ/ *adj* preparing for sth; introductory 准备的; 预备的; 筹备的: *preparatory investigations, measures, training* 为准备做某事而进行的调查、而采取的措施、而进行的训练.

□ **preˈparatory school** (also *infml* 口语作 ˈ**prep school**) **1** (*Brit*) private school for pupils aged between 7 and 13 whose parents pay fees for their education 私立小学. Cf 参看 PUBLIC SCHOOL (PUBLIC). **2** (*US*) (usu private) school that prepares students for college (通常为私立的)大学预科学校.

pre·pare /prɪˈpeə(r); prɪˈpɛr/ *v* **1** [I, Ipr, Tn, Tn·pr, Cn·t] ~ (**sb/sth**) (**for sb/sth**) get or make (sb/sth) ready 使(某人)有准备; 把(某事物)准备好; 预备: *I had no time in which to prepare.* 我已来不及做准备了. ○ *prepare for trouble* 准备应付麻烦事 ○ *prepare a meal*, ie get food ready to be eaten 预备饭菜 ○ *have everything prepared beforehand* 事先把一切都准备好 ○ *prepare children for an examination* 指导儿童准备考试 ○ *The troops were being prepared for battle/to go into battle.* 部队已作好战斗准备[已准备好投入战斗]. **2** (idm 习语) **be prepared for sth** be ready for sth (esp sth unpleasant) 对某事物(尤指令人不愉快者)作好准备: *I knew there were problems, but I was not prepared for this!* 我知道有些问题, 却未料到这一点! ○ *She was prepared for anything to happen.* 她已准备好应付一切. **be prepared to do sth** be able and willing to do sth 能够

并愿意做某事: *I am prepared to lend you the money if you promise to pay it back.* 我愿意把钱借给你, 你得答应还给我. ○ *I am not prepared to stay and listen to these outrageous insults.* 我可不愿意在这儿受这种奇耻大辱. **prepare the ground (for sth)** make it possible or easier to develop sth 为发展某事物准备了条件: *Early experiments with military rockets prepared the ground for space travel.* 早期进行的军用火箭试验为宇航事业的发展打下了基础. **3** (phr v) **prepare sb for sth** cause sb to expect sth (esp sth unpleasant) 使某人对某事物(尤指令人不愉快者)有所准备: *Prepare yourself for a nasty shock!* 有件令人十分震惊的事, 你要有所准备!

▷ **pre·pared·ness** /prɪˈpeərɪdnɪs; prɪˋpɛrɪdnɪs/ *n* [U] being prepared 有所准备: *a state of preparedness* 有准备的状态.

pre·pay /ˌpriːˈpeɪ; priˋpe/ *v* (*pt, pp* **prepaid** /-ˈpeɪd; -ˋped/) [Tn esp passive 尤用于被动语态] pay (sth) in advance 预先支付(某费用); 预付: *a prepaid envelope*, ie one on which the postage has already been paid 邮资已付的信封 ○ *The telegram was sent reply prepaid.* 电报已发出并已预付复电费用. ▷ **pre·pay·ment** *n* [C, U].

pre·pon·der·ant /prɪˈpɒndərənt; prɪˋpɑndərənt/ *adj* (*fml* 文) greater in influence, importance, quantity, etc (影响力、重要性、数量等方面)处于上风的, 占优势的: *Melancholy is the preponderant mood of the poem.* 忧郁的感情是该诗的基调. ▷ **pre·pon·der·ance** /-əns; -əns/ *n* [sing]: *a preponderance of blue-eyed people in the population* 蓝眼睛的人占居民的大多数. **pre·pon·der·antly** *adv*: *preponderantly optimistic* 乐观主义占了上风的.

pre·pon·der·ate /prɪˈpɒndəreɪt; prɪˋpɑndəˌret/ *v* [I, Ipr] **~ (over sth)** (*fml* 文) be greater in influence, importance, quantity, etc (than sth else) (在影响力、重要性、数量等方面较其他事物)处于上风, 占优势: *Christians preponderate in the population of that part of the country.* 基督教徒在该国那一地区的人口中居多.

pre·posi·tion /ˌprepəˈzɪʃn; ˌprɛpəˋzɪʃən/ *n* (*grammar*) (abbreviated as *prep* in this dictionary 本词典中略作 prep) word or group of words (eg *in*, *from*, *to*, *out of*, *on behalf of*) used esp before a noun or pronoun to show place, position, time, method, etc 介词(包括复合介词, 尤用于名词或代词前, 表示处所、位置、时间、方法等, 如 in、from、to、out of、on behalf of).

▷ **pre·posi·tional** /-ʃənl; -ʃənl̩/ *adj* of or containing a preposition 介词的; 含介词的.

□ ˌ**prepositional** ˈ**phrase** preposition and the noun or noun phrase that follows it, eg *in the night*, *after breakfast* 介词词组(介词连同其后的名词或名词词组, 如 in the night、after breakfast).

pre·pos·sess·ing /ˌpriːpəˈzesɪŋ; ˌpripəˋzɛsɪŋ/ *adj* making a good impression; attractive 给人良好印象的; 有吸引力的: *a prepossessing smile, manner, child* 讨人喜欢的微笑、举止、孩子 ○ *He/His appearance is not at all prepossessing.* 他[他的外表]毫无吸引力.

pre·pos·ter·ous /prɪˈpɒstərəs; prɪˋpɑstərəs/ *adj* completely contrary to reason or common sense; absurd or outrageous 完全违背理性或常识的; 荒谬的; 反常的; 愚蠢的; 无法容忍的: *That is a preposterous accusation!* 那样的指责简直荒谬可笑! ○ *They are asking a preposterous price for the work.* 他们为该作品漫天要价. ▷ **pre·pos·ter·ously** *adv*: *That is a preposterously high price!* 那价格高得出奇!

pre·puce /ˈpriːpjuːs; ˋpripjus/ *n* (*anatomy* 解) **1** foreskin (阴茎的)包皮. ⇨illus at MALE 见 MALE 插图. **2** similar fold of skin at the tip of the clitoris (阴蒂的)包皮.

Pre-Raphaelite /ˌpriːˈræfəlaɪt; ˌpriˋræfəˌlaɪt/ *n* (*art* 美术) member of a group of British 19th-century artists who painted in a style considered to be that of Italian painting before the time of Raphael 拉斐尔前派画家(指英国19世纪一种流派的成员, 其作品被认为具有拉斐尔以前之意大利绘画风格).

▷ **Pre-Raphaelite** *adj* of, concerning or in the style of the Pre-Raphaelites 拉斐尔之前的; 拉斐尔前派的; 具有拉斐尔前派风格的: *a Pre-Raphaelite portrait* 具有拉斐尔前派风格的肖像画.

pre-record /ˌpriːrɪˈkɔːd; ˌpririˋkɔrd/ *v* [Tn esp passive 尤用于被动语态] (*esp broadcasting* 尤用于广播) record (film, sound, a television programme, etc) in advance, for use later 预先录制(影像、声音、电视节目等): *The sound effects had been pre-recorded and were added to the dialogue.* 音响效果经预录后已加入对话中. ○ *The interview was pre-recorded.* 采访过程是预先录制好的. Cf 参看 LIVE[1] 7.

▷ **pre-recorded** *adj* (of tape) with film or sound already recorded on it (指磁带)已录影的, 已录音的.

pre·requis·ite /ˌpriːˈrekwɪzɪt; priˋrɛkwəzɪt/ *adj* **~ (for/to sth)** (*infml* 口) required as a condition (for sth) 必备的; 作为先决条件的: *A degree is prerequisite for employment at this level.* 必须具备大专院校的学位才能从事这一级的工作. ○ *A sense of humour is prerequisite to understanding her work.* 要理解她的作品就必须具有幽默感.

▷ **pre·requis·ite** (also **pre-condition**) *n* **~ (for/of sth)** thing required as a condition for sth to happen or exist 必备条件; 先决条件; 前提: *Careful study of the market is a prerequisite for success.* 仔细研究市场情况是取得成功的先决条件. ○ *Good muscles are one of the prerequisites of physical fitness.* 肌肉发达是身体健康的一个必备条件.

pre·rog·at·ive /prɪˈrɒgətɪv; prɪˋrɑgətɪv/ *n* right or privilege, esp one belonging to a particular person or group 权利; (尤指)特权: *It is the Prime Minister's prerogative to decide when to call an election.* 决定大选的日期是首相的职权. ○ *A monarch has the prerogative of pardoning criminals.* 君主享有对罪犯的赦免权. ○ *the* ˌ*royal prerogative*, ie (in Britain), the (theoretical) right of the sovereign to act without the approval of Parliament 皇家的特权(在英国, 指国君名义上享有的不经议会认可而采取行动的权利).

Pres *abbr* 缩写 = President: *Pres (Ronald) Reagan* (罗纳德·)里根总统.

pres·age /ˈpresɪdʒ; ˋprɛsɪdʒ/ *n* (*fml* 文) (**a**) sign that sth (esp sth unpleasant) will happen; omen 预兆; 兆头; (尤指)恶兆, 凶兆. (**b**) feeling that sth unpleasant will happen; presentiment (不祥的)预感; 预知.

▷ **pres·age** /ˈpresɪdʒ, *rarely* 罕读作 prɪˈseɪdʒ; prɪˋsedʒ/ *v* [Tn] be a sign of (sth that will happen); foretell 预示; 预言: *Those clouds presage a storm.* 那样的密云预示着暴风雨将要来临.

Pres·by·ter·ian /ˌprezbɪˈtɪərɪən; ˌprɛzbəˋtɪrɪən/ *adj* (of a Church, esp of the national Church of Scotland) governed by elders (ˈ**pres·by·ters**) who are all equal in rank (指基督教教会, 尤指苏格兰国立教会)长老制的. Cf 参看 EPISCOPAL.

▷ **Pres·by·ter·ian** *n* person who is a member of the Presbyterian Church 长老会教友.

Pres·by·teri·an·ism /-ɪzəm; -ˌɪzəm/ *n* [U] **1** beliefs of Presbyterians 长老会教义. **2** Presbyterian system of church government 长老制.

pres·by·tery /ˈprezbɪtrɪ; *US* -terɪ; ˋprɛzbəˌtɛrɪ/ *n* **1** (regional) administrative court of the Presbyterian Church (基督教长老会的)教务评议会; 长老区会. **2** house where a Roman Catholic parish priest lives 天主教堂区神甫的居所. **3** (in a church) eastern part of the chancel beyond the choir; sanctuary (教堂内的)司祭席, 内殿.

pre-school /ˌpriːˈskuːl; priˋskul/ *adj* of the time or age before a child is old enough to go to school 学龄前的; 学前的: *a* ˌ*pre-school* ˈ*child/a child of pre-school age* 学龄前儿童 ○ ˌ*pre-school* ˈ*learning* 入学前的学习.

pres·ci·ent /ˈpresɪənt; ˋprɛsɪənt/ *adj* (*fml* 文) knowing about things before they take place; able to see into the future 有先见之明的; 能预知未来的. ▷ **pres·ci·ence** /-əns; -əns/ *n* [U].

pre·scribe /prɪˈskraɪb; prɪˋskraɪb/ *v* (*fml* 文) **1** [Tn, Tn·pr] **~ sth (for sth)** advise or order the use of (esp a medicine, remedy, etc) 建议或吩咐采用(尤指药物、疗法等); 开(药方): *She prescribed some pills to help me to sleep.* 她让我吃些药片以利睡眠. ○ *Do not exceed the prescribed dose*, ie quantity of medicine to be taken at one time. 勿超过规定剂量(药物的一次用量). ○ *Ask the doctor to prescribe something for that cough.* 请医生开点咳嗽药. ○ (*fig* 比喻) *The doctor prescribed a holiday as the best cure for his depression.* 医生认为要治好他的抑郁症最好是去度假. ○ *a prescribed text*, ie one that has to be studied, eg for an examination 指定学习的课文(如为应试). **2** [Tn, Tn·pr, Tf, Tw] declare with authority

P

that (sth) should be done or is a rule to be followed 规定做(某事); 指定遵守(某事物): *The law prescribes heavy penalties for this offence.* 法律规定对这种不法行为从严惩处. ○ *Police regulations prescribe that an officer's number must be clearly visible.* 警员条例要求执行职务者的号码标志必须清楚易见. ○ *Army regulations prescribe how rifles must be carried.* 军规中对持枪方式有明文规定. ⇨Usage at DECREE 用法见 DECREE.

pre·script /ˈpriːskrɪpt; ˋpriskrɪpt/ *n* (*fml* 文) law, rule or command 法律; 规章; 命令.

pre·scrip·tion /prɪˈskrɪpʃn; prɪˋskrɪpʃən/ *n* **1** [C] (**a**) doctor's written instruction for the composition and use of a medicine 处方; 药方: *The doctor gave me a prescription for pain-killers.* 医生给我开了个止痛药方. ○ (*fig* 比喻) *His prescription for economic recovery was not well received.* 他为使经济复苏提出的对策反应不佳. (**b**) medicine prescribed in this way 处方上开的药: *The chemist made a mistake when making up the prescription.* 药剂师配错了药. ○ [attrib 作定语] *prescription charges*, ie (in Britain) money to be paid by the patient for drugs supplied on the National Health Service 处方收费(在英国指病人为获得国民保健署所提供的药品而缴纳的费用). **2** [U] action of prescribing 开处方: *The prescription of drugs is a doctor's responsibility.* 开药方是医生的职责.

pre·script·ive /prɪˈskrɪptɪv; prɪˋskrɪptɪv/ *adj* (*fml* 文) **1** (**a**) making rules or giving orders or directions 规定的; 指定的; 规范的: *prescriptive teaching methods* 规定的教学法. (**b**) (*grammar*) telling people how they ought to use a language (在指导语言运用方面)规定性的, 规范性的: *a prescriptive grammar of the English language* 英语规范语法. Cf 参看 DESCRIPTIVE 2. **2** made legal or acceptable by long-standing custom 因长期使用而合法或认可的; 约定俗成的: *prescriptive rights* 因时效而获得的权利. ▷ **pre·script·ively** *adv*.

pres·ence /ˈprezns; ˋprɛzn̩s/ *n* **1** [U] being present in a place 出席; 在场; 存在: *The dogs were trained to detect the presence of explosives.* 那些狗是训练来查寻爆炸物的. ○ *Your presence is requested at the shareholders' meeting.* 敬请您出席股东会议. ○ *Her presence during the crisis had a calming effect.* 在危难中有了她就稳定了人心. Cf 参看 ABSENCE. **2** [U, sing] (*approv* 褒) person's way of standing, moving, etc, esp as it affects other people 仪态; (尤指)风度: *a man of great presence* 潇洒的男子 ○ *The power of his stage presence could never be forgotten.* 他的舞台表演才能令人难忘. **3** [C] person or thing that is or seems to be present in a place (似乎)在场的人或事物: *There seemed to be a ghostly presence in the room.* 屋里像是有个鬼似的. **4** [sing] number of eg soldiers or policemen in a place for a special purpose (执行某种使命的)一群在场人员(如军警等): *a massive police presence at the meeting* 大会期间在场的大批警察 ○ *The United Nations maintains a military presence in the area.* 联合国在该地区驻有军队. **5** (idm 习语) **be admitted to sb's presence** ⇨ ADMIT. **in the presence of sb/in sb's presence** in the place where sb is; with sb there 当着某人; 有某人在场: *He made the accusation in the presence of witnesses.* 他在有见证人在场的情况下提出了控告. ○ *She asked them not to discuss the matter in her presence.* 她请求他们不要当着她讨论这个问题. **make one's ˈpresence felt** make others aware of one's presence or existence by the strength of one's personality, one's superior ability, etc 凭本身的实力、长处等使别人注意自己: *The new chairman is certainly making his presence felt!* 那位新任主席确是在突出自己! **ˌpresence of ˈmind** ability to remain calm and act quickly and sensibly in a crisis 危难中镇定自若; 遇事不慌: *The child showed great presence of mind by grabbing the falling baby.* 那孩子毫不慌张一把抓住了摔下的婴儿.

pres·ent[1] /ˈpreznt; ˋprɛzn̩t/ *adj* **1** [pred 作表语] **~ (at sth)** (**a**) (of a person) being in the place in question (指人)出席, 在场: *Were you present when the news was announced?* 宣布那消息时你在场吗? ○ *The mistake was obvious to all (those) present.* 所有(那些)在场者一眼就看出那个错误. ○ *Everybody present welcomed the decision.* 出席的人都欢迎那个决议. ○ *There were 200 people present at the meeting.* 有200人到会. (**b**) **~ (in sth)** being in a place, substance, etc 存在的; 含有的: *He suspected that a leak was present somewhere along the pipe.* 他猜疑管道里什么地方漏了. ○ *Analysis showed that cocaine was present in the mixture.* 分析的结果表明混合物中含有可卡因. Cf 参看 ABSENT[1]. **2** [attrib 作定语] existing or happening now 现存的; 现有的: *the present difficulties, problems, uncertainties, etc* 目前存在的困难、问题、不稳定性等 ○ *the present administration, government, council, etc* 现在的行政当局、政府、政务委员会等 ○ *the present climate of opinion* 当前的舆论 ○ *You can't use it in its present condition.* 照它目前这种情形, 是无法使用的. **3** [attrib 作定语] now being considered, dealt with or discussed 正在考虑、处理或讨论中的: *the present proposal for increasing taxation* 正在讨论中的增税提案. **4** (idm 习语) **present company exˈcepted/excepting present ˈcompany** (used as a polite comment when making a critical remark 用作发表批评性言论时的礼貌用语) what I am saying does not apply to you 我不是指在座的诸位: *People seem to have drunk far too much tonight, present company excepted of course.* 今晚大家似乎喝酒喝得太多了, 当然在座的各位除外. **the ˌpresent ˈday** the present age; modern times 当今; 现今: *After being taken back 200 years, we were suddenly returned to the present day.* 我们刚才还处在200年前的历史场景之中, 一下子又回到了现在. ○ [attrib 作定语] *ˌpresent-day ˈattitudes, conˈditions, ˈfashions* 现时的态度、条件、流行款式. **on ˈpresent form** (of a judgement) based on sb/sth's previous and/or current actions, behaviour, progress, etc (指评价)基于某人[某事物]先前的和[或]现时的行动、行为、进步等的: *He would not be elected on present form.* 鉴于他的现时表现, 他不可能当选.

▷ **pres·ent** *n* **1 the present** [sing] (**a**) the time now passing; the present time 当前; 目前: *the past, the present and the future* 过去、现在和未来 ○ *Historical romances offer an escape from the present.* 沉浸于历史传奇故事借以逃避现实. (**b**) (*grammar*) = PRESENT TENSE. **2** (idm 习语) **at ˈpresent** at this time; now 此刻; 现在: *I'm afraid I can't help you just at present — I'm too busy.* 很抱歉, 我现在帮不了你——实在太忙了. **ˌby these ˈpresents** (*law* 律) by this document 根据此文件. **for the moment/present** ⇨ MOMENT. **no time like the present** ⇨ TIME[1].

□ **ˌpresent ˈparticiple** (*grammar*) form of the verb that ends in *-ing*, eg *going, having, swimming* 现在分词(以-ing结尾的动词形式, 如going、having、swimming). **ˌpresent ˈtense** (*grammar*) one of the verb tenses (eg *present, present continuous, present perfect*) that express an action or state in the present at the time of speaking 现在时态(动词时态之一, 表示说话此时的动作或状态, 如一般现在时态、现在进行时态、现在完成时态): *The verb is in the present tense.* 这个动词使用的是现在时态. Cf 参看 PAST[1] 4.

pres·ent[2] /ˈpreznt; ˋprɛzn̩t/ *n* **1** thing given or received as a gift 礼物; 赠品: *wedding, Christmas, birthday, etc presents* 结婚、圣诞、生日等礼物 ○ *This book was a present from my brother.* 这本书是哥哥赠送给我的. **2** (idm 习语) **make sb a present of sth** give sth to sb as a gift 将某物赠送给某人: *He admired my old typewriter so much, I made him a present of it.* 他非常喜欢我的旧打字机, 所以我就送给他了. ○ (*ironic* 反语) *Let's not make our opponents a present of any goals*, ie allow them to score easily. 咱们别给对方送分(别让他们轻易得分).

pre·sent[3] /prɪˈzent; prɪˋzɛnt/ *v* **1** [Tn, Tn·pr, Dn·pr] **~ sb with sth; ~ sth (to sb)** give or hand over sth to sb, esp formally at a ceremony 将某物赠予或交给某人; (尤指在仪式上)授予: *Colleagues presented the retiring chairman with a cheque/presented a cheque to the retiring chairman.* 同事们把一张支票交给退休的主席. ○ *They presented a sum of money to the college in memory of their son.* 他们向学院赠送了一笔款项以纪念他们的儿子. **2** [Tn, Dn·pr] **~ sb (to sb)** introduce (sb) formally, esp to sb of higher rank, status, etc 正式介绍, 引见(某人)(尤指向级别、地位等较高的人): *May I present my new assistant (to you).* 请允许我(向你)介绍我的新助手. ○ *The custom of young ladies being presented at court* (ie formally introduced to the monarch) *has disappeared.* 年轻女子被举荐入宫(觐见君主)的风俗已不复存在. **3** [Tn, Tn·pr, Dn·pr] **~ sth (for sth); ~ sth (to sb)** offer sth for consideration 将某事物提请考虑: *a well-*

presented analysis 条理清楚的分析报告 ○ *present one's designs for approval/consideration* 提出自己的计划呈请批准[考虑] ○ *They presented a petition to the governor.* 他们向总督递交了一份请愿书. ○ *She presented* (ie argued) *her case to the committee.* 她提出了自己的理由供委员们考虑. **4** [Tn, Dn·pr] **~ sth (to sb)** (*fml* 文) offer sth 提出某事物: *present one's apologies, compliments, greetings, etc (to sb)* (向某人)致歉、致意、致以问候. **5** (**a**) [Tn, Tn·pr] **~ oneself (for sth)** (of a person) appear or attend (指人)出现, 出席: *You will be asked to present yourself for interview.* 将要求你到场面试. ○ *I have to present myself in court on 20 May.* 我须于5月20日出庭. (**b**) [Tn, Dn·pr] **~ itself (to sb)** (of an opportunity, a solution, etc) show itself (to sb); occur (指机会、解决办法等)(对某人)显露, 产生: *A wonderful opportunity suddenly presented itself.* 突然有了个绝妙的机会. ○ *The answer presented itself to him when he looked at the problem again.* 那问题他再一考虑, 答案就在眼前. **6** [Tn, Tn·pr, Dn·pr] **~ sb with sth; ~ sth (to sth)** show or reveal sth to sb 向某人显示某事物: *This job presents many difficulties to the new recruit.* 这件工作对新手来说困难重重. ○ *Falling interest rates present the firm with a new problem.* 利息一下降给公司带来了一个新的问题. **7** [Tn, Tn·pr] **~ sth (for sth)** offer (a bill or cheque) in order to be paid 提交, 交付(票据或支票): *Has the builder presented his bill yet?* 营造商把帐单送来了吗? ○ *The cheque was presented for payment on 21 March.* 这张支票是在3月21日兑现的. **8** [Tn] (**a**) show (eg a play) to the public 公演(戏剧等): *The National Theatre presents 'Hamlet' in a new production.* 国家剧院上演新戏《哈姆雷特》. (**b**) cause (eg an actor) to perform in public 使(演员等)演出: *Starlight Productions present the Chinese Children's Choir in concert.* 星光剧团主办中国儿童合唱团演出音乐会. (**c**) introduce (a performance) to an audience in the theatre or (a programme) on radio or television (在剧院中)主持上演(节目); (在广播或电视中)主持播出(节目): *Who will present his show* (eg on television) *while he's away?* 他不在场时, 将由谁主持播放他的节目(如电视节目)? ○ *Our review of this week's papers is presented by the editor of 'The Times'.* 我们的本周报纸要闻回顾由《时代》周刊编辑主持. **9** [Tn] hold (a rifle, etc) upright in front of the body as a salute 举(枪枝等)表示敬意: *Present arms!* 举枪敬礼! ○ *The soldiers were ordered to present arms.* 士兵们奉命举枪致敬.

▷ **pre·sent** *n* [sing] upright position of a weapon in a salute 敬礼时枪枝竖举的位置: *rifles at the present,* ie with the weapon held in an upright positon 枪枝竖举着.

pre·senter *n* (esp on radio or television) person who presents (PRESENT³ 8c) a programme (尤指广播或电视)节目主持人.

pre·sent·able /prɪˈzentəbl; prɪˈzɛntəbl̩/ *adj* fit to appear or be shown in public 拿得出去的; 像样的; 体面的: *He's got dozens of suits but not one of them is presentable.* 他有几十套衣服, 却没有一套像样的. ○ *I must go and make myself presentable before the guests arrive.* 趁客人没到, 我得去打扮得像点样子. ○ (*approv* 褒) *She was seen at the opera with an extremely presentable escort.* 她出现在歌剧院里, 有个十分体面的人陪伴着她. ▷ **pre·sent·ably** /-əblɪ; -əblɪ/ *adv*: *He was dressed quite presentably for a change.* 他为了变化变化, 穿得相当体面.

pre·senta·tion /ˌpreznˈteɪʃn; *US* ˌpriːzen-; ˌprizɛnˈteʃən/ *n* **1** [U] (**a**) presenting or being presented 赠送; 引见; 提出; 出席; 显示; 演出; 举枪致敬: *They are preparing for the presentation of a new musical.* 他们正准备上演新的歌舞喜剧. ○ *The cheque is payable on presentation,* ie at the bank. 本支票见票即付. (**b**) way in which sth is presented 赠送、引见、提出、出席、显示、演出等的方式: *The presentation of the material was untidy.* 所提交的资料缺乏条理. ○ *She needs to improve her presentation of the arguments.* 她需要改进阐述其论点的方式. **2** [C] (**a**) thing presented 所赠送、引见、提出、显示、演出等的事物: *We went to the première of their new presentation.* 我们去观看了他们的新剧目的首场演出. (**b**) gift, esp one given at a formal ceremony 赠品; 礼物; (尤指经仪式)授予之物: *We want to make her a presentation to celebrate her jubilee.* 我们想送她一件礼物以庆贺她的纪念日. ○ *The Queen will make the presentation* (ie will hand over the gift) *herself.* 女王将亲自授予礼品. ○ [attrib 作定语] *a presentation ceremony,* ie one at which a presentation is made 赠礼仪式 ○ *a presentation copy,* ie a free book presented by the publisher or by the author (出版者或作者免费提供的)赠阅本. **3** [C, U] position of a baby in the mother's body just before birth 胎位.

pre·sen·ti·ment /prɪˈzentɪmənt; prɪˈzɛntəmənt/ *n* (*fml* 文) vague feeling that sth (esp sth unpleasant) will happen; foreboding 预感(尤指不祥的); 凶兆: *a presentiment of trouble ahead* 要出乱子的预感.

pres·ently /ˈprezntlɪ; ˈprɛzn̩tlɪ/ *adv* **1** after a short time; soon 不久; 立刻: *I'll be with you presently.* 我马上就来. **2** (*esp US*) at the present time; now 现在; 目前: *The Secretary of State is presently considering the proposal.* 国务卿目前正在考虑该项建议.

NOTE ON USAGE 用法: When **presently** means 'soon' it usually comes at the end of the sentence ☆ **presently** 作'立即'解时通常位于句末: *She'll be here presently.* 她马上就来. When it means 'after a short time' it sometimes comes at the beginning 作'很短时间之后'解时有时位于句首: *Presently I heard her leave the house.* 不一会儿我就听到了她离开屋子的声音. Increasingly in British as well as US English it means 'now' or 'currently' and is placed with the verb 不仅在美式英语中, 而且在英式英语中也逐渐广泛用以指'现在'或'当前', 位置紧靠动词: *She's presently working on her PhD.* 她目前在攻读哲学博士学位.

pre·ser·va·tion /ˌprezəˈveɪʃn; ˌprɛzɚˈveʃən/ *n* [U] **1** action of preserving 保护; 维护; 保存; 保留; 保持: *the preservation and conservation of wildlife* 对野生动物的保护 ○ *the preservation of food, one's health, works of art* 食物的保鲜、健康的保持、艺术作品的保存 ○ *The aim of the policy is the preservation of peace.* 这一政策旨在维护和平. ○ [attrib 作定语] *a preserˈvation order,* ie (in Britain) one that makes it illegal to destroy a building, etc because of its historical value (英国的)文物保护法令. **2** degree to which sth has been unaffected by age, weather etc 保存完好之程度: *The paintings were in an excellent state of preservation.* 这些画保存得非常好.

pre·ser·vat·ive /prɪˈzɜːvətɪv; prɪˈzɝvətɪv/ *adj* (used for) preserving (用来)保护的, 保存的: *He painted the posts with a preservative liquid.* 他在柱子上涂上了起保护作用的液体. ○ *Salt has a preservative effect on food.* 盐对食物有防腐作用.

▷ **pre·ser·vat·ive** *n* [C, U] (type of) substance used for preserving 保护剂; 防腐剂: *food free from preservatives* 不含防腐剂的食品 ○ *Alcohol is used as a preservative in certain foods.* 酒精用作某些食物的保护剂. ○ *Preservative is usually added to tinned meat.* 防腐剂通常加在肉类罐头里.

pre·serve /prɪˈzɜːv; prɪˈzɝv/ *v* **1** (**a**) [Tn] keep or maintain (sth) in an unchanged or perfect condition 保护, 维护(某事物): *preserve one's eyesight* 保护视力 ○ *a very well-preserved man of eighty* 一个保养得很好的八十老翁 ○ *Wax polish preserves wood and leather.* 上光蜡可以保护木料和皮革. ○ *Efforts to preserve the peace have failed.* 维护和平的努力已经失败了. (**b**) [Tn, Tn·pr] **~ sth (for sth)** keep sth safe or alive for the future 保存或保留某事物: *Few of the early manuscripts have been preserved.* 早期的手稿保存下来的不多. ○ *His work must be preserved for posterity.* 他的作品当传诸后世. (**c**) [Tn, Tn·pr] **~ sb (from sb/sth)** keep sb safe from harm or danger 保护某人: *The calm courage of the pilot preserved the lives of the passengers.* 飞行员临危不惧的勇气保住了乘客们的生命. ○ *God preserve us!* 上帝保佑我们吧! **2** [Tn] avoid losing (sth); retain 使(某事物)不受损失; 保持: *She managed despite everything to preserve her sense of humour.* 她不管遇到什么情况都竭力保持着幽默感. ○ *It is difficult to preserve one's self-respect in that job.* 做那样的工作很难保持自尊. **3** [Tn] keep (food) from decay (by bottling, drying, freezing, etc) (用装瓶装罐、干燥、冷冻等法)保存(食物): *Salt and spices help to preserve meat.* 盐和调味品有助于保藏肉类. ○ *In the summer, large crops of fruit may be preserved by freezing or bottling.* 夏天收获的大量水果可冷藏或装瓶装罐加以保存. **4** [Tn esp passive 尤用于被动语态] keep (fishing, game, land, part of a river, etc) for private use 禁止外人(捕猎等); 将(土地、河流区段等)保留以供私用: *The fishing in this stretch of the river is strictly preserved.* 此段河流严禁外人捕鱼. Cf 参看 CONSERVE.

▷ **pre·serve** *n* **1** (**a**) [C usu *pl* 通常作复数] preserved fruit 经加工保存的水果: *apricot preserves* 杏脯. (**b**) [U] jam 果酱: *strawberry preserve* 草莓酱. Cf 参看 CONSERVE *n*. **2** [C] area where game or fish are preserved (PRESERVE 4) for private hunting or fishing 专供私人行猎或捕鱼的保留区. **3** [sing] activities, interests, etc regarded as belonging to a particular person 被认为某人所专有的活动、爱好等: *She regards negotiating prices with customers as her special preserve.* 她把与顾客讨价还价看作自己的专长.

pre·server *n* person or thing that preserves 保护者; 维护者; 保藏食品者; 防护用品; 私人保留地: *a* ˈ*life-preserver* 救生用品.

pre-set /ˌpriːˈset; ˌpriˋsɛt/ *v* (**-tt-**; *pt, pp* **pre-set**) [Tn, Cn·t] set (a clock, timer, etc) beforehand 预先调整(时钟、定时器等): *She pre-set the cooker to come on at 6.30.* 她把炊具预先调好在6点30分钟操作. ○ *The video was pre-set to record the match.* 录像机已预调好以便录下比赛情况.

pre-shrunk /ˌpriːˈʃrʌŋk; ˌpriˋʃrʌŋk/ *adj* (of cloth) shrunk before being made into garments, so that they will not shrink when they are washed (指布料)缩过水的, 防缩的: *ˌpre-shrunk* ˈ*jeans* 防缩牛仔裤.

pres·ide /prɪˈzaɪd; prɪˋzaɪd/ *v* **1** [I, Ipr] **~ (at sth)** be chairman (at a conference, meeting, etc) (在会上)担任主席; 主持(会议等): *the presiding officer* 主持会议的官员 ○ *Whoever presides will need patience and tact.* 无论谁作主席, 都需既要有耐性, 又要机敏老练. ○ *The Prime Minister presides at meetings of the Cabinet.* 首相主持内阁会议. **2** (phr v) **preside over sth** (**a**) be head or director of sth 掌管或领导某事物: *The city council is presided over by the mayor.* 市政委员会由市长领导. (**b**) control or be responsible for sth 管理某事物; 对某事物负有责任: *The present director has presided over a rapid decline in the firm's profitability.* 现任领导对公司利润的急剧下降负有责任.

pres·id·ency /ˈprezɪdənsɪ; ˋprɛzədənsɪ/ *n* (**a**) **the presidency** (also **the Presidency**) [sing] office(4) of a president 总统、主席、行政部门首长、院长、会长、行长、总经理、董事长等的职位: *She hopes to win the presidency.* 她希望争取到会长职位. (**b**) [C] term of office as a president 上述各职位的任期: *the last days of his presidency* 他当主席的最后几天 ○ *He was elected to a second presidency.* 他获选连任总统.

pres·id·ent /ˈprezɪdənt; ˋprɛzədənt/ *n* **1 President** elected head of state in the US and many modern republics 总统; 国家主席: *the President of the United States* 美国总统 ○ *President De Gaulle* 戴高乐总统. **2** (also **President**) head of some colleges, government bodies or departments, societies, etc (学院的)院长、(政府部门或机构的)首长、(社会团体等的)会长等: *the President of the Board of Trade* 贸易委员会主席 ○ *He was made president of the cricket club.* 他被任命为板球俱乐部会长. **3** (*US*) head of a bank, business firm, etc (银行的)行长、(公司等的)总经理、总裁、董事长等.

▷ **pres·id·en·tial** /ˌprezɪˈdenʃl; ˌprɛzəˋdɛnʃəl/ *adj* of a president or presidency 总统(职位)的; 最高领导者(职位)的: *a presidential candidate, election, policy* 总统候选人、选举、政策 ○ (*US*) *a presidential year*, ie one in which an election for president is held 总统选举年.

pre·si·dium (also **prae·si·dium**) /prɪˈsɪdɪəm; prɪˋsɪdɪəm/ *n* (*pl* **~s**) permanent executive committee of the administration, esp in Communist countries 常务委员会, 主席团(尤指共产党国家政府的): *the presidium of the Supreme Soviet* 最高苏维埃主席团.

press[1] /pres; prɛs/ *n* **1** [C usu *sing* 通常作单数] act of pushing steadily with (sth held in) the hand 用手(持物)按、压、挤、榨、捏等: *Flatten the dough with a press of the hand.* 用手把生面团压平. ○ *Those trousers need a press*, ie with a hot iron. 那条裤子该熨一熨. **2** [C] (esp in compounds 尤用以构成复合词) any of various devices or machines used for compressing or shaping things, extracting juice, etc 任何压榨或挤压成形之器具或机器: *a* ˈ*winepress* (制酒的)葡萄榨汁机 ○ *a* ˈ*cider-press* 苹果榨汁机 ○ *an* ˈ*olive-press* 橄榄榨油机 ○ *keep one's tennis racket in a press* 把网球拍放在球拍夹中 ○ *a hydraulic press* 水压机. **3** (**a**) (also ˈ**printing-press**) [C] machine for printing 印刷机: *He took a copy of the newspaper as it came off the press.* 报纸在印刷机上印出来后他拿了一份. (**b**) [U] printing or being printed (used esp as in the following phrases) 印刷(尤用于以下词组中): *pass sth for press*, ie give final approval for sth before it goes to be printed 核准稿件以备付印 ○ *go to press*, ie start to be printed 付印(开始印刷) ○ *Prices are correct at the time of going to press, but may be changed.* 付印前价目无误, 之后或有变化. ○ *stop press* 停印. **4** (often 常作 **the Press**) [Gp] (journalists who work for) newspapers, periodicals and the news sections of radio and television 报刊; 定期刊物; 广播和电视的新闻节目; 报界; 新闻界; 记者们: *The Press were not allowed to attend the trial.* 新闻界人士不得出庭旁听. ○ *The majority of the press support the Government's foreign policy.* 舆论界多数支持政府的外交政策. ○ *the local/national/provincial press* 地方[全国性/省级]报刊 ○ *the gutter press*, ie newspapers that concentrate on sensational stories about people's personal lives 低级报纸(专门宣扬别人隐私者) ○ *The freedom of the press* (ie right of journalists to report events, express opinions, etc freely) *must be protected.* 新闻报道的自由(记者自由报道新闻、表达观点等的权利)应该得到保障. ○ [attrib 作定语] *press advertising, comment, freedom* 报刊上的广告、报刊评论、出版自由. **5** [sing] treatment given to a person, a group, an event, etc in radio, newspaper, etc reports (广播、报刊等对个人、团体、事件等的)报道, 评论: *be given/have a good/bad press* 受到舆论界的好评[批评]. **6** [C] business for printing (and publishing) books or periodicals 印刷业; 出版业; 出版社: *Oxford University Press* 牛津大学出版社 ○ *a small press specializing in illustrated books* 专印有插图的书的小出版社. **7** [sing] (**a**) crowd or crowding of people 人群; 人群拥挤: *The child got lost in the press of people leaving the match.* 在看完比赛后散场的人群中把孩子挤丢了. (**b**) pressure of affairs; hurry or stress 事务的压力; 匆忙; 紧迫: *the press of modern life* 现代生活的压力. **8** [C] large cupboard, usu with shelves, for clothes, books, etc 大柜橱(通常有架以放置衣物、书籍等): *a linen press* 衣物柜.

□ ˈ**press agent** person employed by a theatre, etc to organize advertising and publicity in the press (剧院等雇用在报刊等上做宣传和登广告的)宣传员. ˈ**press agency** **1** office or business of a press agent 剧院等的宣传员的办事处或业务. **2** business firm that gathers news and supplies it to journalists 通讯社.

the ˈ**Press Association** (*abbr* 缩写 **PA**) (*Brit*) press agency that gathers home news and supplies it to the British press[1](4) 新闻协会(英国负责采集国内新闻并向本国新闻媒介供稿的通讯社).

ˈ**press baron** (*infml* 口) powerful newspaper proprietor 报业大王.

ˈ**press-box** *n* place reserved for reporters, eg at a football or cricket match 记者席(如足球或板球比赛时设置的).

ˈ**press conference** interview given to journalists in order to announce a decision, an achievement, etc 记者招待会: *The Minister called a press conference as soon as the results were known.* 结果一见分晓, 部长立即举行了记者招待会.

ˈ**press cutting** (also *esp US* ˈ**press clipping**) paragraph, article, etc cut out from a newspaper or periodical 剪报.

ˈ**press-gallery** *n* place reserved for reporters, esp in Parliament or in a lawcourt 记者席(尤指议会里或法庭上的).

pressman /ˈpresmən, -mæn; ˋprɛsmən, -ˌmæn/ *n* (*pl* **-men** /ˈpresmən, -men; ˋprɛsmən/) **1** (*Brit*) journalist 记者. **2** (*US*) person who operates a printing-press 印刷工人.

ˈ**press officer** person employed by a business firm, political party, etc to provide information to the press and to answer journalists' questions (企业、政党等雇用向新闻界发布消息并回答记者问题的)新闻代言人, 新闻发布官.

ˈ**press photographer** newspaper photographer 摄影记者.

ˈ**press release** official announcement or account of sth given to the press by a government department, political party, etc (政府机构、政党等发布的)新闻稿: *The company issued a press release to try to stop speculation in its shares.* 公司发布了新闻稿以期遏止对其股票的投机活动.

press[2] /pres; prɛs/ *v* **1** (**a**) [Tn, Tn·p] move (sth) by pushing steadily against it 对(某物)施以压力使之移动; 按动(某物): *press the trigger of a gun* 扣枪的扳机 ○ *press (down) the accelerator of a car* 踩(下)汽车的油门 ○ *press (in) a button* 按电钮 ○ *press a switch (up)* (向上)扳开关. (**b**) [Ipr, Tn·pr] **~ (sth/sb/oneself) against/on sth; ~ sth to sth** (cause sth/sb/oneself to) push steadily against sth (使某物[某人/自己])对某物施以压力; 压、挤、推或顶某物: *My boot is pressing against a blister on my toe.* 我的靴子挤压了我脚趾上的水疱. ○ *I had to press myself against the wall to let them pass.* 我得贴紧墙壁好让他们过去. ○ *The child pressed her nose against the window.* 那小女孩把鼻子贴在窗户上. ○ *He pressed a handkerchief to his nose.* 他用手帕捂着鼻子. (**c**) [Tn·pr] **~ sth into sth** put sth in a place by pushing steadily against it 对某物施以压力使其进入某位置; 将某物压入、按入或塞入: *press money into sb's hand* 把钱塞进某人手中 ○ *press putty into a hole* 把油灰塞入洞中. **2** [Tn, Cn·a] apply force or weight to (sth) in order to get juice, etc from it 挤出(某物)的汁等; 榨(某物): *press apples, olives, oranges, etc* 挤压苹果、橄榄、橙子等 ○ *press grapes to make wine* 榨葡萄制酒 ○ *press fruit dry*, ie obtain all its juice 把水果榨干(取其全部汁液). **3** [Tn, Cn·a] (**a**) make (sth) flat or smooth (by using force or weight) 压扁, 压平(某物): *press flowers*, eg between pages of a book 把花压扁(如夹在书里) ○ *press the soil flat with the back of a spade* 用铲子的背面平整土地. (**b**) shape or remove creases from (clothes) by applying pressure with an iron 熨平(衣物): *That suit ought to be pressed.* 那套衣服得熨一熨. ○ *Press the pleats flat.* 把褶子熨平. **4** (**a**) [Tn·pr] **~ sb/sth to one** hold sb/sth close; embrace sb/sth 抱紧某人[某物]; 拥抱某人[某物]: *She pressed the child to her.* 她把那孩子搂在怀里. (**b**) [Tn] squeeze (a person's arm, hand, etc) as a sign of affection 紧握(某人之臂、手等)表示情意: *Overcome with emotion, he pressed her hand and left her.* 他感慨万千, 用力握了一下她的手, 离开了她. **5** [Tn, Tn·pr, Cn·t] **~ sb (for sth)** try repeatedly to persuade sb (to do sth) 一再劝说某人(做某事); 催促; 催逼; 敦促: *I don't want to press you, but shouldn't you be leaving?* 我不想逼你, 但你还不该走吗? ○ *The bank is pressing us for repayment of the loan.* 银行催我们偿还贷款. ○ *They are pressing us to make a quick decision.* 他们正在敦促我们迅速作出决定. **6** [Tn] make (one's case, etc) urgently or repeatedly (used esp with the *ns* shown) 急于做或坚持做(某事等)(尤与以下句中名词连用): *I don't wish to press the point, but you do owe me £200.* 我是不愿老提这一点的, 可你还欠着我200英镑呢. ○ *She is still pressing her claim for compensation.* 她仍然坚持要求赔偿. ○ *They were determined to press their case at the highest level.* 他们决定把他们那事向最高层反映. **7** [Tn] make a pressing(*n* a) of (a gramophone record) 压制(唱片). **8** (idm 习语) **be pressed for sth** have barely enough of sth 缺少某事物: *Please hurry — we're a bit pressed for time.* 请快点 —— 我们时间不多了. ○ *I'm very pressed for cash at the moment — can I pay you next week?* 我现在手头很紧 —— 下周再付给你行吗? **press sth home** (**a**) push sth into place 用压力使某物就位: *He locked the door and pressed the bolt home.* 他锁上房门, 并插好插销. (**b**) obtain as much advantage as possible from sth by being determined in attacking, arguing, etc (在进攻、争辩等方面)坚持不懈以多获益: *press home one's advantage* 坚决维护自己的利益 ○ *press home an argument, an attack, a point, etc* 把争论、进攻、某一论点等坚持到底. **press sth into ˈshape** flatten, smooth or shape sth by pushing against it 压平某物; 施加压力使某物平整; 将某物压制成型. **time presses** ⇨ TIME[1]. **9** (phr v) **press across, against, around, etc (sth)** (of people) move in the specified direction by pushing (指人们)挤着走; 拥挤着前进: *The people pressed round the royal visitors.* 人们把那些王室贵宾团团围住. ○ *The crowds were pressing against the barriers.* 人群向着栅栏推挤. ○ *She had to press through the throng to reach the stage.* 她不得不穿过拥挤的人群走上舞台. **press ahead/forward/on (with sth)** continue (doing sth) in a determined way; hurry forward 坚决地继续(进行某事物); 坚持(做某事); 加紧: *The firm is pressing ahead with the modernization plan.* 公司竭力实施现代化计划. ○ *We must press on with the project without wasting time.* 我们要不失时机地加紧进行这项工程. **press for sth** make repeated and urgent requests for sth 一再迫切要求某事物: *The chairman is pressing for a change in the procedure.* 主席一再要求改变程序. ○ *The unions are pressing for improved working conditions.* 工会再三要求改善工作条件. **press sth from sth; press sth out of/in sth** make sth by applying force or weight to a surface 压制某物: *press car bodies out of sheets of steel* 把钢板冲压成汽车车身 ○ *press holes in a piece of leather* 在一块皮革上打出许多洞 ○ *press out shapes from a piece of card* 从一张纸板上压出各种花样. **press sth from/out of sth; press sth out** remove (juice, etc) from fruit by squeezing 挤出(果汁等); 榨出(汁液): *press the juice from oranges* 挤橙子汁 ○ *press oil from olives* 榨橄榄油 ○ *press the seeds out of a tomato* 挤出西红柿的籽. **press (down) on sb** weigh heavily on sb; oppress sb 对某人施重压; 压迫某人: *His responsibilities press heavily on him.* 他身负重任. **press sth on sb** insist that sb accepts sth (against his will) 硬要某人接受某事物: *They pressed gifts on their benefactors.* 他们硬要赞助人接受礼物. ○ *I didn't want to take the money but he pressed it on me.* 我不愿接受那笔钱, 但是他却硬塞给我. **press sth on/onto sth** attach sth to sth by pressing 把某物紧贴在另物上: *press a label on a parcel* 把标签贴在包裹上 ○ *press a clean pad onto a wound* 把一块干净的纱布敷在伤口上.

▷ **press·ing** *adj* (**a**) urgent 紧迫的; 迫切的: *a pressing engagement* 急迫的约会. (**b**) (of a person, request, etc) insistent (指人、要求等)坚持的: *a pressing invitation to dinner* 十分恳切的赴宴邀请 ○ *He was so pressing I couldn't refuse.* 他这样坚持, 我实在难以拒绝. **press·ingly** *adv*.

press·ing *n* (**a**) thing made by pressing, esp a gramophone record 模压制品; (尤指)唱片: *10 000 pressings of a symphony* 10 000张交响乐的唱片. (**b**) number of gramophone records made at one time 同一批制成的唱片: *a pressing of several thousand records* 同批制成的几千张唱片.

□ **press-stud** /ˈprestʌd; ˈprɛsˌstʌd/ *n* (also *infml* 口语作 **popper**, *esp US* ˈ**snap fastener**) small fastener for clothes made of two parts that can be pressed together 子母扣儿; 揿扣儿.

ˈ**press-up** (*US* ˈ**push-up**) *n* (usu *pl* 通常作复数) exercise in which a person lies facing the floor and, keeping his back straight, raises his shoulders and trunk by pressing down on his hands 俯卧撑.

press[3] /pres; prɛs/ *v* **1** [Tn esp passive 尤用于被动语态] (formerly) force (sb) to serve in the army or navy (旧时)强征(某人)入伍. **2** (idm 习语) **press sb/sth into ˈservice** use sb/sth because he/it is urgently needed; use sth as a temporary measure (因急需)征用某人[某物]; 临时使用某物: *Her whole family were pressed into service when the shop was busy.* 店里忙时, 她全家都来干. ○ *Old buses were pressed into service as emergency housing for the refugees.* 用旧公共汽车应急来安置难民.

□ ˈ**press-gang** *n* [CGp] (**a**) (formerly) group of people employed to force men to join the army or navy (旧时)强行拉人的征兵队, 抓壮丁队. (**b**) group who force others to do sth 强拉他人做某事的一伙人. — *v* [Tn] force (sb) into service 强迫(某人)做事: (*joc* 谑) *We were press-ganged into serving the drinks.* 抓了我们当差斟酒.

pres·sure /ˈpreʃə(r); ˈprɛʃɚ/ *n* **1** [U] (**a**) force or weight of sth pressing continuously on or against sth that it touches 压力; 挤压: *the pressure of the crowd against the barriers* 人群推挤栅栏的力量 ○ *The pressure of the water caused the wall of the dam to crack.* 水的压力使堤坝决口. (**b**) amount of this 压力之量; 压强: *The tyre is too hard — reduce the pressure a bit.* 这轮胎太硬, 要减少一点压力. ○ *Your blood pressure* (ie force of the blood in the veins and arteries) *is too high.* 你的血压过高. ○ *a pressure of 6 lb to the square inch* 每平方英寸6磅的压力 ○ [attrib 作定语] *a pressure gauge*, ie an instrument for measuring the pressure of liquid, gas, air, etc 压力计 ○ (*fig* 比喻) *work at high pressure* 在很大压力下工作. **2** [U] weight of the air in the atmosphere 大气的压力: *atmospheric pressure* 气压 ○ *A band of low pressure is moving across the country.* 一个低压带正横越该国. **3** [U, C] **~ (of sth); ~ (to do sth)** strong or oppressive influence 强大的影响; 压迫(感): *She left home to escape the pressure to conform to her family's way of life.* 她离家出走以求摆脱她家生活方式对她的束缚. ○ *The pressures of city life forced him to move to the country.* 都市生活的艰难迫使他迁往乡村. **4** (idm 习语) **bring pressure to bear on sb (to do sth)** use force or strong persuasion (to make sb do sth) 对某人施加压力(使之做某事): *The bank will bring pressure to bear on you if you don't pay.* 你要是不付款, 银行就对你施加压力. ○ *The council brought pressure to bear on the landlord to improve his property.* 市政会向房主施加了压力, 促使其改善房子的居住条件. **put pressure on sb (to do sth)** (try to) force sb (to do sth, esp quickly) (试图)迫使某人(做某事); (尤指)催逼某人: *The birth of twins put pressure on them to find a bigger flat.* 他们生了双胞胎, 不得不寻找一套较大的住房. ○ *I don't want to put pressure on you to make a decision, but we haven't much time left.* 我并不想催你做决定, 只是我们剩下的时间已经不多了. **under 'pressure** (**a**) (of a liquid or gas held in a container) subject to pressure; compressed (指容器中所含的液体或气体)受有压力的, 压缩的: *The gas is stored under pressure in the tank.* 该气体在压缩状态下贮存于罐中. ○ *The beer comes out of the barrel under pressure.* 啤酒受到压力从桶中流出. (**b**) influenced by urgency or compulsion 被催逼的; 被迫的: *work under pressure* 在压力下工作 ○ *put sb under pressure (to do sth)* 迫使某人(做某事) ○ *come under pressure (to do sth)* 被迫(做某事). (**c**) suffering stress 承受压力的: *She is constantly under pressure and it is affecting her health.* 她经常负担很重, 因而影响了健康.

▷ **pres·sure** *v* = PRESSURIZE.

□ **'pressure-cooker** *n* strong tightly-closed pot in which food can be cooked quickly by steam under high pressure 压力锅. ⇨illus at PAN 见 PAN 插图.

'pressure group [CGp] (in politics, business, etc) organized group who try to influence policy, esp by intensive propaganda and campaigning; lobby 压力集团(尤指藉大力宣传及开展活动谋求对政策施加影响的政治、工商业等组织); (议院)院外活动集团.

pres·sur·ize, -ise /ˈpreʃəraɪz; ˋprɛʃə,raɪz/ (also **pressure**) *v* **1** [Tn·pr, Cn·t] **~ sb into sth/doing sth** use force, influence or strong persuasion to make sb do sth 强使某人做某事: *She was pressurized into agreeing to a merger.* 她被迫同意将公司合并. ○ *He felt that he was being pressurized to resign.* 他感到有压力逼他辞职. **2** [Tn esp passive 尤用于被动语态] keep (the compartment of a submarine, the cabin of an aircraft, etc) at a constant atmospheric pressure 使(潜艇的水密舱、飞机的座舱等)保持恒定的气压: *a pressurized cabin* 增压舱 ○ *The compartments are fully pressurized.* 水密舱均已增压完毕. ▷ **pres·sur·iza·tion, -isa·tion** /ˌpreʃəraɪˈzeɪʃn; *US* -rɪˈz-; ˌprɛʃərəˋzeʃən/ *n* [U].

□ **ˌpressurized-ˈwater reactor** type of nuclear reactor that uses water under pressure as a coolant 压力水冷反应堆.

pres·ti·di·git·ator /ˌprestɪˈdɪdʒɪteɪtə(r); ˌprɛstɪˋdɪdʒɪ,tetɚ/ *n* (*fml or joc* 文或谑) conjurer 变戏法的人; 耍把戏的人.

▷ **pres·ti·di·gita·tion** /ˌprestɪˌdɪdʒɪˈteɪʃn; ˌprɛstɪ,dɪdʒɪˋteʃən/ *n* [U] (skill in) performing tricks by conjuring; sleight of hand (变)戏法.

pres·tige /preˈstiːʒ; prɛsˋtiʒ/ *n* [U] **1** respect based on good reputation, past achievements, etc 威望; 威信: *lose/regain prestige* 失去[恢复]威望 ○ *He suffered a loss of prestige when the scandal was publicized.* 这件丑事公开后他便威信扫地. **2** power to impress others, esp as a result of wealth, distinction, glamour, etc 影响力: *have, enjoy, earn prestige in the community* 在社会上很有影响 ○ [attrib 作定语] *the prestige value of owning a Rolls Royce* 拥有劳斯·莱斯汽车的威风.

▷ **pres·ti·gi·ous** /preˈstɪdʒəs; prɛˋstɪdʒəs/ *adj* having or bringing prestige 有威望的; 有威信的; 有影响力的; 带来声望的: *one of the world's most prestigious orchestras* 世界上最负盛名的管弦乐队之一.

presto /ˈprestəʊ; ˋpresto/ *adj, adv* **1** (*music* 音) quick(ly) 以急板(的). **2** (idm 习语) **hey presto** ⇨ HEY.

▷ **presto** *n* (*pl* **~s**) movement or passage of music (to be) played quickly 急板; 急板乐段.

pre-stressed /ˌpriːˈstrest; priˋstrɛst/ *adj* (of concrete) strengthened by having stretched cables inside it (指混凝土)预加应力的.

pre·sum·able /prɪˈzjuːməbl; *US* -ˈzuː-; prɪˋzuməbl̩/ *adj* (*fml* 文) that may be presumed 可假定的; 可推测的: *the presumable result is an election defeat* 推测结果可能竞选失败.

▷ **pre·sum·ably** /-əblɪ; -əblɪ/ *adv* it may be presumed 可假定; 可推测: *She is aware of the difficulties, presumably?* 她对这些困难大概了解吧? ○ *He will presumably resign in view of the complete failure of his policy.* 由于他所推行的政策彻底失败了, 他很可能辞职.

pre·sume /prɪˈzjuːm; *US* -ˈzuːm; prɪˋzum/ *v* **1** [Tf, Cn·a, Cn·t] suppose (sth) to be true; take (sth) for granted 假定(某事物)是事实; 认定(某事物); 假设; 推测: *I presume that an agreement will eventually be reached.* 我想最终是会达成协议的. ○ *'Are the neighbours away on holiday?' 'I presume so.'* '邻居们去度假了吗?' '我想是的.' ○ *In English law, an accused man is presumed (to be) innocent until he is proved guilty.* 根据英国的法律, 被告未经证明有罪即认为是清白的. ○ *Twelve passengers are missing, presumed dead.* 十二名乘客失踪, 据信已经死亡. **2** [It] venture to do sth; be so bold as to do sth 冒昧地做某事; 胆敢做某事: *I won't presume to disturb you.* 我不敢打扰你. ○ *May I presume to advise you?* 我可以冒昧向你进一言吗? **3** (phr v) **presume on sth** (*fml* 文) make a wrong use of sth; take unfair advantage of sth 不正当地利用某事物; 占某事物的便宜: *presume on sb's good nature*, eg by asking for help 利用某人的好心肠(如请求帮助).

pre·sump·tion /prɪˈzʌmpʃn; prɪˋzʌmpʃən/ *n* **1** (**a**) [U] **~ (of sth)** presuming sth to be true or the case 假定; 认定; 假设; 推测: *presumption of her innocence by the court* 法庭对她无罪的推定. (**b**) [C] thing presumed to be true or very probable 假定属实的事物; 被认定的事物; 极为可能的事物: *The article makes too many false presumptions.* 这篇文章中凭空臆测的成分太多. ○ *We're having the party in the garden on the presumption that it's not going to rain.* 我们认为不会下雨, 所以在花园里举行宴会. **2** [U] behaviour that is too bold; arrogance 放肆; 傲慢: *She was infuriated by his presumption in making the travel arrangements without first consulting her.* 他事先没和她商量便做好旅行安排, 她对他自作主张很生气.

pre·sumpt·ive /prɪˈzʌmptɪv; prɪˋzʌmptɪv/ *adj* (*fml esp law* 文, 尤用于法律) (**a**) based on reasonable belief 基于合理之推测的; 推定的: *presumptive evidence* 推定的证据. (**b**) probable 可能的; 假定的: *the presumptive heir/the heir presumptive*, ie the person who will inherit the throne unless sb with a stronger claim is born 假定继承人(除非有更具继承权资格的人出生, 否则即由其继承王位).

pre·sump·tu·ous /prɪˈzʌmptʃʊəs; prɪˋzʌmptʃʊəs/ *adj* (**a**) (of a person or his behaviour) too bold or self-confident (指人或其行为)胆大妄为的, 放肆的, 冒失的, 专横的: *Would it be presumptuous of me to ask you to contribute?* 可否冒昧请求你出一份力? (**b**) (of a person) acting without the necessary authority (指人)自行其是的, 自作主张的: *He was presumptuous in making the announcement before the decision had been approved.* 决议尚未通过他已径自宣布. ▷ **pre·sump·tu·ously** *adv*.

pre·sup·pose /ˌpriːsəˈpəʊz; ˌprisəˋpoz/ *v* [Tn, Tf] (not used in the continuous tenses 不用于进行时态) **1** assume (sth) to be true beforehand 预先假定(某事物)属实; 预料: *We cannot presuppose the truth of his statements.* 我们不能预先假定他的话属实. **2** require (sth) as a condition; imply 以(某事物)为先决条件; 意味着: *Effects presuppose causes.* 有其果必有其因. ○ *Approval of the plan presupposes that the money will be made available.* 批准该计划先要有可用的资金.

▷ **pre·sup·posi·tion** /ˌpriːsʌpəˈzɪʃn; ˌprisʌpəˋzɪʃən/ *n* (*fml* 文) (**a**) [U] (action of) presupposing (PRESUPPOSE 1) 预先假定; 预料: *Bail was refused on the presupposition of* *his guilt.* 已料到他罪名成立而不准保释. (b) [C] thing that is presupposed 预先假定的事物; 预测之事; 先决条件: *You have made several unjustified presuppositions.* 你作了一些毫无根据的假设.

pre-tax /ˌpriːˈtæks; ˋpriˋtæks/ *adj* before tax has been deducted 未扣除税款的; 纳税前的: *pre-tax ˈincome, ˈprofits, ˈsurplus, etc* 税前收入、利润、盈余等.

pre·tence (*US* **pre·tense**) /prɪˈtens; prɪˋtɛns/ *n* **1** (a) [U] deception; make-believe 虚假; 虚伪; 虚饰; 假装; 做作: *Their friendliness was only pretence.* 他们的友谊完全是虚假的. ○ *Their way of life was all pretence.* 他们的生活方式都很做作. (b) [sing] **~ of sth** false show of sth 假象; 假相: *a pretence of strength, grief, sleep* 有力量、伤心、睡觉的假象. **2** (a) [C] **~ to sth** claim to (merit, honour, etc) 声称; 自称; 自诩; 标榜: *I have no pretence to being an expert on the subject.* 我并不自命是这方面的专家. (b) [U] (*fml* 文) ostentation; pretentiousness 炫耀; 虚夸: *an honest, kindly man without pretence* 诚实而不做作的好心人. **3** (idm 习语) **on/under false pretences** ⇨ FALSE.

pre·tend /prɪˈtend; prɪˋtɛnd/ *v* **1** [I, Tf, Tt] make oneself appear to be (doing) sth in order to deceive others or in play 假装; 佯作: *The time has come to stop pretending!* 够了, 别再装蒜了! ○ *She pretended (that) she was not at home when we rang the bell.* 我们按门铃时, 她假装不在家. ○ *The children pretended to eat the mud pies.* 孩子们假装吃泥饼. **2** [Tn] claim (sth) falsely, esp as an excuse 伪称(某事物)(尤用作借口): *She pretended illness as an excuse.* 她佯称有病以为借口. ○ *His pretended friendship was part of the deception.* 他所谓的友谊是一种骗局. **3** [Ipr, Tt] **~ to sth** (*fml* 文) make a claim to (do) sth 声称做某事; 自称为某事物: *Surely he doesn't pretend to any understanding of music!* 谅他不会自以为懂得什么音乐吧! ○ *I don't pretend to know as much as he does about it.* 我不敢说我对此事的了解有他那样多.

▷ **pre·tender** *n* person whose claim (to a throne, title, etc) is disputed 觊觎王位、爵位等者.

pre·ten·sion /prɪˈtenʃn; prɪˋtɛnʃən/ *n* **1** [C usu *pl* 通常作复数] **~ (to sth/doing sth)** (making of a) claim 声称; 自命; 主张; 要求; 权利: *a poet with serious pretensions to literary greatness* 完全有资格称作文学泰斗的诗人 ○ *He has/makes no pretensions to being an expert on the subject.* 他并不以这方面的专家自居. ○ (*derog* 贬) *His social pretensions* (ie behaving as if he was of a higher class) *make him appear ridiculous.* 他冒充上流社会人士而出尽洋相. **2** [U] being pretentious 自负; 狂妄; 炫耀; 标榜: *Readers may find the pretension and arrogance of her style irritating.* 读者可以感觉到她文章中的狂妄自负令人反感.

pre·ten·tious /prɪˈtenʃəs; prɪˋtɛnʃəs/ *adj* claiming (esp without justification) merit or importance; pompous or showy 自负的; 自命不凡的; 炫耀的; 自我标榜的: *expressed in pretentious language* 用狂妄的语言表达的 ○ *a pretentious writer, book, style* 自我炫耀的作家、书、文风. ▷ **pre·ten·tious·ness** *n* [U].

pret·er·ite (*US* **pret·erit**) /ˈpretərət; ˋprɛtərɪt/ *adj, n* (*grammar*) (of the) past simple tense (of a verb) (动词的)过去式(的): *'Ran' is the preterite of 'run'.* ran是run的过去式.

pre·ter·nat·ural /ˌpriːtəˈnætʃrəl; ˌpritəˋnætʃrəl/ *adj* (*fml* 文) beyond what is natural or normal; unusual 超自然的; 异乎寻常的; 不可思议的: *preternatural power, force, ability, etc* 超乎一般的能量、力量、能力等 ○ *a preternatural gift for knowing what others are thinking* 知道别人在想什么的特异禀赋. ▷ **pre·ter·nat·urally** *adv*.

pre·text /ˈpriːtekst; ˋpritɛkst/ *n* **~ (for sth/doing sth)** reason given (for doing sth) that is not the real reason; excuse 借口; 托辞: *He came to see me on/under the pretext of asking my advice when he really wanted to borrow money.* 他以请我指教为借口前来看我, 其实是想借钱. ○ *We'll have to find a pretext for not going to the party.* 我们不去参加聚会得找个借口才是.

pret·tify /ˈprɪtɪfaɪ; ˋprɪtɪˌfaɪ/ *v* (*pt, pp* **-fied**) [Tn] (*usu derog* 通常作贬义) make (sth) pretty in a superficial way 为(某物)装门面; 粉饰, 点缀(某物): *The old farm workers' cottages are being prettified as holiday homes.* 这些农场工人的旧房屋都装饰成了度假别墅. Cf 参看 BEAUTIFY.

pretty /ˈprɪtɪ; ˋprɪtɪ/ *adj* (**-ier**, **-iest**) **1** pleasing and attractive, without being beautiful or magnificent 漂亮的, 可爱的, 精致的(并非华丽的或堂皇的): *a pretty child, pattern, tune* 可爱的孩子、好看的花样、好听的曲调 ○ *a pretty* (ie effeminate-looking) *boy* 俊俏的男孩儿 ○ *What a pretty dress!* 多漂亮的连衣裙哪! ○ *She looks very pretty in that hat.* 她戴着那顶帽子真是漂亮极了. ○ *The bodies of the victims were not a pretty sight.* 这些受害者的尸体惨不忍睹. ⇨Usage at BEAUTIFUL 用法见BEAUTIFUL. **2** (a) (*esp dated* 尤作旧) fine; good 美好的; 良好的: *a pretty wit, compliment, turn of phrase* 敏捷的头脑、动听的恭维话、巧妙的措辞. (b) (*ironic* 反语) not pleasing 糟糕的: *You've got yourself into a pretty mess now!* 你现在可惹了麻烦了! ○ *This a pretty state of affairs!* 事情糟透了! **3** (idm 习语) **(as) ˌpretty as a ˈpicture** very pretty 非常漂亮. **come to such a pass/a pretty pass** ⇨ PASS[1]. **not just a pretty ˈface** not just sb who is superficially attractive without having other qualities or abilities 不仅相貌好(尚有其他优点): *His good looks won him the election but he has still to prove that he's not just a pretty face.* 他由于仪表堂堂而当选, 但他尚须证明决非徒有其表. **a pretty ˈpenny** a lot of money 大量金钱: *Renovating that house will cost you a pretty penny.* 为了整修那所房子, 你得花很多钱.

▷ **pretty** *adv* **1** fairly or moderately 相当; 颇: *The situation seems pretty hopeless.* 这情况似乎没有多大希望了. ○ *She seemed pretty satisfied with the result.* 她对那结果似乎相当满意. ⇨Usage at FAIRLY 用法见FAIRLY. **2** (idm 习语) **pretty much/nearly/well** almost 几乎; 差不多: *The two are pretty much the same.* 这两个简直一模一样. ○ *The car is pretty nearly new.* 那辆车跟新的差不多. ○ *My patience is pretty well exhausted.* 我几乎忍无可忍. **sitting pretty** ⇨ SIT.

pret·tily /ˈprɪtɪlɪ; ˋprɪtɪlɪ/ *adv* in a pretty or charming way 漂亮地; 可爱地; 精致地; 迷人地: *She decorated the room very prettily.* 她把房间装饰得漂亮极了. ○ *She smiled prettily as she accepted the flowers.* 她在接受鲜花时, 笑得真迷人.

pret·ti·ness *n* [U]: *People commented on the prettiness of the cottage.* 大家都夸那小屋很精致.

□ **ˈpretty-pretty** *adj* (*infml derog* 口, 贬) too pretty 过分漂亮的: *a pretty-pretty colour scheme of pale pinks and blues* 浅的粉红色和蓝色过于漂亮的色彩设计 ○ *a frilly, pretty-pretty dress* 有褶边的十分华丽的连衣裙.

pret·zel /ˈpretsl; ˋprɛtsl̩/ *n* crisp salty biscuit made in the shape of a knot or stick 椒盐脆饼干(做成纽结状或棒状).

pre·vail /prɪˈveɪl; prɪˋvel/ *v* **1** [I] **~ (among/in sth/sb)** exist or happen generally; be widespread 普遍存在; 普遍发生; 盛行; 流行: *conditions prevailing in the region* 该地区的普遍状况 ○ *The use of horses for ploughing still prevails among the poorer farmers.* 用马耕作的现象在贫苦农民中仍然十分普遍. **2** [I, Ipr] **~ (against/over sb/sth)** (*fml* 文) fight successfully (against sb/sth); defeat 战胜(某人[某事物]); 击败: *Virtue will prevail against evil.* 美德定将战胜邪恶. ○ *The invaders prevailed over the native population.* 入侵者打败了土著居民. **3** (phr v) **prevail on sb to do sth** (*fml* 文) persuade sb to do sth 劝说某人做某事: *May I prevail on you to make a speech after dinner?* 可以请你在用餐后讲几句话吗?

▷ **pre·vail·ing** *adj* [attrib 作定语] (a) most usual or widespread 普遍的; 盛行的; 流行的: *the prevailing customs, fashions, style, etc* 流行的风俗、式样、款式等. (b) (of a wind) that blows in an area most frequently (指风)某一区域里最常刮的: *The prevailing wind here is from the south-west.* 这里最常刮的风是西南风.

pre·val·ent /ˈprevələnt; ˋprɛvələnt/ *adj* (*fml* 文) **~ (among/in sth/sb)** existing or happening generally; widespread 普遍存在的; 普遍发生的; 盛行的; 流行的: *The prevalent opinion is in favour of reform.* 一般舆论都支持改革. ○ *Is malaria still prevalent among the population here?* 疟疾是否仍为此地居民的多发病?

▷ **pre·val·ence** /-əns; -əns/ *n* [U] being prevalent 普遍; 盛行; 流行: *They were very surprised by the prevalence of anti-government sentiments.* 他们对普遍存在的反政府情绪感到很吃惊.

pre·var·ic·ate /prɪˈværɪkeɪt; prɪˋværəˌket/ *v* [I] (*fml* 文) try to avoid telling the (whole) truth by speaking in an evasive or a misleading way; equivocate 支吾; 搪塞; 闪

烁其辞: *Tell us exactly what happened and don't prevaricate.* 有什么就原原本本地告诉我们吧, 别躲躲闪闪的.

▷ **pre·var·i·ca·tion** /prɪˌværɪˈkeɪʃn; ˌprɪværəˈkeʃən/ *n* (**a**) [U] prevaricating 支吾; 搪塞. (**b**) [C] instance of this 支吾; 搪塞: *The report was full of lies and prevarications.* 这篇报道不是颠倒黑白就是含糊其辞.

pre·var·ic·ator *n* person who prevaricates 支吾搪塞的人.

pre·vent /prɪˈvent; prɪˈvɛnt/ *v* [Tn, Tn·pr, Tsg] **~ sb/sth (from doing sth)** stop or hinder sb/sth 阻止或妨碍某人[某事物]: *prevent the spread of a disease/a disease from spreading* 防止某种疾病的蔓延 ○ *Nobody can prevent us/our getting married.* 谁也阻止不了我们结婚. ○ *Your prompt action prevented a serious accident.* 你由于动作敏捷而防止了一次严重事故.

P

▷ **pre·vent·able** *adj* that can be prevented 可防止的; 可预防的: *preventable accidents, deaths, diseases, etc* 可避免的事故、死亡、疾病等.

pre·ven·tion /prɪˈvenʃn; prɪˈvɛnʃən/ *n* **1** [U] (action of) preventing 阻止; 防止; 妨碍; 预防: *the prevention of crime* 防止犯罪行为 ○ *the prevention of cruelty to animals* 防止虐待动物. **2** (idm 习语) **preˌvention is ˌbetter than ˈcure** (*saying* 谚) it is easier to prevent sth happening than to undo the damage or cure the disease later 预防胜于治疗; 宜未雨绸缪.

pre·vent·ive /prɪˈventɪv; prɪˈvɛntɪv/ (also **pre·vent·ative** /prɪˈventətɪv; prɪˈvɛntətɪv/) *adj* (**a**) preventing or intended to prevent sth; precautionary 预防(性)的; 防备的: *preventive measures* 预防性措施. (**b**) (of medicine) preventing or intended to prevent disease; prophylactic (医学上)预防疾病的, 预防性的: *research into preventive medicine*, ie ways of preventing disease 研究防治学.

▷ **pre·vent·ive** (also **pre·vent·ative**) *n* thing (esp a medicine) used or designed to prevent sth 预防物; 预防性措施; (尤指)预防药.

□ **preˌventive deˈtention** (*law* 律) imprisonment of sb because it is thought likely that he will commit a crime (对有可能犯罪者采取的)预防性拘留.

pre·view /ˈpriːvjuː; ˈpriˌvju/ *n* (**a**) showing of a film, an exhibition, a play, etc before it is shown to the general public (电影、戏剧、展览会等的)预映, 预演, 预展: *a press preview*, ie one for journalists only 为新闻界举办的预映 ○ *We attended a sneak preview of the winter fashion collection.* 我们参观了一次对内的冬季时装预展. (**b**) report or description of a film, performance of a play, etc before it is shown to the general public (电影、戏剧表演等的)预告性述评: *a preview of next week's viewing/listening* 下周节目预告述评.

▷ **pre·view** *v* [Tn] have or give a preview of (sth) 举行(某事物)的预演、预映或预展等.

pre·vi·ous /ˈpriːvɪəs; ˈprivɪəs/ *adj* **1** [attrib 作定语] coming before in time or order (时间或顺序上)先的, 前的: *We had met on a previous occasion.* 我们上次见过面. ○ *He was there the previous day.* 他前一天还在那儿呢. ○ *Who was the previous owner?* 谁是以前的属有人? ○ *I am unable to attend because of a previous engagement.* 我因有约在先故不能出席. ○ *The criminal had had four previous convictions.* 这名罪犯有四次前科. ○ *Applicants for the job must have previous experience.* 申请这份工作的人须先前有过这种工作经验. **2** [pred 作表语] (*infml* 口) done or acting too hastily; presumptuous 操之过急; 自行其是: *Aren't you rather previous in assuming I am going to pay?* 你以为我会付款未免太自作聪明了吧? ▷ **pre·vi·ously** *adv*: *She had previously worked in television.* 她以前干过电视这一行.

pre-war /ˌpriːˈwɔː(r); ˌpriˈwɔr/ *adj* [esp attrib 尤作定语] occurring or existing before a war, esp the Second World War (发生或存在于)战前的; (尤指)第二次世界大战以前的: *in the pre-war period* 在战前 ○ *ˌpre-war ˈcars, ˈhousing, maˈchinery, etc*, ie built or made before the Second World War 第二次世界大战以前造的汽车、房屋、机器等 ○ *ˌpre-war ˈgovernments* 战前的各国政府.

prey /preɪ; pre/ *n* **1** [U] (**a**) animal, bird, etc hunted and killed by another for food 被捕食的动物; 捕获物: *a beast/bird of prey*, ie one that kills and eats others, eg a tiger, an eagle 食肉猛兽[禽](如虎、鹰) ○ *The lion stalked its prey through the long grass.* 那狮子在很深的草丛里潜步逼近猎物. ○ *Mice and other small creatures are the owl's prey.* 老鼠以及其他小动物都是猫头鹰的捕食物. (**b**) (*fig* 比喻) person who is exploited or harmed by another; victim 被剥削者; 受损害者; 牺牲品: *She was easy prey for dishonest salesmen.* 她很容易地让奸商敲了竹杠. **2** (idm 习语) **be/fall prey to sth** (**a**) (of an animal) be hunted and killed for food by another (指动物)被捕食, 成为其他动物的捕获物: *The zebra fell prey to the lion.* 那斑马被狮子捕食. (**b**) (of a person) be greatly troubled or tormented by sth (指人)为某事物所苦, 受到某事物的折磨: *She was prey to irrational fears.* 她遭受着无端恐惧的折磨.

▷ **prey** *v* **1** (idm 习语) **prey on sb's ˈmind** trouble sb greatly 烦扰某人: *Fear of the consequences preyed on her mind.* 她担心其后果而惴惴不安. ○ *The thought that he was responsible for her death preyed on his mind.* 他一想到自己对她的死负有责任就感到心如刀割. **2** (phr v) **prey on sb/sth** (**a**) hunt or catch (an animal, etc) as prey 捕食(动物等): *hawks preying on small birds* 捕食小鸟的老鹰. (**b**) make sb one's victim; exploit or attack 使某人成为受害者; 剥削; 掠夺: *a confidence trickster preying on rich widows* 一个玩弄花招使一些阔寡妇上当的骗子 ○ *The villagers were preyed on by bandits from the hills.* 村民们受到山里强盗抢劫.

price /praɪs; praɪs/ *n* **1** amount of money for which sth is (to be) bought or sold 价格; 价钱: *What is the price of this table?* 这张桌子多少钱? ○ *a woollen sweater, price £19.95* 毛衣, 定价19.95英镑 ○ *Prices are rising, falling, going up, going down, shooting up, plummeting, etc.* 物价在上涨、下跌、上升、下落、猛然上涨、骤然下跌等. ○ *I can't afford it at that price.* 我可出不起那样的价钱. ○ *charge high prices* 要价高 ○ *He sold the house at/for a good price.* 他以很高的价钱卖了那所房子. ○ *Ask the builder to give you a price* (ie say how much he will charge) *for the work.* 请营造商就那工程给你开个价. ○ [attrib 作定语] *the fixing of price levels* 价格水准的制定. ⇨Usage 见所附用法. **2** what must be done, given or experienced to get or keep sth 代价: *Loss of independence was a high price to pay for peace.* 以丧失独立来换取和平是极高的代价. ○ *Being recognized wherever you go is the price you pay for being famous.* 出名所付出的代价是不管你走到哪里, 都会被人认出来. ○ *No price is too high for winning their support.* 为了获得他们的支持, 任何代价均在所不惜. **3** the odds in betting 投注赔率: *Six to one is a good price for that horse.* 那匹马有六比一的赔率很不错. ○ *the starting price*, ie odds offered by a bookmaker on a race just before it starts 赌马经纪人临赛前定的赔率. **4** (idm 习语) **at a ˈprice** at a (fairly) high price 以(相当)高的价格: *Fresh strawberries are now available — at a price!* 鲜草莓现已上市——价钱很高! **at ˈany price** whatever the cost 不惜任何代价: *The people wanted peace at any price.* 人民不惜付出任何代价也要争取和平. **beyond/above/without ˈprice** (*esp rhet* 尤作修辞) extremely valuable; so valuable that it cannot be bought 极其贵重的; 无价的. **cheap at the ˈprice** worth more than the price paid or quoted 物有所值: *'You're surely not asking £40 for this book?' 'Yes — it's cheap at the price!'* '这本书你绝不会要价40英镑吧?' '是40英镑——物有所值啊!' ○ (*joc* 谑) *'It'll cost a fortune to go on holiday there!' 'It'll be cheap at the price if it keeps the family happy.'* '去那里度假可得要一大笔开销哇!' '只要能让一家人快乐, 再贵也值得.' **everyone has his ˈprice** (*saying* 谚) everyone can be bribed in some way 人皆有价(都能以某种方式加以收买). **not at ˈany price** in no circumstances, however favourable 无论如何; 即使有天大的好处: *I wouldn't have my sister's children to stay again — not at any price!* 我可不愿意再让我姐姐的孩子留下来住了——说什么也不行! **of great ˈprice** (*rhet* 修辞) extremely valuable 极其宝贵的. **pay a/the price** ⇨ PAY[2]. **a ˈprice on sb's head** reward offered for sb's capture or for killing him 悬赏缉拿或杀死某人所定之赏格: *The authorities put a price on the outlaw's head.* 当局悬赏缉拿歹徒. ○ *He knew it was dangerous to be seen — there was a price on his head.* 他知道被人发现是很危险的——正在悬赏要他的脑袋呢. **put a price on sth** value sth in terms of money 给某事物定价: *You can't put a price on that sort of loyalty.* 那样的忠心是不能用金钱来衡量的. **what price...?** (*Brit infml* 口) (**a**) (used when sneering at the failure of sth 用于嘲笑失败) see how worthless it was 多么不值得; 有什么用: *What price* *peaceful protest now?* 现在搞和平抗议有个屁用! ○ *What price all your promises now?* 你现在所答应的话又有什么用呢? (**b**) what is the chance of...? ...的可能性如何? *What price he'll offer to pay the fine for us?* 他有可能为我们支付罚金吗?

▷ **price** *v* **1** [Tn, Tn·pr] **~ sth (at sth)** fix the price of sth (at a particular level) 给某物定价: *The agent priced the house at the right level for the market.* 代理商按市场价格给这所房子定了价. ○ *These goods are priced too high.* 这些货物定价过高. ○ *Even the cheapest was priced at £5.* 即使最便宜的也标价5英镑. **2** [Tn] find or estimate the price of (sth) 查明或估计出(某事物)的价钱: *I don't know enough about porcelain to be able to price these plates.* 我不太懂得瓷器, 估计不出这些盘子的价钱. **3** [Tn] mark (goods) with a price 给(货物)标价: *The assistant priced the garments before putting them on display.* 营业员先给服装标好价格再摆出来卖. **4** (idm 习语) **price oneself/sth out of the 'market** charge such a high price for one's goods, services, etc that nobody buys them 漫天要价以致无人问津.

price·less *adj* **1** too valuable to be priced 无价的; 极其贵重的: *priceless jewels, paintings, treasures, etc* 极其贵重的首饰、画、珍宝等 ○ (*fig* 比喻) *Her one priceless asset is her unflappability.* 她有一点是非常难能可贵的, 就是她遇事冷静. ⇨Usage at INVALUABLE 用法见 INVALUABLE. **2** (*infml* 口) very amusing or absurd 非常有趣的; 十分荒唐的: *a priceless joke* 非常有趣的笑话 ○ *You look absolutely priceless in that hat!* 你戴着那顶帽子很滑稽!

pricey (also **pricy**) /ˈpraɪsɪ; ˋpraɪsɪ/ *adj* (**-ier**, **-iest**) [usu pred 通常作表语] (*Brit infml* 口) expensive 昂贵: *This restaurant is a bit pricey for me.* 这家饭馆的价钱对我来说贵了些.

□ **'price control** control of price levels, esp by a government 价格管制(尤指政府所实行的).

'price-fixing *n* [U] (**a**) (*usu derog* 通常作贬义) setting prices by agreement among producers, esp so as to keep them artificially high 价格垄断(制造商之间的协议定价, 尤指人为抬高价格者). (**b**) = PRICE CONTROL.

'price-list *n* list of current prices for goods on sale 价目表; 价格单.

'price-tag *n* (**a**) label showing the price of sth 价格标签. (**b**) **~ (on sth)** (*fig* 比喻) cost of sth 价值; 费用: *The price-tag on the new fighter plane was too high for the government.* 新型战斗机的费用太高, 政府难以负担.

'price war situation in which competing sellers repeatedly reduce their prices in order to attract buyers 价格战(卖方在竞争中不断削价以吸引买主).

NOTE ON USAGE 用法: The **price** and **cost** of something is the amount of money needed to buy it. ☆ **price**和**cost**均指购买某物需要的钱数. **Price** is generally used of objects which can be bought or sold; **cost** usually relates to services or processes ☆ **price**一般指商品的售价; **cost**则通常指服务收费或进行某程序需要的费用: *the price of vegetables, houses, land* 蔬菜、房屋、土地的价格 ○ *the cost of growing vegetables, decorating the house, building on land* 栽培蔬菜、装修房子、建筑施工需要的费用 ○ *the cost of a holiday in France* 在法国度假需要的费用. **Charge** is the amount of money asked, usually for a service ☆ **charge**指索取的费用, 通常用于服务收费: *electricity charges* 电费 ○ *the charge for parking* 存车费. **Price, cost** and **charge** can also be verbs ☆ **price**、**cost**、**charge**这三个词亦可用作动词: *They've priced their house very high,* ie They're asking a high price. 他们出售房子要价很高. ○ *How much did your holiday cost?* 你度假花了多少钱? ○ *How much do they charge for advertising?* 他们索取多少广告费?

prick[1] /prɪk; prɪk/ *n* **1** (**a**) act of pricking 刺; 戳: *I gave my finger a prick with a needle.* 我的手指叫针给扎了一下. (**b**) small hole or mark caused by this 戳出的小孔或记号; 刺痕: *You can see the pricks where the stitches were.* 你可以看见缝针扎出的小洞. **2** pain caused by pricking 刺痛(感): *I can still feel the prick.* 我还有那刺痛的感觉. ○ (*fig* 比喻) *the pricks of conscience*, ie mental uneasiness 良心上的不安. **3** (⚠ *sl* 讳, 俚) (**a**) penis 屌, 鸡巴(阴茎). (**b**) (*derog* 贬) (stupid) man (蠢)人: *What a stupid prick you are!* 你真是个大傻瓜! **4** (idm 习语) **kick against the pricks** ⇨ KICK[1].

prick[2] /prɪk; prɪk/ *v* **1** (**a**) [Tn, Tn·pr] **~ sth (with sth)** pierce sth with a sharp point; make a tiny hole in sth 刺或戳某物; 在某物上穿孔: *The child pricked the balloon and it burst.* 那孩子在气球上刺了个洞, 气球就爆了. ○ *He pricked the blister on his heel with a sterilized needle.* 他用一根消过毒的针扎破他脚后跟上的水疱. ○ *prick holes in paper with a pin* 用大头针在纸上穿孔. (**b**) [Tn, Tn·pr] **~ sth (on/with sth)** cause pain in sth by pricking 刺痛某物; 把某物刺伤: *She pricked her finger on/with a needle.* 她的手指叫针给扎伤了. ○ *Be careful — the thorns will prick you.* 小心——刺会扎伤你的. (**c**) [Tn] (*fig* 比喻) cause mental discomfort to (sb) 使(某人)感到不安: *His conscience is pricking him now that he realizes what he has done.* 他因为已经认识到了自己的所作所为, 所以在良心上深感不安. **2** [I] feel a sharp pain or a sensation of being pricked 感到剧痛; 有刺痛感: *My fingers are beginning to prick after touching that paste.* 我的手指接触那软膏之后就疼起来了. ○ *The vapour made his eyes prick.* 水气熏得他眼睛发痛. **3** (idm 习语) **prick the bubble (of sth)** destroy sb's illusion about sth 使某人对某事物的幻想破灭: *The latest trade figures will surely prick the bubble of government complacency about the economic situation.* 最新的贸易统计数字无疑要惊扰了政府经济情势大好的美梦. **prick up one's ears** (**a**) (of an animal, esp a horse or dog) raise the ears (指动物, 尤指马或狗)竖起耳朵. (**b**) (of a person) suddenly begin to pay attention to what is being said (指人)突然开始注意听: *The children pricked up their ears when they heard the word 'ice-cream'.* 孩子们听到'冰激凌'这个词, 立刻注意起来. **4** (phr v) **prick sth out/off** plant (young plants) in small holes made in the soil with eg a pointed stick 将(幼苗)移植到用尖棒等在土壤中钻的小孔里.

▷ **prick·ing** *n* (usu *sing* 通常作单数) (**a**) act of pricking 刺; 戳. (**b**) sensation of being pricked 刺痛(感): *She felt a pricking on her scalp.* 她感到头皮上被扎了一下.

prickle /ˈprɪkl; ˋprɪkl/ *n* **1** (**a**) small pointed growth on the stem or leaf of a plant; thorn (植物的茎或叶上的)刺. (**b**) small pointed growth on the skin of certain animals, eg a hedgehog; spine (某些动物如刺猬等身上的)皮刺, 刺毛. **2** pricking sensation on the skin (皮肤上的)刺痛(感).

▷ **prickle** *v* [I, Tn] (cause sb/sth to) have a feeling of being pricked 刺痛某人[某物]; (使某人[某物])感到刺痛: *The woollen cloth prickles (my skin).* 穿毛料衣服(使我的皮肤)有被扎的感觉. ○ *My scalp began to prickle as I realized the horrible truth.* 我了解到了那令人恐惧的事实, 顿时感到不寒而栗.

prickly /ˈprɪklɪ; ˋprɪklɪ/ *adj* (**-ier**, **-iest**) **1** (**a**) covered with prickles (PRICKLE 1a) 多刺的: *prickly rose-bushes* 多刺的玫瑰丛. (**b**) having or causing a sensation of prickling 刺痛的; 引起刺痛的: *My skin feels prickly.* 我的皮肤有刺痛感 ○ *a prickly feeling, sensation, etc* 刺痛感. **2** (*infml* 口) (of a person) easily angered; irritable; touchy (指人)易怒的, 脾气暴躁的, 动辄发火的: *You're a bit prickly today!* 你今天动不动就发火! **prick·li·ness** *n* [U]. **prickly 'heat** skin condition common in hot climates, with inflammation of the skin near the sweat glands which causes a prickly sensation 痱子. **prickly 'pear** (**a**) type of cactus covered with prickles 仙人果(一种仙人掌, 多刺). (**b**) its pear-shaped edible fruit 仙人果的果实(像梨, 可食).

pride /praɪd; praɪd/ *n* **1** (**a**) [U] **~ (in sb/sth)** feeling of pleasure or satisfaction which one gets from doing sth well, from owning sth excellent or widely admired, etc 得意; 自豪: *She looked with pride at the result of her work.* 她自豪地看着自己的工作成果. ○ *Her pride in her achievements is justified.* 她为自己的成就而自豪, 这是理所当然的. ○ *He felt a glow of pride as people admired his new car.* 人们夸他的新汽车时, 他得意得很. ○ *the pride of parenthood* 身为父母的骄傲. (**b**) [sing] **the ~ of sth** person or thing that is an object or source of this 引以自豪的人或事物: *The new car was the pride of the whole family.* 新汽车是全家人引以自豪之物. ○ *He was the pride of the village after winning the championship.* 他获得冠军之后成了全村的骄傲. **2** [U] (*derog* 贬) unjustifiably high opinion of oneself or one's achievements;

arrogance 高傲; 倨傲; 骄傲; 傲慢: *the sin of pride* 傲慢的过错 ○ *He was puffed up with pride.* 他傲气十足. **3** [U] knowledge of one's own worth or character; dignity and self-respect 自尊(心): *Her pride was hurt.* 她的自尊心受到了伤害. ○ *He has no pride if he lets the children talk to him so rudely.* 他要是允许孩子们对他说话这样无礼, 就会有失自己的尊严. ○ *Having to accept the money was a blow to her pride.* 她不得不接受这笔钱, 这是对她自尊心的打击. ○ *He refused to accept help out of a false sense of pride.* 他由于死要面子而不肯接受帮助. **4** [CGp] group of (esp) lions 一群(尤指狮子). **5** (idm 习语) **pocket one's pride** ⇨ POCKET *v*. **pride comes/goes before a 'fall** (*saying* 谚) if you behave arrogantly, sth will happen to make you look foolish 骄者必败. **pride of 'place** the most prominent or important position, because of being the best or best-liked 最突出或最重要的位置: *The painting has pride of place in his collection.* 这幅画在他的收藏品中最为珍贵. **sb's pride and 'joy** person or thing that sb is very proud of 使某人感到无比骄傲的人或事物: *Their baby is their pride and joy.* 他们的婴儿是他们的快乐和骄傲. **put one's pride in one's pocket** do sth that would normally make one feel ashamed and humiliated 姑且忍辱含垢. **take (a) pride in sb/sth** be proud of sb/sth 对某人[某事物]感到自豪: *She takes great pride in her children's success.* 她为自己的孩子取得的成绩感到无比骄傲. **take pride in sth** do sth carefully or well because it is important to one 认真做好某事物(因对自己很重要): *He takes no pride in his work.* 他对待工作马马虎虎. ○ *You should take more pride in your appearance.* 你应该多注意一点仪表.

▷ **pride** *v* (phr v) **pride oneself on sth/doing sth** be proud of sth 以某事物而自豪; 得意于某事物: *She prides herself on her garden/on her skill as a gardener.* 她对自己的花园[对自己的园艺]非常得意. ○ *He prides himself on remaining calm in an emergency.* 他在紧急关头十分镇静为此感到骄傲.

priest /priːst; prist/ *n* **1** person appointed to perform religious duties and ceremonies in the Christian Church, esp one who is between a deacon and a bishop in the Roman Catholic, Orthodox or Anglican Church (more usu called a *clergyman* in the Anglican Church) 基督教会的神职人员(尤指助祭或会吏以上主教以下者); 司铎, 司祭, 教士, 牧师, 神甫, 神父(英国国教通常多称为 clergyman): *a parish priest* 牧区牧师 ○ *the ordination of women priests* 女司铎的授圣职仪式. Cf 参看 MINISTER[1] 3, VICAR. **2** (*fem* 阴性作 **priest·ess** /ˈpriːstes; ˋpristɪs/) person who performs religious ceremonies in a non-Christian religion (基督教会以外的)神职人员.

▷ **the priest·hood** /-hʊd; -hud/ *n* **(a)** [sing] office or position of a priest 司铎、司祭、教士、牧师或神甫的职务或职位: *enter the priesthood* 任司铎之职. **(b)** [Gp] whole body of priests (esp of a particular Church or country) 全体神职人员(尤指某一教会或国家的): *the Catholic priesthood* 天主教全体神甫 ○ *the Spanish priesthood* 西班牙神职人员.

priest·like *adj* like a priest 似神职人员的.

priestly *adj* [usu attrib 通常作定语] of, like or relating to a priest (似)神职人员的; 与神职人员有关的: *his priestly duties* 他作为神职人员的责任.

prig /prɪg; prɪg/ *n* (*derog* 贬) person who behaves as if he were morally superior to everyone else, and disapproves of what others do; self-righteous person 自以为道德高尚的人; 道学先生.

▷ **prig·gish** *adj* of or (behaving) like a prig (似)道学先生的. **prig·gishly** *adv*. **prig·gish·ness** *n* [U].

prim /prɪm; prɪm/ *adj* (**-mmer**, **-mmest**) (*usu derog* 通常作贬义) **1** (of a person) disliking anything that is improper, rude or rough; prudish (指人)循规蹈矩的, 拘谨的, 古板的, 假正经的: *You can't tell that joke to her — she's much too prim and proper.* 可别给她讲那样的笑话——她这人过于古板和认真. **2** stiffly formal in appearance, behaviour or manner (外观、行为或举止上)庄重的: *a prim little dress with a white collar* 带有白色衣领的十分端庄的连衣裙. ▷ **primly** *adv*: *He didn't reply, but just smiled primly.* 他没回答, 只是拘谨地笑了笑. **prim·ness** *n* [U].

prima bal·ler·ina /ˌpriːmə ˌbæləˈriːnə; ˋprimə ˌbæləˋrinə/ leading woman dancer in (a) ballet 芭蕾舞中首席女演员.

pri·macy /ˈpraɪməsɪ; ˋpraɪməsɪ/ *n* **1** [U] (*fml* 文) leading position; pre-eminence 首位; 至高无上: *the primacy of moral values, the monarchy, the House of Commons* 道德价值的高于一切、君权的凌驾一切、下议院的支配地位. **2** [C] office or position of an archbishop 大主教的职务或职位.

prima donna /ˌpriːmə ˈdɒnə; ˌprimə ˋdɑnə/ **1** leading woman singer in (an) opera 歌剧中担任主角的女演员. **2** (*derog* 贬) person who easily gets into a bad temper when others do not do as he wants, when his idea of his own importance is challenged, etc (因气量狭小、妄自尊大等)爱发脾气的人.

prim·aeval = PRIMEVAL.

prima facie /ˌpraɪməˈfeɪʃiː; ˌpraɪməˋfeʃɪ/ *adj* [attrib 作定语], *adv* (*esp law* 尤用于法律) based on what seems to be so without further or deeper investigation 似乎如此(的); 未作进一步或深入调查(的): *prima facie evidence*, ie sufficient to establish sth legally (unless it is disproved later) 初步证据 ○ *Prima facie he would appear to be guilty.* 初步证据表明他有罪.

primal /ˈpraɪml; ˋpraɪml/ *adj* [attrib 作定语] (*fml* 文) **1** first or original; primeval 最初的; 原始的: *the loss of their primal innocence* 他们原有的天真素质之丧失. **2** chief or most important; fundamental; primary(2) 主要的; 首要的; 基础性的; 根本的: *of primal importance* 至为重要的.

prim·ary /ˈpraɪmərɪ; *US* -merɪ; ˋpraɪˌmɛrɪ/ *adj* **1 (a)** [usu attrib 通常作定语] earliest in time or order of development (在时间或发展顺序上)初始的, 最早的, 开端的, 起步阶段的: *in the primary stage of development* 在发展的最初阶段 ○ *The disease is still in its primary stage.* 此病尚处于初期阶段. ○ *primary causes* 始发原因. **(b)** (also **Primary**) of the lowest or earliest series of geological strata 最下面的或最早形成的岩层的; 原生的: *Primary rocks* 原生岩石. **2** [usu attrib 通常作定语] most important; fundamental 首要的; 基础性的; 根本的: *The primary reason for advertising is to sell more goods.* 做广告的根本目的是要多出售货物. ○ *the primary* (ie basic) *meaning of a word* 词的基本意义 ○ *This is of primary importance.* 这是最重要的. ○ *primary stress/accent*, ie the strongest stress given to a syllable in a word or compound (shown in this dictionary by the mark ˈ) 主重音, 第一重音(标注于单词或复合结构的音节上的最强的重音, 本词典中以 'ˈ' 号表示). Cf 参看 PRINCIPAL. **3** [attrib 作定语] of or for primary education 初等教育的: *primary teachers* 小学教师. Cf 参看 SECONDARY.

▷ **prim·ar·ily** /ˈpraɪmərəlɪ; *US* praɪˈmerəlɪ; ˋpraɪˌmɛrəlɪ/ *adv* mainly 主要地: *The purpose of the programme is primarily educational.* 演出该节目的主要目的是为了进行教育.

prim·ary *n* (also **primary e'lection**) (in the US) election in which voters select party candidates for a coming election (美国)(为大选推举党内候选人而进行的)初选: *the presidential primaries* 提名总统候选人的初选.

□ **primary 'colour** any one of the colours from which all other colours can be obtained by mixing, ie (of dye or paint) red, yellow and blue and (of light) red, green and violet 原色, 基色(指能混合生成其他各种颜色的基本颜色之一, 染料或颜料中的原色是红、黄、蓝, 光的原色是红、绿、紫).

ˌprimary edu'cation education in the first years of school, for children of (usu) 5-11 years 初等教育(指通常为5至11岁儿童的小学教育).

'primary school **1** (*Brit*) first school for children of (usu) 5-11 years 小学(儿童年龄通常为5至11岁). **2** (*US* **grade school**, **grammar school**) part of an elementary school, for children of (usu) 6-9 years 初级学校(小学之初级阶段, 儿童年龄通常为6至9岁).

prim·ate[1] /ˈpraɪmeɪt; ˋpraɪmet/ *n* archbishop 大主教; 主教长: *the Primate of all England*, ie the Archbishop of Canterbury 全英主教长(坎特伯雷大主教).

prim·ate[2] /ˈpraɪmeɪt; ˋpraɪmet/ *n* member of the most highly developed order of mammals that includes human beings, apes, monkeys and lemurs 灵长目动物.

prime[1] /praɪm; praɪm/ *adj* [attrib 作定语] **1** most important; chief; fundamental 最重要的; 主要的; 基本的: *Her prime motive was personal ambition.* 她的主要动机是为了实现个人的志向. ○ *Her prime concern is to* *protect the property.* 她最为关心的是保护财产. ○ *It is a matter of prime importance.* 此事至为重要. ○ *The prime cause of the trouble was bad management.* 造成麻烦的根本原因在于管理不善. **2** of the best quality; excellent 质量最好的; 第一流的: *prime (cuts of) beef* 上等牛肉(块) ○ *a prime site for development* 最适于发展的场地. **3** having all the expected or typical qualities 最理想的; 最典型的: *That's a prime* (ie very typical, excellent) *example of what I was talking about.* 这就是一个恰能印证我所谈的内容的极好的例子.

□ **ˌprime ˈcost** basic cost of producing or manufacturing sth (ie the cost of materials and labour) not including such additional items as rent and insurance for premises 主要成本(生产或制造所需的基本费用, 包括材料费和劳务费, 而不包括附加费用如场地的租金和保险金).

ˌprime meˈridian line of longitude which passes through Greenwich near London, numbered zero, from which the other lines of longitude are calculated 本初子午线(通过伦敦附近之格林尼治的经线, 度数为零, 是计算东西经度的起点).

ˌprime ˈminister chief minister in a government 首相; (政府)总理.

ˌprime ˈmover (**a**) fundamental source of power for providing movement, such as wind or water 原动力(产生动力的力, 如风力或水力). (**b**) person who originates a plan, course of action, etc and has it put into practice (计划、行动等的)发起者, 推动者: *He was the prime mover in the revolt against the government.* 他是这场反政府叛乱的煽动者.

ˌprime ˈnumber (*mathematics* 数) number which can be divided exactly only by itself and 1 (eg 7, 17, 41) 质数, 素数(只能被1和这个数本身整除的数, 如7、17、41).

ˌprime ˈtime (in broadcasting) time when the highest number of people are watching or listening (广播或电视的)黄金时间(观众或听众最多的时间): [attrib 作定语] *ˌprime-time ˈadvertising, ˈshows, ˈslots* 安排在黄金时间播出的广告、黄金时间的表演、黄金时间.

prime[2] /praɪm; praɪm/ *n* [sing] **1** (**a**) state or time of greatest strength, beauty, vigour, etc 最强壮、最美丽、最具有活力等的状态或时期: *When is a man in his prime?* 一个人的盛年在什么时候? ○ *She is past her prime.* 她的大好时光已经过去. (**b**) state of highest perfection; the best part 最完美的状态; 最佳部分; 精华: *be in the prime of life/youth* 正当年富力强[青春大好年华]. **2** (*rhet* 修辞) first or earliest part 第一部分; 最早的部分: *the prime of the year*, ie spring 第一季度(春季).

prime[3] /praɪm; praɪm/ *v* [Tn, Tn·pr] **~ sth/sb (with sth)** **1** make sth ready for use or action 将某物准备好(以便投入使用或起动): *prime a pump*, ie put liquid in it to make it start working 给水泵注水使之起动 ○ *prime an explosive device*, ie set the trigger 使爆炸装置准备起爆(将引爆器置于待触发状态). **2** prepare (wood, etc) for painting by covering it with a substance that prevents the paint from being absorbed 给(木料等)上底色(以便涂漆). **3** supply sb with facts or information in advance, sometimes dishonestly, so that he can deal with a situation 事先向某人(有时指以不正当手段)提供情况或讯息(供其采取对策): *The witness had been primed by a lawyer.* 这证人曾经受到律师的指点. ○ *The party representative had been well primed with the facts by party headquarters.* 党代表已经掌握了总部提供的事实. ○ *The witness seemed to have been primed* (ie instructed) *about what to say.* 这证人看来经人指点过该说什么不该说什么. **4** (*infml* 口) give sb plenty of food and drink (in preparation for sth) 给某人充足饮食(以备从事某事): *We were well primed for the journey with a large breakfast.* 为了去旅行, 我们早餐都吃得饱饱的. **5** (idm 习语) **prime the ˈpump** encourage the growth of a new or inactive business or industry by investing money in it 将资金投入新的或不景气的公司或行业以刺激其发展.

primer[1] /ˈpraɪmə(r); ˋprɪmɚ/ *n* (*dated* 旧) textbook for people just starting to study a subject 初级读本; 入门书: *a Latin primer* 拉丁文入门.

primer[2] /ˈpraɪmə(r); ˋpraɪmɚ/ *n* **1** [U, C] substance used to prime[3](2) a surface for painting (上油漆用的)底层涂料, 底漆. **2** [C] amount of explosive in a small container used to explode the main charge of gunpowder in a cartridge, bomb, etc 底火; 火帽; 点火药.

prim·eval (also **prim·aeval**) /praɪˈmiːvl; praɪˋmivl/ *adj* [usu attrib 通常作定语] (**a**) of the earliest period of the history of the world 太古时代的: *primeval rocks* 太古的岩石. (**b**) very ancient 远古的; 原始的: *primeval forests*, ie natural forests, where trees have never been cut down 原始森林. (**c**) based on instinct rather than reason, as if from the earliest period of the human race 出于原始之天性的; 基于人类固有之本能的: *It aroused strange primeval yearnings in him.* 这使他产生了奇怪的、基于人类固有之本能的强烈欲望.

prim·it·ive /ˈprɪmɪtɪv; ˋprɪmətɪv/ *adj* **1** [usu attrib 通常作定语] of or at an early stage of social development 社会发展之早期的; 上古的; 原始的: *primitive culture, customs, tribes* 原始文化、习俗、部落 ○ *primitive man* 原始人 ○ *primitive weapons*, eg bows and arrows, spears 原始的武器(如弓箭、矛). **2** (*often derog* 常作贬义) simple and unsophisticated, as if from an earlier period of history 简陋的; 原始性的: *They built a primitive shelter out of tree trunks.* 他们用一些树干建造了一个简陋的棚子. ○ *Living conditions in the camp were pretty primitive.* 营地的生活条件甚为原始.

▷ **prim·it·ive** *n* (**a**) painter or sculptor of the period before the Renaissance 文艺复兴前的画家或雕刻家. (**b**) artist of the modern period who paints in a simple childlike style (as if) without any formal artistic training (现代的)原始派艺术家(绘画风格简单且带有稚气, 或似未经专业训练者). (**c**) example of the work of a primitive 文艺复兴前的画家或雕刻家之作品; 现代的原始派艺术家之作品.

prim·it·ively *adv*.

prim·it·ive·ness *n* [U].

pri·mo·gen·it·ure /ˌpraɪməʊˈdʒenɪtʃə(r); *US* -tʃʊər; ˌpraɪməˋdʒɛnətʃɚ/ *n* [U] **1** fact of being a first-born child 长嗣身分. **2** (also **right of primogeniture**) (*law* 律) system of inheritance by which an eldest son receives his parents' property 长子继承权.

prim·or·dial /praɪˈmɔːdɪəl; praɪˋmɔrdɪəl/ *adj* [attrib 作定语] (*fml* 文) existing at or from the beginning, esp of the world or the universe; primeval (从)一开始便存在的(尤指世界或宇宙之始); 原始的; 原生的: *The universe was created out of a primordial ball of matter.* 宇宙是从一个本来就存在着的球体中产生出来的. ▷ **prim·or·di·ally** /-dɪəlɪ; -dɪəlɪ/ *adv*.

primp /prɪmp; prɪmp/ *v* (*dated* 旧) **1** [I, Tn] (*derog* 贬) tidy (oneself, one's hair, etc) in a fussy way 过于讲究地打扮(自己)、整理(毛发等): *primp and preen in front of a mirror* 对着镜子精心打扮. **2** (phr v) **primp oneself up** make oneself look smart 把自己打扮得漂漂亮亮.

prim·rose /ˈprɪmrəʊz; ˋprɪmˌroz/ *n* **1** [C] (**a**) wild plant that has pale yellow flowers in spring 报春花. ⇨illus at App 1 见附录1插图, page ii. (**b**) one of its flowers 一朵报春花. **2** [U] pale yellow colour 报春花色; 淡黄色. **3** (idm 习语) **the primrose ˈpath** (*rhet* 修辞) the pursuit of pleasure or an easy life 对安乐或享受的追求: *the primrose path to ruin* 因贪图享受而走向堕落的道路.

▷ **prim·rose** *adj* of a pale yellow colour 报春花色的; 淡黄色的.

prim·ula /ˈprɪmjʊlə; ˋprɪmjulə/ *n* any of various types of plant of the primrose family with clusters of flowers of various colours and sizes, commonly grown in gardens 报春花.

Primus /ˈpraɪməs; ˋpraɪməs/ *n* (*pl* **~es**) (also **ˈprimus stove**) (*propr* 专利名) type of portable oil-burning stove for cooking on, used eg by campers 普赖默斯油炉(便携式燃油炉, 如野营使用的).

prince /prɪns; prɪns/ *n* **1** (**a**) male member of a royal family who is not the king, esp (in Britain) a son or grandson of the sovereign 君王家族(除国王外)的男性成员; (在英国尤指)王子, 王孙: *the Prince of Wales*, ie (in Britain, the title often given to the) heir to the throne 威尔士王储(英国常授予王位继承人的封号). (**b**) hereditary royal ruler, esp of a small state 世袭的王室统治者(尤指小国的): *Prince Rainier of Monaco* 摩纳哥国王雷尼尔. (**c**) (in some countries) nobleman (某些国家的)贵族. **2** (*fig* 比喻) excellent or outstanding man in a particular field 某领域中的优秀的或杰出的人物: *Bocuse, a prince among chefs* 博卡斯, 厨师中的佼佼者.

▷ **prince·dom** /-dəm; -dəm/ *n* (**a**) [U] rank of a prince

P

君王家族男性成员的或小国君主的权位. (**b**) [C] area ruled by a prince(1b); principality 小国君主的领地; 公国; 侯国; 封邑.

princely *adj* (**a**) [usu attrib 通常作定语] of, like or ruled by a prince (似)王公贵族的; (似)王子王孙的; 王公贵族统治的: *princely states* 由王公贵族统治的小国. (**b**) (**-ier**, **-iest**) splendid or generous 豪华的; 慷慨的: *a princely gift, sum* 丰厚的礼物、充裕的款项 ○ (*ironic* 反语) *They paid me the princely sum of 50p.* 他们付给我一笔50便士的巨款.

prin·cess /prɪn'ses; ˋprɪnsɪs/ *n* (**a**) female member of a royal family who is not the queen, esp (in Britain) the daughter or granddaughter of the sovereign 君王家族(除女王或王后外)的女性成员; (在英国尤指)公主, 孙公主: *Princess Margaret* 玛格丽特公主. (**b**) wife of a prince 王公贵族的夫人; 王妃. ˌ**Princess** ˈ**Royal** (in Britain) (title often given to the) eldest daughter of the sovereign 大公主(英国常授予君主之长女的封号).

□ ˌ**Prince** ˈ**Consort** (title often given to the) husband of a reigning queen 王夫(女王的丈夫); 王夫的封号.

prin·cipal /ˈprɪnsəpl; ˋprɪnsəpḷ/ *adj* [attrib 作定语] first in rank or importance; chief; main 级别最高的; 最重要的; 为首的; 主要的: *the principal members of the government* 政府高级官员 ○ *The Danube is one of the principal rivers of Europe.* 多瑙河是欧洲的主要河流之一. ○ *The principal aim of the policy is to bring peace to the area.* 该政策的主要目的是为给这一地区带来和平. ○ *The low salary is her principal reason for leaving the job.* 工资太低是她辞去那工作的最重要的原因. ○ *the principal beneficiaries of a will* 遗嘱中继承遗产的主要受益人. Cf 参看 PRIMARY 2.

▷ **prin·cipal** *n* **1** (title of the) person with the highest authority in an organization, esp in certain schools and colleges 某组织的最高领导人(之称号); (尤指某些学校和学院的)校长, 院长: *the Principal of St James' College* 圣詹姆斯学院院长. **2** person who takes a leading part in a play, an opera, etc (话剧、歌剧等中的)主角, 主要演员. **3** (usu *sing* 通常作单数) (*finance* 财) money lent or invested on which interest is paid; capital sum 本金; 资本: *repay principal and interest* 付还本金和利息. **4** person for whom another acts as his agent, eg in business or law 被代理人, 委托人(如于商务或法律事务等): *I must consult my principals before agreeing to your proposal.* 我得同委托人商量后才能接受你的建议. **5** (*law* 律) person directly responsible for a crime (contrasted with an accessory or abetter) 主犯.

prin·cip·ally /-plɪ; -plɪ/ *adv* for the most part; chiefly 多半; 主要地: *The dialect is spoken principally in the rural areas.* 该方言主要通行于农村地区. ○ *Weymouth is principally a holiday resort.* 韦茅斯主要来说是个度假胜地.

□ ˌ**principal** ˈ**boy** leading male role in a pantomime, traditionally played by a woman 童话剧中的男主角(一向由女演员扮演).

ˌ**principal** ˈ**parts** (in English) those forms of a verb (ie the infinitive, past tense and past participle) from which all other forms can be derived (英语中动词的)主要部分(即不定式、过去式和过去分词).

NOTE ON USAGE 用法: Note that **principle** is a noun relating to rules of behaviour 注意: **principle** 是名词, 指行为的规范: *She leads her life according to Christian principles.* 她以基督教教义作为生活的准则. **Principal** is a (rather formal) adjective meaning 'main' or 'most important' ☆ **principal** 是(较文的)形容词, 意为'主要的'或'最重要的': *My principal concern is my family's welfare.* 我至为关心的是我一家的幸福. ○ *the principal objections to the proposal* 对该项建议的主要反对意见. As a noun it is used for the director of certain educational institutions (usually in further education) 该词若用作名词则指某些教育机构(通常属继续教育性质)之领导人: *The principal and the vice-principal of the college both attended the meeting.* 学院的正副院长均出席了会议.

prin·cip·al·ity /ˌprɪnsɪˈpælətɪ; ˌprɪnsəˈpælətɪ/ *n* **1** country ruled by a prince 由王公贵族统治的小国; 公国; 侯国: *the principality of Monaco* 摩纳哥公国. **2 the Principality** [sing] (*Brit*) Wales 威尔士.

prin·ciple /ˈprɪnsəpl; ˋprɪnsəpḷ/ *n* **1** [C] basic general truth that underlies sth (eg a subject or a system of morality) 原理; 原则: *a textbook which teaches the basic principles of geometry* 讲解几何学基本原理的教科书 ○ *the principle of equality of opportunity for all* 人人机会均等的原则 ○ *Discussing all these details will get us nowhere: we must get back to first principles.* 讨论这些枝节问题是毫无用处的, 我们必须回到基本原则上来. **2** (**a**) [C usu *pl* 通常作复数] guiding rule for personal behaviour (行为的)准则, 规范: *principles of conduct* 行为的准则 ○ *live according to/up to one's principles* 按自己的标准行事 ○ *She seems to have no principles at all* (ie behaves immorally) *when it is a question of making money.* 一碰到赚钱的事, 她就好像完全不顾自己的人格了. ○ *It would be against my principles to lie to you.* 对你说假话是违背我的行为准则的. (**b**) [U] these rules 操守; 道义; 为人之道: *a woman of (high) principle* 操守好的女人 ○ *He is quite without principle,* ie behaves immorally. 他完全没有道德观念(做的事不道德). ○ *It is a matter of principle with her to answer her children's questions honestly.* 如实地答复孩子们的询问对她来说是关系到做人的大问题. **3** [sing] general or scientific law shown in the way a thing works, or used as the basis for constructing a machine, etc (事物的)工作原理; (机器等的)构造原理: *These machines both work on the same principle.* 这两台机器的工作原理是相同的. ○ *The system works on the principle that heat rises.* 该项装置是按照热力上升的原理运转的. ⇨Usage at PRINCIPAL 用法见 PRINCIPAL. **4** (idm 习语) **in principle** (**a**) as far as basic principles are concerned 原则上: *There's no reason in principle why people couldn't travel to Mars,* ie It is possible, though it has not yet been done. 从理论上讲, 没有理由认为人不能到火星上去(尽管目前还做不到, 但却是可能的). (**b**) in general but not in detail 大体上; 基本上: *They have agreed to the proposal in principle but we still have to negotiate the terms.* 他们基本上同意了那项提议, 但我们仍须商定条件. **on principle** because of one's (moral) principles or a fixed belief 依据自己的(道德)原则或所确定的信念: *Many people are opposed to the sale of arms on principle.* 许多人根据自己的是非观反对出售武器.

▷ **prin·cipled** *adj* (esp in compounds 尤用以构成复合词) based on or having (esp good) principles (PRINCIPLE 2) of behaviour 依据或有(尤指良好的)行为准则的; 按原则的; 有原则性的: *a (high-)principled man* 品格高尚的人 ○ *low-principled behaviour* 品格低下的行为 ○ *I have no principled objection to it,* ie no objection based on moral scruples. 从道德上来说, 我并不反对此事.

print[1] /prɪnt; prɪnt/ *n* **1** [U] letters, words, numbers, etc in printed form 印出的字母、词、数字等; 印刷字体: *Headlines are written in large print.* 标题是用大号字体印刷的. ○ *The print is too small for me to read without glasses.* 印刷字体太小, 我不戴眼镜就看不清. **2** [C] (esp in compounds 尤用以构成复合词) mark left on a surface where sth has (been) pressed on it 印痕; 印记: *ˈfingerprints* ○ *ˈfootprints.* **3** [C] (**a**) picture or design made by printing from an inked surface (印成的)图画, 图案, 版画: *an old Japanese print* 古老的日本版画 ○ *a series of prints of London life* 一组伦敦生活的画片. (**b**) photograph printed from a negative (由底片印出的)照片: *colour prints* 彩色照片. **4** [U, C] printed cotton fabric 印花布: *She bought a/some flowery print to make a summer dress.* 她买了一块[一些]有花卉图案的印花布做夏天的连衣裙. ○ [attrib 作定语] *a print dress* 印花布连衣裙. **5** (idm 习语) **in print** (**a**) (of a book) available for sale from the publisher (指书)已印好, 可买到: *Is that volume still in print?* 那册书还能买到吗? (**b**) (of a person's work) printed in a book, newspaper, etc (指作品)已印出, 已出版: *It was the first time he had seen himself/his work in print.* 这是他第一次看见自己的作品出版. ˌ**out of** ˈ**print** (of a book) no longer available from the publisher (指书)已销售一空的, 绝版的: *Her first novel is out of print now but you may find a second-hand copy.* 她的第一部小说现已绝版, 不过你可以找本旧的. **rush into print** ⇨ RUSH[1]. **the small** ˈ**print** ⇨ SMALL.

print[2] /prɪnt; prɪnt/ *v* **1** (**a**) [Tn] make letters, pictures, etc on (paper) by pressing an inked surface against it 在(纸)上印字母、图画等; 印在(纸)上: *The first 64 pages* of the book have been printed. 该书的前64页已印出. ○ *They bought a new machine to print the posters.* 他们购置了一台新机器, 用来印海报. **(b)** [Tn, Tn·pr] **~ sth (in/on sth)** make (letters, pictures, etc) on paper by pressing an inked surface against it 在纸上印(字母、图画等): *The poems were printed on a small hand press.* 这些诗是在一台小型手动印刷机上印的. ○ *You surely won't print* (ie publish, esp in a newspaper) *such a scandalous allegation.* 你绝不会让这种造谣中伤的言论披露见报的吧. ○ (*fig* 比喻) *The events printed themselves on her memory*, ie could not be forgotten. 这些事铭刻在她的记忆中. **(c)** [Tn] make (books, pictures, etc) in this way 印刷(书籍、图画等): *The publisher has printed 10 000 copies of the book.* 这本书出版社已印了10 000册. ○ *The firm specializes in printing advertisements.* 这家公司专印广告. **2** [I, Tn] write (with) separated letters like those used in printing (rather than joined together as in handwriting) 用印刷体写; 写印刷体: *Children learn to print when they first go to school.* 儿童刚入学时学习用印刷体写字. ○ *The child carefully printed his name in capitals at the bottom of his picture.* 那孩子在他那张图画的下面用印刷体大写字母仔细地书写了自己的名字. **3** [Tn, Tn·pr] **~ sth (in/on sth)** press (a mark or design) on a surface 打上(印记); 印(图案): *print letters in the sand* 在沙上画出字母 ○ *print a flower design on cotton fabric* 在棉织品上印花卉图案. **4** [Tn] make a design on (a surface or fabric) by pressing a surface against it which has been coloured with ink or dye 将图案印在(某表面或织物)上: *printed cotton, wallpaper* 印花棉布、壁纸. **5** [Tn, Tn·p] **~ sth (off)** make (a photograph) from a negative film or plate 由底片或感光板印(照片): *How many copies shall I print (off) for you?* 你要我印多少份? **6** [I] **(a)** (of a photograph) be produced from a negative film or plate (指照片)由底片或感光板印出: *This snapshot hasn't printed very well.* 这张快照印出来不太清楚. **(b)** (of a plate or film) produce a picture (指感光板或胶片)印出照片: *This plate has been damaged — it won't print very well.* 这感光板坏了——印出来好不了. **7** (idm 习语) **a licence to print money** ⇨ LICENCE. **the ˌprinted ˈword** what is published in books, newspapers, etc 刊在书、报等上的文字: *the power of the printed word to influence people's attitudes* 书刊文字对人们态度的影响力. **8** (phr v) **print (sth) out** (*computing* 计) (of a machine) produce (information from a computer) in printed form (指机器)打印出(计算机中的信息).

▷ **print·able** /-əbl; -əbḷ/ *adj* fit to be published or printed 可印刷的; 可刊印的; 适于出版的: *The article is too badly written to be printable.* 这篇文章写得很糟糕, 不宜发表. ○ *His comment when he heard the news was not printable!* ie was too rude to be printed. 他在得知这消息时所发的议论不宜见诸报端(语言粗俗难登大雅之堂).

printer *n* **1 (a)** person whose job is printing 印刷工人; 印刷业者. **(b)** owner of a printing firm 印刷商. **2** machine for printing, esp one attached to a computer, word processor, etc 打印机(尤指计算机、文字处理机等配用的).

print·ing *n* **(a)** [U] action or art of printing 印刷(术): *They have made a good job of the printing.* 他们干印刷工作很出色. ○ *The invention of printing caused important changes in society.* 印刷术的发明在社会上引起了重大的变化. ○ [attrib 作定语] *a printing error* 印刷上的错误. **(b)** [C] number of copies of a book printed at one time; impression (书的)一次印数, 印次: *a printing of 5 000 copies* 5 000册的印数. **ˈprinting-ink** ink used for the printing of books, newspapers, etc 印刷油墨. **ˈprinting-press** (also **ˈprinting-machine**) *n* machine for printing books, newspapers, etc 印刷机.

□ **ˌprinted ˈcircuit** electric circuit with thin strips of conducting material (instead of wires) on a flat sheet 印刷电路; 印制电路.

ˈprinted matter (also **ˌprinted ˈpapers**) printed material (eg newspapers, magazines) which may be sent by post at a reduced rate 印刷品(如报刊, 邮费较廉).

printout /ˈprɪntaʊt; ˋprɪntˌaʊt/ *n* [C, U] (piece of) material produced in printed form from a computer or teleprinter (计算机或电传打字机的)打印出的资料: *Get me a printout of the statistics.* 给我一份打印出的统计资料.

prior[1] /ˈpraɪə(r); ˋpraɪɚ/ *adj* [attrib 作定语] coming before in time, order or importance 较早的; 居先的; 较重要的: *They have a prior claim to the property*, ie one which invalidates any other claim(s), eg because based on an earlier legal agreement. 他们有优先获得该房地产的权利(如根据先前的合法契约). ○ *My children have a prior claim on my time.* 我的时间首先得用来照顾我的孩子. ○ *I shall have to refuse your invitation because of a prior engagement.* 我因有约在先, 所以只好谢绝你的邀请. ○ *You need no prior knowledge to be able to do this test.* 不必预先学习, 就能做这项测试. Cf 参看 POSTERIOR 1.

□ **prior to** *prep* (*fml* 文) before 在...之前: *We received no notification prior to today's date*, ie before today. 我们在今日之前未获通知.

prior[2] /ˈpraɪə(r); ˋpraɪɚ/ *n* (*fem* 阴性作 **pri·or·ess** /ˈpraɪərɪs, *also* ˌpraɪəˈres; ˋpraɪərɪs/) **(a)** person who is head of a religious order, or of a monastery or convent (教派的)首领; (小的修道院的)院长. **(b)** (in an abbey) person next in rank below an abbot or abbess (大的修道院的)副院长.

▷ **pri·ory** /ˈpraɪərɪ; ˋpraɪərɪ/ *n* monastery governed by a prior or convent governed by a prioress 小的修道院.

pri·or·ity /praɪˈɒrətɪ; *US* -ˈɔːr-; praɪˋɔrətɪ/ *n* **1** [U] **~ (over sb/sth) (a)** (state of) being more important (in rank) 居要位; 居领导地位: *Japan's priority (over other countries) in the field of microelectronics* 日本在微电子学领域中的领先(于其他国家). **(b)** right to have or do sth before others 优先权: *I have priority over you in my claim.* 在要求此事方面, 我比你有优先权. **(c)** right to proceed ahead of other traffic (车辆的)优先通行权: *Vehicles coming from the right have priority.* 从右边驶来的车辆享有优先通行权. **2 (a)** [C] thing that is (regarded as) more important than others (被视为)优先的事物: *You must decide what your priorities are.* 你应该分清轻重缓急. ○ *Housework is low on her list of priorities.* 在她那些非做不可的事情中, 家务活并不重要. ○ *Rebuilding the area is a (top) priority.* 重建这一地区是当务之急. **(b)** [U] **~ (over sth)** high or top place among various things to be done (工作的)重点; 应优先解决的问题: *The Government gave (top) priority to reforming the legal system.* 政府将改革法制列为工作的重点. ○ *The search for a new vaccine took priority over all other medical research.* 在各种医药研究中, 应首先解决寻找新疫苗的问题. ○ [attrib 作定语] *Priority cases, such as homeless families, get dealt with first.* 重点事项如缺房户问题, 要首先着手解决. **3** (idm 习语) **get one's priorities right, wrong, etc** know/not know what is most important and act accordingly 能[不能]按轻重缓急行事: *Your trouble is you've got your priorities back to front!* 你因为本末倒置才出了麻烦!

prise (also *esp US* **prize**) /praɪz; praɪz/ *v* **1** [Tn·p, Cn·a] **~ sth off/up** use force to open (a box, etc) or remove (a lid, etc) 强行打开(箱子等)或移去(盖等): *She used a chisel to prise off the lid.* 她用錾子来把盖子凿开. ○ *The box had been prised open.* 箱子撬开了. **2** (phr v) **prise sth out of sb** force sb to reveal sth 强迫某人披露某事物: *She'd promised not to talk, and nothing we could do could prise the information out of her.* 她答应保守秘密, 无论我们用什么方法她也不说出来. Cf 参看 PRY[2].

prism /ˈprɪzəm; ˋprɪzəm/ *n* **1** solid geometric shape with ends that are parallel and of the same size and shape, and with sides that are parallelograms 棱柱(体). **2** transparent object of this shape, usu triangular and made of glass, which breaks up ordinary light into the colours of the rainbow 棱柱体透明物; (通常指)棱镜, 三棱镜. ⇨illus at SPECTRUM 见 SPECTRUM 插图.

pris·matic /prɪzˈmætɪk; prɪzˋmætɪk/ *adj* **1** of, like or being a prism (似)棱柱或棱镜的; 棱柱形的. **2** (of colours) bright, clear and varied; rainbow-like (指色彩)光彩夺目的, 五光十色的. **3** that uses a prism 使用棱镜的; 含棱柱体的: *a prismatic compass* 棱镜罗盘 ○ *prismatic binoculars* 棱镜式双目望远镜.

prison /ˈprɪzn; ˋprɪzṇ/ *n* **1** [C] **(a)** place where people are kept locked up as a punishment for crimes they have committed or while awaiting trial 监狱; 看守所: *The prisons are overcrowded.* 监狱人满为患. ○ *A modern prison has replaced the Victorian one.* 一所现代化的监狱取代了那所维多利亚时代的监狱. ○ [attrib 作定语] *the*

P

prison population, ie the total number of prisoners in a country 监押人数(一个国家的囚犯总数). **(b)** (*derog* 贬) place from which sb cannot escape 某人无法逃脱的地方; 牢笼: *Now that he was disabled, his house had become a prison to him.* 因为他残废了, 他的房子就成了他的牢笼. ○ (*fig* 比喻) *the prison of one's mind* 思想上的束缚. **2** [U] being kept in a prison, esp as a punishment for crime; imprisonment 被监禁; (尤指)服刑; 坐牢: *She's gone to/is in prison.* 她已入狱[在狱中]. ○ *escape from, be released from, come out of prison* 越狱、释放、出狱 ○ *He was sent to prison for five years.* 他判了五年监禁. ○ *Does prison do anything to prevent crime?* 采取关押方法对制止犯罪有作用吗? ⇨Usage at SCHOOL[1] 用法见SCHOOL[1].

P

▷ **prisoner** *n* **1 (a)** person kept in prison, as a punishment or awaiting trial 犯人; 囚犯; 被拘押的刑事被告: *a prison built to hold 500 prisoners* 可容纳500名囚犯的监狱 ○ *political prisoners*, ie those put in prison because of their political beliefs 政治犯(由于政治信仰而被监禁者) ○ *Prisoner at the bar, do you plead guilty or not guilty?* 接受审讯的刑事被告, 你认罪不认罪? **(b)** person, animal, etc that has been captured and is being kept in confinement; captive 被抓起来的人; 被捕获的动物等: *You are our prisoner now and we won't release you until a ransom is paid.* 你现已遭我们禁锢, 要到交出赎金以后, 才能放你走. ○ *He spent two years as the prisoner of rebel soldiers in the mountains.* 他被山里的叛军抓走有两年之久. ○ (*fig* 比喻) *The wretched man is the prisoner of* (ie controlled by) *his own greed.* 这个坏傢伙完全被贪心所支配. **2** (idm 习语) **hold/take sb captive/prisoner** ⇨ CAPTIVE. ˌ**prisoner of ˈconscience** person kept in prison because of an act of social or political protest 政治犯(因从事社会或政治反抗活动而被监禁的人). ˌ**prisoner of ˈwar** (*abbr* 缩写 **POW**) person (usu a member of the armed forces) captured during a war by the enemy and kept in prison (usu a prison camp) until the end of the war 战俘.

□ ˈ**prison camp** guarded camp where prisoners, esp prisoners of war or political prisoners, are kept 集中营, 劳改营(尤指监禁战俘或政治犯的).

prissy /ˈprɪsɪ; ˋprɪsɪ/ *adj* **(-ier, -iest)** (*derog* 贬) annoyingly precise and fussy, and (claiming to be) easily shocked by improper things 谨小慎微的; 过于认真的; 大惊小怪的. ▷ **pris·sily** *adv*. **pris·si·ness** *n* [U].

pris·tine /ˈprɪsti:n, *also* ˈprɪstaɪn; ˋprɪstin/ *adj* **1 (a)** in its original condition; unspoilt 原始状态的; 未受损的: *a pristine copy of the book's first edition* 保持第一版之原貌的一本书. **(b)** (*approv* 褒) fresh and clean, as if new 新鲜而纯净的; 清新的: *in pristine condition* 处于全新的状况 ○ *The ground was covered in a pristine layer of snow.* 地上覆盖着一层皑皑积雪. **2** [attrib 作定语] (*rhet* 修辞) primitive; ancient 原始的; 远古的: *a remnant of some pristine era* 某原始时期的残迹.

priv·acy /ˈprɪvəsɪ, ˈpraɪv-; ˋpraɪvəsɪ/ *n* [U] **1** state of being alone or undisturbed 独处或不受干扰的状况: *A high wall round the estate protected their privacy.* 庄园周围有一堵高墙, 使他们不受外界打扰. ○ *He preferred to read the documents in the privacy of his study.* 他比较喜欢在书房里无干扰的情况下阅读文件. **2** freedom from interference or public attention 不受干扰或不受公众注目的自由; 私人权利; 个人自由: *Newspapers often don't respect the individual's right to privacy.* 报纸的报道往往不尊重私人权利. ○ *She complained that the questions were an invasion of (her) privacy.* 她投诉这些问题侵犯了她的个人自由.

pri·vate /ˈpraɪvɪt; ˋpraɪvɪt/ *adj* **1** [esp attrib 尤作定语] of, belonging to or for the use of one particular person or group only; personal 私人的; 私有的; 私用的; 个人的: *father's own private chair, which no one else is allowed to use* 父亲专用的椅子, 别人一概不许使用 ○ *a private letter*, ie about personal matters 私人信件 ○ *private property* 私有财产 ○ *a private income/private means*, ie money not earned as a salary, etc but coming from personal property, investments, etc 私产所得(由个人财产、投资等获得而非来自工资等之收入) ○ *private fishing* 私人捕鱼活动 ○ *'Is this a hotel?' 'No, it's a private house.'* '这是旅馆吗?' '不是, 这是私人住宅.' **2 (a)** not (to be) revealed to others; secret 不公开的; 秘密的: *I'm not going to tell you about it; it's private.* 我不打算把此事告诉你; 这是私事. ○ *That's my private opinion.* 这是我私下持有的见解. **(b)** not liking to share thoughts and feelings with others 不喜欢与他人交流思想感情的: *He's a rather private person.* 他不太喜欢和别人交流思想感情. **3** (of a conversation, meeting, etc) with only a small number of participants, esp two, and kept secret from others (指谈话、会议等)只有少数人(尤指两人)参加并对其他人保密的: *I'd like a private chat with you.* 我想跟你私下谈谈. **4 (a)** (of a place) quiet and free from intruders (指场所)清静的, 不受侵扰的: *Let's find some private spot where we can discuss the matter.* 咱们找个清静的地方谈谈这个问题吧. **(b)** [usu pred 通常作表语] (of people) undisturbed by others; alone together (指人们)不受他人打扰; 无外人: *Let's go upstairs where we can be a bit more private.* 咱们上楼吧, 那里没什么外人. **5 (a)** [attrib 作定语] having no official job or position 无官方职务或职位的: *She is acting as a private individual in this matter.* 她在这个问题上只代表她个人意见. ○ *a private citizen* 平民. **(b)** not connected with one's work or official position 与工作或官职无关的: *The Queen is making a private visit to Canada.* 女王正对加拿大进行私人访问. ○ *The public is fascinated by the private lives of public figures.* 公众对社会名流的私生活具有浓厚的兴趣. **6** of, belonging to or carried out by an individual or an independent company rather than the State; not state-controlled 个体(经营)的; 私营的; 民办的; 不受国家控制的: *private industry* 私营企业 ○ *the private sector*, ie of the economy 私营部门 ○ *private education, medicine, medical treatment, etc* 民办教育、私人行医、民间疗法 ○ *a private school* 私立学校 ○ *a private patient*, ie (in Britain) not on the National Health Service 自费病人(英国不享受国民保健署资助者) ○ *a private pension plan* 私营企业的养老金制 ○ *a private detective/investigator*, ie one not employed by the police 私人侦探. Cf 参看 PUBLIC.

▷ **pri·vate** *n* **1** [C] soldier of the lowest rank 士兵; 列兵: *He enlisted as a private.* 他入伍当了士兵. ○ *Private Smith* 列兵史密斯. ⇨App 9 见附录9. **2 privates** [pl] (*infml* 口) = PRIVATE PARTS. **3** (idm 习语) **in private** with no one else present 无他人在场; 私下地: *She asked to see him in private.* 她请求单独与他见面.

pri·vately *adv*: *The matter was arranged privately.* 事情已私下作了安排. ○ *He supported the official policy in public, but privately he knew it would fail.* 他在公开的场合里拥护官方的政策, 而在私下里却明白那是行不通的. ○ *a privately-owned firm* 私有的公司.

□ ˌ**private ˈcompany** business firm that does not issue shares to the general public 私人公司(不向公众发行股票者); 股分不公开公司.

ˌ**private ˈenterprise** management of business by independent companies or private individuals, as opposed to state control 私营企业.

ˌ**private ˈeye** (*infml* 口) private detective 私人侦探.

ˌ**private ˈmember** (*Brit*) member of the House of Commons who is not a minister 普通议员(下议院中非内阁成员者). ˌ**private ˈmember's bill** bill presented to Parliament by a private member 普通议员向议会提交的法案.

ˌ**private ˈparts** (*euph* 婉) genitals 私处, 阴部(生殖器).

ˌ**private ˈsoldier** (*fml* 文) = PRIVATE *n* 1.

pri·vat·eer /ˌpraɪvəˈtɪə(r); ˌpraɪvəˋtɪr/ *n* (formerly) (captain of or sailor on a) ship used for attacking and robbing other ships; pirate (ship) (旧时)(用来攻击和劫掠其他船只的)私人武装船, 私掠船, 私掠船的船长或船员, 海盗(船).

pri·va·tion /praɪˈveɪʃn; praɪˋveʃən/ *n* (*fml* 文) **1** [C usu *pl*, U 作可数名词时通常作复数, 亦作不可数名词] lack of things necessary for life; deprivation (生活必需品的)匮乏; 贫困: *The survivors suffered many privations before they were rescued.* 那些生还者在获救以前备尝艰辛. ○ *a life of privation and misery* 贫苦的生活. **2** [C] state of being deprived of sth (not necessarily sth essential) (某事物之)被剥夺(不一定为必需之事物); 丧失: *She didn't find the lack of a car any great privation.* 她觉得没有汽车并非重大缺憾. ○ *It would be the greatest imaginable privation for her to have to leave London.* 对她来说, 不得不离开伦敦大概是能想像到的最大的损失.

pri·vat·ize, -ise /ˈpraɪvɪtaɪz; ˋpraɪvətˌaɪz/ *v* [Tn] transfer (sth) from state ownership to private ownership;

denationalize 将(某物)由国家所有转为私人所有; 使(某物)私有化. Cf 参看 NATIONALIZE 1. ▷ **pri·vat·iza·tion, -isation** /ˌpraɪvɪtaɪˈzeɪʃn; US -tɪˈz-; ˌpraɪvətəˈzeʃən/ *n* [U]: *the privatization of the steel industry* 钢铁工业的私有化.

privet /ˈprɪvɪt; ˋprɪvɪt/ *n* [U] evergreen bush with small leaves and small white flowers, often used for garden hedges 女贞(常绿灌木, 长有小叶子, 开小白花, 常用作园篱): [attrib 作定语] *a privet hedge* 女贞树篱.

priv·il·ege /ˈprɪvəlɪdʒ; ˋprɪvḷɪdʒ/ *n* **1** (**a**) [C] special right or advantage available only to a particular person, class or rank, or to the holder of a certain position 特有的权利、利益或好处: *Parking in this street is the privilege of the residents.* 在这条街上停车是此处居民特有的权利. ○ *the privileges of birth*, eg the benefits of belonging to a wealthy family 与生俱来的优越(如生于富贵之家而有的利益). (**b**) [U] (*derog* 贬) rights and advantages possessed by the rich and powerful people in a society (有钱有势者的)特权, 特别待遇: *They fought against privilege in order to create a fairer society.* 他们进行反对特权的斗争以便建立较为公平的社会. ○ *She had led a life of luxury and privilege.* 她过着养尊处优的生活. **2** [C] (**a**) special benefit given to sb as a favour 特别给予的好处或待遇: *Older pupils enjoy special privileges.* 岁数较大的学童受到优待. ○ *'Thank you for showing us your collection of paintings.' 'It's my privilege* (ie I am honoured to do so).' '感谢你让我们观赏你所收藏的画.' '同欢共赏, 不胜荣幸.' ○ *Use of the library is a privilege, not a right.* 使用该图书馆是一项特殊的照顾, 而不是一种权利. (**b**) thing that gives one great enjoyment and that most people do not have the opportunity to do 特别的荣幸: *It was a privilege to hear her sing/hearing her sing.* 能听她唱歌十分荣幸. **3** [C, U] right to do or say things without risking punishment (无受惩之虞的)言行自由权: *an Act which granted the trade unions certain legal privileges* 特准工会享有某些合法言行自由权的法案 ○ *parliamentary privilege*, ie the right of Members of Parliament to say things in the House of Commons which might result in an accusation of libel if said outside it 议会言论自由权(国会议员在下议院自由发言的特权, 若在国会以外发表则可能被控以诽谤罪) ○ *a breach of privilege*, ie breaking the rules of parliamentary behaviour 违反议会言论自由权.

▷ **priv·il·eged** *adj* **1** (**a**) (*sometimes derog* 有时作贬义) having privilege(s) 享有特权的; 享受特殊待遇的; 获得优待的: *She came from a privileged background.* 她出身于特权阶层. ○ *a policy of making higher education available to all and not just a privileged few* 使高等教育面向全民而并非少数人的特权的一项政策. (**b**) [pred 作表语] honoured 荣幸: *We are very privileged to have Senator Dobbs with us this evening.* 今晚有多布斯参议员光临, 我们感到十分荣幸. **2** that need not be revealed; legally secret 无须公开的; 有权保守秘密的: *a privileged communication* 特许保密通讯 ○ *This information is privileged.* 这项消息无须公开.

privy /ˈprɪvɪ; ˋprɪvɪ/ *adj* **1** [attrib 作定语] (*arch* 古) private; secret 个人的; 私人的; 秘密的: *a privy matter* 私事. **2** [pred 作表语] **~ to sth** (*fml* 文) sharing in the secret of sth 私下知情; 参与秘事: *They were accused of being privy to the plot against the king.* 他们被控欺君谋反、知情不举. ○ *I wasn't privy to the negotiations.* 我对那些谈判并不知情.

▷ **priv·ily** *adv* (*arch* 古) privately; secretly 私下地; 秘密地.

privy *n* primitive lavatory, esp out of doors 简陋厕所(尤指室外的).

□ ˌ**Privy** ˈ**Council** body of statesmen, politicians, etc appointed by the sovereign formerly as advisers on affairs of State, but now (in Britain) more as a personal honour for its members 枢密院. ˌ**Privy** ˈ**Councillor** (also ˌ**Privy** ˈ**Counsellor**) member of the Privy Council 枢密院官员.

ˌ**privy** ˈ**purse** amount of money given by the British government for the Sovereign's private expenses (英国政府拨付给国君的)私用金.

ˌ**privy** ˈ**seal** British national seal formerly fixed to documents of minor importance (英国的)王玺(旧时用于次要的文件上): *Lord Privy Seal*, ie the senior British government minister without official duties (英国)掌玺大臣(无正式职务的资深官员).

prize[1] /praɪz; praɪz/ *n* **1** award given to the winner of a competition, race, etc (给予获胜者的)奖, 奖励, 奖赏, 奖品, 奖金: *She won first prize in the 100 metres race.* 她在百米赛跑中获头奖. ○ *Her book gained several literary prizes.* 她写的书获得好几种文学奖. **2** thing (that can be) won in a lottery or a gambling game (在抽彩或赌博中所中的)奖, 彩金: *He won the £20 000 prize on the football pools.* 他赢得足球普尔彩金20 000英镑. ○ *She had the prize-winning lottery ticket.* 她抽到了得奖的彩票. ○ [attrib 作定语] *prize money* 奖金. **3** (*fig* 比喻) thing of value worth struggling for 值得争取的有价值的事物: *The greatest prize of all — world peace — is now within our grasp.* 我们为之奋斗的最可贵的事物——世界和平——已指日可待. **4** (esp formerly) ship or its cargo captured at sea during a war (尤指旧时)战时捕获的敌船或其货物, 海上战利品.

▷ **prize** *adj* [attrib 作定语] (**a**) winning or likely to win a prize; excellent of its kind (可能)获奖的; 该得奖的; 出类拔萃的: *prize cattle* 优选的牛 ○ *a prize exhibit in the flower show* 在花展中获奖的展品. (**b**) (*infml ironic* 口, 反语) outstandingly bad; complete 糟透了的; 十足的: *a prize ass, fool, idiot, etc* 不折不扣的笨蛋、傻瓜、白痴等.

prize *v* [Tn] value (sth) highly 对(某事物)高度重视; 珍视(某事物): *The portrait of her mother was her most prized possession.* 她母亲的这张肖像是她最珍爱的物品. ○ *I prize my independence too much to go and work for them.* 我决不愿意丧失自己的独立性去为他们效劳.

□ ˈ**prize day** (also ˈ**prize-giving day**) annual school ceremony at which prizes are given to the best pupils 颁奖日(学校一年一度的仪式).

ˈ**prize-fight** *n* boxing match fought for money 职业拳击赛. ˈ**prize-fighter** *n*.

prize[2] (*esp US*) = PRISE.

pro[1] /prəʊ; pro/ *n* (idm 习语) **the pros and cons** arguments for and against sth 赞成和反对的论据: *Let's add up the pros and cons.* 咱们把正反两方面的意见总结一下吧.

pro[2] /prəʊ; pro/ *n* (*pl* **~s**) (*infml* 口) professional, esp a professional sportsman 从事某种职业的人; (尤指)职业运动员: *a golf pro* 高尔夫球职业选手 ○ (*approv* 褒) *He's a real pro.* 他够得上专业水平. ○ [attrib 作定语] *a pro footballer* 职业足球运动员.

pro- *pref* 前缀 **1** (with *ns* and *adjs* 与名词和形容词连用) in favour of; supporting 亲; 支持: *pro-abortion* ○ *pro-American*. Cf 参看 ANTI-. **2** (with *ns* 与名词连用) acting as 代; 代理: *pro-vice-chancellor* ○ *pronoun*.

PRO *abbr* 缩写 = **1** Public Record Office 档案局. **2** /ˌpiː ɑːr ˈəʊ; ˌpi ɑr ˈo/ (*infml* 口) public relations officer 公共关系人员.

prob·ab·il·ity /ˌprɒbəˈbɪlətɪ; ˌprɑbəˋbɪlətɪ/ *n* **1** [U] likelihood 可能性: *There is little probability of his succeeding/that he will succeed.* 他不大可能成功. ○ *What is the probability of its success?* 其成功的可能性如何? **2** [C] thing that is (most) probable; probable event or result (很)可能有的事物; 可能发生的事; 可能出现的结果: *What are the probabilities?* 可能发生什么事? ○ *A fall in interest rates is a probability in the present economic climate.* 从目前的经济情势看, 很有可能降低利率. **3** [C] (*mathematics* 数) ratio expressing the chances that a certain event will occur 概率; 或然率. **4** (idm 习语) **in** ˌ**all proba**ˈ**bility** very probably 极有可能: *In all probability he's already left.* 他很可能已经离开了.

prob·able /ˈprɒbəbl; ˋprɑbəbl/ *adj* that may be expected to happen or to be so; likely 有望发生或实现的; 可能的: *With England leading 3-0, the probable result is an England victory/England are the probable winners.* 由于英格兰队以3比0领先, 最后的结果可能是英格兰队获胜[英格兰队可能成为优胜者]. ○ *Rain is possible but not probable this evening.* 今晚可能有雨, 但不一定准下. ○ *It seems probable that he will arrive before dusk.* 他似乎有可能黄昏前到达.

▷ **prob·able** *n* **~ (for sth)** person or thing most likely to be chosen, eg for a sports team or as the winner; probable candidate, winner, etc 很有可能被选中(如选拔运动队员)的人; 很有可能获胜的人; 大有希望的候选者、竞争者等: *He is a probable for the national team.* 他很有可能被选入国家队. ○ *The book is a probable for the prize.* 该书很有希望获奖.

prob·ably /-əblɪ; -əblɪ/ *adv* almost certainly 几乎肯定; 很可能; 大概: *He's late — he's probably stuck in a traffic jam.* 他迟到了——很可能是由于交通阻塞耽误了. ○ *'Will you be coming?' 'Probably.'* '你来吗?' '很可能来.' ○ *'Can he hear us?' 'Probably not.'* '他听得见我们的话吗?' '大概听不见.'

pro·bate /ˈprəʊbeɪt; ˈprobet/ *n* (*law* 律) **1** [U] official process of proving that a will is correct 遗嘱检验; 遗嘱认证: *apply for/take out probate* 申请检验遗嘱 ○ *grant probate* 通过对遗嘱的认证 ○ [attrib 作定语] *a probate court* 遗嘱检验法庭. **2** [C] copy of a will with an official certificate that it is correct 经认证的遗嘱.

▷ **pro·bate** *v* [Tn] (*US*) = PROVE 2.

P

pro·ba·tion /prəˈbeɪʃn; *US* prəʊ-; proˈbeʃən/ *n* [U] **1** (*law* 律) (system of) keeping an official check on the behaviour of (esp young) people found guilty of crime as an alternative to sending them to prison 缓刑(制)(尤指对年轻犯人施行的): *sentenced to three years' probation* 被判处缓刑三年. **2** testing of a person's abilities or behaviour to find out if he or she is suitable (对人的)试用(期): *There's a three-month period of probation/probation period for new recruits.* 新加人的人员有三个月试用期. **3** (idm 习语) **on probation** (**a**) (of a law-breaker) undergoing a period of probation(1) (指违法者)服缓刑: *He's been released from prison on probation*, ie If he does not behave satisfactorily he will be sent back. 他获释服缓刑(若表现不好则重新收监). (**b**) being tested before being finally accepted in employment, etc (受雇者)在试用期中.

▷ **pro·ba·tion·ary** /prəˈbeɪʃnrɪ; *US* prəʊˈbeɪʃənerɪ; proˈbeʃənˌɛrɪ/ *adj* of or for probation 缓刑的; (指人)试用的: *a probationary period* 试用期.

pro·ba·tioner /-ʃənə(r); -ʃənɚ/ *n* **1** hospital nurse being trained and still on probation(2) 见习护士. **2** law-breaker sentenced to a period of probation(1) or released from prison on probation 缓刑犯; 获释而服缓刑者.

□ **proˈbation officer** person whose job is to supervise law-breakers who are on probation 监视缓刑犯的官员; 缓刑监督官.

probe /prəʊb; prob/ *n* **1** tool for examining a place which cannot be reached otherwise, esp a thin implement with a blunt end used by a doctor for examining a wound 探查工具; 探测器; (尤指医生用的)探子, 探针. **2** (also **ˈspace probe**) unmanned spacecraft which obtains information about space and transmits it back to earth 航天探测器(一种不载人的宇宙飞船, 用以搜集有关宇宙的资料, 并发送回地球): *information about Venus obtained by Russian probes* 由俄国航天探测器获得的有关金星的信息. **3 ~ (into sth)** (esp in journalism) thorough and careful investigation of sth (尤作新闻用语)探究, 深入的调查: *a probe into the disappearance of government funds* 对政府资金流失一事的调查. **4** act of probing 探查; 探测; 调查.

▷ **probe** *v* **1** [Tn] explore or examine (sth) with or as if with a probe(1) (用或似用探针等)探查, 探测: *He probed the swelling anxiously with his finger.* 他很担心地用手指触摸肿处. ○ *Searchlights probed the night sky.* 探照灯探查夜空. **2** [I, Ipr, Tn] **~ (into sth)** investigate or examine (sth) closely 细查, 探究(某事物): *The journalist was probing into several financial scandals.* 那记者正在调查几起财务丑事. ○ *She tried to probe his mind to find out what he was thinking.* 她想深入了解他的思想, 好知道他在想什么. **prob·ing** *adj* intended to discover the truth; searching 追根究底的; 探索的: *He was asking probing questions.* 他提出了一些盘根究底的问题. **prob·ingly** *adv*.

prob·ity /ˈprəʊbətɪ; ˈprobətɪ/ *n* [U] (*fml* 文) quality of being honest and trustworthy; integrity 正直; 诚实; 刚正不阿.

prob·lem /ˈprɒbləm; ˈprɑbləm/ *n* **1** thing that is difficult to deal with or understand 难以处理的事情; 难以了解的事物; 难题: *How do you cope with the problem of poor vision?* 怎样解决视力不好这一难题呢? ○ *a knotty problem* 错综复杂的事情 ○ *get to the root/heart of a problem* 触及问题的根本[核心] ○ *We've got a problem with the car — it won't start!* 我们的汽车出故障了——发动不起来! ○ *You'll have to mend that leak or it will cause problems later.* 你得修补那个裂缝, 不然以后会出问题. ○ *the housing problem in the inner cities* 城市中心区的住房问题 ○ (*infml* 口) *'Will you be able to get me tickets for the match?' 'Of course, no problem* (ie I shall easily be able to).' '你能给我弄到比赛的票吗?' '当然可以, 没问题.' ○ *'I can't come to the party.' 'Why, what's the problem?'* '我不能来参加聚会.' '呦, 怎么了?' ○ [attrib 作定语] *a problem novel, play, etc*, ie one dealing with a social or moral problem 问题小说、问题剧(探讨社会或道德问题的) ○ *a newspaper's problem page*, ie with readers' letters about their problems, and suggested solutions 报纸的读者问题专版. **2** question to be answered or solved (待答复或待解决的)问题: *a mathematical problem* 数学题 ○ *She has found the answer to/solved the problem.* 她找到了那问题的答案[解决了那个难题].

▷ **prob·lem·atic** /ˌprɒbləˈmætɪk; ˌprɑbləˈmætɪk/ (also **prob·lem·at·ical**) *adj* **1** difficult to deal with or to understand 难处理的; 难了解的; 成问题的; 疑难的. **2** (esp of a result) that cannot be foreseen; doubtful or questionable (尤指结果)难以预料的; 有疑问的; 令人不解的. **prob·lem·at·ic·ally** /-klɪ; -klɪ/ *adv*.

□ **ˈproblem child** child who continually behaves badly, does not learn well, etc 有问题的儿童(一贯行为不端、功课不佳等的).

pro·bos·cis /prəˈbɒsɪs; proˈbɑsɪs/ *n* (*pl* **~es** /-sɪsi:z; -sɪsɪz/) **1** (**a**) elephant's trunk 象的鼻子. (**b**) long flexible nose of certain animals, eg the tapir 某些动物(如貘)的能弯曲的长鼻. **2** elongated part of the mouth of certain insects, used for sucking things 某些昆虫用以吸食的长嘴; 吻部.

pro·ced·ure /prəˈsi:dʒə(r); prəˈsidʒɚ/ *n* **1** [C, U] (regular) order or way of doing things, esp in business, law, politics, etc 程序(尤指工商、法律、政治等事务的): *(the) agreed/correct/established/normal/usual procedure* 商定的[正确的/确定的/正常的/一般的]程序 ○ *Stop arguing about (questions of) procedure and let's get down to business.* 别再为程序(问题)争辩了, 咱们着手议正事吧. ○ *parliamentary procedure* 议会议事程序. **2** [C] **~ (for sth)** action or series of actions (to be) completed in order to achieve sth 办事程序; 手续; 步骤: *Registering a birth or death is a straightforward procedure.* 登记出生或死亡的手续很简单. ○ *Obtaining a refund from the company is a complicated procedure.* 向公司索取退款手续很复杂. ○ *What's the procedure for opening a bank account?* 在银行开个帐户要办什么手续?

▷ **pro·ced·ural** /prəˈsi:dʒərəl; prəˈsidʒərəl/ *adj* of procedure(s) 程序上的; 手续的: *The business of the committee was delayed by procedural difficulties.* 委员会的事务因程序上有困难而耽搁了.

pro·ceed /prəˈsi:d, prəʊ-; prəˈsid, pro-/ *v* **1** (**a**) [I, Ipr, It] **~ (to sth)** go to a further or the next stage; go on 继续前进; 继续进行; 继续下去: *Work is proceeding slowly.* 工作正在慢慢地继续进行着. ○ *What is the best way of proceeding?* 最好采取什么方式继续下去? ○ *Let us proceed (to the next item on the agenda).* 让我们继续进行(下一个议程)吧. ○ *Having said how much she liked it, she then proceeded to criticize the way I'd done it.* 她先表明她非常喜欢这个, 然后批评我方法不当. (**b**) [Ipr] (*fml* 文) make one's way; go 前进; 行进: *I was proceeding along the High Street in a northerly direction when...* 我那时正沿着大街向北去, 走着走着.... (**c**) [I, Ipr] **~ (with sth)** begin or continue (sth) 开始或继续做(某事物): *Please proceed with your report.* 请继续作你的报告吧. ○ *Shall we proceed with the planned investment?* 我们着手进行有计划的投资好吗? **2** [Ipr] **~ against sb** (*law* 律) take legal action against sb; start a lawsuit against sb 起诉某人; 对某人提起诉讼. **3** [Ipr] **~ from sth** (*fml* 文) arise or originate from sth 由某事物引起; 源于某事物: *the evils that proceed from war* 战争所带来的灾祸. **4** [Ipr] **~ to sth** (*fml* 文) go on to obtain a higher university degree after obtaining a first degree (获得学士学位后)攻读高级学位: *He was allowed to proceed to an MA.* 他获准攻读文学硕士学位.

pro·ceed·ings /prəˈsi:dɪŋz; prəˈsidɪŋz/ *n* [pl] **1 ~ (against sb/for sth)** lawsuit 诉讼(程序): *start proceedings (against sb) for divorce* 提出(与某人)离婚的诉讼 ○ *institute divorce proceedings* 提出离婚诉讼. **2** what takes place, esp at a meeting, ceremony, etc 进程; 过程; (尤指会议、仪式等的)议程: *The proceedings will begin with a speech to welcome the guests.* 大会议程首先

是向来宾致欢迎辞. ○ *The proceedings were interrupted by the fire alarm.* 会议的进程被火灾警报打断了. **3 ~ (of sth)** (published) report or record of a discussion, meeting, conference, etc; minutes (讨论会、会议、大会等的)报道, 记录, 公报, 纪要: *His paper was published in the proceedings of the Kent Archaeological Society.* 他的论文已在肯特考古学会学报上发表.

pro·ceeds /ˈprəʊsiːdz; ˈprosidz/ *n* [pl] **~ (of/from sth)** money obtained by selling sth, presenting a performance, etc; profits (售物或从事某种表演活动等所获得的)收入, 收益: *They gave a concert and donated the proceeds to charity.* 他们举办了一次音乐会, 把收入捐给了慈善机构.

pro·cess[1] /ˈprəʊses; *US* ˈprɒses; ˈprɑsɛs/ *n* **1** [C] series of actions or operations performed in order to do, make or achieve sth 步骤; 程序; 过程: *Unloading the cargo was a slow process.* 卸货的过程很缓慢. ○ *Reforming the education system will be a difficult process.* 改革教育制度将是一个艰难的过程. ○ *Teaching him Greek was a painful* (ie slow and difficult) *process.* 教他希腊文是很吃力的事. **2** [C] method, esp one used in industry to make sth 方法; (尤指)工艺流程: *the Bessemer process of steel production* 贝塞麦炼钢法 ○ *They have developed a new process for rustproofing car bodies.* 他们研究出了车身抗锈的新方法. **3** [C] (series of) changes, esp ones that happen naturally and unconsciously 变化(过程)(尤指自然发生的和不知不觉的): *the processes of digestion/the digestive processes* 消化过程 ○ *the process of growing old* 逐渐变老的过程. **4** [C] (*law* 律) **(a)** legal action; lawsuit 诉讼. **(b)** summons; writ 传票; 法院令状. **5** [C] (*biology* 生) small projecting part of a plant or of the body of an animal (动植物体上的)小的凸起部分, 突, 突起. **6** (idm 习语) **in the ˈprocess** while doing sth previously mentioned 在进行中: *I started moving the china ornaments but dropped a vase in the process.* 我动手搬那些瓷制饰物, 但在移动时摔了一只花瓶. **in the process of sth/doing sth** performing a particular task 在从事某任务的过程中: *We're still in the process of moving house.* 我们还正在搬着家呢.

▷ **pro·cess** *v* [Tn] **1** put (a raw material, food, etc) through an industrial or manufacturing process in order to change it; treat 对(原材料、食物等)进行加工; 处理: *process leather to make it softer* 鞣制皮革使其变得柔软 ○ *processed cheese*, ie specially treated to preserve it 经加工的干酪(以便保存) ○ *process* (ie develop) *photographic film* 冲洗摄影胶片. **2** deal with (a document, etc) officially 审查, 审阅, 处理(文件等): *It may take a few weeks for your application to be processed.* 审查你的申请书也许要等几个星期. **3** perform operations on (sth) in a computer 用计算机处理(某事物): *How fast does the new micro process the data?* 这新微型计算机处理数据有多快? **pro·cessor** *n* machine that processes things 加工机械; 处理机: *a food processor* 食品加工机. Cf 参看 MICROPROCESSOR.

pro·cess[2] /prəˈses; proˈsɛs/ *v* [I, Ipr, Ip] walk or move (as if) in procession 列队(似地)行进或移动: *The bishops, priests and deacons processed into the cathedral.* 主教、司铎以及助祭列队走进大教堂.

pro·ces·sion /prəˈseʃn; prəˈsɛʃən/ *n* **1** [C] **(a)** number of people, vehicles, etc moving along in an orderly way, esp as part of a ceremony or demonstration (人、车等的)行列; (尤指仪式或游行之)队伍: *a ˈfuneral procession* 送葬行列 ○ *The procession moved slowly down the hill.* 游行队伍缓慢地走下坡路. **(b)** (*fig* 比喻) large number of people who come one after the other 川流不息的人群: *A procession of visitors came to the house.* 参观者川流不息地向这所房子走来. **2** [U] action of moving forward in this way 列队行进: *The congregation entered the church in procession.* 教徒们排着队进入教堂.

▷ **pro·ces·sional** /-ʃənl; -ʃənḷ/ *adj* of, for or used in a (religious) procession (宗教)行列的; 适于列队行进的; 列队行进时用的. **pro·ces·sional** *n* processional hymn 教徒列队行进时唱的圣诗.

pro·claim /prəˈkleɪm; proˈklem/ *v* **1** [Tn, Tf, Tw, Cn·n] make (sth) known officially or publicly; announce 宣告, 公布(某事物); 声明: *proclaim the good news* 宣布好消息 ○ *proclaim a public holiday* 宣布定某日为公众假日 ○ *After its independence India was proclaimed* (ie officially declared to be) *a republic.* 印度独立之后宣布成立共和国. **2** [Tf, Cn·n] (*fml* 文) show (sth) clearly; reveal 表明(某事物); 显示: *His accent proclaimed him a Scot/that he was a Scot.* 他的口音表明他是苏格兰人.

▷ **pro·clama·tion** /ˌprɒkləˈmeɪʃn; ˌprɑkləˈmeʃən/ *n* **1** [U] action of proclaiming 宣告; 公布; 声明: *by public proclamation* 公开声明. **2** [C] thing that is proclaimed 公告; 布告; 声明: *issue/make a proclamation* 发布公告.

pro·cliv·ity /prəˈklɪvətɪ; proˈklɪvətɪ/ *n* **~ (for/to/towards sth/doing sth)** (*fml* 文) natural inclination to do sth (esp sth bad); tendency 倾向性(尤指坏的); 癖性: *a proclivity towards sudden violent outbursts* 动不动就发火的癖性 ○ *his unusual sexual proclivities* 他对性方面的异常癖好.

pro·cras·tin·ate /prəʊˈkræstɪneɪt; proˈkræstəˌnet/ *v* [I] (*fml derog* 文, 贬) delay or postpone action 拖延; 耽搁; 因循: *He procrastinated until it was too late to do anything at all.* 他因循坐误, 一事无成.

▷ **pro·cras·tina·tion** /prəʊˌkræstɪˈneɪʃn; proˌkræstəˈneʃən/ *n* **1** [U] (*fml derog* 文, 贬) procrastinating 拖延; 耽搁; 因循. **2** (idm 习语) **procrastination is the thief of ˈtime** (*saying* 谚) procrastinating wastes time 因循延宕是时间的窃贼(拖延就是浪费时间).

pro·cre·ate /ˈprəʊkrɪeɪt; ˈprokrɪˌet/ *v* [I] (*fml* 文) reproduce offspring sexually 生育; 生殖. ▷ **pro·cre·ation** /ˌprəʊkrɪˈeɪʃn; ˌprokrɪˈeʃən/ *n* [U].

proc·tor /ˈprɒktə(r); ˈprɑktɚ/ *n* **1** (*Brit*) (at the universities of Oxford and Cambridge) either of two officials with responsibility for discipline (牛津和剑桥大学的)学监(共两名, 主管纪律). **2** (*US*) person responsible for supervising students in an examination, esp so that they do not cheat 监考人.

pro·cur·ator fiscal /ˌprɒkjʊreɪtə ˈfɪskl; ˌprɑkjəˌretɚ ˈfɪskəl/ (in Scotland) public official whose job is to decide whether sb suspected of crime should be prosecuted (苏格兰)地方检察官.

pro·cure /prəˈkjʊə(r); proˈkjʊr/ *v* **1** [Tn, Dn·n, Dn·pr] **~ sth (for sb)** (*fml* 文) obtain sth, esp with care or effort; acquire 取得某事物(尤指费心或费力); 获得: *The book is out of print and difficult to procure.* 那书已绝版, 很难弄到手. ○ *Can you procure some specimens for me/procure me some specimens?* 你能替我弄到一些标本吗? ○ *He was responsible for procuring supplies for the army.* 他的职责是为部队采办军需品. **2** [I, Tn, Dn·pr] **~ sb (for sb)** (*derog* 贬) find (prostitutes) for clients 为宿娼者介绍(娼妓); 拉皮条: *He was accused of procuring women for his business associates.* 他被指控为其生意合伙人招妓.

▷ **pro·cure·ment** *n* [U] (*fml* 文) obtaining 获得: *the procurement of goods, raw materials, supplies, weapons* 货物、原料、供应品、武器之获得.

pro·curer /-ˈkjʊərə(r); -ˈkjʊrɚ/ (*fem* 阴性作 **pro·curess** /-ˈkjʊərɪs; -ˈkjʊrɪs/) *n* (*derog* 贬) person who finds prostitutes for clients 拉皮条者.

prod /prɒd; prɑd/ *v* **(-dd-)** **1** [I, Ipr, Tn] **~ (at sb/sth)** push or poke (sb/sth) with a finger or some other pointed object (用手指或其他尖物)刺, 戳, 捅(某人[某物]): *They prodded (at) the animal through the bars of its cage.* 他们隔着笼子的栏杆用尖东西捅那动物. ⇨Usage at NUDGE 用法见 NUDGE. **2** [Tn, Tn·pr, Cn·t] **~ sb (into/doing sth)** (*infml* 口) (try to) make (a slow or unwilling person) do sth; urge (试图)促使或推动(某人)做某事; 激励: *She is a fairly good worker, but she needs prodding occasionally.* 她干起活来倒是相当不错, 不过有时需要加以督促. ○ *He needs a crisis to prod him into action.* 他要事到临头才被迫采取行动. ○ *I shall have to prod him to pay me what he owes.* 我将不得不催促他把欠我的钱还给我.

▷ **prod** *n* **1** poke or thrust 刺; 戳; 捅: *She gave the man a prod with her umbrella.* 她用伞捅了那男子一下. **2** (*infml* 口) stimulus to action 激励; 激发; 促进; 推动: *If you don't receive an answer quickly, give them a prod.* 你要是不能很快得到答复, 不妨催他们一下. **3** instrument for prodding 刺或戳所用的工具.

prod·ding *n* [U] action of prodding 刺; 戳; 捅; 激励; 促进: *A little gentle prodding may be necessary at this stage.* 在这一阶段或有必要稍微督促一下.

prod·igal /ˈprɒdɪgl; ˈprɑdɪgḷ/ *adj* **1** (*fml derog* 文, 贬) spending money or resources too freely; extravagant 浪费的; 铺张的; 挥霍的: *a prodigal administration* 铺张浪

费的行政机关 ○ *prodigal housekeeping* 大手大脚的持家之道. **2 ~ (of sth)** (*fml* 文) generous or lavish (with sth) 慷慨的; 不吝惜的: *Nature is prodigal of her gifts.* 大自然不吝惜其恩赐. **3** (idm 习语) **the prodigal (son)** person who leaves his home or community to lead a life of pleasure or extravagance, but who later regrets this and returns home 回头的浪子: *the return of the prodigal son* 浪子的回头 ○ *So, the prodigal has returned!* 这么说, 浪子回头了!

▷ **prod·ig·al·ity** /ˌprɒdɪˈgælətɪ; ˌprɑdɪˈgælətɪ/ *n* [U] (*fml* 文) (**a**) (*derog* 贬) wasteful spending; extravagance 浪费; 铺张; 挥霍. (**b**) generosity; lavishness 慷慨; 大方: *the prodigality of the sea*, ie in providing fish 海洋的富饶(大量鱼产).

P

prod·ig·ally /-gəlɪ; -glɪ/ *adv*: *use resources prodigally* 浪费资源.

pro·di·gi·ous /prəˈdɪdʒəs; prəˈdɪdʒəs/ *adj* very great in size, amount or degree, so as to cause amazement or admiration; enormous (在体积、数量或程度上)大得令人惊叹; 巨大的: *a prodigious achievement* 巨大的成就 ○ *It cost a prodigious amount (of money).* 这用了一笔巨款. ▷ **pro·di·gi·ously** *adv*: *The costs are mounting prodigiously.* 价格扶摇直上, 令人吃惊. ○ *She is a prodigiously talented pianist.* 她是才华横溢的钢琴家.

prod·igy /ˈprɒdɪdʒɪ; ˈprɑdədʒɪ/ *n* **1** person with unusual or remarkable qualities or abilities (在素质或能力上)了不起的人; 奇才; 天才: *a child/infant prodigy*, ie one who is unusually talented for his age, eg in music or mathematics 天才儿童[神童](如在音乐或数学方面早慧者). **2** (*rhet* 修辞) (**a**) amazing or wonderful thing, esp a natural phenomenon 令人惊异的事物(尤指自然现象); 奇观: *the prodigies of nature* 大自然的奇观. (**b**) **~ of sth** outstanding example of sth 某方面的出类拔萃者: *The man is a prodigy of learning*, ie knows a lot. 此人学识渊博.

pro·duce /prəˈdjuːs; *US* -ˈduːs; prəˈdus/ *v* **1** [Tn, Tn·pr] **~ sth (from sth)** create sth by making, manufacturing, growing, etc 制造、生产、出产或创造某事物: *America produced more cars this year than last year.* 美国今年生产的汽车比去年多. ○ *She has produced very little (work) recently.* 她近来作品很少. ○ *Linen is produced from flax.* 亚麻布是以亚麻纤维为原料制造的. ○ *He worked hard to produce good crops from poor soil.* 他辛勤耕作, 为使瘠薄的土地上长出好庄稼. ○ *a well-produced book*, ie one that is printed, bound, etc well 印制得很好的书. **2** [Tn] cause (sth) to occur; create 引起(某事物); 产生: *The medicine produced a violent reaction.* 这药物引起了剧烈的反应. ○ *His announcement produced gasps of amazement.* 他宣布的消息引起了一片惊叹声. **3** [I, Tn] bear or yield (offspring or crops) 生育(子女); 产(崽); 出产(农产品): *The silkworms are producing well.* 这些蚕的吐丝量很大. ○ *The cow has produced a calf.* 这母牛生了一头小牛. ○ *The soil produces good crops.* 这种土壤能长出好庄稼来. ○ *The cows are producing a lot of milk.* 这些母牛的产奶量很大. **4** [Tn, Tn·pr] **~ sth (from/out of sth)** bring out or show sth so that it can be examined or used 拿出或出示某事物(以供检验或使用): *produce a railway ticket for inspection* 出示火车票以供查验 ○ *The man produced a revolver from his pocket.* 那人从衣袋里掏出一支左轮手枪. ○ *He can produce evidence to support his allegations.* 他能提出证据以表明他的指控属实. **5** [Tn] arrange the performance of (a play, an opera, etc) or the making of (a film, TV programme, record, etc) 安排上演(戏剧、歌剧等); 制作(影片、电视节目、唱片等): *She is producing 'Romeo and Juliet' at the local theatre.* 她正在当地的剧院里安排演出《罗密欧与朱丽叶》. ○ *He hopes to find the money to produce a film about Japan.* 他希望筹集到资金以便拍一部关于日本的影片. **6** [Tn, Tn·pr] **~ sth (to sth)** (*mathematics* 数) make (a line) longer (so that it reaches a particular point) 将(一线)延长(至某点): *produce the line AB to C* 把线段AB延长到C点.

▷ **pro·duce** /ˈprɒdjuːs; *US* -duːs; ˈprɑdus/ *n* [U] things that have been produced (PRODUCE 1), esp by farming 产品; (尤指)农产品: *fresh produce* 新鲜的农产品 ○ *agricultural, farm, garden produce* 农业的、农场的、园圃的产品 ○ *It says on the bottle 'Produce of France'.* 瓶上标有'法国制造'的字样.

pro·du·cer /prəˈdjuːsə(r); *US* -ˈduː-; prəˈdusɚ/ *n* **1** person, company, country, etc that produces (PRODUCE 1) goods or materials 生产者(可指个人、公司、国家等); 制造者; 产地: *The firm is Britain's main producer of electronic equipment.* 该公司为英国主要的电子设备制造厂家. ○ *The producers of the radios could not find a market for them.* 这些收音机制造厂产品打不开销路. ○ *the conflicting interests of producers and consumers* 生产者与消费者的利害冲突. Cf 参看 CONSUMER. **2** (**a**) person in charge of a film or theatrical production, who obtains the money to make the film or put on the play, and arranges the schedules, publicity, etc (影片的)制片人; (戏剧的)主管人, 制作总监. Cf 参看 DIRECTOR 2. (**b**) person who arranges the making of a TV or radio programme, a record, etc (电视或广播节目、唱片等的)制作人, 监制. (**c**) (esp in the amateur theatre) person who arranges the performance of a play, telling the actors what to do; director (尤指业余剧团的)舞台监督, 导演. (**d**) director of an opera performance 歌剧导演.

prod·uct /ˈprɒdʌkt; ˈprɑdʌkt/ *n* **1** (**a**) [C, U] thing or substance produced by a natural or manufacturing process 产品, 产物(自然的或人工的); 出品; 制品: *a firm known for its high-quality products* 以产品优良而负盛名的公司 ○ *the products of manufacturing industry* 制造业的出品 ○ *pharmaceutical products*, eg drugs, medicines 药品 ○ *the finished product*, ie one that has reached the end of the manufacturing process 制成品 ○ *waste products*, ie waste material produced by eg the body's digestive system 废物(如粪便). (**b**) [U] (*commerce* 商) goods produced by a firm, country, etc 产品(总称): *a campaign to increase sales of the firm's product* 为促进公司产品的销售而开展的运动 ○ *gross national product*, ie the annual total value of goods produced and services provided in a country 国民生产总值 ○ [attrib 作定语] *product development* 产品开发. **2** [C] **~ of sth** (**a**) state or thing that is the result of sth 产物: *Flower power was a product of the sixties.* 戴花嬉皮士的信仰是六十年代的产物. ○ *the products of genius*, eg great works of art 天才的产物(如伟大的艺术作品) ○ *Low morale among the work force is the product of bad management.* 工人干劲不足是管理不善所致. (**b**) person who has been influenced by sth 在某事物影响下产生的人物; (某事物的)产儿: *She is the product of a broken home.* 她是一个破裂家庭的产儿. ○ *They are the products of post-war affluence.* 他们是战后富裕生活的产物. **3** [C] (**a**) (*mathematics* 数) quantity obtained by multiplying one number by another (乘)积: *The product of 4 and 10 is 40.* 4与10的乘积是40. (**b**) (*chemistry* 化) new chemical compound produced by chemical reaction (化学反应的)生成物. Cf 参看 REACTANT.

pro·duc·tion /prəˈdʌkʃn; prəˈdʌkʃən/ *n* **1** [U] action of manufacturing, extracting, etc, esp in large quantities 制造, 生产(尤指大批量): *oil production* 采油 ○ *Production of the new aircraft will start next year.* 明年开始制造新型的飞机. ○ *Production must become more efficient.* 必须提高生产效率. ○ *mass* (ie very large-scale) *production* 大量生产 ○ *Defects in design cannot be put right during production.* 设计上的缺陷是无法在生产过程中加以纠正的. ○ *He has moved from acting to film production.* 他由演员变成了制片人. ○ [attrib 作定语] *production costs, managers, processes, schedules, difficulties* 生产的成本、生产经理、生产过程、生产计划、生产的难题. **2** [U] quantity produced 产量: *increase production by using more efficient methods* 采用更有效的方法提高产量 ○ *a fall/increase in production* 产量的减少[增加]. **3** [C] thing that has been produced, esp a play, film, etc 推出的作品(尤指戏剧、影片等): *They saw several National Theatre productions.* 他们看了国家剧院上演的几出戏. ○ *'King Lear' in a controversial new production* 可能引起争论的新剧《李尔王》. **4** (idm 习语) **go ˌinto/ˌout of proˈduction** start/stop being manufactured 投产[停产]: *The system will have to be tested before it goes into production.* 这套装置必须经过试验之后才能投产. ○ *That car went out of production five years ago.* 那种汽车已经停产五年了. **in proˈduction** being manufactured (in large quantities) 在(大量)生产中: *The device will be in production by the end of the year.* 该装置将于年底投入生产. **on production of sth** by/when showing sth 通过[一经]出示某物: *On production of your membership* *card, you will receive a discount on purchases.* 持会员证购物可享受折扣优待.

□ **pro'duction line** sequence of groups of machines and workers, in which each group carries out part of the production process 生产线: *Cars are checked as they come off the production line.* 汽车经装配线组装完毕后即进行校验.

pro·duct·ive /prəˈdʌktɪv; prəˈdʌktɪv/ *adj* **1** producing or able to produce goods or crops, esp in large quantities 生产(性)的; 有生产能力的; (尤指)多产的: *They work hard, but their efforts are not very productive.* 他们很努力, 但效率不太高. ○ *productive farming land, manufacturing methods* 肥沃的农田、富有成效的生产方法 ○ *a productive worker* 多产的工作者. **2** achieving a lot; useful 富有成效的; 有益的: *It wasn't a very productive meeting.* 这个会议成效不太大. ○ *I spent a very productive hour in the library.* 我在图书馆里这一小时收获很大. **3** [pred 作表语] **~ of sth** (*fml* 文) resulting in sth; causing sth 造成某种结果; 产生某事物: *The changes were not productive of better labour relations.* 这些改变并未能使劳资关系获得改善. ▷ **pro·duct·ively** *adv*: *spend one's time productively* 时间用得有成效.

pro·duc·tiv·ity /ˌprɒdʌkˈtɪvətɪ; ˌprɑdʌkˈtɪvətɪ/ *n* [U] **1** ability to produce (eg goods or crops); state of being productive 生产力; 生产能力; 多产性: *The size of the crop depends on the productivity of the soil.* 作物的产量取决于土地的肥沃程度. **2** efficiency, esp in industry, measured by comparing the amount produced with the time taken or the resources used to produce it 生产率, 生产效率(尤指工业的): *The management are looking for ways of improving productivity.* 管理部门正在设法提高生产率. ○ [attrib 作定语] *a productivity bonus for workers* 发给工人的增产奖.

□ **produc'tivity agreement** agreement between management and unions that the cost of higher wages will be paid for by an increase in productivity (资方与工会订立的)增产协议(生产率提高则工资亦提高).

prof /prɒf; prɑf/ *n* (*infml* 口) = PROFESSOR.

Prof *abbr* 缩写 = Professor (as a title 用作称谓).

pro·fane /prəˈfeɪn; *US* prəʊ-; prəˈfen/ *adj* (*fml* 文) **1** [attrib 作定语] not sacred; secular 世俗的(非宗教的): *sacred and profane music* 圣乐与世俗音乐 ○ *profane* (ie not biblical) *literature* 世俗的(非圣经的)文学作品. **2** (**a**) having or showing contempt for God or holy things; blasphemous 亵渎上帝或神圣事物的; 不敬神的: *profane behaviour in church* 做礼拜时亵渎上帝的行为 ○ *a profane oath* 亵渎上帝的言语. (**b**) offensive; obscene 冒犯的; 无礼的; 下流的: *profane language* 下流语言.

▷ **pro·fane** *v* [Tn] (*fml* 文) (**a**) treat (a sacred thing) with irreverence or contempt 亵渎, 冒犯(神圣事物): *profane the name of God* 亵渎上帝之名 ○ *Their behaviour profaned the holy place.* 他们的行为玷污了这处圣地. (**b**) treat or use (sth worthy of respect) disrespectfully 对(可敬之事物)无礼; 玷污; 滥用: *His action profaned the honour of his country.* 他的行为玷污了国家的荣誉.

prof·ana·tion /ˌprɒfəˈneɪʃn; ˌprɑfəˈneʃən/ *n* [C, U] (*fml* 文) (instance of) profaning 亵渎; 冒犯; 玷污.

pro·fanely *adv*.

pro·fan·ity /prəˈfænətɪ; *US* prəʊ-; proˈfænətɪ/ *n* (*fml* 文) **1** [U] profane behaviour, esp the use of profane language 亵渎行为; (尤指)使用亵渎语言. **2** [C esp *pl* 尤作复数] profane word or phrase; obscenity 亵渎的话; 下流话: *He uttered a stream of profanities.* 他说出了一连串下流话.

pro·fess /prəˈfes; prəˈfɛs/ *v* (*fml* 文) **1** [Tn, Tf, Tt, Cn·a] claim (sth), often falsely 声称, 自称, 伪称, 妄称(某事物): *I don't profess expert knowledge of/to be an expert in this subject.* 我并不自诩对这一问题内行[是这一问题的专家]. ○ *She professed total ignorance of the matter.* 她自称对那事一无所知. ○ *He professed that he knew nothing about the plot.* 他声称对该阴谋毫不知情. **2** [Tn, Cn·a] state openly that one has (a belief, feeling, etc) 公开表明(信仰、感情等): *They professed optimism about the outcome.* 他们对结果表示乐观. ○ *He professed himself satisfied with the progress made.* 他表明自己对所取得的进步感到满意. **3** [Tn] (**a**) publicly declare one's faith in (a religion) 宣布自己的(宗教)信仰: *Christians profess their faith when they say the Creed.* 基督教徒在念信经时就表明了他们的宗教信仰. (**b**) have or belong to (the specified religion) 具有, 忠于(某宗教信仰): *profess Islam* 信仰伊斯兰教.

▷ **pro·fessed** *adj* [attrib 作定语] **1** (falsely) claimed; alleged 声称的; 自称的; 伪称的; 妄称的; 靠不住的; 所谓的: *her professed love of children* 她所谓的对孩子们的爱 ○ *She was betrayed by her professed friends and supporters.* 她被那些自称是她的朋友和支持她的人出卖了. **2** openly acknowledged by oneself; declared 公开承认的; 公开表明的: *a professed Christian* 公开表明信仰的基督教徒 ○ *a professed supporter of disarmament* 倡言裁军的人. **3** having made religious vows (宗教上)已立誓的, 已受戒的: *a professed nun* 已立誓终生为修女者. **pro·fess·edly** /-ɪdlɪ; -ɪdlɪ/ *adv* (*fml* 文) according to one's own claim (whether true or false) or admission 自称; 自我表明; 自己承认: *She is professedly a feminist.* 她自称是女权运动者.

P

pro·fes·sion /prəˈfeʃn; prəˈfɛʃən/ *n* **1** (**a**) [C] paid occupation, esp one that requires advanced education and training, eg architecture, law or medicine 职业(尤指须受高深教育及专业训练者, 如建筑师、律师或医师之职业): *advising college leavers on their choice of profession* 给予院校毕业生以择业上的指导 ○ *the acting, legal, medical, etc profession* 演员、律师、医师等职业. (**b**) **the profession** [CGp] body of people working in a particular profession (某)职业界; 同业: *The legal profession* (ie lawyers) *has/have always resisted change.* 法律界人士对变革总是加以抵制. ⇨Usage at TRADE[1] 用法见 TRADE[1]. **2** [C] **~ of sth** public statement or claim of sth 表示; 表白; 宣言: *a profession of belief, faith, loyalty, etc* 信念、信仰、忠诚等的表白 ○ *His professions of concern did not seem sincere.* 他所表示的关心看来并非出自内心. **3** (idm 习语) **by profession** as one's paid occupation 作为职业: *She is a lawyer by profession.* 她的职业是律师. ○ *The author of the guidebook is an architect by profession.* 该手册的作者任职建筑师.

pro·fes·sional /prəˈfeʃənl; prəˈfɛʃənl̩/ *adj* **1** (**a**) [attrib 作定语] of or belonging to a profession 职业(上)的; 从事某职业的; 属于某专业的: *a professional man, woman, practitioner* 从事某职业的男子、女子、开业者 ○ *professional associations, codes of practice, conduct* 专业协会、职业道德规范、职业道德 ○ *You will need to seek professional advice about your claim for compensation.* 你在索赔的问题上需要内行人士作指导. ○ *The doctor was accused of professional misconduct.* 那医生被控有违行医道德. (**b**) having or showing the skill or qualities of a professional person 具有专门知识的; 表现专门技能的; 内行的: *Many of the performers were of professional standard.* 许多表演者都具有专业水平. ○ *He was complimented on a very professional piece of work.* 他由于一件表现出精湛技艺的作品而受到赞扬. ○ *She is extremely professional in her approach to her job.* 她对工作极为精通. Cf 参看 UNPROFESSIONAL. **2** (**a**) doing as a full-time job sth which others do as a hobby or as a part-time job 职业性的; 专业的; 非业余的: *a professional boxer, footballer, golfer, tennis player, etc* 职业的拳击手、足球运动员、高尔夫球运动员、网球运动员等 ○ *a professional cook, dressmaker, musician, etc* 职业厨师、裁缝、乐师等 ○ *After he won the amateur championship he turned professional*, ie began to earn money for his sport. 他获得业余比赛的冠军后便转为职业运动员了. (**b**) (of sport, etc) practised as a full-time job (指运动等)职业性质的: *professional football, golf, tennis, etc* 职业的足球赛、高尔夫球赛、网球赛等 ○ *She had been on the professional stage* (ie a professional actress) *in her youth.* 她年轻时当过职业演员. Cf 参看 AMATEUR 1. **3** [attrib 作定语] (*derog* 贬) repeatedly doing the specified annoying thing 不断制造麻烦的: *a professional complainer, gossip, moaner, trouble-maker, etc* 专门发牢骚、散布流言蜚语、发泄不满情绪、惹事生非等的人.

▷ **pro·fes·sional** *n* **1** person qualified or employed in one of the professions 具有某专业资格的人; 从事某专业的人; 专业人士: *studio flats suitable for young professionals* 年轻的专业人员适用的单间公寓 ○ *You need a professional to sort out your finances.* 你需要专业人士替你管理财务. **2** (also *infml* 口语作 **pro**) professional (2a) player or performer, esp a sportsman employed by a club to teach and advise its members 职业运动员; 职业演员; (尤指受雇于俱乐部的)职业教练,

职业顾问: *a golf professional* 高尔夫球职业运动员. **3** (also *infml* 口语作 **pro**) (*approv* 褒) highly skilled and experienced person 技术精湛经验丰富的人; 内行; 专家: *She's a true professional!* 她真不愧为专家! ○ *This survey is the work of a real professional.* 这份调查是真正内行人做的.

pro·fes·sion·al·ism /-ʃənəlɪzəm; -ʃənəlɪzəm/ *n* [U] **1** (*approv* 褒) (**a**) skill or qualities of a profession or its members 专业技能; 特长; 职业特性: *You can rely on your solicitor's professionalism in dealing with the house purchase.* 你尽可依靠律师处理购房事宜. (**b**) great skill and competence 精湛的技艺; 娴熟的功夫: *They were impressed by the sheer professionalism of the performance.* 他们赞佩表演炉火纯青. **2** practice of employing professionals (PROFESSIONAL 2) in sport 在体育竞赛中雇用职业选手的做法.

pro·fes·sion·ally /-ʃənəlɪ; -ʃənlɪ/ *adv* (**a**) in a professional way 专业的; 有职业道德的: *A doctor who gives away confidential information about patients is not behaving professionally.* 医生把病人的私人资料透露出来是违反职业道德的. (**b**) by a professional person 由专业人员; 由内行人: *The plans had been drawn professionally.* 那计划是由专家制定的. ○ *Her voice should be professionally trained.* 她在运嗓上应接受专业训练. (**c**) as a paid occupation 作为职业; 职业性地: *He plays cricket professionally.* 他以打板球为职业.

□ **pro,fessional 'foul** (*euph* 婉) (in sport, esp football) deliberate foul, esp one committed in order to stop the game when a member of the opposing team seems certain to score (体育竞赛, 尤指足球比赛中)故意犯规 (尤指藉犯规动作中断比赛以避免对方得分之做法).

pro·fessor /prəˈfesə(r); prəˈfɛsɚ/ *n* (*abbr* 缩写 **Prof**) **1** (*US* also **full professor**) (title of a) university teacher of the highest grade who holds a chair(3) in a subject (大学)教授(的头衔): *He is Professor of Moral Philosophy at Oxford.* 他是牛津大学伦理学教授. ○ *She was made professor at the age of 40.* 她40岁就当了教授. ○ *Professor Smith, may I introduce one of my students to you?* 史密斯教授, 请让我介绍一下我的一个学生. **2** (*US*) teacher at a university or college (大学的)教师, 教员. **3** (*joc* 谑) title taken by instructors in various subjects 师傅 (对各行业中传授技艺者的称呼): *Professor Pate, the famous phrenologist.* 著名的颅相学家佩特师傅.

▷ **pro·fess·or·ial** /ˌprɒfɪˈsɔːrɪəl; ˌprɑfəˈsorɪəl/ *adj* of or like a professor (似)教授的: *a professorial post* 教授的职位 ○ *professorial duties* 教授的职责.

pro·fess·or·ship *n* position of a university professor; chair (3) (大学)教授职位: *The professorship of zoology is vacant and has been advertised.* 动物学教授的职位空缺, 已登广告征聘.

prof·fer /ˈprɒfə(r); ˈprɑfɚ/ *v* [Tn, Dn·n, Dn·pr] **~ sth (to sb)** (*fml* 文) offer sth 提供、提出某事物: *He refused the proffered assistance.* 他拒绝接受向他提供的帮助. ○ *She proffered (him) her resignation.* 她(向他)提交了辞呈. ○ *May we proffer you our congratulations?* 请让我们向你表示祝贺.

▷ **prof·fer** *n* (*fml* 文) offer 提供; 提议: *a proffer of help* 给予援助的建议.

pro·fi·cient /prəˈfɪʃnt; prəˈfɪʃənt/ *adj* **~ (in/at sth/doing sth)** doing or able to do sth in a skilled or an expert way because of training and practice 精通的; 熟练的: *a proficient driver* 开车的好手 ○ *proficient in the use of radar equipment* 精通雷达设备之使用的 ○ *proficient at operating a computer terminal* 善于操作计算机终端设备的.

▷ **pro·fi·ciency** /-nsɪ; -nsɪ/ *n* [U] **~ (in sth/doing sth)** being proficient (in sth) 精通; 熟练: *a test of proficiency (in English)* (英语)水平测试 ○ *show proficiency in operating a switchboard* 操作配电板十分熟练.

pro·fi·ciently *adv*.

pro·file /ˈprəʊfaɪl; ˈprofaɪl/ *n* **1** side view esp of the human face 侧面所见; (尤指人面部的)侧面(像): *his handsome profile* 他漂亮的侧面轮廓 ○ [attrib 作定语] *a profile drawing* 侧面图像. **2** edge or outline of sth seen against a background 轮廓; 外形: *the profile of the tower against the sky* 天空衬托下的塔的轮廓. **3** brief biography of sb or description of sth in a newspaper article, broadcast programme, etc (报刊文章、广播节目等中的)人物或事物之简介, 概况, 传略: *The newspaper publishes a profile of a leading sportsman every week.* 该报每周刊登一篇关于一个优秀运动员的简介. ○ *The BBC are working on a profile of the British nuclear industry.* 英国广播公司正在报道英国核工业概况. **4** (idm 习语) **a ,high/,low 'profile** noticeable/inconspicuous way of behaving, so as to attract/avoid public attention 极力[避免]显示自己的做法; 高[低]姿态: *adopt/keep/maintain a low profile* 采取[保持/维持]低姿态 ○ [attrib 作定语] *high-profile politicians* 引人注目的政治家们. **in profile** (seen) from the side 由侧面(看的): *In profile she is very like her mother.* 由侧面看她很像她母亲. ○ *The Queen's head appears in profile on British stamps.* 英国邮票上有女王的侧面头像.

▷ **pro·file** *v* **1** [Tn esp passive 尤用于被动语态] show (sth) in profile against a background 显出(某物)的轮廓: *The huge trees were profiled against the night sky.* 在夜空的映衬下显出大树的轮廓. **2** [Tn] write or make a profile(3) of (sb/sth) 写(某人[某事物])的简介.

profit[1] /ˈprɒfɪt; ˈprɑfɪt/ *n* **1** (**a**) [C, U] financial gain (财务上的)收益; 利润; 赢利: *do sth for profit* 为营利而做某事 ○ *There's no profit in running a cinema in this town.* 这个镇里电影院是无利可图的. ○ *They're only interested in a quick profit.* 他们急功近利. ○ [attrib 作定语] *The capitalist system is based on the profit motive.* 资本主义制度是以赢利动机为基础建立起来的. (**b**) [C] amount of money gained in business, esp the difference between the amount earned and the amount spent (企业等的)赢利; (尤指)盈余, 纯利润: *They make a profit of ten pence on every copy they sell.* 他们每售出一本获利十便士. ○ *sell at a profit* 销售获利 ○ *operate at a profit*, ie be profitable 经营获利 ○ *The company has declared an increase in profits/increased profits.* 该公司宣布利润增加. ○ *a clear profit of 20 per cent* 百分之二十的净利. **2** [U] (*fml* 文) advantage or benefit gained from sth 利益; 好处: *You could with profit spend some extra time studying the text.* 你多花点时间学习课文是有好处的.

▷ **prof·it·less** *adj* without profit[1](2) 无利的; 无益的: *Revising the procedure was an entirely profitless exercise.* 对程序进行修改是徒劳无功的. **prof·it·lessly** *adv*: *I seem to have spent my day quite profitlessly.* 我这一天过得好像没什么收获.

□ **,profit and 'loss account** (in bookkeeping) account showing income and expenditure for a particular period, with the profit or loss made (簿记)损益帐(反映某时期赢利或亏损的收支情况).

'profit-margin *n* difference between the cost of buying or producing sth and the price for which one sells it 利润率(购物本金或制造成本与售价之差额): *a gross profit-margin of 25%* 25%的毛利率.

'profit-sharing *n* [U] system of dividing a portion of a company's profits amongst its employees 分红制(将公司部分利润分配给雇员的制度): [attrib 作定语] *a profit-sharing scheme* 利润分成办法.

profit[2] /ˈprɒfɪt; ˈprɑfɪt/ *v* (phr v) **profit by sth** (no passive 不用于被动语态) learn from (one's experience, mistakes, etc) so that one does not repeat them 从(经验、失误等)中吸取教益: *He's getting married again, after two divorces, so he obviously hasn't profited by his experiences.* 他两次离婚之后又结婚, 显然没有吸取以往的教训. **profit from sth** benefit from or be helped by sth 得益于某事物; 得到某事物的帮助: *He profited greatly from his year abroad.* 他在国外一年获益匪浅. ○ *I have profited from your advice.* 你的建议对我很有好处.

prof·it·able /ˈprɒfɪtəbl; ˈprɑfɪtəbl/ *adj* bringing profit or advantage; beneficial 可获利润或好处的; 有利可图的; 有益的: *profitable investments* 有利的投资 ○ *The deal was profitable to all of us.* 这笔生意对我们大家都有利. ○ *It would be more profitable to combine the two factories.* 把这两家工厂联合起来更能赚钱. ○ *She spent a profitable afternoon in the library.* 她一下午在图书馆里收获不小.

▷ **prof·it·ab·il·ity** /ˌprɒfɪtəˈbɪlətɪ; ˌprɑfɪtəˈbɪlətɪ/ *n* [U].

prof·it·ably /-əblɪ; -əblɪ/ *adv*: *They invested the money very profitably.* 他们的投资大有赚头. ○ *She spent the weekend profitably.* 她的周末过得很有益.

prof·it·eer /ˌprɒfɪˈtɪə(r); ˌprɑfəˈtɪr/ *v* [I] (*derog* 贬) make too large a profit, esp by exploiting people in difficult times (eg in a war or famine) 牟取暴利; (尤指于困难时期, 如战争或饥荒)剥削, 投机倒把: *Rent controls were introduced to prevent profiteering.* 为了防止牟取暴利而

实行了租金管制.

▷ **prof·it·eer** *n* person who does this 牟取暴利者; 大发不义之财者; 投机商人.

pro·fit·er·ole /prɒˈfɪtərəʊl; prəˈfɪtə,rol/ *n* small hollow bun of light pastry with a sweet or savoury filling 一种甜馅或其他美味馅的酥皮空心小点心.

prof·lig·ate /ˈprɒflɪgət; ˋprɑfləgɪt/ *adj* (*fml derog* 文, 贬) **1** recklessly extravagant or wasteful 恣意挥霍的; 极其浪费的: *profligate spending* 挥霍 ○ *a profligate use of scarce resources* 对稀少的资源的恣意挥霍. **2** (of a person or his behaviour) shamelessly immoral; dissolute (指人或其行为)无耻的, 放荡的.

▷ **prof·lig·acy** /ˈprɒflɪgəsɪ; ˋprɑfləgəsɪ/ *n* [U] (*fml derog* 文, 贬) being profligate 恣意挥霍; 放荡.

prof·lig·ate *n* (*fml derog* 文, 贬) profligate(2) person 无耻的人; 放荡的人.

pro forma /ˌprəʊ ˈfɔːmə; proˈfɔrmə/ *adj, adv* as a matter of convention 作为惯例; 形式上(的).

▷ **pro forma** (also **pro forma invoice**) invoice that gives details of goods that have been sent, but does not request payment 形式发票, 估价单(开列所发货物之清单, 但不要求付款).

pro·found /prəˈfaʊnd; prəˈfaʊnd/ *adj* **1** [usu attrib 通常作定语] (*fml* 文) deep, intense or far-reaching; very great 深的; 深切的; 深远的; 极度的; 极大的: *a profound sigh, silence, sleep, shock* 一声长叹、一片死寂、一阵酣睡、一次沉重的打击 ○ *take a profound interest in sth* 对某事物产生极大的兴趣 ○ *profound ignorance* 极度的无知 ○ *profound changes* 深刻的变化. **2** (**a**) [usu attrib 通常作定语] having or showing great knowledge or insight (into a subject) 知识渊博的; 见解深刻的: *a profound awareness of the problem* 对问题的深刻理解 ○ *a profound thinker* 学识渊博的思想家 ○ *a man of profound learning* 博学的人. (**b**) needing much study or thought 需要研究或思考的; 深奥的: *profound mysteries* 难解之谜.

▷ **pro·foundly** *adv* (**a**) deeply; extremely 深深地; 深刻地; 极度地: *profoundly disturbed, grateful, shocked* 极其不安的、感激的、震惊的. (**b**) in a profound(2a) manner 渊博地; 见多识广地; 深奥地.

pro·fund·ity /prəˈfʌndətɪ; prəˈfʌndətɪ/ *n* (*fml* 文) **1** [U] depth (esp of knowledge, thought, etc) 深度, 渊深, 深刻, 深奥(尤指知识、思想等): *He impressed his audience by the profundity of his knowledge.* 他知识渊博给听众留下了深刻的印象. **2** [C esp *pl* 尤作复数] profound meaning, statement or thought 深刻的含义、言语或思想: *a poem full of profundities* 寓意深长的诗.

pro·fuse /prəˈfjuːs; prəˈfjus/ *adj* **1** in large amounts; abundant 大量的; 丰富的: *profuse blossoms, flowers, apologies, gratitude, thanks* 大量的花朵、数不清的鲜花、再三的道歉、深深的感激、千谢万谢 ○ *profuse bleeding, sweating, tears* 血流如注、大汗淋漓、泪如泉涌. **2** [pred 作表语] **~ in sth** expressing or giving sth freely or generously; lavish with sth 对某事物一再表示或慷慨给予; 某事上滥施: *profuse in one's apologies, thanks* 一再表示歉意、谢意.

▷ **pro·fusely** *adv*: *bleed, sweat profusely* 大出血、出大汗 ○ *thank sb profusely* 一再感谢某人.

pro·fuse·ness *n* [U] state of being profuse 大量; 丰富: *The profuseness of his thanks was embarrassing.* 他再三表示感谢使人很不好意思.

pro·fu·sion /prəˈfjuːʒn; prəˈfjuʒən/ *n* **1** [sing] **~ of sth** abundant supply of sth 大量的某事物: *a profusion of colour, patterns, flowers, good wishes* 许多的颜色、花样、鲜花、美好祝愿. **2** (idm 习语) **in profusion** in large quantities or abundance 大量地; 丰富地: *Roses were growing in profusion against the old wall.* 紧挨着旧墙长着很多玫瑰花.

pro·gen·itor /prəʊˈdʒenɪtə(r); proˈdʒɛnətɚ/ *n* (*fml* 文) **1** ancestor (of a person, an animal or a plant) (人或动植物的)祖先. **2** (*fig* 比喻) originator (of an idea, an intellectual or political movement, etc) (思想、学术或政治运动的)创始人, 前辈, 先驱: *Marx was the progenitor of Communism.* 马克思是共产主义的创始人.

pro·geny /ˈprɒdʒənɪ; ˋprɑdʒənɪ/ *n* [pl *v*] (*fml* 文) (**a**) offspring 子女; 幼崽: (*joc* 谑) *He appeared, surrounded by his numerous progeny.* 他出现时, 子女前呼后拥不计其数. (**b**) descendants 后代; 后裔.

pro·ges·ter·one /prəˈdʒestərəʊn; proˈdʒɛstə,ron/ *n* [U] one of the sex hormones, that prepares and maintains the uterus for pregnancy and is used in the contraceptive pill because it prevents ovulation 孕酮; 黄体酮. Cf 参看 OESTROGEN.

pro·gnosis /prɒgˈnəʊsɪs; prɑgˈnosɪs/ *n* (*pl* **-ses** /-siːz; -siz/) (**a**) (*medical* 医) forecast of the likely course of a disease or an illness (对病情的)预断, 预后: *make one's prognosis* 预断病情 ○ *The prognosis is not good.* 预后不良. Cf 参看 DIAGNOSIS. (**b**) (*fig* 比喻) forecast of the probable development of sth; outlook (对发展情况的)预测; 展望: *The prognosis for the future of the electronics industry is encouraging.* 预测电子工业的前途一片大好.

pro·gnost·ic·ate /prɒgˈnɒstɪkeɪt; prɑgˈnɑstɪ,ket/ *v* (*fml* 文) **1** [I, Tn, Tf] tell (sth) in advance; predict 预言(某事物); 预报: *prognosticate disaster* 预言灾难. **2** [Tn, Tf] be a sign of (a future event) 成为(未来事件)的预兆; 预示.

▷ **pro·gnost·ica·tion** /prɒgˌnɒstɪˈkeɪʃn; prɑg,nɑstɪˋkeʃən/ *n* (*fml* 文) (**a**) [U] prognosticating 预言; 预报. (**b**) [C] thing that is prognosticated 预言或预报的事物; 预兆: *His gloomy prognostications proved to be false.* 他那悲观的预测已证明是错误的.

pro·gram /ˈprəʊgræm; *US* -grəm; ˋprogrəm/ *n* **1** (*US*) = PROGRAMME. **2** (*computing* 计) series of coded instructions to control the operations of a computer 程序; 编码指令: *write a program for producing a balance sheet* 为编制资产负债表而编写程序.

▷ **pro·gram** *v* (**-mm-**; *US* also **-m-**) [Tn, Cn·t] (*computing* 计) instruct (a computer) (to do sth) by putting a program into it 用程序指令(计算机)(执行某任务): *The computer has been programmed (to calculate the gross profit margin on all sales).* 计算机已输入了程序指令(以计算各项销售的毛利率). **pro·gram·mer** (*US* also **pro·gramer**) *n* person who writes programs for a computer (计算机)程序编制员, 程序设计师.

pro·gramme (*US* **pro·gram**) /ˈprəʊgræm; *US* -grəm; ˋprogrəm/ *n* **1** broadcast item (eg a play, discussion or documentary) (广播或电视)节目(如戏剧、讨论或纪实): *There is an interesting programme on television tonight.* 今晚有个好看的电视节目. ○ *They're putting on a programme about/on wine-making.* 他们正推出一个介绍酿酒方法的节目. **2** plan of what is (intended) to be done 工作计划; 活动安排; 行动方案: *a political programme* 政治纲领 ○ *What's (on) the programme for* (ie What are we going to do) *tomorrow?* 明天安排了什么活动? ○ *launch a programme to redevelop the inner cities* 提出一项改建市中心区的方案. **3** (**a**) (notice or list of a) series of items in a concert, on a course of study, etc (音乐会等的)节目单, 节目表; 教学大纲; 课程: *The programme includes two Mozart sonatas.* 节目单中有两首莫扎特的奏鸣曲. ○ *plan a programme of lectures for first-year students* 为大学一年级新生拟制教学大纲. (**b**) (booklet with a) list of the names of the actors in a play, singers in an opera, etc 戏剧演员、歌剧歌唱演员等的名单; (载有演员阵容的)演出说明书.

▷ **pro·gramme** (*US* **pro·gram**) *v* (**-mm-**; *US* also **-m-**) **1** [usu passive 通常用于被动语态: Tn, Tn·pr] **~ sth (for sth)** make a programme of or for sth; put sth on a programme; plan or arrange sth 编排某事物的节目单; 将某事物编入节目单; 计划或安排某事物: *programme a music festival* 为音乐会演编排节目 ○ *A trip to the museum is programmed for next Tuesday.* 已计划下星期二去参观博物馆. **2** [usu passive 通常用于被动语态: Tn, Cn·t] cause (sb/sth) to do sth or behave in a particular way, esp automatically or in an unthinking way 使(某人[某事物])按预定的步骤进行(尤指自动地或不假思索地): *Their early training programmes them to be obedient and submissive.* 他们早先受过的教育已把他们训练得俯首帖耳、唯命是从. ○ *The video is programmed to switch itself on at ten o'clock.* 这台录像机已调好在十点钟自动开机. ˌ**programmed** ˈ**course** educational course in which the material to be learnt is presented in small, carefully graded, amounts 程序教程(一种以循序渐进的方法施教的课程). ˌ**programmed** ˈ**learning** self-instruction using a programmed course 程序学习(按程序教程循序渐进的自学方式).

□ ˈ**programme music** music intended to suggest a story, picture, etc 标题音乐(旨在以音乐表现某情节、图像等).

ˈ**programme note** short description or explanation in a

programme(3b) of a musical work, a play, an actor's career, etc (演出说明书中对音乐、戏剧作品、演员经历等的)简介.

pro·gress /ˈprəʊgres; US ˈprɒg-; ˋprɑgrɛs/ *n* **1** [U] forward or onward movement 前进; 行进: *The walkers were making slow progress up the rocky path.* 行人沿着岩石小道慢慢往上走. ○ *The yacht made good progress with a following wind.* 那小帆船顺风行驶得很快. **2** [U] advance or development, esp towards a better state 进步, 进展, 发展(尤具改进之意): *the progress of civilization* 文明的进展 ○ *There has been very little progress this term.* 这学期没有什么进步. ○ *The patient is making good progress* (ie is getting better) *after her operation.* 这个女病人动过手术后病情大为好转. ○ *Strike leaders have reported some progress in the talks to settle the dispute.* 罢工的领导人汇报了在解决争端的谈判中所取得的某些进展. ○ [attrib 作定语] *a ˈprogress report* 进行情况的报告. **3** [C] (*arch* 古) journey made by a sovereign or ruler (帝王等的)巡行, 巡游: *a royal progress around the country* 国王之全国巡游. **4** (idm 习语) **in progress** being done or made 进行中: *An inquiry is now in progress.* 调查工作此刻正在进行中. ○ *Please be quiet — recording in progress.* 正在录音——请勿喧哗.

▷ **pro·gress** /prəˈgres; prəˋgrɛs/ *v* **1** [I] make progress 前进; 行进; 进步; 进展: *The work is progressing steadily.* 工作在稳步地取得进展. ○ *She is progressing in her studies.* 她学习有进步. ○ *In some ways, civilization does not seem to have progressed much in the last century.* 在某些方面, 上个世纪文明似乎进展不大. **2** [Tn] cause (work, etc) to make regular progress towards completion 使(工作等)正常进行、有进步或取得进展.

pro·gres·sion /prəˈgreʃn; prəˋgrɛʃən/ *n* **1** [U] **~ (from sth) (to sth)** (process of) moving forward or developing, esp in stages or gradually; progressing 进行, 进展, 进程, 进步(尤指按步骤的或渐次的): *the team's progression to the first division* 该队的晋级为甲级队 ○ *Adolescence is the period of progression from childhood to adulthood.* 青春期是由童年到成年的过渡期. **2** [C] sequence or series 连续; 一系列: *a long progression of sunny days* 连续的晴天.

pro·gress·ive /prəˈgresɪv; prəˋgrɛsɪv/ *adj* **1** making a continuous forward movement 前进的; 进步的; 有进展的. **2** increasing steadily or in regular degrees 逐步增加的; 逐级上升的: *a progressive disease*, ie one that gradually increases in its effect 进行性的疾病(逐渐严重) ○ *progressive taxation*, ie at rates that increase as the sum taxed increases 累进税 ○ *Her condition is showing a progressive improvement.* 她的情况已逐步改进. **3** (*approv* 褒) (**a**) advancing in social conditions or efficiency (社会状况)不断改善的; (效率)不断提高的: *a progressive firm, nation* 发展中的企业、国家. (**b**) favouring or showing rapid progress or reform (主张)进步或改革的; 先进的: *progressive schools, views* 先进的学校、进步的观点 ○ *a progressive education policy* 革新的教育政策 ○ *a progressive political party* 进步的政党.

▷ **pro·gress·ive** *n* person who supports a progressive(3b) policy or adopts progressive methods 支持进步的政策或采用进步的方法的人; 进步人士; 改革派人士.

pro·gress·ively *adv* increasingly; by degrees 逐渐地; 逐步地: *His eyesight is becoming progressively worse.* 他的视力越来越差.

pro·gress·ive·ness *n* [U].

□ **progressive ˈtense** (also **continuous ˈtense**) (*grammar*) any of the verb tenses which express action that continues over a period of time, using the *-ing* form, as in 'I am/was/will be/have been writing' 进行时态(动词时态, 表示某一期间持续的动作, 使用-ing形式, 如I am/was/will be/have been writing中者): *the present progressive tense* 现在进行时态.

pro·hibit /prəˈhɪbɪt; US prəʊ-; proˋhɪbɪt/ *v* (*fml* 文) **1** [Tn, Tn·pr] **~ sth/sb (from doing sth)** forbid sth or sb from doing sth esp by laws, rules or regulations 禁止某事物或某人做某事(尤指以法令、规章或条例): *Smoking is prohibited.* 禁止吸烟. ○ *a regulation to prohibit parking in the city centre* 禁止在市中心区停车的规定 ○ *The law prohibits tobacconists from selling cigarettes to children.* 法律禁止烟贩向儿童出售香烟. **2** [Tn] make (sth) impossible; prevent 使(某事物)成为不可能; 阻止: *The high cost prohibits the widespread use of the drug.* 该药昂贵而影响广泛应用.

pro·hibi·tion /ˌprəʊhɪˈbɪʃn; US ˌprəʊəˈbɪʃn; ˌproəˋbɪʃən/ *n* **1** [U] forbidding or being forbidden 禁止; 阻止: *They voted in favour of the prohibition of smoking in public areas.* 他们投票赞成禁止在公共场所吸烟. ○ *Use of the drug has not declined since its prohibition.* 自从禁用该药以来, 该药的使用并未减少. **2** [C] **~ (against sth)** edict or order that forbids sth 禁令; 禁律: *a prohibition against the sale of firearms* 禁止出售火器的法令. **3** **Prohibition** [U] period of time (1920-1933) when the making and selling of alcoholic drinks was forbidden by law in the US 禁酒时期(1920-1933年间美国以法律禁止酿酒及售酒的时期).

▷ **pro·hibi·tion·ist** /-ʃənɪst; -ʃənɪst/ *n* person who supports the prohibition of sth by law, esp the sale of alcoholic drinks 赞成以法律禁止某事物者; (尤指)赞成禁止售酒者.

pro·hib·it·ive /prəˈhɪbətɪv; US prəʊ-; proˋhɪbɪtɪv/ *adj* **1** (**a**) intended to or tending to prevent the use or purchase of sth 禁止使用或购买的; 禁止性的: *a prohibitive tax on imported cars* 对进口小汽车征收的寓禁税. (**b**) (of prices, etc) so high that one cannot afford to buy (指价格等)高得买不起的: *The cost of property in the city is prohibitive.* 城里房地产的价格高得使人望而却步. **2** that prohibits 禁止的: *prohibitive laws, road signs* 禁律、禁止通行的路标. ▷ **pro·hib·it·ively** *adv*: *prohibitively expensive* 昂贵得买不起.

pro·hib·it·ory /prəˈhɪbɪtərɪ; US prəʊˈhɪbətɔːrɪ; proˋhɪbəˌtorɪ/ *adj* (*fml* 文) intended to prohibit sth 意在禁止的: *regulations of a prohibitory nature* 意在禁止的规定.

pro·ject[1] /ˈprɒdʒekt; ˋprɑdʒɛkt/ *n* **1** (plan for a) scheme or undertaking 计划; 规划; 工程; 事业: *a housing development project* 住房建设方案 ○ *a project to establish a new national park* 建立一个新的国家公园的工程 ○ *carry out, fail in, form a project* 执行、未能实施、拟订一项计划. **2** task set as an educational exercise which requires students to do their own research and present the results (学校的)科研习作项目, 课题: *The class are doing a project on the Roman occupation of Britain.* 这个班在进行一项关于古罗马人占领不列颠的研究.

pro·ject[2] /prəˈdʒekt; prəˋdʒɛkt/ *v* **1** [Tn esp passive 尤用于被动语态] plan (a scheme, course of action, etc) 拟制(方案、行动步骤等); 计划; 规划; 设计: *a demonstration of the projected road improvement scheme* 对拟定的道路改善方案的论证 ○ *Our projected visit had to be cancelled.* 我们计划中的访问不得不取消. **2** (**a**) [Tn, Tn·pr] **~ sth (on/onto sth)** cause (light, shadow, a photographic image, etc) to fall on a surface 投射(光线、影子、影像等): *project a slide on a screen* 在银幕上放映幻灯片 ○ *project a beam of light onto a statue* 把一道光线投射在雕像上 ○ *project spotlights on a performer* 把聚光灯对准一位表演者. (**b**) [Tn] show (a film) on a screen using a film projector 放映(影片): *Will you be able to project the film for us?* 你能为我们放映那部影片吗? **3** [I, Tn, Tn·pr] **~ sth (into sth)** send or throw sth outward or forward 发射或投掷某物: *an apparatus to project missiles into space* 将导弹发射到宇宙空间的装置 ○ *An actor must learn to project (his voice).* 演员必须学习(使声音)扩及远处的发声法. ○ (*fig* 比喻) *project one's thoughts into the future* 思想未来. **4** [I, Ipr] extend outward beyond a surface; jut out 伸出; 突出: *a projecting beam* 突出的横梁 ○ *a balcony that projects over the street* 伸展到街道上的阳台. **5** [Tn·pr] **~ sth on to sb** (*psychology* 心) think, esp unconsciously, that sb shares (one's own feelings, usu unpleasant ones) 将(自己的感情, 通常为不愉快者)投射给某人; 以为(尤指潜意识地)某人也存在(与自己同样的、通常为不愉快的感情): *You mustn't project your guilt on to me*, ie assume that I feel as guilty as you do. 你不要以为我也和你一样内疚. **6** [Tn] represent (sth/sb/oneself) to others in a way that creates a strong or favourable impression 向他人表现(某事物[某人/自己])以使其产生深刻的或良好的印象: *Does the BBC World Service project a favourable view of Great Britain?* 英国广播公司的对外广播是否使听众对英国产生了好感? ○ *The party is trying to project a new image of itself as caring for the working classes.* 这个党竭力装出一付关心工人阶级的新形象. **7** [Tn] (**a**) make a systematic drawing of (a solid, esp curved, object) on a flat surface, as maps of the earth are made 作(固体物, 尤指曲线状物)之投影图. (**b**) make (a map) in this way 用投影法制作(地图). **8** [Tn, Tn·pr] **~ sth (to sth)** predict (results) based on known data; extrapolate (根据现有资料)预测(结果); 推断: *project population growth to the year 2000* 预测到2000年人口增长状况.

pro·ject·ile /prəˈdʒektaɪl; *US* -tl; prəˈdʒɛktḷ/ *n* (**a**) object (to be) shot forward, esp from a gun 抛射物; 投掷物; 发射物; (尤指)子弹, 炮弹. (**b**) self-propelling missile, eg a rocket 自行推进的发射物; 导弹; 火箭.

▷ **pro·ject·ile** *adj* that can send objects or be sent forward through air, water, etc 可投射物体的; 可通过大气、水等发射的: *projectile force* 投掷力 ○ *projectile missiles* 可发射的导弹.

pro·jec·tion /prəˈdʒekʃn; prəˈdʒɛkʃən/ *n* **1** (**a**) [U] projecting or being projected 计划; 设计; 投掷; 发射; 投射; 投影放映; 突出; 推断: *the projection of images on a screen* 影像在屏幕上的投影 ○ *film projection* 影片放映 ○ *the projection of one's feelings onto others* 把自己的感情投射给别人 ○ *the projection of a missile through the air* 导弹的发射升空. (**b**) [C] thing that is projected, esp a mental image viewed as reality (制定的)规划; (尤指)设想, 设计. **2** [C] thing that juts out from a surface 凸出物: *a projection of rock on a cliff-face* 悬崖表面凸出的岩石. **3** [C] representation of the surface of the earth on a plane surface (地图)投影图. **4** [C] estimate of future situations or trends, etc based on a study of present ones 对未来形势的估计; 预测; 推断: *sales projections for the next financial year* 对下一财政年度销售情况的预测.

▷ **pro·jec·tion·ist** /-ʃənɪst; -ʃənɪst/ *n* person whose job is to project films onto a screen, esp in a cinema 电影放映员(尤指电影院的).

□ **proˈjection room** room (esp in a cinema) from which films are projected onto a screen 放映室(尤指电影院的).

pro·jector /prəˈdʒektə(r); prəˈdʒɛktɚ/ *n* apparatus for projecting photographs or films onto a screen 放映机: *a ˈcinema projector* 电影放映机 ○ *a ˈslide projector* 幻灯机.

pro·lapse /prəʊˈlæps; proˈlæps/ *v* [I] (*medical* 医) (of an organ in the body, eg the bowel or uterus) slip forward or down so that it is out of place (指器官, 如直肠或子宫)脱垂, 脱出.

▷ **pro·lapse** /ˈprəʊlæps; ˈprolæps/ *n* (*medical* 医) (condition caused by) this movement 脱垂; 脱出.

prole /prəʊl; prol/ *n* (*infml derog* 口, 贬) member of the proletariat 无产者.

pro·let·ariat /ˌprəʊlɪˈteərɪət; ˌproləˈtɛrɪɪt/ *n* **the proletariat** [Gp] **1** class of (esp industrial and manual) workers who do not own the means of production and earn their living by working for wages 无产阶级; (尤指)工人阶级(包括产业工人和体力劳动者, 他们不占有生产资料, 依靠工资为生): *one of the proletariat* 无产阶级的一员. Cf 参看 BOURGEOISIE (BOURGEOIS). **2** (in ancient Rome) lowest class of citizen, owning no property (古罗马)民众中一无所有的最下层阶级.

pro·lif·er·ate /prəˈlɪfəreɪt; *US* prəʊ-; proˈlɪfəˌret/ *v* **1** [I] produce new growth or offspring rapidly; multiply (迅速地)繁殖; 增殖; 增生. **2** [Tn] reproduce (cells, etc) 分裂, 繁殖(细胞等). **3** [I] increase rapidly in numbers (数量)激增.

▷ **pro·lif·era·tion** /prəˌlɪfəˈreɪʃn; *US* prəʊ-; proˌlɪfə-ˈreʃən/ *n* **1** [U] proliferating or being proliferated (迅速的)繁殖; 增殖; 增生: [attrib 作定语] *a nuclear non-proliferation treaty*, ie one aimed at preventing the spread of nuclear weapons to countries that do not already possess them 禁止核扩散条约. **2** [C usu *sing* 通常作单数] rapid growth or increase 迅速的繁殖或增长.

pro·lific /prəˈlɪfɪk; prəˈlɪfɪk/ *adj* **1** (of plants, animals, etc) producing much fruit or many flowers or offspring (指动植物等)多产的, 多育的: *prolific growth* 多产植物. **2** (of a writer, an artist, etc) producing many works (指作家、艺术家等)多创作的: *a prolific author* 多产的作者 ○ *a prolific period in the composer's life* 作曲家一生中创作丰收的时期. ▷ **pro·lific·ally** /-klɪ; -klɪ/ *adv*.

pro·lix /ˈprəʊlɪks; *US* prəʊˈlɪks; proˈlɪks/ *adj* (*fml* 文) (of a speech, writer, etc) using too many words and so boring to listen to or read (指讲话、作家等)冗长而乏味的, 啰唆的: *a prolix speaker* 说话啰唆的人 ○ *Her style is tediously prolix.* 她的文章冗长而乏味. ▷ **pro·lix·ity** /prəʊˈlɪksətɪ; proˈlɪksətɪ/ *n* [U].

pro·logue (*US* also **pro·log**) /ˈprəʊlɒg; *US* -lɔːg; ˈprolɔg/ *n* **~ (to sth)** **1** introductory part of a poem or play 序诗; 开场白: *the 'Prologue' to the 'Canterbury Tales'* 《坎特伯雷故事集》的《序诗》. Cf 参看 EPILOGUE. **2** act or event that is an introduction to sth or leads up to sth; first in a series of events 引出或引致某事物的行动或事件; 一系列事件的开端; 序幕: *The signing of the agreement was a prologue to better relations between the two countries.* 签订这一协定更促进了两国的关系.

pro·long /prəˈlɒŋ; *US* -ˈlɔːŋ; prəˈlɔŋ/ *v* **1** [Tn] make (sth) longer, esp in time; extend 延长(某事物)(尤指时间); 使延伸: *drugs that help to prolong life* 延年益寿的药物 ○ *They prolonged their visit by a few days.* 他们把访问时间延长了几天. **2** (idm 习语) **prolong the ˈagony** make an unpleasant experience, a tense situation, etc last longer than necessary 延长痛苦; 将不愉快的经历、紧张局势等拖长: *Don't prolong the agony — just tell us the result!* 别再让我们着急了——快告诉我们结果吧!

▷ **pro·longa·tion** /ˌprəʊlɒŋˈgeɪʃn; *US* -lɔːŋ-; ˌprolɔŋ-ˈgeʃən/ *n* **1** [U] prolonging or being prolonged 延长; 延伸. **2** [C] addition or extension that prolongs sth 增加或延长的部分.

pro·longed *adj* [usu attrib 通常作定语] continuing for a long time 持续很久的; 长时间的: *After prolonged questioning, she finally confessed.* 她受到长时间的盘问之后, 终于承认了. ○ *There will be prolonged delays for rail travellers.* 乘火车的旅客要长时间受阻.

prom /prɒm; prɑm/ *n* (*infml* 口) **1** (*Brit*) = PROMENADE 1a. **2** (*Brit*) = PROMENADE CONCERT (PROMENADE). **3** (*US*) (often formal) dance, esp one held by a class in high school or college (通常为隆重的)舞会(尤指高中或大学班级举办的).

prom·en·ade /ˌprɒməˈnɑːd; *US* -ˈneɪd; ˌprɑməˈned/ *n* **1** (**a**) (also *Brit infml* 英式英语口语作 **prom**) public place for walking, esp a paved area along the waterfront at the seaside 公共散步场所(尤指海滨经铺筑者). (**b**) (*fml* 文) walk or ride taken in public for exercise or pleasure (为运动或消遣的)散步, 骑马, 开车兜风. **2** (*US*) formal dance or ball (隆重的)舞会.

▷ **prom·en·ade** *v* (*dated or fml* 旧或文) **1** [I] take a leisurely walk or ride in public (esp along a promenade) (在公共场所)散步, 骑马, 开车兜风(尤指于海滨区). **2** [Tn, Tn·pr] (**a**) take (sb) up and down a promenade for exercise 带着(某人)在散步场所走动: *She promenaded the children along the sea front after lunch.* 她午饭后领着孩子们沿着海滨区散步. (**b**) walk with (sb) in public, esp in order to show him off 带着(某人)散步(尤指为招摇): *He proudly promenaded his elegant companion in the park.* 他得意地领着他那标致的伴侣遛公园.

prom·en·ader *n* **1** person who promenades 在公共场所(尤指海滨区)散步、骑马或开车兜风的人. **2** person who (regularly) attends a promenade concert (经常)参加逍遥音乐会的人.

□ **promeˈnade concert** (also *infml* 口语作 **prom**) (*Brit*) concert at which part of the audience is in an area without seats where they listen to the music standing up 逍遥音乐会(部分听众在不设座位的场区站着欣赏音乐).

promeˈnade deck covered upper deck of a passenger ship, where passengers may walk (客轮的上层有篷顶的)散步甲板.

prom·in·ent /ˈprɒmɪnənt; ˈprɑmənənt/ *adj* **1** jutting out; projecting 突出的; 凸出的: *prominent cheek-bones* 突出的颧骨. **2** easily seen; conspicuous 显著的; 惹人注目的: *the most prominent feature in the landscape* 风景中最显著的特色 ○ *The house is in a prominent position on the village green.* 那房子坐落在村中草地最显眼的地方. **3** distinguished or important 杰出的; 卓越的; 重要的: *play a prominent part in public life* 在公共事务中起重要的作用 ○ *a prominent political figure* 杰出的政治人物.

▷ **prom·in·ence** /-əns; -əns/ *n* **1** [U] state of being prominent 突出; 明显; 卓越; 重要: *a young writer who has recently come to/into prominence* 近来崭露头角的青年作家 ○ *The newspapers are giving the affair considerable prominence.* 各报都以相当显著的地位报道了那件事.

2 [C] (*fml* 文) prominent thing, esp part of a landscape or building 突出的事物; 惹人注目的事物; (尤指)风景或建筑物之突出部分: *a small prominence in the middle of the level plain* 平坦的原野中央的一块小小的凸地. **prom·in·ently** *adv*: *The notice was prominently displayed.* 通知已张贴在很醒目的地方.

pro·mis·cu·ous /prəˈmɪskjʊəs; prəˋmɪskjʊəs/ *adj* **1** (*derog* 贬) not carefully chosen; indiscriminate or casual 不加选择的; 不加区别的; 随便的: *promiscuous friendships*, ie ones made without careful choice 滥交. **2** (*derog* 贬) having (esp casual) sexual relations with many people 与多人发生性行为的; (尤指)性关系随便的: *promiscuous behaviour* 性乱行为 ○ *a promiscuous lover* 有性乱行为的人. **3** (*dated fml* 旧, 文) mixed and disorderly; unsorted 混杂的; 杂乱的; 一团糟的: *piled up in a promiscuous heap* 杂乱地堆作一团. ▷ **pro·mis·cu·ity** /ˌprɒmɪˈskju:ətɪ; ˌpramɪsˋkjuətɪ/ *n* [U]: *sexual promiscuity* 性乱行为. **pro·mis·cu·ously** *adv*

P

prom·ise[1] /ˈprɒmɪs; ˋpramɪs/ *n* **1** [C] **~ (of sth)** written or spoken declaration that one will give or do or not do sth 承诺; 许诺; 诺言; 保证书: *We received many promises of help.* 许多人答应帮助我们. ○ *break/carry out/fulfil/give/keep/make a promise* 违背诺言[履行诺言/实现诺言/给予保证/遵守诺言/作出允诺] ○ *I told him the truth under a promise of secrecy.* 我在他答应保守秘密之后把真相告诉了他. ○ *I shall keep you/hold you to your promise.* 我得让你遵守诺言. ○ *'I'll come and see you soon.' 'Is that a promise?'* '我不久再来看你.' '这话算数吗?' **2** [C, U] **~ of sth** indication that sth may be expected to come or occur; likelihood or hope of sth 可指望出现或发生某事物的迹象; 可能性; 希望: *There is a promise of better weather tomorrow.* 明天天气可能更好. ○ *There seems little promise of success for the expedition.* 看来这次探险的成功希望不大. **3** [U] indication of future success or good results 将获得成就、成果或成绩的迹象: *Her work/She shows great promise.* 她的作品[她]大有前途. ○ *a scholarship for young musicians of promise* 为有发展前途的青年音乐家提供的奖学金. **4** (idm 习语) **a lick and a promise** ⇨ LICK *n*.

prom·ise[2] /ˈprɒmɪs; ˋpramɪs/ *v* **1** [I, Tn, Tf, Tt, Dn·n, Dn·pr, Dn·f] **~ sth (to sb)** make a promise (to sb); assure (sb) that one will give or do or not do sth (向某人)许诺; 答应(某人)给予某物、做或不做某事: *I can't promise, but I'll do my best.* 我不能保证做到, 但我一定尽力而为. ○ *He has promised a thorough investigation into the affair.* 他已答应彻查此事. ○ *'Do you promise faithfully to pay me back?' 'Yes, I promise.'* '你能切实保证把钱退还给我吗?' '是的, 我保证.' ○ *I have promised myself a quiet weekend.* 我打算过个清静的周末. ○ *She promised me her help.* 她答应过帮助我. ○ *The firm promised a wage increase to the workers/promised the workers a wage increase.* 公司答应给工人增加工资. ○ *She promised me (that) she would be punctual.* 她向我保证一定准时. ○ *'Promise (me) you won't forget!' 'I promise.'* '你可得答应我你别忘了!' '我答应你.' **2** [Tn, Tt] make (sth) seem likely 使(某事物)很有可能: *The clouds promise rain.* 阴云预示有雨. ○ *It promises to be warm this afternoon.* 今天下午可望转暖. **3** (idm 习语) **I (can) ˈpromise you** (*infml* 口) I assure you 我向你保证: *You won't regret it, I promise you.* 我包你满意. **promise (sb) the ˈearth/ˈmoon** (*infml* 口) make extravagant or rash promises that one is unlikely to be able to keep 作不切实际的或轻率的许诺: *Politicians promise the earth before an election, but things are different once they are in power.* 政治家在选举前空口许愿, 一旦上台就根本不是那么回事了. **the promised ˈland (a)** (in the Bible) the fertile country promised to the Israelites by God; Canaan (《圣经》)上帝许给以色列人的肥沃土地, 迦南. **(b)** any place or situation in which one expects to find happiness and security 期望中的乐土或安乐境界. **promise ˈwell** seem likely to give good results 可望产生良好结果; 大有希望: *The new sales policy promises well.* 新的销售办法可望取得良好效果.

▷ **prom·is·ing** *adj* **(a)** likely to do well; full of promise[1] (3) 有出息的; 有前途的: *a promising young pianist* 有前途的青年钢琴家. **(b)** indicating future success or good results; hopeful 大有可为的; 有希望的: *The results of the first experiments are very promising.* 第一次实验的结果充满了希望. ○ *It's a promising sign.* 这是个很好的迹象. **prom·is·ingly** *adv*.

prom·is·sory /ˈprɒmɪsərɪ; *US* -sɔ:rɪ; ˋpraməˌsorɪ/ *adj* (*fml* 文) conveying a promise 应允的; 约定的; 许诺的.
□ **ˈpromissory note** signed document containing a promise to pay a stated sum of money on demand or on a specified date 本票; 期票.

prom·on·tory /ˈprɒməntrɪ; *US* -tɔ:rɪ; ˋpramənˌtorɪ/ *n* area of high land jutting out into the sea or a lake; headland (伸入海中或湖中的)悬崖; 岬; 海角. ⇨illus at COAST 见 COAST 插图.

pro·mote /prəˈməʊt; prəˋmot/ *v* **1 (a)** [esp passive 尤用于被动语态: Tn, Tn·pr] **~ sb (to sth)** raise sb to a higher position or rank 提升、晋升或擢升某人: *She worked hard and was soon promoted.* 她工作很努力, 很快便获得提升. ○ *His assistant was promoted over his head*, ie above him. 他的助手获得提升, 地位超过了他. ○ *The football team was promoted to the first division.* 该足球队已晋升为甲级队. **(b)** [Tn·pr, Cn·n esp passive 尤用于被动语态] **~ sb (from sth) (to sth)** (*esp Brit*) raise sb to the rank of (sth) 提升某人至(某职位): *He was promoted to sergeant.* 他已提升为中士. Cf 参看 DEMOTE. **2** [Tn] help the progress of (sth); encourage or support 促进, 增进(某事物); 鼓励; 支持: *The organization works to promote friendship between nations.* 该组织旨在促进各国之间的友谊. ○ *promote a bill in Parliament*, ie take the necessary steps for it to be passed 促使某法案在议会通过. **3** [Tn] publicize (sth) in order to sell it 宣传(某物)以促进销售: *a publicity campaign to promote her new book* 为推销她的新书而开展的宣传活动.
▷ **pro·moter** *n* **(a)** person who organizes or finances (esp a business company or a sporting event) 发起人, 创办人, 筹办人, 赞助人(尤指对企业或体育比赛): *a boxing promoter* 拳击比赛的筹办人. **(b) ~ of sth** supporter of sth 某事物的支持者、倡导者: *an enthusiastic promoter of good causes* 有益活动的热心支持者.

pro·mo·tion /prəˈməʊʃn; prəˋmoʃən/ *n* **1 (a)** [U] raising or being raised to a higher rank or position 提升; 晋级: *gain/win promotion* 获得晋级 ○ *If you are successful, you can expect promotion.* 你只要做出成绩, 就能指望获得提升. ○ [attrib 作定语] *promotion prospects* 晋升的可能性. **(b)** [C] instance of this 提升; 晋升: *The new job is a promotion for her.* 这份新工作对她来说是一次提升. **2** [U] **~ of sth** encouragement or aid to the progress of (a cause) (对某事业的)促进, 提倡, 赞助: *They worked for the promotion of world peace.* 他们为促进世界和平而努力. **3 (a)** [U] advertising or other activity intended to increase the sales of a product (为推销商品而作的)广告宣传, 推销活动: *She is responsible for sales promotion.* 她负责推销工作. ○ *Advertising is often the most effective method of promotion.* 做广告往往是最有效的推销方法. **(b)** [C] advertising or publicity campaign for a particular product (某商品的)推销广告或宣传活动: *We are doing a special promotion of our paperback list.* 我们正在搞推销平装书的特别宣传活动.
▷ **pro·mo·tional** /-ʃənl; -ʃənl̩/ *adj* of or relating to promotion(3b) 推销的; 推销广告或宣传的: *a promotional tour by the author* 作者以推销作品为目的的巡游.

prompt[1] /prɒmpt; prampt/ *adj* **1** done without delay; punctual 及时的; 迅速的; 准时的: *a prompt reply* 及时的答复 ○ *Prompt payment of the invoice would be appreciated.* 即付发票款项则不胜感谢. **2 ~ (in doing sth/to do sth)** (of a person) acting without delay (指人)敏捷的, 动作迅速的: *She was very prompt in answering my letter.* 她给我写回信非常及时. ○ *They were prompt to respond to our call for help.* 他们对我们的求助迅即回应.
▷ **prompt** *adv* punctually 准时地: *at 6 o'clock prompt* 在6点正.
prompt·it·ude /ˈprɒmptɪtju:d; *US* -tu:d; ˋpramptəˌtud/ *n* [U] (*fml* 文) quality of being prompt; readiness to act 迅速; 敏捷.
promptly *adv*: *She replied promptly to my letter.* 她立即给我写了回信.
prompt·ness *n* [U].

prompt[2] /prɒmpt; prampt/ *v* **1** [Tn, Dn·t] cause or incite (sb) to do sth 促使或激励(某人)做某事: *What prompted him to be so generous?* 是什么原因使得他如此

大方呢? ○ *The accident prompted her to renew her insurance.* 这一事故促使她为投保续期. **2** [Tn] inspire or cause (a feeling or an action) 激起(感情); 唤起(行动): *Her question was prompted by worries about her future.* 她提出那个问题是因为她对前途十分忧虑. ○ *What prompted that remark?* 那话是怎么勾起来的? **3** (**a**) [Tn] help (a speaker) by suggesting the words that could or should follow 给(发言者)作提示: *The speaker was rather hesitant and had to be prompted occasionally by the chairman.* 那发言者讲话结结巴巴的, 有时得由主席提示. (**b**) [I, Tn] follow the text of a play and help (an actor) if he forgets his words, by saying the next line quietly 给(演员)提词: *Will you prompt for us at the next performance?* 下场演出时你给我们提词好吗? ○ *The actor needed to be prompted frequently.* 那演员经常需要提词.

▷ **prompt** *n* act of prompting or words spoken to prompt an actor, a speaker, etc (给予演员、发言者等的)提示, 提词: *She needed an occasional prompt.* 她需要不时给予提示.

prompter *n* person who prompts in a play 提词员.

prompt·ing *n* [C, U] (act of) urging or persuading 推动; 激励; 敦促; 驱使: *Despite several promptings from his parents the boy refused to apologize.* 尽管那男孩的父母三番五次要他认错, 那男孩就是不听. ○ *He did it without any prompting from me.* 他做这事完全不用我督促.

pro·mul·gate /ˈprɒmlgeɪt; prəˈmʌl,get/ *v* [Tn] (*fml* 文) **1** make (sth) widely known; disseminate 宣扬(某事物); 传播: *promulgate a belief, an idea, a theory, etc* 传播信仰、思想、理论等. **2** announce officially (a decree, new law etc); proclaim 公布, 颁布(法令、新法律等); 宣布.

▷ **pro·mul·ga·tion** /ˌprɒmlˈgeɪʃn; ˌprɑməlˈgeʃən/ *n* [U]: *the promulgation of a treaty* 条约的公布.

prone /prəʊn; pron/ *adj* **1** (of a person or his position) lying flat, esp face downwards (指人或其姿势)平卧的, (尤指)俯卧的: *lying prone* 俯卧的 ○ *in a prone position* 成卧倒姿势. Cf 参看 PROSTRATE 1, SUPINE 1. **2** (**a**) [pred 作表语] **~ to sth/to do sth** liable to sth or likely to do sth; inclined to do sth 易于某事物; 很可能做某事; 有做某事的倾向: *prone to infection after a cut scratch* 割伤之后易受感染 ○ *prone to fall asleep on long car journeys* 乘汽车走长路时容易打盹 ○ *He is prone to lose his temper when people disagree with him.* 人家一不同意他的意见, 他就发脾气. (**b**) (in compounds 用以构成复合词) liable or susceptible to sth specified (esp sth undesirable) 对某事物(尤指厌恶的事)有倾向或可能性的: *The child is rather ˈaccident-prone.* 那个小孩很容易出事儿. ○ *ˈstrike-prone industries* 易闹罢工的行业. ▷ **prone·ness** /ˈprəʊnnɪs; ˈpronnɪs/ *n* [U]: *proneness to injury* 易受伤的特性.

prong /prɒŋ; *US* prɔːŋ; prɔŋ/ *n* each of the two or more long pointed parts of a fork (叉的)尖齿: *One of the prongs of the garden fork went through his foot.* 园艺叉子的一个尖齿把他的脚扎了. ⇨illus at FORK 见 FORK 插图.

▷ **-pronged** (forming compound *adjs* 用以构成复合形容词) having the number or type of prongs specified 有某数量或类型的尖齿的: *a four-pronged ˈfork* ○ (*fig* 比喻) *a three-pronged atˈtack*, ie one made by three separate forces, usu advancing from different directions.

pro·nom·inal /prəʊˈnɒmɪnl; prəˈnɑmənl̩/ *adj* (*grammar*) of or like a pronoun 代词(性)的.

▷ **pro·nom·in·ally** /-nəlɪ; -nl̩ɪ/ *adv* (*grammar*) as a pronoun 作为代词: *a word used pronominally* 用作代词的词.

pro·noun /ˈprəʊnaʊn; ˈpronaʊn/ *n* (*grammar*) word used in place of a noun or noun phrase, eg *he, it, hers, me, them*, etc 代词(代替名词或名词词组者, 如he、it、hers、me、them等): *demonstrative/interrogative/personal/possessive/relative pronouns* 指示[疑问/人称/物主/关系]代词.

pro·nounce /prəˈnaʊns; prəˈnaʊns/ *v* **1** [Tn] make the sound of (a word or letter) (in a particular way) 发(词或字母)的音: *People pronounce the word differently in this part of the country.* 在国内这一地区, 这个单词的发音不同. ○ *How do you pronounce p-h-l-e-g-m? Look up 'phlegm' in the dictionary if you don't know.* 怎样念p-h-l-e-g-m这个词? 你要是不会念, 可查词典中phlegm的注音. ○ *The 'b' in 'debt' is not pronounced.* debt中的b不发音. **2** (**a**) [Tn, Tn·pr, Tf, Cn·a] declare or announce (sth) esp formally, solemnly or officially 宣称, 宣布(某事物)(尤指正式地、郑重地或以官方形式): *pronounce judgement on the issue* 宣布对这一问题的判决 ○ *The doctors pronounced him to be/that he was no longer in danger.* 医生宣称他已脱离危险. (**b**) [Cn·a esp passive 尤用于被动语态] declare (sth) as a considered opinion 断言(某事物); 表示: *The dinner was pronounced excellent by all the guests.* 所有的客人都说这顿饭好极了. ○ *She pronounced herself satisfied with the results.* 她对那结果表示满意. **3** [Ipr] (**a**) **~ for/against sb/sth** (*law* 律) pass judgement in court in favour of/against sb/sth 判决有利于[不利于]某人[某事物]: *The judge pronounced against her appeal.* 法官驳回了她的上诉请求. ○ *The inquiry pronounced for the protesters against the scheme.* 调查结果断定反对这一方案者获胜. (**b**) **~ on/upon sth** express one's opinion on sth, esp formally 就某事物发表意见; (尤指)正式表态: *The minister was asked to pronounce on the proposed new legislation.* 要求部长对提出的新法案表态.

▷ **pro·nounce·able** /-əbl; -əbl̩/ *adj* (of sounds or words) that can be pronounced (指声音)发得出的; (指词)可发音的: *I find some of the place-names barely pronounceable.* 我发现有些地名简直没法念.

pro·nounced *adj* **1** very noticeable 非常明显的: *a pronounced limp* 明显的跛行. **2** (of opinions, views, etc) strongly felt; definite (指意见、观点等)被充分感知的, 明确的: *She has very pronounced views on the importance of correct spelling.* 她极力主张拼写正确是十分重要的. **pro·nouncedly** *adv*.

pro·nounce·ment *n* **~ (on sth)** formal statement or declaration 公告; 声明: *There has been no official pronouncement yet on the state of the president's health.* 官方尚未就总统的健康状况发表公告.

pronto /ˈprɒntəʊ; ˈprɑnto/ *adv* (*infml* 口) at once; quickly 立刻; 马上; 很快地: *I want this rubbish cleared away pronto!* 把这些垃圾立即给我弄走!

pro·nun·ci·ation /prəˌnʌnsɪˈeɪʃn; prəˌnʌnsɪˈeʃən/ *n* **1** (**a**) [U] way in which a language is spoken (一种语言的)发音(法): *She had difficulty learning English pronunciation.* 她学习英语发音有困难. (**b**) way a person speaks (the words of) a language (一个人的)发音, 发音方式: *Their English pronunciation is not good, but it is improving.* 他们的英语发音不够好, 但正在改进. **2** [C] way in which a word is pronounced (一个字的)发音(法), 读法: *Which of these three pronunciations is the most usual?* 这三种读法中, 哪一种最常用?

proof[1] /pruːf; pruf/ *n* **1** [C, U] (piece of) evidence that shows, or helps to show, that sth is true or is a fact 证据; 证物; 证言: *What proofs have you that the statement is correct?* 你有什么证据可以证明这种说法是正确的呢? ○ *Have you any proof that you are the owner of the car?* 你有证据证明这汽车是属于你的吗? ○ *written proof* 书面证明 ○ *documentary proof of his ownership of the land* 证明他领有该地的文件. **2** [U] testing of whether sth is true or a fact; demonstration or proving 验证; 证明; 证实: *Is the claim capable of proof?* 这要求能证明是合理的吗? **3** [U] standard of strength in distilled alcoholic liquors on a scale in which proof spirit is 100% (酒的)标准酒精度: *The liquor is 80% proof.* 这种酒为标准度数的80%. ○ *The rum is 30% below proof.* 朗姆酒低于标准度数30%. **4** (**a**) [C esp *pl* 尤作复数] trial copy of printed material produced so that corrections may be made 校样: *check/correct/read the proofs of a book* 校对[修改/审阅]某书的校样 ○ *pass the proofs for press*, ie approve them, so that printing may begin 同意清样付印 ○ *galley-/page-proofs* 长条[分页]校样 ○ [attrib 作定语] *a proof copy* 校样稿. (**b**) [C] trial print of a photograph 照相样片: *proofs of the wedding photos* 结婚照的样片. (**c**) [U] stage in book production when proofs have been made 校样阶段: *I read the book in proof.* 我审阅了这书的样稿. **5** [C] (*mathematics* 数) sequence of steps or statements that shows the truth of a proposition 验算; 验证: *the proof of a theorem*, ie in geometry (几何)定理的证明. **6** (idm 习语) **be living proof of sth** ⇨ LIVING. **the proof of the ˈpudding (is in the ˈeating)** (*saying* 谚) the real value of sb/sth can be judged only from practical experience and not from appearance or theory 布丁好不好, 吃了才知道(评价人或事物只能凭

P

实际体验不能凭表象或理论): *The new machine is supposed to be the solution to all our production problems, but the proof of the pudding is in the eating.* 新机器按说能够解决我们生产上的一切问题, 然而能否做到这一点还有待于实践的检验. **put sb/sth to the 'proof/'test** test sb/sth; test the truth of sth 考验某人[某事物]; 对某事物的真实性加以检验: *Let's put his theory to the proof.* 让我们来检验一下他的说法吧. ○ *The crisis put his courage and skill to the test.* 这次危难是对他的勇气和技能的考验.

□ **'proof-read** *v* [I, Tn] read and correct (proofs) 校对: *It is part of your duties to proof-read.* 校对是你的分内之事. ○ *proof-read twenty pages* 校对二十页. **'proof-reader** *n*.

,proof 'spirit mixture of alcohol and water at standard strength 标准烈度的酒.

proof[2] /pru:f; pruf/ *adj* **1** [attrib 作定语] **~ against sth** (**a**) providing protection against sth 可防某事物的; 有防护作用的: *The shelter was proof against the bitter weather.* 这个棚子可以避寒. (**b**) that can resist sth 能抵御某事物的: *proof against temptation* 能抵制诱惑的. **2** (in compounds 用以构成复合词) that can resist sth or protect against sth specified 抗…的; 防…的; 耐…的: *,leak-proof 'batteries* 防漏电池 ○ *Are these batteries 'leak-proof?* 这些电池能防止漏电吗? ○ *,bullet-proof 'glass* ○ *a ,sound-proof 'room* ○ *,waterproof 'clothing.*

▷ **proof** *v* [Tn] (*fml* 文) treat (sth) in order to make it proof against sth (esp fabric in order to make it waterproof) 对(某物)进行处理使具有耐防某事物之特性; (尤指)对(织物)作防水处理.

prop 支撑物

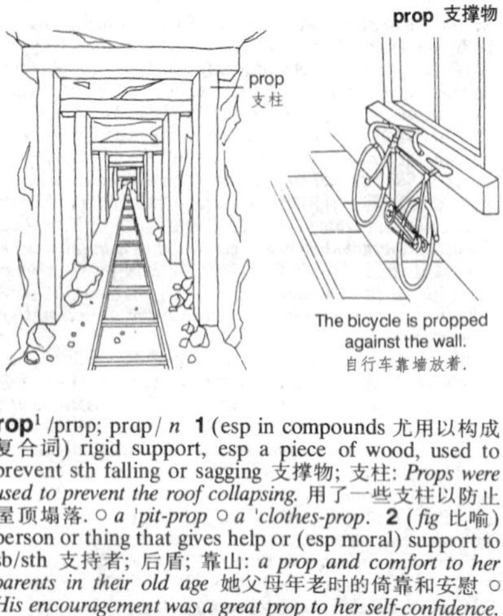

The bicycle is propped against the wall.
自行车靠墙放着.

prop[1] /prɒp; prɑp/ *n* **1** (esp in compounds 尤用以构成复合词) rigid support, esp a piece of wood, used to prevent sth falling or sagging 支撑物; 支柱: *Props were used to prevent the roof collapsing.* 用了一些支柱以防止屋顶塌落. ○ *a 'pit-prop* ○ *a 'clothes-prop.* **2** (*fig* 比喻) person or thing that gives help or (esp moral) support to sb/sth 支持者; 后盾; 靠山: *a prop and comfort to her parents in their old age* 她父母年老时的倚靠和安慰 ○ *His encouragement was a great prop to her self-confidence.* 有了他的鼓励, 她的自信心大大增强了.

▷ **prop** *v* (**-pp-**) **1** (**a**) [Tn, Tn·pr, Cn·a] support (sth) or keep (sth) in position with a prop 支住(某物); 用支撑物固定(某物): *The invalid lay propped on the pillows.* 那病弱者倚靠在枕头上. ○ *He used a box to prop the door open.* 他用盒子顶住门, 让门开着. (**b**) [Tn·pr] **~ sb/sth against sth** lean sb/sth against sth (so that it does not fall down) 使某人[某物]倚靠在某物上: *She propped her bicycle against the wall.* 她把自行车靠墙放好. ○ *He propped himself against the gatepost.* 他倚着门柱. ⇨illus 见插图. **2** (phr v) **prop sth up** (**a**) use a prop or props to raise sth and prevent it from falling 支撑起某物; 支住某物: *The roof will have to be propped up while repairs are carried out.* 那屋顶在修理时要用东西支住. ○ *The baby cannot sit unaided — she has to be propped up on pillows.* 那婴儿还不会坐——得让她倚着枕头才行. (**b**) (*often derog* 常作贬义) support sth that would otherwise fail 支持某事物: *The government refuses to prop up inefficient industries.* 政府拒绝补贴效益不佳的行业. ○ *The regime had been propped up by foreign aid.* 该政权是靠外国援助维持着的.

□ **'prop-word** *n* (*grammar*) the word *one* (or *ones*) when used to stand for a noun, esp a noun that has been mentioned previously, as in *'Which piece would you like?' 'I'd like the bigger one.'* 代替词(即 one 或 ones, 用以代替名词, 尤其是代替前面提到的某名词, 如'Which piece would you like?' 'I' d like the bigger one.').

prop[2] /prɒp; prɑp/ *n* (*infml* 口) = PROPELLER.

prop[3] /prɒp; prɑp/ *n* (*infml* 口) = PROPERTY 5.

pro·pa·ganda /,prɒpə'gændə; ,prɑpə'gændə/ *n* [U] (**a**) publicity that is intended to spread ideas or information which will persuade or convince people (观念的)宣传; (信息的)传播: *There has been so much propaganda against smoking that many people have given it up.* 反对吸烟的宣传很多, 许多人因而戒了烟. (**b**) (*derog* 贬) ideas or statements that are intended as publicity for a particular (political) cause but are (often) presented as being unbiased 为某(政治)利益服务却(常作)貌似不含偏见的宣传: *The play is sheer political propaganda.* 那出戏剧纯属政治宣传. ○ *The people want information from the government, not propaganda.* 人民要政府讲实话, 而不是玩弄宣传伎俩. ○ [attrib 作定语] *propaganda films, plays, posters, etc* 宣传的影片、戏剧、海报等.

▷ **pro·pa·gand·ist** /-dɪst; -dɪst/ *n* (*often derog* 常作贬义) person who creates or spreads propaganda 宣传者; 鼓吹者: *anti-smoking propagandists* 宣传戒烟者 ○ *political propagandists* 政治宣传家.

pro·pa·gand·ize, -ise /-daɪz; -daɪz/ *v* (*fml often derog* 文, 常作贬义) (**a**) [I] spread or organize propaganda (进行)宣传; 搞宣传活动. (**b**) [Tn] spread (sth) by propaganda 宣传(某事物): *propagandize political ideology* 宣传政治观点. (**c**) [Tn] spread propaganda to (a group, class, nation, etc) 向(某团体、阶级、国家等)宣传.

prop·ag·ate /'prɒpəgeɪt; 'prɑpə,get/ *v* **1** [Tn] increase the number of (plants, animals, etc) by a natural process from the parent stock 繁殖(动植物等); 使增殖: *propagate plants from seeds and cuttings* 由种子和枝条繁殖植物 ○ *propagate plants by taking cuttings* 藉插枝繁殖植物. **2** [I, Tn] (of plants) reproduce (themselves) (指植物)繁殖, 繁衍, 增殖: *Plants won't propagate in these conditions.* 植物在这种条件下不能繁殖. ○ *Trees propagate themselves by seeds.* 树木靠种子繁衍. **3** [Tn] (*fml* 文) spread (views, knowledge, beliefs, etc) more widely 传播(观点、知识、信仰等): *Missionaries went far afield to propagate their faith.* 传教士到远方去传播其信仰. **4** [Tn] (*fml* 文) cause or allow (sth) to pass through sth; transmit 促使或准许(某物)通过他物; 传导; 传送: *propagate vibrations through rock* 通过岩石传导震动.

▷ **pro·pa·ga·tion** /,prɒpə'geɪʃn; ,prɑpə'geʃən/ *n* [U] propagating or being propagated 繁殖; 增殖; 传播; 传送: *the propagation of plants from cuttings* 植物的插枝繁殖.

prop·ag·ator person or thing that propagates 繁殖者; 传播者: *tomato plants growing in a propagator* 在繁育场中栽培的西红柿植株.

pro·pane /'prəʊpeɪn; 'propen/ *n* [U] (*chemistry* 化) type of colourless gas, found in natural gas and petroleum and used as a fuel 丙烷.

pro·pel /prə'pel; prə'pɛl/ *v* (**-ll-**) [Tn, Tn·pr] move, drive or push (sth) forward 推进, 驱动, 推(某物): *mechanically propelled vehicles* 机动车辆 ○ *a boat propelled by oars* 用桨划的船 ○ (*fig* 比喻) *His addiction to drugs propelled him towards a life of crime.* 他吸毒成瘾使他走上犯罪的道路.

▷ **pro·pel·lant** (also **pro·pel·lent**) /-ənt; -ənt/ *n* [C, U] propelling agent, eg an explosive that propels a bullet from a weapon, a fuel that provides thrust for a rocket, or compressed gas that forces out the contents of an aerosol container 推进剂(如武器的发射火药、火箭的燃料、喷雾容器中用以产生压力的压缩气体等).

pro·pel·lent /-ənt; -ənt/ *adj* that propels 推进的; 起推动作用的: *a propellent agent* 推进剂.

pro·pel·ler (also **'screw-propeller**, *infml* 口语作 **prop**) *n* two or more spiral blades fixed to a revolving shaft for propelling a ship or an aircraft (轮船或飞机的)推进器, 螺旋桨.

□ **pro,pelling 'pencil** pencil with a lead that can be moved forwards by turning the outer case 自动铅笔.

pro·pen·sity /prə'pensətɪ; prə'pɛnsətɪ/ *n* **~ (for/to/**

towards sth); ~ (**for doing/to do sth**) (*fml* 文) inclination or tendency 倾向; 习性: *a propensity to exaggerate/towards exaggeration* 浮夸的倾向 ○ *a propensity for getting into debt* 借债的习性.

proper /ˈprɒpə(r); ˋprɑpɚ/ *adj* **1** (**a**) that fits, belongs or is suitable; fitting or appropriate 适合的; 适当的; 适宜的; 适用的; 恰当的: *clothes proper for the occasion* 适于那种场合的衣服 ○ *the proper tool for the job* 适用于这种工作的工具 ○ *The teapot has lost its proper lid but this one will do instead.* 茶壶盖儿不见了, 但这个可代替使用. (**b**) [attrib 作定语] according to the rules; right or correct 遵守规则的; 正确的; 对的: *the proper way to hold the bat* 正确的执拍方法 ○ *The reels of film were not in the proper order.* 电影胶片卷盘的顺序弄错了. **2** according to or respecting social conventions; respectable 遵照或尊重社会习俗的; 可敬的; 体面的: *After a very proper upbringing he chose to lead the Bohemian life of an artist.* 他受过正统的教育, 却立意过着艺术家我行我素的生活. ○ *She's not at all a proper person for you to know.* 她可不是正派人, 你不应该结识她. Cf 参看 IMPROPER. **3** (**a**) [attrib 作定语] (*infml* 口) being in fact what it is called; genuine 名副其实的; 真正的: *She hadn't had a proper holiday for years.* 多年来她都没有过真正的假期. ○ *It was discovered that he was not a proper* (ie qualified) *doctor.* 已经发现他并不是合格的医生. (**b**) (placed after the *n* 置于名词之后) strictly so called; itself 严格而言的; 本身的: *You have to wait in a large entrance hall before being shown into the court proper.* 进入皇宫时先要在入口大厅等候, 由人带领进入正殿. ○ *Students have to do a year's preparation before they start the degree course proper.* 学生要先念一年预科, 然后才能开始攻读学位课程. **4** [attrib 作定语] (*infml* 口) thorough; complete 彻底的; 十足的: *We're in a proper mess now.* 我们现在真是一团糟. ○ *He gave the burglar a proper hiding,* ie beat him thoroughly. 他给了那窃贼一顿痛打. **5** (idm 习语) **do the proper/right thing (by sb)** ⇨ THING. **prim and proper** ⇨ PRIM.

▷ **properly** *adv* **1** in a proper manner 适当地; 恰当地; 循规蹈矩地; 正确地; 可敬地; 真正地; 严格地: *She will have to learn to behave properly.* 她要懂得检点些. ○ *Do it properly or don't do it at all.* 要干就得好好干. ○ *He is not properly* (ie strictly) *speaking a member of the staff.* 严格说来, 他不算是职员. **2** (*infml* 口) thoroughly 彻底地: *He got properly beaten by the world champion.* 他被那个世界冠军打得惨败.

□ ˌ**proper** ˈ**fraction** (*mathematics* 数) fraction that has a lower number above the line than below 真分数: $\frac{1}{2}$, $\frac{3}{4}$, $\frac{19}{20}$ *are proper fractions.* $\frac{1}{2}$、$\frac{3}{4}$、$\frac{19}{20}$都是真分数. Cf 参看 IMPROPER FRACTION (IMPROPER).

ˈ**proper name** (also ˈ**proper noun**) (*grammar*) name of an individual person, place, etc (written with an initial capital letter), eg *Jane, Mr Smith, London, Europe, the Thames* 专有名词(人、地等的专用称呼, 书写时以大写字母开头, 如Jane简、Mr Smith史密斯先生、London伦敦、Europe欧洲、the Thames泰晤士河).

prop·erty /ˈprɒpətɪ; ˋprɑpɚtɪ/ *n* **1** [U] thing or things owned; possession (s) 所有物; 财产; 资产: *Don't touch those tools — they are not your property.* 不要动那些工具——那不是你的东西. ○ *The jewels were her personal property.* 这些首饰是她的私人财产. **2** (**a**) [U] land and buildings; real estate 房地产; 不动产: *a man/woman of property,* ie one who owns property 有房地产的男人[女人] ○ *She invested her money in property.* 她进行房地产投资. ○ [attrib 作定语] *property development, management, speculation* 房地产开发、管理、投机. (**b**) [C] (*fml* 文) piece of land and its buildings (一处)房地产: *He has a property in the West Country.* 他在英格兰西南部有一处房地产. ○ *A fence divides the two properties.* 有一道栅栏隔着这两处房地产. **3** [U] (*fml* 文) owning or being owned; ownership 所有; 所有权: *Property brings duties and responsibilities.* 有了财产也就有了义务和责任. **4** [C esp *pl* 尤作复数] (*fml* 文) special quality or characteristic of a substance, etc (物质等的)特性, 性质: *Certain plants have medicinal* (ie healing) *properties.* 某些植物具有药物效用. ○ *the soothing properties of an ointment* 一种油膏的止痛性能 ○ *Paraffin has the property of dissolving grease.* 石蜡具有溶解油脂的特性. **5** [C usu *pl* 通常作复数] (also *infml* 口语作 **prop**) (on a stage or a film set) movable object, eg a piece of furniture or a costume, used in a performance (舞台上或电影布景中)表演用的可移动物件(道具或服装): *She was responsible for buying the properties for the television series.* 她负责采购电视系列片所用的道具. **6** (idm 习语) **public property** ⇨ PUBLIC.

▷ **prop·er·tied** /ˈprɒpətɪd; ˋprɑpɚtɪd/ *adj* (*fml* 文) owning property, esp land 有产的; (尤指)有地产的: *The tax will affect only the propertied classes.* 该税项仅影响有房地产的阶层.

proph·ecy /ˈprɒfəsɪ; ˋprɑfəsɪ/ *n* **1** [U] (power of) saying what will happen in the future 预言(能力): *He seemed to have the gift of prophecy.* 他似乎有预言的天赋. ○ *All these events had been revealed by prophecy.* 所有这些事以前都有过预言. **2** [C] statement that tells what will happen in the future 预言: *prophecies of disaster* 对灾祸的预言 ○ *Her prophecy was proved to be correct.* 她的预言都已实现.

proph·esy /ˈprɒfəsaɪ; ˋprɑfəˌsaɪ/ *v* (*pt, pp* **-sied**) **1** [I, Ip] ~ (**of sth**) foretell future events; speak as a prophet; make prophecies 预告未来; 作预言. **2** [Tn, Tf, Tw] say (what will happen in the future); foretell 预告(某事); 预言: *He prophesied the strange events that were to come.* 他预言要有怪事发生. ○ *They prophesied correctly that the Conservatives would win the election.* 他们预言保守党人在选举中获胜, 果然不出所料. ○ *He refused to prophesy when the economy would begin to improve.* 他不愿推测经济何时好转.

prophet /ˈprɒfɪt; ˋprɑfɪt/ *n* (*fem* 阴性作 **proph·et·ess** /ˈprɒfɪtes, *also* ˌprɒfɪˈtes; ˋprɑfɪtɪs/) **1** [C] person who tells, or claims to be able to tell, what will happen in the future 预言者; 预言家: (*joc* 谑) *I'm afraid I'm no weather prophet.* 我可不会预测天气. **2** (**a**) (also **Prophet**) [C] (in the Christian, Jewish and Muslim religions) person who teaches religion and is, or claims to be, inspired by God (基督教、犹太教及伊斯兰教的)先知(宣讲教义并称受到神灵启示者): *the Prophets of the Old Testament* 《旧约》中的先知. (**b**) **the Prophet** [sing] the founder of the Muslim religion, Mohammed 穆罕默德(伊斯兰教创立人). (**c**) **the Prophets** [pl] the prophetical books of the Old Testament (《旧约》中的)先知书. **3** [C] ~ (**of sth**) spokesman or advocate of a new belief, cause, theory, etc (一种新的信仰、事业、理论等的)鼓吹者, 提倡者: *William Morris was one of the early prophets of socialism.* 威廉·莫里斯是社会主义的早期鼓吹者之一. **4** (idm 习语) **a** ˌ**prophet of** ˈ**doom** person who holds or expresses pessimistic views about sth, esp about the future of the world 对某事物(尤指对世界的未来)持悲观看法或散布悲观言论者: *If we had listened to the prophets of doom, we would never have started the project.* 要是我们听信那些悲观者的论调, 那工程就永远不可能上马.

proph·etic /prəˈfetɪk; prəˋfɛtɪk/ (also **proph·et·ical** /prəˈfetɪkl; prəfɛtɪkḷ/) *adj* (*fml* 文) **1** of or like a prophet or prophets (似)预言家的; (似)先知的. **2** ~ (**of sth**) predicting or containing a prediction 预言的; 预告的; 含预言成分的: *prophetic remarks* 带有预言性质的话 ○ *Her early achievements were prophetic of her future greatness.* 她早期的成就预示了她日后卓尔不群.

▷ **proph·et·ic·ally** /-klɪ; -klɪ/ *adv*: *We were to realize years later how prophetically he spoke on that occasion.* 若干年后我们就能体会他当时说的话多有预见.

pro·phy·lactic /ˌprɒfɪˈlæktɪk; ˌprɑfəˋlæktɪk/ *adj* (*fml* 文) tending to prevent a disease or misfortune 预防(疾病或灾祸)的.

▷ **pro·phy·lactic** *n* (*fml* 文) **1** prophylactic medicine, device or course of action 有预防作用的药物、器具、措施或方法. **2** (*esp US*) = CONDOM.

pro·phy·laxis /-ˈlæksɪs; -ˋlæksɪs/ *n* [U] (*fml* 文) preventive treatment against disease, etc (疾病等的)预防.

pro·pin·quity /prəˈpɪŋkwətɪ; proˋpɪŋkwətɪ/ *n* [U] (*fml* 文) (**a**) nearness in space or time (空间或时间上的)接近, 邻近: *The neighbours lived in close propinquity to each other.* 这些邻居住得很近. (**b**) close blood relationship; consanguinity 近亲关系; 血亲.

pro·pi·ti·ate /prəˈpɪʃɪeɪt; prəˋpɪʃɪˌet/ *v* [Tn] (*fml* 文) win the favour or forgiveness of (sb) (esp when he is angry) by a pleasing act; appease or placate 讨好(某人); 求得(某人)原谅; (尤指)哄(某人)息怒; 劝解; 抚慰: *They* *offered sacrifices to propitiate the gods.* 他们供奉祭品以求神息怒.

▷ **pro·pi·ti·ation** /prəˌpɪʃɪˈeɪʃn; prəˌpɪʃɪˈeʃən/ *n* [U] **~ (of sb); ~ (for sth)**: *propitiation of the gods* 求神饶恕 ○ *in propitiation for their sins* 以宽恕他们的罪过.

pro·pi·ti·at·ory /prəˈpɪʃɪətrɪ; *US* -tɔːrɪ; prəˈpɪʃɪəˌtɔrɪ/ *adj* (*fml* 文) serving or intended to propitiate 谋求好感的; 请求原谅的; 哄人息怒的; 劝解的; 抚慰的: *a propitiatory gift, remark, smile* 赔礼道歉的礼物、言语、微笑.

pro·pi·tious /prəˈpɪʃəs; prəˈpɪʃəs/ *adj* **~ (for sth)** (*fml* 文) giving or indicating a good chance of success; favourable 吉利的; 有利的: *It was not a propitious time to start a new business.* 这时候开张不吉利. ○ *The circumstances were not propitious for further expansion of the company.* 这些情况不利于公司的进一步发展. ▷ **pro·pi·tiously** *adv*.

P

prop-jet /ˈprɒpdʒet; ˈprɑpˌdʒɛt/ *n* = TURBO-PROP.

pro·ponent /prəˈpəʊnənt; prəˈponənt/ *n* **~ (of sth)** person who supports a cause, theory, etc (某事业、理论等的)支持者, 拥护者, 倡导者: *one of the leading proponents of the Channel Tunnel* 修建英吉利海峡隧道的主要倡议者之一.

pro·por·tion /prəˈpɔːʃn; prəˈpɔrʃən/ *n* **1** [C] comparative part or share of a whole; fraction 部分; 分儿; 局部: *a large proportion of the earth's surface* 地球表面的大部分 ○ *The proportion of the population still speaking the dialect is very small.* 只有少数居民仍使用这种方言. ○ *A fixed proportion of the fund is invested in British firms.* 资金中有一固定部分是投资于英国企业的. **2** [U] **~ (of sth to sth)** relation of one thing to another in quantity, size, etc; ratio 一物与他物在数量、大小等方面的关系; 比例; 比: *The proportion of imports to exports* (ie excess of imports over exports) *is worrying the government.* 进口与出口的比例(入超)令政府担忧. ○ *the proportion of passes to failures in the final examination* 期末考试中及格者与不及格者的比例 ○ *What is the proportion of men to women in the population?* 人口中男女的比例是多少? **3** [U, C usu *pl* 作不可数名词或可数名词, 后者通常作复数] correct or ideal relation in size, degree, etc between one thing and another or between the parts of a whole 均衡; 匀称; 协调; 和谐: *the classical proportions of the room* 这房间的匀称协调 ○ *The two windows are in admirable proportion.* 这两扇窗户十分相称. **4 proportions** [pl] measurements or dimensions; size 面积; 体积; 规模; 程度; 大小: *a ship of impressive proportions* 巨大的船 ○ *a painting of huge proportions* 一幅巨画. **5** [U] (*mathematics* 数) relationship between four numbers in which the ratio of the first two equals the ratio of the second two 比例: *'4 is to 8 as 6 is to 12' is a statement of proportion.* '4比8与6比12的比例相等'是一种有关比例的陈述. **6** (idm 习语) ˌ**in** ˈ**proportion (a)** in the correct relation to other things 相称; 符合比例: *Try to draw the figures in the foreground in proportion.* 要把前景中的人物画得合比例. ○ *Her features are in proportion*, ie are of the correct size relative to each other. 她五官端正. ○ *get/see things in proportion* 办事情[看问题]恰如其分 ○ *Try to see the problem in proportion — it could be far worse.* 看问题要恰如其分——事情有可能糟得多. **(b)** (*mathematics* 数) having equal ratios 有相同的比值: $\frac{5}{8}$ *and* $\frac{10}{16}$ *are in proportion.* $\frac{5}{8}$ 和 $\frac{10}{16}$ 比值相同. **in proportion to sth** relative to sth 相对于某事物来说; 与某物成比例: *The room is wide in proportion to its height.* 这房间就其高度的比例而言是很宽的. ○ *Payment will be in proportion to the work done, not to the time spent doing it.* 报酬将与工作量成比例, 而不是与花费的时间成比例. ˌ**out of** ˈ**proportion (to sth)** in the wrong relation (to other things) 不相称; 不成比例: *The figures of the horses in the foreground are out of proportion.* 前景中的马画得不成比例. ○ *Her head is out of proportion to the size of her body.* 她的头部与身体大小不成比例. **out of (all) proportion to sth** too large, serious, etc in relation to sth 对某事物来说过大、过于严重等: *prices out of all proportion to income* 与收入完全脱节的高价 ○ *punishment that was out of all proportion to the offence committed* 罚不当罪.

▷ **pro·por·tioned** *adj* (esp in compounds 尤用以构成复合词) having the proportions (PROPORTION 4) specified (面积、体积、规模、程度、大小)有某种比例关系的: *a well-proportioned room* 各方面都很匀称的房间.

pro·por·tional /prəˈpɔːʃənl; prəˈpɔrʃənl̩/ *adj* **~ (to sth)** (*fml* 文) corresponding in size, amount or degree (to sth); in the correct proportion (与某事物在大小、数量或程度上)相称的, 成比例的: *Payment will be proportional to the amount of work done.* 酬金将与工作量成比例. ▷ **pro·por·tion·ally** /-ʃənəlɪ; -ʃnəlɪ/ *adv*.

□ **proˌportional ˌrepresenˈtation** (*abbr* 缩写 **PR**) electoral system that gives each party a number of seats in proportion to the number of votes its candidates receive 比例代表制(按各政党候选人所得票数之比例分配席位的选举制度). Cf 参看 FIRST PAST THE POST (FIRST[1]).

pro·por·tion·ate /prəˈpɔːʃənət; prəˈpɔrʃənɪt/ *adj* **~ (to sth)** (*fml* 文) in proportion (to sth); corresponding to sth (与某事物)成比例的; 与某事物相称的: *The price increases are proportionate to the increases in the costs of production.* 价格的上涨与生产成本的增加成比例. ▷ **pro·por·tion·ately** *adv*: *Costs have risen, and prices will rise proportionately.* 成本增加了, 价格也要相应提高.

pro·posal /prəˈpəʊzl; prəˈpozl̩/ *n* **1** [U] action of suggesting or putting forward 提议; 建议: *the proposal of new terms for a peace treaty* 缔结和平条约新条款的建议. **2** [C] **~ (for sth/doing sth); ~ (to do sth)** thing that is suggested; plan or scheme 提案; 建议; 计划; 方案: *a proposal for uniting the two companies* 将两公司联合起来的建议 ○ *Various proposals were put forward for increasing sales.* 为提高销售额而提出了各种的建议. ○ *a proposal to offer a discount to regular customers* 对经常性的主顾予以折扣优惠的方案. **3** [C] suggestion or request, esp from a man to a woman, that the two should marry 求婚(尤指男向女): *She had had many proposals (of marriage) but preferred to remain single.* 许多人向她求过婚, 但她愿过独身生活.

pro·pose /prəˈpəʊz; prəˈpoz/ *v* **1** [Tn, Tf, Tg] offer or put forward (sth) for consideration; suggest 提议, 建议(某事物): *The motion* (ie for debate) *was proposed by Mr X and seconded by Mrs Y.* 那动议经X先生提出有Y夫人附议. ○ *The committee proposed that new legislation should be drafted.* 委员会建议着手起草新法规. Cf 参看 SECOND[3] 2. **2** [Tn, Tt, Tg] have (sth) as one's plan or intention; intend 打算, 计划(某事物); 意欲: *I propose an early start/to make an early start/making an early start tomorrow.* 我打算明天早早出发. **3** [I, Ipr, Tn, Dn·pr] **~ (sth) (to sb)** suggest or offer marriage (to sb), esp formally (向某人)求婚(尤指正式地): *He was trying to decide whether he should propose (to her).* 他反复思量是否该(向她)求婚. ○ *He had proposed marriage, unsuccessfully, twice already.* 他已经两次求婚, 均未成功. **4** [Tn·pr, Cn·n/a] **~ sb for sth; ~ sb as sth** put forward (sb/sb's name) for an office, membership of a club, etc; nominate sb 推荐(某人)(担任某职、成为某俱乐部之成员等); 提名某人: *propose him for membership of the society* 推荐他为协会会员 ○ *I propose Mary Davies as a candidate for the presidency.* 我提名玛丽·戴维斯为总裁候选人. **5** (idm 习语) **propose sb's** ˈ**health/a** ˈ**toast** ask people to drink to sb's health and happiness 提议为某人的健康和幸福而干杯: *I should like to propose a toast to the bride and bridegroom.* 我提议为新娘新郎的幸福干杯.

▷ **pro·poser** *n* person who proposes (esp a motion, a candidate for office, etc) 提议人; 建议人; (尤指)提出动议者, 推荐者. Cf 参看 SECONDER (SECOND[3]).

pro·posi·tion /ˌprɒpəˈzɪʃn; ˌprɑpəˈzɪʃən/ *n* **1 ~ (that...)** statement that expresses a judgement or an opinion; assertion 观点; 见解; 主张: *The proposition is so clear that it needs no explanation.* 观点十分明确, 无须解释. **2 ~ (to do sth/that...)** thing that is proposed, esp in business; suggestion 提议, 建议(尤指业务上的): *I made what I hoped was an attractive proposition.* 我希望我提的建议能吸引买家. ○ *a proposition to merge the two firms/that the two firms should merge* 将两家商行合并的提议. **3** (*infml* 口) matter to be dealt with; problem or task 要处理的事; 问题; 任务: *It's a tough/not an easy proposition.* 这是一件棘手的[不好办的]事. ○ *Keeping a shop in this village is not a paying proposition*, ie not profitable. 在这个村子里开设商店是一桩亏本的买卖. **4** (*geometry* 几) formal statement of a theorem or problem, usu containing its proof 定理; 命题.

▷ **pro·posi·tion** *v* [Tn] propose sexual intercourse to

(a woman), esp in a direct and offensive way 向(女方)提出性交要求(尤指直言而放肆); 求欢: *She was propositioned several times in the course of the evening.* 整个晚上有人几次向她提出非分要求.

pro·pound /prə'paʊnd; prə'paund/ *v* [Tn] (*fml* 文) put (sth) forward for consideration or solution 将(某事物)提请考虑; 提出(某事物)以求解决: *propound an idea, a problem, a question, a theory, etc* 提出一个主意、一个问题、一个疑问、一种理论等.

pro·pri·et·ary /prə'praɪətrɪ; US -terɪ; prə'praɪə,tɛrɪ/ *adj* [usu attrib 通常作定语] **1** (**a**) (of goods) manufactured and sold by a particular firm, usu under patent (指货物)独家制造和销售的, (通常指)专利的: *proprietary medicines* 专卖药品 ○ *proprietary brands* 专利商标. (**b**) (in this dictionary abbreviated as **propr**) (of a brand name) owned and used exclusively by a particular firm (本词典略作**propr**专利名)(指商标名称)专利的: *a proprietary name*, eg Kodak for cameras and films 专利名称(如照相机及胶片所用的柯达牌商标) ○ *'Xerox' is a proprietary name and may not be used by other makers of photocopiers.* '施乐'为专利名称, 制造复印机的其他厂家不得采用. **2** of or relating to an owner or ownership 所有的; 所有权的: *proprietary rights* 所有权.

pro·pri·etor /prə'praɪətə(r); prə'praɪətə/ *n* (*fem* 阴性作 **pro·pri·et·ress** /prə'praɪətrɪs; prə'praɪətrɪs/) owner, esp of a business firm, hotel or patent 所有者, 业主, 老板(尤指商行、旅馆或专利): *Complaints about standards of service should be addressed to the proprietor.* 对服务态度有意见者可向老板投诉. ○ *a newspaper proprietor* 报纸老板.

▷ **pro·pri·et·or·ial** /prə,praɪə'tɔːrɪəl; prə,praɪə'tɔrɪəl/ *adj* (*often derog* 常作贬义) of, like or relating to a proprietor 所有者的; 俨然如所有者的; 与所有者有关的: *She resented the proprietorial way he used her car for trips about town.* 他把她的汽车当成自己的车在城里开着到处跑, 她对此十分不满.

pro·pri·ety /prə'praɪətɪ; prə'praɪətɪ/ *n* (*fml* 文) **1** (**a**) [U] state of being correct in one's social or moral behaviour 合乎社交或道德规范的举止; 得体: *behave with perfect propriety* 举止极为得体 ○ *The way tourists dress offends local standards of propriety.* 这些游客的穿着在当地人的眼中简直不成体统. (**b**) **the proprieties** [pl] details of the rules of correct behaviour 行为规范; 礼节; 规矩: *Her use of obscene language offends against the proprieties.* 她使用下流的语言是很失礼的事. ○ *Be careful to observe the proprieties.* 注意遵守礼仪. **2** [U] **~ (of sth)** rightness or suitability; fitness 正确; 适当; 合宜: *I am doubtful about the propriety of granting such a request*, ie doubt whether it is right. 我怀疑答应这项要求是否合适.

pro·pul·sion /prə'pʌlʃn; prə'pʌlʃən/ *n* [U] driving (sth) forward or being driven forward 推进: *changes in the fuel used for propulsion* 用以产生推进力的燃料之改变 ○ *jet propulsion*, ie by means of jet engines 喷气推进(使用喷气式发动机).

▷ **pro·puls·ive** /prə'pʌlsɪv; prə'pʌlsɪv/ *adj* (*fml* 文) that drives sth (esp a vehicle) forward 对某物(尤指机动交通工具)起推进作用的, 推进的, 有推进力的: *propulsive power, forces, gases* 起推进作用的动力、力量、气体.

pro rata /,prəʊ 'rɑːtə; pro'retə/ *adj, adv* (*fml* 文) proportional(ly) 成比例(的): *If production costs go up, there will be a pro rata increase in prices/prices will increase pro rata.* 若生产成本增加, 则价格也要相应提高.

pro·rogue /prə'rəʊg; prə'rog/ *v* [Tn] (*fml* 文) bring (a session of Parliament) to an end without dissolving Parliament (so that unfinished business may be continued in the next session) 使(议会)休会.

▷ **pro·roga·tion** /,prəʊrə'geɪʃn; ,prorə'geʃən/ *n* [C, U] (*fml* 文) (instance of) proroguing (议会的)休会.

pro·saic /prə'zeɪɪk; pro'zeɪk/ *adj* (**a**) uninspired; unimaginative 无灵感的; 无想像力的: *a prosaic metaphor, style, writer* 平庸的比喻、风格、作家 ○ *a prosaic description of the scene* 枯燥无味的场景描写. (**b**) dull and commonplace; unromantic 无聊的; 平凡的; 乏味的: *her prosaic life as a housewife* 她身为家庭妇女的平淡生活. ▷ **pro·sa·ic·ally** /-klɪ; -klɪ/ *adv*.

pro·scen·ium /prə'siːnɪəm; pro'sinɪəm/ *n* (in a theatre) the part of the stage in front of the curtain (剧院)幕布前的舞台部分, 舞台前部. ⇨illus at App 1 见附录1插图, page ix.

□ **pro,scenium 'arch** arch above this space, which forms a frame for the stage when the curtain is opened 舞台上的拱形框架; 台口.

pro·scribe /prə'skraɪb; US prəʊ-; pro'skraɪb/ *v* [Tn] (*fml* 文) **1** state officially that (sth) is dangerous or forbidden 正式宣布(某事物)有危险或被禁止: *The sale of narcotics is proscribed by law.* 法律禁止贩卖毒品. **2** (formerly) place (sb) outside the protection of the law; outlaw (旧时)剥夺对(某人)的法律保护, 使失去法律保障.

▷ **pro·scrip·tion** /prə'skrɪpʃn; US prəʊ-; pro'skrɪpʃən/ *n* [C, U] (*fml* 文) (instance of) proscribing or being proscribed 禁止; 剥夺权利: *the proscription of newspapers critical of the government* 批评政府的报纸被禁.

prose /prəʊz; proz/ *n* [U] written or spoken language that is not in verse form 散文(区别于韵文): *a page of well-written prose* 一篇写得很好的散文 ○ [attrib 作定语] *the great prose writers of the 19th century* 19世纪的伟大散文作家. Cf 参看 POETRY 1, VERSE.

pro·sec·ute /'prɒsɪkjuːt; 'prɑsɪ,kjut/ *v* **1** [Tn, Tn·pr] **~ sb (for sth/doing sth)** bring a criminal charge against sb in a court of law 检举、告发某人; 对某人提起公诉: *Trespassers will be prosecuted.* 闲人免进, 违者必究. ○ *He was prosecuted for exceeding the speed limit.* 他因超速行车而被起诉. ○ *the prosecuting lawyer*, ie the one representing the prosecution 代表原告的律师. **2** [Tn] (*fml* 文) continue to be occupied with (sth) 继续从事(某事物): *prosecute a war, one's inquiries, one's studies* 进行战争、调查、研究.

▷ **pro·secu·tor** /'prɒsɪkjuːtə(r); 'prɑsɪ,kjutə/ *n* person who prosecutes in a court of law 检举人; 告发人; 起诉人; 公诉人; 原告.

pro·secu·tion /,prɒsɪ'kjuːʃn; ,prɑsɪ'kjuʃən/ *n* **1** (**a**) [U] prosecuting (PROSECUTE 1) or being prosecuted for a criminal offence (被)检举; (被)告发; (被)起诉: *Failure to pay your taxes will make you liable to prosecution.* 不缴纳税款就可能被起诉. (**b**) [C] instance of this (被)检举; (被)告发; (被)起诉: *There have been several successful prosecutions for drug smuggling recently.* 近来有几起毒品走私活动被检举立案. **2 the prosecution** [Gp] person or body that prosecutes in a lawcourt together with lawyers, advisers, etc 原告; 原告方面, 控方(包括律师、法律顾问等): *Mr Smith acted as counsel for the prosecution.* 史密斯先生担任原告的律师. ○ *The prosecution based their case on the evidence of two witnesses.* 原告方面以两名证人所提供的证据提起诉讼. Cf 参看 DEFENCE 2. **3** [U] **the ~ of sth** (*fml* 文) carrying out or being occupied with sth 实行; 进行; 从事: *In the prosecution of his duties he had met with a good deal of resistance.* 他在执行职务中遇到许多阻力.

pros·elyte /'prɒsəlaɪt; 'prɑsl,aɪt/ *n* (*fml* 文) person who has been converted from one set of religious, political, etc beliefs to another 改变宗教、政治等信仰的人.

▷ **pros·elyt·ize, -ise** /'prɒsəlɪtaɪz; 'prɑsəlɪt,aɪz/ *v* [I, Tn] (*fml* 文) (try to) persuade (others) to accept one's own beliefs, religion, etc (尽量)劝诱(他人)接受自己的信仰、宗教等: *going round the country proselytizing* 到全国各地进行信仰宣传活动 ○ *attempts to proselytize the younger generation* 向年轻一代进行信仰方面的宣传.

pros·ody /'prɒsədɪ; 'prɑsədɪ/ *n* [U] **1** science of verse forms and poetic metres 韵文学; 诗体学. **2** (study of the) rhythm, pause, tempo, stress and pitch features of a language (某语言的)韵律(学). ▷ **pros·odic** /prə'sɒdɪk; prə'sɑdɪk/ *adj*.

pro·spect[1] /'prɒspekt; 'prɑspɛkt/ *n* **1** [C] (**a**) (*dated* 旧) wide view of a landscape, etc 景象; 景色; 景观: *a magnificent prospect of mountain peaks and lakes* 山峰和湖泊的壮丽景色. (**b**) picture in the mind or imagination, esp of a future event 意境; 想像; (尤指)前景, 展望: *She viewed the prospect of a week alone in the house without much enthusiasm.* 她想像在那所房子里孤身一人百无聊赖地呆上一个星期的情景. **2 prospects** [pl] chance of success; outlook 成功的机会; 前景; 前程: *The prospects for this year's wine harvest are poor.* 今年的葡萄酒产量前景不佳. ○ *The job has no prospects*, ie offers little possibility of promotion. 这工作毫无前途

(晋升的机会很小). **3** [U] **~ (of sth/doing sth)** reasonable hope that sth will happen; expectation 有根据的希望; 期望: *I see little prospect of an improvement in his condition.* 我看他的情况没有什么改进的希望. ○ *There is no prospect of a settlement of the dispute.* 这场纠纷根本不可能获得解决. ○ *have little prospect of succeeding* 没有什么成功的希望 ○ *He is unemployed and has nothing in prospect* (ie no expectation of finding work) *at the moment.* 他失业了, 此刻也没有找到工作的希望. **4** [C] (**a**) candidate or competitor likely to be successful 有望的候选人或竞赛者: *She's a good prospect for the British team.* 她很有可能被选入英国队. (**b**) possible or likely customer or client 可能成为主顾或委托者的人: *He was an experienced car salesman and recognized an easy prospect when he saw one!* 他是个很有经验的汽车推销员, 一眼就能看出谁是容易劝说的买主!

P

pro·spect[2] /prə'spekt; *US* 'prɒspekt; 'prɑspɛkt/ *v* [I, Ipr] **~ (for sth)** search for minerals, gold, oil, etc 勘探; 勘查: *a licence to prospect in the northern territory* 在北部地区从事勘探的许可证 ○ *The company are prospecting for gold in that area.* 这家公司在那地区勘探金矿.

▷ **pro·spector** *n* person who explores a region looking for gold, ores, etc 勘探者; 探矿者.

pro·spect·ive /prə'spektɪv; prə'spɛktɪv/ *adj* [esp attrib 尤作定语] expected to be or to occur; future or possible 预期的; 未来的; 可能的: *prospective changes in the law* 法律上将进行的一些更改 ○ *his prospective mother-in-law* 他未来的岳母 ○ *the prospective Labour candidate at the next election* 下届选举中英国工党可能推出的候选人 ○ *showing the house to a prospective buyer* 带领可能买房子的人看房子.

pro·spectus /prə'spektəs; prə'spɛktəs/ *n* printed document, leaflet, etc giving details of and advertising sth, eg a private school or a new business (私立学校、新办企业等的)章程, 简章, 广告宣传资料: *prospectuses from several universities* 几所大学的学校简介.

pros·per /'prɒspə(r); 'prɑspɚ/ *v* [I] be successful; thrive 成功; 兴旺: *The business is prospering.* 生意兴隆.

pros·per·ity /prɒ'sperətɪ; prɑs'pɛrətɪ/ *n* [U] (**a**) state of being successful or rich; good fortune 成功; 富足; 幸运; 顺利: *He wished the young couple a life of happiness and prosperity.* 他祝这对年轻人生活幸福、万事如意. (**b**) state of being economically successful (经济的)繁荣: *The increase in the country's prosperity was due to the discovery of oil.* 该国经济之日趋繁荣是由于发现了石油的缘故.

pros·per·ous /'prɒspərəs; 'prɑspərəs/ *adj* successful or thriving, esp financially 成功的, 兴旺的, 繁荣的(尤指经济上): *a prosperous country, businessman, industry* 繁荣昌盛的国家、事业成功的实业家、兴旺发达的工业 ○ *a prosperous-looking businessman* 看来事业有成的商人.

▷ **pros·per·ously** *adv*.

pro·state /'prɒsteɪt; 'prɑstet/ *n* (also ˌ**prostate** '**gland**) (*anatomy* 解) (in male mammals) gland at the neck of the bladder (雄性哺乳动物的)前列腺: *in hospital for an operation on his prostate* 为做前列腺手术而住院. ⇨illus at MALE 见 MALE 插图.

pros·thesis /'prɒsθɪsɪs, prɒs'θi:sɪs; 'prɑsθɪsɪs, ˌprɑs'θisɪs/ *n* (*pl* **-theses** /'prɒsθɪsi:z, prɒs'θi:si:z; 'prɑsθɪˌsiz, prɑs'θiˌsiz/) (*medical* 医) **1** [C] artificial part of the body, eg a limb, an eye or a tooth 假体(如假肢、假眼或假牙等): *A prosthesis was fitted after the amputation.* 截肢之后安装了义肢. **2** [U] replacement of a missing part of the body, eg after surgery, by an artificial one 人体修复(术). ▷ **pros·thetic** /prɒs'θetɪk; prɑs'θɛtɪk/ *adj*: *a prosthetic appliance* 用作假体的器械.

pros·ti·tute /'prɒstɪtju:t; *US* -tu:t; 'prɑstəˌtut/ *n* person who offers herself/himself for sexual intercourse for money 卖淫者; 娼妓; 妓女; 男妓.

▷ **pros·ti·tute** *v* [Tn] (*derog* 贬) **1 ~ oneself** act as a prostitute 卖淫; 为娼; 当男妓: *She prostituted herself in order to support her children.* 她为养活子女而操皮肉生涯. **2** use (oneself or one's abilities, etc) wrongly or unworthily, esp in order to earn money 作践(自己), 滥用(自己的才能等)(尤指为图利): *poets prostituting their talent by writing jingles for advertisements* 为广告写顺口溜而折辱才华的诗人.

pros·ti·tu·tion /ˌprɒstɪ'tju:ʃn; *US* -'tu:ʃn; ˌprɑstə'tuʃən/ *n* **1** [U] (practice of) working as a prostitute 卖淫; 当男妓; 操皮肉生涯; 作践自己; 滥用才能: *Prostitution is on the increase in the city.* 城里卖淫活动越来越多. **2** [C, U] **~ of sth** unworthy use of sth 滥用某事物: *He refused the job, saying it would be (a) prostitution of his talents.* 他拒不做那工作, 说那是大材小用.

pros·trate /'prɒstreɪt; 'prɑstret/ *adj* **1** (lying) stretched out on the ground face downward, esp because of exhaustion or in order to show submission, respect, etc 卧倒的, 俯卧的, 拜倒的(尤指因筋疲力尽或为表示顺从、敬意等): *The prisoners were forced to lie prostrate in front of their captors.* 囚犯们被迫在逮捕他们的那些人面前卧倒. ○ *She was found prostrate on the floor of the cell.* 有人发现她趴在小屋的地板上. Cf 参看 PRONE 1, SUPINE 1. **2 ~ (with sth)** overcome by sth; defeated or helpless 被某事物所制服的; 瓦解的; 无能为力的: *She was prostrate with grief after his death.* 她在他死后因悲伤而憔悴了. ○ *The country, prostrate after years of war, began slowly to recover.* 这个国家连年战争元气尽失后, 已开始慢慢恢复正常状态. ○ *The illness left her prostrate for several weeks.* 这场病把她拖倒了几个星期.

▷ **pros·trate** /prɒ'streɪt; *US* 'prɒstreɪt; 'prɑstret/ *v* **1** [Tn] (**a**) **~ oneself** throw oneself on the floor and lie face down, esp as a sign of submission or worship 俯伏在地; (尤指表示顺从或崇拜)拜倒: *The slaves prostrated themselves at their master's feet.* 奴隶们拜倒在主子的脚下. ○ *The pilgrims prostrated themselves before the altar.* 朝圣者都匍伏在圣坛前. (**b**) (*fml* 文) force (sb/sth) to the ground; flatten 使(某人[某物])倒下; 弄倒: *trees prostrated by the gales* 被大风刮倒的树木. **2** [Tn esp passive 尤用于被动语态] (of illness, weather, etc) make (sb) helpless (指疾病、天气等)使(某人)无能为力: *The competitors were prostrated by the heat.* 竞赛者们由于天气炎热而力不从心. **pros·tra·tion** /prɒ'streɪʃn; prɑ'streʃən/ *n* **1** [C, U] (act of) lying face downwards in submission or worship (为表示恭顺或崇拜)俯伏在地, 拜倒, 屈服. **2** [U] state of extreme physical weakness; total exhaustion 身体极度衰竭; 虚脱; 筋疲力尽: *Two of the runners collapsed in a state of prostration.* 有两名赛跑选手因虚脱而倒下了.

prosy /'prəʊzɪ; 'prozɪ/ *adj* (**-ier, -iest**) (of a writer, speaker, book, speech, style, etc) dull or commonplace; unimaginative (指作者、演说者、书、讲话、风格等)单调乏味的, 平淡无奇的; 无想像力的. ▷ **pro·sily** *adv*. **pro·si·ness** *n* [U].

Prot *abbr* 缩写 = Protestant.

prot·ag·on·ist /prə'tægənɪst; pro'tægənɪst/ *n* **1** (**a**) (*fml* 文) chief character in a drama; hero (戏剧的)主角. (**b**) chief person in a story or chief participant in an actual event, esp a conflict or dispute (故事的)主人公; 现实事件(尤指冲突或争端的)主要参与者, 主要人物. **2 ~ (of sth)** leader or advocate of a cause 领导者; 倡导者; 拥护者: *an outspoken protagonist of electoral reform* 对改革选举制度直抒己见的鼓吹者 ○ *a leading protagonist of the women's movement* 妇女运动的领导者.

pro·tean /'prəʊtɪən, prəʊ'ti:ən; 'protɪən, pro'tiən/ *adj* (*fml* 文) that can change quickly and easily; variable 多变的; 易变的; 变化多端的.

pro·tect /prə'tekt; prə'tɛkt/ *v* **1** [Tn, Tn·pr] **~ sb/sth (against/from sth)** keep sb/sth safe from harm, injury, etc; defend sb/sth 保护、保卫某人[某事物]: *You need warm clothes to protect you against the cold.* 你需要穿暖些以免着凉. ○ *The vaccine was used to protect the whole population against infection.* 这种疫苗用以为全体居民预防传染病. ○ *The union was formed to protect the rights and interests of miners.* 建立起工会是为保护矿工的权利和利益. **2** [Tn] guard (one or more industries of a country) against competition by taxing foreign goods (以征收进口税)保护(国内工业): *The country's car industry is so strongly protected that foreign cars are rarely seen there.* 该国对汽车工业严加保护, 外国汽车甚为罕见.

pro·tec·tion /prə'tekʃn; prə'tɛkʃən/ *n* **1 ~ (for sb) (against sth)** (**a**) [U] protecting or being protected 保护; 防卫: *appeal for protection from the police* 请求警方给予保护 ○ *The shady trees provide protection against the burning rays of the sun.* 树木成阴可以遮挡炽热的阳光. ○ *Our medical insurance offers protection* (ie payment for medical treatment) *for the whole family in the event of illness.* 我们的医疗保险可为生病的任何家庭成员提供保障. (**b**) [C] thing that protects 防护物: *He wore a thick overcoat as a protection against the bitter cold.* 他穿着厚实的大衣以抵御严寒. **2** [U] system of protecting (PROTECT 2) home industries by taxing foreign goods 贸易保护措施(藉征收进口税以保护国内工业): *Textile workers favoured protection because they feared an influx of cheap cloth.* 纺织工人拥护贸易保护措施, 因为他们担心涌入廉价纺织品. **3** [U] (**a**) (system of) paying money to gangsters so that one's business will not be attacked by them (为免生意受歹徒袭扰而向其)缴纳保护费(的做法): [attrib 作定语] *The gang were running protection rackets in all the big cities.* 这帮歹徒在各大城市里干着勒索保护费的勾当. (**b**) (also **protection money**) money paid to gangsters for this purpose (为免受袭扰而向歹徒缴纳的)保护费: *He was paying out half his profits as protection.* 他把所得利润的一半交给歹徒作为保护费.

▷ **pro·tec·tion·ism** /-ʃənɪzəm; -ʃənɪzm̩/ *n* [U] principle or practice of protecting (PROTECT 2) home industries (贸易上的)保护主义; 贸易保护制度: *accuse rival countries of protectionism* 指责对方国家实行贸易保护主义. **pro·tec·tion·ist** /-ʃənɪst; -ʃənɪst/ *n* supporter of or believer in protectionism 贸易保护主义者.

pro·tect·ive /prəˈtektɪv; prəˈtɛktɪv/ *adj* **1** [esp attrib 尤作定语] that protects or is intended to protect 保护的; 防护的; 意在保护或防护的: *a protective layer of varnish* 一层保护清漆 ○ *Workers who handle asbestos need to wear protective clothing.* 接触石棉的工人需穿防护衣. ○ *wearing protective headgear on a motor cycle* 骑摩托车时戴保护头盔 ○ *pro,tective ˈcolouring*, ie on the bodies of birds, animals and insects, making it difficult for predators to see them (鸟、兽及昆虫身上之)保护色 ○ *protective duties/tariffs on imported goods* 加于进口货物的保护性关税. **2 ~ (towards sb)** having or showing a wish to protect 有保护之意愿的; 显示保护之意愿的: *A mother naturally feels protective towards her children.* 母亲对自己的孩子自然会悉心保护. ○ *He put his arm round her in a protective gesture.* 他用一只手臂围住她做出保护的姿势.

▷ **pro·tect·ive** *n* (*US*) contraceptive sheath; condom 避孕套; 阴茎套.

pro·tect·ively *adv*.

□ **pro,tective ˈcustody** keeping a person in prison (supposedly) for his own safety 保护性监禁.

pro·tector /prəˈtektə(r); prəˈtɛktɚ/ *n* **1** person who protects 保护者; 防御者: *their guardian and protector* 他们的监护人和保护人. **2** thing made or designed to give protection 保护装置; 保护器; 防护物: *The swordsmen wore chest protectors.* 那些剑客都披着护具.

pro·tect·or·ate /prəˈtektərət; prəˈtɛktərɪt/ *n* country that is controlled and protected by a more powerful country 受较强之国家支配和保护的国家或地区; 受保护国; 受保护领地: *He had been Governor of a British Protectorate.* 他做过英国保护领地的总督. Cf 参看 COLONY 1.

pro·tégé (*fem* 阴性作 **pro·tégée**) /ˈprɒtɪʒeɪ; *US* ˌprəʊtɪˈʒeɪ; ˌprotəˈʒe/ *n* person whose welfare and career are looked after by an influential person, esp over a long period 受有权势人物提携或扶掖的人: *a young protégé of a famous violinist* 某著名小提琴家的年轻门生 ○ *As the protégé of the most powerful man in the country, his success was guaranteed.* 他有该国最有势力的人作靠山, 准能成功.

pro·tein /ˈprəʊtiːn; ˈprotin/ *n* [C, U] substance found in meat, eggs, fish, etc that is an important body-building part of the diet of humans and animals 蛋白质; 朊: *essential proteins and vitamins* 必不可少的蛋白质和维生素 ○ *They were weakened by a diet that was low in protein.* 他们日常饮食中蛋白质含量不足, 因而身体虚弱. ○ [attrib 作定语] *protein deficiency* 蛋白质缺乏.

pro tem /ˌprəʊ ˈtem; proˈtɛm/ *abbr* 缩写 = (*infml* 口) for the time being; temporarily (Latin *pro tempore*) 暂时, 临时(源自拉丁文 *pro tempore*): *This arrangement will have to do pro tem.* 暂时只好这样安排.

pro·test[1] /ˈprəʊtest; ˈprotɛst/ *n* **1** [C] statement or an action that shows one's strong dispproval or disagreement 抗议; 抗议书; 抗议活动: *enter/lodge/make/register a protest about/against sth* 对某事物提出抗议 ○ *Loud protests were heard when the decision was announced.* 这决定一经宣布, 抗议之声不绝于耳. ○ *stage a protest* (ie organize a demonstration) *against management's handling of the dispute* 举行抗议活动(组织示威游行)以反对资方对争端的处理办法. **2** [U] strong disapproval or disagreement that is expressed by a statement or an action 抗议; 异议; 反对: *The minister resigned in protest against the decision.* 这位部长为反对那项决策而辞职. ○ [attrib 作定语] *a protest demonstration, march, movement, etc*, ie one organized by people who disagree with official policy 抗议示威、游行、运动等. **3** (idm 习语) **under ˈprotest** unwillingly and after making protests (经抗议后)心有不甘地: *She paid the fine under protest.* 她争执一番后, 无可奈何地缴纳了罚金.

pro·test[2] /prəˈtest; prəˈtɛst/ *v* **1** [I, Ipr, Tn] **~ (about/against/at sth)** express strong disagreement or disapproval about (sth) 抗议, 反对(某事物); 对(某事物)提出异议: *She protested strongly at being called a snob.* 她极力反对别人说她势利眼. ○ *Demonstrators protested outside the country's embassies all over Europe.* 该国驻欧洲各国的大使馆外都有群众进行示威抗议. ○ *They are holding a rally to protest against the government's defence policy.* 他们正举行集会以抗议政府的防务政策. ○ (*US*) *A demonstration was planned to protest the mistreatment of prisoners.* 为抗议虐待犯人已计划好进行示威活动. **2** [Tn, Tf] declare (sth) solemnly or firmly, esp in reply to an accusation 严正地或坚决地申明(某事物); (尤指)声辩: *He protested his innocence.* 他坚决声辩自己无罪. ○ *She protested that she had never seen the accused man before.* 她坚持说她以前从未见过这一被指控的男子. **3** (idm 习语) **proˈtest too much** affirm or deny sth so strongly that one's sincerity is doubted 对某事物肯定或否定过激而失实; 过犹不及.

▷ **pro·tester** *n* person who protests 抗议者; 反对者: *A group of protesters gathered outside the firm's office.* 有些抗议的人聚集在这家商行的办公室外面.

pro·test·ingly *adv*: *They denied the claim protestingly.* 他们拒不承认对方提出的事.

Prot·est·ant /ˈprɒtɪstənt; ˈprɑtɪstənt/ *n*, *adj* (member) of any of the Christian bodies that separated from the Church of Rome in the 16th century, or of their branches formed later 新教徒(指16世纪脱离罗马天主教之基督教团体或后来由其形成的教派成员); 新教(徒)的: *a Protestant church, minister, service* 新教教会、牧师、礼拜式. Cf 参看 ROMAN CATHOLIC (ROMAN).

▷ **Prot·est·ant·ism** /-ɪzəm; -ˌɪzəm/ *n* [U] (**a**) system of beliefs, teachings, etc of the Protestants 新教的信条、教义等. (**b**) Protestants as a body 新教.

prot·esta·tion /ˌprɒteˈsteɪʃn; ˌprɑtəsˈteʃən/ *n* (*fml* 文) solemn declaration (严正的)声明: *protestations of friendship, innocence, loyalty, etc* 关于友好、无罪、忠诚等的郑重声明 ○ *Despite their protestations, they were glad to accept our help.* 尽管他们严肃地表明了态度, 但他们仍乐于接受我们的援助.

prot(o)- *comb form* 构词成分 first, original or primitive 第一的; 最初的; 原始的: *protozoa* ○ *prototype* ○ *protoplasm*.

pro·to·col /ˈprəʊtəkɒl; *US* -kɔːl; ˈprotəˌkɔl/ *n* **1** [U] system of rules governing formal occasions, eg meetings between governments, diplomats, etc; official etiquette 礼仪; 外交礼节: *The organizer was familiar with the protocol of royal visits.* 组织者熟悉国王出访的礼仪. ○ *The delegates have to be seated according to protocol.* 代表们须按礼仪要求就座. ○ *a breach of protocol* 违反礼仪的行为. **2** [C] (*fml* 文) first or original draft of a diplomatic agreement, esp of the agreed terms for a treaty (外交条约的)草案, 草约; (尤指)议定的条款, 议定书.

pro·ton /ˈprəʊtɒn; ˈprotɑn/ *n* elementary particle with a positive electric charge, which is present in the nuclei of all atoms 质子. Cf 参看 ELECTRON, NEUTRON.

pro·to·plasm /ˈprəʊtəplæzəm; ˈprotəˌplæzəm/ (also **plasma**) *n* [U] (*biology* 生) colourless jelly-like substance that forms the basis of all animal and plant cells and tissues 原生质.

pro·to·type /ˈprəʊtətaɪp; ˈprotəˌtaɪp/ *n* first or original example of sth that has been or will be copied or developed; model or preliminary version 事物之原始形态; 原型; 雏形; 模型; 蓝本: *the prototype for future* *school buildings* 未来的学校建筑的模型 ○ [attrib 作定语] *a prototype supersonic aircraft* 超音速飞机的样机.

pro·to·zoon (also **pro·to·zoan**) /ˌprəʊtəˈzəʊən; ˌprotəˈzoən/ *n* (*pl* **-zoa** /-ˈzəʊə; -ˈzoə/) any of a large group of very small, usu one-celled, living things, that can be seen only under a microscope 原生动物.

▷ **pro·to·zoan** /ˌprəʊtəˈzəʊən; ˌprotəˈzoən/ *adj* of or like a protozoon (似)原生动物的.

pro·tract /prəˈtrækt; *US* prəʊ-; proˈtrækt/ *v* [Tn esp passive 尤用于被动语态] (*often derog* 常作贬义) make (sth) last a long time or longer; lengthen or prolong 延长, 拖延(某事物): *Let's not protract the debate any further.* 我们不要再继续争论下去了. ○ *a protracted lunch break* 延长了的午餐时间 ○ *protracted delays, discussions, questioning* 长时间的耽搁、讨论、询问.

▷ **pro·trac·tion** /prəˈtrækʃn; *US* prəʊ-; proˈtrækʃən/ *n* [C, U] (instance of) making sth last longer; extending 延长; 拖延; 伸展: *Further protraction of the discussion will not achieve anything.* 继续讨论下去并不能解决任何问题.

pro·tractor /prəˈtræktə(r); *US* prəʊ-; proˈtræktɚ/ *n* instrument, usu in the form of a semi-circle with degrees (0° to 180°) marked on it, used for measuring and drawing angles 量角器; 分度规.

pro·trude /prəˈtruːd; *US* prəʊ-; proˈtrud/ *v* [I, Ipr, Tn, Tn·pr] **~ (sth) (from sth)** (cause sth to) jut or stick out from a surface; (cause sth to) project (使某物)(自一表面)伸出; (使某物)突出: *He managed to hang on to a piece of rock protruding from the cliff face.* 他设法抓住悬崖表面向外伸出的岩石. ○ *protruding eyes, lips, teeth* 凸出的眼睛、嘴唇、牙齿 ○ *a protruding chin* 尖突的下巴.

▷ **pro·tru·sion** /prəˈtruːʒn; *US* prəʊ-; proˈtruʒən/ *n* (**a**) [U] protruding 伸出; 突出: *Thumb-sucking can cause protrusion of the teeth.* 经常吮吸拇指能使牙齿向外突出. (**b**) [C] thing that protrudes 伸出物; 突出物; 隆起物: *rocky protrusions on the surface of the cliff* 悬崖表面突出的岩石.

pro·trus·ive /prəˈtruːsɪv; *US* prəʊ-; proˈtrusɪv/ *adj* (*fml* 文) protruding 伸出的; 突出的.

pro·tu·ber·ant /prəˈtjuːbərənt; *US* prəʊˈtuː-; proˈtubərənt/ *adj* (*fml* 文) bulging, curving or swelling outwards from a surface; prominent 突出的; 凸出的; 隆起的: *a protuberant stomach* 膨胀的肚子.

▷ **pro·tu·ber·ance** /-əns; -əns/ *n* (*fml* 文) (**a**) [U] being protuberant 突出; 凸出; 隆起. (**b**) [C] protuberant thing; bulge or swelling 突出物; 凸出物; 隆起物: *The diseased trees are marked by protuberances on their bark.* 有病的树木可由其树皮上的结节看出.

proud /praʊd; praʊd/ *adj* (**-er, -est**) **1** (*approv* 褒) (**a**) **~ (of sb/sth); ~ (to do sth/that...)** feeling or showing justifiable pride (1a) 感到得意的; 自豪的; 荣耀的: *proud of her new car* 为她的新车而颇觉得意 ○ *His proud parents congratulated him.* 他的父母感到光彩向他表示祝贺. ○ *They were proud of their success/of being so successful.* 他们为自己的成功[为取得了这样的成功]而骄傲. ○ *They were proud to belong/that they belonged to such a fine team.* 他们为属于[为自己属于]这么好的一个队而自豪. ○ *She is a remarkable person — I am proud* (ie honoured) *to know her.* 她是位杰出人物——认识她我感到很荣幸. ○ (*ironic* 反语) *I hope you feel proud of yourself — you've ruined the game!* 你可真露脸了——你把比赛搅得一塌糊涂! ○ *the proud owners of a new house* 得意洋洋的新宅主人. (**b**) having or showing self-respect, dignity or independence 有自尊心的; 自尊的; 自主的: *They were poor but proud.* 他们虽然穷, 但很有骨气. ○ *He had been too proud to ask for help.* 他自尊心太强, 从不求助于人. ○ *They are a proud and independent people.* 他们是独立自主的民族. (**c**) causing justifiable pride (1a) 值得自豪的; 足以夸耀的; 引以为荣的: *It was a proud day for us when we won the trophy.* 我们夺得奖杯那一天是值得我们骄傲的日子. ○ *The portrait was his proudest possession.* 那肖像是他最为珍贵的东西. **2** (*derog* 贬) self-important; haughty or arrogant 骄傲自大的; 自负的; 傲慢的: *He was too proud to join in our fun.* 他很高傲, 不屑同我们一起玩儿. ○ *He is too proud now to be seen with his former friends.* 他现在忘乎所以了, 觉得跟以前的朋友在一起有失他的脸面. **3** (*fml* 文) imposing or splendid 壮观的; 辉煌的: *soldiers in proud array* 雄赳赳的列队士兵. **4 ~ of sth** jutting out from or extending above sth 凸出于某物之上的; 自某物上隆起的: *be, rise, stand proud of sth* 自某物上隆起 ○ *The cement should stand proud of the surface and then be smoothed down later.* 施用水泥时应先高出于表面然后再将其抹平. **5** (idm 习语) **(as) ˌproud as a ˈpeacock** extremely proud 骄傲如孔雀(极骄傲).

▷ **proud** *adv* (idm 习语) **do sb ˈproud** (*infml* 口) treat sb with great honour or hospitality; entertain sb lavishly 使某人受到隆重礼遇; 盛情款待某人: *The college did us proud at the centenary dinner.* 院方在一百周年校庆设宴款待我们.

proudly *adv* in a proud(1a) manner 自豪地; 得意地: *proudly displaying the trophy* 自豪地展示奖杯.

Prov *abbr* 缩写 = (esp on a map 尤作地图标记) Province.

prove /pruːv; pruv/ *v* (*pp* **proved**; *US* **proven** /ˈpruːvn; ˈpruvən/) ⇨Usage 见所附用法. **1** [Tn, Tf, Dn·pr, Dpr·f] **~ sth (to sb)** show that sth is true or certain by means of argument or evidence 证明某事物属实; 证实某事物: *prove sb's guilt/(that) sb is guilty* 证明某人有罪 ○ *Can you prove it to me?* 你能向我证实吗? ○ *I shall prove to you that the witness is not speaking the truth.* 我将向你证明, 证人说的不是真话. **2** (*US* **probate**) [Tn] establish that (a will) is genuine 认证(遗嘱): *The will has to be proved before we can inherit.* 遗嘱要先认证, 然后我们才能继承遗产. **3** [La, Ln, Cn·a, Cn·n, Cn·t] **~ (oneself) sth** be seen or found to be sth; turn out to be sth 显现出是某事物; 被发现是某事物: *The old methods proved best after all.* 采用老方法结果反而是某事物最好. ○ *The task proved (to be) more difficult than we'd thought.* 这项任务原来比我们预想的难得多. ○ *He proved himself (to be) a better driver than the world champion.* 他的表现说明他的驾驶技术胜过世界冠军. **4** [I] (of dough) rise because of the action of yeast (指面团)发酵: *leave the dough to prove for half an hour* 让面团发酵半小时. **5** (idm 习语) **the exception proves the rule** ⇨ EXCEPTION. **prove one's/the ˈcase/ˈpoint** demonstrate that one's/the statement, argument, criticism, etc is true or valid 表明自己的[该]言论、论据、批评等是符合事实的或确有根据的: *He quoted figures to prove his case.* 他援引数字以表明自己的说法确有根据. ○ *She claimed that money had been wasted and our financial difficulties seemed to prove her point.* 她断定那笔钱用得不是地方, 而我们在经济上遇到的困难却也似乎说明她言之有理.

▷ **prov·able** /-əbl; -əbl/ that can be proved 可证明的; 可证实的: *a provable case of negligence* 证据确凿的玩忽职守事件. **prov·ably** /-əblɪ; -əblɪ/ *adv*.

NOTE ON USAGE 用法: **Prove** and **shave** have alternative past participle forms ☆ **prove** 和 **shave** 均有两种过去分词形式: **proved/proven; shaved/shaven.** The irregular forms are more common in US than in British English. 不规则形式在美式英语中比在英式英语中用得多. **Shaven** and **proven** are mostly used adjectivally ☆ **shaven** 和 **proven** 多用作形容词性的修饰成分: *a well-proven method* 充分证明行之有效的方法 ○ *a shaven head* 剃光的头.

proven /ˈpruːvn; *Scot* 苏格兰英语读作 ˈprəʊvn; ˈpruvən/ *adj* **1** (*approv* 褒) that has been tested or demonstrated 经过验证或证实的: *a man of proven ability* 已证明确有才干的人. **2** (idm 习语) **not ˈproven** (verdict in a criminal trial in Scottish law that) there is insufficient evidence to prove that the accused is innocent or guilty, and he must therefore be set free 证据不足(根据苏格兰法律在刑事审判中对没有充分证据证明被告有罪或无罪之案件所作的裁定, 据此被告应予开释).

prov·en·ance /ˈprɒvənəns; ˈprɑvənəns/ *n* [U] (*fml* 文) (place of) origin 起源; 出处: *the provenance of the word* 该词的来源 ○ *antique furniture of doubtful provenance*, eg that may not be genuinely antique 出处不明的古董家具(如可能是假古董).

prov·ender /ˈprɒvɪndə(r); ˈprɑvəndɚ/ *n* [U] **1** food for horses and cattle, eg hay or oats; fodder (牛马的)饲料. **2** (*infml or joc* 口或谑) food 食物: *enough provender for the party* 足够会餐的食物.

pro·verb /ˈprɒvɜːb; ˈprɑvɝb/ *n* short well-known saying that states a general truth or gives advice, eg 'It takes two to make a quarrel' or 'Don't put all your eggs in one basket' 谚语, 格言(精练的俗语, 或为普遍道理或为劝戒语, 如'一个巴掌拍不响'或'不要把全部家当放在一处'): *the Book of Proverbs*, ie one of the books of the Old Testament containing the proverbs of Solomon《箴言》(《圣经·旧约》中的一卷书).

▷ **pro·ver·bial** /prəˈvɜːbɪəl; prəˈvɝbɪəl/ *adj* **1** of, like or expressed in a proverb 谚语的; 如同谚语的; 谚语所表达的: *proverbial sayings, wisdom* 谚语、谚语表达的智慧 ○ *He is the proverbial square peg in a round hole.* 他正是谚语中所说的那种方枘圆凿不得其所的人. **2** widely known and talked about 众所周知的: *His stupidity is proverbial.* 他其蠢无比是人所共知的. ○ *I decided not to ask her for a loan in view of her proverbial meanness.* 因为她小气得出了名, 我决定不找她借钱. **pro·ver·bi·ally** /-bɪəlɪ; -bɪəlɪ/ *adv*.

pro·vide /prəˈvaɪd; prəˈvaɪd/ *v* **1** [Tn, Tn·pr, Dn·pr] **~ sb (with sth); ~ sth (for sb)** (**a**) make sth available for sb to use by giving, lending or supplying it 向某人提供某事物; 供给; 供应: *The management will provide food and drink.* 管理部门将供应饮食. ○ *Please put your litter in the bin provided.* 请你把废物扔到预备好的垃圾箱里. ○ *The firm have provided me with a car.* 公司供给我一辆汽车. ○ *Can you provide accommodation for thirty people?* 你能为三十人提供住宿吗? (**b**) (*fig* 比喻) offer or present (an answer, example, opportunity, etc) 提供(答案、范例、机会等): *Let us hope his research will provide the evidence we need.* 但愿他作的研究能提供我们所需要的证据. ○ *The painting provides us with one of the earliest examples of the use of perspective.* 那幅画给我们提供了采用透视画法的最早的范例. **2** [Tf] (*fml* 文) give as a condition; stipulate 作为条件提出; 规定: *A clause in the agreement provides that the tenant shall pay for repairs to the building.* 协议中有一条规定, 承租人负担建筑物的修理费. **3** (phr v) **provide against sth** (*fml* 文) make preparations in case sth happens 防备发生某事物; 预防某事物: *The government has to provide against a possible oil shortage in the coming months.* 政府须为未来几个月中可能出现的油荒作好准备. **provide for sb** supply sb with what he needs, esp the basic necessities of life 供应某人所需(尤指基本的生活必需品): *They worked hard to provide for their large family.* 他们努力工作以供养一大家子人. ○ *He didn't provide for his wife and children in his will*, ie didn't leave them money to live on. 他在遗嘱中没有给妻子儿女留下钱财. **provide for sth** (**a**) make arrangements or decisions which can be carried out if sth occurs 为某事物可能发生作准备: *provide for every eventuality in the budget* 在预算中为可能出现的一切情况作好准备 ○ *The planners had not provided for a failure of the power system.* 计划制定者未对动力系统可能出现故障一事制定应变措施. (**b**) (of a bill, legal agreement, etc) establish the legal basis or authority for sth to be done later (指法案、法律协议等)为其后之某事物提供法律依据: *The right of individuals to appeal to a higher court is provided for in the constitution.* 个人可向上级法院提出上诉, 这是宪法所赋予的权利.

▷ **pro·vider** *n* person who provides, esp one who supports a family 供应者; 提供者; (尤指)维持家庭生计者: *The eldest son is the family's only provider.* 那长子是唯一挣钱养家的人.

pro·vided /prəˈvaɪdɪd; prəˈvaɪdɪd/ (also **provided that**, **providing** /prəˈvaɪdɪŋ; prəˈvaɪdɪŋ/, **providing that**) *conj* on the condition or understanding that 在…情况或条件下; 假若; 倘若; 除非: *I will agree to go provided/providing (that) my expenses are paid.* 假如为我负担费用, 我就同意去. ○ *Provided we get good weather it will be a successful holiday.* 如果天气良好, 我们的假日将过得非常好.

prov·id·ence /ˈprɒvɪdəns; ˈprɑvədəns/ *n* **1** [sing, U] (instance that shows the) way in which God or nature cares for and protects all creatures 天道; 天意; 天佑: *trusting in (a) divine providence* 相信天命. **2** [U] (*fml* 文) being provident; foresight 远见; 卓识; 先见之明. **3** (idm 习语) **tempt fate/providence** ⇨ TEMPT.

prov·id·ent /ˈprɒvɪdənt; ˈprɑvədənt/ *adj* (*fml approv* 文, 褒) having or showing wisdom for future needs; thrifty 顾及未来的; 未雨绸缪的; 节俭的: *Some of the farmers had been provident in the good years but others were ruined by the bad harvests.* 有些农民在丰年节衣缩食有备无患, 但也有些农民由于歉收而陷入绝境.

□ ˈ**Provident Society** = FRIENDLY SOCIETY (FRIENDLY).

prov·id·en·tial /ˌprɒvɪˈdenʃl; ˌprɑvəˈdɛnʃəl/ *adj* (*fml* 文) occurring just at the right time when needed 正合时宜的; 及时的: *Their departure just before the floods was providential.* 他们恰在发洪水之前离开, 走得真是时候.

▷ **prov·id·en·tially** /-ʃəlɪ; -ʃlɪ/ *adv*.

pro·vid·ing ⇨ PROVIDED.

prov·ince /ˈprɒvɪns; ˈprɑvɪns/ *n* **1** [C] any of the main administrative divisions in certain countries (某些国家的)大行政区; 省份: *Canada has ten provinces.* 加拿大有十个省. Cf 参看 COUNTY, STATE[1] 3. **2 the provinces** [pl] all the parts of a country except the capital city 首都以外的地方: *The show will tour the provinces after it closes in London.* 这一表演在伦敦结束以后, 还将在全国各地巡回举行. ○ (*derog* 贬) *He found life in the provinces boring.* 他觉得首都以外的生活很无聊. **3** [sing] (*fml* 文) area of learning, activity or responsibility (学问、活动或责任的)范围: *The matter is outside my province*, ie I cannot or need not deal with it. 那不是我分内之事. ○ *Medieval painting is not his province.* 中世纪的绘画不属于他的研究范围. **4** [C] group of dioceses for which an archbishop has overall responsibility 大主教辖区(由几个教区组成).

pro·vin·cial /prəˈvɪnʃl; prəˈvɪnʃəl/ *adj* **1** [attrib 作定语] (**a**) of a province (1) 大行政区的; 省的: *the provincial government* 省政府 ○ *provincial taxes* 省的税收. (**b**) of the provinces (PROVINCE 2) 首都以外的: *provincial newspapers, theatres, towns* 首都以外的报纸、剧院、城镇. **2** (*usu derog* 通常作贬义) narrow-minded or old-fashioned; not modern or sophisticated 偏狭的; 守旧的; 过时的; 迂腐的: *display provincial attitudes to the theatre* 以旧眼光看待戏剧界.

▷ **pro·vin·cial** *n* (*usu derog* 通常作贬义) native or inhabitant of the provinces 首都以外的人; 地区居民: *Whenever I go to London I feel like a provincial.* 我一去伦敦, 就总是觉得自己像个乡巴佬.

prov·in·cial·ism /-ɪzəm; -ˌɪzəm/ *n* (*derog* 贬) **1** [U] provincial (2) attitude or outlook, esp one that indicates an (excessive) attachment to one's own small area 狭隘的观念; 偏狭; (尤指)地方主义: *He wanted to escape from the provincialism of the small university where he taught.* 他所执教是一所规模很小的大学, 他想摆脱存在于其中的地方主义桎梏. **2** [C] example of provincial(2) behaviour, manners, speech, etc 偏狭守旧的行为、举止、言语等: *embarrassed by his provincialisms* 他偏狭守旧而使人感到难为情.

pro·vin·cially /-ʃəlɪ; -ʃəlɪ/ *adv*.

pro·vi·sion /prəˈvɪʒn; prəˈvɪʒən/ *n* **1 ~ of sth** (**a**) [U] giving, lending, supplying or making sth available; providing sth 供应; 供给; 提供: *The government is responsible for the provision of medical services.* 政府负责提供医疗服务. (**b**) [C usu *sing* 通常作单数] amount of sth that is provided 提供的量; 供应量: *The provision of specialist teachers is being increased.* 配备专业教员的人数有所增加. **2** [U] **~ for/against sth** (**a**) preparation that is made to meet future needs or in case sth happens (为将来或为防万一而做的)准备: *make provision for one's old age* 为他日养老而预做准备 ○ *provision for his wife and children* 为妻子儿女的将来所做的安排 ○ *provision against possible disaster* 为防备可能发生的灾难而采取的措施. (**b**) **~ for sth** dealing with sth (in advance) (预先采取的)对策: *The present law makes no provision for this.* 现行的法律对此未作任何规定. **3** [C usu *pl* 通常作复数] (supply of) food and drink 食物和饮料; 饮食之供应: *She had a plentiful store of provisions.* 她贮存了大量的食物和饮料. ○ [attrib 作定语] *a provision merchant* 食品商人. **4** [C] condition or stipulation in a legal document (法律文件中的)规定, 条款: *under the provisions of the agreement* 根据协议的条文 ○ *She accepted the contract with the provision that it would be revised after a year.* 她同意签订这合同, 其中规定一年之后得加以修订.

▷ **pro·vi·sion** *v* [esp passive 尤用于被动语态: Tn, Tn·pr] **~ sb/sth (with sth)** (*fml* 文) supply sb/sth with provisions of food 向某人[某事物]供应食物: *provisioned for a long voyage* 为远航备足食粮.

pro·vi·sional /prəˈvɪʒənl; prəˋvɪʒənl/ *adj* for the present time only, with the possibility of being changed, etc later; temporary 临时的; 暂时性的: *a provisional appointment, contract, government* 暂定的职务、暂时性的契约、临时政府 ○ *a provisional driving licence*, ie (in Britain) one that has to be obtained before one can start to learn to drive 实习驾驶执照. ▷ **pro·vi·sion·ally** /-nəlɪ; -nlɪ/ *adv*: *The meeting has been provisionally arranged for 3.00 pm next Friday.* 会议时间暂定为下星期五下午三时.

pro·viso /prəˈvaɪzəʊ; prəˋvaɪzo/ *n* (*pl* **~s**; *US* also **~es**) clause, etc that is insisted on as a condition of an agreement 限制性条款; 附文; 但书: *He accepted, with one proviso*, ie on one condition. 他同意了, 但有一个附带条件.

P

pro·vis·ory /prəˈvaɪzərɪ; prəˋvaɪzərɪ/ *adj* (*fml* 文) containing a proviso; conditional 有附带条款的; 附有条件的: *a provisory clause* 附有条件的条文.

pro·voca·tion /ˌprɒvəˈkeɪʃn; ˌprɑvəˋkeʃən/ *n* **1** [U] making sb angry by deliberately doing sth annoying or offensive; provoking or being provoked 挑衅; 激怒; 刺激: *the incessant provocation of the hostile crowd* 抱有对立情绪的群众受到接二连三的煽动 ○ *react with violence only under provocation*, ie when provoked 只有受到挑衅时才以暴力还击 ○ *She loses her temper at/on the slightest provocation.* 只要稍一惹她, 她就大发脾气. **2** [C] cause of annoyance; thing that provokes 恼怒的原因; 激怒人的事: *He hit her after repeated provocations.* 她一次次招惹他, 他就打了她.

pro·voc·at·ive /prəˈvɒkətɪv; prəˋvɑkətɪv/ *adj* **1** tending or intended to arouse anger, annoyance, controversy, etc 激起愤怒、恼恨、争论等的; 挑衅的; 煽动性的: *a provocative comment, remark, speech, etc* 挑衅性的评论、言语、讲话等. **2** tending or intended to arouse sexual desire 引起性欲的; 挑逗的: *a dress with a provocative slit at the side* 开有撩人边缝的连衣裙 ○ *She was sitting in a highly provocative pose.* 她坐在那里姿势非常撩人. ▷ **pro·voc·at·ively** *adv*.

pro·voke /prəˈvəʊk; prəˋvok/ *v* **1** (**a**) [Tn] make (sb) angry or annoyed 激怒(某人); 惹(某人)气恼: *I am not easily provoked, but this behaviour is intolerable!* 我这人不爱生气, 但是这种行为使人忍无可忍! ○ *If you provoke the dog, it will bite you.* 你招惹那条狗, 它会咬你的. (**b**) [Tn·pr, Cn·t] **~ sb into doing sth/to do sth** cause sb to react to sth esp by making him angry 使某人对某事物作出反应(尤指使用刺激手段): *His behaviour finally provoked her into leaving him.* 他把她气得终于离开了他. ○ *He was provoked by their mockery to say more than he had intended.* 他受到他们嘲笑恼羞成怒, 说了一些过头的话. **2** [Tn] cause (sth) to occur or arouse (a feeling, etc) 使(某事物)产生; 引起(某种感情等): *provoke laughter, riots, smiles, violence* 引起大笑、暴乱、微笑、暴力行为.

▷ **pro·vok·ing** *adj* (*dated or fml* 旧或文) annoying 气人的; 恼人的: *It is very provoking of her to be so late.* 她到得这么晚真叫人生气.

prov·ost /ˈprɒvəst; *US* ˈprəʊ-; ˋprovəst/ *n* **1** (**a**) (*Brit*) (title of the) head of certain university colleges (大学中某些学院的)院长(的称号). (**b**) (*US*) senior administrator in certain universities (某些大学的)教务长. **2** (*Scot* 苏格兰) (title of the) head of a town council or burgh 市长(的称号). **3** (*Brit*) (title of the) head of the chapter in certain cathedrals 座堂主任, 教区长(的称号).

prow /praʊ; praʊ/ *n* (*esp fml* 尤作正规语) projecting front part of a ship or boat; bow 船首.

prow·ess /ˈpraʊɪs; ˋpraʊɪs/ *n* [U] (*fml* 文) outstanding skill or ability; expertise 高超的技艺; 非凡的才能; 专长: *We had to admire his prowess as an oarsman/his rowing prowess.* 我们不能不佩服他那了不起的划桨本领.

prowl /praʊl; praʊl/ *v* **1** (**a**) [I, Ip] **~ (about/around)** move quietly and cautiously 小心地悄悄移动: *wild animals prowling in the forest* 在森林里轻轻行走的野兽 ○ *burglars prowling (around) in the grounds of the house* 在房子的庭院里蹑足行走的窃贼. (**b**) [Tn] move about, through or in (a place) in this way 悄悄行经(某处): *thieves prowling the streets at night* 夜里在街上鬼鬼祟祟的小偷. **2** [I, Ip] **~ (about/around)** walk or wander restlessly 徘徊; 逡巡: *I could hear him prowling around in his bedroom all night.* 我听到他整夜在卧室里踱来踱去.

▷ **prowl** *n* (idm 习语) **(be/go) on the ˈprowl** (be/go) prowling 小心而悄悄的移动; 徘徊: *There was a fox on the prowl near the chicken coop.* 有只狐狸在鸡舍附近踅来踅去. ○ (*joc* 谑) *The soldiers went on the prowl hoping to meet some girls.* 这些大兵逛来逛去, 希望碰上花姑娘.

prowler *n* person or animal that prowls 悄悄行走的人或动物.

NOTE ON USAGE 用法: The following verbs indicate the slow, quiet movement of people or animals who do not want to be noticed by others. 下列动词均表示人或动物为免受注意而做出的缓慢而无声的动作. They suggest a variety of reasons for this secrecy. 这些动词暗示的行动隐秘原因不尽相同. **Prowl (about, around, etc)** suggests a wild animal or criminal looking for food or for something to steal ☆ **prowl (about、around、etc)** 指野兽觅食或罪犯伺机行窃: *I saw someone prowling around among the trees.* 我见有人在树林里鬼鬼祟祟地走动. ○ *Wolves prowled the forest in search of prey.* 狼在森林里潜行觅食. **Skulk (about, around, etc)** refers to someone angrily or guiltily waiting out of sight, possibly intending to do something bad ☆ **skulk (about、around、etc)** 指含怒或含罪恶目的窥伺可乘之机: *He skulked around outside until the police had gone.* 他窥探着四周, 直至见到警察走开. **Lurk** is used with similar meaning ☆ **lurk**的意义大体相同: *Somebody's lurking in the bushes.* 有人在灌木丛里窥视动静. A person **slinks (off, away, etc)** when he or she feels ashamed or frightened. 因羞怯或恐惧而悄悄走开用 **slink (off、away、etc).** ☆ It usually suggests that the head is low 此字通常含有垂头之意: *Don't slink away without apologizing.* 不要不道歉就偷偷溜走. ○ *The dog slunk off to lick its wounds.* 那狗耷拉着脑袋溜掉, 去舔伤口去了. People **sneak in, out, etc** when they are doing something wrong but not seriously criminal 偷偷摸摸做坏事, 但还够不上犯罪, 用**sneak in、out、etc**: *She was caught sneaking into the show without paying.* 她不买票就想混进场内看演出, 被当场捉住. **Sidle** is to move furtively, especially if nervous about one's purpose ☆ **sidle** 指悄悄地移动, 尤含惴惴不安之意: *He sidled up/over to her and asked her to dance.* 他忸忸怩怩走到她跟前请她跳舞. ○ *The boy sidled past the teacher and then ran out of the door.* 那男孩怯生生地走过老师身边, 然后便一溜烟跑出门外. We **steal, in, out, etc** in great secrecy 偷偷地走动用**steal in、out、etc**: *She stole out of the house in the middle of the night.* 她在半夜里偷偷地走出那所房子. **Creep** also suggests secrecy and, in animals especially, indicates a crouching position ☆ **creep**亦指偷偷地或悄悄地走动, 并有蜷身或爬行之意, 尤用于动物为然: *The cat crept up on the bird and pounced.* 那只猫悄悄地爬近那只鸟, 接着便猛扑过去. **Tiptoe** is the most neutral verb. ☆ **tiptoe**最无褒贬区别. The purpose in tiptoeing may be to avoid disturbing other people 用这一动词可作为避免惊扰他人之意: *They tiptoed upstairs so as not to wake the baby.* 他们踮着脚上楼, 生怕把孩子吵醒.

prox·im·ate /ˈprɒksɪmət; ˋprɑksəmɪt/ *adj* (*fml* 文) next before or after (in time, order, etc); nearest (时间、顺序等方面)紧邻的, 最接近的.

prox·im·ity /prɒkˈsɪmətɪ; prɑkˋsɪmətɪ/ *n* [U] (*fml* 文) **~ (to sth)** nearness in space or time; closeness (空间或时间上的)邻近, 接近: *in the proximity* (ie neighbourhood) *of the building* 那座大楼附近 ○ *houses built in close proximity to each other* 紧挨在一起的房子 ○ *The restaurant benefits from its proximity to several cinemas.* 那家餐馆位于几家影院附近因而沾光.

proxy /ˈprɒksɪ; ˋprɑksɪ/ *n* **1** [C] person authorized to act on behalf of another 代理人; 代表: *act as sb's proxy* 充当某人的代理人 ○ *He made his wife his proxy.* 他让妻子作他的代表. **2** (**a**) [U] authority to represent sb else (esp in voting at an election) 代理权; (尤指)代表他人投票之权利: *vote by proxy* 由他人代为投票 ○ [attrib 作定语] *a proxy vote* 委托他人代理的投票. (**b**) [C] document that gives such authority 委托书; 委托他人投票的授权书.

prude /pru:d; prud/ *n* (*derog* 贬) person who behaves in an extremely or unnaturally proper manner, esp one who is (too) easily shocked by sexual matters 极端或过分拘谨的人；（尤指对性问题）大惊小怪的人: *She was such a prude that she was even embarrassed by the sight of naked children.* 她正经得出了格，甚至见了赤身露体的孩子也难为情.

▷ **prudery** /ˈpruːdərɪ; ˋprudərɪ/ *n* [U] behaviour or attitude of a prude 拘谨；（尤指对性问题）大惊小怪，假正经.

prud·ish /ˈpruːdɪʃ; ˋprudɪʃ/ *adj* of or like a prude 过分拘谨的；（尤指对性问题）大惊小怪的，假正经的: *a prudish refusal to enjoy rude jokes* 拘谨得听不得粗俗的笑话. **prud·ishly** *adv*. **prud·ish·ness** *n* [U].

pru·dent /ˈpruːdnt; ˋprudn̩t/ *adj* acting with or showing care and foresight; showing good judgement 审慎的；有先见之明的；判断力强的: *prudent housekeeping* 精明的治家 ○ *a prudent saver of money* 很会精打细算的储蓄者 ○ *It would be prudent to save some of the money.* 存点钱是有远见的. ○ *That was a prudent decision.* 那是一个审慎的决定.

▷ **pru·dence** /-dns; -dn̩s/ *n* [U] (*fml* 文) (quality of) being prudent; forethought or wisdom 审慎；远见；智慧: *One can rely on the prudence of his decisions.* 可以相信他所作的决定，都是非常英明的.

prune[1] /pruːn; prun/ *n* dried plum 西梅脯；西梅干: *a dish of stewed prunes* 一碟煮西梅脯.

prune[2] /pruːn; prun/ *v* **1** (a) [Tn, Tn·p] **~ sth (back)** trim the shape of (a tree, bush, etc) by cutting away some of the branches, etc, esp to encourage new growth 修剪(树木等): *She has been pruning the roses.* 她一直在修剪玫瑰. (b) [Tn, Tn·pr, Tn·p] **~ sth (from/off sth); ~ sth (away/back/off)** remove (dead wood, branches, etc) by cutting 剪去(枯木、枯枝等): *These straggly stems should be pruned off the bush.* 这些灌木的蔓生枝条该剪了. ○ *Prune back the longer branches.* 剪掉过长的树枝. ⇨Usage at CLIP[2] 用法见 CLIP[2]. **2** [Tn, Tn·pr, Tn·p] **~ sth of sth; ~ sth down** reduce the extent of sth by cutting unnecessary parts 精简某事物；除去某事物的多余部分: *Next year's budget will have to be drastically pruned.* 下一年度的预算将大幅度削减. ○ *Try to prune your essay of irrelevant detail.* 尽量删去你那文章中无关的细节. ○ *She's pruning down the novel at the publisher's request.* 她按出版商的要求对小说进行删改.

▷ **prun·ing** *n* [U]: *Careful pruning at the right time is the secret of success with roses.* 养玫瑰花的秘诀就是适时细心修剪. ˈ**pruning-hook** *n* tool with a curved blade used for pruning 修枝镰.

pruri·ent /ˈprʊərɪənt; ˋprʊrɪənt/ *adj* (*fml derog* 文，贬) having or showing excessive interest in sexual matters 好色的；迷恋淫欲的: *She showed a prurient interest in the details of the rape case.* 她对那强奸案的细节津津乐道.

▷ **pruri·ence** /-əns; -əns/ *n* [U] (*fml derog* 文，贬) quality or state of being prurient 好色；迷恋淫欲.

pruri·ently *adv*.

Prus·sian /ˈprʌʃn; ˋprʌʃən/ *adj* (esp formerly) of or relating to Prussia in Germany (尤指旧时)普鲁士的，与普鲁士有关的: *the Prussian army* 普鲁士军队.

▷ **Prus·sian** *n* (formerly) inhabitant or native of Prussia (旧时)普鲁士居民，普鲁士人.

□ ˌ**Prussian** ˈ**blue** (of a) deep blue colour 普鲁士蓝(的)；深蓝色(的).

prussic acid /ˌprʌsɪk ˈæsɪd; ˌprʌsɪk ˋæsɪd/ highly dangerous poison 氢氰酸.

pry[1] /praɪ; praɪ/ *v* (*pt, pp* **pried** /praɪd; praɪd/) [I, Ipr] **~ (into sth)** inquire too curiously or rudely about other people's private affairs 打听，刺探(他人的私事): *safe from prying eyes* 闲人无从偷窥 ○ *I don't want them prying into my affairs.* 我不愿意他们打听我的私事.

pry[2] /praɪ; praɪ/ *v* (*pt, pp* **pried** /praɪd; praɪd/) [Tn·pr, Tn·p, Cn·a] (*esp US*) = PRISE: *pry the lid off a tin* 把罐头的盖子撬掉 ○ *pry the tin open* 把罐头撬开 ○ (*fig* 比喻) *pry information out of sb* 从某人嘴里弄到消息.

PS **1** (*Brit*) police sergeant 警长；巡佐: *PS (Bill) Jones* (比尔·)琼斯警长. Cf 参看 WPS. **2** (also **ps**) /ˌpiː ˈes; ˌpi ˋɛs/ *abbr* 缩写 = (esp at the end of a letter 尤用于信末) postscript (Latin *postscriptum* 源自拉丁文 *postscriptum*): *Love from Tessa. PS I'll bring the car.* 爱你的泰萨. 我把车开来. 又及. Cf 参看 PPS.

psalm /sɑːm; sɑm/ *n* sacred song or hymn, esp one of those in the Book of Psalms in the Old Testament 圣歌；圣诗；赞美诗；（尤指）《旧约·诗篇》中之任何一篇: *The choir sang the 23rd Psalm.* 唱诗班唱《旧约·诗篇》之第23篇.

▷ **psalm·ist** /-ɪst; -ɪst/ writer of psalms 赞美诗作者；《旧约·诗篇》作者.

psal·ter /ˈsɔːltə(r); ˋsɔltɚ/ *n* book containing a collection of psalms with their music, for use in public worship 诗篇集；(礼拜时用的)诗篇歌集.

psal·tery /ˈsɔːltərɪ; ˋsɔltərɪ/ *n* musical instrument of ancient and medieval times, played by plucking strings that are stretched over a board 萨泰利琴(古代及中世纪使用的一种拨弦乐器).

psepho·logy /seˈfɒlədʒɪ; *US* siːˈf-; siˋfɑlədʒɪ/ *n* [U] study of the way in which people vote in elections, esp by means of opinion polls 选举学.

▷ **psepho·logical** /ˌsefəˈlɒdʒɪkl; *US* ˌsiːf-; ˌsifəˋlɑdʒɪkəl/ *adj* of or relating to psephology 选举学的；与选举学有关的.

psepho·logist /seˈfɒlədʒɪst; *US* siːˈf-; siˋfɑlədʒɪst/ *n* expert in or student of psephology 选举学专家；选举学的研究者.

pseud /sjuːd; *US* ˈsuːd; sud/ *n* (*infml derog* 口，贬) person who tries to appear more knowledgeable, fashionable or cultured than he really is; pretentious and affected person 假充有知识、合乎潮流或有教养的人；伪君子: *She's just a pseud; she knows nothing about art really.* 她不过是假充内行罢了，实际上对艺术一窍不通.

pseudo /ˈsjuːdəʊ; *US* ˈsuː-; ˋsudo/ *adj* (*infml* 口) not genuine; sham or insincere 假的；虚伪的；不真诚的: *This apparent interest of his in modern music is completely pseudo.* 他对现代音乐显露出的雅兴纯属自欺欺人.

pseud(o)- *comb form* 构词成分 not authentic; false or pretended 假；伪: *pseudonym* ○ *pseudo-intellectual* ○ *pseudo-science*.

pseud·onym /ˈsjuːdənɪm; *US* ˈsuːdənɪm; ˋsudn̩ˌɪm/ *n* (also ˈ**nom de plume**) person's name that is not his real name, esp one used by an author; pen-name 假名；化名；（尤指）笔名: *George Eliot was the pseudonym of Mary Ann Evans.* 乔治·艾略特是玛丽·安·埃文斯的笔名. ○ *She writes under a pseudonym.* 她用笔名发表作品.

▷ **pseud·onym·ous** /sjuːˈdɒnɪməs; *US* suː-; suˋdɑnəməs/ *adj* (*fml* 文) writing or written under a pseudonym 用假名的；用笔名写作的；署笔名的.

psi *abbr* 缩写 = pounds (pressure) per square inch (eg on tyres) 磅/平方英寸(压力标志，如轮胎上的字样).

psit·tac·osis /ˌsɪtəˈkəʊsɪs; ˌsɪtəˋkosɪs/ *n* [U] serious viral disease causing fever and pneumonia in humans, who can catch it from parrots and other birds 鹦鹉热(由鹦鹉等传染给人的疾病).

psori·asis /səˈraɪəsɪs; səˋraɪəsɪs/ *n* [U] skin disease that causes red scaly patches 牛皮癣；银屑病.

psst /pst; pst/ *interj* (used to attract sb's attention secretly or furtively 用以暗中或悄悄提起他人注意): *'Psst! Let's get out now before they see us!'* '嘘！趁着现在他们没看见，咱们走吧！'

PST /ˌpiː es ˈtiː; ˌpi ɛs ˋti/ *abbr* 缩写 = (*US*) Pacific Standard Time 太平洋标准时.

psych (also **psy·che**) /saɪk; saɪk/ *v* (*infml* 口) **1** [Tn, Tn·p] **~ sb (out)** make sb nervous or less confident, etc, esp by psychological means 使某人精神紧张或丧失信心等(尤指用攻心方法): *Her arrogant behaviour on court psyched her opponent (out) completely.* 她在法庭上那盛气凌人的样子把对方完全镇慑住了. **2** (phr v) **psych sb/oneself up** prepare sb/oneself mentally for sth 使某人[自己]对某事物作好思想准备: *She had really psyched herself up for the big match.* 她为大赛作了充分的心理准备.

psy·che /ˈsaɪkɪ; ˋsaɪkɪ/ *n* human soul or mind 灵魂；心灵: *Is aggression an essential part of the human psyche?* 损人利己是否是人心灵的主宰？

psy·che·delic /ˌsaɪkɪˈdelɪk; ˌsaɪkɪˋdɛlɪk/ *adj* **1** (of drugs) producing hallucinations (指药物)引起幻觉的，致幻觉的: *Mescalin and LSD are psychedelic drugs.* 仙人球毒碱和麦角酸二乙基酰胺都是迷幻药. **2** having intensely vivid colours, sounds, etc like those experienced while hallucinating (色彩、声音等)产生迷幻效果的: *psychedelic music* 使人精神恍惚的音乐. ▷ **psy·che·del·ic·ally**

/-klɪ; -klɪ/ *adv*.

psy·chi·atry /saɪˈkaɪətrɪ; *US* sɪ-; səˋkaɪətrɪ/ *n* [U] study and treatment of mental illness 精神病学; 精神病治疗. Cf 参看 PSYCHOLOGY 1.

▷ **psy·chi·at·ric** /ˌsaɪkɪˈætrɪk; ˌsaɪkɪˋætrɪk/ *adj* of or concerning psychiatry 精神病学的; 治疗精神病的: *a psychiatric clinic* 精神病诊所 ○ *psychiatric treatment* 精神病的治疗.

psy·chi·at·rist /-ɪst; -ɪst/ *n* specialist in psychiatry 精神病专家; 精神科医生.

psychic /ˈsaɪkɪk; ˋsaɪkɪk/ *adj* **1** (also **psych·ical** /ˈsaɪkɪkl; ˋsaɪkɪkḷ/) (**a**) concerned with processes and phenomena that seem to be outside physical or natural laws 关于通灵的; 超自然的: *psychical research*, ie the study and investigation of psychical phenomena, eg telepathy 通灵研究(研究心灵现象, 如心灵感应). (**b**) of the soul or mind 灵魂的; 心灵的. **2** (claiming to be) able to respond to or exercise supernatural or occult powers (自称)通灵的, 有特异功能的: *She claims to be psychic and to be able to foretell the future.* 她自称有特异功能, 能预知未来.

▷ **psychic** *n* person claiming or appearing to be responsive to supernatural powers (自称)通灵的或有特异功能的人; 巫师.

psych(o)- *comb form* 构词成分 of the mind 精神的; 心灵的; 心理的: *psychiatry* ○ *psychology* ○ *psychotherapy*.

psy·cho·ana·lysis /ˌsaɪkəʊəˈnæləsɪs; ˌsaɪkoəˋnæləsɪs/ (also **ana·lysis**) *n* [U] (method of treating mental disorders by) repeatedly interviewing a person in order to make him aware of experiences in his early life and trace the connection between them and his present behaviour or feelings 精神分析(治疗法); 心理分析(治疗法).

▷ **psy·cho·ana·lyst** /ˌsaɪkəʊˈænəlɪst; ˌsaɪkoˋænḷɪst/ (also **ana·lyst**) *n* person who practises psychoanalysis 采用精神分析治疗法的专家; 精神分析学家.

psy·cho·ana·lytic, psy·cho·ana·lyt·ical /ˌsaɪkəʊˌænəˈlɪtɪk, -kl; ˌsaɪkoˌænḷˋɪtɪk, -ɪkḷ/ *adjs* relating to psychoanalysis 精神分析(治疗法)的; 心理分析(治疗法)的. **psy·cho·ana·lyt·ically** /-ɪklɪ; -ɪklɪ/ *adv*.

psy·cho·ana·lyse /ˌsaɪkəʊˈænəlaɪz; ˌsaɪkoˋænḷˌaɪz/ (also **ana·lyse**, *US* **-lyze**) *v* [Tn] treat or investigate (sb) by means of psychoanalysis 用精神分析法治疗(某人); 给(某人)作精神分析.

psy·cho·logy /saɪˈkɒlədʒɪ; saɪˋkɑlədʒɪ/ *n* **1** [U] science or study of the mind and how it functions 心理学: *child psychology* 儿童心理学 ○ *industrial psychology* 工业心理学. Cf 参看 PSYCHIATRY. **2** [sing] (*infml* 口) mental characteristics of a person or group 心理; 心理特点: *the psychology of the adolescent* 青春期心理特点.

▷ **psy·cho·lo·gical** /ˌsaɪkəˈlɒdʒɪkl; ˌsaɪkəˋlɑdʒɪkḷ/ *adj* **1** of or affecting the mind 心理的; 精神上的: *the psychological development of a child* 儿童的心理成长. **2** of or relating to psychology 心理学的; 关于心理学的: *psychological methods, research* 心理学的方法、研究. **3** (idm 习语) **the ˌpsychological ˈmoment** the most appropriate time to do sth, in order to achieve success (做某事的)最适当的时机: *We're going to have to ask for more money — it's just a question of finding the (right) psychological moment.* 我们准备要求多加点钱——问题是得找个(最)适当的机会. **psy·cho·lo·gic·ally** /-klɪ; -klɪ/ *adv*. ˌ**psychological ˈwarfare** (waging war by) weakening an enemy's morale or by trying to change his attitudes, beliefs, etc 心理战.

psy·cho·lo·gist /-ɪst; -ɪst/ *n* student of or expert in psychology 心理学研究者; 心理学家.

psy·cho·path /ˈsaɪkəʊpæθ; ˋsaɪkəˌpæθ/ *n* person suffering from a severe mental or emotional disorder, esp one who behaves in a violently aggressive or antisocial way 精神变态者, 精神病患者(尤指行为有破坏性或危害社会者).

▷ **psy·cho·pathic** /ˌsaɪkəʊˈpæθɪk; ˌsaɪkəˋpæθɪk/ *adj* of or suffering from a severe emotional or mental disorder 精神变态的; 患精神病的.

psych·osis /saɪˈkəʊsɪs; saɪˋkosɪs/ *n* (*pl* **-choses** /-ˈkəʊsiːz; -ˋkosiz/) [C, U] severe mental illness that affects the whole personality 精神病.

psycho·so·matic /ˌsaɪkəʊsəˈmætɪk; ˌsaɪkəsəˋmætɪk/ *adj* **1** (of disease) caused or made worse by mental stress (指疾病)由精神压力引起的, 因有精神压力而恶化的. **2** dealing with the relationship between the mind and the body 治疗身心失调之疾病的: *psychosomatic medicine* 心身医学. ▷ **psycho·so·matic·ally** /-klɪ; -klɪ/ *adv*.

psy·cho·ther·apy /ˌsaɪkəʊˈθerəpɪ; ˌsaɪkoˋθɛrəpɪ/ *n* [U] treatment of mental disorders by psychological methods 精神疗法; 心理疗法.

▷ **psy·cho·ther·ap·ist** /-ɪst; -ɪst/ *n* person who treats people by using psychotherapy 采用精神疗法的医生.

psych·otic /saɪˈkɒtɪk; saɪˋkɑtɪk/ *adj* of or suffering from psychosis 精神病的; 患精神病的: *a psychotic disorder* 精神错乱.

▷ **psych·otic** *n* person suffering from psychosis 精神病患者.

PT /ˌpiː ˈtiː; ˌpi ˋti/ *abbr* 缩写 = physical training 体育锻炼: *do PT* 进行体育锻炼 ○ *a PT lesson* 一堂体育课. Cf 参看 PE.

pt *abbr* 缩写 = **1** (also **Pt**) part: *Shakespeare's Henry IV Pt 2* 莎士比亚的《亨利四世》第二部分. **2** (*pl* **pts**) pint: *2 pts today please, milkman*, eg on a notice. 送奶员注意, 本日请送 2 品脱(如便条字样). **3** (*pl* **pts**) point: *The winner scored 10 pts.* 胜者获得 10 分. **4** (also **Pt**) (esp on a map 尤作地图标记) port: *Pt Moresby* 摩斯比港.

PTA /ˌpiː tiː ˈeɪ; ˌpi ti ˋe/ *abbr* 缩写 = parent-teacher association (eg in schools) 家长教师联谊会(如中小学的).

pta (*pl* **ptas**) *abbr* 缩写 = peseta.

ptar·migan /ˈtɑːmɪgən; ˋtɑrməgən/ *n* bird of the grouse family, with black or grey feathers in summer and white feathers in winter 雷鸟(松鸡科鸟, 夏季羽毛呈黑色或灰色, 冬季呈白色).

Pte *abbr* 缩写 = (*Brit*) (*US* **Pvt**) Private (soldier): *Pte (Jim) Hill* 二等兵(吉姆·)希尔.

ptero·dac·tyl /ˌterəˈdæktɪl; ˌtɛrəˋdæktɪl/ *n* extinct flying reptile 翼指龙, 翼手龙(绝灭的飞行爬行动物).

PTO (also **pto**) /ˌpiː tiː ˈəʊ; ˌpi ti ˋo/ *abbr* 缩写 = (eg at the bottom of a page) please turn over 见反面, 见下页(如页末字样).

pto·maine /ˈtəʊmeɪn; ˋtomen/ *n* [C, U] any of a group of substances formed by decaying animal and vegetable matter 尸碱, 尸毒(动物和蔬菜腐烂后产生的物质).

□ ˈ**ptomaine poisoning** (*dated* 旧) = FOOD POISONING (FOOD).

pub /pʌb; pʌb/ *n* (*Brit infml* 口) public house 酒店; 酒馆: *They've gone down/round to the pub for a drink.* 他们到酒店喝酒去了.

□ ˈ**pub crawl** (*Brit infml* 口) tour of several pubs or bars with drinking at each of them 连着光顾几家酒店或酒吧: *go on a pub crawl* 接连到好几家酒店喝酒.

pu·berty /ˈpjuːbətɪ; ˋpjubɚtɪ/ *n* [U] stage at which a person's sexual organs are maturing and he or she becomes capable of having children 青春期: *reach the age of puberty* 到达青春期.

pu·bic /ˈpjuːbɪk; ˋpjubɪk/ *adj* [usu attrib 通常作定语] of or on the lower part of the abdomen, near the sexual organs 阴部的; 近阴部的; 性器官附近的: *pubic hair* 阴毛 ○ *the pubic bone* 耻骨. ⇨ illus at MALE 见 MALE 插图.

pub·lic /ˈpʌblɪk; ˋpʌblɪk/ *adj* **1** (esp attrib 尤作定语) (**a**) of or concerning people in general 公众的; 与公众有关的: *a danger to public health* 对公众健康的威胁 ○ *The campaign was designed to increase public awareness of the problem.* 这个运动目的在于提高公众对这一问题的认识. ○ *public expenditure* 公共事业开支. (**b**) provided, esp by central or local government, for the use of people in general 为公众的, 公用的, 公共的(尤指由中央或地方政府提供的): *public education, libraries, parks* 民众教育、公共图书馆、公园 ○ *the public highway* 公路. (**c**) of or engaged in the affairs, entertainment, service, etc of the people (从事)公共事务、群众娱乐活动、社会服务等的: *He is one of the most admired public figures/figures in public life today.* 他是当今公众事务中最受大家爱戴的人. **2** open or known to people in general 向大众公开的; 众所周知的: *She decided to make her views public.* 她决定把自己的观点公开. ○ *a public admission of guilt* 公开承认有罪 ○ *a public place* 公共场所. Cf 参看 PRIVATE. **3** (idm 习语) **be public knowledge** be generally known 众所周知: *It's public knowledge she's expecting a baby.* 大家都知道她已怀孕了. **go ˈpublic**

(of a company) become a public company by selling shares to the public (指公司)向公众出售股分. **in the public 'eye** well known to or often seen by the public (in newspapers, on television, etc) (报刊、电视等上)公众熟悉的, 公众常见的. **ˌpublic 'property** (thing that is) known to everybody or anybody 人人皆知的(事物): *Their financial problems are public property now.* 他们在经济上出现的问题现已尽人皆知了.

▷ **pub·lic** *n* **1** [Gp] (**a**) **the public** (members of) the community in general 公众; 民众: *the British public* 英国公众 ○ *The public is/are not allowed to enter the court room.* 一般民众不准进入审判室. (**b**) part of the community having a particular interest in common (有共同爱好的)一群人: *the theatre-going public* 爱看戏的人 ○ *She knows how to keep her public* (eg the readers of her books) *satisfied.* 她知道怎样迎合她那些读者的需要. **2** (idm 习语) **in 'public** not in private; openly 公开地; 公然: *She was appearing in public* (ie in front of people in general) *for the first time since her illness.* 她自从患病以来第一次公开露面. **wash one's dirty linen in public** ⇨ WASH[2].

pub·licly /-klɪ; -klɪ/ *adv.*

□ **ˌpublic-ad'dress system** (*abbr* 缩写 **P'A system**) system of microphones and loudspeakers used at public meetings, sports events, etc 扩音系统.

ˌpublic 'bar (*Brit*) bar in a public house with simpler or less comfortable furniture than other bars (酒店中的)酒吧(设备较其他酒吧简陋). Cf 参看 LOUNGE BAR (LOUNGE).

ˌpublic 'company (also **ˌpublic ˌlimited 'company**) (*abbrs* 缩写 **ˌPL'C, plc**) company that sells shares in itself to the public 向公众出售股分的公司: *The pension fund owns shares in several major public companies.* 该养老基金在几家主要出售股分给公众的公司中均有股分.

ˌpublic con'venience (*Brit*) toilet provided for the public to use 公共厕所. ⇨Usage at TOILET 用法见TOILET.

ˌpublic 'house (*Brit fml* 文) building (not a club, hotel, etc but often serving meals) where alcoholic drinks are sold and drunk 酒店, 酒馆(常供应饭菜): *Public houses are licensed to sell alcoholic drinks for a certain number of hours per week.* 酒店执有酒类经销许可证, 每周可按一定时数出售. Cf 参看 INN, TAVERN.

ˌpublic 'lending right (*abbr* 缩写 **ˌPL'R**) right of authors to receive payment when their books are borrowed from public libraries 作者对公共图书馆出借其著作所享有的获得报酬的权利.

ˌpublic 'nuisance 1 (*law* 律) illegal act that is harmful to people in general 妨害公众利益的违法行为: *charged with committing a public nuisance* 因妨害公众利益而受到指控. **2** (*infml* 口) person who behaves in a way that annoys people in general 大家厌恶的人: *People who park on the pavement are a public nuisance.* 把汽车停在人行道上的人很讨人嫌.

ˌpublic o'pinion opinions or views of the public in general 舆论; 民意: *Public opinion was opposed to the war.* 舆论是反对那场战争的. **ˌpublic o'pinion poll** ⇨ POLL[1] 2.

ˌpublic 'ownership ownership and management of an industry by the State 公有(制); 国家所有(制): *Socialist policy favours public ownership of the coal industry.* 社会主义的政策有利于在煤炭工业中推行公有制.

ˌpublic 'prosecutor (*law* 律) legal official who conducts prosecutions on behalf of the State or in the public interest 检察官; 公诉人.

ˌPublic 'Record Office (*Brit*) place where official records are kept and made available to the public 档案局(保存官方档案可供公众查阅).

ˌpublic re'lations (*abbr* 缩写 **ˌP'R**) **1** work of presenting a good image of an organization, a commercial firm, etc to the public, esp by distributing information 公关工作; 公关活动: *She works in public relations.* 她从事公关工作. **2** relationship (esp a friendly one) between an organization, etc and the public 公共关系: *We support local artistic events; it's good for public relations.* 我们赞助本地的艺术活动; 这有利于促进公共关系. **ˌpublic re'lations officer** (*abbr* 缩写 **ˌPR'O**) person employed in public relations 公共关系人员.

ˌpublic 'school 1 (in Britain, esp England) private school (usu a boarding-school) for pupils aged between 13 and 18 whose parents pay fees for their education 公学(英国, 尤指英格兰之私立付费学校, 通常实行寄宿制, 学生年龄为13岁至18岁). Cf 参看 PREPARATORY SCHOOL (PREPARATORY). **2** (esp in the US) local state school providing free education (尤指美国地方开办的免费的)公立学校.

ˌpublic 'spirit readiness to do things that help the community 热心公益的精神. **ˌpublic-'spirited** *adj*: *It's very public-spirited of you to offer to take the old people to the shops each week.* 你每星期都主动领老年人去商店购物, 真有助人为乐的精神.

ˌpublic 'transport buses, trains, etc available to the public according to a published timetable 公共交通工具(公共汽车、火车等): *travel by public transport* 乘公共车辆旅行.

ˌpublic u'tility (*fml* 文) public service such as the supply of water, electricity, gas or a bus or rail network 公用事业: [attrib 作定语] *public utility companies* 公用事业公司.

pub·lican /ˈpʌblɪkən; ˋpʌblɪkən/ *n* person who owns or manages a public house 酒店老板.

pub·lica·tion /ˌpʌblɪˈkeɪʃn; ˌpʌblɪˋkeʃən/ *n* **1** (**a**) [U] action of making a book or periodical, available to the public 出版; 刊行: *the date of publication* 出版日期 ○ *It was clear, even before publication, that the book would be a success.* 该书将驰誉天下, 这一点甚至在出版发行以前就已十分清楚. (**b**) [C] book, periodical, etc that is published 出版物: *There are many publications on the subject.* 关于这一问题的出版物有很多. **2** [U] action of making sth known to the public 发表; 公布: *publication of the exam results* 考试成绩的公布 ○ *The government have delayed publication of the trade figures.* 政府已将贸易统计数字延后公布.

pub·li·cist /ˈpʌblɪsɪst; ˋpʌblɪsɪst/ *n* **1** person whose job is to make sth widely known; press or publicity agent 宣传人员; 宣传代理人. **2** writer or specialist in current affairs, eg a political journalist 政论家; 时事评论员.

pub·li·city /pʌbˈlɪsətɪ; pʌbˋlɪsətɪ/ *n* [U] **1** state of being known to, seen by, etc the public 为公众所知、所见等之状况: *avoid/shun/seek publicity* 避免[不愿/一心要]引起公众注意 ○ *Their marriage took place amid a blaze of publicity.* 他们举行婚礼轰动一时. **2** (business of) providing information in order to attract public attention; advertising 宣传(业务); 广告: *Her new play has attracted a lot of publicity.* 她的新剧作获得广泛宣传. ○ *The publicity for the book was poor and sales were low.* 该书宣传工作没有做好, 所以销量不大. ○ [attrib 作定语] *a publicity campaign*, ie special effort to publicize and promote sth 宣传运动. **3** (idm 习语) **the glare of publicity** ⇨ GLARE[2].

□ **pub'licity agent** person whose job is to make a performer, book, play, product, etc successful by informing the public about him or it (推荐表演者、书籍、剧作、产品等的)宣传代理人.

pub·li·cize, -ise /ˈpʌblɪsaɪz; ˋpʌblɪˌsaɪz/ *v* [Tn] inform the public about (sth), esp by advertising it 宣传(某事物)(尤指用广告): *an advertising campaign to publicize the new train service* 为新投入运营的铁路路线而开展的宣传活动 ○ *a well-publicized attempt to break the world speed record* 为打破世界速度纪录的尝试进行了充分的宣传.

pub·lish /ˈpʌblɪʃ; ˋpʌblɪʃ/ *v* **1** [Tn] (**a**) prepare, have printed and distribute to the public (a book, periodical, etc) 出版, 发行(书籍、期刊等): *This book is published by Oxford University Press.* 这本书是牛津大学出版社出版的. ○ *The journal is published monthly.* 那本杂志是月刊. (**b**) (of an author) have (one's work) printed and distributed (指作者)使(作品)印行, 发表: *He publishes articles in various newspapers.* 他在许多报纸上发表文章. ○ *She is publishing a history of the war period.* 她有一部战争时期的历史著作正在印行. **2** [Tn] make (sth) known to the public 公布, 宣布(某事物): *The firm publishes its accounts in August.* 该商行于八月份公布会计帐目. ○ *publish the banns of marriage*, ie announce formally (in church) the names of people who are soon to be married 公布结婚预告(教堂正式宣布即将结婚者的名单). **3** (idm 习语) **ˌpublish and be 'damned** (*catchphrase* 警语) (said eg to a blackmailer) make your accusation public if you like; I refuse to be blackmailed (对例如敲诈者说的话)你愿意宣扬就宣扬去吧，我可不吃你那一套.

▷ **pub·lish·ing** *n* [U] profession or business of publishing books 出版(业): *She chose publishing as a career.* 她选择的职业是出版工作.

pub·lisher *n* person or firm that publishes (PUBLISH 1a) books, newspapers, etc 出版者; 出版商; 出版社: *Several publishers are competing in the same market.* 几家出版公司正在同一市场上进行竞争.

puce /pju:s; pjus/ *adj*, *n* [U] (of a) purple-brown colour 紫褐色(的): *The man's face was puce with rage.* 那人的脸都气紫了.

puck /pʌk; pʌk/ *n* hard rubber disc struck by players in ice hockey (冰球运动用的)冰球(饼状, 用硬橡胶做成).

pucker /ˈpʌkə(r); ˋpʌkɚ/ *v* [I, Ip, Tn, Tn·p] **~ (sth) (up)** (cause sth to) form small folds or wrinkles (使某物)起褶子或皱纹: *The dress fitted badly and puckered at the waist.* 这件连衣裙不合身, 腰部很皱. ○ *The child's face puckered (up) and he began to cry.* 那孩子脸一皱哭了起来. ○ *pucker one's brows* 皱起眉头.

▷ **pucker** *n* small wrinkle, esp an unwanted one, in a garment (衣服上的)皱纹, 褶子(尤指不应有的): *an obvious pucker in the seam of her dress* 她衣缝上的一处明显的皱纹.

puck·ish /ˈpʌkɪʃ; ˋpʌkɪʃ/ *adj* mischievous, esp in a playful way; impish 恶作剧的; 胡闹的; 顽皮的: *a puckish grin* 调皮的一笑. ▷ **puck·ishly** *adv*: *smiling puckishly* 嬉笑.

pud·ding /ˈpʊdɪŋ; ˋpʊdɪŋ/ *n* **1** [C, U] (also *infml* 口语作 **pud** /pʊd; pʊd/) (*Brit*) (dish of) sweet food eaten at the end of a meal; dessert (一道)甜食(于餐末食用); 甜点心: *There isn't a pudding today.* 今天没有甜食. ○ *What's for pudding?* 甜点吃什么? Cf 参看 AFTERS. **2 (a)** [C, U] (also *Brit infml* 英式口语作 **pud**) sweet or savoury dish usu made with flour and cooked by baking, boiling or steaming 布丁(通常用面粉经烘烤或蒸煮做成的美味甜食品): *bread and butter pudding* 面包黄油布丁 ○ *rice pudding* 大米布丁 ○ *steak and kidney pudding* 牛排腰子布丁 ○ *Christmas/plum pudding* 圣诞布丁. **(b)** [C] thing like this in texture or appearance; (person with a) large, fat face 材料或外观似布丁之物; 肥胖而大的脸; 面孔肥胖而大的人: [attrib 作定语] *pudding face* 大胖脸. **3** [C, U] any of various types of sausage 香肠: *black pudding*, ie a type of blood sausage made with oatmeal 黑香肠(用燕麦片与血制成). **4** [C] (also ˈ**pudding head**) (*infml* 口) fat and slow or stupid person 肥胖而迟钝的人; 笨蛋. **5** (idm 习语) **the proof of the pudding** ⇨ PROOF[1].

puddle /ˈpʌdl; ˋpʌdl/ *n* [C] small pool of water, esp of rain-water on the road 水坑; (尤指道路上的)雨水坑.

▷ **puddle** *v* [Tn] stir (molten iron) in order to expel carbon and produce wrought iron 搅炼(熔铁).

pu·denda /pju:ˈdendə; pjuˋdɛndə/ *n* [pl] (*fml* 文) external genitals, esp of a woman 外生殖器(尤指女性的).

pudgy /ˈpʌdʒɪ; ˋpʌdʒɪ/ *adj* (**-ier, -iest**) (*infml* 口) short and fat; podgy 矮胖的; 短而粗的: *pudgy fingers* 短而粗的手指 ○ *a pudgy child* 胖乎乎的小孩. ▷ **pudgi·ness** *n* [U].

pu·er·ile /ˈpjʊəraɪl; *US* -rəl; ˋpjuə,rɪl/ *adj* (*derog* 贬) showing immaturity; childish and silly 幼稚的; 孩子气的; 愚蠢的: *puerile behaviour, concerns, objections, tasks* 幼稚的行为、无谓的操心、徒劳的反对、无聊的工作 ○ *She was tired of answering these puerile questions.* 她回答这些幼稚的问题觉得不胜其烦.

▷ **pu·er·il·ity** /pjʊəˈrɪlətɪ; ,pjuəˋrɪlətɪ/ *n* (*fml derog* 文, 贬) **(a)** [U] puerile behaviour; childishness 幼稚; 愚蠢. **(b)** [C esp *pl* 尤作复数] (*fml* 文) childish and foolish act, idea, statement, etc 幼稚、愚蠢的言行、想法等.

pu·er·peral /pju:ˈɜ:pərəl; pjuˋɝpərəl/ *adj* [attrib 作定语] (*medical* 医) of or related to childbirth 分娩的; 与分娩有关的: *puerperal fever* 产褥热.

puff[1] /pʌf; pʌf/ *n* **1** [C] **(a)** (sound of a) short light blowing of breath or wind (呼吸或风的)呼, 吹, 喷(之声): *a puff of wind* 一阵风 ○ *She blew out the candles in one puff.* 她噗的一声把蜡烛都吹灭了. **(b)** amount of smoke, steam, etc sent out at one time 一缕(烟、蒸气等): *There was a puff of steam from the engine before it stopped.* 机车喷出一股蒸气后就停了下来. ○ (*fig* 比喻) *puffs of cloud in the sky* 天空中朵朵的浮云 ○ (*joc* 谑) *vanish in a puff of smoke*, ie disappear quickly 一溜烟就不见了. **(c)** (*infml* 口) short drawing in of breath when smoking a pipe or cigarette (烟斗或香烟的)一吸, 一口: *She stubbed out the cigarette after the first puff.* 她只吸了一口就把香烟掐灭了. **2** [C] = POWDER-PUFF (POWDER). **3** [C] (esp in compounds 尤用以构成复合词) hollow piece of pastry filled with cream, jam, etc (有奶油、果酱等馅的)酥皮点心: *a cream puff* 奶油酥. **4** [U] (*infml* 口) = BREATH[1] 1a: *out of puff*, ie breathless 气喘吁吁的.

▷ **puffy** *adj* (**-ier, -iest**) forming or covered with a soft swelling or swellings 膨胀的; 肿胀的: *Beat the mixture until it has a light, puffy texture.* 把混合料搅拌到发起来为止. ○ *Her skin is puffy round her eyes.* 她眼圈浮肿. **puf·fily** *adv*. **puf·fi·ness** *n* [U] state of being puffy 膨胀; 肿胀: *Puffiness round the eyes is a sign of poor health.* 眼圈浮肿是不健康的样子.

□ ˈ**puff-adder** *n* large poisonous African viper that puffs out the upper part of its body when it is excited 鼓腹巨蝰(非洲产的大毒蛇, 受刺激时身体上半部即膨胀).

ˈ**puff-ball** *n* type of fungus with a ball-shaped spore-case that bursts open when it is ripe 马勃菌(有球状孢子囊, 成熟时即裂开).

ˌ**puff** ˈ**pastry** type of light flaky pastry used for pies, cakes, etc (做馅饼、糕饼等用的)油酥面团.

puff[2] /pʌf; pʌf/ *v* **1** [Ipr, Tn, Tn·pr] **(a)** (cause sth to) come out in puffs (PUFF[1] 1b) (使某物)阵阵喷出: *Smoke puffed from the chimney.* 烟从烟囱里一股一股地喷出来. ○ *Don't puff smoke into people's faces.* 别把烟往别人脸上喷. **(b)** [Ipr, Ip, Tn] **~ at/on sth** smoke (a pipe, cigarette, etc) in puffs (PUFF[1] 1c) 一口口地吸(烟斗、香烟等)或喷烟: *puff away at/on a cigarette* 一口一口地喷着香烟 ○ *He sat puffing his pipe.* 他坐着抽烟斗. **2** [I] (*infml* 口) breathe loudly or rapidly as after running, etc; pant 喘气; 喘息: *He was puffing hard when he reached the station.* 他到达车站时喘得很厉害. **3** (idm 习语) **huff and puff** ⇨ HUFF[2]. ˌ**puff and** ˈ**blow (a)** (also ˌ**puff and** ˈ**pant**) breathe noisily after physical effort 气吁吁: *puffing and panting at the top of the hill* 在山顶上气吁吁的. **(b)** = HUFF AND PUFF (HUFF[2]). **(be) puffed up with** ˈ**pride, etc** (be) very conceited 傲气十足. **4** (phr v) **puff along, in, out, up, etc** (*infml* 口) move in the specified direction, sending out small clouds of smoke or breathing heavily 喷着一股股的烟向某方向移动; 气喘吁吁地行进: *The train puffed out of the station.* 火车吐着烟驶出了车站. ○ *She puffed up the hill.* 她气喘吁吁地爬上山顶. **puff sb out** (usu passive 通常用于被动语态) (*infml* 口) cause sb to be out of breath 使某人气喘不止: *That run has puffed me out.* 那场赛跑累得我喘不过气来. ○ *He was puffed out after climbing all those stairs.* 他登完楼梯后已经上气不接下气了. **puff sth out** extinguish (a candle, etc) by blowing 吹灭(蜡烛等). **puff sth out/up** (cause sth to) swell (as) with air (使某物)膨胀(如有空气): *The bird puffed out/up its feathers.* 那鸟膨起了羽毛. ○ *She puffed up the cushions.* 她给垫子充了气. ○ *puff out one's cheeks* 鼓起双颊.

▷ **puffed** *adj* [usu pred 通常作表语] (*infml* 口) (of a person) breathing with difficulty; out of breath (指人)呼吸困难, 气吁吁: *He was quite puffed by the time he reached the top.* 他登上顶端时气喘得很厉害.

puf·fin /ˈpʌfɪn; ˋpʌfɪn/ *n* type of N Atlantic sea-bird with a large brightly-coloured bill 海鹦(海鸟, 产于北大西洋, 嘴大而颜色鲜艳). ⇨illus at App 1 见附录1插图, page v.

pug /pʌg; pʌg/ (also ˈ**pug-dog**) *n* small dog with a short flattish nose like that of a bulldog 哈巴狗.

□ ˈ**pug-nose** *n* short, squat or snub nose 短平的翘鼻子; 狮子鼻. ˈ**pug-nosed** *adj* having a pug-nose 长有狮子鼻的.

pu·gil·ist /ˈpju:dʒɪlɪst; ˋpjudʒəlɪst/ *n* (*fml* 文) professional boxer (职业的)拳击手.

▷ **pu·gil·ism** /-lɪzəm; -lɪzəm/ *n* [U] (*fml* 文) professional boxing (职业)拳击.

pu·gil·istic /ˌpju:dʒɪˈlɪstɪk; ,pjudʒəˋlɪstɪk/ *adj* (*fml* 文) **(a)** of or like a pugilist (似)职业拳击手的. **(b)** of pugilism (职业)拳击的.

pug·na·cious /pʌgˈneɪʃəs; pʌgˋneʃəs/ *adj* (*fml* 文) inclined or eager to fight; aggressive 好战的; 好斗的;

好寻衅的: *in a pugnacious mood* 有好斗的情绪. ▷ **pug·na·ciously** *adj*. **pug·na·city** /pʌgˈnæsətɪ; pʌgˋnæsətɪ/ *n* [U].

puke /pju:k; pjuk/ *v* [I, Ip, Tn, Tn·p] **~ (sth) (up)** (*sl* 俚) vomit 呕吐: *The baby puked (up) all over me.* 这小孩儿吐了我一身. ○ *It makes me want to puke* (ie It disgusts me)! 这真让人恶心(使我感到厌恶)!

▷ **puke** *n* [U] vomit 呕吐.

pull[1] /pʊl; pʊl/ *n* **1** [C] **~ (at/on sth)** act of pulling; tug 拉; 拖; 扯; 拽; 牵: *A pull on the rope will make the bell ring.* 一拉绳子钟就响. ○ *I felt a pull at my sleeve and turned round.* 我觉得有人扯我的袖子, 便转过身来. **2** [sing] **the ~ of sth** (**a**) physical force or magnetic attraction found in nature (自然界的)力, 磁力, 引力: *The tides depend on the pull of the moon.* 潮汐是月亮引力作用的结果. ○ *the pull of the current carrying us downstream* 使我们顺流而下的冲力. (**b**) (*fig* 比喻) force that influences a person's behaviour, career, etc (对人的行为、事业等的)影响(力), 吸引(力): *the pull of the wandering life* 漫游生活之令人神往 ○ *He felt the pull of the sea again.* 他又感到了海上生活的吸引力. **3** [U] (*infml* 口) influence over other people (对他人的)影响(力): *He has a lot of pull with the managing director.* 他对总经理有很大的影响力. **4** [C] **~ (at sth)** (**a**) action of drinking deeply 大口喝: *take a pull at a bottle* 从瓶中喝一大口. (**b**) action of inhaling smoke from a cigarette, pipe, etc 吸, 抽(香烟、烟斗等): *She took a long pull at her cigarette.* 她深深地吸了一口烟. **5** [sing] prolonged effort (in walking, rowing etc) (行走、划船等)持续的努力: *It was a hard pull up to the mountain hut.* 费了很大力气才到达山上的小屋. ○ *It was a long pull to the shore.* 费了半天劲才划到岸边. **6** [C] (esp in compounds 尤用以构成复合词) handle for pulling sth 拉手; 拉线; 拉环: *a bell-pull*. **7** [C] (in printing) single impression; proof (印刷)样张, 校样. **8** [C] (in cricket or golf) type of stroke (板球或高尔夫球的)一种击球方式. Cf 参看 PULL[2] 11.

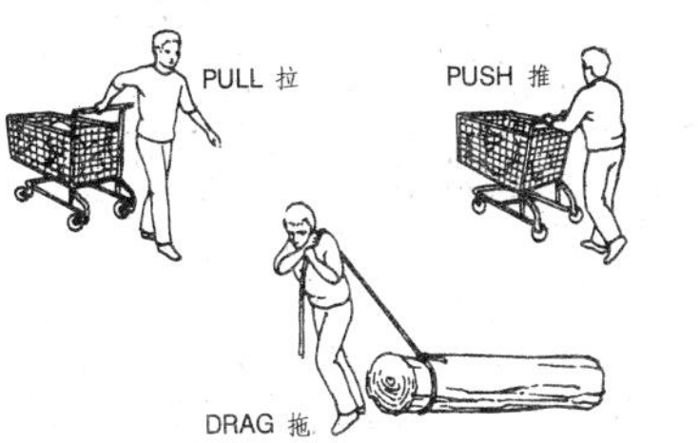

pull[2] /pʊl; pʊl/ *v* **1** (**a**) [I] use force on sth in order to move it towards oneself 拉; 拖; 扯; 拽; 牵: *In a tug-of-war, the competitors pull as hard as they can.* 在拔河比赛中, 双方队员都拼命地拉. ○ *You push and I'll pull.* 你来推, 我来拉. (**b**) [Tn] use this force on (sth); tug 拉, 拖, 扯, 拽(某物): *Fred pulled his sister's hair and made her cry.* 弗雷德揪他妹妹的头发, 把她弄哭了. ○ *He pulled my ears/me by the ears.* 他扯我的耳朵. ○ *pull* (ie draw) *the blinds/curtains* 拉窗帘[帘子]. (**c**) [Tn, Tn·pr, Tn·p, Cn·a] cause (sth) to move (in a specified direction) by using this force; draw sth 拖拉(某物); 牵引某物: *How many coaches can that locomotive pull?* 那个火车头能拉多少节车厢? ○ *Would you rather push the barrow or pull it?* 这辆小车你愿意推呢, 还是愿意拉呢? ○ *The horse was pulling a heavy cart (up a steep slope).* 马拉着一辆沉重的车子(走上陡坡). ○ *Pull your chair up to/nearer to the table.* 把你的椅子拉到桌子跟前来. ○ *Pull the plug out.* 把塞子拔掉. ○ *The child was pulling the toy along behind her.* 那小女孩拖着玩具走. ○ *pull the door shut/to* 带上门 ○ *pull off/on one's shoes, socks, etc* 脱掉[穿上]鞋、袜子等. ⇨Usage 见所附用法. **2** [Tn] (**a**) remove (sth) by using force; draw sth out 使用拉力移动(某物); 拔出、抽出某物: *pull a cork, tooth, stopper* 拔软木塞、牙、塞子 ○ *pull a gun (on sb)*, ie from a pocket, holster, etc (从衣袋、枪套等中)掏出枪(对付某人) ○ *pull (a pint of beer)*, ie draw it out from a barrel (从桶中)汲取(一品脱啤酒) ○ *She spent the afternoon pulling weeds in the garden.* 她一下午都在花园里拔草. ○ *pull a chicken*, ie remove its innards before cooking it 掏出鸡的内脏(以备烹调). (**b**) damage (sth) by using too much force; strain or tear 拉伤(某物); 扭伤; 扯伤: *pull a ligament/muscle/tendon* 扭伤韧带[肌肉/腱]. **3** [I, Ipr, Tn] **~ (for sth)** (cause a boat to) move through the water by the action of oars 划(船): *They pulled hard and reached the shore quickly.* 他们用力划船, 很快就到了岸边. ○ *Pull for shore!* 向岸边划! ○ *They pulled (the boat) to the shore.* 他们(把船)划向岸边. **4** [Ipr] **~ at/on sth** (**a**) give a tug on sth 拉某物一下: *pull at/on a rope* 拉一下绳子. (**b**) draw or suck sth 抽或吸某物: *pull at/on a pipe*, ie draw breath and smoke through a tobacco pipe 吸烟斗 ○ *pull at* (ie have a drink from) *a bottle* 从瓶中喝. **5** [Tn] move (a switch, lever, etc) in order to operate a mechanism 扳动(开关、手柄等)以操纵机械: *pull the trigger*, ie fire a gun 扣扳机(开枪). **6** [Tn] (*sl* 俚) attract (sb) sexually (在性方面)吸引(某人): *He can still pull the girls.* 他还能吸引女性. **7** [Tn] (*sl* 俚 *esp US*) succeed in committing (a crime, esp stealing) or in playing a (trick) on sb 犯下(罪行, 尤指盗窃); 对某人耍(花招): *They pulled a bank (job).* 他们抢了银行. ○ *He's pulling some sort of trick.* 他不定在耍什么花招. **8** [I] (of a horse) struggle against the bit, esp habitually (指马)甩嚼子(尤指习惯地). **9** [I, Tn] (cause a vehicle to) move sideways; veer or steer (sth) (使机动车)打斜; 使(某物)转向; 操纵(某物): *The car seems to be pulling to the left.* 那汽车似乎在向左偏. ○ *She pulled the van to the left to avoid a dog.* 她把客货车向左一闪以免轧着狗. **10** [Tn] (**a**) hold back (a horse) in a race in order to avoid winning (赛马中存心要输)控制(马)(放慢). (**b**) (in boxing) hold back a blow in order to avoid hurting sb (拳击中为避免伤着对方)收住拳. **11** [Tn] (**a**) (in golf) hit (the ball) wrongly to the left (高尔夫球)击(球)误向左偏. Cf 参看 SLICE 4. (**b**) (in cricket) strike (the ball) forward and to the left of the wicket by striking across the ball's path (板球)击(球)向前至三柱门的左方. **12** (idm 习语) **bring/pull sb up ˈshort/ˈsharply** make sb stop suddenly 使某人突然停止: *Her remark pulled me up short.* 我听到她的话后一下子愣住了. **make/pull ˈfaces/a ˈface** ⇨ FACE[1]. **pick/pull sb/sth to pieces** ⇨ PIECE[1]. **pull the ˌcarpet/ˌrug (out) from under sb's ˈfeet** (*infml* 口) take the help or support away from sb suddenly 突然停止对某人的援助或支持: *His mother pulled the carpet from under his feet by announcing that she was selling the house.* 他母亲说要把那所房子卖了, 他顿时感到失去了依靠. **pull a ˈfast one (on sb)** (*infml* 口) gain an advantage (over sb) by a trick; deceive (对某人)耍手段占便宜; 蒙骗. **pull sb's ˈleg** (*infml* 口) make fun of sb, esp by making him believe sth that is untrue; tease sb 开某人的玩笑(尤指使其信以为真); 耍弄某人. **pull the ˈother one (— it's got ˈbells on)** (*infml* 口) (expression used when one believes that the person one is talking to is pulling one's leg 认为对方在耍弄自己时的用语). **pull out all the ˈstops** (*infml* 口) use all one's power or resources in order to achieve sth 竭尽全力; 全力以赴: *The airline pulled out all the stops to get him there in time.* 航空部门已想尽一切办法好让他及时赶到那里. **pull the ˈplug on sb/sth** (*sl* 俚) destroy sb/sth 毁掉某人[某事物]. **pull one's ˈpunches** (usu negative 通常用于否定式) (*infml* 口) attack (sb) less vigorously than one is able to 不全力攻击(某人)(留有余地): *He certainly didn't pull any punches when it came to criticizing the work.* 他批评这项工作时可绝不留情. **pull ˈrank (on sb)** make use of one's place or status in society or at work to gain advantages (over sb) to which one is not really entitled 利用地位权势占(某人)便宜. **pull one's ˈsocks up** (*infml* 口) try harder or improve one's behaviour 多加把劲; 努力改进: *The class were told that there would be no outing unless they pulled their socks up.* 已告诉这班的学生, 要是他们不努力, 就不能去游玩. **pull ˈstrings/ˈwires (for sb)** (*infml* 口) use influential friends, indirect pressure, etc in order to obtain an advantage (for sb) 凭借私人关系、间接压力等(为某人)谋取好处; 走后门: *My father pulled a few strings to get me into the Civil Service.* 我父亲凭借一些私人关系把我弄到政府机关任职. **pull the ˈstrings/ˈwires** control events or the actions of other people 幕后操纵或牵线. **pull oneself up by one's (own) 'bootstraps** (*infml* 口) try to improve one's position by one's own unaided efforts 依靠自己的努力改善处境; 自力更生. **pull up one's 'roots** move from a settled home, job, etc to start a new life elsewhere 离开家、工作等另创新生活; 迁居; 改行. **pull one's 'weight** do one's fair share in a job, project, etc 尽本分: *We can succeed only if everyone in the team pulls his weight.* 我们全队只有人人各尽所能才能取得成功. **pull the 'wool over sb's eyes** (*infml* 口) hide one's real actions or intentions from sb; deceive 对某人隐瞒真实举动或意图; 掩人耳目: *It's no use trying to pull the wool over my eyes — I know exactly what's going on.* 要想瞒我是多此一举的 —— 我对所发生的事一清二楚.

P

13 (phr v) **pull ahead (of sb/sth)** move in front (of sb/sth) 领先(于某人[某事物]): *The car pulled ahead as soon as the road was clear.* 路上稍一有空, 那辆汽车就抢到前面去了. ○ *The team has pulled well ahead of the rest in the championship.* 这个队在锦标赛中遥遥领先于其他各队.

pull (sb) back (cause sb to) retreat; withdraw (sb) (使某人)退却; 撤回(某人): *The army pulled back after the battle.* 部队在结束战斗以后撤走了.

pull sb down (*infml* 口) (of an illness) leave sb in a weak condition (指疾病)使某人虚弱: *His long illness had pulled him down.* 他因长期患病身体很虚弱. (**a**) **pull sth down** (**a**) destroy or demolish (eg an old building) 毁坏, 拆毁(如旧建筑物): *The cinema she used to visit had been pulled down.* 她常去的那家电影院已经拆除了. (**b**) ⇨ PULL STH IN.

pull sb in (**a**) (*infml* 口) bring sb to a police station for questioning; detain sb 把某人带到警察局问话; 拘留某人. (**b**) attract (audiences, supporters, etc) 吸引(观众、支持者等): *How many voters can he pull in?* 能有多少人投他的票? ○ *The new show is certainly pulling in the crowds.* 新的表演一定很吸引人. **pull sth in** (*US* **pull sth down**) (*infml* 口) earn (money, a salary, etc) 挣(钱、薪水等): *He's pulling in £50 000 a year.* 他一年挣50 000英镑.

pull into sth; pull in (to sth) (**a**) (of a train) enter a station (指火车)进站: *The train pulled in right on time.* 这列火车正点到站. ○ *Passengers stood and stretched as the train pulled into the station.* 火车进站时旅客们站起来伸了伸懒腰. (**b**) (of a motor vehicle) move in towards sth (指机动车辆)驶近某处: *The bus pulled in to the side of the road.* 那辆公共汽车驶近路边.

pull off (sth) (of a motor vehicle) leave (the road) (and park in a lay-by, etc) (指机动车辆)驶离(道路)(至路侧停车处停下). **pull sth off** (*infml* 口) succeed in sth 做成某事: *pull off a coup, deal, scoop, etc* 做好一件漂亮事、做成一笔生意、抢先获得独家新闻.

pull out (of a motor vehicle, boat, etc) move out or sideways (指机动车辆、船只等)驶出, 划出或打斜: *The boat pulled out into the middle of the river.* 那只船划出到了河中央. ○ *A car suddenly pulled out in front of me.* 一辆汽车突然横冲到我面前. **pull sth out** remove (sth) by pulling; detach 拉掉, 拔掉(某物); 使分离: *He pulled out a gun.* 他掏出一枝枪. **pull out (of sth)** (of a train) leave (a station) (指火车)驶离(车站): *I arrived as the last train was pulling out.* 我到达时, 末班列车刚刚开出.

pull (sb/sth) out (of sth) (cause sb/sth to) withdraw from sth (使某人[某事物])从某事物中退出: *They are pulling their troops out of the battle zone.* 他们正把部队调离战区. ○ *The project became so expensive that we had to pull out.* 这个计划耗资太大, 我们只好退出.

pull (sth) over (cause a vehicle, boat, etc to) move or steer to one side (eg in order to let another boat or vehicle pass) (使车船等)闪到一边(如以便让其他车船通过): *Pull (your car) over and let me pass!* 把你的车闪开, 让我过去!

pull (sb) round/through (*infml* 口) (help sb to) recover consciousness or from an illness (帮助某人)恢复知觉或康复: *She was so ill that it seemed unlikely that she would pull through.* 她病得很厉害, 看来不大可能康复了. ○ *A sip of brandy helped to pull him round.* 给他喝一口白兰地酒有助于使他苏醒.

pull together act, work, etc with combined effort in a well-organized way 同心协力; 通力合作: *After the shock of their electoral defeat, the party really began to pull together.* 该党在受到选举失败的打击之后, 才真正地团结起来. **pull oneself together** get control of oneself, one's feelings etc 控制自己、控制感情等: *You must try to pull yourself together — your family depend on you.* 你应该振作起来 —— 你的家庭都指着你呢.

pull (sth) up (cause a vehicle to) come to a halt (使车辆)停下: *The driver pulled up at the traffic lights.* 司机在红绿灯前把车停住. **pull sb up** (*infml* 口) correct or reprimand sb 纠正某人; 训斥某人: *He was pulled up by the chairman.* 他挨了主席一顿训. **pull up (to/with sb/sth)** improve one's position (in relation to sb/sth) 改善自己(相对于某人[某物]的)地位; 赶上: *At first the new boy was at the bottom of the class but he soon pulled up (with the others).* 起初那新来的男孩是班上成绩最差的, 但他很快便追上了(其他同学).

□ **'pull-in** *n* (*Brit infml* 口) roadside café 路边小餐馆.

'pull-up (*Brit*) (*US* **'pull-off**) *n* place where vehicles may leave the road and park 路旁停车处.

'pull-out *n* part of a magazine, etc that can be pulled out and kept separately 杂志等之可拆下单独保存的部分; 附页; 附件: [attrib 作定语] *a 'pull-out supplement* 可从报刊中抽出的增刊.

NOTE ON USAGE 用法: **Pull, drag, haul, tow, trail** and **draw** all indicate the using of strength or force to move something, especially behind oneself. ☆ **pull**、**drag**、**haul**、**tow**、**trail**、**draw** 均指用力移动某物, 尤指物在人后. **Pull** has the widest use and its meaning covers that of all the other verbs in this group. ☆ **pull** 用途最广, 兼有这一组中所有其他动词的意义. A vehicle/animal/person can pull any movable object 车辆[动物/人]拉动任何可移动的物体均可使用 **pull**: *You sometimes see oxen pulling carts in southern Europe.* 在南欧, 有时可看到用牛拉车. **Drag** and **haul** suggest that the object is heavy and usually pulled along the ground. ☆ **drag** 和 **haul** 指所拉者为重物, 通常为在地面上移动. It is therefore difficult to move and requires (great) effort. 因较困难, 故需用(极大之)力. **Drag** suggests greater friction ☆ **drag** 暗指具较大摩擦力: *He dragged the heavy chest across the floor.* 他在地板上拉着沉重的箱子. ○ *The police dragged the football fans off the pitch.* 警察把足球迷拖出了球场. **Haul** often indicates the pulling or raising of a heavy object, especially by pulling on a rope ☆ **haul** 常表示拖拉或提升重物, 尤指使用绳索: *After a good day's fishing they hauled in the nets and went home.* 他们捕了一天的鱼, 收起鱼网满载而归. ○ *Elephants are used in some countries for hauling timber.* 有的国家用大象来拖运木材. **Haul** also has the specific meaning of 'transport goods by lorry/truck' ☆ **haul** 还另有一种含义, 指用卡车运送货物: *road haulage* 公路运输. **Tow** suggests less effort and is used mainly of vehicles. ☆ **tow** 含不甚费力之意, 主要指车辆. The object being pulled is often damaged and firmly attached to the vehicle by a rope or chain 用此字指所牵引之物常为坏的, 以绳索或链条与车辆固着在一起: *My car broke down and had to be towed to a garage.* 我的汽车出故障了, 得拉到修理厂去. ○ *The ship needed two tugs to tow it into port.* 这艘船需用两艘拖船把它拖进港. People **trail** objects behind them, carelessly or for no particular reason. 漫不经心地或无所谓地把物体拖在后面用 **trail**. ☆ They may also **trail** their arms or hands in the water when travelling in a boat 船在航行时把胳膊或手伸进水中, 亦可用 **trail**: *The little boy went upstairs trailing his teddy bear behind him.* 那小男孩儿走上楼去, 还拖着他的玩具熊. ○ *She lay back in the boat trailing her fingers in the water.* 她仰靠在船上, 把手指伸进水里. **Draw** is more formal than **pull** ☆ **draw** 比 **pull** 较文些: *Draw/Pull your chair a little closer.* 把你的椅子拉近一点. ○ *The men drew/pulled the boat onto the beach.* 那些人把船拖上了海滩. **Draw** is commonly used to mean 'open/close curtains/blinds'. ☆ **draw** 常用以指'拉开[拉上]帘子[窗帘]'. It is also used in adjectival compounds 这一词还可用以构成复合形容词: *a horse-drawn carriage* 马拉的车子.

pul·let /ˈpʊlɪt; ˋpʊlɪt/ *n* young domestic hen, esp at the time she begins to lay eggs 小母鸡(尤指开始生蛋的).

pul·ley /ˈpʊlɪ; ˋpʊlɪ/ *n* **1** (apparatus consisting of a) wheel or wheels with grooves for ropes or chains, used for lifting things 滑轮(组); 滑车. **2** wheel or drum fixed on a shaft and turned by a belt, used esp to increase speed or power 皮带轮.

□ ˈ**pulley-block** wooden block in which a pulley(1) is fixed 装有滑轮的木架.

Pull·man /ˈpʊlmən; ˋpʊlmən/ (also ˈ**Pullman car**, *US* ˈ**parlor car**) *n* (esp formerly) luxurious type of railway carriage without compartments, and with seats grouped at tables (尤指旧时)豪华型列车车厢(无隔间, 设有桌椅).

pull·over /ˈpʊləʊvə(r); ˋpʊlˌovɚ/ *n* = JERSEY 1.

pul·mon·ary /ˈpʌlmənərɪ; *US* -nerɪ; ˋpʌlməˌnɛrɪ/ *adj* [usu attrib 通常作定语] (*medical* 医) of, in or affecting the lungs 肺的; 肺部的; 侵袭肺部的: *pulmonary diseases* 肺部疾病 ○ *the pulmonary arteries*, ie those that carry blood to the lungs 肺动脉.

pulp /pʌlp; pʌlp/ *n* **1** (**a**) [U] soft fleshy inner part of fruit; flesh 水果的肉质部分; 果肉: *Scoop out the pulp and serve it with sugar.* 把果肉挖出来和糖一起食用. ○ *tomato pulp* 西红柿瓤. (**b**) [U] soft mass of wood fibre, used for making paper 纸浆: ˈ*wood pulp* 木浆. (**c**) [U, sing] substance with a soft texture similar to these 柔软似果肉或浆状之物质: *reduce the garlic to a pulp*, ie beat or crush it until it becomes pulp 把蒜捣成蒜泥 ○ *The beans need to be mashed into (a) pulp.* 豆子需压成豆沙. ○ (*fig* 比喻) *The gang threatened to beat him to a pulp* (ie injure him badly) *if he gave any more trouble.* 匪徒威胁他说再不服就把他打个稀巴烂. **2** [U] (*derog* 贬) books, magazines that are of poor quality, esp popular sensational literature 低级书刊; (尤指)有刺激性的通俗读物: *She writes pulp.* 她写低级趣味的书. ○ [attrib 作定语] *pulp fiction, magazines* 庸俗的小说、杂志.

▷ **pulp** *v* [I, Tn] (cause sth to) become pulp (使某物)成为浆状: *pulp grapes, olives, raspberries, etc* 把葡萄、橄榄、悬钩子...弄烂 ○ *pulp* (ie make pulp from) *old books* 把旧书制成纸浆.

pulpy *adj.* (**-ier, -iest**) like or containing a lot of pulp(1c) 像果肉或浆的; 多果肉的; 多汁的: *a pulpy consistency* 浆的黏稠度 ○ *pulpy food* 糊状食品.

pul·pit /ˈpʊlpɪt; ˋpʊlpɪt/ *n* **1** [C] (usu small) raised and enclosed platform in a church, where a clergyman stands when he is preaching (教堂中的)讲坛(通常指小型的). ⇨illus at App 1 见附录1插图, page viii. **2 the pulpit** [sing] (*fml* 文) (religious teaching of) the clergy 神职人员(的讲道): *The policy was condemned* (ie by clergymen) *from the pulpit.* 该项政策受到神职人员的谴责.

pulsar /ˈpʌlsɑː(r); ˋpʌlsɑr/ *n* star that cannot be seen but can be detected by pulsating radio signals 脉冲星; (快速)脉冲射电源.

puls·ate /pʌlˈseɪt; *US* ˈpʌlseɪt; ˋpʌlset/ *v* **1** (also **pulse**) [I] expand and contract rhythmically; throb 有节奏地舒张及收缩; 跳动; 搏动; 脉动: *blood pulsating in the body* 体内血脉搏动. **2** [I, Tn] (cause sth to) shake with regular movements or sounds; vibrate (使某物)有规律地振动; 颤动: *a pulsating rhythm* 均匀的节奏 ○ *The needle pulsates when the engine is running.* 发动机开动时指针就颤动. **3** [Ipr] **~ with sth** be moved by (strong emotion); be thrilled 受(激情)震动, 感动; 激动: *pulsate with desire, excitement, joy, etc* 因满怀欲望、激情、喜悦等而激动.

▷ **pulsa·tion** /pʌlˈseɪʃn; pʌlˋseʃən/ *n* (**a**) [C] single beat or throb; heartbeat 一次跳动或搏动; 心跳: *a rate of 60 pulsations per minute* 每分钟60次的脉率. (**b**) [U] pulsating; throbbing 有节奏的舒张及收缩; 跳动; 搏动; 脉动; 振动; 颤动: *the pulsation of the blood in the body* 血液在体内的涌动.

pulse[1] /pʌls; pʌls/ *n* **1** (usu *sing* 通常作单数) (**a**) regular beating of the arteries as blood is pumped through them by the heart, esp as felt at the wrist 脉搏: *have a low, irregular, strong, weak, etc pulse* 脉搏很慢、不规则、很强、很弱等 ○ *His pulse raced as he faced the armed intruder.* 他面对携带武器的闯入者, 顿时血脉偾张. ○ [attrib 作定语] *one's* ˈ*pulse rate*, ie the number of times per minute that one's heart beats, as felt at the wrist 脉率(按脉所得每分钟的心跳数). (**b**) regular beat in music (音乐的)节拍: *the throbbing pulse of the drums* 鼓的打击节拍. **2** (**a**) single vibration of sound, light, electric current, etc (声波、光波、电流等的)一次脉动: *The machine emits sound pulses.* 这台机器可发出声脉冲信号. (**b**) (usu *sing* 通常作单数) series of these 连续的脉动; 脉冲波: *The machine is operated by an electronic pulse.* 这台机器由电子脉冲信号操纵. **3** (idm 习语) **feel/take sb's** ˈ**pulse** find out the speed of the heartbeat by feeling the pulse in the wrist and counting the number of beats per minute 诊脉; 按脉; 把脉. **have/keep one's finger on the pulse** ⇨ FINGER.

▷ **pulse** *v* (**a**) [I, Ipr] **~ (through sth)** move with strong regular movements; beat or throb 强烈而有规律地跳动; 搏动; 振动: *The news sent the blood pulsing through his veins.* 这消息使他的血液都沸腾起来了. ○ (*fig* 比喻) *the life pulsing through a great city* 大都市里紧张繁忙的生活. (**b**) [I] = PULSATE 1.

pulse[2] /pʌls; pʌls/ *n* (usu *pl* 通常作复数) seed(s) of various plants (eg beans, lentils, peas), that grow in pods and are dried and used as food 豆类植物的种子; (用作食物的)豆子(如蚕豆、扁豆、豌豆): *Pulses are a good source of protein for vegetarians.* 对于素食者来说, 豆类食物是蛋白质的理想来源.

pul·ver·ize, -ise /ˈpʌlvəraɪz; ˋpʌlvəˌraɪz/ *v* **1** (*fml* 文) (**a**) [Tn] grind or smash (sth) to powder or dust 将(某物)磨成粉或捣成末; 粉碎, 摧毁(某物): *a machine that pulverizes nuts, coffee beans, etc* 研磨果仁、咖啡豆等的机器. (**b**) [I] become powder or dust 成为粉状; 成末. **2** [Tn] (*infml or joc* 口或谑) destroy or defeat (sb/sth) completely 彻底粉碎或摧毁(某人[某事物]): *He pulverized the opposition with the force of his oratory.* 他能言善辩把对方驳得体无完肤. ▷ **pul·ver·iza·tion, -isation** /ˌpʌlvəraɪˈzeɪʃn; *US* -rɪˈz-; ˌpʌlvərəˋzeʃən/ *n* [U].

puma /ˈpjuːmə; ˋpjumə/ *n* (also **cougar**, ˌ**mountain** ˈ**lion**) large brown American animal of the cat family 美洲狮.

pum·ice /ˈpʌmɪs; ˋpʌmɪs/ (also ˈ**pumice-stone**) *n* [C, U] (piece of) light porous lava used for removing stains or rough patches of skin and (in powder form) for cleaning and polishing 浮岩, 浮石, 轻石(轻而多孔, 可用以去除皮肤污垢或使皮肤光滑, 其粉剂可作清洁剂或抛光剂).

pum·mel (also **pomm·el**) /ˈpʌml; ˋpʌml̩/ *v* (**-ll-**; *US* also **-l-**) [Tn] strike (sb/sth) repeatedly, esp with the fist(s); beat 连击(某人[某物])(尤指用拳); 打: *The child pummelled his mother angrily as she carried him home.* 那孩子因其母带他回家而生气地捶打着母亲.

▷ **pum·mel·ling** /ˈpʌməlɪŋ; ˋpʌməlɪŋ/ *n* [sing] severe beating 沉重的打击: *The boxers gave each other a terrific pummelling.* 那两名拳击手彼此都以重拳出击. ○ (*fig* 比喻) *The team took a real pummelling in their last match.* 这个队在最后的比赛中受到了沉重的打击.

pump[1] /pʌmp; pʌmp/ *n* **1** (esp in compounds 尤用以构成复合词) machine or device for forcing liquid, gas or air into, out of or through sth, eg water from a well, petrol from a storage tank, air into a tyre or oil through a pipe-line 泵; 唧筒; 抽水机; 抽气机; 打气筒: *A pump in the boiler sends hot water round the central heating system.* 热水器中的水泵将热水输送给集中供热设备. ○ *a petrol pump* 汽油泵 ○ *She blew up the flat tyre with a bicycle pump.* 她用自行车打气筒给瘪了的轮胎打气. ○ *The doctor removed the contents of her stomach with a stomach pump.* 医生用胃唧筒给她洗胃. ⇨illus at App 1 见附录1插图, page xiii. **2** pumping (PUMP[1] *v* 1) action 泵的抽吸、压送、充气等动作: *After several pumps, the water began to flow.* 用泵抽了几下之后, 水流出来了. ○ *give sb's hand a pump*, ie shake it energetically up and down 握住某人的手用力上下摇动. **3** (idm 习语) **all hands to the pump** ⇨ HAND[1]. **parish pump** ⇨ PARISH. **prime the pump** ⇨ PRIME[3].

▷ **pump** *v* **1** [Tn, Tn·pr, Cn·a] cause (air, gas, water, etc) to move in a specified direction by using a pump[1](1) 用泵等抽出或压入气体、液体等: *pump air into a tyre* 给轮胎打气 ○ *The heart pumps blood round the body.* 心脏将血液压送到全身. **2** [I] (**a**) use a pump[1](1) 使用泵等: *You will need to pump hard for several minutes to fill the tank.* 你需用泵着实抽吸几分钟, 才能把油箱灌满. (**b**) (of the heart or blood) beat (指心脏)跳动; (指血液)脉动: *Her heart was pumping very fast.* 她的心脏跳得很快. **3** [Tn, Tn·p] (*infml* 口) move (sb's hand) up and down like the handle of a pump 握住(某人的手)上下摇动(如唧筒的手柄): *He pumped my hand (up and down)* *vigorously.* 他握住我的手用力地(上下)摇晃. **4** [Tn, Tn·pr] **~ sb (for sth); ~ sth out of sb** (*infml* 口) try to obtain (information) from sb by asking persistent questions 追问某人以探知(信息): *He tried to pump the secretary for information.* 他极力向秘书打探消息. ○ *She succeeded in pumping the name of the winner out of him.* 她从他的口中打听到了获胜者的名字. **5** (phr v) **pump sth in; pump sth into sth/sb (a)** invest much money (in sth) 将大量资金投入(某事物): *The firm pumped money into the development of the new product.* 这家企业投入大量资金以开发这种新产品. **(b)** (*infml* 口) persuade or force sb to learn sth 劝说或驱使某人学习某事物: *She tried to pump some facts into his head before the examination.* 在考试前她极力向他灌输一些知识. **pump sth up** inflate (a tyre, etc) by pumping (PUMP^{1} *v* 1) air into it 给(轮胎等)充气.

'pump-room *n* (esp formerly) room (at a spa) where mineral water is available for drinking (尤指旧时)(矿泉疗养地的)矿泉水饮用室.

pump^{2} /pʌmp; pʌmp/ *n* **1** = PLIMSOLL. **2** light soft shoe worn for dancing, etc (跳舞等穿的)轻而软的鞋. **3** (*esp US*) woman's low-heeled shoe without a fastening 无带的矮跟女鞋.

pum·per·nickel /'pʌmpənɪkl; 'pʌmpɚ,nɪkl/ *n* [U] type of (esp German) wholemeal rye bread (尤指德国的)全麦的黑麦面包.

pump·kin /'pʌmpkɪn; 'pʌmpkɪn/ *n* **(a)** [C] (plant that bears a) large round orange-coloured fruit with many seeds 南瓜; 倭瓜: *Some children make lanterns out of pumpkins at Hallowe'en.* 有些儿童在万圣节前夕用南瓜做灯笼. **(b)** [U] flesh of this fruit, used as a vegetable and (esp in the US) as a filling for pies 南瓜的果肉, 南瓜瓤(用作蔬菜, 亦作饼馅, 尤其在美国): [attrib 作定语] *pumpkin pie* 南瓜馅饼.

pun /pʌn; pʌn/ *n* **~ (on sth)** humorous use of a word that has two meanings or of different words that sound the same, eg 'She told the child to *try* not to be so *trying*'; play on words 双关(语)(利用词的一词多义现象或同音异义现象产生出的词的诙谐用法): *The slogan was a pun on the name of the product.* 那广告用语与其产品名称一语双关.

▷ **pun** *v* **(-nn-)** [I, Ipr] **~ (on sth)** make a pun or puns (on a word) 使用双关语: *He's always punning and I don't find it funny.* 他老是使用双关语, 我觉得很没意思.

Punch /pʌntʃ; pʌntʃ/ *n* **1** [sing] (name of a) grotesque humpbacked figure in a traditional puppet show called *Punch and Judy* 庞奇(传统木偶戏《庞奇和朱迪》中的驼背丑角). **2** (idm 习语) **as pleased as Punch** ⇨ PLEASED (PLEASE).

punch^{1} /pʌntʃ; pʌntʃ/ *n* **1 (a)** tool or machine for cutting holes in leather, metal, paper, etc 打孔器; 穿孔机; 冲床. **(b)** tool for forcing nails beneath a surface or bolts out of holes 压钉器. **2** tool for stamping designs on surfaces 压印器; 冲头; 戳子.

▷ **punch** *v* **1** [Tn, Tn·pr] **~ sth (in sth)** make (a hole) in sth with a punch^{1}(1a); perforate sth 打(孔); 给某物穿孔: *punch a train ticket* 在火车票上打孔 ○ *punch holes in a sheet of metal* 在金属板上冲孔. **2** (phr v) **punch (sb) in/out** (*US*) = CLOCK (SB) IN/OUT (CLOCK 2).

'punch card (also **'punched card**) card on which information is recorded by punching holes in it, used for giving instructions or data to a computer, etc 穿孔卡片(以穿孔方法记录信息, 用以向计算机等输入指令或数据).

punch^{2} /pʌntʃ; pʌntʃ/ *n* [U] drink made of wine or spirits mixed with hot or cold water, sugar, lemons, spice, etc 伴汁酒(以酒、热水或冷水、糖、柠檬、香料等混合而成的饮料).

□ **'punch-bowl** *n* bowl in which punch is mixed or from which it is served 伴汁酒钵: *a glass punch-bowl* 玻璃的伴汁酒钵.

punch^{3} /pʌntʃ; pʌntʃ/ *v* **1** [Tn, Tn·pr] strike (sb/sth) hard with the fist 用拳猛击(某人[某物]): *punch a man on the chin* 挥拳猛击一男子的下巴 ○ *He has a face I'd like to punch.* 他那张脸我真想打它一拳. **2** [Tn] (*US*) herd (cattle) 放牧(牛).

▷ **punch** *n* **1 (a)** [C] blow given with the fist (用拳的)一击; 一拳: *give sb a hard punch on the nose* 向某人的鼻子猛击一拳. **(b)** [sing] ability to give such a blow effectively 拳击的能力: *a boxer with a strong punch* 出拳很重的拳击手. **2** [U] (*fig* 比喻) effective force or vigour 力量; 活力: *a speech with plenty of punch* 很有力量的演说. **3** (idm 习语) **pack a punch** ⇨ PACK^{2}. **pull one's punches** ⇨ PULL^{2}.

punchy *adj* **(-ier, -iest)** (*infml* 口) having punch^{3}(*n* 2); forceful 有力的: *a punchy argument, debate, etc* 有力的论据、辩论等.

□ **'punch-ball** *n* (*US* **punching ball**) inflated or stuffed leather ball held on a stand or hung from above and punched for exercise or training, esp by boxers (练习拳击用的)梨球, 吊球.

,punch-'drunk *adj* **(a)** (in boxing) dazed or stupefied by being severely punched (拳击中)因受重击而昏眩的, 被打得晕头转向的. **(b)** (*fig* 比喻) dazed or confused, eg after working intensely 头昏眼花的(如劳累之后): *The negotiators seemed punch-drunk after another all-night session.* 谈判者又经过一次通宵会谈, 似乎都已头晕眼花.

'punch-line *n* words that form the climax of a joke or story 笑话或故事中形成高潮的语句; 画龙点睛的妙语: *He forgot the punch-line of his after-dinner speech.* 他在宴会之后的讲话中把那句最绝妙的话给忘了.

'punch-up *n* (*Brit infml* 口) fight with the fists; brawl 用拳头打斗; 打架: *The argument ended in a punch-up.* 争论到最后双方大打出手.

punc·tilio /pʌŋk'tɪlɪəʊ; pʌŋk'tɪlɪ,o/ *n* (*pl* **~s**) [C, U] (*fml* 文) (instance of) giving careful attention to every small point of ceremony, good conduct, honour, etc (对礼仪、操守、荣誉等的)谨慎, 一丝不苟, 拘泥, 拘谨, 拘礼.

punc·tili·ous /pʌŋk'tɪlɪəs; pʌŋk'tɪlɪəs/ *adj* (*fml* 文) very careful to carry out one's duties, etc correctly; very attentive to details of behaviour or ceremony (在履行职责等上)一丝不苟的; (在行为或礼节上)谨慎的: *a punctilious attention to detail* 对细节一丝不苟 ○ *a punctilious observance of the formalities* 礼节上的拘谨.

▷ **punc·tili·ously** *adv*. **punc·tili·ous·ness** *n* [U].

punc·tual /'pʌŋktʃʊəl; 'pʌŋktʃʊəl/ *adj* happening or doing sth at the agreed or proper time 按时的; 准时的; 守时的: *a punctual start to the meeting* 会议准时开始 ○ *be punctual for an appointment* 准时赴约 ○ *The tenants are punctual in paying the rent.* 房客都能按时缴纳房租.

▷ **punc·tu·al·ity** /,pʌŋktʃʊ'ælətɪ; ,pʌŋktʃʊ'ælətɪ/ *n* [U] being punctual 及时; 准时; 守时.

punc·tu·ally /'pʌŋktʃʊəlɪ; 'pʌŋktʃʊəlɪ/ *adv*: *arrive, depart, etc punctually* 准时到达、离去等.

punc·tu·ate /'pʌŋktʃʊeɪt; 'pʌŋktʃʊ,et/ *v* **1** [I, Tn] put full stops, commas, colons, question marks, etc into (a piece of writing) (在文字中)加标点符号, 加标点: *The children have not yet learned to punctuate correctly.* 这些小学生尚未学会正确使用标点符号. ○ *The transcription of his speech must be punctuated.* 他的讲话文本得加上标点符号. **2** [Tn, Tn·pr] **~ sth (with sth)** interrupt sth (by/with sth) at intervals 不时打断某事物: *The announcement was punctuated by cheers from the crowd.* 在宣布过程中, 群众的欢呼声此起彼伏. ○ *He punctuated his remarks with thumps on the table.* 他讲话时不时地捶着桌子.

▷ **punc·tu·ation** /,pʌŋktʃʊ'eɪʃn; ,pʌŋktʃʊ'eʃən/ *n* [U] (art, practice or system of) punctuating 标点符号的使用; 标点符号用法: *The children have never been taught punctuation.* 这些孩子从未学过使用标点符号.

□ **punctu'ation mark** any of the marks (eg full stop, comma, question mark, etc) used in a written or printed text to separate sentences, etc and to make the meaning clear 标点符号. ⇨App 3 见附录 3.

punc·ture /'pʌŋktʃə(r); 'pʌŋktʃɚ/ *n* small hole made by a sharp point, esp one made accidentally in a tyre (尖物刺成的)小孔; (尤指)轮胎穿孔: *I got a puncture on the way and arrived late.* 我在路上扎破了轮胎, 所以迟到了.

▷ **punc·ture** *v* **1 (a)** [Tn] make a puncture in (sth) 在(某物)上穿孔; 刺穿(某物): *puncture a tyre, an abscess, a balloon* 刺破轮胎、脓肿、气球 ○ *She was taken to hospital with a punctured lung.* 她因肺部被刺破而送进了医院. **(b)** [I] (of a tyre, etc) get a puncture (指轮胎等)被刺穿: *Two of the tyres punctured on the stony road.* 有两个车胎在碎石路上扎破了. **2** [Tn] reduce (sb's pride, confidence, etc); deflate 削弱(某人的傲气、信心等); 泄某人的气: *I wish something would happen to puncture her ego*, ie lessen her conceit. 她自以为是, 我希望让她碰个钉子.

pun·dit /ˈpʌndɪt; ˋpʌndɪt/ *n* **1** very learned Hindu 博学的印度人. **2** (*often joc* 常作戏谑语) person who is an authority on a subject; expert 某一学科的权威; 专家: *The pundits disagree on the best way of dealing with the problem.* 如何妥善处理这一问题, 专家众说纷纭. ○ *a panel of well-known television pundits* 由著名电视专家组成的专家小组.

pun·gent /ˈpʌndʒənt; ˋpʌndʒənt/ *n* **1** having a sharp or strong taste or smell (味道或气味)有刺激味的, 辛辣的, 刺鼻的: *a pungent odour, sauce, spice, etc* 刺鼻的气味、辛辣的沙司、有刺激味的香料. **2** (of remarks) sharply critical; biting or caustic (指言语)尖刻的, 刺人的, 刻薄的: *pungent comments, criticism, satire, etc* 尖刻的评语、批评、讽刺等.

▷ **pun·gency** /-nsɪ; -nsɪ/ *n* [U] quality or state of being pungent 刺激味; 辛辣; 尖刻.

pung·ently *adv*.

pun·ish /ˈpʌnɪʃ; ˋpʌnɪʃ/ *v* **1** [Tn, Tn·pr] (**a**) **~ sb (for sth) (by/with sth)** hurt, imprison, fine, etc sb for wrongdoing 罚、处罚或惩罚某人: *punish those who break the law* 惩罚违法者 ○ *He punished the children for their carelessness by making them pay for the damage.* 他让孩子赔偿损失, 惩罚他们粗心大意. (**b**) [Tn, Tn·pr] **~ sth (by/with sth)** hurt, imprison, fine, etc sb for (wrongdoing) 以(过错)为由处罚某人: *Serious crime must be punished by longer terms of imprisonment.* 重罪须处以长期监禁. **2** [Tn] (*infml* 口) treat (sb) roughly, esp by giving hard blows 粗暴地对待(某人); (尤指)痛打: *He punished his opponent with fierce punches to the body.* 他猛击对手的身体. ○ *Chapman punished the bowling*, ie (in cricket) scored freely from weak bowling. 查普曼把投球手给治了(板球比赛中轻易得分, 因对方投球手技术差).

▷ **pun·ish·able** *adj* **~ (by sth)** that can be punished (esp by law) 可处罚的; 该处罚的; (尤指)该法办的: *punishable by death* 该处以死罪 ○ *Giving false information is a punishable offence.* 谎报资料可以论罪.

pun·ish·ing *adj* [usu attrib 通常作定语] that makes one very tired or weak; severe 十分吃力的; 使人筋疲力尽的; 严厉的: *a punishing climb up the hill* 十分吃力的登山活动 ○ *a punishing defeat* 惨重的失败. — *n* [sing] (*infml* 口) severe defeat or damage 极大的失败或损坏: *My boots have taken quite a punishing recently — I need a new pair.* 我的靴子近来已经破得不得了了 —— 我需要一双新的. **pun·ish·ingly** *adv*.

pun·ish·ment *n* (**a**) [U] punishing or being punished 处罚; 受罚: *corporal punishment*, ie punishment by physical beating, etc 体罚 ○ *capital punishment*, ie punishment by death 极刑(死刑). (**b**) [C] penalty inflicted on sb who has done sth wrong 罚; 处罚; 惩罚: *The punishments inflicted on the children were too severe.* 对这些孩子的处罚过于严厉. ○ *The punishment should fit* (ie be appropriate for) *the crime.* 罪与罚应相当.

pun·it·ive /ˈpju:nətɪv; ˋpjunətɪv/ *adj* (*fml* 文) (**a**) intended as punishment 处罚的; 惩罚性的: *punitive action, measures, restrictions, etc* 惩罚性的行动、措施、限定等 ○ *a punitive expedition*, ie a military one intended to punish rebels, etc 讨伐. (**b**) causing hardship; severe 令人受苦的; 严厉的: *punitive taxation* 重税 ○ *punitive increases in the cost of living* 生活费用之急剧增加. ▷ **pun·it·ively** *adv*.

punk /pʌŋk; pʌŋk/ *n* **1** (**a**) (also **punk ˈrock**) [U] type of loud violent rock[3] music popular since the late 1970's and associated with protest against conventional attitudes 蓬克(一种摇滚乐, 自70年代末期起流行, 是对传统的反叛): [attrib 作定语] *a punk band, concert, fan* 蓬克摇滚乐队、摇滚音乐会、摇滚乐迷. (**b**) [C] (also **punk ˈrocker**) (esp young) person who likes punk music and imitates the appearance of punk musicians, eg by wearing metal chains, clothes with holes in and brightly coloured hair 蓬克摇滚乐迷(喜爱蓬克摇滚乐、模仿蓬克摇滚乐师打扮者, 尤指青年, 如佩带金属链、穿破烂衣服、将头发染成鲜艳的颜色等): [attrib 作定语] *a punk hairstyle* 蓬克发式. **2** (*infml derog* 口, 贬) (**a**) [C] (*esp US*) badly-behaved young man or boy; lout 行为不端的男性青少年; 小流氓. (**b**) [U] worthless stuff; rubbish 无用的东西; 废物: [attrib 作定语] *punk material* 废料.

pun·net /ˈpʌnɪt; ˋpʌnɪt/ *n* (*esp Brit*) small basket made of very thin wood, plastic, etc and used as a container for fruit (用细木条、塑料等制的很小的)水果篮子: *Strawberries cost 60p a punnet.* 草莓60便士一小篮.

pun·ster /ˈpʌnstə(r); ˋpʌnstɚ/ *n* person who habitually makes puns 爱用双关语的人.

punt[1] /pʌnt; pʌnt/ *n* long shallow flat-bottomed boat with square ends that is moved by pushing the end of a long pole against the bottom of a river (用篙撑的)长而浅的方头平底船.

▷ **punt** *v* (**a**) [I, Ipr, Ip] move a punt with a pole (in the specified direction) 用篙撑方头平底船: *She soon learned to punt.* 她很快就学会了撑方头平底船. ○ *They punted along the river.* 他们撑着方头平底船沿河航行. (**b**) [I] (often 常作 **go punting**) go along a river in a punt, esp for pleasure 乘方头平底船沿河航行(尤指游览).

punt[2] /pʌnt; pʌnt/ *v* [Tn] kick (a football) after it has dropped from the hands and before it touches the ground 踢(从手中落下而未着地之足球); 踢(悬空球).

▷ **punt** *n* kick made in this way 踢悬空球.

punt[3] /pʌnt; pʌnt/ *v* [I] **1** (in some card-games) lay a stake against the bank (在某些牌戏中)对庄家下赌注. **2** (*infml* 口 *esp Brit*) speculate in shares, bet money on a horse, etc; gamble 进行股票投机、对赛马下赌注等; 赌博.

▷ **punter** *n* (*Brit*) (**a**) person who punts (PUNT[3] 1, 2) 对庄家或赛马下赌注的人; 搞股票投机的人. (**b**) (*infml derog* 口, 贬) foolish or unthinking person who can be persuaded to buy goods or services of poor quality 冤大头: *You can write what you like, as long as it keeps the punters happy.* 你可以想怎么写就怎么写, 只要能让那些花冤枉钱的人高兴就行. ○ *Your average punter* (ie The ordinary uncultured person) *does not go to the opera.* 一般没什么文化的人是不会去看歌剧的.

puny /ˈpju:nɪ; ˋpjunɪ/ *adj* (**-ier, -iest**) (*usu derog* 通常作贬义) (**a**) small, weak and underdeveloped 弱小的; 发育不良的; 未充分发展的: *puny limbs, muscles, stature* 细弱的肢体、不发达的肌肉、瘦小的身材 ○ *What a puny little creature!* 多么瘦小哇! (**b**) feeble or pathetic 虚弱的; 可怜的: *They laughed at my puny efforts at rock-climbing.* 他们取笑我在攀岩活动中的那种可怜劲儿.

pup /pʌp; pʌp/ *n* **1** (**a**) = PUPPY 1. (**b**) young of various other animals, eg otters, seals 幼小动物(如小水獭、小海豹): *a mother seal and her pup* 一只母海豹和一只小海豹. **2** = PUPPY 2. **3** (idm 习语) **in pup** (of a bitch) pregnant (指母狗)怀胎的. **sell sb a pup** ⇨ SELL.

▷ **pup** *v* (**-pp-**) [I] give birth to a pup or pups 生小狗等小动物.

pupa /ˈpju:pə; ˋpjupə/ *n* (*pl* **~s** or **pupae** /ˈpju:pi:; ˋpjupi/) insect in the stage of development between a larva and an adult insect 蛹. ⇨illus at BUTTERFLY 见 BUTTERFLY 插图. Cf 参看 CHRYSALIS.

▷ **pu·pal** *adj*.

pu·pate /pju:ˈpeɪt; *US* ˈpju:peɪt; ˋpjuˌpet/ *v* [I] (*fml* 文) (of an insect larva) develop into a pupa (指昆虫的幼虫)化蛹.

pu·pil[1] /ˈpju:pl; ˋpjupl̩/ *n* (**a**) person, esp a child, who is taught in school or privately 学生; (尤指)小学生: *There are 30 pupils in the class.* 这个班有30名学生. ○ *She takes private pupils as well as teaching in school.* 她除在学校任教外, 也私自教授学生. (**b**) person who is taught by an expert; follower 弟子; 门生; 追随者: *The painting is the work of a pupil of Rembrandt.* 这幅画是伦勃朗的一位弟子的作品. ○ *The tenor was a pupil of Caruso.* 这位男高音歌手师承卡鲁索.

pu·pil[2] /ˈpju:pl; ˋpjupl̩/ *n* circular opening in the centre of the iris of the eye that regulates the amount of light passing to the retina by becoming larger or smaller 瞳孔. ⇨illus at EYE 见 EYE 插图.

pup·pet /ˈpʌpɪt; ˋpʌpɪt/ *n* **1** doll or small figure of an animal, etc, either a *marionette* that can be made to move by pulling wires or strings attached to its jointed limbs, or a *glove puppet* that fits one's hand so that one can move the head and arms with one's fingers 木偶: [attrib 作定语] *a puppet theatre* 木偶剧院. ⇨illus 见插

puppets 木偶

GLOVE PUPPET 手套式木偶　　MARIONETTE 牵线木偶

图. **2** (*usu derog* 通常作贬义) person or group whose actions are controlled by another 傀儡: *The union representative was accused of being a puppet of the management.* 那名工会代表受到了指责, 说他是资方的傀儡. ○ [attrib 作定语] *a puppet government/state*, ie one that is controlled by another power 傀儡政府[不能自主的国家].

▷ **pup·pet·eer** /ˌpʌpɪ'tɪə(r); ˌpʌpɪ`tɪr/ *n* person who performs with or controls a puppet(1) or puppets 演木偶剧的人; 操纵木偶的人.

pup·petry /'pʌpɪtrɪ; `pʌpɪtrɪ/ *n* art of making and handling puppets (PUPPET 1) 制作木偶或演木偶剧的技艺.

□ '**puppet-play** (also '**puppet-show**) *n* type of entertainment with puppets 木偶剧.

puppy /'pʌpɪ; `pʌpɪ/ (also **pup** /pʌp; pʌp/) *n* **1** young dog 小狗; 幼犬. **2** (*infml derog* 口, 贬) conceited or insolent young man 自负或傲慢的年轻人: *You insolent young puppy!* 你这个目中无人的小子!

□ '**puppy-fat** *n* [U] (*infml* 口) fatness, esp of a female child or adolescent, which disappears as the child grows up 儿童(尤指女性青少年)的肥胖(长大即消失): *After Jane lost her puppy-fat she became very slim.* 简发育期间出现的肥胖消除之后, 显得十分苗条.

'**puppy-love** (also '**calf-love**) *n* [U] (*infml* 口) immature infatuation of an adolescent 未成年男女不成熟的爱情: *He's mad about his biology teacher, but it's only puppy-love.* 他迷恋着生物学老师, 但那只不过是孩子的一片痴情罢了.

pur·chase[1] /'pɜ:tʃəs; `pɝtʃəs/ *n* **1** (*fml* 文) (**a**) [U] (action of) buying sth 购买: *the date of purchase* 购买日期 ○ *The receipt is your proof of purchase.* 这张发票是你购物的凭据. ○ *They began to regret the purchase of such a large house.* 他们开始后悔不该买这么大的房子. ○ *hire-purchase* 分期付款购买. (**b**) [C usu *pl* 通常作复数] thing bought 购买之物: *I have some purchases to make in town.* 我要去城里买些东西. ○ *It was the most extravagant purchase I have ever made.* 这是我买过的最奢侈的东西. **2** [U, sing] (*fml* 文) firm hold or grip for pulling or raising sth, preventing it from slipping, etc; leverage (为拉动或升举某物、防止滑落等的)紧握, 紧抓; 杠杆作用: *The climbers had difficulty getting a/any purchase on the rock face.* 攀登者很难抓住岩石表面的什么东西.

□ '**purchase price** *n* price (to be) paid for sth 买价: *The purchase price is less if you pay by cash.* 付现金的话, 价钱便宜些.

'**purchase tax** tax charged on several types of goods, at varying rates, collected by the retailer (and since 1973 replaced in Britain by VAT) 购买税(1973 年以后在英国由增值税取代). Cf 参看 SALES TAX (SALE).

pur·chase[2] /'pɜ:tʃəs; `pɝtʃəs/ *v* **1** [Tn, Dn·pr] **~ sth (with sth); ~ sth (for sb)** (*fml* 文) buy sth 购买某物: *houses purchased with loans from building societies* 由房屋建筑协会贷款购置的房屋 ○ *Employees are encouraged to purchase shares in the firm.* 该企业号召职工购买其股票. **2** [Tn, Tn·pr] **~ sth (with sth)** (*rhet* 修辞) obtain or achieve sth (at a cost or with sacrifice) (以某种代价或牺牲)换得或实现某事物: *a dearly purchased victory*, ie one for which many lives were lost 以巨大的代价换来的胜利(许多人为此牺牲了生命).

▷ **pur·chaser** *n* (*fml* 文) person who buys sth 购买人; 买主: *The purchaser of the house will pay the deposit next week.* 买房者下周付定金. Cf 参看 VENDOR (VEND).

□ '**purchasing power** [U] (**a**) wealth and the ability to buy goods with it (人的)购买力: *Inflation reduces the purchasing power of people living on fixed incomes.* 靠固定收入生活的人其购买力因通货膨胀而下降. (**b**) value (of a unit of money) in terms of what it can buy (货币的)购买力: *a decline in the purchasing power of the dollar* 美元的贬值.

pur·dah /'pɜ:də; `pɝdə/ *n* [U] (system in Muslim and Hindu societies of) keeping women from public view by means of a veil, curtain, etc 妇女用面纱、帘幕等隔开公众视线的做法; 穆斯林社会和印度社会的深闺制度: *keep sb/be/live in purdah*, ie concealed in this way 使某人身处于深闺之中[身居深闺] ○ (*fig infml* 比喻, 口) *I've got a lot of urgent work to do at home and will have to go into purdah for a couple of weeks.* 我有许多紧要的工作须在家里做, 因此要有几个星期足不出户.

pure /pjʊə(r); pjʊr/ *adj* (in senses 1b, 1c, 2 and 4 用于下述第 1b、1c、2、4 义时比较级作 **-r, -st** /'pjʊərə(r), 'pjʊərɪst; `pjʊrɚ, `pjʊrɪst/) **1** (**a**) not mixed with any other substance 纯的; 纯净的; 纯粹的: *pure cotton, gold, silk, wool, etc* 纯棉、纯金、纯丝、纯毛 ○ *The room was painted pure white.* 这房间漆成了纯白色. ○ (*fig* 比喻) *pure bliss, happiness, etc* 极乐、至福. (**b**) without harmful substances; clean or unadulterated 无有害物质的; 洁净的; 不搀杂的: *pure water* 洁净的水 ○ *The air is so pure in these mountains.* 这些山区里的空气格外清新. (**c**) [usu attrib 通常作定语] of unmixed origin or race 血统纯的; 纯种的: *She has pure gypsy blood in her veins.* 她血管里流的是纯吉卜赛人的血液. ○ *He is a pure Red Indian.* 他是血统纯正的北美印第安人. **2** without evil or sin, esp sexual sin; virtuous, chaste 无邪的; 清白的; 有操守的; (尤指)贞洁的: (*rhet* 修辞) *pure in body and mind* 身心纯洁 ○ *pure thoughts* 纯洁的思想 ○ *a pure young girl* 纯真无邪的年轻姑娘 ○ *keep oneself pure* 洁身自好 ○ *His motives were pure.* 他的动机很单纯. **3** [attrib 作定语] nothing but; mere or sheer 单纯的; 仅仅的; 完全的: *They met by pure accident.* 他们的相见纯属偶然. ○ *pure folly, extravagance, nonsense* 愚蠢透顶、十足的浪费、一派胡言 ○ *do sth out of pure kindness, malice, mischief, etc* 完全出于好意、恶意、戏弄人的动机等而做某事 ○ *It was pure chance that I was there.* 我刚巧在那儿. **4** (of sound) clear and unwavering (指声音)清晰的, 不发颤的: *a pure note, voice, etc* 纯音、纯正的嗓音. **5** [attrib 作定语] (*fml* 文) dealing with or studied for the sake of theory only; without practical application 纯理论的; 非实用的: *pure mathematics* 理论数学 ○ *pure art*, ie art created for its own sake, and not for decoration, eg painting, sculpture, etc 纯艺术(为艺术而艺术而不以装饰为目的, 如绘画、雕塑等). Cf 参看 APPLIED (APPLY). **6** (idm 习语) **(as) pure as the driven snow** extremely pure(2) 纯真无邪的; 玉洁冰清. ˌ**pure and** '**simple** (*infml* 口) (used after the *n* referred to 用于所指名词之后) and nothing else; sheer 纯粹的; 十足的: *It's laziness, pure and simple.* 这纯粹是懒惰. ○ *The reason for the change is lack of money, pure and simple.* 进行更改的原因就是缺少经费.

▷ **purely** *adv* merely or entirely 纯粹地; 仅仅; 完全地: *purely by accident* 纯属偶然 ○ *He bought it purely as an investment.* 他纯粹是作为投资而购买的.

pure·ness *n* [U] = PURITY.

□ '**pure-bred** *adj*, *n* = THOROUGHBRED.

purée /'pjʊəreɪ; *US* pjʊə'reɪ; pjʊ`re/ *n* [U, C] (often in compounds 常用以构成复合词) thick liquid made by pressing fruit or cooked vegetables through a sieve; pulp (水果或熟的蔬菜经挤压、过滤后的)泥, 酱: *Make a purée of the vegetables.* 做蔬菜泥吧. ○ *apple, potato, raspberry, etc purée* 苹果、土豆、悬钩子...泥.

▷ **purée** *v* [Tn] make (fruit or vegetables) into a purée 将(水果或蔬菜)做成泥: *She fed the baby on puréed carrots.* 她用胡萝卜泥喂养那婴儿. ○ *a machine for puréeing vegetables* 制作蔬菜泥的机器.

pur·ga·tion /pɜ:'geɪʃn; pɝ`geʃən/ *n* [U] (*fml* 文) purging or purification 净化; 洗涤.

pur·gat·ive /'pɜ:gətɪv; `pɝgətɪv/ *n, adj* (substance, esp a medicine) that causes the bowels to empty; strong(ly) laxative 通便的; 催泻的; 泻药: *This oil acts as a purgative/has a purgative effect.* 这种油有催泻作用. ○ *He was given a purgative before the operation.* 他在手术前用了通便药.

pur·gat·ory /ˈpɜːgətrɪ; US -tɔːrɪ; ˋpɝgəˌtɔrɪ/ *n* [U] **1** (usu 通常作 **Purgatory**) (in Roman Catholic teaching) place or condition in which the souls of the dead are purified by suffering in preparation for Heaven (天主教教义中的)炼狱: *a prayer for the souls in Purgatory* 为炼狱中的灵魂作的祈祷. **2** (*esp infml or joc* 尤作口语或戏谑语) any place or condition of suffering 任何受难的处所或情况: *He's so impatient that waiting in a queue is sheer purgatory for him!* 他毫无耐性, 对他来说排队等候完全是活受罪!

▷ **pur·gat·orial** /ˌpɜːgəˈtɔːrɪəl; ˌpɝgəˋtɔrɪəl/ *adj* (*fml* 文) of or like purgatory (似)炼狱的: *purgatorial agony, fires* 炼狱般的痛苦、大火.

purge /pɜːdʒ; pɝdʒ/ *v* **1** [Tn, Tn·pr, Tn·p] **~ sb (of/from sth); ~ sth (away)** make sb clean or pure by removing (evil, sin, etc) 为某人(免罪、赦罪等): *Catholics go to confession to be purged of sin/purge (away) their sin/purge their souls of sin.* 天主教徒透过告解以获得赦罪[净化灵魂]. **2** [Tn] (*dated or joc* 旧或谑) empty the bowels (of a person) 给(某人)通便: *A dose of this stuff will purge you!* 这种药只须一剂就能让你通便! **3** [Tn, Tn·pr] **~ sth (of sb)/~ sb (from sth)** rid (esp a political party) of (people thought to be undesirable); remove (such people) from (a party) 清除(尤指政党的)(异己分子); 清洗(党员): *So-called traitors were purged (from their ranks).* 所谓的叛徒均已(从队伍中)清洗出去. ○ *They promised that the party would be purged of racists/that racists would be purged from the party.* 他们保证该党一定把种族主义分子清除掉[把种族主义分子从党内清洗出去]. **4** [Tn] (*law* 律) atone for (an offence, esp contempt of court) 弥补(罪过, 尤指藐视法庭罪): *purge one's contempt* 于藐视法庭后认错以求得免罪.

▷ **purge** *n* **1** action of ridding (a political party, state, etc) of people who are considered undesirable (政党、国家等之)清洗行动; 整肃: *a purge of disloyal members* 对不忠诚分子的整肃行动 ○ *the political purges that followed the change of government* 随政权之改变而来的政治上的清洗. **2** (esp formerly) medicine that empties the bowels; purgative (尤指旧时的)泻药, 泻剂.

pur·ify /ˈpjʊərɪfaɪ; ˋpjurəˌfaɪ/ *v* (*pt, pp* **-fied**) [Tn, Tn·pr] (a) **~ sth (of sth)** make sth pure by removing dirty, harmful or foreign substances 使某物纯净; 净化某物: *Water is purified by passing through rock.* 水在穿透岩石的过程中获得了净化. ○ *purified salts* 精制的盐 ○ *The soil has to be purified of all bacteria.* 要消灭这土壤的所有细菌使之净化. ○ *an air-purifying plant*, eg for providing pure air in a factory 净化空气的设备(如在工厂中用以供给新鲜空气者). (b) **~ sb (of sth)** make sb pure by removing his sins, esp in a religious ceremony 洗刷某人的罪恶; (尤指在宗教仪式上)给某人涤罪.

▷ **puri·fica·tion** /ˌpjʊərɪfɪˈkeɪʃn; ˌpjurəfəˋkeʃən/ *n* [U] (action of) purifying 净化; 提纯; 涤罪: *purification of water* 水的净化 ○ *the purification of souls* 心灵的净化.

pur·ist /ˈpjʊərɪst; ˋpjurɪst/ *n* person who pays great attention to correctness, esp in the use of language or in the arts 纯粹主义者, 力求纯正的人(尤指在语言的运用或艺术方面): *Purists were shocked by the changes made to the text of the play.* 抱有纯粹主义观点的人对该剧语言中的更改感到震惊. ▷ **pur·ism** /ˈpjʊərɪzəm; ˋpjurɪzəm/ *n* [U] (*fml* 文).

pur·itan /ˈpjʊərɪtən; ˋpjurətn̩/ *n* **1 Puritan** member of the party of English Protestants in the 16th and 17th centuries who wanted simpler forms of church ceremony 清教徒(16世纪和17世纪英国基督教新教徒之一派, 主张简化宗教仪式): [attrib 作定语] *the Puritan settlers in New England* 移民到新英格兰的英国清教徒. **2** (*usu derog* 通常作贬义) person who is extremely strict in morals and who tends to regard pleasure as sinful 道德上极拘谨, 视享乐为罪恶的人; 禁欲者; 苦行者: *the puritans who wish to clean up television* 希望净化电视内容的道学先生.

▷ **pur·itan** *adj* **1 Puritan** of or relating to a Puritan or Puritanism 清教徒的; 清教主义的; 禁欲的; 苦行的. **2** = PURITANICAL.

pur·it·an·ical /ˌpjʊərɪˈtænɪkl; ˌpjurəˋtænɪkl/ *adj* (*derog* 贬) very strict and severe in morals 清教徒式的; 道德上极拘谨的: *a puritanical attitude, conscience, upbringing* 清教徒式的态度、良心、教养 ○ *pursue vice with puritanical zeal* 道学先生般地疾恶如仇. **pur·it·an·ically** /-klɪ; -klɪ/ *adv*: *puritanically opposed to pleasure* 清教徒式地反对享乐.

pur·it·an·ism /ˈpjʊərɪtənɪzəm; ˋpjurətn̩ˌɪzəm/ *n* [U] practices and beliefs of a Puritan or a puritan 清教徒的行为和教义; 清教主义.

pur·ity /ˈpjʊərətɪ; ˋpjurətɪ/ (also **pureness**) *n* [U] state or quality of being pure 纯净; 纯洁; 纯粹; 纯正; 纯度: *test the purity of the water* 检测水的纯度 ○ *question the purity of their motives* 对他们的动机是否纯洁存有疑问 ○ *purity of colour, form, sound, etc* 颜色、形式、声音等的纯正.

purl /pɜːl; pɝl/ *n* [C, U] (also ˈ**purl stitch**) stitch in knitting that produces ridges on the upper side (编织的)反针: *knitted in purl* 用反针编织 ○ *Knit two plain, two purl.* 两针平织, 两针反织. Cf 参看 PLAIN[3].

▷ **purl** *v* [I, Tn] knit (sth) in this stitch 用反针编织(某物): *Knit one* (ie make one plain stitch), *purl one.* 平织一针, 反织一针.

pur·lieus /ˈpɜːljuːz; ˋpɝlɪuz/ *n* [pl] (*fml or rhet* 文或修辞) outlying parts; outskirts 边缘部分; 外围部分; 郊区: *the purlieus of the capital* 首都的郊区.

pur·loin /pɜːˈlɔɪn, ˈpɜːlɔɪn; pɝˋlɔɪn, ˋpɝˌlɔɪn/ *v* [Tn] (*fml or joc* 文或谑) steal (sth) 偷窃(某物): *food purloined from her employer's kitchen* 从雇主的厨房里偷来的食物.

purple /ˈpɜːpl; ˋpɝpl̩/ *adj* **1** having the colour of red and blue mixed together 紫的: *a purple flower, dress, sunset* 紫色的花朵、连衣裙、晚霞 ○ *go purple (in the face) with rage* 气得脸色铁青. **2** (*fml* 文) (of literature) elaborate in style; overwritten (指文章)刻意雕琢的, 词藻华丽的: *purple passages/patches/prose* 词藻华丽的段落[节段/散文].

▷ **purple** *n* **1** [U] purple colour 紫色: *dressed in purple* 穿紫色衣服. **2 the purple** [sing] the purple robes of a Roman emperor or the crimson robes of a cardinal (古罗马帝国皇帝的)紫袍; (红衣主教的)大红袍.

purp·lish /ˈpɜːpəlɪʃ; ˋpɝplɪʃ/ *adj* rather purple in colour 略带紫色的: *a purplish complexion* 略微发紫的肤色.

□ ˌ**purple** ˈ**heart** **1 Purple Heart** (*US*) medal awarded to a soldier who has been wounded in battle (授予作战负伤之军人的)紫心勋章. **2** (*infml* 口) heart-shaped pill containing amphetamine, used as a stimulant 紫心片(一种心形的含有苯丙胺的药片, 用作兴奋剂).

pur·port /ˈpɜːpət; ˋpɝport/ *n* [sing] **~ (of sth)** (*fml* 文) general meaning or intention (of sth) 主要意义; 大意; 意图: *The purport of the statement is that the firm is bankrupt.* 该项声明大意是该商行已破产.

▷ **pur·port** /pəˈpɔːt; pɚˋport/ *v* [Tt] (*fml* 文) be meant to seem (to be); claim or pretend 意思似乎是; 声称; 伪称: *The document purports to be an official statement.* 该文件据称是一项正式声明.

pur·pose /ˈpɜːpəs; ˋpɝpəs/ *n* **1** [C] thing that one intends to do, get, be, etc; intention 目的; 意图: *What is the purpose of the meeting?* 这会议的目的是什么? ○ *What is your purpose in going to Canada?* 你到加拿大干什么去? ○ *Getting rich seems to be her only purpose in life.* 她生活的唯一目的似乎是发财. **2** [U] (*fml* 文) ability to form plans and carry them out; determination 意志; 毅力; 决心: *Her approach to the job lacks purpose.* 她干这项工作缺乏毅力. **3** (idm 习语) **for practical purposes** ⇨ PRACTICAL. **on** ˈ**purpose** not by accident; intentionally 并非偶然地; 故意地: *'Did he break it accidentally?' 'No, on purpose.'* '他是无意中损坏的吗?' '不, 是故意的.' ○ *She seems to do these things on purpose.* 她似乎是有意地做这些事. **serve one's/the** ˈ**purpose** (*fml* 文) do what is necessary or required; be satisfactory 适合需要; 适合要求; 令人满意: *We have found a meeting-place that will serve our purpose.* 我们找到了一个很合适的会址. **to little/no/some** ˈ**purpose** (*fml* 文) with little/no/some result or effect 几乎徒劳地[毫无成效地/有一定效果地]: *Money has been invested in the scheme to very little purpose.* 资金已投入那计划中却几无成效.

▷ **pur·pose** *v* [Tt, Tg] (*dated* 旧) intend 有意; 打算: *They purpose making/to make a further attempt.* 他们有意做进一步的尝试.

pur·pose·ful /-fl; -fəl/ *adj* having or showing determination or will-power; resolute 有决心的; 有毅力的; 坚定的; 果

P

断的: *They dealt with the problem in a purposeful way.* 他们处理这问题很果断. **pur·pose·fully** /-fəlɪ; -fəlɪ/ *adv*: *He strode purposefully into the meeting.* 他迈着坚定的步伐走进会场.

pur·pose·less *adj* without (a) purpose 毫无目的的; 缺乏毅力的; 没有决心的: *a purposeless existence* 毫无目的的生活. **pur·pose·lessly** *adv*.

pur·posely *adv* on purpose; intentionally 故意地; 蓄意地: *He was accused of purposely creating difficulties.* 有人指责他故意制造麻烦.

□ ˌ**purpose-ˈbuilt** *adj* (*esp Brit*) made for a particular purpose 特地建造的: *a* ˌ*purpose-built* ˈ*factory* 特地兴建的工厂.

P

purr /pɜː(r); pɝ/ *v* [I, Ipr] **(a)** (of a cat) make a low continuous vibrating sound (指猫)发低而连续的呼噜声: *purring happily* 快活地呼噜作声. **(b)** (of machinery) make a similar smooth vibrating sound (指机器)发低沉而连续的呼隆声: *a car engine purring smoothly* 汽车发动机平隐地呼隆作响.

▷ **purr** *n* purring sound (猫的)呼噜声; (机器的)呼隆声: *the contented purrs of the cat* 猫表示满足的呼噜声.

purse[1] /pɜːs; pɝs/ *n* **1** [C] small bag for money (formerly closed by drawing strings together and now usu with a clasp) 小钱袋, 小钱包(旧时用绳抽拢袋口, 现多用扣合起): *a leather/plastic purse* 皮的[塑料的]钱包 ○ *Her purse was stolen from her handbag.* 她的钱包放在手提包里被人偷走了. Cf 参看 WALLET. **2** [sing] money available for spending; funds or resources 备用款; 资金; 财源: *the public purse* 国库 ○ *the privy Purse* 国王私用金. **3** [C] sum of money collected and given as a gift or prize (为用作礼物或奖金而筹集的)款项: *a purse of £50 000*, eg for the winner of a boxing match 筹集得50 000英镑的奖金(如为颁赠拳击赛获胜者). **4** [C] (*US*) handbag 女用手提包. **5** (idm 习语) **hold the** ˈ**purse-strings** have control of spending 控制开支: *I can't offer you any more money because I don't hold the purse-strings.* 我不能再多给你钱了, 因为我在经济上做不了主. **loosen/tighten the** ˈ**purse-strings** increase/reduce expenditure 增加[紧缩]开支.

purse[2] /pɜːs; pɝs/ *v* [Tn, Tn·p] **~ sth (up)** draw together or pucker (one's lips) in wrinkles esp as a sign of disapproval or displeasure 缩拢或噘起(嘴唇)(尤指表示反对或不悦): *with pursed lips* 噘着嘴 ○ *purse (up) one's lips* 噘起嘴来.

purser /ˈpɜːsə(r); ˈpɝsɚ/ *n* ship's officer responsible for the accounts, stores, passengers, etc (轮船上的)事务长.

pur·su·ance /pəˈsjuːəns; *US* -ˈsuː-; pɚˈsuəns/ *n* (idm 习语) **in (the) pursuance of sth** (*fml* 文) while performing sth; in the course of sth 在实行某事时; 在某过程中: *injuries suffered in the pursuance of one's duties* 在执行任务时受的伤.

pur·sue /pəˈsjuː; *US* -ˈsuː; pɚˈsu/ *v* [Tn] (*fml* 文) **1** follow (sb/sth), esp in order to catch or kill; chase 追赶, 追逐(某人[某物]); (尤指)追捕, 追杀; 追寻; 追求: *pursue a wild animal, one's prey, a thief* 追捕野兽、被捕食的动物、窃贼 ○ *The police pursued the stolen vehicle along the motorway.* 警察在高速公路上追赶被盗的车辆. **2** (continue to) be occupied or busy with (sth); go on with (继续)从事或忙于(某事物); 进行: *She decided to pursue her studies after obtaining her first degree.* 她决定在获得学士学位之后继续深造. ○ *I have decided not to pursue* (ie investigate) *the matter any further.* 我决定不再追查那事.

▷ **pur·suer** *n* person who pursues (PURSUE 1) 追赶者; 追捕者; 追击者: *He managed to avoid his pursuers.* 他设法甩掉了那些追捕者.

pur·suit /pəˈsjuːt; *US* -ˈsuːt; pɚˈsut/ *n* (*fml* 文) **1** [U] **~ of sth** action of pursuing (PURSUE 2) sth 追求; 寻求; 从事; 进行: *The pursuit of profit was the main reason for the changes.* 作出这些改变主要是为了追求利润. ○ *She devoted her life to the pursuit of pleasure.* 她一生都在寻求享乐. **2** [C usu *pl* 通常作复数] thing to which one gives one's time, energy, etc; occupation or activity 花时间、精力等做的事; 职业: *artistic, literary, scientific pursuits* 艺术的、文学的、科学的研究 ○ *be engaged in/devote oneself to worthwhile pursuits* 从事[献身于]有意义的活动. **3** (idm 习语) **in pursuit (of sb/sth)** with the aim of catching sb/sth 追捕某人[某物]: *thirty grown men in pursuit of a single fox* 追猎一只狐狸的三十名成年男子. **in pursuit of sth** with the aim of obtaining sth 追求某事物: *people travelling about the country in pursuit of work* 到全国各地寻找工作的人们. **in (hot) purˈsuit** pursuing (closely and with determination) 穷追不舍: *a fox with the hounds in hot pursuit* 被猎犬穷追的狐狸.

puru·lent /ˈpjʊərələnt; ˈpjʊrələnt/ *adj* (*medical* 医) of, containing or discharging pus 脓的; 含脓的; 化脓的; 流脓的. ▷ **puru·lence** /-əns; -əns/ *n* [U].

pur·vey /pəˈveɪ; pɚˈve/ *v* [Tn, Dn·pr] **~ sth (to sb)** (*fml* 文) provide or supply (esp food, etc) to sb as a trader (商人)向某人提供或供应(尤指食品等): *butchers who have purveyed meat to the royal household for generations* 世世代代向王室供应肉食品的肉商 ○ *a bureau that purveys information about the stock market to potential investors* 向可能投资的人提供股票市场信息的机构.

▷ **pur·vey·ance** /-əns; -əns/ *n* [U].

pur·veyor *n* (*fml* 文) person or firm that supplies goods or services 供应货物或提供服务的人或公司: *Brown and Son, purveyors of fine wines* 布朗父子公司, 美酒供应商.

pur·view /ˈpɜːvjuː; ˈpɝvju/ *n* [U] (*fml* 文) range of operation or activity; scope (工作或活动的)范围: *These are questions that lie outside/that do not come within the purview of our inquiry.* 这些问题不在我们的调查范围之内.

pus /pʌs; pʌs/ *n* [U] thick yellowish matter formed in and coming out from an infected wound 脓: *The doctor lanced the boil to let the pus out.* 医生把皮下脓肿切开让脓流出.

push[1] /pʊʃ; pʊʃ/ *n* **1** [C] act of pushing; shove 推; 搡: *Give the door a hard push.* 用力推那门. ○ *He opened the gate with/at one push.* 他一下子就把大门推开了. **2** [C] large-scale attack made to break through enemy positions 为突破敌人阵地而发起的大规模攻势: *The commander decided to postpone the big push until the spring.* 指挥官决定把大规模的进攻推迟到春天进行. **3** [U] (*infml* 口) determination to succeed; drive 毅力; 推动力: *He hasn't enough push to be a successful salesman.* 他缺乏优秀推销员应有的闯劲. **4** (idm 习语) **at a** ˈ**push** (*infml* 口 *esp Brit*) if one is forced to do so 不得已时: *We can provide accommodation for six people at a push.* 如情况需要, 我们可以安排六个人的住处. **give sb/get the** ˈ**push** (*esp Brit infml* 口) **(a)** dismiss sb/be dismissed from one's job; give sb/get the sack 解雇某人[被解雇]; 开除某人[被开除]: *He got the push when the new manager came.* 新经理到任后, 他被解雇了. **(b)** bring/have brought to an end one's relationship with sb 与某人断绝关系: *He gave his girl-friend the push.* 他跟女朋友吹了. **if/until/when it comes to the** ˈ**push** if/until/when a special effort is necessary or a special need arises 如[到/在]需作出特别努力或有特别需要时: *If it comes to the push, we shall have to use our savings.* 遇有急用时, 我们只好动用积蓄.

□ ˈ**push-start** *v* [Tn] start (a motor vehicle) by pushing it along to make the engine turn 推车起动(机动车). — *n*: *We'll have to give it a push-start, I'm afraid.* 我看我们得用助推的办法起动这辆车了.

push[2] /pʊʃ; pʊʃ/ *v* **1** **(a)** [I] use force in order to move sth away from oneself 推; 搡: *You push from the back and I'll pull at the front.* 你在后面推, 我在前面拉. ○ *Push hard and the lever will go down.* 用力推就能把控制杆按下去. **(b)** [Tn, Tn·pr, Cn·a] use force on (sth) in order to move it away from oneself, forward or to a different position 推动(某物): *You can pull a rope, but you can't push it!* 绳子能拉不能推! ○ *push the pram up the hill* 推着婴儿车上山 ○ *push the table a bit nearer the wall* 把桌子推得离墙近一点 ○ *He pushed the door open.* 他把门推开了. ○ (*fig* 比喻) *push a problem to the back of one's mind* 把某问题置诸脑后. ⇨illus at PULL 见PULL插图. **(c)** [Ipr, Ip, Tn·pr, Tn·p] move forward using force 推进; 往前挤: *The crowd pushed past (us).* 人群从(我们)旁边挤了过去. ○ *We had to push our way through (the crowd).* 我们只好从(人群)中挤了过去. **2** [Ipr, Tn] **~ (on/against) sth** exert pressure on sth; press 对某物施加压力; 按: *He pushed hard against the door with his shoulder.* 他用肩膀用力顶那房门. ○ *Push the doorbell.* 按门铃. ○ *You can stop the machine by pushing the red button.* 按红色的按钮就能把机器停住.

3 (a) [Tn, Tn·pr, Cn·t] (*infml* 口) try to make (sb) do sth (that he does not want to do); drive or urge 逼迫(某人)做某事; 驱策; 敦促: *One has to push the child or she will do no work at all.* 这孩子要有人督促, 否则她什么也不干. ○ *She was pushed into going to university by her parents.* 她是父母逼着上大学的. ○ *We pushed him hard to take up science.* 我们极力让他学习自然科学. (b) [Tn·pr] **~ sb for sth** try to obtain sth from sb by putting pressure on him 对某人施加压力以图获得某事物: *push sb for payment* 催逼某人付款 ○ *We shall have to push them for a quick decision.* 我们须敦促他们迅速决断. 4 [Tn] (*infml* 口) persuade people to buy (goods, etc) or accept (an idea, etc) 劝人购买(物品等)或接受(某意见等): *You will have to push the new product to win sales — there's lots of competition.* 你要努力打开新产品的销路 —— 市场上竞争很激烈. ○ *Unless you push your claim, you will not get satisfaction.* 不努力争取就得不到满意的结果. 5 [Tn] (*infml* 口) sell (illegal drugs) to drug-users 向嗜毒者贩卖(毒品): *She was arrested for pushing heroin.* 她因贩卖海洛因而被捕. ⇨Usage at SELL 用法见SELL. 6 (idm 习语) **be pushed for sth** (*infml* 口) not have enough of sth 缺少某事物; 某事物不足: *be pushed for money, time, etc* 缺少金钱、时间等. **be pushed to do sth** (*infml* 口) have difficulty doing sth 做某事有困难: *We'll be pushed to get there in time.* 我们很难及时赶到那儿. **push the 'boat out** (*infml* 口) celebrate regardless of the expense 不惜费用地庆贺: *This is the last party we shall give, so let's really push the boat out.* 这是咱们要举行的最后一次聚会了, 所以豁出点钱来热闹一下吧. **push one's 'luck** (*infml* 口) risk sth in a bold and often foolish way, hoping that one's good fortune will continue 莽撞冒险以期再交好运: *You didn't get caught last time, but don't push your luck!* 上次没把你抓住, 可别再碰运气了! **push up (the) 'daisies** (*infml joc* 口, 谑) be dead and in one's grave 入土: *I shall be pushing up daisies by the time the project is finished.* 等到这项目完成时, 我早已入土了. 7 (phr v) **push sb about/around** (*infml* 口) order sb to do things in a bullying way; order sb about/around 蛮横地指使某人做某事; 摆布某人. **push ahead/forward/on** continue on one's way 继续前进: *Let's push on — it's nearly nightfall.* 咱们继续往前走吧 —— 天快黑了. **push ahead/forward/on (with sth)** continue doing sth, in a determined way 毅然继续做某事: *push ahead with one's plans* 坚决按自己的计划行事. **push along** (*infml* 口) leave 离开: *Goodbye — I'd better be pushing along now.* 再见吧 —— 我现在该走了. **push for sth** make repeated and urgent requests for sth; press for sth 一再地或迫切地要求某事物; 催促某事物: *They are pushing for electoral reform.* 他们迫切要求改革选举制度. **push sth forward** force others to consider or notice sth 迫使他人考虑或注意某事物; 提出某事物: *He repeatedly pushed forward his own claim.* 他不断地提出自己的要求. **push oneself forward** ambitiously draw attention to oneself 引人注意自己; 出风头. **push off** (*infml* 口) (often as an impolite command 常作不客气的命令语) go away 走开: *Push off! We don't want you here.* 走开! 我们这儿用不着你. **push (sth) off/out** push against a bank, etc with an oar or a pole, so that a boat, etc moves away (用桨或篙顶岸等)把船等撑开. **push sb/sth over** cause sb/sth to fall or overturn 使某人[某事物]倒下或被推翻: *Several children were pushed over in the rush to leave.* 大家都争先恐后跑着离开时有几个孩子被推倒了. **push sth through** get sth accepted or completed quickly 使某事物迅速地被通过或完成: *push a plan through the committee stage* 使一项计划先在委员会中迅速通过. **push sth up** cause (esp prices) to rise steadily 使(尤指物价)稳步上升: *A shortage of building land will push property values up.* 建筑用地缺乏将造成房地产价格逐渐上升.

▷ **pusher** 1 (*infml derog* 口, 贬) person who tries constantly to gain an advantage for himself 讨便宜的人. 2 (*sl* 俚) person who sells drugs illegally; drug-pedlar 非法贩卖毒品的人; 毒品贩子.

push·ing *adj* 1 = PUSHY. 2 [pred 作表语] (*infml* 口) having nearly reached (a certain age) 接近(某一年龄)的: *pushing forty, fifty, sixty, etc* 将近四十岁、五十岁、六十岁等.

□ **'push-bike** *n* (*infml* 口) bicycle that is operated by pressing the pedals and not by a motor 自行车; 脚踏车.

'push-button *adj* [attrib 作定语] operated automatically by pressing a button 用按钮操纵的: *a radio with push-button tuning* 使用按钮调谐的无线电收音机.

'push-cart *n* small cart pushed by hand, eg a barrow for selling fruit, etc 手推车.

'push-chair (*Brit*) (also *esp US* **stroller**) *n* small folding chair on wheels for a baby or small child to be pushed around in (折叠式)幼儿车.

'push-over *n* (*sl* 俚) (a) thing that is very easily done, esp a contest that is easily won 极容易做的事; (尤指)容易获胜的竞赛: *Winning that match was a push-over.* 那场比赛赢得易如反掌. (b) client, opponent, etc who is easily convinced or won over 容易被劝诱或争取过来的顾客、对手等: *Getting money from her is easy — she's a push-over.* 挣她的钱很容易 —— 她是个好说话的顾客.

ˌpush-'pull *adj* (of electrical equipment) containing two valves, etc operated alternately by alternating current (指电气设备)推挽式的: *a push-pull amplifier* 推挽放大器.

'push-up *n* (*esp US*) = PRESS-UP (PRESS[2]).

pushy /ˈpʊʃɪ; ˈpʊʃɪ/ (**-ier, -iest**) (also **push·ing**) *adj* (*infml derog* 口, 贬) trying constantly to draw attention to oneself and gain an advantage; self-assertive 爱出风头的; 爱讨便宜的; 坚持己见的: *He made himself unpopular by being so pushy.* 他特别喜欢出风头, 所以人缘不好. ▷ **push·ily** /-ɪlɪ; -ɪlɪ/ *adv.* **pushi·ness** *n* [U].

pu·sil·lan·im·ous /ˌpju:sɪˈlænɪməs; ˌpjuslˈænəməs/ *adj* (*fml derog* 文, 贬) cowardly; timid 胆小的; 怯懦的. ▷ **pu·sil·lan·im·ity** /ˌpju:sɪləˈnɪmətɪ; ˌpjusləˈnɪmətɪ/ *n* [U]. **pu·sil·lan·im·ously** *adv.*

puss /pʊs; pʊs/ *n* 1 (word used to call a) cat 咪咪, 猫咪(呼唤用语). 2 (*infml* 口) playful or coquettish girl 调皮的或卖俏的姑娘: *She's a sly puss.* 她是个刁滑的姑娘. ▷ **pussy** /ˈpʊsɪ; ˈpʊsɪ/ *n* 1 (also **'pussy-cat**) (used by and to young children) cat (小儿语)猫咪. 2 (⚠ *sl* 讳, 俚) female genitals; vulva 屄; 阴门.

□ **'pussyfoot** *v* [I, Ip] **~ (about/around)** (*infml usu derog* 口, 通常作贬义) act (too) cautiously or timidly (过于)谨慎或胆小地行事: *Stop pussyfooting around and say what you mean.* 别那么缩手缩脚的, 说说你到底是什么意思吧.

'pussy willow willow tree with soft furry catkins 褪色柳.

pus·tule /ˈpʌstju:l; *US* -tʃu:l; ˈpʌstʃʊl/ *n* (*medical* 医) pimple or blister, esp one containing pus 丘疹; 水疱; (尤指)脓疱.

put /pʊt; pʊt/ *v* (**-tt-**, *pt, pp* **put**) 1 (a) [Tn·pr, Tn·p] move (sth/sb), esp away from oneself, so that it/he is in the specified place or position 将(某物[某人])置于某处所或位置; 放; 放置: *She put the book on the table.* 她把书放在桌子上了. ○ *'Where did you put the scissors?' 'I put them (back) in the drawer.'* '你把剪刀放在哪儿了?' '我把它放(回)到抽屉里了.' ○ *Did you put sugar in my tea?* 你在我的茶里加糖了吗? ○ *He put his hands in his pockets.* 他把双手插在口袋里. ○ *She put her arm round his shoulders.* 她的一只手臂搭在他的双肩上. ○ *She put her hand to her mouth.* 她用一只手捂住嘴. ○ *You've put the picture too high up (on the wall).* 你把这幅画挂得太高了. ○ *The Americans put a man on the moon in 1969.* 美国人于1969年把人送上了月球. ○ *It's time to put the baby to bed.* 该让那婴儿上床睡觉了. ○ *Maradona put the ball in the net*, ie scored a goal in a football match. 马拉多纳把球踢进了网内. (b) [Tn·pr] fit or fix (sth) to sth else 使(某物)与他物配合; 将(某物)固定于他物上: *Will you please put* (ie sew) *a patch on these trousers?* 请你在这条裤子上缝个补丁好吗? ○ *We must put a new lock on the front door.* 我们得在前门上安一把新锁. (c) [Tn·pr] thrust (sth) in a specified direction 猛推(某物); 使(某物)刺向...: *She put a knife between his ribs.* 她举起一把刀子刺进了他的肋骨间. ○ *He put his fist through a plate-glass door.* 他挥拳打穿了一扇玻璃门. (d) [Tn·pr, Tn·p] write or mark (sth) on sth 在某物上书写或标上(某事物): *put one's signature to a document* 在文件上签字 ○ *put a cross against sb's name* 在某人的名字上打叉 ○ *Put your name here.* 把你的名字签在这里. 2 [Tn·pr] cause (sb/sth) to be in the specified state or condition 使(某人[某事物])处于某状: *The incident put her in a bad mood.* 这件事使她心情很不好. ○ *Your*

P

decision puts me in an awkward position. 你的决定把我弄得很尴尬. ○ *The injury to her back will put her out of action for several weeks.* 她背部受了伤, 几个星期都活动不了. ○ *The Russians plan to put a satellite into orbit round Mars.* 俄国人计划把一颗人造卫星送入环绕火星的轨道. **3** [Tn·pr] rate or classify (sb/sth) in the specified way 将(某人[某事物])看作或列为...: *I wouldn't put him among the greatest composers.* 我认为他算不上一个最伟大的作曲家. ○ *I put her in the top rank of modern novelists.* 我把她看做是当代第一流的小说家. ○ *As a writer I'd put him on a par/level with Joyce.* 我认为他这位作家与乔伊斯实乃伯仲之间. **4** [Tn, Tn·pr] (used esp with a following *adv* or in questions after *how* 尤与以下副词连用或用于以 how 开始的问句中) express or state (sth) 表达或表述(某事物): *She put it very tactfully.* 她说得很有技巧. ○ *That's very well put.* 那话十分得体. ○ *How shall I put it?* 我该怎么说才好呢? ○ *As T.S. Eliot puts it...* 正如T.S.艾略特所说... ○ *'The election result was a disaster for the country.' 'I wouldn't put it quite like that.'* '这次选举的结果对国家来说是个灾难.' '我看未必如此.' **5** [Tn] throw (esp the shot) with an upward movement of the arm, as an athletic exercise 以手臂向上抛掷(尤指铅球). Cf 参看 SHOT-PUT (SHOT[1]). **6** (idm 习语) **not put it past sb (to do sth)** (*infml* 口) (used with *would* 与would连用) consider sb capable of doing sth malicious, illegal, etc 认为某人有可能做坏事、不合法的事等: *I wouldn't put it past him to steal money from his own grandmother!* 我认为他偷他祖母的钱这事不是不可能的! **put it to sb that...** suggest to sb that it is true that...; invite sb to agree that... 向某人表明事实是...; 请某人同意...: *I put it to you that you are the only person who had a motive for the crime.* 我让你明白你是唯一具有犯罪动机的人. **put sb 'through it** (*infml* 口) force sb to undergo sth demanding or unpleasant 强使某人承担费力的或讨厌的事: *They really put you through it* (ie ask you difficult questions, etc) *at the interview.* 他们在面试时提的问题的确够你受的. **put to'gether** (used after a *n* or *ns* referring to a group of people or things 用于名词之后, 指人或事物之群体) combined 加在一起; 汇总: *Your department spent more last year than all the other departments put together.* 你们部门去年的花销比其他所有部门的加起来还多. (For other idioms containing **put**, see entries for *ns, adjs*, etc 查阅与 **put** 搭配的其他习语见有关名词、形容词等的词条, 如 **put one's foot in it** ⇨ FOOT[1]; **put sth right** ⇨ RIGHT[1].)
7 (phr v) **put (sth) a'bout** (*nautical* 海) (cause sth to) change direction (使某物)改变方向: *The ship put slowly about.* 那船慢慢改变了航向. ○ *The captain put the ship about.* 船长更改了船的航向. **put sth about** spread or circulate (false news, rumours, etc) 散布, 传播(假消息、谣言等): *He's always putting about malicious rumours.* 他老是散布别有用心的谣言. ○ *It's being put about that the Prime Minister may resign.* 有谣传说首相可能辞职.
put sth above sth ⇨ PUT STH BEFORE/ABOVE STH.
put sth across sb (*infml* 口) trick sb into accepting a claim, etc that is worthless or untrue 哄骗某人接受无谓的或虚假的说法等: *Are you trying to put one across me?* 你想蒙我吧? **put oneself/sth a'cross/'over (to sb)** communicate or convey (one's personality, an idea, etc) to sb 让某人认识(自己的个性); 沟通或传达(思想等): *He doesn't know how to put himself across at interviews.* 他不知道在面试时怎样把自己的意思讲清楚. ○ *She's very good at putting her ideas across.* 她非常善于表达思想.
put sth a'side (**a**) place sth to one side 把某物放到一边: *She put the newspaper aside and picked up a book.* 她把报纸放下, 拿起了一本书. (**b**) save (a sum of money) to use later; reserve (an item) for a customer to collect later 储存(某钱数)以备他日之需; 为顾客保留(物品): *She's put aside a tidy sum for her retirement.* 她存了一笔相当可观的钱以备退休之用. ○ *We'll put the suit aside for you, Mr Parkinson.* 帕金森先生, 我们暂时为你保留这套衣服. (**c**) disregard, ignore or forget sth 不顾、忽视或不再想某事物: *They decided to put aside their differences.* 他们决定抛开彼此的分歧.
put sth at sth calculate or estimate (the size, cost, etc of sth) to be (the specified weight, amount, etc) 计算, 估计(某物之大小、价值等): *I would put his age at about sixty.* 我估计他大概有六十岁. ○ *'What would you put the price of this car at?' 'I'd put it at £15 000.'* '你看这辆汽车值多少钱?' '我看值15 000英镑.'
put sb a'way (often passive 常用于被动语态) (*infml* 口) confine sb in a prison or mental hospital 把某人关进监狱或精神病院: *He was put away for ten years for armed robbery.* 他因持械抢劫而关押了十年. ○ *She went a bit odd and had to be put away.* 她有点不正常, 只好送进了疯人院. **put sth a'way** (**a**) put sth in a box, drawer, etc because one has finished using it (使用完毕)将某物收起或放入箱子、抽屉等中: *Put your toys away in the cupboard, when you've finished playing.* 你把玩具玩儿完了以后放进柜子里去. ○ *I'm just going to put the car away*, ie in the garage. 我正要把车开进车库里去. (**b**) save (money) to use later 存(钱)以备他日之需: *She's got a few thousand pounds put away for her retirement.* 她已存了几千镑以备退休之用. (**c**) (*infml* 口) eat or drink (a large quantity of food or drink) 吃, 喝(大量食物或饮料): *He must have put away half a bottle of whisky last night.* 昨晚他大概喝了半瓶威士忌酒. ○ *I don't know how he manages to put it all away!* 我真不知道他怎么吃得这样多!
put sth 'back (**a**) return sth to its proper place; replace sth 把某物放回原处; 放回某物: *Please put the dictionary back on the shelf when you've finished with it.* 词典用完后请放回到书架上. (**b**) move (the hands of a clock) back to give the correct time 把(钟表指针)倒拨(校准): *My watch is fast; it needs putting back five minutes.* 我的表快了, 需要拨回五分钟. (**c**) move sth to a later time or date; postpone sth 使某事物延期或延迟; 推迟某事物: *This afternoon's meeting has been put back to next week.* 今天下午的会议已延至下星期举行. (**d**) cause sth to be delayed 使某事物延误: *The lorry drivers' strike has put back our deliveries by over a month.* 因卡车司机罢工, 我们的交货日期延误了一个多月. (**e**) (*infml* 口) drink (a large quantity of alcohol) (大量地)喝(酒): *By midnight he had put back nearly two bottles of wine.* 到半夜时分他已喝了近两瓶酒.
put sth before/above sth treat or regard sth as more important than sth else 把某事物看得比其他事物重要: *He puts his children's welfare before all other considerations.* 他把子女的幸福看得比什么都重要.
put sth 'by save (money) to use in the future 存(钱)以备未来之需: *She has a fair amount of money put by.* 她存了不少钱.
put (sth) 'down (of an aeroplane or its pilot) land; land (an aeroplane, etc) (指飞机或飞行员)着陆; 将(飞机等)降落: *He put (the glider) down in a field.* 他(把滑翔机)降落在田地里了. **put sb down** (**a**) (of a bus, coach, etc) allow sb to get off (指公共汽车、长途汽车等)让某人下车: *The bus stopped to put down some passengers.* 公共汽车停下来让一些旅客下车. (**b**) (*infml* 口) humiliate or snub sb 羞辱或怠慢某人: *He's always putting his wife down in public.* 他老是当众羞辱妻子.
put sth down (**a**) place sth on a table, shelf, etc; set down sth that is dangerous or a nuisance to others 把某物放到桌子、架子等上; 把对别人有危险或有妨碍之某物放下: *Put down that knife before you hurt somebody!* 把那刀子放下, 以免伤人! ○ *I can't put this novel down*, ie because I am enjoying it so much. 这本小说我实在撂不下(因为我读上了瘾). (**b**) place sth in storage; place (wine) in a cellar to mature 把某物储藏起来; 窖(酒): *I put down a couple of cases of claret last year.* 去年我把几箱红葡萄酒放进地窖使之香醇. (**c**) write sth down; make a note of sth 把某事物写下来; 记下某事物: *I'm having a party next Saturday; put it down in your diary so you don't forget.* 本星期六我有个聚会; 把这事记在你的日记里吧, 以免忘了. (**d**) stop, suppress or abolish sth by force or authority 使用力量或权威禁止、压制或废止某事物: *put down a rebellion, a revolt, an uprising, etc* 镇压叛乱、反叛、起义等 ○ *The military junta is determined to put down all political opposition.* 这个军人集团决心镇压政治上的一切反对派. (**e**) (often passive 常用于被动语态) kill (an animal) because it is old or sick; destroy sth 宰杀(衰老或有病的动物); 破坏某事物: *The horse broke a leg in the fall and had to be put down.* 这马跌断了一条腿, 不得不杀掉. ○ *Our cat was getting so old and sick that we had her put down.* 我们的老猫病成这个样子, 该把它杀掉了. (**f**) (esp in

Parliament) include sth on the agenda for a meeting or debate （尤指议会中）将某事列入议程，将某事提交会议辩论：*The Opposition plan to put down a censure motion on the Government's handling of the affair.* 反对党拟将谴责政府处理该事的动议提交议会辩论. **put sb down as sb** consider sb to be (the specified type of person); take sb to be sb 认为某人是（某种类型的人）；把某人当作某种人：*I put him down as a retired naval officer.* 我看他是个退役的海军军官. **put sb down for sth (a)** write down that sb is willing or wishes to buy or contribute sth 登记某人预购或认捐某物：*Put me down for three tickets for Saturday's performance.* 给我登记购买三张星期六的演出票. **(b)** put (sb's name) on the waiting-list for admission to a private school 为（某人）预约报名（进入私立学校）：*They've put their son down for Eton.* 他们已为儿子预约报名入伊顿公学. **put sth down to sth (a)** charge (an amount or item) to a particular account 把（数额或项目）记在某帐户上：*Would you put these shoes down to my account, please?* 请你把这双鞋记在我的帐上好吗？**(b)** consider that sth is caused by sth; attribute sth to sth 认为某事物系由另事物所引起；把某事物归因于另事物：*What do you put her success down to?* 你认为她成功的原因是什么？○ *I put it all down to her hard work and initiative.* 我把这一切归因于她工作又勤奋又主动.

put sth forth (*fml* 文) (of trees and plants) send out or produce (buds, shoots, etc) （指花草树木）长出（花蕾）或发（芽等）：*Spring has come and the hedges are putting forth new leaves.* 春天到了，树篱长出了新叶子.

put oneself/sb forward present oneself or propose or recommend sb as a candidate for a job, position, etc 自荐或提名或推荐某人为某职务、职位等的候选人：*Two left-wingers have been put forward for the Labour Party's National Executive.* 两名左翼成员被提名为工党全国执行委员会的委员. ○ *Can I put you/your name forward for golf club secretary?* 我推荐你［提名让你］担任高尔夫球俱乐部的秘书好吗？**put sth forward (a)** move (the hands of a clock) forward to give the correct time 把（钟表指针）顺拨（校准）：*Put your watch forward; you're five minutes slow.* 把你的表往前拨拨；你的表慢了五分钟. **(b)** move sth to an earlier time or date 将某事物提前：*We've put forward (the date of) our wedding by one week.* 我们将婚礼（日期）提前了一周. **(c)** advance, propose or suggest sth for discussion 提出某事供讨论；提请审议某事：*put forward an argument, a plan, a suggestion, etc* 提出一论据、一计划、一建议等 ○ *She is putting forward radical proposals for electoral reform.* 她为选举制度的改革提出极为激进的建议.

put 'in interrupt another speaker in order to say sth; interject 插话；插嘴：*'But what about us?' he put in.* ‘可是我们怎么办呢？’他插嘴问道. **put sb in (a)** give duties to sb (eg in an office building) 指派某人担任职务（如在办公楼内）：*put in a caretaker, a security man, etc* 指派管理员、保安员等. **(b)** elect (a political party) to govern a country 选举（某政党）执掌政权：*The electorate put the Tories in with an increased majority in 1983.* 1983年选民选举保守党执政，其票数超过了上届的多数票. **(c)** (of the team that wins the toss in cricket) ask (the opposing team) to bat first （指板球戏于掷钱币中获胜的队）请（对方）首先击球：*Australia won the toss and put England in (to bat).* 澳大利亚队于掷币中获胜，要求英格兰队首先击球. **put sth in (a)** install or fit sth 安装或设置某物：*We put new central heating in when we moved here.* 我们搬到这儿的时候安装了集中供暖设备. ○ *We're having a new shower put in.* 我们正在安装新的淋浴器. **(b)** include or insert sth in a story, narrative, etc （在故事、叙述等中）包括或插入某事物：*If you're writing to your mother, don't forget to put in something about her coming to stay.* 你要是正在给你母亲写信，可别忘了加上几句请她来住上几天. **(c)** present sth formally; submit sth 正式提出某事物；呈交某事物：*put in a claim for damages, higher wages* 提出赔偿损失、提高工资的要求. **(d)** manage to strike (a blow) or say sth 给予（打击）；说某话：*Tyson put in some telling blows to Tucker's chin.* 泰森重击了塔克的下巴儿拳. ○ *Could I put in a word* (ie say sth) *at this point?* 我现在说几句行吗？**(e)** spend (a period of time) working at sth 花费（一段时间）做某事物：*She often puts in twelve hours' work a day.* 她常常一天工作十二小时. ○ *I must put in an hour's gardening this evening.* 今晚我得用一个小时干些园艺活儿. **put sth in; put sth into sth/doing sth** devote (time, effort, etc) to sth 用（时间、精力等）做某事：*Thank you for all the hard work you've put in.* 谢谢你的这一切努力. ○ *We've put a great deal of time and effort into this project.* 我们为这一项目付出了大量的时间和精力. ○ *She's putting a lot of work into improving her French.* 她正在下功夫进修法语. **put in (at...)/put into...** (of a ship, its crew, etc) enter (a port or harbour) （指船、全体船员等）进入（港口）：*The boat put in at Lagos/put into Lagos for repairs.* 那船进了拉各斯港进行检修. **put in for sth** apply formally for sth 申请某事物：*Are you going to put in for that job?* 你打算申请那份工作吗？**put oneself/sb/sth in for sth** enter oneself/sb/sth for (a competition) 使自己［某人/某物］参加（竞赛）：*She's put herself in for the 100 metres and the long jump.* 她参加了百米赛跑和跳远. **put sb in for sth** recommend sb for (a job, an award, etc) 推荐某人获（职位、奖励等）：*The commanding officer put Sergeant Williams in for a medal for bravery.* 指挥官推荐威廉斯中士获勇敢勋章.

put 'off (of a boat, its crew, etc) move away from a pier, jetty, etc （指船、全体船员等）驶离码头等：*We put off from the quay.* 我们驶离了码头. **put sb off (a)** (of a vehicle, boat, etc) stop in order to allow sb to get off （指车船等）停住让某人下去：*I asked the bus driver to put me off near the town centre.* 我请公共汽车司机在快到市中心时让我下车. **(b)** postpone or cancel a meeting or an engagement with sb 推迟或取消会议或与某人的约会：*We've invited friends to supper and it's too late to put them off now*, ie to tell them not to come. 我们已邀请朋友来吃晚饭，现在取消已来不及了. ○ *She put him off with the excuse that* (ie said that she could not see him because) *she had too much work to do.* 她以工作太忙为借口取消了跟他的约会. **(c)** make sb feel dislike; displease, repel or disgust sb 使某人不高兴；惹某人不悦、厌恶或反感：*He's a good salesman, but his offhand manner does tend to put people off.* 他是个很好的推销员，可是他那随便的态度容易使人产生反感. ○ *Don't be put off by his gruff exterior; he's really very kind underneath.* 别介意他表现粗野，其实他心地很善良. **put sb off (sth)** disturb sb who is doing sth; distract sb 打搅某人；使某人注意力不集中：*Don't put me off when I'm trying to concentrate.* 我正要集中注意力呢，别打搅我. ○ *The sudden noise put her off her game.* 突如其来的嘈杂声分散了她比赛时的注意力. **put sb off sth/doing sth** cause sb to lose his interest in or liking or appetite for sth 使某人对某事物失去兴趣、不再喜欢或倒了胃口：*The accident put her off driving for life.* 这次事故使她一辈子不愿意再开车了. ○ *She was put off maths by a bullying and incompetent teacher.* 她对数学失去了兴趣，因为老师仗势欺人又没教学能力. **put sth off** switch sth off 关掉某物：*Could you put the lights off before you leave?* 你走的时候把灯关掉好吗？**put sth off; put off doing sth** postpone, delay or defer sth 推迟、延缓或拖延某事物：*We've had to put our wedding off until September.* 我们得把婚礼延期到九月举行. ○ *This afternoon's meeting will have to be put off.* 今天下午的会议得延期. ○ *She keeps putting off going to the dentist.* 她老是拖延着不去看牙病.

put it 'on (esp in the continuous tenses 尤用于进行时态) pretend to be angry, sad, remorseful, etc 假装生气、伤心、悔恨等：*She wasn't angry really; she was only putting it on.* 她不是真的生气，只不过故作姿态而已. **put sth on (a)** clothe oneself with (a garment) 穿上（衣服）：*put on one's coat, gloves, hat, skirt, trousers, etc* 穿上外套、戴上手套、戴上帽子、穿上裙子、穿上裤子 ○ *What dress shall I put on for the party?* 我穿什么衣服去参加聚会呢？**(b)** apply sth to one's skin 在皮肤上涂某物：*put on lipstick, hand-cream, etc* 涂唇膏、擦润手油脂 ○ *She's just putting on her make-up.* 她正在化妆. **(c)** switch sth on; operate sth 打开开关启动某物；操作某物：*put on the light, oven, radio, television, etc* 打开灯、烤箱、收音机、电视机等 ○ *Let's put the kettle on and have a cup of tea.* 咱们坐壶水沏杯茶吧. ○ *She put on the brakes suddenly.* 她突然刹住了车. **(d)** make sth begin to play 使（视听设备）开始播放：*put on a record, tape, compact disc, etc* 放唱片、磁带、激光唱片等 ○ *Do you mind if I put some music on?* 我放放音乐你不介意吧？

(**e**) grow fatter or heavier (by the specified amount) 长胖或增加若干体重: *put on a stone in weight* 增加一呫的重量 ○ *How many pounds did you put on over Christmas?* 你过完圣诞节后体重增加了多少磅? (**f**) add (a train, coach, etc) to an existing service 增加(运营的火车、长途汽车等): *British Rail are putting on extra trains during the holiday period.* 英国铁路公司于假期里额外增加火车投入运营. (**g**) produce or present (a play, an exhibition, etc) 演出(戏剧); 举办(展览等): *The local drama group are putting on 'Macbeth' at the Playhouse.* 当地的剧团正在普赖豪斯剧院演出《麦克佩斯》. (**h**) move (the hands of a clock) forward to show a later time 把(钟表指针)向前拨. (**i**) pretend to have sth; assume or adopt sth 装作有某事物; 假装或采纳某事物: *put on a silly face, a Liverpool accent, a wounded expression* 装傻的面容、假操利物浦的口音、扮出受伤的样子 ○ *Don't put on that innocent look; we know you ate all the biscuits.* 别装作没事的样子了, 我们知道你把饼干都吃光了. ○ *He seems very sincere, but it's all put on.* 他看样子很诚恳, 但那都是假装的. **put sth on sth** (**a**) add (an amount of money) to the price or cost of sth 将某物提价(若干): *The government has put ten pence on the price of a gallon of petrol.* 当局已将每加仑汽油涨价十便士. (**b**) impose or place (a tax, etc) on sth 对某事物征收或确定(税等): *put a duty on wine* 对酒征税. (**c**) place (a bet) on sth 把(赌注)压在某事物上: *I've put £10 on 'Black Widow' in the 3.45 at Newmarket.* 在纽马基特马场3时45分那场赛事中, 我在名叫'黑寡妇'的马上压了10英镑. ○ *I've never put money on a horse.* 我从未赌过马. **put sb on to sb/onto sb** help sb to find, meet or see sb; put sb in touch with sb 帮助某人寻找、会晤或晤见某人; 安排某人与某人接触: *put sb onto a dentist, lawyer, plumber, etc* 帮某人找牙医、律师、管子工等 ○ *Could you put me on to a good accountant?* 你能帮我找个好的会计师吗? (**a**) inform (the police, etc) where sb is, so he can be caught 向(警方等)提供某人的线索(以便追捕): *Detectives hunting the gang were put on to them by an anonymous telephone call.* 缉捕歹徒的侦探接到向他们提供线索的匿名电话. **put sb on to sth/onto sth** inform sb of the existence of (sth interesting or advantageous); tell sb about sth 向某人提供(有趣或有利之事物)的信息; 将某事物告诉某人: *'Who put you on to this restaurant? It's superb!' 'Friends put us on to it.'* '你是从谁那里知道有这家餐馆的? 这餐馆棒极了!' '是朋友告诉我们的.'

put oneself 'out (*infml* 口) do sth even though it is inconvenient for oneself 虽对自己不便而仍做某事: *Please don't put yourself out on our account.* 请你不要为了我们而难为你自己. ○ *She's always ready to put herself out to help others.* 她总是乐于舍己助人. **put sb out** (**a**) make sb unconscious (by striking him, with an anaesthetic, etc) 使某人失去知觉(予以打击、使用麻醉剂等): *He put his opponent out in the fifth round.* 他在第五个回合中将对手击昏. (**b**) cause inconvenience to sb 使某人感到不便: *I hope our arriving late didn't put them out.* 我希望我们迟到一事不致给他们带来麻烦. (**c**) upset or offend sb 使某人不安; 得罪某人: *She was most put out by his rudeness.* 她非常厌恶他行为粗鲁. ○ *He looked rather put out.* 他看来不太高兴. **put sth out** (**a**) take sth out of one's house and leave it, esp for sb to collect 将某物置于门外(尤指待人取走): *put out the dustbins, the empty milk bottles, etc* 把垃圾箱、空奶瓶等放到外面去 ○ *Have you put the cat out yet?* 你把猫赶出去了吗? (**b**) place sth where it will be noticed and used 把某物放在看得见用得着的地方: *put out ashtrays, bowls of peanuts* 摆出烟灰缸、盛有花生的碗 ○ *put out clean towels for a guest* 为客人预备好干净的毛巾. (**c**) (of a plant) sprout or display (leaves, buds, etc) (指植物)生长出(叶、芽等): *The trees are beginning to put out shoots.* 这些树正在发芽. (**d**) produce or generate sth 生产或产生某物: *The plant puts out 500 new cars a week.* 该厂每周生产500辆新汽车. (**e**) issue, publish or broadcast sth (usu for a particular purpose) 发布、出版或广播某事物(通常为有某目的): *Police have put out a description of the man they wish to question.* 警方公布了那男子的特征, 希望找他问话. (**f**) cause sth to stop burning 使某物停止燃烧: *Firemen soon put the fire out.* 消防队员很快把火扑灭了. ○ *put out a candle, cigarette, pipe* 把蜡烛、香烟、烟斗熄灭. (**g**) switch sth off 关掉某物: *put out the lamp, light, gas fire* 关灯、熄灯、关掉煤气取暖器. (**h**) dislocate (a part of the body) 使(身体某部)脱位: *She fell off her horse and put her shoulder out.* 她从马上摔了下来, 肩关节脱臼了. (**i**) cause (a figure, result, calculation, etc) to be wrong 使(数字、结果、计算等)出错: *The devaluation of the pound has put our estimates out by several thousands.* 英镑一贬值使我们的估计数差了几千镑. **put sth out (to sb)** (**a**) give (a job, task, etc) to a worker or manufacturer who is not one's employee and will do the work in another place 把(工作、活儿等)送出去请别人做: *A lot of proof-reading is put out to freelancers.* 校对工作有很多是请外人做的. ○ *All repairs are done on the premises and not put out.* 一切修理工作都在场址内进行, 不送到外面去做. (**b**) lend (money) to sb in order to get interest on it 贷(款)给某人: *Banks are putting out more and more money to people buying their own homes.* 银行向买房者放款越来越多了. **put 'out (to.../from...)** (of a boat or its crew) move out to sea from a harbour, port, etc (指船只或全体船员)出海: *put out to sea* 出海 ○ *We put out from Liverpool.* 我们自利物浦起航.

put oneself/sth over (to sb) ⇨ PUT ONESELF/STH ACROSS/OVER (TO SB). **put sth over on sb** (*infml* 口) persuade sb to accept a claim, story, etc that is untrue or worthless 诱劝某人接受虚假的或无价值的事物: *He's not the sort of man you can put one over on.* 他可不是能用花言巧语打动的人.

put sth through complete or conclude (a plan, programme, etc) successfully 完成或达成(计划、方案等): *put through a business deal* 做成交易 ○ *The government is putting through some radical social reforms.* 政府正在实行某些彻底的社会改革. **put sb through sth** (**a**) cause sb to undergo (an ordeal, a test, etc) 使某人经受(苦难、考验等): *You have put your family through much suffering.* 你让你全家受了不少苦. ○ *Trainee commandos are put through an exhausting assault course.* 受训的突击队员要参加令人筋疲力尽的突击课程. (**b**) pay for sb to attend (the specified school, college, etc) 供某人上(某学校): *He put all his children through boarding-school.* 他把孩子都送进了寄宿学校. **put sb/sth through (to sb/...)** allow sb to speak to sb by making a telephone connection 为某人接通电话: *Could you put me through to the manager, please.* 劳驾请经理接电话. ○ *I'm trying to put a call through to Paris.* 我正要给巴黎通个电话.

put sb to sth make sb undergo or suffer (inconvenience, trouble, etc) 使某人遭(不便、麻烦等): *I do hope we're not putting you to too much trouble.* 但愿我们不致使你太为难. ○ *We've already been put to great inconvenience.* 我们已很感不便. **put sth to sb** express, communicate or submit sth to sb 向某人表达、传达或提交某事物: *Your proposal will be put to the board of directors.* 你的建议将呈交董事会. (**a**) ask sb (a question) 问某人(问题): *The audience are now invited to put questions to the speaker.* 现在请听众向讲演者提问题. (**b**) ask sb to vote on (an issue, a proposal, etc) 请某人对(某问题、提议等)进行表决: *Let's put the resolution to the meeting.* 咱们将此决议提请会议表决吧. ○ *The question of strike action must be put to union members.* 举行罢工这一问题须提请工会会员表决.

put sth together construct or repair sth by fitting parts together; assemble sth 装配或修配某物; 把某物结合成一整体: *put together a model aeroplane* 装配模型飞机 ○ *He took the machine to pieces and then put it together again.* 他把机器拆开后又组装起来了. ○ (*fig* 比喻) *put together an essay, a meal, a case for the defence* 组织好一篇文章、调配好一顿饭、汇集起辩护理由. Cf 参看 PUT TOGETHER (PUT[1] 6).

put sth towards sth give (money) as a contribution to sth 凑(钱)做某事物: *He puts half of his salary each month towards the skiing holiday he's planning.* 他把每月工资的一半攒起来作计划中的滑雪度假之用.

put up sth offer or present (resistance, a struggle, etc) in a battle, game, etc (在战斗、比赛等中)进行(抵抗、斗争等): *They surrendered without putting up much of a fight.* 他们没怎么抵抗就投降了. ○ *The team put up a splendid performance*, ie played very well. 这个队表现极佳. **put sb up** (**a**) provide food and accommodation for sb 向某人提供食宿: *We can put you up for the night.* 我们可以招待你过夜. (**b**) present sb as a candidate in an election 提名某人为候选人: *The Green Party hopes to* put up a number of candidates in the General Election. 绿党希望提出若干候选人参加大选. **put sth up** (**a**) raise or hoist sth 升起或举起某物: *put up a flag* 升旗 ○ *Put your hand up if you want to ask a question.* 若要提问题就把手举起来. ○ *She's put her hair up*, ie She is wearing it coiled on top of her head. 她把头发挽在头上. (**b**) build or erect sth 建造或设立某物: *put up a fence, memorial, shed, tent* 筑起篱笆、建立纪念碑、搭起小棚、支起帐篷 ○ *Many ugly blocks of flats were put up in the 1960's.* 许多难看的公寓式建筑群都是六十年代建造的. (**c**) fix or fasten sth in a place where it will be seen; display sth 把某物固定或紧固于某处俾人注目; 展示某物: *put up Christmas decorations, a notice, a poster* 展出圣诞节装饰品、发布通告、张贴海报 ○ *The team will be put up on the notice-board.* 该队名单将张榜公布. (**d**) raise or increase sth 提高或增加某事物: *My landlord's threatening to put the rent up by £10 a week.* 我的房东要挟说要把每周租金提高10英镑. (**e**) provide or lend (money) 提供(资金); 借给(款项): *A local businessman has put up the £500 000 needed to save the football club.* 当地的一位商人提供所需的500 000英镑以助足球俱乐部度过难关. (**f**) present (an idea, etc) for discussion or consideration 提出(意见等)供讨论或考虑: *put up an argument, a case, a proposal, etc* 提出一论点、事实、建议等. **put ˈup (at...)** obtain food and lodging (at a place); stay (在某处)获得食宿安排; 暂住: *They put up at an inn for the night.* 他们在一家小客栈里过夜. **put (oneself) up for sth** offer oneself as a candidate for sth 自荐为某事物候选人; 参加竞选: *She is putting (herself) up for election to the committee.* 她参加委员竞选. **put sb up (for sth)** propose or nominate sb for a position 推荐或提名某人就任某职务: *We want to put you up for club treasurer.* 我们想请你担任俱乐部的司库. ○ *To join the club you have to be put up by an existing member.* 要加入俱乐部必须有一位会员做介绍人. **put sb up to sth/doing sth** (*infml* 口) urge or encourage sb to do sth mischievous or illegal 怂恿或唆使某人做坏事或干非法勾当: *I can't believe he'd do a thing like that on his own. He must have been put up to it by some of the older boys.* 我不相信他会主动干那种事, 一定是有些年龄大的男孩子叫他干的. **put up with sb/sth** tolerate or bear sb/sth 忍受或容忍某人[某事物]: *I don't know how she puts up with him/his cruelty to her.* 我不明白她怎么能容忍他[忍受他的虐待].

□ ˈ**put-down** *n* humiliating remark; snub 羞辱的言语; 怠慢.

ˌ**put-up ˈjob** (*infml* 口) scheme to cheat or deceive sb 骗局; 欺诈行为.

ˈ**put-upon** *adj* (of a person) badly treated; misused or exploited (指人)受到不良对待的, 受虐待的, 受剥削的: *a much put-upon person* 受尽虐待的人 ○ *I'm beginning to feel just a little put-upon.* 我开始感到有点受人利用了.

pu·tat·ive /ˈpjuːtətɪv; ˋpjutətɪv/ *adj* [attrib 作定语] (*fml* 文) generally supposed to be; reputed 公认的; 普遍认为的: *his putative father* 公认是他父亲的那个人.

pu·trefy /ˈpjuːtrɪfaɪ; ˋpjutrəˌfaɪ/ *v* (*pt, pp* **-fied**) [I, Tn] (cause sth to) rot or decay; become or make putrid (使某物)腐烂, 腐败, 腐坏, 变质.

▷ **pu·tre·fac·tion** /ˌpjuːtrɪˈfækʃn; ˌpjutrəˋfækʃən/ *n* [U] **1** (process of) putrefying 腐烂; 腐败; 腐坏; 变质. **2** rotting matter 腐败之物.

pu·tres·cent /pjuːˈtresnt; pjuˋtrɛsn̩t/ *adj* (*fml* 文) (**a**) in the process of rotting 正在腐烂的; 正在变质的: *a putrescent corpse* 腐烂的尸体. (**b**) of or accompanying this process 腐烂的; 因腐烂而产生的: *a putrescent smell* 腐臭味. ▷ **pu·tres·cence** /-sns; -sn̩s/ *n* [U].

pu·trid /ˈpjuːtrɪd; ˋpjutrɪd/ *adj* **1** (**a**) (esp of animal or vegetable matter) that has become rotten; decomposed (尤指动物或蔬菜之机体)腐烂的, 腐败的. (**b**) (rotting and therefore) foul-smelling; noxious (因腐烂)发臭的, 有害的, 有毒的: *a pile of rotten, putrid fish* 一堆腐烂、发臭的鱼 ○ *the putrid smell of rotting fish* 腐烂的鱼发出的臭味. **2** (*infml* 口) very distasteful or unpleasant or of poor quality 令人厌恶的; 使人不愉快的; 不好的: *putrid weather* 很坏的天气 ○ *Why did you paint the room that putrid colour?* 你怎么把房间刷成那么难看的颜色?

putsch /pʊtʃ; pʊtʃ/ *n* attempt to overthrow a government by force; political revolution 以武力推翻政府的企图; 武装起义; 造反; 政治革命.

putt /pʌt; pʌt/ *v* [I, Tn] (in golf) hit (the ball) with a light stroke so that it rolls across the ground into or nearer to the hole, usu from a position on the green[2](5) (高尔夫球)轻击(球): *You need to practise putting (the ball).* 你需要练习轻击(球).

▷ **putt** *n* putting stroke (高尔夫球)轻击: *She took three putts* (ie to get the ball into the hole) *from the edge of the green.* 她从球穴区的边缘轻击三次(以图将球打入穴中).

putter *n* **1** golf club used for putting (高尔夫球的)轻击球棒. **2** person who putts 轻击高尔夫球者.

□ ˈ**putting-green** *n* area of smooth closely-cut grass for putting on, esp one with several holes like a miniature golf course (高尔夫球的)轻击区; (尤指)如小型高尔夫球场有几个洞孔之处.

put·tee /ˈpʌtɪ; ˋpʌtɪ/ *n* (esp *pl* 尤作复数) long narrow strip of cloth that is wound round the leg from the ankle to the knee for protection and support, esp as part of an army uniform 绑腿, 裹腿(尤指军人的).

put·ter (*US*) = POTTER[1].

putty /ˈpʌtɪ; ˋpʌtɪ/ *n* **1** [U] soft paste, a mixture of chalk powder and linseed oil, which is used for fixing glass in window frames, etc and becomes hard when it has set 油灰; 泥子; 腻子. **2** (idm 习语) **(be) putty in sb's ˈhands** (be) easily influenced or controlled by sb 易受某人影响或操纵: *She was a woman of such beauty and charm that men were putty in her hands.* 她美艳绝伦, 男人在她手心任其摆布.

▷ **putty** *v* (*pt, pp* **puttied**) **1** [Tn, Tn·p] **~ sth (up)** fill (a hole, gap etc) with putty 用油灰填塞(洞孔、缝隙等). **2** (phr v) **putty sth in** fix sth in place with putty 用油灰把某物固定住: *putty a pane of glass in* 用油灰镶玻璃.

puzzle /ˈpʌzl; ˋpʌzl̩/ *n* **1** [C usu *sing* 通常作单数] question that is difficult to understand or answer; mystery 难题; 谜一般的事物: *Their reason for doing it is still a puzzle to me.* 他们为什么要做此事我仍莫名其妙. **2** [C] (often in compounds 常用以构成复合词) problem or toy that is designed to test a person's knowledge, ingenuity, skill, etc 用以测验人的知识、智力、技巧等的问题或玩具; 谜: *crossword puzzles* 纵横字谜 ○ *a jigsaw puzzle* 拼图玩具 ○ *find the answer to/solve a puzzle* 找到谜底[解开一个谜] ○ *set a puzzle for sb/set sb a puzzle* 出个谜叫某人猜.

▷ **puzzle** *v* **1** [Tn] make (sb) think hard; perplex 让(某人)动脑筋; 使困惑: *Her reply puzzled me.* 她的回答把我弄糊涂了. ○ *I am puzzled by his failure to reply/that he hasn't replied to my letter.* 他不给我回信使我百思不解. ○ *He puzzled his brains* (ie thought hard) *to find the answer.* 他绞尽脑汁以寻求答案. ○ *The sudden fall in the value of the dollar has puzzled financial experts.* 美元突然贬值, 财经专家无不大伤脑筋. ○ *They are puzzled (about) what to do next/how to react.* 他们不知道下一步怎么办[如何作出反应]. **2** [Ipr] **~ over sth** think deeply about sth in order to understand it 对某事物苦苦思索(以便理解): *She's been puzzling over his strange letter for weeks.* 她几个星期也琢磨不透他那封奇怪的来信. **3** [Tn·p] **~ sth out** (try to) find the answer or solution to sth by thinking hard 开动脑筋(试图)找出某事物的答案或解决方法: *The teacher left the children to puzzle out the answer to the problem themselves.* 老师让学生动脑筋自行寻找问题的答案. **puzz·led** *adj* unable to understand; perplexed or confused 无法了解的; 困惑的; 茫然的: *She listened with a puzzled expression on her face.* 她脸上带着困惑的表情在倾听着. **puzz·ler** /ˈpʌzlə(r); ˋpʌzlɚ/ *n* (*infml* 口) person or thing that puzzles 使人困惑的人或事物: *That question is a real puzzler!* 那个问题真难! **puz·zle·ment** /ˈpʌzlmənt; ˋpʌzl̩mənt/ *n* [U] (state of) being puzzled; bewilderment 困惑; 大惑不解: *He stared at the words in complete puzzlement.* 他注视着那些语句, 茫然不解. **puzz·ling** /ˈpʌzlɪŋ; ˋpʌzlɪŋ/ *adj*: *a puzzling statement, affair, attitude* 令人费解的说法、事情、态度.

PVC /ˌpiː viː ˈsiː; ˌpi vi ˋsi/ *abbr* 缩写 = polyvinyl chloride (a type of plastic) 聚氯乙烯(一种塑料): *The seat covers were (made of) PVC.* 座椅的外罩是聚氯乙烯(做)的.

Pvt *abbr* 缩写 (*US*) PTE.

PW /ˌpiː ˈdʌbljuː; ˌpi ˋdʌbljʊ/ *abbr* 缩写 = (*Brit*) Policewoman: *PW (Christine) Bell* 女警察(克里斯廷·)贝尔. Cf 参看 WPC.

PX /ˌpiː ˈeks; ˌpi ˋɛks/ *abbr* 缩写 = (*US*) Post Exchange 军人消费合作社. Cf 参看 NAAFI.

pygmy (also **pigmy**) /ˈpɪgmɪ; ˋpɪgmɪ/ *n* **1 Pygmy** member of a tribal group of very short people living in equatorial Africa 俾格米人(赤道非洲部族的人, 属矮小人种). **2** very small person or species of animal; dwarf 矮小的人或动物种类; 矮子; 侏儒: [attrib 作定语] *the pygmy shrew* 小鼩鼱.

py·ja·mas (also *esp US* **pa·ja·mas**) /pəˈdʒɑːməz; *US* -ˈdʒæm-; pəˋdʒæməz/ *n* [pl] **1** loose-fitting jacket and trousers worn for sleeping in, esp by men 睡衣裤(尤指男人的): *a pair of pyjamas* 一套睡衣 ○ *He was wearing striped pyjamas.* 他穿着带条纹的睡衣裤. **2** loose trousers tied round the waist, worn by Muslims of both sexes in India and Pakistan (印度和巴基斯坦穆斯林男女穿的)肥大的裤子. **3** (idm 习语) **be the cat's whiskers/pyjamas** ⇨ CAT[1]. ▷ **py·jama** (*US* **pa·jama**) *adj* [attrib 作定语]: *pyjama bottom(s)/top/trousers/jacket* 睡衣下身[上身/裤子/上衣].

py·lon /ˈpaɪlən; *US* ˈpaɪlɒn; ˋpaɪlɑn/ *n* **1** tall steel framework used for carrying overhead high-voltage electric cables 电缆塔. **2** tall tower or post that marks a path for aircraft landing (机场的)标塔, 标杆.

py·or·rhoea (also *esp US* **py·or·rhea**) /ˌpaɪəˈrɪə; ˌpaɪəˋriə/ *n* [U] diseased condition of the gums that causes them to shrink and the teeth to become loose 齿槽脓溢.

pyr·amid /ˈpɪrəmɪd; ˋpɪrəmɪd/ *n* **1** structure with a flat square or triangular base and sloping sides that meet in a point at the top, esp one of those built of stone by the ancient Egyptians as tombs 金字塔(尤指古埃及的). **2** (esp in geometry) solid figure of this shape with a base of three or more sides (尤指几何学中的)锥体. ⇨illus at CUBE 见CUBE插图. **3** thing or pile of things that has the shape of a pyramid 金字塔形之物或一堆东西: *a pyramid of tins in a shop window* 商店橱窗中摆成金字塔形的罐头.

▷ **pyr·am·idal** /pɪˈræmɪdl; pɪˋræməd̩l/ *adj* having the shape of a pyramid 金字塔形的; 锥体形的.

□ **pyramid ˈselling** (*commerce* 商) method of selling goods in which a distributor pays a premium for the right to sell a company's goods and then sells part of that right to other distributors 金字塔式销售(商品销售方法, 一经销商购得经销权后将部分转售给其他经销商).

pyre /ˈpaɪə(r); paɪr/ *n* large pile of wood, etc for burning a dead body as part of a funeral ceremony (火葬用的)大堆供燃烧之木材等.

Pyrex /ˈpaɪreks; ˋpaɪrɛks/ *n* [U] (*propr* 专利名) type of heat-resistant glass used esp for cooking and serving food in 耐热玻璃(尤用于制造烹炊具): [attrib 作定语] *a Pyrex dish* 耐热玻璃盘子.

pyr·ites /paɪˈraɪtiːz; *US* pɪˈraɪtiːz; pəˋraɪtiz/ *n* [U] mineral that is a sulphide of iron (*iron pyrites*) or copper and iron (*copper pyrites*) 硫化矿类(黄铁矿或黄铜矿).

pyro·mania /ˌpaɪrəʊˈmeɪnɪə; ˌpaɪrəˋmenɪə/ *n* [U] illness that causes an uncontrollable desire to start fires 放火狂; 纵火狂.

▷ **pyro·ma·niac** /-nɪæk; -nɪæk/ *n* person who suffers from pyromania 放火狂者; 纵火狂者.

pyro·tech·nics /ˌpaɪrəˈteknɪks; ˌpaɪrəˋtɛknɪks/ *n* **1** [sing *v*] art of making fireworks 烟火制造术. **2** [pl] (*fml* 文) public display of fireworks as an entertainment 烟火的施放; 放烟火. **3** [pl] (*fig sometimes derog* 比喻, 有时作贬义) brilliant display of skill, eg by an orator, a musician, etc 技艺(如口才、演奏技巧等)的出色表现; 炫耀技巧. ▷ **pyro·tech·nic** *adj* [usu attrib 通常作定语].

Pyr·rhic vic·tory /ˌpɪrɪk ˈvɪktərɪ; ˌpɪrɪk ˋvɪktərɪ/ victory that was not worth winning because the winner has lost so much in winning it 得不偿失的胜利.

py·thon /ˈpaɪθn; *US* ˈpaɪθɒn; ˋpaɪθɑn/ *n* large snake that crushes and kills its prey by twisting itself round it 巨蛇; 蟒蛇; 蚺蛇.

pyx /pɪks; pɪks/ *n* (in the Christian Church) container in which bread that has been consecrated for Holy Communion is kept (基督教)圣饼盒.

Q q

Q, q /kju:; kju/ *n* (*pl* **Q's, q's** /kju:z; kjuz/) **1** the seventeenth letter of the English alphabet 英语字母表中的第十七个字母: *'Queen' starts with (a) Q/'Q'.* Queen 字以 Q 字母开始. **2** (idm 习语) **mind one's p's and q's** ⇨ MIND[2].

Q /kju:; kju/ *abbr* 缩写 = question: *Q and A*, ie question and answer 问题和答案 ○ *Qs 1-5 are compulsory*, eg in an exam paper. 1-5 题为必答题(如试卷说明). Cf 参看 A 2.

QB /ˌkju: ˈbi:; ˌkju ˈbi/ *abbr* 缩写 = (*Brit law* 律) Queen's Bench. Cf 参看 KB.

QC /ˌkju: ˈsi:; ˌkju ˈsi/ *abbr* 缩写 = (*Brit law* 律) Queen's Counsel: *Mr Justice Norman QC* 王室法律顾问诺曼法官. Cf 参看 KC.

QED /ˌkju: i: ˈdi:; ˌkju i ˈdi/ *abbr* 缩写 = which was to be proved (Latin *quod erat demonstrandum*) 证明完毕(源自拉丁文 *quod erat demonstrandum*).

QE2 /ˌkju: i: ˈtu:; ˌkju i ˈtu/ *abbr* 缩写 = Queen Elizabeth the Second (a cruise liner) '伊丽莎白女王'2 号(邮船): *a holiday on the QE2* 乘'伊丽莎白女王'2 号邮船度假.

qr *abbr* 缩写 = quarter(s).

qt *abbr* 缩写 = quart(s).

qto (also **4to**) *abbr* 缩写 = quarto.

qty *abbr* 缩写 = (*commerce* 商) (esp on order forms) quantity (尤用于订货单).

qua /kweɪ; kwe/ *prep* (*fml* 文) in the capacity or character of (sb/sth); as 以(某人[某事物])的身分或特性; 作为: *I don't dislike sport qua sport — I just think it's rather a waste of time.* 我倒不是不喜欢运动本身 —— 而是觉得有些浪费时间.

quack[1] /kwæk; kwæk/ *interj, n* harsh sound made by a duck (鸭叫的)嘎嘎声.
▷ **quack** *v* [I] make the sound of a duck 作鸭叫.
□ ˈ**quack-quack** *n* (used by and to small children 儿语) duck 鸭鸭; 鸭子.

quack[2] /kwæk; kwæk/ *n* (*infml* 口) person who pretends to have special knowledge and skill, esp in medicine 冒充有专门知识和技能的人; (尤指)庸医, 江湖医生: *Don't be taken in — he's just a quack.* 可别上当 —— 他纯粹是江湖医生. ○ [attrib 作定语] *a quack cure for arthritis* 庸医治关节炎的疗法.
▷ ˈ**quack·ery** /-ərɪ; -ərɪ/ *n* [U] methods or practices of a quack 庸医的医术或行医.

quad /kwɒd; kwɑd/ *n* (*infml* 口) **1** = QUADRANGLE 2. **2** = QUADRUPLET.

Quad·ra·ges·ima /ˌkwɒdrəˈdʒesɪmə; ˌkwɑdrəˈdʒɛsəmə/ *n* the first Sunday in Lent 大斋期的第一个星期日.

quad·rangle /ˈkwɒdræŋgl; ˈkwɑdræŋgl/ *n* **1** plane figure with four sides, esp a square or rectangle 四边形; (尤指)正方形, 长方形. **2** (*fml* 文) four-sided courtyard surrounded by large buildings, eg in an Oxford college (四周由大型建筑物围绕的)方形庭院(如于牛津大学学院的).
▷ **quad·ran·gu·lar** /kwɒˈdræŋgjʊlə(r); kwɑdˈræŋgjʊlɚ/ *adj* having four sides 有四边的; 四边形的.

quad·rant /ˈkwɒdrənt; ˈkwɑdrənt/ *n* **1** quarter of a circle or of its circumference 圆的或圆周的四分之一; 象限. ⇨illus at CIRCLE 见 CIRCLE 插图. **2** instrument with an arc of 90° marked off in degrees, for measuring angles 象限仪; 四分仪.

quad·ra·phonic (also **quad·ro·phonic**) /ˌkwɒdrəˈfɒnɪk; ˌkwɑdrəˈfɑnɪk/ *adj* (of sound-reproduction) using four transmission channels (指录音放音)四声道的.
▷ **quad·ra·phony** (also **quad·ro·phony**) /kwɒˈdrɒfənɪ; kwɑˈdrɑfənɪ/ *n* [U] system for recording and reproducing sound in this way 四声道录音放音系统或设备.

quad·ratic equa·tion /kwɒˌdrætɪk ɪˈkweɪʒn; kwɑdˈrætɪk ɪˈkweʒən/ (*algebra* 代数) equation that uses the square (and no higher power) of an unknown quantity, eg $x^2 + 2x - 8 = 0$ 二次方程式(如 $x^2 + 2x - 8 = 0$).

quad·ren·nial /kwɒˈdrenɪəl; kwɑˈdrɛnɪəl/ *adj* **1** lasting for four years 持续四年的. **2** happening every fourth year 每四年一次的.

quadr(i)- *comb form* 构词成分 **1** having four parts 有四部分的: *quadrilateral* ○ *quadruped*. **2** being one of four parts 四部分之一的: *quadrant* ○ *quadruplet*.

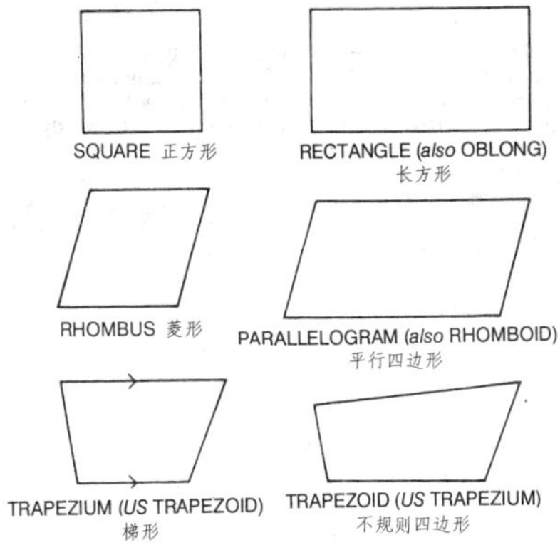

quadrilaterals 四边形

quad·ri·lat·eral /ˌkwɒdrɪˈlætərəl; ˌkwɑdrəˈlætərəl/ *n, adj* (plane figure) with four sides 四边形(的).

quad·rille /kwəˈdrɪl; kwəˈdrɪl/ *n* (music for a) square dance for four couples 四对方舞(曲): *play/dance a quadrille* 演奏四对方舞曲[跳四对方舞].

quad·ril·lion /kwɒˈdrɪlɪən; kwɑdˈrɪljən/ *pron, det, n* (*pl* unchanged or **~s** 复数或不变或作 **quadrillions**) (after *a* or *one*, a number, or an indication of quantity 用于 a 或 one 之后或用于数目或表示数量的词语之后) **1** (*Brit*) number shown by 1 followed by 24 zeros; one million to the power of 4 ☆ 1 后有 24 个 0 的数; 一百万的 4 次幂. **2** (*US*) number shown by 1 followed by 15 zeros; one thousand to the power of 5 ☆ 1 后有 15 个 0 的数; 一千的 5 次幂.

quad·ro·phonic, quad·ro·phony ⇨ QUADRAPHONIC.

quad·ru·ped /ˈkwɒdrʊped; ˈkwɑdrəˌpɛd/ *n* four-footed animal 四足动物.

quad·ruple /ˈkwɒdrʊpl; US kwɒˈdru:pl; kwɑdˈrupl̩/ *adj* consisting of four parts, individuals or groups 由四个部分、四个个体或四个群体组成的: *a tune in quadruple time* 四拍的曲调 ○ *a quadruple alliance* 四方联盟.
▷ **quad·ruple** *n, adv* (number or amount) four times as great as (sth) 四倍; 四倍的数或量: *20 is the quadruple of 5.* 20 是 5 的四倍. ○ *We need quadruple the number of players we've got for a full orchestra.* 我们要组成完整的管弦乐队需要有四倍于现有的演奏人员.
quad·ruple /kwɒˈdru:pl; kwɑdˈrupl̩/ *v* [I, Tn] become multiplied or multiply (sth) by four 变成四倍; 以四乘(某数): *Their profits have quadrupled/They have quadrupled their profits in ten years.* 他们的利润十年中增长至四倍[他们使利润在十年中增长至四倍].

quad·ru·plet /ˈkwɒdru:plet; US kwɒˈdru:p-; kwɑdˈruplɪt/ (also *infml* 口语作 **quad**) *n* (usu *pl* 通常作复数) one of four children born to the same mother at one birth 四胞胎中的一个孩子.

quad·ru·plic·ate /kwɒˈdru:plɪkət; kwɑdˈruplɪkɪt/ *n* (idm 习语) **in quadruplicate** in four exactly similar examples or copies 一式四份: *Please submit your application form in quadruplicate.* 请交申请表一式四份.

quaff /kwɒf; US kwæf; kwæf/ *v* [Tn] (*dated or rhet* 旧或修辞) drink (sth) by swallowing large amounts at a time, not taking small sips 大口地喝(某物): *quaffing his beer* *by the pint* (他)论品脱地大喝啤酒.

quag·mire /ˈkwæɡmaɪə(r), *also* kwɒɡ-; ˋkwæɡ,maɪr, kwɑɡ-/ *n* area of soft wet ground; bog or marsh 泥沼; 泥塘; 沼泽: (*fig* 比喻) *The heavy rain had turned the pitch into a quagmire.* 大雨滂沱, 球场变成了泥沼.

quail[1] /kweɪl; kwel/ *n* (*pl* unchanged or **~s** 复数或不变或作 **quails**) (**a**) [C] small bird, similar to a partridge 鹌鹑. ⇨illus at App 1 见附录1插图, page v. (**b**) [U] its meat as food (食用的)鹌鹑肉.

quail[2] /kweɪl; kwel/ *v* [I, Ipr] **~ (at/before sb/sth)** feel or show fear; flinch 感到或显露恐惧、害怕或胆怯; 畏缩: *His heart quailed.* 他心惊胆战. ○ *She quailed at the prospect of addressing such a large crowd.* 她想到要在大庭广众之中讲话心里就发毛.

quaint /kweɪnt; kwent/ *adj* attractively odd or old-fashioned 离奇有趣的; 古色古香的: *quaint old customs* 稀奇古怪的旧风俗 ○ *quaint little cottages on the village green* 在村中草地上的古朴的小房子. ▷ **quaintly** *adv*. **quaint·ness** *n* [U].

Q

quake /kweɪk; kwek/ *v* [I] **1** (of the earth) shake (指地)震动, 颤动: *They felt the ground quake as the bomb exploded.* 炸弹爆炸时, 他们觉得地都震动了. **2** (of persons) tremble (指人)颤抖, 哆嗦: *quaking with fear/cold* 因恐惧[寒冷]而颤抖. ▷ **quake** *n* (*infml* 口) = EARTHQUAKE.

Quaker /ˈkweɪkə(r); ˋkwekɚ/ *n* member of the Society of Friends, a religious sect that worships Christ without any formal ceremony or stated creed and is strongly opposed to violence and war 公谊会教徒, 贵格会教徒, 教友会教徒(基督教的教派, 既无任何正式仪式又无固定教义, 其信条为强烈反对暴力与战争).

quali·fica·tion /ˌkwɒlɪfɪˈkeɪʃn; ˌkwɑləfəˋkeʃən/ *n* **1** [U] qualifying or becoming qualified 赋予资格; 获得资格. **2** [C] (**a**) training, examination or experience that qualifies (QUALIFY 1) sb for work, further training, etc 资格; 资历. (**b**) degree, diploma, certificate, etc awarded for this (获得的)学位, 文凭, 证书, 执照等: *What sort of qualifications do you need for the job?* 做这项工作需要什么资格? ○ *He's got all the right qualifications but is temperamentally unsuitable.* 他具备所需要的一切合格证件, 惟独性情不适合. **3** [C, U] statement that modifies or restricts a previous statement (对前述言语或文字的)限定条件: *She gave her approval to the scheme but not without several qualifications.* 她批准了这项计划, 但附加了几项意见. ○ *I can recommend him without qualification.* 我可以毫无保留地推荐他.

qual·ify /ˈkwɒlɪfaɪ; ˋkwɑlə,faɪ/ *v* (*pt, pp* **-fied**) **1** [I, Ipr, Tn, Tn·pr, Cn·n/a, Cn·t] **~ (sb) (for/as sth)** have or give (sb) the qualities, training, etc that are necessary or suitable (for sth) (使)(某人)具有资格; 给(某人)某种资格; (使)合格: *I won't qualify until next year.* 我明年才具备资格. ○ *Our team has qualified for the semi-final.* 我队已有资格进入半决赛. ○ *A stroll round the garden hardly qualifies as exercise!* 在花园转转算不上锻炼! ○ *The training course qualifies you to be/as a driving instructor.* 参加了训练课程就有资格成为[当]驾驶教练. **2** [I, Ipr, It, Tn, Tn·pr, Cn·t] **~ (sb) (for sth)** have or give (sb) a legal right (to sth/to do sth) 具有或给(某人)(某种)合法权利: *After three years here you'll qualify for a rise.* 你在这里三年就可获加薪. ○ *Eighteen-year-olds qualify to vote.* 年满十八岁者有选举权. ○ *Residence in the area qualifies you for membership.* 只要在本区居住就可入会. ○ *Your passport qualifies you to receive free medical treatment.* 你所持的护照可使你享有免费医疗. **3** [Tn] make (a statement, etc) less general or extreme 使(言语等)不过于笼统或极端: *I feel I must qualify my earlier remarks in case they are misinterpreted.* 我觉得我得把我说的话改得具体些, 以免产生误解. **4** [Tn] (*grammar*) name the qualities of (sth); describe in a particular way 限定; 修饰: *In 'the open door', 'open' is an adjective qualifying 'door'.* 在 the open door 这一词组中, open 是修饰 door 的形容词.

▷ **quali·fied** *adj* **1** having completed the relevant training or examination 经过训练或考试的; 有资格的; 合格的; 及格的: *a qualified doctor* 合格的医生 ○ *She's extremely well qualified for the job.* 她极胜任这一工作. ○ *It takes three years to become qualified.* 需时三年才具备资格. **2** limited 有限制的; 有限度的: *give the scheme only qualified approval* 有所保留地批准此计划.

quali·fier /-faɪə(r); -,faɪɚ/ *n* **1** (*grammar*) word, esp an adjective or adverb, that qualifies another word 修饰词; (尤指)形容词, 副词. **2** person who becomes entitled to compete in the next round of a competition, etc (有资格进入下一轮竞赛等的)合格者: *The final brings together four qualifiers from each heat.* 有四名初赛获胜者进入决赛.

qual·it·at·ive /ˈkwɒlɪtətɪv; *US* -teɪt-; ˋkwɑlə,tetɪv/ *adj* of or concerned with quality 性质的; 质量的; 与性质或质量有关的: *qualitative analysis* 定性分析 ○ *little qualitative improvement in their work* 他们的工作质量没什么改进. Cf 参看 QUANTITATIVE. ▷ **qual·it·at·ively** *adv*.

qual·ity /ˈkwɒlətɪ; ˋkwɑlətɪ/ *n* **1** (**a**) [U, C] degree of goodness or worth 质量; 品质: *goods of the highest quality* 质量最高的货物 ○ *This material is very poor quality.* 这种材料质量很差. ○ *There are many different qualities of gold and silver.* 金银的成色有很多种. (**b**) [U] general excellence 优质; 优点: *As an actor she shows real quality.* 她表现出演员的真正才华. ○ *This company is more concerned with quality than with quantity.* 这家公司对质量比对产量更重视. ○ [attrib 作定语] *We specialize in quality furniture.* 我们专门经营优质家具. **2** [C] (**a**) attribute; characteristic 属性; 特征; 特性: *He possesses the quality of inspiring confidence.* 他有本事能让别人信任他. ○ *She had many good qualities despite her apparent rudeness.* 她粗鲁是粗鲁, 但还有许多优秀品质. (**b**) special or distinguishing feature 特点; 特色: *One quality of this plastic is that it is almost unbreakable.* 这种塑料有个特点是不易断裂. ○ *His voice had a rich melodic quality.* 他的音色浑厚而优美.

qualm /kwɑːm; kwɑm/ *n* feeling of doubt, esp about whether what one is doing is right; misgiving 怀疑(尤指对自己正做的事是否正确); 疑虑: *He had/felt no serious qualms about concealing the information from the police.* 他向警方隐瞒实情而并未感到十分不妥.

quan·dary /ˈkwɒndərɪ; ˋkwɑndərɪ/ *n* state of not being able to decide what to do; awkward or difficult situation 困惑; 窘况: *I've been offered a better job but at a lower salary — I'm in a quandary about what to do.* 有人要给我一份更好的工作, 但薪水较低——我很为难, 不知如何是好.

quango /ˈkwæŋɡəʊ; ˋkwæŋɡo/ *n* (*pl* **~s**) administrative organization that operates independently but with support from the government (formed from the initials of 'quasi-autonomous, non-governmental organization') (由政府赞助的)自治机构(此字由 'quasi-autonomous, non-governmental organization' 之首字母组成).

quant·ify /ˈkwɒntɪfaɪ; ˋkwɑntə,faɪ/ *v* (*pt, pp* **-fied**) [Tn] express or measure the quantity of (sth) 表示或测量(某事物)的数量: *The cost of the flood damage is impossible to quantify.* 这次水灾的损失是无可估量的. ▷ **quan·ti·fi·able** *adj*. **quan·ti·fica·tion** /ˌkwɒntɪfɪˈkeɪʃn; ˌkwɑntəfəˋkeʃən/ *n* [U].

quant·it·at·ive /ˈkwɒntɪtətɪv; *US* -teɪt-; ˋkwɑntə,tetɪv/ *adj* of or concerned with quantity 数量的; 关于数量的: *quantitative analysis* 定量分析. Cf 参看 QUALITATIVE.

quant·ity /ˈkwɒntətɪ; ˋkwɑntətɪ/ *n* **1** [U] that which makes it possible to measure things through having number, size, weight, etc 量; 大小; 重量: *His reputation as a writer depends more on quantity than quality*, ie He writes a lot but he doesn't write very well. 他获得作家的名气靠的是作品的数量而不是质量. ○ *Mathematics is the science of pure quantity.* 数学是研究纯数量的科学. **2** [C, U] number or amount, esp a large one 数目, 数量(尤指巨大的): *What quantity* (ie How many) *do you require?* 你要求多大的数量? ○ *a small quantity of cutlery* 少量的刀叉餐具 ○ *It's cheaper to buy goods in quantity/in large quantities.* 大批量购货较便宜. **3** (idm 习语) **an unknown quantity** ⇨ UNKNOWN.

□ ˈ**quantity surveyor** person who estimates the quantity of materials needed for constructing buildings, etc and how much they will cost 估算员(估算建筑材料等用量及其成本者).

quantum /ˈkwɒntəm; ˋkwɑntəm/ *n* (*pl* **quanta** /-tə; -tə/) (*fml* 文) amount that is required or desired (需要的或想要的)数量.

□ **quantum** ˈ**leap** sudden progress; breakthrough 突飞猛进; 突破: *This discovery marks a quantum leap forward in the fight against cancer.* 这一发现标志着治疗癌症的

一大突破.

'**quantum theory** (*physics* 物) theory based on the assumption that in radiation the energy of electrons exists in units that cannot be divided 量子论.

quar·ant·ine /'kwɒrəntiːn; US 'kwɔːr-; 'kwɔrən,tin/ *n* [C usu *sing*, U 作可数名词时通常作单数, 亦作不可数名词] (period of) isolation for people or animals that may carry an infectious disease, until it is known that there is no danger of the disease being passed on to others (对可能患传染病的人或动物的)隔离(期间): *kept in quarantine for a week* 接受一星期的检疫隔离 ○ *be out of quarantine after five days* 五天后解除检疫隔离 ○ [attrib 作定语] *quarantine regulations, restrictions, etc* 检疫隔离的规定、限制等.

▷ **quar·ant·ine** *v* [Tn] put (sb/sth) into quarantine 对(某人[某物])进行检疫隔离: *quarantined because of rabies* 因怀疑患狂犬病而被检疫隔离.

quark /kwɑːk; kwɑrk/ *n* (*physics* 物) any of several very small parts of which elementary particles are thought to consist 夸克(组成基本粒子的更小的粒子).

quar·rel /'kwɒrəl; US 'kwɔːrəl; 'kwɔrəl/ *n* **1 ~ (with sb) (about/over sth)** angry argument or disagreement 争吵; 吵架; 不和; 口角: *pick* (ie provoke or seize the opportunity for) *a quarrel with sb* 向某人寻衅(找茬儿) ○ *I had a quarrel with my flat-mate about who should do the housework.* 我与和我同住一单元的人关于谁应做家务事吵了一架. ○ *Their quarrel wasn't serious.* 他们吵架吵得不厉害. ⇨Usage at ARGUMENT 用法见 ARGUMENT. **2 ~ with/against sb/sth** reason for complaining about sb/sth 抱怨某人[某事物]的原因或理由: *I have no quarrel with him.* 我没有理由责怪他.

▷ **quar·rel** *v* (**-ll-**; *US* **-l-**) **1** [I, Ipr] **~ (with sb) (about/over sth)** break friendly relations; argue angrily 吵嘴; 吵架; 争吵; 口角: *Stop quarrelling, children!* 孩子们, 别吵架了! ○ *She quarrelled with her brother about the terms of their father's will.* 她和哥哥为父亲遗嘱条款一事争吵起来. **2** [Ipr] **~ with sth** disagree with sth; find fault with sth 不同意或挑剔某事物: *quarrel with a statement, an account, an estimate, etc* 寻找结算、帐目、预算等的漏洞 ○ *You can't quarrel with the court's decision — it's very fair.* 你不能反对法院的判决 —— 判得很公平.

quar·rel·some /-səm; -səm/ *adj* likely to start a quarrel; quick-tempered 爱争吵的; 急脾气的.

quarry[1] /'kwɒrɪ; US 'kwɔːrɪ; 'kwɔrɪ/ *n* (**a**) animal or bird that is being hunted 正在被捕猎的鸟兽: *The hunters lost sight of their quarry in the forest.* 猎人失去了在林中追捕的鸟兽踪影. (**b**) person or thing that is being looked for or pursued eagerly 被寻找或追逐的人或事物: *It took the police several days to track down their quarry.* 警方用了几天时间追查到案中目标.

quarry[2] /'kwɒrɪ; US 'kwɔːrɪ; 'kwɔrɪ/ *n* place where stone, slate, etc is extracted from the ground 采石场; 石矿. Cf 参看 MINE[2] 1.

▷ **quarry** *v* (*pt, pp* **quarried**) **1** [Tn, Tn·pr, Tn·p] **~ A for B/B from A; ~ sth out (of sth)** extract (stone, etc) from (a quarry) 从(采石场)采(石等): *quarrying the hillside for granite* 从山坡上采花岗石 ○ *quarry out a block of marble* 挖出一块大理石. **2** [Ipr] search with great effort for information, etc 大力搜寻资料等: *quarrying in old documents for historical evidence* 查阅旧文件以寻找历史证据.

quart /kwɔːt; kwɔrt/ *n* **1** (*abbr* 缩写 **qt**) measure of capacity for liquids, equal to 2 pints or approximately 1.14 litres 夸脱(液体容量单位, 等于2品脱或约1.14升). ⇨App 5 见附录5. **2** (idm 习语) **put a quart into a pint 'pot** (try to) do sth that is impossible, esp to put sth into a space that is too small for it (试图)做不可能做到的事(尤指将某物置于容纳不下之处).

quar·ter /'kwɔːtə(r); 'kwɔrtər/ *n* **1** [C] each of four equal or corresponding parts of sth 四分之一; 四等分: *a quarter of a mile* 四分之一英里 ○ *three and a quarter* (ie $3\frac{1}{4}$) *inches* 三又四分之一($3\frac{1}{4}$)英寸 ○ *The programme lasted an hour and a quarter.* 节目持续了一小时十五分钟. ○ *Divide the apples into quarters.* 把这些苹果分成四分. ○ *Three quarters of the theatre was full.* 剧院的座位坐满了四分之三. ○ (*infml* 口) *A quarter* (ie of a pound) *of coffee, please.* 请给我四分之一磅的咖啡. ⇨App 4, 5 见附录4、5. ⇨Usage at HALF[1] 用法见 HALF[1]. **2** [C] point of time fifteen minutes before or after every hour 每小时之前或之后的第十五分钟: *It's (a) quarter to (US of) four now — I'll meet you at quarter past (US after).* 现在是差一刻四点 —— 我四点一刻见你. ○ *The clock strikes the hours, the half-hours and the quarters.* 这个钟在正点、半点和一刻钟都打点. ○ *The buses leave twice every hour on the quarter,* eg at 10.15 and 10.45. 公共汽车在每小时的第一刻钟和第三刻钟各开出一班车(如10时15分及10时45分). ⇨App 4 见附录4. **3** [C] three months, esp as a period for which rent or other payment is made, or a firm's earnings are calculated 季度, 三个月(尤指作为偿付租金或公司收益结算等的阶段): *The rent is due at the end of each quarter.* 缴纳租金以每季度末为期限. ○ *Our gas bill for the last quarter was unusually high.* 我们上季度的煤气费异常高. ○ *Sales of the dictionary are twice what they were in the same quarter last year.* 这部词典的销售量是去年同季度的两倍. **4** [C] (**a**) direction 方向: *The wind blew from all quarters.* 风从四面八方吹来. ○ *Her travels had taken her to every quarter of the globe.* 她游遍了世界各地. (**b**) district; part of a town 地区; 城镇的一部分: *a residential quarter* 住宅区 ○ *the student quarter of the city*, ie the part mainly inhabited by students 城里的学生居住区. **5** [C] person or group of people, esp as a possible source of help, information, etc 人, 团体(尤指可能提供援助、消息等的): *As her mother was now very poor she could expect no help from that quarter.* 她母亲已很贫困, 她无法指望得到母亲的帮助. ○ *The minister's speech is interpreted in some quarters* (ie by some people) *as an admission that the Government was wrong.* 部长的讲话有人认为是承认政府错了. **6** [C] (*US*) (coin worth) 25 cents; fourth part of a dollar 两角五分(的硬币); 四分之一元: *It'll cost you a quarter.* 你得花两角五分钱. ⇨App 4 见附录4. **7** [C] one fourth of a lunar month; position of the moon at the end of the first and third of these 太阴月的四分之一; 月球上弦或下弦的位相: *The moon is in its last quarter.* 月球现处于下弦. **8** [C usu *sing* 通常作单数] rear part of a ship's side 船舷的后部: *on the port/starboard quarter* 在左舷[右舷]后部. **9** [C] fourth part of a hundredweight, ie (in UK) 28 lb or (in US) 25 lb 夸特(四分之一英担, 即英国为28磅, 美国为25磅). ⇨App 4, 5 见附录4、5. **10 quarters** [pl] accommodation, esp for soldiers 住处; (尤指)营房: *take up quarters in the nearest village* 在最近的村中驻扎 ○ *married/single quarters*, ie place where a soldier with/without a family can lodge 已婚军人[单身军人]营房 ○ *ordered to return to their quarters* 被命令回营房. **11** [U] (*dated or fml* 旧或文) mercy shown towards an enemy who has surrendered or to an opponent who is one's power (对降敌或对手的)慈悲, 宽恕: *His business rivals knew they could expect no quarter from such a ruthless adversary.* 他的业务对手都知道不可指望他这样无情的人会手软. **12** (idm 习语) **at close quarters** ⇨ CLOSE[1].

▷ **quar·ter** *v* **1** [Tn] divide (sb/sth) into four parts 将(人[事物])分成四部分: *quarter an apple* 把苹果切成四瓣儿 ○ *sentenced to be hung, drawn and quartered*, ie executed by hanging, the body then being opened and cut up 被判处绞刑并剖尸裂肢. **2** [Tn, Tn·pr] **~ sb (on sb)** provide sb with lodgings 供某人住宿: *troops quartered on the local villagers* 驻扎在当地村民家中的部队.

□ '**quarter-day** *n* first day of a quarter(3) when payments become due 季度结帐日(一季度的第一天, 为付款到期日).

'**quarterdeck** *n* part of the upper deck of a ship near the stern, usu reserved for officers 上层后甲板区(通常为高级船员专用处).

,**quarter-'final** *n* (in sport, etc) any of four competitions or matches to choose the players or teams for the semifinals (运动等的)四分之一决赛.

'**quarter-light** *n* small triangular section of a window in a car, which can be opened to admit air without opening the main section 边窗(汽车窗中的三角形小窗).

'**quartermaster** *n* **1** (in the army) regimental officer in charge of stores and accommodation for a battalion (陆军的)军需官(负责营的物资及住宿的团级军官). **2** (in the navy) petty officer in charge of steering, signals, etc (海军的)航信士官(负责掌舵、信号等).

,**Quartermaster-'General** *n* staff officer in charge of supplies for an army 陆军军需总长.

Q

ˈ**quarter-note** *n* (*US*) = CROTCHET.
ˈ**quarter sessions** (formerly) court of law with limited power to try criminal and civil cases, held every three months (旧时)(按季开庭的)初级法院.
ˈ**quarterstaff** *n* strong pole, 6 to 8 feet long, formerly used as a weapon (旧时用作武器的6至8英尺长的)棍棒.

quar·terly /ˈkwɔːtəlɪ; ˋkwɔrtɚlɪ/ *adj*, *adv* produced or occurring once every three months 季度的, 按季度(每三个月一次): *I receive quarterly bank statements.* 我每三个月都收到一份银行结单. ○ *Subscriptions should be paid quarterly.* 订费按季度交付.
▷ **quar·terly** *n* periodical published four times a year 季刊.

quar·tet /kwɔːˈtet; kwɔrˋtɛt/ *n* **1** (piece of music for) four players or singers 四重奏(曲); 四重唱(曲); 四重奏演奏者; 四重唱演唱者: *a string quartet*, ie players of or music for two violins, a viola and a cello 弦乐四重奏(两个小提琴、一个中提琴和一个大提琴的演奏者或其乐曲). **2** set of four people or things 四人一组; 四件一套: *a quartet of novels with a linking theme* 主题连贯的四部小说.

Q

quarto /ˈkwɔːtəʊ; ˋkwɔrto/ *n* (*pl* **~s**) (**a**) (*abbrs* 缩写 **4to, qto**) size of page made by folding a standard sheet of paper twice to form eight pages 四开(标准纸张折叠两次而成八页的大小). (**b**) book made of these folded sheets 四开本: *the first quarto of 'Hamlet'* 《哈姆雷特》的第一种四开本 ○ [attrib 作定语] *Quarto volumes are too large to fit on this shelf.* 这架子上放不下四开本的书.

quartz /kwɔːts; kwɔrts/ *n* [U] any of various types of hard mineral (esp crystallized silica) 石英: [attrib 作定语] *a quartz clock/watch*, ie one that is operated, very accurately, by the electric vibrations of a quartz crystal 石英钟[表].

quasar /ˈkweɪzɑː(r); ˋkwezɑr/ *n* (*astronomy* 天) very distant object like a star that is the source of intense electromagnetic radiation 类星体.

quash /kwɒʃ; kwɑʃ/ *v* [Tn] **1** reject (sth) (by legal procedure) as not valid; declare (sth) not to be enforceable by law (依法)撤销(某事物); 宣布(某事物)无效: *quash a verdict* 宣布裁决无效 ○ *They had their sentence quashed by the appeal court judge.* 上诉法院的法官撤销了对他们的判决. **2** put an end to (sth); suppress or crush 制止(某事物); 镇压; 捣碎: *The rebellion was quickly quashed.* 叛乱被迅速平息.

quasi- /ˈkweɪzaɪ-, ˈkweɪsaɪ; ˋkwezaɪ, ˋkwesaɪ/ *pref* 前缀 (forming *adjs* and *ns* 用以构成形容词和名词) **1** to a certain extent 达到某种程度: *a quasi-official body* 半官方团体. **2** seemingly but not really 类似; 准; 半: *a quasi-scientific explanation* 类似科学的解释 ○ *a quasi-scholar* 似学者的人.

quat·er·cen·ten·ary /ˌkwɒtəsenˈtiːnərɪ; *US* -ˈsentənerɪ; ˌkwɑtɚˋsɛntəˌnɛrɪ/ *n* 400th anniversary 第400周年: *celebrate the quatercentenary of Shakespeare's birth* 纪念莎士比亚诞生四百周年.

quat·rain /ˈkwɒtreɪn; ˋkwɑtren/ *n* poem, or verse of a poem, consisting of four lines 四行诗; 四行的诗节.

qua·ver /ˈkweɪvə(r); ˋkwevɚ/ *v* **1** [I] (of a voice or a musical sound) shake; tremble (指嗓音或乐音)颤抖: *in a quavering voice* 以颤抖的嗓音 ○ *Her top notes quavered a little.* 她唱的高音有些颤. **2** [Tn, Tn·p] **~ sth (out)** say or sing sth in a trembling voice (以颤抖的声音)说出, 唱出: *The children quavered out their little song.* 孩子们颤悠悠地唱出了一支歌.
▷ **qua·ver** *n* **1** (usu *sing* 通常作单数) trembling sound 颤抖的声音: *You could hear the quaver in her voice.* 她的声音中能听出有些颤抖. **2** (*US* **eighth note**) note in music that lasts half as long as a crotchet 八分音符. ⇨ illus at MUSIC 见 MUSIC 插图.
qua·very /ˈkweɪvərɪ; ˋkwevərɪ/ *adj* (of a voice) shaking; tremulous (指嗓音)颤抖的, 发颤的.

quay /kiː; ki/ *n* landing-place, usu built of stone or iron, for loading and unloading ships 码头.
□ ˈ**quayside** *n* [sing] land situated at the side or edge of a quay 码头边: *crowds waiting at the quayside to welcome them* 等候在码头边上欢迎他们的人群.

queasy /ˈkwiːzɪ; ˋkwizɪ/ *adj* (**-ier, -iest**) having a tendency to feel sick; feeling sick 使人作呕的; 易呕吐的; 易眩晕的: *Travelling on a bus makes me feel queasy.* 我坐公共汽车感到头晕. ○ *She complained of a queasy stomach*, ie a feeling in her stomach that made her want to be sick. 她说觉得反胃(要呕吐). ▷ **queas·ily** *adv*. **queasi·ness** *n* [U].

queen /kwiːn; kwin/ *n* **1** (title of the) female ruler of an independent state, usu inheriting the position by right of birth (独立政体的)女王, 女酋长, 女首领(的头衔)(通常为世袭的): *Queen Elizabeth II* 英女王伊丽莎白二世 ○ *the Queen of the Netherlands* 荷兰女王 ○ *be made/crowned queen* 被立[加冕]为女王. Cf 参看 KING. **2** wife of a king 王后: *King George VI and Queen Elizabeth* 英王乔治六世及王后伊丽莎白. **3** (**a**) woman, place or thing regarded as best or most important in some way 最好的或最重要的女子、地方或事物: *Agatha Christie, the queen of detective-story writers* 阿加莎·克里斯蒂, 侦探小说杰出女作家 ○ *Marilyn Monroe is the most famous of all American movie queens*, ie leading film actresses. 玛丽莲·梦露是全美最著名的影后. ○ *Venice, the queen of the Adriatic* 威尼斯, 亚得里亚海沿岸的名城. (**b**) woman or girl chosen to hold the most important position in a festival or celebration 节日或庆典中最重要的女子: *Queen of the May*, ie girl chosen to lead a procession, dance, etc to celebrate spring 五朔节小姐(带领庆祝春季节日者) ○ *a carnival queen* 狂欢节小姐 ○ *a beauty queen* 选美赛的冠军. **4** fertile female insect (eg ant, bee or wasp) that produces eggs for the whole group (为群体产卵的雌性昆虫, 如蚂蚁、蜜蜂、黄蜂等的)王; 蚁王; 蜂王: *A hive cannot exist without a queen.* 蜂房不可无蜂王. ○ [attrib 作定语] *The queen bee never leaves the hive.* 蜂王从不离开蜂房. **5** (**a**) (in chess) the most powerful piece on the board, used for attack and defence (国际象棋的)后. ⇨ illus at CHESS 见 CHESS 插图. (**b**) (in a pack of playing-cards) any of the four cards with the picture of a queen on (纸牌中的)王后, Q: *the queen of hearts* 红桃Q. **6** (*sl derog* 俚, 贬) effeminate male homosexual 女性化的男同性恋者. **7** (idm 习语) **the King's/Queen's English** ⇨ ENGLISH. **turn King's/Queen's evidence** ⇨ EVIDENCE. **the uncrowned king/queen of sth** ⇨ UNCROWNED.
▷ **queen** *v* **1** (**a**) [Tn] (in chess) change (a pawn) into a queen by moving it across the board to the opponent's end (国际象棋中)使(卒)升变为后(至对方底线者). (**b**) [I] (of a pawn) be changed in this way (指卒)升变为后. **2** (idm 习语) **queen it (over sb)** behave as if in a position of power (over sb) (对某人)似掌权者行事: *Since her promotion she queens it over everyone else in the office.* 她获提升后对办事处所有的人都发号施令.
queenly *adj* of, like or suitable for a queen; majestic (似)女王的; 适合女王的; 堂皇的: *her queenly duties* 她的女王职权 ○ *give a queenly wave* 像女王那样挥手 ○ *dressed in queenly robes* 穿着华丽的(女装)礼服.
□ **queen** ˈ**bee** **1** ⇨ QUEEN 4. **2** (*fig* 比喻) woman who behaves as if she is the most important person in a particular place or group (在某场合或某些人中, 举止宛如最重要人物的)女子.
queen ˈ**consort** wife of a king 王后.
queen ˈ**dowager** widow of a king 孀居的王后.
queen ˈ**mother** widow of a king and mother of a reigning king or queen 孀居的王后及执政王之母: *The queen mother waved to the crowd.* 王太后向人群挥手.
Queen's ˈ**Bench (Division)** ⇨ KING'S BENCH (KING).
Queen's ˈ**Counsel** ⇨ KING'S COUNSEL (KING).
the Queen's ˈ**English** form of written and spoken English generally regarded as the most correct 标准英语.

queer /kwɪə(r); kwɪr/ *adj* **1** (**a**) different from what is expected; strange, esp in an unpleasant way (与预期的)不同的; 奇怪的; (尤指)古怪的: *The fish had a queer taste.* 那鱼有一股怪味道. ○ *His behaviour seemed queer.* 他的举动似乎有些古怪. ○ *I think she's gone a bit queer in the head*, ie slightly crazy. 我看她精神不太正常. (**b**) causing doubt or suspicion 使人生疑的; 可疑的: *I heard some very queer noises in the garden.* 我听到花园里有些可疑的声音. ○ *There's something queer about him.* 他有些可疑. **2** (*sl derog* 俚, 贬) homosexual 同性恋的. **3** (*dated infml* 旧, 口) unwell; faint 不舒服的; 眩晕的: *I woke up feeling rather queer.* 我醒来觉得有些头晕. **4** (idm 习语) **be in** ˈ**Queer Street** (*dated Brit sl* 旧, 俚) be in (esp financial) trouble 处于(尤指财务)困境; 拮

据: *He lost all his money gambling and now he's really in Queer Street.* 他把钱都输光了，现在可真狼狈了. **an odd/a queer fish** ⇨ FISH[1].

▷ **queer** *n* (*sl derog* 俚, 贬) homosexual man 男同性恋者.

queer *v* (idm 习语) **queer sb's 'pitch** (*infml* 口) cause sb's plans to go wrong 破坏或阻挠某人的计划: *I think I'm likely to get the job, but if Bob applies for it too it/he could queer my pitch.* 我想我很可能得到这份工作, 可是假设鲍勃也申请的话, 那[他]可能使我的计划落空.

queerly *adv.*

queer·ness *n* [U].

quell /kwel; kwɛl/ *v* [Tn] put an end to (sth); suppress 制止(某事物); 镇压; 压制: *quell the rebellion, opposition, uprising, etc* 镇压叛乱、反抗、起义等 ○ *quell sb's fears, anxieties, etc* 消除某人的恐惧、忧虑等.

quench /kwentʃ; kwɛntʃ/ *v* [Tn] **1** extinguish (fire, flames, etc), esp with water 扑灭(火焰等)(尤指用水): (*fig* 比喻) *quench sb's ardent passion* 使某人的热情冷却下来. **2** satisfy (sth) by drinking 解(渴): *quench one's thirst with cold water* 喝冷水止渴. **3** put an end to (sth) 终止(某事物): *Nothing could quench her longing to return home again.* 她重返家园的念头怎么也打消不掉. **4** cool (a hot substance) rapidly by placing it in water 将(热物体)放人水中急速冷却; 淬火; 蘸火.

queru·lous /ˈkwerʊləs; ˋkwɛrʊləs/ *adj* complaining; irritable 抱怨的; 易怒的: *in a querulous tone* 以发牢骚的腔调. ▷ **queru·lously** *adv.* **queru·lous·ness** *n* [U].

query /ˈkwɪərɪ; ˋkwɪrɪ/ *n* **1** question 疑问; 问题: *answer readers' queries* 答读者问 ○ *Your interesting report raises several important queries.* 你的精彩报告引发出了几个重要问题. **2** question mark (?) 问号(?): *Put a query against that.* 在那儿加一个问号.

▷ **query** *v* (*pt, pp* **queried**) **1** [Tn, Tn·pr] **~sb (about sth)** ask sb a question or questions 向某人提出问题: *'Will it be too late?' she queried.* '是否太晚呢?'她问道. ○ *The minister was queried about his plans for the industry.* 有人向部长提出了工业计划问题. **2** [Tn, Tw] express doubt about sth 对某事物表示怀疑: *query a statement, suggestion, conclusion, etc* 对一言论、建议、决议等表示怀疑 ○ *query the amount charged*, ie say that one thinks it is wrong 对索要的数额质疑(称认为有误) ○ *I query whether he can be trusted.* 我怀疑他是否可靠.

quest /kwest; kwɛst/ *n* (*fml or rhet* 文或修辞) **1 ~ (for sth)** act of seeking sth; search or pursuit 寻求; 寻找; 搜索; 追求: *the quest for gold, knowledge, happiness* 勘探黄金、寻求知识、追求幸福. **2** (idm 习语) **in quest of sth** trying to find sth; seeking sth 试图找到某事物; 寻求某事物: *She had come in quest of advice.* 她曾来征求意见.

▷ **quest** *v* [I, Ipr] **~ (for sth)** (*fml or rhet* 文或修辞) try to find sth; search 试图找到某事物; 搜索: *His questing fingers found the light switch.* 他用手指摸到了灯的开关. ○ *continue to quest for clues* 继续寻找线索.

ques·tion[1] /ˈkwestʃən; ˋkwɛstʃən/ *n* **1** [C] form of expression in speech or writing that requests an answer from sb 问题: *ask a lot of questions* 问很多问题 ○ *Question 3 is quite difficult.* 第3个问题很难. ○ *I will be happy to answer questions at the end.* 我愿在最后回答一些问题. ○ *I'd like to put a question to the speaker.* 我想向发言者提一个问题. **2** [C] topic that is being or needs to be discussed; problem that needs to be solved 议题; 难题: *What about the question of security?* 安全的问题怎么办? ○ *We have to consider the question of where to sleep.* 我们得考虑在何处安歇的问题. ○ *The question of choosing a successor has arisen.* 挑选后继人的问题已经提出. **3** [U] raising of doubt 质疑: *There is no/some question about his honesty.* 他的诚实没有[有些]问题. ○ *Her sincerity is beyond question.* 她态度诚恳, 毋庸置疑. ○ *His suitability for the post is open to question.* 对这一职位他是否适宜很成问题. **4** (idm 习语) **beg the question** ⇨ BEG. **bring sth/come into 'question** (cause sth to) be discussed or considered as a matter of importance (使某事物)被讨论, 被考虑: *My promotion brings into question the status of certain other members of staff.* 提升我后某些职员的地位就成了问题. **call sth in/into 'question** express doubt about sth 对某事物表示怀疑: *His moral standards have been called into question.* 他的道德标准令人生疑. **a fair question** ⇨ FAIR[1]. **in 'question** being considered or discussed 正被考虑或讨论: *The woman in question is sitting over there.* 提到的那个女的就在那里坐着呢. ○ *The job in question is available for three months only.* 所谈到的这一工作空缺为时仅三个月. **it is a question of** what is really involved is 问题在于: *It isn't a question of whether we can afford a holiday — I'm just too busy at the moment.* 问题倒不是我们是否有钱度假——而是目前我实在太忙了. ○ *She is so talented that her success can only be a question of time.* 她才华横溢, 事业成功只是时间问题. **a loaded question** ⇨ LOAD[2]. **a moot point/question** ⇨ MOOT. **out of the 'question** not worth discussing; impossible 不值得讨论的; 不可能的: *Missing school to watch the football match is out of the question.* 为看足球比赛而旷课, 那可不行. ○ *A new bicycle is out of the question — we can't afford it.* 买新自行车的事谈不到——我们买不起. **pop the question** ⇨ POP[4]. **a/the sixty-four thousand dollar question** ⇨ DOLLAR. **there is some/no question of** there is a/no possibility of 有[没有]...的可能性: *There was some question of selling the business.* 有可能将公司转让. ○ *There will be no question of anyone being made redundant.* 决不可能裁掉任何人. **a vexed question** ⇨ VEX.

□ **'question mark** the symbol (?) used in writing after a question 问号(?). ⇨App 3 见附录3. Cf 参看 QUERY 2.

'question-master (also **'quiz-master**) *n* person who asks the questions in a quiz, esp on TV or radio 测试中问问题的人; (尤指电视或电台中)问答节目主持人.

'question time (*Brit*) (in the House of Commons) period of time during which ministers answer questions from MPs (下议院中的)质询时间(大臣答复议员提问的时间).

ques·tion[2] /ˈkwestʃən; ˋkwɛstʃən/ *v* **1** [Tn] ask (sb) a question or questions 问(某人)问题: *They questioned her closely about her friendship with the dead man.* 他们仔细查问她与死者的情谊. ○ *I was questioned by the police for six hours.* 警方把我盘问了六个小时. ○ *I'd like to question you on your views about the housing problem.* 我想问问你对住房问题的看法. **2** [Tn, Tw] express or feel doubt about (sth) 对(某事物)表示或感到怀疑: *Her sincerity has never been questioned.* 她的诚意从未受到怀疑. ○ *Do you question my right to read this?* 你是否怀疑我无权看这份材料? ○ *We must question the value of our link with the university.* 我们要斟酌一下与这所大学联系有何价值. ○ *I seriously question whether we ought to continue.* 我真正怀疑我们是否应该继续下去.

▷ **ques·tion·able** *adj* that can be doubted; not certainly true or advisable or honest 有问题的; 可疑的; 不见得真实的; 不太可取的; 不一定诚实的: *Such a questionable assertion is sure to provoke criticism.* 这种有问题的主张肯定会招致非议. ○ *an object of questionable value, usefulness, authenticity* 价值、用途、真实性有问题的物件. **ques·tion·ably** /-əblɪ; -əblɪ/ *adv.*

ques·tioner *n* person who asks questions, esp in a broadcast programme or a public debate 问问题的人; (尤指广播节目或公开辩论中的)发问者.

ques·tion·ingly *adv* using a questioning gesture or tone of voice 表示怀疑地: *She looked at me questioningly.* 她用怀疑的目光看着我.

ques·tion·naire /ˌkwestʃəˈneə(r); ˌkwɛstʃənˋɛr/ *n* written or printed list of questions to be answered by a number of people, esp to collect statistics or as part of a survey 问卷; (尤指为作统计或调查用的)问题单, 调查表, 征求意见表: *Please complete and return the enclosed questionnaire.* 所附问卷请填妥交回.

queue /kjuː; kju/ *n* **1** line of people, vehicles, etc waiting for sth or to do sth (人或车辆等的)长列, 行列: *By 7 o'clock a long queue had formed outside the cinema.* 到7点钟时, 电影院门外已经排成了长队. ○ *People had to stand in a queue for hours to buy a ticket.* 人们买票得排几小时的队. ○ *Is this the queue for the bus?* 这是等候公共汽车的队吗? ○ *a queue of cars at the traffic-lights* 交通灯前的一长列汽车. **2** (idm 习语) **jump the queue** ⇨ JUMP[2].

▷ **queue** *v* [I, Ipr, Ip] **~ (up) (for sth)** wait in a queue 排队等候: *We queued for an hour but didn't get in.* 我们排队等候一小时也没进去. ○ *Queue here for a taxi.* 等候出租汽车在此排队. ○ *They're queuing up to see a*

Q

film. 他们排着队等候看电影.

quibble /ˈkwɪbl; ˋkwɪbl/ *n* **1** objection or criticism, esp a trivial one 反对或批评的意见; (尤指)吹毛求疵: *quibbles over the exact amount* 斤斤计较 ○ *Basically it was a fine performance — I have only minor quibbles to make about her technique.* 表演基本上很精彩——我只对她的技巧稍有意见. **2** remark, etc made in order to evade the main point of an argument 回避正题的话等; 遁词: *She's only introducing this as a quibble.* 她提出此点, 纯属遁词.

▷ **quibble** *v* [I, Ipr] **~ (over/about sth)** argue about small differences or disagreements (对小的差别或分歧)争论: *Stop quibbling about the use of the comma.* 别再争辩逗号的用法了. ○ *50p isn't worth quibbling about.* 50便士不值一争.

quiche /kiːʃ; kiʃ/ *n* open pastry tart with a savoury filling, esp of eggs, bacon, cheese, etc 一种糕饼(上层多为鸡蛋、腌肉、干酪等).

quick /kwɪk; kwɪk/ *adj* **(-er, -est)** **1 (a)** (capable of) moving fast or doing sth in a short time 快的; 迅速的: *a quick worker, reader* 工作速度快的人、阅读速度快的人 ○ *quick to respond, react, learn* 回应、反应、学得快的 ○ *Taxis are quicker than buses.* 计程车比公共汽车快. ○ *Go and find the tickets and be quick about it*, ie hurry. 去把票弄来, 快点儿. ○ *The thief got away — he was too quick for me.* 小偷溜掉了——我没追上. ○ *We must move at a quicker pace or we'll be late.* 我们动作得快些, 不然就晚了. **(b)** done in a short time 短时间做成的: *have a quick meal* 吃快餐 ○ *We've just got time for a quick one*, ie a quick (usu alcoholic) drink. 我们的时间不多, 只够匆匆喝上一口(通常指酒). ○ *with a quick flick of the wrist* 用手腕急速一抖 ○ *Are you sure this is the quickest way?* 你肯定这条路最快吗? ○ *He fired three shots in quick succession.* 他快速连发三枪. **2 (a)** [attrib 作定语] lively; active; alert 灵活的; 灵敏的; 伶俐的; 机警的: *a quick ear for music* 对音乐灵敏的耳朵 ○ *a quick eye for imperfections* 能挑毛病的锐利的眼睛 ○ *Her quick wits saved the boy's life.* 她靠急智救了那男孩一命. **(b)** easily roused; sensitive 易受激发的; 敏感的: *Be careful not to annoy him — he's got a quick temper*, ie he becomes angry very readily. 小心别惹他——他脾气急. ○ *She's always very quick to take offence*, ie easily offended. 她动不动就生气. **(c) ~ (at sth)** intelligent; competent 聪明的; 有能力的: *He's not as quick as his sister.* 他没有妹妹那么聪明. ○ *His spelling's poor but he's very quick at figures.* 他拼写差, 但算术好. **3** (idm 习语) **the ˌquick and the ˈdead** (*arch* 古) all people alive or dead 活的或死的所有的人. **(as) quick as a ˈflash; (as) quick as ˈlightning** very quick(ly) 极快: *He got the answer to the riddle as quick as a flash.* 他一下子就猜中了谜底. ○ *She's as quick as lightning on the tennis court.* 她在网球场上疾如闪电. **(be) ˌquick off the ˈmark** making a prompt start 迅速开始: *You have to be quick off the mark when you answer a newspaper advertisement.* 回应报纸的广告得说办就办. **quick/slow on the draw** ⇨ DRAW[1]. **quick/slow on the uptake** ⇨ UPTAKE.

▷ **quick** *adv* **(-er, -est)** quickly 快地; 迅速地: *Come as quick as you can.* 你要尽快来. ○ *Everyone is trying to get rich quick nowadays.* 现在每个人都想要尽快发财致富. ○ *Who ran quickest?* 谁跑得最快? ○ *quick-drying paint* 快干漆.

quick *n* **1** [sing] soft tender flesh, esp below the finger-nails 软而嫩的肉(尤指指甲下的): *She has bitten her nails (down) to the quick.* 她咬指甲(一直)咬到肉. **2** (idm 习语) **cut sb to the ˈquick** hurt sb deeply by speaking or acting unkindly 用恶劣的语言或行动深深伤害某人: *She was cut to the quick by his insults.* 她受他侮辱而十分伤心.

quickly *adv*: *speak, write, run, learn very quickly* 说得、写得、跑得、学得很快.

quick·ness *n* [U]: (*saying* 谚) *The quickness of the hand deceives the eye.* 手疾骗眼快.

□ **ˌquick-ˈchange** *adj* [attrib 作定语] (of an actor, etc) quickly changing his costume or appearance to play another part (指演员等)瞬变的(迅速换装或改变相貌而演另一角色): *a quick-change artist* 瞬变的演员.

quick-ˈfreeze *v* (*pt* **-froze** /-frəʊz; -froz/, *pp* **-frozen** /-frəʊzn; -frozən/) [Tn] freeze (food) very quickly for storing so that it keeps its natural qualities 速冻(食物).

ˌquick ˈmarch (used as a military command to march at the usual pace (用作军令)齐步行进).

ˈquickstep *n* (music for a) ballroom dance with quick steps 快步舞(曲): *play/dance a quickstep* 演奏快步舞曲[跳快步舞].

ˌquick-ˈtempered *adj* likely to become angry very quickly 易怒的; 性情急躁的.

ˌquick-ˈwitted *adj* able to think quickly; intelligent 机智的; 聪明的.

quicken /ˈkwɪkən; ˋkwɪkən/ *v* [I, Tn] **1** (cause sth to) become quicker (使某事物)加快, 变快: *His pace quickened.* 他的步伐加快了. ○ *We quickened our steps.* 我们加快了脚步. **2** (*fml* 文) (cause sth to) become more active (使某事物)变得更活跃, 更加活泼: *The child quickened in her womb*, ie She felt the movements of the foetus. 她感到了胎动. ○ *Her pulse quickened.* 她的脉搏加快了. ○ *His interest was quickened by an article he had read.* 他读了一篇文章便兴趣大增了.

quickie /ˈkwɪkɪ; ˋkwɪkɪ/ *n* (*infml* 口) thing that is made or done very quickly 迅速做成的事物: *I've just made some coffee — have you time for a quickie?* 我刚煮好咖啡——你能抽空儿喝点儿吗?

quick·lime /ˈkwɪklaɪm; ˋkwɪkˌlaɪm/ *n* [U] = LIME[1] 1.

quick·sand /ˈkwɪksænd; ˋkwɪkˌsænd/ *n* [C often *pl*, U 作可数名词时常作复数, 亦作不可数名词] (area of) loose wet deep sand into which people or things will sink 流沙(区).

quick·sil·ver /ˈkwɪksɪlvə(r); ˋkwɪkˌsɪlvɚ/ *n* [U] = MERCURY: *like quicksilver*, ie very quick(ly) 极快.

quid[1] /kwɪd; kwɪd/ *n* (*pl* unchanged 复数不变) (*Brit infml* 口) **1** one pound sterling 一英镑: *Can you lend me five quid?* 你能借给我五英镑吗? ○ *It costs a quid (ie £1) to get in.* 进去要花一英镑(£1). **2** (idm 习语) **quids ˈin** in a position to profit from sth 处于从某事物中获利的地位: *Having sold the film and TV rights to his new best seller he's absolutely quids in.* 他售出了最新畅销小说的电影和电视版权, 现在单等坐收厚利了.

quid[2] /kwɪd; kwɪd/ *n* lump of tobacco for chewing (供咀嚼的)烟草块.

quid pro quo /ˌkwɪd prəʊ ˈkwəʊ; ˌkwɪdproˋkwo/ *n* (*pl* **quid pro quos**) thing given in return for sth else 补偿物; 交换物: *Please accept the use of our cottage as a quid pro quo for lending us your car.* 请尽管使用我们的村舍, 以酬谢借给我们汽车之事.

qui·es·cent /kwaɪˈesnt, kwɪˈesnt; kwaɪˋɛsn̩t, kwɪˋɛsn̩t/ *adj* (*fml* 文) inactive; passive; quiet 不活动的; 被动的; 静止的: *It is unlikely that such an extremist organization will remain quiescent for long.* 这种过激的组织是不太可能长期沉默的. ▷ **qui·es·cence** /-sns; -sn̩s/ *n* [U].

quiet /ˈkwaɪət; ˋkwaɪət/ *adj* **(-er, -est)** **1** with little or no sound; not noisy or loud 轻声的; 无声的; 安静的: *her quiet voice, footsteps* 她那轻轻的嗓音、脚步声 ○ *Be quiet* (ie silent), *please!* 请安静! ○ *Can't you keep the children quiet? I'm trying to concentrate.* 你能不能让孩子们静一静? 我做事需要精神集中. **2** with little or no movement or disturbance (几乎)不动的; 静止的; 平静的; 安定的: *The roads are usually quiet in the afternoon.* 下午路面通常很清静. ○ *The sea looks quieter now.* 现在海面看起来平静些了. ○ *Business is quiet at this time of the year.* 一年中的这个时候生意很淡. **3** without excitement, activity or interruption 无感情波动的; 无活动的; 不受干扰的: *lead a quiet life* 过着平淡的生活 ○ *have a quiet smoke* 悠闲地吸着烟 ○ *have a quiet evening at home* 在家度过恬静的夜晚 ○ *Their wedding was very quiet.* 他们的婚礼很平淡. **4** gentle; not forceful 文静的; 温和的; 温顺的: *a lady of a quiet disposition* 文静的女士. **5** (of colours) not bright; unobtrusive (指颜色)不鲜艳的, 暗淡的, 素净的: *a quiet shade of blue* 暗淡的蓝色. **6** not expressed loudly; restrained 不大声表达的; 克制的: *have a quiet laugh about sth* 轻声笑某事物 ○ *Her manner concealed quiet resentment.* 她心中怨恨而不形于色. ⇨Usage 见所附用法. **7** (idm 习语) **keep quiet about sth; keep sth quiet** say nothing about sth 对某事物缄默不语: *I've decided to resign but I'd prefer you to keep quiet about it.* 我已决定辞职, 你先别声张. **(as) quiet as a ˈmouse** making very little sound 不出声; 无声响.

▷ **quiet** *n* [U] **1** state of being quiet; tranquillity 寂静; 平静: *the quiet of the countryside* 乡村的寂静 ○ *live in peace and quiet* 过着平静、安定的生活. **2** (idm 习语)

on the quiet secretly 秘密地; 私下; 暗地里: *have a drink on the quiet* 偷偷地喝酒.
quiet *v* [I, Ip, Tn, Tn·p] **~ (sb/sth) (down)** (*esp US*) become or make (sb/sth) quiet 安静下来; 使(某人[某事物])安静, 平静: *quiet a frightened horse* 使受惊的马静下来.
qui·eten /ˈkwaɪətn; ˋkwaɪətn̩/ *v* [I, Ip, Tn, Tn·p] **~ (sb/sth) (down)** (*esp Brit*) (cause sb/sth to) become less disturbed, noisy, etc (使某人[某事物])平静些, 安静些: *Quieten down and get on with your work.* 静下心来继续工作吧. ○ *quieten a screaming baby* 哄着惊叫的小孩儿 ○ *quieten* (ie allay, calm) *sb's fears/suspicions* 消除某人的恐惧[怀疑].
quietly *adv*: *This car engine runs very quietly.* 这辆汽车的发动机噪音很小. ○ *She died quietly in her bed.* 她在床上安然去世.
quiet·ness *n* [U]: *the quietness of the chapel* 教堂中的寂静.

NOTE ON USAGE 用法: **Quiet, silent** and **calm** can all be applied to both people and things and generally indicate the absence of a quality rather than the presence of something. ☆ **quiet**、**silent**、**calm** 三词用于人和事物均可, 通常指不具有某种性质, 而不指具有某种性质. A **silent** film has no speech and a **silent** machine makes no noise. ☆ **silent** 影片没有言语, 而 **silent** 机器没有噪声. The opposite of *reading silently* (or *to oneself*) is *reading aloud.* 与 reading silently (或 to oneself) (默读) 相对的是 reading aloud (读出声来). **Quiet** can mean silent ☆ **quiet** 可意为 silent: *Quiet! Don't make any noise!* 静一静! 不要出声! It can also indicate a lack of disturbance 这个词还可指没有骚扰: *a quiet road with few cars* 没有什么汽车经过的平静的道路. ○ *Politicians must sometimes long for a quieter life.* 政治家有时巴不得能过些清静日子. The opposite of *quiet music* is *loud music.* 与 quiet music (轻柔的音乐) 相对的是 loud music (喧闹的音乐). **Still** indicates the absence of movement ☆ **still** 意思是不动: *Stand still!* 站着别动! It may also suggest a lack of noise 这个词也可指没有噪声: *a still night after a stormy day* 白天风暴过后的寂静的夜晚. A **calm** person shows no agitation in difficult circumstances. ☆ **calm** 形容人, 意为在困难情况下不慌里慌张. A **calm** sea has no, or only small, waves. ☆ **calm** 形容海洋, 意为没有波浪或只有波纹.

quiet·ism /ˈkwaɪətɪzəm; ˋkwaɪətɪzm̩/ *n* [U] form of religious devotion based on a calm and passive acceptance of life and the abandonment of all desires 寂静主义(主张清心寡欲的宗教形式).
▷ **quiet·ist** /-ɪst; -ɪst/ *n* person who practises this 寂静主义者.
quiet·ude /ˈkwaɪətju:d; *US* -tu:d; ˋkwaɪə,tud/ *n* (*fml* 文) stillness; calm 平静; 宁静; 寂静.
qui·etus /kwaɪˈi:təs; kwaɪˋitəs/ *n* (usu *sing* 通常作单数) (*fml* 文) release from life; extinction 死亡; 灭绝: *give sb his quietus*, ie put an end to his life 结束某人的生命 ○ *The plan has finally got its quietus*, ie been abandoned. 这一计划终于胎死腹中(遭放弃).
quiff /kwɪf; kwɪf/ *n* (*Brit*) lock of hair, esp of a man, brushed up above the forehead 额前向上梳的一束头发(尤指男子的).
quill /kwɪl; kwɪl/ *n* **1** (**a**) (also ˈ**quill-feather**) large feather from the wing or tail (翅膀或尾部的)大羽毛. ⇨ illus at FEATHER 见 FEATHER 插图. (**b**) (also **quill-pen**) (formerly) pen made from the hollow stem of this (旧时)(用羽毛管做的)羽毛笔. **2** (usu *pl* 通常作复数) long sharp stiff spine of a porcupine (豪猪的长而硬的)刺.
quilt /kwɪlt; kwɪlt/ *n* thick covering for a bed, made of cloth padded with soft material 被褥; 被子; 褥子. Cf 参看 DUVET, EIDERDOWN.
▷ **quilt** *v* [Tn] line (a garment or coverlet) with padding held in place by lines of stitches (用线绗着絮好的材料) 给(衣服或床罩)做衬里: *a quilted anorak, dressing-gown, etc* 用线绗着絮好的材料做衬里的皮猴儿、晨衣等.
quin /kwɪn; kwɪn/ (*US* **quint** /kwɪnt; kwɪnt/) *n* (*infml* 口) = QUINTUPLET.
quince /kwɪns; kwɪns/ *n* **1** hard yellowish pear-shaped fruit used for making jam, etc 榅桲(梨状淡黄色坚硬水果, 可制果酱等): [attrib 作定语] *quince jelly* 榅桲果冻. **2** tree bearing this fruit 榅桲树.
quin·cen·ten·ary /ˌkwɪnsenˈti:nərɪ; *US* -ˈsentənerɪ; kwɪnˋsɛntn̩ˌɛrɪ/ *n* 500th anniversary 第500周年: [attrib 作定语] *quincentenary celebrations* 第五百周年庆典.
quin·ine /kwɪˈni:n; *US* ˈkwaɪnaɪn; ˋkwaɪnaɪn/ *n* [U] bitter liquid made from the bark of a tree and used in drinks or as a medicine against fever 奎宁; 金鸡纳霜.
Quin·qua·ges·ima /ˌkwɪŋkwəˈdʒesɪmə; ˌkwɪŋkwəˋdʒɛsəmə/ *n* the Sunday before Lent (50 days before Easter) 大斋节前的星期日(复活节前50天).
quinsy /ˈkwɪnzɪ; ˋkwɪnzɪ/ *n* [U] inflammation of the throat, esp with an abscess on one of the tonsils 扁桃体周脓肿.
quint·es·sence /kwɪnˈtesns; kwɪnˋtɛsn̩s/ *n* [sing] **the ~ of sth** (*fml* 文) **1** essential part of (a theory, speech, condition, etc) (理论、讲话、条件等)的精髓, 精华: *Her book captures the quintessence of Renaissance humanism.* 她的书抓住了文艺复兴时期人文主义的精髓. **2** perfect example of (a quality) 典范: *He is the quintessence of tact and politeness.* 他处世谦恭得体. ▷ **quint·es·sen·tial** /ˌkwɪntɪˈsenʃl; ˌkwɪntəˋsɛnʃəl/ *adj*. **quint·es·sen·tially** /-ʃəlɪ; -ʃəlɪ/ *adv*: *a sense of humour that is quintessentially British* 典型的英式幽默感.
quin·tet /kwɪnˈtet; kwɪnˋtɛt/ *n* (piece of music for) five players or singers 五重奏(曲); 五重唱(曲); 五重奏演奏者; 五重唱演唱者: *They're playing Schubert's 'Trout' Quintet.* 他们正演奏着舒伯特的《鳟鱼五重奏》.
quin·tu·plet /ˈkwɪntju:plet; *US* kwɪnˈtu:plɪt; kwɪnˋtuplɪt/ (also **quin**, *US* **quint**) *n* (usu *pl* 通常作复数) any of five children born to the same mother at one birth 五胞胎中的一个孩子.
quip /kwɪp; kwɪp/ *n* witty or sarcastic remark 妙语; 讽刺话: *He ended his speech with a merry quip.* 他以十分风趣的话结束了演讲.
▷ **quip** *v* (**-pp-**) [I] make a quip or quips 说风趣的或讽刺的话: *'Who overslept this morning?' She quipped.* '今天早晨谁睡过头了?' 她风趣地问.
quire /ˈkwaɪə(r); kwaɪr/ *n* 25 (formerly 24) sheets of paper (纸的)一刀(25张纸, 旧时为24张): *buy/sell paper by the quire/in quires* 按刀数买[卖]纸. Cf 参看 REAM 1.
quirk /kwɜ:k; kwɝk/ *n* **1** habit or action that is peculiar to sb/sth (某人[某事物]特有的)习惯, 举动: *He had a strange quirk of addressing his wife as Mrs Smith.* 他很怪, 把自己的妻子称作史密斯夫人. **2** accident; coincidence 偶然的事; 巧合: *one of those odd historical quirks* 偶发的历史事件 ○ *By a quirk of fate they had booked into the same hotel.* 由于命运的捉弄, 他们住进同一家旅馆.
quis·ling /ˈkwɪzlɪŋ; ˋkwɪzlɪŋ/ *n* traitor, esp one who helps an enemy occupying his country 卖国贼, 内奸, 叛徒(尤指助敌侵占本国者).
quit /kwɪt; kwɪt/ *v* (**-tt-**; *pt, pp* **quit** or, in British use, 英式英语作 **quitted**) **1** [I, Tn] go away from (a place); leave 从(某处)离开; 离去: *He got his present job when he quitted/quit the army.* 他退伍后得到现在这份工作. ○ *If I don't get a pay rise I'll quit.* 若不给我加薪, 我就不干了. ○ *I have received your notice to quit*, ie to leave the accommodation I am renting. 我已收到你让我搬家的通知. **2** [Tn, Tg] (*infml* 口) stop (sth/doing sth) 停止(某事物[做某事物]): *quit work for five minutes* 停止工作五分钟 ○ *Quit fooling around!* 别胡闹了! **3** (idm 习语) **be quit of sb/sth** be rid of sb/sth; be released from the company or addition of sb/sth 摆脱某人[某事物]; 脱离某人[某事物]: *I'd like to be quit of the responsibility.* 我很想摆脱这个责任. ○ *You're well quit of him*, ie fortunate because he has left. 你可摆脱他了(很幸运, 他已离去).
▷ **quit·ter** *n* (*often derog* 常作贬义) person who does not finish a task he has started, esp one that is done as a duty 对工作半途而废的人; (尤指对职责)不善始善终的人: *I've asked you to do this for me because I know you're not a quitter.* 我要求你为我做这件事, 因为我知道你做事不虎头蛇尾.
quite /kwaɪt; kwaɪt/ *adv* **1** (not used with a negative 不与否定词连用) (**a**) (used esp with *adjs* or *advs* that refer to a gradable quality 尤与表示程度的形容词或副词连用) to some extent; not very; fairly 达到某种程度; 不很; 相当: *quite big, small, good, cold, warm, interesting,*

etc 相当大、小、好、冷、热、有趣等 ○ *The girl sang quite a long song.* 这女孩儿唱了一首很长的歌. ○ *He plays quite well.* 他表演得挺不错. ○ *I quite like some opera music.* 我颇喜欢某些歌剧乐曲. ⇨Usage at FAIRLY 用法见 FAIRLY. **(b)** (used as an intensifier with *adjs* or *advs* that express an extreme opinion 与表示极度的形容词或副词连用, 以加强语气): *quite awful, delicious, dazzling, amazing, unbelievable, etc* 太糟糕、好吃、耀眼、奇妙、不可置信等 ○ *a quite extraordinary experience* 极不平凡的经历 ○ *The view was quite breathtaking.* 那景色美极了. ○ *That was quite the nicest meal I've ever had.* 那可真是我吃过的最好的一顿饭. ○ *She performed quite brilliantly.* 她表演得确实很优美. **2** (used with absolute measures 与表示绝对的词语连用) completely; entirely 完全地; 整体地; 十分地: *quite empty, perfect, unique, flawless, enough* 完全空的、完美的、独特的、无瑕的、充足的 ○ *The theatre was not quite* (ie almost) *full.* 戏院尚未全满. ○ *Cheer up, it's not quite hopeless yet.* 振作起来, 并非毫无希望. ○ *Are you sure you're quite satisfied?* 你真十分满意吗? ○ *He has quite recovered from his illness.* 他已痊愈. ○ *The answer is 62 — quite right.* 答案是 62 —— 完全正确. ○ *I quite agree/understand.* 我完全同意[理解]. ○ *talking on the telephone for quite 2 hours* 打电话整整谈了两小时 ○ *'I made myself a cup of tea while I was waiting.' 'Oh don't worry, that's quite all right.'* '我等候的时候, 自己沏了一杯茶.' '噢, 没关系, 当然可以了.' **3** (used as an *interj* to express agreement or understanding 用作叹词表示同意或理解): *'It's not something we want to have talked about.' 'Quite (so).'* '那不是我们要谈的事.' '的确(如此).' ○ *'He's bound to feel shaken after his accident.' 'Quite.'* '他出事之后一定心有余悸.' '不错.' **4** (idm 习语) **quite a 'few; quite a 'lot (of)** a considerable number or amount 相当多: *Quite a few people came to the lecture.* 有相当多的人来听讲. ○ *We drank quite a lot of wine.* 我们喝了不少葡萄酒. **quite a; quite some** /sʌm; sʌm/ (*approv* 褒 *esp US*) (used to indicate that a person or thing is unusual 用以指某人或物不寻常): *It must be quite some car.* 那辆汽车可不比寻常. ○ *We had quite a party.* 我们的聚会很不一般. **ˌquite some** /sʌm; sʌm/ **'time** a considerable length of time 相当长的时间: *It happened quite some time ago.* 那是很久以前的事.

▷ **quite** *det* **1** (used before *a/the + n* or before a name, as an intensifier 用于 a/the + 名词前或用于名字前, 以加强语气): *quite a beauty, hero, swimmer* 真是个美女、英雄、游泳健将 ○ *We found it quite a change when we moved to London.* 我们搬到伦敦, 真有天壤之别. ○ *It's not quite the Lake District but the countryside's very pretty.* 这儿虽说比不上湖区, 但郊外的景色倒也十分漂亮. **2** (idm 习语) **(not) ˌquite the (done) 'thing** (not) that which is considered socially acceptable (不)得体: *It wasn't quite the done thing for women to drink in pubs in those days.* 那年月女的到酒店喝酒可不成体统. **ˌquite the 'fashion, 'rage, etc** extremely popular or fashionable 极为流行或时髦: *Black leather trousers seem to be quite the rage these days.* 近来黑色皮裤似乎风靡一时.

NOTE ON USAGE 用法: In British English **quite** can have different meanings partly depending on the intonation of the sentence. 在英式英语中, **quite** 一词有时靠句中的语调可表达不同的意思. **1** If **quite** carries the main stress when used with gradable words (ie those describing qualities which can be of different strengths or degrees) it has a negative meaning such as 'not very' 若 **quite** 有主要重音, 与之连用的是表示程度的词(即其性质可有强弱或程度差别者), 则 **quite** 有否定含义, 如'不很': *He's 'quite handsome.* 他不太漂亮. ○ *She played 'quite well.* 她表演得不怎么好. **2** If **quite** receives secondary or no stress the sentence expresses more approval and possibly surprise 如 **quite** 有次重音或无重音, 则全句较具褒义, 也可能表示惊奇: *I was quite 'pleased.* 我挺高兴. ○ *I think he's quite 'handsome.* 我认为他够漂亮的了. **3** When **quite** is used with a word expressing an absolute quality, it means 'completely' and does not usually carry the main stress 若 **quite** 与表示绝对的词连用时, 其意为'完全', 通常不带主要重音: *It was quite 'wonderful.* 那可太妙了. ○ *She played quite 'brilliantly.* 她表演得优美极了. But compare 试比较 *I ˌquite a'gree with you* (= I entirely agree with you). 我完全同意你的意见.

quits /kwɪts; kwɪts/ *adj* (idm 习语) **be quits (with sb)** be on even terms after a debt of money, etc has been repaid (因已偿清财物等)抵消的, 对等的: *Are we quits or do you still owe me a pound?* 咱们是已经两相抵消了呢, 还是你仍欠我一镑呢? **call it quits** ⇨ CALL². **double or quits** ⇨ DOUBLE⁴.

quiver¹ /'kwɪvə(r); 'kwɪvɚ/ *v* [I, Tn] (cause sth to) tremble slightly or vibrate (使某事物)轻微颤动, 抖动: *The moth quivered its wings.* 蛾子抖动着翅膀. ○ *a quivering leaf* 颤动着的叶子 ○ *Quivering with rage she slammed the door shut.* 她气得浑身发抖, 砰的一声使劲把门关上了.

▷ **quiver** *n* quivering sound or movement 颤抖的声音或动作: *A quiver of expectancy ran through the audience.* 全场引颈以待, 群情鼎沸. ○ *the quiver of an eyelid* 眼跳.

quiver² /'kwɪvə(r); 'kwɪvɚ/ *n* case used by archers for carrying arrows 箭筒; 箭壶. ⇨illus at ARCHERY 见 ARCHERY 插图.

qui vive /ˌki: 'vi:v; ˌki 'viv/ (idm 习语) **on the qui 'vive** watching for sth to happen; alert; watchful 注视某事物发生; 警惕着; 注意着.

quix·otic /kwɪk'sɒtɪk; kwɪk'sɑtɪk/ *adj* noble, unselfish or gallant in an extravagant or impractical way 堂吉诃德式的; 空想而侠义的. ▷ **quix·ot·ic·ally** /-klɪ; -klɪ/ *adv*.

quiz /kwɪz; kwɪz/ *n* (*pl* **quizzes**) competition, esp on TV or radio, in which people try to answer questions to test their knowledge 竞赛, 比赛(尤指电视或电台中人们竞相回答问题以测验其知识者): *take part in a quiz* 参加知识竞赛 ○ *a sports, music, general knowledge, etc quiz* 运动、音乐、一般知识等的竞赛 ○ [attrib 作定语] *a quiz game/programme/show* 问答竞赛[游戏/节目].

▷ **quiz** *v* (**-zz-**) [Tn, Tn·pr] **~ sb (about sb/sth)** ask sb questions 问某人问题: *She quizzed him all night about the people he'd seen.* 她整夜盘问他都见到谁了.

□ **'quiz-master** *n* = QUESTION-MASTER (QUESTION¹).

quiz·zical /'kwɪzɪkl; 'kwɪzɪkl/ *adj* in a questioning manner, esp when amused 疑问的; (尤指)戏弄的, 揶揄的: *with a quizzical smile* 带着嘲弄的微笑 ○ *He continued in a quizzical tone.* 他以揶揄的声调继续说. ▷ **quiz·zic·ally** /-klɪ; -klɪ/ *adv*: *She looked at me quizzically.* 她疑惑地看着我.

quod /kwɒd; kwɑd/ *n* [U] (*sl* 俚 *esp Brit*) prison (used esp in the expressions shown) 监狱(尤用于以下示例): *go to quod* 进监狱 ○ *in/out of quod* 入[出]狱.

quoit /kɔɪt; *US* kwɔɪt; kwɔɪt/ *n* **(a)** [C] ring, made of eg metal, rubber or rope, that is thrown onto an upright peg (掷向桩子用的)环(如用金属、橡胶、绳等制成的). **(b) quoits** [sing *v*] game in which this is done, esp when on board a ship 掷环游戏(尤指在船上玩的): *play deck quoits* 在甲板上玩掷环游戏.

quorum /'kwɔ:rəm; 'kwɔrəm/ *n* (usu *sing* 通常作单数) minimum number of people who must be present at a meeting (of a committee, etc) before it can proceed and its decisions, etc can be considered valid (会议的)法定人数: *have/form a quorum* 具备[构成]法定人数.

quota /'kwəʊtə; 'kwotə/ *n* **1** fixed share that must be done or contributed or received 定额; 限额; 配额: *have one's full quota of rations* 有自己全份的配给量 ○ *I'm going home now — I've done my quota of work for the day.* 我现在回家了 —— 我已经完成了今天的工作定额. **2** maximum number or amount of people or things allowed, eg to enter a country (人或事物的)最高限额(如准予人境者): *Grain imports are controlled by strict quotas.* 谷物进口量受最高限额的严格控制.

quo·ta·tion /kwəʊ'teɪʃn; kwo'teʃən/ *n* **1** [U] quoting or being quoted (对他人语言或文字的)引用, 引述, 引证: *Support your argument by quotation.* 引用他人的话来支持你的论点. **2** (also *infml* 口语作 **quote**) [C] group of words taken from a book, play, speech, etc and used again, usu by sb other than the original author 语录; 引文; 引用语: *a dictionary of quotations* 语录汇编 ○ *She finished her speech with a quotation from Shakespeare.* 她讲话结束时引用了莎士比亚的语录. ⇨App 3 见附录 3. **3** [C] (statement of the) current price of stocks or commodities 行情; 牌价: *the latest quotations from the Stock Exchange* 股票交易所的最新行情. **4** (also *infml* 口语作 **quote**) [C] estimate of the likely cost of a piece of work 估价; 报价: *The insurance company requires three quotations for repairs to the car.* 保险公司要三家修理这辆汽车的报价单. Cf 参看 ESTIMATE[1] 2.

□ **quo'tation-marks** (also **quotes**) *n* [pl] pair of punctuation marks (' ' or " ") used at the beginning and end of words that are being quoted 引号(' '或" "). ⇨App 3 见附录 3. Cf 参看 INVERTED COMMAS (INVERT).

quote /kwəʊt; kwot/ *v* **1** [I, Ipr, Tn, Tn·pr] **~ (sth) (from sb/sth)** repeat in speech or writing (words previously said or written by another person) 引用, 引述, 引证(他人的语言或文字): *You said (and I quote): 'I have always loved her.'* 你曾说过(我引用你的原话): '我一直爱着她.' ○ *He's always quoting verses from the Bible.* 他经常引用《圣经》中的章节. ○ *She is quoted as saying she disagrees with the decision.* 用她的话说, 她不同意这一决定. ○ *I think he's going to resign, but please don't quote me*, ie because I am not sure if it is true. 我想他要辞职了, 可请不要说是我说的(因为我没有把握是否确实). **2** [Tn, Dn·n] mention (sb/sth) in support of a statement 提到(某人[某事物])以支持某论点: *Can you quote (me) an example of what you mean?* 你能否(给我)举个例子, 以说明你的意思? **3** [Tn, Tn·pr, Dn·n] **~ sth (at sth)** name (an amount) as the price of sth 报(价); 开(价): *The shares are currently being quoted at 54 pence a share.* 该股票现在的报价是每股54便士. ○ *This is the best price I can quote you.* 这是我给你开出的对你最有利的价钱了. Cf 参看 ESTIMATE[2] 2.

▷ **quote** *n* (*infml* 口) **1** [C] = QUOTATION 2. **2 quotes** [pl] = QUOTATION-MARKS (QUOTATION): *His words are in quotes.* 他的话是加了引号的. **3** (idm 习语) **'quote (... 'unquote)** (used when speaking to show the beginning (and end) of a passage being quoted, esp when the speaker disagrees with it 用于说话时表示一段引文的开始(和结尾), 尤指说话人不以为然者): *This quote startlingly original novel unquote is both boring and badly written.* 这部所谓的'不同凡响的小说'云云, 内容既枯燥、文笔又拙劣. **4** (*infml* 口) = QUOTATION 4.

quot·able *adj* that can be or that deserves to be quoted 可引用的; 值得引用的: *full of quotable quotes* 充满了值得引用的语录.

quoth /kwəʊθ; kwoθ/ *v* [Tn] (1st and 3rd person singular past tense only 仅用于过去式单数第1及第3人称) (*arch* 古) said 说过: *quoth I/he/she* 我[他/她]说过.

quo·tient /'kwəʊʃnt; 'kwoʃənt/ *n* (*mathematics* 数) number obtained when one number is divided by another 商(除数除以被除数的得数).

qv /ˌkju: 'vi:; ˌkju 'vi/ *abbr* 缩写 = (*fml* 文) which may be referred to (Latin *quod vide*), eg showing a cross-reference 见该项, 参看该条(源自拉丁文 *quod vide*)(如表示相互参看条目).

Q

R r

R, r /ɑ:(r); ɑr/ *n* (*pl* **R's, r's** /ɑ:z; ɑrz/) **1** the eighteenth letter of the English alphabet 英语字母表的第十八个字母: *'Rabbit' begins with (an) R/'R'.* rabbit一字是以r字母开始的. **2** (idm 习语) **roll one's r's** ⇨ ROLL². **the three 'R's** reading, (w)riting and (a)rithmetic, as the basis of an elementary education 基本三会(指作为初等教育基础的读、写、算).

R *abbr* 缩写 = **1** Queen; King (Latin *Regina*; *Rex*) 女王, 国王(源自拉丁文*Regina*、*Rex*): *Elizabeth R* 伊丽莎白女王. **2** (also *symb* 符号为 ®) (*commerce* 商) registered (trademark) (商标): *Scotch* ® 苏格兰威士忌 ®. **3** (*US politics* 政) Republican (party): *James W Sistino (R)* 詹姆斯·W·西斯提诺(共和党人). Cf 参看 D. **4** River: *R Thames*, eg on a map 泰晤士河(如地图上的标示).

r *abbr* 缩写 = **1** recto. **2** right. Cf 参看 L 1.

RA /ˌɑ:r 'eɪ; ˌɑr 'e/ *abbr* 缩写 = (*Brit*) **1** Royal Academy; Royal Academician 英国皇家艺术学会; 英国皇家艺术学会会员: *George Tophill RA* 英国皇家艺术学会会员乔治·托普希尔 ○ *be an RA* 为英国皇家艺术学会会员. **2** Royal Artillery 英国皇家炮兵.

R

rabbi /'ræbaɪ; 'ræbaɪ/ *n* (*pl* **~s**) (title of a) spiritual leader of a Jewish congregation; teacher of the Jewish law 拉比(犹太教教士及其头衔; 犹太教法学导师): *the Chief Rabbi*, eg of Jewish communities in Britain 首席拉比(例如英国犹太人社区的教会领袖).

▷ **rab·bin·ical** /rə'bɪnɪkl; rə'bɪnɪkḷ/ *adj* of rabbis; of Jewish doctrine or law 犹太教教士的; 犹太教教义或法规的.

rab·bit /'ræbɪt; 'ræbɪt/ *n* **1** [C] small burrowing animal of the hare family with long ears and a short furry tail 兔; 兔子. ⇨illus at App 1 见附录1插图, page iii. Cf 参看 HARE. **2** [U] (**a**) its fur 兔的毛皮: *gloves lined with rabbit* 兔毛衬里的手套. (**b**) its flesh used as meat (食用的)兔肉: [attrib 作定语] *rabbit pie* 兔肉馅饼. **3** [C] (*Brit infml* 口) poor player of a game, esp tennis 竞技活动(尤指网球)的蹩脚运动员.

▷ **rab·bit** *v* **1** [Ipr, Ip] **~ on (about sb/sth)** (*infml derog* 口, 贬) talk lengthily or in a rambling and pointless way 冗长地或信口开河、无针对性地谈: *What are you rabbiting on about?* 你在胡诌些什么? **2** [I] (usu 通常作 **go rabbiting**) hunt rabbits 去猎兔.

rab·bity *adj* like a rabbit in appearance, smell or taste (外貌、气味或味道)像兔子一般的.

□ **'rabbit-hutch** *n* wooden cage for rabbits (木制)兔笼, 兔棚.

'rabbit punch sharp blow made with the edge of the hand on the back of sb's neck (用掌边对某人颈背的)重击.

'rabbit-warren *n* (**a**) area of land full of connected burrows made by wild rabbits 野兔繁殖区(有野兔挖的相接的洞穴). (**b**) (*fig usu derog* 比喻, 通常作贬义) building or district full of narrow winding passages 有许多弯曲狭窄通道的建筑物或地方.

rabble /'ræbl; 'ræbḷ/ *n* **1** [C] disorderly crowd; mob 乱纷纷的人群; 乌合之众; 暴民. **2 the rabble** [sing] (*derog* 贬) the common people; the lowest social classes 平民百姓; 社会最低阶层: *speeches, etc appealing to the rabble* 对民众很有吸引力的讲话等.

□ **'rabble-rouser** *n* person who tries to rouse the passions of the mob, eg for political aims 煽动民众的人(如为达到政治目的). **'rabble-rousing** *adj*, *n* [U]: *a rabble-rousing speaker, speech* 作煽动性宣传的演说者、演说.

Rab·el·ais·ian /ˌræbə'leɪzɪən; ˌræbḷ'ezɪən/ *adj* full of bawdy humour, in the style of the French writer Rabelais 法国幽默讽刺作家拉伯雷风格的; 富有拉伯雷式的粗俗幽默情趣的: *Rabelaisian prose* 具有拉伯雷风格的散文.

ra·bid /'ræbɪd; *US also* 'reɪbɪd; 'ræbɪd, 'rebɪd/ *adj* **1** suffering from rabies 患狂犬病的: *a rabid dog, fox, etc* 发疯的狗、狐狸等. **2** (*fig* 比喻) (of feelings or opinions) violent or extreme; fanatical (指情绪或见解)疯狂的, 极端的, 狂热的: *rabid hate, greed, etc* 极其愤恨、贪心等 ○ *a rabid racist* 极端的种族主义者.

ra·bies /'reɪbi:z; 'rebiz/ *n* [U] fatal virus disease causing madness in dogs, foxes and other animals, transmitted to humans usu by a bite 狂犬病, 恐水症, 瘈咬病. Cf 参看 HYDROPHOBIA.

RAC /ˌɑ:r eɪ 'si:; ˌɑr e 'si/ *abbr* 缩写 = (*Brit*) Royal Automobile Club 英国皇家汽车俱乐部.

rac·coon (*esp US*) (*Brit* also **ra·coon**) /rə'ku:n; *US* ræ-; ræ'kun/ (also *US infml* 美式口语作 **coon**) *n* **1** [C] small N American flesh-eating mammal with a pointed snout and a bushy black-ringed tail 浣熊(北美产的食肉的哺乳动物). **2** [U] (*US*) its fur 浣熊的毛皮.

race¹ /reɪs; res/ *n* **1 ~ (against/with sb/sth); ~ (between A and B)** (**a**) [C] contest of speed between runners, horses, vehicles, etc to see which reaches a certain place first, or does sth first (人、马、车等的)速度竞赛: *a 'horse-race* 赛马 ○ *a 'boat-race* 划船比赛 ○ *a half-'mile race* 半英里赛跑 ○ *run a race with sb* 同某人赛跑 ○ *We had a race* (ie a great hurry) *to repair the house before winter.* 我们争取在冬季到来以前修好房子. (**b**) **the races** [pl] =RACE-MEETING: *a day at the races* 赛马大会的一天. ⇨Usage at SPORT 用法见SPORT. **2** competition or rivalry 比赛; 竞争: *the race for the presidency* 总统竞选. **3** [C] strong fast current of water in a river, the sea, etc (河、海等的)急流: *a tidal race* 潮汐引起的急流 ○ *a 'mill-race*, ie a channel taking water to the wheel of a water-mill 磨坊水磨的进水槽. **4** (idm 习语) **a ˌrace against 'time** desperate effort to do or finish sth before a certain time 和时间赛跑: *It was a race against time to stop people dying from starvation.* 为抢救那些即将饿死的人而分秒必争. **the rat race** ⇨ RAT.

□ **'racecard** *n* programme of the races, times and runners at a race-meeting 赛马项目单.

'racecourse *n* (*esp Brit*) (*US* usu 美式英语通常作 **'race-track**) ground where horse-races are run 赛马跑道; 赛马场.

'racegoer *n* person who regularly attends horse-races 经常观看赛马的人.

'racehorse *n* horse bred or kept to run in races 赛马用的马.

'race-meeting *n* (*Brit*) series of horse-races at one course held at fixed times on one or several days (一天或几天中时间固定的)赛马大会.

'race-track *n* **1** (usu oval) track, esp for vehicle races (通常为椭圆形的)跑道(尤指赛车的). **2** (*US*) = RACECOURSE.

race² /reɪs; res/ *v* **1** (**a**) [I, Ipr, It] **~ (against/with sb/sth)** take part in a race 参加速度竞赛: *race for the prize/to win the prize* 参加有奖速度比赛 ○ *The lorries were racing against each other.* 一辆辆的卡车在争先恐后地行驶. ○ *The cars raced round the track.* 汽车围着跑道进行比赛. (**b**) [Tn, Tn·pr] compete with (sb/sth) in speed 与(某人[某事物])进行速度竞赛: *I'll race you to school*, ie try to get there before you do. 我要和你比赛看谁先到学校. **2** (**a**) [I, Ipr, Ip, It] move very fast 急速移动: *race along (the road)* (沿路)飞奔 ○ *The policeman raced after the thief.* 警察追着那个贼. ○ *The days seemed to race by/past.* 光阴似箭. ○ *We had to race to catch the train.* 我们得快走, 好赶上火车. ⇨Usage at RUN¹ 用法见RUN¹. (**b**) [Tn, Tn·pr] cause (sb/sth) to move very fast 使(某人[某物])急速移动: *The patient had to be raced to hospital.* 病人得火速送往医院. **3** [I, Tn] compete in (esp) horse-racing or cause (eg a horse, vehicle) to compete in races 赛(尤指赛马); 使(马、车等)进行速度竞赛: *She races at all the big meetings.* 她参加所有大规模的赛马比赛. ○ *race pigeons, dogs, etc* 信鸽比赛、赛狗 ○ *race saloon cars, bikes, etc in rallies* 在公路赛车会上赛轿车、自行车等 ○ *The filly has been raced twice this season.* 这匹小牝马本季度曾两次参赛. **4** [I, Tn] (cause sth to) operate at high speed (使某物)高速

运转: *Don't race your engine*, ie make it run fast when not in gear. 不要让发动机空转. ○ *The driver waited for the green light, his engine racing.* 那司机等候绿灯放行, 让发动机空转着.

▷ **ra·cer** *n* horse, boat, car, etc used for racing 比赛用的马、小船、汽车等.

ra·cing *n* [U] hobby, sport or profession of competing in horse or vehicle races 赛马或赛车的嗜好、运动或职业: [attrib 作定语] *a 'racing man* 赛马迷(或赛车迷) ○ *a 'racing car, yacht, etc*, ie designed for racing 比赛用的汽车、快艇等 ○ *keep/run a 'racing stable*, ie for horses trained to race 经营[管理]赛马马厩.

race³ /reɪs; res/ *n* **1** [C, U] **(a)** any of several large subdivisions of mankind sharing physical characteristics, eg colour of skin, colour and type of hair, shape of eyes and nose 人种; 种族: *the Caucasian, Mongolian, Negro, etc race* 高加索、蒙古、黑色等人种 ○ *people of mixed race* 混血种的人. **(b)** [C] any of the main species, breeds or varieties of animals or plants (动植物的)类, 属, 种, 族: *the human race*, ie mankind 人类 ○ *breed a race of cattle that can survive drought* 饲养能耐干旱的一种牛. **2** [C] group of people with a common culture, history, language, descent, etc 民族: *the Anglo-Saxon, Germanic, Nordic, etc races* 盎格鲁一撒克逊、日耳曼、北欧日耳曼等民族 ○ *The British are an island race.* 英国人是以岛为家的民族. **3** [U] (*fml* 文) ancestry; descent 世系; 血统: *people of ancient and noble race* 古老贵族的后裔.

□ **'race relations** relations between two or more races in the same community (同一社区中的)种族关系: *Race relations are good here.* 此地种族关系良好. ○ *Race relations is a sensitive issue.* 种族关系是敏感的问题.

'race-riot *n* outbreak of violence due to hostility between races in the same community 种族骚乱(同一社区中的种族由于相互仇视而产生的暴力事件).

ra·ceme /'ræsi:m, *also* rə'si:m; *US* reɪ-; re'sim/ *n* (*botany* 植) flower cluster having separate flowers on stalks evenly spaced along a central stem, with the lower flowers opening first (as in lupins, hyacinths, etc) 总状花序, 串状花(如羽扇豆属植物、风信子等的花序).

ra·cial /'reɪʃl; 'reʃəl/ *adj* characteristic of race³(1a); due to or resulting from race 人种的; 种族的; 由种族引起的: *a racial feature, type, difference, etc* 人种特征、类型、差异等 ○ *racial conflict, harmony, hatred, pride* 种族冲突、和睦、仇恨、优越感 ○ *racial discrimination* 种族歧视.

▷ **ra·cial·ism** /-ʃəlɪzəm; -ʃəl,ɪzəm/ (also **racism**) *n* [U] **1** belief that human abilities, etc depend on race and that some races are superior to others 种族主义; 种族偏见; 种族优越感. **2** (aggressive behaviour, speech, etc showing) hostility between races 种族仇视; 表现种族仇视的挑衅行为、讲话等.

ra·cial·ist /-ʃəlɪst; -ʃəlɪst/ (also **racist**) *n, adj* (of or like a) believer in racialism, esp one who is hostile to races thought to be inferior 种族主义者; (似)种族主义的: *a racialist theory, book, speech* 宣扬种族主义的理论、书、讲话.

ra·cially /-ʃəlɪ; -ʃəlɪ/ *adv*: *a racially diverse community* 多种族的社区.

ra·cily, ra·ci·ness ⇨ RACY.

ra·cism /'reɪsɪzəm; 'resɪzəm/ *n* [U] =RACIALISM. ▷ **ra·cist** /'reɪsɪst; 'resɪst/ *n, adj* =RACIALIST.

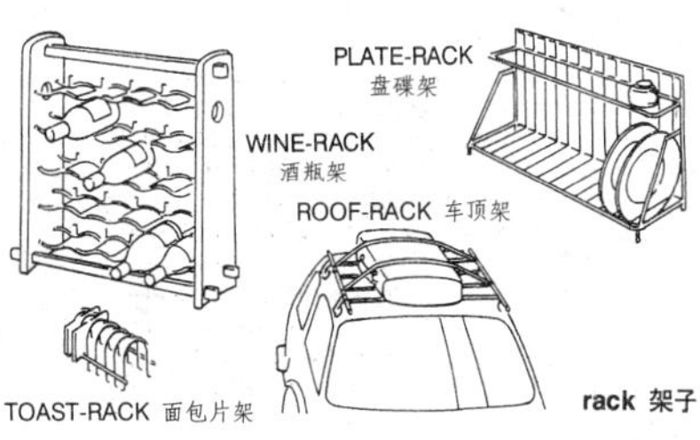

rack 架子

rack¹ /ræk; ræk/ *n* **1** (often in compounds 常用以构成复合词) framework, usu with bars or pegs, for holding things or for hanging things on (放东西或挂东西用的)架子: *a 'plate-rack* 盘碟架 ○ *a 'wine-rack*, ie for holding wine bottles 酒瓶架 ○ *a 'toast-rack* 面包片架 ○ *a 'hat-rack* 帽架. **2** type of shelf for light luggage, coats, etc over the seats of a bus, train, plane, etc (公共汽车、火车、飞机等座位上方放置轻便行李、衣物等的)行李架: *a 'luggage-rack* 行李架. **3** rod, bar or rail with teeth or cogs, into which those of a wheel, gear, etc fit 齿条; 齿板; 齿轨: *a 'steering rack*, eg on a cable car 转向齿条(如缆车上的). Cf 参看 PINION².

□ **'rack-railway** (also *esp US* **cog-railway**) *n* railway that has a cogged central rail with which a cogged wheel on the train engages to drive the train up a steep slope 齿轨铁道(设有带齿的中轨, 与列车带齿的车轮啮合, 将列车送上陡坡).

rack² /ræk; ræk/ *n* **1** (usu 通常作 **the rack**) (formerly) instrument of torture consisting of a frame with rollers to which a person's wrists and ankles were tied so that his joints were stretched when the rollers were turned (旧时)拉肢拷问台(一种刑具): *put sb on the rack* 对某人施以拉肢之刑. **2** (idm 习语) **on the 'rack** in severe pain or mental distress (肉体或精神上)受极大折磨.

▷ **rack** *v* **1** [Tn] torture (sb) on the rack 以拉肢之刑拷问或折磨(某人). **2** [Tn esp passive 尤用于被动语态] (of disease, pain or mental distress) cause agony to (sb) (指疾病、疼痛、苦恼等)使(某人)极为痛苦: *racked with pain, fever, etc* 因疼痛、发烧等而痛苦 ○ *A coughing fit racked her whole body.* 她一阵咳嗽全身都十分难受. ○ *a voice racked by sobs/weeping* 抽抽搭搭[哭哭啼啼]的痛苦的声音 ○ *racked by (feelings of) guilt, remorse, doubt, etc* 深受内疚、悔恨、怀疑等之苦. **3** (idm 习语) **rack one's 'brain(s)** try very hard to think of sth or recall sth 苦思某事; 努力回忆某事: *We racked our brains for an answer.* 我们为寻找答案而绞尽脑汁. ○ *I've been racking my brains (trying) to remember his name.* 我一直在回想他的名字.

□ **'rack-rent** *n* [C, U] unfairly high rent 过高的租金.

rack³ /ræk; ræk/ *n* (idm 习语) **go to ,rack and 'ruin** fall into a ruined or disorganized state through neglect 因忽视而致毁坏、混乱或瓦解: *The old empty house soon went to rack and ruin.* 这所旧的空房子很快就毁坏了. ○ *This country is going to rack and ruin; we need a change of government.* 这个国家正在分崩离析, 我们需要更换政府.

racket¹ (also **rac·quet**) /'rækɪt; 'rækɪt/ *n* **1** [C] bat with a round or oval stringed frame, used for hitting the ball in tennis, badminton, etc (网球、羽毛球等的)球拍. ⇨ illus at SQUASH, TENNIS 见 SQUASH、TENNIS 插图. **2** **rackets** (also **racquets**) [sing *v*] ball-game for two or four people played with rackets and a small hard ball in a four-walled court 墙网球(二人或四人玩的球戏, 使用球拍和一质硬小球, 场地四面有围墙): [attrib 作定语] *a rackets court, ball, match* 墙网球的球场、球、比赛. Cf 参看 SQUASH *n* 3.

□ **'racket-press** *n* frame worked by a spring, used for holding a racket tightly when not in use, to prevent warping, etc 球拍夹(有弹簧的架框, 用以保存球拍).

racket² /'rækɪt; 'rækɪt/ *n* (*infml* 口) **1** [sing] loud noise; uproar or noisy disturbance 喧嚷; 吵闹: *What a racket the children are making!* 这些孩子太吵了! ○ *The students kicked up no end of a racket* (ie were very noisy and boisterous) *in the street.* 这些学生在街上大吵大闹. **2** [C] **(a)** dishonest or illegal way of getting money 敲诈; 勒索; 诈骗: *the gambling/protection/drugs racket* 赌博[收取保护费/贩毒]的勾当 ○ *Police investigating the fraud suspected him of being in on* (ie profiting by) *the racket.* 警方调查这一诈骗案时怀疑他涉嫌参与诈骗活动. **(b)** business or occupation 生意; 职业: *What's your racket?* 你是干哪一行的? ○ *How did she get into the modelling racket?* 她是怎样当上模特儿的?

▷ **racket** *v* [I, Ip] **~ (about/around)** (*infml* 口) move about noisily; join in wild social activities 到处闹腾; 参加喧闹的社交活动.

rack·et·eer /,rækə'tɪə(r); ,rækɪt'ɪr/ *n* (*derog* 贬) person involved in or controlling a racket²(2) 敲诈勒索的骗子或主谋. **rack·et·eer·ing** *n* [U] (*derog* 贬) activity of racketeers 敲诈勒索活动.

rack·ety *adj* (*infml* 口) noisy 嘈杂的; 吵闹的: *a rackety old bicycle* 嘎吱嘎吱响的旧自行车.

ra·con·teur /ˌrækɒnˈtɜ:(r); ˌrækɑnˈtɝ/ *n* person who tells stories skilfully and wittily 善于讲故事的人: *She's a brilliant raconteur.* 她是讲故事的高手.

ra·coon =RACCOON.

racy /ˈreɪsɪ; ˈresɪ/ *adj* (**-ier, -iest**) **1** (of speech, writing, etc) lively or spirited; vivid (指语言、文字等)生动的, 活泼的, 有活力的: *a racy account of his adventures* 对他冒险经历的生动叙述. **2** (*infml* 口) slightly improper or indecent 有失体统的; 不雅的: *Her racy stories can be rather shocking.* 她那些下流的故事讲起来有时很让人吃惊. **3** strong and distinctive in flavour 味浓而富有特色的: *a racy wine* 醇厚的酒. ▷ **ra·cily** /-ɪlɪ; -ɪlɪ/ *adv.* **ra·ci·ness** *n* [U].

RADA /ˈrɑ:də; ˈrɑdə/ *abbr* 缩写 = (*Brit*) Royal Academy of Dramatic Art 英国皇家戏剧艺术学院: *a student at RADA* 英国皇家戏剧艺术学院的学生.

ra·dar /ˈreɪdɑ:(r); ˈredɑr/ *n* [U] (**a**) system for detecting the presence, position or movement of solid objects within its range by sending out short radio waves which they reflect 雷达: *locate an aircraft by radar* 用雷达测定一飞机的位置. (**b**) equipment used for this 雷达装置: *Enemy ships were detected on the radar (screen).* 敌舰的影像已显现在雷达(屏幕)上. ○ [attrib 作定语] *a radar operator, installation, scanner* 雷达手、设备、扫描天线. Cf 参看 SONAR.

R

□ ˈ**radar trap** (also ˈ**speed trap**) section of road where the police use a radar device to detect vehicles travelling faster than the speed limit 雷达监测路段(警方用雷达装置监测超速车辆的路段).

ra·dial /ˈreɪdɪəl; ˈredɪəl/ *adj* of or arranged like rays or radii; having bars, lines, etc that radiate from a central point 放射(式)的; 辐射(状)的; 径向的; 星形的: *radial spokes*, eg in a bicycle wheel 径向辐(如自行车的辐条) ○ *a radial engine*, ie one with cylinders pointing outwards from a central crankshaft 星形发动机.

▷ **ra·dial** *n* (also **radial-ply tyre**) tyre with the cords in its outer casing arranged radially to the hub of the wheel, so making it stronger and able to grip better on wet road surfaces 径向帘布轮胎; 子午(线轮)胎; 辐射状轮胎. Cf 参看 CROSS-PLY.

ra·di·ally /-ɪəlɪ; -ɪəlɪ/ *adv.*

ra·di·ant /ˈreɪdɪənt; ˈredɪənt/ *adj* **1** [attrib 作定语] sending out rays of light; shining brightly 光芒四射的; 光辉灿烂的: *the radiant sun* 光辉灿烂的太阳. **2** ~ **(with sth)** (of a person, his eyes, look, etc) bright with joy, hope or love (指人、人的眼睛、面容等)容光焕发的; 喜形于色的: *a radiant face, smile* 容光焕发的脸、喜气洋洋的微笑 ○ *radiant beauty* 解颐美人 ○ *She was radiant with joy at her wedding.* 她在举行婚礼时喜气洋洋. ○ *You look absolutely radiant!* 你看上去真是满面春风! **3** (*physics* 物) [attrib 作定语] (**a**) transmitting heat or energy by radiation 发出辐射热或能的: *a radiant heater* 辐射加热器. (**b**) (of heat or energy) transmitted by radiation (指热或能)辐射的.

▷ **ra·di·ance** /-əns; -əns/ *n* [U] quality of being radiant (1, 2) 发光; 灿烂; 容光焕发.

ra·di·antly *adv*: *smiling radiantly* 喜笑颜开.

ra·di·ate /ˈreɪdɪeɪt; ˈredɪˌet/ *v* **1** (**a**) [Tn] send out rays of (light or heat) 发出(光或热): *a stove that radiates warmth* 发出热量的火炉. (**b**) [Ipr] ~ **from sth** (of light or heat) be sent out from sth by radiation (指光或热)从某物中发出: *warmth radiating from the stove* 从火炉中散发出来的热量. **2** (**a**) [Tn] (*fig* 比喻) (of a person) give forth a feeling of (sth) (指人)显露(某种神情或样子): *radiating confidence, enthusiasm, health, etc* 显示出信心、热情、健康等. (**b**) [Ipr] ~ **from sb/sth** (*fig* 比喻) (of a feeling) be given forth by sb/sb's eyes, etc (指感情)自某人[某人的眼睛]等处流露出来. **3** (of lines, etc) spread out like radii from a central point (指线路等)自中心向各方伸展: *Five roads radiate from this roundabout.* 有五条道路以这个环状交叉路为中心向各方伸展开.

ra·di·ation /ˌreɪdɪˈeɪʃn; ˌredɪˈeʃən/ *n* **1** [U] (**a**) (the sending out of) heat, energy, etc in the form of rays (热、能等的)放射; 辐射的热、能等: *a combination of radiation and convection*, eg in a gas fire 辐射和对流的结合(如在煤气炉中). (**b**) (the sending out of) rays and atomic particles from radioactive substances (自放射性物质中放射出的)射线和原子粒子; 放射; 放射现象: *a low/high level of radiation* 低[高]强度辐射 ○ [attrib 作定语] *Some cancers are treated by radiation therapy.* 有些癌症可用放射疗法治疗. **2** [C] thing that is radiated, esp radioactive particles 放射物; (尤指)放射性微粒, 放射线: *radiations emitted by an X-ray machine* X射线机放射出来的放射线.

□ **radiˈation sickness** illness caused when the body is exposed to high radiation, eg from radioactive material or X-rays 放射病; 辐射病.

ra·di·ator /ˈreɪdɪeɪtə(r); ˈredɪˌetɚ/ *n* **1** apparatus for radiating heat into rooms, etc, esp a metal casing through which hot water or steam is circulated (取暖用的)散热器; (尤指以热水或蒸汽循环供热的)暖气装置. **2** device for cooling the engine of a vehicle or an aircraft (车辆或飞机之发动机的)冷却器: *This car has a fan-cooled radiator.* 这辆汽车有一个风扇冷却器. ⇨ illus at App 1 见附录1插图, page xii.

rad·ical /ˈrædɪkl; ˈrædɪkl/ *adj* [usu attrib 通常作定语] **1** of or from the root or base; fundamental 根本的; 基本的: *a radical flaw, error, fault, etc in the system* 制度中的基本缺陷、错误、缺点等. **2** thorough or complete; drastic 彻底的; 完全的; 激烈的: *radical reforms, changes, etc* 彻底的改革、改变等. **3** favouring thorough political or social reform; holding extreme views 赞成实行彻底的政治或社会改革的; 持激进观点的: *a radical politician, thinker, writer, etc* 思想激进的政治家、思想家、作家等 ○ *She is radical in her demands.* 她的要求十分偏激.

▷ **rad·ical** *n* **1** person with radical(3) opinions 激进分子. **2** (*mathematics* 数) quantity forming or expressed as the root of another 根数; 根式; 根号. **3** (*chemistry* 化) group of atoms forming part of a compound and not changing during chemical reactions 基; 根; 原子团.

rad·ic·al·ism /-kəlɪzəm; -klˌɪzm/ *n* [U] (belief in) radical (3) ideas and principles 激进主义; 激进的思想和原则.

rad·ic·ally /-klɪ; -klɪ/ *adv*: *radically altered, improved, etc* 根本地改变、改善等.

rad·icle /ˈrædɪkl; ˈrædɪkl/ *n* part of a plant embryo that develops into the main root 幼根; 胚根.

radii *pl* of RADIUS.

ra·dio /ˈreɪdɪəʊ; ˈredɪˌo/ *n* (*pl* **~s**) **1** [U] process of sending and receiving messages, etc by electromagnetic waves without a connecting wire 无线电传送: *contact a ship at sea by radio* 用无线电与海上的船只联络 ○ [attrib 作定语] ˈ*radio waves*, *communiˈcations* 无线电波、无线电通讯 ○ *a radio ˈtelephone* 无线电话. **2** [C] (**a**) (also ˈ**radio set**) apparatus, eg on ships or planes, for sending and receiving messages in this way 无线电收发报机(如船只、飞机等的): *hear a gale warning on/over a ship's radio* 在船上的无线电收发报机中听到大风警报 ○ [attrib 作定语] *a radio receiver, transmitter* 无线电接收机、发射机. (**b**) (also *dated* 旧作 **wireless**) apparatus, eg in the house, for receiving sound broadcasting 无线电; 收音机: *a portable, transistor radio* 便携式的、晶体管的收音机. **3** (often 常作 **the radio**) [U, sing] sound broadcasting by this means 无线电广播: *I heard it on the radio.* 我从无线电广播中听到了这消息. ○ *She always listens to the radio.* 她经常听无线电广播. ○ *a play specially written for radio* 专为无线电广播编写的剧本 ○ *Do you prefer radio or television?* 你喜欢听广播, 还是喜欢看电视? ○ [attrib 作定语] *a radio programme, announcer, station* 无线电广播节目、播音员、电台.

▷ **ra·dio** *v* (*pt, pp* **radioed**) [Ipr, Tn, Tn·pr, Tf, Dn·f, Dpr·f, Dpr·w, Dpr·t no passive 不用于被动语态] send a message by radio 用无线电发送讯息; 发报: *radio (to sb) for help* 用无线电(向某人)呼救 ○ *radio (sb) one's position* 用无线电告知(某人)自己的位置 ○ *We radioed (to) headquarters that we were in trouble.* 我们向大本营发报, 说我们遇到了困难. ○ *Radio to them to come/where we are.* 用无线电通知他们前来[告知他们我们所在的地方].

□ ˌ**radio asˈtronomy** branch of astronomy in which radio waves from space are received and analysed 射电天文学.

ˈ**radio car**, ˈ**radio cab** car or cab equipped with a radio for communication 装有无线电通讯设备的汽车或计程车.

ˌ**radio-conˈtrolled** *adj* controlled from a distance by radio signals 由无线电控制的: *a ˌradio-controlled ˈtaxi* 由无线电控制的计程车.

ˌ**radio-ˈfrequency** *n* frequency of electromagnetic waves used in radio and TV transmission, between 10 kilocycles per second and 3000000 megacycles per second 射频, 无线电频率(无线电传递和电视发送所用电磁波的频率, 其范围从每秒10千周到3 000 000兆周之间).

ˈ**radiogram** *n* **1** telegram sent by radio 无线电报. **2** (*Brit*) (esp formerly) combined radio and record player (尤指旧时)收音电唱两用机.

ˌ**radio ˈtelescope** apparatus for finding stars, tracking spacecraft, etc by means of radio waves from outer space 射电望远镜(藉来自外层空间的无线电波发现星体、追踪宇宙飞船等).

radio- *comb form* 构词成分 of radiation or radioactivity 放射的; 辐射的; 放射性的: *radioactive* ○ *radiologist* ○ *radio-therapy*.

ra·dio·act·ive /ˌreɪdɪəʊˈæktɪv; ˌredɪoˈæktɪv/ *adj* having atoms that break up and send out radiation which can penetrate opaque bodies and sometimes produce harmful electrical effects 放射性的; 有辐射能的: *Radium and uranium are radioactive elements.* 镭和铀是放射性元素. ○ ˌ*radioactive ˈfall-out*, ie dust carried by winds around the earth after a nuclear explosion, etc 放射性微粒回降(核爆炸等之后放射性尘埃随风散落到地面) ○ *radioactive waste*, ie waste material from nuclear power-stations, etc 放射性废料(核电站等产生的核废料). ▷ **ra·dio·ac·tiv·ity** /ˌreɪdɪəʊækˈtɪvətɪ; ˈredɪˌoækˈtɪvətɪ/ *n* [U].

radio-carbon /ˌredɪəʊ ˈkɑːbən; ˌredɪoˋkɑrbən/ *n* [U] radioactive form of carbon present in organic materials, used in carbon dating 放射性碳(有机材料中碳元素的放射性形式, 用以测定某物的年代).

ra·dio·graph /ˈreɪdɪəʊgrɑːf; *US* -græf; ˋredɪəˌgræf/ *n* =X-RAY 2.

▷ **ra·dio·grapher** /ˌreɪdɪˈɒgrəfə(r); ˌredɪˈɑgrəfɚ/ *n* person who takes radiographs X射线摄影师.

ra·dio·graphy /ˌreɪdɪˈɒgrəfɪ; ˌredɪˈɑgrəfɪ/ *n* [U] production of X-ray photographs X射线照相(术).

ra·dio·iso·tope /ˌreɪdɪəʊˈaɪsətəʊp; ˌredɪoˈaɪsəˌtop/ *n* radioactive form of an element, used in medicine, industry, etc to study the path and speed of substances through bodies and objects 放射性同位素.

ra·di·ology /ˌreɪdɪˈɒlədʒɪ; ˌredɪˈɑlədʒɪ/ *n* [U] scientific study of X-rays and other radiation, esp as used in medicine 放射学(尤指用于医学的).

▷ **ra·di·olo·gist** /ˌreɪdɪˈɒlədʒɪst; ˌredɪˈɑlədʒɪst/ *n* expert in radiology 放射学家.

radio-therapy /ˌreɪdɪəʊ ˈθerəpɪ; ˈredɪoˈθɛrəpɪ/ *n* [U] treatment of disease by radiation, esp X-rays 放射疗法; (尤指)X射线疗法.

▷ ˌ**radio-ˈtherapist** *n* expert in radio-therapy 放射治疗专家.

rad·ish /ˈrædɪʃ; ˋrædɪʃ/ *n* (**a**) plant with a crisp hot-tasting root 萝卜. (**b**) this root, eaten raw in salads 萝卜(于色拉中生吃的): *bunches of radishes* 成捆的萝卜.

ra·dium /ˈreɪdɪəm; ˋredɪəm/ *n* [U] chemical element, a shining white radioactive metal used in the treatment of some diseases, eg cancer 镭: [attrib 作定语] *radium therapy* 镭疗法. ⇨App 10 见附录10.

ra·dius /ˈreɪdɪəs; ˋredɪəs/ *n* (*pl* **-dii** /-dɪaɪ; -dɪˌaɪ/) **1** (length of a) straight line from the centre of a circle or sphere to any point on its circumference or surface 半径(距离). ⇨App 5 见附录5. ⇨illus at CIRCLE 见CIRCLE插图. **2** circular area measured by its radius 用半径度量的圆形面积; 半径范围: *Police searched all the woods within a six-mile radius/within a radius of six miles.* 警方搜索了在周围六英里以内的树林各处. **3** (*anatomy* 解) outer shorter bone in the human forearm; corresponding bone in an animal's foreleg or a bird's wing (人与兽的)桡骨; 鸟翼中相当于桡骨的骨. ⇨illus at SKELETON 见SKELETON插图. Cf 参看 ULNA.

ra·don /ˈreɪdɒn; ˋredɑn/ *n* [U] chemical element, a radioactive gas produced by the decay of radium 氡. ⇨App 10 见附录10.

RAF /ˌɑːr eɪ ˈef, *or, in infml use,* 俗读作 ræf; ˌɑr e ˋɛf, ræf/ *abbr* 缩写 = (*Brit*) Royal Air Force 皇家空军.

raf·fia /ˈræfɪə; ˋræfɪə/ *n* [U] soft fibre from the leaves of a type of palm-tree, used for tying up plants, weaving table-mats, etc 酒椰叶纤维(由酒椰棕榈树叶制成, 质软, 用于捆扎植物、编织桌席等).

raff·ish /ˈræfɪʃ; ˋræfɪʃ/ *adj* (esp of men, their appearance or behaviour) flashy or slightly disreputable; rakish (尤指男子、其外表或行为)花里胡哨的, 有失体面的, 放荡不羁的: *He was drinking cheap champagne with a raffish air.* 他喝着廉价的香槟酒, 样子十分放荡. ▷ **raff·ishly** *adv*. **raff·ish·ness** *n* [U].

raffle /ˈræfl; ˋræfl/ *n* lottery (esp for charity) with an article as the prize 抽彩(尤指为慈善捐款): *win a video in a raffle* 在抽彩中得了一台录像机 ○ [attrib 作定语] *a raffle ticket* 抽彩的彩券. Cf 参看 DRAW[1] 1.

▷ **raffle** *v* [Tn, Tn·p] **~ sth (off)** offer (goods) as a prize in a raffle 在抽彩中奖给(货物).

raft[1] /rɑːft; *US* ræft; ræft/ *n* (**a**) flat floating structure of logs, barrels, etc tied together, used esp as a substitute for a boat 筏; 筏子: *shipwrecked sailors on a makeshift raft* 在临时代用的筏子上的遇难船员. (**b**) number of logs tied together to be floated down a river 木排.

▷ **raft** *v* (**a**) [Tn·pr, Tn·p] carry (people or goods) on a raft 用筏子载运(人或货物): *raft people across/over/up/down (a river)* 用筏子载运人过河[到对岸/逆流而上/顺流而下]. (**b**) [Ipr, Ip] cross a river, etc on a raft 乘筏过河等.

raft[2] /rɑːft; *US* ræft; ræft/ *n* (usu *sing* 通常作单数) **~ (of sth)** (*US infml* 口) large number or amount 大量; 许多: *She got a raft of presents.* 她收到了许多礼物.

raf·ter /ˈrɑːftə(r); *US* ˈræf-; ˋræftɚ/ *n* any of the parallel sloping beams supporting the tiles, slates, etc of a roof 椽: *hams hanging from the rafters*, eg in an old inn 悬挂在椽子上的火腿(如在昔时酒店所见).

▷ **raf·tered** /ˈrɑːftəd; *US* ˈræf-; ˋræftɚd/ *adj* having rafters, esp ones that are exposed, eg because there is no ceiling 有椽的; (尤指)椽暴露在外面的(如因无天花板).

rag[1] /ræg; ræg/ *n* **1** [C, U] odd (scrap of) cloth, usu torn, frayed, etc 碎布(通常指撕碎、磨破的): *I use an oily rag to clean my bike with.* 我用沾满油污的碎布擦我的自行车. ○ *Instead of a handkerchief he had an old (piece of) rag.* 他拿一块旧布当作手绢用. ○ [attrib 作定语] *a rag doll*, ie one stuffed with rags 碎布娃娃(以碎布做填塞物的). **2 rags** [pl] (**a**) old, worn or torn clothes 破旧衣服: *a tramp dressed in rags and tatters* 衣衫褴褛的流浪汉 ○ *trade in rags and waste paper* 做破旧衣服和废纸生意. (**b**) pieces of waste cloth used to make good quality paper 用以制造优质纸的废旧布片: [attrib 作定语] ˈ*rag paper* (以破布做原料的)优质纸. **3** [C] (*infml usu derog* 口, 通常作贬义) newspaper or journal 报纸; 杂志: *I read it in the local rag.* 我从本地的报纸上看到了这条消息. **4** (idm 习语) **chew the fat/rag** ⇨ CHEW. **from** ˌ**rags to** ˈ**riches** from extreme poverty to wealth 从赤贫到巨富: [attrib 作定语] *Hers was a rags-to-riches story.* 她的经历可谓白手起家. **glad rags** ⇨ GLAD. **like a wet rag** ⇨ WET. **lose one's rag** ⇨ LOSE. **a red rag to a bull** ⇨ RED[1].

□ **rag-and-ˈbone man** (*Brit*) person who goes round buying and selling old clothes, discarded furniture, etc 四处买卖旧衣物、废弃家具等的人.

ˈ**rag-bag** *n* **1** [C] bag in which scraps of fabric are kept, eg to mend clothes 存放碎布的袋子(如供修补衣物用的). **2** [sing] (*fig* 比喻) confused assortment; hotchpotch 杂七杂八的东西; 杂凑: *a rag-bag of strange ideas, theories, etc* 奇思、怪论等的大杂烩.

the ˈ**rag trade** (*infml* 口) business of designing, making and selling (esp women's) clothes 设计、制造和销售服装的行业(尤指女装): *go into the rag trade* 从事服装业.

rag[2] /ræg; ræg/ *v* (**-gg-**) [Tn, Tn·pr] **~ sb (about/for sth)** (*Brit infml* 口) play practical jokes on sb; tease sb 拿某人取乐; 戏弄某人: *They are always ragging the teacher about his accent.* 他们总是取笑这位老师的口音.

▷ **rag** *n* **1** practical joke; prank 恶作剧; 玩笑: *We hid her clothes for a rag.* 我们开了个玩笑, 把她的衣服藏了起来. **2** annual entertainment held by students to collect money for charity 学生一年一度为募集慈善基金举行的娱乐活动: *the college* ˈ*rag* 学院的募捐联欢 ○ [attrib 作定语] *hold a* ˈ*rag week* 举办募捐联欢周.

rag[3] /ræg; ræg/ *n* piece of ragtime music 雷格泰姆音乐的曲子.

rag·amuf·fin /ˈrægəmʌfɪn; ˋrægə,mʌfɪn/ *n* person, esp a small boy, in dirty untidy clothes 衣衫褴褛的人(尤指小男孩).

rage /reɪdʒ; redʒ/ *n* **1** [U, C] (**a**) (fit of) violent anger (一阵)狂怒; 盛怒(之爆发): *trembling with rage* 气得直哆嗦 ○ *white/livid with rage* 气得脸色发白[发青] ○ *be in/fly into a (towering) rage* 勃然大怒 ○ *Her rages don't last long.* 她发脾气很快就消气. (**b**) (*fig* 比喻) (instance of) violence in nature 大自然的狂暴: *The storm's rage continued.* 暴风雨肆虐不已. **2** (idm 习语) **all the fashion/rage** ⇨ FASHION.

▷ **rage** *v* **1** (**a**) [I, Ipr] **~ (at/against sb/sth)** show violent anger 大发脾气; 动怒: *He raged against me for disagreeing.* 他因我有异议对我大发雷霆. ○ *I raged for hours at the decision.* 我对这个决定几小时怒不可遏. (**b**) [I] (of storms, fires, battles, etc) continue violently (指暴风雨、火势、战斗等)猛烈地继续下去. **2** [I, Ipr] (esp of illnesses) spread rapidly (尤指疾病)迅速蔓延: *A flu epidemic raged through the school for weeks.* 流感在这所学校里蔓延了几个星期.

ra·ging *adj* [attrib 作定语] extreme or painful 极端的; 痛苦的: *raging hunger, thirst, passion* 极其饿、渴、热情 ○ *have a raging headache, toothache, etc* 头痛、牙痛…已极.

R

rag·ged /ˈrægɪd; ˋrægɪd/ *adj* **1** (**a**) (of clothes) badly worn or in rags; tattered (指衣服)破旧的; 褴褛的: *a ragged coat, suit, etc* 破旧的大衣、西服等 ○ *His sleeves were ragged at the cuffs.* 他的袖口磨破了. (**b**) (of people) wearing badly worn or torn clothes (指人)衣衫褴褛的: *a ragged old man* 衣衫褴褛的老人. **2** (*fig* 比喻) having an uneven outline, edge or surface; jagged (外形)不规则的; (边缘)锯齿状的; (表面)凹凸不平的: *the ragged profile of the cliffs* 参差不齐的峭壁 ○ *ragged clouds driven by the wind* 被风吹散的残云. **3** (*fig* 比喻) lacking smoothness or uniformity; imperfect 不流畅的; 不一致的; 不完美的: *The choir gave a ragged performance,* ie The singers were not following the conductor. 合唱队演唱得很不和谐(歌唱者不听从指挥). ○ *A ragged shout went up from the small crowd.* 这一小群人发出了刺耳的喊叫. ▷ **rag·gedly** *adv.* **rag·ged·ness** *n* [U].

rag·lan /ˈræglən; ˋræglən/ *n, adj* [attrib 作定语] (**a**) (sleeve) that is joined to the body of a garment by sloping seams from the armpit to the neckline 插肩的(袖子). (**b**) (coat, sweater, etc) having sleeves of this kind 插肩袖的(大衣、毛衣等).

rag·out /ˈræguː; *US* ræˈguː; ræˋgu/ *n* [C, U] (dish of) meat and vegetable stew (一道)蔬菜炖肉.

rag·tag /ˈrægtæg; ˋræg,tæg/ *n* (idm 习语) ˌ**ragtag and** ˈ**bobtail** disreputable people; riff-raff 声名狼藉之辈; 流氓.

rag·time /ˈrægtaɪm; ˋræg,taɪm/ *n* [U] type of popular 1920's jazz music first played by Blacks in the US, in which the beat of the melody just precedes the beat of the accompaniment 雷格泰姆音乐(二十世纪二十年代流行的美国黑人爵士音乐): [attrib 作定语] *a* ˌ*ragtime* ˈ*band* 演奏雷格泰姆音乐的乐队.

rag·weed /ˈrægwiːd; ˋræg,wid/ *n* [U, C] N American weed producing large amounts of pollen which causes hay fever 豚草(产于北美, 其花粉能使人患枯草热).

rag·wort /ˈrægwɜːt; ˋræg,wɝt/ *n* [C, U] wild plant with yellow daisy-like flowers and ragged leaves 千里光(野生植物, 开黄花似雏菊, 叶呈不规则齿形).

raid /reɪd; red/ *n* **~ (on sth)** **1** sudden surprise attack and withdrawal by troops, ships or aircraft (部队、舰艇或飞机的)突袭, 突击: *make/launch a bombing raid* (ie by aircraft) *on enemy bases* 对敌方基地进行突然的空袭. **2** sudden surprise attack in order to steal or do harm (突如其来的)抢劫, 行凶: *an armed raid* 持械抢劫 ○ *A security guard was killed in the bank raid.* 这次银行劫案中有一名保安员遇害. **3** sudden surprise visit by the police, etc, eg to arrest people or seize illicit goods (警方等的)突然搜查或搜捕(如为捕人或搜寻违禁品): *carry out a dawn raid* 破晓时进行的搜捕 ○ *a police drugs raid* 警方进行的毒品搜查. **4** (*finance* 财) attempt by a group of people to lower eg share prices by selling at the same time (为使价格如股价下跌)集体抛售.

▷ **raid** *v* [Tn] make a raid on (a place) 对(某处)进行突然袭击、抢劫或搜查: *Customs men raided the house.* 海关人员突然搜查了这所房子. ○ (*fig* 比喻) *raid the larder,* ie take food from it, usu between meals 翻柜橱找吃的(通常指两顿饭之间) ○ *boys raiding an orchard,* ie to steal fruit 在果园里偷水果的男孩子. **raider** *n* person, ship, aircraft, etc that makes a raid 进行袭击、抢劫或搜捕的人; 进行突袭的舰艇、飞机等.

rail[1] /reɪl; rel/ *n* **1** [C] (**a**) level or sloping bar or connected series of bars of wood or metal, eg forming part of a fence, the top of a banister, a protective barrier, etc (护栏等的)横条, 横挡, 扶手: *wooden rails in front of an altar* 祭坛前的木栏杆 ○ *the horses on the rails,* ie those on the inside curve of a racecourse 挨近围栏的马(在跑道内圈一侧的) ○ *Hold the* ˈ*handrail for safety,* eg while descending steps. 抓住扶手以防摔倒(如下楼时). ○ *leaning on the ship's (guard-)rail looking out to sea* 倚着船上的护栏眺望大海. (**b**) level bar fixed to a wall for hanging things on (固定在墙上用来挂东西的)横杆: *a* ˈ*towel-rail,* eg beside a wash-basin 挂毛巾的横杆(如脸盆旁的) ○ *a* ˈ*curtain rail* 窗帘横杆. ⇨illus at App 1 见附录1插图, page xvi. **2** (**a**) [C esp *pl* 尤作复数] steel bar or continuous line of steel bars fixed to the ground as one side of a track for trains or trams 铁轨; 轨道. ⇨illus at FLANGE 见 FLANGE 插图. (**b**) [U, often attrib 常作定语] railways as a means of transport 铁路(交通); 铁路运输: *a rail strike* 铁路员工罢工 ○ *rail travel, freight, etc* 乘火车的旅行、铁路货运 ○ *send sth by rail* 由铁路运输某物 ○ *British Rail* 英国铁路. **3** (idm 习语) **free on board/rail** ⇨ FREE[1]. **go off the** ˈ**rails** (*Brit infml* 口) (**a**) become disorganized or out of control 陷于混乱; 失去控制: *Our schedule went completely off the rails during the strike.* 我们的预定计划在罢工期间完全被打乱了. (**b**) become mad or crazy 发疯; 发狂. **jump the rails/track** ⇨ JUMP[2].

▷ **rail** *v* (phr v) **rail sth in/off** surround or separate sth with rails 用栏杆围住或隔开某物: *rail off a field (from a road)* 用栏杆把场地(与道路)隔开 ○ *The winners' enclosure was railed in.* 授奖区有栏杆围着.

□ ˈ**railhead** *n* (**a**) furthest point reached by a railway that is being built 修建中的铁路已到达的最远点. (**b**) point on a railway at which road transport begins or ends 铁路运输的起点或终点.

ˈ**railroad** *n* (*US*) railway 铁路. — *v* (phr v) **railroad sb into (doing) sth** (*infml* 口) force sb to do sth 强迫某人做某事: *I won't be railroaded into buying a car I don't want!* 谁也不能强迫我购买我根本不想要的汽车! **railroad sth through (sth)** (*infml* 口) get sth passed, accepted, etc quickly by applying pressure 施加压力促使某事物迅速通过、获准等: *railroad a bill through Congress* 强使法案在国会中迅速通过.

rail[2] /reɪl; rel/ *v* [I, Ipr] **~ (at/against sb/sth)** complain, protest or reproach sb/sth strongly 极力抱怨、挑剔或责备某人[某事物]: *railing against fate* 抱怨命运不好 ○ *She railed at (him for) his laziness.* 她因他懒惰而责备他.

rail·ing /ˈreɪlɪŋ; ˋrelɪŋ/ *n* (often *pl* 常作复数) fence or barrier made of rails (RAIL[1] 1a), supported by upright bars (有立柱支撑的)横条的栏杆、栅栏或扶手.

rail·lery /ˈreɪlərɪ; ˋrelərɪ/ *n* [U] good-humoured mockery or ridicule 善意的嘲讽或揶揄.

rail·way /ˈreɪlweɪ; ˋrel,we/ (*US* **rail·road**) *n* **1** track with rails (RAIL[1] 2a) for trains to run on 铁路; 铁道: *railways under construction* 修建中的铁路. **2** (often *pl* 常作复数) system of such tracks, together with the trains, etc running on them, and the organization and people needed for their operation 铁路系统; 铁路部门: *work on/for the railway(s)* 在铁路部门工作 ○ *a network of railways run by the state* 国营铁路网 ○ [attrib 作定语] *a railway station, carriage, engineer* 火车站、火车车厢、铁路工程师.

□ ˈ**railwayman** /-mən; -mən/ *n* (*pl* **-men**/-mən; -mən/) man who works for a railway company 铁路员工.

rai·ment /ˈreɪmənt; ˋremənt/ *n* [U] (*arch* 古) clothing 衣物.

rain[1] /reɪn; ren/ *n* **1** [U] condensed moisture of the atmosphere falling as separate drops; fall of these drops 雨; 下雨: *heavy/light rain* 大[小]雨 ○ *Don't go out in the rain.* 不要冒着雨出去. ○ *Come in out of the rain.* 快进来, 别让雨淋着. ○ *It looks like* (ie as if there will be a fall of) *rain.* 像是要下雨了. **2 the rains** [pl] season of heavy continuous rain in tropical countries (热带地区

的)雨季: *The rains come in September.* 雨季于九月到来. **3** [sing] (preceded by an *adj* 用于形容词之后) shower of rain of the specified type 某种类型的雨: *There was a heavy rain during the night.* 夜间下了一场大雨. **4** [sing] **~ of sth** (*esp fig* 尤作比喻) great number of things falling like rain 像雨点般降落的东西: *a rain of arrows, bullets, etc* 箭、子弹等如雨点一般 ○ *a rain of ashes*, eg from a volcano 如雨点般落下的灰尘(如从火山口中喷出者). **5** (idm 习语) **come ˌrain, come ˈshine; (come) ˌrain or ˈshine** whether there is rain or sunshine; whatever happens 不论晴雨; 不管发生什么事情: *The fête will take place on Sunday, rain or shine.* 游园义卖会定于星期日举行, 风雨无阻. **right as rain** ⇨ RIGHT. ▷ **rain·less** *adj*: *a rainless day* 无雨天.

□ **rainbow** /ˈreɪnbəʊ; ˈrenˌbo/ *n* arch containing the colours of the spectrum, formed in the sky when the sun shines through rain or spray 虹; 彩虹: *silks dyed in all (the) colours of the rainbow* 染成彩虹那样七种颜色的丝绸服装. ˈ**rainbow trout** black-spotted trout with two reddish bands from nose to tail 虹鳟鱼(身上有黑点, 从鼻到尾有两条红线).

ˈ**rain-check** *n* (*US*) **1** ticket for later use when a match, show, etc is cancelled because of rain (比赛、表演等)因雨延期有效票. **2** (idm 习语) **take a rain-check (on sth)** (*infml* 口) decline an offer, etc but promise to accept it later 谢绝一项好意, 但答应日后接受: *Thanks for the invitation, but I'll have to take a rain-check on it.* 你的邀请我心领了, 感谢盛意改日一定践约.

ˈ**raincoat** *n* light waterproof or water-resistant coat 雨衣.

ˈ**raindrop** *n* single drop of rain 雨点.

ˈ**rainfall** *n* [U] total amount of rain falling within a given area in a given time 降雨量: *an annual rainfall of 10 cm* 年降雨量10厘米. ⇨App 4 见附录4.

ˈ**rain forest** thick evergreen forest in tropical regions with heavy rainfall 雨林(热带地区多雨的茂密常绿森林).

ˈ**rain-gauge** *n* instrument for measuring rainfall 雨量计.

ˈ**rainproof** *adj* that can keep rain out 防雨的: *a rainproof jacket* 防雨短上衣.

ˈ**rain-water** *n* soft water that has fallen as rain, eg not taken from wells, etc 雨水(软水, 如并非井水等).

rain[2] /reɪn; ren/ *v* **1** [I] (used with *it* 与it连用) fall as rain 下雨; 降雨: *It is raining*, ie Rain is falling. 下着雨呢. ○ *It rained hard all day.* 下了一整天的大雨. **2** [Ipr] **~ on sb/sth** (*fig* 比喻) fall like rain on sb/sth 像雨点般落在某人[某物]上: *Blows rained on the door.* 敲门声像雨点一样. ○ *The suitcase burst open and its contents rained on the floor.* 手提箱裂开了, 里面的东西纷纷落在地板上. **3** (idm 习语) **it ˌnever ˌrains but it ˈpours** (*saying* 谚) misfortunes, etc usually come in large numbers 不雨则已, 一雨倾盆; 灾祸等不发生则已, 一发生便接踵而至: *First my car broke down, then I lost my key: it never rains but it pours!* 先是我的汽车出了故障, 接着又丢了钥匙, 真是祸不单行! **rain ˈbuckets; rain cats and ˈdogs** (esp in the continuous tenses 尤用于进行时态) rain very heavily 下倾盆大雨. **4** (phr v) **rain down (sth)** flow or come down in large quantities 大量流下; 大量落下: *Tears rained down her cheeks.* 她泪流满面. ○ *Loose rocks rained down (the hillside).* 松动的岩石大量滚下(山坡). **rain down (on sb/sth)** come down on sb/sth 传给某人[某事物]: *Abuse rained down on the noisy students from the open windows.* 穿过敞开的窗户传来对那些喧闹学生的责骂声. ○ *Invitations rained down on the visiting writer.* 来访的这位作家收到了许多邀请信. **rain in** (used with *it* 与it连用): *It is raining in*, ie Rain is coming through the roof, tent, etc. 漏雨了. **rain sth off**; *US* **rain sth out** (usu passive 通常用于被动语态) (*infml* 口) prevent (eg an event) from taking place because of rain 因雨而使(事情等)受阻: *The match was rained off twice.* 比赛因雨而被迫两次改期.

rainy /ˈreɪnɪ; ˈrenɪ/ *adj* (**-ier, -iest**) **1** (of a day, period, etc) on or in which much rain falls; (of sky, weather, etc) bringing much rain (指某日、某段时间等)多雨的; (指天空、天气等)下雨的: *a rainy afternoon, month, etc* 多雨的下午、月份等 ○ *the ˈrainy season* 雨季 ○ *a rainy climate, sky* 多雨的气候、雨中阴沉的天空. **2** (idm 习语) **save, keep, etc sth for a ˌrainy ˈday** save (esp money) for a time when one may need it 节省(尤指金钱)以备不时之需; 未雨绸缪.

raise /reɪz; rez/ *v* **1** [Tn, Tn·pr, Tn·p] (**a**) lift or move (sth) to a higher level; cause to rise 举起, 升起, 提起, 抬起(某物): *raise one's hand* 举手 ○ *He raised his eyes from his work.* 他停下工作举目观看. ○ *raise a sunken ship (up) to the surface* 把沉船打捞出水面 ○ *raise one's hat to sb*, ie as a sign of respect 向某人举帽致敬. (**b**) move (sth/sb) to an upright position 竖起, 立起, 扶起(某物[某人]): *raise a man from his knees* 把跪着的男子搀起来 ○ *We raised the fence and fixed it in position.* 我们把篱笆竖立起来并固定住. **2** [Tn, Tn·pr] **~ sth (to sth)** increase the amount or volume or heighten the level of sth 增加某物之数量或容量; 提高某事物的水平: *raise salaries, prices, profits, etc* 增加薪水、提高价格、加大利润 ○ *He raised his offer to £500.* 他把出价提高到500英镑. ○ *raise one's voice*, ie speak more loudly 提高嗓门 ○ *raise the temperature to 80°* 使温度升高到80° ○ *raise standards of service* 提高服务水平 ○ *raise sb's hopes*, ie make sb more hopeful 点燃某人的希望. **3** [Tn] cause (sth) to arise or appear 引起, 激起(某事物); 使(某事物)产生或出现: *raise doubts, fears, suspicions, etc in people's minds* 引起人们的怀疑、恐惧、猜疑等 ○ *The horses' hooves raised a cloud of dust.* 马蹄扬起了一片尘土. ○ *raise the spirits of the dead* 使死者显灵 ○ *The dirty joke raised a blush on her cheek.* 这个下流笑话羞得她脸通红. **4** [Tn] (**a**) cause (sth) to be heard 使(某事)尽人皆知: *raise a commotion, fuss, protest, stink, etc* 搞出骚乱、纷扰、抗议、纠纷等 ○ *raise the alarm/alert* 发出警报 ○ *The retort raised a cheer in support of the speaker.* 发言人这一反驳博得了一片支持的欢呼声. (**b**) bring (sth) up for discussion or attention; put forward 将(某事物)提出讨论或引起注意: *The book raises many important issues (for our consideration).* 该书提出了许多重要问题(值得考虑). ○ *I'm glad you raised that point.* 你能把那一点指出来, 我感到很高兴. **5** [Tn] bring or collect (sth) together; manage to obtain 召集或集结(某事物); 筹措: *raise an army* 招募军队 ○ *raise a loan, a subscription, etc* 借款、募捐 ○ *raise funds for charity*, eg by holding a bazaar 筹集慈善基金(如借助于举行义卖活动) ○ *a fund-raising event* 筹款活动. **6** [Tn] (**a**) (*esp US*) bring up (a child, etc) 养育(孩子等): *I was raised by my aunt on a farm.* 我是在农场由姨妈抚养大的. ○ *It's difficult raising a family on a small income.* 依靠微薄的收入是很难养家的. (**b**) breed (farm animals); grow or produce (crops) 饲养(家畜); 种植或生产(作物). Cf 参看 REAR[2]. **7** [Tn, Tn·pr] **~ sth (to sb/sth)** build or erect (a monument, statue, etc) 建造或树立(纪念碑、雕像等): *raise a memorial to those killed in war* 立碑纪念战争中的死难者. **8** [Tn] end (a siege, etc) 解除(包围等): *raise a blockade, a ban, an embargo* 解除封锁、禁令、禁运. **9** [Tn] (*infml* 口) get in contact with (sb); find (sth) 与(某人)接触; 与(某人)建立联系; 找到(某人): *I can't raise her on the phone.* 我打电话找不到她. ○ *I've been trying to raise this spare part everywhere.* 我一直在到处寻找, 想弄到这种备件. **10** [Tn] (in card-games, esp poker) bet more than (another player) (纸牌戏, 尤指扑克牌戏中)下赌注超过(对手): *I'll raise you!* 我超过你(的赌注)! **11** (idm 习语) **kick up/raise a dust** ⇨ DUST[1]. **lift/raise a finger/hand** ⇨ LIFT. **raise ˈCain/ˈhell/the ˈroof** (*infml* 口) be very angry; cause an uproar 大怒; 大吵大闹: *He raised Cain when he found he had been cheated.* 他发觉受骗而勃然大怒. **raise one's ˈeyebrows (at sth)** (esp passive 尤用于被动语态) show disdain or surprise 表示轻蔑或惊讶: *Eyebrows were raised/There were many raised eyebrows when he shaved all his hair off.* 他把头发剃光了, 人人见了都大吃一惊. **raise one's glass (to sb)** drink a toast (to sb) 向(某人)祝酒. **raise sb's hackles** ⇨ HACKLES. **raise/start a hare** ⇨ HARE. **raise a ˈlaugh/ˈsmile** amuse people enough to make them laugh/smile 逗得人大笑[发笑]. **raise/lower one's sights** ⇨ SIGHT[1]. **raise sb's ˈspirits** make sb feel more cheerful or brave 使某人感到振奋或受到鼓舞; 鼓起某人的勇气: *My win at chess raised my spirits a little.* 我赢了这盘国际象棋才打起了一点精神. **raise the ˈtemperature** increase tension, hostility, etc 加剧紧张气氛、敌对情绪等: *This insult raised the temperature of the discussion.*

R

这种侮辱的言语使讨论的气氛顿时紧张起来. **raise one's voice aˈgainst sb/sth** speak firmly and boldly against sb/sth 坚决而勇敢地发言反对某人[某事物].

▷ **raise** *n* (*US*) =RISE¹ 3: *get a raise of £200* 获得加薪200英镑.

-raiser (forming compound *ns* 用以构成复合名词) person or thing that raises (RAISE 5) 进行召集或筹措的人或事物: *a ˈcurtain-raiser*, ie a short play before the main one ○ *ˈfire-raisers*, ie arsonists ○ *a ˈfund-raiser*.

raisin /ˈreɪzn; ˋrezn̩/ *n* dried sweet grape, used in cakes, puddings, etc 葡萄干. Cf 参看 SULTANA 1.

raison d'être /ˌreɪzɒn ˈdetrə; ˋrezɔnˋdɛt/ *n* [sing] (*French* 法) reason for or justification of sb's/sth's existence (某人[某事物])存在的原因或理由: *Work seems to be her raison d'être.* 工作似乎就是她生活的目的.

raj /rɑːdʒ; rɑdʒ/ *n* [U] **the raj** (also **the Raj, the British Raj**) (period of) British rule in India 英国在印度的统治(时期): *life under the Raj*, ie before 1947 英国统治印度时期的生活(1947年之前).

rajah (also **raja**) /ˈrɑːdʒə; ˋrɑdʒə/ *n* (formerly) (title of an) Indian king or prince (旧时)印度的君主或王子(的称号). Cf 参看 RANEE.

rake 耙子

rake¹ /reɪk; rek/ *n* **1** (**a**) long-handled tool with a row of prongs at the end for drawing together fallen leaves, smoothing soil, etc 耙子. (**b**) similar mechanical farm tool on wheels, usu for gathering hay, etc 耙机(有轮, 通常用以收集干草等). **2** similar implement, used eg by a croupier for drawing in money at a gambling table 钱耙(赌桌主持人收取钱用的).

▷ **rake** *v* **1** [I, Tn, Cn·a] use a rake on (sth); level (sth) with a rake 用耙子耙(某物); 用耙子耙平(某物): *I was busy raking.* 我在忙着用耙子干活. ○ *rake the soil (smooth)*, eg before planting seeds 把地耙平(如在播种以前). **2** [Tn, Tn·p] **~ sth (out)** remove ashes from (a fire, kiln, etc) 将灰从(炉、窑等)里耙出来. **3** [Tn] fire a gun at or point a camera, telescope, etc at (sth) while moving it from one side to the other (用枪、照相机、望远镜等)扫射, 扫拍, 扫视(某物): *rake the enemy lines with machine-gun fire* 用机枪扫射敌人的防线 ○ *The bird-watcher raked the trees with his binoculars.* 观察野鸟的人用双筒望远镜扫视树木. **4** (idm 习语) **rake over old ˈashes** revive (usu unpleasant) memories of the past 回想起(通常指不愉快的)往事. **5** (phr v) **rake about/around (for sth)** search carefully 仔细搜寻: *We raked around in the files, but couldn't find the letter.* 我们翻遍了文件夹, 怎么也找不到那封信. **rake sth/it in** (*infml* 口) earn a lot of (money, etc) 挣大量的(钱等): *raking in the profits* 挣得大量利润 ○ *She gets tips as well as her wages, so she's really raking it in.* 她又领工资又收小费, 真赚了不少钱. **rake sth together, up, etc** move sth together, up, etc with a rake 用耙把某物耙在一起、耙成一堆等: *rake together dead leaves (into a heap)* 把枯叶耙到一起(聚成一堆) ○ *rake hay up* 把干草耙成一堆 ○ *rake the cut grass off the lawn* 把刈下的草耙出草坪. **rake sb/sth together/up** (*infml* 口) collect (people or things) with difficulty 费力地凑集(人或物): *We need to rake up two more players to form a team.* 我们需要物色两名队员才能凑成一个队. ○ *I couldn't rake together enough money for a new bike.* 我凑不够买一辆新自行车的钱. **rake sth up** (*infml* 口) remind people of (sth that it would be better to forget) 使人回想起(最好不再想起的事): *rake up old quarrels, grievances, etc* 重新提起旧日的争吵事、冤情等 ○ *Don't rake up the past.* 别再提那些往事了.

□ **ˈrake-off** *n* (*infml* 口) share of profits or commission, esp from dishonest or illegal activity 利润的分成或回扣(尤指从不正当或非法活动中获取者): *She got a rake-off of 5 per cent from the deal.* 她从这笔交易中获得百分之五的回扣.

rake² /reɪk; rek/ *n* (*dated* 旧) man, esp a rich and fashionable one, who lives a wild immoral life 过放荡生活的男子(尤指时髦的富人); 浪子.

▷ **rak·ish** /ˈreɪkɪʃ; ˋrekɪʃ/ *adj* **1** of or like a rake (似)浪子的; 放荡的: *a rakish appearance, look, etc* 浪荡的外表、样子等. **2** jaunty or dashing 得意洋洋的; 潇洒的: *a hat set at a rakish angle*, eg on the back of the head or sideways 神气地歪戴着帽子. **rak·ishly** *adv* **rak·ish·ness** *n* [U].

rake³ /reɪk; rek/ *n* [sing] (**a**) backward slope, eg of a ship's mast or funnel or of a driver's seat 后倾(如船的桅杆或烟囱或司机座椅等的). (**b**) downward slope of a stage in a theatre, ie towards the audience (剧院舞台的)前倾(即向观众一方倾斜).

▷ **rake** *v* [I, Tn] be or place (sth) at a sloping angle 倾斜; 使(某物)倾斜: *The stage rakes steeply.* 这舞台坡度很大. ○ *The seat back is raked for extra comfort.* 这椅背向后倾斜更加舒适.

ral·lent·ando /ˌrælənˈtændəʊ; ˌrælənˋtændo/ *adj, adv, n* (*pl* **-dos** or **-di** /-diː; -di/) (*music* 音) (passage performed) with gradually decreasing speed 渐慢; 渐慢的乐段. Cf 参看 ACCELERANDO.

rally¹ /ˈrælɪ; ˋrælɪ/ *v* (*pt, pp* **rallied**) **1** (**a**) [I, Ipr, Ip] **~ (round/to sb/sth); ~ (round)** (of people) come together, esp to make new efforts, eg after a defeat or when there is danger, need, etc (指人)集合起来(尤指重新努力, 如失败后或有危险、需要等时): *The troops rallied (round their leader/the flag).* 部队重新集结(在指挥官[旗帜]周围). ○ *They rallied to their leader's cause.* 他们团结一致支持领袖的事业. ○ *When their mother was ill, the children all rallied round.* 母亲生病时, 孩子们都来到她身旁. (**b**) [Tn, Tn·pr, Tn·p] **~ sb (round sb); ~ sb (together)** bring (people) together in this way (重新)召集(人): *The leader rallied his men (round him).* 指挥官重新集结其部属. **2** [I, Tn] (cause sb/sth to) recover health, strength, etc; revive; rouse (使某人[某事物])恢复健康、力量等; 复苏; 振作: *rally from an illness* 康复 ○ *Her spirits rallied on hearing the good news.* 她听到这好消息精神又振作起来. ○ *The team rallied after the first half.* 该队在上半场过后士气大增. **3** [I] (of share prices, etc) increase after a fall (指股票价格等)跌后回升.

▷ **rally** *n* **1** [sing] act of rallying 集合; 集结; 重整: *Bugler, sound the rally!* 司号兵, 吹集合号! **2** [C] large gathering of people with a common (usu political) purpose (具有共同目的的人们参加的, 通常为政治性的)群众大会: *a party rally* 政党集会 ○ *hold/stage a ˈpeace rally* 举行拥护和平的群众大会. **3** [sing] recovery of health, strength, etc, eg after an illness; revival (健康、力量等的)恢复, 康复; 复苏: *an unexpected rally* (ie increase in the price) *of tin shares on the Stock Market* 股票市场上锡股价格的意外回升. **4** [C] (in tennis, squash, etc) series of strokes before a point is scored (网球、壁球等)得分前的连续对打: *a fifteen-stroke rally* 连续对打了十五下. **5** [C] driving competition for motor vehicles over public roads 公路赛车.

rally² /ˈrælɪ; ˋrælɪ/ *v* (*pt, pp* **rallied**) [Tn] (*dated* 旧) mock (sb) in a good-humoured way; tease 善意地嘲讽(某人); 揶揄.

ram /ræm; ræm/ *n* **1** uncastrated male sheep (未阉割的)公羊. ⇨illus at SHEEP 见SHEEP插图. Cf 参看 EWE, TUP. **2** =BATTERING RAM (BATTER¹). **3** any of several devices in machines for plunging or striking with great force, eg the falling weight of a pile-driver 撞击装置(如打桩机的夯锤).

▷ **ram** *v* (**-mm-**) **1** (**a**) [Ipr, Tn] **~ (against/into) sth** crash against sth; strike or push sth with great force 撞击某物; 猛击或猛推某物: *The car rammed against/into the lorry.* 小汽车撞了卡车. ○ *The ice skater rammed* *into the barrier.* 溜冰者撞到护栏上了. ○ *They rammed the door to smash it down.* 他们使劲把门撞破. (**b**) [Tn] (of a ship) strike or run into (another ship) in an attempt to sink it (指船)撞击(另一船)(企图撞沉): *The frigate rammed the submarine.* 护卫舰撞击了潜艇. **2** [Tn·pr] **~ sth in, into, on, etc sth** drive sth into place by ramming 将某物打入、夯入、压入或填入某物: *ram piles into a river bed* 把桩子打入河床 ○ (*infml* 口) *ram clothes into a suitcase* 把衣服塞进衣箱 ○ *He rammed his hat on his head.* 他把帽子扣在头上. **3** (phr v) **ram sth down** flatten (eg a surface) by ramming 夯平, 压平(如某物表面): *ram down the soil*, eg when building roads 把地面夯实(如筑路时). **ram sth home** (**a**) force sth into place by ramming 填实; 塞满: *ram a charge* (ie of gunpowder) *home* 装好火药. (**b**) (*fig* 比喻) emphasize (eg a point, an argument) to make it more convincing 强调(如某论点、论据)使之更具说服力.

□ **'ram-jet** *n* (also **ram-jet engine**) type of jet engine that uses air forced in by the speed of flight to burn fuel 冲压式喷气发动机.

RAM /ˌɑːr eɪ 'em; ˌɑr e 'ɛm/ *abbr* 缩写 = **1** (*computing* 计) random access memory 随机存取存储器: *a RAM software component* 随机存取存储器软件. Cf 参看 ROM. **2** (*Brit*) Royal Academy of Music 英国皇家音乐学院.

Ram·adan /ˌræmə'dæn; *Brit also* -'dɑːn; ˌræmə'dɑn/ *n* the ninth month of the Muslim year, when Muslims fast during the hours of daylight 赖买丹月(伊斯兰教历的第九月); 斋月.

ramble /'ræmbl; 'ræmbḷ/ *v* **1** [I, Ip] walk for pleasure with no special destination 漫步; 闲逛: *I like rambling (around/about) in the country.* 我喜欢在乡间漫步. Cf 参看 HIKE 1. **2** [I, Ipr, Ip] **~ (on) (about sb/sth)** (*fig* 比喻) wander in one's talk or writing by not keeping to the subject 漫谈; 闲聊; 漫笔: *The old man rambled (on) about the past.* 这位老者在聊过去的事情. **3** [I] (of plants) grow or climb over other plants, hedges, etc with long trailing shoots (指植物)蔓生, 攀缘生长.

▷ **ramble** *n* rambling walk 漫步: *go for/on a ramble in the country* 去乡间漫步.

ram·bler /'ræmblə(r); 'ræmblɚ/ *n* **1** person who rambles (RAMBLE 1) 漫步者. **2** rambling plant 蔓生植物: [attrib 作定语] *rambler roses* 攀缘蔷薇.

ram·bling *adj* **1** (esp of buildings, streets, towns, etc) extending in various directions irregularly (尤指建筑物、街道、城镇等)无规则地向各方延伸的, 布局凌乱的. **2** (of a plant) growing or climbing with long trailing shoots (指植物)蔓生的, 攀缘的. **3** (of a speech, essay, etc) not keeping to the subject; disconnected (指讲话、文章等)不切题的, 不连贯的.

ram·bunc·tious /ræm'bʌŋkʃəs; ræm'bʌŋkʃəs/ *adj* (*infml* 口 *esp US*) =RUMBUSTIOUS.

ram·ekin /'ræməkɪn; 'ræməkɪn/ *n* (**a**) small mould for baking and serving an individual portion of food (烘烤一人分量的食物用的)小模子, 小烤盘: [attrib 作定语] *a 'ramekin dish* 一人分量的烤盘食物. (**b**) food served in this 小烤盘中的食物: *a cheese 'ramekin* 一烤盘有干酪的食物.

ram·ify /'ræmɪfaɪ; 'ræməˌfaɪ/ *v* (*pt, pp* **-fied**) [I, Tn esp passive 尤用于被动语态] (*fml* 文) (cause sth to) branch out in many directions; make or become a network (使某物)向各方分枝; (使)成网状: *a ramified system*, eg of railways 网状系统(如铁路的).

▷ **ra·mi·fica·tion** /ˌræmɪfɪ'keɪʃn; ˌræməfə'keʃən/ *n* (usu *pl* 通常作复数) part of a complex structure; secondary consequence, esp one that complicates 某复杂系统之部分; 分支(尤指形成复杂结构者): *widespread ramifications of trade* 广布各地的贸易分支机构 ○ *I couldn't follow all the ramifications of the plot.* 我并不完全明白故事的所有情节.

ramp[1] /ræmp; ræmp/ *n* **1** slope joining two levels of ground, a floor, a road, etc (地面、地板、道路等两水平面之间的)斜面, 斜坡, 斜道: *push a wheelchair up/down a ramp* 把轮椅推上[下]坡道 ○ *Beware ramp*, eg seen on a road sign. 注意斜坡(如路标所示). **2** movable set of steps for entering and leaving an aircraft (上下飞机用的)移动式舷梯.

ramp[2] /ræmp; ræmp/ *n* (*dated Brit sl* 旧, 俚) swindle, esp one that involves charging excessively high prices 诈骗; (尤指)敲诈, 敲竹杠.

ram·page /ræm'peɪdʒ; ræm'pedʒ/ *v* [Ipr, Ip] rush around wildly or violently 狂暴地乱冲乱闯: *The mob rampaged through the village.* 这伙暴徒在村中横冲直撞.

▷ **ram·page** *n* (idm 习语) **be/go on the 'rampage** go about behaving violently or destructively 到处进行暴力或破坏活动: *drunken soldiers on the rampage* 喝醉酒而到处闹事的大兵.

ramp·ant /'ræmpənt; 'ræmpənt/ *adj* **1** (of disease, crime, etc) flourishing excessively; unrestrained (指疾病、罪恶等)猖獗的, 遏制不住的: *Cholera was rampant in the district.* 这个区里霍乱蔓延十分严重. ○ *a city of rampant violence* 暴力活动失去控制的城市. **2** (of plants) growing too luxuriantly or thickly (指植物)过于繁茂的: *Rampant ivy had covered the wall.* 密密的常春藤遮住了这面墙. **3** (usu directly after a *n* 通常直接用于名词之后) (*heraldry* 纹) (of an animal on a coat of arms) standing on one hind leg with forelegs raised (指盾形纹章上的动物)用一只后腿站立前脚跃起的: *lions rampant* 立狮纹章. Cf 参看 COUCHANT. ▷ **ramp·antly** *adv*.

ram·part /'ræmpɑːt; 'ræmpɑrt/ *n* **1** (esp *pl* 尤作复数) defensive wall round a fort, etc consisting of a wide bank of earth with a path for walking along the top (城堡等周围宽阔的)防御土墙. **2** (esp *sing* 尤作单数) defence; protection 防御; 保护: *a rampart against infection* 对传染病的预防.

ram·rod /'ræmrɒd; 'ræmˌrɑd/ *n* **1** iron rod formerly used for ramming the charge into muzzle-loading guns 推弹杆(旧时前膛枪炮装火药用的铁棒). **2** (idm 习语) **(as) stiff/straight as a 'ramrod** (of a person) very erect (指人)挺立的: *The soldier stood stiff as a ramrod.* 这士兵站得笔直.

ram·shackle /'ræmʃækl; 'ræmʃækḷ/ *adj* (of houses, vehicles, etc) almost collapsing (指房屋、车辆等)破烂不堪的: *a ramshackle old bus* 快要报废的公共汽车 ○ (*fig* 比喻) *a ramshackle organization* 即将解体的组织.

ran *pt* of RUN[1].

ranch /rɑːntʃ; *US* ræntʃ; ræntʃ/ *n* (**a**) large farm, esp in the US or Canada, where cattle are bred; similar farm producing crops, fruit, chickens, etc 大牧牛场(尤指美国或加拿大的); 农场、果园、养鸡场等: [attrib 作定语] *a ranch house* 大农场主的住宅. (**b**) farm where certain other animals are bred 牧场; 饲养场: *a mink ranch* 水貂饲养场.

▷ **rancher** *n* person who owns, manages or works on a ranch 大农场等的主人、管理人或工人.

ran·cid /'rænsɪd; 'rænsɪd/ *adj* **1** (of fatty foods) tasting or smelling bad because of staleness (指含油脂食物)因变质而有陈腐味道或气味的: *The butter has gone/turned rancid.* 这黄油已经哈喇了. **2** (of smells or tastes) like stale fat (指气味或味道)如陈腐脂肪味的: *the rancid stench of dirty drains* 脏水沟发出的腐臭味. ▷ **ran·cid·ness** *n* [U].

ran·cour (*US* **-cor**) /'ræŋkə(r); 'ræŋkɚ/ *n* [U] deep long-lasting bitterness or ill-will; spite 深仇; 积怨; 怨恨: *feel full of rancour against sb* 对某人怀有深仇大恨. ▷ **ran·cor·ous** /'ræŋkərəs; 'ræŋkərəs/ *adj*. **ran·cor·ously** *adv*.

rand /rænd; rænd/ *n* unit of money in the Republic of South Africa; 100 cents 兰特(南非共和国货币单位, 等于100分).

NOTE ON USAGE 用法: The pronunciation of **rand** varies. ☆ **rand**一字的读音有多种. In South Africa commonly heard variants are 在南非常可听到以下异读形式: /rɑːnd, rɑːnt, rɒnt; rænd, rɑnd, rɑnt/.

R and D /ˌɑːr ən 'diː; ˌɑr ən 'di/ *abbr* 缩写 = (*commerce* 商) research and development 研究与开发.

ran·dom /'rændəm; 'rændəm/ *adj* [usu attrib 通常作定语] done, chosen, etc without method or conscious choice; haphazard 随便的; 任意的; 胡乱的: *a random sample, selection, etc* 随意抽取的样品、任意选择的东西 ○ *a few random remarks* 随便说的话.

▷ **ran·dom** *n* (idm 习语) **at 'random** without method or conscious choice 随便; 任意: *draw the winning numbers at random* 任意抽出的中奖数字 ○ *open a book at random*, ie not at any particular page 打开一本书的

任何一页 ○ *The terrorists fired into the crowd at random.* 恐怖分子向人群胡乱射击.

ran·domly *adv*: *people randomly chosen*, eg to carry out a survey 任意选择的人(如为进行抽样调查).

□ **random 'access** (also **direct 'access**) (*computing* 计) process that allows information in a computer to be stored or retrieved without reading through items stored previously 随机存取. Cf 参看 READ ONLY (READ). **ˌrandom access 'memory** (*abbr* 缩写 **RAM**) computer memory used temporarily to store data (usu found by random access) that can be changed or removed 随机存取存储器. Cf 参看 READ ONLY MEMORY (READ).

randy /ˈrændɪ; `rændɪ/ *adj* (**-ier**, **-iest**) (*infml* 口 *esp Brit*) sexually excited; lustful 性欲冲动的; 好色的: *a randy tom-cat* 闹春的雄猫 ○ *I feel really randy.* 我的确有些性冲动. ▷ **randily** *adv*. **ran·di·ness** *n* [U].

ranee (also **rani**) /ˈrɑːniː; `rɑni/ *n* (formerly) Hindu queen or princess; rajah's wife or widow (旧时)印度的女王或公主, 印度君主之妻或遗孀.

rang *pt* of RING².

range¹ /reɪndʒ; rendʒ/ *n* **1** [C] connected line or row of mountains, hills, etc (山、丘等连贯而成的)脉, 排, 列, 行: *a mountain-range* 山脉. **2** [C] group or series of similar things; selection or variety 成套或成系列的东西; 种类: *sell/stock a whole range of tools, dresses, foods* 出售[备有]各种各样的工具、服装、食品 ○ *The new model comes in an exciting range of colours.* 这种新式样有各种鲜艳的颜色. ○ *have a wide/narrow range of interests, hobbies, etc* 兴趣、爱好等甚广[不广]. **3** [C] limits between which sth varies; extent (种类或变化的)限度, 范围, 幅度, 程度: *a soprano's range*, ie between her top and bottom notes 女高音的音域 ○ *What is the salary range for the post?* 这一职位的薪金幅度是多少? ○ *The annual range of temperature is from -10°C to 40°C.* 全年的温度较差为-10°C至40°C. ○ *There's a wide range of ability in the class.* 这班的水平差距很大. ○ *That subject is outside my range*, ie one I have not studied. 那个问题已超出了我的研究范围. **4** (**a**) [U] distance within which one can see or hear; distance over which sounds will travel 视力或听力所达到的距离; 声音所能传送的距离: *It came within my range of vision.* 该物体进入了我的视野. ○ *take a long-range shot*, eg with a camera 进行远距离拍摄 ○ *They live within range of the transmitter.* 他们住在无线电发射机的有效范围以内. ○ *She was out of range (of my voice).* 她在那地方听不见(我的声音). (**b**) [U, sing] distance to which a gun will shoot, or over which a missile, shell, etc will travel (枪炮、导弹等的)射程: *The gun has a range of five miles.* 这炮的射程为五英里. ○ *in/within/out of/beyond (firing) range* 在射程以内[以外] ○ *He shot the lion at point-blank range*, ie when it was so near that he could not miss. 他在近距离平射射程内向狮子射击. ○ *fire at close/long range* 进行近[远]距离射击. (**c**) [C] distance that a vehicle, aircraft, etc will travel before it needs to be refuelled (车辆、飞行器等)不再次加油可抵达的距离. **5** [C] (**a**) area of ground with targets for soldiers, etc to practise shooting 射击场; 靶场: *an army range* 军用射击场 ○ *a 'rifle-range* 步枪靶场. (**b**) area within which rockets and missiles are fired (火箭和导弹的)发射场. **6** [C] area within which a particular plant, animal, etc may be found (某类植物、动物等的)生长区, 分布区. **7** [sing] (*US*) large open area for hunting or grazing (大面积空旷的)狩猎场, 放牧场. **8** [C] (esp formerly) cooking stove with ovens and hotplates for pans, etc (尤指旧式的)炉灶: *a kitchen range* 厨房中的炉灶.

□ **'range-finder** *n* device for finding the distance of sb/sth to be shot at or photographed (射击或摄影用的)测距仪, 测远计.

range² /reɪndʒ; rendʒ/ *v* **1** (**a**) [esp passive 尤用于被动语态: Tn, Tn·pr] arrange (sb/sth) in a line or in ranks, or in a specified way 使(某人[某物])排成行或队: *troops ranged facing each other* 面对面排列的部队 ○ *The spectators ranged themselves along the route of the procession.* 观众沿队伍行进的路线排成行. ○ *flowerpots ranged in rows on the window-sill* 窗台上一排排摆放着的花盆. (**b**) [Tn·pr] **~ sb/oneself with sb/sth** place sb/oneself in a certain group 使某人[自己]站在某一方面: *On this issue, she has ranged herself with the Opposition.* 在这个问题上, 她站在反对派一边. **2** [Ipr] **~ between A and B/from A to B** vary or extend between specified limits 在A和B之间变化或变动; 从A延伸到B: *Their ages range from 25 to 50.* 他们的年龄在25岁到50岁之间. ○ *Prices range between £7 and £10.* 售价在7英镑和10英镑之间. ○ *The frontier ranges from the northern hills to the southern coast.* 边界从北部山地一直延伸到南部海岸. ○ *His interests ranged from chess to canoeing.* 他的爱好从下国际象棋到划独木舟, 范围很广. **3** [I, Ipr, Tn] **~ (over/through sth)** wander over/through (an area) freely; roam 漫游(某地); 漫步: *cattle ranging over the plains* 在平原上来回走动的牛 ○ (*fig* 比喻) *research ranging over a number of fields* 涉及若干领域的研究 ○ *a wide-ranging discussion*, ie covering many topics 内容广泛的讨论 ○ *range the hills, countryside, etc* 漫游山地、乡村等. **4** [Ipr] **~ over sth** (**a**) (of guns) fire bullets, etc over (a distance) (指枪炮)射程达到(某距离): *This rifle ranges over a mile.* 这种步枪射程达一英里. (**b**) (of bullets, missiles, etc) travel (a distance) (指子弹、导弹等)射程达到(某距离).

ranger /ˈreɪndʒə(r); `rendʒɚ/ *n* **1** (**a**) (*Brit*) keeper of a royal park, estate, etc who enforces forest laws 皇家园林、地产等的管理员. (**b**) (*esp US*) guard who patrols and protects a forest, etc 担任巡逻和警戒任务的护林员. **2** (*US*) member of a body of armed mounted men acting as police, eg in thinly populated areas 武装骑警(如驻守人口稀少地区的): *the Texas Rangers* 得克萨斯州骑警. **3** (*US*) commando 突击队员. **4 Ranger** (*Brit*) senior Girl Guide 高年级的女童子军.

rani =RANEE.

rank¹ /ræŋk; ræŋk/ *n* **1** [C, U] position in a scale of responsibility, quality, social status, etc (职务、身分、社会地位等的)等级: *ministers of Cabinet rank* 内阁各大臣 ○ *a painter of the first/top rank*, ie one of the very best 第一流的画家 ○ *people of (high) rank* 地位高的人 ○ *people of all ranks and classes* 各阶层各阶级的人. **2** [C, U] position or grade in the armed forces 军阶; 军衔: *promoted to the rank of captain* 晋升到上尉军衔 ○ *above/below a major in rank* 军衔高于[低于]少校 ○ *officers of high rank* 高级军官 ○ *reach the rank of colonel* 高达上校军衔. **3** [C] line or row of things (物体的)行, 列, 排: *a 'cab/'taxi rank* 一排计程车 ○ *Take the taxi at the head of the rank*, ie the first in the line. 乘坐排在前头的那辆计程车. **4** (**a**) [C] line or row of soldiers, policemen, etc standing side by side (士兵、警察等肩并肩站成的)行列, 横列: *ranks of marching infantry* 横排行进的步兵 ○ *keep/break ranks*, ie remain/fail to remain in line 保持[打乱]队形. (**b**) **the ranks** [pl] (also **'other ranks**) ordinary soldiers, ie privates, corporals, etc, not officers 士兵(即二等兵、下士等, 非军官): *join, serve in, etc the ranks* 当兵 ○ *rise from the ranks*, ie be made an officer after serving as an ordinary soldier 行伍出身(由士兵升为军官) ○ *be reduced to the ranks*, ie (of a sergeant, etc) be made an ordinary soldier as a punishment (指中士等)降级为士兵(作为处罚) ○ (*fig* 比喻) *join the ranks of the unemployed*, ie become unemployed 加入失业者大军(沦为失业者). **5** (idm 习语) **close ranks** ⇨ CLOSE⁴. **pull rank** ⇨ PULL².

▷ **rank** *v* (not in the continuous tenses 不用于进行时态) **1** [Tn, Tn·pr, Cn·n/a] **~ sb/sth (as sth)** place sb/sth in a rank; grade sb/sth according to quality, achievement, etc 将某人[某事物]置入行列中; (按特性、成就等)将某人[某事物]分等级: *I rank her achievement very highly.* 我对她的成就评价很高. ○ *Where/How do you rank Karpov as a chess player?* 你把卡尔波夫列为哪一级的棋手? ○ *I rank her among the country's best writers.* 我认为她可属全国最优秀作家之列. **2** [Ipr] have a rank or place 属某等级; 居某地位: *Does he rank among/with the failures?* 他可以算作失败的那一类人吗? ○ *A major ranks above a captain.* 少校比上尉军衔高. ○ *a high-ranking official, delegate, etc* 高级官员、代表等. **3** [Tn] (*US*) have a higher rank than (sb) 比(某人)级别高.

□ **the ˌrank and 'file** **1** the ordinary soldiers, not officers 士兵(非军官). **2** (*fig* 比喻) the ordinary members of an organization (某组织的)普通成员: *the rank and file of the party* 普通党员 ○ [attrib 作定语] *rank-and-file workers* 普通工作者.

'ranking officer (*US*) officer of the highest rank present 在场的最高级军官.

rank[2] /ræŋk; ræŋk/ *adj* **1** (**a**) (of plants, etc) growing too thickly; over-luxuriant (指植物等)生长过盛的; 过于繁茂的: *rank grass, ivy, etc* 蔓生的杂草、常春藤等 ○ *roses that grow rank* 过于茂盛的玫瑰. (**b**) **~ (with sth)** (of land) full of or likely to produce many weeds (指土地)长满杂草的, 易生杂草的: *rank soil, earth, etc* 杂草滋生的土壤、土地等 ○ *a field rank with nettles and thistles* 一块长满荨麻和大蓟的土地. **2** smelling or tasting bad; offensive 气味或味道不好的; 讨厌的: *rank tobacco* 呛人的烟叶 ○ *the rank stench of rotting meat* 腐肉的臭味. **3** [attrib 作定语] (*esp derog* 尤作贬义) complete and utter; unmistakable 完全的; 不折不扣的: *a rank traitor, lie* 十足的卖国贼、谎言 ○ *rank insolence, stupidity, injustice, etc* 极端的无礼、愚蠢、不公等 ○ *The winning horse was a rank outsider.* 获胜的马是一匹完全不起眼儿的冷门马. ▷ **rankly** *adv*. **rank·ness** *n* [U].

rankle /ˈræŋkl; ˋræŋkl/ *v* [I] cause lasting bitterness or resentment 使痛苦不已; 使怨恨不已: *The insult still rankled in his mind.* 他对那次受辱仍耿耿于怀.

ran·sack /ˈrænsæk; *US* rænˈsæk; ˋrænsæk/ *v* **1** [Tn, Tn·pr] **~ sth (for sth)** search (a place) thoroughly 彻底搜索(某处): *I've ransacked the house for those papers, but I can't find them.* 我满房子各处寻找那些文件, 但却找不到. **2** [Tn] plunder (sth); pillage 抢劫(某物); 掠夺: *Burglars ransacked the stately home.* 盗贼洗劫了这所富丽堂皇的住宅.

ran·som /ˈrænsəm; ˋrænsəm/ *n* **1** [U] release of a captive in return for money, etc demanded by his captors (劫持者要求)付赎金等使被劫持者获释; 赎身: [attrib 作定语] *ransom money* 赎金. **2** [U, C] money, etc paid for this 赎金; 用以赎身之物: *pay ransom to the kidnappers* 付给绑架者赎金 ○ *The kidnappers demanded a ransom of £10000 for his release.* 绑架者要10 000英镑赎金才释放他. **3** (idm 习语) **hold sb to ˈransom** (**a**) keep sb captive and demand ransom for him 禁锢被绑架者以勒索赎金. (**b**) (*fig* 比喻) demand concessions from sb by using threats 以威胁手段逼某人让步: *The unions are holding the country to ransom*, eg by a national strike. 工会正在挟制国家以逼迫政府让步(如否则采取全国大罢工). **a king's ransom** ⇨ KING.

▷ **ran·som** *v* [Tn] (**a**) obtain the release of (a captive) in return for payment 以赎金赎回(被劫持者). (**b**) hold (a captive) and demand ransom for him 禁锢(被劫持者)以勒索赎金.

rant /rænt; rænt/ *v* [I, Ipr, Ip, Tn] **~ (at sb/sth)** (*derog* 贬) **1** speak loudly, violently or theatrically 大声地、激昂地或拿腔拿调地说话: *He ranted (on) at me about my mistakes.* 他大声数落我. ○ *This actor rants his lines.* 这演员背台词拿腔拿调. **2** (idm 习语) **ˌrant and ˈrave (at sb/sth)** condemn or censure sb/sth loudly and forcefully 大声地、狠狠地责备或训斥某人[某事物]: *You can rant and rave at the fine, but you'll still have to pay it.* 你闹也好, 骂也好, 罚金还是得交. ▷ **ranter** /ˈræntə(r); ˋræntɚ/ *n*.

rap[1] /ræp; ræp/ *n* **1** [C] (sound of a) quick sharp blow or knock (轻快的)敲击(声); 急敲(声): *a sharp rap on the elbow* 碰了一下胳膊肘 ○ *There was a rap at/on the door.* 有敲门声. **2** [U] (*US sl* 俚) rapid talk; chatter 速度快的谈话; 唠叨. **3** (idm 习语) **beat the rap** ⇨ BEAT[1]. **give sb/get a ˌrap on/over the ˈknuckles** (*infml* 口) reproach or rebuke sb 责备或训斥某人: *He got a rap over the knuckles from the teacher for not doing enough work.* 他没做完功课挨了老师一通训. **take the rap (for sth)** (*infml* 口 *esp US*) be punished, esp for sth one has not done 受罚; (尤指)背黑锅.

▷ **rap** *v* (**-pp-**) **1** (**a**) [Tn] strike (sth) quickly and smartly (轻而快地)敲击(某物); 急敲(某物): *She rapped my knuckles.* 她轻而快地敲打我的指节. (**b**) [Ipr, Tn] knock or tap lightly and quickly 轻敲; 急敲: *rap (on) the table* 轻敲桌子 ○ *rap (at) the door* 轻轻叩门. **2** [Tn] (*infml* 口) reproach or rebuke (sb) 责备或训斥(某人): *She rapped the Minister publicly for his indiscreet remarks.* 她公开斥责那位大臣言论失当. **3** [I] (*US sl* 俚) talk or chatter rapidly 快速地说; 唠叨. **4** (phr v) **rap sth out** (**a**) say sth abruptly and sharply 突然厉声说出某事: *The officer rapped out the orders.* 那军官厉声发出命令. (**b**) express sth by taps 用敲击表达某事物: *The prisoner rapped out a message on the cell wall.* 那囚犯敲打囚室的墙来传达讯息.

rap[2] /ræp; ræp/ *n* (idm 习语) **not care/give a rap (about/for sb/sth)** (*infml* 口) not care at all 毫不在乎.

ra·pa·cious /rəˈpeɪʃəs; rəˋpeʃəs/ *adj* (*fml* 文) **1** greedy, esp for money; grasping 贪婪的; (尤指)贪财的: *fall into the clutches of a rapacious landlord* 落入一个贪婪的地主手中 ○ *rapacious business methods* 唯利是图的生意经. **2** plundering and robbing others 抢劫的; 掠夺的: *rapacious marauders, invaders, etc* 肆意掠夺的强盗、侵略者等.

▷ **ra·pa·ciously** *adv*.

ra·pa·city /rəˈpæsətɪ; rəˋpæsətɪ/ *n* [U] greed; desire to rob and plunder 贪婪; 贪心; 劫掠的欲望.

rape[1] /reɪp; rep/ *v* [Tn] commit the crime of forcing (a woman or girl) to have sexual intercourse against her will 强奸(女子).

▷ **rape** *n* [C, U] **1** (act of) raping; being raped 强奸: *commit two rapes* 犯两次强奸罪 ○ *Is rape on the increase?* 强奸案是否越来越多了? ○ *Her rape had a profound psychological effect on her.* 她被强奸这件事造成了她心理上的严重创伤. **2** (*fig* 比喻) act of violently interfering with sth 肆意损坏某事物: *the rape of the countryside*, eg by removing ancient hedges 对乡村的破坏(如拆除古老的树篱).

rap·ist /ˈreɪpɪst; ˋrepɪst/ *n* person who commits rape 强奸者; 强奸犯.

rape[2] /reɪp; rep/ *n* [U] plant grown as food for farm animals and for its seed, from which oil is made 油菜, 芸薹(可作饲料, 种子可榨油): *a field of rape* 一块油菜田 ○ ˌ*rape-seed* ˈ*oil* 油菜籽油 ○ ˌ*oilseed* ˈ*rape* 油料作物油菜.

R

rapid /ˈræpɪd; ˋræpɪd/ *adj* **1** (**a**) moving or acting with great speed; fast 迅速的; 快的: *a rapid pulse, heartbeat* 过快的脉搏、心搏 ○ *ask several questions in rapid succession* 快速连续提出几个问题 ○ *the rapid to-and-fro movements of a piston* 活塞快速的往复运动. (**b**) happening in a short time; prompt 短时间内发生的; 敏捷的: *a rapid decline in sales* 销售额的急剧下降 ○ *Cats have rapid reflexes.* 猫的反应很敏捷. **2** (of a slope) descending steeply (指斜坡)陡的. **3** (idm 习语) **make great/rapid strides** ⇨ STRIDE *n*.

▷ **ra·pid·ity** /rəˈpɪdətɪ; rəˋpɪdətɪ/ *n* [U].

rapidly *adv*.

rapids *n* [pl] swift current in a river caused by a steep downward slope in the river bed (河的)急流, 湍流: *shoot the rapids*, eg in a canoe 穿过急流(如乘独木舟).

□ **rapid-fire** *adj* [attrib 作定语] (**a**) (of a gun) firing bullets, etc in quick succession (指枪炮)速射的. (**b**) (*fig* 比喻) (of questions, etc) spoken very quickly, one after the other (指问题等)连珠炮似的: *the rapid-fire jokes of a comedian* 喜剧演员连续说出的笑话.

ˌ**rapid** ˈ**transit** (*US*) (system of) fast urban public transport, eg by underground or overhead railway 城市高速交通(系统)(如地铁或高架铁路).

ra·pier /ˈreɪpɪə(r); ˋrepɪɚ/ *n* light thin double-edged sword, used for thrusting 一种轻巧细长的剑(用以刺戳): [attrib 作定语] (*fig* 比喻) *rapier wit* 机智的言语. ⇨ illus at SWORD 见SWORD插图.

□ ˈ**rapier-thrust** *n* (*fig* 比喻) witty remark or reply 机智巧妙的言语或回答.

ra·pine /ˈræpaɪn; *US* ˈræpɪn; ˋræpɪn/ *n* [U] (*fml or rhet* 文或修辞) act of seizing property by force; plundering 劫掠; 强夺: *land ravaged by pillage and rapine* 遭劫掠蹂躏的国土.

rap·port /ræˈpɔː(r); *US* -ˈpɔːrt; ræˋpɔrt/ *n* [U, sing] **~ (with sb/between A and B)** sympathetic and harmonious relationship 融洽和谐的关系: *He is in rapport with his pupils.* 他与学生关系很好. ○ *The actor developed a close rapport with his audience.* 该演员与观众建立了密切的关系. ○ *Father and son have a great rapport.* 父子情深.

rap·proche·ment /ræˈprɒʃmɒŋ, ræˈprəʊʃ-; *US* ˌræprəʊʃˈmɒŋ; ˌræprɔʃˋmɑ̃/ *n* (*French* 法) **~ (with sb/between A and B)** renewal of friendly relations, esp between countries 友好关系的恢复(尤指国家间): *bring about a rapprochement between warring states, factions, etc* 交战国、派系等恢复友好关系.

rap·scal·lion /ræpˈskæljən; ræpˋskæljən/ *n* (*arch or joc* 古或谑) rascal; rogue 流氓; 坏蛋.

rapt /ræpt; ræpt/ *adj* **~ (in sth)** so intent or absorbed that one is unaware of other things; spellbound 全神贯注的; 入迷的: *a rapt expression, look, smile, etc* 着迷的表情、样子、微笑等 ○ *rapt in contemplation, thought, devotion, etc* 一心一意地沉思、思考、奉献等 ○ *He listened to the music with rapt attention.* 他屏气凝神地听着音乐. ▷ **raptly** *adv*.

rap·ture /ˈræptʃə(r); ˋræptʃɚ/ *n* **1** [U] intense delight 极度的欢喜: *gazing in/with rapture at the girl he loved* 喜不自胜地注视着他心爱的姑娘. **2** (idm 习语) **be in, go into, etc raptures (about/over sb/sth)** feel or express great delight or enthusiasm 狂喜; 狂热: *I'm in raptures about my new job.* 我对这一新工作喜不可言.

▷ **rap·tur·ous** /ˈræptʃərəs; ˋræptʃərəs/ *adj* causing or expressing rapture (使人)欣喜若狂的: *rapturous applause* 热烈的掌声 ○ *give sb a rapturous welcome/reception* 热情洋溢地欢迎[接待]某人 ○ *a rapturous sigh, look* 欣喜若狂的惊叹、神情. **rap·tur·ously** *adv*.

rare[1] /reə(r); rɛr/ *adj* **(-r, -st) 1** not often happening or seen, etc; unusual 稀有的; 罕见的; 不寻常的: *a rare occurrence, sight, visitor* 稀罕事、罕见的景象、稀客 ○ *a rare book, plant, butterfly*, ie one of only a few that exist 珍本书、珍奇的植物、稀有的蝴蝶 ○ *With rare exceptions, he does not appear in public now.* 除了极其个别的情况外, 他现在不公开露面. ○ *It is rare for her to arrive late.* 她很少有迟到的时候. **2** [attrib 作定语] (*dated* 旧) unusually good or great 极好的; 极大的: *be shy, tolerant, etc to a rare degree* 极为腼腆、宽容等 ○ *We had a rare (old) time at the party.* 我们在聚会时玩得高兴极了. **3** (of gases, esp the atmosphere) of less than usual density (指气体, 尤指空气)稀薄的.

▷ **rarely** *adv* not often; seldom 不常: *I rarely eat in restaurants.* 我很少在饭馆吃饭. ○ (*fml* 文) *Only rarely do I eat in restaurants.* 我极少到饭馆就餐.

rare·ness *n* [U].

□ ˌ**rare** ˈ**earth** any of a group of metallic elements with similar chemical properties 稀土元素.

NOTE ON USAGE 用法: A thing or an event may be **rare** when it is found or occurs infrequently. 很少见到的东西或很少发生的现象, 可用 **rare** 一词来表达. It may once have been common 这类东西或现象可能在过去很普通: *The panda is now a rare animal.* 熊猫现在是稀有动物. ○ *A top hat is a rare sight these days.* 高顶大礼帽现在已不多见. It may have a special value 这类事物有的可能有特殊价值: *a painting of rare distinction* 一幅希世之珍的画儿. Something, usually a thing in daily use, is **scarce** when it is hard to get because it is in short supply 有些东西, 通常为日用品, 因匮乏而难以得到, 即是 **scarce**: *Water is scarce in the desert.* 在沙漠里水是很难得到的. ○ *Strawberries are scarce this year.* 今年草莓很少.

rare[2] /reə(r); rɛr/ *adj* (usu of beef) cooked so that the inside is still red and juicy; underdone (通常指牛肉)半熟的(里面色红肉嫩的): *a (medium-) rare steak* 半生半熟的牛排.

rare·bit /ˈreəbɪt; ˋrɛrˌbɪt/ *n* =WELSH RAREBIT (WELSH).

rar·efy /ˈreərɪfaɪ; ˋrɛrəˌfaɪ/ *v* (*pt, pp* **-fied**) [I, Tn esp passive 尤用于被动语态] (cause sth to) become thinner or less dense (使某物)变薄, 变稀, 变稀薄: *rarefying gases* 变得稀薄的气体.

▷ **rar·efied** *adj* [usu attrib 通常作定语] **1** (of gases) less dense than is normal; thin (指气体)稀薄的: *the rarefied air* (ie with little oxygen) *of the Andes* 安第斯山脉的稀薄空气(缺氧). **2** (*fig* 比喻) (of ideas, etc) subtle and refined; lofty and exclusive (指思想等)缜密而纯正的, 清高的: *dons living in a rarefied academic atmosphere* 生活在纯净的学术气氛中的大学教师.

rar·ing /ˈreərɪŋ; ˋrɛrɪŋ/ *adj* [pred 作表语] (*infml* 口) **1 ~ to do sth** so eager or willing to do sth that restraint is difficult 渴望做某事而难以阻止: *The horses were raring to have a gallop.* 这些马都急不可耐地要飞跑起来. ○ *She is raring to try out her new skates.* 她很想试试她那双新溜冰鞋. **2** (idm 习语) ˌ**raring to** ˈ**go** keen to start 巴不得马上开始.

rar·ity /ˈreərətɪ; ˋrɛrətɪ/ *n* **1** [U] rareness 稀有; 罕见. **2** [C] thing that is uncommon or unusual; thing valued because it is rare 稀有的事物; 因稀少而珍贵的东西: *Rain is a rarity in the desert.* 在沙漠中雨是很少见的. ○ *ancient scrolls and other rarities* 古书卷等珍品.

ras·cal /ˈrɑːskl; *US* ˈræskl; ˋræskḷ/ *n* **1** dishonest person 不诚实的人; 流氓; 无赖. **2** (*joc* 谑) mischievous or cheeky person who likes playing tricks, esp a child 喜欢恶作剧的人, 爱捣蛋的傢伙(尤指儿童): *Give me my keys back, you little rascal!* 把钥匙还给我, 你这个小淘气!

▷ **ras·cally** /-kəlɪ; -klɪ/ *adj* of or like a rascal; dishonest (似)流氓的, 无赖的: *a rascally person, trick* 奸诈的人、奸计.

rase =RAZE.

rash[1] /ræʃ; ræʃ/ *n* **1** [C usu *sing* 通常作单数] patch of tiny red spots on the skin 疹; 皮疹: *a* ˈ*nettle-rash* 荨麻疹 ○ *I break out/come out in a rash* (ie A rash appears on my skin) *if I eat chocolate.* 我一吃巧克力, 就出皮疹. ○ *The heat brought her out in* (ie caused) *a rash.* 她热得出了痱子. **2** [sing] **~ of sth** (*fig* 比喻) sudden widespread appearance of sth unpleasant 令人不快的事物突然大量出现: *a rash of ugly new houses* 一下子冒出来的一大片难看的房子 ○ *a rash of strikes in the steel industry* 钢铁工业突如其来的一连串大罢工.

rash[2] /ræʃ; ræʃ/ *adj* (**-er, -est**) acting or done without careful consideration of the possible consequences; impetuous 未仔细虑及后果的; 轻率的: *a rash young student* 鲁莽的年轻学生 ○ *Don't make rash promises*, ie ones you may regret. 勿轻易许诺(以免后悔). ○ *It was rash of you to sign the form without reading it.* 你看也不看就在表格上签字真太轻率了. ▷ **rashly** *adv*. **rash·ness** *n* [U]: *I lent him £5 in a moment of rashness.* 我一时不慎借给了他5英镑.

rasher /ˈræʃə(r); ˋræʃɚ/ *n* thin slice of bacon or ham 腌猪肉片; 火腿片: *a fried egg and a couple of rashers of bacon for breakfast* 早餐吃的一个煎鸡蛋和两片腌猪肉.

rasp /rɑːsp; *US* ræsp; ræsp/ *n* **1** [C] coarse file with rows of sharp points on its surface(s) 粗锉刀. **2** [sing] unpleasant grating sound 刺耳的锉磨声: *the rasp of a saw on wood* 刺耳的锯木声.

▷ **rasp** *v* **1** [Tn, Cn·a] scrape (sth) with, or as if with, a rasp 用粗锉刀锉(某物); (如锉一般)刮削(某物): *rasp the surface (smooth)* 把表面锉(平). **2 (a)** [Tn, Tn·p] **~ sth (out)** say sth in an unpleasant grating voice 以刺耳的粗声说出某事: *rasp (out) orders, insults, etc* 粗声粗气发出命令、辱骂之词等. **(b)** [I, Ip] make an unpleasant grating sound 发出刺耳的锉磨声: *a learner rasping (away) on his violin* 用小提琴拉出刺耳声音的初学者 ○ *a rasping voice* 粗声粗气. **3** (phr v) **rasp sth away/off** remove sth with a rasp (用粗锉刀)锉掉某物: *rasp off the rough edges* 把粗糙的边锉掉.

rasp·berry /ˈrɑːzbrɪ; *US* ˈræzberɪ; ˋræzˌbɛrɪ/ *n* **1 (a)** type of bramble 悬钩子; 复盆子: [attrib 作定语] *raspberry canes* 悬钩子的新枝. **(b)** its edible sweet red berry 悬钩子的红色聚合果(味甜, 可食): *raspberries and ice-cream* 悬钩子加冰激凌 ○ [attrib 作定语] *raspberry jam* 悬钩子果酱. **2** (*US* also **razz, Bronx cheer**) (*infml* 口) sound made with the tongue and lips to show dislike, contempt, etc 用舌与唇发出的表示憎恶、鄙夷等的声音: *give/blow sb a raspberry* 用舌与唇发声嘲笑某人 ○ *The teacher got a raspberry as she turned her back.* 该教师转过身去时有人用舌与唇发出嘲笑她的声音.

Ras·ta·far·ian /ˌræstəˈfeərɪən; ˌræstəˋfærɪən/ *n, adj* (member) of a Jamaican sect regarding Blacks as a people chosen by God for salvation 拉斯塔法里(牙买加的教派, 认为黑人是上帝将拯救的人); 该教派的成员.

rat /ræt; ræt/ *n* **1** rodent that looks like, but is larger than, a mouse 大鼠. ⇨illus at App 1 见附录1插图, page iii. **2** (*infml fig* 口, 比喻) **(a)** disloyal person, esp one who deserts a cause in times of difficulty 不忠的人; (尤指困难时)背弃事业的人: *So you've changed sides, you dirty rat!* 那么, 你改变立场了, 你这可耻的叛徒! **(b)** unpleasant or despicable man 讨厌的人; 卑鄙的人. **3** (idm 习语) **like a drowned rat** ⇨ DROWN. **the rat race** (*infml derog* 口, 贬) fiercely competitive struggle, esp to keep one's position in work or life 激烈的竞争(尤指为保住职位或地位): *opt out of* (ie withdraw from) *the rat race* 决定退出这场竞争. **smell a rat** ⇨ SMELL[2].

▷ **rat** *v* (**-tt-**) **1** [I] (usu 通常作 **go ratting**) hunt rats

去捕鼠. **2** [I, Ipr] (*infml* 口) (**a**) **~ (on sb/sth)** break an agreement, a promise, etc; fail to do sth one has undertaken to do 违背协议、诺言等; 未履行责任. (**b**) **~ (on sb)** reveal a secret; betray sb 泄露秘密; 背叛某人: *She's ratted on us — here comes the head teacher!* 她把我们出卖了——瞧校长都来了!

rats *interj* (*dated infml* 旧, 口) (used to express annoyance or contempt 用以表示恼怒或鄙视).

rat·ter *n* dog or cat that catches rats 捕鼠的狗或猫: *Terriers are good ratters.* 㹴是善于捕鼠的狗.

ratty *adj* (**-ier, -iest**) **1** (*Brit infml* 口) easily made angry; irritable 易怒的; 暴躁的: *be/feel in a ratty mood* 心烦气躁. **2** (*US infml* 口) shabby or dilapidated 破旧的; 破烂的. **3** of, like or full of rats (似)老鼠的; 有很多老鼠的.

□ ˈ**ratbag** *n* (*sl esp Austral or NZ* 俚, 尤用于澳大利亚或新西兰) contemptible person 卑鄙的傢伙.

ˈ**ratfink** *n* (*US sl derog* 俚, 贬) **1** unpleasant person 讨厌的傢伙. **2** informer 告密者.

rat·a·tat, rat-a-tat-tat =RAT-TAT.

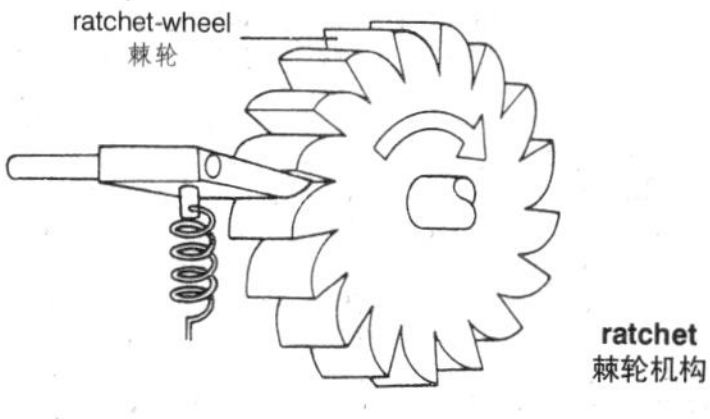

ratchet /ˈrætʃɪt; ˈrætʃɪt/ *n* **1** device consisting of a toothed wheel or bar with a catch that fits between the teeth allowing movement in one direction only 棘轮机构. **2** (also ˈ**ratchet-wheel**) wheel that forms part of this device 棘轮. ⇨illus 见插图.

rate[1] /reɪt; ret/ *n* **1** standard of reckoning obtained by expressing the quantity or amount of one thing in relation to another 比率; 率: *walk at a/the rate of 3 miles an hour* 以每小时3英里的速度行走 ○ *produce cars at a rate of 50 a/per week* 以每周50辆的速度生产汽车 ○ *the annual ˈbirth/ˈmarriage/ˈdeath rate* 年出生[结婚/死亡]率 ○ *a high ˈpass/ˈfailure rate*, eg in an exam 高的及格[不及格]率 ○ *the exˈchange rate/the rate of exˈchange*, ie the number of units of one currency given in exchange for one unit of another 兑换率. **2** measure of value, charge or cost 价值、费用或价格的量度: *a ˌfirst-, ˌsecond-, ˌthird-rate ˈjob* 一等、二等、三等的工作 ○ *postal, advertising, insurance, etc rates* 邮资、广告费、保险费 ○ *a low/high hourly rate of pay* 按小时收取的低[高]报酬 ○ *special reduced rate for children, students, etc* 儿童、学生等的特惠价格 ○ *Surveys offered at reasonable rates.* 提供测定服务收费廉宜. ○ *What's the going* (ie current) *rate for baby-sitters?* 请临时保姆的费用现在是多少? **3** speed of movement, change, etc; pace (运动、变化等的)速度; 进度: *at a great, dreadful, steady, etc rate* 以很高的、惊人的、稳定的...速度 ○ *His pulse-rate dropped suddenly.* 他的脉搏突然放慢了. ○ *double the rate of production, development, etc* 使生产、发展等速度提高一倍 ○ *At the rate you work, you'll never finish.* 按你这样的工作速度, 你绝对做不完. **4** (usu *pl* 通常作复数) (*Brit*) tax on land and buildings paid to local authorities (地方当局征收的)房地产税: *set a rate of 66p in the pound*, ie 66 pence for every pound of a property's value 规定按财产价值每英镑纳税66便士 ○ *an extra £5 on/off* (ie added to/deducted from) *the rates* 在房地产税中增加[扣除]5英镑. **5** (idm 习语) **at ˈany rate** whatever may happen; in any case 无论如何; 不管怎样: *That's one part of the job done at any rate.* 不管怎么说, 这个工作已经做了一部分了. **at a rate of ˈknots** (*infml* 口) very rapidly 极快地. **at ˈthis/ˈthat rate** (*infml* 口) if this/that continues; doing things this/that way; if this/that is typical 照这样[那样]下去; 照这样[那样]做; 如果情况就是这样[那样]的话: *At this rate, we shall soon be bankrupt.* 这样下去的话, 我们很快就要破产了.

□ ˈ**rate-capping** *n* [U] (in Britain) limit on the amount of money a local authority can raise through the rates, imposed by the Government to curb overspending (英国)政府为遏制超支, 限制地方当局征收房地产税不得超过的最高限额.

ˈ**ratepayer** *n* (*Brit*) person liable to pay rates 房地产税的纳税人.

rate[2] /reɪt; ret/ *v* **1** [Tn, Tn·pr, Cn·n/a] **~ sth at sth**; **~ sb/sth as sth** estimate the worth or value of sb/sth 评定某人[某事物]的价值: (*infml* 口) *I don't rate this play* (ie think it is good) *at all.* 我认为这出戏一点都不好. ○ *What do you rate his income at?* 你估计他的收入有多少? ○ *She is highly rated as a novelist.* 她这位小说家受到很高的评价. **2** [Tn·pr] regard (sb/sth) as; consider 把(某人[某事物])看成是; 认为: *Do you rate Tom among your friends?* 你认为汤姆是你的朋友吗? **3** [esp passive 尤用于被动语态: Tn, Tn·pr] **~ sth (at sth)** (*Brit*) value (property) in order to assess rates (RATE[1] 4) 核定(财产)的价值以确定应纳的税额: *a house rated at £500 per annum* 按财产核定每年应纳税500英镑的房子. **4** [La] rank or be regarded in a specified way 以某方式划分等级或对待: *That task rates low on my priority list.* 那件事情并不是我的当务之急. **5** [Tn] (*US infml* 口) be worthy of (sth); deserve 有(某事物)的价值; 值得: *That joke didn't rate a laugh.* 那笑话不值一笑.

rate·able /ˈreɪtəbl; ˈretəbḷ/ *adj* (*Brit*) (of property) liable for payment of rates (RATE[1] 4) (指财产)应纳税的: *the rateable value of a house*, ie the value at which a house is assessed for rates 对一所房子的课税估价.

rather /ˈrɑːðə(r); *US* ˈræ-; ˈræðɚ/ *adv* **1** (usu indicating criticism, disappointment or surprise 通常表示批评、失望或惊奇) to a certain extent; fairly 在一定程度上; 颇. (**a**) (used before *adjs* and *advs* 用于形容词和副词之前): *We're having rather cold weather for June.* 在六月里, 这样的天气未免有点冷. ○ *The book is rather long.* 这本书有点长. (Cf 参看 *This is a rather long book.*) ○ *You've done rather badly in the test.* 你考得够糟的. ○ *For an Englishman he speaks French rather well.* 他作为英国人, 法语说得很不错. (**b**) (used before comparatives 用于比较级之前): *This hotel is rather more expensive than that.* 这家旅馆的收费比那家贵得多. ○ *She drives rather faster than she ought.* 她开车的速度比她正常的速度快多了. (**c**) (used before *too* 用于 too 之前): *The exercise was rather too difficult.* 这练习未免太难了. ○ *He spoke rather too quickly for me to understand.* 他说得有些太快了, 我听不懂. **2** to a moderate extent; quite 或多或少; 有几分; 相当地. (**a**) (used before a *det* 用于限定词之前): *It seems rather a good idea.* 这似乎是个相当不错的主意. ○ *It's rather a shame that Joyce missed the concert.* 乔伊斯未能参加音乐会, 有些可惜. (**b**) (used before a *v* 用于动词之前): *I rather suspect we're making a big mistake.* 我有些怀疑我们可能犯了个大错. ○ *We were rather hoping you'd be free on Friday.* 我们很希望你星期五能有空. ○ *The weather rather spoiled our trip to the seaside.* 我们去海滨玩却因天气不太好而颇为扫兴. ⇨ Usage at FAIRLY 用法见FAIRLY. **3** (idm 习语) **or rather** (used to introduce a more precise expression 用以提出更确切的说法): *I worked as a secretary, or rather, a typist.* 我担任秘书工作, 说得准确些是打字员. ○ *He had to walk — or rather run — to the office.* 他得走着——应该说是跑着——去上班. **would rather... (than)**; *US* also **had rather... (than)** (usu shortened to 通常略作 *'d rather*) prefer to 宁愿; 宁可; 较喜欢: *I'd rather walk than take a bus.* 我愿意走路而不愿意坐公共汽车. ○ *She'd rather die than lose the children.* 她宁可死也不愿失去孩子们. ○ *'Some more wine?' 'Thank you, I'd rather not. I have to drive home.'* '再来一点酒好吗?' '不要了, 我不能再喝了. 我还得开车回家呢.'

▷ **rather** *interj* (*dated* 旧 *Brit*) (used when replying to a suggestion, etc and always stressed 用以回答提议等, 须重读) certainly 好哇; 当然: *'How about a trip to the coast?' 'Rather!'* '去海滨玩玩好吗?' '好极了!'

□ **rather than** *prep* in preference to (sb/sth); instead of 与其(某人[某事物]); 不愿; 不要; 不是: *I think I'll have a cold drink rather than coffee.* 我想喝冷饮, 不想喝咖啡. ○ *It's management that's at fault rather than the work-force.* 错在资方而不在劳方. ○ *Rather than risk breaking up his marriage he told his wife everything.* 他惟

恐婚姻破裂, 把一切都告诉了妻子.

rat·ify /ˈrætɪfaɪ; ˋrætəˌfaɪ/ *v* (*pt, pp* **-fied**) [Tn] make (an agreement, a treaty, etc) officially valid, usu by signing it 使(协议、条约等)正式生效(通常为经签署); 正式批准.

▷ **rati·fica·tion** /ˌrætɪfɪˈkeɪʃn; ˌrætəfəˋkeʃən/ *n* [U] ratifying or being ratified 批准; 认可.

rat·ing /ˈreɪtɪŋ; ˋretɪŋ/ *n* **1** (**a**) [C, U] classification or ranking of sb/sth according to quality, etc (人或事物按品质、特性等划分的)等级, 级别: *a high/low popularity, credibility, etc rating* 受欢迎、信用等程度高的[低的] ○ *The critics' rating of the film was low.* 评论电影的人对这部影片评价很低. ○ *give medical research a high-priority rating* 把医学研究置于高度优先的地位. (**b**) [C often *pl* 常作复数] (in the media) popularity of a programme, record, etc, as measured by the number of viewers, buyers, etc (传播媒介)(根据观众、购买者等的人数得出的节目、唱片等的)收视率, 收听率, 普及率: *Our show has gone up in the ratings.* 我们节目的收视率提高了. ○ *Blue Funk's new hit has had good ratings in the charts.* 布鲁·芬克新灌录的唱片在流行音乐最畅销的每周目录上排名很高. **2** [C, U] (*Brit*) (calculation of the) amount payable as a local rate[1](4) 房地产税征收额(的计算): *a rating of 60p in the pound* 按财产估价每英镑60便士的房地产税征收额. **3** [C] status of a person or business with regard to financial responsibility and trustworthiness (个人或公司在财务上的)信誉, 信用程度: *have/enjoy a high credit rating* 信贷方面信誉良好. **4** (*esp Brit*) (in the navy) non-commissioned sailor (海军)士兵: *officers and ratings* 海军官兵.

R

ra·tio /ˈreɪʃɪəʊ; ˋreʃɪˌo/ *n* (*pl* **~s**) relation between two amounts determined by the number of times one contains the other 比; 比率: *The ratios of 1 to 5 and 20 to 100 are the same.* 1与5之比和20与100之比相同. ○ *Men outnumber women here in the ratio of three to one.* 此地男子数量以三比一超过女子. Cf 参看 PROPORTION.

ra·ti·ocina·tion /ˌrætɪˌɒsɪˈneɪʃn; *US* ˌræʃɪ-; ˌræʃɪˌɑsn̩ˋeʃən/ *n* [U] (*fml* 文) process of logical and methodical reasoning 推论; 推理.

ra·tion /ˈræʃn; ˋræʃən/ *n* **1** [C] fixed quantity, esp an official allowance of food, etc in times of shortage 定量; (尤指食物等短缺时的)配给限额: *the weekly butter, coal, petrol, etc ration*, eg during a war 黄油、煤炭、汽油等的每周配给量(如在战争期间) ○ [attrib 作定语] *a ration card/book*, ie entitling the holder to a ration 配给卡[簿](持有者获配给品供应的凭证). **2 rations** [pl] fixed daily allowance of food in the armed forces, etc (军队等每日的)口粮: *draw rations* 领取口粮. **3** (idm 习语) **be on short rations** ⇨ SHORT[1].

▷ **ra·tion** *v* **1** [esp passive 尤用于被动语态: Tn, Tn·pr] **~ sb/sth (to sth)** limit sb/sth to a fixed amount of sth 按定量向某人[某事物]供应某物; 配给: *People were rationed to one egg a week.* 每周配给一个鸡蛋. ○ *Bread was rationed to one loaf per family.* 每户供应一个面包. **2** (phr v) **ration sth out** distribute (food, etc) in fixed quantities 按定量分发(食品等): *ration the remaining water out among the survivors* 把剩余的水分发给幸存者.

ra·tion·ing *n* [U] system of limiting and sharing food, clothing, etc in times of shortage (食品、衣物等短缺时实行的)配给制度: *The Government may have to introduce petrol rationing.* 政府可能不得不实行汽油限量供应.

ra·tional /ˈræʃnəl; ˋræʃənl̩/ *adj* **1** able to reason 能推理的: *Man is a rational being.* 人是有理性的生物. **2** not foolish or absurd; sensible; reasonable 出于理性的; 理智的; 明事理的; 讲道理的: *rational conduct* 合理的行为 ○ *a rational argument, explanation, solution, etc* 合乎情理的论证、解释、解决方法等. **3** lucid or sane 头脑清醒的; 神志正常的: *Despite her recent stroke, she is quite rational.* 她尽管最近曾患中风, 但头脑仍很清醒. ○ *No rational person would go to work in his pyjamas.* 任何神志正常的人都不会穿着睡衣去上班.

▷ **ra·tion·al·ity** /ˌræʃəˈnælətɪ; ˌræʃəˋnælətɪ/ *n* [U] quality of being rational; reasonableness 理性; 合理性; 理智; 推理能力.

ra·tion·ally /-ʃnəlɪ; -ʃənl̩ɪ/ *adv*: *think, behave, argue rationally* 思考、行为、辩论合情合理.

ra·tion·ale /ˌræʃəˈnɑːl; *US* -ˈnæl; ˌræʃəˋnæl/ *n* fundamental reason for or logical basis of sth 基本原理; 理论基础: *the rationale behind a decision* 一项决定的理论根据.

ra·tion·al·ism /ˈræʃnəlɪzəm; ˋræʃənl̩ˌɪzəm/ *n* [U] practice of testing all religious belief and knowledge by reason and logic 理性主义; 唯理主义; 唯理论.

▷ **ra·tion·al·ist** /-lɪst; -lɪst/ *adj, n* (typical of a) person practising rationalism 理性主义者(的); 唯理论者(的).

ra·tion·al·istic /ˌræʃnəˈlɪstɪk; ˌræʃənl̩ˋɪstɪk/ *adj* of rationalism or rationalists 理性主义(者)的; 唯理论(者)的.

ra·tion·al·ize, -ise /ˈræʃnəlaɪz; ˋræʃənl̩ˌaɪz/ *v* **1** [I, Tn] (try to) justify (one's actions, emotions, etc) by giving a rational explanation for them (试图)使(自己的行动、情感等)有合理依据: *He's constantly rationalizing.* 他总是不断反省是否言行合理. ○ *She rationalized her decision to abandon her baby by saying she could not afford to keep it.* 她为抛弃婴儿事辩称自己抚养不起. **2** [Tn] make (sth) more logical and consistent 使(某事物)更合理、更一致: *an attempt to rationalize English spelling* 使英语拼法更趋合理的做法. **3** [Tn] reorganize (a process, an industry, etc) in order to increase efficiency and reduce waste (为提高效率、降低损耗而)改进(工序、产业等); 使合理化: *rationalize production, distribution, etc* 使生产、分配等合理化. ▷ **ra·tion·al·iza·tion, -isation** /ˌræʃnəlaɪˈzeɪʃn; *US* -lɪˈz-; ˌræʃənəlɪˋzeʃən/ *n* [C, U].

rat·line (also **rat·lin**) /ˈrætlɪn; ˋrætlɪn/ *n* (usu *pl* 通常作复数) short rope fixed between the shrouds of a sailing-ship, like a rung of a ladder, and used for climbing up or down 绳梯横索(轮船支索间作梯级用的横索).

rat·tan /ræˈtæn; ræˋtæn/ *n* **1** [C] (long thin cane-like stem of an) E Indian palm 白藤(东印度棕榈树); 藤条. **2** [C] walking-stick or cane made from a rattan stem 藤杖. **3** [U] rattan stems used for weaving baskets, furniture, chair seats, etc 藤条(用于编篮筐、家具、座椅子等).

rat-tat /ˌræ ˈtæt; ˌræˋtæt/ (also **rat-a-tat** /ˌræt ə ˈtæt; ˌrætəˋtæt/, **rat-a-tat-tat** /ˌræt ə tæt ˈtæt; ˌrætəˌtætˋtæt/) *n* [sing] sound of rapping or knocking, esp on a door 砰砰的敲击声; (尤指)敲门声: *a sharp rat-tat at/on the front door* 敲击正门的响亮声音.

rattle /ˈrætl; ˋrætl̩/ *v* **1** [I, Tn] (cause sth to) make short sharp sounds quickly, one after the other; (cause sth to) shake while making such sounds (使某物)发出一连串的短促而尖利的声音; (使某物)颤动出声: *The windows were rattling in the wind.* 风刮得窗户格格作响. ○ *Hailstones rattled on the tin roof.* 冰雹落在铁皮屋顶上发出砰砰声. ○ *The wind rattled the windows.* 风把窗户刮得颤悠悠地格格作响. **2** [Tn esp passive 尤用于被动语态] (*infml* 口) make (sb) nervous; frighten or alarm 使(某人)紧张; 使恐惧; 使惊慌: *The policeman's visit really got her rattled.* 警察来访可把她吓了一跳. **3** (phr v) **rattle along, off, past, etc** move with a rattling sound 移动时发出嘈杂声: *The old bus rattled along the stony road.* 那辆旧公共汽车格登格登地沿碎石路行驶. ○ *A cart rattled past (us).* 一辆大车发出嘎吱嘎吱声经过我们身边. **rattle away/on** talk idly and at length; chatter 神聊; 喋喋不休: *He rattled on about his job, not noticing how bored she was.* 他只顾喋喋不休地说自己工作上的事, 没注意到她有多么腻烦. **rattle sth off** say or repeat sth quickly and meaninglessly 急促而不假思索地说或重述某事: *The child rattled off the poem he had learnt.* 那孩子把学到的那首诗背得滚瓜烂熟. **rattle through sth** tell (a story), repeat (a list, etc) quickly 急急巴巴地讲(故事)或念(表册等): *He rattled through the list of names.* 他口中像爆豆一般念那名单.

▷ **rattle** *n* **1** [U, C] rattling sound 一连串的短促而尖利的声音: *the rattle of bottles, chains, etc* 瓶子哐啷哐啷响、链子当啷当啷响 ○ *the harsh rattle of machine-gun fire* 机关枪射击时的刺耳的格格声 ○ *The car has several irritating rattles at the back.* 这辆汽车后部有几处发出烦人的嘈杂声. **2** [C] toy or device for producing a rattling sound 产生连续声音的玩具或器具: *a baby's rattle* 拨浪鼓 ○ *Football fans sounded their rattles.* 足球迷们弄响了他们那用来助阵的发声器. **3** [C] horny rings on a rattlesnake's tail that make a rattling noise when shaken 响环(响尾蛇尾部的角质环, 摆动时格格作响).

rat·tling /ˈrætlɪŋ; ˋrætlɪŋ/ *adj* [attrib 作定语] (*dated infml* 旧, 口) fast or brisk 快的; 轻快的: *set a rattling pace* 定出快速. — *adv* very 非常: *spin a rattling good yarn*, ie tell a very good story 讲一个非常好听的故事.

□ **ˈrattle·snake** (also *US infml* 美式口语作 **rat·tler**

/ˈrætlə(r); ˋrætlɚ/ *n* poisonous American snake that makes a rattling noise with its tail when alarmed or threatened 响尾蛇(美洲毒蛇).

ratty ⇨ RAT.

rauc·ous /ˈrɔ:kəs; ˋrɔkəs/ *adj* loud and hoarse; harsh-sounding 粗厉沙哑的; 刺耳的: *the raucous cries of the crows* 乌鸦粗哑的叫声 ○ *a raucous voice, laugh, etc* 沙哑的声音、笑声等. ▷ **rauc·ously** *adv*. **rauc·ous·ness** *n* [U].

raunchy /ˈrɔ:ntʃɪ; ˋrɔntʃɪ/ *adj* (*infml* 口 *esp US*) having or showing sexual desire; coarse or obscene 有性欲的; 淫秽的; 猥亵的: *feel raunchy* 有性欲 ○ *a raunchy joke, story, etc* 淫秽的笑话、故事等. ▷ **raunch·ily** *adv*. **raunchi·ness** *n* [U].

rav·age /ˈrævɪdʒ; ˋrævɪdʒ/ *v* [Tn] **1** damage (sth) badly; destroy 严重损坏(某物); 毁坏: *forests ravaged by fire* 毁于火灾的森林 ○ (*fig* 比喻) *a face ravaged by disease*, eg covered with marks after smallpox 因疾病而破相(如患天花后留有麻子). **2** (of armies, etc) rob and plunder (sth) with violence (指军队等)抢劫, 掠夺(某物): *Bands of soldiers ravaged the countryside.* 成群的士兵洗劫了乡村.

▷ **the rav·ages** *n* [pl] **~s of sth** destructive effect of sth; damage done by sth 某事物的破坏力或造成的破坏: *the ravages of deforestation on the hills* 滥伐山林的恶果 ○ (*fig* 比喻) *The ravages of time had spoilt her looks.* 岁月摧残了她的容貌.

rave /reɪv; rev/ *v* **1** [I, Ipr] **~ (at/against/about sb/sth)** talk wildly or furiously as if in a fever or mad 胡言乱语; 说胡话; 说疯话: *The patient began to rave incoherently at the nurses.* 病人对护士说起胡话来. **2** [Ipr] **~ about sb/sth** (*infml* 口) speak or write about sb/sth with enthusiasm or admiration 热情地或赞赏地说或写到某人[某事物]: *She simply raved about French cooking.* 她对法国烹调赞不绝口. **3** (idm 习语) **rant and rave** ⇨ RANT.

▷ **rave** *n* **1** [esp attrib 尤作定语] (*infml* 口) enthusiastic praise 热情的赞美: *The play got rave reviews/notices in the papers.* 该剧在报刊上受到热烈的好评. **2** (also **ˈrave-up**) (*dated Brit infml* 旧, 口) lively party, dance, etc 活跃的聚会、舞会等: *have a rave-up* 举办一次娱乐活动.

raver *n* (*infml esp ironic* 口, 尤作反语) person leading a wild and exciting social life 放荡不羁的人: *be a real/right little raver* 是个真正的小放荡鬼.

rav·ing *adj* [attrib 作定语] talking wildly or furiously 胡言乱语的; 说胡话的: *a raving lunatic* 说胡话的疯子. — *adv* (*infml* 口) utterly or completely 十足地; 完全地: *You must be stark raving mad!* 你简直疯了!

rav·ings *n* [pl] wild or delirious talk 胡话; 疯话; 谵语: *the ravings of a madman* 疯子的胡话.

ravel /ˈrævl; ˋrævl/ *v* (**-ll-**; *US* also **-l-**) **1** [I, Ip, Tn, Tn·p] **~ (sth) (up)** (cause threads or fibres to) tangle and become knotted (使线或纤维)缠结. **2** [I] (of woven or knitted fabric) separate into threads; become untwisted; fray (使编织物或编结物)散成线, 绽线: *Bind the edge of the rug so that it won't ravel.* 给地毯镶个边以免开线. Cf 参看 UNRAVEL 1.

raven /ˈreɪvn; ˋrevən/ *n* large bird like a crow with glossy black feathers and a hoarse cry 渡鸦(较乌鸦大, 羽毛黑色而有光泽, 叫声嘶哑).

▷ **raven** *adj* [attrib 作定语] (of hair) glossy and black (指毛发)乌亮的: *silky raven hair* 柔软乌亮的毛发.

rav·en·ing /ˈrævənɪŋ; ˋrævənɪŋ/ *adj* [attrib 作定语] (esp of wolves) hungrily seeking prey or food (尤指狼群)觅食的: *a ravening beast* 觅食的野兽.

rav·en·ous /ˈrævənəs; ˋrævənəs/ *adj* **1** very hungry 极饿的: *The ravenous lions tore at the carcass.* 这些饥饿的狮子撕碎了那动物的尸体. ○ (*infml* 口) *Where's dinner? I'm ravenous!* 饭呢? 我饿极了! **2** (of hunger, etc) very great (指饥饿等)极度的: *a ravenous appetite* 嚣然思食.

▷ **rav·en·ously** *adv* very hungrily; as if starving 饥肠辘辘; 象要饿死: *eat ravenously* 如饿狼般地吃.

ra·vine /rəˈvi:n; rəˋvin/ *n* deep narrow steep-sided valley between mountains 既深且狭、坡度很大的山谷.

ra·vi·oli /ˌrævɪˈəʊlɪ; ˌrævɪˋolɪ/ *n* [U] (Italian dish of) small square cases of pasta filled with meat, cheese, etc and usu served with a sauce (意大利式)方形饺(用肉、乳酪等做馅, 通常加调味汁食用).

rav·ish /ˈrævɪʃ; ˋrævɪʃ/ *v* **1** [Tn esp passive 尤用于被动语态] fill (sb) with delight; enchant 使(某人)欣喜若狂; 使着迷; 使心醉: *I was ravished by her beauty.* 我被她的美貌迷住了. **2** [Tn] (*arch or fml* 古或文) rape (a woman or girl) 强奸(女子).

▷ **rav·ish·ing** *adj* (*infml* 口) delightful or enchanting; lovely 使人欣喜若狂的; 使人入迷的; 可爱的: *a ravishing view, smile* 醉人的景色、笑容 ○ *Darling, you look simply ravishing in that dress!* 亲爱的, 你穿上那件连衣裙真漂亮!

rav·ish·ingly *adv*.

raw /rɔ:; rɔ/ *adj* **1** uncooked 未经烹调的; 生的: *raw meat, vegetables, etc* 生的肉、蔬菜等 ○ *eat oysters raw* 吃生牡蛎. **2** [usu attrib 通常作定语] **(a)** in the natural state; not yet processed or manufactured 自然状态的; 未经加工或制造的: *raw silk, sewage* 生丝、原污水 ○ *raw* (ie unrefined) *sugar* 粗糖(未精炼的) ○ *raw* (ie undiluted) *spirit/alcohol* 无水酒精(未经稀释的). **(b)** not yet analysed or corrected 未进行分析或改正的: *processing raw data, statistics, etc* 处理原始数据、统计资料等 ○ *feed raw data into a computer* 把原始数据输入计算机. **3** [usu attrib 通常作定语] (*fig* 比喻) (of people) not yet skilled or trained; inexperienced (指人)不熟练的, 未经训练的, 无经验的: *raw recruits*, eg in the army, etc 新成员(如新兵等) ○ *a mistake made by a very raw reporter* 毫无经验的记者犯的错误. **4** **(a)** (of wounds) unhealed; bloody (指创伤)未愈的, 流血的: *a raw cut, blister, etc* 未愈的伤口、水疱等. **(b)** (of a place on the skin) with the skin rubbed away and therefore sore (指皮肤某处)擦掉皮因而疼痛的: *The stirrup leathers rubbed raw patches on his legs.* 马蹬皮带把他腿上的皮肤擦伤引起疼痛. **5** **(a)** artistically crude; lacking finish 技艺不娴熟的; 不完美的: *His literary style is still rather raw.* 他的文学风格还很不成熟. **(b)** frank or realistic 如实的; 实际的: *a raw portrayal of working-class life* 工人阶级生活的真实写照. **6** (of the weather) damp and cold (指天气)潮湿而寒冷的: *raw north-east winds* 阴冷的东北风 ○ *a raw February morning* 二月里一个阴冷的早晨. **7** (of an edge of cloth) not hemmed or finished to prevent fraying (指布的边缘)未缝折边的, 未包缝的. **8** (idm 习语) **a raw/rough deal** ⇨ DEAL[4].

▷ **raw** *n* (idm 习语) **in the ˈraw** **(a)** not made to seem better, pleasanter, etc than it is; unrefined 不加粉饰的; 未加工的: *life, nature, etc seen in the raw* 生活、自然界等的原貌. **(b)** (*infml* 口) without clothes; naked 无衣着的; 裸体的. **touch sb on the raw** ⇨ TOUCH[2].

raw·ness *n* [U].

□ **ˌraw-ˈboned** *adj* (*usu derog* 通常作贬义) with little flesh on the bones; gaunt 皮包骨头的; 骨瘦如柴的: *a ˌraw-boned ˈhorse, ˈpeasant* 骨瘦如柴的马、农民.

ˈrawhide *n* [U] untanned leather 生皮: [attrib 作定语] *rawhide boots, whips, etc* 生皮制成的皮靴、皮鞭等.

ˌraw maˈterial (often *pl* 常作复数) natural product which manufacturing processes turn into another 原料: *Coal, oil and minerals are the raw materials of industry.* 煤、石油和矿产品都是工业原料. ○ (*fig* 比喻) *The writer's raw material is life.* 作家从生活中汲取素材.

ray[1] /reɪ; re/ *n* **1** **(a)** narrow beam or line of light or other radiation, eg energy or heat (光或其他辐射, 如能或热的)线, 射线: *the rays of the sun* 太阳的光线 ○ *ˈX-rays* X射线 ○ *ˈheat-rays* 热辐射线 ○ [attrib 作定语] *a ˈray gun*, eg in science fiction 光线枪(如科学幻想小说中的). **(b)** **~ of sth** (*fig* 比喻) slight indication of sth good or hoped for (好事或所希望的事物的)点滴迹象: *a ray of comfort (for us) in these troubled times* 在这些忧心的日子里(给予我们)的一丝安慰 ○ *a few rays of hope* 一线希望. **2** any one of a number of lines, bands, etc coming out from a centre (从中心向外发出的)线、条、带等. **3** (idm 习语) **a ray of ˈsunshine** (*infml often ironic* 口, 常作反语) person or thing that makes sb's life brighter or more cheerful 给某人的生活带来光明或快乐的人或事物.

ray[2] /reɪ; re/ *n* any of various types of large broad flat sea-fish related to the shark, eg the skate 魟; 鳐: *a ˈsting-ray* 刺鳐.

ray[3] (also **re**) /reɪ; re/ *n* (*music* 音) second note in the sol-fa scale (首调唱法的)任何大音阶的第二音.

rayon /ˈreɪɒn; ˋreɑn/ *n* [U] silk-like fibre or fabric made from cellulose 人造丝; 人造丝纤维: [attrib 作定语]

R

rayon shirts 人造丝衬衫.

raze (also **rase**) /reɪz; rez/ *v* [esp passive 尤用于被动语态: Tn, Tn·pr] destroy (a building, town, etc) completely, usu by leaving no walls, etc standing (used esp in the expression shown) 彻底破坏或摧毁(建筑物、城镇等)(尤用于以下示例): *raze sth to the ground* 将某物夷为平地.

razor /ˈreɪzə(r); ˋrezɚ/ *n* instrument with a sharp blade, or with electrically-driven revolving cutters, used for shaving hair from the skin 剃刀; 刮脸刀; 电动剃胡刀: *a ˈsafety razor*, ie with guards protecting the blade 保险剃刀 ○ *Vandals had slashed the tyres with a razor.* 恣意破坏公物的人用剃刀把轮胎割破了. ○ *a ˈrazor socket*, eg in a bathroom 剃刀插座(如浴室中的). Cf 参看 SHAVER (SHAVE).

□ **ˈrazor-back** *n* (*US*) hog of the southern US with a spinal ridge on its back 美国南部的一种猪, 背上有脊骨隆起.

ˈrazor-blade *n* blade (esp one that is disposable) used in a safety razor 保险刀片(尤指供一次使用的).

ˌrazor-ˈedge *n* (also **ˌrazor's ˈedge**) (*fig* 比喻) **1** sharp line of division 明显的分界线: *a razor-edge of difference between genius and madness* 天才和疯狂之截然不同. **2** (idm 习语) **on a razor-edge/razor's edge** in a dangerous or critical situation 处于危险的境地; 处于紧要关头: *Since he escaped from gaol, Tom has been living on a razor's edge, terrified of recapture.* 汤姆越狱后, 时时如惊弓之鸟, 生怕再次被捕.

ˌrazor-ˈsharp *adj* extremely sharp 极锐利的: (*fig* 比喻) *ˌrazor-sharp ˈwit, reparˈtee, ˈcriticism, etc* 极敏锐的智力、极巧妙的回答、极尖锐的批评.

razz /ræz; ræz/ (*US infml* 口) *v* [Tn] make fun of (sb); ridicule 取笑(某人); 嘲弄; 奚落: *kids razzing the teacher* 拿老师取笑的小学生.

▷ **razz** *n* (*US infml* 口) = RASPBERRY 2.

razzle /ˈræzl; ˋræzl/ *n* (idm 习语) **be/go (out) on the razzle** (*infml* 口) be/go out to celebrate and enjoy oneself; be/go on a spree 外出庆祝和找乐; 寻欢作乐.

razz·ma·tazz /ˌræzməˈtæz; ˌræzməˈtæz/ (also **razza·ma·tazz** /ˌræzəməˈtæz; ˋræzəməˌtæz/) *n* [U] (*infml* 口) glamour and excitement; extravagant publicity 魅力; 刺激; 令人眼花缭乱的场面: *all the razzamatazz of showbiz* 娱乐行业令人眼花缭乱的一切.

RC /ˌɑː ˈsiː; ˌɑr ˋsi/ *abbr* 缩写 = **1** Red Cross 红十字(会). **2** Roman Catholic 天主教: *St Mary's Church (RC)*, eg on a street map 圣马利亚教堂(天主教)(如街道地图的标示).

RCM /ˌɑː siː ˈem; ˌɑr si ˋɛm/ *abbr* 缩写 = (*Brit*) Royal College of Music 皇家音乐学院.

RD /ˌɑː ˈdiː; ˌɑr ˋdi/ *abbr* 缩写 = (*US*) (in postal addresses) rural delivery (作邮递标记)乡村投递: *RD2 West Stockbridge, Massachusetts* 马萨诸塞州西斯托克布里奇乡村投递2区.

Rd *abbr* 缩写 = (in street names) road (用于街名中)路: *12 Ashton Rd* 阿什顿路12号.

re[1] = RAY[3].

re[2] /riː; ri/ *prep* (*fml* 文) with reference to (sb/sth); concerning; about 关于(某人[某事物]): *Re your letter of 1 September...* 关于您9月1日的来信....

re- *pref* (used widely with *vs* and related *ns, adjs* and *advs* 可作许多动词及由动词派生的名词、形容词和副词的前缀) again 再; 又; 重新: *reapply* ○ *redecoration* ○ *re-entered* ○ *reassuringly.*

NOTE ON USAGE 用法: In many verbs beginning with **re-** the prefix is pronounced /rɪ-; rɪ-/ or /re-; rɛ-/ and it may have lost its original meaning of 'again' or 'back' 在以**re-**开始的许多动词中, 这个前缀读作/rɪ-; rɪ-/或/re-; rɛ-/, 并有可能已失去原来的'再、又'或'回'等意义: /rɪ-; rɪ-/ *recall, repair,* /re-; rɛ-/ *represent.* ☆ Other verbs have had **re-** added to them with the meaning of 'again' and it is pronounced /riː-; ri-/ 另有一些动词加**re-**表示'再、又'之意, 读作/riː-; ri/: *reopen; recreate.* ☆ There are a few verbs which fit into both groups and a hyphen may be used to show the distinction 还有一些动词适合于上述两种情况, 可用连接号表示这种区别: *recount* /rɪˈkaʊnt; rɪˋkaʊnt/ = 'tell a story', *re-count* /ˌriːˈkaʊnt; ˌriˋkaʊnt/ = 'count again'; *recover* /rɪˈkʌvə(r); rɪˋkʌvɚ/ = 'get back' or 'become well again', *re-cover* /ˌriːˈkʌvə(r); ˌriˋkʌvɚ/ = 'supply with a new cover'.

reach /riːtʃ; ritʃ/ *v* **1** [Ipr, Ip] **~ for sth; ~ out (to sb/sth)** stretch out (one's hand) in order to touch, grasp or take sth 伸出(手)以触到、抓到或拿到某物: *He reached for his gun.* 他伸手去拿枪. ○ *I reached across the table for the jam.* 我伸手到桌子那端去拿果酱. ○ (*fig* 比喻) *We must reach out to those in need.* 我们应该伸出援助之手, 帮助有困难的人. **2** [Tn·p, Dn·n, Dn·pr] **~ sth down/over; ~ sth (down/over) for sb** (*infml* 口) stretch one's hand out or up and take sth; get and give sth (to sb) 伸手取某物; 把某物递给(某人): *Please reach (me) the atlas down from the bookshelf.* 请把那本地图册从书架上取下来(递给我). ○ *Can you reach me (over) my slippers? They're under the bed.* 你能把我的拖鞋递给我吗? 拖鞋在床底下呢. **3** [Ipr, Tn] **~ (to) sth** extend to sth; be able to stretch up, out, etc and touch sth 延伸到某处; 够得着某物: *I can just about reach the apples on the top branch.* 我只差一点就能够着最上边树枝上的苹果. ○ *My feet can hardly reach the pedals.* 我的脚怎么也够不着踏板. ○ *Her hair nearly reached down to her waist.* 她的头发几乎垂到了腰部. **4** [Tn] communicate with (sb) esp by telephone 与(某人)取得联系; (尤指)给(某人)打电话: *reach her at home on 0355-694162* 拨0355-694162号码打电话到她家与她联系 ○ *I can't reach him by phone/on the phone.* 我打电话找不到他. **5** [Tn] (**a**) go as far as (sb/sth/a place); get to or arrive at 到达(某人[某物])那里; 到达(某处): *reach York by one o'clock* 一点钟到约克 ○ *reach the end of the chapter* 读到这一章的末尾 ○ *reach a speed of 500 mph* 达到每小时500英里的速度 ○ *Not a sound reached our ears.* 我们一点声音都听不见. ○ *The rescuers reached him just in time.* 救援人员及时赶到他那里. (**b**) achieve (sth); attain 达成(某事物); 达到; 获得: *reach a conclusion, decision, verdict, etc* 做出结论、决定、判决等 ○ *You'll know better when you reach my age.* 你到了我这样的年纪就明白多了. ○ *The appeal fund has reached its target of £10 000.* 吁请捐助的款项已达到10 000英镑这一预定目标. ○ *We can never reach perfection.* 我们不可能做到尽善尽美. **6** (idm 习语) **sth comes to/reaches sb's ears** ⇨ EAR[1]. **hit/make/reach the headlines** ⇨ HEADLINE (HEAD[1]). **reach for the stars** be very ambitious 雄心壮志; 野心勃勃.

▷ **reach** *n* **1** [sing] extent to which a hand, etc can be stretched out 伸手等可达到的距离: *a boxer with a long reach* 出拳距离远的拳击手. **2** [C usu *pl* 通常作复数] continuous extent of a river between two bends or of a canal between two locks (河流两弯曲处或运河两船闸之间的)河段: *the upper/lower reaches of the Thames* 泰晤士河的上[下]游. **3** (idm 习语) **beyond/out of/within (one's) ˈreach** (**a**) outside or inside the distance that a hand, etc can be stretched out 手不能及[伸手可及]: *have a dictionary within (arm's) reach* 把词典放在(伸手)够得着的地方 ○ *The shelf is so high it is well out of/beyond my reach.* 架子太高, 我根本够不着. ○ *Keep those medicines out of reach of the children/out of the children's reach.* 把那些药放在孩子够不着的地方. (**b**) (*fig* 比喻) beyond or within sb's/sth's capability, authority, effectiveness, etc 非[为]某人的[某事物的]能力、权力、影响等所能及: *concepts beyond the reach of one's intelligence* 本人不能理解的概念 ○ *Such highly-paid jobs are out of his reach.* 这类报酬高的工作没有他的份儿. ○ *The gang live abroad, beyond reach of the British police.* 这帮匪徒住在国外, 英国警方鞭长莫及. **within (easy) ˈreach (of sb/sth)** inside a distance that can be travelled (easily) 在可(易于)前往的距离以内: *The hotel is within easy reach of the beach.* 这家旅馆离海滩很近.

reach·able *adj* that can be reached 可到达的; 可达到的; 能及的; 够得着的.

□ **ˈreach-me-downs** *n* [pl] = HAND-ME-DOWNS (HAND).

re·act /rɪˈækt; rɪˋækt/ *v* **1** [I, Ipr] **~ (to sb/sth)** behave differently or change as a result of sth; respond 作出反应; 回应: *Pinch me and I will react.* 你要掐我我就有反应. ○ *People can react badly to certain food additives.* 有的人对某些食物添加剂产生严重变态反应. ○ *react positively/negatively to a suggestion* 对一项建议作出赞成的[反对的]回应 ○ *She reacted to the insult by turning her back on him.* 她受他侮辱之后就不再理睬他了. **2** [I, Ipr] **~ (against sb/sth)** respond to sb/sth with hostility, resistance, etc 反对; 反抗; 反动: *react strongly* *against tax increases* 强烈反对增税 ○ *Will the people ever react against this dictator?* 有朝一日人民会起来反抗这个独裁者吗? **3** (*chemistry* 化) (**a**) [I, Ipr, Ip] **~ with sth; ~ (together)** (of substances) undergo changes by coming into contact with sth (指物质)起化学反应: *Iron reacts with water and air to produce rust.* 铁与水和空气起化学反应而生锈. ○ *Sodium and water react (together).* 钠和水能起反应. (**b**) [Ipr] **~ on sth** have an effect on sth or produce a change in sth 对某事物有影响; 使某事物产生变化: *How do acids react on metals?* 酸对金属起什么反应?

re·act·ant /rɪˈæktənt; rɪˋæktənt/ *n* (*chemistry* 化) substance taking part in a chemical reaction 反应物. Cf 参看 PRODUCT 3.

re·ac·tion /rɪˈækʃn; rɪˋækʃən/ *n* **1** [C, U] **~ (to sb/sth)** response to a situation, an act, an influence, etc (对情况、行动、影响等做出的)反应, 回应: *What was his reaction to the news?* 他对这消息的反应如何? ○ *Her arrest produced an immediate/a sudden reaction from the press.* 她被捕的事立刻[突然]在新闻界引起反响. ○ *the shocked reaction of schools to education cuts* 学校对削减教育经费的激烈反应 ○ *Reaction to his taunts will only encourage him.* 别理会他恶言寻衅, 一理他更来劲儿. **2** [sing] physical response, usu a bad one, to a drug, chemical substance, etc (由药物、化学物质等引起的)生理上的反应(通常指不良反应): *an allergic reaction to animals, birds, etc* 对兽类、鸟类等的变态反应 ○ *I had a bad reaction after my typhoid injection.* 我注射伤寒针剂后产生了不良反应. **3** [sing, U] return to a previous state after a period of the opposite condition 回复到原来的状态; 复旧: *After all the excitement there was (an inevitable) reaction,* eg a time when life seemed dull again. 热闹一番过后, (不可避免地)又恢复了旧观(生活沉闷如故). **4** [U] opposition to (esp political) progress or reform 反对(尤指政治的)进步或改革; 反动: *The forces of reaction made reform difficult.* 反动势力给改革造成了困难. **5** [C, U] chemical change produced by two or more substances acting upon each other 化学反应: *nuclear reaction,* ie change within the nucleus of an atom 核反应.

▷ **re·ac·tion·ary** /rɪˈækʃənrɪ; *US* -ənerɪ; rɪˋækʃən,ɛrɪ/ *n, adj* (person) opposing (esp political) progress or reform 反对(尤指政治的)进步或改革的(人); 反动的(人).

re·act·iv·ate /ˌriːˈæktɪveɪt; riˋæktə,vet/ *v* [Tn] bring (sth) back into operation; make active again 使(某物)重新运转; 使恢复活力: *reactivate an old generator* 使旧发电机重新运转 ○ *reactivate a spacecraft's defence system* 使宇宙飞船防卫系统重新进入工作状态 ○ *reactivate our links/contacts with China* 恢复我们与中国的联系.

re·actor /rɪˈæktə(r); rɪˋæktɚ/ *n* **1** (also **nuclear reactor**) apparatus for the controlled production of nuclear energy 反应器; 反应堆. **2** substance taking part in or undergoing a chemical reaction 反应物; 反应剂.

read /riːd; rid/ *v* (*pt, pp* **read** /red; rɛd/) **1** [I, Tn] (used in the simple tenses or with *can/be able* 用于简单时态, 或与can/be able 连用) (be able to) understand the meaning of (written or printed words or symbols) 理解(文字或印刷符号)的意义; 阅读: *be able to/know how to read and write well* 有很好的读写能力 ○ *I can't read your untidy writing.* 你的字太乱, 我看不懂. ○ *read shorthand, Chinese (characters), Braille, music* 理解速记符号、看懂汉字、辨认盲文、阅读乐谱 ○ *A motorist must be able to read traffic signs.* 机动车辆驾驶员必须能看懂交通标志. **2** [I, Ipr, Ip, Tn, Tn·p, Tw no passive 不用于被动语态, Dn·n, Dn·pr] **~ sth (to sb)** go through (written or printed words, etc) silently or aloud to others 读, 默读, 朗诵(文字等): *I haven't enough time to read/for reading.* 我没有足够的时间读书. ○ *He was reading silently/to himself.* 他正在默读. ○ *His work is not much read* (ie Few people read it) *nowadays.* 他的作品现在很少有人看. ○ *She read (to us) from her book.* 她(向我们)朗诵她的书. ○ *Read (the letter) aloud, please.* 请大声念(这封信). ○ *read proofs,* ie read and correct the proofs of a book, etc 读校样(校对) ○ *He read the article through twice.* 他把那篇文章通读了两遍. ○ *Read this over for mistakes.* 把这校阅一下. ○ *Read what the instructions say.* 看看说明书上是怎样说的. ○ *She read a story to us/read us a story.* 她给我们读了一篇故事. **3** [Ipr, Tn, Tf, Tw no passive 不用于被动语态] **~ about/of sb/sth** discover or find out about sb/sth by reading 借助阅读发现某人[某事物]的情况: *I read about/of her in today's paper.* 我在今天的报纸上读到关于她的消息. ○ *read the news, the share prices, etc* 看新闻、了解股票行情 ○ *I read that he had resigned.* 我看到他已辞职的报道. ○ *We read how it was done.* 我们看到了资料, 知道是怎么做的了. **4** [Ipr, Tn] **~ (for) sth** study (a subject), esp at a university 研究(某学科); (尤指在大学)攻读, 学习: *read classics, law, etc at Oxford* 在牛津大学学古典文学、法律等 ○ *read for a physics degree/a degree in physics* 攻读物理学位 ○ *read for the Bar,* ie study law to become a barrister 学习法律准备当律师. **5** (**a**) [Tn] learn the significance of (sth); interpret 领会(某事物)的意义; 解释: *read sb's mind/thoughts* 了解某人的想法 ○ *read (sb's fortune in) the cards* 解(某人吉凶的)纸牌含义 ○ *A gypsy read my hand/palm,* ie told me about myself and my future by looking at the lines on the palm of my hand. 一个吉卜赛人为我看手相. ○ *Doctors must be able to read symptoms correctly.* 医生要有正确诊断症状的能力. ○ *How do you read the present situation?* 你对当前的形势怎样看? (**b**) [Cn·n/a esp passive 尤用于被动语态] **~ sth as sth** (of a statement, action, etc) convey meaning(s) which may not be intended (指言语、行动等)有别的意思(可能并非有意表达的): *Silence must not always be read as consent.* 沉默并不见得一定意味着同意. **6** [I] have a certain wording 有某字样: *The sign reads 'Keep Left.'* 路标上写着'靠左行驶.' ○ *The clause reads thus/as follows...* 该条款内容如下.... **7** (**a**) [In/pr] (of measuring instruments) indicate a certain weight, pressure, voltage, etc (指测量仪器)显示某一重量、压力、电压等数值: *What does the scale, dial, gauge, etc read?* 刻度尺、刻度盘、量规等显示的读数是多少? ○ *The meter reads 5 500 units.* 仪表标明为5 500单位. (**b**) [Tn, Tw] receive information from instruments (从仪器中)得到信息: *read the gas/electric meter* 从煤气[电]表中看到读数 ○ *I can't read what the thermometer says.* 我不会看温度表上的度数. **8** [I] give a certain impression 给予某种印象: *The story reads well/badly.* 这篇小说读起来很不错[不好]. ○ *The poem reads like* (ie sounds as if it is) *a translation.* 这首诗听起来像是翻译作品. **9** [Tn] hear and understand (sb speaking on a two-way radio) 听明白(某人在双向无线电通讯中说的话): *'Are you reading me?' 'Reading you loud and clear.'* '你听得清我的话吗?''听清了, 声音又大又清楚.' **10** [Tn·pr, Cn·n/a] **~ A for B; ~ B for A** (of corrections in text) replace (one word, etc) with another (指勘误)将(某词语等)改作另一词语等: *For 'neat' in line 3 read 'nest'.* 把第3行中的'neat'改为'nest'. **11** (idm 习语) **ˌread between the ˈlines** look for or discover a meaning in sth written or spoken that is not openly stated 找出或发觉字里行间的言外之意. **ˌread sb like a ˈbook** (*infml* 口) understand clearly sb's motives, thoughts, etc 清楚地了解某人的动机、思想等: *I can read you like a book: you're not sorry at all.* 我可以看透你的心思: 你根本就不感到懊悔. **ˌread (sb) the ˈRiot Act** declare authoritatively (to sb) that sth must stop (向某人)宣布不得再做某事: *When he came home drunk again, she read him the Riot Act.* 他又一次醉醺醺地回到家里, 她立刻警告他下不为例. **ˌread oneself/sb to ˈsleep** read until one/sb falls asleep 读着读着就使自己[某人]睡着了. **ˌtake it/sth as ˈread** assume sth without a need for discussion 不妨认定某事: *We can take it as read that she will object.* 我们可以肯定她一定反对. ○ *You can take his agreement as read.* 你可以确信他一定会同意. **12** (phr v) **read on** continue reading 继续读; 读下去: *Will Tom and Sue's quarrel mean divorce? Now read on...* 汤姆和休争吵是不是要离婚呢? 往下读吧.... **read sth back** read (a message, etc) aloud so that its accuracy can be checked 读出(信息内容等)以供校验: *Read me back that telephone number.* 把那个电话号码念给我听听. **read sth into sth** assume that sth means more than it does 将本来没有的意思加进去解释; 自以为有某种含义: *You have read into her letter a sympathy that she cannot possibly feel.* 你误解她信中有同情的意思, 她根本不可能有这种感觉. **read sth out** read sth aloud, esp to others 读出(文字内容)(尤指为别人): *She read out the letter to all of us.* 她给我们大家念了那封信. **read sb/sth up; read up on sb/sth** read extensively about or make a special study of (a

R

subject) 广泛阅读(某学科的著作); 对(某学科)作专门研究: *I must read Nelson up/read up on Nelson for the history exam.* 我为准备历史考试得专门研究一下纳尔逊的生平事迹.

▷ **read** /riːd; rid/ *n* [sing] (*infml* 口 *esp Brit*) **1** period or act of reading 阅读: *have a long, quiet, little, etc read* 长时间、静静、短时间等的阅读 ○ *Can I have a read of that timetable?* 我可以看一下那张时间表吗? **2** (with an *adj* 与形容词连用) writer, book, etc that is interesting to read 使人感兴趣的书、某作家的著作等: *This author/novel is a very good read.* 这位作家的著作[这部小说]非常好.

read /red; rɛd/ *adj* (preceded by an *adv* 用于副词之后) having knowledge gained from reading 博学的: *a well-read person* 博览群书的人 ○ *be widely read in the classics* 有渊博的古典文学知识.

read·able /ˈriːdəbl; ˈridəbl/ *adj* **1** that can be read easily or enjoyably 易读的; 读起来令人愉快的: *a highly readable style, essay, article, etc* 脍炙人口的风格、随笔、文章等. **2** (of handwriting, etc) that can be read (指笔迹等)能辨认的. Cf 参看 LEGIBLE. **read·ab·il·ity** /ˌriːdəˈbɪlətɪ; ˌridəˈbɪlətɪ/ *n* [U].

□ ˌ**read** ˈ**only** (*computing* 计) (of information) that a person can read but not change (指信息)只读: *I have read-only access to my bank files.* 我用只读方式存取我的银行文件. Cf 参看 RANDOM ACCESS (RANDOM). ˌ**read only** ˈ**memory** (*abbr* 缩写 **ROM**) computer memory storing data that cannot be altered or removed and that can be found by random access 只读存储器: *The most important programs are in the read only memory.* 最重要的程序都存在只读存储器中. Cf 参看 RANDOM ACCESS MEMORY (RANDOM).

ˈ**read-out** *n* [C, U] (*computing* 计) (act of extracting) information from a memory or storage device 读出.

re·ad·dress /ˌriːəˈdres; ˌriəˈdrɛs/ (also **redirect**) *v* [Tn, Tn·pr] **~ sth (to sb/sth)** change the address on (a letter, etc) 更改(信件等)的地址: *readdress the parcel to her new home* 把包裹上的地址改写成她新居的地址.

reader /ˈriːdə(r); ˈridɚ/ *n* **1** person who reads, esp one who is fond of reading 读者; (尤指)爱好读书的人: *an avid, slow, etc reader* 废寝忘食的读者、看书看得慢的人 ○ *Happy Christmas to all our readers!* eg as a notice in a newspaper, magazine, library, etc 祝全体读者圣诞快乐! (如报刊、图书馆等的贺词) ○ *He's a great reader of science fiction.* 他很喜欢看科学幻想小说. **2** book intended to give students practice in reading 阅读教材; 读物; 读本: *graded English readers,* eg for foreign learners 分级英语读本(如供外国学习者使用的). **3** **Reader ~ (in sth)** (*Brit*) senior university teacher of a rank immediately below a professor 教授(职位仅次于讲座教授): *Reader in English Literature* 英国文学教授. **4** (also **publisher's reader**) person employed to read and report on the suitability of manuscripts for publication (出版部门的)审稿人. **5** person employed to read and correct proofs at a printer's 校对员. **6** (also **lay reader**) person appointed to read aloud parts of a service in church (教堂仪式中指定的)朗诵经文者.

▷ **read·er·ship** *n* **1** [C] **~ (in sth)** (*Brit*) position of a Reader(3) 教授的职位: *hold, have a readership in Maths* 担任数学教授. **2** [sing] (**a**) number of readers of a newspaper, periodical, etc (报刊等的)读者人数: *The Daily Echo has a readership of over ten million.* 《每日回声报》拥有读者逾一千万人. (**b**) number of readers of an author, journalist, etc (作家、新闻工作者的)读者人数: *Len Deighton has/commands a large readership.* 莱恩·戴顿有很多读者.

read·ily, readi·ness ⇨ READY.

read·ing /ˈriːdɪŋ; ˈridɪŋ/ *n* **1** [U] (**a**) action of a person who reads 阅读; 朗读: *be fond of reading* 喜欢读书 ○ [attrib 作定语] *reading matter,* ie books, newspapers, etc 阅读材料(书、报等) ○ *have a reading knowledge of French,* ie understand it when written 有阅读法语的能力. (**b**) books, etc intended to be read 读物; 读本: *heavy/light reading,* ie for study/entertainment 学习[消遣]读物 ○ *Her articles make/are interesting reading for travellers.* 她的文章旅行的人很喜欢看. (**c**) knowledge gained from books 书本知识: *a pupil of wide reading* 有丰富书本知识的学生. **2** [C] amount indicated or registered by a measuring instrument (仪器上的)读数: *readings on a thermometer, dial, etc* 温度计、刻度盘等的读数 ○ *The readings we took were well above average.* 我们记录的读数远远高于平均数. **3** [C] way in which sth is interpreted or understood (对某事物的)解释, 理解: *my reading of this clause in the contract,* ie what I think it means 我对合同中这一条款的理解 ○ *Give me your reading of the situation.* 告诉我你对局势的看法. **4** [C] variant wording of a text, esp when more than one version of it exists 异文(尤指不同版本的): *different readings* (eg by editors) *of a speech in Hamlet* 《哈姆雷特》剧中一段台词的异文(如经编者改动过的). **5** [C] (**a**) entertainment at which sth is read to an audience; passage read in this way 朗诵会; 朗诵的章节: *a poetry-/play-reading* 诗歌[剧本]朗诵会 ○ *readings from Dickens* 狄更斯作品的朗诵片段. (**b**) formal announcement of sth to an audience 向公众正式宣布的事物; 告白: *the reading of a will, marriage banns, etc* 遗嘱、结婚等的启事. (**c**) formal reading aloud of a passage from the Bible (在仪式上朗读的)《圣经》中的章节: *a reading from St John's gospel* 选自《约翰福音》的朗读. **6** [C] (in the British parliament) one of the three stages of debate through which a Bill must pass before it is ready for royal assent (英国议会中)一法案在提交国王批准以前须通过的三读之任何一次.

□ ˈ**reading age** one's ability to read, measured by comparing it with the average ability of children of the specified age 阅读年龄(与某年龄儿童的平均阅读能力相比较而测定的某人的阅读能力): *adults with a reading age of eight* 有相当于八岁儿童阅读能力的成年人.

ˈ**reading-desk** *n* desk for supporting a book that is being read (读书用的)书桌.

ˈ**reading-glasses** *n* [pl] glasses for reading (as contrasted with those for seeing things at a distance) 阅读眼镜(与一般视物所用者有别).

ˈ**reading-lamp** (also ˈ**reading-light**) *n* lamp designed or placed to give light so that a person can read 供阅读使用的灯.

ˈ**reading-room** *n* room in a library, club, etc set aside for reading 阅览室.

re·ad·just /ˌriːəˈdʒʌst; ˌriəˈdʒʌst/ *v* **1** [I, Ipr, Tn, Tn·pr no passive 不用于被动语态] **~ (oneself) (to sth)** adapt (oneself) again 使(自己)重新适应: *It's hard to readjust (oneself) to life in Britain after working abroad.* 在国外工作之后, 很难重新适应英国的生活. ○ *You need time to readjust (to living alone).* 你需要些时间才能重新习惯(过单身生活). **2** [Tn] set or adjust (sth) again 重新安排或调整(某事物): *readjust the engine tuning, TV set, lighting* 调节发动机、电视机、灯光.

▷ **re·ad·just·ment** *n* **1** [U] readjusting or being readjusted 重新适应; 重新调整: *go through a period of readjustment* 经过一段重新适应的时期. **2** [C] act of readjusting 重新适应; 重新调整: *make minor readjustments to the wiring* 对线路作些微调整.

ready /ˈredɪ; ˈrɛdɪ/ *adj* (**-ier, -iest**) **1** [pred 作表语] **~ (for sth/to do sth)** (**a**) in a fit state for immediate use or action; fully prepared or completed 准备好: *get ready for a journey* 准备旅行 ○ *I've got my overalls on, so I'm ready to start work.* 我已经穿上了长罩衣, 准备开始工作了. ○ *Your dinner is ready.* 你的饭已经准备好了. ○ *Ready, steady, go!* ie said at the start of a race. 各就各位, 预备, 跑! ○ *'Shall we go?' 'I'm ready when you are!'* '咱们走吗?' '我准备好了, 就等你了!' (**b**) (of a person) resolved to do sth; willing and eager (指人)决心做某事的, 愿意并急欲采取行动的: *He's always ready to help his friends.* 他总是乐于帮助朋友. ○ *Don't be so ready to find fault.* 不要动不动就挑毛病. ○ *The troops were ready for anything.* 部队已做好了一切准备. **2** [pred 作表语] **~ to do sth** on the point of doing sth; about to do sth 即将做某事; 正要做某事: *She looked ready to collapse at any minute.* 她看样子随时都可能垮下来. **3** (**a**) [attrib 作定语] quick and facile; prompt 敏捷的; 立刻行动的: *have a ready wit, mind, tongue* 头脑机敏、脑子快、口齿伶俐 ○ *a ready answer to the question* 对问题的随口而出的回答 ○ *a ready solution to the problem* 对问题的当场解决. (**b**) [pred 作表语] **~ with sth** (of a person) quick to give sth (指人)敏于某事物: *be too ready with excuses, criticisms, etc* 很会找借口、挑毛病等. **4** within reach; easily available 在可及范围内; 容易得到: *Keep your dictionary ready (to hand) at all times.* 把词典时时

放在手边. ○ *This account provides you with a ready source of income.* 这个户头为你提供了一个现成的收入来源. ○ *There's a ready market for antiques,* ie Buyers are easily found for them. 古董的销路很好(很容易找到买主). **5** (idm 习语) **make ready (for sth)** prepare 做好准备: *make ready for the Queen's visit* 为女王莅临做好准备. ˌ**ready and ˈwaiting** fully prepared and available for a particular task, activity, etc 做好充分准备以执行某任务、进行某活动等. **rough and ready** ⇨ ROUGH.

▷ **read·ily** /-ɪlɪ; -ɪlɪ/ *adv* **1** without hesitation; willingly 毫不迟疑地; 欣然: *answer questions readily* 毫不迟疑地回答问题. **2** without difficulty; easily 无困难地; 不费事地; 容易地: *The sofa can be readily converted into a bed.* 这张沙发可以很容易改成床.

readi·ness /ˈredɪnɪs; ˈrɛdɪnɪs/ *n* [U] **1** state of being ready or prepared 有准备; 准备就绪: *the troops' readiness for battle* 部队的临战状态 ○ *have everything in readiness for an early start* 为及早出发做好一切准备 ○ *hold oneself in readiness to take control* 准备好以便控制. **2** willingness or eagerness 愿意; 乐意: *her readiness to help* 她乐于助人的品性. **3** quickness and facility; promptness 敏捷; 迅速: *readiness of wit* 机智.

ready *n* **1 the ready** [sing] (also **readies** [pl]) (*infml* 口) available money; cash 现款; 现金: *not have enough of the ready* 现金不足. **2** (idm 习语) **at the ˈready** (**a**) (of a rifle) in the position for aiming and firing (指步枪)瞄准目标准备射击. (**b**) ready for immediate action or use 准备立即行动; 随时可用: *reserve troops held at the ready* 准备投入战斗的预备役部队 ○ *He had his camera at the ready.* 他把照相机准备好, 可随时拍摄.

ready *adv* (used before a past participle 用于过去分词之前) beforehand; already 预先; 已经: *ready cooked, mixed, etc* 预先做熟的、混合好的等.

ready *v* (*pt, pp* **-died**) [Tn, Tn·pr] **~ sb/sth (for sth)** make sb/sth ready; prepare sb/sth 使某人[某事物]做好准备: *ships readied for battle* 作好战斗准备的舰艇.

□ ˌ**ready-ˈmade** *adj* **1** (esp of clothes) made in standard sizes, not to any particular customer's measurements (尤指衣服)现成的: *a ˌready-made ˈsuit* 一套成衣. **2** (**a**) of a standard type 标准型的: *buy ˌready-made ˌChristmas decoˈrations* 购买配套的圣诞节饰物. (**b**) (*fig derog* 比喻, 贬) not original 非独创的; 陈腐的: *come to a subject with ready-made ideas* 用旧思想来对待问题. **3** very appropriate; ideal 恰当的; 理想的: *a ready-made answer to the problem* 对该问题的妥善解决办法.

ˌ**ready ˈmoney** (also ˌ**ready ˈcash**) (*infml* 口) actual coins and notes; immediate payment (instead of credit) 现款; (立即支付的)现金: *payment in ready money* 现金支付.

ˌ**ready ˈreckoner** book, table, etc of answers to calculations of the type most commonly needed in business 计算便览; 简便计算表.

re·af·firm /ˌriːəˈfɜːm; ˌriəˈfɝm/ *v* [Tn, Tf] state (sth) positively again; affirm again 重申(某事物); 再确认: *reaffirm one's loyalty* 重申个人的忠诚 ○ *She reaffirmed that she was prepared to help.* 她再次表明她乐于提供帮助.

re·af·for·est /ˌriːəˈfɒrɪst; *US* -ˈfɔːr-; ˌriəˈfɔrəst/ (*US* **reforest** /ˌriːˈfɒrɪst; *US* -ˈfɔːr-; riˈfɔrɪst/) *v* [Tn] replant (an area of land) with forest trees 在(某地)重新造林. ▷ **re·af·for·esta·tion** /ˌriːəˌfɒrɪˈsteɪʃn; *US* -ˌfɔːr-; ˌriəfɔrəsˈteʃən/ (*US* **re·for·esta·tion** /ˌriːˌfɒr-; *US* -ˌfɔːr-; ˌrifɔr-/) *n* [U].

re·agent /riːˈeɪdʒənt; riˈedʒənt/ *n* (*chemistry* 化) substance used to cause a chemical reaction, esp to detect another substance 试药; 试剂; 反应物.

real /rɪəl; ˈriəl/ *adj* **1** (**a**) existing as a thing or occurring as a fact; not imagined or supposed 确实的; 实在的: *real and imagined fears, illnesses, achievements* 确实的和想像的恐惧、疾病、成就 ○ *Was it a real person you saw or a ghost?* 你看见的是真人还是鬼? ○ *The growth of violent crime is a very real problem.* 暴力犯罪的增加是个非常现实的问题. (**b**) [attrib 作定语] not apparent; actual or true 真实的; 真正的: *Real life is sometimes stranger than fiction.* 现实生活有时比小说还离奇. ○ *Who is the real manager of the firm* (ie the person who effectively runs it)? 谁是这家商行真正管事的经理? ○ *The doctors couldn't bring about a real* (ie permanent) *cure.* 这些医生都无根治良方. ○ *Tell me the real reason.* 把真正的原因告诉我. **2** not imitation; genuine 非模仿的; 真的: *real silk, gold, pearls, etc* 真丝、真金、真正的珍珠 ○ *Is that real hair or a wig?* 那是真发还是假发? **3** [attrib 作定语] (of incomes, values, etc) assessed by their purchasing power (指收入、价值等)按购买力衡量的: *Real incomes have gone up by 10% in the past year.* 去年实际收入提高了10%. ○ *This represents a reduction of 5% in real terms,* ie when inflation, etc has been allowed for. 这相当于实际上减少了5%(考虑到通货膨胀等因素). **4** (idm 习语) **for ˈreal** (*infml* 口) (**a**) seriously; in earnest 严肃地; 认真地: *This isn't a practice game; we're playing for real.* 这可不是练习; 我们是在认真地比赛. (**b**) genuine 真正的: *I don't think her tears were for real.* 我认为她的眼泪不是真的. **the** ˌ**real ˈthing/McˈCoy** /məˈkɔɪ; məˈkɔɪ/ (*infml* 口) (**a**) the ultimate experience, achievement, etc 了不起的经历、成就等: *Marathons are the real McCoy — these little jogs are no challenge at all.* 马拉松赛跑才是真玩意儿 —— 这些慢跑根本不算回事. (**b**) the authentic article 真货色: *Bottled lemon juice is no good — you must use the real thing.* 瓶装柠檬汁可不行 —— 你得用真货.

▷ **real** *adv* (*US or Scot infml* 用于美国或苏格兰, 口) very; really 非常; 的确: *have a real fine time, a real good laugh* 玩得、笑得非常痛快 ○ *I'm real sorry.* 我非常抱歉.

□ ˌ**real ˈale** (*Brit*) draught ale or beer that is made and stored in the traditional way (按传统方法酿造及储存的)散装麦芽啤酒或普通啤酒.

ˈ**real estate** **1** (also **realty**, **real property**) (*law* 律) immovable property, consisting of land, buildings, etc 不动产. Cf 参看 PERSONAL PROPERTY (PERSONAL). **2** (*US*) (business of selling) houses, land for building, etc 房屋、建房用地等(的销售业务).

ˌ**real ˈnumber** (*mathematics* 数) number that has no imaginary part 实数.

ˌ**real ˈtennis** (also ˌ**royal ˈtennis**) ancient form of tennis played in an indoor court 纯网球, 宫廷网球, 皇家网球(古时在室内场地进行的).

ˌ**real ˈtime** (*computing* 计) (of a system) that can receive continually changing data from outside sources, process this rapidly, and supply results that influence the sources 实时.

re·align /ˌriːəˈlaɪn; ˌriəˈlaɪn/ *v* **1** [Tn] bring (sth) into a new or former arrangement; align again 使(某事物)(按新的或原先的方式)重新排列: *realign ranks of troops* 重整部队队形 ○ *The chairs were realigned to face the stage.* 椅子已重新排好面向舞台. **2** [I, Ipr, Tn, Tn·pr no passive 不用于被动语态] **~ (oneself) (with sth)** (*esp politics* 尤用于政治) form into new groups; reorganize 重组; 改组; 整编: *The party may realign (itself) with Labour in a new coalition.* 该党可能与工党重新组成新的联盟. ▷ **re·align·ment** *n* [U, C]: *the realignment of car wheels* 对汽车轮的重新校整 ○ *various realignments in political parties* 政治派别中各种各样的重新组合.

real·ism /ˈrɪəlɪzəm; ˈrɪəlˌɪzəm/ *n* [U] **1** attitudes and behaviour based on the acceptance of facts and the rejection of sentiment and illusion 现实主义的态度和行为. **2** (in art and literature) portrayal of familiar things as they really are without idealizing them (文艺的)现实主义, 写实主义. Cf 参看 CLASSICISM, ROMANTICISM (ROMANTIC). **3** (*philosophy* 哲) theory that matter has real existence independent of our perception of it 唯实论; 实在论. Cf 参看 IDEALISM.

▷ **real·ist** *n* **1** writer, painter, etc whose work shows realism(2) 现实主义的作家、画家等: [attrib 作定语] *a realist writer, novel, style* 现实主义的作家、小说、风格. **2** person who shows realism(1) in his attitudes and behaviour 现实主义者: *I'm a realist — I know you can't change people's attitudes overnight.* 我是实事求是的人 —— 知道不可能在一夜之间改变人们的看法.

real·istic /ˌrɪəˈlɪstɪk; ˌrɪəˈlɪstɪk/ *adj* **1** (in art and literature) showing realism(2) (文艺的)现实主义的, 写实主义的. **2** based on facts rather than on sentiment or illusion; practical 实事求是的: *a realistic person, attitude* 实事求是的人、态度 ○ *Be realistic — you can't expect a big salary at eighteen.* 实际一点吧 —— 你别指望十八岁就能挣高薪. **3** (of wages or prices) high enough to pay the worker or seller adequately (指工资或价格)够高的: *Is this a realistic salary for such a responsible job?* 这种工

作责任重大, 这份薪水够高吗? **real·ist·ic·ally** /-klɪ; -klɪ/ *adv*.

real·ity /rɪˈælətɪ; rɪˈælətɪ/ *n* **1** [U] quality of being real or of resembling an original 真实(性): *the lifelike reality of his paintings* 他的绘画作品中表现的真实性. **2** [U] all that is real; the real world, as contrasted with ideals and illusions 现实; 现实世界: *bring sb back to reality*, ie make him give up his illusions 使某人面对现实 ○ *escape from the reality of everyday existence* 逃避现实 ○ *face (up to)* (ie accept) *reality* 正视(承认)现实. **3** [C often *pl* 常作复数] thing that is actually experienced or seen; thing that is real 实际经历或目睹过的事物: *the harsh realities* (eg poverty, misery, etc) *of unemployment* 失业的严酷现实 ○ *He cannot grasp the realities of the situation.* 他未能掌握实际情况. ○ *The plan will soon become a reality*, ie will be carried out. 这计划不久就要化为现实. **4** (idm 习语) **in reˈality** in actual fact; really 事实上; 实际上: *The house looks very old, but in reality it's quite new.* 这房子看起来很旧, 实际上很新.

real·ize, -ise /ˈrɪəlaɪz; ˋrɪəˌlaɪz/ *v* **1** [Tn, Tf, Tw no passive 不用于被动语态] (not used in the continuous tenses 不用于进行时态) be fully aware of or accept (sth) as a fact; understand 认识到或承认(某事物)属实; 了解到: *realize one's mistake* 认识到自己的错误 ○ *realize the extent of the damage* 了解到破坏的程度 ○ *She realized that he had been lying.* 她明白了他一直在说谎. ○ *I fully realize why you did it.* 我完全了解你为什么要做这事. **2** [Tn esp passive 尤用于被动语态] convert (plans, etc) into reality 实现(计划等): *realize one's hopes, ambitions, etc* 实现自己的希望、抱负等 ○ *Her worst fears were realized*, ie The things she was most afraid would happen did happen. 她最担心的事情终于发生了. **3** (*fml* 文) **(a)** [Tn] convert (property, shares, etc) into money by selling 变卖(财产、股票等): *realize one's assets* 变卖自己的财产 ○ *Can these bonds be realized at short notice?* 这些债券能在短期内兑现吗? **(b)** [Tn, Tn·pr] **~ sth (on sth)** (of goods, etc) be sold for (a price); (of a person) sell sth for (a price) (指货物等)卖得(某价钱); (指人)将某物卖得(某价钱): *The furniture realized £900 at the sale.* 拍卖这家具获900英镑. ○ *How much did you realize on those paintings?* 那些画你卖了多少钱?

▷ **real·iz·able, -isable** /-əbl; -əbl̩/ *adj* that can be realized (REALIZE 2) 可实现的.

real·iza·tion, -isation /ˌrɪəlaɪˈzeɪʃn; *US* -lɪˈz-; ˌrɪələˋzeʃən/ *n* **1** [U] realizing (facts, hopes, plans, etc) (事情等)发生; (希望、计划等)实现: *I was struck by the sudden realization that I would probably never see her again.* 我突然意识到可能再也见不到她了. **2** [U] converting property into money 变卖财产.

really /ˈrɪəlɪ; ˋrɪəlɪ/ *adv* **1** in reality; truly 事实上; 实际上; 真正地; 真实地; 的确; 确实: *What do you really think about it?* 你对那件事究竟是怎样想的? ○ *Your name is on the car's documents, but who really owns it?* 汽车登记证上倒是写着你的名字, 但真正的车主是谁? ○ *Do you love him — really (and truly)?* 你爱他吗——确实爱他吗? **2** thoroughly; very 完全地; 非常: *a really charming person* 很讨人喜欢的人 ○ *a really cold, fast, long, etc journey* 非常冷、快、长等的一次旅行. **3** (used to express interest, surprise, mild protest, doubt, etc 用以表示兴趣、惊奇、异议、怀疑等): *'We're going to Japan next month.' 'Oh, really?'* '我们下个月要去日本.' '啊, 真的吗?' ○ *You ˈreally shouldn't smoke.* 你真不该吸烟. ○ *'Shut up!' 'Well, really!'* '住口!' '哎呀, 怎么啦!' ○ *'She's going to resign.' 'Really? Are you sure?'* '她打算辞职了.' '真的? 这话有把握吗?'

realm /relm; rɛlm/ *n* **1** (*fml or rhet* 文或修辞) kingdom 王国: *the defence of the realm* 捍卫国家 ○ *coins, peers, laws of the realm* 王国的钱币、贵族、法律. **2** (*fig* 比喻) field of activity or interest; sphere (活动或兴趣的)领域, 范围: *in the realm of literature, science, etc* 在文学、科学等领域里 ○ *the realms of the imagination* 想像的境界.

real·po·li·tik /ˌreɪælˈpɒlɪtɪk; reˋɑlˌpolɪˌtik/ *n* [U] (*German* 德) approach to politics based on realities and material needs, not on morals or ideals 现实政治, 实力政策(从现实及物质需要出发而不顾及道义与理想).

re·altor /ˈrɪəltə(r); ˋrɪəltɚ/ *n* (*US*) = ESTATE AGENT (ESTATE).

re·alty /ˈrɪəltɪ; ˋriəltɪ/ *n* = REAL ESTATE (REAL).

ream /riːm; rim/ *n* **1** [C] 500 or 516 (formerly 480) sheets of paper 令(纸张的计数单位, 旧为480张, 现为500或516张). Cf 参看 QUIRE. **2 reams** [pl] (*infml fig* 口, 比喻) large quantity (of writing) 许多(文字): *write reams (and reams) of bad verse* 写出很多(很多)坏诗.

reap /riːp; rip/ *v* **1** [I, Tn] cut and gather (a crop, esp grain) as harvest 收割(庄稼, 尤指谷物); 收获: *reap (a field of) barley* 收割(田里的)大麦. **2** [Tn] (*fig* 比喻) receive (sth) as a result of one's own or others' actions (因自己或他人所为)获得(某事物): *reap the reward of years of study* 从多年研究中获得报偿 ○ *reap the fruits of one's actions* 获得自己努力的成果. **3** (idm 习语) **(ˌsow the ˈwind and) ˌreap the ˈwhirlwind** (*saying* 谚) (start sth that seems fairly harmless and) have to suffer unforeseen consequences that are serious or disastrous 播种的是风, 收割的是暴风; (原无大害的事)后果却不堪设想.

▷ **reaper** *n* **1** person who reaps 收割者; 收获者. **2** machine for reaping 收割机.

□ ˈ**reaping-hook** *n* sickle 镰刀.

re·appear /ˌriːəˈpɪə(r); ˌriəˋpɪr/ *v* [I] appear again (after being absent or not visible) 再出现; 再现. ▷ **re·appear·ance** /-rəns; -rəns/ *n* [U, C].

re·appraisal /ˌriːəˈpreɪzl; ˌriəˋprezl̩/ *n* [U, C] action of re-examining sth to see whether it or one's attitude to it should be changed; re-evaluation 重新考虑; 重新评价: *a reappraisal of the situation, problem, etc* 对情况、问题等的重新考虑 ○ *a radical reappraisal of our trade with China* 对我们同中国的贸易彻底的重新估价.

rear[1] /rɪə(r); rɪr/ *n* **1** (usu 通常作 **the rear**) [sing] the back part 后部; 后面; 背后: *a kitchen in/at/to the rear of the house* 在房子后部的厨房 ○ *a view of the house taken from the rear* 房子的后视景 ○ *attack the enemy's rear* 攻击敌人的后部 ○ [attrib 作定语] *a car's rear doors, lights, wheels, window* 汽车的后门、尾灯、后轮、后窗. **2** [C] (*infml euph* 口, 婉) buttocks 臀部; 屁股: *a kick in/on the rear* 踢屁股一脚. **3** (idm 习语) ˌ**bring up the ˈrear** be or come last, eg in a procession, race, etc 处于在最后的位置, 殿后(如列队行进、赛跑等).

▷ **rear·most** /ˈrɪəməʊst; ˋrɪrˌmost/ *adj* furthest back 最后的: *the rearmost section of the aircraft* 飞机的最后一段机身.

rear·ward /ˈrɪəwəd; ˋrɪrwɚd/ *n* [U] the rear (used esp in the expressions shown) 后部, 后面(尤用于以下示例): *to rearward of* (ie some distance behind) *sth* 在某物之后 ○ *in the rearward*, ie at the back 在后部.

rear·wards /ˈrɪəwədz; ˋrɪrwɚdz/ (also **rear·ward**) *adv* towards the rear 向后: *move the troops rearwards* 使部队向后移动.

□ ˌ**rear-ˈadmiral** /ˌrɪər ˈædmərəl; ˌrɪrˋædmərəl/ *n* naval officer holding a rank between those of commodore and vice-admiral 海军少将: *Rear Admiral (Tom) King* (汤姆·)金海军少将. ⇨App 9 见附录9.

ˈ**rearguard** *n* (usu 通常作 **the rearguard**) [CGp] body of troops sent to guard the rear of an army, esp when it is retreating 后卫部队(尤指军队撤退时的). Cf 参看 VANGUARD. ˈ**rearguard action** **1** fight between an army in retreat and the enemy 后卫战斗(后撤的部队与敌军之间的战斗). **2** (*fig* 比喻) struggle continued even when it is unlikely to succeed 即使无望取胜也要继续进行的斗争: *The government is fighting a rearguard action against the mass of public opinion.* 政府冒天下之大不韪负隅顽抗.

ˌ**rear-view** ˈ**mirror** mirror in which a driver can see traffic, etc behind him 后视镜(供司机观察后面情况的). ⇨illus at App 1 见附录1插图, page xii.

rear[2] /rɪə(r); rɪr/ *v* **1** [Tn] **(a)** (*esp Brit*) bring up and educate (children, etc) 养育(子女等): *rear a family* 养家. **(b)** breed and look after (sheep, poultry, etc); grow or produce (crops) 饲养(羊、家禽等); 种植(作物). Cf 参看 RAISE 6. **2** [I, Ip] **~ (up)** (of a horse, etc) raise itself on its hind legs (指马等)用后腿站立: *The horse reared (up) in fright.* 那马因受惊而用后腿直立(起来). **3** [Tn] raise (esp one's head) 抬起(尤指头): *The snake reared its head.* 那蛇扬起了头. ○ (*fig* 比喻) *terrorism rearing its ugly head again* 再次嚣张起来的恐怖主义.

re·arm /ˌriːˈɑːm; riˋɑrm/ *v* [I, Ipr, Tn, Tn·pr] **~ (sb/sth) (with sth)** supply (an army, etc) with weapons again or with better weapons 重新武装或装备(军队

等); 给(军队等)更新装备. ▷ **re·arma·ment** /riːˈɑːməmənt; riˋɑrməmənt/ *n* [U].

re·arrange /ˌriːəˈreɪndʒ; ˌriəˋrendʒ/ *v* [Tn] **1** place (sth) in a different way or order 重新安排(某物); 改变(某物)的秩序: *rearrange the furniture, one's books, etc* 重新摆放家具、重新整理自己的书 ○ *Do you like the way I've rearranged the room?* 我把房间这样重新布置了一下, 你觉得怎样? **2** change (plans, etc) that have already been made 改变既定的(计划等): *Let's rearrange the match for next Saturday.* 咱们把比赛重新安排在下星期六举行吧. ▷ **re·arrange·ment** *n* [U, C]: *make some rearrangements* 做些新安排.

reason[1] /ˈriːzn; ˋrizn̩/ *n* **1** [C, U] **~ (for sth/doing sth); ~ (to do sth); ~ (why.../that...)** (fact put forward as or serving as the) cause of, motive for or justification for sth 原因; 动机; 理由: *for one/some reason or other* 由于某种原因 ○ *have adequate/sufficient reason for doing sth* 有充分的[足够的]理由做某事 ○ *all the more reason for doing/to do sth* 做某事的更为充足的理由 ○ *Give me your reasons for going/the reasons for your going.* 告诉我你去的动机. ○ *There is/We have (good) reason to believe that he is lying.* 有[我们有](充分的)理由认为他说谎. ○ *Is there any (particular) reason why you can't come?* 你有什么(特殊的)原因不能来? ○ *The reason why I'm late is that/because I missed the bus.* 我迟到的原因是没赶上公共汽车. ○ *My reason is that the cost will be too high.* 我的理由是费用太高. ○ *We aren't going, for the simple reason that we can't afford it.* 我们不去, 原因很简单: 我们负担不起. ○ *She complained, with reason* (ie rightly), *that she had been underpaid.* 她抱怨她工资一直很低, 这也不无道理. ⇨Usage 见所附用法. **2** [U] power of the mind to think, understand, form opinions, etc 思考、理解、推想等的能力; 理性: *Only man has reason.* 只有人类才有理性. **3 one's/sb's reason** [sing] one's/sb's sanity 自己的[某人的]理智: *lose one's reason/senses*, ie go mad 失去理智(即发疯) ○ *We feared for her reason*, ie were afraid that she might go mad. 我们担心她可能失去理智. **4** [U] what is right or practical or possible; common sense or judgement 道理; 情理; 明智; 常识; 常理: *see/listen to/hear/be open to* (ie be prepared to accept) *reason* 讲道理(服理) ○ *There's a good deal of reason in what you say.* 你的话很有道理. **5** (idm 习语) **beˌyond/ˌpast all ˈreason** not reasonable or acceptable 不合道理的; 无法接受的: *Her outrageous remarks were/went beyond all reason.* 她那些无礼的话全无道理. **ˌbring sb to ˈreason; ˌmake sb see ˈreason** make sb stop acting foolishly, resisting uselessly, etc 使某人停止愚蠢的举动、无谓的抵抗等. **by reason of sth** (*fml* 文) because of sth 因为或由于某事物: *He was excused by reason of his age.* 他因年高而获宥. **for reasons/some reason best known to oneˈself** (*esp joc* 尤作戏谑语) for reasons that are hard for others to understand or discover 出于惟本人才知道的原因: *For reasons best known to himself, he drinks tea from a beer glass.* 谁都猜不透他为什么要用啤酒杯子喝茶. **(do anything) in/within ˈreason** sensible or reasonable 理智的; 合理的: *I'll do anything within reason to earn my living.* 为了谋生, 只要是正当的事我什么事都做. **lose all reason** ⇨ LOSE. **rhyme or reason** ⇨ RHYME *n*. **it/that ˌstands to ˈreason** it/that is obvious to everyone 这是人人都清楚的: *It stands to reason that nobody will work without pay.* 做工作不能白做, 这是明摆着的事.

NOTE ON USAGE 用法: A **cause** (of something) is what makes something happen ☆ **cause** 指事物发生的原因: *The police are investigating the cause of the explosion.* 警方正在调查爆炸的原因. ○ *The causes of the First World War.* 第一次世界大战的起因. **Reason** (for something) has a wider use. ☆ **reason** 一词用法较广. It can be the explanation that people give for why something is done 可用以解释做某事的原因或理由: *What was the reason for his resignation?* 他辞职的原因是什么? ○ *She didn't give any reasons for leaving.* 她未做任何解释就走了. **Reason, justification** and **cause** (for something) can indicate that the explanation is acceptable to people in general, or **reasonable** ☆ **reason**、**justification**、**cause** 三词均指用以解释的理由是一般人都可以接受的, 或曰 **reasonable**: *The police had no reason to suspect him/no justification for suspecting him/no cause for suspicion* (ie They didn't suspect him or shouldn't have suspected him). 警方是没有理由怀疑他的(即: 警方未怀疑他或不该怀疑他). **Ground** is the formal, especially legal, justification for an action. ☆ **ground** 是用于较庄重场合的另一同义词, 尤用于法律文件中. It is commonly used in the plural 此词常用作复数: *Boredom is not a ground for divorce.* 日久生厌不能成为离婚的理由. ○ *I left my job on medical grounds.* 我由于健康原因而辞去了工作. A **motive** for doing something is a feeling or desire within people which makes them act ☆ **motive** 指想做某事的感觉或愿望: *He claimed that his motive for stealing was hunger.* 他说他因为饿才去偷东西. ○ *The crime seemed to have been committed without (a) motive.* 这一罪案似乎并无作案动机.

reason[2] /ˈriːzn; ˋrizn̩/ *v* **1 (a)** [I] use one's power to think, understand, form opinions, etc 思考; 理解; 推理: *man's ability to reason* 人的思考能力. **(b)** [Tf no passive 不用于被动语态] conclude or state as a step in this process 推论; 推断: *He reasoned that if we started at dawn, we would be there by noon.* 他推断, 我们要是黎明出发, 中午就能到. **2** (phr v) **reason sb into/out of sth** persuade sb by argument to do/not to do sth 以理说服某人做[不做]某事: *reason sb out of his fears* 劝说某人消除恐惧 ○ *She was reasoned into a sensible course of action.* 她听人劝而采取了理智的做法. **reason sth out** find an answer to (a problem, etc) by considering various possible solutions 考虑各种可能性以找出对(问题等)的解决办法: *The detective tried to reason out how the thief had escaped.* 这个侦探反复琢磨想弄明白那个窃贼是怎样逃跑的. **reason with sb** argue in order to convince or persuade sb 为说服某人而与之理论: *I reasoned with her for hours about the danger, but she would not change her mind.* 我跟她争辩了几个小时, 想让她认识到危险性, 但她就是不听. ○ *There's no reasoning with that woman*, ie She won't listen to arguments. 那个女人简直不可理喻.

▷ **reas·oned** *adj* [attrib 作定语] (of an argument, etc) presented in a logical way (指论据等)合乎逻辑的: *a reasoned approach to the problem* 处理该问题的合理的方法 ○ *She put a (well-)reasoned case for increasing the fees.* 对于提高费用, 她提出了(非常)充分的理由.

reas·on·ing *n* [U] act or process of using one's reason[1](2); arguments produced when doing this 运用思考、理解、推想等能力的做法或过程; 推理: *great power/strength of reasoning* 极强的推理能力 ○ *Your reasoning on this point is faulty.* 你在这一点上的推论是错误的.

reas·on·able /ˈriːznəbl; ˋriznəbl̩/ *adj* **1 (a)** (of people) ready to use or listen to reason; sensible (指人)讲理的, 明事理的: *No reasonable person could refuse.* 凡是明事理的人都不会拒绝此事. ○ *She's perfectly reasonable in her demands.* 她的要求完全合情合理. **(b)** (of emotions, opinions, etc) in accordance with reason; not absurd; logical (指情感、见解等)合情理的, 不荒谬的, 合逻辑的: *a reasonable suspicion, fear, belief, etc* 不无道理的怀疑、恐惧、信念等 ○ *a reasonable attitude, conclusion* 合乎情理的态度、结论 ○ *It's not reasonable to expect a child to understand sarcasm.* 希望孩子明白讽刺的意义, 未免脱离实际. ○ *Is the accused guilty beyond all reasonable doubt?* 判定被告有罪是否毫无怀疑余地? **2 (a)** not unfair or expecting too much; moderate 公平的; 不过分的; 适度的: *a reasonable fee, offer, claim* 公平合理的费用、出价、要求. **(b)** (of prices, etc) not too expensive; acceptable (指价格等)不太贵的, 公道的: *Ten pounds for a good dictionary seems reasonable enough.* 花十镑买一部好词典算是够公道的了. **3** [esp attrib 尤作定语] tolerable; average 还可以的; 平均水平的: *reasonable weather, health, food* 过得去的天气、健康状况、食物 ○ *There's a reasonable chance that he'll come.* 他还是有可能来的. ○ *reasonable expectations of success* 对取得成功所抱有的并非捕风捉影的希望.

▷ **reas·on·able·ness** *n* [U].

reas·on·ably /-əblɪ; -əblɪ/ *adv* **1** in a reasonable way 合理地; 合乎逻辑地; 有理由地: *discuss the matter calmly and reasonably* 冷静而有理性地讨论问题. **2** moderately, acceptably or tolerably; fairly or quite 适度地; 尚可; 过得去; 公平地; 相当地: *reasonably good, cheap, intelligent* 相当好、便宜、聪明 ○ *a reasonably-priced book* 售价公

道的书 ○ *He seems reasonably satisfied with it.* 他看来对此相当满意.

re·as·sure /ˌriːə'ʃɔː(r); US -'ʃʊər; ˌriə'ʃʊr/ *v* [Tn, Tn·pr, Dn·f] **~ sb (about sth)** remove sb's fears or doubts; make sb confident again 消除某人的恐惧或疑虑; 恢复某人的信心; 使某人放心: *The police reassured her about her child's safety.* 警方让她放心, 她的孩子很安全. ○ *A glance in the mirror reassured him that his tie wasn't crooked.* 他照了一下镜子, 领带确实没有戴歪.

▷ **re·as·sur·ance** /-rəns; -rəns/ *n* **1** [U] reassuring or being reassured 消除恐惧或疑虑; 恢复信心; 放心: *want, need, demand, etc reassurance*, eg from a doctor about one's health 需要消除疑虑(如经医生证实身体健康). **2** [C] thing that reassures 使人消除恐惧或疑虑的事物; 使人恢复信心的事物: *numerous reassurances that we were safe* 消除我们的疑虑使我们感到安全的事物.

re·as·sur·ing *adj* that reassures 使人消除恐惧或疑虑的; 使人放心的: *a reassuring glance, word, pat on the back* 使人恢复信心的目光、话、轻拍一下背部. **re·as·sur·ingly** *adv*.

re·bate /'riːbeɪt; 'ribet/ *n* amount by which a debt, tax, etc can be reduced; discount or partial refund (债、税等的)可减免的款额; 折扣; 部分退款: *qualify for a rate/rent/tax rebate* 有资格获得房地产税[租金/所得税]的部分退款 ○ *offer a rebate of £1.50 for early settlement*, ie of an account, a bill, etc 及早结帐有1.50英镑的折扣. Cf 参看 DISCOUNT[1].

R

rebel /'rebl; 'rɛbl/ *n* (**a**) person who fights against, or refuses to serve, the established government 反政府的人; 拒不为政府效劳的人; 反叛者; 造反者: [attrib 作定语] *rebel forces* 叛军. (**b**) person who resists authority or control 反抗权威的人; 抗拒控制的人; 叛逆者: *She has always been a bit of a rebel.* 她总是有点桀骜不驯.

▷ **rebel** /rɪ'bel; rɪ'bɛl/ *v* (**-ll-**) [I, Ipr] **~ (against sb/sth)** **1** fight against or resist the established government 反抗政府; 反叛; 造反. **2** resist authority or control; protest strongly 反抗权威; 抗拒控制; 叛逆; 强烈抗议: *Such treatment would make anyone rebel.* 谁受这样的对待都得反抗. ○ *He finally rebelled against his strict upbringing.* 他终于起来反抗那种严厉管教他的方式.

re·bel·lion /rɪ'belɪən; rɪ'bɛljən/ *n* **~ (against sb/sth)** **1** [U] open (esp armed) resistance to the established government; resistance to authority or control 对政府的公开(尤指武装)反抗; 对权威的反抗; 对控制的抗拒; 反叛; 造反; 叛逆: *rise (up) in open rebellion* 起来造反. **2** [C] act of rebelling 反叛行动: *five rebellions in two years* 两年中的五次叛乱.

re·bel·li·ous /rɪ'belɪəs; rɪ'bɛljəs/ *adj* showing a desire to rebel; not easily controlled 显示反叛欲望的; 叛逆的; 难以控制的: *rebellious tribes* 反叛部落 ○ *rebellious acts, activities, behaviour, etc* 叛逆的行动、活动、行为等 ○ *a child with a rebellious temperament* 倔强的孩子. **re·bel·liously** *adv*. **re·bel·lious·ness** *n* [U].

re·bind /ˌriː'baɪnd; ri'baɪnd/ *v* (*pt, pp* **rebound** /ˌriː'baʊnd; ri'baʊnd/) [Tn] put a new binding on (a book, etc) 重新装订(书等).

re·birth /ˌriː'bɜːθ; ri'bɝθ/ *n* [sing] **1** spiritual renewal or enlightenment caused by religious conversion, etc (皈依后等精神上的)再生, 新生, 启蒙. **2** revival 复活; 复兴: *the rebirth of learning*, eg in the Renaissance 学术之再度繁荣(如文艺复兴时期的).

re·born /ˌriː'bɔːn; ri'bɔrn/ *adj* [pred 作表语] **1** spiritually renewed or enlightened (精神上)再生, 新生, 启蒙. Cf 参看 BORN-AGAIN (BORN). **2** brought back to life; revived 重新获得生命; 复活: *The old man felt reborn in his children.* 这个老人觉得在他的孩子们身上获得了新生.

re·bound[1] /rɪ'baʊnd; rɪ'baʊnd/ *v* **1** [I, Ipr] **~ (against/from/off sth)** spring or bounce back after hitting sth 弹回; 反弹: *The ball rebounded from/off the wall into the pond.* 球从墙上弹回来掉进池里. **2** [I, Ipr] **~ (on sb)** have an adverse effect on (the doer); misfire 对(施动者)产生反作用; 未能奏效: *The scheme rebounded on her in a way she had not expected.* 她未曾想到这计谋反倒使她自食其果.

▷ **re·bound** /'riːbaʊnd; 'riˌbaʊnd/ *n* (idm 习语) **on the 'rebound (from sth)** (**a**) while bouncing back 在弹回时: *hit a ball on the rebound* 击弹回的球. (**b**) (*fig* 比喻) while still affected by disappointment, depression, etc 失望、沮丧等之余: *She quarrelled with Paul and then married Peter on the rebound.* 她和保罗争吵后愤而嫁给了彼得.

re·bound[2] *pt, pp* of REBIND.

re·buff /rɪ'bʌf; rɪ'bʌf/ *n* unkind or contemptuous refusal or rejection (of an offer, request, friendly gesture, etc); snub (对好意、请求、友好表示等的)粗暴拒绝, 轻蔑回绝, 冷落: *Her kindness to him was met with a cruel rebuff.* 她一片好心却遭到他冷酷的拒绝.

▷ **re·buff** *v* [Tn] give a rebuff to (sb); snub 粗暴拒绝(某人); 冷落.

re·build /ˌriː'bɪld; ri'bɪld/ *v* (*pt, pp* **rebuilt** /ˌriː'bɪlt; ri'bɪlt/) [Tn] **1** build or put (sth) together again 重建(某事物); 重新组装(某物): *rebuild the city centre after an earthquake* 地震后重建城市中心区 ○ *We rebuilt the engine* (ie took it to pieces and put it together again) *using some new parts.* 我们用了一些新零件重新装配了这台发动机. **2** (*fig* 比喻) form (sth) again; restore 再形成(某事物); 恢复: *rebuild sb's confidence, hopes, health* 恢复某人的信心、希望、健康 ○ *After his divorce, he had to rebuild his life completely.* 他离婚后得完全重新安排生活.

re·buke /rɪ'bjuːk; rɪ'bjuk/ *v* [Tn, Tn·pr] **~ sb (for sth)** express sharp or severe disapproval to sb, esp officially; reprove sb 指摘或非难某人: *My boss rebuked me for coming to work late.* 我的上司指摘我上班迟到.

▷ **re·buke** *n* act of rebuking sb; reproof 指摘; 非难; 责难: *administer a stern rebuke* 予以严厉的谴责.

re·bus /'riːbəs; 'ribəs/ *n* puzzle in which a word or phrase has to be guessed from pictures or diagrams representing the letters or syllables in it (以画或图代表字母或音节的)画谜.

re·but /rɪ'bʌt; rɪ'bʌt/ *v* (**-tt-**) [Tn] prove (a charge, piece of evidence, etc) to be false; refute 证明(指控、证据等)不实; 反驳; 驳斥.

▷ **re·but·tal** /-tl; -tl/ *n* **1** [U] act of rebutting or being rebutted 反驳; 反证: *produce evidence in rebuttal of the charge* 提出反驳指控的证据. **2** [sing] evidence that rebuts a charge, etc 用以反驳指控等的证据; 反证.

rec /rek; rɛk/ *abbr* 缩写 = recreation ground 游乐场.

re·cal·cit·rant /rɪ'kælsɪtrənt; rɪ'kælsɪtrənt/ *adj* (*fml* 文) resisting authority or discipline; disobedient 反抗权威的; 不守纪律的; 不服从的: *a recalcitrant child, attitude* 倔强的孩子、态度.

▷ **re·cal·cit·rance** /-əns; -əns/ *n* [U] (*fml* 文) quality of being recalcitrant 抗拒; 不服从.

re·call /rɪ'kɔːl; rɪ'kɔl/ *v* **1** (**a**) [Tn, Tn·pr] **~ sb (from...) (to...)** order sb to return (from a place) (从某处)召回某人: *recall an ambassador (from his post)* 将大使(从驻在国)召回 ○ *recall (members of) Parliament*, eg for a special debate 召回国会议员(如举行特别辩论会). (**b**) [Tn] order (sth) to be returned 要求归还(某物): *recall library books*, eg for stock-taking 要求归还图书馆的书(如以便清点). **2** [Tn, Tf, Tw, Tg, Tsg] bring (sth/sb) back into the mind; recollect 回忆(某事物[某人]); 记起: *I can't recall his name.* 我想不起他的名字了. ○ *She recalled that he had left early.* 她回忆起他走得很早. ○ *Try to recall (to mind) exactly what happened.* 把发生的事情尽可能仔细地回忆一下. ○ *I recall seeing him.* 我记得见过他. ○ *I recall her giving me the key.* 我记得她给过我那把钥匙. Cf 参看 REMEMBER 1. **3** (phr v) **recall sb to sth** make sb aware or conscious again of sth 使某人重新注意到或意识到某事物: *The danger recalled him to a sense of duty.* 这危险的事唤起了他的责任感.

▷ **re·call** /*also* 'riːkɔːl; 'riˌkɔl/ *n* **1** [sing] order to sb/sth to return 召回; 唤回: *the temporary recall of embassy staff* 使馆人员的临时召回. **2** [U] ability to remember; recollection 记忆力; 记性: *a person gifted with total recall* 有本事把全部细节都能记住的人 ○ *My powers of recall are not what they were.* 我的记忆力已大不如前. **3** [C] signal, esp a bugle-call, to troops, etc to return 军队等的归队信号; (尤指)归队号: *sound the recall* 吹归队号. **4** (idm 习语) **beyond/past re'call** that cannot be brought back or cancelled 想不起来的; 不能取消的.

re·cant /rɪ'kænt; rɪ'kænt/ *v* [I, Tn] (*fml* 文) (**a**) formally reject (a former opinion, belief, etc) as being wrong 宣布放弃(以前的意见、信仰等): *recant one's former beliefs, heresies* 宣布放弃以前的信仰、异教信仰.

(**b**) take back or withdraw (a statement, an opinion, etc) as being false 撤回, 撤销(声明、意见等)(因不正确).

▷ **re·canta·tion** /ˌriːkænˈteɪʃn; ˌrikænˋteʃən/ *n* (*fml* 文) **1** [U] recanting 放弃; 撤销. **2** [C] act of recanting; statement that one's former beliefs were wrong 放弃; 撤销; 承认以前信仰错误的声明.

re·cap[1] /ˈriːkæp; ˋrikæp/ *v* **(-pp-)** [I, Tn, Tw] (*infml* 口) = RECAPITULATE. ▷ **re·cap** *n* [C, U] (*infml* 口) = RECAPITULATION (RECAPITULATE).

re·cap[2] /ˌriːˈkæp; riˋkæp/ *v*, *n* **(-pp-)** = RE-TREAD.

re·cap·itu·late /ˌriːkəˈpɪtʃʊleɪt; ˌrikəˋpɪtʃəˌlet/ (also *infml* 口语作 **recap**) *v* [I, Tn, Tw] state again or summarize the main points of (a discussion, etc) 重述或概括(讨论等)的要点: *Let me just recapitulate (on) what we've agreed so far.* 让我仅扼要重述一下到目前为止我们已取得的一致意见.

▷ **re·cap·itu·la·tion** /ˌriːkəpɪtʃʊˈleɪʃn; ˌrikəˌpɪtʃəˋleʃən/ (also *infml* 口语作 **recap**) *n* [C, U] (act of) recapitulating 扼要的重述; 概述: *a brief recapitulation* 摘要.

re·cap·ture /ˌriːˈkæptʃə(r); riˋkæptʃɚ/ *v* [Tn] **1** capture again (a person or an animal that has escaped, or sth taken by an enemy) 重新捕获(逃跑的人或动物); 夺回(敌人夺走的事物): *recapture escaped prisoners, bears* 重新捕获逃脱的犯人、熊 ○ *The town was recaptured from the enemy.* 该城已从敌人手中收复. **2** (*fig* 比喻) experience again or reproduce (past emotions, etc) 再次经历、体验或产生(往日的情感等): *recapture the joys of youth* 重新体验年轻时的欢乐 ○ *recapture a period atmosphere*, eg in a play, film, etc 再现某历史时期的气氛(如在戏剧、电影等中).

▷ **re·cap·ture** *n* [U] recapturing; being recaptured 重新捕获; 再次体验: *What led to the prisoner's recapture?* 靠什么线索把那个逃犯捉回的?

re·cast /ˌriːˈkɑːst; *US* -ˈkæst; riˋkæst/ *v* (*pt*, *pp* **recast**) **1** [Tn, Cn·n/a] **~ sth (as sth)** put (sth written or spoken) into a new form 改动(文字或言语): *recast a sentence, chapter, paragraph, etc* 改写一个句子、一章、一段等 ○ *She recast her lecture as a radio talk.* 她把讲义改动后用作电台的讲话. **2** (**a**) [Tn] change the cast of (a play, etc) 改变(戏剧等)的演员阵容. (**b**) [Tn] change the role of (an actor) 改变(演员)的角色: *I've been recast as Brutus.* 我改演布鲁特斯一角.

recce /ˈrekɪ; ˋrɛkɪ/ *n* [C, U] (*infml* 口) = RECONNAISSANCE: *make a quick recce of the area* 对该地区进行快速侦察.

▷ **recce** *v* [I, Tn] (*infml* 口) = RECONNOITRE.

recd *abbr* 缩写 = received: *recd £9.50* 收到 9.50 英镑.

re·cede /rɪˈsiːd; rɪˋsid/ *v* **1** [I, Ipr] **~ (from sth)** (seem to) move back from a previous position or away from an observer (似)自原处后退或避开别人的注视: *As the tide receded (from the shore) we were able to look for shells.* 潮水(自岸边)退去, 我们就能寻找贝壳了. ○ *We reached the open sea and the coast receded into the distance.* 我们驶抵公海, 海岸似乎退到了远方. ○ (*fig* 比喻) *The prospect of bankruptcy has now receded*, ie is less likely. 破产的危险现已减少了. **2** [I] slope backwards 向后倾斜: *a receding chin* 向后缩的下巴 ○ *Tom has a receding hairline*, ie His hair has stopped growing at the forehead and temples. 汤姆的前发际已渐渐后移(前额和太阳穴不再长头发).

re·ceipt /rɪˈsiːt; rɪˋsit/ *n* **1** [U] **~ (of sth)** (*fml* 文) act of receiving or being received 收到: *acknowledge receipt of a letter, an order, etc* 签收信件、订单等 ○ *On receipt of the news, he left.* 他一接到消息就走了. **2** [C] **~ (for sth)** written statement that sth (esp money or goods) has been received 收条; 收据: *get a receipt for your expenses* 对开销要索取收据 ○ *sign a receipt* 在收据上签字 ○ [attrib 作定语] *a receipt book* 收据簿. **3 receipts** [pl] money received by a business (营业)收到的款项, 收入: *net/gross receipts* 纯[总]收入. Cf 参看 EXPENDITURE. **4** [C] (*arch* 古) recipe 食谱; 烹饪法; 处方. **5** (idm 习语) **(be) in receipt of sth** (*commerce* 商) having received sth 已收到某物: *We are in receipt of your letter of the 15th.* 我们收到了您 15 日来函.

▷ **re·ceipt** *v* [Tn] mark (a bill) as having been paid, eg with a rubber stamp saying 'Paid' or 'Received with thanks' 在(帐单)上盖注有'收讫'字样的图章(以示款已付清).

re·ceiv·able /rɪˈsiːvəbl; rɪˋsivəbl̩/ *adj* (usu following *ns* 通常用于名词之后) (*commerce* 商) (of bills, accounts, etc) for which money has not yet been received (指票据、帐款等)应收的: *bills receivable* 应收票据.

▷ **re·ceiv·ables** *n* [pl] assets of a business represented by accounts that still have to be paid 应收款项.

re·ceive /rɪˈsiːv; rɪˋsiv/ *v* **1** (**a**) [Tn, Tn·pr] **~ sth (from sb/sth)** get, accept or take (sth sent, given, etc) 收到, 得到, 接到, 领取(邮寄、赠送等之物): *receive a letter, present, phone call, grant* 接到信、礼物、电话、补助金 ○ *receive a good education* 受到良好教育 ○ *receive severe injuries, blows* 受重伤、打击 ○ *receive insults, thanks, congratulations* 受到侮辱、感谢、祝贺 ○ *Your comments will receive our close attention.* 你的意见我们一定认真考虑. ○ *You will receive a warm welcome when you come to England.* 你到英国时一定受到热烈欢迎. (**b**) [I, Tn] (*esp Brit*) buy or accept (stolen goods) knowingly (有意)购买或接受(赃物). **2** (**a**) [Tn, Tn·pr] **~ sb (into sth)** allow sb to enter, eg as a guest, member, etc; admit sb 接待(如客人、成员等); 接纳或承认某人: *rooms* (eg in a hotel) *ready to receive their new occupants* 准备接待新房客的房间(如旅馆的) ○ *He has been received into the Church.* 他已入教. (**b**) [esp passive 尤用于被动语态: Tn, Tn·pr, Cn·n/a] **~ sb (with sth) (as sth)** (*fml* 文) welcome or entertain (guests, etc), esp formally 欢迎或招待(客人等)(尤指正式地): *The chief was received by the Prime Minister.* 该领导人受到了首相的接见. ○ *She was received with warm applause.* 大家以热烈的掌声欢迎她. ○ *He was received as an honoured visitor.* 他以贵宾的身分受到款待. **3** [esp passive 尤用于被动语态: Tn, Tn·pr] **~ sb/sth (with sth)** react in a specified way to sb/sth (以某方式)对某人[某事物]做出反应: *How was the play received?* 对这出戏反应如何? ○ *My suggestion was received with disdain.* 我的建议人家不屑一顾. ○ *The reforms have been well received by the public.* 公众对改革反应良好. **4** [Tn] convert (broadcast signals) into sounds or pictures 将(无线电讯号)转变为声音或图像: *receive a programme via satellite* 通过卫星接收节目 ○ *Are you receiving me?* ie Can you hear me (said to sb to whom one is speaking on a radio transmitter)? 你能收听到我的声音吗(通过无线电发报机呼叫对方)? **5** (idm 习语) **be at/on the receiving end (of sth)** (*infml* 口) be the one who suffers sth unpleasant 承受不愉快事物的人: *The party in power soon learns what it's like to be on the receiving end of political satire.* 执政党很快就尝到了遭受政治讽刺的滋味.

▷ **re·ceived** *adj* [attrib 作定语] widely accepted as correct 公认为正确而普遍接受的: *received opinion, pronunciation* 公认为正确的看法、规范读音 ○ *change received ideas about education* 改变对教育的一贯看法.

re·ceiver /rɪˈsiːvə(r); rɪˋsivɚ/ *n* **1** (**a**) person who receives sth 接受者. (**b**) (*esp Brit*) person who buys or accepts stolen goods knowingly 购买或接受分明是赃物的人. **2** (also **Receiver**, **Of,ficial Re'ceiver**) official appointed by law to look after the property and affairs of a minor, bankrupt, etc or to administer disputed property 破产管理官: *call in the receiver* 申请委派破产管理官 ○ *put the business in the hands of a receiver* 把公司交由破产管理官管理. **3** part of an instrument that receives sth, esp the part of a telephone that receives the incoming sound and is held to the ear 接收器; 受话器; (尤指)电话听筒: *lift, replace, etc the receiver* 拿起、放下...听筒. **4** radio or TV set that converts broadcast signals into sound or pictures 无线电接收机; 收音机; 电视机.

▷ **re·ceiv·er·ship** /-ʃɪp; -ˌʃɪp/ *n* [U] (*law* 律) **1** (period of) office of a Receiver 破产管理官的职务或任期. **2** (idm 习语) **in receivership** (esp of bankrupt companies) under the control of an Official Receiver (尤指破产公司)受破产管理官管理: *go into/be in receivership* 交由[受]破产管理官管理.

re·cent /ˈriːsnt; ˋrisn̩t/ *adj* [usu attrib 通常作定语] (that existed, happened, began, was/were made, etc) not long ago or before 不久前的; 近来的: *a recent event, development, occurrence, etc* 不久前的事件、发展、事情等 ○ *In recent years there have been many changes.* 最近几年有了许多变化. ○ *Ours is a recent acquaintance*, ie We only met a short time ago. 我们是最近才认识的. ⇨ Usage at NEW 用法见 NEW.

▷ **re·cently** *adv* not long ago or before; lately 不久前;

R

近来: *until quite recently* 直到不久以前 ○ *a recently painted house* 最近粉刷过的房子.

NOTE ON USAGE 用法: **Recently, not long ago, lately** indicate that the action spoken about took place in the recent past. ☆ **recently**、**not long ago**、**lately** 均指最近发生过的事. **1 Recently** has the widest use, in positive and negative statements and questions, with the past tense and the present perfect tense ☆ **recently** 用法最广, 可用于肯定式陈述句、否定式陈述句及疑问句中, 与过去时态和现在完成时态连用: *Did she have a party recently?* 她最近举办过聚会吗? ○ *They've recently bought a new car.* 他们不久前买了一辆新汽车. **2 Not long ago** is only used in positive statements with the verb in the past tense ☆ **not long ago** 仅用于肯定式陈述句中, 与动词过去时态连用: *They arrived in Britain not long ago/recently.* 他们不久以前[最近]到达英国. ○ *It's not long ago that they arrived in Britain.* 他们是不久以前到达英国的. **3 Lately** is used in questions and negative statements. ☆ **lately** 用于疑问句和否定式陈述句中. In positive statements it is used generally with **only, much** and **a lot.** 若用于肯定式陈述句中, 通常与 **only**、**much**、**a lot** 连用. The verb must be in the present perfect tense 动词必须用现在完成时态: *Have you seen him lately/recently?* 你近来[最近]见过他吗? ○ *They haven't written lately/recently.* 他们近来[最近]没有写信. ○ *She's only lately/recently begun working here.* 她只是近来[最近]才开始在这里工作的. ○ *I've seen a lot of her lately/recently.* 我近来[最近]常见到她.

R

re·cept·acle /rɪˈseptəkl; rɪˋsɛptəkl̩/ *n* (*fml* 文) container, space, etc for placing or storing sth 容器; 放置物品的地方: *a receptacle for litter, washing, waste paper* 垃圾箱、待洗衣物袋、废纸箱.

re·cep·tion /rɪˈsepʃn; rɪˋsɛpʃən/ *n* **1** [U] action of receiving or being received 接受; 接待; 接纳; 接收: *The bridal suite was prepared for the reception of the honeymooners.* 新婚套间已准备好以接待度蜜月的人. ○ *prepare rooms for the reception of guests* 准备房间以接待宾客 ○ *her reception into the religious order* 接纳她进修道会 ○ [attrib 作定语] *a reception area, camp, centre, etc,* ie where refugees, immigrants, etc are received and accommodated 接待区、营、中心等(接纳和安置难民、移民等的处所) ○ *a* ˈ*reception committee* 接待委员会. **2** [sing] way in which sb/sth is received (RECEIVE 3) 反应: *The play got a favourable reception from the critics.* 该剧获评论界好评. ○ *His talk met with/was given a warm* (ie enthusiastic) *reception.* 他的讲话受到热烈的欢迎. **3** [sing] (*Brit*) area in a hotel or an office building where guests or clients are received, registered, etc (旅馆或事务所的)接待处: *Wait for me at reception.* 在接待处等我吧. **4** [C] formal social occasion to welcome sb 正式的欢迎场合; 欢迎会; 招待会; 宴会: *hold a wedding reception* 举办结婚宴会 ○ *official receptions for the foreign visitors* 欢迎外宾的招待会. **5** [U] receiving of broadcast signals; efficiency of this (无线电信号的)接收, 接收效果: *a radio with excellent reception* 接收性能极好的收音机 ○ *Reception* (eg of TV programmes) *is poor here.* 这里的接收情况欠佳(如电视节目的).

▷ **re·cep·tion·ist** /-ʃənɪst; -ʃənɪst/ *n* person employed to make appointments for and receive clients at a hotel, an office building, a doctor's or dentist's surgery, a hairdressing salon, etc (旅馆、事务所、诊所、理发馆等雇用的)接待员.

□ **re**ˈ**ception desk** (*Brit*) (in a hotel, an office building, etc) counter where guests, clients, etc are received, where they ask for rooms, etc (旅馆、事务所等的)服务台.

reˈ**ception room** **1** (used esp when advertising houses for sale 尤用于房屋出售广告) living-room; room other than a kitchen, bathroom or bedroom 客厅; 起居室. **2** room (eg in a hotel) suitable for large social functions (适于大型活动的)客厅(如旅馆中的).

re·cept·ive /rɪˈseptɪv; rɪˋsɛptɪv/ *adj* **~ (to sth)** able or quick to receive new ideas, suggestions, etc (对新的思想、建议等)易于接受的, 接受得快的: *a receptive person, mind, attitude* 敏于接受新思想的人、头脑、态度 ○ *receptive to new developments* 对新事物接受得快的. ▷ **re·cept·ive·ness, re·cep·tiv·ity** /ˌriːsepˈtɪvətɪ; ˌrisɛpˋtɪvətɪ/ *ns* [U].

re·cess /rɪˈses; *US* ˈriːses; ˋrisɛs/ *n* **1** [C, U] (**a**) (*US* also **vacation**) period of time when work or business is stopped, esp in Parliament, the lawcourts, etc (工作或业务活动的)中止或暂停期间; (尤指国会、法庭等的)休会期, 休庭期: *the summer recess* 暑假 ○ *Parliament is in recess.* 议会处于休会期. (**b**) (*US*) break between classes at school (学校的)课间休息. ➪Usage at BREAK[2] 用法见 BREAK[2]. **2** [C] space in a room where part of a wall is set back from the main part; alcove 壁凹(墙壁的凹进处); 凹室; 壁龛: *a door, window, cupboard, etc recess* 可供安门、窗、橱柜等的壁凹. **3** [C] hollow space inside sth 某物内部的凹形空间: *a drawer with a secret recess* 有隐秘槽子的抽屉. **4** [C usu *pl* 通常作复数] remote or secret place 遥远或隐秘的地方: *the dark recesses of a cave* 洞中隐秘的暗处 ○ (*fig* 比喻) *in the innermost recesses of the heart/mind* 在内心[思想]的最深处.

▷ **re·cess** *v* **1** [Tn esp passive 尤用于被动语态] place (sth) in a recess(2) 把(某物)放在墙壁的凹处: *recessed shelves, windows, etc* 在墙壁的凹处设置的搁架、窗户等. **2** [Tn esp passive 尤用于被动语态] set (a wall) back; provide (a wall) with recesses 将(墙)做成凹形; 在(墙)上做壁龛. **3** [I] (*US*) take a recess(1a) 休息; 休假; 休会; 休庭.

re·ces·sion /rɪˈseʃn; rɪˋsɛʃən/ *n* **1** [C] temporary decline in economic activity or prosperity (经济)衰退; 不景气: *an industrial, a trade, etc recession* 工业、贸易等的衰退. Cf 参看 SLUMP *n* 1. **2** [U] movement back from a previous position; withdrawal 后退; 撤退; 撤回: *the gradual recession of flood waters* 洪水的逐渐消退.

▷ **re·ces·sion·ary** *adj* **1** [attrib 作定语] of a slowing of economic activity (经济)萧条的, 疲软的: *in the present recessionary period, conditions* 在当前经济萧条的时期里、情况下. **2** likely to bring about a slowing of economic activity 可能使经济活动减慢的: *a recessionary effect on the economy* 可能使经济衰退的影响 ○ *introduce recessionary measures* 采取防止经济过热的措施.

re·ces·sional /rɪˈseʃənl; rɪˋsɛʃənəl/ *n* (also **recessional hymn**) hymn sung while the clergy and choir withdraw after a church service (礼拜仪式完毕后牧师和唱诗班退场时唱的)退场赞美诗.

re·cess·ive /rɪˈsesɪv; rɪˋsɛsɪv/ *adj* **1** (*biology* 生) (of characteristics inherited from a parent, such as the colour of the eyes or of the hair) not appearing in a child but remaining hidden because of the presence of stronger characteristics (指遗传性状, 如眼睛或毛发的颜色)隐性的, 潜性的. Cf 参看 DOMINANT. **2** having a tendency to recede or go back (倾向于)后退的, 倒退的.

re·charge /ˌriːˈtʃɑːdʒ; riˋtʃɑrdʒ/ *v* [Tn] **1** charge (a battery, a gun, etc) again 给(电池)再充电; 给(枪)再装弹药. **2** (idm 习语) **recharge one's** ˈ**batteries** (*infml* 口) have a period of rest and relaxation during which one's energy is built up again 休整. ▷ **re·charge·able** *adj*: *rechargeable batteries* 可再充电的电池.

re·cher·ché /rəˈʃeəʃeɪ; rəˋʃɛrʃe/ *adj* (*fml* 文) **1** (*usu derog* 通常作贬义) much too studied or refined; affected 过分刻意求工的; 矫揉造作的: *a recherché idea, writing style, image* 煞费苦心的念头、矫揉造作的文风、挖空心思的比喻. **2** chosen or planned with great care; choice 精心选择的; 精心设计的: *a recherché menu,* eg for gourmets 佳肴菜单.

re·cid·iv·ist /rɪˈsɪdɪvɪst; rɪˋsɪdəvɪst/ *n* person who commits crimes repeatedly and seems unable to be cured of criminal tendencies; persistent offender 本性难移的惯犯; 累犯. ▷ **re·cid·iv·ism** /-ɪzəm; -ɪzəm/ *n* [U].

re·cipe /ˈresəpɪ; ˋrɛsəpɪ/ *n* **1 ~ (for sth)** set of instructions for preparing a food dish, including the ingredients required 烹饪法; 食谱: [attrib 作定语] *recipe books, cards* 烹饪书、食谱卡片. **2 ~ for sth** (*fig* 比喻) method of achieving sth 方法; 秘诀; 诀窍: *What is your recipe for success?* 你取得成功有什么窍门? ○ *His plans are a recipe for* (ie are likely to lead to) *disaster.* 他的计划后患无穷.

re·cipi·ent /rɪˈsɪpɪənt; rɪˋsɪpɪənt/ *n* **~ (of sth)** person who receives sth 接受者.

re·cip·rocal /rɪˈsɪprəkl; rɪˋsɪprəkl/ *adj* given and received in return; mutual 互相给与的; 互惠的; 相互

的: *reciprocal affection, help, trade* 互爱、互助、互惠贸易 ○ *have a reciprocal agreement to combat terrorism* 有相互配合的协定, 共同与恐怖主义作斗争. ▷ **re·cip·roc·ally** /-klɪ; -klɪ/ *adv*.

□ **re͵ciprocal ˈpronoun** (*grammar*) pronoun expressing a mutual action or relation, eg *each other, one another* 相互代词(表示相互之行为或关系, 如each other、one another).

re·cip·roc·ate /rɪˈsɪprəkeɪt; rɪˋsɪprə͵ket/ *v* **1** [I, Tn] (*fml* 文) (**a**) give and receive (sth) in return; exchange (sth) mutually 互给(某物); 互换(某物). (**b**) return (sth done, given or felt) 回报以(某种动作、物品或感情): *He reciprocated by wishing her good luck.* 他也祝她交好运. ○ *I reciprocate your good wishes.* 我也同样祝福你. **2** [I] (of parts of a machine) move alternately backwards and forwards in a straight line (指机件)沿直线往复移动: *a reciprocating saw* 往复式锯 ○ *reciprocating pistons* 往复式活塞. Cf 参看 ROTARY 2. ▷ **re·cip·roca·tion** /rɪ͵sɪprəˈkeɪʃn; rɪ͵sɪprəˋkeʃən/ *n* [U].

□ **reˈciprocating engine** engine in which pistons move backwards and forwards inside cylinders 往复式发动机.

re·ci·pro·city /͵resɪˈprɒsətɪ; ͵rɛsəˋprɑsətɪ/ *n* [U] principle or practice of mutual exchange, esp of making concessions or granting privileges, etc in return for concessions or privileges received 相互交换的原则或实践; (尤指)互相让步或互惠: *reciprocity in trade (between countries)* (国与国之间的)贸易互惠.

re·cital /rɪˈsaɪtl; rɪˋsaɪtl̩/ *n* **1** [C] public performance of music, dance, etc by a soloist or a small group 独唱会; 独奏会; (小型团体的)音乐演奏会、舞蹈表演会等: *give a piˈano recital* 举行钢琴独奏会 ○ *a ˈsong/ˈdance/ˈpoetry recital* 歌曲演唱会[舞蹈表演会/诗歌朗诵会]. Cf 参看 CONCERT. **2** [C] detailed account of a series of events, etc 一系列事件等的详述: *I had to listen to a long recital of all his complaints.* 我得听他那些没完没了的牢骚. **3** [U] action of reciting 背诵, 朗诵(尤指向听众): *his recital of the poem* 他的诗歌朗诵 ○ *music recorded in recital* 在演奏现场录制的音乐.

re·cita·tion /͵resɪˈteɪʃn; ͵rɛsəˋteʃən/ *n* **1** [C, U] (instance of) public delivery of passages of prose or poetry learnt by heart (散文或诗歌的)当众吟诵, 背诵: *recitations from Dickens* 狄更斯作品选段的背诵 ○ *the recitation of a ballad, an ode, etc* 叙事歌谣、颂诗等的背诵. **2** [C] piece of prose or poetry (to be) recited (要)背诵的散文或诗歌. **3** [C] (*US*) student's oral responses to questions on a lesson, etc (学生对课文等作的)口头答问.

re·cit·at·ive /͵resɪtəˈtiːv; ͵rɛsətəˋtiv/ *n* [C, U] (passage of) narrative or dialogue in an opera or oratorio sung in the rhythm of ordinary speech with many words on the same note 宣叙调, 朗诵调(歌剧或清唱剧中近似说话的歌唱风格).

re·cite /rɪˈsaɪt; rɪˋsaɪt/ *v* **1** [I, Ipr, Tn, Tn·pr] **~ (sth) (to sb)** say (a poem, passage, etc) aloud from memory, esp to an audience 背诵, 朗诵(诗文等)(尤指向听众): *recite a speech from 'Hamlet' to the class* 向班上同学背诵《哈姆雷特》中的一段话. **2** [Tn, Tn·pr] **~ sth (to sb)** state (names, facts, etc) one by one; give a list of 说出一连串(名字、事情等); 列举: *recite one's grievances* 叙述自己的苦难 ○ *recite the names of all the European capitals* 一一说出欧洲各国首都的名称.

reck·less /ˈreklɪs; ˋrɛklɪs/ *adj* **~ (of sth)** (of people or their actions) not thinking of the consequences or of danger; rash or impulsive (指人或其行为)不考虑后果的, 不顾危险的, 鲁莽的, 由冲动引起的: *a reckless spender, gambler, etc* 乱花钱的人、乱赌博的人 ○ *fined £100 for reckless driving* 因鲁莽驾驶罚款100英镑 ○ *He's quite reckless of his own safety.* 他完全不顾及自己的安全. ▷ **reck·lessly** *adv*. **reck·less·ness** *n* [U].

reckon /ˈrekən; ˋrɛkən/ *v* **1** [Tn·pr, Tf, Cn·a esp passive 尤用于被动语态, Cn·n esp passive 尤用于被动语态, Cn·n/a esp passive 尤用于被动语态, Cn·t esp passive 尤用于被动语态] **~ sb/sth among sth; ~ sb/sth as sth** (*infml* 口) (not used in the continuous tenses 不用于进行时态) be of the opinion or consider that sb/sth is as specified 认为某人[某事物]是…: *We reckon her among our best reporters.* 我们认为她是我们最好的记者. ○ *I reckon (that) he is too old for the job.* 我认为他年龄太大, 不适于做这工作. ○ *The price was reckoned high.* 价钱未免太高了. ○ *She is reckoned (to be) the cleverest pupil in the class.* 她是班上最聪明的学生. ○ *One quarter of the country is reckoned as unproductive.* 全国四分之一的土地是不毛之地. **2** (**a**) [Tf no passive 不用于被动语态] (*infml* 口) assume; think 假定; 想; 思忖; 认为: *I reckon we'll go next week.* 我想我们下星期去. ○ *The news won't worry her, I reckon.* 我看这消息不会使她不安. ○ *What do you reckon our chances are of arriving on time?* 你认为我们有没有可能按时到达? (**b**) [Tf, Tt] calculate (time, price, age, etc) approximately; guess 约略地计算(时间、价格、年龄等); 猜想: *I reckon it will cost about £100.* 我估计大约要100英镑. ○ *We reckon to arrive in Delhi at noon.* 我们估计正午抵达德里. **3** [Tn] find out (the quantity, number, cost, etc) by using numbers; calculate 算出(数量、数目、费用等); 计算: *reckon the total volume of imports* 计算进口商品的总量 ○ *Hire charges are reckoned from the date of delivery.* 租金由货到之日起计算. **4** (phr v) **reckon sth in** include sth in a calculation 将某事物计算在内: *When you did your expenses, did you reckon in your taxi fares?* 你计算费用时, 把计程车费算进去了吗? **reckon on sb/sth** base one's plans on sb doing sth or on sth happening; rely on sb/sth 指望或依赖某人[某事物]: *Can I reckon on you to help?* 你能帮助我吗? ○ *We're reckoning on moving house in May.* 我们指望着五月份搬家. ○ *You can't always reckon on (having) good weather.* 总依赖(有)好天气是靠不住的. **reckon sth up** find the sum or total of sth; count sth up 计算; 结算: *reckon up bills, accounts, costs, etc* 结算帐单、帐目、费用等. **reckon with sb/sth** take sb/sth into account; consider sb/sth as important 考虑到或重视某人[某事物]: *They had many difficulties to reckon with.* 他们有许多困难要考虑. ○ *a force, fact, person to be reckoned with*, ie that cannot be ignored 不可忽视的力量、事实、人物. **reckon without sb/sth** not take sb/sth into account; not consider sb/sth as important 未考虑到或未重视某人[某事物]: *We wanted a quiet holiday, but we had reckoned without the children.* 我们原想安安静静地度假, 却没有把孩子考虑在内.

▷ **reck·oner** /ˈrekənə(r); ˋrɛkənɚ/ *n* device or table (of figures, etc) used as an aid to reckoning 计算器; 计算表. Cf 参看 READY RECKONER (READY).

reck·on·ing /ˈrekənɪŋ; ˋrɛkənɪŋ/ *n* **1** [U] calculation; estimation 计算; 估计: *the reckoning of debts, accounts, etc* 债务、帐目等的计算 ○ *By my reckoning, this short cut will save us five miles.* 据我估计, 我们走这条近道可少走五英里. ○ *You were £5 out* (ie over or under the correct sum) *in your reckoning.* 你计算差了5英镑. **2** [sing] (*dated* 旧) (settlement of an) account or a bill, eg at a hotel or restaurant 帐目或帐单(的结算)(如旅馆或饭馆中): *ask for the reckoning* 要求结帐 ○ (*fig* 比喻) *There'll be a heavy reckoning to pay!* ie The consequences will be serious. 后果不堪设想! **3** (idm 习语) **a day of reckoning** ⇨ DAY.

re·claim /rɪˈkleɪm; rɪˋklem/ *v* [Tn, Tn·pr] **1 ~ sth (from sb/sth)** recover possession of sth 恢复或收回某事物: *reclaim tax, rent, lost property* 取回税款、租金、失去的财物. **2 ~ sth (from sth)** make (land) suitable for cultivation, eg by draining or irrigating it 开垦(土地)(如排水、灌溉以利耕种): *reclaimed marshland, desert, etc* 经治理的沼泽地、沙漠等 ○ *reclaim an area from the sea* 填海造地. **3 ~ sb (from sth)** (*fml* 文) win sb back or away from sin, error, etc; reform sb 挽救某人(不再犯罪、犯错等); 改造某人: *reclaim young offenders from a life of crime* 挽救失足少年脱离罪恶的生活. **4 ~ sth (from sth)** recover (raw material) from waste products (从废品中)回收(原料): *reclaim glass from old bottles* 回收旧瓶子用以再造玻璃. Cf 参看 RECYCLE. ▷ **re·clama·tion** /͵rekləˈmeɪʃn; ͵rɛkləˋmeʃən/ *n* [U].

re·cline /rɪˈklaɪn; rɪˋklaɪn/ *v* **1** [I, Ipr] lean or lie back in a horizontal or near-horizontal position 向后倚靠或躺: *recline on a pillow, a sofa, a grassy bank* 躺在枕头、沙发、草坡上 ○ *recline in a deck-chair, a punt, a hammock* 斜躺在折叠帆布椅、平底船、吊床上 ○ *a reclining chair*, ie one with a back that tilts 躺椅 ○ *a reclining seat*, eg in a train, plane, etc 躺式座椅(如火车、飞机等的) ○ *a reclining figure*, eg in a painting 躺卧着的人像(如绘画

中的). **2** [Tn·pr] **~ sth against/on sb/sth** put or lay (one's head, arms) in a position of rest 将(头、臂)倚着某人[某物]. **3** [Tn] tilt (a seat, etc) backwards 使(座位等)向后倾斜.

re·cluse /rɪˈklu:s; rɪˋklus/ *n* person who lives alone and avoids other people 隐居者; 隐士: *live/lead the life of a recluse* 过隐居生活.

re·cog·ni·tion /ˌrekəgˈnɪʃn; ˌrɛkəgˋnɪʃən/ *n* **1** [U] recognizing or being recognized 认识; 认出; 承认: *an award in recognition of one's services, achievements, etc* 为表彰某人的贡献、成就等而授予的奖励 ○ *He has won wide recognition in the field of tropical medicine.* 他在热带疾患这一医学领域里广获赞誉. ○ (*fml* 文) *Britain's recognition of* (ie establishment of diplomatic relations with) *the new regime is unlikely.* 这个新政权不大可能获英国承认. **2** (idm 习语) **change, etc beyond/out of (all) recogˈnition** change so much that recognition is very difficult 变化大得难以认出: *The town has altered out of all recognition since I was last here.* 自从我上次离开这里以来, 这小城已变得认不出来了.

re·cog·niz·ance, -nisance /rɪˈkɒgnɪzns; rɪˋkɑgnɪzəns/ *n* (*law* 律) (**a**) formal promise made to a court or magistrate that one will observe certain conditions (eg keep the peace), appear when summoned or pay a debt 具结; 保证书: *enter into recognizances (for sb)* (为某人)具结 ○ *bail in one's own recognizance of £500* 自付500英镑保证金获得保释 ○ *be released on one's own recognizance* 经本人具结获释. (**b**) sum of money pledged as a guarantee that this promise will be kept (交付法院的)保证金.

R

re·cog·nize, -ise /ˈrekəgnaɪz; ˋrɛkəgˌnaɪz/ *v* (not used in the continuous tenses 不用于进行时态) **1** [Tn, Tn·pr] **~ sb/sth (by sth)** be able to identify (sb/sth that one has seen, heard, etc before); know sb/sth again 认出或识别某人[某事物]: *recognize a tune, an old friend, a signal* 听出一首听过的曲子、认出一个老朋友、识别一个熟悉的信号 ○ *I recognized her by her red hat.* 我根据她的红色帽子认出了她. **2** [Tn, Cn·n/a, Cn·t] **~ sb/sth (as sth)** be willing to accept sb/sth as valid or genuine; approve 承认某人[某事物]有效或属实; 认可: *recognized* (ie qualified or official) *instructors, schools, charities* 获得承认的教员、学校、慈善团体 ○ *recognize sb's claim to ownership* 承认某人提出的所有权要求 ○ (*fml* 文) *Britain has recognized* (ie established diplomatic relations with) *the new regime.* 英国已承认了这个新政权. ○ *Everyone recognized him to be the lawful heir/as the lawful heir.* 大家都承认他为合法继承人. **3** [Tn, Tf] be prepared to admit or be aware of (sth); realize 承认或认清(某事物); 认识到: *He recognized his lack of qualifications/that he was not qualified for the post.* 他承认自己不够条件[没有资格]担任那个职务. **4** [Tn] show gratitude or appreciation of (sb's ability, service, etc) by giving him an honour or reward 给予某人以荣誉或奖励以对(其能力、贡献等)表示感激或赏识: *The firm recognized Tom's outstanding work by giving him an extra bonus.* 公司发给汤姆一笔额外奖金以表彰他工作出色. ○ *His services to the State were recognized*, eg by a knighthood. 他对国家的贡献获得了奖赏(如被封为爵士).

▷ **re·cog·niz·able, -isable** /ˈrekəgnaɪzəbl, *also* ˌrekəgˈnaɪzəbl; ˋrɛkəgˌnaɪzəbl/ *adj* that can be recognized 可认出的; 可识别的; 可承认的; 可认可的: *She was barely recognizable as the girl I had known at school.* 我几乎认不出她就是我上学时认识的那个女孩儿. **re·cog·niz·ably, -isably** /-əblɪ; -əblɪ/ *adv*.

re·coil /rɪˈkɔɪl; rɪˋkɔɪl/ *v* **1** [I, Ipr] **~ (from sb/sth); ~ (at sth)** (**a**) draw oneself back in fear, disgust, etc (因恐惧、厌恶等)畏缩, 退缩: *She recoiled from the gunman in terror.* 她面对持枪歹徒吓得直往后缩. ○ *He recoiled at the sight of the corpse.* 他见到尸体厌恶得止步不前. (**b**) (*fig* 比喻) withdraw mentally 畏怯: *recoil from murder, violence, etc* 畏惧凶杀、暴力等. **2** [I] (**a**) (of guns) jerk back when fired (指枪炮)反冲, 产生后座力. (**b**) (of springs) move or jump back suddenly after impact (指弹簧)弹回. **3** (phr v) **recoil on sb** (of harmful actions) return to hurt the person who does them (指有害行动)还治其人之身; 报应.

▷ **re·coil** /ˈri:kɔɪl; ˋrikɔɪl/ *n* [U, sing] sudden backward movement, esp of a gun when fired 反冲(力); (尤指枪炮的)后座(力).

re·col·lect /ˌrekəˈlekt; ˌrɛkəˋlɛkt/ *v* [I, Tn, Tf, Tw, Tg, Tsg no passive 不用于被动语态] succeed in calling (sth) back to the mind; remember 想起; 记得; 回忆起: *As far as I recollect, you came late.* 我记得你来晚了. ○ *recollect one's childhood, sb's name* 回忆起童年时代、某人的名字 ○ *I recollect that you denied it.* 我记得你曾否认此事. ○ *Can you recollect how it was done?* 你还记得是怎么做的吗? ○ *She can recollect meeting the king.* 她能回忆起觐见国王的事. ○ *No one can recollect her leaving.* 谁也想不起她走的事.

re·col·lec·tion /ˌrekəˈlekʃn; ˌrɛkəˋlɛkʃən/ *n* **1** (**a**) [U] ability to recollect; action of recollecting 记忆力; 回忆: *have amazing powers of recollection* 有惊人的记忆力 ○ *I have some/no recollection of that day.* 那天的事我还记得一些[不记得了]. ○ *lost in quiet recollection of the past* 沉浸在对往事的幽思之中 ○ *to the best of my recollection*, ie if I remember correctly 就我记忆所及(假若我没记错的话) ○ *My recollection of events differs from hers.* 这些事, 我记得的情况与她的说法不同. (**b**) [C usu *pl* 通常作复数] thing, event, etc recollected 回忆的事物: *vague, clear, distant, etc recollections of childhood* 依稀记得的、历历在目的、遥远的...童年往事 ○ *The old letters brought back many happy recollections.* 这些旧信使人想起许多愉快的往事. **2** time over which sb's memory goes back 记忆所及的时间: *Such a problem has never arisen within my recollection.* 我不记得有过这样的问题.

re·com·mend /ˌrekəˈmend; ˌrɛkəˋmɛnd/ *v* **1** [Tn, Cn·n/a, Dn·n, Dn·pr] **~ sb/sth (to sb) (for sth/as sth)** praise sth as suitable for a purpose; praise sb as suitable for a post, etc; speak favourably of sb/sth 推许某事物; 推荐某人; 赞许某人[某事物]: *recommend a car, film, plumber, etc* 推荐某汽车、影片、管子工等 ○ *What would you recommend for removing ink stains?* 你看用什么方法可除去墨迹? ○ *She was strongly recommended for the post.* 她获大力推荐担任这个职务. ○ *I can recommend him as an extremely good accountant.* 我推荐他一定能当个极好的会计. ○ *Can you recommend me a good novel?* 你给我介绍一本好的小说行吗? **2** [Tn, Tf, Tw, Tg, Tsg, Dn·t, Dpr·f] suggest (a course of action, treatment, etc); advise 建议(采取某种做法、对策等); 劝告: *I'd recommend extreme caution.* 我奉劝多加小心. ○ *I recommend that you resign.* 我建议你辞职. ○ *I'm not the person to recommend how the job should be done.* 我不是能为做此事出主意的人. ○ *I recommended (you) meeting him first.* 我建议(你)先见见他. ○ *I wouldn't recommend you to go there alone.* 我劝你不要孤身一人到那里去. **3** [Tn, Dn·pr] **~ sb/sth (to sb)** (of a quality, etc) make sb/sth seem attractive (指特质等)使某人[某事物]显得可取: *a plan with nothing, little, something, much, etc to recommend it* 毫无、没有什么、有某种、有许多...可取之处的计划 ○ *His integrity recommended him to his employers.* 他很正直, 雇主对他都有好感.

▷ **re·com·mend·able** /-əbl; -əbl̩/ *adj*: *a highly recommendable film, restaurant, camping site* 备受推荐的影片、餐厅、露营地.

re·com·menda·tion /ˌrekəmenˈdeɪʃn; ˌrɛkəmɛnˋdeʃən/ *n* **1** [U] action of recommending 推许; 推荐; 赞许; 建议; 劝告: *speak in recommendation of sb/sth* 口头推荐某人[某事物] ○ *I bought it on your recommendation*, ie because you recommended it. 我是经你推荐买的. **2** [C] (**a**) statement, letter, etc that recommends sb/sth, esp a person for a job 推荐; (尤指)推荐信, 求职介绍信: *write, give sb a recommendation* 为某人写推荐信、给某人一封介绍信. (**b**) course of action, etc that is recommended 建议采取的做法等: *The judge made recommendations to the court.* 法官向审判人员提出建议. ○ *a recommendation that the offer of 5% be rejected* 对5%这一出价应予拒绝的建议. **3** quality, etc that makes sb/sth seem attractive 使某人[某事物]显得有可取之处的特质等: *The cheapness of coach travel is its only recommendation.* 乘长途汽车唯一可取之处就是旅费便宜.

re·com·pense /ˈrekəmpens; ˋrɛkəmˌpɛns/ *v* [Tn, Tn·pr] **~ sb (for sth)** (*fml* 文) reward sb (for his work, efforts, etc); compensate sb (for his losses, etc) 酬谢或报答某人(因其工作、尽力等); 赔偿或补偿某人(受的

损失等): *recompense employees for working overtime* 给雇员发加班费 ○ *recompense her for the loss of her job* 赔偿她失去工作的损失.

▷ **re·com·pense** *n* [sing, U] ~ **(for sth)** (*fml* 文) thing that rewards; thing that compensates 报酬; 赔偿; 补偿: *receive adequate recompense for one's services, labours, efforts, etc* 因工作、劳动、尽力等而获得合适的报酬 ○ *award the victim £500 in recompense for damages* 给予受害者500英镑损害赔偿金.

re·con·cile /ˈrekənsaɪl; ˈrɛkən,saɪl/ *v* **1 (a)** [esp passive 尤用于被动语态: Tn, Tn·pr] ~ **sb (with sb)** cause (people) to become friends again, eg after quarrelling 使(人)重新和好(如争吵后); 使和解; 使复交: *We were finally reconciled when he apologized.* 他道歉以后我们终于言归于好了. ○ *She refused to be reconciled with her brother.* 她拒不同她的弟弟和解. **(b)** [Tn] bring (a quarrel, disagreement, etc) to an end; settle 化解(争吵、分歧等); 调解; 调停: *They can't reconcile their differences.* 他们无法调和彼此的分歧. **2** [Tn, Tn·pr] ~ **sth (with sth)** make (aims, statements, ideas, etc) agree when they seem to conflict 使(似有分歧的目标、说法、意见等)一致, 和谐: *reconcile the evidence with the facts* 使证据符合事实 ○ *Can eating fish be reconciled with vegetarianism?* 吃鱼与素食主义有矛盾吗? **3** [Tn·pr] ~ **sb/oneself to sth** (cause sb to) accept reluctantly sth unwelcome, unpleasant, etc (使某人)无可奈何地接受某事物: *The high salary reconciled me to living abroad.* 我为获高薪也只好在国外生活. ○ *Could you reconcile yourself to a lifetime of unemployment?* 你能甘心一辈子失业吗?

▷ **re·con·cil·able** /-əbl, *also* ˌrekənˈsaɪləbl; -əbḷ, ˌrɛkənˈsaɪləbḷ/ *adj*. **re·con·cili·ation** /ˌrekənˌsɪlɪˈeɪʃn; ˌrɛkən-ˌsɪlɪˈeʃən/ *n* **1** [U] reconciling or being reconciled 和解; 调和; 一致; 和谐; 勉强接受: *the reconciliation of ideas, opinions, etc* 思想、见解等的一致. **2** [sing] end to a quarrel, etc (争吵等的)止息; 和解; 复交: *bring about a reconciliation between former enemies* 使旧时的仇敌和解.

re·con·dite /ˈrekəndaɪt; ˈrɛkən,daɪt/ *adj* (*fml* 文) **1** (of subjects) little known or understood; obscure (指学科)不甚了解的, 不甚理解的, 深奥的. **2** (of writers, etc) dealing with subjects that are little known or understood (指作者等)研究鲜为人知的或难以理解的专题的.

re·con·di·tion /ˌriːkənˈdɪʃn; ˌrikənˈdɪʃən/ *v* [Tn esp passive 尤用于被动语态] repair (sth) and put it into good condition again; overhaul or restore 修理(某物); 彻底检修; 修复: *a reconditioned engine, cooker* 修复的发动机、炉具 ○ *reconditioned furniture, leather* 修整过的家具、皮革.

re·con·nais·sance /rɪˈkɒnɪsns; rɪˈkɑnəsəns/ (also *infml* 口语作 **recce**) *n* [C, U] (patrol, flight, etc that carries out an) exploration or a survey of an area, esp for military purposes (对某地区的)侦察或观测(尤指为军事目的); (执行侦察任务的)巡逻队、飞行队等: *make an aerial reconnaissance of an island* 对一岛进行空中侦察 ○ *troops engaged in reconnaissance* 执行侦察任务的部队 ○ [attrib 作定语] *a reconnaissance plane, party, mission* 侦察机、小组、任务.

re·con·noitre (*US* **-ter**) /ˌrekəˈnɔɪtə(r); ˌrɛkəˈnɔɪtɚ/ (also *Brit infml* 英式口语作 **recce**) *v* [I, Tn] explore or survey (an enemy area, position, etc) 侦察或观测(敌人的地区、位置等): *The platoon was sent to reconnoitre the village before the attack.* 在发动进攻前, 这个排奉命侦察该村.

re·con·sider /ˌriːkənˈsɪdə(r); ˌrikənˈsɪdɚ/ *v* [I, Tn] consider (sth) again, esp to change an earlier opinion, decision, etc 重新考虑(某事物): *reconsider one's position, view, decision, etc* 重新考虑自己的立场、观点、决定等 ○ *The jury was called upon to reconsider its verdict.* 召集陪审团重新审议其裁定. ▷ **re·con·sid·era·tion** /ˌriːkənˌsɪdəˈreɪʃn; ˌrikənˌsɪdəˈreʃən/ *n* [U].

re·con·stit·ute /ˌriːˈkɒnstɪtjuːt; *US* -tuːt; riˈkɑnstə,tut/ *v* [Tn esp passive 尤用于被动语态] **1** restore (dried food) to its original state, eg by adding water 使(脱水食物)复原(如加水): *reconstitute dried milk, powdered soup, etc* 加水使奶粉、汤粉等复原. **2** (*fml* 文) reorganize or change the membership of (sth) 重新组织或改组(某事物): *a reconstituted board, panel, committee, etc* 经过改组的董事会、专门小组、委员会等. ▷ **re·con·stitu·tion** /ˌriːˌkɒnstɪˈtjuːʃn; *US* -tuːʃn; ri,kɑnstəˈtuʃən/ *n* [U].

re·con·struct /ˌriːkənˈstrʌkt; ˌrikənˈstrʌkt/ *v* **1** [Tn] construct or build again, eg after damage 重建, 修复(如破坏之后). **2** [Tn, Tn·pr, Tw] ~ **sth (from sth)** create again (sth that has existed or happened) by using evidence or imagination (根据证据或想像)重现(存在过的或发生过的事物): *Police are trying to reconstruct the crime*, eg by using actors at the place where it was committed or by assembling the known facts. 警方正在重组作案经过(如派员到案发现场重演作案过程或汇集事实资料综合思考). ○ *We reconstructed what the dinosaur looked like from a few of its bones.* 我们根据恐龙的一些骨头重组恐龙的原貌.

▷ **re·con·struc·tion** /-ˈstrʌkʃn; -ˈstrʌkʃən/ *n* **1** [C, U] (act of) reconstructing or being reconstructed 重建; 再现: *plans for the reconstruction of the city centre* 重建城市中心的计划 ○ *a reconstruction of events by detectives* 侦探对事情经过的设想. **2 Reconstruction** [sing] (*US*) period of occupation and reform in the Southern States after their defeat in the American Civil War 重建时期(美国南北战争末期南部各州的改革重建期).

rec·ord[1] /ˈrekɔːd; *US* ˈrekərd; ˈrɛkɚd/ *n* **1** [C] ~ **(of sth)** permanent account, esp in writing, of facts, events, etc (对事实、事件等的)记录; (尤指)记载: *a record of school attendances, road accidents* 学生出席、交通事故记录 ○ *records of births, marriages and deaths* 出生、婚姻和死亡记录 ○ *public, parish, medical, etc records* 公共事务、教区事务、医疗等记录 ○ *make/keep a record of one's expenses* 记自己开支的帐. **2** [sing] ~ **(for sth)** facts, events, etc known (but not always written down) about the past of sb/sth (已知的有关某人[某事物]过去的)事实、事件等(不一定有文字记载); 功过; 经历; 履历: *He had a good 'war record*, eg fought bravely. 他有良好的作战经历(如作战勇敢). ○ *have a (previous) criminal 'record*, ie have already been convicted for a crime or crimes 有前科 ○ *The airline has a bad safety record*, ie Its aircraft often crash. 这家航空公司安全情况历来不好(班机常失事). ○ *The school has a poor record for examination passes*, ie Many of its pupils fail. 这所学校考试成绩历来欠佳(许多学生不及格). **3** [C] (also **'gramophone record, disc**) ~ **(of sb/sth)** thin circular piece of plastic on which sound has been recorded 唱片: *a pop, jazz, hit record* 通俗歌曲、爵士音乐、流行歌曲唱片 ○ *the band's latest record* 该乐队最新录制的唱片 ○ *put on/play some records* 放一些唱片 ○ [attrib 作定语] *a record sleeve, album, library* 唱片的封套、唱片集、唱片库. **4** [C] best performance or highest or lowest level ever reached, esp in sport 最好的成绩, (最高的或最低的)水平, 记录(尤指体育运动): *beat/break* (ie surpass) *a record* 打破一项记录 ○ *an Olympic, world, all-time record* 奥林匹克运动会、世界、空前的记录 ○ *She holds the world record in/for the 100 metres.* 她保持着100米世界记录. ○ [attrib 作定语] *a record performance, score, time* 刷新记录的表现、得分、时间 ○ *record profits, sales, crops* 创记录的利润、销售额、收成. **5** [C] (*computing* 计) set of related data forming a unit in a computer file 记录(计算机文件中形成一个单元的一组相关的数据). **6** (idm 习语) **(just) for the 'record** so that it should be noted; for the sake of accuracy (仅)供记录在案; 为准确起见: *Just for the record, the minister's statement is wrong on two points.* 必须明确指出, 部长的言论有两点是错误的. **ˌoff the 'record** (*infml* 口) (of statements, opinions, etc) not for publication or not to be officially noted (指说法、意见等)不得发表的, 不可正式记录的: *The Prime Minister admitted, (strictly) off the record, that the talks had failed.* 首相承认会谈失败, 此消息(绝)不可发表. **on 'record (a)** (of facts, events, etc) noted or recorded, esp officially (指事实、事件等)记载下来的; (尤指)正式记录的: *Last summer was the wettest on record for 50 years.* 刚过去的这个夏季是50年来记录中雨水最多的. **(b)** (of statements, opinions, etc) publicly known or officially noted (指说法、意见等)公开发表的, 正式记录的: *be/go on record as saying that the law should be changed* 公开说该法规应予更改 ○ *put one's views, objections, etc on record*, ie publish or broadcast them 公开发表自己的观点、反对意见等. **put/set the 'record straight** give a correct account of facts, events, etc; put right a

R

misunderstanding (对事实、事件等)作正确的陈述, 纠正误解: *To set the record straight, I must say now that I never supported the idea.* 我必须在此表明, 我从未支持过那种意见.

□ ˈ**record-breaker** *n* person, car, boat, etc that breaks a record[1](4) 打破记录者(人、汽车、船等).

ˈ**record-breaking** *adj* [attrib 作定语]: *a record-breaking attendance, flight, jump, time* 破记录的出席率、飞行、跳跃、时间.

ˈ**record-holder** *n* person holding a sports record (某项运动的)记录保持者.

ˈ**record-player** (also *dated* 旧作 **gramophone**) *n* instrument for reproducing sound from records (RECORD[1] 3) 唱机.

re·cord[2] /rɪˈkɔːd; rɪˋkɔrd/ *v* **1** (**a**) [Tn, Tf, Tw] write down (facts or events) for later use or reference 将(事实或事件)记录下来以备他日使用或参考; 记录; 记载: *record progress, developments, etc* 记载进展、发展等情况 ○ *record the minutes/proceedings of a meeting* 做会议记录[记录会议事项] ○ *The papers record that inflation has dropped.* 报纸刊载通货膨胀已下降. ○ *Historians record how Rome fell.* 历史学家记载了罗马帝国衰亡的经过. (**b**) [I, Ipr, Tn, Tn·pr, Tng] **~ (sth) (from sth) (on sth)** preserve (sound or images) on a disc or magnetic tape for later reproduction 将(声音或图像)保存在磁盘或磁带上以便重放; 录(音); 录(像): *To record, press both buttons.* 录音时须按双钮. ○ *My voice records quite well.* 我的声音录下来很好听. ○ *record music from the radio* 录下无线电广播中的音乐 ○ *record a speech, piece of music, TV programme (on tape/video)* (在磁带[录像带]上)录演讲、乐曲、电视节目 ○ *a recorded* (ie not live) *programme, concert, interview, etc* 录制的节目、音乐会、访问记等(非现场直播的) ○ *record sb playing the guitar* 为某人的吉他演奏录音. **2** [Tn] (of measuring instruments) mark or indicate (sth); register (指测量仪器)标明或显示(某事物); 自动记下: *The thermometer recorded 40°C.* 温度计上显示出40°C.

□ reˌ**corded deˈlivery** (*Brit*) postal service in which delivery is confirmed by the receiver signing a form 挂号邮递: *send a letter by recorded delivery* 寄挂号信. Cf 参看 REGISTERED POST (REGISTER[2]).

re·corder /rɪˈkɔːdə(r); rɪˋkɔrdɚ/ *n* **1** apparatus for recording sound or pictures, or both 录音机; 录像机: *a* ˈ*tape-recorder* 磁带录音机 ○ *a* ˈ*video-recorder* 录像机. **2** wooden or plastic wind instrument of the flute family, played like a whistle, with eight holes for the fingers 竖笛(木制或塑料制的管乐器, 有八个指孔). ⇨ illus at App 1 见附录1插图, page x. **3** (*Brit*) judge in certain lawcourts (某些法院的)法官.

re·cord·ing /rɪˈkɔːdɪŋ; rɪˋkɔrdɪŋ/ *n* **1** [U] action of preserving sound or images on magnetic tape, etc (音像的)录制; 录音; 录像: *during the recording of the show* 在录制节目时 ○ [attrib 作定语] *a reˈcording studio, session, company* 音像录制室、时间、公司. **2** [C] sound or images that have been preserved in this way (录制的)音像; 录音; 录像: *make a video recording of a wedding* 为婚礼录像 ○ *a good recording of the opera on tape/video* 将该歌剧录制得很好的录音带[录像带].

recount /rɪˈkaʊnt; rɪˋkaʊnt/ *v* [Tn, Tw, Dn·pr, Dpr·w] **~ sth (to sb)** give a detailed account of sth; tell about sth 详细叙述某事; 讲述某事: *recount one's adventures, experiences, misfortunes, etc* 叙述自己的冒险事、经历、不幸等 ○ *He recounted how he had shot the lion.* 他讲述他射死那只狮子的经过.

re-count /ˌriːˈkaʊnt; ˌriˋkaʊnt/ *v* [Tn] count (esp votes) again 重新计算(尤指选票); 重数.

▷ **re-count** /ˈriːkaʊnt; ˋriˌkaʊnt/ *n* another count, esp of votes in an election 重新计算(尤指选票的): *The unsuccessful candidate demanded a re-count.* 那个落选的候选人要求重新计算选票.

re·coup /rɪˈkuːp; rɪˋkup/ *v* [Tn, Tn·pr, Tw] **~ sb/oneself for sth** get back (what one has spent, lost, etc); give sb/oneself back (what has been spent, lost, etc) 获得(补偿); 付给某人[自己](补偿): *We recouped the show's expenses from ticket sales.* 我们从门票收入中赚回演出的费用. ○ *He recouped himself for his losses.* 他挽回了自己的损失. ○ *recoup what the project has cost* 补偿该项目花去的费用.

re·course /rɪˈkɔːs; rɪˋkɔrs/ *n* [U] **1** possible source of help, eg in an emergency 求助的对象(如情况紧急时): *They managed without recourse to* (ie without seeking) *outside help.* 他们不寻求外援也能应付过去. ○ *Your only recourse is legal action.* 你只有靠诉讼了. **2** (idm 习语) **have recourse to sb/sth** (*fml* 文) turn to sb/sth for help; get help from sb/sth 求助于某人[某事物]; 获得来自某人[某事物]的援助: *I hope the doctors won't have recourse to surgery.* 我希望医生可别非动手术不可.

re·cover /rɪˈkʌvə(r); rɪˋkʌvɚ/ *v* **1** [Tn, Tn·pr] **~ sth (from sb/sth)** find again (sth stolen, lost, etc); regain possession of sth 找回(被盗、遗失等之物); 重新获得某事物(的所有权): *recover stolen goods, lost property, etc* 找回被盗的货物、失去的财物等 ○ *Six bodies were recovered from the wreck.* 从交通工具的残骸中找到了六具尸体. ○ *recover what was lost* 重新获得失去的东西. **2** [Tn] (**a**) get back the use of (one's faculties, health, etc) 恢复(能力、健康等): *recover one's sight, hearing, etc* 恢复视力、听力等 ○ *recover one's senses/consciousness*, eg after fainting 恢复知觉(如晕倒后) ○ *I'm slowly recovering my strength after a bout of flu.* 我得过流感后体力正在慢慢恢复. (**b**) get back the control of (oneself, one's actions, one's emotions, etc) 重新控制(自己、自己的行动、自己的情绪等): *The skater quickly recovered his balance.* 那个滑冰的人很快恢复了平衡. ○ *She recovered herself/her composure and smiled.* 她恢复了常态[镇静], 笑了笑. ○ *The murderer never recovered his peace of mind.* 这个杀人凶手心里再也没平静过. **3** [Tn, Tn·pr] **~ sth (from sb/sth)** regain (money, time or position) 重新获得(金钱、时间或地位): *They sought to recover damages, costs, expenses, etc from the firm.* 他们设法向那家公司索取损害赔偿金、用费、费用等. ○ *We recovered lost time by setting out early.* 我们提前出发从而把损失的时间补了回来. ○ *The team recovered its lead in the second half.* 该队在下半场重新领先. **4** [I, Ipr] **~ (from sb/sth)** return to a normal state, eg of health, mind, prosperity 回复到正常状态(如健康、神智、繁荣): *He's now fully recovered from his stroke.* 他现已从中风病完全康复了. ○ *recover from the shock, surprise, strain, etc* 从震惊、惊讶、紧张等中恢复过来 ○ *Trade soon recovered from the effects of the war.* 贸易摆脱了战争的影响而很快复苏了.

▷ **re·cov·er·able** /-rəbl; -rəbl/ *adj* that can be recovered (RECOVER 1) 能找回的; 能重新获得的: *recoverable deposits, losses, assets* 能索回的定金、能挽回的损失、能收回的资产.

re-cover /ˌriːˈkʌvə(r); ˌriˋkʌvɚ/ *v* [Tn, Tn·pr] **~ sth (in/with sth)** put a new cover on sth 给某物换上新的覆盖物: *re-cover a cushion (in/with velvet)* 给垫子换(天鹅绒的)套子.

re·cov·ery /rɪˈkʌvərɪ; rɪˋkʌvərɪ/ *n* **1** [U] **~ (of sth/sb)** recovering (RECOVER 1) or being recovered 找回; 重新获得: *the recovery of the missing diamonds* 丢失钻石的寻回 ○ [attrib 作定语] *a recovery vehicle*, ie one for taking broken-down cars, etc to a garage 维修拖车(把毁坏的汽车等拉回修理厂的车). **2** [sing, U] **~ (from sth)** return to a normal state, eg of health or prosperity 恢复正常状态(如康复或复兴); 复原: *make a quick, speedy, good, slow, etc recovery (from illness)* (从疾病中)很快、迅速、完全、缓慢...康复 ○ *be well on the way/road to recovery* 正在顺利恢复 ○ *the team's recovery from defeat* 这个队失败后的重新振作. **3** [U] (*esp US*) area of a hospital where patients are kept immediately after an operation 监护部(医院中监护刚做过手术的病人的地方): *The patient is in recovery.* 该病人在手术后的监护部.

□ **reˈcovery room** (*US*) room in a hospital where patients are kept for observation after an operation 恢复室(医院中护理做过手术的病人的屋子).

rec·re·ant /ˈrekrɪənt; ˋrɛkrɪənt/ *n, adj* [usu attrib 通常作定语] (*dated* 旧) (person who is) cowardly, unfaithful or treacherous 怯懦的、不忠的或叛逆的(傢伙); 懦夫; 叛徒: *You recreant knave!* 你这个不义之徒!

re-create /ˌriːkrɪˈeɪt; ˌrikrɪˋet/ *v* [Tn] create (sth past) again; reproduce 再创(已成为过去的事物); 再创造; 再现: *The play re-creates life before the war.* 该剧再现了战前的生活景象. ▷ **re-cre·ation** /-ˈeɪʃn; -ˋeʃən/ *n* [U, C].

re·cre·ation /ˌrekrɪˈeɪʃn; ˌrɛkrɪˋeʃən/ *n* [C, U] (means of) refreshing or entertaining oneself after work; relaxation 业余消遣或娱乐(的方式); (身心的)放松;

休憩: *My favourite recreation is chess.* 我最喜欢的娱乐是下国际象棋. ○ *walk and climb mountains for recreation* 为消遣而散步和爬山 ○ *Gardening is a form of recreation.* 园艺活动是一种消遣方式.

▷ **re·cre·ational** /-ʃənl; -ʃənl/ *adj* of or for recreation 消遣的; 娱乐的: *take part in recreational activities* 参加娱乐活动 ○ *recreational facilities*, eg sports grounds, swimming-pools 娱乐设施(如运动场、游泳池).

□ **recre'ation ground** (*abbr* 缩写 **rec**) publicly-owned area of land used for adult sports or games, or having swings, slides, etc for children (公共的)游乐场.

recre'ation room (also **rec room**) (*US*) room in a private house used for games, relaxation, entertainment, etc (私人住宅中的)康乐室.

re·crim·in·ate /rɪˈkrɪmɪneɪt; rɪˋkrɪmə,net/ *v* [I, Ipr] **~ (against sb)** (*fml* 文) accuse or blame (sb by whom one has been accused or blamed) 反诉或反责(某人).

▷ **re·crim·ina·tion** /rɪˌkrɪmɪˈneɪʃn; rɪ,krɪməˋneʃən/ *n* [C usu *pl*, U 作可数名词时通常作复数, 亦作不可数名词] (act of making an) accusation in response to an accusation from sb else; countercharge 反诉; 反告: *bitter, angry, furious, etc recriminations* 激烈的、愤怒的、猛烈的…反诉 ○ *Let's not indulge in (mutual) recrimination.* 咱们不要总是互相指责吧.

re·crim·in·at·ory /rɪˈkrɪmɪnətrɪ; *US* -tɔ:rɪ; rɪˋkrɪmənə,torɪ/ *adj* of recrimination 反诉的; 反责的: *recriminatory remarks, comments, etc* 反唇相稽的话、评语等.

re·cru·desce /ˌri:kru:ˈdes; ,rikruˋdɛs/ *v* [I] (*fml* 文) (of diseases, violence, etc) break out again; recur (指疾病、暴力活动等)复发, 再次发生.

▷ **re·cru·des·cence** /-ˈdesns; -ˋdɛsns/ *n* [C, U] (*fml* 文) new outburst; recurrence 新发作; 再发生: *a recrudescence of influenza* 流行性感冒的新发作 ○ *prevent the recrudescence of civil disorder* 防止内乱再次爆发.

re·cru·des·cent /-ˈdesnt; -ˋdɛsənt/ *adj*.

re·cruit /rɪˈkru:t; rɪˋkrut/ *n* **~ (to sth) (from sth)** **1** person who has just joined the armed forces or police and is not yet trained (未经训练的)新兵或新警察: *new, recent, raw* (ie inexperienced) *recruits* 新兵 ○ *drilling recruits on the parade ground* 在练兵场上训练新兵. **2** new member of a club, society, etc (俱乐部、会社等的)新成员, 新会员: *gain/seek new recruits* (eg to training schemes) *from among the young unemployed* 从年轻的失业者中吸收[招收]新成员(如实施培训计划).

▷ **re·cruit** *v* [I, Tn, Tn·pr, Cn·n/a] **~ (sb) (to sth) (from sth); ~ sb (as sth)** **1** gain (sb) as a recruit; enlist 吸收(某人)为新成员; 征募: *recruit on a regular basis* 定期招募 ○ *a re'cruiting officer, poster, drive* 征募新兵的军官、布告、运动 ○ *recruit new members (to the club)* 吸收新成员(进入俱乐部) ○ *recruit sb as a spy* 招募某人为特工. **2** form (an army, a party, etc) by gaining recruits (吸收新成员)组成(军队、党派等): *recruit a task force* 为特遣部队招募新兵. **re·cruit·ment** *n* [U].

rectal /ˈrektəl; ˋrɛktl/ *adj* (*anatomy* 解) of the rectum 直肠的.

rect·angle /ˈrektæŋgl; ˋrɛktæŋgl/ *n* four-sided geometric figure with four right angles, esp one with unequal adjacent sides 方形; (尤指)长方形, 矩形. ⇨illus at QUADRILATERAL 见 QUADRILATERAL 插图.

▷ **rect·an·gu·lar** /rekˈtæŋgjʊlə(r); rɛkˋtæŋgjələ/ *adj* having the shape of a rectangle 长方形的; 矩形的.

rect·ify /ˈrektɪfaɪ; ˋrɛktə,faɪ/ *v* (*pt, pp* **-fied**) **1** [Tn] put (sth) right; correct 改正(某事物); 纠正: *rectify an error, omission, etc* 修订错处、疏漏处等 ○ *mistakes that cannot be rectified* 无法改正的错误. **2** [Tn esp passive 尤用于被动语态] (*chemistry* 化) purify or refine, esp by repeated distillation 净化或精炼; (尤指)分馏, 精馏: *rectified spirits* 精馏酒精. **3** [Tn] convert (alternating current) to direct current 将(交流电)变成直流电; 整(流).

▷ **rec·ti·fi·able** /-faɪəbl, *also* ˌrektɪˈfaɪəbl; -,faɪəbl/ *adj* that can be rectified 可改正的; 可精馏的; 可整流的: *an error that is easily rectifiable* 容易改正的错误.

rec·ti·fica·tion /ˌrektɪfɪˈkeɪʃn; ,rɛktəfəˋkeʃən/ *n* **1** [U] rectifying or being rectified 改正; 精炼; 整流: *the rectification of errors, alcohol* 错误的改正、酒精的精馏. **2** [C] thing that has been rectified; correction 被改正的事物; 经过精炼之物; 矫正.

rec·ti·fier *n* device that converts alternating current to direct current 整流器.

rec·ti·lin·ear /ˌrektɪˈlɪnɪə(r); ,rɛktəˋlɪnɪə/ *adj* **1** in or forming a straight line 直线的; 形成直线的: *rectilinear motion* 直线运动. **2** bounded by or having straight lines 用直线围着的; 有直线的: *a rectilinear figure* 直线图形.

rect·it·ude /ˈrektɪtju:d; *US* -tu:d; ˋrɛktə,tud/ *n* [U] (*fml* 文) moral correctness or straightforwardness; honesty 正直; 刚正; 诚实: *a person of stern (moral) rectitude* 刚正不阿的人.

recto /ˈrektəʊ; ˋrɛkto/ *n* (*pl* **~s**) right-hand page of an open book (打开的书的)右页: *on the recto* (*page*) 在右页上. Cf 参看 VERSO.

rector /ˈrektə(r); ˋrɛktə/ *n* **1** (**a**) (in the Church of England) clergyman in charge of a parish from which he receives his income directly (formerly entitled to receive all the tithes of his parish) (英国国教的)牧区司铎, 牧区长. Cf 参看 VICAR. (**b**) (in the Roman Catholic Church) head of a church or a religious community (天主教的)教区首席神甫. **2** (*esp Brit*) head of certain universities, colleges, schools or religious institutions (某些学校或宗教机构的)校长、院长或领导人.

▷ **rect·ory** /ˈrektərɪ; ˋrɛktərɪ/ *n* rector's house 牧区长、教区长、某些学校或宗教机构领导人的住所.

rectum /ˈrektəm; ˋrɛktəm/ *n* (*pl* **~s** or **recta**) (*anatomy* 解) lower end of the large intestine, through which solid waste passes to the anus 直肠. ⇨illus at DIGESTIVE 见 DIGESTIVE 插图.

re·cum·bent /rɪˈkʌmbənt; rɪˋkʌmbənt/ *adj* [usu attrib 通常作定语] (*fml* 文) (esp of a person) lying down; reclining (尤指人)躺着的, 斜倚的: *a recumbent figure*, eg in a painting or sculpture 卧像(如绘画或雕塑中的).

re·cu·per·ate /rɪˈku:pəreɪt; rɪˋkupə,ret/ *v* **1** [I, Ipr, Tn] **~ (from sth)** (*fml* 文) recover from illness, exhaustion or loss, etc 复原; 恢复(体力); 挽回(损失等): *He is still recuperating from his operation.* 他动手术后仍在恢复中. ○ *recuperate one's strength after a climb* 攀登之后恢复体力. **2** [Tn] get back (money spent or lost) 复得(花掉或失去的钱): *recuperate costs, expenses, etc* 索回用费、费用等.

▷ **re·cu·pera·tion** /rɪˌku:pəˈreɪʃn; rɪ,kupəˋreʃən/ *n* [U] (*fml* 文) recuperating 复原; 恢复; 挽回.

re·cu·per·at·ive /rɪˈku:pərətɪv; rɪˋkupə,retɪv/ *adj* (*fml* 文) of or aiding recuperation (有助于)复原的, 恢复的, 挽回的: *the recuperative powers of fresh air* 新鲜空气可助人康复的作用.

re·cur /rɪˈkɜ:(r); rɪˋkɝ/ *v* (**-rr-**) **1** [I] happen again; happen repeatedly 再发生; 复发: *a recurring problem, error, illness* 反复出现的问题、错误、疾病 ○ *The symptoms tend to recur.* 这种症状有可能复发. ○ *This theme recurs constantly throughout the opera.* 这一主旋律在该歌剧中不断出现. **2** (phr v) **recur to sb/sth** (*fml* 文) (of ideas, events, etc) come back into the mind (指想法、事情等)在头脑中重现: *Our first meeting often recurs to me/my mind.* 我们初次见面的情形时常浮现于我的脑海.

▷ **re·cur·rence** /rɪˈkʌrəns; rɪˋkʌrəns/ *n* [C, U] (instance of) recurring; repetition 复发; 反复; 重现: *the recurrence of an illness, error, problem, theme* 疾病、错误、问题、主旋律的一再反复.

re·cur·rent /-ənt; -ənt/ *adj* [usu attrib 通常作定语] recurring often or regularly 经常发生的; 周期性的: *recurrent attacks, fits, headaches, etc* 周期性发作的疾病、痉挛、头痛等 ○ *a recurrent problem, theme* 经常出现的问题、主旋律.

□ **recurring decimal** decimal fraction in which the same figure(s) are repeated indefinitely, eg 3.999, 4.014014 循环小数(如: 3.999、4.014014): *The recurring decimal 3.999... is also described as 3.9 recurring.* 循环小数'3.999...'亦作'3.9循环'.

re·cus·ant /ˈrekjʊznt; ˋrɛkjʊznt/ *n* (formerly) Roman Catholic who refused to attend Anglican services as required by law (旧时)拒绝按照法律规定参加英国国教礼拜式的天主教徒.

re·cycle /ˌri:ˈsaɪkl; riˋsaɪkl/ *v* [Tn] (**a**) treat (used material) so that it can be used again 回收(废旧材料): *recycle newspaper*, ie by de-inking and pulping it 回收旧报纸(以脱墨和制浆方式处理). (**b**) get (natural products) back from used material by treating it (利用废旧材料)再造(原始成品): ˌ*recycled* ˈ*glass*, ie from old bottles 再造的玻璃(利用旧瓶再制的). Cf 参看 RECLAIM 4.

red[1] /red; rɛd/ *adj* (**-dder, -ddest**) **1** (**a**) of the colour of fresh blood or a similar colour 红的; 红色的: *a red sky, door, car* 红色的天空、门、汽车 ○ *ruby-red lips* 深红的嘴唇 ○ *Maple leaves turn red in the autumn.* 枫叶在秋天变红了. ⇨illus at SPECTRUM 见SPECTRUM插图. (**b**) (of the eyes) sore and having red veins and rims; bloodshot (指眼睛)布满血丝的, 眼眶发红的, 充血的: *Her eyes were red with weeping.* 她的眼睛哭红了. (**c**) (of the face) flushed with shame, anger, etc (指脸)(因羞惭、愤怒等)涨红的: *turn, go, be red in the face* 脸红. **2** (of hair or an animal's fur) of a reddish-brown colour; ginger or tawny (指毛发或动物皮毛)红褐色的, 黄褐色的, 茶色的: *red deer, squirrels* 马鹿、红松鼠. **3** (**a**) **Red** [attrib 作定语] Soviet or Russian 苏维埃的; 俄国的: *The Red Army*, ie that of the former USSR 红军(前苏联军队). (**b**) (*infml sometimes derog* 口, 有时作贬义) revolutionary; communist 革命的; 共产主义的. **4** (idm 习语) **neither fish, flesh, nor good red herring** ⇨ FISH[1]. **not (be) worth a red** ˈ**cent**; **not give a red** ˈ**cent for sth** (*US infml* 口) (be) worthless; regard sth as being worthless 没有价值; 认为某事物毫无价值. **paint the town red** ⇨ PAINT[2]. **(as) red as a beetroot** very red in the face, esp because one is embarrassed 满脸通红(尤因受窘): *He went as red as a beetroot when I asked about his new girl-friend.* 我问起他那新女友, 他就满脸通红. **a red** ˈ**herring** fact, argument, etc that leads attention away from the matter being considered 转移注意力的事情、言语等: *Stop chasing red herrings and get back to the point.* 别东拉西扯了, 说正事吧. **(like) a red rag to a bull** likely to cause strong resentment, anger, violence, etc 可能激起强烈的憎恨、愤怒、暴力行动等: *Her remarks were like a red rag to a bull: he was furious with her.* 她的话惹得他对她暴跳如雷. ▷ **redly** *adv*: *The fire glowed redly.* 火烧得通红. **red·ness** *n* [U].

□ ˌ**red-**ˈ**blooded** *adj* [usu attrib 通常作定语] (*infml* 口) full of vigour or sexual desire; virile 充满活力的; 性欲旺盛的; 有男子气的: ˌ*red-blooded* ˈ*males* 精力充沛的男子.

ˈ**redbreast** *n* ⇨ ROBIN.

ˈ**redbrick** *adj* (*Brit sometimes derog* 有时作贬义) (of universities) founded near the end of the 19th century or later (指大学)接近19世纪末或19世纪末以后建立的: *redbrick colleges, campuses, etc* 19世纪末建立的学院、大学校园等. Cf 参看 OXBRIDGE.

ˌ**red** ˈ**cabbage** type of cabbage with red leaves 红色卷心菜.

ˈ**redcap** *n* (*infml* 口) **1** (*Brit*) member of the military police 宪兵. **2** (*US*) railway porter (火车站的)搬运工.

ˌ**red** ˈ**card** (in football, etc) card shown by the referee to a player that he is sending off the field (足球等)(比赛时裁判向球员出示的)红牌(罚球员下场). Cf 参看 YELLOW CARD (YELLOW).

ˌ**red** ˈ**carpet** strip of red carpet laid out for the reception of an important visitor (为迎接贵宾铺的)红地毯: [attrib 作定语] (*fig* 比喻) *We must give our guests the red-carpet treatment.* 我们得隆重接待贵宾.

ˈ**redcoat** *n* (formerly) British soldier (旧时)英国士兵.

ˌ**red** ˈ**corpuscle** (also ˈ**red** ˈ**blood cell**) blood cell that carries oxygen to the body tissues and carbon dioxide from them 红血球. Cf 参看 WHITE CORPUSCLE (WHITE[1]).

ˌ**Red** ˈ**Crescent** (emblem of the) organization in Muslim countries that corresponds to the Red Cross 红新月会(穆斯林国家中相当于红十字会的组织); 红新月会的会徽.

ˌ**Red** ˈ**Cross** (emblem of the) international organization that works to relieve suffering caused by natural disasters, etc and to help the victims of war 红十字会(的会徽).

ˌ**red**ˈ**currant** *n* (shrub producing) a small round edible berry 红醋栗(小而圆的可食用的小果子); 红醋栗灌木: [attrib 作定语] ˌ*redcurrant* ˈ*jelly* 红醋栗果子冻.

ˌ**red** ˈ**ensign** red flag of the British merchant navy with a Union Jack in the top left corner 英国商船旗(红色, 左上角标有英国国旗). Cf 参看 WHITE ENSIGN (WHITE[1]).

ˌ**red** ˈ**flag** **1** flag used as a symbol of danger, eg on roads, railways, etc (表示危险的)红色信号旗(如用于公路、铁路等). **2** symbol of revolution or communism (象征革命或共产主义的)红旗.

ˌ**red** ˈ**giant** large star near the middle of its life that gives out a reddish light 红巨星(发微红色光, 其寿命已近中期). Cf 参看 WHITE DWARF (WHITE[1]).

ˌ**red-**ˈ**handed** *adj* (idm 习语) **catch sb red-handed** ⇨ CATCH[1].

ˈ**redhead** *n* person, esp female, with red[1](2) hair 红褐色头发的人(尤指女子).

ˌ**red-**ˈ**hot** *adj* **1** (of a metal) so hot that it glows red (指金属)热得通红的, 炽热的. **2** (*fig* 比喻) very great 极其: ˌ*red-hot* ˈ*anger, en*ˈ*thusiasm, etc* 非常愤怒、热情等. **3** (*fig infml* 比喻, 口) (of news) completely new; fresh (指新闻)全新的, 最新的: *The reporter had a red-hot story.* 那个记者掌握着最新消息.

ˌ**Red** ˈ**Indian** (*Brit* ˈ**redskin**) (⚠ *infml offensive* 讳, 口, 蔑) N American Indian 北美印第安人.

ˌ**red** ˈ**lead** red oxide of lead, used in paint 铅丹(用做颜料).

red-ˈ**letter day** day that is important or memorable because sth good happened on it 重要的或值得纪念的日子.

ˌ**red** ˈ**light** road signal meaning 'stop'; danger signal on railways, etc 红灯(表示'停'的道路信号; 铁路等的危险信号): *go through, jump a red light*, ie not stop 闯红灯. **red-**ˈ**light district** part of a town where there are many prostitutes, sex-shops, etc 红灯区(城市中妓女、性用品商店等集中的地方).

ˌ**red** ˈ**meat** beef, lamb or mutton 牛羊肉. Cf 参看 WHITE MEAT (WHITE[1]).

ˌ**red** ˈ**pepper** **1** (red fruit of the) capsicum plant 红辣椒. **2** = CAYENNE PEPPER.

ˌ**red** ˈ**setter** = IRISH SETTER (IRISH).

ˈ**redskin** *n* ⇨ RED INDIAN.

ˌ**red** ˈ**tape** (*derog* 贬) excessive bureaucracy, esp in public business 繁文缛节; (尤指)官僚作风: *procedures hedged about with red tape* 繁琐拖拉的办事程序 ○ *It takes weeks to get through the red tape.* 办完这些繁琐的手续得需要几个星期.

ˌ**red** ˈ**wine** wine made from black grapes and coloured red by contact with their skins 红葡萄酒. Cf 参看 ROSÉ, WHITE WINE (WHITE[1]).

ˈ**redwood** *n* any type of tree with reddish wood, esp a Californian conifer that sometimes grows to a great height 红木; (尤指加利福尼亚的)红杉(有些极高).

red[2] /red; rɛd/ *n* **1** [U, C] (shade of) red colour (深浅不同的)红色: *light, clear, deep, dark, etc red* 浅、纯、深、暗等红色 ○ *There's too much red in the painting.* 这幅画中用的红色太多. ○ *the reds and browns of the woods in autumn*, ie of the leaves, undergrowth, etc 秋天树林中呈现的红色和褐色(指树叶和矮树丛的颜色). **2** [U] red clothes 红衣服: *dressed in red* 穿着红衣服 ○ *Don't wear red tonight.* 今晚别穿红衣服. **3** [C] (**a**) **Red** person supporting Socialism or Communism 拥护社会主义或共产主义的人: *the conflict between Reds and Whites*, ie during the Russian Revolution 拥护和反对共产主义的人之间的冲突(俄国革命期间). (**b**) (*infml or derog* 口或贬) person supporting revolution or radical policies 赤色分子; 革命分子; 激进分子: *a union organized by reds* 由激进分子组织的工会. Cf 参看 PINK[1]. **4** (idm 习语) **be in the** ˈ**red**; **get (sb) into the** ˈ**red** (*infml* 口) have more liabilities than assets; (cause sb to) owe money 负债; (使某人)欠债: *My bank account is £50 in the red.* 我的银行帐户有50英镑的亏空. Cf 参看 BE IN THE BLACK (BLACK[2] 4). **be out of the red**; **get (sb) out of the red** (*infml* 口) (help sb to) be no longer in debt (帮助某人)偿清债务: *This payment will get me out of the red*, ie into a state of credit. 这一笔报酬能帮我偿清欠债了. **see** ˈ**red** (*infml* 口) become very angry 大怒: *Her criticisms were enough to make anyone see red.* 她那些批评任谁都得火冒三丈.

red·den /ˈredn; ˈrɛdn/ *v* **1** [I, Tn] (cause sth to) become red (使某物)变红. **2** [I] (of the face) flush with shame, anger, etc (指脸)(因羞涩、愤怒等)发红.

red·dish /ˈredɪʃ; ˈrɛdɪʃ/ *adj* rather red 略呈红色的; 微红的: *reddish fur, hair* 略带红色的皮毛、毛发.

re·deem /rɪˈdi:m; rɪˈdim/ *v* **1** (**a**) [Tn, Tn·pr] **~ sth (from sb/sth)** buy back sth by paying the required sum; recover sth 买回或赎回某物: *I redeemed my watch from the pawn shop.* 我把手表从当舖里赎回来了. **(b)** [Tn] pay off (eg a debt); clear 偿清(债务等); 结清: *redeem a mortgage, loan, etc* 偿还抵押借款、贷款等. **(c)** [Tn] convert (bonds, shares, etc) into cash or goods 将(债券、股票等)兑换为现金或货物: *This coupon can be redeemed at any of our branches.* 这种息票可在我们的任何分行兑现. **2** [Tn] (*fml* 文) keep (a promise); fulfil 遵守(诺言); 履行: *redeem one's pledges, obligations* 履行誓约、义务. **3** [Tn, Tn·pr] **~ sb (from sth)** **(a)** obtain the freedom of sb, esp by payment; rescue sb 使某人获得自由; (尤指)为某人赎身; 解救某人: *redeem hostages from captivity* 营救禁锢的人质. **(b)** (*fig* 比喻) (of Christ) free or save (mankind) from sin (指耶稣)将人类从罪孽中拯救出来. **4** [Tn] **(a)** make up for faults or deficiencies in (sth); compensate for 补救或弥补(某事物); 补偿: *The sole redeeming feature of this job is the salary.* 这份工作唯其薪水尚可弥补一切之不足. ○ *The acting was not good enough to redeem the (awfulness of the) play.* 该剧(很糟糕), 演得好也于事无补. ○ *Jones redeemed his earlier poor performance by scoring two goals.* 琼斯射入两球方弥补其初时表现之不足. **(b)** save (sb/sth/oneself) from blame; vindicate 使(某人[某事物/自己])免受责难; 维护: *redeem one's honour* 挽回名誉 ○ *The minister redeemed himself in the eyes of the public by resigning.* 这位大臣毅然辞职, 维护了自己在公众心目中的声誉.

▷ **re·deem·able** /-əbl; -əbḷ/ *adj* that can be redeemed 可赎回的; 可补救的; 可偿清的; (债券等)可兑现的.

the Re·deemer *n* [sing] Jesus Christ 救世主; 耶稣基督.

re·demp·tion /rɪˈdempʃn; rɪˈdɛmpʃən/ *n* [U] (*fml* 文) **1** redeeming or being redeemed 赎回; 补救; 偿清; 兑现: *the redemption of one's property, debts, shares, promises* 财产的赎回、债务的偿清、股票的兑现、诺言的履行. **2** (idm 习语) **beyond/past reˈdemption** (*esp joc* 尤作戏谑语) in such a poor state that there is no chance of improvement or recovery 无可救药; 不可挽回: *When the third goal was scored against us, we knew the match was past redemption.* 对方一射进第三个球, 我们就知道这场比赛算是输定了. ○ *Joan's career with the firm is really beyond redemption.* 琼在该公司的工作确实没有回旋余地了. ▷ **re·dempt·ive** *adj* /rɪˈdemptɪv; rɪˈdɛmptɪv/ *adj* (*fml* 文) of redemption; serving to redeem (用以)赎回的, 补救的, 偿还的.

re·deploy /ˌriːdɪˈplɔɪ; ˌridɪˈplɔɪ/ *v* [Tn] give new positions or tasks to (sb) 给予(某人)新的职位或任务; 重新调派: *redeploy troops, workers, scientists, etc* 调动部队、工作人员、科学家等 ○ *redeploy teachers into industry* 把教师调入工业部门.

▷ **re·deploy·ment** *n* [U] redeploying 调动; 调配; 重新部署: *the redeployment of staff, labour, manpower, etc* 工作人员、劳动力、人力等的调配.

re·develop /ˌriːdɪˈveləp; ˌridɪˈvɛləp/ *v* [Tn] replan or rebuild (an area of land or building(s)) in a different way 重新规划或重新建设(某一地区或建筑物); 改造: *redevelop a city centre, housing estate, slum area, etc*, eg modernize them, improve conditions, etc 改造市中心、住宅区、贫民区等.

▷ **re·devel·op·ment** *n* [U] redeveloping or being redeveloped 重新规划; 重新建设; 改造: *an area ripe for redevelopment* 条件成熟即可重建的地方.

re·dif·fu·sion /ˌriːdɪˈfjuːʒn; ˌridɪˈfjuʒən/ *n* [U] (*esp Brit*) relaying of broadcast radio or TV programmes esp by wire from a central receiver to public places (eg cinemas, etc) (无线电广播或电视节目的)转播(尤指向电影院等公共场所的有线转播).

re·dir·ect /ˌriːdɪˈrekt; ˌridəˈrɛkt/ *v* = READDRESS.

re·dis·trib·ute /ˌriːdɪˈstrɪbjuːt; ˌridɪsˈtrɪbjʊt/ *v* [Tn] give (sth) out in a different way 重新分配(某事物): *redistribute jobs, power, land* 重新分配工作、权力、土地. ▷ **re·dis·tribu·tion** /ˌriːdɪstrɪˈbjuːʃn; ˌridɪstrəˈbjuʃən/ *n* [U]: *the redistribution of wealth, labour, resources, etc* 财富、劳力、资源等的重新分配.

redo /ˌriːˈduː; riˈdu/ *v* (*pt* **redid** /-ˈdɪd; -ˈdɪd/, *pp* **redone** /-ˈdʌn; -ˈdʌn/) [Tn] **1** do (sth) again 再做或重做(某事物). **2** (*infml* 口) redecorate (a room, building, etc); repair 重新装饰(房间、建筑物等); 修理: *have the kitchen redone*, ie wallpapered, painted, etc 重新装修厨房(贴壁纸、粉刷等) ○ *The roof needs redoing*, eg retiling. 屋顶需要修理(如重新铺瓦).

red·ol·ent /ˈredələnt; ˈrɛdḷənt/ *adj* [pred 作表语] **~ of/with sth** (*fml* 文) **1** smelling strongly of sth 有强烈气味: *have breath redolent of garlic, whisky, tobacco* 口中有强烈的大蒜、威士忌、烟草气味 ○ *a room redolent of roses* 弥漫着玫瑰花香的房间. **2** (*fig* 比喻) strongly suggestive or reminiscent of sth 使人联想或回想起某事物的: *a town redolent of the past* 使人对往事触景生情的小城. ▷ **red·ol·ence** /-əns; -əns/ *n* [U].

re·double /ˌriːˈdʌbl; riˈdʌbḷ/ *v* [I, Tn] **1** (cause sth to) become greater, stronger, more intense, etc (使某事物)变得更大、更强、再加倍: *Her zeal redoubled.* 她热情倍增. ○ *We must redouble our efforts.* 我们应该加倍努力. **2** (in the card-game of bridge) double again (a bid already doubled by an opponent) (桥牌中)将(对方已加倍的叫牌)再加倍.

re·doubt /rɪˈdaʊt; rɪˈdaʊt/ *n* **(a)** last defensive position within a system of fortifications (防御系统中的)最后阵地. **(b)** isolated fortified outpost 孤立的前哨站.

re·doubt·able /rɪˈdaʊtəbl; rɪˈdaʊtəbḷ/ *adj* (*fml or joc* 文或谑) to be feared and respected; formidable 令人敬畏的; 可怕的: *a redoubtable opponent, fighter* 令人敬畏的对手、战士.

re·dound /rɪˈdaʊnd; rɪˈdaʊnd/ *v* (phr v) **redound on sb/sth** (*fml* 文) come back on sb/sth; rebound or recoil on sb/sth 返回或报应到某人[某事物]上: *Your practical jokes will redound on you/your own head one day.* 你那些恶作剧总有一天会使你自食其果. **redound to sth** (*fml* 文) contribute greatly to (one's/sb's reputation, etc); promote sth 提高(自己的[某人的]声誉等); 促进某事物: *Her hard work redounds to her credit/to the honour of the school.* 她工作努力从而提高了自己的声誉[为学校增添了荣誉]. ○ *This course of action will redound to our advantage.* 这种做法对我们很有好处.

re·dress /rɪˈdres; rɪˈdrɛs/ *v* **1** [Tn] (*fml* 文) put right (a wrong); compensate for (sth) 纠正(过错); 补偿(某事物): *redress an injustice, an abuse, etc* 纠正不公的现象、弊端等 ○ *redress a grievance* 申冤 ○ *redress the damage done* 赔偿损失. **2** (idm 习语) **redress the ˈbalance** make things equal again 使各事物重新相等或均衡: *The team has more men than women so we must redress the balance*, ie include more women in it. 这个队男的多女的少, 所以我们得平衡一下(招收女队员).

▷ **re·dress** *n* [U] **~ (for sth)** (*fml* 文) redressing or being redressed; thing that redresses 纠正; 补偿; 有改正或补偿作用的事物: *seek legal redress for unfair dismissal* 对不合理的解雇一事提起诉讼以求匡正 ○ *Under the circumstances, you have no redress*, ie You cannot demand compensation. 在此情况下, 你不能索赔.

re·duce /rɪˈdjuːs; *US* -ˈduːs; rɪˈdus/ *v* **1** [Tn, Tn·pr] **~ sth (from sth) (to/by sb)** make sth smaller in size, number, degree, price, etc 缩减(体积、数量、程度、价格等); 减小; 减少; 减低; 降低: *reduce volume, quantity, pressure, speed* 缩小体积、减少数量、降低压力、减低速度 ○ *increase profits by reducing costs* 降低成本以增加利润 ○ *reduce one's weight from 98 to 92 kilos/by 6 kilos* 把体重从98公斤减少到92公斤[减少6公斤] ○ *Antibiotics will reduce the swelling.* 使用抗菌素能消肿. ○ *This shirt was greatly/drastically reduced in the sale.* 这种衬衣在大减价时降价很多. **2** [I] (*infml* 口 *esp US*) lose weight intentionally; diet (有意识地)减轻体重; 节食. **3** [Tn·pr] **~ sb (from sth) to sth** make sb lower in rank or status; demote sb 降低某人的级别或地位; 降职: *reduce a sergeant to the ranks*, ie make him an ordinary soldier 把一名中士降为士兵 ○ *The reform has reduced us to servants of the State.* 这一改革把我们都降为公务员了. **4** [Tn·pr] **~ sb/sth (from sth) to sth** bring sb/sth into a specified (usu worse) state or condition 使某人[某事物]陷入某种(通常指更坏的)状态或状况中: *be reduced to begging, borrowing* 沦落到得要饭、借债 ○ *reduce sb to tears, silence, despair, obedience* 使某人流泪、沉默、绝望、顺从 ○ *reduce the chaos in one's office to some form of order* 改变办公室的混乱状况, 使之有些条理 ○ *Overwork has reduced him to a physical wreck.* 他过度劳累而损害了健康. ○ *The fire reduced the house to ashes.* 这场火灾把那所房子化为灰烬. **5** [Tn·pr] **~ sth to sth** change sth to a more general or basic form 将

某事物概括或简化成某种形式: *reduce an equation, argument, issue to its simplest form* 把某方程式、论据、问题化为最简单形式 ○ *reduce a problem to two main issues* 把某问题归纳成两个要点. **6** [Tn, Tn·pr] **~ sth (to sth)** (*chemistry* 化) remove oxygen from or add hydrogen or electrons to (a compound) 将(化合物)还原: *reduce water* (ie to hydrogen) *by electrolysis* 用电解法把水还原(为氢) ○ *reduce a compound to its constituent elements* 将一化合物还原为构成该化合物的元素. Cf 参看 OXIDIZE (OXIDE).

▷ **re·du·cible** /-əbl; -əbl/ *adj* **~ (to sth)** that can be reduced 可缩减的; 可降低的; 可化简的; 可还原的.

re·duc·tio ad ab·surdum /rɪˌdʌktɪəʊ æd əbˈsɜːdəm; rɪˈdʌktɪoˌædəbˈsɝdəm/ (*Latin* 拉) method of disproving a proposition by showing that, if interpreted literally and precisely, it would lead to an absurd result 归谬法; 反证法.

re·duc·tion /rɪˈdʌkʃn; rɪˈdʌkʃən/ *n* **1** (**a**) [U] reducing or being reduced 缩减; 降低; 简化; 还原: *the reduction of tax* 税金的减少 ○ *reduction of an argument to its essentials* 将论据归纳成为一些要点. (**b**) [C] instance of reducing 缩减; 降低; 简化; 还原: *a reduction in size, weight, etc* 体积的缩小、重量的减少 ○ *a price reduction* 价格的降低. (**c**) [C] amount by which sth is reduced, esp in price 缩减之量; (尤指)减去的价钱: *sell sth at a huge reduction* 大幅度降价出售某物 ○ *make/offer reductions on certain articles* 对某些商品减价. **2** [C] copy of a map, picture, etc made by reducing the size of the original (地图、图片等的)缩版, 缩图. Cf 参看 ENLARGEMENT (ENLARGE).

R

re·dund·ant /rɪˈdʌndənt; rɪˈdʌndənt/ *adj* **1** (usu of language or art) not needed; superfluous; unnecessary (通常指语言或艺术)不必要的, 冗赘的, 多余的: *a paragraph without a redundant word* 无一冗词的一段文字 ○ *The illustration had too much redundant detail.* 解说中不必要的细节太多. **2** (*esp Brit*) (of industrial workers) no longer needed for any available job and therefore dismissed (指工人)(因人员过剩)被解雇的, 失业的: *become/be made/find oneself redundant* 成为冗员而被裁 ○ *the plight of redundant miners* 被裁减的矿工的困境 ○ *Fifty welders were declared redundant.* 已公布削减五十名焊工.

▷ **re·dund·ancy** /-ənsɪ; -ənsɪ/ *n* **1** [U] (**a**) state of being redundant(2) 人浮于事; 裁员; 成为冗员被裁: *a high level of redundancy among unskilled workers* 非熟练工人的大量裁减 ○ [attrib 作定语] *redundancy pay, money, etc,* ie given to sb made redundant 遣散费(给予被裁减人员的). (**b**) material that is redundant(1) (通常指语言或艺术)多余的材料: *express oneself without redundancy* 精练地表达意思. **2** [C] worker made redundant(2) 遭裁减的工人: *Two hundred redundancies were announced in the shipyards.* 造船厂公布削减二百名工人.

re·dund·antly *adv*.

re·du·pli·cate /rɪˈdjuːplɪkeɪt; rɪˈduplə͵ket/ *v* [Tn] (*fml* 文) repeat (esp a word or syllable), as in *bye-bye*; double 重复(尤指词或音节)(如bye-bye); 使加倍. ▷ **re·du·plica·tion** /rɪˌdjuːplɪˈkeɪʃn; *US* -ˌduː-; rɪˌdupləˈkeʃən/ *n* [U].

re-echo /riːˈekəʊ; riˈɛko/ *v* [I] echo again and again 反复发出回声; 反复回响: *Their shouts re-echoed through the valley.* 他们的喊声在山谷中回荡.

reed /riːd; rid/ *n* **1** (**a**) [C] (tall hollow stem of) any of various types of grass-like plants growing near water 芦苇(秆). (**b**) [U] mass of such plants growing together 芦苇丛. **2** [C] strip of metal or cane that vibrates to produce sound in eg an oboe, a bassoon, or a clarinet 簧片(如双簧管、低音管、单簧管中的): [attrib 作定语] *reed instruments* 簧乐器. ⇨ illus at App 1 见附录1插图, page x. **3** (idm 习语) **a broken reed** ⇨ BROKEN[2].

▷ **reedi·ness** *n* [U] state of being reedy(2) (声音的)尖利刺耳: *an unpleasant reediness of tone* 声调的刺耳尖利.

reedy *adj* (**-ier, iest**) **1** having many reeds (REED 1) 多芦苇的; 芦苇丛生的. **2** (*derog* 贬) (of voices, sounds) high and scratchy instead of full and clear (指嗓音、声响)尖利刺耳的: *a thin, reedy tenor* 音色尖细刺耳的男高音.

re-educate /riːˈedʒʊkeɪt; riˈɛdʒə͵ket/ *v* [Tn, Cn·t] train (sb) to think or behave in a new or different way 对(某人)再培训或再教育: *We must re-educate people (to eat more healthily).* 我们应该对人们进行再教育(使之重视饮食卫生). ▷ **re-education** /ˌriːedʒʊˈkeɪʃn; riˌɛdʒəˈkeʃən/ *n* [U].

reef[1] /riːf; rif/ *n* part of the top or bottom of a sail that can be rolled or folded to reduce the area exposed to the wind 缩帆部, 叠帆部(帆的顶部或底部可卷起或折起的部分).

▷ **reef** *v* [Tn] reduce the area of (a sail) by drawing in a reef or reefs 卷起或折起(缩帆部).

□ ˈ**reef-knot** (*US* **square-knot**) *n* type of symmetrical double-knot that will not slip or come undone easily 平结, 方结(对称的双结, 不容易滑脱或松开).

reef[2] /riːf; rif/ *n* ridge of rock, shingle, sand, etc at or near the surface of the sea 礁; 礁脉: *The ship was wrecked on a coral reef.* 那艘船触珊瑚礁失事.

reefer /ˈriːfə(r); ˈrifɚ/ *n* **1** (also **reefer-jacket**) close-fitting thick double-breasted jacket 厚布制的双排钮上衣. **2** (*sl* 俚) hand-rolled cigarette containing marijuana 手卷的大麻烟.

reek /riːk; rik/ *n* [sing] **1** (*derog* 贬) strong bad smell 浓烈的臭味: *the reek of stale tobacco (smoke)* 发霉烟草的臭(烟)味. **2** (*Scot* 苏格兰) thick smoke, usu from fires or chimneys 浓烟(通常指燃烧产生的或烟囱中喷发的).

▷ **reek** *v* **1** [Ipr] **~ (of sth)** (*derog* 贬) (**a**) smell unpleasantly of sth 发出难闻气味: *His breath reeked of tobacco.* 他口中带有烟草的臭味. ○ *The room reeked of cheap perfume.* 房间里弥漫着劣质香水的呛鼻气味. (**b**) (*fig* 比喻) strongly suggest sth unpleasant or suspicious 明显带有令人不快的或令人生疑的特质: *Their actions reek of corruption.* 他们的举动显然有贪污之嫌. **2** [I, Tn] (*Scot* 苏格兰) (usu of fires or chimneys) give out (thick smoke) (通常指火或烟囱)冒出(浓烟).

reel (*US* **spool**) 卷轴类

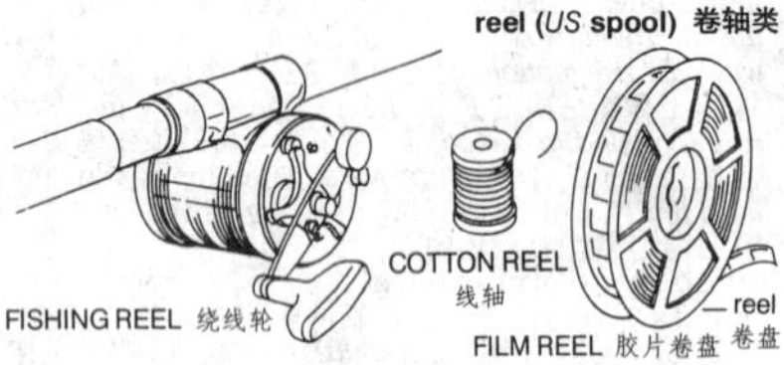

reel[1] /riːl; ril/ *n* (*US* **spool**) **1** cylinder, roller or similarly shaped object on which thread, wire, fishing line, photographic film, magnetic tape, etc is wound (线绳、金属丝、钓丝、摄影胶片、磁带等的)卷轴, 卷筒, 卷盘: *a cotton reel* 绵线轴 ○ *a cable reel* 电缆卷轴. **2** quantity of thread, etc wound on such a cylinder, roller, etc 一卷轴、卷筒、卷盘等的量: *a six-reel film* 一部有六盘胶片的电影.

▷ **reel** *v* **1** [Tn·p] **~ sth in/out** wind (sth) on or off a reel; pull (sth) in by using a reel 在卷轴等上缠绕(某物); 从卷轴等上抽出(某物); 用卷轴等拉拽(某物): *reel the line, the hosepipe, etc out* 从卷轴上放出线绳、水龙带等 ○ *The angler reeled the trout in slowly.* 钓鱼的人慢慢地收绕钓丝钓起鳟鱼. **2** (phr v) **reel sth off** say or repeat sth rapidly without pause or apparent effort 一口气说或重复某事: *reel off a poem, list of names, set of instructions* 一口气背出一首诗、说出许多名字、发出一系列指令.

reel[2] /riːl; ril/ *v* **1** [I, Ipr, Ip] move unsteadily or sway; stagger 摇摇晃晃地移动; 摇摆; 蹒跚: *reel drunkenly down the road* 醉得东倒西歪沿路走去 ○ *She reeled (back) from the force of the blow.* 她受此一击(向后)打了个趔趄. ○ *I reeled round in a daze.* 我头昏眼花走不稳. **2** [I, Ipr] (*fig* 比喻) (of the mind or head) be or become dizzy or confused; be in a whirl (指心智或头脑)眩晕, 迷乱, 发昏: *The very idea sets my head reeling.* 就是那念头把我弄得头昏脑胀. ○ *His mind reeled when he heard the news/at the news.* 他听到那消息后感到头发蒙. ○ *be reeling from/with/under the shock* 吓得晕头转向 ○ (*fig* 比喻) *The street reeled* (ie seemed to go round and round) *before her eyes.* 她感到街道在眼前打旋.

reel[3] /riːl; ril/ *n* (music for a) lively Scottish or Irish dance, usu for two or four couples 里尔舞(轻快的苏格兰或爱尔兰舞, 通常由两对或四对舞者共舞); 里尔舞曲.

re-elect /ˌriːɪˈlekt; ˌriəˈlɛkt/ *v* [Tn, Tn·pr, Cn·n/a] **~ sb (to sth); ~ sb (as sth)** elect sb again 再选某人: *re-elect sb to the Presidency/(as) President* 再度选举某人担任总统职位[为总统]. ▷ **re-election** /-ˈlekʃn; -ˈlɛkʃən/ *n* [C, U].

re-enter /ˌriːˈentə(r); riˈɛntɚ/ *v* **1** [I, Tn] come in or into (sth) again 再次进入或加入(某事物)中; 重返: *re-enter (the room) by another door* 由另一个门再进入(该房间). **2** [I, Ipr] **~ (for sth)** put one's name forward again, esp for an exam 重新报名或再次报名(尤指参加考试).

▷ **re-entry** /ˌriːˈentrɪ; riˈɛntrɪ/ *n* [C, U] **1** (act of) re-entering 重新进入或加入; 重返; 重新报名; 再次报名. **2** return of a spacecraft into the earth's atmosphere (宇宙飞船)重返地球大气层: *The capsule gets very hot on re-entry.* 航天舱在重返大气层时产生高热.

reeve /riːv; riv/ *n* **1** (*Brit*) (**a**) (formerly) chief magistrate of a town or district (旧时)市镇或区的司法官. Cf 参看 SHERIFF 1. (**b**) (in medieval times) steward of a manor (中世纪时期)庄园的管家. **2** (in Canada) elected head of a village or town council (加拿大)乡镇议会的议长.

re-examine /ˌriːɪgˈzæmɪn; ˌriɪgˈzæmɪn/ *v* [Tn] (*law* 律) examine or question (one's own witness) again 再诘问(己方证人). ▷ **re-examination** /ˌriːɪgˌzæmɪˈneɪʃn; ˌriɪgˌzæmɪˈneʃən/ *n* [C, U].

re-export /ˌriːekˈspɔːt; ˌriɪkˈspɔrt/ *v* [Tn, Tn·pr] **~ sth (to...)** export (imported goods) again, esp after reprocessing 将(进口货物)再输出(尤指经加工后); 将(某物)转口.

ref /ref; rɛf/ *n* (*infml* 口) = REFEREE 1.

ref /ref; rɛf/ *abbr* 缩写 = (*commerce* 商) reference: *ref no 369* 函件编号369 ○ *our ref 14A; your ref 392*, eg at the top of a business letter 我方编号: 14A; 你方编号: 392 (如商务信件页首所注).

re·face /ˌriːˈfeɪs; riˈfes/ *v* [Tn] put a new surface on (a wall, building, etc) 装修(墙壁、建筑物等的)外表.

re·fect·ory /rɪˈfektrɪ *or, rarely,* 罕读作 ˈrefɪktrɪ; rɪˈfɛktərɪ/ *n* dining-hall in a monastery, convent, college, school, etc (修道院、学校等的)食堂, 餐厅.

re·fer /rɪˈfɜː(r); rɪˈfɝ/ *v* **(-rr-)** **1** [Ipr] **~ to sb/sth** (**a**) mention or speak of sb/sth; allude to sb/sth 提到、说到或涉及到某人[某事物]: *When I said some people are stupid, I wasn't referring to you.* 我说有些人很愚蠢, 并不是指你. ○ *Don't refer to this matter again, please.* 请不要再提这件事了. ○ *This incident in his childhood is never again referred to.* 他小时候的这件事永远不再提了. (**b**) be relevant to sb/sth; concern sb/sth 与某人[某事物]有关; 关系到某人[某事物]: *What I have to say refers to all of you.* 我要说的事和你们大家都有关. **2** [Ipr] **~ to sth/sb** turn to sth/sb for information, etc 向某事物[某人]查询信息等: *refer to a dictionary, an expert* 查词典、询问专家 ○ *I referred to my watch for the exact time.* 我看了一下手表好知道准确的时间. ○ *The speaker often referred to his notes.* 那个讲演的人不时地看发言稿. **3** [Tn·pr esp passive 尤用于被动语态] **~ sb/sth to sb/sth** send sb/sth to sb/sth for help, advice, action, etc 将某人[某事物]送交某人[某事物]以谋求帮助、指点、行动支持等: *refer a patient to a specialist for treatment* 把病人交给专科医生治疗 ○ *The dispute was referred to the United Nations/to arbitration.* 该项争端已提交联合国处理[予以仲裁]. ○ *I was referred to the manager/the enquiry office.* 人家叫我去找经理[去问讯处]. ○ *The reader is referred to page 3.* 请读者参看第3页. **4** (phr v) **refer sth back (to sb)** return (a document, etc) to the sender for further clarification 将(文件等)退给送件人予以澄清: *The letter was referred back (to us) with a query.* 该函已退给(我方)要求对某问题加以解释.

▷ **re·fer·able** /rɪˈfɜːrəbl; rɪˈfɝəbl/ *adj* **~ (to sb/sth)** that can be referred (REFER 3) to sb/sth 可送交某人[某事物]的.

re·fer·ral /rɪˈfɜːrəl; rɪˈfɝəl/ *n* **1** [U] referring (REFER 3) or being referred to sb/sth 送交: *the referral of such cases to a doctor* 将此类病人转给某医生诊治. **2** [C] person or thing referred (REFER 3) to sb/sth 送交给某人[某事物]的人或事物: *several referrals from the clinic* 从诊所转来的几个病人.

ref·eree /ˌrefəˈriː; ˌrɛfəˈri/ *n* **1** (also *infml* 口语作 **ref**) (in football, boxing, etc) official who controls matches, prevents rules being broken, etc (足球、拳击等的)裁判员. ⇨illus at HOCKEY 见 HOCKEY 插图. Cf 参看 UMPIRE. **2** person to whom disputes, eg between employers and employees, are referred for decision (争端, 如劳资纠纷的)仲裁者, 调解者, 公断者. **3** (*Brit*) person willing to make a statement about the character or ability of sb applying for a job (愿为求职者提供证明的)证明人, 介绍人, 推荐人: *The head teacher often acts as (a) referee for his pupils.* 这位校长常为求职学生做证明人.

▷ **ref·eree** *v* [I, Tn] act as a referee(1) in (sth) 当裁判: *Who refereed (the match)?* 谁当(这场比赛的)裁判?

ref·er·ence /ˈrefərəns; ˈrɛfərəns/ *n* **1 ~ (to sb/sth)** (**a**) [U] act of referring (REFER 1a) to sb/sth 提到; 说到; 涉及: *Avoid (making) any reference to his illness.* 千万别提起他的病. ○ *The original text is here for ease of reference.* 谨附原文以便查考. (**b**) [C] statement, etc speaking of or mentioning sb/sth; allusion 说到或提到某人[某事物]的言语或文字等; 暗示: *He made pointed* (ie obvious) *references to the recent scandal.* 他有针对性地提到最近的丑闻. ○ *The book is full of references to places I know.* 这本书里提到许多我熟悉的地方. **2** [C] **~ (to sb/sth)** note, etc telling a reader in what other book, article, etc information may be found; book, passage, etc referred to in this way or as an authority (向读者指示参考书、文章等的)附注, 旁注; (做此种用途的)书, 章节: *a thesis crowded with references to other sources* 有旁征博引附注的论文 ○ *check your references* 要核对引证的资料 ○ *cite Green 1986 as a reference* 引用1986年格林的论述作参考资料. **3** [C] (*abbr* 缩写 **ref**) (*commerce* 商) (on letters, etc) means of identification (书信等的)编号: *Please quote our reference when replying.* 回信时请注明我方函件编号. **4** [C] (person willing to make a) statement about a person's character or abilities (有关某人品格或能力的)证明文书, 介绍信; 证明人: *quote sb/sb's name as a reference* 提出某人[某人的名字]做可咨询的证明人 ○ *provide a reference for sb* 为某人出具证明 ○ *supply sb with a reference* 向某人提供愿做证明的人 ○ *She has excellent references from former employers.* 她持有以前的雇主写的很好的证明书. ○ *a banker's reference*, ie a note from one's bank saying that one's financial position is sound 银行证明(证明某人财务状况良好). Cf 参看 TESTIMONIAL 1. **5** (idm 习语) **bear/have some/no reference to sth** (not) be connected with sth 与某事物有关[无关]: *This has no reference to what we were discussing.* 这与我们讨论的问题无关. **a frame of reference** ⇨ FRAME[1]. **in/with reference to sb/sth** (*esp commerce* 尤用于商业) about or concerning sb/sth 关于某人[某事物]: *I am writing with reference to your job application.* 敬复者, 关于您申请工作一事. Cf 参看 TERMS OF REFERENCE (TERM). **without reference to sb/sth** not taking account of sb/sth 不考虑某人[某事物]; 置某人[某事物]于不顾: *She issued all these invitations without any reference to her superiors.* 她未请示上级擅自把所有这些请柬都发了出去.

□ **ˈreference book** book, eg an encyclopedia or a dictionary, which is consulted for information, not read right through 参考书, 工具书(如百科全书或词典).

ˈreference library (also **ˈreference room**) library or room having books that may be consulted on the premises, but not borrowed 参考书阅览室(藏书仅供室内参阅, 不外借).

ˈreference marks marks, eg *, †, ‡, §, used to direct the reader to eg a footnote, where information may be found 参照符号(如*、†、‡、§, 用以指示读者参看脚注等).

ref·er·en·dum /ˌrefəˈrendəm; ˌrɛfəˈrɛndəm/ *n* (*pl* **~s**) [C, U] referring of a political issue to a general vote by all the people of a country for a decision; vote thus taken 全民投票(以表决某政治问题); 全民投的票: *hold a referendum on ending conscription* 就结束征兵问题举行全民投票 ○ *settle a national issue by referendum* 以全民投票来解决一项国家大事. Cf 参看 PLEBISCITE.

re·fill /ˌriːˈfɪl; riˈfɪl/ *v* [Tn] fill again 再装满; 再充满: *refill a glass, (petrol) tank, (cigarette) lighter, etc* 把玻璃杯、汽

油箱、打火机等重新灌满.

▷ **re·fill** /ˈri:fɪl; ˋriˌfɪl/ *n* new material used to refill a container; container thus refilled 用以重新装人一容器的新添材料; 重新装入新添材料的容器: (*infml* 口) *Would you like a refill* (ie another glass of beer, wine, etc)? 您还要再添一杯吗? ○ *two refills for a cartridge pen* 两支替换笔芯.

re·fine /rɪˈfaɪn; rɪˋfaɪn/ *v* [Tn] **1** remove impurities from (sth); purify 从(某物)中除去杂质; 精制; 精炼; 提纯: *refine sugar, oil, ore, etc* 制糖、炼油、提炼矿石 ○ *refining processes* 提炼过程. **2** improve (sth) by removing defects and attending to detail (去粗取精、一丝不苟)改良(某事物): *refine one's working methods* 改进自己的工作方法 ○ *refine earlier systems, designs, theories* 改良原先的制度、设计、理论. **3** (*fig* 比喻) make (sb/sth) more cultured or elegant; remove what is coarse or vulgar from 使(某人[某事物])更有教养或更文雅; 使去掉粗俗言行: *refine one's manners, taste, language* 使举止更优雅、趣味更高雅、语言更文雅.

▷ **re·fined** *adj* **1** cultured or elegant; free from what is coarse or vulgar 有教养的; 文雅的; 不粗俗的: *Her tastes are very refined.* 她的趣味十分高雅. **2** freed from impurities 纯净的; 精炼的: *refined sugar, oil, etc* 精制的糖、精炼的油.

re·finer *n* person, firm or machine that refines (REFINE 1) 做精炼加工的人、企业或机器: *sugar refiners* 精糖制造者.

re·finery /-nərɪ; -nərɪ/ *n* factory, etc where sth is refined 精炼加工厂: *a ˈsugar refinery* 制糖厂 ○ *an ˈoil refinery* 炼油厂.

re·fine·ment /rɪˈfaɪnmənt; rɪˋfaɪnmənt/ *n* **1** [U] refining or being refined 精炼; 精制; 提纯: *the refinement of oil, sugar, etc* 油、糖等的精炼 ○ *the gradual refinement of her taste in music* 她音乐修养的逐步提高. **2** [U] culture or elegance of manners, taste, language, etc (仪态、趣味、语言等的)高雅, 文雅: *a person of great refinement* 温文尔雅的人 ○ *lack of refinement* 缺乏教养. **3** [C esp *pl* 尤作复数] (**a**) clever development of eg machinery, technique; improvement (机器、技术等的)精巧的改进; 改良: *all the refinements of 20th-century technology* 20世纪技术上的一切进步 ○ *The oven has an automatic timer and other refinements.* 这个烤箱有自动定时器及其他改进装置. ○ *make further refinements to our original model* 对我们最初的型号作进一步的改进. (**b**) subtle or ingenious development of eg thought, behaviour 精妙, 精细(思想、行为的): *refinements of meaning, cruelty* 意义的精细入微、残酷之极.

re·fit /ˈri:fɪt; ˋriˌfɪt/ *n* repair or renewal of parts (of a ship, etc) (船等的)修理或更换零部件: *The liner is in dock for a refit.* 班轮正在船坞修理.

▷ **re·fit** /ˌri:ˈfɪt; riˋfɪt/ *v* (**-tt-**) (**a**) [Tn, Cn·n/a] **~ sth (as sth)** give a refit to (a ship, etc) 修理(船等)或更换其零部件: *The ferry was refitted as a troop-ship and joined the fleet.* 那艘渡轮已改装为运兵船编人舰队. (**b**) [I] (of a ship, etc) be given a refit (指船等)被修理或更换零部件: *put into port to refit* 进港修理.

re·flate /ˌri:ˈfleɪt; riˋflet/ *v* [I, Tn] increase the amount of money and credit circulating in (an economy) to restore the system (after a period of deflation) to its previous condition (增加流通货币及贷款)使经济(在通货紧缩后)复苏. Cf 参看 DEFLATE 2, INFLATE 3.

▷ **re·fla·tion** /ri:ˈfleɪʃn; riˋfleʃən/ *n* [U] reflating or being reflated 放宽银根使经济复苏. **re·fla·tion·ary** /ri:ˈfleɪʃnrɪ; *US* -nerɪ; riˋfleʃəˌnɛrɪ/ *adj*: *adopt reflationary policies, measures, etc* 采取增加流通货币使经济复苏的政策、措施等.

re·flect /rɪˈflekt; rɪˋflɛkt/ *v* **1** [esp passive 尤用于被动语态: Tn, Tn·pr] (**a**) **~ sb/sth (in sth)** (of a mirror, etc) make a visible image of sb/sth (指镜子等)映出某人[某物]的影像: *trees reflected in a window/lake* 窗上[湖中]映出的树影 ○ *He looked at his face reflected in the mirror.* 他照镜子看看脸. (**b**) **~ sth (from sth)** (of a surface) throw back (light, heat, sound) (指物体表面)反射(光、热、声): *The heat reflected from the white sand formed a mirage.* 热气经白色的沙面反射形成了蜃景. ○ *The moon shines with reflected light.* 月球是藉反射阳光而发光的. **2** [Tn] (*fig* 比喻) show the nature of or express (sth); correspond to 表现(某事物)的性质; 表达(某事物); 符合: *Her sad looks reflected the nature of her thoughts.* 她面带忧伤显出心事重重. ○ *The literature of a period reflects its values and tastes.* 某一时期的文学可反映出该时期的价值观念和审美观念. ○ *Increased sales were reflected in higher profits.* 销售量的增加带来了更大的利润. **3** [I, Ipr, Tf, Tw no passive 不用于被动语态] **~ (on/upon sth)** think deeply about, or remind oneself of, past events; consider 沉思或思忆(往事); 思考: *I need time to reflect (on your offer/on what you offered).* 我需要时间来考虑(你的建议[你提出的建议]). ○ *She reflected that his argument was probably true.* 她心想他的理由也可能对. ○ *How distant those times seemed now, he reflected.* 他在想那些日子现在已显得多么遥远. **4** (idm 习语) **reflect (well, badly, etc) on sb/sth** show or suggest that sb/sth is sound, unsound, etc 表明或显出某人[某事物]健全、不健全等: *This scandal will reflect badly on the Party as a whole.* 这件丑闻可以说明这个党在整体上不健康. **reflect credit, discredit, etc on sb/sth** (of actions, results, etc) bring honour, dishonour, etc to sb/sth (指行为、结果等)给某人[某事物]带来光荣、耻辱等: *These excellent results reflect great credit on all our staff.* 这些优异的成绩给我们全体工作人员带来了莫大的光荣. ○ *Stealing reflects dishonour on your family.* 偷窃行为会使家人蒙羞.

re·flec·tion (*Brit* also **reflexion**) /rɪˈflekʃn; rɪˋflɛkʃən/ *n* **1** (**a**) [U] reflecting or being reflected 反映; 反射; 表现; 沉思: *heat transmitted by reflection* 由反射传导的热. (**b**) [C] thing reflected, esp an image in a mirror, still water, etc 被反映或反射之物; (尤指镜中、静水等中的)映像: *see one's reflection in a polished table-top* 在光亮的桌面上看见自己的映像 ○ *the reflection of the trees in the lake* 湖面映出的树的倒影 ○ (*fig* 比喻) *be a pale reflection of one's former self*, eg after an illness 与自己以前相比, 面容憔悴(如病后). **2** [C] (*fig* 比喻) thing reflecting the nature of eg a person, task, etc 可反映人、任务等的本质的事物: *Your clothes are a reflection of your personality.* 一个人的衣着可反映出其个性. **3** (**a**) [U] thought or memory of past events; consideration 沉思; 回忆; 思考: *lost in reflection* 陷入沉思中 ○ *act without sufficient reflection* 未经深思即采取行动 ○ *A moment's reflection will show you are wrong.* 只要略加考虑就可看出你错了. (**b**) [C] **~ (on sth)** (often *pl* 常作复数) (spoken or written expression of an) idea arising from this 经沉思而产生的想法(表达出的语言或文字): *idle reflections on the past* 回忆往事的遐想 ○ *publish one's reflections on sexism* 发表对性别歧视的看法. **4** (idm 习语) **be a (bad/poor/adverse) reflection on sb/sth** harm the good reputation of sb/sth; imply blame or criticism of sb/sth 损害某人[某事物]的名声; 暗含责难或批评: *Your remarks are a reflection on me/my character.* 你的话是对我[我的人格]的污辱. ○ *This mess is a (poor) reflection on her competence.* 这种混乱情况说明她难当此任. **on reflection** after reconsidering (sth) 再经考虑: *On further reflection, I saw that she might be right, after all.* 我再一考虑, 反倒觉得可能还是她对. ○ *She decided, on reflection, to accept the offer.* 她重新考虑后, 决定接受那个建议.

re·flect·ive /rɪˈflektɪv; rɪˋflɛktɪv/ *adj* **1** (of a person, mood, etc) thoughtful (指人、心情等)思考的, 沉思的: *in a reflective frame of mind* 在沉思中. **2** (of a surface, etc) reflecting (esp light) (指物体表面等)反射的, 反映的; (尤指)反光的: *reflective number plates*, eg on cars 反光的号码牌(如汽车上的). ▷ **re·flect·ively** *adv*: *answer, comment, etc reflectively* 经过思考而答复、评论等.

re·flector /rɪˈflektə(r); rɪˋflɛktɚ/ *n* **1** thing that reflects heat, light or sound 反射热、光或声音的东西; 反射器; 反射物. **2** red disc fitted to the back of a vehicle; disc or strip fitted to cycle wheels, etc making them visible in the dark by reflecting the lights of other vehicles 机动车辆尾部的红色反光器; 自行车轮等上的圆形或条形反光镜. ⇨ illus at App 1 见附录1插图, page xiii.

re·flex /ˈri:fleks; ˋriflɛks/ *n* (also ˈ**reflex action**) involuntary action (eg sneezing or shivering) made instinctively in response to a stimulus 反射作用(受刺激后的本能反应, 如打喷嚏或发抖): *Sorry I hit you; it was a pure reflex.* 对不起我撞着你了; 这完全是无意的. ○ *have quick, slow, normal, etc reflexes* 产生迅速的、缓慢的、正常的…反射动作 ○ *test/control one's reflexes* 测验[控制]自己的反射动作 ○ [attrib 作定语] *a reflex movement, response,* *etc*, ie one arising from a reflex 反射运动、反射性反应.

□ **reflex 'angle** angle of more than 180° 优角(大于180°的角).

'reflex camera camera in which the object or scene to be photographed is reflected by a mirror, and focused on a large viewfinder for adjustment up to the moment of exposure 反射式照相机.

re·flexion (*Brit*) = REFLECTION.

re·flex·ive /rɪˈfleksɪv; rɪˋflɛksɪv/ *n, adj* (*grammar*) (word or form) showing that the action of the verb is performed on its subject 反身的(词或形式)(表示动词的动作及于施动者): *a reflexive verb, pronoun*, eg as in 'He 'cut himself.' 反身动词、代词(如 He cut himself).

NOTE ON USAGE 用法: The reflexive verb is usually stressed. For emphasis, the syllable *-self/-selves* of the reflexive pronoun may be stressed. 反身动词通常须重读. 为加强语气, 反身代词中的 -self/-selves 这个音节可以重读.

re·float /ˌriːˈfləʊt; riˋflot/ *v* [I, Tn] (cause a ship, etc to) float again after sinking, running aground, etc (使船只等)(沉没、搁浅等之后)再浮起.

re·for·est (*US*) = REAFFOREST.

re·form /rɪˈfɔːm; rɪˋfɔrm/ *v* [I, Tn] become or make better by removing or putting right faults, errors, etc 变好; 改善; 改进; 改良; 改革; 改造: *There are signs that he's reforming.* 有迹象表明他在变好. ○ *reform one's ways, habits* 改变作风、习惯 ○ *reform an unfair salary structure* 改革不合理的工资结构 ○ *He's given up drink and is now a reformed character.* 他戒了酒, 现已判若两人.

▷ **re·form** *n* **1** [U] reforming or being reformed 改善; 改进; 改良; 改革; 改造: *agitate for, bring about, effect social reform* 鼓吹、带来、实行社会改革 ○ *the reform of teaching methods* 教学法的改进 ○ [attrib 作定语] *reform laws, bills, measures, etc* 改革法律、法案、措施等. **2** [C] change that removes or puts right faults, errors, etc (缺点等的)克服; (错误等的)改正, 纠正: *make, carry out reforms in education* 进行、实行教育改革.

re·former *n* person who brings about or advocates reform 改进者; 改革者; 改造者: *a social, political, religious reformer* 社会的、政治的、宗教的改革者.

re-form /ˌriː ˈfɔːm; ˌriˋfɔrm/ *v* **1** [I] form again 重新组成; 重新形成: *Ice re-formed on the plane's wings.* 飞机的机翼上又结冰了. **2** [I, Tn] (make soldiers, etc) get into ranks again (使士兵等)重新编队.

re·forma·tion /ˌrefəˈmeɪʃn; ˌrɛfɚˋmeʃən/ *n* **1 (a)** [U] reforming or being reformed 改善; 改进; 改良; 改革; 改造: *the reformation of criminals* 对罪犯的改造. **(b)** [C] great change for the better in social, religious or political affairs (社会、宗教或政治事务的)改革, 改良, 变革: *a reformation in state education* 国家教育事业的改革. **2 the Reformation** [sing] 16th-century European movement for reform of the Roman Catholic Church, which resulted in the establishment of Reformed or Protestant Churches 宗教改革(16 世纪欧洲改革天主教会的运动, 产生了新教).

re·form·at·ory /rɪˈfɔːmətrɪ; *US* -tɔːrɪ; rɪˋfɔrməˌtorɪ/ *n* (*US*) place where young offenders are sent to be trained and reformed (失足少年的)管教所, 教养所. Cf 参看 APPROVED SCHOOL (APPROVE), BORSTAL.

▷ **re·form·at·ory** *adj* (*fml* 文) tending or intended to produce reform (为)改善的, 改革的, 改造的.

re·fract /rɪˈfrækt; rɪˋfrækt/ *v* [Tn] bend (a ray of light) where it enters eg water or glass at an oblique angle from a medium of different density 使(光线)折射: *Light is refracted when passed through a prism.* 光线经过棱镜时产生折射现象.

▷ **re·frac·tion** /rɪˈfrækʃn; rɪˋfrækʃən/ *n* [U] refracting or being refracted 折射(现象). ⇨illus at SPECTRUM 见 SPECTRUM 插图.

re·fract·ory /rɪˈfræktərɪ; rɪˋfræktərɪ/ *adj* **1** (*fml* 文) difficult to control or discipline; wilful or unmanageable 难控制的; 不听管教的; 任性的; 难管理的: *a very refractory child* 很不听话的孩子. **2** (of a disease, etc) not yielding to treatment (指疾病等)难治的. **3** (of substances, metals, etc) difficult to fuse or work; resistant to heat (指物质、金属等)难熔的; 难处理的; 耐热的: *refractory brick*, eg in furnace linings 耐火砖.

re·frain[1] /rɪˈfreɪn; rɪˋfren/ *n* **1** lines of a song or poem which are repeated, esp at the end of each verse (歌曲或诗歌的)叠句; (尤指每节末的)反复部分, 副歌: *Will you all join in singing the refrain, please?* 请大家一道来唱副歌好吗? **2** tune accompanying this 副歌曲调: *a haunting refrain* 萦绕于心头的副歌曲调 ○ (*fig* 比喻) *the familiar refrain of her husband's snoring* 她丈夫的习惯的鼾声.

re·frain[2] /rɪˈfreɪn; rɪˋfren/ *v* [I, Ipr] **~ (from sth)** (*fml* 文) keep oneself from doing sth 克制; 抑制: *refrain from comment, criticism, etc* 避免评论、批评等 ○ *refrain from smoking* 克制而不吸烟 ○ *Let's hope they will refrain (from hostile action).* 希望他们能克制(不采取敌对行动).

re·fresh /rɪˈfreʃ; rɪˋfrɛʃ/ *v* [Tn] **1** give new strength or vigour to (sb/sth); restore or revive 给(某人[某事物])新的力量或活力; 使恢复; 使振作: *refresh oneself with a cup of tea/a hot bath* 喝杯茶[洗个热水澡]以提神 ○ *She felt refreshed after her sleep.* 她睡了一觉就精神了. **2** (idm 习语) **refresh one's/sb's memory (about sb/sth)** remind oneself/sb of facts by referring to notes, etc (借助笔记等)使自己[某人]想起: *Just refresh my memory: were you born in York?* 请再告诉我一次: 你是在约克郡出生的吧?

▷ **re·fresh·ing** *adj* **1** giving new strength or vigour; restoring or reviving 给人以新的力量或活力的; 提神的; 使人重新振作的: *a refreshing bath, sleep, cup of tea* 使人恢复精力的一个澡、一觉、一杯茶 ○ *This breeze is very refreshing.* 这微风使人心旷神怡. **2** (*fig* 比喻) welcome and interesting because unusual or novel (因少见或新奇)令人欣喜的, 使人耳目一新的: *a refreshing sense of humour* 别具一格的幽默感 ○ *a new and refreshing approach to a problem* 对某问题别辟蹊径的处理方法 ○ *The holiday was a refreshing change for us.* 这次假日别开生面, 我们都感到新奇. **re·fresh·ingly** *adv*: *refreshingly honest, original, different* 极其老实的、新颖的、不同的.

□ **re'fresher course** course of instruction for eg teachers to learn about new techniques and developments in their field 进修课程(如为教师等设的业务知识更新课).

re·fresh·ment /rɪˈfreʃmənt; rɪˋfrɛʃmənt/ *n* **1** [U] refreshing or being refreshed (精力的)恢复; (身心的)爽快. **2 (a)** [U] (*fml or joc* 文或谑) food and drink 食物和饮料: *partake of some refreshment* 吃些东西 ○ [attrib 作定语] *a refreshment room*, eg at a railway station where food and drink are sold 小吃部(如火车站等处的). **(b) refreshments** [pl] snacks 小吃; 点心: *Light refreshments* (eg ice-cream, crisps, chocolate) *are available during the interval.* 中间休息时有些点心(如冰激凌、炸土豆片、巧克力).

re·fri·ger·ate /rɪˈfrɪdʒəreɪt; rɪˋfrɪdʒəˌret/ *v* [Tn] make (food, etc) cold in order to freeze or preserve it 冷冻, 冷藏(食物等): *keep meat, milk, etc refrigerated* 冷藏肉、牛奶等.

▷ **re·fri·ger·ant** /-rənt; -rənt/ *n* substance that refrigerates, eg liquid carbon dioxide 致冷剂(如液态二氧化碳); 冷冻剂.

re·fri·gera·tion /rɪˌfrɪdʒəˈreɪʃn; rɪˌfrɪdʒəˋreʃən/ *n* [U] (of food, etc) refrigerating or being refrigerated, in order to freeze or preserve (指食物等)冷冻, 冷藏: *Keep perishable foods under refrigeration.* 把容易变质的食物冷藏起来. ○ [attrib 作定语] *the refrigeration industry* 制冷工业.

re·fri·ger·ator /rɪˈfrɪdʒəreɪtə(r); rɪˋfrɪdʒəˌretɚ/ *n* (also *esp US* **ice-box**, *infml* 口语作 **fridge** /frɪdʒ; frɪdʒ/) cabinet or room in which food is kept cold 冰箱; 冷藏室; 冷藏库. Cf 参看 FREEZER.

re·fuel /ˌriːˈfjuːəl; riˋfjuəl/ *v* (**-ll-**; *US* **-l-**) [I, Tn] (cause a car, plane, etc to) be filled up with fuel (给汽车、飞机等)加燃料: *stop, land, dock, etc for refuelling* 停车、着陆、靠码头等以便加燃料.

ref·uge /ˈrefjuːdʒ; ˋrɛfjudʒ/ *n* **1** [C, U] **~ (from sb/sth)** (place giving) shelter or protection from danger, trouble, pursuit, etc 避难(处); 庇护(所): *a place of refuge* 避难处 ○ *seek refuge from the storm* 躲避暴风雨 ○ *take refuge in the cellar* 在地下室里避难 ○ *a refuge* (eg a safe house) *for battered wives, alcoholics, etc* 遭受殴打的

R

妻子、酗酒者等的藏身处 ○ (*fig* 比喻) *For her, poetry is a refuge from the world.* 她把诗歌当作逃避现实的慰藉物. **2** [C] (*Brit*) = TRAFFIC ISLAND (TRAFFIC).

re·fu·gee /ˌrefjʊˈdʒiː *US* ˈrefjʊdʒiː; ˌrɛfjʊˋdʒi/ *n* person who has been forced to leave his country, home, etc and seek refuge, esp from political or religious persecution 难民, 避难者, 流亡者(尤指因遭政治上或宗教上的迫害): [attrib 作定语] *set up ˌrefuˈgee camps* 建立难民营.

re·ful·gent /rɪˈfʌldʒənt; rɪˋfʌldʒənt/ *adj* (*fml* 文) gloriously bright; shining 光辉的; 灿烂的; 明亮的. ▷ **re·ful·gence** *n* [U].

re·fund /riːˈfʌnd; rɪˋfʌnd/ *v* [Tn, Dn·n, Dn·pr esp passive 尤用于被动语态] **~ sth (to sb)** pay back (money received); reimburse (expenses incurred) 退还(所收的钱); 偿付(花去的费用): *refund a deposit* 退还保证金 ○ *Postage costs will be refunded (to you).* 邮费将退还(给你). ○ *I'll refund you the full cost of your fare.* 我来偿付你的全部旅费.

▷ **re·fund** /ˈriːfʌnd; ˋriˌfʌnd/ *n* [C, U] repayment; reimbursement 退款; 偿还金额: *a tax, pension, etc refund* 税金、年金等的退款 ○ *claim, obtain, pay, etc a refund* 要求、获得、支付…退款 ○ *He demanded a refund on the unused tickets.* 他要求对未使用之票给予退款.

re·fund·able *adj* that can be refunded 可退还的; 可偿还的: *a non-refundable deposit* 不予退还的保证金.

re·fur·bish /ˌriːˈfɜːbɪʃ; riˋfɝbɪʃ/ *v* [Tn] make (sth) clean or bright again; redecorate 将(某物)弄干净; 使(某物)恢复光亮; 重新装饰: *The flat will be refurbished for the new tenants.* 这套房间将重新粉刷以接纳新房客.

re·fusal /rɪˈfjuːzl; rɪˋfjuzl̩/ *n* **1** (**a**) [U] refusing or being refused 拒绝: *refusal of a request, an invitation, an offer, etc* 回绝一请求、邀请、建议等. (**b**) [C] act of refusing 拒绝: *a blunt, flat, curt, etc refusal* 干脆的、断然的、粗率的…拒绝. **2 the refusal** [sing] right to accept or refuse sth before it is offered to others; option 优先取舍权(决定是否接受某事物的优先权): *have the refusal on a car, house, etc* 对是否购买某汽车、房子等, 有优先取舍权. Cf 参看 FIRST REFUSAL (FIRST[1]).

re·fuse[1] /ˈrefjuːs; ˋrɛfjus/ *n* [U] waste or worthless material; rubbish 废料; 废物; 垃圾: *kitchen, garden, household, etc refuse* 厨房里的、花园里的、家里的…垃圾 ○ [attrib 作定语] *a refuse bag, dump, bin, etc* 垃圾袋、堆、箱等 ○ *refuse disposal* 废料的处理.

□ ˈ**refuse collector** (*fml* 文) = DUSTMAN (DUST).

re·fuse[2] /rɪˈfjuːz; rɪˋfjuz/ *v* [I, Tn, Tt, Dn·n] say or show that one is unwilling to give, accept, grant or do sth 拒绝; 回绝: *refuse one's consent, help, permission* 不同意、不愿帮助、不允许 ○ *refuse a gift, an offer, an invitation* 拒绝接受一礼物、建议、邀请 ○ *She refused him/his proposal of marriage.* 他向她求婚, 她拒绝了. ○ *Our application for visas was refused.* 我们的签证申请没有获得批准. ○ *The car absolutely refused to start.* 这辆汽车完全发动不起来. ○ *I was refused admittance.* 未准许我进去. Cf 参看 AGREE 1.

re·fute /rɪˈfjuːt; rɪˋfjut/ *v* [Tn] prove (a statement, an opinion, etc or a person) to be wrong 证明(某说法、意见等或某人)不对; 反驳; 驳斥: *refute a claim, a theory, an argument* 驳斥某要求、理论、论点 ○ *refute an opponent* 反驳对方.

▷ **re·fut·able** /-əbl, *also* ˈrefjʊtəbl; -əbl̩/ *adj* that can be refuted 可反驳的; 可驳斥的.

re·futa·tion /ˌrefjuːˈteɪʃn; ˌrɛfjuˋteʃən/ *n* **1** [U] refuting or being refuted 反驳; 驳斥; 辩驳. **2** [C] argument that refutes sth; counter-argument 作辩驳用的论据; 反驳性论据.

re·gain /rɪˈgeɪn; rɪˋgen/ *v* **1** [Tn] get (sth) back again after losing it; recover 重新获得(失去之事物); 恢复: *regain consciousness* 恢复知觉 ○ *regain one's freedom, health, sight* 恢复自由、健康、视力 ○ *Our troops soon regained possession of the town.* 我部队不久重克该镇. **2** [Tn no passive 不用于被动语态] reach (a place or position) again 再到(某地或某位置): *regain the river bank* 返回河岸 ○ *regain one's footing/balance*, eg after slipping, stumbling, etc 重新站稳[恢复平衡](如滑了一下、绊了一下等之后).

regal /ˈriːgl; ˋrigl̩/ *adj* of, like or fit for a king or queen; royal (似)帝王的; 为帝王而设的; 王室的: *regal dignity, splendour, power* 帝王的威严、豪华、权力 ○ (*fig* 比喻) *The developers made a regal* (ie generous) *offer for the land.* 地产商出高价购买该地. ▷ **reg·ally** /-gəlɪ; -gl̩ɪ/ *adv*.

re·gale /rɪˈgeɪl; rɪˋgel/ *v* [Tn·pr] (*fml or joc* 文或谑) (**a**) **~ sb with sth** amuse or entertain sb (with stories, jokes, etc) (用故事、笑话等)使某人快乐或喜悦: *She regaled us with an account of her school-days.* 她讲她上学时的往事把我们逗得不亦乐乎. (**b**) **~ oneself/sb on/with sth** give (esp choice) food and drink to oneself/sb 以(尤指上等的)食物和饮料供自己[某人]享用: *regale an invalid with fruit and other dainty morsels* 给病人吃水果和美味佳肴 ○ *We regaled ourselves on caviar and champagne.* 我们尽情地享用鱼子酱和香槟酒.

re·galia /rɪˈgeɪlɪə; rɪˋgelɪə/ *n* [U] **1** emblems or robes of royalty used at coronations, eg crown, orb and sceptre (加冕礼中用的)王权的标志(如王冠、宝球和权杖); 王袍: *the king in full regalia* 王袍加身的君王. **2** emblems and costumes of an order (eg the Order of the Garter), or of a certain rank or office 某种勋位(如英国嘉德勋位)或某种官阶或官职的标志和服装: *wearing the mayoral regalia*, ie the mayor's chain of office, etc 戴着市长的职务标志(官职链等).

re·gard[1] /rɪˈgɑːd; rɪˋgɑrd/ *v* **1** [Tn] (*fml* 文) look steadily at (sb/sth) in the specified way 注视, 凝视(某人[某物]): *She regarded him closely, intently, curiously, etc.* 她紧紧地、目不转睛地、好奇地…注视着他. **2** [Tn, Tn·pr, Cn·n/a] **~ sb/sth (with sth); ~ sb/sth as sth** consider or think about sb/sth in the specified way 将某人[某事物]视为; 认为某人[某事物]是: *How is he regarded locally?* 当地的人对他看法如何? ○ *Your work is highly regarded.* 你的工作很受重视. ○ *We regard her behaviour with suspicion.* 我们对她的行为有怀疑. ○ *regard sb unfavourably/with disfavour* 对某人没有好感 ○ *I regard your suggestion as worth considering/as worthy of consideration.* 我觉得你的建议值得考虑. ○ *We regard your action as a crime/as criminal.* 我们认为你这种行为是犯罪行为. ○ *She's generally regarded as a nuisance.* 大家都很讨厌她. **3** [Tn] (usu in negative sentences or questions 通常用于否定句或疑问句) pay attention to (sth); heed 注意(某事物); 留意: *He seldom regards my advice.* 他很少听我的话. ○ *He booked the holiday without regarding my wishes.* 他不考虑我的意愿就把假日的一切都定下来了. **4** (idm 习语) **as regards sb/sth** concerning or connected with sb/sth 关于或至于某人[某事物]: *I have little information as regards his past.* 我对他过去的情况不太了解. ○ *As regards the second point in your letter…* 关于你信中的第二点….

▷ **re·gard·ing** *prep* with reference to (sb/sth); concerning 对于(某人[某事物]); 关于; 至于: *She said nothing regarding your request.* 她对你的要求只字不提.

re·gard[2] /rɪˈgɑːd; rɪˋgɑrd/ *n* **1** [U] **~ to/for sb/sth** attention to or concern for sb/sth; care for sb/sth (对某人[某事物]的)注意或关心: *drive without regard for/to speed limits* 不顾速度限制开快车 ○ *have, pay, show little regard for the feelings of others* 不大顾及别人的感情. **2** [U] **~ (for sb/sth)** esteem or consideration; respect 尊重; 敬重; 尊敬: *hold sb in high/low regard*, ie have a good/bad opinion of sb 尊重[不尊重]某人 ○ *have a great regard for sb's judgement, intelligence, achievements* 极为尊重某人的判断、才智、成就. **3 regards** [pl] (used esp at the end of a letter 尤用于信函的结尾) kind wishes; greeting 致意; 问候: *With kind regards, Yours sincerely…* 谨此致意, …敬上 ○ *Please give/send my regards to your brother.* 请代为向令兄致意. **4** (idm 习语) **in/with regard to sb/sth; in this/that/one regard** in connection with sb/sth; in this/that connection; concerning sb/sth 关于某人[某事物]; 在这[那]点上: *I have nothing to say with regard to your complaints.* 对于你的投诉, 我无可奉告. ○ *He is very sensitive in this regard*, ie concerning this. 他在这方面非常敏感. ○ *We have succeeded in one crucial regard: making this scandal public.* 我们办成了一件大事: 将这件丑事公之于众.

▷ **re·gard·less** *adv* (*infml* 口) paying no attention to sb/sth 不加理会; 不顾: *I protested, but she carried on regardless.* 我极力反对, 但她置之不理仍一意孤行. **regardless of** *prep* paying no attention to (sb/sth); heedless of 不理会(某人[某事物]); 不顾: *regardless of the consequences, danger, expense* 不顾后果、危险、代价

○ *He continued speaking, regardless of my feelings on the matter.* 他不顾及我在此事上的感情继续往下说.

re·gatta /rɪ'gætə; rɪ'gætə/ *n* sporting event at which races are held between rowing-boats or yachts 划船比赛; 赛艇会.

regd *abbr* 缩写 = (*commerce* 商) registered.

re·gency /'ri:dʒənsɪ; 'ridʒənsɪ/ *n* **1** [C] (period of) office of a regent 摄政(期). **2 the Regency** [sing] (in Britain) the period 1810-20, when George, Prince of Wales acted as regent (英国)摄政时期(1810-1820年, 威尔士亲王乔治摄政时期): [attrib 作定语] *Regency architecture, furniture* 英国摄政时期的建筑风格、家具.

re·gen·er·ate /rɪ'dʒenəreɪt; rɪ'dʒɛnə,ret/ *v* **1** [Tn] give fresh strength or life to (sb/sth); restore 赋予(某人[某事物])新的力量或生命; 使恢复: *After his holiday he felt regenerated.* 他休假之后觉得又有了精神. ○ *Their aim is to regenerate British industry.* 他们的目的是复兴英国的工业. **2** [I, Tn] (cause a person or an institution to) reform or improve, esp morally or spiritually 改造或改进(人或机构)(尤指在道德上或精神上): *The party soon regenerated under her leadership.* 该党在她的领导下很快焕然一新.

▷ **re·gen·er·ate** /rɪ'dʒenərət; rɪ'dʒɛnərɪt/ *adj* [usu attrib 通常作定语] (*fml* 文) morally or spiritually reformed (道德上或精神上)新生的, 更新的: *a regenerate society* 观念更新的社会.

re·gen·era·tion /rɪ,dʒenə'reɪʃn; rɪ,dʒɛnə'reʃən/ *n* [U].

re·gen·er·at·ive /rɪ'dʒenərətɪv; rɪ'dʒɛnə,retɪv/ *adj*: *enjoy the regenerative powers of sea air* 享受清新宜人的海上空气.

re·gent /'ri:dʒənt; 'ridʒənt/ (often 常作 **Regent**) *n* person appointed to rule a country while the monarch is too young, old, ill, etc, or is absent 摄政者.

▷ **re·gent** (often 常作 **Regent**) *adj* (following *n*s 用于名词之后) performing the duties of a Regent 摄政的: *the Prince Regent* 摄政王.

reg·gae /'regeɪ; 'rɛge/ *n* [U] type of West Indian popular music and dance with strong rhythms 西印度群岛的节奏很强的流行音乐和舞蹈.

re·gi·cide /'redʒɪsaɪd; 'rɛdʒə,saɪd/ *n* **1** [U] crime of killing a king 弑君罪. **2** [C] person who commits or helps to commit this crime 弑君者; 弑君罪犯或从犯.

re·gime /reɪ'ʒi:m, *also* 'reʒi:m; re'ʒim/ *n* **1 (a)** method or system of government 统治方式或制度; 政体; 政权: *a fascist, military, etc regime* 法西斯、军事统治等政权. **(b)** prevailing method or system of administration (eg in a business) 盛行的管理方式或制度(如商业中的): *changes made under the present regime* 现行管理方法带来的变化 ○ *the old regime versus the new* 新管理制度对旧管理制度. **2** regimen 养生法; 摄生法.

re·gi·men /'redʒɪmən; 'rɛdʒəmən/ *n* (*medical or fml* 医或文) set of rules about diet, exercise, etc aimed at improving sb's health and physical well-being (以增进健康及强身为目的, 在饮食、锻炼等方面规定的)生活制度; 养生法; 摄生法: *follow a strict regimen* 严格地遵守养生之道 ○ *put a patient on a regimen* 为某病人安排生活制度.

re·gi·ment /'redʒɪmənt; 'rɛdʒəmənt/ *n* **1** [CGp] **(a)** (artillery and armour) unit divided into batteries or squadrons (炮兵的和装甲兵的)团: *an attack by three tank regiments* 以三个坦克团的进攻. **(b)** (British infantry) unit, usu based on a city or county, and represented in the field by battalions (英国步兵的)团队(以营编制的作战单位, 通常为从一市或一郡中征集的): *the 1st battalion of the Lancashire Regiment* 兰开夏郡团队第1营 ○ *enlist in a crack* (ie outstanding) *infantry regiment* 加入赫赫有名的团队. **2** [CGp] **~ of sth/sb** (*fig* 比喻) large number of things or people 大量的物或人: *a whole regiment of volunteers* 大批志愿者.

▷ **re·gi·ment** /'redʒɪment; 'rɛdʒə,mɛnt/ *v* [Tn esp passive 尤用于被动语态] (*esp derog* 尤作贬义) force strict discipline on (sb/sth); organize rigidly into groups, patterns, etc 严格地管制(某人[某事物]); 严密地编组、编队等: *regimented school outings* 控制极严的校外远足活动 ○ *tourists regimented into large parties for sightseeing* 编成大组进行观光的游客. **re·gi·menta·tion** /,redʒɪmen'teɪʃn; ,rɛdʒəmɛn'teʃən/ *n* [U].

re·gi·mental /,redʒɪ'mentl; ,rɛdʒə'mɛntl/ *adj* [attrib 作定语] of a regiment 团的; (英国步兵)团队的: *a regimental mascot, band, parade, etc* 团队的吉祥物、乐队、队列 ○ *regimental headquarters, colours, etc* 团指挥部、团旗.

▷ **re·gi·mentals** *n* [pl] uniform of a regiment 团的制服; (英国步兵的)团队制服: *dressed in full regimentals* 身穿全套团队制服.

Re·gina /rɪ'dʒaɪnə; rɪ'dʒaɪnə/ *n* (*Latin* 拉) (used esp in signatures on proclamations or in the titles of lawsuits 尤用于文告之签署或诉讼案件之名称中) reigning queen 女王: *Elizabeth Regina* 伊丽莎白女王 ○ (*law* 律) *Regina v Hay*, ie the Crown versus Hay 王国政府对海伊的讼案. Cf 参看 REX.

re·gion /'ri:dʒən; 'ridʒən/ *n* **1** part of a surface or body or space with or without definite boundaries or characteristic features 物体表面、身体或空间的部分(可有可无边缘或特征); 范围; 部位; 地方; 地区; 区域: *the Arctic, desert, tropical, etc regions* 北极、沙漠、热带等地区 ○ *the northernmost regions of England* 英格兰的最北部地区 ○ *pains in the abdominal region* 腹部的疼痛. **2** administrative division of a country 行政区. **3** (idm 习语) **in the region of sth** approximately (a number, weight, price, etc) 大约(某数量、重量、价格等): *earn (somewhere) in the region of £20 000 a year* 一年约挣20 000英镑.

▷ **re·gional** /-nl; -nl/ *adj* [usu attrib 通常作定语] of a region 局部范围的; 部位的; 地方的; 地区的; 区域的: *the regional wines of France* 法国各地出产的葡萄酒 ○ *organized, listed, etc on a regional basis* 按地区组织的、列出的等. **re·gion·ally** /-nəlɪ; -nlɪ/ *adv*.

re·gis·ter[1] /'redʒɪstə(r); 'rɛdʒɪstɚ/ *n* **1** (book containing an) official list or record of names, items, attendances, etc 登记; 注册; 注册簿; 登记表; 登记簿: *a parish register*, ie listing births, marriages and deaths 牧区登记册(记载出生、婚丧等事项) ○ *Lloyd's Register (of Shipping)* 劳埃德船级社 ○ *the electoral register/the register of voters*, ie of people entitled to vote 选民名册 ○ *make entries in a register* 登记入册 ○ *The class teacher called the (names on the) register.* 任课教师点了名. **2** mechanical device for indicating or recording speed, force, numbers, etc automatically 记录器(自动显示或记录速度、力度、数量等的装置): *a cash register* 现金出纳机. **3** (part of the) range of a human voice or a musical instrument (人声或乐器的)声区: *notes in the upper/middle register* 高[中]声区 ○ *the lower register of a clarinet, tenor, etc* 单簧管、男高音等的低声区. **4** (*linguistics* 语言) range of vocabulary, grammar, etc used by speakers in particular social circumstances or professional contexts 语域(在特定社交场合或专业领域中人们使用的词汇、语法等的范围): *the informal register of speech* 通俗语体 ○ *specialist registers of English*, eg for legal, financial, etc matters 英语的专门术语(如法律、金融等术语). **5** adjustable metal plate for widening or narrowing an opening and regulating draught, esp in a fire-grate 节气门, 调风器(尤指炉箅中的).

□ **'register office** ⇨ REGISTRY OFFICE (REGISTRY).

re·gis·ter[2] /'redʒɪstə(r); 'rɛdʒɪstɚ/ *v* **1** [I, Ipr, Tn, Tn·pr, Cn·a only passive 只用于被动语态, Cn·n/a esp passive 尤用于被动语态] **~ (at/for/with sth); ~ sth (in sth); ~ sb as sth** formally record (a name, an event, a sale, etc) in a list 登记(姓名、事项、销售额等); 注册; 记录: *register at a hotel*, ie book in as a guest 登记入住旅馆 ○ *You must register with the police, the embassy, etc.* 你应该向警方、使馆等登记. ○ *Where can I register* (ie enrol as a student) *for the Arabic course?* 我学习阿拉伯语课程到哪里注册? ○ *register one's car, the birth of a child, a patent* 登记自己的汽车、小孩的出生日、专利 ○ *a State Registered Nurse*, ie one who is officially registered 国家注册护士 ○ *register the house in your name* 把房子登记在你的名下 ○ *She is registered (as) disabled.* 她已登记为伤残者. **2** [Tn, Tn·pr] **~ sth (with sb); ~ sth (at sth)** present sth formally in writing for consideration (以书面形式)提出某事以便考虑: *register a complaint with the authorities* 向当局提出申诉 ○ *register a strong protest at the government's action* 对政府的行动提出强烈抗议. **3 (a)** [I, Tn] (of figures, etc) be indicated or recorded; (of measuring instruments) indicate or record (figures, etc) automatically (指数字等)被显示或记录; (指测量仪器)自动显示或记录(数

字等): *Loss of pressure had not registered on the dials.* 刻度盘未记录压力下降. ○ *The thermometer registered 32°C.* 温度计显示的读数为32°C. (**b**) [Tn] (of a person, his face, his actions, etc) show (emotion, etc) (指人、人的面孔、动作等)显出, 流露(情绪等): *He slammed the door to register his disapproval.* 他砰的一声把门关上以示不满. ○ *Her face registered dismay.* 她脸上流露出惊慌的神色. **4** [I, Ipr, Tn, Tf] **~ (with sb)** (*infml* 口) (of facts, etc) be mentally recorded or fully realized; (of people) remember or notice (sth) (指事实等)铭记在心, 充分了解; (指人)记住或注意到(某事物): *Her name didn't register (with me).* 我没记住她的名字. ○ *I registered (the fact) that he was late.* 我注意到他迟到了. **5** (**a**) [Tn] send (letters, etc) by post, paying extra for compensation against loss or damage 挂号邮寄(信等): *It's wise to register letters containing banknotes.* 信中夹钞票最好寄挂号. (**b**) [esp passive 尤用于被动语态: Tn, Tn·pr] **~ sth (to sth)** send (luggage) by rail or sea, paying extra for compensation against loss or damage (由铁路或海路)挂号托运(行李): *sea baggage registered to Rio* 由海路挂号托运到里约热内卢的行李.

□ **ˌregistered ˈnurse** (*US*) trained nurse licensed by a state authority 注册护士.

ˌregistered ˈpost (*US* **ˌcertified ˈmail**) service by which the sender pays extra for compensation against loss or damage 挂号邮寄. Cf 参看 RECORDED DELIVERY (RECORD[2]).

ˌregistered ˈtrade mark (*abbr* 缩写 **R**; *symb* 符号为 ®) emblem or name, etc of a manufacturer or trader which is officially recorded as identifying his goods 注册商标.

re·gis·trar /ˌredʒɪˈstrɑː(r), ˈredʒɪstrɑː(r); ˌrɛdʒɪˋstrɑr, ˋrɛdʒɪˌstrɑr/ *n* **1** (**a**) official keeper of records or registers, eg of births, marriages and deaths 户籍员. (**b**) official responsible for admissions, examinations, etc at a university 注册主任(大学中主管招生、考试等事务的负责人): *an assistant registrar* 助理注册主任. **2** (*Brit*) senior hospital doctor being trained as a specialist or consultant(2) 专科住院医师.

re·gis·tra·tion /ˌredʒɪˈstreɪʃn; ˌrɛdʒɪˋstreʃən/ *n* **1** [U] registering or being registered 登记; 注册; 挂号: *registration of letters, parcels, trunks, etc* 信件、包裹、衣箱等的挂号 ○ *registration of students for a course/examination* 学生之选课[考试]登记 ○ [attrib 作定语] *registration fees* 注册费. **2** [C] entry in a register 登记或注册的项目: *an increase in registrations for ballet classes* 芭蕾舞班注册人数的增加.

□ **regiˈstration number** series of letters and numbers displayed at the front and back of a vehicle to identify it 机动车的登记号码; 牌照号码. ⇨ illus at App 1 见附录1插图, page xii.

re·gis·try /ˈredʒɪstrɪ; ˋrɛdʒɪstrɪ/ *n* place, eg in a church or university, where registers are kept 登记处, 注册处(如教堂或大学等的).

□ **ˈregistry office** (also **ˈregister office**) place where civil marriages are performed before a registrar, and where records of births, marriages and deaths are made 户籍登记处(由户籍员登记并主持结婚仪式处, 无宗教仪式, 该处并负责记录出生、婚丧等事项).

Re·gius pro·fessor /ˌriːdʒɪəs prəˈfesə(r); ˌridʒɪəs prəˋfɛsɚ/ (*Brit*) professor (esp at Oxford or Cambridge) holding a university chair which was founded by a king or queen, or is filled with the monarch's approval 钦定讲座教授(尤指牛津大学或剑桥大学的)(该职由君主钦定设立或由君主批准任命).

reg·nant (often 常作 **Regnant**) /ˈregnənt; ˋrɛgnənt/ *adj* (*fml* 文) (following *ns* 用于名词之后) reigning 在位的; (君主)统治的, 执政的: *Queen Regnant*, ie one ruling in her own right, not as a consort 执政的女王.

re·gress /rɪˈgres; rɪˋgrɛs/ *v* [I, Ipr] **~ (to sth)** (*fml* 文) return to an earlier or less advanced form or state 退步; 倒退; 回归; 退化.

▷ **re·gres·sion** /rɪˈgreʃn; rɪˋgrɛʃən/ *n* regressing 退步; 倒退; 回归; 退化.

re·gress·ive *adj* regressing or tending to regress 退步的; 倒退的; 回归的; 退化的.

re·gret[1] /rɪˈgret; rɪˋgrɛt/ *n* **1** [U, C] feeling of sadness at the loss of sb/sth; feeling of annoyance, disappointment or repentance 痛惜; 懊悔; 遗憾; 失望; 悔恨: *express, feel regret at/about a missed opportunity* 对错过良机表示、感到懊悔 ○ *I heard of his death with profound/deep/great regret.* 我听到他去世的消息感到万分悲痛. ○ *Much to my regret, I am unable to accept your invitation.* 很抱歉, 我不能接受你的邀请. ○ *I have no regrets about leaving.* 我对离去一事毫不后悔. **2 regrets** [pl] (*fml* 文) (used in polite expressions of refusal, apology, etc 用以表示拒绝、歉意等的客气说法): *give/send one's regrets*, eg in answer to a wedding invitation 深表歉意(如谢绝婚礼邀请) ○ *Please accept my regrets at refusing/that I must refuse.* 有拂雅意, 深以为憾.

▷ **re·gret·ful** /-fl; -fl/ *adj* feeling or expressing regret 痛惜的; 悔恨的; 遗憾的: *a regretful smile, look, etc* 抱歉的笑容、样子等. **re·gret·fully** /-fəlɪ; -fəlɪ/ with regret; sadly 痛惜地; 悔恨地; 遗憾地; 哀伤地: *smile regretfully* 遗憾地微笑 ○ *Regretfully, I must decline.* 很抱歉, 我不得不辞谢.

re·gret[2] /rɪˈgret; rɪˋgrɛt/ *v* (**-tt-**) **1** [Tn, Tf, Tw, Tt, Tg, Tsg] feel regret about (sth sad, annoying, disappointing, etc) 对(伤心、恼人、失望等事)感到惋惜、懊悔、遗憾: *If you go now, you'll regret it*, ie You will wish you had stayed. 假若你现在就走, 一定得后悔. ○ *I regret that I cannot help.* 很抱歉, 此事爱莫能助. ○ *It is to be regretted that...* 遗憾的是... ○ *I regret what I said.* 我很后悔不该说那话. ○ *I regret to say the job has been filled.* 十分抱歉, 那个工作已经有人做了. ○ *We regret to inform you...*, ie used in letters when giving bad news.兹奉告..., 甚以为憾.(用于以书信通知坏消息) ○ *I regret (his) ever having raised the matter.* (他)竟然提出此事, 令人遗憾. **2** [Tn] feel sorrow about (the loss of sb/sth); wish to have (sb/sth) again 对(失去某人[某事物])感到悲伤或惋惜: *regret lost/missed opportunities* 对失去[错过]机会感到惋惜 ○ *His death was regretted by all.* 他去世了, 大家都很悲痛.

▷ **re·gret·table** /-əbl; -əbl/ *adj* that is or should be regretted 令人痛惜的; 令人遗憾的; 可悲的; 不幸的: *regrettable failures, losses, mistakes, etc* 令人惋惜的失败、损失、错误等 ○ *Her rudeness was most/highly regrettable.* 她粗俗无礼, 令人遗憾. **re·gret·tably** /-əblɪ; -əblɪ/ *adv* **1** in a regrettable way 惋惜地; 遗憾地; 可悲地: *a regrettably small income* 少得可怜的收入. **2** it is to be regretted that 十分遗憾; 遗憾的是: *Regrettably, the experiment ended in failure.* 很遗憾, 该试验最后失败了.

re·group /ˌriːˈgruːp; riˋgrup/ *v* [I, Ipr, Tn, Tn·pr] **~ (sth) (for sth)** form into groups again; form (sth) into new groups 重新编组; 重组(某事物): *The enemy regrouped (their forces) for a new attack.* 敌人重新聚集(兵力)准备发起新的进攻.

Regt *abbr* 缩写 = Regiment.

regu·lar /ˈregjʊlə(r); ˋrɛgjəlɚ/ *adj* **1** [esp attrib 尤作定语] happening, coming or done repeatedly at times or places which are the same distance apart 有规律的; 定期的; 定时的: *regular breathing* 均匀的呼吸 ○ *a regular pulse, heartbeat, etc* 正常的脉搏、心跳等 ○ *have regular bowel movements* 大便正常 ○ *have regular habits/be regular in one's habits*, ie do the same things at the same times every day 作息时间有规律 ○ *lampposts placed at regular intervals* 按等距离设置的路灯柱. **2** conforming to a principle or standard of procedure; proper 合乎原则的; 符合规定的; 正当的; 适合的: *He applied for the job through the regular channels*, ie in the accepted way. 他通过正常的途径申请这一工作. ○ *You should sign a contract to make your job situation regular.* 你应该签个合同使你任职合乎规定手续. **3** evenly or systematically arranged; symmetrical 均匀的; 整齐的; 对称的; 匀称的: (*approv* 褒) *her regular teeth, features* 她那整齐的牙齿、匀称的五官 ○ *jets flying in (a) regular formation* 编成整齐队形飞行的喷气式飞机 ○ *a regular geometrical figure*, eg a polygon, with sides and angles equal 规则的几何图形. **4** [esp attrib 尤作定语] (**a**) normal or usual 正常的; 经常的: *my regular doctor, dentist, etc* 经常给我看病的医生、牙医等 ○ *our regular customers, readers, listeners, etc* 我们的老主顾、读者、听众等. (**b**) continuous or habitual; constant 连续的; 习惯性的; 固定不变的: *have no regular work, employment, etc* 没有固定的工作、职业等 ○ *a regular offender*, ie against the law 惯犯 ○ *He was a regular visitor of hers.* 他是她家的常客. **5** [attrib 作定语] belonging to the permanent armed forces of a country 常备军的; 正规军的: *a regular soldier, army, battalion* 正规士兵、军、营. **6** (*grammar*) (of verbs, nouns, etc) having normal inflected forms (指动词、名词等)按规则变化的: *The verb 'go' is not regular, but 'walk' is.* go是不规则动词, walk是规则动词. **7** (*infml often ironic* 口, 常作反语) thorough; complete 彻底的; 完全的: *a regular hero, rascal, genius* 真正的英雄、流氓、天才 ○ *This is a regular mess.* 真是乱七八糟. ○ *You're a regular little charmer, aren't you?* 你真是个小迷人精, 对不对? **8** [attrib 作定语] (*dated US infml* 旧, 口) likeable; good 可爱的; 好的: *He's a regular guy.* 他是个好人. **9** (idm 习语) **(as) ˌregular as ˈclockwork** (*infml* 口) doing sth or occurring at set times in a way that can be depended upon 极有规律: *She arrives every day at five, (as) regular as clockwork.* 她每天五点钟到, 极有规律.

▷ **regu·lar** *n* **1** member of the permanent armed forces of a country 正规军人. **2** (*infml* 口) regular customer or client at a shop, pub, etc (商店、酒馆等的)老主顾, 常客: *He's one of our regulars.* 他是我们的老主顾.

re·gu·lar·ity /ˌregjʊˈlærətɪ; ˌrɛgjəˈlærətɪ/ *n* [U] state of being regular 规律性; 规则性; 经常性: *regularity of attendance at church* 经常去教堂做礼拜 ○ *They meet with great regularity.* 他们定期会面.

regu·larly *adv* **1** at regular intervals or times 有规律地; 经常地; 定期地: *The post arrives regularly at eight every morning.* 邮件每天上午八点钟按时送到. **2** in a regular manner 整齐地; 匀称地: *a garden laid out regularly* 布局很整齐的花园.

regu·lar·ize, -ise /ˈregjʊləraɪz; ˈrɛgjələˌraɪz/ *v* [Tn] make (sth) lawful or correct 使(某事物)合法化或合乎规律: *Illegal immigrants can regularize their position by obtaining the necessary residence permit.* 非法移民获得必要的居留证后即可使身分合法. ▷ **regu·lar·iza·tion, -isation** /ˌregjʊləraɪˈzeɪʃn; *US* -rɪˈz-; ˌrɛgjələrɪˈzeʃən/ *n* [U].

regu·late /ˈregjʊleɪt; ˈrɛgjəˌlet/ *v* [Tn] **1** control or direct (sth) by means of rules and restrictions (以规章制度)控制或管理(某事物): *regulate one's conduct, expenditure, lifestyle* 约束行为、限制消费、节制生活方式 ○ *regulate the traffic* 管理交通 ○ *The activities of credit companies are regulated by law.* 信贷公司的业务受法律制约. **2** adjust (an apparatus, a mechanism, etc) so that it functions as desired; control (speed, pressure, etc) in this way 调校, 校准(仪器、机械等); 控制(速度、压力等): *regulate a clock, radiator, etc* 校准时钟、调节散热器 ○ *This valve regulates the flow of water.* 这个阀门控制着水的流量.

▷ **regu·lator** *n* device that regulates, esp the time 调节器; (尤指)整时器: *a pressure, temperature, etc regulator* 压力、温度等调节器.

re·gu·la·tion /ˌregjʊˈleɪʃn; ˌrɛgjəˈleʃən/ *n* **1** [U] regulating or being regulated; control 管理; 调校; 校准; 调节; 控制: *the regulation of share prices* 股票价格的管制. **2** [C usu *pl* 通常作复数] rule or restriction made by an authority 规章; 规则; 法规; 条例: *regulations laid down for your guidance* 为指导工作而制定的规章制度 ○ *too many rules and regulations* 过多的规章制度 ○ *fire, flood regulations* 防火、防洪条例 ○ *ˈsafety regulations*, eg in factories 安全规则(如工厂中的) ○ *ˈtraffic regulations*, ie made by the police 交通规则 ○ *contrary to/against (the) regulations* 违章. **3** [attrib 作定语] required by the regulations; correct 规定的; 正规的: *in regulation dress, uniform, etc* 穿规定的服装、制服等 ○ *drive at the regulation speed*, eg on motorways 按规定速度行车(如在高速公路上).

re·gur·git·ate /rɪˈgɜːdʒɪteɪt; riˈgɝdʒəˌtet/ *v* (*fml* 文) **1** [Tn] bring (swallowed food) up into the mouth again 使(咽下的食物)反回到口中; 反刍. **2** [I] (of liquid, etc) gush back (指液体等)回涌, 回流. **3** [Tn] (*fig* 比喻) give (opinions, etc gained from others) as if they were one's own 将(别人的意见等)当作自己的表达出: *He's simply regurgitating stuff remembered from lectures.* 他只不过是照背讲义而已. ▷ **re·gur·gita·tion** /rɪˌgɜːdʒɪˈteɪʃn; riˌgɝdʒəˈteʃən/ *n* [U].

re·hab·il·it·ate /ˌriːəˈbɪlɪteɪt; ˌriəˈbɪləˌtet/ *v* [Tn] **1** restore (sb) to a normal life by retraining, medical treatment, etc, esp after imprisonment or illness (通过重新培训、治疗等)使(某人)恢复正常生活(尤指出狱者或病愈者): *rehabilitate the mentally/physically disabled in the community* 使社区中智力[身体]有缺陷的人恢复正常的生活. **2** (*fig* 比喻) restore (sb who has suffered loss of rank, reputation, etc) to his former position; reinstate 恢复(某人)原有的地位、名誉等; 使恢复原状: *rehabilitate a disgraced former leader* 为蒙受耻辱的原领导人恢复名誉.

▷ **re·hab·il·ita·tion** /ˌriːəˌbɪlɪˈteɪʃn; ˌriəˌbɪləˈteʃən/ *n* [U] rehabilitating or being rehabilitated 恢复; 复原: *the patient's slow rehabilitation* 病人的缓慢康复 ○ [attrib 作定语] *a rehabilitation centre*, eg for psychiatric patients 康复中心(如为精神病人设立的).

re·hash /ˌriːˈhæʃ; riˈhæʃ/ *v* [Tn, Tn·pr] **~ sth (into sth)** (*infml derog* 口, 贬) put (ideas, material, etc) into a new form with no great change or improvement 使(意见、材料等)改变形式(并无实质改变): *rehash newspaper articles into a book* 把报上的文章编辑成册 ○ *His answer was just a rehashed version of my lecture.* 他的回答只不过是把我的讲义重复了一遍.

▷ **re·hash** /ˈriːhæʃ; ˈriˌhæʃ/ *n* **1** [sing] rehashed material 只在形式上经过变动的材料: *a rehash of familiar ideas* 对旧思想的翻新. **2** [U] rehashing (形式上的)改变, 翻新.

re·hear /ˌriːˈhɪə(r); riˈhɪr/ *v* (*pt, pp* **reheard** /ˌriːˈhɜːd; riˈhɝd/) [Tn] hear or consider (a case, etc in a lawcourt) again 重新审理或复审(案件等).

▷ **re·hear·ing** *n* reconsideration (of a case, etc) (案件等的)重新审理或复审: *get, be given, demand a rehearing* 获得、被给予、要求重新审理.

re·hearse /rɪˈhɜːs; rɪˈhɝs/ *v* **1** (**a**) [I, Tn] practise (a play, piece of music, etc) for public performance 排练(戏剧、乐曲等); 排演: *rehearse with a full cast, orchestra, etc* 与全体演出人员、管弦乐队等进行预演 ○ *rehearse an opera* 排练歌剧. (**b**) [Tn] supervise or train (sb) by practising in this way (通过排演)指导或训练(某人): *rehearse the actors for the fight scene* 指导演员排练武打场面. **2** [Tn] (*fml* 文) give an account of (sth), esp to oneself; recite 讲述(某事物); (尤指)自述, 背诵: *rehearse one's grievances* 诉苦 ○ *He rehearsed the interview in his mind beforehand.* 他把面试时要说的话预先想好了.

▷ **re·hearsal** /-sl; -sl/ *n* **1** [U] rehearsing 排练; 排演; 训练; 讲述; 背诵: *put a play into rehearsal* 排练一出戏 ○ *have two plays in rehearsal*, ie being rehearsed 有两出戏正在排演. **2** [C] practice performance of a play, opera, etc (戏剧、歌剧等的)排练, 排演: *have/hold/stage a ˈdress rehearsal* 进行彩排. **3** [C] (*fml* 文) account or recital of sth, esp in the mind 讲述; 背诵; (尤指)默诵: *a rehearsal of what he would say* 对要说的话的默诵.

re·house /ˌriːˈhaʊz; riˈhaʊz/ *v* [Tn] give (sb) a new house, flat, etc 向(某人)提供新房子、寓所等: *tenants rehoused during building repairs* 在修房期间予以安排新住处的房客 ○ *the need to rehouse people in the inner cities* 给旧城区的居民提供新住房的需要.

Reich /raɪk; raɪx/ *n* [sing] the former German state (旧时的)德国; (德意志)帝国: *the Third Reich*, ie Germany under the Nazi regime (1933-1945) 第三帝国(1933-1945年纳粹统治下的德国).

reign /reɪn; ren/ *n* (period of) rule of a king or queen 君主的统治; 君主统治时期: *in/during the reign of King Alfred* 在阿尔弗烈德大王统治时期 ○ (*fig* 比喻) *The revolution was followed by a reign of terror*, ie a time of violence. 革命之后随即出现了恐怖统治(暴政时期).

▷ **reign** *v* **1** [I, Ipr] **~ (over sb/sth)** be king, queen or regent; rule 成为国君或摄政王; 当政; 统治: *reign over the country/over one's subjects* 统治国家[臣民]. **2** [I] (*esp fig* 尤作比喻) be dominant; prevail 君临; 支配; 盛行: *Silence reigned*, ie There was complete silence. 万籁俱寂. ○ *the reigning champion, Miss World, etc* 本届的冠军、世界小姐等 ○ *Chaos reigns supreme in our new house.* 我们的新房子里乱极了.

re·im·burse /ˌriːɪmˈbɜːs; ˌriɪmˈbɝs/ *v* [Tn, Tn·pr esp passive 尤用于被动语态, Dn·n, Dn·pr] **~ sth (to sb); ~ sb (for sth)** (*usu fml* 通常作庄重语) pay back to sb (money that he has spent, lost, etc); refund sth 补偿某人(花费、损失等的钱); 偿还某物: *I was reimbursed in full.* 我已得到全部补偿. ○ *All expenses will be reimbursed (to you).* 一切费用都能(给你)报销. ○ *We will reimburse the customer for any loss or damage.* 我们愿赔偿顾客受到的一切损失和损害.

▷ **re·im·burse·ment** *n* [C, U] repayment (of expenses,

R

etc)(费用等的)偿还, 报销.

rein /reɪn; ren/ *n* **1** (**a**) [C often *pl* 常作复数] long narrow strap fastened to the bit of a bridle and used to guide and control a horse 缰绳: *ride on a short/long rein*, ie use more/less control 骑马时拉紧[放松]缰绳. (**b**) **reins** [pl] similar device for restraining a small child 成人牵着幼儿走路用的保护带. **2 reins** [pl] (*fml* 文) means of control 控制手段: *hold, take up, assume, etc the reins of government*, ie (begin to) govern 掌握、取得、执掌...政权. **3** (idm 习语) **give, etc free rein to sb/sth** ⇨ FREE[1]. **keep a tight rein on sb/sth** ⇨ TIGHT.

▷ **rein** *v* (phr v) **rein sth in** slow down or stop (a horse) by pulling back the reins (用缰绳)勒住(马)(使之放慢或止住脚步).

re·in·carn·ate /ˌriːˈɪnkɑːneɪt; ˌriɪnˋkɑrnet/ *v* [esp passive 尤用于被动语态: Tn, Tn·pr, Cn·n/a] **~ sb/sth (in/as sb/sth)** bring back (a soul after death) in another body 使(灵魂)转世; 使(灵魂)投胎: *Some people believe they may be reincarnated in the form of an animal.* 有些人相信他们死后可能转生为动物.

▷ **re·in·carn·ate** /ˌriːɪnˈkɑːneɪt; ˌriɪnˋkɑrnet/ *adj* (*dated* 旧) born again in a new body 转生的; 再生的.

re·in·carna·tion /ˌriːɪnkɑːˈneɪʃn; ˌriɪnkɑrˋneʃən/ *n* (**a**) [U] belief that the soul enters a new (human or animal) body after death 转世说(认为人死后灵魂可投入另一人或动物之躯体内). (**b**) [C] instance of this; new body inhabited in this way 转世; (灵魂的)转世化身.

rein·deer /ˈreɪndɪə(r); ˋrenˌdɪr/ *n* (*pl* unchanged 复数不变) type of large deer with branched antlers, living in the arctic regions 驯鹿(体型较大, 生有枝状角, 生活在北极地区): *a herd of reindeer* 一群驯鹿 ○ [attrib 作定语] *reindeer meat* 驯鹿肉. Cf 参看 CARIBOU.

re·in·force /ˌriːɪnˈfɔːs; ˌriɪnˋfɔrs/ *v* [Tn] **1** make (sth) stronger by adding material, etc (以添加材料等)加固(某物): *reinforce the sleeves of a jumper*, eg with elbow patches 在套头毛衣肘部加补钉 ○ *reinforce a wall, bridge, dyke, etc* 把墙、桥、堤坝等加固. **2** (*fig* 比喻) give more support to (sth); emphasize 给(某事物)更多的支持; 加强: *reinforce sb's opinion, argument, conviction, etc* 支持某人的意见、论点、信念等 ○ *This evidence reinforces my view that he is a spy.* 这个证据证实了我认为他是间谍的这一看法. **3** increase the numbers or military strength of (sth) 增加(某事物)的数量或军事力量: *reinforce a garrison, fleet, etc* 增援驻军、舰队等 ○ *Our defences must be reinforced against attack.* 我们必须加强防御设施以抵抗敌人的进攻.

▷ **re·in·force·ment** *n* **1** [U] reinforcing or being reinforced 加固; 加强; 增援. **2 reinforcements** [pl] extra soldiers, ships, tanks, etc sent to reinforce armed forces, etc 用以增援武装力量等的士兵、舰船、坦克等; 援军.

□ ˌ**reinforced** ˈ**concrete** (also **ferroconcrete**) concrete with metal bars or wires embedded in it to give greater strength 钢筋混凝土.

re·in·state /ˌriːɪnˈsteɪt; ˌriɪnˋstet/ *v* [Tn, Tn·pr, Cn·n/a] **~ sb (in/as sth)** restore sb to a previous (esp important) position 使某人恢复原先的(尤指重要的)职位或地位: *reinstate sb in the post of manager/as manager* 恢复某人的经理职位 ○ (*fig* 比喻) *Sue is now reinstated in his affections*, eg after a quarrel. 休现在又重新得到了他的爱(如在争吵之后). ▷ **re·in·state·ment** *n* [U].

re·is·sue /ˌriːˈɪʃuː; riˋɪʃu/ *v* **1** [Tn, Tn·pr, Cn·n/a] **~ sb (with sth); ~ sth (as sth)** issue again (esp sth that has been temporarily unavailable) 重新发行(尤指暂无之物): *reissue a stamp, coin, magazine, etc* 重新发行邮票、硬币、杂志等 ○ *The novel was reissued as a paperback.* 该小说以平装本的形式再版. **2** [Tn] issue (sth) again, esp after it has been recalled 再发出(某物)(尤指曾收回的): *reissue library books after stocktaking* 经清点后重新出借图书馆的书.

▷ **re·is·sue** *n* thing reissued, esp a reprint of a book in a new format 重新发行之物; (尤指形式一新的)再版书.

re·it·er·ate /riːˈɪtəreɪt; riˋɪtəˌret/ *v* [Tn, Tf] (*fml* 文) say or do (sth) again or repeatedly 再次或反复说或做(某事物): *reiterate a command, question, offer, etc* 重申一项命令、重复一个问题、重提一个建议. Cf 参看 ITERATE.

▷ **re·it·era·tion** /riːˌɪtəˈreɪʃn; riˌɪtəˋreʃən/ *n* [C, U] (instance of) reiterating or being reiterated 重复或反复的话语或行为: (*a*) *reiteration of past excuses* 旧借口的重新搬出.

re·ject /rɪˈdʒekt; rɪˋdʒɛkt/ *v* **1** [Tn, Cn·n/a] refuse to accept (sb/sth) 拒绝接受(某人[某事物]): *reject a gift, a possibility, an opinion, a suggestion* 拒绝接受一件礼物、一种可能性、一条意见、一项建议 ○ *a rejected candidate, applicant, etc* 遭到拒绝的候选人、申请人等 ○ *She rejected his offer of marriage.* 他向她求婚, 她拒绝了. ○ *After the transplant his body rejected* (ie failed to adapt to) *the new heart.* 他的身体对新移植的心脏产生排斥作用. ○ *The army doctors rejected several recruits as unfit.* 军医拒收几名新兵, 认为身体不合格. **2** [Tn] put (sth) aside or throw (sth) away as not to be used, chosen, done, etc; discard 抛弃(某事物); 摈弃; 剔除: *Imperfect articles are rejected by our quality control.* 我们进行质量检验时, 有缺陷的产品均予剔除. ○ *reject over-ripe fruit*, eg when making jam 除去熟透的水果(如制果酱时). **3** [Tn] not give due affection to (sb/sth); rebuff 不给予(某人[某事物])应有的爱; 慢待: *The child was rejected by its parents.* 这孩子未受到父母的疼爱.

▷ **re·ject** /ˈriːdʒekt; ˋridʒɛkt/ *n* rejected person or thing 被拒绝或被抛弃的人或事物: *rejects from an officers' training course* 军官培训课程的不合格者 ○ *export rejects*, ie damaged or imperfect goods 被拒收的出口货物 ○ [attrib 作定语] *reject china, earthenware, etc* 不合格的瓷器、陶器等.

re·jec·tion /rɪˈdʒekʃn; rɪˋdʒɛkʃən/ *n* (**a**) [U] rejecting or being rejected 拒绝; 抛弃. (**b**) [C] instance of this 拒绝; 抛弃: *Her proposal met with continual rejections.* 她的建议一再遭到拒绝.

□ **reˈjection slip** formal note from an editor or a publisher accompanying a rejected article, book, etc 退稿通知单(编辑或出版者附在退稿等上的).

re·jig /ˌriːˈdʒɪɡ; ˌriˋdʒɪɡ/ *v* (**-gg-**) [Tn] **1** re-equip (a factory, plant, etc) for a new type of work 重新装备(工厂等). **2** (*infml* 口) rearrange (sth) 重新布置(某物): *rejig the kitchen to fit in the new cooker* 重新布置厨房以安装新炉具.

re·joice /rɪˈdʒɔɪs; rɪˋdʒɔɪs/ *v* **1** [I, Ipr, It] **~ (at/over sth)** (*fml* 文) feel or show great joy 极欢喜; 极高兴: *rejoice over a victory* 为胜利而欣喜 ○ *rejoice at sb's success* 为某人的成功而高兴 ○ *I rejoice to hear that you are well again.* 得知你身体康复, 甚为欣慰. ○ *We rejoiced that the war was over.* 我们为战争结束而欢欣鼓舞. **2** (phr v) **rejoice in sth** (*joc* 谑) have or glory in (a title, etc) 有(某种称号等); 以(有某种称号等)为荣: *She rejoices in the name of Cassandra Postlethwaite.* 她为有卡桑德拉·波斯尔思韦特这样的名字而引以为荣.

▷ **re·joi·cing** *n* **1** [U] happiness; joy 快乐; 欢喜; 高兴. **2 rejoicings** [pl] expressions of joy; celebrations 欢乐的表现; 庆祝: *loud rejoicings after the victory* 胜利之后的欢呼声.

re·join[1] /ˌriːˈdʒɔɪn; ˌriˋdʒɔɪn/ *v* [Tn] **1** join (sb/sth) again; be reunited with 与(某人[某事物])重新在一起: *rejoin one's group, ship, regiment* 重新回到组里、船上、团里 ○ *She made a detour and rejoined us on the other side of the wood.* 她绕道在树林的另一边与我们重新会合. ○ *This lane rejoins the main road further on.* 这条小巷前端与大路相连. **2** join (sth) together again 使(某物)重新接合: *rejoin the broken pieces* 把碎片重新接好.

re·join[2] /rɪˈdʒɔɪn; rɪˋdʒɔɪn/ *v* [Tf no passive 不用于被动语态] (*fml* 文) say in answer or reply; retort 回答; 反驳: *'You're wrong!' she rejoined.* '你错了!'她答道. ○ *He rejoined that this was quite right.* 他反驳说这很正确.

▷ **re·join·der** /-də(r); -dɚ/ *n* what is said in reply; retort 回答; 反驳: *'No!' was his curt rejoinder.* 他草率地回答了一声'不!'

re·ju·ven·ate /rɪˈdʒuːvəneɪt; rɪˋdʒuvəˌnet/ *v* [Tn esp passive 尤用于被动语态] restore youthful appearance, strength, etc to (sb) 使(某人)恢复青春容貌、活力等: *feel rejuvenated after a holiday* 度假之后感到又有了精神. ▷ **re·ju·vena·tion** /rɪˌdʒuːvəˈneɪʃn; rɪˌdʒuvəˋneʃən/ *n* [U, C]: *undergo a total rejuvenation* 完全恢复了活力.

re·kindle /ˌriːˈkɪndl; riˋkɪndl/ *v* [I, Tn] (cause sth to) light again (将某物)重新点燃: *rekindle the fire by blowing on the ashes* 向灰烬吹气使火复燃 ○ (*fig* 比喻) *rekindle love, enthusiasm, hope, etc* 再次燃起爱情、热

情、希望...之火.

re-laid *pt, pp* of RE-LAY.

re·lapse /rɪˈlæps; rɪˋlæps/ *v* [I, Ipr] **~ (into sth/doing sth)** fall back into a previous condition or a worse state after making an improvement 退回到原来的或更坏的状态; 退步: *relapse into bad habits* 重染恶习 ○ *relapse into unconsciousness, silence, crime* 再度昏迷、恢复平静、再次犯罪 ○ *relapse into smoking twenty cigarettes a day* 又恢复到一天吸二十枝香烟的地步.

▷ **re·lapse** *n* act of relapsing, esp after partial recovery from an illness 倒退; (尤指疾病好转后的)复发: *have/suffer a relapse* 旧病复发.

re·late /rɪˈleɪt; rɪˋlet/ *v* **1** [Tn, Tw, Dn·pr, Dpr·w] **~ sth (to sb)** (*fml* 文) give an account of (facts, experiences, etc); tell (a story, etc) 叙述(事实、经历等); 讲(故事等): *relate the events of the last week* 叙述上周发生的事 ○ *She related (to them) how it happened.* 她(给他们)讲那事发生的经过. **2 (a)** [Tn, Tn·pr] **~ sth to/with sth** connect (two things) in thought or meaning; associate sth with sth (在思想上或意义上)将(两事物)联系起来; 将某事物与另一事物相联系: *It is difficult to relate cause and effect in this case.* 这个案件中的动机与效果很难联系起来. ○ *The report relates high wages to/with labour shortages.* 该报告把工资高与劳动力短缺联系在一起了. **(b)** [Ipr] **~ to sb/sth** be connected with sb/sth else; refer to sb/sth 与他人[他事物]有关; 涉及某人[某事物]: *Wealth is seldom related to happiness.* 财富鲜与幸福相关. ○ *statements relating to his resignation* 与他辞职一事有关的说法 ○ *Does the new law relate only to theft?* 新法规是否只涉及盗窃案? **3** [Ipr] **~ to sb/sth** be able to understand and sympathize with sb/sth 能理解并同情某人[某事物]: *Some adults can't relate to children.* 有些成年人不理解儿童的想法. ○ *I just can't relate to* (ie appreciate) *punk music.* 我对蓬克摇滚音乐简直一窍不通. **4** (idm 习语) **strange to relate/say** ⇨ STRANGE.

▷ **re·lated** *adj* **~ (to sb/sth)** **1** connected or associated with sb/sth (与某人[某事物])有关的, 相联系的: *crime related to drug abuse* 与滥用麻醉药品有关的罪案 ○ *chemistry, biology and other related sciences* 化学、生物学及其他相关的科学. **2** [esp pred 尤作表语] in the same family or class, etc 属于同一家族或种类等: *be closely/distantly related (to sb)* (与某人)是近[远]亲 ○ *two related species of ape* 有亲缘关系的两种猿 ○ *He is related to her by marriage.* 他与她是姻亲. **re·lated·ness** *n* [U] being related 有关; 相关.

re·la·tion /rɪˈleɪʃn; rɪˋleʃən/ *n* **1** [U] **~ (between sth and sth); ~ (to sth)** way in which one person or thing is related to another; similarity, contrast or connection between people, things or events (人或事物与他者的)联系, 关联, 关系: *the relation between rainfall and crop production* 降雨量与作物产量之间的关系 ○ *The cost of this project bears/has/shows no relation to the results*, ie It does not justify them. 此项目的费用与其成果不相称. **2 (a)** [C] person who is related to another; relative 亲戚; 亲属: *a close/near/distant relation of mine* 我的近亲[较近的亲戚/远亲] ○ *a relation by marriage/law* 姻亲. **(b)** [U] family connection; kinship 亲戚关系; 亲属关系: *Is he any relation (to you)?* 他(跟你)是亲戚吗? ○ *He's no relation (to me).* 他(跟我)不是亲戚. ○ *What relation are you (to each other)?* ie How are you related? 你们(彼此之间)是什么亲属关系? **3 relations** [pl] **~s (between sb/sth and sb/sth); ~s (with sb/sth)** links or contacts between people, groups, countries, etc; dealings (人、团体、国家等之间的)关系, 联系; 交往: *diplomatic, international, business relations* 外交、国际、业务关系 ○ *the friendly relations (existing) between our countries* 我们国家之间(存在的)友好关系 ○ *Relations are rather strained* (ie difficult or awkward) *at present.* 目前关系有些紧张. ○ *break off (all) relations with one's family* 与家庭断绝了(一切)联系. **4** (idm 习语) **have (sexual) relations (with sb)** have intercourse (with sb) 与(某人)发生(性)关系; 与(某人)性交. **in/with relation to sb/sth** (*fml* 文) concerning sb/sth; with reference to sb/sth 与某人[某事物]有关; 涉及某人[某事物]. **a poor relation** ⇨ POOR.

▷ **re·la·tion·ship** *n* **1 ~ (between A and B); ~ (of A to/with B)** state of being connected 关系; 关联: *the close relationship between industry and trade/of industry to trade* 工业与贸易间的密切关系. **2 (a) ~ (between A and B); ~ (of A to B)** state of being related by birth or marriage 血缘关系; 姻亲关系: *a father-son relationship* 父子关系. **(b) ~ (between A and B); ~ (of A with B)** emotional or sexual liaison 感情的或性的关系: *have a relationship with sb* 与某人有情 ○ *Their affair did not develop into a lasting relationship.* 他们的暧昧交往未能发展成为持久的关系. **3 ~ (between A and B); ~ (of A with B)** links or contacts; dealings 关系; 联系; 交往: *a purely business relationship* 纯业务关系 ○ *The author had a good working relationship with his editor.* 该作者与编辑之间工作关系很融洽.

NOTE ON USAGE 用法: Compare **relation, relations** and **relationship**. 试比较**relation**、**relations**、**relationship**这三个词. **Relationship** has the widest use, covering many of the meanings of **relation** and **relations.** ☆ **relationship**用法最广, 包括了**relation**和**relations**的许多含义. **1 Relation** and **relationship** can be used of family connections ☆ **relation**和**relationship**可用以表示亲属关系: *A relation of mine is coming to stay.* 我有个亲戚要来此暂住. ○ *'What's your relationship to her?' 'She's my cousin.'* '你跟她是什么亲戚?' '她是我的表妹.' **2 Relationship** can indicate a strong emotional association ☆ **relationship**可以指强烈的感情联系: *Their relationship has lasted many years.* 他们的感情已有很多年了. **3** When speaking about less personal associations or friendships, **relations** or **relationship** is used 若不侧重个人关系或友谊时, 可用**relations**或**relationship**: *Relations with the USSR are improving.* 与苏联的关系正在改善. ○ *Britain has a unique relationship with the USA.* 英国与美国之间的关系很特殊. **4 Relation** and **relationship** can indicate a similarity or correspondence between things ☆ **relation**和**relationship**可以表示事物之间的相似处或一致性: *Some people say that there's no relation/relationship between violence on television and crimes of violence.* 有些人说电视中的暴力镜头与生活中的暴力犯罪并无关系.

rel·at·ive /ˈrelətɪv; ˋrɛlətɪv/ *adj* **1 ~ (to sth)** considered in relation or proportion to sb/sth else; comparative (与他人[他事物])相对的, 成比例的, 比较的: *the relative merits of the two plans, candidates, cars* 两种方案、两个候选人、两辆汽车在相比之下显示出的长处 ○ *Supply is relative to demand.* 供应要与需求保持一定比例. ○ *They are living in relative comfort*, ie compared with other people or with themselves at an earlier time. 他们现在生活比较舒适(与他人或与过去相比而言). Cf 参看 ABSOLUTE 4. **2 ~ to sth** (*fml* 文) (following *ns* 用于名词之后) having a connection with sth; referring to sth 与某事物有关的; 关于或涉及某事物的: *the facts relative to the problem* 与这问题有关的事实 ○ *the papers relative to the case* 关于此案的文件. **3** [attrib 作定语] (*grammar*) referring to an earlier noun, clause or sentence 与前面的名词、主句、从句或句子相关联的: *a relative pronoun, clause, adverb* 关系代词、从句、副词 ○ *The word 'who' in 'the man who came' is a relative pronoun.* 在the man who came这一片语中who这个词是关系代词.

▷ **rel·at·ive** *n* person who is related to another; relation 亲戚; 亲属: *a close/near/distant relative of hers* 她的近亲[较近的亲戚/远亲].

rel·at·ively *adv* **1** in relation or proportion to sb/sth else; comparatively (与他人[他事物])相对地, 比较地: *Considering the smallness of the car, it is relatively roomy inside.* 别看这辆汽车小, 里面还比较宽敞. ○ *Relatively speaking, this matter is unimportant.* 相对来说, 这事并不重要. **2** (*infml* 口) quite; moderately 相当地; 适度地: *In spite of her illness, she is relatively cheerful.* 她尽管有病, 但仍很快乐.

rel·at·iv·ism /ˈrelətɪvɪzəm; ˋrɛlətɪvɪzəm/ *n* [U] belief that truth is not always and generally valid, but is limited by the nature of the human mind 相对主义(认为真理并非在任何时候、任何地方都站得住脚, 而是受到人的认识水平的局限).

re·lat·iv·ity /ˌreləˈtɪvətɪ; ˌrɛləˋtɪvətɪ/ *n* [U] **1** state of being relative(1) 相对性. **2** (*physics* 物) Einstein's theory of the universe, which shows that all motion is relative and treats time as a fourth dimension related to

R

space 相对论.

▷ **re·lat·iv·istic** /ˌreləti'vɪstɪk; ˌrɛlətɪ'vɪstɪk/ *adj* (*esp physics* 尤用于物理学) based on relativity 相对论的.

re·lax /rɪ'læks; rɪ'læks/ *v* **1** (**a**) [I, Tn] (make sth) become less tight, stiff, etc (使某事物)松弛、放松等: *Let your muscles relax slowly.* 让你的肌肉慢慢放松. ○ *relax one's grip, hold, grasp (on sth)* 放松(对某物的)掌握. (**b**) [I, Ipr] **~ (into sth)** become less anxious, worried or formal in manner; be at ease 缓和下来; 变得轻松: *Her features suddenly relaxed.* 她的表情一下子变得轻松了. ○ *I'll only relax when I know you're safe.* 我惟有知道你平安无事才能放心. ○ *His face relaxed into a smile.* 他解颜一笑. **2** [Tn] let (rules, regulations, etc) become less strict or rigid 使(制度、规则等)变得不严或放宽: *We could relax the procedure slightly in your case.* 我们可以根据你的情况通融一些. ○ *Discipline is often relaxed at weekends.* 一到周末纪律往往松弛下来. **3** [I, Tn no passive 不用于被动语态] (make sb) rest after work or effort; calm down (使某人)休息, 放松; 镇定: *A holiday will help you relax after your exams.* 考试之后放个假有助于弛缓紧张情绪. ○ *These pills will relax you and make you sleep.* 这些药丸有镇静催眠作用. **4** [I, Tn] (cause effort, concentration, etc to) become less intense (使干劲、注意力等)松懈, 涣散: *His attention never relaxes.* 他总是精神十分集中. ○ *You cannot afford to relax your vigilance for a moment.* 警惕性是万万不可放松的.

▷ **re·laxa·tion** /ˌri:læk'seɪʃn; ˌrilæks'eʃən/ *n* **1** [U] relaxing or being relaxed 松弛; 放松; 休息; 松懈: *some relaxation of the rules* 对规则的某些放宽. **2** [C, U] (thing done for) recreation or amusement 消遣; 娱乐: *Fishing is his favourite relaxation.* 他最喜爱的消遣是钓鱼.

re·laxed *adj* not feeling or showing worry, anxiety, tenseness, etc 不烦恼的、不焦急的、不紧张的; 轻松的: *look, feel, seem relaxed (about sth)* (对某事物)看起来、感到、似乎很轻松 ○ *a relaxed smile* 轻松的微笑 ○ *a relaxed style of teaching* 使人感到轻松的教学方式.

re·lax·ing *adj* (*derog* 贬) (of climate) making people feel lacking in energy or sluggish; enervating (指气候)使人无精打采的; 使人懒洋洋的.

re·lay /'ri:leɪ; 'rile/ *n* **1** fresh set of people or animals taking the place of others who have finished a period of work 接班的人员或动物: *Rescuers worked in relays to save the trapped miners.* 救援人员轮班工作以营救遇难的矿工. ○ *A new relay of horses was harnessed to the cart.* 用作轮换的马都已套到了那辆马车上. Cf 参看 SHIFT² 2. **2** (also '**relay race**) race between teams in which each member runs, swims, etc part of the total distance, the second, etc member starting when the first, etc finishes (赛跑、游泳等的)接力赛: [attrib 作定语] *a relay team, runner, etc* 接力队、赛跑运动员等. **3** (**a**) (*radio* 无) electronic device for receiving signals and transmitting them again with greater strength, thus increasing the distance over which they are carried 中继设备: [attrib 作定语] *a relay station* 中继站. (**b**) broadcast, programme or telegraph message sent out in this way 无线电转播; 转播的节目; 无线电中继通讯: *a relay from Radio Hamburg* 汉堡广播电台的转播.

▷ **re·lay** /'ri:leɪ, rɪ'leɪ; 'rile, rɪ'le/ *v* (*pt, pp* **relayed**) [Tn, Tn·pr] **~ sth (from...) (to...)** **1** receive and pass on (eg a message) 收到并传出(如信息): *relay the colonel's orders to the troops* 向部队传达上校的命令. **2** (*Brit*) broadcast (sth) by passing signals through a transmitting station 转播(某事): *a concert relayed live from the Royal Albert Hall* 从皇家艾伯特大厅实况转播的音乐会 ○ *The pop festival was relayed all round the world.* 流行音乐会的实况已向全世界转播.

re-lay /ˌri:'leɪ; ˌri'le/ *v* (*pt, pp* **re-laid** /-'leɪd; -'led/) [Tn] lay (a cable, carpet, lawn, etc) again 重新铺设(电缆、地毯、草坪等).

re·lease /rɪ'li:s; rɪ'lis/ *v* **1** [Tn, Tn·pr] **~ sb/sth (from sth)** (**a**) allow (a person or an animal) to go; set free or liberate sb/sth 放走(人或动物); 释放或解放某人[某事物]: *release a prisoner, hostage, kidnap victim, etc (from captivity)* 释放囚犯、人质、被劫持者等 ○ *release a rat from a trap* 把老鼠从夹子上放走 ○ *release the horses into the paddock* 把马放入围场 ○ *She gently released herself from his arms/embrace.* 她轻轻地从他的双臂[拥抱]中挣脱. ○ (*law* 律) *The robber was released on bail.* 该劫犯交保释金后获释. ○ (*fig* 比喻) *Death released him from his sufferings.* 死神解脱了他的痛苦. (**b**) (*fig* 比喻) free (sb) from an obligation 免除(某人)的义务或责任: *release sb from a promise, duty, undertaking, etc* 不要某人履行诺言、尽义务、承担任务等 ○ *release a monk from his vows* 准许一僧人还俗. **2** (**a**) [Tn] remove (sth) from a fixed position; cause (sth) to move freely 将(某物)从固定位置上移走; 使(某事物)自由移动: *release the clutch, handbrake*, eg of a lorry 松开离合器、手闸(如卡车上的) ○ *release a switch, catch, lever, etc* 断开开关、松开掣子、放松手柄 ○ *release the trigger*, eg of a rifle 松开扳机(如步枪上的) ○ *use oil to release a rusted lock* 给生锈的锁加油使之松动. (**b**) [Tn, Tn·pr] (used esp in the expressions shown 尤用于以下示例) let go (one's hold of sb/sth) 放弃(对某人[某事物]的掌握或控制): *release one's grip (on sth)* 松开手(不再抓紧某物) ○ *release one's grasp (of sth)* 松开手(不再抓住某物). **3** [Tn, Tn·pr] **~ sth (from sth)** (*fml* 文) allow sth to fly, fall, etc 让某物飞走、落下等: *release an arrow, bomb, etc* 射箭、投掷炸弹 ○ *The bullet is released from the gun at very high speed.* 子弹自枪膛中高速射出. **4** [Tn, Tn·pr] **~ sth (to sb/sth)** (**a**) allow (news, etc) to be made known 发布(新闻等): *The latest developments have just been released to the media.* 最新的进展情况已向大众传播媒介发表. ○ *The police have released no further details about the crime.* 警方没有透露这一罪案进一步的详情. (**b**) make sth available to the public 向公众提供某事物: *release a film, book, record, etc* 发行影片、书、唱片等 ○ *The new model has now been released for sale (to export markets).* 新型号的产品现已(向出口市场)出售. **5** [Tn] (*law* 律) give up (a right, title, property, etc) to sb else 将(权利、头衔、财产等)让与他人.

▷ **re·lease** *n* **1** [U, C] **~ (from sth)** releasing or being released 放走; 释放; 解脱; 免除; 放松; 投掷; 发表; 让与: *an order for sb's release from prison/captivity* 释放某人出狱[解除某人监禁]的命令 ○ *a feeling of release*, ie of freedom 获得解脱的感觉 ○ (*fig* 比喻) *Death is often a welcome release from pain.* 死神往往是解除痛苦的救星. ○ *the release of a film, record, book, newsflash* 影片的发行、唱片的发行、书籍的发行、简要新闻的发表 ○ *The film is on general release*, ie is being shown widely at local cinemas. 该影片发行面很广(当地影院普遍放映). **2** [C] thing released (RELEASE 4b) 发行或发表的事物: *the latest releases*, ie records, films, etc 最新的发行物(唱片、影片等) ○ *a 'press release*, ie of news, etc for printing or broadcasting 新闻稿(供报道或广播). **3** [C] handle, lever, catch, etc that releases part of a machine 松开机件用的把手、手柄、掣子等; 释放器; 脱扣器; 松脱器: *the 'carriage release*, ie on a typewriter 滑架释放杆(打字机的) ○ [attrib 作定语] *a re'lease gear* 释放装置 ○ *the re'lease button, knob, etc* 释放按钮、旋钮等.

re·leg·ate /'relɪgeɪt; 'rɛləˌget/ *v* [esp passive 尤用于被动语态: Tn, Tn·pr] **~ sb/sth (to sth)** **1** dismiss sb/sth to a lower or less important rank, task or state 使某人[某事物]降级、降职或降低地位: *I have been relegated to the role of a mere assistant.* 已经把我降到只任助手的工作了. ○ *relegate old files to the storeroom* 把旧文件存入储藏室. **2** (*esp Brit*) transfer (a sports team) to a lower division 将(运动队)降至较低等级: *Will Spurs be relegated to the third division?* 斯珀尔斯队会降为丙级队吗? ▷ **re·lega·tion** /ˌrelɪ'geɪʃn; ˌrɛlə'geʃən/ *n* [U]: *teams threatened with relegation* 有降级危险的队.

re·lent /rɪ'lent; rɪ'lɛnt/ *v* [I] **1** decide to be less strict, determined or harsh 决定采取较为温和、缓和或宽容的态度和做法: *Afterwards she relented and let the children stay up late to watch TV.* 后来她宽容了些, 让孩子们晚睡看电视. ○ *The police will not relent in their fight against crime.* 警方在跟犯罪分子的斗争中决不手软. **2** (of the speed or rate of doing sth, etc) become less intense (指做某事等的速度或进度)减弱, 缓和: *The pressure on us to finish this task will not relent.* 我们为完成此项任务受到的压力不会减轻. **3** (of bad weather) improve (指坏天气)变好: *The rain relented just long enough for me to go shopping.* 雨小了一阵, 刚好够我去买东西的时间.

▷ **re·lent·less** *adj* **1** not relenting; strict or harsh 不留

情的; 严格的; 苛刻的: *be relentless in punishing offenders* 惩处犯罪者不手软. **2** not ceasing; constant 不停的; 不间断的: *driven by a relentless urge, ambition, quest, etc for power* 为得到权力一直受到欲望、野心、追求等所驱使 ○ *relentless pursuit, questioning, criticism* 不断的探索、询问、批评 ○ *the relentless pressure of her life as a politician* 她身为政治家一生不断受到的压力. **re·lent·lessly** *adv*. **re·lent·less·ness** *n* [U].

rel·ev·ant /ˈreləvənt; ˋrɛləvənt/ *adj* **~ (to sth/sb)** connected with what is being discussed, what is happening, what is being done, etc 有关的; 切题的: *a highly relevant argument, point, suggestion, etc* 密切相关的论据、论点、建议等 ○ *have all the relevant documents ready* 已把一切有关文件准备妥当 ○ *supply the facts (directly) relevant to the case* 提供与该案(直接)有关的事实 ○ *Colour and sex are hardly relevant when appointing somebody to a job.* 肤色和性别对于任命某人担任某职来说是没有什么关系的. ▷ **rel·ev·ance** /-əns; -əns/ (also **rel·ev·ancy** /-ənsɪ; -ənsɪ/) *n* [U]: *have/bear some relevance to the matter in hand* 与要做的事情有一些关系.

re·li·able /rɪˈlaɪəbl; rɪˋlaɪəbḷ/ *adj* consistently good in quality or performance, and so deserving trust; dependable 可信赖的; 可靠的: *a reliable assistant, witness, report, watch, battery, firm* 可靠的助手、可信的证人、合乎事实的报道、走得准的手表、耐用的电池、有信用的公司 ○ *be a reliable source of information (about sth)* 成为(某事物的)可靠信息来源 ○ *My memory's not very reliable these days.* 近来我的记性不太好.

▷ **re·li·ab·il·ity** /rɪˌlaɪəˈbɪlətɪ; rɪˌlaɪəˋbɪlətɪ/ *n* [U] state or quality of being reliable 可靠(性); 可信(性).

re·li·ably /-əblɪ; -əblɪ/ *adv*: *I am reliably informed that he's about to resign.* 我获得可靠消息说他就要辞职了.

re·li·ance /rɪˈlaɪəns; rɪˋlaɪəns/ *n* [U] **~ on sb/sth** confidence or trust in sb/sth; dependence on sb/sth (对某人[某事物]的)信任, 信赖, 信心: *Don't place too much reliance on his advice.* 别太相信他的意见. ○ *his total, absolute, complete reliance on his colleagues* 他对同事毫无保留的、绝对的、完全的信任.

▷ **re·li·ant** /-ənt; -ənt/ *adj* **~ on sb/sth** [pred 作表语] having reliance on sb/sth; dependent on sb/sth 对某人[某事物]有信心; 信任或依赖某人[某事物]: *He's heavily reliant on bank loans.* 他离不开银行贷款. Cf 参看 SELF-RELIANT.

relic /ˈrelɪk; ˋrɛlɪk/ *n* **1** [C] trace or feature surviving from a past age and serving to remind people of it 遗物; 遗迹; 遗风; 遗俗: *relics of ancient civilizations, rituals, beliefs* 古代文明、礼仪、信仰的遗迹. **2** [C] part of the body, clothes, belongings, etc of a holy person kept after his death as sth to be deeply respected 圣者遗物(圣者的部分遗骸、衣物、所有物等供人崇奉者). ⇨Usage at REST[3] 用法见 REST[3]. **3 relics** [pl] (parts of a) dead body surviving destruction or decay; remnants 遗骸(的部分); 残存部分.

re·lief[1] /rɪˈliːf; rɪˋlif/ *n* **1** [U, sing] **~ (from sth)** lessening or removing of pain, distress, anxiety, etc (痛苦、困苦、忧虑等的)减轻或解除: *bring, seek, find, give, feel relief* 带来、寻求、得到、予以、感到解脱 ○ *doctors working for the relief of suffering, hardship, etc* 为解除病痛、痛苦等而工作的医生 ○ *The drug gives some relief from pain.* 这种药可以减轻一些痛苦. ○ *I breathed/heaved a sigh of relief when I heard he was safe.* 我听到他平安的消息时才松了一口气. ○ *To my great relief/Much to my relief, I wasn't late.* 我最庆幸的是没有迟到. ○ *It's a great relief to find you here.* 见到你在这儿也就放心了. ○ *'What a relief!' she said, as she took her tight shoes off.* 她把夹脚的鞋脱下时说: '可松快了!' **2** [U] that which brings relief(1); assistance given to people in need or to a disaster area 减轻或解除痛苦等的事物; 向需要帮助者或灾区提供的援助: *send relief* (eg food, tents, money, etc) *to those made homeless by floods* 给水灾中无家可归的人发送救援物资(如食品、帐篷、金钱等) ○ *provide relief for refugees* 赈济难民 ○ *go/come to the relief of earthquake victims* 救济地震灾民 ○ *committees for famine relief* 饥荒赈灾委员会 ○ [attrib 作定语] *reˈlief funds, projects, supplies* 救济金、赈灾计划、救济品. **3** [U] **~ (from sth)** thing that reduces tension, relieves monotony or brings pleasing variety 缓和紧张、克服单调或带来可喜的变化的事物: *His jokes provided some comic relief in what was really a dull speech.* 他说的笑话给极沉闷的讲话增加几分轻松气氛. ○ *Two comedians followed* (eg in a variety show) *by way of light relief.* 两名喜剧演员接着上场使观众轻松一下(如杂耍演出中). **4** [C] **(a)** person taking over or following after another's turn of duty 换班人; 接替人; 轮班人: *stand in as Peter's relief* 准备接替彼得 ○ [attrib 作定语] *a reˈlief driver, crew, etc* 轮换的驾驶员、乘务组人员等. **(b)** bus, train, etc supplementing a regular service (正常运营之外)增开的公共汽车、火车等; 加班车: *The coach was full so a relief was put on.* 长途汽车已满员, 所以增开了一辆. ○ [attrib 作定语] *a reˈlief bus, service, etc* 增加的公共汽车、运营服务等. **5** [sing] **~ (of sth)** ending or raising of the siege (of a town, fort, etc) (城镇、要塞等的)解围: *the relief of Mafeking* 马弗京城的解围.

□ **reˈlief road** bypass or other road that vehicles can use to avoid an area of heavy traffic (为免交通阻塞使用的)备用车道, 旁道.

re·lief[2] /rɪˈliːf; rɪˋlif/ *n* **1 (a)** [U] method of carving or moulding in which a design stands out from a flat surface 浮雕(法): *in high/low relief*, ie with the background cut out deeply/shallowly 深[浅]浮雕. **(b)** [C] design or carving made in this way 浮雕图; 浮雕品. **2** [U] (in drawing, etc) appearance of being done in relief by the use of shading, colour etc (绘画等中)凸现(用明暗、色彩等方法造成的如浮雕般的效果): (*fig* 比喻) *The hills stood out in sharp relief against the dawn sky.* 拂晓时, 群山的轮廓在天空的映衬下显得很突出. ○ *The MI5 scandal throws the security issue into stark relief*, ie draws attention to its real nature. 英国安全局丑闻发生后, 安全问题显得格外突出. **3** [U] differences of height between hills and valleys, etc 山和山谷等的高度的差异: *a reˈlief map* 地形图 ○ *The relief is clearly shown on this plan.* 在这张平面图上, 地势的起伏表示得很清楚.

□ **reˈlief map** map showing hills, valleys, etc either by shading or by their being moulded in relief (用晕渲法或凸现法显示山、山谷等的)地形图.

re·lieve /rɪˈliːv; rɪˋliv/ *v* [Tn] **1** lessen or remove (pain, distress, anxiety, etc) 减轻或解除(痛苦、困苦、忧虑等): *relieve suffering, hardship, etc among refugees* 解除难民的痛苦、苦难等 ○ *This drug will relieve your discomfort.* 这种药可减轻你的病痛. **2 ~ oneself** (*euph* 婉) empty one's bladder or bowels 解小便或大便. **3** provide aid or assistance for (people in need, a disaster area, etc) 给(需要帮助者、灾区等)提供帮助或救援: *relieve famine in Africa* 救济非洲的饥荒灾区 ○ *The bypass relieves traffic jams in our city centre.* 这条旁道缓解了我们城市中心的交通阻塞情况. **4** introduce variety into (sth) 调剂(某事物): *relieve the tedium/boredom/monotony of waiting* 调剂等候时的乏味[无聊/单调] ○ *Not a single tree relieved the flatness of the plain.* 平原上单调得毫无变化, 连一棵树都没有. **5** release (sb) from a duty or task by taking his place (or finding sb else to do so) 接替(某人)工作; 将(某人)从岗位上轮换下来: *relieve the guard/the watch* 给卫兵[警卫]换岗 ○ *relieve a sentry, workmate, driver* 接替一哨兵、同事、司机 ○ *I'm to be relieved at six.* 六点钟有人来换我的班. **6** end or raise the siege of (a town, fort, etc) 给(某城市、要塞等)解围. **7** (idm 习语) **relieve one's ˈfeelings** make one's emotions easier to bear by weeping, shouting, behaving violently, etc 发泄感情(如藉哭、叫、粗暴行为等). **8** (phr v) **relieve sb of sth** **(a)** (*fml* 文) take (a burden, responsibility, etc) away from sb 解除某人的(负担、责任等): *relieve Mr Brett of his post as manager* 解除布雷特先生的经理职务 ○ *The general was relieved of his command.* 这位将军的指挥权被解除了. **(b)** (*joc* 谑) carry, take charge, etc of sb's personal effects 替某人拿、照管...私人财物: *Let me relieve you of your coat and hat.* 让我替你拿外衣和帽子吧. **(c)** (*infml joc* 口, 谑) rob sb of sth 抢劫或盗取某人的某物: *The thief relieved him of his wallet.* 那小偷把他的钱包偷走了.

▷ **re·lieved** *adj* feeling or showing relief(1) (感到或显出)宽慰的, 放心的: *a relieved smile, look, expression, etc* 宽慰的笑容、样子、表情等 ○ *We were/felt relieved to hear you were safe.* 我们听说你平安无恙而如释重负.

re·li·gion /rɪˈlɪdʒən; rɪˋlɪdʒən/ *n* **1** [U] belief in the existence of a god or gods, who has/have created the universe and given man a spiritual nature which continues to exist after the death of the body 宗教信仰.

R

2 [C] particular system of faith and worship based on such a belief 宗教: *the Christian, Buddhist and Hindu religions* 基督教、佛教和印度教 ○ *practise one's religion* 用自己的宗教信仰指导行动. **3** [sing] (*fig* 比喻) controlling influence on one's life; sth one is devoted or committed to 支配自己生活的大事; 一心追求的或务必做到的事情: *Football is like a religion for Bill.* 对比尔来说, 足球就是他天大的乐趣. ○ *make a religion of always being punctual* 把遵守时间奉为圭臬.

re·li·gious /rɪˈlɪdʒəs; rɪˈlɪdʒəs/ *adj* **1** [attrib 作定语] of religion 宗教的; 宗教上的: *religious worship, belief, faith* 宗教礼拜、信仰 ○ *a religious service* 宗教仪式. **2** (of a person) believing in and practising a religion; devout (指人)笃信宗教的, 虔诚的. **3** [attrib 作定语] of a monastic order 苦修会的: *a religious house*, ie a monastery or convent 苦修院. **4** (*fig* 比喻) scrupulous or conscientious 审慎的; 认真的: *pay religious attention to detail* 对细节一丝不苟 ○ *be religious in one's observance of protocol* 十分讲究礼节.

▷ **re·li·giously** *adv* **1** in a religious(2) way 虔诚地. **2** (*fig* 比喻) scrupulously or conscientiously; regularly 审慎地; 认真地; 有规律地: *I followed the instructions religiously.* 我认真地按指示办事. ○ *She phones him religiously every day.* 她每天照例给他打电话.

re·li·gious·ness *n* [U].

R

re·lin·quish /rɪˈlɪŋkwɪʃ; rɪˈlɪŋkwɪʃ/ *v* (*fml* 文) **1** [Tn] give up or cease to practise, feel, etc (sth); abandon 不再采取(某行动); 不再有(某种感觉); 放弃: *relinquish the struggle for power* 放弃追求权力的斗争 ○ *relinquish bad habits* 戒除坏习惯 ○ *He had relinquished all hope that she was alive.* 他已经放弃了她还活着的一切希望. **2** [Tn, Tn·pr] **~ sth (to sb)** give up or renounce (a claim, etc); surrender sth 放弃(要求等); 让出某事物: *relinquish a right, privilege* 放弃权利、特权 ○ *She relinquished possession of the house to her sister.* 她把房子的所有权让给了她的妹妹. ○ *relinquish a post to one's successor* 把职位让给接替自己的人. **3** [Tn, Tn·pr] (used esp in the expressions shown 尤用于以下示例) cease to hold (sb/sth); release 松手放开(某人[某物]); 放松: *relinquish one's grip (on sb/sth)* 松手放开(某人[某物]) ○ *relinquish one's hold (on sb/sth)* 松手放开(某人[某物]).

rel·iquary /ˈrelɪkwərɪ; *US* -kwerɪ; ˈrɛlə,kwɛrɪ/ *n* container for a relic or relics of a holy person 盛放圣者遗骨或遗物的容器; 圣骨箱; 圣物箱.

rel·ish /ˈrelɪʃ; ˋrɛlɪʃ/ *n* **1** [U] **~ (for sth)** great enjoyment of food, etc; zest (美食等的)享受; 滋味; 美味; 乐趣: *eat, drink with (great) relish* 津津有味地吃、喝 ○ *She savoured the joke with relish.* 她对这个笑话很感兴趣. **2** [U] (used esp in negative sentences 尤用于否定句中) attractive quality; appeal 兴趣; 吸引力; 感染力: *Tennis loses its relish when one gets old.* 人老了就觉得打网球没意思了. ○ *Routine office jobs have no relish at all for me.* 我对坐办公室那种刻板的工作毫无兴趣. **3** [C, U] spicy or strongly-flavoured appetizer served with plain food (有香料或辛辣调料的)开胃小菜, 调味品(加于淡味食物上): *cucumber, sweetcorn, etc relish*, ie for hamburgers, etc 黄瓜、甜玉米等调味品(汉堡包等中的). Cf 参看 PICKLE 1, SAUCE 1.

▷ **rel·ish** *v* [Tn, Tg, Tsg] enjoy or get pleasure out of (sth) 享受(某事物); 从(某事物)中获得乐趣: *relish a meal, drink, joke* 津津有味地吃饭、喝饮料、听笑话 ○ *I don't relish having to get up so early.* 我可不乐意这么早就起床.

re·live /ˌriːˈlɪv; riˋlɪv/ *v* [Tn] go through (an experience, a period of time, etc) again, esp in one's imagination 再体验(某种经历), 再经历(某时期)(尤指在想像中): *relive the horrors of war* 再体验战争的恐怖 ○ *I relived that fateful day over and over in my mind.* 我在思想上不断地重温着那决定不幸命运的日子.

re·lo·cate /ˌriːləʊˈkeɪt; *US* ˌriːˈləʊkeɪt; riˋloket/ *v* [I, Ipr, Tn, Tn·pr] **~ (sb/sth) (from...) (to...)** move (sb/sth) to, or build (sth) in, another place 将(某人[某物])迁往别处; (在新地方)重建(某物): *We're relocating just south of Newcastle.* 我们将迁往纽卡斯尔南部. ○ *The company is to relocate its headquarters in the Midlands.* 公司将把总部迁往英格兰中部. ▷ **re·lo·ca·tion** /ˌriːləʊˈkeɪʃn; ˌriloˋkeʃən/ *n* [U]: *the relocation of industry* 工业区的迁移 ○ [attrib 作定语] *relocation allowances, expenses*, eg for those taking up a new job in a different area 搬迁津贴、搬迁费(如发给调往新地方工作之人员的).

re·luct·ant /rɪˈlʌktənt; rɪˋlʌktənt/ *adj* **~ (to do sth)** unwilling and therefore slow to co-operate, agree, etc 不情愿的; 勉强的: *a reluctant helper, recruit, admirer* 勉强来帮忙的人、勉强入伍的新兵、勉强说好话的人 ○ *She was very reluctant to admit the truth.* 她很不情愿地承认了这事实. ▷ **re·luct·ance** /-əns; -əns/ *n* [U]: *She made a great show of reluctance, but finally accepted our offer.* 她对我们的建议做出极不满意的样子, 但最后还是接受了. ○ *He left us with (some) reluctance.* 他(有些)依依不舍地离开了我们. **re·luct·antly** *adv*: *After much thought, we reluctantly agreed.* 我们考虑再三之后, 勉强同意了.

rely /rɪˈlaɪ; rɪˋlaɪ/ *v* (*pt, pp* **relied**) [Ipr] **~ on/upon sb/sth (to do sth)** **1** count or depend on sb/sth 指望或依赖某人[某事物]: *Nowadays we rely increasingly on computers for help/to help us.* 现今人们越来越依赖计算机协助工作. ○ *I relied on you(r) coming early.* 我指望你早来. ○ *You can rely upon it that it will rain this weekend.* 你放心好了, 本周末一定下雨. ○ *She cannot be relied on to tell the truth.* 别指望她能说真话. **2** have trust or confidence in sb/sth 信任或信赖某人[某事物]: *You can rely on me to keep your secret.* 你尽管相信我一定为你保密.

re·main /rɪˈmeɪn; rɪˋmen/ *v* (usu not used in the continuous tenses 通常不用于进行时态) **1** [I] be left or still present after other parts have been removed or used or dealt with 剩下; 剩余; 遗留: *After the fire, very little remained of my house.* 火灾过后, 寒舍所剩无几. ○ *If you take 3 from 8, 5 remains.* 8减3剩5. ○ *The fact remains that she was lying.* 事实表明她说的是假话. ○ *leave the remaining points for our next meeting* 余下的各点留待下次会议再议. **2** [It] (*fml* 文) be left to be seen, done, said, etc 留待以后去看、去做、去说等: *It remains to be seen* (ie We shall know later) *whether you are right.* 你是否正确, 以后可见分晓. ○ *Much remains to be done.* 要做的事情还很多. ○ *Nothing remains except for me to say goodbye.* 最后我该说一声再见了. **3** [I, Ipr, Ip] (*esp fml* 尤作庄重语) stay in the same place; stay behind 停留; 逗留; 留下: *I remain in London until May.* 我在伦敦一直呆到五月. ○ *The aircraft remained on the ground.* 那飞机仍停在地面. ○ *She left, but I remained (behind).* 她走了, 我没走. **4** [La, Ln] continue to be; stay in the same condition 仍然是; 保持不变: *remain standing, seated, etc* 一直站着、坐着等 ○ *He remained silent.* 他保持沉默. ○ *Let things remain as they are.* 一切保持现状吧. ○ *In spite of their quarrel, they remained the best of friends.* 他们尽管吵过架, 却仍不失为最好的朋友.

re·main·der /rɪˈmeɪndə(r); rɪˋmendɚ/ *n* **1** (usu 通常作 **the remainder**) [Gp] remaining people, things or time; the rest 剩下的人、事物或时间; 剩余部分: *Ten people came but the remainder stayed away.* 来了十个人, 其余的没来. ○ *We spent the remainder of the day sightseeing.* 这天剩下的时间我们到各处观光. **2** [C usu *sing* 通常作单数] (*mathematics* 数) quantity left after subtraction or division 差数; 余数: *Divide 2 into 7, and the answer is 3, (with) remainder 1.* 2除7, 商3余1. ⇨Usage at REST[3] 用法见REST[3]. **3** [C] number of copies of a book left unsold after demand has almost ceased (某书因滞销而积压的)全部剩余册数: [attrib 作定语] *a remainder merchant* 买卖剩余图书的书商.

▷ **re·main·der** *v* [Tn esp passive 尤用于被动语态] sell (unsold copies of a book) at a reduced price 削价出售(滞销的某书).

re·mains /rɪˈmeɪnz; rɪˋmenz/ *n* [pl] **1** what is left after other parts have been removed or used or dealt with 剩余物; 残余: *the remains of a meal, a chicken* 吃剩下的饭、鸡 ○ *the remains of a defeated army* 败军的残余部队 ○ *I rescued the remains of my slipper from the dog.* 我从那狗的口中夺回了我拖鞋的残留部分. **2** ancient buildings, etc that have survived when others were destroyed; ruins (古建筑等的)遗迹, 遗址, 废墟: *the remains of an abbey, of ancient Rome* 寺院、古罗马的遗迹. **3** (*fml* 文) dead body; corpse 遗体; 遗骸: *His mortal remains are buried in the churchyard.* 他的遗体埋葬在教堂的墓地里. ○ *Investigators found a trench* *containing human remains*. 调查人员发现一条沟中有人的尸体. ⇨Usage at REST[3] 用法见 REST[3].

re·make /ˌriːˈmeɪk; riˋmek/ *v* (*pt, pp* **remade** /-meɪd; -ˋmed/) make (esp a film) again or differently 重新制作(尤指影片); 改造; 重做.

▷ **re·make** /ˈriːmeɪk; ˋriˌmek/ *n* thing remade 重制之物; 改制品: *produce a remake of the 1932 original* 重新摄制1932年原拍的影片.

re·mand /rɪˈmɑːnd; *US* -ˈmænd; rɪˋmænd/ *v* [Tn esp passive 尤用于被动语态] send (an accused person) back (from a lawcourt) into custody, esp while further evidence is being gathered 将(被告)还押(尤指为进一步搜集证据时): *The accused was remanded in custody for a week.* 被告还押候审一星期.

▷ **re·mand** *n* [U] **1** remanding or being remanded 还押; 押候: [attrib 作定语] *a remand prisoner* 还押候审的犯人. **2** (idm 习语) **on remand** in a state of being remanded 还押中: *prisoners on remand* 还押中的犯人 ○ *detention on remand* 还押监禁.

□ **reˈmand centre**, **reˈmand home** (*Brit*) place where young offenders are sent temporarily 青少年拘留所.

re·mark /rɪˈmɑːk; rɪˋmɑrk/ *v* **1** [Ipr, Tn, Tf] **~ on/upon sth/sb** say or write (sth) by way of comment; observe 谈论或评论(某事物); 评述: *I couldn't help remarking on her youth.* 我脱口而出说她那么年轻. ○ *The similarity between them has often been remarked on.* 他们之间很相似, 这是常有人提到的事. ○ *'I thought it was odd,' he remarked.* '我觉得很奇怪,'他说. ○ *Critics remarked that the play was not original.* 评论家指出该剧缺乏创意. **2** [Tn] (*dated or fml* 旧或文) take notice of (sth/sb); perceive 注意到(某事物[某人]); 察觉: *remark the likeness between father and son* 注意到父子之间的相似之处.

▷ **re·mark** *n* **1** [C] thing said or written as a comment; observation 评论; 评述; 注意; 察觉: *pointed, cutting* (ie sarcastic) *remarks* 直言不讳的、尖刻的评论 ○ *make a few remarks about sb/on a subject* 讲几句有关某人[某问题]的话 ○ *In the light of* (ie Considering) *your remarks, we rejected her offer.* 鉴于你的评语, 我们拒绝了她的提议. **2** [U] (*dated or fml* 旧或文) notice 注意: *Nothing worthy of remark happened.* 没有发生值得注意的事.

re·mark·able /-əbl; -əbḷ/ *adj* **~ (for sth)** worth noticing or unusual; exceptional 值得注意的; 不寻常的; 独特的: *a remarkable person, feat, event, book* 出类拔萃的人、非凡的业绩、引人瞩目的事件、特别好的书 ○ *a boy who is remarkable for his stupidity* 笨得出奇的男孩. **re·mark·ably** /-əblɪ; -əblɪ/ *adv*.

re·marry /ˌriːˈmærɪ; riˋmærɪ/ *v* (*pt, pp* **-ried**) (**a**) [I] marry sb different 再婚: *The widower did not remarry.* 那鳏夫未曾再娶. (**b**) [Tn] marry (sb) again 与(某人)复婚: *She remarried her former husband ten years after their divorce.* 她与原来的丈夫离婚十年后又复婚了. ▷ **re·mar·riage** /ˌriːˈmærɪdʒ; riˋmærɪdʒ/ *n*.

rem·edy /ˈremədɪ; ˋrɛmədɪ/ *n* **~ (for sth)** **1** [C] (*fml* 文) treatment, medicine, etc that cures or relieves a disease or pain 祛除或减轻病痛的治疗(法)、药物等: *a popular remedy for flu, toothache, cramp* 流感、牙痛、痉挛的常用疗法 ○ *I often use herbal remedies.* 我常用草药治病. ○ *The remedy seems worse than the disease.* 这种疗法比疾病本身更让人难受. **2** [C, U] (*fig* 比喻) means of countering or removing sth undesirable 纠正、矫正或消除某不良事物之方法: *seek a remedy for injustice* 寻求纠正不公之办法 ○ *He found a remedy for his grief in constant hard work.* 他找到了排忧解愁的方法, 就是一刻不停地努力工作. ○ *The mistake is beyond/past remedy*, ie cannot be put right. 这个错误是无法补救的.

▷ **re·med·ial** /rɪˈmiːdɪəl; rɪˋmidɪəl/ *adj* [attrib 作定语] **1** providing, or intended to provide, a remedy or cure 治疗的; 纠正的; 矫正的; 补救的: *undergo remedial treatment/therapy*, eg for backache 接受缓解治疗[疗法](如治疗背痛) ○ *take remedial measures against unemployment* 采取对付失业现象的补救措施. **2** (of education) for slow learners or pupils suffering from disadvantages (指教育)(为后进学生提供)辅导的, 补习的: *remedial classes, lessons, groups, etc* 补习班、课、小组等 ○ *a remedial French course/a course in remedial French* 法语补习课程.

re·medi·able /rɪˈmiːdɪəbl; rɪˋmidɪəbḷ/ *adj* that can be remedied 可治疗的; 可纠正的; 可矫正的; 可补救的.

rem·edy *v* (*pt, pp* **-died**) [Tn] provide a remedy for (sth undesirable); rectify 治理(不良事物); 纠正; 补救: *remedy injustices, mistakes, losses, deficiencies* 消除不公、纠正错误、弥补损失、克服缺点 ○ *The situation could not be remedied*, ie saved. 情况已无可挽救.

re·mem·ber /rɪˈmembə(r); rɪˋmɛmbɚ/ *v* (not usu used in the continuous tenses 通常不用于进行时态) **1** [I, Tn, Tf, Tw, Tt, Tg, Tsg, Cn·n/a] have or keep (sth) in the memory; recall to one's memory 记着或记住(某事物); 回想起: *If I remember rightly the party starts at 8 pm.* 我记得聚会是在下午8点开始. ○ *Have you met my brother? Not as far as I remember.* 你见过我弟弟吗? 我不记得见过他. ○ *I can't/don't remember his name.* 我想不起他的名字了. ○ *Robert's contribution should also be remembered.* 罗伯特的贡献同样应该久志不忘. ○ *Remember (that) we're going out tonight.* 别忘了我们今晚出去. ○ *Do you remember where you put the key?* 你记得你把钥匙放在什么地方了吗? ○ *Remember* (ie Don't forget) *to lock the door.* 别忘了锁门. ○ *I remember posting the letters*, ie I have the memory of doing so in my mind. 我记得把信都寄出去了. ○ *I remember his objecting to the scheme.* 我记得他曾经反对该计划. ○ *I remember her* (ie picture her in my mind) *as a slim young girl.* 我想起她那时还是个苗条的少女. **2** [Tn] give money, etc to (sb/sth) 给(某人[某事物])钱等: *Please remember* (ie Don't forget to tip) *the waiter.* 别忘了给服务员小费. ○ *remember sb in one's will* 在遗嘱中给某人遗赠 ○ *Auntie Jill always remembers my birthday*, eg with a card or present. 吉尔姨在我的生日总送给我礼物. **3** [Tn] **~ oneself** (*fml* 文) stop behaving badly 约束自己的言行: *Bill, remember yourself! Don't swear in front of the children.* 比尔, 注意检点! 别在孩子们面前骂人. **4** [Tn] mention or commemorate (sb), esp in one's prayers 提及或纪念(某人)(尤指在祈祷中): *remember the sick, the old and the needy* 为病人、老人、穷人祈祷 ○ *a church service to remember the war dead* 为纪念战争中的死难者而举行的宗教仪式. **5** (phr v) **remember sb to sb** pass greetings from one person to another 代某人向他人问候: *Please remember me to Jenny.* 请代我问候珍妮. ○ *He asked me to remember him to you.* 他要我代他向你问好.

re·mem·brance /rɪˈmembrəns; rɪˋmɛmbrəns/ *n* (*fml* 文) **1** [U] remembering or being remembered; memory 记忆; 回忆; 记性: *have no remembrance of sth* 不记得某事物 ○ *a service in remembrance of those killed in the war* 纪念战争中死难者的仪式. **2** [C] thing given or kept in memory of sb/sth; memento 纪念物; 纪念品: *He sent us a small remembrance of his visit.* 他送给我们一件他观光的小纪念品.

□ **Reˈmembrance Sunday** (*Brit*) (nearest Sunday to) 11 November, on which those killed in the wars of 1914-18 and 1939-45 are commemorated 阵亡将士纪念日(纪念在1914-1918和1939-1945两次大战中的死难者, 时间在11月11日或最临近该日的星期日). Cf 参看 ARMISTICE DAY (ARMISTICE).

re·mind /rɪˈmaɪnd; rɪˋmaɪnd/ *v* **1** [Tn, Dn·f, Dn·w, Dn·t] inform (sb) of a fact or tell (sb) to do sth he may have forgotten 提醒(某人)注意某事或做某事: *Do I have to remind you yet again?* 还需要我再次提醒你吗? ○ *That* (eg What you've just said, done, etc) *reminds me. I must feed the cat.* 对了, 我该喂猫了(如你刚说的话、刚做的事等提醒了我). ○ *Travellers are reminded that malaria tablets are advisable.* 旅客须知要服用预防疟疾药. ○ *I reminded her how much the fare was.* 我提醒她车票的价钱. ○ *Remind me to answer that letter.* 提醒我回复那封信. **2** [Tn·pr] **~ sb of sb/sth** cause sb to remember or be newly aware of sb/sth 使某人回想起或意识到某人[某事物]: *He reminds me of his brother.* 我见到他便回想起了他的哥哥. ○ *This song reminds me of France.* 我一听到这首歌就想起了法国.

▷ **re·minder** *n* **1** thing which reminds sb of a fact or person 使某人回想起某事或某人的事物; 帮助记忆或起提醒作用的东西: *The statue is a lasting reminder of Churchill's greatness.* 这尊塑像使人永远缅怀邱吉尔的伟大功绩. **2** way of reminding sb to do sth 提醒某人做某事的方式; 提示: *send, give sb a gentle reminder*, eg to pay a bill 婉言提醒某人(如付帐) ○ *The waiters were clearing the tables, which served as a reminder that it was* *time to leave.* 服务员在收拾桌子, 提醒顾客该走了.

re·min·isce /ˌremɪˈnɪs; ˌrɛməˈnɪs/ *v* [I, Ipr] **~ (about sth/sb)** think or talk about past events and experiences, usu with enjoyment 缅怀过去或叙谈往事(通常为愉快地); 回忆; 话旧.

re·min·is·cence /ˌremɪˈnɪsns; ˌrɛməˈnɪsn̩s/ *n* **1** [U] recalling of past events and experiences; reminiscing 回忆; 话旧; 怀旧. **2 reminiscences** [pl] spoken or written account of one's remembered experiences 经验谈; 回忆录: *reminiscences of my youth* 我青年时代的回忆.

re·min·is·cent /ˌremɪˈnɪsnt; ˌrɛməˈnɪsn̩t/ *adj* **1** [pred 作表语] **~ of sb/sth** reminding one of or suggesting sb/sth 使人回想或联想起某人[某事物]: *His style is reminiscent of Picasso's.* 他的艺术风格很像毕加索的. **2** having a tendency to reminisce 怀旧的; 好缅怀往事的: *in a reminiscent mood* 以怀旧的心情. ▷ **re·min·is·cently** *adv*.

re·miss /rɪˈmɪs; rɪˋmɪs/ *adj* [pred 作表语] **~ (in sth)** (*fml* 文) careless of one's duty; lax 玩忽职守; 松懈; 马虎: *You have been very remiss in fulfilling your obligations.* 你一向太不负责了. ○ *It was remiss of her to forget to pay the bill.* 她忘了付帐, 真粗心大意. ▷ **re·missly** *adv*: *act very remissly* 做得极马虎. **re·miss·ness** *n* [U].

re·mis·sion /rɪˈmɪʃn; rɪˋmɪʃən/ *n* **1** [U] pardoning or forgiveness of sins by God (上帝对罪恶的)宽恕, 赦免. **2** [U, C] (**a**) shortening of a prison sentence because of good behaviour (囚犯因表现良好而获得的)刑期减免, 减刑: *get (a) remission of six months/six months' remission* 获减刑六个月. (**b**) freeing from a debt, payment, penalty, etc; exemption (债务、费用、处分等的)免除, 豁免: *gain remission from tax payments* 获准免税 ○ *remission of exam fees* 考试费的免除. **3** [U] lessening or weakening (of pain, disease, etc) (病痛等的)缓解, 减轻: *slight remission of a fever* 体温的稍退.

re·mit /rɪˈmɪt; rɪˋmɪt/ *v* (**-tt-**) (*fml* 文) **1** [Tn esp passive 尤用于被动语态] (**a**) refrain from inflicting (a punishment, etc) 赦免(惩罚等); 宽恕: *His prison sentence has been remitted.* 他的监禁刑罚已获得赦免. (**b**) cancel (a debt, payment, penalty, etc) 取消(债务、费用、处罚等): *The taxes have been remitted.* 税款已免除. ○ *Your fees cannot be remitted.* 你的费用不能免除. **2** [Tn] make (sth) less intense; relax 使(某事物)缓和; 放松: *We must not remit our efforts.* 我们不可松劲. **3** [Tn, Dn·n, Dn·pr] **~ sth (to sb)** send (money, etc) to a person or place, esp by post 汇(款等): *Remit a fee, cheque, payment, etc* 汇寄费用、支票、款项等 ○ *Kindly remit us the balance without delay.* 请立即将余额寄来. ○ *Remit the interest to her new address.* 将利息寄到她的新地址. **4** [Tn·pr] **~ sth to sb** (*law* 律) send (a matter to be decided) to an authority 将(待决事项)提交当局处理: *The case has been remitted from the appeal court to a lesser tribunal.* 此案已由上诉法庭转给下级法庭处理.

▷ **re·mit·tance** /-ns; -n̩s/ *n* **1** [U] remitting of money 汇款. **2** [C] sum of money remitted 所汇的款项: *return the completed form with your remittance* 把填写好的表格连同汇款一并寄回.

re·mit·tent /rɪˈmɪtnt; rɪˋmɪtn̩t/ *adj* (of a fever or disease) becoming less severe at intervals (指发烧或疾病)弛张的, 忽轻忽重的.

rem·nant /ˈremnənt; ˋrɛmnənt/ *n* **1** (often *pl* 常作复数) (**a**) small remaining quantity or part or number of things or people (事物或人)剩余的小部分, 余下的数量: *remnants of a meal* 残羹剩饭 ○ *the remnants of a shattered army* 被击溃的军队的残余部分. (**b**) (*fig* 比喻) surviving trace of sth 遗留的痕迹: *remnants of one's former glory* 自己过去的光荣见证. ⇨Usage at REST[3] 用法见 REST[3]. **2** small piece of cloth or carpet left over from a roll and sold at a reduced price (减价出售的布料或地毯织料的)零头: [attrib 作定语] *a remnant sale* 布头的减价出售.

re·mold (*US*) ⇨RETREAD.

re·mon·strance /rɪˈmɒnstrəns; rɪˋmɑnstrəns/ *n* [U] (*fml* 文) remonstrating; protest 抗议; 抱怨; 反对.

re·mon·strate /ˈremənstreɪt; *US* rɪˈmɒnstreɪt; rɪˋmɑnstret/ *v* [Ipr] **~ with sb**; **~ against sth** (*fml* 文) make a protest or complaint about sb/sth 对某人[某事物]提出抗议; 抱怨: *I remonstrated with him about his rudeness.* 他粗暴无礼, 我给他提了意见. ○ *remonstrate against cruelty to children* 反对虐待儿童.

re·morse /rɪˈmɔːs; rɪˋmɔrs/ *n* [U] **1 ~ (for sth)** sense of deep and bitter regret for having done sth wrong 悔恨; 懊悔; 自责: *He was filled with remorse for having refused to visit his dying father.* 他因不肯去看他垂死的父亲而深怀内疚. ○ *In a fit of remorse she burnt all her lover's letters.* 她在一阵悔恨之中把情人的信都烧了. ○ *The prisoner shows no remorse for his crimes.* 那囚犯对其罪行毫无悔改之意. **2** mercy or pity; compunction 慈悲; 怜惜 (used esp with the *prep* shown 尤与以下示例中之介词连用): *The captives were shot without remorse.* 这些俘虏惨遭枪杀.

▷ **re·morse·ful** /-fl; -fəl/ *adj* filled with remorse(1) 悔恨的; 懊悔的; 自责的: *a remorseful confession, mood* 痛悔的自白、心情. **re·morse·fully** /-fəlɪ; -fəlɪ/ *adv*. **re·morse·ful·ness** *n* [U].

re·morse·less *adj* **1** without mercy or pity 无慈悲心的; 无同情心的: *remorseless cruelty* 残酷无情的虐待. **2** that does not slacken; relentless 不放松的; 持续的: *a remorseless urge, ambition, etc* 永无休止的欲望、野心等. **re·morse·lessly** *adv*: *The police pursued the criminal remorselessly.* 警方追捕那罪犯毫不松劲. ○ *Drugs drove him remorselessly to an early death.* 毒品毫不留情, 过早地夺去了他的生命.

re·mote /rɪˈməʊt; rɪˋmot/ *adj* (**-r**, **-st**) **1** (**a**) **~ (from sth)** far away from other communities, houses, etc; isolated (与其他社区、房子等)远离的, 遥远的, 隔离的: *a remote region, village, farmhouse, etc* 偏僻的地区、村子、农舍等 ○ *in the remotest* (ie most distant) *parts of Asia* 在亚洲的最偏远的地方 ○ *in a house remote from any town or village* 在远离任何城镇或村庄的房子里. (**b**) [attrib 作定语] far away in time (时间上)遥远的, 久远的: *in the remote past/future* 在遥远的过去[未来]. (**c**) [attrib 作定语] distant in relationship or kinship (亲属关系)远的: *a remote ancestor of mine* 我的远祖. (**d**) **~ (from sth)** separate (in feeling, interest, etc); not connected (with sth) (感情、关注的事等方面)距离很大的; (与某事物)无关的: *Your comments are rather remote from the subject we are discussing.* 你的评论跟我们正谈的问题关系不大. ○ *remote causes, effects, etc* 不相干的原因、后果等. **2** (of a person or his manner) cold and unfriendly; aloof (指人或态度)冷淡的, 疏远的, 漠不关心的. **3** small; slight 微小的; 轻微的: *a remote possibility/chance* 微乎其微的可能性[机会] ○ *I haven't the remotest idea who did it.* 是谁做的我一点都不知道. ○ *The connection between the two events is remote.* 这两件事之间没有什么联系.

▷ **re·motely** *adv* (usu in negative sentences 通常用于否定句中) to a very small or slight degree (程度)极微地, 极轻地: *It isn't remotely possible that you will be chosen to go.* 挑选你去的可能性并非很小. ○ *The essay isn't even remotely relevant to the topic.* 这篇文章毫不切题.

re·mote·ness *n* [U].

□ **reˌmote conˈtrol** control of an apparatus, eg a model aircraft, car, etc, from a distance, usu by radio or electrical signals 遥控: *The bomb was exploded by remote control.* 这颗炸弹是遥控引爆的. ○ [attrib 作定语] *a remote conˈtrol panel*, eg for switching channels on a TV set 遥控器(如电视机转换频道用的).

re·mould ⇨RETREAD.

re·mount /ˌriːˈmaʊnt; riˋmaʊnt/ *v* **1** [I, Tn no passive 不用于被动语态] get on (a horse, bicycle, etc) again 重新骑上(马、自行车等). **2** [Tn no passive 不用于被动语态] go up (a ladder, hill, etc) again 再次登(梯、山等). **3** [Tn] put (a picture, photograph, etc) on a new mount 重新装裱(画片、照片等).

▷ **re·mount** /ˈriːmaʊnt; ˋriˌmaʊnt/ *n* fresh horse for a rider 为骑马者新配备的马.

re·move[1] /rɪˈmuːv; rɪˋmuv/ *v* **1** (*esp fml* 尤作庄重语) (**a**) [Tn, Tn·pr] **~ sth/sb (from sth)** take sth/sb away from one place to another 将某物[某人]移到别处; 移开: *remove the dishes (from the table)* (从餐桌上)撤去碗碟 ○ *remove one's hand from sb's shoulder* 把放在某人肩上的手移开 ○ *The statue was removed to another site.* 塑像已挪到另一地方. ○ *They were removed from the English class*, eg to have special lessons. 他们已从英语班转走(如上专设课). (**b**) [Tn, Tn·pr] **~ sb (from sth)** dismiss sb from a post, etc 免去某人的职务等:

remove a diplomat from office 免除一外交官的职务 ○ *He was removed from his position as chairman.* 他被撤去主席的职务. (**c**) [Tn] take off (clothing, etc) from the body 脱下(衣服等): *remove one's hat, coat, gloves, etc* 摘下帽子、脱掉大衣、摘下手套 ○ *remove the bandages/plaster from sb's arm* 解掉某人手臂上的绷带[揭掉某人臂膀上的橡皮膏]. **2** [Tn, Tn·pr] **~ sth (from sth)** (**a**) get rid of sth by cleaning 去掉或清除某物: *remove graffiti from the subway walls* 除去人行隧道墙上乱涂乱画的痕迹 ○ *Washo removes stains!* Washo一到, 污迹全掉! ○ *She removed her make-up with a tissue.* 她用纸巾擦掉脂粉. (**b**) cause sth to disappear; eliminate sth 使某物消失; 消除某物: *remove superfluous hair* 剪去多余的毛发 ○ (*fig* 比喻) *remove problems, difficulties, objections, etc* 解决问题、克服困难、消除反对意见 ○ *remove doubts, fears, etc from sb's mind* 消除某人的疑虑、恐惧等 ○ *The threat of redundancy was suddenly removed.* 裁员的危险顿时消除了. **3** [Ipr] **~ (from sth)** (*fml* 文) go to live or work in another place; move 移居; 迁移: *We are removing from London to the country.* 我们正从伦敦迁往乡下. ○ *Our suppliers have removed to Bath.* 我们的供应厂商已迁往巴斯. **4** (idm 习语) **once, twice, etc removed** (of cousins) belonging to a different generation (指堂、表亲戚)隔一代、两代...的: *a first cousin once removed*, ie a first cousin's child 堂或表兄弟姐妹的子或女.

▷ **re·mov·able** /-əbl; -əbḷ/ *adj* (**a**) that can be removed or detached 可移动的; 可除去的; 可拆卸的: *This coffee-maker has two removable parts.* 这个煮咖啡器有两个部分, 可以拆开. (**b**) [pred 作表语] (of a person) that can be dismissed from office (指人)可免职.

re·moval /-vl; -vḷ/ *n* **1** [U] removing or being removed 移动; 迁移; 免职; 去除. **2** [C] transfer of furniture, etc to a different home 搬迁: [attrib 作定语] *a re'moval van, firm, specialist, etc* 搬迁用车、公司、专门人员等.

re·moved *adj* [pred 作表语] **~ (from sth)** (*fig* 比喻) distinct or different; remote 有区别; 不同; 遥远; 关系远: *an accent not far removed from Cockney* 与伦敦土话差不多的口音 ○ *an explanation far removed from the truth* 与事实相去甚远的解释.

re·mover *n* **1** (in compounds 用以构成复合词) thing that removes sth 移动或去除某物之物: *a stain, paint, nail-varnish, etc remover* 污斑、油漆、指甲油等清除剂. **2** (esp *pl* 尤作复数) person or business that moves sb's furniture, etc, to a new house 代人搬迁的人员或公司: *a firm of removers* 搬运公司.

re·move[2] /rɪˈmuːv; rɪˋmuv/ *n* **1 ~ (from sth)** (*fml* 文) stage or degree of difference or distance (from sth) 差别或距离的阶段或程度; 差距; 间距: *Your story is several removes from the truth.* 你的说法与事实有些距离. ○ *feel a child's suffering at one remove*, ie as a parent 身为父母感受到孩子的痛苦. **2** (*Brit*) class or division in some schools, esp for pupils of about 14 (某些学校的)班或组(尤指约14岁学生的).

re·mu·ner·ate /rɪˈmjuːnəreɪt; rɪˋmjunəˌret/ *v* [Tn, Tn·pr] **~ sb (for sth)** (*fml* 文) pay or reward sb for work or services 酬报某人(为其工作或服务).

▷ **re·mu·nera·tion** /rɪˌmjuːnəˈreɪʃn; rɪˌmjunəˋreʃən/ *n* [U] (*fml or rhet* 文或修辞) payment; reward 酬金; 报酬.

re·mu·nerat·ive /rɪˈmjuːnərətɪv; *US* -nəreɪtɪv; rɪˋmjunəˌretɪv/ *adj* profitable 有报酬的; 付酬的; 有利益的: *a highly remunerative job, post, position, etc* 报酬很高的工作、职务、职位等.

re·nais·sance /rɪˈneɪsns; *US* ˈrenəsɑːns; ˌrɛnəˋsɑns/ *n* **1 the Renaissance** [sing] (period of the) revival of art and literature in the 14th, 15th and 16th centuries, based on classical forms (14、15、16世纪的)文艺复兴; 文艺复兴时期: [attrib 作定语] *Renaissance art, literature, etc* 文艺复兴时期的艺术、文学等. **2** [C] any similar revival 任何类似的复兴; 再生: *Folk music is currently enjoying a renaissance.* 民间音乐现在又时兴起来了.

renal /ˈriːnl; ˋrinḷ/ *adj* [usu attrib 通常作定语] (*anatomy* 解) of, in or near the kidneys 肾脏的; 肾脏中的; 肾脏部位的: *a renal artery* 肾动脉 ○ *renal dialysis* 肾透析.

re·name /ˌriːˈneɪm; riˋnem/ *v* [Tn, Cn·n] give a new name to (sb/sth); name again 给(某人[某事物])重新取名; 改名: *rename a street, a country, a racehorse* 给一条街道、一个国家、一匹赛马重新命名 ○ *The ship was renamed ('Nimrod').* 该船已改名(为尼姆罗德号).

re·nas·cent /rɪˈnæsnt; rɪˋnæsṇt/ *adj* (*fml* 文) becoming active again; reviving 复兴的; 复活的; 再生的: *a renascent interest in medieval times* 对中世纪重新产生的兴趣.

rend /rend; rɛnd/ *v* (*pt, pp* **rent** /rent; rɛnt/) (*arch or fml* 古或文) **1** [Tn, Tn·pr, Tn·p] tear (sth) apart forcibly; split (用力)撕开或撕裂(某物); 使分离: *rend one's garments*, eg (formerly) to show grief or frustration 撕扯自己的衣服(如在旧时表示悲痛或失意之举) ○ *The tiger rent its prey to pieces.* 老虎把猎物撕成碎块. ○ *a country rent in two by civil war* 由于内战而分裂为两部分的国家 ○ *The stone was rent asunder/apart.* 那石块碎裂了. ○ (*fig* 比喻) *Loud cries rent the air.* 吼声冲破云霄. ○ *heart-rending appeals for help* 令人心碎的求助. **2** [Tn·pr] **~ sb/sth (from sb/sth)** pull or wrench sb/sth violently 猛拉或猛夺某人[某物]: *Children were rent from their mothers' arms by the brutal soldiers.* 凶残的士兵把孩子们从母亲的怀抱中夺走了.

ren·der /ˈrendə(r); ˋrɛndɚ/ *v* (*fml* 文) **1** [Tn, Tn·pr, Dn·n, Dn·pr] **~ sth (for sth); ~ sth (to sb)** give sth in return or exchange, or as sth which is due 给予某物作为报偿或用以交换; 回报; 归还: *render homage, obedience, allegiance, etc* 表示敬意、顺从、效忠等 ○ *a reward for services rendered* 服务的酬金 ○ *render good for evil* 以德报怨 ○ *render insult for insult* 以侮辱对侮辱 ○ *render sb a service/render a service to sb* 为某人服务 ○ *render help to disaster victims* 向灾民提供援助 ○ *render thanks to God* 感谢上帝. **2** [Tn] present or send in (an account) for payment 递交或开出(帐单): *account rendered £50* 开出50英镑的帐单. **3** [Cn·a] cause (sb/sth) to be in a certain condition 使(某人[某事物])处于某种状况: *rendered helpless by an accident* 因出事故而束手无策 ○ *Your action has rendered our contract invalid.* 你们的这种做法导致双方的合同失效. **4** [Tn esp passive 尤用于被动语态] give a performance of (music, a play, a character, etc); give a portrayal of (sb/sth) in painting, etc 演奏(音乐); 演出(戏剧); 扮演(角色); 以绘画等表现(某人[某物]): *The piano solo was well rendered.* 那支钢琴独奏曲弹得真好. ○ *'Othello' was rendered rather poorly.* 《奥赛罗》这出戏演得不好. ○ *The artist had rendered her gentle smile perfectly.* 该艺术家把她那温柔的笑容表现得惟妙惟肖. **5** [Tn, Tn·pr] **~ sth (into sth)** express sth in another language; translate sth 翻译某事物: *How would you render 'bon voyage' (into English)?* bon voyage怎样翻译(成英语)? ○ *Rendering poetry into other languages is difficult.* 翻译诗歌是很困难的. **6** [Tn] cover (stone or brick) with a first layer of plaster 在(石或砖)上抹灰泥打底: *render walls* 在墙上抹底灰. **7** (idm 习语) **render an account of oneself, one's behaviour, etc** (*fml* 文) explain or justify what one has said, done, etc 为自己的言行等作解释或辩护. **8** (phr v) **render sth down** make (eg fat, lard) liquid by heating it; melt sth down 将(脂肪、猪油等)熬成油; 熔化某物. **render sth up** (*fml* 文) hand over or surrender sth; yield sth 移交或交出某物; 放弃某事物: *render up a fort, town, etc to the enemy* 放弃要塞、城市等被敌人占领 ○ (*fig* 比喻) *He rendered up his soul to God*, ie died. 他魂归天国了.

▷ **ren·der·ing** /ˈrendərɪŋ; ˋrɛndərɪŋ/ *n* **1** [C, U] (instance of) performing a piece of music or a dramatic role 演奏; 演唱; 扮演; 表演: *a moving rendering of a Brahms song* 勃拉姆斯歌曲动人的演唱 ○ *his rendering of Hamlet* 他扮演的哈姆雷特. **2** [C, U] (instance of) translating (sth written) (文字的)翻译; 译文: *a Spanish rendering/a rendering in Spanish of the original Arabic* 阿拉伯文的西班牙文译文. **3** [C] first layer of plaster (on stone or brick) (石或砖上)打底的灰泥, 底灰.

ren·dez·vous /ˈrɒndɪvuː; ˋrɑndəˌvu/ *n* (*pl* unchanged 复数不变 /-z; -z/) **1 ~ (with sb)** (place chosen for a) meeting at an agreed time 约会; 约会地点: *arrange/make a rendezvous with Bill at the pub at two o'clock* 与比尔约定两点钟在酒馆会面. **2** place where people often meet (经常的)聚会处: *This café is a rendezvous for writers and artists.* 这家小餐馆是作家和艺术家经常聚会的地方.

▷ **ren·dez·vous** *v* [I, Ipr] **~ (with sb)** meet (sb) at a rendezvous 与(某人)在约定地点相会: *The two platoons will rendezvous (with each other) in the woods as planned.* 这两个排按计划在树林里会合.

R

ren·di·tion /ren'dɪʃn; rɛn`dɪʃən/ *n* (*fml* 文) way in which a dramatic role or piece of music, etc is performed; rendering （戏剧角色或音乐作品等的）表演，扮演，演奏，演唱，演出: *give a spirited rendition of a Bach chorale* 充满生气地演唱巴赫的众赞歌.

ren·eg·ade /'renɪgeɪd; `rɛnɪ,ged/ *n* (*fml derog* 文，贬) **1** person that deserts a cause, political party, religious group, etc（事业、政党、宗教团体等的）背叛者，叛党者，叛教者，叛徒，变节分子: [attrib 作定语] *a renegade priest, spy, soldier* 背教的牧师、叛变的间谍、倒戈的士兵. **2** any outlaw or rebel 亡命徒；造反者: *bands of renegades in the mountains* 山区的匪帮.

re·nege (also **re·negue**) /rɪ'ni:g, rɪ'neɪg; rɪ`nig, rɪ`nɛg/ *v* (*fml* 文) **1** [I, Ipr] **~ (on sth)** fail to keep a promise, one's word, etc 违背诺言等；食言；背信. **2** [I] (in card-games) revoke(2)（纸牌戏中）有牌而违例不跟.

re·new /rɪ'nju:; *US* -'nu:; rɪ`nu/ *v* **1** [Tn] replace (sth) with sth new of the same kind 将（某物）换成新的；更新（某物）: *renew worn tyres, bearings, brake-blocks, etc* 更换磨损的轮胎、轴承、闸瓦等 ○ *renew the water in the goldfish bowl* 给金鱼缸换水 ○ *renew* (ie replenish) *one's stock of coal* 补充煤的储存量 ○ *The light bulb needs renewing.* 灯泡该换新的了. **2** [Tn esp passive 尤用于被动语态] (*fig* 比喻) put new life and vigour into (sb/sth); restore 赋予（某人[某事物]）新的生命和活力；使复元: *work with renewed enthusiasm* 以新的热情工作 ○ *The brandy renewed his strength/energy.* 他喝了白兰地后就又恢复了体力. ○ *After praying, I felt spiritually renewed.* 我祷告之后觉得精神焕然一新. ○ *Her kindness made him regard her with renewed affection.* 她十分体贴，使他对她重生情愫. **3** (**a**) [Tn] take up or begin (sth) again, eg after a break or pause; resume 重新做或开始（某事物）（如中断或休止之后）；恢复: *renew an attack* 重新发起进攻 ○ *We renewed our journey the next day.* 次日我们继续旅行. ○ *renewed outbreaks of terrorist violence* 恐怖分子的暴行又卷土重来 ○ *renew one's efforts/attempts to break a record* 为破纪录而再接再厉. (**b**) [Tn, Tn·pr] **~ sth (with sb/sth)** make or form sth again; re-establish sth 重新缔造或重又形成某事物；重建: *renew a friendship, relationship, acquaintance, etc* 重新建立友谊、关系等 ○ *The pilot renewed contact with the control tower.* 飞行员同指挥塔恢复了联系. (**c**) [Tn] say or state (sth) again; reaffirm 再说或重述（某事物）；重申: *renew a request, complaint, criticism, protest* 再次提出要求、申诉、批评、抗议 ○ *We renewed our marriage vows.* 我们又一次重复了我们的婚誓. ○ *I renewed my offer of help.* 我重申愿给予帮助. **4** [Tn] arrange for (sth) to be valid without a break; extend 使（某事物）延期，续期，延长，延伸: *renew a passport, permit, lease, contract* 延长护照、许可证、租约、合同的期限 ○ *renew one's subscription to a journal, membership of a club, etc* 续订一份刊物、办理俱乐部会员的延期手续 ○ *renew one's library books* (ie extend the period during which one can borrow them) *for another week* 把图书馆的书续借一周.

▷ **re·new·able** /-əbl; -əbl/ *adj* that can be renewed (RENEW 4) 可延长有效期的；可续期的: *Is the permit renewable?* 这个许可证可以延期吗?

re·newal /-'nju:əl; *US* -'nu:əl; -`nuəl/ *n* **1** [U] renewing or being renewed 更新；恢复；重新开始；重建；重申；续期: *Any renewal of negotiations will be welcomed.* 为恢复谈判的任何做法都值得欢迎. ○ *urban renewal,* eg clearing slums to build better housing 市区的重建（如改造贫民区）○ [attrib 作定语] *the renewal date,* eg of a library book, licence, lease, etc 续期日（如图书、执照、租约等）. **2** [C] act of renewing 更新；恢复；重建；延期: *We've dealt with several renewals this week.* 我们本周内处理了几件续约的事.

ren·net /'renɪt; `rɛnɪt/ *n* [U] substance used to curdle milk in making cheese and junket 凝乳酶.

re·nounce /rɪ'naʊns; rɪ`naʊns/ *v* (*fml* 文) **1** [Tn] (**a**) agree to give up ownership or possession of (sth), esp formally 同意放弃（某事物）的所有权或占有权（尤指正式地）: *renounce a claim, title, right, privilege* 宣布放弃要求、头衔、权利、特权. (**b**) give up (esp a habit) voluntarily; abandon 自愿放弃（尤指习惯）；抛弃: *renounce strong drink, cigarettes, dangerous driving* 戒酒、戒烟、改掉危险驾驶的习惯 ○ *They've renounced their old criminal way of life.* 他们已改变了过去那种罪恶的生活方式. ○ *I soon renounced all thought of getting home before dark.* 我不久就完全打消了天黑以前赶到家里的想法. **2** [Tn, Tn·pr] **~ sb/sth (for sth)** reject or stop following sb/sth; repudiate sb/sth 摈弃或背弃某人[某事物]；拒绝承认: *renounce Satan and all his works* 摈弃撒旦及一切罪恶 ○ *renounce terrorism, drugs, etc* 唾弃恐怖主义、毒品等 ○ *renounce a treaty, an agreement, etc* 废除条约、协定等 ○ *renounce one's earlier ideals, principles, convictions, etc* 背弃原先的理想、原则、信仰等 ○ *She renounced Islam for/in favour of Christianity.* 她不再信伊斯兰教而改信基督教. **3** [Tn] refuse to associate with or acknowledge (esp sth/sb with a claim to one's care, affection, etc) 拒绝与（某事物[某人]）发生联系；与（某事物[某人]）断绝关系: *renounce a friendship* 绝交 ○ *He renounced his son (as an unworthy heir).* 他与儿子断绝了父子关系（认为他不配作继承人）.

▷ **re·nounce·ment** *n* [U] = RENUNCIATION 1.

ren·ov·ate /'renəveɪt; `rɛnə,vet/ *v* [Tn] restore (esp old buildings) to good condition 修复（尤指旧建筑物）；整修.

▷ **re·nova·tion** /,renə'veɪʃn; ,rɛnə`veʃən/ *n* **1** [U] renovating or being renovated 修复；整修: *be under renovation* 在修复中 ○ *The college is closed for renovation.* 这所学院停课进行整修. ○ [attrib 作定语] *renovation works, plans, schemes, etc* 整修作业、计划、方案等. **2** [C usu *pl* 通常作复数] act of renovating 修复；整修: *The castle will undergo extensive and costly renovations.* 那城堡要用巨资进行全面整修.

ren·ov·ator /-tə(r); -tɚ/ *n*.

re·nown /rɪ'naʊn; rɪ`naʊn/ *n* [U] (*fml* 文) fame or distinction 名望；声誉: *win renown (as a singer)* 获得（歌唱家的）声誉 ○ *an artist of great renown* 极有名望的艺术家.

▷ **re·nowned** *adj* **~ (as/for sth)** famous; celebrated 著名的；有声望的: *renowned as an actress/for her acting* 出名的女演员[演技].

rent[1] /rent; rɛnt/ *n* **1** [U, C] regular payment made for the use of land, premises, a telephone, machinery, etc; sum paid in this way 租金；地租；房租；（电话、机器等的）租赁费: *owe three weeks' rent/be three weeks behind with the rent* 欠三个星期的租金 ○ *live in a house free of rent,* ie without paying rent 住免缴租金的房子 ○ *Non-payment of rent can mean eviction.* 不交租金就可能被赶出去. ○ *pay a high/low rent for farming land* 缴纳耕地的高昂的[低廉的]地租 ○ *Rents are going up again.* 租金又涨了. ○ [attrib 作定语] *a rent book, agreement, collector* 租金登记簿、租赁协定、收租人. **2** (idm 习语) **for rent** (*esp US*) available to be rented 供租用的；招租的.

▷ **rent** *v* **1** [Tn, Tn·pr] **~ sth (from sb)** pay for the occupation or use of (land, premises, a telephone, machinery, etc) 租借或租用（土地、房屋、电话、机器等）: *rent a holiday cottage from an agency* 向代理公司租用度假村舍 ○ *Do you own or rent your video?* 你的录像机是自己的呢，还是租来的? **2** [Tn, Tn·pr, Tn·p, Dn·n] **~ sth (out) (to sb)** allow sb to occupy or use (land, premises, a telephone, machinery, etc) in return for payment 将（土地、房屋、电话、机器等）出租给某人: *Mr Hill rents this land (out) to us at £500 a year.* 希尔先生把这块地租给我们，租金每年500英镑. ○ *Will you rent me this television?* 你把这台电视机租给我行吗? ⇨ Usage at LET[2] 用法见LET[2]. **3** [I, Ipr] **~ (at/for sth)** be let at a specified rent 以一定租金出租: *The building rents at £3 000 a year.* 这座建筑物以每年3 000英镑的租金出租. ○ (*US*) *an apartment renting for $900 a month* 每月租金为900美元的一套公寓.

rent·able *adj* that can be rented or that yields a rent 可出租的；可收租金的.

rental /'rentl; `rɛntl/ *n* **1** [C] amount of rent paid or received 缴付或收取的租金数额: *pay a telephone rental of £20 a quarter* 每季度缴付电话租金20英镑. **2** [U] renting 租赁: [attrib 作定语] *rental charges* 租赁费.

□ ,**rent-'free** *adj, adv* for which no rent is charged 不收租金（的）: *a* ,*rent-free* '*house* 不收租金的房子 ○ *occupy rooms rent-free* 占用不收租金的房间.

,**rent** '**rebate** rebate of rent payable, given by a local authority to low wage-earners, esp council tenants 租金减免款（地方当局给予低工资者的）.

rent[2] /rent; rɛnt/ *n* torn place in cloth, etc; tear; split

(布的)破裂处; 撕裂; 破裂: (*fig* 比喻) *The sun shone through a rent in the clouds.* 太阳透过云间的缝隙照射出来.

rent[3] *pt, pp* of REND.

re·nun·ci·ation /rɪˌnʌnsɪˈeɪʃn; rɪˌnʌnsɪˈeʃən/ *n* **1** [U] (also **renouncement**) (formal declaration of) giving sth/sb up; renouncing 放弃; 断绝联系; 拒绝承认; 放弃权利或断绝关系的声明: *the king's renunciation of the throne* 国王之宣布退位. **2** [U] habit of renouncing things; self-denial 忘我; 克己: *the virtues of renunciation* 忘我的美德.

re·open /ˌriːˈəʊpən; riˈopən/ *v* [I, Tn] (cause sth to) open again after closing or being closed for a while (使某事物)再开, 再开始, 再打开: *School/Parliament reopens next week.* 下周学校复课[议会复会]. ○ *reopen a shop under a new name* 使某商店换个招牌重开张 ○ *reopen a discussion/debate/dialogue* 重新开始讨论[辩论/对话] ○ *The murder inquiry/case/trial was reopened.* 对此谋杀案的调查[审理/审讯]重新开始了. ○ (*fig* 比喻) *reopen old wounds*, ie cause suffering by referring to painful experiences, disagreements, etc in the past 揭旧伤疤(提及以往的苦难经历、争吵等使人痛苦).

re·order /ˌriːˈɔːdə(r); riˈɔrdɚ/ *v* **1** [I, Tn] order (sth) again; order fresh supplies of (sth) 再订购(某物); 添加订购(同类的某物). **2** [Tn] put (sth) in a new order; rearrange 重新整理或排列(某物); 重安排: *reorder the furniture* 重新布置家具.

▷ **re·order** *n* demand for more or fresh supplies 再订购; 添加订购: *put in a reorder for Oxford dictionaries* 添购牛津词典 ○ [attrib 作定语] *a reˈorder form* 重新订购单.

re·or·gan·ize, -ise *v* /ˌriːˈɔːgənaɪz; riˈɔrgəˌnaɪz/ [I, Tn] organize (sth) again or in a new way 重新组织、改组或整顿(某事物). ▷ **re·or·gan·iza·tion, -isation** /ˌriːˌɔːgənaɪˈzeɪʃn; *US* -nɪˈz-; riˌɔrgənəˈzeʃən/ *n* [U, C].

rep[1] (also **repp**) /rep; rɛp/ *n* [U] textile fabric with a corded effect, used in upholstery and curtains 棱纹平布(用作家具被覆材料及帘幕).

rep[2] /rep; rɛp/ *n* (*infml* 口) = REPRESENTATIVE *n* 2: *working as a rep for a printing firm* 做印刷公司的营业代表.

rep[3] /rep; rɛp/ *n* (*infml* 口) = REPERTORY: *act/appear in rep* 在轮演剧目中演出.

Rep *abbr* 缩写 = (*US*) **1** Representative (in Congress). **2** Republican (party). Cf 参看 DEM.

re·paid *pt, pp* of REPAY.

re·pair[1] /rɪˈpeə(r); rɪˈpɛr/ *v* [Tn] **1** restore (sth damaged or badly worn) to good condition 修理或修补(某物): *repair a road, puncture, watch, shirt* 修路、补洞、修表、补衬衣. **2** put right or make amends for (sth); remedy 纠正或修正(某事物); 补救: *repair an error, omission, etc* 修正错误、弥补疏漏 ○ *repair a broken marriage* 使破裂的夫妻关系和好 ○ *Can the damage done to international relations be repaired?* 国际关系受到的损害还能够弥补吗? Cf 参看 FIX[1] 4, MEND 1.

▷ **re·pair** *n* **1** [U] restoring or being restored to good condition 修理; 修补: *a road under repair* 维修中的道路 ○ *The vase was (damaged) beyond repair*, ie could not be repaired. 这个花瓶已(破得)不能修复了. ○ [attrib 作定语] *a bike repair shop* 自行车修配店. **2** [C usu *pl* 通常作复数] **~ (to sth)** act or result of repairing 修理; 修补: *The shop is closed for repairs*, ie while repair work is being done. 该店停止营业进行整修. ○ *Heel repairs while you wait*, eg in a shoe shop. 修理鞋后跟, 当时修好. **3** (idm 习语) **in good, bad, etc reˈpair; in a good, bad, etc state of reˈpair** in good, bad, etc condition 维修良好、失修: *keep a car in good repair* 对汽车善为保养 ○ *The house is in a shocking state of repair.* 这所房子亟须维修.

re·pair·able /-rəbl; -rəbl̩/ *adj* that can be repaired 可修理的; 可补救的.

re·pairer *n* person who repairs things 修理者; 修理工: *a watch repairer* 修表匠.

re·pair[2] /rɪˈpeə(r); rɪˈpɛr/ *v* [Ipr] **~ to...** (*fml or rhet* 文或修辞) visit, esp frequently or in large numbers 去, 赴(尤指经常地或成群地): *repair to seaside resorts in the summer* 经常前往海滨胜地避暑 ○ *Let's repair to the pub.* 咱们大伙上酒馆去吧.

rep·ar·able /ˈrepərəbl; ˈrɛpərəbl̩/ *adj* (*fml* 文) (of a loss, etc) that can be made good (指损失等)可补救的, 可弥补的. Cf 参看 REPAIRABLE (REPAIR1).

re·para·tion /ˌrepəˈreɪʃn; ˌrɛpəˈreʃən/ *n* (*fml* 文) **1** [U] **~ (for sth)** compensating for damage; making amends for loss 补偿; 赔偿: *make reparation (to God) for one's sins* (向上帝)赎罪. **2 reparations** [pl] compensation for war damages, demanded from a defeated enemy (向战败者索取的)赔偿, 赔款: *exact heavy reparations* 索取巨额赔款.

re·par·tee /ˌrepɑːˈtiː; ˌrɛpɚˈti/ *n* [U] **1** (skill in making) sharp clever retorts 机智而巧妙的应答或反驳; 巧辩的才能: *be good at (the art of) repartee* 善于巧辩. **2** conversation, dialogue, etc consisting of such retorts 妙语如珠的对话、对答等: *indulge in brilliant, witty, etc repartee* 热中于巧妙、机智等的对答 ○ *The repartee flew back and forth across the dinner table.* 宴会上妙语连珠对答如流.

re·past /rɪˈpɑːst; *US* rɪˈpæst; rɪˈpæst/ *n* (*fml* 文) meal 餐; 饭食: *partake of a light, sumptuous, etc repast* 参加便宴、盛宴等.

re·pat·ri·ate /riːˈpætrieɪt; *US* -ˈpeɪt-; riˈpetrɪˌet/ *v* [Tn, Tn·pr] **~ sb (to sth)** send or bring sb back to his own country 将某人遣送回国: *repatriate refugees, prisoners-of-war, immigrants, etc to their homeland* 把难民、战俘、外来移民等遣送回国. ▷ **re·pat·ri·ation** /ˌriːpætrɪˈeɪʃn; *US* riːˌpeɪt-; riˌpetrɪˈeʃən/ *n* [U].

re·pay /rɪˈpeɪ; rɪˈpe/ *v* (*pt, pp* **repaid** /rɪˈpeɪd; rɪˈped/) **1** (**a**) [Tn, Dn·n, Dn·pr] **~ sth (to sb)** pay (money) back; refund sth 付还(钱); 偿还某物: *repay a debt, mortgage, loan, etc* 清偿债务、抵押借款、贷款等 ○ *If you lend me £2, I'll repay it (to you) tomorrow.* 你要是借给我两英镑, 我明天就还(给你). (**b**) [Tn, Dn·n] pay (sb) back; reimburse 将钱付还给(某人); 偿还: *Has she repaid you (the £2)?* 她把(那两英镑)钱还给你了吗? **2** [Tn, Tn·pr] **~ sb (for sth); ~ sth (with sth)** give sb sth in return (for a service); reward sb/sth 以某物酬报某人; 报答某人[某事物]: *How can I ever repay (you for) your kindness?* 我怎么能报答你的恩惠呢? ○ *The firm repaid her hard work with a bonus.* 公司发给她奖金以酬谢她工作努力.

▷ **re·pay·able** /-əbl; -əbl̩/ *adj* that can or must be repaid 可偿还的; 应偿还的; 应报答的.

re·pay·ment *n* **1** [U] repaying 偿还; 付还; 回报: *bonds due for repayment* 到期应偿还的债券 ○ *repayment for your services, efforts* 对你提供的服务、做出的努力的酬报. **2** [C] thing repaid 偿还或回报之物; 付还之款: *make two more repayments to clear the debt* 再付两笔款把债还清 ○ *Repayments can be spread over two years.* 偿还款项可分期于两年偿清. ○ *mortgage/loan repayments* 抵押借款[贷款]的偿还款项.

re·peal /rɪˈpiːl; rɪˈpil/ *v* [Tn] withdraw (a law, etc) officially; revoke 废止(法规等); 撤消; 取消. ▷ **re·peal** *n* [U].

re·peat /rɪˈpiːt; rɪˈpit/ *v* **1** (**a**) [Tn, Tf, Tw] say or write (sth) again once or more than once; reiterate 重复说或写(某事物); 反复重申: *I repeat: the runway is not clear for take-off.* 我再说一遍: 跑道尚未畅通, 不能起飞. ○ *repeat a comment, promise, demand* 重复一个评论、承诺、要求 ○ *Am I repeating myself?* ie Did I say this before? 我以前说过这件事吗? ○ *She repeated what she had said.* 她重复了自己说过的话. (**b**) [Tn] do or make (sth) again once or more than once 重做或重复(某事物): *repeat an action, attempt, attack* 重做一动作、重复一尝试、再次发动进攻 ○ *Such bargain offers can't be repeated.* 这么便宜的价钱不会再有了. ○ *She repeated the waltz as an encore*, eg at a piano recital. 她应听众的要求把华尔兹舞曲又演奏了一遍(如在钢琴独奏会上). (**c**) [I, Tn] **~ (itself)** occur again once or more than once 重复发生; 反复出现: *a repeating decimal* 循环小数 ○ *Does history/the past repeat itself?* ie Do similar events or situations recur? 历史[过去的事件]还会重演吗? (类似的事情或情况还会发生吗?) **2** (**a**) [Tn, Tw] say aloud (sth heard or learnt by heart); recite 复述或背诵(某事物); 朗诵: *Repeat the oath after me.* 跟着我宣誓. ○ *He repeated her statement word for word.* 他一字不差地重复她的话. (**b**) [Tn, Tw, Dn·pr, Dpr·w] **~ sth (to sb)** tell sb else (sth one has heard or been told) 向某人转述(某事物): *His language won't bear repeating*, eg because it's too obscene. 他的话别人实在说不出口(如因太下

流). ○ *Don't repeat what I said (to anyone) — it's confidential.* 别把我的话告诉别人——这是秘密. **3** [I, Ipr] **~ (on sb)** (of food) continue to be tasted from time to time after being eaten, esp as a result of belching (指食物)吃后仍留有余味(尤指因打嗝): *Do you find that onions repeat (on you)?* 你感觉到吃洋葱后口中留有余味吗? **4** [Tn] (*commerce* 商) supply a further consignment of (sth) 再次供应(某物): *repeat an order, a deal* 再次供应同样一批货、一笔交易.

▷ **re·peat** *n* [C] **1** act of repeating; thing repeated 重复; 反复; 复述; 背诵: *a second, etc repeat of a broadcast, TV series, etc* 广播节目、电视系列节目等的第二次...重播 ○ [attrib 作定语] *a repeat performance, showing* 重演、重映 ○ (*commerce* 商) *a repeat order*, ie for another consignment of the same goods (同样货物的)再次订购. **2** (*music* 音) mark indicating a passage that is to be repeated 反复记号.

re·peat·able *adj* [usu pred 通常作表语] that can be repeated 可重复; 可复述: *His comments are not repeatable*, eg because they were rude, obscene, etc. 他的话别人实在说不出口(如因粗俗、下流等).

re·peated *adj* [attrib 作定语] done, said or occurring again and again 反复做的; 反复说的; 反复发生的: *repeated blows, warnings, accidents* 多次的打击、警告、事故. **re·peat·edly** *adv* again and again 一再; 多次; 反复地: *He begged her repeatedly to stop.* 他一再求她停下来.

re·peater *n* (*dated* 旧) **1** revolver or rifle that can be fired many times without being reloaded 转轮手枪; 连发步枪. **2** watch or clock that can strike the last quarter hour or hour again 打簧表; 打簧钟. **3** device that repeats a signal 转播器; 中继器; 增音机.

re·pel /rɪˈpel; rɪˋpɛl/ *v* **(-ll-)** **1** [Tn] drive (sb/sth) back or away; repulse 赶走或驱除(某人[某事物]); 击退: *repel an attacker, attack, invasion* 击退进攻者、进攻、入侵 ○ (*fig* 比喻) *The surface repels moisture*, ie does not allow it to penetrate. 这表层能防潮. **2** [Tn] refuse to accept (sb/sth); spurn 拒绝(某人[某事物]); 唾弃: *She repelled him/his advances*, ie discouraged him/them. 她拒绝了他[他的追求]. ○ *She repelled all offers of help.* 她断然拒绝一切援助. **3** [I, Tn] push (sth) away from itself by an unseen force 排斥(某事物): *North magnetic poles repel (each other).* 磁北极与磁北极互相排斥. **4** [I, Tn] cause a feeling of distaste or disgust in (sb/sth) 使(某人[某事物])厌恶或反感: *Gratuitous violence repels (most people).* 无端使用暴力则激起民愤. ○ *His greasy hair repelled her.* 他头发油腻很讨她嫌.

▷ **re·pel·lent** /-ənt; -ənt/ *adj* **1 ~ (to sb)** arousing distaste or disgust; repulsive 令人厌恶的; 使人反感的; 可憎的: *the repellent smell of rotting meat* 腐肉的难闻气味 ○ *I find his selfishness repellent.* 我很讨厌他那么自私. ○ *The very idea of sniffing glue is repellent to me.* 我一想到吸胶毒就感到恶心. **2** that cannot be penetrated by a specified substance 某种物质无法穿透的; 防...的: *a water-repellent fabric* 防水织物. — *n* [U] **1** chemical that repels insects 驱虫剂: *Rub some of this mosquito-repellent on your legs.* 你在腿上搽点驱蚊剂吧. **2** substance used to make fabric, leather, etc waterproof (涂在织物、皮革等上的)防水剂.

re·pent /rɪˈpent; rɪˋpɛnt/ *v* **1** [I, Ipr, Tn, Tg] **~ (of sth)** (*fml esp religion* 文, 尤用于宗教) feel regret or sorrow about (sth one has done or failed to do) 对(自己的所为)感到懊悔、痛心、悔悟或忏悔: *Repent (of your sins) and ask God's forgiveness.* 你要忏悔, 请求上帝宽恕. ○ *He bitterly repented his folly.* 他对自己干的蠢事后悔已极. ○ *I repent having been so generous to that scoundrel.* 我后悔不该对那坏傢伙如此宽宏大量. **2** (idm 习语) **marry in haste, repent at leisure** ⇨ MARRY.

▷ **re·pent·ance** /-əns; -əns/ *n* [U] **~ (for sth)** regret or sorrow for wrongdoing 懊悔; 痛悔; 悔悟; 悔改; 忏悔: *show signs of repentance* 表现悔改之意.

re·pent·ant /-ənt; -ənt/ *adj* **~ (of sth)** feeling or showing repentance 感到或表示懊悔、悔悟、悔改等的: *a repentant sinner, expression, mood* 表示悔改的罪人、神情、心情 ○ *repentant of his folly* (他)对自己愚蠢的行为感到懊悔.

re·per·cus·sion /ˌriːpəˈkʌʃn; ˌripɚˋkʌʃən/ *n* **1** [C usu *pl* 通常作复数] indirect effect or result (esp unpleasant) of an event, etc; consequence (间接的)影响(尤指不良的); 后果: *His resignation will have serious repercussions on/for the firm.* 他辞职一事对公司影响很大. ○ *the endless repercussions of living on credit* 靠赊欠过日子的无穷后患. **2** (**a**) [U] recoil after an impact (碰撞后)弹回. (**b**) [C] thing thrown back, esp a sound; echo 被弹回的或反弹的事物; (尤指)回响, 回声.

rep·er·toire /ˈrepətwɑː(r); ˋrɛpɚˌtwɑr/ *n* all the plays, songs, pieces, etc which a company, actor, musician, etc knows and is prepared to perform (某一艺术团体、演员、音乐家等可随时演出的)全部节目: *extend one's repertoire*, ie learn sth new 丰富自己的演出项目(学新节目) ○ *That tune is not in my repertoire.* 我演出的节目中没有这个曲子. ○ (*fig* 比喻) *He has a wide repertoire of dirty jokes.* 他一肚子下流笑话.

rep·er·tory /ˈrepətrɪ; *US* -tɔːrɪ; ˋrɛpɚˌtorɪ/ (also *infml* 口语作 **rep**) *n* **1** [U] performance of various plays for short periods by one company (instead of one play for a long time with changes of cast) 轮演剧目(一剧团的多项剧目在短期的轮换演出): *act/work in repertory* 参加轮演剧目演出 ○ *play repertory for two years* 演出两年轮演剧目 ○ [attrib 作定语] *a repertory actor* 参加轮演剧目演出的演员. **2** [C] (*fml* 文) = REPERTOIRE.

□ **ˈrepertory company** permanent company in which each actor plays a variety of parts in a number of plays 轮演剧目剧团.

ˈrepertory theatre theatre in which repertory is performed 上演轮演剧目的剧院.

re·pe·ti·tion /ˌrepɪˈtɪʃn; ˌrɛpɪˋtɪʃən/ *n* **1** (**a**) [U] repeating or being repeated 重复; 反复; 重说; 重写; 重做; 背诵: *learn by repetition* 反复学习. (**b**) [C] act of repeating; recurrence 重复; 反复; 重说; 重写; 重做; 背诵: *after numerous repetitions* 经多次反复 ○ *Let there be no repetition of this behaviour*, ie Don't do it again. 别再干这种事了. **2** [C] copy or replica 复制件; 副本; 拷贝: *a repetition of a previous talk* 前次会谈的副本.

▷ **re·pe·ti·tious** /ˌrepɪˈtɪʃəs; rɛpɪˋtɪʃəs/, **re·pet·it·ive** /rɪˈpetətɪv; rɪˋpɛtɪtɪv/ *adjs* (*usu derog* 通常作贬义) characterized by repetition 重复的; 反复的: *a repetitive job, tune* 重复性的工作、反复的曲调 ○ *repetitive questions* 翻来复去的老问题. **re·pe·ti·tiously**, **re·pet·it·ively** *advs*. **re·pe·ti·tious·ness**, **re·pet·it·ive·ness** *ns* [U].

re·phrase /ˌriːˈfreɪz; riˋfrez/ *v* [Tn] say (sth) again in different words, esp to make the meaning clearer 换用词语说(某事)(尤指深入浅出): *rephrase a remark, question, point, etc* 改换措辞说清一段话、一问题、一要点等.

re·pine /rɪˈpaɪn; rɪˋpaɪn/ *v* [I, Ipr] **~ (at/against sth)** (*fml* 文) feel or show discontent; fret 不满; 埋怨; 发牢骚; 苦恼: *repine at one's misfortune* 哀怨自己的不幸 ○ *repine against Fate* 抱怨命运女神.

re·place /rɪˈpleɪs; rɪˋples/ *v* **1** [Tn] put (sth) back in its place 将(某物)放回原处: *replace the book on the shelf* 把书放回书架上 ○ *replace the receiver*, ie after telephoning 把听筒放回原处(打电话后). **2** [Tn, Cn·n/a] take the place of (sb/sth) 代替, 取代(某人[某事物]): *Robots are replacing people on assembly lines.* 机器人逐渐代替了装配线上的工人. ○ *Can anything replace a mother's love?* 有什么东西能代替母爱吗? ○ *His deputy replaced him as leader.* 他的副手接替他当了领导. **3** [Tn, Tn·pr] **~ sb/sth (with sb/sth)** provide a substitute for sb/sth 更换、替换某人[某事物]: *He is inefficient and must be replaced.* 他不称职, 必须撤换. ○ *replace a broken window (with a new one)* (用新窗户)更换破了的窗户.

▷ **re·place·able** /-əbl; -əbl/ *adj* that can be replaced 可回归原位的; 可代替的; 可更换的.

re·place·ment *n* **1** [U] replacing or being replaced 回归原位; 代替; 更换: *the replacement of worn parts* 磨损零件的更换. **2** [C] **~ (for sb/sth)** person or thing that replaces another 代替或替换他者的人或事物: *find a replacement for Sue* (ie sb to do her work) *while she is ill* 苏珊生病时找个代她工作的人 ○ [attrib 作定语] *replacement staff* 替补人员.

re·play /ˌriːˈpleɪ; riˋple/ *v* [Tn] **1** play (eg a football match that was drawn) again 重新(比赛)(如足球赛之平局后). **2** play (sth recorded) again on a tape-recorder, video recorder, etc 重放(录音、录像等).

▷ **re·play** /ˈriːpleɪ; ˋriˌple/ *n* **1** replayed match 重赛. **2** replaying of a recorded incident or sequence in a game, etc (录制内容的)重放: *an action replay of a penalty kick* 罚点球镜头的重放.

re·plen·ish /rɪˈplenɪʃ; rɪˋplɛnɪʃ/ *v* **1** [Tn, Tn·pr] **~ sth (with sth)** fill sth again 再将某物充满: *Let me replenish your glass*, eg with more wine. 我给你把杯子再斟满吧. ○ *replenish one's wardrobe* 添置衣服. **2** [Tn] get a further supply of (sth) 补充某物: *replenish one's stocks of pet food, timber, notepaper, light bulbs* 添置宠物的食物、木材、信纸、灯泡. ▷ **re·plen·ish·ment** *n* [U].

re·plete /rɪˈpliːt; rɪˋplit/ *adj* [pred 作表语] **~ (with sth)** (*fml* 文) **1** well-fed or full; gorged 饱食; 吃饱喝足: *lions replete with their kill* 捕获猎物后吃得饱饱的狮子 ○ *feel replete after a large meal* 吃一大顿饭后觉得很饱. **2** well stocked or supplied 备足的; 供应充分的: *a house replete with every modern convenience* 现代化设备一应俱全的房子.

▷ **re·ple·tion** /rɪˈpliːʃn; rɪˋpliʃən/ *n* [U] (*fml* 文) state of being replete(1) 充满; 充足; 饱足: *be full to repletion* 很饱.

rep·lica /ˈreplɪkə; ˋrɛplɪkə/ *n* **(a)** exact copy, esp one made by an artist of one of his own pictures, etc 精确的复制品(尤指出自图画等之原作者之手的). **(b)** model, esp one made on a smaller scale 模型; (尤指)按比例缩小的复制品: *make a replica of the Eiffel Tower* 制作埃菲尔铁塔的模型.

▷ **rep·lic·ate** /ˈreplɪkeɪt; ˋrɛplɪ͵ket/ *v* [Tn] (*fml* 文) be or make a copy of (sth); reproduce 复现或复制(某物); 再制造; 再生出: *The chameleon's skin replicates the pattern of its surroundings.* 变色龙的皮肤可随环境改变颜色. **rep·lica·tion** /͵replɪˈkeɪʃn; ͵rɛpləˋkeʃən/ *n* [U].

re·ply /rɪˈplaɪ; rɪˋplaɪ/ *v* (*pt, pp* **replied**) **(a)** [I, Ipr, Tf] **~ (to sb/sth)**; **~ (with sth)** say or make an answer, in speech or writing; respond (以口头或书面形式)回答, 答复: *fail to reply to a question, letter, accusation* 未能回答问题、回信、抗辩指控 ○ *I replied with a short note.* 我回了一封短信. ○ *'Certainly not,' she replied.* '当然不行,'她答道. ○ *He replied that he was busy.* 他答称很忙. **(b)** [I, Ipr] **~ (to/with sth)** give an answer in the form of an action; respond (以行动)作答, 回答: *He replied with a nod.* 他点了点头作为回答. ○ *The enemy replied to our fire*, ie fired back at us. 敌人向我方还击.

▷ **re·ply** *n* **1** [U] act of replying 回答; 答复: *She made no reply.* 她没有回答. ○ *What did he do in reply to your challenge?* 你提出与他较量, 他作何反应? **2** [C] what is replied; response 回答; 答复: *get/have/receive several replies to an advertisement* 收到回应广告的来信 ○ [attrib 作定语] *a reply-paid telegram, envelope, etc*, ie paid for by the sender or addressee 已付回电费的电报、邮资已付的回邮信封. Cf 参看 ANSWER[1].

re·port[1] /rɪˈpɔːt; rɪˋpɔrt/ *v* **1** [I, Ipr, Tn, Tn·pr, Tw, Tg, Tsg, Cn·a] **~ (on sb/sth) (to sb/sth)**; **~ sth (to sb)** give a spoken or written account of (sth heard, seen, done, studied, etc); describe (以口头或书面形式)报告或报道(所闻、所见、所做、研究所得等); 记述; 叙述: *report on recent developments* 报告近况 ○ *report (on) progress made* 报告所取得的进展 ○ *report a debate, strike, kidnapping* 报道辩论情况、罢工事件、绑架事件 ○ *Tom reported his discoveries to the professor.* 汤姆向教授汇报了自己的发现. ○ *I reported how he had reacted.* 我把他的反应做了汇报. ○ *She reported (her) having seen the gunman.* 她叙述说曾看见那持枪歹徒. ○ *The doctor reported the patient fit and well.* 医生说患者情况良好. **2 (a)** [Tn, Tf, Tnt, Tg, Tsg, Cn·a] make (sth) known, esp by publishing or broadcasting; announce 公布(某事物)(尤指藉出版或广播); 发布; 宣告: *Police reported the closure of the road/that the road was closed.* 警方宣布那条道路禁止通行. ○ *The poll reported Labour to be leading.* 民意测验显示工党领先. ○ *They reported sighting the plane.* 他们宣称看见了那架飞机. ○ *The judge reported the case closed.* 法官宣布结案. **(b)** [I, Ipr] **~ (for sth)** work as a reporter 从事新闻报道工作; 当记者: *report for the Times, the BBC, etc* 任《泰晤士报》、英国广播公司等记者. **3** [Tn, Tn·pr] **~ sb (for sth)**; **~ sb/sth (to sb)** make a formal complaint or accusation about (an offence or offender) 告发; 举报: *report an official for insolence* 告一公职人员傲慢无礼 ○ *report a burglary, car crash, fraud, etc to the police* 因失窃、汽车车祸、受人诈骗等向警方报案 ○ *report sb/sb's lateness to the manager* 向经理告发某人[某人迟到一事]. **4 (a)** [I, Ipr] **~ (to sb/sth) for sth** present oneself as arrived, returned, ready for work, etc 报到; 复命: *report to the receptionist/reception* (eg in a hotel) *for one's room key* 向接待员[接待处]报到以索取房间钥匙(如在旅馆中) ○ *report for duty at 7 am* 上午7点钟报到上班. **(b)** [La, Cn·n/a] declare or show oneself or sb to be in a certain state or place 宣布或表明自己或某人处于某种状况或身在某处: *report sick, absent, fit* 表明有病、缺席、健康 ○ *The child was reported missing* (ie was said to have disappeared) *on Friday.* 据说那孩子星期五失踪了. ○ *The officer reported his men in position.* 那军官报告其部下已到位. **5** [Ipr] **~ to sb/sth** be responsible to a certain person or department that supervises one's work 对上司或上级部门负责: *All representatives report (directly) to the sales department.* 所有营业代表均须向销售部(直接)承担责任. **6** (phr v) **report back (from sth)** return 归来报到: *The officer reported back from leave on Sunday night.* 那军官于星期日晚上报到销假. **report back (to sb/sth)** give a spoken or written account of sb/sth one has been asked to investigate 将调查的某人[某事物]的情况做口头或书面报告: *He was requested to report back to the committee about/on the complaint.* 委员会要求他对投诉事件做出调查报告.

▷ **re·port·age** /͵repɔːˈtɑːʒ, *also* rɪˈpɔːtɪdʒ; ͵rɛpɔrˋtɑʒ, rɪˋpɔrtɪdʒ/ *n* [U] (typical style of) reporting news for the media 新闻报道; 报道文体: *the skilful reportage of sports journalists* 体育记者十分拿手的报道工作.

re·port·edly *adv* according to reports (REPORT 1) 据报道; 据说: *The star is reportedly very ill.* 据说该明星病重.

re·porter *n* person who reports news for the media 记者; 新闻通讯员: *press/TV/radio reporters* 报刊[电视台/广播电台]记者 ○ *an on-the-spot reporter*, ie one who is at the scene of the event 现场记者. Cf 参看 JOURNALIST (JOURNAL).

□ **re͵ported ˈspeech** = INDIRECT SPEECH (INDIRECT).

re·port[2] /rɪˈpɔːt; rɪˋpɔrt/ *n* **1** [C] spoken or written account of sth heard, seen, done, studied, etc, esp one that is published or broadcast (口头或书面的)报告, 报道(尤指经传播媒介发表者): *reliable, conflicting, detailed reports* 可靠的、互相矛盾的、详细的报道 ○ *positive/negative reports* 持肯定[否定]态度的报道 ○ *produce, submit, draw up regular progress reports* 提出、呈交、写出定期的进度报告 ○ *a report on the state of the roads*, eg from an automobile association 路况报告(如汽车协会提出者) ○ *a firm's annual, monthly, etc reports*, ie on its profitability 公司的年度、月度等报告(关于营利情况的) ○ *ˈlaw reports*, ie written records of trials, etc in the lawcourts 案例报告(法庭办案等情况的书面记录) ○ *radio/TV/press reports on the crash* 广播电台[电视台/报刊]对这一碰撞事故的报道. **2** [C] (*Brit*) periodical written statement about a pupil's or an employee's work and conduct (学生的)成绩报告单; (雇员的)工作鉴定书: *a ˈschool report* 学生成绩报告单 ○ *get a good report from one's boss* 得到老板的好评. **3 (a)** [U] (*fml* 文) common talk or rumour 传闻; 谣言: *Report has it that...*, ie People are saying that... 据说.... **(b)** [C] piece of gossip 流言蜚语; 道听途说: *I have only reports to go on.* 我的依据只是谣传而已. **4** [U] (*fml* 文) way in which sb/sth is spoken of; repute 名誉; 名声: *be of good/bad report* 名声好[坏]. **5** [C] explosive sound, like that of a gun being fired (似枪炮声的)爆炸声: *the sharp report of a pistol, firework, etc* 手枪、爆竹等的尖锐的响声 ○ *The tyre burst with a loud report.* 轮胎砰的一声巨响爆裂了.

□ **reˈport card** (*US*) school report 学生成绩报告单.

re·pose[1] /rɪˈpəʊz; rɪˋpoz/ *v* (*fml* 文) **1** [I] rest; lie 休息; 躺: *repose from toil* 劳累后休息一下 ○ *The picture shows a nude reposing on a couch.* 这幅画表现的是一个人赤身裸体躺在长沙发上. ○ *Beneath this stone repose the poet's mortal remains*, ie lies the poet's corpse. 在此石块下面埋葬着诗人的遗骸. **2** [Tn·pr] **~ sth on sb/sth** lay (an arm, etc) on sb/sth for support 将(手臂等)靠在某人[某物]上: *repose one's head on a cushion* 把头靠在垫子上.

▷ **re·pose** *n* [U] (*fml* 文) **1** rest; sleep 休息; 睡眠: *disturb sb's repose* 打扰某人的休息 ○ *Her face is sad in repose.* 她在睡眠时脸上显露出忧伤. **2 (a)** peaceful state; tranquillity 安静; 安宁: *win repose after months of*

R

suffering 经历几个月的苦难才获得安宁. (**b**) ease of manner; composure 安详; 沉静: *He lacks repose.* 他这人心浮气躁.

re·pose·ful /-fl; -fl/ *adj* calm; quiet 平静的; 安静的.

re·pose[2] /rɪˈpəʊz; rɪˋpoz/ *v* [Tn·pr] **~ sth in sth/sb** (*fml* 文) place (trust, etc) in sb/sth 将(信赖等)寄托于某人[某事物]: *He reposed too much confidence in her/her promises.* 他过于相信她[她的诺言].

re·pos·it·ory /rɪˈpɒzɪtrɪ; *US* -tɔːrɪ; rɪˋpɑzəˌtorɪ/ *n* **1** place where things are stored or may be found, esp a warehouse or museum 贮藏或存放物品之处所; (尤指)仓库, 栈房, 博物馆: *a furniture repository* 家具贮藏室. **2** (*fig* 比喻) person or book that receives and stores confidences, secrets, information, etc 可信任的人; 心腹; 知己; 知识宝库: *My father is a repository of interesting facts.* 我父亲有说不完的趣事. ○ *My diary is the repository of all my hopes and plans.* 我在日记中记载着我的一切希望和计划.

re·pos·sess /ˌriːpəˈzes; ˌripəˋzɛs/ *v* [Tn] regain possession of (esp hire-purchase goods or mortgaged property on which repayments have not been kept up) 收回(尤指未按分期付款规定付款的货物或抵押物): *repossess furniture* 收回未按分期付款规定付款的家具 ○ *repossess a flat, site, smallholding, etc* (因抵押借款人未按分期还款规定付款, 贷款人)收回公寓、建筑用地、小农田等.

▷ **re·pos·ses·sion** /ˌriːpəˈzeʃn; ˌripəˋzɛʃən/ *n* [U].

repp = REP[1].

rep·re·hend /ˌreprɪˈhend; ˌrɛprɪˋhɛnd/ *v* [Tn] (*fml* 文) criticize or rebuke (sb or sb's behaviour) 批评或指责(某人或某人的行为).

▷ **rep·re·hens·ible** /ˌreprɪˈhensəbl; ˌrɛprɪˋhɛnsəbl/ *adj* (*fml* 文) deserving to be reprehended 应受指责的: *Your conduct/attitude is most reprehensible.* 你的行为[态度]的确应该受到批评. **rep·re·hens·ibly** /-səblɪ; -səblɪ/ *adv*.

rep·res·ent[1] /ˌreprɪˈzent; ˌrɛprɪˋzɛnt/ *v* **1** [Tn, Cn·n/a] make an image of or show (sb/sth) in a picture, sculpture or play; depict (在绘画、雕塑或戏剧中)表现(某人[某事物]); 描绘; 塑造: *The picture represents a hunting scene.* 这是一幅行猎图. ○ *The king is represented as a villain in the play.* 在这出剧中把国王刻画成一个反面人物. **2** [Tn, Cn·n/a, Cn·t] describe (sb/sth), often misleadingly, as having a certain character or qualities 将(某人[某事物])(常指歪曲性地)描述为有某特点或性质: *Why do you represent the matter in this way?* 你为什么把这事说成这样? ○ *He represented himself as an expert.* 他把自己说成是专家. ○ *The risks were represented as negligible.* 把这么冒险的事说得微不足道. ○ *I am not what you represent me to be.* 我不是像你说的那种人. **3** [Tn, Tf, Dn·pr, Dpr·f] **~ sth (to sb)** (*fml* 文) state sth as a protest or appeal 陈述某事物(作为抗议或申诉): *represent the rashness of a plan, the seriousness of an accusation* 抗议某计划过于粗率、某指控过于严厉 ○ *They represented their grievances to the Governor.* 他们向总督申诉冤情. ○ *The barrister represented to the court that the defendant was mentally unstable.* 讼务律师向法庭陈述被告精神不正常. **4** [Tn] (**a**) stand for or be a symbol or equivalent of (sb/sth); symbolize 代表, 象征, 等于(某人[某事物]); 标志: *Phonetic symbols represent sounds.* 语音符号是标音的符号. ○ *What does x represent in this equation?* 这个方程式中的x代表什么? ○ *The rose represents England.* 玫瑰花是英格兰的象征. (**b**) be an example or embodiment of (sth); typify 是(某事物)的一个例子; 体现(某事物); 作为...典型: *This quartet represents a major new trend in modern music.* 这首四重奏的曲子反映了现代音乐中一种主要的新趋向. ○ *Fonteyn represents the best traditions of ballet.* 芳廷承袭了芭蕾舞艺术的最优秀的传统. **5** [Tn] be the result of (sth); correspond to 是(某事物)的结果; 相当于: *This new car represents years of research.* 这种新型汽车是多年研究的成果. ○ *A wage rise of 5% represents an annual increase of £250 for the lowest-paid workers.* 工资提高5%对收入最低的工人来说相当于全年收入增加250英镑. **6** (**a**) [Tn esp passive 尤用于被动语态] act as a substitute or deputy for (sb) 作为(某人)的代表或代理人: *The Queen was represented at the funeral by the British ambassador.* 英国大使代表女王参加了葬礼. (**b**) [Tn, Dpr·f] act as a spokesman for (sb) 作为(某人)的代言人: *Members* (ie of Parliament) *representing Welsh constituencies* 代表威尔士各选区的国会议员 ○ *Our firm is represented in India by Mr Hall.* 我公司驻印度代表是霍尔先生. ○ *Who is representing you* (ie acting as your lawyer) *in the case?* 这一案中谁是你的辩护律师? ○ *He represented to the court that the accused was very remorseful.* 他代被告向法庭陈情说被告十分懊悔.

▷ **rep·res·enta·tion** /ˌreprɪzenˈteɪʃn; ˌrɛprɪzɛnˋteʃən/ *n* **1** [U] act of representing or state of being represented 表现; 表示; 代表; 代理: *The firm needs more representation in China.* 这家公司需要在中国多设些代理机构. ○ *effective representation* (ie in Parliament) *of voters' interests* (在议会中)代表选民利益的反映. **2** [C] (*fml* 文) thing, esp a picture, sculpture or play, that represents sb/sth 表现某人[某事物]的事物; (尤指)图画, 雕塑, 戏剧: *stained-glass representations of saints* 彩色玻璃的圣徒画像 ○ *an unusual representation of Hamlet* 在演出上别具一格的《哈姆雷特》. **3** (idm 习语) **make representations to sb** (*fml* 文) protest or appeal to sb (about sth) (就某事物)向某人提出抗议或呼吁: *make representations to the council about the state of the roads* 就路况问题提请市政当局解决 ○ *The ambassador made forceful representations to the White House.* 该大使向白宫提出了强烈抗议.

rep·res·ent[2] /ˌriːprɪˈzent; ˌrɛprɪˋzɛnt/ *v* [Tn] submit (a cheque, bill, etc) again for payment 再提交或递送(支票、帐单等).

rep·res·ent·at·ive /ˌreprɪˈzentətɪv; ˌrɛprɪˋzɛntətɪv/ *adj* **1 ~ (of sb/sth)** (**a**) serving to show or portray a class or group 有代表性的; 典型的: *Is a questionnaire answered by 500 people truly representative of national opinion?* 一份调查问卷有500人作答, 是否能真正代表全国人民的意见? (**b**) containing examples of a number of types 包含多种类型的样品的: *a representative sample, selection, survey, etc* 有多种类型的样品、锦集、调查等 ○ *a representative collection of British insects* 英国各类昆虫的标本. **2** consisting of elected deputies; based on representation by these 由选出之代表组成的; 代议制的: *representative elections, governments, institutions* 代议制的选举、政府、机构.

▷ **rep·res·ent·at·ive** *n* **~ (of sb/sth)** **1** typical example of a class or group 典型; 有代表性的人或事物: *Many representatives of the older generation were there.* 老一辈的各类人都在那里. **2** (also *infml* 口语作 **rep**) (*commerce* 商) agent of a firm, esp a travelling salesman (公司的)代理者; (尤指)派出的推销员: *act as sole representatives of XYZ Oil* 充当XYZ石油公司的总代理. **3** (**a**) person chosen or appointed to represent[1] (6) another or others; delegate 代表他人的人; 代表: *the Queen's representative at the ceremony* 参加典礼的女王代表 ○ *send a representative to the negotiations* 派代表参加谈判. (**b**) person elected to represent others in a legislative body (被选入立法机构的)代表: *our representative* (ie MP) *in the House of Commons* 我们在下议院的代表.

re·press /rɪˈpres; rɪˋprɛs/ *v* [Tn] **1** (**a**) restrain or suppress (an impulse); check 约束或抑制(冲动); 压抑: *repress an urge to scream* 强忍着不喊出来 ○ *repress a sneeze, smile, cough* 强抑着不打喷嚏、不笑、不咳嗽 ○ *He repressed his natural sexual desires as sinful.* 他压抑着本能的性欲, 视之为罪恶. (**b**) (usu passive 通常用于被动语态) cause (sb) to restrain or suppress emotion, thoughts, etc 使(某人)在感情、思想等上受压抑: *His childhood was repressed and solitary.* 他童年经受到压抑很孤独. **2** (**a**) prevent (a revolt, etc) from breaking out; quell 防止(暴乱等); 平息; 镇压: *All protest is brutally repressed by the regime.* 一切抗议活动都遭到当局的野蛮镇压. (**b**) prevent (sb) from protesting or rioting; subjugate 防止(某人)反对或作乱; 压制: *The dictator represses all opposition as illegal.* 这个独裁者把所有反对他的活动均视为非法加以镇压.

▷ **re·pressed** *adj* suffering from suppression of the emotions 受压抑的.

re·pres·sion /rɪˈpreʃn; rɪˋprɛʃən/ *n* **1** [U] repressing or being repressed 约束; 抑制; 压抑; 压制; 镇压. **2** (*psychology* 心) (**a**) [U] action of forcing desires and urges, esp those in conflict with accepted standards of conduct, into the unconscious mind, often resulting in abnormal behaviour 压抑: *sexual repression* 性欲的压抑. (**b**) [C] desire or urge repressed in this way 被压抑的欲望或冲动.

re·press·ive /rɪˈpresɪv; rɪˋprɛsɪv/ *adj* tending to repress; harsh or severe 抑制的; 压制的; 严厉的; 严格的: *a repressive regime, tendency, law* 严酷的政权、压抑的倾向、严厉的法律 ○ *Parliament condemned the repressive measures taken by the police.* 议会谴责了警方采取的镇压措施. **re·press·ively** *adj.* **re·press·ive·ness** *n* [U].

re·prieve /rɪˈpriːv; rɪˋpriv/ *v* [Tn] **1** postpone or cancel a punishment for (sb), esp the death sentence 缓期执行或撤消对(某人)的惩罚(尤指死刑): *reprieve a condemned prisoner* 缓期执行已决犯的死刑. **2** (*fig* 比喻) give temporary relief from danger, trouble, etc to (sb/sth) 暂时缓解(某人[某事物])的危险、困难等: *The tree that was due to be cut down has been reprieved for six months.* 原定砍伐的那棵树已经推迟六个月再砍.
▷ **re·prieve** *n* **1** (**a**) [U] postponement or cancellation of a punishment, esp the death sentence 刑罚(尤指死刑)的缓期执行或撤消: *the reprieve of the hostages* 对人质的暂缓处决. (**b**) [C] order for this to happen 缓刑令(尤指死刑的): *grant (sb) a reprieve/a reprieve to sb* 准许(某人)缓期受刑 ○ *The prisoner won a last-minute reprieve.* 那囚犯在临刑前获得了缓刑. **2** [U, C] (*fig* 比喻) temporary relief from danger, trouble, etc (危险、困难等的)暂时缓解.

rep·rim·and /ˈreprɪmɑːnd; *US* -mænd; ˋrɛprə,mænd/ *v* [Tn, Tn·pr] **~ sb (for sth)** rebuke sb (for a fault, etc), esp officially 训斥、申斥或斥责某人(尤指对下属).
▷ **rep·rim·and** *n* [C, U] rebuke, esp an official one 训斥, 申斥, 斥责(尤指对下属): *receive a stiff, severe, sharp, etc reprimand* 受到严厉的、严格的、尖刻的…训斥 ○ *His negligence passed without reprimand.* 他玩忽职守并未受到斥责.

re·print /ˌriːˈprɪnt; riˋprɪnt/ *v* (**a**) [Tn] print (a book, etc) again, with few or no changes 重印, 再版(书等). (**b**) [I] (of a book, etc) be printed again (指书等)重印, 再版: *The dictionary is reprinting with minor corrections.* 这部词典稍作修改后正在重印.
▷ **re·print** /ˈriːprɪnt; ˋri,prɪnt/ *n* (**a**) reprinting or new impression of a book with few or no changes 重印; 再版: *The work is into its third reprint.* 这部著作已是第三次重印了. (**b**) such a reprinted book 重印本; 再版本. Cf 参看 EDITION.

re·prisal /rɪˈpraɪzl; rɪˋpraɪzl/ *n* [C, U] (act of) returning an injury, esp political or military, done to oneself; retaliation 报复(行动)(尤指政治或军事的): *suffer heavy reprisals* 遭到严厉的报复 ○ *take reprisals against terrorism* 对恐怖主义进行报复 ○ *Civilian targets were bombed in reprisal (for the raid).* 轰炸了民用目标作为(对曾受袭击的)报复.

re·proach /rɪˈprəʊtʃ; rɪˋprotʃ/ *v* [Tn, Tn·pr] (**a**) **~ sb/oneself (for sth)** criticize sb/oneself, esp for failing to do sth 责备某人[自己](尤指因未做成某事): *She reproached him for forgetting their anniversary.* 她责备他竟把他们的结婚周年纪念日忘了. ○ *I have nothing to reproach myself for*, ie that I need regret. 我问心无愧. (**b**) **~ sb/oneself (with sth)** name a fault as a reason for criticizing sb/oneself 指出过失而责备某人[自己]: *reproach the government with neglect* 指责政府疏忽.
▷ **re·proach** *n* **1** (**a**) [U] reproaching 责备: *a word, look, sigh of reproach* 责备的话、目光、叹息. (**b**) [C] word, remark, etc that reproaches 责备的言词、话语等: *heap reproaches on sb* 对某人诸多指责. **2** (**a**) [U] (*fml* 文) state of disgrace or discredit 耻辱; 丢脸: *bring reproach upon oneself* 给自己蒙羞. (**b**) [sing] **~ (to sb/sth)** person or thing that disgraces or discredits sb/sth 使某人[某事物]蒙羞或丢丑的人或事物: *Poverty is/The poor are a constant reproach to our society.* 贫穷现象[穷人]是我们社会长期存在的耻辱. **3** (idm 习语) **above/beyond reproach** perfect; blameless 尽善尽美的; 无可指摘的: *Her manners are above reproach.* 她的举止无可非议.
re·proach·ful /-fl; -fl/ *adj* expressing reproach(1) 表示责备的: *a reproachful look, remark, sigh* 表示责备的目光、话语、叹息. **re·proach·fully** /-fəlɪ; -fəlɪ/ *adv*.

rep·rob·ate /ˈreprəbeɪt; ˋrɛprə,bet/ *adj, n* [attrib 作定语] (*fml or joc* 文或谑) immoral or unprincipled (person) 道德败坏的(人); 堕落的(人): *have reprobate tendencies* 有堕落的倾向 ○ *You sinful old reprobate!* 你这个作恶多端的无赖! ○ *He has always been a bit of a reprobate.* 他一向不很规矩.

re·pro·duce /ˌriːprəˈdjuːs; *US* -ˈduːs; ,riprəˋdus/ *v* **1** [Tn] make a copy of (a picture, etc) 复制(图画等): *This copier can reproduce colour photographs.* 这台复印机可复制彩色照片. **2** [Tn, Tn·pr] **~ sth (as sth)** cause sth to be seen or heard again, or to occur again 再现某事物的形象或声音; 放映或播放某事物: *a portrait that reproduces every detail of the sitter's face* 把那被画像的人的容貌表现得惟妙惟肖的画像 ○ *Her stereo system reproduces every note perfectly.* 她的立体声音响设备放音效果极佳. ○ *Can this effect be reproduced in a laboratory?* 这种效果能在实验室里产生吗? ○ *The computer reproduced the data as a set of diagrams.* 计算机用一组图表把那些数据重新显示出来. **3** [I] have a specified quality when copied 达到某种复制效果: *Some colours reproduce well/badly.* 有的颜色复制效果好[差]. **4** [I, Tn] (of humans, animals, insects, etc) produce (offspring) by natural means (指人、兽、昆虫等)生殖, 繁殖: *Ferns reproduce (themselves) by spores.* 蕨类植物用孢子繁殖.
▷ **re·pro·du·cible** /-əbl; -əbl/ *adj* that can be reproduced 可复制的; 可重现的; 能繁殖的.
re·pro·duc·tion /ˌriːprəˈdʌkʃn; ,riprəˋdʌkʃən/ *n* **1** [U] reproducing or being reproduced 复制; 重现; 繁殖: *Compact disc recordings give excellent sound reproduction.* 激光唱片播放的声音保真度很高. **2** [U] process of reproducing (REPRODUCE 4) 繁殖过程: *study reproduction in shellfish* 研究水生有壳动物的繁殖方法. **3** [C] thing reproduced, esp a copy of a work of art 复制品(尤指艺术作品的): *Is that painting an original or a reproduction?* 那幅画是原作还是复制品? ○ [attrib 作定语] *reproduction furniture*, ie made in imitation of an earlier style 仿制的旧式家具.
re·pro·duct·ive /ˌriːprəˈdʌktɪv; ,riprəˋdʌktɪv/ *adj* of or for reproduction of offspring 生殖的; 繁殖的; 起生殖作用的: *reproductive organs, systems, urges* 生殖器官、系统、欲望.

re·proof /rɪˈpruːf; rɪˋpruf/ *n* [C, U] (*fml* 文) (remark, etc expressing) blame or disapproval 责备; 非难; 责备的话语等: *administer a stern reproof* 给予严厉的斥责 ○ *conduct deserving a stern reproof* 应该受到严厉斥责的行为 ○ *Tom swept up the broken glass without a word of reproof to his son.* 汤姆把碎玻璃扫干净, 没说一句责备儿子的话.

re·prove /rɪˈpruːv; rɪˋpruv/ *v* [Tn, Tn·pr] **~ sb (for sth)** (*fml* 文) blame or rebuke sb; censure 责备或指责某人; 谴责: *The priest reproved people for not coming to church.* 牧师责备那些不做礼拜的人.
▷ **re·prov·ing** *adj* [usu attrib 通常作定语] expressing reproof 表示责备的: *a reproving glance, remark, etc* 表示责备的一瞥、话语等. **re·prov·ingly** *adv*.

rep·tile /ˈreptaɪl; *US* -tl; ˋrɛptl/ *n* any of the class of cold-blooded, egg-laying animals including lizards, tortoises, crocodiles, snakes, etc with relatively short legs or no legs at all 爬行动物(冷血, 卵生, 如蜥蜴、龟、鳄鱼、蛇等); 爬虫.
▷ **rep·ti·lian** /repˈtɪlɪən; rɛpˋtɪlɪən/ *adj, n* (of or like a) reptile 爬行动物(的); 爬虫(似的).

re·pub·lic /rɪˈpʌblɪk; rɪˋpʌblɪk/ *n* (country with a) system of government in which supreme power is held not by a monarch but by the (elected representatives of the) people, with an elected President 共和国; 共和政体: *a constitutional republic*, eg the US, Canada 立宪共和国(如美国、加拿大). Cf 参看 MONARCHY (MONARCH).

re·pub·lican /rɪˈpʌblɪkən; rɪˋpʌblɪkən/ *adj* of or like a republic; supporting the principles of a republic 共和国的; 共和政体的; 拥护共和政体的: *a republican movement, party, government* 共和运动、党、政体 ○ *republican sympathies* 对共和制的拥护.
▷ **re·pub·lican** *n* **1** person favouring republican government 拥护共和政体的人; 共和主义者. **2 Republican** member of one of the two main political parties in the US (美国)共和党党员. Cf 参看 DEMOCRAT 2.
re·pub·lic·an·ism /-ɪzəm; -,ɪzəm/ *n* [U] (support for) republican principles 共和主义; 共和制; 对共和制的拥护.
□ **Reˈpublican Party** one of the two main political parties in the US (美国)共和党. Cf 参看 DEMOCRATIC PARTY (DEMOCRATIC).

R

re·pu·di·ate /rɪˈpju:dɪeɪt; rɪˋpjudɪˌet/ *v* [Tn] **1** refuse to have any more to do with (sb); disown 与(某人)断绝来往; 否认…是自己的: *repudiate a son, lover, former friend, etc* 与儿子、情人、旧友等断绝关系. **2** (**a**) refuse to accept or acknowledge (sth); reject 拒绝接受或承认(某事物); 回绝: *repudiate a charge, view, claim, suggestion* 拒绝一项指控、一种观点、一项权利要求、一项建议 ○ *He utterly repudiated my offer of friendship.* 他完全拒绝接受我的友好表示. (**b**) refuse to abide by (the ruling of an authority or an agreement) 拒不服从(权威); 拒不遵守(协议): *He repudiated the court's decision to offer bail.* 他不接受法庭的保释裁决. ○ *repudiate a treaty, contract, vow, etc* 不履行条约、合同、誓约等. **3** refuse to discharge (a debt or an obligation) 拒绝偿付(债款); 拒不履行(义务). ▷ **re·pu·di·ation** /rɪˌpju:dɪˈeɪʃn; rɪˌpjudɪˋeʃən/ *n* [U, C].

re·pug·nant /rɪˈpʌgnənt; rɪˋpʌgnənt/ *adj* **~ (to sb)** (**a**) (*fml* 文) causing a feeling of strong opposition or dislike; abhorrent 令人厌恶的; 使人极反感的; 讨厌的: *I find his racist views totally repugnant.* 我十分厌恶他的种族主义观点. ○ *The idea of accepting a bribe was repugnant to me.* 我一想到受贿这种事就非常反感. (**b**) causing a feeling of strong disgust; nauseating 使人作呕的; 恶心的: *All food was repugnant to me during my illness.* 我生病时吃什么都恶心.

▷ **re·pug·nance** /-nəns; -nəns/ *n* [U] **~ (to sth/doing sth)** strong aversion or disgust 厌恶; 强烈的反感; 恶心: *She has a deep repugnance to the idea of accepting charity.* 她认为接受救济的想法是要不得的. ○ *I cannot overcome my repugnance to eating snails.* 吃蜗牛真恶心, 我可受不了.

re·pulse /rɪˈpʌls; rɪˋpʌls/ *v* [Tn] (*fml* 文) **1** drive back (an attacker or an attack) by fighting; repel 击退(进攻者或进攻); 驱逐. **2** (*fig* 比喻) (**a**) refuse to accept (an offer, help, etc); reject 拒绝接受(提议、帮助等); 回绝: *repulse kindness, sympathy, assistance, etc* 拒绝接受好意、同情、帮助等 ○ *She repulsed his advances.* 他向她求爱, 她拒绝了. (**b**) discourage (sb making an offer, wanting to help, etc) by being rude or unfriendly; rebuff (粗暴或无礼地)顶回(提议者、想要给予帮助者等); 冷落. Cf 参看 REPEL 1, 2.

▷ **re·pulse** *n* [sing] **1** defeat of an attack by fighting 击退. **2** (*fig* 比喻) rude or unfriendly rejection of an offer, etc; rebuff (对提议等, 粗暴或无礼的)拒绝; 回绝; 冷落: *Her request for a donation met with a repulse.* 她要求赞助却遭到粗暴拒绝.

re·pul·sion /rɪˈpʌlʃn; rɪˋpʌlʃən/ *n* [U] **1 ~ (for sb/sth)** feeling of loathing or aversion; disgust 厌恶; 憎恶; 反感: *feel repulsion for sb* 厌恶某人. **2** (*physics* 物) tendency of bodies (eg magnetic poles) to repel each other 排斥, 斥力(如磁极的). Cf 参看 ATTRACTION.

re·puls·ive /rɪˈpʌlsɪv; rɪˋpʌlsɪv/ *adj* **1** causing a feeling of loathing or aversion; disgusting 令人厌恶的; 使人反感的; 讨厌的: *a repulsive sight, smell, person* 使人厌恶的情景、气味、人 ○ *Picking your nose is a repulsive habit.* 挖鼻孔这种习惯很讨厌. ○ *The sight of him is repulsive to me.* 我一看见他就十分反感. **2** (*physics* 物) causing repulsion(2); repelling 排斥的; 斥力的: *repulsive forces* 斥力.

▷ **re·puls·ively** *adv* in a repulsive manner 令人厌恶地; 排斥地: *repulsively ugly* 丑陋得令人厌恶.

re·puls·ive·ness *n* [U].

rep·ut·able /ˈrepjʊtəbl; ˋrɛpjətəbl/ *adj* having a good reputation; respected or trustworthy 声誉好的; 有名望的; 受尊敬的; 值得信赖的: *a highly reputable firm, shop, accountant* 有名气的公司、商店、会计. ▷ **rep·ut·ably** /-əblɪ; -əblɪ/ *adv*.

re·pu·ta·tion /ˌrepjʊˈteɪʃn; ˌrɛpjəˋteʃən/ *n* [U, C] **~ (for sth)** what is generally said or believed about the abilities, qualities, etc of sb/sth 名声; 名誉; 名气: *a school with an excellent, enviable, fine, etc reputation* 享有盛誉的学校 ○ *a good/bad reputation as a doctor* 医疗信誉好[坏] ○ *have a reputation for laziness/for being lazy* 以懒惰出名 ○ *compromise, ruin sb's reputation* 损害、败坏某人的名誉 ○ *establish, build up, make a reputation (for oneself)* (为自己)树立声誉, 博得名声 ○ *live up to one's reputation*, ie behave, perform, etc as one is expected to 不负盛名(行为、表现等与声誉相符).

re·pute /rɪˈpju:t; rɪˋpjut/ *v* (idm 习语) **be reputed as/to be sb/sth** be generally said or considered to be sb/sth 普遍称为或当作是某人[某事物]: *He is reputed as/to be the best surgeon in Paris.* 他是公认的巴黎最好的外科医生. ○ *She is reputed to be very wealthy.* 大家说她很富有.

▷ **re·pute** *n* (*fml* 文) **1** [U] reputation 名声; 名誉; 名气: *know sb only by repute* 对某人仅闻其名声 ○ *an inn of good/evil repute* 名声好的[坏的]小旅馆 ○ *He has little repute as an academic.* 他是个名不见经传的大学教师. **2** (idm 习语) **of repute** (*fml* 文) having a good reputation 名声好的: *wines of repute* 名酒 ○ *a doctor of repute* 名医.

re·puted *adj* [attrib 作定语] generally said or considered to be sth/sb (but with some element of doubt) 一般人所谓的, 普遍认为的(略含怀疑成分): *the reputed father of the child* 据说是那孩子的父亲的人 ○ *her reputed learning* 她那所谓不错的学问. **re·putedly** *adv*.

re·quest /rɪˈkwest; rɪˋkwɛst/ *n* **1 ~ (for sth/that...)** (**a**) act of asking for sth in speech or writing, esp politely (口头或书面的)要求; (尤指)请求: *make repeated requests for help* 一再请求帮助 ○ *your request that I should destroy the letter* 你要求我销毁那封信一事. (**b**) thing asked for in this way 要求或请求的事物: *Your requests will be granted.* 你的请求能够获准. ○ [attrib 作定语] *a request programme, show, etc*, ie in which music is played that has been requested by listeners 点播的节目、演出等. **2** (idm 习语) **at sb's request/at the request of sb** because of sb's wish 应某人之请求; 鉴于某人之请求: *I came at your (special) request.* 我是(特别)应你要求而来的. **by request (of sb)** in response to a request (from sb) 应(某人的)请求; 经(某人之)要求: *By popular request, the chairman was re-elected.* 徇众要求, 主席获重选连任. **on reˈquest** when asked for 一经要求: *Catalogues are available on request.* 备有目录供索取.

▷ **re·quest** *v* [Tn, Tn·pr, Tf, Dn·t] **~ sth (from/of sb)** (*fml* 文) ask sb, esp politely, in speech or writing to do sth (以口头或书面形式)要求, (尤指)请求某人做某事: *request compliance with the rules*, eg on a notice 请遵守规则(如告示用语) ○ *All I requested of you was that you came early.* 我只要求你早点来. ○ *I requested him to help.* 我请求他帮忙. ○ *You are (kindly) requested not to smoke.* 请不要吸烟. ⇨Usage at ASK 用法见 ASK.

□ **reˈquest stop** (*Brit*) place where buses will only stop if a passenger signals (公共汽车的)招手即停车站.

re·quiem /ˈrekwɪəm; ˋrɛkwɪəm/ *n* (**a**) (also **requiem ˈmass**) special mass for the repose of the soul of a dead person (为死者举行的)安魂弥撒, 追思弥撒. (**b**) musical setting for this 安魂弥撒曲.

re·quire /rɪˈkwaɪə(r); rɪˋkwaɪr/ *v* (not used in the continuous tenses 不用于进行时态) **1** [Tn, Tf, Tnt, Tg] depend on (sb/sth) for success, fulfilment, etc; need 有赖于(某人[某事物]); 需要: *We require extra help.* 我们需要额外的帮助. ○ *The situation requires that I should be there.* 情况需要我在那里. ○ *The manuscript requires an expert to understand it.* 这份手稿只有专家才看得懂. ○ *All cars require servicing regularly.* 所有汽车都需要定期检修. **2** [esp passive 尤用于被动语态: Tn, Tn·pr, Tf, Dn·t] **~ sth (of sb)** (*fml* 文) order or command (sth), esp from a position of authority 命令或指示(某事物): *I have done all that is required by law.* 我已按照法律规定把一切做好. ○ *It is required (of me) that I give evidence.* 要求我提供证据. ○ *Civil Servants are required to sign the Official Secrets Act.* 公务员须签署遵守公务保密条例. **3** [esp passive 尤用于被动语态: Tn, Tn·pr] demand (sth) as being obligatory; stipulate (强制性地)要求(某事物); 规定: *Hamlet is required reading* (ie must be read) *for the course.* 《哈姆雷特》为本课程指定读物. ○ *You must satisfy the required conditions to get your voucher.* 必须具备所需条件方可获发凭证. ○ *He only did what was required (of him).* 他只是照章办事. **4** [Tn] (*fml* 文) wish to have 想要: *Will you require tea?* 你要茶吗? ○ *Is that all that you require, sir?* 先生, 您还要别的吗?

▷ **re·quire·ment** *n* (esp *pl* 尤作复数) **1** thing depended on or needed 依赖的或需要的事物: *Our immediate requirement is extra staff.* 我们亟需增加工作人员. ○ *stock surplus to requirements*, ie more than is needed 超过需要的存货 ○ *Our latest model should meet* *your requirements exactly*, ie be just what you want. 我们的最新型号包你满意. **2** thing ordered or demanded 规定的或要求的事物: *Not all foreign visitors satisfy/fulfil legal entry requirements.* 并非所有外宾均符合入境规定.

re·quis·ite /ˈrekwɪzɪt; ˋrɛkwəzɪt/ *adj* [attrib 作定语] (*fml* 文) required by circumstances or necessary for success (情况)需要的; (成功)必要的: *Have you the requisite visa to enter Canada?* 你有进入加拿大必备的签证吗? ○ *have/lack the requisite capital to start a business* 有[没有]创业所需的资金.

▷ **re·quis·ite** *n* **~ (for sth)** thing needed for a purpose 必需的事物: *toilet requisites*, eg soap, perfume, etc 梳妆用品(如肥皂、香水等) ○ *We supply every requisite for travel/all travelling requisites.* 本处供应旅行必备的一切用品.

re·quisi·tion /ˌrekwɪˈzɪʃn; ˌrɛkwəˋzɪʃən/ *n* **1** [C] **~ (on sb) (for sth)** official, usu written, demand for (esp) the use of property or materials by an army in wartime or by certain people in an emergency 正式要求; (尤指军队)征用; (通常指)征用文书: *make a requisition on headquarters for supplies* 向司令部申请补给品. **2** [U] action of demanding in this way 正式要求; 征用: *The farm was in/under constant requisition as a base for the rescue team.* 这农场一再征用作救援队的活动基地. ○ [attrib 作定语] *a requisition form, order, etc* 征用单、征用令.

▷ **re·quisi·tion** *v* **1** [Tn, Tn·pr, Cn·n/a] **~ sth (from sb); ~ sth as sth** demand (the use of sth) by a requisition 正式要求(使用某物); 征用: *requisition billets, blankets, horses (from the villagers)* (向村民)征用部队用的住房、毯子、马 ○ *The town hall was requisitioned as army headquarters.* 市政厅征用作了军队的指挥部. **2** [Tn·pr, Tnt] **~ sb (for sth)** command sb officially to do sth 命令或指示某人做某事: *requisition the villagers for billets/to provide billets* 命令村民为部队提供住房.

re·quite /rɪˈkwaɪt; rɪˋkwaɪt/ *v* [Tn, Tn·pr] (*fml* 文) **1 ~ sth (with sth)** give sth in return for sth else; repay sth 回报; 报答某事物: *Will she ever requite my love?* 她会回报我对她的爱吗? ○ *The Queen requited his services with a knighthood.* 女王为表彰他的贡献封他为爵士. **2 ~ sb (for sth)** take vengeance on sb 向某人报复; 报仇: *requite sb for wrongs, evils, etc* 向某人报怨、报仇等 ○ *requite him for the injury he has done me* 因他伤害了我而向他报复.

▷ **re·quital** /-tl; -tl/ *n* [U] (*fml* 文) **1** repayment 回报或报答: *the requital of her love* 对她的爱的回报 ○ *make full requital to sb for his help* 因得到某人的帮助而给予厚礼回报. **2** revenge 报复; 报仇.

re-route /ˌriːˈruːt; riˋrut/ *v* [Tn, Tn·pr] send or carry (sb/sth) by a different route 以另一路线运送(某人[某事物]): *re-route traffic, shipping, freight, luggage* 按新规定的路线行驶、航行、运送货物、寄运行李 ○ *My flight was re-routed via Athens.* 我乘坐的航班改变航线途经雅典.

re·run /ˌriːˈrʌn; riˋrʌn/ *v* (**-nn-**; *pt* **reran**, *pp* **rerun**) [Tn] **1** show (a cinema or television film), broadcast (a programme) or play (a tape) again 重映, 重播, 重放(影片、电视片、广播节目、录音或录像). **2** run (a race) again 重新举行(赛跑或赛马等).

▷ **re·run** /ˈriːrʌn; ˋriˌrʌn/ *n* film or programme that is shown or broadcast again; repeat (影片或节目的)重映, 重放, 重播: *a rerun of a popular play, series, etc* 受欢迎的戏剧之重演、系列节目之重播等 ○ (*fig* 比喻) *We don't want a rerun of Monday's fiasco.* 我们可别让星期一的惨败重演.

re·sale /ˈriːseɪl, riːˈseɪl; ˋriˌsel, riˋsel/ *n* [U] sale to another person of sth that one has bought 转卖; 转售: *a house up for resale* 准备转卖的房子.

res·cind /rɪˈsɪnd; rɪˋsɪnd/ *v* [Tn] (*law* 律) cancel or repeal (a law, contract, etc); annul 取消, 废除或撤消(法规、合同等); 废止: *rescind an agreement, order, act, etc* 废除协定、收回成命、撤消法案.

res·cue /ˈreskjuː; ˋrɛskju/ *v* [Tn, Tn·pr] **~ sb/sth (from sth/sb)** save or bring away sb/sth from danger, captivity, etc (从危险、囚禁等中)搭救或救出某人[某物]: *Police rescued the hostages.* 警方救出了人质. ○ *rescue a man from drowning, attack, bankruptcy* 援救一男子使之免遭溺毙、攻击、破产 ○ (*fig* 比喻) *rescue sb's name from oblivion*, ie prevent him from being forgotten 使某人名声长在 ○ *You rescued me from an embarrassing situation.* 是你给我解了围.

▷ **res·cue** *n* **1** [U] rescuing or being rescued 搭救; 解救; 援救: [attrib 作定语] *a rescue party, bid, operation* 救援队、叫牌、行动. **2** [C] instance of this 搭救; 解救; 援救: *an attempt at a rescue* 一次营救行动. **3** (idm 习语) **come/go to the/sb's ˈrescue** rescue or help sb 援救或帮助某人: *A wealthy sponsor came to our rescue with a generous donation.* 有个富有的赞助人慷慨捐赠来解救我们.

res·cuer *n*.

re·search /rɪˈsɜːtʃ, ˈriːsɜːtʃ; rɪˋsɝtʃ, ˋrisɝtʃ/ *n* [U] (also **researches** [pl]) **~ (into/on sth); ~ (on sb)** careful study or investigation, esp in order to discover new facts or information 研究; 探讨; 调查: *medical, scientific, historical, etc research* 医学、科学、历史等研究 ○ *a startling piece of research into the causes of cancer/on cancer* 研究致癌[癌症]的一项惊人成果 ○ *be engaged in, carry out, do research* 从事、进行、作研究 ○ (*infml* 口) *My researches into adventure holidays were very fruitful.* 我在琢磨让假期过得有刺激性, 在这一点上已大有收获. ○ [attrib 作定语] *a research worker, grant, degree* 研究人员、经费、学位.

▷ **re·search** /rɪˈsɜːtʃ; rɪˋsɝtʃ/ *v* [I, Ipr, Tn] **~ (into/on sth); ~ (on sb)** do research on (sth/sb) 对(某事物[某人])进行研究、探讨或调查: *researching into/on the spread of AIDS* 研究艾滋病的传播 ○ *The subject has already been fully researched.* 这个课题已进行过充分的研究. ○ *a well-researched book* 研究得很透彻的书.

re·searcher *n*.

re·seat /ˌriːˈsiːt; riˋsit/ *v* [Tn] **1** supply (sth) with a new seat 给(某物)装设新座: *reseat a cane chair* 换藤椅的座. **2** place (sb/oneself) on a seat again, or on a new seat 使(某人[自己])重新就座或坐在新座位上: *reseat oneself more comfortably* 换个更舒服的座位坐下.

re·sell /ˌriːˈsel; riˋsɛl/ *v* (**-ll-**; *pt*, *pp* **resold** /ˌriːˈsəʊld; riˋsold/) [Tn] sell (sth one has bought) to another person 转卖(某物): *resell the goods at a profit* 转卖货物赢利.

re·semble /rɪˈzembl; rɪˋzɛmbl/ *v* [no passive 不用于被动语态: Tn, Tn·pr] **~ sb/sth (in sth)** (not used in the continuous tenses 不用于进行时态) be like or similar to (another person or thing) 与(他人或他物)相似; 像...: *a small object resembling a pin* 像大头针的小物件 ○ *She resembles her brother in looks.* 她和她弟弟长得很像.

▷ **re·semb·lance** /rɪˈzembləns; rɪˋzɛmbləns/ *n* [C, U] **~ (to sb/sth); ~ (between A and B)** (instance of) likeness or similarity 相似; 相像: *a marked, strong, notable, faint resemblance* 明显的、显著的、能觉察出的、略微的相似之处 ○ *There is a degree of resemblance between the two boys.* 这两个男孩有某些相似之处. ○ *Your story bears/has/shows little or no resemblance to the facts.* 你说的与事实相去甚远, 或谓根本不符.

re·sent /rɪˈzent; rɪˋzɛnt/ *v* [Tn, Tg, Tsg] feel bitter, indignant or angry about (sth hurtful, insulting, etc) (因受到伤害、侮辱等)对(某事物)感到愤恨、怨恨或气愤: *I bitterly resent your criticism.* 我对你批评我的话十分反感. ○ *Does she resent my being here?* 她讨厌我呆在这里吗?

▷ **re·sent·ful** /-fl; -fl/ *adj* feeling or showing resentment 感到或表示愤恨的; 憎恨的: *a resentful silence, stare, comment* 充满怨恨的沉默、凝视、评语 ○ *He was deeply resentful of/at her interference.* 他非常讨厌她从中干预.

re·sent·fully /-fəlɪ; -fəlɪ/ *adv*. **re·sent·ful·ness** *n* [U].

re·sent·ment *n* [U, sing] (act of) resenting sb/sth 愤恨; 怨恨: *bear, feel, show, etc no resentment against/towards anyone* 对任何人均无怨恨 ○ *a deep-seated resentment at/of/over the way one has been treated* 因受到如此对待而深怀怨恨.

re·ser·va·tion /ˌrezəˈveɪʃn; ˌrɛzɚˋveʃən/ *n* **1** [C] reserved seat or accommodation, etc; record of this 保留的座位、住处等; (座位、住处等的)预订: *a coach, hotel reservation* 预订的客车座位、旅馆房间 ○ *make, hold reservations (in the name of T Hill)* (以T·希尔的名字)预订. Cf 参看 BOOKING (BOOK[2]). **2** [U, C esp *pl* 作不可数名词或可数名词, 后者尤作复数] spoken or unspoken limitation which prevents one's agreement with a plan, acceptance of an idea, etc 保留意见; 保留态度: *I support this measure without reservation*, ie completely, wholeheartedly. 我毫无保留地支持这一措施. ○ *express certain (mental) reservations about an offer* 对某项提议表示(有)一定的保留意见 ○ *I have my reservations* (ie doubts) *about his ability to do the job.* 我对于他做该项工作的能力持保留看法(怀疑他能否胜任). **3** [C] (*Brit*) strip of land between the two carriageways of a road 道路中央双向交通的分隔带: *the central reservation* 路中双向交通分隔带. **4** [C] area of land reserved in the US for occupation by an Indian tribe (美国印第安部落的)居留地.

re·serve[1] /rɪˈzɜːv; rɪˋzɝv/ *v* [Tn, Tn·pr] **~ sth (for sb/sth)** **1** put aside or keep sth for a later occasion or special use 保留或储备某物: *Reserve your strength for the climb.* 留点力气准备攀登吧. ○ *These seats are reserved for special guests.* 这些座位是留给贵宾的. **2** have or keep (a specified power); retain 具有或保持(某种权利); 保留: *The management reserves the right to refuse admission.* 资方有权拒绝接纳. ○ (*law* 律) *All rights reserved*, eg for the publisher of the book, record, etc. 版权所有. **3** order or set aside (seats, accommodation, etc) for use by a particular person at a future time; book 预订或保留(座位、住处等); 订购: *reserve tickets, rooms, couchettes* 预订票、房间、卧舖 ○ *reserve a table for two in the name of Hill* 以希尔的名字预订一个双座的桌位 ○ *Is your holiday a reserved booking, sir?* 先生, 您来度假办理预订手续了吗? **4** (idm 习语) **reserve (one's) ˈjudgment (on sb/sth)** (*fml* 文) delay giving an opinion, eg until the matter has become clearer 暂不表态(如有待事情明朗化).

re·serve[2] /rɪˈzɜːv; rɪˋzɝv/ *n* **1** [C usu *pl* 通常作复数] thing put aside or kept for later use; extra amount available when needed 储备(物); 储备量: *dwindling oil reserves* 日渐减少的石油储量 ○ *have great reserves of capital, energy, stock* 储备有大量资金、能源、物资 ○ *the ˈgold reserve*, ie to support the issue of banknotes 黄金储备 ○ [attrib 作定语] *a reserve (petrol) tank* 备用(汽)油箱 ○ *The champion drew on his reserve strength to win in the last 50 yards.* 那个冠军在最后的50码使出全部力气争取胜利. **2** (**a**) **the Reserve** [sing] forces outside the regular armed services and liable to be called out in an emergency 预备役部队; 后备军. (**b**) **reserves** [pl] military forces kept back, for use when needed 后备部队: *commit one's reserves to the battle* 将后备部队投入战斗. **3** [C] extra player chosen in case a substitute is needed in a team 替补队员. **4** [C] (**a**) area of land reserved esp as a habitat for nature conservation 保留用地; (尤指)自然保护区: *a ˈbird, ˈgame, ˈwildlife, etc reserve* 鸟类、猎物、野生动物等保护区. (**b**) similar area of land reserved for occupation by a native tribe (土著部落的)专用居留地: *ˈIndian reserves*, eg on the Amazon 印第安部落的居留地(如亚马逊河沿岸的). **5** [U] limitation on one's agreement with a plan, acceptance of an idea, etc (在同意某计划、接受某意见时所加的)限制条件, 保留: *We accept your statement without reserve*, ie fully. 我们毫无保留地接受你的意见. ○ *He spoke without reserve* (ie freely) *of his time in prison.* 他毫无保留地(直言不讳地)述说了他在监狱中的事. **6** [C] (also **reserve price**) (*Brit*) (*US* **upset price**) lowest price that will be accepted, esp for an item at an auction 底价(尤指拍卖时的): *put a reserve of £95 000 on a house* 把一所房子的底价定为95 000英镑 ○ *The Van Gogh failed to reach its reserve and was withdrawn.* 凡高的画因出价未达拍卖底价而收回. **7** [U] tendency to avoid showing one's feelings and appear unsociable to other people; restraint 矜持; 落落寡合; 自制: *For once, she lost/dropped her customary reserve and became quite lively.* 这次, 她一反平素的沉默寡言, 表现得很活跃. ○ *A few drinks broke through his reserve.* 他喝了点酒之后那矜持态度消失了. **8** (idm 习语) **in reˈserve** kept back unused, but available if needed 储存; 留以备用: *funds kept/held in reserve* 备用金.

▷ **re·serv·ist** /rɪˈzɜːvɪst; rɪˋzɝvɪst/ *n* member of a country's reserve forces 预备役军人.

re·served /rɪˈzɜːvd; rɪˋzɝvd/ *adj* (of a person or his character) slow to show feelings or express opinions (指人或性格)矜持的, 寡言的, 内向的: *a reserved disposition, manner, etc* 矜持的性格、态度等. Cf 参看 COMMUNICATIVE. ▷ **re·served·ness** /rɪˈzɜːvɪdnɪs; rɪˋzɝvɪdnɪs/ *n* [U].

res·er·voir /ˈrezəvwɑː(r); ˋrɛzɚˏvwɑr/ *n* **1** natural or artificial lake used as a source or store of water for a town, etc (天然的或人工的)水库, 蓄水池. **2 ~ of sth** (*fig* 比喻) large supply or collection of sth 储藏; 汇集: *a reservoir of information, facts, knowledge, etc* 信息、事实、知识等的蓄积 ○ *The show is a veritable reservoir of new talent.* 这次演出真是新秀荟萃.

re·set /ˌriːˈset; riˋsɛt/ *v* (**-tt-**; *pt*, *pp* **reset**) [Tn] **1** (**a**) place (sth) in position again 重新安放或安置(某物): *reset a diamond in a ring* 在戒指上重镶钻石 ○ *reset a broken bone* 重接断骨 ○ *reset type*, ie in printing 重新排版. (**b**) place (the indicator of a measuring instrument) in a new position 重拨(测量仪器指针): *reset one's watch to local time* 把手表调到当地时间 ○ *reset a dial, gauge, control, etc at zero* 把刻度盘、仪表、控制器指针拨回至零位. **2** devise a new set of questions for (an exam, a test, etc) 为(考试、测试等)出一套新题.

re·settle /ˌriːˈsetl; riˋsɛtl/ *v* (**a**) [I, Tn] help (esp refugees) to settle again in a new country 帮助(尤指难民)定居他国: *resettle refugees in Canada* 帮助难民定居加拿大. (**b**) [Tn] cause (land, a country, etc) to be inhabited again 使(土地、地区等)重新成为定居点: *resettle an island* 使岛上重新有人住. ▷ **re·set·tle·ment** *n* [U]: [attrib 作定语] *a government resettlement programme* 政府重新安置居民的计划.

re·shuffle /ˌriːˈʃʌfl; riˋʃʌfl/ *v* **1** [Tn] interchange the posts or responsibilities of (a group of people) 对(某集体)作岗位或职责的调整; 改组(某团体). **2** [I, Tn] shuffle (playing-cards) again 重新洗(牌).

▷ **ˈre·shuffle** *n* [C] act of reshuffling (esp a political team) 改组(尤指政治组织的): *carry out a Cabinet reshuffle* 进行内阁改组.

res·ide /rɪˈzaɪd; rɪˋzaɪd/ *v* [I, Ipr] (*fml* 文) **1 ~ (in/at...)** have one's home (in a certain place); live 定居(于某处); 居住: *reside abroad* 定居国外 ○ *reside at 10 Elm Terrace* 住在埃尔姆街10号 ○ *reside in college* 住在校内. **2** (phr v) **reside in sb/sth** (of power, rights, etc) be present or vested in sb/sth (指权力、权利等)归于或属于某人[某事物]: *Supreme authority resides in the President/State.* 最高权力属于总统[国家].

res·id·ence /ˈrezɪdəns; ˋrɛzədəns/ *n* (*fml* 文) **1** [C] (**a**) house, esp a large or impressive one 房子; (尤指)大宅, 宅邸, 官邸: *10 Downing Street is the British Prime Minister's official residence.* 唐宁街10号是英国首相的官邸. (**b**) (esp as used by house-agents) house (尤作房屋经纪人用语)房子, 住宅: *a desirable country, family, Georgian, etc residence for sale* 理想的乡间、家居、乔治王朝时期风格等住宅待售. **2** [U] (**a**) process of residing 居住: *hall of residence*, eg for university students 宿舍楼(如大学生的) ○ *take up (one's) residence* (ie go and live) *in college* 住校. (**b**) period of residing 居留期间: *Foreign visitors are only allowed one month's residence.* 外国访客只准逗留一个月. **3** (idm 习语) **in ˈresidence** living in a specified place because of one's work or duties (因工作或职责关系)驻于某处: *The royal standard flies when the Queen is in residence.* 女王的王宫及驻跸处均有王旗为识. ○ *Students must remain in residence during term.* 学生于学期中必须住校. ○ *writer, artist, etc in residence*, eg at a college or in a community, etc which pays him to work there for a period of time 常驻作家、艺术家等(如驻在学校、社区等处者, 为驻地服务获酬).

res·id·ent /ˈrezɪdənt; ˋrɛzədənt/ *n* **1** person who lives or has a home in a place, not a visitor 居民(非来访者): *a (local) residents' association* (本地)居民联合会. **2** (in a hotel) person staying overnight (旅馆的)住宿者: *Restaurant open to non-residents.* 餐厅对非住宿者开放. **3** (*US* also **resident physician**) doctor living at a hospital where he is receiving advanced training 住院医生.

▷ **res·id·ent** *adj* having a home in a place; residing 定居的; 常驻的: *the town's resident population*, ie not tourists or visitors 该城居民人口(不包括游客或来访者) ○ *be resident abroad/in the UK* 常驻国外[英国] ○ (*joc* 谑) *Stanley is our resident crossword fanatic.* 斯坦利是我们中间的填纵横字谜的游戏迷.

res·id·en·tial /ˌrezɪˈdenʃl; ˌrɛzəˋdɛnʃəl/ *adj* [esp attrib 尤作定语] **1** containing or suitable for private houses 住宅的; 适于作住宅的: *a residential area, suburb,* *district, etc*, ie one having no offices, factories, etc 住宅区、近郊住宅区等. **2** connected with or based on residence 与居住有关的: *I often go on residential summer courses.* 我经常去学习必须住校的暑期课程. ○ *residential qualifications for voters*, ie requiring that they should reside in the constituency 选民须为选区居民之资格.

res·idue /ˈrezɪdjuː; *US* -duː; ˋrɛzə,du/ *n* (usu *sing* 通常作单数) **~ (of sth)** **1** what remains after a part or quantity is taken or used 剩余物; 残余. **2** (*law* 律) part of an estate remaining after all debts, charges, bequests, etc have been settled (扣除债款、各种费用、遗赠等之后的)剩余遗产. ⇨Usage at REST³ 用法见 REST³.

▷ **re·sid·ual** /rɪˈzɪdjʊəl; *US* -dʒʊ-; rɪˋzɪdʒʊəl/ *adj* [usu attrib 通常作定语] left over as a residue(1); remaining (作为剩余物)存留下来的; 剩余的; 残余的: *residual chalk deposits*, ie left after rocks have been eroded 残余白垩沉积(岩石经侵蚀后的) ○ *a few residual faults in the computer program* 计算机程序中的少许残留误差.

re·sid·uary /rɪˈzɪdjʊərɪ; *US* -dʒʊerɪ; rɪˋzɪdʒʊ,ɛrɪ/ *adj* **1** of a residue(1); residual 剩余物的; 残余的. **2** (*law* 律) of the residue(2) of an estate 剩余遗产的: *a residuary legatee, clause, bequest* 剩余遗产的承受人、条款、遗赠.

resign /rɪˈzaɪn; rɪˋzaɪn/ *v* **1** [I, Ipr, Tn, Tn·pr] **~ (from sth)** give up (one's job, position, etc) 放弃或辞去(工作、职位等); 辞职: *The Minister resigned (from office).* 那部长辞职了. ○ *She resigned her directorship and left the firm.* 她放弃了董事职务, 离开了公司. ○ *resign (one's post) as chairman* 辞去主席职务. Cf 参看 RETIRE 1. **2** (phr v) **resign oneself to sth/doing sth** be ready to accept and endure sth as inevitable 听任; 顺从: *be resigned to one's fate* 听天由命 ○ *The team refused to resign themselves to defeat/to being defeated.* 该队不甘失败.

▷ **resigned** *adj* **1** [attrib 作定语] having or showing patient acceptance of sth unwelcome or unpleasant 听任的; 顺从的; 逆来顺受的: *a resigned look, smile, gesture* 表示顺从的脸色、微笑、姿势. **2** (idm 习语) **be, etc resigned to sth/doing sth** be ready to endure or tolerate sth 准备忍受或容忍某事物; 甘心情愿: *She seems resigned to not having a holiday this year.* 她对今年不休假似乎并无怨言. **resign·edly** /-nɪdlɪ; -nɪdlɪ/ *adv* in a resigned manner 顺从地; 听之任之.

resig·na·tion /ˌrezɪgˈneɪʃn; ,rɛzɪgˋneʃən/ *n* **1 ~ (from sth)** **(a)** [C, U] (instance of) resigning (职务等的)放弃; 辞职: *Further resignations are expected.* 预料还会有人辞职. ○ *He is considering resignation (from the Board).* 他正考虑辞去(委员会中的)职务. **(b)** [C] letter, etc to one's employers stating one's wish to resign 辞呈: *offer, tender, send in, give in, hand in one's resignation* 提交辞呈 ○ *We haven't yet received his resignation.* 我们尚未收到他的辞呈. **2** [U] patient acceptance or endurance 听任; 顺从: *accept failure with resignation* 情愿承认失败.

re·si·li·ent /rɪˈzɪlɪənt; rɪˋzɪlɪənt/ *adj* **1** (of an object or material) springing back to its original form after being bent, stretched, crushed, etc; springy (指物体或材料)能复原的, 弹性的, 有弹力的. **2** (of a person or character) quickly recovering from shock or depression; buoyant (指人或性格)能迅速恢复或重新振作的, 达观的, 适应性强的: *physically/mentally resilient* 肉体上[精神上]迅速复原的 ○ *She is very resilient to change.* 她对变化有很强的适应力.

▷ **re·si·li·ence** /-əns; -əns/ (also **re·si·li·ency** /-nsɪ; -nsɪ/) *n* [U] **1** quality of being springy 弹性; 弹力; 迅速恢复的能力; 适应性: *an alloy combining strength and resilience* 既有强度又有弹性的合金. **2** (of people) quality of being buoyant (指人)乐观的性情: *Her natural resilience helped her overcome the crisis.* 她生性乐观有助于她渡过难关. **re·si·li·ently** *adv*.

resin /ˈrezɪn; *US* ˈrezn; ˋrɛzn̩/ *n* [C, U] **1** sticky substance that oozes esp from fir and pine trees and is used in making varnish, medicine, etc 树脂(尤指冷杉树脂和松脂). **2** similar substance made synthetically, used as a plastic or in making plastics 合成树脂.

▷ **res·in·ous** /ˈrezɪnəs; *US* ˈrezənəs; ˋrɛzn̩əs/ *adj* of or like resin (似)树脂的.

res·ist /rɪˈzɪst; rɪˋzɪst/ *v* **1** [I, Tn] use force in order to prevent sth happening or being successful; oppose 使用武力以阻止某事物发生或取得成功; 抵抗; 对抗: *He could resist no longer.* 他再也抵抗不住了. ○ *resist an enemy, attack* 抵抗敌人、进攻 ○ *He was charged with resisting arrest.* 他被控拒捕. **2** [I, Tn] regard (a plan, an idea, etc) unfavourably 抵制, 抗拒(计划、主张等): *resist the call for reform* 抗拒实行改革的号召. **3** [Tn] be undamaged or unaffected by (sth) 不受(某事物)的损害或影响; 抗; 耐: *ovenware, glass, etc that resists heat* 耐热的烤箱器皿、玻璃等 ○ *resist corrosion, damp, frost, disease* 抗腐蚀、防潮、防霜冻、防病. **4** [Tn, Tg] succeed in not yielding to (sth/sb) 不屈从(某事物[某人]); 经得住: *resist temptation, chocolate* 经得起诱惑、忍住不吃巧克力 ○ *Jill couldn't resist making jokes about his baldness.* 吉尔忍不住拿他的秃顶开玩笑.

▷ **res·ister** *n* person who resists 抵抗者; 对抗者: *passive resisters* 消极抵抗者.

res·ist·ible *adj* that can be resisted 可抵抗的; 可抗拒的.

res·ist·ance /rɪˈzɪstəns; rɪˋzɪstəns/ *n* **1** [U, sing] **~ (to sth/sb)** (action of) using force to oppose sth/sb 抵抗; 对抗: *break down, overcome, put an end to armed resistance* 粉碎、战胜、停止武装抵抗 ○ *The demonstrators offered little or no resistance to the police.* 示威群众对警方没怎么抵抗. ○ *put up (a) passive resistance* 进行消极抵抗. **2** [U, sing] **~ (to sth)** influence or force that hinders or stops sth 起阻碍或阻止作用的力量; 阻力: *The firm has to overcome its resistance to new technology.* 这家公司必须克服对采用新技术的阻力. ○ *a low wind resistance*, eg in the aerodynamic of planes, cars, etc 低风阻(如飞机、汽车等的空气动力学中者). **3** [U, sing] **~ (to sth)** power to remain undamaged or unaffected (or only slightly so) by sth 抵抗力; 抗力: *the body's natural resistance to disease* 身体对疾病的自然抵抗力 ○ *build up (a) resistance to infection* 增强对传染病的抵抗力. **4** [U] (*physics* 物) (measure of the) property of not conducting heat or electricity 热阻; 电阻. **5** [U] **~ (to sth)** desire to oppose sth; antagonism 反对; 抗拒; 抵制: *make, offer, put up, etc resistance to the proposed changes* 对改革建议进行抵制 ○ *The idea met with some resistance.* 这种意见受到某种抵制. ○ (*commerce* 商) *market resistance*, eg to a new product 市场抗拒(如对新产品). **6** (often 常作 **the Resistance**) [Gp] secret organization resisting the authorities, esp in a conquered or an enemy-occupied country 抵抗运动; (尤指在被征服或敌占区的)秘密抵抗组织: [attrib 作定语] *a resistance fighter* 地下军的战士. **7** (idm 习语) **the line of least resistance** ⇨ LINE¹.

res·ist·ant /rɪˈzɪstənt; rɪˋzɪstənt/ *adj* **~ (to sth)** offering resistance 抵抗的; 对抗的; 抗拒的; 有阻力的: *insects that have become resistant to DDT* 对滴滴涕已有抗药性的昆虫 ○ *a resistant strain of virus* 病毒抵抗株 ○ *be resistant to change* 抗拒变革. ▷ **-resistant** (forming compound *adjs* 用以构成复合形容词): *ˈwater-/ˈheat-/ˈrust-resistant*.

res·istor /rɪˈzɪstə(r); rɪˋzɪstɚ/ *n* device providing resistance to electric current in a circuit 电阻器.

re·sit /ˌriːˈsɪt; riˋsɪt/ *v* (**-tt-**; *pt, pp* **resat**) [Tn] (*Brit*) sit (an examination or test) again, usu after failing 再行(考试或测验); (通常指)补考.

▷ **re·sit** /ˈriːsɪt; ˋrisɪt/ *n* second, etc sitting (of an examination or test) 重考; 补考: *candidates for the September resit* 参加九月份补考的考生.

res·ol·ute /ˈrezəluːt; ˋrɛzə,lut/ *adj* **~ (in sth)** having or showing great determination or firmness 坚决的; 坚定的; 有决心的: *a resolute refusal, approach, measure* 断然的拒绝、坚决的手段、果断的措施 ○ *be resolute in one's demands for peace* 坚决要求和平. ▷ **res·ol·utely** *adv*. **res·ol·ute·ness** *n* [U].

res·olu·tion /ˌrezəˈluːʃn; ,rɛzəˋluʃən/ *n* **1** [U] quality of being resolute or firm; determination 坚决; 坚定; 坚毅: *show great resolution* 表现得十分坚定 ○ *a man lacking in resolution* 缺乏毅力的人 ○ *His speech ended on a note of resolution.* 他演讲结束时语调很坚决. **2** [C] decision or mental pledge to do or not to do sth; resolve 决定; 决心: *make, keep good resolutions* 下定决心 ○ *her resolution never to marry* 她永远不嫁的决心 ○ *New Year resolutions*, eg not to smoke in the new year ahead 新年伊始下的决心(如来年戒烟). **3** [C] formal statement of opinion agreed on by a committee or assembly, esp by means of a vote 正式决定; 决议: *pass, carry, adopt, reject*

R

a resolution 通过、赞同、采纳、否决一决议 ○ *a resolution in favour of/demanding better conditions* 赞成[要求]改善环境的决议 ○ *a resolution that conditions should be improved* 改善环境的决议. **4** [U] (*fml* 文) solution 解决; 解答: *the resolution of a problem, question, difficulty, doubt, etc* 难题、问题、困难、疑问等的解决. **5** [U] **~ (into sth)** process of separating sth or being separated into constituent parts 分解; 解析: *the resolution of white light into the colours of the spectrum* 将白色的光分解成光谱的各种颜色.

re·solve /rɪˈzɒlv; rɪˋzɑlv/ *v* (*fml* 文) **1** [Ipr, Tf, Tt] **~ on/upon/against sth/doing sth** decide firmly; determine 决定; 决心: *He resolved on/against (making) an early start.* 他决定[反对]尽早出发. ○ *She resolved that she would never see him again/never to see him again.* 她决心不再见他. **2** [Tf, Tt] (of a committee or assembly) make a decision by a formal vote (指委员会或集会)表决: *The senate resolved that...* 参议院决议如下... ○ *The union resolved to strike by 36 votes to 15.* 工会以36票对15票通过决议举行罢工. **3** [Tn] solve or settle (problems, doubts, etc) 解决(问题、疑问等): *resolve an argument, a difficulty, a crisis* 解决争端、困难、危机 ○ *Her arrival did little to resolve the situation.* 她来后也未能解决什么问题. **4** [Tn, Tn·pr] **~ sth (into sth)** separate (sth) into constituent parts 分解或解析(某物): *resolve a complex argument into its basic elements* 将复杂的论证内容分为若干要点 ○ *the resolving power of a lens*, ie its ability to magnify things distinctly 透镜的解象能力.

▷ **re·solv·able** *adj* that can be solved or settled 可解决的; 可解答的.

re·solve *n* (*fml* 文) **1** [C] thing one has decided to do; resolution(2) 决定要做的事; 决定; 决心: *make a resolve not to smoke* 决定不吸烟 ○ *show, keep, break one's resolve* 表现出、持有、改变决心. **2** [U] firmness or determination; resolution(1) 坚决; 坚定; 坚毅: *be strong/weak in one's resolve* 很[不]坚决 ○ *His opposition served only to strengthen our resolve.* 他一反对反而增强了我们的决心.

re·solved *adj* [pred 作表语] (of a person) resolute or determined (指人)下定决心, 坚定: *I was fully/firmly resolved to see him.* 我打定主意要去见他.

res·on·ant /ˈrezənənt; ˋrɛzənənt/ *adj* **1** (of sound) continuing to echo; resounding (指声音)回响的, 回荡的, 洪亮的: *deep resonant notes, voices* 深沉而洪亮的声调、声音. **2** (of rooms, bodies, etc) tending to prolong sounds, esp by vibration (指房间、物体等)激起回响的, 引起共鸣的, 产生共振的: *a resonant hall* 产生共鸣的大厅 ○ *the resonant body of a guitar* 吉他的共鸣腔. **3 ~ with sth** (of places) resounding or echoing with sth (指处所)产生某种回响的, 回荡着某种声音的: *Alpine valleys resonant with the sound of church bells.* 回荡着教堂钟声的阿尔卑斯山谷.

▷ **res·on·ance** /-əns; -əns/ *n* [U] quality of being resonant 回响; 回荡; 洪亮; 共鸣; 共振.

res·on·antly *adv*.

res·on·ate /ˈrezəneɪt; ˋrɛzəˌnet/ *v* [I] produce or show resonance 使起回声、共鸣或共振; 产生回响、共鸣或共振. **res·on·ator** /-tə(r); -tɚ/ *n* appliance or system for giving resonance to sound 共鸣器; 共鸣腔; 共振器; 谐振腔.

re·sort /rɪˈzɔːt; rɪˋzɔrt/ *v* [Ipr] **1 ~ to sth** make use of sth for help; adopt sth as an expedient 求助于或诉诸某事物; 采取某手段或方法应急或作为对策: *If negotiations fail we shall have to resort to strike action.* 假若谈判失败, 我们就采取罢工行动. ○ *resort to violence, deception, trickery, etc* 靠暴力、欺骗、欺诈等. **2** [Tn] (*fml* 文) visit (a place) frequently or habitually; frequent 常去, 常到(某处): *The police watched the bars which he was known to resort.* 警方监视着他常去的酒吧.

▷ **re·sort** *n* **1** [C] person or thing that is turned to for help; expedient 可求助的人或事物; 采取的应急手段或对策: *Our only resort is to inform the police.* 我们唯一的办法就是向警方报案. **2** [U] **~ to sth** resorting to sth 求助; 诉诸; 采取; 凭靠: *talk calmly, without resort to threats* 心平气和地说, 不取威胁手段. **3** [C] **(a)** popular holiday centre 度假胜地: *seaside, skiing, health, etc resorts* 海滨、滑雪、休养等度假胜地 ○ *Brighton is a leading south coast resort.* 布赖顿是南部地区最著名的海滨胜地. **(b)** (*US*) hotel or guest-house for holiday-makers 专门接待度假者的旅店或宾馆. **4** (idm 习语) **a/one's last resort** ⇨ LAST[1]. **in the last resort** ⇨ LAST[1].

re·sound /rɪˈzaʊnd; rɪˋzaund/ *v* **1** [I, Ipr] **(a) ~ (through/throughout sth)** (of a sound, voice, etc) fill a place with sound; produce echoes (指声音等)回荡于某处, 产生回响: *The organ resounded (through the church).* 风琴的声音(在教堂里)回荡着. **(b) ~ (with sth)** (of a place) be filled with sound; echo (指某处)回荡着声音, 回响: *The hall resounded with applause.* 大厅里回荡着掌声. **2** [Ipr] **~ (throughout sth)** (*fig* 比喻) (of fame, an event, etc) be much talked of; spread far and wide (指名声、事件等)被广为传颂, 广泛传播: *Her name resounded throughout Europe.* 她名扬全欧洲. Cf 参看 REVERBERATE.

▷ **re·sound·ing** *adj* [attrib 作定语] **1** sounding or echoing loudly 鸣响的; 回响的; 回荡的; 响亮的: *resounding cheers, shouts, laughs* 响亮的欢呼声、叫声、笑声. **2** (of an event, etc) notable; famous (指事件等)令人瞩目的, 闻名的: *win a resounding victory* 获得大胜 ○ *The film was/scored a resounding success.* 那部电影十分成功.

re·sound·ingly *adv*.

re·source /rɪˈsɔːs, *also* -ˈzɔːs; *US* ˈriːsɔːrs; ˋrisɔrs/ *n* **1** [C usu *pl* 通常作复数] supply of raw materials, etc which bring a country, person, etc wealth 资源: *rich in natural, mineral, agricultural, etc resources* 自然的、矿产的、农业的...资源丰富 ○ *The mortgage is a drain on our financial resources.* 偿还抵押借款是我们财务上的一大负担. ○ *We agreed to pool our resources*, ie available assets. 我们同意共用我们现成的资产. ○ *Is there any resource that we have left untapped?* 还有什么资源我们尚未发掘吗? **2** [C usu *pl* 通常作复数] thing that can be turned to for help, support or consolation when needed 必要时可给予帮助、支持或安慰的事物: *He has no inner resources and hates being alone.* 他没有内在的精神寄托, 因而害怕孤独. ○ *An only child is often left to his own resources*, ie left to amuse himself. 独生子女往往要自寻乐趣. ○ [attrib 作定语] *a resource file, room*, eg containing materials for teachers 资料库、室(如供教师使用者). **3** [U] (*fml* 文) ingenuity or quick wit; initiative 才智; 机敏; 创造精神: *a man of great resource* 足智多谋的男子.

▷ **re·source·ful** /-fl; -fəl/ *adj* clever at finding ways of doing things 善于随机应变的; 机敏的; 办法多的. **re·source·fully** /-fəlɪ; -fəlɪ/ *adv*. **re·source·ful·ness** *n* [U].

re·spect[1] /rɪˈspekt; rɪˋspɛkt/ *n* **1** [U] **~ (for sb/sth)** admiration felt or shown for a person or thing that has good qualities or achievements; regard 尊敬; 敬重; 钦敬: *a mark, token, etc of respect* 尊敬的标志、表示等 ○ *have a deep, sincere, etc respect for sb* 深深地、由衷地...敬重某人 ○ *I have the greatest respect for you/hold you in the greatest respect.* 我非常尊敬您. ○ *The new officer soon won/earned the respect of his men.* 那新来的军官很快博得了士兵的钦敬. **2** [U] **~ (for sb/sth)** politeness or consideration arising from admiration or regard 尊敬之表示; 尊重之情: *Children should show respect for their teachers.* 学生要尊敬老师. ○ *Out of respect, he took off his hat.* 他脱帽以示敬意. ○ *have some, little, no, etc respect for sb's feelings* 相当、不太、毫不...尊重某人的感情 ○ *With (all due) respect, sir, I disagree.* 先生, 恕我直言, 我不能同意. **3** [U] **~ (for sb/sth)** protection or recognition 维护; 承认; 尊重: *very little respect for human rights* 极不尊重人权. **4** [C] particular aspect or detail 方面; 着眼点: *in this one respect* 在这一点上 ○ *in some/all/many/several/few respects* 在某些[各个/许多/几个/极少]方面 ○ *In what respect do you think the film is biased?* 你认为影片在哪一方面失之偏颇? **5** (idm 习语) **in respect of sth** (*fml or commerce* 文或商) as regards sth; with special reference to sth 关于某事物; 就某方面而言: *The book is admirable in respect of style.* 这本书风格极佳. ○ *price rises in respect of gas and water costs* 煤气费和水费涨价. **with respect to sth** (*fml or commerce* 文或商) concerning sth 涉及、提到或关于某事物: *This is true with respect to English but not to French.* 这一点在英语属实而在法语则不同. ○ *With respect to your enquiry, I enclose an explanatory leaflet.* 关于你的询问, 兹附上有关说明资料.

▷ **re·spects** *n* [pl] (*fml* 文) **1** polite greetings 敬意; 问候: *Give/send/offer him my respects.* 代我向他致意. **2** (idm 习语) **pay one's respects** ⇨ PAY[2].

re·spect[2] /rɪˈspekt; rɪˋspɛkt/ *v* **1** [Tn, Tn·pr] **~ sb/sth (for sth)** admire or have a high opinion of sb/sth (because of sth) (因某事物)尊敬或敬重某人[某事物]: *I respect you for your honesty.* 由于你为人正直, 我对你十分敬重. **2** [Tn] show consideration for (sb/sth) 重视、考虑或尊重(某人[某事物]): *respect sb's wishes, opinions, feelings, etc* 尊重某人的意愿、意见、感情等 ○ *respect the environment*, eg by protecting it 重视环境问题(如保护环境) ○ *People won't respect my (desire for) privacy.* 大家都不顾及我(希望享有的)个人自由. **3** [Tn, Cn·n/a] **~ sth (as sth)** avoid interfering with or harming sth; agree to recognize 不干预或不损害某事物; 承认某事物: *respect sb's rights, privileges, etc* 承认某人的权利、特权等 ○ *respect a treaty, contract, etc* 遵守条约、合同等 ○ *respect diplomatic immunity* (eg of foreign embassy staff to British law) *as valid* 承认外交豁免权有效. **4** [Tn] **~ oneself** have proper respect for one's own character and behaviour 自重; 自尊: *If you don't respect yourself, how can you expect others to respect you?* 自己不自重, 又怎能受到别人尊重呢?

▷ **re·specter** *n* (idm 习语) **be no/not be any respecter of ˈpersons** treat everyone in the same way, without being influenced by their importance, wealth, etc 不问贫富贵贱, 一视同仁: *Death is no respecter of persons.* 死神不区分贫富贵贱.

re·spect·ing *prep* (*fml* 文) relating to (sth); concerning 关于, 至于(某事物): *laws respecting property* 关于财产的法律 ○ *information respecting the child's whereabouts* 关于那孩子的下落的消息.

re·spect·able /rɪˈspektəbl; rɪˋspɛktəbl/ *adj* **1** of acceptable social position; decent and proper in appearance or behaviour 体面的; 有身分的; 正派的; 值得尊敬的: *a respectable married couple* 一对值得尊敬的夫妻 ○ *a respectable middle-class background, upbringing, etc* 体面的中产阶级的出身、正派人所受的教养 ○ *She looked perfectly respectable in her bathrobe at breakfast.* 她用早餐时穿着浴衣, 真够风雅的. ○ (*ironic* 反语) *He's a bit too respectable* (ie staid and conventional) *for my tastes.* 他老成持重未免过分, 我可不欣赏. **2** of a moderately good standard or size, etc; not bringing disgrace or embarrassment 达到一定标准或规模的; 不丢脸的: *There was quite a respectable crowd at the match on Saturday.* 星期六观看比赛的人相当多. ○ *£20 000 is a very respectable salary.* 20 000 英镑的薪金是非常可观的. ○ *Hunt jumped a respectable round although his horse was unfit.* 亨特的马状态欠佳, 但他纵马跳障碍这一轮还算不错.

▷ **re·spect·ab·il·ity** /rɪˌspektəˈbɪlətɪ; rɪˌspɛktəˋbɪlətɪ/ *n* [U] quality of being socially respectable; decency 名望; 体面; 得体.

re·spect·ably /-əblɪ; -əblɪ/ *adv* in a respectable manner 体面地; 得体地; 可敬地; 相当地: *respectably dressed, behaved, spoken, etc* 衣着、举止、言语等得体的.

re·spect·ful /rɪˈspektfl; rɪˋspɛktfəl/ *adj* **~ (to/towards sb); ~ (of sth)** feeling or showing respect 恭敬的; 表示尊敬或尊重的: *listen in respectful silence* 必恭必敬地静听着 ○ *stand at a respectful distance* 表示尊敬地保持距离站着 ○ *respectful of other people's opinions* 尊重他人的意见. ▷ **re·spect·fully** /-fəlɪ; -fəlɪ/ *adv.* **re·spect·ful·ness** *n* [U].

re·spect·ive /rɪˈspektɪv; rɪˋspɛktɪv/ *adj* [attrib 作定语] of or for or belonging to each as an individual 各自的; 各个的; 分别的: *They each excel in their respective fields.* 他们在各自领域里都是出类拔萃的. ○ *After the party we all went off to our respective rooms.* 聚会之后我们回到各自的房间.

▷ **re·spect·ively** *adv* separately or in turn, in the order mentioned 各自地; 分别地; 轮流地: *German and Italian courses are held in Munich and Rome respectively.* 德语和意大利语课程分别设于慕尼黑和罗马.

res·pira·tion /ˌrespəˈreɪʃn; ˌrɛspəˋreʃən/ *n* **1** [C, U] (*fml* 文) (single act of) breathing air 呼吸; 一次呼吸: [attrib 作定语] *respiration rate* 呼吸率. **2** [U] plant's absorption of oxygen and release of carbon dioxide (植物的)呼吸.

res·pir·ator /ˈrespəreɪtə(r); ˋrɛspəˌretɚ/ *n* [C] **1** apparatus for giving artificial respiration over a long period 人工呼吸器: *put the patient on a respirator* 给患者戴上人工呼吸器. **2** device worn over the nose and mouth to warm, filter or purify air before it is breathed 口罩; 呼吸保护罩; 防毒面具.

re·spire /rɪˈspaɪə(r); rɪˋspaɪr/ *v* [I] **1** (*fml* 文) breathe air 呼吸: *respire deeply* 深呼吸. **2** (of plants) absorb oxygen and release carbon dioxide (指植物)呼吸.

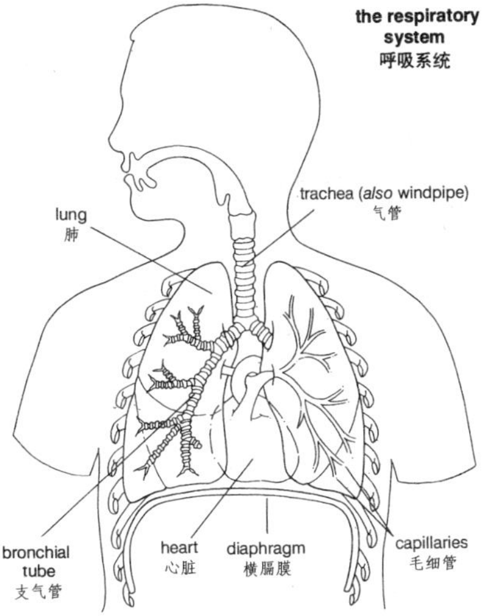

▷ **res·pir·at·ory** /rɪˈspaɪərətrɪ, ˈrespɪrətrɪ; *US* -tɔːrɪ; rɪˋspaɪrəˌtɔrɪ/ *adj* [esp attrib 尤作定语] (*medical* 医) of or for breathing air 呼吸的; 呼吸用的: *respiratory diseases*, eg bronchitis, asthma 呼吸道疾病(如支气管炎、气喘) ○ *respiratory organs, systems* 呼吸器官、系统.

res·pite /ˈrespaɪt, ˈrespɪt; ˋrɛspɪt/ *n* **1** [U, sing] **~ (from sth)** interval of rest or relief 休息(时间); 暂时的缓解或放松: *longing for a moment of respite* 恨不得歇会儿 ○ *work without respite* 不停地工作 ○ *a brief, welcome respite* 短暂的、愉快的休息 ○ *(a) respite from pain, worry, stress, etc* 痛苦、忧虑、压力等的暂时减轻. **2** [C] delay allowed before an obligation must be fulfilled or a penalty suffered; reprieve (义务的)暂缓履行; (刑罚的)缓期执行; 缓刑: *grant sb a respite* 准予某人缓刑.

re·splen·dent /rɪˈsplendənt; rɪˋsplɛndənt/ *adj* [usu pred 通常作表语] **~ (in sth)** (*fml* 文) brilliant with colour or decorations; splendid 华丽灿烂; 辉煌: *resplendent in coronation robes* 身穿加冕礼服而光彩夺目 ○ (*ironic* 反语) *resplendent in her curlers and a face-pack* 戴着发卷抹着美容霜而臭美的. ▷ **re·splen·dence** /-əns; -əns/ *n* [U]. **re·splen·dently** *adv*.

re·spond /rɪˈspɒnd; rɪˋspɑnd/ *v* [I, Ipr] **1 ~ (to sb/sth) (with sth)** give a verbal or written answer (以口头或书面方式)回答: *She asked where he'd been, but he didn't respond.* 她问他到什么地方去了, 他却不回答. ○ *She responded to my letter with a phone call.* 她收到我的信, 给我回了个电话. **2 ~ (to sth) (with sth)** act in answer to (sth) or because of the action of another; behave in a similar way (对某事物或对他人的行动)反应, 回应, 响应: *He responded to my volley with a backhand*, ie in tennis. 他反手一击把我截击的空中球打了回来(网球中). ○ *I kicked the dog, which responded by growling/with a growl.* 我踢了那条狗, 它便狂吠起来. **3 ~ (to sb/sth)** react quickly or favourably (to or because of sb/sth); be easily controlled (by sb/sth) (对某人[某事物])反应灵敏; 易(为某人[某事物])控制: *The car responds well to the controls.* 这辆汽车操纵灵敏. ○ *The patient did not respond to treatment.* 病人经治疗后未见起色. ○ *Animals respond to kindness.* 动物受到善待能做出反应. **4 ~ (to sb/sth)** (of people at a church service) make the responses (指在教堂做礼拜的人)应答.

re·spond·ent /rɪˈspɒndənt; rɪˈspandənt/ *n* (*law* 律) defendant, esp in a divorce case 被告(尤指离婚案的).

re·sponse /rɪˈspɒns; rɪˈspans/ *n* **~ (to sb/sth)** **1** [C, U] answer 回答; 答复: *She made no response.* 她没有回答. ○ *In response to your inquiry...* 兹答复您的询问... ○ *His accusations brought an immediate response.* 他提出指控后迅即得到答复. **2** [C, U] act or feeling produced in answer to a stimulus; reaction 反应; 响应: *a poor, generous, united, etc response to the appeal for funds* 对征集资金的呼吁反应甚微、积极响应、群起响应等 ○ *Her cries for help met with no, some, little, etc response.* 她那求救的呼声没有激起任何、激起了一些、没有激起什么...反应. ○ *The tax cuts produced a favourable response from the public.* 税额削减受到了公众的欢迎. **3** [C usu *pl* 通常作复数] (*religion* 宗) part of the liturgy said or sung by the people at a church service in answer to the priest (礼拜时会众对牧师的)应答, 唱和. Cf 参看 VERSICLE.

re·spons·ib·il·ity /rɪˌspɒnsəˈbɪlətɪ; rɪˌspansəˈbɪlətɪ/ *n* **1** [U] **~ (for sb/sth)** being responsible or accountable 责任; 负责: *a position of real, great, major, etc responsibility* 负实际的、很大的、主要的...责任的职务 ○ *have, show a sense of responsibility* 有、显示出责任感 ○ *take, assume, accept, bear full responsibility for the consequences* 对后果承担全部责任 ○ *The manufacturers disclaim all responsibility for damage caused by misuse.* 使用不当而造成的损坏, 生产厂家不负任何责任. **2** [C] **~ (to sb)** commitment or duty for which a person is responsible 职责; 任务; 义务: *Our business is a joint/shared responsibility.* 我们的公司实行共同责任制. ○ *It's my responsibility to lock the doors.* 我负责锁门. ○ *the various responsibilities of the post* 这一职位的多种责任.

res·pons·ible /rɪˈspɒnsəbl; rɪˈspansəbl/ *adj* **1** [pred 作表语] **~ (for sb/sth); ~ (for doing sth)** legally or morally obliged, eg to take care of sb/sth or to carry out a duty, and liable to be blamed if one fails (在法律上或道义上)须负责任, 承担责任: *All pilots are responsible for their passengers' safety.* 凡是飞机驾驶员均应对乘客的安全负责. ○ *I am wholly/partly responsible for the confusion.* 我对此混乱情况负有全部[部分]责任. ○ *You must make yourself personally responsible for paying these bills.* 你应该个人支付这些帐. **2** [pred 作表语] **~ to sb/sth** having to account for one's actions to an authority or a superior 对自己的行动向主管者或上级承担责任: *be directly/indirectly responsible to the President* 直接[间接]向总统负责. **3** [pred 作表语] **~ (for sth)** answerable for one's behaviour 应对自己的行为负责: *A drunk man cannot be held/considered fully responsible for his actions.* 醉汉不能为其行为负全部责任. **4** (**a**) (of people) capable of being relied on; trustworthy (指人)可靠的, 可信赖的: *behave like responsible citizens, adults, committee members* 做有责任心的公民、成年人、委员 ○ *She is very responsible for* (ie considering that she is) *a six-year-old.* 对于六岁的孩子来说, 她算是很靠得住的. Cf 参看 IRRESPONSIBLE. (**b**) [esp attrib 尤作定语] (of jobs, etc) needing sb who can be relied on; involving important duties (指工作等)需可靠的人来做的; 责任重大的: *a highly responsible position, appointment, role* 极其重要的职位、职务、职责. **5** [pred 作表语] **~ (for sth)** being the cause (of sth) 作为(某事物的)原因; 应归咎或归功(于某事物): *Who's responsible for this mess?* 是谁弄得这么乱? ○ *Smoking is responsible for many cases of lung cancer.* 吸烟是许多人患肺癌的致病因素.

▷ **re·spons·ibly** /-əblɪ; -ablɪ/ *adv* in a rational or trustworthy way 明事理地; 合乎理性地; 可信赖地: *act, behave responsibly* 行动、行事靠得住.

re·spons·ive /rɪˈspɒnsɪv; rɪˈspansɪv/ *adj* **1 ~ (to sb/sth)** (**a**) responding warmly or favourably; sympathetic 反应热烈的或良好的; 赞同的; 支持的: *a responsive class, audience, etc* 积极应答的班级、反应很热烈的观众 ○ *be responsive to suggestions, ideas, criticisms, etc* 对建议、意见、批评等表示欢迎. (**b**) [usu pred 通常作表语] reacting quickly or favourably; easily controlled 反应灵敏; 易受控制: *These brakes should be more responsive.* 这些制动器应该更灵敏些. ○ *a flu virus that is not responsive to treatment* 不易治疗的流感病毒 ○ *a horse responsive to the needs of its rider* 很好骑的马. **2** [esp attrib 尤作定语] given or made as an answer 回答的; 应答的: *a responsive smile, gesture, wink, etc* 表示回应的微笑、手势、眨眼等. ▷ **re·spons·ively** *adv.* **re·spons·ive·ness** *n* [U].

rest[1] /rest; rɛst/ *v* **1** (**a**) [I, Ipr] **~ (from sth)** be still or asleep; stop moving or working, esp in order to regain one's strength 静止; 睡眠; 停止活动或工作; (尤指)休息: *lie down and rest (for) an hour after lunch* 午饭后躺下休息一小时 ○ *resting from our exertions, efforts, etc* 劳作、工作后休息一下 ○ (*fig* 比喻) *He will never rest* (ie never have peace of mind) *until he knows the truth.* 他不获真相是不会安心的. (**b**) [Tn, Tn·pr] cause or allow (sth/sb) to do this 使或让(某物[某人])静止、睡眠或休息: *You should rest your eyes after a lot of reading.* 长时间阅读后应该让眼睛休息一下. ○ *Sit down and rest your legs.* 坐下歇歇腿儿吧. ○ *Are you rested enough to go on?* 你是否歇够了可以接着干了? **2** [Ipr, Tn·pr] **~ (sth) on/against sth** lie or be placed on/against sth for support 躺或倚靠在某物上; 靠某物支撑: *Her elbows rested/She rested her elbows on the table.* 她的肘部[她把肘部]靠在桌子上. ○ *Rest the ladder against the wall.* 把梯子靠在墙上. **3** [Ipr] **~ on sb/sth** depend or rely on sb/sth 依靠或依赖某人[某事物]: *British hopes of a medal rested on Ovett.* 英国把获得奖牌的希望寄托在奥维特的身上. **4** [Ipr] **~ on sb/sth** (of a look, etc) be directed steadily at sb/sth (指目光等)停留在某人[某物]上: *His gaze/eyes rested on her face.* 他双眼凝视着她的脸. **5** [I] (*fml* 文) (of a subject under discussion) be left without further investigation or pursuit (指问题的探讨)中止: *let the matter, topic, affair, etc rest* 使事情、话题、事务等到此为止 ○ *The matter cannot rest there — I demand an apology.* 事情不能就此罢了 —— 我要求向我道歉. **6** [I, Tn] (*esp law* 尤用于法律) conclude (one's case); have no more to say about (sth) 停止(举证); 自动停止陈述(某事): *The defence rests.* 被告陈述完毕. ○ *I rest my case.* 本人对案情陈述完毕. **7** [I] (*euph or fig* 婉或比喻) be buried 长眠; 安息: *May he rest* (ie lie in his grave) *in peace.* 愿他安息. **8** [I, Tn] (cause land to) be free from disturbance, etc (使土地)休耕: *Let this field rest/Rest this field for a year.* 让这块田地休耕一年. **9** (idm 习语) **rest assured (that...)** (*fml* 文) be certain that... 放心...: *You may rest assured that everything possible is being done.* 你尽管放心, 正在尽力把一切都做好. **rest on one's 'laurels** (*esp derog* 尤作贬义) stop trying to achieve further successes; become complacent 满足于既有的成绩而不思进取; 自满. **10** (phr v) **rest on sth** (no passive 不用于被动语态) be based on sth 建立在某事物的基础上; 基于某事物: *His fame rests more on his plays than on his novels.* 他出名是靠他的戏剧, 并不是靠小说. ○ *an argument, a claim, a theory, etc resting on a false assumption* 根据凭空设想而提出的论点、要求、理论等. **rest with sb (to do sth)** (*fml* 文) be sb's responsibility (to do sth) (做某事)是某人的责任: *The choice rests entirely with you.* 这完全由你来选择. ○ *It rests with the committee to decide.* 这事要由委员会来决定.

□ **'resting-place** *n* (*euph* 婉) grave 安息处; 坟墓: *His last resting-place is on that hill.* 他的长眠处就在那座山上.

rest[2] /rest; rɛst/ *n* **1** [C, U] **~ (from sth)** (period of) sleep or inactivity as a way of regaining one's strength 睡眠或休息(的时间): *have a good night's rest* 睡一宿好觉 ○ *stop for a well-earned/-deserved rest* 停下来该好好休息一下 ○ *have/take a rest from all your hard work* 放下繁重的工作休息一下 ○ *get some, no, more, etc rest* 稍事、得不到、再多...休息(一下) ○ *Sunday is a day of rest.* 星期日休息. ⇨Usage at BREAK[2] 用法见 BREAK[2]. **2** [C] (often in compounds 常用以构成复合词) support for an object; prop 支承物; 支撑物; 支架; 支座; 托; 台: *a rest for a billiard cue, telescope, telephone receiver* 台球杆的搁架、望远镜的支架、电话听筒的托架 ○ *an 'arm-, 'head-, 'foot-rest* 扶手、头枕、搁脚物. **3** [C] (*music* 音) (sign making an) interval of silence between notes 休止(符): *The trumpets have six bars' rest.* 小号有六小节休止. ⇨illus at MUSIC 见 MUSIC 插图. **4** (idm 习语) **at 'rest** (**a**) not moving 静止; 不动. (**b**) free from trouble or anxiety 安宁: (*euph* 婉) *be/lie at rest* (ie be buried) *in a country churchyard* 安息在乡间的教堂墓地里. **come to 'rest** (of a moving object) stop moving (指运动中的物体)停止, 不再移动: *The mine finally came to rest on the sea bed.* 那水雷最后沉入海底. **lay sb to 'rest**

(*euph* 婉) bury sb 安葬某人: *She was laid to rest beside her late husband.* 她安葬在亡夫的墓旁. **put/set sb's mind at ease/rest** ⇨ MIND[1].

▷ **rest·ful** /-fl; -fəl/ *adj* **~ (to sb/sth)** giving (a feeling of) rest 让人得到休息的; 令人有宁静感的: *a restful Sunday afternoon* 可以好好休息一下的星期日下午 ○ *Pastel colours are restful to the eye.* 清淡柔和的颜色可以养目. **rest·fully** /-fəlɪ; -fəlɪ/ *adv*. **rest·ful·ness** *n* [U].

□ ˈ**rest area**, ˈ**rest stop** (*US*) = LAY-BY.

ˈ**rest-cure** *n* long period of rest, usu in bed, as medical treatment for stress, anxiety, etc 休养疗法(通常须卧床, 用以治疗因紧张、焦急等所致的疾病).

ˈ**rest-day** *n* day spent resting, esp during an international cricket match 休息日(尤指国际板球赛期间的).

ˈ**rest-home** *n* place where old or convalescent people are cared for 养老院; 疗养院.

ˈ**rest-room** *n* (*US euph* 婉) public lavatory in eg a theatre, store 盥洗室, 洗手间, 公共厕所(如剧院、商店内的). ⇨Usage at TOILET 用法见 TOILET.

rest[3] /rest; rɛst/ *n* **the ~ (of sth)** **1** [sing] the remaining part; the remainder of some amount 剩余部分; 其余: *the rest of the world, my life, her money* 世界的其他地方、我的余生、她剩下的钱 ○ *watch the rest of a film* 观看一部影片的剩余部分 ○ *Take what you want and throw the rest away.* 把你要的拿走, 剩下的扔掉. **2** [pl *v*] the remaining individuals or number; the others 其余的人或数目; 其他人; 其他事物: *While we play tennis what will the rest of you do?* 我们打网球, 你们其余的人做什么呢? ○ *Her hat was red, like the rest of her clothes.* 她的帽子是红色的, 跟她衣服的颜色一样. **3** (idm 习语) **for the** ˈ**rest** (*fml* 文) as far as other matters are concerned; apart from that 至于其他; 除此之外: *Ensure that our traditional markets are looked after; for the rest, I am not much concerned.* 一定要满足我们传统市场的需要, 其他方面倒无所谓.

NOTE ON USAGE 用法: When speaking about who or what remains from an original total, we use **the rest** or (more formal) **the remainder** 表示在原有总体中剩下的人或事物, 可用**the rest**, 在较庄重场合可用**the remainder**: *Some boys stay on after school; the rest/remainder (of them) go home.* 放学后总有些男孩子不走, 其余的人回家. ○ *The rest/remainder of the time was spent swimming.* 剩下的时间用来游泳. If something has been partly used or destroyed, we use **remains** or **remnants.** 若某物的一部分已用掉或毁掉, 其剩余或残存部分可用 **remains**或**remnants**表示. Of food **left-overs** is often used 若为食物, 则多用**left-overs**: *The remains/remnants/left-overs of the meal* (ie the bits of food left uneaten) *were fed to the dog.* 剩饭喂狗了. **Remains** is also used of old buildings or dead bodies ☆ **remains**还可指古旧建筑物或尸体: *the remains of an old castle* 古堡的废墟 ○ *human remains* 人的遗体. A **relic** is a historical object and reminder of the past. ☆ **relic**指历史遗物、遗迹以及纪念物品. A **residue** is what is left after a process, especially a chemical one, has taken place. ☆ **residue**指某一过程(尤指化学反应)的残余物. *There is a green residue in the bottom of the test tube.* 试管底部有绿色的沉淀. In a mathematical calculation the **remainder** (in arithmetic) or the **balance** (in accounting) is the amount left after subtraction or division. 在数学计算中**remainder**指(算术中的)差数或余数, **balance**指(会计学中的)余额或差额.

re·state /ˌriːˈsteɪt; riˋstet/ *v* [Tn] state (sth) again or in a different way 重述或以另一方式重申(某事物): *restate one's position, case, argument, etc* 重新阐述立场、情况、论点等. ▷ **re·state·ment** *n* [C, U]: *make a restatement of current policy* 重申现行的政策.

res·taur·ant /ˈrestrɒnt; *US* -tərənt; ˋrɛstərənt/ *n* public place where meals can be bought and eaten 餐馆; 饭店. Cf 参看 CAFÉ.

▷ **res·taur·at·eur** /ˌrestərəˈtɜː(r); ˌrɛstərəˋtɝ/ (*US* also **res·taur·ant·eur** /-tərən-; -tərən-/) *n* (*fml* 文) manager or owner of a restaurant 餐馆的经理或老板.

□ ˈ**restaurant car** (*Brit*) = DINING-CAR (DINE).

res·ti·tu·tion /ˌrestɪˈtjuːʃn; *US* -ˈtuː-; ˌrɛstəˋtuʃən/ *n* [U] **~ (to sb/sth)** **1** (*fml* 文) restoration of a thing to its proper owner or original state (物之)归还原主; (事物之)恢复原状: *restitution of the deeds to the owner* 契据归还原主 ○ *the full restitution of property, conjugal rights, diplomatic status* 财产的全部归还、婚姻权的完全恢复、外交地位的完全恢复. **2** (*law* 律) reparation, esp in the form of money, for injury, etc (对损害等的)赔偿, 补偿(尤指用钱): *make restitution for the damage done* 赔偿所造成的损失.

rest·ive /ˈrestɪv; ˋrɛstɪv/ *adj* **1** restless or uneasy 焦躁不安的; 不安宁的: *Another hour passed and the crowd grew/became restive.* 又过了一个小时, 人们有些不耐烦了. **2** (esp of horses) resisting control, esp by refusing to move forwards or by moving sideways or backwards (尤指马)难驾驭的, (尤指)不肯前行的, 逡巡不前的. ▷ **rest·ively** *adv*: *move, shuffle, fiddle about restively* 焦急地走来走去、踱来踱去、荡来荡去. **rest·ive·ness** *n* [U].

rest·less /ˈrestlɪs; ˋrɛstlɪs/ *adj* **1** constantly moving 运动不止的: *the restless motion of the sea* 大海的不停的翻腾. **2** unable to be still or quiet, esp because of boredom, impatience, anxiety, etc 静不下来的, 不能安宁的(尤指因厌烦、烦躁、焦虑等): *The audience was becoming restless.* 观众渐渐地不耐烦了. ○ *The children grew restless with the long wait.* 孩子们等了很久便着急了. ○ *After only a month in the job, he felt restless and decided to leave.* 那工作他只干了一个月就厌倦了, 决定不干了. **3** without rest or sleep 得不到休息或睡眠的: *spend/pass/have a restless night* 度过一个不眠之夜. ▷ **rest·lessly** *adv*: *The wind moved restlessly through the trees.* 风不停地吹过树林. ○ *The lion paced restlessly up and down in its cage.* 狮子在笼子里不安地来回走动. **rest·less·ness** *n* [U].

re·stock /ˌriːˈstɒk; riˋstɑk/ *v* **1** [Tn, Tn·pr] **~ sth (with sth)** fill sth with new or different things to replace those used, sold, etc 补充新的或他种物品以替换用掉、售出…之物品; 补足货源: *restock the freezer for Christmas* 把新食物装入冰箱冷冻室为圣诞节做准备 ○ *restock the library shelves with new books* 进一些新书补充到图书馆的书架上 ○ *restock a lake/river with trout* 在湖[河]里再放养一些鳟鱼. **2** [Tn] take (a supply of sth) again, eg after an interval 补充(供应物)(如隔一段时间后): *restock the dictionary in its new edition* 重新购置该词典的新版本.

res·tora·tion /ˌrestəˈreɪʃn; ˌrɛstəˋreʃən/ *n* **1** [U] **~ (to sb/sth)** return of sth lost, etc to its owner (遗失等物的)归还原主: *the restoration of stolen property, goods, etc* 失窃财物、物品等的归还. **2** [U] **~ (to sth)** restoring or being restored to a former place or condition 回复到原处或原状; 恢复: *the restoration of the Elgin marbles to Greece* 埃尔金大理石雕塑品的交还给希腊 ○ *her restoration to complete health* 她的完全康复 ○ *the restoration of order after the riots* 骚乱之后秩序的恢复. **3** [U, C] **~ (to sb/sth)** reintroduction of sth, eg after it has lapsed or been withdrawn 重新采用, 恢复(如消失或取消后): *the restoration of old customs* 旧习俗的恢复 ○ *We demand an immediate restoration of our right to vote.* 我们要求立即恢复我们的选举权. **4** [C, U] (example of the) work of restoring a ruined building, work of art, etc to its original condition (损坏的建筑物、艺术品等的)修复, 整修: *undergo a lengthy process of restoration* 经过漫长的修复过程 ○ *The palace is closed during restorations/for restoration.* 宫殿于整修期间[因整修]停止开放. ○ [attrib 作定语] *the museum restoration fund* 整修博物馆的资金 ○ *(a) full/complete restoration of the damaged painting, vase, mosaic, etc* 受到损坏的画、花瓶、镶嵌画等的完全修复. **5** [C] building formerly ruined and now rebuilt; reconstruction (毁坏后重建的)建筑物; 重建: *The castle is largely a restoration,* ie little of the original is left. 该城堡大部分是重建的. **6** [C] model representing the supposed form of an extinct animal, a ruined building, etc (绝种动物、已毁建筑物等的)模型: *a restoration of an Iron-Age cave dwelling* 模拟铁器时代穴居生活的洞穴. **7 the Restoration** [sing] (period following) the re-establishment of the monarchy in Britain in 1660, when Charles II became king (1660年英王查理二世的)王政复辟(时期): [attrib 作定语] *Restoration comedy, poetry* 王政复辟时期的喜剧、诗.

res·tor·at·ive /rɪˈstɔːrətɪv; rɪˋstɔrətɪv/ *adj* [esp attrib 尤

作定语] tending to restore health and strength 有助于恢复健康和体力的: *restorative drugs, exercises, tonics* 促进健康恢复的药物、运动、滋补品 ○ *the restorative powers of sea air* 海上空气可使人恢复体力的作用.

▷ **res·tor·at·ive** *n* [C, U] restorative food, medicine or treatment 有助于恢复健康或体力的食物、药品或疗法: *The brandy acted as a restorative.* 喝白兰地酒消除了疲劳.

re·store /rɪˈstɔː(r); rɪˈstɔr/ *v* **1** [Tn, Tn·pr] **~ sth (to sb/sth)** (*fml* 文) give back (sth lost, etc) to its owner 将(某失物等)归还原主: *Police restored the stolen jewels to the showroom.* 警方将被盗的珠宝交还给了陈列室. **2** (**a**) [Tn·pr] **~ sb/sth to sth** bring sb/sth back to a former place or position 使某人[某物]回复到原处或原位: *restore sacked workers to their old jobs* 使被解雇的工人复工 ○ *restore an officer to his command* 恢复一军官的指挥权 ○ (*fml* 文) *He restored the dictionary to the shelf.* 他把词典放回到书架上. (**b**) [Tn, Tn·pr] **~ sb (to sth); ~ sth (to sb)** bring sb/sth back to a former condition 使某人[某物]恢复原先的状况: *restore my health/me to health* 使我恢复健康 ○ *restore sb's beauty, sight, confidence, etc* 恢复某人的姿色、视力、信心等 ○ *The brandy fully/completely restored him.* 他喝了白兰地酒以后完全恢复了体力. ○ *Law and order were quickly restored after the riots.* 骚乱过后很快恢复了治安. ○ *The deposed chief was restored (to power/to his throne).* 废黜的酋长重新掌了权. **3** [Tn, Tn·pr] **~ sth (to sb)** bring sth back into use, eg after it has lapsed or been withdrawn 重新采用某事物(如终止或取消后): *restore ancient traditions, rights, ceremonies, etc* 恢复古已有之的传统、权利、礼仪等 ○ *restore old laws, taxes, charges, etc* 恢复旧时的法律、税制、收费等 ○ *Our Christmas bonus should be restored.* 我们发圣诞节赠金的做法应予恢复. **4** [Tn, Tn·pr] **~ sth (to sth)** rebuild or repair (a ruined building, work of art, etc) so that it is like the original 重建或修复(被毁之建筑物、艺术品等): *restore a Roman fort, a vintage car, an oil painting, a china vase, etc* 修复罗马的要塞、老式汽车、油画、瓷花瓶等 ○ *The mill was restored to full working order.* 这工厂已完全恢复生产. Cf 参看 RENOVATE.

▷ **re·storer** *n* (esp in compounds 尤用以构成复合词) [C] (**a**) person who restores (RESTORE 4) things 做修复工作的人: *picture, furniture restorers* 修复画、家具的人. (**b**) [C, U] substance, etc that restores (RESTORE 2b) things 用以恢复原状的物质; 恢复剂: *hair-restorer*, ie to cure baldness 生发剂.

re·strain /rɪˈstreɪn; rɪˈstren/ *v* [Tn, Tn·pr] **~ sb/sth (from sth/doing sth)** hold back sb/sth from movement or action; keep sb/sth under control or in check 抑制或遏制某人[某事物]; 管制; 约束: *restrain one's anger, laughter, tears* 抑制住愤怒、笑声、眼泪 ○ *restrain one's natural urges, impulses, etc* 克制住欲望、冲动等 ○ *I must learn to restrain myself*, eg not say what I think. 我得学会约束自己. ○ *The police had difficulty in restraining the crowd from rushing on to the pitch.* 警方难以阻止人群涌入球场.

▷ **re·strained** *adj* keeping one's feelings, language or behaviour in check; controlled (感情、言语或行为)克制的, 节制的, 受到控制的: *a restrained rebuke, protest, discussion* 有节制的斥责、抗议、讨论 ○ *He was furious, but his manner was very restrained.* 他十分恼火, 但在态度上却很能克制.

re·straint /rɪˈstreɪnt; rɪˈstrent/ *n* (*fml* 文) **1** [U] restraining or being restrained 抑制; 遏制; 管制; 约束: *submit to/break loose from restraint* 忍受[摆脱]束缚 ○ *The child's affections were kept under/suffered continual restraint.* 那孩子的感情一直受到压抑. **2** [C] **~ (on sb/sth)** thing that checks or controls; restriction 起遏制作用的事物; 管制措施; 约束力: *the restraints on the family budget of a limited income* 有限的收入对家庭开支预算的约束 ○ *throw off the restraints of convention* 打破常规 ○ *impose restraints on wage settlements* 对工资的协议加以限制. **3** [U] **~ (in sth)** avoidance of exaggeration or excess; moderation 克制; 节制; 适度: *He showed/exercised considerable restraint in not suing for a divorce.* 他极力克制自己, 不提出离婚诉讼. **4** (idm 习语) **without reˈstraint** without control; freely 无拘无束地; 自由地: *talk, weep without restraint* 畅谈、痛哭.

re·strict /rɪˈstrɪkt; rɪˈstrɪkt/ *v* [Tn, Tn·pr] **~ sb/sth (to sth)** put a limit on sb/sth 限制或约束某人[某事物]: *Fog restricted visibility.* 雾天能见度很低. ○ *measures restricting one's freedom, authority, rights* 限制自由、权力、权利的措施 ○ *Speed is restricted to 30 mph in towns.* 市内车速每小时不得超过30英里. ○ *families restricted to (having) one child* 受限制只能有一个孩子的家庭 ○ *restrict oneself to one meal a day* 限制自己一天吃一顿饭 ○ *You are restricted to eight litres of duty-free wine.* 携带的免税酒不得超过八升.

▷ **re·stricted** *adj* **1** having certain limitations 有一定限制的; 有限的; 受约束的: *restricted access, development, potential* 受限制的接触、发展、潜力 ○ *The drug has only a restricted commercial use.* 这种麻醉药用作商品是极受限制的. ○ (*Brit*) *a restricted area*, ie where speed or parking is strictly controlled 车速或停车限制区. **2** [esp attrib 尤作定语] (**a**) (*Brit*) (of land) not fully open to the public (指土地)对公众不完全开放的: *enter a restricted zone* 进入禁区. (**b**) (*esp US*) (of land) not fully open to military personnel (指土地)对军人不完全开放的.

re·stric·tion /rɪˈstrɪkʃn; rɪˈstrɪkʃən/ *n* **1** [U] restricting or being restricted 限制; 约束: *restriction of expenditure* 对开支的限制. **2** [C esp *pl* 尤作复数] **~ (on sth)** instance of this; law, etc that restricts 限制; 约束; 限制性规定: *raise, lift, ban, abolish, etc a restriction* 撤消限制 ○ *place, impose, enforce, etc a restriction* 实行限制 ○ *speed, price, import, etc restrictions* 速度、价格、进口等限制 ○ *There are currency restrictions on the sums allowed for foreign travel.* 到国外旅行允许携带的款额有所限制. ○ *The sale of firearms is subject to many legal restrictions.* 出售枪枝受到许多法律限制.

re·strict·ive /rɪˈstrɪktɪv; rɪˈstrɪktɪv/ *adj* **1** restricting 限制(性)的; 约束(性)的: *restrictive rulings, measures, etc* 限制性的规定、措施等. **2** (*grammar*) of a relative clause or phrase that limits or defines the noun which it follows 限制性的: *'My friends who live in London' contains a restrictive clause; 'my parents, who live in Leeds' does not.* ☆ my friends who live in London 这一结构中含有限制性从句; my parents, who live in Leeds 这一结构中无限制性成分. ▷ **re·strict·ively** *adv*. **re·strict·ive·ness** *n* [U].

□ **reˌstrictive ˈpractices** (*Brit*) (in industry) practices that hinder the most effective use of labour, technical resources, etc and hamper efficient production (工业方面的)限制性条条框框(妨碍有效利用劳动力、技术资源等阻碍提高生产效率的做法).

re·struc·ture /ˌriːˈstrʌktʃə(r); ˌriˈstrʌktʃɚ/ *v* [Tn] give a new or different structure or arrangement to (sth) 重建, 改建, 重组, 改组, 重新安排(某事物): *restructure an organization, a proposal, the plot of a novel* 改组组织、调整计划、重新安排小说的情节. ▷ **re·struc·tur·ing** *n* [U, C usu *sing* 作不可数名词或可数名词, 后者通常作单数]: *The rating system is undergoing some/a complete restructuring.* 房地产税制正在进行某些[全面的]调整.

res·ult /rɪˈzʌlt; rɪˈzʌlt/ *n* **1** (**a**) [C, U] **~ (of sth)** effect or outcome (of sth) 结果; 效果: *The flight was delayed as a result of fog.* 因有雾该航班误点. ○ *His limp is the result of an accident.* 他腿瘸是事故所致. ○ (*fml* 文) *I was late, with the result that* (ie so that) *I missed my train.* 我迟到了, 没能赶上火车. ○ *All our hard work produced little or no result.* 我们辛苦努力无甚结果. ○ *My investigations were without result.* 我的调查毫无结果. (**b**) **results** [pl] significant and pleasing outcome 成果; 成效: *That trainer knows how to get results from his horses.* 那个驯马师掌握行之有效的驯马技巧. ○ *begin to show, produce, achieve results* 开始显示、产生、获得成果. **2** [C] (**a**) (esp *pl* 尤作复数) **~ (of sth)** statement of the score, marks or name of the winner in a sporting event or a competition or an examination, etc (运动、竞赛、考试等的)结果, 比分, 成绩, 优胜者: *'football, racing, etc results* 足球比赛、速度竞赛等的结果 ○ *have good/bad exam results* 考试成绩优良[不佳] ○ *The result of the match was a draw.* 比赛结果不分胜负. ○ *announce the results of an election* 宣布选举结果. (**b**) (esp *sing* 尤作单数) (*Brit infml* 口) (esp in football) win (尤指足球比赛)获胜, 赢: *We desperately need a result from this match.* 这场比赛我们务必获胜. **3** [C] answer to a mathematical problem, etc found by calculation (数学问题等通过计算而获得的)答案.

▷ **res·ult** /rɪˈzʌlt; rɪˋzʌlt/ *v* **1** [I, Ipr] **~ (from sth)** occur as a result(1a) (因而)发生, 产生, 出现: *injuries resulting from a fall* 因摔倒而受的伤. **2** (phr v) **result in sth** have a specified effect or consequence 产生某种作用或结果: *Our efforts resulted in success/failure.* 我们的努力终于成功[失败]了. ○ *The talks resulted in reducing the number of missiles/missile reduction.* 谈判结果削减了导弹数量.

res·ult·ant /-ənt; -ənt/ *adj* [attrib 作定语] (*fml* 文) happening as a result or consequence 因而发生的; 必然产生的: *the resultant profit from reducing staff and increasing sales* 因裁员和增加销量而获得的收益.

re·sume /rɪˈzjuːm; *US* -ˈzuːm; rɪˋzum/ *v* (*fml* 文) **1** [I, Tn, Tg] begin (sth) again or continue (sth) after stopping for a time 重新开始(某事物); (停顿后)继续进行(某事物): *Hostilities resumed after the cease-fire.* 停火过后, 战事再度爆发. ○ *resume a flight, voyage, trip, etc* 继续飞行、航海、旅行等 ○ *resume (one's) work, efforts, labours, etc* 重新开始工作、努力、劳动等 ○ *Resume reading where you left off.* 从停下的地方接着往下读吧. **2** [Tn] take or occupy (sth) again 重新得到或占有(某事物): *She resumed her maiden name after the divorce.* 她离婚后重新使用娘家的姓. ○ *resume one's seat*, ie sit down again 重新坐下 ○ *resume possession of a title* 恢复头衔.

ré·sumé /ˈrezjuːmeɪ; *US* ˌrezʊˈmeɪ; ˌrɛzʊˋme/ *n* **1** summary 摘要; 概要: *give a résumé of the evidence, plot, meeting* 作证言的摘要、情节的梗概、会议的纪要. **2** (*US*) = CURRICULUM VITAE (CURRICULUM).

re·sump·tion /rɪˈzʌmpʃn; rɪˋzʌmpʃən/ *n* [U, sing] (*fml* 文) (instance of) resuming (RESUME 1) (停顿后的)重新开始, 继续进行; 重新取得或占有; 恢复: *no immediate resumption of building work* 建筑施工没有立即恢复 ○ *a resumption of hostilities, activites, negotiations* 战事、活动、谈判的重新开始.

re·sur·face /ˌriːˈsɜːfɪs; riˋsɝfɪs/ *v* **1** [Tn] put a new surface on (a road, etc) 给(路等)铺设新路面: *resurfacing work on the motorway* 高速公路更新路面的作业. **2** [I] come to the surface again 重新升至表面; 重新露面: *The submarine resurfaced.* 潜艇重新浮出水面. ○ (*fig* 比喻) *Old prejudices began to resurface.* 旧的偏见又冒了出来.

re·sur·gent /rɪˈsɜːdʒənt; rɪˋsɝdʒənt/ *adj* [usu attrib 通常作定语] (*fml* 文) rising or reviving after destruction, defeat, disappearance, etc 复苏的; 复兴的; 恢复生机或活力的: *a resurgent economy* 复苏的经济 ○ *resurgent hope, nationalism* 重新燃起的希望、重新抬头的民族主义. ▷ **re·sur·gence** /-əns; -əns/ *n* [U, sing]: *a sudden resurgence of interest in Victorian art* 对维多利亚时代的艺术重新激发起的兴趣.

re·sur·rect /ˌrezəˈrekt; ˌrɛzəˋrɛkt/ *v* [Tn] (*usu fig* 通常作比喻) **1** bring (sb) back to life again 使(某人)复活: *That noise is enough to resurrect the dead!* 那噪音都能把死人吵活! **2** revive (a practice, etc); bring back into use 使(某种做法)复兴; 重新使用: *resurrect old customs, habits, traditions, etc* 恢复旧的习俗、习惯、传统等 ○ (*joc* 谑) *resurrect an old dress from the sixties* 让六十年代的旧式连衣裙起死回生.

▷ **re·sur·rec·tion** /ˌrezəˈrekʃn; ˌrɛzəˋrɛkʃən/ *n* **1 the Resurrection** [sing] (*religion* 宗) **(a)** the rising of Jesus from the tomb 耶稣复活. **(b)** the rising of all the dead at the Last Judgement (最后审判日)所有死者之复活. **2** [U, sing] (*fml fig* 文, 比喻) revival after disuse, inactivity, etc 恢复使用、活动等: *a resurrection of hope* 希望的复萌.

re·sus·cit·ate /rɪˈsʌsɪteɪt; rɪˋsʌsəˌtet/ *v* [Tn] (*fml* 文) bring (sb/sth) back to consciousness 使(某人[某物])恢复知觉; 苏醒: *resuscitate a boy rescued from drowning* 使溺水获救的男孩苏醒过来. ▷ **re·sus·cita·tion** /rɪˌsʌsɪˈteɪʃn; rɪˌsʌsəˋteʃən/ *n* [U]: *their efforts/attempts at resuscitation* 他们为使人苏醒过来而做的努力[尝试].

ret (also **retd**) *abbr* 缩写 = **1** retired. **2** returned.

re·tail /ˈriːteɪl; ˋritel/ *n* [U] selling of goods, which are usu not for resale, in small quantities to the general public 零售; 零卖: *outlets* (ie shops) *for the retail of leather goods* 皮革制品零售店 ○ [attrib 作定语] *retail businesses, traders* 零售生意、零售商 ○ *manufacturer's recommended retail price £9.99* 厂家建议的零售价格为9.99英镑 ○ *the retail price index*, ie the record of average retail prices 零售价格指数. Cf 参看 WHOLESALE.

▷ **re·tail** *adv* by retail 零售: *Do you buy wholesale or retail?* 你是整批买还是零买?

re·tail *v* **1** [Ipr, Tn·pr] **~ (sth) at/for sth** be sold or sell (sth) retail at (a price) 以(某价格)零售(某物): *These biros retail at/for 70p.* 这些圆珠笔零售价为70便士. **2** [Tn, Tn·pr] **~ sth (to sb)** (*fml* 文) give (details of gossip, scandal, etc) to others, usu repeatedly 传播(闲话、流言蜚语等)(通常指屡次地).

re·tailer *n* tradesman who sells by retail 零售商.

re·tain /rɪˈteɪn; rɪˋten/ *v* [Tn] (*esp fml* 尤作文雅语) **1** keep (sth) in one's possession or use 保持或保留(某物): *We retained the original fireplace when we decorated the room.* 我们装修房间时保留了原有的壁炉. **2** continue to have (sth); not lose 仍然有(某事物); 未丧失; 保住: *Despite losing his job he retains his pension.* 他虽然失去了工作, 但仍然享有养老金. ○ *These roses retain their scent.* 这些玫瑰花仍有余香. ○ *He is 90 but still retains (the use of) all his faculties.* 他已90高龄, 但身体功能都很好. ○ *The police retained control of the situation.* 警方仍然控制着局势. **3** keep (sth) in one's memory 记住(某事物): *be able to retain numbers, dates, facts, etc* 能记住数目、日期、事实等 ○ *She retains a clear impression/memory of the incident.* 她对那件事印象很深[记得很清楚]. **4** keep (sth) in place; hold or contain 止住(某物); 保持; 容纳: *A dyke was built to retain the floods.* 修了一道堤坝挡住洪水. ○ *Clay soil retains water.* 黏土能保持水分. **5** (*law* 律) book the services of (esp a barrister) by making a payment 付定金聘请(尤指讼务律师): *a retaining fee* 聘用定金.

▷ **re·tainer** *n* **1** fee paid to sb (esp a barrister) in advance for services as and when one may need them 聘用定金(尤指预付给讼务律师的): [attrib 作定语] *a retainer agreement* 预付聘用费的协议. **2** reduced rent paid to reserve a flat, etc for one's use while one is absent from it (为外出期间保留租房等而付的)定金. **3** (*arch* 古) servant, esp one who has been with a family or person for a long time 仆人(尤指服务多年的): (*joc* 谑) *an old family retainer* 老家仆.

□ **re'taining wall** wall built to support a mass of earth or to confine water 挡土墙; 挡水墙; 拥壁.

re·take /ˌriːˈteɪk; riˋtek/ *v* (*pt* **retook** /-ˈtʊk; -ˋtʊk/, *pp* **retaken** /-ˈteɪkən; -ˋtekən/) [Tn] **1** capture (sth) again 再拿, 再取, 夺回(某物): *retake a fortress, ship, town* 夺回要塞、轮船、城市. **2** photograph or film (sth) again 重拍(照片、影片等): *retake a shot, scene, etc* 重拍一个镜头、场面等. **3** sit (an examination, etc) again; resit 重新(考试等); 补考: *retake the physics paper* 补考物理.

▷ **re·take** /ˈriːteɪk; ˋriˌtek/ *n* (*infml* 口) **1** second, etc filming of a scene (电影镜头的)重拍: *do several retakes* 多次重拍. **2** (person attending a) second, etc sitting of an examination; resit 重考; 补考; 参加重考或补考的人.

re·tali·ate /rɪˈtælɪeɪt; rɪˋtælɪˌet/ *v* [I, Ipr] **~ (against sb/sth)** repay an injury, insult, etc with a similar one 报复: *He slapped his sister, who retaliated by kicking him.* 他打了妹妹一巴掌, 他妹妹回敬他一脚. ○ *If we impose import duties, other countries may retaliate against us.* 我们若征收进口税, 别的国家就可能报复我们.

▷ **re·tali·ation** /rɪˌtælɪˈeɪʃn; rɪˌtælɪˋeʃən/ *n* [U] **~ (against sb/sth); ~ (for sth)** retaliating 报复: *immediate retaliation against the striking miners* 对罢工的矿工立即采取的报复行动 ○ *a terrorist bomb attack in retaliation for recent arrests* 恐怖分子为报复最近的逮捕行动而进行的炸弹袭击.

re·tali·at·ory /rɪˈtælɪətrɪ; *US* -tɔːrɪ; rɪˋtælɪəˌtɔrɪ/ *adj* done or meant as retaliation 报复的; 报复性的: *take retaliatory measures, actions, etc* 采取报复手段、行动等 ○ *The raid was purely retaliatory.* 这次袭击完全是报复性的.

re·tard /rɪˈtɑːd; rɪˋtɑrd/ *v* [Tn] (*fml* 文) **1** make (sth) slow or late 使(某物)放慢或迟缓: *retard the mechanism*, eg of a clock 使机械装置减速(如时钟的) ○ *retard the spark*, eg of an engine 使点火延迟(如发动机的). **2** slow the progress or development of (sb/sth); hinder 阻碍(某人[某事物])的进步或发展; 妨碍: *Lack of sun retards plant growth.* 光照不足则植物生长缓慢.

▷ **re·tarda·tion** /ˌriːtɑːˈdeɪʃn; ˌritɑrˋdeʃən/ *n* [U]: *mental retardation* 智力迟钝.

re·tarded *adj* backward in physical or (esp) mental development 身体或(尤指)精神发育迟缓的; 智力迟钝

的: *be severely (mentally) retarded* (智力)发育极为迟缓.

retch /retʃ; rɛtʃ/ *v* [I] make the sounds and movements of vomiting, esp involuntarily, but without bringing anything up from the stomach 干哕; 干呕.

retd *abbr* 缩写 = RET.

re·tell /ˌriːˈtel; riˈtɛl/ *v* (*pt, pp* **retold** /-ˈtəʊld; -ˈtold/) [Tn, Tn·pr] **~ sth (to sb)** tell (a story, etc) again, in a different way or in a different language (以不同方式或语言)复述(故事等): *Greek myths retold for children* 为儿童讲的希腊神话.

re·ten·tion /rɪˈtenʃn; rɪˈtɛnʃən/ *n* [U, sing] (*fml* 文) **1** possession or use of sth 具有; 具备; 享有; 享用: *retention of one's rights, privileges, etc* 权利、特权等的享有 ○ *the full retention of one's (mental) faculties* (心智)能力的健全. **2** ability to remember things 记忆力; 记性: *her limited/extraordinary powers of retention* 她那有限的[非凡的]记忆力 ○ *show an amazing retention of facts, details, childhood impressions, etc* 显示出对事实、细节、儿时情景等的惊人记忆力. **3** action of holding sth in position or containing it 挡住; 拦阻; 保持; 保留; 容纳: *the retention of flood waters, crowds* 拦住洪水、人群 ○ *suffer from retention of urine*, ie failure to pass it out from the bladder 患尿潴留(不能排尿).

re·tent·ive /rɪˈtentɪv; rɪˈtɛntɪv/ *adj* **1** (of the memory) having the ability to remember facts, impressions, etc (指记忆力)有记性的, 记忆力强的. **2** having the ability to hold or contain liquid, etc 能保持或容纳液体等的: *retentive soil*, ie that does not dry out quickly 能保持水分的土壤. ▷ **re·tent·ively** *adv*. **re·tent·ive·ness** *n* [U].

R

re·think /ˌriːˈθɪŋk; riˈθɪŋk/ *v* (*pt, pp* **-thought** /-ˈθɔːt; -ˈθɔt/) [I, Tn] reconsider or think about (sth) again, esp in order to change it 重新考虑或再想(某事物)(尤指意在更改): *rethink a policy, plan, situation, verdict* 重新考虑一政策、计划、情况、裁定 ○ *A good deal of rethinking is needed on this question.* 这个问题需要多加考虑.

▷ **re·think** /ˈriːθɪŋk; ˈriθɪŋk/ *n* [sing] (*infml* 口) act of thinking again 再思考; 反思: *have a quick rethink before deciding* 再很快考虑一下再做决定.

re·ti·cent /ˈretɪsnt; ˈrɛtəsn̩t/ *adj* **~ (about/on sth)** not revealing one's thoughts or feelings easily; reserved 不轻易暴露思想或感情的; 有保留的: *be reticent about one's plans* 不愿谈自己的计划 ○ *He seemed unduly reticent on the subject of his past.* 他似乎对他过去的事情讳莫如深.

▷ **re·ti·cence** /-sns; -sn̩s/ *n* [U]: *He always displays a certain reticence in discussing personal matters.* 他在谈论个人问题时总显得有些保留. **re·ti·cently** *adv*.

re·ticu·lated /rɪˈtɪkjʊleɪtɪd; rɪˈtɪkjəˌletɪd/ (also **re·ticu·late** /rɪˈtɪkjʊleɪt; rɪˈtɪkjəˌlet/) *adj* (*fml* 文) divided into a network of small squares or intersecting lines 网状的: *the reticulated skin of a snake* 蛇的网状的皮.

▷ **re·ticu·la·tion** /rɪˌtɪkjʊˈleɪʃn; rɪˌtɪkjəˈleʃən/ *n* [U, C esp *pl* 作不可数名词或可数名词, 后者尤作复数] net-like pattern or structure 网状图案; 网状结构.

ret·ic·ule /ˈretɪkjuːl; ˈrɛtɪˌkjul/ *n* (*arch or joc* 古或谑) woman's small bag, usu made of net, etc and shaped like a pouch with a drawstring neck (女用)小手提包(通常为网兜式, 可收口).

ret·ina /ˈretɪnə; *US* ˈretənə; ˈrɛtn̩ə/ *n* (*pl* **~s** or **-ae** /-niː; -n̩ˌi/) layer of membrane at the back of the eyeball, sensitive to light 视网膜. ⇨illus at EYE 见 EYE 插图.

ret·inue /ˈretɪnjuː; *US* ˈretənuː; ˈrɛtn̩ˌu/ *n* [CGp] group of attendants accompanying an important person (要人的)一批随员: *The Queen was flanked by a retinue of bodyguards and policemen.* 女王左右有保镖和警察护卫着. ○ (*joc* 谑) *the fête organizer and her retinue of helpers* 游乐义卖会的组织人和她的一群助手.

re·tire /rɪˈtaɪə(r); rɪˈtaɪr/ *v* **1 (a)** [I, Ipr] **~ (from sth)** give up one's regular work, esp because of age 退职; 退役; (尤指)退休: *retire early*, ie before reaching retirement age 提前退休(未达退休年龄) ○ *retire on a pension at 65* 于65岁时退休领取养老金 ○ *He will retire from the army/his directorship next year.* 他明年从部队退役[从主管职位上退休]. ○ *the retiring union leader* 行将退休的工会领导人. **(b)** [Tn esp passive 尤用于被动语态] cause (an employee) to do this 使(雇员)退职或退休: *I was retired on full pay.* 给我全薪让我退休了. Cf 参看 RESIGN 1. **2** [I, Ipr] **~ (from...) (to...)** (*fml* 文) (of an army, etc) withdraw voluntarily, esp in order to reorganize, etc (指军队等)主动撤退(尤指以休整等为目的): *Our forces retired to prepared positions.* 我们的部队撤退到既设阵地上. Cf 参看 RETREAT. **3** [I, Ipr] **(a) ~ (from...) (to...)** (*fml* 文) retreat or go away, esp to somewhere quiet or private 退下, 退出, 离开(尤指到僻静处): *The jury retired (from the courtroom) to consider their verdict.* 陪审团退庭以考虑如何裁断. ○ *After lunch he retired to his study.* 他午饭后就到书房去了. **(b) ~ (to sth)** (*fml or joc* 文或谑) go to bed 就寝: *I decided to retire early with a book.* 我决定带本书早点就寝. **4** [La, I, Ipr] **~ (from sth)** (in sport) withdraw voluntarily from a game, match, etc (体育运动中)主动退出比赛等: *The boxer retired from the contest with eye injuries.* 该拳击手因眼部受伤而退出比赛. ○ *The batsman retired hurt.* 击球员因伤退场.

▷ **re·tired** *adj* having retired from work 退职的; 退休的; 退役的: *a retired Civil Servant* 退休的公务员.

re·tir·ing /rɪˈtaɪərɪŋ; rɪˈtaɪrɪŋ/ *adj* avoiding society; shy 过隐居生活的; 孤僻的; 害羞的: *Joanna had a gentle retiring disposition.* 乔安娜性格温柔而腼腆.

re·tire·ment /rɪˈtaɪəmənt; rɪˈtaɪrmənt/ *n* **1** [C, U] (instance of) retiring or being retired from work 退职; 退役; 退休: *There have been several retirements in my office recently.* 最近我那办公室里有几个人退休了. ○ *announce/give notice of one's retirement* 宣布[通知]退休 ○ *urge older staff to take early retirement*, ie retire before the usual age 敦促年纪较大的职员提前退休 ○ *be well above/below the age of retirement* 远远超过[低于]退休年龄 ○ [attrib 作定语] *retirement benefits* 退休补助金 ○ *a retirement pension* 退休金. **2** [U, sing] condition of being retired from work 退职、退役、退休之状况: *He lives in retirement in Cornwall.* 他在康沃尔郡过退休生活. ○ *a happy and profitable retirement* 愉快而有益的退休生活. **3** (idm 习语) **go into/come out of retirement** leave/return to one's regular work 离[复]职.

□ **re'tirement age** age at which people normally retire 退休年龄: *reach retirement age* 达到退休年龄 ○ *reduce the retirement age for teachers to 55* 把教师的退休年龄降低到55岁.

re·tort[1] /rɪˈtɔːt; rɪˈtɔrt/ *v* [Tn, Tf] make a quick, witty or angry reply, esp to an accusation or challenge 反驳; 回嘴: *'Nonsense!' she retorted.* 她反驳说, '一派胡言!' ○ *He retorted that it was my fault as much as his.* 他反驳说我的错误并不比他的错误小.

▷ **re·tort** *n* **(a)** [U] retorting 反驳; 回嘴: *He made a rude sign by way of retort.* 他做出粗鲁动作表示反驳. **(b)** [C] reply of this kind 反驳的回答: *make an insolent retort* 做出侮慢的答复.

re·tort[2] /rɪˈtɔːt; rɪˈtɔrt/ *n* **1** glass vessel with a long narrow neck turned downwards, used for distilling liquids 曲颈甑; 蒸馏甑. **2** receptacle used in making gas or steel (制煤气、炼钢用的)蒸馏罐.

re·touch /ˌriːˈtʌtʃ; riˈtʌtʃ/ *v* [Tn] improve or alter (a photograph, painting, etc) by removing flaws or making minor changes 修整(照片、画等)(以除去瑕疵或作一些微小的改变).

re·trace /riːˈtreɪs; rɪˈtres/ *v* [Tn] **1** go back over or repeat (a journey, route, etc) exactly 折返或重行(原路程、路线等): *retrace one's steps*, ie return the way one came 顺原路折回. **2** recall a series of (past actions, etc) 回忆, 回顾, 追溯(经过情形等): *Police retraced the movements of the murder victim.* 警方追溯了那被谋杀者当时的情形.

re·tract /rɪˈtrækt; rɪˈtrækt/ *v* [I, Tn] (*fml* 文) **1** withdraw (a statement, charge, etc) 撤回或撤消(声明、指控等): *The accused refused to retract (his statement).* 那被告拒不撤消(其供述). **2** refuse to honour or keep (an agreement, etc) 拒绝执行或遵守(协议等): *retract a promise, an offer, etc* 食言、撤消提议. **3** move or pull (sth) back or in 缩回或拉回(某物): *The undercarriage on light aircraft does not always retract in flight.* 轻型飞机飞行时起落架不一定缩回.

▷ **re·tract·able** /-əbl; -əbl̩/ *adj* that can be drawn in 可缩进的; 可拉入的: *a retractable undercarriage* 伸缩式起落架.

re·tract·ile /rɪˈtræktaɪl; *US* -tl; rɪˈtræktl̩/ *adj* that can be retracted (RETRACT 3) 可缩回的; 可拉回的: *A cat's* *claws are retractile.* 猫的爪能缩回.

re·trac·tion /rɪˈtrækʃn; rɪˋtrækʃən/ *n* (**a**) [U] retracting 撤回; 撤消; 缩回; 拉入. (**b**) [C] instance of this 撤回; 撤消; 缩回; 拉入: *publish a retraction of the charge* 宣布撤回指控.

re·tread /ˌriːˈtred; riˋtrɛd/ *v* (*pt, pp* **-ed**) (also **remould**, *US* **remold** /ˌriːˈməʊld; riˋmold/, *US* also ˌ**reˈcap**) [Tn] provide (an old tyre) with a new tread(*n* 3) 给(旧轮胎)装新胎面.

▷ **re·tread** /ˈriːtred; ˋriˌtrɛd/ (also **remould**, *US* **remold** /ˈriːməʊld; ˋriˌmold/, *US* also ˈ**recap**) *n* tyre made by moulding rubber onto an old foundation 翻新的旧轮胎.

re·treat /rɪˈtriːt; rɪˋtrit/ *v* [I, Ipr, In/pr] **1** (esp of an army, etc) withdraw after being defeated or when faced with danger or difficulty (尤指军队等)(战败后或面临危险或困难时)撤退, 退却: *force the enemy to retreat (behind their lines)* 迫使敌人退却(至其阵线后) ○ *crowds retreating before police fire hoses* 面对警方的消防水龙而退却的群众 ○ *We retreated half a mile.* 我们后撤了半英里. Cf 参看 ADVANCE[2] 2. **2** (*fig* 比喻) go away to a place of shelter or privacy 退避; 回避至自己的范围: *retreat into a world of fantasy* 遁入幻想世界 ○ *retreat from the public eye* 避开公众的眼睛. Cf 参看 RETIRE.

▷ **re·treat** *n* **1** [C usu *sing*, U 作可数名词时通常作单数, 亦作不可数名词] act or instance of retreating 撤退; 退却: *The minister made an undignified retreat from his earlier position.* 那部长很不光彩地背离了他原先的立场. ○ *an orderly retreat from the camp* 秩序井然的撤营 ○ *The army was in full retreat.* 军队已全线撤退. **2 the retreat** [sing] military signal for this 撤退信号: *sound the retreat*, eg on a drum or bugle 发出撤退信号(如击鼓或吹号). **3** (**a**) [U] withdrawal into privacy or seclusion 退避; 隐遁. (**b**) [C] place suitable for this 静居处; 隐居处: *spend weekends at my country retreat* 在我的乡间僻静处过周末. (**c**) [U, C] (*religion* 宗) period of withdrawal from worldly activities for prayer and meditation 静修(期间): *go into/be in retreat* 去静修[于静修中] ○ *make an annual retreat* 进行一年一度的静修. **4** (idm 习语) **beat a retreat** ⇨ BEAT[1].

re·trench /rɪˈtrentʃ; rɪˋtrɛntʃ/ *v* (*fml* 文) **1** [I] make economies or reduce expenses 节省; 削减费用; 紧缩开支: *Inflation has forced us to retrench.* 因通货膨胀我们不得不紧缩开支. **2** [Tn] reduce the amount of (money spent) 削减(费用); 紧缩(开支): *retrench one's expenditure* 减少花费.

▷ **re·trench·ment** *n* (**a**) [U] retrenching 节省; 削减; 紧缩开支. (**b**) [C] instance of this 节省; 削减; 紧缩开支.

re·trial /ˌriːˈtraɪəl; riˋtraɪəl/ *n* action of trying a lawsuit again; new trial 再审; 复审: *The judge ordered a retrial because of irregularities.* 因初审不合规则, 法官下令复审.

re·tri·bu·tion /ˌretrɪˈbjuːʃn; ˌrɛtrəˋbjuʃən/ *n* [U] ~ (**for sth**) (*fml* 文) deserved punishment or compensation for injury, etc (由于伤害等)应得的惩罚或赔偿: *jailed in retribution for his crimes* (他)因犯罪而受监禁 ○ *make retribution to God for one's sins* 向上帝赎罪 ○ *the day, hour, moment, etc of retribution* 报应的日子、时刻、瞬间等.

▷ **re·tribu·tive** /rɪˈtrɪbjʊtɪv; rɪˋtrɪbjətɪv/ *adj* [attrib 作定语] happening or inflicted as retribution 作为惩罚而发生或施予的; 惩罚性的; 报应的: *reˌtributive ˈjustice* 因果报应.

re·trieve /rɪˈtriːv; rɪˋtriv/ *v* **1** [Tn, Tn·pr] ~ **sth (from sb/sth)** (*esp fml* 尤作庄重语) get possession of sth again 重新获得某物; 取回某物: *retrieve one's suitcase from the left luggage office* 从行李寄存处取回衣箱 ○ (*joc* 谑) *I must retrieve my credit card from the waiter.* 我得向服务员要回信用卡. **2** [Tn, Tn·pr] (*esp computing* 尤作计算机术语) find again or extract (stored information) 检索(储存的信息): *retrieve data from a disk* 检索储存在磁盘中的资料 ○ *retrieve an address from the files* 从文件中检索地址. **3** [Tn] (*fml* 文) set right (a loss, an error, etc) 挽回(损失); 纠正(错误等): *He retrieved his losses by betting on a succession of winners.* 他下的赌注连续获胜才挽回了损失. ○ *We can only retrieve the situation by reducing our expenses.* 我们只有缩减开支才能扭转这种状况. **4** [I, Tn] (of a trained dog) find and bring back (dead or wounded birds, etc) (指经过训练的狗)找到并衔回(被打死或打伤的鸟等). **5** [Tn, Tn·pr] ~ **sth (from sth)** (*fml* 文) restore sth to a flourishing state; revive sth 使某事物恢复旺盛状态; 复兴某事物: *retrieve one's fortunes* 恢复自己丰裕的生活.

▷ **re·triev·able** /-əbl; -əbl̩/ *adj* (*esp computing* 尤作计算机术语) that can be retrieved 可检索的.

re·trieval /-vl; -vl̩/ *n* [U] (*fml* 文) retrieving or being retrieved 重获; 取回; 检索; 挽回; 恢复: *the retrieval of the company's fortunes* 该公司之挽回财产损失 ○ *a match lost beyond all hope of retrieval* 毫无挽回获胜希望而输定的比赛 ○ (*computing* 计) *information retrieval* 信息检索.

re·triever *n* dog of a breed which is often trained to retrieve game 经训练常用以寻回猎物的一种猎犬.

retro- *pref* 前缀 (with *adjs* and *ns* 与形容词和名词结合) back or backwards 后; 向后; 在后: *retroactive* ○ *retrograde* ○ *retro-rocket*.

ret·ro·act·ive /ˌretrəʊˈæktɪv; ˌrɛtroˋæktɪv/ *adj* (*fml* 文) effective from a past date 溯及既往的; 有追溯效力的: *The new law was made retroactive to 1 January*, ie as if it had come into effect then. 新法令生效日期可追溯到1月1日. ▷ **ret·ro·act·ively** *adv*.

ret·ro·flex /ˈretrəfleks; ˋrɛtrəˌflɛks/ (also **ret·ro·flexed** /-kst; -kst/) *adj* [attrib 作定语] (*phonetics* 语音) (of a sound) made by bending the tip of the tongue upwards and backwards (指声音)卷舌的, 卷舌音的.

ret·ro·grade /ˈretrəgreɪd; ˋrɛtrəˌgred/ *adj* (*fml* 文) **1** going backwards 向后的; 后退的: *retrograde motion* 逆向运动. **2** getting worse; returning to a less good condition 退化的; 恶化的; 衰退的: *a retrograde policy, step* 倒退的政策、一步.

ret·ro·gress /ˌretrəˈgres; ˌrɛtrəˋgrɛs/ *v* [I, Ipr] ~ (**to sth**) (*fml* 文) **1** go backwards 后退; 倒退. **2** get worse or deteriorate 恶化; 衰退.

▷ **ret·ro·gres·sion** /ˌretrəˈgreʃn; ˌrɛtrəˋgrɛʃən/ *n* [U] return to a less advanced state; decline 退步; 退化; 衰退; 衰落.

ret·ro·gress·ive *adj*. **ret·ro·gress·ively** *adv*.

retro-rocket /ˈretrəʊrɒkɪt; ˋrɛtroˌrɑkɪt/ *n* rocket engine providing power in the opposite direction to the path of flight and used to slow down or alter the course of a spacecraft, etc 制动火箭; 减速火箭.

ret·ro·spect /ˈretrəspekt; ˋrɛtrəˌspɛkt/ *n* (idm 习语) **in retrospect** looking back on a past event or situation 回顾; 追溯: *In retrospect, it's easy to see why we were wrong.* 回顾过去就很容易明白我们的错处了.

▷ **ret·ro·spec·tion** /ˌretrəˈspekʃn; ˌrɛtrəˋspɛkʃən/ *n* [U] action of looking back on past events, experiences, etc 回顾; 追溯.

ret·ro·spect·ive /ˌretrəˈspektɪv; ˌrɛtrəˋspɛktɪv/ *adj* **1** looking back on the past 回顾的: *retrospective views, thoughts, etc* 回顾过去的观点、想法等 ○ *a retrospective exhibition of the painter's work* 那画家作品的回顾展. **2** (of laws, payments, etc) applying to the past as well as the future; retroactive (指法律、支付关系等)溯及既往的, 有追溯效力的: *The legislation was made retrospective.* 该项法规具有追溯效力. ○ *a retrospective* (ie back-dated) *pay rise* 有追溯效力的加薪. — *n* exhibition tracing the development of a painter, sculptor, etc (画家、雕塑家等作品的)回顾展. **ret·ro·spect·ively** *adv*.

re·troussé /rəˈtruːseɪ; *US* ˌretruˈseɪ; ˌrɛtruˋse/ *adj* (*French esp approv* 法, 尤作褒义) (of the nose) turned up at the end (指鼻子)尖端上翘的.

re·try /ˌriːˈtraɪ; riˋtraɪ/ *v* (*pt, pp* **retried**) [Tn] try (a lawsuit or a defendant) again 重审, 复审(案件或被告): *There are calls for the case to be retried.* 该案有必要重审.

ret·sina /retˈsiːnə; *US* ˈretsɪnə; ˋrɛtsɪnə/ *n* [U, C] Greek wine flavoured with resin 一种带有松香味的希腊葡萄酒.

re·turn[1] /rɪˈtɜːn; rɪˋtɝn/ *v* **1** [I, Ipr] (**a**) ~ (**to...**) (**from...**) come or go back to a place 回; 返回: *return (home) from a holiday* 度假归来 ○ *return to Paris from London* 从伦敦回巴黎 ○ *She returned to collect her umbrella.* 她回来取伞. (**b**) ~ (**to sb/sth**) come or go back to an earlier activity or condition 恢复原先的活动或情况: *doubts, symptoms, suspicions that return constantly* 经常反复出现的疑惑、症状、怀疑 ○ *My good humour/spirits soon* *returned.* 我的心情[情绪]很快又好起来了. ○ *I shall return to this point* (ie discuss it again) *later.* 我稍后再谈这个问题. ○ *return to one's old habits* 恢复旧习惯 ○ *The bus service has returned to normal after the strike.* 罢工结束后公共汽车恢复了正常的运营. **2** (**a**) [Tn, Tn·pr, Cn·a, Dn·n, Dn·pr] **~ sth (to sth/sb)** bring, give, put or send sth back 带回、归还、放回或送回某物: *Please return all empties*, ie empty milk bottles. 请把空瓶全部退回. ○ (*fml* 文) *She returned the bird to its cage.* 她把鸟放回笼子里. ○ *I returned the letter unopened.* 我把那封信原封退回了. ○ *Please return me my £5/return my £5 to me.* 请把我的5英镑还给我. (**b**) [Tn] give (sth) in response; reciprocate 给予(某事物)作为报答; 回报; 回礼: *return an invitation, a visit* 回请、回访 ○ *return a greeting, stare, salute, etc* 回应问候、回瞪一眼、还礼 ○ *return a compliment/favour* 回应赞语[报答恩惠] ○ *I cannot return your love/affection.* 我无法回报你的爱[情意]. ○ *The enemy returned our fire.* 敌人向我们还击. ○ *He returned the blow smartly.* 他狠狠地还击了一拳. (**c**) [Tn] (in cricket, tennis, etc) send (a ball) back (板球、网球等)回击(球): *return a shot, service, volley, etc* 把对方的抽球、发球、凌空球击回. **3** [Tn] (*fml* 文) state or describe (sth) officially, esp in reply to a formal demand for information 正式宣布或表明(某事物)(尤指回应正式的询问): *return the details of one's income*, ie to a tax inspector 申报个人收入细目(报税) ○ *The jury returned a verdict of guilty.* 陪审团宣布裁决被告有罪. **4** [Tn] give (sth) as profit 产生(利润): *Our investment accounts return a high rate of interest.* 我们的投资项目利润回报很高. **5** [esp passive 尤用于被动语态: Tn, Tn·pr, Cn·n/a] **~sb (to sth); ~ sb (as sth)** elect sb as a Member of Parliament 选举某人为议员: *He was returned to Parliament with a decreased majority.* 他以有所减少的多数票当选为议员. ○ *Smith was returned as MP for Bath.* 史密斯当选为巴斯市的议员. **6** [Tn] (*dated* 旧) say (sth) in answer; reply 回答说(某话); 答复: *'Never!' he returned curtly.* '决不!'他唐突地答道. **7** (idm 习语) **return to the 'fold** (*fml* 文) rejoin a group of people, esp a religious or political group with similar beliefs or aims 重新加入组织(尤指具有相同之信仰或目标的宗教或政治组织).

▷ **re·turn·able** /-əbl; -əbḷ/ *adj* that can or must be returned 可以或必须返回、归还、退还、送回等的: *returnable bottles, crates, etc* 可回收的瓶子、板条箱等.

re·turnee /ˌrɪtɜːˈniː; rɪˌtɝˈni/ *n* (*US*) person who returns from military service abroad, esp after a war 从国外服役归来的军人(尤指战后).

□ **re'turning officer** (*Brit*) official who conducts an election in a constituency and announces the result 选举监察官(负责选区内选举事宜并宣布选举结果者).

re·turn[2] /rɪˈtɜːn; rɪˈtɝn/ *n* **1** [sing] (**a**) **~ (to...) (from...)** coming or going back to a place 返回: *on my return home (from Italy)*, ie when I got/get back 我(从意大利)回国时 ○ [attrib 作定语] *a return trip, voyage, flight, etc* 陆上、海上、空中等的回程. (**b**) **~ (to sth)** coming or going back to an earlier activity or condition 恢复原先的活动或情况: *a return of my doubts, symptoms, suspicions* 我的疑惑、症状、怀疑再次出现 ○ *the return of spring* 春之归来 ○ *a return to normal working hours, old habits* 正常工作时间、旧习惯的恢复. **2** [C, U] **~ (to sb/sth)** bringing, giving, putting or sending back 带回; 归还; 放回; 送回: *the return of library books, milk bottles, faulty goods* 图书馆借阅书籍的归还、牛奶瓶的回收、残货的退货 ○ *The deposit is refunded on return of the vehicle.* 押金于归还车辆时退还. ○ *no deposit, no return*, eg as a notice on a non-returnable bottle, etc 不收押金亦不退瓶等(告示用语) ○ *These flowers are a small return* (ie token of thanks) *for your kindness.* 向您献花聊表谢忱. ○ *Her return of service* (ie at tennis) *was very fast.* 她击回发球很快(在网球赛中). ○ [attrib 作定语] *return shots* 击回抽球. **3** [C] official report or statement, esp one made in reply to a formal demand 正式报告或陈述(尤指回应正式要求的): *make one's '(income-)tax return* 做所得税的申报 ○ *the e'lection returns*, ie figures of the voting at an election 选举结果报告(公布票数). **4** [C esp *pl* 尤作复数] **~ (on sth)** profit from a transaction, etc 赢利; 收益: *disappointing returns on capital, investment, etc* 令人失望的资本、投资等的收益 ○ *You'll get a good return on these shares.* 投资这种股票可获优厚利润. ○ *small profits and quick returns*, ie the theory behind businesses that rely on large sales and a quick turnover 薄利多销. **5** [C] (*Brit*) (*US* **round trip**) ticket for a journey to a place and back again 来回票; 往返票; 双程票: *weekend, period, etc returns* 周末的、定期的…双程票 ○ *a ˌday-'return to London*, ie valid only for the day of issue 去伦敦的当日往返票. Cf 参看 SINGLE 5. **6** [C] theatre ticket bought and then sold back to the box-office (购买后又退还票房的)退票: *queuing for returns* 排队购买退票. **7** (idm 习语) **by re'turn (of 'post)** (*Brit*) by the next post 由下一班邮递: *Please reply by return.* 请即赐复. ○ *Write now to this address and we will send you a free sample by return.* 按此地址函索即免费寄奉样品. **in return (for sth)** as payment or reward (for sth) 作为(对某物)的付款或回报: *I bought him a drink in return for his help.* 我请他喝酒以酬谢他的帮助. **many happy returns** ⇨ HAPPY. **the point of no return** ⇨ POINT[1]. **sale or return** ⇨ SALE.

□ **reˌturn 'fare** (*Brit*) fare needed for a journey to a place and back again 往返路费.

return 'game, return 'match second game or match between the same opponents (原对手的)再次交锋.

return 'ticket (*US* **ˌround-trip 'ticket**) = RETURN 5.

re·union /ˌriːˈjuːnɪən; riˈjunjən/ *n* **1** [U] reuniting or being reunited 再联合; 重聚: *a reunion between the two sisters* 姊妹俩的重聚 ○ *the reunion of the Democrats with the Liberals* 民主党人与自由党人的再次联合. **2** [C] social gathering of people who were formerly friends, colleagues, etc (昔日朋友、同事等的)团聚, 联谊活动: *emotional, touching, etc reunions* 令人感动的、激动的…团聚 ○ *a family reunion at Christmas* 圣诞节的合家团聚 ○ *have/hold an annual reunion of war veterans* 举行一年一度的老战友联欢会 ○ [attrib 作定语] *a reunion dinner, celebration* 重聚宴会、庆祝会.

re·unite /ˌriːjuːˈnaɪt; ˌrijuˈnaɪt/ *v* [I, Ipr, Tn, Tn·pr] **~ (sb/sth) (with sb/sth)** (cause sb/sth to) come together again (使某人[某事物])再次联合, 重聚: *her hopes of reuniting with her family* 她与家人团聚的希望 ○ *attempts to reunite the Labour Party* 为使工党重新团结起来的努力 ○ *Parents were reunited with their lost children.* 父母与失散的孩子们团圆了.

re·use /ˌriːˈjuːz; riˈjuz/ *v* [Tn] use (sth) again 再用, 重新使用(某物): *reuse an old envelope* 使用旧信封.

▷ **re·use** /ˌriːˈjuːs; riˈjus/ *n* [U] using or being used again 再用; 重新使用.

re·usable /ˌriːˈjuːzəbl; riˈjuzəbḷ/ *adj* that can be used again 可再次使用的; 可重复使用的: *reusable envelopes* 可再次使用的信封 ○ *reusable* (ie rechargeable) *batteries* 可重复使用的电池(可充电的).

rev /rev; rɛv/ *n* (usu *pl* 通常作复数) (*infml* 口) revolution of an engine (发动机的)旋转: *run at maximum revs* 开动发动机至最高转速 ○ *doing a steady 4 000 revs (per minute)* 达到(每分钟)4 000转的恒定转速.

▷ **rev** *v* (**-vv-**) **1** [I, Ip] **~ (up)** (of an engine) revolve; increase the speed of revolution (指发动机)旋转, 加快转速. **2** [Tn, Tn·p] **~ sth (up)** cause (an engine) to run esp quickly, as when starting a car 使(发动机)运转(尤指快速, 如起动汽车时): *Don't rev the engine so hard.* 别让发动机转得太快. ○ *Rev it up to warm the engine.* 让发动机转起来预热.

Rev (also **Revd**) *abbr* 缩写 = Reverend: *Rev George Hill* (乔治·)希尔牧师. Cf 参看 RT REV.

re·value /ˌriːˈvæljuː; riˈvælju/ *v* **1** [Tn] reassess the value of (sth) 对(某物)重新估价: *have your house revalued at today's prices* 把你的房子按今日价格重新估价. **2** [I, Tn] increase the exchange value of (a currency) 调高(货币)的兑换价; 使(货币)升值: *The franc is to be revalued.* 法郎的兑换价要调高. Cf 参看 DEVALUE.

▷ **re·valu·ation** /ˌriːvæljuːˈeɪʃn; ˌrivæljuˈeʃən/ *n* [C, U] (instance of) revaluing 重新估价; (货币的)升值: *property revaluation* 房地产的重新估价 ○ *(a) further revaluation of the yen* 日元的进一步升值.

re·vamp /ˌriːˈvæmp; riˈvæmp/ *v* [Tn] (*infml* 口) renew (sth), esp superficially; improve the appearance of 将(某物)更新(尤指外观); 翻新: *revamp an old comedy routine with some new jokes* 修改一个旧的喜剧节目使之增加些新笑料 ○ *The department was revamped to try to improve its performance.* 该部门进行了改组以改进工

作. ○ *revamp a kitchen, study, etc*, ie decorate or modernize it 装修厨房、书房等.

re·veal /rɪ'vi:l; rɪ'vil/ *v* **1** [Tn, Tf, Tw, Cn·t, Dn·pr, Dpr·f, Dpr·w] **~ sth (to sb)** make (facts, etc) known 使(事实等)显露出来; 透露; 泄露; 揭露: *reveal secrets, details, methods, faults, feelings* 泄露秘密、披露详情、透露方法、揭露错误、流露感情 ○ *The survey revealed that the house was damp.* 那所房子经检视表明很潮湿. ○ *I can't reveal who told me.* 我不能透露是谁告诉我的. ○ *Her answers revealed her to be innocent.* 她的回答显示出她无辜. ○ *The doctor did not reveal the truth to him.* 医生没有向他透露真相. ○ *Teachers revealed to the press that they were going on strike/what action they were taking.* 教师向报界透露他们将举行罢教[正在采取的行动]. **2** [Tn] cause or allow (sth) to be seen 展现或显示(某物): *The open door revealed an untidy kitchen.* 透过敞开的房门可以看见凌乱的厨房. ○ *Close examination revealed a crack in the vase.* 花瓶经仔细检查发现有裂璺.

▷ **re·veal·ing** *adj* **1** making (facts, etc) known 揭露(事实等)的; 暴露真相的: *a revealing slip of the tongue, disclosure, comment* 暴露真相的失言、揭发、评论 ○ *This document is extremely revealing.* 这份文件揭露出大量事实. **2** (usu preceded by *very, most, rather*, etc 通常用于very、most、rather等之后) causing or allowing (sth) to be seen 展现或显示(某物)的; 显露的: *The X-ray was very revealing.* 在X射线照射下问题十分清楚. ○ *a rather revealing* (ie low-cut) *dress* 袒胸露肩的连衣裙.

□ **re,vealed re'ligion** religion believed to have been revealed to mankind directly by God 天启教(据信为直接由上帝启示于人类的宗教).

re·veille /rɪ'vælɪ; *US* 'revəlɪ; 'rɛvḷɪ/ *n* (also **the reveille**) [sing] military bugle, drum, etc signal to soldiers to get up in the morning (军队的)起床号、鼓等: *sound (the) 5.30 reveille* 5点30分吹起床号.

revel /'revl; 'rɛvḷ/ *v* (**-ll-**; *US* **-l-**) **1** [I, Ipr] (*dated or joc* 旧或谑) make merry; celebrate noisily 作乐; 狂欢: *revelling until dawn* 狂欢达旦. **2** (phr v) **revel in sth/doing sth** take great delight in sth 尽情享受某事情; 沉迷于某事物: *revelling in her new-found freedom* 充分享受她新获得的自由 ○ *revel in wielding power* 醉心于行使权力.

▷ **rev·el** *n* (usu *pl* 通常作复数) (*dated* 旧) noisy celebrations 狂欢: *holding midnight revels* 举行午夜狂欢会.

rev·el·ler (*US* **rev·eler**) /'revələ(r); 'rɛvlɚ/ *n* (*dated or joc* 旧或谑) merry-maker 寻欢作乐的人: *late-night revellers leaving the pubs* 夜深时分离开酒馆的寻欢作乐者.

rev·ela·tion /,revə'leɪʃn; ,rɛvḷ'eʃən/ *n* **1** [U] making known sth that was secret or hidden; revealing 显露; 泄露; 透露; 揭露: *divine revelation of truth* 上帝对真理的启示 ○ *the revelation of his identity* 他的身分之暴露. **2** [C] that which is revealed, esp sth surprising 被揭露的事, 暴露出来的事(尤指出人意料者): *scandalous revelations in the press* 新闻界对丑闻的揭露 ○ *His Hamlet was a revelation to the critics*, ie They did not expect him to act so well. 他扮演的哈姆雷特使评论界耳目一新(未料到演得如此之好). **3 Revelation** (*Bible* 《圣经》) the last book of the New Testament, also called *The Revelation of St John the Divine*, or (incorrectly) *Revelations* 《启示录》(《圣经·新约》的最后一卷).

rev·elry /'revlrɪ; 'rɛvlrɪ/ *n* [C usu *pl*, U 作可数名词时通常作复数, 亦作不可数名词] noisy celebrations; revels 狂欢; 作乐: *The revelries went on all night.* 狂欢活动通宵达旦. ○ *sounds of drunken revelry* 酗酒作乐的吵闹声.

re·venge /rɪ'vendʒ; rɪ'vɛndʒ/ *n* **1** [U] deliberate punishment or injury inflicted in return for what one has suffered 复仇; 报复: *thirsting for revenge* 渴望报仇雪恨 ○ (*saying* 谚) *Revenge is sweet.* 报仇的滋味是甜的. **2** [U] desire to inflict this; vindictiveness 复仇的欲望; 报复心: *done in the spirit of revenge* 在报复心驱使下干的. **3** [U] opportunity given to an opponent in a return game to reverse the result of an earlier one 使败方有机会获胜的再次比赛: *give Leeds their revenge* 让利兹队有雪耻机会的比赛. **4** (idm 习语) **get/have/take one's revenge (on sb) (for sth); take revenge (on sb) (for sth)** return an injury 报仇; 报复: *They swore to take their revenge on the kidnappers.* 他们发誓要向绑架者报仇. **out of/in revenge (for sth)** in order to return an injury 为了报复: *Terrorists bombed the police station in revenge for the arrests.* 恐怖分子用炸弹袭击了警察局报复逮捕行动.

▷ **re·venge** *v* **1** [Tn] (**a**) do sth to get satisfaction for (an offence, etc) 为(某事)报仇; 洗雪(耻辱等): *revenge an injustice, injury, insult, etc* 对受到的冤屈、伤害、侮辱进行报复. (**b**) avenge (sb) 为(某人)报仇: *determined to revenge his dead brother* 决心替他死去的哥哥报仇. **2** [Tn·pr] **~ oneself on sb** get satisfaction by deliberately inflicting injury on sb in return for injury inflicted on oneself 向某人报仇. **3** (idm 习语) **be revenged on sb** revenge oneself on sb 向某人报仇.

re·venge·ful /-fl; -fḷ/ *adj* feeling or showing a desire for revenge 复仇的; 报复的. **re·venge·fully** /-fəlɪ; -fəlɪ/ *adv*. **re·venge·ful·ness** *n* [U].

rev·enue /'revənju:; *US* -ənu:; 'rɛvə,nu/ *n* **1** [U] income, esp the total annual income of the State from taxes, etc 收入; (尤指)岁入: *sources, channels of revenue* 岁入的来源、渠道 ○ *public/private revenue* 公共的[私人的]收入 ○ [attrib 作定语] *a 'revenue tax*, ie one producing revenue contrasted with one protecting a country's trade 财政税. **2 revenues** [pl] separate items of revenue put together 各项收入; 总收入: *the revenues of the City Council* 市议会的总收入 ○ *rising/falling oil revenues* 逐渐增加的[逐渐减少的]石油收入.

re·ver·ber·ate /rɪ'vɜ:bəreɪt; rɪ'vɝbə,ret/ *v* [I, Ipr] **~ (with sth)** echo or resound repeatedly (反复地)发出回声, 回响; 回荡: *The roar of the train reverberated in the tunnel.* 火车的轰隆声在隧道里回荡. ○ *The room reverberated with the noise of the shot.* 房间里回响着枪声. ○ (*fig* 比喻) *Shock waves reverberated round the department from the manager's resignation.* 经理辞职一事在该部门引起轩然大波.

▷ **re·ver·ber·ant** /-bərənt; -bərənt/ *adj* (*fml* 文).

re·ver·bera·tion /rɪ,vɜ:bə'reɪʃn; rɪ,vɝbə'reʃən/ *n* **1** [U] reverberating or being reverberated 回声; 回响; 回荡; 反响. **2** [C usu *pl* 通常作复数] repeated echo 反复的回声: *the reverberations of the explosion* 爆炸的回声 ○ (*fig* 比喻) *the continuing reverberations* (ie repercussions) *of the scandal* 该丑闻引起的一连串的反响.

re·vere /rɪ'vɪə(r); rɪ'vɪr/ *v* [Tn, Tn·pr] **~ sb/sth (for sth)** (*fml* 文) feel deep respect or (esp religious) veneration for sb/sth 深为尊敬或(尤指宗教上)崇敬某人[某事物]: *revere virtue, human life, the church's teaching* 崇尚美德、尊重人的生命、崇奉教义 ○ *The professor was revered for his immense learning.* 那教授学识渊博备受敬重.

rev·er·ence /'revərəns; 'rɛvərəns/ *n* **1** [U] **~ (for sb/sth)** feeling of deep respect or (esp religious) veneration 尊敬; (尤指宗教的)崇敬: *He removed his hat as a sign of reverence.* 他脱下帽子表示敬意. ○ *He felt/had/showed great reverence for Leonardo.* 他非常崇拜列奥纳多. **2** [C] (*dated or joc* 旧或谑) title used in speaking to or about a clergyman 对牧师的尊称: *your/his reverence* 牧师 ○ *Their reverences will have tea.* 牧师要用茶.

▷ **rev·er·ence** *v* [Tn] (*fml* 文) treat (sb/sth) with reverence; revere 尊敬, 敬重(某人[某事物]); 崇敬.

rev·er·end /'revərənd; 'rɛvərənd/ *adj* [attrib 作定语] **1** deserving to be treated with respect, esp because of age, etc 应受尊敬的, 值得敬重的(尤指因年纪大等). **2 the Reverend** (*abbrs* 缩写 **Rev, Revd**) (used as the title of a clergyman 用作神职人员的尊称): *the Rev John/J/Mr Smith* 约翰[J]史密斯牧师 (but not 但不可作 *the Rev Smith*); *the Very Reverend*, of a dean (指教长); *the Right Reverend*, of a bishop (指主教); *the Most Reverend*, of an archbishop or Irish Roman Catholic bishop (指大主教或爱尔兰天主教的主教); *the Reverend Father*, of a Roman Catholic priest (指天主教的司铎).

□ **,Reverend 'Mother** (title of a) Mother Superior of a convent 女修道院院长(的称号).

rev·er·ent /'revərənt; 'rɛvərənt/ *adj* feeling or showing reverence 虔敬的; 恭敬的: *reverent attitudes, gestures, etc* 恭敬的态度、姿势等. ▷ **rev·er·ently** *adv*: *wreaths laid reverently on the coffin* 端端正正摆放在灵柩上的花圈.

rev·er·en·tial /,revə'renʃl; ,rɛvə'rɛnʃəl/ *adj* (*fml* 文) caused by or showing reverence 出于尊敬的; 恭敬的: *ushered in with a reverential bow* 以鞠躬礼相迎. ▷

R

rev·er·en·tially /-ʃəlɪ; -ʃəlɪ/ *adv.*

rev·erie /ˈrevərɪ; ˋrɛvərɪ/ *n* [U, C] (state of having) idle and pleasant thoughts 幻想; 空想; 遐想: *be deep, sunk, lost in reverie* 沉浸在、沉溺于、陷入幻想中 ○ *She fell into a reverie about her childhood.* 她沉浸在对童年往事的遐思中.

re·vers /rɪˈvɪə(r); rəˋvɪr/ *n* (*pl* unchanged 复数不变 /-ɪəz; -ɪrz/) (usu *pl* 通常作复数) edge of a coat, jacket, etc, turned back to show the reverse side (eg on a lapel or cuff) (大衣、外套等的)翻边(如翻领或翻袖口的).

re·versal /rɪˈvɜ:sl; rɪˋvɝsḷ/ *n* [C, U] **1** (instance of) making sth the opposite of what it was; turning around 反转; 倒向; 颠倒: *a dramatic reversal of her earlier decision* 她的突然改变决定 ○ *a reversal of the usual procedures, tendencies, opinions* 常规的颠倒、趋势的扭转、意见的转变 ○ (*fig* 比喻) *His luck suffered a cruel reversal*, ie change for the worse. 他遭逢厄运. **2** (instance of) exchanging two positions, functions, etc (位置、功能等的)转换: *role reversal/reversal of roles*, eg between husband and wife when the husband looks after the house and children while the wife works 角色的转换(如夫妻之间由男方料理家务、照看小孩而女方工作).

re·verse[1] /rɪˈvɜ:s; rɪˋvɝs/ *adj* **1** [attrib 作定语] **~ (of/to sth)** contrary or opposite to what is expected (与预期的事)相反的; 未料到的: *reverse tendencies, processes* 相反的趋势、过程 ○ *Statistics showed a reverse trend to that recorded in other countries.* 统计数字表明这种趋向与其他国家所示情况迥异. **2** (idm 习语) **in/into reverse ˈorder** from the end towards the start; backwards 顺序相反; 反向: *Count down in reverse order — 10, 9, 8...* 倒数——10、9、8... ○ *Put the letters in 'madam' into reverse order and they still read 'madam'.* 把 madam 这个字的字母排列顺序颠倒过来, 仍读作 madam.

□ **reverse gear** = REVERSE[2] 4a.
reverse turn = REVERSE[2] 4b.

re·verse[2] /rɪˈvɜ:s; rɪˋvɝs/ *n* **1** [sing] **the ~ (of sth)** thing that is the contrary or opposite to what is expected (与预期的事)相反的事物; 未料到的情况: *In hot weather, the reverse happens/applies.* 在热天, 情况相反. ○ *Children's shoes aren't cheap — quite the reverse.* 儿童的鞋并不便宜——反而更贵. ○ (*fml* 文) *You were the (very) reverse of polite*, ie You were rude. 你(非常)无礼貌. **2** [sing] (**a**) (design on the) underside or back of a coin, medal, etc (钱币、徽章等的)反面, 背面(的图案): *The 50p coin has a crowned lion on its reverse.* 50便士硬币反面的图案是个戴皇冠的狮子. Cf 参看 OBVERSE. (**b**) underside or back of sth 底面; 反面; 背部: *flaws on the reverse of the silk* 这丝织品背面的瑕疵 ○ *a maker's mark on the reverse of a plate* 盘子底部的厂家标记. **3** [C] (*fml* 文) (**a**) change for the worse; misfortune 逆转; 挫折; 不幸; 灾难: *We suffered some serious (financial) reverses.* 我们(在财务上)受到一些严重挫折. (**b**) defeat 失败; 失利: *a sudden reverse in the guerrilla campaign* 游击战的突然失败 ○ *a reverse at the polls*, ie a poor election result 选举中的失利. **4** (**a**) [U, C usu *sing* 作不可数名词或可数名词, 后者通常作单数] (also **reverse ˈgear**) control used to make a vehicle travel backwards (机动车的)倒挡: *Put the car into reverse.* 汽车挂上倒挡. ○ *cars with five forward gears and a reverse* 有五个前进挡和一个倒挡的汽车. (**b**) [C] (also **reverse ˈturn**) turn made while driving backwards 倒车转弯: *I can't do reverses.* 我不会倒车转弯. **5** [C] device that reverses sth 换向装置; 回动装置; 反向齿轮: *an automatic ribbon reverse*, ie on a typewriter 色带自动换向装置(打字机上的). **6** (idm 习语) **in/into reˈverse** from the end towards the start; backwards 顺序相反; 反向: *Ambulances have 'AMBULANCE' printed in reverse on their bonnets.* 救护车发动机罩盖上标有逆序反向字母的 AMBULANCE 字样. ○ (*fig* 比喻) *The superpowers are putting the arms race into reverse.* 超级大国正在把军备竞赛转换成相继裁军.

re·verse[3] /rɪˈvɜ:s; rɪˋvɝs/ *v* **1** [Tn] turn (sth) the other way round or up, or inside out 使(某物)反转; 将(某物)翻转: *Writing is reversed in a mirror.* 写出来的字在镜子里是倒着的. ○ *reverse the collar and cuffs on a shirt*, ie to hide frayed edges 把衬衫的领子和袖口翻过来(以遮盖破边). **2** (**a**) [I, Ipr, Ip, Tn, Tn·pr, Tn·p] (cause a vehicle to) travel backwards (使车辆)倒退行驶: *reverse round a corner, up a hill, across a side street,etc* 开车倒退转弯、上山、穿过小街等 ○ *He reversed (the car) into a tree.* 他开倒车撞到了树上. ○ *The garage is open, so you can reverse in.* 车房的门开着呢, 你可以倒着开进去. (**b**) [I, Tn] (make an engine, etc) work in the opposite direction (使发动机等)逆向运转: *reverse the thrust of the rocket motors* 使火箭发动机产生逆向推力 ○ *brake (eg a fixed-wheel cycle) by reversing the pedalling action* 倒蹬踏板制动(如脚蹬闸自行车). **3** [Tn] (**a**) make (sth) the opposite of what it was; change around completely 使(某物)转化为其自身的对立面; 彻底转变: *reverse a procedure, process, trend, etc* 使程序、过程、趋向等完全相反. (**b**) exchange (two functions, positions, etc) 互换(功能、位置等): *Husband and wife have reversed roles.* 丈夫和妻子互换了责任. ○ *Their situations are now reversed as employee has become employer.* 他们双方的地位转换了, 雇员成了雇主. **4** [Tn] revoke or annul (a decree, etc) 撤消或废除(法令等): *reverse the decision of a lower court* 撤消下级法院的判决 ○ *reverse a decree, judgement, verdict, etc* 撤消法令、判决、裁决等. **5** (idm 习语) **reverse (the) ˈcharge(s)** (*US* **call ˈcollect**) make a telephone call that will be charged to the person receiving it, not the caller 由接电话一方付费: *reverse the charges on/for a call* 电话费转由受话人支付 ○ *make a reversed-ˈcharge call to New York* 打电话至纽约, 由受话人付费.

▷ **re·vers·ible** /-əbl; -əbḷ/ *adj* that can be reversed 可反转的; 可翻转的; 可倒退的; 可转变的; 可撤消的; 可逆的: *a reversible coat, scarf, cap, etc*, ie one that can be worn with either side turned out 可正反两面使用的大衣、围巾、帽子等. **re·vers·ib·il·ity** /rɪˌvɜ:səˈbɪlətɪ; rɪˌvɝsəˋbɪlətɪ/ *n* [U].

□ **reˈversing light** white light at the back of a vehicle showing that it is in reverse gear 倒车灯(倒车时使用的白色灯).

re·vert /rɪˈvɜ:t; rɪˋvɝt/ *v* [Ipr] **1 ~ to sth** (**a**) return to (a former state or condition) 恢复(原状): *fields that have reverted to moorland*, ie are no longer cultivated 重又变成高沼池的田地(不再耕作的). (**b**) (*fml* 文) return to (a former practice or habit) 恢复(原先的作法或习惯): *revert to smoking when under stress* 因受到压力又恢复了吸烟的习惯 ○ *After her divorce she reverted to (using) her maiden name.* 她离婚后又重新使用娘家的姓. **2 ~ to sth** (*fml* 文) return to (a topic in talk or thought) 回到(原话题或思路): *To revert/Reverting to your earlier question,...* 谈到你原先提的那个问题, ... ○ *The conversation kept reverting to the subject of money.* 谈话的内容总是离不开钱的事. ○ *Her thoughts often reverted to Italy.* 她念念不忘意大利. **3 (~ to sb/sth)** (*law* 律) (of property, rights, etc) return or pass to the original owner, the State, etc (指财产、权利等)复归或归属于(原主、国家等): *If he dies without an heir, his property reverts to the state.* 他死后若无继承人, 其财产则归国家所有. **4** (idm 习语) **revert to type** return to a natural or an original condition 回复到自然的或原先的状况: *Once a socialist, she has now reverted to type and votes Tory like her parents.* 她一度信仰社会主义, 但现已回归家族传统, 像她父母一样投票支持保守党了.

▷ **re·ver·sion** /rɪˈvɜ:ʃn; *US* -ʒn; rɪˋvɝʒən/ *n* **1** [U, sing] reverting 恢复; 回复; 回归; 复归: *(a) reversion to swamp, old methods, former habits* 以前之沼泽状况、老方法、旧习惯之恢复. **2** (*law* 律) (**a**) [C] right to possess property, etc when its present owner dies or gives it up 未来所有权(目前财产等所有者死后或放弃所有权的). (**b**) [U] returning of a right or property to the original owner, the State, etc 复归权(权利或财产的复归原主或国家等): *succeed to an estate in reversion* 获得一地产的复归权. **re·ver·sion·ary** /rɪˈvɜ:ʃənərɪ; *US* -ʒənerɪ; rɪˋvɝʒənˌɛrɪ/ *adj* [attrib 作定语] (*law* 律): *reversionary rights* 未来所有权或复归权.

re·vert·ible /rɪˈvɜ:təbl; rɪˋvɝtəbḷ/ *adj*.

re·vet·ment /rɪˈvetmənt; rɪˋvɛtmənt/ *n* **1** facing of masonry, concrete, sandbags, etc on a wall or an embankment, esp of a fortification 铺面, 砌面(护墙或护堤所用的砖石、混凝土、沙袋等结构)(尤指用于工事的). **2** retaining wall 挡土墙; 拥壁.

re·view /rɪˈvju:; rɪˋvju/ *n* **1** [U, C] (act of) re-examination or reconsideration 复查; 重新考虑: *The terms of the contract are subject to review.* 合同的条款有待复查决定. ○ *a radical review of manufacturing methods* 对生产方法

的彻底检查. **2** [C] survey or report of past events or a subject 回顾; 检讨; 述评; 汇报: *an annual, monthly, etc review of progress* 年度、月度等进展情况的报告 ○ *a review of the year's sport* 全年体育活动回顾 ○ *a wide-ranging review of recent developments in wildlife conservation* 在保护野生动植物方面最新进展的面面观. **3** [C] (**a**) published report that assesses the merits of a book, film, etc 书评、影评等: *The play got splendid, excellent, unfavourable, etc reviews.* 该剧受到高度的、极好的、很糟的评价. ○ [attrib 作定语] *a review copy*, ie a copy of a book, etc sent by the publishers to a periodical for review 供评论用的赠阅本(出版者赠给期刊的). (**b**) (section of a) periodical containing reviews, etc 有评论文章等的期刊(的专栏): *a scientific, musical, etc review* 科学的、音乐的 ... 期刊 ○ *the London Review of Books* 《伦敦书评》. **4** [C] ceremonial display and inspection of troops, a fleet, etc (部队、舰队等的)检阅, 阅兵式: *hold a review* 举行阅兵式. **5** (idm 习语) **be/come under re'view; be/come up for re'view** be (due to be) re-examined or reconsidered 在复查或重新考虑中: *Our contracts are currently under review.* 我们的合同正在复查. ○ *Your case is coming up for review in May.* 你的事情将在五月再研究. **keep sth under re'view** re-examine sth continually 不断复查某事物: *Salaries are kept under constant review.* 薪金问题要一直不断审订.

▷ **re·view** *v* **1** [Tn] (**a**) re-examine or reconsider (sth) 复查或重新考虑(某事物): *The government is reviewing the situation.* 政府正在重新检讨形势. (**b**) go over (esp past events) in one's mind; survey 思考(尤指往事); 回顾: *review one's successes and failures* 反省自己的成败 ○ *review one's progress* 回顾自己的进程. **2** [I, Ipr, Tn] write a review of (a book, film, etc) for publication 写(书、影片等)的评论文章: *She reviews for 'The Spectator'.* 她为《观众》杂志写评论. ○ *The play was well/favourably reviewed.* 该剧受到好评. **3** [Tn] inspect (troops, a fleet, etc) ceremonially 检阅(部队、舰队等). **4** [Tn] (*esp US*) go over (work already learnt) in preparation for an exam; revise 复习(功课).

re·viewer *n* person who writes reviews of books, etc 书评等的撰写人; 评论家: *a play which reviewers have praised highly* 评论家高度评价的剧.

re·vile /rɪˈvaɪl; rɪˋvaɪl/ *v* [Tn] (*fml* 文) criticize (sb/sth), in angry and abusive language 痛斥, 谩骂(某人[某事物]).

re·vise /rɪˈvaɪz; rɪˋvaɪz/ *v* **1** [Tn] re-examine (sth), esp in order to correct or improve it 复查(某事物); (尤指)复核, 校订, 修正: *revised proposals, estimates, rules, figures* 修正的提案、估计、规则、数字 ○ *revise a manuscript before publication* 审校手稿以备出版 ○ *revise one's opinion of sb* 改变对某人的看法. **2** [I, Ipr, Tn, Tn·pr] **~ (sth) (for sth)** (*Brit*) go over (work already done) in preparation for an examination 复习(功课): *She's revising (her history notes) for the test.* 她正在复习(历史课笔记)准备测验.

▷ **re·vise** *n* (usu *pl* 通常作复数) (in printing) proof-sheet in which errors marked in an earlier proof have been corrected (印刷业务中的)再校样, 二校样.

re·vi·sion /rɪˈvɪʒn; rɪˋvɪʒən/ *n* (**a**) [U] **~ (for sth)** revising or being revised 复查; 校订; 修正; 改正; 复习: *Our budget needs drastic revision.* 我们的预算需作重大修改. ○ (*Brit*) *do some revision for the exam/some exam revision* 为准备考试而复习. (**b**) [C] instance of this 复查; 校订; 修正; 改正; 复习: *undergo a final revision* 经最后修订. (**c**) [C] thing that has been revised 经修订或改正之物; 修订本; 修订版: *submit the revision of a novel for publication* 送交小说的修订本准备出版.

□**the Re,vised ,Standard 'Version** revision of the Bible made in 1946-57 《圣经》修订标准本(1946-1957年间修订而成).

the Re,vised 'Version revision by British scholars in 1870-84 of the Authorized Version of the Bible 《圣经》修订本(英国学者于1870-1884年间根据《圣经》钦定本修订而成).

re·vi·sion·ism /rɪˈvɪʒənɪzəm; rɪˋvɪʒən,ɪzəm/ *n* [U] (*esp derog* 尤作贬义) changes to, or questioning of, orthodox political doctrines or practices, esp Marxism 修正主义(尤指针对马克思主义的). ▷ **re·vi·sion·ist** /-ʒənɪst; -ʒənɪst/ *n* [attrib 作定语]: *revisionist tendencies* 修正主义倾向.

re·vit·al·ize, -ise /riːˈvaɪtəlaɪz; riˋvaɪtḷ,aɪz/ *v* [Tn] put new life into (sth); regenerate 使(某事物)恢复生机; 使新生; 使再兴: *revitalize industry, the economy, education, etc* 振兴工业、经济、教育等 ○ *Her appointment as leader revitalized the party.* 她担任领袖后, 该党获得了转机. ▷ **re·vit·al·iza·tion, -isation** /riːˌvaɪtəlaɪˈzeɪʃn; *US* -lɪˈz-; ˌrivaɪtḷɪˋzeʃən/ *n* [U].

re·vival /rɪˈvaɪvl; rɪˋvaɪvḷ/ *n* **1** [U, C] coming or bringing back to health, strength or consciousness; recovery (健康、力量或知觉的)恢复, 复原, 重振, 苏醒: *the patient's speedy revival after her operation* 女病人在手术后的迅速康复 ○ (*fig* 比喻) *the revival of hope, interest, ambition* 希望、兴趣、雄心的恢复 ○ *Our economy is undergoing a revival.* 我们的经济正处于复兴阶段. **2** (**a**) [U] coming or bringing back into use, activity, fashion, etc 重新使用; 恢复活动; 重新流行: *the revival of old customs, values, skills* 旧的习俗、价值观念、技艺的恢复 ○ *the revival of the Welsh language* 威尔士语的重新流行. (**b**) [C] instance of this 重新使用; 恢复活动; 重新流行: *a religious, commercial, political revival* 宗教的、商业的、政治上的复兴. **3** [C] new production of a play, etc that has not been performed for some time (戏剧等的)重演: *stage a revival of a Restoration comedy* 重新上演英国王政复辟时期的喜剧. **4** [U, C] (*religion* 宗) (series of public meetings, etc to promote a) reawakening of (esp Christian) faith 奋兴活动, 奋兴大会(尤指旨在促进基督教信仰的): *preach (the spirit of) revival* 作奋兴布道 ○ [attrib 作定语] *televised revival meetings* 用电视播放的宗教奋兴大会.

▷ **re·viv·al·ism** /-vəlɪzəm; -vḷɪzəm/ *n* [U] process of reawakening religious faith 宗教奋兴运动.

re·viv·al·ist /-vəlɪst; -vḷɪst/ *n* person who organizes or conducts religious revival meetings 宗教奋兴大会的组织者或主持者: [attrib 作定语] *revivalist campaigns, missions, etc* 宗教奋兴家的宣传活动、布道等.

re·vive /rɪˈvaɪv; rɪˋvaɪv/ *v* **1** [I, Tn] come or bring (sb/sth) back to health, strength or consciousness (使某人[某物])恢复健康、力量或知觉: *The flowers will revive in water.* 这些花一浇水就能活过来. ○ *She fainted but the brandy soon revived her.* 她昏迷了, 但喂她些白兰地酒就很快醒过来了. ○ (*fig* 比喻) *Our failing hopes/spirits revived.* 我们破灭的希望又重新燃起[低落的情绪又重新振作起来]. **2** [I, Tn] come or bring (sth) back into use, activity, fashion, etc 重新使用(某事物); 使(某事物)恢复活动或重新流行: *revive old practices, customs, trends, etc* 恢复旧做法、再兴旧习俗、重现某倾向 ○ *efforts to revive the mini-skirt* 为使超短裙重新流行而做的努力. **3** [Tn] stage again a play, etc that has not been performed for some time 重新上演(戏剧等): *revive a 1930's musical* 重新上演20世纪30年代的歌舞喜剧.

re·viv·ify /riːˈvɪvɪfaɪ; riˋvɪvə,faɪ/ *v* (*pt, pp* **-fied**) [Tn] (*fml* 文) give new life or liveliness to (sth); revitalize 给予(某事物)新生命或活力; 复兴.

re·voca·tion /ˌrevəˈkeɪʃn; ˌrɛvəˋkeʃən/ *n* [C, U] (*fml* 文) (instance of) revoking or being revoked 撤消; 取消; 废除: *the revocation of laws, contracts, etc* 法规的废除、合同的取消.

re·voke /rɪˈvəʊk; rɪˋvok/ *v* **1** [Tn] (*fml* 文) withdraw or cancel (a decree, permit, etc) 撤消或废除(法令等); 吊销(许可证): *revoke orders, promises* 撤消命令、允诺 ○ *His driving licence was revoked after the crash.* 他撞车后驾驶执照吊销了. **2** [I] (of a player in a card-game) fail to play a card of the same suit as the leading player although able to do so (指玩纸牌者)藏牌, 有牌不跟.

re·volt /rɪˈvəʊlt; rɪˋvolt/ *v* **1** [I, Ipr] **~ (against sb/sth)** (**a**) rise in rebellion (against authority) 反叛(当权者): *The people revolted against the military dictator/dictatorship.* 人民反抗军事独裁者[的统治]. (**b**) express protest or defiance 反抗; 违抗: *revolt against parental discipline* 抗拒父母的教导. **2** [Ipr, Tn usu passive 通常用于被动语态] **~ against/at sth** (cause sb to) feel horror or disgust (使某人)憎恶或讨厌: *Human nature revolts against/at such cruelty.* 人出自本性厌恶这种暴行. ○ *I was revolted by his dirty habit of spitting.* 我很讨厌他随地吐痰的恶习.

▷ **re·volt** *n* **1** (**a**) [U] act or state of rebelling or defying authority 叛乱; 反叛; 反抗; 违抗: *a period of open, armed, political revolt* 公开的、武装的、政治的叛乱时期 ○ *stir, incite, etc militant party members to revolt*

R

鼓动、煽动…激进的党员反党 ○ *quell, put down, etc a revolt* 镇压、平息…叛乱. (**b**) [C] instance of this 叛乱; 反叛; 违抗: *The army has put down/suppressed the revolt.* 军队镇压[平息]了叛乱. ○ *a revolt against conformity* 对习俗的反抗. **2** (idm 习语) **in revolt** state of having revolted (REVOLT 1a) 叛乱; 反叛; 反抗; 违抗: *The people broke out/rose in revolt.* 人民起来造反了.

re·volt·ing /rɪˈvəʊltɪŋ; rɪˋvoltɪŋ/ *adj* (**a**) causing disgust or horror 使人讨厌或憎恶的: *revolting atrocities* 使人憎恨的暴行. (**b**) (*infml* 口) nasty or unpleasant 令人作呕的; 令人不愉快的: *His feet smelt revolting.* 他双脚散发的气味让人恶心. ○ *a revolting mixture of pasta and curry* 令人作呕的面食和咖喱的混合食品. ▷ **re·volt·ingly** *adv*: *revoltingly wet weather* 潮湿得让人难受的天气.

re·volu·tion /ˌrevəˈluːʃn; ˌrɛvəˋluʃən/ *n* **1** [C, U] (instance of the) overthrow of a system of government, esp by force 革命: *He has lived through two revolutions.* 他经历了两次革命. ○ *the French Revolution*, ie in 1789 法国大革命(1789年) ○ *foment, stir up revolution* 激起、鼓动革命 ○ *the dispute over the question of evolution and revolution* 关于渐进和革命问题的争论. **2** [C] **~ (in sth)** (*fig* 比喻) complete or drastic change of method, conditions, etc (方法、情况等的)彻底改变, 重大变革: *a revolution in the treatment of cancer* 在癌症治疗上的重大突破 ○ *a genetic, technological, etc revolution* 遗传学的、技术上的飞跃 ○ *Credit cards have brought about a revolution in people's spending habits.* 信用卡的使用给人们的消费习惯带来巨大改变. **3** [C, U] **~ (on/round sth)** (**a**) (act of) revolving or rotating, esp of one planet round another 旋转, 运行(尤指行星绕另一行星的): *make, describe a full revolution* 旋转、转动一周 ○ *the revolution of the earth on its axis round the sun* 地球以太阳为轴的旋转. (**b**) (process of making a) single complete movement or turn round a central point (围绕中心点)旋转一周: *a record designed to be played at 45 revolutions per minute* 每分钟45转的唱片.

▷ **re·volu·tion·ary** /-ʃənərɪ; *US* -nerɪ; -ʃənˌɛrɪ/ *adj* **1** [usu attrib 通常作定语] of political revolution 革命的: *revolutionary parties, leaders, activities* 革命政党、领袖、活动. **2** involving complete or drastic change 彻底改变的; 重大变革的: *Genetic engineering will have revolutionary consequences for mankind.* 遗传工程将对人类产生深远的影响. — *n* person who begins or supports a political revolution 革命者; 革命活动家.

re·volu·tion·ize, -ise /-ʃənaɪz; -ʃənˌaɪz/ *v* [Tn] cause (sth) to change completely or drastically 使(某事物)发生根本性的或巨大的改变: *Computers have revolutionized banking.* 计算机的运用彻底改变了银行业务运作.

re·volve /rɪˈvɒlv; rɪˋvɑlv/ *v* **1** [I, Ipr] **~ (around/round sth) (on sth)** (of a planet, etc) move in a circular orbit (指行星等)在轨道上运行: *The earth revolves round the sun (on its axis).* 地球(以太阳为轴)绕太阳公转. **2** [I, Ipr, Tn] **~ (around/round/on sth)** (cause sth to) go round in a circle; rotate (使某物)作圆周运动, 旋转, 转动: *A wheel revolves round/on its axis.* 轮子是绕轴旋转的. ○ *The mechanism that revolves the turntable is broken.* 带动转盘旋转的机械装置坏了. ○ (*fig fml* 比喻, 文) *revolve sth in one's mind*, ie consider sth carefully 仔细考虑某事物. **3** (phr v) **revolve around sb/sth** have sb/sth as its chief concern; centre on sb/sth 以某人[某事物]为中心: *My life revolves around my job.* 我的工作是我生活的中心. ○ *He thinks that everything revolves around him.* 他认为一切事情都要以他为主.

▷ **re·volv·ing** *adj* [usu attrib 通常作定语] that rotates 旋转的; 转动的: *a revolving chair, hat-stand* 转椅、旋转帽架 ○ *This theatre has a revolving stage.* 这家戏院的舞台是旋转式的. **reˌvolving ˈcredit** (*finance* 财) credit that is automatically renewed up to a fixed amount, as part of the debt is paid 循环信贷(一俟偿还部分债款即自动恢复到原定数额). **revolving ˈdoor** door with four or more partitions turning on a central axis to keep out draughts 旋转门.

re·volver /rɪˈvɒlvə(r); rɪˋvɑlvɚ/ *n* pistol with a revolving chamber from which bullets are fed into the breech for firing 左轮手枪: *draw one's revolver* 掏出左轮手枪. ⇨ illus at GUN 见 GUN 插图.

re·vue /rɪˈvjuː; rɪˋvju/ *n* [C, U] (type of) theatrical entertainment consisting of a mixture of dialogue, song and dance, esp of a topical and satirical nature 时事讽刺剧: *a political revue* 政治讽刺剧 ○ *act, appear, perform, etc in revue* 演出时事讽刺剧 ○ [attrib 作定语] *revue artistes* 时事讽刺剧表演者.

re·vul·sion /rɪˈvʌlʃn; rɪˋvʌlʃən/ *n* [U, sing] **1 ~ (against/at/from sth)** feeling of disgust or horror 厌恶; 憎恶: *feel a sense of revulsion at the bloodshed* 对伤害人的行为深恶痛绝 ○ *She stared at the snake in revulsion.* 她盯着那条蛇, 感到很厌恶. **2** (*fml* 文) sudden violent change of feeling; reaction 感情的急剧转变; 剧烈反应: *a revulsion of public feeling in favour of the accused* 舆论之突然转向同情被告.

re·ward /rɪˈwɔːd; rɪˋwɔrd/ *n* **1** [U] recompense for work, merit or services 报答; 报偿: *work without hope of reward* 没有希望获得报偿的工作 ○ *He received a medal in reward for his bravery.* 他因表现勇敢而获得了一枚奖章. **2** [C] something given or received in return for work, merit or services 报酬; 酬金: *reap, receive one's just reward* 获得应有的报酬 ○ *emotional, intellectual, financial rewards* 感情方面的、知识方面的、财务方面的报酬 ○ *One reward of my job is meeting people.* 我在工作中的一个收获是能认识许多人. **3** [C] sum of money offered for the capture of a criminal, return of lost property, etc (为捉捕罪犯、寻回失去财物等的)赏金, 奖赏: *A £1 000 reward has been offered for the return of the stolen painting.* 悬赏1 000英镑寻找失窃的画. **4** (idm 习语) **virtue is its own reward** ⇨ VIRTUE.

▷ **re·ward** *v* [esp passive 尤用于被动语态: Tn, Tn·pr] **~ sb (for sth/doing sth)** give a reward to sb 给某人报酬; 奖赏某人: *Is this how you reward me for helping/my help?* 你就这样报答我对你的帮助吗? ○ *She rewarded him with a smile.* 她向他报之以一笑. ○ *His persistence was rewarded when the car finally started.* 他那些力气没有白费, 汽车终于启动了. ○ *Anyone providing information which leads to the recovery of the painting will be rewarded.* 凡提供线索有助于寻回该画者可获报酬.

re·ward·ing *adj* (of an activity, etc) worth doing; satisfying (指活动等)值得做的, 令人满意的: *a rewarding film, study, trip* 有益的影片、研究、旅行 ○ *Gardening is a very rewarding pastime.* 园艺劳动是非常有益的消遣. ○ *Teaching is not very rewarding financially*, ie not very well paid. 教书的工作报酬不太高.

re·wire /ˌriːˈwaɪə(r); riˋwaɪr/ *v* [Tn] renew the electrical wiring of (a building, etc) 给(建筑物等)换新电线: *The house has been completely rewired.* 这所房子已全部换上了新电线.

re·word /ˌriːˈwɜːd; riˋwɝd/ *v* [Tn] change the wording of (sth spoken or written) 改变…的措辞; 改说; 改写: *reword a telegram to save money* 改写电文以节省费用.

re·write /ˌriːˈraɪt; riˋraɪt/ *v* (*pt* **rewrote** /-ˈrəʊt; -ˋrot/, *pp* **rewritten** /-ˈrɪtn; -ˋrɪtn/) [Tn, Tn·pr, Cn·n/a] **~ sth (for sth)**; **~ sth (as sth)** write (sth) again in a different form or style 重写; 改写: *rewrite the script for radio/as a radio play* 把原稿改写成广播稿[广播剧] ○ *The essay needs to be rewritten.* 这篇文章需要重写.

▷ **re·write** /ˈriːraɪt; ˋriˌraɪt/ *n* thing rewritten 重写或改写的文稿: *do a complete rewrite of the original speech* 把原讲稿全面改写.

Rex /reks; rɛks/ *n* (*Latin* 拉) (used esp in signatures on proclamations or in the titles of lawsuits 尤用于签署文告或诉讼案之标题) reigning king (在位)君主, 国王: *George Rex* 乔治国王 ○ (*law* 律) *Rex v Hill* 王国政府诉讼希尔案. Cf 参看 REGINA.

RFC *abbr* 缩写 = (*Brit*) Rugby Football Club 橄榄球俱乐部.

rh *abbr* 缩写 = right hand 右手. Cf 参看 LH.

rhaps·ody /ˈræpsədɪ; ˋræpsədɪ/ *n* **1** (*music* 音) (often in titles 常用于标题) romantic composition in irregular form 狂想曲: *Liszt's Hungarian Rhapsodies* 李斯特的《匈牙利狂想曲》. **2** (idm 习语) **go into rhapsodies (over sb/sth)** express enthusiasm or delight in speech or writing (言语或文字中)表现热情或喜悦: *The guests went into rhapsodies over the food.* 宾客对食物交口称赞.

▷ **rhaps·odic** /ræpˈsɒdɪk; ræpˋsɑdɪk/ *adj* (*esp ironic* 尤作反语) expressing enthusiasm or delight 热情的; 欣喜的: *The rejection of their pay claim was given a less than rhapsodic reception by the miners.* 矿工要求提高工资遭到拒绝而甚为恼火.

rhaps·od·ize, -ise /ˈræpsədaɪz; ˋræpsəˌdaɪz/ *v* [I, Ipr] **~ (about/over sb/sth)** (*esp ironic* 尤作反语) talk or write with great enthusiasm (about sb/sth) 极热情地说或写(某人[某事物]的事).

rhea /rɪə; ˋriə/ *n* three-toed ostrich of S America 鹈鹕, 美洲鸵鸟(南美洲产之三趾鸵鸟).

rheo·stat /ˈri:əstæt; ˋriə,stæt/ *n* instrument used to control the current in an electrical circuit by varying the resistance in it 变阻器.

rhesus /ˈri:səs; ˋrisəs/ *n* (also ˈ**rhesus monkey**) small monkey common in N India, often used in biological experiments 恒河猴(印度北部产, 常用于生物学实验).

□ ˈ**Rhesus factor** (also **Rh factor** /ɑ:rˈeɪtʃ fæktə(r); ,ɑr ˋetʃ ,fæktɚ/) (*medical* 医) substance present in the blood of most people and some animals, causing a blood disorder in a new-born baby whose blood is *Rhesus-positive* (ie containing this substance) while the mother's is *Rhesus-negative* (ie not containing it) Rh因子.

rhet·oric /ˈretərɪk; ˋrɛtərɪk/ *n* [U] **1** (art of) using language impressively or persuasively, esp in public speaking 修辞; 修辞艺术; 修辞学: *impassioned rhetoric* 富有表现力的修辞. **2** (*derog* 贬) elaborate language which is intended to impress but is often insincere, meaningless or exaggerated 华丽的词藻(常含华而不实之意); 虚夸的言辞: *the empty rhetoric of politicians* 政客们的花言巧语.

rhet·or·ical /rɪˈtɒrɪkl; *US* -ˈtɔ:r-; rɪˋtɔrɪkl/ *adj* **1** of the art of rhetoric 修辞的; 修辞学的: *rhetorical figures such as hyperbole* 修辞手段, 如夸张法. **2** (*derog* 贬) in or using rhetoric(2) 词藻华丽的; 虚夸的: *rhetorical speeches* 词藻华丽的台词. ▷ **rhet·or·ic·ally** /-klɪ; -klɪ/ *adv.*

□ **rhe,torical ˈquestion** question asked only for dramatic effect and not to seek an answer, eg *Who cares?* (ie Nobody cares) 反问(如 Who cares? 即 Nobody cares).

rheum·atic /ru:ˈmætɪk; ruˋmætɪk/ *adj* of, causing or affected by rheumatism 风湿病的; 引起风湿病的; 风湿病造成的: *a rheumatic condition, pain, joint* 风湿病、风湿痛、患风湿病的关节.

▷ **rheum·atic** *n* person who suffers from rheumatism 风湿病患者.

rheum·at·icky *adj* (*infml* 口) rheumatic 风湿病的.

rheum·atics *n* [pl] (*infml* 口) rheumatism 风湿病.

□ **rheumatic ˈfever** serious form of rheumatism with fever, chiefly in children 风湿热.

rheum·at·ism /ˈru:mətɪzəm; ˋrumə,tɪzəm/ *n* [U] any of several diseases causing pain, stiffness and inflammation in the muscles and joints 风湿病: *contract, develop rheumatism* 患、得风湿病. Cf 参看 ARTHRITIS, FIBROSITIS.

rheum·at·oid /ˈru:mətɔɪd; ˋrumə,tɔɪd/ *adj* of rheumatism 类风湿病的; 风湿性的.

□ ,**rheumatoid arˈthritis** chronic progressive form of arthritis causing inflammation, esp in the joints of the hands, wrists, knees and feet 风湿性关节炎.

rhine·stone /ˈraɪnstəʊn; ˋraɪn,ston/ *n* imitation diamond 莱茵石(仿钻石制品).

rhino /ˈraɪnəʊ; ˋraɪno/ *n* (*pl* unchanged or **~s** 复数或不变或作 **rhinos** /-nəʊz; -noz/) (*infml* 口) rhinoceros 犀牛: *black/white rhino* 黑[白]犀牛 ○ [attrib 作定语] *rhino horn* 犀牛角. ➪illus 见插图.

rhinoceros 犀牛

rhi·no·ceros /raɪˈnɒsərəs; raɪˋnɑsərəs/ *n* (*pl* unchanged or **~es** 复数或不变或作 **rhinoceroses**) **1** large thick-skinned heavily-built animal of Africa and S Asia, with either one or two horns on its nose 犀牛(产于非洲及亚洲南部). **2** (idm 习语) **have, etc a hide/skin like a rhiˈnoceros** show insensitivity to attack, criticism, insults, etc (对受攻击、批评、侮辱等)麻木不仁.

rhiz·ome /ˈraɪzəʊm; ˋraɪzom/ *n* (*botany* 植) root-like stem of some plants, growing along or under the ground and sending out both roots and shoots 根茎; 根状茎. ➪ illus at App 1 见附录1插图, page ii.

rho·do·den·dron /,rəʊdəˈdendrən; ,rodəˋdɛndrən/ (*US* also **rosebay**) *n* evergreen shrub with large clusters of trumpet-shaped red, purple, pink or white flowers 杜鹃花.

rhom·bus /ˈrɒmbəs; ˋrɑmbəs/ *n* geometric figure with four equal sides and angles which are not right angles (eg the diamond or lozenge shape on playing cards) 菱形. ➪illus at QUADRILATERAL 见 QUADRILATERAL 插图.

▷ **rhomb·oid** /ˈrɒmbɔɪd; ˋrɑmbɔɪd/ *adj* in the shape of a rhombus 菱形的. — *n* rhombus of which only the opposite sides and angles are equal 长菱形; 长斜方形. ➪illus at QUADRILATERAL 见 QUADRILATERAL 插图.

rhu·barb /ˈru:bɑ:b; ˋrubɑrb/ *n* [U] **1** (garden plant with) fleshy reddish leaf-stalks that are cooked and eaten like fruit 大黄; 大黄茎: [attrib 作定语] *rhubarb pie* 大黄馅饼. **2** (*infml* 口) (word that crowd actors repeat to simulate the babble of voices on stage 为制造人声嘈杂的舞台效果, 群众演员反复说的道白).

rhyme /raɪm; raɪm/ *n* **1** [U] sameness of sound between words or syllables, esp the endings of lines of verse, as in *day, away; visit, is it; puff, rough* 韵, (尤指)韵脚(如 day 和 away、visit 和 is it、puff 和 rough). **2** [C] **~ (for/to sth)** word that provides a rhyme for another 押韵词; 同韵词: *Is there a rhyme for/to 'hiccups'?* 有和 hiccups 押韵的词吗? **3** [C] verse or verses with rhymes 押韵的诗; 韵文: *sing nursery rhymes to the children* 给孩子们唱儿歌. **4** [U] rhyming form 押韵的形式; 韵律: *a story told in rhyme* 用韵文讲的故事 ○ *Can you put that into rhyme?* 你能把它改写成韵文吗? **5** (idm 习语) **neither, no, little, etc ,rhyme or ˈreason** no sense or logic 毫无道理: *a decision without rhyme or reason* 毫无道理的决定 ○ *There's neither rhyme nor reason in his behaviour.* 他的举动莫名其妙. ○ *English spelling has little rhyme or reason.* 英文字的拼法没什么规律.

▷ **rhyme** *v* **1** [Tn, Tn·pr] **~ sth (with sth)** put (words) together to form a rhyme 使(词)押韵: *You can rhyme 'hiccups' and/with 'pick-ups'.* 用 hiccups 可和 pick-ups 押韵. ○ *rhymed verse* 押韵的诗. **2** [I, Ipr] **~ (with sth)** (of words or lines of verse) form a rhyme (指词或诗句)押韵: *'Though' and 'through' don't rhyme, and neither rhymes with 'tough'.* though 和 through 不押韵, 这两个词跟 tough 也不押韵. **rhymed** *adj* having rhymes 押韵的: *rhymed couplets* 押韵的对句.

□ ˈ**rhyming slang** form of slang which replaces words with rhyming words or phrases, eg *apples and pears* for *stairs* 同韵俚语(以同韵的词或短语作为替代语的俚语形式, 如以 apples and pears 代替 stairs).

rhythm /ˈrɪðəm; ˋrɪðəm/ *n* **1** (**a**) [U] pattern produced by emphasis and duration of notes in music or by stressed and unstressed syllables in words (音乐或词语的)节奏. (**b**) [C] instance of this 节奏: *play the same tune in/with a different rhythm* 用不同节奏演奏同一个曲子 ○ *Latin-American rhythms* 拉丁美洲的音乐节奏. (**c**) [U, C] movement with a regular succession of strong and weak elements 节律: *the rhythm of her heart/pulse beating* 她的心跳[脉搏]的节律. **2** [U] (*infml* 口) ability to move, dance, etc in time with a fixed beat 节奏感: *a natural sense of rhythm* 天生的节奏感. **3** [U, C] (*fig* 比喻) constantly recurring sequence of events or processes (事件或过程)有规律的反复出现: *the rhythm of the tides, seasons* 潮汐的涨落、四季的循环 ○ *biological rhythms*, eg of the human body 生物节律(如人体的).

▷ **rhyth·mic** /ˈrɪðmɪk; ˋrɪðmɪk/ (also **rhyth·mical**) /ˈrɪðmɪkl; ˋrɪðmɪkl/ *adj* having rhythm 有节奏的; 有规律的: *rhythmic breathing* 有规律的呼吸 ○ *the rhythmic tread of marching feet* 有节奏的行进步伐. **rhyth·mic·ally** /-klɪ; -klɪ/ *adv.*

□ ,**rhythm and ˈblues** type of popular music based on the blues 节奏与布鲁斯(由布鲁斯演变的流行音乐).

ˈ**rhythm method** method of contraception by avoiding sexual intercourse near the time of ovulation 安全期避孕法.

RI *abbr* 缩写 = (*Brit*) (on coins) Queen and Empress; King and Emperor (Latin *Regina et Imperatrix*; *Rex et*

R

Imperator) (钱币上的)女王和女皇, 国王和皇帝(源自拉丁文 *Regina et Imperatrix; Rex et Imperator*).

rib /rɪb; rɪb/ *n* **1** (**a**) [C] any one of the 12 pairs of curved bones extending from the backbone round the chest in humans (人的)肋骨: *broken, fractured, bruised, etc ribs* 折断的、断裂的、挫伤的...肋骨 ○ *dig sb/give sb a dig* (ie nudge or poke sb) *in the ribs* 触某人的肋部. ⇨ illus at SKELETON 见SKELETON插图. (**b**) [C] corresponding bone in animals (动物的)肋骨, 肋条. **2** [U, C] cut of meat from the ribs of an animal (肋部的)排骨: *barbecued spare-ribs* 烤猪排骨. **3** [C] curved part of the structure of sth resembling a rib 类似肋骨的结构: *the ribs of a leaf, an umbrella, a fan, a boat* 叶主脉、伞骨、扇骨、船的肋材. **4** [U, C] (stitch producing a) raised line in knitting (织物的)凸起条纹, 罗纹: *cuffs knitted in rib* 织成罗纹的袖口.

▷ **rib** *v* (**-bb-**) [Tn, Tn·pr] **~ sb (about/for sth)** (*infml* 口) make fun of sb in a good-natured way; tease 逗弄某人; 戏弄: *She was constantly ribbed about her accent.* 人家总拿她的口音开玩笑. ○ *rib sb for being shy* 取笑某人害羞. **rib·bed** *adj* (esp of fabrics) having raised lines (尤指织物)有凸起条纹的, 有罗纹的: *ribbed tights/stockings* 罗纹裤袜[长统袜] ○ *ribbed corduroy trousers* 条绒裤子. **rib·bing** *n* [U] **1** pattern of raised lines in knitting (织物的)凸条花样, 罗纹. **2** (*infml* 口) good-natured teasing 逗乐; 戏弄: *He takes a good ribbing*, ie can accept being teased. 他不怕人家拿他取笑.

□ **'rib-cage** *n* framework of ribs round the chest 胸廓. **'rib-tickling** *adj* (*infml* 口) funny or amusing 滑稽的; 有趣的.

rib·ald /ˈrɪbld; ˋrɪbḷd/ *adj* humorous in a vulgar, obscene or disrespectful way (以粗俗、下流或无礼的方式)幽默的: *ribald humour, talk, laughter* 粗俗可笑的幽默、谈话、笑声.

▷ **rib·aldry** /ˈrɪbldrɪ; ˋrɪbḷdrɪ/ *n* [U] ribald language or behaviour 粗俗可笑的言语或行为.

rib·bon /ˈrɪbən; ˋrɪbən/ *n* **1** [C, U] (length of) silk, nylon, etc woven in a narrow strip and used for tying sth or for ornament (丝、尼龙等的)捆扎带, 装饰带: *Her hair was tied back with a black ribbon.* 她的头发用黑缎带扎在后面. ○ *lengths of ribbon hung from the bride's bouquet* 从新娘的花束上垂下来的丝带 ○ [attrib 作定语] *ribbon bows/rosettes* 丝带蝴蝶结[玫瑰花结] ○ (*fig* 比喻) *a ribbon of land stretching out into the sea* 伸入海中的狭长陆地. **2** [C] ribbon of a special colour, pattern, etc worn to show the award of a medal, an order, etc (奖章、勋章、勋位等的)绶带, 勋带, 勋表. **3** [C] long narrow inked strip of material used in a typewriter, etc (打字机等的)色带: *change the typewriter ribbon* 更换打字机的色带. **4** [pl] ragged strips 碎布条 (used esp with the *vs* and *preps* shown 尤与以下示例中的动词和介词连用): *The wind tore the sail to ribbons.* 大风把帆刮成了碎片. ○ *Vandals had slashed/cut the train seats to ribbons.* 恣意破坏公物的人把火车座位割碎了. ○ *Her clothes hung in ribbons (about her).* 她的衣服褴褛不堪.

□ **ˌribbon deˈvelopment** (*Brit esp derog* 尤作贬义) (building of) long lines of houses along a main road leading from a town or village (and thought to spoil the countryside) 带状发展(的建筑物)(自都市沿干线向乡村延伸者, 视为破坏风景之举).

ri·bo·flavin /ˌraɪbəʊˈfleɪvɪn; ˌraɪbəˋflevɪn/ *n* [U] vitamin B2, which is found in meat, fish, milk and green vegetables, and also produced synthetically, and which helps growth in man 核黄素.

rice /raɪs; raɪs/ *n* [U] **1** type of grass grown on wet land in hot countries, esp in E Asia, producing seeds that are cooked and used as food 稻: [attrib 作定语] *rice fields/paddies* 稻田. **2** these seeds 稻米; 大米: *a bowl of boiled/fried rice* 一碗米饭[炒饭] ○ *long-/short-grain rice* 长粒[短粒]米 ○ *brown rice*, ie without the husks removed 稻谷 ○ [attrib 作定语] *rice pudding*, ie dessert made by cooking rice in milk and sugar 大米布丁(大米加牛奶和糖制成的餐后甜食).

□ **'rice-paper** *n* [U] **1** type of thin paper made from the pith of an oriental plant and used by Chinese artists to paint on 宣纸. **2** similar type of thin edible paper made from rice straw and used as a base for small cakes, etc 米纸(垫点心等用的可食薄纸).

rich /rɪtʃ; rɪtʃ/ *adj* (**-er, -est**) (in meanings 1, 3 and 4 the opposite of **poor** 第1、3、4义为**poor**之反义词) **1** having much money or property; wealthy 富的; 富裕的; 富有的: *a rich film star* 很有钱的电影明星 ○ *America is a rich country.* 美国很富. **2** valuable or expensive; splendid or luxurious 贵重的; 昂贵的; 华丽的; 豪华的: *rich clothes, furnishings* 华丽的衣服、豪华的家具 ○ *the rich interior of the church* 教堂富丽堂皇的内景. **3** [pred 作表语] **~ in sth** producing or having a large supply of sth (某物)盛产, 丰富, 多: *Oranges are rich in vitamin C.* 橙子含有丰富的维生素C. ○ *The baroque style is rich in ornament.* 巴罗克风格极具装饰性. ○ *a play rich in humour* 富于幽默的剧 ○ *soil rich in minerals* 矿物质多的土壤. **4** producing or produced abundantly 丰产的; 肥沃的: *rich soil* 沃土 ○ *a rich harvest* 丰收 ○ (*fig* 比喻) *a rich supply of ideas* 多谋 ○ *a rich display of talent* 才华横溢的表现. **5** (of food) containing a large amount of fat, butter, eggs, spices, etc (指食物)脂肪、黄油、蛋类、调料等含量大的, 油腻的, 味浓的: *a rich fruit cake* 油腻的水果蛋糕 ○ *a rich curry, casserole, sauce* 味道很浓的咖喱菜、砂锅菜、沙司. **6** (of colours, sounds or smells) pleasantly deep, full, mellow or strong (指色彩)深的, 鲜艳的; (指声音)深沉的, 洪亮的; (指气味)浓烈的, 馥郁的: *cloth dyed a rich purple* 被染成深紫色的布 ○ *a rich soothing voice* 深沉柔和的声音 ○ *the rich bouquet of mature brandy* 酿熟的白兰地的醇厚香味. **7** (idm 习语) **(as) rich as ˈCroesus** extremely wealthy 极富有的. **strike it rich** ⇨ STRIKE[2]. **ˌthat's ˈrich** (*Brit infml* 口) (**a**) that is very amusing 真有趣; 真逗. (**b**) (*ironic* 反语) that is ludicrous or preposterous 真好笑; 真荒唐.

▷ **the rich** *n* [pl *v*] rich people 富人; 有钱人: *take from the rich and give to the poor* 取自富人, 接济穷人.

richly *adv* **1** in a splendid or generous manner 富丽地; 富裕地: *a richly-ornamented design* 装饰华丽的图案 ○ *I was richly rewarded for my trouble.* 我好心做的事得到了优厚的报酬. **2** (idm 习语) **richly deserve sth** fully or thoroughly deserve sth 完全值得某事物; 某事物是完全应该的: *He richly deserved the punishment he received.* 他受到的处罚是罪有应得. ○ *a richly-deserved success* 完全应得到的成功 ○ *a novel richly deserving (of) praise* 值得大加赞扬的小说.

rich·ness *n* [U] quality or state of being rich 富裕; 富有; 贵重; 昂贵; 富丽; 豪华; 丰饶; 肥沃.

riches /ˈrɪtʃɪz; ˋrɪtʃɪz/ *n* [pl] **1** being rich; wealth 富有; 财富: *He claims to despise riches.* 他声称视财富为粪土. ○ *amass great riches* 积聚大量的财产 ○ (*fig* 比喻) *the riches of Oriental art* 东方艺术的丰富 ○ *the natural riches of the soil* 土壤的肥沃. **2** (idm 习语) **an embarrassment of riches** ⇨ EMBARRASSMENT (EMBARRASS). **from rags to riches** ⇨ RAG[1].

Richter scale /ˈrɪktə ˌskeɪl; ˋrɪktɚ ˌskel/ (*geology* 地质) scale from 0 to 8 for measuring the intensity of earthquakes 里克特震级, 里氏震级(测定地震强度的标度, 从0到8级).

rick[1] /rɪk; rɪk/ *n* [C] (*Brit*) slight sprain or strain 轻度扭伤.

▷ **rick** *v* [Tn] sprain or strain (a joint, etc) slightly 轻度扭伤(关节等): *rick one's ankle, wrist, back* 扭伤足踝、手腕、背.

rick[2] /rɪk; rɪk/ *n* large stack of hay, straw, corn, etc which is built up in the open and covered to protect it from rain (露天堆放并有防雨之遮挡物的)干草堆, 禾堆.

rick·ets /ˈrɪkɪts; ˋrɪkɪts/ *n* [sing or pl *v*] children's disease caused by a lack of vitamin D, resulting in softening and deformity of the bones and enlargement of the liver and spleen 佝偻病.

rick·ety /ˈrɪkətɪ; ˋrɪkətɪ/ *adj* (*infml* 口) weak or shaky, esp in the joints; likely to fall or collapse 不牢靠的, 不稳固的(尤指连接处); 摇晃的; 摇摇欲坠的: *rickety wooden stairs* 摇摇晃晃的木楼梯 ○ *a rickety stool, table, bed, etc* 快要散架的凳子、桌子、床等 ○ *a rickety shelter for the bikes* 摇摇欲坠的自行车棚.

rick·shaw /ˈrɪkʃɔː; ˋrɪkʃɔ/ *n* **1** light two-wheeled covered vehicle used in India and the Far East, pulled by one or more men 人力车: *ride in a rickshaw* 坐人力车. **2** similar three-wheeled vehicle like a bicycle with seats attached behind the driver 三轮车. Cf 参看 PEDICAB.

ri·co·chet /ˈrɪkəʃeɪ; *US* ˌrɪkəˈʃeɪ; ˌrɪkəˋʃe/ *v* (*pt, pp*

ricocheted, ricochetted /-ˈʃeɪd; -ˈʃed/) [I, Ipr] **~ (off sth)** (of a bullet, etc) strike a surface and rebound at an angle (指子弹等)击中物体表面后弹起: *The stone ricocheted off the wall and hit a passer-by.* 石头击中那面墙弹回打着了过路的人.

▷ **ri·co·chet** *n* [U, C] **~ (off sth)** (hit made by a) rebound of this kind 弹回: *the constant ricochet of bricks and bottles off police riot shields* 砸在警察防暴盾牌上的砖块和瓶子不断弹回来.

rid /rɪd; rɪd/ *v* (**-dd-**; *pt, pp* **rid**) **1** [Tn·pr] **~ sb/sth of sb/sth** make sb/sth free from (sb/sth unpleasant or unwanted) 使某人[某事物]摆脱(讨厌的或不想要的人[事物]): *rid the world of famine* 使世界不再有饥荒 ○ *rid the house of mice* 把房子里的老鼠消灭光. **2** (idm 习语) **be/get rid of sb/sth** be/become free of 摆脱: *He was a boring nuisance! I'm glad to be rid of him.* 他这人真讨厌! 我很庆幸能摆脱他的纠缠. ○ *The shop ordered 20 copies of the book and now it can't get rid of* (ie sell) *them.* 该店定购了20本这种书, 现在却无法脱手.

rid·dance /ˈrɪdns; ˋrɪdn̩s/ *n* (idm 习语) **good riddance (to sb/sth)** (said to express relief, etc at being free of an unwanted or unpleasant person or thing 用以表达摆脱不想要的或讨厌的人或事物后的如释重负感): *He's gone at last, and good riddance (to him)!* 他终于走了, 谢天谢地!

rid·den /ˈrɪdn; ˋrɪdn̩/ **1** *pp* of RIDE[2]. **2** *adj* (usu in compounds 通常用以构成复合词) full of or dominated by sth specified 满是某事物的; 受某事物支配或控制的: *a flea-ridden ˈbed* 满是跳蚤的床 ○ *ˈguilt-ridden* 罪孽深重的 ○ (*fml* 文) *She was ridden by/with guilt.* 她罪孽深重.

riddle[1] /ˈrɪdl; ˋrɪdl̩/ *n* [C] **1** puzzling question, statement or description, esp one intended to test the cleverness of those wishing to solve it 谜; (尤指)谜语: *ask/tell sb a riddle* 出个谜语叫某人猜 ○ *know the answer to/solve a riddle* 知道谜底 ○ *She speaks/talks in riddles — it's very difficult to know what she means.* 她说话含糊其辞——实在令人费解. **2** puzzling person, thing, event, etc 谜一般的人、东西、事情等: *She's a complete riddle, even to her parents.* 她是个很难了解的人, 连她父母都无法了解她. ○ *the riddle of how the universe originated* 宇宙起源之谜.

riddle[2] /ˈrɪdl; ˋrɪdl̩/ *n* [C] coarse sieve for earth, gravel, cinders, etc (筛泥土、碎石、煤渣等用的)粗筛.

▷ **riddle** *v* **1** [Tn] **(a)** pass (gravel, etc) through a riddle 用粗筛筛(碎石等). **(b)** shake (a grate, eg in a stove) in order to make ashes, cinders, etc fall through 摇动(炉箅子等)使灰、煤渣等落下. **2 (a)** [esp passive 尤用于被动语态: Tn, Tn·pr] **~ sb/sth (with sth)** make many holes in sb/sth 将某人[某物]弄得满是窟窿: *The car was riddled from end to end.* 那汽车前前后后都是窟窿. ○ *The roof was riddled with bullet holes.* 房顶满是子弹打的窟窿. **(b)** [Tn·pr esp passive 尤用于被动语态] **~ sb/sth with sth** affect sb/sth completely 严重影响或侵袭某人[某事物]: (*derog* 贬) *They are riddled with disease.* 他们饱受病痛之苦. ○ *an administration riddled with corruption* 极其腐败的政府.

ride[1] /raɪd; raɪd/ *n* [C] **1 (a)** (period of) being carried on or in sth, esp as a passenger 乘骑, 乘坐, 搭乘(尤指乘客): *'Give me a ride on your shoulders, Daddy.'* '爸爸, 让我在你肩膀上骑一会儿吧.' ○ *We went for a ride in her new car.* 我们坐了一趟她的新汽车. ○ *It's a ten-minute ride on the bus.* 乘公共汽车要用十分钟. ○ *Can I hitch a ride with you?* 我可以顺路搭乘你的车吗? **(b)** (in compounds 用以构成复合词) journey (in the specified vehicle, etc) (搭乘交通工具的)旅行: *It's only a 5-minute ˈbus-ride to the park.* 坐公共汽车去公园仅需5分钟. ○ *go for a ˈdonkey-ride on the beach* 在沙滩上骑驴兜风. **2** feel of riding in a car, etc 乘坐汽车等时的感觉: *The luxury model gives a smoother ride.* 坐这种豪华型汽车感觉很平稳. **3** track for riding (usu a horse) on, esp through woods 可供骑行(通常指骑马)的小路(尤指林间). **4** (idm 习语) **take sb for a ˈride** (*infml* 口) deceive or swindle sb 欺骗或诈骗某人.

ride[2] /raɪd; raɪd/ *v* (*pt* **rode** /rəʊd; rod/, *pp* **ridden** /ˈrɪdn; ˋrɪdn̩/) **1** [Ipr, Ip] **~ on sth; ~ away, off, etc** sit on a horse, etc and be carried along 骑马等: *children riding on donkeys* 骑着驴的孩子 ○ *ride off into the distance* 骑马奔向远方 ○ *riding on her father's shoulders* 骑在她父亲的肩上. **2** [Tn] sit on and control (sth) 骑(某物): *ride a pony, bicycle, etc* 骑小马、自行车等 ○ *a jockey who has ridden six winners* (ie winning horses) *this season* 在本赛季中已六次夺标的赛马骑师. **3** [Ipr] **~ in/on sth** be carried along (in a vehicle) as a passenger 搭乘(交通工具): *ride in a bus, on a train, etc* 坐公共汽车、火车等 ○ *You ride in the back (of the car) with your brother.* 你跟你弟弟坐(汽车的)后座. ⇨Usage at TRAVEL 用法见 TRAVEL. **4** [I] go out regularly on horseback (as a pastime, etc) 经常骑马外出(消遣等): *Do you ride much?* 你常骑马吗? ○ *She hasn't been out riding since the accident.* 她自从出了事故以后, 一直没有骑马外出过. **5** [Tn, Tn·pr] go through or over (sth) on a horse, bicycle, etc 骑马、骑自行车等通过(某物): *ride the prairies* 骑马过草原 ○ *I've been riding these trails for 40 years.* 我40年来一直骑自行车走这条小路. **6** [I, Ipr, Tn] float or be supported on (water, etc) 漂浮于(水等)之上: *surfers riding the waves* 正在作冲浪运动的人 ○ *gulls riding (on) the wind* 乘风翱翔的海鸥 ○ (*fig* 比喻) *The moon was riding* (ie appeared to be floating) *high (in the sky).* 月亮高高挂在天空. **7** [Tn] yield to (a punch, etc) so as to reduce its effect 顺势躲避(来拳等). **8** (idm 习语) **let sth ˈride** (*infml* 口) take no further (immediate) action on sth 对某事物不(立即)采取进一步的行动: *I'll let things ride for a week and see what happens.* 我先让事情任其发展一星期再说. **ride at ˈanchor** (of a ship) remain secured by an anchor (指船)抛锚停泊. **ride for a ˈfall** (used esp in the continuous tenses 尤用于进行时态) act in a risky way which makes disaster likely 鲁莽行事. **ride ˈhigh** (used esp in the continuous tenses 尤用于进行时态) be successful 获得成功: *The company is riding high this year.* 公司今年生意很好. **ride out/weather the/a storm** ⇨ STORM. **ride roughshod over sb/sth** treat sb/sth harshly, thoughtlessly or with contempt 粗暴地、轻率地或盛气凌人地对待某人[某事物]: *He rode roughshod over all opposition to his ideas.* 他恣意压制所有与他相左的意见. **ride to ˈhounds** (*fml* 文) go fox-hunting 去猎狐. **9** (phr v) **ride sb down** direct one's horse at sb to knock him down 策马撞倒某人. **ride up** (of an article of clothing) move gradually upwards, out of position (指衣物)逐渐向上拥(脱离正常位置): *Your shirt's riding up.* 你的衬衫拥到上边来了.

▷ **rider** *n* **1** person who rides a horse, bicycle, etc 骑马、骑自行车等的人: *a poor, an excellent, an average, etc rider* 骑术不佳、极好、一般...的人 ○ *She's no rider*, ie cannot ride well. 她不善骑马. **2 ~ (to sth)** additional remark following a statement, verdict, etc 供述、裁定等后面附加的评论; 附文: *We should like to add a rider to the previous remarks.* 我们想在原有的意见后面再加上一条. **rider·less** *adj* without a rider 无骑乘者的: *a riderless horse* 没人骑的马.

ridge /rɪdʒ; rɪdʒ/ *n* **1** raised line where two sloping surfaces meet; narrow raised strip 脊; 脊梁; 脊状物: *the ridge of a roof* 屋脊 ○ *There are ridges on the soles to help the boots grip the surface.* 靴底有凸起的条纹防滑. ○ *a series of ridges in a ploughed field* 犁过的田地上的垅. Cf 参看 FURROW. **2** narrow stretch of high land along the top of a line of hills; long mountain range 山脊; 山脉. ⇨illus at MOUNTAIN 见 MOUNTAIN 插图. Cf 参看 PLATEAU. **3** (in meteorology) elongated region of high pressure (气象学用语)高压脊. Cf 参看 TROUGH 4.

▷ **ridge** *v* [Tn] cover (sth) with or make (sth) into ridges 给(某物)加脊状物; 使(某物)成脊状: *a slightly ridged surface* 略呈脊状的表面.

□ **ˈridge-pole** *n* horizontal pole at the apex of the roof of a long tent (长形帐篷的)横梁.

ˈridge-tile *n* any of the tiles placed on the apex of the sloping roof of a building 脊瓦.

ˈridgeway *n* (*Brit*) road or track along the ridge of a hill 山脊路; 山脊小径.

ri·di·cule /ˈrɪdɪkju:l; ˋrɪdɪkjul/ *n* [U] (process of) making sb/sth appear foolish or absurd; scorn 嘲弄; 戏弄; 嘲笑: *incur ridicule* 遭受嘲弄 ○ *attempt to escape ridicule* 力图避免他人耻笑 ○ *be held up to ridicule* 被嘲弄 ○ *He's become an object of ridicule*, ie People say he is foolish/absurd. 他成了大家嘲笑的对象.

▷ **ri·di·cule** *v* [Tn] make fun of (sb/sth); mock 嘲弄

R

(某人[某事物]); 嘲笑: *The opposition ridiculed the government's proposals, saying they offered nothing new.* 反对派揶揄政府的建议, 说成是老调重弹.

ri·dicu·lous /rɪˈdɪkjʊləs; rɪˈdɪkjələs/ *adj* **1** deserving to be laughed at; absurd 可笑的; 荒谬的; 荒唐的: *You look ridiculous in those tight jeans.* 你穿上那紧身牛仔裤样子真可笑. ○ *What a ridiculous idea!* 多么荒谬的念头! **2** (idm 习语) **(go) from the sublime to the ridiculous** ⇨ SUBLIME. ▷ **ri·dicu·lously** *adv*. **ri·dicu·lous·ness** *n* [U].

rid·ing[1] /ˈraɪdɪŋ; ˋraɪdɪŋ/ *n* [U] **1** sport or pastime of going about on a horse 骑马(运动或消遣): *enjoy, take up riding* 骑马玩、骑马消遣. **2** (in compounds 用以构成复合词) concerned with or used in riding 骑马的; 骑马用的: *ˈriding-boots* 马靴.

□ **ˈriding-crop** *n* = CROP 5.

ˈriding-school *n* school for teaching and practising horse-riding 骑术学校.

rid·ing[2] /ˈraɪdɪŋ; ˋraɪdɪŋ/ *n* **1 Riding** (*Brit*) any of the three administrative divisions of Yorkshire until 1974 1974 年以前约克郡所设之三个行政区之一: *East/North/West Riding (of Yorkshire)* (约克郡的)东[北/西]区. **2** (in Canada) electoral constituency (加拿大的)选区.

rife /raɪf; raɪf/ *adj* [pred 作表语] (*fml* 文) **(a)** (esp of bad things) widespread; common (尤指不良事物)流行, 普遍: *an area where crime is rife* 犯罪现象十分普遍的地区. **(b) ~ with sth** full of (esp sth bad) (尤指不良事物)充满, 充斥: *the country was rife with rumours of war* 这个国家流传着要发生战争的谣言.

R

riff /rɪf; rɪf/ *n* short repeated pattern of notes in popular music (流行音乐中的)重复乐段.

riffle /ˈrɪfl; ˋrɪfl/ *v* **1** [Tn] shuffle (playing-cards) by holding part of the pack in each hand and releasing cards alternately so that they form one pack again 洗(纸牌)(搀和整理). **2** (phr v) **riffle through sth** turn the pages of (a book, etc) quickly and casually 迅速而随意地翻动(书等)的页.

▷ **riffle** *n* (*US*) **1** (stretch of) choppy water in a stream, caused by a rocky shoal or shallow (礁石、浅滩或浅水处的)急流, 湍流, 湍急流段. **2** shoal or shallow 浅滩; 浅水处.

riff-raff /ˈrɪf ræf; ˋrɪf ˌræf/ (esp 尤作 **the riff-raff**) *n* [U] (*derog* 贬) ill-behaved people of the lowest social class; the rabble 下等社会的为非作歹者; 乌合之众: *Don't bring any riff-raff into my house!* 别把不三不四的人领到我家来!

rifle[1] /ˈraɪfl; ˋraɪfl/ *n* type of gun with a long barrel which has spiral grooves inside, usu fired from the shoulder 步枪; 来复枪. ⇨ illus at GUN 见 GUN 插图.

▷ **rifle** *v* [Tn] cut spiral grooves in (a gun-barrel) 在(枪管)内制出来复线. **rif·ling** /ˈraɪflɪŋ; ˋraɪflɪŋ/ *n* [U] these grooves 来复线; 膛线.

□ **ˈrifleman** /-mən; -mən/ *n* (*pl* **-men** /-mən; -mən/) soldier in a regiment armed with rifles (配备步枪的)步兵.

ˈrifle-range *n* **1** [C] place for practising shooting with rifles 步枪射击场. **2** (also **ˈrifle-shot**) [U] distance that a rifle-bullet will travel 步枪射程: *out of/within rifle-range* 在步枪的射程外[内].

rifle[2] /ˈraɪfl; ˋraɪfl/ *v* [Tn] search and rob (sth) 搜劫(某物): *The safe had been rifled and many documents taken.* 保险箱遭到搜劫, 许多文件被盗走了.

rift /rɪft; rɪft/ *n* **1** split, crack, break, etc 裂缝; 裂口; 破裂处: *a rift in the clouds* 云中的缝隙. **2** serious disagreement between friends, members of a group, etc (朋友、成员等之间的)不和, 裂痕: *a growing rift between the two factions* 两派日益扩大的裂痕.

□ **ˈrift valley** *n* steep-sided valley caused by subsidence of the earth's crust 地堑; 裂谷.

rig[1] /rɪg; rɪg/ *v* **(-gg-)** **1** [Tn, Tn·pr] **~ sth (with sth)** fit (a ship or boat) with masts, spars, ropes, sails, etc 给(船)装备桅樯、帆樯、索具、帆等. **2** (phr v) **rig sb out (in/with sth)** **(a)** provide sb with clothes or equipment 向某人提供衣物或装备: *The sergeant will rig you out (with everything you need).* 中士将发给你(一切必需的)物品. **(b)** (*infml* 口) dress sb up 给某人穿衣打扮: *rigged out in her best clothes* 身穿她最漂亮的衣服. **rig sth up** set up (a structure, etc) quickly and/or with makeshift materials 用临时替代材料迅速搭起(某物): *rig up a shelter for the night* 匆匆搭篷过夜 ○ *rig up some scaffolding for the workmen* 为工人搭个脚手架.

▷ **rig** *n* **1** way that a ship's masts, sails, etc are arranged 船桅、船帆等的装置: *the fore-and-aft rig of a schooner* 纵帆船的纵向帆装. **2** (esp in compounds 尤用以构成复合词) equipment for a special purpose 作某用途的设备: *an ˈoil rig* 油井钻探设备 ○ *a ˈtest-rig*, ie on which motor-vehicles, electrical appliances, etc are tested 试验架(测试机动车辆、电器等的装置). **3** (*infml* 口) style of dress 服装式样.

rig·ging *n* [U] arrangement of ropes, etc that support a ship's masts and sails 支撑船桅和船帆的索具装置: *The sailors climbed up into the rigging.* 水手沿帆索往上攀. ⇨ illus at YACHT 见 YACHT 插图.

□ **ˈrig-out** *n* (*Brit infml* 口) outfit of clothes 一套服装: *wearing a bizarre rig-out* 穿着一套奇装异服.

rig[2] /rɪg; rɪg/ *v* **(-gg-)** [Tn] manage or control (sth) fraudulently (以欺诈手段)操纵或控制(某事物): *He claimed (the result of) the election was rigged.* 他断言选举(的结果)有假. ○ *rig the market*, ie cause an artificial rise or fall in share prices, etc in order to make (illegal) profits 操纵股票市场.

right[1] /raɪt; raɪt/ *adj* **1** [usu pred 通常作表语] (of conduct, actions, etc) morally good; required by law or duty (指行为、行动等)正当, 适当, 合法, 符合要求: *Is it ever right to kill?* 杀害生命是正当的吗? ○ *You were quite right to refuse/in deciding to refuse/in your decision to refuse.* 你予以拒绝[决定予以拒绝/予以拒绝的决定]是恰当的. ○ *It seems only right to warn you that...* 似乎应该警告你.... Cf 参看 WRONG 1. **2** true or correct 对的; 正确的; 准确的: *Actually, that's not quite right.* 实际上, 那不完全对. ○ *Did you get the answer right?* 你找到正确的答案了吗? ○ *Have you got the right money* (ie exact fare) *for the bus?* 你有买公共汽车票(那个数)的零钱吗? ○ *What's the right time?* 现在准确的时间是几点? **3** best in view of the circumstances; most suitable 最切合实际的; 最适宜的; 最恰当的: *Are we on the right road?* 我们走的路对吗? ○ *Is this the right way to the zoo?* 去动物园是走这条路吗? ○ *He's the right man for the job.* 他是最适合做这件工作的人. ○ *That coat's just right for you.* 那件大衣你穿正合适. ○ *the right side of a fabric*, ie the side meant to be seen or used 织物的正面. **4** (also **all right**) in a good or normal condition 情况良好或正常: *'Do you feel all right?' 'Yes, I feel quite all right/No, I don't feel (quite) right.'* '你感觉好吗?' '很好[不(太)好].' **5** [attrib 作定语] (*Brit infml* 口) (esp in derogatory phrases 尤用于含贬义的词组) real; complete 真实的; 完全的: *you made a right mess of that!* 你把那事完全弄糟了! ○ *She's a right old witch!* 她是个不折不扣的老妖婆! **6** (idm 习语) **all ˈright** (used to indicate agreement, approval, etc 用以表示同意、赞成等): *'Do you want to join us for dinner?' 'All right!'* '你愿意和我们一起吃晚饭吗?' '好哇!' **all ˌright on the ˈnight** (*saying* 谚) (of a performance, etc) satisfactory when the time comes for it to be done, etc (指表演等)到时候准能使人满意: *The hall isn't quite ready for the ceremony yet, but it will be all right on the night.* 举行典礼的大厅尚未完全布置好, 但到时候定能准备就绪. **a bit of all right** ⇨ BIT[1]. **do the right/wrong thing** do sth that is/is not honourable, socially acceptable, etc in the circumstances 做得对[不对]、得当[不得当]等. **get sth ˈright/ˈstraight** understand sth clearly, without error 清楚无误地了解某事物: *Let's get this right once and for all.* 咱们把这个问题彻底弄清楚吧. ○ *Let's get one thing straight — I give the orders round here, OK?* 咱们得先弄清楚一件事 — 在这儿得听我的, 懂吗? **have one's heart in the right place** ⇨ HEART. **hit/strike the right/wrong note** ⇨ HIT[1]. **(not) in one's right ˈmind** (not) mentally normal; (not) sane 精神(不)正常的; 神志(不)清醒的. **might is right** ⇨ MIGHT[2]. **not (quite) right in the/one's ˈhead** (*infml* 口) foolish; eccentric; (slightly) mad 愚蠢的; 古怪的; (有些)疯癫的. **on the right/wrong side of forty, etc** ⇨ SIDE[1]. **on the right/wrong side of sb/sth** ⇨ SIDE[1]. **on the right/wrong track** ⇨ TRACK *n*. **put/set sb/sth right** restore sb/sth to order; correct sb/sth 使某人[某事物]恢复正常; 改正、纠正某人[某事物]的错误: *put a ˈwatch right*, ie to the correct time 把手表拨准 ○ *I want to set/put you ˈright on one or two matters.* 我想给你

纠正一两个错误. **right (you are)!** (*Brit* also **right-oh!**) (*infml* 口) (used to indicate agreement to an order or with a suggestion or (esp *US*) with a request 用以表示同意一项命令、建议或请求, 尤用于美式英语表示同意请求). **(as) right as 'rain/as a 'trivet** (*infml* 口) in excellent health or working order 十分健康或正常. **start off on the right/wrong foot** ⇨ START². **touch the right chord** ⇨ TOUCH¹.

▷ **rightly** *adv* justly; correctly; properly; justifiably 公正地; 正确地; 恰当地: *act rightly* 做得对 ○ *Did I hear rightly?* 我听到的消息准确吗? ○ *She's been sacked, and rightly so.* 她被解雇了, 这件事做得对. ○ *He was rightly furious at the decision.* 他对那个决定大发雷霆, 这是很自然的.

right·ness *n* [U]: *the rightness* (ie justice) *of their cause* 他们的事业的正义性.

□ **'right angle** angle of 90° 直角; 90度角: *at right angles/at a right angle (to the wall)* (与墙)成直角. ⇨illus at ANGLE 见 ANGLE 插图. ⇨App 5 见附录 5. **'right-angled** *adj* having/consisting of a right angle 有[成]直角的: *a right-angled triangle* 直角三角形 ○ *a right-angled bend in the road* 道路上成90度的转弯.

ˌright-'minded having proper or honest opinions, based on what is right 见解正确的; 有正义感的; 正直的: *All ˌright-minded 'people will be surely shocked by this outrage.* 凡是有正义感的人都一定会对这种暴行感到震惊. **ˌright-'mindedness** *n* [U].

right² /raɪt; raɪt/ *adv* **1** exactly (in position, time, etc); directly (位置、时间等)准确地; 直接地: *sitting right beside you* 就坐在你的旁边 ○ *The wind was right in our faces.* 风迎面吹来. **2** all the way; completely 从头到尾; 彻底地; 完全地: *Go right to the end of the road.* 一直走到这条路的尽头. ○ *I fell right to the bottom of the stairs.* 我从楼梯上一直摔到楼梯下面. ○ *a fence right around the garden* 严严实实环绕着花园的围栏 ○ *The pear was rotten right through.* 这个梨烂透了. ○ *turn right round and go in the opposite direction* 向后转走 ○ *The handle came right off in my hand.* 这个把手脱落时还在我手中攥着. **3** correctly; satisfactorily; properly 正确地; 令人满意地; 恰当地: *Have I guessed right or wrong?* 我猜得对不对? ○ *Nothing seems to be going right for me at the moment*, ie I'm having a lot of problems. 我现在好像事事不顺心. **4** immediately 立即; 马上: *I must answer that phone, but I'll be right back.* 我得去接电话, 马上就回来. **5** (idm 习语) **'right/'straight away/off** without hesitation or delay 毫不犹豫地; 毫不耽搁地: *I want it typed right away, please.* 请立刻把它打印出来. ○ *I told her right/straight off what I thought of her.* 我把我对她的看法直截了当地告诉了她. **right 'now** immediately; at this moment 立即; 此刻. **see sb 'right** ensure that sb has all he needs or wants 保证某人的一切需要或愿望得到满足: *You needn't worry about running out of money — I'll always see you right.* 你不必担心钱花光了怎么办—— 我随时关照你的需要. **serve sb right** ⇨ SERVE. **ˌtoo 'right!** (*infml esp Austral* 口, 尤用于澳大利亚) (used to indicate enthusiastic agreement 用以表示欣然同意).

□ **ˌRight 'Honourable** title of earls, viscounts, barons, Cabinet Ministers, and certain others 阁下(对伯爵、子爵、男爵、内阁大臣及其他人士的尊称): *the Right Honourable James Smith, Foreign Secretary* 外交大臣詹姆斯·史密斯阁下. Cf 参看 HONOURABLE 2.

ˌRight 'Reverend title of a bishop 对主教的尊称: *the Right Reverend Richard Harries, Bishop of Oxford* 牛津主教理查德·哈里斯大人.

right³ /raɪt; raɪt/ *n* **1** [U] what is good, just, honourable, etc 正确; 正当; 公正; 正义: *know the difference between right and wrong* 明辨是非 ○ *You did right to tell me the truth.* 你把真相告诉了我, 这事做得对. **2 (a)** [U] **~ to sth/to do sth** proper claim to sth, or authority to do sth 对某事物的正当要求; 做某事的权利: *What right have you to do that?* 你有什么权利做那事? ○ *What gives you the right to do that?* 谁给你的权利做那事? ○ *have no right/not have any right to do sth* 无权[没有任何权利]做某事. **(b)** [C] **~ (to sth)** thing one may do or have by law 依法可做的或可有的事物: *Everyone has a right to a fair trial.* 人人有权要求获得公正审判. ○ *have no rights as a UK citizen* 没有英国公民所享有的权利 ○ *Do the police have the right of arrest in this situation?* 在此情况下警方有逮捕权吗? **3 rights** [pl] legal authority or claim 法定权力或要求: *the film, translation, foreign rights (of a book)*, ie authority to make a film of it, translate it, sell it abroad, etc (某书的)改编成电影的制片权, 翻译权, 向国外发行权 ○ *all rights reserved*, ie protected or kept for the owners of the book, film, etc 版权所有. Cf 参看 COPYRIGHT. **4** (idm 习语) **as of 'right/by 'right** (*fml* 文) justly; correctly; because of having the proper/legal claim 公正地; 正确地; 基于正当的[合法的]权利: *The property belongs to her as of right.* 这财产按理说是属于她的. **be in the 'right** have justice and truth on one's side 正义与真理在自己这边. **by right of sth** (*fml* 文) because of sth 因为; 由于: *The Normans ruled England by right of conquest.* 诺曼人征服了英格兰成了统治者. **by 'rights** if justice were done (which, by implication, seems unlikely); in justice 要是公正的话(言外之意不大可能); 公正地: *By rights, half the reward should be mine.* 按理说, 有一半奖赏应该是我的. **do right by sb** treat sb fairly 公正地对待某人. **in one's own 'right** because of a personal claim, qualification, etc 凭本身的权利、资格等: *She's a peeress in her own right*, ie not merely by marriage to a peer. 她本身就是贵族(并非因嫁给了贵族). **put/set sb/sth to 'rights** correct sb/sth; put (things) in order 纠正某人[某事物]的错误; 使(事物)就绪: *It took me ages to put things to rights after the workmen had finished.* 工人干完活儿后, 我用了很长时间才收拾好. **the rights and 'wrongs of sth** true facts 事实; 真相. **stand on one's 'rights** insist on being treated in a way that one can properly claim one is entitled to 坚持自己的权利. **two wrongs don't make a right** ⇨ WRONG *n*. **within one's 'rights (to do sth)** not exceeding one's authority or entitlement 不超越自己权力或权利的范围: *He's quite within his rights to demand an enquiry.* 他完全有权要求进行调查.

□ **ˌright of 'way 1 (a)** right to pass over another person's land (在他人土地上通过的)通行权: *Is there a right of way across these fields?* 人们有权通过这些田地吗? **(b)** path subject to such a right 有通行权的道路: *public rights of way* 公众有通行权的道路. **2** (in road traffic) right to proceed while another vehicle must wait (路上的车辆)优先通行权: *It's my right of way, so you should have stopped and let me go.* 我有优先通行权, 你本应当停车让我先过.

'rights issue (*commerce* 商) offer of new shares in a company at a reduced price to existing shareholders 股权股发行(公司以优惠价格向现有股东发售新股).

right⁴ /raɪt; raɪt/ *v* [Tn] **~ itself/sth 1** return itself/sth to a proper, correct or upright position 使某物回复到适当的、正确的或直立的位置: *I managed to right the car after it skidded.* 汽车滑向一侧, 我立即控制住了. ○ *The ship righted itself after the big wave had passed.* 大浪过后, 船又平稳了. **2** correct itself/sth 纠正或改正某事物: *right a wrong* 改正错误 ○ *The fault will right itself* (ie will correct itself without help) *if you give it time.* 只要过一些时候, 这个毛病就能自行更正了.

right⁵ /raɪt; raɪt/ *adj* of, on or towards the side of the body which is towards the east when a person faces north 右边的; 右面的; 右方的: *my right eye* 我的右眼 ○ *In Britain we drive on the left side of the road, not the right side.* 在英国, 车辆是靠路的左侧行驶而不是靠右侧行驶. Cf 参看 LEFT².

▷ **right** *adv* **1** to the right side 向右; 往右: *He looked neither right nor left.* 他既不向右看也不向左看. ○ *Turn right at the end of the street.* 在这条街的尽头向右拐. **2** (idm 习语) **eyes right/left/front** ⇨ EYE¹. **left, right and centre** ⇨ LEFT². **ˌright and 'left** everywhere 到处; 各处: *She owes money right and left.* 她到处欠债.

right *n* **1** [U] right-hand side or direction 右边; 右面; 右方: *the first turning to/on the right* 向右转的第一个弯. **2** [C] (blow given with the) right hand 右手; 右手拳: *He was hit with a succession of rights.* 他遭受到右手拳的连续攻击. ○ *Defend yourself with your right.* 要用右手护卫自己. **3 the Right** [Gp] (*politics* 政) right wing of a party or group (政党或团体的)右翼, 右派.

right·ist *n, adj* (*dated* 旧) (member) of a right-wing political party or group 右派政党或组织的(成员); 右派人士; 右派分子.

□ **ˌright 'bank** bank of a river on the right side of a person facing downstream 右岸(以面向河的下游为准).

R

ˈ**right-hand** *adj* [attrib 作定语] of or towards the right side of a person or thing 右手的; 右边的; 向右的: *a right-hand glove* 右手的手套 ○ *make a right-hand turn* 向右转. ˌ**right-ˈhanded** *adj* **1** (of a person) using the right hand more, or with more ease, than the left hand (指人)惯用右手的. **2** (of a blow) made with the right hand (指打击)用右手击出的, 右手拳的. **3** (of a tool) designed for use with the right hand (指工具)供右手使用的. **4** (of a screw) designed to be tightened by turning towards the right (指螺丝钉)右旋的, 向右旋紧的. — *adv* with the right hand 用右手: *play tennis right-handed* 用右手打网球. ˌ**right-ˈhandedness** *n* [U]. ˌ**right-ˈhander** *n* right-handed person or blow 惯用右手的人; 右手的一击. ˌ**right-hand ˈman** chief assistant; most reliable helper 得力助手; 极可靠的帮手; 左右手.

ˌ**right ˈturn** turn to the right into a position at right angles (90°) to the original one 向右转.

ˌ**right ˈwing** (*politics* 政) those who support more conservative or traditional policies than others in a group, party, etc (组织、政党等的)右翼, 右派: *on the right wing of the Labour Party* 在工党的右翼. ˌ**right-ˈwing** *adj*: *ˌright-wing oˈpinions* 右翼观点 ○ *This newspaper's views are very right-wing.* 这家报纸的观点很右. ˌ**right-ˈwinger** *n* person on the right wing of a group, etc (组织等的)右翼成员, 右翼人士. Cf 参看 WING 7, WINGER (WING).

R

right·eous /ˈraɪtʃəs; ˋraɪtʃəs/ *adj* **1** (*fml* 文) doing what is morally right 正直的; 公正的. **2** morally justifiable 正义的; 正当的: *righteous anger, indignation, wrath* 义愤 ○ (*derog* 贬) *Don't adopt that righteous tone of voice!* 别用那种一本正经的腔调说话! ▷ **right·eously** *adv*. **right·eous·ness** *n* [U].

right·ful /ˈraɪtfl; ˈraɪtfəl/ *adj* [attrib 作定语] just, proper or legal 正义的; 正当的; 合法的: *a rightful claim* 正当的要求 ○ *his rightful punishment* 他受到的应有的处罚 ○ *the rightful owner, king, father, etc* 合法的所有人、国王、父亲等. ▷ **right·fully** /-fəlɪ; -fəlɪ/ *adv*.

ri·gid /ˈrɪdʒɪd; ˋrɪdʒɪd/ *adj* **1** stiff; not bending or yielding 坚硬的; 不弯曲的; 刚性的: *a rigid support for the tent* 帐篷的坚硬的支柱 ○ (*fig* 比喻) *Her face was rigid with terror.* 她吓得目瞪口呆. **2** strict; firm; unchanging 严格的; 坚强的; 不变的: *a man of very rigid principles* 原则性很强的人 ○ *practise rigid economy*, ie be very frugal 厉行节约. ▷ **ri·gid·ity** /rɪˈdʒɪdətɪ; rɪˋdʒɪdətɪ/ *n* [U]: *The rigidity of the metal caused it to crack.* 这金属因刚度强而产生裂纹. ○ *He deplored the rigidity of her views.* 他痛感她的观点僵化. **ri·gidly** *adv*: *rigidly constructed buildings* 建造得很坚固的建筑物 ○ *rigidly opposed to any change* 顽固地反对一切变革.

rig·mar·ole /ˈrɪgmərəʊl; ˋrɪgməˌrol/ *n* [C usu *sing* 通常作单数] (*derog* 贬) **1** (unnecessarily) complicated procedure (不必要的)复杂手续: *go through the whole rigmarole of filling out forms* 通过填表这一整套繁琐的程序. **2** long wandering story or statement 冗长而离题的故事或叙述: *I've never heard such a rigmarole.* 我从来没听过象这样的长篇废话.

rigor mor·tis /ˌrɪgə ˈmɔːtɪs; ˌrɪgɚˋmɔrtɪs/ stiffening of the body after death 尸僵; 死后强直: *Rigor mortis had already set in.* 尸体已经僵硬.

rig·our (*US* **rigor**) /ˈrɪgə(r); ˋrɪgɚ/ *n* (*fml* 文) **1** [U] severity; strictness; (esp mental) discipline 严格; 严厉; (尤指思想的)严谨, 严密: *the utmost rigour of the law* 法律的苛严 ○ *intellectual rigour* 思想的缜密. **2** [C often *pl* 常作复数] harshness (of weather, conditions, etc) (气候、条件等的)严酷; 艰苦: *the rigour(s) of an Arctic winter, of prison life, etc* 北极冬季的严寒、监狱生活的艰苦.

▷ **rig·or·ous** /ˈrɪgərəs; ˋrɪgərəs/ *adj* (*fml* 文) **1** severe; strict 严厉的; 严格的: *rigorous discipline* 严明的纪律. **2** strictly accurate or detailed 精确的; 严密的: *rigorous attention to detail* 一丝不苟 ○ *a rigorous search, examination, analysis, etc* 彻底的搜寻、严密的检查、精确的分析. **3** (of weather, etc) harsh (指天气等)严酷的: *a rigorous climate* 严酷的气候. **rig·or·ously** *adv*. **rig·or·ous·ness** *n* [U].

rile /raɪl; raɪl/ *v* [Tn] (*infml* 口) annoy (sb); irritate 使(某人)恼火; 激怒: *Don't get riled.* 别生气. ○ *It riles me that he won't agree.* 他就是不同意, 真气人.

rim /rɪm; rɪm/ *n* **1** edge or border of sth that is (approximately) circular 圆形(或近似圆形)物体的边缘: *the rim of a cup, bowl, etc* 杯、碗等的边 ○ *a pair of spectacles with gold rims* 一副金框眼镜. **2** outer edge of a wheel, on which the tyre is fitted (安装轮胎的)辋圈, 轮圈. ⇨illus at App 1 见附录1插图, page xiii.

▷ **rim** *v* (**-mm-**) [Tn] provide (sth) with a rim; be a rim for (sth) 给(某物)镶边; 形成(某物)的边缘: *Mountains rimmed the valley.* 群山环绕着这个山谷.

rim·less *adj* (of spectacles) having lenses which have no frames round them (指眼镜)无框的.

-rimmed (forming compound *adjs* 用以构成复合形容词) having a rim or rims of the type specified 有某种边缘或边框的: *steel-rimmed glasses* 钢框眼镜 ○ *red-rimmed eyes*, eg from weeping 眼眶发红(如因哭泣).

rime /raɪm; raɪm/ *n* [U] (*esp rhet* 尤作修辞) frost 霜.

rind /raɪnd; raɪnd/ *n* [C, U] hard outer skin or covering on some fruits (eg oranges, lemons) and some types of cheese, bacon, etc 某些水果(如橘子、柠檬)的硬皮; 干酪、腌肉等的外皮: *cut off the ˈbacon rind* 切掉腌肉的皮. Cf 参看 PEEL *n*, SKIN 4, ZEST 3.

ring[1] /rɪŋ; rɪŋ/ *n* **1** small circular band of precious metal, often set with a gem or gems, worn esp on the finger 用贵金属制造的(常镶有珠宝的)小环, 小圈; (尤指)戒指: *a diamond ˈring* 钻戒 ○ *an enˈgagement ring* 订婚戒指 ○ *a ˈwedding ring* 结婚戒指 ○ *a ˈnose ring* 鼻环. **2** (esp in compounds 尤用以构成复合词) circular band of any kind of material (任何材料制的)环形物: *a ˈnapkin ring* 餐巾环 ○ *a ˈkey-ring* 钥匙环 ○ *inflatable rubber rings*, eg as worn by children on their arms when learning to swim 充气橡皮圈(如儿童学游泳时戴在胳膊上的) ○ *the rings of Saturn* 土星的光环. **3** circle 圆圈; 圆环: *the rings in/of a tree*, ie the concentric circles seen when the trunk is cut straight across, showing the tree's age 树的年轮 ○ *puff out ˈsmoke-rings*, ie rings of tobacco smoke 喷出烟圈儿(吸烟时) ○ *The men were standing in a ring.* 那些人站成一个圆圈. ○ *dark rings round her eyes from lack of sleep* 她那因睡眠不足而发黑的眼圈. **4** combination of people working together, esp secretly 集团(尤指秘密的): *a ˈspy ring* 间谍网 ○ *a ring of dealers controlling prices at an antiques auction* 操纵古物拍卖价格的一帮买卖人. **5 (a)** (also ˈ**circus ring**) (esp circular) enclosure in which a circus is held (尤指圆形的)马戏场. **(b)** (also ˈ**boxing ring**) raised square space enclosed by ropes for boxing matches 拳击场: *knock sb out of the ring* 把某人击出场地. **6** (idm 习语) **run ˈrings round sb** (*infml* 口) do things much better than sb 做事比某人好得多.

▷ **ring** *v* (*pt, pp* **-ed**) **1** [Tn, Tn·pr esp passive 尤用于被动语态] **~ sb/sth (with sth)** surround sb/sth 围绕、环绕或包围某人[某物]: *A high fence ringed the prison camp.* 有一道高高的铁丝网围着战俘营. ○ *ringed about with enemies* 被敌人包围. **2** [Tn] make a circular mark round (sth) 环绕(某物)做圆形标记; 将(某物)圈出: *Ring the correct answer with your pencil.* 用铅笔圈出正确的答案. **3** [Tn] put a metal ring on the leg of (a bird) to identify it, or in the nose of (a bull, etc) 给(鸟)的腿套上金属环(以供识别); 给(牛等)戴鼻圈.

□ ˈ**ring binder** folder for papers, in which metal rings go through holes in the edges of the pages, holding them in place 活页夹; 活页簿.

ˈ**ring-finger** *n* third finger, usu of the left hand, on which a wedding-ring is traditionally worn 无名指(通常指左手的, 结婚戒指多戴于该指). ⇨illus at HAND 见 HAND 插图.

ˈ**ringleader** *n* (*esp derog* 尤作贬义) person who leads others in crime or opposition to authority 犯罪或叛乱活动的头目; 罪魁; 祸首; 元凶.

ˈ**ring mains** main electrical circuit in a house, etc, off which branch supplies are taken (房子等配电线路的)环形主线.

ˈ**ringmaster** *n* person in charge of a circus performance 马戏演出的领班.

ˈ**ring-pull** *n* small piece of metal with a ring attached which is pulled to open certain types of tin can, etc (易拉罐等的)拉环: [attrib 作定语] *a ring-pull can* 易拉罐罐头.

ˈ**ring road** (*Brit*) road built around a town to reduce traffic in the centre 环路, 环城公路(为疏导城市中心区之交通而设).

ˈ**ringside** *n* **1** (esp 尤作 **the ringside**) [U] area

immediately beside a boxing or wrestling ring (拳击或摔跤竞技场的)台边区, 近台座席. **2** (idm 习语) **have a ringside 'seat** be favourably placed for seeing sth 获得近台座席; 处于便于看清之位置.

'ringworm *n* [U] skin disease, esp of animals or children, producing round red patches 癣.

ring[2] /rɪŋ; rɪŋ/ *v* (*pt* **rang** /ræŋ; ræŋ/, *pp* **rung** /rʌŋ; rʌŋ/) **1** [I] make a clear resonant sound, usu like that of a bell being struck 发出清晰响亮的声音(通常指似铃声): *Will you answer the telephone if it rings?* 电话铃声响时请你接电话好吗? ○ *The metal door rang as it slammed shut.* 金属门猛一关上时发出咣的响声. ○ *The buzzer rang when the meal was ready.* 饭做好时蜂鸣器发出嗞嗞的响声. **2** [Tn, Tn·pr] cause (a bell, etc) to sound 使(钟铃等)发声: *ring the fire alarm* 鸣响火警警报 ○ *ring the bell for school assembly* 敲钟通知全校集合. **3** [La] produce a certain effect when heard 产生某种声音效果; 听起来: *Her words rang hollow*, ie What she said sounded insincere. 她的话听起来很虚(言不由衷). ○ *His story may seem incredible, but it rang* (ie seemed likely to be) *true.* 他说的事情尽管难以置信, 但听起来却似有其事. **4** [I, Ipr] ~ **(for sb/sth)** make a bell sound to call, warn, etc sb 鸣铃召唤、警告...某人: *'Did you ring, sir?' asked the stewardess.* '先生, 是您按铃叫人吗?' 女服务员问道. ○ *Someone is ringing at the door*, ie ringing the doorbell. 有人在按门铃. ○ *ring for the maid, for room service, etc* 按铃召唤女仆、召唤客房用餐服务部等. **5** [I, Ipr] ~ **(with sth)** (*fig* 比喻) be filled with (sounds, etc) 响着(声音等): *The playground rang with children's shouts.* 游戏场上到处都是儿童的喊叫声. ○ (*rhet* 修辞) *The village rang with the joy of Christmas.* 村里洋溢着圣诞节的欢乐气氛. **6** [I, Ipr] (of ears) be filled with a ringing or humming sound (指耳朵)嗡嗡作响: *The music was so loud it made my ears ring.* 音乐的声音太大了, 把我耳朵震得直响. **7** (*US* **call**) [Tn, Tn·p] ~ **sb/sth (up)** telephone (sb/sth) 给(某人[某处])打电话: *I'll ring you tonight.* 我今晚给你打电话. ○ *Ring (up) the airport and find out when the plane leaves.* 给机场打个电话, 问清楚什么时候起飞. **8** [Tn] (of a chime of bells) mark (the time) by striking (指钟的报时装置)敲出(钟点): *ring the hours but not the quarters*, ie ring on the hour but not at quarter or half past or quarter to 每小时响一次而不是每刻钟响一次. **9** (idm 习语) **ring a 'bell** (*infml* 口) bring sth vaguely back to mind; sound familiar 模糊地记得; 听起来耳熟: *His name rings a bell; perhaps we've met somewhere.* 他的名字听起来耳熟, 也许我们在什么地方见过面. **ring the 'changes** ring church bells in various different orders (以不同顺序)敲教堂的钟. **ring the changes (on sth)** vary one's routine, choices, actions, etc 改变常规、选择、行动等: *She likes to ring the changes (on how her office is arranged).* 她喜欢经常换换(布置自己办公室的)方式. **ring up/down the 'curtain (on sth)** (**a**) (in a theatre) give the signal for the curtain to be raised/lowered (戏院)响铃升[落]幕: *ring down the curtain on the first act* 第一幕结束时响铃落幕. (**b**) mark the beginning/end of (an enterprise, etc) 开幕[闭幕]: *ring up the curtain on a new football season* 新的足球赛季正式开始. **ˌring out the 'old year and ˌring in the 'new** announce and celebrate the end of one year and the beginning of the next 辞旧岁迎新年. **10** (phr v) **ring off** (*Brit*) end a telephone conversation 挂断电话: *He rang off before I could explain.* 我还没来得及解释, 他就把电话挂上了. **ring out** sound loudly and clearly 发出响亮而清晰的声音: *A pistol shot rang out.* 响起了手枪的声音. **ring sth up** record (an amount, etc) on a cash register 将(款额等)记入现金出纳机: *ring up all the items, the total, £6.99* 把所有款项、总额、6.99英镑的一笔钱记入现金出纳机.

▷ **ring** *n* **1** [C] act of ringing a bell; sound of a bell 按铃; 敲钟; 铃声; 钟声: *give two rings of the bell* 敲两下钟 ○ *There was a ring at the door.* 有人按门铃. **2** [sing] loud clear sound 响亮而清晰的声音: *the ring of happy voices* 欢声响亮. **3** [sing] ~ **of sth** tone or feeling of a particular kind 某种语气或感觉: *That has a/the ring of truth about it*, ie sounds true. 那件事听起来像是确有其事. **4** [C] (*Brit infml* 口) (*US* **call**) telephone call 电话; 通话: *I'll give you a ring tomorrow.* 我明天给你打电话.

ringer *n* **1** person who rings bells 按铃的人; 敲钟的人. **2** (*US*) racehorse, etc entered in a race under a false name 冒名顶替参赛的马等. **3** (idm 习语) **be a dead ringer for sb** ⇨ DEAD.

ring·let /'rɪŋlɪt; 'rɪŋlɪt/ *n* [C esp *pl* 尤作复数] long curl of hair hanging down from sb's head 下垂的长鬈发.

rink ⇨ ICE-RINK (ICE[1]), SKATING-RINK (SKATE[1]).

rinse /rɪns; rɪns/ *v* [Tn] **1** wash (sth) lightly 略微洗(某物): *He rinsed his hands quickly before eating.* 他吃东西以前很快洗了一下手. **2** remove dirt, soap, etc from (sth) with water 冲洗掉(某物)上的污垢、肥皂沫等: *Rinse your hair thoroughly after shampooing it.* 用洗发剂洗头后, 要把头发冲洗干净. **3** (phr v) **rinse sb/sth down** (*infml* 口) have a drink after eating sth 吃食物后再用饮料送下: *a sandwich and a glass of beer to rinse it down* 一份三明治用一杯啤酒送下. **rinse sth out** remove dirt, etc from sth with water 用水冲洗污垢等: *He rinsed the teapot out under the tap, to get rid of the tea-leaves.* 他在水龙头下面冲洗茶壶, 以便把茶叶冲掉. **rinse sth out of/from sth** remove (dirt, soap, etc) from sth with water 用水冲洗某物上的(污垢、肥皂沫等): *I rinsed the shampoo out of my hair.* 我把头发上的洗发剂冲洗干净了.

▷ **rinse** *n* **1** [C] act of rinsing 洗涤; 冲洗: *Give your hair a good rinse after shampooing it.* 用洗发剂洗头后, 要把头发好好冲洗干净. **2** [C, U] solution for tinting or conditioning the hair 染发液; 护发液: *a blue rinse* 蓝色染发液.

riot /'raɪət; 'raɪət/ *n* **1** [C] wild or violent disturbance by a crowd of people 暴乱; 骚乱: *Riots broke out in several areas.* 有几个地方发生了骚乱. ○ *The police succeeded in quelling the riot.* 警方把暴乱镇压了下去. ○ (*fig* 比喻) *There'll be a riot* (ie People will be very angry) *if the government doesn't invest more in this service.* 倘若政府不对此公用事业增加拨款, 就要天下大乱了. **2** [sing] ~ **of sth** profuse display (of sth) 充分的表现或展示: *The flower-beds were a riot of colour.* 花坛里色彩缤纷. ○ *a riot of emotion* 感情的宣泄. **3 a riot** [sing] (*infml* 口) very amusing thing or person 极有趣的事物或人: *She's an absolute riot!* 她这个人真逗! **4** (idm 习语) **read the Riot Act** ⇨ READ. **run 'riot** behave in a wild, violent or uncontrolled way 撒野; 闹事: *Football hooligans ran riot through the town.* 闹事的足球迷在城里胡作非为. ○ (*fig* 比喻) *weeds running riot in the garden* 园中蔓延滋长的杂草 ○ *Inflation is running riot and prices are out of control.* 通货极度膨胀, 物价失去控制.

▷ **riot** *v* [I, Ipr] take part in a riot 暴动; 闹事: *There's rioting in the streets.* 街上有人闹事. ○ *renewed outbreaks of rioting* 骚乱的再度爆发. **rioter** *n* person who riots 参加暴乱者; 闹事者.

ri·ot·ous /-əs; -əs/ *adj* **1** (*fml or law* 文或律) disorderly; unruly 无秩序的; 不守规矩的; 混乱的; 闹事的: *a riotous assembly*, ie of people 秩序混乱的集会 ○ *charged with riotous behaviour* 被控聚众闹事. **2** [attrib 作定语] (*usu derog* 通常作贬义) boisterous; unrestrained 喧闹的; 不受约束的: *a riotous party* 喧闹的聚会 ○ *riotous laughter* 放声大笑. **ri·ot·ously** *adv* extremely 极端地: *riotously funny* 非常可笑. **ri·ot·ous·ness** *n* [U] violent disorderly behaviour 暴乱; 骚乱; 闹事.

□ **'riot police** police trained in dealing with rioters 防暴警察.

'riot shield shield for use by police or soldiers dealing with riots 防暴盾牌(警察或士兵对付暴乱用的).

rip /rɪp; rɪp/ *v* (**-pp-**) **1** (**a**) [Tn, Tn·pr] divide or make a hole in (sth) by pulling sharply 撕裂或拉破(某物): *I've ripped my trousers.* 我把裤子撕破了. ○ *rip a piece of cloth (in two)* 把一块布撕成两半. (**b**) [Cn·a] ~ **sth open** open sth by pulling in this way 拉开或撕开某物: *rip open a letter* 撕开一封信 ○ *My cat had its ear ripped open by a dog.* 我的猫的耳朵被狗咬破了. (**c**) [I] (of material) become torn (指材料)破, 裂: *Be careful with that dress; it rips easily.* 小心那件连衣裙, 很容易破. **2** (idm 习语) **let 'rip (about/against/at sb/sth)** speak violently or passionately 激烈或激昂地说话: *let rip against the government* 激烈地抨击政府. **let sth 'rip** (*infml* 口) (**a**) allow (a car, machine, etc) to go at its top speed 让(汽车、机器等)以最高速度行驶或运转: *Let her/it rip!* 让车全速前进! (**b**) allow (things) to develop naturally, without attempting to control them 让(事物)自由发展而不加控制: *They just let inflation rip.* 他们对

R

通货膨胀完全不加控制. **3** (phr v) **rip sb off** (*sl* 俚) cheat sb, esp financially 欺骗某人(尤指钱财): *The shop tried to rip me off.* 那商店想欺骗我. **rip sth off** (**a**) remove sth by pulling sharply 撕掉某物: *rip the cover off (a book)* 撕掉(书的)封面. (**b**) (*sl* 俚) steal sth 偷窃某物: *Somebody's ripped off my wallet.* 有人把我的钱包偷走了.

▷ **rip** *n* **1** uneven or ragged tear or cut (参差不齐的)裂口, 裂缝: *There's a big rip in my sleeve.* 我的袖子破了一大块. **2** stretch of rough water in a river or the sea (河流或海洋的)激流, 激浪. Cf 参看 RIP-TIDE.

□ ˈ**rip-cord** *n* cord that releases a parachute from its pack (降落伞的)开伞索: *pull the rip-cord* 拉动开伞索.

ˈ**rip-off** *n* (usu *sing* 通常作单数) (*sl* 俚) act of defrauding, stealing, overcharging, etc 欺诈; 偷窃; 索要高价: *80p for a cup of coffee? What a rip-off!* 一杯咖啡要80便士? 真是敲竹杠!

ˈ**rip-roaring** *adj* [attrib 作定语] (*infml* 口) (**a**) wild and noisy 喧闹的; 闹嚷嚷的. (**b**) great, huge, etc 大的; 巨大的: *The film was a rip-roaring success.* 这部影片极为成功.

ˈ**rip-saw** *n* saw with large coarse teeth, used for cutting wood along the grain 纵切锯; 粗齿锯.

RIP /ˌɑːr aɪ ˈpiː; ˌɑr aɪ ˋpi/ *abbr* 缩写 = (on tombstones, etc) (may he, she, they) rest in peace (Latin *requiescat/requiescant in pace*) (墓碑等用语)(愿他、她、他们)安息(源自拉丁文 *requiescat/requiescant in pace*): *James Dent RIP* 愿詹姆斯·登特安息.

R

ri·par·ian /raɪˈpeərɪən; raɪˋpɛrɪən/ *adj* (*law or fml* 律或文) of or inhabiting the banks of a river, lake, etc 河边的; 湖滨的; 岸上的; 栖于水滨的: *riparian rights*, eg to fish in a river 河岸权(如在某河中的捕鱼权) ○ *riparian creatures* 水滨生物.

ripe /raɪp; raɪp/ *adj* **1** (of fruit, grain, etc) ready to be gathered and used, esp for eating (指水果、谷物等)成熟的: *Are the apples ripe enough to eat yet?* 这些苹果已经熟了吗? ○ *harvest the ripe corn* 收割已成熟的谷物 ○ (*fig* 比喻) *Her lips were ripe as cherries*, ie full and red like ripe cherries. 她的嘴唇像樱桃一样红润. **2** (of cheese) fully matured or developed (指干酪)已成熟的: *ripe cheese* 成熟的干酪 ○ (*rare fig* 罕, 比喻) *ripe judgement, scholarship* 成熟的判断力、丰富的学识. **3** (of a person's age) advanced (指人)成年的, 上年纪的: *men of riper years* 已成年的男子 ○ *lived to a ripe old age* 活到高龄 ○ (*ironic* 反语) *at the ripe old age of 21* 正值21岁高龄. **4** [pred 作表语] **~ (for sth)** ready; fit; prepared 时机成熟; 适宜; 准备就绪: *land that is ripe for development* 适合开发的土地 ○ *a nation ripe for revolution* 革命时机已成熟的国家. **5** (idm 习语) **the time is ripe** ⇨ TIME[1].

▷ **ripen** /ˈraɪpən; ˋraɪpən/ *v* [I, Tn] (cause sth to) become ripe (使某物)成熟: *ripening corn* 即将成熟的谷物 ○ *peaches ripened by the sun* 经日晒而成熟的桃.

ripe·ness *n* [U].

ri·poste /rɪˈpɒst; rɪˋpost/ *n* **1** quick verbal reply or retort, esp to criticism 迅速的回答或反驳(尤指对于批评): *a witty riposte* 巧妙的回答. **2** (in fencing) quick return thrust after parrying (剑术)挡开对方的剑后迅速还刺.

▷ **ri·poste** /rɪˈpɒst; rɪˋpost/ *v* [I, Ipr] **~ (with sth)** deliver a riposte 还刺; 还击.

ripple /ˈrɪpl; ˋrɪpl̩/ *n* [C] **1** small wave or series of waves 波纹; 涟漪: *She threw a stone into the pond and watched the ripples spread.* 她把一块石头扔进池塘里, 看着水的波纹扩散开. **2** thing like this in appearance or movement 外观或运动如波纹的事物: *slight ripples on the surface of the metal* 金属表面上的小波纹. **3** gentle rising and falling sound 轻柔的起伏声: *a ripple of laughter, voices, applause* 一阵轻柔起伏的笑声、说话声、掌声.

▷ **ripple** *v* [I, Tn] (cause sth to) move in ripples (使某物)起伏: *corn rippling in the breeze* 在微风中起伏如波浪的庄稼 ○ *rippling muscles* 一条条凸起的肌肉 ○ *wind rippling the lake* 吹皱湖水的风.

rip-tide /ˈrɪptaɪd; ˋrɪpˌtaɪd/ *n* tide causing strong currents and rough water (造成巨浪和急流的)大潮.

rise[1] /raɪz; raɪz/ *n* **1** (**a**) upward movement or progress 上升; 升起; 进展; 振兴: *His rise to power was very rapid.* 他很快掌握了大权. ○ *the rise and fall of the British Empire* 大英帝国的兴衰. (**b**) increase in amount, number or intensity (金额、数量或强度的)增加: *a rise in the price of meat, the value of the dollar, the average temperature* 肉类价格的上涨、美元的升值、平均温度的增高. **2** upward slope; small hill 斜坡; 小山; 岗; 丘: *At the top of the rise they paused for a rest.* 他们在小山的顶部停下来休息. ○ *a church situated on a small rise* 座落在小山上的教堂. **3** (*Brit*) (*US* **raise**) increase (in wages) (工资的)增加: *demand a rise (in wages) from next October* 要求从下个十月份起增加工资. **4** (idm 习语) **get/take a rise out of sb** cause sb to show annoyance or make an angry response by teasing, etc 戏弄某人使之厌烦或愤怒. **give rise to sth** (*fml* 文) cause sth 引起、导致某事物: *Her disappearance gave rise to the wildest rumours.* 她失踪一事引起了各种流言蜚语.

▷ **riser** *n* **1** vertical piece between two treads of a staircase 梯级竖板. **2** person who habitually gets up early or late in the morning (as specified) 惯于早起或晚起的人: *an early/a late riser* 早起[晚起]的人.

rise[2] /raɪz; raɪz/ *v* (*pt* **rose** /rəʊz; roz/, *pp* **risen** /ˈrɪzn; ˋrɪzn̩/) **1** [I, Ipr, Ip, In/pr] come or go upwards; reach a high or higher level, position, etc 上升; 达到较高的水平、位置等: *The cost of living continues to rise.* 生活费用继续上涨. ○ *The river has risen (by) several metres.* 河水上涨了好几米. ○ *smoke rising from the chimney* 从烟囱里冒出的烟 ○ *Her voice rose in anger.* 她因愤怒而提高了嗓门. ○ *new tower-blocks rising nearby* 在附近新建起的高层建筑. **2** [I] (*fml* 文) get up from a lying, sitting or kneeling position; get out of bed (躺、坐或跪后)起立, 起身; 起床: *accustomed to rising early* 习惯于早起 ○ *He rose (in order) to welcome me.* 他起身欢迎我. ○ *unable to rise because of his injuries* (他)因受伤而起不了床. **3** [I] (*fml* 文) (of the people taking part in a meeting or other assembly) disperse (指参加会议或其他集会的人)散开, 散去: *The House* (ie Members of the House of Commons) *rose at 10 pm.* 下议院已于晚上10点钟散会. ○ *Parliament rises* (ie ends its current session) *on Thursday.* 国会星期四休会. **4** [I] become upright or erect 竖立; 竖起: *The hair on the back of my neck rose when I heard the scream.* 我听到那尖叫声不禁毛骨悚然. **5** [I, Ipr, Ip] **~ (up) (against sb/sth)** (*fml* 文) rebel 反叛; 造反; 起义: *rise (up) in revolt* 起来造反 ○ *rise (up) against the foreign invaders* 反抗外国侵略者. **6** [I] (of the wind) begin to blow (more strongly) (指风)刮起来(更猛): *The wind is rising — I think there's a storm coming.* 风越刮越猛——大概要来暴风雨了. **7** [I] (of the sun, moon, etc) appear above the horizon (指太阳、月亮等)从地平线上升起: *The sun rises in the east and sets in the west.* 太阳从东方升起, 至西方落下. Cf 参看 SET[2] 19. **8** [I] increase in cheerfulness (情绪)增高: *Her spirits* (ie her mood, feelings, emotions) *rose at the news.* 她听到那消息异常兴奋. **9** [I, Ipr] reach a higher rank, status or position (in society, one's career, etc) (在社会上、职业上等)升至较高的级别、地位或职位: *He rose from the ranks to become an officer.* 他由士兵升为军官. ○ *rise from nothing to become a great leader* 由无名小卒一跃而为伟大领袖 ○ *a rising young politician* 平步青云的年轻政治家. **10** [I] (of dough, bread, etc) swell under the action of yeast, baking powder, etc (指生面团、面包等)发酵胀起: *My cake is a disaster — it hasn't risen.* 我的蛋糕做坏了——面没发起来. **11** [I, Ipr] (of a river) begin to flow; have its source (指河流)发源: *The Thames rises in the Cotswold Hills.* 泰晤士河发源于科茨沃尔德丘陵. **12** (idm 习语) **early to bed and early to rise** ⇨ EARLY. **make sb's gorge rise** ⇨ GORGE[1]. **make one's hackles rise** ⇨ HACKLES. ˌ**rise and** ˈ**shine** (*Brit catchphrase* 警语) (usu imperative 通常用于祈使句) get out of bed and be active 快起床. ˈ**rise again/from the** ˈ**dead** come to life again after death 复活; 再生: *Christians believe that Jesus rose from the dead on Easter Sunday.* 基督徒相信耶稣在那个星期日(后定为复活节)里复活了. **rise to the** ˈ**bait** succumb to a lure or temptation 上钩; 中圈套: *As soon as I mentioned money he rose to the bait, and became really interested.* 我一提钱他便怦然心动, 上了我的钩. **rise to the ocˈcasion, ˈchallenge, ˈtask, etc** prove oneself able to deal with an unexpected situation, problem, etc 有随机应变、克服困难、完成任务等的能

力. **13** (phr v) **rise above sth** (show oneself to) be superior to sth, capable of dealing with it, etc (表明自己)优于某事物、有能力处理等: *She rose above her difficulties and became a tremendous success.* 她战胜了重重困难，取得了巨大的成功.

▷ **ris·ing** *n* [C] armed rebellion; revolt 武装反叛; 造反; 起义: *Troops put down a rising in the capital.* 部队平息了发生在首都的叛乱. — *adv* (idm 习语) **ˌrising ˈfive, twelve, etc** (of a child) nearly five, twelve, etc years old (指儿童)近五岁、十二岁等.

□ **ˌrising ˈdamp** dampness rising from the ground into the walls of a building (从地面渗入墙中的)潮气.

ˌrising ˈfives, etc children of nearly five, etc years old 接近五岁等的儿童: *Mrs Smith teaches the rising fives.* 史密斯夫人教那些快五岁的儿童.

the ˌrising geneˈration young people who are growing up 年轻的一代.

ris·ible /ˈrɪzəbl; ˋrɪzəbḷ/ *adj* (*fml or joc* 文或谑) fit to be laughed at; ridiculous 引人笑的; 可笑的; 滑稽的: *The entire proposal is risible: it will never be accepted.* 这个建议完全是荒唐可笑的，根本不可能采纳.

risk /rɪsk; rɪsk/ *n* **1** [C, U] **~ (of sth/that...)** (instance of the) possibility of meeting danger or suffering harm, loss, etc 危险; 风险: *Is there any risk of the bomb exploding?* 这个炸弹有爆炸的危险吗? ○ *You shouldn't underestimate the risks of the enterprise.* 你不应低估这一计划的风险. ○ *There's no risk of her failing/that she'll fail.* 她不会有失败的危险. ○ *insure a house for all risks*, ie fire, theft, etc 给房子保综合险(火险、盗窃险等) ○ [attrib 作定语] *an all-risks policy* 综合保险保单 ○ *an investment involving a high degree of risk* 风险很大的投资. **2** [C] person or thing insured or representing a source of risk 被保险的人或物; 保险对象; 产生危险的根源: *He's a good/poor risk.* 他是个风险很小[很大]的保险对象. ○ *All the people who know this secret represent a security risk.* 凡是知道这个秘密的人都对安全造成危险. **3** (idm 习语) **at one's own risk** agreeing to make no claims for any loss, injury, etc 自担风险(同意不要求赔偿损失、损害等): *Persons swimming beyond this point do so at their own risk*, ie No one else will take responsibility for whatever happens to them. 游泳者超越此界限若有意外后果自负. **at ˈrisk** threatened by the possibility of loss, failure, etc; in danger 有危险; 冒风险: *put one's life at risk* 冒生命危险 ○ *The whole future of the company is at risk.* 公司的整个前途受到威胁. ○ *My job is at risk*, ie I may be made redundant. 我的工作保不住了(我遭受到裁减的危险). **at the risk of (doing sth)** with the possibility of (doing sth) 冒可能(做某事)的危险: *At the risk of sounding ungrateful, I must refuse your offer.* 我甘受拂逆盛情之嫌，也必须谢绝你的提议. **at risk to sb/sth** with the possibility of losing or injuring sb/sth 冒失去或殃及某人[某事物]的危险: *He saved the child at considerable risk to himself/to his own life.* 他冒着极大的生命危险救了那个孩子. **a calculated risk** ⇨ CALCULATE. **run the risk (of doing sth)**; **run ˈrisks** do sth that exposes one to a danger, possibility, etc 冒自身危险做某事: *We can't run the risk (of losing all that money).* 我们不能冒(失掉全部钱的)风险. ○ *He runs more risk of being arrested.* 他冒的被逮捕的危险更大. ○ *She runs the same risks.* 她也在冒这样的风险. **take a ˈrisk/ˈrisks** do sth that involves the possibility of failure, danger, etc 冒险做可能失败、有危险等的事: *You can't get rich without taking risks.* 人不冒险不富. ○ *That's a risk I'm prepared to take.* 那是我愿意冒险做的事情.

▷ **risk** *v* **1** [Tn] expose (sb/oneself) to danger 使(某人[自己])面临危险: *risk one's health, fortune, neck* (ie life) 冒丧失健康、财富、生命之险. **2** [Tn, Tg] accept the possibility of (sth) 甘愿承受可能发生的(某事): *risk failure* 失败亦在所不惜 ○ *risk getting caught in a storm* 不怕赶上暴风雨.

risky *adj* (**-ier, -iest**) full of danger; full of potential for failure, loss, etc 充满危险或风险的; 有很大危险或风险的: *a risky undertaking* 多风险的事业. **risk·ily** /-ɪlɪ; -ɪlɪ/ *adv*. **riski·ness** *n* [U].

ris·otto /rɪˈzɒtəʊ; rɪˋzɑto/ *n* (*pl* **~s**) [C, U] Italian dish of rice cooked in stock, to which vegetables, seafood, etc may be added 意大利汤饭(有时有蔬菜、海味等).

risqué /ˈri:skeɪ; *US* rɪˈskeɪ; rɪsˋke/ *adj* (of a story, remark, item of clothing, etc) slightly indecent (指故事、言语、衣着等)颇为下流的，有伤风化的.

ris·sole /ˈrɪsəʊl; ˋrɪsol/ *n* small flat cake or ball of minced meat or fish mixed with potato or breadcrumbs and fried (用肉末或鱼末混以马铃薯或面包屑煎炸而成的)炸肉饼，炸丸子.

rite /raɪt; raɪt/ *n* [C] religious or some other solemn ceremony (宗教等的)隆重的仪式或典礼: *marriage/funeral rites* 结婚[丧葬]仪式 ○ *initiation rites*, eg those performed when a new member joins a secret society 入会仪式(如秘密社团为新会员举行的).

rit·ual /ˈrɪtʃʊəl; ˋrɪtʃʊəl/ *n* **1** (**a**) [U] series of actions used in a religious or some other ceremony (宗教等仪式的)程序，仪节: *the ritual of the Catholic Church* 天主教的礼仪 ○ *Some religions employ ritual more than others.* 有的宗教举行仪式时特别注重礼则. (**b**) [C] particular form of this 具体的礼仪: *the ritual of the Japanese tea ceremony* 日本茶道的仪式. **2** [C] (*esp joc* 尤作戏谑语) procedure regularly followed in precisely the same way each time 固定方式; 老习惯: *He went through the ritual of filling and lighting his pipe.* 他照例填满烟斗，然后点着了.

▷ **rit·ual** *adj* [attrib 作定语] of or done as a ritual 仪式上的; 作为仪式而进行的; 惯常的: *a ritual dance* 仪式上的舞蹈 ○ *ritual phrases of greeting* 例行的客套话. **ritu·ally** /ˈrɪtʃʊəlɪ; ˋrɪtʃʊəlɪ/ *adv*.

ritu·al·ism /-ɪzəm; -ˌɪzəm/ *n* [U] (*esp derog* 尤作贬义) fondness for or insistence on ritual 对仪式的热衷或拘泥; 仪式主义. **ritu·al·istic** /ˌrɪtʃʊəˈlɪstɪk; ˌrɪtʃʊəlˋɪstɪk/ *adj*.

ritzy /ˈrɪtsɪ; ˋrɪtsɪ/ *adj* (**-ier, -iest**) (*dated infml* 旧，口) luxurious; elegant 豪华的; 优美的; 文雅的.

ri·val /ˈraɪvl; ˋraɪvḷ/ *n* **~ (for/in sth)** person or thing competing with another 竞争或相比的人或事物: *ˈbusiness rivals* 商业上的竞争对手 ○ *rivals in love* 情敌 ○ *a new rival for the title of champion* 争夺冠军的新对手 ○ [attrib 作定语] *a rival firm* 竞争的商行 ○ *a violinist without rival*, ie better than any other 无与伦比的小提琴家 ○ *She has no rival* (ie no one is as good as she is) *in the field of romantic fiction.* 她写的浪漫小说谁也比不了.

▷ **ri·val** *v* (**-ll-**; *US also* **-l-**) [Tn, Tn·pr] **~ sb/sth (for/in sth)** seem or be as good as sb/sth; be comparable to sb/sth 堪与某人[某事物]竞争; 比得上某人[某事物]: *a view rivalling anything the Alps can offer* 可以与阿尔卑斯山的任何景物相媲美的景色 ○ *Cricket cannot rival football for/in excitement.* 板球不如足球有刺激性.

ri·valry /ˈraɪvlrɪ; ˋraɪvḷrɪ/ *n* [C, U] (instance of) being rivals; competition 竞争; 竞赛; 对抗; 较量: *a country paralysed by political rivalries* 由于政治对抗而陷于瘫痪的国家 ○ *the usual rivalry between brother and sister* 兄妹之间常见的钩心斗角.

riven /ˈrɪvn; ˋrɪvən/ *adj* [pred 作表语] (*fml or rhet* 文或修辞) split; torn violently 分裂; 撕裂: *a family riven by ancient feuds* 由于世代结仇而分裂的家族.

river /ˈrɪvə(r); ˋrɪvɚ/ *n* [C] **1** large natural stream of water flowing in a channel 河; 江; 水道: *the River Thames* 泰晤士河 ○ *the Mississippi River* 密西西比河 ○ [attrib 作定语] *the river mouth* 河口 ○ *river traffic* 内河航运. Cf 参看 CANAL 1. **2** any large flow of similar form 巨流: *a river of lava* 熔岩流 ○ (*fig rhet* 比喻, 修辞) *rivers of blood*, ie great bloodshed in war, etc 血流成河. **3** (idm 习语) **sell sb down the river** ⇨ SELL.

□ **ˈriver-bed** *n* ground over which a river usu flows 河床: *It's so long since it rained that the river-bed is dry.* 很久没有下雨了，河床都已干涸.

ˈriverside *n* ground along the bank of a river 河边; 河畔: *go for a walk along the riverside* 沿着河边散步 ○ [attrib 作定语] *a riverside pub* 江滨酒店.

rivet /ˈrɪvɪt; ˋrɪvɪt/ *n* metal pin or bolt for fastening two pieces of metal together, its headless end being hammered or pressed flat to prevent slipping 铆钉.

▷ **rivet** *v* **1** [Tn, Tn·pr, Tn·p] fasten (sth) with a rivet or rivets 铆, 铆接(某物): *riveted together/down/in place* 铆接在一起[铆紧/铆好]. **2** [Tn, Tn·pr usu passive 通常用于被动语态] make (sth) immobile; fix 将(某物)固定住: *We stood riveted (to the spot).* 我们寸步不移地(在那地方)站着. **3** [Tn esp passive 尤用于被动语态] attract and strongly hold the attention of (sb) 吸引(某人); 吸

R

引住(某人)的注意力: *I was absolutely riveted by her story.* 她的故事完全把我吸引住了. **riv·eter** *n.* **riv·et·ing** *adj* (*approv* 褒) that holds the attention; enthralling 吸引人的; 饶有兴味的: *an absolutely riveting performance* 极为精彩的演出.

Ri·vi·era /ˌrɪvɪˈeərə; ˌrɪvɪˋɛrə/ *n* [sing] **1 the Riviera** region along the Mediterranean coast of SE France, Monaco and NW Italy, famous for its climate and beauty and containing many holiday resorts 里维埃拉(位于法国东南部、摩纳哥及意大利西北部的地中海沿岸地区, 以景色优美气候宜人驰名, 有许多度假胜地). **2** region thought to resemble this 像里维埃拉那样的海滨度假胜地: *the Cornish Riviera* 康沃尔海滨度假胜地.

rivu·let /ˈrɪvjʊlɪt; ˋrɪvjəlɪt/ *n* small stream 小溪; 细流: *rivulets running down the mountainside* 从山上流下来的小溪 ○ *rivulets of sweat on his forehead* 他前额上淌着的汗水.

riyal /riːˈɑːl; riˋɑl/ *n* **1** unit of money in Dubai and Qatar 里亚尔(迪拜酋长国和卡塔尔国的货币单位). **2** (also **rial**) unit of money in Saudi Arabia and the Yemen Arab Republic 里亚尔(沙特阿拉伯和阿拉伯也门共和国的货币单位).

rly *abbr* 缩写 = (eg on a map 如地图上的标示) railway.

RM /ˌɑːr ˈem; ˌɑr ˋɛm/ *abbr* 缩写 = (*Brit*) Royal Marines 皇家海军陆战队: *Capt Tom Pullen RM* 皇家海军陆战队上尉汤姆·普伦.

rm *abbr* 缩写 = room: *rm 603*, eg in a hotel 603 号房间(如旅馆中的).

RN /ˌɑːr ˈen; ˌɑr ˋɛn/ *abbr* 缩写 = **1** (*US*) registered nurse 注册护士. **2** (*Brit*) Royal Navy 皇家海军: *Capt L J Grant RN* 皇家海军上校 L·J·格兰特.

RNA /ˌɑːr en ˈeɪ; ˌɑr ɛn ˋe/ *abbr* 缩写 = (*chemistry* 化) ribonucleic acid 核糖核酸.

RNIB /ˌɑːr en aɪ ˈbiː; ˌɑr ɛn aɪ ˋbi/ *abbr* 缩写 = (*Brit*) Royal National Institute for the Blind 皇家全国盲人协会.

RNLI /ˌɑːr en el ˈaɪ; ˌɑr ɛn ɛl ˋaɪ/ *abbr* 缩写 = (*Brit*) Royal National Lifeboat Institution 皇家全国救生艇协会.

R

roach[1] /rəʊtʃ; rotʃ/ *n* (*pl* unchanged 复数不变) small freshwater fish of the carp family 拟鲤(一种鲤科淡水小鱼).

roach[2] /rəʊtʃ; rotʃ/ *n* (*pl* **~es**) (*esp US*) **1** (*infml* 口) = COCKROACH. **2** (*sl* 俚) stub of a marijuana cigarette 大麻卷烟的烟蒂.

road /rəʊd; rod/ *n* **1** (**a**) way between places, esp one with a prepared surface for the use of motor vehicles 路; 道路; 公路: *the road to Bristol/the Bristol road* 通往布里斯托尔的公路[布里斯托尔公路] ○ *main/major/minor roads* 公路干线[大路/支路] ○ *a quiet suburban road* 清静的郊区道路 ○ [attrib 作定语] *ˈroad junctions* 道路交叉处 ○ *ˈroad signs* 道路标志牌. (**b**) (in compounds 用以构成复合词) of or concerning such a way or ways 道路或公路的; 与道路或公路有关的: *a ˈroad-map of Scotland* 苏格兰公路交通图 ○ *be considerate to other ˈroad-users* 礼让行车. **2 Road** (*abbr* 缩写 **Rd**) (in names of roads, esp in towns 用于道路的名称, 尤用于城镇): *35 York Rd, London SW16* 伦敦SW16 约克路 35 号. ⇨Usage 见所附用法. **3** (usu *pl* 通常作复数) stretch of water near the shore where ships may be anchored (供船只停泊的)近岸水域, 近岸锚地: *the Southampton Roads* 南安普敦港外锚地. **4** (idm 习语) **all roads lead to ˈRome** (*saying* 谚) any of the methods, means, etc being considered will bring about the same result in the end 条条道路通罗马; 殊途同归. **by ˈroad** in or on a road vehicle (乘车)在公路上, 由公路: *It's a long way by road — the train is more direct.* 走公路很远——乘火车近. ○ *It's cheaper to ship goods by road than by rail.* 公路运输比铁路运输便宜. **the end of the line/road** ⇨ END[1]. **hit the road** ⇨ HIT[1]. **one for the road** (*infml* 口) final drink before leaving for home, on a journey, etc 离别酒; 饯别酒. **on the ˈroad** travelling, esp as a salesman, performer or tramp 在旅途中(尤指推销员、表演者或流浪者): *The band has been on the road for almost a month.* 那乐队进行巡回演出近一个月了. **the road to sth** way towards achieving sth, reaching a goal, etc 实现某事、达到某目标等的途径: *the road to success/ruin* 成功[毁灭]之途. **the road to hell is paved with good intentions** (*saying* 谚) people may be blamed or punished as a result of not putting into practice their original good motives 通往地狱的道路是由良好的意图铺成的(只有良好动机而不付诸实践, 徒遭埋怨或惩罚). **rule of the road** ⇨ RULE. **take to the ˈroad** (*fml* 文) become a tramp 成为流浪者.

▷ **ˈroadie** *n* (*infml* 口) person who works with a pop group, etc on tour, esp moving and setting up equipment 巡回演出的流行音乐乐队等的工作人员(尤指搬道具和布置场地者).

□ **ˈroad-block** *n* barricade across a road, set up by the police or army to stop traffic for search 路障(军警设置的).

ˈroad-hog *n* (*infml* 口) reckless or inconsiderate driver 鲁莽而不顾他人的司机.

ˈroad-house *n* pub, restaurant, etc on a main road in the country (郊外主要公路上的)路边酒店、饮食店等.

ˈroad-metal (also **metal**) *n* [U] broken stone used for the making and repairing of roads 筑路和修路用的碎石; 道砟.

ˈroadrunner *n* type of cuckoo of Mexico and southern US 走鹃(一种杜鹃鸟, 产于墨西哥及美国南部).

ˈroad safety safety from traffic accidents 公路交通安全: *a campaign for road safety*, ie to encourage the prevention of road accidents 公路交通安全运动.

ˈroad sense ability to behave safely on roads, esp while driving 避免发生路面事故的能力; (尤指)安全行车的能力.

ˈroad show play, musical, etc performed by a company on tour 巡回演出的戏剧、歌舞喜剧等.

ˈroadside *n* edge/border of a road 路边; 路旁: *parked by/at the roadside* 停靠在路边的 ○ [attrib 作定语] *a ˌroadside ˈcafé* 路边小餐馆.

ˈroad tax tax paid by the owner of a motor vehicle to allow him to drive it on public roads 公路税(机动车车主缴纳的). **ˈroad tax disc** (also **ˈroad fund licence**) (*Brit*) certificate of payment of road tax, displayed on the vehicle 公路税付讫证(标示于车辆上).

ˈroad test test of a vehicle (esp a new model) by using it on a road 车辆(尤指新型号车)的道路试验: *The new sports model achieved 100 miles an hour in road tests.* 这种新型号赛车于道路测试中时速达100英里. **ˈroad-test** *v* [Tn] test (a vehicle) in this way 对(车辆)进行道路测试.

the ˈroadway *n* part of the road used by vehicles, contrasted with the footpath, pavement, etc 车行道.

ˈroad-works *n* [pl] work involving the construction or repair of roads 道路施工: *We were delayed by road-works for two hours.* 我们因道路施工耽搁了两个小时.

ˈroadworthy *adj* (of a vehicle) fit to be driven on a public road (指车辆)适于在公路上行驶的. **ˈroadworthiness** *n* [U].

NOTE ON USAGE 用法: In a town, **street** is the most general word for a road lined with buildings 在城镇, **street**是指道路时用得最广的词, 其两侧有建筑物: *a street-map of London* 伦敦街道图. In British English **street** is not used for roads outside towns but streets in towns may have the word **Road** in their names 在英式英语中, **street**不用以指城镇外的道路, 而 **Road**一词却可用于城镇街道的名称中: *Edgware Road* 埃奇韦尔路. An **alley** or **lane** is a narrow street between buildings. ☆ **alley**和**lane**均指小街或小巷. An **avenue** is usually a wide street of houses, often in the suburbs and lined with trees. ☆ **avenue**通常指两旁有房子的宽阔街道, 常指郊区的林阴道. (In US cities **avenues** often run at right angles to **streets**. 在美国城市中, **avenue**与**street**的走向常有纵横之分.) **Roads** (*US* **highways**) connect towns and villages ☆ **road**(美国用**highway**)指连接城乡的公路: *a road-map of Ireland* 爱尔兰公路交通图. **Motorways** (*US* **freeways/expressways**) are built for long-distance traffic to avoid towns. ☆ **motorway**(美国用**freeway/expressway**)指避开城镇的长距离高速公路. A **lane** is a narrow country road which winds between fields, connecting villages. ☆ **lane**亦指郊外的狭窄小路, 蜿蜒穿过田间, 连接各个村落. **Highway** is seldom used in British English except in certain official phrases ☆ **highway**—

词在英式英语中很少使用，除非用于某些官方用语中: *the Highway Code* 公路法规. **Road, Street, Lane** and **Avenue** are the most common words in street names and are often abbreviated in addresses to **Rd, St, La, Ave.** ☆ **Road**、**Street**、**Lane**、**Avenue** 是用于街道名称中最常用的词，书写地址时常缩写为 **Rd**、**St**、**La**、**Ave**.

roam /rəʊm; rom/ *v* **1** [Ipr, Ip, Tn] walk or travel without any definite aim or destination 漫无目的地走动; 漫步; 漫游; 闲逛: *roam through the deserted village* 漫步于空寂无人的村庄 ○ *just roaming around* 只是随便走走 ○ *He used to roam the streets for hours on end.* 他过去常逛大街，一逛就是几个小时. **2** (phr v) **roam over sth** talk about various things, or various aspects of sth 漫谈某事: *The speaker roamed freely over the events of the past week.* 那个人东拉西扯地谈了一些上周的事.
▷ **roam** *n* [sing] walk, etc of this kind 漫步; 漫游; 闲逛.
roamer *n* person or animal who does this 漫步行走的人或动物: *He's a bit of a roamer*, ie he tends not to stay in one place for very long. 他在哪儿都呆不长.

roan /rəʊn; ron/ *n, adj* [attrib 作定语] (animal, esp a horse or cow) with a coat of mixed colour, esp brown with white or grey hairs in it 杂色毛皮的(尤指棕色中混杂白色或灰色毛的); 杂色毛动物; (尤指)杂色马或牛: *a roan mare* 杂色母马.

roar /rɔː(r); rɔr/ *n* long loud deep sound (like that) made by a lion (狮子的)吼叫声; 似狮子的吼叫声: *the roar of traffic* 车辆的隆隆声 ○ *a roar of applause, anger, etc* 雷鸣般的掌声、怒吼声等 ○ *roars of laughter* 哈哈大笑声.
▷ **roar** *v* **1** (**a**) [I, Ipr, Ip] make such long loud deep sounds 吼叫; 咆哮: *tigers roaring in their cages* 在笼中吼叫的老虎 ○ *roar with laughter, pain, rage, etc* 放声大笑、痛得大叫、怒吼 ○ *He just roared* (ie laughed loudly) *when he heard that joke!* 他听了那笑话就哈哈地笑起来. ○ *a roaring* (ie large, bright and noisy) *fire* 熊熊烈火. (**b**) [Tn, Tn·p] **~ sth (out)** express sth in this way 大声表达某事物: *The crowd roared its approval.* 群众高呼赞成. ○ *roar out an order* 高声发出命令. **2** (idm 习语) **roar oneself ˈhoarse, etc** make oneself hoarse, etc by roaring 喊得嗓子发哑等. **3** (phr v) **roar along, down, past, etc** move in the specified direction making a loud, deep sound 发出洪亮、深沉的声音而行、而去、而过等: *Cars roared past (us).* 汽车隆隆地驶过(我们身边). **roar/shout sb down** silence a speaker by shouting loudly so that he cannot be heard 大声喊叫以压倒某人的讲话声(使其讲不下去).
roar·ing /ˈrɔːrɪŋ; ˈrɔrɪŋ/ *adj* [attrib 作定语] **1** noisy; rough or stormy 吼叫的; 喧闹的; 狂暴的; 狂风暴雨的: *roaring thunder* 震耳的雷声 ○ *a roaring night* 狂风暴雨之夜. **2** (idm 习语) **do a roaring ˈtrade (in sth)** sell (sth) very quickly; do excellent business (in sth) 畅销; 生意兴隆. **the roaring ˈforties** part of the Atlantic Ocean, often very stormy, between latitudes of 40° and 50° S (大西洋的)风暴带(在南纬 40° 和 50° 之间). **a roaring sucˈcess** a very great success 巨大的成功; 辉煌的胜利. — *adv* extremely and noisily 极度且喧闹地: *roaring mad*, ie very angry 大发雷霆 ○ *roaring drunk* 大耍酒疯.

roast /rəʊst; rost/ *v* **1** (**a**) [Tn, Tn·pr] cook (meat, etc) in an oven, or over or in front of a fire 烤(肉等): *roast a joint of meat, a chicken, some potatoes* 烤一大块肉、鸡、一些土豆. (**b**) [I, Ipr] be cooked in this way 烤; 烘; 焙: *the delicious smell of meat roasting in its own juices* 原汁烤肉的香味. ⇨Usage at COOK 用法见 COOK. **2** [Tn] dry (sth) and turn it brown using intense heat 烘干或烤(某物): *roast coffee beans, peanuts, chestnuts* 烘焙咖啡豆、花生、栗子. **3** [I, Tn] expose (sb/oneself) to the heat of a fire, the sun, etc 烤火; 晒太阳: *We're going to lie in the sun and roast for two weeks.* 我们打算躺着晒太阳，晒上两个星期. ○ *roast one's toes in front of the fire* 在火前烤脚趾. **4** [Tn] (*US infml* 口) criticize (sb/sth) harshly, esp in jest; ridicule 严厉批评(某人[某事物])(尤指以取笑方式); 嘲讽: *The critics roasted her new play.* 评论家狠狠挖苦她的新剧.
▷ **roast** *adj* [attrib 作定语] cooked in an oven, etc 烘烤的; 烤制的: *roast beef* 烤牛肉. — *n* **1** [C] joint of meat that has been roasted or is meant for roasting 烤过的或适于烤食的大块肉: *order a roast from the butcher* 向肉商订购一块烤着吃的大块肉. **2** [C] (*esp US*) outdoor picnic or barbecue at which food is roasted 户外烧烤野餐. **3** [C, U] (*US infml* 口) (occasion of) harsh criticism or ridicule, esp in jest 严厉的批评; 嘲讽; (尤指)挖苦.
roaster *n* type of chicken, etc suitable for roasting 适于烤食的鸡等. Cf 参看 BROILER (BROIL).
roast·ing *adj* (*infml* 口) very hot 极热的; 火烫的: *It's roasting today!* ie The weather is very hot. 今天热极了! — *n* (idm 习语) **give sb/get a (good, real, etc) ˈroasting** scold sb/be scolded severely 严厉批评某人[受到严厉批评].

rob /rɒb; rɑb/ *v* (**-bb-**) [Tn, Tn·pr] **~ sb/sth (of sth)** **1** take property from (a person or place) illegally 抢夺; 抢劫; 盗窃: *I was robbed (of my cash and cheque-book).* 我(的现金和支票簿)被抢了. ○ *accused of robbing a bank (of one million pounds)* 被控抢劫银行(一百万镑). ⇨Usage 见所附用法. **2** deprive sb/sth (of what is expected or normal) 剥夺某人[某事物](想要的或应有的事物): *Those cats robbed me of my sleep.* 那些猫吵得我无法入睡. ○ (*fig* 比喻) *The fact that he had lied before robbed his words of any credibility.* 由于他过去说过谎话，他的话已经没有人相信了. **3** (idm 习语) ˌ**rob** ˌ**Peter to** ˌ**pay** ˈ**Paul** pay one debt, etc with money borrowed from somewhere else, thus creating another debt 借新债还旧债; 拆东墙补西墙.
▷ **rob·ber** *n* person who robs; thief 抢劫者; 强盗; 盗贼.
rob·bery /ˈrɒbərɪ; ˈrɑbərɪ/ *n* [C, U] **1** (instance of) stealing; theft 抢劫; 盗窃; 偷盗; 失窃: *three robberies in one week* 一周内的三起劫案 ○ *Armed robbery is on the increase everywhere.* 持械劫案各地均有增无已. **2** (idm 习语) **daylight robbery** ⇨ DAYLIGHT.

NOTE ON USAGE 用法: Compare **rob, steal** and **burgle.** 试比较 **rob**、**steal**、**burgle** 这三个词. A robber or thief **robs** a place, eg a bank, or a person (of things, especially money) and he **steals** things (from a place or person). 劫匪或强盗 **rob** 的对象是'某处所(如银行)或某人'; 他们劫的'物(尤指钱)'要用'of + 物'来表达. 他们 **steal** 的对象是'物'; 受损失的'处所或人'要用'from + 处所或人'来表达. A burglar **burgles** a house by forcing a way into it and stealing from it. 窃贼 **burgle** 的对象是'房子', 指以破门、撬锁等手段强行入户行窃.

robe /rəʊb; rob/ *n* **1** (esp in compounds 尤用以构成复合词) long loose outer garment 长袍: *a beach-robe* 海滩罩袍 ○ *Many Arabs wear long flowing robes.* 许多阿拉伯人身穿松垂的长袍. **2** (esp *pl* 尤作复数) such a garment worn as a sign of rank or office, or for a ceremony (作为级别或职位标志的)袍服, 礼袍: *coroˈnation robes*, ie of a king or queen 加冕礼袍(国王或女王穿的) ○ *cardinals in scarlet robes* 身穿红袍的红衣主教. **3** (*US* also ˈ**bathrobe**) dressing-gown 晨衣.
▷ **robe** *v* [esp passive 尤用于被动语态: Tn, Tn·pr] **~ sb/oneself (in sth)** (*fml* 文) dress sb/oneself in a robe, etc 给某人[自己]穿上长袍、袍服、晨衣等: *black-robed judges* 穿黑袍的法官 ○ *robed in a ceremonial gown* 穿礼袍的.

robin /ˈrɒbɪn; ˈrɑbɪn/ *n* **1** (also ˌ**robin** ˈ**redbreast**) small brown red-breasted bird 鸲, 欧洲鸲(褐色小鸟, 胸部红色). ⇨illus at App 1 见附录1插图, page iv. **2** (*US*) type of N American thrush resembling this (北美的)鸫(似欧洲鸲).

ro·bot /ˈrəʊbɒt; ˈrobɑt/ *n* [C] **1** (also **automaton**) machine that (resembles and) can perform the actions of a person, operated automatically or by remote control 机器人: *Many production-line tasks in car factories are now performed by robots.* 在汽车制造厂里, 生产线上的许多工作现在是由机器人来完成的. **2** (*esp derog* 尤作贬义) person who seems to behave like a machine 行动像机器般的人. Cf 参看 AUTOMATON 2. **3** (in Southern Africa) an automatic traffic-light (非洲南部)自动交通信号灯.
▷ **ro·botic** /rəʊˈbɒtɪk; roˈbɑtɪk/ *adj* like a robot; stiff and mechanical 像机器人的; 呆板而机械的: *robotic movements* 呆板而机械的动作. **ro·botics** *n* [sing *v*]

(study of the) use of robots in manufacturing 机器人的应用; 机器人学.

ro·bust /rəʊˈbʌst; roˈbʌst/ *adj* **1** vigorous; healthy and strong 有活力的; 强健的: *a robust young man* 身强力壮的青年男子 ○ *a robust appetite* 旺盛的食欲. **2** (*derog* 贬) not delicate or refined 粗野的; 粗鲁的: *a rather robust sense of humour* 颇为粗俗的幽默感. **3** (of wine) full-bodied (指酒)浓烈的, 醇厚的. ▷ **ro·bustly** *adv*. **ro·bust·ness** *n* [U].

rock[1] /rɒk; rɑk/ *n* **1** (**a**) [U] (usu solid) part of the earth's crust 岩层; 岩: *They drilled through several layers of rock to reach the oil.* 他们钻透了几层岩石以寻找石油. ○ *The volcano poured out molten rock.* 火山喷出了熔岩. (**b**) [C] mass of this standing out from the earth's surface or from the sea 岩石; 礁石: *The ship hit some rocks and sank.* 那船触到了一些暗礁沉没了. ○ *the Rock of Gibraltar* 直布罗陀山. **2** [C] (**a**) large detached stone or boulder 大石块; 大圆石: *The sign said, 'Danger: falling rocks'.* 告示牌上写着: '危险, 前面有滚石'. (**b**) (*US*) small stone or pebble 小石子; 卵石: *That boy threw a rock at me.* 那男孩朝我扔了一块石子. **3** [U] (*Brit*) type of hard sugar sweet, usu made in cylindrical sticks and flavoured with peppermint 硬棒糖(通常含薄荷味): *a stick of rock* 一条硬棒糖. **4** (idm 习语) **(as) firm/solid as a ˈrock** immovable; dependable 稳固如磐石的; 可靠的. **on the ˈrocks** (**a**) (of a ship) wrecked on rocks (指船)触礁. (**b**) (*infml* 口) (of a marriage, business, etc) in danger of failing; in a severe crisis (指婚姻等)濒于破裂; (指生意等)濒于破产. (**c**) (*infml* 口) (of drinks) served with ice cubes but no water (指饮料)加冰块而不加水的: *Scotch* (ie whisky) *on the rocks* 加冰块的威士忌酒.

▷ **rock·ery** /ˈrɒkərɪ; ˈrɑkərɪ/ (also **rock-garden**) *n* artificial or natural mound or bank containing large stones, planted with rock-plants (天然的)岩石庭园; 假山庭园. ⇨illus at App 1 见附录1插图, page vii.

rocky *adj* (**-ier, -iest**) **1** of or like rock (似)岩石的: *a rocky outcrop* 露出地面的岩石. **2** full of rocks 多岩石的: *rocky soil* 多石的土壤. **rocki·ness** *n* [U].

□ ˌ**rock-ˈbottom** *n* [sing] (used without *a*/*the* 不用a/the) lowest point 最低点: *Prices have reached rock-bottom.* 物价已下降到最低点. ○ [attrib 作定语] ˌ*rock-bottom* (ie bargain) ˈ*prices* 最低的价格.

ˈ**rock-cake** *n* small cake or bun with a hard rough surface 一种表皮粗硬的小糕饼或小圆面包.

ˈ**rock-climbing** *n* [U] sport of climbing rock surfaces 攀岩运动.

ˈ**rock-crystal** *n* [U] pure natural transparent quartz 水晶.

ˈ**rock-garden** *n* = ROCKERY.

ˈ**rock-plant** *n* any of various types of plant found growing on or among rocks 岩生植物.

ˌ**rock ˈsalmon** (*Brit*) (piece of) dogfish sold as food (作为食物出售的)角鲨, 角鲨鱼片.

ˈ**rock-salt** *n* [U] common salt as mined in crystal form 岩盐; 石盐.

ˌ**rock-ˈsteady** *adj* unlikely to fall over, be changed, etc 稳固的; 不动摇的; 不改变的: *a* ˌ*rock-steady* ˈ*chair,* ˈ*friendship* 结实的椅子、牢不可破的友谊 ○ *Prices in the shares market are rock-steady.* 股票市场的价格非常平稳.

rock[2] /rɒk; rɑk/ *v* **1** [I, Ipr, Tn, Tn·pr] (cause sb/sth to) move gently (backwards and forwards, or from side to side) (使某人[某物])(前后或左右)轻轻摆动, 摇动, 摇晃: *He sat rocking (himself) in his chair.* 他坐在椅子上前后摇动着. ○ *rock a baby to sleep* 摇晃婴儿使其入睡 ○ *Our boat was rocked (from side to side) by/on the waves.* 我们的船被波浪冲得[在波浪中](左右)摇摇晃晃. **2** [I, Ipr, Tn, Tn·pr] (cause sth to) shake violently (使某物)剧烈震动或摇摆: *The whole house rocked (to and fro) when the bomb exploded.* 炸弹爆炸时整座房子都震得(前后)直晃. ○ *The town was rocked by an earthquake.* 该城遭地震而发生剧烈震动. **3** [Tn] (*fig* 比喻) disturb or shock (sb/sth) greatly 使(某人[某事物])极为不安或震惊: *The scandal rocked the government.* 这件丑闻把政府搅得十分狼狈. **4** (idm 习语) **rock the ˈboat** (*infml* 口) do sth that upsets the balance of a situation, etc 做某事从而使局面等失去平衡: *Things are progressing well — don't (do anything to) rock the boat.* 事情进行得很顺利——(千万)不要无风生浪.

▷ **rocker** *n* **1** either of the curved pieces of wood on which a rocking-chair, etc rests (摇椅等下面的)弧形摇板. ⇨illus at App 1 见附录1插图, page xvi. **2** = ROCKING-CHAIR. **3** (also ˈ**rocker switch**) switch that changes from 'on' to 'off' by means of a rocking action 摇臂式开关; 摇压开关. **4 Rocker** (*Brit*) member of a 1960's teenage gang or their later followers, wearing leather jackets and riding motor bikes 洛可帮(20世纪60年代的青少年帮派, 好穿皮夹克和骑摩托车)的成员或其追随者. Cf 参看 MOD. **5** (idm 习语) **off one's ˈrocker** (*sl* 俚) out of one's mind; crazy 精神失常; 发疯: *You must be off your rocker!* 你简直疯了!

rocky /ˈrɒkɪ; ˈrɑkɪ/ *adj* (**-ier, -iest**) shaky; unsteady 摇摆的; 摇晃的; 不稳的: *This chair is a trifle rocky.* 这把椅子有点摇晃. ○ (*fig* 比喻) *Their marriage seems a bit rocky.* 他们的婚姻好像有些问题. **rocki·ness** *n* [U].

□ ˈ**rocking-chair** (also **rocker**) *n* chair mounted on rockers or with springs so that it can be rocked by the sitter 摇椅. ⇨illus at App 1 见附录1插图, page xvi.

ˈ**rocking-horse** *n* wooden horse mounted on rockers or springs so that it can be rocked by a child sitting on it (儿童游戏用的)木马.

rock[3] /rɒk; rɑk/ *n* [U] (also ˈ**rock music**) type of modern popular music with a strong beat, played on electric guitars, etc 摇滚乐: [attrib 作定语] *a* ˈ*rock star* 摇滚乐歌星.

▷ **rock** *v* [I, Ipr] dance to this music 跳摇滚舞.

□ ˌ**rock and ˈroll** (also ˌ**rock 'n' ˈroll**) earlier (and usu simpler) form of this (初期的, 通常较简单的)摇滚乐: [attrib 作定语] *Jerry Lee Lewis was a rock 'n' roll singer.* 杰里·李·刘易斯是初期摇滚乐歌手. — *v* [I] dance to rock and roll music 跳初期的摇滚舞.

rocket 火箭

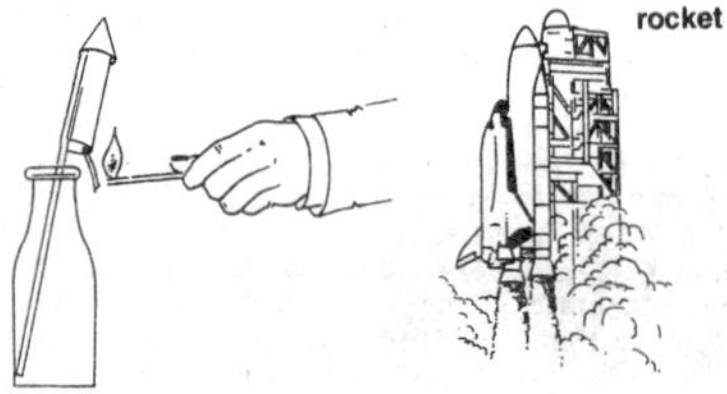

rocket /ˈrɒkɪt; ˈrɑkɪt/ *n* **1** firework or similar device that shoots into the air when lit and then explodes 火箭式烟火或类似装置: *a diˈstress rocket,* ie used to signal for help 呼救信号火箭. **2** (**a**) cylindrical device that flies by expelling gases produced by combustion, used to propel a warhead or spacecraft 火箭(发射器). (**b**) bomb or shell together with the rocket propelling it 火箭(弹): [attrib 作定语] *a* ˈ*rocket attack* 火箭攻击. ⇨ illus 见插图. **3** (idm 习语) **give sb/get a ˈrocket** (*Brit infml* 口) reprimand sb/be reprimanded severely 严厉斥责某人[受到严厉斥责].

▷ **rocket** *v* **1** [I, Ipr, Ip] **~ (up)** increase very rapidly 迅速增加: *Unemployment levels have rocketed (to new heights).* 失业率猛然上升(到新的水平). ○ *House prices are rocketing (up).* 房价在飞涨. **2** [Ipr, Ip] move extremely quickly 飞快地移动: *He rocketed to stardom* (ie became famous) *overnight.* 他转瞬间成了明星. ○ *rocket along, away, off, past, etc* 飞快地行进、离开、离去、越过等.

rock·etry /ˈrɒkɪtrɪ; ˈrɑkɪtrɪ/ *n* [U] (science or practice of) using rockets for propelling missiles or spacecraft 火箭学; 火箭技术.

rocky ⇨ ROCK[1], ROCK[2].

ro·coco /rəˈkəʊkəʊ; rəˈkoko/ *adj* of a style of decoration in furniture, architecture, music, etc with much elaborate decoration, common in Europe in the 18th century 洛可可式的(18世纪盛行于欧洲的家具、建筑、音乐等精致的装饰艺术风格).

rod /rɒd; rɑd/ *n* **1** (often in compounds 常用以构成复合词) thin straight piece of wood or metal (木质或金属的)杆, 竿, 棍, 棒: ˈ*curtain-rods* 挂帘子的杆子 ○ *a* '*measuring rod* 测杆 ○ '*piston-rods* 活塞杆. **2** stick used for hitting people as a punishment; cane(3a) (责打用的)棍棒. **3** = FISHING-ROD (FISH[2]). **4** (*US sl* 俚) hand gun 手枪. **5** = PERCH[1] 3. **6** (idm 习语) **make a rod for one's own 'back** do sth likely to cause oneself difficulties later 自讨苦吃; 自找麻烦. **a rod/stick to beat sb with** ⇨ BEAT[1]. **rule with a rod of iron** ⇨ RULE *v*. **spare the rod and spoil the child** ⇨ SPARE[2].

rode *pt* of RIDE[2].

ro·dent /'rəʊdnt; 'rodn̩t/ *n* type of small animal that gnaws things with its strong front teeth, eg a rat, squirrel or beaver 啮齿目动物(如鼠、松鼠或海狸).

ro·deo /rəʊ'deɪəʊ; *US* 'rəʊdɪəʊ; 'rodɪ,o/ *n* (*pl* **~s**) **1** rounding up of cattle on a ranch, for branding, etc (在牧场中)驱集牛群(为打烙印等). **2** exhibition or contest of cowboys' skill in lassoing and riding cattle, untamed horses, etc 牛仔竞技表演或比赛(表演掷套索、骑牛、驯马等).

ro·do·mont·ade /ˌrɒdəmɒn'teɪd, -'tɑːd; ˌrɑdəmɑn'ted, -'tɑd/ *n* [U] (*fml derog* 文, 贬) boastful bragging talk 狂言; 大话; 吹嘘; 吹牛.

roe[1] /rəʊ; ro/ *n* [U, C] (mass of) eggs in a female fish's ovary (*hard roe*) or a male fish's milt (*soft roe*) 雌鱼的卵块(硬鱼子); 雄鱼的精块或精液(软鱼子).

roe[2] /rəʊ; ro/ *n* (*pl* unchanged or **~s** 复数或不变或作 **roes**) (also '**roe deer**) type of small deer 狍(鹿的一种, 体小).

□ '**roebuck** *n* male roe 雄狍.

roent·gen (also **röntgen**) /'rɒntjən; *US* 'rentgən; 'rɛntgən/ *n* unit of ionizing radiation (eg in X-rays) 伦琴(电离辐射单位, 如X射线的).

roga·tions /rəʊ'geɪʃnz; ro'geʃənz/ *n* [pl] special litany sung on the three days (**Ro'gation Days**) before Ascension Day (耶稣升天节前三天即祈祷日所唱的)祈祷文.

□ **Roˌgation 'Sunday** the Sunday before Ascension Day 耶稣升天节之前的星期日.

roger[1] /'rɒdʒə(r); 'rɑdʒɚ/ *interj* **1** (in radio communications) your message has been received and understood (无线电通讯用语)信息收到, 明白. **2** (*Brit infml or joc* 口或谑) okay 好的; 可以; 行; 对.

roger[2] /'rɒdʒə(r); 'rɑdʒɚ/ *v* [Tn] (⚠ *Brit sl euph* 讳, 俚, 婉) (of a male) have sexual intercourse with (sb) (指男子)与(某人)性交.

rogue /rəʊg; rog/ *n* **1** (*dated* 旧) dishonest or unprincipled man 不诚实或不道德的男子; 无耻之徒. **2** (*joc esp approv* 谑, 尤作褒义) mischievous person 调皮捣蛋的人: *He's a charming rogue.* 他是淘气鬼. **3** wild animal driven or living apart from the herd 离群的野兽: [attrib 作定语] *a ˌrogue 'elephant* 离群的野象.

▷ **roguery** /'rəʊgərɪ; 'rogərɪ/ *n* [C, U] (instance of) dishonest, unprincipled or mischievous behaviour 不诚实的、不道德的或调皮捣蛋的行为.

roguish /'rəʊgɪʃ; 'rogɪʃ/ *adj* mischievous in a playful way 调皮的; 淘气的; 恶作剧的: *He gave her a roguish look.* 他调皮地看了她一眼. **roguishly** *adv*. **roguish·ness** *n* [U].

□ ˌ**rogues' 'gallery** police collection of photographs of criminals, used for identifying suspects, etc (警方存档的)罪犯照片集.

rois·ter·ing /'rɔɪstərɪŋ; 'rɔɪstərɪŋ/ *adj* [attrib 作定语], *n* [U] (*dated* 旧) noisy merrymaking 喧闹作乐(的). ▷ **rois·terer** /'rɔɪstərə(r); 'rɔɪstərɚ/ *n*.

role (also **rôle**) /rəʊl; rol/ *n* **1** actor's part in a play 角色: *play a variety of roles* 扮演各种的角色 ○ *the title-role* 主角. **2** function or importance of sb/sth 作用; 重要性: *the key role of the teacher in the learning process* 教师在教学中的关键作用 ○ *the declining role of the railways in the transport system* 在运输系统中, 铁路的重要性逐渐下降.

□ '**role-play** *n* [U, C] activity (esp in language teaching or treating mentally ill people) in which a person acts a part 角色扮演; (尤指语言教学或治疗精神病患者的)角色演习. — *v* [I, Tn]: *to role-play a situation* 演习处理某情况.

roll[1] /rəʊl; rol/ *n* **1** (**a**) cylinder made by turning flexible material over and over on itself without folding it 卷状物: *Wallpaper is bought in rolls.* 壁纸是成卷买的. ○ *a roll of carpet, film, cloth* 一卷地毯、胶卷、布. (**b**) person or

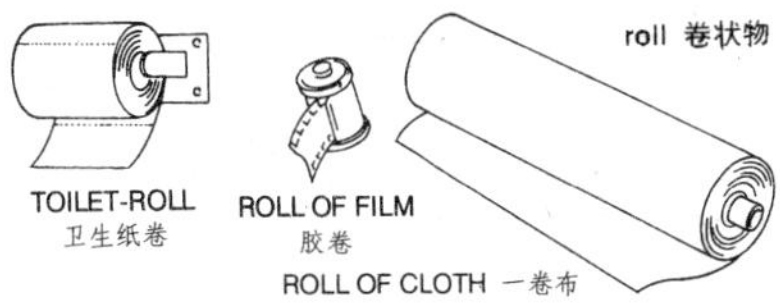

thing with this shape 带有卷状物的人或物: *a man with rolls of fat around his stomach* 腹部有层层肥肉的男子. **2** (**a**) small individual portion of bread baked in a rounded shape 小圆面包: *Six brown rolls, please.* 请给我来六个黑面包. ⇨illus at BREAD 见 BREAD 插图. Cf 参看 BUN 1. (**b**) (with a preceding *n* or *ns* 用于名词之后) one of these containing the stated filling 有某种馅的小圆面包: *a ham roll* 火腿面包 ○ *a bacon and tomato roll* 腌猪肉加西红柿馅的面包. **3** swaying movement; action of turning (over) from side to side 摇摆; 摇晃; (左右)翻滚: *The slow, steady roll of the ship made us feel sick.* 船老是晃晃悠悠的, 弄得我们很恶心. ○ *walk with a nautical roll*, ie like a sailor 走路摇摇晃晃(像海员似的) ○ *a horse enjoying a roll in the grass* 在草地上尽情打滚的马. Cf 参看 PITCH[3] 6. **4** official list or register, esp of names 正式的表册; 登记表; (尤指)名单, 花名册: *the electoral roll*, ie the list of people eligible to vote in an election 选举人名单 ○ *call/read the roll in school, class, etc*, ie read aloud a list of names to check whether everyone is present 在学校、班…里点名. **5** long steady vibrating sound 持续而平稳的振动声: *A 'drum roll preceded the most dangerous part of the performance.* 演出快进行到最惊险的部分时响起了咚咚的鼓声. ○ *the distant roll of thunder* 远处传来的隆隆雷声. **6** (*US infml* 口) (*Brit* '**bankroll**) wad of paper money 一卷或一叠钞票.

□ '**roll-bar** *n* bar used to strengthen the roof of a car and protect the occupants if the car rolls over 翻车保护杠(汽车顶部的加固杠, 翻车时可保护乘车人).

'**roll-call** *n* (time of) reading aloud of a list of names to check whether everyone is present 点名(时间): *Roll-call will be at 7 am.* 上午7时点名.

ˌ**roll of 'honour** list of people whose achievements are honoured, esp those who have died in battle 荣誉名册; (尤指)阵亡将士名册.

ˌ**roll-top 'desk** desk with a flexible cover that rolls up into a compartment at the top 卷盖式书桌(顶盖可卷起).

roll[2] /rəʊl; rol/ *v* **1** [Ipr, Ip, Tn·pr, Tn·p] (cause sth to) move on wheels or rollers or by turning (over and over) (使某物)滚动: *The ball rolled down the hill.* 球滚下了山. ○ *The hoop rolled along the pavement.* 圆环沿人行道滚动. ○ *The coin fell and rolled away.* 硬币掉下滚走了. ○ *men rolling barrels across a yard* 滚着圆桶经过院子的人 ○ *Roll it over and look at the other side.* 把它翻滚过来看看另一面. **2** [I, Ipr, Ip, Tn, Tn·pr, Tn·p] (cause sth to) turn on an axis, over and over or round and round (使某物)转动, 旋转, 转圈: *a porpoise rolling in the water* 在水中翻滚的鼠海豚 ○ *His eyes rolled strangely/He rolled his eyes strangely.* 他那双眼睛滴溜溜地转动, 甚是古怪 [他滴溜溜转动着眼睛, 甚是古怪]. ○ *rolling a pencil between his fingers* 把铅笔夹在他的指头上捻. **3** [Ipr, Ip, Tn, Tn·pr, Tn·p, Dn·n] **~ (sth) (up)** make (sth) or be made into the shape of a ball or cylinder; fold (sth) over on itself (将某物)卷或绕成球形或圆柱形; 卷起(某物): *The hedgehog rolled up into a spiky ball.* 刺猬卷起身子成了一个刺球. ○ *I always roll my own (cigarettes).* 我总是抽自己卷的(烟). ○ *roll string, wool, etc (up) into a ball* 把细绳、毛线等绕成线团 ○ *roll up a carpet, a map, a towel* 把地毯、地图、毛巾卷起来 ○ *He rolled himself a cigarette.* 他自己卷了一枝烟. Cf 参看 UNROLL. **4** [Tn, Tn·pr] wrap or cover (sb/sth) in sth 将(某人[某物])包或裹在某物内: *He rolled himself (up) in his blanket.* 他用毛毯裹住身体. ○ *roll the sausages in batter* 把香肠放在蛋奶面糊里滚一下. **5** [Tn, Tn·pr, Tn·p, Cn·a] flatten (sth) with a roller(1) 用碾子轧平(某物); 将(某物)碾平: *roll a lawn* 把草坪碾平 ○ *roll out*

R

the dough 擀面团 ○ *roll the ground flat* 把地碾平. **6** (**a**) [I, Ipr, Ip, Tn, Tn·pr, Tn·p] (cause sb/sth to) sway or rock (from side to side) (使某人[某物])(左右)摇摆或摇晃: *The ship was rolling heavily to and fro.* 那船晃来晃去很不平稳. ○ *walk with a rolling gait* 走起路来摇摇晃晃 ○ *The huge waves rolled the ship from side to side.* 巨浪把船打得左右摇晃. Cf 参看 PITCH[2] 4. (**b**) [I, Ipr] sway or rock helplessly 不由自主地摇摆或摇晃: *rolling with laughter* 笑得前仰后合 ○ *rolling drunk* 醉得东倒西歪. **7** [I, Ipr, Ip] (appear to) rise and fall; undulate 起伏; 作起伏状; 波动: *rolling hills* 绵延起伏的丘陵地带 ○ *waves rolling in to the beach* 湧向海滩的滚滚浪涛. **8** [I] make a long continuous vibrating sound 发出持续颤动的声音: *The thunder rolled.* 雷声隆隆. ○ *rolling drums* 咚咚的鼓声. **9** [I, Tn] (*infml* 口) (cause film cameras to) begin working (使电影摄影机或电视摄像机)开拍, 开机: *Let them roll!/Roll 'em!* 开机! **10** [Tn] (*US infml* 口) rob (esp sb drunk or asleep) 抢劫(某人, 尤指抢喝醉的或睡觉的人). **11** (idm 习语) **be ˈrolling (in money/it/cash)** (*sl* 俚) have lots (of money) 有许多(钱): *What do you mean, he can't afford it? He's absolutely rolling (in money)!* 你这是怎么说, 他负担不起? 他可有的是钱! **heads will roll** ⇨ HEAD[1]. **keep/start the ball rolling** ⇨ BALL[1]. **rolled into ˈone** combined in one person or thing 合为一体; 兼于一身: *He's an artist, a scientist and a shrewd businessman (all) rolled into one.* 他既是艺术家, 又是科学家, 同时还是个精明的生意人. **ˌrolling in the ˈaisles** much amused; helpless with laughter 乐不可支; 捧腹大笑: *The comedian soon had them rolling in the aisles.* 那滑稽演员很快就逗得他们捧腹大笑. **roll one's ˈr's** pronounce the sound of the letter **'r'** with vibration of the tongue against the palate 发 **r** 的舌尖颤音. **roll ˈup! roll ˈup!** (used to invite passers-by to join an audience, etc 邀请过往行人进入观看等之用语). **roll up one's ˈsleeves** (*fig* 比喻) prepare to work or fight 卷起袖子(准备工作或战斗). **12** (phr v) **roll sth back** (**a**) turn or force back (eg enemy forces) 赶回或击退(如敌军). (**b**) (*esp US*) reduce (prices, etc) 降低(价格等): *roll back inflation* 缓解通货膨胀. **roll in** (*infml* 口) (**a**) arrive in great numbers or quantities 滚滚而来; 大量涌来: *Offers of help are still rolling in.* 仍不断有人提出愿予以帮助. (**b**) arrive casually 不期然到达: *She rolled in for work twenty minutes late.* 她懒懒散散地来上班, 迟到了二十分钟. **roll (sth) on** (**a**) apply, spread, etc (sth) by rolling 用滚动方法敷、涂...(某物): *This paint is easy to roll on/rolls on easily.* 这种颜料用滚轴涂布很容易. (**b**) (of time) pass steadily (指时间)不断地流逝: *The years rolled on.* 岁月流逝. (**c**) (used in the imperative 用于祈使句) come soon 赶快来到: *Roll on the holidays!* 假期快来吧! **roll up** (*infml* 口) (of a person or vehicle) arrive (指人或车辆)到达: *Bill finally rolled up two hours late.* 比尔终于来了, 迟到了两个小时.

□ **rolled ˈgold** thin coating of gold applied to the surface of another metal 金箔; 包金.

rolled ˈoats oats that have had the husks removed and have been crushed 燕麦片.

ˈrolling-mill *n* machine or factory in which metal is rolled into sheets, bars, etc 轧钢机; 轧钢厂.

ˈrolling-pin *n* cylinder of wood, glass, etc used for rolling out dough, pastry, etc 擀面棍; 擀面杖. ⇨illus at KITCHEN 见 KITCHEN 插图.

ˈrolling-stock *n* [U] railway engines, carriages, wagons, etc collectively 铁路各种车辆的总称.

ˌrolling ˈstone **1** person who does not settle down to live and work in one place 无固定住处和工作的人. **2** (idm 习语) **a ˌrolling ˌstone ˌgathers no ˈmoss** (*saying* 谚) sb of this type is free of responsibilities, family ties, etc and has no wealth 滚石不生苔(喻人既无责任、无家室等, 又无钱财).

ˈroll-on **1** *n* cosmetic applied by means of a ball that rotates in the neck of the container 滚抹式化妆品(容器口有可转动涂布的圆球): [attrib 作定语] *roll-on deodorants* 滚抹除臭剂. **2** (*dated* 旧) woman's elastic corset rolled on over the hips 女用弹力紧身内裤.

ˌroll-on roll-ˈoff (*abbr* 缩写 **roro**) designed to allow vehicles to be driven onto and off it 供车辆驶进驶出的; 滚装: *a roll-on roll-off ferry* 驶进驶出式渡船.

ˈroll-up *n* (*infml* 口) cigarette rolled by hand 手卷的纸烟: *He always smokes roll-ups.* 他总是抽手卷的纸烟.

roller /ˈrəʊlə(r); *US* ˈrolɚ/ *n* [C] **1** (**a**) cylinder used for flattening or spreading things (碾轧或涂布用的)磙子: *a garden roller*, ie for use on a lawn 园圃滚压机(碾草坪用) ○ *a ˈroad-roller*, ie for levelling tarmac on roads, etc 压路机. (**b**) cylinder on which sth is placed to enable it to be moved 滚柱, 滚轴(物体置于其上便于移动): *The huge machine was moved to its new position on rollers.* 那台巨型机器用滚柱移到了新的地方. (**c**) cylinder on which sth is wound (缠绕东西的)滚筒, 滚轴: *a ˈroller-blind*, ie a type of window blind wound on a roller 卷式窗帘. (**d**) small cylinder of plastic around which hair is wound to make it curl 塑料发卷: *put her hair in rollers* (她)用发卷卷发. **2** long swelling wave 翻滚的巨浪: *rollers crashing on the beach* 冲击海滩的巨浪.

□ **ˈroller bandage** long surgical bandage which is rolled up before being unrolled onto a limb, etc 绷带卷.

ˈroller-coaster (*Brit* also **switchback**) *n* type of railway with open cars, tight turns and very steep slopes (found in funfairs, amusement parks, etc) 过山车, 云霄飞车(游乐场、娱乐园等处的惊险游戏车).

ˈroller-skate (also **skate**) *n* type of shoe with small wheels fitted to the bottom, allowing the wearer to glide over hard surfaces 旱冰鞋; 轱辘鞋: *a pair of roller-skates* 一双旱冰鞋. ⇨illus at SKATE 见 SKATE 插图. — *v* [I, Ipr, Ip] roll about smoothly wearing a pair of these 穿旱冰鞋滑行: *She roller-skated across rather unsteadily.* 她穿着旱冰鞋晃晃悠悠地滑了过去. **ˈroller-skating** *n* [U].

ˌroller ˈtowel continuous loop of towel hung over a roller 滚带毛巾(套在滚筒上连续使用的毛巾).

rol·lick·ing /ˈrɒlɪkɪŋ; ˈrɑlɪkɪŋ/ *adj* [attrib 作定语] (*dated* 旧) noisy and jolly 喧闹而欢乐的: *have a rollicking time* 尽情欢乐.

roll·mop /ˈrəʊlmɒp; ˋrolˌmɑp/ *n* (also **ˌrollmop ˈherring**) herring fillet rolled up and pickled in vinegar 醋渍鲱鱼卷.

roly-poly /ˌrəʊlɪˈpəʊlɪ; ˋrolɪˌpolɪ/ *n* [C, U] **1** (also **roly-poly pudding**) (*Brit*) pudding made from suet pastry spread with jam, rolled up and boiled (有果酱的)布丁卷. **2** (*infml* 口) short and plump person 矮胖的人: *She's a real roly-poly.* 她可真是又矮又胖.

ROM /rɒm; rɑm/ *abbr* 缩写 = (*computing* 计) read only memory 只读存储器: *a ROM software component* 只读存储器软件元件. Cf 参看 RAM 1.

Ro·man /ˈrəʊmən; ˋromən/ *adj* **1** (**a**) of ancient or modern Rome 古罗马的; 现代罗马的. (**b**) of the ancient Roman republic or empire 古罗马共和国的; 古罗马帝国的: *ˌRoman reˈmains* 古罗马的遗迹 ○ *an old Roman road* 古罗马的道路. **2** of the Christian Church of Rome; Roman Catholic 罗马基督教会的; 天主教的: *the Roman rite*, eg contrasted with Greek or Russian Orthodox 天主教仪式(如与希腊或俄国东正教之仪式相对). **3 roman** (of printing type) in ordinary upright form, like that used for this definition (指印刷字体)罗马字体的, 正体的: *The words in the definition are roman/are set in roman type.* 本定义中的英文字使用的是罗马字体. Cf 参看 ITALIC.

▷ **Ro·man** *n* **1** [C] member of the ancient Roman republic or empire 古罗马共和国或帝国的人; 古罗马人: *after the Romans invaded Britain* 在古罗马人入侵不列颠之后. **2** [C] native or inhabitant of the city of Rome 罗马市民. **3** [C] Roman Catholic 天主教教徒. **4 roman** [U] plain upright type (not italic) like that used for the definitions in this dictionary 罗马字体, 正体(如本词典英文定义使用的字体): *The above definition is set in roman; this example is in italics.* 上面的定义用的是正体字排印的, 本例句用的是斜体. **5** (idm 习语) **when in Rome, do as the Romans do** (*saying* 谚) one should change one's habits to suit the customs of the place one is living in or of the people one is living with 入乡随俗.

□ **the ˌRoman ˈalphabet** the letters A to Z, used esp in West European languages 罗马字母(表)(尤用于西欧语言). Cf 参看 CYRILLIC.

ˌRoman ˈcandle tubular firework that emits coloured sparks 罗马烟火筒(能喷发彩色火花).

ˌRoman ˈCatholic (also **Catholic**) (member) of the Church that acknowledges the Pope as its head 天主教的; 天主教徒: *He's (a) Roman Catholic.* 他是天主教徒.

Cf 参看 PROTESTANT. ˌ**Roman Caˈtholicism** the faith of the Roman Catholic Church 天主教: *convert to Roman Catholicism* 皈依天主教.

ˌ**Roman ˈnose** nose with a high bridge[1](4a) 鹰钩鼻(高鼻梁).

ˌ**Roman ˈnumerals** (system of) letters representing numbers 罗马数字(体系)(以字母记数) ⇨App 4 见附录4. Cf 参看 ARABIC NUMERALS (ARABIC).

Ro·mance /rəʊˈmæns; roˈmæns/ *adj* [attrib 作定语] of those languages (the Romance languages) which are descended from Latin, eg French, Italian, Spanish 罗曼语的(由拉丁语演变而成的语言, 如法语、意大利语、西班牙语). Cf 参看 LATIN 2.

ro·mance /rəʊˈmæns; roˈmæns/ *n* **1** [C, U] imaginative story; literature of this kind 富于想像力的故事; 浪漫故事; 浪漫作品; 传奇文学: *(a) medieval romance* 中世纪的传奇故事. **2** [U] romantic atmosphere or feeling 浪漫气氛; 传奇色彩: *There was an air of romance about the old castle.* 那座古堡颇有传奇色彩. **3** [C] love story; love affair resembling this 爱情故事; 风流韵事: *She writes romances about rich men and beautiful women.* 她写的是富翁美女的爱情故事. ○ *a holiday romance* 假日的风流事. **4** [C, U] (instance of) colourful exaggeration or make-believe 绘声绘色的夸张或虚构; 虚构的情节: *The story he told was complete romance.* 他说的那件事纯属虚构.

▷ **ro·mance** *v* [I] exaggerate or distort the truth in an imaginative way; romanticize 凭借想像夸张、歪曲或捏造事实; 赋予浪漫色彩: *given to colourful romancing* 爱绘声绘色地夸张事实.

Ro·man·esque /ˌrəʊməˈnesk; ˌromənˋɛsk/ *adj, n* [U] (of the) style of architecture current in Europe from about 1050 to 1200, with round arches, thick walls, huge vaulting, etc 罗马风格(的), 罗马式(的)(约1050年至1200年流行于欧洲的建筑风格, 以使用圆拱、厚墙、巨大拱顶等为特征).

Romano- *comb form* 构词成分 Roman; of Rome 罗马的: *Romano-British settlements* 罗马人在英国的居民点.

ro·man·tic /rəʊˈmæntɪk; roˈmæntɪk/ *adj* **1** appealing to the emotions by its imaginative, heroic or picturesque quality (因有想像力、侠义气概或生动性)动人的, 有浪漫色彩的, 传奇的: *romantic scenes, adventures, tales* 富于传奇色彩的场面、冒险、故事 ○ *The Lake District is a very romantic area.* 英国湖区很有浪漫色彩. **2** [esp attrib 尤作定语] involving a love affair 爱情的; 罗曼蒂克的: *a romantic involvement* 堕入情网 ○ *romantic complications* 爱情上的纠葛. **3** (of people, their characters, etc) enjoying emotional situations (指人、性格等)多情的, 浪漫的: *She has a dreamy romantic nature.* 她爱幻想又多情. **4** (also **Romantic**) [esp attrib 尤作定语] (of music, literature, etc) marked by feeling rather than intellect; preferring wild nature, passion, etc to order and proportion (指音乐、文学等)浪漫主义的: *Keats is one of the greatest Romantic poets.* 济慈是伟大的浪漫主义诗人. ○ *a masterpiece of the Romantic school/movement* 浪漫派[浪漫主义运动]的杰作.

▷ **ro·man·tic** *n* **1** person who enjoys romantic situations 浪漫的人. **2** (also **Romantic**) romantic artist 浪漫派艺术家. **ro·man·tic·ally** /-klɪ; -klɪ/ *adv*.

ro·man·ti·cism /rəʊˈmæntɪsɪzəm; roˈmæntəˌsɪzəm/ *n* [U] **1** romantic feelings, attitudes or behaviour 浪漫的感情、态度或行为. **2** (also **Romanticism**) Romantic tendency in literature, art and music (文艺及音乐中的)浪漫主义. Cf 参看 CLASSICISM, IDEALISM 2, REALISM 2. **ro·man·ti·cist** /-tɪsɪst; -təsɪst/ *n*.

ro·man·ti·cize, -ise /-tɪsaɪz; -təˌsaɪz/ *v* [I, Tn] (*esp derog* 尤作贬义) exaggerate or distort (the truth) in an imaginative, falsely heroic, etc way (以想像的、虚构英雄事迹等方式)夸大或歪曲(事实): *Don't romanticize — stick to the facts.* 别夸夸其谈了——说实际的吧. ○ *a novel that refuses to romanticize the grim realities of war* 毫不掩盖战争中残酷现实的小说.

Ro·many /ˈrɒmənɪ; ˋrɑmənɪ/ *n* **1** [C] gipsy 吉卜赛人. **2** [U] language of the gipsies 吉卜赛语.

▷ **Ro·many** *adj* [usu attrib 通常作定语] of gipsies or their language 吉卜赛人的; 吉卜赛语的.

romp /rɒmp; rɑmp/ *v* **1** [I, Ipr, Ip] (esp of children or animals) play about together in a lively way, running, jumping, etc (尤指儿童或动物)在一起玩耍、跑跳、嬉戏等: *puppies romping around in the garden* 在园子里跑来跑去的小狗. **2** (idm 习语) **romp home/in** win, succeed, etc easily 轻易地取胜、成功等: *romp home in a race* 在速度比赛中轻易取胜 ○ *The Liberal candidate romped in with thousands of votes to spare.* 自由党候选人轻易获胜, 超出所需选票数以千计. **3** (phr v) **romp through (sth)** (*infml* 口) succeed easily (in a test, etc) (在考核等中)轻易通过: *She romped through her exams.* 她毫不费力就考及格了.

▷ **romp** *n* [sing] instance of romping 玩耍; 嬉戏: *have a romp about* 四处玩耍嬉戏.

rompers /ˈrɒmpəz; ˋrɑmpəˑz/ *n* [pl] (also ˈ**romper-suit** [C]) one-piece suit worn by a small child or baby (幼儿穿的)连衫裤.

rondo /ˈrɒndəʊ; ˋrɑndo/ *n* (*pl* **~s**) piece of music in which the main theme returns a number of times 廻旋曲.

rönt·gen = ROENTGEN.

rood /ru:d; rud/ *n* crucifix, esp one erected on the middle of a rood-screen 有耶稣受难像的十字架(尤指竖立在圣坛屏中央的).

□ ˈ**rood-screen** *n* carved wooden or stone screen separating the nave and choir(2) of a church 圣坛屏(教堂中分隔中堂和唱诗班席位的木雕或石雕屏风).

roof /ru:f; ruf/ *n* (*pl* **~s**) **1** structure covering or forming the top of a building, vehicle, etc (建筑物、车辆等的)顶部; 屋顶; 车顶: *a flat/sloping roof* 平的[斜的]顶 ○ *fly above the roofs of the city* 在城市上空飞行 ○ *Although divorced, they continued to live under the same roof,* ie in the same house. 他们已经离婚了, 但仍然同住在一所房子里. ○ *a library and concert-hall both under one roof,* ie in the same building 设在同一座建筑物内的图书馆和音乐厅 ○ *have a/no roof over one's head,* ie have a/no place to live 有[没有]住处 ○ *The roof of the mine passage collapsed.* 巷道的顶部塌了. ○ *a painful sore in the roof of her mouth,* ie the palate 她腭部的痛处 ○ (*rhet* 修辞) *the roof of the world,* ie the highest part, esp a mountain (range) or plateau 世界屋脊(最高的部分, 尤指山脉或高原). ⇨illus at App 1 见附录1插图, pages vi, xii. **2** (idm 习语) **go through the roof** (*infml* 口) become very angry 怒气冲天: *She went through the roof when I told her I'd crashed her car.* 我告诉她我把她的汽车撞坏了, 她气得大发雷霆. Cf 参看 HIT THE CEILING/ROOF (HIT[1]). **raise the roof** ⇨ RAISE.

▷ **roof** *v* (*pt, pp* **~ed** /ru:ft; ruft/) [Tn, Tn·pr, Tn·p] **~ sth (over/in) (with sth)** cover sth with a roof; be a roof for sth 给某物装上顶部; 作某物的顶部: *roof (over) a yard (with sheets of plastic)* (用塑料板)给院子搭顶篷 ○ *a plan to roof in the stadium* 给露天体育场加盖顶篷的计划 ○ *a hut crudely roofed with strips of bark* 简简单单用树皮作顶的小屋.

roof·ing *n* [U] material used for roofs 作顶部用的材料: [attrib 作定语] ˈ*roofing material, tiles, slates, felt, etc* 盖屋顶用的材料、瓦、石板、油毡等.

□ ˈ**roof-garden** *n* garden on the flat roof of a building (建筑物平顶上的)屋顶花园.

ˈ**roof-rack** (also ˈ**luggage-rack**) *n* frame for carrying luggage, etc attached to the roof of a vehicle 车顶架(机动车顶部供装载行李等用的). ⇨illus at App 1 见附录1插图, page xii.

ˈ**roof-top** *n* **(a)** outer surface of a roof 屋顶的外层. **(b)** (*esp rhet* 尤作修辞) top of a building 建筑物的顶部: *flying swiftly over the roof-tops* 迅速飞越屋顶.

ˈ**roof-tree** *n* strong horizontal main beam at the highest point of a roof 脊檩; 大梁; 正梁.

rook[1] /rʊk; rʊk/ *n* large black crow that nests in colonies 秃鼻乌鸦.

▷ **rook·ery** /-ərɪ; -ərɪ/ *n* **1 (a)** colony of rooks 秃鼻乌鸦群. **(b)** group of trees where rooks nest 秃鼻乌鸦结巢的丛林. **2** colony or breeding-place of penguins or seals 企鹅群; 海豹群; 企鹅或海豹繁殖地.

rook[2] /rʊk; rʊk/ *v* [Tn, Tn·pr] **~ sb (of sth)** (*infml* 口) **(a)** overcharge sb 向某人索高价: *That hotel really rooked us.* 那家旅馆可真敲了我们竹杠. **(b)** cheat or swindle sb at cards, etc 在纸牌等戏中欺骗或欺诈某人: *They rooked him of £100.* 他们在纸牌戏中骗走他100英镑.

rook[3] /rʊk; rʊk/ *n* = CASTLE 2.

rookie /ˈrʊkɪ; ˋrʊkɪ/ *n* (*infml* 口) inexperienced newcomer to a team, an organization, etc 无经验的新成员；新手；生手：[attrib 作定语] *a rookie half-back* 新来的前卫队员.

room /ru:m, rʊm; rum, rʊm/ *n* **1** (**a**) [C] part of a building enclosed by walls or partitions, and with a floor and ceiling 房间；室：*a large airy room on the first floor* 二楼的宽敞通风的房间 ○ *He's in the next room.* 他在隔壁房间. (**b**) **rooms** [pl] set of these for living in, usu rented; lodgings 一套房间(通常指租的)；寓所：*He's staying in rooms in West Kensington.* 他住在肯辛顿西区的寓所里. **2** [U] **~ (for sb/sth); ~ (to do sth)** space that is or could be occupied, or is enough for a purpose (可)占用的空间或地方：*Is there enough room for me in the car?* 汽车里还有我坐的地方吗？○ *This table takes up too much room.* 这张桌子太占地方了. ○ *Can you make room on that shelf for more books?* 你能在那个架子上腾出些地方再放些书吗？○ *There's no room to work here.* 这里没有可工作的空间. ○ *standing room only*, ie no room to sit down, eg in a bus, theatre, etc 仅有站位(无坐位，如在公共汽车、戏院等内). ⇨Usage at SPACE 用法见SPACE. **3** [U] **~ (for sth)** opportunity; scope 机会；范围：*There's (plenty of) room for improvement in your work*, ie It is not as good as it could be. 你的工作还有(许多)改进的余地. ○ *There's no room for doubt*, ie It is quite certain. 没有怀疑的余地. **4** (idm 习语) **cramped for room/space** ⇨ CRAMP[2]. **leave the room** ⇨ LEAVE[1]. **no room to swing a 'cat** (*infml saying* 口，谚) not enough space to live, work, etc in 没有生活、工作等的足够空间：*There's no room/There isn't (enough) room to swing a cat in here.* 这里地方过于狭窄.

▷ **room** *v* [Ipr] (*US*) occupy a room or rooms in sb else's house; lodge[2](2) (在别人家中)占一间或一套房间；租住；寄宿：*He's rooming with my friend Alan.* 他住在我的朋友艾伦家里.

-roomed (forming compound *adjs* 用以构成复合形容词) having the stated number of rooms 有所示数目的房间的：*a ten-roomed house* 有十个房间的一所房子.

roomer *n* (*US*) person who rooms; lodger (在别人家中住的)房客；寄宿者.

room·ful /-fʊl; -,fʊl/ *n* amount or number a room will hold 一室所能容纳的数量：*a whole roomful of antiques* 满室的古董.

roomy *adj* (**-ier**, **-iest**) (*approv* 褒) having plenty of space to contain things or people 宽敞的：*a surprisingly roomy car* 极其宽敞的汽车. **roomi·ness** *n* [U].

□ **'rooming-house** *n* (*US*) building where furnished rooms can be rented 连家具出租的公寓.

'room-mate *n* person living in the same room or set of rooms as another, eg in a college or lodgings 同住一室的人(如学校或寄宿舍中的).

'room service (those who provide) service of food, etc to a guest in his hotel room (旅馆的)送食物到客房的服务(人员)：*Call room service and ask for some coffee.* 叫客房服务员送些咖啡来.

roost /ru:st; rust/ *n* **1** place where birds perch or settle for sleep 禽鸟栖息处：*One of the main starling roosts is on top of the Town Hall.* 市政厅的房顶是欧椋鸟的一个主要栖息处. **2** (idm 习语) **come home to roost** ⇨ HOME[3]. **rule the roost** ⇨ RULE *v*.

▷ **roost** *v* [I, Ipr] (of birds) settle for sleep; perch (指鸟)栖息.

rooster /'ru:stə(r); 'rustɚ/ *n* (*esp US*) = COCK[1] 1.

root[1] /ru:t; rut/ *n* **1** [C] part of a plant that keeps it firmly in the soil and absorbs water and food from the soil (植物的)根(部)：*a plant with very long roots* 根部很长的植物 ○ *pull a plant up by the roots* 把一植物连根拔起. **2 roots** [pl] family ties, feelings, etc that attach a person emotionally and culturally to the society or community where he grew up and/or lives or where his ancestors lived (家族的)根：*Many Americans have roots in Europe.* 许多美国人祖籍在欧洲. ○ *She has no real roots in this area.* 她原籍不在这儿. **3** [C] part of a hair, tooth, nail or tongue that attaches it to the rest of the body (毛发、牙齿、指甲或舌头的)根部：*pull hair out by* (ie complete with) *the roots* 把头发连根拔掉. **4** [C esp *sing* 尤作单数] (*fig* 比喻) source or basis 根源；根基；根本；基础：*The root of the problem is lack of trust.* 产生这问题的根源在于缺乏信任. ○ *Money is often said to be the root of all evil.* 金钱常常说成是万恶之源. **5** [C] (also **base form**) (*grammar*) form of a word on which its other forms are said to be based 词根：*'Walk' is the root of 'walks', 'walked', 'walking' and 'walker'.* walk 是 walks、walked、walking、walker 的词根. **6** [C] (*mathematics* 数) quantity which, when multiplied by itself a certain number of times, produces another quantity 方根；根：*4 is the square root of 16 (4 x 4 = 16), the cube root of 64 (4 x 4 x 4 = 64) and the fourth root of 256 (4 x 4 x 4 x 4 = 256).* 4是16的平方根、是64的立方根、是256的四次方根. ⇨App 4 见附录4. **7** (idm 习语) **get at/get to/strike at the 'root(s) of sth** discover the source of sth (usu problematic or unpleasant) and tackle it there 找到某事物(通常指棘手的或讨厌的事物)的根源并加以解决. **pull up one's roots** ⇨ PULL[2]. **put down (new) 'roots** establish oneself in a place to which one has moved 在新的地方立足. **,root and 'branch** thorough(ly); complete(ly) 彻底(的)；完全(的)：*destroy an organization root and branch* 彻底摧毁一个组织 ○ [attrib 作定语] *root-and-branch reforms* 全面的改革. **the root cause (of sth)** the fundamental cause 根本原因：*He argues that one of the root causes of crime is poverty.* 他认为犯罪的一个根本原因是贫穷. **take/strike root** (**a**) (of a plant) send down a root or roots (指植物)生根，扎根. (**b**) (*fig* 比喻) become established 建立；确立：*a country where democracy has never really taken root* 从未真正建立起民主制度的国家.

▷ **root·less** *adj* having no root or roots 无根的；无根基的：*a rootless wandering life* 飘泊无依的生活. **root·less·ness** *n* [U].

□ **'root beer** (*esp US*) non-alcoholic drink flavoured with the roots of various plants 根汁饮料(用植物根茎调味的不含酒精的饮料).

'root-crop *n* crop grown for its edible roots, eg turnips, carrots, etc 根用作物，块根植物(如萝卜等).

'root vegetable edible root eaten as a vegetable, eg a turnip, carrot, etc 块根蔬菜(如萝卜等).

root[2] /ru:t; rut/ *v* **1** (**a**) [I, Ipr] (of a plant) send down roots and begin to grow (指植物)生根成长：*This type of plant roots easily.* 这种植物容易生根成长. (**b**) [Tn, Tn·pr] plant (sth) 种植(某物)：*Root the cuttings in peat.* 把插枝扦插泥炭中. **2** [Tn·pr esp passive 尤用于被动语态] cause (sb) to stand fixed and unmoving 使(某人)站立不动：*be/stand rooted to the spot/ground* 站在那里不动 ○ *Fear rooted him to the spot.* 他吓得呆若木鸡. **3** [usu passive 通常用于被动语态：Tn, Tn·pr] establish (sth) deeply and firmly 使(某事物)深深扎根；牢固地树立(某事物)：*a story firmly rooted in reality* 深深扎根于现实中的小说 ○ *Her affection for him is deeply rooted.* 她对他矢志不渝. ○ *He has a rooted objection to cold baths.* 他一向反对冷水浴. **4** (phr v) **root sth out** destroy sth completely 根除某事物：*determined to root out corruption* 决心根除腐败现象. **root sth up** dig or pull up (a plant, etc) with the roots 将(植物等)连根挖出或拔起.

root[3] /ru:t; rut/ *v* (phr v) **root about/around (for sth)** (**a**) (of pigs) turn up the ground with the snout in search of food (指猪)用鼻拱土觅食：*rooting for acorns* 用鼻拱土寻觅橡实. (**b**) (of people) turn things over when searching, esp in an untidy way (指人)翻寻，(尤指)乱翻：*What are you doing rooting around in my desk?* 你在我的书桌里乱翻什么呀？ **root for sb/sth** (no passive 不用于被动语态) (*infml* 口) cheer for sb/sth; support sb/sth wholeheartedly 给某人[某事物]打气；全力支持某人[某事物]：*We're rooting for the college baseball team.* 我们在给学院的棒球队加油. ○ *We're all rooting for you — good luck with your job interview!* 我们全都支持你——祝你求职面试成功！ **root sth out** (*infml* 口) find sth after hard searching 终于找到某物：*I managed to root out a copy of the document.* 我好不容易才找到了文件的副本.

rope /rəʊp; rop/ *n* **1** [C, U] (length of) thick cord or wire made by twisting finer cords or wires together (由多股拧成的)粗绳或金属缆：*We tied his feet together with (a) rope.* 我们用绳子把他的双脚捆在一起. ○ *The kids tied a (piece of) rope to the tree and used it as a swing.* 孩子们把(一根)绳子系在树上当作秋千玩. **2** [C] number of similar things twisted or strung together 缠结或串连成绳状的东西：*a rope of onions, pearls, etc* 一串

洋葱、珍珠等. **3 the rope** [sing] (*infml or rhet* 口或修辞) death by hanging 绞刑: *bring back the rope*, ie the death penalty 恢复死刑. **4** (idm 习语) **give sb enough ˈrope (and he'll hang himself)** (*saying* 谚) allow sb enough freedom of action (and he will bring about his own downfall) 任由某人为所欲为(终将自作自受). **give sb plenty of/some ˈrope** allow sb much/some freedom of action 给某人以充分的[一定程度的]行动自由. **money for jam/old rope** ⇨ MONEY. **show sb/know/learn the ˈropes** explain to sb/know/learn the procedures or rules for doing sth 向某人解释[弄清楚/学习]做某事的程序或规则: *She's just started — it'll take her a week or two to learn the ropes.* 她是新手——要用一两个星期的时间熟悉情况.

▷ **rope** *v* **1** [Tn, Tn·pr, Tn·p] fasten or bind (sb/sth) with (a) rope 用绳系住或捆绑(某人[某物]): *rope* (ie lasso and tie up) *cattle* 用套索套牛 ○ *They roped him to a tree.* 他们把他绑在树上. ○ *climbers roped together* 用绳联结在一起的登山者. **2** (phr v) **rope sb in (to do sth)** (*infml* 口) (esp passive 尤用于被动语态) persuade sb (to take part in an activity) 说服某人(参与一项活动): *All her friends have been roped in to help organize the event.* 她所有的朋友都已动员来协助组织这一活动. **rope sth off** enclose sth with rope(s) 用绳围起某物: *rope off the scene of the accident* 把事故现场用绳子拦起来.

□ **rope-ladder** *n* ladder made of two long ropes connected by short cross-pieces 绳梯.

ropy (also **ropey**) /ˈrəʊpɪ; ˋropɪ/ *adj* (**-ier**, **-iest**) (*Brit infml* 口) poor in quality, health, etc (质量、健康等)糟糕的, 差劲的: *ropy old furniture* 破旧的家具 ○ *I'm feeling pretty ropey.* 我觉得身体很不舒服. ▷ **ro·pi·ness** *n* [U].

Roque·fort /ˈrɒkfɔ:(r); *US* ˈrəʊkfərt; ˋrokfɚt/ *n* [U] type of blue cheese made from ewes' milk 罗克福尔干酪(用羊奶制成, 有蓝色霉菌花纹).

ro·ro /ˈrəʊrəʊ; ˋro,ro/ *abbr* 缩写 = roll-on roll-off.

ros·ary /ˈrəʊzərɪ; ˋrozərɪ/ *n* **1 the rosary** [sing] (book containing a) set series of prayers used in the Roman Catholic Church (天主教的)玫瑰经, 玫瑰经经文书: *say the rosary* 念玫瑰经. **2** [C] (**a**) string of beads for keeping count of these prayers (念玫瑰经时用的)数珠, 念珠. (**b**) similar string of beads used in other religions (其他宗教用的)数珠, 念珠.

rose[1] *pt* of RISE[2].

rose[2] /rəʊz; roz/ *n* **1** [C] (bush or shrub, usu with thorns on its stems, bearing an) ornamental and usu sweet-smelling flower, growing in cultivated and wild varieties 蔷薇科植物; 蔷薇(花); 玫瑰(花): *I found him pruning his roses.* 我看见他在修剪玫瑰. ○ *a bunch of red roses* 一束红玫瑰花 ○ [attrib 作定语] *a ˈrose bush* 玫瑰丛. ⇨ illus at App 1 见附录1插图, page ii. **2** [C] pink colour 粉红色: *the rose (colour) of clouds at dawn* 黎明时分云彩所呈现的粉红的颜色. **3** [C] perforated nozzle of a watering-can or hose-pipe, used for sprinkling plants, etc (喷壶或水管的)莲蓬式喷嘴. **4** [C] (also ˈ**ceiling rose**) (esp plaster) decoration on a ceiling around the point where the main light is fitted 天花板上主灯周围的花饰(尤指灰泥制的). **5** (idm 习语) **a bed of roses** ⇨ BED[1]. **not all ˈroses** having some discomforts or disadvantages; not perfect 也有不如意或不利的地方; 并非完美: *Being an opera star is not all roses by any means.* 当上了歌剧明星也决非事事如意. **look at/see sth through rose-coloured/rose-tinted ˈspectacles, etc** think of/regard sth (esp life in general) too optimistically 看问题(尤指生活的整体)过于乐观.

□ ˈ**rosebay** *n* (*US*) = RHODODENDRON.

ˈ**rose-bud** *n* bud of a rose 玫瑰花蕾: [attrib 作定语] *a rose-bud mouth*, ie one having this shape 玫瑰花蕾般的嘴.

ˈ**rose-hip** *n* = HIP[2].

ˈ**rose-water** *n* [U] perfume made from roses 玫瑰香水.

ˌ**rose-ˈwindow** *n* ornamental circular window, usu in a church 圆花窗(通常为教堂中的).

ˈ**rosewood** *n* [U] type of high-quality hardwood used for making furniture 黄檀木(木材坚硬, 质地优良, 用以制造家具): [attrib 作定语] *a rosewood table* 黄檀木的桌子.

rosé /ˈrəʊzeɪ; *US* rəʊˈzeɪ; roˋze/ *n* [U] any of several types of pink wine 粉红色葡萄酒: *an excellent (bottle of) rosé* (一瓶)优质红葡萄酒. Cf 参看 RED WINE (RED[1]), WHITE WINE (WHITE[1]).

ros·eate /ˈrəʊzɪət; ˋrozɪɪt/ *adj* [usu attrib 通常作定语] (*rhet* 修辞) deep pink 深粉红色的: *the roseate hues of dawn* 黎明时分天空呈现的深粉红色.

rose·mary /ˈrəʊzmərɪ; *US* -merɪ; ˋroz,mɛrɪ/ *n* [U] (**a**) fragrant leaves of a type of evergreen shrub, used for flavouring food 迷迭香(一种常绿灌木的叶子, 有香味, 用作调味品). (**b**) this shrub 迷迭香(指灌木).

ros·ette /rəʊˈzet; roˋzɛt/ *n* **1** rose-shaped badge, usu of silk or ribbon 玫瑰形标志; (通常指丝带或缎带做的)玫瑰花结: *The fans are all wearing Arsenal rosettes*, ie showing their support for Arsenal football team. 球迷全都佩带着表示支持阿塞纳尔球队的玫瑰花结. ○ *the Tory candidate with his big blue rosette* 佩带着蓝色大玫瑰花结的保守党候选人. **2** rose-shaped carving on stonework, etc 石制品等上雕刻的玫瑰形花样.

rosin /ˈrɒzɪn; *US* ˈrɒzn; ˋrɑzn̩/ *n* [U] type of resin(1) used on the strings and bows of stringed musical instruments 松香.

▷ **rosin** *v* [Tn] rub (sth) with rosin 用松香涂(某物).

ros·ter /ˈrɒstə(r); ˋrɑstɚ/ *n* (*esp US*) (esp in the army, etc) list of names showing duties to be performed and the times at which those named are to perform them (尤指军队等的)值勤人员名单.

▷ **ros·ter** *v* [Tn] (*esp US*) place (sb) on a roster 将(某人)列入值勤人员名单中: *proposals for more flexible rostering* 较灵活的值勤安排建议 ○ *I've been rostered to work all weekend!* 给我安排整个周末都要值班!

rost·rum /ˈrɒstrəm; ˋrɑstrəm/ *n* (*pl* **~s** or **-tra** /-trə; -trə/) raised platform from which public speeches are made 演讲台; 讲坛: *mount the rostrum* 登上讲坛.

rosy /ˈrəʊzɪ; ˋrozɪ/ *adj* (**-ier**, **-iest**) **1** of the colour of red roses; deep pink 玫瑰红的; 深粉红色的: *rosy cheeks*, ie indicating good health 红润的脸颊. **2** (*fig* 比喻) very encouraging; very hopeful 令人鼓舞的; 极有希望的: *The prospects couldn't be rosier.* 前景好得不能再好了. ○ *She painted a rosy picture of the firm's future.* 她认为这家公司前途十分美好. ▷ **rosi·ness** *n* [U].

rot /rɒt; rɑt/ *v* (**-tt-**) (**a**) [I, Ip] decay naturally through the action of bacteria, fungi, etc 腐烂; 腐坏: *a heap of rotting leaves* 一堆腐烂的叶子 ○ *The wood has rotted away completely.* 那木头已完全朽了. ○ (*fig* 比喻) *He was thrown into prison and left to rot.* 他被关进监牢任其苟延残喘. (**b**) [Tn, Tn·p] cause (sth) to decay or become useless; damage 使(某物)腐烂或无用; 损坏: *Oil and grease will rot the rubber of your tyres.* 油污能腐蚀轮胎橡胶. ○ *Too much sugar will rot your teeth away.* 吃糖太多就要损坏牙齿.

▷ **rot** *n* **1** [U] rotting; rottenness 腐烂; 腐坏: *a tree affected by rot* 枯朽的树 ○ *Rot has set in*, ie started. 已经逐渐腐烂了. ○ *There's dry rot in the floor.* 地板已经朽了. **2** [U] (*dated Brit sl* 旧, 俚) nonsense; absurd statement(s) or argument(s) 胡说; 谬论: *Don't talk such utter rot!* 别说这种荒唐话了! ○ *'They're bound to win.' 'Rot! They haven't a chance!'* '他们一定赢.' '胡说! 他们毫无希望!' **3 the rot** [sing] liver disease of sheep (羊的)肝蛭病. **4** (idm 习语) **the rot sets ˈin** conditions begin to get worse 情况开始变坏: *The rot set in when we lost that important customer in Japan.* 我们失去了日本的那家重要客户后, 情况越来越糟了. **stop the rot** ⇨ STOP.

□ ˈ**rot-gut** *n* [U] (*sl* 俚) cheap and unpleasant alcoholic drink, esp inferior spirits that can harm the stomach 廉价而难喝的酒(尤指伤胃的劣质烈酒).

rota /ˈrəʊtə; ˋrotə/ *n* (*pl* **~s**) (*Brit*) (*US* **roster**) list showing duties to be done or names of people to do them in turn 勤务轮值表.

ro·tary /ˈrəʊtərɪ; ˋrotərɪ/ *adj* [esp attrib 尤作定语] **1** (*fml* 文) (of motion) moving round a central point; circular (指运动)旋转的. **2** (of a machine, an engine, etc) using this type of motion (指机器、发动机等)转动的: *a rotary drill, clothes drier, switch, etc* 旋转式钻机、干衣机、开关等 ○ *a rotary printing machine/press*, ie one which prints from metal plates attached to revolving cylinders 轮转印刷机. Cf 参看 RECIPROCATE 2.

▷ **ro·tary** *n* (*US*) = ROUNDABOUT 2.

ro·tate /rəʊˈteɪt; *US* ˈrəʊteɪt; ˋrotet/ *v* [I, Ipr, Tn, Tn·pr] **1** (cause sth to) move in circles round a central point

(使某物)旋转或转动: *Danger: rotating blades.* 危险: 叶片旋转, 注意安全. ○ *rotate the handle gently* 轻轻转动手柄. **2** (cause sb/sth to) take turns or recur in a particular order (使某人[某事物])轮流或按顺序循环: *The post of chairman rotates among members of the committee.* 主席一职由委员会的成员轮流担任. ○ *the technique of rotating crops* 轮种作物的技术.

▷ **ro·ta·tion** /rəʊˈteɪʃn; roˈteʃən/ *n* **1** (**a**) [U] rotating or being rotated 旋转; 转动: *the rotation of the Earth* 地球的自转. (**b**) [C] one complete movement of this type (旋转的)一圈; (一)转: *five rotations per hour* 每小时旋转五圈. **2** [C, U] regular organized sequence of things or events 轮流; 轮换: *the rotation of crops/crop rotation*, ie varying the crops grown each year on the same land to avoid exhausting the soil 作物的轮作[轮种]. **3** (idm 习语) **in rotation** in turn; in regular succession 轮流地; 轮番地; 循环地: *The chairmanship of the committee changes in rotation.* 委员会主席一职是轮流担任的.

ro·ta·tional /-ʃənl; -ʃənl/ *adj*.

ro·tat·ory /ˈrəʊtətərɪ, rəʊˈteɪtərɪ; *US* ˈrəʊtətɔːrɪ; ˈrotə,torɪ/ *adj* (*fml* 文) rotating; of rotation 旋转的; 轮流的: *rotatory motion* 旋转运动.

rote /rəʊt; rot/ *n* (idm 习语) **by ˈrote** by heart; from memory, without thinking of the meaning 凭记忆: *do, say, know, learn, etc sth by rote* 机械地做某事、脱口而出、凭记忆、死记硬背.

□ **ˈrote learning** method of study based on learning facts, etc by heart without considering their meaning 死记硬背的学习方法.

ro·tis·serie /rəʊˈtiːsərɪ; roˈtisərɪ/ *n* cooking device for roasting meat, etc on a revolving spit²(1) 旋转式烤炉.

ro·tor /ˈrəʊtə(r); ˈrotɚ/ *n* rotating part of a machine, esp on a helicopter 机器的旋转部分; (尤指直升飞机的)旋翼. ⇨illus at HELICOPTER 见 HELICOPTER 插图.

rot·ten /ˈrɒtn; ˈrɑtn̩/ *adj* **1** decayed; having gone bad 腐烂的; 变质的: *rotten eggs* 已坏的蛋 ○ *The wood was so rotten you could put your finger through it.* 木头已经朽了, 用手指一捅就是一个窟窿. **2** morally corrupt 道德败坏的; 腐化的: *an organization, a person, a policy that is rotten to the core*, ie completely rotten 腐败透顶的组织、人、政策. **3** (*infml* 口) very bad; very unpleasant 极坏的; 极讨厌的: *The film was pretty rotten.* 这部影片简直糟透了. ○ *She's a rotten cook.* 她做的饭菜真差劲. ○ *What rotten luck!* 真倒霉! ○ *rotten weather* 讨厌的天气.

▷ **rot·tenly** *adv* (*infml* 口) very badly 极坏地: *Her husband treated her rottenly all their married life.* 他们结婚以来, 她丈夫待她坏极了.

rot·ten·ness *n* [U].

rot·ter /ˈrɒtə(r); ˈrɑtɚ/ *n* (*sl joc* 俚, 谑) nasty or worthless person 可恶的人; 无赖: *He's a complete rotter!* 他是个十足的大坏蛋!

ro·tund /rəʊˈtʌnd; roˈtʌnd/ *adj* (*euph or joc* 婉或谑) (of a person) rounded; plump; fat (指人)肥胖的, 胖墩墩的, 胖的.

▷ **ro·tund·ity** /-ətɪ; -ətɪ/ *n* [U] (*euph or joc* 婉或谑) state of being rotund 肥胖; 胖.

ro·tundly *adv*.

ro·tunda /rəʊˈtʌndə; roˈtʌndə/ *n* type of round building or hall, esp one with a domed roof 圆形建筑物或大厅(尤指有半球形屋顶的).

rouble (also **ruble**) /ˈruːbl; ˈrubl̩/ *n* unit of money in the former USSR; 100 kopecks 卢布(前苏联发行的货币的单位, 合100戈比).

roué /ˈruːeɪ; ruˈe/ *n* (*dated derog* 旧, 贬) dissolute or lecherous man, esp an elderly one 放荡的或好色的男子(尤指年长的).

rouge /ruːʒ; ruʒ/ *n* [U] **1** reddish cosmetic for colouring the cheeks 胭脂. **2** fine red powder used for polishing metal 铁丹; 红铁粉: *jewellers' rouge* 抛光铁丹.

▷ **rouge** *v* [Tn] colour (the cheeks) with rouge 用胭脂搽(脸颊).

rough¹ /rʌf; rʌf/ *adj* (**-er, -est**) **1** having an uneven or irregular surface; not level or smooth 高低不平的; 参差不齐的; 不平滑的; 粗糙的: *A jeep is ideal for driving over rough terrain.* 吉普车很适合在高低不平的路面上行驶. ○ *a rough stone wall* 里出外进的石墙 ○ *rough hands* 粗糙的手 ○ *rough woollen cloth* 粗糙的毛料布. Cf 参看 SMOOTH¹. **2** not gentle or calm; moving or acting violently 粗鲁的; 粗暴的; 粗野的; 剧烈的: *rough behaviour* 粗暴的行为 ○ *His children are very rough with their toys.* 他的孩子很不爱惜玩具. ○ *Rugby is a rough sport.* 橄榄球是一种很剧烈的运动. ○ *That area of the city is quite rough* (ie dangerous) *after dark.* 那一带市区天黑之后很危险. ○ *This suitcase has had some rough handling*, ie has been badly treated. 这个手提箱用得很不在意. ○ *He has a rough tongue*, ie often speaks rudely or sharply. 他讲话很不中听(言语粗野或尖刻). ○ *rough seas* 风浪大的海 ○ *have a rough crossing from Dover to Calais* 在大风大浪中从多佛港横渡到加莱港. **3** made or done without (much) attention to detail, esp in haste or as a first attempt; approximate 粗制的; 粗略的; (尤指)粗率的或初步的; 概略的: *a rough sketch, calculation, translation* 草图、概略的计算、粗略的翻译 ○ *a rough draft of his speech* 他的演讲草稿 ○ *Give me a rough idea of your plans.* 请把你那计划的大概意思告诉我. ○ *I'll give you a rough estimate of the costs.* 我给你大致估计一下费用. ○ *rough justice*, ie more or less fair, but not necessarily strictly according to law 勉强的公正. **4** harsh (in taste, sound, etc) (味道、声音等)令人不快的; 难吃的; 刺耳的: *a rough red wine* 难喝的红葡萄酒 ○ *Your engine sounds a bit rough — you'd better have it checked.* 你的发动机声音有点不正常 —— 最好检查检查. ○ *a rough voice* 粗厉的嗓音. **5** (*infml* 口) unwell 不舒服: *I feel a bit rough — I'm going to bed.* 我有点儿不舒服 —— 想去睡觉了. **6** (idm 习语) **be rough (on sb)** (*infml* 口) be unpleasant or unlucky (for sb) (对某人来说)不愉快的, 不幸的: *Losing his job was rough (on him).* 他失业了, 真倒霉. **give sb/have a rough ˈtime** (cause sb to) experience hardship, be treated severely, etc (使某人)受苦、受到严厉的对待等: *She had a really rough time when her father died.* 她在父亲去世以后受了很多罪. **a raw/rough deal** ⇨ DEAL⁴. **ˌrough and ˈready** adequate but unrefined; crude but effective 能满足需要但不精美; 简陋但有效: *The accommodation is rather rough and ready, I'm afraid.* 依我看, 这个住处还算差强人意. ○ [attrib 作定语] *rough and ready methods* 原始但实用的方法. **a rough ˈdiamond** person who is good-natured but lacking polished manners, education, etc 心地善良但粗俗、缺乏教养等的人.

▷ **roughly** *adv* **1** in a rough manner 粗鲁地; 粗暴地; 粗略地: *treat sb roughly* 粗暴地对待某人 ○ *a roughly made table*, ie not finely finished 做工粗糙的桌子. **2** approximately 大概; 大约: *It should cost roughly £10.* 这大约10英镑. ○ *about forty miles, roughly speaking* 大致说来, 约四十英里.

rough·ness *n* [U] quality or state of being rough 粗糙; 粗略; 粗率; 粗鲁; 粗厉: *the roughness of his chin* 他下巴的粗糙不光滑.

□ **ˌrough-and-ˈtumble** *n*, *adj* (fight, struggle, etc that is) boisterous and disorganized, but usu not serious 吵闹而混乱的(打、斗等)(通常不很严重): *All the pups were having a rough-and-tumble in the garden.* 小狗都正在花园里又叫又闹.

ˈrough house (*infml* 口) disturbance with violent and noisy behaviour 大吵大闹.

ˌrough ˈluck bad luck, worse than is deserved (不该有的)坏运气.

ˈroughneck *n* (*US infml* 口) **1** rowdy person; hooligan 粗暴而好吵闹的人; 流氓. **2** worker on an oil rig 油井工人.

rough² /rʌf; rʌf/ *adv* **1** in a rough manner 粗鲁地; 粗暴地; 粗略地: *a team that is notorious for playing rough*, ie in a (physically) somewhat violent way 因动作粗野而声名狼藉的运动队. **2** (idm 习语) **cut up ˈrough** (*infml* 口) become angry or violent 发脾气; 暴跳如雷: *I hope he doesn't cut up rough when I tell him what I've done.* 我把我做的事情告诉他, 但愿他别发火. **live rough** ⇨ LIVE². **sleep rough** ⇨ SLEEP².

□ **ˈroughcast** *n* [U] coarse plaster containing gravel, used for covering the outside walls of buildings (含沙石的)粗灰泥(用以抹建筑物的外墙).

ˈrough-hewn *adj* (*fml or rhet* 文或修辞) shaped or carved roughly 初步成形的; 粗雕的: *a rough-hewn statue* 粗凿的雕像.

ˈroughshod *adv* (idm 习语) **ride roughshod over sb/sth** ⇨ RIDE².

rough³ /rʌf; rʌf/ *n* **1** (also **the rough**) [U] part of a golf-course where the ground is uneven and the grass uncut (高尔夫球场的)深草区(场地不平、杂草不修剪). ⇨illus at GOLF 见GOLF插图. Cf 参看 FAIRWAY 1. **2** [C] rough drawing or design, etc 草图、草样等: *Have you seen the (artwork) roughs for the new book?* 你看到那本新书的(插图)草稿了吗? **3** [C] (*infml* 口) violent lawless person; (usu male) hooligan 无法无天的人; (通常指男性)流氓: *beaten up by a gang of young roughs* 遭一帮小流氓殴打. **4** (idm 习语) **in 'rough** without great accuracy; approximately 不太精确地; 大约: *I've drawn it in rough, to give you some idea of how it looks.* 我已经把它草草画了出来, 好让你有个大概的印象. **in (the) 'rough** in an unfinished state 尚未完成: *We only saw the new painting in the rough.* 我们只见过那幅新画未完成时的样子. **take the ˌrough with the 'smooth** accept what is unpleasant or difficult as well as what is pleasant or easy 好坏一齐接受.

rough[4] /rʌf; rʌf/ *v* **1** (idm 习语) **'rough it** (*infml* 口) live without the usual comforts and conveniences of life 在没有一般的舒适和便利的条件下生活: *roughing it in the mountains* 在山区因陋就简地生活 ○ *You may have to rough it a bit if you come to stay.* 你要来住可能得吃点苦. **2** (phr v) **rough sth out** shape, plan or sketch sth roughly 拟定某事物的草案或纲要: *He roughed out some ideas for the new buildings.* 他为新建筑物提出了一些初步设想. **rough sb up** (*infml* 口) treat sb roughly, with physical violence 对某人施用暴力; 殴打某人. **rough sth up** make sth untidy or uneven 将某物弄乱或弄得不平整: *Don't rough up my hair!* 别把我的头发弄乱了!

rough·age /ˈrʌfɪdʒ; ˋrʌfɪdʒ/ *n* [U] indigestible material in certain plants used as food (eg bran) that stimulates the action of the intestines, and helps the digestion of other foods 粗糙食物(不易吸收的粗纤维, 如糠、麸, 可刺激肠蠕动, 有助于消化他种食物).

roughen /ˈrʌfn; ˋrʌfən/ *v* [I, Tn] (cause sth to) become rough (使某物)变得粗糙或不平整: *Roughen the surface before applying the paint.* 先把表面弄毛糙再涂颜料.

roul·ette /ruːˈlet; ruˋlɛt/ *n* [U] gambling game in which a small ball falls at random into one of the numbered compartments on a revolving wheel 轮盘赌: *play roulette* 玩轮盘赌 ○ [attrib 作定语] *a roulette wheel* 轮盘赌具上的轮盘.

round[1] /raʊnd; raʊnd/ *adj* **1** shaped like a circle or a ball 环形的; 球形的; 圆的: *a round plate, window, table* 圆盘、窗、桌 ○ *round cheeks*, ie plump and curved 圆而胖的脸. **2** full; complete 满的; 完全的: *a round dozen*, ie not less than twelve 整整一打 ○ *a round* (ie considerable) *sum of money* 一笔很可观的钱. **3** (idm 习语) **in round 'figures/'numbers** (given) in 10's, 100's, 1000's etc, without using the other digits 取整数的, 不计尾数的(仅以几十、几百、几千等表示): *Add £2.74 to £7.23 and you get £10.00, in round figures.* 7.23英镑加上2.74英镑取整数为10英镑. **a square peg in a round hole** ⇨ SQUARE[1].

▷ **round·ish** *adj* approximately round 近似圆形的.

roundly *adv* thoroughly; pointedly 彻底地; 直率地: *She was roundly rebuked for what she had done.* 她做出了这种事因而受到严厉的指责. ○ *We told her roundly that she was unwelcome.* 我们坦率地告诉她大家不欢迎她.

round·ness *n* [U].

□ **round brackets** parentheses 圆括号.

ˌround-'eyed *adj* with the eyes wide open in wonder, etc (因惊奇等)眼睛睁大的.

'Roundhead *n* supporter of Parliament in the English Civil War 圆颅党人(英国内战时期的议会派人士). Cf 参看 CAVALIER.

ˌround 'robin **1** statement, petition, etc signed by a number of people, often with signatures arranged in a circle to conceal who signed first 圆形签名陈情书、请愿书等(签名排列成圆形, 故分不清先后). **2** letter sent in turn to members of a group, each of whom adds sth before sending it on to the next 传阅的信件(各成员传阅并签注意见).

ˌround-'shouldered *adj* (*derog* 贬) (walking, standing, etc) with the shoulders bent forward (行走、站立等)弓背曲肩的. Cf 参看 SQUARE-SHOULDERED (SQUARE[1]).

ˌround-'table *adj* [attrib 作定语] (of a meeting, etc) in which the participants meet more or less as equals (指会议等)圆桌的(与会者平等): *a ˌround-table disˈcussion, ˈconference, etc* 圆桌讨论会、会议等.

ˌround 'trip (**a**) journey to one or more places and back again, often by a different route 环程旅行(常不循原路线返回). (**b**) (*US*) = RETURN[2] 5: [attrib 作定语] *a ˌround-trip ˈticket* 一张往返票.

round[2] /raʊnd; raʊnd/ *adv part* (For special uses with many *vs*, eg *bring round, get round*, see the *v* entries 可与许多动词连用, 如bring round、get round, 其释义见各动词词条.) **1** so as to be facing in a different (usu the opposite) direction 朝另一方向(通常指反方向): *turn the car round* 使汽车掉头 ○ *Stop turning (your heads) round to look at people.* 别再(把头)扭过去看人. **2** making the completion of a full cycle 转一整圈: *How long does it take the minute hand of the clock to go round once?* 钟的分针转一圈要多长时间? ○ *Spring will soon come round again.* 春天又快到了. **3** measuring or marking the circumference of sth 周长: *a young tree measuring only 18 inches round* 周长仅18英寸的小树 ○ *They've built a fence all round to stop the children falling in.* 他们在四周围起一圈栅栏防止儿童掉进去. **4** to all members of a group in turn 依次、逐个轮到: *Hand the biscuits round.* 把饼干分给大家. ○ *The news was quickly passed round.* 消息很快就传开了. ○ *Have we enough cups to go round?* 我们的杯子够大家用吗? **5** by a route that is longer than the most direct one 绕道地; 迂回地: *It's quickest to walk across the field — going round by road takes much longer.* 穿过田地路途最近——绕行公路要远得多. ○ *We decided to come the long way round in order to see the countryside.* 我们决定绕远路来, 为的是看看野外的景色. **6** (*infml* 口) to or at a specified place, esp where sb lives 至某处, 在某处(尤指某人的住处): *I'll be round in an hour.* 我在一小时后就到. ○ *We've invited the Frasers round this evening.* 我们邀请了弗雷泽一家今晚来作客. **7** (idm 习语) **ˌround a'bout** in the surrounding district 在附近; 在周围: *the countryside round about* 附近的郊外 ○ *all the villages round about* 附近的所有村庄. Cf 参看 AROUND[2].

R

round[3] /raʊnd; raʊnd/ *n* **1** (**a**) complete slice of bread (整片的)面包片: *a round of toast* 整片的烤面包片 ○ *two rounds* (ie sandwiches) *of ham and one of beef* 两个火腿三明治和一个牛肉三明治. (**b**) (of food) sth round; a round piece/shape (指食物)圆形食物(圆片[形]): *Cut the pastry into small rounds, one for each pie.* 把油酥面团切成小圆片, 每个馅饼用一片. **2** regular series, succession, route, etc 有规律的系列、路线等: *the daily round*, ie the ordinary occupations of every day 日常工作 ○ *His life is one long round of meetings.* 他的生活内容就是一个会议接着一个会议. ○ *the postman's round*, ie the route he takes to deliver letters 邮递员的投递路线 ○ *a doctor's rounds*, ie his series of daily visits to patients or wards 医生的巡回出诊或查房. **3** stage in a game, competition, etc (游戏、比赛等的)一轮, 一局, 一场, 一回合: *a boxing-match of ten rounds* 十回合的一场拳击比赛 ○ *He was knocked out in the third round/in Round Three.* 他在第三个回合就被击倒了. ○ *have a round of cards* 玩一局牌 ○ *play a round* (ie 18 holes) *of golf* 打一场高尔夫球(18个穴). **4** (any one of a) set or series 一连串, 一系列, 一套, 一组(中之一): *a round of drinks*, ie one for each person in a group 每人一份饮料 ○ *It's my round*, ie my turn to pay for the next set of drinks. 轮到我了(该由我付下一回饮料的费用). ○ *a new round of pay bargaining* 新的一轮增加工资的谈判. **5** burst (of applause, cheering, etc) (掌声、欢呼声等的)一阵: *Let's have a good round of applause for the next performer.* 咱们为下一个表演者热烈鼓掌吧. **6** musical composition for two or more voices in which each sings the same melody but starts at a different time 轮唱曲. **7** single shot or volley of shots from one or more guns; ammunition for this (枪炮的)一次射击或群射; 一发子弹或炮弹: *They fired several rounds at us.* 他们向我们射击了几次. ○ *We've only three rounds* (ie shells or bullets) *left.* 我们只剩下三发炮弹(或子弹)了. **8** (idm 习语) **do/go the 'rounds (of sth)** (*infml* 口) make a tour; visit places one after another 到各处玩乐; 到一处又一处: *We did/went the rounds of all the pubs in town.* 我们逐一光顾了城里所有的酒店. **go the round of** circulate in or among 流传; 散播: *The news quickly went the round of the village.* 消息很快传遍了全村. **in the 'round** (**a**) (of a theatre, play, etc) with the audience (almost) all around the stage (指剧场、演出等)舞台设

在场地中央的. (**b**) (of sculpture) made so that it can be viewed from all sides (指雕塑)圆雕的(能从各面观看的). **make one's 'rounds** make one's usual visits, esp of inspection 例行巡视; (尤指)巡查: *the production manager making his rounds* 正在进行巡查的生产部经理.

round[4] /raʊnd; raʊnd/ *prep* **1** having (sth) as the central point of a circular movement; circling (sth) 以(某物)为中心(作圆周运动); 围绕, 环绕(某物): *The earth moves round the sun.* 地球环绕太阳运行. ○ *Drake sailed round the world.* 德雷克扬帆环游世界. ○ *goldfish swimming round the bowl* 在鱼缸里转圈游动的金鱼. **2** to or at a point on the other side of (sth) 至或在(某物)另一面的某一点; 绕过(某物): *walk round a corner* 步行绕过拐角 ○ *There's a garage round the next bend.* 在下一个转弯处有个汽车服务站. ○ *Go round the roundabout and take the third exit.* 绕着环状交叉路, 从第三个出口出去. **3** covering or at points close to the edge of (sth) 围着(某物)的边缘或在其近处: *a scarf round his neck* 他脖子上围着的围巾 ○ *sitting round the table* 围桌而坐. **4** to or at various points in (sth) 至或在(某物)中之各点: *look round the room* 环视房间 ○ *show sb round* (ie all the different rooms in) *the house* 领某人参观房子(中的各个房间) ○ *There were soldiers positioned all round the town.* 城里到处都驻守着士兵. **5 ~ (about) sth** approximately (a time, amount, etc) 大约(某时刻、数量等): *We're leaving round about midday.* 我们要在中午前后走. ○ *A new roof will cost round about £1 000.* 换新顶篷需要1000英镑左右.

R

round[5] /raʊnd; raʊnd/ *v* [Tn] **1** make (sth) into the shape of a circle, a ball, an oval, etc 使(某物)成圆形、球形、卵形等: *round the lips*, eg when making the sound /uː; u/ 把嘴唇撮成圆形(如发/uː; u/音时) ○ *stones rounded by the action of water* 由于水的冲刷而变圆的石块. **2** go round (sth) 环绕(某物)而行; 绕过(某物): *We rounded the corner at high speed.* 我们以高速度绕过拐角. **3** (phr v) **round sth off** (**a**) end or complete sth satisfactorily 使某事物圆满结束或完成: *round off a sentence, speech, etc* 把句子、演说等修饰好 ○ *He rounded off his career by becoming Home Secretary.* 他担任内政大臣一职, 在事业上已登峰造极了. (**b**) take the sharp edges off sth 将某物的棱角修钝: *She rounded off the corners of the table with sandpaper.* 她用砂纸把桌角打磨光了. **round on/upon sb** attack sb (esp verbally) in sudden anger 突然发怒而攻击某人(尤指抨击): *She was amazed when he rounded on her and called her a liar.* 他突然怒斥她说谎, 她大吃一惊. **round sth out** supply sth with more explanation, detail, etc 对某事进一步解释、说明等: *John will tell you the plan in outline, and then I'll round it out.* 约翰要告诉你那个计划的梗概, 然后我再详谈. **round sb/sth up** cause sb/sth to gather in one place 使某人[某物]集合在一起: *The guide rounded up the tourists and led them back to the coach.* 导游把游客集合在一起, 领他们回到车上. ○ *cowboys rounding up cattle* 把牛赶到一起的牛仔 ○ *I spent the morning trying to round up the documents I needed.* 我用上午的时间尽力搜集所需要的文件. **round sth up/down** increase/decrease (a figure, price, etc) to the nearest whole number 将(数字、价格等)调高[降低]为整数: *A charge of £1.90 will be rounded up to £2, and one of £3.10 rounded down to £3.* 把1.90英镑的费用上调为整数2英镑, 把3.10英镑下调为整数3英镑.

□ **'round-up** *n* **1** act of gathering together people, animals or things into one place (人、动物或事物的)聚集; 聚拢: *a round-up of stray cattle* 将走失的牛群驱赶到一起. **2** summary 总结; 摘要: *Here is a round-up of the latest news.* 以下是最新的新闻综合报道.

round·about /ˈraʊndəbaʊt; ˋraʊndəˌbaʊt/ *adj* [usu attrib 通常作定语] not using the shortest or most direct route, form of words, etc 绕道的; 兜圈子的; 拐弯抹角的: *take a roundabout route* 绕远道 ○ *I heard the news in a roundabout way.* 我是间接听到这消息的. ○ *a roundabout way of saying sth* 拐弯抹角的说某事.

▷ **round·about** *n* **1** (*US* also **carousel**, **'merry-go-round**, **whirligig**) revolving platform with model horses, cars, etc for children to ride on in a playground or at a funfair 旋转木马. **2** (*US* **traffic circle**, **rotary**) multiple road junction in the form of a circle round which all traffic has to pass in the same direction 环状交叉路(多条道路的交叉口, 车辆均须按相同方向绕行). ⇨illus at App 1 见附录1插图, page xiii. Cf 参看 CIRCUS 3. **3** (idm 习语) **swings and roundabouts** ⇨ SWING[2].

roundel /ˈraʊndl; ˋraʊndl/ *n* circular identifying mark showing nationality, used on military aircraft of some countries 圆形标志(表示国别的符号, 用于某些国家的军用飞机上).

round·ers /ˈraʊndəz; ˋraʊndɚz/ *n* [sing *v*] (*Brit*) game for two teams, played with a bat and ball, in which players have to run round a circuit of bases 一种似棒球的游戏. Cf 参看 BASEBALL.

Round·head ⇨ ROUND[1].

rounds·man /ˈraʊndzmən; ˋraʊndzmən/ *n* (*pl* **-men** /-mən; -mən/) tradesman's employee delivering goods, etc on a regular route (有固定路线的)送货员: *Ask your roundsman for extra milk over Christmas.* 请贵店送货员在圣诞节多送些牛奶来.

rouse /raʊz; raʊz/ *v* **1** (**a**) [Tn, Tn·pr] **~ sb (from/out of sth)** cause sb to wake 唤醒某人: *I was roused by the sound of a bell.* 钟声把我吵醒了. ○ *It's time to rouse the children.* 该叫醒孩子们了. ○ (*fig* 比喻) *rouse him from his depression* 使他不再消沉. (**b**) [I, Ipr] **~ (from/out of sth)** (*fml* 文) wake (oneself) 醒来: *I roused slowly from a deep sleep.* 我从熟睡中慢慢地醒来. **2** [Tn, Tn·pr] **~ sb/sth (from sth) (to sth)** cause sb/sth to become active, interested, etc 使某人[某事物]活跃起来、产生兴趣等: *rouse sb/oneself to action* 激励某人[自己]行动起来 ○ *roused to anger by their insults* 被他们的侮辱所激怒 ○ *When he's roused, he can get very angry.* 要是惹着了他, 他有时大发脾气. Cf 参看 AROUSE.

▷ **rous·ing** *adj* [usu attrib 通常作定语] vigorous; giving encouragement (esp to action) 充满活力的; 激励人的(尤指使之付诸行动): *a rousing speech* 振奋人心的讲话 ○ *three rousing cheers for the winner* 向获胜者热烈地表示祝贺的三次欢呼声.

roust·about /ˈraʊstəbaʊt; ˋraʊstəˌbaʊt/ *n* labourer on an oil rig 石油钻台上的工人.

rout[1] /raʊt; raʊt/ *n* [C, U] **1** utter defeat (ending in disorder) 彻底的失败; 溃败; 大败: *After our fifth goal the match became a rout.* 我队进了第五个球以后, 对方一败涂地. **2** (idm 习语) **put sb to 'rout** (*dated fml* 旧, 文) defeat sb completely 彻底打败某人.

▷ **rout** *v* [Tn] defeat (sb) completely; make (sb) retreat in confusion 彻底打败(某人); 使(某人)溃退: *He resigned after his party was routed in the election.* 他所在的那个党在选举中遭到惨败, 他随之辞职了.

rout[2] /raʊt; raʊt/ *v* (phr v) **rout sb out (of sth)** fetch sb out abruptly, forcibly, etc 生硬地、强制地…使某人出去: *We were routed out of our beds at 4 am.* 清晨4点钟就把我们从床上叫起来了.

route /ruːt; *US* raʊt; raʊt/ *n* way taken or planned to get from one place to another 路; 路途; 路线: *We drove home by a roundabout route.* 我们开车绕道回的家. ○ *the main shipping routes across the Atlantic* 穿越大西洋的主要海运路线 ○ (*US*) *take Route 66* 走66号公路.

▷ **route** *v* (*pres p* **routeing**, *pp* **routed**) [Tn·pr esp passive 尤用于被动语态] send (sth) by a specified route 按某路线发送(某物): *This flight is routed to Chicago via New York.* 这班机是经纽约飞往芝加哥的.

□ **'route march** long march made by soldiers in training (部队操练中的)长途行军.

rou·tine /ruːˈtiːn; ruˋtin/ *n* **1** [C, U] fixed and regular way of doing things 固定而有规则性的程序; 例行公事; 常规: *She found it difficult to establish a new routine after retirement.* 她退休后觉得很难建立起新的生活秩序. ○ *do sth as a matter of routine* 按常规办事 ○ [attrib 作定语] *routine tasks, chores, duties, etc* 日常工作、日常事务、例行职责. **2** [C] set sequence of movements in a dance or some other performance 舞蹈等表演的成套动作: *go through a dance routine* 做一套舞蹈动作.

▷ **rou·tine** *adj* usual; habitual; regular 通常的; 惯例的; 例行的: *the routine procedure* 例行手续 ○ *routine maintenance* 定期的保养 ○ (*derog* 贬) *a rather routine* (ie ordinary, undistinguished) *performance* 很一般的(平淡无奇的)演出. **rou·tinely** *adv*.

roux /ruː; ru/ *n* (*pl* unchanged 复数不变) (in cooking) mixture of melted fat and flour blended together and used as the basis for sauces 油脂面糊(用以制沙司).

rove /rəʊv; rov/ *v* **1 (a)** [Ipr, Ip, Tn] (*esp rhet* 尤作修辞) wander without intending to reach a particular destination; roam 漂泊; 流浪; 漫游: *a roving reporter* 到处奔走的记者 ○ *bands of hooligans roving (round) the streets* 成群结伙在街上东游西逛的流氓. **(b)** **~ about/around (sth)** [Ipr, Ip] (of eyes) look in one direction after another (指眼睛)环顾, 扫视. **2** (idm 习语) **have a roving eye** be always looking for a chance to flirt or have love affairs 时刻寻找调情或做风流事的机会.
▷ **rover** *n* wanderer 流浪者; 漂泊者; 漫游者: *She's always been a rover.* 她一向到处流浪.
□ ˌ**roving comˈmission** authority to travel as much as necessary in order to carry out enquiries, duties, etc (为进行调查、工作等之需而有的)自由旅行权.

row[1] /rəʊ; ro/ *n* **1** number of people or things arranged in a line 一行; 一排; 一列: *a row of books, houses, desks* 一排书、房子、书桌 ○ *standing in a row/in rows* 站成行 ○ *plant a row of cabbages* 种植一行洋白菜. **2** line of seats across a theatre, etc (戏院等的)成排坐位: *the front two rows* 前两排坐位 ○ [attrib 作定语] *a front-row ˈseat* 前排坐位. **3** (idm 习语) **in a row** one after another; in unbroken sequence 一个接一个地; 连续不断地: *This is the third Sunday in a row that it's rained.* 这是接连着的第三个星期天下雨了.

row[2] /rəʊ; ro/ *v* **1** [I, Ipr, Ip, Tn, Tn·pr, Tn·p] propel (a boat) by using oars 划(船): *Can you row?* 你会划船吗? ○ *They rowed (the boat) across (the river).* 他们划(船)过了河. **2** [Tn, Tn·pr, Tn·p] carry (sb/sth) in a rowing-boat 用划艇运载(某人[某物]): *Row me across (the river).* 划船把我送到对岸去吧. **3 (a)** [Tn, Tn·pr] perform in a race, etc against (sb) by rowing 与(某人)进行划船比赛等: *We're rowing Cambridge in the next race.* 我们在下一次划船比赛中要跟剑桥大学队较量. **(b)** [I, Ipr] be an oarsman in a racing-boat's crew (在赛艇上)当划桨队员, 划船: *row for Cambridge* 在剑桥队当划船运动员 ○ *He rows (at) No 5* (ie in this position) *for Oxford.* 他是牛津大学船队的5号队员.
▷ **row** *n* (usu *sing* 通常作单数) outing in a boat that one rows; period of rowing 划船游玩; 划船时间: *go for a row* 去划船 ○ *a long and tiring row* 划船很长很累的一段时间.
rower *n* person who rows a rowing-boat 划船者. Cf 参看 OARSMAN (OAR).
□ ˈ**rowing-boat** (also *esp US* ˈ**row-boat**) *n* small boat propelled by rowing (usu not competitively) 划艇(通常指非比赛用艇).

row[3] /raʊ; raʊ/ *n* (*infml* 口) **1** [U, sing] loud noise; uproar 大的噪声; 吵闹: *How can I read with all this row going on?* 吵闹的声音这样大, 我怎能读书呢? ○ *Could you please make less (of a) row?* 请你别那么大声嚷嚷好吗? ○ *kick up a row* 大声吵闹. **2** [C] noisy or violent argument; quarrel 大声而激烈的争论; 吵架: *I think they've had a row.* 我想他们一定吵架了. ○ *the continuing row over the Government's defence policy* 关于政府防务政策的无休止的争论. ⇨Usage at ARGUMENT 用法见 ARGUMENT. **3** [C] instance of being criticized, scolded, etc 受批评、挨骂等: *I got/She gave me a row for being late.* 因为我迟到了, 我挨了批评[她批评了我].
▷ **row** *v* [I, Ipr] **~ (with sb)** quarrel noisily 大声争吵: *They're always rowing,* ie with each other. 他们总是吵架. ○ *rowing (with his employers) over money* (与雇主)在钱的问题上争吵.

rowan /ˈrəʊən, ˈraʊən; ˋroən, ˋraʊən/ *n* (also ˈ**rowan tree**) type of tree that bears hanging clusters of scarlet berries; mountain ash 花楸树(结鲜红色的浆果, 成串下垂).

rowdy /ˈraʊdɪ; ˋraʊdɪ/ *adj* (**-ier, -iest**) (*derog* 贬) noisy; disorderly 吵闹的; 混乱的; 无秩序的: *a group of rowdy teenagers* 一群吵吵嚷嚷的青少年 ○ *The meeting broke up amid rowdy scenes.* 会议在混乱中结束了.
▷ **row·dily** *adv*.
row·di·ness, **row·dy·ism** *ns* [U] rowdy behaviour 吵闹行为.
rowdy *n* (*dated derog* 旧, 贬) rowdy person 大吵大闹的人; 好争吵者.

row·lock /ˈrɒlək; *US* ˈrəʊlɒk; ˋroˌlɑk/ (*US* also ˈ**oarlock**) *n* device on the side of a rowing-boat for keeping an oar in place (划艇边缘的)桨架. ⇨illus at ROWING-BOAT (ROW[2]) 见 ROWING-BOAT(ROW[2])插图. Cf 参看 THOLE.

royal /ˈrɔɪəl; ˋrɔɪəl/ *adj* [usu attrib 通常作定语] **1** of a king or queen 国王的; 女王的: *limitations on royal power* 对王权的限制 ○ *the royal visit to Canada* 国王对加拿大的访问 ○ *the royal prerogative* 国王的特权. **2** belonging to the family of a king or queen (属于)王室的, 王族的: *the royal princesses* 国王的(除王后之外的)女眷. **3** in the service or under the patronage of a king or queen 为国王或女王效力的; 国王或女王赞助的: *the Royal ˈAir Force* 皇家空军 ○ *the Royal Marines* 皇家海军陆战队 ○ *the Royal Society for the Protection of Birds* 皇家鸟类保护协会. **4** suitable for a king, etc; splendid 适于国王的; 盛大的: *a royal welcome* 盛大的欢迎. **5** (idm 习语) **the royal 'we'** monarch's use of the plural pronoun to refer to himself or herself 朕, 寡人(君主用于自称): (*joc* 谑) *'We've never liked Italy.' 'Is that the royal "we"? I think Italy's great!'* '我们向来不喜欢意大利.' '你说的"我们"是指你孤家寡人吧? 我认为意大利好极了!'
▷ **royal** *n* (usu *pl* 通常作复数) (*infml* 口) member of the royal family 王室成员.
roy·al·ist /ˈrɔɪəlɪst; ˋrɔɪəlɪst/ *n* person who favours monarchy as a form of government 保皇主义者; 保皇党成员.
roy·ally /ˈrɔɪəlɪ; ˋrɔɪəlɪ/ *adv* in a splendid manner 盛大地: *We were royally entertained.* 我们受到了盛情的款待.
□ ˌ**royal ˈblue** (*Brit*) deep bright blue colour 宝蓝; 藏蓝.
ˌ**Royal Comˈmission** (*Brit*) group of people officially appointed by the monarch to investigate and report on a particular matter 皇家调查委员会(由君主指派的).
ˌ**Royal ˈHighness** (used as the title of a royal person, esp a prince or princess 用作王室成员(尤指王子、王孙或公主、孙公主)的尊称): *Her Royal Highness, the Princess of Wales* 储妃殿下 ○ *Their Royal Highnesses, the Duke and Duchess of York* 约克公爵及公爵夫人殿下 ○ *Thank you, Your Royal Highness.* 感谢殿下.
ˌ**royal ˈjelly** substance secreted by worker bees and fed by them to future queen bees 蜂王浆.

roy·alty /ˈrɔɪəltɪ; ˋrɔɪəltɪ/ *n* **1** [U] royal person or people 王室成员; 王族: *in the presence of royalty* 在御前 ○ *a shop patronized by royalty* 王族成员光顾的商店. **2** [U] being a member of a royal family 王室成员的身分: *the duties of royalty* 王室成员的责任. **3** [C] **(a)** sum paid to the owner of a copyright or patent, eg to an author for each copy of his book sold 版税; 专利权使用费. **(b)** sum paid by a mining or oil company to the owner of the land being mined, etc (矿业或石油公司付给土地所有者的)矿区使用费: *oil royalties* 石油开采地使用费.

rpm /ˌɑː piː ˈem; ˌɑr pi ˋɛm/ *abbr* 缩写 = revolutions per minute (esp as a measure of engine speed) 每分钟的转数(尤指发动机的): *2 500 rpm* 2 500转/分.

RRP /ˌɑːr ɑː ˈpiː; ˌɑr ɑr ˋpi/ *abbr* 缩写 = (*commerce* 商) recommended retail price 建议零售价格: *RRP £35.00, our price £29.95,* eg in a sales catalogue. 建议零售价格为35.00英镑, 本公司实际售价为29.95英镑(如商品目录表所载的).

RSA /ˌɑːr es ˈeɪ; ˌɑr ɛs ˋe/ *abbr* 缩写 = Republic of South Africa 南非共和国.

RSC /ˌɑːr es ˈsiː; ˌɑr ɛs ˋsi/ *abbr* 缩写 = (*Brit*) Royal Shakespeare Company 皇家莎士比亚剧团: *an RSC production* 皇家莎士比亚剧团演出.

RSM /ˌɑːr es ˈem; ˌɑr ɛs ˋɛm/ *abbr* 缩写 = **1** Regimental Sergeant-Major 准尉. **2** Royal School of Music 皇家音乐学校.

RSPB /ˌɑːr es piː ˈbiː; ˌɑr ɛs pi ˋbi/ *abbr* 缩写 = (*Brit*)

Royal Society for the Protection of Birds 皇家鸟类保护协会.

RSPCA /ˌɑːr es ˌpiː siː ˈeɪ; ˌɑr ɛs ˌpi si ˋe/ *abbr* 缩写 = (*Brit*) Royal Society for the Prevention of Cruelty to Animals 皇家防止虐待动物协会.

RSV /ˌɑːr es ˈviː; ˌɑr ɛs ˋvi/ *abbr* 缩写 = Revised Standard Version (of the Bible)《圣经》修订标准本.

RSVP /ˌɑːr es viː ˈpiː; ˌɑr ɛs vi ˋpi/ *abbr* 缩写 = (esp on invitations) please reply (French *répondez s'il vous plaît*) (尤用于请柬)请赐复(源自法文 *répondez s'il vous plaît*).

Rt Hon *abbr* 缩写 = (*Brit*) Right Honourable: *(the) Rt Hon Richard Scott* 理查德·斯科特阁下. Cf 参看 HON 2.

Rt Rev (also **Rt Revd**) *abbr* 缩写 = Right Reverend: *(the) Rt Rev George Hill* 乔治·希尔主教大人. Cf 参看 REV.

RU *abbr* 缩写 = Rugby Union 橄榄球联合会.

rub[1] /rʌb; rʌb/ *v* (**-bb-**) **1** [I, Tn, Tn·pr, Tn·p] **~ (sth) (with sth)** (cause sth to) press against (a surface) with a to-and-fro sliding movement (用某物)擦, 磨, 揉, 搓(另一物): *If you keep rubbing, the paint will come off.* 你再多擦擦颜色就能掉了. ○ *He rubbed his chin thoughtfully.* 他抚摩着下巴, 陷入沉思. ○ *rub the glass (with a cloth)* (用布)擦玻璃 ○ *rubbing his hands together* (他)搓着手. **2** (**a**) [Tn·pr, Tn·p] apply (sth) in this way 搽上、抹上或涂上(某物): *Rub the lotion on(to the skin).* (在皮肤上)搽上涂剂. (**b**) [Tn·pr] move (one's hand, etc) in this way 用(手等)擦, 抹, 抚摩, 按摩: *He rubbed his palm across his forehead.* 他用手掌揉了揉前额. **3** (**a**) [Cn·a] cause (sth) to reach the specified condition by rubbing 用擦、磨等方法使(某物)达到某种状况: *rub the surface smooth, clean, dry, etc (with a cloth)* (用布)把表面擦光、净、干等. (**b**) [Tn·pr] **~ sth in sth** make (a hole, etc) in sth by rubbing 在某物上磨出(洞等): *rub a bald patch in one's trousers* 裤子上磨出一片斑痕. **4** [I, Ipr] **~ (on/against sth)** be pressed (against sth) and sliding about on it (与某物)摩擦: *The heel of my shoe keeps rubbing*, ie against the heel of my foot. 我的鞋后跟磨脚. ○ *The wheel's rubbing on the mudguard.* 车轮蹭着了挡泥板. **5** (idm 习语) **rub sb's ˈnose in it** (*infml derog* 口, 贬) remind sb cruelly of their past mistakes, etc 无情地提及某人已往的错误等. **rub salt into the wound/sb's wounds** make a painful experience even more painful for sb 在某人的伤口上撒盐(给某人增加痛苦); 给某人雪上加霜. **rub shoulders with sb** meet sb socially or professionally 与某人作社交上或职业上的来往: *In his job he's rubbing shoulders with film stars all the time.* 他在工作中一直与电影明星有来往. **rub sb up the wrong ˈway** (*infml* 口) annoy sb 惹恼某人.

6 (phr v) **rub along** (*infml* 口) (of a person) manage without too much difficulty (指人)(生活等)勉强过得去. **rub along with sb/together** (*infml* 口) (of two or more people) live together in a reasonably friendly way (指人)相处得还不错.

rub (sb/oneself/sth) down rub (sb/oneself/a horse, etc) vigorously with eg a towel to make the skin dry and clean (用毛巾等)将(某人[自己/马匹]等)用力擦干净: *The players paused to rub (themselves) down between games.* 运动员在比赛中间休息时擦汗. **rub sth down** make sth smooth or level by rubbing 磨光或磨平某物: *Rub the walls down well before painting them.* 先把墙面打磨光滑再粉刷.

rub sth in/into sth force (ointment, etc) into sth by rubbing 将(油膏等)揉搓进某物中: *Rub the cream in well.* 搽上乳膏后揉匀. **rub it in** emphasize or remind sb constantly of an unpleasant fact 不断地向某人提及令人不快的事: *I know I made a mistake but there's no need to rub it in.* 我知道自己做了错事, 可也不必老提这个.

rub (sth) off (sth) (cause sth to) be removed from (a surface) by rubbing (将某物)擦掉: *Rub the mud off your trousers.* 把你裤子上的泥擦掉. ○ *Who's rubbed my figures off the blackboard?* 谁把我写在黑板上的数字擦掉了? ○ *These stains won't rub off.* 这些污迹擦不掉. **rub off (on/onto sb)** be transferred (to sb) as a result of sb else's example 从他人的榜样中汲取到…: *Let's hope some of her patience rubs off on her brother.* 希望她的弟弟也能有点她那样的耐性.

rub sb out (*US sl* 俚) murder sb 谋杀某人. **rub (sth) out** (cause sth, esp pencil marks, to) be removed by using a rubber[1](2) 用橡皮擦掉(某物, 尤指铅笔痕迹等): *rub out a mistake, figure, drawing* 用橡皮把一错处、数字、图画擦掉 ○ *I can't get it to rub out.* 我用橡皮擦不掉它.

rub sth up polish sth by rubbing 将某物擦亮. **rub up against sb** (*infml* 口) meet sb by chance 偶然遇到某人.

▷ **rub·bing** *n* impression of sth, eg a brass decoration on a grave, made by rubbing paper laid over it with wax, chalk or charcoal 摹拓; 拓印.

rub[2] /rʌb; rʌb/ *n* **1** [C usu *sing* 通常作单数] act or process of rubbing 擦; 磨; 摩擦: *Give the spoons a good rub to get them clean.* 把这些匙擦干净. **2 the rub** [sing] (*dated* 旧) difficulty or drawback (used esp in the expressions shown) 困难, 障碍(尤用于以下示例): *There's the rub/Therein lies the rub.* 难就难在这里.

rubber[1] /ˈrʌbə(r); ˋrʌbɚ/ *n* **1** [U] tough elastic substance made from the milky juice of certain tropical plants, or synthetically 橡胶; 合成橡胶: *an electric cable insulated with rubber* 用橡胶作绝缘材料的电缆 ○ [attrib 作定语] *a pair of rubber gloves* 一副橡皮手套 ○ *rubber car tyres* 橡胶汽车轮胎. **2** [C] (*Brit*) (also *esp US* **eraser**) (**a**) piece of this or some other substance for rubbing out pencil or ink marks (擦铅笔或墨水痕迹的)橡皮: *a pencil with a rubber on the end* 一端带橡皮的铅笔. (**b**) piece of material for rubbing out chalk marks on a blackboard 黑板擦. **3** [C] (*infml* 口 *esp US*) contraceptive sheath; condom 避孕套; 阴茎套. **4 rubbers** [pl] (*esp US*) waterproof rubber coverings worn over the shoes; galoshes (防水的)橡胶套鞋.

▷ **rub·ber·ize, -ise** /ˈrʌbəraɪz; ˋrʌbəˌraɪz/ *v* [Tn] treat or coat (sth) with rubber 用橡胶处理(某物); 在(某物)上复上橡胶: *rubberized material* 复有橡胶层的材料.

rub·bery /ˈrʌbərɪ; ˋrʌbərɪ/ *adj* like rubber in consistency or texture 似橡胶的: *chewing a rubbery piece of meat* 嚼着一块嚼不烂的肉.

□ ˌ**rubber ˈband** (also **elastic band**, *US* **elastic**) loop of rubber used for holding things together 橡皮筋; 橡皮圈: *a pack of cards with a rubber band round them* 用橡皮筋捆着的一副纸牌.

ˈ**rubber goods** (*euph* 婉) contraceptive devices and sexual aids 避孕用具及性生活辅助用具.

ˈ**rubber plant** type of plant with thick shiny green leaves, often grown indoors for decoration 橡胶植物(叶厚而有光泽, 常作室内盆栽).

ˌ**rubber ˈstamp** **1** small device for printing dates, signatures, etc on a surface by hand 橡皮图章. **2** (*fig* 比喻) person or group that automatically gives approval to the actions or decisions of others 机械地赞同他人的行动或决定的人或团体. ˌ**rubber-ˈstamp** *v* [Tn] (*often derog* 常作贬义) approve (sth) automatically and without proper consideration 未经适当考虑便机械地赞同(某事物).

rubber[2] /ˈrʌbə(r); ˋrʌbɚ/ *n* match of (the best of) three games at bridge, whist, etc (桥牌、惠斯特等牌戏的)(三局两胜的)比赛: *Let's play another rubber.* 咱们再赛个三局两胜吧. ○ *We can win the rubber 2 games to nil or 2-1.* 我们可以以2比零或2比1赢得这三局两胜的比赛.

rubber-neck /ˈrʌbənek; ˋrʌbɚˌnɛk/ *v* [I] (*US sl derog* 俚, 贬) stare or gape inquisitively (好奇地)注视, 张望.

▷ **rubber-neck** *n* person who does this, esp a tourist or sightseer (好奇地)东张西望的人(尤指旅游者或观光者).

rub·bish /ˈrʌbɪʃ; ˋrʌbɪʃ/ *n* [U] **1** waste or worthless material 垃圾; 废物: *The dustmen haven't collected the rubbish yet.* 清洁工人还没把垃圾收走. ○ [attrib 作定语] *a ˈrubbish dump/heap/tip* 垃圾场[堆/倾倒处] ○ *a ˈrubbish bin* 垃圾箱. **2** (*derog* 贬) (often used as an *interj* 常用作感叹语) worthless ideas, etc; nonsense 无聊的想法等; 胡说: *His book is (a load of) rubbish.* 他的书简直是废话(连篇). ○ *Don't talk rubbish!* 别胡说八道! ○ *What he says is all rubbish.* 他满口胡言.

▷ **rub·bish** *v* [Tn] (*Brit or Austral sl* 英或澳, 俚) criticize (sb/sth) contemptuously; treat as worthless 贬损(某人[某事物]); 把…看得一文不值: *The film was rubbished by the critics.* 影评家把这部影片贬得一无是处. ○ *She is often accused of rubbishing her opponents.* 她经常因诋毁对手而受到指责.

rub·bishy *adj* (*infml* 口) worthless 毫无价值的.

rubble /ˈrʌbl; ˋrʌbl̩/ *n* [U] bits of broken stone, rock or bricks 碎石; 碎砖: *a road built on a foundation of rubble* 用碎石做路基修筑的道路 ○ *The explosion reduced the building to (a pile of) rubble*, ie totally demolished it. 那次爆炸把那建筑物毁成(一堆)瓦砾.

ru·bella /ruːˈbelə; ruˋbɛlə/ *n* [U] (*medical* 医) = GERMAN MEASLES (GERMAN).

Ru·bi·con /ˈruːbɪkən; US -kɒn; ˋrubɪˌkɑn/ *n* (idm 习语) **cross the Rubicon** ⇨ CROSS².

rubi·cund /ˈruːbɪkənd; ˋrubəˌkʌnd/ *adj* (*fml* 文) (of a person's complexion) red; ruddy (指人的肤色)发红的, 红润的: *fat rubicund cheeks* 丰满红润的脸颊.

ruble = ROUBLE.

rub·ric /ˈruːbrɪk; ˋrubrɪk/ *n* [C] words put as a heading, esp to show or explain how sth should be done, etc 标题(尤指提示或说明做法等的).

ruby /ˈruːbɪ; ˋrubɪ/ *n* **1** [C] type of red jewel 红宝石: [attrib 作定语] *ruby red* 红宝石色. **2** [U] colour of a ruby; deep red 红宝石的颜色; 深红色.

▷ **ruby** *adj* [esp attrib 尤作定语] deep red 深红色的: *ruby lips* 深红色的嘴唇.

□ ˌ**ruby** ˈ**wedding** 40th anniversary of a wedding 红宝石婚(结婚40周年纪念).

RUC /ˌɑː juː ˈsiː; ˌɑr ju ˋsi/ *abbr* 缩写 = Royal Ulster Constabulary 北爱尔兰皇家警察.

ruche /ruːʃ; ruʃ/ *n* gathered trimming on a garment, etc 褶饰; 褶边.

▷ **ruched** /ruːʃt; ruʃt/ *adj* trimmed with gathered material (eg lace) 用褶饰材料(如花边)装饰的; 有褶边的: *a dress with ruched sleeves* 袖子上有褶饰花边的连衣裙.

ruck¹ /rʌk; rʌk/ *n* **1** [C] (*sport* 体) (**a**) (*Brit*) (in Rugby football) loose scrum with the ball on the ground (橄榄球)自由密集争球. (**b**) disorganized group (of players, competitors, etc) (运动员、竞赛者等的)散乱的一群. **2** **the ruck** [sing] ordinary commonplace people or things 普通人; 寻常事物: *He was eager to get out of the (common) ruck and distinguish himself in some way.* 他渴望出人头地, 在某方面与众不同.

ruck² /rʌk; rʌk/ *n* irregular unintentional fold or crease (esp in cloth) (非有意形成的)皱, 褶(尤指布上的): *smooth out the rucks in the bedclothes* 把床单上的褶子弄平.

▷ **ruck** *v* (phr v) **ruck up** form rucks 起皱; 起褶: *The sheets on my bed have rucked up.* 我床上的床单有褶子了.

ruck·sack /ˈrʌksæk; ˋrʌkˌsæk/ (also **knapsack**, *US* also ˈ**backpack**) *n* bag strapped to the back from the shoulders, used by hikers, climbers, etc 背包(远足者、登山者等用的). ⇨illus at LUGGAGE 见 LUGGAGE 插图. Cf 参看 HAVERSACK.

ruckus /ˈrʌkəs; ˋrʌkəs/ *n* (usu *sing* 通常作单数) (*infml* 口 *esp US*) noisy disturbance; uproar 吵闹; 争吵: *cause a ruckus* 引起争吵.

ruc·tions /ˈrʌkʃnz; ˋrʌkʃənz/ *n* [pl] (*infml* 口) angry protests; noisy argument 愤怒的抗议; 争吵; 吵架: *There'll be ructions if you don't do as you're told.* 你要是不照办就要吵架了.

rud·der /ˈrʌdə(r); ˋrʌdɚ/ *n* (**a**) broad flat piece of wood or metal hinged vertically at the stern of a boat or ship, used for steering (船的)舵. ⇨illus at YACHT 见 YACHT 插图. (**b**) similar piece of metal on the rear of an aircraft, for the same purpose (飞机的)方向舵. ⇨illus at AIRCRAFT 见 AIRCRAFT 插图.

ruddy¹ /ˈrʌdɪ; ˋrʌdɪ/ *adj* (**-ier, -iest**) **1** (*approv* 褒) (of a person's face) having a fresh healthy colour (指人的脸)红润的, 气色好的: *ruddy cheeks* 红润的脸颊. **2** reddish 发红的; 淡红色的: *a ruddy glow in the sky* 天空的红光.

▷ **rud·dily** *adv*. **rud·di·ness** *n* [U].

ruddy² /ˈrʌdɪ; ˋrʌdɪ/ *adj* [attrib 作定语], *adv* (*Brit sl euph* 俚, 婉) bloody²; damned 极度的; 该死的: *What the ruddy hell are you doing?* 你到底在搞什么鬼? ○ *He's a ruddy idiot.* 他是个大傻瓜. ○ *I work ruddy hard.* 我非常努力.

rude /ruːd; rud/ *adj* (**-r, -st**) **1** (of a person or his behaviour) showing no respect or consideration; impolite (指人或人的行为)粗鲁的, 粗野的, 无礼的: *He's very rude/a very rude man.* 他这人非常粗野. ○ *It's rude to interrupt.* 打断别人的话是不礼貌的. ○ *What a rude reply!* 多么粗鲁无礼的回答! **2** (*euph* 婉) (of a story, etc) slightly indecent; risqué (指故事等)近乎下流的, 有伤风化的: *a rather rude joke* 颇为粗鄙的笑话. **3** [attrib 作定语] primitive; simple 原始的; 简单的: *rude stone implements* 原始的石制工具. **4** [attrib 作定语] violent; startling; abrupt 狂暴的; 惊人的; 突然的: *a rude awakening to the realities of life* 突然觉醒而回到现实生活中来 ○ *a rude reminder of the danger they were in* 使他们突然觉察到所处的危险之事. **5** (idm 习语) **in rude** ˈ**health** (*fml or rhet* 文或修辞) vigorously healthy 十分健壮的.

▷ **rudely** *adv* **1** impolitely 无礼地; 粗暴地: *behave rudely* 举动无礼. **2** in a primitive manner 原始地; 简单地: *rudely-fashioned weapons* 原始式的武器. **3** roughly; abruptly 粗暴地; 突然地: *rudely awakened by screams and shouts* 突然被尖叫声和呼喊声惊醒.

rude·ness *n* [U].

ru·di·ment /ˈruːdɪmənt; ˋrudəmənt/ *n* **1** **rudiments** [pl] **~s (of sth)** (**a**) basic or elementary principles (of a subject) (某一学科的)基础, 基本原理: *master the rudiments of economics* 精通经济学的基本原理. (**b**) imperfect beginning of sth that is not yet fully developed 初级形态: *working on the rudiments of a new idea* 研究一种新思想的萌芽. **2** [C] part or organ that is incompletely developed 未充分发展的部分; 发育不成熟的器官: *the rudiment(s) of a tail* 未完全发育的尾巴.

▷ **ru·di·ment·ary** /ˌruːdɪˈmentrɪ; ˌrudəˋmɛntrɪ/ *adj* **1** existing in an imperfect or undeveloped form 未充分发展的; 发育不成熟的; 退化的: *Some breeds of dog have only rudimentary tails.* 有些品种的狗只有退化了的短尾巴. **2** (*derog* 贬) elementary; (not more than) basic 初步的; (充其量)基本的: *I have only a rudimentary grasp of physics.* 我对物理学仅有初步的了解.

rue¹ /ruː; ru/ *n* [U] type of evergreen shrub with bitter leaves formerly used in medicine 芸香(常绿灌木, 叶味苦, 旧时用以人药).

rue² /ruː; ru/ *v* (*pres p* **rueing** or **ruing**, *pt, pp* **rued**) [Tn] (*dated or fml* 旧或文) repent or regret (sth) (used esp in the expressions shown) 对(某事物)感到懊悔(尤用于以下示例): *You'll live to rue it*, ie You will regret it one day. 总有一天你得后悔. ○ *He's rueing the day he joined the Army!* 他后悔参了军!

▷ **rue·ful** /ˈruːfl; ˋrufəl/ *adj* showing or feeling good-humoured regret 表示或感到后悔的(但很看得开): *a rueful smile* 抱憾的微笑. **rue·fully** /ˈruːfəlɪ; ˋrufəlɪ/ *adv*. **rue·ful·ness** *n* [U].

ruff¹ /rʌf; rʌf/ *n* **1** ring of differently coloured or marked feathers or fur round the neck of a bird or animal 鸟兽颈部的羽或毛形成的彩环. **2** wide stiff frill worn as a collar, esp in the 16th century 飞边(宽而硬的皱领, 16世纪尤为流行).

ruff² /rʌf; rʌf/ *v* [I, Tn] trump (a card or a player) in a card-game (纸牌戏中)打出王牌胜(另一牌或他家).

ruf·fian /ˈrʌfɪən; ˋrʌfɪən/ *n* (*dated derog* 旧, 贬) violent lawless man 无法无天的暴徒; 恶棍: *a gang of ruffians* 一帮暴徒.

ruffle /ˈrʌfl; ˋrʌfl̩/ *v* **1** [Tn, Tn·p] **~ sth (up)** disturb the smoothness or evenness of sth 弄皱或弄乱某物: *a breeze ruffling the surface of the lake* 吹皱了湖面的微风 ○ *Don't ruffle my hair, I've just combed it.* 别把我的头发弄乱了, 我刚刚梳好了的. ○ *The bird ruffled up its feathers.* 那只鸟竖起了羽毛. **2** [Tn esp passive 尤用于被动语态] upset the calmness or even temper of (sb); disconcert 扰乱(某人)的情绪; 激怒(某人): *Anne is easily ruffled by awkward questions.* 安妮遇到难堪的问题很容易发脾气. **3** (idm 习语) **ruffle sb's** ˈ**feathers** (*infml* 口) annoy sb 惹某人生气. **smooth sb's ruffled feathers** ⇨ SMOOTH².

▷ **ruffle** *n* strip of material gathered into a frill and used to ornament a garment, esp at the wrist or neck 褶饰, 花边(尤用于袖口或衣领).

rug /rʌg; rʌg/ *n* **1** thick floor-mat (usu smaller than a carpet) 厚地毯(通常比 carpet 小): *a* ˈ*hearth-rug* 壁炉前的小地毯. **2** piece of thick warm fabric used as a blanket or covering 厚毯子: *a* ˈ*travelling-rug*, ie for covering a passenger's knees in a car, etc 旅行毯(乘坐汽车等时, 盖住膝部的). **3** (idm 习语) **pull the carpet/rug from under sb's feet** ⇨ PULL². **snug as a bug in a rug** ⇨ SNUG.

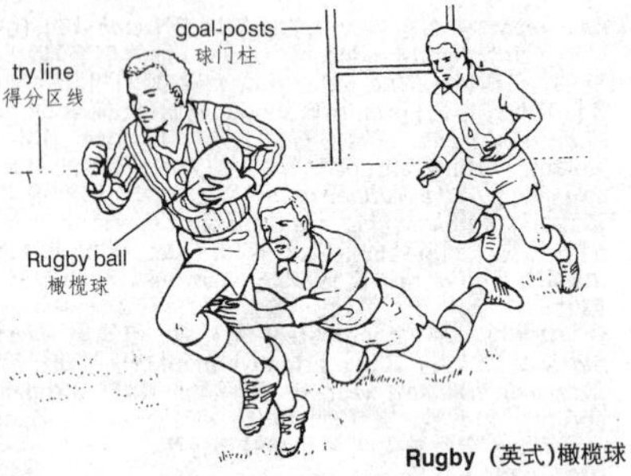

Rugby (英式)橄榄球

Rugby /ˈrʌgbɪ; ˋrʌgbɪ/ *n* [U] (also ˌ**Rugby** ˈ**football**) form of football played with an oval ball which may be kicked or carried (英式)橄榄球(运动): [attrib 作定语] *a Rugby ball, club, match, player* 橄榄球的球、俱乐部、比赛、运动员. ⇨App 4 见附录 4.

□ ˌ**Rugby** ˈ**League** partly professional form of Rugby, with 13 players in a team 联盟橄榄球(半职业性质, 每队 13 人).

ˌ**Rugby** ˈ**Union** amateur form of Rugby, with 15 players in a team 联合会橄榄球(业余性质, 每队 15 人).

rug·ged /ˈrʌgɪd; ˋrʌgɪd/ *adj* **1** rough; uneven; rocky 粗糙的; 不平的; 多岩石的: *a rugged coastline* 多岩石的海岸线 ○ *rugged country* 地势起伏的地区. **2** (*esp approv* 尤作褒义) sturdy; robust; tough(-looking) 强健的; 结实的; (看上去)坚强的: *a rugged player* 强健的运动员 ○ *a car famous for its rugged qualities* 以坚固耐用驰名的汽车 ○ *a rugged face* 健康的脸 ○ *rugged features* 刚毅的相貌. **3** not refined or gentle 粗野的; 不文雅的: *a rugged individualist* 无教养只顾自己的人 ○ *rugged manners* 粗鲁的举止. ▷ **rug·gedly** *adv*. **rug·ged·ness** *n* [U].

rug·ger /ˈrʌgə(r); ˋrʌgɚ/ *n* [U] (*infml* 口 *esp Brit*) Rugby (esp Rugby Union) football (英式)橄榄球(运动)(尤指联合会橄榄球).

ruin /ˈruːɪn; ˋruɪn/ *n* **1** [U] severe damage or destruction 毁坏; 毁灭; 灭亡: *a city reduced to a state of ruin by war* 由于战争而遭到严重破坏的城市 ○ *The news meant the ruin of all our hopes.* 这消息使我们的一切希望都破灭了. **2** [U] (**a**) complete loss of all one's money, resources or prospects (金钱、资财的)完全丧失; (前途的)断送: *Ruin was staring her in the face.* 她眼看就要倾家荡产了. ○ *brought to ruin by drugs* 因吸毒而断送了前程. (**b**) cause of this 毁灭、破产等的原因; 祸根: *Gambling was his ruin.* 他堕落是因为好赌. **3** [U] state of being decayed, collapsed or destroyed 破败、坍塌或毁坏的状态: *The castle has fallen into ruin.* 那城堡已破败不堪. **4** [C] remains of sth that has decayed or collapsed or been destroyed 破败、坍塌或毁坏之残余物; 废墟: *The abbey is now a ruin.* 那修道院现已成废墟. ○ *the ruins of Pompeii* 庞贝城的遗迹. **5** (idm 习语) **go to rack and ruin** ⇨ RACK[3]. **in** ˈ**ruins** in a severely damaged or decayed condition 严重受损; 破败不堪: *An earthquake left the whole town in ruins.* 那次地震过后, 全城到处是颓垣断壁. ○ *His career is/lies in ruins.* 他已前途尽毁.

▷ **ruin** *v* [Tn] **1** cause the destruction of (sth/sb) 毁坏, 毁灭(某事物[某人]): *He ruined his prospects by carelessness.* 他因疏忽大意而断送了前途. ○ *The storm ruined the crops.* 暴风雨毁坏了庄稼. ○ *He's a ruined man*, ie has lost all his money, prospects, etc. 他已不名一文(损失了全部钱财、断送了前途等). ○ *a ruined building* 毁坏的建筑物. **2** (*infml* 口) spoil (sth/sb) 毁坏, 损害(某事物[某人]): *The island has been ruined by tourism.* 该岛毁在旅游业上了. ○ *It poured with rain and my dress got/was ruined.* 大雨倾盆, 我的连衣裙已淋得不成样子了. ○ *You're ruining that child*, eg by being too indulgent. 你把孩子宠坏了.

ru·ina·tion /ˌruːɪˈneɪʃn; ˌruɪnˋeʃən/ *n* [U] (cause of) being ruined 损害, 毁坏(的起因); 祸根: *Late frosts are ruination for the garden.* 晚霜能冻死园中的植物. ○ *You'll be the ruination of me!* 你早晚得把我毁了!

ru·in·ous /ˈruːɪnəs; ˋruɪnəs/ *adj* bringing (esp financial) ruin 带来巨大损失的(尤指财务上): *ruinous expenditure* 倾家荡产的花费 ○ (*joc* 谑) *The prices in that restaurant are absolutely ruinous.* 那家饭馆的价钱贵得能把人坑死. **ru·in·ously** *adv*: *a ruinously expensive meal, restaurant, coat* 价钱贵得令人咋舌的饭食、餐馆、大衣.

rule /ruːl; rul/ *n* **1** [C] statement of what can, should or must be done in certain circumstances or when playing a game 规则; 规章; 规定; 条例: *The rule is that someone must be on duty at all times.* 按照规定, 任何时候均需有人值班. ○ *the rules of the game* 游戏规则 ○ *rules and regulations* 规章制度. **2** [C usu *sing* 通常作单数] usual practice or habit; normal state of things 惯常的做法; 习惯: *My rule is to get up at seven every day.* 我习惯每天七点起床. ○ *He makes it a rule never to borrow money.* 他无论如何也不向别人借钱. ○ *She made a rule of eating an apple a day.* 她每天一定要吃一个苹果. ○ *Cold winters here are the exception rather than the rule*, ie are comparatively rare. 这里冬天很少有冷的时候. **3** [U] authority; government 统治; 管理: *the rule of law* 法治 ○ *majority rule* 多数裁定原则 ○ *a country formerly under French rule* 以前由法国统治的国家 ○ *mob rule*, ie the state that exists when a mob takes control 暴民统治. **4** [C] straight measuring device, often jointed, used by carpenters, etc (木工等用的)尺, (常指)折尺. **5** [C] (usu straight) line drawn by hand or printed (通常指直的)线条(手画的或印刷的). **6** (idm 习语) **as a (general)** ˈ**rule** (*fml* 文) in most cases; usually 在多数情况下; 通常: *As a rule I'm home by six.* 我通常六点钟到家. **bend the rules** ⇨ BEND[1]. **the exception proves the rule** ⇨ EXCEPTION. **a rule of** ˈ**thumb** rough practical method of assessing or measuring sth, usu based on past experience rather than on exact measurement, etc (and therefore not completely reliable in every case or in every detail) (对事物)粗略但实用的估计方法(通常指凭经验而不作精确的计量等, 故并非时时处处均可靠): *As a rule of thumb, you should cook a chicken for 20 minutes for each pound that it weighs.* 凭经验估计, 每磅鸡肉应烹调 20 分钟. **rule(s) of the** ˈ**road** rules regulating the movement of vehicles, ships, etc when meeting or passing each other 交通规则. **work to** ˈ**rule** follow the rules of one's occupation with excessive strictness in order to cause delay, as a form of industrial protest 照章工作(以严格遵守规章为名而行怠工之实的抗议形式).

▷ **rule** *v* **1** [I, Ipr, Tn] **~ (over sb/sth)** govern (sb/sth); have authority (over) 统治(某人[某事物]); 管理: *She once ruled over a vast empire.* 她曾统治过一个版图辽阔的帝国. ○ *Charles I ruled (England) for eleven years.* 查理一世统治了(英国)十一年. **2** [Tn usu passive 通常用于被动语态] have power or influence over (sb, sb's feelings, etc); dominate 控制或影响(某人、某人的感情等); 支配; 操纵: *Don't allow yourself to be ruled by emotion.* 不要感情用事. ○ *She let her heart rule her head*, ie acted according to her emotions, rather than sensibly. 她感情超越了理智(以感情而不以理智支配行动). **3** [Ipr, Tf, Cn·a, Cn·t] give a decision as a judge or as some other authority 作出裁决或裁定: *rule in favour of the plaintiff* 判原告胜诉 ○ *The chairman ruled that the question was out of order/ruled the speaker out of order.* 主席裁定该问题不合议事规则[裁定该发言者违反了议事规则]. ○ *The court ruled the action to be illegal.* 法庭判定该项行动非法. **4** [Tn] draw (a line) using a ruler, etc; mark parallel lines on (writing-paper, etc) 用尺等画(线); 在(书写纸等)上画平行线: *Do you want ruled paper or plain?* 你要有格的纸还是白纸? **5** (idm 习语) **rule the** ˈ**roost** be the dominant person in a group 为首; 主宰. **rule (sb/sth) with a rod of** ˈ**iron/with an iron hand** govern (a group of people, a country, etc) very harshly 以高压手段[铁腕]统治(人群、国家等). **6** (phr v) **rule sth off (from sth)** separate sth from everything else by drawing a line below it, round it, etc 在下面、周围等处画线将某部分隔开: *rule the photographs off from the text* 画线把照片与文字隔开. **rule sb/sth out (as sth)** exclude sb/sth (as irrelevant, ineligible, etc) 排除某人[某事物](因其无关、不合格等): *That possibility can't be ruled out*, ie It must continue to be considered. 不能排除这种可能性(有待继续研究). ○ *He was ruled out as a possible candidate.* 他已经没有可能成为候选人.

ruler /ˈruːlə(r); ˋrulɚ/ *n* **1** person who rules or governs 统治者; 主宰者. **2** straight strip of wood, plastic, metal, etc used for measuring or for drawing straight lines 尺; 直尺.

rul·ing /ˈruːlɪŋ; ˋrulɪŋ/ *adj* [attrib 作定语] that rules; prevalent; dominant 统治的; 占主导地位的; 居支配地位的: *the ruling class, party, faction, etc* 统治阶级、执政党、居支配地位的派别 ○ *His ruling passion was ambition.* 他一心要实现自己的抱负.

▷ **rul·ing** *n* decision made by a judge or by some other authority 裁决; 裁定; 判决: *When will the committee give/make its ruling?* 委员会什么时候做出裁决?

rum[1] /rʌm; rʌm/ *n* [U] **1** strong alcoholic drink distilled from sugar-cane juice 朗姆酒(用甘蔗汁蒸馏制成). **2** (*US*) any type of alcoholic liquor 酒.

rum[2] /rʌm; rʌm/ *adj* (**-mmer, -mmest**) (*dated Brit infml* 旧, 口) peculiar; odd 古怪的; 奇特的: *He's a rum character.* 他这个人真古怪.

rumba /ˈrʌmbə; ˋrʌmbə/ *n* (piece of music for a) type of ballroom dance that originated in Cuba 伦巴舞(一种交际舞, 起源于古巴); 伦巴舞曲: *dance/do the rumba* 跳伦巴舞.

rumble[1] /ˈrʌmbl; ˋrʌmbl̩/ *v* (**a**) [I] make a deep heavy continuous sound 发出持续的低沉的声音: *thunder rumbling in the distance* 远方发出的隆隆雷声 ○ *I'm so hungry that my stomach's rumbling.* 我饿得肚子咕咕叫. (**b**) [Ipr, Ip] move (in the specified direction) making such a sound 发着低沉声音(沿某方向)行进: *trams rumbling through the streets* 发着辘辘声驶过大街的电车.

▷ **rumble** *n* **1** [U, C usu *sing* 作不可数名词或可数名词, 后者通常作单数] rumbling sound 低沉而连续的声音: *the rumble of drums* 咚咚的鼓声. **2** [C] (*US sl* 俚) street fight between gangs (在街上)打群架.

rumble[2] /ˈrʌmbl; ˋrʌmbl̩/ *v* [Tn] (*Brit sl* 俚) detect the true character of (sb/sth); see through (a deception) 察觉(某人[某事物])的真实性质; 看穿(诡计): *He looks suspicious — do you think he's rumbled us/what we're up to?* 他好像起了疑心——你觉得他看穿我们[我们要干的事]了吗?

rum·bus·tious /rʌmˈbʌstɪəs; rʌmˋbʌstʃəs/ (also esp *US* **rambunctious**) *adj* (*infml* 口) cheerful in a noisy energetic way; boisterous 热闹的; 闹得欢的.

ru·min·ant /ˈruːmɪnənt; ˋrumənənt/ *n, adj* (animal) that chews the cud, eg a cow 反刍的; 反刍动物(如牛).

ru·min·ate /ˈruːmɪneɪt; ˋruməˌnet/ *v* **1** [I, Ipr] ~ **(about/on/over sth)** think deeply; meditate; ponder 深思; 沉思; 思索: *ruminating on recent events* 思考最近发生的事. **2** [I] (of animals) chew the cud (指动物)反刍.

▷ **ru·mina·tion** /ˌruːmɪˈneɪʃn; ˌruməˋneʃən/ *n* [U].

ru·min·at·ive /ˈruːmɪnətɪv; *US* -neɪtɪv; ˋruməˌnetɪv/ *adj* inclined to meditate; thoughtful 好沉思的; 思考的: *in a ruminative mood* 在冥思苦索中. **ru·min·at·ively** *adv*: *gazing ruminatively out of the window* 若有所思地凝视着窗外.

rum·mage /ˈrʌmɪdʒ; ˋrʌmɪdʒ/ *v* [I, Ipr, Ip] ~ **(among/in/through sth) (for sth)**; ~ **(about/around)** turn things over or disarrange them while searching for sth 翻找或搜寻某物: *rummaging through (the contents of) a drawer for a pair of socks* 在抽屉里(的东西中)翻找一双袜子 ○ *rummage around in the attic* 在顶楼上到处寻找.

▷ **rum·mage** *n* search of this kind 翻找; 搜寻: *have a good rummage around* 到处翻遍.

□ ˈ**rummage sale** = JUMBLE SALE (JUMBLE).

rummy /ˈrʌmɪ; ˋrʌmɪ/ *n* [U] any of various types of simple card-game in which players try to form sets or sequences of cards 拉米纸牌戏(玩法是组成套牌或顺牌).

ru·mour (*US* **ru·mor**) /ˈruːmə(r); ˋrumɚ/ *n* [C, U] (instance of) information spread by being talked about but not certainly true 传说; 传闻; 谣言: *Rumour has it* (ie says) *that he was fired.* 据说他给解雇了. ○ *There are rumours of an impending merger.* 有谣传说是快要合并了. ○ *I heard a rumour (that) he was leaving.* 我听人说他要走了.

▷ **ru·moured** (*US* **rum·ored**) *adj* reported as a rumour 传说的; 谣传的: *They bought the house at a rumoured price of £200 000.* 他们据说是以200 000英镑的价格购置的那所房子. ○ *It's rumoured that she's going to resign/She is rumoured to be on the point of resigning.* 听说她打算辞职[听说她就要辞职了].

rump /rʌmp; rʌmp/ *n* **1** [C] (**a**) animal's buttocks; tail-end of a bird (兽的)臀部; (鸟的)尾梢, 尾端. (**b**) (*joc* 谑) person's bottom (人的)屁股. **2** [C, U] (also ˌ**rump** ˈ**steak**) (piece of) beef cut from near the rump 臀肉牛排. **3** [C] (*derog* 贬) small or insignificant remnant (of a larger group) 少量的或无足轻重的残余部分: *The election reduced the Party to a rump.* 这次选举后该党已沦为微不足道的少数党.

rumple /ˈrʌmpl; ˋrʌmpl̩/ *v* [Tn] make (sth) creased or untidy; crumple 弄皱或弄乱(某物); 使起皱纹: *rumple one's clothes, hair* 弄皱衣服、弄乱头发.

rum·pus /ˈrʌmpəs; ˋrʌmpəs/ *n* (usu *sing* 通常作单数) disturbance; noise; uproar 骚乱; 喧闹; 喧嚣: *kick up/make/cause/create a rumpus* 激起[制造/引起/产生]骚乱.

□ ˈ**rumpus room** (*US dated* 旧) room in a private house (often in the basement) used esp for games, parties, etc; recreation room (私人住宅的)游艺室(常设于地下室); 娱乐室.

run[1] /rʌn; rʌn/ *v* (**-nn-**; *pt* **ran** /ræn; ræn/, *pp* **run**) **1** [I, Ipr, Ip] move at a speed faster than a walk, never having both or all the feet on the ground at the same time 跑; 奔跑: *He cannot run because he has a weak heart.* 他有心脏病, 不能跑. ○ *Can you run fast?* 你跑得快吗? ○ *They turned and ran* (ie in order to escape) *when they saw he had a gun.* 他们看见他有枪, 转身就跑. ○ *She ran/came running to meet us.* 她跑着来接我们. ○ *I had to run to catch the bus.* 我得赶快跑, 好赶上公共汽车. ○ *She ran out (of the house) to see what was happening.* 她(从房子里)跑出去, 看看出了什么事. ○ *The boys ran off as soon as we appeared.* 我们一来, 孩子就都跑了. ○ *He ran home in tears to his mother.* 他流着泪跑回家去找妈妈. ⇨Usage 见所附用法. **2** (**a**) [Tn] cover (the specified distance) by running 跑(一段距离): *Who was the first man to run a mile in under four minutes?* 谁第一个在四分钟以内跑完了一英里? (**b**) [I, Tn] (in cricket) score (a run or runs) by running between the wickets (板球)击球跑动得(分): *run a quick single* 击球后快跑得到1分 ○ *The batsmen ran two.* 击球员得了两分. **3** (**a**) [I] practise running as a sport 跑步锻炼; 跑步运动: *You're very unfit; you ought to take up running.* 你身体很弱, 应该练练跑步. ○ *She used to run when she was at college.* 她上大学时经常练跑步. (**b**) [I, Ipr, Tn] ~ **(in sth)** take part or compete in (a running race) (参加)赛跑: *Aouita will be running (in the 1500 metres) tonight.* 奥依塔今晚参加(1500米)赛跑. ○ *run the mile* 参加一英里赛跑 ○ *Cram ran a fine race to take the gold medal.* 克拉姆在赛跑中成绩突出夺得金牌. (**c**) [Tn] cause (a horse or dog) to take part in a race 使(马或狗)参加赛跑: *run two horses in the Derby* 让两匹马参加德比马赛. (**d**) [Tn esp passive 尤用于被动语态] cause (a race) to take place 举行(赛跑): *The Grand National will be run in spite of the bad weather.* 尽管天气不好, 一年一度的全国大马赛仍将举行. **4** [Ipr, Ip] go quickly or hurry to the specified place or in the specified direction 迅速地或急迫地前往某处: *run across to a neighbour's house to borrow some sugar* 急忙到邻居家去借些糖 ○ *I've been running around (town) all morning looking for Christmas presents.* 我(在城里)跑了一上午寻购圣诞节礼物. **5** [Ipr] move forward smoothly or easily, esp on wheels 平稳地或不很费力地向前移动(尤指用轮): *Trains run on rails.* 火车在轨道上行驶. ○ *Sledges run well over frozen snow.* 雪橇在冻硬了的雪上顺利滑行. **6** [Ipr, Ip] (of a ship or its crew) sail or steer in the specified direction (指船)行驶; (指船员)驾船航行: *We ran into port for supplies.* 我们驶进港口装补给品. ○ *The ship ran aground.* 船搁浅了. **7** (**a**) [I, Ipr] (of buses, ferries, trains, etc) travel to and fro on a particular route (指公共汽车、渡船、火车等)(沿规定路线)往来行驶: *Buses to Oxford run every half hour.* 去牛津的公共汽车每半小时开一班. ○ *The trains don't run on Christmas Day.* 圣诞节火车停驶. ○ *There are frequent trains running between London and Brighton.* 伦敦与布莱顿之间火车班次很多. (**b**) [Tn] cause (buses, trains, etc) to be in service 使(公共汽车、火车等)运营: *London Transport run extra trains during the rush-hour.* 伦敦运输公司在交通高峰时

R

间增开加班列车. **8** [Ipr, Tn·pr, Tn·p] drive (sb) to a place in a car 开车至某处; 开车送(某人): *It's a lovely sunny day; why don't we run down to the coast?* 天气多好哇, 咱们何不开车到海边玩玩? ○ *Can I run you* (ie give you a lift) *to the station?* 我开车送你去车站好吗? **9** (**a**) [Ipr] move, esp quickly, in the specified direction 向某方向移动(尤指快速): *The lorry ran down the hill out of control.* 卡车失去控制直往山下冲去. ○ *The car ran off the road into a ditch.* 汽车驶离道路跌进沟中. ○ *The ball ran* (ie rolled) *to the boundary.* 球向着边线滚去. ○ *Her eyes ran critically over her friend's new dress.* 她以挑剔的眼光打量朋友的新连衣裙. ○ *A shiver ran down her spine.* 她浑身哆嗦了一下. (**b**) [Tn·pr] cause (sth) to move in the specified direction 使(某物)向某方向移动: *She ran her fingers nervously through her hair.* 她紧张地用手指拢着头发. ○ *She ran her fingers lightly over the keys of the piano.* 她用手指轻轻地弹着钢琴. ○ *He ran his eyes over the page.* 他把这一页看了一遍. **10** [Tn, Tn·pr] bring or take (sth) into a country illegally and secretly; smuggle 非法地秘密运送或携带(某物)进入某国; 走私: *He used to run guns across the border.* 他过去经常偷运枪枝过境. ○ *run contraband goods/liquor into a country* 走私违禁物品[偷运私酒]进入某国. ⇨Usage at SMUGGLE 用法见SMUGGLE. **11** [I] (of salmon) move up a river in large numbers from the sea (指鲑鱼)洄游: *The salmon are running.* 鲑鱼正在洄游. **12** [Ipr] (of plants) grow or spread in the specified direction (指植物)蔓生: *Ivy ran over the walls of the cottage.* 村舍的墙壁上爬满了常春藤. **13** [Ipr] extend in the specified direction 伸展; 延伸: *A fence runs round the whole field.* 有一道篱笆围着这一整块地. ○ *The road runs parallel to the railway.* 这条公路与铁路平行. ○ *He has a scar running across his left cheek.* 他左脸上有一道很长的疤痕. **14** [Ipr] **~ (for...)** continue for the specified period of time without stopping 持续; 延续: *The play ran* (ie was performed regularly) *for six months on Broadway.* 这出戏在百老汇连续演了半年. ○ *Election campaigns in Britain run for three weeks.* 英国选举活动持续三周. **15** [Ipr] operate or be valid for the specified period of time (在一定期限内)起作用, 有效: *The lease on my house has only a year to run.* 我那房子的租期只有一年了. **16** [I] (of a story, an argument, etc) have the specified wording, content, etc (指叙述、陈述等)有某样言词、内容等: *The story runs that she poisoned her husband/She poisoned her husband, or so the story runs.* 据报道说, 她把丈夫毒死了. ○ *'Ten shot dead by gunmen,' ran the newspaper headline.* 报纸标题为'枪手击毙十人'. **17** (**a**) [Ipr] (of a liquid) flow (指液体)流动: *The River Rhine runs into the North Sea.* 莱茵河流人北海. ○ *The tears ran down her cheeks.* 她的脸上淌着眼泪. ○ *Water was running all over the bathroom floor/The bathroom floor was running with water.* 洗澡间水流了一地. (**b**) [Tn, Tn·pr, Dn·n, Dn·pr] **~ sth (for sb)** cause (a liquid) to flow 使(液体)流动: *She ran hot water into the bowl.* 她用碗接点热水. ○ *run the hot tap* 打开热水的水龙头 ○ *Could you run me a hot bath/run a hot bath for me?* 你给我放一盆热的洗澡水好吗? (**c**) [I] (of a tap, etc) send out a liquid (指水龙头等)流出液体: *Who left the tap running?* 谁忘了关水龙头了? ○ *Your nose is running*, ie Mucus is flowing from it. 你流鼻涕了. ○ *The smoke makes my eyes run.* 烟熏得我直流眼泪. ⇨Usage at DRIP[1] 用法见DRIP[1]. (**d**) [Ipr] **~ with sth** (usu in the continuous tenses 通常用于进行时态) be covered with (a flowing liquid) 流满(液体): *The streets were running with blood after the massacre.* 那场大屠杀后街上血流成河. ○ *His face was running with sweat.* 他汗流满面. **18** [I] (of dye or colour in a garment) dissolve and spread (指衣服上的染料或颜色)掉色, 扩散: *I'm afraid the colour ran when I washed your new skirt.* 很遗憾, 你那条新裙子我洗的时候掉色了. **19** [I] melt 融化: *It was so hot that the butter ran.* 天气太热, 黄油都化了. ○ *The wax began to run.* 蜡开始融化了. **20** [La, I] (of the sea, the tide, a river, etc) rise higher or flow faster (指海水、潮水、河水等)上涨, 流动加快: *The tide was running strong.* 潮水涨得很猛. **21** [La] pass into or reach the specified state; become 进入或达到某种状态; 变成: *The water ran cold when I turned the tap on.* 我把水龙头打开, 水就凉了. ○ *The river ran dry* (ie stopped flowing) *during the drought.* 大旱期间这条河都干了. ○ *Supplies are running short/low.* 供应品短缺. ○ *I have run short of money.* 我缺钱. **22** [Tn] be in charge of (sth); manage 负责(某事物); 经营; 管理: *run a hotel, a shop, a language school* 管理旅馆、商店、语言学校 ○ *He has no idea of how to run a successful business.* 他不知道把企业办好的方法. ○ *Stop trying to run* (ie organize) *my life for me!* 我的生活用不着你来管! **23** [Tn] make (a service, course of study, etc) available to people; organize 开办(服务项目、课程等); 举办: *The college runs summer courses for foreign learners of English.* 这所学院为学习英语的外国人开设了暑期班. **24** [I, Ipr, Tn, Tn·pr] (cause sth to) operate or function (使某物)运转, 起作用: *Your new car seems to run very nicely.* 你的新汽车开起来还很不错. ○ (*fig* 比喻) *Her life has run smoothly up to now.* 她的生活到目前仍一帆风顺. ○ *Could you run the engine for a moment?* 你让发动机转一会儿好吗? ○ *I can run my electric razor off* (ie with power from) *the mains.* 我的电动剃刀可以使用交流电. **25** [Tn] own and use (esp a vehicle) 有并使用(尤指交通工具): *I can't afford to run a car on my salary.* 凭我的薪水我是开不起汽车的. ○ *A bicycle is cheap to run.* 使用自行车是很经济的. **26** [I, Ipr] **~ (for sb/sth); ~ (in sth)** (*esp US*) be a candidate in an election (for a political position); stand (for sth) 竞选(某一政治职位); 当(某职务的)候选人: *Reagan ran (for the Presidency) a second time in 1980.* 里根于1980年再次竞选(总统). ○ *How many candidates are running in the Presidential election?* 有多少候选人参加总统竞选? **27** [Tn] present or nominate (sb) as a candidate in an election 提出(某人)参加竞选: *How many candidates is the Liberal Party running in the General Election?* 自由党在这次大选中提出了多少个候选人? **28** [Tn] (of a newspaper or magazine) print and publish (sth) as an item or a story (指报刊)刊登, 发表: *The 'Guardian' is running a series of articles on Third World Economics.* 《卫报》发表了论《第三世界的经济》的一系列文章. **29** [I] (*esp US*) (of a woven or knitted garment) become unwoven or unravelled (指编织的或针织的服装)脱针, 脱线, 抽丝: *Nylon tights sometimes run*, ie ladder. 尼龙裤袜有时候抽丝. **30** [La, Ipr] (esp in the continuous tenses 尤用于进行时态) (of an event, a train, etc) happen, arrive, etc at the specified time (指事情等)(在某时候)发生; (指火车等)(在某时刻)到达: *The trains are running an hour late.* 火车晚点一个小时. ○ *Programmes are running a few minutes behind schedule this evening.* 今晚的节目演出比预定的时间晚了几分钟. **31** (idm 习语) **come running** be eager to do what sb wants 渴望做某人想做的事: *If you offer the children rewards for helping they'll all come running.* 要是让孩子帮忙做事, 给他们点奖品, 他们就巴不得都来帮忙了. **'run for it** run in order to escape from sb/sth 逃跑: *Run for it — he's got a gun!* 快逃吧——他带着枪呢! (For other idioms containing **run**, see entries for *ns, adjs*, etc 查阅与**run**搭配的其他习语, 见有关名词、形容词等的词条, 如 **run/take its course** ⇨ COURSE[1]; **run riot** ⇨ RIOT.)

32 (phr v) **run across sb/sth** meet sb or find sth by chance 偶然遇见某人或发现某事物: *I ran across my old friend Jean in Paris last week.* 上周我在巴黎遇见了老朋友琼.

run after sb (no passive 不用于被动语态) (**a**) run to try to catch sb; chase sb 追赶某人; 追逐某人: *The dog was running after a rabbit.* 狗在追一只兔子. (**b**) (*infml* 口) (esp of a woman) seek sb's company (in order to have a romantic or sexual relationship with him) (尤指女性)追求(男子): *She runs after every good-looking man she meets.* 凡是漂亮的男子, 她见一个追一个.

run a'long (*infml* 口) (used in the imperative to tell sb, esp a child, to go away 用以叫某人(尤指小孩)离开): *Run along now, children, I'm busy.* 走开吧, 孩子们, 我正忙着呢.

run at sb (no passive 不用于被动语态) run towards sb (as if) to attack him 向某人冲去: *He ran at me with a knife.* 他持刀向我冲来. **run at sth** (no passive 不用于被动语态, usu in the continuous tenses 通常用于进行时态) (of a statistic or figure) be at the specified level or rate (指统计或数字)达到一定水平或比率: *Inflation is running at 25%.* 通货膨胀率达25%. ○ *Interest rates are running at record levels.* 利率达到创记录的水平.

run a'way (from sb/...) suddenly leave sb/a place;

escape from sb/a place 突然离开某人[某处]; 从某人处[某处]逃走: *Don't run away — I want your advice.* 请不要走——我需要你的意见. ○ *He ran away from home at the age of thirteen.* 他十三岁那年就离家出走了. **run away from sth** try to avoid sth because one is shy, lacking in confidence, etc 因羞怯、缺乏信心等而极力回避某事物; 逃避: *run away from a difficult situation* 尽力摆脱困境 ○ *Her suicide bid was an attempt to run away from reality.* 她想自杀就是要逃避现实. **run a'way with one** (of a feeling) gain complete control of one; dominate one (指感情)完全控制自己, 支配自己: *Don't let your temper run away with you.* 要控制住自己, 不要发脾气. ○ *Her imagination tends to run away with her.* 她的想像力如脱缰之马难以驾驭. **run away with sb; run a'way (together)** (also *infml* 口语作 **run off with sb; run 'off (together)**) leave home, one's husband etc with sb, in order to have a relationship with him or marry him 与某人私奔: *She ran away with her boss/She and her boss ran away (together).* 她与老板私奔了. **run away with sth** (**a**) steal sth and carry it away 偷走某物: *A cashier ran away with the day's takings.* 出纳员偷走了当天的进款. (**b**) use up or consume a lot of sth 用尽或大量消耗某物: *My new car really runs away with the petrol.* 我的新汽车耗油太多了. (**c**) win sth clearly or easily 轻易赢得某事物: *The champion ran away with the match.* 这个冠军获得的不费吹灰之力.

run sth back rewind (a film, tape, etc) in order to see or hear it again 倒回(影片、录音带等). **run back over sth** discuss or consider sth again; review sth 重新讨论或研究某事物; 回顾某事物: *I'll run back over the procedure once again.* 我把这个程序再复查一次.

run (sth) down (**a**) (cause sth to) lose power or stop functioning (使某物)耗尽能源或失去作用: *My car battery has run down; it needs recharging.* 我的汽车电池没电了, 需要充电. ○ *If you leave your headlights on you'll soon run down the battery.* 停车后不关前灯, 电池的电很快就会耗尽. (**b**) (often in the continuous tenses 常用于进行时态) (cause sth to) stop functioning gradually or decline in size or number (使某事物)逐渐失去作用, 衰退, 衰减, 萎缩: *British manufacturing industry has been running down for years.* 英国的制造业多年来一直在走下坡路. ○ *The local steelworks is being run down and is likely to close within three years.* 当地的这家钢铁厂越来越不景气, 有可能在三年内关闭. ○ *The company is running down its sales force.* 这家公司正在裁减推销人员. **run sb/sth down** (**a**) (of a vehicle or its driver) hit sb/sth and knock him/it to the ground; (of a ship) collide with sth (指车辆或驾驶人)撞倒某人[某物]; (指船)与某物相撞: *run down a pedestrian* 撞倒一行人 ○ *The cyclist was run down by a lorry.* 卡车把骑自行车的人撞倒了. ○ *The liner ran down a fishing-boat in thick fog.* 班轮在浓雾中撞上了渔船. (**b**) criticize sb/sth unkindly; disparage sb/sth 说某人[某事物]的坏话; 贬低某人[某事物]: *He's always running down his wife's cooking.* 他总嫌妻子做的饭菜不好. ○ *She's always running her children down in public.* 她总是当着人说自己的孩子不懂事. (**c**) find sb/sth after looking for him/it for a long time (寻找很长时间后)找到某人[某物]: *I finally ran the book down in the university library.* 我终于在大学图书馆找到了那本书. ○ *The criminal was eventually run down in the woods near his home.* 那罪犯终于落网, 就在他家附近的树林里被捕.

run sb in (*infml* 口) arrest sb and take him to a police station 逮捕某人押送警察局: *He was run in for drunk and disorderly behaviour.* 他因酗酒滋事而被拘留. **run sth in** prepare (the engine of a new car) for normal use by driving slowly and carefully 进行(新汽车的发动机的)磨合运转, 磨合试车: *Don't drive your new car too fast until you've run it in.* 新汽车未经磨合运转不要开得太快.

run into sb meet sb by chance 偶然遇见某人: *Guess who I ran into today.* 你猜我今天碰见谁了. ○ *I ran into an old schoolfriend at the supermarket this morning.* 今天早上我在超级市场碰见了一个老同学. **run into sth** (**a**) meet or enter (an area of bad weather) while travelling (旅行中)遇到(坏天气): *We ran into a patch of thick fog just outside Edinburgh.* 我们就在爱丁堡城外遇到了浓雾. (**b**) encounter (difficulties, problems, etc) 遭遇(困难、问题等): *The project is running into financial difficulties.* 这一项目遇到了财务困难. ○ *run into debt, danger, trouble* 陷入债务、危险、困境之中. (**c**) (no passive 不用于被动语态) reach (the specified level or amount) 达到(某一水平或数额): *Her income runs into six figures*, ie is more than £100 000. 她的收入达到六位数字(超过 100 000 英镑). ○ *Her last novel ran into three reprints in its first year of publication.* 她最近的一部小说在出版当年就印行了三次. **run (sth) into sb/sth** (cause a car, etc to) collide with or crash into sb/sth (使汽车等)撞及某人[某物]: *The bus went out of control and ran into a shop front.* 那公共汽车失去控制, 撞到了一家商店的门脸. ○ *She ran* (ie drove) *her car into a tree while reversing.* 她倒车时撞着了一棵树.

run (sth) off (cause liquid to) drain or flow out of a container (使液体)流尽, 排出: *Why don't you ever run the water off after you've had a bath?* 你洗完澡后为什么老是不把水放掉? **run sth off** (**a**) cause (a race) to be contested 进行(速度比赛): *The heats of the 200 metres will be run off tomorrow.* 明天举行 200 米预赛. (**b**) copy, reproduce or duplicate sth, eg on a photocopying machine 复印或复制某物: *Could you run (me) off twenty copies of the agenda?* 你把议事日程表给(我)复印二十份好吗? **run off with sb; run off (together)** (*infml* 口) = RUN AWAY WITH SB; RUN AWAY (TOGETHER). **run off with sth** steal sth and carry it away 偷走某物: *The treasurer has run off with the club's funds.* 会计拐走了俱乐部的资金.

run 'on continue without stopping; go on 连续不断; 继续下去: *The meeting will finish promptly — I don't want it to run on.* 会议要按时结束——不要拖延下去. ○ *She does run on so!* 她简直没完没了! **run (sth) on** (of a line of type) continue without being indented to show the beginning of a paragraph; continue (a line of type) without indenting it to show the beginning of a paragraph (指印刷文字的一行)接下去不分段; 使(印刷文字的一行)接下去不分段. **run on sth** (no passive 不用于被动语态) (of thoughts, a discussion, etc) have sth as a subject; be concerned with sth (指思想、议论等)以某事物为主题, 涉及某事物: *Her talk ran on developments in computer software.* 她谈的是计算机软件的开发问题. ○ *His thoughts kept running on recent events in India.* 他一直想着最近在印度发生的事.

run 'out (of an agreement, a document, etc) become no longer valid; expire (指协议、文件等)失效, 过期: *The lease on our flat runs out in a few months.* 我们公寓的租约还有几个月就到期了. ○ *My passport has run out.* 我的护照已失效. **run out (of sth)** (of a supply of sth) be used up, finished or exhausted; (of a person) use up or finish (a supply of sth) (指供应品)用完, 耗尽; (指人)用完, 耗尽(供应品): *The petrol is running out/We are running out of petrol.* 汽油快用光了[我们的汽油快用光了]. ○ *Our time is running out/We are running out of time.* 我们剩下的时间不多了. ○ *Could I have a cigarette? I seem to have run out (of them).* 给我一枝烟好吗? 我的(烟)已经抽完啦. **run (sth) out** (of a rope, etc) be passed out; pass (a rope, etc) out (指绳索等)放出, 拉出; 将(绳等)放出, 拉出: *The rope ran out smoothly.* 绳子顺顺当当地拉出来了. ○ *The sailor ran the line out neatly.* 水手很利落地把绳子放出去了. **run sb out** (often passive 常用于被动语态) (in cricket) dismiss (a batsman who is trying to make a run) by striking the wicket with the ball before he has reached his crease (板球)将(跑动中可能得分的击球员)杀出局(即在其到位前用球击中三柱门): *Border was (brilliantly) run out by Botham for 41.* 博德获 41 分后, 博瑟姆一个漂亮球把他杀出局了.

run 'over (of a container or its contents) overflow (指容器或所盛之物)溢出: *The bath/The bath water is running over.* 浴缸[浴缸的水]溢出来了. **run over sb; run sb over** (of a vehicle or its driver) knock sb down and pass over (a part of) his body (指车辆或驾驶人)撞倒某人并轧过其身体(之一部分): *I ran over a cat last night.* 我昨晚开车轧着了一只猫. ○ *Two children were run over by a lorry and killed.* 有两个孩子被一辆卡车轧死了. **run over sth** read through sth quickly; revise or rehearse sth 快速阅读某物; 温习或演习某事物: *I always run over my lines before going on stage.* 我登台演出前总要温习一下台词. ○ *She ran over her notes before giving the lecture.* 她讲课前把讲稿匆匆看了一遍. **run**

over with sth show a lot of (energy, enthusiasm, etc); overflow with sth 充满(活力、热情等); 洋溢: *She's running over with health and vitality.* 她非常健康, 充满活力.

run through sth (**a**) (no passive 不用于被动语态) pass quickly through sth 快速地穿过或传遍: *An angry murmur ran through the crowd.* 群众纷纷气愤地抱怨着. ○ *Thoughts of revenge kept running through his mind.* 他脑海里时刻萦绕着复仇的念头. (**b**) (no passive 不用于被动语态) be present in every part of sth; permeate sth 遍布于某事物; 贯穿着某事物: *A deep melancholy runs through her poetry.* 她的诗中贯穿着悲伤的情调. ○ *There is a deep-seated conservatism running through our society.* 我们社会中普遍存在着根深蒂固的保守思想. (**c**) discuss, examine or read sth quickly 匆匆讨论、检查或阅读: *He ran through the names on the list.* 他把名单匆匆地看了一遍. (**d**) review or summarize sth 复查或总结某事物: *run through the main points of the news* 把新闻要点归纳一下 ○ *Could we run through your proposals once again?* 我们再来审议一下你的建议好吗? (**e**) perform, act or rehearse sth 表演; 扮演; 排练: *Could we run through Act 3 again, please?* 请大家把第3幕再排练一遍好吗? (**f**) use up or spend (money) carelessly or wastefully 挥霍(金钱): *She ran through a lot of money in her first term at university.* 她上大学第一个学期就花了很多钱. **run sth through** play (part of a film or tape) by passing it through a machine 播放(电影或录音带片段): *Could we run that sequence through again?* 咱们再把那一段重放一遍好吗?

R

run to sth (no passive 不用于被动语态) (**a**) extend to or reach (the specified amount or size) 达到(某一数额或规模): *The book runs to 800 pages.* 该书长达800页. ○ *Her latest novel has already run to three impressions.* 她最近出版的一部小说已经印行三次了. (**b**) (of a person) have enough money for sth; (of money) be enough for sth (指人)有够作某事物用的钱; (指钱)足够某事物之用: *We can't/Our funds won't run to a holiday abroad this year.* 今年我们没有钱[我们的钱不够]去国外度假.

run ˈup (of a bowler in cricket, a long-jumper, etc) gather speed by running before releasing the ball, jumping, etc (指板球投球手、跳远运动员等)助跑: *Hadlee is now running up to bowl.* 哈德利正在助跑投球.

run sth up (**a**) raise or hoist sth 升起某物: *run up a flag on the mast* 在旗杆上升起旗子. (**b**) make (a garment) quickly, esp by sewing 赶做(衣服)(尤指缝纫): *run up a blouse, dress, skirt, etc* 赶做女衬衣、连衣裙、裙子等. (**c**) allow (a bill, debt, etc) to accumulate 积欠(帐款、债务等): *You'll run up a huge gas bill if you leave the heater on.* 热水器要是总开着, 煤气费就很高了. **run up against sth** meet or encounter (a difficulty, problem, etc) 遇到(困难、问题等): *The government is running up against considerable opposition to its privatization plans.* 政府的私有化计划遇到了很大的阻力.

□ ˈ**runabout** *n* (*infml* 口) small light car, esp one for making short journeys in towns 轻型小汽车(尤指市内用的).

ˈ**run-around** *n* (*infml* 口) (idm 习语) **give sb/get the ˈrun-around** treat sb/be treated in a deceitful or evasive manner 欺骗、瞒哄或搪塞某人[被欺骗、瞒哄或搪塞]: *He's been giving his wife the run-around*, eg sleeping with other women. 他一直蒙蔽着妻子(如与别的女人发生性关系).

ˈ**runaway** *adj* [attrib 作定语] **1** who has run away 逃跑的; 逃避的; 私奔的: *a runaway child* 离家出走的孩子. **2** (of an animal or a vehicle) no longer under the control of its rider or driver (指动物或车辆)失去控制的: *a runaway horse, lorry, train* 脱缰的马、失去控制的卡车、煞不住闸的火车. **3** happening very rapidly or easily 来得快的; 来得容易的: *the runaway success of her last play* 她最近那出戏的一炮而红 ○ *a runaway victory, win, etc* 轻而易举的胜利、成功等. — *n* person who has run away; fugitive 逃跑者; 逃亡者.

ˌ**run-down** *n* (usu *sing* 通常作单数) **1** act of running down (an industry, a company, etc); reduction of the size of an industry, etc (工业、公司等的)紧缩, 缩减: *the government's gradual run-down of the coal industry* 政府对煤炭工业所采取的逐渐紧缩的做法. **2 ~ (of/on sth)** (*infml* 口) detailed analysis or description (of sth) 详细的分析或描述: *give sb/get a run-down on sth* 做出[得到]某事物的详细汇报 ○ *I want a complete run-down on the situation.* 我需要一份有关形势的全面的分析报告.

ˌ**run-ˈdown** *adj* **1** in bad condition; dilapidated; neglected 破损的; 破败的; 失修的: *a ˌrun-down ˈarea, ˈtown, ˈindustry, ˈhouse* 衰败的地区、衰落的城市、衰退的工业、破损的房子 ○ *The whole district is in a terribly run-down state.* 这整个地区都已破败不堪. **2** tired and slightly ill, esp from working hard 疲惫的, 衰弱的(尤指因劳累): *be, feel, get run-down* 筋疲力尽 ○ *You look pretty run-down; why don't you take a holiday?* 你看上去气色不佳, 何不去度假?

ˈ**run-in** *n* **1 ~ (to sth)** period of time leading to (an event) (事件的)准备时期: *during the run-in to the election* 在选举的酝酿期间. **2 ~ (with sb)** (*infml* 口 *esp US*) quarrel or disagreement (with sb) (与某人)争吵, 争论: *have a run-in with sb* 与某人争吵.

ˈ**run-off** *n* extra race held to decide the winner when a race has ended in a tie (平局后的)加赛.

ˈ**run-through** *n* **1** review or summary (of sth) 复查; 总结: *Could we have a run-through of the main points discussed?* 我们把讨论的要点归纳一下好吗? **2** rehearsal or practice 排练; 练习: *There will be a run-through of the whole play tonight.* 今天晚上要把全剧排练一次.

ˈ**run-up** *n* **1** (**a**) (of a bowler in cricket, an athlete, etc) running in order to gain speed before releasing the ball, jumping, etc (指板球的投球手、田径运动员等的)助跑: *a fast, smooth, short, etc run-up* 快速的、稳健的、短距离的...助跑. (**b**) distance run in this way 助跑距离: *Pole vaulters need long run-ups.* 撑竿跳需要长距离助跑. **2 ~ (to sth)** period of time leading to an event (事件的)准备时期: *the run-up to the election* 选举前的酝酿时期.

NOTE ON USAGE 用法: Compare **run, trot, jog, gallop, sprint** and **race**. 试比较**run**、**trot**、**jog**、**gallop**、**sprint**、**race**这几个词. When describing movement that is faster than walking, **run** is the most general verb. 描述比行走快的动作, 最常用的动词是**run**. People usually **run** in a race or when they are in a hurry 通常**run**用于赛跑或有急事的场合: *I was late for the train so I had to run.* 我要赶不上火车了, 所以得跑着去. We generally **jog** for physical exercise, running steadily and not very fast. ☆ **jog**一般用于健身运动, 跑得稳但不太快. **Trot** and **gallop** are mainly used of horses. ☆ **trot**和**gallop**主要指马跑. When people **trot,** they run quite quickly with short steps 若以**trot**指人, 则意为小步快跑: *The girls spent the afternoon trotting up and down the beach.* 姑娘们一下午都在海滩上轻快地跑来跑去. Informally, **trot** can mean simply to 'go' 在口语中, **trot**可直接地表示go之意: *I'll just trot round to the shops for some bread.* 我就到附近商店去买些面包. **Gallop** is to run fast ☆ **gallop**指快跑: *He came galloping up the road.* 他沿路飞快跑来. **Race** suggests a need to run very fast, not always in competition ☆ **race** 指有快速跑的必要, 但不一定总是指比赛: *She raced to the window to stop the child jumping out.* 她一个箭步跑到窗前, 制止那孩子往外跳. **Sprint** is to run as fast as possible, usually over a short distance ☆ **sprint**指尽力快跑, 通常距离较短: *You'll have to sprint if you want to catch the train.* 你要想赶上火车, 就得快跑几步.

run[2] /rʌn; rʌn/ *n* **1** [C] act or period of running on foot 跑; 跑步; 奔跑; 奔跑的一段时间: *go for a run every morning* 每天早晨跑步 ○ *Catching sight of her, he broke into a run.* 他一看见她, 赶紧就跑. **2** instance or period of travelling by car, train, etc 乘汽车、火车等的旅行; 乘车旅行期间: *take the car out for a run in the country* 乘汽车去郊外一游 ○ *Oxford to London is about an hour's run by train.* 从牛津到伦敦乘火车大约有一小时行程. **3** [C] route taken by vehicles, ships, etc 车、船等行驶的路线: *The boat operates on the Dover-Calais run.* 这艘船运行多佛——加莱航线. **4** [C] series of performances 持续的演出: *The play had a good run/a run of six months.* 那出戏演了很久[演了半年]. ○ *It's just finished its West End run*, ie in the West End of London. 在伦敦西区的长期演出刚刚结束. **5** [C] period or succession; spell 时期; 一段时间: *We've enjoyed an exceptional run of fine weather recently.* 我们这里最近天气好极了. ○ *a run of bad luck*, ie a series of misfortunes 一连串的不幸. **6** [C usu *sing* 通常作单数] **~ on sth** sudden demand for sth by many people 许多人一时对某物的需求: *a run on sterling following its rise in value against the dollar* 英镑对美元升值后引起的抢购英镑的热潮 ○ *a run on the bank*, ie a sudden withdrawal of deposits by many customers 挤兑. **7** [C] (often in compounds 常用以构成复合词) space for domestic animals, fowl, etc (家畜、家禽等的)饲养场: *a 'chicken-run* 养鸡场 ○ *a 'sheep-run*, ie an area of pasture for sheep 牧羊场. **8** [C] point scored in cricket or baseball (板球或棒球中所得的)分. **9** [sing] **the ~ of sth** tendency or trend of sth 趋势; 趋向: *After 40 minutes Spurs scored, against the run of play*, ie although they had been playing poorly. 斯珀尔斯队每况愈下, 40分钟后却得了分. ○ *The run of the cards favoured me*, ie I was dealt good cards. 我得到的牌非常好. ○ *in accordance with the recent run of events*, ie the way things have been going recently 按照最近的情况发展. **10** [C] (*music* 音) series of notes sung or played quickly up or down the scale 急唱; 急奏. **11** [C] track for some purpose 有某种用途的小道: *a 'ski-run* 滑雪道. **12** [C] = LADDER 2. **13** [C] large number of fish in motion 游动的鱼群: *a run of salmon*, eg on their way upstream 游动的鲑鱼群(如在溯江洄游途中). **14 the runs** [pl] (*sl* 俚) diarrhoea 腹泻; 拉肚子. **15** (idm 习语) **at a 'run** running 跑(着): *He started off at a run but soon tired and slowed to a walk.* 他跑步出发, 但很快就累得慢下来成了步行. **the common, general, ordinary, etc run (of sth)** the average type or class 普通的类型或等级: *the common run of mankind*, ie ordinary average people 普通人 ○ *a hotel out of the ordinary run*, ie better than average 较好的旅馆. **give sb/get/have the run of sth** give sb/get/have permission to make full use of sth 允许某人[得到许可/获准]充分使用某物: *gave me the run of his library* 允许我自由使用他的书房 ○ *He has the run of the house.* 他获准使用那所房子. **in the long run** ⇨ LONG[1]. **make a bolt/dash/run for it/sth** ⇨ BOLT[2]. **on the 'run** (**a**) fleeing from pursuit or capture 奔逃; 逃跑: *He's on the run from the police.* 他正在逃避警方的追缉. ○ *have/keep the enemy on the run* 逼得敌人奔窜. (**b**) continuously active and moving about 忙碌; 奔波: *I've been on the run all day and I'm exhausted.* 我整天忙个不停, 疲于奔命. ○ *on the run from one office to another* 从一个公司的部门到另一个公司的部门. **a (good, etc) run for one's 'money** (**a**) challenging competition or opposition 较量; 竞争; 对抗: *They may win the game, but we'll give them a good run for their money.* 他们即使能赢得这场比赛, 我们也不会让他们轻易取胜. (**b**) reward, interest, enjoyment, etc, esp in return for effort 报偿、利益、满足等(尤指付出努力后所获得者): *I feel I've had an excellent run for my money* (ie a rewarding career) *and now I'm happy to retire.* 我对我一生的事业十分满意, 现在退休甚为欣慰.

□ **ˌrun-of-the-'mill** *adj* (*often derog* 常作贬义) not special; ordinary 一般的; 普通的: *a ˌrun-of-the-mill de'tective story* 平淡无奇的侦探小说.

rune /ru:n; run/ *n* **1** any of the letters in an ancient Germanic alphabet used by the Scandinavians and Anglo-Saxons for carving on wood or in stone 古日耳曼字母(斯堪的纳维亚人和盎格鲁撒克逊人刻于木石上的). **2** similar mark with a mysterious or magic meaning 神秘的或有魔力的符号.

▷ **ru·nic** /'ru:nɪk; 'runɪk/ *adj* of runes; written in or inscribed with runes 古日耳曼字母的; 有神秘符号的; 用古日耳曼字母写成或刻成的: *a runic calendar, alphabet, sign* 用古日耳曼字母写成的历书、古日耳曼字母表、有魔力的神秘符号.

rung[1] /rʌŋ; rʌŋ/ *n* [C] **1** cross-piece forming a step in a ladder (梯子的)横档, 梯级. ⇨illus at LADDER 见LADDER插图. **2** cross-piece joining the legs of a chair, etc to strengthen it (椅子等腿间的)横档. **3** (*fig* 比喻) level or rank in society, one's career, an organization, etc (社会、职业、组织等的)阶层, 等级: *start on the lowest/bottom rung of the salary scale* 从最低级别的薪金开始 ○ *His promotion has moved him up several rungs on the management ladder.* 他获得提升, 在管理阶层中提高了好几级.

rung[2] *pp* of RING[2].

run·nel /'rʌnl; 'rʌnl/ *n* (*fml* 文) small trickle or stream 细流; 小溪: *The rain ran in shallow runnels alongside the path.* 雨水流进路边的小河沟里.

run·ner /'rʌnə(r); 'rʌnɚ/ *n* **1** person or animal that runs; one taking part in a race 奔跑的人或动物; 赛跑的人或动物: *a long-distance runner* 长跑者 ○ *There are eight runners* (ie horses competing) *in the final race.* 有八匹马参加决赛. **2** messenger, esp for a bank or stockbroker 信差; 送信人; (尤指银行或股票经纪人的)跑外. **3** (esp in compounds 尤用以构成复合词) person smuggling the goods stated into or out of an area 偷运某货物出入某地的人; 走私者: *'drug-runners* 偷运毒品的人 ○ *'gun-runners* 走私枪枝的人. **4** metal or wood strip on which sth slides or moves along (金属制的或木制的)条状滑行装置: *the runners* (ie blades) *of my ice-skates* 我的冰鞋上的冰刀 ○ *sledge runners* 雪橇的滑板. **5** creeping plant stem that can take root 匍匐茎; 纤匐枝: *strawberry runners* 草莓纤匐枝. **6** long narrow strip of embroidered cloth, lace, etc placed on a sideboard, table, etc for ornament or protection (铺于餐具柜、桌子等上的)长条绣花饰布、饰带等.

□ **ˌrunner 'bean** (also **string bean**) (*Brit*) (*US* **'pole bean**) (**a**) type of climbing bean-plant 红花菜豆(攀缘豆科植物). (**b**) long green pod growing from this 红花菜豆(此种植物的绿色长豆荚).

runner-up /ˌrʌnər'ʌp; ˌrʌnɚ'ʌp/ *n* (*pl* **runners-up** /ˌrʌnəz'ʌp; ˌrʌnɚz'ʌp/) **~ (to sb)** person or team finishing second in a race or competition (竞赛中的)第二名, 亚军.

run·ning /'rʌnɪŋ; 'rʌnɪŋ/ *n* [U] **1** action or sport of running 跑; 跑步; 赛跑: *take up running* 开始跑步 ○ [attrib 作定语] *running shoes* 跑鞋. **2** management, maintenance or operation 管理; 经营; 维持; 操作: *the day-to-day running of a shop, business, machine, country* 商店的日常经营、事务的日常料理、机器的日常运转、国家的日常管理 ○ [attrib 作定语] *the running costs of a car*, eg of fuel, repairs, insurance 汽车的消费(如燃料费、保养费、保险费). **3** (idm 习语) **in/out of the 'running (for sth)** (*infml* 口) having some/no chance of succeeding or achieving sth 有[无]达到或实现某目的之机会: *be in the running for a management post, a company car* 有可能获得管理职位、公司的汽车. **make the 'running** (*infml* 口) set the pace or standard 定步调; 带头; 做榜样: *Wall Street made Friday's running on the international stock exchange.* 在国际股票交易中, 华尔街星期五率先确定了走势行情. ○ *Mike is rather timid with women, so Sue has to make all the running in their relationship.* 迈克在女子面前很腼腆, 所以苏珊只好对迈克主动一些.

▷ **run·ning** *adj* **1** [attrib 作定语] performed while running 边跑边做的; 在奔跑中完成的: *a running jump, kick* 跑跳步、跑动踢球. **2** [attrib 作定语] continuous or uninterrupted 连续的; 不断的: *a running battle for control of the party* 为控制该党而进行的持续斗争 ○ *The police kept up a running fire of questions during their interrogation of the suspect.* 警方审问嫌疑犯时提出了一连串的问题. **3** [pred 作表语] (following a number and a *pl n* 用于数字及复数名词之后) in succession; consecutively 接连; 连续: *win three times running* 连胜三次 ○ *For the sixth day running, my car wouldn't start.* 我的汽车已连续六天发动不起来了. **4** [attrib 作定语] (of water) flowing (指水)流动的: *I can hear running water.* 我听见有流水的声音. ○ *All our rooms have hot and cold running water*, ie from taps. 我们所有的房间都有冷热自来水. **5** [attrib 作定语] (of sores, etc) exuding liquid or pus (指伤口等)排出液体的, 流脓的. **6** (idm 习语) **in running/working order** ⇨ ORDER[1]. **take a running 'jump** (**a**) run up to the point where one jumps 助跑起跳. (**b**) (*sl* 俚) (used as a command 用作命令语) go away 走开: *I refused to lend him any more money and told him to take a running jump.* 我不愿再借给他钱, 便叫他走开.

□ **'running-board** *n* (formerly) foot-board under the doors of a car (旧时)汽车车门下方的踏板.

ˌrunning 'commentary spoken description of events as they occur, esp by a broadcaster 现场报道(尤指广播的): *From the passenger seat, he kept up a running*

R

commentary on her driving. 他坐在乘客座位上评论她的驾驶技术.

ˈrunning mate 1 (*politics* 政 *esp US*) candidate for a supporting position in an election, esp for the Vice-Presidency 竞选伙伴; (尤指)副总统候选人. **2** horse used to set the pace for another in a race (赛马中)领跑的马.

ˌrunning reˈpairs minor repairs or replacement of parts 小修; 修配: *Our photocopier is in continual need of running repairs.* 我们的复印机经常需要检修.

ˈrunning stitch line of evenly-spaced stitches made by a straight thread passing in and out of the material 直行针脚.

ˌrunning ˈtotal total (eg of costs, expenses) which includes each new item as it occurs 累积总计(如费用、开支的).

runny /ˈrʌnɪ; ˋrʌnɪ/ *adj* (**-ier, -iest**) (*infml* 口) **1** (*sometimes derog* 有时作贬义) more liquid than is usual or expected 水分过多的; 太稀的: *runny jam, sauce, cake-mixture, etc* 很稀的果酱、沙司、糕饼混合料等 ○ *Omelettes should be runny* (ie not fully cooked) *in the middle.* 荷包蛋要煎成溏心儿的. **2** (of the nose or eyes) tending to exude mucus (指鼻子)流鼻涕的; (指眼睛)流泪的: *You've got a runny nose!* 你流鼻涕了!

runt /rʌnt; rʌnt/ *n* **1** undersized animal, esp the smallest and weakest of a litter 发育不良的小动物(尤指一胎中最弱小的). **2** (*derog* 贬) insignificant or worthless person 小人物; 卑微小人.

run·way /ˈrʌnweɪ; ˋrʌnˌwe/ *n* prepared surface along which aircraft take off and land (飞机的)跑道.

ru·pee /ruːˈpiː; ruˋpi/ *n* [C] unit of money in India, Pakistan and certain other countries 卢比(印度、巴基斯坦等国的货币单位).

rup·ture /ˈrʌptʃə(r); ˋrʌptʃɚ/ *n* **1** [C, U] (*fml* 文) (instance of) breaking apart or bursting 破裂; 断裂: *the rupture of a blood-vessel, seed-pod, membrane* 血管、豆荚、薄膜的破裂. **2** [C, U] (*fig fml* 比喻, 文) (instance of) ending of friendly relations (友好关系的)破裂, 决裂; 绝交: *deep ruptures within the party* 党内严重的分裂. **3** [C] (*medical* 医) swelling in the abdomen caused when some organ or tissue breaks through the wall of its retaining cavity 疝. Cf 参看 HERNIA.

▷ **rup·ture** *v* **1** (**a**) [I, Tn] (cause tissue, an organ, etc to) burst or break (使身体组织、器官等)破裂, 裂开: *a ruptured appendix, spleen* 阑尾穿孔、脾破裂. (**b**) [Tn] **~ oneself** cause such a burst or break to happen to oneself 发生疝; 出现疝: *He ruptured himself lifting a bookcase.* 他抬书柜时出现了疝. **2** [I, Tn] (*fml* 文) (cause a connection, union, etc to) end (使关系等)破裂, 断绝: *the risk of rupturing East-West relations* 可能破坏东西方关系的危险.

rural /ˈrʊərəl; ˋrʊrəl/ *adj* [esp attrib 尤作定语] of, in or suggesting the countryside 乡村的; 在乡村的; 有乡村特点的: *rural areas, scenes, smells, accents* 农村地区、乡村风光、乡土气息、乡下口音 ○ *rural bus services, MPs, pastimes* 乡间公共汽车运营、下议院议员、娱乐活动 ○ *life in rural Britain* 英国的乡村生活. Cf 参看 RUSTIC 1, URBAN.

□ **ˌrural ˈdean** = DEAN 2.

ˌrural deˈlivery, ˌrural ˈroute, (*US*) delivery of mail in rural areas 乡村投递(路线).

Ru·ri·ta·nian /ˌrʊərɪˈteɪnɪən; ˌrʊrəˋtenɪən/ *adj* (of a State, its politics) full of plots and intrigues (as in two melodramatic novels about an imaginary country called *Ruritania*) (指国家、政治)玩弄阴谋诡计的.

ruse /ruːz; ruz/ *n* deceitful way of doing sth or getting sth; trick 骗术; 诈术; 诡计: *think up a ruse for getting into the cinema without paying* 想个不花钱进电影院的花招 ○ *My ruse failed.* 我的计谋落空了.

rush[1] /rʌʃ; rʌʃ/ *v* **1** [I, Ipr, Ip, It, Tn·pr, Tn·p, Dn·n, Dn·pr] (cause sb/sth to) go or come with great speed (使某人[某物])急速去或来: *Don't rush: take your time.* 别急急忙忙的, 慢慢来. ○ *Water went rushing through the lock gates.* 水流经水闸时十分湍急. ○ *The children rushed out of school.* 孩子们飞快跑出学校. ○ *Don't rush away/off — I haven't finished.* 别急着要走 —— 我还没完呢. ○ *People rushed to buy the shares.* 人们抢着购买股票. ○ *Ambulances rushed the injured to hospital.* 救护车把受伤的人火速送到医院. ○ *Relief supplies were rushed in.* 救济品已急速送到. ○ *Please rush me* (ie send me immediately) *your current catalogue.* 请将你方现有目录尽速寄来为盼. **2** [I, Ipr, Tn, Tn·pr] **~ (sb) (into sth/doing sth)** (cause sb to) act hastily (使某人)仓促行事: *regret rushed decisions* 对贸然做出的决定感到懊悔 ○ *rush into marriage* 仓促结婚 ○ *Don't rush me — this needs thinking about.* 别催我 —— 这事得考虑考虑. ○ *rush sb into signing a contract* 催促某人匆匆签署合同. **3** [Tn] attack or capture (sb/sth) by a sudden assault 突袭(某人[某事物]): *rush the enemy's positions, defences, etc* 向敌人的阵地、防御工事等突然发起进攻 ○ *Fans rushed the stage after the concert.* 音乐会结束后乐迷涌向舞台. **4** [Tn, Tn·pr] **~ sb/sth (for sth)** (*infml* 口) charge (a customer, etc) a high or exorbitant price 向(顾客等)索高价, 敲竹杠: *How much did the garage rush you for those repairs?* 汽车服务站敲了你多少修理费? **5** (idm 习语) **run/rush sb off his feet** ⇨ FOOT[1]. **rush into ˈprint** publish sth without proper care or consideration 草率出版某物. **6** (phr v) **rush sth out** produce sth very quickly 匆促生产某物; 赶制某物: *Editors rushed out a piece on the crash for the late news.* 编辑迅速将失事消息编入晚间新闻. **rush sth through (sth)** cause sth to become official policy, etc very quickly 使某事物很快通过成为官方政策: *rush a bill through Parliament* 使一项法案在议会中仓促通过.

rush[2] /rʌʃ; rʌʃ/ *n* **1** [sing] (instance of) rapid headlong movement or swift advance 急促的动作; 冲; 奔: *The tide comes in with a sudden rush here.* 这里潮水来势汹涌. ○ *make a rush for the door* 冲到门前 ○ *People were trampled in the headlong rush.* 大家拼命向前涌, 踩着了很多人. **2** [sing] sudden onset or surge of sth 突发; 突现: *a rush of blood to the cheeks* 脸一下子红起来 ○ *work in a rush of enthusiasm* 凭着一股热情工作 ○ *a rush of cold air*, eg as a window is opened 一股冷空气(如开窗时). **3** [sing, U] (*infml* 口) (period of) great activity 繁忙的活动(时刻): *Why all this mad rush?* 为什么要这样急急忙忙的? ○ *the Christmas rush*, ie the period before Christmas when crowds of people go shopping 圣诞节前的购物热 ○ *I'm in a dreadful/tearing rush* (ie hurry) *so I can't stop.* 我忙得不可开交. ○ *have a bit of a rush on* 要忙一阵子 ○ [attrib 作定语] *a rush job*, ie one done as quickly or as soon as possible 要尽快做妥的工作. **4** [C] **~ on/for sth** sudden great demand for goods, etc (对货物等的)大量急需, 争购: *a rush on umbrellas*, eg when there is heavy rain 争购雨伞(如下大雨时). **5 rushes** [pl] (*infml* 口) first print of a cinema film before it is cut and edited (电影)样片(未经剪辑者).

□ **ˈrush-hour** *n* time each day when traffic is busiest because people are going to or coming from work (上下班时的)交通拥挤时间, 高峰时刻: *morning/evening rush-hours* 早上[晚上]交通拥挤时间 ○ [attrib 作定语] *I got caught in the rush-hour traffic.* 我遇上了高峰时刻的车辆, 寸步难行.

rush[3] /rʌʃ; rʌʃ/ *n* marsh plant with a slender pithy stem which is dried and used for making chair-seats, baskets, etc 灯心草(干燥后用于编制椅面、篮子等): [attrib 作定语] *rush matting* 灯心草编织的席子.

▷ **rushy** *adj* full of rushes 长满灯心草的.

rusk /rʌsk; rʌsk/ *n* type of biscuit or bread baked hard and crisp, esp one used for feeding babies 脆饼干, 硬而脆的面包干(尤指婴儿食用的): *ˈteething rusks* 婴儿出牙期磨牙的饼干.

rus·set /ˈrʌsɪt; ˋrʌsɪt/ *adj* soft reddish-brown (柔和的)赤褐色的: *russet autumn leaves* 秋天赤褐色的叶子.

▷ **rus·set** *n* **1** [U] russet colour 柔和的赤褐色. **2** [C] type of rough-skinned apple of this colour 一种赤褐色的粗皮苹果.

Rus·sian /ˈrʌʃn; ˋrʌʃən/ *adj* of Russia, its culture, its language or its people 俄罗斯的; 俄国的; 俄罗斯文化的; 俄语的; 俄罗斯人的; 俄国人的: *Russian folklore, dancing* 俄罗斯民俗、舞蹈.

▷ **Rus·sian** *n* **1** [C] person from Russia or, loosely, the former Soviet Union 俄罗斯人; 俄国人; (泛指旧时的)苏联人. **2** [U] principal language of the former Soviet Union 俄罗斯语; 俄语.

□ **ˌRussian rouˈlette** (**a**) act of bravado in which a person holds to his head a revolver of which one (unknown) chamber contains a bullet, and pulls the trigger 俄罗斯轮盘赌(逞能冒险举动, 用只装一发子弹

的左轮手枪对准自己头部扣动扳机): *play (at) Russian roulette* 玩俄罗斯轮盘赌. (**b**) (*fig* 比喻) any action or situation involving serious and unpredictable risks 严重而不可预测的冒险行动或情况.

Russo- *comb form* 构词成分 Russian; of Russia or, loosely, the former Soviet Union 俄罗斯的; 俄国的; 俄罗斯文化的; 俄语的; 俄罗斯人的; 俄国人的; (泛指旧时)苏联的: *the Russo-Japanese war* 日俄战争 ○ *Russophiles*, ie people who are friendly to Russia or impressed by Russian achievements 亲俄的人.

rust /rʌst; rʌst/ *n* [U] **1** reddish-brown coating formed on iron or steel by the action of water and air 铁锈: *badly corroded with rust* 严重锈蚀的 ○ [attrib 作定语] *rust patches* 锈斑 ○ *rust remover* 除锈剂. **2** reddish-brown 赤褐(色): [attrib 作定语] *rust colour* 赤褐色. **3** (fungus causing a) plant disease with rust-coloured spots 锈病(植物疾病, 呈现铁锈色斑点); 锈菌.

▷ **rust** *v* [I, Ip, Tn, Tn·p esp passive 尤用于被动语态] **~ (sth) (away/through)** (cause sth to) be affected with rust (使某物)生锈; (使某植物)生锈病: *Brass doesn't rust.* 黄铜不生锈. ○ *The hinges had rusted away*, ie been destroyed by rust. 铰链锈坏了. ○ *The underneath of the car was badly rusted.* 汽车底部锈得很厉害.

rusty *adj* (**-ier**, **-iest**) **1** affected with rust 生锈的; 锈蚀的; 生锈病的: *rusty nails* 生锈的钉子. **2** [esp pred 尤作表语] (*fig* 比喻) of a poor quality or standard through lack of practice (因缺乏实践)质量或标准下降; 荒疏: *My German, tennis, singing is rather rusty.* 我久未练习, 德语、网球、唱歌水平低了很多. **rust·ily** *adv*. **rusti·ness** *n* [U].

□ ˈ**rust-proof** *adj* (of metal) treated to prevent rusting (指金属)经防锈处理的, 不锈的. — *v* [Tn] treat (metal) this way 对(金属)作防锈处理.

rus·tic /ˈrʌstɪk; ˋrʌstɪk/ *adj* [usu attrib 通常作定语] **1** (*approv* 褒) typical of the country or country people 有农村或村民特色的: *rustic charm, peace, simplicity* 乡村的秀丽、宁静、简朴 ○ *lead a rustic existence* 过乡村生活. Cf 参看 RURAL. **2** rough and unrefined 粗野的; 不雅的: *rustic accents, manners* 粗俗的腔调、举止. **3** made of rough timber or untrimmed branches 用粗糙的木材或树枝制作的: *a rustic bench, bridge, fence, etc* 用粗糙木料制的长凳、桥、栅栏等.

▷ **rus·tic** *n* (*esp derog* 尤作贬义) peasant or yokel 乡巴佬儿: *country rustics* 乡下佬儿.

rus·tic·ally /-klɪ; -klɪ/ *adv*.

rus·ti·city /rʌˈstɪsətɪ; rʌsˋtɪsətɪ/ *n* [U] being typical of the country in appearance or character 乡村的特点、风格或气息.

rus·tic·ate /ˈrʌstɪkeɪt; ˋrʌstɪˌket/ *v* **1** [Tn] (*Brit*) send (a student) away from university temporarily, as a punishment 罚(大学生)暂时停学离校. **2** [I] (*fml* 文) settle in the country and lead a rural life 在农村定居. ▷ **rus·tica·tion** /ˌrʌstɪˈkeɪʃn; ˌrʌstɪˋkeʃən/ *n* [U].

rustle /ˈrʌsl; ˋrʌsl̩/ *v* **1** [I, Ipr, Tn, Tn·pr] (cause sth to) make a dry light sound, esp by friction or rubbing together (使某物)发出轻而爽的声音(尤指摩擦或挤磨声): *Her silk dress rustled as she moved.* 她走起路来, 丝质的连衣裙窸窣作响. ○ *Leaves rustled gently in the breeze.* 树叶迎着微风策策作响. ○ *I wish people wouldn't rustle their programmes during the solos.* 在独奏进行时, 我希望人们不要把节目单翻得沙沙地响. **2** [Ipr, Ip] move along making such a sound 发着轻而爽的声音移动: *Did you hear something rustling through the bushes?* 你听见有东西在灌木丛中窸窸窣窣地移动吗? **3** [Tn] (*US*) steal (cattle or horses that are grazing in the wild) 偷盗(放牧中的牛或马). **4** (phr v) **rustle sth/sb up** (*infml* 口) prepare or provide sth/sb, esp at short notice 准备, 提供, 张罗(尤指仓促间): *I'll rustle up some eggs and bacon for you.* 我给你弄些鸡蛋和腌猪肉. ○ *I rustled up a few helpers to hand out leaflets.* 我找到几个助手散发传单.

▷ **rustle** *n* [sing] rustling sound 轻而爽的声音: *the rustle of banknotes, petticoats* 钞票、衬裙的窸窣声.

rust·ler /ˈrʌslə(r); ˋrʌslɚ/ *n* (*US*) cattle or horse thief 偷牛贼; 盗马贼.

rust·ling /ˈrʌslɪŋ; ˋrʌslɪŋ/ *n* **1** [C, U] (instance of the) sound made by sth that rustles 轻而爽的声音: *mysterious rustlings at night* 夜里神秘的瑟瑟声 ○ *the rustling of dry leaves, sweet-papers* 枯叶、糖果纸的沙沙声. **2** [U] stealing of cattle or horses 偷牛; 偷马.

rut[1] /rʌt; rʌt/ *n* [C] **1** deep track made by a wheel or wheels in soft ground; furrow 车辙; 犁沟: *My bike bumped over the ruts.* 我的自行车在凹凸不平的车辙道上颠颠簸簸. **2** (idm 习语) **be (stuck) in a ˈrut** have a fixed and boring way of life 囿于刻板而乏味的生活方式. **get into/out of a ˈrut** start/stop leading a routine existence 开始[不再]过刻板的生活: *It's time to get out of the 9 to 5 rut*, ie of the normal working day. 应该摆脱开9点上班5点下班那种刻板的生活了.

▷ **rut** *v* (**-tt-**) [Tn esp passive 尤用于被动语态] mark (sth) with ruts 在(某物)上形成车辙; 使(某物)留下凹痕: *The lane was rutted with tyre tracks.* 这小巷有车胎轧出的凹痕. ○ *a deeply rutted road* 留有很深车辙的路.

rut[2] /rʌt; rʌt/ *n* (also **the rut**) [U] periodic sexual excitement of a male deer, goat, ram, etc (雄性的鹿、羊等的周期的)性冲动: *stags fight during the rut* 雄鹿之间在交配期的格斗.

▷ **rut** *v* (**-tt-**) [I] be affected by this (雄性的鹿、羊等周期地)性冲动: *a rutting stag* 准备交配的雄鹿.

ru·ta·baga /ˌruːtəˈbeɪgə; ˌrutəˋbegə/ *n* [C, U] (*US*) = SWEDE.

ruth·less /ˈruːθlɪs; ˋruθlɪs/ *adj* **1** having or showing no pity or compassion; cruel 无怜悯心或同情心的; 残忍的: *show ruthless disregard for other people's feelings* 对别人的感情漠不关心 ○ *a ruthless dictator* 残酷的独裁者 ○ *be utterly ruthless in one's determination to succeed* 下决心争取成功对一切毫不留情. **2** never slackening or stopping; unremitting 决不松懈的; 永不停止的; 持久的: *set off at a ruthless pace* 勇往直前 ○ *ruthless schedules, demands* 决不放松的时间安排、要求. ▷ **ruth·lessly** *adv*: *be ruthlessly efficient* 永远保持高效率. **ruth·less·ness** *n* [U]: *The terrorists' ruthlessness shocked the population.* 恐怖分子极其残忍, 全体人民无不感到震惊.

-ry ⇨ -ERY.

rye /raɪ; raɪ/ *n* **1** [U] (grain of a) type of cereal plant used for making flour or as food for cattle 黑麦; 黑麦粒: [attrib 作定语] *rye bread* 黑面包. ⇨illus at CEREAL 见 CEREAL 插图. **2** [C, U] (also **rye whisky**) (*esp US*) (glass of) whisky made from rye (一杯)黑麦威士忌酒.

S s

S, s /es; ɛs/ *n* (*pl* **S's, s's** /ˈesɪz; ˋɛsɪz/) the nineteenth letter of the English alphabet 英语字母表的第十九个字母: *'Say' begins with (an) 'S'.* say一字以s字母开始.
□ ˈ**S-bend** *n* bend in a road shaped like an S S形的弯路.

S *abbr* 缩写 = **1** (*pl* **SS**) Saint. Cf 参看 ST 1. **2** (esp on clothing) small (size) (尤用于衣物)小(号). **3** (*US* also **So**) south(ern): *S Yorkshire* 约克郡南部.

s *abbr* 缩写 = **1** (in former British currency) shilling(s) (旧时英国货币的)先令. **2** (esp on forms) single (status) (尤用于表格中)单身.

SA *abbr* 缩写 = **1** (*religion* 宗) Salvation Army. **2** /ˌes ˈeɪ; ˌɛs ˋe/ (*infml* 口) sex appeal. **3** South Africa.

Sab·bat·arian /ˌsæbəˈteərɪən; ˌsæbəˋtɛrɪən/ *n* Christian who believes that on the sabbath one should go to church and not work, take part in sports, etc 严守安息日的基督徒(认为安息日只应去做礼拜而不应工作、参加体育运动等者). ▷ **Sab·bat·arian** *adj* [attrib 作定语]: *Sabbatarian beliefs, principles* 严守安息日的教徒的信仰、教义.

sab·bath /ˈsæbəθ; ˋsæbəθ/ *n* **the sabbath** [sing] day of the week intended for rest and worship of God (Saturday for Jews and Sunday for Christians) 安息日(犹太教为星期六, 基督教为星期日): *keep/break the sabbath*, ie (not) work or play on the sabbath 守[不守]安息日 ○ [attrib 作定语] *the sabbath day* 安息日.

S

sab·bat·ical /səˈbætɪkl; səˋbætɪkḷ/ *adj* **1** [attrib 作定语] (of leave) given at intervals to academics for travel, study, etc (指假期)给大学教师的(用于旅行、研究等): *a sabbatical term, year, etc* 大学教师的休假学期、学年等. **2** (*fml* 文) of or like the sabbath (似)安息日的.
▷ **sab·bat·ical** *n* [C, U] (period of) sabbatical leave (大学教师的)休假(期间): *a one-year sabbatical* 为期一年的休假 ○ *be on sabbatical* 在休假.

sable /ˈseɪbl; ˋsebḷ/ *n* **1** [C] small Arctic mammal, valued for its dark fur 紫貂; 黑貂. **2** [U] fur of this mammal 紫貂皮: [attrib 作定语] *a sable coat, stole, etc* 紫貂皮大衣、披肩等. ▷ **sable** *adj* [usu attrib 通常作定语] (*fml* 文) black; dark; gloomy 黑色的; 暗的; 阴暗的.

sabot /ˈsæbəʊ; *US* sæˈbəʊ; sæˋbo/ *n* shoe hollowed out of a single piece of wood, or having a wooden sole 木鞋(用整块木头挖成的); 木底鞋.

sab·ot·age /ˈsæbətɑːʒ; ˋsæbəˌtɑʒ/ *n* [U] damage done secretly to prevent an enemy, a competitor, etc succeeding, esp by destroying his weapons or equipment and spoiling his plans 阴谋破坏(尤指摧毁对方武器或装备以及挫败对方计划等行为): *Was the fire an accident or (an act of) sabotage?* 这场大火是意外事故还是有人破坏?
▷ **sab·ot·age** *v* [Tn] secretly damage, destroy or spoil (sth) 阴谋破坏(某事物): *sabotage a missile, a ship, an engine, etc* 毁坏导弹、船、发动机等 ○ *sabotage sb's plans, business* 破坏某人的计划、生意 ○ *They tried to sabotage my party by getting drunk.* 他们想藉要酒疯来破坏我的宴会.
sa·bot·eur /ˌsæbəˈtɜː(r); ˌsæbəˋtɝ/ *n* person who commits sabotage 搞阴谋破坏的人.

sabra /ˈsɑːbrə; ˋsɑbrə/ *n* (*esp US*) Israeli Jew born in Israel 在以色列出生的犹太人.

sabre (*US* **saber**) /ˈseɪbə(r); ˋsebɚ/ *n* **1** heavy cavalry sword with a curved blade (骑兵用的弯刃的)军刀, 马刀. ⇨illus at SWORD 见SWORD插图. **2** light sword with a tapering blade, used in fencing (FENCE[2]) (击剑时用的)尖细的轻剑. Cf 参看 ÉPÉE, FOIL[3].
□ ˈ**sabre-rattling** *n* [U] attempts to frighten sb by threatening to attack or punish him 武力威胁; 炫耀武力: *Her speech is mere sabre-rattling*, ie She will not carry out her threats. 她讲的话只不过是吓唬人而已. ○ [attrib 作定语] *sabre-rattling tactics* 武力威胁手段.
ˌ**sabre-toothed** ˈ**tiger** tiger, now extinct, having (usu two) sabre-like teeth 剑齿虎(已绝种).

sac /sæk; sæk/ *n* bag-like part of an animal or plant (动植物组织中的)囊, 液囊.

SAC *abbr* 缩写 = (*US*) Strategic Air Command 战略空军司令部.

sac·charin /ˈsækərɪn; ˋsækərɪn/ *n* [U] very sweet substance used as a substitute for sugar 糖精.
▷ **sac·char·ine** /-riːn; -ˌrin/ *adj* (*esp derog* 尤作贬义) very sweet; too sweet 极甜的; 太甜的: *a saccharine taste* 极甜的味道 ○ (*fig* 比喻) *a saccharine smile* 谄笑 ○ *I found the film far too saccharine.* 我觉得这部电影太缠绵了.

sa·cer·dotal /ˌsæsəˈdəʊtl; ˌsæsɚˋdotḷ/ *adj* (*fml* 文) **1** of a priest or priests 牧师的; 神甫的; 司铎的. **2** (of a doctrine, etc) claiming supernatural powers for ordained priests (指教义等)认为神职人员有超自然力的. ▷ **sa·cer·dot·al·ism** /-təlɪzəm; -tḷˌɪzəm/ *n* [U].

sachet /ˈsæʃeɪ; *US* sæˈʃeɪ; sæˋʃe/ *n* **1** sealed plastic or paper pack containing a small amount of a product (用以装少量物品的)封口的塑料袋或纸袋: *a sachet of sugar, sauce, shampoo, etc* 一小袋食糖、沙司、洗发剂等. **2** small bag containing a sweet-smelling substance, placed among clothes, etc to scent them (置于衣物等中的)香囊, 香料袋.

sack[1] /sæk; sæk/ *n* **1** (contents of) any large bag of strong material used for storing and carrying eg cement, coal, flour, potatoes 大口袋(用以存放或装运水泥、煤、面粉、马铃薯等的); 大口袋所装之物: *The sack split and the rice poured out.* 口袋裂开了, 大米撒出来了. **2** (*US*) (contents of) any bag (任何的)口袋(所盛之物): *a sack of candies* 一包糖果 ○ *two sacks of groceries* 两袋杂货. **3** (also ˈ**sack dress**) short loose straight dress 布袋装(宽松直筒短装). **4** (idm 习语) **hit the hay/sack** ⇨ HIT[1].
▷ **sack·ful** /-fʊl; -fʊl/ *n* quantity held by a sack 一袋的量: *two sackfuls of flour* 两袋面粉.
sack·ing *n* [U] cloth, eg coarse flax or hemp, used for making sacks 做口袋用的布(如麻布).
□ ˈ**sackcloth** *n* [U] **1** = sacking. **2** (idm 习语) ˌ**sackcloth and** ˈ**ashes** signs of repentance or mourning 忏悔; 哀悼.
ˈ**sack-race** *n* race in which competitors put both legs in a sack and move forward by jumping 套袋赛跑(双腿套入袋内跳跃前进的竞赛).

sack[2] /sæk; sæk/ *v* [Tn] (*infml* 口 *esp Brit*) dismiss (sb) from a job; fire 解雇(某人): *be sacked for incompetence* 因能力不够而被解雇.
▷ **the sack** *n* [sing] dismissal from a job 解雇: *give sb/get the sack* 解雇某人[遭解雇] ○ *It's the sack for you!* ie You are going to be dismissed. 要把你解雇了!

sack[3] /sæk; sæk/ *v* [Tn] steal or destroy property in (a captured town, etc) 劫掠, 毁坏(一占领的城市等).
▷ **the sack** *n* [sing] act or process of sacking a town, etc (对占领的城市等的)劫掠, 毁坏: *the sack of Troy* 对特洛伊的洗劫.

sack[4] /sæk; sæk/ *n* [U] (*arch* 古) dry white wine made in Spain or the Canary Islands (西班牙或加那利群岛产的)干白葡萄酒.

sac·ra·ment /ˈsækrəmənt; ˋsækrəmənt/ *n* **1** [C] ritual act in the Roman Catholic, Anglican and other Christian Churches through which those who take part believe they receive a special grace from God 圣事; 圣礼: *the sacraments of baptism, confirmation, confession, etc* 洗礼、坚信礼、告解. **2 the** ˈ**sacrament** [sing] (also **the** ˌ**Blessed** ˈ**Sacrament, the** ˌ**Holy** ˈ**Sacrament**) the consecrated bread and wine of the Eucharist; Holy Communion圣餐; 圣餐礼: *receive the sacrament* 领圣餐.
▷ **sac·ra·mental** /ˌsækrəˈmentl; ˌsækrəˋmɛntḷ/ *adj* [esp attrib 尤作定语] of or connected with the sacraments圣餐的; 圣礼的: *sacramental wine* 圣餐中的葡萄酒.

sac·red /ˈseɪkrɪd; ˋsekrɪd/ *adj* **1** connected with or dedicated to God or a god; connected with religion 神圣的; 宗教的: *a sacred rite, place, image* 宗教仪式、圣地、圣像 ○ *a sacred building*, eg a church, mosque, synagogue or temple 宗教建筑物(如教堂、回教寺、犹太教会堂或寺庙) ○ *sacred music,* ie for use in religious services 圣乐(宗教仪式中用的音乐) ○ *sacred writings,* eg the Koran, the Bible 宗教经典(如古兰经、圣经). **2 ~ (to sb)** regarded with great respect or reverence 受崇敬的; 不可冒犯的: *In India the cow is a sacred animal.* 在印度, 牛是神圣的动物. ○ *Her marriage is sacred to her.* 她认为自己的婚姻至高无上. ○ (*joc* 谑) *They've changed the time of the news — is nothing sacred?*把新闻时间改了——什么都不当一回事了? **3** (*fml* 文) (of an obligation, etc) regarded as very important; solemn (指义务等)认为重要的, 庄严的: *a sacred promise, task* 郑重的诺言、重大的任务 ○ *hold a promise sacred* 信守诺言 ○ *regard sth as a sacred duty* 视某事为神圣的职责. **4 ~ to sb/sth** (phrase seen on tombstones and monuments to the dead 用于墓碑及对死者的纪念碑上的词语) dedicated to sb/sth 献给某人[某事物]: *sacred to the memory of...* 献给.... **5** (idm 习语) **a sacred 'cow** an idea, institution, etc that many think should not be criticized神圣不可侵犯的思想、机构、制度等: *Let's not make a sacred cow of the monarchy.* 咱们别把君主政体奉若神明. ▷ **sac·redly** *adv*. **sac·red·ness** *n* [U].

sac·ri·fice /ˈsækrɪfaɪs; ˋsækrə,faɪs/ *n* **1 ~ (to sb) (a)** [U] offering of sth valuable, often a slaughtered animal, to a god 供奉; 献祭; 祭祀: *the sacrifice of an ox to Jupiter* 用牛祭祀古罗马主神朱庇特. **(b)** [C] such an offering; thing offered in this way 供品; 祭品; 牺牲: *kill a sheep as a sacrifice* 宰羊用作祭品. **2 (a)** [U] giving up of sth, usu in return for sth more important or valuable 放弃某事物(通常指为获得更重要或更有价值的东西): *Getting rich isn't worth the sacrifice of your principles.* 为致富而牺牲原则是不值得的. ○ *He became a top sportsman at some sacrifice to himself,* ie by training very hard, giving up many pleasures, etc. 他付出了一些代价才成为优秀运动员. **(b)** [C] thing given up in this way 牺牲的事物: *Her parents made many sacrifices so that she could go to university.* 她父母为她上大学在多方面作了牺牲.

▷ **sac·ri·fice** *v* **1** [Ipr, Tn, Tn·pr] **~ to sb; ~ sth (to sb) make a sacrifice(1) of (sth) to sb** 供奉; 献祭; 祭祀: *sacrifice to idols* 供奉偶像 ○ *sacrifice a lamb to the gods* 以羊羔祭祀众神. **2** [Tn, Tn·pr] **~ sth (to sb/sth)** give up sth as a sacrifice(2) 牺牲某事物: *She sacrificed her career to marry him.* 她为了嫁给他牺牲了自己的事业. ○ *The car's designers have sacrificed comfort to economy,* ie have made the car less comfortable in order to sell it at a low price. 汽车设计人员为降低造价舍弃了汽车舒适方面的一些设想. ○ *I'm not sacrificing my day off just to go shopping with Jane.* 我可不愿意牺牲一天休假日单单陪简去买东西.

sac·ri·fi·cial /ˌsækrɪˈfɪʃl; ˌsækrəˈfɪʃəl/ *adj* [usu attrib 通常作定语] of or like a sacrifice (似)供奉(品)的, 献祭(品)的, 祭祀(品)的, 牺牲(品)的. **sac·ri·fi·cially** /-ʃəlɪ; -ʃəlɪ/ *adv*.

sac·ri·lege /ˈsækrɪlɪdʒ; ˋsækrəlɪdʒ/ *n* [C usu *sing*, U 作可数名词时通常作单数, 亦作不可数名词] (act of) treating a sacred thing or place with disrespect 渎圣(亵渎圣物或圣地的行为): *It is (a) sacrilege to steal a crucifix from an altar.* 从圣坛窃取耶稣受难像是亵渎神灵的行为. ○ (*fig* 比喻) *She regarded the damage done to the painting as sacrilege.* 她认为毁坏了那幅画是大逆不道的事. ▷ **sac·ri·le·gious** /ˌsækrɪˈlɪdʒəs; ˌsækrɪˋlɪdʒəs/ *adv*. **sac·ri·le·giously** *adv*.

sac·ristan /ˈsækrɪstən; ˋsækrɪstən/ *n* person who looks after the contents of a church and prepares the altar for services 圣器保管员.

sac·risty /ˈsækrɪstɪ; ˋsækrɪstɪ/ *n* room in a church where a priest puts on his vestments and where the vestments, candles, etc are kept (教堂的)圣器收藏室.

sac·ro·sanct /ˈsækrəʊsæŋkt; ˋsækro,sæŋkt/ *adj* (*often ironic* 常作反语) considered too important to be changed, argued about, etc 神圣不可侵犯的: *You can't cut spending on defence — that's sacrosanct!* 国防开支可削减不得——那可是关天关地的事!

sad /sæd; sæd/ *adj* **(-dder, -ddest) 1** showing or causing sorrow; unhappy 悲哀的; 忧愁的; 难过的: *a sad look, event, story* 忧愁的表情、伤心的事件、悲惨的故事 ○ *John is sad because his dog has died.* 约翰因为自己的狗死了非常伤心. ○ *I'm sad you're leaving.* 你要走了, 我很难过. ○ *It was a sad day for us all when the school closed down.* 学校关闭那天, 我们都很悲痛. ○ *Why is she looking so sad?* 她为什么愁容满面? **2** [attrib 作定语] worthy of blame or criticism; bad 该受责备或批评的; 坏的: *a sad state of affairs* 很糟糕的情况 ○ *a sad case of cruelty* 非常残忍的事. **3** making one feel pity or regret 令人遗憾或惋惜的: *This once beautiful ship is in a sad condition now.* 那么漂亮的船现在成了这种样子了. **4** (idm 习语) **ˌsadder but ˈwiser** having learnt sth important from a disappointing mistake or failure 从错误和失败吸取重要教训: *The divorce left him a sadder but a wiser man.* 他离婚是吃一堑长一智. **sad to say** (used esp at the beginning of a sentence 尤用于句首) unfortunately 不幸的是: *Sad to say, she hasn't given us permission to do it.* 不幸的是, 她没准许我们做这件事.

▷ **sad·den** /ˈsædn; ˋsædn̩/ *v* [I, Tn] (cause sb to) become sad (使某人)悲哀, 忧愁: *He saddened at the memory of her death.* 他想到她已死去就很难过. ○ *The bad news saddened us.* 我们得知这个坏消息后非常伤心.

sadly *adv* **1** in a sad manner 悲哀地; 忧愁地: *She looked at him sadly.* 她很难过地看着他. **2** regrettably 令人遗憾地; 惋惜地: *a sadly neglected garden* 荒废得很可惜的花园. **3** unfortunately 不幸地: *Sadly, we have no more money.* 我们可惜没有钱了. ⇨Usage at HOPEFUL 用法见 HOPEFUL.

sad·ness *n* **1** [U] being sad 悲哀; 忧伤. **2** [C usu *pl* 通常作复数] thing that makes one sad 令人悲哀或忧伤的事物: *One of the many sadnesses in his life was that he never had children.* 他一生中的一大憾事就是膝下犹虚.

saddle /ˈsædl; ˋsædl̩/ *n* **(a)** seat, often of leather, for a rider on a horse, donkey, etc or on a bicycle or motor cycle 鞍; 鞍座; (自行车或摩托车的)车座. ⇨illus at App 1 见附录1插图, page xiii. **(b)** part of a horse's back on which this is placed 马背装鞍的部位. **2** ridge of high land rising to high points at each end 两峰间的凹下部分; 鞍状山脊. ⇨ illus at MOUNTAIN 见 MOUNTAIN 插图. **3** joint of meat from the back of an animal, together with part of the backbone and ribs (动物的)带脊骨和肋骨的大块肉: *a saddle of lamb, venison, beef, etc* 羊脊肉、鹿脊肉、牛脊肉. **4** (idm 习语) **in the ˈsaddle (a)** on horseback 骑着马: *spend hours in the saddle* 骑马数小时. **(b)** (*fig* 比喻) in a position of control 处于控制地位: *The director hopes to remain in the saddle* (ie in his job) *for a few more years.* 该董事希望再多留任几年.

▷ **saddle** *v* **1** [Ip, Tn, Tn·p] **~ up; ~ sth (up)** put a saddle on (a horse) 给(马)装鞍: *saddle up and ride off* 套上鞍骑走 ○ *saddle one's pony (up)* 给小马套上鞍. **2** (phr v) **saddle sb with sth** give sb an unwelcome responsibility, task, etc 让某人承担使人厌恶的责任、任务等: *I've been saddled with the job of organizing the conference.* 组织会议这件倒霉事交给我了. ○ *The boss saddled her with all the most difficult customers.* 老板把那些最难应付的顾客全推给她了.

sad·dler /ˈsædlə(r); ˋsædlɚ/ *n* maker of saddles and leather goods for horses 鞍匠; 马具师. **sad·dlery** /ˈsædlərɪ; ˋsædlərɪ/ *n* **1** [U] **(a)** goods made or sold by a saddler 马具. **(b)** the art of making these 马具制造术. **2** [C] saddler's business 马具业.

□ **ˈsaddle-bag** *n* **1** either of a pair of bags laid over the back of a horse or donkey 马褡子; 驴褡子. **2** bag attached to the back of a bicycle saddle (自行车后座上的)挂包.

ˈsaddle-sore *adj* (of a rider) sore and stiff after riding (指骑马人)(骑马后)疼痛并发僵的.

ˈsaddle stitching long running-stitch made with thick thread, used decoratively 鞍形针迹.

sadhu /ˈsɑːduː; ˋsɑdu/ *n* Hindu holy man who lives an ascetic life 衣食简朴的印度教圣人.

sad·ism /ˈseɪdɪzəm; ˋsedɪzəm/ *n* [U] **(a)** enjoyment of watching or inflicting cruelty 施虐狂: *sadism in the treatment of prisoners* 从虐待囚犯中得到的乐趣. **(b)** getting sexual pleasure from this 性施虐狂. Cf 参看 MASOCHISM.

▷ **sad·ist** /ˈseɪdɪst; ˋsedɪst/ person who practises sadism 有施虐狂的人; 有性欲施虐狂的人. **sad·istic** /səˈdɪstɪk; səˋdɪstɪk/ *adj* of or showing sadism 有施虐狂的; 表现性欲施虐的: *sadistic laughter* 施虐狂般的笑声 ○ *a sadistic teacher* 以虐待学生为乐的教师. **sad·ist·ic·ally** /-klɪ; -klɪ/ *adv*.

S

sado-masochism /ˌseɪdəʊˈmæsəkɪzəm; ˌsedoˈmæsəkɪzm/ *n* [U] combination of sadism and masochism in one person, each type of behaviour being displayed at different times 施虐受虐狂; 性施虐受虐狂. ▷ **sado-masochist** /ˌseɪdəʊˈmæsəkɪst; ˌsedoˈmæsəkɪst/ *adj*, *n*.

sae /ˌes eɪ ˈiː; ˌɛs e ˋi/ *abbr* 缩写 = stamped addressed envelope 贴有邮票并写好地址的信封: *enclose sae for reply* 附贴有邮票并写明地址的信封以便作复.

sa·fari /səˈfɑːrɪ; səˋfɑrɪ/ *n* (*pl* **-ris**) [U, C] **1** hunting expedition or overland journey, esp in E or Central Africa 游猎, 陆路旅行(尤指在东非或中非): *on safari* 在东非游猎 ○ *return from (a) safari* 中非陆路旅行归来. **2** similar expedition organized as a holiday tour 类似游猎的假日旅行.

□ **sa·fari park** park where wild animals are kept in the open for visitors to see from their cars as they drive around (可开车四处观赏的)野生动物园.

saˈfari suit casual suit in linen or a similar fabric 游猎便装.

safe[1] /seɪf; sef/ *adj* (**-r**, **-st**) **1** [pred 作表语] **~ (from sth/sb)** protected from danger and harm; secure 安全; 平安; 无危险: *You'll be safe here.* 你在这里很安全. ○ *safe from attack/attackers* 免受攻击[他人攻击]. **2** [pred 作表语] not or unlikely to be damaged, hurt, lost, etc 不会或不致受到损害、伤害、损失等: *The missing child was found safe and well.* 失踪的孩子已经找到, 平安无事. ○ *She got back safe from her adventure.* 她有惊无险已安全返回. ○ *The plane crashed but the crew are safe.* 那架飞机失事了, 但机组人员都安然无恙. ○ *Will the car be safe outside?* 汽车停在外面安全吗? ○ *Your secret is safe with me*, ie I will not tell it to anyone. 我一定给你保密. **3** not likely to cause or lead to damage, injury, loss, etc 不致引起或导致损害、损伤、损失等的: *a safe car, speed, road* 安全的汽车、速度、道路 ○ *safer methods of testing drugs* 检验药物的更可靠的方法 ○ *Is that ladder safe?* 那梯子结实吗? ○ *It's not safe to go out at night.* 夜晚出门不安全. ○ *Are the toys safe for small children?* 小孩儿玩儿这样的玩具有危险吗? ○ *a safe investment*, ie that will not lose money 无风险的投资 ○ *Put it in a safe place*, ie where it will not be stolen, lost, etc. 把它放在安全的地方. **4** (**a**) [usu attrib 通常作定语] (of a person) unlikely to do dangerous things; cautious (指人)不冒险的, 小心的: *a safe driver, worker, goalkeeper* 谨慎的驾驶员、工人、守门员. (**b**) (*often derog* 常作贬义) showing a cautious attitude 谨小慎微的: *a safe choice* 过于小心的选择 ○ *They appointed a safe person as the new manager*, eg one unlikely to make changes, offend people, etc. 他们任命了一个谨小慎微的人担任新经理. **5** (idm 习语) **better safe than sorry** ⇨ BETTER[2]. **for safe ˈkeeping** to be kept safely, protected, etc 妥善保管、保护等: *Before the game I gave my watch to my wife for safe keeping.* 我在比赛前把手表交妻子保管. **in (sb's) safe ˈkeeping** being kept safely, protected, etc (by sb) 由(某人)保管、保护等: *Can I leave the children in your safe keeping?* 我把孩子交给你看管行吗? **on the ˈsafe side** taking no risks 为慎重起见; 以防万一: *Although the sun was shining, I took an umbrella (just) to be on the safe side.* 虽然有太阳, 但我仍带了雨伞以防万一. **play (it) ˈsafe** carefully avoid risks 小心避开危险; 稳重行事: *The bus might be early, so we'd better play safe and leave now.* 公共汽车可能早到, 因此我们得稳妥点, 现在就动身. **ˌsafe and ˈsound** unharmed 平安无事: *The rescuers brought the climbers back safe and sound.* 救援人员把登山的人都平安地救了回来. **(as) safe as ˈhouses** very safe 非常安全: *If you fix the brakes the car will be as safe as houses.* 把制动器修好, 汽车就非常安全了. **a safe bet** thing that is certain to be successful 肯定成功的事情: *I'm wearing black for the party — it's always a safe bet.* 我穿黑色礼服参加聚会——万无一失. ▷ **safely** *adv*. **safe·ness** *n* [U]: *a feeling of safeness* 安全感.

□ **ˌsafe ˈconduct** (document granting) freedom from the danger of attack, arrest, etc when passing through an area 安全通行权; 安全通行证: *The robbers wanted safe conduct to the airport for themselves and their hostages.* 劫匪要求保证他们自己以及他们劫持的人质去机场的安全.

ˈsafe deposit (*US* **ˌsafe deˈposit**) building containing strong-rooms and safes which people may rent separately for storing valuables 贵重物品保管处(其保险箱可供人租用). **safe-deposit box** small safe in such a building (贵重物品保管处的)保险箱.

ˈsafe house house used by criminals, secret agents, etc, where sb can be kept without being discovered or disturbed 罪犯、特务等用来藏匿人的房子.

the ˈsafe period time just before and during a woman's period when sexual intercourse is unlikely to make her pregnant 安全期(妇女受孕可能性极小的时期).

ˌsafe ˈseat (*Brit*) Parliamentary seat which a candidate for a particular party cannot lose 保险席位(一政党候选人肯定可以得到的国会议席).

safe[2] /seɪf; sef/ *n* strong lockable box, cabinet, etc for storing valuables 保险箱; 保险柜.

□ **ˈsafe-breaker** (*Brit*) (also *esp US* **ˈsafe-cracker**) *n* person who breaks into safes to steal valuables 破开保险箱的盗贼.

safe·guard /ˈseɪfgɑːd; ˋsef,gɑrd/ *n* **~ (against sb/sth)** thing that serves as a protection from harm, risk or danger 安全设施; 保护性措施: *We make copies of our computer disks as a safeguard against accidents.* 我们复制了计算机磁盘以防意外. ○ *We will introduce legal safeguards against fraud.* 我们为制止诈骗活动要采取法律保护措施.

▷ **safe·guard** *v* [Tn, Tn·pr] **~ sb/sth (against sb/sth)** protect or guard sb/sth 保护或保卫某人[某事物]: *We have found a way of safeguarding our money.* 我们已有了保护钱财的办法. ○ *a high fence that safeguards (the house) against intruders* 防止外人擅入(房子)的高栅栏 ○ *new ways of safeguarding personal data*, ie so that it will remain private 保护私人资料的新方法.

safety /ˈseɪftɪ; ˋseftɪ/ *n* [U] **1** being safe; not being dangerous or in danger 安全; 平安: *I'm worried about the safety of the children*, ie I'm afraid something may happen to them. 我为孩子们的安全担心. ○ *I'm worried about the safety of the product*, ie I'm afraid it may be dangerous. 我担心使用这种产品是否安全. ○ *We reached the safety of the river bank*, ie a place where we would be safe. 我们到了河岸的安全地带. ○ *We're keeping you here for your own safety.* 我们让你呆在这里是为了你自身的安全. ○ *road safety*, ie stopping accidents on the roads 道路安全 ○ [attrib 作定语] *safety precautions* 安全保护措施 ○ *a safety harness, bolt* 安全带、保险螺栓. **2** (idm 习语) **ˌsafety ˈfirst** (*saying* 谚) safety is the most important thing 安全第一. **there's ˌsafety in ˈnumbers** (*saying* 谚) being in a group makes one feel more confident 人多势众: *We decided to go to see the boss together; there's safety in numbers.* 我们决定一起去找老板, 人多胆壮.

□ **ˈsafety-belt** *n* **1** = SEAT-BELT (SEAT). **2** strap securing a person, eg sb working on a high building 安全带(如高空作业用的).

ˈsafety-catch *n* device that prevents the dangerous or accidental operation of a machine, etc, esp one that stops a gun being fired accidentally 安全制动装置; (尤指枪炮上的)保险栓: *Is the safety-catch on?* 保险栓拉上了吗?

ˈsafety curtain fireproof curtain that can be lowered between the stage and the auditorium of a theatre (剧院舞台与观众席之间可降落的)防火幕.

ˈsafety glass glass that does not shatter or splinter when broken 安全玻璃(不易破碎或破碎时不易散落的).

ˈsafety island (also **ˈsafety zone**) (*US*) = TRAFFIC ISLAND (TRAFFIC).

ˈsafety lamp miner's lamp in which the flame is protected so that it will not ignite dangerous gases (矿工的)安全灯.

ˈsafety match match that will only ignite when rubbed against a special surface, eg on the side of the matchbox 安全火柴.

ˈsafety net **1** net placed to catch an acrobat, etc if he should fall (杂技演员等用的)安全网. **2** (*fig* 比喻) arrangement that helps to prevent disaster if sth goes wrong 安全保障措施: *If I lose my job, I've got no safety net.* 我丢掉这份工作就无计可施了.

ˈsafety-pin *n* pin like a brooch, with the point bent back towards the head and covered by a guard when closed 别针.

S

'safety razor razor with a guard to prevent the blade cutting the skin 安全剃刀; 保险刀.

'safety-valve *n* **1** valve that releases pressure in a steam boiler, etc when it becomes too great 安全阀. ⇨ illus at PAN 见 PAN 插图. **2** (*fig* 比喻) way of releasing feelings of anger, resentment, etc harmlessly (无害地)发泄怒气、怨恨等的方式: *My hobby is a good safety-valve for the tension that builds up at work.* 我用业余爱好来消除工作中产生的紧张情绪.

saf·fron /ˈsæfrən; ˋsæfrən/ *n* [U] (colour of the) bright orange strands obtained from the flowers of the autumn crocus, used in cooking 藏红花的橘黄色色丝(用于烹饪); 橘黄色. ▷ **saf·fron** *adj*: *saffron robes* 橘黄色长袍.

sag /sæg; sæg/ *v* (**-gg-**) [I] **1** sink or curve down in the middle under weight or pressure (因负重或受压)向下凹或中间下陷: *a sagging roof* 下陷的屋顶 ○ *The tent began to sag as the canvas became wet.* 帐篷因帆布湿了中间有些下坠. **2** hang loosely or unevenly 松弛或不整齐地悬着: *old torn curtains sagging at one end* 垂在一端的破旧窗帘 ○ *Your skin starts to sag as you get older.* 人一老皮肤就松弛了.

▷ **sag** *n* [U, sing] extent to which sth sags; sagging 下陷或松弛的程度; 下陷或松弛: *too much sag in the mattress* 床垫过于松弛 ○ *a sag in the seat of the chair* 椅子座位部分的凹陷.

saga /ˈsɑːgə; ˋsɑgə/ *n* **1** long story of heroic deeds, esp of Icelandic or Norwegian heroes 长篇英雄故事, 萨迦(尤指冰岛或挪威的英雄的). **2** story of a long series of events or adventures, esp one involving several generations of people (情节曲折或惊险的)长篇故事(尤指家世小说): *The Forsyte Saga*《福赛特世家》○ *His biography is a saga of scientific research.* 他的传记就是一部科研记实. ○ (*joc* 谑) *the latest episode in her house-hunting saga* 在她寻找住房漫长过程中最近发生的新鲜事.

sa·ga·cious /səˈgeɪʃəs; səˋgeʃəs/ *adj* (*fml* 文) showing wisdom and good judgement 睿智的; 精明的; 有判断力的: *a sagacious person, remark, decision* 精明的人、精辟的论断、英明的决定.

▷ **sa·ga·ciously** *adv*.

sa·ga·city /səˈgæsətɪ; səˋgæsətɪ/ *n* [U] (*fml* 文) quality of being sagacious; wisdom and good judgement 睿智; 精明; 精确的判断: *Sagacity, unlike cleverness, may increase with age.* 睿智与聪明不同, 前者可与年龄俱增.

sage[1] /seɪdʒ; sedʒ/ *n* (*fml* 文) very wise man 圣人; 贤哲; 智者: *consult the sages of the tribe* 向部落的智者求教.

▷ **sage** *adj* [usu attrib 通常作定语] (*fml often ironic* 文, 常作反语) wise or wise-looking 贤明的; 貌似聪明的: *a sage judge, priest, ruler, etc* 贤明的法官、牧师、统治者等 ○ *in the sage opinion of experienced journalists* 根据有经验记者的高见. **sagely** *adv*.

sage[2] /seɪdʒ; sedʒ/ *n* [U] herb with fragrant greyish-green leaves used to flavour food 鼠尾草(叶色灰绿, 用于调味): *sage and onion stuffing*, ie used to stuff a goose, duck, etc 鼠尾草和洋葱填料(用作烹调鹅、鸭等者).

□ **'sage-brush** *n* [U] plant with a fragrance like sage growing in the US 灌木蒿(产于美国, 有鼠尾草味).

Sa·git·tarius /ˌsædʒɪˈteərɪəs; ˌsædʒɪˋtɛrɪəs/ *n* **1** [U] the ninth sign of the zodiac, the Archer 人马宫(黄道第九宫). **2** [C] person born under the influence of this sign 属人马宫星座的人. ⇨ illus at ZODIAC 见 ZODIAC 插图.

▷ **Sa·git·tarian** /-ˈteərɪən; -ˋtɛrɪən/ *n, adj.* ⇨ Usage at ZODIAC 用法见 ZODIAC.

sago /ˈseɪgəʊ; ˋsego/ *n* [U] starchy food in the form of hard white grains, used in puddings, obtained from the pith of a type of palm-tree (the **sago-palm**) 西米, 西谷米(用棕榈茎髓制的白色硬粒状的淀粉质食物).

sahib /sɑːb, ˈsɑːɪb; ˋsɑɪb/ *n* (often used in India, formerly, to address or refer to a) male European, usu with some social or official status (常用于印度, 旧时用作对欧洲男子直接或间接的称呼)老爷(通常用以指有社会地位或官职者).

said /sed; sɛd/ **1** *pt, pp* of SAY. **2** *adj* [attrib 作定语] (*fml* 文) = AFOREMENTIONED.

sail[1] /seɪl; sel/ *n* **1** (**a**) [C] (often in compounds 常用以构成复合词) sheet of canvas spread to catch the wind and drive a ship or boat along 帆: *hoist/lower the sails* 扬[下]帆 ○ *the 'foresail* 前桅帆 ○ *the 'mainsail* 主帆. (**b**) [U] sails; propulsion by means of sails 帆(总称); (扬帆)航行: *put on more sail* 多扯起些帆 ○ *take in sail* 收回些帆 ○ *the age of sail*, ie when ships all used sails 帆船时代. **2** [sing] (**a**) voyage or excursion on water for pleasure 航行游览: *go for a sail* 乘船游玩. (**b**) voyage of a specified length 航程: *a three-day sail to get to Brest* 到布雷斯特的三天航程 ○ *How many days' sail is it from Hull to Oslo?* 从赫尔到奥斯陆有几天的航程? **3** [C] (*pl* unchanged 复数不变) (*nautical* 海) ship 船: *a fleet of twenty sail* 有二十艘船的船队 ○ *There wasn't a sail in sight.* 一条船也看不见. **4** [C] set of slats attached to the arm of a windmill to catch the wind 风车的翼板. ⇨ illus at WINDMILL 见 WINDMILL 插图. **5** (idm 习语) **crowd on sail** ⇨ CROWD[2]. **in full sail** ⇨ FULL. **set sail (from/to/for...)** begin a voyage 起航: *We set sail (for France) at high tide.* 我们在涨潮时起航(去法国). **take the wind out of sb's sails** ⇨ WIND[1]. **under 'sail** (moving) with sails spread 扬着帆(行进): *The yacht wasn't under sail because the wind wasn't strong enough.* 风不够大, 赛艇未能扬起风帆.

□ **'sailboat** *n* (*US*) boat driven by sails 帆船.

'sailcloth *n* [U] canvas for sails 帆布.

sail[2] /seɪl; sel/ *v* **1** (**a**) [Ipr, Ip] travel on water in a ship, yacht, etc using sails or engine power; move forward on ice, a sandy beach, etc in a wheeled vehicle with sails (乘船或机帆船、游艇等)作水上旅行; (坐带帆的轮式运载工具)在冰上或沙滩上滑行: *sail up/along the coast* 向[沿]海岸航行 ○ *sail into the harbour* 驶入海港 ○ *an oil tanker sailing by* 驶过的油轮. (**b**) [I] (usu 通常作 **go sailing**) travel on water in a boat with sails, esp as a sport 乘帆船航行; (尤指)帆船运动. ⇨ Usage at TRAVEL 用法见 TRAVEL. **2** [I, Ipr] ~ **(from...) (for/to...)** (of a ship or the crew and passengers) begin a voyage (指船或船员和乘客)起航: *When does the ship sail?* 这船何时起航? ○ *He has sailed (from Southampton) for New York.* 他已乘船(从南安普顿)去纽约了. **3** [Tn] travel by ship across or on (a sea, an ocean, etc) 乘船在(海洋等)上或越过(海洋等)旅行: *sail the Aegean in a cruiser* 乘游艇在爱琴海上旅游. **4** [I, Tn, Tn·pr, Tn·p] (be able to) control (a ship or boat) (能)驾驶(船): *Do you sail?* 你会驾驶船吗? ○ *She sails her own yacht.* 她驾驶自己的游艇. ○ *He sailed the boat between the islands.* 他驾驶着船在两岛之间航行. **5** (idm 习语) **run/sail before the wind** ⇨ WIND[1]. **sail close/near to the 'wind** behave in a way that is dangerous or nearly illegal 干危险或近乎违法的事: *He never actually tells lies, but he often sails pretty close to the wind.* 他实际上从不撒谎, 但说的话常迹近撒谎. **6** (phr v) **sail across, into, past, etc sb/sth** move in a smooth or very confident way in the direction specified 顺利地或极有信心地沿某方向行进: *clouds sailing across the sky* 轻快地飘过天空的云彩 ○ *The manager sailed into the room.* 经理神态自若地走进房间. ○ *She sailed past (me), ignoring me completely.* 她从我身旁翩然走过, 全然不理会我. **sail in** enter an argument or dispute energetically 参与激烈争论或辩论: *Ann then sailed in with a furious attack on the chairman.* 安随后严词抨击董事长. **sail into sb** attack sb in words 抨击某人: *He sailed into the witness, accusing him of lying.* 他指责证人撒谎. **sail through (sth)** come through (an examination, a test, etc) without difficulty 顺利通过(考试、测验等): *She sailed through her finals.* 她顺利通过期末考试.

▷ **sail·ing** *n* **1** [U] travelling in a yacht, dinghy, etc, esp as a sport 驾驶帆船航行(尤指作为运动): *I love sailing.* 我喜欢帆船运动. ○ [attrib 作定语] *a sailing club, dinghy* 帆船俱乐部、帆船. **2** [C] voyage made regularly; departure of a ship on a voyage (轮船的)航班; 起船: *three sailings a day from here to Calais* 从这里到加来每日三次轮船航班. **3** (idm 习语) **plain sailing** ⇨ PLAIN[1].

'sailing-boat, 'sailing-ship *ns* boat or ship that uses sails 帆船. ⇨ illus at DINGHY 见 DINGHY 插图.

sailor /ˈseɪlə(r); ˋselɚ/ *n* **1** member of a ship's crew, esp one below the rank of officer; seaman 海员; 水手. **2** (idm 习语) **a good/bad 'sailor** person who seldom/often becomes seasick in rough weather (风浪大时)不大[常易]晕船的人.

□ **'sailor hat** straw hat with a flat top and straight brim 平顶直边草帽.

S

ˈ**sailor suit** suit for a child made in the style of a sailor's uniform（儿童的）水手装.

saint /seɪnt *or, in British use, before names,* 用于姓名前, 英式英语读作 snt; sent/ *n* **1** (**a**) (*abbr* 缩写 **St**, esp before the names of places, churches, etc 尤用于地名、教堂名称等专名之前) person who has been declared by the Christian Church to have deserved veneration through holy living, performing miracles, etc（基督教会宣布的）圣徒: *the gospel of St John* 圣约翰所记载的福音 ○ *St Andrew's Road* 圣安德鲁路. (**b**) holy person 圣人. **2** (usu *pl* 通常作复数) person who has died and is in heaven 死亡后已在天国的人; 死者: *in the company of the saints* 已死亡. **3** unselfish or patient person 无私的人; 有耐心的人: *You must be a saint to be able to stand his temper!* 能受得了他的脾气, 一定得非常有涵养!

▷ **sainted** *adj* [usu attrib 通常作定语] (*dated or joc* 旧或谑) declared to be or regarded as a saint 被宣布为圣徒的; 被视为圣人的: *My sainted aunt!* ie as an exclamation expressing surprise. 我的妈呀!（表示惊讶的用语）.

saint·hood *n* [U].

saintly *adj* (**-ier, -iest**) of or like a saint; very holy or good（似）圣徒的;（似）圣人的; 神圣的; 崇高的: *a saintly way of life* 圣洁的生活方式 ○ *a saintly expression on her face* 她面部圣徒般慈祥的表情. **saint·li·ness** *n* [U].

□ ˈ**saint's day** day of the year when a saint is celebrated, and on which (in some countries) people who are named after that saint also have celebrations 圣徒纪念日（纪念某一圣徒者, 有些国家亦同时庆祝以该圣徒之名命名的人）.

S

sake[1] /seɪk; sek/ *n* (idm 习语) **for God's, goodness', Heaven's, pity's, etc sake** (used as an interjection before or after a command or request, or to express irritation 用作感叹语, 可置于表示命令或要求的词语之前或之后, 或表示恼怒): *For God's sake, stop that whining!* 看在上帝面上, 别号叫了! ○ *For goodness' sake! How can you be so stupid?* 天哪! 你怎么这么笨哪? **for old times' sake** ⇨OLD. **for the sake of argument** as the basis of a discussion 为便于讨论: *Let's assume, for the sake of argument, that inflation will remain at 5% per year for two years.* 为便于讨论, 咱们先假设通货膨胀率连续两年均为5%. **for the sake of sb/sth; for sb's/sth's sake** in order to help sb/sth or because one likes sb/sth 为了某人[某事物]（起见）: *do sth for the sake of one's family* 为家庭做某事 ○ *I'll help you for your sister's sake*, eg because I want to save her trouble. 看在你姐姐面上, 我来帮你. **for the sake of sth/doing sth** in order to get or keep sth 为获得或保持某事物: *We made concessions for the sake of peace.* 为了和平我们做出了让步. ○ *She argues for the sake of arguing*, ie because she likes arguing. 她因为好辩而与人争论. ○ *Let's not spoil the job for the sake of a few pounds.* 咱们不要为了几英镑而把工作弄糟.

sake[2] (also **saki**) /ˈsɑːkɪ; ˈsɑkɪ/ *n* [U] Japanese alcoholic drink made from fermented rice 日本米酒.

sa·laam /səˈlɑːm; səˈlɑm/ *n, interj* **1** Muslim greeting used in the East 东方的穆斯林问候语. **2** low bow with the right hand touching the forehead 额手鞠躬礼（右手触额深鞠躬）.

▷ **sa·laam** *v* [I, Ipr] make a salaam 行额手鞠躬礼: *salaam to sb* 向某人行额手鞠躬礼.

sal·able (also **sale·able**) /ˈseɪləbl; ˈseləbl̩/ *adj* fit for sale; that sb will want to buy 适于销售的; 有销路的: *not in a saleable condition* 不适于销售 ○ *The houses are highly salable.* 这些房子销路很好.

sa·la·cious /səˈleɪʃəs; səˈleʃəs/ *adj* (*derog* 贬) (of speech, books, pictures, etc) treating sexual activity, nudity, etc in an obscene way; indecent; lewd（指言语、书籍、图画等）猥亵的, 淫秽的. ▷ **sa·la·ciously** *adv*. **sa·la·cious·ness** *n* [U]. **sa·la·city** /səˈlæsətɪ; səˈlæsətɪ/ *n* [U] (*fml* 文).

salad /ˈsæləd; ˈsæləd/ *n* **1** (**a**) [C, U] (dish of) chopped, usu raw, vegetables such as lettuce, tomatoes, cucumber, often seasoned with oil, vinegar, etc 色拉;（一盘）凉拌生菜: *prepare/mix a salad* 调配[调拌]色拉 ○ *cold beef and salad* 牛肉和生菜冷盘 ○ [attrib 作定语] *a salad bowl, shaker, etc* 色拉碗、搅拌器等. (**b**) [C, U] (dish of

salad 色拉

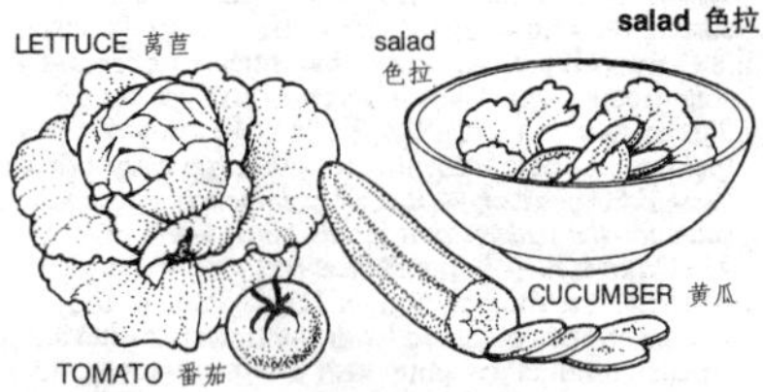

a) specified food served with salad（一盘）有色拉的凉拌食品: *a/some chicken, ham, lobster, etc salad* 一盘[一些]凉拌鸡肉、火腿、龙虾等色拉. **2** [U] lettuce, endive or other green vegetable suitable for eating raw 生菜（适于生吃的）. ⇨illus 见插图. **3** (idm 习语) **one's ˈsalad days** time when one is young and inexperienced 少不更事的时期: *I was in my salad days then, and fell in love easily.* 我那时年纪轻、涉世未深, 极易堕入情网.

□ ˈ**salad cream** type of mayonnaise, usu sold in jars 色拉酱（通常瓶装出售）.

ˈ**salad-dressing** *n* [U] sauce usu made of oil, vinegar and herbs for putting on salad 色拉调味汁（通常为油、醋、香草之混合物）.

ˈ**salad-oil** *n* [U] oil used for salad-dressing 色拉油.

sala·mander /ˈsæləmændə(r); ˈsælə,mændɚ/ *n* lizard-like animal living on land and in water, once thought to be capable of living in fire 火蜥蜴（两栖类动物, 曾认为能生活于火中）.

sa·lami /səˈlɑːmɪ; səˈlɑmɪ/ *n* [U] sausage salted and flavoured with spices, usu eaten cold 萨拉米香肠（通常冷食）.

sal·ary /ˈsælərɪ; ˈsælərɪ/ *n* fixed regular (usu monthly) payment to employees doing other than manual or mechanical work（非体力劳动雇员的）薪金, 薪水（通常按月计）: *a salary of 12 000 a year* 12 000 英镑的年薪 ○ *Has your salary been paid yet?* 你发薪了吗? ○ *Should doctors' salaries be higher?* 医生的薪水应该高些吗? ○ [attrib 作定语] *a salary agreement, scale, cheque* 薪金协议、级别、支票. ⇨Usage at INCOME 用法见 INCOME.

▷ **sal·ar·ied** *adj* receiving a salary; (of employment) paid for by means of a salary 领薪水的;（指职业）付给薪水的: *a salaried employee, post* 有薪的雇员、职务.

sale /seɪl; sel/ *n* **1** [U] selling or being sold 卖; 出售; 销售: *the sale of cars, clothes, machinery* 汽车、服装、机器的销售 ○ *The money was raised by the sale of raffle tickets.* 这笔款是通过出售购物彩券筹集的. **2** (**a**) [C] act of selling sth 卖; 出售; 销售: *I haven't made a sale all week.* 我整个星期没有卖出东西. ○ *She gets £10 commission on each sale.* 她每出售一批货可得10英镑的佣金. (**b**) **sales** [pl] amount sold 销售额; 销售量: *vast sales of ice-cream in the hot weather* 天热时冰激凌的巨大销量 ○ *Sales are up* (ie More goods have been sold) *this month.* 本月销售量增加. **3** [C] (in a shop, etc) occasion when goods are sold at lower prices than usual（商店等的）廉售, 贱卖: *hold an end-of-season sale* 举办季末大减价 ○ *the January sales*, ie when many shops reduce their prices 元月大减价 ○ *buy goods at/in the sales* 减价期间购物 ○ [attrib 作定语] *sale prices, goods, etc* 廉价、廉价货. **4** [U, sing] desire to buy goods; demand 销路; 市场需求: *There's always a ready sale for high-quality furniture.* 高档家具总是很畅销. ○ *They found no sale for their goods*, ie could not sell them. 他们的商品没有销路. **5** [C] auction 拍卖. **6** (idm 习语) **for sale** intended to be sold (usu by or on behalf of the owners) 待售（通常由物主或代理人经手）: *I'm sorry this painting's not for sale.* 很抱歉, 这幅画是非卖品. ○ *She has put her house up for sale.* 她的房子现在出售. **on sale** (**a**) (esp of goods in shops, etc) available to be bought（尤指商店等的货物）出售, 上市: *on sale at your local post office* 在你们当地邮局出售 ○ *The new model is not on sale in the shops.* 这种新款式商店尚未上市. (**b**) (*US*) being offered at a reduced price 廉价出售. **(on) ˌsale or reˈturn** (of goods) supplied to a retailer, who can send back without paying for them any items that he does not sell（指货物）批发给零售商, 卖不掉可

退还批发商. ▷ **sale·able** *adj* = SALABLE.

□ ˌ**sale of** ˈ**work** sale of items, eg cakes or knitting, made by members of a church, club, etc for charity 教会、俱乐部等为慈善事业所做物品(如糕点、针织品)的义卖.

ˈ**sale-room** (*US* ˈ**salesroom**) *n* room where goods are sold by public auction 拍卖处.

ˈ**salesclerk** *n* (*US*) = SHOP-ASSISTANT (SHOP).

ˈ**sales department** department of a firm concerned with selling its products 营业部.

ˈ**salesman** /-mən; -mən/, ˈ**saleswoman**, ˈ**saleslady**, ˈ**salesperson** *ns* person whose job it is to sell goods, eg in a shop or in people's homes 售货员; 推销员. ˈ**salesmanship** *n* [U] skill in selling goods 推销术; 销售技巧.

ˈ**sales slip** (*US*) receipt recording a sale 售货单; 售货收据.

ˈ**sales talk** talk aimed at persuading sb to buy sth 推销货物的说辞.

ˈ**sales tax** tax paid by a customer who buys retail goods 销售税(由购买零售商品的顾客所付者). Cf 参看 PURCHASE TAX (PURCHASE[1]).

sa·li·ent /ˈseɪlɪənt; ˋselɪənt/ *adj* [attrib 作定语] **1** most noticeable or important; main 显著的; 重要的; 主要的: *the salient points of a speech* 讲话的要点 ○ *She pointed out all the salient features of the building.* 她指出了该建筑物的全部显著特征. **2** (of an angle) pointing outwards (指角)凸出的.

▷ **sa·li·ent** *n* **1** salient angle 凸角. **2** (*military* 军) bulge in a military line of attack or defence 进攻或防卫阵地的突出部分.

sa·line /ˈseɪlaɪn; *US* -liːn; ˋselaɪn/ *adj* [attrib 作定语] (*fml* 文) containing salt; salty 含盐的; 咸的: *a saline lake* 盐湖 ○ *saline springs* 盐泉 ○ *saline solution*, eg as used for gargling, storing contact lenses, etc 盐溶液(如用于漱喉、存放隐形眼镜等).

▷ **sa·line** *n* [U] (*medical* 医) solution of salt and water 盐水.

sa·lin·ity /səˈlɪnətɪ; səˋlɪnətɪ/ *n* [U] *the high salinity of sea water* 海水的高含盐量.

sa·liva /səˈlaɪvə; seˋlaɪvə/ (also **slaver**) *n* [U] liquid produced in the mouth that helps one chew and digest food; spittle 唾液; 口水.

▷ **sa·liv·ary** /ˈsælɪvərɪ, səˈlaɪvərɪ; *US* ˈsæləverɪ; ˋsæləˌverɪ/ *adj* [attrib 作定语] of or producing saliva 唾液的; 分泌唾液的: *the* ˈ*salivary glands* 唾液腺.

sal·iv·ate /ˈsælɪveɪt; ˋsæləˌvet/ *v* [I] (*fml* 文) produce saliva, esp excessively 分泌唾液(尤指大量地): *A dog salivates when it sees a bone.* 狗见到骨头就大量分泌唾液. **sal·iva·tion** /ˌsælɪˈveɪʃn; ˌsæləˋveʃən/ *n* [U].

sal·low[1] /ˈsæləʊ; ˋsælo/ *adj* (**-er, -est**) (of a person's skin or complexion) yellowish (指人的皮肤或面色)蜡黄色的. ▷ **sal·low·ness** *n* [U].

sal·low[2] /ˈsæləʊ; ˋsælo/ *n* type of willow that does not grow to be very tall 黄华柳.

sally /ˈsælɪ; ˋsælɪ/ *n* **1 (a)** sudden attack, esp by troops surrounded by the enemy 出击; (尤指)突围: *make a successful sally* 进行突围成功. **(b)** (*joc* 谑) quick journey 短途旅行: *a brief sally to the shops* 逛逛商店. **2** lively or witty, usu good-humoured, remark 俏皮话.

▷ **sally** *v* (*pt, pp* **sallied**) (phr v) **sally out/forth** (*fml* 文) **(a)** emerge suddenly, usu from a place where one is surrounded, to attack an enemy 出击; 突围: *sally out against the besiegers* 向包围的敌人出击. **(b)** (*joc* 谑) set out somewhere or to do sth 出发; 着手做某事: *Party workers sallied forth in a drive to find new members.* 党的工作人员发起了纳新运动.

sal·mon /ˈsæmən; ˋsæmən/ *n* (*pl* unchanged 复数不变) **1 (a)** [C] large fish with pinkish flesh, sometimes fished for with rod and line as a sport 鲑; 大马哈鱼. **(b)** [U] its flesh as food 食用的鲑肉; 大马哈鱼肉: *smoked salmon* 熏制的大马哈鱼 ○ [attrib 作定语] *a salmon salad, mousse, etc* 鲑肉色拉、奶油冻等. **2** [U] the colour of its flesh; orange-pink 鲑肉色; 橙红色.

□ ˌ**salmon-**ˈ**pink** *adj* orange-pink, the colour of the salmon's flesh 橙红色的; 鲑肉色的. ˌ**salmon-**ˈ**trout** *n* trout resembling a salmon 欧鳟; 马苏大马哈鱼.

sal·mon·ella /ˌsælməˈnelə; ˌsælməˋnɛlə/ *n* [U] type of bacteria causing food poisoning 沙门氏菌: [attrib 作定语] *salmonella poisoning* 沙门氏菌中毒.

salon /ˈsælɒn; *US* səˈlɒn; səˋlɑn/ *n* **1** place where customers go to see a hairdresser, beauty consultant, etc (营业性质的)店, 厅, 院: *a* ˈ*beauty salon* 美容院 ○ *a* ˈ*hairdressing salon* 美发厅. **2** (formerly) regular gathering of notable guests at the house of a lady of high society; room used for this 沙龙(旧时知名人士在上流社会女主人家的例行聚会或聚会场所): *a literary salon*, ie with writers and critics as guests 文学沙龙.

sa·loon /səˈluːn; səˋlun/ *n* **1** public room on a ship, in a hotel, etc (轮船、旅馆等的)大厅, 交谊厅: *the ship's dining-saloon* 轮船的餐厅. **2** public room or building for a specified purpose 有某用途的公共大厅或建筑物: *a* ˈ*billiard*/ˈ*dancing saloon* 台球室[舞厅]. **3** (*US*) place where alcoholic drinks may be bought and drunk; bar 酒店; 酒吧间. **4** (also **sa**ˈ**loon-car**) (*Brit*) (*US* **sedan**) motor car where the area for the driver and passengers is closed off from the luggage and engine areas 轿车. ⇨ illus at CAR 见 CAR 插图.

□ **sa**ˈ**loon bar** = LOUNGE BAR (LOUNGE).

sal·sify /ˈsælsɪfɪ; ˋsælsəfɪ/ *n* [U] plant with a long fleshy root cooked as a vegetable 蒜叶婆罗门参, 牡蛎草, 蔬菜牡蛎(根长而肉厚, 可作蔬菜).

salt /sɔːlt; sɔlt/ *n* **1** [U] (also **common salt**) common white substance obtained from mines, present in sea water (from which it is obtained by evaporation), used esp for flavouring and preserving food; sodium chloride 盐; 食盐; 氯化钠: *a grain of salt* 一粒盐 ○ *too much salt in the soup* 汤里盐太多 ○ ˈ*table salt*, ie powdered so that it can be sprinkled on food 餐桌食盐 ○ ˈ*sea salt* 海盐. **2** [C] chemical compound of a metal and an acid (化学)盐. **3 salts** [pl] substance like salt in taste, form, etc, esp such a substance used as a laxative 味道、外观等像盐的物质; (尤指)泻盐: *a dose of (Epsom) salts* 一剂泻盐 ○ ˈ*bath salts*, ie used to scent bath water 浴盐(用以使洗澡水芳香者). **4** [C] (*dated infml* 旧, 口) experienced sailor 有经验的水手: *an old salt* 老水手. **5** [U] (*fig* 比喻) thing that makes sth more interesting, lively, etc 增添趣味或活跃气氛的事物: *Her humour adds salt to her conversation.* 她很幽默, 谈起话来妙趣横生. Cf 参看 SPICE 2. (idm 习语) **like a dose of salts** ⇨ DOSE. **rub salt into the wound/sb's wounds** ⇨ RUB[1]. **the salt of the** ˈ**earth** very decent, honest, etc person or people 非常正派、诚实等的人: *You can trust her: she's the salt of the earth.* 你可以信任她, 她这人很诚实. **take sth with a pinch of salt** ⇨ PINCH *n*. **worth one's salt** ⇨ WORTH.

▷ **salt** *v* **1** [Tn] put salt on or in (food) to season it 在(食物)中加盐. **2** [Tn, Tn·p] ~ **sth (down)** preserve (food) with salt 用盐腌(食物): *salt (down) pork* 腌猪肉 ○ *salted beef* 腌制的牛肉. **3** [Tn] sprinkle salt on (roads, etc) to melt ice or snow 将盐撒在(路等)上使冰或雪融化. **4** [Tn] make (a mine) seem rich by putting ore into it, usu so as to trick sb who wants to buy it 将矿石投入(矿区)使矿样显得有价值(通常为欺骗买矿人). **5** (phr v) **salt sth away** save (money, etc) secretly and usu dishonestly 私下并且通常指不正当地积蓄(钱等): *She salted away most of the profit from the business.* 她把做生意赚的利润大部分都私自蓄存起来了.

salt *adj* [attrib 作定语] containing, tasting of or preserved with salt 含盐的; 咸的; 腌的: *salt beef, pork, etc* 腌牛肉、猪肉等 ○ *salt water* 咸水 ○ *salt marshes* 盐沼 ○ *the* ˈ*salt flats of Utah* 犹他州的盐地.

salty *adj* (**-ier, -iest**) **1** containing or tasting of salt 含盐的; 咸的. **2** (*fig* 比喻) (of wit, speech, etc) vigorous, vivid, etc (指才智、言语等)活泼的, 生动的: *her salty humour* 她那机智的幽默话. **sal·ti·ness** *n* [U].

□ ˈ**salt-cellar** (*US* ˈ**salt-shaker**) *n* small container for salt at the table, either open or enclosed with a hole or holes at the top for sprinkling (餐桌上用的)小盐瓶. Cf 参看 PEPPER-POT (PEPPER). ˈ**salt-lick** (also **lick**) *n* place where animals go to lick salty rock or earth 动物舐食天然岩盐或咸土的地方.

ˈ**salt-mine** *n* mine from which salt is obtained 盐矿.

ˈ**salt-pan** (also **pan**) *n* hollow near the sea where salt is obtained by evaporation 盐田.

ˈ**salt-water** *adj* [attrib 作定语] of the sea 海的; 咸水的: *a salt-water fish* 咸水鱼. Cf 参看 FRESHWATER (FRESH).

SALT /sɔːlt; sɔlt/ (also **Salt**) *abbr* 缩写 = Strategic Arms

Limitation Talks 限制战略武器会谈: *the Salt treaties* 限制战略武器会谈协议.

salt·petre (*US* **-peter**) /sɔːlt'piːtə(r); 'sɔlt'pitɚ/ *n* [U] salty white powder used in making gunpowder, for preserving food and as medicine 硝酸钾; 硝石.

sa·lu·bri·ous /sə'luːbrɪəs; sə'lubrɪəs/ *adj* (*fml* 文) (esp of the climate) health-giving (尤指气候)有益健康的: *the salubrious mountain air* 有益健康的山间空气. ▷ **sa·lu·bri·ous·ness** *n* [U].

sal·ut·ary /'sæljʊtrɪ; *US* -terɪ; 'sæljʊ,tɛrɪ/ *adj* having a good effect 有益的: *salutary exercise, advice* 有益的锻炼、劝告 ○ *The accident is a salutary reminder of the dangers of climbing.* 这一事故有益的一面是提醒了我们攀登活动是有许多危险的.

sa·lu·ta·tion /,sæljuː'teɪʃn; ,sæljə'teʃən/ *n* (*fml* 文) **1** (**a**) [U] greeting or respect 问候; 致意; 致敬: *raise one's hat in salutation* 举帽行礼. (**b**) [C] sign or expression of this, eg a bow or a kiss 问候或致意的表示(如鞠躬或亲吻): *the polite salutations of the courtier* 朝臣的谦恭致意. **2** [C] (in a letter, etc) words used to address the person being written to, eg *Dear Sir* (信函等中的)称呼语(如Dear Sir).

sa·lute /sə'luːt; sə'lut/ *n* **1** (**a**) action performed to show honour, respect or welcome to sb 致敬; 欢迎: *fire a salute of ten guns* 鸣礼炮十响. (**b**) (esp military) gesture of respect to a senior officer, etc, often a raising of the right hand to the forehead in a certain way (尤指军队)(向上级长官等)敬礼,(常为)举手礼: *give a salute* 敬礼 ○ *The officer returned the sergeant's salute*, ie saluted in reply to such a gesture. 军官向中士还了礼. **2** polite gesture of greeting, eg a bow 行礼(如鞠躬): *raised his hat as a friendly salute* 举帽行礼. **3** (idm 习语) **in sa'lute** as a salute 以表示敬意: *They took off their hats by the grave in silent salute.* 他们在墓旁脱帽默哀. ○ *They raised their fists in salute to their leader.* 他们举起拳头向领袖致敬. **take the sa'lute** acknowledge with a salute the salutes of soldiers marching past (在前进通过的士兵敬礼时)行答礼, 还礼.

▷ **sa·lute** *v* (**a**) [I, Tn] give (sb) a salute; greet (sb) 向(某人)致敬, 致意; 问候或欢迎(某人): *The guard saluted (the general) smartly.* 卫兵非常精神地(向将军)行礼. ○ *The royal visitor was saluted by a fanfare of trumpets.* 皇室贵宾在嘹亮的铜管乐曲中受到热烈欢迎. (**b**) [Tn, Cn·n/a] **~ sb/sth (as sth)** (*fml or rhet* 文或修辞) publicly notice (an important person, achievement, etc) 颂扬(一重要人物、成就等): *We salute you for your tireless efforts for peace.* 我们为您在寻求和平方面做出的不懈努力向您表示敬意. ○ *Today should be saluted as the beginning of a new era.* 应把今天看作是一个新时代的开始来庆祝.

sal·vage /'sælvɪdʒ; 'sælvɪdʒ/ *n* [U] **1** rescue of a damaged ship or its cargo; rescue of property from damage caused by fire, floods, etc (对船、船上货物的)海上营救; (对火灾、水灾等的)财物抢救: *Salvage of the wreck was made difficult by bad weather.* 船遇难后因天气恶劣救援工作十分困难. ○ [attrib 作定语] *a salvage company*, ie one that salvages wrecked ships, recovers valuables from sunken ships, etc 沉船打捞公司 ○ *a salvage tug*, ie for towing a disabled ship to port 救难拖船. **2** (money paid for such rescue or the) property rescued in this way 抢救出的财产; (为抢救财产付的)救援费. **3** (saving of) waste material that can be used again after being processed 经加工可重新利用的废物; 废料回收: *collect old newspapers and magazines for salvage* 回收旧报纸和杂志. ▷ **sal·vage** *v* **1** [Tn] save (sth) from loss, fire, wreck, etc (从火灾、海难等中)抢救(某物). **2** [Tn] save (sth) as salvage(3) 回收利用(某物). **3** [Tn, Tn·pr] **~ sth (from sth)** recover sth (from a wreck, damaged vehicle, etc) (从失事的船、车辆等中)抢救某物: *Valuable raw materials were salvaged (from the sunken freighter).* (从沉船中)打捞起许多贵重的原料. ○ (*fig* 比喻) *How can she salvage her reputation after the scandal?* 她出了这件丢人的事以后还怎么能挽回名誉呢?

sal·va·tion /sæl'veɪʃn; sæl'veʃən/ *n* [U] **1** (*religion* 宗) saving of a person's soul from sin and its consequences; state of being saved in this way (对人的灵魂的)拯救, 超度: *pray for the salvation of sinners* 祈求拯救道德上的罪人. **2** way of avoiding loss, disaster, etc 避免损失、躲避灾难等的途径或方法: *I get so depressed about life; work is my salvation*, ie helps me forget my worries. 我对生活十分悲观, 埋头工作才可寻求解脱.

□ **Sal,vation 'Army** missionary Christian organization whose members wear military-style uniforms, and who work esp to help the poor 救世军.

salve /sælv; *US* sæv; sæv/ *n* **1** [C, U] (esp in compounds 尤用以构成复合词) oily substance used on wounds, sores or burns 药膏; 软膏: *'lip-salve* 唇用药膏. Cf 参看 OINTMENT. **2** [sing] **~ to sth** action or thought that makes sb feel less guilty, anxious, angry, etc 使人宽慰的行为或想法; 慰藉: *She paid the repair bill as a salve to her conscience.* 她付了维修费以减轻内疚感.

▷ **salve** *v* [Tn] make (esp one's conscience) feel better 使(尤指某人的良心)得到安慰: *It's too late to salve your conscience by apologizing.* 现在想凭借道歉获得良心上的安慰已经太晚了.

salver /'sælvə(r); 'sælvɚ/ *n* (usu metal) tray on which letters, drinks, etc are placed for handing to people (用于递送信件、饮料等的)盘子(通常为金属的).

salvo /'sælvəʊ; 'sælvo/ *n* (*pl* **~s** or **~es**) **1** firing of several guns at the same time, esp as a salute 数炮齐发; (尤指)礼炮齐鸣. Cf 参看 VOLLEY 1. **2** outburst of applause 齐声欢呼喝彩.

sal vo·la·tile /,sæl və'lætəlɪ; ,sæl vo'lætḷ,i/ *n* [U] sharp-smelling solution of ammonium carbonate given to sb to sniff if he is faint or unconscious; smelling-salts 碳酸铵水; 挥发盐; 嗅盐.

SAM /sæm; sæm/ *abbr* 缩写 = surface-to-air missile 地[舰]对空导弹.

Sa·mar·itan /sə'mærɪtən; sə'mærətṇ/ *n* **1 the Samaritans** [pl] organization devoted to giving help and friendship to people in despair 撒马利亚会(援助及安慰绝望者的慈善组织). **2** (idm 习语) **a ,good Sa'maritan** a person who gives sympathy and help to people in trouble 同情并援助苦难者的善人.

samba /'sæmbə; 'sæmbə/ *n* (music for a) ballroom dance that originated in Brazil 桑巴舞(曲)(源于巴西): *dance the samba* 跳桑巴舞.

same[1] /seɪm; sem/ *adj* **1 the ~ sb/sth (as sb/sth/that...)** (also sometimes preceded by *this/that/these/those* 有时亦可用于this/that/these/those之后) exactly the one (or ones) referred to or mentioned; not different; identical 就是前面提到的那(些)个; 同一的: *They both said the same thing.* 他们俩说的一样. ○ *We have lived in the same house for twenty years.* 我们二十年来一直住在这所房子里. ○ *He took it off the top shelf and put it back in the same place.* 他把它从架子顶层上取下来, 然后又放回到原处. ○ *He is the same age as his wife.* 他和他妻子同岁. ○ *The cinema is showing the same film as last week.* 电影院演的还是上星期的那部影片. ○ *I saw the mistake at the (very) same moment that she did.* 我与她(恰恰)同时发现了这一错误. ○ *I resigned on Friday and left that same day.* 我星期五辞职后当天就离开了. **2 the ~ sb/sth (as sb/sth/that...)** one that is exactly like the one referred to or mentioned; exactly matching 与前面提到的一模一样的; 相同的: *I saw the same shoes in a shop last week.* 我上星期在一家商店看到了同一式样的鞋. ○ *Men with moustaches all look the same to me.* 在我看来, 凡是留须的人模样都很像. ○ *I bought the same car as yours/that you did*, ie another car of that type. 我买的汽车和你买的一样. ○ *The two recipes are very much the same*, ie only slightly different. 这两分食谱几乎一个样. ○ (*derog or joc* 贬或谑) *You men are all the same!* eg have the same faults, obsessions, etc. 你们男人都是一路货! **3** (idm 习语) **amount to/come to/be the same 'thing** not be different; have the same result, meaning, etc 无不同; 结果、意义等相同: *You can pay by cash or cheque: it comes to the same thing.* 你可付现金或支票, 都一样. **at the same 'time** (**a**) at once; together 同时; 一起: *Don't all speak at the same time.* 大家别同时说. ○ *She was laughing and crying at the same time.* 她一面笑一面哭. (**b**) (introducing a fact, etc that must be considered 提出须予考虑的事实等) nevertheless; yet 但是; 然而: *You've got to be firm, but at the same time you must be sympathetic.* 你态度要强硬, 但还必须有同情心. **be in the same boat** be in the same (usu unfortunate) circumstances 处于同样(通常指不幸的)境地: *She and I* *are in the same boat: we both failed the exam.* 我和她一样, 考试都没及格. **be of the same 'mind (about sb/sth)** (*fml* 文) having the same opinion 意见一致: *We're all of the same mind: opposed to the proposal.* 我们想法一样, 都反对这项提议. **by the same 'token** in a corresponding way; following from the same argument 相应地; 基于同一理由: *She must be more reasonable, but by the same token you must try to understand her.* 她得讲点理, 可你也得尽量体谅她. **in the same breath** immediately after saying sth else (说完某些话后)紧接着: *He praised my work and in the same breath told me I would have to leave.* 他称赞我工作好, 刚说完这话就让我离职. **lightning never strikes in the same place twice** ⇨ LIGHTNING[1]. **not in the same street (as sb/sth)** of a much lower standard (than sb/sth) 远不如(某人[某事物]). **one and the same** the same person or thing 同一人或事物: *It turns out that her aunt and my cousin are one and the same (person).* 原来她姑姑就是我表姐. **on the same wavelength (as sb)** sharing the same way of thinking and the same interests, etc (as sb) and therefore able to understand him (与某人)志趣相同: *I find him difficult to talk to — we're on completely different wavelengths.* 我觉得很难和他谈得来——我们完全没有共通之处. **pay sb in his own/the same coin** ⇨ PAY[2]. **the ˌsame old 'story** what usually happens 常常发生的事: *It's the same old story: everybody wants the house tidy, but nobody wants to tidy it himself.* 还是老生常谈的事: 谁都想让房子整洁, 可谁也不愿意亲自整理. **speak the same language** ⇨ SPEAK. **tarred with the same brush** ⇨ TAR[1].

▷ **the same** *adv* in the same way; similarly 同样地; 相同地: *I still feel the same about it.* 我对此事看法仍和原来一样. ○ *The two words are spelled differently, but pronounced the same.* 这两个字拼写不同, 但发音相同.

same·ness *n* [U] quality of being the same; lack of variety 同一性; 相同性; 无变化: *the tedious sameness of winter days indoors* 冬天室内那种漫长而又单调乏味的生活.

samey /'seɪmɪ; 'semɪ/ *adj* (*infml* 口) not changing enough 变化不大的: *The food we get here is terribly samey.* 我们这里吃的食物差不多总是老一套.

same[2] /seɪm; sem/ *pron* **1 (a) the ~ (as sb/sth ...)** the same thing 同一事物: *He and I said the same.* 我和他说的是同一件事. ○ *Their ages are the same.* 他们年龄相同. ○ *I think the same (as you do) about the matter.* 我对此事的看法也是(和你)一样. ○ *I would do the same again.* 那我就再来一遍. ○ (*infml* 口) *'I'll have a coffee.' 'Same for me, please* (ie I will have one too).' '我要一杯咖啡.' '我也要一杯.' **(b) the ~** (*fml or joc* 文或谑) the same person 同一人: *'Was it George who telephoned?' 'The same.'* ie Yes, it was George. '是乔治打的电话吗?' '是他.' **2** (without *the*; used in bills, etc 用于招贴等, 不与 the 连用) (*fml or joc* 文或谑) the previously mentioned thing 前面提到的事物: *To dry-cleaning suit, £3; to repairing same, £2.* 干洗一套衣服, 3英镑; 修补一套衣服, 2英镑. **3** (idm 习语) **ˌall/ˌjust the 'same** in spite of this; nevertheless 尽管如此; 仍然: *All the same, there's some truth in what she says.* 即便这样, 她的话也还是有些道理. ○ *He's not very reliable, but I like him just the same.* 他是不太可靠, 但我仍很喜欢他. ○ *I wasn't able to use your screwdriver, but thanks all the same*, ie for lending it. 我没用上您的改锥, 还是要谢谢您. **(the) same again** (request to sb to serve the same drink as before 再要刚刚喝的同一种饮料): *Same again, please!* 请再来一杯! **ˌsame 'here** (*infml* 口) the same thing applies to me; I agree 我也一样; 我同意: *'I hate this book.' 'Same here.'* '我不喜欢这本书.' '我也不喜欢.' ○ *'I'm not very good at history.' 'Same here.'* '我历史学得不太好.' '我也是.' **(the) ˌsame to 'you** (used as an answer to an insult, a greeting, etc 用以反唇相讥、回敬问候等): *'Stupid!' 'Same to you!'* '愚蠢!' '你愚蠢!' ○ *'Happy Christmas!' 'And the same to you!'* '圣诞快乐!' '圣诞快乐!'

sa·mosa /sə'məʊsə; sə'mosə/ *n* spicy snack with a meat or vegetable filling in a triangular case of crisp fried pastry 炸馅角(有肉或菜馅的三角形面食小吃).

samo·var /'sæməʊvɑ:(r); 'sæməˌvɑr/ *n* container for heating water used esp in Russia for making tea 茶炊(尤指俄式的).

sam·pan /'sæmpæn; 'sæmpæn/ *n* small flat-bottomed boat used along the coasts and rivers of China 舢板.

sample /'sɑ:mpl; *US* 'sæmpl; 'sæmpḷ/ *n* **1** one of a number of things, or part of a whole, that can be looked at to see what the rest is like; specimen 货样; 样品; 标本: *a sample of his handwriting* (他的)手写的样本 ○ *a blood, urine, tissue, etc sample* 血、尿、组织等的样 ○ *The survey covers a representative sample of the population*, ie people of all levels of society. 这项调查涉及到社会各阶层的人士. ○ *a sample of the kind of cloth I want to buy* 我想买的那种布的货样. **2** small amount of a product given away free 免费分发的小量试(货)样; 赠样: *hand out free samples of the perfume* 送出香水的赠样 ○ [attrib 作定语] *a sample pack, sachet, etc* 馈赠的小包、小袋等样品.

▷ **sample** *v* [Tn] try out or examine (sth) by taking a sample or by experiencing it 抽样检查(某物); 取(某物)样; 试用(某物): *sample a new type of flour for oneself* 试样选择一种新的面粉 ○ *sample the delights of Chinese food* 品尝中国美食 ○ *We sampled opinion among the workers about* (ie asked some of them about) *changes in working methods.* 我们抽样调查工人对改变工作方法的看法.

sam·pler /'sɑ:mplə(r); *US* 'sæm-; 'sæmplɚ/ *n* piece of cloth embroidered to show skill in needlework and often displayed on a wall 刺绣样品(用以展示刺绣技艺, 常贴于墙上).

sam·urai /'sæmʊraɪ; 'sæmʊˌraɪ/ *n* (*pl* unchanged 复数不变) **1 the samurai** [pl] the military caste in feudal Japan (日本封建时代的)武士阶级. **2** [C] member of this caste (日本的)武士.

san·at·orium /ˌsænə'tɔ:rɪəm; ˌsænə'tɔrɪəm/ *n* (*US* also **san·it·arium** /ˌsænə'teərɪəm; ˌsænə'tɛrɪəm/, **san·it·orium** /ˌsænə'tɔ:rɪəm; ˌsænə'tɔrɪəm/) (*pl* **~s** or **-ria** /-rɪə; -rɪə/) clinic where patients suffering or recovering from a long illness are treated 疗养院.

sanc·tify /'sæŋktɪfaɪ; 'sæŋktəˌfaɪ/ *v* (*pt, pp* **-fied**) **1** [Tn] make (sb/sth) holy 使(某人[某事物])神圣化: *a life sanctified by prayer* 因祈祷而变得神圣的生活. **2** [Tn esp passive 尤用于被动语态] (*fig* 比喻) make (sth) seem right, legal, etc; justify; sanction 使(某事物)正当、合法、有理等; 认可: *a practice sanctified by tradition* 为传统所认可的做法. ▷ **sanc·ti·fica·tion** /ˌsæŋktɪfɪ'keɪʃn; ˌsæŋktəfə'keʃən/ *n* [U].

sanc·ti·mo·ni·ous /ˌsæŋktɪ'məʊnɪəs; ˌsæŋktə'monɪəs/ *adj* (*derog* 贬) showing that one feels morally better than other people 假装高尚、正经的: *a sanctimonious smile, remark, person, letter of protest* 假仁假义的微笑、言词、人、抗议信. ▷ **sanc·ti·mo·ni·ously** *adv*. **sanc·ti·mo·ni·ous·ness** *n* [U].

sanc·tion /'sæŋkʃn; 'sæŋkʃən/ *n* **1** [U] permission or approval for an action, a change, etc (对某种行动、变化等的)认可, 批准: *The book was translated without the sanction of the author.* 这本书未经作者许可就给翻译了. ○ *The government gave its sanction to what the Minister had done.* 政府对这位部长的做法均已认可. ○ *These measures have the sanction of tradition*, ie seem justified because they have often been taken before. 这些措施已约定俗成. **2** [C] reason that stops people disobeying laws, rules, etc 使人们不违背法律、规定等的因素或约束力: *Is prison the best sanction against a crime like this?* 为遏止这类罪行, 监禁手段是否是上策? ○ *The fear of ridicule is a very effective sanction.* 人们不做违法乱纪的事, 其中一个重要因素就是怕人耻笑. **3** measure taken to force a country to obey international law (迫使某国服从国际法的)处罚措施, 制裁: *apply economic sanctions against that country* 对那个国家实行经济制裁.

▷ **sanc·tion** *v* [Tn, Tg, Tsg] give one's permission for (sth); authorize or approve 同意(某事); 批准; 认可: *I can't sanction your methods.* 我不能同意你的办法. ○ *Who sanctioned bombing the town?* 是谁批准轰炸那座城的? ○ *They won't sanction our spending on this scale.* 他们不会同意我们这么大的开支.

sanc·tity /'sæŋktətɪ; 'sæŋktətɪ/ *n* [U] holiness; sacredness 神圣; 庄严: *She gives us a living example of sanctity.* 她给我们树立了一个圣洁的活榜样. ○ *the sanctity of an oath* 誓约的严肃性.

sanc·tu·ary /'sæŋktʃʊərɪ; *US* -ʊerɪ; 'sæŋktʃʊˌɛrɪ/ *n*

S

1 [C] sacred place, eg a church, temple or mosque 圣所, 圣地(如教堂、庙宇或回教寺院). **2** [C] (**a**) chancel of a church 圣坛. (**b**) (*esp US*) room where general religious services are held 圣堂. **3** (**a**) [C] sacred place where sb is protected from people wishing to arrest or attack him (为受逮捕、攻击威胁的人提供的)庇护所: *The fleeing rebels found a sanctuary in the nearby church.* 叛乱后逃跑的人躲入附近教堂寻求庇护. (**b**) [U] (the right to offer) such protection 庇护; (为他人提供的)庇护权: *claim/seek/take/be offered sanctuary* 要求[寻求/接受/受到]庇护. **4** [C] any place where refuge is provided 避难所: *This country is a sanctuary for political refugees from all over the world.* 该国是全世界政治难民的避难所. **5** [C] area where birds and wild animals are protected from hunters, etc and are encouraged to breed 禁猎区; 鸟兽保护区: *a* '*bird sanctuary* 鸟类禁猎区.

sanc·tum /'sæŋktəm; 'sæŋktəm/ *n* **1** holy place 圣地; 圣所. **2** (*fig* 比喻) room, office, etc where sb may not be disturbed (不受人打扰的)房间、办公室等: *I was allowed once into his inner sanctum.* 我有一次获准进入他的内室.

sand /sænd; sænd/ *n* **1** [U] (mass of) very fine fragments of rock that has been worn down, found on beaches, in river-beds, deserts, etc 沙; 沙粒: *mix sand and cement to make concrete* 把沙子和水泥混合制成混凝土. **2** [U, C usu *pl* 作不可数名词或可数名词, 后者通常作复数] area of sand, eg on a beach 沙地(如沙滩): *children playing on the sand(s)* 在沙滩上玩耍的儿童. **3** **sands** [pl] (used in names 用于地名) sandbank 沙坝; 沙滩; 沙洲: *the Goodwin Sands* 古德温沙洲. **4** (idm 习语) **bury/hide one's head in the sand** ⇨ HEAD. **the sands are running** '**out** there is not much time left 剩下的时间不多了: *The sands are running out: we must have the money by tomorrow.* 剩下的时间不多了: 我们明天得弄到这笔钱.

▷ **sand** *v* **1** [Tn, Tn·p, Cn·a] **~ sth (down)** smooth or polish sth with sandpaper, etc 用砂纸等擦平或磨光某物: *The bare wood must be sanded down.* 这个没有皮的木料得用砂纸磨光. ○ *The floor has been sanded smooth.* 地板已用砂纸磨光. **2** [Tn] sprinkle sand on (sth) or cover (sth) with sand 在(某物)上撒沙; 用沙覆盖(某物). **sander** (also '**sanding-machine**) *n* machine for sanding surfaces, eg by means of a rotating pad with sandpaper attached 砂轮打磨机. **sandy** *adj* (**-ier, -iest**) **1** like sand; covered with sand 沙状的; 覆盖着沙的: *a surface with a sandy texture* 有沙粒样的表面 ○ *The floor of the beach-hut was sandy.* 那海滨小屋的地面上净是沙子. **2** (of hair, etc) yellowish-red (指毛发等)沙色的. **sandi·ness** *n* [U].

□ '**sandbag** *n* bag filled with sand, used as a defence (eg in war, against rising flood-water, etc) 沙袋, 沙包(如用于作战、防洪等). — *v* (**-gg-**) [Tn] put sandbags in or around (sth) 在(某物)内或四周堆上沙袋: *sandbag the doorway in case of flooding* 在门口堆上沙袋以防洪水.

'**sandbank** *n* bank or shoal of sand in a river or the sea (河或海的)沙坝, 沙滩, 沙洲.

'**sand-bar** *n* sandbank at the mouth of a river or harbour (河口或港口的)沙洲.

'**sand-blast** *v* [Tn] clean or decorate (a stone wall, etc) by aiming a jet of sand at it 喷沙清洗或装饰(石墙等).

'**sandboy** *n* (idm 习语) **happy as a sandboy** ⇨ HAPPY.

'**sand-castle** *n* pile of sand shaped to look like a castle, usu made by a child on a beach 用沙子堆的城堡(通常指儿童在沙滩堆筑的).

'**sand-dune** *n* = DUNE.

'**sand-fly** *n* type of midge common on seashores 白蛉.

the '**sandman** *n* [sing] imaginary person who makes children feel sleepy 睡魔(神话中能催儿童入睡的人): *The sandman's coming!* ie It's time for bed! 睡魔来了! (该睡觉了!)

'**sandpaper** *n* [U] strong paper coated with sand or a similar substance, used for rubbing surfaces smooth 砂纸. — *v* [Tn, Tn·p] smooth (sth) with sandpaper 用砂纸磨光(某物).

'**sandpiper** *n* small bird living in wet sandy places near streams 矶鹬.

'**sand-pit** *n* hole in the ground partly filled with sand for children to play in (儿童游戏用的)沙坑.

'**sand-shoes** *n* [pl] light shoes with rubber or hemp soles for wearing on beaches 沙地鞋(在沙滩上用的轻便鞋).

'**sandstone** *n* [U] rock formed of compressed sand 沙岩.

'**sandstorm** *n* storm in a desert in which sand is blown through the air by the wind 沙暴.

'**sand trap** (*esp US*) = BUNKER 2.

'**sand-yacht** *n* vehicle with wheels and a sail, driven over sand by the wind 沙地帆车(有轮及帆, 藉风力在沙地行驶).

sandal 凉鞋类

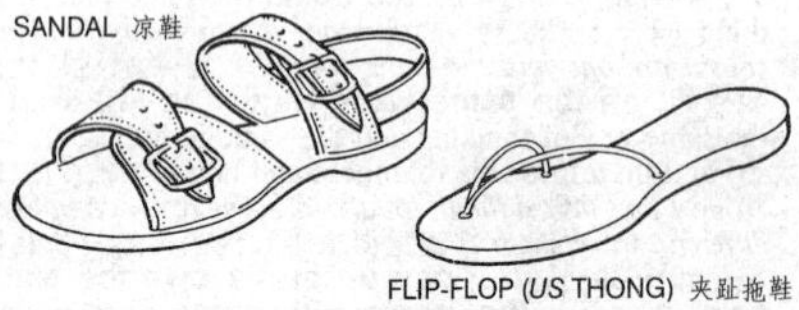

san·dal /'sændl; 'sændḷ/ *n* type of open shoe consisting of a sole held on to the foot by straps or cords 凉鞋. Cf 参看 BOOT[1] 1, SHOE 1. ▷ **san·dalled** *adj* wearing sandals 穿凉鞋的.

san·dal·wood /'sændlwʊd; 'sændḷ,wʊd/ *n* [U] hard scented wood used for making fans, caskets, etc 檀香木: [attrib 作定语] *sandalwood soap*, ie smelling like this wood 檀香皂.

sand·wich /'sænwɪdʒ; *US* -wɪtʃ; 'sænwɪtʃ/ *n* two or more slices of bread with meat, cheese, etc between 三明治: *ham, chicken, cucumber, etc sandwiches* 火腿、鸡肉、黄瓜等三明治 ○ [attrib 作定语] *a sandwich bar, box, filling* 三明治柜台、盒、夹心.

▷ **sand·wich** *v* [Tn, Tn·pr] **~ sb/sth (between sb/sth)** put sb/sth between two other people or things, esp in a restricted space 将某人[某物]夹在另两人或两物之间(尤指受空间限制): *I sandwiched myself between two fat men on the bus.* 我在公共汽车上, 一边一个胖子把我夹在中间不能动.

□ '**sandwich board** either of two connected boards, usu carrying advertisements and hung over the shoulders of a person (a '**sandwich man**) who walks about the streets to display them 夹板广告牌(游街宣传员胸前背后挂的广告牌, 这种宣传员称 **sandwich man** 夹板广告员).

'**sandwich course** course of training in which periods of instruction and practical work alternate 工读交替制课程.

sane /seɪn; sen/ *adj* (**-r, -st**) **1** having a healthy mind; not mad 心智健全的; 神志正常的: *It's hard to stay sane under such awful pressure.* 处于这种可怕的压力之下, 不疯才怪呢. **2** (*fig* 比喻) showing good judgement; moderate; sensible 明智的; 稳健的; 理智的: *a sane person, decision, policy* 明智的人、决定、政策 ○ *her sane, democratic views* 她的理智、民主的见解. ▷ **sanely** *adv*.

sang *pt* of SING.

sang-froid /ˌsɒŋ 'frwɑ:; sɑŋ'frwɑ/ *n* [U] calmness in a situation of danger or in an emergency; composure (面临危险或危急时的)冷静, 沉着, 镇定: *They showed great sang-froid in dealing with the fire.* 他们处理这场火灾时极为镇定.

san·gria /'sæŋgrɪə; *US* sæŋ'gri:ə; sæŋ'griə/ *n* [U] (*Spanish* 西) drink made of red wine with fruit, lemonade, etc 桑格里酒(由红葡萄酒、水果汁、汽水等配制而成).

san·guin·ary /'sæŋgwɪnərɪ; *US* -nerɪ; 'sæŋgwɪn,ɛrɪ/ *adj* (*dated fml* 旧, 文) **1** with much bloodshed; bloody 血腥的; 血淋淋的: *a sanguinary battle* 血战. **2** fond of bloodshed; cruel 嗜杀的; 残酷的: *a sanguinary ruler* 残暴的统治者.

san·guine /'sæŋgwɪn; 'sæŋgwɪn/ *adj* (*fml* 文) **1** **~ (about sth/that...)** hopeful; optimistic 充满希望的;

乐观的: *not very sanguine about our chances of success* 对我们成功的机会不很乐观 ○ *sanguine that we shall succeed* 自信我们将成功. **2** having a red complexion 面色红润的. ▷ **san·guinely** *adv*. **san·guine·ness** *n* [U].

san·it·arium, san·it·orium (*US*) = SANATORIUM.

san·it·ary /ˈsænɪtrɪ; *US* -terɪ; ˋsænə,tɛrɪ/ *adj* **1** free from dirt or substances that may cause disease; hygienic 清洁的; 卫生的; 保健的: *Conditions in the kitchen were not very sanitary.* 厨房环境不太卫生. **2** [attrib 作定语] of or concerned with protecting health 保健的; 有关保健的: *sanitary ware*, ie toilet bowls, etc 洁具(抽水马桶等) ○ *a ˈsanitary inspector*, ie an official who checks that the conditions in shops, restaurants, etc are hygienic 卫生检查员.

□ **ˈsanitary towel, ˈsanitary pad** absorbent pad used by a woman during her period 卫生巾; 月经带.

san·ita·tion /ˌsænɪˈteɪʃn; ˌsænəˋteʃən/ *n* [U] systems that protect people's health, esp those that dispose efficiently of sewage 卫生系统或设备(尤指下水道设备).

san·it·ize, -ise /ˈsænɪtaɪz; ˋsænə,taɪz/ *v* [Tn] **1** make (a place) hygienic 使(某处)卫生. **2** (*fig derog* 比喻, 贬) make (a story, news, etc) less disturbing, shocking, etc 净化(陈述、报道、新闻等)(以免引起不安、惊慌等): *They've sanitized my report on army atrocities.* 他们删除了我那篇报道中记述军队暴行的内容.

san·ity /ˈsænətɪ; ˋsænətɪ/ *n* [U] **1** state of being sane; health of mind 神志正常; 心智健康: *doubt/question sb's sanity* 怀疑某人神志是否正常. **2** soundness of judgement; state of being sensible or moderate 明智; 理智; 稳健: *try to bring some sanity into a difficult situation* 在困难情况下, 力求理智.

sank *pt* of SINK[1].

san·serif /ˌsænˈserɪf; sænˋsɛrɪf/ *n* [U] (in printing) form of type without serifs (印刷)无衬线的铅字. ⇨illus at SERIF 见SERIF 插图.

Santa Claus /ˈsæntə klɔːz; ˋsæntə,klɔz/ (also *esp Brit* **Father Christmas**) man with a white beard and dressed in red, who, children are told, comes down chimneys at Christmas to bring presents 圣诞老人.

sap[1] /sæp; sæp/ *n* [U] **1** liquid in a plant that carries food to all its parts 树液: *The sap rises in trees in springtime.* 春天树中的汁液向上流动. **2** (*fig* 比喻) vigour or energy 元气; 精力: *He's full of sap and ready to start.* 他精神抖擞准备出发.

▷ **sappy** *adj* (**-ier, -iest**) full of sap 多树液的; 精力充沛的.

□ **ˈsapwood** *n* [U] soft outer layers of wood 边材, 白木质(木之柔软的外层).

sap[2] /sæp; sæp/ *n* (*infml* 口) stupid person 傻瓜; 笨蛋: *You poor sap!* 你这个可怜的傻瓜!

sap[3] /sæp; sæp/ *v* (**-pp-**) **1** [esp passive 尤用于被动语态: Tn, Tn·pr] **sb/sth (of sth)** gradually weaken sb/sth by taking away (strength, vitality, etc) 逐渐削弱某人[某事物](力量、活力等): *I was sapped by months of hospital treatment.* 我住院治疗几个月, 大伤元气. ○ *She's been sapped of her optimism.* 她的乐观情绪已逐渐消失了. **2** [Tn] gradually take away (sb's strength, vitality, etc) 逐渐消耗(某人的力量、活力等): *Stop sapping her confidence!* 别动摇她的信心! ○ *Lack of planning is sapping the company's efficiency.* 公司缺乏计划性已逐渐降低了工作效率.

sap[4] /sæp; sæp/ *n* tunnel or covered trench dug to get nearer to the enemy (借以接近敌人的)地道, 地下战壕.

▷ **sap·per** *n* soldier carrying out engineering work, eg road and bridge building 工程兵; 工兵.

sapi·ent /ˈseɪpɪənt; ˋsepɪənt/ *adj* (*fml* 文) wise 有智慧的. ▷ **sapi·ence** /-əns; -əns/ *n* [U]. **sapi·ently** *adv*.

sap·ling /ˈsæplɪŋ; ˋsæplɪŋ/ *n* young tree 幼树.

Sap·phic (also **sap·phic**) /ˈsæfɪk; ˋsæfɪk/ *n* form of four-line verse typical of the Greek lesbian poetess Sappho 希腊女同性恋诗人萨福式的四行诗体. ▷ **Sap·phic** *adj* **1** of such verse 萨福四行诗体的. **2** (*fml* 文) lesbian 女同性恋的.

sap·phire /ˈsæfaɪə(r); ˋsæfaɪr/ *n* **1** [C] clear, bright blue jewel 蓝宝石. **2** [U] its colour 蔚蓝色.

▷ **sap·phire** *adj* bright blue 蔚蓝色的.

sap·ro·phyte /ˈsæprəʊfaɪt; ˋsæpro,faɪt/ *n* fungus or similar plant living on dead organic matter 腐生植物; 死物寄生菌. ▷ **sap·ro·phytic** /ˌsæprəʊˈfɪtɪk; ˌsæproˋfɪtɪk/ *adj*.

Sara·cen /ˈsærəsn; ˋsærəsn̩/ *n* Arab or Muslim at the time of the Crusades 萨拉森人(十字军东征时的阿拉伯人或穆斯林).

sar·casm /ˈsɑːkæzəm; ˋsɑrkæzəm/ *n* [U] (use of) bitter, esp ironic, remarks intended to wound sb's feelings 讥讽; 讽刺; 挖苦: *her constant sarcasm about his poor work* 她对他作品拙劣的一贯嘲讽.

▷ **sar·castic** /sɑːˈkæstɪk; sɑrˋkæstɪk/ (also *infml* 口语作 **sarky**) *adj* of or using sarcasm 讥讽的; 讽刺的; 挖苦的: *a sarcastic person, tone, remark* 好讥讽的人、讽刺的语调、挖苦的话. **sar·cast·ic·ally** /-klɪ; -klɪ/ *adv*.

sar·co·phagus /sɑːˈkɒfəgəs; sɑrˋkɑfəgəs/ *n* (*pl* **-gi** /-gaɪ; -gaɪ/ or **~es** /-gəsɪz; -gəsɪz/) stone coffin, esp one with carvings, etc, used in ancient times (古代的)石棺(尤指有雕刻的).

sar·dine /sɑːˈdiːn; sɑrˋdin/ *n* **1** young pilchard or a similar fish, usu tinned in oil or tomato sauce 沙丁鱼(通常为罐装). **2** (idm 习语) **(packed, squashed, etc) like sardines** (*infml* 口) pressed tightly together 拥挤: *The ten of us were squashed together like sardines in the lift.* 我们十个人在电梯里拥成一团.

sar·donic /sɑːˈdɒnɪk; sɑrˋdɑnɪk/ *adj* expressing scorn, usu in a grimly humorous way; mocking 嘲笑的; 讥笑的: *a sardonic smile, laugh, expression, etc* 嘲弄的微笑、大笑、表情等. ▷ **sar·don·ic·ally** /-klɪ; -klɪ/ *adv*.

sari /ˈsɑːrɪ; ˋsɑrɪ/ *n* length of cotton or silk cloth draped round the body, worn as the main garment by Hindu women 莎丽(印度女子裹在身上的棉布或绸布, 作主要外衣).

sarky /ˈsɑːkɪ; ˋsɑrkɪ/ *adj* (*Brit infml* 口) = SARCASTIC: *She's a sarky little madam.* 她是个爱讽刺人的小姐.

sa·rong /səˈrɒŋ; *US* -ˈrɔːŋ; səˋrɔŋ/ *n* long strip of cotton or silk cloth worn as a skirt tucked in at the waist or under the armpits by Malay and Indonesian men and women 莎笼(马来人及印尼人用以裹住身体的长条布或绸缎, 在腰部或腋下系住, 似裙, 男女皆穿).

sar·tor·ial /sɑːˈtɔːrɪəl; sɑrˋtɔrɪəl/ *adj* [attrib 作定语] (*fml* 文) of (usu men's) clothes or a way of dressing 服装的; (通常指)男式服装的; 衣着的: *sartorial elegance* 衣着的大方雅致. ▷ **sar·tor·ially** /-rɪəlɪ; -rɪəlɪ/ *adv*.

SAS /ˌes eɪ ˈes; ˌɛs e ˋɛs/ *abbr* 缩写 = (*Brit*) Special Air Service (of the army) (陆军的)特种空勤部队.

sash[1] /sæʃ; sæʃ/ *n* long strip of cloth worn around the waist or over one shoulder as an ornament or as part of a uniform 腰带; 肩带.

sash[2] /sæʃ; sæʃ/ *n* either of a pair of window frames, one above the other, opening and closing by sliding up and down in grooves (垂直拉窗的)窗框.

□ **ˈsash-cord** *n* cord with a weight at one end running over a pulley and attached to a sash, allowing the window to be kept open in any position 吊窗绳(一端有坠, 另一端固着于垂直拉窗的窗框, 中间有滑轮, 可使窗户停留在任何开启位置).

ˌsash-ˈwindow *n* window consisting of two sashes 垂直拉窗. ⇨illus at App 1 见附录1插图, page vi.

sashay /ˈsæʃeɪ; sæˋʃe/ *v* [Ipr, Ip] (*US infml* 口) walk or move in a casual but showy way 大摇大摆地或神气活现地走: *sashay into the room* 大摇大摆地走进房间 ○ *She sashayed past, not condescending to look at us.* 她神气活现地走了过去, 连看也不愿看我们一眼.

sass /sæs; sæs/ *n* [U] (*US infml* 口) disrespectful rudeness; sauce(2) 无礼; 莽撞: *Just listen to her sass!* 你听听她那些无礼的话!

▷ **sass** *v* [Tn] (*US infml* 口) **1** be disrespectfully rude to (sb) 对(某人)粗鲁无礼: *Don't you dare sass me!* 你竟敢对我这样无礼! **2** (phr v) **sass sb back** answer sb rudely 与某人顶嘴: *I asked her to go and brush her teeth and she just sassed me back.* 我叫她去刷牙, 她就跟我顶起嘴来.

sassy *adj* (**-ier, -iest**) (*US infml* 口) **1** disrespectfully rude 无礼的; 莽撞的. **2** lively or stylish 活泼的; 时髦的: *a real sassy dresser* 衣着十分时髦的人.

Sas·sen·ach /ˈsæsənæk; ˋsæsn,æk/ *n* (*Scot derog or joc* 苏格兰, 贬或谑) English person 英格兰人.

Sat *abbr* 缩写 = Saturday: *Sat 2 May* 5月2日星期六.

sat *pt, pp* of SIT.

Satan /ˈseɪtn; ˋsetn̩/ *n* the Devil 撒旦; 魔鬼.

▷ **sa·tanic** /səˈtænɪk; *US* seɪ-; seˋtænɪk/ *adj* **1** (often 常作 **Satanic**) of or like Satan (似)撒旦的, 魔鬼的:

S

satanic rites, eg involving the worship of Satan 崇拜撒旦的仪式 ○ (*joc* 谑) *His Satanic Majesty*, ie Satan 撒旦陛下. **2** (*esp rhet* 尤作修辞) wicked; evil 邪恶的; 罪恶的. **sa·tan·ic·ally** /-klɪ; -klɪ/ *adv*.

Sa·tan·ism /ˈseɪtənɪzəm; ˋsetn̩,ɪzəm/ *n* [U] worship of Satan 撒旦崇拜; 魔鬼崇拜. ▷ **Sa·tan·ist** /ˈseɪtənɪst; ˋsetnɪst/ *n* worshipper of Satan 撒旦崇拜者; 魔鬼崇拜者.

satchel /ˈsætʃəl; ˋsætʃəl/ *n* small leather or canvas bag, usu carried over the shoulders and used for carrying school books, etc 小的皮包或帆布包; (通常指背在肩上的)书包.

sated /seɪtɪd; setɪd/ *adj* [usu pred 通常作表语] **~ (with sth)** (*fml* 文) having had so much (of sth) that one does not want any more; satiated 厌腻: *sated with pleasure* 享乐得生厌.

sat·el·lite /ˈsætəlaɪt; ˋsætl̩,aɪt/ *n* **1** (**a**) natural body in space orbiting round a larger body, esp a planet 卫星: *The moon is the Earth's satellite.* 月球是地球的卫星. (**b**) man-made device, eg a space station, put in orbit round a planet 人造卫星: *a comˌmuniˈcations satellite*, ie one that relays back to the Earth telephone messages or radio and TV signals received from another part of the Earth 通信卫星. ⇨ illus at ORBIT 见ORBIT插图. **2** (also ˈ**satellite state**) (*usu derog* 通常作贬义) country dependent on another more powerful country and controlled by it 卫星国(依附于某大国并受其控制者): *the great powers and their satellites* 列强及其卫星国.

sa·tiate /ˈseɪʃɪeɪt; ˋseʃɪ,et/ *v* [Tn usu passive 通常用于被动语态] (*fml* 文) provide (sb) with so much of sth that he wants no more 使(某人)充分满足(而不再需要某物): *She pushed her chair back from the table, satiated.* 她把椅子从餐桌处向后挪了挪, 再也吃不下了. ○ *satiated with pleasure* 享乐得生厌. ▷ **sa·ti·ation** /ˌseɪʃɪˈeɪʃn; ˌseʃɪˋeʃən/ *n* [U].

sa·ti·ety /səˈtaɪətɪ; səˋtaɪətɪ/ *n* [U] (*fml* 文) condition or feeling of being satiated 满足; 饱足: *feel full to satiety* 感到过于满足.

satin /ˈsætɪn; *US* ˈsætn; ˋsætn̩/ *n* [U] silk material that is shiny and smooth on one side 缎; 缎子: [attrib 作定语] *a satin dress, ribbon, etc* 缎子连衣裙、缎带.

▷ **satin** *adj* [usu attrib 通常作定语] smooth like satin 像缎子一样光滑的: *The paint has a satin finish.* 漆面光滑如缎.

sat·iny *adj* having the appearance or texture of satin (外观或质地)似缎的, 光滑的: *her satiny skin* 她的光滑的皮肤.

sat·in·wood /ˈsætɪnwʊd; *US* ˈsætn-; ˋsætn̩,wʊd/ *n* [U] smooth hard wood of a tropical tree, used for making furniture 缎木.

sat·ire /ˈsætaɪə(r); ˋsætaɪr/ *n* **1** [U] attacking foolish or wicked behaviour by making fun of it, often by using sarcasm and parody 讽刺; 讥讽: *a work of bitter satire* 充满尖刻讽刺的作品 ○ *Is there too much satire on TV?* 电视上讽刺内容是否太多了? **2** [C] **~ (on sb/sth)** piece of writing, play, film, etc that makes fun of foolish or wicked behaviour in this way 讽刺作品(文章、戏剧、电影等): *Her novel is a satire on social snobbery.* 她的小说是描写势利小人的讽刺作品.

▷ **sa·tir·ical** /səˈtɪrɪkl; səˋtɪrɪkl/ (also **sa·tiric** /səˈtɪrɪk; səˋtɪrɪk/) *adj* containing or using satire 含讽刺意味的; 嘲讽的: *a satirical play, poem, sketch, etc* 讽刺剧、诗、小品等. **sa·tir·ic·ally** /-klɪ; -klɪ/ *adv*.

sat·ir·ist /ˈsætərɪst; ˋsætərɪst/ *n* person who uses or writes satire 进行讽刺的人; 创作讽刺作品的作家.

sat·ir·ize, -ise /ˈsætəraɪz; ˋsætə,raɪz/ *v* [Tn] make fun of (sb/sth) by means of satire 讽刺或讥讽(某人[某事物]): *Politicians are often satirized on TV and radio.* 政客常遭到电视与无线电广播的讥讽.

sat·is·fac·tion /ˌsætɪsˈfækʃn; ˌsætɪsˋfækʃən/ *n* **1** [U] feeling of contentment felt when one has or achieves what one needs or desires 满意; 满足: *She can look back on her career with great satisfaction.* 她回顾自己的经历觉得心满意足. ○ *get/obtain/derive satisfaction from one's work* 从自己的工作中得到满足 ○ *a look of smug satisfaction* 自鸣得意的表情 ○ *In old age he finally had the satisfaction of seeing the quality of his work recognized.* 他在暮年终于目睹自己的作品得到赞赏深感欣慰. ○ *do the work to the satisfaction of the client*, ie so that he is pleased with it 工作做得让顾客满意 ○ *job satisfaction* 从工作中得到的满足感. **2** [U] fulfilment (of a need, desire, etc) (需要、愿望等的)实现: *the satisfaction of one's hunger* 解饿 ○ *the satisfaction of a hope, desire, ambition, etc* 希望、愿望、抱负等的实现. **3** [C] thing that gives contentment or pleasure 令人满足或带来乐趣的事物: *the satisfactions of doing work that one loves* 做自己喜欢的工作从中得到的乐趣. **4** [U] (*fml* 文) (**a**) adequate response (eg compensation or an apology) to a complaint (对投诉做出的)满意的回应(如补偿或道歉): *When I didn't get any satisfaction from the local people I wrote to the head office.* 当地部门做出的回应我十分不满, 因而向其总部投书. (**b**) revenge for an insult, etc, esp (formerly) by means of duelling (受辱后的)复仇, (尤指旧时)决斗: *You have insulted my wife; I demand satisfaction!* 你侮辱了我的妻子, 我要与你决斗!

sat·is·fact·ory /ˌsætɪsˈfæktərɪ; ˌsætɪsˋfæktərɪ/ *adj* good enough for a purpose (but not outstanding) 满意的, 满足的, 如意的(但并非十全十美): *a satisfactory attempt, meal, book, piece of work* 满意的尝试、饭菜、书、作品 ○ *The result of the experiment was satisfactory.* 实验结果令人满意. ○ *Her school report says her French is satisfactory.* 她成绩单上记载法语尚可. ○ *We want a satisfactory explanation of your lateness.* 我们想让你解释一下你迟到有什么充分理由.

▷ **sat·is·fact·or·ily** /-tərəlɪ; -tərəlɪ/ *adv* in a satisfactory manner 令人满意地; 令人满足地: *The patient is getting on satisfactorily.* 病人康复情况令人满意.

sat·is·fact·ori·ness *n* [U].

sat·isfy /ˈsætɪsfaɪ; ˋsætɪs,faɪ/ *v* (*pt, pp* **-fied**) **1** [Tn] give (sb) what he wants, demands or needs; make contented 使(某人)满意或满足: *Nothing satisfies him: he's always complaining.* 他对什么都不满意, 总是抱怨. ○ *She's not satisfied with anything but the best.* 她事事都要最好的方才罢休. **2** [Tn] fulfil (a need, desire, etc); do enough to meet (a requirement, etc) 满足(需要、愿望等); 达到(要求等): *satisfy sb's hunger, demands, curiosity* 解饿、符合要求、满足好奇心 ○ *She has satisfied the conditions for entry into the college.* 她已符合进入这所学院的条件. **3** [Tn, Tn·pr, Dn·f] **~ sb (as to/of sth)** give sb proof, information, etc; convince sb 向某人提供证据、消息等; 使某人信服: *My assurances don't satisfy him: he's still sceptical.* 我说的确确实实他都不信, 仍有疑虑. ○ *satisfy the police that one is innocent/as to one's innocence* 向警方证实自己是清白的. **4** (idm 习语) ˌ**satisfy the eˈxaminers** pass an exam 考及格.

▷ **sat·is·fied** *adj* feeling satisfaction; contented 满意的; 满足的: *I felt quite satisfied after my big meal.* 我这顿饭吃得很多, 觉得很饱. ○ (*ironic* 反语) *Look! You've broken my watch. Now are you satisfied?* 看! 你把我的手表弄坏了. 现在该满意了吧?

sat·is·fy·ing *adj* giving satisfaction 令人满意的; 令人满足的: *a satisfying meal, result* 令人满意的饭菜、结果. **sat·is·fy·ingly** *adv*.

sat·suma /sætˈsuːmə; ˌsætˋsumə/ *n* small loose-skinned edible fruit like a mandarin orange 蜜橘.

sat·ur·ate /ˈsætʃəreɪt; ˋsætʃə,ret/ *v* **1** [Tn, Tn·pr] **~ sth (with/in sth)** make sth very wet; soak sth 浸湿或浸透某物: *clothes saturated with water* 浸湿的衣服 ○ *Saturate the meat in the mixture of oil and herbs.* 把肉浸泡在油和作料的卤汁里. **2** [Tn·pr esp passive 尤用于被动语态] **~ sth/sb with/in sth** cause sth/sb to absorb a lot of sth; fill sth/sb completely with sth 使某物[某人]大量吸收或充满某物: *We lay on the beach, saturated in sunshine.* 我们躺在沙滩上, 沐浴在阳光里. ○ *The market is saturated with good used cars*, ie There are too many of them for sale. 市场上质量好的旧汽车供过于求.

▷ **sat·ur·ated** *adj* **1** [usu pred 通常作表语] very wet; soaked 极湿; 湿透: *I went out in the rain and got saturated.* 我冒着雨出门, 浑身都淋透了. **2** [usu attrib 通常作定语] (*chemistry* 化) (of a solution) containing the greatest possible amount of the dissolved substance (指溶液)饱和的: *a saturated solution of salt* 饱和的食盐溶液. **3** [usu attrib 通常作定语] (of fats and oils, eg butter) containing chemicals bonded in such a way that eating them is bad for the health (指油脂, 如黄油)含饱和脂肪酸的(不利健康). Cf 参看 POLYUNSATURATED.

sat·ura·tion /ˌsætʃəˈreɪʃn; ˌsætʃəˋreʃən/ *n* [U] saturating or being saturated 浸湿; 浸透; 饱和. — *adj* [attrib 作定

语] (of an attack) carried out in such a way that the whole of an area is affected (指攻击)呈饱和状态的, 遍及各处的: *saturation bombing of the town* 对该城的饱和轰炸.

□ ˌ**satuˈration point** **1** (*chemistry* 化) stage at which no more of a substance can be absorbed into a solution 饱和点. **2** (*fig* 比喻) stage at which no more can be absorbed, accepted, etc 饱和(状态): *So many refugees have arrived that the camps have reached saturation point.* 来了那么多的难民, 营房都饱和了.

Sat·ur·day /ˈsætədɪ; ˈsætɚdɪ/ *n* [U, C] (*abbr* 缩写 **Sat**) the seventh and last day of the week, next after Friday 星期六.

For the uses of *Saturday* see the examples at *Monday*. 关于 Saturday 的用法见 Monday 词条中的示例.

Sat·urn /ˈsætən; ˈsætɚn/ *n* (*astronomy* 天) the planet sixth in order from the sun, large and with rings round it 土星.

sat·ur·na·lia /ˌsætəˈneɪlɪə; ˌsætɚˈnelɪə/ *n* (*pl* unchanged or **~s** 复数或不变或作 **saturnalias**) (*rhet* 修辞) wild revelry 纵情狂欢.

sat·ur·nine /ˈsætənaɪn; ˈsætɚˌnaɪn/ *adj* (*fml* 文) (of a person or his appearance) gloomy (指人或人的外貌)忧郁的, 阴沉的: *a saturnine face, frown* 愁容、颦蹙.

satyr /ˈsætə(r); ˈsætɚ/ *n* **1** (in Greek and Roman myths) god of the woods, half man and half goat (希腊及罗马神话)(半人半羊的)森林之神. **2** (*rhet* 修辞) man with very strong sexual desires 性欲极强的男子.

sauce /sɔːs; sɔs/ *n* **1** [C, U] (type of) liquid or semi-liquid mixture served with food to add flavour 沙司; 调味汁; 酱: *tomato, soy, cranberry, etc ˈsauce* 番茄酱、酱油、越橘沙司 ○ *fruit pudding and brandy sauce* 水果布丁和白兰地调味汁 ○ *What sauces go best with fish?* 吃鱼配哪种调味汁最好? ○ [attrib 作定语] *a ˈsauce bottle* 沙司瓶. Cf 参看 PICKLE 1, RELISH 3. **2** [U] (*infml* 口) disrespectful rudeness, often of a harmless kind 无礼, 莽撞(常指无伤大雅的): *We'll have no more of your sauce, young man!* 小伙子, 别对我们这么不客气! Cf 参看 SASS. **3 the sauce** [sing] (*US infml* 口) alcoholic drink 烈酒: *Keep off the sauce!* 别喝烈酒! **4** (idm 习语) **in the ˈsauce** (*US infml* 口) having had a lot of alcohol; drunk 饮酒过多的; 醉的. **what is ˌsauce for the ˈgoose is ˌsauce for the ˈgander** (*saying* 谚) what applies to one person must apply to another in similar circumstances 适用于一人也一定适用于另一人: *If you can arrive late, then so can I: what's sauce for the goose is sauce for the gander.* 你可以迟到, 那我也可以晚来: 一视同仁嘛. ▷ **sauce** *v* [Tn] (*infml* 口) be disrespectfully rude to (sb) 对(某人)无礼或粗鲁: *Don't you dare sauce me!* 你竟敢对我无礼! Cf 参看 SASS *v*.

saucy *adj* (**-ier**, **-iest**) **1** disrespectfully rude 无礼的; 莽撞的: *You saucy little thing!* 你这个鲁莽的小东西! **2** (esp of clothes) smart and cheerful; jaunty (尤指衣物)时髦的, 漂亮的: *a saucy little hat* 漂亮的小帽. **sau·cily** /-ɪlɪ; -əlɪ/ *adv*. **sau·ci·ness** *n* [U].

□ ˈ**sauce-boat** *n* container for serving sauce (船形的)沙司碟.

sauce·pan /ˈsɔːspən; *US* -pæn; ˈsɔsˌpæn/ *n* metal cooking pot, usu round and with a lid and a handle, used for cooking things over heat 锅(通常指有盖及柄的). ⇨ illus at PAN 见 PAN 插图.

sau·cer /ˈsɔːsə(r); ˈsɔsɚ/ *n* **1** small shallow curved dish on which a cup stands 茶托; 茶杯碟: *Where's my cup and saucer?* 我的茶杯和茶托在哪儿呢? **2** anything shaped like this, eg the dish of a radio telescope 碟形物(如射电望远镜的碟形盘).

sauer·kraut /ˈsaʊəkraʊt; ˈsaʊrˌkraʊt/ *n* [U] (*German* 德) chopped pickled cabbage 泡洋白菜丝.

sauna /ˈsɔːnə, *also* ˈsaʊnə; ˈsɔnə, ˈsaʊnə/ *n* **(a)** period of sitting or lying in a special room heated to a very high temperature, often followed by a quick bath in cold water 桑拿浴; 蒸气浴. **(b)** room for this 蒸气浴室.

saun·ter /ˈsɔːntə(r); ˈsɔntɚ/ *v* [Ipr, Ip] walk in a leisurely way; stroll 漫步; 闲逛: *saunter down the avenue* 沿着林阴道漫步 ○ *He sauntered by with his hands in his pockets.* 他双手插在口袋里悠闲地走了过去.

▷ **saun·ter** *n* [sing] leisurely walk or pace 漫步; 闲逛: *a casual saunter around the shops* 逛商店.

saur·ian /ˈsɔːrɪən; ˈsɔrɪən/ *n, adj* (animal) of the lizard family including crocodiles, lizards and some extinct species (eg dinosaurs) 蜥蜴亚目的(动物)(包括鳄鱼、蜥蜴及一些已绝种的品种, 如恐龙).

sausage 香肠

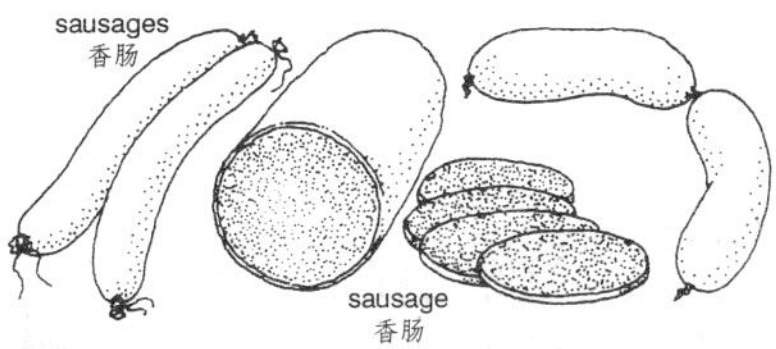

saus·age /ˈsɒsɪdʒ; *US* ˈsɔːs-; ˈsɔsɪdʒ/ *n* **1** [C, U] mixture of minced meat (esp pork or beef) and flavouring, etc in a thin tube-like casing (either cooked and eaten whole or served cold and in slices) 香肠; 腊肠: *grill some sausages* 烤些香肠 ○ *a pound of garlic sausage* 一磅蒜味香肠. **2** (idm 习语) **not a sausage** (*infml* 口) nothing at all 一点也不; 毫无.

□ ˈ**sausage-dog** *n* (*Brit infml* 口) dachshund 猎獾狗.

ˈ**sausage meat** minced meat with cereal, flavourings, etc used for making sausages (做香肠的)肉馅.

ˌ**sausage ˈroll** sausage meat baked in a tube of pastry 香肠卷(面皮卷香肠肉馅烤的点心).

sauté /ˈsəʊteɪ; *US* səʊˈteɪ; soˈte/ *adj* [attrib 作定语] (*French* 法) (of food) quickly fried in a little fat (指食物)煎的, 炒的: *sauté potatoes* 煎马铃薯.

▷ **sauté** *v* (*pt, pp* **~ed** or **~d**, *pres p* **~ing**) [Tn] fry (food) in this way 煎, 炒(食物): *Sauté the onions.* 炒洋葱. ⇨ Usage at COOK 用法见 COOK.

S

sav·age /ˈsævɪdʒ; ˈsævɪdʒ/ *adj* **1 (a)** wild and fierce 野性的; 凶猛的: *a savage lion, wolf, etc* 猛狮、恶狼 ○ *a savage attack by a big dog* 凶猛的大狗的攻击. **(b)** cruel, vicious or hostile 残酷的; 恶毒的; 敌意的: *savage criticism, remarks* 粗暴的批评、恶毒的言语 ○ *The article was a savage attack on her past actions.* 那篇文章对她过去的行为进行了恶毒的攻击. ○ *He has a savage temper.* 他脾气暴躁. ○ *The savage ruler ordered that the prisoner be executed.* 那残暴的统治者命令将囚犯处死. **(c)** extremely severe 极严重的: *savage cuts in our budget* 对我们的预算做的大幅度削减. **2** (⚠ *offensive* 讳, 蔑) at an early stage of civilization; primitive 野蛮的; 未开化的: *savage tribes* 这帮野蛮人.

▷ **sav·age** *n* (⚠ *offensive* 讳, 蔑) savage(2) person 野蛮人; 野人: *an island inhabited by savages* 野蛮人居住的岛 ○ (*derog or joc* 贬或谑) *Those children can be real little savages.* 那些孩子简直是小野人.

sav·age *v* [Tn] **1** attack (sb) savagely; maul 残暴地攻击(某人); 残害: *She was badly savaged by a mad dog.* 她让疯狗咬得伤势很重. **2** (*fig* 比喻) criticize (sb/sth) severely 猛烈批评(某人[某事物]): *a novel savaged by the reviewers* 遭评论家猛烈抨击的小说. **sav·agely** *adv*. **sav·age·ness** *n* [U] being savage 野性; 残酷; 野蛮.

sav·agery /ˈsævɪdʒrɪ; ˈsævɪdʒrɪ/ *n* [U] savage behaviour 野蛮或残酷的行为: *treat prisoners with brutal savagery* 残酷野蛮地对待囚犯.

sa·van·nah (also **sa·vanna**) /səˈvænə; səˈvænə/ *n* [C, U] (expanse of) treeless grassy plain in tropical and subtropical regions (热带和亚热带的)无树大草原. Cf 参看 PAMPAS, PRAIRIE, STEPPE, VELD.

sav·ant /ˈsævənt; *US* sæˈvɑːnt; səˈvɑnt/ *n* (*fml* 文) person of great learning 博学之士; 学者; 专家.

save[1] /seɪv; sev/ *v* **1** [Tn, Tn·pr] **~ sb/sth (from sth/ doing sth)** make or keep sb/sth safe (from harm, loss, etc) 救; 拯救; 援救; 保全(以免伤害、损失等): *save sb's life* 救某人的命 ○ *save sb from drowning* 救溺水的人 ○ *save a person from himself*, eg from the results of his own foolishness 使某人免于自食恶果 ○ *It was too late to save the sick woman, and she died.* 病妇未获及时抢救而死亡. ○ *Can the school be saved from closure?* 能保全这所学校不致关闭吗? ○ *She saved the set* (ie at tennis) *by winning the next game.* 她因下一局获胜从而赢了这一盘(网球)比赛. **2 (a)** [I, Ipr, Ip, Tn, Tn·pr, Tn·p] **~ (sth) (up) (for sth)**; **~ (with sth)** keep (money) for future use; not spend 储存(钱); 储蓄: *It's prudent to* *save.* 储蓄是有远见的. ○ *save (up) for a new bike/to buy a new bike* 攒钱买新自行车 ○ *I save with* (ie keep my savings in) *the Brighton Building Society.* 我把钱存在布赖顿房屋建筑协会里. ○ *save part of one's salary each month* 把每月薪水存起一部分来. **(b)** [Tn, Dn·n, Dn·pr] **~ sth (for sb/sth)** keep sth for future use; not use up sth completely 储存某物; 不将某物用完: *Don't eat all the cake now; save some for tomorrow.* 现在别把蛋糕都吃了, 留些明天吃. ○ *Save your strength for the hard work you'll have to do later.* 留着点儿劲儿, 你一会儿还得干重活儿呢. ○ *save one's eyes,* ie protect one's eyesight, eg by not reading too much 保护视力 ○ *Don't drink all the wine; save me some/save some for me!* 别把酒喝光了, 给我留些! **(c)** [Ipr, Tn] **~ (on) sth** avoid wasting sth 避免浪费某物; 节省; 节约: *save on time and money by shopping at the supermarket* 到超级市场购物省时省钱 ○ *save fuel by insulating one's house* 给房子作隔热处理以节省燃料. **3** [Tn, Tg, Tsg, Dn·n] make (sth) unnecessary; make it unnecessary for sb to use sth, spend sth, etc 省去(某事物); 使某人不必使用、花费...: *Order the goods by phone and save (yourself) a journey.* 打电话购物免得(亲自)跑一趟. ○ *Walking to the office saves (me) spending money on bus fares.* 步行上班可省(我)公共汽车费. ○ *The gift of money saved our having to borrow from the bank.* 有了这笔赠款我们就不用向银行借钱了. ○ *That will save us a lot of trouble.* 那就省了我们很多麻烦. ○ *We've been saved a lot of expense by doing the work ourselves.* 我们自己做那工作, 节省了一大笔开销. **4** [I, Tn, Tn·pr] **~ sb (from sth)** set sb free (from the power of sin or its bad consequences) 拯救, 挽救某人(摆脱罪愆或罪孽); 赦罪: *Jesus saves!* 耶稣拯救世人! ○ *Jesus Christ came into the world to save us from our sins.* 基督降世拯救我们摆脱罪恶. **5** [Tn] (in football, etc) prevent an opponent from making (a scoring shot, etc) (足球等)阻碍对方得(分等), 救球: *The goalie managed to save a shot struck at close range.* 守门员救起一个近距离射的球. **6** (idm 习语) **pinch and save/scrape** ⇨ PINCH. **risk/save one's neck** ⇨ NECK. **save sb's 'bacon** (*infml* 口) prevent sb from failing, losing, being harmed, etc 使某人免于失败或免受损失、伤害等: *I was nearly bankrupt, but your loan saved my bacon.* 我已濒于破产, 是你借给我的钱使我幸免于难. **save one's 'breath** not bother to speak when it is useless 不必白费唇舌: *You can save your breath: you'll never persuade her.* 别白费唇舌了, 你决说服不了她. **save (sb's) 'face** preserve one's/sb's pride, reputation, etc 保全面子: *Though she'd lost her job, she saved face by saying she'd left it willingly.* 她失去了工作, 却说是自愿离职以保全面子. **save one's (own) 'hide/'skin** (*infml usu derog* 口, 通常作贬义) escape harm, injury, punishment, loss, etc 免受伤害、损失、惩罚等: *When the rest of the gang were arrested, he saved his own skin by giving evidence against them.* 他那一伙人都已被捕, 他因提供指控他们的证据而保全了自己. **save the situ'ation** deal successfully with a situation which seems hopeless 挽回局势; 渡过难关: *Disagreements threatened to wreck the peace talks, but the president's intervention saved the situation.* 讲和谈判因意见分歧危如累卵, 而会长从中斡旋方转危为安. **scrimp and save** ⇨ SCRIMP. **a stitch in time saves nine** ⇨ STITCH *n.*

▷ **save** *n* (in football, etc) act of preventing a goal from being scored (足球等)阻碍对方得分的动作, 救球.

saver *n* **1** **(a)** person who saves 拯救者; 储蓄者; 储存者; 救星; 救球的运动员: *Good news for all savers — a rise in interest rates!* 储蓄者的好消息——利率提高了! ○ *a saver of souls,* eg a priest 灵魂的拯救者(如牧师). **(b)** (esp in compounds 尤用以构成复合词) thing that saves 用以节省的装置: *a boiler that is a good fuel-saver* 非常节省燃料的锅炉. **2** (*Brit*) ticket, etc that costs less than the usual price 廉价的票、券等: [attrib 作定语] *an off-peak saver ticket* 非高峰时期的优惠票.

sav·ing *adj* (idm 习语) **a saving 'grace** thing that makes up for the poor qualities in sb/sth 可弥补某人[某事物]缺点的特质: *He may be stupid and mean, but his one saving grace is his humour.* 他虽说又愚蠢又吝啬, 但他有幽默的长处.

-saving (forming compound *adjs* 用以构成复合形容词) that saves (SAVE[1] 3) the thing specified 节省的; 节约的: *Modern houses have many labour-saving devices,* eg washing-machines, dishwashers, etc which make housework easier. 现代化的房屋有许多省力的设备(如洗衣机、洗碗机等). ○ *energy-saving modifications* 为节能做的改装.

□ **,save-as-you-'earn** *n* (*abbr* 缩写 **SAYE**) (*dated* 旧 *Brit*) method of saving one's money by having some of it deducted from one's salary each month 薪金扣存储蓄法.

save[2] /seɪv; sev/ (also **sav·ing** /ˈseɪvɪŋ; ˋsevɪŋ/) *prep, conj* (*fml* 文) except 除了(表示所说的不包括在内): *all save him* 除他以外所有的人 ○ *We know nothing about her save that her surname is Jones.* 我们除了知道她姓琼斯外, 对她全不了解.

sav·ing /ˈseɪvɪŋ; ˋsevɪŋ/ *n* **1** [C] amount saved 节省或储存的量: *a useful saving of time and money* 在时间和金钱方面有价值的节省 ○ *big savings on fuel through greater efficiency* 通过提高效率节省大量燃料. **2 savings** [pl] money saved up 储蓄金; 存款; 积蓄: *keep one's savings in the bank* 把储蓄的钱存在银行里.

□ **'savings account** **1** (*Brit*) any type of bank account that earns more interest than a deposit account 储蓄帐户(可获利息高于定期存款帐户的任何类型的银行帐户). **2** (*US*) any type of account that earns interest 储蓄帐户(可获利息的任何类型的帐户). Cf 参看 CURRENT ACCOUNT (CURRENT[1]), DEPOSIT ACCOUNT (DEPOSIT[2]).

'savings bank bank that pays interest on money deposited but does not provide other services for its customers 储蓄银行.

sa·viour (*US* **sa·vior**) /ˈseɪvɪə(r); ˋsevjɚ/ *n* **1** person who rescues or saves sb from danger 救助者; 拯救者; 救星. **2 the Saviour, Our Saviour** Jesus Christ 救世主(耶稣基督).

savoir-faire /ˌsævwɑːˈfeə (r); ˌsævwɑrˋfɛr/ *n* [U] (*French approv* 法, 褒) ability to behave appropriately in social situations 处世的能力: *possess, display, lack savoir-faire* 有、表现出、没有社交本领.

sa·vory /ˈseɪvərɪ; ˋsevərɪ/ *n* **1** [U] herb of the mint family used in cooking 香薄荷(用于烹饪的). **2** [C] (*US*) = SAVOURY *n.*

sa·vour (*US* **sa·vor**) /ˈseɪvə(r); ˋsevɚ/ *n* [C, U] (pleasant) taste or flavour (美)味; 味道; 滋味; 风味: *soup with a slight savour of garlic* 略带蒜味的汤 ○ *meat that has lost its savour* 已失去原有香味的肉 ○ (*fig* 比喻) *His political views have a savour of fanaticism.* 他的政治观点有些偏激. ○ *Life seems to have lost some of its savour,* ie its enjoyable quality. 生活中似乎已失去了一些值得享受的乐趣. ▷ **sa·vour** *v* **1** [Tn] enjoy the taste or flavour of (sth), esp by eating or drinking it slowly 欣赏(某物)的味道或风味(尤指慢慢地品尝): *savour the finest French dishes* 品尝最好的法国菜 ○ (*fig* 比喻) *Now the exams are over, I'm savouring my freedom.* 因为考试结束了, 我现在自由自在了. **2** (phr v) **savour of sth** (no passive 不用于被动语态) have a suggestion or trace of sth (esp sth bad) 有某种迹象或痕迹(尤指坏事): *Her remarks savour of hypocrisy.* 她说的话听起来有点儿虚伪.

sa·voury (*US* **sa·vory**) /ˈseɪvərɪ; ˋsevərɪ/ *adj* **1** (of food) having a salty or sharp flavour, not a sweet one (指食物)咸的, 辣的: *a savoury pancake* 咸的烙饼. **2** having an appetizing taste or smell 开胃的(可口的或香喷喷的). **3** (usu in negative sentences 通常用于否定句) morally wholesome or respectable 道德高尚的; 可敬的: *I gather his past life was not altogether savoury.* 我猜想他过去的生活并非十分正派. Cf 参看 UNSAVOURY.

▷ **sa·voury** (*US* **sa·vory**) *n* (*Brit*) savoury(1) dish, usu served at the end of a meal 咸的或辣的食物(通常为一顿饭最后吃的).

sa·voy /səˈvɔɪ; səˋvɔɪ/ *n* type of cabbage with wrinkled leaves 皱叶甘蓝.

savvy /ˈsævɪ; ˋsævɪ/ *n* [U] (*sl* 俚) common sense; understanding 常识; 理解: *Where's your savvy?* 你的常识到哪里去了?

▷ **savvy** *v* (*pt, pp* **savvied**) [I] (*sl* 俚) (usu in the imperative or present tense 通常用于祈使句或现在时态) understand; know 理解; 知道: *Keep your mouth shut! Savvy?* 闭上嘴! 懂吗? ○ *No savvy,* ie I do not know/understand. 我不知道[懂].

saw[1] *pt of* SEE[1].

saw[2] /sɔː; sɔ/ *n* (often in compounds 常用以构成复合词) cutting tool that has a long blade with a sharp-toothed edge, worked by hand (by pushing it backwards and forwards) or mechanically, and used for cutting wood, metal, stone, etc 锯: *cutting logs with a 'power saw* 用电锯锯原木 ○ *a ˌcircular 'saw* ○ *a 'handsaw* ○ *a 'chainsaw.*

▷ **saw** *v* (*pt* **sawed**, *pp* **sawn** /sɔːn; sɔn/; *US* **sawed**) **1** [I, Ipr, Tn, Tn·pr, Tn·p] use a saw; cut (sth) with a saw; make (logs, etc) by using a saw 用锯; 锯(某物); 锯成(原木段等): *spend half an hour sawing* 锯半小时 ○ *saw into the branch* 把锯锯进树枝 ○ *saw wood* 锯木材 ○ *saw a log into planks/in two* 把原木锯成板[两截] ○ *saw the plank right through* 把木板锯开. ⇨Usage at CUT[1] 用法见CUT[1]. **2** [Ipr, Ip, Tn] **~ (away) (at sth)** make to-and-fro movements as if with a saw 像拉锯一样来回移动: *sawing at his fiddle*, ie using the bow as if it were a saw 拉提琴 ○ *She was sawing (away at) the bread with a blunt knife.* 她正在用一把钝刀拉锯般地切着面包. **3** [I] be capable of being sawn 可被锯开: *This wood saws easily.* 这木材很容易锯开. **4** (phr v) **saw sth down** bring sth to the ground using a saw 锯倒某物: *saw a tree, pole, etc down* 锯倒树、杆等. **saw sth off (sth)** cut sth off with a saw 锯掉某物: *saw a branch off (a tree)* 锯掉树枝 ○ *a sawn-off shotgun*, ie one with most of the barrel sawn off, used esp by criminals because it is easier to carry and conceal 枪管锯短的枪(尤指罪犯为便于携带或隐藏用的). **saw sth up** saw sth into pieces 将某物锯成小块: *All the trees have been sawn up into logs.* 所有的树都已锯成原木.

saw·yer /'sɔːjə(r); 'sɔjɚ/ *n* person whose job is sawing wood 锯木工.

□ **'sawdust** *n* [U] tiny pieces of wood falling as powder from wood as it is sawn 锯末.

'saw-horse (*US* also **'sawbuck**) *n* wooden frame on which wood is supported while it is being sawn 锯木架.

'sawmill *n* mill with power-operated saws for cutting timber into planks, etc 锯木厂.

saw[3] /sɔː; sɔ/ *n* (*dated* 旧) saying; proverb 格言; 谚语: *the old saw 'More haste, less speed.'* 语云, '欲速则不达.'

sax /sæks; sæks/ *n* (*infml* 口) = SAXOPHONE.

saxi·frage /'sæksɪfreɪdʒ; 'sæksəfrɪdʒ/ *n* [U] any of various Alpine or rock plants with white, yellow or red flowers 虎耳草(生于高山或岩石间, 花呈白色、黄色或红色).

Saxon /'sæksn; 'sæksn̩/ *n* **1** [C] member of a people once living in NW Germany, some of whom conquered and settled in Britain in the 5th and 6th centuries 撒克逊人(早期居住在德意志西北部的人, 有些人于5世纪及6世纪时征服了不列颠而定居下来). **2** [U] their language 撒克逊语.

▷ **Saxon** *adj* of this people or their language 撒克逊人的; 撒克逊语的: *Saxon tribes, customs, grammar* 撒克逊的部落、习俗、语法.

saxo·phone /'sæksəfəʊn; 'sæksəˌfon/ (also *infml* 口语作 **sax**) *n* metal musical instrument played by blowing, with keys worked by the player's fingers, typically shaped like a long thin letter S and used mainly for jazz 萨克管(铜管乐器): *a tenor/bass saxophone* 次中音[低音]萨克管 ○ [attrib 作定语] *a saxophone solo* 萨克管独奏. ⇨illus at App 1 见附录1插图, page x.

▷ **saxo·phon·ist** /sæk'sɒfənɪst; *US* 'sæksəfəʊnɪst; 'sæksəˌfonɪst/ *n* saxophone player 萨克管吹奏者.

say /seɪ; se/ *v* (*3rd pers sing pres t* **says** /sez; sɛz/, *pt, pp* **said** /sed; sɛd/) **1** (**a**) [Tn, Tn·pr, Tf, Dn·pr, Dpr·f, Dpr·w] **~ sth (to sb)** tell sth (to sb), usu in words 说; 讲: *Did you say 'Please'?* 你说'请'这个字了吗? ○ *'Hello!' I said.* '喂!'我说. ○ *She said nothing to me about it.* 这件事她完全没对我说过. ○ *He said (that) his friend's name was Sam.* 他说他朋友的名字叫山姆. ○ *Everyone said how awful the weather was.* 大家都说天气糟透了. ○ *He finds it hard to say what he feels.* 他觉得很难说出自己的感受. ○ *She said to meet her here.* 她说在这里与她见面. ○ *I said to myself* (ie thought), *'That can't be right!'* 我心说, '这不对呀!' ○ *They say/It's said* (ie People claim) *that he's a genius.* 据说他很有才华. ○ *So you say*, ie I think you may be wrong. 你是这么说的(我认为你可能错了). ○ *Who said I can't cook?* ie Of course I can! 谁说我不会做饭? ○ *Be quiet, I've got something to say.* 请安静, 我有话要说. ○ *Having said that* (ie Despite what I have just said), *I agree with your other point.* 我虽然这么说, 我还是同意你的另一说法. ○ (*euph* 婉) *If you damage the car, your father will have plenty to say about it*, ie he will be angry. 你要是把汽车弄坏了, 你父亲非说你不可(他一定得生气). (**b**) [Tn] pronounce (eg words one has learned) 念, 背诵(如学过的词语): *say a short prayer* 背诵简短的祈祷文 ○ *Try to say that line with more conviction.* 念这一行时, 要尽量带出坚定的语气. (**c**) [Tn, Tn·pr] **~ sth (to sb)** make (thoughts, feelings, etc) clear to sb by using words, or else by gestures, behaviour, etc (用言语、手势、行为等)表达(思想、情感等): *This poem doesn't say much to me.* 我体会不出这首诗好在什么地方. ○ *Just what is the artist trying to say in her work?* 那艺术家在她的作品中究竟想表达什么? ○ *Her angry glance said everything.* 她愤怒的目光足以说明了一切. (**d**) [no passive 不用于被动语态: Tn, Tf, Tw, Tt] (of a book, sign, etc) give (information or instructions) (指书、符号等)表示(信息或指示): *a notice saying 'Keep Out'* 写有'禁止入内'的告示 ○ *The clock says three o'clock.* 这个钟三点了. ○ *The law says (that) this is quite legitimate.* 从法律上说, 这是合法的. ○ *The book doesn't say where he was born.* 书上没说他是在哪里出生的. ○ *The guidebook says to turn left.* 旅游指南上说向左转. ⇨Usage 见所附用法. **2** (**a**) [Tn, Tf, Tw] give (an opinion, answer, etc) 表明(看法、意见等): *I'll say this (for them)*, (ie I'll admit that) *they're efficient.* 我得(为他们)说句话, 他们很有能力. ○ *I can't say I blame her for resigning*, ie I think she was justified. 我不能说她辞职是错的(我认为她有她的道理). ○ *I would say he's right.* 我认为他对. ○ *My wife thinks I'm too fat — what do you say?* 我妻子认为我太胖——你说呢? ○ *I say* (ie suggest) *we stay here.* 我看我们就待在这里吧. ○ *I wouldn't say they were rich*, ie In my opinion they aren't rich. 我看他们算不上阔气. ○ *Say all you want about her* (ie Despite any criticism you can make), *she's still a fine singer.* 不管你怎么说, 她唱得还算不错. ○ *It's hard to say who it was.* 很难说是谁. ○ *There is no saying* (ie Nobody knows) *when the war will end.* 谁也说不上战争什么时候能结束. ○ *'When will the meal be ready?' 'I couldn't say.'* '饭什么时候做好?''我说不准.' (**b**) [no passive 不用于被动语态: Tn, Tf] suppose (sth) as an example or a possibility 假定; 比如说: *You could learn to play chess in, (let's) say, three months.* 学下国际象棋要用, 比如说, 三个月吧. ○ *Let's take any writer, say* (ie for example) *Dickens...* 咱们可以随便拿个作家为例, 比方说狄更斯... ○ *Say you have an accident: who would look after you?* 假如你出了事故, 谁来照顾你呢? **3** (idm 习语) **before you can/could say Jack Robinson** very quickly or suddenly 立刻; 马上; 一下子. **easier said than done** ⇨ EASY[2]. **ˌgo without 'saying** be very obvious or natural 不用说; 显而易见: *It goes without saying that I'll help you.* 用不着说, 我一定帮助你. **have a good word to say for sb/sth** ⇨ WORD. **have something, nothing, etc to 'say for oneself** be ready, unwilling, etc to talk, eg to give one's views or justify oneself 有话要说、没话可说等(如表达自己的观点或作自我辩解): *She hasn't got much to say for herself*, ie doesn't take part in conversation. 她没什么话说. ○ *You've got too much to say for yourself*, ie You think you are more interesting than you really are. 你有些自我标榜. ○ *You've lost your games kit again — what have you got to say for yourself?* 你又把运动用具给丢了——看你还有什么话好说? **I dare say** ⇨ DARE[1]. **'I'll say!** (*infml* 口) yes indeed 当然; 的确: *'Does he come often?' 'I'll say! Nearly every day.'* '他常来吗?''可不! 差不多每天都来.' **I 'must say** (used when making a comment 用于作评论时): *Well that's daft, I must say!* 依我看, 那可太蠢了! **I say** (*dated* 旧) (used to express surprise, shock, etc or (unstressed) to start a conversation 用以表示惊讶、震惊等; 若不重读时, 用以引起话题): *I 'say! What a huge cake!* 好家伙! 这么大的蛋糕! ○ *I say, can you lend me five pounds?* 我说, 能借我五英镑吗? **it says a 'lot, very 'little, etc for sb/sth** (used to present a revealing fact about sb/sth 用以揭示关于某人[某事物]的事实): *It says a lot for her that she never lost her temper*, ie It shows how patient she is. 她从没发过脾气, 这足以说明她多有耐性. ○ *It doesn't say much for*

S

our efficiency that (ie We are not efficient because) *the order arrived a week late.* 定单晚了一个星期才到，我们的工作效率未免说不过去了. **I ˌwouldn't say ˈno (to sth)** (*infml* 口) used to show one wants sth, or to accept sth when it is offered 表示想要或接受某事物: *'Fancy some coffee?' 'I wouldn't say no.'* '想来点咖啡吗?' '好哇.' ○ *I wouldn't say no to a pizza.* 我想来块意大利饼. **least said soonest mended** (*saying* 谚) a particular situation will be most quickly remedied if nothing more is said about it 说得越少，境况越好. **the less/least said the better** the best thing to do is to say as little as possible (about sth) 少说为妙. **let us say** for example 比如说; 例如. **needless to say** ⇨NEEDLESS (NEED[3]). **ˌnever say ˈdie** (*saying* 谚) don't give up hope 不可气馁; 不要泄气: *Never say die: we might still get there on time.* 别泄气，我们仍有可能按时赶到那里. **no sooner said than done** ⇨ SOON. **not be saying much** (used to point out that sth is not really remarkable 用以指出某事物没什么了不起): *She's taller than me, but as I'm only five foot, that's not saying much.* 她比我高，可我只有五英尺，不能说明她很高. **not say boo to a goose** be very or too timid or gentle 非常胆小或温顺: *He's such a nervous chap he wouldn't/couldn't say boo to a goose.* 他很怯懦，胆小如鼠. **not say a dicky-bird** (*sl* 俚) say nothing 不吭气; 不作声. **not to say** (used to suggest that a stronger way of describing sth is justified 用以表示退一步着想的让步关系): *a difficult, not to say impossible, task* 这一任务即使不说办不到，也得说是十分艰巨的. **sad to say** ⇨ SAD. **say/ be one's last word** ⇨ LAST[1]. **say no (to sth)** refuse (an offer, a suggestion, etc) 谢绝(好意等); 拒绝(建议等): *If you don't invest in these shares, you're saying no to a fortune.* 要是不买这种股票，就是放着发财的机会都不要. **ˌsay no ˈmore** (**a**) (used to interrupt sb when one wishes to react to what he is saying 用以打断某人的话以便插入自己的反应意见): *Say no more! How much do you want to borrow?* 别再说了! 你想借多少钱吧? (**b**) I understand what you mean 我明白你的意思: *'He came home with lipstick on his face.' 'Say no more!'* '他回到家时脸上还带着口红印呢.' '我明白了!' **say one's piece** say what one wants to say 说自己要说的话. Cf 参看 HAVE ONE'S SAY (SAY *n*). **says ˈyou** (*sl* 俚) I do not believe what you say 我不相信你的话: *'I'll beat him.' 'Says you, you haven't got a chance!'* '我要把他打败.' '我不信，你决办不到!' **say ˈwhen** (used to ask sb to show when one should stop doing sth, esp when one has poured enough to drink 在为对方做某事的过程中，用以请求对方于满意时做出表示，尤指已斟入不少饮料时). **say the ˈword** give an order; make a request 下命令; 提要求: *Just say the word, and I'll ask him to leave.* 只要你开口，我就叫他走. **strange to say** ⇨ STRANGE. **suffice it to say** ⇨ SUFFICE. **to ˌsay the ˈleast** without any exaggeration 至少可以这样说; 不夸张地说: *I was surprised at what he said, to say the least.* 毫不夸张地说，我对他的话感到吃惊. **to say nothing of sth** without even mentioning sth 更不用说; 何况: *He had to go to prison for a month, to say nothing of the fine.* 他得入狱一个月，更不用说罚款了. **that is to say** in other words (也)就是说; 换言之; 即: *three days from now, that's to say Friday* 三天之后，也就是说星期五. **what do/ would you say (to sth/doing sth)?** would you like sth/to do sth? (对某事物[做某事物])你觉得怎样?: *We'll go on holiday together. What do you say?* 我们一起去度假吧. 你觉得怎么样? ○ *What do you say to going to the theatre tonight?* 今晚去看戏，你说好吗? ○ *What would you say to a chocolate?* 吃块巧克力吧? **what/ whatever sb says goes** (*infml* 口) the specified person has total authority and must be obeyed 某人说了算; 照某人说的办: *My wife wants the kitchen painted white, and what she says goes.* 我妻子要把厨房刷成白色的，这事就得照她的意思办. **you can say ˈthat again** I agree with you 我同意你的意见: *'She's a violent woman.' 'You can say that again. She's hit me more than once.'* '她是个悍妇.' '你说得太对了. 她打我可不止一次了.' **you don't ˈsay!** (*infml* 口) (used to express surprise 用以表达惊奇): *'We're going to get married.' 'You don't say!'* '我们要结婚了.' '真的吗?' **you ˈsaid it!** (*infml* 口) that is very true 真是这样; 千真万确: *'The food was awful!' 'You said it!'* '这食物很糟糕!' '一点不假!' ○ *'I looked a fool.' 'You said it!'* (ie I am glad you realized it.) '我活像个傻瓜.' '算你说着了!'

▷ **say** *n* **1** [sing, U] **~ (in sth)** power to decide 决定权: *have no, not much, some, any, etc say (in a matter)* (对某事)没有、不大有、有些、有...决定权 ○ *I want a say in the management of the business.* 我想要在业务管理方面有决定权. **2** (idm 习语) **have one's ˈsay** express one's view 表达意见: *Don't interrupt her: let her have her say.* 别打断她的话，让她把意见说出来.

say *interj* (*US infml* 口) (used to express mild surprise or to introduce a remark 用以表示轻度惊讶或引起话题): *Say! How about a Chinese meal tonight?* 喂! 今晚吃顿中餐好不好?

say·ing /ˈseɪɪŋ; ˋseɪŋ/ *n* well-known phrase, proverb, etc; remark often made 谚语; 格言; 俗话: *'More haste, less speed,' as the saying goes.* 常言道: '欲速则不达.'

□ **ˈsay-so** *n* [sing] (*infml* 口) **1** statement made by sb without proof 无充分根据的话: *Don't just accept his say-so: find out for yourself.* 别听他信口开河，你得自己去弄清楚. **2** permission (to do sth); power (to decide sth) (做某事物的)许可; (决定某事物的)权力: *You don't need my say-so to change things.* 你不必向我请示可自行做些变动.

NOTE ON USAGE 用法: **1 Say** and **tell** are transitive verbs. ☆ **say** 和 **tell** 均为及物动词. The direct object of **say** is usually the words spoken. ☆ **say** 的直接宾语通常是所说的话. The direct object of **tell** is usually the information given and the indirect object is the person that it is given to ☆ **tell** 的直接宾语通常是提供的信息，其间接宾语是接受信息的人: *He sat in a corner and said nothing all evening,* ie spoke no words. 他坐在角落里，整晚一句话也没说. ○ *She told me nothing about herself,* ie she gave me no information. 她没向我透露她个人的情况. **Say** is commonly used with direct speech ☆ **say** 多用以表达出直接引语: *He said, 'Goodnight,' and went to bed.* 他说了声'晚安'，就去睡觉了. **Say** and **tell** often report speech. ☆ **say** 和 **tell** 常用以表达间接引语. **Tell** must normally be followed by a personal direct object; **say** is used without a personal object ☆ **tell** 后面一般须有一表示人的直接宾语，而 **say** 后则无表示人的宾语: *He hasn't told me/said that he's leaving.* 他还没告诉我[说]他要走. **Tell sb** + infinitive is used for commands ☆ **tell sb** +不定式，这一结构用以表达命令或指示: *She told him to hurry up.* 她叫他快点. **2 Speak** and **talk** are used intransitively and transitively. ☆ **speak** 和 **talk** 既可用作不及物动词也可用作及物动词. They are often used with similar meaning, **speak** being more formal 这两个词的意思相近，只是 **speak** 较为文些: *Can I talk to Susan, please?* 请问，我和苏珊说句话行吗? ○ *I'd like to speak to Mrs Jones, please.* 劳驾，我想和琼斯夫人说句话. **Talk** suggests that two or more people are having a conversation with each other, while **speak** is often used of one person addressing a group ☆ **talk** 指两人或两人以上相互交谈，而 **speak** 常用以指一人讲大家听: *We talked for hours about the meaning of life.* 我们谈人生的意义谈了几个小时. ○ *He spoke to the class about the dangers of smoking.* 他给班上学生讲了吸烟的危害性.

SAYE /ˌes eɪ waɪ ˈiː; ˌɛs e waɪ ˋi/ *abbr* 缩写 = (*dated* 旧 *Brit*) (of a Post Office savings scheme) save-as-you-earn.

sc *abbr* 缩写 = **1** (also **Sc**) scene: *Act I Sc IV* 第一幕第四场. **2** namely (Latin *scilicet* 源自拉丁文 *scilicet*).

scab /skæb; skæb/ *n* **1** [C, U] dry crust formed over a wound or sore as it heals 痂. **2** [U] disease of skin or plants causing scab-like roughness 疥癣: *sheep-scab* 羊疥癣. **3** [C] (*infml derog* 口, 贬) worker who refuses to join a strike or a trade union, or who takes the place of a striker; blackleg 拒绝参加罢工的工人; 拒不参加工会的工人; 顶替罢工者工作的人; 工贼.

▷ **scabby** *adj* (**-ier**, **-iest**) (**a**) covered with scabs (SCAB 1) 结痂的; 有痂的. (**b**) (*sl derog* 俚, 贬) contemptible 卑鄙的; 下贱的: *You scabby liar!* 你这个卑鄙的撒谎的人!

scab·bard /ˈskæbəd; ˋskæbəd/ *n* cover for the blade of a sword, dagger or bayonet; sheath (剑、匕首或刺刀的)鞘. ⇨illus at SWORD 见 SWORD 插图.

sca·bies /ˈskeɪbiːz; ˋskebiz/ *n* [U] contagious skin

disease causing scabs and itching 疥疮；疥螨病.

sca·bi·ous /ˈskeɪbɪəs; ˋskebɪəs/ *n* [U] wild or cultivated plant with thick clusters of blue, pink or white flowers 山萝卜.

scab·rous /ˈskeɪbrəs; *US* ˈskæb-; ˋskebrəs/ *adj* (*fml* 文) **1** (of animals, plants, etc) having a rough surface (指动植物等)表面粗糙的, 不平滑的. **2** indecent; obscene 猥亵的; 淫秽的: *Her scabrous novels shocked the public.* 她的小说淫秽不堪, 公众十分震惊.

scads /skædz; skædz/ *n* [pl] **~s (of sth)** (*US infml* 口) large numbers or amounts 许多; 大量: *scads of money, people* 许多钱、人.

scaffold 脚手架

scaf·fold /ˈskæfəʊld; ˋskæfold/ *n* **1** frame made of long metal tubes put up next to a building so that builders, painters, etc can work on it, or to support a platform 脚手架; 建筑架. **2** platform on which criminals are executed 绞架; 断头台: *go to the scaffold*, ie be executed 上断头台.

▷ **scaf·fold·ing** /ˈskæfəldɪŋ; ˋskæfl̩dɪŋ/ *n* [U] (materials for a) scaffold(1), eg poles and planks 脚手架; 搭脚手架的材料: *tubular scaffolding*, ie metal tubes to be bolted together 管子脚手架.

scalar /ˈskeɪlə(r); ˋskelɚ/ *n*, *adj* (*mathematics* 数) (quantity) having size but no direction 标量(的); 纯量(的). Cf 参看 VECTOR 1.

scala·wag (*US*) = SCALLYWAG.

scald /skɔːld; skɔld/ *v* **1** [Tn, Tn·pr] burn (oneself or part of one's body) with boiling liquid or steam (用沸腾的液体或蒸汽)烫伤(自己或自己身体的部位): *scald one's hand with hot fat* 热油把手烫伤 ○ *She was scalded to death when the boiler exploded.* 锅炉爆炸把她烫死了. **2** [Tn] heat (esp milk) almost to boiling-point 将(尤指奶)加热至接近沸点. **3** [Tn] clean (pans, etc) with boiling water 用沸水烫洗(锅等).

▷ **scald** *n* injury to the skin from boiling liquid or steam (沸腾的液体或蒸汽对皮肤的)烫伤: *an ointment for burns and scalds* 治疗烧伤和烫伤的药膏.

scald·ing *adj* hot enough to scald 滚烫的; 灼热的: *scalding water, fat, etc* 滚烫的水、油等. — *adv* extremely 极: *scalding hot* 极热.

scale[1] /skeɪl; skel/ *n* **1** [C] any of the thin overlapping plates of hard material covering the skin of many fish and reptiles 鳞; 鳞片: *scrape the scales from a herring* 刮去鲱鱼的鳞. ➪ illus at FISH 见 FISH 插图. **2** [C] thing resembling this, esp a loose flake of diseased skin 鳞状物; (尤指皮肤的)鳞屑. **3** [U] **(a)** (also *esp Brit* **fur**) chalky material deposited by hard water inside boilers, kettles, water-pipes, etc 水碱; 水锈. **(b)** tartar on teeth 牙垢. **4** (idm 习语) **the scales fall from sb's ˈeyes** someone suddenly realizes the truth after having been deceived 受骗后突然发觉真相; 发觉上当: *Then the scales fell from my eyes: he had been lying all the time.* 我恍然大悟: 他一直在撒谎.

▷ **scale** *v* **1** [Tn] remove the scales from (fish) 刮(鱼)鳞. **2** (phr v) **scale off** (sth) come off in flakes 呈片状剥落或脱落: *paint/plaster scaling off (a wall)* (墙壁)脱落下来的油漆[灰泥].

scaly *adj* (**-ier**, **-iest**) covered with scale or scales; coming off in scales 覆有鳞的; 有鳞屑的; 有水碱的; 有牙垢的; 呈鳞片状脱落的: *a scaly skin, surface* 有鳞屑的皮肤、表面 ○ *a kettle that's scaly inside* 有水锈的水壶.

sca·li·ness *n* [U].

scale[2] /skeɪl; skel/ *n* **1** [C] **(a)** series of marks at regular distances for the purpose of measuring (eg on a ruler or thermometer) 标度; 刻度: *This ruler has one scale in centimetres and another in inches.* 这把尺上有厘米的刻度和英寸的刻度. **(b)** measuring instrument marked in this way 有刻度的量具. **2** [C] system of units for measuring 量度制; 进位制: *the ˈdecimal scale* 十进制. **3** [C] system of grading people or things according to how big, important, rich, etc, they are 等级; 级别: *a scale of wages, taxation* 工资、税率的等级 ○ *a person who is high on the social scale* 社会地位高的人 ○ *The salary scale goes from £8 000 to £20 000.* 薪金级别为8 000英镑至20 000英镑. **4** [C] relation between the actual size of sth and the map, diagram, etc which represents it 比例; 比率: *a scale of ten kilometres to the centimetre, a scale of one to a million* 一厘米代表十公里的比例、一比一百万的比例 ○ *a large-scale map*, ie one showing a relatively small area in detail 大比例的地图(较小范围的详图) ○ *Sheet maps use a much larger scale.* 单张地图用的比例大得多. ○ [attrib 作定语] *a scale model, drawing, etc* 成比例的模型、图等. ➪ illus at MAP 见 MAP 插图. **5** [U, C] relative size, extent, etc 规模; 程度; 范围: *entertain on a large scale*, eg hold expensive parties with many guests 举办大规模的招待会 ○ *The scale of his spending — £50 000 in a year — amazed us all.* 他开销之大——一年50 000英镑——把我们都吓了一跳. ○ *We achieve economies of scale in production*, ie Producing many items reduces the price of each one. 我们取得了大规模生产的经济效益. **6** [C] (*music* 音) series of notes arranged at fixed intervals in order of pitch, esp a series of eight starting on a keynote 音阶: *the scale of F*, ie with F as the keynote F音阶 ○ *practise scales on the piano* 练习弹奏钢琴的连续音阶. Cf 参看 OCTAVE 1. **7** (idm 习语) **to scale** in a fixed proportion to the actual size 按比例: *draw a map of an area to scale* 按比例绘制某地的地图.

▷ **scale** *v* (phr v) **~ sth down/up** reduce/increase sth 缩减[增加]某事物: *We are going to scale down the number of trees being felled.* 我们要减少砍伐的树的数量. ○ *We've scaled up production to meet demand.* 我们已经扩大了生产以满足需求.

scales 台秤

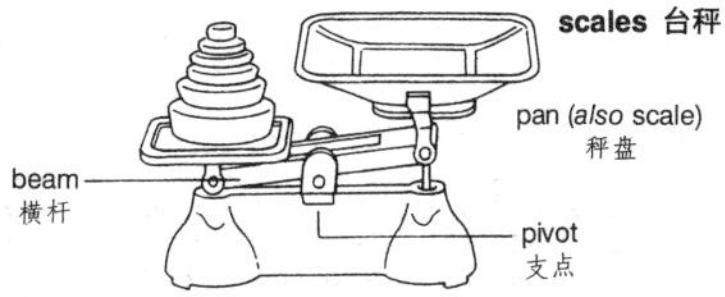

scale[3] /skeɪl; skel/ *n* **1** [C] either of the two pans on a balance 天平盘. **2 scales** [pl *v*] balance or instrument for weighing 天平; 磅秤: *a pair of scales* 一台天平 ○ *bathroom scales*, ie for weighing oneself 浴室磅秤. ➪ illus 见插图. **3** (idm 习语) **tip the balance/scale** ➪ TIP[2]. **tip/turn the scale(s) at sth** (*infml* 口) weigh (a specified amount) 称得重量为(某量): *The jockey turned the scales at 80 lb.* 那赛马骑师体重为80磅.

▷ **scale** *v* [In/pr] weigh (a specified amount) 称得重量为(某量): *The boxer scaled 90 kilos.* 那拳击手体重为90公斤.

scale[4] /skeɪl; skel/ *v* [Tn] climb up (a wall, cliff, etc) 攀登, 爬(墙、悬崖等).

sca·lene /ˈskeɪliːn; skeˋlin/ *adj* (*geometry* 几) (of a triangle) having no two sides of equal length (指三角形)不等边的, 不规则的.

scal·lion /ˈskælɪən; ˋskæljən/ *n* (*US*) = SPRING ONION (SPRING[2]).

scal·lop (also **scollop**) /ˈskɒləp; ˋskɑləp/ *n* **1** **(a)** shellfish with two fan-shaped shells 扇贝. **(b)** (also **ˈscallop-shell**) one shell of this used as a container in which food is cooked and served 扇贝壳(用以烤制及盛放食物的单扇壳). **2** any one of a series of scallop-shaped curves cut on the edge of fabric, pastry, etc 扇形饰边.

▷ **scal·lop** (also **scollop**) *v* [Tn] **1** decorate (sth) with scallops (SCALLOP 2) 用扇形饰边装饰(某物): *a scalloped hem* 扇形的衣物饰边. **2** cook (eg oysters) in a scallop-shell 在扇贝壳里烤制(如牡蛎).

scal·ly·wag /ˈskælɪwæg; ˋskælɪˌwæg/ (*US* **scalawag**

S

/ˈskæləwæg; ˋskælə,wæg/) *n* (used playfully) person, esp a child, who behaves mischievously (戏谑用语)搞恶作剧的人(尤指儿童): *You naughty little scallywag!* 你这个小淘气鬼!

scalp /skælp; skælp/ *n* **1** skin of the head excluding the face 头皮(头顶及其周围的皮肤): *dandruff flaking off one's scalp* 从头皮上脱落下的头皮屑. **2** this and the hair rooted in it, formerly cut off a dead enemy as a trophy by some N American Indians 带发头皮(旧时北美印第安人取自敌人头颅作为战利品的): (*fig* 比喻) *be after sb's scalp,* ie want to punish, take revenge on sb, etc 想整治某人(惩罚、报复等).

▷ **scalp** *v* [Tn] take the scalp(2) from (an enemy) 剥(敌人)的头皮: (*joc* 谑) *You've just about scalped me!* ie cut my hair very short. 你把我的头发剪得真短!

scal·pel /ˈskælpəl; ˋskælpəl/ *n* small light knife used by surgeons 手术刀; 解剖刀.

scam /skæm; skæm/ *n* (*US infml* 口) dishonest scheme 骗局; 欺诈: *a betting scam* 赌博骗局.

scamp[1] /skæmp; skæmp/ *n* (often used playfully) mischievous child (常作戏谑用语)顽皮的孩子: *That little scamp Jimmy has hidden my slippers again!* 这个调皮的小吉米又把我的拖鞋藏起来了!

scamp[2] = SKIMP.

scamper /ˈskæmpə(r); ˋskæmpɚ/ *v* [Ipr, Ip] run quickly and often playfully as children and some small animals do (儿童及某些小动物)奔跑, 蹦蹦跳跳: *scamper up the steps* 蹦跳着上台阶 ○ *The rabbit scampered away in fright.* 兔子惊慌地跑了. ⇨Usage at SCURRY 用法见SCURRY.

▷ **scamper** *n* [sing] scampering movement; act of scampering 奔跑; 蹦蹦跳跳: *a little scamper round the garden* 在花园里绕着圈蹦蹦跳跳奔跑一阵.

S

scampi /ˈskæmpɪ; ˋskæmpɪ/ *n* **1** [pl] large prawns 大虾. **2** [U] dish of these as food, usu fried in breadcrumbs 烹调的大虾(通常为裹面包屑炸的): *have some scampi* 吃些炸大虾.

scan /skæn; skæn/ *v* (**-nn-**) **1** Tn] look at every part of (sth) carefully; examine (sth) with great attention 细看(某物)的各部; 仔细检查(某物): *He scanned the horizon, looking for land.* 他细看天水相连的地方, 寻找陆地. **2** [Tn] (**a**) (of a searchlight, etc) pass across (an area) (指探照灯等)扫掠(某处): *The flashlight's beam scanned every corner of the room.* 手电筒的光束扫遍屋内各个角落. (**b**) (*medical* 医) obtain an image of (a body or part of the body) with a scanner 用扫描器扫描(身体或身体的部位). **3** [Tn] glance at (eg a document) quickly but not very thoroughly 匆匆而粗略地看(如文件): *She scanned the newspaper over breakfast.* 她吃着早饭把报纸大略看了一遍. **4** (**a**) [Tn] analyse the metre of (a line of verse) by noting how it is stressed and how many syllables it has, as in ˈ*Mary* /ˈ*had a*/ˈ*little*/ˈ*lamb* 划分(诗句)的音步(如'Mary/'had a/'little/'lamb.) (**b**) [I] (of verse) have a proper metrical pattern (指诗句)符合韵律: *a line that does not scan* 一行不合韵律的诗句 ○ *The verses scan well.* 这些诗句韵律严谨. **5** [Tn] (in television, etc) pass an electronic beam over (sth), esp so as to produce a picture on a screen (电视等)扫描.

▷ **scan** *n* act of scanning (SCAN 2b) 扫描: *a* ˈ*body scan,* ie done by a scanner 全身扫描 ○ *a* ˈ*brain scan* 脑扫描.

scan·ner *n* machine for scanning (SCAN 2b), esp one used by doctors, which uses a computer to give a picture of the inside of the body from a series of X-rays or other techniques 扫描器(尤指医疗用的).

scan·sion /ˈskænʃn; ˋskænʃən/ *n* [U] scanning of verse; way in which verse scans 韵律分析; 韵律法.

scan·dal /ˈskændl; ˋskændḷ/ *n* **1** (**a**) [C, U] (act, behaviour, etc that causes) public feelings of outrage or indignation 民愤; 公愤; 引起公愤的举动: *cause (a) scandal* 激起民愤 ○ *A series of corruption scandals led to the fall of the government.* 一系列贪污腐化事件激起民愤导致政府垮台. ○ *Her theft from the shop caused (a) scandal in the village.* 她因偷商店的东西引起全村的义愤. (**b**) [sing] action, attitude, etc that is disgraceful or shameful 丑行; 丑事; 丑闻: *It is a scandal that the defendant was declared innocent.* 宣判被告无罪, 这真是可耻的事. ○ *The council's failure to act is a scandal.* 市议会未能采取行动是一件丑闻. **2** [U] talk about the bad things people are thought to have done; gossip 流言蜚语; 闲话: *spread scandal* 散布流言蜚语 ○ *Most of us enjoy a bit of scandal.* 我们大多愿意知道一点别人的坏事. ○ *Have you heard the latest scandal?* 你听到最近这段闲话了吗?

▷ **scan·dal·ize, -ise** /ˈskændəlaɪz; ˋskændḷ,aɪz/ *v* [Tn] shock (sb) by sth immoral or outrageous 使(某人)愤慨或震惊: *scandalize the neighbours by sunbathing naked on the lawn* 在草坪上作裸体日光浴教邻居触目惊心.

scan·dal·ous /ˈskændələs; ˋskændḷəs/ *adj* **1** disgraceful; shocking 丢脸的; 令人震惊的: *scandalous behaviour, talk, books* 令人愤慨的举止、谈话、书. **2** [attrib 作定语] (of reports or rumours) containing scandal(1a) (指报道或谣传)含有引起公愤内容的. **scan·dal·ously** *adv.*

□ ˈ**scandalmonger** /-mʌŋgə(r); -,mʌŋgɚ/ *n* (*derog* 贬) person who spreads scandal(2) 传闲话的人. ˈ**scandalmongering** /-mʌŋgərɪŋ; -,mʌŋgərɪŋ/ *n* [U].

Scan·din·avian /ˌskændɪˈneɪvɪən; ,skændəˋnevɪən/ *n, adj* (native) of Scandinavia (ie Denmark, Norway, Sweden, Iceland) 斯堪的纳维亚的(人)(即丹麦、挪威、瑞典、冰岛的).

scan·sion ⇨ SCAN.

scant /skænt; skænt/ *adj* [attrib 作定语] (*fml* 文) hardly enough; not very much (used esp with the *ns* shown) 不足的, 缺少的(尤与下列示例中的名词连用): *pay scant attention to sb's advice* 不甚重视某人的劝告 ○ *with scant regard for my feelings* 不大理会我的感情.

▷ **scanty** *adj* (**-ier, -iest**) small in size or amount; hardly large enough (大小或数量)不足的, 勉强够大的: *a scanty supply of soap* 肥皂供应不足 ○ *a scanty bikini* 勉强穿得下的比基尼泳装. **scant·ily** *adv*: *scantily dressed* 穿得单薄. **scanti·ness** *n* [U].

-scape *suff* 后缀 (with *ns* forming *ns* 与名词结合构成名词) (picture of a) view of 景色(的画): *landscape* ○ *seascape.*

scape·goat /ˈskeɪpgəʊt; ˋskep,got/ *n* (also *esp US* **fall guy**) person who is blamed or punished for the wrongdoing of sb else 替罪羊: *I was made the scapegoat, but it was the others who started the fire.* 是别人放的火, 让我背了黑锅.

scap·ula /ˈskæpjʊlə; ˋskæpjələ/ *n* (*anatomy* 解) shoulder-blade 肩胛骨. ⇨illus at SKELETON 见SKELETON插图.

scar /skɑː(r); skɑr/ *n* **1** mark left on the skin by a wound, sore, etc 伤痕; 疤: *Will the cut leave a scar?* 这伤口能留下疤痕吗? ○ (*fig* 比喻) *scars on the cupboard from burning cigarettes* 香烟在柜橱上烧的痕迹. **2** feelings of great sadness, guilt, etc after an unpleasant experience (精神上的)创伤: *Her years in prison left a scar.* 她在狱中的岁月留下了精神创伤.

▷ **scar** *v* (**-rr-**) **1** [Tn] leave a scar or scars on (sb) 给(某人)留下伤痕: *a face scarred by smallpox* 出过天花的脸 ○ (*fig* 比喻) *scarred by the death of his daughter* 他因女儿死亡精神受创. **2** [I, Ip] **~ (over)** heal by forming a scar; form a scar or scars 痊愈(留下疤痕); 结疤: *Will the cut scar?* 伤口能结疤吗? ○ *The wound gradually scarred over.* 伤口逐渐痊愈结了疤.

scarab /ˈskærəb; ˋskærəb/ *n* **1** type of beetle regarded as sacred in ancient Egypt 圣甲虫(古埃及人奉为神圣的甲虫). **2** carving of a scarab, worn as an ornament or a charm 甲虫形雕饰(作饰物或护符佩带).

scarce /skeəs; skɛrs/ *adj* **1** not easily obtained and much less than is needed 难获得而不足的: *scarce resources, supplies, etc* 资源、供应等不足 ○ *It was wartime and food was scarce.* 那时是战争时期, 食物短缺. Cf 参看 PLENTIFUL. **2** [pred 作表语] not often found; rare 稀有; 罕见: *This book is now scarce.* 这书现在很难得. ⇨ Usage at RARE[1] 用法见RARE[1]. **3** (idm 习语) **make oneself** ˈ**scarce** (*infml* 口) go away; avoid others 走开; 溜走; 不露面: *He's in a bad mood, so I'll make myself scarce.* 他情绪不好, 我得躲着点.

▷ **scar·city** /ˈskeəsətɪ; ˋskɛrsətɪ/ *n* [C, U] (instance of) shortage 不足; 缺乏: *frequent scarcities of raw materials* 原料经常供不应求 ○ *The scarcity of food forced prices up.* 食物短缺促使价格上涨.

scarcely /ˈskeəslɪ; ˋskɛrslɪ/ *adv* **1** only just; hardly 仅仅; 几乎不: *There were scarcely a hundred people present.* 出席的不足一百人. ○ *I scarcely know him.* 我不大认识他. ○ *Scarcely had she entered the room when the phone rang.*

她一进屋电话就响了. **2** surely not 决不: *You can scarcely expect me to believe that.* 别以为我能相信那件事. ⇨Usage at ALMOST 用法见 ALMOST.

scare /skeə(r); skɛr/ *v* **1** (**a**) (also *infml* 口语作 **scarify**) [Tn] frighten (sb) 恐吓(某人): *That noise scared me.* 那响声把我吓坏了. (**b**) [I] (used esp with an *adv* 尤与副词连用) become frightened 受惊吓; 感到害怕: *He scares easily.* 他动不动就害怕. **2** (idm 习语) **frighten/scare the daylights out of sb** ⇨ DAYLIGHTS. **frighten/scare sb to death/out of his wits** ⇨ FRIGHTEN. **scare sb ˈstiff** (*infml* 口) make sb very nervous; alarm sb 使某人精神紧张; 惊吓某人: *The thought of my exams next week scares me stiff.* 我一想到下星期要考试就很紧张. ○ *He's scared stiff of women.* 他一见女的就发慌. **3** (phr v) **scare sb away/off** make sb leave, stay away, etc by frightening or alarming him 将某人吓跑: *light a fire to scare off the wolves* 点起火来把狼吓跑 ○ *He scares people away by being so brash.* 他狂妄自大把别人都吓跑了. **scare sb into/out of sth/doing sth** make sb do/not do sth by frightening him 吓得某人做[不敢做]某事: *They scared him into handing over the keys.* 他们把他吓得交出了钥匙. ○ *We'll scare her out of telling the police.* 我们要把她吓得不敢报警.

▷ **scare** *n* sudden fright; alarm caused by a rumour, etc 惊恐; 恐慌: *You did give me a scare, creeping up on me like that!* 你那样悄悄地过来, 真把我吓了一大跳! ○ *The explosion at the chemical factory caused a major pollution scare.* 化工厂发生爆炸引起了害怕污染的巨大恐慌. ○ [attrib 作定语] *a scare story*, eg a newspaper report that spreads panic 引起恐慌的报道.

scared *adj* **~ (of sb/sth)**; **(of doing sth/to do sth)** frightened 惊恐的; 恐惧的: *I'm scared (of ghosts).* 我害怕(鬼). ○ *scared of being attacked, to go out alone* 害怕受到攻击、独自外出 ○ *a very scared man* 吓怕了的人.

scary /ˈskeərɪ; ˈskɛrɪ/ *adj* (**-ier, -iest**) (*infml* 口) causing fear or alarm 引起恐慌的: *a scary ghost story* 吓人的鬼故事.

□ **ˈscarecrow** *n* figure resembling a person that is dressed in old clothes and set up in a field to frighten away birds 稻草人.

ˈscaremonger /-mʌŋgə(r); -ˌmʌŋgɚ/ *n* (*derog* 贬) person who frightens people by spreading alarming news, rumours, etc 散布引起恐慌的消息、谣言等的人.

scarf /skɑːf; skɑrf/ *n* (*pl* **scarfs** /skɑːfs; skɑrfs/ or **scarves** /skɑːvz; skɑrvz/) piece of material worn for ornament or warmth round the neck or (by women) over the shoulders or hair 围巾; 头巾; 披肩.

scar·ify[1] /ˈskærɪfaɪ; ˈskærəˌfaɪ/ *v* (*pt, pp* **-fied**) [Tn] **1** loosen the surface of (soil, etc) by using a tool or machine with prongs 翻松(土地等). **2** (*medical* 医) (in surgery) make small cuts in (skin, etc); cut off skin from (a part of the body) (外科)在(皮肤等)上做小切口或划痕, 割去(身体部位)的皮肤.

scar·ify[2] /ˈskeərɪfaɪ; ˈskɛrəˌfaɪ/ *v* (*pt, pp* **-fied**) [Tn] (*infml* 口) = SCARE 1a.

scar·let /ˈskɑːlət; ˈskɑrlət/ *adj, n* [U] bright red 猩红的; 鲜红的: *dressed all in scarlet* 穿着一身鲜红的衣服 ○ *She blushed scarlet when I swore.* 她听到我骂街, 羞得脸通红.

□ ˌ**scarlet ˈfever** infectious disease causing scarlet marks on the skin 猩红热.

ˌ**scarlet ˈrunner** bean plant with scarlet flowers 红花菜豆.

ˌ**scarlet ˈwoman** (*dated derog or joc* 旧, 贬或谑) immoral woman; prostitute 荡妇; 妓女.

scarp /skɑːp; skɑrp/ *n* steep slope; escarpment 陡坡; 悬崖.

scarper /ˈskɑːpə(r); ˈskɑrpɚ/ *v* [I] (*Brit sl* 俚) run away; leave 逃跑; 溜走: *Scarper! The cops are coming!* 快跑! 警察来了!

scary ⇨ SCARE.

scat /skæt; skæt/ *v* (**-tt-**) [I] (usu imperative 通常用于祈使句) (*infml* 口) go away; leave 走开: *I don't want you here, so scat!* 我这里用不着你, 走开!

scath·ing /ˈskeɪðɪŋ; ˈskeðɪŋ/ *adj* **1** (of criticism, ridicule, etc) severe; harsh (指批评、嘲笑等)严厉的, 刻薄的: *a scathing remark, rebuke, etc* 严厉的言语、指责等 ○ *a scathing review of a new book* 对一本新书的尖锐评论. **2** [pred 作表语] **~ (about sb/sth)** very critical (of sb/sth); scornful (对某人[某事物])非常挑剔, 嘲笑: *The report was scathing about the lack of safety precautions.* 该报道对缺乏安全预防措施一事严加指责.

scato·logy /skæˈtɒlədʒɪ; skæˈtɑlədʒɪ/ *n* [U] (*derog* 贬) excessive interest in excrement or obscenity 过分对粪便或淫秽言行感兴趣. ▷ **scato·lo·gical** /ˌskætəˈlɒdʒɪkl; ˌskætəˈlɑdʒɪkəl/ *adj*: *scatological conversation, humour* 有淫秽言语的谈话、幽默.

scat·ter /ˈskætə(r); ˈskætɚ/ *v* **1** [I, Tn] (cause people or animals to) move, usu quickly, in different directions (使人或动物)散开: *The crowd scattered.* 人群散开了. ○ *The police scattered the crowd.* 警察驱散了人群. **2** (**a**) [Tn, Tn·pr, Tn·p] throw (sth) in different directions; put here and there 撒(某物); 散布: *scatter seed (over the ground)* 播种 ○ *scatter grit on the road* 把沙砾撒在路面上 ○ *We scattered plates of food around the room before the party.* 我们在聚会前把一盘盘食物摆放在屋中各处. ○ (*fig* 比喻) *Don't scatter your money around.* 别到处挥霍. (**b**) [Tn·pr] **~ sth with sth** cover (a surface, etc) with sth by throwing it in different directions 将某物撒在(某物表面)上: *scatter the lawn with grass seed* 把草籽撒在草坪上.

▷ **scat·ter** (also **scat·ter·ing** /ˈskætərɪŋ; ˈskætərɪŋ/ *n* [sing] amount or number of things scattered; sprinkling 散布之物的数量; 少量: *a scatter of hailstones* 稀疏的冰雹.

scat·tered *adj* lying far apart; not close together 分散的; 稀疏的: *a few scattered settlements* 几处分散的居民点 ○ *a thinly scattered population* 散布得很稀疏的居民 ○ *sunshine with scattered showers* 晴朗, 间有零星阵雨.

□ **ˈscatter-brain** *n* (*infml* 口) person who cannot concentrate on one thing for very long, is forgetful, etc 精神不集中的人; 健忘的人. **ˈscatter-brained** *adj*.

NOTE ON USAGE 用法: When we **scatter** something we throw it in different directions. ☆ **scatter** 指将某物向四面八方扔去. We can also scatter an area (the ground, a field, etc) with something 这个词也可指将某物撒在一处(地上、田里等): *scatter seeds on the fields/scatter the fields with seeds* 在田里播种[把种子撒在田地里]. **Scatter over/about** suggests that the throwing is done carelessly and causes a mess ☆ **scatter over/about** 指随便扔, 弄得乱七八糟: *Who's scattered my papers all over the floor?* 谁把我的文件扔得满地都是? ○ *We came home to find our belongings scattered about the room.* 我们回到家里看到东西扔得满屋都是. **Strew** is most commonly used in the past participle form **strewn**. ☆ **strew** 多见于其过去分词形式 **strewn**. ☆ It can suggest both intentional and careless throwing 这一动作既可为有意识的, 也可为随随便便的: *The streets were strewn with flowers for the royal visit.* 街道布满了花朵以迎接王室成员莅临. ○ *There was litter strewn all over the pavement.* 人行道上到处都是扔的垃圾. **Sprinkle** is used with water, sand, salt, etc and indicates intentional scattering, usually over a small area ☆ **sprinkle** 用以指洒水、撒沙子、撒盐等, 且指有意识地散布在通常为一小块范围内: *Sprinkle a little salt on the rice.* 在米饭上撒点盐. ○ *The priest sprinkled holy water on the baby's forehead.* 神父把圣水洒在婴儿的额头上. ○ *The grass was sprinkled with dew.* 草上沾满了露珠.

scatty /ˈskætɪ; ˈskætɪ/ *adj* (**-ier, -iest**) (*Brit infml* 口) **1** mad; crazy 发疯的; 疯狂的: *The noise would drive anyone scatty.* 那噪音简直能把人逼疯. **2** scatter-brained; absent-minded 精神不集中的; 心不在焉的: *Your scatty son has forgotten his key again.* 你那儿子丢三落四又把钥匙给忘了. ▷ **scat·tily** *adv*. **scat·ti·ness** *n* [U].

scav·enge /ˈskævɪndʒ; ˈskævɪndʒ/ *v* **1** [I, Ipr] **~ (for sth)** (of an animal or a bird) search for decaying flesh as food; use decaying flesh for food (指兽或鸟)觅食腐肉, 以腐肉为食: *a crow scavenging for carrion* 寻找腐肉吃的乌鸦. **2** [I, Ipr, Tn] **~ (for) sth** (of a person) search through waste for items that one can use (指人)在垃圾堆里寻找有用之物: *tramps scavenging through dustbins* 在垃圾堆里找东西的流浪汉 ○ *a tramp scavenging in dustbins for food* 在垃圾箱里寻找食物的流浪汉 ○ *You can often scavenge nice bits of old furniture from skips.* 从废物堆里往往能捡到一些挺好的旧家具.

S

▷ **scav·en·ger** *n* animal, bird or person that scavenges 食腐肉的兽或鸟; 捡破烂的人.

SCE /ˌes siː ˈiː; ˌɛs si ˈi/ *abbr* 缩写 = Scottish Certificate of Education 苏格兰教育证书.

scen·ario /sɪˈnɑːrɪəʊ; *US* -ˈnær-; sɪˈnærɪˌo/ *n* (*pl* **~s**) **1** written outline of a film, play, etc with details of the scenes and plot (电影、戏剧等的)脚本、剧情概要等. **2** imagined sequence of future events 想像中的未来事情的顺序: *a possible scenario for war* 战争中可能出现的情况.

▷ **scen·ar·ist** /sɪˈnɑːrɪst; *US* -ˈnær-; sɪˈnærɪst/ *n* writer of scenarios 电影、戏剧等的脚本的作者.

scene /siːn; sin/ *n* **1** place of an actual or imagined event (实际或想像中的)事发地点: *the scene of the accident, crime, etc* 事故、犯罪等的现场 ○ *The scene of the novel is set in Scotland.* 小说中的事是在苏格兰发生的. **2** situation or incident in real life (现实生活中的)情景, 事件: *the horrific scenes after the earthquake* 地震后的惨状 ○ *There were hilarious scenes when the pig ran into the shop.* 猪闯进商店以后, 滑稽情景令人啼笑皆非. **3** (incident where there is an) outburst of emotion or anger 吵闹; 发脾气: *make a scene* 大吵大闹 ○ *There was quite a scene when she refused to pay.* 她拒不付款引起了一场争吵. ○ *We had a big scene when I fired him.* 我解雇他时, 我们大吵起来. **4** (**a**) sequence of continuous action in a play, film, etc (戏剧或电影中的)片段, 场面: *The scene in the hospital was very moving.* 在医院的那一场面十分感人. (**b**) (*abbr* 缩写 **sc**) part of an act in a play or opera; episode within such a part (戏剧或歌剧的)场, (一场中的)一段情节: *Act 1, Scene 2 of 'Macbeth'* 《麦克佩斯》第一幕第二场 ○ *the duel scene in 'Hamlet'* 《哈姆雷特》中决斗的一场. **5** place represented on the stage of a theatre; the painted background, woodwork, etc representing such a place; scenery (舞台上的)场景, 布景: *The first scene of the play is the king's palace.* 剧中的第一个场景是王宫. ○ *The scenes are changed during the interval.* 剧间休息时更换布景. **6** view as seen by a spectator 景色; 景象; 景致: *a delightful rural scene* 赏心悦目的乡村景色 ○ *The boats in the harbour make a beautiful scene.* 港湾中的船只构成了美丽的景象. ○ *They went abroad for a change of scene*, ie to see and experience new surroundings. 他们出国换换环境. **7** **the scene** [sing] (modified by a *n* 受名词修饰) (*infml* 口) the current situation in a particular area of activity or way of life 某一活动范围或生活方式的现状: *the 'drug scene* 吸毒问题的现状 ○ *the 'gay scene* 同性恋活动的情况 ○ *a newcomer on the 'fashion scene* 时装界的新人 ○ *the entertainment scene in the West End of London* 伦敦西区的娱乐场所. **8** (idm 习语) **behind the 'scenes** (**a**) out of sight of the audience; behind the stage 在后台; 在幕后. (**b**) in secret; without being known to the public 秘密的; 暗中: *political deals done behind the scenes* 秘密的政治交易. **come on the 'scene** arrive 到场: *By the time I came on the scene, it was all over.* 我来到时, 一切都结束了. **not one's scene** (*infml* 口) not sth one knows about, is interested in, etc 非某人所熟悉的事物; 非某人兴趣之所在: *I'm not going to the disco: it's just not my scene.* 我不想去跳迪斯科舞, 我完全不感兴趣. **on the 'scene** present 在场: *Reporters were soon on the scene after the accident.* 那事故发生后不久记者就都赶到了现场. **set the 'scene (for sth)** (**a**) describe a place or a situation in which sth is about to happen 作事前的现场或情况描述: *Radio reporters were in the church to set the scene.* 电台记者在教堂里作事前的现场介绍. (**b**) prepare for sth; help to cause sth 为某事物作准备; 促使: *His arrival set the scene for another argument.* 他一来就要另有一场争论了. **steal the scene/show** ⇨ STEAL.

□ **'scene-shifter** *n* person who changes the scenery in a theatre (剧场中)更换布景的人.

scenery /ˈsiːnərɪ; ˈsinərɪ/ *n* [U] **1** general natural features of an area, eg mountains, valleys, rivers, forests 景色; 风景; 风光: *mountain scenery* 山景 ○ *stop to admire the scenery* 停下来欣赏风景. **2** furniture, woodwork, canvas, etc used on a theatre stage to represent the place of action 舞台布景. ⇨illus at App 1 见附录1插图, page ix.

scenic /ˈsiːnɪk; ˈsinɪk/ *adj* [usu attrib 通常作定语] **1** having or showing beautiful natural scenery 风景优美的: *the scenic splendours of the Rocky Mountains* 落基山脉的壮丽景色 ○ *a scenic route across the Alps* 穿越阿尔卑斯山的风景优美的路径 ○ *a scenic railway* 游览小铁路. **2** of stage scenery 舞台布景的. ▷ **scen·ic·ally** /-klɪ; -klɪ/ *adv*.

scent /sent; sɛnt/ *n* **1** (**a**) [U] characteristic smell of sth, esp a pleasant one (某物特有的)气味; (尤指)香味: *the scent of new-mown hay* 新刈青草的气味 ○ *Modern roses have no scent.* 现在的玫瑰不香. (**b**) [C] particular type of smell 某种气味: *scents of lavender and rosemary* 薰衣草和迷迭香的气味. **2** [U] (*esp Brit*) sweet-smelling (usu liquid) substance obtained from flowers, plants, etc; perfume 香精(通常为液体); 香水: *a bottle of scent* 一瓶香精 ○ *put some scent on before going out* 先搽点香水再出门 ○ [attrib 作定语] *a 'scent bottle* 香水瓶. **3** (**a**) [C usu *sing* 通常作单数] smell left behind by an animal, that allows dogs, etc to track it (动物的)臭迹, 遗臭: *follow, lose, recover the scent* 追踪、失去、重新发现臭迹 ○ *a strong/hot scent*, ie one that is easy for dogs to follow 强烈的[新留下的]臭迹 ○ *a poor/cold scent*, ie one that is difficult for dogs to follow 微弱的[时间久的]臭迹 ○ *a false* (ie misleading) *scent* 并非所追踪的臭迹. (**b**) [U] sense of smell, esp in dogs 嗅觉(尤指狗的): *hunt by scent* 藉嗅觉追猎. **4** [sing] **~ of sth** feeling of the presence of sth 察觉出某事物: *a scent of danger, fear, trouble* 察觉出有危险、恐惧感、麻烦事. **5** (idm 习语) **on the scent (of sb/sth)** likely to find sb/sth soon 循某人[某事物]的线索: *The police are now on the scent of the culprit.* 警方已获得罪犯的线索. **put/throw sb off the 'scent** mislead sb, esp by giving him false information 使某人失去线索(尤指为其提供错误信息): *The false alibi threw the police off the scent.* 那个不在犯罪现场的伪证使警方失去了线索.

▷ **scent** *v* **1** [Tn] (**a**) discover (sth) by the sense of smell 嗅出(某物)的存在; 闻到(某物): *The dog scented a rat.* 那狗嗅出有老鼠的气味. (**b**) (*fig* 比喻) begin to suspect the presence or existence of (sth) 怀疑有(某事物); 觉察出: *scent a crime* 察觉出有犯罪的事 ○ *scent treachery, trouble, etc* 怀疑有背叛行为、麻烦事等. **2** [esp passive 尤用于被动语态: Tn, Tn·pr] **~ sth (with sth)** give sth a certain scent 使某物有香味: *scented notepaper, soap* 有香味的信纸、肥皂 ○ *a handkerchief scented with lavender* 用薰衣草薰香的手帕 ○ *roses that scent the air* 香味四溢的玫瑰.

scepter (*US*) = SCEPTRE.

scep·tic (*US* **skep·tic**) /ˈskeptɪk; ˈskɛptɪk/ *n* **1** person who doubts that a claim, statement, etc is true 持怀疑态度的人: *The government must still convince the sceptics that its policy will work.* 政府仍须使持怀疑态度的人相信其政策可行. **2** person who does not think religious teachings are true 怀疑宗教教义的人.

▷ **scep·tical** (*US* **skep-**) /-kl; -kl̩/ *adj* **~ (of/about sth)** unwilling to believe sth; often doubting that claims, statements, etc are true (对某事物)不肯相信的, 常怀疑的: *I'm rather sceptical about their professed sympathy for the poor.* 他们声称同情穷人, 我对此有些怀疑. **scep·tic·ally** (*US* **skep-**) /-klɪ; -klɪ/ *adv*. **scep·ti·cism** (*US* **skep-**) /ˈskeptɪsɪzəm; ˈskɛptəˌsɪzəm/ *n* [U] sceptical attitude 怀疑态度; 怀疑主义: *her healthy scepticism towards authority* 她对权威所持的善意的怀疑态度 ○ *reports treated with scepticism* 受到怀疑的报道.

sceptre (*US* **scepter**) /ˈseptə(r); ˈsɛptɚ/ *n* staff or rod carried by a ruler as a sign of royal power, eg at a coronation ceremony 王节, 权杖(象征王权的标志, 如用于加冕仪式中).

sch *abbr* 缩写 = school.

sched·ule /ˈʃedjuːl; *US* ˈskedʒʊl; ˈskɛdʒʊl/ *n* **1** [C, U] (**a**) programme of work to be done or of planned events 进度表; 预定计划表: *a factory production schedule* 工厂生产进度表 ○ *have a full schedule*, ie have many things to do 预定计划表排得很满 ○ *a project that is ahead of/on/behind schedule* 提前[按期/未按期]完成的计划 ○ *Everything is going according to schedule.* 一切都在按预定计划进行. (**b**) = TIMETABLE (TIME[1]): *The fog disrupted airline schedules.* 这场大雾扰乱了航空公司的时刻表. **2** list of items, etc 清单; 明细表; 一览表: *a spare parts schedule* 零件一览表 ○ *The attached schedule gives details of the shipment.* 装运货物的细目见所附清单.

▷ **sched·ule** *v* [esp passive 尤用于被动语态: Tn,

Tn·pr, Cn·t] ~ **sth (for sth)** include sth in a schedule; arrange sth for a certain time 将某事列入进度表; 为某事安排时间: *One of the scheduled events is a talk on flower arranging.* 安排的活动中有一项是插花艺术讲座. ○ *The sale is scheduled for tomorrow.* 大减价定于明日举行. ○ *She is scheduled to give a speech tonight.* 她定于今晚演讲. ○ *a scheduled flight, service, etc*, ie one that an airline, etc organizes and carries out regularly 定期航班、服务等.

schema /ˈskiːmə; ˋskimə/ *n* (*pl* **-mata** /-mətə; -mətə/) (*fml* 文) diagram or representation of sth 图表; 图解; 纲要; 概要.

schem·atic /skiːˈmætɪk; skiˋmætɪk/ *adj* in the form of a diagram or chart 图表的; 图解的: *a schematic representation of the structure of the organization* 该组织结构的示意图. ▷ **schem·at·ic·ally** /-klɪ; -klɪ/ *adv*.

scheme /skiːm; skim/ *n* **1** ~ **(for sth/to do sth)** (**a**) plan for doing or organizing sth 计划; 方案: *a scheme for manufacturing paper from straw* 用麦秆造纸的计划 ○ *an imaginative scheme to raise money* 富创意的筹款方案 ○ *a pension scheme* 养老金方案. (**b**) secret or devious plan 阴谋; 诡计: *a scheme for not paying tax* 逃税的诡计. **2** ordered system; arrangement 组合; 配合: *a ˈcolour scheme*, eg for a room, so that the colours in its decor match 色彩的调配. **3** (idm 习语) **the ˈscheme of things** the way things are or are planned 事物的规律; 安排: *In the scheme of things it is hard for small businesses to succeed.* 一般来说, 小本生意较难做.

▷ **scheme** *v* **1** [I, Ipr, It] ~ **(for sth/against sb)** make (esp secret or devious) plans 策划; 图谋: *rebels scheming for the overthrow of the leadership* 图谋推翻领导的叛乱者 ○ *They are scheming to get her elected as leader.* 他们正策划让她当选领导. **2** [Tn] plan (sth) in a devious way 策划(某事): *Her enemies are scheming her downfall.* 她的对头正在策划把她搞垮. **schemer** *n* person who schemes in a devious way 策划阴谋诡计的人. **schem·ing** *adj* often making devious schemes 常搞阴谋诡计的: *scheming rivals* 诡计多端的竞争对手.

scherzo /ˈskeətsəʊ; ˋskɛrtso/ *n* (*pl* ~**s**) lively vigorous piece of music; such a passage in a larger work 诙谐曲.

schism /ˈsɪzəm; ˋsɪzəm/ *n* [U, C] strong disagreement, esp in a religious organization over doctrine, in which one group stops recognizing the authority of the other 分歧; (尤指)教会分裂.

▷ **schis·matic** /sɪzˈmætɪk; sɪzˋmætɪk/ *adj* of or causing schism 分歧的, 造成分裂的(尤指教会). — *n* person who takes part in a schism 搞分裂的人; 分裂教会的人.

schist /ʃɪst; ʃɪst/ *n* [U] (*geology* 地质) any of various types of rock which split easily into thin plates 页岩; 片岩.

schizo /ˈskɪtsəʊ; ˋskɪtso/ *n* (*pl* ~**s**) (*infml often derog* 口, 常作贬义) = SCHIZOPHRENIC *n*.

schiz·oid /ˈskɪtsɔɪd; ˋskɪtsɔɪd/ *adj* resembling or suffering from schizophrenia 类精神分裂症的; 精神分裂样的.

▷ **schiz·oid** *n* schizoid person 有分裂性人格的人.

schizo·phre·nia /ˌskɪtsəʊˈfriːnɪə; ˌskɪtzəˋfrinɪə/ *n* [U] (*medical* 医) mental illness that causes the sufferer to act irrationally, have delusions, withdraw from social relationships, etc 精神分裂症.

▷ **schizo·phrenic** /ˌskɪtsəʊˈfrenɪk; ˌskɪtzəˋfrɛnɪk/ *adj* **1** of or suffering from schizophrenia 精神分裂症的; 患精神分裂症的. **2** (*infml* 口) behaving in an odd way, esp when circumstances keep changing 行为古怪的(尤指于环境不断变化时): *Living half the time in Oxford and half in Paris makes me feel quite schizophrenic.* 我有一半时间住在牛津, 一半时间住在巴黎, 弄得我晕头转向. — *n* (also *infml often derog* **schizo** 口语作 **schizo**, 常作贬义) person suffering from schizophrenia or behaving in a schizophrenic way 精神分裂症患者; 行为古怪的人. **schizo·phrenic·ally** /-klɪ; -klɪ/ *adv*.

schmaltz (also **schmalz**) /ʃmɔːlts; ʃmɔlts/ *n* [U] (*infml* 口) excessive sentimentality, esp in literature or music 过分感伤(尤指文学或音乐作品). ▷ **schmaltzy** (also **schmalzy**) *adj* (**-ier, -iest**).

schnapps /ʃnæps; ʃnæps/ *n* [U] strong alcoholic drink distilled from grain (谷物酿制的)烈酒.

schnit·zel /ˈʃnɪtsl; ˋʃnɪtsl/ *n* [C, U] (*US*) veal cutlet covered with breadcrumbs and fried in butter 炸小牛肉片(裹面包屑于黄油中炸成).

scholar /ˈskɒlə(r); ˋskɑlɚ/ *n* **1** student who has been awarded money after a competitive exam, etc, to be used to finance his education 获奖学金的学生: *a British Council scholar* 获英国文化协会奖学金的学生. **2** person who studies an academic subject deeply 学者: *a Greek, classical, history scholar* 研究希腊问题的、研究古典著作的、研究历史的学者.

▷ **schol·arly** *adj* **1** showing the learning, care and attention typical of a scholar 有学者风度的; 博学的; 好学的: *be more scholarly in one's approach to a problem* 在处理问题上更有学者风度 ○ *a scholarly young woman* 好学的女青年. **2** involving or connected with academic study 学术性的: *a scholarly journal* 学术刊物 ○ *scholarly pursuits* 学术研究.

schol·ar·ship /ˈskɒləʃɪp; ˋskɑlɚˌʃɪp/ *n* **1** [C] (award of a) grant of money to a scholar(1) 奖学金; 获得奖学金的资格: *win a scholarship to the university* 获得该大学的奖学金. **2** [U] great learning; care and attention in carrying out scholarly work 学问; 学识; 学术成就: *a teacher of great scholarship* 很有学问的教师 ○ *The book shows meticulous scholarship.* 这本书的写作态度很慎重.

schol·astic /skəˈlæstɪk; skəˋlæstɪk/ *adj* **1** [usu attrib 通常作定语] (*fml* 文) of schools and education 学校的; 教育的; 学业的: *my scholastic achievements*, eg examination passes, prizes 我的学习成绩. **2** of scholasticism 经院哲学的; 烦琐哲学的. ▷ **schol·as·ti·cism** /skəˈlæstɪsɪzəm; skəˋlæstəˌsɪzəm/ *n* [U] system of philosophy taught in the universities in the Middle Ages, based in theological dogma (中世纪的)经院哲学, 烦琐哲学.

school[1] /skuːl; skul/ *n* **1** [C] (**a**) institution for educating children 学校: *ˈprimary and ˈsecondary schools* 小学和中学 ○ *ˈSunday schools* 主日学校 ○ *attend a good school* 上一所好学校 ○ *the use of computers in schools* 学校中计算机的使用 ○ [attrib 作定语] *a school bus, building, report* 校车、校舍、学生成绩报告单. (**b**) institution for teaching a particular subject 专科学校: *ˈart school* 艺术学校 ○ *secreˈtarial school* 秘书专科学校. **2** [C] (*US*) college or university 学院; 大学: *famous schools like Yale and Harvard* 像耶鲁、哈佛这样的著名大学. **3** [U] (used without *the* 不与冠词 the 连用) (**a**) process of being educated in a school[1](1a) 上学: *I hate school!* 我讨厌上学! ○ *two more years of school* 再上两年学 ○ *old enough for/to go to school* 到了上学年龄 ○ *the school-ˈleaving age*, ie the age until which children must attend school 中学毕业的年龄 ○ *Are you still at school?* 你还在上学吗? ○ *He left school when he was sixteen.* 他十六岁时中学毕业了. (**b**) time when teaching is done in a school; lessons 上课时间; 上课: *meet friends before school* 上课前会见朋友 ○ *School begins at 9 am.* 上午9点钟上课. ○ *There will be no school* (ie no lessons) *tomorrow.* 明天不上课. ○ *Will you come for a walk after school?* 放学后你愿意来散散步吗? ⇨Usage 见所附用法. **4 the school** [sing] all the pupils or all the pupils and teachers in a school 全校学生; 全校师生: *The head teacher told the school at assembly.* 校长在全校学生大会上讲话. ○ *Soon, the whole school knew about her win.* 不久, 全校师生都知道她获胜了. **5** [C] department of a university concerned with a particular branch of study 大学的院、系: *the ˈlaw, ˈmedical, ˈhistory school* 法学院、医学院、历史系 ○ *the School of ˈDentistry* 牙医学系. **6** [C] course, usu for adults, on a particular subject 专门学科课程(通常指为成人设的): *a ˈsummer school for music lovers* 音乐爱好者暑期班. **7** [C usu *sing* 通常作单数] (*infml* 口) experience or activity that provides discipline or instruction 锻炼; 磨炼: *the hard school of adversity* 逆境的磨炼. **8** [C] group of writers, thinkers, etc sharing the same principles or methods, or of artists having a similar style 学派; 流派: *the Dutch, Venetian, etc school of painting* 荷兰、威尼斯等绘画流派 ○ *the Hegelian school*, ie of philosophers influenced by Hegel 黑格尔学派. **9** [C] group of card-players, gamblers, etc 一伙玩纸牌的人、赌徒等: *a ˈpoker school* 一伙打扑克的人. **10** (idm 习语) **one of the old school** ⇨ OLD. **a school of ˈthought** group of people with similar views 有类似观点的一批人; 学派: *I don't belong to the school of thought that favours radical change.* 我不属于激进派. **teach school** ⇨ TEACH.

S

▷ **school** *v* [Tn, Tn·pr, Cn·t] **~ sb/sth (in sth)** train, discipline or control sb/oneself/an animal 训练、磨练或控制某人[自己/动物]: *school a horse* 训练马 ○ *school oneself in patience/to be patient* 培养自己的忍耐力 ○ *a child who is well-schooled in good manners* 有教养懂礼貌的孩子. **school·ing** *n* [U] education 教育: *He had very little schooling.* 他没受过什么教育. ○ *Who's paying for her schooling?* 谁在供她读书?

□ ˈ**school age** age between starting and finishing school 学龄: *a child of school age* 学龄儿童.

ˈ**schoolboy** *n* boy at school (中小学的)男生: [attrib 作定语] *a schoolboy joke, prank, etc* (中小学)男生的玩笑、恶作剧等.

ˈ**school-days** *n* [pl] time when sb is at school 学生时代.

ˈ**schoolfellow** (also ˈ**schoolmate**) *n* member of the same school, either now or in the past 同学; 校友.

ˈ**schoolgirl** *n* girl at school (中小学的)女生.

ˈ**schoolhouse** *n* building of a school, esp a small one in a village 校舍(尤指乡村的小校舍).

ˌ**school-ˈleaver** *n* person who has recently left school 中学毕业生.

ˈ**schoolman** /-mən; -mən/ *n* (*pl* **-men**) teacher in a university in the Middle Ages, esp one teaching scholastic philosophy (中世纪大学里的)教师(尤指教经院哲学的).

ˈ**school-marm** /ˈskuːlmɑːm; ˋskulˌmɑrm/ *n* (*infml* 口) **1** (*esp US*) schoolmistress (中小学的)女教师. **2** (*derog or joc* 贬或谑) woman who is domineering, prim or easily shocked 专横、古板或大惊小怪的女子.

ˈ**schoolmaster** *n* (*fem* 阴性作 ˈ**schoolmistress**) teacher in a school (in Britain, esp one in a private school) (中小学)教师(在英国, 尤指私立学校教师).

ˈ**schoolmate** *n* = SCHOOLFELLOW.

ˈ**schoolteacher** *n* teacher in a school (中小学)教师.

NOTE ON USAGE 用法: When a **school, hospital,** etc is being referred to as an institution, we do not use the definite article after a preposition 当**school**、**hospital**等词指机构时, 在介词后不加定冠词: *She went to school/university/college in York.* 她在约克上学. ○ *He's coming out of hospital on Friday.* 他星期五要出院了. ○ *She's been sent to prison for a year.* 她入狱已经一年了. When we are talking about the place as a building, the definite article is used 这类词若用以指建筑物所在地, 前面就要加定冠词: *We went to the school to discuss our daughter's progress.* 我们去学校谈谈女儿的进步情况. ○ *I saw her coming out of the hospital/the church.* 我看见她从医院[教堂]出来.

school² /skuːl; skul/ *n* large number of fish, whales, etc swimming together; shoal (鱼、鲸等的)群.

schooner /ˈskuːnə(r); ˋskunɚ/ *n* **1** type of sailing-ship with two or more masts and sails set lengthways rather than from side to side 斯库纳纵帆船(两桅或多桅的纵帆船). **2** (**a**) (*Brit*) tall glass for sherry (盛雪利酒的)大玻璃杯. (**b**) (*US*) tall glass for beer (盛啤酒的)大玻璃杯.

schwa /ʃwɑː; ʃwɑ/ *n* (*phonetics* 语音) **1** sound occurring in unstressed syllables and diphthongs in English, eg the 'a' in 'about' 非重读央元音, 混元音(英语里出现在非重读音节和复合元音中的中性元音, 如 about 中的 a). **2** phonetic symbol for this, /ə; ə/ 国际音标中的 /ə/.

sci·atic /saɪˈætɪk; saɪˋætɪk/ *adj* [usu attrib 通常作定语] (*anatomy* 解) of the hip or of the **sciatic nerve**, which goes from the pelvis to the thigh 臀部的; 坐骨神经的.

▷ **sci·at·ica** /saɪˈætɪkə; saɪˋætɪkə/ *n* [U] pain in or near the sciatic nerve 坐骨神经痛.

sci·ence /ˈsaɪəns; ˋsaɪəns/ *n* **1** (**a**) [U] organized knowledge, esp when obtained by observation and testing of facts, about the physical world, natural laws and society; study leading to such knowledge 科学; 科学研究: *an interest in science* 对科学的爱好 ○ *a man of science* 科学家 ○ *Science is an exact discipline.* 研究科学可以锻炼人思维严谨. (**b**) [C, U] branch of such knowledge 某一门科学; 学科: *the natural sciences*, eg biology and geology 自然科学(如生物学和地质学) ○ *the physical sciences*, eg physics, chemistry 自然科学(如物理学、化学) ○ *the study of social science* 对社会科学的研究. (**c**) [U] these sciences taken as a whole 自然科学(统称); 理科: *I prefer science to the humanities.* 我喜爱自然科学, 不喜欢人文科学. ○ *more funding for science in the universities*, ie for the work of those studying it 为大学的理科多提供些经费 ○ [attrib 作定语] *a science teacher, textbook, subject* 理科教师、教科书、科目. Cf 参看 ART¹ 3. **2** (**a**) [U] skill of an expert 专门技术或技巧: *In this game, you need more science than strength.* 在这项比赛中, 技巧比力气更重要. (**b**) [sing] activity needing this 需运用技巧的活动: *Getting these children to do what you want is a science, I can tell you!* 我敢说, 要做到让这些孩子百依百顺那可是一门艺术! **3** (idm 习语) **blind sb with science** ⇨BLIND².

▷ **sci·ent·ist** /ˈsaɪəntɪst; ˋsaɪəntɪst/ *n* expert in or student of one or more of the natural or physical sciences 自然科学家; 研究自然科学的人.

□ ˌ**science ˈfiction** (also *infml* 口语作 **sci-fi**) fiction often based on future or recent scientific discoveries, and dealing with imaginary worlds, space travel, or life on other planets 科学幻想小说.

sci·ent·if·ic /ˌsaɪənˈtɪfɪk; ˌsaɪənˋtɪfɪk/ *adj* **1** (**a**) [attrib 作定语] of, used in or involved in science 科学的; 用于科学研究的; 关于科学的: *a scientific discovery, instrument, textbook, researcher* 科学发现、科学仪器、理科教科书、科学研究人员. (**b**) using methods based on those of science 采用科学方法的: *scientific farming* 科学种田 ○ *They are very scientific in their approach.* 他们的方法很科学. **2** having, using or needing skill or expert knowledge 具有、采用或需要技术或专门知识的: *a scientific player, game* 有专门技术的选手、需要技巧的游戏. ▷ **sci·en·tif·ic·ally** /-klɪ; -klɪ/ *adv*.

sci-fi /ˈsaɪfaɪ; ˋsaɪˋfaɪ/ *n* [U] (*infml* 口) = SCIENCE FICTION (SCIENCE).

scim·itar /ˈsɪmɪtə(r); ˋsɪmətɚ/ *n* short curved sword with one sharp edge, formerly used by Arabs, Persians, Turks, etc 短弯刀(旧时阿拉伯人、波斯人、土耳其人等用的). ⇨illus at SWORD 见 SWORD 插图.

scin·tilla /sɪnˈtɪlə; sɪnˋtɪlə/ *n* (idm 习语) **not a scintilla of sth** (*fml* 文) not the slightest amount of sth 一点儿也没有: *not a scintilla of truth in the claim* 这种说法中没有丝毫的真实性 ○ *not a scintilla of evidence to prove it* 没有一点儿证据可以证实此事.

scin·til·late /ˈsɪntɪleɪt; *US* -təleɪt; ˋsɪntḷˌet/ *v* **1** [I] give off sparks; sparkle 发出火花; 闪烁: *diamonds scintillating in the candlelight* 在烛光下闪烁的钻石. **2** [I, Ipr] (*fig* 比喻) be brilliant, witty, etc 焕发才智: *scintillate with wit* 才智敏锐.

▷ **scin·til·lat·ing** *adj* brilliant and witty 焕发才智的: *scintillating repartee* 机敏的应答 ○ *You were scintillating on TV last night.* 您昨晚在电视上妙语如珠.

scin·til·la·tion /ˌsɪntɪˈleɪʃn; *US* -tlˈeɪʃn; ˌsɪntḷˋeʃən/ *n* [U].

scion /ˈsaɪən; ˋsaɪən/ *n* **1** (*fml* 文) young member of a family, esp a noble one 子孙, 后裔(尤指贵族的). **2** shoot of a plant, esp one cut for grafting or planting 幼枝; 幼芽; (尤指)接穗.

scissors 剪刀

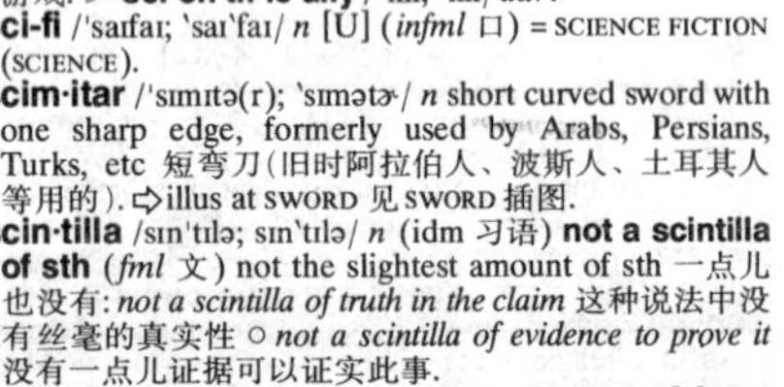

scis·sors /ˈsɪzəz; ˋsɪzɚz/ *n* **1** [pl] cutting instrument with two blades, pivoted in the middle, which cut as they come together 剪刀; 剪子: *a pair of scissors* 一把剪刀 ○ *Scissors won't cut through wire.* 剪刀剪不断铁丝. **2** (idm 习语) **scissors and ˈpaste** (of articles, books, etc) compiled from parts of others (指文章、书籍等)从其他文章或书上剪辑拼凑而成的: [attrib 作定语] *the programme's a real scissors-and-paste job.* 这个节目真可谓是东拼西凑的.

scler·osis /skləˈrəʊsɪs; sklɪˋrosɪs/ *n* [U] (*medical* 医) condition in which there is abnormal hardening of soft tissue, eg the walls of the arteries 硬化(症)(如动脉硬化).

SCM /ˌes siː ˈem; ˌɛs si ˋɛm/ *abbr* 缩写 = (*Brit*) State Certified Midwife 国家注册助产士: *be an SCM* 是国家注册助产士 ○ *Janet Cox SCM* 珍妮特·考克斯国家注册助产士.

scoff[1] /skɒf; *US* skɔːf; skɔf/ *v* I, Ipr] **~ (at sb/sth)** speak contemptuously (about or to sb/sth); jeer or mock 嘲弄; 嘲笑: *Don't scoff: he's quite right.* 别讥笑, 他没错. ○ *scoff at other people's beliefs* 嘲笑别人的信仰.

▷ **scoff** *n* (usu *pl* 通常作复数) scoffing remark; taunt 嘲弄的话; 嘲笑: *She ignored the scoffs of her workmates.* 她对同事的嘲弄不屑一顾. **scoffer** *n* person who scoffs 嘲弄者; 嘲笑者.

scoff·ingly *adv*.

scoff[2] /skɒf; *US* skɔːf; skɔf/ *v* [Tn] (*sl* 俚) eat (sth) greedily 贪婪地吃(某物): *Who scoffed all the biscuits?* 是谁把饼干全都吃光了?

▷ **scoff** *n* (*sl* 俚) **1** [sing] act of scoffing 狼吞虎咽: *have a good scoff* 大吃一顿. **2** [U] food 食物; 食品: *Where's all the scoff gone?* 食物都到哪儿去了?

scold /skəʊld; skold/ *v* [I, Tn, Tn·pr] **~ sb (for sth/doing sth)** express anger, criticism, etc, esp to a child; rebuke sb 骂, 责骂(尤指对儿童); 叱责某人: *If I walk in with muddy boots, Dad always scolds (me).* 我的靴子上要是有泥, 一进屋爸爸就骂(我). ○ *Did you scold her for breaking it?* 她把那件东西打破了, 你骂她了吗?

▷ **scold** *n* (*dated* 旧) person who scolds 爱骂人的人.

scold·ing *n*: *give sb/get a scolding for being late* 因迟到叱责某人[受到叱责].

scol·lop = SCALLOP.

scone /skɒn; *US* skəʊn; skon/ *n* soft flat cake of wheat flour or barley meal baked quickly 司康饼, 烤饼(用小麦面或大麦面快速烘烤的).

scoop 铲

scoop /skuːp; skup/ *n* **1** (**a**) deep shovel-like tool used for picking up and moving grain, flour, sugar, coal, etc (铲谷物、面粉、糖、煤等的)铲状工具, 铲子, 勺. (**b**) similar small tool with a round bowl, used eg for serving ice-cream 圆形小勺(如用以舀冰激凌的). **2** (**a**) (*infml* 口) movement made with, or as if with, a scoop 铲; 舀: *After three scoops the jar was nearly empty.* 舀了三勺后, 罐子就快空了. (**b**) (also **scoop·ful**) amount picked up by a scoop 一铲或一勺的量: *two scoops of mashed potato* 两勺土豆泥. **3** (**a**) piece of news made public by a newspaper, radio station, etc before its rivals 抢先报道的新闻. (**b**) (*commerce* 商) large profit made by acting before one's competitors do 抢先赚得的巨额利润.

▷ **scoop** *v* **1** [Tn, Tn·p] **~ sth (out)** make (a hole, etc) with, or as if with, a scoop 用铲、勺等挖(洞等): *scoop a hole in the sand* 用铲子在沙子上挖洞. **2** [Tn] (**a**) act before (a rival, etc) to get a scoop(3a) 抢在(对手等)之前报道新闻: *She scooped all the national newspapers to get the story.* 她抢在全国各报之前发表了这一消息. (**b**) get (news, a profit, etc) as a scoop(3b) 抢先获得(新闻、利润等): *He scooped £1 000 in the lottery.* 他在抽彩中捷足先登赢得1 000英镑. **3** (phr v) **scoop sth out/up** lift sth with, or as if with, a scoop 铲起; 舀出: *He scooped the coins up in his hands.* 他用手把硬币捧了起来.

scoot /skuːt; skut/ *v* [I, Ipr, Ip] (esp in commands and in the infinitive 尤用于命令句和不定式) (*infml joc* 口, 谑) run away quickly 赶快跑开: *Get out of here! Scoot!* 躲开这儿! 快走开! ○ *You'll have to scoot or you'll be late.* 你快跑吧, 不然就要迟到了. ○ *She scooted (off) down the road after them.* 她沿路飞奔追赶他们.

scooter /ˈskuːtə(r); ˈskutɚ/ *n* **1** (also ˈ**motor-scooter**) light motor cycle, usu with small wheels, a low seat and a metal shield protecting the driver's legs 小型摩托车. ⇨ illus at MOTOR 见MOTOR插图. **2** toy vehicle with two wheels, which a child moves forward by pushing against the ground with one foot 踏板车(儿童游戏用具, 有双轮, 一脚蹬地一脚踏板行进).

scope /skəʊp; skop/ *n* **1** [U] **~ (for sth/to do sth)** opportunity to do or achieve sth (做某事物的)机会, 余地: *a job with (a lot of) scope for self-fulfilment* 有机会(充分)发挥自己的能力的工作 ○ *a house with some scope for improvement* 尚可改进的房子. **2** [sing] range of matters being dealt with, studied, etc (处理、研究事物的)范围: *Does feminist writing come within the scope of your book?* 你这本书是否涉及到女权主义内容? ○ *This subject is outside the scope of our inquiry.* 这个问题不在我们探讨的范围之内.

-scope *comb form* 构词成分 (forming *ns* 用以构成名词) instrument for looking through or observing with 观察用的仪器: *microscope* ○ *oscilloscope* ○ *telescope*.

▷ **-scopic(al)** *comb form* 构词成分 (forming *adjs* 用以构成形容词): *microscopic(al)* ○ *telescopic*.

-scopy *comb form* 构词成分 (forming *ns* 用以构成名词) **1** observing 观察: *spectroscopy*. **2** use of an instrument like a microscope, telescope, etc 使用显微镜、望远镜等仪器: *microscopy*.

scorch /skɔːtʃ; skɔrtʃ/ *v* **1** (**a**) [Tn] burn or discolour (a surface) by dry heat 将(物体表面)烫焦、烫煳或烫得变色: *I scorched my shirt when I was ironing it.* 我把衬衫烫煳了. (**b**) [I] (of a surface) be burned or discoloured in this way (指物体表面)烧焦、烫煳或烫得变色: *The meat will scorch if you don't lower the gas.* 你不把煤气调小一点肉就煳了. **2** [Tn] cause (a plant) to dry up and wither 使(植物)枯萎: *The lawn looked scorched after days of sunshine.* 草坪晒了几天以后好像有些枯萎了. **3** (phr v) **scorch off, away, down, etc** (*sl* 俚) go in the direction specified at a very high speed 疾驶: *motorcyclists scorching down the road* 沿路疾驶的摩托车手.

▷ **scorch** (also ˈ**scorch-mark**) *n* mark made on a surface (esp cloth) by scorching 焦痕(尤指布上的).

scorcher *n* (*Brit infml* 口) **1** very hot day 炎热的天: *Whew! It's a real scorcher today!* 哟! 今天可太热了! **2** remarkable thing, esp a fast ball at cricket, tennis, etc 绝妙的事物; (尤指板球、网球等的)快球: *The bowler let go a couple of scorchers.* 投球手投出了几个快球.

scorch·ing *adj* very hot 极热的: *a scorching day* 炎热的天 ○ *It's scorching outside.* 外面骄阳似火. — *adv* extremely 极其: *scorching hot* 极热.

□ **scorched** ˈ**earth policy** policy of destroying anything that may be useful to an advancing enemy 焦土政策.

score[1] /skɔː(r); skɔr/ *n* **1** [C] (**a**) number of points, goals, etc made by a player or team in a game, or gained in a competition, etc (比赛中一方得的)分数: *a high/low score* 高[低]分 ○ *make a good score of 50 points* 获得50分的好成绩 ○ *What's my score?* 我得了多少分? ○ [attrib 作定语] *a score-keeper, score-sheet* 记分员、记分单. ⇨App 4 见附录4. (**b**) number of points made by both players or teams in such a game, etc (比赛中双方得的)分数, 比分: *keep the score*, ie keep a record of the score as it is made 记分数 ○ *The final score was 4-3.* 最后的比分是4比3. (**c**) number of marks gained in a test, examination, etc (考试、测验得的)分数: *a score of 120 in the IQ test* 智商测验中获得的120分. **2** [C] cut, scratch or scrape on a surface 刻痕; 划痕: *deep scores on the rock*, eg made by a glacier 岩石上深深的凹痕(如冰川留下的) ○ *scores made by a knife on the bark of a tree* 用刀在树皮上划的痕迹. **3** [sing] (*dated infml* 旧, 口) amount of money owed, eg in a restaurant 欠帐, 欠款(如于餐馆中): *pay the score at the hotel* 付旅店费. **4** (**a**) [C] (*pl* unchanged 复数不变) set or group of twenty 二十: *a score of people* 二十人 ○ *three score and ten*, ie 70 七十. (**b**) **scores** [pl] very many 很多: *'How many people were there?' 'There were scores (of them).'* '那里有多少人?''有很多(人).' **5** [C] (**a**) written or printed version of a piece of music showing what each instrument is to play or what each voice is to sing 总谱; 乐谱: *the piano score of the opera*, ie with the orchestra's music arranged for a piano 歌剧中的钢琴乐谱. (**b**) music for a film, play, etc (电影、戏剧等的)配乐: *a* stirring film score by William Walton 由威廉·沃尔顿创作的感人的电影配乐. **6** (idm 习语) **know the score** ⇨ KNOW. **on more scores than 'one** for many good reasons 由于许多原因; 为了许多理由: *I want revenge against her on more scores than one.* 我有种种理由要向她报复. **on 'that score** with regard to that; as far as that is concerned 关于那一点; 为了这一点: *You need have no worries on that score.* 你不必担心那件事. **pay/settle an old score** ⇨ OLD.

□ **'score-board** *n* board on which a score (eg at cricket) is shown 记分牌(如板球的).

'score-card *n* card on which a score is recorded 记分卡.

score[2] /skɔ:(r); skɔr/ *v* **1** (**a**) [I, Tn] gain (points, goals, etc) in a game or competition, etc (比赛中)得(分): *The home team has yet to score.* 主队还没有得分. ○ *Hughes scored two goals before half-time.* 休斯在上半场进了两个球. ○ *He scored a century*, ie 100 runs in cricket. 他得了一百分(板球赛中). (**b**) [I, Tn] gain (marks, etc) in a test or an examination (在测验或考试中)得(分): *score well/high at bridge* 桥牌比赛得分很高 ○ *She scored 120 in the IQ test.* 她在智商测验中得了120分. (**c**) [I] keep a record of the points, etc gained in a game or competition, etc (在比赛中)记分: *Who's going to score?* 谁来记分? (**d**) [Dn·n] give a certain number of marks, points, etc to (a competitor) 给(参赛者)分数: *The Russian judge scored our skaters 5.8.* 那个俄国裁判给我们的滑冰运动员5.8分. **2** [I, Ipr, Tn, Tn·pr] **~ (sth) (against sb)** achieve (a success, etc); succeed 获得(成功等); 获胜: *He has really scored with his latest book; it's selling very well.* 他的新书很成功, 十分畅销. ○ *She scored against him by quoting his earlier statement.* 她引用他以前的话把他驳倒了. ○ *score an instant success* 迅速获胜 ○ *The programme scored a real hit with the public.* 那节目备受群众欢迎. **3** [I, Ipr] **~ (with sb)** (*sl* 俚) have sex with a new partner 与新伙伴发生性关系: *Do you think you'll score at the party?* 你能不能在聚会上与新伙伴发生性关系? **4** [Tn] make a cut, scratch or scrape on (a surface) 在(某物)上刻痕, 划痕: *rocks scored by a glacier* 有冰川划痕的岩石 ○ *They scored the floor-boards by pushing furniture about.* 他们推动家具, 在地板上留下了划痕. ○ *score the trees that are due to be felled* 在待砍伐的树上刻痕做记号. **5** [Tn] (*US*) criticize (sb); scold 批评(某人); 骂; 叱责: *Critics scored him for his foolishness.* 评论家批评他愚蠢. **6** [I] (*sl* 俚) succeed in obtaining illegal drugs 弄到毒品: *You need a lot of money to score every day.* 每天弄到毒品可得花很多钱. **7** [esp passive 尤用于被动语态: Tn, Tn·pr] **~ sth (for sth)** arrange (music) for one or more musical instruments; write sth as a musical score[1](5) (为乐器演奏)改编(乐曲); 编写总谱或配乐曲: *scored for violin, viola and cello* 为小提琴、中提琴、大提琴的演奏改编乐曲. **8** (idm 习语) **score a point/points (against/off/over sb)** = SCORE OFF SB. **9** (phr v) **score off sb** make sb appear foolish, eg by making a witty remark 使某人出丑: *She knows how to score off people who ask difficult questions.* 她很会让那些给她出难题的人自讨没趣. **score sth out/through** draw a line or lines through sth 划线删去(文字等): *Her name had been scored out on the blackboard.* 她的名字已从黑板上划掉.

▷ **scorer** *n* **1** person who keeps a record of points, goals, etc scored in a game (比赛中的)记分员. **2** player who scores goals, runs, etc 得分的运动员: *a prolific goal-scorer* (球类运动)命中率高的得分者.

scorn /skɔ:n; skɔrn/ *n* **1** [U] **~ (for sth)** strong contempt 鄙视; 轻蔑: *be filled with scorn* 十分鄙视 ○ *dismiss a suggestion with scorn* 对一建议不屑一顾 ○ *He had nothing but scorn for my ideas.* 对于我的想法他嗤之以鼻. **2** [sing] **the ~ of sb** (*fml* 文) person or thing that is treated with scorn by sb 受某人鄙视的人或事物: *She was the scorn of her classmates.* 她常受同学们的鄙视. **3** (idm 习语) **laugh sb/sth to scorn** ⇨ LAUGH. **pour scorn on sb/sth** ⇨ POUR.

▷ **scorn** *v* **1** [Tn] feel or show scorn for (sb/sth) 鄙视(某人[某事物]): *As a professional painter, she scorns the efforts of amateurs.* 她是专业画家, 看不起业余画家的创作. **2** (**a**) [Tn] refuse (sth) proudly 傲慢地拒绝(某事物): *scorn sb's invitation, advice, offer* 轻蔑地回绝某人的邀请、劝告、好意. (**b**) [Tt, Tg] (*fml* 文) reject (sth one is too proud to do) 不屑做(某事): *scorn to ask for help* 不屑于求助 ○ *He scorns telling lies.* 他鄙夷说谎的行为.

scorn·ful /-fl; -fəl/ *adj* showing or feeling scorn 鄙视的; 轻蔑的: *a scornful remark, smile, look, gesture, etc* 鄙夷的言语、微笑、神情、姿势等 ○ *scornful of the greed of others* 看不起别人那么贪心. **scorn·fully** /-fəlɪ; -fəlɪ/ *adv*.

Scor·pio /'skɔ:pɪəʊ; 'skɔrpɪ,o/ *n* **1** [U] the eighth sign of the zodiac, the Scorpion 天蝎宫(黄道第八宫). **2** [C] (*pl* **~s**) person born under the influence of this sign 属天蝎宫星座的人. ⇨illus at ZODIAC 见 ZODIAC 插图.

▷ **Scor·pian** *n, adj.* ⇨Usage at ZODIAC 用法见 ZODIAC.

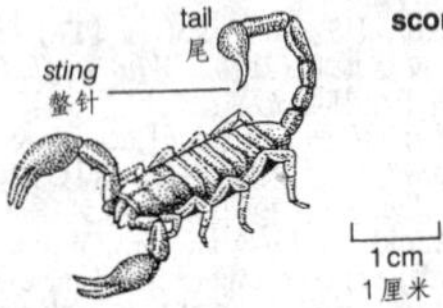

scor·pion /'skɔ:pɪən; 'skɔrpɪən/ *n* small creature of the spider group with lobster-like claws and a poisonous sting in its long jointed tail 蝎子.

Scot /skɒt; skɑt/ *n* native of Scotland 苏格兰人: *(The) Scots are an adventurous and inventive people.* 苏格兰人既富于冒险精神又富于创造精神.

Scotch /skɒtʃ; skɑtʃ/ *adj* **1** (also **Scots**) of Scottish people 苏格兰人的. **2** (also **Scottish**, except in certain fixed combinations 除用于固定词组外, 亦作 **Scottish**) of Scotland 苏格兰的. ⇨Usage at SCOTTISH 用法见 SCOTTISH.

▷ **Scotch** *n* (**a**) [U] Scotch whisky 苏格兰威士忌. (**b**) [C] type of this 苏格兰威士忌类的酒: *only the best Scotches* 上好的苏格兰威士忌. (**c**) [C] glass of this 一杯苏格兰威士忌: *Have a Scotch!* 喝一杯苏格兰威士忌!

□ **Scotch 'broth** soup or stew containing pearl barley and vegetables 苏格兰浓汤.

Scotch 'cap man's wide beret, esp as worn with Highland costume 苏格兰男子戴的无边帽.

Scotch 'egg boiled egg enclosed in sausage meat 苏格兰式鸡蛋(外裹香肠肉先煮后炸的).

Scotch 'tape (*US propr* 专利名) transparent adhesive tape made of cellulose or plastic 透明胶带. Cf 参看 SELLOTAPE.

Scotch 'terrier small terrier with rough hair and short legs 苏格兰㹴狗. ⇨illus at App 1 见附录1插图, page iii.

Scotch 'whisky type of whisky distilled in Scotland 苏格兰威士忌.

scotch /skɒtʃ; skɑtʃ/ *v* [Tn] (**a**) stop (esp a rumour, etc) being believed 遏止, 阻止(尤指谣言等): *His arrival in the capital scotched reports that he was dead.* 他抵达首都一事止住了说他已死的传言. (**b**) stop (a plan, etc) being accepted or carried out 阻止(计划等).

scot-free /ˌskɒt 'fri:; ˌskɑt 'fri/ *adv* without punishment or harm 免受惩罚; 免受伤害: *The accused got off/escaped scot-free because of lack of evidence.* 由于证据不足, 被告未受惩罚.

Scot·land Yard /ˌskɒtlənd 'jɑ:d; 'skɑtlənd'jɑrd/ headquarters of the London police, now officially called *New Scotland Yard*; its Criminal Investigation Department 伦敦警察厅(现称New Scotland Yard新伦敦警察厅); 伦敦警察厅侦缉处: *They called in Scotland Yard*, ie asked for the help of this Department. 他们向伦敦警察厅侦缉处报了案. ○ *Scotland Yard is/are investigating the crime.* 伦敦警察厅正在对该罪案进行调查.

Scots /skɒts; skɑts/ *adj* of Scotland, its people or its dialect of English 苏格兰的; 苏格兰人的; 苏格兰英语的: *Scots law* 苏格兰的法律. ⇨Usage at SCOTTISH 用法见 SCOTTISH.

▷ **Scots** *n* dialect of English traditionally spoken in Scotland 苏格兰英语.

□ **'Scotsman** /-mən; -mən/, **'Scotswoman** /-wʊmən; -wʊmən/ *ns* native of Scotland 苏格兰人.

Scot·tish /ˈskɒtɪʃ; ˈskɑtɪʃ/ *adj* of Scotland, its people or its dialect of English 苏格兰的; 苏格兰人的; 苏格兰英语的.

NOTE ON USAGE 用法: Compare **Scottish, Scots** and **Scotch.** 试比较**Scottish**、**Scots**、**Scotch**这三个词. The adjective **Scottish** is used of the people and things of Scotland, **Scots** only of its people, its law and language. ☆ **Scottish**这一形容词用以指苏格兰的人和事物, 而**Scots**则仅指苏格兰的人、法律和语言. **Scotch** is mainly used of certain products such as whisky and broth. ☆ **Scotch**主要用于某些产品, 如苏格兰的威士忌和汤. It is sometimes used for **Scottish** or **Scots**, but this is generally regarded as offensive or old-fashioned by Scottish people themselves. ☆ **Scotch**这个词有时用以代替**Scottish**或**Scots**, 但苏格兰人本身普遍认为这是侮辱性的或是旧式用法. The noun **Scots** refers to the Scottish dialect of the English language and **Scotch** is whisky. ☆ **Scots**作名词时, 指英语中的苏格兰方言或称苏格兰英语; **Scotch**则专指苏格兰威士忌. A native of Scotland is a **Scot** (or **Scotsman/woman**). 苏格兰本土的人称作**Scot**(或**Scotsman/woman**).

scoun·drel /ˈskaʊndrəl; ˈskaʊndrəl/ *n* person who has no moral principles and no conscience; villain 无赖; 恶棍.

scour[1] /ˈskaʊə(r); skaʊr/ *v* **1** [Tn, Tn·p] **~ sth (out)** make the dirty surface of sth clean or bright by rubbing it with sth rough 将某物刷净或擦亮: *scour the pots and pans* 把壶和锅刷干净 ○ *scour out a saucepan*, ie with a scourer 擦亮长柄锅 ○ *scour the pipe (out)* 把烟斗掏干净. **2** [Tn, Tn·pr, Tn·p] **~ sth (out)** (of a river, etc) clear out or make (a channel, etc) by flowing at high speed (指河流等)冲刷成(水道等): *The torrent scoured a gully down the hillside.* 那急流顺山坡而下冲出一条水沟. **3** (phr v) **scour sth away/off** remove (dirt) by rubbing with sth rough 擦掉, 刷去(污垢): *scour the grease off (the floor)* 刷掉(地板上的)油渍.

▷ **scour** *n* [sing] act of scouring 刷; 擦; 冲刷: *give the pan a good scour* 把锅好好刷刷.

scourer /ˈskaʊərə(r); ˈskaʊrɚ/ *n* (**a**) [C] pad of stiff nylon or wire used for scouring saucepans, etc 刷锅等用的尼龙丝或金属丝. (**b**) [U] powder for this 去污粉.

scour[2] /ˈskaʊə(r); skaʊr/ *v* **1** [Tn, Tn·pr] **~ sth (for sb/sth)** go over (an area) thoroughly searching for sb/sth 走遍(某地)以搜寻某人[某物]: *Police scoured the woods (looking) for the body.* 警方到树林各处(寻)找那具尸体. **2** (phr v) **scour about, through, etc (sth)** move around quickly in search of sb/sth 搜寻某人[某物]: *hounds scouring about in the copse (after the fox)* 在矮树林中追寻着(狐狸)的猎犬 ○ *We scoured through the fields, looking for stray sheep.* 我们在田地里搜寻走失的绵羊.

scourge /skɜːdʒ; skɝdʒ/ *n* **1** whip for flogging people (用以打人的)鞭子. **2** (*fig* 比喻) person or thing that causes suffering 造成灾难的人或事物: *The new boss was the scourge of the inefficient.* 新老板来了以后, 不称职的人就遭殃了. ○ *the scourge of war* 战争的苦难.

▷ **scourge** *v* [Tn] **1** flog (sb) with a scourge 鞭打(某人). **2** (*fml* 文) cause (sb) to suffer 使(某人)受痛苦: *scourged by guilt* 受内疚的煎熬.

scout /ˈskaʊt; skaʊt/ *n* **1** person, ship or aircraft sent out to get information about the enemy's position, strength, etc 侦察员; 侦察舰; 侦察机. **2 Scout** (also formerly 旧时作 **Boy ˈScout**) member of the **Scout Association**, an organization which aims to teach boys self-reliance, discipline and public service through outdoor activities 童子军: [attrib 作定语] *a scout troop, hut* 童子军的部队、营房. Cf 参看 GIRL GUIDE (GIRL). **3** person whose job is to find talented performers (eg footballers, stage artists, etc) and offer them work 物色(运动员、演员等)人材的工作人员: *a ˈtalent scout* 物色演员或运动员的人. **4** servant at an Oxford college 牛津大学的校工.

▷ **scout** *v* [Ipr, Ip] **~ around/about (for sb/sth)** **1** look in various places to find sb/sth 到处寻找某人[某事物]: *We'd better start scouting about for a new secretary.* 我们最好着手物色一个新秘书. ○ *I've been scouting around town for a better house.* 我跑遍了全城想找个好一点的房子. **2** act as a scout(1) 侦察: *scouting around (looking) for enemy troops* 到各处侦察寻找敌军.

□ **ˈscoutmaster** *n* person who leads a troop of Scouts 童子军队长.

scowl /skaʊl; skaʊl/ *n* bad-tempered or angry look on the face 怒容.

▷ **scowl** *v* [I, Ipr] **~ (at sb/sth)** look (at sb/sth) with a scowl 怒视(某人[某物]): *The receptionist scowled at me.* 接待员横眉怒目地看着我. ⇨Usage at SMIRK 用法见SMIRK.

Scrabble[1] /ˈskræbl; ˈskræbl̩/ *n* [U] (*propr* 专利名) game in which words are built up on a board marked with squares, using letters printed on blocks of wood, etc 一种拼字游戏: *be good at Scrabble* 擅长拼字游戏 ○ [attrib 作定语] *a Scrabble board, player, tournament* 拼字游戏板、参加者、比赛.

scrabble[2] /ˈskræbl; ˈskræbl̩/ *v* (phr v) **~ about (for sth)** grope about with the fingers, trying to get hold of sth 用手指摸索着抓某物: *scrabble about under the table for the dropped sweets* 在桌子底下摸索着找掉在地上的糖块.

▷ **scrabble** *n* [sing] act of scrabbling 用手指摸索着抓: *a noisy scrabble for coins on the floor* 摸索着抓地板上的硬币而发出的响声.

scrag /skræg; skræg/ *n* **1** (also ˌ**scrag-ˈend**) [C, U] bony part of a sheep's neck, used for making soups and stews 羊颈肉(用以煮汤和炖食): *buy a ˌscrag-end of ˈmutton* 买羊颈肉 ○ *a bit of scrag* 一小块羊颈肉. **2** [C] skinny person or animal 皮包骨的人或动物.

▷ **scrag** *v* (**-gg-**) [Tn] **1** strangle or hang (sb) 勒或吊(某人). **2** (*infml* 口) treat (sb) roughly 粗暴对待(某人): *Alan's always getting scragged at school.* 艾伦在学校里总受欺负.

scraggly *adj* (**-ier, -iest**) (*infml* 口 *esp US*) rough, untidy or irregular 散乱的; 不整齐的; 不规则的: *scraggly weeds* 蓬乱的杂草.

scraggy *adj* (**-ier, -iest**) (*derog* 贬) thin and bony 瘦的; 皮包骨的: *a scraggy neck* 瘦脖子. **scrag·gi·ness** *n* [U].

scram /skræm; skræm/ *v* (**-mm-**) [I] (esp in commands and in the infinitive 尤用于命令句和不定式) (*sl* 俚) go away quickly 快走开: *Scram! I don't want you here!* 走开! 别呆在这儿! ○ *Tell those boys to scram.* 叫那些男孩子快走开.

scramble /ˈskræmbl; ˈskræmbl̩/ *v* **1** [Ipr, Ip] climb or crawl quickly, usu over rough ground or with difficulty; clamber 攀登; 爬: *scramble up the embankment* 爬上堤岸 ○ *The girl scrambled over the wall.* 那个女孩儿翻过了墙. ○ *The children scrambled out of the hollow tree.* 孩子都从树洞里爬出来了. **2** [I, Ipr, It] **~ (for sth)** struggle or compete with others, esp to get sth or a share of sth 争夺, 竞争(尤指为得到某事物): *players scrambling for possession of the ball* 争着抢球的运动员 ○ *The children scrambled for the coins.* 孩子们争夺硬币. ○ *They were all scrambling to get the bargains.* 他们都争先恐后抢购廉价货. **3** [Tn, Tn·p] **~ sth (up)** mix (things) together in an untidy way; jumble sth up 将(东西)乱混在一起; 搅乱某事物: *Who has scrambled up my sewing things?* 谁把我的针线活儿弄乱了? **4** [Tn] mix the whites and yolks of (eggs) together while cooking them in a saucepan with milk and butter (用牛奶和黄油)炒(蛋). **5** [Tn] change the way (a telephone conversation, etc) sounds by altering the wave frequency, so that only sb with a special receiver can understand it 扰频或倒频使(电话通话等)只可由有特殊接收器的人收听. **6** [I, Tn] (cause a military aircraft to) take off suddenly, eg to repel an enemy raid (使军用飞机)紧急起飞.

▷ **scramble** *n* **1** [sing] climb or walk done with difficulty or over rough ground 攀登; 爬行: *a scramble over the rocks at the seashore* 攀登海边的岩石. **2** [sing] **~ (for sth)** rough struggle (to get sth) 争夺; 抢夺: *There was a scramble for the best seats.* 大家都在抢最好的座位. **3** [C] motor-cycle race over rough ground 摩托车越野赛.

scrambler /ˈskræmblə(r); ˈskræmblɚ/ *n* device for scrambling telephone conversations, etc 扰频器; 倒频器.

scrap[1] /skræp; skræp/ *n* **1** (**a**) C] small, usu unwanted, piece; fragment 碎片; 碎屑; 小块: *scraps of paper, cloth, wood, etc* 纸片、布头、木屑 ○ (*fig* 比喻) *Only a few scraps of news about the disaster have emerged.* 那场灾祸的情况只获知一些零星的消息. (**b**) **scraps** [pl] items of left-over food 剩下的食物: *Give the scraps to the dog.* 把剩下的东西喂狗吧. **2** [U] waste or unwanted articles, esp those still of some value for the material they contain 废弃材料(尤指其中仍有些价值的): *sell an old car for scrap*, ie so that any good parts can be used again 把旧汽车当废弃材料卖掉 ○ *A man comes round regularly collecting scrap.* 有个男子按时来收破烂. ○ [attrib 作定语] *scrap iron* 废铁 ○ *a scrap (metal) merchant* 收破烂(金属)的人 ○ *a scrap car* 报废的汽车. **3** [sing] (usu with a negative 通常与否定词连用) small amount of sth 少量; 一点儿: *There's not a scrap of truth in the claim.* 这种说法毫无真实性. ○ *'Does he have evidence to support this?' 'Not a scrap!'* '他有证据证明此事吗?''完全没有!'

▷ **scrap** *v* (**-pp-**) [Tn] throw away (sth useless or worn-out) 抛弃, 抛掉(无用的或用坏的东西): *scrap a car, ship, bicycle, etc* 遗弃报废的汽车、船、自行车等 ○ (*fig* 比喻) *Lack of cash forced us to scrap plans for a new house.* 我们现款不足, 只好打消买新房子的念头.

scrappy *adj* (**-ier, -iest**) **1** made up of bits and pieces; not well organized; not complete 零碎拼凑起来的; 杂乱的; 不完全的: *a scrappy book consisting of articles published elsewhere* 把别处发表过的文章拼凑一起而成的书 ○ *It was a scrappy, rambling speech.* 那篇讲话杂乱无章, 毫无条理. **2** (*US infml* 口) liking quarrels; aggressive 爱吵架的; 好争斗的. **scrap·pily** /-ılı; -ılı/ *adv*. **scrap·pi·ness** *n* [U].

□ ˈ**scrap-book** *n* book with blank pages in which newspaper cuttings, etc are pasted 剪贴簿; 剪报资料簿.

ˈ**scrap-heap** *n* **1** heap of scrap 废料堆; 废物堆. **2** (idm 习语) **on the** ˈ**scrap-heap** no longer wanted 不再需要的: *Unemployed people often feel they are on the scrap-heap.* 失业的人常有遭遗弃的感觉.

ˈ**scrap paper** (*US* also ˈ**scratch paper**) loose bits of paper, often partly used, for writing notes on 零散的便条纸(常指部分已用过的).

ˈ**scrap-yard** *n* place where scrap[1] (2) is collected 废弃材料存放处.

scrap[2] /skræp; skræp/ *n* ~ **(with sb)** (*infml* 口) fight; quarrel 打架; 吵架: *get into a scrap* 吵起嘴来 ○ *He had a scrap with his sister.* 他和妹妹吵了一架.

▷ **scrap** *v* (**-pp-**) [I, Ipr] ~ **(with sb)** fight; quarrel 打架; 吵架: *He was always scrapping at school.* 他在学校总打架.

scrape[1] /skreıp; skrep/ *v* **1** (**a**) [Tn, Tn·p, Cn·a] ~ **sth (down/out/off)** make (a surface, etc) clean, level or smooth by drawing a sharp tool or sth rough across it 擦净, 削平, 磨光(某物): *scrape the floor with a stiff brush* 用硬毛刷子刷地板 ○ *scrape out a sticky saucepan* 把锅垢刮掉 ○ *scrape the walls clean* 把墙擦干净 ○ *She is scraping the path clear of snow.* 她正在把路上的积雪铲掉. (**b**) [Tn·pr, Tn·p] ~ **sth from/off sth; ~ sth away/off** remove (mud, grease, paint, etc) in this way 除掉(泥、油渍、油漆等): *scrape the rust off (sth)* 把锈刮掉 ○ *scrape paint from a door* 铲掉门上的油漆. **2** (**a**) [Tn, Tn·pr] ~ **sth (against/on/along/sth)** injure or damage sth by rubbing with sth rough, sharp, etc 擦伤或刮坏某物: *I fell and scraped my knee.* 我跌倒时擦伤了膝盖. ○ *I scraped the side of my car against a wall.* 我的汽车车身蹭墙划坏了. (**b**) [Tn·pr, Tn·p] ~ **sth from/off sth; ~ sth away/off** remove (skin, paint, etc) accidentally in this way 擦伤, 刮坏(皮肤、油漆等): *She's scraped the skin off her elbow.* 她把胳膊肘的皮肤擦破了. ○ *I must have scraped some of the paint off when I was parking the car.* 我准是停放汽车的时候刮掉了一些油漆. **3** [Ipr, Tn·pr] ~ **(sth) against/along/on sth** (cause sth to) rub against sth (使某物)擦着某物: *Bushes scraped against the car windows.* 矮小的树擦着了汽车的窗户. ○ *The ship's hull scraped along the side of the dock.* 船行时船身擦着码头的边. ○ *Don't scrape your feet on the floor.* 别用脚蹭着地板. **4** [Tn, Tn·p] ~ **sth (out)** make sth by scraping 刮成或挖成某物: *scrape a hole (out) in the soil for planting* 挖个土坑栽种. **5** (idm 习语) **bow and scrape** ⇨ BOW[2]. **pinch and save/scrape** ⇨ PINCH. **scrape (up) an ac**ˈ**quaintance with sb** (*infml* 口) get to know sb not very well and with difficulty 挖空心思与某人结识: *I slowly scraped (up) an acquaintance with my neighbours.* 我慢慢设法认识了邻居. **scrape (the bottom of) the** ˈ**barrel** use the least satisfactory items or people available 勉强使用现有的物品或人: *We had to scrape the barrel to get a full team, and then we lost 6-1.* 我们勉强凑成一个队, 结果以6比1输了. **scrape a** ˈ**living** earn with difficulty just enough to live on 勉强维持生活: *I manage to scrape a living by selling my pictures.* 我靠卖画餬口. **6** (phr v) **scrape along/by (on sth)** manage to live with difficulty 勉强活下去: *I can just scrape along on what my parents give me.* 我靠父母扶养勉强过活. **scrape in; scrape into sth** get in/into (eg a job or a school) with difficulty 勉强获得(工作); 勉强进入(学校): *She just scraped into university with the minimum qualifications.* 她刚刚及格, 勉强进了大学. **scrape through (sth)** succeed with difficulty in doing sth, esp in passing an exam 勉强做成某事物; (尤指)勉强及格: *She only just scraped through the test.* 她测验勉强及格. **scrape sth together/up** obtain sth with difficulty, or by being careful 费力地或小心翼翼地获得某事物: *We scraped together an audience of fifty for the play.* 我们张罗来五十个观众看这出戏. ○ *Can you scrape up enough money for a holiday?* 你能凑够了钱去度假吗?

▷ **scraper** *n* tool used for scraping, eg for scraping mud from one's shoes 刮刀; 刮削器.

scrap·ing *n* (usu *pl* 通常作复数) small bit produced by scraping 刮屑: *scrapings from the bottom of the pan* 从锅底刮下的碎屑.

scrape[2] /skreıp; skrep/ *n* **1** (esp *sing* 尤作单数) act or sound of scraping 刮擦声: *the scrape of sb's pen on paper, of sb's fingernail on a blackboard* 某人的钢笔尖在纸上划出的沙沙声、某人的指甲在黑板上刮出的嚓嚓声. **2** injury or mark made by scraping 擦伤; 擦痕: *a scrape on the elbow*, eg as a result of a fall 胳膊肘上的擦伤 ○ *a scrape along the paintwork* 油漆面上的划痕. **3** (*infml* 口) awkward situation caused by foolish behaviour or by not thinking carefully (因举动愚蠢或考虑不周而陷入的)尴尬处境: *She's always getting into scrapes.* 她总是作茧自缚. ○ *Don't expect me to get you out of your scrapes.* 你自讨苦吃可别指望我来帮你.

scrappy ⇨ SCRAP[1].

scratch[1] /skrætʃ; skrætʃ/ *v* **1** (**a**) I, Ipr, Tn] make marks on or in (a surface) with a sharp tool, nails, claws, etc; make a shallow wound in (the skin) in this way 刮, 划, 抓(物体表面或皮肤)(呈现伤或痕): *That cat scratches.* 那只猫爱用爪子乱抓. ○ *The dog is scratching at the door.* 狗正在抓门. ○ *The knife has scratched the table.* 刀子把桌子划出了道子. ○ *She won't scratch you.* 她不会把你抓伤的. (**b**) [Tn, Tn·pr, Tn·p] make (sth) by scratching 抓、划或刮等而成(某状态): *scratch a line on a surface* 在物体表面划出一条线 ○ *scratch (out) a hole in the soil* 在土里挖(出)一个洞 ○ *He'd scratched his name in the bark of the tree.* 他把名字刻在树皮上了. **2** [I, Tn] scrape or rub (the skin), esp with the nails to relieve itching 挠或擦(皮肤); (尤指)搔痒: *Stop scratching (yourself).* 别再搔痒了. ○ *Scratching the rash will make it worse.* 丘疹越挠越坏. **3** [Tn, Tn·pr] ~ **sb/sth (on sth)** get (oneself or a part of the body) scratched by accident 使(自己或身体某部)意外划伤: *She scratched herself badly while pruning the roses.* 她修剪玫瑰花时把自己划伤了一大片. ○ *He's scratched his hand on a nail.* 他的手让钉子刮破了. **4** [I] make an unpleasant scraping sound 发出刮或擦的声音: *My pen scratches.* 我的钢笔在写字时发出刮纸声. **5** [I, Ipr, Tn, Tn·pr] ~ **(sb/sth) (from sth)** withdraw (sb/sth) from competing in a race, competition, etc (使自己[某物])退出比赛: *I had to scratch (from the marathon) because of a bad cold.* 我患了重感冒, 只好退出马拉松比赛. ○ *The horse had to be scratched (from its first race).* 只好把那匹马撤出了(第一场比赛). **6** (idm 习语) **scratch one's** ˈ**head** think hard in a puzzled way about what to do or say 挠头; 伤脑筋; 费思量: *We've been scratching our heads for a solution to the problem.* 我们一直苦苦思索, 想找到解决这一问题的方法. **scratch the** ˈ**surface (of sth)** treat a subject or deal with a problem without being thorough 对待或处理一问题不深入彻底: *This essay is so short that it can only scratch the surface of the* *topic.* 这篇文章很短，只能对这一问题作肤浅的探讨. ○ *The famine is so bad, aid can only scratch the surface.* 饥荒十分严重，援助也只是杯水车薪. ˌ**you scratch** ˈ**my back and** ˌ**I'll scratch** ˈ**yours** (*saying* 谚) you help me and I'll help you, esp in an unfair way 你给我搔背，我也给你搔背(你帮我，我也帮你，尤指不正当的事): *The contract went to a friend of the chief accountant: it's (a case of) you scratch my back and I'll scratch yours.* 承包合同批给了总会计师的朋友，(可谓)各有好处、串通一气. **7** (phr v) **scratch about (for sth)** search here and there using sth sharp, one's nails etc (用尖物、指甲等)各处抓挠寻找: *The monkey scratched about in its mate's fur for fleas.* 那只猴子在另一只猴子身上找跳蚤. **scratch sth away, off, etc** remove sth by scratching 刮去某物: *scratch the paint away from the lock* 把锁头上的油漆刮掉. ○ *scratch the rust off the wheel* 把轮子上的锈刮掉 ○ *I'll scratch your eyes out!* 我要把你的眼睛挖出来! **scratch sth out (of sth)** erase sth by scratching with sth sharp 用尖物划掉某物: *Her name had been scratched out of the list.* 她的名字已从名单上划掉了. **scratch sth together/up** = SCRAPE STH TOGETHER/UP (SCRAPE[1]). **scratch sth up** get sth out of the ground by scratching 从地上刮出某物: *The dog scratched up a bone in the garden.* 那条狗在花园里刨出一根骨头.

□ ˈ**scratch pad** (*esp US*) pad of scrap paper 便条纸簿.

ˈ**scratch paper** (*US*) = SCRAP PAPER (SCRAP[1]).

scratch[2] /skrætʃ; skrætʃ/ *n* **1** [C] mark, cut, injury or sound made by scratching (SCRATCH[1] 1a) 刮、划、抓等的痕、伤或声音: *scratches on old records* 旧唱片发出的沙沙声 ○ *Her hands were covered with scratches from the thorns.* 她手上有很多棘刺划的伤痕. ○ *It's only a scratch*, ie a very slight injury. 那只是一点擦伤. ○ *He escaped without a scratch*, ie completely unhurt. 他安全逃脱了. **2** [sing] act or period of scratching (SCRATCH[1] 2) 挠; 搔; 搔痒: *The dog gave itself a good scratch.* 那条狗使劲地搔痒一番. **3** (**a**) [C] line from which competitors start in a race when they receive no handicap (无让步条件的)起跑线. (**b**) [U] status of a player who receives no handicap 无让步条件的参赛者的资格或身分: *play to scratch*, ie without any handicap 平权比赛 ○ [attrib 作定语] *a scratch player, golfer, etc* 无让步条件比赛的参加者、高尔夫球员等. **4** (idm 习语) **(start sth) from** ˈ**scratch** (begin sth) at the beginning, not using any work that was done before 从没有任何基础开始; 从零开始: *There were so many spelling mistakes, I had to write the letter out again from scratch.* 这封信的拼写错误太多，我得重写一遍. **(be/come) up to** ˈ**scratch**; **(bring sb/sth) up to** ˈ**scratch** as good as sb/sth should be; satisfactory (使某人[某事物])合格; 令人满意: *Is her schoolwork up to scratch?* 她的功课行吗? ○ *We'll have to bring the house up to scratch before we sell it.* 我们得把这所房子维修一下再出售.

▷ **scratch** *adj* [attrib 作定语] made up with whatever people or materials are available 用现有的人或材料拼凑的: *a scratch meal, team, crew* 现凑成的饭菜、队、工作人员. **scratchy** *adj* (**-ier**, **-iest**) **1** making the skin feel itchy or irritated 使皮肤发痒的; 刺激皮肤的: *scratchy clothes, wool, etc* 使皮肤发痒的衣物、毛织品等. **2** (of a record) making clicks and hisses when played because of scratches on its surface (指唱片)发沙沙声的. **3** (of a pen) making a scratching sound (指钢笔)发刮纸声的. **4** (of writing or drawings) untidy or carelessly done (指文字或图画)潦草的. **scratch·ily** *adv*. **scratchi·ness** *n* [U].

scrawl /skrɔːl; skrɔl/ *v* [I, Ipr, Tn, Tn·pr] **1** write or draw (sth) in an untidy, careless or unskilful way 写或画(某内容)(不工整、不仔细或无技法): *Who's scrawled all over the wall?* 是谁把墙画得这么难看? ○ *She scrawled a few words on a postcard.* 她在明信片上草草地写了几个字. **2** make (meaningless or illegible marks) on sth 在某物上乱画(无意义或无法辨认): *The baby scrawled on the table-top.* 那小孩儿在桌上乱画.

▷ **scrawl** *n* **1** [sing] untidy or unskilful handwriting 潦草的笔迹: *the typical doctor's scrawl* 医生惯常的潦草笔迹 ○ *I could hardly read her childish scrawl.* 我简直认不出她那歪七扭八的字. **2** [C] piece of such writing; scrawled note or letter 潦草的文字或便条、书信: *Her signature was an illegible scrawl.* 她的签字潦草难辨.

scrawny /ˈskrɔːnɪ; ˋskrɔnɪ/ *adj* (**-ier**, **-iest**) (*derog* 贬) not having much flesh; scraggy 瘦的; 皮包骨的: *the scrawny neck of a turkey* 火鸡的瘦脖子. ⇨Usage at THIN 用法见 THIN.

scream /skriːm; skrim/ *v* **1** [I, Ipr, Ip, Tn, Tn·pr, Tn·p, Tf, Cn·a] **~ (sth) (out) (at sb)**; **~ (with sth)** give a long piercing cry of fear, pain or excitement; cry (sth) in this way (因恐惧、痛苦或兴奋)尖声喊叫; 喊出: *Those cats have been screaming for hours.* 那些猫叫了半天了. ○ *She screamed (out) (at me) in anger.* 她愤怒地(对我)尖声喊叫. ○ *The fans screamed with excitement when they saw him.* 球迷一看见他都激动得大喊大叫. ○ *We all screamed with laughter*, ie laughed noisily. 我们都大笑起来. ○ *'Help!' she screamed.* 她高声喊叫'救命啊!' ○ *He screamed (out) that there was a fire.* 他叫嚷失火了. ○ *The baby was screaming himself red in the face.* 那小孩儿哭叫得脸都红了. ⇨Usage at SHOUT 用法见 SHOUT. **2** [I] (of the wind, a machine, etc) make a loud piercing sound (指风、机器等)发出大而尖的声音: *The hurricane screamed outside.* 外面飓风呼啸着. ○ *I pressed the accelerator until the engine screamed.* 我猛踩油门踏板，发动机发出了尖利的声音. **3** (phr v) **scream past, through, round, etc** move quickly with a loud, piercing sound 尖叫着移动: *The wind screamed through the trees.* 风呼啸着穿过树林. ○ *Racing cars screamed past.* 汽车赛车呼啸而过.

▷ **scream** *n* **1** [C] loud shrill piercing cry or noise 大而尖的声音: *the screams of tortured prisoners* 犯人受折磨时的尖叫声 ○ *a scream of pain, laughter, excitement, etc* 痛苦、大笑、激动等时的尖叫声. **2** [sing] (*infml* 口) person or thing that causes laughter 令人大笑的人或事物: *He's an absolute scream.* 他非常滑稽. ○ *The play's a scream.* 这个剧十分可笑. **scream·ingly** *adv* enough to cause screams of laughter 极其可笑: *screamingly funny* 滑稽得令人大笑.

scree /skriː; skri/ *n* [U, C] (area on a mountainside covered by) small loose stones, which slide when trodden on 山坡上的碎石(地带); 岩屑堆.

screech /skriːtʃ; skritʃ/ *v* **1** I, Ipr, Ip, Tn, Tn·pr, Tn·p] **~ (sth) (out) (at sb)** give a harsh high-pitched cry; call out (sth) in such a way 尖叫; 尖声喊出: *screech (out) in pain* 痛苦地尖叫 ○ *monkeys screeching in the trees* 在树丛中尖叫的猴子 ○ *old ladies screeching hymns* 用尖声唱着赞美诗的老妇人 ○ *The child screeched insults at us.* 那孩子尖着嗓子骂我们. **2** [I] make a harsh high-pitched sound 发出尖利的声音: *The brakes screeched as the car stopped.* 汽车停下时刹车发出尖利的声音. ○ *The gate screeched as it opened.* 大门打开时发出刺耳的声音. **3** (phr v) **screech along, past, through, etc** move with a loud harsh high-pitched sound 发出大而尖利的声音移动: *jets screeching over the house-tops* 在房顶上呼啸而过的喷气式飞机 ○ *screech to a halt* 发出尖利的声音停下.

▷ **screech** *n* [sing] screeching cry or sound 尖利刺耳的声音: *the screech of tyres*, eg when a car is cornering fast 轮胎发出的刺耳声音(如汽车急转弯时).

□ ˈ**screech-owl** *n* type of owl that makes a screeching cry, rather than a hoot 鸣角鸮.

screed /skriːd; skrid/ *n* **1** [C] long (and usu uninteresting) speech or piece of writing 冗长的(通常为乏味的)讲话或文字. **2** [C, U] layer of cement, mortar, etc spread over a floor to make it smooth 找平层(铺在地面上的水泥砂浆等的).

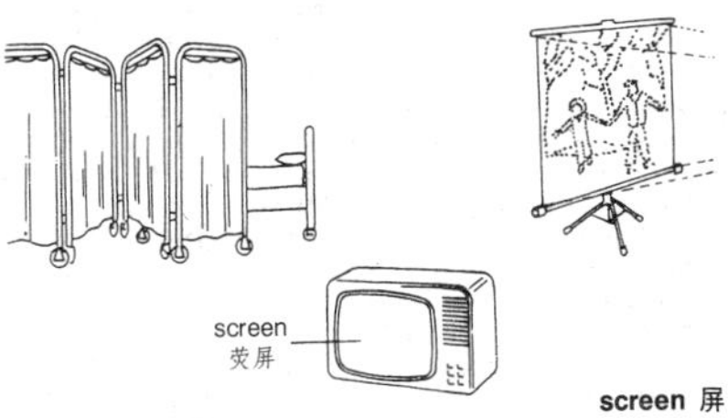

screen 屏

screen /skriːn; skrin/ *n* **1** [C] upright, fixed or movable, sometimes folding framework used for dividing a room, concealing sth, protecting sb from excessive heat, light, etc 隔板; 屏; 幕; 帘; 帐: *a screen in front of the fire* 炉前的隔板 ○ *get undressed behind a screen* 在屏风后脱衣服. **2** [C] anything that conceals sb or sth or gives protection, eg from the weather 掩蔽物: *a screen of trees*, eg hiding a house from a road 树林形成的屏障 ○ *use the blanket as a screen to keep the wind off* 用毯子挡风 ○ *a 'sunscreen*, ie used to protect the skin from harmful rays from the sun 防晒剂(保护皮肤用的) ○ *He was using his business activities as a screen for crime.* 他用生意活动作掩护干着犯罪的勾当. **3** [C] (esp in old churches) wood or stone structure that partially separates the main part of a church from the altar, or the nave of a cathedral from the choir (尤指旧教堂的)圣坛屏幕, 唱诗班屏幕. ⇨illus at App 1 见附录1插图, page viii. **4** (**a**) [C] blank surface onto which still pictures or films are projected 银幕. ⇨illus 见插图. (**b**) [C] blank surface, esp on a TV or computer monitor, on which pictures or data are shown 屏幕, 荧光屏, 荧屏(尤指电视机或计算机的). (**c**) (often 常作 **the screen**) [sing] the film industry or cinema films 电影业; 电影界; 电影: *write for the screen*, ie write the dialogue for films 为电影写对白 ○ *a star of stage and screen*, ie appearing in plays and films 戏剧兼电影明星 ○ *I work for both the big and the small screen*, ie for both films and TV. 我从事影视工作. ○ [attrib 作定语] *a screen actor, performance, writer* 电影的演员、上演、脚本作者. (**d**) [C] cinema, esp one that is part of a complex of cinemas 电影院(尤指影院集中区的): *Two smaller screens will be opening in May.* 五月份将有两家小型电影院开业. **5** [C] frame with fine wire netting to keep out flies, mosquitoes, etc 纱门、纱窗等: *a 'door-screen* 纱门 ○ *a 'window-screen* 纱窗. **6** [C] large sieve or riddle used for separating coal, gravel, etc into different sizes by passing it through holes of different sizes (筛煤、砾石等的)筛子. **7** [C] = SIGHT-SCREEN (SIGHT[1]). **8** (idm 习语) **the silver screen** ⇨ SILVER.

▷ **screen** *v* **1** [Tn, Tn·pr, Tn·p] **~ sth/sb (off) (from sth/sb)**; **~ sth/sb (against sth)** conceal, protect or shelter sth/sb with a screen (用隔板、屏、幕等)隐藏、掩护或遮蔽某物[某人]: *The bushes will screen us while we change.* 我们用灌木丛遮挡着换衣服. ○ *The trees screen the house from view.* 有这些树隔着看不见那所房子. ○ *The camera lens must be screened from direct sunlight.* 照相机的镜头不可受到阳光的直射. ○ *The wall screens us against the wind.* 这堵墙能给我们挡风. ○ *A bookcase screens off part of the room.* 有个书柜把房间隔开了一部分. **2** [Tn, Tn·pr] **~ sb (from sth/sb)** (*fig* 比喻) protect sb (from blame, punishment, etc) 保护某人(不受责备、惩罚等); 包庇; 袒护: *Everyone's angry with you, and I can't screen you (from their anger).* 大家都生你的气, 我无法护着你. ○ *You can't screen your children from real life for ever.* 不能总护着孩子不让他们接触实际生活. **3** Tn] pass (coal, gravel, etc) through a screen(6) 筛(煤、砾石等). **4** [Tn, Tn·pr] **~ sb/sth (for sth)** examine or test sb/sth to find out if there is any disease, defect, etc 检查或测试某人[某事物](有无疾病、缺陷等): *screen women for breast cancer* 检查女子是否患有乳腺癌 ○ *The applications were carefully screened in case any of them contained false information.* 仔细审查了所有的申请资料以防弄虚作假. ○ *Government employees are often screened by the security services*, ie Their past history is checked, to ensure that they are not likely to be disloyal or subversive. 政府雇员经常受到保安部门审查. **5** [Tn] show (a film, scene, etc) on a screen(4a) 放映(影片、片段等): *The film has been screened in the cinema and on TV.* 这部电影已在电影院及电视上放映. **screen·ing** *n* showing of a film, TV programme, etc (电影、电视等的)放映: *the film's first screening in this country* 该影片在本国之首映.

□ **'screenplay** *n* script for a film 电影剧本.

'screen test test to see if sb is suitable to appear in a cinema film 试镜头(以挑选电影演员).

screw /skru:; skru/ *n* **1** [C] metal pin with a slot or cross cut into its head, and a spiral groove around its shaft, that can be turned and forced into wood, metal, etc so as to fasten and hold things together 螺丝钉; 螺钉; 螺丝. **2** [C] (often in compounds 常用以构成复合词) thing that is turned like a screw and is used for tightening, gripping, etc 螺旋状物: *tighten the screw on a fruit press* 旋紧水果榨汁机的螺丝 ○ *a 'corkscrew*, ie for taking corks out of bottles 瓶塞钻(拔软木瓶塞用的). **3** [C] act of turning; turn 拧; 转动: *The nut isn't tight enough yet: give it another screw.* 螺母不太紧, 再拧一下吧. ⇨illus 见插图. **4** [C] propeller, esp of a ship or motor boat 螺旋桨(尤指船的): *a twin-screw cruiser* 双螺旋桨的机动游艇. **5** [C] (*dated* 旧 *esp Brit*) small twisted piece of paper and its contents (拧口的)小纸包及所盛之物: *a screw of salt, tea, tobacco, etc* 一小纸包盐、茶、烟草等. **6** [sing] (*Brit sl* 俚) salary or wages 薪水; 工资: *be on/be paid a good screw* 薪水挣得不少. **7** [C] (*Brit sl* 俚) prison warder 监狱看守. **8** [sing] (△ *sl* 讳, 俚) (**a**) act of sexual intercourse 性交: *have a screw with sb* 与某人性交. (**b**) partner in sexual intercourse 性交的对象: *be a good screw* 是个性交的好对象. **9** (idm 习语) **have a 'screw loose** be slightly mad or eccentric 有点疯癫或古怪: *She eats nothing but nuts: she must have a screw loose!* 她这个人除了干果, 什么都不吃, 准是有毛病! **put the 'screw(s) on (sb)** force sb to do sth by intimidating him 威逼某人做某事: *The landlord's putting the screws on to get her out of the house.* 房东正在逼她搬家. **a turn of the screw** ⇨ TURN[2].

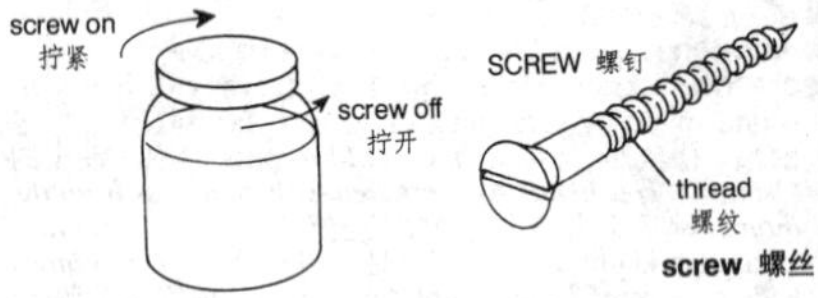

screw 螺丝

▷ **screw** *v* **1** [Tn, Tn·pr, Tn·p] fasten or tighten (sth) with a screw or screws 用螺丝钉将(某物)拧紧: *a tightly screwed joint* 用螺钉拧得很紧的接头 ○ *screw a bracket to the wall* 用螺丝把托架固定到墙上 ○ *screw a lock on the door* 用螺丝把锁拧在门上 ○ *screw all the parts together* 用螺丝钉把所有部件都拧在一起. **2** (**a**) [Tn·pr, Tn·p, Cn·a] twist (sth) round; make tighter by twisting 拧动(某物); 拧紧: *screw the lid on/off (the jar)* 拧上[拧开](罐子)盖 ○ *screw the joints together* 把接头拧在一起 ○ *screw a bulb in* 把灯泡拧上 ○ *screw one's head round*, ie in order to look over one's shoulder 转过头去 ○ *screw the nut (up) tight* 把螺母拧紧. (**b**) [Ipr, Ip] be attached by screwing 拧牢: *This type of bulb screws into the socket.* 这种灯是拧到灯座上的. ○ *Does this lid screw on, or does one press it down?* 这个盖子是拧的还是按的? **3** [Tn, Tn·pr] **~ sb (for sth)** (*sl* 俚) cheat sb 欺骗某人: *We got screwed when we bought this house.* 我们买这所房子上当了. ○ *How much did they screw you for?* ie How much did you have to pay? 他们敲了你多少钱? (你付了多少?) **4** (△ *sl* 讳, 俚) (**a**) [I] (of two people) have sexual intercourse (指二人)性交: *a couple screwing in the back of a car* 正在汽车后排座位上性交的两个人. (**b**) [Tn] (esp of a man) have sexual intercourse with (尤指男子)与...性交: *He accused me of screwing his wife.* 他控告我奸淫他的妻子. **5** (idm 习语) **have one's head screwed on** ⇨ HEAD[1]. **screw him, you, that, etc** (△ *sl* 讳, 俚) (used in the imperative to express one's irritation about sb/sth 用于祈使句, 对某人[某事物]表示愤怒): *Screw you, mate!* 去你妈的, 你这个家伙! **screw up one's 'courage** force oneself to be brave 鼓起勇气: *I screwed up my courage and went to the dentist.* 我鼓起勇气去找牙科医生. **6** (phr v) **screw sth out of sth** remove sth from sth by twisting 从某物中拧出某物: *screw the water out of the sponge* 把水从海绵里拧出. **screw sth out of sb** force sb to give sth 逼某人交出某事物: *They screwed the money out of her by threats.* 他们威胁她把钱交出来. **screw up** (*sl* 俚) handle a situation very badly 弄糟某事: *I was trying to help, but I screwed up again.* 我原想帮忙, 反而又把事情搞糟了. **screw sth up** (**a**) fasten sth with screws 用螺丝钉将某物拧紧: *screw up a crate* 用螺丝钉把板条箱拧紧. (**b**) make (paper, etc) into a tight ball 将(纸等)揉成团: *I screwed up the note and threw it on the fire.* 我把便条揉成团扔进火里了. (**c**) tense the muscles of (the face, the eyes) when the light is too strong, when one feels pain, etc (因光强、疼痛等)扭曲(面孔、眼睛): *The taste of the lemon made her screw up her face.* 柠檬把她酸得龇牙咧嘴. (**d**) (*sl* 俚) handle (a situation) very badly; make a mess of sth 把(某物)弄糟; 搞乱某事: *Don't ask them to organize the trip, they'll only screw everything up.* 别让他们组织此行, 他们准得把一切都搞糟了.

screwy *adj* (**-ier**, **-iest**) (*infml* 口) strange, eccentric or crazy 奇怪的; 古怪的; 疯狂的: *She's really screwy!* 她简直疯了! ○ *What a screwy idea!* 多奇怪的主意!

□ **'screwball** *n* (*US infml* 口) eccentric or crazy person 古怪的人; 疯狂的人: [attrib 作定语] *a screwball comedy* 一出离奇的喜剧.

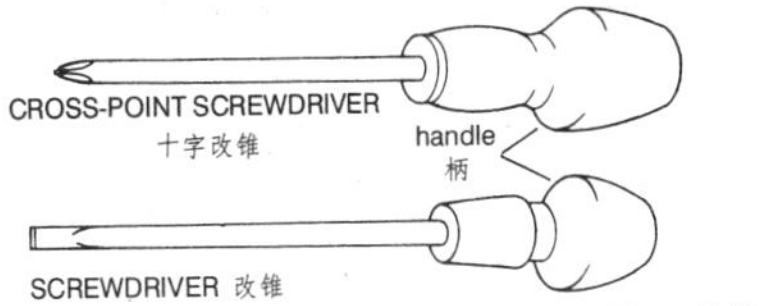

screwdriver 改锥

'screwdriver *n* tool with a handle and a blade that fits into a slot, etc in the head of a screw to turn it 改锥; 螺丝刀; 螺丝起子. **ˌscrewed-'up** *adj* (*sl* 俚) upset and not completely able to cope with problems in life 烦乱而无法处理生活问题的: *ˌscrewed-up 'kids* 烦乱而不能自理的孩子 ○ *I'm still screwed-up about the accident.* 我仍对那次事故耿耿于怀.

'screw-topped (also **'screw-top**) *adj* (of a jar, etc) having a top or lid that screws onto it (指罐子等)旋盖的.

scribble /'skrɪbl; ˋskrɪbḷ/ *v* [I, Tn, Tn·pr] **1** write (sth) very fast or carelessly 匆匆或草草书写(某内容): *scribbling (figures) on an envelope* 在信封上乱写(数字). **2** make (meaningless marks) on sth 在某物上画(无意义的东西): *a child scribbling all over a book* 在本子上到处乱画的孩子.

▷ **scribble** *n* **1** [U, sing] very fast or careless handwriting 潦草的笔迹: *I can't read this scribble.* 我看不懂这种潦草的字. **2** [C] meaningless marks 乱画的无意义的东西: *scribbles all over the page* 整页上乱画的东西.

scrib·bler /'skrɪblə(r); ˋskrɪblɚ/ *n* **1** person who scribbles 写字潦草的人. **2** (*derog* 贬) untalented author, journalist, etc 无天分的作家、新闻工作者等: *the scribblers of Fleet Street* 伦敦弗利特街报馆区庸碌无能的记者.

□ **'scribbling-block** *n* pad of cheap paper for making notes (质劣的)拍纸簿.

scribe /skraɪb; skraɪb/ *n* **1** person who made copies of writings before printing was invented (印刷术发明之前的)抄写员. **2** (in Biblical times) professional religious scholar (圣经时代的)文士, 经师.

scrim·mage /'skrɪmɪdʒ; ˋskrɪmɪdʒ/ *n* **1** (also **scrummage**) confused struggle or fight; tussle 混战; 争夺: *a scrimmage round the bargain counter in the store* 在商店廉价品柜台周围你争我夺. **2** (in US football) period between the moment the ball goes into play and the moment it goes out of play (美国橄榄球中的)比赛开始至死球期间.

▷ **scrim·mage** *v* [I] take part in a scrimmage(1) 混战.

scrimp /skrɪmp; skrɪmp/ *v* (idm 习语) **scrimp and save** manage to live on very little money, esp so as to afford sth 节衣缩食, 节省(尤指为攒钱): *We had to scrimp and save to pay the bills.* 我们得省吃俭用来付帐.

scrip /skrɪp; skrɪp/ *n* **1** [C] extra share in a business company issued instead of a dividend (代股息的)股分: [attrib 作定语] *a scrip issue* 以股代息. **2** [U] shares issued in this way (代股息的)股分.

script /skrɪpt; skrɪpt/ *n* **1** [C] text of a play, film, broadcast, talk, etc (戏剧、电影、广播、讲话等的)剧本, 脚本, 讲稿: *That line isn't in the script.* 脚本上没有那一段词. ○ [attrib 作定语] *a script editor* 脚本编辑. **2** [U] (**a**) handwriting 笔迹. (**b**) printed or typewritten cursive characters resembling this 书写体的字. **3** system of writing 文字体系: *a letter in Cyrillic script* 西里尔文字的字母. **4** [C] (*Brit*) candidate's written answer or answers in an examination 笔试答卷: *The examiner had to mark 150 scripts.* 主考人须评阅150分试卷.

▷ **script** *v* [Tn esp passive 尤用于被动语态] write a script for (a film, a TV or radio play, etc) 为(电影、电视或广播剧等)写脚本: *a film scripted by a famous novelist* 由著名小说家撰写脚本的电影. **scrip·ted** *adj* read from a script 照稿子念的: *a scripted talk on the radio* 广播中照稿子念的谈话.

□ **'script-writer** *n* person who writes scripts for films, TV and radio plays, etc (电影、电视及广播剧等的)撰稿人.

scrip·ture /'skrɪptʃə(r); ˋskrɪptʃɚ/ *n* **1 Scripture** [U] (also **the Scriptures** [pl]) the Bible《圣经》: [attrib 作定语] *a 'Scripture lesson*《圣经》课. **2 scriptures** [pl] holy writings of a religion other than Christianity (基督教以外的)经典, 经文: *Vedic scriptures* 吠陀经文.

▷ **scrip·tural** /'skrɪptʃərəl; ˋskrɪptʃərəl/ *adj* of or based on the Bible 圣经的; 根据圣经的: *wide scriptural knowledge* 精通圣经.

scrof·ula /'skrɒfjʊlə; ˋskrɑfjələ/ *n* [U] disease causing swelling of the glands, probably a form of tuberculosis 淋巴结核; 瘰疬. ▷ **scrofu·lous** /'skrɒfjʊləs; ˋskrɑfjələs/ *adj*.

scroll /skrəʊl; skrol/ *n* **1** (**a**) roll of parchment or paper for writing on (供书写用的)羊皮纸卷, 纸卷. (**b**) ancient book written on such a roll 用羊皮纸写的古籍. **2** anything curved like a scroll, esp an ornamental design cut in stone or a flourish in writing 卷形物; (尤指)卷形石雕饰物或字体.

▷ **scroll** *v* **1** [I, Ipr, Ip] (of text on a computer screen) move gradually up or down (指计算机荧屏上的文本)逐渐上下移动. **2** [I, Tn] (of a computer) show (text) moving in this way (指计算机)显示(上下移动的)文本: *This model scrolls far too slowly.* 这种型号的计算机文本上下移动得实在太慢.

Scrooge /skru:dʒ; skrudʒ/ *n* (*derog* 贬) person who is miserly and mean-spirited 斯克鲁奇; 吝啬鬼.

scro·tum /'skrəʊtəm; ˋskrotəm/ *n* (*pl* **scrotums** or **scrota** /'skrəʊtə; ˋskrotə/) pouch of skin enclosing the testicles in most male mammals 阴囊. ⇨ illus at MALE 见 MALE 插图.

scrounge /skraʊndʒ; skraʊndʒ/ *v* [I, Ipr, Tn, Tn·pr] **~ (sth) (from/off sb)** (*infml often derog* 口, 常作贬义) get (sth) by borrowing or taking it without permission 借得或擅取(某物): *She's always scrounging (money) off her brother.* 她总找哥哥借钱. ○ *I managed to scrounge the materials to build a shed.* 我设法弄来点材料搭个棚子.

▷ **scrounge** *n* (idm 习语) **on the 'scrounge** (*infml* 口) trying to borrow or get sth by scrounging 设法借得或擅取某物: *If you're on the scrounge again, I've no money.* 你要是再想借钱, 我可没有了. **scroun·ger** *n*.

scrub[1] /skrʌb; skrʌb/ *n* [U] (land covered with) underdeveloped trees or shrubs 发育不良的矮树丛(地带): *clear the scrub and plough the land* 消除矮树丛后开垦这片地 ○ [attrib 作定语] *'scrub-oak* 矮栎, *'scrub-pine*, ie dwarf or underdeveloped types 矮松.

▷ **scrubby** /'skrʌbɪ; ˋskrʌbɪ/ *adj* (**-ier**, **-iest**) **1** covered with scrub; (of trees, etc) underdeveloped 长有矮树丛的; (指树木)发育不良的. **2** small or mean 矮小的; 卑劣的: *a scrubby little shed in a back street* 在后街上的破棚子.

scrub[2] /skrʌb; skrʌb/ *v* (**-bb-**) **1** [I, Ip, Tn, Tn·p, Cn·a] **~ sth (down/out)** clean sth thoroughly by rubbing hard, esp with a brush and soap and water 彻底擦洗某物; (尤指用肥皂和水)刷洗: *He's down on his knees, scrubbing (away).* 他跪在地上擦洗(起来). ○ *scrub the floor* 刷洗地板 ○ *Scrub the walls down before painting them.* 先把墙刷干净再上漆. ○ *scrub out a saucepan* 把长柄锅刷干净 ○ *Scrub the table-top clean.* 把桌面擦洗干净. **2** [Tn] (*infml* 口) cancel (a plan, etc) 取消(计划等): *We wanted to go for a picnic, but we had to scrub it because of the rain.* 我们原想去野餐, 后来因为下雨而取消了. ○ *It costs £10 per metre, no, scrub that* (ie ignore what I've just said), *it costs £12 per metre.* 每米的价钱是10英镑, 不, 应该说是每米12英镑. **3** (phr v) **scrub**

sth away/off remove sth by scrubbing 将某物擦洗掉或刷洗掉: *scrub the grease away* 把油渍刷洗掉 ○ *scrub the dirt off the shelf* 把书架上的土擦掉. **scrub up** (*medical* 医) (of a surgeon) wash one's hands and arms thoroughly before an operation (指外科医生)(施行手术前)擦洗手和胳膊.

▷ **scrub** *n* [sing] act of scrubbing 擦洗; 刷洗: *give the floor a good scrub* 把地面好好刷洗一番.

□ 'scrubbing-brush *n* stiff brush for scrubbing floors, etc (刷地面等的)硬刷子. ⇨illus at BRUSH 见 BRUSH 插图.

scrub·ber /ˈskrʌbə(r); ˈskrʌbɚ/ *n* (*Brit infml derog* 口, 贬) prostitute or woman who has sexual intercourse with many partners 妓女; 与很多人性交的女子.

scrudge /skrʌdʒ; skrʌdʒ/ *n* (*Brit*) small bent nail for holding roofing-tiles in place 房倒板钩(固着房倒板用的).

scruff /skrʌf; skrʌf/ *n* (idm 习语) **by the scruff of the/one's 'neck** (grasping or lifting) by the back of an animal's or a person's neck (抓住或拎起)动物或人的颈背: *The cat picked up the kitten by the scruff of its neck.* 大猫叼着小猫的颈背. ○ *She grabbed me by the scruff of my neck and threw me out.* 她抓着我的颈背把我扔了出去.

scruffy /ˈskrʌfɪ; ˈskrʌfɪ/ *adj* (**-ier, -iest**) (*infml* 口) dirty and untidy 邋遢的: *You can't go to a job interview looking so scruffy!* 你求职去面试不能这样邋里邋遢的!

▷ **scruff** *n* (*infml* 口) dirty and untidy person 邋遢的人: *He's a dreadful scruff!* 他真邋遢!

scruff·ily *adv*.

scruf·fi·ness *n* [U].

scrum /skrʌm; skrʌm/ *n* **1** = SCRUMMAGE 1. **2** (*fig* 比喻) confused struggle; tussle 混战; 争夺: *Shoppers got into a scrum round the bargain counter.* 顾客在廉价品柜台周围你争我夺.

▷ **scrum** *v* (**-mm-**) (phr v) **scrum down** form a scrummage 混战; 争夺.

□ ˌ**scrum-'half** *n* half-back who puts the ball into the scrummage 争球前卫.

scrum·mage /ˈskrʌmɪdʒ; ˈskrʌmɪdʒ/ *n* **1** (also **scrum**) part of a Rugby football game when the forwards of both sides pack together with their heads down to push against the other side, while the ball is thrown between them and they try to kick it back to their own team; all the forwards taking part in this (橄榄球赛的)并列争球, 并列争球的全体前锋: *... and it's a scrummage just inside the Welsh half.* ...而且这是在威尔士队半场内的并列争球. **2** = SCRIMMAGE 1.

scrump·tious /ˈskrʌmpʃəs; ˈskrʌmpʃəs/ *adj* (*infml* 口) (esp of food) delicious (尤指食物)美味的: *What a scrumptious meal!* 多香的饭菜!

scrunch /skrʌntʃ; skrʌntʃ/ *n, v* = CRUNCH.

scruple /ˈskru:pl; ˈskrupl̩/ *n* **1** [U, C often *pl* 作不可数名词或可数名词, 后者常作复数] feeling that prevents one from doing or allowing sth that one thinks may be wrong 顾忌; 顾虑: *Have you no scruples about buying stolen goods?* 你买赃物就毫无顾忌吗? ○ *She tells lies without scruple.* 她撒谎肆无忌惮. **2** [C] weight unit of 20 grains 重量单位(等于 20 格令).

▷ **scruple** *v* [It] (usu in negative sentences 通常用于否定句) hesitate (to do sth) because of scruples (因有顾忌)犹豫: *She wouldn't scruple to tell a lie if she thought it would be useful.* 她只要认为说谎有利, 就连犹豫都不犹豫.

scru·pu·lous /ˈskru:pjʊləs; ˈskrupjələs/ *adj* **1** extremely careful and thorough; paying great attention to details 极仔细彻底的; 一丝不苟的: *a scrupulous examiner* 认真仔细的检查员 ○ *a scrupulous inspection of the firm's accounts* 对公司的帐目彻底审核. **2 ~ (in sth/doing sth)** careful not to do wrong; absolutely honest 审慎的; 极诚实的: *scrupulous in all her business dealings* (她)对所有交易都十分老实 ○ *behave with scrupulous honesty* 表现极为正直. ▷ **scru·pu·lously** *adv*: *scrupulously exact, careful, honest, clean* 极为精确、细心、诚实、清洁.

scru·tin·eer /ˌskru:tɪˈnɪə(r); *US* -tnˈɪər; ˌskrutn̩ˈɪɚ/ *n* (*Brit*) person who checks that an election or other vote is carried out correctly 监票人.

scru·tin·ize, -ise /ˈskru:tɪnaɪz; *US* -tənaɪz; ˈskrutn̩ˌaɪz/ *v* [Tn] look at or examine (sth) carefully or thoroughly 仔细或彻底检查(某事物): *scrutinize all the documents relating to the trial* 仔细审阅与该案审判有关的所有文件.

scrutiny /ˈskru:tɪnɪ; *US* ˈskru:tənɪ; ˈskrutn̩ɪ/ *n* [C, U] (instance of) careful and thorough examination 仔细而彻底的检查: *a close scrutiny of the election results* 彻底检查选举结果 ○ *subject the thesis to careful scrutiny* 认真仔细审阅论文.

scuba /ˈsku:bə; ˈskubə/ *n* underwater breathing apparatus consisting of a cylinder or cylinders of compressed air, attached by a hose to a mouthpiece 水肺(水下呼吸器): [attrib 作定语] '*scuba diving* 戴水肺潜水.

scud /skʌd; skʌd/ *v* (**-dd-**) [I, Ipr, Ip] (esp of ships, etc or clouds) move straight, fast and smoothly (尤指船、舰或云彩)笔直、高速而平稳地移动: *The yacht was scudding along before the wind.* 那只帆船正乘风笔直疾驶. ○ *clouds scudding across the sky* 在天空中掠过的飞云.

scuff /skʌf; skʌf/ *v* **1** [Tn] (**a**) mark or scrape (a surface) with one's shoes 用鞋踩或蹭(物体表面): *a badly scuffed door* 用鞋蹭旧的门. (**b**) mark, scrape or wear away (a shoe) 蹭、磨损或穿坏(鞋): *I scuffed the heel of my boot on the step.* 我的靴子后跟在台阶上磨坏了. **2** [I, Ipr, Ip, Tn no passive 不用于被动语态] drag (one's feet) while walking; shuffle 拖着(脚)走; 拖着脚走: *If you scuff (your feet) like that, you'll wear the heels out.* 你那么拖着脚走路, 就要把鞋跟磨坏了. ○ *She scuffed past in her mother's slippers.* 她趿拉着她母亲的拖鞋走过去了.

▷ **scuff** (also '**scuff-mark**) *n* mark made by scuffing 用鞋踩出的或蹭出的痕迹: *scuffs on the skirting-board* 壁脚板上用鞋蹭出的痕迹.

scuffle /ˈskʌfl; ˈskʌfl̩/ *n* confused struggle between people who are close together 扭打; 混战: *Scuffles broke out between police and demonstrators.* 警察和示威群众扭打起来了.

▷ **scuffle** *v* [I, Ipr] **~ (with sb)** take part in a scuffle 扭打: *scuffle with reporters* 与记者厮打起来.

scull /skʌl; skʌl/ *n* **1** either of a pair of small oars used by a single rower, one in each hand (双桨船上的)短桨. **2** oar placed over the stern of a boat to drive it with twisting strokes (船尾的)橹. **3** light racing boat rowed by a single rower with two sculls (单人双桨)赛艇.

▷ **scull** *v* [I, Ipr, Ip, Tn, Tn·pr, Tn·p] row (a boat) with a scull or sculls (用桨)划(船); (用橹)摇(船): *be able to scull* 会划船 ○ *scull (the boat) past the boat-house* 划(船)经过船库. **sculler** *n* person who sculls 划桨的人; (在船尾)摇橹的人.

scull·ery /ˈskʌlərɪ; ˈskʌlərɪ/ *n* small room (usu in a large house) beside the kitchen, where dishes, etc are washed up (厨房旁的)洗涤室(通常设于大宅中).

scul·lion /ˈskʌlɪən; ˈskʌljən/ *n* (formerly) boy or man who did simple tasks, eg washing-up, in a kitchen (旧时)做粗活儿的男子(如在厨房洗碗).

sculpt = SCULPTURE *v*.

sculptor /ˈskʌlptə(r); ˈskʌlptɚ/ *n* (*fem* 阴性作 **sculp·tress** /ˈskʌlptrɪs; ˈskʌlptrɪs/) person who makes sculptures 做雕塑或雕刻的人.

sculp·ture /ˈskʌlptʃə(r); ˈskʌlptʃɚ/ *n* **1** [U] art of making figures, objects, etc by carving wood or stone, shaping clay, making metal casts, etc 雕塑; 雕刻: *the techniques of sculpture in stone* 石雕技术. **2** [C, U] a work or works made in this way 雕塑品: *a sculpture of Venus* 维纳斯雕像 ○ *a collector of sculpture* 雕塑收藏家.

▷ **sculp·tural** /ˈskʌlptʃərəl; ˈskʌlptʃərəl/ *adj* [esp attrib 尤作定语] of, like or connected with sculpture (似)雕塑的: *a sculptural quality* 雕塑的特色.

sculp·ture (also **sculpt** /skʌlpt; skʌlpt/) *v* **1** (**a**) [Tn, Tn·pr] represent (sb/sth) in sculpture; make (a sculpture) 为(某人[某物])做塑像或雕像; 做(塑像或雕像): *saints sculptured in marble* 用大理石雕刻的圣徒像 ○ *sculpture a statue out of hard wood* 用硬木做雕像. (**b**) [Tn, Tn·pr] make (sth) into a sculpture 将(某物)制成雕塑品: *sculpture the clay into a vase* 用黏土做成花瓶. (**c**) [Tn] decorate (sth) with sculptures 用雕塑装饰(某物): *sculptured columns* 用雕刻装饰的柱子. **2** [I] make sculptures; be a sculptor 做雕塑; 作雕塑师: *learn to* *sculpture* 学习雕塑.

scum /skʌm; skʌm/ *n* **1** [U] layer of froth on the surface of a boiling liquid; layer of dirt on a pond or other area of still water (煮沸的液体表面的)泡沫; (池塘或其他静止水面上的)浮垢, 浮渣. **2** [pl *v*] (*fig derog* 比喻, 贬) people considered to be bad or contemptible 一群坏人或卑贱的人: *You scum!* 你们这群坏蛋! ○ *She treats smokers like the scum of the earth*, ie as the worst people there are. 她把吸烟的人都当作败类. ○ *I wouldn't have anything to do with those scum.* 我才不跟那些无耻之徒来往呢.

▷ **scummy** *adj* (**-ier**, **-iest**) of, like or containing scum(1) (似)泡沫或浮渣的; 含有泡沫或浮渣的.

scup·per /ˈskʌpə(r); ˋskʌpɚ/ *n* (often *pl* 常作复数) opening in a ship's side to allow water to run off the deck (船舷上的)排水孔(用以排除甲板上的水).

▷ **scup·per** *v* (*Brit*) **1** Tn] sink (one's ship) deliberately 故意弄沉(自己的船). **2** [Tn esp passive 尤用于被动语态] (*infml* 口) cause (sth) to fail; ruin 使(某事物)失败; 摧毁: *We're scuppered!* 我们完蛋了! ○ *The project was scuppered by lack of money.* 那个计划因缺钱而告吹.

scurf /skɜ:f; skɝf/ *n* [U] flakes of dead skin, esp on the scalp, that comes off as new skin grows; dandruff 皮屑; (尤指)头皮屑: *clean hair that's free of scurf* 没有头皮屑的干净头发.

▷ **scurfy** *adj* having or covered with scurf 有皮屑的; 有头皮屑的.

scur·ril·ous /ˈskʌrələs; ˋskʌrələs/ *adj* abusive and insulting, esp in a crude or obscene way 辱骂的(尤指粗俗下流的): *a scurrilous rumour, attack, book* 粗俗污秽的流言蜚语、攻击、书 ○ *She was often quite scurrilous in her references to me.* 她一提起我, 常常骂骂咧咧的.

▷ **scur·ril·ity** /skəˈrɪlətɪ; skəˋrɪlətɪ/ *n* (*fml* 文) **1** [U] (**a**) quality of being scurrilous 粗俗下流: *the scurrility of their journalism* 他们新闻内容中使用的淫言秽语. (**b**) scurrilous language 辱骂的语言: *a book full of scurrility and slander* 内容充满辱骂和诽谤的书. **2** [C often *pl* 常作复数] scurrilous remark 辱骂的言辞: *I refused to listen to these scurrilities.* 我不听这些骂人的话.

scur·ril·ously *adv*.

scur·ri·lous·ness *n* [U].

scurry /ˈskʌrɪ; ˋskʌrɪ/ *v* (*pt, pp* **scurried**) [I, Ipr, Ip] run with short quick steps 小步疾跑: *mice scurrying across the floor* 在地面很快跑过的老鼠 ○ *scurry along the road* 在路上匆匆小跑 ○ *They scurried in out of the cold.* 他们冻得很快跑进来了. ○ *Crowds scurried past.* 很多人匆匆地跑过去了. ○ *The rain sent everyone scurrying for shelter.* 这阵雨把大家浇得纷纷找地方躲避.

▷ **scurry** *n* **1** (**a**) [sing] act or sound of scurrying 小步疾跑; 小跑的脚步声: *a/the scurry of feet in the room above* 楼上房间里小跑的脚步声. (**b**) [U] anxious or excited movement; bustle 不安的或兴奋的移动; 热闹的活动: *the scurry and scramble of town life* 城市生活的匆忙. **2** [C] windy shower of rain, snow, etc or cloud of dust; flurry 风雨、风雪等交加; 飞扬的灰尘.

NOTE ON USAGE 用法: **Scamper, scurry** and **scuttle** indicate people or animals running with short, quick steps. ☆ **scamper**、**scurry**、**scuttle**三词均指人或动物小步奔跑. **Scamper (around, away, off, etc)** is only used of small animals (puppies, mice, etc) and children. ☆ **scamper**(**around**、**away**、**off**等)仅用于小动物(小狗、老鼠等)和儿童. It suggests them playing happily or running away when startled 这个词指玩耍嬉戏或受惊逃跑: *The children were scampering around the garden.* 孩子们在花园里嬉戏奔跑. ○ *The rabbits scampered away as we approached.* 我们一走近就把兔子吓跑了. **Scuttle/scurry (about, away, off, etc)** indicate running in order to escape from danger, bad weather, etc ☆ **scuttle/scurry**(**about**、**away**、**off**等)指为躲避危险、坏天气等而奔跑: *The beetle scuttled away when I lifted the stone.* 我把石头搬起来, 那甲虫就逃跑了. ○ *The spectators scurried for shelter as soon as it began to rain.* 一下起雨来, 观众就纷纷找地方躲避. **Scurry** can indicate great or hurried activity ☆ **scurry** 可指重大的或仓促的活动: *We were scurrying about until the last minute before the party.* 聚会开始前我们一直不停地忙忙碌碌.

scurvy /ˈskɜ:vɪ; ˋskɝvɪ/ *n* [U] disease of the blood caused by a lack of vitamin C in the diet 坏血病.

▷ **scurvy** *adj* [attrib 作定语] (*dated sl* 旧, 俚) contemptible; worthless; mean 可鄙的; 无价值的; 卑劣的: *He's a scurvy wretch.* 他是个卑鄙的家伙. ○ *That was a scurvy trick to play on an old lady.* 用那样的花招欺负一个老太太, 可真卑鄙. **scur·vily** /-ɪlɪ; -əlɪ/ *adv*.

scut /skʌt; skʌt/ *n* short upright tail, esp of a hare, rabbit or deer 短而上翘的尾巴(尤指兔或鹿的).

scuttle[1] /ˈskʌtl; ˋskʌtl̩/ *v* [I, Ipr, Ip] run with short quick steps 用小而快的步子跑: *small animals scuttling about* 各处奔跑的小动物. ⇨Usage at SCURRY 用法见 SCURRY.

▷ **scuttle** *n* [sing] act of scuttling 小跑: *a scuttle down the passage* 沿通道小跑.

scuttle[2] /ˈskʌtl; ˋskʌtl̩/ *n* small opening with a lid on a ship's deck or side, or in a roof or wall of a building 舷窗; 天窗; 气窗.

▷ **scuttle** *v* [Tn] sink (a ship) deliberately by opening valves or making holes in its side or bottom 故意将(船)弄沉(凿穿船舷或船底或打开阀门).

scuttle[3] /ˈskʌtl; ˋskʌtl̩/ *n* = COAL-SCUTTLE (COAL).

Scylla /ˈsɪlə; ˋsɪlə/ *n* (idm 习语) **between Scylla and Cha'rybdis** (*fml* 文) faced by a problem or danger that one can only avoid by facing another, equally unpleasant problem or danger 进退维谷.

scythe /saɪð; saɪð/ *n* tool with a slightly curved blade on a long pole, sometimes with two handles, used (esp formerly) for cutting long grass, corn, etc 长柄大镰刀. Cf 参看 SICKLE.

▷ **scythe** *v* [I, Tn, Tn·p] cut (grass, etc) with a scythe (用长柄大镰刀)割(草等): *workers scything in the meadow* 用长柄大镰刀在草地上割草的工人 ○ *scythe the grass (down)* 用长柄大镰刀割草.

SDLP /ˌes di: el ˈpi:; ˌɛs di ɛl ˋpi/ *abbr* 缩写 = (*Brit politics* 政) (in N Ireland) Social and Democratic Labour Party (北爱尔兰的)社会民主工党.

SDP /ˌes di: ˈpi:; ˌɛs di ˋpi/ *abbr* 缩写 = (*Brit politics* 政) Social Democratic Party 社会民主党: *the SDP-Liberal alliance* 社会民主党—自由党联盟.

SE *abbr* 缩写 = South-East(ern): *SE Asia* 东南亚 ○ *London SE9 2BX*, ie as a postal code 伦敦 SE9 2BX(邮政编码).

sea /si:; si/ *n* **1** (often 常作 **the sea**) [U] (also **seas** [pl]) the salt water that covers most of the earth's surface and encloses its continents and islands; any part of this, in contrast to areas of fresh water and dry land 海; 海洋: *fly over land and sea* 飞越陆地海洋 ○ *travel by sea* 乘船过海 ○ *sail the seas* 航海 ○ *the high seas*, ie parts away from the land, where no single country can impose its laws 公海 ○ *the cold sea(s) of the Antarctic* 南极冰冷的海洋 ○ *Most of the earth's surface is covered by (the) sea.* 地球表面大部分是海洋. ○ *Ships sail on the sea.* 轮船能在海上航行. ○ *Fish swim in the sea.* 有些鱼生活在海洋里. ○ *The river flows into the sea near Portsmouth.* 这条河在朴次茅斯附近入海. ○ [attrib 作定语] *a sea animal, fish, voyage* 海洋动物、海鱼、海上航行. **2** (often **Sea**, esp as part of a proper name 常大写作 **Sea**, 尤用于专有名称) [C] (**a**) particular area of the sea, smaller than an ocean 海(比洋小的水域): *the Mediterranean Sea* 地中海 ○ *The Caribbean Sea* 加勒比海 ○ *the South China Sea* 中国的南海. (**b**) large inland lake of fresh water or salt water 内海, 湖(可为淡水或咸水): *the Caspian Sea* 里海 ○ *the Sea of Galilee* 加利利海. **3** [C] (also **seas** [pl]) (state or movement of the) waves of the sea 海浪(的起伏状况): *a heavy/light sea*, ie with big/small waves 浪大的[小的]海面 ○ *The ship was struck by a heavy sea*, ie a large wave. 那艘船遇到了巨浪. ○ *The liner foundered in heavy seas.* 那艘班轮遇到巨大海浪而沉没. **4 ~ of sth** (*fig* 比喻) large amount of sth covering a large area 在大范围中的大量事物: *I stood amid a sea of corn.* 我站在茫茫一片庄稼之中. ○ *The lecturer looked down at the sea of faces beneath him.* 讲演的人俯视着下面无数的面孔. **5** (idm 习语) **at 'sea** (**a**) on a ship, etc on the sea 在海上的轮船等之上: *spend three months at sea* 在海上度过了三个月. (**b**) not knowing what to do; confused 不知所措; 茫然; 糊涂: *I'm all at sea; I've no idea how to repair cars.* 我手足无措, 不知道怎样修理汽车. ○ *She tried to understand the instructions, but she was completely at sea.* 她费尽力气想

看懂那些说明文字，却全然不知所云. **between the devil and the deep blue sea** ⇨ DEVIL[1]. **beyond/over the 'sea(s)** (*fml or rhet* 文或修辞) to or in countries on the other side of a sea or seas; overseas; abroad 到海外; 在海外: *our cousins beyond the seas* 我们那些在海外的表兄弟姐妹. **go to 'sea** be a sailor 当水手. **on the 'sea** at the seaside 在海边; 在海滨: *a town on the sea in Devon* 在德文郡海边的市镇 ○ *Mudford-on-Sea*, ie as a place-name 穆德福特海滨. **put (out) to 'sea** leave port or land travelling on a ship, etc (离港或离岸)出海, 起航. **the seven seas** (*rhet* 修辞) all the seas of the world 七大洋: *He's sailed the seven seas in search of adventure.* 他闯荡七大洋去历险. **there are more/other fish in the sea** ⇨ FISH.

▷ **'sea·ward** /-wəd; -wɚd/ *adj, adv* towards the sea; in the direction of the sea 向海(的).

'sea·wards /-wədz; -wɚdz/ *adv*.

□ **,sea 'air** air at the seaside, thought to be good for the health 海边的空气(认为于健康有益): *a breath of sea air* 呼吸海边的空气.

'sea anemone tube-shaped sea animal with petal-like tentacles round its mouth 海葵.

'sea bed floor of the sea 海底; 海床.

'sea-bird *n* any of several species of bird which live close to the sea, eg on cliffs, islands, etc 海鸟. ⇨ illus at App 1 见附录1插图, page v.

'seaboard *n* coastal region; sea-shore 沿海地区; 海滨; 海岸: *on the Atlantic seaboard* 大西洋沿岸地区.

'sea-borne *adj* (esp of trade) carried in ships (尤指贸易)海运的: *sea-borne commerce, goods, etc* 海运的贸易、货物等 ○ *airborne and sea-borne missiles*, ie carried by aircraft and ships or submarines 机载及海上导弹.

S

'sea-bream *n* = BREAM 2.

'sea-breeze *n* breeze blowing from the sea towards the land, esp during the day, followed by a land-breeze at night 海风(尤指白天刮向内陆的).

'sea-cow *n* type of warm-blooded creature living in the sea and feeding its young with milk 海牛; 儒艮.

'sea-dog *n* old sailor 老水手.

'seafarer /-feərə(r); -,fɛrɚ/ *n* sailor 水手.

'seafaring /-feərɪŋ; -,fɛrɪŋ/ *adj* [attrib 作定语], *n* [U] (of) work or travel on the sea 海上工作或航海(的): *a seafaring man* 海员 ○ *a life of seafaring* 海上生活.

'sea fog fog along the coast, caused by the difference between the temperatures on land and at sea 海雾(因陆海温差所致).

'seafood *n* [U] edible fish or shellfish from the sea 海味: [attrib 作定语] *a 'seafood restaurant* 海味餐厅 ○ *a ,seafood 'cocktail* 海味什锦. **'sea front** part of a town facing the sea (市镇的)滨海区: *a hotel on the sea front* 滨海区的旅馆 ○ [attrib 作定语] *a sea-front restaurant* 滨海餐厅.

'seagoing *adj* [attrib 作定语] **1** (of ships) built for crossing the sea, not for coastal voyages only (指船)适于航海的, 远洋航行的. **2** (of a person) seafaring (指人)以航海为业的.

,sea-'green *adj, n* bluish-green, like the colour of the clean sea 海绿色(的).

'seagull *n* = GULL[1].

'sea-horse *n* small fish with a horse-like head 海马.

,sea-island 'cotton long-stapled cotton of high quality 海岛棉.

'sea-kale *n* coastal plant whose young white shoots are used as a vegetable 海甘蓝.

'sea-legs *n* [pl] ability to walk easily on the deck of a moving ship or to avoid seasickness (航行时)在甲板上行走自如或不晕的能力: *I feel a bit odd; I haven't got my sea-legs yet.* 我稍觉不适, 在船上还走不稳.

'sea-level *n* level of the sea half-way between high and low tide 海平面: *50 metres above/below sea-level* 海拔[低于海平面]50米.

'sea-lion *n* large seal of the N Pacific Ocean 海狮(产于北太平洋).

'Sea Lord (*Brit*) any of the four naval members of the Board of Admiralty 海军部四位海军首长之一.

'seaman /-mən; -mən/ *n* (*pl* **-men** /-mən; -mən/) **1** sailor, esp one in a navy below the rank of an officer 水兵. ⇨ App 9 见附录9. **2** any skilled sailor (熟练的)水手, 海员. **'seamanlike** /-mənlaɪk; -mənl,aɪk/ *adj*.

'seamanship /-mənʃɪp; -mən,ʃɪp/ *n* [U] skill in managing a boat or ship 船舶驾驶术.

'sea mile = NAUTICAL MILE (NAUTICAL).

'sea-pink *n* [U] = THRIFT 2.

'seaplane *n* aircraft designed so that it can take off from and land on water 水上飞机.

'seaport *n* town with a harbour used by seagoing ships 海港市镇.

'sea power **1** [U] ability to control the seas with a strong navy 海军实力. **2** [C] country with a strong navy 海军强国.

'seascape *n* picture of a scene at sea 海景画.

'sea shell shell of any mollusc living in the sea 海贝壳.

'sea-shore *n* [U] **1** land next to the sea 海岸; 海滨: *a walk on/along the sea-shore* 在海滨散步. **2** (*law* 律) area between high and low-water marks 海岸(高潮线与低潮线之间的地带).

'seasick *adj* feeling sick or wanting to vomit as the result of the motion of a ship, etc 晕船的. **'seasickness** *n* [U].

'seaside *n* (often 常作 **the seaside**) [U] land, place, town, etc by the sea, esp a holiday resort 海边, 海滨, 海滨市镇(尤指度假胜地): *two weeks at the seaside* 在海滨的两个星期 ○ *own a house at the seaside* 在海滨有自己的房子 ○ [attrib 作定语] *a seaside town, hotel, holiday* 海滨的市镇、旅馆、度假. ⇨Usage at COAST[1] 用法见COAST[1].

'sea-urchin (also **urchin**) *n* small sea animal with a prickly shell 海胆.

,sea-'wall *n* wall built to stop the sea flowing onto or eroding the land 海堤; 海岸防波堤.

'sea water salt water from the sea 海水.

'sea-way *n* **1** [C] deep inland waterway along which ocean-going ships can sail 海道(海轮可驶入的内陆深水航道). **2** [U] progress by a ship on the sea (海轮的)航进: *The liner made good sea-way because of the fine weather.* 因天气好, 班轮在海上航行顺利.

'seaweed *n* [U, C] plant growing in the sea, esp on rocks at the edge of the sea 海藻, 海草(尤指海边岩石上的).

'seaworthy *adj* (of a ship) in a fit state for a sea voyage (指船)适于航海的: *make a damaged ship seaworthy again* 使损坏的船能再度出海. **'seaworthiness** *n* [U].

seal 海豹

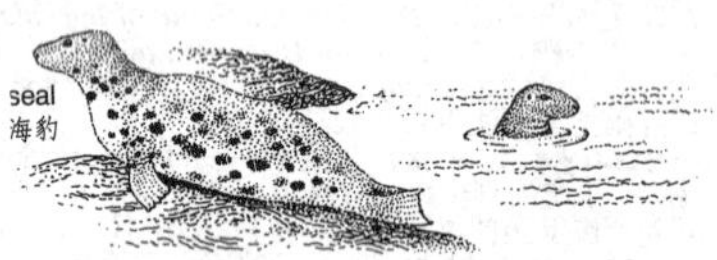

seal[1] /si:l; sil/ *n* animal with flippers that lives near and in the sea and eats fish 海豹.

▷ **seal·ing** *n* [U] hunting seals 捕海豹: [attrib 作定语] *a sealing expedition* 捕海豹之行.

□ **'sealskin** *n* [U] skin or fur of a seal used as clothing material 海豹皮(用作衣料的): [attrib 作定语] *a sealskin jacket* 海豹皮夹克.

seal 封

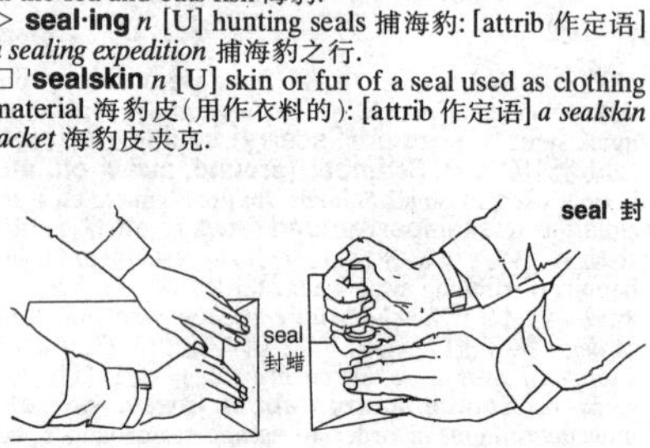

seal[2] /si:l; sil/ *n* **1 (a)** piece of wax, lead or other soft material, usu stamped with a design and fixed to a document to show that it is genuine, or to a letter, packet, container, etc to prevent it being opened by the wrong person; design stamped in this way 封蜡; 封铅; 火漆; 封条; 封印: *The letter bears the seal of the king.* 这封信有国王的封印. **(b)** piece of metal, ring, etc with an engraved design used for stamping a seal 印章; 图章.

⇨ illus 见插图. **2** thing used instead of a seal, eg a paper disc stuck to a document, or an impression stamped on it 代替封印之物(如纸签或印记). **3** (**a**) substance or device used to fill a gap, crack, etc so that gas or fluid cannot enter or escape (用以填充的)密封物质或装置: *a rubber seal in the lid of a jar* 罐子盖儿里的橡皮密封圈 ○ *I've bought a seal to put around the edge of the bath.* 我买了一种密封胶涂在浴缸边缘上. (**b**) closure made by this 密封: *The putty gives a good seal round the window.* 窗户四周泥的油灰密封效果很好. **4** small decorative sticker like a postage stamp, esp one sold in aid of charity 印花贴签(尤指出售以捐助慈善事业的). **5** (idm 习语) **a ˌseal of apˈproval** formal approval 正式认可: *The deal needs the government's seal of approval.* 这一交易需经政府批准. **set the seal on sth** (*fml* 文) be the high point in sth; complete sth 为某事物之顶点; 完成某事物: *This award has set the seal on a successful stage career.* 获此奖标志着舞台生涯成就的顶峰.

▷ **seal** *v* **1** [Tn] put a seal[2] (1,2) on (eg a legal document) 在(尤指法律文件)上加封或盖印. **2** [Tn, Tn·p] (**a**) **~ sth (down)** stick down (an envelope, etc) 粘住(信封等). (**b**) **~ sth (up)** fasten or close sth securely 封住某物: *sealed orders* 密封指令 ○ *seal the parcel (up) with adhesive tape* 用胶带把包裹封住. (**c**) **~ sth (up)** close tightly or put a substance, etc on sth to stop gas or fluid entering or escaping 将某物密封住: *The jar must be well sealed.* 这个罐子得封严实了. ○ *Seal (up) the window to prevent draughts.* 把窗户封起来以防风. **3** [Tn] coat or surface (sth) with a protective substance, sealant, etc 给(某物)加保护层或面, 或涂上密封胶等: *seal the boat's hull with special paint* 给船体涂上特种油漆. **4** [Tn] (*fml* 文) settle (sth); decide 解决(某事物); 决定: *seal a bargain* 成交 ○ *Her fate is sealed,* ie No one can stop what is going to happen to her. 她的命运已定. **5** (idm 习语) **one's lips are sealed** ⇨ LIP. **6** (phr v) **seal sth in** keep sth in by sealing 将某物封住: *Our foil packets seal the flavour in.* 我们用锡纸包装以保持原味. **seal sth off** prevent anybody or anything entering or leaving (an area, etc) 防止某人或某物进入或离开(某范围等): *Police sealed off all the exits from the building.* 警方把建筑物的所有出口都封锁住了.

seal·ant /ˈsiːlənt; ˈsilənt/ *n* [U, C] substance used for waterproofing, stopping leaks, etc 密封胶; 密封剂: *mend the hole and paint some sealant on* 先把洞补好, 再涂上一些密封胶.

□ ˌ**sealed ˈorders** instructions given to an officer in the armed forces in a sealed envelope to be opened at a certain time or place, usu in wartime 密封指令(给军官的命令, 封合于信封内, 在某时或某处方可开启, 通常用于战时).

ˈ**sealing-wax** *n* [U] type of wax that melts quickly when heated and hardens quickly when cooled, used for sealing letters, etc 封蜡; 火漆.

seal·skin ⇨ SEAL[1].

Sea·ly·ham /ˈsiːlɪəm; ˈsilɪəm/ *n* breed of terrier with short legs and wiry hair 锡利哈姆狗.

seam /siːm; sim/ *n* **1** (**a**) line along which two edges, esp of cloth, are joined or sewn together (两边缘相接合的)缝(尤指布的): *the seams down the side of his trousers* 他裤子的边缝. ⇨illus at SEW 见SEW插图. (**b**) line where two edges meet, eg of boards forming a ship's deck (两边缘相接合的)线(如甲板间的). **2** layer, eg of coal, between layers of other materials, eg rock, clay (夹层中的)层(如石层、黏土层之间的煤层); 矿层. **3** line on a surface, eg a wrinkle or scar on skin (物体表面的)纹, 线(如皮肤上的皱纹或伤疤). **4** (idm 习语) **be bursting at the seams** ⇨ BURST[1].

▷ **seam** *v* [Tn] join (two pieces of cloth, etc) by means of a seam 将(两块布等)缝合, 接合.

seamed *adj* **~ (with sth)** having a seam or seams 有接合缝的; 有层的; 有纹的: *seamed stockings* 有接合缝的长袜 ○ *rock seamed with gold* 有金矿层的岩石 ○ *a face seamed with wrinkles* 有皱纹的脸.

seam·less *adj* without a seam(1a)无缝的: *seamless stockings* 无缝长袜.

seam·stress (*Brit* also **sempstress**) /ˈsemstrɪs; ˈsimstrɪs/ *n* woman who sews, esp as a paid job 缝纫女工; 女裁缝.

seamy /ˈsiːmɪ; ˈsimɪ/ *adj* (**-ier, -iest**) unattractive and sordid 难看而污秽的: *the seamy side of life,* ie corruption, crime, etc 生活中丑陋的一面(如腐败、犯罪等) ○ *a seamy bribery scandal* 肮脏的受贿丑闻.

se·ance (also **sé·ance**) /ˈseɪɑːns; ˈseɑns/ *n* meeting, esp of spiritualists, at which people try to talk with the spirits of the dead 降神会(尤指招魂术士的).

sear /sɪə(r); sɪr/ *v* **1** (also **sere**) [Tn] scorch or burn (a surface) 烧灼, 烧焦(物体表面): *a cloth seared by the heat of the oven* 被烤箱烤焦的布 ○ *sear a wound to prevent infection* 烧灼伤口以防感染. **2** [Tn esp passive 尤用于被动语态] (*fig rhet* 比喻, 修辞) affect (sb) with strong emotion 用强烈情感影响(某人): *a soul seared by injustice* 因受到不公平对待而极度痛苦的心灵 ○ *The novel is a searing indictment of urban poverty.* 这部小说是对城市贫困的震撼心灵的控诉.

search /sɜːtʃ; sɝtʃ/ *v* **1** [I, Ipr, Ip, Tn, Tn·pr] **~ (sb/sth) (for sb/sth); ~ through sth (for sth)** empty the pockets, etc of (sb) and examine his body and clothes to see if anything is concealed there; look at, examine or go over (a thing or place) carefully in order to find sb/sth 搜查(某人); 细查(某物或某处)以搜寻某人[某物]; 搜索: *We searched (around) for hours, but couldn't find the book.* 我们(各处)找了半天, 却找不到那本书. ○ *search (the woods) for escaped prisoners* 搜查(树林)寻找逃犯 ○ *search (through) the drawers for the missing papers* 翻遍抽屉寻找遗失的文件 ○ *The police searched her for drugs.* 警察搜查她, 看她身上是否有毒品. ○ (*fig* 比喻) *I searched my memory, but couldn't remember her name.* 我想来想去也想不起她的名字. **2** (idm 习语) **search one's ˈheart/ˈconscience** (*fml* 文) think carefully about one's motives, actions, feelings, etc 反躬自问: *Search your heart and ask if you're not equally to blame.* 你扪心自问是否自己也同样要承担责任. ˌ**search ˈme** (*infml* 口) I don't know 我不知道: *'Where's the newspaper?' 'Search me, I haven't seen it.'* '报纸在哪儿呢?' '不知道, 我没看见.' **3** (phr v) **search sb/sth out** find sb/sth by searching 找出某人[某事物]: *We've searched out some of your favourite recipes.* 我们找出了你喜欢的几个菜谱. ○ *I want to search out an old school friend.* 我想寻找我的一个老同学.

▷ **search** *n* **1** act of searching 搜查; 搜寻: *a search for a missing aircraft* 搜寻失踪的飞机 ○ *make repeated searches for concealed weapons* 反复搜查暗藏的武器 ○ *Volunteers joined the search for the lost child.* 有人自告奋勇也来寻找那失踪的孩子. **2** (idm 习语) **in search of sb/sth** searching for sb/sth 寻找某人[某物]: *go in search of a cheap hotel* 寻找便宜的旅馆 ○ *Scientists are in search of a cure for the disease.* 科学家想研究出治疗这种疾病的方法.

search·ing *adj* (of an examination, a question, etc) keen and penetrating; seeking the truth (指考试、问题等)尖锐而深刻的, 探究的: *She gave me a searching look and asked if I was lying.* 她用锐利的目光看着我, 问我是否说谎了. ○ *a searching interview technique* 面试深入提问技巧. **search·ingly** *adv.*

□ ˈ**searchlight** *n* powerful lamp whose beam can be turned in any direction, used esp to discover enemy aircraft at night 探照灯.

ˈ**search-party** *n* group of people brought together to search for a person or thing 搜索队.

ˈ**search-warrant** *n* official document allowing a building, etc to be searched, eg for stolen property 搜查证; 搜查令.

sea·son /ˈsiːzn; ˈsizn̩/ *n* **1** part of the year distinguished according to its particular type of weather, esp one of the four traditional periods into which the year is divided, ie spring, summer, autumn and winter 季, 季节(尤指四季之一): *the ˈdry/ˈrainy season* 旱季[雨季] ○ *Plants grow fast in the warmest season.* 植物在最暖和的季节生长很快. ○ *Spring is my favourite season.* 春天是我最喜欢的季节. **2** (**a**) time of the year when sth is easily available or common, or when a certain activity takes place (一年中有某事物或有某活动的)时期, 时候; 旺季: *the ˈstrawberry, ˈapple, etc season* 草莓、苹果等当令 ○ *the ˈgrowing season* 生长时期 ○ *the ˈfootball, ˈtheatre, ˈopera, etc season* 足球联赛期、戏剧会演期、歌剧荟萃 ○ *the ˈnesting season,* ie when birds build nests and lay their eggs 筑巢产卵期 ○ *the ˈoff season,* ie (at holiday resorts, etc) the time when there are very few visitors 淡

季 ○ *the* ˈ*holiday*/ˈ*tourist season* 度假[旅游]旺季 ○ *the season of goodwill*, ie Christmas 圣诞节. (**b**) (usu *sing* 通常作单数) (*fml* 文) time of the year during which most fashionable social events are held 社交繁忙时期: *The ball was the highlight of the London season.* 那次舞会是伦敦社交活动时期的高潮. (**c**) series of concerts, plays, etc with a particular theme, eg works by certain artists 系列专题音乐会、戏剧会演等: *a short season of silent film classics on Saturday afternoons* 每星期六下午放映的无声电影经典作品拾零. **3** (idm 习语) **in ˈseason** (**a**) (of food) available in large quantities (指食物)上市, 当令, 在旺季: *Strawberries are cheaper when they're in season.* 草莓当令时便宜些. (**b**) (of a female animal) ready for mating (指雌性动物)在发情期. (**c**) at the time when most people take their holidays 在很多人度假的时期: *Hotels are often full in season.* 在度假旺季, 旅馆经常客满. (**d**) at the time of year when certain animals may be legally hunted 一年中在准许捕猎某些动物的时期: *Grouse will soon be in season again.* 允许捕猎松鸡的时期又快到了. ˌ**out of ˈseason** (**a**) (of food) not in season (指食物)未上市, 不当令, 不在旺季. (**b**) at the time when most people do not take their holidays 在多数人不度假期间: *Holiday prices are lower out of season.* 在度假淡季, 度假费用较低. **the season's ˈgreetings** (used as a greeting at Christmas 用作圣诞节问候语). **the silly season** ⇨SILLY.

▷ **sea·son** *v* **1** [Tn, Tn·pr] **~ sth (with sth)** flavour (food) with salt, pepper, etc (用盐、胡椒等)给(食物)调味: *highly seasoned sauces* 味道很浓的沙司 ○ *lamb seasoned with garlic and rosemary* 用蒜和迷迭香调味的羊肉 ○ (*fig* 比喻) *conversation seasoned with wit* 妙语如珠的谈话. **2** (**a**) [I, Tn] (of wood) become fit for use by exposure to the weather; make (wood) fit for use in this way (指木材)风干后适用; (使木材)风干后适用: *well-seasoned oak, birch, etc* 充分风干可用的栎木、桦木等. (**b**) [Tn esp passive 尤用于被动语态] (*fig* 比喻) make (sb) experienced by practice 使(某人)通过实践而有经验: *a politician seasoned by six election campaigns* 经历六次竞选锻炼而富经验的政治家 ○ *a seasoned boxer, traveller* 有经验的拳击手、旅行者.

□ ˈ**season-ticket** (also *Brit infml* 英式口语作 **season**) *n* ticket that allows a person to make as many journeys, go to as many concerts, etc as he wishes within a specified period 长期票. Cf 参看 COMMUTATION TICKET (COMMUTE).

sea·son·able /ˈsiːznəbl; ˋsiznəbl̩/ *adj* **1** (of the weather) suitable for the time of year (指天气)合时的: *seasonable snow showers* 合时的一阵阵雪. **2** (of help, advice, gifts, etc) coming at the right time; opportune (指帮助、劝告、礼物等)及时的, 合时宜的. ▷ **sea·son·ably** /-nəblɪ; -nəblɪ/ *adv*.

sea·son·al /ˈsiːzənl; ˋsizn̩əl/ *adj* happening during a particular season; varying with the seasons 季节的; 季节性的; 随季节而变化的: *seasonal work*, eg fruit-picking 季节性的工作(如采集水果) ○ *a seasonal trade*, eg selling Christmas cards 节令性的生意(如出售圣诞卡) ○ *a seasonal increase in unemployment* 季节性的失业率增长. ▷ **sea·son·ally** /-nəlɪ; -n̩əlɪ/ *adv*.

sea·son·ing /ˈsiːzənɪŋ; ˋsizənɪŋ/ *n* [U, C] herb, spice, etc used to season food 调味品; 作料: *not enough seasoning in the stew* 炖菜里作料不够 ○ *adventurous seasonings, like paprika and turmeric* 有刺激味的调料, 如辣椒粉和郁金.

seat[1] /siːt; sit/ *n* **1** [C] thing made or used for sitting on, eg a chair, bench or box 坐具或用作坐具之物(如椅子、凳子或箱子): *take a seat*, ie sit down 坐下 ○ *a stone seat in the garden* 花园里的石凳 ○ *The furniture hadn't arrived so we were using crates as seats.* 家具还没运来, 所以我们坐在大木箱上. ○ *The back seat of the car is wide enough for three people.* 汽车的后座很宽, 可以坐三个人. ○ *She rose from her seat to protest.* 她从座位上站起来提出抗议. ⇨illus at App 1 见附录1插图, page xii. **2** [C] that part of a chair, bench, stool, etc on which one sits (contrasted with the back, legs, etc) (椅子、凳子等的)座部: *a chair with a cane seat* 藤座的椅子. **3** [C] (**a**) (*fml* 文) the buttocks 臀部. (**b**) part of a garment covering these 裤子的臀部: *a hole in the seat of his trousers* 他的裤子臀部上的洞. **4** [C] place where one pays to sit in a vehicle or in a theatre, concert-hall, etc (车辆或戏院、音乐厅等的)坐位, 座: *There are no seats left on the flight.* 班机上没有剩余的座位了. ○ *book two seats for the concert* 订两张音乐会的票 ○ *expensive opera seats* 很贵的歌剧票. ⇨Usage at SPACE 用法见SPACE. **5** [C] place as a member of a law-making assembly, council, committee, etc (立法会、议会、委员会等的)席位: *a seat on the council, in Parliament, etc* 议会等的席位 ○ *take one's seat*, ie begin one's duties, eg in the House of Commons 在议会中就职(如在下议院中) ○ *win a/lose one's seat*, ie win/lose a place in a parliament, etc in an election 当选[未再当选]议员 ○ *a majority of 21 seats in the Senate* 在参议院中占21席位的多数. **6** [C] (*esp Brit*) parliamentary constituency 议会议员的选区: *a seat in Devon* 德文郡选区. **7** [C] (*fml* 文) place where sth is based, or where an activity is carried on (某事物或活动的)所在地, 中心: *In the US, Washington is the seat of government and New York City is the chief seat of commerce.* 在美国, 华盛顿是政府所在地, 纽约是主要的商业中心. ○ *seats of learning*, ie universities 学府. **8** [C] (also ˌ**country ˈseat**) (*dated* 旧) large house in the country, usu the centre of a large estate 宅第(通常为大片地产的中心): *the family seat in Norfolk* 在诺福克郡的祖传宅第. **9** [sing] way in which sb sits on a horse 骑马的方式或姿势: *an experienced rider with a good seat* 姿势好的有经验的骑手. **10** (idm 习语) **(drive/fly) by the seat of one's ˈpants** (do sth) by instinct rather than careful thought 凭直觉而不仔细思考(做某事): *None of us had seen an emergency like this and we were all flying by the seat of our pants.* 我们谁都没有遇到过这种紧急情况, 只好凭感觉驾驶飞机. **have a ringside seat** ⇨RINGSIDE (RING[1]). **the hot seat** ⇨HOT. **in the driver's seat** ⇨DRIVER. **take a back seat** ⇨BACK[2].

▷ **-seater** (forming compound *ns* and *adjs* 用以构成复合名词和形容词) (vehicle, etc) with the specified number of seats 有某数量座位的(车辆等): *a* ˌ*ten-seater* ˈ*minibus* 有十个座位的小型公共汽车 ○ *a fast little* ˌ*two-*ˈ*seater*, ie car 速度快的双座汽车.

□ ˈ**seat-belt** (also ˈ**safety-belt**) *n* strap worn as a belt, attached to a seat in an aircraft, car, etc to prevent a passenger being thrown forward if an accident happens (飞机、汽车等的)安全带: *Fasten your seat-belts!* 系好安全带! ⇨illus at App 1 见附录1插图, page xii.

seat[2] /siːt; sit/ *v* **1** [Tn esp passive 尤用于被动语态] (*fml* 文) make (sb/oneself) sit 使(某人[自己])就坐, 坐下: *Seat the boy next to his brother.* 让那个孩子坐在他哥哥旁边. ○ *a statue of a woman seated on a horse* 一个女子骑着马的塑像 ○ *Please be seated, ladies and gentlemen.* 女士们、先生们, 请就座. ○ *She seated herself on the sofa.* 她坐在长沙发上. **2** [Tn] have seats for (a specified number of people) 有(某数量的人)的座位; 可坐(某数量的人): *a hall that seats 500* 可坐500人的大会堂.

▷ **seat·ing** *n* [U] (arrangement of) places to sit; seats 坐位(的安排); 坐位设置: *renew the seating in the theatre* 重新安排戏院的坐位 ○ [attrib 作定语] *seating arrangements* 座位安排 ○ *How much seating room do we have?* 我们有多少可坐的地方?

SEATO /ˈsiːtəʊ; ˋsiˌto/ *abbr* 缩写 = (formerly) South-East Asia Treaty Organization (旧时)东南亚条约组织. Cf 参看 NATO.

se·ba·ceous /sɪˈbeɪʃəs; sɪˋbeʃəs/ *adj* [attrib 作定语] producing an oily or greasy substance 分泌脂质的: *the sebaceous glands in the skin* 皮脂腺 ○ *a sebaceous cyst* 皮脂囊肿.

sec /sek; sɛk/ *n* (*Brit infml* 口) = SECOND[3] 2.

sec *abbr* 缩写 = **1** secondary. **2** secretary.

se·ca·teurs /ˈsekətɜːz, ˌsekəˈtɜːz; ˋsɛkə,tɝz, ˌsɛkəˋtɝz/ *n* [pl] (*Brit*) clippers used for pruning bushes, etc 修枝剪: *a pair of secateurs* 一把修枝剪. ⇨illus at CLIPPERS 见CLIPPERS插图.

se·cede /sɪˈsiːd; sɪˋsid/ *v* [I, Ipr] **~ (from sth)** (*fml* 文) withdraw (from membership of an organization, state, etc) 退出, 脱离(组织等): *the Southern States which seceded from the Union* (ie from the United States) *in 1860-61* 在1860-1861年脱离联邦的南方各州.

▷ **se·ces·sion** /sɪˈseʃn; sɪˋsɛʃən/ *n* [C, U] **~ (from sth)** (*fml* 文) (instance of) seceding 退出; 脱离.

se·clude /sɪˈkluːd; sɪˋklud/ *v* [Tn, Tn·pr] **~ sb/oneself (from sb)** (*fml* 文) keep sb/oneself apart (from others) 使某人[自己](与他人)隔离: *She secludes herself in her study to work.* 她把自己关在书房里埋头研究. ○ *You can't seclude yourself from the world.* 人不能与世隔绝.

▷ **se·c luded** *adj* (**a**) (of a place) not visited or seen by many people (指地方)很少有人去的或见的: *a secluded garden behind high walls* 高墙后面无人去的花园. (**b**) away from the company of others 与他人隔离的: *lead a secluded life* 过离群索居的生活.

se·clu·sion /sɪ'klu:ʒn; sɪ`kluʒən/ *n* [U] (**a**) secluding or being secluded 隔离. (**b**) secluded place; privacy 很少有人去的地方; 私人的范围: *in the seclusion of one's own home* 在家中自己的天地.

sec·ond[1] /'sekənd; `sɛkənd/ *det* **1** 2nd; next after first in time, order, importance, etc 第二的: *February is the second month of the year.* 二月是一年的第二个月份. ○ *Tom is the second son — he has an elder brother.* 汤姆是次子——他有一个哥哥. ○ *Osaka is the second largest city in Japan.* 大阪是日本的第二大城市. ○ *Who was second in the race?* 赛跑谁得了第二名? ⇨App 4 见附录4. Cf 参看 TWO. **2** another after the first; additional; extra (除第一个外)再一个的; 加上的; 额外的: *a second helping of soup* 又一份汤 ○ *You will need a second pair of shoes.* 你需要再有一双鞋. **3** of an inferior or a less important kind 次等的; 次要的: *We never use second quality ingredients.* 我们决不使用次等配料. ○ (*sport* 体) *the second eleven*, ie a team of reserves 后补队. **4** of the same quality, merit, etc as a previous one (与前一个)同样好的: *He thinks he's a second Churchill!* ie believes he has Churchill's abilities. 他认为他是第二个丘吉尔(自信有丘吉尔的才能). **5** (idm 习语) ˌ**second ˈonly to sb/sth** having only one person or thing that is better, more important, etc 仅次于某人或某事物: *He is second only to my own son in my affections.* 我除了爱我的儿子, 最爱他. ˌ**second to ˈnone** as good as the best 不亚于任何人或事物: *As a dancer, he is second to none.* 他的舞艺无出其右. (For other idioms containing **second**, see the other major words in each idiom 查阅其他含有**second**一词的习语, 见该习语中含有其他主要词的词条, 如 **get one's second wind** ⇨WIND[1].)

▷ **sec·ond** *adv* in second place; second in order or importance 以第二位: *The English swimmer came second.* 英国游泳选手得了第二名. ○ *I agreed to speak second.* 我同意让我第二个发言. **sec·ondly** *adv* in the second place; furthermore 第二; 其次: *First(ly), it's too expensive; and secondly, it's very ugly.* 一来太贵, 二来很难看. ⇨Usage at FIRST[2] 用法见 FIRST[2].

□ ˌ**second-ˈbest** *adj* **1** next after the best 仅次于最好的: *my ˌsecond-best ˈsuit* 我的这身套装, 仅次于最好的那套 ○ *the second-best performance of the tournament* 联赛中仅次于最好的那一场. **2** not as good as one would really like 未达到最喜欢的程度的: *I like live music: for me, records are definitely second-best.* 我喜欢现场演奏的音乐, 听唱片可没那么好. **3** (idm 习语) **come off ˌsecond-ˈbest** fail to win; fail to do as well as sb else 未获胜的; 做得不如他人的: *When they have to choose between quality and price, quality usually comes off second-best.* 他们在质量和价格作取舍时, 往往要牺牲质量. — *n* [U] person or thing that is not as good as the best 第二等的人或事物: *I'm used to high quality and won't take second-best.* 我用惯高质量的东西, 差一点儿的都不行. ˌ**second ˈchamber** upper house in a law-making body 议会的上议院. ˌ**second ˈclass** (**a**) standard of accommodation, etc that is of lower quality than first class (住宿等的级别的)二等: [attrib 作定语] *a second-class carriage on the train* 火车的二等车厢. (**b**) category of mail that is given less priority than first-class mail 二等邮件(次于获优先处理的一等邮件): *Second class is cheaper.* 二等邮件较便宜. ○ [attrib 作定语] *ˌsecond-class ˈletters* 二等邮件的信. ˌ**second-ˈclass** *adj* **1** of the second-best group or category 第二等的; 第二级的: *a second-class degree in history* 乙等荣誉历史学位. **2** (*derog* 贬) much less good than the best; second-rate 次等的; 二流的: *a ˌsecond-class hoˈtel* 次等旅馆 ○ *The old are treated as ˌsecond-class ˈcitizens*, ie not as well as other members of society. 老人遭次等公民待遇. — *adv*: *go/travel second-class* 乘坐二等车 ○ *It takes longer if you send it second-class.* 按二等邮件寄, 花的时间长.

the ˌ**second ˈcoming** the return of Jesus Christ at the Last Judgement 基督复临(最后审判时).

ˌ**second ˈcousin** child of one of one's parents' first cousins or first cousin of one of one's parents 父或母的堂或表兄弟姐妹的子女; 父或母的堂或表兄弟姐妹. Cf 参看 COUSIN.

ˌ**second-deˈgree** *adj* [attrib 作定语] (of burns) of the type that is next to the most serious (指烧伤)二度的.

ˌ**second ˈfloor** floor above the first (in Britain two floors, in US one floor, above the ground) 三楼(英国用法); 二楼(美国用法): [attrib 作定语] *a ˌsecond-floor aˈpartment* 二楼的一套公寓.

ˌ**second-ˈguess** *v* [Tn] (*esp US infml* 口) **1** comment on or criticize (an action, a decision, etc) after its results have become clear (事后)评论或批评(某行动、决定等): *It's easy to second-guess the casting of the film*, eg say that the wrong actors were chosen. 事后指摘影片选角不当确很容易. **2** make a better guess than (sb) 比(某人)猜得准: *The papers have all been trying to second-guess each other about the President's next move.* 各报一直在竞相猜测总统的下一步行动. **3** guess (what is going to happen) 猜测(要发生的事): *Don't try to second-guess the outcome.* 不要猜测结果.

ˌ**second-ˈhand** *adj, adv* **1** previously owned by sb else 二手(的)(曾属于他人的): *a ˌsecond-hand ˈcar, ˈsuit, ˈcamera* 二手的汽车、套装、照相机 ○ *a ˌsecond-hand ˈbookshop*, ie a shop selling second-hand books 旧书店 ○ *I rarely buy anything second-hand.* 我很少买二水货. **2** (of news, information, etc) obtained from others, not from personal experience, etc (指新闻、信息等)二手(的), 得自他人(的): *ˌsecond-hand ˈgossip* 辗转听到的流言蜚语 ○ *get news second-hand* 间接得到的消息.

ˌ**second lieuˈtenant** army officer next below lieutenant 陆军少尉. ⇨App 9 见附录9.

ˌ**second-ˈrate** *adj* of poor quality; not very good 二流的; 次等的; 劣质的: *a ˌsecond-rate ˈactor, ˈscript, perˈformance* 二流的演员、剧本、表演 ○ *His novels are very second-rate.* 他写的小说很不怎么样.

ˌ**second ˈsight** ability to know what is going to happen, or to see events happening far away (as if one were present) 预知未来或见到遥远事物的能力.

ˌ**second-ˈstring** *adj* [attrib 作定语] (of a sports player) being a substitute, rather than a regular player (指运动员)替补的.

sec·ond[2] /'sekənd; `sɛkənd/ *n, pron* **1 the second** [sing] person or thing that comes next after the first 第二个人或事物: *the second of May* 五月二日 ○ *George the Second*, ie King George II 乔治二世 ○ *I was the first to arrive, and she was the second.* 我是第一个到的, 她是第二个. **2** [sing] person or thing additional to one already mentioned 另一个人或事物: *She published her first book last year, and has now written a second.* 她去年出版了第一本书, 现在写了第二本. ○ *You're the second to ask me that.* 你是第二个问我这件事的人. **3** [C] **~ (in sth)** (*Brit*) second-class university degree 大学的乙等荣誉学位: *get an upper, a lower second (in economics)* 获得(经济学的)乙等一级、乙等二级荣誉学位. **4** [U] second gear on a car, bicycle, etc (汽车、自行车等的)二挡: *Are you in first or second?* 你用的是一挡还是二挡? ○ *Change from second to third.* 从二挡换到三挡. **5** [C usu *pl* 通常作复数] manufactured article that has a fault and is therefore sold cheaper 剔装货: *These plates are seconds.* 这些盘子是剔装货. **6 seconds** [pl] second helping of food 第二份食物: *I'm going to ask for seconds.* 我想再要一份吃的. **7** [C] person who assists a boxer or sb fighting a duel (拳击者或决斗者的)助手.

□ ˌ**second in comˈmand** person next below the commanding officer, most senior official, etc in rank 级别仅次于指挥官、最高级负责人等的人: *the sales director and her second in command* 销售部经理和她的助理.

sec·ond[3] /'sekənd; `sɛkənd/ *n* **1** (*symb* 符号为 ″) 60th part of a minute of time or of angular measurement (时间或角度计量单位的)秒: *The winning time was 1 minute 5 seconds.* 获胜的时间是1分零5秒. ○ *1°6′10″*, ie one degree, six minutes, and ten seconds (1度6分10秒). ⇨App 4, 5, 11 见附录4、5、11. **2** (also *Brit infml* 英式口语作 **sec**) short time; moment 一会儿; 片刻: *I'll be ready* *in a sec(ond).* 我马上就准备好. ○ *The food was on the table in seconds.* 吃的东西一转眼就摆在桌上了.

□ **'second hand** hand on some watches and clocks that records seconds 秒针. Cf 参看 SECOND-HAND (SECOND[1]).

sec·ond[4] /'sekənd; `sɛkənd/ *v* [Tn] **1** support or assist (sb), esp in a boxing-match or duel 支持或协助(某人)(尤指拳击比赛或决斗中): *I was ably seconded in this research by my son.* 在这项研究中, 我儿子帮了我很大忙. **2** formally support (a motion, resolution, etc already proposed by sb else) to show that he is not the only person in favour of it 附议(某动议、决议等): *Mrs Smith proposed the vote of thanks, and Mr Jones seconded (it).* 史密斯夫人提议大家鼓掌表示感谢, 琼斯先生附议. ○ (*joc* 谑) *'Let's go away this weekend.' 'I'll second that.'* '咱们本周末离开吧.' '我同意.' Cf 参看 PROPOSE 1.

▷ **sec·onder** *n* person who seconds a motion, resolution, etc 赞成某动议、决议等的人; 附议者. Cf 参看 PROPOSER (PROPOSE).

se·cond[5] /sɪ'kɒnd; sɪ`kɑnd/ *v* [Tn, Tn·pr] **~ sb (from sth) (to sth)** (*esp Brit*) transfer (sb) from his normal duties to other duties 调任, 调派(某人)做其他工作: *an officer seconded from the Marines to staff headquarters* 从海军陆战队调往总参谋部的军官. ▷ **se·cond·ment** *n* [C, U]: *a two-month secondment* 两个月的借调 ○ *an officer on secondment* (ie seconded) *overseas* 调往海外的军官.

sec·ond·ary /'sekəndrɪ; *US* -derɪ; `sɛkən,dɛrɪ/ *adj* **1 ~ (to sth)** coming after sth that is first or primary; of less importance, value, etc than what is primary 第二的; 次要的: *Such considerations are secondary to our main aim of improving efficiency.* 对于我们提高效率的主要目的来说, 这些想法都是次要的. ○ *Her age is of secondary interest.* 她的年龄不太重要. ○ *secondary stress*, eg on the first syllable of ',sacri'ficial' 次重音 ○ *secondary picketing*, eg of a company that is thought to be helping the employers of the workers on strike 第二纠察线(协助罢工工人的雇主的). **2** dependent on, caused by or derived from sth that is original or primary 从属的; 引伸出的; 次生的; 继发性的: *secondary literature*, eg criticism or reviews of an author's work 二次文献(如对某作者作品的评论) ○ *a secondary colour*, ie one produced by mixing two primary colours 二次色(由两原色混合而成的) ○ *a secondary infection*, ie one which occurs as a result of another illness 继发感染. **3** [attrib 作定语] following primary or (in the US) elementary or junior high schools 中等教育的: *a secondary school* 中学 ○ *secondary education* 中等教育. Cf 参看 PRIMARY. ▷ **sec·ond·ar·ily** /-drəlɪ; *US* ,sekən'derəlɪ; ,sɛkən`dɛrəlɪ/ *adv*.

se·crecy /'si:krəsɪ; `sikrəsɪ/ *n* **1** [U] keeping secrets; ability or tendency to keep secrets; state of being secret 保密; 保密能力: *rely on sb's secrecy* 信赖某人的保密能力 ○ *his obsessive secrecy about his work* 他对工作的强迫性保密观念 ○ *The meeting was arranged with the utmost secrecy*, ie very secretly. 会议绝对保密. ○ *the secrecy that still surrounds the accident* 对该事故仍讳莫如深. **2** (idm 习语) **swear sb to secrecy** ⇨SWEAR.

se·cret /'si:krɪt; `sikrɪt/ *adj* **1 ~ (from sb)** kept or intended to be kept from the knowledge or view of others; not known by others 秘密的; 保密的; 机密的: *a secret marriage, document, meeting* 秘密结婚、文件、会议 ○ *keep sth secret from one's family* 不让家人知道某事 ○ *She escaped through a secret door.* 她通过暗道逃走了. ○ *The party was given secret financial support by some foreign backers.* 该党得到外国一些支持者的秘密资助. **2** [attrib 作定语] not openly declared or admitted 不公开说的; 不公开承认的: *I'm a secret fan of soap operas on TV.* 我从不声张我是电视连续剧迷. **3** [attrib 作定语] (of a place) secluded or quiet (指地方)人迹罕至的, 幽静的: *my secret cottage in the country* 我在郊野的寂静小舍. **4** [esp pred 尤作表语] (*fml* 文) fond of keeping secrets; secretive 爱保密.

▷ **se·cret** *n* **1** fact, decision, etc that is or must be kept secret 秘密; 机密: *keep a secret*, ie not tell it to anyone else 保守秘密 ○ *The wedding date's a big secret.* 举行婚礼的日期是一大秘密. ○ *Are you going to let him in on* (ie tell him) *the secret?* 你想让他知道这个秘密吗? ○ *He made no secret of his dislike for me*, ie made it very clear. 他并不讳言他不喜欢我. **2** method of doing or achieving sth that not many people know 秘诀; 诀窍; 窍门: *the secret of success* 成功的秘诀 ○ *What's your secret for this wonderful pastry?* 你做的酥馅饼真好, 有什么诀窍? **3** anything not properly understood or difficult to understand; mystery 奥秘; 神秘的事物: *the secrets of nature* 自然界的奥秘. **4** (idm 习语) **in 'secret** without others knowing 偷偷的; 暗地的: *meet in secret* 私下会见 ○ *leave the country in secret* 秘密去国. **in the 'secret** (*dated* 旧) among those who know the secret 知道秘密或内情: *Is your brother in the secret?* 你哥哥知道内情吗? **an open secret** ⇨OPEN[1]. **se·cretly** *adv*.

□ **,secret 'agent** (also **agent**) person working secretly for a government and trying to find out secret information, esp the military secrets of another government; spy 特工人员; 特务; 间谍.

,secret po'lice police force that works in secret to ensure that citizens behave as their government wants 秘密警察.

,secret 'service government department dealing with espionage and counter-espionage 特务机关.

sec·ret·ariat /,sekrə'teərɪət; ,sɛkrə`tɛrɪət/ *n* **1** administrative department of a large organization 秘书处; 书记处. **2** staff or office of a Secretary-General or of a government Secretary 秘书长、国务大臣或国务卿的全体工作人员或办公厅: *the UN secretariat in New York* 在纽约的联合国秘书处.

sec·ret·ary /'sekrətrɪ; *US* -rəterɪ; `sɛkrə,tɛrɪ/ *n* **1** employee in an office, usu working for another person, dealing with letters, typing, filing, etc and making appointments and arrangements 秘书; 书记: *I sometimes think my secretary runs the firm.* 我有时认为是我的秘书经管着公司. **2** official of a club, society, etc who deals with its correspondence, records, or business affairs (俱乐部、协会等的)干事, 文书. **3 Secretary (a)** = SECRETARY OF STATE. **(b)** (*Brit*) senior Civil Servant 高级文职官员. **(c)** (*US*) head of a government department 部长: *Secretary of the Treasury* 财政部长.

▷ **sec·ret·arial** /,sekrə'teərɪəl; ,sɛkrə`tɛrɪəl/ *adj* of (the work of) secretaries 秘书(的工作)的: *secretarial staff, duties, training, colleges* 任秘书的工作人员、秘书工作、秘书培训、秘书专科学校.

□ **,Secretary-'General** *n* (*pl* **Secretaries-General**) chief official in charge of a large organization (eg the UNO) 秘书长(如联合国的).

,Secretary of 'State 1 (also **Secretary, minister**) (*Brit*) head of one of the major government departments 大臣: *the Secretary of State for Home Affairs, Defence, etc* 内政、国防等大臣 ○ *the Home, Defence, etc Secretary* 内政、国防等大臣. **2** (*US*) head of the Foreign Affairs department 国务卿.

se·crete /sɪ'kri:t; sɪ`krit/ *v* (*fml* 文) **1** [Tn] (of an organ) produce (a substance, usu liquid) either as waste material or for use within the body (指器官)分泌(某物质): *The kidneys secrete urine.* 肾脏是分泌尿液的器官. ○ *Saliva is secreted by glands in the mouth.* 唾液是由口腔的唾液腺分泌出来的. **2** [Tn, Tn·pr] put or keep (sth) in a secret place; hide 隐藏(某物); 藏匿: *money secreted in a drawer* 藏在抽屉里的钱.

▷ **se·cre·tion** /sɪ'kri:ʃn; sɪ`kriʃən/ *n* (*fml* 文) **1** [U] secreting (SECRETE 1) or being secreted 分泌: *the secretion of bile by the liver* 肝脏分泌出的胆汁. **2** [C] substance that is secreted, eg saliva, bile, etc 分泌物(如唾液、胆汁等). **3** [U] secreting (SECRETE 2) or being secreted 隐藏; 藏匿.

se·cret·ive /'si:krətɪv; `sikrətɪv/ *adj* liking to keep things secret or to hide one's thoughts, feelings, etc 爱保密的; 爱把思想、感情等深藏不露的: *a secretive nature* 事事保密的天性. ▷ **se·cret·ively** *adv*. **se·cret·ive·ness** *n* [U].

sect /sekt; sɛkt/ *n* (*sometimes derog* 有时作贬义) group of people who share (esp religious) beliefs or opinions which differ from those of most people 派别; 宗派; (尤指)教派: *a minor Christian sect* 基督教的一个小教派.

sect *abbr* 缩写 = section (esp of a document) 条, 款, 项(尤指文件的): *clause 3 sect 2* 第3条第2款.

sec·tar·ian /sek'teərɪən; sɛk`tɛrɪən/ *adj* **1** of a sect or sects 派别的; 宗派的; (尤指)教派的: *sectarian violence*, ie between members of different religious sects 教派之

间的暴力斗争. **2** (*derog* 贬) showing a lack of tolerance or concern for those outside one's own sect, class, etc 派性的; 闹宗派的: *sectarian views* 派性观点 ○ *Sectarian politics are ruining the country's economy.* 派系政治危害着国家的经济.

▷ **sec·tari·an·ism** /-ɪzəm; -ɪzəm/ *n* [U] (*often derog* 常作贬义) tendency to split up into sects; tendency to be sectarian(2) 宗派主义.

sec·tion /ˈsekʃn; ˋsɛkʃən/ *n* **1** [C] any of the parts into which sth may be or has been divided 部分: *This section of the road is closed.* 这段路已经封闭. ○ *White lines divide the playing area into sections.* 这些白线把赛区分成各个部分. ○ *the practical sections of the course* 该课程的实践部分. **2** [C] any one of a number of parts that can be fitted together to make a structure 部件; 零件: *the three sections of a fishing-rod* 钓鱼杆的三节 ○ *The shed comes in sections that you assemble yourself.* 这个棚子有几个部分, 要由自己组装起来. **3** [C] separate group within a body of people 集体中的小团体; 小集团: *Farm workers make up only a small section of the population.* 农民只占人口的一小部分. ○ *a discontented section of the army* 军队里心怀不满的人. **4** [C] department of an organization, institution, etc (组织、机构等的)部门, 处, 科, 组, 股: *the library's extensive biology section* 图书馆中有大量图书的生物学部 ○ *the woodwind section of the orchestra*, ie players of woodwind instruments 乐队中的木管乐组. **5** [C] separate part of a document, book, etc (文件、书等的)节, 款, 项, 段: *section 4, subsection 2 of the treaty* 条约中的第4节第2小节 ○ *the financial section of the newspaper* 报纸上的金融栏 ○ *The report has a section on accidents at work.* 报告中有一段谈到工作中的事故问题. **6** [C] (**a**) (*US*) piece of land one mile square, equal to 640 acres (about 260 hectares) 一平方英里的面积(等于640英亩或约260公顷). (**b**) (*esp US*) area of a town 市镇的范围; 市区: *the business, residential, shopping section* 商业区、住宅区、购物区. **7** [C] view or representation of sth seen as if cut straight through from top to bottom 纵剖面; 纵断面; 纵切面: *This illustration shows a section through the timber.* 本图所示为木材的纵剖面. **8** (*medical* 医) (**a**) [U] process of cutting or separating sth surgically 切除; 切开: *the section of a diseased organ* 切除患病器官. (**b**) [C] piece cut or separated in this way 切除或切开的部分; 切片: *put a section of tissue under the microscope* 把组织的切片放在显微镜下.

▷ **sec·tion** *v* **1** [Tn, Tn·pr] divide (sth) into sections 将(某物)分成部分: *a library sectioned into subject areas* 按科目划分的图书馆. **2** [Tn] (*medical* 医) cut or separate (tissue, etc) 切除或切开(组织等).

sec·tional /-ʃənl; -ʃənl̩/ *adj* **1** made or supplied in sections (SECTION 2) 组装的; 组合的: *a sectional fishing-rod* 分节的钓鱼杆 ○ *sectional furniture* 组合家具. **2** [usu attrib 通常作定语] of a group or groups within a community, etc 社会中某群体的: *sectional interests*, ie the different and often conflicting interests of various parts of the community 不同群体的利益 ○ *sectional jealousies, rivalry, etc* 不同群体之间的倾轧、竞争等.

sec·tion·al·ism /-ʃənəlɪzəm; -ʃənl̩ˌɪzəm/ *n* [U] (*usu derog* 通常作贬义) too much concern for the good of one's own section of the community, rather than that of everybody 本位主义.

sec·tor /ˈsektə(r); ˋsɛktɚ/ *n* **1** part of a circle lying between two straight lines drawn from the centre to the circumference 扇形. ⇨ illus at CIRCLE 见 CIRCLE 插图. **2** part or branch of a particular area of activity, esp of a country's economy (活动领域的)部门; (尤指)经济领域: *the manuˈfacturing sector*, ie all the manufacturing industries of a country 制造业 ○ *the ˈservice sector*, eg hotels, restaurants, etc 服务性行业. **3** any of the parts of a battle area, or of an area under military control 战区; 防区: *an enemy attack in the southern sector* 敌军对南部战区的进攻.

secu·lar /ˈsekjʊlə(r); ˋsɛkjəlɚ/ *adj* **1** not concerned with spiritual or religious affairs; worldly 现世的; 世俗的: *secular education, art, music* 世俗教育、艺术、音乐 ○ *the secular power*, ie the State contrasted with the Church 政权(非教会之权). **2** (of priests) not belonging to a community of monks (指教士)不属修道院的: *the secular clergy*, ie parish priests, etc 教区神职人员.

▷ **secu·lar·ism** /-lərɪzəm; -lərˌɪzəm/ *n* [U] belief that morality, education, etc should not be based on religion 现世主义; 世俗主义. **secu·lar·ist** /-lərɪst; -lərɪst/ *n* believer in or supporter of secularism 现世主义者; 世俗主义者.

secu·lar·ize, -ise /-ləraɪz; -lərˌaɪz/ *v* [Tn] (*fml* 文) make (sth) secular 使(某事物)现世化, 世俗化: *secularize church property, courts, education* 使教会财产、法院、教育不受教会控制 ○ *Is the country more secularized nowadays?* 现在该国的宗教影响力减弱了吗?

se·cure /sɪˈkjʊə(r); sɪˋkjʊr/ *adj* **1 ~ (about sth)** not feeling worry, doubt, etc 无忧虑的; 无疑虑的: *feel secure about one's future* 对自己的前途无忧无虑 ○ *a secure faith, belief, etc* 明确的信仰、信念. **2** not likely to be lost or to fail; certain; guaranteed 有把握的; 确切的; 有保证的: *a secure investment* 无风险的投资 ○ *have a secure job in the Civil Service* 在政府部门有一份稳定的工作 ○ *Her place in the history books is secure.* 她一定名垂青史. **3** firmly fixed; not likely to fall, be broken, etc; reliable 牢固的; 稳固的; 可靠的: *A climber needs secure footholds.* 攀登的人脚踩的地方要很牢固. ○ *Is that ladder secure?* 那个梯子安全吗? **4 ~ (against/from sth)** (*fml* 文) safe; protected 安全的; 受保护的: *The strong-room is as secure as we can make it.* 我们的保险库建造得十分安全. ○ *Are we secure from attack here?* 我们这里受不到攻击吧? ○ *When you're insured, you're secure against loss.* 只要买了保险就不会遭受损失.

▷ **se·cure** *v* **1** [Tn] fix (sth) firmly; fasten 将(某物)固定住; 缚住; 系住: *Secure all the doors and windows before leaving.* 要把所有门窗关好再出门. ○ *secure the ladder with ropes* 用绳子把梯子捆好. **2** [Tn, Tn·pr] **~ sth (against/from sth)** make sth safe; protect 使某事物安全; 保护: *secure a building (from collapse)* 将建筑物加固(以免倒塌) ○ *Can the town be secured against attack?* 能保护这个市镇不受攻击吗? ○ (*fig* 比喻) *The new law will secure the civil rights of the mentally ill.* 这一新法则可保障精神病患者享有公民权. **3** [Tn, Dn·n, Dn·pr] **~ sth (for sb/sth)** (*fml* 文) obtain sth, sometimes with difficulty 得到某事物(有时有困难): *We'll need to secure a bank loan.* 我们需获银行贷款. ○ *They've secured government backing* (for the project). 他们得到政府(对该计划)的支持.

se·curely *adv*.

se·cur·ity /sɪˈkjʊərətɪ; sɪˋkjʊrətɪ/ *n* **1** [U] freedom or protection from danger or worry 安全; 保护; 保障: *children who lack the security of a good home* 缺乏良好家庭照顾的儿童 ○ *have the security of a guaranteed pension* 有保证可获养老金的保障. **2** [U] measures taken to prevent spying, attacks, theft, etc (防刺探、攻击、偷盗等的)安全措施: *There was tight security for the Pope's visit*, eg Many police officers guarded him. 为教皇到访采取了严密的保安措施. ○ *We need greater security in car parks.* 我们需要加强停车场的安全措施. ○ *national security*, ie the defence of a country 国家的防卫 ○ [attrib 作定语] *security forces*, eg police, troops, etc fighting terrorism 保安部队 ○ *a security van*, eg for transporting money 保安车(如解送金钱的) ○ *a high security prison*, ie for dangerous criminals 戒备森严的监狱. **3** [C, U] jewellery, insurance policies, etc that can be used to guarantee that one will pay back borrowed money or keep a promise 抵押品: *lend money on security*, ie in return for sth given as security 收取抵押品贷出款项 ○ *give sth as (a) security* 以某物作抵押. Cf 参看 GUARANTEE[1] 1. **4 securities** [pl] documents or certificates showing who owns stock, bonds, shares, etc 证券: *government securities*, ie for money lent to a government 政府证券.

□ **the Seˈcurity Council** the permanent peace-keeping body of the United Nations, with five permanent and ten elected members (联合国)安全理事会.

seˈcurity risk person who, because of his political beliefs, personal habits, etc may endanger the security of the state, eg by revealing secrets to an enemy (威胁国家安全的)危险人物: *She's a poor/good security risk.* 她是个不太[十分]危险的人.

seˈcurity guard guard who wears a uniform and

S

provides protection, eg in a public building or when money is being moved between banks 保安人员; 护卫员.

se·dan /sɪˈdæn; sɪˈdæn/ *n* **1** = SALOON 4. **2** (also **se,dan-ˈchair**) box containing a seat for one person, carried on poles by two people, esp in the 17th and 18th centuries 轿子(尤指17及18世纪的).

sed·ate[1] /sɪˈdeɪt; sɪˈdet/ *adj* (of a person or his behaviour) calm and dignified; composed (指人或人的行为)安静的, 庄重的, 镇静的, 沉着的. ▷ **sed·ately** *adv*. **sed·ate·ness** *n* [U].

sed·ate[2] /sɪˈdeɪt; sɪˈdet/ *v* [Tn] (*medical* 医) give (sb) a drug that calms the nerves or reduces stress 给(某人)镇静剂.

▷ **seda·tion** /sɪˈdeɪʃn; sɪˈdeʃən/ *n* [U] sedating or being sedated; condition resulting from being sedated 镇静作用; 镇静状态: *the sedation of a hysterical patient* 癔病患者用药后的镇静状态 ○ *under (heavy) sedation* 在(大剂量的)镇静剂的作用下.

sed·at·ive /ˈsedətɪv; ˈsɛdətɪv/ *n* drug or medicine that sedates 镇静药: *give sb a sedative* 给某人镇静剂. Cf 参看 TRANQUILLIZER (TRANQUIL). — *adj* [usu attrib 通常作定语]: *a sedative drug, injection, etc* 镇静药、镇静注射剂.

sed·ent·ary /ˈsedntrɪ; *US* -terɪ; ˈsɛdn̩,tɛrɪ/ *adj* **1** (of work) done sitting down (指工作)坐着做的: *a sedentary job, occupation, etc* 坐着做的工作、坐着做工作的职业. **2** (of people) spending a lot of time seated (指人)久坐的: *a sedentary worker* 工作上需要久坐的人 ○ *lead a sedentary life* 过着久坐不动的生活.

sedge /sedʒ; sɛdʒ/ *n* [U] grass-like plant growing in marshes or near water 莎草; 蔗草.

S

▷ **sedgy** *adj* covered or bordered with sedge 长着莎草或蔗草的; 周围有莎草或蔗草的.

sedi·ment /ˈsedɪmənt; ˈsɛdəmənt/ *n* [U] **1** matter that settles to the bottom of a liquid 沉淀物: *a wine with a gritty sediment* 有沙粒状沉淀物的葡萄酒. **2** matter (eg sand, gravel, mud, etc) carried by water or wind and deposited on the surface of the land 沉积物(如沙、砾石、泥等).

▷ **sedi·ment·ary** /ˌsedɪˈmentrɪ; ˌsɛdəˈmɛntərɪ/ *adj* of or like sediment; formed from sediment (似)沉淀物的; 由沉淀物形成的: *sedimentary rocks*, eg sandstone, limestone, slate 沉积岩(如砂岩、石灰岩、板岩).

sedi·menta·tion /ˌsedɪmenˈteɪʃn; ˌsɛdəmɛnˈteʃən/ *n* [U] (*geology* 地质) process of depositing sediment 沉淀; 沉积.

se·di·tion /sɪˈdɪʃn; sɪˈdɪʃən/ *n* [U] words or actions intended to make people rebel against the authority of the State 煽动叛乱的言论或行动: *speeches advocating open sedition* 鼓动公开叛乱的讲话.

▷ **se·di·tious** /sɪˈdɪʃəs; sɪˈdɪʃəs/ *adj* of, causing or spreading sedition 煽动性的; 叛乱性的: *seditious actions, speeches, writings, etc* 煽动性的行为、言语、文字等. **se·di·tiously** *adv*.

se·duce /sɪˈdjuːs; *US* -ˈduːs; sɪˈdus/ *v* **1** [Tn] tempt (esp sb younger or less experienced) to have sexual intercourse 引诱(尤指年轻或无经验的人)性交: *He's trying to seduce his secretary.* 他竭力勾引他的秘书. ○ (*fig* 比喻) *Men are seduced* (ie charmed) *by her beauty and wit.* 她才貌双全倾倒众生. **2** [Tn, Tn·pr] **~ sb (from sth); ~ sb (into sth/doing sth)** (*fml* 文) persuade sb to do sth wrong, or sth he would not normally do, esp by offering sth desirable as a reward, etc 唆使某人做坏事或不至于做的事(尤指提供好处): *I won't be seduced from my duty.* 我不会受人怂恿做渎职的事. ○ *Higher salaries are seducing many teachers into industry.* 在高薪利诱之下, 许多教师改行进入工业界. ○ *I let myself be seduced into buying a new car.* 我情不自禁买了一辆新汽车.

▷ **se·du·cer** *n* person who seduces sb, esp into sexual intercourse 引诱者, 勾引者(尤指为性交).

se·duc·tion /sɪˈdʌkʃn; sɪˈdʌkʃən/ *n* **1** [C, U] (act of) seducing or being seduced 引诱; 勾引: *the art of seduction* 诱惑之术 ○ *her seduction by an older man* 她受到年纪较大男子的勾引. **2 seductions** [pl] (*fml* 文) charming or attractive features 诱惑力; 吸引力: *the seductions of country life* 田园生活的魅力.

se·duct·ive /sɪˈdʌktɪv; sɪˈdʌktɪv/ *adj* tending to seduce, charm or tempt sb; attractive 诱人的; 有魅力的; 有吸引力的: *a seductive woman, smile, look* 有魅力的女子、微笑、样子 ○ *This offer of a high salary and a free house is very seductive.* 这种高薪加免费住房的条件十分诱人. ▷ **se·duct·ively** *adv*. **se·duct·ive·ness** *n* [U].

sedu·lous /ˈsedjʊləs; *US* ˈsedʒʊləs; ˈsɛdʒələs/ *adj* (*fml* 文) showing much hard work, steady effort or care 勤勉的; 不懈的; 细心的: *a sedulous researcher, journalist, etc* 勤奋的研究人员、新闻工作者等 ○ *sedulous work, study, etc* 细心的工作、研究等 ○ *pay sedulous attention to details* 一丝不苟. ▷ **sedu·lously** *adv*.

see[1] /siː; si/ *v* (*pt* **saw** /sɔː; sɔ/, *pp* **seen** /siːn; sin/)

▸ USING THE EYES 见到 **1** [Tn, Tf, Tw, Tng, Tni] (not in the continuous tenses 不用于进行时态) become aware of (sb/sth) by using the eyes; perceive 看见(某人[某物]); 察觉: *He looked for her but couldn't see her in the crowd.* 他寻找她, 但人群中看不见有她. ○ *I looked out of the window but saw nothing.* 我向窗外望去, 什么也没看见. ○ *He could see (that) she had been crying.* 他察觉到她哭过. ○ *If you watch carefully you will see how I do it/how it is done.* 你要是仔细观察, 就能看出我是怎么做的[这是怎么做的]. ○ *Did you see what happened?* 你看见有什么事了吗? ○ *I hate to see you so unhappy*, ie in such an unhappy state. 我可不愿意看见你这么不高兴. ○ *She was seen running away from the scene of the crime.* 有人看见她从犯罪现场跑开. ○ *I saw him put the key in the lock, turn it and open the door.* 我看见他把钥匙插进锁孔、转动钥匙, 然后打开了门. ○ *She was seen to enter the building about the time the crime was committed.* 有人看见她约在案发时进入了该建筑物. **2** [I, Ipr, Ip] (not usu in the continuous tenses; often used with *can* and *could* 通常不用于进行时态, 常与can和could连用) have or use the power of sight 看; 看见: *If you shut your eyes you can't see.* 要是把眼睛闭上就什么也看不见了. ○ *On a clear day you can see for miles from the top of the tower.* 天气晴朗时, 从塔顶上能看到很远的地方. ○ *It was getting dark and I couldn't see to read.* 天渐渐黑了, 我看不见字, 无法再阅读了. ○ *She'll never (be able to) see again*, ie She has become blind. 她再也看不见东西了(她失明了). ○ *Move out of the way, please: I can't see through you!* 请借光, 你挡着我就看不见了! ⇨Usage at FEEL[1] 用法见 FEEL[1].

▸ LOOKING AT 观看 **3** [Tn] (not usu in the continuous tenses 通常不用于进行时态) look at or watch (sth)看(某物): *In the evening we went to see a film.* 晚上我们去看了一场电影. ○ *Have you seen the new production of 'Hamlet' at the Playhouse?* 你在大剧院看过新排演的《哈姆雷特》吗? ○ *Fifty thousand people saw the match.* 有五万人观看了这场比赛. **4** [Tn] (only in the imperative 仅用于祈使句) look at (sth) in order to find information 参看; 参见; 见: *See page 158.* 参看第158页.

▸ MEETING 遇见或会晤 **5** [Tn] (not usu in the continuous tenses 通常不用于进行时态) be near and recognize (sb); meet (sb) by chance 遇见, 碰见(某人): *I saw your mother in town today.* 我今天在城里碰见你母亲了. ○ *Guess who I saw at the party yesterday?* 你猜我昨天在聚会上遇见谁了? **6 (a)** [Tn] visit 看望; 探望: *Come and see us again soon.* 有空儿再到我们这儿来坐坐. **(b)** [Tn, Tn·p] **~ sb (about sth)** have a meeting with sb 会晤某人: *I'm seeing my solicitor tomorrow.* 我明天去见律师. ○ *You ought to see* (ie consult) *a doctor.* 你应该去看看病. ○ *What is it you want to see* (ie talk with) *me about?* 你来找我有什么事? **7** [Tn] receive a call or visit from (sb) 接见(访客): *The manager can only see you for five minutes.* 经理只能接待你五分钟. ○ *She's too ill to see anyone at present.* 她现在病得不能会客. **8** [Tn] (used esp in the continuous tenses 尤用于进行时态) spend time in the company of (sb) 与(某人)在一起: *She doesn't want to see him any more.* 她不想再和他来往了. ○ *She's seeing* (ie having a relationship with) *a married man.* 她现在总和一个结了婚的男子在一起.

▸ GRASPING WITH THE MIND OR IMAGINATION 理解或想像 **9** [I, Tn, Tf, Tw] (not usu in continuous tenses 通常不用于进行时态) perceive (sth) with the mind; understand (sth) 领会; 理解; 明白: *'The door* *opens like this.' 'Oh, I see.'* '这门是这样开的.' '噢, 我明白了.' ○ *He didn't see the joke.* 他没听懂这个笑话. ○ *I don't think she saw the point of the story.* 我看她没有明白那故事的意思. ○ *I can see* (ie recognize) *the advantages of the scheme.* 我意识到这个计划的优点. ○ *Can't you see (that) he's deceiving you?* 你还不明白他是欺骗你吗? ○ *Do you see what I mean?* 你明白我的意思吗? **10** [Tn] (not usu in the continuous tenses 通常不用于进行时态) have an opinion of (sth); interpret (sth) 有对(某事物)的看法; 解释(某事物): *I see things differently now.* 我现在的看法不同了. ○ *Try to see the matter from her point of view.* 尽量用她的观点来看这件事. **11** [Tng, Cn·n/a] **~ sb/sth as sth** (not in the continuous tenses 不用于进行时态) visualize; imagine; envisage 设想; 想像: *I can't see her changing her mind.* 我无法想像她会改变主意. ○ *Her colleagues see her as a future Prime Minister.* 她的同事设想她将来能当首相.

▸ DISCOVERING OR CHECKING 发觉或查看 **12** (not usu in the continuous tenses 通常不用于进行时态) **(a)** [I, Tf, Tw no passive 不用于被动语态] find out or discover by looking or searching or asking (经观看、寻找、询问)了解或发觉: *'Has the postman been yet?' 'I'll just go and see.'* '邮递员来过了吗?' '我去看看.' ○ *Go and see if/whether the postman has been yet.* 去看看邮递员来过了吗. ○ *I see (that)* (ie I have read in the newspapers that) *there is going to be a general election in France.* 我了解到法国要举行大选了. ○ *Could you go and see what the children are doing?* 你去看看孩子们干什么呢, 好吗? ○ *'Is he going to recover?' 'I don't know, we'll just have to wait and see.'* '他的病能好吗?' '我不知道, 我们只能等着瞧了.' **(b)** [I, Tw] find out or discover by thinking or considering (经思考)了解或发觉: *'Do you think you'll be able to help us?' 'I don't know; I'll have to see.'* '你看你能帮助我们吗?' '我不知道, 我得先考虑一下.' ○ *I'll see what I can do to help.* 我要考虑考虑看能帮上忙吗. **13** [Tf] (not usu in the continuous tenses 通常不用于进行时态) make sure; ensure; check 一定注意到; 保证; 检查: *See that all the doors are locked before you leave.* 你一定要查看一下门都锁好再走. ○ *Could you see (that) the children are in bed by 8 o'clock?* 你务必让孩子们8点钟上床睡觉, 行吗? ○ *I'll see that it's done.* 我管保这件事情能办好.

▸ EXPERIENCING OR WITNESSING 经历或目睹 **14** [Tn] (not in the continuous tenses 不用于进行时态) experience or undergo (sth) 经历或进行(某事): *This coat of mine has seen hard wear*, ie has been worn a lot. 我这件大衣穿了很久了. ○ *He has seen a great deal in his long life.* 他在漫长的一生中经历过很多事. **15** [Tn] (not in the continuous tenses 不用于进行时态) **(a)** be the time when (an event) happens; witness 为(某事)发生之时; 目睹: *This year sees the tercentenary of Handel's birth.* 今年是韩德尔诞辰三百周年. **(b)** be the scene or setting of (sth) 为(某事)的现场或背景: *This stadium has seen many thrilling football matches.* 在这个体育场里举行过很多精彩的足球赛.

▸ OTHER MEANINGS 其他意义 **16** [Tn·pr, Tn·p] accompany or escort 陪伴; 护送: *He saw her to the door.* 他把她送到门口. ○ *I saw the old lady across* (ie helped her to cross) *the road.* 我搀扶着老太太穿过马路. ○ *May I see you home* (ie go with you as far as your house)? 我送你回家好吗? ○ *My secretary will see you out.* 我让秘书送你出去. **17** [Tn] (in gambling games) equal (a bet); equal the bet of (another player) (赌博中)下相同(赌注); 下与(另一人)相同的赌注. **18** (idm 习语) **for all (the world) to ˈsee** clearly visible 显眼; 醒目. **ˌsee for oneˈself** find out or witness sth in order to be convinced or satisfied 亲眼看; 亲自去看: *If you don't believe that it's snowing, go and see for yourself!* 你要是不相信正在下雪, 你去看看! **seeing that...** in view of the fact that...; since...; because... 鉴于...; 由于...; 因为...: *Seeing that he's ill, he's unlikely to come.* 因为他病了, 他大概不来了. **see a lot, nothing, etc of sb** be often, never, etc in the company of sb 经常、从不...和某人在一起: *They've seen a lot/nothing/little/more/less of each other recently.* 他们最近经常[从不/很少/频频/减少]来往. **ˈsee you; (I'll) be ˈseeing you** (*infml* 口) goodbye 再见: *I'd better be going now. See you!* 我得走了. 回见! **see you aˈround** (*infml* 口) = SEE YOU. (For other idioms containing **see**, see entries for *ns*, *adjs*, etc 查阅与**see**搭配的其他习语见有关名词、形容词等的词条, 如 **see the light** ⇨LIGHT¹; **see red** ⇨RED².)

19 (phr v) **see about sth/doing sth** deal with sth; attend to sth 处理或照看某事物: *I must see about* (ie prepare) *lunch soon.* 我得马上去做午饭了. ○ *I'll have to see about getting the roof mended.* 我得去照料修理屋顶这件事. ○ *He says he won't co-operate, does he? Well, we'll soon see about that!* ie I will insist that he does co-operate. 他说他不愿意合作, 是吗? 好, 我们非办办这件事不可! (我一定得让他合作.)

see sth in sb/sth find sb/sth attractive or interesting 觉得某人[某事物]有吸引力或有意思: *I can't think what she sees in him.* 我想不通她看上他什么了.

see sb off (a) go to a railway station, airport, etc to say goodbye to sb who is about to start a journey 到火车站、飞机场等处为某人送行: *We all went to the airport to see her off.* 我们都去飞机场为她送行了. **(b)** force sb to leave a place, eg by chasing him 强迫某人离开某处(如赶走): *The farmer saw the boys off with a heavy stick.* 农场主拿着大棍子把那些男孩子赶跑了.

see sth out (not in the continuous tenses 不用于进行时态) last until the end of sth 持续到某事物结束: *We have enough coal to see the winter out.* 我们有足够的煤过冬.

see over sth visit and examine or inspect (a place) carefully 仔细查看、检查或观察(某处): *I shall need to see over the house before I can make you an offer.* 我得先看看房子, 然后才能给你出个价钱.

see through sb/sth (not in the continuous tenses 不用于进行时态) not be deceived by sb/sth 看穿或看透某人[某事物](不受骗); 识破: *We all saw through him*, ie realized what type of man he really was. 我们都看透了他的为人. ○ *I can see through your little game*, ie am aware of the trick you are trying to play on me. 我已经看穿了你的鬼把戏. **see sth through** (not usu in the continuous tenses 通常不用于进行时态) not abandon a task, undertaking, etc until it is finished 把某任务、事情等进行到底: *She's determined to see the job through.* 她决心把这项工作干到底.

see sb through (sth) (not in the continuous tenses 不用于进行时态) satisfy the needs of, help or support sb for a particular (esp difficult) period of time 满足某人的需要, 帮助或支持某人(尤指困难时): *Her courage and good humour saw her through the bad times.* 她有志气、性格刚强, 有助于她渡过难关. ○ *That overcoat should see me through the winter.* 有那件大衣我应该能过冬了. ○ *I've only got £10 to see me through until pay-day!* 我只有10英镑, 要熬到发薪那天了!

see to sth attend to or deal with sth 照看或处理某事物: *This machine isn't working; get a mechanic to see to it.* 这台机器坏了, 找技工来修理一下吧. ○ *Will you see to the arrangements for the next committee meeting?* 你来处理下次委员会会议安排, 好吗? **see to it that...** make sure that... 一定注意到...; 务必...: *See to it that you're ready on time!* 到时候你千万要准备好!

see² /siː; si/ *n* (*fml* 文) district for which a bishop or an archbishop is responsible; office or jurisdiction of a bishop or an archbishop 主教或大主教的辖区、职务或管辖权: *the See of Canterbury* 坎特伯雷大主教的辖区 ○ *the Holy See/the See of Rome*, ie the Papacy 罗马教廷.

seed /siːd; sid/ *n* **1 (a)** [C] part of a plant from which a new plant of the same kind can grow 种子: *a tiny poppy seed* 小小的罂粟籽 ○ *sow a row of seeds* 播种一行种子. **(b)** [U] quantity of these for planting, feeding birds, etc (种植、喂鸟等的)种子: *a handful of grass seed* 一把草籽 ○ *Sweet pea seed can be sown in May.* 香豌豆籽可在五月份种上. **(c)** [attrib 作定语] (to be) used for planting 用作种子的: *seed corn, potatoes, etc* 作种子用的谷物、马铃薯等. **2** [U] (*dated fml* 旧, 文) semen 精液: *the fruit of his seed*, ie his child or children 他的孩子. **3** [C] (esp in tennis) seeded (SEED *v* 4) player (尤指网球的)种子选手: *a final between the first and second seeds* 一号和二号种子选手的决赛. **4** (idm 习语) **go/run to seed (a)** (of a plant) stop flowering as seed is produced (指植物)花谢结子. **(b)** (*fig* 比喻) begin to look shabby or become less able, efficient, etc 衰败; (能

S

力、效力等)减弱: *He started to drink too much and gradually ran to seed.* 他喝酒过多, 身体逐渐衰弱了. **(plant/sow) the seeds of sth** the cause or origin of sth 某事物的起因或根源: *Are the seeds of criminal behaviour sown early in life?* 犯罪行为的根源是否始自幼时?

▷ **seed** *v* **1** [I] (of a plant) produce seed (指植物)结子. **2** [Tn, Tn·pr] **~ sth (with sth)** sow seed in sth 将种子种在某处: *a newly-seeded lawn* 新近撒上草籽的草坪 ○ *seed a field with wheat* 在地里播种小麦. **3** [Tn esp passive 尤用于被动语态] remove the seeds from (sth) 除去(某物)的种子: *seeded raisins* 除去子的葡萄干. **4** [Tn esp passive 尤用于被动语态] (esp in tennis) select (a good player) to play against a poorer player in the early rounds of a knock-out competition, so that all the good players have a chance to reach the later rounds (尤指网球中)挑选(种子选手)与较弱选手比赛(使种子选手不至过早遭淘汰): *The seeded players all won their matches.* 这些种子选手已全部获胜.

seed·less *adj* having no seeds 无子的: *seedless raisins* 无子葡萄干.

seed·ling /ˈsiːdlɪŋ; ˈsidlɪŋ/ *n* young plant newly grown from a seed 幼苗.

□ **ˈseed-bed** *n* **1** bed of fine soil for sowing seeds 苗床. **2** (*fig* 比喻) place or situation in which sth develops 某事物借以发展的处所或环境: *The tennis club is a seed-bed for young talent.* 这个网球俱乐部是培养年轻选手的场所.

ˈseed-cake [C, U] *n* cake containing seeds, eg caraway, as a flavouring 带有芳香种子(如葛缕子)的糕饼.

ˈseed capsule capsule holding a plant's seed (包种子的)外壳.

S

ˈseed-pearl *n* small pearl 小珍珠.

ˈseedsman /-mən; -mən/ *n* (*pl* **-men**) dealer in seeds 种子商.

seedy /ˈsiːdɪ; ˈsidɪ/ *adj* (**-ier, -iest**) **1** shabby-looking; disreputable 衰败的; 破旧的; 破烂的: *a seedy old tramp* 衣服破烂的流浪者 ○ *a cheap hotel in a seedy part of town* 在城里破烂地区的廉价旅店. **2** [usu pred 通常作表语] (*infml* 口) unwell 身体不舒服: *feeling seedy* 觉得不舒服. **3** full of seeds 种子多的; 多籽的: *The grapes are delicious but very seedy.* 葡萄好吃是好吃, 就是子儿太多. ▷ **seedi·ness** *n* [U]: *the seediness of his lodgings* 他居住处之破旧状况.

see·ing /ˈsiːɪŋ; ˈsiɪŋ/ *conj* (also **seeing that**, *infml* 口语作 **seeing as**) in view of the fact that; because 由于; 因为: *Seeing (that) the weather is bad, we'll stay at home.* 因为天气不好, 我们要呆在家里了.

seek /siːk; sik/ *v* (*pt, pp* **sought** /sɔːt; sɔt/) (*fml* 文) **1** (**a**) [I, Ipr esp passive 尤用于被动语态, Tn] **~ (after/for sth)** look (for sth); try to find or obtain (sth) 寻找; 找到或得到(某事物): *We sought long and hard but found no answer.* 我们费力多时也未找到答案. ○ *seeking (for) solutions to current problems* 寻找对目前问题的解决办法 ○ *the long sought-for cure for the disease* 长期寻求的治疗该疾病的方法 ○ *young graduates seeking (after) success in life* 探索人生成功之途的年轻毕业生 ○ *It's a very/highly/much sought-after* (ie popular) *make of car.* 这是一种极受欢迎的汽车型号. ○ *seek happiness, comfort, wealth, etc* 追求幸福、安逸、财富等 ○ *seek shelter from the rain* 寻找避雨之处 ○ *seek safety in flight* 逃生 ○ *The explanation is not far to seek*, ie is very clear. 这种解释不难理解. (**b**) [Tn] try to reach (a place or point); move towards (sth) 设法到达或达到(某处或某点); 向(某物)移动: *Water seeks its own level.* 水能自行流平. ○ *The flood started and we had to seek higher ground.* 发大水了, 我们得到高的地方去. **2** [Tn, Tn·pr] **~ sth (from sb)** ask sb for sth 向某人寻求某事: *seek help, advice, information, etc* 请求帮助、征求意见、寻找信息 ○ *You must seek permission from the manager.* 你需请求经理批准. **3** [It] attempt (to do sth); try 设法(做某事); 试图: *seek to bring the conflict to an end* 试图结束冲突 ○ *They are seeking to mislead us.* 他们竭力误导我们. **4** (idm 习语) **seek one's ˈfortune** try to find a way to become rich and successful 寻找致富及成功之道. **5** (phr v) **seek sb/sth out** look for and find sb/sth 找出或找到某人[某事物]: *We sought her out to tell her of her success.* 我们找到她, 告诉她她成功了. ○ *She sought out and acquired all his early paintings.* 她找到并获得了他早期画的所有的画儿.

seem /siːm; sim/ **1** *v* [La, Ln, Ipr, It] **~ (to sb) (to be) sth; ~ like sth** (not used in progressive tenses 不用于进行时态) have or give the impression or appearance of being or doing sth; appear 似乎; 好像; 仿佛: *She seems happy (to me).* (我看)她好像很愉快. ○ *Do whatever seems best.* 只要觉察出是最好的, 就去做. ○ *It seems (to me) (to be) the best solution.* (依我看)这似乎是最好的解决办法. ○ *It seemed like a disaster at the time.* 在当时那就像是一场灾难. ○ *She seems (to me) to be right/It seems (to me) that she's right.* (我看)她做得对. ○ *It would seem that...*, ie a cautious way of saying, 'It seems that...' 看来似乎是…(为 It seems that…的含蓄说法) ○ *'She's leaving.' 'So it seems'*, ie People say so. '她要走了.' '据说是这样.' ○ *They seem to know what they're doing.* 他们好像明白他们做的事情. ○ *I can't seem to* (ie It seems that I can't) *stop coughing.* 我的咳嗽看来止不住了. ⇨Usage at APPEAR 用法见 APPEAR. **2** (idm 习语) **it seems/seemed as if.../as though...** the impression is/was given that... 看样子…; 看起来…; 似乎…; 好像…: *It always seemed as though they would marry in the end.* 久而久之, 看来他们终归得结婚.

▷ **seem·ing** *adj* [attrib 作定语] appearing to be sth, but perhaps not being this in fact; apparent 似是而非的; 看上去的; 貌似的: *seeming intelligence, interest, anger* 貌似聪明、有兴趣、气愤 ○ *Despite his seeming deafness, he could hear every word.* 别看他好像耳背, 他每个字都听得见. **seem·ingly** *adv* in appearance; apparently 看上去; 表面上: *They were seemingly unaware of the decision.* 他们似乎并不了解这个决定.

seemly /ˈsiːmlɪ; ˈsimlɪ/ *adj* (**-ier, -iest**) (*dated or fml* 旧或文) proper and suitable by the standards of polite society 恰当的, 得体的, 适宜的(合乎礼仪的): *seemly conduct, modesty* 适度的举止、谦虚 ○ *It would be more seemly to tell her after the funeral.* 待葬礼过后再告诉她较合适. ▷ **seem·li·ness** *n* [U].

seen *pp* of SEE[1].

seep /siːp; sip/ *v* [Ipr, Ip] **~ through (sth)/into sth/out (of sth)** (of liquids) flow slowly and in small quantities through a substance (指液体)漏出, 渗出, 渗漏: *water seeping through the roof of the tunnel* 从隧道顶部渗出的水 ○ *Oil is seeping out through a crack in the tank.* 油箱的裂缝漏出油来了. ⇨Usage at DRIP[1] 用法见 DRIP[1].

▷ **seep·age** /ˈsiːpɪdʒ; ˈsipɪdʒ/ *n* **1** [U, C] process of seeping 漏; 渗; 渗漏: *some seepage* 有点渗漏 ○ *reported seepages from the pipe* 据称管道渗漏. **2** [U] liquid that seeps 渗漏出的液体: *a bowl to catch the seepage* 承接渗出液体的盆.

seer·sucker /ˈsɪəsʌkə(r); ˈsɪrˌsʌkɚ/ *n* [U] thin striped fabric with a crinkled surface 绉条纹薄织物; 泡泡纱: [attrib 作定语] *a seersucker table-cloth* 泡泡纱桌布.

see-saw 跷跷板

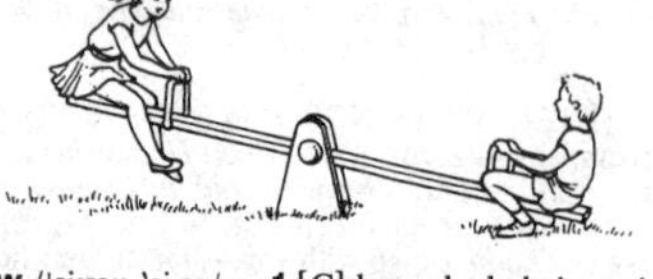

see-saw /ˈsiːsɔː; ˈsiˌsɔ/ *n* **1** [C] long plank, balanced on a centre support, and with a person sitting at each end, which can rise and fall alternately 跷跷板: *have a go on the see-saw* 玩跷跷板. **2** [sing] (**a**) up-and-down or to-and-fro motion 上下或往复的移动: *the slow see-saw of the branch in the wind* 树枝在风中缓缓摇动. (**b**) (*fig* 比喻) long series of rises and falls 一长串的起伏: *Changing demand causes a see-saw in prices.* 需求不断变化造成价格反复涨跌.

▷ **see-saw** *v* [I] **1** play on a see-saw 玩跷跷板. **2** (**a**) move up and down or to and fro 上下或往复移动: *a branch see-sawing in the wind* 随风摇曳的树枝. (**b**) (*fig* 比喻) rise and fall in turn, or move from one position, opinion, etc to another repeatedly 反复升降; 反复改变位置、意见等: *Prices see-saw according to demand.* 物价随需求变化而反复涨跌. ○ *public opinion see-sawing* *continuously* 不断变来变去的舆论.

seethe /siːð; sið/ *v* **1** [I] (of liquids) bubble and froth as if boiling (指液体)起泡, 冒泡(似沸腾): *They fell into the seething waters of the rapids.* 他们跌进了翻腾的急流中. **2** [I, Ipr] **~ (with sth)** (**a**) be crowded 拥挤: *streets seething with excited crowds* 群情激动十分拥挤的街道. (**b**) (usu in the continuous tenses 通常用于进行时态) be very angry, agitated, etc 非常气愤、激动等: *She was seething (with rage) at his remarks.* 对于他的说法, 她(气得)火冒三丈.

seg·ment /ˈsegmənt; ˋsɛgmənt/ *n* **1** (**a**) (*geometry* 几) part of a circle cut off by a line 弦(一直线切割圆, 在圆周内的部分). ⇨illus at CIRCLE 见 CIRCLE 插图. (**b**) part of sth separated or marked off from the other parts; part of sth that can be separated off in the mind 分出的或标出的一部分; 想像中可分出的一部分: *She cleaned a small segment of the painting.* 她把画儿上的一小部分擦干净了. ○ *Lines divided the area into segments.* 这几条线把这个面分割成了几个部分. **2** any one of the several sections of which an orange, lemon, etc is made up (橙子、柠檬等的)瓣: *grapefruit segments* 葡萄柚瓣.

▷ **seg·ment** /segˈment; sɛgˋmɛnt/ *v* [I, Tn] (cause sth to) separate into segments (将某事物)分割成弦、部分或瓣. **seg·menta·tion** /ˌsegmenˈteɪʃn; ˌsɛgmɛnˋteʃən/ *n* [U, C] division into segments 分割成弦、部分或瓣.

se·greg·ate /ˈsegrɪgeɪt; ˋsɛgrɪˌget/ *v* [Tn, Tn·pr] **~ sb/sth (from sb/sth)** **1** put sb/sth in a place away from the rest; isolate 将某人[某事物]隔离、分离或分开: *segregate cholera patients* 把霍乱病人隔离开 ○ *The two groups of fans must be segregated in the stadium.* 必须把体育场中这两部分球迷隔开. **2** separate (esp a racial or religious group) from the rest of the community and treat them unfairly 将(尤指某种族或宗教团体)与社区其他人隔开并作不公平对待: *Why should the handicapped be segregated from the able-bodied?* 为什么要把伤残人士和身体健康的人分开? ○ *a segregated society*, ie one in which some groups are segregated 有种族隔离的社会. Cf 参看 INTEGRATE.

▷ **se·grega·tion** /ˌsegrɪˈgeɪʃn; ˌsɛgrɪˋgeʃən/ *n* [U] segregating or being segregated; state of being segregated 隔离; 隔离状况: *a policy of racial segregation* 种族隔离政策 ○ *We oppose segregation on religious grounds.* 我们反对基于宗教不同的隔离状况. Cf 参看 INTEGRATION (INTEGRATE).

seis·mic /ˈsaɪzmɪk; ˋsaɪzmɪk/ *adj* [usu attrib 通常作定语] of earthquakes 地震的: *seismic research, tremors, waves* 地震的研究、震动、震波.

▷ **seis·mo·graph** /ˈsaɪzməgrɑːf; *US* -græf; ˋsaɪzməˌgræf/ *n* instrument for detecting earthquakes and recording how strong they are and how long they last 地震仪.

seis·mo·logy /saɪzˈmɒlədʒɪ; saɪzˋmɑlədʒɪ/ *n* [U] science of earthquakes 地震学. **seis·mo·lo·gist** /saɪzˈmɒlədʒɪst; saɪzˋmɑlədʒɪst/ *n*.

seize /siːz; siz/ *v* **1** [Tn, Tn·pr] (**a**) take hold of (sth), suddenly and violently; grab 抓住, 捉住(某物); 攫取: *an eagle seizing its prey* 捉住猎物的雕 ○ *seize hold of sth* 抓住某物 ○ *She seized me by the wrist.* 她抓住我的手腕. ○ *He seized the bag and ran off with it.* 他把那个包抢跑了. (**b**) (of the police, customs, etc) take (stolen goods, illegal drugs, etc) away from sb (指警方、海关等)扣押, 没收(赃物、毒品等): *20 kilos of heroin were seized yesterday at Heathrow.* 昨日在希思罗机场扣押了20公斤的海洛因. (**c**) capture (sth); take 夺取(某物); 占领; 获得: *seize the airport in a surprise attack* 突袭而占领机场 ○ *The army has seized power.* 军队夺取了政权. **2** [Tn] see (an opportunity, etc) and make use of it eagerly and at once 抓住, 把握(机会等): *seize the chance to make some money* 抓住时机赚一些钱 ○ *Seize any opening you can.* 只要有机会就要抓住. **3** [Tn esp passive 尤用于被动语态] (of a strong feeling, desire, etc) affect (sb) suddenly and overwhelmingly (指强烈的感情、愿望等)突然影响或控制(某人): *Panic seized us.* 我们惊恐万状. ○ *We were seized by a sudden impulse to run.* 我们身不由己突然想跑. **4** (phr v) **seize on/upon sth** recognize sth and exploit it, use it, etc eagerly and at once 意识到某事物而立即加以利用: *She seized on my suggestion and began work immediately.* 她采纳了我的建议, 马上干了起来. ○ *The critics seized on my mistake and said I was ignorant.* 批评我的人抓住了我的错误就硬说我一无所知. **seize up** (of moving machinery) become stuck or jammed because of overheating, etc (指开动着的机器)卡住(因过热等所致): *Your engine will seize up if you don't put some more oil in.* 你再不加些润滑油, 发动机就要卡住了. ○ (*fig* 比喻) *My joints seize up in the cold weather.* 天气寒冷, 我的关节都冻僵了.

▷ **seiz·ure** /ˈsiːʒə(r); ˋsiʒɚ/ *n* **1** (**a**) [U] act of seizing by force or legal authority 扣押; 没收: *the seizure of contraband by Customs officers* 海关官员对违禁品的扣押. (**b**) [C] instance of this 扣押; 没收: *impressive seizures of drugs* 轰动一时的毒品扣押案. **2** [C] sudden attack of apoplexy, etc (中风等的)发作.

sel·dom /ˈseldəm; ˋsɛldəm/ *adv* not often; rarely 不常; 罕见; 难得: *I have seldom seen such brutality.* 我很少见到这种暴行. ○ *We seldom go out.* 我们不常出门. ○ *We go out very seldom.* 我们绝少外出. ○ *The island is seldom, if ever, visited by ships.* 这个岛难得有船停靠.

se·lect /sɪˈlekt; səˋlɛkt/ *v* [Tn, Tn·pr, Cn·n/a, Cn·t] **~ sb/sth (as sth)** choose sb/sth, esp as being the best or most suitable 选择, 挑选, 选拔(尤指最好的或最合适的): *select a gift, candidate, wine* 挑选礼物、候选人、葡萄酒 ○ *select a card from the rack* 从架子上选择贺卡 ○ *selected as the team leader* 被选中作队长 ○ *Who has been selected to take part in the project?* 挑上谁来参与这项计划? ⇨Usage at CHOOSE 用法见 CHOOSE.

▷ **se·lect** *adj* **1** [usu attrib 通常作定语] carefully chosen, esp as the best out of a larger group 仔细挑选的; (尤指)精选的: *select passages of Milton's poetry* 弥尔顿诗选. **2** (of a society, club, gathering, etc) admitting only certain people; exclusive (指会社、俱乐部、集会等)选择成员严格的: *a select group of top scientists* 最优秀科学家小组 ○ *a film shown to a select audience* 给内部观众放映的影片 ○ *This area is very select*, ie Only the most wealthy, respectable, etc people live here. 这个地方住的人很有来头(非富即贵的人住的地方).

se·lector *n* **1** person who selects (eg members of a national team) 负责挑选的人(如挑选国家队队员的人). **2** device that selects (eg the correct gear) 选择器(如选择适当排挡的).

□ **seˌlect comˈmittee** (in the House of Commons) committee that checks the activities of a particular ministry or that is appointed to conduct a special investigation (下议院中的)特别委员会.

se·lec·tion /sɪˈlekʃn; səˋlɛkʃən/ *n* **1** [U] selecting or being selected 挑选; 选择; 选拔: *the selection of a football team* 选拔足球队员 ○ *I'm delighted about my selection as leader.* 选中了我作领导, 十分欣喜. ○ [attrib 作定语] *the selection process* 选择的过程. **2** [C] (**a**) number of selected items or people 挑选出的事项或人: *selections from 18th century English poetry* 18世纪英国诗歌精选 ○ *a selection of milk and plain chocolates* 精选的牛奶巧克力和纯巧克力. (**b**) number of items from which some can be selected 可供挑选的事项: *a shop with a huge selection of paperbacks* 有大量平装书可供选购的书店.

□ **seˈlection committee** committee appointed to select eg the members of a sports team 选拔委员会(如选拔运动员的).

se·lect·ive /sɪˈlektɪv; səˋlɛktɪv/ *adj* **1** using or based on selection 选择的; 选择性的: *the selective training of recruits*, ie the training of specially chosen recruits 对挑选出的新成员的培训 ○ *a selective weed-killer*, ie one that kills weeds but not other plants 选择性除草剂(专除杂草而不伤及其他植物的). **2 ~ (about sb/sth)** tending to choose carefully 挑拣的: *I'm very selective about the people I associate with.* 我与他人来往极慎重, 不滥交.

▷ **se·lect·ively** *adv*.

se·lect·iv·ity /ˌsɪlekˈtɪvətɪ; səˌlɛkˋtɪvətɪ/ *n* [U] **1** quality of being selective 选择性. **2** the power of a radio to receive broadcasts from one station without interference from other stations (收音机排除干扰的)选择性能.

□ **seˌlective ˈservice** (*US*) selection of people for compulsory military service 义务兵役.

sel·en·ium /sɪˈliːnɪəm; səˋlinɪəm/ *n* [U] (*chemistry* 化) non-metallic element whose power to conduct electric current increases as the light reaching it becomes more intense 硒. ⇨App 10 见附录10.

S

□ **seˈlenium cell** cell containing a strip of selenium, used in photo-electric devices, eg the exposure meter of a camera 硒光电池(如照相机曝光计中的).

self /self; sɛlf/ *n* (*pl* **selves** /selvz; sɛlvz/) **1** (**a**) [U] one's own nature, special qualities, etc; one's personality (个人的)本性, 本质; 自我; 自己: *the commitment of the whole self to a relationship* 对一种关系全身心的奉献 ○ *analysis of the self* 对自己的分析 ○ *the conscious self* 意识到的自我. (**b**) [C] particular part of one's nature 个人本性的某一方面: *one's better self*, ie one's generous qualities 个人好的一面 ○ *By doing that he showed his true self*, ie what he is really like. 他那样做显示了他的本性. ○ *She's her old self again*, ie has recovered her usual health, composure, etc. 她又恢复了老样子. **2** [U] one's own interest, advantage or pleasure 私利: *You always put self first.* 你总是把个人利益放在首位. ○ *She has no thought of self*, ie is always more concerned for other people. 她从不为自己打算. **3** [C] (*commerce or fml or joc* 商或文或谑) myself, yourself, himself, etc 我自己、你自己、他自己等: *a cheque payable to self*, ie to the person whose signature is on it 付给自己的支票 ○ *Mr Jones, your good self* (ie you) *and I* 琼斯先生, 您和我. **4** (idm 习语) **a shadow of one's/its former self** ⇨SHADOW.

self- *comb form* 构词成分 of, to or by oneself or itself 自己的; 向自己; 由自己: ˌ*self-conˈtrol* ○ ˌ*self-adˈdressed* ○ ˌ*self-ˈtaught* ○ ˌ*self-closing ˈdoors*, ie ones that close automatically.

self-abnegation /ˌself æbnɪˈgeɪʃn; ˌsɛlfæbnɪˈgeʃən/ *n* [U] (*fml* 文) = ABNEGATION.

self-absorbed /ˌself əbˈsɔːbd; ˌsɛlfəbˈsɔrbd/ *adj* only concerned about or interested in oneself 只顾自己的: *He's too self-absorbed to care about us.* 他只顾自己, 不关心我们. ▷ **self-absorption** /-əbˈsɔːpʃn; -əbˈsɔrpʃən/ *n* [U].

self-abuse /ˌself əˈbjuːs; ˌsɛlfəˈbjus/ *n* [U] (*euph* 婉) masturbation 手淫.

self-addressed /ˌself əˈdrest; ˌsɛlfəˈdrɛst/ *adj* [usu attrib 通常作定语] (of an envelope that will be used for a reply) addressed to oneself (指回信信封)写有寄给自己的姓名地址的.

self-appointed /ˌself əˈpɔɪntɪd; ˌsɛlfəˈpɔɪntɪd/ *adj* [usu attrib 通常作定语] having decided to be sth, usu without the agreement of others 自封的(通常指未经他人认可的): *a self-appointed judge, expert, critic, etc* 自封的裁判、专家、评论家等.

self-assembly /ˌself əˈsemblɪ; ˌsɛlfəˈsɛmblɪ/ *adj* [attrib 作定语] (esp of furniture) that has to be fitted together by the buyer from a kit (尤指家具)顾客自己组装的.

self-assertive /ˌself əˈsɜːtɪv; ˌsɛlfəˈsɝtɪv/ *adj* expressing one's views, demands, etc confidently 有信心表达自己的看法、要求等的. ▷ **self-assertion** /-əˈsɜːʃn; -əˈsɝʃən/, **self-assertiveness** *ns* [U].

self-assured /ˌself əˈʃɔːd; *US* -ˈʃʊərd; ˌsɛlfəˈʃurd/ *adj* = ASSURED (ASSURE). ▷ **self-assurance** /-əˈʃɔːrəns; *US* -ʃʊər-; -əˈʃurəns/ *n* [U] = ASSURANCE 1.

self-catering /ˌself ˈkeɪtərɪŋ; ˌsɛlfˈketərɪŋ/ *adj* [usu attrib 通常作定语] (of a holiday, accommodation, etc) during or in which one has to cook for oneself (指假日、住宿等)自己举炊的: *self-catering chalets* 自己举火的度假木屋.

self-centred (*US* **-centered**) /ˌself ˈsentəd; ˌsɛlfˈsɛntɚd/ *adj* (*derog* 贬) thinking too much about oneself and too little about others 自我中心的: *her self-centred attitude* 她那自我中心的态度. ▷ **self-centredness** (*US* **-centered-**) *n* [U].

self-confessed /ˌself kənˈfest; ˌsɛlfkənˈfɛst/ *adj* [attrib 作定语] having confessed that one is (usu sth bad) 自己承认的; (通常指)自己坦白的: *a* ˌ*self-confessed alcoˈholic, ˈliar, ˈthief, etc* 自己承认的酒鬼、说谎的人、窃贼等.

self-confident /ˌself ˈkɒnfɪdənt; ˈsɛlfˈkɑnfədənt/ *adj* having confidence in oneself, one's abilities, etc 自信的: *a self-confident person, manner, reply* 自信的人、态度、回答 ○ *learn to be more self-confident* 锻炼得更加自信. ▷ **self-confidence** /-dəns; -dəns/ *n* [U].

self-conscious /ˌself ˈkɒnʃəs; ˈsɛlfˈkɑnʃəs/ *adj* **1** seeming nervous or unnatural because one is worried about other people's opinions or reactions (因顾虑他人的看法或反应)扭怩的, 不自然的: *a* ˌ*self-conscious ˈsmile* 局促不安的微笑 ○ *be self-conscious about one's appearance* 对自己的外貌很在意. **2** aware of one's own existence, thoughts and actions (对自己的存在、思想和行为)自觉的. ▷ **self-consciously** *adv*. **self-consciousness** *n* [U].

self-contained /ˌself kənˈteɪnd; ˌsɛlfkənˈtend/ *adj* **1** [usu attrib 通常作定语] (*esp Brit*) (of accommodation) having no shared facilities, and usu having its own private entrance (指住所)有独立设施的, (通常指)门户独立的: *a* ˌ*self-contained ˈflat, maisonette, etc* 有独立设施的公寓、二层楼的公寓等. **2** (of a person) not needing the company of others; reserved (指人)不需与他人来往的, 拘谨的.

self-control /ˌself kənˈtrəʊl; ˌsɛlfkənˈtrol/ *n* [U] ability to control one's behaviour or not to show one's feelings 自制力; 控制感情的能力: *show/exercise great self-control in moments of stress* 在有压力时表现出[运用]很强的自制力 ○ *lose one's self-control* 失去控制感情的能力. ▷ **self-controlled** *adj* showing self-control 有自制力的; 喜怒不形于色的.

self-defeating /ˌself dɪˈfiːtɪŋ; ˌsɛlfdɪˈfitɪŋ/ *adj* (of a course of action, etc) likely to achieve the opposite of what it should achieve (指步骤等)适得其反的: *Punishing the demonstrators is self-defeating because it only encourages further demonstrations.* 惩治示威群众可谓事与愿违, 因为这反而会激发起更多的示威游行.

self-defence /ˌself dɪˈfens; ˌsɛlfdɪˈfɛns/ *n* [U] defence of one's body, property, rights, etc 自卫: *kill sb in self-defence*, ie while defending oneself against attack 为自卫而杀死某人 ○ *the art of self-defence*, ie boxing, judo, etc 自卫术(如拳术、柔道等).

self-denial /ˌself dɪˈnaɪəl; ˌsɛlfdɪˈnaɪəl/ *n* [U] choosing not to do or have the things one would like to, esp as a religious practice 克己; (尤指宗教的)苦行.

self-determination /ˌself dɪtɜːmɪˈneɪʃn; ˌsɛlfdɪˌtɝmɪˈneʃən/ *n* [U] right of a nation, people, etc to decide what form of government it will have or whether it will be independent of another country or not (国家、民族等的)自决权.

self-discipline /ˌself ˈdɪsɪplɪn; ˌsɛlfˈdɪsəplɪn/ *n* [U] (power of) controlling one's own desires, feelings, etc, usu so as to improve oneself 自律(力); 自我约束(通常指为提高个人修养的): *an athlete's self-discipline* 运动员的自律力 ○ *Dieting demands self-discipline.* 节食需有自我约束力.

self-drive /ˌself ˈdraɪv; ˌsɛlfˈdraɪv/ *adj* [attrib 作定语] (*Brit*) (of a hired vehicle) driven by the hirer (指租赁的车)由承租人驾驶的: *a* ˌ*self-drive ˈcar, ˈvan, etc* 由承租人驾驶的汽车、客货车等 ○ ˌ*self-drive ˈhire* 由承租人驾驶的汽车之租赁.

self-educated /ˌself ˈedʒʊkeɪtɪd; ˌsɛlfˈɛdʒəˌketɪd/ *adj* educated more by one's own efforts than by schools, teachers, etc 自我教育的; 自学的; 自修的.

self-effacing /ˌself ɪˈfeɪsɪŋ; ˌsɛlfɪˈfesɪŋ/ *adj* not trying to impress people; modest 不求闻达的; 谦逊的: *She's brilliant but self-effacing.* 她才华横溢而不露锋芒. ▷ **self-effacement** /-ɪˈfeɪsmənt; -ɪˈfesmənt/ *n* [U].

self-employed /ˌself ɪmˈplɔɪd; ˌsɛlfɪmˈplɔɪd/ *adj* working independently for customers or clients and not for an employer 自己经营的; 个体户的. ▷ **self-employment** /-ɪmˈplɔɪmənt; -ɪmˈplɔɪmənt/ *n* [U]: *a person in self-employment* 个体户.

self-esteem /ˌself ɪˈstiːm; ˌsɛlfəˈstim/ *n* [U] good opinion of one's own character and abilities 自尊; 自负: *high/low self-esteem* 很强的[弱的]自尊心 ○ *injure sb's self-esteem* 伤某人的自尊心.

self-evident /ˌself ˈevɪdənt; ˌsɛlfˈɛvɪdənt/ *adj* clear without any need for proof, explanation, or further evidence; obvious 不证自明的; 不言而喻的; 明显的: *a* ˌ*self-evident ˈtruth, ˈstatement, ˈfact* 不证自明的真相、不言而喻的说法、明摆着的事实 ○ *Her sincerity is self-evident.* 她真心实意, 这是显而易见的.

self-explanatory /ˌself ɪkˈsplænətrɪ; *US* -tɔːrɪ; ˌsɛlfɪkˈsplænəˌtɔrɪ/ *adj* without any need for (further) explanation; clear 毋需(多加)解释的; 清楚的: *The diagram is self-explanatory.* 该图表本身即很清楚.

self-help /ˌself ˈhelp; ˌsɛlfˈhɛlp/ *n* [U] use of one's own efforts, resources, etc to achieve things, without the help of others 自助; 自立: *Self-help is an important element in* *therapy for the handicapped.* 伤残人士在治疗中, 自助自立是个重要因素. ○ [attrib 作定语] *a self-help group* 自助小组.

self-important /ˌself ɪmˈpɔːtənt; ˌsɛlfɪmˈpɔrtn̩t/ *adj* (*derog* 贬) thinking that one is much more important than one really is; pompous 自视过高的; 妄自尊大的. ▷ **self-importance** /-təns; -tn̩s/ *n* [U].

self-imposed /ˌself ɪmˈpəʊzd; ˌsɛlfɪmˈpozd/ *adj* (of a duty, task, etc) imposed upon oneself (指责任、任务等)自愿承担的: *a ˌself-imposed ˈdiet, ˈexile* 自愿的节食、自我流放.

self-indulgent /ˌself ɪnˈdʌldʒənt; ˌsɛlfɪnˈdʌldʒənt/ *adj* (*derog* 贬) allowing oneself to do or have what one enjoys, instead of controlling one's desires, etc 放纵自己的: *The novel is too long and self-indulgent.* 这部小说冗长芜杂. ▷ **self-indulgence** /-dʒəns; -dʒəns/ *n* [U]: *a life of gross self-indulgence* 极其放纵的生活.

self-interest /ˌself ˈɪntrɪst; ˌsɛlfˈɪntrɪst/ *n* [U] (concern for) one's own interests or personal advantage 私利; 利己(之心): *do sth purely from/out of self-interest* 纯粹从私利出发做某事.

self·ish /ˈselfɪʃ; ˈsɛlfɪʃ/ *adj* (*derog* 贬) thinking first of one's own interests, needs, etc without concern for others; not sharing what one has with others; (of an action) done from selfish motives 自私的; 不顾他人的; 不与他人共享的; (指行动)出于自私动机的: *He's too selfish to think of lending me his car.* 他很自私, 不想把汽车借给我. ○ *a selfish refusal* 出于自私动机的拒绝. ▷ **self·ishly** *adv.* **self·ish·ness** *n* [U].

self·less /ˈselflɪs; ˈsɛlflɪs/ *adj* (*fml* 文) thinking more of others' needs and welfare than of one's own; unselfish 无私的; 不自私的: *selfless devotion to one's children* 一心一意为自己的孩子. ▷ **self·lessly** *adv.* **self·less·ness** *n* [U].

self-locking /ˌselfˈlɒkɪŋ; ˌsɛlfˈlɑkɪŋ/ *adj* (eg of a door) locking automatically when closed (如指门)(关闭时)自动锁上的.

self-made /ˌself ˈmeɪd; ˌsɛlfˈmed/ *adj* [usu attrib 通常作定语] having become successful, rich, etc by one's own efforts 靠自己的努力而成功、致富等的: *a ˌself-made ˈman/ˈwoman* 白手起家的男子[女子].

self-opinionated /ˌself əˈpɪnjəneɪtɪd; ˌsɛlfəˈpɪnjəˌnetɪd/ *adj* (*derog* 贬) always wanting to express one's own strong views without considering that they could be wrong 固执己见的.

self-pity /ˌself ˈpɪtɪ; ˌsɛlfˈpɪtɪ/ *n* [U] (*often derog* 常作贬义) pity for oneself 自怜: *a letter full of complaints and self-pity* 充满怨言和自怜的信.

self-portrait /ˌselfˈpɔːtreɪt, *also* -trɪt; ˌsɛlfˈpɔrtret, -trət/ *n* portrait of oneself 自画像: *a self-portrait by Van Gogh* 凡高的自画像 ○ (*fig* 比喻) *The book's hero is a self-portrait of the author.* 书中的主人公就是作者的自我写照.

self-possessed /ˌself pəˈzest; ˌsɛlfpəˈzɛst/ *adj* calm and confident, esp at times of stress or difficulty 冷静而自信的(尤指在有压力或困难时): *self-possessed in front of the TV cameras* 在电视摄影机前泰然自若. ▷ **self-possession** /-pəˈzeʃn; -pəˈzɛʃən/ *n* [U] calmness; composure 冷静; 沉着: *keep/lose/regain one's self-possession* 保持[不再有/恢复]冷静的情绪.

self-preservation /ˌself prezəˈveɪʃn; ˌsɛlfˌprɛzəˈveʃən/ *n* [U] protection of oneself from harm or destruction; natural urge to survive 自我保护; 自身保存: *the instinct for self-preservation* 自我保存的本能.

self-raising flour /ˌself reɪzɪŋ ˈflaʊə(r); ˌsɛlfˌrezɪŋ ˈflaʊr/ (*US* **self-rising flour** /-ˈraɪzɪŋ; -ˌraɪzɪŋ/) flour containing a substance which makes dough rise during baking without needing baking-powder 自发面粉(已含酵母的). Cf 参看 PLAIN FLOUR (PLAIN[1]).

self-reliant /ˌself rɪˈlaɪənt; ˌsɛlfrɪˈlaɪənt/ *adj* relying on one's own abilities and efforts; independent 依靠自己的; 独立的: *too self-reliant to want to borrow from anyone* 过甚依靠自己而不想借贷. ▷ **self-reliance** /-ˈlaɪəns; -ˈlaɪəns/ *n* [U].

self-respect /ˌselfrɪˈspekt; ˌsɛlfrɪˈspɛkt/ *n* [U] feeling that one is behaving and thinking in ways that will not make one ashamed of oneself 自尊(心); 自重: *lose all self-respect* 完全丧失自尊心. ▷ **self-respecting** *adj* [attrib 作定语] (usu in negative sentences 通常用于否定句) having self-respect 有自尊心的: *No self-respecting doctor would refuse to treat a sick person.* 凡是有自尊心的医生都不会对病人置之不顾的.

self-righteous /ˌselfˈraɪtʃəs; ˌsɛlfˈraɪtʃəs/ *adj* (*derog* 贬) showing in a smug way that one believes that what one does, thinks, etc is right 自以为是的: *a self-righteous person, attitude, remark* 自以为是的人、态度、言语 ○ *self-righteous anger, condemnation* 自以为是的气愤、指责. ▷ **self-righteously** *adv.* **self- righteousness** *n* [U].

self-rule /ˌselfˈruːl; ˌsɛlfˈrul/ *n* [U] government of a people by its own representatives 自治.

self-sacrifice /ˌselfˈsækrɪfaɪs; ˌsɛlfˈsækrəˌfaɪs/ *n* [U] giving up or willingness to give up things that one wants, in order to help others or for a good purpose 放弃个人利益; 自我牺牲精神: *Her self-sacrifice saved our lives.* 她以自我牺牲精神救了我们的性命. ▷ **self-sacrificing** *adj* [usu attrib 通常作定语].

self·same /ˈselfseɪm; ˈsɛlfsem/ *adj* [attrib 作定语] (used after *the, this, that,* etc 用于 the、this、that 等之后) very same; identical 同一的; 完全相同的: *She said the selfsame thing to me.* 她对我讲的是完全一样的事情. ○ *They were both born on that selfsame day.* 他们俩都是那一天出生的.

self-satisfied /ˌself ˈsætɪsfaɪd; ˈsɛlfˈsætɪsˌfaɪd/ *adj* (*derog* 贬) too pleased with oneself and one's own achievements; smug 沾沾自喜的; 自鸣得意的: *a self-satisfied person, attitude, grin* 得意忘形的人、态度、傻笑.

self-sealing /ˌselfˈsiːlɪŋ; ˌsɛlfˈsilɪŋ/ *adj* [usu attrib 通常作定语] (usu of envelopes) that can be sealed by pressure only (通常指信封)压合封口的.

self-seeking /ˌselfˈsiːkɪŋ; ˌsɛlfˈsikɪŋ/ *adj, n* (*derog* 贬) (having or showing) concern for one's own interests and advantage before those of others 先为自己打算的.

S

self-service /ˌselfˈsɜːvɪs; ˌsɛlfˈsɝvɪs/ *n* [U] system of service in a restaurant, filling-station, etc in which customers take what they want and pay a cashier for it (饭店、加油站等的)自我服务, 自助式. ▷ **self-service** *adj*: *a ˌself-service canˈteen* 自助食堂 ○ *Are these pumps self-service?* 这些加油泵是自助式的吗?

self-starter /ˌselfˈstɑːtə(r); ˌsɛlfˈstɑrtɚ/ *n* **1** person showing initiative and not needing others to make him work, etc 有主动性的人; 有积极性的人: *The advertisement read 'Young self-starter wanted as salesperson'.* 广告称'聘请有积极性的年轻人任推销员'. **2** (*dated* 旧) (usu electrical) device for starting an engine (发动机的)(通常指电动的)自动起动器.

self-styled /ˌself ˈstaɪld; ˌsɛlfˈstaɪld/ *adj* [attrib 作定语] (*sometimes derog* 有时作贬义) using a name, title, etc which one has given oneself, esp without having any right to do so 自封的; 自称的: *the self-styled leader of the sect, Mr Baker* 自封为这一宗派领袖的贝克先生 ○ *The self-styled 'Reverend' Harper is not a real clergyman at all.* 这位自称'教士'的哈珀根本就不是真正的教士.

self-sufficient /ˌself səˈfɪʃnt; ˌsɛlfsəˈfɪʃənt/ *adj* **~ (in sth)** able to fulfil one's own needs, without help from others 自给自足的: *She's handicapped but very self-sufficient.* 她身体有缺陷, 但很有自立的能力. ○ *a country self-sufficient in coal,* ie producing all the coal it needs 煤炭自给自足的国家. ▷ **self-sufficiency** /-fənsɪ; -fənsɪ/ *n* [U].

self-supporting /ˌself səˈpɔːtɪŋ; ˌsɛlfsəˈpɔrtɪŋ/ *adj* (eg of a person or a business) earning enough to support oneself or itself, without help from others (指人)自食其力的; (指生意)足以维持的.

self-willed /ˌselfˈwɪld; ˈsɛlfˈwɪld/ *adj* (*derog* 贬) determined to do what one wants; stubborn 任性的; 固执的: *a troublesome ˌself-willed ˈchild* 调皮捣蛋而又任性的孩子.

self-winding /ˌself ˈwaɪndɪŋ; ˌsɛlfˈwaɪndɪŋ/ *adj* (of a watch) winding itself automatically from the movements of the wearer's wrist (指手表)自动的.

sell /sel; sɛl/ *v* (*pt, pp* **sold** /səʊld; sold/) **1** [I, Ipr, Tn, Tn·pr, Dn·n, Dn·pr] **~ (sth) (to sb) (at/for sth)** give (goods, etc) to sb who becomes their owner after paying one money 卖; 售; 销: *Can she be persuaded to sell (the house)?* 能劝得她把房子卖了吗? ○ *I won't sell to a stranger.* 我不卖给生人. ○ *sell (sth) at a high price, a loss, a discount* 高价、赔钱、减价出售(某物) ○ *sell (one's* *bike) for £80* 以80英镑的价钱转让(自己的自行车) ○ *sell sth by auction* 拍卖某物 ○ *sell sb into slavery*, ie as a slave 把某人卖作奴隶 ○ *I sold my car (to a friend) for £750.* 我把汽车以750英镑卖(给朋友)了. ○ *Will you sell me your camera?* 你把照相机卖给我行吗? **2** [Tn] (**a**) have a stock of (sth) for sale; be a dealer in (sth) 备有(某物)出售; 经销(某物): *a shop that sells fruit, clothes, electrical goods* 出售水果、服装、电器的商店 ○ *Do you sell stamps?* 你们这儿卖邮票吗? (**b**) (of a salesperson) persuade people to buy (sth) (指推销员)推销(某物): *I sell insurance.* 我是保险业推销员. **3** [Tn] make people want to buy (sth); cause (sth) to be sold 使人买(某物); 将(某物)卖出: *It is not price but quality that sells our shoes.* 我们的鞋好卖不是因为价钱低而是因为质量好. ○ *Her name will help to sell the film.* 有她的名字, 这部影片就卖座. ⇨Usage 见所附用法. **4** [I, Ipr, In/pr] **~ (at/for sth)** be sold; find buyers 被出售; 有销路; 有人买: *Will such a long novel sell?* 这么长的小说有人买吗? ○ *The car is selling well.* 这种汽车卖得很好. ○ *Umbrellas sell best in winter.* 雨伞在冬季最好卖. ○ *The badges sell at 50p each.* 这种纪念章50便士一个. ○ *The group's record has sold millions.* 他们的唱片已经售出了千千万万张了. **5** (*infml* 口) (**a**) [Tn, Dn·n, Dn·pr] **~ sth/sb (to sb)** make sb believe that sth/sb is good, useful, worth having, etc 使某人相信某事物[某人]好、有用、可取等: *You'll never sell changes like that to the workforce.* 那样的改革, 工人决不买你的帐. ○ *a big poster campaign selling the new party* 对这一新党派的大海报宣传活动 ○ *You have to sell yourself* (ie show that you are the most suitable applicant) *at a job interview.* 在接受求职面试时, 要毛遂自荐. (**b**) [Dn·n, Dn·pr] **~ sth to sb** make sb believe that sth is true 使某人相信某事属实: *sell sb an excuse, story, etc* 使某人对一借口、一套说法等信以为真 ○ *He tried to sell me a line about losing his wallet.* 他一个劲儿地想让我相信他真把钱包丢了. **6** [Tn, Dn·pr] **~ oneself (to sb)** accept a bribe, reward, etc (from sb) for doing sth bad (从某人处)接受贿赂、报酬等而做坏事: *Are artists who work in advertising selling themselves?* 艺术家做广告是不是作践自己? ○ *The police had sold themselves to the gang leaders.* 那些警察已卖身投靠匪首. **7** [Tn esp passive 尤用于被动语态] (*dated infml* 旧, 口) cheat (sb) 欺骗(某人): *You've been sold again. That car you bought is a wreck.* 你又上当了. 你买的那辆汽车是个废物. **8** (idm 习语) **be sold on sth/sb** (*infml* 口) be enthusiastic about sth/sb 看中某事物[某人]: *I like the house but I'm not sold on the area.* 我喜欢这所房子, 但相不中这个地区. **be sold 'out (of sth)** have sold all the stock, tickets, etc 卖光存货、票等: *The match was completely sold out.* 比赛的票已售清. ○ *We're sold out of Sunday papers, sir.* 先生, 星期日的报纸我们全卖光了. **sell one's 'body** (*rhet* 修辞) work as a prostitute 卖身(卖淫). **sell sb down the 'river** (*infml* 口) betray sb, usu for one's own advantage 出卖某人(尤指为个人利益). **sell one's life 'dearly** (*fml* 文) kill or wound a number of one's enemies before being killed 杀伤若干敌人后死去. **sell like hot cakes** ⇨ HOT. **sell the pass** betray one's cause or one's allies 背叛自己的事业或盟友. **sell sb a 'pup** (*infml* 口) sell sb sth that is worthless, or worth less than the price paid 卖给某人不值钱的或不值那么多钱的东西: *You've been sold a pup — that house is nearly falling down!* 你上当了——那所房子都要塌了! **sell sth/sb 'short** (**a**) (*commerce* 商) sell (shares, etc) that one does not yet own in the hope of being able to buy them soon at a lower price 以买空卖空方式卖(股票等). (**b**) not recognize the true value of sth/sb/oneself 认识不到某事物[某人/自己]的真实价值: *Don't sell her short: she's very gifted in some areas.* 别小看她, 她有些方面很有天赋. (**c**) cheat sb in value or quantity 在质或量方面欺骗某人. **sell one's 'soul (to the devil)** do sth dishonourable or unworthy in return for money, fame, etc (为名利等)出卖灵魂, 做不名誉的或不合身分的事: *She'd sell her soul to get the job.* 她为了得到那份工作可以出卖灵魂. **9** (phr v) **sell sth off** sell (esp items which are unwanted or have not sold well) often at very low prices 甩卖(尤指要处理的或滞销的货物): *sell off old stock* 甩卖旧存货. **sell out** be all sold 售完: *The show has sold out*, ie There are no tickets left. 演出的票已售清. **sell out (of sth)** sell one's whole supply of sth 售完某物的全部现货: *We've sold out (of milk) but we'll be getting some more in later.* 我们(的牛奶)都卖光了, 但还要陆续进货. **sell out (to sb)** betray one's principles 背弃自己的宗旨: *She's sold out and left the party.* 她背弃了原有信仰而脱党了. **sell (sth) out (to sb)** sell all or part of (one's share in a business) 出卖全部或部分(股分): *She had decided to sell out (her share of the company) and retire.* 她已决定卖掉她的公司股分然后退休. **sell sb out** betray sb 背叛某人: *They've sold us out by agreeing to work during the strike.* 他们背叛了我们, 竟同意罢工期间仍上班. **sell (sth) up** sell (all one's property, one's home, etc) eg when leaving the country or retiring 卖掉(全部家产等)(如于出国或退休时).

▷ **sell** *n* [sing] **1** (*infml* 口) deception; disappointment 欺骗; 失望: *It's a real sell: the food seems cheap but you pay extra for vegetables.* 真骗人, 饭食好像很便宜, 可是吃菜还得另付钱呢. **2** (idm 习语) **the hard/soft 'sell** aggressive/persuasive way of selling sth 硬[软]推销术(以死缠[劝诱]方式推销): *They're certainly giving the book the hard sell, with advertisements every night on TV.* 他们用硬推销术宣传这本书, 每天晚上都在电视上登广告.

□ **'sell-by date** date (esp one marked on food products) by which sth must be sold in shops (商店中的)某物必须售出的截止日期(尤指标在食品上的).

'selling-point *n* feature of sth that makes it attractive to buyers (吸引顾客的)商品特色: *Double glazing is often a good selling-point for houses.* 镶有双层玻璃门窗的房子往往好出售.

'selling price price to be paid by the customer 售价. Cf 参看 COST PRICE (COST^2).

'sell-out *n* **1** event (eg a concert) for which all the tickets have been sold 满座的演出(如音乐会). **2** (*infml* 口) betrayal 背叛: *The agreement is a compromise, not a sell-out.* 这个协议是双方妥协的产物而不是一方让步.

NOTE ON USAGE 用法: Compare **sell, vend, peddle, push** and **flog.** 试比较**sell**、**vend**、**peddle**、**push**、**flog**这几个词. **1 Sell** is the most general verb, meaning 'give in exchange for money' ☆ **sell**使用最广, 意为'拿东西换钱': *They are selling their house and moving to the country.* 他们打算把房子卖掉, 搬到乡下去. ○ *Do you sell magazines here?* 你们这儿卖杂志吗? **2 Vend** is formal and indicates the selling of small articles. ☆ **vend**较文, 指出售小件商品. The noun **vendor** is much more common than the verb 由这个动词派生出的名词**vendor**, 比其动词本身较为常用: *a street vendor, a news-vendor* 街上的摊贩、报贩. It is also a legal term used especially in the selling of a house ☆ **vendor**还是个法律术语, 用以指房产的卖方: *The vendor signs a contract with the purchaser.* 卖方须与买方签订契约. **Vending-machine** is also common and is a coin-operated slot machine for the sale of small items. ☆ **vending-machine**也较常用, 是一种投币式出售小商品的自动售货机. **3 Peddle** indicates the selling of small, inexpensive goods by going from house to house ☆ **peddle**指挨门挨户地推销廉价的小商品: *He peddled small household articles around the town.* 他在城里挨家挨户兜售日用百货. **4 Push** is informal and is used for the selling of illegal drugs ☆ **push**是口语用词, 指出售违禁毒品: *He was caught pushing heroin to schoolchildren.* 他在向小学生贩卖海洛因时被捕. **5 Flog** is slang. ☆ **flog**是俚语用词. It often suggests that what is to be sold is of little value, possibly stolen and therefore difficult to sell 这个词常指出售的东西无甚价值, 或可为赃物, 故难以售出: *He tried to flog me a broken TV set.* 他一个劲儿向我兜售一个破电视机.

seller /'selə(r); 'sɛlɚ/ *n* **1** (often in compounds 常用以构成复合词) person who sells 卖者; 卖方: *a 'bookseller* 书商 ○ *the buyer and the seller* 买方和卖方. **2** (esp following an *adj* 尤用于形容词之后) item that is sold (esp in the manner specified) 售出之物(尤指以修饰词语描述之方式售出): *This model is a poor seller*, ie Not many have been sold. 这种型号的不好卖. ○ *This dictionary is a best seller.* 这部词典是畅销书.

□ **ˌseller's 'market** situation in which goods are in

demand, so that sellers have an advantage 卖方市场(供不应求而有利卖方的): *It's a seller's market for vintage cars*, ie Many people will pay high prices for them. 1917年到1930年制造的汽车有卖方市场(很多人愿高价收购).

Sel·lo·tape /ˈseləʊteɪp; ˈsɛlo,tep/ *n* [U] (*Brit propr* 专利名) (also **sticky tape**) (usu transparent) cellulose or plastic sticky tape (通常为透明的)胶带: *mend a torn map with Sellotape* 用透明胶带修补破损的地图.
▷ **sel·lo·tape** *v* [Tn, Tn·pr, Tn·p] stick Sellotape on (sth); mend or fix (sth) with Sellotape 用(透明)胶带粘、贴或修补(某物): *sellotape the parcel (up)* 用胶带把包裹粘好 ○ *sellotape torn pieces of paper (together)* 用透明胶带把碎纸粘在一起 ○ *sellotape a notice to the wall* 用胶带把通知贴在墙上.

sel·vage (also **sel·vedge**) /ˈselvɪdʒ; ˈsɛlvɪdʒ/ *n* edge of cloth woven so that it will not unravel or fray (布的)织边.

selves *pl* of SELF.

se·mantic /sɪˈmæntɪk; səˈmæntɪk/ *adj* [usu attrib 通常作定语] of the meaning of words; of semantics 语义的; 语义学的: *the semantic content of a sentence* 句子的含义.
▷ **se·mant·ics** *n* [sing *v*] branch of linguistics dealing with the meanings of words and sentences 语义学.

sema·phore /ˈseməfɔː(r); ˈsɛmə,fɔr/ *n* **1** [U] system of sending signals by holding the arms or two flags in certain positions to indicate letters of the alphabet 旗语: *send a message by semaphore* 用旗语发送信息. **2** [C] device with red and green lights on mechanically moved arms, used for signalling on railways (铁路的)臂板信号机.
▷ **sema·phore** *v* [I, Tn, Tf, Dpr·f, Dpr·w, Dpr·t no passive 不用于被动语态] send (messages) by semaphore 用旗语发送(信息): *semaphore (to sb) that help is needed/to send help* (向某人)打旗语求救.

semb·lance /ˈsembləns; ˈsɛmbləns/ *n* [sing, U] **~ of sth** appearance of being sth; likeness to sth 外表; 外观; 外貌; 与某物相似: *put on a semblance of cheerfulness* 装出愉快的样子 ○ *bring the meeting to some semblance of order* 把会议维持得像是有些秩序的样子.

se·men /ˈsiːmen; ˈsimən/ *n* [U] whitish fluid containing sperm produced by male animals 精液.
▷ **sem·inal** /ˈsemɪnl; ˈsɛmənl/ *adj* **1** [usu attrib 通常作定语] of seed or semen 种子的; 精液的: *the seminal fluid* 精液 ○ *a seminal duct* 精管. **2** (*fig often approv* 比喻, 常作褒义) strongly influencing later developments 对以后发展有巨大影响的: *a seminal idea, essay, speech* 有巨大影响的思想、文章、讲话 ○ *Her theories were seminal for educational reform.* 她的理论对教育改革影响很大.

se·mes·ter /sɪˈmestə(r); səˈmɛstɚ/ *n* (esp in US universities and colleges) either of the two divisions of the academic year (尤指美国的大专院校的)学期(半学年): *the summer/winter semester* 夏季[冬季]学期. Cf 参看 TERM 3.

semi /ˈsemɪ; ˈsɛmɪ/ *n* (*pl* **semis** /ˈsemɪz; ˈsɛmɪz/) (*Brit infml* 口) semi-detached house 半独立式住宅.

semi- *pref* 前缀 (used fairly widely with *adjs* and *ns* 与形容词和名词连用, 使用很广) half; partially 半; 部分: *semicircular* ○ *semi-detached* ○ *semifinal*.

semi·breve /ˈsemɪbriːv; ˈsɛmə,briv/ *n* (*US* ˈ**whole note**) the longest written musical note in common use, equal to two minims in length 全音符. ⇨ illus at MUSIC 见MUSIC 插图.

semi·circle /ˈsemɪsɜːkl; ˈsɛmɪ,sɝkl/ *n* half of a circle or of its circumference; thing arranged like this 半圆形; 半圆形的周长; 半圆形的东西: *a semicircle of chairs* 排列成半圆形的椅子 ○ *sitting in a semicircle round the fire* 围着火坐成半圈. ⇨ illus at CIRCLE 见 CIRCLE 插图.
▷ **semi·cir·cu·lar** /ˌsemɪˈsɜːkjʊlə(r); ˌsɛmɪˈsɝkjəlɚ/ *adj* having the shape of a semicircle 半圆形的.

semi·co·lon /ˌsemɪˈkəʊlən; *US* ˈsemɪk-; ˈsɛmə,kolən/ *n* the punctuation mark (;) used in writing and printing, between a comma and a full stop in value 分号(;). ⇨ App 3 见附录3. Cf 参看 COLON[2].

semi·con·ductor /ˌsemɪkənˈdʌktə(r); ˌsɛmɪkənˈdʌktɚ/ *n* substance that conducts electricity in certain conditions, but not as well as metals 半导体.

semi-conscious /ˌsemɪˈkɒnʃəs; ˌsɛmɪˈkɑnʃəs/ *adj* partly conscious 半清醒的; 半意识的: *a semi-conscious patient recovering from an anaesthetic* 经麻醉后逐渐恢复的半清醒的病人.

semi-detached /ˌsemɪ dɪˈtætʃt; ˌsɛmɪdɪˈtætʃt/ *adj* (of a house) joined to another house by one shared wall (指房子)与另一所房子共用一堵墙的, 半独立式的. ⇨ illus at App 1 见附录1插图, page vi.

semi·final /ˌsemɪˈfaɪnl; ˌsɛmɪˈfaɪnəl/ *n* match or round preceding the final, eg in football 半决赛(如足球赛的).
▷ **semi·fin·al·ist** /-ˈfaɪnəlɪst; -ˈfaɪnəlɪst/ *n* person or team taking part in a semifinal 参加半决赛的人或队.

sem·inal ⇨ SEMEN.

sem·inar /ˈsemɪnɑː(r); ˈsɛmə,nɑr/ *n* small group of students at a university, etc meeting to discuss or study a particular topic with a teacher (大学生与教师的)(专题)研讨会.

sem·in·ary /ˈsemɪnərɪ; *US* -nerɪ; ˈsɛmə,nɛrɪ/ *n* **1** college for training priests or rabbis 神学院. **2** (*dated fml* 旧, 文) school for older children or young people 中等学校: *a seminary for young ladies* 女子中学.
▷ **sem·in·ar·ist** /ˈsemɪnərɪst; ˈsɛmə,nɛrɪst/ *n* person studying at a seminary 神学院学生; 中学生.

se·mi·ot·ics /ˌsemɪˈɒtɪks; ˌsɛməˈɑtɪks/ *n* [sing *v*] study of signs and symbols, esp in writing, and of what they mean and how they are used 符号学(研究符号和符号使用行为的学科).

semi·pre·cious /ˌsemɪˈpreʃəs; ˌsɛməˈprɛʃəs/ *adj* [usu attrib 通常作定语] (of a gem) less valuable than a precious stone (指宝石)半宝石的, 次贵重的.

semi·qua·ver /ˈsemɪkweɪvə(r); ˈsɛmə,kwevɚ/ *n* (*US* **six'teenth note**) musical note equal to half a quaver 十六分音符. ⇨ illus at MUSIC 见 MUSIC 插图.

semi-skilled /ˌsemɪ ˈskɪld; ˌsɛməˈskɪld/ *adj* [usu attrib 通常作定语] (of a worker) having some special training or qualifications, but less than a skilled worker; (of work) for such a worker (指工作者)半熟练的; (指工作)为半熟练工作者的: *a ˌsemi-skilled maˈchine operator, ˈjob* 半熟练机床工人、半熟练工人的工作.

Sem·ite /ˈsiːmaɪt; ˈsimaɪt/ *n* member of the group of races including the Jews and Arabs, and formerly the Phoenicians and Assyrians 闪米特人(包括犹太人和阿拉伯人以及从前的腓尼基人和亚述人). ▷ **Sem·itic** /sɪˈmɪtɪk; səˈmɪtɪk/ *adj*: *Semitic languages, tribes* 闪米特语言、部族.

semi·tone /ˈsemɪtəʊn; ˈsɛmə,ton/ *n* (*US* ˈ**half tone**) half of a tone on the musical scale 半音.

semi·trop·ical /ˌsemɪˈtrɒpɪkl; ˌsɛməˈtrɑpɪkəl/ *adj* [attrib 作定语] (of regions) near but not in the tropics (指地区)亚热带的, 副热带的, 半热带的: *ˌsemitropical ˈweather, vegeˈtation, ˈcountries* 亚热带的天气、植物、国家.

semi·vowel /ˈsemɪvaʊəl; ˈsɛmə,vaʊəl/ *n* (letter representing a) sound like a vowel that functions as a consonant, eg /w/, /j/ 半元音(字母)(如 /w/、/j/).

se·mo·lina /ˌseməˈliːnə; ˌsɛməˈlinə/ *n* [U] hard grains of wheat left after it has been ground and sifted, used for making pasta, milk puddings, etc 粗粒面粉(精制硬小麦粗粉, 用于制作意大利面食、牛奶布丁等): [attrib 作定语] *semolina pudding* 粗粒面粉布丁.

semp·stress /ˈsemstrɪs; ˈsɛmstrɪs/ *n* (*Brit*) = SEAMSTRESS.

SEN /ˌes iː ˈen; ˌɛs i ˈɛn/ *abbr* 缩写 = (*Brit*) State Enrolled Nurse (with 2 years' training): *be an SEN* 为国家登记护士 ○ *Judy Green SEN* 朱迪·格林, 国家登记护士. Cf 参看 SRN.

Sen *abbr* 缩写 = **1** Senate. **2** Senator: *Sen John K Nordqvist* 约翰·K·诺德维斯参议员. **3** (also **Snr, Sr**) Senior: *John F Davis Sen*, ie to distinguish him from his son with the same name 老约翰·F·戴维斯(用以区别同名的儿子). Cf 参看 JNR.

sen·ate /ˈsenɪt; ˈsɛnɪt/ *n* (often 常作 **Senate**) **1** [CGp] upper house of the law-making assembly in some countries, eg France, the US and Australia 参议院(如法国、美国、澳大利亚的): [attrib 作定语] *a Senate committee, decision* 参议院委员会、决议. Cf 参看 CONGRESS 2, THE HOUSE OF REPRESENTATIVES (HOUSE[1]). **2** [CGp] governing council of certain universities (某些大学的)教务委员会, 理事会. **3** [Gp] (in ancient Rome) highest council of state (古罗马的)元老院.
▷ **sen·ator** /ˈsenətə(r); ˈsɛnətɚ/ *n* (often 常作

S

Senator, *abbr* 缩写 **Sen**) member of the senate 参议员. **sen·at·orial** /ˌsenəˈtɔ:rɪəl; ˌsɛnəˈtɔrɪəl/ *adj* [attrib 作定语]: *senatorial rank, powers, office* 参议员的级别、权力、办事处.

send /send; sɛnd/ *v* (*pt, pp* **sent** /sent; sɛnt/) **1** [Tn, Tn·pr, Tn·p, Dn·n, Dn·pr] **~ sth/sb (to sb/sth)** cause sth/sb to go or be taken without going oneself 送或寄某物; 派或遣某人: *send a letter, telegram, message, etc* 寄信、发电报、传送信息 ○ *send goods, documents, information* 发送货物、文件、资料 ○ *I've sent the children to bed.* 我把孩子打发上床了. ○ *Send out the invitations to the party.* 发出宴会的请帖. ○ *His mother sent him to the shop to get some bread.* 他母亲让他去商店买些面包. ○ *We sent him a letter/We sent a letter to him.* 我们给他寄了一封信. **2** [Tn, Tn·p] **~ sth (out)** transmit (a signal, etc) by radio waves 用无线电波发送(信号): *The radio operator sent (out) an appeal for help to headquarters.* 无线电报务员向司令部发出求救信号. **3** [Tn·pr, Tn·p, Cn·g] cause (sth) to move sharply or quickly, often by force 使(某物)猛然或迅速移动(常指靠外力): *Whenever he moved, the wound sent pains all along his arm.* 他只要一动, 伤口就连带整个胳膊都疼. ○ *Space rockets are being sent up all the time.* 现在随时都有火箭发射. ○ *She bumped against the table and sent the crockery crashing to the ground*, ie knocked it to the ground. 她碰到了桌子, 把杯子、盘子都撞碎在地上了. ○ *The explosion sent us running in all directions.* 那次爆炸把我们轰得东奔西逃. ○ (*fig* 比喻) *The difficult word sent me to my dictionary*, ie to find its meaning. 这个词把我难住了, 只好去查词典. ○ *The bad weather has sent vegetable prices up.* 天气不好, 影响到蔬菜价格上涨. ○ *The storm sent the temperature down.* 暴风雨袭来, 气温随之下降. **4** (**a**) [Cn·a] cause (sb) to become 使(某人)变得: *send sb mad/crazy/insane/berserk* 使某人发疯[发狂/神经失常/勃然大怒]. (**b**) [Tn·pr] **~ sb to/into sth** make sb enter a specified state 使某人进入某种状态: *send sb to sleep* 使某人入睡 ○ *send sb into a rage, a frenzy, fits of laughter* 使某人大怒、发狂、哈哈大笑 ○ *The news sent the Stock Exchange into a panic.* 这个消息把证券交易所里的人吓得惊慌失措. **5** [It] (*fml* 文) send a message 发出信息: *She sent to say that she was safe and well.* 她送来消息说她安然无恙. **6** [Tn] (*dated infml* 旧, 口) excite (sb); thrill 使(某人)兴奋; 使激动: *That music really sends me!* 我听到这种音乐非常兴奋! **7** (idm 习语) **give/send sb one's love** ⇨ LOVE[1]. **send sb about his business** = SEND SB PACKING. **send sb/sth flying** hit or knock sb/sth so that he/it falls over or backwards 将某人[某物]打倒、打翻或打得向后退: *The blow sent him flying.* 这一击把他打倒了. **send things flying** cause things to be thrown violently in all directions 使东西被抛向各处. **send sb ˈpacking** (*infml* 口) tell sb (roughly or rudely) to go away (粗暴地)叫某人走开: *She tried to interfere, but I sent her packing!* 她想多管闲事, 我把她赶走了! **send sb to ˈCoventry** refuse to speak to sb, esp as a punishment by other members of a group 拒不与某人谈话(尤指集体以此惩罚某人): *Men who refused to strike were sent to Coventry by their colleagues.* 凡是不参加罢工的人, 同事都不理睬他们. **8** (phr v) **send away (to sb) (for sth)** = SEND OFF (FOR STH). **send sb down** (*Brit*) (**a**) expel (a student) from a university (大学中)开除(某学生). (**b**) (*infml* 口) sentence sb to imprisonment 判某人入狱: *He was sent down for ten years for armed robbery.* 他因持械抢劫被判入狱十年. **send for sth; send for sb (to do sth)** ask or order that sth be brought or delivered, or that sb should come 要求或指示将某物取来或送到, 或使某人来到: *send for a fresh supply of paper* 要求再送些纸来 ○ *send for a taxi, an ambulance, a doctor* 找计程车、叫救护车、请医生来 ○ *send for sb to repair the TV* 请人来修理电视机. **send sb in** order sb to go to a place in order to deal with a situation 指示某人去某地处理某局面: *Soldiers were sent in to quell the riots.* 已派士兵去镇压动乱. **send sth in** send sth by post to a place where it will be dealt with 将某物寄至某处进行处理: *Have you sent in your application for the job?* 你的求职申请书寄出去了吗? **send off (for sth)** write to sb to ask for sth to be sent to one by post 写信要求某人将某物寄来: *I've sent off for those bulbs I saw advertised in the paper.* 我已写信订购我在报纸广告上看到的那种灯泡. **send sb off** (*Brit*) (of a referee, etc) send a footballer, etc off the playing field for breaking the rules of play (指裁判等)将犯规的足球运动员等判罚下场. **send sth off** send sth by post; dispatch sth 寄出或发出某物: *Have you sent that letter off yet? There's something I want to add to it.* 你把那封信寄出去了吗? 我还想再附上一句话. **send sth out** (**a**) give sth out from itself; emit sth 从某事物本身发出或放出某事物; 射出某物: *The sun sends out light and warmth.* 太阳不断放出光和热. (**b**) produce sth 生出或长出某物: *The trees send out new leaves in spring.* 树在春天长出新叶子. **send sb to....** cause sb to attend a particular place or institution 使某人进入某处或某机构: *They send their daughter to one of the best schools in the country.* 他们把女儿送进国内最好的学校. ○ *He was sent to hospital/to prison.* 他被送进医院[监狱]. **send sb up** (*US infml* 口) send sb to prison 把某人关进监狱. **send sb/sth up** (*Brit infml* 口) make fun of sb/sth, esp by copying in a comical way 取笑某人[某事物](尤指用滑稽的模仿方式): *comedians who send up members of the government* 用滑稽模仿动作取笑政府官员的喜剧演员 ○ *Bill is constantly being sent up by his children.* 比尔经常遭自己孩子耍笑.

□ ˈ**send-off** *n* act of saying goodbye to sb 送行; 送别: *She was given a good send-off at the airport.* 她在飞机场受到了热情的欢送.

ˈ**send-up** *n* imitation intended to make fun of sth or sb 旨在取笑的模仿: *Her book is a hilarious send-up of a conventional spy story.* 她写的书用的是取笑传统侦探小说的笔法, 令人捧腹.

sender /ˈsendə(r); ˈsɛndɚ/ *n* person who sends 发送或邮寄物品的人: *If undelivered, return to sender*, eg on a letter. 若无法投递, 请退还寄件人(如信件上的字样).

sen·es·cent /sɪˈnesnt; səˈnɛsn̩t/ *adj* (*fml or medical* 文或医) becoming old 衰老的; 变老的.

▷ **sen·es·cence** /sɪˈnesns; səˈnɛsn̩s/ *n* [U] (*fml or medical* 文或医) process of becoming old 衰老的过程.

sen·ile /ˈsi:naɪl; ˈsinaɪl/ *adj* suffering from bodily or mental weakness because of old age 衰老的: *He keeps forgetting things: I think he's getting senile.* 他总忘事, 我看他是老了.

▷ **sen·il·ity** /sɪˈnɪlətɪ; səˈnɪlətɪ/ *n* [U] state of being senile 衰老的状态.

□ **senile dementia** /ˌsi:naɪl dɪˈmenʃə; ˌsinaɪl dɪˈmɛnʃə/ illness of old people resulting in loss of memory, loss of control of bodily functions, etc 老年痴呆.

se·nior /ˈsi:nɪə(r); ˈsinjɚ/ *adj* **1 ~ (to sb)** (**a**) older 较年长的: *He is ten years senior to me.* 他比我大十岁. (**b**) higher in rank, authority, etc (级别、权位等)较高的: *There are separate rooms for senior and junior officers.* 高级军官和下级军官的房间是分着的. ○ *He is the senior partner in* (ie the head of) *the firm.* 他是公司的老板. (**c**) having been in a job, etc longer (做某工作等)年资较深的: *She is senior to me, since she joined the firm before me.* 她比我资格老, 因为她加入公司比我早. **2** (often 常作 **Senior**, *abbr* 缩写 **Sen**) (placed immediately after sb's name 置于姓名之后) being the parent of sb with the same name (父或母与子女同名情况下的)父或母: *John Brown Senior* 老约翰·布朗. **3** [attrib 作定语] (of a school) for children over the age of 11 (指学校)高年级的(学生年龄在11岁以上的). Cf 参看 JUNIOR.

▷ **se·nior** *n* **1** senior person 较年长的人: *She is my senior by two years/two years my senior*, ie is two years older than me. 她比我大两岁. **2** member of a senior school 高年级学生: *a football match between the juniors and the seniors* 低年级学生和高年级学生之间的足球赛. **3** (*US*) student in the year before graduation from a high school or college (中学或大学的)毕业班的学生: [attrib 作定语] *her senior year at college* 她在大学毕业班那一年.

se·ni·or·ity /ˌsi:nɪˈɒrətɪ; *US* -ˈɔ:r-; sinˈjɔrətɪ/ *n* [U] **1** being senior in age, rank, etc 年长; 级别高; 资格老: *Should promotion be through merit or seniority?* 晋升应该凭成绩还是靠年资? **2** extent to which sb is senior 年长、级别高或资格老的程度: *a doctor with five years' seniority over his colleague* 比同事多五年资历的医生.

□ ˌ**senior ˈcitizen** (*euph* 婉) old or retired person 老人; 退休的人.

senna /ˈsenə; ˋsɛnə/ *n* [U] dried leaves of a tropical plant, used as a laxative 旃那叶, 山扁豆叶, 番泻叶(热带一种植物的干叶, 用作通便剂).

señor /seˈnjɔ:(r); senˋjɔr/ *n* (*pl* **señores** /seˈnjɔ:reɪz; seˋnjɔrez/) (before a name, 用于人名前作 **Señor**) (title of a) Spanish-speaking man; Mr or sir 说西班牙语的男子; (对说西班牙语男子的称呼)先生(相当于 Mr或 sir).

▷ **señ·ora** /seˈnjɔ:rə; senˋjɔrə/ *n* (before a name, 用于人名前作 **Señora**) (title of a) Spanish-speaking woman; Mrs or madam 说西班牙语的女子; (对说西班牙语女子的称呼)夫人, 太太(相当于 Mrs或 madam).

señ·or·ita /ˌsenjɔ:ˈri:tə; ˌsenjəˋritə/ *n* (before a name, 用于人名前作 **Señorita**) (title of an) unmarried Spanish-speaking woman or girl; Miss or madam 说西班牙语的未婚女子; (对说西班牙语未婚女子的称呼)小姐(相当于 Miss或 madam).

sen·sa·tion /senˈseɪʃn; sɛnˋseʃən/ *n* **1** (**a**) [C] feeling in one's body resulting from sth that happens or is done to it 感觉; 感受: *a sensation of warmth, dizziness, falling* 温暖、眩晕、下降的感觉 ○ *Massage produces wonderful sensations.* 按摩可产生舒适的感觉. (**b**) [C] general awareness or impression not caused by anything that can be seen or defined 下意识的感觉: *I had the sensation that I was being watched.* 我觉得有人监视着我. (**c**) [U] ability to feel through the sense of touch 知觉; 触觉: *lose all sensation in one's legs* 腿部完全失去知觉 ○ *Some sensation is coming back to my arm.* 我的胳膊逐渐恢复一些知觉. **2** [C, U] state of great surprise, excitement, interest, etc among many people 轰动; 群情激动: *The news caused a great sensation.* 这个消息十分轰动. ○ (*derog* 贬) *Sensation-seeking newspapers tried to cash in on her misery.* 专登危言耸听内容的报纸竭力渲染她的苦境来卖钱.

▷ **sen·sa·tional** /-ʃənl; -ʃənḷ/ *adj* **1** (**a**) causing sensation(2) 轰动的; 群情激动的: *a sensational crime, victory, etc* 骇人听闻的罪案、轰轰烈烈的胜利. (**b**) (*derog* 贬) trying to cause a sensation(2) 耸人听闻的: *a sensational newspaper, writer* 刊登耸动视听消息的报纸、写耸人听闻内容的作家. **2** (*infml* 口) extraordinarily good; wonderful 极好的; 绝妙的: *You look sensational in that dress.* 你穿着那件连衣裙漂亮极了. ○ *That music is sensational!* 这段乐曲太优美了! **sen·sa·tion·al·ism** /-ʃənəlɪzəm; -ʃənḷˌɪzəm/ *n* [U] (*derog* 贬) deliberate use of shocking words, scandalous stories, etc in order to produce a sensation(2) 为耸动视听而使用的词语、描绘的丑事等: *Avoid sensationalism in reporting crime.* 报道罪案时要避免使用耸动视听的手段. ○ *the sensationalism of the popular press* 为大众服务的新闻界所使用的耸动视听的做法. **sen·sa·tion·al·ist** /-ʃənəlɪst; -ʃənḷɪst/ *n*. **sen·sa·tion·al·ize, -ise** /-ʃənəlaɪz; -ʃənəˌlaɪz/ *v* [Tn] (*derog* 贬) treat (sth) in a way that is likely to cause public excitement 用耸动视听的方法处理(某事物): *a sensationalized account of a squalid crime* 用耸人听闻的方式描绘的卑劣罪行. **sen·sa·tion·ally** /-ʃənəlɪ; -ʃənḷɪ/ *adv*: *Newspapers reported the incident sensationally, making it appear worse than it really was.* 报纸大肆渲染这件事, 描述得更不像话.

sense /sens; sɛns/ *n* **1** [C] any of the five powers of the body by which a person, an animal, etc receives knowledge of things in the world around, ie sight, hearing, smell, taste and touch 感觉官能; 视觉; 听觉; 嗅觉; 味觉; 触觉: *the five senses* 五种感觉官能 ○ *have a keen sense of hearing* 听觉灵敏. **2** [U, sing] (**a**) appreciation or understanding of the value or worth of sth (对价值的)辨别, 理解, 领悟: *a sense of the* (ie the ability to know what is) *absurd, ridiculous, etc* 对荒唐、可笑等事物的识别力 ○ *not have much sense of humour*, ie a liking for jokes, funny situations, etc 没什么幽默感 ○ *a person with no sense of direction*, ie who cannot find his way easily 无方向感的人. (**b**) consciousness of sth; awareness 觉察; 觉悟: *a sense of one's own importance, worth, etc* 对自身的重要性、价值等的觉察 ○ *have no sense of shame, guilt, etc* 无羞耻心、无罪恶感 ○ *feel a sense of security in her arms* 在她怀里感到安全. **3** [U] ability to make reasonable judgements; practical wisdom 识别力; 常识; 见识: *have the sense to come in out of the rain* 懂得进来避雨 ○ *There's a lot of sense in what she says.* 她说的话很有见地. **4 senses** [pl] normal state of mind; ability to think 健全的心智; 思维的能力: *lose/regain one's senses* 失去[恢复]理智. **5** [U] reason; purpose 道理; 目的: *What's the sense of doing that?* 为什么要做那件事呢? ○ *There's no sense in going alone*, ie It would be better not to. 一个人去没有好处. **6** [C] (**a**) meaning of a word, phrase, etc (词语等的)意义: *a word with several senses* 有几个意思的词 ○ *The sense of the word is not clear.* 这个词的意思不清楚. (**b**) way in which a word, sentence, etc is to be understood (词句等)被理解的意义: *in the strict/literal/figurative sense of the expression* 按照严格的[字面的/比喻的]意义来说 ○ *I am a worker only in the sense that I work; I don't get paid for what I do.* 我是工作人员, 这是仅就我做工作而言的; 我并无报酬. **7** [sing] **the ~ of sth** (*fml* 文) general feeling or opinion among a group of people (集体的)普遍感觉或意见: *The sense of the meeting was* (ie Most people present thought) *that he should resign.* 与会者普遍认为他应该辞职. **8** (idm 习语) **beat, knock, drive, etc (some) sense into sb** (*infml* 口) change sb's behaviour, views, etc by severe or sometimes violent methods 改变某人的行为、看法等(用严厉的, 有时为粗暴的方式): *She's a wild uncontrollable girl, but that new school should knock some sense into her.* 她是个很不听话的女孩儿, 那所新学校应该能管管她了. **bring sb to his/come to one's ˈsenses** (**a**) (make sb) stop behaving foolishly or irrationally (使某人)不再做傻事或不理智的事: *He was finally brought to his senses and agreed to let the hostages go.* 他最后恢复些理智, 同意释放人质. (**b**) wake (sb) up from unconsciousness 使(某人)苏醒: *When I came to my senses, I was lying on the floor.* 我苏醒过来的时候是在地板上躺着呢. **in a ˈsense** if the statement, etc is understood in a particular way 在某种意义上: *What you say is true in a sense.* 你的话在某种意义上属实. **in one's ˈsenses** in one's normal state of mind; sensible 头脑健全; 神志清醒: *No one in their right senses would let a small child go out alone.* 凡是有理智的人, 谁都不会让那么小的孩子独自出门. **make ˈsense** (**a**) have an understandable meaning 有意义; 有道理; 讲得通: *What you say makes no sense.* 你说的话没有道理. ○ *These words are jumbled up and don't make sense.* 这些词藻堆砌在一起讲不通. (**b**) be sensible 是明智的; 是合情理的: *It doesn't make sense to buy that expensive coat when these cheaper ones are just as good.* 这些便宜的大衣也很好, 何必非买那件贵的不可. ○ *It would make sense to leave early.* 还是早点儿走好. **make sense of sth** understand sth difficult or apparently meaningless 理解或弄懂困难的或似无法理解的事物: *Can you make sense of this poem?* 你看得懂这首诗吗? **out of one's ˈsenses** not in one's normal state of mind; foolish 精神不正常; 愚蠢: *You sold it? You must be out of your senses!* 你把它卖了? 你简直是疯了! **see ˈsense** start to be sensible 明白事理: *I hope she soon sees sense and stops fighting a battle she cannot win.* 我希望她能很快明白过来, 别再打这场打不赢的仗了. **a sense of occasion** special feeling produced in sb by a special event, etc 遇到某种情况而产生的某种感觉. **a sixth sense** awareness of things one cannot actually see, hear, etc 第六感觉; 第六感官: *A sixth sense told her that he would be waiting for her when she got home.* 她有一种第六感觉, 就是她到家时他一定在那儿等候她呢. **take leave of one's senses** ⇨ LEAVE[2]. **talk sense** ⇨TALK[2].

▷ **sense** *v* **1** [Tn, Tf, Tw] become aware of (sth); feel 意识到(某事物); 感觉到: *sense sb's sorrow, hostility, etc* 感觉到某人的忧愁、敌意等 ○ *Although she didn't say anything, I sensed (that) she didn't like the idea.* 她虽然什么也没说, 但我已意识到她不喜欢这个主意. **2** [Tn] (of a machine, etc) detect (sth) (指机器等)检测出(某事物): *an apparatus that senses the presence of toxic gases* 能检测出有毒气体存在的仪器.

□ **ˈsense-organ** bodily organ, eg the ear or the eye, by which the body becomes aware of what is happening around it 感觉器官(如耳朵、眼睛).

sense·less /ˈsenslɪs; ˋsɛnslɪs/ *adj* **1** pointless; foolish 无意义的; 无针对性的; 愚蠢的: *a senseless idea, action* 愚蠢的主意、行为 ○ *I condemn this senseless violence.* 我谴责这种无谓的暴行. ○ *It would be senseless to continue any further.* 再继续下去就没意义了. **2** [usu pred 通常作表语] unconscious 失去知觉; 无感觉: *fall senseless to* *the ground* 倒在地上不省人事. ▷ **sense·lessly** *adv*. **sense·less·ness** *n* [U].

sens·ibil·ity /ˌsensəˈbɪlətɪ; ˌsɛnsəˈbɪlətɪ/ *n* **1** [C usu *pl* 通常作复数] ability to receive and appreciate delicate impressions; sensitivity 识别力; 敏感性; 灵敏度: *the sensibility of a poet* 诗人的鉴赏力 ○ *a man of subtle and refined sensibilities* 感情细腻的男子. **2 sensibilities** [pl] capacity for being easily offended or shocked (易生气或易受刺激的)感情: *wound/offend/outrage readers' sensibilities* 伤害[挫伤/触怒]读者的感情.

sens·ible /ˈsensəbl; ˈsɛnsəbl/ *adj* **1** (**a**) (*approv* 褒) having or showing good sense(3); reasonable 识别力强的; 合理的: *a sensible person, idea, course of action, suggestion* 通情达理的人、主意、做法、建议 ○ *It was sensible of you to lock the door.* 你把门锁上了, 做得对. (**b**) [attrib 作定语] (of clothing, etc) practical rather than fashionable (指衣着等)实用而不时髦的: *wear sensible shoes for long walks* 为走长路而穿舒适的鞋. **2** [pred 作表语] **~ of sth** (*fml* 文) aware of sth 觉察到某事物: *Are you sensible of the dangers of your position?* 你觉察出你处境中的危险了吗? **3** [attrib 作定语] (*dated* 旧) that can be perceived by the senses (SENSE 1); perceptible 可感觉到的: *a sensible rise in temperature* 可以感觉到的温度升高.

▷ **sens·ibly** /-əblɪ; -əblɪ/ *adv* in a sensible(1) way 有识别力地; 合情理地: *sensibly dressed for hot weather* 天热时穿得很合时宜.

NOTE ON USAGE 用法: The noun **sense** can mean **1** 'the way the body experiences its surroundings': *the sense of touch, sight, etc*, or **2** 'reason, good judgement': *She talks a lot of good sense.* ☆ **sense** 作名词时可指 **1** '身体感受周围事物的方式': the sense of touch, sight, etc(触觉、视觉等), 也可指 **2** '道理、识别力': She talks a lot of good sense. (她说得很有道理.) The adjective **sensitive** usually relates to meaning **1** 与这个词有关的形容词 **sensitive** 含上述第1义: *She's got very sensitive hearing, skin, etc.* 她的听觉、触觉等很灵敏. ○ *Don't laugh at him; he's very sensitive.* 千万别笑他, 他很敏感. **Sensible** relates to meaning **2** 另一个形容词 **sensible** 含上述第2义: *She gave me some sensible advice.* 她给我提的建议很有道理. ○ *You must try to be more sensible.* 你得懂点儿好歹.

S

sens·it·ive /ˈsensətɪv; ˈsɛnsətɪv/ *adj* **1** (**a**) easily hurt or damaged 易受伤害的; 易损坏的: *the sensitive skin of a baby* 婴儿娇嫩的皮肤 ○ *A sensitive nerve in a tooth can cause great pain.* 牙神经易受损伤, 可产生巨痛. (**b**) **~ (to sth)** affected greatly or easily by sth 很受影响的; 易受影响的; 敏感的: *Photographic paper is highly sensitive to light.* 感光纸对光十分敏感. ○ *This material is heat-sensitive*, ie responds quickly to changes in temperature. 这种材料对温度变化很敏感. **2 ~ (about/to sth)** easily offended or emotionally upset 易生气的; 感情容易冲动的; 神经质的: *a frail and sensitive child* 脆弱而娇气的孩子 ○ *He's very sensitive about being small, so don't mention it.* 他对自己个子矮小神经过敏, 可别提这件事. ○ *A writer mustn't be too sensitive to criticism.* 作家不可对批评意见反应过激. **3** (*approv* 褒) having or showing perceptive feeling or sympathetic understanding 有细腻感情的; 同情理解的: *an actor's sensitive reading of a poem* 演员富于感情的诗朗诵 ○ *When I need advice, he is a helpful and sensitive friend.* 我一没了主意他就帮助我, 是个体贴人的朋友. **4 ~ (to sth)** (of instruments, etc) able to measure very small changes (指仪器等)灵敏的: *a sensitive thermometer, balance, ammeter, etc* 灵敏的温度计、天平、安培计等 ○ (*fig* 比喻) *The Stock Exchange is sensitive to likely political changes.* 证券交易所对潜在的政治变化很敏感. **5** needing to be treated with great secrecy or tact 需极秘密或慎重处理的: *sensitive military information* 需秘密处理的军事情报 ○ *a sensitive issue like race relations* 需慎重对待的种族关系问题. ⇨Usage at SENSIBLE 用法见 SENSIBLE.

▷ **sens·it·ively** *adv*.

sens·it·iv·ity /ˌsensəˈtɪvətɪ; ˌsɛnsəˈtɪvətɪ/ *n* [U] **~ (to sth)** quality or degree of being sensitive 易受伤害的特性; 敏感性; 灵敏度: *sensitivity to pain, light, heat* 对疼痛、光、热的敏感 ○ *the sensitivity of a writer* 作家的细腻感情.

sens·it·ize, -ise /ˈsensɪtaɪz; ˈsɛnsəˌtaɪz/ *v* [esp passive 尤用于被动语态: Tn, Tn·pr] **~ sth/sb (to sth) 1** make sth or sb sensitive 使某事物或某人敏感: *sensitize students to a poet's use of language* 培养学生对诗人语言运用的感受能力. **2** (in photography) make (film, paper, etc) sensitive to light (摄影)使(胶片、纸等)易于感光.

sensor /ˈsensə(r); ˈsɛnsɚ/ *n* device (eg a photoelectric cell) that detects light, heat, humidity, etc 探测光、热、湿度等的装置(如光电池): *Smoke sensors warned us of the fire.* 烟雾探测器已向我们发出火警警报.

sens·ory /ˈsensərɪ; ˈsɛnsərɪ/ *adj* [usu attrib 通常作定语] of the senses (SENSE 1) or of sensation 感觉官能的; 感觉的; 感受的: *sensory organs/nerves* 感觉器官[神经] ○ *a sensory stimulus* 感官刺激 ○ *sensory deprivation* 感觉丧失.

sen·sual /ˈsenʃʊəl; ˈsɛnʃʊəl/ = *adj* (*sometimes derog* 有时作贬义) of, suggesting, enjoying or giving physical (often sexual) pleasure 肉体上享乐的; (常指)性快感的: *the sensual feel of a warm bath* 洗温水澡的舒服感觉 ○ *a life devoted entirely to sensual pleasure* 耽于肉欲的一生 ○ *the sensual curves of her body* 她体形的性感的曲线.

▷ **sen·su·al·ist** *n* person who enjoys physical pleasures, esp to excess 喜欢感官享受的人; (尤指)耽于肉欲的人.

sen·su·al·ity /ˌsenʃʊˈælətɪ; ˌsɛnʃʊˈælətɪ/ *n* [U] (excessive) love or enjoyment of physical pleasure (过分的)肉欲.

sen·su·ally /-ʃʊəlɪ; -ʃʊəlɪ/ *adv*.

sen·su·ous /ˈsenʃʊəs; ˈsɛnʃʊəs/ *adj* affecting, noticed by or giving pleasure to the senses 刺激感官的; 感觉官能的; 给感官以快感的: *the sensuous appeal of her painting* 她的画儿之使人赏心悦目 ○ *his full sensuous lips* 他那丰满漂亮的嘴唇. ▷ **sen·su·ously** *adv*: *She swayed her hips sensuously as she danced.* 她跳舞时扭动着臀部十分诱人. **sen·su·ous·ness** *n* [U].

sent *pt, pp* of SEND.

sen·tence /ˈsentəns; ˈsɛntəns/ *n* **1** [C] (*grammar*) largest unit of grammar, usu containing a subject, a verb, an object, etc and expressing a statement, question or command 句子; 句. **2** [C, U] (*law* 律) (statement of the) punishment given by a lawcourt 判决; 宣判; 判刑: *The judge passed/pronounced sentence (on the prisoner)*, ie said what his punishment would be. 法官宣布了(对犯人的)判决. ○ *She has served her sentence, and will now be released.* 她已服刑期满, 现即将获释. ○ *under sentence of death*, ie to be officially killed as a punishment 判处死刑 ○ *a sentence of ten years' imprisonment* 十年监禁之刑.

▷ **sen·tence** *v* [Tn, Tn·pr, Dn·t] **~ sb (to sth)** state that sb is to have a certain punishment 判决; 宣判: *sentence a thief to six months' imprisonment* 判处窃贼六个月监禁 ○ *He has been sentenced to pay a fine of £1 000.* 他被判罚款1 000英镑. ○ (*fig* 比喻) *a crippling disease which sentenced him to a lifetime in a wheelchair* 把他终生束缚在轮椅上的残疾.

sen·ten·tious /senˈtenʃəs; sɛnˈtɛnʃəs/ *adj* (*fml derog* 文, 贬) expressing pompous moral judgements 说教的: *a sententious speaker, speech, remark, book* 说教式的演讲者、演说、言语、书. ▷ **sen·ten·tiously** *adv*: *'He should have thought of the consequences before he acted,' she concluded sententiously.* 她最后以说教的口吻说: '他应该先想到后果然后再做.' **sen·ten·tious·ness** *n* [U].

sen·tient /ˈsenʃnt; ˈsɛnʃənt/ *adj* [attrib 作定语] (*fml* 文) capable of perceiving or feeling things 能感知或感觉事物的: *a sentient being* 有感觉的生物.

sen·ti·ment /ˈsentɪmənt; ˈsɛntəmənt/ *n* **1** [U] (*usu derog* 通常作贬义) tender feelings of pity, nostalgia, etc, which may be exaggerated or wrongly directed (contrasted esp with reason) (对怜悯、怀旧等的)柔情情感(可为夸张的或滥施的, 尤与理智相对): *act from rational motives rather than sentiment* 行事出于理智而非出于怜悯之情 ○ *a love story full of cloying sentiment* 通篇缠绵伤感的爱情小说 ○ *There's no room for sentiment in business.* 做生意不能婆婆妈妈的感情用事. **2** [U, C usu *pl* 作不可数名词或可数名词, 后者通常作复数] (expression of an) attitude or opinion, usu influenced by emotion 态度或意见(的表示)(通常指受感情影响的): *a speech full of lofty sentiments* 充分表达高尚情操的演

讲 ○ *Sentiment in the City* (ie the financial centre of London) *is now in favour of a cut in taxes.* 在伦敦金融中心，群情期于减税. **3 sentiments** [pl] (*fml or rhet* 文或修辞) point of view; opinion 观点；意见：*What are your sentiments on this issue?* 你对这个问题有什么看法？○ *My sentiments exactly!* ie I agree! 我完全同意！

sen·ti·mental /ˌsentɪˈmentl; ˌsɛntəˋmɛntl̩/ *adj* **1** of or concerning the emotions, rather than the reason 情感的，情绪的（非理智的）：*do sth for sentimental reasons* 由于感情的原因而做某事 ○ *have a sentimental attachment to one's birth-place* 对出生地有眷恋之情 ○ *a watch with sentimental value*, ie which is precious eg because it was given by sb one loves 有怀念价值的手表（因所爱的人所赠）. **2** (*usu derog* 通常作贬义) **(a)** (of things) expressing or arousing tender emotions, such as pity, romantic love or nostalgia, which may be exaggerated or wrongly directed （指事物）表达或引起柔懦情感的（可为夸张的或滥施的）：*sentimental music* 令人感伤的音乐 ○ *a sloppy, sentimental love story* 伤情感心的爱情小说. **(b) ~ (about sb/sth)** (of people) having such emotions （指人）有柔懦情感的：*She's too sentimental about her cat.* 她对她的猫未免太牵肠挂肚了. ▷ **sen·ti·ment·al·ist** /-təlɪst; -təlɪst/ *n* (*derog* 贬) person who is sentimental(2b) 情感柔懦的人.

sen·ti·ment·al·ity /ˌsentɪmenˈtæləti; ˌsɛntəmɛnˋtælətɪ/ *n* [U] (*derog* 贬)quality of being too sentimental(2a) 情感过于柔懦的特性：*the sickly sentimentality of a romantic novel* 一部浪漫小说中无病呻吟的柔懦情调.

sen·ti·ment·al·ize, -ise /-təlaɪz; -tl̩ˌaɪz/ *v* [I, Tn] (*derog* 贬) speak or write sentimentally; treat (sb/sth) sentimentally 说或写时表达柔懦情感；以柔懦的情感对待（某人［某事物］）：*Don't sentimentalize when you talk about animals.* 谈论动物不必忧形于色. ○ *This book sentimentalizes the suffering of the disabled.* 这本书以柔懦的笔调渲染了残疾人的痛苦.

sen·ti·ment·ally /-təlɪ; -tl̩ɪ/ *adv*.

sen·tinel /ˈsentɪnl; ˋsɛntənl̩/ *n* (*fml or dated* 文或旧) sentry 岗哨；哨兵：(*fig* 比喻) *The Press is a sentinel of* (ie guards or protects) *our liberty.* 新闻界是捍卫我们自由的卫士.

sen·try /ˈsentrɪ; ˋsɛntrɪ/ *n* soldier posted outside a building, etc in order to watch or guard it 岗哨；哨兵：*People approaching the gate were challenged by the sentry.* 向大门走去的人受到了哨兵的查问. ○ [attrib 作定语] *sentry duty* 哨兵的值勤.

□ ˈ**sentry-box** *n* small hut for a standing sentry 岗亭.

sepal /ˈsepl; ˋsɛpl̩/ *n* (*botany* 植) any of the leaf-like parts which lie under and support the petals of a flower 萼片.

sep·ar·able /ˈsepərəbl; ˋsɛpərəbl̩/ *adj* **~ (from sth)** that can be separated 可分开的；可分隔的：*The lower part of the pipe is separable from the upper part.* 管子的下部可与上部分开. ▷ **sep·ar·ably** /-əblɪ; -əblɪ/ *adv*.

sep·ar·ab·il·ity /ˌseprəˈbɪlətɪ; ˌsɛprəˋbɪlətɪ/ *n* [U].

sep·ar·ate[1] /ˈseprət; ˋsɛprɪt/ *adj* **1 ~ (from sth/sb)** forming a unit by itself; existing apart 自成一单元的；单独存在的；分开的：*The children sleep in separate beds.* 孩子都睡在各自的床上. ○ *Violent prisoners are kept separate from the others.* 有暴力行为的囚犯隔离囚禁. ○ *They lead separate lives*, ie do not live or do things together. 他们各自单独生活. ○ *We can't work together any more; I think it's time we went our separate ways*, ie parted. 我们再也不能在一起工作了，我看得各奔东西了. **2** [usu attrib 通常作定语] different or distinct 不同的；有区别的：*It happened on three separate occasions.* 这件事在三个不同场合都发生过. ○ *That is a separate issue and irrelevant to our discussion.* 这是另一个问题，同我们的讨论无关.

▷ **sep·ar·ately** *adv* as separate people or things; not together 分着地；不在一起：*They are now living separately.* 他们现在分居了. ○ *Can the engine and the gearbox be supplied separately?* 发动机和变速箱能分开供应吗？**sep·ar·ates** *n* [pl] individual items of clothing designed to be worn together in different combinations （可与不同衣物配合使用的）单件衣物.

sep·ar·at·ism /ˈsepərətɪzəm; ˋsɛpərəˌtɪzəm/ *n* [U] policy of staying or becoming a separate group from other people, esp through political independence 分离主义，独立主义（尤指通过政治独立的）.

sep·ar·at·ist /ˈsepərətɪst; ˋsɛpəˌretɪst/ *n* [attrib 作定语]: *the Basque separatist organization ETA* 西班牙巴斯克分离主义组织埃塔（埃塔ETA为巴斯克语'巴斯克祖国与自由'的缩写）.

sep·ar·ate[2] /ˈsepəreɪt; ˋsɛpəˌret/ *v* **1** [I, Ipr, Ip, Tn, Tn·pr, Tn·p] **(a) ~ (sb/sth) (from sb/sth); ~ sth (up) (into sth)** (cause things or people to) come apart; divide （使事物或人与人）分离，分开：*The two parts of the pipe have separated at the joint.* 这个管子从接口处分成两截了. ○ *The branch has separated from the trunk of the tree.* 这个树枝已从树干上脱落了. ○ *This patient should be separated from the others.* 这个病人应该隔离. ○ *The land has been separated (up) into small plots.* 这块地已经分成小块了. ○ *The children were separated into groups for the game.* 那些儿童分成小组做游戏. **(b) ~ (sth) (out) (from sth)** (cause sth to) stop being combined in a liquid mixture （使混合液）分离，离析：*Oil and water always separate out.* 油和水总是分开的. **2** [Tn, Tn·pr] **~ sth (from sth)** lie or stand between (two countries, areas, etc), keeping them apart 从中隔开（两国、两地等）：*A deep gorge separates the two halves of the city.* 有一道深谷把这座城市分成两部分. ○ *England is separated from France by the Channel.* 英国和法国之间隔着英吉利海峡. ○ (*fig* 比喻) *Politics is the only thing which separates us*, ie on which we disagree. 我们只是政治观点相左. **3** [I] (of people) leave each other's company （指人与人）分开，分手：*We talked until midnight and then separated.* 我们一直谈到深夜才分手. **4** [I] stop living together as a married couple （有婚姻关系的双方）分居：*After ten years of marriage they decided to separate.* 他们婚后十年决定分居了. **5** (idm 习语) **separate the sheep from the goats** distinguish good people from bad people 把好人同坏人分开. **separate the ˌwheat from the ˈchaff** distinguish valuable people or things from worthless ones 把有价值的人或事物同无价值的分开：*We have to sift through the application forms very carefully to separate the wheat from the chaff.* 我们得把申请书仔细筛选一下以甄别优劣.

▷ **sep·ar·ated** *adj* [pred 作表语] **~ (from sb)** no longer living together as a married couple (but not necessarily divorced) 分居（未必离婚）：*I'm separated from my wife.* 我和妻子分居了. ○ *We're separated.* 我们分居了.

sep·ar·ator *n* device that separates things, esp cream from milk 分离器；（尤指分离奶油的）脱脂器.

sep·ara·tion /ˌsepəˈreɪʃn; ˌsɛpəˋreʃən/ *n* **1 ~ (from sb/sth) (a)** [U] separating; state of being separate 分离；分开；隔开：*the separation of infectious patients from other patients* 传染病人与其他病人之隔离 ○ *Separation from his friends made him sad.* 他离开了朋友，十分难过. **(b)** [C] instance or period of being separated 分离；分开的期间：*after a separation of five years from his parents* （他）离开父母五年以后. **2** [U, sing] legal arrangement by which a married couple live apart but do not end the marriage （有婚姻关系的双方按法律程序的）分居：*decide on (a) separation* 决定按法律程序分居.

se·pia /ˈsiːpɪə; ˋsipɪə/ *n* [U] **1** brown colouring-matter used in inks and water-colour paints and (esp formerly) for printing photographs 斯比亚褐色颜料（用作墨水或水彩画颜料，尤指旧时印照片用的）. **2** rich reddish-brown colour 浓艳的红褐色.

▷ **se·pia** *adj* [usu attrib 通常作定语] of sepia colour 红褐色的：*an old sepia photograph* 一张旧的红褐色照片.

sep·sis /ˈsepsɪs; ˋsɛpsɪs/ *n* [U] (*medical* 医) infection of (part of) the body by bacteria 脓毒病；脓毒症. Cf 参看 SEPTIC.

Sept *abbr* 缩写 = September: *12 Sept 1969* 1969年9月12日.

Sep·tem·ber /sepˈtembə(r); sɛpˋtɛmbɚ/ *n* [U, C] (*abbr* 缩写 **Sept**) the ninth month of the year, next after August 九月.

For the uses of *September* see the examples at *April.* 关于September的用法见April词条中的示例.

sep·tet /sepˈtet; sɛpˋtɛt/ *n* (piece of music written for a) group of seven instruments or singers 七重奏（曲）；七重唱（曲）.

sept(i)- *comb form* 构词成分 having or made up of seven of sth 有七个的；由七个组成的：*septuagenarian.*

S

sep·tic /'septɪk; ˋsɛptɪk/ *adj* caused by or causing infection with harmful bacteria 由病菌引起或感染的; 脓毒性的: *a septic wound* 染毒创伤 ○ *A dirty cut may become septic*, ie affected by bacteria. 伤口不洁可受感染. Cf 参看 SEPSIS.

□ ˌ**septic 'tank** tank into which sewage flows and where it remains until the action of bacteria makes it liquid enough to drain away 化粪池.

sep·ti·caemia (*US* **-cemia**) /ˌseptɪ'si:mɪə; ˌsɛptəˋsimɪə/ *n* [U] (*medical* 医) blood-poisoning 败血症.

sep·tua·gen·arian /ˌseptjuədʒɪ'neərɪən; *US* -tʃʊdʒə-; ˌsɛptʃuədʒəˋnɛrɪən/ *n*, *adj* [attrib 作定语] (*fml* 文) (person) between the ages of 70 and 79 70到79岁的(人).

sep·ul·chre (*US* **sep·ul·cher**) /'seplkə(r); ˋsɛplkɚ/ *n* (*arch* 古) **1** tomb, esp one cut in rock or built of stone 坟墓, 塚(尤指石凿的或石砌的): *the Holy Sepulchre*, ie the one in which Jesus Christ was laid 圣墓(耶稣的墓). **2** (idm 习语) **a whited sepulchre** ⇨ WHITE[1] *v*. ▷ **se·pul·chral** /sɪ'pʌlkrəl; səˋpʌlkrəl/ *adj* (*fml* 文) **1** [usu attrib 通常作定语] of a tomb or of burial 坟墓的; 埋葬的. **2** looking or sounding gloomy 阴森森的; 阴郁的; 阴沉的: *a sepulchral face* 阴沉的脸色 ○ *speak in sepulchral tones* 用低沉的语调说话 ○ *look quite sepulchral* 看上去阴沉沉的.

se·quel /'si:kwəl; ˋsikwəl/ *n* **~ (to sth)** **1** thing that happens after or as a result of an earlier event 继之而来的事物; 有前因的事物: *His speech had an unfortunate sequel, in that it caused a riot.* 他的演说产生了不幸的后果, 由之引发一场骚乱. ○ *Famine is often the sequel to war.* 饥荒往往是战争造成的. **2** novel, film, etc that continues the story of an earlier one, often using the same characters (小说、电影等的)续篇, 续集: *He is writing a sequel to his latest best seller.* 他正在写他的最新畅销书的续集.

S

se·quence /'si:kwəns; ˋsikwəns/ *n* **1** [U, C] set of events, numbers, actions, etc with each following the one before continuously or in a particular order 有次序的事情、数字、行动等: *deal with events in historical sequence* 按照历史上的先后顺序研究大事件 ○ *describe the sequence of events*, ie in the order in which they occurred 按时间顺序叙述事情 ○ *a sequence of dance movements* 连续的舞蹈动作 ○ *a sequence of playing-cards*, ie three or more next to each other in value, eg 10, 9, 8 纸牌的顺牌(至少为三张点数相连的牌如10、9、8). **2** [C] part of a cinema film dealing with one scene or topic (影片中描述一个场景或主题的)连续镜头: *a thrilling sequence that includes a car chase* 含有汽车追逐镜头的紧张片段.

□ ˌ**sequence of 'tenses** (*grammar*) principles according to which the tenses of subordinate clauses are suited to the tenses of principal clauses 时态序列, 时态一致(从句时态须与主句时态相合的原则).

se·quen·tial /sɪ'kwenʃl; sɪˋkwɛnʃəl/ *adj* following in order of time or place; forming a sequence 按次序的; 顺序的; 序列的; 构成连续镜头的. ▷ **se·quen·tially** /-ʃəlɪ; -ʃəlɪ/ *adj*: *files of correspondence arranged sequentially* 按顺序排列的信件档案.

se·ques·ter /sɪ'kwestə(r); sɪˋkwɛstɚ/ *v* (*fml* 文) **1** [Tn, Tn·pr] **~ sb/oneself (from sth)** keep sb/oneself away or apart from other people; seclude 使某人[自己]与他人分开或隔离; 使隔绝: *sequester oneself from the world* 避世. **2** [Tn] (*law* 律) = SEQUESTRATE.

▷ **se·ques·tered** *adj* [usu attrib 通常作定语] (*fml* 文) quiet and secluded 僻静而与世隔绝的: *lead a sequestered life* 过离群索居的生活 ○ *a sequestered island far from the mainland* 远离大陆的僻静孤岛.

se·quest·rate /'si:kwestreɪt; sɪˋkwɛstret/ *v* [Tn] **1** (*law* 律) take temporary possession of (a debtor's property, funds, etc) until a debt has been paid or other claims met 扣押(债务人的财产、资金等)(至还清债务等时). **2** confiscate (sth) 没收; 充公. ▷ **se·quest·ra·tion** /ˌsi:kwe'streɪʃn; ˌsikwɛsˋtreʃən/ *n* [U].

se·quin /'si:kwɪn; ˋsikwɪn/ *n* small circular shiny disc sewn onto clothing as an ornament (衣物上作装饰用的)圆形小光片: *Her dress was covered in sequins which twinkled as she moved.* 她的连衣裙上镶着小光片, 身体一动就闪闪发光.

se·quoia /sɪ'kwɔɪə; sɪˋkwɔɪə/ *n* either of two types of large evergreen coniferous trees of California, the *redwood* or the *giant sequoia* 红杉, 巨杉(高大常绿树, 产于美国加利福尼亚州).

se·ra·glio /se'rɑ:lɪəʊ; sɪˋrɑljo/ *n* (*pl* **~s**) part of a Muslim household reserved for women; harem 穆斯林住宅中女眷居住的内室或闺房.

ser·aph /'serəf; ˋsɛrəf/ *n* (*pl* **~s** or **~im** /-fɪm; -fɪm/) (in the Bible) member of the highest order of angels (《圣经》中的)撒拉弗(级别最高的天使). Cf 参看 CHERUB.

▷ **ser·aphic** /se'ræfɪk; sɛˋræfɪk/ *adj* (*fml* 文) **1** like an angel in beauty or purity 似天使般美丽或纯洁的: *a seraphic child, nature* 天使般可爱的孩子、性格. **2** feeling or showing great happiness 极愉快的: *a seraphic smile* 极愉快的微笑.

sere = SEAR 1.

ser·en·ade /ˌserə'neɪd; ˌsɛrəˋned/ *n* song or tune (suitable to be) sung or played at night, esp by a lover outside the window of the woman he loves 小夜曲(尤指男子在所爱慕的女子窗外唱的或演奏的).

▷ **ser·en·ade** *v* [Tn] sing or play a serenade to (sb) 为(某人)唱或奏小夜曲.

se·ren·dip·ity /ˌserən'dɪpətɪ; ˌsɛrənˋdɪpətɪ/ *n* [U] (talent for) making pleasant and unexpected discoveries entirely by chance 全然无意中有所新奇发现(的本事).

se·rene /sɪ'ri:n; səˋrin/ *adj* calm and peaceful; tranquil 平静的; 宁静的: *a serene sky* 晴朗的天空 ○ *a serene look, smile, etc* 安详的神情、笑容等 ○ *In spite of the panic, she remained serene and in control.* 尽管人心惶惶, 但她却泰然自若. ▷ **se·renely** *adv*: *He seemed serenely unaware that anything had gone wrong.* 他神色平静, 似乎并不知道已出事了. **se·ren·ity** /sɪ'renətɪ; səˋrɛnətɪ/ *n* [U].

serf /sɜ:f; sɝf/ *n* **1** (formerly) person forced by a landowner to work on the land in a feudal system (旧时)(封建制度中的)农奴. **2** (*fig* 比喻) worker treated harshly or like a slave 像奴隶般受奴役的人.

▷ **serf·dom** /-dəm; -dəm/ *n* [U] **1** social and economic system under which land was cultivated by serfs 农奴制: *abolish serfdom* 废除农奴制. **2** conditions of a serf's life 农奴的处境: *released from his serfdom* 脱离他那农奴困境.

serge /sɜ:dʒ; sɝdʒ/ *n* [U] strong woollen cloth used for making clothes 毛哔叽: [attrib 作定语] *a blue serge suit* 蓝色毛哔叽套服.

ser·geant /'sɑ:dʒənt; ˋsɑrdʒənt/ *n* (often 常作 **Sergeant**; *abbrs* 缩写 **Sergt, Sgt**) **1** non-commissioned army officer ranking above a corporal and below a warrant officer 中士. ⇨App 9 见附录9. **2** (**a**) (*Brit*) police officer with a rank below that of an inspector 巡佐(级别低于巡官). (**b**) (*US*) police officer with a rank below that of a captain or sometimes a lieutenant 警佐(级别低于队长或副队长).

□ ˌ**sergeant-'major** *n* (**a**) (*Brit*) warrant officer assisting the adjutant of a regiment or battalion 准尉副官. ⇨App 9 见附录9. (**b**) (*US*) highest rank of non-commissioned army officer 军士长. ⇨App 9 见附录9.

Sergt (also **Sgt**) *abbr* 缩写 = Sergeant: *Sergt (Colin) Hill* (科林·)希尔中士 ○ *Sgt-Maj*, ie Sergeant-Major 准尉副官.

serial /'sɪərɪəl; ˋsɪrɪəl/ *adj* **1** [usu attrib 通常作定语] of, in or forming a series 连续的; 一系列的: *number files in serial order* 把档案按顺序编上号 ○ *a serial murderer*, ie one who kills several people one after another 连续杀人犯. **2** [attrib 作定语] (of a story, etc) appearing in parts in a periodical, etc or on TV or radio (指故事等)(在杂志、电视或广播等中)连续刊登或播出的: *Our new serial thriller begins at 7.30 this evening.* 我们的新系列惊险故事于今晚7时30分开始播出.

▷ **serial** *n* serial play, story, etc 连续剧; 连载故事: *a detective, romantic, thriller, etc serial* 侦探的、浪漫的、惊险的...连续剧 ○ [attrib 作定语] *serial rights*, ie rights to make a serial out of a novel, story, etc 连载权. **seri·al·ize, -ise** /-rɪəlaɪz; -rɪəlˌaɪz/ *v* [Tn] publish or broadcast (sth) as a serial 连载或连播(某内容): *serialized on radio in twelve parts* 分十二集在电台播出. **seri·al·iza·tion, -isation** /ˌsɪərɪəlaɪ'zeɪʃn; *US* -lɪ'z-; ˌsɪrɪələˋzeʃən/ *n* [C, U]. **seri·ally** /-əlɪ; -əlɪ/ *adv*.

□ ˈ**serial number** number identifying one item in a series, eg on a banknote or a cheque 顺序号, 编号(如纸币或支票上的).

seri·atim /ˌsɪərɪˈeɪtɪm; ˌsɪrɪˈetɪm/ *adv* (*fml* 文) one thing after another; point by point 依次地; 逐一地.

series /ˈsɪəri:z; ˈsɪriz/ *n* (*pl* unchanged 复数不变) **1** number of things, events, etc of a similar kind, esp placed or occurring one after another 一系列的事物: *a series of good harvests* 接连的丰收 ○ *a series of brilliant leaders* 一个接一个的杰出领袖 ○ *a series of interconnected caves* 一连串相互连接的洞 ○ *a television/radio series*, ie a number of programmes, each complete in itself, linked to each other by characters, theme, etc 电视[广播]系列节目 ○ *a series of stamps/coins*, eg of different values, but issued all at one time 一套邮票[硬币] ○ *publish a new series of readers for students of English* 出版一套新的英语学习读物 ○ *the world series*, eg of important baseball or football games in the US 世界联赛(如美国棒球或橄榄球的重要大赛). **2** [C, U] electrical circuit with the supply of current flowing directly through each component 串联: *batteries connected in series* 串联电池 ○ [attrib 作定语] *a series circuit, connection, etc* 串联电路、串联. Cf 参看 PARALLEL.

serif /ˈserɪf; ˈsɛrɪf/ *n* small line at the end of the stroke of a printed letter in certain type-faces 衬线(某些印刷体字母各端部的短线): [attrib 作定语] *printed in a serif type-face* 用字母带衬线的字体印刷. Cf 参看 SANSERIF.

serio-comic /ˌsɪərɪəʊ ˈkɒmɪk; ˌsɪrɪoˈkɑmɪk/ *adj* partly serious and partly comic 半严肃半滑稽的: *a serio-comic remark, style, play* 半严肃半滑稽的言语、风格、话剧.

ser·ious /ˈsɪərɪəs; ˈsɪrɪəs/ *adj* **1** solemn and thoughtful; not frivolous 严肃的; 庄重的; 正经的: *a serious person, mind, appearance* 严肃的人、心情、外表 ○ *Her face was serious as she told us the bad news.* 她告诉我们这个坏消息时脸色很严肃. ○ *He seems very serious, but in fact he has a delightful sense of humour.* 他看上去很严肃, 其实他十分诙谐. ○ *Please be serious for a minute, this is very important.* 请严肃点儿, 这事很重要. **2** [usu attrib 通常作定语] (of books, music, etc) intended to provoke thought; not merely for amusement (指书、音乐等)启发思考的, 不仅为消遣的: *a serious essay about social problems* 关于社会问题的发人深省的文章 ○ *Do you ever read serious works?* 你看不看理论性的著作? **3** important because of possible danger or risk; grave 严重的(可能有危险或风险的); 重大的: *a serious illness, mistake, accident* 严重的疾病、错误、事故 ○ *a serious decision about giving up a steady job* 要放弃一份稳定工作的重大决定 ○ *That could cause serious injury.* 那可能造成重伤. ○ *The international situation is extremely serious.* 国际形势极为严峻. **4** ~ **(about sb/sth)** in earnest; sincere 认真的; 真诚的: *a serious suggestion* 诚恳的建议 ○ *Are you really serious about him?* ie Do you have sincere affection for him? 你真对他有意吗? (是否真心爱他?) ○ *Is she serious about learning to be a pilot?* 她真想学开飞机吗?

▷ **ser·iously** *adv* **1** in a serious way 严肃地; 庄重地; 启发性地; 严重地; 认真地: *speak seriously to her about it* 跟她认真地谈谈这件事 ○ *seriously ill, injured, etc* 病得、伤得...很重. **2** (*infml* 口) (used at the beginning of a sentence when turning to a serious matter 用以将话题转到正经事上, 置于句首): *Seriously though, you could really hurt yourself doing that.* 说正经的, 你那样做可真要自讨苦吃了. ⇨Usage at HOPEFUL 用法见 HOPEFUL. **3** (idm 习语) **take sb/sth seriously** regard sb/sth as important and worth treating with respect 认真对待某人[某事物]: *You can't take her promises seriously: she never keeps her word.* 她答应的事不必当真, 她从来说话不算数. ○ *I take this threat very seriously.* 我认为这种威胁非同小可.

ser·ious·ness *n* [U] **1** state of being serious 严肃; 庄重; 严重; 认真: *the seriousness of his expression* 他的表情严肃 ○ *the seriousness of the crisis* 危机的严重性. **2** (idm 习语) **in all** ˈ**seriousness** (*infml* 口) very seriously; not as a joke 极严肃、庄重、严重或认真; 并非玩笑: *You can't in all seriousness go out in a hat like that!* 你戴着那种帽子出门不是开玩笑嘛!

serjeant-at-arms /ˌsɑ:dʒənt ət ˈɑ:mz; ˌsɑrdʒəntət ˈɑrmz/ *n* official who performs ceremonial duties for a lawcourt, city council or parliament (在法庭、市议会、议会上的)仪仗官.

ser·mon /ˈsɜ:mən; ˈsɝmən/ *n* **1** (**a**) talk on a moral or religious subject, usu given by a clergyman from the pulpit during a religious service 讲道(通常指教士在讲坛上做出的). (**b**) such a talk in printed form (印刷的)讲道文章: *a book of sermons* 讲道集. **2** (*fig infml* 比喻, 口) long talk about moral matters or about sb's faults, etc (对某人的错误等的)一大通教训: *We had to listen to a long sermon about not wasting money.* 我们硬着头皮听了一通别浪费钱的大道理.

▷ **ser·mon·ize, -ise** /-aɪz; -aɪz/ *v* [I, Ipr] (*derog* 贬) give (often unwanted) moral advice in a pompous way 作长篇大论的说教(常指不中听的).

ser·ous /ˈsɪərəs; ˈsɪrəs/ *adj* [usu attrib 通常作定语] of or like serum; watery (似)浆液的, 血清的; 水的; 多水的.

ser·pent /ˈsɜ:pənt; ˈsɝpənt/ *n* (*dated* 旧) **1** snake, esp a large one 蛇(尤指大的). **2** person who tempts others to do wrong; sly person 诱人犯错的人; 狡猾的人: *the old Serpent*, ie the Devil 魔王(魔鬼).

▷ **ser·pent·ine** /ˈsɜ:pəntaɪn; *US* -ti:n; ˈsɝpənˌtin/ *adj* (*fml* 文) twisting and curving like a snake 像蛇般蜷曲的; 蜿蜒的: *the serpentine course of the river* 蜿蜒的河道.

S

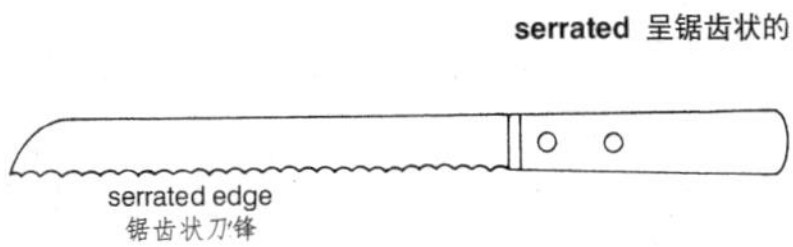

ser·rated /sɪˈreɪtɪd; *US* ˈsereɪtɪd; ˈsɛretɪd/ *adj* having notches on the edge like a saw; having a toothed edge 边缘呈锯齿状的; 有锯齿形边缘的: *a knife with a serrated blade* 有锯齿形刃的刀子 ○ *serrated leaves* 有锯齿形边缘的叶子.

ser·ra·tion /sɪˈreɪʃn; sɛˈreʃən/ *n* **1** [U] being serrated 锯齿状. **2** [C] notch on a serrated edge 锯齿形边缘的凹口.

ser·ried /ˈserɪd; ˈsɛrɪd/ *adj* [usu attrib 通常作定语] (*dated or fml* 旧或文) (of rows of people or things) arranged close together in order (指人或物的行列)排紧的, 密集的: *serried rows/ranks/lines* 密集的排[列/行].

serum /ˈsɪərəm; ˈsɪrəm/ *n* (*pl* **sera** /ˈsɪərə; ˈsɪrə/ or ~ **s**) (*medical* 医) **1** [U] (**a**) watery liquid in animal bodies (动物体内的)浆液. (**b**) thin yellowish liquid that remains from blood after it has clotted 血清. **2** [C, U] (dose of) such liquid taken from an animal that is immune to a disease, used for inoculations (一剂)免疫血清(用于接种或预防注射). Cf 参看 VACCINE.

ser·vant /ˈsɜ:vənt; ˈsɝvənt/ *n* **1** person who works in sb else's household for wages, and often for food and lodging 用人; 仆人; 佣人: *have/employ a large staff of servants* 有[雇用]大批用人. **2** ~ **(of sb/sth)** (**a**) employee, esp a faithful and devoted one 雇员(尤指忠心耿耿的): *a trusted servant of the company* 公司里可靠的雇员. (**b**) person devoted to sb/sth 忠于某人[某事物]的人: *a servant of Jesus Christ*, eg a Christian priest 耶稣基督的忠仆(如牧师). **3** (idm 习语) **your obedient servant** ⇨ OBEDIENT.

serve /sɜ:v; sɝv/ *v* **1** [I, Tn] ~ **(sb) (as sth)** work for (sb), esp as a servant 为(某人)工作; (尤指)当用人: *served as (a) gardener and chauffeur* 做园艺工人兼司机 ○ *He has served his master for many years.* 他伺候主人很多年了. **2** [I, Ipr, Tn] ~ **(in sth/as sth)** perform duties, eg in the armed forces 供职, 服役(如在军队里): *serve (a year) in the Army* 在陆军服役(一年) ○ *served as a naval officer during the war* 战时在海军当军官 ○ *serve on* (ie be a member of) *a committee, board, etc* 担任委员、董事等 ○ *serve under sb*, ie be under the command of (a superior officer, leader, etc) 在某人手下任职 ○ *She has served her country well*, eg as a civil servant, Member of Parliament, etc. 她为国尽职(如作公务员、议员等). ○ (*fig* 比喻) *This desk has served me well* (ie been very useful to me) *over the years.* 这张办公桌多年来对我的用处可大了. **3** (**a**) [I, Ipr, Tn, Tn·pr, Tn·p, Dn·n, Dn·pr] **~ sb (with sth); ~ sth (up) (to sb)** give food to (sb) at a meal; place (food) on the table at a meal 供(某人)饭菜; 将(饭菜)摆上桌: *learn to serve at table*, ie as a waiter 学习端饭上菜(当服务员) ○ *Who's going to serve?* 谁来布菜? ○ *Dinner is served*, ie is ready. 开饭了. ○ *We serve coffee in the lounge.* 我们起居室里有咖啡奉客. ○ *Have all the guests been served (with) food and drink?* 给所有的客人都上了饭菜饮品了吗? ○ *Four waiters served lunch to us/served us lunch.* 有四个服务员招待我们吃午饭. (**b**) [I, Tn, Tn·pr, Dn·n, Dn·pr] **~ sb (with sth); ~ sth (to sb)** attend to (a customer) or supply (sth) in a shop, etc (在商店等处)接待(顾客)或为顾客取来(货物): *He serves in a shoeshop.* 他在鞋店卖鞋. ○ *Are you being served?* 有售货员接待您吗? ○ *He served some sweets to the children.* 他为孩子们拿来他们要买的糖果. (**c**) [esp passive 尤用于被动语态: Tn, Tn·pr] **~ sb/sth (with sth)** provide sb/sth with a facility 为某人[某事物]提供设施: *The town is well served with public transport.* 这个市镇公共交通设施很完善. **4** [I, Ipr, It, Tn, Tn·pr, Cn·n/a no passive 不用于被动语态] **~ (sb) (for/as sth)** (*fml* 文) satisfy (a need or purpose); be suitable (for) 满足(需要); 达到(目的); 适合(于): *This room can serve as/for a study.* 这个房间可作书房用. ○ *This serves to show how foolish you have been.* 这足以说明你有多蠢. ○ *It's not exactly what I wanted but it will serve my purpose.* 这个跟我想要的不太一样, 但也算可以. **5** [Tn] (of a portion of food) be enough for (指一份食物)够...: *This packet of soup serves two.* 这包汤料可供两人用. **6** [Tn] (*fml* 文) treat (sb) in a specified way 以某方式对待(某人): *They have served me shamefully*, ie have treated me very badly. 他们待我很坏. **7** [In/pr, Tn] (**a**) spend (a period of time) learning a trade, etc 用(某段时间)习艺等: *serve two years as an apprentice/a two-year apprenticeship* 当两年学徒. (**b**) pass (a period of time) in prison 在狱中服(某段时间)刑: *serve ten years for armed robbery* 因持械抢劫罪服刑十年 ○ (*infml* 口) *serve time for fraud* 因诈骗罪服刑. **8** [Tn, Tn·pr] **~ sth (on sb); ~ sb with sth** (*law* 律) formally deliver sth to sb 将某物正式送达某人: *serve a summons, writ, warrant, etc* 送达传票、书面命令、授权命令等 ○ *serve a court order on sb/sb with a court order* 把法院的命令送达某人. **9** [I, Ipr, Tn, Tn·pr] **~ (sth) (to sb)** (in tennis, etc) put the ball into play by striking it to one's opponent (网球等)发球: *It's your turn to serve (to me).* 该你发(给我)球了. ○ *She's already served two aces this game.* 她在这一局中已两次发球得分. **10** [Tn] (of a male animal) copulate with (a female animal), esp after being hired for this purpose (指雄性动物)与(雌性动物)交配(尤指为此而租用动物): *His bull will come to serve our cows tomorrow.* 明天我们用他的公牛与我们的母牛配种. **11** [no passive 不用于被动语态: I, Tn] assist a priest at (a religious service) 在(宗教仪式上)担任助祭: *Who will serve (at) Mass today?* 今天谁任助祭? **12** (idm 习语) **first come, first served** ⇨FIRST[2]. **if memory serves** ⇨MEMORY. **serve sb 'right** (of a misfortune, etc) be deserved by sb (指不幸事等)应由某人承受: *'I got soaked in the rain.' 'It serves you right — I told you to take an umbrella.'* '我让雨浇坏了.' '活该——我早就告诉你得带雨伞.' **serve one's/its turn** be useful for a purpose or for a particular period 于某目的或某时期有用: *I finally had to sell the car, but it had served its turn.* 我最后只好把汽车卖了, 不过也算是物尽其用了. **serve sb's turn** be good or useful enough for sb's purpose 对某人(之需)有好处或有用处. **serve two 'masters** (usu in negative sentences 通常用于否定句) follow two conflicting parties, principles, etc 伺候两个主人(追随两个敌对的党派或奉行两种相互矛盾的原则等). **13** (phr v) **serve sth out** (**a**) give portions of (food) to several people 把(食物)分给大家: *Shall I serve out the soup or would you like to help yourselves?* 是我来给你们盛汤, 还是你们愿意自己来? (**b**) serve, work, etc until the end of (a fixed period) 工作到(规定期限)的末尾: *You'll have to serve out your notice before you leave the firm.* 你必须工作到你辞职通知的最后期限才能离开这个公司. **serve sth up** (*infml derog* 口, 贬) offer sth 提出: *She served up the usual excuses for being late.* 她又端出老一套借口为迟到辩解.

▷ **serve** *n* (in tennis, etc) act or manner of serving the ball (网球等的)发球或发球方式: *Whose serve is it?* ie Whose turn is it to serve? 该谁发球了? ○ *a fast serve* 快速发球.

server *n* **1** person who serves, eg at Mass or in tennis (做弥撒时的)助祭; (网球等的)发球人. **2** tray for dishes; salver 放菜碟的浅盘; 托盘. **3** (usu *pl* 通常作复数) utensil used for putting a portion of food onto sb's plate 向个人碗碟中盛取食物的餐具: *salad servers* 盛取色拉用的叉匙.

ser·ving *n* portion of food for one person (供一人食用的)一份食物: *This recipe will be enough for four servings.* 本食谱为四人食用分量.

ser·vice /'sɜːvɪs; 'sɝvɪs/ *n* **1** [U] **~ (to sth)** performing duties, eg in the armed forces, or working for a government, company, etc 任职; 执行任务: *ten years' service in the navy, police force, etc* 在海军、警界等服务十年 ○ *conditions of service* 任职条件 ○ *a life of public service* 为公共事业服务的一生 ○ *many years of faithful service to the company* 为公司忠实工作多年. **2** [U] (*fig* 比喻) work done by a vehicle, machine, etc (车辆、机器等的)用处: *My car has given me excellent service.* 我的汽车很好用. ○ *You will get good service from this typewriter.* 这个打字机对你很有用. **3** [C] (**a**) department of people employed by the government or a public organization 政府部门; 公用机构: *the ˌCivil 'Service* 政府的行政部门 ○ *the ˌDiplo'matic Service* 外交部门 ○ *the ˌNational 'Health Service* 国民保健署. (**b**) branch of the armed forces 军种: *the three services*, ie the Navy, the Army, the Air Force 三军(海军、陆军、空军) ○ *Which service is she in?* 她在哪个军种服役? ○ [attrib 作定语] *a service rifle, family, house* 军用步枪、军人家庭、军人用房. **4** [U] (*dated* 旧) being a servant; position as a servant 当仆人; 仆人的地位: *be in/go into service*, ie be/become a domestic servant 当仆人. **5** [C usu *pl* 通常作复数] **~ (to sb/sth)** work done for another or others; helpful act; favour 服务; 帮助; 益处: *You did me a great service by showing me the truth.* 你把实情告诉我了, 这对我很有好处. ○ *They need the services of a good lawyer.* 他们需要找个能干的律师协助处理. ○ *Her services to the state have been immense.* 她对国家的贡献极大. **6** [C] (**a**) system or arrangement that meets public needs, esp for communication 公用事业的业务或工作状况(尤指交通及通讯): *a 'bus/'train service* 公共汽车[火车]营运 ○ *the 'telephone service* 电话网络 ○ *a good 'postal service* 良好的邮政业务 ○ *Essential services* (ie the supply of water, electricity, etc) *will be maintained.* 基本的公用业务(水电等的供应)一定得到保障. (**b**) business that does work or supplies goods for customers, but does not make goods; such work or goods 不生产货物而以工作或提供货物的形式为顾客服务的业务; 这类工作或货物; 劳务: *We get export earnings from goods and services.* 我们用货物和劳务创收外汇. ○ *banking and 'insurance services* 银行业务和保险业务 ○ *a new 'carpet-cleaning service* 新兴的地毯清洗业务 ○ [attrib 作定语] *a 'service industry* 服务行业 ○ *the 'service sector* 服务部门. **7** [U] serving of customers in hotels, restaurants, etc; work done by domestic servants, hotel staff, etc 旅馆、饭馆等的业务; 用人、旅馆职员等做的工作: *The food is good at this hotel, but the service is poor.* 这家旅馆饭菜很好, 但服务很差. ○ *An extra 10% was added to the restaurant bill for service.* 饭馆帐单上已加了10%的服务费. ○ [attrib 作定语] *a quick-service restaurant* 上菜快的饭馆 ○ *a service entrance*, ie one for staff, rather than the public 服务人员入口. **8** [C] ceremony of religious worship or the prayers, etc used at this 礼拜仪式; 祈祷仪式: *three services every Sunday* 每星期日三次礼拜 ○ *attend morning/evening 'service* 参加早[晚]祷 ○ *the 'marriage, 'burial, com'munion, etc service* 婚礼、葬礼、

圣餐仪式. **9** [C, U] maintenance and repair of a vehicle, machine, etc at regular intervals (车辆、机器等定期的)维修: *take a car in for (a) service every 3 000 miles*, eg to have the oil changed, the brakes checked, etc 汽车每行驶3 000英里要进厂维修一次(如换机油、检查刹车等) ○ *a service for a gas boiler* 煤气锅炉维修 ○ *We offer (an) excellent after-sales service.* 我们提供完备的售后服务. ○ [attrib 作定语] *a service department, engineer* 维修部、技师. **10** [C] set of dishes, etc for serving food at table 吃饭用的一套盘碗等餐具: *a 30-piece 'dinner service* 30件一套的盘碗餐具. **11** [U] (*law* 律) delivering of a writ, summons, etc (书面命令、传票等的)送达. **12** [C] (**a**) (in tennis, etc) act or manner of serving the ball; person's turn to serve (网球等的)发球, 发球方式, 轮到的发球权: *a fast service* 快速发球 ○ *Her service has improved.* 她的发球技术已经改进了. ○ *Whose service is it?* 该谁发球了? (**b**) game in which sb serves 某人有发球权的一局: *win/hold/lose/drop one's service* 赢得[保住/失去/输掉]有发球权的一局 ○ *break sb's service*, ie win a game in which one's opponent serves 破某人有发球权的一局 ○ [attrib 作定语] *a service game* 有发球权的一局. **13** [U] serving (SERVE 10) of a female animal by a male animal (用雄性动物与雌性动物的)配种. **14** (idm 习语) **at sb's 'service** ready to help sb 随时帮助某人: *If you need advice, I am at your service.* 你要是需要参考意见, 我随时可以帮你点儿忙. **(be) of service (to sb)** useful or helpful 有用; 有帮助: *Can I be of service to you in organizing the trip?* 你组织这次旅行需要我帮忙吗? **press sth into service** ⇨PRESS[3]. **see service (in sth)** (**a**) serve in the armed forces 在军队中服役: *He saw service as an infantry officer in the last war.* 他在上次战争中当过步兵军官. ○ *He has seen service in many different parts of the world.* 他当兵到过世界各地. (**b**) (*infml* 口) be very useful, dependable, etc 很有用、可靠等: *These old boots have certainly seen some service.* 这双旧靴子可真禁穿.

▷ **ser·vice** *v* [Tn] **1** maintain and repair (a vehicle, machine, etc) at regular intervals (定期)维修(车辆、机器等): *service a car, boiler, washing-machine* 检修汽车、锅炉、洗衣机 ○ *Has this mower been regularly serviced?* 这个刈草机定期维修了吗? **2** supply a service(6a) or services to (sth) (公用事业)向(某处)提供服务: *The power station is serviced* (ie Fuel is delivered to it) *by road transport.* 这座发电站的燃料是通过公路运送的. **3** pay interest on (a loan) 支付(贷款)的利息: *The company hasn't enough cash to service its debts.* 这家公司没有支付债务利息的现款. **4** = SERVE 4. **ser·vice·able** *adj* **1** in usable condition 可使用的: *The tyres are worn but still serviceable.* 这些轮胎已磨损, 但尚可用. **2** suitable for ordinary use or hard wear (and not designed to be ornamental); durable; long-lasting 适于一般用途的, 禁磨的(非装饰性的); 耐用的: *serviceable clothes for children* 耐穿的儿童衣物. **ser·vice·ably** /-əblɪ; -əblɪ/ *adv*.

□ **'service area** area beside a motorway where petrol and refreshments, etc are sold (高速公路旁的)服务区(出售汽油、茶点等的). ⇨illus at App 1 见附录1插图, page xiii.

'service break = BREAK[2] 6.

'service charge sum added to a restaurant bill, eg 10% of the total, to pay for the service given by the waiters, etc (加于饭馆帐单上的)服务费, 小费(如全部费用的10%): *Does my bill include a service charge?* 我的帐单包括服务费了吗?

'service flat (*Brit*) flat in which domestic service and sometimes meals, etc are provided and charged for in the rent 有室内服务的公寓(有时包括饭食等, 均计入房租中).

'serviceman /-mən; -mən/ *n* (*pl* **-men** /-mən; -mən/) man in the armed forces 军人.

'service road minor road, off a main road, giving access to houses, etc (大路旁的)侧路(通向建筑物等的).

'service station = PETROL STATION (PETROL).

'servicewoman *n* (*pl* **-women**) woman in the armed forces 女军人.

ser·vi·ette /ˌsɜːvɪ'et; ˌsɝvɪ'ɛt/ *n* (*esp Brit*) table napkin 餐巾: *paper serviettes* 纸餐巾.

serv·ile /'sɜːvaɪl; *US* -vl; 'sɝvl̩/ *adj* **1** (*derog* 贬) too ready to obey others; lacking independence 过分屈从的; 缺乏独立性的: *servile flattery* 卑躬屈膝的谄媚 ○ *I don't like his servile manner.* 我不喜欢他那低三下四的样子. **2** of, like or for a servant (似)仆人的; 为仆人的: *made to do servile tasks* 被迫做仆人的工作.

▷ **serv·ilely** /-aɪllɪ; -əllɪ/ *adv*.

serv·il·ity /sɜː'vɪlətɪ; sɝ'vɪlətɪ/ *n* [U] (*usu derog* 通常作贬义) servile behaviour or attitude 过分屈从的行为或态度.

ser·vit·ude /'sɜːvɪtjuːd; *US* -tuːd; 'sɝvəˌtud/ *n* [U] (*fml* 文) condition of being forced to work for others and having no freedom 奴役(状况): *Such ill-paid farm work is a form of servitude.* 这种农活儿工资低得可怜, 简直是苦役.

servo /'sɜːvəʊ; 'sɝvo/ *n* (*pl* **~s**) (*infml* 口) = SERVO-MECHANISM.

servo- *comb form* 构词成分 (of machinery) having a power unit controlling a larger mechanism (指机器)有伺服机构的(有控制较大机械装置的动力部件的): *servo-assisted brakes*, eg in a large car 继动闸(如大型汽车的).

servo-mechanism /ˌsɜːvəʊ 'mekənɪzəm; ˌsɝvo-'mɛkəˌnɪzəm/ *n* any mechanism that controls a larger mechanism 伺服机构.

servo-motor /'sɜːvəʊ məʊtə(r); 'sɝvoˌmotɚ/ *n* motor that controls a larger mechanism 伺服电动机.

ses·ame /'sesəmɪ; 'sɛsəmɪ/ *n* **1** [U] tropical plant with seeds which are used as food and which give an oil used in salads and in cooking 芝麻; 脂麻; 胡麻: [attrib 作定语] *sesame seeds, oil* 芝麻种子、芝麻油. **2** (idm 习语) **open sesame** ⇨ OPEN[1].

ses·sion /'seʃn; 'sɛʃən/ *n* **1** meeting or series of meetings of a parliament, lawcourt, etc for discussing or deciding sth (议会的)会议; (法庭的)开庭: *the morning session of the Crown Court* 英国地方刑事法庭的上午开庭 ○ *the next session of arms negotiations* 军备谈判的下一届会议 ○ *the autumn session* (ie sitting) *of parliament* 议会的秋季会议. **2** (**a**) school or university year 学年. (**b**) (*US*) school term or period of study 学期. **3** single continuous period spent in one activity (进行某活动连续的)一段时间: *a re'cording session*, ie one at which material is recorded on tape or discs, etc 录制时间(把材料录在磁带、唱片等上用的时间) ○ *After several sessions at the gym, I feel a lot fitter.* 我在健身房锻炼了几次以后, 觉得身体好多了. **4** governing body of a Presbyterian church 长老会的管理机构. **5** (idm 习语) **in 'session** (**a**) assembled for business 开会; 开庭: *The court is now in session.* 法院现在开庭. (**b**) not on vacation 不在休假期: *Is Parliament in session during the summer?* 议会在夏季是开会期吗?

set[1] /set; sɛt/ *n* **1** [C] **~ (of sth)** group of similar things that belong together in some way (类似物品的)一组, 一套, 一副, 一对: *a set of cutlery, golf clubs, hand tools* 一套刀叉匙餐具、高尔夫球杆、手用工具 ○ *a set of six dining chairs* 六把一套的餐椅 ○ *a set of Dickens novels* 一套狄更斯的小说 ○ *a set of false teeth* 一副假牙 ○ *a tea set*, ie teapot, cups, saucers, etc 一套茶具 ○ *a new set of rules to learn* 要学的一套新规则. **2** [CGp] group of people who spend much time together socially or have similar tastes and interests 经常来往、意气相投的一些人: *the literary, racing, golfing set* 爱好文学、赛马、高尔夫球的一伙人 ○ *the smart set*, ie rich fashionable people 追求时髦的一批阔人 ○ *the fast set*, eg people who gamble, spend a lot of money, etc 放荡不羁的一群人(如赌博、挥霍等的). **3** [C] group of pupils with similar ability in a particular subject 在某学科上能力相当的一批学生: *She's in the top set in maths.* 她在数学成绩最好的班上. **4** [C] (*mathematics* 数) group of things having a shared quality 集; 集合. **5** [C] device for receiving radio or television signals 收音机; 电视机: *a transistor set* 晶体管收音机 ○ *Do not adjust your (TV) set.* 请勿自行调整电视机. **6** [sing] **~ (of sth)** way in which sth is placed or arranged; position or angle (某物摆放的)样子; 位置; 角度: *She admired the firm set of his shoulders.* 她喜欢他的肩膀很结实. **7** [sing] way in which sth sets (SET[2] 13) 凝结、凝固或固定的样子: *You won't get a good set if you put too much water in the jelly.* 果冻搀水太多就凝固不好了. **8** [C] (in a tennis match) group of

S

games in which one side must win the greater number of games in order to win that part of the match (网球赛中的)盘. **9** (also **sett**) [C] rectangular paving stone (铺路用的)长方形石板. **10** (also **sett**) [C] badger's burrow 獾洞. **11** [C] (**a**) scenery being used for a play, film, etc (戏剧、电影等的)布景, 场景: *We need volunteers to help build and paint the set.* 我们需要有人自愿帮忙把布景搭起、画好. (**b**) stage or place where a play or (part of) a film is performed 表演戏剧或拍摄电影(片断)的舞台或场地: *The cast must all be on (the) set by 7 pm.* 所有演员必须在下午7时到达拍摄场地. **12** [C] young plant, shoot, etc for planting 幼苗; 树苗: *onion sets* 洋葱苗. **13** [C] act of setting (SET² 15) hair 固定发型; 做头发: *A shampoo and set costs £8.* 洗头、做头发共8英镑. **14** (idm 习语) **the jet set** ⇨ JET¹.

□ **'set theory** (*mathematics* 数) study or use of sets (SET¹ 4) 集合论.

set² /set; sɛt/ *v* (**-tt-**, *pt*, *pp* **set**)

► PLACING IN POSITION 摆放 **1** [Tn·pr, Tn·p] put (sth) in the specified place or position; place 将(某物)放在某处或某位置; 置; 摆放: *She set a tray down on the table.* 她把托盘放在桌子上了. ○ *He set a post in the ground.* 他在地上树起了一根杆子. ○ (*fml* 文) *We set food and drink before the travellers.* 我们把食物和饮料摆在旅客面前. ○ *The house is set* (ie situated) *in fifty acres of rolling parkland.* 那所房子周围有五十英亩的起伏不平的草地. ○ *Her eyes are set very close together.* 她的两只眼睛长得距离很近. **2** [Tn·pr] **~ sth to sth** move or place sth so that it is near to or touching sth 将某物移至或放置在接近或接触到另一物处: *She set the glass to her lips/her lips to the glass.* 她把玻璃杯送到嘴边[用嘴唇触及玻璃杯]. ○ *He set a match to the dry timber,* ie in order to burn it. 他用火柴去点燃那干木头. ○ *set pen to paper,* ie begin to write 动笔. **3** [Tn, Tn·pr] represent the action of (a play, novel, etc) as happening in a specified place or at a specified time 设置(戏剧、小说等)的背景: *The novel is set in pre-war London.* 这部小说以战前的伦敦为背景.

► CAUSING TO BE IN A PARTICULAR STATE OR TO HAPPEN 使处于某状态或使发生 **4** [Tn·pr, Cn·a] cause (sb/sth) to be in or reach the specified state 使(某人[某事物])处于或达到某状态: *The revolution set the country on the road to democracy.* 这场革命把国家引上了通往民主的道路. ○ *The firm's accounts need to be set in order.* 公司的帐目需要清理. ○ *She untied the rope and set the boat adrift.* 她把绳索解开, 放开小船. ○ *The hijackers set the hostages free,* ie released them. 劫机者释放了人质. **5** (**a**) [Cn·g] cause (sb/sth) to begin to do sth 使(某人[某事物])开始做某事: *set a pendulum swinging* 让摆摆动起来 ○ *The sudden noise set the dog barking.* 这突然的声响惊得狗汪汪叫起来. ○ *The sight of her set his heart beating faster.* 他一见到她, 不由得心就怦怦直跳. ○ *Her remarks set me thinking.* 我听了她的话不禁沉思起来. (**b**) [Cn·t] cause (oneself/sb) to do the specified task 使(自己[某人])做某事: *We set them to chop wood/set them to work chopping wood in the garden.* 我们让他们在花园里劈木柴. ○ *I've set myself* (ie resolved) *to finish the job by the end of the month.* 我决心月底以前把这件工作干完.

► ADJUSTING OR ARRANGING 调整或安排 **6** [Tn, Tn·pr] adjust (sth) so that it is ready for use or in position 调整好(某事物)(使之随时可用或置于某位置): *set the controls,* eg of a machine 调整好控制装置(如机器的) ○ *She set the camera on automatic.* 她把照相机调到自动位置. **7** Tn] (**a**) adjust the hands of (a clock or watch) to show the right time 拨动(钟或表)的指针至准确时间: *I always set my watch by the time-signal on the radio.* 我一向按照收音机的报时信号对表. (**b**) adjust (an alarm-clock) so that it sounds at a particular time 调好(闹钟)(使之按时响闹): *She set her alarm for 7 o'clock.* 她把闹钟调到7点钟. **8** [Tn] arrange knives, forks, etc on (a table) for a meal; lay¹(1b) 在(桌子)上摆好刀叉等餐具准备开饭; 铺桌子: *Could you set the table for supper?* 你铺好桌子准备吃晚饭好吗? ○ *The table is set for six guests.* 桌子上摆好了六位客人的餐具. **9** [Tn·pr esp passive 尤用于被动语态] **~ A in B/~ B with A** fix (sth, esp a precious stone) firmly into (a surface or an object) 将(某物, 尤指宝石)镶嵌到(某物)上: *She had the sapphire set in a gold ring.* 她把那枚蓝宝石镶在金戒指上了. ○ *Her bracelet was set with emeralds.* 她的手镯上镶着绿宝石. **10** [Tn, Tn·pr] arrange or fix (sth); decide on (sth) 安排、确定或决定(某事物): *They haven't set a date for their wedding yet.* 他们的婚期还没定下来. ○ *The government plans to set strict limits on public spending this year.* 政府计划严格限制今年公费开支.

► CREATING 创造 **11** [Tn] (used esp with the *ns* shown 尤与所示名词连用) establish (sth) 建立(某事物): *Imposing a lenient sentence for such a serious crime sets a dangerous precedent.* 对这样严重的罪行轻判就开了个危险的先例. ○ *She set a new world record for the high jump.* 她创下跳高的新世界纪录. ○ *Rock stars often set fashions in clothes.* 摇滚乐歌星往往创出时装的潮流. ○ *I rely on you to set a good example.* 我全靠你来树立个好榜样. **12** [Tn, Dn·n, Dn·pr] **~ sth (for oneself/sb)** present or impose (a task, piece of work, problem, etc) to be done, dealt with, etc (by oneself/sb) (给自己[某人])提出或规定(任务、工作、问题等)来处理、解决等: *Who will be setting* (ie writing the questions in) *the French exam?* 谁负责出法语试题? ○ *What books have been set* (ie are to be studied) *for the Cambridge First Certificate next year?* 剑桥大学主办的明年的中学会考要读哪些书? ○ *She's set herself a difficult task/set a difficult task for herself.* 她给自己提出一个艰巨的任务. ○ *The sudden drop in share prices has set the government a tricky problem.* 股票价格突然下跌给政府出了一个难题. ○ *We must set ourselves precise sales targets for the coming year.* 我们要为明年定出准确的销售指标.

► MAKING OR BECOMING FIRM OR FIXED (使)凝固或固定 **13** [I, Tn] (cause sth to) become firm, hard or rigid from a soft or liquid state (使某物)由软变硬或由液态变成固态: *Some kinds of concrete set more quickly than others.* 有些种类的混凝土凝结硬化快, 有的较慢. ○ *The jelly hasn't set yet.* 果冻尚未凝固. **14** [Tn esp passive 尤用于被动语态] fix (one's face or part of the body) into a firm expression 使(脸或身体某部)呈呆板表情或姿势: *He set his jaw in a determined fashion.* 他挺着下巴显得很坚决. **15** [Tn] fix (hair) while it is wet so that it will dry in the desired style 固定发型; 做头发: *She's having her hair set for the party this evening.* 她正在为参加今晚的聚会做头发. **16** [Tn] put (a broken bone) into a fixed position so that it will mend 将(断骨)接好或复位: *The surgeon set her broken arm.* 外科医生为她接好断臂.

► PRESENTING IN THE RIGHT FORM 以适当的形式表现 **17** [Tn] choose a specific type² for printing (a book, etc) 选用某字体为(书等)排版: *This dictionary is set in Press Roman.* 本词典的英文排版用的是Press Roman字体. **18** [Tn, Tn·pr] **~ sth (to sth)** provide music for (words, a poem, etc) so that it can be sung 为(词句、诗等)谱曲, 配乐: *Schubert set many of Goethe's poems (to music).* 舒伯特为歌德的许多诗谱了曲.

► MOVING OR FLOWING 移动或流动 **19** [I] (of the sun, moon or stars) go down below the horizon (指日、月或星)落到地平线以下: *In Britain the sun sets much later in summer than in winter.* 在英国, 夏季日落时间比冬季晚得多. ○ *We sat and watched the sun setting.* 我们坐在那里看日落. Cf 参看 RISE² 7. **20** [Ipr, Ip] (of the tide, a current, etc) move or flow in the specified direction (指潮水、潮流等)流动: *The current sets strongly eastwards.* 急流迅猛东去. ○ *The current sets in towards the shore.* 潮水向岸边涌来. ○ (*fig* 比喻) *The tide of public opinion has set in his favour,* ie He has the support and approval of the public. 舆论的倾向是支持他的. ○ (*fig* 比喻) *Opinion seems to be setting against* (ie People are not in favour of) *the proposal.* 人们似乎不赞成这个建议.

21 (idm 习语) **be all 'set (for sth/to do sth)**; **be set for sth/to do sth** be ready or prepared for sth/to do sth 准备好某事[做某事]: *Are we all set?* 我们都准备好了吗? ○ *We were all set to go when the telephone rang.* 我们都准备好要走时电话铃响了. ○ *The socialists look set* *for victory in/set to win the general election.* 社会党人似已决意要在大选中获胜. (For other idioms containing **set**, see entries for *ns, adjs,* etc 查阅与 **set** 搭配的其他习语, 见有关名词、形容词等的词条, 如 **set the pace** ⇨PACE[1]; **set fair** ⇨FAIR[1].)

22 (phr v) **set about sb** (*infml* 口) attack sb with blows or words 攻击或抨击某人: *He set about the intruders with a stick.* 他用棍子打那些私闯进来的人. **set about sth/doing sth** (no passive 不用于被动语态) begin (a task); start doing sth 开始(某工作); 着手做某事: *I must set about my packing.* 我得开始收拾行李了. ○ *I don't know how to set about this job.* 这工作我不知如何入手. ○ *The new government must set about finding solutions to the country's economic problems.* 新政府必须立即找出解决国家经济问题的办法.

set sb against sb (no passive 不用于被动语态) make sb oppose or be hostile to (a friend, relative, etc) 使某人反对或敌视(朋友、亲戚等): *The civil war set brother against brother.* 因内战引起兄弟反颜. ○ *She accused her husband of setting their children against her.* 她责怪丈夫鼓动孩子反对她. **set sth (off) against sth** consider (sth good or positive) as balancing or outweighing (sth bad or negative) 视(某好的事物)可抵消或抵偿(某坏的事物): *You must set the initial cost of a new car against the saving you'll make on repairs.* 你得想到买新汽车先花这一笔钱可省下日后修车的费用. ○ *Set against her virtues, her faults don't seem nearly so bad.* 考虑到她的优点, 她的缺点还不算太糟.

set sb/sth apart (from sb/sth) make sb/sth different from or superior to others 使某人[某事物]与众不同或优于其他的: *Her clear and elegant prose sets her apart from most other journalists.* 她的散文凝练高雅, 多数新闻工作者无出其右.

set sth aside (**a**) place sth to one side 将某事物放在一边: *She set aside her book and lit a cigarette.* 她把书放在一旁, 点了一枝香烟. (**b**) save or keep (money or time) for a particular purpose (为某目的)节省或保留(钱或时间): *She sets aside a bit of money every month.* 她每月都存一点儿钱. ○ *I try to set aside a few minutes each day to do some exercises.* 我每天尽量腾出一些时间锻炼一下身体. (**c**) disregard or ignore sth; abandon or reject sth 不理会或不顾某事物; 放弃或回绝某事物: *Let's set aside my personal feelings.* 不必顾及我个人的感情. ○ *Set aside for a moment your instinctive dislike of the man.* 暂且不要考虑你从直觉上憎恶他这一因素. (**d**) (*law* 律) cancel or reject (a verdict, sentence, etc) 撤消或驳回(某裁决、判决等): *The judge's decision was set aside by the Appeal Court.* 法官的判决被上诉法庭驳回.

set sth back (sth) delay or hinder the progress of sth (by the specified time) 耽搁或阻碍某事物的进展(之时间): *Financial problems have set back our building programme.* 财务上出现问题延误了我们的建设计划. ○ *Work on the new theatre has been set back three months.* 兴建新剧院的工作误了三个月. **set sb back sth** (*infml* 口) cost sb (the specified amount of money) 使某人花费(某数量的钱): *The meal is likely to set us back £15 each.* 这顿饭我们可能每人要花15英镑. **set sth back (from sth)** (often passive 常用于被动语态) place or situate sth (esp a building) at a distance from sth 将某物(尤指建筑物)置于距另一物一定距离处: *The house is set well back from the road.* 这所房子与公路很有一段距离.

set sb down (of a vehicle or its driver) stop and allow (a passenger) to get off (指车辆或司机)停下来让(乘客)下车: *The bus stopped to set down an old lady.* 公共汽车停下来让一个老太太下车. ○ *I'll set you down on the corner of your street.* 我在你说的那条街的拐角处停下来让你下车. **set sth down** note or record sth on paper; write sth down 将某事物记在纸上; 写下来: *Why don't you set your ideas down on paper?* 你怎么不把你的想法写在纸上呢?

set 'forth (*fml* 文) start a journey; set out 起程; 出发; 动身. **set sth forth** (*fml* 文) make sth known; declare or present sth 公布某事物; 宣布或提出某事物: *The Prime Minister set forth the aims of his government in a television broadcast.* 首相在电视广播中公布了内阁的工作目标.

set 'in (of rain, bad weather, infection, etc) begin and seem likely to continue (指雨、坏天气、传染等)开始并可能继续下去: *I must get those bulbs planted before the cold weather sets in.* 我得在天气转冷之前把这些球茎秧种上. ○ *Those beams will need to be replaced; it looks as though woodworm has set in.* 那些大梁该换了, 看样子里面生了蛀虫了.

set 'off begin (a journey, race, etc) 开始(旅行、赛跑等): *What time are you planning to set off tomorrow?* 你打算明天几点钟启程? ○ *They've set off on a journey round the world.* 他们已经开始环游世界. ○ *If you want to catch that train we'd better set off for the station immediately.* 你要是想赶上那班火车, 咱们就最好马上动身去火车站. **set sth off** (**a**) cause (a bomb, mine, etc) to explode 使(炸弹、地雷等)爆炸: *Do be careful with those fireworks; the slightest spark could set them off.* 这些烟火要格外小心, 稍有火星就能引起爆炸. (**b**) cause or prompt sth 引起或激发某事物: *Panic on the stock market set off a wave of selling.* 股票市场上人心惶惶, 掀起抛售浪潮. (**c**) make sth appear more attractive by contrast (通过对比)使某事物更有吸引力: *That jumper sets off the blue of her eyes.* 在这件毛衣衬托下, 她眼睛的蓝色显得更漂亮了. **set sb off (doing sth)** cause sb to start (doing sth) 使某人开始做(某事物): *Don't set him off talking politics or he'll go on all evening.* 可别让他谈起政治来, 要不然他一谈就得一个晚上. ○ *Her imitations always set me off (laughing).* 她模仿别人的动作, 每次都把我逗得哈哈大笑.

set on sb attack sb 攻击某人: *I was set on by their dog as soon as I opened the gate.* 我刚一开大门, 他们的狗就朝我扑来. **set sb/sth on sb** cause (a person or an animal) to attack sb 使(人或动物)攻击某人: *The farmer threatened to set his dogs on us.* 那个农场主威胁着要让狗咬我们.

set 'out leave a place and begin a journey 从某地出发上路: *She set out at dawn.* 她天一亮就动身了. ○ *They set out on the last stage of their journey.* 他们开始了旅行的最后一程. **set sth out** (**a**) arrange or display (items) 安排或摆放(物件): *We'll need to set out chairs for the meeting.* 我们要为会议摆好椅子. ○ *She set out the pieces on the chess-board.* 她把国际象棋的棋子摆在棋盘上了. ○ *Her work is always very well set out.* 她的工作总是很有条理. ○ (*fig* 比喻) *You haven't set out your ideas very clearly in this essay.* 在你这篇文章里, 你没把意思说清楚. (**b**) state or declare sth 陈述或宣布某事: *He set out his objections to the scheme.* 他说他反对这项计划. ○ *She set out the reasons for her resignation in a long letter.* 她在一封长信里阐明了辞职原因. **set out to do sth** begin a job, task, etc with a particular aim or goal (带着某目的)开始做某事: *She set out to break the world land speed record.* 她决心要打破陆上速度的世界纪录. ○ *They succeeded in what they set out to do.* 他们打算做的事已经做成了.

set 'to (**a**) begin doing sth energetically 精力充沛地开始做某事: *The engineers set to on repair work to the bridge.* 工程师奋力进行修桥工作. ○ *If we really set to we can get the whole house cleaned in an afternoon.* 我们要是认真干, 一个下午就能把房子打扫干净. (**b**) begin to fight or argue 开始打斗或争吵: *The boys set to and had to be separated by a teacher.* 那些男生大打出手, 来个老师才把他们拉开.

set sb up (*infml* 口) (**a**) make sb healthier, stronger, more lively, etc 使某人更健康、强壮、活跃等: *A hot drink will soon set you up.* 你喝杯热饮料马上就精神了. ○ *A week in the country will set her up nicely after her operation.* 她手术后在郊外住上一个星期一定能复原. (**b**) provide sb with the money to start a business, buy a house, etc 使某人有钱创业、买房子等: *Her father set her up in business.* 她父亲出钱帮她创业. ○ *His father set him up as a bookseller.* 他父亲资助他做了书商. ○ *Winning all that money on the pools set her up for life.* 她赢得足球普尔的那些彩金已够她一生花用不尽. **set sth up** (**a**) place sth in position; erect sth 摆放或竖起某物: *set up a memorial, monument, statue, etc* 竖起纪念物、纪念碑、塑像等 ○ *Police set up road-blocks on routes leading out of the city.* 警方在通往城外的路上设置了路障. (**b**) make (an apparatus, a machine, etc) ready for use 使(器械、机器等)准备使用: *How long will it take to set up the projector?* 把这个放映机安放好需要多长时间? (**c**) establish or create sth 建立或开创某事物: *The government has set up a working party to*

S

look into the problem of drug abuse. 政府已成立工作组调查滥用毒品问题. ○ *A fund will be set up for the dead men's families.* 抚恤死难工人家属的基金会即将建立起来. (**d**) establish (a record speed, time or distance in a sport) 创(体育)记录: *She set up a new world record time in the 100 metres.* 她创下了新的百米世界记录. (**e**) cause or produce sth 造成或产生某事物: *The slump on Wall Street set up a chain reaction in stock markets around the world.* 华尔街金融滑坡引起世界股票市场的连锁反应. (**f**) begin to make (the specified loud noise) 开始发出(很大的噪声): *set up a commotion, din, row, etc* 发出骚乱声、嘈杂声、争吵声等 ○ *The cats set up a frightful yowling when the dog appeared.* 猫看到那条狗就都大声叫起来. **set (oneself) up as sb** establish oneself in business as (a shopkeeper, craftsman, etc) 当上(店主、手艺人等): *He moved to Leeds and set up as a printer.* 他搬到利兹干起了印刷业. **set oneself up as sb** regard oneself as or claim to be (the specified type of person) 将自己视为或称作(某种人): *He likes to set himself up as an intellectual.* 他喜欢自命为知识分子.

□ **ˈset-back** *n* thing that hinders the progress of sth 妨碍发展的事物: *Hopes of an early end to the strike received/suffered a severe set-back yesterday.* 希望罢工早些结束, 这一愿望昨日严重受挫. ○ *Defeat in the by-election is a major set-back to the ruling party.* 执政党在补缺选举中落选, 是一极大挫折. **ˌset ˈbook** (also **ˌset ˈtext**) book on which students must answer questions in an examination 必修课本: *What are your set books for English A Level?* 你们参加高级程度英语考试要读哪些必修课本?

setline = TRAWL LINE (TRAWL).

ˌset-ˈto *n* (*pl* **set-tos**) fight or argument 打斗; 争吵: *They had the most frightful set-to.* 他们大打出手, 从来没有这么厉害.

ˈset-up *n* (usu *sing* 通常作单数) (*infml* 口) structure of an organization 组织的结构: *What's the set-up (like) in your company?* 你们公司的机构是怎样的? ○ *I've only been here for a couple of weeks and don't really know the set-up.* 我才刚来俩星期, 还不大了解这里的组织结构.

set³ /set; sɛt/ *adj* **1** [usu pred 通常作表语] having the specified position 处于某位置: *a house set on a wooded hillside* 在树木丛生的山坡上的房子 ○ *She has deep-set eyes.* 她的眼窝很深. **2** [usu attrib 通常作定语] (of a person's expression) fixed; stiff (指人的表情)凝滞的, 呆板的: *Her face wore a grim, set look.* 她脸上显出严厉、木然的神情. ○ *a set* (ie insincere) *smile* 假笑. **3** [usu attrib 通常作定语] fixed or arranged in advance 固定的; 事先安排的: *The meals in this hotel are at set times.* 这家旅馆的用餐时间是固定的. ○ *There is a set procedure for making formal complaints.* 要正式提出投诉是有固定程序的. ○ *Are there set hours of work in your company?* 你们公司有固定的办公时间吗? **4** fixed and unchanging 固定不变的: *He's a man of set opinions.* 他是个有固定见解的人. ○ *She has very set ideas about politics.* 她在政治问题上有自己的固定看法. ○ *As people get older they become more set in their ways.* 人越老越有一定之规. **5** [attrib 作定语] deliberate; specific 故意的; 具体的: *We've come here for a set purpose.* 我们来到这里是有目的的. **6** (idm 习语) **be (dead) ˈset against sth/doing sth** be (firmly) opposed to sth (坚决)反对某事: *The government are set against (the idea of) raising taxes.* 内阁坚决反对增加税收(的意见). **be set on sth/doing sth** be determined to do sth 决定做某事: *He's set on going to university.* 他决心要上大学. ○ *She's absolutely set on publishing as a career.* 她决意从事出版事业.

□ **ˌset ˈpiece** scene in a novel, film, play, etc arranged in a fixed or typical pattern or style (小说、电影、戏剧等中)以固定模式或风格安排的场景: *The play contains a number of typical Stoppard set pieces.* 这出戏里有若干典型的斯托帕特式的场景.

ˈset square /ˈset skweə(r); ˈsɛtskwɛr/ triangular piece of plastic, metal or wood with angles of 90°, 60° and 30° (or 90°, 45° and 45°), used for drawing straight lines, esp at these angles 三角板; 三角尺.

sett /set; sɛt/ *n* = SET¹ 9, 10.

set·tee /seˈtiː; sɛˈti/ *n* long soft seat with a back and usu with arms, for two or more people 长沙发. ⇨illus at App 1 见附录1插图, page xvi.

set·ter /ˈsetə(r); ˈsɛtɚ/ *n* **1** any of several breeds of long-haired dog, trained to stand motionless when it scents animals or birds being hunted 蹲伏猎狗(毛长, 经训练嗅到猎物蹲伏不动以助猎). ⇨illus at App 1 见附录1插图, page iii. **2** (often in compounds 常用以构成复合词) person or thing that sets sth (in various meanings of SET) (SET各词义所指的)人或事物: *the setter of an examination paper* 试卷命题人 ○ *a ˈtype-setter* 排字工人 ○ *a trend-setter* 新潮倡导人.

set·ting /ˈsetɪŋ; ˈsɛtɪŋ/ *n* **1** [C] way or place in which sth is fixed or fastened 镶嵌; 镶嵌底座: *The ring has a ruby in a silver setting.* 这枚戒指的银底座上镶着一块红宝石. **2** [C] (**a**) surroundings; environment 环境: *The castle stands in a picturesque setting surrounded by hills.* 这座城堡四周环山, 风景如画. (**b**) place and time at which an event occurs or a play, novel, etc is set (某事、戏剧、小说等的)背景: *The setting of the story is a hotel in Paris during the war.* 故事发生在战时巴黎的一家旅馆里. ○ *a gruesome setting for the murder* 那谋杀案令人毛骨悚然的背景. **3** [C] speed, height, temperature, etc at which a device, machine, etc is or can be set to operate 装置、机器等(可调)定的速度、高度、温度等; 挡: *The cooker has several temperature settings.* 这个炉具有几个温度定位挡. **4** [C] music composed for a poem, etc (为诗等谱写的)乐曲: *Schubert's setting of a poem by Goethe* 舒伯特为歌德的诗谱写的乐曲. **5** [sing] descent (of the sun, moon, etc) below the horizon (日、月等的)落(在地平线以下).

settle¹ /ˈsetl; ˈsɛtl̩/ *n* wooden seat for two or more people, with a high back and arms, the seat often being the lid of a chest 木制有扶手的高背长椅(座位下常为柜橱, 座位即盖儿).

settle² /ˈsetl; ˈsɛtl̩/ *v* **1** (**a**) [I, Ipr, Tn esp passive 尤用于被动语态] make one's permanent home in (a country, etc) as a colonist 在(某国等)殖民: *The Dutch settled in South Africa.* 荷兰人在南非殖民. ○ (*fml* 文) *This area was settled by immigrants over a century ago.* 这一带在一个世纪以前是移民的殖民地. (**b**) [I, Ipr] make one's home in a place 定居; 安家落户: *After years of travel, we decided to settle here.* 我们旅行多年后, 决定在此定居. ○ *settle in London, in Canada, in the country, near the coast* 在伦敦、在加拿大、在乡村、在沿海安家. **2** [I, Ipr] **~ (on/over sth)** come to rest on sth; stay for some time on sth 在某处停歇或停留一时: *Will the snow settle?* ie Will it remain on the ground without melting? 这雪呆得住吗? (能落在地上不融化吗?) ○ *The bird settled on a branch.* 那只鸟落在树枝上了. ○ *Clouds have settled over the mountain tops.* 那些云彩在山顶上空停留不散. ○ *The dust had settled on everything.* 到处都是积尘. ○ *The cold has settled on my chest,* ie It is making me cough, etc. 我患感冒已引起胸部不适(咳嗽等). ○ (*fig* 比喻) *A tense silence had settled over the waiting crowd.* 在等候的人群中有一种紧张的寂静感. **3** [I, Ip, Tn] **~ (back)** make (sb/oneself) comfortable in a new position 使(某人[自己])在新位置上觉得舒适: *settle (back) in one's armchair* 舒适地(仰)坐在单座沙发上 ○ *The nurse settled her patient for the night,* ie made him comfortable, gave him medicine, etc. 护士安顿病人过夜(让他舒适、给他药等). ○ *He settled himself on the sofa to watch TV.* 他舒舒服服地坐在长沙发上看电视. **4** [I, Tn] (cause sb/sth to) become calm, composed or relaxed (使某人[某事物])平静、镇静或放松: *Wait until all the excitement has settled.* 等到激动情绪平静下来再说. ○ *Have a drink to settle your stomach.* 喝点饮料胃里就舒服些. ○ *The thunderstorm may settle the weather.* 这场雷暴过后天气可能反而好些. ○ *This pill will help to settle your nerves.* 你吃了这片药神经就不那么紧张了. ○ *He had been quite anxious, but I managed to settle his mind.* 他原来很着急, 我总算把他的情绪稳定下来了. **5** (**a**) [Tn, Tn·pr, Tf, Tw] **~ sth (with sb)** make an agreement about sth; arrange sth finally or satisfactorily; deal with sth 对某事物达成一致意见; 终于或满意地安排好某事物; 解决; 处理: *settle a dispute, an argument, an issue, etc* 解决一争端、争论、问题等 ○ *That settles the matter.* 事情就那样解决了. ○ *Nothing is settled yet.* 什么也没定下来. ○ *You should settle your affairs* (eg by making a will) *before you leave.* 你应该把你的事情处理好再走(如先写好遗嘱). ○ *It's time you settled your dispute with him.* 现在你该跟他把争端解决了. ○ *We have settled that we will leave next*

week. 我们已经安排好下星期走. ○ *Have you settled how it will be done?* 对于如何处理这件事, 你们是否已达成协议了? (**b**) [I, Ipr] **~ (with sb)** resolve a legal dispute by mutual agreement 相互同意解决一法律上的争端: *The parties in the lawsuit settled (with each other) out of court,* ie reached an agreement before the case was heard in court. 涉讼双方(相互)达成协议庭外和解. **6** (**a**) [I, Ipr, Ip, Tn] **~ (up) (with sb)** pay (what is owed, a bill, etc) 偿付, 结算(欠债、帐单等): *You owe a lot, and it's now time to settle (with your creditors).* 你欠了很多债, 现在该偿还(给债权人)了. ○ *Have you settled (up) with her for the goods?* 你跟她结算货款了吗? ○ *If you pay for both of us now, we can settle up later.* 你要是现在先付清咱们两人的帐, 事后咱们俩再细算. ○ *The insurance company has settled her claim.* 保险公司已经清偿了她的索赔款额. ○ *Please settle your bill before leaving the hotel.* 离开旅馆前请先结帐. (**b**) [Ipr, Tn, Tn·pr] **~ (sth) (with sb)** (*fig* 比喻) punish sb for (an injury, insult, etc that one has suffered) 为(所受的伤害、侮辱等)惩罚某人: *He thinks he can laugh at me, but I'll settle with him soon.* 他以为他嘲笑我之后就算完事了, 我马上就要找他算这笔帐. ○ *settle a score, grievance, etc* 清算旧仇、积怨等. **7** (**a**) [I, Tn] (cause sth to) sink to a lower level (使某物)下沉, 下降: *The dregs have settled at the bottom of the bottle.* 渣滓都沉到瓶底了. ○ *Stir the coffee to settle the grounds.* 把咖啡搅一搅好让渣滓沉淀. ○ *The shower of rain has settled the dust.* 这一阵雨把尘土都赶到地上了. (**b**) [I, Tn] (cause sth to) become clear as solid matter sinks (使某物)清澈(因固体下沉所致): *Has the beer settled?* 啤酒澄清了吗? ○ *Leave the wine on a shelf for a week to settle it.* 把酒搁在架子上放一个星期好让它澄清. (**c**) [I] become more compact; subside 变得更紧实或坚实; 下陷: *The wall sagged as the earth beneath it settled.* 由于墙基的土下陷, 墙也凹陷了. ○ *The contents of the packet have settled in transit,* ie come closer together, so that there appears to be less. 小包装袋里的东西在运输中已经压实了(显得少了). **8** (idm 习语) **pay/settle an old score** ⇨ OLD. **settle one's/an ac'count (with sb)** get revenge for an injury, insult, etc 为受到的伤害、侮辱等复仇: *She insulted my mother, so I have an account to settle with her.* 她侮辱我的母亲, 我得跟她算这笔帐. **settle sb's 'hash** (*infml* 口) deal finally with sb who is being awkward, aggressive, etc 终于整治一下那个闹别扭、找麻烦等的人. **when the dust has settled** ⇨ DUST[1].
9 (phr v) **settle down** (**a**) sit or lie in a comfortable position 舒适地坐或躺: *She settled down in an armchair to read her book.* 她舒适地坐在单座沙发上看书. (**b**) adopt a more stable or quiet way of life; get used to a new way of life, job, etc 过更安定或宁静的生活; 习惯于新的生活方式、工作等: *When are you going to marry and settle down?* 你什么时候结婚过上安定生活? ○ *She is settling down well in her new job.* 她很能适应这份新工作. **settle (sb) down** (cause sb to) become calm, less restless, etc (使某人)安静、安顿、安心等: *Wait until the children settle down before you start the lesson.* 等学生都静下心来再开始上课. ○ *After all the recent excitement things have begun to settle down again.* 经过最近这些激烈事情之后, 一切又都平静下来了. ○ *The chairman tried to settle the audience down,* ie get them to stop talking, etc. 主席尽力让听众安静下来. **settle (down) to sth** begin to give one's attention to sth 开始注意某事物: *The constant interruptions stopped me settling (down) to my work.* 我受到不断打扰, 无法定下心来工作.
settle for sth accept sth that is seen as not quite satisfactory 勉强认可某事物: *I had hoped to get £1000 for my old car but had to settle for a lot less.* 我那辆旧汽车原指望卖上1000英镑, 后来少卖了很多也认了.
settle (sb) in/into sth (help sb to) move into a new home, job, etc and become established there (帮助某人)迁入新居、做新工作等, 并安顿下来: *We only moved house last week and we haven't settled in yet.* 我们上星期才搬的家, 还没安顿下来呢. ○ *We settled the children into new schools when we moved to London.* 我们搬到伦敦后就给孩子们转好了新学校.
settle on sth choose sth; decide to take sth 选择某事物; 决定做某事: *Have you settled on the wallpaper you prefer?* 你选好你喜欢的壁纸了吗? ○ *We must settle on a place to meet.* 咱们得把见面的地点定下来. **settle sth on sb** (*law* 律) transfer (property, etc) to sb's ownership 将(财产等)转让给某人: *He settled part of his estate on his son.* 他把部分财产转让给儿子了.

set·tled /ˈsetld; ˋsɛtld/ *adj* not changing or likely to change; stable 不变的; 不大可能改变的; 稳定的: *a settled spell of weather* 持续一阵的天气 ○ *lead a more settled life* 过着安定些的生活.

set·tle·ment /ˈsetlmənt; ˋsɛtlmənt/ *n* **1** (**a**) [U] settling or being settled 解决; 处理; 决定; 和解: *the settlement of a debt, dispute, claim* 债务的偿还、争端的解决、索赔的清偿. (**b**) [C] agreement, etc that settles sth 解决某事物之协议等: *a lasting settlement of the troubles* 一劳永逸的解决纠纷的办法 ○ *The strikers have reached a settlement with the employers.* 罢工的人已同雇主达成协议. **2** [C] (*law* 律) (document stating the) terms on which money or property is given to sb; money or property given in this way 金钱或财产的转让(契约); 转让的金钱或财产: *a 'marriage settlement,* ie one made by a spouse in favour of his/her spouse when they get married 婚姻财产协议(结婚时一方向配偶转让财产的协议). **3** (**a**) [U] process of settling in a colony 殖民(过程): *the gradual settlement of the American West* 向美国西部逐渐伸展的殖民过程. (**b**) [C] place where colonists have settled 殖民地: *Dutch and English settlements in North America* 荷兰人和英国人在北美的殖民地 ○ *penal settlements in Australia* 澳大利亚流放地. **4** (idm 习语) **in settlement (of sth)** as payment (for sth) 对(债务等的)清偿: *I enclose a cheque in settlement of your account.* 兹附支票一张以结清贵处帐目.

set·tler /ˈsetlə(r); ˋsɛtlɚ/ *n* person who comes to live permanently in a new, developing country; colonist 移民到新的发展中国家的人; 殖民者: *Welsh settlers in Argentina* 移居阿根廷的威尔士人.

S

seven /ˈsevn; ˋsɛvən/ *pron, det* 7; one more than six 7, 七(个). ⇨App 4 见附录4.
▷ **seven** *n* **1** the number 7 ☆ 7; 七. **2** (idm 习语) **at sixes and sevens** ⇨ SIX.
seven- (in compounds 用以构成复合词) having seven of the thing specified 有七个...的: *a seven-line poem* 一首七行诗.
sev·enth /ˈsevnθ; ˋsɛvənθ/ *pron, det* 7th; next after sixth 第7, 第七(个). — *n* one of seven equal parts of sth 七分之一. **sev·enthly** *adv.*
For the uses of *seven* and *seventh* see the examples at *five* and *fifth.* 关于seven和seventh的用法见five和fifth词条中的示例.
□ **the seventh 'day** the Sabbath (Saturday for Jews, Sunday for Christians) 安息日(犹太教徒之星期六; 基督教徒之星期日).

sev·en·teen /ˌsevnˈtiːn; ˌsɛvənˋtin/ *pron, det* 17; one more than sixteen 17, 十七(个). ⇨App 4 见附录4.
▷ **sev·en·teen** *n* the number 17 ☆ 17; 十七.
sev·en·teenth /ˌsevnˈtiːnθ; ˌsɛvənˋtinθ/ *pron, det* 17th; next after sixteenth 第17, 第十七(个). — *n* one of seventeen equal parts of sth 十七分之一.
For the uses of *seventeen* and *seventeenth* see the examples at *five* and *fifth.* 关于seventeen和seventeenth的用法见five和fifth词条中的示例.

sev·enty /ˈsevntɪ; ˋsɛvəntɪ/ *pron, det* 70; one more than sixty-nine 70, 七十(个). ⇨App 4 见附录4.
▷ **sev·en·ti·eth** /ˈsevntɪəθ; ˋsɛvəntɪəθ/ *pron, det* 70th; next after sixty-ninth 第70, 第七十(个). — *n* one of seventy equal parts of sth 七十分之一.
sev·enty *n* **1** [C] the number 70 ☆ 70; 七十. **2 the seventies** [pl] numbers, years or temperature from 70 to 79 从70到79的数目、年数或温度. **3** (idm 习语) **in one's 'seventies** between the ages of 70 and 80 在70到80岁之间.
For the uses of *seventy* and *seventieth* see the examples at *five* and *fifth.* 关于seventy和seventieth的用法见five和fifth词条中的示例.
□ **ˌseventy-'eight** *n* old-fashioned type of gramophone record to be played at 78 revolutions per minute 每分钟78转的旧式电唱机唱片.

sever /ˈsevə(r); ˋsɛvɚ/ *v* (*fml* 文) **1** (**a**) [Tn, Tn·pr] **~ sth (from sth)** divide or break or separate sth by cutting 切断, 割断(某物): *sever a rope* 割断绳子 ○ *a severed limb, artery* 截断的一肢、动脉 ○ *His hand was* *severed from his arm.* 他的手切下与胳膊分离了. (**b**) [Tn] (*fig* 比喻) break off; end 中止; 结束: *sever relations with sb* 与某人断绝关系 ○ *She has severed her connection with the firm.* 她已同那家公司脱离了关系. **2** [I] break 断; 裂: *The rope severed under the strain.* 绳子拉断了.

▷ **sev·er·ance** /ˈsevərəns; ˈsɛvərəns/ *n* (*fml* 文) [U] cutting or being cut; discontinuation 切; 割; 中断: *the severance of diplomatic relations, of communications, of family ties* 外交关系、通讯、家庭关系的断绝.

□ ˈ**severance pay** money paid to an employee whose contract is terminated 遣散费; 离职金; 解雇费.

sev·eral /ˈsevrəl; ˈsɛvrəl/ *indef det, indef pron* more than three; some, but fewer than many 三个以上; 一些(但不多); 几个. (**a**) (*det*) : *Several letters arrived this morning.* 今天上午来了几封信. ○ *He's written several books about India.* 他已经写了几本关于印度的书. ○ *Several more people than usual came to the lunchtime concert.* 来参加午餐时间音乐会的人比平日多了几个. (**b**) (*pron*) : *If you're looking for a photograph of Alice you'll find several in here.* 你要是想找艾丽斯的照片, 这儿有几张. ○ *There was a fire in the art gallery and several of the paintings were destroyed.* 美术馆失了场火, 烧毁了几张画. ○ *Several of you need to work harder.* 你们有几个人还需要努力.

▷ **sev·er·ally** /ˈsevrəlɪ; ˈsɛvrəlɪ/ *adv* (*dated or fml* 旧或文) separately 分开地: *They had all severally reached the same conclusion.* 他们分别得出了同一结论.

se·vere /sɪˈvɪə(r); səˈvɪr/ *adj* (**-r**, **-st**) **1** ~ **(on/with sb/sth)** strict or harsh in attitude or treatment; imposing stern discipline 严格的; 严厉的; 苛刻的; 纪律严明的: *a severe look, punishment, measure* 严厉的样子、惩罚、措施 ○ *a severe critic of modern drama* 严厉批评现代戏剧的评论家 ○ *be severe with one's children* 对子女很严 ○ *Was the judge too severe on the thief?* 这个法官对小偷是不是太严厉了? **2** very bad, intense, difficult, etc 非常恶劣、紧张、困难等: *a severe storm* 猛烈的风暴 ○ *severe pain, injuries, etc* 剧痛、重伤 ○ *a severe attack of toothache* 牙齿的剧痛 ○ *The drought is becoming increasingly severe.* 旱灾日趋严重. **3** demanding great skill, ability, patience, etc (对技巧、能力、耐心等)要求很高的: *a severe test of climbers' stamina* 对攀登者耐力的严峻考验 ○ *severe competition for university places* 考大学的激烈竞争 ○ *The pace of the race was too severe to be maintained for long.* 比赛的速度极快, 很难持久. **4** (of style, appearance, clothing, etc) unadorned; simple (指风格、外貌、衣物等)无装饰的, 简单的, 朴素的: *Her plain black dress was too severe for such a cheerful occasion.* 她穿着黑色连衣裙, 在这种欢乐的场合未免太素了.

▷ **se·verely** *adv*: *punish sb severely* 严厉惩罚某人 ○ *severely handicapped* 严重伤残 ○ *dress very severely* 穿得很朴素.

se·ver·ity /sɪˈverətɪ; səˈvɛrətɪ/ *n* **1** [U] quality of being severe 严格; 严厉; 苛刻; 剧烈; 朴素: *punish sb with severity* 严厉惩罚某人 ○ *the severity* (ie extreme cold) *of the winter* 冬天的严寒. **2 severities** [pl] (*fml* 文) severe treatment or conditions 严厉的对待; 艰苦的环境: *the harsh severities of life in the desert* 沙漠生活的艰苦.

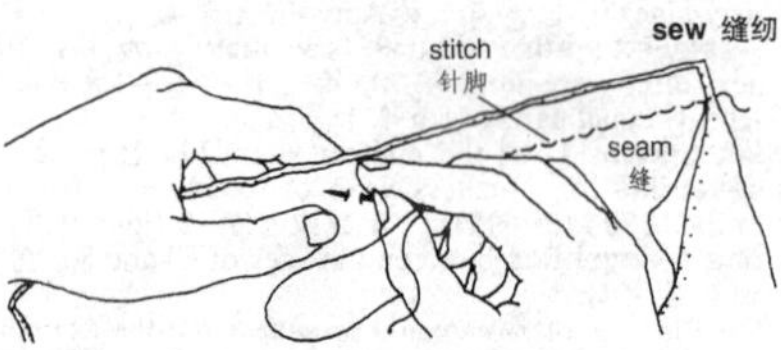

sew /səʊ; so/ *v* (*pt* **sewed**, *pp* **sewn** /səʊn; son/ or **sewed**) **1** (**a**) [I, Ipr] make stitches in cloth, etc with a needle and thread (用针线)缝: *sitting sewing by the fire* 坐在火炉旁不停地缝着 ○ *sew by hand/by machine* 用手[用机器]缝 ○ *sew round the hem* 缝边 ○ *sew over the seam again* 在缝合处再缝一次. (**b**) [Tn, Tn·pr, Tn·p] make or attach or fasten (sth) by stitching 缝制或缝上或缝合(某物): *sew a dress, skirt, etc* 缝制连衣裙、裙子等 ○ *a hand-sewn shirt* 手工缝的衬衫 ○ *sew a button onto the shirt* 把钮扣缝在衬衫上 ○ *sew the parts of the shirt together* 把衬衫各部分缝在一起 ○ *sew the flap of the pocket down* 缝上衣服口袋的盖儿. **2** (phr v) **sew sth in/into sth** enclose sth by sewing 将某物缝进去: *sew money into the lining of a coat* 把钱缝在大衣的衬里儿里. **sew sth up** (**a**) join or mend sth by sewing 缝合或缝补某物: *sew up a hole in a sock* 把袜子上的洞缝补好 ○ *The suit was sewn up along the seams by hand.* 这套衣服是手工缝的. (**b**) (esp passive 尤用于被动语态) (*infml* 口) arrange sth; settle sth 安排或解决某事: *sew up a deal, project, etc* 安排一交易、计划等 ○ *By the end of the meeting everything should be nicely sewn up.* 到会议结束时, 一切均应妥善解决.

▷ **sewer** /ˈsəʊə(r); ˈsoɚ/ *n*. **sew·ing** *n* [U] **1** activity of sewing (用针线的)缝, 缝合, 缝纫. **2** work (clothes, etc) that is being sown 缝制的东西(衣物等): *Where is my sewing?* 我的针线活儿在哪儿呢? ○ *I've got a pile of sewing to do.* 我有很多东西要缝. ○ *a sewing table, basket, etc* 裁缝案子、篮子等. ˈ**sewing-machine** *n* machine for sewing 缝纫机.

sew·age /ˈsuːɪdʒ *or, in British use,* 英式英语读作 ˈsjuː-; ˈsuɪdʒ/ *n* [U] waste matter from human bodies, factories, towns, etc that flows away in sewers (SEWER[1]) (下水道里的)污物: *chemical treatment of sewage* 对下水道污物的化学处理 ○ [attrib 作定语] *sewage disposal* 下水道污物处理.

□ ˈ**sewage farm** place where sewage is treated, esp for use as manure (下水道的)污物处理场(尤指用作肥料的).

ˈ**sewage works** place where sewage is purified so that it can be allowed to flow away safely into a river, etc (对下水道的)污物处理厂.

sewer[1] /ˈsuːə(r) *or, in British use,* 英式英语读作 ˈsjuː-; ˈsuɚ/ *n* underground pipe or passage that carries sewage away to be treated or purified 下水道; 阴沟; 污水管; 排水管.

▷ **sew·er·age** /-ɪdʒ; -ɪdʒ/ *n* [U] system of sewers; drainage 排水系统.

sewer[2] ⇨SEW.

sewn *pp* of SEW.

sex /seks; sɛks/ *n* **1** (**a**) [U] condition of being male or female; gender 性别; 性: *differences of sex* 性的区别 ○ *What sex is your dog?* 你的狗是公的还是母的? ○ *Everyone is welcome, regardless of age or sex.* 欢迎大家, 无论男女老幼一律欢迎. ○ [attrib 作定语] *sex discrimination*, ie treating sb differently because of his/her sex 性别歧视. (**b**) [C] either of the two main groups (*male* and *female*) into which living things are placed according to their functions in the process of reproduction (REPRODUCE 4) 男性, 女性, 雄性, 雌性(指生殖功能而言的): *Is this behaviour typical of the male sex?* 这种行为是雄性特有的吗? ○ *There has always been some conflict between the sexes.* 两性之间从来就有矛盾. **2** [U] ~ **(with sb)** sexual intercourse 性交: *have sex (with sb)* (与某人)性交 ○ *They often had sex together.* 他们常发生性关系. ○ [attrib 作定语] *sex organs*, ie penis, vagina, etc 性器官. **3** [U] activities that lead to and include sexual intercourse; mutual physical attraction between people 性行为; 性吸引; 性感: *a film with lots of sex in it* 有很多性行为镜头的电影 ○ *During puberty, young people become more interested in sex.* 年轻人在青春期对性逐渐产生较大兴趣. ○ [attrib 作定语] *a sex manual*, ie giving information on sexual behaviour 性知识手册 ○ *a sex shop*, ie selling pornography, devices to make sex more enjoyable, etc 性用品商店. **4** (idm 习语) **the weaker sex** ⇨ WEAK.

▷ **sex** *v* [Tn] find out the sex(1) of (a creature) 鉴别(某生物)的性别: *sexing very young chicks* 识别小雏鸡的性别.

-sexed (forming compound *adjs* 用以构成复合形容词) having the specified amount of sexual desire 有某程度的性欲的: *a highly-sexed youth* ○ *over-sexed*, ie too interested in sexual matters.

sex·less *adj* **1** lacking sexual desire, attractiveness or activity 缺乏性欲、性感或性行为的: *a dry, sexless person* 冷淡、无性感的人 ○ *a sexless relationship* 无性行为的关系. **2** neither male nor female; having neither masculine nor feminine characteristics; neuter 无性的; 无雌雄特

征的; 中性的.

sexy *adj* (**-ier, -iest**) (*infml* 口) **1** of or about sex(2,3) (关于)性交的, 性行为的, 性吸引的: *a sexy book, film, etc* 关于性行为的书、影片等 ○ *making sexy suggestions* 提出性交的想法. **2** (**a**) causing sexual desire 引起性欲的; 性感的: *You look very sexy in that dress.* 你穿着那件连衣裙很性感. (**b**) feeling sexual desire 有性欲的: *get/feel sexy* 产生性欲[感到有性欲]. **sex·ily** *adv*. **sexi·ness** *n* [U].

□ ˈ**sex act** sexual intercourse 性交.

ˈ**sex appeal** sexual attractiveness 性的魅力; 性感: *a man with lots of sex appeal* 极性感的男子.

ˈ**sex life** person's sexual activities 性生活: *How's your sex life?* 你的性生活怎样?

ˈ**sex-starved** *adj* (*infml* 口) not having enough opportunities for sexual intercourse 缺少性交机会的; 性饥饿的.

sex- *comb form* 构词成分 six 六: *sexcentenary*, ie 600th anniversary.

sexa·gen·arian /ˌseksədʒɪˈneərɪən; ˌsɛksədʒəˈnɛrɪən/ *n*, *adj* [attrib 作定语] (*fml* 文) (person who is) of any age from 60 to 69 60到69岁之间的(人).

sex·ism /ˈseksɪzəm; ˋsɛksɪzəm/ *n* [U] (*derog* 贬) prejudice or discrimination against people (esp women) because of their sex 性别偏见或歧视(尤指对女性): *blatant sexism in the selection of staff* 在挑选职员时明显的性别歧视.

▷ **sex·ist** /ˈseksɪst; ˋsɛksɪst/ *adj* (*derog* 贬) of or showing sexism (表现)性别偏见的, 性别歧视的(尤指对女性): *a sexist person, attitude, remark, book* 有性别歧视的人、态度、言语、书 ○ *It is sexist to say that women are less intelligent than men.* 所谓女性没有男性聪明的说法是对性别的偏见. — *n* (*derog* 贬) person who shows sexism or has a sexist attitude 有性别偏见或性别歧视的人(尤指对女性).

sex·ology /sekˈsɒlədʒɪ; sɛkˋsɑlədʒɪ/ *n* [U] scientific study of human sexual behaviour 性学.

▷ **sex·olo·gist** /sekˈsɒlədʒɪst; sɛkˋsɑlədʒɪst/ *n* expert in sexology 性学专家.

sex·tant /ˈsekstənt; ˋsɛkstənt/ *n* instrument used for measuring the altitude of the sun, eg in order to determine the position of one's ship 六分仪(测量太阳高度的仪器, 如用以为船定位).

sex·tet (also **sex·tette**) /seksˈtet; sɛksˋtɛt/ *n* (piece of music for a) group of six singers or players 六重唱(曲); 六重奏(曲).

sex·ton /ˈsekstən; ˋsɛkstən/ *n* person who takes care of a church and its churchyard, rings the church bell, etc 教堂司事(负责看管教堂及其墓地、敲钟等).

sexual /ˈsekʃʊəl; ˋsɛkʃʊəl/ *adj* **1** (**a**) of sex(2,3) or the sexes or the physical attraction between them 性交的; 性行为的; 性吸引的; 两性的; 肉体吸引的: *sexual feelings, activity, desire* 性吸引的感受、性活动、性欲 ○ *Her interest in him is primarily sexual.* 她喜欢他主要是肉体上的. (**b**) of sex(1) or gender 性别的; 性的; 男性或女性的; 雄性或雌性的: *sexual differences, characteristics, etc* 性的区别、特征等. **2** [attrib 作定语] concerned with the reproduction of offspring 生殖的; 有性生殖的: *sexual organs*, ie penis, vagina, etc 生殖器官 ○ *sexual reproduction in plants* 植物的有性生殖.

▷ **sexu·al·ity** /ˌsekʃʊˈælətɪ; ˌsɛkʃʊˋælətɪ/ *n* [U] sexual nature or characteristics 性别的特性或特征; 性吸引; 性感; 性能力.

sexu·ally /-əlɪ; -əlɪ/ *adv*: *sexually active* 在性方面活跃 ○ *a sexually transmitted disease* 性传染病.

□ **sexual** ˈ**intercourse** (also **intercourse**) insertion of a man's penis into a woman's vagina, usu leading to the ejaculation of semen; copulation 性交; 交媾.

SF /ˌes ˈef; ˌɛs ˋɛf/ *abbr* 缩写 = (*infml* 口) science fiction.

sgd *abbr* 缩写 = signed (on a form, etc).

Sgt *abbr* 缩写 = SERGT.

sh /ʃ; ʃ/ *interj* be quiet!; be silent! 安静! ; 静一静!: *Sh! You'll wake the baby!* 嘘! 你要把孩子吵醒的!

shabby /ˈʃæbɪ; ˋʃæbɪ/ *adj* (**-ier, -iest**) **1** (**a**) (of things) in poor condition through much use or being badly cared for (指东西)因使用过久或照管不善而破旧的: *a shabby dress, chair, room* 破旧的连衣裙、椅子、房间 ○ *a tramp in shabby old clothes* 衣衫褴褛的流浪者. (**b**) (of people) poorly dressed (指人)衣着寒酸的: *You look rather shabby in those clothes.* 你穿着那种衣服显得很寒酸. **2** (*fig* 比喻) (of behaviour) mean and unfair; dishonourable (指行为)卑鄙而不正当的, 不光彩的: *a shabby excuse* 卑劣的借口 ○ *play a shabby trick on sb* 对某人耍鬼花招. ▷ **shab·bily** /ˈʃæbɪlɪ; ˋʃæblɪ/ *adv*: *I think you have been shabbily treated.* 我看是人家亏待你了. **shab·bi·ness** *n* [U].

shack /ʃæk; ʃæk/ *n* roughly built shed, hut or house 简陋的棚子、小屋或房子.

▷ **shack** *v* (phr v) **shack up (with sb/together)** (*Brit sl* 俚) (esp of a couple) live together although not married (尤指情侣)未婚而同居: *They've decided to shack up together in her flat.* 他们决定在她的公寓里同居.

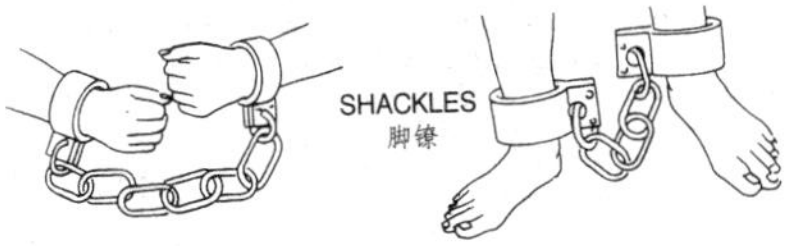

shackle /ˈʃækl; ˋʃækḷ/ *n* **1** [C usu *pl* 通常作复数] either of a pair of metal rings linked by a chain, used for fastening a prisoner's wrists or ankles together 手铐; 脚镣; 镣铐. **2 shackles** [pl] **the ~s of sth** (*fig* 比喻) conditions, circumstances, etc that prevent one from acting or speaking freely 束缚; 羁绊: *the shackles of convention* 习俗的束缚.

▷ **shackle** *v* **1** [Tn] put shackles on (sb) 给(某人)带上手铐或脚镣. **2** [Tn esp passive 尤用于被动语态] (*fig* 比喻) prevent (sb) from acting or speaking freely 束缚(某人): *shackled by outdated attitudes* 受旧观念的束缚.

shad /ʃæd; ʃæd/ *n* (*pl* unchanged 复数不变) large edible fish of the N Atlantic coast of N America 西鲱(体大, 食用鱼, 产于北美北大西洋沿岸).

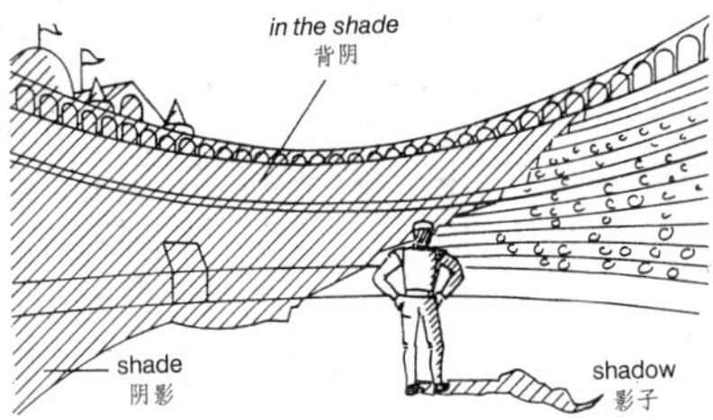

shade /ʃeɪd; ʃed/ *n* **1** [U] **~ (from sth)** (place where there is) comparative darkness and often coolness caused by sth blocking direct light or heat, esp of the sun 荫; 阴凉处: *a temperature of 35°C in the shade* 阴凉处35°C的温度 ○ *sit in the shade of a tree, wall, etc* 坐在树、墙等的阴凉处 ○ *Stay in the shade — it's cooler.* 呆在背阴处吧——那儿凉快些. ○ *The trees give some welcome shade from the sun.* 这些树遮住了阳光, 很舒适凉快. **2** [C] (often in compounds 常用以构成复合词) thing that shuts out light or makes it less bright 遮光物: *an* ˈ*eye-shade* 遮光帽檐 ○ *a new shade for the* ˈ*lamp/*ˈ*lampshade* 新灯罩. **3 shades** [pl] **the ~s of sth** (*fml* 文) the darkness of sth 黑暗: *the shades of evening/night* 暮[夜]色. **4 shades** [pl] (*infml* 口 *esp US*) sun-glasses 墨镜. **5** [U] darker part(s) of a picture, etc (图画、照片等的)较阴暗部分: *There is not enough light and shade in your drawing.* 你这幅画的明暗色调不够. **6** [C] (degree or depth of) colour; hue 颜色; 色度: *material in several shades of blue* 几种色度的蓝色材料 ○ *choose a lighter shade* 选择淡些的颜色 ○ *Do you like the blouse in this shade?* 你喜欢这种色度的女衬衫吗? **7** (**a**) [C] **~**

of sth slight difference in sth 细微的差别: *a word with many shades of meaning* 有许多相近意思的一个词 ○ *people with all shades of opinion* 意见不一的人们. (**b**) [sing] **a ~ (better, worse, etc)** a small amount 少量; 些微: *I think it's a shade warmer today.* 我觉得今天暖和一点儿. ○ *She feels a shade better than yesterday.* 她感觉比昨天好一些. **8 shades** [pl] **~ s of sb/sth** (*infml* 口) reminders of sb/sth 对某人[某事物]的联想: *'Shades of Hitler!' I thought, as I listened to the dictator haranguing the crowd.* 那个独裁者向群众声嘶力竭地训话, 我一听就想到, '真像希特勒!' ○ *In some modern fashions we can see shades of the 1930s.* 在有些摩登时装中可以看到三十年代的影子. **9** [C] (*fml* 文) soul after death; ghost 灵魂; 鬼魂; 阴魂: *the shades of my dead ancestors* 我的先祖的幽魂. **10** (idm 习语) **put sb/sth in the 'shade** be very superior to sb/sth 使某人[某事物]相形失色: *I thought I was quite a good artist, but your painting puts mine in the shade.* 我原以为为自己画得不错, 可比起你的画儿来未免相形见绌.

▷ **shade** *v* **1** [Tn, Tn·pr] **~ sb/sth (from sth)** block off light from sb/sth; give shade to sb/sth 给某人[某物]遮住光线; 给某人[某物]阴凉: *She shaded her eyes (from the sun) with her hand.* 她把手放在眼睛上方挡住阳光. **2** [Tn] screen (a lamp, light, etc) to reduce its brightness 遮挡(灯、光等)以减弱亮度: *shade the bulb with a dark cloth* 用深色布遮挡灯泡使光暗些. **3** [Tn, Tn·p] **~ sth (in)** darken (a part of a drawing, etc), eg with parallel pencil lines, to give an effect of light and shade 将(图画等的某部)颜色加深(如加铅笔线条以显出明暗效果): *shade (in) this area to represent the person's shadow* 把这部分画暗些以显出人影 ○ *the shaded areas on the map* 地图上颜色深的地方. **4** [Ipr, Ip] **~ from sth into sth; ~ (off) into sth** (esp of colours) change gradually into (another colour or variety) (尤指颜色)逐渐变成(其他颜色): *scarlet shading (off) into pink* 猩红色逐渐变成粉色 ○ *a colour that shades from blue into green* 由蓝逐渐变绿的颜色 ○ (*fig* 比喻) *socialism shading into communism* 逐渐向共产主义过渡的社会主义. **shad·ing** *n* [U] (use of) pencil marks, etc that give an effect of darkness in a part of a picture (绘画的)明暗(运用).

S

shadow /ˈʃædəʊ; ˈʃædo/ *n* **1** [C, U] (patch of) shade caused by an object blocking direct rays of light 阴影; 影子: *The chair casts a shadow on the wall.* 椅子的影子映到墙上了. ○ *Shadows are longer when the sun is low in the sky.* 太阳很低时, 物体的影子就很长. ○ *Her face was in deep shadow.* 她的脸部在一片很暗的阴影中. ○ (*fig* 比喻) *The bad news cast a shadow on/over our meeting,* ie made us sad. 那个坏消息给会议蒙上了阴影. ⇨ illus at SHADE 见SHADE插图. **2** [C] dark patch or area 深色的斑; 深色部分: *have shadows under/round the eyes,* eg because of illness or lack of sleep 眼睛下面[周围]有黑圈(如因病或缺觉). **3** [U] shaded part of a picture (绘画的)阴暗部分: *areas of light and shadow* 明暗的部分 ○ *The light from one side leaves half the subject's face in shadow.* 因光线来自一边, 画中人的脸有一半成为阴暗部分. **4 shadows** [pl] partial darkness 不完全的黑暗: *a figure standing in the shadows* 站在较暗处的人 ○ *the shadows of evening* 暮色. **5** [C] (**a**) person's constant attendant or companion 如影随形的随从或伙伴: *The dog is his master's shadow.* 这条狗和主人形影不离. (**b**) person who secretly follows and watches sb, eg a criminal 跟踪盯梢的人(如对罪犯的): *The police put a shadow on the suspected robber.* 警方派探员盯住那个抢劫疑犯. **6** [C] thing that is weak or unreal 微弱的或虚幻的东西: *catch at shadows,* ie try to obtain sth that does not exist 捕捉虚无缥缈的东西 ○ *You can't spend your life chasing after shadows.* 你不能一辈子追求不存在的东西. **7** [sing] **~ of sth** (usu in negative sentences 通常用于否定句) slight trace of sth 某事物的痕迹: *not a shadow of (a) doubt* 毫无疑义 ○ *There's not a shadow of justification for your behaviour.* 你的举动毫无道理. **8** [sing] **the ~ of sb/sth** the strong influence of sb/sth 某人[某事物]的巨大影响: *the shadow of the approaching catastrophe* 灾难即将降临的威胁 ○ *For years he lived in the shadow of his famous mother.* 他多年受母亲盛名所累难露头角. ○ *The shadow of this early tragedy has affected her whole life.* 她年纪轻轻遭此劫难, 影响了她一生. **9** (idm 习语) **be afraid of one's own shadow** ⇨ AFRAID. **a 'shadow of one's/its former self** not having the strength, influence, etc that one/it formerly had 已不再有以前的力量、影响力等: *She used to be a great player, but now she's only a shadow of her former self.* 她以前是个健将, 现在已不及当年了.

▷ **shadow** *v* [Tn] **1** cast a shadow on (sb/sth) 使阴影或影子映在(某人[某物])上: *The wide brim of his hat shadowed his face.* 他的大帽檐的影子映在他的脸上. **2** follow and watch (sb) secretly 跟踪盯住(某人): *A policeman in plain clothes shadowed the criminal all day.* 有个便衣警察整天秘密监视那个罪犯.

shadow *adj* [attrib 作定语] (*Brit politics* 政) denoting leading members of the Opposition party who would probably be Cabinet ministers if their party became the Government, and who act as spokesmen on matters for which they would then be responsible 影子内阁的(指在野党若组阁, 有望成为内阁各大臣的人对各自应负责的事务发表言论方面): *the Shadow Cabinet* 影子内阁 ○ *the Shadow Foreign Secretary* 影子外交大臣.

shad·owy *adj* **1** full of shadows or shade 有影子的; 多阴凉的: *the shadowy interior of the barn* 谷仓阴凉的内部 ○ *cool, shadowy woods* 凉爽、多阴凉的树林. **2** (*fig* 比喻) like a shadow; indistinct 似影子的; 模糊的: *a shadowy figure glimpsed in the twilight* 在暮色中闪现出的一个人影.

□ **'shadow-box** *v* [I] box with an imaginary opponent 与假想对手打拳: *shadow-boxing alone in the ring* 在拳击台上自己练习打拳. **'shadow-boxing** *n* [U].

shady /ˈʃeɪdɪ; ˈʃedɪ/ *adj* (**-ier, -iest**) **1** giving shade from sunlight; situated in the shade 遮阳的; 背阴的; 成阴的; 在背阴处的: *a shady orchard* 成阴的果园 ○ *a shady corner of the garden* 花园背阴的一角. **2** (*infml derog* 口, 贬) not entirely honest; disreputable 不太正直的; 名声不好的: *a shady business, deal, organization* 不正当的生意、交易、组织机构 ○ *a shady-looking person* 鬼头鬼脑的人. ▷ **sha·dily** /-ɪlɪ; -ɪlɪ/ *adv*. **sha·di·ness** *n* [U].

shaft /ʃɑːft; *US* ʃæft; ʃæft/ *n* **1** [C] (**a**) long slender stem of an arrow or a spear 箭杆; 矛杆. (**b**) [C] (*arch* 古) arrow; spear 箭; 矛. **2** [C] **~ (of sth)** (*fig* 比喻) remark intended to wound or stimulate 旨在伤人或刺激人的话: *shafts of malice* 恶意挖苦人的话 ○ *her brilliant shafts of wit* 她的机智犀利的词锋. **3** [C] long handle of an axe or other tool, or eg of a golf-club 长柄(如斧、高尔夫球杆等用具的). **4** [C] either of the two bars or poles between which a horse is harnessed to pull a cart, etc 辕; 辕子. **5** [C] main part of a column, between the base and the capital 柱身. ⇨ illus at COLUMN 见COLUMN插图. **6** [C] (often in compounds 常用以构成复合词) bar or rod joining parts of a machine or transmitting power in a machine (机器的)连杆, 传动轴, 旋转轴: *a 'crankshaft* ○ *a 'drive-shaft.* **7** [C] (often in compounds 常用以构成复合词) long narrow (usu vertical) space, eg for a lift to move up and down in, for entry into a mine, or for ventilation 通道(通常指垂直的, 如为电梯、矿井升降机等上下移动的, 或通风用的): *a 'lift-shaft* 升降机井 ○ *a 'mine-shaft* 井筒 ○ *sink a shaft* 挖竖井. Cf 参看 GALLERY 6. **8 the shaft** [sing] (*US infml* 口) unfair treatment; trickery 苛待; 诡计: *give sb/get the shaft* 亏待某人[受到亏待] ○ *We were given the shaft, and lost a lot of money.* 我们上了大当, 损失了很多钱. **9** [C] **~ (of sth)** long thin beam (of light, etc) (光线等的)束: *a shaft of light/sunlight/moonlight/lightning* 一道光[阳光/月光/闪光].

▷ **shaft** *v* [Tn] (*US infml* 口) treat (sb) unfairly or harshly; cheat 苛待(某人); 欺骗.

shag[1] /ʃæg; ʃæg/ *n* [U] strong coarse type of cut tobacco 浓味粗烟丝.

shag[2] /ʃæg; ʃæg/ *v* [I, Tn] (⚠ *Brit sl* 讳, 俚) have sexual intercourse with (sb) 与(某人)性交.

shagged /ʃægd; ʃægd/ *adj* [pred 作表语] (also **shagged 'out**) (*Brit sl* 俚) very tired 非常累; 精疲力竭.

shaggy /ˈʃægɪ; ˈʃægɪ/ *adj* (**-ier, -iest**) **1** rough, thick and untidy 粗糙、浓密而不整齐的: *shaggy hair, eyebrows* 蓬乱的头发、粗眉 ○ *a shaggy beard* 蓬乱的胡子. **2** covered with rough untidy hair or fibres, etc 有粗糙而不整齐的毛发或纤维的: *a shaggy dog, mat, coat* 粗毛的狗、垫子、大衣. ▷ **shag·gily** /-ɪlɪ; -ɪlɪ/ *adv*. **shag·gi·ness** *n* [U].

□ **shaggy-'dog story** long rambling joke, often with a pointless and not very funny ending 冗长杂乱的笑话(结尾常为平淡无趣的).

shah /ʃɑː; ʃɑ/ *n* (title of a) former ruler of Iran 沙(旧时伊朗国王或其称号).

shake[1] /ʃeɪk; ʃek/ *v* (*pt* **shook** /ʃʊk; ʃuk/, *pp* **shaken** /'ʃeɪkən; 'ʃekən/) **1 (a)** [La, I, Tn, Tn·p, Cn·a] **~ sb/sth (about/around)** (cause sb/sth to) move quickly and often jerkily from side to side or up and down (使某人[某物])急速摇动或颠簸(常指猛然产生或停止): *a bolt shaking loose in an engine* 发动机上震松的螺栓 ○ *The earth shook under us*, eg in an earthquake. 大地在我们脚下抖动(如地震时). ○ *The table shook when she banged her fist on it.* 她用拳头把桌子敲得直颤. ○ *Shake the bottle before taking the medicine.* 服药前先将药瓶摇一摇. ○ *He shook the carpet to get rid of the dust.* 他把地毯上的尘土抖掉了. ○ *He shook her violently as a dog shakes a rat.* 他使劲把她推来推去, 像狗玩老鼠似的. ○ *Great sobs shook his whole body.* 他哭得浑身发抖. ○ *The bumpy car ride shook us around a bit.* 汽车把我们颠得有些摇摇晃晃. ○ *Vibrations shook the panel loose.* 仪表板震松了. **(b)** [I, Ipr] **~ (with sth)** (of a person) tremble; quiver (指人)发抖, 打颤: *laughed until their sides shook* 笑得他们浑身直颤 ○ *shaking with laughter, fear, rage, etc* 笑得、吓得、气得...打颤 ○ *shaking with cold* 冻得发抖. **2 (a)** [Tn, Tn·p] **~ sb (up)** disturb the calmness of sb; trouble or shock sb 使某人心绪不宁; 烦扰或惊吓某人: *shaken by the news of her death* 受到她死讯的震惊 ○ *They were badly shaken (up) in the accident.* 他们在这次事故中受到很大打击. ○ *This surprising development quite shook me.* 这一惊人的新情况把我吓坏了. **(b)** [Tn] make (sth) less certain; weaken 动摇(某人)的想法; 减弱: *shake sb's faith, courage, belief, etc* 动摇某人的信仰、削弱某人的勇气、动摇某人的信念 ○ *Her theory has been shaken by this new evidence.* 这一新证据动摇了她的理论. **3** [I, Ipr] **~ (with sth)** (of sb's voice) become weak or faltering; tremble (指某人的嗓音)变弱, 发颤, 颤抖: *His voice shook (with emotion) as he announced the news.* 他宣布这一消息时, 声音(因激动)有些颤抖. **4** [I, Ipr] **~ (on sth)** (*infml* 口) shake hands 握手: *We're agreed, so let's shake (on it).* 咱们意见一致了, 握握手吧. **5** (idm 习语) **shake the dust (of...) off one's feet** leave a place one does not like, hoping not to return 离开厌恶之处, 但愿不再返回: *After a year of misery here, I'm finally shaking the dust of this town off my feet.* 我在这个市镇受了一年罪, 总算离开这里了. **shake one's 'fist (at sb)** show that one is angry with sb or threaten sb by shaking one's fist 向某人挥拳表示愤怒或恐吓. **shake sb's 'hand/shake 'hands (with sb)/shake sb by the 'hand** grasp sb's hand and move it up and down as a greeting, or to express agreement, etc 握手(表示问候或同意等). **shake one's 'head** turn one's head from side to side as a way of indicating 'no', or to express doubt, sorrow, disapproval, etc 摇头(表示否定、怀疑、悲伤、不赞成等). **shake in one's 'shoes** (*infml* 口) be very frightened 非常害怕: *He was shaking in his shoes at the thought of flying for the first time.* 他想到这是他第一次乘飞机就吓得要命. **shake a 'leg** (*dated Brit sl* 旧, 俚) (esp imperative 尤用于祈使句) get moving; start to act; hurry 出发; 动手; 赶快; 快点儿: *Come on, shake a leg, we're late already.* 好啦, 快点儿吧, 我们已经晚啦. **shake like a leaf** tremble with fear, nervousness, etc 因害怕、紧张...而发抖.

6 (phr v) **shake down (a)** settle down and function properly 安顿下来, 一切就绪: *The new office staff are shaking down well.* 新职员各方面都很顺利. **(b)** sleep somewhere where there is no proper bed 睡在没有正式床的地方: *You can shake down on the floor.* 你可以临时睡在地板上. **shake sb down** (*US infml* 口) get money from sb by threats, violence, etc 勒索或敲诈某人. **shake sb/sth down** (*US infml* 口) search sb/sth thoroughly 彻底搜查某人[某处]: *Police shook the club down, looking for narcotics.* 警方为搜索毒品把那个俱乐部彻底搜查了一遍.

shake sth from, into, onto, out of, etc sth move sth in the specified direction by shaking 摇动某物使之沿某方向移动: *shake scouring powder into the bath* 把去污粉撒进浴缸里 ○ *shake salt from the salt-cellar onto one's food* 摇晃盐瓶把盐撒在食物上 ○ *shake sand out of one's shoes* 把鞋里的沙子抖落出来.

shake sb off rid oneself of (sb unwanted); escape from sb 摆脱(某人); 从某人处逃脱: *shake off one's pursuers* 甩掉跟踪的人 ○ *She tried to shake him off but he continued to pester her.* 她想甩开他, 但他仍不断缠着她.

shake sth off get rid of sth 摆脱某事物: *shake off a cold, a fit of depression* 治好感冒、消除沮丧的情绪.

shake sth off (sth) remove sth by shaking 用摇动等方法除掉某物: *shake the snow off (one's coat)* 抖掉(大衣上的)雪.

shake sth out open or spread sth by shaking 用摇动等方法打开或展开某物: *shake out a sheet, sail, etc* 抖开床单、帆等.

shake sth up mix sth thoroughly by shaking 用摇动等方法将某物混合均匀: *Shake up the salad-dressing before you put it on.* 把色拉调味汁摇匀再洒在色拉上.

shake sb up rouse sb from a state of lethargy, apathy, etc 使某人振作起来、积极起来等: *We've got to shake up all these people with old-fashioned ideas.* 我们得让这些老脑筋的人清醒清醒了.

▷ **shaker** *n* (often in compounds 常用以构成复合词) container in which or from which sth is shaken 摇动的容器; 可摇出东西的容器: *a 'cocktail-shaker* 鸡尾酒摇动器 ○ *a 'dice-shaker* 色子摇盒.

shak·ing *n* [sing] act of shaking 摇动; 震动; 颠簸: *give sth a good shaking*, ie shake it well 把某物摇匀.

□ **'shakedown** *n* **1** improvised bed 临时床铺: *a shakedown on the floor* 地铺. **2** (*US infml* 口) act of getting money by violence, threats, etc 勒索; 敲诈. **3** (*US infml* 口) thorough search 彻底的搜查: *a shakedown of drug dealers* 对毒贩进行的彻底搜查. **4** final test, eg of a ship, aircraft, etc 最后的测试(如对船、飞行器等的): [attrib 作定语] *a shakedown voyage, flight, trial, etc* 最后试航、试飞、试用等.

'shake-up (also **'shake-out**) *n* major reform or reorganization 大改革; 大改组: *The only thing that will save the company is a thorough shake-up of the way it is run.* 挽救该公司的唯一办法是彻底改变其经营方式.

shake[2] /ʃeɪk; ʃek/ *n* **1** [C usu *sing* 通常作单数] act of shaking or being shaken 摇动; 震动; 颠簸: *a shake of the head*, ie indicating 'no' 摇一下头(表示否定) ○ *I gave my purse a shake, and a coin fell out.* 我摇了一下钱包, 掉出一枚硬币. **2 the shakes** [sing *v*] (*infml* 口) fit of trembling or shivering 哆嗦; 寒战: *a high temperature and a fit of the shakes* 发高烧打哆嗦. **3** (idm 习语) **a fair shake** ⇨ FAIR[1]. **in a couple of 'shakes/in two 'shakes (of a lamb's tail)** (*infml* 口) in a moment; very soon 马上; 立刻: *Hang on! I'll be back in two shakes!* 电话先不要挂! 我马上就来! **no great shakes** ⇨ GREAT.

Shake·spear·ian (also **Shake·spear·ean**) /ʃeɪk'spɪərɪən; ʃek'spɪrɪən/ *adj* (in the style) of Shakespeare 莎士比亚的(风格的): *Shakespearean sonnets* 莎士比亚十四行诗 ○ *Shakespearian quotations* 莎士比亚语录.

shaky /'ʃeɪkɪ; 'ʃekɪ/ *adj* (**-ier**, **-iest**) **1** shaking or trembling through weakness, illness, etc (因病、体弱等)摇晃的, 发抖的, 颤抖的: *a shaky walk, voice* 摇摇晃晃的步子、颤抖的声音 ○ *Her hands are shaky because she's nervous.* 她紧张得双手发抖. ○ *He looks a bit shaky on his feet.* 他像是站不稳的样子. **2** not firm and steady; not safe and reliable 不坚定的; 不稳定的; 不安全的; 不可靠的: *a shaky chair, table, wall* 不安全的椅子、桌子、墙 ○ *The tripod is too shaky.* 这个三角架太不稳了. ○ (*fig* 比喻) *a shaky argument* 站不住脚的论点 ○ *The government is looking very shaky at the moment.* 政府目前看来很不稳固. ○ *My French is a bit shaky*, ie I don't speak it very well. 我的法语不太好. ▷ **sha·kily** /-ɪlɪ; -ɪlɪ/ *adv*. **sha·ki·ness** *n* [U].

shale /ʃeɪl; ʃel/ *n* [U] type of soft rock that splits easily into thin flat pieces 页岩. ▷ **shaly** *adj*.

□ **'shale-oil** *n* [U] oil extracted from shale 页岩油.

shall /ʃəl; ʃl strong form 强读式 ʃæl; ʃæl/ *modal v* (*esp Brit*) (*neg* 否定式 **shall not**, *contracted form* 缩约式 **shan't** /ʃɑːnt; ʃænt/; *pt* **should** /ʃʊd; ʃud/, *neg* 否定式 **should not**, *contracted form* 缩约式 **shouldn't** /'ʃʊdnt; 'ʃudnt/) **1** (indicating future predictions 表示预言): *We shan't know the results until next week.* 我们下星期才能知道结果. ○ *Shall we be there in time for tea?* 咱们能及

S

时赶到那里吃下午茶点吗? ○ *This time next week I shall be sitting on a beach in Greece.* 下星期此时此刻我正坐在希腊海滨呢. ○ *I said I should be glad to help.* 我说过我很愿意帮忙. ⇨Usage 1 见所附用法第1项. **2** (*fml* 文) (indicating will or determination 表示意愿或决心): *I shall write to you again at the end of the month.* 我月底给你再写一封信. ○ *You shall have a new dress for your birthday.* 你过生日一定得有件新连衣裙. ○ *He insisted that the papers should be destroyed.* 他坚持那些文件得销毁. ○ *She was determined that we should finish on time.* 她坚决要我们按时完成. **3** (indicating offers or suggestions 表示提供意见或建议): *Shall I* (ie Would you like me to) *do the washing-up?* 我来洗餐具好吗? ○ *What shall we do this weekend?* 我们本周末干什么呢? ○ *Let's look at it again, shall we?* 咱们再看一看好吗? ⇨ Usage 3 见所附用法第3项. **4** (*fml* 文) (indicating orders or instructions 表示命令或指示): *Candidates shall remain in their seats until all the papers have been collected.* 试卷全部收回后应试人才可离开座位. ○ *The lease stated that tenants should maintain the property in good condition.* 租约规定承租人必须保持房产完好无损.

NOTE ON USAGE 用法: **1** PREDICTIONS 预言 (**shall, will**[1]) (**a**) **Shall** is used with *I* or *we* to predict a future event ☆ **shall** 与I或we连用, 预示将要发生的事情: *I shall be in touch with you again shortly.* 我很快再和你联系. **Will** (when speaking usu contracted to **'ll**) is used with *you, he, she, it, they* as well as *I* and *we*, often in more informal contexts than **shall** ☆ **will** (口语中通常缩略成 **'ll**) 与I和we连用, 也与you、he、she、it、they连用, 与**shall**相比, 多用于口语或较随便的场合: *She'll never finish in time.* 她决不能按时完成. ○ *It'll be our first holiday for years.* 这(将)是我们多年来的第一次假期. (**b**) In indirect speech, **should** and **would** (when speaking usu contracted to **'d**) are used 在间接引语中用**should**和**would** (口语中通常缩略成**'d**): *I estimated that I should finish in ten days.* 我估计我十天能完成. ○ *Bill said he'd soon be back.* 比尔说他很快就回来. **2** VOLITION 决定 (**shall, will**[1]) (**a**) Both **shall** and **will** can express determination. ☆ **shall** 和 **will** 均可用以表示决心. **Shall** is more formal, especially when used with pronouns other than *I* or *we* ☆ **shall** 词义较文, 与除I或we的其他代词连用时, 尤其来得庄重: *He shall be given a fair trial.* 他一定可以得到公平审判的. ○ *You'll have your radio back on Tuesday.* 星期二你就能取回收音机了. ○ *We 'will get the thing right!* 我们决心要把这件事弄对! (**b**) **Should** and **would** are used in clauses after *be certain, be determined, insist*, etc ☆ **should** 和 **would** 用于从句中的be certain、be determined、insist等词语之后: *He insisted that we should make a fresh start.* 他硬要我们重新开始. **3** SUGGESTIONS 建议 (**shall, can**[2], **could**[1]) (**a**) **Shall I** and **shall we** are used to make suggestions ☆ **shall I** 和 **shall we** 可用以提出建议: *Shall I drive?* 我来开车好吗? ○ *Shall we take our swim-suits?* 我们带着游泳衣好不好? **Can** (often with *of course* and/or *always*) is also used for this purpose ☆ **can**(常与of course和[或] always连用)也可用以提出建议: *We can always come back tomorrow if you prefer.* 只要你愿意的话, 我们反正明天还可以回来. **Could** is used to make more tentative suggestions ☆ **could** 可用以提出较试探性的建议: *You could try pushing the car.* 你不妨推推这辆汽车试试看. ○ *Couldn't we ask a policeman?* 我们问问警察行吗? (**b**) Any of these verbs can be used to ask for suggestions 这些动词均可用以征询意见: *Where shall we go now?* 我们现在上哪儿去? ○ *Can we perhaps try another route?* 我们是不是可以另试试别的路线? ○ *How could we make them listen?* 我们怎样才能让他们听呢?

shal·lot /ʃəˈlɒt; ʃəˈlɑt/ *n* type of onion that grows as a cluster of small bulbs 青葱.

shal·low /ˈʃæləʊ; ˈʃælo/ *adj* (**-er, -est**) **1** not deep 浅的: *shallow water* 浅水 ○ *a shallow saucer, dish, bowl, etc* 浅的茶托、碟子、盆等 ○ *the shallow end*, eg of a swimming-pool 水浅的一端(如游泳池的) ○ *shallow breathing* 浅呼吸. **2** (*derog* 贬) (of a person) not thinking or capable of thinking seriously; (of ideas, remarks, etc) not showing serious thought (指人)肤浅的, 浅薄的; (指思想言语等)肤浅的, 浅显的: *a shallow writer, argument, conversation, book* 浅薄的作家、议论、交谈、书. Cf 参看 DEEP[1].

▷ **shal·low** *v* [I] become shallow 变浅.

shal·lowly *adv.*

shal·low·ness *n* [U].

shal·lows *n* [pl] shallow place in a river or in the sea (河或海的)浅水处.

sham /ʃæm; ʃæm/ *v* (**-mm-**) [I, Tn] pretend (sth); feign 装作(某事物); 假装: *He's only shamming.* 他只是假装而已. ○ *sham illness, death, sleep* 装病、装死、装睡 ○ *sham dead*, ie pretend to be dead 装死.

▷ **sham** *n* (*usu derog* 通常作贬义) **1** [C] (**a**) person who pretends to be what he is not 装成与自己实际情况不符的人: *She claims to know all about computers but really she's a sham.* 她自称精通计算机, 其实她是假充内行. (**b**) (usu *sing* 通常作单数) thing, feeling, etc that is not what sb pretends that it is 装出的事物、感情等: *His love was a sham; he only wanted her money.* 他爱她是假的, 他只想要她的钱. ○ *Their marriage had become a complete sham.* 他们的婚姻关系已虚有其表. **2** [U] pretence 假装: *What he says is all sham.* 他说的都是假的.

sham *adj* [attrib 作定语] (*usu derog* 通常作贬义) pretended; not genuine 假装的; 假的: *sham piety, sympathy, anger, etc* 假虔诚、同情、生气等 ○ *sham jewellery* 假珠宝.

shamble /ˈʃæmbl; ˈʃæmbl̩/ *v* [I, Ipr, Ip] walk or run awkwardly, without raising one's feet properly 笨拙地走或跑(拖着脚): *a shambling gait* 蹒跚的脚步 ○ *The old tramp shambled up to me.* 那个老流浪者拖着脚向我走来. ○ *The hungry marchers shambled slowly along (the road).* 行军的人饿得步履蹒跚在路上慢慢走着. ⇨ Usage at SHUFFLE 用法见SHUFFLE.

▷ **shamble** *n* [sing] shambling walk 拖着脚走的步态.

shambles /ˈʃæmblz; ˈʃæmbl̩z/ *n* [sing *v*] (*infml* 口) scene of complete disorder; muddle; mess 混乱的场面; 凌乱; 杂乱: *Your room is (in) a shambles. Tidy it up!* 你的房间乱七八糟. 把它整理一下吧!

sham·bolic /ʃæmˈbɒlɪk; ʃæmˈbɑlɪk/ *adj* (*Brit infml joc* 口, 谑) disorganized; chaotic 凌乱的; 混乱的.

shame /ʃeɪm; ʃem/ *n* **1** [U] painful feeling caused by wrong, dishonourable, improper or ridiculous behaviour (by oneself, one's family, etc) 羞耻; 羞愧; 惭愧: *feel shame at having told a lie* 说谎后感到羞愧 ○ *hang one's head in shame* 惭愧得低下了头 ○ *To my shame* (ie I feel shame that) *I never thanked him for his kindness.* 我感到惭愧的是对他的好意我从未表示过感谢. **2** [U] ability to feel shame 羞愧感: *How could you do such a thing? Have you no shame?* 你怎么竟然做出这种事? 你难道不知羞耻吗? ○ *She is completely without shame.* 她恬不知耻. **3** [U] dishonour 耻辱: *bring shame on sb/oneself*, eg by doing sth wrong or unworthy 使某人[自己]丢脸 ○ *How can we make people forget the family's shame?* 我们怎么能让人忘记这一家庭耻辱呢? **4 a shame** [sing] (*derog infml* 贬, 口) (**a**) person or thing that causes shame or is unworthy 可耻的人或事物: *It's a shame to take money from those who can't afford it.* 拿别人的钱使人家无以自立是十分可耻的. (**b**) thing that is regrettable; a pity 遗憾的事; 可惜: *What a shame you didn't win.* 你没赢, 真遗憾. ○ *Isn't it a shame that the rain spoiled our picnic?* 这场雨把我们的野餐给搅了, 可惜不可惜? **5** (idm 习语) **put sb/sth to 'shame** be greatly superior to sb/sth 大大优越于某人[某事物]: *Your beautiful handwriting puts my untidy scrawl to shame.* 你漂亮的字体把我的潦草字迹比得见不得人. **'shame on you** you should feel shame (about what you have done or said) 你(对做的事或说的话)应该感到羞耻: *How could you treat her so badly? Shame on you!* 你怎么能待她那么坏? 真可耻!

▷ **shame** *v* **1** [Tn] (**a**) cause (sb) to feel shame(1) 使(某人)感到羞愧: *He was shamed by how much more work the others had done.* 别人做得多得多, 他感到很难为情. (**b**) bring shame(3) upon (sb); dishonour 给(某人)带来耻辱; 使丢脸: *You've shamed your family.* 你给你们家丢脸了. ○ *It's quite shaming that our society cares so little for the poor.* 我们这个社会对穷人很不关心, 是很难堪的事. **2** (phr v) **shame sb into/out of doing sth** cause sb to do/not to do sth by making him feel shame 使某人感到惭愧而做[不做]某事: *shame sb into apologizing* 使某人惭愧得赔礼道歉.

shame·ful /-fl; -fəl/ *adj* causing shame; disgraceful 可耻的; 丢脸的: *shameful conduct, deceit, etc* 可耻的行为、骗局等. **shame·fully** /-fəlɪ; -fḷɪ/ *adv*. **shame·ful·ness** *n* [U].

shame·less *adj* (*derog* 贬) having or showing no feeling of shame; immodest or impudent 无羞耻感的; 无耻的; 不要脸的: *a shameless hussy* 不知羞耻的荡妇 ○ *a shameless cheat, liar, etc* 无耻的骗子、说谎的人等 ○ *She's quite shameless about wearing sexy clothes at work.* 她穿着性感的衣服上班而不觉羞耻. **shame·lessly** *adv*. **shame·less·ness** *n* [U].

□ **shamefaced** /ˌʃeɪmˈfeɪst; ˋʃemˌfest/ *adj* showing feelings of shame 羞愧的; 羞怯的: *a ˌshame-faced exˈpression, aˈpology, ˈculprit* 感到惭愧的表情、致歉、罪犯. **shamefacedly** /-ˈfeɪstlɪ; -ˋfestlɪ/ *adv*.

shammy /ˈʃæmɪ; ˋʃæmɪ/ *n* [U, C] (also **shammy leather**) (*infml* 口) = CHAMOIS-LEATHER (CHAMOIS).

sham·poo /ʃæmˈpuː; ʃæmˋpu/ *n* (*pl* **~s**) **1** [C, U] (**a**) (type of) soapy liquid, cream, etc for washing the hair 洗发剂; 洗发液; 洗发膏: *a new perfumed shampoo* 新出的香型洗发液 ○ *Don't use too much shampoo.* 使用洗发剂不要过多. ○ *dry shampoo*, ie a powder brushed into the hair to clean it without wetting it 洗发粉(刷入头发中而不用水洗的粉剂). (**b**) (type of) liquid or chemical for cleaning carpets, upholstery, etc or for washing a car (清洗地毯、室内饰物、汽车等的)洗涤剂. **2** [C] (**a**) act of washing the hair 洗发: *give sb a shampoo* 给某人洗头发 ○ *a shampoo and set* 洗头发并做头发. (**b**) act of cleaning a carpet, etc 清洗地毯等.

▷ **sham·poo** *v* (*pt, pp* **-pooed**, *pres p* **-pooing**) [Tn] wash (hair, carpets, upholstery, etc) 洗(毛发、地毯、室内饰物等).

sham·rock /ˈʃæmrɒk; ˋʃæmrɑk/ *n* [C, U] clover-like plant with three leaves on each stem, the national emblem of Ireland 白花酢浆草(爱尔兰的国花): *wearing some shamrock on his lapel* 他西装翻领上戴着白花酢浆草.

shandy /ˈʃændɪ; ˋʃændɪ/ *n* (*Brit*) (**a**) [U] drink made by mixing beer with ginger-beer or lemonade 啤酒与姜汁汽水或其他汽水混合而成的饮料. (**b**) [C] glass of this 一杯啤酒与姜汁汽水或其他汽水混合而成的饮料: *Two lemonade shandies, please.* 请来两杯啤酒与汽水混合的饮料.

shang·hai /ʃæŋˈhaɪ; ʃæŋˋhaɪ/ *v* (*pt, pp* **-haied** /-ˈhaɪd; -ˋhaɪd/, *pres p* **-haiing** /-ˈhaɪɪŋ; -ˋhaɪɪŋ/) **1** [Tn, Tn·pr] **~ sb (into doing sth)** (*infml* 口) trick or force sb into doing sth 诱骗或强迫某人做某事: *tourists shanghaied into buying expensive fakes* 被诱骗买昂贵假货的游客. **2** [Tn] (*sl* 俚) (formerly) make (a man) unconscious with drink or drugs and take him away to be a sailor (旧时)用酒或麻醉剂使(男子)失去知觉后将其掳走当水手.

shank /ʃæŋk; ʃæŋk/ *n* **1** straight slender part of an implement, etc; shaft 工具等的长柄; 杆: *the shank of an anchor, a key, a golf-club* 锚杆、钥匙柄、高尔夫球棒的杆. **2** (usu *pl* 通常作复数) (*often joc or derog* 常作戏谑语或作贬义) leg, esp the part between the knee and the ankle 腿; (尤指)小腿: *long thin shanks* 细长的腿. **3** (idm 习语) **on Shanks's ˈpony/ˈmare** (*dated infml joc* 旧, 口, 谑) on foot (not by car, etc) 步行; 徒步: *If you won't drive me, I'll have to get there on Shanks's pony.* 要是你不开车送我去, 那我就只好走着去了.

shan't *contracted form* of SHALL NOT (SHALL) ☆ SHALL NOT 的缩约式(参看 SHALL).

shan·tung /ʃænˈtʌŋ; ʃænˋtʌŋ/ *n* [U] type of heavy silk material, usu undyed 茧绸(通常未染色); 山东绸.

shanty[1] /ˈʃæntɪ; ˋʃæntɪ/ *n* poorly-built hut, shed or cabin; shack 简陋的棚、舍或小屋.

□ ˈ**shanty town** area inside or just outside a town, where poor people live in shanties (城镇中或近郊的)贫民窟.

shanty[2] (*US* **chantey**, **chanty**) /ˈʃæntɪ; ˋʃæntɪ/ *n* (also ˈ**sea-shanty**) song formerly sung by sailors while hauling ropes, etc (旧时水手拉绳索时唱的)劳动号子.

shape[1] /ʃeɪp; ʃep/ *n* **1** [C, U] outer form or appearance; outline of an area, a figure, etc 外形; 形状; 样子: *clouds of different shapes in the sky* 天空中各种形状的云彩 ○ *a garden in the shape of a semicircle* 半圆形的花园 ○ *trees in all shapes and sizes* 大大小小形状各异的树 ○ *the odd shape of his nose* 他那鼻子的怪模样 ○ *a dress that hasn't got much shape* 外形欠佳的连衣裙 ○ *The picture is round in shape.* 这幅画是圆形的. ○ (*fig* 比喻) *He's a devil in human shape.* 他是披着人皮的魔鬼. **2** [C] thing that is difficult to see properly; vague form 模糊的东西; 朦胧的形状: *I made out two dim shapes in the gloom.* 我在朦胧中看出有两个模糊的影子. ○ *A huge shape loomed up out of the fog.* 在雾中隐约出现一个巨大的影像. **3** [U] (*infml* 口) condition; state 情况; 状态: *She's in good shape* (ie fit) *after months of training.* 她经过几个月训练身体好了. ○ *What shape is the team in after its defeat?* 这个队失败后情况如何? ○ *The illness has left him in rather poor shape.* 他经过这场大病已形容枯槁. **4** (**a**) C] mould, etc in which sth, eg jelly, is given a particular form 模; 模子. (**b**) [C, U] jelly, etc shaped in such a mould 模制的果子冻等: *Have some more shape.* 再吃点果子冻. **5** (idm 习语) **get (oneself) into ˈshape** take exercise, etc in order to become fit 为健美而进行锻炼等: *I've been jogging a lot to get myself into shape.* 我长期慢跑锻炼身体. **get/knock/lick sth/sb into ˈshape** get sth/sb into an orderly state; arrange sth/sb properly 使某事物[某人]有条理; 恰当地安排某事物[某人]: *We need a new manager to get the business into shape.* 我们需要有个新经理来把业务安排妥当. ○ *A sergeant soon knocks new recruits into shape.* 中士很快就把新兵训练得规规矩矩. **give shape to sth** express sth clearly 清晰地表达某事: *I'm having trouble giving shape to my ideas in this essay.* 我在这篇文章中表达不清自己的想法. **in ˈany shape (or form)** (*infml* 口) in whatever form sth appears or is presented 某事物的任何形式: *I don't drink alcohol in any shape or form.* 我什么酒都不喝. **in ˈshape** fit 健康: *You'll never be in shape until you eat less and take more exercise.* 只有少吃多锻炼才能健美. **in the shape/form of sb/sth** (*infml* 口) appearing specifically as sb/sth 以某人[某事物]的形式: *Help arrived in the shape of our next-door neighbours.* 来帮助我们的是隔壁的邻居. ○ *I received a nasty surprise in the shape of a letter from the taxman.* 我收到税务局的来信, 把我吓得六神无主. **out of ˈshape** (**a**) not having the usual shape 变形; 走样: *The children have been playing with my hat — they've knocked it out of shape.* 孩子们一直玩着我的帽子——把它弄得不成样子了. (**b**) unfit 不健康: *Take exercise if you're out of shape.* 身体不好就要锻炼. **press sth into shape** ⇨ PRESS[2]. **the ˌshape of ˌthings to ˈcome** sign that shows how the future is likely to develop 未来事物可能呈现的状况. **take ˈshape** take on a definite form; become more organized 成形; 变得更有条理: *The plan is beginning to take shape in my mind.* 这个计划在我脑子里逐渐有了眉目. ○ *After months of work, the new book is gradually taking shape.* 经过多月的努力, 这本新书渐渐像个样子了.

▷ **shape·less** *adj* having no definite shape; not elegant in shape 无定形的; 形状不雅致的: *The book is rather shapeless.* 这本书不太像样子. ○ *a shapeless mass, form, dress* 不成形的一堆、不雅观的形态、不成样式的连衣裙. **shape·lessly** *adv*. **shape·less·ness** *n* [U].

shape[2] /ʃeɪp; ʃep/ *v* **1** [Tn, Tn·pr] **~ sth (into sth)** give a shape or form to sth 做成某物的形状: *shape the wet clay on a potter's wheel* 在陶钧上用湿黏土制坯 ○ *shape the sand into a mound* 把沙堆成小丘. **2** [Tn] have a great influence upon (sb/sth); determine the nature of (sth) 对(某人[某事物])有重大影响; 决定(某事物)的性质: *These events helped to shape her future career.* 这些事促成了她后来从事的事业. ○ *His attitudes were shaped partly by early experiences.* 他的想法在一定程度上是由他早期的经历决定的. **3** [I, Ip] **~ (up)** develop in a certain way 进展: *Our plans are shaping (up) well*, ie giving signs that they will be successful. 我们的计划进展顺利. ○ *How is the new team shaping up?* 新队的表现怎样? **4** [Tn esp passive 尤用于被动语态] make (a garment) conform to the shape of the body 使(衣服)合身: *The jacket is shaped* (ie becomes narrower) *at the waist.* 这件外衣腰部很贴身(较窄).

▷ **-shaped** (in compounds 用以构成复合词) having the specified shape 具有某形状的: *a ˌkidney-shaped ˈswimming-pool* 肾形的游泳池 ○ *His figure is somewhat*

ˈ*pear-shaped.* 他的体形有点像梨. ○ *Rugby is played with an* ˌ*egg-shaped* ˈ*ball.* 英式橄榄球运动使用的是卵形的球.

SHAPE (also **Shape**) /ʃeɪp; ʃep/ *abbr* 缩写 = Supreme Headquarters of Allied Powers in Europe 欧洲盟军最高司令部.

shapely /ˈʃeɪplɪ; ˈʃeplɪ/ *adj* (**-ier, -iest**) (*approv* 褒) (esp of a woman's body) having an attractive shape; well formed (尤指女子的身材)漂亮的, 匀称的: *a shapely bosom* 线条优美的胸部 ○ *shapely legs* 匀称的腿. ▷ **shape·li·ness** *n* [U].

shard /ʃɑːd; ʃɑrd/ (also **sherd** /ʃɜːd; ʃɝd/) *n* broken piece of pottery, glass, etc (陶器、玻璃等的)碎片. Cf 参看 POTSHERD.

share[1] /ʃeə(r); ʃɛr/ *n* **1** [C] **~ (in/of sth)** part or portion of a larger amount which is divided among several or many people, or to which several or many people contribute (分享到的或贡献出的)一份: *a fair share of the food* 应得的一份食物 ○ *the robber's share of the stolen money* 劫匪的一份赃款 ○ *Your share of the cost is £10.* 你这一份费用是10英镑. ○ *Everyone who helped gets a share in the profits.* 凡是帮过忙的就得到一份利润. **2** [U, sing] **~ (in/of sth)** person's part in sth done, received, etc by several people (参与、得到等的)份儿: *What share did he have in their success?* 在他们的成绩中他有何贡献? ○ *She must take her share of the blame*, ie accept that she was partly responsible. 她必须承担事故的部分责任. ○ *You're not taking much share in the conversation*, ie you're saying little. 在交谈中你没怎么说话. **3** [C] any of the equal parts into which the capital of a business company is divided, giving the holder a right to a portion of the profits 股; 股分: *stocks and shares* 股分 ○ *buy/hold 500 shares in a shipping company* 购买[持有]某航运公司的500股股分 ○ *£2 shares are now worth £2.75.* 2英镑的股分现值2.75英镑. ○ [attrib 作定语] *share capital, dealing, prices* 股本、股票交易、股票价格 ○ *a share certificate* 股票. **4** (idm 习语) **get, etc a/one's fair share of sth** ⇨ FAIR[1]. **get, etc a slice/share of the cake** ⇨ CAKE. **go** ˈ**shares (with sb) (in sth)** (*Brit infml* 口) share (profits, costs, etc) equally with others 与他人分享(利润)或分摊(费用): *Let me go shares with you in the taxi fare.* 我和你分摊计程车费吧. **the lion's share** ⇨ LION.

▷ **share** *v* **1** (**a**) [Tn·pr, Tn·p] **~ sth (out) (among/between sb)** give a share of sth to others 将某物平均分配: *share £100 equally between five people*, ie by giving them £20 each 把100英镑平分给五个人(每人得20英镑) ○ *share the sweets among the children* 把糖分给孩子们 ○ *The profits are shared (out) equally among the partners.* 合伙人均分利润. (**b**) [I, Ipr, Tn, Tn·pr] **~ (sth) (with sb)** have a share of (sth) with another or others 与别人分享(某物): *Let's share (the last cake); you have half and I'll have half.* 咱们分了(最后这块蛋糕)吧, 你一半我一半. ○ *He would share his last pound with me.* 他要是剩下最后一镑也会和我分着用. **2** [I, Ipr, Tn, Tn·pr] **~ (sth) (with sb)** have or use (sth) with others; have (sth) in common 与别人共有或合用(某物); 在(某方面)有共同之处: *There's only one bedroom, so we'll have to share.* 只有一个卧室, 所以我们得合着用. ○ *share a bed, room, house, etc* 合用一张床、一个房间、一所房子等 ○ *share sb's belief, faith, optimism, etc* 与某人有共同的信仰、信念、乐观态度等 ○ *He shares my fears about a possible war.* 他和我一样害怕有可能发生战争. ○ *We both share the credit for* (ie were both responsible for) *this success.* 做成这件事我们俩都有功劳. ○ *Will you share your pen with me?* 我能与你合用你的笔吗? **3** [Ipr, Tn] **~ (in) sth** have a share in sth; participate in sth 分摊或分享某事物; 参与某事物: *I will share (in) the cost with you.* 我愿与你分摊费用. ○ *She shares (in) my troubles as well as my joys.* 她与我同甘共苦. **4** [Tn, Tn·pr] **~ sth (with sb)** tell sb about sth 将某事告诉某人: *She won't share her secret (with us).* 她不肯把她的秘密告诉我们. ○ *I want to share my news with you.* 我想把我得到的消息告诉你. **5** (idm 习语) **share and share a**ˈ**like** (*saying* 谚) share things equally 事事均分: *Don't be so selfish — it's share and share alike in this house.* 别这么自私 — 在这所房子里要事事均分.

□ ˈ**share-cropper** *n* (*esp US*) tenant farmer who gives part of his crop as rent to the owner of the land 佃农.

ˈ**shareholder** *n* owner of shares in a business company 股东.

ˈ**share index** number used to show the current value of shares on the stock market, based on the prices of a selected number of shares 股票指数: *The Financial Times share index went up five points yesterday.*《金融时报》的股票指数昨天上升了五点.

ˈ**share-out** *n* [sing] distribution 分配; 分摊: *After the robbery the crooks had a share-out (of the stolen money).* 歹徒们打劫后把赃款分掉了.

share[2] /ʃeə(r); ʃɛr/ *n* = PLOUGHSHARE (PLOUGH).

shark 鲨

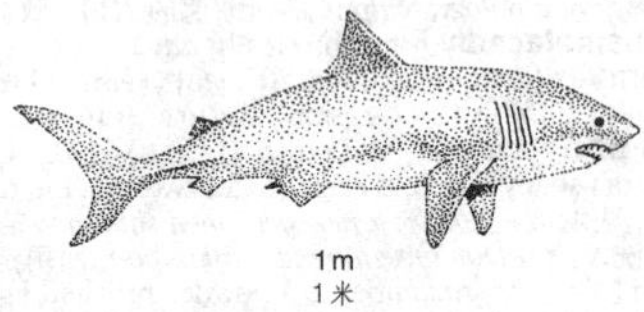

shark /ʃɑːk; ʃɑrk/ *n* **1** any of various types of sea-fish with a triangular fin on its back, some of which are large and dangerous to bathers 鲨鱼. **2** (*infml derog* 口, 贬) person who extorts money from others or lends money at very high interest rates; swindler 敲诈勒索的人; 放高利贷的人; 骗子.

□ ˈ**shark-skin** *n* [U] textile fabric with a smooth, slightly shiny surface, used for outer clothing 雪克斯金细呢, 鲨皮布(表面光滑发亮、用作面料的织物): [attrib 作定语] *a shark-skin jacket, suit, etc* 鲨皮布外衣、套装等.

sharp /ʃɑːp; ʃɑrp/ *adj* (**-er, -est**) **1** having a fine edge or point; capable of cutting or piercing; not blunt 锋利的; 尖锐的: *a sharp knife, pin, needle, etc* 锋利的刀、尖的大头针、尖的针 ○ *The shears aren't sharp enough to cut the grass.* 这把大剪刀不够快, 剪不动草. **2** (**a**) (of curves, bends, slopes, etc) changing direction suddenly; abrupt (指曲线、弯、斜坡等)急转的, 陡峭的: *a sharp bend in the road* 路上的急转弯 ○ *a sharp turn to the left* 向左的急转. (**b**) [usu attrib 通常作定语] sudden; abrupt 突然的; 急剧的: *a sharp drop in prices* 价格的暴跌 ○ *a sharp rise in crime* 犯罪率的急剧上升. **3** well-defined; distinct; clear 轮廓鲜明的; 明显的; 清晰的: *a sharp outline* 清晰的轮廓 ○ *a sharp photographic image*, ie one with clear contrasts between areas of light and shade 反差大的影像 ○ *in sharp focus* 锐聚焦 ○ *The TV picture isn't very sharp.* 电视图像不太清晰. ○ *There is a sharp contrast between the lives of the poorest and the richest members of society.* 社会上贫富悬殊. **4** [usu attrib 通常作定语] (of sounds) shrill; piercing (指声音)尖锐的, 刺耳的: *a sharp cry of distress* 痛苦的尖叫声 ○ *the sharp raucous cawing of a crow* 乌鸦的粗哑而刺耳的叫声. **5** (of tastes or smells) producing a smarting sensation; pungent (指味道或气味)强烈的, 辛辣的, 刺鼻的: *the sharp taste of lemon juice* 柠檬汁的强烈酸味 ○ *the sharp smell of the acid* 酸的刺鼻气味 ○ *The cheese is a little too sharp for me*, ie tastes too strong. 我觉得这干酪味道太重了点. **6** producing a physical sensation of cutting or piercing; keen 刺骨的; 凛冽的; 剧烈的: *a sharp frost/wind* 严寒的霜[风] ○ *a sharp pain in the back* 背部的剧痛. **7** quickly aware of things; acute; alert 灵敏的; 敏锐的; 机警的: *sharp eyes, ears, reflexes* 灵敏的眼睛、耳朵、反应 ○ *a sharp person, mind, intelligence* 机灵的人、敏锐的头脑、机智 ○ *a sharp sense of smell* 敏锐的嗅觉 ○ *keep a sharp look-out* 严密警戒 ○ *It was very sharp of you to notice that detail straight away.* 你真机灵, 一下子就注意到这一细节. **8** **~ (with sb)** (*derog* 贬) intended or intending to criticize, injure, etc; harsh; severe 蓄意批评、中伤等的; 尖刻的; 严厉的: *a sharp criticism, rebuke, remark, etc* 尖锐的批评、严厉的指责、刻薄的言语 ○ *She was very sharp with me* (ie rebuked me) *when I forgot my book.* 我忘带书了, 她把我训斥了一顿. ○ *He has a sharp tongue*, ie often speaks harshly or angrily. 他说话尖酸刻薄. **9** [usu attrib 通常作定语] quick; brisk;

vigorous 迅速的；敏捷的；活跃的：*a sharp struggle, contest, etc* 激烈的斗争、竞赛等 ○ *sharp competition for the job* 为获得这一工作而产生的剧烈竞争 ○ *That was sharp work*, ie It was done quickly or energetically. 这件工作干得很利索. **10** (*often derog* 常作贬义) quick to take advantage of sb/sth; unscrupulous 过分精明的；狡猾的；不择手段的：*a sharp lawyer, accountant, etc* 精明的律师、会计等 ○ *She was too sharp for me*, ie outwitted me. 她太精明（我斗不过她）. **11** [usu attrib 通常作定语] (*infml* 口) (too) smart or stylish（过分）时髦的，漂亮的：*a gambler in a sharp suit* 衣着入时的赌徒 ○ *be a very sharp dresser* 是个衣着漂亮的人. **12** (*music* 音) (**a**) (of a sound, an instrument, etc) above the normal or correct pitch（指声音、乐器的音调等）偏高的：*That note sounded sharp.* 那个音调听起来偏高. (**b**) (usu following *ns* 通常用于名词之后) (of notes) raised half a tone in pitch（指音符）升半音的：*in the key of C sharp minor* 用升 C 小调. ⇨illus at MUSIC 见 MUSIC 插图. Cf 参看 FLAT[2] 10. **13** (idm 习语) **look 'sharp** be brisk; hurry 赶紧；赶快：*You'd better look sharp or you'll be late.* 你得赶快，不然就晚了. **(as) sharp as a needle** very intelligent and quick-witted 非常聪敏的. **sharp 'practice** business dealings that are not entirely honest 不够诚实的交易手段.

▷ **sharp** *n* (*symb* 符号为 #) (*music* 音) (symbol used to indicate a) sharp note 升半音；升半音号：*a difficult piano piece full of sharps and flats* 有很多升半音、降半音难度很大的钢琴曲. Cf 参看 FLAT[4] 4, NATURAL 6.

sharp *adv* **1** (*infml* 口) punctually 准时地：*Please be here at seven (o'clock) sharp.* 请七点整到这里. **2** (*infml* 口) suddenly; abruptly 突然地；急剧地：*stopped sharp* 突然停住 ○ *turn sharp left* 向左急转. **3** (*music* 音) above the correct pitch 偏高：*sing sharp* 唱得偏高.

sharpen /ˈʃɑːpən; ˋʃɑrpən/ *v* [I, Tn] (cause sth to) become sharp（使某物）锋利，尖锐，陡峭，清晰，强烈：*The tone of his letters has sharpened* (ie become less friendly) *recently.* 他最近来信的口气变得刻薄起来. ○ *sharpen a pencil* 削铅笔 ○ *This knife needs sharpening.* 这把刀要磨一下. ○ *This incident has sharpened public awareness of the economic crisis.* 这件事提高了公众对经济危机的认识. ○ *sharpen sb's wits*, ie make sb more mentally alert 使某人更机智. **sharp·ener** /ˈʃɑːpnə(r); ˋʃɑrpənɚ/ *n* (usu in compounds 通常用以构成复合词) device that sharpens 磨具；削具：*a 'pencil-sharpener* ○ *a 'knife-sharpener*.

'sharper (also **'card-sharper**) *n* swindler, esp one who makes a living by cheating at cards 骗子（尤指以赌纸牌行骗为生者）.

sharp·ish *adj* rather sharp 相当尖锐的；相当敏锐的. — *adv* (*infml* 口) quickly; briskly 迅速地；敏捷地.

sharply *adv* **1** in a sharp way 尖锐地；急剧地：*sharply pointed* 尖尖的 ○ *The road bends sharply.* 这条路的弯转得很急. ○ *prices dropping sharply* 暴跌的价格 ○ *sharply contrasted styles* 迥然不同的风格 ○ *speak sharply to sb* 斥责某人. **2** (idm 习语) **bring/pull sb up short/sharply** ⇨ SHORT[2].

sharp·ness *n* [U].

□ ˌ**sharp-'eyed** *adj* having good eyesight; quick to notice things 眼快的；目光敏锐的：*A ˌsharp-eyed po'lice officer spotted the stolen car.* 那个目光敏锐的警察发现了那辆被盗的汽车.

'sharpshooter *n* person who is skilled at shooting with a gun, etc 神射手；神枪手.

ˌ**sharp-'sighted** *adj* having good eyesight 眼快的；目光敏锐的.

ˌ**sharp-'witted** *adj* able to think quickly; alert 思维敏捷的；机智的：*She was sharp-witted enough to dodge her attacker.* 她才思敏捷足以避开别人的攻击.

shat *pt, pp of* SHIT.

shat·ter /ˈʃætə(r); ˋʃætɚ/ *v* **1** I, Tn] (cause sth to) break suddenly and violently into small pieces（使某物）突然而剧烈地裂成碎片，粉碎：*The pot shattered as it hit the floor.* 罐子掉在地板上摔了个粉碎. ○ *The explosion shattered all the windows.* 这次爆炸把所有窗户都震碎了. ○ (*fig* 比喻) *What an ear-shattering noise!* 这声音能把耳朵震聋！ **2** [Tn] (*infml* 口) destroy (sth) completely 粉碎（某事物）：*shatter sb's hopes* 使某人的希望破灭 ○ *This event shattered all my previous ideas.* 这件事把我以前所有的想法都摧毁了. **3** [Tn esp passive 尤用于被动语态] (*infml* 口) disturb the calmness of (sb); shock 扰乱（某人）的心境；使震骇：*We were shattered by the news.* 这一消息震动了我们. **4** [Tn esp passive 尤用于被动语态] (*Brit infml* 口) exhaust (sb) completely 使（某人）筋疲力尽：*We were totally shattered after the long journey.* 我们经过长途旅行都已精疲力竭.

▷ **shat·ter·ing** /ˈʃætərɪŋ; ˋʃætərɪŋ/ *adj* very disturbing; shocking 令人极度不安的；令人震惊的：*a shattering experience* 令人恐慌的事 ○ *The news was shattering.* 这个消息令人震惊.

□ **'shatterproof** *adj* designed not to shatter 防碎的：*shatterproof glass for car windscreens* 用作汽车挡风玻璃的防碎玻璃.

shave /ʃeɪv; ʃev/ *v* **1** [I, Tn, Tn·pr, Tn·p] ~ **sth (off sth/ off)** cut (hair) off the face, etc with a razor; cut hair off the face, etc of (sb) in this way（用剃刀）刮（胡须等）；为（某人）剃毛发：*I shave every morning.* 我每天早上刮脸. ○ *The nurse washed and shaved the patient.* 护士给病人清洗皮肤、刮去毛发. ○ *Buddhist priests shave their heads.* 和尚都剃光头. ○ *She sometimes shaves the hair off her legs.* 她有时剃腿上的寒毛. ○ *Why don't you shave your beard off?* 你怎么不把胡子刮掉？ **2** [Tn] cut or scrape thin slices from the surface of (wood, etc) 刨（木头等）；削；刮. ⇨ Usage at CLIP[2] 用法见 CLIP[2]. **3** [Tn] (*infml* 口) pass very close to (sb/sth), or touch (sb/sth) slightly in passing 掠过，擦过（某人[某物]）：*The bus just shaved me by an inch.* 那辆公共汽车从我身边掠过，离我只有一英寸. ○ *The ball narrowly shaved his off stump.* 那个球紧贴着他的三柱门的外柱掠过. ○ *The lorry shaved the barrier, scraping its side.* 那辆卡车掠过路障，刮坏了车身. **4** (phr v) **shave sth off (sth)** remove (a thin layer) from the surface of sth by cutting or scraping 从某物表面削去或刮掉（薄薄的一层）：*shave a millimetre (of wood) off the block* 把木块刨去一毫米.

▷ **shave** *n* **1** act of shaving 剃；刮：*A sharp razor gives a close shave.* 剃刀锋利刮得就干净. ○ *Have a shave before you go out.* 把胡子刮刮再出门. **2** (idm 习语) **a close shave** ⇨ CLOSE[1].

shaven /ˈʃeɪvn; ˋʃevən/ *adj* shaved 剃过的；刮过的：ˌ*clean-'shaven* 剃得干净的 ○ *Their heads were shaven.* 他们的头都剃了. ⇨Usage at PROVE 用法见 PROVE.

shaver *n* **1** (also **electric razor**) razor with an electric motor, operated from the mains or by a battery 电动剃刀. **2** (*dated infml* 旧，口) lad; youngster 小伙子；年轻人：*You cheeky young shaver!* 你这个毛头小伙子！

shav·ings *n* [pl] thin pieces of wood shaved off, esp with a plane 薄木屑；（尤指）刨花：*The floor of the carpenter's shop was covered with shavings.* 木匠店的地板上满是刨花. ⇨illus at PLANE 见 PLANE 插图.

□ **'shaving-brush** *n* brush for spreading lather over the face, etc before shaving 胡刷.

'shaving-cream, **'shaving-foam** *ns* cream or foam spread over the face, etc before shaving 剃须膏.

'shaving-stick *n* cylindrical piece of soap for making lather to be used for shaving 剃须皂条.

shawl /ʃɔːl; ʃɔl/ *n* large (usu square or oblong) piece of material worn round the shoulders or head of a woman, or wrapped round a baby（女用）披肩，围巾；襁褓.

she /ʃiː; ʃi/ ⇨Detailed Guide 6.2, 3 见词条使用详细说明 6.2、6.3. *pers pron* 人称代词 (used as the subject of a *v* 用作动词的主体) female person or animal mentioned earlier or being observed now 她；（指雌性动物）它：*My sister's very strong — she can swim 5 miles.* 我姐姐身体很棒——她能游 5 英里. ○ *Doesn't she* (ie the woman we are looking at) *look like her mother?* 她长得是不是很像她母亲？ ○ *Do you remember our cat? She had kittens last week.* 你还记得我们那只猫吗？上星期生小猫了. Cf 参看 HER[1]. ⇨Usage at HE 用法见 HE.

▷ **she** *n* [sing] female animal 雌性动物：*We didn't know it was a she until it had puppies.* 我们原来不知道这条狗是母的，后来这狗下了小狗才知道.

she- (forming compound *ns* 用以构成复合名词) female 雌的：*a 'she-goat* 母山羊.

sheaf /ʃiːf; ʃif/ *n* (*pl* **sheaves** /ʃiːvz; ʃivz/) **1** bundle of stalks of corn, barley, etc tied together after reaping（谷物等收割后的）束，捆. **2** bundle of papers, etc laid lengthwise and often tied together（文件等的）束，扎.

shear /ʃɪə(r); ʃɪr/ *v* (*pt* **~ed**, *pp* **shorn** /ʃɔːn; ʃɔrn/ or **~ed**) **1** [Tn] cut the wool off (a sheep) with shears 剪

S

(羊)的毛: *sheep shearing time* 剪羊毛的时节. **2** [I, Ip, Tn, Tn·p] **~ (sth) (off)** (cause sth to) become twisted or break under pressure (使某物)弯曲或折断: *The bolt sheared (off) and the wheel came off.* 螺栓折了, 轮子脱了出来. ○ *The bar fell into the machinery and sheared a connecting-rod.* 那根棒掉进机器里把连杆给打弯了. **3** (phr v) **be shorn of sth** be stripped or deprived of sth 被剥夺或除去某物: *The room looked bare, shorn of its rich furnishings.* 这个房间除去了豪华的家具以后, 看上去光秃秃的. ○ *a deposed king shorn of his former power* 被剥夺了权力遭废黜的国王. **shear sth off (sb/sth)** remove (fur, hair, etc) by cutting with shears 剪掉(毛发等): *All her beautiful tresses have been sheared/shorn off.* 她那长长的秀发都给剪掉了.

▷ **shearer** *n* person who shears sheep 剪羊毛的人.

shears /ʃɪəz; ʃɪrz/ *n* [pl] large cutting instrument shaped like scissors, used for shearing sheep, cutting hedges, etc and usu operated with both hands (剪羊毛、修树篱等用的)大剪刀(通常需用双手使用): *a pair of shears* 一把大剪刀 ○ *'gardening shears* 园艺剪刀 ○ *'pinking shears* 有锯齿的剪刀. ⇨illus at CLIPPER 见 CLIPPER 插图.

sheath /ʃi:θ; ʃiθ/ *n* (*pl* **~ s** /ʃi:ðz; ʃiðz/) **1** (**a**) close-fitting cover for the blade of a weapon or tool 鞘; (工具的)套: *Put the dagger back in its sheath.* 把短剑插回鞘内. ⇨illus at KNIFE 见 KNIFE 插图. (**b**) any similar covering 鞘状物: *the sheath round an electric cable* 电缆的护皮 ○ *the 'wing-sheath of an insect* 昆虫的鞘翅. **2** close-fitting (usu rubber) covering for wearing on the penis during intercourse as a contraceptive; condom (男用)避孕套, 保险套, 阴茎套: *a contraceptive sheath* 避孕套. **3** woman's close-fitting dress (女用)紧身连衣裙: [attrib 作定语] *a sheath gown* 紧身长袍.

□ **'sheath-knife** *n* (*pl* **-ves**) knife with a fixed blade that fits in a sheath 有鞘的刀. ⇨illus at KNIFE 见 KNIFE 插图.

S

sheathe /ʃi:ð; ʃið/ *v* **1** [Tn] (*fml* 文) put (sth) into a sheath 将(某物)插入鞘或套中: *He sheathed his sword.* 他把剑插进鞘里. **2** [esp passive 尤用于被动语态: Tn, Tn·pr] **~ sth (in/with sth)** put a protective covering or casing on sth 给某物加上保护套: *electric wire sheathed with plastic* 有塑料护皮的电线.

▷ **sheath·ing** *n* [U, C] protective covering or casing, eg on parts of a building 盖板, 望板(如建筑物的).

sheaves *pl* of SHEAF.

she·bang /ʃɪ'bæŋ; ʃə'bæŋ/ *n* (idm 习语) **the whole shebang** ⇨ WHOLE.

she·been /ʃɪ'bi:n; ʃɪ'bin/ *n* place selling alcoholic liquor illegally, esp in Ireland and Africa 非法卖酒的地方(尤指在爱尔兰和非洲的).

shed[1] /ʃed; ʃɛd/ *n* (often in compounds 常用以构成复合词) one-storey building used for storing things, sheltering animals, vehicles, etc or as a workshop (用以储物、关牲口、停车辆等或作车间的)平房, 棚: *a 'tool-shed* 工具房 ○ *a 'wood-shed* 柴房 ○ *a 'coal-shed* 煤库 ○ *a 'cattle-shed* 牲口棚 ○ *an 'engine-shed* 机车库 ○ *a 'bicycle-shed* 自行车棚. ⇨illus at App 1 见附录1插图, page vii. Cf 参看 HUT.

shed[2] /ʃed; ʃɛd/ *v* (**-dd-**; *pt, pp* **shed**) **1** [Tn] lose (sth) by its falling off; let (sth) fall or come off 使(某物)脱落、剥落、蜕下或脱下: *Trees shed their leaves and flowers shed their petals.* 到时候树就落叶、花就掉瓣. ○ *Some kinds of deer shed their horns.* 鹿有些种类能脱换鹿角. ○ *The snake sheds its skin regularly.* 蛇到时候会蜕皮. ○ *The lorry has shed its load,* ie Its load has accidentally fallen off onto the road. 那辆卡车把货物掉在路上了. **2** [Tn] (*fml* 文) allow (sth) to pour out 使(某物)流出: *shed tears,* ie weep 流泪 ○ *shed blood,* ie wound or kill another person or other people 流血(使他人受伤或丧命) ○ *shed one's blood,* ie be wounded or killed 流血(受伤或被杀死). **3** [Tn] take or throw (sth) off; remove 去掉(某物); 除掉: *shedding one's clothes on a hot day* 天热时脱掉衣服 ○ *The duck's feathers shed water immediately.* 鸭子的羽毛沾不住水. ○ (*fig* 比喻) *You must learn to shed* (ie get rid of) *your inhibitions.* 你应该尽量摆脱抑制心态. **4** [Tn, Tn·pr] **~ sth (on sb/sth)** spread or send sth out 散发出(某物): *a fire shedding warmth* 向外散热的火 ○ *The lamp shed soft light on the desk.* 台灯柔和的光线照射在桌面上. ○ (*fig* 比喻) *She sheds happiness all around her.* 她焕发着喜悦的神采. **5** (idm 习语) **cast/shed/throw light on sth** ⇨ LIGHT[1].

she'd /ʃi:d; ʃid/ *contracted form* 缩约式 **1** she had ⇨ HAVE. **2** she would ⇨ WILL[1], WOULD[1].

sheen /ʃi:n; ʃin/ *n* [U] gleaming brightness; shiny quality 光辉; 光彩; 光泽: *the sheen of silk* 丝绸的光泽 ○ *hair with a glossy golden sheen* 金灿灿的毛发.

sheep 绵羊

sheep /ʃi:p; ʃip/ *n* (*pl* unchanged 复数不变) **1** grass-eating animal with a thick fleecy coat, kept in flocks for its flesh as food and for its wool 羊; 绵羊. Cf 参看 EWE, LAMB 1, RAM 1, BLACK SHEEP (BLACK[1]). **2** (idm 习语) **like 'sheep** too easily influenced or led by others 易受他人影响; 易受他人左右. **make 'sheep's eyes at sb** (*infml* 口) look at sb in a loving but foolish way 傻乎乎地向某人送秋波. **one may/might as well be hanged/hung for a sheep as a lamb** ⇨ HANG[1]. **separate the sheep from the goats** ⇨SEPARATE[2]. **a wolf in sheep's clothing** ⇨ WOLF.

□ **'sheep-dip** *n* [U, C] (liquid used in a) bath in which sheep are immersed to kill the insects, etc in their wool 羊消毒浴(液).

'sheep-dog *n* dog trained to guard and herd sheep; dog of a breed suitable for this 牧羊犬: [attrib 作定语] *sheep-dog trials*, ie contests for trained sheep-dogs 牧羊犬比赛.

'sheep-fold *n* enclosure for sheep 羊栏; 羊圈.

'sheepskin *n* **1** [C] (**a**) rug consisting of a sheep's skin with the wool on it 羊皮毯(一只羊的整张毛皮). (**b**) garment made of two or more such skins 羊皮袄. **2** [U] leather or parchment made from the skin of sheep 绵羊皮革; 羊皮纸. **3** [C] (*US joc* 谑) diploma 毕业证书.

sheep·ish /'ʃi:pɪʃ; ʃipɪʃ/ *adj* (feeling) foolish and embarrassed through shame 羞怯的; 局促不安的: *a sheepish smile, grin, look, expression, etc* 腼腆的微笑、粲然一笑、样子、表情等. ▷ **sheep·ishly** *adv.* **sheep·ish·ness** *n* [U].

sheer[1] /ʃɪə(r); ʃɪr/ *adj* **1** [attrib 作定语] complete; thorough; utter 完全的; 彻底的; 十足的: *sheer nonsense* 一派胡言 ○ *a sheer waste of time* 纯粹浪费时间 ○ *by sheer chance* 完全出于偶然地. **2** [usu attrib 通常作定语] (of textiles, etc) thin, light and almost transparent (指织物等)薄的、轻的、几乎透明的: *sheer nylon* 薄而透明的尼龙. **3** almost vertical; very steep 近乎垂直的; 陡峭的: *a sheer rock, cliff, etc* 陡峭的巉岩、悬崖等 ○ *a sheer drop of 50 feet* 50英尺垂直降落.

▷ **sheer** *adv* straight up or down 垂直地; 陡峭地: *a cliff that rises sheer from the beach* 矗立于海滩上的悬崖 ○ *The ground dropped away sheer at our feet.* 我们眼前的地面垂直地陷落下去.

sheer[2] /ʃɪə(r); ʃɪr/ *v* (phr v) **sheer away (from sth)/ sheer off (sth)** turn suddenly away from a course, topic, etc that one wishes to avoid 突然改变路线、转换话题等; 避开: *When he saw me coming he sheered off in the opposite direction.* 他一看到我过来, 掉头就走了. ○ *She tends to sheer away from any discussion of her divorce.* 一谈到她离婚的事她就尽量转换话题.

sheet[1] /ʃi:t; ʃit/ *n* **1** large rectangular piece of cotton, linen, etc, usu used in pairs between which a person sleeps 被单; 褥单; 床单: *put clean sheets on the bed* 把干净的被单铺在床上. **2** (**a**) broad thin piece of any material 薄板; 薄片: *a sheet of glass, tin, copper, paper* 一块玻璃、一块镀锡铁皮、一块铜片、一张纸 ○ [attrib 作定语] *sheet metal, copper, tin, etc*, ie rolled or hammered into thin sheets 金属薄板、薄铜板、镀锡铁皮. (**b**) piece of paper for writing or printing on, usu in a standard size（书写或打印用的）纸（通常指大小有一定规格的）: *two sheets of A4* 两张A4的纸 ○ *put a fresh sheet in the typewriter* 把一张纸放进打字机中. **3** wide expanse (of water, ice, snow, flame, etc)（水、冰、雪、火等的）一片: (*infml* 口) *The rain came down in sheets*, ie very heavily. 大雨滂沱. ○ *After the heavy frost the road was a sheet of ice.* 浓霜过后，路面结了一层冰. **4** (idm 习语) **a clean sheet/slate** ⇨ CLEAN¹. **white as a sheet** ⇨ WHITE¹.

▷ **sheet·ing** *n* [U] material used for making sheets (SHEET¹ 1) 用作被单、褥单或床单等的料子.

□ ˈ**sheet lightning** lightning that appears as a broad expanse of light in the sky 片状闪电.

ˈ**sheet music** music published on separate sheets and not bound in a book 活页乐谱.

sheet² /ʃiːt; ʃit/ *n* rope or chain fastened to the lower corner of a sail to hold it and control the angle at which it is set 帆脚索.

□ ˈ**sheet anchor** person or thing that one depends on in a difficult situation（困难时）可依靠的人或事物: *I have a small income from shares, which is my sheet anchor if my business should fail.* 我有点股票收入，万一生意赔了还有个退步. ○ [attrib 作定语] *She played a sheet anchor role for the team when things were going badly.* 情况不妙时，队里就指望她了.

sheikh (also **sheik**) /ʃeɪk; *US* ʃiːk; ʃik/ *n* **1** Arab chief; head of an Arab village, tribe, etc（阿拉伯的）酋长;（阿拉伯村庄、部落等的）首领. **2** Muslim religious leader（伊斯兰教的）教长.

▷ **sheikh·dom** (also **sheik·dom**) /-dəm; -dəm/ *n* area of land ruled by a sheikh 酋长统辖的领土; 酋长国.

sheila /ˈʃiːlə; ˈʃilə/ *n* (*Austral or NZ sl* 澳或新西兰，俚) girl or young woman 少女; 少妇.

shekel /ˈʃekl; ˈʃɛkḷ/ *n* **1** [C] (**a**) ancient silver coin used by the Jews 谢克尔（古时犹太人用的银币）. (**b**) unit of money in Israel 新谢克尔（以色列的货币单位）. **2** **shekels** [pl] (*infml joc* 口，谑) money 钱: *She's raking in the shekels* (ie earning a lot of money) *in her new job.* 她做这份新工作可捞着钱了.

shel·drake /ˈʃeldreɪk; ˈʃɛl,drek/ *n* (*pl* **shel·duck** /ˈʃeldʌk; ˈʃɛl,dʌk/) type of wild duck with brightly coloured feathers that lives in coastal areas 翘鼻麻鸭.

shel·duck /ˈʃeldʌk; ˈʃɛl,dʌk/ *n* (*pl* unchanged 复数不变) female sheldrake（雌的）翘鼻麻鸭.

shelf /ʃelf; ʃɛlf/ *n* (*pl* **shelves** /ʃelvz; ʃɛlvz/) **1** flat rectangular piece of wood, metal, glass or other material fastened horizontally to a wall or in a cupboard, bookcase, etc for things to be placed on（柜橱、书架等的）搁架，搁板: *put up a shelf* 搭搁板 ○ *a shelf full of crockery* 摆满了陶器的架子 ○ *a ˈbookshelf* 书架. ⇨illus at App 1 见附录1插图, page xvi. **2** thing resembling a shelf, esp a piece of rock projecting from a cliff, etc or from the edge of a mass of land under the sea 搁板状物;（尤指）悬崖等上突出的岩石，大陆架: *the continental shelf* 大陆架. **3** (idm 习语) **on the ˈshelf** (*infml* 口) (**a**) (of a person) put aside as if no longer useful（指人）被闲置（似已无用）: *A retired person should not be made to feel he's on the shelf.* 不应该让退休的人感到自己是个闲人. (**b**) (*often sexist* 常含性别偏见) (of an unmarried woman) regarded as being too old to be likely to be asked to marry sb（指未婚女子）被认为年龄较大因而不太可能有人向她求婚: *Women used to think they were on the shelf at 30.* 过去女人一到30岁就认为是过了结婚年龄.

□ ˈ**shelf-life** *n* (usu *sing* 通常作单数) time for which a stored item remains usable 贮藏寿命（物品的保存期限）: *packets of biscuits with a shelf-life of two or three weeks* 保存期为二至三星期的袋装饼干.

ˈ**shelf-mark** *n* number marked on a book to show where it should be kept in a library 排架号（图书馆标于书上指示置于书架位置的编号）.

shell /ʃel; ʃɛl/ *n* **1** [C, U] hard outer covering of eggs, of nut-kernels, of some seeds and fruits, and of animals such as oysters, snails, crabs and tortoises（卵、坚果、种子、果实以及牡蛎、蜗牛、蟹、龟等的）壳: *collecting sea-shells on the beach* 在海滩捡贝壳 ○ *empty coconut shells* 空的椰子壳 ○ *broken pieces of shell* 贝壳的碎片. ⇨illus 见插图. **2** [C] (**a**) walls, outer structure, etc of an unfinished or burnt-out building, ship, etc（尚未完工的或被火烧毁房子或船等的）骨架、框架等: *Only the shell of the factory was left after the fire had been put out.* 大火扑灭之后，工厂只剩下个空架子了. (**b**) any structure that forms a firm framework or covering（任何形式的）坚固框架或外罩: *the metal shell of the aircraft engine* 飞机发动机的金属外壳 ○ *the rigid body shell of a car* 汽车坚固的车体外壳. **3** [C] (**a**) metal case filled with explosive, to be fired from a large gun 炮弹: *The building was destroyed by an artillery shell.* 这座建筑物被炮弹炸毁了. Cf 参看 CARTRIDGE 1, SHOT¹ 4. (**b**) (*US*) = CARTRIDGE 1. **4** [C] light rowing-boat for racing（轻型的）赛艇. **5** (idm 习语) **come out of one's ˈshell** become less shy, reserved, etc 不再羞怯、沉默等: *She used to be so quiet, but now she's really coming out of her shell and chatting to everyone.* 她一向沉默寡言，但现在可真活了，跟谁都能谈得来. **go, retire, withdraw, etc into one's ˈshell** become more shy, reserved, etc 越发羞怯、沉默等: *Her rejection of him seems to have made him go back into his shell.* 他遭她拒绝后就更不爱吭声了.

▷ **shell** *v* **1** [Tn] (*US* also **shuck**) remove the shell of (sth) 除去（某物）的壳: *shell peas, peanuts, almonds, etc* 剥豌豆、花生、杏仁等 ○ (*saying* 谚) *It's as easy as shelling peas*, ie very easy. 这事非常容易. **2** [Tn] fire shells (SHELL 3) at (sb/sth) 炮击（某人[某物]）: *shell the enemy positions* 炮击敌人阵地. **3** (phr v) **shell out (sth) (for sth)** (*infml* 口) pay out, often reluctantly 付款（常指不情愿地）: *I shall be expected to shell out (the money) for the party.* 这次聚会可能要让我花钱.

□ ˈ**shell bean** (*US*) bean of which the seed is eaten and not the pod 不连豆荚吃的豆类.

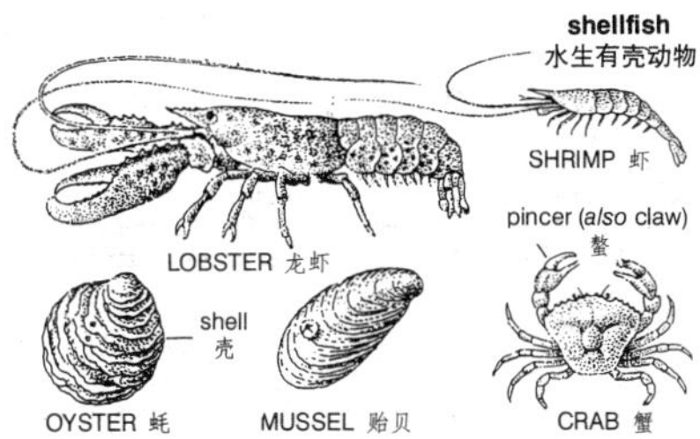

ˈ**shellfish** *n* (*pl* unchanged 复数不变) (**a**) [C] type of water animal with a shell, esp one of the edible types, eg oysters, mussels, crabs and shrimps 水生有壳动物（如牡蛎、贻贝、蟹及虾等可食用者）. (**b**) [U] such animals as food（作食物用的）水生有壳动物: *I eat lots of shellfish.* 我常吃虾、蟹及贝类食物.

ˈ**shell-shock** *n* [U] nervous illness that can affect soldiers who have been in battle for a long time 炮弹休克（士兵因久战而患的神经病）.

ˈ**shell-shocked** *adj* **1** suffering from shell-shock 患炮弹休克的. **2** (*fig* 比喻) shocked; confused; dazed 震惊的; 慌乱的; 眩晕的: *I felt totally shell-shocked after coping with five boisterous children all day.* 我和五个吵闹的孩子周旋了一整天，觉得头昏脑胀.

she'll /ʃiːl; ʃil/ *contracted form* 缩约式 she will ⇨ WILL¹.

shel·lac /ʃəˈlæk, *also* ˈʃelæk; ʃəˈlæk/ *n* [U] resinous substance in the form of thin sheets or flakes, used in making varnish 虫胶; 紫（胶虫）胶.

▷ **shel·lac** *v* (**-ck-**) [Tn] **1** varnish (sth) with shellac 给（某物）涂上虫胶清漆. **2** (*US infml* 口) defeat (sb) soundly or severely 彻底击败（某人）. **shel·lack·ing** *n* (usu *sing* 通常作单数) (*US infml* 口) sound or severe defeat 彻底的失败: *We gave their team a real shellacking.* 我们把他们队打得落花流水.

shel·ter /ˈʃeltə(r); ˈʃɛltɚ/ *n* **1** [U] **~ (from sth)** condition of being protected, kept safe, etc, eg from rain, danger, attack; refuge 遮蔽，庇护（如避雨、脱险、免受攻击等）: *seek/take shelter from the rain*, eg under a tree 避雨（如在树下）○ *get under shelter*, eg when bombs are dropping during an air-raid 隐蔽起来（如在空袭时）○ *They found shelter from the storm in a barn.* 他们在谷仓里躲避暴风雨. ○ *The high fence gives/affords (us)* *some shelter from the wind.* 这道高栅栏(给我们)挡住了风. **2** [C] (often in compounds 常用以构成复合词) **(a)** structure built to give protection, esp from rain, wind or attack 遮蔽物, 庇护物(尤指避雨、避风或免受攻击者): *a ˈbus shelter*, ie one in which people wait for buses 公共汽车站的候车亭 ○ *an ˈair-raid shelter* 防空掩蔽所. **(b)** building providing refuge, esp for homeless people 收容所(尤指为无家可归的人提供的).

▷ **shel·ter** *v* **1** [Tn, Tn·pr] **~ sb/sth (from sb/sth)** give shelter to sb/sth; protect sb/sth 给某人[某物]提供庇护处; 保护某人[某事物]: *trees that shelter a house from the wind* 给房子挡风的树 ○ *shelter* (ie hide, protect) *an escaped prisoner* 窝藏逃犯 ○ *The wall sheltered the soldiers from gunfire.* 这堵墙挡住了攻击士兵的炮火. ○ *He is trying to shelter his boss from criticism.* 他极力为老板顶住外界的批评. ○ *Is our country's industry sheltered from foreign competition?* 我国的工业在与外国竞争时是否有足够保障? **2** [I, Ipr] **~ (from sth)** find a place that gives shelter; take shelter 躲避; 避难: *shelter under the trees* 躲在树下 ○ *shelter from the rain* 避雨. **shel·tered** *adj* **1** (of a place) not exposed to wind, rain, etc (指地方)可避风、雨等的: *find a sheltered spot for a ˌpicnic* 找个有遮蔽的地方野餐. **2** kept away from or not exposed to unhappiness or harmful influences 与不幸的或有害的事物隔绝的; 不受坏事影响的: *a sheltered childhood* 未受到坏事物影响的童年时代 ○ *He has led a sheltered life in the countryside.* 他在乡村生活, 避免了很多烦恼.

shelve[1] /ʃelv; ʃɛlv/ *v* [Tn] **1** put (books, etc) on a shelf or shelves 将(书等)放在搁架上. **2** (*fig* 比喻) abandon or postpone consideration of (a plan, project, problem, etc); delay dealing with (sth) 放弃或搁置(计划、方案、问题等); 缓议(某事物): *The plans for a new theatre have had to be shelved because of lack of money.* 兴建新剧院的计划因资金短缺只好搁置起来.

▷ **shel·ving** *n* [U] (material for) shelves 搁板; 制造搁板的材料: *wooden shelving* 木板架.

shelve[2] /ʃelv; ʃɛlv/ *v* [I, Ip] **~ (away/down/off)** (of land) slope gradually (in the specified direction) (指陆地)呈缓坡倾斜: *The river-bottom shelves here.* 河底从这里呈缓坡倾斜. ○ *The shore shelves down to the sea.* 海岸向海面的倾斜角度很小.

shelves *pl* of SHELF.

she·mozzle /ʃɪˈmɒzl; ʃəˈmɑzl/ *n* (usu *sing* 通常作单数) (*infml* 口) noisy disturbance; rumpus; brawl 喧嚷; 吵闹: *I've never heard such a shemozzle!* 我从来没听过这么吵闹的!

she·nan·igans /ʃɪˈnænɪɡənz; ʃəˈnænəɡəns/ *n* [pl] (*infml* 口) **1** mischievous or high-spirited behaviour 恶作剧; 胡闹. **2** trickery; deception 诡计; 诈骗.

shep·herd /ˈʃepəd; ˈʃɛpəd/ *n* person who takes care of sheep 牧羊人.

▷ **shep·herd** *v* [Tn, Tn·pr, Tn·p] guide or direct (people) as if they were sheep 带领, 引导(人群): *A guide shepherded the tourists into the coach.* 导游把游客领进旅游车里. ○ *The children were shepherded around by two teachers.* 这些小学生是由两位老师带领的.

shep·herd·ess /ˌʃepəˈdes; *US* ˈʃepərdɪs; ˈʃɛpədɪs/ *n* woman who takes care of sheep 女牧羊人.

□ **shepherd's ˈpie** (also **cottage ˈpie**) dish of minced meat baked with mashed potatoes on top 羊馅肉饼(用碎肉做的饼覆以土豆泥烘烤而成).

Sher·aton /ˈʃerətən; ˈʃɛrətn̩/ *n* [usu attrib 通常作定语] late 18th century style of English furniture 谢拉顿家具式样(英国18世纪的家具式样): *Sheraton chairs* 谢拉顿式椅子.

sher·bet /ˈʃɜːbət; ˈʃɝbɪt/ [C, U] **1** refreshing drink of weak sweet fruit-juice 带甜味的果汁饮料. **2** (*esp Brit*) sweet fizzy drink, or the powder from which it is made 甜味汽水; 制甜味汽水的粉. **3** (*US*) = SORBET.

sherd = SHARD.

sher·iff /ˈʃerɪf; ˈʃɛrɪf/ *n* **1** (often 常作 **High ˈSheriff**) chief officer of the Crown in counties and certain cities of England and Wales, with legal and ceremonial duties (英格兰和威尔士某些地区或城市的)行政长官, 郡长. Cf 参看 REEVE 1. **2** chief judge of a district in Scotland (苏格兰的)司法长官. **3** (in the US) chief officer responsible for enforcing the law in a county (美国的)县治安官.

sherry /ˈʃerɪ; ˈʃɛrɪ/ *n* **(a)** [U, C] type of yellow or brown fortified wine, originally from S Spain 雪利酒(西班牙南部产的黄色或褐色加度葡萄酒): *Do you like sweet or dry sherry?* 你喜欢甜的还是不甜的雪利酒? ○ *high-quality sherries* 上等雪利酒. **(b)** [C] glass of this 一杯雪利酒: *have a sherry before dinner* 饭前喝杯雪利酒.

she's /ʃiːz; ʃiz/ *contracted form* 缩约式 **1** she is ⇨BE. **2** she has ⇨HAVE.

Shet·land /ˈʃetlənd; ˈʃɛtlənd/ *n* (also **the Shetlands** [pl]) group of islands off the north coast of Scotland 设得兰群岛(苏格兰北部).

□ ˌ**Shetland ˈpony** pony of a small rough-coated breed 设得兰小型马.

ˌ**Shetland ˈwool** soft fine kind of wool from Shetland sheep 设得兰羊毛(质地柔软).

shew /ʃəʊ; ʃo/ *v* (*arch* 古) = SHOW[2].

shib·bol·eth /ˈʃɪbəleθ; ˈʃɪbəlɪθ/ *n* old slogan or principle that is no longer regarded by many as very important 陈旧的口号或原则(很多人认为已不太重要的): *elderly politicians still clinging to the outmoded shibboleths of party doctrine* 仍然抱着党性教条的陈词滥调不放的年迈的政治家.

shied *pt, pp* of SHY[1], SHY[2].

shield /ʃiːld; ʃild/ *n* **1 (a)** piece of (usu metal or leather) armour formerly carried on the arm to protect the body when fighting 盾. **(b)** (in heraldry) drawing or model of a shield displaying a coat of arms (COAT) (纹章中的)盾形纹徽, 盾形徽章. ⇨illus at COAT OF ARMS (COAT) 见 COAT OF ARMS (COAT) 插图. **(c)** trophy in the form of a shield 盾形锦标: *win the school boxing shield* 赢得学校拳击赛盾形锦标. **2 ~ (against sth)** (*fig* 比喻) person or thing that protects 起保护作用的人或物: *This car polish is an effective shield against rust.* 这种汽车上光蜡很有防锈作用. **3** (in machinery, etc) plate or screen that protects the operator or the machine; thing used to keep out wind, dust, etc (机器等的)护板, 挡风板, 防尘板: *a shield around the grip of a chainsaw* 链锯手柄的护套 ○ *the ˈheat-shield on a space capsule* 宇宙飞船密封舱的隔热屏 ○ *a welder's ˈeye-shield*, ie to stop sparks getting into the eye 电焊工的护目罩.

▷ **shield** *v* [Tn, Tn·pr] **~sb/sth (against/from sb/sth)** protect sb/sth from harm; defend sb/sth from criticism, attack, etc 保护或庇护某人[某事物]: *shield one's eyes (from the sun) with one's hand* 用手(挡住阳光)保护眼睛 ○ *The police officer shielded the child with her body.* 那警察用她的身体保护了小孩. ○ *You can't shield this criminal from prosecution.* 你不能包庇该罪犯而不起诉他. ○ *I tried to shield him against prying journalists.* 我竭力为他挡驾, 拦住那些锲而不舍的记者.

shift[1] /ʃɪft; ʃɪft/ *v* **1 (a)** [I, Ipr, Ip, Tn, Tn·pr, Tn·p] **~ (sth/sb/oneself) (from.../to...)**; **~ (sth/sb/oneself) (about/around)** (cause sth/sb/oneself to) change or move from one position or direction to another (使某事物[某人/自己])改变位置或方向: *The cargo has shifted*, ie has been shaken out of place by the movement of the ship. 货物移动了位置(因船颠簸). ○ *The wind shifted from east to north.* 风由东转向北. ○ *The tools shift around in the car boot every time we turn a corner.* 我们每次转弯, 汽车行李箱里的工具就来回动. ○ *The audience shifted uneasily in their seats.* 观众在座位上不安地动来动去. ○ (*infml* 口) *Soap won't shift that stain*, ie wash it off. 肥皂洗不掉那个污迹. ○ *Help me to shift the sofa away from the fire.* 帮我把这沙发挪得离炉火远些. ○ *You'll have to shift yourselves to another room — I want to clean in here.* 你得到另一个房间去——我要打扫这里. ○ *The teacher shifted the chairs around in the classroom.* 那个教师挪动了教室里的椅子. **(b)** [Tn, Tn·pr] **~ sth (from A to/onto B)** transfer sth 转移或转换某事物: *Don't try to shift the responsibility onto others: you must do the job yourself.* 别想把责任推给别人, 你得自己干这件事. ○ *He shifted the load from his left to his right shoulder.* 他把重物从左肩换到右肩. **2** [Ipr, Ip, Tn] **~ out of sth/into sth**; **~ up/down** (*esp US*) change (gear) in a vehicle 换(挡): *shift out of first into second* 从一挡换到二挡 ○ *Shift up when you reach 30 mph.* 车速达到每小时30英里时要换高挡. ○ *You have to shift down to climb steep hills.* 汽车爬陡坡得换低挡. ○ *Learn to shift gear at the right moment.* 要学会掌握在什么时候换挡. **3** [I] (*Brit infml* 口) move quickly 迅速移

动: *You'll have to shift if you want to get there by nine o'clock.* 你要想九点钟到那儿, 就得快点. ○ *That car can really shift!* 那辆汽车要是快开的话还真够快! **4** (idm 习语) **shift one's 'ground** take a new position or a different way of approaching a subject during an argument (辩论中)改变立场或方法. **5** (phr v) **shift for oneself** manage one's life without help from others 自谋生计: *When their parents died, the children had to shift for themselves.* 孩子们在父母死后只好自谋生路.

□ **'shift-key** *n* key on a typewriter, etc which, when pressed, causes the machine to type capital letters (打字机等的)大小写字体转换键.

shift[2] /ʃɪft; ʃɪft/ *n* **1 ~ (in sth)** change of place, nature, form, etc (位置、性质、形式等的)改变, 转变: *a gradual shift of people from the country to the town* 人们由乡村向市镇的逐渐转移 ○ *shifts in public opinion* 公众舆论的转变 ○ *There has been a shift in fashion from formal to more informal dress.* 服装的式样已经有了转变, 以前很拘谨现在较随便. **2** (period of time worked by a) group of workers which starts work as another group finishes 轮班职工; 轮值的班(工作时间): *the 'day/'night shift* 日班[夜班] ○ *work an eight-hour shift* 八小时轮班工作 ○ *working in shifts* 轮班工作 ○ [attrib 作定语] *a shift worker* 轮班工作的人 ○ *shift work, pay* 轮班的工作、工资. Cf 参看 RELAY 1. **3** trick or scheme for achieving sth or avoiding a difficulty (为获得某事物或逃避困难的)计谋, 手段: *use some dubious shifts to get money* 用某种值得怀疑的手段赚钱 ○ *As a temporary shift, he covered up the leak with a plastic bag.* 作为权宜之计, 他用塑料袋把漏洞给包上了. **4 (a)** woman's straight narrow dress 狭窄的直筒式连衣裙. **(b)** (*arch* 古) woman's undergarment like a dress; chemise 连衣裙式女内衣. **5** mechanism on a typewriter, etc that allows capitals to be typed 换字键(打字机等的大小写字体转换键): *Press 'Shift' and type 'A'.* 按'换字键'然后打字母'A'. **6** (idm 习语) **make 'shift (with sth)** (*becoming dated* 渐旧) use what is available, though it is seen as barely adequate; manage 勉强使用; 将就: *We haven't really got enough food for everyone but we'll have to make shift (with what we've got).* 我们的食物其实并不够分的, 只好(用现有的东西)将就了.

▷ **shift·less** *adj* (*derog* 贬) lazy and unambitious; lacking the ability to find ways of getting things done 没出息的; 无能的: *a shiftless individual who never works and constantly borrows from others* 从不工作、专靠向人借钱度日的懒家伙. **shift·less·ness** *n* [U].

shifty /ˈʃɪftɪ; ˈʃɪftɪ/ *adj* (**-ier, -iest**) untrustworthy; deceitful; seemingly dishonest 不可靠的; 诡诈的; 不诚实的: *a shifty-looking person* 看上去不可靠的家伙 ○ *shifty behaviour* 不正直的行为 ○ *shifty eyes, looks* 诡诈的眼睛、表情. ▷ **shif·tily** /-ɪlɪ; -ɪlɪ/ *adv*. **shif·ti·ness** *n* [U].

shil·ling /ˈʃɪlɪŋ; ˈʃɪlɪŋ/ *n* **1** (until 1971) British coin worth twelve old pennies; one twentieth of a pound (到1971年止)先令(英国货币, 值旧币十二便士, 为一镑的二十分之一). **2** basic unit of money in Kenya, Uganda and Tanzania; 100 cents 先令(肯尼亚、乌干达、坦桑尼亚的基本货币单位, 等于100分).

shilly-shally /ˈʃɪlɪ ʃælɪ; ˈʃɪlɪˌʃælɪ/ *v* (*pt, pp* **-shallied**) [I] (*infml derog* 口, 贬) be unable to make up one's mind; be undecided; hesitate 犹豫不决; 踌躇; 优柔寡断: *If you keep shilly-shallying like this we'll be late.* 要是你老这样举棋不定, 我们就来不及了.

shim·mer /ˈʃɪmə(r); ˈʃɪmɚ/ *v* [I] shine with a soft light that seems to waver 发闪烁的微光: *moonlight shimmering on the lake* 湖面上闪烁的月光 ○ *The surface of the road shimmered in the heat of the sun.* 路面在烈日的热气中发出闪烁的微光.

▷ **shim·mer** *n* [U] shimmering light 微光; 闪光: *the shimmer of pearls* 珍珠的闪光.

shin /ʃɪn; ʃɪn/ *n* front part of the leg below the knee 胫; 胫部: *get kicked on the shin* 小腿上被踢了一脚. ⇨illus at HUMAN 见 HUMAN 插图.

▷ **shin** *v* (**-nn-**) (phr v) **shin up/down (sth)** climb up/down (sth), using the hands and legs to grip (手脚并用沿某物)向上[下]爬: *shin up a tree* 爬树 ○ *shin down a rope* 沿绳索爬下来.

□ **'shin-bone** (also **tibia**) *n* inner and (usu) larger of the two bones from the knee to the ankle 胫骨.

'shin-pad (also **'shin-guard**) *n* pad worn to protect the shin when playing football, etc 护胫(踢足球等用的).

shin·dig /ˈʃɪndɪg; ˈʃɪndɪg/ *n* (*infml* 口) **1** lively and noisy party 热闹的聚会. **2** = SHINDY.

shindy /ˈʃɪndɪ; ˈʃɪndɪ/ (also **shindig**) *n* (usu *sing* 通常作单数) (*infml* 口) noisy disturbance; brawl 吵闹; 争吵; 打架: *kick up* (ie cause) *a shindy* 引起一场争吵 ○ *There was a dreadful shindy in the pub last night.* 昨天晚上酒馆里有人大打出手.

shine /ʃaɪn; ʃaɪn/ *v* (*pt, pp* **shone** /ʃɒn; *US* ʃəʊn; ʃon/ or, in sense 3, 用于下述第3义时作 **~d**) **1** [I, Ipr, Ip] give out or reflect light; be bright 发光; 反射光; 照耀: *Clean the glasses until they shine.* 把眼镜擦亮. ○ *The moon is shining (through the window).* 月光(通过窗户)照了进来. ○ *The clouds parted and the sun shone (out).* 云开了, 太阳出来了. ○ *The hot sun shone down on the scene.* 烈日照射着这个地方. ○ (*fig* 比喻) *His face shone with excitement.* 他脸上焕发着兴奋的光芒. **2** [Tn·pr, Tn·p] aim the light of (a torch, etc) in a specified direction 用(手电筒等)的光向某方向照射: *The police shone a searchlight on the house.* 警察用探照灯照射这所房子. ○ *Shine your torch into the drawer.* 你用手电筒照一下这抽屉里面. ○ *I hate lights being shone in my face.* 我不喜欢灯光正对着我的脸. **3** [Tn] (*infml* 口) polish (sth) 擦亮(某物): *shine shoes, brassware* 擦鞋、铜器. **4** [I, Ipr] **~ (at/in sth)** excel in some way 表现突出; 出众: *He's a shining* (ie outstanding, excellent) *example of a hard-working pupil.* 他是用功的学生, 是优秀的榜样. ○ *She does not shine in conversation*, ie is not a good talker. 她不擅长谈话. ○ *I've never shone at tennis.* 我从来就打不好网球. **5** (idm 习语) **a knight in shining armour** ⇨KNIGHT. **make hay while the sun shines** ⇨HAY. **rise and shine** ⇨RISE[2].

▷ **shine** *n* **1** [sing, U] brightness; polished appearance 光亮; 光泽: *Give your shoes a good shine.* 把你的鞋好好擦一下. ○ *There's too much shine on the seat of these old trousers.* 这条裤子臀部磨得太亮了. **2** (idm 习语) **come rain, come shine; rain or shine** ⇨ RAIN[1]. **take a shine to sb/sth** (*infml* 口) suddenly begin to like sb/sth 突然间喜欢上某人[某事物]: *I think that dog has taken a shine to me: it follows me everywhere.* 我想这狗已经喜欢上我了, 我走到哪儿它跟到哪儿.

shiner *n* (*dated sl* 旧, 俚) black eye 黑眼圈: *That's quite a shiner you've got there.* 你眼睛那儿可青了一块.

shiny *adj* (**-ier, -iest**) shining; rubbed until bright 发亮的; 磨光的: *the shiny head of a bald man* 秃头男子发亮的脑袋 ○ *shiny black leather* 乌黑发亮的皮革 ○ *All the cups are clean and shiny.* 杯子都很干净明亮.

shingle[1] /ˈʃɪŋgl; ˈʃɪŋgl/ *n* [U] small rounded pebbles on the sea-shore 海滨的小圆石.

▷ **shingly** /ˈʃɪŋglɪ; ˈʃɪŋglɪ/ *adj* covered with or consisting of shingle 遍布小圆石的; 由小圆石组成的: *I prefer a sandy beach to a shingly one.* 我喜欢沙滩, 不喜欢遍布小圆石的海滩.

shingle[2] /ˈʃɪŋgl; ˈʃɪŋgl/ *n* **1** small, flat, square or oblong piece of wood used as a covering on roofs and walls 盖板; 屋顶板; 木瓦; 墙面板. **2** (*US infml* 口) small wooden signboard put up outside the office of a doctor, dentist, etc (医生等挂在办事处外面的)木质小招牌.

▷ **shingle** *v* [Tn esp passive 尤用于被动语态] cover (a roof, etc) with shingles 用盖板覆盖(屋顶等): *a shingled church spire* 用屋顶板覆盖的教堂尖顶.

shingles /ˈʃɪŋglz; ˈʃɪŋglz/ *n* [sing *v*] (also ˌ**herpes 'zoster**) disease caused by a virus, with a band of painful spots on the skin, esp around the waist 带状疱疹(尤多生于腰部).

ship[1] /ʃɪp; ʃɪp/ *n* **1** large vessel carrying people or goods by sea 船; 舰: *a 'sailing-ship* 帆船 ○ *a 'merchant ship* 商船 ○ *a 'warship* 战舰 ○ *the ship's company*, ie the entire crew 全体船员 ○ *board a ship for India* 登上去印度的船. **2** (*infml* 口) **(a)** spacecraft 宇宙飞船; 太空船: *aboard an alien ship* 在外星飞船上. **(b)** (*US*) aircraft 飞行器. **3** (idm 习语) **jump ship** ⇨JUMP[2]. **(like) ˌships that ˌpass in the 'night** people who meet each other briefly and usu only once 短暂相遇的人(通常指只遇此一次). **when one's 'ship comes home/in** when one has become successful 等自己成功时: *I'll buy a house in the country when my ship comes in.* 等我有钱时, 我要在

S

乡间买一所房子.

□ **ship 'biscuit** (also **ship's 'biscuit**) hard coarse biscuit used formerly as food during long voyages 硬饼干(旧时远航备用的): *a diet of ship biscuit* 以硬饼干作固定食物.

'shipboard *adj* [attrib 作定语] used or occurring on a ship 在船上的; 在船上使用的; 在船上发生的: *a shipboard romance* 船上的艳情. — *n* (idm 习语) **on shipboard** on a ship; on board ship 在船上.

'shipbuilding *n* [U] building ships 造船业; 造船术: [attrib 作定语] *a shipbuilding company, yard* 造船公司、造船厂. **'shipbuilder** *n*.

'ship-canal *n* canal that is wide and deep enough for seagoing vessels (可供海船通行的)运河.

'shipload *n* as much cargo or as many passengers as a ship can carry 船载量: *set sail with a shipload of grain* 载着一船谷物起航.

'shipmate *n* person travelling or working on the same ship as another 同船旅客; 同船船员: *He and I were shipmates on a trawler once.* 我与他一度同在一艘拖网船上工作.

'shipowner *n* person who owns a ship or ships, or has shares in a shipping company 船主; 船股东.

,ship's 'chandler person who deals in supplies and equipment for ships 船具商.

'shipwreck *n* (**a**) [U] loss or destruction of a ship at sea by storm, collision, etc 海难: *suffer shipwreck* 遭遇海难. (**b**) [C] instance of this 海难: *He died in a shipwreck off the south coast.* 他在南部海岸一带的海难中死亡. — *v* [Tn usu passive 通常用于被动语态] cause (sb) to suffer shipwreck 使(某人)遭遇海难: *shipwrecked sailors* 遭海难的水手 ○ *We were shipwrecked on a deserted island.* 我们遭遇海难而困在荒岛上.

S

'shipwright *n* person employed in building or repairing ships 造船工; 修船工.

'shipyard *n* place where ships are built or repaired 造船厂.

ship[2] /ʃɪp; ʃɪp/ *v* (**-pp-**) **1** [Tn, Tn·pr, Tn·p] send or transport (sth/sb), esp in a ship 运送(某人[某物])(尤指用船): *Are the goods to be flown or shipped?* 这些货物是空运还是海运? ○ *We ship grain to Africa.* 我们把谷物运往非洲. ○ *Fresh supplies were shipped (out) by lorry.* 新到的货已由卡车运出. **2** [Tn] take (oars) out of the water into the boat 将(船桨)收进船内: *We shipped (the) oars and moored alongside the bank.* 我们收起桨, 把船泊在岸边. **3** [Tn] (of a boat) take in (water) over the side, eg in a storm (指船)舷侧进(水)(如在风暴中): *The waves were very high, and the boat began to ship water.* 浪很大, 船舷开始进水. **4** [I] become a member of a ship's crew 当船员: *ship* (ie take a post) *as a steward on an Atlantic liner* 在航行大西洋的班轮上当乘务员. **5** (phr v) **ship sb/sth off** (*infml* 口) send sb/sth away 将某人[某物]送走: *The children had been shipped off to boarding-school at an early age.* 孩子们很小就送进了寄宿学校.

▷ **ship·ment** /'ʃɪpmənt; 'ʃɪpmənt/ *n* **1** [U] placing of goods on a ship; transport of goods by any means 装船; 装运: *immediate shipment of the cargo* 货物立即装运 ○ *safe shipment by air* 安全空运. **2** [C] items shipped; consignment 装载的货物; 运输的货物: *a shipment of grain for West Africa* 运往西非的一批谷物.

ship·per *n* person who arranges for goods to be shipped 托运人; 发货人.

ship·ping *n* [U] **1** ships, esp those of a country or port 船舶(尤指一国或一海港的): *The canal is now open to shipping.* 该运河现已通航. ○ [attrib 作定语] *a shipping office* 海运事务所 ○ *busy shipping lanes* 繁忙的海上航道 ○ *the shipping forecast*, ie a report on the weather conditions at sea 海洋气象预报. **2** transporting goods by ship 船运; 海运: *the shipping of oil from the Middle East* 从中东经水路运送石油. **'shipping-agent** *n* shipowner's representative at a port 船舶业务代理人.

-ship *suff* 后缀 (with *ns* forming *ns* 与名词结合构成名词) **1** state of being; status; office 状态; 地位; 身分; 职位: *friendship* ○ *ownership* ○ *professorship*. **2** proficiency as; skill 技能; 技巧: *musicianship* ○ *scholarship*. Cf 参看 -MANSHIP (MAN[1]).

ship·shape /'ʃɪpʃeɪp; 'ʃɪp,ʃep/ *adj* [usu pred 通常作表语] in good order; tidy 有秩序; 整齐: *get the room all nice and shipshape* 把房间收拾得井井有条.

shire /'ʃaɪə(r); ʃaɪr *or, in compounds,* 在复合词中读作 -ʃə(r); -ʃɚ/ *n* **1** [C] (*arch* 古) county (now chiefly used in the names of certain counties, eg *Hampshire, Yorkshire*) 郡(现主要用于地名, 如 Hampshire, Yorkshire). **2 the shires** [pl] certain midland counties of England and parts of these well known for fox-hunting 英格兰中部几个郡(其中有些以猎狐区著名).

□ **'shire-horse** *n* large powerful breed of horse used for pulling carts and wagons 英格兰中部的大挽马.

shirk /ʃɜ:k; ʃɝk/ *v* [I, Tn, Tg] (*derog* 贬) avoid doing (work, one's duty, etc) through laziness, cowardice, etc (因偷懒、胆怯等)逃避(工作、责任等): *You're supposed to tidy up, so stop shirking and do it!* 要你来整理就别躲着了, 干吧! ○ *He always shirks the unpleasant tasks.* 他总是逃避那些厌恶性工作. ○ *She is shirking going to the dentist.* 她躲着不愿意去治牙. ▷ **shirker** *n*.

shirt /ʃɜ:t; ʃɝt/ *n* **1** loose-fitting garment (usu worn by men) for the upper part of the body, made of cotton, linen, silk, etc, with long or short sleeves 衬衫, 衬衣(通常指男用的): *a 'sports shirt*, ie one with short sleeves for casual wear 短袖衬衫 ○ *a 'dress shirt*, ie a formal one worn with a dinner-jacket, etc 礼服衬衫. ⇨illus at JACKET 见 JACKET 插图. **2** (idm 习语) **keep one's 'shirt on** (*infml* 口) (usu imperative 通常用于祈使句) not lose one's temper 不生气; 不发脾气: *Keep your shirt on! Nobody meant to offend you.* 别发火! 没人想惹你. **lose one's shirt** ⇨LOSE. **put one's shirt on sth** (*sl* 俚) bet all one's money on (a horse, etc) 将全部钱财作赌注压在(马、狗等上); 孤注一掷: *He has put his shirt on his team winning the trophy.* 他孤注一掷, 赌自己的队一定能赢得锦标. **a stuffed shirt** ⇨STUFF[2].

▷ **shirt·ing** *n* [U] material for making shirts 做衬衫用的料子.

□ **'shirt-front** *n* front part of a shirt, esp the stiffened and starched front part of a formal white shirt 衬衫的胸部(尤指礼服白衬衫浆硬的部分).

'shirt-sleeve *n* sleeve of a shirt 衬衫的袖子: *in one's shirt-sleeves*, ie not wearing a jacket over one's shirt 穿着衬衫(未穿外衣).

'shirt-tail *n* part of a shirt that extends below the waist 衬衫的下摆.

'shirtwaist *n* (*US*) woman's dress that buttons down the front to the waist 衬衫式连衣裙(胸部有扣至腰部的).

shirty /'ʃɜ:tɪ; 'ʃɝtɪ/ *adj* (**-ier**, **-iest**) (*infml* 口) annoyed; angry; bad-tempered 发怒的; 生气的; 脾气坏的: *Don't get shirty with me!* 别冲着我发脾气! ▷ **shirt·ily** *adv*. **shirti·ness** *n* [U].

shish ke·bab /,ʃɪʃ kɪ'bæb; *US* 'ʃɪʃ kəbæb; 'ʃɪʃ kə,bɑb/ = KEBAB.

shit /ʃɪt; ʃɪt/ *n* (⚠ *sl* 讳, 俚) **1** [U] waste matter from the bowels; excrement 粪便; 屎: *a pile of dog shit on the pavement* 便道上的一堆狗屎. **2** [sing] act of emptying the bowels 拉屎: *have/need a shit* 拉[要拉]屎. **3** [U] stupid remarks or writing; nonsense 胡说; 胡言; 废话: *You do talk a load of shit!* 你胡说八道! **4** [C] (*derog* 贬) contemptible person 讨厌的家伙; 可鄙的人: *That little shit stole my money.* 那个小混蛋把我的钱偷走了. **5** (idm 习语) **in the 'shit** in trouble 遇到麻烦事. **not give a 'shit (about sb/sth)** not care at all 毫不关心: *He doesn't give a shit about anybody else.* 他对别人漠不关心. **scare the shit out of sb** ⇨SCARE.

▷ **shit** *v* (**-tt-**; *pt, pp* **shitted** or **shat** /ʃæt; ʃæt/) (⚠ *sl* 讳, 俚) **1** [I, Tn] empty (solid waste) from the bowels 拉(屎). **2** [Tn] **~ oneself** (**a**) soil oneself by emptying solid waste from the bowels accidentally 突然拉出屎来把自己弄脏. (**b**) be very frightened 极害怕.

shit *interj* (⚠ *sl* 讳, 俚) (used to express annoyance 用以表示恼怒): *Shit! I've missed the train!* 妈的! 我没赶上火车!

shitty /'ʃɪtɪ; 'ʃɪtɪ/ *adj* (**-ier, -iest**) (⚠ *sl* 讳, 俚 *esp Brit*) **1** nasty; disgusting 令人厌恶的; 令人作呕的; 讨厌的: *I'm not going to eat this shitty food.* 我可不吃这种恶心东西. **2** contemptible; mean; unworthy 卑鄙的; 无耻的; 无足取的: *What a shitty way to treat a friend!* 这样对待一个朋友, 真不像话!

shiver[1] /'ʃɪvə(r); 'ʃɪvɚ/ *v* [I, Ipr] **~ (with sth)** tremble, esp from cold or fear 颤抖(尤指因寒冷或恐惧); 哆嗦:

She shivered at the thought of going into the dark house alone. 她想到要独自走进那所黑洞洞的房子里去就不寒而栗. ○ *shivering all over with cold* 冷得浑身发抖.

▷ **shiver** *n* **1** [C] act of shivering 颤抖; 哆嗦: *The gruesome sight sent a shiver down my spine.* 那可怕情景使我的背脊发凉. **2 the shivers** [pl] fit of trembling, resulting from fever or fear (因高烧或恐惧而引起的)颤抖, 战栗: *lying in bed with a bout of the shivers* 躺在床上浑身打战 ○ *Having to make a speech always gives me the shivers.* 一让我演讲我就吓得直哆嗦.

shiv·ery /ˈʃɪvərɪ; ˋʃɪvərɪ/ *adj* tending to shiver; having or causing a feeling of cold, horror, fear, etc 令人颤抖的; 令人毛骨悚然的: *feel shivery in the damp atmosphere* 在潮湿的空气中感到毛骨悚然 ○ *a cold, shivery breeze* 凛冽的寒风.

shiver[2] /ˈʃɪvə(r); ˋʃɪvɚ/ *n* (usu *pl* 通常作复数) any of the many small fragments of sth, esp of glass, that has been broken 碎片(尤指玻璃的): *break sth into shivers* 把某物打碎 ○ *cut one's foot on a small shiver of glass* 玻璃碎片把脚划破了.

▷ **shiver** *v* [I, Tn] (cause sth to) break into shivers; shatter (使某物)裂成碎片; 打碎.

shoal[1] /ʃəʊl; ʃol/ *n* great number of fish swimming together 鱼群: *a shoal of herring, cod, etc* 一群鲱鱼、鳕鱼等 ○ *swimming in shoals* (鱼)成群地游着 ○ (*fig* 比喻) *Shoals of tourists come here in the summer.* 这里夏季游人如鲫.

▷ **shoal** *v* [I] (of fish) form a shoal or shoals (指鱼)成群.

shoal[2] /ʃəʊl; ʃol/ *n* **1** [C] shallow place in the sea; sandbank, esp one that can be seen when the water level is low 海的浅水处; 沙洲(尤指水位降落时可见者); 浅滩: *run aground on a shoal* 搁浅 ○ *steer away from the shoals* 绕开浅水处. **2 shoals** [pl] (*fig* 比喻) hidden dangers or difficulties 隐伏的危险或困难; 隐患.

▷ **shoal** *v* [I] become shallow(er) 变浅.

shock[1] /ʃɒk; ʃɑk/ *n* **1** [C] violent blow or shake, caused eg by a collision or an explosion 强烈的冲击或震动(如因碰撞或爆炸造成的): *earthquake shocks* 地震 ○ *The shock of the blast shattered many windows.* 许多窗户在爆炸中震碎了. ○ *I felt the shock as the aircraft hit the ground.* 飞机着陆时我感觉到震了一下. **2** [C] = ELECTRIC SHOCK (ELECTRIC): *If you touch this live wire, you'll get a shock.* 摸这条带电的导线, 就会触电. **3** [C] sudden violent disturbance of the mind or emotions caused eg by bad news, a frightening event, etc 震惊; 震骇; 惊愕: *The news of his mother's death was a terrible shock to him.* 他母亲去世的噩耗使他非常震惊. ○ *The result of the election came as a shock to us all*, ie None of us expected it. 选举的结果令我们惊愕. ○ *It gave me quite a shock to be told I was seriously ill.* 听说我的病很严重, 我吃了一惊. **4** [U] state of extreme weakness caused by physical injury, pain, fright, etc 休克: *be in/go into shock* 处于休克状态 ○ *suffering from shock* 已休克 ○ *What is the correct medical treatment for shock?* 在医学上怎样处理休克才对? ○ *She died of shock following an operation on her brain.* 她作脑科手术后因休克死亡.

□ ˈ**shock absorber** device fitted to a motor vehicle to absorb vibration caused by the unevenness of the road surface, etc (汽车的)减震器. ⇨illus at App 1 见附录1插图, page xii.

ˈ**shock-proof** *adj* (esp of a watch) designed to resist damage when knocked, dropped, etc (尤指手表)防震的.

ˈ**shock tactics** sudden, violent or outrageous action taken to achieve a purpose 为达到某目的而采取的突然的、激烈的或不道德的行动; 出奇制胜战术: *The group used shock tactics to get publicity: one of them took his clothes off on TV.* 这伙人为了扬名做出了惊人的举动, 其中一人在电视上当众脱下了衣服.

ˈ**shock therapy** (also ˈ**shock treatment**) way of treating mental illness by giving electric shocks or a drug having a similar effect 电震疗法; 休克疗法.

ˈ**shock-troops** *n* [pl] troops specially trained for violent assaults 突击队; 奇袭队.

ˈ**shock wave** moving region of very high air pressure caused by an explosion or an aircraft moving faster than sound 激震波, 冲击波, 激波(由爆炸或超音速飞机引起的): (*fig* 比喻) *As soon as news of the tragedy was announced, shock waves spread rapidly to all parts of the country.* 这可悲的消息一发表, 震撼人心的冲击波迅速传遍全国各地.

shock[2] /ʃɒk; ʃɑk/ *n* (usu 通常作 **shock of hair**) rough untidy mass of hair on the head 蓬乱的头发.

□ ˌ**shock-ˈheaded** *adj* (*dated* 旧) having such hair 头发蓬乱的.

shock[3] /ʃɒk; ʃɑk/ *v* [Tn esp passive 尤用于被动语态] cause a shock[1](3) to (sb); cause (sb) to feel disgust, indignation, horror, etc 使(某人)震惊; 使(某人)感到厌恶、愤怒、恐惧等: *I was shocked at the news of her death.* 我听到她去世的消息十分震惊. ○ *He was shocked to hear his child swearing.* 他听见他孩子骂人非常生气. ○ *I'm not easily shocked, but that book really is obscene.* 我并不是大惊小怪的人, 但那本书淫秽之甚确实让我大吃一惊.

▷ **shocker** *n* **1** person who shocks 引起震惊、厌恶、愤怒的人. **2** (*infml* 口) (**a**) thing that shocks, eg a sensational novel 引起震惊、厌恶、愤怒等的事物(如摄人心魄的小说): *Some of these horror stories are real shockers.* 这些恐怖小说有的十分吓人. (**b**) very bad example of sth 极坏的典型: *You've written bad essays before, but this one is a shocker!* 你以前也写过差劲的文章, 但这篇可糟透了!

shock·ing *adj* **1** causing indignation, disgust, etc; very bad or wrong 令人气愤的; 令人厌恶的; 极坏的; 非常错误的: *shocking behaviour, words, insults* 恶劣的行为、恶毒的言语、极大的侮辱 ○ *What she did was so shocking that I can hardly describe it.* 她的行为太过分了, 我简直无法形容. **2** causing a shock[1](3) 令人震惊的: *shocking news*, eg of an accident in which many died 令人震惊的消息. **3** (*infml* 口) very bad 很糟的: *shocking luck, weather, handwriting, work* 很糟的运气、天气、笔迹、作品 ○ *The food here is shocking.* 这儿的食物糟透了.

shock·ingly *adv* **1** badly 糟糕地: *You're playing shockingly.* 你演奏得很糟糕. **2** (*infml* 口) extremely 极; 非常: *a shockingly expensive dress* 特贵的连衣裙.

shod *pt, pp* of SHOE *v*.

shoddy[1] /ˈʃɒdɪ; ˋʃɑdɪ/ *adj* (**-ier**, **-iest**) of poor quality or badly made 劣质的; 粗制滥造的: *shoddy goods, clothes, etc* 劣质的货物、服装等 ○ *shoddy workmanship* 劣等工艺. ▷ **shod·dily** *adv*: *shoddily made* 做得很糟. **shod·di·ness** *n* [U].

shoddy[2] /ˈʃɒdɪ; ˋʃɑdɪ/ *n* [U] (poor-quality cloth made from) fibre obtained from old cloth 再生布; 长弹毛(织物); 软再生毛(织物).

shoe 鞋

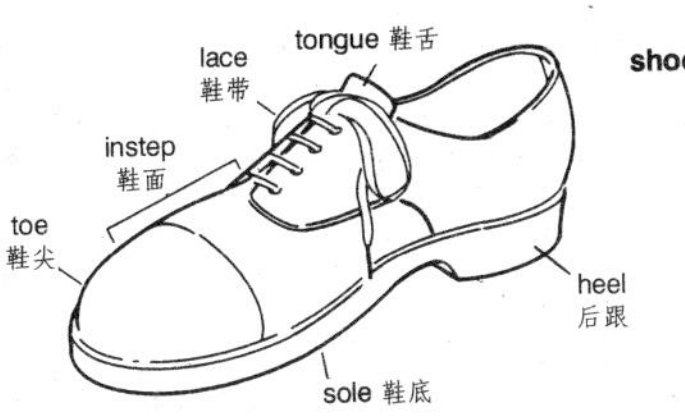

shoe /ʃuː; ʃu/ *n* **1** outer covering for a person's foot, usu with a stiff sole and not reaching above the ankle 鞋: *a pair of shoes* 一双鞋 ○ *walking shoes* 轻便鞋 ○ *tennis shoes* 网球鞋 ○ *put on/take off one's shoes* 穿[脱]鞋 ○ [attrib 作定语] *a shoe brush, shop* 鞋刷、鞋店 ○ *shoe polish, leather* 鞋油、制鞋用的皮革. Cf 参看 BOOT[1] 1, SANDAL. **2** = HORSESHOE (HORSE): *cast/throw a shoe*, ie lose one 掉了一块马蹄铁. **3** part of a brake that presses against the wheel or its drum (on a bicycle, in a motor vehicle, etc) (自行车、汽车等的)煞车瓦, 闸瓦. **4** any object like a shoe in appearance or use 在外观或用途上似鞋之物. **5** (idm 习语) **be in/put oneself in sb's shoes** be in/imagine oneself to be in sb else's position (设想)处于某人的地位或处境: *I wouldn't like to be in your shoes if they find out what you're doing.* 要是人家发现你现在干的这件事, 我可不愿设想你得有多倒霉. **dead men's shoes** ⇨DEAD. **fill sb's shoes** ⇨FILL[1]. **shake in one's shoes** ⇨SHAKE[1]. **step into sb's shoes** ⇨STEP[1].

▷ **shoe** *v* (*pt, pp* **shod** /ʃɒd; ʃɑd/) [Tn] fit (a horse) with a shoe or shoes 给(马)钉马蹄铁: *a blacksmith shoeing a pony* 给小马钉马蹄铁的铁匠.

shod *adj* [attrib 作定语] (of a person) wearing shoes of a specified type or quality (指人)穿着某种(式样或质量)鞋的: *shod in leather* 穿着皮鞋 ○ *well shod for wet weather* 穿好了雨鞋以防下雨 ○ (*fig* 比喻) *an iron-shod stick*, ie one with an iron tip 包有铁头的手杖.

□ ˈ**shoehorn** *n* device with a curved blade used to help the heel slide easily into a shoe 鞋拔子.

ˈ**shoe-lace** *n* cord fastened to the edges of a shoe's uppers to hold it tightly on the foot 鞋带.

ˈ**shoemaker** *n* [C], ˈ**shoemaking** *n* [U] (person whose trade is) making or repairing boots and shoes 鞋匠; 制鞋; 补鞋; 制鞋业.

ˈ**shoeshine** *n* (*esp US*) person whose job is polishing other people's shoes 以擦皮鞋为业的人: [attrib 作定语] *a shoeshine boy* 擦鞋男童.

ˈ**shoe-string** *n* **1** (*esp US*) shoe-lace 鞋带. **2** (idm 习语) **on a ˈshoe-string** using very little money 以极少的钱: *living on a shoe-string* 过着极节俭的生活.

ˈ**shoe-tree** *n* shaped piece of wood, plastic or metal placed inside a shoe so that it keeps its shape 鞋楦.

shone *pt, pp* of SHINE

shoo /ʃu:; ʃu/ *interj* (said to make animals or people, esp children, go away 为将动物或人, 尤指儿童, 赶走时发出的声音): *Shoo, all of you, I'm busy.* 嘘, 都走开, 我正忙着呢.

▷ **shoo** *v* (*pt, pp* **shooed**) (phr v) **shoo sb/sth away, off, out, etc** make sb/sth go away, etc, by saying 'shoo' 发嘘声将某人[某物]赶走: *shooing the chickens away/into the barn* 发出嘘声把鸡轰走[进饲养棚] ○ *He shooed the little children out of the shop.* 他发出嘘声把小孩儿都赶出了商店.

shoo-in /ˈʃu:ɪn; ˈʃu,ɪn/ *n* (*US infml* 口) person, team, etc that is thought certain to win 被认为肯定可以取胜的人、队等.

shook *pt* of SHAKE[1].

shoot[1] /ʃu:t; ʃut/ *v* (*pt, pp* **shot** /ʃɒt; ʃɑt/) **1 (a)** [I, Ipr, Tn, Tn·pr, Tn·p] **~ (sth) (at sb/sth); ~ sth (from sth); ~ sth (off)** fire (a gun or some other weapon); fire (a bullet, an arrow, etc) at sb/sth 开(枪或其他武器); 向某人[某物]发射(子弹、箭等): *Aim carefully before shooting.* 仔细瞄准后再射击. ○ *Don't shoot — I surrender.* 别开枪——我投降. ○ *What are you shooting (your gun) at?* 你(用枪)射击什么呢? ○ *He shot an arrow from his bow.* 他拉弓放了一箭. ○ *The police only rarely shoot to kill*, ie try to kill the people they shoot at. 警察开枪很少打死人. ○ *The missiles were shot at the aircraft from a ship.* 从军舰上向飞机发射导弹. ○ *He shot (off) several bullets before hitting the target.* 他射出好几发子弹才击中目标. **(b)** [I] use a gun, etc; hunt with a gun, etc 使用枪等; 用枪等打猎: *Can you shoot (well)?* 你会放枪吗(你枪打得准吗)? ○ *learn to shoot straight* 练习枪法 ○ *I need more practice at shooting.* 我需要多练习射击. ○ *He enjoys riding, fishing and shooting*, ie as sport. 他喜欢骑马、钓鱼和射击. **(c)** [Tn, Cn·a] kill or wound (sb/sth) with a bullet, an arrow, etc (用子弹、箭等)击毙或射伤(某人[某物]): *She went out shooting rabbits.* 她打兔子去了. ○ *The soldier was shot* (ie executed by shooting) *for desertion.* 那士兵因开小差儿而被处死. ○ *She was shot in the leg.* 她腿上中了一枪. ○ *The hunter shot the stag dead.* 猎人把雄鹿射死了. **(d)** [I] (of a gun, bow, etc) fire bullets, arrows, etc (指枪、弓等)发射子弹、箭等: *This is just a toy gun: it doesn't shoot.* 这只是玩具枪, 不能发射子弹. ○ *Get a rifle that shoots straight.* 找一杆射得准的步枪来. **(e)** [Tn·pr] make (sth) by shooting 由射击造成(某现象): *The gun/gunman shot a hole in the door.* 这枪[持枪歹徒]在门上射出一个洞. **2** [Tn] go over (an area) shooting game animals 去(某地)打猎: *shoot a covert, an estate, etc* 去丛林、庄园等打猎. ⇨Usage at HUNT[1] 用法见 HUNT[1]. **3 (a)** [Ipr, Ip, Tn·pr, Tn·p] (cause sth to) move suddenly or quickly in the specified direction (使某物)沿某方向突然或迅速运动: *The sports car shot past us.* 赛车从我们前面飞驰而过. ○ *A meteor shot across the sky.* 流星划过天空. ○ *He shot out of the door after her.* 他冲出门去追赶她. ○ *The runner shot ahead (of the rest).* 那个赛跑的人向前飞奔而去(把其他人抛在后面). ○ *Flames were shooting (up) from the burning house.* 从燃烧着的房子里喷射出火舌. ○ *The snake's tongue shot out.* 蛇飞快地吐出芯子. ○ *The driver was shot out of the open car as it crashed.* 那辆敞篷汽车撞车时把司机抛出车外. ⇨Usage at WHIZ 用法见 WHIZ. **(b)** [I, Ipr] **~ (down, up, etc sth)** (of pain) move suddenly and quickly with a stabbing sensation (指疼痛)刺痛, 剧痛: *a shooting pain in my back* 我背部的刺痛感 ○ *The pain shot up her arm.* 她手臂一阵剧痛. **(c)** [no passive 不用于被动语态: Tn·pr, Dn·n] **~ sth at sb** direct sth at sb suddenly or quickly 突然或迅速向某人抛出某物: *journalists shooting questions at the minister* 向部长发出连珠炮般问题的记者 ○ *She shot an angry glance at him/shot him an angry glance.* 她愤怒地扫了他一眼. **4** [I] (of plants and bushes) put forth new twigs or branches from a stem; sprout (指花草或灌木)发芽, 生枝: *Rose bushes shoot again after being cut back.* 玫瑰丛修剪后还能再长出新枝. **5** [I, Tn, Tng no passive 不用于被动语态] (*esp cinema* 尤用于电影) photograph (an object, a scene, etc) 拍摄(物、景等): *Cameras ready? OK, shoot!* 摄影机准备好了吗? 好, 开拍! ○ *We're ready to shoot (the ballroom sequence).* 我们已经准备好拍摄(舞厅的连续镜头). ○ *The film was shot in black and white.* 这部电影拍成了黑白片. ○ *shoot a woman riding a horse* 拍摄一个骑着马的女子. **6** [Tn] (of a boat or a person in a boat) move quickly through, past, etc (sth) (指船或船中人)迅速穿过(某物): *shooting the rapids* 迅速穿过激流 ○ *shoot the bridge*, ie pass quickly underneath it 迅速从桥下穿过. **7** [Tn] push (the bolt of a door) into or out of its slot 插上或打开(门闩). **8** [Tn] (*infml* 口) (in golf) achieve (a specified number of strokes) in a game (高尔夫球)击出(杆数): *shot a 75 in the first round* 第一场击出75杆. **9** [Tn] (*esp US*) play (certain games) 玩(某些游戏): *shoot craps/pool/dice* 玩双色子[台球/掷色子]游戏. **10 (a)** [I, Ipr] **~ (at sth)** (in football, hockey, etc) try to kick, hit, etc the ball directly into the goal (足球、曲棍球等中)射门: *She's looking for an opportunity to shoot (at goal).* 她正在寻找机会射门. **(b)** [Tn no passive 不用于被动语态] score (a goal) 射中(一球)得分: *He shot a goal from twenty yards out.* 他从二十码外射门得分. **11** [I] (*US infml* 口) (only imperative 只用于祈使句) say what one has to say 说出(要说的话): *You want to tell me something? Well, shoot!* 你有事告诉我吗? 那好, 说吧! **12** [Tn no passive 不用于被动语态] (*sl* 俚) inject (a drug) into one's bloodstream 注射(毒品): *shoot heroin* 注射海洛因. **13** (idm 习语) **be/get shot of sth/sb** (*infml* 口) be/get rid of sth/sb 摆脱某事物[某人]. **shoot one's ˈbolt** (*infml* 口) make one's final effort, so that there is nothing further one can do to achieve one's aim 竭尽全力. **shoot the ˈbreeze** (*US infml* 口) talk casually; gossip 聊天; 闲聊: *We sat around in the bar, shooting the breeze.* 我们坐在酒吧里谈天说地. **shoot it out (with sb)** (*infml* 口) settle a contest, dispute, etc, using guns 用枪来解决竞争、争端等: (*fig* 比喻) *rival politicians shooting it out in a television debate* 在电视辩论中决一雌雄的政界敌手. **shoot a ˈline** (*infml* 口) exaggerate; tell lies 夸张; 说谎: *She said she was an expert skier but I think she was just shooting a line.* 她说自己是滑雪行家, 但我认为她说大话. **shoot one's ˈmouth off (about sth)** (*infml* 口) **(a)** exaggerate; boast 夸张; 吹牛: *He's always shooting his mouth off about his success with women.* 他总是瞎吹他如何能赢得女子芳心. **(b)** talk indiscreetly 轻率地谈话: *It's a secret, so don't go shooting your mouth off about it.* 这是秘密, 别随便乱说. **shoot pool** (*US*) play pool[2](4) 打台球. **shoot one's way in/into sth; shoot one's way out/out of sth** get into/out of sth by shooting 开枪杀进[杀出]某处: *The gangster stole a gun and shot his way out of prison.* 歹徒偷到一枝枪一路杀出监狱. **shoot the ˈworks** (*US infml* 口) gamble or use up all one's money, resources, effort, etc 孤注一掷; 竭尽钱财; 不遗余力. **14** (phr v) **shoot sb down** kill sb, esp cruelly, by shooting 击毙某人; (尤指)残酷枪杀某人: *His victims were all shot down in cold blood.* 他杀害的那些人都是遭他疯狂枪杀的. **shoot sth/sb down** cause (an aircraft or its pilot) to fall to the ground by shooting eg a missile 击落(飞机或其驾驶员)(如用导弹): *ships shooting down fighter planes* 把战斗机击落的舰艇 ○ (*fig* 比喻) *His latest theories have been shot down in flames by the experts.* 他的最新理论被

专家们批驳得一无是处. **shoot sth off (a)** sever sth by shooting it with a gun, etc (用枪等)射断(某物): *His arm was shot off in the war.* 他的手臂在战争中打断了. **(b)** shoot (a gun, fireworks, etc) into the air 朝天放(枪、焰火等): *People were shooting off pistols in the streets to celebrate the victory.* 人们在街上朝天鸣枪庆祝胜利. **shoot sth up** terrorize (a place) by going through it firing guns 在(某地)胡乱放枪制造恐怖: *The gangsters ran into the bar and started shooting it up.* 歹徒们冲进酒吧胡乱扫射一通.

□ **'shooting-brake** *n* (*Brit dated* 旧) = ESTATE CAR (ESTATE).

'shooting-gallery *n* building or room where people practise shooting rifles, etc at targets 室内射击场; 打靶场.

'shooting match (idm 习语) **the whole shooting match** ⇨ WHOLE

,shooting 'star (also **falling star**) small meteor that burns up as it enters the earth's atmosphere, appearing as a bright streak in the sky 流星.

'shooting-stick *n* stick with a spiked end (to be stuck into the ground) and a handle which unfolds to form a small seat 折叠座手杖(可插在地上, 上端可打开成为坐凳).

'shoot-out *n* battle fought with guns 相互开枪; 枪战: *The robbery led to a shoot-out between the robbers and the police.* 这次打劫酿成一场警匪枪战.

shoot[2] /ʃu:t; ʃut/ *n* **1** new young growth on a plant or bush, eg a bud (花草或灌木的)嫩芽, 幼苗, 新枝: *train the new shoots of a vine* 修整藤蔓的新枝. **2** (*Brit*) **(a)** (expedition made by a) group of people shooting game animals for sport 狩猎队; 狩猎: *members of a grouse shoot* 狩猎松鸡的队员. **(b)** area of land over which game animals are shot in this way 狩猎场. **3** (idm 习语) **the whole (bang) 'shoot** (*infml* 口) everything 一切; 全体.

-shooter (in compound *ns* 用以构成复合名词) **1** person who shoots 射手: *a 'sharpshooter* 神枪手. **2** thing that shoots 发射装置: *a 'pea-shooter* 豆子枪 ○ *a 'six-shooter* 装六发子弹的手枪.

shop /ʃɒp; ʃɑp/ *n* **1** (*US* **store**) building or room where goods or services are sold to the public 商店; 店铺: *a butcher's, chemist's, etc shop* 肉店、药房 ○ *a sweet-shop* 糖果店 ○ *a bookshop* 书店 ○ *serve in a shop* 当店员. **2** (also **'workshop**) (esp in compounds 尤用以构成复合词) place where things are manufactured or repaired 工厂; 车间: *an engineering shop* 机械加工车间 ○ *a machine shop* 机械工厂 ○ *a paint shop*, eg where cars are painted 油漆车间(如汽车喷漆车间). **3** (*infml* 口) place of business; institution; establishment 办事处; (工商业)机构; 企业: *I want this shop to run as smoothly as possible.* 我想让这个机构办得尽可能顺利. **4** (idm 习语) **all 'over the shop** (*sl* 俚) **(a)** in great disorder; scattered everywhere 纷乱; 零乱: *His clothes lay all over the shop.* 他衣服扔得到处都是. **(b)** everywhere 各处: *I've looked for it all over the shop.* 我到处都找过了. **a bull in a china shop** ⇨ BULL[1]. **come/go to the wrong shop** ⇨ WRONG. **keep 'shop** look after a shop, serve customers, etc 照管商店; 接待顾客等: *Will you keep shop while I go out for lunch?* 我去吃午饭, 你照看一下商店好吗? **set up 'shop** start a business 开店; 开业: *She set up shop as a bookseller in the High Street.* 她在大街开了一家书店. **shut up shop** ⇨ SHUT. **talk shop** ⇨ TALK[2].

▷ **shop** *v* **(-pp-)** **1** [I, Ipr] **~ (for sth)** (usu 通常作 **go shopping**) go to a shop or shops to buy things 去买东西; 购物: *go shopping every day* 每天去店铺买东西 ○ *I'm shopping for Christmas presents.* 我正在买圣诞礼物. **2** [Tn] (*US*) visit (a shop) to buy things 去(商店)买东西: *shopping the stores looking for bargains* 逛商店找便宜货. **3** [Tn] (*Brit sl* 俚) give information about (sb), esp to the police 告发(某人)(尤指向警方): *The gang leader was shopped by one of the robbers.* 有个劫匪向警方告发了匪首. **4** (phr v) **shop around (for sth)** (*infml* 口) search carefully for goods that are the best value, or for the best services, etc 仔细寻找(物美价廉的东西或最佳服务项目等): *Don't buy the first car you see: shop around a bit.* 买汽车时别见到一辆就买, 多转几家挑一挑. ○ *People must shop around for the best school for their children.* 人们都要为子女找最好的学校.

shop·per *n* person who is shopping 到商店买东西的人: *crowds of Christmas shoppers* 成群的购买圣诞节物品的人. **shop·ping** *n* [U] **1** activity of shopping 买东西; 购物: *do one's shopping* 去买东西. ○ [attrib 作定语] *a 'shopping street*, ie one with many shops 商业街 ○ *a 'shopping bag, basket, etc* 购物袋、篮等. **2** goods bought 买到的东西: *Where did I leave my shopping?* 我把买到的东西忘在哪儿了? **'shopping centre** area where there are many shops 购物中心; 商业区. **'shopping mall** (*US*) area, closed to traffic and usu covered, where there are many shops (禁行车辆的)商业网点(通常有篷顶).

□ **'shop-assistant** (*US* **salesclerk**) *n* person who serves customers in a shop 店员; 售货员.

,shop-'floor *n* [sing] **1** area in a factory where goods are made (工厂里的)生产区: *working on the shop-floor* 在工厂的生产区工作 ○ [attrib 作定语] *a shop-floor worker* 工厂里生产区的工人. **2** workers in a factory (contrasted with the management) 工厂的劳方(相对于资方): *How does the shop-floor feel about these changes?* 劳方对这些改革有何想法?

'shopkeeper (*US* **'storekeeper**) *n* person who owns or manages a shop, usu a small one 店主, 零售商(通常指小店的).

'shoplift *v* [I] steal goods from a shop while pretending to be a customer 入店行窃, 高买(假装买东西趁机行窃): *started to shoplift as a fifteen-year-old* 十五岁就开始到商店里偷东西. **'shoplifter** *n*. **'shoplifting** *n* [U]: *arrested for shoplifting* 因在商店偷东西被捕.

'shop-soiled *adj* dirty or faded from being on display in a shop 在店中摆脏的或摆旧的: *a sale of shop-soiled goods at half price* 店里脏旧货的半价出售.

,shop-'steward *n* trade union official elected by his fellow-workers as their spokesman (同厂工人选出的)工会发言人.

shore[1] /ʃɔ:(r); ʃɔr/ *n* [C, U] land along the edge of the sea or of any large body of water (海或湖等大水域的)岸, 滨: *a house on the shore(s) of Lake Geneva* 日内瓦湖畔的房子 ○ *swim from the ship to the shore* 由船边游到岸边 ○ *go on shore*, eg of sailors from a ship 上岸(如海员离船登岸) ○ *This island is two miles off shore.* 这个岛离岸两英里. ⇨illus at COAST 见 COAST 插图. ⇨Usage at COAST[1] 用法见 COAST[1].

shore[2] /ʃɔ:(r); ʃɔr/ *v* (phr v) **shore sth up** support sth with a wooden beam, etc propped against it (以支柱等)支撑: *shore up the side of an old house to stop it falling down* 支撑旧屋墙壁以防倒塌 ○ (*fig* 比喻) *She used this evidence to shore up her argument.* 她用该证据来支持自己的论点.

▷ **shore** *n* wooden beam, etc used to support sth 支柱; 撑柱.

shorn *pp* of SHEAR.

short[1] /ʃɔ:t; ʃɔrt/ *adj* **(-er, -est)** **1 (a)** measuring little from one end to the other (长度方面)短的: *a short stick, line, dress, journey* 短棒、短线、短连衣裙、短途旅行 ○ *short grass, fur* 短的草、毛皮 ○ *a short distance between the two houses* 两所房子间的短距离 ○ *You've cut my hair very short.* 你把我的头发剪得太短了. ○ *She walked with short quick steps.* 她以小而快的步子走路. ○ *The coat is rather short in the sleeves.* 这件大衣的袖子有点短. Cf 参看 LONG[1] 1. **(b)** below the average height 矮的; 低的: *a short person* 身材矮的人 ○ *short in stature* 身材矮小 ○ *too short to become a police officer* 因身材矮而不能当警察. Cf 参看 TALL. **(c)** not lasting long; brief (时间方面)短的, 短暂的; 简短的: *a short holiday, speech, film, ceremony* 短暂的假期、简短的发言、短片、简短的仪式 ○ *have a short memory*, ie remember only things that have happened recently 短暂的记忆(只能记住最近发生的事) ○ *The days get shorter as winter approaches.* 冬天来临, 白天越来越短了. Cf 参看 LONG[1] 1. **2 ~ (of sth)** not reaching the usual standard or required weight, length, quantity, etc (在重量、长度、数量等方面)未达到通常标准的, 短缺的: *Water is short at this time of year.* 每年这个时候缺水. ○ *The shopkeeper gave us short weight: we got 7.5 kilos instead of 10 kilos.* 店主给我们的分量不足: 应该10公斤我们只得到7.5公斤. ○ *The soldiers complained that they were getting short rations.* 士兵们抱怨他们得到的配给不够数. ○ *These*

S

goods are in short supply, ie There are not enough to satisfy the demand for them. 这些货物短缺(供不应求). ○ *This packet is supposed to contain ten screws, but it's two short.* 这包应装有十个螺丝钉, 可是短了两个. ○ *The missile landed ten miles short (of its target).* 那枚导弹落在离目标十英里的地方. ○ *We've only raised £2 000 so far; we're still £500 short (of the amount we need).* 我们到目前为止才筹集到2 000英镑, (离所需数目)还差500英镑. **3** [pred 作表语] **(a)** **~ (of sth)** not having much or enough of sth; lacking sth (某物)不够; 缺乏(某物): *short of time, money, ideas* 缺少时间、钱、主意 ○ *The hospital is getting short of clean linen.* 这所医院现在缺少干净的被服用品. ○ *We can't lend you any sugar, we're a bit short (of it) ourselves.* 我们无法借给你糖, 我们自己(的糖)也不太够. ○ (*infml* 口) *I'm a bit short* (ie of money) *this week.* 我这星期手头不宽裕(缺钱). **(b)** **~ on sth** (*infml* 口) lacking (a certain quality) 缺少(某种特质): *He's short on tact.* 他处事不够圆通. ○ *Her speeches are rather short on wit.* 她的讲话不够风趣. **4** [pred 作表语] **~ for sth** serving as an abbreviation of sth 作某事物的简略形式、缩写或简称: *'Ben' is usually short for 'Benjamin'.* Ben 通常为 Benjamin 的简称. **5** **(a)** [pred 作表语] **~ (with sb)** (of a person) speaking sharply and briefly; curt; abrupt (指人)说话尖刻而简短, 简单粗暴, 唐突无礼: *She was rather short with him when he asked for help.* 他请她帮帮忙, 她却不客气地把他顶了回去. **(b)** (of a remark or sb's manner of speaking) expressed in few words; curt (指言语或说话方式)简短的, 唐突无礼的: *He gave her a short answer.* 他给了她一个简短生硬的回答. ○ *All his observations were short and to the point.* 他的观察报告都很简单扼要. **6** **(a)** (of a fielder or his position in cricket) relatively near the batsman (指板球运动的外场员或其位置)距击球员较近的: *short leg, slip, etc* 距击球员近的在其左侧的、在其右后侧的 ... 外场员. **(b)** (of a bowled ball in cricket) bouncing relatively near to the bowler (指板球中投出的球)反弹至较近投球手的位置. **7** (of vowels or syllables) pronounced for a relatively brief time (指元音或音节)短音的: *the short vowel in 'pull' and the long vowel in 'pool'* 在 pull 一字中的短元音和在 pool 一字中的长元音. **8** (of an alcoholic drink) small and strong, made with spirits (指烈性酒)少而浓的, 烈性的: *I rarely have short drinks.* 我很少喝烈性酒. **9** [usu attrib 通常作定语] (*commerce* 商) (of a bill of exchange, etc) maturing at an early date (指汇票等)短期的, 即将兑现的: *a short bill, bond, etc* 短期票据、债券等 ○ *a short date*, ie an early date for the maturing of a bill, bond, etc 短期(兑现票据、债券等的). **10** [usu attrib 通常作定语] (of cake or pastry) rich and crumbly as a result of containing much fat (指饼或面点心)油酥的: *a flan with a short crust* 果馅酥饼. **11** (idm 习语) **be on short ˈrations** be allowed or able to have less than the usual quantity of food 食物配给量不足; 靠不足的食物配给量生活. **by a short ˈhead** **(a)** (in horse-racing) by a distance of less than the length of a horse's head (赛马)以不到一个马头的距离: *win/lose by a short head* 以不到一个马头的距离之差获胜[失败]. **(b)** by only a little 以极少的量: *I got 96 per cent, he got 94, so I beat him by a short head.* 我得96分, 他得94分, 我仅超过他一点. **for ˈshort** as an abbreviation 简略形式; 缩写; 简称: *Her name is 'Frances', or 'Fran' for short.* 她叫'弗朗西丝'或简称'弗朗'. **get/have sb by the short ˈhairs** (*infml* 口) get/have sb in a difficult position or at one's mercy 使某人处境困难; 完全操纵某人. **give full/short measure** ⇨MEASURE². **give sb/sth/get short ˈshrift** /ʃrɪft; ʃrɪft/ give sb/sth/get curt treatment or attention 怠慢某人[某事物]; 受冷遇: *He went to complain to the boss, but got very short shrift: she told him to get out and stay out* 他到老板那儿去投诉, 但老板态度冷淡: 她叫他出去上一边呆着去. **in long/short pants** ⇨PANTS. **in the long/short term** ⇨TERM. **in ˈshort** in a few words; briefly 总之; 简言之: *Things couldn't be worse, financially: in short, we're bankrupt.* 在财务方面已经糟得不能再糟了: 总之一句话, 我们破产了. **in short ˈorder** quickly and without fuss 迅速而直截了当地: *When the children are naughty she deals with them in very short order: they're sent straight to bed.* 孩子们一淘气她有个干脆的办法: 马上打发他们上床睡觉. **in short supply** not plentiful; scarce 不充裕; 供应不足. **little/nothing short of sth** little/nothing less than sth; almost sth 不亚于某事物; 几乎就是: *Our escape was little short of miraculous.* 我们能够逃出来简直是奇迹. **make short work of sth/sb** deal with, or dispose of sth/sb quickly 迅速处理某事物或对付某人: *make short work of one's meal* 很快吃完饭 ○ *The team made short work of their opponents.* 这个队一下子就把对方压倒了. **on a short ˈfuse** likely to get angry quickly and easily 易怒的; 脾气暴躁的: *Don't irritate her, she's on a short fuse today.* 别惹她, 她今天动不动就发火. **out of/short of breath** ⇨BREATH. **(on) short ˈcommons** (*dated* 旧) not having enough to eat 没有足够的食物吃. **a short ˈcut** **(a)** route that makes a journey, walk, etc shorter 近路; 捷径: *I took a short cut across the field to get to school.* 我穿过田野抄近路去上学. **(b)** way of doing sth more efficiently, quickly, etc 更快、更有效等的办事方法: *Becoming a doctor requires years of training — there are really no short cuts.* 当医生需要多年的学习和锻炼 —— 实无捷径可言. **ˌshort and ˈsweet** (*often ironic* 常作反语) brief but pleasant 简短而愉快的: *I only needed two minutes with the doctor — the visit was short and sweet.* 我找医生治病只用了两分钟 —— 别管受罪不受罪, 反正时间短. **thick as two short planks** ⇨THICK. ▷ **short·ness** *n* [U].

□ **ˈshortbread** *n* [U] crumbly dry cake made with flour, sugar and much butter 油酥甜饼(由面粉、糖、黄油制成).

ˈshortcake *n* [U] **(a)** (*Brit*) = SHORTBREAD. **(b)** dessert made from a biscuit dough or sponge mixture with cream and fruit on top 油酥糕饼(在发酵面团上覆奶油、水果做成的甜食): *strawberry shortcake* 草莓油酥糕饼.

ˌshort-ˈchange *v* [Tn] cheat (sb), esp by giving him less than the correct change²(4) (故意)少找给(某人)钱.

ˌshort ˈcircuit (also *infml* 口语作 **short**) (usu faulty) connection in an electric circuit, by which the current flows along a shorter route than the normal one 电路短路. **ˌshort-ˈcircuit** (also *infml* 口语作 **short**) *v* **1** [I, Tn] (cause sth to) have a short circuit (使某用电器)短路: *The lights short-circuited when I joined up the wires.* 我一接上电线, 电灯就短路了. ○ *You've short-circuited the washing-machine.* 你把洗衣机弄短路了. **2** [Tn] (*fig* 比喻) avoid (sth); bypass 避开(某事物); 绕过: *short-circuit the normal procedures to get sth done quickly* 为尽快办成某事不循正常手续.

ˈshortcoming *n* (usu *pl* 通常作复数) failure to be of a required standard; fault 缺点; 缺陷: *a system/person with many shortcomings* 有许多缺点的体系[人].

ˈshortfall *n* **~ (in sth)** deficit 赤字; 亏空: *a shortfall in the annual budget* 年度预算中的不足.

ˈshorthand (also *esp US* **stenography**) *n* [U] method of writing rapidly, using special quickly-written symbols 速记法: [attrib 作定语] *a shorthand course, typist, letter* 速记课程、打字员、信.

ˌshort-ˈhanded *adj* [usu pred 通常作表语] not having enough workers, helpers, etc 人手不足: *The shop is short-handed, so we are all having to work harder.* 店里人手不足, 所以我们都得勤奋些.

ˈshorthorn *n* breed of cattle with short curved horns 短角牛.

ˈshort list small number, esp of candidates for a job, selected from a larger number, and from which the final selection is to be made 决选名单(从多数人中挑出的少数候选人, 以备从中选出所需的人, 尤指应征职务者): *draw up a short list* 拟定一份决选名单 ○ *Are you on the short list?* 你在决选名单上吗? **ˈshort-list** *v* [Tn, Tn·pr] **~ sb (for sth)** put sb on a short list 将某人列入决选名单: *Have you been short-listed for the post?* 已经把你列入该工作的决选名单上了吗?

short-lived /ˌʃɔːtˈlɪvd; *US* ˈlaɪvd; ʃɔrtˈlaɪvd/ *adj* lasting for a short time; brief 短命的; 短暂的: *a short-lived triumph, relationship* 短暂的胜利、关系 ○ *Her interest in tennis was very short-lived.* 她喜好网球只是昙花一现.

ˌshort ˈodds (in betting) nearly even odds, indicating a horse, etc that is likely to win (赌博中)可能赢的机会几乎均等.

ˌshort ˈorder (*US*) order for food that can be cooked quickly (点叫)快餐: [attrib 作定语] *a ˌshort-order ˈchef*

专做快餐的厨师.

ˌ**short-ˈrange** *adj* [usu attrib 通常作定语] **1** designed for or applying to a limited period of time 短期间的: *a ˌshort-range ˈplan, ˈproject, etc* 短期计划、项目等 ○ *ˌshort-range ˈweather forecasts*, ie for one or two days ahead 短期天气预报. **2** (of missiles, etc) designed to travel over relatively short distances (指导弹等)短程的, 近程的. ˌ**short ˈsight** ability to see clearly only what is close 近视. ˌ**short-ˈsighted** *adj* **1** suffering from short sight 近视的. **2** (*fig* 比喻) having or showing an inability to foresee what will happen 目光短浅的; 无远见的: *a short-sighted person, attitude, plan* 目光短浅的人、看法、计划.

ˌ**short-ˈstaffed** *adj* [usu pred 通常作表语] not having enough staff; understaffed 人员不足: *We're very short-staffed in the office this week.* 本星期我们办公室人手不够.

ˌ**short ˈstory** piece of prose fiction that is shorter than a novel, esp one that deals with a single event or theme 短篇小说.

ˌ**short ˈtemper** tendency to become angry quickly and easily 易怒; 脾气暴躁: *He has a very short temper.* 他脾气很暴躁.

ˌ**short-ˈtempered** *adj*: *Being tired often makes me short-tempered.* 我一累就容易发脾气.

ˌ**short-ˈterm** *adj* [usu attrib 通常作定语] of or for a short period 短期的: *a ˌshort-term ˈplan, ˈloan, aˈgreement, apˈpointment* 短期计划、贷款、协议、任命.

ˌ**short ˈtime** employment for less than the full working week 短工时雇用工作(每周开工不足者): *workers on short time* 短工时雇用的工人 ○ [attrib 作定语] *ˌshort-time ˈworking* 短工时的工作.

ˌ**short ˈwave** (*abbr* 缩写 **SW**) radio wave with a length between 100 and 10 metres 短波(波长在100米与10米之间的无线电波): [attrib 作定语] *a ˌshort-wave ˈradio, ˈbroadcast, etc* 短波收音机、广播等.

ˌ**short-ˈwinded** *adj* easily getting breathless after exerting oneself, running, etc (用力、跑步等后就)容易气喘的.

short[2] /ʃɔːt; ʃɔrt/ *adv* **1** suddenly; abruptly 突然; 唐突地: *He stopped short when he heard his name called.* 他听到有人叫他, 就突然停了下来. **2** (idm 习语) **be caught/taken ˈshort** (*infml* 口) suddenly feel the need to go to the lavatory urgently 突然感到要去厕所. **bring/pull sb up short/sharply** ⇨ PULL[2]. **cut a long story short** ⇨ LONG[1]. **cut sth/sb ˈshort** bring sth/sb to an end before the usual or natural time; interrupt sth/sb 结束或中断某事物: *a career tragically cut short by illness* 因疾病而不幸中断的事业 ○ *The interviewer cut short his guest in mid-sentence.* 采访的人没等客人把那句话说完就打断了他的话. **fall short of sth** not reach sth 未达到(某目的): *The money collected fell short of the amount required.* 筹集的资金没达到所需的数额. ○ *His achievements had fallen short of his hopes.* 他的成就没有达到他期望的那么大. **go short (of sth)** not have enough (of sth) 缺少(某物); 欠缺: *If you earn well, you'll never go short.* 钱挣多了就什么都不缺了. ○ *The children must not go short of food.* 儿童不可缺少食物. **run short (of sth)** use up most of one's supply (of sth) 已快用完(某物): *Go and get some more oil so we don't run short.* 去多弄些油来以免到时候用光了. ○ *I'm late for work every day, and I'm running short of excuses.* 我每天迟到, 现在找不到什么借口了. **sell sth/sb short** ⇨ SELL. **short of sth** without sth; unless sth happens 没有(某事物); 除非(发生某事): *Short of a miracle, we're certain to lose now.* 除非出现奇迹, 不然我们现在是输定了. **stop short of sth/doing sth** ⇨ STOP[1].

short[3] /ʃɔːt; ʃɔrt/ *n* (*infml* 口) **1** = SHORT CIRCUIT (SHORT[1]). **2** short film, esp one shown before the main film at a cinema 短片(尤指正片之前放映的). **3** (esp *pl* 尤作复数) small strong alcoholic drink, esp of spirits 少量烈性酒精饮料; (尤指)烈酒. **4** (idm 习语) **the long and short of it** ⇨ LONG[2]. ▷ **short** *v* [I, Tn] (*infml* 口) = SHORT-CIRCUIT (SHORT[1]).

short·age /ˈʃɔːtɪdʒ; ˈʃɔrtɪdʒ/ *n* [C, U] lack of sth needed; deficiency 缺少; 不足; 短缺: *food, fuel, housing shortages* 食物、燃料、住房短缺 ○ *a shortage of rice, funds, equipment* 大米、资金、设备不足 ○ *owing to (a) shortage of staff* 由于人员缺乏 ○ *a shortage of 50 tons* 缺少50吨 ○ *There was no shortage of helpers.* 不缺帮手.

shorten /ˈʃɔːtn; ˈʃɔrtn̩/ *v* [I, Tn] (cause sth to) become shorter (使某物)变短: *The days are beginning to shorten*, eg in autumn. 白天开始变短了(如在秋季). ○ *take two links out of the chain to shorten it* 取下两个链环把链子弄短 ○ *They want to shorten the time it takes to make the car.* 他们想把生产汽车的时间缩短. Cf 参看 LENGTHEN (LENGTH).

short·en·ing /ˈʃɔːtnɪŋ; ˈʃɔrtn̩ɪŋ/ *n* [U] fat used to make pastry light and crumbly 用以使糕饼松脆的油脂.

shortly /ˈʃɔːtlɪ; ˈʃɔrtlɪ/ *adv* **1** in a short time; not long; soon 马上; 立刻; 不久: *shortly afterwards* 不久以后 ○ *coming shortly* 很快就来 ○ *shortly before noon* 中午前不久 ○ *I'll be with you shortly.* 我马上就来. **2** in a cross way; curtly 无礼地; 唐突地: *spoke to me rather shortly* 很不客气地和我说话.

shorts /ʃɔːts; ʃɔrts/ *n* [pl] **1** short trousers that do not reach the knee, eg as worn by children, or by adults playing sports or in hot weather 短裤: *a pair of tennis shorts* 一条网球短裤. **2** (*US*) men's underpants (男用)短内裤.

shorty /ˈʃɔːtɪ; ˈʃɔrtɪ/ *n* (*infml* 口) (**a**) (*sometimes derog* 有时作贬义) (used esp as a term of address 尤用作称谓) person who is shorter than average 矮个子. (**b**) garment that is shorter than average (比一般的)短的衣服: [attrib 作定语] *a shorty mackintosh* 短雨衣.

shot[1] /ʃɒt; ʃɑt/ *n* **1** [C] **~ (at sb/sth)** act of shooting a gun, etc; sound of this 射击; 发射; 枪炮声: *fire a few shots* 放几枪 ○ *hear shots in the distance* 听到远处的枪声 ○ *take a shot at the enemy* 朝敌人开枪 ○ *Two of her shots hit the centre of the target.* 她有两枪打中靶心. ○ (*fig* 比喻) *His remark was meant as a shot at me.* 他的话是冲着我来的. **2** [C] **~ (at sth/doing sth)** attempt to do sth; try 试图; 设法: *have a shot at (solving) this problem* 设法解决这一问题 ○ *After a few shots at guessing who did it, I gave up.* 到底是谁干的, 我猜了几次没猜着就不再猜了. **3** [C] stroke in cricket, tennis, billiards, etc or a kick in football (板球、网球、台球等中的)击球; (足球中的)踢: *a backhand shot* 反手抽击 ○ *Good shot!* 好球! ○ *The striker had/took a shot at goal*, ie tried to score. 前锋射门. **4** [C] (**a**) (*pl* unchanged 复数不变) (formerly) non-explosive ball of stone or metal shot from a cannon or gun (旧时)大炮或枪使用的无炸药的石弹丸或金属弹丸. Cf 参看 CARTRIDGE 1, SHELL 3. (**b**) (often 常作 **the shot**) [sing] heavy iron ball used in shot-put competitions (运动竞赛用的)铅球: *put* (ie throw) *the shot* 推铅球. **5** [U] (also **lead ˈshot**) large number of tiny balls or pellets of lead packed inside cartridges fired from shotguns (猎枪用的)铅沙弹. **6** [C] person with regard to his skill in shooting a gun, etc 射手; 枪手; 炮手: *a first-class, good, poor, etc shot* 第一流的、好的、差劲的…射手. **7** [C] (**a**) photograph or scene photographed 镜头; 景: *a long shot*, ie taken with a long distance between the camera and the thing photographed 远镜头 ○ *a shot of the politician making a speech* 政治家演讲的镜头. (**b**) single continuous film sequence photographed by one camera (电影中以同一摄影机拍摄的)连续镜头: *an action shot of a car chase* 汽车追赶动作的连续镜头. **8** [C] launch of a space rocket, missile, etc (宇宙火箭、导弹等的)发射: *the second space shot this year* 今年的第二次空间发射. **9** [C] (*infml* 口) injection of a drug, etc with a hypodermic needle 皮下注射(药物等): *Have you had your typhus shots yet?* 你打过斑疹伤寒防疫针了吗? **10** [C] (*infml* 口) small amount of whisky, gin, etc (威士忌、杜松子酒等的)少量: *a shot of vodka* 一点伏特加. **11** (idm 习语) **a big noise/shot** ⇨ BIG **call the shots/tune** ⇨ CALL[2]. **a leap/shot in the dark** ⇨ DARK[1]. **like a ˈshot** (*infml* 口) (**a**) at once; without hesitation 立刻; 毫不犹豫地: *If I had the chance to go, I'd take it like a shot.* 我要是有机会去, 我就不犹豫. (**b**) very fast 飞快地: *The dog was after the rabbit like a shot.* 那只狗飞快地追赶兔子. **a long shot** ⇨ LONG[1]. **not by a long chalk/shot** ⇨ LONG[1]. **a parting shot** ⇨ PARTING. **a shot in the ˈarm** thing that encourages or gives fresh energy to sb/sth 起鼓舞或振奋作用的事物: *The improved trade figures are a much-needed shot in the arm for the economy.* 贸易数额增长是当前极需的推动国民经济的因素.

□ ˈ**shotgun** *n* **1** gun for firing cartridges containing shot[1](5), eg at birds, rabbits, etc (发射铅沙弹的)猎枪(如用于打鸟、兔者). ⇨illus at GUN 见 GUN 插图. **2** (idm 习语) **a shotgun ˈwedding** wedding of two people who are or feel forced to marry, usu because the woman is pregnant 被迫举行的结婚(通常指已怀孕).

ˈshot-put *n* [sing] (also ˌ**putting the ˈshot**) sports contest in which athletes try to throw a shot[1](4b) as far as possible 推铅球; 掷铅球.

shot[2] /ʃɒt; ʃɑt/ *adj* **1 ~ (with sth)** (of cloth) woven or dyed so as to show different colours when looked at from different angles (指织物)(织得或染得)颜色闪变的(从不同角度看颜色不同): *shot silk* 闪光绸 ○ *a black curtain shot with silver* 闪银光的黑色帷幔 ○ (*fig* 比喻) *brown hair shot with grey* 花白的棕色头发. **2** [usu pred 通常作表语] (*infml* 口 *esp US*) worn out; used up; wrecked 筋疲力尽; 用旧; 耗尽; 毁坏: *Her patience was completely shot.* 她已忍无可忍. **3** (idm 习语) **shot through with sth** containing much of (a quality); suffused with sth 很有(某特质); 充满着: *conversation shot through with humour* 富于幽默的交谈 ○ *comedy shot through with sadness* 充满心酸的喜剧.

shot[3] *pt, pp* of SHOOT[1].

should[1] /ʃəd; ʃəd; *strong form* 强读式 ʃʊd; ʃud/ *modal v* (*neg* 否定式 **should not**, *contracted form* 缩约式 **shouldn't** /ˈʃʊdnt; ˈʃʊdn̩t/) **1** (**a**) (indicating obligation 用以表示义务或责任): *You shouldn't drink and drive.* 你不应该喝酒后开车. ○ *Visitors should inform the receptionist of their arrival.* 来宾在到达时应当知会接待员. ○ *We should have bought a new lock for the front door.* 我们本该买把新锁安在前门上. ⇨Usage 1 at MUST 见 MUST 所附用法第1项. (**b**) (indicating advice or recommendation 用以表示劝告或推荐): *He should stop smoking.* 他应该戒烟. ○ *You shouldn't leave a baby alone in the house.* 你不应该把幼儿一个人留在家里. ○ *They should have called the police.* 他们本应该叫警察的. ⇨ Usage 2 at MUST 见 MUST 所附用法第2项. **2** (drawing a tentative conclusion 用以表示试探性的推断): *We should arrive before dark.* 我们按说能在天黑前到达. ○ *The roads should be less crowded today.* 今天路上不致于那么拥挤了. ○ *I should have finished reading it by Friday.* 我大概到星期五能把它看完. ⇨ Usage 3 at MUST 见 MUST 所附用法第3项. **3** (*fml* 文) (used to describe the consequence of an imagined event 用以表达假定的结果): *If I was asked to work on Sundays I should resign.* 要是叫我星期天上班, 我就辞职. ○ *We should move to a larger house if we had the money.* 我们要是有钱就找个大房子住了. **4** (used in a *that*-clause after the *adjs anxious, sorry, concerned, happy, delighted,* etc 用在形容词 anxious、sorry、concerned、happy、delighted 等后接的 that 从句中): *I'm anxious that he should be well cared for.* 我盼望他能受到很好的照顾. ○ *We're sorry that you should feel uncomfortable.* 你觉得在这儿不舒服, 我们非常抱歉. ○ *That he should speak to you like that is quite astonishing.* 他竟然这样对你说话, 实在让人吃惊. ○ *I am delighted that he should take that view.* 他有那种看法, 我十分高兴. **5** (used after *if* and *in case*, or with subject and *v* reversed, to suggest that an event is unlikely to happen 用于 if 和 in case 之后或将主语与动词倒置, 表示某事不太可能发生): *If you should change your mind, do let me know.* 万一你要改变主意, 一定要告诉我. ○ *If he should have forgotten to go to the airport, nobody will be there to meet her.* 要是他忘了去机场, 就没人去那儿接她了. ○ *Should anyone phone* (ie If anyone phones), *please tell them I'm busy.* 有人打电话来, 就说我很忙. **6** (*fml* 文) (used after *so that/in order that* to express purpose 用于 so that/in order that 之后表示目的或动机): *He put the cases in the car so that he should be able to make an early start.* 他把箱子放在汽车里, 这样他就可以早点动身了. ○ *She repeated the instructions slowly in order that he should understand.* 她把那些指示慢慢重复了一遍好让他听明白. **7** (**a**) (used to make polite requests 用作表示请求的客气说法): *I should like to make a phone call, if possible.* 劳驾, 我想打个电话. ○ *We should be grateful for your help.* 承您协助, 不胜感激. Cf 参看 WOULD[1] 2a. (**b**) (used with *imagine, say, think,* etc to give tentative opinions 与 imagine、say、think 等连用, 表达不成熟的意见): *I should imagine it will take about three hours.* 我想得花大约三个钟头. ○ *I should say she's over forty.* 我说她有四十多岁了. ○ *'Is this long enough?' 'I should think so.'* '这个够长吗?' '我看可以了.' **8** (**a**) (used with question words to express lack of interest, disbelief, etc 与疑问词连用, 表示不感兴趣、难以相信等): *How should I know?* 我怎么知道呢? ○ *Why should he think that?* 他怎么那么想呢? (**b**) (used with question words to express surprise 与疑问词连用表示惊讶): *I was thinking of going to see John when who should appear but John himself.* 我还想去看约翰, 想不到约翰来了. ○ *I turned round on the bus and who should be sitting behind me but my ex-wife.* 我在公共汽车上转过身来, 谁料后面坐的竟是我的前妻.

should[2] *pt* of SHALL.

shoulder /ˈʃəʊldə(r); ˈʃoldɚ/ *n* **1** [C] (**a**) part of the body where an arm, a foreleg or a wing is attached; part of the human body from this point to the neck 胳膊、前腿或翅膀与身体相连接的部位; 肩; 肩膀; 肩胛: *look back over one's shoulder* 回头看 ○ *shrug one's shoulders* 耸肩 ○ *This coat is too narrow across the shoulders.* 这件大衣肩部太窄. ⇨illus at HUMAN 见 HUMAN 插图. ⇨ Usage at BODY. (**b**) part of a garment covering this (衣服的)肩部: *a jacket with padded shoulders* 有垫肩的夹克. (**c**) [C, U] piece of meat cut from the upper foreleg of an animal 前腿肉(从动物前腿上部切下的肉): *some shoulder of lamb, beef, etc* 羊、牛等的前腿肉. **2** **shoulders** [pl] (**a**) part of the back between the shoulders 背的上部; 肩胛: *a person with broad shoulders* 肩宽的人 ○ *a coalman carrying a sack on his shoulders* 肩上扛着麻袋的送煤人 ○ *give a child a ride on one's shoulders* 让子孩骑在肩膀上. (**b**) (*fig* 比喻) a person, with regard to the responsibilities, blame, etc he must bear 有责任的或须承担责任的人: *shift the blame onto sb else's shoulders* 把责任推给别人承担 ○ *The burden of guilt has been lifted from my shoulders.* 我已卸下了负疚的重担. ○ *The duty fell upon her shoulders.* 这一责任落在了她的肩上. **3** [C] part of a thing resembling a human shoulder in shape or position, eg on a bottle, tool, mountain 形状或部位似肩的部分(如瓶、工具、山的). ⇨illus at MOUNTAIN 见 MOUNTAIN 插图. **4** (idm 习语) **be/stand head and shoulders above sb/sth** ⇨ HEAD[1] **a chip on one's shoulder** ⇨ CHIP[1]. **give sb/get the cold shoulder** ⇨COLD[1]. **have a good head on one's shoulders** ⇨HEAD[1]. **an old head on young shoulders** ⇨OLD. **put one's shoulder to the ˈwheel** work hard at a task 努力工作: *Come on, everyone, shoulders to the wheel — we've got a lot to do.* 快, 各位, 加把劲——我们有很多事情要做. **rub shoulders with sb** ⇨RUB[1]. ˌ**shoulder to ˈshoulder** (**a**) side by side 肩并肩: *soldiers standing shoulder to shoulder* 肩并肩站着的士兵. (**b**) working, fighting, etc together; united 并肩工作、战斗等; 团结一致: *shoulder to shoulder with one's fellow-workers in the dispute* 辩论中与同事齐心协力. **straight from the shoulder** ⇨ STRAIGHT[2].

▷ **shoulder** *v* **1** [Tn] (**a**) put (sth) on one's shoulder(s) 扛, 担, 挑, 掮(某物): *She shouldered her rucksack and set off along the road.* 她背起帆布背包就上路了. (**b**) (*fig* 比喻) take (guilt, responsibility, etc) upon oneself 承担(罪责、责任等): *shoulder the duties of chairman* 负起主席的责任 ○ *She won't shoulder all the blame for the mistake.* 她不承担该过失的全部责任. **2** [Tn·pr, Tn·p] push (sb/sth) with one's shoulder 用肩顶(某人［某物］): *shoulder sb to one side* 用肩膀把某人顶到一旁 ○ *He shouldered off a defender and shot at goal.* 他用肩膀挡开防守队员后射门. **3** (phr v) **shoulder one's way in, through, past, etc** move in the specified direction by pushing with one's shoulder(s) 用肩膀沿某方向挤出一条路: *shoulder one's way into the room* 用肩膀挤着进入房间 ○ *shoulder one's way through (the crowd)* 用肩膀挤着穿过人群.

□ ˈ**shoulder-bag** *n* bag hung over the shoulder by a long strap 背在肩上的手提包.

ˈ**shoulder-blade** *n* either of the two large flat bones at the top of the back; scapula 肩胛骨. ⇨illus at SKELETON 见 SKELETON 插图.

ˈ**shoulder-strap** *n* (**a**) narrow strip of material that goes over the shoulder to support a bra, nightdress, etc (乳罩上、睡衣裙上及儿童服装等的)肩带. (**b**) narrow strap on the shoulder of a military uniform, a raincoat, an overcoat, etc (军服、雨衣、大衣等的)肩带.

shout /ʃaʊt; ʃaʊt/ *n* **1** loud call or cry 呼喊; 喊叫: *shouts of joy, alarm, excitement, etc* 欢呼、惊叫、激动的喊叫 ○ *Her warning shout came too late.* 她发出的警告呼喊声来得太晚了. ○ *She was greeted with shouts of 'Long live the President!'* 大家欢迎她, 高呼着'总统万岁!' **2** (*sl esp Austral or NZ* 俚, 尤用于澳大利亚或新西兰) person's turn to buy drinks 轮到某人请喝饮料: *What will you have? It's my shout.* 你要喝什么? 该我请客了.

▷ **shout** *v* **1** (**a**) [I, Ipr, Ip, Cn·a, Dpr·f, Dpr·t no passive 不用于被动语态, Dpr·w] **~ (at/to sb)**; **~ (out)** speak or call out in a loud voice 大声说; 喊; 呼; 叫: *shout for joy* 欢呼 ○ *shout (out) in pain* 痛得大叫 ○ *We had to shout because the music was so loud.* 因为音乐音量太大, 我们只好大声叫喊. ○ *Don't shout at me!* 别冲着我喊! ○ *She shouted to me across the room.* 她在房间的另一端向我喊. ○ *She shouted herself hoarse cheering on the team.* 她为该队喝彩把嗓子都喊哑了. ○ *He shouted to me that the boat was sinking.* 他对我大声喊叫说船要沉了. ○ *I shouted to him to shut the gate.* 我大声告诉他把门关上. (**b**) [Tn, Tn·pr, Tn·p, Tf no passive 不用于被动语态] **~ sth (at/to sb)**; **~ sth (out)** say sth in a loud voice 大声说(某事): *I shouted (out) my name to the teacher.* 我向老师大声说出我的名字. ○ *'Go back,' she shouted.* '回去,'她喊道. ○ *They shouted their disapproval*, ie expressed it by shouting. 他们大声喊着反对. ○ *She shouted that she couldn't hear properly.* 她大声说她听不清楚. **2** (phr v) **shout sb down** shout to prevent sb from speaking 大声喊叫以阻止某人说话: *The crowd shouted the speaker down.* 群众高声喊叫把演讲人的声音压了下去. **shout·ing** *n* [U] **1** shouts 叫; 喊: [attrib 作定语] *within shouting distance*, ie near enough to hear sth shouted 在能听到彼此喊声的距离. **2** (idm 习语) **be all over ˌbar the ˈshouting** (of a performance, contest, etc) be concluded or decided, with only the applause, the official announcement, etc to follow (指演出、竞赛等)大局已定, 胜负已分(只剩下欢呼声、大会正式宣布等): *Now that most of the election results have been declared, it's all over bar the shouting.* 因为选举结果多已公布, 可谓大局已定.

NOTE ON USAGE 用法: Compare **cry (out), shout, yell** and **scream.** 试比较**cry (out)**、**shout**、**yell**、**scream**的用法. These verbs indicate people making different kinds of noise for various reasons. 这四个动词指人们因不同原因而发出各种声音. We **cry out** by making a sharp noise as an automatic reaction to pain, surprise, etc ☆ **cry out** 指发出尖利的声音, 是痛苦、惊讶等的自然反应: *He cried out in fright as the dark figure approached.* 那个黑影向他逼近, 他吓得叫了出来. We **shout** in anger or to get attention ☆ **shout** 是因愤怒或为引起注意而发出的声音: *I don't like our teacher; he's always shouting at us.* 我不喜欢我们的老师, 他动不动就大声说我们. ○ *I had to shout to make myself heard.* 我得大声嚷, 否则根本听不见我的声音. **Yell** is to make a high-pitched shout of pain, fear or excitement ☆ **yell** 是指因痛苦、恐惧或激动而尖叫: *We heard him yelling for help.* 我们听见他高呼救命. It can also indicate loud shouting 这个词还可指大声呼喊: *You don't have to yell; I can hear you.* 你用不着喊, 我听得见. People **scream** in pain, fear or excitement. ☆ **scream** 指因痛苦、恐惧或激动而喊叫. It is a very loud, high-pitched noise 这种喊叫, 声音大而尖利: *The baby woke up screaming.* 那婴儿醒来时尖声哭叫. These verbs can all be used instead of 'say' to indicate ways of speaking 这几个动词都可用以替换say, 表示说话的方式: *'Get out!' she screamed/yelled/shouted.* '走开!'她高声喊道. ○ *'Who's there?' he cried (out).* '谁呀?'他嚷道.

shove /ʃʌv; ʃʌv/ *v* **1** [I, Tn, Tn·pr, Tn·p] push (sb/sth) roughly 乱推, 挤, 撞(某人[某物]): *a crowd pushing and shoving to get in* 推推搡搡往里挤的人群 ○ *Who shoved me?* 谁撞我了? ○ *He shoved her out of the way.* 他把她推到了一边. ○ *The policeman shoved me aside.* 警察把我挤到一旁. **2** [Tn·pr, Tn·p] (*infml* 口) put (sth) casually (in a place) 随意将(某物)放在(某处): *shove papers (away) in a drawer* 把文件往抽屉里胡乱一塞 ○ *'Where shall I put the case?' 'Shove it on top of the car.'* '我把箱子放在哪里?''先放在汽车顶上吧.' **3** (idm 习语) **put/shove/stick one's oar in** ⇨OAR. **4** (phr v) **shove off** (**a**) push a boat out onto the water away from the shore (eg by pushing the shore with a pole) 将船推离岸边(如用篙撑). (**b**) (*infml* 口) (often imperative 常用于祈使句) leave; go away 离开; 走开: *You aren't wanted here, so shove off!* 这儿不需要你, 走开! **shove up** (*infml* 口) move along, esp in order to make more room 向前移动(尤指为腾出地方): *We can get one more in if you shove up.* 向前挤一挤, 我们还能再进一个人.

▷ **shove** *n* (usu *sing* 通常作单数) rough push 乱推; 挤; 撞: *give sb/sth a good shove* 猛推某人[某物].

□ **shove-halfpenny** /ʃʌv ˈheɪpnɪ; ˈʃʌvˈhepənɪ/ *n* [U] game played in pubs, etc, in which coins are pushed with the hand along a marked board (在酒馆等玩的)推硬币游戏.

shovel /ˈʃʌvl; ˈʃʌvḷ/ *n* **1** tool like a spade with curved edges, used for moving earth, snow, sand, etc 铲; 铁锹. ⇨illus at SPADE 见SPADE插图. **2** part of a large earth-moving machine that scoops up earth, etc like a shovel 挖土机或推土机前的铲形部分.

▷ **shovel** *v* (**-ll-**; *US* **-l-**) **1** [Tn, Tn·pr, Tn·p] lift or move (sth) with a shovel (用铲子或铁锹)铲(某物): *spend hours shovelling snow* 用几个小时铲雪 ○ *shovel sand into the hole* 把沙子铲进洞里 ○ *shovel up coal into the container* 把煤铲起来放进箱子里 ○ (*fig derog* 比喻, 贬) *shovelling food into their mouths* (他们)把食物大块大块地塞进嘴里. **2** [Tn, Cn·a] make or clear (sth) by shovelling 铲成, 铲净(某物): *shovel a path through the snow* 在雪中铲出一条路 ○ *shovel the pavement clear of snow* 把人行道上的雪铲干净.

shov·el·ful /-fʊl; -fʊl/ *n* amount that a shovel can hold 一铲或一锹之量: *two shovelfuls of earth* 两铲的土.

S

show[1] /ʃəʊ; ʃo/ *n* **1** [C] any type of public entertainment, eg a circus, a theatre performance, or a radio or TV programme 演出; 表演; 节目: *a TV quiz show* 电视上的智力竞赛节目 ○ *a comedy show on radio* 收音机里的喜剧节目 ○ *She has her own chat show.* 她有个个人漫谈节目. ○ *The most successful shows in the London theatre are often musicals.* 伦敦剧院最叫座的剧目往往是歌舞喜剧. **2** [C] public display or exhibition, eg of things in a competition, new products, etc 展览; 展览会: *a flower, horse, cattle show* 花卉、马、牛的展览会 ○ *the motor show*, ie where new models of cars, etc are displayed 汽车展览会 ○ *the Lord Mayor's Show*, ie a procession through the streets of London when a new Mayor is appointed 伦敦市长的就职游行. ⇨Usage at DEMONSTRATION 用法见DEMONSTRATION. **3** [C, U] (**a**) thing done to give a certain impression, often a false one; outward appearance 表面上做出的样子(常指虚伪的); 外观: *a show of defiance, strength, friendship, sympathy* 做出的蔑视、强大、友好、同情的样子 ○ *His public expressions of grief are nothing but show.* 他公开表示悲痛只不过是做做样子而已. (**b**) splendid or pompous display 炫耀; 夸示: *a fine show of blossom on the apple trees* 苹果树上盛开的花朵 ○ *all the glitter and show of the circus* 马戏团的光彩华丽的洋洋大观 ○ *They are too fond of show*, ie too ostentatious. 他们太好炫耀. **4** [C usu *sing* 通常作单数] (*Brit infml* 口) thing done or performed in a specified way 表现: *a poor show*, ie sth done badly 表现不佳 ○ *put up a good show*, eg do well in examinations or a contest 表现良好. **5** [C] (*infml* 口) anything that is happening; organization, business or undertaking 事情; 组织; 事业; 企业: *She runs the whole show.* 她负责全部业务. ○ *Let's get this show moving*, ie start work. 咱们先干起来吧. ○ *This is the manager's show: you must ask him about it.* 这是经理的事: 你得问他. **6** (idm 习语) **for ˈshow** intended to be seen but not used 为了给人看而不是为了使用: *She only has those books for show — she never reads them.* 她的那些书只是装门面的——她从来不看. **ˌgood ˈshow!** (*Brit infml* 口) (used to express approval or congratulation when sth has been done well 用以表示赞成或祝贺某事干得好): *You passed your exams? Good show!* 你考试及格了? 好极了! **on ˈshow** being displayed 在展览中; 陈列着: *All the new products were on show at the exhibition.* 展览会上陈列着所有的新产品. **a show of ˈhands** raising of hands by a group of people to vote for or against sth 举手表决(赞成或反对某事): *The issue was* *decided by a show of hands.* 这件事是通过举手表决决定的. ○ *Who is in favour of the proposal? Can I have a show of hands, please?* 谁赞成这项建议? 请大家举手表决好吗? **steal the scene/show** ⇨STEAL. **stop the show** ⇨STOP[1].

▷ **showy** *adj* (**-ier**, **-iest**) (*often derog* 常作贬义) attracting attention through being bright, colourful or exaggerated 夸示的; 炫示的: *a showy dress, hair-style, manner* 花哨的连衣裙、招眼的发型、做作的态度. **show·ily** /-ɪlɪ; -əlɪ/ *adv*: *dress very showily* 穿得十分艳丽. **showi·ness** *n* [U].

□ **showbiz** /ˈʃəʊbɪz; ˈʃobɪz/ *n* [U] (*infml* 口) = SHOW BUSINESS.

ˈ**show business** business of professional entertainment, esp in the theatre, in films, in TV, etc 演艺业, 娱乐界(尤指戏剧、电影、电视等): *working in show business* 在娱乐界工作 ○ [attrib 作定语] *show-business people, news* 娱乐界人士、新闻.

ˈ**show-case** *n* **1** case with a glass top or sides, for displaying articles in a shop, museum, etc (商店、博物馆等的)玻璃柜橱, 陈列橱. **2** (*fig* 比喻) any means of showing sth favourably 显示某事物优点的方法: *The programme is a show-case for young talent.* 该计划旨在展示年轻人的才华.

ˈ**show-down** *n* final test, argument or fight to settle a dispute (为解决争端的)最后的较量: *The two contenders for the world championship will meet for a show-down next month.* 两位世界冠军竞争者将于下月一决雌雄. ○ *Management are seeking a show-down with the unions on the issue of illegal strikes.* 资方正在就非法罢工问题与工会摊牌.

ˈ**showgirl** *n* girl (usu one of a group) who sings and dances in a musical show (歌舞喜剧中的)歌舞女演员.

ˈ**show-jumping** *n* [U] sport of riding a horse to jump over barriers, fences, etc 骑马跳越障碍运动: [attrib 作定语] *a show-jumping competition* 骑马跳越障碍比赛.

showman /-mən; -mən/ *n* (*pl* **-men** /-mən; -mən/) **1** person who organizes public entertainments, eg musicals, pop concerts, etc 演出主持人(如歌舞喜剧、流行音乐会等的). **2** person who is skilled in showmanship 善于引起公众注意的人: *He's always been a bit of a showman,* ie fond of drawing attention to himself. 他总是爱出风头.

ˈ**showmanship** *n* [U] skill in attracting public attention, eg to sth one wishes to sell or to one's own abilities 引起大家注意的技巧(如招揽生意或展示能力).

ˈ**show-piece** *n* thing that is an excellent example of its type and is therefore used for display 供展出的样品.

ˈ**show-place** *n* place that is attractive or interesting, eg for tourists 吸引人的或有趣的地方(如游客去处): *old castles, palaces and other show-places* 古老的城堡、皇宫以及其他游览胜地.

ˈ**showroom** *n* place where things, eg goods for sale, are put on display 商品陈列室.

show[2] /ʃəʊ; ʃo/ *v* (*pt* **showed**, *pp* **shown** /ʃəʊn; ʃon/ or, rarely, 罕读作 **showed**) **1** (**a**) [Tn, Cn·a, Cn·g, Dn·n, Dn·pr] **~ sb/sth (to sb)** cause sb/sth to be seen; display sb/sth 使某人[某物]被看见; 显示或展示某人[某物]: *You must show your ticket at the barrier.* 必须在检票处出示票. ○ *The film is being shown at the local cinema.* 本地影院正在上映这部电影. ○ *Her paintings are being shown* (ie exhibited) *at a gallery in London.* 她的画正在伦敦的一个美术馆里展出. ○ *The photo shows her dressed in black.* 在这张照片里, 她穿着黑衣服. ○ *In the portrait he is shown lying on a sofa.* 在这张画像中画着他躺在沙发上. ○ *He showed me his pictures.* 他给我看了他的照片. ○ *She has shown them to all her friends.* 她把那些东西给她所有的朋友都看过了. (**b**) [Tn, Tf, Tw] allow (sth) to be seen; reveal 使(某物)被看见; 显露: *A dark suit doesn't show the dirt so much.* 黑色的套装禁脏. ○ *My shoes are showing signs of wear.* 我的鞋已经显得旧了. **2** [I, Ipr, Ip] be visible or noticeable 看得见; 可察觉出: *Your petticoat is showing, Jane.* 简, 你的衬裙露出来了. ○ *Does the scar still show?* 伤疤还看得出来吗? ○ *His fear showed in his eyes.* 他眼里露出恐惧的目光. ○ *Her laziness showed in her exam results.* 她平时懒惰从她的考试成绩可以看得出来. ○ *His shirt was so thin that his vest showed through (it).* 他的衬衫很薄, 连里面穿的背心都能看见. **3** [Tn no passive 不用于被动语态, Dn·n, Dn·w] point (sth) out; indicate 指出(某物); 指示; 告知: *The clock shows half past two.* 时钟的针指着两点半. ○ *Show me which picture you drew.* 告诉我哪张是你画的. **4** [Tn no passive 不用于被动语态] (**a**) **~ itself** be visible 呈现; 可看出: *His annoyance showed itself in his face.* 从他的脸上可以看出他有烦恼. ○ *The sun didn't show itself all day.* 一整天没出太阳. (**b**) **~ oneself** be present; appear 出席; 出现: *He showed himself briefly at the party.* 他在聚会上匆匆露了一面. ○ *The leader rarely shows herself in public.* 这位领导她很少在公众场合露面. **5** [Tn, Dn·n, Dn·pr] treat (sb) with (kindness, respect, cruelty, etc); give; grant 对(某人)(和蔼、尊敬、残忍等); 给; 施予: *The king often shows mercy (to prisoners).* 这位国王常(对囚犯)大发慈悲. ○ *The priest showed me great understanding.* 神父对我非常理解. ○ *They showed nothing but contempt for him.* 他们对他轻蔑已极. **6** [Tn, Cn·a, Cn·n no passive 不用于被动语态] give evidence or proof of being or having (sth) 证明、证实或表明为或有(某特质): *show no signs of intelligence* 表现得一点也不聪明 ○ *a soldier who showed great courage/showed himself to be very brave* 表现得非常勇敢的士兵 ○ *She showed herself unable to deal with money.* 她做出的事表明她不善理财. ○ *He showed himself (to be) a dishonest rascal.* 他的表现证明他是个无赖. **7** [Tn, Tf, Tw, Tnt, Dn·n, Dn·pr, Dn·f, Dn·w] **~sth (to sb)** make sth clear; demonstrate sth; prove sth 使某事物清楚; 阐明或证明某事物: *show the falseness of her claims/that her claims are false* 证明她的说法不确 ○ *show (him) how to do it/what to do* 告诉(他)如何做[做什么] ○ *His expression shows how unhappy he is.* 他的表情说明他非常不愉快. ○ *Her new book shows her to be a first-rate novelist.* 她的新书表明她是第一流的小说家. ○ *They were shown the tragedy of war.* 他们了解到了战争的悲惨. ○ *She showed her methods of analysis to her pupils.* 她向学生展示自己的分析方法. **8** [Tn·pr, Tn·p] lead or conduct (sb) to the specified place or in the specified direction 引领(某人); 引导; 指引: *We were shown into the waiting-room.* 把我们带到了候客室. ○ *Please show this lady out (of the building).* 请把这位太太送出去. ○ *The usherette showed us to our seats.* 女引座员把我们带到座位上. ○ *Our trained guides will show you round (the museum).* 我们这些训练有素的导游来带你们参观(博物馆). **9** [Tn no passive 不用于被动语态] (*infml* 口) prove one's ability or worth to (sb) 向(某人)证实自己有能力或价值: *They think I can't win, but I'll show them.* 他们认为我赢不了, 但我要让他们看看. **10** (*sl* 俚 *esp US*) appear; show up 出现; 露面: *I waited for you all morning but you never showed.* 我整个上午都在等你, 但是没见到你的影子. **11** [I] (*US*) win a place (third or better) in a horse race 赛马中得名次(前三名). **12** (idm 习语) **do/show sb a kindness** ⇨KINDNESS (KIND[1]). **fly/show/wave the flag** ⇨FLAG[1]. **go to ˈshow** serve to prove or demonstrate 用以证明或显示: *You've got no money now. It all/only goes to show you shouldn't gamble.* 你现在没钱了, 这完全证明你不应该赌博. **show (sb) a clean pair of ˈheels** (*infml often joc* 口, 常作戏谑语) run away 跑掉; 溜之大吉. **show sb the ˈdoor** ask sb to leave 叫某人离开; 逐出: *After having insulted his host, he was shown the door.* 他侮辱了主人, 结果被轰了出去. **show one's ˈface** appear before people 露面: *She daren't show her face in the street.* 她不敢在街上露面. **show one's ˈhand/ˈcards** reveal one's intentions or plans 表明意图或计划: *I suspect they're planning something but they haven't shown their hand yet.* 我怀疑他们在策划什么事, 但是他们还没表露出来. **show sb/know/learn the ropes** ⇨ROPE. **show a ˈleg** (*infml joc* 口, 谑) get out of bed 起床. **show one's teeth** use one's power or authority to intimidate or punish sb 用权力或权威来吓唬或惩罚某人. **show (sb) the ˈway** (**a**) tell sb how to get to a certain place 告诉(某人)怎样到达某处: *show him the way to the station* 告诉他到车站怎么走. (**b**) be an example to sb 成为某人的榜样: *Let's hope her bravery will show the way for other young people.* 希望她的英雄行为能成为年轻人的榜样. **show the white ˈfeather** act in a cowardly way; show fear 示弱; 胆怯. **show ˈwilling** show that one is ready to do sth, eg work hard, help, etc 表示愿意做某事(如努力工作、

帮助别人等): *I don't think I'm needed as a helper, but I'll go anyway, just to show willing.* 我想并不需要我帮忙, 但我还是要去, 以示诚意. **(have) something, nothing, etc to show for sth** (have) something, nothing, etc as a result of sth 在某事物上有些、没有成果等: *All those years of hard work, and nothing to show for it!* 苦干了那么多年, 却拿不出成绩来. ○ *I've only got £100 to show for all the stuff I sold.* 我卖了那么多东西, 只得到区区100英镑. **13** (phr v) **show off** (*infml often derog* 口, 常作贬义) try to impress others with one's abilities, wealth, intelligence, etc 炫耀自己的能力、财富、智慧等: *Do stop showing off — it's embarrassing.* 快别卖弄了——太难为情了. ○ *The child danced around the room, showing off to everybody.* 那个孩子满屋子跳舞, 向大家显摆一番. **show sb/sth off** draw people's attention to sb/sth 吸引大家注意某人[某事物]: *a dress that shows off her figure well* 能充分衬托出她那身段的连衣裙 ○ *She was showing off her new husband at the party.* 她在聚会上引着大家注意她的新郎. ○ *He likes showing off how well he speaks French.* 他喜欢引人注意到他法语说得非常好. **show up** (*infml* 口) arrive, often after a delay; appear 到来(通常在耽搁一段时间后); 出现: *It was ten o'clock when he finally showed up.* 十点钟时他终于到了. ○ *We were hoping for a full team today but only five players showed up.* 今天我们希望全体队员都到齐, 但结果只到了五个人. **show (sth) up** (cause sth to) become visible (使某物)显现出来: *The dust on the shelf shows up in the sunlight.* 在阳光照射下能看见架子上有灰尘. ○ *Close inspection shows up the cracks in the stonework.* 仔细观察就能发现这石雕中有裂缝. **show sb up** (*infml* 口) make sb feel embarrassed by behaving badly in his company 因举止失当使某人羞与为伍: *He showed me up by falling asleep at the concert.* 他在音乐会上睡着了, 弄得我很难为情. **show sb up (as/for sth/to be sth)** show sb to be (dishonest, disreputable, etc) 显露某人(不诚实、不名誉等): *His diary shows him up as/shows him up to have been a greedy, arrogant man.* 他的日记暴露出他又贪婪又傲慢.

▷ **show·ing** *n* **1** act of showing 演出; 表演: *two showings of the film daily* 该电影每天放映两场. **2** (usu *sing* 通常作单数) record or evidence of the success, quality, etc of sb/sth (某人[某事物]的)功过、好坏、表现等: *the company's poor financial showing in recent years* 公司近年来的财务不佳情况 ○ *On* (ie Judging by) *last week's showing, the team is unlikely to win today.* 按上星期的情况判断, 这个队今天不太可能赢.

□ **'show-off** *n* (*derog* 贬) person who tries to impress others in speech or actions 爱炫耀的人: *Take no notice of him — you know what a show-off he is.* 别理睬他——你知道他多喜欢卖弄.

shower /ˈʃaʊə(r); ˋʃaʊɚ/ *n* **1** (**a**) brief fall of rain, sleet or hail; sudden sprinkle of water 一阵的雨、雨夹雪或冰雹; 突然喷洒的水: *be caught in a shower* 遇到阵雨 ○ *a shower of spray* 一阵喷雾. (**b**) large number of things falling or arriving together 大量同时来到的事物: *a shower of stones, arrows, dust, ash* 一阵乱石、乱箭、灰尘、灰烬 ○ (*fig* 比喻) *a shower of insults, blessings* 一番侮辱、祝福. **2** (**a**) (small room or cabinet containing a) device attached to the water supply, which produces a spray of water for washing 淋浴设备; 喷头; 淋浴室: *I'm in the shower.* 我在淋浴室呢. ○ [attrib 作定语] *a shower cap*, ie for keeping the hair dry 淋浴帽(防止头发淋湿的). (**b**) wash in or under this 淋浴: *take a shower* 淋浴. **3** (*US*) party at which presents are given to a person, esp a woman about to get married or have a baby 礼物赠送会(尤指为即将结婚或分娩的女子举行的).

▷ **shower** *v* **1** [Ipr, Ip] **~ (down) on sb/sth; ~ down** fall in a shower 阵雨般地降落: *Small stones showered (down) on us from above.* 小石块阵雨般地落在我们身上. ○ *Good wishes showered (down) on the bride and bridegroom.* 大家纷纷向新娘新郎祝福. **2** [Tn·pr] **~ sb with sth; ~ sth on/upon sb** (**a**) cause (a great number of things) to fall on sb 使(大量东西)落在某人身上: *shower the newly-weds with confetti* 向新婚夫妇撒彩色纸屑 ○ *The falling wall showered dust on us.* 墙倒了, 落了我们一身土. (**b**) send or give sth to sb in great numbers 给某人大量的某物: *The dancer was showered with praise.* 那个跳舞的人备受称赞. ○ *shower gifts on sb* 向某人赠送大量礼物 ○ *Honours were showered upon the hero.* 人们纷纷向那位英雄致敬. ⇨ Usage at SPRAY[2] 用法见 SPRAY[2].

showery /ˈʃaʊərɪ; ˋʃaʊərɪ/ *adj* (of the weather) with frequent showers of rain (指天气)多阵雨的: *a showery day* 有阵雨的一天.

□ **'shower-proof** *adj* (of clothing) that can keep out light rain (指衣服)防小雨的.

shown *pp* of SHOW[2].

shrank *pt* of SHRINK.

shrap·nel /ˈʃræpnəl; ˋʃræpnəl/ *n* [U] small fragments of metal encased in a shell and scattered when the shell explodes 榴霰弹: *be hit by (a piece of) shrapnel* 被榴霰弹(弹片)击中.

shred /ʃred; ʃrɛd/ *n* **1** (esp *pl* 尤作复数) strip or piece torn, cut or scraped from sth (撕下、切下或刮下的)细条, 碎片: *The jacket was torn to shreds by the barbed wire.* 那件夹克让铁丝网给挂碎了. **2** **~ of sth** (usu *sing*, in questions and negative sentences 通常作单数, 用于疑问句与否定句中) (*fig* 比喻) small amount of sth 少量: *not a shred of truth in what she says* 她说的没有一点实话 ○ *Can they find a shred of evidence against me?* 他们能找到丝毫不利于我的证据来吗? ▷ **shred** *v* (**-dd-**) [Tn] tear, cut, etc (sth) into shreds 将(某物)撕成细条、切成碎片等: *shredded cabbage* 切成丝的洋白菜 ○ *shredding top-secret documents* 用碎纸机切碎绝密文件. **shred·der** *n* device that shreds, esp one that cuts documents into very small pieces so that they cannot be read 切碎机; (尤指用以销毁文件的)碎纸机.

shrew /ʃru:; ʃru/ *n* **1** small mouse-like animal that feeds on insects 鼩鼱(似鼠的小动物, 以昆虫为食). **2** (*dated* 旧) bad-tempered scolding woman 脾气坏而好骂人的女子.

▷ **shrew·ish** *adj* bad-tempered; scolding 脾气坏的; 爱骂人的. **shrew·ishly** *adv*. **shrew·ish·ness** *n* [U].

shrewd /ʃru:d; ʃrud/ *adj* (**-er**, **-est**) having or showing good judgement and common sense; astute 有准确判断力和常识的; 精明的; 敏锐的: *a shrewd financier, dealer, politician, etc* 精明的金融家、商人、政治家等 ○ *a shrewd argument, plan, measure, investment* 高明的论点、计划、措施、投资 ○ *make a shrewd guess*, ie one that is likely to be right 猜得相当准. ▷ **shrewdly** *adv*. **shrewd·ness** *n* [U].

shriek /ʃri:k; ʃrik/ *v* (**a**) [Ipr, Ip] **~ with sth; ~ (out)** utter a shrill scream 尖叫: *shrieking with laughter, excitement* 尖声大笑、激动的尖叫 ○ *shriek (out) in fright* 吓得尖叫起来. (**b**) [Tn, Tn·p] **~ sth (out)** utter sth with a shrill scream 尖声说出: *shriek (out) a warning* 尖声警告 ○ *'I hate you,' he shrieked.* '我讨厌你,' 他尖声叫道.

▷ **shriek** *n* shrill scream 尖叫声: *shrieks of laughter* 尖利的笑声 ○ *He gave a loud shriek and dropped the pan.* 他尖叫了一声就把锅扔下了.

shrift /ʃrɪft; ʃrɪft/ *n* (idm 习语) **give sb/sth/get short shrift** ⇨SHORT[1].

shrike /ʃraɪk; ʃraɪk/ *n* bird with a strong hooked bill which often impales its prey (small birds and insects) on thorns 伯劳(鸟, 喙弯而坚, 常将捕捉的小鸟和昆虫穿挂在荆刺上).

shrill /ʃrɪl; ʃrɪl/ *adj* **1** (**-er**, **-est**) (of sounds, voices, etc) high-pitched; piercing; sharp (指声响、嗓音等)高声调的, 尖锐的, 刺耳的: *a shrill cry, whistle* 尖叫声、刺耳的汽笛声 ○ *the shrill call of the parrot* 鹦鹉的尖叫声. **2** (*fig sometimes derog* 比喻, 有时作贬义) making loud, persistent and forceful complaints, demands, etc 大声、执着、强烈地提出申诉、要求等的: *his shrill protests about cruelty* 他大声疾呼反对残酷行为 ○ *The Opposition were shrill in their criticism of the Government's action.* 反对党声嘶力竭地抨击政府的措施. ▷ **shrilly** /ˈʃrɪlɪ; ˋʃrɪlɪ/ *adv*: *scream shrilly* 高声叫喊 ○ *complain shrilly in a letter* 在信中笔锋尖利地表示不满. **shrill·ness** *n* [U].

shrimp /ʃrɪmp; ʃrɪmp/ *n* **1** small marine shellfish that is used for food, becoming pink when boiled 小虾. ⇨illus at SHELLFISH 见 SHELLFISH 插图. **2** (*joc or derog* 谑或贬) very small person 矮小的人: *a pale, skinny shrimp* 面黄肌瘦的小个子.

▷ **shrimp** *v* [I] (usu 通常作 **go shrimping**) try to catch shrimps 去捉小虾.

shrine /ʃraɪn; ʃraɪn/ *n* **1** any place that is regarded as holy because of its associations with a special person or event 神圣的地方或处所; 圣地; 圣坛; 圣祠; 神龛: *He built a chapel as a shrine to the memory of his dead wife.* 他建了一座小教堂作为悼念亡妻的圣所. ○ (*fig* 比喻) *Wimbledon is a shrine for all lovers of tennis.* 温布尔登是所有网球爱好者的圣地. **2** tomb or container in which holy relics are kept 圣陵; 圣骨匣.

shrink /ʃrɪŋk; ʃrɪŋk/ *v* (*pt* **shrank** /ʃræŋk; ʃræŋk/ or **shrunk** /ʃrʌŋk; ʃrʌŋk/, *pp* **shrunk**) **1** [I, Tn] (cause sth to) become smaller, esp because of moisture or heat or cold (使某物)收缩(尤指因受潮、受热或受凉所致); 萎缩: *Will this shirt shrink in the wash?* 这件衬衫洗后缩水吗? ○ *The dough shrank slowly in the cold air.* 面团在冷空气中慢慢收缩了. ○ *Car sales have been shrinking* (ie Fewer have been sold) *recently.* 汽车销量近来一直在下降. ○ *The hot water shrank my pullover.* 我的套头毛衣遇热水后收缩了. **2** (idm 习语) **a ˌshrinking ˈviolet** (*joc* 谑) timid or shy person 胆小的或怕羞的人: *She's no shrinking violet — always ready to speak up for herself.* 她可不胆小——任何场合都能为自己说话. **3** (phr v) **shrink (away/back) from sth/sb** move back or withdraw from sth/sb, esp through fear or disgust 退缩; 畏缩: *As he moved threateningly forward she shrank (back) from him.* 他步步逼近, 把她吓得直(向后)退缩. **shrink from sth/doing sth** be reluctant to do sth 不愿做某事: *He shrinks from hurting animals.* 他很怕伤害了动物.

▷ **shrink** *n* (*sl joc* 俚, 谑 *esp US*) psychiatrist 精神科医生; 精神病学家.

shrink·age /ˈʃrɪŋkɪdʒ; ˋʃrɪŋkɪdʒ/ *n* [U] process of shrinking; amount by which sth shrinks 收缩过程; 收缩量; 收缩程度: *You can expect some shrinkage when the jeans are washed.* 这种牛仔裤洗后要缩些水. ○ *There has been some shrinkage in our export trade.* 我们的出口贸易已有些萎缩.

shrun·ken /ˈʃrʌŋkən; ˋʃrʌŋkən/ *adj* [usu attrib 通常作定语] having shrunk 萎缩的; 收缩的: *an old, shrunken apple* 因放久而蔫了的苹果 ○ *the shrunken body of a starving child* 孩子饿瘦的身体.

□ ˌ**shrink-ˈwrap** *v* (**-pp-**) [Tn esp passive 尤用于被动语态] wrap (eg food) in plastic film that shrinks tightly round it 用收缩性塑料薄膜包装(如食物): *ˌshrink-wrapped ˈcheese* 用收缩塑料薄膜包装的干酪.

shrive /ʃraɪv; ʃraɪv/ *v* (*pt* **shrived** or **shrove** /ʃrəʊv; ʃrov/, *pp* **shrived** or **shriven** /ˈʃrɪvn; ˋʃrɪvən/) [Tn] (*arch* 古) (of a priest) hear (sb) confess his sins and forgive him for them (指教士)听(某人)忏悔并赦其罪.

shrivel /ˈʃrɪvl; ˋʃrɪvḷ/ *v* (**-ll-**; *US* **-l-**) [I, Ip, Tn, Tn·p] ~ **(sth) (up)** (cause sth to) shrink and wrinkle from heat, cold or dryness (使某物)蔫, 萎缩, 枯萎(因热、冷或干所致): *The leaves shrivelled (up) in the sun.* 叶子在阳光下都蔫了. ○ *The dry air shrivels the leather.* 因空气干燥, 皮子已起皱了. ○ *He has a shrivelled face*, ie with many wrinkles. 他脸上有很多皱纹.

shroud /ʃraʊd; ʃraud/ *n* **1** (also ˈ**winding-sheet**) [C] cloth or sheet in which a dead person is wrapped for burial 裹尸布; 寿衣. **2** [C] ~ **(of sth)** (*fig* 比喻) thing that covers and hides 覆盖物; 遮蔽物: *a shroud of fog, smoke, etc* 一片浓雾、烟雾等 ○ *cloaked in a shroud of mystery/secrecy* 笼罩在神秘的[秘密的]气氛中. **3** **shrouds** [pl] ropes supporting a ship's masts 支桅索.

▷ **shroud** *v* [Tn·pr esp passive 尤用于被动语态] ~ **sth in sth** cover or hide sth with sth 用某物覆盖或遮蔽他物: *shrouded in darkness, mist, etc* 笼罩在黑暗、雾霭等中 ○ *a crime shrouded in mystery* 笼罩在神秘气氛中的罪案.

Shrove Tuesday /ʃrəʊv ˈtju:zdɪ, -deɪ; *US* ˈtu:z-; ˋʃrov-ˋtuzdɪ, -de/ day before the beginning of Lent, on which people were often shriven 忏悔节(大斋首日的前一天, 人们曾常在此日忏悔请求赦罪). Cf 参看 ASH WEDNESDAY (ASH[2]).

shrub /ʃrʌb; ʃrʌb/ *n* plant with a woody stem, lower than a tree and often having smaller stems branching off near the ground (有一个主茎的)灌木: [attrib 作定语] *shrub roses* 灌木蔷薇. Cf 参看 BUSH ▷ **shrub·bery** /ˈʃrʌbərɪ; ˋʃrʌbərɪ/ *n* [C, U] area planted with shrubs 灌木丛: *plant a shrubbery* 栽种灌木林 ○ *hiding in some shrubbery* 藏在灌木丛中.

shrug /ʃrʌg; ʃrʌg/ *v* (**-gg-**) **1** [I, Tn] raise (one's shoulders) slightly to express doubt, indifference, ignorance, etc 耸(肩)(以示怀疑、与己无关、不知道等): *I asked her where Sam was, but she just shrugged (her shoulders)*, ie to show she didn't know or didn't care. 我问她萨姆在哪儿, 她只是耸了耸肩(表示不知道或与己无关). **2** (phr v) **shrug sth off** dismiss sth as being unimportant (认为某事物不重要)不予理会: *I admire the way she is able to shrug off unfair criticism.* 我很佩服她能对错误的批评意见不予理会.

▷ **shrug** *n* (usu *sing* 通常作单数) movement of shrugging the shoulders 耸肩: *with a shrug of the shoulders* 耸耸肩 ○ *She gave a shrug and walked away.* 她耸了耸肩就走开了.

shrunk, shrun·ken ⇨SHRINK.

shuck /ʃʌk; ʃʌk/ *n* (*US*) **1** [C] outer covering of a nut, etc; shell; husk (坚果等的)外壳; 荚; 外皮. **2 shucks** [pl] thing of little value 没什么价值的东西: *not worth shucks* 没有价值.

▷ **shuck** *v* [Tn] (*US*) remove the shucks from (sth); shell 剥去(某物)的壳; 去荚: *shuck peanuts, maize, peas* 剥花生、玉米、豆.

shucks *interj* (*US infml* 口) (used to express annoyance, regret, embarrassment, etc 用以表示恼怒、悔恨、尴尬等).

shud·der /ˈʃʌdə(r); ˋʃʌdɚ/ *v* (**a**) [I, Ipr, It] ~ **(with sth)** shiver violently with cold, fear, etc; tremble (因寒冷、恐惧等)发抖, 战栗: *shudder with pleasure in a hot bath* 洗热水澡时舒适得抖动起来 ○ *shudder (with horror) at the sight of blood* 看到血(吓得)发抖 ○ *I shudder to think of the problems ahead of us.* 我想到摆在面前的问题就不寒而栗. (**b**) [I] make a strong shaking movement; vibrate 剧烈地摇晃、摆动; 震动: *The ship shuddered as it hit the rocks.* 船撞到礁石上剧烈地摇晃起来.

▷ **shud·der** *n* shuddering movement 战栗; 发抖; 摆动; 震动: *A shudder of fear ran through him.* 他吓得浑身哆嗦. ○ (*infml* 口) *It gives me the shudders*, ie terrifies me 我害怕极了.

shuffle /ˈʃʌfl; ˋʃʌfḷ/ *v* **1** (**a**) [I, Ipr, Ip] walk without lifting the feet completely clear of the ground 拖着脚步走: *Walk properly — don't shuffle.* 好好走路——脚别蹭地. ○ *The prisoners shuffled along the corridor and into their cells.* 囚犯们沿着走廊拖着脚步进入牢房. ○ *The queue shuffled forward slowly.* 排长队的人拖着脚步往前蹭. (**b**) [I, Tn] change one's position or move (one's feet) about while standing or sitting, because of nervousness, boredom, etc (因紧张、厌烦等)站着或坐着时改变位置或移动(双足): *The audience began to shuffle (their feet) impatiently.* 观众已经不耐烦了, 渐渐跺起脚来. ⇨Usage 见所附用法. **2** (**a**) [I, Tn, Tn·p] slide (playing-cards) over one another to change their order 洗(纸牌): *Who is going to shuffle?* 谁洗牌? ○ *She shuffled the pack (up).* 她把牌洗好了. (**b**) [Tn, Tn·p] move (papers, etc) around to different positions 将(文件等)移来移去: *He shuffled the papers (around) on the desk, pretending to be busy.* 他胡乱翻动桌上文件, 装出很忙的样子. **3** [I] behave as if one is being dishonest, or avoiding responsibility, etc; avoid being definite 显得不诚实或逃避责任等; 闪烁其辞: *Don't shuffle: give us a clear answer.* 别躲躲闪闪的: 给我们一个明确的答复. **4** (phr v) **shuffle sth off (onto sb)**; **shuffle out of sth** avoid doing (what one ought to do) 推卸(应做的事): *He tries to shuffle his work off onto others.* 他想把工作推给别人. ○ *She shuffled out of the chores by saying she felt ill.* 她说她有病, 把杂事都推掉了.

▷ **shuffle** *n* (usu *sing* 通常作单数) **1** shuffling walk or movement 拖着脚步走或移动(的姿态): *walk with an exhausted shuffle* 拖着疲惫不堪的脚步走. **2** act of shuffling playing-cards 洗牌: *give the pack a good shuffle* 把牌好好洗一下. **3** rearrangement; reordering 重新安排; 重新组合: *a shuffle in the Cabinet*, ie reallocating responsibilities among its members, etc 内阁改组. **shuf·fler** /ˈʃʌflə(r); ˋʃʌflɚ/ *n*.

NOTE ON USAGE 用法: There are a number of verbs which describe abnormal ways of walking. 有几个动词可用以表示不正常的行走方式. **Shuffle** and **shamble** indicate moving without lifting the feet completely off the ground. ☆ **shuffle** 和 **shamble** 均指行走时脚不完全离开地面. **Shuffle** suggests a slow, tired movement;

shamble may be faster and more careless ☆ **shuffle** 指缓慢的、疲惫的步子，而 **shamble** 则可来得较快也较随便: *The queue of prisoners shuffled towards the door.* 那队囚犯拖着沉重的步子向门口蹭去. ○ *The beggar shambled past us.* 那个乞丐脚蹭着地从我们身旁走过. **Stagger** and **stumble** suggest unsteady or uncontrolled movement. ☆ **stagger** 和 **stumble** 均指不稳的或身不由己的动作. A person **staggers** when carrying a heavy load or when drunk. 身负重物的人或喝醉的人走起路来即为 **stagger**. We **stumble** when we hit our feet against unseen objects. 因未见到地上的物体，不留心用脚碰到即为 **stumble**. **Waddle** is used humorously to describe someone swaying from side to side like a duck because of fatness or while carrying heavy bags. ☆ **waddle** 的词义很幽默，指因肥胖或因负重走起路来一摇一摆像鸭子似的. **Hobble** and **limp** describe the uneven movement of someone whose legs are injured. ☆ **hobble** 和 **limp** 均指腿受伤时不平稳的步子. **Limp** is used especially when only one leg is damaged or stiff. ☆ **limp** 专用以指单腿受伤或强直.

shufty (also **shufti**) /ˈʃʊftɪ; ˋʃuftɪ/ *n* (idm 习语) **take/have a shufty (at sth/sb)** (*dated Brit sl* 旧，俚) have a look (at sb/sth) (朝某人[某物])看一眼: *Take a shufty at this box and tell me if it's big enough.* 看一下这个盒子，告诉我够大不够大.

shun /ʃʌn; ʃʌn/ *v* (**-nn-**) [Tn, Tg] keep away from (sth/sb); avoid 避开，回避(某事物[某人]); 避免: *shun temptation, publicity, other people* 避开诱惑、避免出风头、躲避别人 ○ *She shuns being photographed.* 她不愿别人给她照相.

'shun /ʃʌn; ʃʌn/ *interj* (*infml* 口) = ATTENTION.

shunt /ʃʌnt; ʃʌnt/ *v* **1** (**a**) [Tn, Tn·pr, Tn·p] move (a railway locomotive, wagons, etc) from one track to another 使(火车头、货车等)转轨、调轨: *shunting a train into a siding* 把火车开到岔轨上. (**b**) [I, Ipr, Ip] (of a train) be shunted (指火车)转轨，调轨. **2** (*fig infml* 比喻，口) (**a**) [Tn·pr, Tn·p] move sb/sth to a different (often less important) place 将(某人[某事物])转至另一(常指次要)地方: *She's been shunted off to an office in the annexe.* 她已调到附属建筑的办事处去了. ○ *The luggage was shunted slowly into the lift.* 已把行李慢慢移进电梯里. (**b**) [Tn·pr] change the direction or course of (sth); divert 改变(某事物)的方向或路线; 转移: *shunt the conversation towards more pleasant topics* 转换话题谈些愉快的事.

shush /ʃʊʃ; ʃʌʃ/ *interj* be silent!; hush! 安静!；嘘!

▷ **shush** *v* [Tn, Tn·p] **~ sb (up)** tell sb to be silent 让某人安静.

shut /ʃʌt; ʃʌt/ *v* (**-tt-**, *pt, pp* **shut**) **1** (**a**) [Tn] move (a door, lid, window, etc) into a position where it blocks an opening 关上(门、盖子、窗户等): *shut the doors and windows at night* 夜晚把门窗都关上 ○ *shut the drawer* 关上抽屉 ○ *I can't shut the suitcase lid when it's so full.* 衣箱装得很满，我盖不上盖子了. ○ *He shut the door on her /in her face*, ie wouldn't let her in. 他把她关在门外了. (**b**) [I] (of a door, etc) move or be able to be moved into such a position (指门等)关上，能关闭: *The window won't shut.* 这窗户关不上. ○ *The supermarket doors shut automatically.* 超级市场的门是自动关的. **2** (**a**) [Tn] cause (sth open) to close; close the door, lid, etc of (sth) 使(开着的东西)关上; 关上(某物)的门、盖等: *shut one's eyes/mouth* 合上眼睛[嘴] ○ *I can't shut my briefcase.* 我关不上公事包. ○ *The cashier shut the till and locked it.* 出纳员把钱柜关好并锁上了. (**b**) [I] (esp of the eyes or mouth) close (尤指眼睛或嘴)闭上，合上: *His eyes shut and he fell asleep.* 他合上眼睛睡着了. ○ *Her mouth opened and shut, but no sound came out.* 她的嘴张开又闭上了，没有发出声音. **3** [Tn] fold together (sth that opens out) 合拢(打开着的东西); 折起: *shut a book, wallet, penknife* 合上书、钱夹、折刀. **4** [I, Tn] (cause a business, etc to) stop functioning, esp temporarily (使公司等)停止营业(尤指暂时的): *It's time to shut the shop.* 商店该关门了. ○ *When do the pubs shut?* 酒馆什么时候关门? ⇨Usage at CLOSE[4] 用法见CLOSE[4]. **5** (idm 习语) **keep one's mouth shut** ⇨ MOUTH[1]. **shut/slam the door in sb's face** ⇨DOOR. **shut the door on sth** refuse to consider sth 拒不考虑某事物: *The union accused the management of closing the door on further negotiation.* 工会指责资方拒绝进一步谈判. **shut one's ears to sth/sb** refuse to listen to sth/sb 拒不听某事[某人的话]: *I begged her for help but she shut her ears to all my appeals.* 我恳求她帮忙，但她完全不理睬我的请求. **shut/close one's eyes to sth** ⇨EYE[1]. **shut one's 'mouth/'face** (*sl* 俚) (esp imperative 尤用于祈使句) be silent 要安静: *Shut your mouth, nobody asked you!* 闭上你的嘴，没人要你说话! **shut sb's 'mouth** (*infml* 口) prevent sb from speaking, revealing secrets, etc 防止某人说话、泄露机密等. **shut up 'shop** close one's business, stop trading, etc 停业; 关张: *I've lost so much money this year that I'm being forced to shut up shop.* 我今年赔了很多钱，只好关门了. **with one's eyes shut/closed** ⇨EYE[1]. **6** (phr v) **shut sb/sth away** put sb/sth in an enclosed place or away from others 将某人[某事物]置于封闭的范围内或隔离开: *shut the letters away where no one will find them* 把信放在谁也找不到的地方 ○ *I hate being shut away in the country.* 我很不喜欢住在闭塞的乡村.

shut (sth) down (cause a factory, etc to) stop working; close (使工厂等)停工，歇业，关闭: *The workshop has shut down and the workers are unemployed.* 工厂关闭后工人失业了. ○ *They've shut down their factory.* 他们把工厂关闭了.

shut sb/oneself in (sth) prevent sb/oneself from getting out of (a place) 将某人[自己]关在(某处): *She shuts herself in her study for hours.* 她一个人关在书房里一呆就是几个小时. ○ *We're shut in* (ie surrounded) *by the hills here.* 我们处在群山环抱之中. **shut sth in sth** trap or pinch sth by closing sth 关闭某物时夹住、卡住、挤住...某物: *I shut my finger in the car door*, ie between the door and the door-pillar. 我的手指让汽车门给夹住了.

shut sth off stop the supply or flow of (eg gas, steam, water) 停止供应(煤气、蒸汽、水): *You must shut the gas supply off if there's a leak.* 煤气泄漏时，必须把截门关上. **shut sb/sth off (from sth)** keep sb/sth away from sth 将某人[某物]与他物分开或隔开: *His deafness shuts him off from the lives of others.* 他耳聋阻碍了他与别人的交往. ○ *The village is shut off from the world by lakes and marshes.* 这个村子周围有湖泊与沼泽地，隔断了与外界的联系.

shut sb/sth out (of sth) keep sb/sth out; exclude sb/sth; block sb/sth 将某人[某物]关在外面; 排除; 遮住: *The government wants to shut the refugees out.* 政府不愿接收难民. ○ *These trees shut out the view.* 这些树把景色遮住了. ○ *He tried to shut all thoughts of her out of his mind.* 他尽力不再想与她有关的任何事情.

shut (sb) up (*infml* 口) (cause sb to) stop talking (使某人)不再谈话: *Oh, shut up, you fool!* 喂，住嘴，你这个傻瓜! ○ *Tell her to shut up.* 叫她不要再说了. ○ *Can't you shut him up?* 你能不能叫他别再说了? **shut sth up** close all the doors and windows of (a house, etc) 将(房子等)的所有门窗都关上: *We shut up the house before going on holiday.* 我们去度假之前把所有门窗都关好了. **shut sb/sth up (in sth)** confine sb; put sth away 将某人关在(某处); 将某物藏在(某处): *We shut him up in his room.* 我们把他关在他的房间里. ○ *Shut the jewels up in the safe.* 把这些宝石藏在保险箱里.

□ **'shut-down** *n* process of closing a factory, etc, either temporarily or permanently (工厂等的)关闭(临时或永久的): *strikes causing shut-downs in the steel industry* 造成钢铁工业中一些企业倒闭的罢工.

'shut-eye *n* [U] (*infml* 口) sleep 睡觉: *get a bit of shut-eye* 睡一会儿觉.

shut·ter /ˈʃʌtə(r); ˋʃʌtɚ/ *n* **1** movable panel or screen that can be closed over a window to keep out light or thieves 活动的窗板或窗帘; 百叶窗; 遮板: *The shop-front is fitted with rolling shutters.* 那商店的店面装有卷动门帘. **2** device that opens to allow light to come through the lens of a camera (照相机镜头的)快门. **3** (idm 习语) **put up the 'shutters** (*infml* 口) stop doing business at the end of the day or permanently 停止营业(一日结束时的或永久性的): *After managing the shop for thirty years she decided it was time to put up the shutters.* 她经营这个商店已三十年了，认为应该停业了.

▷ **shut·ter** *v* [Tn esp passive 尤用于被动语态] close the shutters of (a building); provide with shutters 关闭(建筑物)的窗板; 装上窗板: *The house was empty and* *shuttered.* 这所房子是空的, 窗板都关上了.

shuttle /ˈʃʌtl; ˋʃʌtl̩/ *n* **1** (**a**) (in a loom) instrument that pulls the thread of weft between the threads of warp (织机的)梭, 梭子. (**b**) (in a sewing-machine) holder that carries the lower thread to meet the upper thread to make a stitch (缝纫机的)滑梭, 摆梭. **2** aircraft, bus, etc that travels regularly between two places 穿梭班机、公共汽车等(定时往返两地的): *I'm flying to Boston on the shuttle.* 我将乘穿梭班机去波士顿. **3** (*infml* 口) = SHUTTLECOCK.

▷ **shuttle** *v* [I, Tn] (cause sth to) move or travel backwards and forwards, or to and fro (使某物)穿梭般往返移动.

shuttlecock 羽毛球

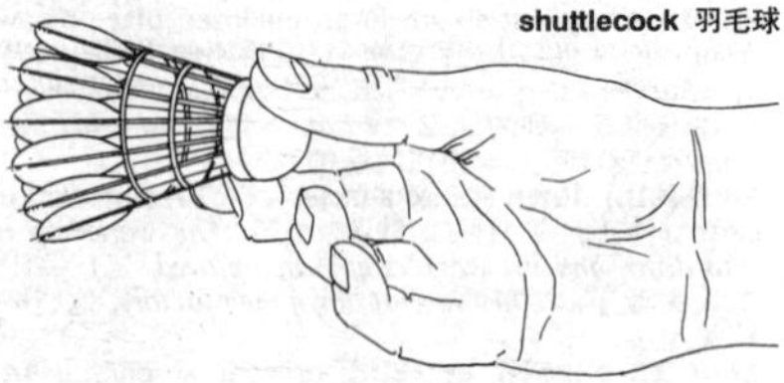

□ ˈ**shuttlecock** *n* round piece of cork, etc with a ring of feathers or of a light synthetic material attached, struck to and fro in badminton 羽毛球.

ˌ**shuttle di**ˈ**plomacy** diplomacy that requires the diplomat(s) to travel to and fro between the two groups involved 穿梭外交.

ˈ**shuttle service** service of buses, aircraft, etc travelling regularly between two places 穿梭业务, 穿梭营运(公共汽车、飞机等往返于两地之间的定期班次).

shy[1] /ʃaɪ; ʃaɪ/ *adj* (**shyer, shyest**) **1** (**a**) (of people) timid and nervous in the presence of others; reserved (指人)羞怯的, 腼腆的: *He was too shy to speak to her.* 他很怕羞, 连话都不敢跟她说. ○ *The child isn't at all shy with adults.* 这小孩在大人面前一点也不羞怯. (**b**) (of behaviour, etc) showing that one is timid, reserved, etc (指行为等)羞怯的, 腼腆的: *a shy look, smile, etc* 羞怯的表情、微笑等. **2** (of animals, birds, etc) unwilling to be seen by or be near to humans; easily frightened (指鸟兽等)不愿近人的, 易受惊的, 胆怯的. **3** ~ **of sb/doing sth** wary or afraid of (a person or an action) 对(某人或某行为)存戒心的或有顾忌的: *The dog is shy of strangers.* 这狗怕生人. ○ *I'm shy of buying shares, in case I lose money.* 我不敢买股票, 怕赔钱. **4** ~ **(on/of sth/sb)** (*US infml* 口) short of or lacking sth/sb 短、少或缺某事物[某人]: *We've plenty of wine, but we're shy on beer.* 我们有很多葡萄酒, 但啤酒不够. ○ *We are still two men shy (of a full team).* 我们还少两个人(才能凑成一个队). **5** (idm 习语) **fight shy of sb/sth** ⇨ FIGHT[1]. **once bitten, twice shy** ⇨ BITE[1].

▷ **shy** *v* (*pt, pp* **shied** /ʃaɪd; ʃaɪd/) **1** [I, Ipr] ~ **(at sth)** (of a horse) turn aside or hold back in fear or alarm (指马)受惊, 惊: *The colt shied at the fence and refused to jump over it.* 这马驹到障碍物前害怕不敢跳过去. **2** (phr v) **shy away from sth/doing sth** avoid or move away from (doing) sth because of shyness, fear, etc (因害羞、恐惧等)避免或逃避(做某事): *I've always shied away from close friendships.* 我总是避免与人深交.

-shy (forming compound *adjs* 用以构成复合形容词) avoiding or not liking the thing specified 避开或厌恶某事物的: ˈ*camera-shy*, ie reluctant to be photographed ○ *a pubˌlicity-shy poliˈtician* ○ *You've been* ˈ*work-shy all your life.* 你这辈子就是不喜欢工作. **shyly** *adv.* **shy·ness** *n* [U].

shy[2] /ʃaɪ; ʃaɪ/ *v* (*pt, pp* **shied** /ʃaɪd; ʃaɪd/) [Tn, Tn·pr] (*dated infml* 旧, 口) throw (sth) 投, 掷, 扔(某物): *shy stones (at a bottle, over a wall, etc)* (朝瓶子、墙那边等)扔石头.

▷ **shy** *n* (*infml* 口) act of throwing 投; 掷; 扔: *have/take a couple of shies at the tin can in the lake* 朝着湖里的白铁罐砍了两下. Cf 参看 COCONUT SHY (COCONUT).

shy·ster /ˈʃaɪstə(r); ˋʃaɪstɚ/ *n* (*infml* 口 *esp US*) unscrupulous and dishonest person, esp a lawyer 不道德、不诚实的人(尤指律师): [attrib 作定语] *shyster politicians* 奸诈的政客.

SI /ˌes ˈaɪ; ˌɛs ˋaɪ/ *abbr* 缩写 = International System (of units of measurement) (French *Système International*) 国际单位制(源自法文 *Système International*): *SI units* 国际单位.

Si·ame·se /ˌsaɪəˈmi:z; ˌsaɪəˋmiz/ *adj* of Siam (now called Thailand), its people or its language 暹罗(现称泰国)的; 暹罗人的; 暹罗语的.

▷ **Si·ame·se** *n* **1** (**a**) [C] (*pl* unchanged 复数不变) native of Siam 暹罗人. (**b**) [U] language of Siam 暹罗语. **2** [C] (*pl* unchanged 复数不变) = SIAMESE CAT.

□ ˌ**Siamese** ˈ**cat** cat of an oriental breed having short pale fur with darker face, ears, tail and feet 暹罗猫.

ˌ**Siamese** ˈ**twins** twins born with their bodies joined together in some way 连体双胞胎.

sib·il·ant /ˈsɪbɪlənt; ˋsɪbl̩ənt/ *adj* like or produced with a hissing sound (似)发咝咝声的: *the sibilant noise of steam escaping* 蒸汽逸出时发出的咝咝声.

▷ **sib·il·ant** *n* sibilant letter or speech-sound, eg /s, z, ʃ, ʒ, tʃ, dʒ/ 发咝音的字母或语音(如/s/、/z/、/ʃ/、/ʒ/、/tʃ/、/dʒ/).

sib·ling /ˈsɪblɪŋ; ˋsɪblɪŋ/ *n* (*fml* 文) any one of two or more people with the same parents; brother or sister 兄弟姊妹: *I have two brothers and a sister: three siblings in all.* 我有两个哥哥和一个妹妹: 共有三个兄妹. ○ [attrib 作定语] *sibling rivalry* 同胞兄弟姊妹间的竞争.

sibyl /ˈsɪbl; ˋsɪbl̩/ *n* any of a group of women in the ancient world thought to be able to foresee the future (古代的)女预言家.

▷ **sibyl·line** /ˈsɪbəlaɪn, sɪˈbɪlaɪn *or, rarely, US* 罕, 美亦读作 ˋsɪbəliˈn; ˋsɪblˌin/ *adj* spoken by or characteristic of a sibyl; mysteriously prophetic 女预言家(所言)的; 神秘预言的: *a sibylline utterance* 女预言家的预言.

sic /sɪk; sɪk/ *adv* (placed in brackets after a quoted word or phrase that seems to be or is incorrect, in order to show that it is quoted accurately 置于括号中, 表示前面引文非笔者之误): *The notice read: 'Skool (sic) starts at 9 am.'* 布告上写的是: 'Skool(原文如此)starts at 9 am.'

sick /sɪk; sɪk/ *adj* (**-er, -est**) **1** physically or mentally unwell; ill (身体或精神)不适; 患病的: *a sick person, animal, plant* 患病的人、动物、植物 ○ *She has been sick for weeks.* 她已病了好几个星期了. ○ *He's off (work) sick.* 他因病而未上班. **2** [usu pred 通常作表语] likely to vomit; nauseous 作呕; 恶心: *feeling sick* 觉得恶心 ○ *a sick feeling in the stomach* 胃里恶心的感觉 ○ *You'll make yourself sick if you eat all those sweets.* 要是你把这些糖都吃下去就要恶心. ⇨Usage 见所附用法. **3** [pred 作表语] ~ **of sb/sth/doing sth** (*infml* 口) bored with sb/sth; not liking sb/sth through having had too much of him/it 厌倦或腻烦某人[某事物]: *I'm sick of waiting around like this.* 我腻烦像这样在一旁等着. ○ *She has had the same job for years and is heartily sick of it.* 她做这一工作已多年, 因此从心底里感到厌烦. ○ *Get out! I'm sick of the sight of you!* 滚出去! 一见到你我就觉得讨厌! **4** [pred 作表语] ~ **(at/about sth/doing sth)** distressed or disgusted 苦恼; 憎恶: *We were pretty sick about losing the match.* 我们比赛输了感到很恼火. **5** (*infml* 口) cruel, morbid or perverted; offensive 残酷的; 病态的; 反常的; 讨厌的: *a sick joke, mind* 可怖的笑话、病态的心理 ○ *sick humour* 残酷的幽默 ○ *She made a sick remark about dead babies.* 关于那些死的婴儿, 她说了些令人反感的话. **6** (idm 习语) **be** ˈ**sick** throw up food from the stomach; vomit 呕吐: *The cat's been sick on the carpet.* 猫在地毯上吐了. **eat oneself sick** ⇨ EAT. **fall sick (with sth)**; (*fml* 文) **take** ˈ**sick** become ill 生病: *He fell sick with malaria on a trip to Africa.* 他在去非洲时患了疟疾. **laugh oneself silly/sick** ⇨ LAUGH. **make sb** ˈ**sick** outrage or disgust sb 使某人愤慨或厌恶: *His hypocrisy makes me sick.* 我很讨厌他那么虚伪. ○ *It makes me sick to see her being treated so badly.* 我看到她受到这样虐待非常愤怒. **on the** ˈ**sick-list** (*infml* 口) sick and absent from work, duty, etc 因病缺勤或缺席: *She's not at her desk today: she's on the sick-list.* 她今天没上班: 因病缺勤. **(as) sick as a parrot** (*Brit joc catchphrase* 谑, 警语) disgusted 憎恶的. **sick at** ˈ**heart** (*fml* 文) full of disappointment, fear or grief; unhappy 极为失望、恐惧或悲伤; 感到不快: *She left her home reluctantly and sick at heart.* 她依依不舍地离开了家, 心情很沉重. **sick to death of/sick**

and tired of sb/sth (*infml* 口) wearied, bored or annoyed by sb/sth; fed up with sb/sth (因某人[某事物])厌倦, 厌恶; 厌烦某人[某事物]: *sick to death of eating boiled cabbage with every meal* 顿顿都吃煮洋白菜, 腻死了 ○ *I'm sick and tired of your constant complaints.* 我厌烦你没完没了的抱怨. **sick to one's 'stomach** (*US*) outraged or disgusted 愤慨的; 厌恶的.

▷ **sick** *n* **1** [U] (*infml* 口) vomit 呕吐物: *The basin was full of sick.* 盆里全是吐的东西. **2 the sick** [pl *v*] people who are ill 病人; 患者: *all the sick and wounded* 所有的病人和伤者 ○ *visit the sick in hospital* 看望住院的病人.

sick *v* (phr v) **sick sth up** (*infml* 口) throw (food) up from the stomach; vomit sth 吐出(食物); 呕吐某物: *The baby sicked up a little milk.* 婴儿吐出了一点奶.

-sick (forming compound *adjs* 用以构成复合形容词) feeling sick(2) as a result of travelling on a ship, plane, etc 晕船、晕飞机等: *'seasick* ○ *'airsick* ○ *'travel-sick* ○ *'carsick.*

□ **'sick-bay** *n* room or rooms in a ship, boarding-school, etc for people who are ill (船上、寄宿学校等的)病室.

'sick-bed *n* bed of a person who is ill 病床: *lying pale on his sick-bed* (他)躺在病床上, 面色苍白 ○ *The President left his sick-bed to attend the ceremony*, ie attended it although he was ill. 总统带病参加了典礼.

'sick-leave *n* [U] permission to be absent from work, duty, etc because of illness; period of such absence 病假: *be granted sick-leave* 准予休病假 ○ *two weeks' sick-leave* 两周病假. **'sick-pay** *n* [U] pay given to an employee who is absent because of illness 病假工资.

'sick-room *n* room that is occupied by or kept ready for sb who is ill 病室: *You should go to the sick-room if you're not feeling well.* 要是觉得不舒服就应该到病室里去休息.

NOTE ON USAGE 用法: **1 (Be) sick** in informal British English means 'bring food up from the stomach' (*US* **vomit**) 在英式英语的口语中, **(be) sick**意为'呕吐'(美式英语中用**vomit**): *Johnny's been sick again — should we call the doctor?* 约翰尼又吐了——我们应该请医生来吗? ○ *Do you get seasick/airsick?* 你晕船[晕机]吗? ○ *I feel sick — I think it was that fish I ate.* 我很恶心——大概是吃那鱼的缘故. **Sick** in British English is used only before a noun when it means 'ill' 在英式英语中, **sick**只有用在名词前时才作ill解: *a sick child* 患病的孩子 ○ *He's looking after his sick mother.* 他正在看护生病的母亲. **2 Sick** in US English and **ill** in British English mean 'not well' or 'in bad health', usually as a result of a disease 美式英语中的**sick**和英式英语中的**ill**均指'不适'或'身体不好', 通常指因疾病引起的: *I've been too sick/ill to go to work for the last few months.* 我近几个月身体不好没上班. **3 Poorly** (informal British English) means 'ill'. ☆ **poorly**(在英式英语的口语中)意为ill. ☆ It is often used of or by children 这个词常用于儿童或是儿童经常使用: *My daughter's a bit poorly today, so she didn't go to school.* 我女儿今天有点不舒服, 所以她没去上学.

sicken /ˈsɪkən; ˋsɪkən/ *v* **1** [Tn] cause (sb) to feel disgusted 使(某人)感到厌恶或恶心: *Cruelty sickens most of us.* 我们大多数人都对残暴行为十分愤慨. ○ *Their business methods sicken me.* 我很讨厌他们做生意的手法. ○ *I was sickened at/by the sight of the dead body.* 我看到那死尸感到很恶心. **2** [I, Ipr] **~ (for sth)** (*Brit*) begin to be ill; become ill 生病; 患病: *slowly sickened and died* 慢慢病死了 ○ *She looks so pale. Is she sickening for something?* 她气色很不好. 是不是得了什么病了? **3** (phr v) **sicken of sth** (*fml* 文) become weary of or disgusted with sth 厌倦或厌恶某事物: *I began to sicken of the endless violence shown on television.* 我逐渐对电视上无尽无休的暴力镜头感到厌恶.

▷ **sick·en·ing** *adj* disgusting 令人厌恶的: *a sickening sight, smell* 令人厌恶的场面、气味 ○ *sickening cruelty* 令人憎恶的残酷行为 ○ *The car hit the tree with a sickening crash.* 那辆汽车撞在树上发出让人难受的撞击声. **sick·en·ingly** *adv*.

sickle /ˈsɪkl; ˋsɪkl̩/ *n* short-handled tool with a curved

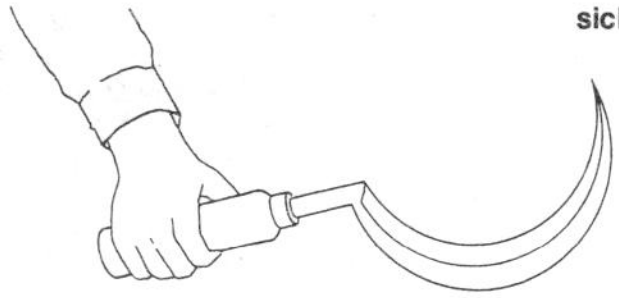

sickle 镰刀

blade for cutting grass, corn, etc 镰刀. Cf 参看 SCYTHE.

□ ˌ**sickle 'cell** sickle-shaped red blood-corpuscle found esp in a severe type of hereditary anaemia 镰形红细胞.

sickly /ˈsɪklɪ; ˋsɪklɪ/ *adj* (**-ier**, **-iest**) **1** often ill 常病的: *a sickly child* 多病的孩子. **2** looking unhealthy 不健康的: *sickly, dried-out plants* 长势不好、枯槁的植物 ○ *a pale, sickly complexion* 苍白的病容 ○ *He looked weak and sickly.* 他看上去虚弱有病态. **3** [usu attrib 通常作定语] expressing unhappiness; weak; faint 显示不愉快的; 虚弱的; 无力的: *a sickly smile, look* 苦笑、苦相. **4** causing or likely to cause a feeling of sickness or distaste 令人作呕的; 令人厌恶的: *a sickly smell, taste, etc* 令人作呕的气味、味道等 ○ *a sickly green colour* 令人生厌的绿色 ○ (*fig* 比喻) *a sickly, sentimental story* 无病呻吟的伤感故事.

sick·ness /ˈsɪknɪs; ˋsɪknɪs/ *n* [U] **1** illness; ill health 疾病; 患病; 不健康: *Is there much sickness in the village now?* 这村庄现在患病的多吗? ○ *They were absent because of sickness.* 他们因病缺席. **2** [U, C usu *sing* 作不可数名词或可数名词, 后者通常作单数] particular type of illness or disease 病; 疾病: *sleeping sickness* 昏睡病 ○ *suffering from altitude sickness* 患高空病 ○ *air-/sea-/travel-/car-sickness* 晕机[晕船/晕(机、船、车等)/晕车] ○ *a sickness common in the tropics* 热带常见病. **3** [U] feeling that one is likely to vomit; vomiting 作呕; 呕吐: *The sickness passed after I lay down for a while.* 我躺下一会后就不恶心了. ○ *The symptoms of this disease are fever and sickness.* 这种病的症状是发烧与呕吐.

□ **'sickness benefit** (*Brit*) money paid by the State to sb who is absent from work because of illness 病假补助(政府付给生病员工的钱): *entitled to sickness benefit* 享受病假补助.

side[1] /saɪd; saɪd/ *n* **1** [C] **(a)** any of the flat or nearly flat surfaces of a solid object (固体的平的或近似平的)面: *the six sides of a cube* 立方体的六个面. **(b)** any of the surfaces that is not the top or bottom 侧面(不包括顶面或底面): *A box has a top, a bottom and four sides.* 盒子有顶面、底面和四个侧面. **(c)** any of the surfaces that is not the top or bottom, front or back 侧面(不包括顶面、底面、前面或后面): *There is a garage built onto the side of the house.* 这所房子的一侧建有一个车库. ○ [attrib 作定语] *a side door, entrance, window* 边门、侧门、边窗. **2** [C] (*mathematics* 数) any of the lines that form the boundaries of a plane figure, such as a triangle or a rectangle (组成三角形、矩形等平面图形的)边. **3** [C] (area near the) edge or boundary of sth 边缘或边界(的地方): *a table by one's bedside/by the side of one's bed* 床边的桌子 ○ *people sitting on both sides of the table*, ie on the two longer sides of a rectangular one 坐在桌子两(长)边的人 ○ *standing at the side of the road* 站在路边 ○ *the south side of the field* 田地的南边 ○ *We planted tulips along the side of the lawn.* 我们沿草坪的边缘种上了郁金香. **4** [C] either of the two surfaces of sth flat and thin, eg paper, cloth, sheet metal (平而薄的东西, 如纸、布、金属片两面之一的)面: *Write on one side of the paper only.* 只在纸的一面写字. ○ *Which is the right side of the cloth* (ie the one intended to be seen)? 这块布哪一面是正面? ○ *This side of the glass is filthy.* 玻璃的这一面很脏. **5** [C] inner or outer surface of sth more or less upright (垂直或近似垂直物的)内侧或外侧: *the side of the mountain, tower, haystack* 山、塔、草堆的坡面 ○ *a steep hillside* 陡峭的山坡 ○ *paint the sides of the cylinder* 把圆筒的外面漆一下 ○ *paintings on the sides* (ie walls) *of the cave* 在洞穴内壁上的图画 ○ *a puncture in the side of the tyre* 轮胎上的小孔. **6** [C] **(a)** either the right or the left part of a person's body, esp from the armpit to the hip (人体的)左侧或右侧(尤指腋至臀的部分); 肋: *wounded in the left side* 左肋受伤 ○ *lying on one's side* 侧卧. **(b)** region near to this 身边; 身旁: *sit at/by sb's side*

坐在某人旁边 ○ *On my left side stood Fred.* 我的左侧站着弗雷德. **7** [C] either of the two halves of an animal that has been killed for meat (已宰杀供食用动物的)半边躯体, 胁肉: *a side of beef, bacon, etc* 牛的胁肉、腌的猪胁肉. **8** [C] (**a**) either of the two halves of a surface or an object divided by an imaginary central line (一物体或物体表面从中以假想线分为两半之一的)面, 半, 边: *the left side of the brain* 脑的左半部 ○ *the left, right, shady, sunny, etc side of the street* 大街的左、右、背阴、向阳等面 ○ *the eastern side of the town* 城镇的东区 ○ *the debit/credit side of the account* 帐簿中的借[贷]方 ○ *Go over to the other/far side of the room.* 到房间的另一边去. ○ *Which side of the theatre would you like to sit?* 你喜欢坐在剧院的哪一边? (**b**) either of the two areas, etc divided by a line or boundary (由一界线分成两部分之一的)面, 边, 部分: *She stood on the other side of the fence.* 她站在篱笆的另一边. ○ *He crossed the bridge to this side of the river.* 他过桥来到河的这一边. **9** [C] (*Brit dated infml* 旧, 口) television channel 电视频道: *Switch over to the other side.* 转到另一个频道看看. **10** [C] (**a**) either of two parties or groups involved in a dispute, contest, etc with each other (辩论、竞赛等双方的)一方: *the two sides in the strike*, ie employers and workers 罢工事件中的双方(雇主和工人) ○ *There are faults on both sides.* 双方都有错. (**b**) position or opinion held in an argument; attitude or activity of one person or group with respect to another (辩论中所持的)立场或观点; (个人或团体相对于另一个人或团体采取的)态度或行动: *She argued her side of the case well.* 她有理有据地陈述了自己的意见. ○ *You must hear his side of things now.* 你现在得听听他这方面的看法. ○ *Will you keep your side of the bargain?* 你那一方能遵守协议吗? **11** (*Brit*) sports team (运动)队: *five-a-side football* 五人一队的足球比赛 ○ *the winning/losing side* 胜[败]方 ○ *pick sides*, ie choose who will play on each side 双方各自挑选队员 ○ *Austria has a good side, and should win.* 奥地利队阵容强, 很可能赢. **12** [C] aspect of sth that is different from other aspects; point of view (与其他方面不同的)方面, 观点: *study all sides of a question* 研究一问题的各个方面 ○ *the gentle side of her character* 她性格中温柔的一面 ○ *approach the problem from a different side* 从另一角度来探讨这一问题. **13** [C] line of descent through a father or mother 父系或母系; 世系; 血统: *a cousin on my father's side*, ie a child of my father's brother or sister 堂兄弟姐妹之一或父系的表兄弟姐妹之一. **14** [U] (*dated infml* 旧, 口) behaviour showing that one thinks one is better than others; arrogance 自大; 傲慢: *a person quite without side* 不摆架子的人 ○ *There's absolutely no side to him.* 他非常谦虚. **15** (idm 习语) **born on the wrong side of the blanket** ⇨BORN. **come down on one side of the fence or the other** make a choice between two alternatives 在两者之间做出选择; 支持两方中之一方: *The jury is considering its verdict and we're waiting to see which side of the fence they'll come down on.* 陪审团正在考虑裁决, 我们等着看他们支持哪一方. **err on the side of sth** ⇨ERR. **get on the right/wrong side of sb** please/ displease sb 使某人愉快[使某人不愉快]. **have got out of bed on the wrong side** ⇨BED[1]. **know which side one's bread is buttered** ⇨KNOW. **laugh on the other side of one's face** ⇨LAUGH. **let the 'side down** not give one's colleagues, etc the help and support they expect, or behave in a way that disappoints them 不帮助、不支持同事; 使同事感到失望: *You can always rely on Angela — she'd never let the side down.* 你尽可完全信赖安吉拉——她从不使同事感到失望. **look on the bright side** ⇨BRIGHT. **on/ from all sides; on/from every side** in/from all directions; everywhere 在[从]各个方向; 到处: *soldiers attacking on all sides* 从各个方向发动进攻的士兵 ○ *There was devastation on every side.* 到处都是破坏的创伤. **on the 'big, 'small, 'high, etc side** (*infml* 口) rather or too big, small, high, etc 偏大、偏小、偏高等: *These new trousers are a bit on the large side.* 这条新裤子有点大. **on the distaff side** ⇨DISTAFF. **on the ˌright/ ˌwrong side of 'forty, 'fifty, etc** (*infml often joc* 口, 常作戏谑语) younger/older than forty, fifty, etc years of age 不足[已过]四十、五十岁等. **on the safe side** ⇨SAFE[1]. **on the 'side** (*infml* 口) (**a**) as a sideline 作为兼职或副业: *a mechanic who buys and sells cars on the side* 兼营买卖汽车的技工. (**b**) secretly 秘密地; 暗地里: *He's married but he has a girl-friend on the side.* 他虽有妻室, 但暗地里还有一个女朋友. **(be) on the side of sb** (be) a supporter of sb; holding the same views as sb (成为)某人的支持者; 与某人观点相同: *Whose side are you on anyway?* ie You should be supporting me. 你究竟支持谁? (你应该支持我.) ○ *I'm on George's side in this debate.* 这场辩论中我和乔治的观点相同. **on/from the wrong side of the tracks** ⇨WRONG. **the other side of the 'coin** the opposite or contrasting aspect of a matter 事情的另一面: *Everyone assumes he's to blame but they don't know the other side of the coin.* 大家都认为是他的错, 但他们都不知道事情的另一面. **put sth on/ to one 'side** (**a**) put sth aside 将某物置于一边: *I put the broken glass to one side.* 我把破玻璃杯搁在一旁. (**b**) leave sth to be dealt with later 搁置某事; 暂缓处理: *I put his complaint on one side until I had more time.* 我把他的申诉暂搁一边, 待有时间时再处理. **ˌside by 'side** (**a**) close together, facing in the same direction 肩并肩地: *two children walking side by side* 两个并肩走路的小孩. (**b**) supporting each other 相互支持: *We stand side by side with you in this dispute.* 在这场辩论中我们与你们相互支持. **split one's sides** ⇨SPLIT. **take sb on(to) one 'side** have a private talk with sb 将某人拉到一边以便私下交谈: *I took her on one side to ask about her odd behaviour.* 我把她带到一旁问她为什么有这种奇怪举动. **take 'sides (with sb)** express support for sb in a dispute, etc 在辩论等中表示支持某人; 偏袒: *You mustn't take sides in their argument.* 在他们的争论中你不要偏袒任何一方. ○ *She took sides with me against the teacher.* 她支持我反对老师. **a thorn in one's flesh/ side** ⇨THORN. **time is on sb's side** ⇨TIME[1]. **wrong side out** ⇨WRONG.

▷ **-sided** (forming compound *adjs* 用以构成复合形容词) having a specified number or type of sides (有某数目或类型的)面的, 边的: *a six-sided object* ○ *a glass-sided container.*

□ **'sideboard** *n* **1** [C] table, usu with drawers and cupboards, for crockery, etc 餐具柜. **2 'sideboards** (*US* **'sideburns**) [pl] patches of hair growing on the side of a man's face in front of the ears (男子的)鬓角. ⇨ illus at HAIR 见 HAIR 插图.

'side-car *n* small vehicle attached to the side of a motor cycle, to seat a passenger (摩托车的)跨斗.

'side-dish *n* extra dish or course at a meal, usu served with another course (正菜外的)小菜(通常指配菜).

'side-drum *n* small double-sided drum 小鼓. ⇨illus at App 1 见附录1插图, page xi.

'side-effect *n* (often *pl* 常作复数) secondary, usu unpleasant or unwanted, effect of a drug, etc (药物等的)副作用.

'side-issue *n* issue that is less important than the main one 次要问题: *What I earn is a side-issue. What really matters is that I don't like my work.* 我挣多少钱倒不重要. 真正重要的是我不喜欢这个工作.

'sidekick *n* (*infml* 口 *esp US*) assistant or close companion 助手; 亲密伙伴: *the gangster and his two sidekicks* 匪徒与他的两个帮凶.

'sidelight *n* **1** either of a pair of small lights at the front of a vehicle (车辆前面的)侧灯. ⇨illus at App 1 见附录1插图, page xii. **2 ~ (on sb/sth)** (*fig* 比喻) minor or casual piece of information that helps one to understand a subject, etc (有助于了解某问题等的)小的或偶然的启示: *The article about the theatre gave us a few sidelights on the character of its owner.* 关于该剧院的这篇文章对我们了解其业主的个性带来了意外的启示.

'sidelong *adj* [attrib 作定语], *adv* (directed) to or from the side; sideways 横向(的); 侧面(的): *a sidelong glance* 横扫一眼 ○ *look sidelong at sb* 斜着看某人.

ˌside-'on *adv* with the side of sth towards sth else 以某物的侧面朝着另一物: *The other car hit us side-on*, ie hit us with its side. 那辆汽车的侧面撞到了我们.

'side order (*esp US*) item of food served to a person in addition to the main dish and on a separate plate (主菜之外)另点的菜: *a side order of French fries* 另点了一个炸薯条.

'side-road *n* minor road branching off a main road (从干线分出来的)支线, 叉道, 小道.

ˈ**side-saddle** *n* saddle for a woman rider made so that both legs can be on the same side of the horse 横鞍; 偏座鞍; 女鞍. — *adv* on a side-saddle 在鞍上偏坐着: *riding side-saddle* 偏坐在鞍上.

ˈ**side-show** *n* **1** small show offering a game or some other amusement at a circus, fun-fair, etc (马戏、游乐场等的)杂耍. **2** (*fig* 比喻) activity of less importance than the main activity 次要的活动; 附属事件.

ˈ**side-slip** *n* (**a**) sideways skid of a motor vehicle (机动车)滑向一边, 侧滑, 横滑. (**b**) sideways movement of an aircraft making a turn (飞机转弯时的)侧滑, 横滑. — *v* [I] (**-pp-**) make a side-slip 侧滑; 横滑.

ˈ**side-splitting** *adj* (*infml* 口) extremely funny 极滑稽的: *the clown's side-splitting antics* 小丑令人捧腹大笑的滑稽动作.

ˈ**side-step** *n* step to one side, eg to dodge sb or to avoid a blow 横跨的一步(如避开某人或避免受打击). — *v* (**-pp-**) **1** [Tn] (**a**) avoid (a blow, etc) by stepping to one side 横跨一步以免受(打击等): *The footballer side-stepped the tackle.* 该足球队员向旁边跨步以避开对方拦截动作. (**b**) evade (a question, etc) 回避(问题等): *He side-stepped the issue by saying it was not part of his responsibilities.* 他回避这一问题, 说这不属于他的责任范围. **2** [I] make a side-step 横跨一步.

ˈ**side-street** *n* minor street branching off a major street 小巷.

ˈ**side-stroke** *n* [U] any of various types of swimming stroke in which the swimmer is on his side 侧泳: *Can you do side-stroke?* 你会侧泳吗?

ˈ**side-swipe** *n* (*US*) **1** indirect blow along the side of sth 横击; 侧击. **2** (*infml* 口) critical remark made among remarks of a different kind or on a different subject 旁敲侧击: *When talking about the performance, she couldn't resist (taking) a side-swipe at the orchestra.* 她谈到演出时, 忍不住把管弦乐队批评了一通.

ˈ**side-track** *v* [Tn esp passive 尤用于被动语态] divert (sb) from the main topic or issue 引导(某人)转换话题: *The lecturer was discussing politics but got side-tracked by a question from the audience into talking about religion.* 讲演人正在谈论政治, 但因听众提出问题一岔开而谈起宗教来了.

ˈ**side-view** *n* view of sth from the side 侧面图; 侧景: *The picture is/shows a side-view of the house.* 这幅画画的是房子的侧面.

ˈ**sidewalk** *n* (*US*) = PAVEMENT 1.

ˈ**sideways** *adv*, *adj* [attrib 作定语] **1** to, towards or from the side 斜着(的); 斜向一边(的): *A crab moves sideways.* 螃蟹横着爬行. ○ *He looked sideways at me.* 他斜着眼看我. ○ *a sideways glance* 斜着眼看. **2** with one side facing forwards 以侧面对着(的): *carry the sofa sideways through the door* 把沙发顺过来一端向前抬着通过这道门. **3** (idm 习语) **knock sb sideways** ⇨ KNOCK[2].

ˈ**side-whiskers** *n* [pl] patches of hair growing on the sides of a man's face down to, but not on, the chin (男子的长可至颏的, 但不长在颏上的)长鬓角(与络腮胡子不同).

side-winder /ˈsaɪdwaɪndə(r); ˋsaɪd,waɪndɚ/ *n* type of small rattlesnake that moves sideways in a series of loops 角响尾蛇.

side[2] /saɪd; saɪd/ *v* (phr v) **side with sb (against sb)** support sb in an argument, dispute, etc (在争论、辩论等中)支持(某人), 站在(某人)一边: *She sided with her brother against the others in the class.* 她在班上支持哥哥反对其他同学.

side·line /ˈsaɪdlaɪn; ˋsaɪd,laɪn/ *n* **1** [C] class of goods sold in addition to the main class of goods 附带出售的货物: *a butcher selling groceries as a sideline* 兼卖杂货的肉商. **2** [C] occupation that is not one's main work 副业; 兼职: *I'm a teacher really; my writing is just a sideline.* 我其实是个教师, 写作只是我的兼职. **3 sidelines** [pl] (space immediately outside the) lines forming the boundary of a football pitch, tennis court, etc at the sides (足球场、网球场等的)边线(界外区): *some spectators on the sidelines* 在边线外的一些观众. **4** (idm 习语) **on the ˈsidelines** observing sth but not directly involved in it 旁观; 不直接参与: *As a journalist, I was on the sidelines during the political crisis.* 我是记者, 在这一政治危机时期我是目睹一切的局外人.

▷ **side·line** *v* [Tn] (*esp US*) remove (sb) from a game, team, etc; put out of action 使(某人)退出比赛; 使中止活动: *Our best player has been sidelined by injury.* 我们的主力队员已因受伤而退出了比赛.

si·der·eal /saɪˈdɪərɪəl; saɪˋdɪrɪəl/ *adj* (*fml* 文) of the stars or measured by them 星的; 恒星的; 以恒星为计算标准的: *sidereal time* 恒星时 ○ *the sidereal year*, ie 365 days, 6 hours, 10 minutes 恒星年(即365天6小时10分).

sid·ing /ˈsaɪdɪŋ; ˋsaɪdɪŋ/ *n* short track beside a main railway line, into and from which trains can be shunted (铁路的)侧轨, 旁轨, 岔轨.

sidle /ˈsaɪdl; ˋsaɪdḷ/ *v* [Ipr, Ip] **~ up/over (to sb/sth)**; **~ along, past, away, etc** move (in the specified direction) furtively, or as if shy or nervous 悄悄(沿某方向)移动(或因羞怯或紧张所致): *sidling up to the bar* 悄悄朝酒吧走去 ○ *She sidled over to me and asked if I recognized her.* 她羞怯地向我走来, 问我是否认识她. ○ *He sidled past, trying to seem casual.* 他悄悄地溜了过去, 竭力装作漫不经心的样子. ⇨Usage at PROWL 用法见PROWL.

siege /siːdʒ; sidʒ/ *n* **1** (**a**) surrounding of a town, fortress, etc by armed forces in order to capture it or force it to surrender 围困; 围攻; 围城: *a siege of 50 days* 50天的围困 ○ *be in a state of/under siege* 处于被围状态 ○ *raise/lift* (ie end) *a siege* 撤围 ○ *By the time the siege ended, the citizens were nearly starving.* 围城停止时, 市民已饿得濒于死亡. ○ [attrib 作定语] *siege guns* 攻城炮. (**b**) surrounding by police, etc of a building in which people are living or hiding (警方等对住有或藏有人的建筑物的)包围. **2** (idm 习语) **lay siege to sth** begin a siege of (a town, fortress, etc) 包围(城镇、城堡等).

si·enna /sɪˈenə; sɪˋɛnə/ *n* [U] type of clay used as colouring matter 赭石(用作颜料): *burnt sienna*, ie reddish-brown 煅赭石(赤褐色颜料) ○ *raw sienna*, ie brownish-yellow 生赭石(棕黄颜料).

si·erra /sɪˈerə; sɪˋɛrə/ *n* long range of mountains with steep slopes and a rugged outline (esp in Spain and Spanish America) 锯齿山脊(尤指在西班牙及西班牙语系的美洲国家的).

si·esta /sɪˈestə; sɪˋɛstə/ *n* rest or sleep taken in the early afternoon, esp in hot countries 午睡(尤指在气候炎热国家的); 午后小睡: *have/take a siesta* 睡午觉.

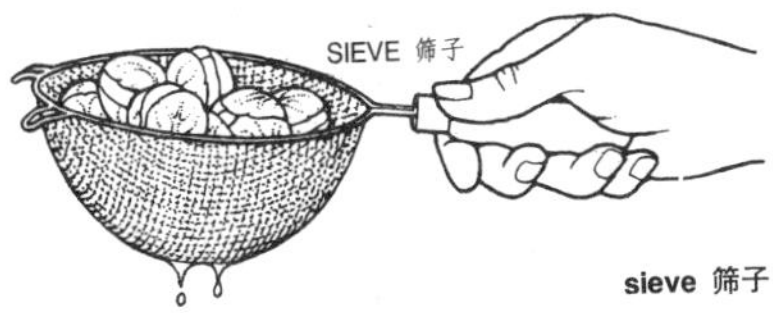

sieve 筛子

sieve /sɪv; sɪv/ *n* **1** utensil consisting of a wire mesh or gauze on a frame, used for separating solids or coarse matter (which do not pass through) from liquids or fine matter (which do pass through) 滤器; 漏勺; 筛子. **2** (idm 习语) **have a memory/ mind like a sieve** have a very bad memory; forget things easily 记性坏; 健忘.

▷ **sieve** *v* [Tn, Tn·pr] put (sth) through a sieve 用漏勺或筛子滤(某物): *sieve the flour into a bowl* 把面粉筛进盆里.

sift /sɪft; sɪft/ *v* **1** (**a**) [Tn] put (sth) through a sieve 筛(某物): *sift the flour, sugar, etc* 筛面粉、糖等. (**b**) [Tn·pr, Tn·p] **~ sth (out) from sth**; **~ sth out** separate sth from sth by putting it through a sieve 筛分(某物): *sift (out) the lumps from the flour, the wheat from the chaff* 把面粉中的面块筛出来、把小麦的壳筛掉. **2** [Tn, Tn·pr] shake or sprinkle (sth) through a sieve 筛下(某物): *sift flour (into the mixture)* 把面粉筛进混合物里 ○ *sift sugar onto a cake* 把糖筛撒在糕饼上. **3** [Ipr, Tn] **~ (through) sth** (*fig* 比喻) examine sth very carefully 详察, 细审(某事物): *sift through the piles of correspondence* 仔细检查成堆的信件 ○ *sift the evidence, data, etc* 认真审查证据、数据等.

▷ **sifter** *n* (often in compounds 常用以构成复合词) small utensil like a sieve, used chiefly in cooking 小筛子(主要用作炊具): *a flour-sifter* 面粉筛子.

sigh /saɪ; saɪ/ *v* **1** [I, Ipr] **~ (with sth)** take a long deep breath that can be heard, expressing sadness, tiredness, relief, etc 叹息；叹气：*She sighed as she lay back on the bed.* 她在床上向后一躺，长叹了一声. ○ *He sighed with pleasure after the excellent meal.* 他美餐一顿之后，满足地叹了口气. **2** [I] (of the wind) make a sound like sighing (指风)哀鸣. **3** [Tn] express or say (sth) with a sigh 叹息地表示；叹息地说：*'I wish I didn't have so much to do,' she sighed.* '我但愿能没有这么多事情做，' 她叹着气说. **4** (phr v) **sigh for sth** (*fml* 文) feel a deep longing for sth that is lost, far away, etc (对失去的、遥远的事物的)思念，热望：*an exile who sighs for home* 想念着家的流放者.

▷ **sigh** *n* act or sound of sighing 叹息；叹息声：*breathe/utter/heave/give a sigh* 发出一声叹息 ○ *with a sigh of relief, sadness, pleasure, etc* 带着欣慰、悲痛、愉快等的一声长吁.

sight[1] /saɪt; saɪt/ *n* **1** [U] ability to see; vision 视力；视觉：*lose one's sight*, ie become blind 失明 ○ *have good, poor, etc sight*, ie eyesight 视力好、差等 ○ *Some drugs can affect your sight.* 有些药物能影响视力. **2** [U] **~ of sb/sth** action of seeing sb/sth 看；看见：*Their first sight of land came after ten days at sea.* 他们在海上十天之后首次看到陆地. ○ *We laughed at the sight of his strange clothes.* 我们看到他那怪模怪样的衣服都笑了起来. ○ (*fml* 文) *When can we have sight of your new house?* 我们什么时候能够看看你的新房子? **3** [U] range within which sb can see or sth can be seen 视野；视界：*in/within/out of (sb's) sight*, ie (of objects, etc) visible/invisible (指物体等)看得见[看不见] ○ *The train is still in sight.* 还能看得见那列火车. ○ *The ship came into sight out of the fog.* 那艘船驶出浓雾，依稀可见. ○ *The plane crashed out of our sight*, ie where we could not see it. 飞机出事时那个地方我们看不见. ○ *The house was out of sight behind a wall.* 房子被墙遮住看不见了. ○ *We are not yet out of sight of land*, ie can still see it. 我们还能看到陆地. ○ *You must keep out of sight*, ie stay where you cannot be seen. 你要呆在别人看不见的地方. ○ *Get out of my sight!* 滚开! ○ (*fig* 比喻) *The end of the project is almost in sight.* 该计划完成之时已遥遥在望. **4** (**a**) [C] thing (to be) seen, or worth seeing, esp sth remarkable 情景；景象；(尤指)奇观，壮观：*The flowers are a lovely sight in spring.* 春天百花盛开十分美丽. ○ *He saw some amazing sights at the zoo.* 他在动物园里看到一些珍禽异兽. ○ *A suffering animal is a distressing sight.* 看到动物受痛苦是很难受的. (**b**) **sights** [pl] interesting buildings, places, features, etc of a place or district 某处或某地令人感兴趣的建筑物、地方、特征；名胜：*Come and see the sights of London.* 来看看伦敦的名胜. **5 a sight** [sing] (*infml* 口) person or thing that looks ridiculous, untidy, etc 显得滑稽可笑、不整洁等的人或物：*What a sight you look in those old clothes!* 你穿上那些旧衣服样子可真怪! ○ *This kitchen is a sight. Clean it up at once!* 这厨房太乱了. 马上整理一下吧! **6** [C usu pl 通常作复数] device that one looks through to aim a rifle, etc or to observe sth through a telescope, etc (步枪等的)瞄准器；观测器：*the sights of a gun* 枪的瞄准器. **7** (idm 习语) **at first glance/sight** ⇨GLANCE. **at/on 'sight** as soon as sb/sth is seen 一见到某人[某事物]立即：*play music at sight*, ie when seen in printed form without previous study or practice 视奏(未经事先学习或练习，见到乐谱即行演奏) ○ *They were told to shoot looters on sight.* 他们奉令见到打劫者立即射击. **catch sight/a glimpse of sb/sth** ⇨CATCH[1]. **hate, loathe, be sick of, etc the sight of sb/sth** (*infml* 口) hate, etc sb/sth very much 不愿见到某人[某物]；讨厌；憎恶：*I can't stand the sight of you any more.* 我再也不愿见到你了. ○ *She hates the sight of that old car.* 她见到那辆旧汽车就讨厌. **heave in sight** ⇨HEAVE. **in the sight of sb/in sb's sight** (*fml* 文) in sb's opinion; in sb's view 依某人的意见；在某人看来：*Do what is right in your own sight.* 做你认为对的事. ○ *All men are equal in the sight of God.* 上帝对所有的人都一视同仁. **keep sight of sb/sth; keep sb/sth in sight** (**a**) remain where one can see sb/sth 看住某人[某物]；监视：*Follow that man and keep him in sight all the time.* 要跟着那个人，一直盯着他. (**b**) remain aware of sth 了解到某事：*You must keep sight of one fact: your life is in danger.* 有一件事你必须明白，你有生命危险. **know sb by sight** ⇨KNOW. **lose sight of sb/sth** ⇨LOSE. **,out of 'sight, ,out of 'mind** (*saying* 谚) we tend to forget people or things that are absent or can no longer be seen 眼不见，心不念. **raise/lower one's 'sights** be more/less ambitious; expect more/less 提高[降低]要求：*They had to lower their sights and buy a smaller house than they would have liked.* 他们原来想买一所大房子，后来不得不降低要求买一所较小的. **set one's sights on sth** decide to achieve sth 立意做成某事物：*I've set my sights on winning the championship.* 我下定决心要赢得冠军. **a (damn, etc) sight better, etc (than...); a (damn, etc) sight too good, etc** (*infml* 口) very much better, etc; far too good, etc 好得多；非常好：*My car goes a (darned) sight faster than yours.* 我的汽车比你的快得多. ○ *That child is a damn sight too cheeky.* 这孩子脸皮太厚. **a ,sight for sore 'eyes** (*infml* 口) person or thing that one is relieved or pleased to see 使人悬念而想见到的人或物；喜欢见到的人或物：*You're a sight for sore eyes — I thought you'd gone for good!* 见到你真高兴——我还以为你一去不复返了呢! **a sight of sth** (*infml* 口) a great amount of sth 大量；许多：*It cost him a sight of money/trouble.* 这花了他一大笔钱[这给他惹来很多麻烦]. **sight un'seen** without an opportunity for previous inspection 事前未得以检查：*You should never buy a car sight unseen.* 买汽车时，事先未检查可千万不要买. **take a 'sight** aim or observe using a sight[1](6) or sights 用瞄准器瞄准；用观测器观测：*take a careful sight before firing* 仔细瞄准再发射 ○ *take a sight with a compass/quadrant* 用罗盘[象限仪]观测.

▷ **sighted** *adj* able to see; not blind 有视力的；不盲的：*the blind and partially sighted* 盲人和有部分视力的人 ○ *Those of us who are sighted don't understand the problems of the blind.* 我们这些有视力的人不理解盲人的困难.

-sighted (in compound *adjs* 用以构成复合形容词) having the specified type of eyesight 有某种视力的：*short-/long-/far-sighted.*

□ **'sight-read** *v* [I, Tn] (be able to) play or sing (music) without previous study or practice (能)视奏或视唱(不经事先学习或练习). **'sight-reading** *n* [U].

'sight-screen (also **screen**) *n* (in cricket) large movable white structure placed at either end of the playing area to help the batsmen see the ball (板球的)屏幕(为击球员看清球而设于球场两端可移动的白色屏幕).

'sightseeing *n* [U] visiting the sights (SIGHT[1] 4b) of a place as a tourist 观光；游览. **'sightseer** *n* person who does this 观光客；游人.

sight[2] /saɪt; saɪt/ *v* [Tn] **1** manage to see (sb/sth), esp by coming near 看见(尤指因接近)：*After three days at sea, we sighted land.* 我们在海上航行三天后见到了陆地. **2** observe (a star, etc) by using sights (SIGHT[1] 6) (用仪器)观测(星等).

▷ **sight·ing** *n* instance of sb/sth being seen 被看见的人或事物；看见；见到：*several reported sightings of the escaped prisoner* 据称有几次见到了那个逃犯 ○ *the first sighting of a new star* 一颗新星首次有人见到.

sight·less /'saɪtlɪs; 'saɪtlɪs/ *adj* unable to see; blind 看不见的；失明的：*a sightless species of bat* 一种无视觉的蝙蝠.

sign[1] /saɪn; saɪn/ *n* **1** mark, symbol, etc used to represent sth 记号；符号：*mathematical signs*, eg +, –, ×, ÷ 数学符号(如+、–、×、÷). **2** board, notice, etc that directs sb towards sth, gives a warning, advertises a business, etc 牌子；牌示；招牌；指示牌：*traffic signs*, eg for a speed limit, a bend in the road, etc 交通标志(如表示速度限制、有弯路等) ○ *a shop-sign, pub-sign, etc* 商店招牌、酒馆招牌 ○ *Look out for a sign to the motorway.* 留意通往高速公路的路标. **3** gesture or movement made with the hand, head, etc, used to give information, a command, etc (用手、头等的)示意动作(用以传递信息、命令等)：*the sign of the cross*, ie a movement made with the hand outlining a cross as a blessing, prayer, etc (用手)画十字(祝福、祈祷等) ○ *She gave us a sign to leave the room*, eg by pointing to the door. 她示意我们离开房间(如以手指门). **4 ~ (of sth)** thing that shows that sb/sth is present or exists, or that sth may happen 痕迹；迹象；征兆：*signs of suffering on his face* 他面部的痛苦表情 ○ *some signs of improvement in her work* 她工作有些改进的迹象 ○ *There wasn't a sign of life in the place*, ie It appeared deserted. 那儿没有生命的迹象. ○

S

She shows no sign of being interested. 她没有表示出有兴趣来. ○ *There are some signs of sales increasing.* 有迹象显示销售额在增长. **5** (also ˌ**sign of the ˈzodiac**) (symbol representing) any of the twelve divisions of the zodiac (黄道十二宫之一的)宫, 星座: *What sign were you born under?* 你是属什么星座的? **6** (idm 习语) **a ˌsign of the ˈtimes** (*often derog* 常作贬义) thing that shows the nature of a particular period 某时期的标志: *The rising level of crime is a sign of the times.* 犯罪率增高是这一时代的特征.

□ ˈ**sign language** language, eg for deaf and dumb people, using gestures instead of words 手势语, 手语(如聋哑人用的).

ˈ**signpost** *n* post at a road junction, etc with arms pointing to places along the roads, and often showing the distances to them 路标. — *v* [Tn usu passive 通常用于被动语态] provide (a road) with signposts; indicate (a route or place) with signposts 为(路)设置路标; 用路标指示(路径或地方): *Is the road well signposted?* 这条路的路标清楚吗? ○ *Our village is so small it's not even signposted.* 我们的村子很小, 连路标都没有.

sign[2] /saɪn; saɪn/ *v* **1** [I, Tn] write (one's name) on (a document, etc), eg to show that one has written it, that it is genuine, or that one agrees with its contents 在(文件等)上签(名); 签字: *Sign (your name) here, please.* 请在这儿签(你的名)字. ○ *sign a letter, cheque, contract, etc* 在信、支票、合同等上签字 ○ *The painting isn't signed so we don't know who it's by.* 这幅画没有签名, 不知道是谁画的. **2** [no passive 不用于被动语态: Dpr·f, Dpr·w, Dpr·t, Dn·t] convey information or a request or an order by making a gesture 示意, 做手势(传达信息、请求或命令): *sign to sb that it is time to go/where to go* 示意某人该走了[去何处] ○ *The policeman signed (for) them to stop.* 警察示意让他们停住. ○ *He signed me to be quiet.* 他示意要我安静. **3** [I, Ipr, Tn] (*esp sport* 尤用于体育) **~ (for/with sb)** be engaged or engage (sb), eg as a footballer, by signing a contract (签约)应聘或受雇, 雇用或聘请(某人)(如足球队员): *He signed for Arsenal yesterday.* 他昨天跟阿塞纳尔队签了约. ○ *Arsenal have just signed a new striker.* 阿塞纳尔队刚雇用了一名新前锋. **4** (idm 习语) **sign on the dotted ˈline** (*infml* 口) sign a document, etc that legally binds one, eg to buy sth 签署文件等(如购买某物): *Just sign on the dotted line and the car is yours.* 你只需签署这份文件, 这辆汽车就是你的了. **sign sb's/one's own ˈdeath-warrant** do sth that will result in one's death, defeat, etc 做出可能使自己致命或失败的事: *By informing on the gang, he was signing his own death-warrant.* 他告发了那帮歹徒, 自己的性命也就难保了. **5** (phr v) **sign sth away** give up (one's rights, property, etc) by signing a document, etc 签字放弃(权利、财产等): *I'll never get married — it's like signing your life away!* 我可不结婚——结婚就像签了卖身契一样! **sign for sth** sign a form, etc to show that one has received sth 签收某物: *The postman asked me to sign for the parcel.* 邮递员叫我签收包裹. **sign (sb) in/out** write one's/sb's name to show arrival or departure 签上名字以示到达或离去: *You must sign guests in when they enter the club.* 客人进入俱乐部你得为他们登记. ○ *Soldiers sign out when they leave the barracks.* 士兵离开营房得登记签字. **sign off (a)** stop work 结束工作: *sign off early to go to the dentist* 提前结束工作去看牙. **(b)** end a letter 结束一封信: *She signed off with 'Yours ever, Janet'.* 她在信的结尾处写上了 'Yours ever, Janet'. **(c)** end a broadcast in some way, eg by playing a short piece of music 结束广播(如放一小段音乐): *This is your resident DJ signing off for another week with our signature tune.* 这是本台流行音乐唱片节目主持人, 现在播放信号曲来结束我们为您安排的这一星期的节目. **sign on** (*Brit infml* 口) register as an unemployed person 登记为失业的人. **sign (sb) on/up** (cause sb to) sign an agreement to work for sb, become a soldier, etc (使某人)签约受雇、应征: *sign on for five years in the army* 签约服兵役五年 ○ *sign up more workers to boost production* 再签约雇用工人以促进生产 ○ *The club has signed up a new goalkeeper this season.* 俱乐部这一季节已签约雇用一名新守门员. **sign sth over (to sb)** formally transfer the ownership of sth to sb by signing a document, etc 正式将所有权签字转让某人: *She has signed her house over to her daughter.* 她已签字把房子转让给女儿了. **sign up (for sth)** join a club, enrol on a course, etc 参加一俱乐部、课程等: *sign up for a secretarial course* 注册参加秘书课程.

sig·nal[1] /ˈsɪgnəl; ˈsɪgnl/ *n* **1** sign, gesture, sound, etc that conveys a message, command, etc (传递信息、命令等的)信号, 手势, 声音, 暗号: *a signal made with a red flag* 用红旗打出的信号 ○ *hand signals*, ie made by the driver of a car, etc to show which way it will turn, etc 手势信号(司机指示转弯等的) ○ *She flashed the torch as a signal.* 她用手电筒发信号. ○ *He raised his arm as a signal for us to stop.* 他抬起手臂示意我们停下. ○ *A red light is usually a signal for/of danger.* 红灯通常是危险的信号. **2** any device or object placed to give people a warning, information, etc (给人警告、信息等的)信号器或信号物: *traffic signals*, ie for cars, etc in the streets 交通信号 ○ *The railway signal* (ie light) *was on red, so the train stopped.* 铁路红灯亮了, 所以火车停下了. **3 (a)** any event or action that causes some general activity 触发某些普遍活动的事情或行动: *The President's arrival was the signal for an outburst of cheering.* 总统来到爆发一阵欢呼声. **(b)** anything indicating that sth exists or is likely to happen 表明某事物存在或可能发生的任何事物: *Her speech yesterday was a signal that her views have changed.* 她昨天的讲话标志着她的观点已经转变. ○ *Is this announcement the signal of better times ahead?* 宣布的这件事是否预示往后日子越过越好了? **4** sequence of electronic impulses or radio waves transmitted or received (电子脉冲或无线电波的)信号: *receive a signal from a satellite* 接收到卫星信号 ○ *an area with a poor/good TV signal* 电视信号弱[强]的地区 ○ [attrib 作定语] *signal strength* 信号强度. ▷ **sig·nal** *v* (**-ll-**; *US* **-l-**) [I, Ipr, Tn, Tn·pr, Tf, Tw, Dn·pr, Dn·f, Dpr·f, Dn·w, Dpr·w, Dn·t, Dpr·t no passive 不用于被动语态] **~ (to sb/sth) (for sth)** make a signal or signals; send or express (sth) in this way; communicate with (sb) in this way 发信号; 用信号传达(某信息); 用信号与(某人)通讯: *He seems to be signalling.* 他似乎正在发送信号. ○ *signal wildly with one's arms* 奋力挥臂打信号 ○ *signal a message (to sb)* 用信号(向某人)传递消息 ○ (*fig* 比喻) *signal one's discontent by refusing to vote* 拒绝投票以示不满 ○ (*fig* 比喻) *an event signalling a change in public opinion* 说明公众舆论变化的事件 ○ *signal that one is going to turn/which way one is going to turn* 打信号示意要转弯[走哪条路] ○ *signal (to) the commanding officer (that...)* 向指挥官发信号(报告...) ○ *signal to the regiment for the attack to begin* 向团部发出开始进攻的信号 ○ *signal (to) sb which way to go* 示意某人走哪条路 ○ *signal (to) the waiter to bring the menu* 示意要服务员把菜单拿来. **sig·nal·ler** (*US* **sig·naler**) /ˈsɪgnələ(r); ˈsɪgnələ˞/ *n* person who signals, esp a soldier specially trained for this purpose 信号员; (尤指)信号兵.

□ ˈ**signal-box** *n* (*Brit*) building beside a railway, from which railway signals are operated (铁路)信号所, 信号房.

ˈ**signalman** /-mən; -ˌmən/ *n* (*pl* **-men** /-mən; -mən/) **1** person who operates signals on a railway (铁路)信号员. **2** person who signals, esp in the army or navy 信号手, 信号兵(尤指陆军或海军的).

sig·nal[2] /ˈsɪgnəl; ˈsɪgnl/ *adj* [attrib 作定语] remarkably good or bad; outstanding (好或坏)显著的; 出色的: *a signal victory, success, failure, etc* 极大的胜利、成功、失败等.

▷ **sig·nally** /-nəlɪ; -nlɪ/ *adv* in a signal way 显著地; 出色地: *You have signally failed to do what was expected of you.* 希望你做的事你显然并没做.

sig·nat·ory /ˈsɪgnətrɪ; *US* -tɔːrɪ; ˈsɪgnəˌtorɪ/ *n* **~ (to sth)** person, country, etc that has signed an agreement 签约的人; 签约国: *the signatories to the treaty* 签约各方 ○ [attrib 作定语] *the signatory powers* 签约的各强国.

sig·na·ture /ˈsɪgnətʃə(r); ˈsɪgnətʃə˞/ *n* **1 (a)** [C] person's name written by himself 签名; 签字; 署名: *a document with two signatures on it* 经两人签署的文件 ○ *Her signature is almost illegible.* 她的签字很难辨认. **(b)** [U] action of signing sth 签名; 签字; 签署: *a contract ready for signature* 准备签字的合同. **2** [C] section of a book made from one sheet of paper folded and cut 书帖(一整张平版纸折叠切割而成的一沓, 为书芯的一部分).

□ ˈ**signature tune** (also **theme tune**) usu brief tune used to introduce a particular broadcast or performer

信号曲，开始曲(通常为短曲，用于一广播前或演出者出场前).

sig·net /ˈsɪgnɪt; ˋsɪgnɪt/ *n* person's seal[2](1a) used with or instead of a signature 图章；私章.

□ ˈ**signet ring** finger-ring with a design engraved on it, formerly used as a seal 图章戒指(旧时用作图章).

sig·ni·fic·ance /sɪgˈnɪfɪkəns; sɪgˋnɪfəkəns/ *n* [U] **1** meaning 意义；意思: *understand the significance of a remark* 了解某句话的意义 ○ *What is the significance of this symbol?* 这个符号是什么意思? **2** importance 重大意义；重要性: *a speech of great significance* 有重大意义的讲话 ○ *Few people realized the significance of the discovery.* 很少有人意识到这一发现的重要性.

sig·ni·fic·ant /sɪgˈnɪfɪkənt; sɪgˋnɪfəkənt/ *adj* **1** (**a**) having a meaning, esp one that is immediately obvious 有意义的(尤指直接而明显的): *Their change of plan is strange but I don't think it's significant.* 他们改变了计划十分奇怪，我觉得没有什么用意. (**b**) full of meaning 意味深长的: *a significant remark, look, smile* 意味深长的话语、一瞥、微笑. **2** important; considerable 重要的；重大的；可观的: *a significant rise in profits* 利润的巨大增长.

▷ **sig·ni·fic·antly** *adv* **1** in a way that conveys a special meaning 意味深长地；意义深远地: *smile, nod, wink significantly* 意味深长地微笑、点点头、眨眨眼 ○ *Significantly, he did not deny that there might be an election.* 颇有意义的是，他没否认可能要进行选举. **2** to an important or considerable degree 重要地；重大地；可观地: *Profits have risen significantly.* 利润已大大提高了.

sig·nif·ica·tion /ˌsɪgnɪfɪˈkeɪʃn; ˌsɪgnəfəˋkeʃən/ *n* (*fml or linguistics* 文或语言) meaning of a word, etc 词等的含义；词义.

S

sig·nify /ˈsɪgnɪfaɪ; ˋsɪgnəˌfaɪ/ *v* (*pt, pp* **-fied**) **1** [Tn] be a sign of (sth); mean 表示(某事物)的意思；意味: *What do these marks signify?* 这些符号表示什么意思? ○ *Do dark clouds signify rain?* 有乌云是否显示要下雨? **2** [Tn, Tf no passive 不用于被动语态] make (sth) known; indicate 表明(某事物)；表示: *signify one's agreement/that one agrees by nodding* 用点头表示同意 ○ *She signified her approval with a smile.* 她笑了笑表示赞成. **3** [I] (used esp in questions and negative sentences 尤用于疑问句与否定句) be of importance; matter 有重要性；有关系: *It doesn't signify, so you needn't worry about it.* 这无所谓，你不必担心.

Sikh /si:k; sik/ *n* member of a religion (**Sikh·ism**) that developed from Hinduism in the 16th century and is based on a belief in only one God 锡克教教徒(源于16世纪印度教的教徒，相信只有一个神).

sil·age /ˈsaɪlɪdʒ; ˋsaɪlɪdʒ/ *n* [U] green fodder stored without drying, esp in a silo, to feed cattle in winter 青贮饲料(尤指贮藏在青贮塔内以备冬季饲牛的).

si·lence /ˈsaɪləns; ˋsaɪləns/ *n* **1** [U] condition of being quiet or silent; absence of sound 寂静；无声: *the silence of the night* 夜的寂静 ○ *A scream shattered the silence.* 一声尖叫打破了寂静. ○ *In the library silence reigned*, ie it was totally silent. 图书馆内十分安静. **2** (**a**) [U] not speaking, answering sth spoken or written, making comments, etc; not mentioning sth or revealing a secret 沉默；缄默；默不作声: *All my questions were met with silence from him.* 我的所有问题他都拒不回答. ○ *The teacher's stern look reduced him to silence.* 教师神情严肃，他便静了下来. ○ *I can't understand her silence on this matter.* 我不明白她为什么对此事默不作声. ○ *I assume that your silence implies consent*, ie that by saying nothing you are showing that you do not disagree. 我想你沉默即表示同意. ○ *After a year's silence* (ie a year during which she didn't write), *I got a letter from her.* 她沉默了一年之后，又给我来了一封信. ○ *They tried to buy his silence*, ie to pay him not to reveal a secret. 他们想收买他让他保持缄默(不泄露秘密). (**b**) [C] period during which sb is silent 沉默的一段时间: *a conversation with many silences* 时断时续的交谈 ○ *There was a brief silence, followed by uproar.* 沉默片刻之后又喧嚣起来了. **3** (idm 习语) **in silence** without speaking or making a sound; silently 安静地；无声地: *listen to sb in silence* 静静地听某人谈话 ○ *The whole ceremony took place in complete silence.* 举行仪式的全过程中寂静无声. **a pregnant pause/silence** ⇨PREGNANT. ˌ**silence is** ˈ**golden** (*saying* 谚) it is often best not to say anything 沉默是上策.

▷ **si·lence** *v* [Tn] cause (sb/sth) to be silent; cause to be quiet(er) 使(某人[某物])沉默；使安静: *try to silence a noisy crowd, a crying baby* 设法使喧闹的人群、啼哭的婴儿静下来 ○ *silence one's critics*, eg by doing sth they cannot criticize 使挑剔的人无话可说 ○ *silence the enemy's guns*, eg by destroying them 把敌人的阵地摧毁 ○ *This insult silenced him completely.* 他受此侮辱后一言不发了.

si·len·cer *n* (**a**) (*Brit*) (*US* **muffler**) device that reduces the noise made by a vehicle's exhaust (机动车的)消声器. ⇨illus at App 1 见附录1插图, page xii. (**b**) device that reduces the noise made by a gun being fired (枪的)消声器. **si·lence** *interj* be quiet 安静；别出声: *'Silence!' shouted the teacher.* '安静!' 教师喊道.

si·lent /ˈsaɪlənt; ˋsaɪlənt/ *adj* **1** (**a**) making no or little sound; not accompanied by any sound 寂静的；无声的: *with silent footsteps* 脚步轻轻地 ○ *the smooth, silent running of the engine* 发动机顺畅而静静的运转 ○ *The children went out, and the room was silent.* 孩子们出去了，房间里十分安静. (**b**) not expressed aloud 不出声或小声表达的: *a silent prayer, curse, etc* 默默的祈祷、诅咒等. **2** (**a**) not speaking; making no spoken or written comments 沉默的；不发表意见的: *He was silent for a moment, then began his answer.* 他沉默了一会儿，然后开始回答. ○ *She was silent for months before I got a letter from her.* 她沉默了几个月，然后给我来了一封信. ○ *On certain important details the report remains strangely silent.* 这份报告在某些重要的细节问题上只字未提，莫名其妙. (**b**) saying little 沉默寡言的: *He is the strong, silent type.* 他是个坚强而沉默的人. **3** (of a letter) written but not pronounced (指字母)不发音的: *The 'b' in 'doubt' and the 'w' in 'wrong' are silent.* doubt一字中的b字母与wrong一字中的w字母都不发音. ⇨Usage at QUIET 用法见QUIET. **4** (idm 习语) **the** ˌ**silent ma**ˈ**jority** the people with moderate views who are unable or unwilling to express them publicly 沉默的多数(不能或不愿公开表达意见的中间群众). ▷ **si·lently** *adv*.

□ ˌ**silent** ˈ**film** film without a sound-track, esp one made before the invention of sound-films 无声电影；默片. ˈ**silent partner** (*US*) = SLEEPING PARTNER (SLEEP[2]).

sil·hou·ette /ˌsɪlu:ˈet; ˌsɪluˋɛt/ *n* **1** (**a**) dark outline of sb/sth seen against a light background 黑色轮廓；侧影: *the silhouettes of the trees against the evening sky* 夜空衬托出树木的轮廓. (**b**) picture showing sb/sth as a black shape against a light background 黑色轮廓像；剪影. **2** (idm 习语) **in silhouette** as a silhouette 以黑色轮廓像或剪影形式: *see sth in silhouette* 看见某物的轮廓 ○ *paint sb in silhouette* 画出某人的黑色轮廓像.

▷ **sil·hou·ette** *v* [usu passive 通常用于被动语态: Tn, Tn·pr] **~ sth (against sth)** cause sth to be seen as a silhouette 使某物现出轮廓或呈黑色轮廓像: *She stood in front of the window, silhouetted against the dawn sky.* 她站在窗前，晨空衬托出她的轮廓.

sil·ica /ˈsɪlɪkə; ˋsɪlɪkə/ *n* [U] compound of silicon occurring as quartz or flint, and in sandstone and other rocks 硅石；二氧化硅.

sil·ic·ate /ˈsɪlɪkeɪt; ˋsɪlɪˌket/ *n* [C, U] any of the insoluble compounds of silica 硅酸盐.

sil·icon /ˈsɪlɪkən; ˋsɪlɪkən/ *n* [U] non-metallic chemical element found combined with oxygen in quartz, sandstone, etc 硅. ⇨App 10 见附录10.

□ ˌ**silicon** ˈ**chip** microchip made of silicon, used to make an integrated circuit 硅片(用以制集成电路).

sil·ic·one /ˈsɪlɪkəʊn; ˋsɪlɪkon/ *n* [U] any of the complex organic compounds of silicon, widely used in paints, varnish and lubricants 硅酮(复合有机化合物，多用以制油漆、清漆和润滑剂).

sil·ic·osis /ˌsɪlɪˈkəʊsɪs; ˌsɪlɪˋkosɪs/ *n* [U] disease caused by breathing in dust containing silica, eg in a coal-mine 硅肺，石末沉着病(因吸入硅尘引起的疾病，如在煤矿中).

silk /sɪlk; sɪlk/ *n* **1** [U] fine soft thread produced by silkworms to make their cocoons, or by certain insects or spiders (蚕、蜘蛛或昆虫吐出的)丝. **2** [U] thread or cloth made from this 丝线；丝绸: *dressed all in silk* 全身穿着绫罗绸缎 ○ [attrib 作定语] *a silk scarf, dress, etc* 丝制的围巾、连衣裙等. **3 silks** [pl] (*dated* 旧) clothes made from silk 丝绸衣服: *dressed in fine silks* 穿着绫罗绸缎. **4** [C] (*Brit infml* 口) Queen's or King's Counsel, who wears a silk gown in court 御用律师. **5** (idm 习语) **smooth as silk** ⇨SMOOTH[1]. **take 'silk** become a Queen's or King's Counsel 任御用律师: *After fifteen years as a barrister, she took silk.* 她当了十五年的讼务律师之后, 担任了御用律师.

□ **ˌsilk-screen 'printing** method of printing by forcing ink through a stencil of finely-woven material 丝网印刷法. **'silkworm** *n* caterpillar that spins silk to form a cocoon 蚕.

silken /ˈsɪlkən; ˋsɪlkən/ *adj* [usu attrib 通常作定语] **1** (*usu approv* 通常作褒义) soft and smooth; shiny like silk 柔软光滑的; 像丝般有光泽的: *a silken voice* 柔和的嗓音 ○ *silken hair* 柔软光滑的头发. **2** (*arch* 古) made of silk 丝制的; 绸的: *a silken gown* 绸袍.

silky /ˈsɪlkɪ; ˋsɪlkɪ/ *adj* (**-ier**, **-iest**) (*usu approv* 通常作褒义) soft, fine, smooth, etc like silk 像丝一样柔软、纤细、光滑等的: *silky hair, skin* 柔软光滑的头发、皮肤 ○ (*fig* 比喻) *a silky manner, voice* 温和的态度、柔和的嗓音. ▷ **silki·ness** *n* [U].

sill /sɪl; sɪl/ *n* piece of wood, or stone, etc forming the base of a window or a door 窗台; 门槛: *a 'window-sill* 窗台 ○ *a 'door-sill* 门槛. ⇨illus at App 1 见附录1插图, page vi.

sil·la·bub = SYLLABUB.

silly /ˈsɪlɪ; ˋsɪlɪ/ *adj* (**-ier**, **-iest**) **1** (**a**) not showing thought or understanding; foolish 愚昧的; 愚蠢的; 傻的: *a silly little boy* 傻小子 ○ *Don't be silly!* 别这么傻! ○ *silly mistakes* 愚蠢的错误 ○ *What a silly thing to say!* 这话说得多蠢! (**b**) ridiculous in appearance, behaviour, etc (外貌、行为等)可笑的, 荒唐的: *made us play silly games* 让我们做荒唐可笑的游戏. **2** [attrib 作定语] (of a fielder in cricket) standing close to the batsman (指板球中的外场员)靠近击球员的: *silly mid-on* 靠近击球员的外场员. **3** (idm 习语) **laugh oneself sick/silly** ⇨LAUGH. **play 'silly buggers** (*Brit sl* 俚) behave in a foolish or irresponsible way 举止愚蠢或不负责任: *Stop playing silly buggers and help me lift this.* 别胡闹了, 快来帮我把这个抬起来. **the 'silly season** time, usu in the summer, when newspapers are full of trivial stories because there is little news 新闻淡季(通常在夏季, 因报上缺少主要新闻而琐事充斥). ▷ **sil·li·ness** *n* [U].

silly (also **silly-billy**) *n* (*infml* 口) (often used to or by children 常用以指儿童或儿童常用) silly person 傻瓜; 笨蛋: *Of course I won't leave you alone, you silly!* 当然我不会把你单独留下, 你这个小傻瓜!

silo /ˈsaɪləʊ; ˋsaɪlo/ *n* (*pl* **~s**) **1** (**a**) tall tower or pit, usu on a farm, in which grass or other food for animals can be kept fresh 青贮塔, 青贮窖(贮藏新鲜饲料的建筑, 通常指农场上的). (**b**) tower or pit for storing grain, cement or radioactive waste 用以贮藏谷物、水泥或放射性废料的高塔或地窖. **2** underground place where missiles are kept ready for firing 导弹发射井.

silt /sɪlt; sɪlt/ *n* [U] sand, mud, etc carried by flowing water and left at the mouth of a river, in a harbour, etc (由流水带到河口、港口等的)淤沙、淤泥等.

▷ **silt** *v* (phr v) **silt (sth) up** (cause sth to) become blocked with silt (使某物)为淤泥堵塞: *The harbour has silted up.* 这港口已被淤泥堵塞. ○ *The sand has silted up the mouth of the river.* 泥沙已把河口堵住了.

silty *adj* (**-ier**, **-iest**) covered with, full of or containing silt 为沙泥覆盖的; 充满或含有泥沙的: *silty rocks* 有泥沙覆盖的岩石 ○ *silty soil* 粉土质土壤.

sil·van (also **syl·van**) /ˈsɪlvən; ˋsɪlvən/ *adj* (*arch or rhet* 古或修辞) (**a**) of the woods 森林的; 林木的: *silvan glades* 森林中的空地. (**b**) having woods; rural 有森林的; 乡村的.

sil·ver /ˈsɪlvə(r); ˋsɪlvɚ/ *n* **1** [U] chemical element, a shiny white precious metal used for ornaments, jewellery, coins, utensils, etc 银: *solid silver* 纯银 ○ [attrib 作定语] *a silver mine* 银矿. ⇨App 10 见附录10. **2** [U] coins made of silver or of an alloy looking like it 银币(银或似银合金铸成的硬币): *£20 in notes and £5 in silver* 20镑纸币和5镑银币 ○ *a handful of silver* 一把银币 ○ *Have you any silver on you?* 你带着银币呢吗? **3** [U] (**a**) dishes, ornaments, etc made of silver 银器(银盘、银首饰等): *have all one's silver stolen by burglars* 所有的银器全被窃贼偷走 ○ *sell the family silver to pay one's debts* 卖掉祖传的银器还债. (**b**) cutlery made of any metal 任何金属制的餐具: *We keep the silver in this sideboard.* 我们把金属餐具放在这个餐具柜里. **4** (idm 习语) **born with a silver spoon in one's mouth** ⇨BORN. **cross sb's palm with silver** ⇨CROSS[2]. **every cloud has a silver lining** ⇨CLOUD[1]. **the silver 'screen** a cinema screen or the cinema industry 银幕; 电影业: *stars of the silver screen* 影星. **a ˌsilver 'tongue** way of speaking that charms or persuades people 口才; 雄辩: *It was his silver tongue that got him the job.* 他因口齿伶俐而获得了这份工作.

▷ **sil·ver** *v* **1** [Tn] coat (sth) with silver or sth that looks like silver 在(某物)上镀银、包银或似银的物质: *metal silvered to make ornaments* 用做饰物的镀银金属 ○ *silver a mirror*, ie coat glass to make it reflect things 制镜(在玻璃上涂似银物质而成). **2** [I, Tn] (cause hair, etc to) become bright like silver (使毛发等)变成银白色: *Her hair had silvered.* 她的头发已变成银白色. ○ *The years have silvered her hair.* 随着岁月流逝她的头发已白了.

sil·ver *adj* made of or looking like silver 银的; 像银的: *a silver plate, dish, watch* 银盘、碟、表 ○ *a silver car, paint, thread* 银色的汽车、颜料、线 ○ *the silver moon* 银色的月亮.

sil·very /ˈsɪlvərɪ; ˋsɪlvərɪ/ *adj* **1** shiny or coloured like silver(1) 光亮的; 银色的: *a silvery surface* 有银色光泽的表面. **2** [attrib 作定语] (*approv* 褒) (of sounds) high-pitched and clear (指声音)清脆的: *the silvery notes of the little bells* 小铃铛的清脆响声.

□ **ˌsilver 'birch** common birch tree with a light grey bark 欧洲桦.

'silver-fish *n* any of various types of small silver-coloured wingless insects feeding on scraps of food, bookbindings, etc 衣鱼, 蠹鱼(银色无翼昆虫, 蛀蚀书籍等).

ˌsilver 'jubilee (celebration of a) 25th anniversary 25周年(纪念). Cf 参看 DIAMOND JUBILEE (DIAMOND), GOLDEN JUBILEE (GOLDEN).

ˌsilver 'paper (*infml* 口) thin light foil of tin or aluminium, used esp for wrapping cigarettes, chocolates, etc 锡纸(尤指用以包装香烟、巧克力等的).

ˌsilver 'plate metal articles coated with silver 镀银或包银的金属器具.

ˌsilver-'plated *adj*: *silver-plated dishes* 镀银的盘子.

'silverside *n* [U] (*Brit*) outer side of the top of a leg of beef 牛腿肉上面的外侧部分.

'silversmith *n* person who makes or sells silver articles 银匠; 银器商.

ˌsilver-'tongued *adj* speaking in a way that charms or persuades people 有口才的; 雄辩的: *a ˌsilver-tongued 'lawyer* 能言善辩的律师.

'silverware *n* [U] articles made of silver 银器.

ˌsilver 'wedding 25th anniversary of a wedding 银婚(结婚25周年纪念). Cf 参看 DIAMOND WEDDING (DIAMOND), GOLDEN WEDDING (GOLDEN).

sim·ian /ˈsɪmɪən; ˋsɪmɪən/ *adj*, *n* (*fml* 文) (of or like a) monkey or ape 猴或猿(的); 似猴或猿的: *a simian appearance, posture, movement* 像猴的外貌、姿势、动作.

sim·ilar /ˈsɪmɪlə(r); ˋsɪmələ˞/ *adj* **~ (to sb/sth)** resembling sb/sth but not the same; alike 相似的; 类似的: *We have similar tastes in music.* 我们在音乐方面爱好相似. ○ *Gold is similar in colour to brass.* 金与黄铜的颜色相似. ○ *The brothers look very similar.* 他们兄弟看上去很相似.

▷ **sim·ilarly** *adv* **1** in a similar way 相似地; 类似地: *The two boys dress similarly.* 两个小男孩穿得差不多一样. **2** also; likewise 也; 同样: *She was late and I similarly was delayed.* 她迟到了, 我也晚了.

sim·il·ar·ity /ˌsɪməˈlærətɪ; ˌsɪməˋlærətɪ/ *n* **1** [U] being similar; likeness 相似; 类似: *points of similarity between the two men* 这两人的相似之点. **2** [C] similar feature or aspect 相似之处; 相似之点: *similarities in age and background* 年龄与背景相似.

sim·ile /ˈsɪmɪlɪ; ˋsɪməˌlɪ/ *n* [U, C] (use of) comparison of one thing with another, eg 'as brave as a lion', 'a face like a mask' 明喻; 明喻的运用(如: '勇猛如狮','像假面具一样的面孔'): *use daring similes* 使用破格的明喻 ○ *Her style is rich in simile.* 她的文体中用很多明喻. Cf 参看 METAPHOR.

S

si·mil·it·ude /sɪˈmɪlɪtju:d; *US* -tu:d; səˈmɪlə,tud/ *n* (*fml* 文) **1** [U] being similar; similarity 相似; 类似. **2** [C] comparison; simile 比喻; 明喻: *talk in similitudes* 说话中用比喻.

sim·mer /ˈsɪmə(r); ˋsɪmɚ/ *v* **1** [I, Tn] (cause sth to) remain almost at boiling-point (使某物)保持在接近沸点; 煨; 炖: *Let the soup simmer (for) a few minutes.* 让汤再煮几分钟. ○ *Simmer the stew for an hour.* 用文火把菜炖一小时. **2** [I, Ipr] **~ (with sth)** be filled with (anger, etc) which one can hardly control 充满难以控制的(怒火等): *She simmered for a minute or two, then began shouting uncontrollably.* 她强忍了一两分钟, 然后情不自禁地大叫起来. ○ *simmer with rage, annoyance, etc about sth* 按捺着对某事物的怒气、烦恼等. **3** [I] (of a quarrel, dispute, etc) continue for a time without any real anger or violence being shown (指争吵、争辩等)处于即将爆发的状态: *This row has been simmering for months.* 这场争吵已憋了好几个月了. **4** (phr v) **simmer down** (*infml* 口) become calm after a period of anger, excitement, violence, etc 变冷静, 安静下来(在愤怒、激动、暴力行为等之后): *Simmer down, now, and stop shouting.* 静下来吧, 别喊了. ○ *Things have simmered down since the riots last week.* 自上周骚动以来, 事态已平静下来了.

▷ **sim·mer** *n* **1** [sing] process of simmering 煨; 炖: *give the vegetables a five-minute simmer* 把菜炖五分钟. **2** (idm 习语) **keep sth at a/on the ˈsimmer** keep sth simmering 使某物保持在接近沸点: *Keep the potatoes on the simmer for ten minutes.* 把马铃薯炖十分钟.

si·mony /ˈsaɪmənɪ; ˋsaɪmənɪ/ *n* [U] (formerly) the buying and selling of church appointments, holy relics, etc (旧时)买卖圣职、圣物等.

S

si·moom /sɪˈmu:m; sɪˋmum/ (also **si·moon** /sɪˈmu:n; sɪˋmun/) *n* [sing] hot dry wind blowing in the Sahara and Arabian deserts carrying clouds of dust 西蒙风(撒哈拉及阿拉伯沙漠地区的干热风沙).

sim·per /ˈsɪmpə(r); ˋsɪmpɚ/ *v* [I] smile in a foolish, affected way 傻笑; 假笑: *a simpering waiter* 面带假笑的侍应生.

▷ **sim·per** *n* [sing] foolish, affected smile 傻笑; 假笑. **sim·per·ingly** /ˈsɪmpərɪŋlɪ; ˋsɪmpərɪŋlɪ/ *adv*.

simple /ˈsɪmpl; ˋsɪmpl̩/ *adj* (**-r**, **-st**) **1** easily done or understood; not causing difficulty 简单的; 简明的: *a simple task, sum, problem* 简单的工作、算题、问题 ○ *written in simple English* 用浅显的英文写出 ○ *The machine is quite simple to use.* 这机器使用很简便. ○ *When speaking to young people, keep it simple*, ie speak in a way they can understand. 对年轻人说话, 要简明易懂. **2** plain in form, design, etc; without much decoration or ornament 式样简朴的; 朴素的: *simple food, furniture* 简单的食物、家具 ○ *a simple style of architecture* 简朴的建筑风格 ○ *the simple life*, ie a way of living without luxury, expensive entertainments, etc 简朴的生活 ○ *I like my clothes to be simple but elegant.* 我喜欢穿朴素大方的衣服. **3** [usu attrib 通常作定语] (**a**) not made up of many parts or elements 单纯的; 非复合的: *a simple substance, mixture* 单纯的物质、混合物 ○ *a simple tool, toy* 简单的工具、玩具 ○ *a simple sentence*, ie one without subordinate clauses 简单句. (**b**) not highly developed; basic in structure or function 未充分发展的; (在结构或功能方面)初级的: *simple forms of life, like one-cell organisms* 生命的原始形式, 如单细胞有机体 ○ *a fairly simple system of classification* 相当初步的分类系统. **4** (**a**) natural and straightforward; not sophisticated 自然的; 率直的; 天真的: *behave in a simple, open way* 行为直率 ○ *as simple as a child* 像儿童一样天真. (**b**) not having a high position in society; ordinary 社会地位不高的; 普通的; 卑微的: *I'm just a simple soldier.* 我只不过是普通士兵. ○ *My father was a simple farm-worker.* 我父亲是个普通的农民. **5** (**a**) easily deceived; inexperienced; naïve 易受欺的; 无经验的; 幼稚的: *Are you simple enough to believe what that liar tells you?* 你会蠢到相信那骗子说的话吗? ○ *I'm not so simple as to think it will be easy.* 我决不致于笨得以为那是容易的事. (**b**) (*infml* 口) not having normal intelligence 头脑简单的; 智能低下的: *She doesn't understand you. She's a bit simple.* 她不明白你的意思. 她有点笨. **6** [attrib 作定语] nothing more or other than 纯粹的; 纯然的: *It's a simple fact.* 这就是事实. ○ *a simple unbiased account of events* 对事情纯然无偏见的叙述 ○ *Was it simple greed that made you steal it?* 你偷这件东西是完全因为贪心作祟吗? **7** (idm 习语) **pure and simple** ⇨PURE.

▷ **simple** *n* (*arch* 古) herb used for treating illness, wounds, etc 草药.

simply /ˈsɪmplɪ; ˋsɪmplɪ/ *adv* **1** in an easy way 简单地; 简明地: *solved quite simply* 很简单就解决了 ○ *Explain it as simply as you can.* 尽可能简单地解释一下. **2** in a plain or unfussy way 朴素地; 朴实地: *dress simply* 穿得朴素 ○ *simply dressed* 衣着朴素 ○ *live simply* 生活朴素. **3** completely; absolutely 完全地; 绝对地: *His pronunciation is simply terrible.* 他的发音实在糟透了. ○ *I simply refuse to go!* 我就是不去! **4** merely; only 仅; 只: *I bought the house simply because it was large.* 就是因为这所房子大我才买的. ○ *Is success simply a matter of working hard?* 是否只要勤奋就能成功?

□ **simple fraction** = VULGAR FRACTION (VULGAR).

ˌ**simple ˈinterest** interest paid on a capital sum only, not on the interest that is added to it 单利. Cf 参看 COMPOUND INTEREST (COMPOUND[1]).

ˌ**simple maˈchine** any simple instrument used as (part of) a machine, eg a wheel, lever, pulley 简单机械(如轮、杠杆、滑轮).

ˌ**simple-ˈminded** *adj* (*often derog* 常作贬义) showing very little intelligence 头脑简单的; 笨的: *her more ˌsimple-minded supˈporters* 她的那些头脑更加简单的支持者 ○ *a simple-minded approach to the problem* 处理该问题愚蠢的办法.

sim·ple·ton /ˈsɪmpltən; ˋsɪmpl̩tən/ *n* person who is foolish, easily deceived or not very intelligent 傻瓜; 笨蛋; 易受骗的人.

sim·pli·city /sɪmˈplɪsətɪ; sɪmˋplɪsətɪ/ *n* [U] **1** being easy, plain or straightforward 简单; 朴素; 率直: *the simplicity of the problem* 该问题的简单性 ○ *the simplicity of her style* 她风格的朴实 ○ *a character marked by frankness and simplicity* 爽直的性格. **2** (idm 习语) **be simˌplicity itˈself** be very easy 极为容易: *Cleaning the light is simplicity itself; just wipe it with a damp cloth.* 把灯弄干净非常容易, 用湿布一擦就行了.

sim·plify /ˈsɪmplɪfaɪ; ˋsɪmplə,faɪ/ *v* (*pt, pp* **-fied**) [Tn] make (sth) easy to do or understand; make simple(1) 使(某事物)简单或简明; 简化: *a simplified text*, eg one for learners of the language 简易读本 ○ *simplify the instructions so that children can understand them* 简化指示便于儿童理解 ○ *That will simplify my task.* 那可简化我的工作.

▷ **sim·pli·fica·tion** /ˌsɪmplɪfɪˈkeɪʃn; ˌsɪmpləfəˋkeʃən/ *n* (**a**) [U] act or process of simplifying 简化. (**b**) [C] instance of simplifying; sth simplified 简化; 简化的事物: *What she said was a useful simplification of the theory.* 她把这一理论讲得深入浅出.

sim·plistic /sɪmˈplɪstɪk; sɪmˋplɪstɪk/ *adj* (*usu derog* 通常作贬义) making difficult problems, issues, ideas, etc seem much simpler than they really are; over-simplifying (使困难的问题、事情、意见等)显得过于简单的; 过分简单化的: *a rather simplistic assessment of a complex situation* 对一复杂局面过于简单化的看法.

si·mu·lac·rum /ˌsɪmjʊˈleɪkrəm; ˌsɪmjəˋlekrəm/ *n* (*pl* **-cra** /-krə; -krə/) (*fml* 文) thing resembling or made to resemble sb/sth 模拟物; 假象; 幻影.

simu·late /ˈsɪmjʊleɪt; ˋsɪmjə,let/ *v* [Tn] **1** pretend to have or feel (esp an emotion) 假装有或感到(尤指情感): *simulate anger, joy, interest, etc* 假装愤怒、高兴、有兴趣等 ○ *her carefully simulated disappointment* 她精心装出的失望. **2** reproduce (certain conditions) by means of a model, etc, eg for study or training purposes (用模型等)模拟(某环境)(如用于研究或训练): *simulate flight using a model plane in a wind tunnel* 用模型飞机在风洞里模拟飞行 ○ *The computer simulates conditions on the sea bed.* 这个计算机能模拟海底环境. **3** take on the appearance of (sth/sb) 模仿, 伪装(某物[某人]): *insects that simulate dead leaves* 伪装成枯叶的昆虫 ○ *change colour to simulate the background* 改变颜色以模仿得与背景一致.

▷ **simu·lated** *adj* [usu attrib 通常作定语] made to look, sound, etc like (sth) 模仿的; 假的: *simulated fur, jewels, etc* 人造毛皮、珠宝等.

simu·la·tion /ˌsɪmjʊˈleɪʃn; ˌsɪmjəˋleʃən/ *n* **1** [U] action of simulating 假装; 伪装; 模拟; 模仿: *the simulation of* *genuine concern* 装出真正关心的样子 ○ *the simulation of flight conditions* 飞行环境模拟. **2** [C] operation in which a real situation, etc is represented in another form 模拟操作: *a computer simulation of the nuclear reaction* 对核反应的计算机模拟.

simu·lator *n* any device designed to simulate certain conditions, eg flight, weightlessness, etc (模拟某环境的)模拟装置(如模拟飞行、失重等).

sim·ul·tan·eous /ˌsɪmlˈteɪnɪəs; *US* ˌsaɪm-; ˌsaɪmlˋtenɪəs/ *adj* **~ (with sth)** happening or done at the same time (as sth) 同时的; 同时发生的; 同时做出的: *simultaneous demonstrations in London and New York* 在伦敦与纽约同时举行的示威游行 ○ *The explosion was timed to be simultaneous with the plane's take-off.* 把爆炸的时间定在正是飞机起飞的时刻. ▷ **sim·ul·tan·eously** *adv*. **sim·ul·tan·eous·ness, sim·ul·tan·eity** /ˌsɪmltəˈni:ətɪ; *US* ˌsaɪm-; ˌsaɪmltəˋniətɪ/ *ns* [U].

sin /sɪn; sɪn/ *n* **1 (a)** [U] the breaking of a religious or moral law 违背宗教或道德原则的恶行: *a life of sin* 不道德的生活. **(b)** [C] offence against such a law (宗教或道德上的)罪, 罪恶, 罪孽: *commit a sin* 犯有罪恶 ○ *confess one's sins to a priest* 向神父认罪忏悔 ○ *the sin of gluttony* 贪食罪. **2** [C] action regarded as a serious fault or offence 严重过失: *Being late is an unforgivable sin round here.* 迟到在这儿是一种不可原谅的过错. ○ (*joc* 谑) *It's a sin to stay indoors on such a fine day.* 这样好的天气呆在家里实在是罪过. **3** (idm 习语) **cover/hide a multitude of sins** ⇨MULTITUDE. **the deadly sins** ⇨DEADLY. **live in sin** ⇨LIVE². **(as) miserable/ugly as ˈsin** (*infml* 口) very miserable/ugly 非常凄惨[丑陋].

▷ **sin** *v* **(-nn-)** [I, Ipr] **~ (against sth)** commit a sin or sins; do wrong 犯有罪恶; 犯过错: *It's human to sin.* 犯过错是人之常情. ○ (*fig* 比喻) *They sinned against the unwritten rules of the school.* 他们违反了学校的不成文规定.

sin·ful /-fl; -fəl/ *adj* (*esp fml* 尤作文雅语) wrong; wicked 有过错的; 有过失的; 邪恶的: *Man is sinful.* 是人就有过错. ○ *sinful deeds* 邪恶的行为 ○ (*infml* 口) *a sinful waste of good wine* 浪费好酒的罪过. **sin·fully** /-fəlɪ; -fəlɪ/ *adv*. **sin·ful·ness** *n* [U]. **sin·less** *adj* (*fml* 文) never sinning; innocent 无罪过的; 无辜的; 清白的. **sin·less·ness** *n* [U].

sin·ner /ˈsɪnə(r); ˋsɪnɚ/ *n*: *saints and sinners* 圣人和有罪过的人.

sin *abbr* 缩写 = (*mathematics* 数) sine. Cf 参看 COS *abbr* 缩写.

since /sɪns; sɪns/ *prep* (used with the present or past perfect tense 与现在完成时态或过去完成时态连用) from (a specified time in the past) till a later past time, or till now 从(过去某时间)以来、以后或到现在: *I haven't eaten since breakfast.* 我吃了早饭后到现在还什么都没吃呢. ○ *She's been working in a bank since leaving school.* 她中学毕业后就一直在一家银行工作. ○ *He had spoken to her only once since the party.* 自从那次聚会以来, 他只跟她说过一次话.

▷ **since** *conj* **1** (used with the present perfect, past perfect or simple present tense in the main clause 与主句中的现在完成时态、过去完成时态或一般现在时态连用) from (a specified event in the past) till a later past event, or till now 从(过去某事)以来、以后或到现在: *Where have you been since I last saw you?* 自从我上次见到你以后, 你到哪儿去了? ○ *It was the first time I'd won since I'd learnt to play chess.* 自从我学会下国际象棋以来, 这是我第一次赢. ○ *How long is it since we visited your mother?* 自从我们看望你母亲以来到现在有多长时间了? **2** because; as 因为; 既然; 由于: *Since we've no money we can't buy a new car.* 因为我们没钱, 没法买新汽车. **3** (idm 习语) **ever since** ⇨EVER.

since *adv* (used with the present or past perfect tense 与现在完成时态或过去完成时态连用) from a specified time in the past till a later past time, or till now 从过去某时间以来、以后或到现在: *He left home two weeks ago and we haven't heard from him since.* 他两星期以前离开了家, 到现在我们一直没有他的消息. ○ *She moved to London last May and has since got a job on a newspaper.* 她去年五月到伦敦, 此后一直在报社工作.

sin·cere /sɪnˈsɪə(r); sɪnˋsɪr/ *adj* **1** (of feelings or behaviour) not pretended; genuine (指感情或行为)真实的, 诚挚的: *sincere friendship, affection, dislike, disagreement, etc* 诚挚的友谊、真诚的爱、真正的厌恶、实质的分歧 ○ *It is my sincere belief that...* 我确信... ○ *His was a sincere offer of help.* 他真心实意愿意协助. **2** (of people) only saying things one really means or believes; straightforward (指人)诚实的, 直率的: *a sincere Christian* 虔诚的基督教徒 ○ *She wasn't entirely sincere when she said she liked me.* 她说她喜欢我, 这话有些言不由衷.

▷ **sin·cerely** *adv*: *thank sb sincerely* 真诚地感谢某人 ○ *yours sincerely* 谨启(用于信件署名前). ⇨Usage at YOUR 用法见 YOUR.

sin·cer·ity /sɪnˈserətɪ; sɪnˋsɛrətɪ/ *n* [U] quality of being sincere; honesty 真诚; 诚挚; 诚实: *the warmth and sincerity of his welcome* 他热情而真诚的欢迎.

sine /saɪn; saɪn/ *n* (*abbr* 缩写 **sin**) (*mathematics* 数) (in a right-angled triangle) the ratio of the length of the side opposite one of the acute angles to the length of the hypotenuse 正弦. Cf 参看 COSINE, TANGENT 2.

sine·cure /ˈsaɪnɪkjʊə(r), ˈsɪn-; ˋsaɪnɪˌkjʊr, ˋsɪn-/ *n* position that requires no work or responsibility, but gives the holder prestige or money 无工作或责任而领干薪的职位; 挂名职位.

sine die /ˌsaɪnɪ ˈdaɪi:, ˌsɪnɪ ˈdi:eɪ; ˋsaɪnɪˋdaɪ·i/ (*fml esp law* 文, 尤用于法律) without a date being fixed; indefinitely 无确定日期地; 无限期地: *adjourn a meeting sine die* 无限期休会.

sine qua non /ˌsɪneɪ kwɑ: ˈnəʊn; ˋsaɪnɪkweˋnɑn/ (*fml* 文) essential condition; thing that is absolutely necessary 必要条件; 必不可少的事物: *Patience is a sine qua non for a good teacher.* 做个优秀教师必不可少的条件是要有耐心.

sinew /ˈsɪnju:; ˋsɪnju/ *n* **1** [C, U] tough cord of tissue joining a muscle to a bone; tendon 腱; 肌腱. **2 sinews** [pl] **(a)** muscles 肌肉: *The athletes waited, with all their sinews tensed.* 运动员都在等待着, 全身肌肉十分紧张. **(b)** (*fml fig* 文, 比喻) source of strength or energy 力量或能量的来源: *A country's sinews are its roads and railways.* 公路和铁路是国家的命脉.

▷ **sin·ewy** *adj* **1** having strong sinews; tough; muscular 肌肉发达的; 坚韧的; 强壮的: *sinewy arms, legs, etc* 粗壮的手臂、腿等. **2** (*fig* 比喻) having or showing strength or vigour 强劲的; 有力的: *her sinewy prose style* 她那强劲有力的散文风格.

sing /sɪŋ; sɪŋ/ *v* (*pt* **sang** /sæŋ; sæŋ/, *pp* **sung** /sʌŋ; sʌŋ/) **1** [I, Ipr, Ip, Tn, Tn·pr, Dn·n, Dn·pr] **~ (sth) (for/to sb)** make musical sounds with the voice; utter (words or notes) with a tune 唱; 歌唱; 唱(歌): *She sings well.* 她很会唱歌. ○ *You're not singing in tune.* 你唱走调了. ○ *Birds sang/were singing away happily outside.* 小鸟在外面愉快地唱个不停. ○ *He sang to a piano accompaniment.* 他演唱由钢琴伴奏. ○ *She was singing a lullaby to her child.* 她在给孩子唱摇篮曲. ○ *He sang the baby to sleep.* 他唱着歌哄孩子入睡. ○ *Will you sing me a song?* 你给我唱支歌好吗? ○ *They sang a song for me.* 他们给我唱了支歌. **2** [I, Ip] make a humming, buzzing or whistling sound 发出哼哼声、嗡嗡声或口哨声: *The kettle was singing (away) on the cooker.* 水壶在炉子上发出呜呜声. ○ *The explosion made my ears sing*, ie made me hear a singing sound. 那爆炸声震得我耳朵嗡嗡作响. **3** [I] (*sl* 俚 *esp US*) become an informer 告密: *She'll sing if we put the pressure on.* 我们给她些压力她就会讲出来. **4** (idm 习语) **sing a different ˈsong/ˈtune** change one's opinion about or attitude towards sb/sth 改变对某人[某事物]的看法或态度: *You say you don't believe in marriage, but I bet you sing a different song when you finally fall in love.* 你说你认为结婚是无谓的, 但我肯定你最终爱上一个人的时候你就不这么说了. **sing sb's/sth's ˈpraises** praise sb/sth greatly 盛赞某人[某事物]: *The critics are singing the praises of her new book.* 评论家高度赞扬她写的新书. **5** (phr v) **sing out (for sth)** (*infml* 口) shout (to get sth) 大声说出(要某物): *If you need anything, just sing out for it.* 你需要什么东西就大声说出来. **sing sth out** (*infml* 口) shout (eg an order) 喊出(如命令): *Just sing out what you want.* 你要什么尽管大声说出来. **sing past, through, etc** move with a humming, buzzing or whistling sound 发着哼哼声、嗡嗡声或口哨声运动: *A bullet sang past my ear.* 一颗子弹嗖的一声从我耳边飞过. **sing up** sing more vigorously or loudly 唱得更有力或声音更大: *Sing up, let's hear you.* 大点声唱, 让我们听听.

▷ **singer** *n* person who sings, esp in public 唱歌的人; (尤指)歌手, 歌唱家: *an opera singer* 歌剧演唱者.

sing·ing *n* [U] **1** art of the singer 唱歌的技巧: *teach singing* 教唱歌 ○ [attrib 作定语] *a singing teacher* 教唱歌的教师 ○ *singing lessons* 唱歌课. **2** action or sound of singing 唱歌; 歌声: *their beautiful singing of the madrigal* 他们的歌唱得很动听 ○ *I heard singing next door.* 我听见隔壁的歌声.

singe /sɪndʒ; sɪndʒ/ *v* (*pres p* **singeing**) **1** (**a**) [Tn] blacken (sth) by burning; scorch 烧焦或烫焦(某物): *The iron's too hot, you'll singe the dress.* 熨斗太热了, 你会把衣服烫焦的. (**b**) [I] be blackened or scorched in this way 被烧焦或被烫焦: *The rug singed because it was too near the fire.* 地毯太靠近壁炉已烤焦了. **2** [Tn] burn off the tips or ends of (hair, feathers, etc) 烧掉(毛发、羽毛等)的梢或根.

▷ **singe** *n* slight burn or scorch on cloth, etc (布等的)轻微烧焦或烫焦.

single /ˈsɪŋgl; ˋsɪŋgl/ *adj* **1** [attrib 作定语] (**a**) one only; not in a pair, group, etc 单一的; 单个的; 仅有一个的: *a single apple hanging from the tree* 树上仅挂着一个苹果 ○ *a single layer of paint* 单层颜料 ○ *one double and one single sink-unit* 一套双的和一套单的洗涤槽组合台. (**b**) considered on its own; separate 唯一的; 单独的: *the single most important event in the history of the world* 世界史上唯一最重要的事件 ○ *She removed every single thing from the box.* 她把箱子里的东西一件不剩地全拿了出来. **2** not married 未婚的; 独身的: *single men and women* 未婚男女 ○ *remain single* 一直单身 ○ *the single state* 独身. **3** [attrib 作定语] designed for, or used or done by, one person 适于一人的; 一人用的; 一人做的: *a single bed, sheet* 单人床、被单 ○ *reserve one single and one double room*, eg at a hotel 预订一个单人房间和一个双人房间. **4** [attrib 作定语] (*botany* 植) having only one set of petals 单瓣的: *a single tulip* 单瓣郁金香. **5** [attrib 作定语] (*Brit*) (*US* **one-way**) (of a journey) only to a place, not there and back (指旅程)单程的: *a single fare, ticket, etc* 单程票价、票等. Cf 参看 RETURN² 5. **6** (idm 习语) **hang by a hair/a single thread** ⇨ HANG¹. **(in) single ˈfigures** figures less than ten 个位数字(小于十): *Interest rates are in single figures*, ie under 10%. 利率为个位数字(10%以下). **(in) single file** ⇨ FILE³.

▷ **single** *n* **1 singles** [sing *v*] game played with one player rather than a pair of players on each side 单打比赛: *play (a) singles* 进行单打比赛 ○ *the men's/women's singles in the golf tournament* 高尔夫球锦标赛男子[女子]单打 ○ [attrib 作定语] *a singles match* 单打比赛. **2** [C] (in cricket) hit for which one run is scored (板球)一分打: *get a quick single* 击球后速跑得一分. **3** [C] = BASE HIT (BASE¹). **4** [C] (*infml* 口) single(5) ticket 单程票: *two second-class singles to Leeds* 两张到利兹的二等的单程票. **5** [C] record with only one short recording on each side 每面只录有一段录音的唱片: *a hit single* 畅销的单曲唱片. Cf 参看 ALBUM 2, EP, LP. **6 singles** [pl] (*esp US*) unmarried people 未婚的人: *a club for singles* 未婚者俱乐部 ○ [attrib 作定语] *a singles bar, holiday* 未婚者的酒吧、假日.

single *v* (phr v) **single sb/sth out (for sth)** select sb/sth from others, eg for special attention 挑出或选出某人[某事物]: *Which would you single out as the best?* 你觉得哪一个最好? ○ *He was singled out for punishment.* 把他挑出来予以处罚.

single·ness *n* [U]: *singleness of mind*, ie single-mindedness 一心一意 ○ *singleness of purpose*, ie concentration on one goal, aim, etc 专心致志.

singly /ˈsɪŋglɪ; ˋsɪŋglɪ/ *adv* one by one; on one's own 一个一个地; 个别地; 单独地: *Do you teach your students singly or in groups?* 你教学生是个别地教还是按组教?

□ ˌ**single ˈcombat** fight, usu with weapons, between two people; duel 两人相斗(通常指用武器); 决斗: *meet in single combat* 两人相斗.

ˌ**single ˈcream** cream that contains relatively little fat 低脂奶油.

ˌ**single-ˈdecker** *n* bus with only one deck 单层公共汽车.

ˌ**single-ˈhanded** *adj, adv* done (by one person) with no help from others 独自(的); 独力(的): *a ˌsingle-handed ˈsailing trip* 单人扬帆航行 ○ *do sth single-handed* 独自做某事.

ˌ**single-ˈminded** *adj* having or concentrating on one aim, purpose, etc 一心一意的; 专心致志的: *too single-minded to be distracted by failures* 专心致志百折不挠. **single-mindedly** *adv*: *work single-mindedly at sth* 一心一意做某事. **single-mindedness** *n* [U].

ˌ**single ˈparent** parent bringing up a child/children on his/her own 单亲(单独养育子女的人): [attrib 作定语] *a ˌsingle-parent ˈfamily* 单亲家庭.

sing·let /ˈsɪŋglɪt; ˋsɪŋglɪt/ *n* (*Brit*) (**a**) man's sleeveless garment worn under or instead of a shirt; vest 男用无袖汗衫; 背心. (**b**) such a garment worn by runners, athletes, etc 无袖运动衫.

sing·song /ˈsɪŋsɒŋ; ˋsɪŋˌsɔŋ/ *adj* (of a voice or way of speaking) having a rising and falling rhythm (指嗓音或说话方式)有起伏节奏的: *in a singsong voice, accent, manner* 语调、声调、腔调有起伏节奏的.

▷ **sing·song** *n* **1** [sing] singsong manner of speaking 有起伏节奏的说话方式: *the tedious singsong of the preacher's voice* 传教士单调乏味的起伏语调 ○ *speak in a singsong* 用有起伏节奏的声音说. **2** [C] (*infml* 口) informal occasion when a group of people sing songs together 即兴歌唱会: *a singsong round the camp-fire* 围着营火的即兴歌唱会.

sin·gu·lar /ˈsɪŋgjʊlə(r); ˋsɪŋgjələ˞/ *adj* **1** (*grammar*) of the form used when speaking about one person or thing 单数的: *a singular verb, noun, ending* 单数动词、名词、词尾. Cf 参看 PLURAL. **2** (*fml* 文) (**a**) (*dated* 旧) unusual; strange 异常的; 奇怪的: *a singular occurrence, event, circumstance, etc* 异常的现象、事件、情况等. (**b**) outstanding; remarkable 突出的; 非凡的: *a person of singular courage and honesty* 极为勇敢和诚实的人.

▷ **sin·gu·lar** *n* (*grammar*) (word in a) singular form 单数形式(的词): *What is the singular of 'children'?* children的单数形式是怎样的? ○ *What is the ending in the singular?* 这个词的单数词尾是怎样的?

sin·gu·lar·ity /ˌsɪŋgjʊˈlærətɪ; ˌsɪŋgjəˋlærətɪ/ *n* [U] (*fml* 文) strangeness 奇怪: *the singularity of the event* 这件事的奇异之处.

sin·gu·larly *adv* (*fml* 文) **1** (*dated* 旧) unusually; strangely 异常地; 奇怪的: *rather singularly attired* 穿着很奇怪. **2** very; remarkably 非常; 非凡地: *a singularly gifted pianist* 非凡的天才钢琴家.

sin·is·ter /ˈsɪnɪstə(r); ˋsɪnɪstə˞/ *adj* **1** suggesting evil, or that sth bad may happen 邪恶的; 险恶的; 不吉祥的; 凶兆的: *a sinister motive, action, place* 邪恶的动机、险恶的行动、不祥之处. **2** suggesting an evil nature 凶恶的; 阴险的: *a sinister face* 凶恶的脸 ○ *sinister looks* 阴险的神情.

sink¹ /sɪŋk; sɪŋk/ *v* (*pt* **sank** /sæŋk; sæŋk/, *pp* **sunk** /sʌŋk; sʌŋk/) **1** [I, Ipr, Ip] go down under the surface of a liquid or soft substance 下沉; 沉没: *Wood does not sink in water, it floats.* 木头在水中不沉, 而是漂在水面. ○ *The ship sank (to the bottom of the ocean).* 船沉(到海底)了. ○ *My feet sank (down) into the mud.* 我的脚陷进了泥里. ○ *It fell onto the wet sand, then sank (in).* 那个东西掉在潮湿的沙子上, 然后沉了下去. **2** [Tn] (**a**) cause (a ship, etc) to go to the bottom of the sea 使(船等)沉到海底: *a carrier sunk by a torpedo* 被鱼雷击沉的航空母舰 ○ *They sank the barge by making a hole in the bottom.* 他们在驳船底部打个洞把它弄沉了. (**b**) (*fig infml* 比喻, 口) prevent (sb or sb's plans) from succeeding; ruin 阻止或搞垮(某人或某人的计划); 毁灭: *The press want to sink his bid for the Presidency.* 新闻界想搞垮他参选总统职位的计划. ○ *We'll be sunk if the car breaks down.* 要是汽车坏了, 我们就糟了. **3** (**a**) [I, Ipr, Ip] become lower; fall slowly downwards 变低; 缓慢下陷或倒下: *The foundations sank (two feet) after the flood.* 洪水退后地基下陷了(两英尺). ○ *The earthquake made the wall sink and start to crumble.* 这次地震把这堵墙震得下陷并开始崩塌. ○ *The soldier sank to the ground badly wounded.* 那士兵受了重伤, 倒在地上. ○ *I sank (down) into an armchair.* 我一下子坐在单座沙发上. (**b**) [Tn, Tn·pr] cause (sth) to be lower; move (sth) downwards 使(某物)变低; 将(某物)下降: *sink the cable into position on the sea bed* 把电缆沉到海底的位置 ○ (*fig* 比喻) *sink one's voice to a whisper* 把自己的声音减小变成耳语.

4 (**a**) [I, Ipr] (of the sun) go down below the horizon (指太阳)落下: *the sun sinking in the west* 西下的太阳 ○ *The sun sank slowly behind the hills.* 太阳慢慢落山了. (**b**) [I, Ipr] lose value, strength, etc gradually; decline 逐渐贬值、变弱等; 衰退: *Stocks and shares are sinking.* 股票正在逐渐贬值. ○ *The value of our currency has sunk to almost nothing.* 我们货币已经毛得简直分文不值了. ○ *He is sinking fast,* ie will soon die. 他快死了. ○ (*fig* 比喻) *sink in the estimation of one's friends* 在朋友中人缘越来越差 ○ (*fig* 比喻) *His voice sank to a whisper.* 他的声音逐渐小得成了耳语. 5 (**a**) place (sth) in a hole made by digging 将(某物)置于掘的洞中: *sink two posts (into the ground) here* 把两根杆子埋到这里(的地上). (**b**) [Tn, Tn·pr] make (sth) by digging 掘, 挖, 凿(某物): *sink a well, shaft, etc* 掘井、矿井等 ○ *sink a tunnel into the side of the mountain* 在山腰挖隧道. 6 [Tn, Tn·pr] send (a ball) into a pocket or hole (in billiards, golf, etc) 将(球)击入袋中或洞中(台球、高尔夫球等): *sink the red (into the top pocket)* 把红球打入顶头的袋中. 7 [Tn] (*infml* 口) drink (esp a large amount of alcohol) 喝(尤指大量的酒): *They sank a bottle of gin between them.* 他们俩喝了一瓶杜松子酒. 8 (idm 习语) **be sunk in sth** be in such a state of (esp despair or deep thought) 陷入或堕入(某状态)(尤指绝望或沉思): *She just sat there, sunk in depression.* 她就坐在那里, 情绪十分低落. **one's heart sinks** ⇨HEART. **sink one's ˈdifferences** agree to forget what one disagrees about 同意放弃不同意见: *We must sink our differences and save the firm.* 我们必须消除分歧以挽救公司. **a/that ˈsinking feeling** (*infml* 口) feeling that sth bad is about to happen 感到要出事: *When they didn't get back by midnight, I got that sinking feeling.* 他们到半夜时还没回来, 我感到心神不定. **sink like a ˈstone** sink straight down immediately 急速下降或下落. **ˌsink or ˈswim** (*saying* 谚) (used of a situation where one will either fail totally or survive by one's own efforts 用以指或完全失败或自力更生的情况): *The refugees had lost their homes and their possessions, and it was now (a case of) sink or swim.* 这些难民失去了家园和财产, 若不自救别无生路. 9 (phr v) **sink in/sink into sth** (**a**) (of liquids) go down into another substance; be absorbed (指液体)渗入(某一物质), 被吸收: *Rub the cream on your skin and let it sink in.* 把这种软膏搽在皮肤上, 让它渗进去. ○ *The rain sank into the dry ground.* 雨水渗入干燥的土地. (**b**) (of words, etc) be fully understood (指话语等)完全理解: *The scale of the tragedy gradually sank in.* 这一悲惨事件涉及的范围已逐渐完全清楚了. ○ *My warning obviously hasn't sunk into your thick skull.* 我对你的警告, 你显然全不理解. **sink into sth** (no passive 不用于被动语态) go into (a less active or happy state) 陷入(消极、不活跃或不愉快的状态): *sink into sleep, a coma, etc* 入睡、陷入昏迷 ○ *Don't let yourself sink into despair.* 别让自己陷入绝望的境地. **sink sth into sth** (**a**) make sth go into sth 使某物进入另一物中: *sink one's teeth into a bun,* ie bite it 咬面包 ○ *sink a knife into butter* 把刀插进黄油里. (**b**) invest (money) in a business, etc 将(钱)投资到某生意等中: *They sank all their profits into* (ie used them to buy) *property.* 他们用全部赢利购买了房地产.

□ **ˈsinking fund** money put aside by a government or company, etc to be used to repay a debt gradually (政府、公司等准备的)偿债基金.

sink² /sɪŋk; sɪŋk/ *n* 1 fixed basin, usu of steel, porcelain, etc, with a water supply and a drain for waste water to flow away, used for washing dishes, cleaning vegetables, etc 洗涤槽(通常由钢、瓷等制成, 配有水源和排水管, 用于洗涤碗碟、蔬菜等): [attrib 作定语] *a sink unit,* ie a sink with drawers and cupboards underneath 洗涤槽组合台(洗涤槽下面有抽屉和柜橱). 2 (*US*) wash-basin 洗脸盆. 3 cesspool 污水坑. 4 (idm 习语) **everything but the kitchen sink** ⇨KITCHEN.

sinker /ˈsɪŋkə(r); ˈsɪŋkɚ/ *n* 1 weight attached to a fishing-line or net to keep it under water (钓丝或鱼网上的)铅坠. 2 (idm 习语) **hook, line and sinker** ⇨HOOK¹.

Sino- (also **sino-**) *comb form* 构词成分 Chinese; of China 中国的: *sinology* ○ *Sino-Japanese.*

si·no·logy /saɪˈnɒlədʒɪ; saɪˈnɑlədʒɪ/ *n* [U] knowledge or study of China and its language and culture 汉学.

▷ **si·no·lo·gist** /-dʒɪst; -dʒɪst/ *n* expert in sinology 汉学家.

sinu·ous /ˈsɪnjʊəs; ˈsɪnjuəs/ *adj* having many curves and twists; winding 弯曲的; 蜿蜒的: *the sinuous movements of the dancer* 舞蹈演员柔美的动作 ○ *the river's sinuous course* 那条河的蜿蜒的河道.

▷ **sinu·os·ity** /ˌsɪnjʊˈɒsətɪ; ˌsɪnjuˈɑsətɪ/ *n* (*fml* 文) 1 [U] quality of being sinuous 弯曲; 蜿蜒. 2 [C] curve or twist 弯曲处; 曲折.

si·nus /ˈsaɪnəs; ˈsaɪnəs/ *n* cavity in a bone, esp any of the air-filled spaces in the skull that are connected to the nostrils 窦(骨骼中的空穴, 尤指颅骨中的).

▷ **si·nus·itis** /ˌsaɪnəˈsaɪtɪs; ˌsaɪnəˈsaɪtɪs/ *n* [U] inflammation of a sinus membrane 窦炎.

-sion ⇨-ION.

sip /sɪp; sɪp/ *v* (**-pp-**) [I, Tn] drink (sth), taking very small quantities each time 小口喝; 抿: *drink one's tea, sipping noisily* 喝茶时小口抿出声 ○ *sip one's coffee* 一小口一小口地喝咖啡.

▷ **sip** *n* act of sipping; amount sipped 小口喝; 抿; 一小口的量: *a few sips of brandy* 抿了几口白兰地.

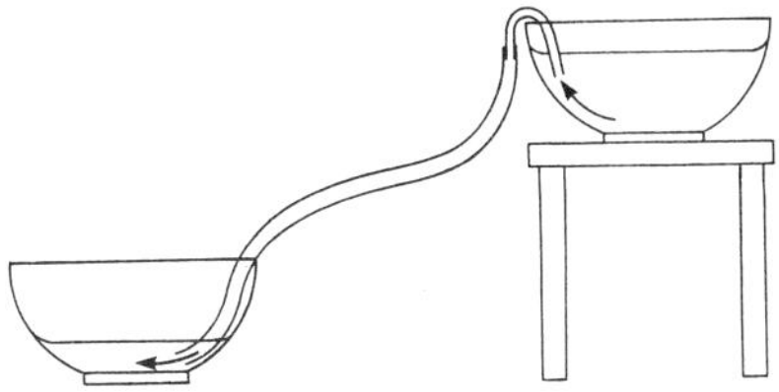

siphon 虹吸(管)

si·phon /ˈsaɪfn; ˈsaɪfən/ *n* 1 pipe, tube, etc in the form of an upside-down U, used for making a liquid flow, eg from one container to another, using atmospheric pressure 虹吸管. 2 (also **soda siphon**) bottle from which soda-water can be forced out by the pressure of gas in the bottle 虹吸瓶. 3 sucking-tube of some insects and animals (某些昆虫和其他动物的)管形口器或吸管.

▷ **si·phon** *v* (phr v) **siphon sth into/out of sth; siphon sth off/out** draw (a liquid) from one place to another using a siphon 用虹吸管将(液体)抽出: *siphon petrol out of a car into a can* 把汽车里的汽油用虹吸管抽进罐里 ○ *siphon off all the waste liquid* 把全部废液用虹吸管抽掉. **siphon sb/sth off** (*infml often derog* 口, 常作贬义) transfer sb/sth from one place to another, often unfairly or illegally 将某人[某物]由一处抽调到另一处(通常指不公正地或非法地): *The big clubs siphon off all the best players.* 大俱乐部把所有最佳选手都抽调走了. ○ *She siphoned off profits from the business into her account.* 她把企业的赢利转到了自己的帐户上.

sir /sɜː(r); sɝ/ *n* 1 (**a**) (used as a polite way of addressing a man 对男子的礼貌称呼): *Yes, sir.* 是的, 先生. ○ *Are you ready to order, sir?* 先生, 要点什么? ○ *Sir, it is my duty to inform you that...* 先生, 我必须通知您.... (**b**) (used as a form of address by schoolchildren to a male teacher 中小学生对男教师的称呼). Cf 参看 MISS² 2. 2 **Sir** (used at the beginning of a formal letter 用于正式信件的开头): *Dear Sir/Sirs* 敬启者. 3 **Sir** /sə(r); sɚ/ (title used before the first name of a knight or baronet 冠于爵士或准男爵的名字之前或名字与姓之前, 但不可只用于姓之前): *Sir ˈEdward* 爱德华爵士 ○ *Sir ˌJohn ˈJackson* 约翰·杰克逊爵士. 4 (idm 习语) **ˌno ˈsir!** (*US infml* 口) certainly not 绝不: *I never smoke, no sir!* 我从来不吸烟, 绝对不吸!

sire /ˈsaɪə(r); saɪr/ *n* male parent of an animal 雄性种兽: *the sire of many successful racehorses* 繁殖了多匹比赛得奖马的雄性种马.

▷ **sire** *v* [Tn] be the sire of (an animal) (雄性种兽)繁殖(幼兽): *a filly sired by a famous racehorse* 一著名雄性赛马的牝驹.

siren /ˈsaɪərən; ˈsaɪrən/ *n* 1 device that makes a long loud sound as a signal or warning 汽笛; 警报器: *an air-raid siren* 空袭警报器 ○ *a police siren* 警察用的警报器 ○ *an ambulance/a fire-engine racing along with its* *sirens wailing* 响着警报器急驰而过的救护车[消防车]. **2** (in Greek mythology) one of a number of winged women whose songs lured sailors to their destruction (希腊神话中的)塞壬(半鸟半女人的怪物, 常用美妙的歌声引诱航海者触礁毁灭). **3** woman regarded as fascinating and dangerous 妖艳而危险的女人.

sir·loin /ˈsɜːlɔɪn; ˋsɝlɔɪn/ *n* [U, C] best part of a loin of beef 牛腰上部的肉: *a slice of sirloin* 一块牛腰肉 ○ *a top-quality sirloin* 上好的牛腰肉.

si·rocco /sɪˈrɒkəʊ; səˋrɑko/ *n* (*pl* **~s**) hot moist wind reaching Italy from Africa (由非洲吹到意大利的)潮湿热风.

sirup (*US*) ⇨SYRUP.

sisal /ˈsaɪsl; ˋsaɪsl̩/ *n* **1** [U] rope-fibre made from the leaves of a tropical plant 西沙尔麻, 剑麻(由热带植物叶制成的纤维, 可制绳): [attrib 作定语] *sisal grass, fibre, rope, etc* 西沙尔草、纤维、绳等. **2** [C] the plant itself 做西沙尔麻的植物.

sissy (also **cissy**) /ˈsɪsɪ; ˋsɪsɪ/ *n* (*infml derog* 口, 贬) effeminate or cowardly boy or man 柔弱或怯懦的男子; 女人腔的男子: *You daren't jump down, you sissy!* 你不敢往下跳, 你不是男子汉! ○ [attrib 作定语] *sissy games, behaviour* 女孩儿的游戏、举止.

sis·ter /ˈsɪstə(r); ˋsɪstɚ/ *n* **1** daughter of the same parents as oneself or another person 姐; 妹: *my, your, his, etc big sister* 我的、你的、他的...姐姐 ○ *She has been like a sister to me,* ie has behaved as a sister does. 她一向待我亲如姐妹. **2** (used esp by feminist women 尤为提倡女权主义的女性使用) fellow woman 姐妹: *They supported their sisters in the dispute.* 她们在辩论中支持她们的姐妹. **3** (*US infml* 口) (used to address a woman 用以称呼女子): *Come on, sister, hurry along!* 好了, 大姐, 快点! **4** (*Brit*) senior hospital nurse 护士长. **5 Sister** member of certain female religious orders; nun 修女: *the Little Sisters of the Poor* 贫民救济修女会. **6** [attrib 作定语] (eg of a ship or an organization) of the same design or type (例如指船或团体)同样类型的: *After the disaster, tests were carried out on the tanker's sister vessels.* 那艘油轮遇难后, 对同类型的油轮都进行了检验. ○ *our sister college in Cambridge* 我们剑桥大学的姐妹学院.

▷ **sis·ter·hood** *n* **1** [U] relationship of sisters(1,2) (esp as claimed by feminist women) 姐妹关系(尤为女权主义者使用). **2** [Gp] society of women with shared interests or aims, esp a religious society 女性社团(尤指宗教社团).

sis·terly *adj* of or like a sister (似)姐妹的: *sisterly love* 姐妹般的爱 ○ *a sisterly kiss* 姐妹般的亲吻.

□ ˈ**sister-in-law** *n* (*pl* **~s-in-law**) sister of one's wife or husband; wife of one's brother 妻或夫的姐或妹(姑子; 姨子); 兄或弟的妻子(嫂子; 弟媳).

sit /sɪt; sɪt/ *v* (**-tt-**; *pt, pp* **sat** /sæt; sæt/) **1 (a)** [I, Ipr, Ip] be in a position in which the body is upright and resting on the buttocks, either on a seat or on the ground 坐; 就座: *Never stand when you can sit.* 能坐着就别站着. ○ *Are you sitting comfortably?* 你坐得舒服吗? ○ *sit on a chair, on the floor, in an armchair, etc* 坐在椅子上、地板上、单座沙发上等 ○ *sit at (a) table to eat* 坐在桌旁吃饭 ○ *sit on a horse* 骑在马上. **(b)** [I, Ip, Tn, Tn·p] **~ (sb) (down)**; **~ oneself down** (cause sb to) take up such a position; place (sb) in a sitting position (使某人)坐, 就座; 将(某人)安置成坐着的姿势: *She sat (down) on the chair and took her shoes off.* 她坐在椅子上, 把鞋脱了. ○ *He lifted the child and sat* (ie seated) *her on the wall.* 他把小孩举起来, 让她坐在墙上. ○ *Sit yourself down and tell us what happened.* 你坐下, 告诉我们怎么回事. ○ (*fig* 比喻) *We must sit down together and settle our differences.* 我们得坐下来解决分歧. **2** [I, Ipr] **~ (for sb)** pose for a portrait 坐着供人画像或拍照: *I sat every day for a week until the painting was finished.* 我每天那样坐着, 一个星期才把我画好. ○ *sit for a famous painter* 坐着供一位名画家画像. **3** [I] (of a parliament, lawcourt, committee, etc) hold a meeting (指国会、法庭、委员会等)开会, 开庭: *The House of Commons was still sitting at 3 am.* 下议院凌晨三时仍在开会. **4** [I, Ipr] **(a)** (of birds) perch (指鸟)栖: *a sparrow sitting on a branch* 栖在树枝上的麻雀. **(b)** (of certain animals, esp dogs) rest with the hind legs bent and the rear end on the ground (指某些动物, 尤指狗)坐: *'Sit!' she told the dog.* '坐下!' 她对狗说. **5** [I] (of birds) stay on the nest to hatch eggs (指禽)孵卵: *The hen sits for most of the day.* 这只母鸡整天大部分时间都在抱窝. **6** [I, Ipr] **~ (on sb)** (usu followed by an *adv* 通常后接副词) (of clothes) fit the body well (指衣服)合身: *a dress that sits well, loosely, etc on sb* 某人穿着合身、宽松等的连衣裙 ○ *The coat sits badly across the shoulders.* 这件大衣肩部不合适. ○ (*fig* 比喻) *His new-found prosperity sits well on him,* ie suits him well. 他别开蹊径十分称心如意. **7** [Ipr] be in a certain position; lie 处于某位置; 位于: *The book's still sitting on my shelf,* ie I haven't read it. 那本书仍在我的书架上搁着呢(我还没看呢). ○ *The farm sits on top of the hill.* 那个农场在山顶上. **8** [Ipr, Tn] **~ (for) sth** be a candidate for (an examination) 参加(考试): *sit (for) an exam/a test* 参加考试[测试] ○ *sit for a scholarship* 为获奖学金而参加考试. **9** (idm 习语) **sit at sb's ˈfeet** be sb's pupil or follower 做某人的弟子或追随者: *She sat at the feet of Freud himself.* 她师承弗洛伊德. **sit in ˈjudgement (on/over sb)** judge sb, esp when one has no right to do so 评论某人(尤指论者无此资格): *How dare you sit in judgement on me?* 你怎么敢对我妄加评论? **sit on the ˈfence** hesitate or fail to decide between two opposite courses of action, sets of beliefs, etc 骑墙; 持观望态度. **sit on one's ˈhands** do nothing 什么都不干: *Are you going to sit on your hands while she does all the work?* 所有的工作都是她做, 你难道什么都不干吗? **a ˌsitting ˈduck** person or thing that is an easy target, or is easy to attack 容易攻击或容易击中的人或事物: *Without my gun, I'm a sitting duck for any terrorist.* 没有这支枪, 我就成了恐怖分子下手的目标. ˌ**sitting ˈpretty** (*infml* 口) in a fortunate situation, esp when others are unlucky 处境幸运(尤指别人不幸时): *I was properly insured so I'm sitting pretty.* 我已经有了一定的保险, 因而有备无患了. ˌ**sit ˈtight** **(a)** remain where one is 留在原处; 不动: *All the others ran away, but I sat tight.* 别人都跑了, 但我在原地没动. **(b)** refuse to take action, yield, etc 不采取行动、不屈服等: *She threatened us with dismissal if we didn't agree, but we all sat tight.* 她威胁说若我们不同意就把我们解雇, 但大家都没理会. **sit ˈup (and take notice)** (*infml* 口) suddenly start paying attention to what is happening, being said, etc 突然注意起发生的事情或说的话等: *I called her a damned hypocrite and that made her sit up.* 我骂她惺惺作态, 她马上警觉起来. ○ *This news made us all sit up and take notice.* 这消息立即引起我们大家的注意. **10** (phr v) **sit around** spend one's time sitting down, unwilling or unable to do anything 闲坐着(什么事都不愿做或不能做): *I've been sitting around waiting for the phone to ring all day.* 我一整天都坐在那儿等着来电话. **sit back (a)** settle oneself comfortably back, eg in a chair 倚着靠背舒服地坐着(如在椅子上): *I sat back and enjoyed a cup of tea.* 我向后靠着舒适地坐着品茶. **(b)** relax after working; do nothing 工作之后歇息; 什么都不做: *I like to sit back and rest in the evenings.* 我喜欢在晚上什么也不做, 好好休息. ○ *Are you going to sit back and let me do everything?* 你什么事都不想做, 所有事都让我干? **sit down under sth** (*fml* 文) suffer (insults, etc) without protest or complaint 忍受(凌辱等)(不反抗或不抱怨): *He should not sit down under these accusations.* 他不应该默默地忍受这类指责. **sit for sth** (no passive 不用于被动语态) (*Brit*) be the Member of Parliament for (a constituency) 任(某选区)的议会议员: *I sit for Bristol West.* 我是西布里斯托尔的议会议员. **sit in** occupy (part of) a building as a protest 静坐示威(占据一建筑物或其中一部分): *The workers are sitting in against the factory closures.* 工人们静坐示威抗议关闭工厂. **sit in on sth** attend (a discussion, etc) as an observer, not as a participant 列席(讨论会等): *The teachers allowed a pupil to sit in on their meeting.* 教师允许有一名学生列席他们的会议. **sit on sth (a)** (no passive 不用于被动语态) be a member of (a committee, jury, etc) 做(委员会、陪审团等)的成员: *How many people sit on the commission?* 委员会有多少成员? **(b)** (*infml* 口) fail to deal with sth 搁置; 积压: *They have been sitting on my application for a month.* 他们把我的申请搁置了一个月. **sit on sb** stop sb's bad or awkward behaviour 制止某人的不良举动: *I have to sit on the class when they get too rowdy.* 班上学生太闹时, 我就得管一管. ○ *She thinks she knows everything, and needs sitting on.* 她认为她什么都

懂, 需要管束一下. **sit out** sit outdoors 坐在户外: *The garden's so lovely, I think I'll sit out.* 花园真漂亮, 我想我还是坐在外面好. **sit sth out** (**a**) stay to the end of (a performance, etc) 坐着直到(演出等)结束: *sit out a boring play* 耐着性子看完一出乏味的话剧. (**b**) not take part in (a particular dance) 不想跳(某种舞): *I think I'll sit out the rumba.* 我不想跳伦巴舞. **sit through sth** remain in a theatre, etc from the beginning to the end of (a performance, etc) (在剧院等)一直坐到(演出等)结束: *I can't sit through six hours of Wagner!* 看六小时的瓦格纳歌剧我可坐不住! **sit up (for sb)** not go to bed until later than the usual time, esp because one is waiting for sb 晚睡(尤指为等候某人): *I shall get back late, so don't sit up (for me).* 我要晚些回来, 别(为等我)晚睡. ○ *The nurse sat up with the patient all night.* 那护士整夜没睡守护着病人. ○ *We sat up late watching a film on TV.* 我们很晚都没睡觉还在看电视影片. **sit (sb) up** (cause sb to) move to an upright position after lying flat, slouching, etc (使某人)坐起来, 坐直, 坐正, 端坐: *The patient is well enough to sit up in bed now.* 病人现在已能在床上坐起来了. ○ *We sat the baby up to feed her.* 我们让那婴儿坐正了好喂她. ○ *Sit up straight!* 坐直了! Cf 参看 SIT UP (AND TAKE NOTICE).

□ **ˈsit-down** *n* **1** (also ˌ**sit-down** ˈ**strike**) strike in which workers occupy a factory, etc until their demands are considered or met 静坐罢工(工人占据厂房, 争取要求获考虑或满足). **2** [attrib 作定语] (of a meal) served to people sitting down (指就餐)由服务员送到座位的, 坐着吃的: *a sit-down lunch* 坐着吃的午餐.

ˈ**sit-in** *n* protest made by sitting in (在建筑物内的)静坐示威: *a sit-in at the city council offices* 在市议会办事处内的静坐示威.

ˌ**sitting** ˈ**member** (*Brit*) candidate at a general election who holds the seat until the next election is called 现任的议员.

ˈ**sitting-room** *n* (*esp Brit*) = LIVING-ROOM (LIVING[2]).

ˌ**sitting** ˈ**tenant** tenant who is actually occupying a flat, house, etc (公寓、房屋等的)正在租用的人: *It's difficult to sell a house with a sitting tenant.* 住着房客的房子很难卖.

sitar /sɪˈtɑː(r), ˈsɪtɑː(r); sɪˈtɑr, ˈsɪˌtɑr/ *n* Indian stringed instrument resembling a guitar, with a long neck 锡塔琴(似吉他的印度弦乐器).

sit·com /ˈsɪtkɒm; ˈsɪtˌkɑm/ *n* (*infml* 口) = SITUATION COMEDY (SITUATION).

site /saɪt; saɪt/ *n* **1** place where a building, town, etc was, is, or will be situated (建筑物、城镇等的)地方, 位置, 遗址, 地基: *built on the site of a Roman fort* 建筑在古罗马城堡的遗址上 ○ *a site for a new school* 选定的新校址 ○ *deliver the materials to a building site* 把建筑材料送到工地去 ○ *I picked a sheltered site for the tent.* 我选了个有遮蔽的地方搭帐篷. **2** place where sth has happened or will happen, or for a particular activity (事情发生的或活动的)地点, 现场: *the site of the battle* 战场 ○ *Rescue workers rushed to the site of the plane crash.* 救护人员急速赶到飞机坠毁的现场.

▷ **site** *v* [Tn, Tn·pr] locate (a building, etc); place 择定(建筑物等)的位置; 设置: *a factory sited next to a railway line* 设置在铁路沿线的工厂 ○ *Is it safe to site the power-station here?* 把发电厂建在这里安全吗?

sit·ter /ˈsɪtə(r); ˈsɪtɚ/ *n* **1** person who is being painted or photographed 被画像或拍照的人. **2** (**a**) bird or animal that is not flying or moving and is therefore easy to shoot 不在飞行中或运动中的鸟或兽(因而容易射中). (**b**) (*sl* 俚) thing that is easy to do, catch, etc 易做的或易捕捉的事物: *The purse in her handbag was a sitter for any thief.* 她手提袋里的钱包小偷很容易偷走. **3** (with an *adj* 与形容词连用) hen that sits (SIT 5) 孵蛋的母鸡: *a good/poor sitter* 孵蛋的[不孵蛋的]母鸡. **4** (*infml* 口) = BABY-SITTER (BABY).

sit·ting /ˈsɪtɪŋ; ˈsɪtɪŋ/ *n* **1** time during which a lawcourt, parliament, etc sits continuously (法庭、议会等)开庭、开会等的期间: *during a long sitting* 在冗长的议会开会期间. **2** period when a group of people eat a meal 一批人就餐的时间: *The dining-hall is small, so there are two sittings for lunch.* 饭厅很小, 所以午饭分两批吃. ○ *About 100 people can be served at one sitting*, ie together, at one time. 约一百人可同时进餐. **3** period spent continuously in one activity 持续进行某一活动的时间: *finish reading a book at one sitting* 一口气读完一本书. **4** period spent by sb being painted or photographed 供人画像或拍照的时间: *The portrait was completed after six sittings.* 这幅画模特儿坐了六次才画完. **5** number of eggs on which a hen sits (一只母鸡等)一次孵的卵数.

situ·ate /ˈsɪtjʊeɪt; *US* ˈsɪtʃʊeɪt; ˈsɪtʃʊˌet/ *v* [Tn·pr esp passive 尤用于被动语态] (*fml* 文) place or locate (eg a building or town) in a certain position 使(如建筑物或城镇)建于或坐落在某处: *The company wants to situate its headquarters in the north.* 公司想把总部设在北方. ○ *The village is situated in a valley.* 那个村子在山谷里. ○ *Where will the school be situated?* 学校要建在哪儿?

▷ **situ·ated** *adj* [pred 作表语] (of a person) in circumstances of a specified kind; placed (指人)处于某种境况: *Having six children and no income, I was badly situated.* 我有六个孩子却没有收入, 生活十分困难. ○ *How are you situated with regard to equipment?* ie Do you have all you need? 你所需的设备都有了吗?

situ·ation /ˌsɪtʃʊˈeɪʃn; ˌsɪtʃʊˈeʃən/ *n* **1** set of circumstances or state of affairs, esp at a certain time 状况, 处境, 局面, 形势(尤指某时期的): *find oneself in an embarrassing situation* 觉得自己处于尴尬的境地 ○ *get into/out of a difficult situation* 陷入[摆脱]困难的状况 ○ *the worsening diplomatic situation* 日趋恶化的外交局面 ○ *The company is in a poor financial situation*, eg is losing money. 公司财务状况不佳. **2** position of a town, building, etc in relation to its surroundings (城镇、建筑物等相对于周围环境的)位置: *a beautiful situation overlooking the valley* 可俯瞰山谷的优美地点. **3** (*fml* 文) paid job 有酬劳的工作; 职业: *find a new situation* 找个新工作 ○ *Situations vacant/Situations wanted*, eg as headings for newspaper advertisements from people offering or looking for jobs. 招聘[求职](如报纸上的广告标题). **4** (idm 习语) **save the situation** ⇨ SAVE.

□ ˌ**situation** ˈ**comedy** (also *infml* 口语作 **sitcom**) comedy, usu a TV or radio programme, based on a set of characters in a particular situation 情景喜剧(一批角色在特定情景中的喜剧表演, 通常指电视或广播剧).

six /sɪks; sɪks/ *pron, det* **1** 6; one more than five 6, 六(个). ⇨App 4 见附录4. **2** (idm 习语) **at** ˌ**sixes and** ˈ**sevens** (*infml* 口) in confusion 乱七八糟: *I haven't had time to arrange everything, so I'm all at sixes and sevens.* 我没来得及把每件事都安排好, 因此心里七上八下的.

▷ **six** *n* the number 6 ☆ 6; 六.

sixth /sɪksθ; sɪksθ/ *pron, det* 6th; next after fifth 第6, 第六(个). **sixthly** *adv.* — *n* one of six equal parts of sth 六分之一: *save a sixth of one's income* 把收入的六分之一储存起来. ˈ**sixth form** (*Brit*) (in secondary schools) class of pupils preparing for A-level examinations (中学)六年级(为准备参加英国普通教育文凭高级程度考试的班级): [attrib 作定语] *a sixth-form pupil, lesson* 中学六年级的学生、课. ˈ**sixth-former** *n* pupil in this form 中学六年级学生.

For the uses of *six* and *sixth* see the examples at *five* and *fifth*. 关于six和sixth的用法见five和fifth词条中的示例.

□ **sixfold** /ˈsɪksfəʊld; ˈsɪksˈfold/ *adj, adv* **1** six times as much or as many; six times as great 六倍(的): *a sixfold increase* 六倍的增加 ○ *increase sixfold* 增加六倍. **2** having six parts 有六个部分的.

ˌ**six-**ˈ**footer** *n* (*infml* 口) **1** person who is six foot tall 身高六英尺的人. **2** thing that is six foot long 六英尺长的东西.

ˈ**six-pack** *n* (*esp US*) case of six bottles or cans, esp of beer 六瓶或六罐装(尤指啤酒).

ˈ**sixpence** /ˈsɪkspəns; ˈsɪkspəns/ *n* **1** former GB coin having a value of six old pennies (before 1971) (英国旧时)面值六便士的硬币(1971年前). **2** sum of six pennies 六便士: *It costs sixpence.* 价值为六便士.

sixpenny /ˈsɪkspənɪ; ˈsɪksˌpənɪ/ *adj* [attrib 作定语] costing six pennies 值六便士的.

ˌ**six-**ˈ**shooter** *n* revolver with six bullets when fully loaded 六发左轮手枪.

six·teen /ˌsɪkˈstiːn; sɪksˈtin/ *pron, det* 16; one more than fifteen 16, 十六(个). ⇨App 4 见附录4.

▷ **six·teen** *n* the number 16 ☆ 16; 十六.

six·teenth /sɪkˈstiːnθ; sɪksˈtinθ/ *pron, det* 16th; next after fifteenth 第16, 第十六(个). — *n* one of sixteen equal

parts of sth 十六分之一. **six'teenth note** (*US*) = SEMIQUAVER.
For the uses of *sixteen* and *sixteenth* see the examples at *five* and *fifth*. 关于 sixteen 和 sixteenth 的用法见 five 和 fifth 词条中的示例.

sixty /'sɪkstɪ; `sɪkstɪ/ *pron, det* 60; one more than fifty-nine ☆ 60, 六十(个). ⇨App 4 见附录 4.
▷ **six·tieth** /'sɪkstɪəθ; `sɪkstɪɪθ/ *pron, det* 60th; next after fifty-ninth 第60, 第六十(个). — *n* one of sixty equal parts of sth 六十分之一.
sixty *n* **1** the number 60 ☆ 60; 六十. **2 the sixties** [pl] numbers, years or temperature from 60 to 69 从60到69的数目、年数或温度. **3** (idm 习语) **in one's 'sixties** between the ages of 60 and 70 在60岁到70岁之间.
For the uses of *sixty* and *sixtieth* see the examples at *five* and *fifth*. 关于 sixty 和 sixtieth 的用法见 five 和 fifth 词条中的示例.

size[1] /saɪz; saɪz/ *n* **1** [U, C] the measurements or amount of sth; degree of largeness or smallness (量度、数量或程度的)大小, 多少: *a building of vast size* 巨大的建筑物 ○ *the car's compact size* 小型的汽车 ○ *people of all shapes and sizes* 各种形体的人 ○ *about the size of* (ie about as large as) *a duck's egg* 约鸭蛋般大小 ○ *the size of the cheque* 支票的数额 ○ *a house of some size*, ie a fairly large house 相当大的房子 ○ *They're both of a size*, ie are the same size. 这两个大小相同. **2** [C] any of a number of standard measurements in which items such as clothes are made (服装等的)号, 码: *a size fifteen collar* 十五号的领子 ○ *trousers three sizes too large* 大了三号的裤子 ○ *I take size nine shoes.* 我穿九号的鞋. ○ *You need a smaller size.* 你需要小点号的. ○ *Try this on for size*, ie to see if it fits, whether or not you like it. 穿上这个试试尺码. **3** (idm 习语) **that's about 'it/about the 'size of it** that is (roughly) how matters stand 大致上就是这样.
▷ **size** *v* **1** [Tn] sort (sth) according to size 将(某物)按大小排列或分类. **2** (phr v) **size sb/sth up** (*infml* 口) form a judgement or opinion of sb/sth 判断或估计某人[某事物]: *We sized each other up at our first meeting.* 我们初次见面时相互打量了一番.
size·able (also **siz·able**) /-əbl; -əbl̩/ *adj* fairly large 相当大的; 颇大的: *a sizeable field, house, sum of money* 相当大的一块地[一所房子/一笔钱].
-sized (forming compound *adjs* 用以构成复合形容词) having the specified size 某种大小的: *a medium-sized garden.*

size[2] /saɪz; saɪz/ *n* [U] sticky substance used to glaze textiles, paper, etc or to seal plaster 胶料, 浆料(用作纺织品、纸张等的上光剂或用作灰泥或石膏的填塞剂).
▷ **size** *v* [Tn] glaze or seal (sth) with size 用胶料或浆料给(某物)上光或填塞(某物).

sizzle /'sɪzl; `sɪzl̩/ *v* [I, Ip] (*infml* 口) make the hissing sound eg of sth frying in fat 发嗞嗞声(如煎炸声): *sausages sizzling (away) in the pan* 在锅里发出嗞嗞声的香肠 ○ *water sizzling as it falls on a hot rock* 落在滚烫的石头上嗞嗞作响的水 ○ (*fig* 比喻) *a sizzling hot day* 炎热的一天.
▷ **sizzle** *n* [sing] this sound 嗞嗞声.
sizz·ler /'sɪzlə(r); `sɪzlɚ/ *n* (*infml* 口) very hot day 炎热的日子; 大热天: *Whew! What a sizzler!* 唷! 多热的天哪!

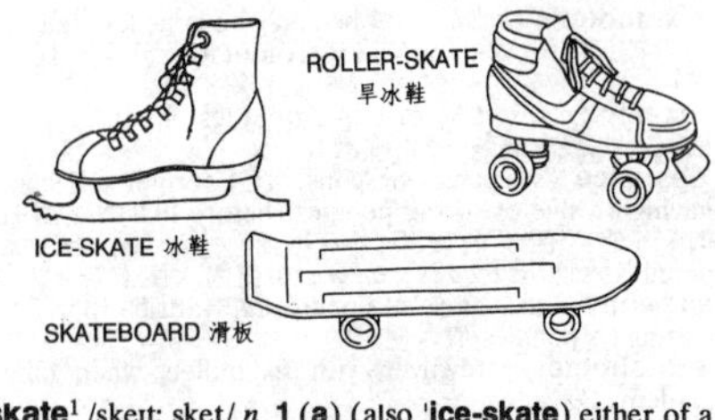

skate[1] /skeɪt; sket/ *n* **1 (a)** (also **'ice-skate**) either of a pair of boots with steel blades fixed to the soles so that the wearer can glide smoothly over ice 溜冰鞋. **(b)** one of these blades 冰刀. **2** = ROLLER-SKATE (ROLLER). **3** (idm 习语) **get/put one's 'skates on** (*infml* 口) hurry up 赶快: *Get your skates on or you'll miss the bus.* 快点儿, 不然你就赶不上公共汽车了.
▷ **skate** *v* [I, Ipr, Ip, Tn] **1** move on skates; perform (sth) while moving in this way 溜冰; 溜冰表演(某动作): *Can you skate?* 你会滑冰吗? ○ *skate along, past, over, etc (sth)* 溜冰沿着、经过、越过...(某物) ○ *skate a figure of eight* 溜8字形. **2** (idm 习语) **be skating on thin 'ice** talk about or do sth that can easily cause disagreement, protest or other trouble 谈论或做易引起分歧、反对意见或其他麻烦的事: *We could ignore him and go direct to the chairman, but we'd be skating on very thin ice.* 我们可以不理会他而直接去找主席, 但那样做我们就如履薄冰了. **3** (phr v) **skate over/round sth** not deal with sth directly 间接处理某事物; 不直接触及某事物: *skate over a difficulty, a delicate issue* 对一困难、敏感问题一带而过 ○ *She skated round the likely cost of the plan.* 她婉转地提到这项计划可能需要的费用.
skater *n* person who skates 滑冰的人. **skat·ing** *n* [U] sport of moving on skates 冰上运动: [attrib 作定语] *a skating competition, club* 滑冰比赛、俱乐部.
□ **'skateboard** *n* narrow board about 50 cm long, with roller-skate wheels fixed to it, which the rider stands on, eg to take part in races, demonstrate skill, etc 滑板(长约50厘米的窄板, 装有滑轮, 可站在上面滑行, 如作比赛或表演等). ⇨illus 见插图. **'skateboarder** *n* person who uses a skateboard 玩滑板的人. **'skateboarding** *n* [U] sport of riding a skateboard 滑板运动.
'skating-rink *n* area of natural or artificial ice for ice-skating; smooth area used for roller-skating 滑冰场; 旱冰场.

skate[2] /skeɪt; sket/ *n* (*pl* unchanged or **~s** 复数或不变或作 **skates**) large flat long-tailed fish that lives in the sea and is eaten as food 鳐(体大扁平、尾长的海鱼, 可食).

ske·daddle /skɪ'dædl; skɪ`dædl̩/ *v* [I] (*Brit infml* 口) (usu imperative 通常用于祈使句) go away quickly 快走开.

skein /skeɪn; sken/ *n* **1** length of wool, thread, etc wound into a loose coil (纱、线等的)一束. **2** group of wild geese, etc in flight (飞行中的)一群(大雁等).

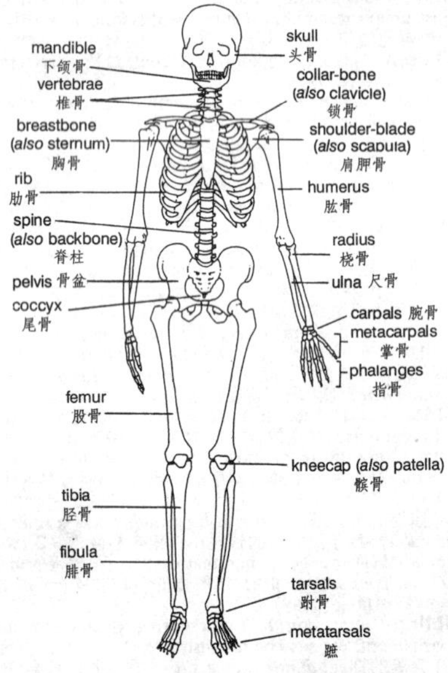

the human skeleton 人体骨骼

skel·eton /'skelɪtn; `skɛlətn̩/ *n* **1 (a)** framework of bones supporting an animal or a human body (动物或人的)全副骨骼, 骨架: *The child was reduced to a skeleton*, ie very thin because of hunger, illness, etc. 这

孩子骨瘦如柴. (**b**) such a framework, or a model of it, fixed in the position it has in the body, used esp for the purposes of study 骨架或骨架模型(尤用于科研): *ape skeletons in the museum* 博物馆里的猿的骨架. **2** (**a**) any supporting structure or framework, eg of a building 框架结构, 骨架结构(如建筑物的): *The block is still just a skeleton of girders.* 这片建筑还只是仅有主梁的骨架. (**b**) outline to which details are to be added 纲要; 提要: *Her notes give us just the bare skeleton of her theory.* 她的笔记只给我们提供了她的理论的梗概. **3** [attrib 作定语] having the smallest possible number of people, vehicles, etc needed to run an operation (进行一项作业所需的)最起码数量的人员、车辆等: *a skeleton crew, staff, etc* 最低数量的船员、职员等 ○ *We only have a skeleton bus service on public holidays.* 在公众假期, 只有最少量的公共汽车营运. **4** (idm 习语) **a skeleton in the ˈcupboard** secret which would embarrass sb if it became known (若揭露出来可能使某人难堪的)秘密: *bribery of officials and other skeletons in the government's cupboard* 政府中的官员受贿以及其他丑事.

□ **ˈskeleton key** key that will open several different locks 万能钥匙.

skep·tic = SCEPTIC.

sketch /sketʃ; skɛtʃ/ *n* **1** rough quickly-made drawing, without many details 素描; 速写; 草图: *make a sketch of a face, place* 作一面部、地方的速写. **2** short account or description, giving only basic details 简短的陈述或描写: *a newspaper sketch of a debate in Parliament* 报上关于议会辩论的简短报道 ○ *give a sketch of one's plans* 概述一项计划. **3** short funny play or piece of writing 诙谐的短剧或短文: *a sketch set in a doctor's surgery* 以医生诊所为背景的诙谐短剧 ○ *She writes satirical sketches for a magazine.* 她为一家杂志撰写讽刺小品.

▷ **sketch** [I, Tn] **1** draw sketches; make a sketch of (sb/sth) 作素描; 画速写; 作(某人[某事物])的素描、速写或草图: *go into the park to sketch (flowers)* 去公园作(花卉)写生. **2** (phr v) **sketch sth out** give a general description or account of sth; outline sth 概述(某事); 草拟: *sketch out proposals for a new road* 草拟修建新路的计划 ○ *Sketch out what you intend to do.* 把你要做的事概括地叙述一下.

sketchy *adj* (**-ier**, **-iest**) (*often derog* 常作贬义) lacking thoroughness and detail; incomplete; rough 概要的; 不完全的; 粗略的: *Your essay gives a rather sketchy treatment of the problem.* 你的文章只粗略地涉及到这个问题. ○ *I have only a sketchy knowledge of geography.* 我对地理只是一知半解. ○ *Information about the crisis was sketchy and hard to get.* 关于这次危机的消息所知甚少并且很难获得. **sketch·ily** *adv*: *The book treats the problem too sketchily.* 该书关于这一问题写得太简略. **ˈsketchi·ness** *n* [U].

□ **ˈsketch-book**, **ˈsketch-pad** *ns* book of sheets of paper for sketching on 素描簿; 速写簿.

ˈsketch-map *n* map, usu drawn by hand, that shows only basic details 略图; (通常指手画的)地图.

skew /skju:; skju/ *adj* [usu pred 通常作表语] not straight; twisted or slanting 歪; 斜; 偏: *The picture is a bit skew.* 这幅画有点歪. Cf 参看 ASKEW.

▷ **skew** *n* (idm 习语) **on the ˈskew** skew 歪; 斜; 偏.

□ **skew-whiff** /ˌskju:ˈwɪf; ˈskjuˌhwɪf/ *adj* (*Brit infml* 口) skew 歪的; 斜的; 偏的: *You've got your hat on skew-whiff.* 你帽子戴歪了.

skew·bald /ˈskju:bɔ:ld; ˈskjuˌbɔld/ *n*, *adj* (animal, esp a horse) having patches of white and another colour (usu not black) 白色与另一颜色(黑色除外)夹杂的(动物, 尤指马). Cf 参看 PIEBALD.

skewer /ˈskju:ə(r); ˈskjuɚ/ *n* pin of wood or metal with a point, pushed through meat to hold it together while cooking 串肉扦, 烤肉扦(烤肉时串肉用的).

▷ **skewer** *v* [Tn] push a skewer or sth similar through (sth) (用串肉扦或类似物)串起, 刺穿: *He skewered his foot on a nail.* 他的脚踩在钉子上了.

ski /ski:; ski/ *n* either of a pair of long narrow strips of wood, plastic, etc fixed to a person's boots so that he can glide smoothly over snow 滑雪板: *a pair of skis* 一副滑雪板 ○ *bind on one's skis* 缚上滑雪板 ○ [attrib 作定语] *a ski suit, slope, club* 滑雪衣、斜坡、俱乐部.

▷ **ski** *v* (*pt*, *pp* **ski'd** or **skied**, *pres p* **skiing**) [I, Ipr, Ip] move over snow on skis, esp as a sport 滑雪(尤指作

为运动): *go skiing in Switzerland* 去瑞士滑雪 ○ *ski into a village* 滑雪滑进一村庄 ○ *ski past, along, down, etc* 滑雪滑过、滑去、滑下.... **skier** /ˈski:ə(r); ˈskiɚ/ *n* person who uses skis 滑雪的人. **ski·ing** *n* [U] activity or sport of moving on skis 滑雪; 滑雪运动: [attrib 作定语] *a skiing course, instructor, resort* 滑雪课程、教练、胜地 ○ *skiing equipment, clothes* 滑雪用具、服装. ⇨illus 见插图.

□ **ˈski-bob** *n* vehicle used for races on snow and resembling a bicycle with skis instead of wheels 滑雪车(状如自行车, 有滑雪板, 无轮).

ˈski-jump *n* **1** jump made by a skier after sliding down a long ramp 滑雪跳跃. **2** ramp for making such jumps 供滑雪跳跃的斜坡. **3** competition in which such jumps are made 滑雪跳跃比赛.

ˈski-lift *n* device for pulling or carrying skiers up a slope 载送滑雪者上坡的装置.

ˈski-plane *n* aircraft fitted with skis instead of wheels, enabling it to land on snow 雪上飞机(装有雪橇、可在雪地降落的飞机).

skid /skɪd; skɪd/ *n* **1** sideways movement made eg by a car slipping on ice or turning a corner too fast 滑向一侧, 打滑(如车在结冰路上或急转弯时的): *try to get out of/correct a skid* 设法纠正打滑现象. **2** log, plank, etc used to make a track over which heavy objects may be dragged or rolled 滑道, 滚道, 滑轨(使重物易于在上面拉或滚动). **3** piece of wood or metal that acts as a brake on the wheel of a cart, etc 制轮器; 刹车. **4** (idm 习语) **put the skids under sb/sth** (*sl* 俚) (**a**) cause sb/sth to fail 使某人[某事]失败: *The government put the skids under the plan by stopping their research grant.* 政府停发研究经费让他们的计划半途而废. (**b**) make sb hurry 催促某人.

▷ **skid** *v* (**-dd-**) [I, Ipr, Ip] (of a car, etc) move or slip sideways (指汽车等)滑向一侧, 打滑: *The car skidded on the ice.* 汽车在冰上打滑了. ○ *The bus skidded (on) into a wall.* 公共汽车打滑撞到墙上.

□ **ˈskid-pan** surface specially prepared for skidding on, so that drivers can practise controlling skids 转向试验场(为司机练习控制车辆打滑的特制路面).

skid row /ˌskɪd ˈrəʊ; ˌskɪdˈro/ (*US sl* 俚) slum area where vagrants live 流浪者住的贫民区: *He ended up on skid row.* 他最后沦落到了流浪人的贫民区.

skies *pl* of SKY.

skiff /skɪf; skɪf/ *n* small light boat for rowing or sculling, usu by one person 轻舟, 小艇(通常指单人划的).

skiffle /ˈskɪfl; ˈskɪfəl/ *n* [U] (*esp Brit*) type of music popular in the 1950's, a mixture of jazz and folk-song often using improvised instruments and a singer with a guitar or a banjo 二十世纪五十年代流行的一种爵士乐: [attrib 作定语] *a skiffle group, song, etc* 爵士乐团、歌曲等.

skil·ful (*US* **skill·ful**) /ˈskɪlfl; ˈskɪlfəl/ *adj* **~ (at sth/doing sth)** having or showing skill 有技巧的; 熟练的: *a skilful painter, driver, performer* 熟练的画家、司机、表演者 ○ *a skilful performance* 娴熟的表演 ○ *skilful at inventing excuses* 很会编造借口. ▷ **skil·fully** /-fəlɪ; -fəlɪ/ *adv*.

skill /skɪl; skɪl/ *n* **1** [U] **~ (at sth/doing sth)** ability to do sth well 技能; 技艺; 技巧: *show great skill at driving,*

S

telling stories, playing billiards 显示出驾驶、讲故事、打台球的高度技巧. **2** [C] particular type of skill 技能; 技艺; 技巧: *the practical skills needed in carpentry* 木工所需的应用技艺.

▷ **skilled** *adj* **1 ~ (in/at sth/doing sth)** (**a**) having skill; skilful 熟练的; 有能力的: *a skilled negotiator* 谈判能手 ○ *skilled at dealing with complaints* 善于处理投诉个案. (**b**) experienced; trained 有经验的; 训练过的: *a skilled worker, salesperson, etc* 有经验的工人、推销员等 ○ *an actor skilled at improvising* 擅长临场发挥的演员. **2** [attrib 作定语] (of work) needing skill (指工作)需要技能的: *a skilled job* 技术性的工作.

skil·let /ˈskɪlɪt; ˋskɪlɪt/ *n* **1** (*esp US*) frying-pan 煎锅. ⇨ illus at PAN 见 PAN 插图. **2** small metal cooking-pot with a long handle and (usu) feet 小的长柄锅(通常带有支脚).

skim /skɪm; skɪm/ *v* (**-mm-**) **1** [Tn] remove cream, scum, etc from the surface of (a liquid) 撇去(液体)表面的油脂、浮沫等: *skim milk* 撇去牛奶上的奶油. **2** (**a**) [Ipr, Tn no passive 不用于被动语态] move or glide lightly over (a surface), not touching it or only occasionally touching it 掠过或擦过(某物的表面): *swallows skimming (over) the water/along the ground* 擦着水面[地面]飞过的燕子 ○ *aircraft skimming the roof-tops* 从屋顶上掠过的飞机. (**b**) [Tn, Tn·pr] cause (a stone, etc) to pass low over water, bouncing several times 使(石块等)擦过水面, 反弹几次; 用(石块等)打水漂: *skimming pebbles (over the lake)* 用小圆石(在湖面上)打水漂. **3** [Ipr, Tn] **~ (through/over) sth** read sth quickly, noting only the main points 略读; 浏览: *skim (through) the report in half an hour* 用半小时浏览这份报告 ○ *skim over the list, looking for one's name* 很快地看着名单, 寻找自己的名字. **4** (phr v) **skim sth from/off sth; skim sth off** remove (cream, scum, etc) from the surface of a liquid (从液体表面)撇去(油脂、浮沫等): *skim the cream from the milk* 从牛奶上撇去奶油 ○ *skim the fat off (the soup)* 把(汤上面的)油撇去.

▷ **skim·mer** *n* **1** type of spoon with holes in, used for skimming liquids (撇油、撇沫用的)漏勺. **2** water bird with long wings 剪嘴鸥(长翼水鸟).

□ ˌ**skimmed** ˈ**milk** (also ˌ**skim** ˈ**milk**) milk from which the cream has been skimmed 脱脂奶.

skimp /skɪmp; skɪmp/ (also **scamp** /skæmp; skæmp/) *v* [I, Ipr, Tn] **~ (on sth)** use or provide less than enough of (what is needed) 使用或供给(所需之物)不敷应用: *Use plenty of oil. Don't skimp!* 多用些油. 别省着! ○ *They have to skimp on fuel in winter.* 冬天他们得节省燃料. ○ *skimp material when making a dress* 做连衣裙时节省布料.

▷ **skimpy** *adj* (**-ier, -iest**) using or having less than enough of what is needed (所需之物)不足的, 不够的: *a rather skimpy meal* 分量不太够的一顿饭 ○ *The dancers wore skimpy dresses*, ie that did not cover much of the body. 那些跳舞的人穿着不足以遮体. **skimp·ily** *adv*: *a skimpily made dress* 做得太小的连衣裙. **skimpi·ness** *n* [U].

skin /skɪn; skɪn/ *n* **1** [U] elastic substance that forms the outer covering of the body of a person or an animal (人或动物的)皮, 皮肤: *a dark, an olive, a fair, etc skin* 黝黑的、橄榄色的、白皙的皮肤 ○ *She has a beautiful skin*, ie complexion. 她肤色很美. ○ [attrib 作定语] *a skin disease, treatment* 皮肤病、皮肤治疗. **2** [U, C] (often in compounds 常用以构成复合词) skin of an animal that has been removed from its body, with or without the fur; hide; fur 毛皮; 皮革; 皮张: ˈ*pigskin*, ˈ*calfskin*, ˈ*sheepskin* 猪皮、小牛皮、羊皮 ○ *a* ˈ*rabbit-skin* 兔皮. **3** [C] (often in compounds 常用以构成复合词) vessel for storing liquids, made from the whole skin of an animal (装液体用的)皮囊(用整个兽皮制成的): *a* ˈ*wineskin* 酒囊. **4** (**a**) [C, U] outer covering of a fruit or plant 果皮; 植物的外皮: *slip on a banana skin* 踩着香蕉皮而滑倒 ○ *grape skins* 葡萄皮. Cf 参看 PEEL *n*, RIND, ZEST 3. (**b**) [C, U] thin covering of a sausage (灌香肠用的)肠衣. (**c**) [C usu *sing* 通常作单数] any outer covering or case 外壳; 外皮: *the metal skin of an aircraft* 飞机的金属外壳 ○ *a waterproof plastic skin on a metal sheet* 金属板的防水塑料外层. **5** [C, U] thin layer that forms on the surface of certain liquids, eg boiled milk 结于某些液面的薄层(如煮过的牛奶的表面): *the skin on a milk pudding* 牛奶布丁上的乳皮 ○ *a skin forming on the paint in the pot* 罐中油漆结的一层皮. **6** (idm 习语) **beauty is only skin deep** ⇨ BEAUTY. **be no skin off one's nose** (*infml* 口) not concern one; not matter to one 与己无关; 事不关己; 满不在乎: *It's no skin off my nose if I lose this job, I can always get another one.* 我失掉这份工作也没有关系, 我随时都能再找到工作. **by the** ˌ**skin of one's** ˈ**teeth** (*infml* 口) only just 仅; 刚刚: *He escaped by the skin of his teeth.* 他险些没逃掉. **get under sb's** ˈ**skin** (*infml* 口) (**a**) annoy or irritate sb 惹恼或激怒(某人): *Don't let him get under your skin!* 别让他惹着你! (**b**) interest or attract sb greatly 深深地打动或吸引(某人): *The charm of the place soon gets under your skin.* 这地方很美丽, 你很快就会爱上这个地方. **have got sb under one** ˈ**skin** (*infml* 口) be strongly attracted to sb 对某人极感兴趣. **have, etc a hide/skin like a rhinoceros** ⇨ RHINOCEROS. **jump out of one's** ˈ**skin** (*infml* 口) be startled 吓一大跳: *I nearly jumped out of my skin when a hand grabbed me in the dark.* 黑暗中有一只手把我抓住, 可真把我吓了一大跳. **save one's (own) skin** ⇨ SAVE. **(nothing but/all) skin and** ˈ**bone** (*infml* 口) very thin 极瘦; 皮包骨: *He was all skin and bone after his illness.* 他病后瘦成皮包骨. ˌ**soaked/**ˌ**wet to the** ˈ**skin** (of a person) completely soaked (指人)湿透: *We were soaked to the skin after the storm.* 暴雨过后我们全都湿透了. **(have) a thin/thick** ˈ**skin** (*infml* 口) (have) a character that makes one easily/not easily hurt by criticism, insults, etc 脸皮薄[厚]; 禁得住[禁不住]批评、侮辱等: *You need a thick skin to be a politician.* 当政客得脸皮厚.

▷ **skin** *v* (**-nn-**) **1** (**a**) [Tn] take the skin off (eg an animal) 剥掉(如动物)的皮: *skin a rabbit, fox, etc* 剥兔子、狐狸等的皮. (**b**) injure by scraping skin off (eg one's knees) 擦破(如膝盖)的皮: *I skinned my elbow against the wall.* 我的肘部撞在墙上擦破了皮. **2** (idm 习语) **keep one's eyes open/peeled/skinned** ⇨ EYE[1]. **skin sb alive** (said as a threat 威胁用语) punish sb severely 严惩某人: *Your father'll skin you alive when he sees this!* 要是让你父亲看见, 他非活剥了你不可!

-skinned (forming compound *adjs* 用以构成复合形容词) having a skin of the specified type 有某种皮肤的: *dark-skinned* ○ *pink-skinned*.

skinny *adj* (**-ier, -iest**) (*infml usu derog* 口, 通常作贬义) very thin 极瘦的; 皮包骨的: *You're skinny enough without going on a diet!* 你不必节食就已经够瘦的了! ⇨ Usage at THIN 用法见 THIN.

□ ˌ**skin-**ˈ**deep** *adj* [pred 作表语] not deeply felt or lasting 肤浅; 不深刻; 不持久: *His political commitment is only skin-deep.* 他政治上的承诺只是表面文章.

ˈ**skin-diving** *n* [U] sport of swimming under water with goggles, flippers and an aqualung or a snorkel to breathe with 轻装潜水(只使用护目镜、脚蹼、水肺或潜水通气管). ˈ**skin-diver** *n*.

ˈ**skin-flick** *n* (*sl* 俚) pornographic film 色情电影.

skinful /ˈskɪnfʊl; ˋskɪn,fʊl/ *n* (*sl* 俚) enough alcohol to make a person drunk 足以使人醉倒的酒的量: *He'd had a skinful and got into a fight.* 他喝得大醉还打了一架.

ˈ**skin-graft** *n* surgical operation in which skin taken from one part of sb's body (or from sb else's body) is placed over another part that is burned, wounded, etc 皮移植(术).

ˈ**skinhead** *n* (*Brit*) young person with very short hair, esp one who is violent 留平头的青少年(尤指暴徒).

ˌ**skin-**ˈ**tight** *adj* (of a garment) fitting very closely to the body (指服装)贴身的, 紧身的.

skin·flint /ˈskɪnflɪnt; ˋskɪn,flɪnt/ *n* (*infml* 口) miser 吝啬鬼; 小气的人.

skint /skɪnt; skɪnt/ *adj* [pred 作表语] (*Brit sl* 俚) without any money 无钱; 身无分文.

skip[1] /skɪp; skɪp/ *v* (**-pp-**) **1** [Ipr, Ip] move lightly and quickly, esp by taking two steps with each foot in turn 轻快地跳(尤指每只脚轮流跳两次): *a child skipping along the road, into the house, etc* 沿路跳着、跳着进屋…的小孩 ○ *skipping along, past, out, etc* 蹦蹦跳跳地走去、走过、走出等 ○ *skip out of sb's way*, ie by making a little jump 跳开给某人让路 ○ *The lambs were skipping about in the fields.* 羊羔在田里跳来跳去. **2** [I] jump over a rope held in both one's hands or by two other people and passed repeatedly over the head and under the feet

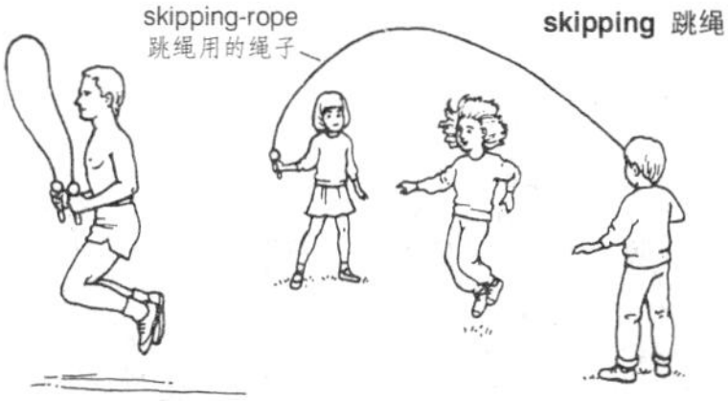

跳绳: *children skipping in the playground* 在操场中跳绳的儿童 ○ *skipping games* 跳绳游戏. ⇨illus 见插图. **3** (**a**) [Ipr, Ip] (*infml* 口) go from one place to another quickly or casually 匆匆地或随便地由一处到另一处: *skip over/across to Paris for the weekend* 匆匆赶到巴黎度周末 ○ (*fig* 比喻) *She skipped from one subject to another.* 她讲得没有条理, 东拉西扯. (**b**) [I, Ipr, Ip, Tn no passive 不用于被动语态] **~ (out of...); ~ off** leave (a place) secretly or in a hurry 悄悄地或匆匆地离开(某地): *skip (out of) the country with the stolen money* 携赃款潜逃国外 ○ *skip off without saying anything to anyone* 一声不吭地匆匆溜走. **4** [Tn] not attend (a meeting, etc) 不参加(会议等): *skip a lecture, an appointment, a class, etc* 未参加讲座、没赴约、旷课. **5** [I, Tn] omit (part of a book when reading, a task, etc) 略过(书中的一部分、任务等): *I read the whole book without skipping (a page).* 我一页不漏地读完了全书. ○ *Skip the first chapter and start on page 25.* 跳过第一章, 从第25页开始看. ○ *He managed to skip the washing-up.* 他变着法地不做洗碗的事. **6** (idm 习语) **'skip it!** (*infml* 口) don't talk about that any more 别再提这件事了: *I've heard enough about your job, so skip it!* 你的工作我已经听够了, 别再提了!

▷ **skip** *n* skipping movement 跳跃; 跳绳; 跳过; 躲过: *a hop, a skip and a jump* 三级跳远.

□ **'skipping-rope** *n* length of rope, usu with handles at each end, used esp by a child or a boxer for skipping 跳绳用的绳子. ⇨illus 见插图.

skip[2] /skɪp; skɪp/ *n* large (usu open) metal container for carrying away rubble, rubbish, etc, esp from a building site 旧料桶(通常无盖, 尤用以装运工地废料的): [attrib 作定语] *skip hire* 旧料桶租赁.

skip·per /ˈskɪpə(r); ˈskɪpɚ/ *n* **1** captain, esp of a small merchant ship or fishing-boat 船长(尤指小商船或渔船的). **2** (*infml* 口) captain of a team, eg in football or cricket 队长(如足球或板球队的). **3** (*esp US*) captain of an aircraft (飞机的)机长.

▷ **skip·per** *v* [Tn] act as skipper of (a boat, team, etc) 担任船长、球队队长等.

skirl /skɜːl; skɝl/ *n* [sing] shrill piercing sound, esp of bagpipes 尖利声(尤指风笛的).

skir·mish /ˈskɜːmɪʃ; ˈskɝmɪʃ/ *n* fight between small groups of soldiers, ships, etc, esp one that is not planned 小规模战斗; 小冲突; (尤指)遭遇战: *a brief skirmish on the frontier* 边界上的小规模冲突 ○ (*fig* 比喻) *a skirmish between the two party leaders* 两党领导人间的摩擦. Cf 参看 PITCHED BATTLE (PITCH[2]).

▷ **skir·mish** *v* [I] take part in a skirmish 进行小规模战斗或冲突. **skir·misher** *n*.

skirt /skɜːt; skɝt/ *n* **1** [C] (**a**) woman's garment that hangs from the waist (女用的)裙子. (**b**) part of a dress or other garment, eg a long coat, that hangs below the waist (连衣裙或大衣等的)下摆. **2** [C] any of various types of guard or covering for the base of a vehicle or machine (车辆或机器基部的)护板: *the rubber skirt round the bottom of a hovercraft* 汽垫船底部四周的橡胶护板. **3 skirts** [pl] = OUTSKIRTS. **4** (*dated sexist sl* 旧, 性别偏见, 俚) (**a**) [U] girls or women in general, seen as sexual objects (被视为性欲对象的)女子: *a bit of skirt* 裙衩. (**b**) [C] girl or woman seen in this way (被视为性欲对象的)女子.

▷ **skirt** *v* [Ipr, Tn] **1** be on or move along the edge of (sth) 位于(某物)的边缘; 沿着(某物)边缘走: *We skirted (round) the field and crossed the bridge.* 我们沿着田边走, 经过了那座桥. ○ *The road skirts the forest.* 那条路在森林的边上. **2** (phr v) **skirt round sth** avoid referring to or treating (a topic, an issue, etc) directly 不直接提及或不直接处理(话题、问题等): *She skirted round the problem of the high cost.* 她避而不谈巨额费用问题.

□ **'skirting-board** (*Brit*) (*US* **'baseboard**) *n* board attached to the wall of a room, next to the floor 壁脚板; 踢脚板.

skit /skɪt; skɪt/ *n* **~ (on sth)** piece of humorous writing or short play that mimics or makes fun of sb/sth serious (模仿或取笑某人[某事物]的)幽默小品文章或短剧: *a skit on Wagner/on 'Macbeth'* 模仿瓦格纳[《麦克佩斯》]的短剧.

skit·tish /ˈskɪtɪʃ; ˈskɪtɪʃ/ *adj* **1** (of horses) lively and playful; difficult to control (指马)活泼的, 难以驾驭的. **2** (of people) fond of flirting; lively and playful (指人)爱调情的, 活泼顽皮的: *She gets very skittish when her boy-friend is around.* 她男朋友在场时, 她就显得格外轻佻. ▷ **skit·tishly** *adv*. **skit·tish·ness** *n* [U].

skittle /ˈskɪtl; ˈskɪtḷ/ *n* **1** [C] bottle-shaped wooden pin used in the game of skittles (撞柱戏用的瓶状的)木柱. **2 skittles** [sing *v*] game in which players try to knock over as many skittles as possible by rolling a ball at them 撞柱戏(以球撞击瓶状木柱的游戏). Cf 参看 NINEPIN, TENPIN BOWLING. **3** (idm 习语) **beer and skittles** ⇨ BEER.

▷ **skittle** *v* (phr v) **skittle sb out** (in cricket) end the turn of (a number of batsmen) quickly (板球中)迅速使(数名击球员)出局, 从而结束对方击球机会: *The whole side was skittled out for 10 runs.* 这个队在跑动得10分时, 全队失去击球机会.

skive /skaɪv; skaɪv/ *v* [I, Ip] **~ (off)** (*Brit sl* 俚) avoid work, esp by staying away or going away from where it is being done 逃避劳动(尤指躲避或离开现场): *He's usually skiving down at the pub when there's gardening to be done.* 他常在需要整理花园时就躲进酒馆去了. ○ *She always skives off early.* 她总是在干活儿时早早溜走.

▷ **skiver** *n* (*Brit sl* 俚) person who skives 逃避劳动的人.

skivvy /ˈskɪvɪ; ˈskɪvɪ/ *n* (*Brit infml derog* 口, 贬) (usu female) servant, esp one who has to do menial jobs like cleaning and washing (通常为女性)仆人, 佣人(尤指专做清洗打杂等粗活儿的): *I'm no better than* (ie I'm treated like) *a skivvy in this house.* 我在这个家里与仆人无异.

▷ **skivvy** *v* (*pt, pp* **skivvied**) [I, Ipr] **~ (for sb)** (*Brit infml* 口) work as a skivvy or as if one is a skivvy 做清洗打杂等粗活儿; 做(似)女佣的工作: *She refused to skivvy for the whole family.* 她不肯给全家当仆人.

skua /ˈskjuːə; ˈskjuə/ *n* large type of seagull 贼鸥(一种大海鸥).

skul·dug·gery (also **skull-**) /skʌlˈdʌgərɪ; skʌlˈdʌgərɪ/ *n* [U] (*often joc* 常作戏谑语) deception and planning of evil acts; trickery 诈骗; 诡计: *a career ruined by political skulduggery* 被政治诡计毁掉的事业.

skulk /skʌlk; skʌlk/ *v* [Ipr, Ip] (*derog* 贬) hide or move around as if one is ashamed or trying to hide, esp when one is planning sth bad 躲躲闪闪; (尤指)鬼鬼祟祟: *I don't want reporters skulking around (my house).* 我不愿看到记者在(我家)周围神出鬼没地来回走动. ⇨Usage at PROWL 用法见 PROWL.

skull /skʌl; skʌl/ *n* **1** bony framework of the head under the skin 脑壳; 头颅骨: *The fall fractured his skull.* 这一跤把他的颅骨摔裂了. ⇨illus at SKELETON 见 SKELETON 插图. **2** (idm 习语) **a thick skull** ⇨ THICK. ▷ **-skulled** (forming compound *adjs* 用以构成复合形容词): *thick-skulled*, ie having a thick skull; stupid.

□ **ˌskull and 'cross-bones** picture of a skull above two crossed bones, once used on the flags of pirates' ships and now to warn of danger, eg on bottles of poison 骷髅画, 骷髅旗(旧时为海盗旗标志, 现作危险标志, 尤用于毒药瓶上).

'skull-cap *n* small round cap with no peak that sits on top of the head, nowadays worn esp by male Jews when praying and by Catholic bishops 无檐便帽(今尤为男性犹太教徒祈祷时或天主教的主教戴用). ⇨illus at HAT 见 HAT 插图.

skunk /skʌŋk; skʌŋk/ *n* **1** (**a**) (also **polecat**) [C] small bushy-tailed N American animal that can send out a strong unpleasant smell as a defence when attacked 臭

skunk 臭鼬

鼬(产于北美, 体小, 尾毛蓬松, 遇敌时放恶臭以自卫). (**b**) [U] its fur 臭鼬毛皮. **2** [C] (*infml* 口) contemptible person 卑鄙的人: *How could you cheat your own children, you skunk!* 你怎么能欺骗自己的孩子, 你这个坏家伙!

▷ **skunk** *v* [Tn] (*US sl* 俚) defeat (sb) completely 彻底击败(某人).

sky /skaɪ; skaɪ/ *n* **1** (**a**) [U, sing] (usu **the sky** when [sing] but **a sky** or **skies** [pl] when modified by an *adj* 用于单数时通常作 **the sky**, 但受形容词修饰时则作 **a sky** 或 **skies**) the space seen when one looks upwards from the earth, where clouds and the sun, moon and stars appear 天; 天空: *a patch of blue sky* 一块蓝天 ○ *birds flying up into the sky* 飞向天空的鸟 ○ *under the open sky*, ie out of doors 在户外 ○ *a clear, blue sky* 晴朗蔚蓝的天空 ○ *clouds moving across the sky* 在天空飘过的浮云 ○ *a starry sky/(the) starry skies* 星斗满天. (**b**) **skies** [pl] climate or weather as shown by this 天气; 气候: *a day of rain and cloudy skies* 有雨、多云的一天 ○ *the sunny skies of Italy* 意大利的晴朗天气. **2** (idm 习语) **pie in the sky** ⇨ PIE. **praise, etc sb/sth to the ˈskies** praise sb/sth very greatly 极力称赞某人[某事物]; 把某人[某事物]捧上了天: *The teacher was extolling her work to the skies.* 教师极力称赞她功课好. **the sky's the limit** (*infml saying* 口, 谚) there is no limit 没有限制: *You could win millions! The sky's the limit!* 你有可能赢数百万. 无尽无休!

▷ **sky** *v* (*pt, pp* **skied** /skaɪd; skaɪd/) [Tn] hit (esp a ball) very high 将(尤指球)击向空中.

□ ˌ**sky-ˈblue** *adj, n* [U] (of the) bright blue colour of the sky on a cloudless day 天蓝色; 天蓝色的.

ˈ**sky-diver** *n* [C], ˈ**sky-diving** *n* [U] (person who takes part in the) sport of jumping from an aircraft and falling for as long as one safely can before opening one's parachute 延缓张伞跳伞运动(员).

ˌ**sky-ˈhigh** *adj, adv* very high 极高(的): *Prices are sky-high at the moment.* 眼下物价高得上了天. ○ *The bomb blew the house sky-high.* 炸弹把房子炸得飞起来了.

ˈ**skylark** *n* type of lark that sings while hovering high in the sky 云雀. ⇨illus at App 1 见附录1插图, page iv. — *v* [I, Ip] = LARK.

ˈ**skylight** *n* window in a roof or ceiling 天窗. ⇨illus at App 1 见附录1插图, page vi.

ˈ**skyline** *n* outline of buildings, trees, hills, etc as seen against the sky 建筑物、树、山等以天空为背景映出的轮廓: *the New York skyline* 纽约市的建筑物在空中的轮廓.

ˈ**sky-rocket** *v* [I] (of prices, etc) rise to a very high level (指物价等)飞涨: *sky-rocketing costs* 猛涨的费用.

ˈ**skyscraper** *n* very tall modern city building 摩天大楼.

ˈ**skywards** /ˈskaɪwədz; ˈskaɪwɚdz/ (also **skyward** /-wəd; -wɚd/) *adj, adv* towards the sky; upwards 向天空(的); 向上(的): *the skywards path of the rocket* 火箭的向上飞行路线 ○ *hit the ball skywards* 把球击向空中.

ˈ**sky-writing** *n* [U] (forming of) legible words in the sky from the smoke-trails of aircraft, usu to advertise sth 飞机放烟组成(的)空中文字(通常为宣传).

slab /slæb; slæb/ *n* thick flat, often rectangular or square, piece of stone, wood or other solid substance 厚板(常指矩形或正方形的石板、木板等): *paved with stone slabs* 以石板铺成的 ○ *massive slabs of rock* 巨大的石板 ○ *a slab of cheese, chocolate* 一块干酪、巧克力.

slack[1] /slæk; slæk/ *adj* (**-er, -est**) **1** not tight or tense; loose 不紧的; 松弛的: *a slack rope* 松弛的绳子 ○ *The boxer's jaw went slack.* 那拳击手的下巴松了下来. ○ *Your grip on the bar is too slack.* 这根棒你握得太松了. **2** (**a**) **~ (at/about sth)** (of a person) giving little care and energy to a task (指人)懈怠的, 疏忽的: *He's been getting slack and making silly mistakes.* 他越来越懒散, 出了些荒谬的错误. ○ *Don't get slack about doing your exercises.* 不要疏于练习. (**b**) not carefully done, planned, etc; lax (做得、计划得)粗心的, 马虎的, 松散的: *Organization of the conference was rather slack.* 会议的组织工作很松散. **3** (of business) not having many customers, sales, etc; not busy (指生意)清淡, 萧条, 不景气: *Trade is slack in winter.* 冬季贸易不景气. ○ *Demand is slack over the summer months.* 夏季的几个月市场滞销. **4** (esp of water) slow-moving; sluggish (尤指水流)缓慢的, 滞缓的.

▷ **slack** *v* **1** [I] be lazy; avoid work 怠惰; 偷懒: *Stop slacking and get on with that digging!* 别偷懒, 继续挖! **2** (phr v) **slack off/up** (**a**) reduce one's level of activity 松懈; 放松: *After intense work in the summer, we are slacking off now.* 夏季紧张的工作过后, 我们现在放松了. (**b**) reduce speed 减速; 放慢: *Slack off/up as you approach the junction.* 接近交叉口时要减速. **slack (sth) up** make (a rope, etc) less tight or tense 将(绳子等)放松.

slacker *n* (*infml* 口) person who is lazy or avoids work 懒惰的人; 偷懒的人.

slackly *adv*: *ropes hanging slackly between the boat and the quay* 在船与码头间系得很松弛的缆绳 ○ *The firm had been run rather slackly.* 那家公司一直经营得松松垮垮.

slack·ness *n* [U].

slack[2] /slæk; slæk/ *n* **1** [U] slack part of a rope, etc (绳等的)松弛部分: *too much slack in the tow-rope* 拖缆很松. **2 slacks** [pl] casual trousers for men or women 宽松的裤子(便装的男裤或女裤): *a pair of slacks* 一条宽松的裤子. **3** [U] coal-dust left over after coal has been screened (煤经筛后剩下的)煤末. **4** (idm 习语) **take up the ˈslack** (**a**) pull on a rope, etc so that it is no longer slack 拉紧绳子: *The tractor took up the slack and pulled the trailer out of the mud.* 拖拉机拉紧拖缆把拖车从泥中拉了出来. (**b**) (in industry) make little-used resources more productive (工业中)充分利用闲置资源.

slacken /ˈslækən; ˈslækən/ *v* **1** [I, Tn] (cause sth to) become slack (使)松弛: *The rope slackened.* 绳子松了. ○ *slacken the reins* 放松缰绳 ○ *slacken one's grip* 松手. **2** [I, Tn, Tn·p] **~ sth (off/up)** (cause sth to) become slower, less active, etc (使某事物)放慢, 迟缓: *The ship's speed slackened.* 船速减慢了. ○ *After hours of digging, we began to slacken up a little.* 我们挖了数小时后, 速度慢了下来. ○ *Slacken (off) your speed as you approach the village.* 接近村庄时要放慢速度.

slag /slæg; slæg/ *n* **1** [U] waste matter that remains after metal has been extracted from ore by smelting 矿渣; 熔渣. **2** [C] (*Brit derog sl* 贬, 俚) woman who does not look respectable and is regarded as sexually immoral 贱妇; 淫妇.

▷ **slag** *v* (**-gg-**) (phr v) **slag sb off** (*Brit sl* 俚) say offensive and critical things about sb, esp unfairly 侮慢或批评某人(尤指无理地): *Now he's left, she's always slagging off her old boss.* 因原老板已走了, 她就一个劲儿地褒贬他.

□ ˈ**slag-heap** *n* heap of slag from a mine 矿渣堆.

slain *pp* of SLAY.

slake /sleɪk; slek/ *v* [Tn] **1** satisfy (one's thirst, or a desire, etc) 解(渴); 满足(欲望等): *slake one's thirst with a cup of tea* 喝杯茶解解渴 ○ (*fml* 文) *Has this murderer slaked his lust for blood yet?* 该杀人犯满足了嗜杀欲了吗? **2** combine (lime) chemically with water 熟化(石灰).

sla·lom /ˈslɑːləm; ˈslɑləm/ *n* **1** ski-race along a zig-zag course marked out by poles with flags 障碍滑雪赛(穿越旗帜标出的弯道): *win the slalom* 在障碍滑雪赛中获胜 ○ [attrib 作定语] *a slalom race, champion, course* 障碍滑雪比赛、冠军、滑道. **2** any similar race, eg in canoes or on water-skis 任何类似的比赛(如划艇或滑水).

slam /slæm; slæm/ *v* (**-mm-**) **1** [I, Ip, Tn, Tn·p, Cn·a] **~ (sth) (to/shut)** (cause sth to) shut forcefully and loudly (使某物)猛然关闭并发出巨响: *The door slammed (to).* 门砰的一声关上了. ○ *Slam the window (shut).* 把窗户使劲关上. ○ *He slammed the lid down.* 他砰的一声盖上了盖子. **2** [Tn·pr, Tn·p] put, push, throw or knock (sth) with great force 猛力地放、推、扔或敲(某物): *slam one's brakes on* 猛力踩闸 ○ *She slammed* *the box down on the table.* 她使劲把盒子摔在桌子上. ○ *The batsman slammed the ball straight at a fielder.* 击球员把球猛击向外场员. **3** [Tn] (*infml* 口) criticize (sb/sth) harshly 猛烈批评(某人[某事物]): *a play slammed by the reviewers* 受到论者猛烈抨击的话剧 ○ *The minister was slammed by the press for the cuts.* 这位部长因削减一事受到报界猛烈抨击. **4** (idm 习语) **shut/slam the door in sb's face** ⇨ DOOR.

▷ **slam** *n* (usu *sing* 通常作单数) noise of sth being slammed 猛然关闭的声音: *the slam of a car door* 关汽车门时发出的声音.

slan·der /ˈslɑːndə(r); *US* ˈslæn-; ˈslændɚ/ *n* [U, C] (offence of making a) false statement intended to damage sb's reputation 诽谤(罪); 诋毁; 中伤: *a vicious slander* 恶毒的诽谤 ○ *a case of slander* 诽谤案 ○ *bring an action against sb for slander*, ie sue sb for slander in a lawcourt 控告某人犯有诽谤罪. Cf 参看 LIBEL.

▷ **slan·der** *v* [Tn] make such a false statement about (sb) 诽谤、诋毁或中伤(某人). **slan·derer** /-dərə(r); -dərɚ/ *n*.

slan·der·ous /-dərəs; -dərəs/ *adj*: *a slanderous attack, accusation* 诽谤性的攻击、指控. **slan·der·ously** *adv*.

slang /slæŋ; slæŋ/ *n* [U] (*abbr* **sl** in this dictionary 本词典中略作 **sl** 俚) very informal words, phrases, etc commonly used in speech, esp between people from the same social group or who work together, not considered suitable for formal contexts and often not in use for long 俚语: *army, prison, railway, etc slang* 军队、监狱、铁路等俚语 ○ *'Grass' is criminal slang for 'informer'.* 'grass' 是罪犯用的俚语, 意思是'告密的人'. ○ [attrib 作定语] *a slang word, expression, etc* 俚语词、词语等. Cf 参看 COLLOQUIAL, INFORMAL 3.

▷ **slang** *v* [Tn] (*infml* 口) **1** attack (sb) using angry, uncontrolled language; abuse 用气愤的、不加控制的语言抨击(某人); 谩骂: *The driver was slanging a pedestrian who had got in his way.* 那司机破口大骂挡他的路的行人. **2** (idm 习语) **a ˈslanging match** quarrel in which each person is angry and uses angry uncontrolled language 相互谩骂.

slangy *adj* typical of or containing slang 使用俚语的; 含有俚语的: *a slangy style* 使用俚语的文体. **slangi·ness** *n* [U].

slant /slɑːnt; *US* slænt; slænt/ *v* **1** [I, Ipr, Tn, Tn·pr esp passive 尤用于被动语态] lean in a particular direction; not be straight 倾斜; 歪: *Her handwriting slants from left to right.* 她写的字从左往右斜. ○ *The picture is slanted to the left.* 这幅画歪向左边了. **2** [Tn] (*usu derog* 通常作贬义) present (news, etc) from a particular point of view 有倾向性地报道(消息等): *slant the story to protect the minister* 歪曲事实以袒护部长 ○ *She slanted the report so that I was made to appear incompetent.* 她作出歪曲报道好让我显得无能.

▷ **slant** *n* **1** slope 斜线; 斜面; 斜坡. **2** (*infml* 口) point of view, sometimes prejudiced, from which sth is seen or presented 观点; 意见; 看法; 见解; (有时指)偏见: *get a new slant on the political situation* 对政治形势有新看法 ○ *gave the report a right-wing slant* 在报告中加入右倾观点. **3** (idm 习语) **on a/the ˈslant** sloping; not straight 倾斜着; 歪着.

slanted *adj* showing a prejudiced slant(2) 有偏见的: *a rather slanted account of the meeting* 对会议作出带有偏见的报道.

slant·ingly, **slant·wise** /-waɪz; -waɪz/ *advs* in a slanting position or direction 倾斜地; 歪斜地: *a picture hanging slantwise* 斜挂着的画.

slap /slæp; slæp/ *v* (**-pp-**) **1** [Tn] strike (sb/sth) with the palm of the hand or with sth flat; smack 掌击(某人[某物]); 掴; 拍: *slap sb's face/sb on the face* 打某人耳光 ○ *People slapped me on the back after the fight*, ie to congratulate me. 拳击比赛后大家拍拍我的背(以示祝贺). **2** [Tn·pr, Tn·p] put (sth) somewhere with a slapping noise 啪的一声将(某物)放在某处: *slapped the money on the counter* 啪的一声把钱放在柜台上 ○ *slap some paint onto a wall* 劈里啪啦把浆涂在墙上 ○ *He slapped the book down (on the table).* 他把书啪的一声放在桌子上. **3** (phr v) **slap sb down** (*infml* 口) stop sb talking, making suggestions, etc in a firm, usu unpleasant, way 严厉制止某人谈话、提建议等(通常指令人不快): *She tried to object, but the chairman slapped her down.* 她想表示反对意见, 但主席喝止住了她. **slap sth on sth** (*infml* 口) add (an extra amount) to the price of sth 在某物原价上加(额外的价): *They've slapped 10p on the price of cigarettes.* 他们把香烟价钱加了10便士.

▷ **slap** *n* **1** (sound of a) blow with the palm of the hand or sth flat 掌击, 掴, 拍(的声音): *I heard a loud slap behind me.* 我听到背后啪的一声. *give sb a slap on the back* 给某人背上一巴掌. **2** (idm 习语) **slap and ˈtickle** (*Brit infml joc* 口, 谑) lively cuddling, kissing, etc between lovers 情人间的热情搂抱、接吻等: *a bit of slap and tickle on the sofa* 在沙发上拥抱接吻. **a slap in the ˈface** snub or insult 冷落; 侮辱: *It was a bit of a slap in the face when she refused to see me.* 她拒绝见我, 这简直是侮辱我.

slap (also ˌ**slap-ˈbang**) *adv* (*infml* 口) **1** directly; straight 直接; 径直: *The car ran slap(-bang) into the wall.* 汽车一头撞到墙上了. **2** right; exactly 正好; 恰恰: *She stood slap(-bang) in the middle of the path, so I couldn't get past.* 她站在路的正中间, 我过不去.

slap·dash /ˈslæpdæʃ; ˈslæpˌdæʃ/ *adj*, *adv* (done or doing things) in a careless and hasty way 匆促(的): *slapdash work* 草率的工作 ○ *a slapdash worker* 粗心的工作者 ○ *do one's work slapdash/in a slapdash way* 工作马马虎虎.

slap-happy /ˌslæp ˈhæpɪ; ˈslæpˌhæpɪ/ *adj* (*infml* 口) cheerfully irresponsible; carefree 马大哈的; 粗心大意的; 无忧无虑的: *too slap-happy in his attitude to schoolwork* (他)对功课太马大哈.

slap·stick /ˈslæpstɪk; ˈslæpˌstɪk/ *n* [U] comedy based on simple visual jokes, eg hitting people, falling over, etc 打闹剧(多打闹等简单滑稽动作): [attrib 作定语] *slapstick comedy* 打闹喜剧.

slap-up /ˈslæpʌp; ˈslæpˌʌp/ *adj* [attrib 作定语] (*Brit infml* 口) (of a meal) excellent (指饭菜)极好的: *a slap-up dinner at an expensive restaurant* 在高档饭馆的一顿美餐.

slash /slæʃ; slæʃ/ *v* **1** [Ipr, Tn, Cn·a] make a cut or cut (sth) with a sweeping stroke; strike (sb/sth) with a whip 砍(某物); 用鞭抽(某人[某物]): *slash through the rope with a sword* 用剑把绳子砍断 ○ *The blade slashed his leg (open).* 刀刃把他的腿划(破)了. ⇨Usage at CUT[1] 用法见CUT[1]. **2** [Tn] cut or reduce (sth) drastically 大幅度裁减或削减(某物): *slash costs, prices, numbers* 大幅度地削减费用、价格、数目 ○ *a government promise to slash taxes* 政府大幅度减税的承诺. **3** [Tn esp passive 尤用于被动语态] make long narrow cuts in (a garment) for ornament 在(衣服)上开长缝作装饰: *slashed sleeves*, ie cut so that the lining or material underneath can be seen 开衩的袖子. **4** [Tn] criticize (sb/sth) harshly 严厉批评(某人[某事物]): *a government plan slashed by the press* 受到新闻界猛烈抨击的政府计划. **5** (phr v) **slash at sth (with sth)** use a stick, sword, etc to make sweeping strokes at sth (用棍棒、刀剑等)砍某物: *slashing at the tall weeds with a stick* 用棍子抽打高高的野草 ○ *slashing wildly at his opponent with a sword* 用剑疯狂地朝对手乱砍. **slash one's way through, past, etc sth** move through, past, etc with sweeping strokes, eg of a sword, etc 挥、砍(如刀剑等)开路: *slashing our way through the jungle with long knives* (我们)在丛林中用长刀砍出一条路.

▷ **slash** *n* **1** [C] (**a**) act of slashing 砍; 抽: *a wild slash with a sword* 用剑乱砍. (**b**) long cut or gash 长的切口或裂口. (**c**) slit made in a garment 衣服的衩. **2** [C] = OBLIQUE *n*. ⇨App 3 见附录3. **3 a slash** [sing] (*Brit sl* 俚) act of urinating 撒尿: *have a quick slash* 很快撒泡尿.

slat /slæt; slæt/ *n* long thin narrow piece of wood, metal or plastic often made to overlap with others, eg in a Venetian blind (木、金属或塑料的)窄而薄的长条(如百叶板). ▷ **slat·ted** *adj*: *a bed with a slatted pine base* 松木板板床.

slate /sleɪt; slet/ *n* **1** (**a**) [U] type of blue-grey rock that splits easily into thin flat layers 板岩; 石板: *slate-coloured*, ie blue-grey 石板色(蓝灰色) ○ [attrib 作定语] *a slate quarry* 板岩采石场. (**b**) [C] small thin piece of this, used as a roof tile 石板瓦: [attrib 作定语] *a slate roof* 石板瓦屋顶. ⇨illus at App 1 见附录1插图, page vi. **2** [C] small sheet of slate in a wooden frame, formerly used by schoolchildren for writing on 石板(旧时学童书写用具). **3** [C] (*US*) list of candidates for nomination or election 提名的或候选人的名单: *on the Democratic slate* 在民主党候选人名单上. **4** (idm 习语) **a clean sheet/slate** ⇨ CLEAN[1]. **(put sth) on the 'slate** (*infml* 口) (note sth down) to be paid for later rather than when it is bought 记在帐上(以后付款): *I've no change, could you put these eggs on the slate?* 我没零钱, 能把这些蛋钱记在帐上吗? **wipe the slate clean** ⇨ WIPE.

▷ **slate** *v* **1** [Tn] cover (a roof, etc) with slates 用石板瓦盖(屋顶等). **2** (*US infml* 口) (**a**) [esp passive 尤用于被动语态: Tn, Tn·pr] **~ sb (for sth)** propose sb (for an office, appointment, etc) 推举某人(任某职位等); 提名: *slated for the Presidency* 被提名作总统候选人. (**b**) [esp passive 尤用于被动语态: Tn·pr, Cn·t] **~ sth (for...)** plan that sth will happen at a specified time 预定; 定于; 安排在: *a meeting slated for Thursday/to take place on Thursday* 定于星期四举行的会议. **3** [Tn, Tn·pr] **~ sb/sth (for sth)** (*Brit infml* 口) criticize sb/sth severely, eg in a newspaper review 严厉批评某人[某事物](如在报纸评论中): *slate a play, book, writer* 猛烈抨击一话剧、书、作者 ○ *The idea got slated by the committee.* 这种意见遭到委员会严厉批评.

slaty *adj* of, like or containing slate(1a) 板岩的; (似)石板的; 含石板的: *slaty coal* 含石板成分的煤.

slat·tern /ˈslætən; ˋslætɚn/ *n* (*fml derog* 文, 贬) dirty untidy woman 不整洁的女子.

▷ **slat·ternly** *adj* (*fml derog* 文, 贬) (of a woman) dirty and untidy (指女子)不整洁的. **slat·tern·li·ness** *n* [U].

slaugh·ter /ˈslɔːtə(r); ˋslɔtɚ/ *n* [U] **1** the killing of animals, esp for food 屠宰(尤指供食用). **2** the killing of many people at once; massacre 屠杀; 杀戮: *the slaughter of innocent civilians* 对无辜平民的屠杀 ○ *the slaughter on the roads*, ie the killing of people in road accidents 路上车祸造成的多人死亡. **3** (*infml* 口) complete defeat 完全失败: *the total slaughter of the home team* 主队的惨败.

▷ **slaugh·ter** *v* [Tn] **1** (**a**) kill (an animal), usu for food 屠宰(动物)(通常为食用): *slaughter pigs by humane methods* 用人道方法杀猪. (**b**) kill (animals or people) in large numbers 大量屠杀(动物或人): *thousands slaughtered by the invading army* 被侵略军杀害的数以千计的人. **2** (*fig infml* 比喻, 口) defeat (sb/sth) completely, esp in sport 彻底打败(某人[某物])(尤指在体育运动中): *We slaughtered them at hockey.* 我们在曲棍球赛中把他们打得一败涂地.

□ **'slaughterhouse** (also **abattoir**) *n* place where animals are killed for food 屠宰场.

slave /sleɪv; slev/ *n* **1** person who is the property of another and is forced to work for him 奴隶: *treat sb like a slave* 像对待奴隶一样对待某人 ○ [attrib 作定语] *slave labour, owners* 奴隶的劳动、奴隶主. **2 ~ of/to sth** person whose way of life is dominated by (a habit, an interest, etc) 生活方式受(习惯、兴趣等)支配的人: *a slave to duty, convention, drink* 被职务、习俗、杯中物所左右的人 ○ *a slave of fashion*, ie person who wears only the latest fashions 赶穿时髦服装的人.

▷ **slave** *v* [I, Ipr, Ip] **~ (away) (at sth)** work very hard 刻苦工作; 苦干: *slaving (away) in the garden for hours* 在花园苦干了数小时 ○ *I've been slaving at the housework all day.* 我整天都在干繁重的家务活儿.

slaver *n* **1** person who buys and sells slaves 奴隶贩子. **2** ship for carrying slaves 贩运奴隶的船.

slavery /ˈsleɪvərɪ; ˋslevərɪ/ *n* [U] **1** condition of being a slave 受奴役的状态: *sold into slavery* 被卖为奴隶. **2** practice of having slaves 奴隶制: *people working to abolish slavery* 为废除奴隶制而奋斗的人们. **3** hard or poorly paid work 苦役; 报酬低的工作. Cf 参看 WHITE SLAVERY (WHITE[1]).

□ **'slave-driver** *n* **1** person in charge of slaves 监管奴隶的监工. **2** (*fig derog* 比喻, 贬) person who makes those under him work very hard 迫使下属拼命干活儿的人.

'slave-trade (also **'slave-traffic**) *n* [sing] the capturing, transporting, buying and selling of people as slaves 奴隶买卖.

slaver /ˈslævə(r); ˋslævɚ/ *v* [I, Ipr] **1 ~ (over sth)** let saliva run out of one's mouth; drool 流口水; 垂涎: *slavering over a plate of spaghetti* 垂涎一盘意大利面条. **2 ~ (over sb/sth)** (*usu derog* 通常作贬义) show great eagerness, desire, etc 热望; 渴望: *Stop slavering over that baby!* 别总看着人家的孩子了! ○ *The dealer was slavering over some precious stones.* 那商人对一些宝石垂涎欲滴.

▷ **slaver** *n* [U] = SALIVA.

slav·ish /ˈsleɪvɪʃ; ˋslevɪʃ/ *adj* (*derog* 贬) lacking in independence or originality 无独立性的; 无创造性的: *slavish devotion to a leader* 对领导的盲目崇拜 ○ *His style is a slavish imitation of his teacher's.* 他一味模仿教师的风格, 毫无创意. ▷ **slav·ishly** *adv*.

slay /sleɪ; sle/ *v* (*pt* **slew** /sluː; slu/, *pp* **slain** /sleɪn; slen/) [Tn] (*fml* 文 *or US*) kill (esp an enemy) in a violent way 杀, 残杀(尤指敌人): *soldiers slain in battle* 在战斗中被杀害的士兵.

SLD /ˌes el ˈdiː; ˌɛs ɛl ˋdi/ *abbr* 缩写 = (*Brit politics* 政) Social and Liberal Democrats 社会自由民主党.

sleazy /ˈsliːzɪ; ˋslizɪ/ *adj* (**-ier, -iest**) (*infml* 口) (esp of a place) dirty and not respectable; sordid (尤指地方)肮脏的, 污秽的, 破烂的: *a sleazy club, hotel, etc* 肮脏的俱乐部、旅馆等 ○ *a rather sleazy appearance* 很脏的外貌.

▷ **sleaz·ily** /-ɪlɪ; -ɪlɪ/ *adv*. **sleazi·ness** *n* [U].

sledge[1] /sledʒ; slɛdʒ/ (also *esp US* **sled** /sled; slɛd/) *n* vehicle with long narrow strips of wood, metal, etc instead of wheels, for travelling over ice and snow (larger types being pulled by horses or dogs and smaller ones used in sport for travelling downhill fast) 雪橇; 雪车. Cf 参看 SLEIGH.

▷ **sledge** (also *esp US* **sled**) *v* **1** [I, Ipr, Ip] (often 常作 **go sledging/sledding**) travel on a sledge, esp downhill for sport 乘雪橇(尤指滑坡, 作为运动): *sledging down the ski slopes* 乘雪橇沿滑雪道下滑. **2** [Tn] carry (sth/sb) on a sledge 用雪橇运载(某物[某人]): *sledging supplies to remote villages* 用雪橇把物资运往偏远的乡村.

sledge[2] /sledʒ; slɛdʒ/ (also **'sledge-hammer**) *n* large heavy hammer with a long handle, used eg for driving posts into the ground 大锤(如用于打桩者).

sleek /sliːk; slik/ *adj* (**-er, -est**) **1** smooth and glossy 光滑而有光泽的: *sleek hair, fur, etc* 光滑而有光泽的毛发、毛皮等. **2** (*often derog* 常作贬义) (of a person) looking well-fed and prosperous (指人)保养得很好的, 脑满肠肥的. **3** well-styled 时髦的: *a sleek, shiny sports-car* 闪闪发亮的时髦跑车.

▷ **sleek** *v* [Tn] make (one's hair, a cat's fur, etc) sleek 使(毛发、猫的毛等)光滑而发亮.

sleekly *adv*.

sleek·ness *n* [U].

sleep[1] /sliːp; slip/ *n* **1** [U] condition that occurs regularly in humans and animals, esp at night, in which the eyes are closed and the muscles, nervous system, etc are relaxed 睡眠: *How many hours' sleep do you need?* 你需要几个小时的睡眠? ○ *He didn't get much sleep.* 他睡眠不足. ○ *Do you ever talk in your sleep?* 你睡觉说梦话吗? ○ *send sb/get to sleep*, ie (make sb) fall asleep (使某人)入睡 ○ *sing/rock a baby to sleep*, ie make the baby fall asleep by singing/rocking 唱歌[摇着]哄孩子入睡. **2** [sing] a period of sleep 睡眠时间: *have a short, good, restful, etc sleep* 短时间的、良好的、安静的...睡眠. **3** [U] (*infml* 口) substance that gathers in the corners of the eyes during sleep 眼眵: *wash the sleep out of one's eyes* 把眼眵洗掉. **4** (idm 习语) **cry/sob oneself to 'sleep** cry/sob until one falls asleep 哭着入睡. **ˌgo to 'sleep** (**a**) fall asleep 入睡: *Go to sleep now, it's late.* 快睡吧, 很晚了. (**b**) (*infml* 口) (eg of a limb) become numb through lack of movement, etc (如肢体)麻木(因

不活动等): *I've been sitting on the floor and my foot's gone to sleep.* 我一直坐在地板上，脚都麻木了. **not get/have a wink of sleep** ⇨ WINK. **not lose sleep/lose no sleep over sth** ⇨ LOSE. **put sb to 'sleep** make sb fall asleep, esp by using an anaesthetic 使某人入睡(尤指用麻醉剂). **put (an animal) to 'sleep** (*euph* 婉) kill (an animal) deliberately, eg because it is ill 杀死(动物)(如因病): *Stray dogs are usually put to sleep if no one claims them.* 走失的狗如无人认领通常就不让它再生存了. **read oneself/sb to sleep** ⇨ READ. **sleep the sleep of the just** ⇨ SLEEP².

▷ **sleep·less** *adj* [usu attrib 通常作定语] without sleep 失眠的; 不眠的: *pass a sleepless night* 度过一个不眠之夜. **sleep·lessly** *adv*. **sleep·less·ness** *n* [U].

□ **'sleep-walker** *n* person who walks around while asleep 梦游者; 患梦行症的人. **'sleep-walking** *n* [U].

sleep² /sli:p; slip/ *v* (*pt*, *pp* **slept** /slept; slɛpt/) **1** [I, Ip, In/pr] be in a state of sleep; be asleep 睡; 睡觉; 睡着: *Try to sleep in spite of the noise.* 尽管有喧闹声也要设法睡着. ○ *sleep well/badly* 睡得好[不好] ○ *I got up early, but he slept on.* 我起得很早，而他还睡呢. ○ *We slept (for) eight hours.* 我们睡了八个小时. ○ *I slept at a friend's house last night.* 我昨晚睡在朋友家里. **2** [Tn no passive 不用于被动语态] have enough beds for (a number of people) 为(某数量的人)提供床位: *Our caravan sleeps six in comfort.* 我们居住的拖车可舒舒服服地睡六个人. ○ *The hotel sleeps 300 guests.* 这旅馆可供三百人住宿. **3** (idm 习语) **let sleeping dogs 'lie** (*saying* 谚) do not try to change a situation that could become a problem if sb interfered 别惊动睡着的狗; 别惹事生非; 别自找麻烦: *We decided to let sleeping dogs lie and not take them to court.* 我们决定不起诉他们，免得惹事生非. **not sleep a wink** ⇨ WINK. **sleep like a 'log/'top** (*infml* 口) sleep soundly 睡得很熟. **sleep 'rough** sleep out of doors wherever one can 在户外睡觉: *He'd been sleeping rough for a week, in ditches and haystacks.* 他在沟里和草堆里露宿了一个星期. **sleep the sleep of the 'just** not be troubled by any guilty feeling 能睡安稳觉; 问心无愧. **sleep 'tight** (*infml* 口) (esp imperative 尤用于祈使句) sleep soundly 睡个好觉: *Good night, sleep tight!* 晚安，睡个好觉! **4** (phr v) **sleep around** (*infml* 口) have sex with many partners 与很多人发生性关系. **sleep in (a)** (*US*) = LIE IN (LIE²): *I get a chance to sleep in at the weekend.* 我在周末才有机会睡个懒觉. **(b)** (esp formerly of servants) sleep at the place where one works (尤指旧时仆人)在工作处住宿: *a housekeeper that sleeps in* 住在雇主家里的管家. **sleep sth off** recover from sth by sleeping 藉睡眠恢复或复原: *sleep off a bad headache, a hangover, etc* 用睡眠来消除头痛、宿醉等 ○ *sleep it off*, ie after being drunk 藉睡眠醒酒. **sleep on sth** (no passive 不用于被动语态) not decide about sth until the next day 将(某事)留待次日再决定: *Don't say now if you'll take the job: sleep on it first.* 你现在先别决定接受这项工作: 考虑一天再说. **sleep out (a)** sleep outdoors 露宿. **(b)** (esp formerly of servants) not sleep at the place where one works (尤指旧时仆人)不在工作处住宿: *a butler who sleeps out* 不在雇主家住宿的男管家. **sleep through sth** (no passive 不用于被动语态) not be woken up by (eg a noise or an alarm clock) 声音(如噪声、闹钟)吵不醒: *You slept right through the thunderstorm.* 你一直睡着，这场雷雨都没把你吵醒. **sleep together; sleep with sb** (*euph* 婉) have sex with sb, esp sb to whom one is not married 与某人发生性关系(尤指并非配偶).

□ **'sleeping-bag** *n* warmly lined bag for sleeping in, esp when camping 睡袋(尤指露营用的).

'sleeping-car *n* railway coach fitted with beds or berths (铁路的)卧车.

'sleeping partner (*US* **'silent partner**) partner who has invested capital in a business company but who does not actually work in it 不参加实际业务的股东.

'sleeping-pill *n* pill containing a drug that helps sb to sleep 安眠药.

,sleeping po'liceman (*infml* 口) bump built across a road to make drivers slow down 路埂(横设于道路上的隆起物，可使司机减速).

'sleeping sickness tropical disease carried by the tsetse fly, causing sleepiness and often death 昏睡病(由采采蝇传染的热带疾病，引起昏睡，常造成死亡).

sleeper /'sli:pə(r); 'slipɚ/ *n* **1** (with an *adj* 与形容词连用) person who sleeps in the specified way 睡觉(呈某种状态)的人: *a good/bad sleeper* 睡得好[睡不好]的人 ○ *a heavy/light sleeper*, ie one whom it is hard/easy to wake up 睡觉沉[轻]的人. **2** (*US* **tie**) beam of wood or other material on which the rails of a railway, etc are fixed 轨枕; 枕木; 道木. **3** (bed or berth in a) sleeping-car 卧车(中的卧铺). **4** (*Brit*) small ear-ring used to keep the hole in a pierced ear open (用以保持耳环孔不封口的)小耳环. **5** (*US infml* 口) play, book, person, etc that has an unexpected success, esp after being overlooked or unnoticed 未料到获得成功的剧、书、人等(尤指未受重视的).

sleepy /'sli:pɪ; 'slipɪ/ *adj* (**-ier**, **-iest**) **1** needing or ready to go to sleep 困的; 欲睡的: *feel, look sleepy* 觉得、看来困了 ○ *That beer made me quite sleepy.* 我喝了那啤酒后昏昏欲睡. **2** (of places) not very busy; without much activity (指地方)冷清的，不热闹的: *a sleepy little village* 冷清的小村庄. ▷ **sleep·ily** /-ɪlɪ; -əlɪ/ *adv*. **sleepi·ness** *n* [U].

sleet /sli:t; slit/ *n* [U] falling snow or hail mixed with rain 雨夹雪或雹: *showers of sleet* 阵阵的雨夹雪. ▷ **sleet** *v* [I] (used with *it*, usu in the continuous tenses 与it连用，通常用于进行时态): *It is sleeting*, ie Sleet is falling. 下着雨夹雪. **sleety** *adj*: *sleety rain* 夹有冰雹的雨.

sleeve /sli:v; sliv/ *n* **1** part of a garment that covers all or part of the arm 袖子: *roll up the sleeves of one's shirt/one's shirt-sleeves* 卷起衬衫的袖子 ○ *a dress with short/long sleeves* 短[长]袖的连衣裙. ⇨illus at JACKET 见JACKET插图. **2** tube that encloses a rod, cable, etc (杆、缆绳等的)套管，套筒: *a metal cable inside a plastic sleeve* 套着塑料管的金属电缆. **3** (*US* **jacket**) stiff envelope for a gramophone record 唱片套: [attrib 作定语] *a sleeve design* 唱片套设计 ○ *sleeve notes*, ie notes about composers, performers, etc on a sleeve 唱片套上的介绍(关于作曲者、演奏者等的). **4** (idm 习语) **an ace up one's sleeve** ⇨ ACE. **a card up one's sleeve** ⇨ CARD¹. **laugh up one's sleeve** ⇨ LAUGH. **roll up one's sleeves** ⇨ ROLL². **a trick up one's sleeve** ⇨ TRICK. **(have sth) up one's sleeve** kept secret for use when needed 暗藏以备不时之需: *Have you any ideas up your sleeve if our money runs out?* 要是我们钱用光了你有什么锦囊妙计? **wear one's heart on one's sleeve** ⇨ WEAR².

▷ **-sleeved** (forming compound *adjs* 用以构成复合形容词) having sleeves of the specified type 有某种样式袖子的: *a long-, short-, loose-sleeved shirt.*

sleeve·less *adj* without sleeves 无袖的.

sleigh /sleɪ; sle/ *n* [attrib 作定语] sledge, esp one drawn by a horse 雪橇(尤指马拉的): [attrib 作定语] *a sleigh ride* 乘雪橇.

▷ **sleigh** *v* [I, Ipr] travel on a sleigh 乘雪橇: *go sleighing* 坐雪橇 ○ *sleigh over to the village* 乘雪橇去那个村庄.

sleight /slaɪt; slaɪt/ *n* (idm 习语) **,sleight of 'hand** great skill in using the hands in performing conjuring tricks, etc (变戏法等的)巧妙的手法: (*fig* 比喻) *The company accounts show a little financial sleight of hand.* 公司帐目显示在财务上耍了一点手腕.

slen·der /'slendə(r); 'slɛndɚ/ *adj* (**-er**, **-est**) **1** (*approv* 褒) **(a)** not very wide but comparatively long or high 细长的; 纤细的: *slender fingers* 纤细的手指 ○ *a slender waist* 细腰 ○ *a wineglass with a slender stem* 高脚杯. **(b)** (of people) slim (指人)瘦长的，苗条的: *a slender girl, figure* 苗条的女孩、身段 ○ *a slender, graceful ballet-dancer* 苗条而动作优美的芭蕾舞演员. ⇨Usage at THIN 用法见THIN. **2** small in amount or size; inadequate; scanty 微薄的; 不足的; 微少的: *a slender income* 微薄的收入 ○ *people of slender means*, ie with little money 贫穷的人们 ○ *win by a slender margin* 险胜. ▷ **slen·derly** *adv*. **slen·der·ness** *n* [U].

slept *pt*, *pp* of SLEEP².

sleuth /slu:θ; sluθ/ *n* (*infml joc* 口，谑) detective 侦探.

▷ **sleuth** *v* [I] (*infml joc* 口，谑) do detective work 侦查: *I had to go out sleuthing to find your address.* 我得出去侦查一番才找到你的住址.

slew¹ *pt* of SLAY.

slew² (*US* also **slue**) /slu:; slu/ *v* [Ipr, Tn·pr] **~ (sth) round** (cause sth to) turn, esp very fast in a new direction; swing (使某物)转动(尤指沿新方向急转); 旋转: *The car slewed round on the icy road.* 汽车在结冰的路上打滑了. ○ *The driver slewed the crane round.* 司机把吊车转了过来.

slew[3] /slu:; slu/ *n* [sing] **~ of sth** (*US infml* 口) great amount of sth 大量; 许多: *a whole slew of problems* 一大堆问题.

slice /slaɪs; slaɪs/ *n* **1** thin wide flat piece cut off an item of food (从食物上切下的)薄片: *a slice of meat, cake, cheese, etc* 一片肉、蛋糕、干酪等 ○ *slices of beef between slices of fresh bread* 夹在新鲜面包片之间的牛肉片. **2** (*infml* 口) portion; share 部分; 份儿: *get a slice of the profit* 得到一份利润 ○ *She takes a large slice of the credit for our success.* 她把我们做成的事大部分算作她的功劳. **3** utensil with a broad flat blade for cutting, serving or lifting food, eg cooked fish or fried eggs (切片、上菜或铲起食物用的)刀, 铲子. **4** (eg in golf) poor stroke that makes the ball spin off in the wrong direction, ie to the right of a right-handed player (如高尔夫球中)(因击偏而成的)同侧旋转球(如右手击球者将球击成右旋球). Cf 参看 PULL[2] 11. **5** (idm 习语) **get, etc a slice/share of the cake** ➪ CAKE. **a piece/slice of the action** ➪ ACTION.

▷ **slice** *v* **1** [Tn, Tn·p] **~ sth (up)** cut sth into slices 将某物切成薄片: *slice the meat, loaf, etc (up)* 把肉、面包等切成薄片 ○ *a sliced loaf* 切片的面包. **2** [Tn·pr, Tn·p, Dn·n no passive 不用于被动语态, Dn·pr] **~ sth off/from sth; ~ sth off** cut sth from a larger piece 将某物切下: *slice a piece off (the meat)* 切下一片(肉) ○ *slice a thin wedge from the cake* 从蛋糕上切下一角 ○ *Slice me a piece of bread/a piece of bread for me.* 给我切一片面包. **3** [Ipr, Tn] **~ through/into sth** cut cleanly or easily through sth (干净利落地)切, 割: *The axe sliced through the wood.* 斧头一下子把木头劈开了. ○ *The falling slate sliced into his arm.* 落下来的一块石片划破了他的手臂. ○ *The bows of the ship sliced the water.* 船头划开水面前进. **4** [Tn] (eg in golf) strike (a ball) with a slice(4) (如在高尔夫球中)将(球)击成同侧旋转球.

S

slick /slɪk; slɪk/ *adj* **(-er, -est)** **1** done smoothly and efficiently, apparently without effort 顺利而有效的; 不费力的: *a slick translation* 流畅的译文 ○ *a slick take-over* 顺利的接管 ○ *gave a slick excuse for staying away* 为未前来找了一个巧妙的借口. **2** (*often derog* 常作贬义) (of people) doing things in a slick(1) way (指人)圆滑的, 油滑的: *a slick performer, salesperson, negotiator, etc* 圆滑的表演者、推销员、谈判者等 ○ *She's very slick, but I don't believe a word she says.* 她很伶俐, 但她的话我一句也不信. **3** smooth and slippery 光滑的: *The roads were slick with wet mud.* 道路上有泥十分滑.

▷ **slick** *n* (also **'oil slick**) thick patch of oil floating on the sea (esp from an oil-tanker after a collision) 海面浮油(尤指从撞毁的油轮中流出的).

slick *v* (phr v) **slick sth down** flatten (hair), using eg hair-oil 使(头发)平滑(如用发油): *curls slicked down with grease* 加润发脂梳平的鬈发.

slicker *n* **1** (*infml* 口 *esp US*) slick(2) person 圆滑的人: *a city slicker*, ie slick by comparison with a person from the country 油头滑脑的城里人. **2** (*US*) long loose waterproof coat (长而宽松的)雨衣.

slide[1] /slaɪd; slaɪd/ *n* **1** [sing] act of sliding 滑; 滑行: *have a slide on the ice* 在冰上滑行. **2** [C] smooth stretch of ice, hard snow, etc used esp by children on sledges (冰、压实的雪等的)滑面(尤为儿童用以乘雪橇的). **3** [C] smooth slope, track or chute down which goods can slide or on which children can play at sliding (运送货物用的)滑坡、滑道或滑槽; (儿童游戏用的)滑梯. **4** [C] **(a)** picture, diagram, etc on photographic film, usu held in a small frame and shown on a screen using a projector; transparency 幻灯片(有框的透明软片). **(b)** (formerly) such a picture on a glass plate (旧时)幻灯片(玻璃的). **5** [C] glass plate on which sth is placed so that it can be looked at under a microscope (显微镜的)载片. **6** [C] part of a machine, etc that slides, eg the U-shaped part of a trombone (机器等的)滑动部件(如长号上的U形管). ➪illus at App 1 见附录1插图, page x. **7** [C] (in compounds 用以构成复合词) sudden fall of a mass of earth, mud, etc (土、泥等的)突然崩落: *a 'landslide* ○ *a 'mudslide.* **8** [C] = HAIR-SLIDE (HAIR).

slide[2] /slaɪd; slaɪd/ *v* (*pt, pp* **slid** /slɪd; slɪd/) **1** [I, Ipr, Ip, Tn·pr, Tn·p, Cn·a] (cause sth to) move smoothly along an even, polished or slippery surface (使某物)滑动: *I was sliding (about) helplessly (on the ice).* 我(在冰上)身不由己地滑起来了. ○ *The ship slid (down) into the water.* 船滑入水中. ○ *The drawers slide in and out easily.* 这些抽屉很容易推进拉出. ○ *We slid down the grassy slope.* 我们顺着草坡滑下去. ○ *I slid the rug in front of the fire.* 我挪了挪铺在炉前的地毯. ○ *Can the car seat be slid forward a little?* 汽车的座位能向前挪一点吗? ○ *She slid the door open.* 她把门推开. **2** [Ipr, Ip, Tn·pr, Tn·p] (cause sth to) move quietly or so as not to be noticed (使某物)悄悄地或偷偷地移动: *The thief slid out (of the door) while no one was looking.* 小偷乘没人注意时溜了出去. ○ *She slid a coin into his hand.* 她把一枚硬币偷偷塞进他的手里. ○ *He lifted the mat and slid the key under (it).* 他掀起垫子把钥匙悄悄放在下面. **3** [I] (eg of prices) fall gradually (如指价格)逐渐降低: *House values may begin to slide.* 房价可能开始逐渐下降了. **4** (idm 习语) **let sth 'slide** (*infml* 口) allow sth to become neglected, less organized, etc 放任某事; 听其自然: *She got depressed and began to let things slide.* 她情绪低落, 一切都听之任之. **5** (phr v) **slide into sth** (no passive 不用于被动语态) gradually pass into (a certain, usu bad, condition) 慢慢进入(某状态, 通常指坏的): *slide into bad habits, debt* 逐渐染上了坏习惯、背上了债 ○ *We mustn't slide into complacency.* 我们决不可产生自满情绪. **slide over sth** avoid dealing with (a topic, etc) in detail 避免深入涉及(某问题等): *She discussed sales, but slid over the problem of how to increase production.* 她谈论了销售情况, 却对增加生产的问题一带而过.

□ **'slide-rule** *n* ruler with a strip sliding in a groove in the middle, marked with logarithmic scales for making rapid calculations 滑尺; 计算尺.

ˌsliding 'door door that slides on runners and is drawn across an opening 滑门; 拉门.

ˌsliding 'scale scale that relates two things, so that they each increase or decrease together 滑动费率, 滑动折算制(相关的两项目相应增减制): *Fees are calculated on a sliding scale according to income*, ie Richer people pay more. 这种费用是根据收入高低滑动折算的(富人多付钱).

slight[1] /slaɪt; slaɪt/ *adj* **(-er, -est)** **1** not serious or important; small 不严重的; 不重要的; 微小的; 轻微的: *a slight slip, error, change, improvement* 些微的失误、错误、变化、改进 ○ *a slight headache* 轻微的头痛 ○ *The differences between the pictures are very slight.* 这两幅画差别很小. ○ *do sth without the slightest difficulty*, ie with no difficulty at all 毫无困难地做某事 ○ *She takes offence at the slightest thing*, ie is very easily offended. 她动不动就生气. ○ *Compared to his early work, this is a rather slight novel*, ie not a major one. 这部小说与他早期作品相比, 不甚重要. **2** not thick and strong; frail; slender 不粗壮的; 脆弱的; 细长的: *a slight figure, girl* 苗条的身材、女孩 ○ *supported by a slight framework* 由纤细的骨架支撑的. **3** (idm 习语) **not in the 'slightest** not at all 毫不; 一点也不: *You didn't embarrass me in the slightest.* 你一点也没让我为难.

▷ **slightly** *adv* **1** to a slight(1) degree 轻微地; 稍稍: *a slightly bigger house* 稍大些的房子 ○ *The patient is slightly better today.* 病人今天稍稍好些. ○ *I know her slightly.* 我对她稍有了解. **2** slenderly 细长; 苗条; 微小: *a slightly-built child* 瘦高的孩子.

slight·ness *n* [U].

slight[2] /slaɪt; slaɪt/ *v* [Tn] treat (sb) without proper respect or courtesy; snub 怠慢(某人); 冷落: *a slighting remark* 怠慢的话 ○ *She felt slighted because no one spoke to her.* 没人跟她说话, 她觉得受到冷落.

▷ **slight** *n* **~ (to/on sb/sth)** act, remark, etc that offends sb 冒犯他人的行为、言语等; 蔑视; 侮辱: *My remark was not meant as a slight on you.* 我的话并没有冒犯你的意思. ○ *She suffered many slights from colleagues.* 她多次遭到同事侮慢.

slight·ingly *adv*.

slim /slɪm; slɪm/ *adj* **(-mmer, -mmest)** **1** (*approv* 褒) not fat or thick; slender 纤细的; 修长的; 苗条的: *a slim person, figure, waist* 瘦高的人、苗条的身材、纤细的腰 ○ *I'm trying to get slim.* 我想要瘦一些. ○ *a slim pocket-book* 小巧的笔记本. ➪Usage at THIN 用法见 THIN. **2** not as big as one would like or expect; small 不够大的;

小的: *slim hopes/chances/prospects of success* 成功的希望[机会/可能性]不大 ○ *condemned on the slimmest of evidence* 根据微不足道的证据被判罪.

▷ **slim** *v* **(-mm-)** 1 [I, Ip] **~ (down)** eat less, take exercise, etc in order to lose weight and become slim (藉节食、运动等)减轻体重使体形苗条: *trying to get fit and slim (down)* 努力使身体健康、体形苗条. **2** (phr v) **slim sth down** reduce sth in size or scale 缩小某事物的大小或规模: *slim down the factory's work-force* 缩减工厂劳力.

slimly *adv*: *a slimly-built person* 身材苗条的人.

slim·mer *n* person who is slimming 减轻体重的人: *a slimmers' magazine*, ie one that gives advice on how to slim 健美杂志.

slim·ness *n* [U].

slime /slaɪm; slaɪm/ *n* [U] **1** thick soft slippery liquid substance, esp mud 稠、软而滑的液态物质; (尤指)泥浆: *There was a coating of slime on the unwashed sink.* 未刷洗的水涤槽上有一层污垢. **2** sticky liquid produced by snails, slugs, etc (蜗牛、蛞蝓等的)黏液: *a trail of slime* 蜗牛的黏液痕迹.

▷ **slimy** /ˈslaɪmɪ; ˋslaɪmɪ/ *adj* **(-ier, -iest)** **1** of, like or covered with slime (似)泥浆的; 有泥浆的: *slip on the slimy steps* 在有泥浆的台阶上滑倒. **2** (*infml* 口) disgustingly dishonest, flattering, hypocritical, etc 奸诈的; 谄媚的; 虚伪的: *You slimy little creep!* 你这个卑鄙无耻的小人! **sli·mi·ness** *n* [U].

sling /slɪŋ; slɪŋ/ *n* **1** bandage, tied over one shoulder or round the neck, used to support a broken arm, wrist, etc 悬带(用以固定断臂、腕等的): *have one's arm in a sling* 用悬带吊着手臂. **2** length of rope, strap, chain, etc looped round an object (eg a barrel) to support or lift it 吊具, 吊索, 吊链(用以悬挂或提起物体, 如圆桶的). **3** strap held in a loop, used for throwing stones, etc 投石器.

▷ **sling** *v* (*pt, pp* **slung** /slʌŋ; slʌŋ/) **1** [Tn, Tn·pr, Tn·p] (*infml* 口) throw (sb/sth) with great force 用力投掷(某人[某物]): *slinging stones at birds* 投石击鸟 ○ *She slung her coat angrily into the car.* 她愤怒地把大衣扔进汽车里. ○ *He was slung out (of the club) for fighting.* 他因打架被人(从俱乐部)驱逐出去. **2** [Tn, Tn·pr, Tn·p] lift or support (sth) so that it can hang loosely 悬或挂(某物): *sling a hammock between two tree-trunks* 把吊床悬在两树干间 ○ *with her bag slung over her shoulder* 她的包挂在肩上. **3** (idm 习语) **fling/sling/throw mud** ⇨ MUD. **sling one's ˈhook** (*Brit sl* 俚) go away 走开; 滚蛋.

□ **ˈsling-shot** *n* (*US*) = CATAPULT.

slink /slɪŋk; slɪŋk/ *v* (*pt, pp* **slunk** /slʌŋk; slʌŋk/) [Ipr, Ip] **1** move as if one feels guilty or ashamed, or does not want to be seen 鬼鬼祟祟地移动; 溜走: *The thief slunk down the dark alley.* 那个贼偷偷钻进黑胡同里. ○ *The dog slunk out when I shouted at him.* 我向那条狗一喊, 它就溜出去了. ⇨Usage at PROWL 用法见 PROWL. **2** move in a seductive way 扭捏招摇地走: *slinking around in a tight black dress* 穿着黑色紧身连衣裙媚态十足地走来走去.

slinky /ˈslɪŋkɪ; ˋslɪŋkɪ/ *adj* **(-ier, -iest)** **1** (esp of a woman) moving in a seductive way (尤指女子)扭捏招摇地移动: *her slinky way of dancing* 她迷人的舞姿. **2** (of clothes) clinging to the curves of the body (指衣服)紧身显出身体线条的: *a slinky night-dress* 显出优美身段的睡衣. ▷ **slinki·ness** *n* [U].

slip[1] /slɪp; slɪp/ *n* **1** [C usu *sing* 通常作单数] act of slipping; false step 滑动; 滑倒; 失足: *One slip and you could fall off the cliff.* 脚下一滑就可能从悬崖上跌下去. **2** [C] minor error caused by carelessness or lack of attention 小错误; 小疏忽: *make a slip* 失误 ○ *There were a few trivial slips in the translation.* 译文中有几个小错误. **3** [C] **(a)** loose sleeveless garment worn under a dress; petticoat (有肩带的)衬裙. **(b)** = GYM-SLIP (GYM). **4** [C] = PILLOWCASE (PILLOW). **5** [C] thin or small piece of paper 纸条: *a salary slip*, ie giving details of earnings, tax paid, etc 薪金单(列有收入、税款等细节) ○ *write a phone number on a slip of paper* 把电话号码写在纸条上. **6** [C] cutting[1](2) taken from a plant for grafting or planting 接穗或插条(嫁接或种植用的). **7 the slips** [pl] = SLIPWAY (SLIP[2]). **8 (a)** [C] (in cricket) (position of a) fielder standing close behind and usu to the off side of the batsman (板球赛中)通常位于击球员右后方的外场员(的位置): *first/second/third slip* 第一[第二/第三]外场员 ○ *Who is (at) first slip?* 谁在第一外场员位置? **(b) the slips** [pl] place where these fielders stand 上述外场员的守球区: *fielding in the slips* 在击球员右后方的位置守球. **9** [U] almost liquid clay for coating earthenware or making patterns on it 泥釉(涂于陶器上作表层或图样的). **10** (idm 习语) **give sb the ˈslip** (*infml* 口) escape from or get away from (sb following or chasing one) 摆脱或避开(尾随者或追逐者): *We managed to give our pursuers the slip.* 我们设法甩掉了后面追来的人. **a ˈslip of a boy, girl, thing, child, etc** a slightly-built boy, etc 瘦削的男孩等: *She's just a slip of a thing, but she can run faster than all of us.* 别看她那么瘦, 跑起来比我们谁都快. **a slip of the ˈpen/ˈtongue** minor error in writing/speech 笔误[口误]: *A slip of the tongue made me say Robert instead of Richard.* 我说走了嘴把理查德说成了罗伯特. **there's ˌmany a ˌslip ˈtwixt (the) ˌcup and (the) ˈlip** (*saying* 谚) things can easily go wrong before one gets what one wants, expects, hopes for, etc 事情往往会功败垂成: *They think they'll win the election easily, but there's many a slip 'twixt cup and lip.* 他们以为能在选举中轻易取胜, 但事情往往会功败垂成.

slip[2] /slɪp; slɪp/ *v* **(-pp-)** **1 (a)** [I, Ipr, Ip] **~ (over) (on sth)** (of a person, an animal, a car, etc) slide accidentally; lose one's balance and fall or nearly fall in this way (指人、动物、汽车等)意外滑动, 失去平衡跌倒或险些跌倒: *The climber's foot slipped, and she fell.* 那个攀登的女子脚下一滑就摔倒了. ○ *She slipped (over) (on the ice) and broke her leg.* 她(在冰上)滑了一跤把腿摔断了. ○ *The van slipped (a few feet) down the embankment.* 那客货车沿堤坝向下滑动了(几英尺). **(b)** [I, Ipr, Ip] (of an object) slide accidentally out of its proper position (指物体)意外滑离原位: *The lorry turned and its load slipped.* 卡车转弯时车上货物滑离了原位. ○ *The razor slipped and cut my cheek.* 剃刀一滑把我脸给割破了. ○ *The straps keep slipping off (my shoulders).* 吊带老是(从我肩上)滑下来. **(c)** [Ipr, Ip] move smoothly and easily in a particular direction 沿某方向顺畅而容易地移动: *The ship slipped through the water.* 船在水上平稳地航行. ○ *I slipped along the bench next to her.* 我沿长凳一下子滑到她的旁边. ○ *This wine slips down easily,* ie is pleasant to drink. 这种葡萄酒很好喝. **2 (a)** [Ipr, Ip] go somewhere quietly or quickly, eg in order not to be noticed, or without being noticed 悄悄或匆匆到某处(如以免受注意或无人注意到): *The thief slipped out (by the back door).* 那个贼偷偷(从后门)溜出去了. ○ *We slipped away to Paris for the weekend.* 我们赶到巴黎去度周末. ○ *The ship slipped into the harbour at night.* 那艘船夜里悄悄开进了港口. ○ (*fig* 比喻) *Errors have slipped into the book.* 书中有些错误. ○ (*fig* 比喻) *The years slipped by.* 岁月在不知不觉中逝去. ○ (*fig* 比喻) *We've slipped behind schedule.* 我们无形中已落后于预定计划. **(b)** [Tn·pr, Tn·p, Dn·n, Dn·pr] **~ sth (to sb)** put sth somewhere, often quietly or secretly 将某物放在某处(常指悄悄地或偷偷地): *slip an envelope into one's pocket* 把信封悄悄塞进口袋 ○ *I slipped a few jokes into the speech.* 我在讲话中巧妙地加了几句笑话. ○ *She opened the letter-box and slipped a newspaper through.* 她打开信箱把报纸塞了进去. ○ *Slip the waiter a tip.* 悄悄给服务员一点小费. ○ *I tried to slip the note to him while the teacher wasn't looking.* 我想趁老师不注意时把条子偷偷递给他. **3** [Ipr, Ip] **~ from/out of/through sth; ~ out/through** fall, get away, escape, etc by being difficult to hold, or by not being held firmly 滑落; 滑脱; 逃走: *The fish slipped out of my hand.* 鱼从我手中滑走了. ○ *He caught the ball, then it slipped through his fingers.* 那球他已接住却又从手中滑脱了. ○ *The mouse slipped quickly from the cat's claws.* 老鼠很快从猫爪下逃走了. ○ (*fig* 比喻) *I didn't mean to say that: it just slipped out.* 我本不想说, 只是无意中漏了出来. **4** [Ipr, Tn·pr, Tn·p] **~ into/out of sth; ~ sth over/round sth; ~ sth on/off** put (a coat, one's shoes, etc) on/off, esp quickly and easily 穿上[脱去](大衣、鞋等)(尤指迅速且容易地): *slip into/out of a dress* 一下子穿上[脱下]连衣裙 ○ *slip a shawl round one's shoulders* 很快披上披肩. **5 (a)** [Tn, Tn·pr] **~ sth (from/off sth)** detach or release sth 放开, 释放(某物): *slip a dog from* *its leash* 松开皮带把狗放开 ○ *slip the rope off the hook* 解开钩上的绳索 ○ *slip a stitch*, ie (in knitting) move a stitch from one needle to another without knitting it 漏针(编织时). (**b**) [Tn] get free from (sth); escape from 逃离(某处); 逃脱; 挣脱: *The ship slipped its moorings.* 那船漂离了系船处. ○ *The dog slipped its collar.* 狗挣脱开了项圈. ○ (*fig* 比喻) *That point slipped my attention.* 那一点我疏忽了. ○ *It had slipped my mind/memory that you were arriving today.* 我把你今天抵达的事忘记了. **6** (idm 习语) **be 'slipping** (*infml* 口) not be as good, alert, strong, etc as usual 不如平时好、机警、强壮等: *I've forgotten your name again — I must be slipping.* 我又把你的名字给忘了 —— 我肯定是不行了. **let sth slip** (**a**) miss or not take advantage of (an opportunity, etc) 错过或放过(机会等): *She let slip a chance to work abroad.* 她错过了出国工作的机会. (**b**) accidentally reveal (a secret, etc); say sth casually 偶然泄露(秘密等); 无意中说出(某事): *She let slip that she had not paid her tax.* 她偶然说出她还没交税呢. ○ *I let it slip that I was expecting a baby.* 我无意中透露了我已怀孕了. **slip 'anchor** (of a ship) become detached from the ropes on the anchor (指船)脱离锚索, 弃锚. **slip a 'disc** suffer from a slipped disc 椎间盘突出. **slip through sb's 'fingers** (esp of an opportunity) be missed by sb (尤指机会)被错过: *We let the last chance of escape slip through our fingers.* 我们错过了最后一次逃走的机会. **7** (phr v) **slip up (on sth)** (*infml* 口) make a careless mistake 疏忽; 出差错: *I slipped up and gave you the wrong phone number.* 我粗心大意给错了你电话号码. ○ *I slipped up on the date.* 我把日期弄错了.

▷ **slip·page** /ˈslɪpɪdʒ; ˋslɪpɪdʒ/ *n* [U] **1** reduction in values, prices, etc (价值、价格等的)降低, 下降. **2** failure to keep to a schedule or target (对计划或指标的)延误: *production delays due to slippage* 因未能执行规定计划而造成的生产延误.

□ **'slip-case** *n* (usu cardboard) case for a book (通常指用硬厚纸板做的)书套.

'slip-cover *n* removable cover for a piece of furniture 家具套.

'slip-knot *n* **1** knot that can slip easily along the rope on which it is tied, to tighten or loosen the loop 滑结(可沿绳滑动改变松紧者). **2** knot that can be undone by pulling one end of a rope 活结(拉绳的一端可解开者).

'slip-on *n*, *adj* [attrib 作定语] (garment or shoe) made to be slipped on without fastening buttons, etc (服装或鞋)便于穿上或脱下的(不用系扣等的).

'slip-over *n*, *adj* (garment) made to be slipped easily over the head 套头的(服装).

ˌslipped 'disc disc between the vertebrae that has moved out of place and causes pain 突出的椎间盘.

'slip-road *n* (*US* **'access road**) road used for driving onto or off a motorway (连接高速公路的)岔道. ⇨ illus at App 1 见附录1插图, page xiii.

'slip-stream *n* **1** stream of air behind a moving object, eg a racing-car 滑流(移动物体的后向气流, 如赛车的). **2** stream of air thrust back by an aircraft's engines 尾流(飞机发动机的后向气流).

'slip-up *n* (*infml* 口) mistake 错误; 疏忽; 失误: *Leaving his name off the list was a bad slip-up.* 名单上没有他的名字是个严重的疏忽.

'slipway [C] (also **the slips** [pl]) *n* sloping track of stone or timber leading down to the water, on which ships are built or pulled up out of the water for repairs 船台(造船或修船用的).

slip·per /ˈslɪpə(r); ˋslɪpɚ/ *n* loose-fitting light soft shoe worn in the house (室内用的)便鞋, 拖鞋: *a pair of slippers* 一双拖鞋.

▷ **slip·pered** *adj* wearing slippers 穿拖鞋的.

slip·pery /ˈslɪpərɪ; ˋslɪpərɪ/ *adj* (**-ier, -iest**) **1** (of a surface) difficult to hold, stand on or move on without slipping because it is smooth, wet, polished, etc (指物体表面)光滑的, 滑的: *a slippery road, floor, etc* 滑的路面、地板等 ○ *Ice made the path slippery underfoot.* 路上结了冰, 走起来很滑. **2** (*infml* 口) (of a person) not to be trusted; unreliable (指人)狡猾的, 不可靠的: *a slippery salesman* 油嘴滑舌的推销员 ○ *She's as slippery as an eel.* 她像狐狸一样狡猾. **3** (*infml* 口) (of a situation, topic, problem, etc) difficult to deal with (指形势、话题、问题等)难处理的, 棘手的: *the rather slippery subject of race relations* 相当棘手的种族关系问题 ○ *be on slippery ground*, ie be dealing with a subject that needs tact, care, etc 处于难以处理的局面. **4** (idm 习语) **the slippery 'slope** (*infml* 口) course of action that can easily lead to disaster, failure, etc 易导致失败、灾难等的情况: *Extreme nationalism can be the start of the slippery slope towards fascism.* 极端民族主义有可能是滑向法西斯主义的起点. ▷ **slip·peri·ness** *n* [U].

slippy /ˈslɪpɪ; ˋslɪpɪ/ *adj* (**-ier, -iest**) (*infml* 口) **1** slippery 光滑的; 滑的; 狡猾的; 棘手的. **2** (*dated* 旧 *Brit*) quick (used esp in the expressions shown) 快(尤用于以下示例): *Be slippy about it!* 快一点! ○ *Look slippy!* ie Hurry up! 赶快!

slip·shod /ˈslɪpʃɒd; ˋslɪpˌʃɑd/ *adj* not done or not doing things carefully; careless 不认真的; 粗心的: *slipshod work* 不经心做的工作 ○ *a slipshod style* 散漫的作风 ○ *a slipshod worker, writer, etc* 马虎的工人、作者等 ○ *You're too slipshod about your presentation.* 你表达得太不认真.

slit /slɪt; slɪt/ *n* long narrow cut, tear or opening 狭长的切口; 裂缝; 开口: *the slit of the letter-box*, ie through which letters are put 信箱的投信口 ○ *eyes like slits* 细长的眼睛 ○ *a long slit in her skirt* 她裙上细长的开口. Cf 参看 SLOT.

▷ **slit** *v* (**-tt-**; *pt*, *pp* **slit**) [Tn, Tn·pr, Cn·a] make a slit in (sth) by cutting; open (sth) by slitting 切开, 划开(某物); 在(某物)上开缝: *slit sb's throat* 切开某人的喉咙 ○ *a jacket slit up the back* 在背部有开缝褶的外衣 ○ *slit cloth into strips* 把布撕成细条 ○ *slit an envelope open* 拆开信封.

slither /ˈslɪðə(r); ˋslɪðɚ/ *v* [I, Ipr, Ip] slide or slip unsteadily 摇晃不稳地滑动或滑行: *slithering dangerously (on the muddy path)* (在泥泞的路上)危险地滑行 ○ *slither down an icy slope* 摇晃着沿结冰的斜坡滑下 ○ *slithering around in the mud* 在泥中滑动着 ○ *The snake slithered off (into the grass) as we approached.* 那蛇在我们走近时扭动身体钻进草丛中去了.

▷ **slith·ery** *adj* slippery 光滑的; 滑的.

sliver /ˈslɪvə(r); ˋslɪvɚ/ *n* long thin piece of sth cut or broken off from a larger piece; splinter (切割或断裂下来的)薄长条, 碎片: *slivers of wood, glass, metal, etc* 木头、玻璃、金属等的碎片 ○ *Cut me just a small sliver of cheese.* 给我切一小片干酪吧.

▷ **sliver** *v* [I, Tn] (cause sth to) break into slivers or break off as a sliver; splinter (使某物)破碎或断裂成碎片: *The glass slivered when it fell.* 玻璃杯掉在地上摔碎了.

slob /slɒb; slɑb/ *n* (*infml derog* 口, 贬) slovenly, untidy, lazy or ill-mannered person 肮脏、不修边幅、懒惰或粗鲁的人: *Get out of bed, you idle slob!* 快起来, 你这懒虫!

slob·ber /ˈslɒbə(r); ˋslɑbɚ/ *v* **1** [I] let saliva fall from the mouth; drool 流口水; 流涎: *a slobbering baby* 流着口水的小孩儿. **2** (phr v) **slobber over sb/sth** (*infml derog* 口, 贬) show one's affection for sb/sth too openly so that it embarrasses other people 露骨地对某人[某事物]示爱(以致使人难为情): *slobbering all over her boyfriend* 对男朋友肉麻地示爱.

▷ **slob·ber** *n* [U] (*infml* 口) saliva 口水.

slob·bery /-ərɪ; -ərɪ/ *adj*: *slobbery kisses* 多口水的接吻.

sloe /sləʊ; slo/ *n* **1** small, bluish-back, very bitter wild plum, fruit of the blackthorn bush 黑刺李(果). **2** the blackthorn bush itself 黑刺李(树).

□ **sloe-'gin** *n* [U] liqueur made from sloes steeped in gin 黑刺李杜松子酒.

slog /slɒg; slɑg/ (also **slug**) *v* (**-gg-**) **1** [I, Ipr, Tn, Tn·pr] hit (sth/sb) hard 猛击(某物[某人]): *slog (at) the ball* 猛击球 ○ *slogging one's opponent (all around the ring)*, eg in boxing (围着拳击台)猛击对手(如拳击赛中) ○ *slog the ball over the boundary* 把球击过边线. **2** (idm 习语) **slog/sweat one's guts out** ⇨ GUT. **slog it out** (*infml* 口) fight or struggle until a conclusion is reached 斗出个胜负: *two boxers slogging it out* 要斗出个胜败的两个拳击手 ○ *The party leaders are slogging it out in a TV debate.* 政党领袖在电视辩论中一决雌雄. **3** (phr v) **slog (away) at sth** (*infml* 口) work hard and steadily at sth 勤劳而塌实的工作: *slogging away at my accounts* 勤勤恳恳地管理着我的帐目. **slog down, up, along, etc** walk steadily, often with difficulty, in the direction specified 稳步地沿某方向走(常指艰难地): *slog up (the hill) in the dark* 在黑暗中吃力地向(山)上

走 ○ *slogging through the snow* 踏着雪走. **slog through sth** (*infml* 口) work hard and steadily to complete sth 勤劳而塌实地工作以完成某事: *slog through a pile of marking* 埋头判一批试卷.

▷ **slog** (also **slug**) *n* (*infml* 口) **1** hard stroke, eg in cricket 猛击(如板球赛中). **2** (usu *sing* 通常作单数) period of hard work or walking 艰难的工作或行走期间: *Marking the exam papers was quite a slog.* 评阅试卷是很辛苦的工作. ○ *It's a long hard slog up the mountain.* 上山的这段路很难走.

slog·ger *n* (*infml* 口) **1** person who slogs, eg at cricket 猛击者(如板球赛中). **2** hard worker 勤劳的工作者.

slo·gan /ˈsləʊgən; ˋslogən/ *n* word or phrase that is easy to remember, used as a motto eg by a political party, or in advertising 标语; 口号: *political slogans* 政治标语 ○ *'Power to the people' is their slogan.* '一切权力归人民'是他们的口号.

sloop /sluːp; slup/ *n* small ship with one mast and sails pointing forward and aft 单桅纵帆船.

slop /slɒp; slɑp/ *v* (**-pp-**) **1** [Ipr, Ip] (of liquids) spill over the edge, esp of a container (指液体)溢出, 泼出(尤指从容器中): *I dropped the bucket, and water slopped out (of it).* 我把桶掉在地上, 水都洒了出来. ○ *The tea slopped (over) into the saucer.* 茶溢出流到茶托里了. **2** [Tn, Tn·pr, Tn·p] cause (sth) to spill 使(某物)溢出或泼出: *slop the beer, paint, etc carelessly (all over the floor)* 不小心把啤酒、油漆等洒了一地 ○ *She slopped the dirty water (out) onto the grass.* 她把污水泼在草地上了. **3** (phr v) **slop about/around** (of liquids) move around in a small space, esp a container (指液体)晃荡(尤指在容器里): *Water was slopping around in the bottom of the boat.* 水在船底晃晃荡荡的. **slop about/around (in sth)** (of people) splash around (指人)用手或脚溅水: *Why do some children like slopping around in puddles?* 为什么有些儿童爱在水坑里泼水玩? **slop out** empty slops (SLOP *n* 1, 2) 倒污水; 倒(尿桶、便盆等).

▷ **slop** *n* (usu *pl* 通常作复数) **1** dirty waste water from sinks, baths, etc (洗涤槽、浴缸等的)污水. **2** urine, excrement and waste water contained in a bucket in prison cells that have no toilet or sink (在无卫生设备的牢房里用便桶盛的)粪便与废水: [attrib 作定语] *a ˈslop-bucket* 便桶. **3** (**a**) swill for pigs (喂猪的)剩菜屑. (**b**) liquid food (eg milk, soup) esp for sick people 流质食物(如牛奶、汤等, 尤指供病人食用的).

slope /sləʊp; slop/ *n* **1** (usu *sing* 通常作单数) slanting line; surface that is at an angle of less than 90° to the earth's surface or a flat surface 斜线; 斜面; 倾斜: *the slope of a roof* 屋顶的斜面 ○ *a 40° slope* 40°的斜线 ○ *a slight/steep slope* 稍稍的[很陡的]倾斜. **2** area of rising or falling ground 斜坡: *mountain slopes* 山坡 ○ *ski slopes* 滑雪斜坡. **3** (idm 习语) **the slippery slope** ➪ SLIPPERY.

▷ **slope** *v* **1** [I, Ipr, Ip] have a slope; slant 有坡度; 倾斜: *a garden sloping gently towards the river* 向河边稍稍倾斜的花园 ○ *The field slopes (away) to the east.* 这片田地向东倾斜. ○ *Does your handwriting slope forwards or backwards?* 你写的字是向前斜还是向后斜? **2** (phr v) **slope off** (*Brit infml* 口) go away, esp without being noticed, in order to avoid doing work, etc 走开(尤指溜走以逃避工作等).

sloppy /ˈslɒpɪ; ˋslɑpɪ/ *adj* (**-ier, -iest**) **1** (*infml* 口) (**a**) (of a person) careless and untidy in dress, or in the way he does things (指人)衣着不整的, 做事马虎的: *a sloppy worker, writer, etc* 做事马虎的工人、作者等 ○ *look sloppy* 看上去不整洁. (**b**) done in a careless and untidy way 草率的; 粗心的: *sloppy typing* 粗心大意打出的字 ○ *a sloppy repair* 马虎的修理工作. **2** (*infml* 口) foolishly sentimental 庸俗伤感的: *sloppy sentiment* 庸俗伤感的情调 ○ *I hate sloppy romantic films.* 我讨厌那些庸俗伤感的爱情片. **3** (*derog* 贬) (**a**) covered with spilled water, etc 溅满水等的: *a sloppy counter, floor* 溅满水的柜台、地板. (**b**) too liquid 太稀的: *sloppy porridge* 很稀的麦片粥.

▷ **slop·pily** /-ɪlɪ; -ɪlɪ/ *adv* (*infml* 口) in a sloppy(1, 2) way 衣着不整; 草率; 庸俗伤感: *sloppily dressed* 衣着邋遢 ○ *talking sloppily about love* 庸俗伤感地谈论着爱情.

slop·pi·ness *n* [U].

slosh /slɒʃ; slɑʃ/ *v* **1** (*infml* 口) (**a**) [I, Ipr, Ip] **~ (about/around)** (of liquid) move around noisily, eg in a bucket (指液体)晃动作响(如在桶内): *water sloshing against the sides of the bath* 溅着浴缸内侧的水 ○ *Milk sloshed around in the flask.* 牛奶在瓶里晃荡作响. (**b**) [Tn·pr, Tn·p] cause (liquid) to move noisily; splash 使(液体)晃动作响; 泼; 溅: *slosh the whitewash all over the floor* 把粉刷涂料溅了一地板 ○ *sloshing the water around in the pail* 搅动桶里的水. **2** [Tn, Tn·pr] (*Brit sl* 俚) hit (sb) 打, 击(某人): *slosh sb on the chin* 打在某人的下颌上. **3** (phr v) **slosh about/around (in sth)** move around noisily in sth liquid 在液体中移动作响: *children sloshing about in puddles* 在水坑里溅水玩的儿童. **slosh sth onto sth** put (paint, etc) on in a careless way 随便涂、抹、洒或泼(颜料等): *sloshing whitewash on the wall* 把粉刷涂料泼在墙上. ➪Usage at SPRAY[2] 用法见 SPRAY[2].

▷ **sloshed** *adj* [pred 作表语] (*sl* 俚 *esp Brit*) drunk 醉.

slot /slɒt; slɑt/ *n* **1** narrow opening through which sth can be put (可投入东西的)窄孔: *put a 10p coin in the slot* 把一枚10便士的硬币投入孔中. **2** slit, groove or channel into which sth fits or along which sth slides (用以安装某物或供某物滑动的)沟, 槽, 滑道: *a slot on a dashboard for a car radio* 汽车仪表板上的收音机的插口 ○ *The curtain hooks run along a slot in the curtain rail.* 窗帘的吊钩可沿轨槽滑动. **3** position for sb/sth, eg in a series of broadcasts, a lecture course, etc 为某人[某事物]安排的位置或时间(如在一系列广播、讲座等中): *find a slot for a talk on the economy* 为经济问题演讲安排时间.

▷ **slot** *v* (**-tt-**) **1** [Tn] make a slot or slots in (sth) 在(某物)中开缺口、狭缝、沟、槽等. **2** (phr v) **slot (sth/sb) in, into, through, etc** (cause sth/sb to) move in, into, through, etc a slot(2, 3) (使某事物[某人])插入或置于某位置: *The bolt slotted smoothly into place.* 插销很容易就插上了. ○ *slot the edge of the panel into the groove* 把嵌板的边插进槽里 ○ *Slot this disk in.* 把这张盘放进去. ○ *Can we slot her into a job in the sales department?* 我们能把她安排在销售部工作吗?

□ **ˈslot-machine** *n* machine with a slot for coins, used for gambling, or selling cigarettes, bars of chocolate, etc 投币机(设有投币孔, 可用于赌博、售香烟、巧克力糖等).

sloth[1] /sləʊθ; sloθ/ *n* [U] (*fml* 文) laziness; idleness 怠惰; 懒散.

▷ **sloth·ful** /-fl; -fəl/ *adj* (*fml* 文) lazy; idle 怠惰的; 懒散的. **sloth·fully** /-fəlɪ; -fəlɪ/ *adv*. **sloth·ful·ness** *n* [U].

sloth[2] /sləʊθ; sloθ/ *n* S American mammal that lives in trees and moves very slowly 树懒(南美洲的哺乳动物, 栖于树上, 行动极缓慢).

slouch /slaʊtʃ; slaʊtʃ/ *v* [I, Ipr, Ip] stand, sit or move in a lazy way, often not quite upright 无精打采地立、坐或行动(常指不直): *Don't slouch! Stand up straight!* 别没精打采的! 起来站直了! ○ *She slouched past me with her hands in her pockets.* 她手插在口袋里懒洋洋地从我身边走了过去. ○ *slouching about all day doing nothing* 终日闲荡无所事事.

▷ **slouch** *n* **1** [sing] slouching posture or way of moving 无精打采的姿态或动作: *walk with a slouch* 没精打采地走. **2** (idm 习语) **be no slouch at sth** (*infml* 口) be very good at sth 善于做某事: *She's no slouch at tennis.* 她网球打得不赖.

slouch·ingly *adv*.

□ **ˌslouch ˈhat** soft hat with a wide turned-down brim 垂边软帽.

slough[1] /slaʊ, *US also* sluː; slaʊ, slu/ *n* **1** [C] swamp; marsh 沼泽; 沼地. **2** [C] (in western Canada) pond formed by rain or melted snow (加拿大西部)(雨水、融雪形成的)水池, 池塘. **3** [sing] **~ of sth** (*fml* 文) bad mental attitude that is hard to change 难以改变的不良心理: *a slough of despair, self-pity, etc* 绝望、自怜等的深渊.

slough[2] /slʌf; slʌf/ *n* skin that has fallen away from a snake; any dead tissue that falls away at regular intervals 蛇蜕下来的皮; 按时脱落的死组织.

▷ **slough** *v* **1** [Tn, Tn·p] **~ sth (off)** let (skin, dead tissue, etc) fall off; cast sth off 使(皮、死组织等)蜕下或脱落; 舍弃某物: *a snake sloughing (off) its skin* 正在蜕皮的蛇. **2** (phr v) **slough sth off** get rid of sth; abandon sth 摆脱, 抛弃(某事物): *slough off one's bad habits, worries, responsibilities, etc* 抛弃坏习惯、摆脱烦恼、卸责.

slov·enly /ˈslʌvnlɪ; ˋslʌvənlɪ/ *adj* (*derog* 贬) careless, untidy, dirty, etc in appearance, dress or habits (仪表、穿着、习惯等方面)疏忽的，不整洁的，邋遢的: *a slovenly waiter, secretary, cook, etc* 邋遢的服务员、秘书、厨师等 ○ *Those terrible overalls would make anyone look slovenly.* 无论谁穿上那种不像样子的长罩衣也是个邋遢相.

▷ **sloven** /ˈslʌvn; ˋslʌvən/ *n* (*dated derog* 旧，贬) slovenly person 不整洁的人; 邋遢的人.

slov·en·li·ness *n* [U].

slow[1] /sləʊ; slo/ *adj* (**-er, -est**) **1** not moving, acting or done quickly; taking a long time; not fast 行动迟缓的; 费时的; 慢的: *a slow runner, vehicle, journey* 跑得慢的人、行驶缓慢的车、费时的旅程 ○ *a slow recovery from illness* 缓慢的康复 ○ *We're making slow progress.* 我们进展缓慢. ○ *a slow poison* 慢性毒药 ○ *They played the overture at a fairly slow tempo.* 他们用相当缓慢的速度演奏那首序曲. **2** not quick to learn; finding things hard to understand 迟钝的; 愚钝的: *a slow child, learner, pupil, etc* 迟钝的孩子、学习者、学生等 ○ *slow at figures*, ie not good at doing calculations, etc 不善于计算. **3** [pred 作表语] **~ to sth/do sth; ~ (in/about) doing sth** not doing things immediately; hesitating to act, speak, etc 迟缓的; 犹豫的: (*fml* 文) *slow to anger* 不轻易发怒 ○ *She's not slow to tell us what she thinks.* 她总是毫不犹豫地把她的想法告诉我们. ○ *They were very slow (about) paying me.* 他们不痛痛快快把钱付给我. **4** not lively or active enough; sluggish 不活跃的; 不景气的: *The film's too slow*, eg does not have enough exciting scenes, etc. 这部影片太没劲了. ○ *Business is rather slow today*, eg not many goods are being sold. 今天生意很清淡. **5** [pred 作表语] (often preceded by *two minutes, one hour*, etc 常用于 two minutes、one hour 等之后) (of watches and clocks) showing a time earlier than the correct time (指钟表)慢: *That clock is five minutes slow*, eg It shows 1.55 when it is 2.00. 那座钟慢了五分. **6** (of a route, etc) not allowing great speed (指路径等)不能快速行进的: *the slow road through the mountains* 只能慢行的山路. **7** (of a surface) causing what moves over it (esp a ball) to move at a reduced speed (指表面)能降低(尤指球)运动速度的: *a slow billiard table, cricket pitch, etc* 能减低球的速度的台球台、板球场等 ○ *Long grass makes the field slower.* 场地上草很长能影响球的速度. **8** (of photographic film) not very sensitive to light (指摄影胶片)感光性低的. **9** (idm 习语) **quick/slow on the draw** ⇨ DRAW[1]. **quick/slow on the uptake** ⇨ UPTAKE.

▷ **slowly** *adv* **1** (preceding or following the *v*, as shown 置于动词前或后，如下列所示) in a slow[1](1) way 缓慢地: *walk, speak, learn, react slowly* 走、说、学、反应得慢 ○ *She slowly opened the door.* 她慢慢地把门打开. ○ *Slowly, things began to improve.* 情况渐渐有了好转. **2** (idm 习语) **slowly but surely** making slow but definite progress 进展缓慢但平稳: *Slowly but surely the great ship glided into the water.* 那艘巨轮缓慢而平稳地下水了.

slow·ness *n* [U].

□ ˈ**slowcoach** (*Brit*) (*US* ˈ**slowpoke**) *n* (*infml* 口) person who moves, acts, works or thinks slowly 动作、行为、工作或思考缓慢的人: *Get on with it, you old slowcoach!* 继续干，你这个慢性子!

ˈ**slow lane** nearside lane of a motorway, along which slow vehicles move 高速公路的慢车道.

ˌ**slow** ˈ**motion** (in cinema photography) method of making action appear slow by filming a scene with a higher number of exposures than usual per second, then showing it at normal speed (电影片的)慢动作: *filmed in slow motion* 拍摄成慢动作的 ○ [attrib 作定语] *a ˌslow-motion ˈsequence* 慢动作连续镜头.

slow[2] /sləʊ; slo/ *adv* (**-er, -est**) **1** (used after *vs*, after *how* or in compounds with participles 用于动词或 how 之后，或与分词构成复合词) at a slow[1](1) speed; slowly 缓慢地; 低速地: *Tell the driver to go slower.* 告诉司机开慢些. ○ *How slow this train goes!* 这列火车开得多慢哪! ○ *slow-moving* 缓慢移动的 ○ *slow-cooked food* 用文火烹调的食物. **2** (idm 习语) **go** ˈ**slow** (**a**) (of workers) work slowly, esp as a protest or to make their employer meet their demands (指工人)怠工(尤指为抗议或迫使雇主答应要求). Cf 参看 GO-SLOW (GO). (**b**) be less active than usual 减少活动: *You ought to go slow until you feel really well again.* 你应该减少活动，要到真正康复以后再说.

slow[3] /sləʊ; slo/ *v* **1** [I, Ipr, Ip, Tn, Tn·pr, Tn·p] **~ (sth) (up/down)** (cause sth to) go at a slower speed (使某事物)缓行，减速: *The train slowed (down) (to a crawl) as it approached the station.* 火车进站时慢了下来. ○ *Output has slowed (up) a little.* 生产已放慢了一点. ○ *She slowed the car down and stopped.* 她把汽车速度减慢后停了下来. ○ *Lack of demand will slow (down) our economic growth.* 市场需求低就要拖慢我们的经济增长速度. **2** (phr v) **slow up/down** work less energetically 松弛下来: *Slow up a bit, or you'll make yourself ill.* 别这么卖力气，不然你要累出病来的.

□ ˈ**slow-down** *n* reduction of activity, esp a deliberate reduction of industrial production by workers or employers 生产放慢(尤指工人或雇主有目的的): *a slow-down in the dairy industry* 奶制品工业的生产放慢.

slow-worm /ˈsləʊwɜːm; ˋsloˌwɝm/ *n* small non-poisonous European reptile with no limbs 蛇蜥蜴(欧洲产，无足、无毒).

SLR /ˌes el ˈɑː(r); ˌɛs ɛl ˋɑr/ *abbr* 缩写 = (of a type of camera) single lens reflex (指一种照相机)单镜头反射.

sludge /slʌdʒ; slʌdʒ/ *n* [U] **1** thick greasy mud or substance resembling this 油泥或类似油泥之物: *some sludge in the bottom of the tank* 桶底的一些淤泥. **2** sewage 污水; 下水道的污物.

slue (*US*) = SLEW.

slug[1] /slʌg; slʌg/ *n* small creature like a snail without a shell that moves slowly and leaves a slimy trail 蛞蝓; 鼻涕虫. ⇨illus at SNAIL 见 SNAIL 插图.

slug[2] /slʌg; slʌg/ *n* **1** (**a**) bullet, esp of irregular shape 子弹(尤指形状不规则的). (**b**) (*infml* 口 *esp US*) any bullet 子弹. **2** (in printing) strip of metal with a line of type along one edge (印刷中的)大嵌条. **3** (*US*) piece of metal for use (esp illegally) in a coin-operated machine 用以(尤指非法地)充硬币启动投币机的金属块. **4** (*infml* 口 *esp US*) small amount of whisky, vodka, etc 少量的威士忌、伏特加等: *swallow a slug of gin* 喝一点杜松子酒.

slug[3] /slʌg; slʌg/ *v* (**-gg-**) (*US*) **1** [I, Ipr, Tn, Tn·pr] = SLOG. **2** (idm 习语) **slug it out** = SLOG IT OUT (SLOG).

▷ **slug** *n* = SLOG.

slug·gard /ˈslʌgəd; ˋslʌgɚd/ *n* (*dated derog* 旧，贬) lazy slow-moving person 懒散而行动迟缓的人.

slug·gish /ˈslʌgɪʃ; ˋslʌgɪʃ/ *adj* slow-moving; not alert or lively; lethargic 行动迟缓的; 不机警或不活泼的; 无精打采的: *a sluggish stream, pulse* 流速缓慢的溪流、跳动缓慢的脉搏 ○ *sluggish traffic, conversation* 缓慢行驶的车辆、无生气的谈话 ○ *These tablets make me feel rather sluggish.* 我吃了这些药片感到困倦无力. ▷ **slug·gishly** *adv*. **slug·gish·ness** *n* [U].

sluice /sluːs; slus/ *n* **1** (also ˈ**sluice-gate**, ˈ**sluice-valve**) sliding gate or other device for controlling the flow of water out of or into a canal, lake, lock, etc 水门; 水闸: *open the sluice-gates of a reservoir* 放开水库的闸门. **2** water controlled by this (水闸内的)蓄水. **3** (also ˈ**sluice-way**) artificial water-channel, esp where gold-miners rinse gold out of sand and dirt 人工水道; (尤指金矿工人用以冲洗金砂的)洗矿槽.

▷ **sluice** *v* **1** [Tn, Tn·p] **~ sth (down/out)** wash or rinse sth with a stream of water 冲洗某物: *sluice ore*, ie to separate it from gravel, etc 冲洗矿砂(使之与砂砾等分开) ○ *sluice out the stables* 冲洗马厩 ○ *We sluiced the muddy wheels (down) with a hose.* 我们用水龙软管冲洗沾满泥浆的轮子. **2** (phr v) **sluice away, out, out of sth, etc** (of water) flow away, out, etc as if from a sluice (指水)(如同从水闸中)流走、泄出等: *water sluicing out of the hole* 从洞口流出的水.

slum /slʌm; slʌm/ *n* **1** [C] (house or rooms in a) street, alley, etc of badly-built, over-crowded buildings 破旧拥挤的建筑物组成的街道、小巷等(里的房屋); 贫民窟: *brought up in a slum* 在贫民窟长大 ○ [attrib 作定语] *a slum area* 贫民区 ○ *slum children* 贫民窟的儿童 ○ (*fig* 比喻) *I can't stand this slum any longer, tidy it up!* 我再也无法忍受这种脏乱的环境了，快整理一下! **2 the slums** [pl] area of a town where such buildings are found 贫民区.

▷ **slum** *v* (**-mm-**) **1** [I] (usu in the continuous tenses

通常用于进行时态) visit places thought socially inferior to those where one usu works or enjoys oneself, esp out of curiosity 到社会地位低下的地方去看看(尤指因好奇): *What are they doing drinking at this end of town? Slumming, I suppose.* 他们为什么到城里这个地方来饮酒? 我猜是想看看这穷地方的吧. **2** (idm 习语) **slum it** (*infml* 口) choose or be forced to live in poor surroundings 自愿地或被迫地在贫民窟般的环境中生活: *While he was studying, Nick had to slum it in a tiny room.* 尼克上学期间只能住在很小的房间里.

slummy *adj* (**-ier**, **-iest**) (*derog* 贬) of or like a slum; dirty or untidy (似)贫民窟的; 脏乱的: *a slummy district* 贫民区 ○ *It looks terribly slummy in this house.* 这房子脏乱不堪.

slum·ber /ˈslʌmbə(r); ˋslʌmbɚ/ *v* [I] (*fml or joc* 文或谑) sleep, esp peacefully and comfortably 睡眠(尤指睡得安稳而舒服): *The baby was slumbering peacefully.* 孩子睡得正香.

▷ **slum·ber** *n* (often *pl* 常作复数) (*fml or joc esp fig* 文或谑, 尤作比喻) sleep 睡眠: *fall into a deep slumber* 酣然入睡 ○ *disturb sb's slumber(s)* 打扰某人的睡眠.

slum·berer /-bərə(r); -bərɚ/ *n* (*fml* 文) person who slumbers 睡觉的人.

slum·ber·ous /-bərəs; -bərəs/ *adj* (*fml* 文) sleepy 昏昏欲睡的; 困的.

slump /slʌmp; slʌmp/ *v* **1** [I, Ipr, Ip] fall or flop heavily 沉重地落下或倒下: *Tired from her walk she slumped (down) onto the sofa.* 她走累了, 一屁股坐在沙发上. ○ *They found her slumped over the steering wheel.* 他们发现她倒伏在方向盘上. **2** [I] (of prices, trade, business activity) fall suddenly or greatly (指价格、贸易、商业活动)突然或大幅度下跌或减少: *What caused share values to slump?* 股价暴跌是什么原因?

▷ **slump** *n* **1** period when business is bad, sales are few, etc; depression(3) 商业萧条期; 不景气; 经济衰退. Cf 参看 RECESSION 1. **2** (*US*) period when a person, a team, etc has little success, poor results, etc (个人、运动队等的)低潮状态(几无进展、成绩不佳等): *a slump in her career* 她事业中的低谷.

slung *pt, pp* of SLING.

slunk *pt, pp* of SLINK.

slur /slɜ:(r); slɝ/ *v* (**-rr-**) [Tn] **1** run (sounds, words) into each other so that they are indistinct 含糊不清地发出(声音)或说(话): *the slurred speech of a drunk* 喝醉的人说的含糊不清的话. **2** play (musical notes) so that each one runs smoothly into the next 连奏(音符). **3** harm (sb's reputation) by making (esp untrue) statements 诋毁(某人的名誉): *slurred by accusations of dishonesty* 遭诽谤被指责为不诚实. **4** (phr v) **slur over sth** avoid dealing with an unpleasant fact, a difficult problem, etc 回避令人不快的事、棘手的问题等: *She slurred over the high cost of her plan.* 她避而不提她这一计划费用之巨.

▷ **slur** *n* **1** [C, U] **~ (on sb/sth)** statement, accusation, etc that may damage sb's reputation, esp when untrue 诋毁; 诽谤; 中伤: *cast a slur on sb* 诽谤某人 ○ *Any suggestion that I accepted bribes would be a monstrous slur.* 谁说我受贿就是对我恶意中伤. ○ (*fml* 文) *She tried to keep her reputation free from slur.* 她极力避免名誉受损. **2** [C] (*music* 音) the mark (⌒) or (‿), used to show that two or more notes are to be sung to one syllable or played smoothly without a break 圆滑线, 连接线(即⌒或‿)(用以表示把一组音符唱成或奏成一个音节). **3** [C] slurred sound 含糊不清的声音.

slurp /slɜ:p; slɝp/ *v* [I, Tn, Tn·p] (*infml* 口) make a loud noise with the lips as one eats or drinks (sth) 吃或喝(某物)时嘴唇发出很响的声音: *Stop slurping!* 吃喝时别发出这么大的声音! ○ *He was slurping (down) his soup.* 他喝汤时嘴唇发出啧啧的声音.

▷ **slurp** *n* (usu *sing* 通常作单数) sound of slurping 吃或喝时嘴唇发出的响声.

slurry /ˈslʌrɪ; ˋslɝɪ/ *n* [U] thin semi-liquid mixture, esp of cement, clay, mud, etc 半流质稀薄混合物(尤指水泥、黏土、泥浆等).

slush /slʌʃ; slʌʃ/ *n* [U] **1** soft, usu dirty, melting snow on the ground 地面上半融化的(通常指脏的)雪. **2** (*infml derog* 口, 贬) silly sentimental speech or writing 庸俗的伤感言语或文字: *a romantic novel full of slush* 庸俗伤感的爱情小说. ▷ **slushy** *adj* (**-ier**, **-est**): *slushy pavements* 有泥有雪的人行道 ○ (*fig* 比喻) *slushy sentiment, stories* 庸俗伤感的情调、故事.

□ ˈ**slush fund** (*derog* 贬) fund created eg by a political party or a business company, for illegal purposes, eg bribing officials (政党、公司等的)用于非法目的的基金(如行贿官员的).

slut /slʌt; slʌt/ *n* (*derog* 贬) woman who is slovenly or sexually immoral 邋遢女子; 放荡女子: *a common slut* 下贱的淫荡女人. ▷ **slut·tish** *adj*: *a sluttish appearance* (女子)邋遢的样子 ○ *sluttish behaviour* (女子)放荡的行为.

sly /slaɪ; slaɪ/ *adj* (**-er**, **-est**) **1** (*often derog* 常作贬义) acting or done in a secret, often cunning and deceitful, way 狡猾的; 狡诈的: *a sly fellow, trick, ruse* 狡诈的家伙、伎俩、计谋 ○ (*joc* 谑) *You sly old devil!* 你这个老奸巨猾的家伙! ○ *It was sly of you not to tell us you'd already met.* 你们真坏, 已经见了面还瞒着我们. **2** [usu attrib 通常作定语] suggesting that one knows sth secret; knowing 会意的; 会心的: *a sly smile, look, etc* 会心的一笑、表情等 ○ *She cast a sly glance at her bridge partner.* 她向桥牌搭档使了个会意的眼色. **3** mischievous; playful 淘气的; 顽皮的: *play a sly trick on a friend* 作弄朋友. **4** (idm 习语) **on the** ˈ**sly** secretly 秘密地: *She must have been having lessons on the sly.* 她准是暗地里一直在上课. ▷ **slyly** *adv.* **sly·ness** *n* [U].

smack[1] /smæk; smæk/ *n* **1** [C] (**a**) (sound of a) blow given with the open hand; slap 掌击(声); 掴: *give a child a smack on the bottom* 给小孩屁股上一巴掌. (**b**) (usu *sing* 通常作单数) loud sound of the lips being parted 嘴唇张开时发出的声音: *a greedy smack of the lips as he cut into the steak* 他切牛排时馋得嘴唇一张发出的声音. (**c**) [C] (*infml* 口) loud kiss 出声的吻; 响吻: *a smack on the lips/cheek* 在嘴唇[面颊]上的响吻. **2** [C usu *sing* 通常作单数] blow; hit 打; 击: *give the ball a hard smack*, eg with a bat in cricket 用力击球(如用板球棒). **3** [U] (*sl* 俚 *esp Brit*) heroin 海洛因. **4** (idm 习语) **a smack at sth/doing sth** (*infml* 口) attempt at doing sth 试做某事物: *have a smack at making an omelette* 试做煎蛋.

▷ **smack** *v* [Tn] **1** strike (sb) with the open hand; slap 用掌击(某人); 掴: *Don't you dare smack my children!* 你敢掴我的孩子! **2** (idm 习语) **lick/smack one's lips/chops** ⇨ LICK.

smack *adv* **1** in a sudden and violent way 突然而猛烈地: *run smack into a brick wall* 猛然撞在砖墙上 ○ *hit sb smack in the eye* 猛然打在某人的眼部. **2** (*US* ˈ**smack-dab**) directly; squarely 直接地; 恰好: *It landed smack (-dab) in the middle of the carpet.* 那东西正好落在地毯的中央.

smacker *n* (*infml* 口) **1** loud kiss 出声的吻; 响吻. **2** (*sl* 俚) pound sterling or US dollar 英镑; 美元: *one hundred smackers* 一百块钱.

smack·ing *n* [sing] hitting or being hit with the open hand 掌掴; 挨的巴掌: *The child needs a good smacking.* 这孩子该好好打一顿.

smack[2] /smæk; smæk/ *n* small sailing-boat for fishing 捕鱼的小帆船.

smack[3] /smæk; smæk/ *v* (phr v) **smack of sth** (no passive 不用于被动语态) **1** have a slight flavour of sth 微带某味: *medicine that smacks of sulphur* 微带硫磺味的药. **2** suggest that sb has unpleasant attitudes or qualities 显示某人有令人不快的态度或品性: *Their comments smack of racism.* 他们的评论有点种族偏见的味道.

▷ **smack** *n* [sing] **~ of sth** **1** slight flavour of sth 某物的轻微之味: *a smack of garlic* 一点大蒜味. **2** suggestion; hint 微含某意; 暗示: *There was a smack of malice in her reply.* 她回答中含有恶意.

small /smɔ:l; smɔl/ *adj* **1** not large in size, degree, number, value, etc (体积、程度、数量、价值等)小的, 少的: *a small house, town, room, audience, sum of money* 小房子、小镇、小房间、少数听众、一小笔钱 ○ *This hat is too small for me.* 这帽子我戴太小. ○ *My influence over her is small, so she won't do as I say.* 我对她起不了多大影响, 她不会按我的话去做. Cf 参看 BIG. ⇨Usage 见所附用法. **2** young 幼小的; 年幼的: *Would a small child know that?* 小孩能懂这种事吗? ○ *I lived in the country when I was small.* 我小时候住在乡下. **3** [usu attrib 通常作定语] (**a**) not as big as sth else of the same kind (在同类事物中)较小的: *the small intestine* 小肠. (**b**) (of letters) not written or printed as capitals (CAPITAL[1] 2)

(指字母)小写的. **4** [usu attrib 通常作定语] not doing things on a large scale 小规模的; 小范围的: *a small farmer, trader, shopkeeper, company, etc* 小农场主、小本商人、小店主、小公司 ○ *more help for small businesses* 对小公司的较多帮助 ○ *a small eater*, ie a person who does not eat much 饭量小的人. **5** unimportant; trivial; slight 不重要的; 微不足道的; 微小的: *a small matter, change, mistake* 小的事情、变化、错误 ○ *There are only small differences between the two translations.* 这两种翻译之间只有些细微的区别. **6** [attrib 作定语] (*derog* 贬) having a mean and petty attitude 小气的; 心胸狭窄的: *a very small man* 心胸非常狭隘的人 ○ *Only somebody with a small mind would have refused to help.* 只有心胸狭窄的人才不肯帮助别人. **7** [attrib 作定语] (used with uncountable nouns 与不可数名词连用) little or no 些微的; 几乎没有的: *have small cause to be glad* 没什么可高兴的 ○ *He failed, and small wonder*, ie it is not surprising. 他失败了, 这没什么奇怪. **8** (idm 习语) **(be) grateful/thankful for small ˈmercies** relieved that a bad situation is not worse 庆幸已然糟糕的情况并未更糟: *It may be cold but it's not raining — let's be thankful for small mercies.* 尽管天气很冷, 但没有下雨—应该知足了. **great and small** ⇨ GREAT. **in a big/small way** ⇨ WAY[1]. **it's a small ˈworld** (*saying* 谚) one is likely to meet, or hear about, sb one knows (however distantly) wherever one goes 世界可真小(无论走到哪里都可能碰到或听说到自己认识的人). **look/feel ˈsmall** be humiliated 感到羞愧: *You made me look so small, correcting me in front of everybody.* 你当众纠正我的错误, 弄得我很难为情. **no/little/small wonder** ⇨ WONDER *n*. **small ˈbeer** (*infml* 口) person or thing of no great importance or value 重要性或价值不大的人或事物: *That grant was pretty small beer: we shall need a lot more money.* 这点补助金是杯水车薪, 我们需要的钱远比这些多. **a small ˈfortune** a lot of money 许多钱: *The car cost me a small fortune.* 这辆汽车花了我很多钱. **ˈsmall fry** (*infml* 口) people thought to be unimportant (被认为)不重要的人. **the ˈsmall hours** period of time soon after midnight 午夜刚过的一段时间: *working until/into the small hours* 工作到深夜. **the small ˈprint** the parts of a legal document, contract, etc which are often printed in small type and contain important details that are easy to overlook 法律文件、契约等中常用小号字体印刷的部分(包括容易忽视的重要细节): *The penalty clause was hidden in the small print.* 惩罚条款印在不起眼的小号字体部分. ○ *Make sure you read all the small print before signing.* 一定要先看清小号字体印刷部分再签字. **the still small voice** ⇨ STILL[1].

▷ **small** *adv* **1** into small pieces 成为小块: *chop the wood small* 把木头劈成碎块. **2** of a small size 很小: *Don't draw the picture too small.* 别把图画得太小.

small *n* **1 smalls** [pl] (*Brit infml* 口) small items of clothing, esp underwear 小件衣物(尤指内衣裤). **2** [sing] the slender part of sth (used esp in the phrase shown) 某物较细的部分(尤用于以下示例): *the small of the back* 背部最窄处.

small·ness *n* [U].

□ **ˈsmall ads** /ædz; ˌædz/ (*Brit infml* 口) = CLASSIFIED ADVERTISEMENTS (CLASSIFY).

small ˈarms weapons light enough to be carried in the hands 轻武器(可随手携带者): [attrib 作定语] *small-arms fire* 轻武器射击.

small ˈchange coins of low value 小面值的硬币: *I dropped some small change into the collecting tin.* 我把一些硬币投进募捐罐里了.

ˈsmallholder, ˈsmallholding *ns* (*Brit*) (owner or tenant of a) piece of land, usu more than one acre and less than 50 acres, used for farming 小片耕地(通常指1至50英亩的); (小片耕地的)地主, 佃农.

the ˈsmall hours the very early hours of the morning eg 3, 4, 5 o'clock 凌晨的几小时(如3、4、5点钟).

ˌsmall-ˈminded *adj* (*derog* 贬) mean and selfish; petty 吝啬自私的; 心胸狭窄的. **ˌsmall-ˈmindedness** *n* [U].

ˈsmallpox *n* [U] serious contagious disease causing high fever and leaving permanent scars on the skin 天花: [attrib 作定语] *a smallpox injection, epidemic* 天花的预防注射、流行.

ˌsmall-ˈscale *adj* **1** (of a map, drawing, etc) drawn to a small scale[2](4) so that few details are shown (指地图、图样等)以小比例绘制的. **2** not great in size, extent, quantity, etc 小规模、小范围、小数量等的: *ˌonly a ˌsmall-scale ˈsurvey of 20 people* 只涉及20人的小范围调查.

ˈsmall talk conversation about everyday matters, usu at a social event 闲谈; 聊天: *I'm afraid I have no small talk*, ie I can't chat about unimportant things. 很抱歉, 我不能聊闲天.

ˈsmall-time *adj* (*infml derog* 口, 贬) unimportant; petty 不重要的; 琐碎的: *a small-time criminal* 轻罪犯.

NOTE ON USAGE 用法: Compare **small** and **little.** 试比较**small**和**little**这两个词. **Small** is the usual opposite of *big* or *large*. ☆ **small**是big和large常见的反义词. It has comparative and superlative forms and can be modified by adverbs such as 'rather' ☆ **small**有比较级和最高级并可受rather一类副词修饰: *Our house is smaller than yours but I think the garden is bigger.* 我们的房子比你们的小, 但花园比你们的大. ○ *I have a fairly small income.* 我的收入相当微薄. The comparative and superlative forms of **little** are rare and it is not usually modified by adverbs. ☆ **little**的比较级和最高级形式很少见, 且**little**通常不受副词修饰. It is generally only used attributively, often following another adjective, to indicate an attitude of affection, dislike, amusement, etc ☆ **little**一般只用作定语, 常置于另一形容词之后, 表示爱、厌恶、欢娱等: *He's a horrid little man.* 他是个讨厌的傢伙. ○ *What a lovely little house!* 多漂亮的房子!

smarmy /ˈsmɑːmɪ; ˈsmɑrmɪ/ *adj* (**-ier, -iest**) (*Brit infml derog* 口, 贬) trying to make oneself popular by flattery and charm 逢迎的; 奉承的; 谄媚的: *a smarmy salesman* 满口甜言蜜语的推销员 ○ *The waiters' manners are always so smarmy.* 那些服务员总是点头哈腰的.

smart[1] /smɑːt; smɑrt/ *adj* (**-er, -est**) **1** bright and new-looking; well-dressed; neat 帅气的; 衣着讲究的; 整齐的: *a smart hat, frock, car* 漂亮的帽子、连衣裙、汽车 ○ *You look very smart in your new suit.* 你穿上新衣服显得很帅. ○ *Make yourself smart before my parents arrive.* 趁我父母未到, 你快去打扮一下. **2** (*esp US*) having or showing intelligence; clever; ingenious 聪明的; 伶俐的; 聪敏的: *a smart student* 聪明的学生 ○ *a smart answer, idea* 巧妙的回答、主意 ○ *It was smart of you to bring a map.* 你很聪明, 能想到带张地图. **3** (**a**) quick; brisk 快的; 敏捷的: *go for a smart walk* 轻松地散散步 ○ *set off at a smart pace* 迈着矫健的步子出发. (**b**) (of a blow or of criticism) forceful (指打击或批评)有力的, 猛烈的: *I gave a smart blow on the lid, and it flew open.* 我朝盖子猛一击, 就把它打开了. ○ *a smart rebuke from the teacher* 教师的严厉指责. **4** fashionable; chic 时髦的; 高雅的: *the smart set* 时髦的阔人 ○ *a smart restaurant* 格调高雅的餐馆.

▷ **smarten** /ˈsmɑːtn; ˈsmɑrtn̩/ *v* (phr v) **smarten (oneself/sb/sth) up** make oneself/sb/sth neater, tidier, etc 使自己[某人/某物]更整洁、更有条理等: *You'll have to smarten (yourself) up a bit before going out.* 你得打扮一下再出门. ○ *Try to smarten the house up before the visitors arrive.* 在客人来到之前要把房子整理一下.

smartly *adv*: *smartly dressed* 衣着整洁 ○ *walk smartly into the room* 迈着矫健的步子走进房间 ○ *hit sth smartly with a hammer* 用锤子猛敲某物.

smart·ness *n* [U].

□ **smart ˈalec** /ˈælɪk; ˌælɪk/ (*infml usu derog* 口, 通常作贬义) person who acts as if he has great ability and knowledge; know-all 自作聪明的人; 万事通.

smart[2] /smɑːt; smɑrt/ *v* [I, Ipr] **~(from sth)** cause or feel a sharp stinging pain (of the body or the mind) 造成或感到(肉体或精神方面的)痛苦: *The bee-sting smarted terribly.* 蜜蜂蜇得很疼. ○ *He smarted from the savage attacks on his film.* 他因自己的影片受到猛烈攻击而感到痛心. ○ *They're still smarting from their defeat in the final.* 他们仍在为决赛失败而伤心.

▷ **smart** *n* [U] (*fml* 文) sharp physical or mental pain 肉体或精神上的痛苦: *the constant smart of the blisters on his feet* 他脚上水泡引起的持续疼痛.

smash /smæʃ; smæʃ/ *v* **1** [I, Ipr, Tn, Tn·pr, Tn·p, Cn·a] **~ sth (up); ~ sth open** (cause sth to) be broken violently into pieces (使某物)粉碎, 破碎: *the sound of a* *glass smashing (into pieces) on the floor* 玻璃杯摔在地板上破碎时发出的声音 ○ *smash a window* 打破一扇窗户 ○ *smash (up) all the furniture* 捣毁所有的家具 ○ *smash the furniture to pieces* 把家具砸碎 ○ *The lock was rusty, so we had to smash the door open.* 锁锈住了，我们得把门砸开. **2 (a)** [Tn, Tn·pr, Tn·p] hit (sth/sb) very hard 重击，痛击，猛击(某物[某人]): *smash the ball (out of the court)* 用力击球(把球击出场外) ○ *I'll smash you in the eye!* 当心我给你眼睛一拳! ○ *The batsman smashed the ball up into the air.* 击球员把球击得很高. **(b)** [Tn, Tn·pr] (in tennis) hit (a ball) downwards over the net with a hard overhand stroke (网球)打出高压(球): *He smashed the lob (straight at his opponent's body).* 他把高球(冲着对手)叩杀过去. **3** [Tn, Tn·p] **~ sth (up)** crash (a vehicle) 撞毁(车): *She smashed (up) her new car in the fog.* 她在大雾中把新汽车给撞毁了. **4** [Tn] (*infml* 口) defeat or destroy (eg an opponent or his activities); end (esp sth bad) 击败或粉碎(如对手或其行动); 结束(尤指坏事): *We are determined to smash terrorism.* 我们一定要消灭恐怖主义. ○ *The champions were completely smashed in the final.* 冠军在决赛中都吃了败仗. ○ *smash a record*, ie (in sport, etc) set a far better record (运动等)大破记录 ○ *Police smashed the drug ring.* 警方粉碎了贩毒集团. **5** (phr v) **smash (sth) against, into, through, etc sth** (cause sth to) move with great force into, against etc, sth (使某物)冲进或撞上某物: *The car smashed into the wall.* 汽车撞在墙上. ○ *The elephant smashed through the trees.* 大象在树林中横冲直撞. ○ *She smashed the hammer down onto the box.* 她用锤子猛击箱子. **smash sth down** make sth fall down by smashing it, eg with a hammer 击倒某物(如用锤子): *The fireman smashed the door down to reach the children.* 消防员破门而入冲向孩子们. **smash sth in** make a hole, dent, etc in sth by hitting it with great force 将某物撞出窟窿、凹痕等: *Vandals smashed the door in.* 那些破坏公物的人把门撞瘪了. ○ (*infml* 口) *I'll smash your head in!* ie said as a threat to hit sb. 当心我砸碎你的脑袋!

▷ **smash** *n* **1** [sing] act or sound of smashing 破碎; 破碎时发出的声音: *the smash of breaking glass* 玻璃摔得粉碎 ○ *The plate hit the floor with a smash.* 盘子摔在地板上啪的一声碎了. **2** (also ˈ**smash-up**) [C] car crash 撞车: *an awful smash(-up) on the motorway* 高速公路上严重的撞车事故. **3** [C] tennis stroke in which a player smashes the ball 网球的高压球: *develop a powerful smash* 训练打出强有力的高压球. **4** [C] (also **smash ˈhit**) (*infml* 口) play, song, film, etc which is suddenly very successful 极为轰动的戏剧、歌曲、影片等.

smash *adv* with a smash (撞)得破碎; 碰撞时发出声音: *land smash on the floor* 掉在地板上摔得粉碎 ○ *go/run smash into the wall* 步行[跑步]时砰的一声撞到墙上.

smashed *adj* [pred 作表语] (*sl* 俚) drunk 喝醉.

smasher *n* (*infml* 口 *esp Brit*) excellent, attractive, etc person or thing 优异的、漂亮的人或事物; 尤物: *She's a real smasher!* 她真是漂亮极了!

smash·ing *adj* (*infml* 口 *esp Brit*) excellent 极好的: *We had a smashing time on holiday!* 我们假期过得真痛快!

□ ˌ**smash-and-ˈgrab** *adj* [attrib 作定语] (of a robbery) in which the thief smashes a shop window to steal the goods on display (指抢劫案)(窃贼)砸破商店橱窗(抢走陈列品之)行劫的: *a ˌsmash-and-ˈgrab raid* 砸破商店橱窗行劫.

smat·ter·ing /ˈsmætərɪŋ; ˋsmætərɪŋ/ *n* [sing] **~ (of sth)** slight knowledge, esp of a language 浅薄的知识(尤指对一语言); 一知半解: *have a smattering of French, German, etc* 懂一点法语、德语等.

smear /smɪə(r); smɪr/ *v* **1** [Tn·pr] **~ sth on/over sth/sb; ~ sth/sb with sth** spread a greasy or sticky substance, eg paint, on sth/sb 将油脂或黏性物质(如油漆)涂于某物[某人]: *smear oil on the machinery* 把油涂在机器上 ○ *smearing mud all over the wall* 在墙上涂满泥浆 ○ *We smeared cream on our faces/smeared our faces with cream.* 我们在脸上搽雪花膏. **2** [Tn] **(a)** make (sth) dirty or greasy; smudge 弄脏(某物); 使(某物)弄上油污: *The window was all smeared after the rain.* 下过雨后窗户都脏了. ○ *Don't smear the lens; I've just polished it.* 别把镜头弄脏了，我刚刚擦过. **(b)** (*fig* 比喻) damage (sb or sb's reputation), eg by suggesting they have acted immorally 玷污(某人或某人的名誉)(如说某人行为不端): *In politics you expect to get smeared by your opponents.* 在政治事务中遭对手诽谤是常有的事. **3** [Tn] blur (a drawing, an outline, etc) eg by rubbing it 将(图画、轮廓等)弄模糊(如经摩擦): *smear the print with one's finger* 手指把印刷品弄得模糊不清.

▷ **smear** *n* **1** mark made by smearing 污点; 污迹: *a smear of paint* 油漆的污迹 ○ *smears of blood on the wall* 墙上的血迹. **2 ~ (on sb/sth)** suggestion or accusation that damages sb's reputation 污蔑; 诽谤: *This accusation of bribery is a vile smear on an honourable citizen.* 这项有关贿赂的指控是对一个正直公民的无耻诽谤. ○ [attrib 作定语] *a smear campaign* 一系列有预谋的诽谤活动 ○ *smear tactics* 污蔑的伎俩. **3** specimen of a substance spread on a slide to be examined under a microscope 涂片(涂在显微镜载片上供检查的物质标本): *a cervical smear*, ie taken from the cervix 子宫颈涂片 ○ [attrib 作定语] *a smear test* 涂片检查.

smeary /ˈsmɪərɪ; ˋsmɪrɪ/ *adj* (**-ier, -iest**) (*infml* 口) **1** smeared 被涂污的; 被弄脏的: *a smeary window* 弄脏的窗户. **2** causing smears 造成污迹的: *a smeary paintbrush* 容易弄出污迹的颜料刷.

smell[1] /smel; smɛl/ *n* **1** [U] ability to smell 嗅觉: *Taste and smell are closely connected.* 味觉与嗅觉是密切相关的. ○ *The dogs can find drugs by smell.* 这些狗能嗅出毒品. **2 (a)** [C, U] thing that is smelled; quality that allows sth to be smelled; odour 气味; 某物特有的气味: *a strong smell of gas* 一股强烈的煤气味 ○ *There's a smell of cooking.* 有一股烹饪的味. ○ *The smells from the kitchen filled the room.* 整个房间都是从厨房飘来的气味. ○ *The cream has no smell.* 这种奶油无特殊气味. **(b)** [sing] unpleasant smell 难闻的气味; 臭味: *There's a bit of a smell in here.* 这里有点难闻的味. ○ *What a smell!* 多难闻的气味! **3** [C *usu sing* 通常作单数] act of smelling sth 嗅; 闻: *Have a smell of this egg and tell me if it's bad.* 闻闻这个蛋，告诉我坏没坏. ○ *One smell of the rotten meat was enough!* 这腐烂的肉闻一下就够受的了!

▷ **smelly** *adj* (**-ier, -iest**) (*infml* 口) having a bad smell 发出难闻气味的; 有臭味的: *a smelly room, car, yard* 有难闻气味的房间、汽车、院子 ○ *smelly feet, breath, fumes* 有臭味的脚、口臭、难闻的烟. **smel·li·ness** *n* [U].

smell[2] /smel; smɛl/ *v* (*pt, pp* **smelt** /smelt; smɛlt/ or **smelled**) ⇨Usage at DREAM[2] 用法见 DREAM[2]. **1 (a)** [Tn, Tf, Tng no passive 不用于被动语态] (not used in the continuous tenses; often with *can* or *could* 不用于进行时态，常与 can 或 could 连用) notice (sth/sb) by using the nose 闻出，嗅出(某物[某人])的气味: *Do you smell anything unusual?* 你闻到有什么怪味吗? ○ *The dog smelt the rabbit a long way off.* 那条狗嗅出远处有兔子. ○ *I could smell (that) he had been smoking.* 我闻得出他抽过烟. ○ *I can smell something burning.* 我闻到燃烧东西的气味. **(b)** [Ipr, Tn] **~ (at) sth** sniff sth in order to test its smell 闻某物以分辨其气味: *a dog smelling (at) a lamp-post* 闻着路灯柱的狗 ○ *Smell this and tell me what it is.* 闻闻这东西，告诉我是什么. **2** [I] (not used in the continuous tenses 不用于进行时态) be able to smell 有嗅觉: *Can fish smell?* 鱼有嗅觉吗? **3 (a)** [I] (not used in the continuous tenses 不用于进行时态) have an unpleasant smell 有难闻的气味; 有臭味: *Your breath smells.* 你呼出的气很难闻. ○ *The fish has begun to smell.* 这鱼已经发臭了. **(b)** [La, Ipr] **~ (of sth)** have a smell of the specified type 有某种气味: *The flowers smell sweet.* 这些花很香. ○ *The dinner smells good.* 这饭菜闻起来真香. ○ *What does the perfume smell like?* 这种香水闻起来怎样? ○ *The meat smells of garlic.* 这肉有大蒜的气味. ○ *Your breath smells of brandy.* 你呼吸中带有白兰地酒味. **4** [Tn, Tng no passive 不用于被动语态] (*fig* 比喻) be able to detect (sth) by instinct 藉本能或直觉察知(某事): *The reporter began to smell a good story.* 那记者意识到要有精彩的报道材料. ○ *I can smell trouble (coming).* 我凭直觉感到(要)有麻烦了. **5** (idm 习语) **smell a ˈrat** (*infml* 口) suspect that sth is wrong 怀疑某事不对头: *I smelt a rat when he started being so helpful!* 他主动帮起忙来，我怀疑其中另有文章. **6** (phr v) **smell sb/sth out (a)** detect sb/sth by smelling 藉嗅觉发现某人[某物]: *Specially-trained dogs can smell out drugs.* 受过特殊训练的狗能嗅出毒品. **(b)** discover sth by finding and interpreting clues 通过对线

S

索的发掘和分析发现某事物: *The Secret Service smelled out a plot to kill the President.* 情报部门抽丝剥茧发现了要行刺总统的阴谋.

□ ˈ**smelling-salts** *n* [pl] sharp-smelling substances sniffed esp as a cure for faintness 嗅盐(尤用于治疗昏厥).

smelt[1] /smelt; smɛlt/ *v* [Tn] **1** heat and melt (ore) in order to obtain the metal it contains 熔炼. **2** obtain (metal) in this way (以熔炼法)提炼(金属): *a copper-smelting works* 炼铜厂.

smelt[2] /smelt; smɛlt/ *n* (*pl* unchanged or **~s** 复数或不变或作 **smelts**) small fish eaten as food 银白鱼.

smelt[3] *pt, pp* of SMELL[2].

smidgen (also **smidgin**) /ˈsmɪdʒən; ˋsmɪdʒən/ *n* [sing] **~ (of sth)** (*infml* 口 *esp US*) small bit or amount 些微; 少量: *'Do you want some sugar?' 'Just a smidgen.'* '你要糖吗?' '只要一点儿.'

smile /smaɪl; smaɪl/ *n* **1** expression of the face, usu with the corners of the mouth turned up, showing happiness, amusement, pleasure, etc 微笑: *with a relieved, amused, cheerful smile on his face* 他面带宽慰、喜悦、欢快的笑容 ○ *give sb a happy smile* 对某人愉快地微笑. **2** (idm 习语) **all** ˈ**smiles** looking very happy 显得非常愉快: *She was all smiles at the news of her win.* 她听到自己获胜的消息喜形于色.

▷ **smile** *v* **1** [I, Ipr] **~ (at sb/sth)** give a smile or smiles 微笑: *smile happily, with pleasure, etc* 幸福地、高兴地...微笑 ○ *He never smiles.* 他从不露笑脸. ○ *I smiled at the child and said 'Hello'.* 我朝那小孩笑了笑说: '你好'. **2** [Tn] express (sth) by means of a smile 以微笑表示(某信息): *She smiled her approval.* 她以微笑表示同意. ○ *I smiled my thanks.* 我以微笑表示谢意. **3** [Tn] give (the specified type of smile) 发出(某种微笑): *She smiled a bitter smile.* 她苦笑了一下. **4** (phr v) **smile on sb/sth** (*fml* 文) approve of or encourage sb/sth 对某人[某事物]表示赞成或鼓励之意: *The council did not smile on our plan*, ie rejected it. 委员会否决了我们的计划. ○ *Fortune smiled on us*, ie We were successful. 幸运之神向我们微笑了(我们成功了). **smil·ingly** *adv* with a smile or smiles 微笑着.

S

smirch /smɜːtʃ; smɝtʃ/ *v* [Tn] = BESMIRCH.

smirk /smɜːk; smɝk/ *n* silly or self-satisfied smile 傻笑; 得意的笑: *Wipe that smirk off your face!* 别那么傻笑了!

▷ **smirk** *v* [I] give a smirk 傻笑.

NOTE ON USAGE 用法: Compare **smirk, sneer, frown, scowl** and **grimace**. 试比较 **smirk**、**sneer**、**frown**、**scowl**、**grimace** 这几个词. These verbs indicate people twisting their faces to express various, usually negative, attitudes. 这几个动词表达的是面部的各种表情, 通常都表示有不好的含义. People **smirk** when they smile in a silly way to show that they are pleased with themselves, usually at the expense of somebody else. ☆ **smirk** 指自鸣得意地傻笑, 通常含幸灾乐祸之意. When we **sneer**, we curl our upper lip to express a superior or contemptuous attitude to other people ☆ **sneer** 指翘起上唇嗤笑, 流露出高人一等的或轻蔑的神情: *He's always sneering at my suggestions.* 他总是对我提出的建议嗤之以鼻. We **frown** by bringing our eyebrows together to indicate displeasure, puzzlement or concentration. ☆ **frown** 指皱眉头, 表示不悦、不解或精神集中. When **scowling** we twist the whole face to express anger, bad temper, etc ☆ **scowl** 指怒容满面, 表示愤怒、发脾气等: *He sits alone all day scowling at passers-by.* 他整天独自坐着, 横眉怒目地瞪着来往的人. We also twist the whole face when we **grimace**. ☆ **grimace** 也指整个面部抽动的表情. We usually **grimace** for a very short time as a reaction to pain or annoyance, or to cause laughter. ☆ **grimace** 通常为时短暂, 是痛苦或烦恼的反应, 或是为引人发笑.

smite /smaɪt; smaɪt/ *v* (*pt* **smote** /sməʊt; smot/, *pp* **smitten** /ˈsmɪtn; ˋsmɪtn̩/) [Tn] (*fml or joc* 文或谑) **1** hit (sb/sth) hard; strike 重击(某人[某物]); 打: *He smote the ball into the grandstand.* 他把球打到看台上去了. **2** have a great effect on (sb) 对(某人)产生重大影响: *His conscience smote him.* 他受到了良心的谴责.

smith /smɪθ; smɪθ/ *n* **1** = BLACKSMITH. **2** (in compounds 用以构成复合词) person who makes metal utensils, ornaments, etc 金属工匠(制金属器皿、饰物等者): *a* ˈ*goldsmith* ○ *a* ˈ*silversmith.*

▷ **smithy** /ˈsmɪðɪ; ˋsmɪðɪ/ *n* blacksmith's workshop 铁匠铺.

smith·er·eens /ˌsmɪðəˈriːnz; ˌsmɪðəˋrinz/ *n* [pl] (used esp with *vs* meaning *break* or *destroy*) small pieces (尤与意为'打破'或'粉碎'之类的动词连用)碎片: *smash, blow, hammer, etc sth (in)to smithereens* 把某物撞、炸、敲...成碎片.

smit·ten[1] *pp* of SMITE.

smit·ten[2] /ˈsmɪtn; ˋsmɪtn̩/ *adj* [pred 作表语] **1 ~ with sth** deeply affected by (an emotion) 深受(某种情感)的影响: *smitten with remorse for one's cruelty* 对自己的残酷行为深感悔恨. **2 ~ (with sb/sth)** (*esp joc* 尤作戏谑语) having taken a sudden, often romantic, liking (to sb) (对某人)突然喜爱(常指情爱): *I met Janet yesterday, and I'm rather smitten with her.* 我昨天遇见了珍妮特, 一下子就爱上她了.

smock /smɒk; smɑk/ *n* **(a)** loose garment (often with smocking on it) worn over other clothes to protect them from dirt, etc 罩衫, 罩衣(常有褶饰): *Smocks were formerly worn by farm-workers.* 这种罩衫是旧时农民穿的. ○ *The artist's smock was covered in paint.* 那艺术家的罩衣上沾满了颜料. **(b)** loose comfortable shirt-like garment worn esp by pregnant women (衬衫式的)宽松舒适的上衣(尤指孕妇服): *a brightly-coloured smock worn over trousers* 罩住裤子的鲜艳上衣.

▷ **smock·ing** *n* [U] type of decoration on a garment made by gathering the cloth tightly with stitches (服装上的)褶饰: *delicate smocking on a baby's dress* 幼儿服装上精致的褶饰.

smog /smɒg; smɑg/ *n* [U] mixture of fog and smoke 雾和烟的混合物; 烟雾: *Smog used to bring London traffic to a standstill.* 过去伦敦的交通常因烟雾而受阻. ⇨ Usage at FOG 用法见 FOG.

smoke[1] /sməʊk; smok/ *n* **1** [U] visible (usu white, grey or black) vapour coming from sth that is burning 烟: *smoke from factory chimneys* 工厂烟囱冒出的烟 ○ *The room was full of cigarette smoke.* 满屋子都是香烟的烟雾. **2** [C] **(a)** (usu *sing* 通常作单数) (*infml* 口) act or period of smoking tobacco 吸烟; 抽烟: *They stopped work to have a smoke.* 他们停下工作吸口烟. ○ *I haven't had a smoke all day.* 我一整天还没抽过烟呢. **(b)** (*dated sl* 旧, 俚) thing (esp a cigar or cigarette) to be smoked 烟(尤指雪茄或香烟): *Has anyone got any smokes?* 哪位有烟? **3** (idm 习语) ˌ**go up in** ˈ**smoke** **(a)** be completely burnt 被烧光: *The whole house went up in smoke in less than an hour.* 整座房子不到一个小时就烧光了. **(b)** (*fig* 比喻) result in failure; leave nothing of value behind 以失败告终; 未剩下有价值的东西: *When he crashed his car all his travel plans went up in smoke.* 他把汽车撞坏了, 他的整个旅行计划都吹了. **(there is)** ˌ**no** ˌ**smoke with**ˌ**out** ˈ**fire** (*saying* 谚) there is always some reason for a rumour 无火不生烟; 谣言也总是事出有因: *He's denied having an affair with his secretary, but of course there's no smoke without fire.* 他不承认和他秘书发生了关系, 但自是空穴来风喽.

▷ **smoke·less** *adj* [usu attrib 通常作定语] **1** burning with little or no smoke (燃烧时)无烟的: *smokeless fuel* 无烟燃料. **2** free from smoke (环境)无烟的: *a smokeless zone*, ie an area where smoke is prohibited 禁止吸烟区.

smo·ki·ness *n* [U]: *He hates the smokiness of pubs and bars.* 他讨厌酒馆和酒吧里弥漫的烟雾.

□ ˈ**smoke-bomb** (also ˈ**smoke-grenade**) *n* bomb that sends out clouds of smoke (used esp in police or military operations) 烟幕弹(尤为警方或于军事行动中使用的): *Smoke-bombs were thrown during the street riots.* 街道上出现骚乱时投放了烟幕弹.

ˈ**smoke-screen** *n* **(a)** clouds of smoke used to hide military, naval, police, etc operations 烟幕(用以掩护陆军、海军、警方等的行动的). **(b)** (*fig* 比喻) action, explanation, etc designed to hide one's real intentions, activities, etc 障眼法(用以遮掩真实意图、行动等的举动、借口等): *The export business was just a smokescreen for his activities as a spy.* 他做出口生意只是为他的间谍活动打掩护.

ˈ**smoke-stack** *n* **(a)** funnel serving as an outlet for steam from a steamship 轮船的烟囱. **(b)** tall chimney

高大的烟囱. (**c**) (*US*) funnel of a steam train 蒸汽火车的烟囱.

smoke[2] /sməuk; smok/ *v* **1** [I] (**a**) give off smoke or other visible vapour 冒烟; 冒气: *a smoking volcano* 冒着烟的火山 ○ *smoking factory chimneys* 冒着烟的工厂烟囱. (**b**) (of a fire or fireplace) give off too much smoke (and send it out into the room instead of up the chimney) (指炉火或壁炉)出烟过多(未经烟囱排出而进入屋内): *This fireplace smokes (badly).* 这个壁炉烟冒得(太)厉害. **2** [I, Tn] draw in smoke from burning tobacco or other substances through the mouth and let it out again; use cigarettes, etc in this way regularly 吸烟; 抽(香烟等): *Do you smoke?* 你抽烟吗? ○ *She has never smoked.* 她从不吸烟. ○ *He smokes a pipe.* 他抽烟斗. ○ *She smokes 20 (cigarettes) a day.* 她一天抽20支(香烟). **3** [Tn esp passive 尤用于被动语态] preserve (meat, fish, etc) with smoke (from wood fires) to give a special taste 用烟熏制(肉、鱼等): *smoked ham, salmon, mackerel, etc* 熏火腿、鲑、鲭等. **4** [Tn esp passive 尤用于被动语态] darken (esp glass) with smoke 熏黑(尤指玻璃): *He looked at the sun through a sheet of smoked glass.* 他透过一片熏黑的玻璃观看太阳. ○ *fit smoked plastic lenses in spectacles* 把烟色的塑料镜片安在眼镜上. **5** (idm 习语) **put that in your pipe and smoke it** ⇨ PIPE[1]. **6** (phr v) **smoke sb/sth out** drive sb/sth out by means of smoke 将某人[某物]熏出: *smoke out snakes from a hole* 把蛇从洞中熏出 ○ (*fig* 比喻) *He was determined to smoke out the leaders of the gang*, ie bring them out of hiding. 他决心要把匪首从躲藏处赶出来. **smoke sth out** fill sth with smoke 使某处充满烟雾: *Turn off that pan — you're smoking the place out!* 快把坐着锅的炉子关上 —— 你把这儿弄得都是烟.

▷ **smoker** *n* **1** person who smokes tobacco regularly 吸烟的人: *a heavy smoker*, ie one who smokes very often 吸烟多的人 ○ *Non-smokers often disapprove of smokers.* 不吸烟的人往往不赞成别人吸烟. **2** carriage on a train where smoking is allowed (火车上的)准予吸烟的车厢: *Shall we sit in a smoker or a non-smoker?* 我们坐吸烟车厢还是非吸烟车厢?

smok·ing *n* [U] activity or habit of smoking cigarettes, etc 吸烟; 抽烟: *'No Smoking'*, eg on a notice in a public place '禁止吸烟' ○ *Smoking isn't allowed in this cinema.* 这家影院不准吸烟. ○ *Smoking damages your health.* 吸烟有害于健康. ○ [attrib 作定语] *the smoking section of an aircraft* 飞机上的吸烟区. **'smoking-jacket** *n* man's comfortable jacket, made of velvet, etc, worn (esp formerly) at home 吸烟服(男用舒适的丝绒等制的外衣, 尤指旧时在家中穿的). **'smoking-room** *n* room (in a hotel, etc) where smoking is allowed (旅馆等的)吸烟室.

smoky /'sməukɪ; 'smokɪ/ *adj* (**-ier, -iest**) **1** giving out or having a lot of smoke; full of smoke 冒烟的; 多烟的; 烟雾弥漫的: *smoky chimneys, fires, etc* 冒烟的烟囱、炉火等 ○ *the smoky atmosphere of an industrial town* 工业城市中混有烟雾的空气 ○ *This room is very smoky.* 这房间里烟雾弥漫. **2** like smoke in smell, taste or appearance (气味、味道或外观)像烟(雾)的: *smoky cheeses* 烟熏味的干酪 ○ *rather a smoky whisky* 带有烟熏味的威士忌. **3** like smoke in colour, appearance, etc (颜色、外观等)像烟(雾)的: *a pretty smoky glass* 小巧的烟色玻璃杯 ○ *a smoky grey coat* 烟灰色的大衣. **smo·ki·ness** *n* [U].

smol·der (*US*) = SMOULDER.

smooch /smu:tʃ; smutʃ/ *v* [I] (*infml* 口) kiss and cuddle, sometimes when dancing slowly with another person 接吻、拥抱(有时于慢舞时): *hours of smooching in the back seat of the car* 在汽车后座上接吻、拥抱数小时 ○ *couples smooching on the dance floor* 在舞池里相拥相吻的对对舞伴.

▷ **smooch** *n* [sing] (*infml* 口) activity of smooching 接吻、拥抱: *having a smooch in the back row of the cinema* 在影院后排接吻、拥抱.

smooth[1] /smu:ð; smuð/ *adj* (**-er, -est**) **1** having an even surface without points, lumps, bumps, etc; not rough 光滑的; 平坦的; 平静的: *a smooth skin* 光滑的皮肤 ○ *a smooth road* 平坦的路面 ○ *a smooth sheet of ice* 光滑的冰 ○ *a smooth sea*, ie calm, free from waves 平静的海面 ○ *Marble is smooth to the touch*, ie feels smooth when touched. 大理石摸起来很光滑. Cf 参看 ROUGH[1]. **2** free from difficulties, problems, etc 顺利的; 无困难的; 无问题的: *as smooth a journey as possible* 极为顺利的旅途 ○ *The new bill had a smooth passage through Parliament.* 新法案在议会顺利通过. ○ *They made things very smooth for me*, ie removed difficulties for me. 他们为我排除了困难. **3** moving evenly, without bumps, jolts, stops, etc 平稳的; 无颠簸的; 不摇晃的: *a smooth ride in a good car* 坐着性能好的汽车平稳的行驶 ○ *a smooth landing in an aircraft* 乘飞机平稳的着陆 ○ *a smooth crossing by sea* 平稳的海上横渡 ○ *smooth breathing* 畅顺的呼吸. **4** (of a liquid mixture) free from lumps; evenly mixed or beaten (指液态混合物)无颗粒的, 搅拌均匀的: *smooth custard* 调匀的牛奶蛋糊 ○ *Mix the butter and sugar to a smooth paste.* 把黄油、糖调匀成糊状. **5** (**a**) tasting pleasant; not bitter 味美的; 不苦的: *a smooth whisky* 味醇的威士忌 ○ *a smooth cigar* 烟味柔和的雪茄. (**b**) (*fig* 比喻) flowing easily and evenly 流畅的: *smooth verse* 流畅的诗句 ○ *a smooth voice* 柔和的嗓音. **6** (*often derog* 常作贬义) (usu used of men) flattering and agreeable (but perhaps insincere); (too) polite (通常指男子)奉承而随和的(但可为虚假的); (过分)礼貌的: *a smooth manner* 圆滑的态度 ○ *a smooth, plausible individual* 八面玲珑、油嘴滑舌的人. **7** (idm 习语) **in smooth 'water(s)** making even and easy progress 进展顺利; 一帆风顺: *The business seems to be in smooth waters these days.* 这些日子生意好像很顺利. **a smooth, slick, etc operator** ⇨ OPERATOR. **(as) smooth as 'silk/a baby's 'bottom/'velvet** very smooth 十分柔软、光滑: *Her skin is still as smooth as a baby's bottom.* 她的皮肤仍然十分柔软、光滑. **take the rough with the smooth** ⇨ ROUGH[3].

▷ **smoothie** (also **smoothy**) (*infml derog* 口, 贬) *n* person (usu a man) who behaves in a smooth[1](6) way 奉承而随和的人(通常指男子): *Don't trust him — he's a real smoothie!* 别相信他 —— 他净顺情说好话!

smoothly *adv* in a smooth manner 光滑地; 平坦地; 平静地; 顺利的: *The engine is running smoothly now.* 发动机现在运转得很顺畅. ○ *Things are not going very smoothly*, ie There are troubles, interruptions, etc. 事情进展得不太顺利.

smooth·ness *n* [U]: *the smoothness of her skin* 她皮肤的柔软光滑 ○ *the smoothness of the sea* 海面的平静 ○ *the smoothness of the negotiations* 谈判的顺利进展.

□ **,smooth-'tongued** (also **,smooth-'spoken**) *adj* (*usu derog* 通常作贬义) speaking in a smooth[1](6) way; persuasive in speech 油腔滑调的; 能言善辩的: *,smooth-tongued 'salesmen* 能说会道的推销员.

S

smooth[2] /smu:ð; smuð/ *v* **1** [Tn, Tn·pr, Tn·p] **~ sth (away, back, down, out, etc)** make sth smooth or flat 使某物光滑、平坦、平静或顺利: *smooth down one's dress* 拉平衣服 ○ *smooth her skirt over her hips* 抚平她裙子的臀部处 ○ *smooth out a sheet on a bed* 把床单铺平 ○ *smooth down wood with sandpaper* 用砂纸把木料打磨光滑. **2** (idm 习语) **smooth sb's path** make progress easier for sb 为某人铺平道路: *Speaking the language fluently certainly smoothed our path.* 我们说这种语言说得很流利, 确实为我们带来许多方便. **smooth sb's ,ruffled 'feathers** make sb feel less angry or offended 平息某人的怒气或怨气. **3** (phr v) **smooth sth away** get rid of (esp problems, difficulties, etc) smoothly and easily, or by smoothing 轻易地摆脱或消除(尤指问题、困难等): *smooth away wrinkles with cream* 用油膏消除皱纹 ○ *We'll smooth away any difficulties when we reach them.* 我们碰到任何困难都能顺利克服. ○ *Money helps to smooth away most problems.* 金钱有助于使许多问题迎刃而解. **smooth sth over** make (problems, etc) seem less important 使(问题等)缓解: *It will be difficult for you to smooth over your differences after so many years.* 经过了这么多年, 你想消除你们之间的分歧谈何容易.

smor·gas·bord /'smɔ:gəsbɔ:d; 'smɔrgəs,bɔrd/ *n* [U] (meal with a) variety of hot or cold savoury dishes served from a buffet 瑞典式自助餐(的各种冷热佳肴): *Help yourself from the smorgasbord.* 请随便用自助餐.

smote *pt* of SMITE.

smother /'smʌðə(r); 'smʌðɚ/ *v* **1** [I, Tn] (cause sb to) die from lack of air, or from not being able to breathe; suffocate (使某人)窒息, 闷死: *He smothered the baby with a pillow.* 他用枕头把婴儿闷死了. ○ (*fig* 比喻) *She felt smothered with kindness.* 她感受到难以消受的热情.

2 [Tn] put out or keep down (a fire) by covering it with ashes, sand, etc 用灰、沙等熄灭或闷住(火): *If you put too much coal on the fire at once you'll smother it.* 在火上一下子添上很多煤, 反而能把火闷死. ○ *Smother the flames from the burning pan with a wet towel.* 用湿毛巾把锅里的火扑灭. ○ (*fig* 比喻) *smother a yawn, smile, laugh, etc*, ie prevent it from developing 忍住哈欠、微笑、大笑等 ○ (*fig* 比喻) *He had to smother a giggle.* 他得抑制住自己, 不咯咯地笑出声来. **3** [Tn·pr] **~ sth/sb with/in sth** cover sth/sb thickly or to too great an extent 厚厚地或大面积地覆盖某物[某人]: *a pudding smothered in cream* 有很厚的奶油的布丁 ○ *smother a child with kisses* 不停地吻着孩子.

smoul·der (*US* **smol·der**) /ˈsməʊldə(r); ˈsmoldɚ/ *v* [I] burn slowly without flame (无火焰)缓慢燃烧: *a cigarette smouldering in the ashtray* 在烟灰缸里慢慢燃烧的香烟 ○ (*fig* 比喻) *Hate smouldered inside him.* 他心中积怨甚久. ○ *She smouldered silently with jealousy*, ie did not express it openly. 她妒火中烧.

smudge /smʌdʒ; smʌdʒ/ *n* dirty or blurred mark, often caused by rubbing 污点, 污迹(常因磨擦造成的): *You've got a smudge of soot on your cheek.* 你脸上有块煤灰污迹. ○ *Wash your hands or you'll make smudges on the writing paper.* 把手洗干净, 别把写字的纸弄脏了.

▷ **smudge** *v* **1** [Tn] make a dirty or blurred mark or marks on (sth) 弄污, 污脏(某物): *paper smudged with fingerprints* 被指印弄脏的纸 ○ *You've smudged my picture!* 你把我的画给弄脏了! **2** [I] become blurred or smeared 变模糊; 弄脏: *Wet ink smudges easily.* 墨水没干很容易弄出污迹.

smug /smʌg; smʌg/ *adj* (**-gger, -ggest**) (*usu derog* 通常作贬义) too pleased with or proud of oneself, one's achievements, etc; self-satisfied 沾沾自喜的; 自满的; 自鸣得意的: *a life of smug respectability* 沾沾自喜的体面生活 ○ *smug optimism* 自鸣得意的乐观态度. ▷ **smugly** *adv*: *smile smugly at the failures of others* 对别人的失败幸灾乐祸. **smug·ness** *n* [U].

smuggle /ˈsmʌgl; ˈsmʌgl/ *v* [Tn, Tn·pr, Tn·p] **~ sth/sb (into/out of/across/through sth); ~ sth/sb in/out/across/through** **1** get (goods) secretly and illegally into or out of a country, esp without paying customs duty 偷运(货物)进出某国(尤指逃避关税); 走私: *smuggle Swiss watches into England* 走私瑞士表运进英国 ○ *smuggle drugs through customs* 偷运毒品过海关 ○ *smuggle goods across a frontier* 偷运货物过境 ○ *arrested for smuggling out currency* 因私携货币出境而被捕. **2** send, take or bring (sth/sb) secretly and in defiance of rules and regulations (违反规章制度)偷运, 偷带(某物[某人]): *smuggle people out of the country* 把人偷偷运送出国 ○ *smuggle a prisoner through the main gates* 把囚犯偷偷带出大门 ○ *smuggle a letter into prison* 把信偷偷带进监狱.

▷ **smug·gler** /ˈsmʌglə(r); ˈsmʌglɚ/ *n* person who smuggles 走私者; 偷运者: *This cave was used by smugglers in the eighteenth century.* 这个洞穴是十八世纪走私的人使用的. *drug smugglers* 走私毒品的人.

smug·gling /ˈsmʌglɪŋ; ˈsmʌglɪŋ/ *n* [U] activity of smuggling 走私活动: *ˈdrug-smuggling* 毒品走私活动 ○ *There's a lot of smuggling across this frontier.* 这段边境走私活动很猖獗.

NOTE ON USAGE 用法: People **smuggle** goods from one country to another when they illegally take things like watches, drugs, cigarettes, etc across a border. ☆ **smuggle** 指将手表、毒品、香烟之类物品从一国非法越过边境运往另一国. These goods may be banned (eg drugs) or they may be more expensive in the second country because of duty (eg jewellery). 这些物品或为禁品(如毒品), 或因关税重(如珠宝)在另一国可能价格更贵. Smugglers **run** guns, drugs and other prohibited dangerous items between countries, possibly as a regular activity. ☆ **run** 指走私者在国与国之间运送枪支、毒品及其他违禁危险品, 可能为经常性的活动. Goods (especially alcohol) are **bootlegged** when they are smuggled or manufactured and sold illegally. ☆ **bootleg** 指非法运送、制造及出售货物(尤指酒). When records, films, books, etc are illegally copied and sold they are **pirated.** ☆ **pirate** 指非法复制及出售唱片、影片、书籍等.

smut /smʌt; smʌt/ *n* **1** [C] (mark or spot made by a) bit of soot, dirt, etc 煤炱、污泥等(造成的污迹或污点): *dozens of smuts on my clean washing* 我洗干净的衣物上的许多污迹. **2** [U] (*infml derog* 口, 贬) indecent or vulgar words, stories, pictures, etc 下流的或猥亵的言语、故事、图片等: *Don't talk smut.* 不要说脏话. ○ *The tabloid papers are full of smut.* 这些小报充斥着下流的东西.

▷ **smutty** *adj* (**-ier, -iest**) **1** marked with smuts (SMUT 1); dirty 有污迹的; 肮脏的: *a child with a smutty face* 满脸污垢的孩子 ○ *smutty marks on the white tablecloth* 白桌布上的斑斑污迹. **2** (*infml derog* 口, 贬) (of talk, pictures, stories, etc) indecent; vulgar (指谈话、图片、故事等)下流的, 猥亵的, 淫秽的: *smutty books* 淫秽的书 ○ *smutty humour* 下流的幽默. **smut·ti·ness** *n* [U]: *the smuttiness of the comedian's jokes* 那滑稽演员说的笑话中的猥亵话.

snack /snæk; snæk/ *n* small meal, usu eaten in a hurry, esp between main meals 小吃, 点心(通常指匆匆食用者, 尤指两正餐之间的): *Usually I only have a snack at lunchtime.* 我中午通常只吃点心. ○ *The children have a mid-morning snack of milk and biscuits.* 这些儿童在早餐与午餐之间有牛奶与饼干作点心. ○ [attrib 作定语] *a snack lunch* 午餐小吃.

▷ **snack** *v* [I] (*infml* 口) eat snacks between or instead of main meals 吃点心或小吃: *I prefer to snack when I'm travelling rather than have a full meal.* 我旅行时喜欢吃小吃而不吃正餐.

□ **ˈsnack-bar** *n* café, counter, etc where snacks may be bought 小餐馆; 小吃店; 小吃部: *We had coffee and sandwiches at the snack-bar.* 我们在小吃店喝咖啡、吃三明治.

snaffle /ˈsnæfl; ˈsnæfl̩/ *v* [Tn] (*Brit infml* 口) take (sth) for oneself, usu quickly and greedily or unlawfully 将(某物)攫为己有(通常指迅速地、贪婪地或非法地): *They snaffled all the food at the party before we got there.* 在我们到那里之前, 他们已经把聚会上的食物全吃光了. ○ *Thieves snaffled all the goods from the burnt warehouse.* 窃贼把失火的仓库里的货物都偷走了.

snag /snæg; snæg/ *n* **1** small difficulty or obstacle, usu hidden, unknown or unexpected 小的困难或障碍(通常指潜在的、未知的或未料到的): *come across a snag* 碰到点困难 ○ *We hit* (ie encountered) *several snags while still at the planning stage.* 我们在计划阶段就遇到了几个困难. ○ *There must be a snag in it somewhere.* 一定是在某处出了个小故障. ○ *The only snag is that I have no money.* 唯一的困难是我没钱. **2** rough or sharp projection, which may be dangerous (可能带来危险的)不平的或尖利的突出部分. **3** tear, hole or thread pulled out of place (esp in tights or stockings) in material that has caught on a snag(2) (尖利物造成的)划破、刺穿或断线处(尤指裤袜或长袜上的): *I have a snag in my best black tights.* 我最好的一条黑裤袜给划破了.

▷ **snag** *v* (**-gg-**) [Tn] catch or tear (sth) on sth rough or sharp 在尖利物上钩住或撕破(某物): *Her tights were badly snagged.* 她的裤袜划破了一大片. ○ *He snagged his sweater on the wire fence.* 他的毛衣在铁丝网上钩破了.

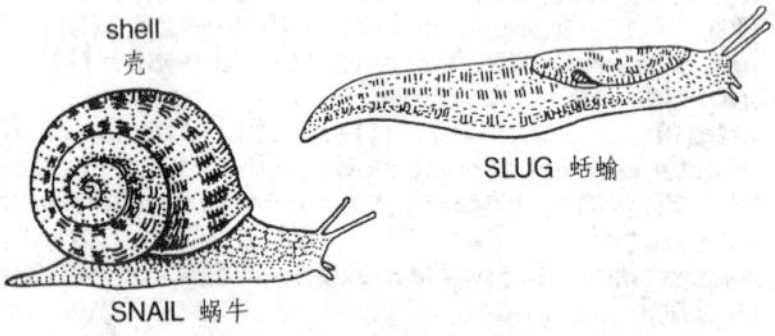

snail /sneɪl; snel/ *n* **1** type of small soft slow-moving animal, usu with a hard spiral shell 蜗牛: *Snails have been eating our lettuces.* 蜗牛一直在吃我们的莴苣. ○ *The snail retreated into its shell.* 蜗牛缩进壳里去了. **2** (idm 习语) **at a ˈsnail's pace** very slowly 极慢的: *The old woman crossed the road at a snail's pace.* 那个老太太横过马路时走得慢极了.

snake /sneɪk; snek/ *n* **1** any of various types of long legless crawling reptile, some of which are poisonous 蛇: *the scaly skin of the snake* 蛇的鳞状皮 ○ *cobras and other*

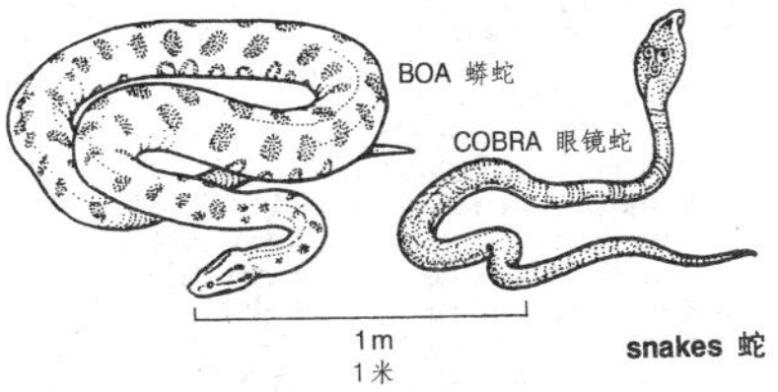

snakes 蛇

dangerous snakes 眼镜蛇及其他毒蛇. **2** treacherous person 阴险的人. **3** (idm 习语) **a ˌsnake in the ˈgrass** deceitful or treacherous person who pretends to be a friend 伪装成朋友的阴险的人: *That snake in the grass reported me to the boss.* 那个口蜜腹剑的傢伙到老板那里告了我一状.

▷ **snake** *v* (phr v) **snake (its way) across, past, through, etc** move in a twisting way like a snake; follow a twisting winding course 蛇行斗折; 沿曲折道路行进: *The road snakes (its way) through the mountains.* 那条路斗折蛇行穿过群山. ○ *The river snaked away into the distance.* 那条河蜿蜒曲折流向远方.

snaky *adj* of or like a snake (似)蛇的: *the snaky movements of the young dancers* 年轻舞蹈演员婀娜的舞姿 ○ *narrow snaky roads through the hills* 穿过群山的羊肠小道.

□ **ˈsnake-bite** *n* [C, U] wound or condition resulting from being bitten by a poisonous snake 毒蛇咬伤: *be ill from a snake-bite* 因毒蛇咬后生病 ○ *an antidote for snake-bite*, ie sth that acts against the poison 治蛇咬伤的解毒药.

ˈsnake-charmer *n* entertainer who can control snakes and make them (seem to) move rhythmically to music 弄蛇者(能驯蛇使蛇随音乐起舞的人).

ˌsnakes and ˈladders board game played with counters which can move up pictures of ladders (to progress) or down pictures of snakes (to go back) 蛇梯棋(一种棋类游戏, 棋子沿梯形图前进、沿蛇形图后退).

ˈsnakeskin *n* skin of a snake, esp when made into leather (for bags, etc) 蛇皮(尤指用于做皮包等的): *shoes made of snakeskin* 蛇皮鞋 ○ [attrib 作定语] *a snakeskin belt* 蛇皮皮带.

snap[1] /snæp; snæp/ *v* **(-pp-)** **1** [I, Ipr, Ip, Tn, Tn·pr, Tn·p] (cause sth to) break suddenly with a sharp noise (使某物)断裂并发出尖利声音: *He stretched the rubber band till it snapped.* 他把橡皮筋啪的一声拉断了. ○ *Suddenly the branch that he was standing on snapped off.* 他踩着的树枝突然啪的一声折断了. ○ *The great weight snapped the metal bar (in two).* 重量很大把金属杆喀吧一声压成两截了. ○ (*fig* 比喻) *After years of hard work and poverty, he finally snapped*, ie had a nervous breakdown, fell ill, etc. 他多年劳累和贫困终因体力不支而病倒. **2** [La, Ip, Tn, Tn·p, Cn·a] open or close (sth) with a sudden sharp noise; (cause sth to) make a sudden sharp noise 打开或关闭(某物)并突然发出尖利声音; (使某物)突然发出尖利声音: *The box snapped open.* 箱子啪的一声打开了. ○ *The circus manager snapped his whip.* 马戏团主管把鞭子抽得很响. ○ *He snapped down the lid of the box.* 他砰的一声把箱子盖合上了. ○ *She snapped her bag shut.* 她喀哒一声把提包关上了. ○ *The shark snapped its jaws shut.* 鲨鱼啪嗒一声把嘴合上了. **3** [I, Tn] speak or say (sth) in a sharp (usu angry) voice 厉声说(话)(通常指生气时): *'Come here at once,' she snapped.* 她高声喊道: '快过来!' ○ *He never speaks calmly — just snaps all the time.* 他从来不心平气和地说话——总是高声喊叫. **4** [Tn] (*infml* 口) take a quick photograph of (sb) (很快地)给(某人)拍照: *I snapped you sunbathing on the beach.* 我给你拍了一张海滩日光浴的照片. **5** (idm 习语) **bite/snap sb's head off** ⇨ HEAD[1]. **snap one's ˈfingers** make a clicking noise by moving the second or third finger quickly against the thumb (eg to attract sb's attention, mark the beat of music, etc) 打榧子(用食指或中指捻碰拇指发声, 如为引人注意或打音乐拍子等): *He snapped his fingers to attract the waiter.* 他打了个榧子招呼服务员. **ˌsnap to atˈtention** come quickly and smartly to the position of attention(4) 利落地立正. **ˌsnap ˈto it** (*infml* 口) (usu as a command 通常作命令语) start moving, working, etc quickly; hurry up 快走; 快干; 赶快: *'I want those bricks moved; come on, snap to it!'* '那些砖得搬走; 来呀, 快!' **ˌsnap ˈout of it** (*infml* 口) (often as a command 常作命令语) get (quickly) out of a (usu bad, unhappy, etc) mood (迅速)摆脱某种(通常指坏的、不愉快的...)情绪. **6** (phr v) **snap at sb** speak to sb sharply and rudely 厉声对某人说: *'Shut up!' she snapped (back) at him.* '住嘴!'她厉声顶(回)了他一句. ○ *I'm sorry I snapped at you just now.* 对不起, 我刚才不该对你嚷嚷. **snap at sth** try to grasp sth with the teeth by closing them quickly and sharply around it 一下子咬住: *The fish snapped at the bait.* 那鱼一下子咬住了鱼饵. ○ (*fig* 比喻) *They snapped at* (ie accepted eagerly) *the chance of a cheap holiday.* 他们欣然抓住这一少花钱度假的机会. **snap sth out** exclaim sth in a sharp or unpleasant way 厉声喊出: *The sergeant snapped out an order.* 中士大声发出命令. **snap sth up** buy or seize sth quickly and eagerly 抢购或迅速抓取某物: *The cheapest articles at the sale were quickly snapped up.* 大减价货物中最便宜的物品很快抢购一空.

snap[2] /snæp; snæp/ *n* **1** [C] act or sound of snapping (物体)断裂、开或关(的声音); (人)厉声说(的)话; 拍照(的快门声); 突然咬住(的声音): *The dog made an unsuccessful snap at the meat.* 那条狗没咬住肉. ○ *The lid shut with a snap.* 盖子啪嗒一声合上了. ○ *The oar broke with a snap.* 桨喀吧一声断了. **2** [C] short spell or period of (usu cold) weather 一阵(通常指寒冷的)天气: *There was a cold snap after Christmas.* 圣诞节后出现一段寒冷天气. **3** (also **snapshot**) [C] photograph (usu one taken quickly with a hand-held camera) 照片(通常指用手提照相机拍摄的): *She showed us her holiday snaps.* 她给我们看了她假期的照片. **4** (usu in compounds 通常用以构成复合词) type of small crisp biscuit 小的脆饼干: *ˈginger-snaps* 姜味饼干 ○ *ˈbrandy-snaps* 白兰地酒味饼干. **5 Snap** [U] (*Brit*) card game in which players call out 'Snap' when two similar cards are laid down together 喊'对儿'纸牌游戏(亮出相同两张牌时, 玩牌者竞先喊出'对儿'): *play a game of Snap* 玩喊'对儿'游戏. **6** [sing] (*US infml* 口) thing that is easy to do 轻而易举的事: *This job's a snap.* 这件工作很容易做.

▷ **snap** *adj* [attrib 作定语] (*infml* 口) done, made, etc quickly and with little or no warning 匆忙的; 仓促的: *a snap election* 临时的选举 ○ *take a snap vote* 匆匆表决 ○ *a snap decision* 仓促的决定.

snap *interj* (*Brit infml* 口) **1** (said in the game of Snap[2](5) when one notices that two similar cards have been laid down 玩喊'对儿'纸牌游戏(Snap[2](5))时, 见到相同两张牌时的呼喊声). **2** (said to draw attention to the similarity of two things 见到相同两事物时, 说 snap 以引起注意): *Snap! You've got the same shoes as me.* 嘿! 你的鞋跟我的一模一样.

snap *adv* with a snapping sound 伴有断裂、开或关等声音: *Suddenly the oar went snap*, ie made a snapping sound as it broke. 桨突然啪的一声断了.

snap·pish *adj* inclined to snap[1](3); bad-tempered or irritable 厉声说话的; 脾气暴躁的; 易怒的: *a snappish small terrier* 暴躁的小狗 ○ *a snappish old man* 爱嚷嚷的男人.

snappy *adj* **(-ier, -iest)** **1** inclined to snap[1](3); irritable 厉声说话的; 易怒的: *a snappy little dog* 暴躁的小狗 ○ *She's always snappy early in the morning.* 她总是一大早就嚷嚷. **2** (*infml* 口) lively; quick 活泼的; 利落的: *snappy on her feet* 她的脚步利索 ○ *a snappy dancer* 活泼的跳舞的人. **3** (*infml* 口) [usu attrib 通常作定语] smart; trendy 帅气的; 漂亮的; 时髦的: *a snappy outfit* 漂亮的全套服装 ○ *She's a very snappy dresser*, ie She dresses very smartly and trendily. 她衣着很入时. **4** (idm 习语) **ˌmake it ˈsnappy** (also **ˌlook ˈsnappy**) (*infml* 口) (often as a command 常作命令语) hurry up; be quick about it 赶快; 快点儿: *Look snappy! The bus is coming.* 快点儿! 公共汽车来了. ○ *You'll have to make it snappy if you want to come too.* 你也想来的话就得快点儿. **snap·pily** *adv*: *'Go away,' she said snappily.* '走开,'她厉声地说. **snap·pi·ness** *n* [U].

□ **ˈsnap fastener** (also **ˈpress stud**, *Brit infml* 英式口语作 **popper**) device made of two small round metal

S

or plastic parts that are pressed together to fasten dresses, skirts, etc 子母扣儿; 揿扣儿: *the press stud on the collar of his evening shirt* 他晚礼服衬衫领口上的揿扣儿 ○ *the poppers on a child's pyjamas* 儿童睡衣上的子母扣儿.

'snapshot *n* = SNAP 3.

snap·dragon /'snæpdrægən; `snæp,drægən/ *n* = ANTIRRHINUM.

snap·per /'snæpə(r); `snæpɚ/ *n* type of large fish that lives in warm seas and is eaten as food 啮鱼(产于热带海区的大型食用鱼).

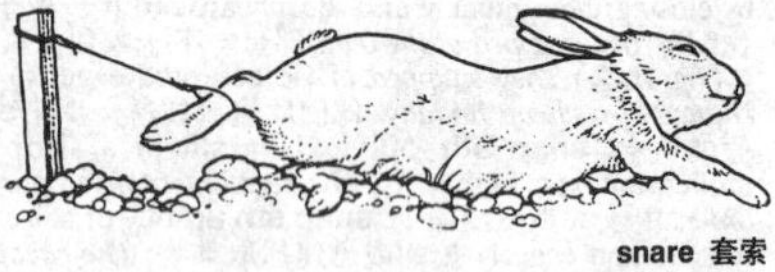

snare 套索

snare /sneə(r); snɛr/ *n* **1** trap for catching small animals and birds, esp one with a noose made of rope or wire 罗网, 陷阱(用于捕捉小野兽及鸟类, 尤指有套索的): *The rabbit's foot was caught in a snare.* 套索把兔子的脚套住了. **2** (*fml* 文) thing likely to trap or injure sb (易使人上当或受害的)圈套: *All his promises were snares and delusions.* 他的许诺都是圈套和骗局. **3** (*music* 音) string of gut stretched underneath a side-drum to produce a sharp rattling sound (绷在小鼓下面的)响弦.

▷ **snare** *v* [Tn] catch (sth) in a snare(1) or as if in a snare (似)用罗网或陷阱捕捉(某物): *snare a rabbit* 设陷阱捕捉兔子 ○ (*fig* 比喻) *snare a rich husband* 设圈套嫁给富人.

snarl[1] /snɑ:l; snɑrl/ *v* **1** [I, Ipr] **~ (at sb/sth)** (of dogs, etc) show the teeth and growl angrily (指狗等)露出牙齿低声怒吠或吼: *The dog snarled at the milkman.* 那条狗对着送牛奶的人低声吠叫. ○ *The tiger snarled frighteningly.* 老虎发出可怕的吼声. **2** [I, Ipr, Tn, Tn·pr] **~ (sth) (at sb)** (of people) speak in an angry bad-tempered voice (指人)咆哮, 厉声喊叫: *'Get out of here,' he snarled (at us).* '滚开,'他(对我们)厉声嚷道. ○ *an unpleasant man who snarled abuse at strangers* 大骂陌生人的讨厌的男子.

▷ **snarl** *n* (usu *sing* 通常作单数) act or sound of snarling 怒吼(声); 咆哮(声): *the sudden snarl of the dog* 那狗突然发出的吠叫声 ○ *answer with an angry snarl* 怒气冲冲地回答.

snarl[2] /snɑ:l; snɑrl/ *n* (*infml* 口) confused state; tangle 混乱; 纠缠: *My knitting was in a terrible snarl.* 我织的东西都乱成一团了.

▷ **snarl** *v* (phr v) **snarl (sth) up** (usu passive 通常用于被动语态) (*infml* 口) (cause sth to) become confused, jammed, tangled, etc (使某物)混乱、阻塞、纠结在一起等: *The machine snarled the material up.* 机器把材料搅在一起了. ○ *Traffic has snarled up the city centre.* 来往车辆把市中心堵得水泄不通. **'snarl-up** *n* (*infml* 口) tangled or jammed state, esp of traffic 拥挤、阻塞的状态(尤指交通): *a big snarl-up on the motorway* 高速公路上严重的交通阻塞.

snatch /snætʃ; snætʃ/ *v* **1** [I, Ipr, Tn, Tn·pr, Tn·p] (try to) seize (sth/sb) quickly and sometimes rudely; grab (设法)迅速地或粗鲁地抓住(某物[某人]); 抢: *It's rude to snatch.* 你争我夺是粗鲁的行为. ○ *She snatched the letter from me/out of my hand.* 她从我这里[从我手中]把信抢走了. ○ *The baby had been snatched from its pram.* 那婴儿被人从婴儿车中劫走了. ○ *He snatched up his gun and fired.* 他迅速拿起枪来射击. **2** [Tn] take or get (sth) quickly, esp when a chance to do so occurs 迅速抓住(某物)(尤指机会): *snatch an hour's sleep* 偷空儿睡一小时觉 ○ *snatch a meal between jobs* 趁工作间歇时吃饭.

▷ (phr v) **snatch at sth 1** try to grasp sth 设法抓住某物: *He snatched at the ball but did not catch it.* 他想抓那个球但没抓住. **2** (*fig* 比喻) grasp sth eagerly and quickly 迫切而迅速地抓住某事物: *snatch at every opportunity* 抓住任何机会.

snatch *n* **1** [sing] sudden attempt to seize (sth) quickly 抓; 抢; 夺: *make a snatch at sth* 抢夺某物. **2** [C esp *pl* 尤作复数] short part or period; brief extract 片刻; 片段: *work in snatches*, ie not continuously 断断续续地工作 ○ *short snatches of song* 歌的片段 ○ *overhear snatches of conversation* 偶尔听到谈话的只言片语.

snatcher *n* (often in compounds 常用以构成复合词) person who snatches (and takes away) 抢夺的人: *a baby snatcher* 抢夺婴儿的人 ○ *a bag snatcher* 抢提包的人.

snazzy /'snæzɪ; `snæzɪ/ *adj* (**-ier**, **-iest**) (*infml* 口) (esp of clothes) smart and stylish (尤指衣物)帅气的, 漂亮的, 时髦的: *a snazzy little hat* 漂亮的小帽子 ○ *a very snazzy new car* 很漂亮的新汽车 ○ *She's a very snazzy dresser*, ie She always dresses fashionably. 她衣着总是很时髦. ▷ **snaz·zily** *adv*: *dress snazzily* 衣着入时. **snaz·zi·ness** *n* [U].

sneak /sni:k; snik/ *v* **1** [I, Ipr] **~ (on sb) (to sb)** (*Brit infml derog* 口, 贬) (used esp by children 尤为儿童用语) tell an adult about the faults, wrongdoings, etc of another child 告状; 打小报告: *She sneaked on her best friend to the teacher.* 她向老师告了她最好的朋友一状. **2** [Tn] (*infml* 口) take (sth) secretly (often without permission) 偷偷地做(某事)或取(某物)(常指未获许可): *sneak a chocolate from the box* 从盒子里偷拿一块巧克力 ○ *sneak a look at the Christmas presents* 朝圣诞礼物偷看一眼. **3** (phr v) **sneak into, out of, past, etc sth; sneak in, out, away, back, past, etc** go quietly and secretly in the direction specified 悄悄地走(向某处); 溜: *He stole the money and sneaked out of the house.* 他偷了钱后从房子里溜了出去. ○ *The cat ate the food and sneaked off.* 猫吃完食物就偷偷跑了. **sneak up (on sb/sth)** approach quietly, staying out of sight until the last moment 悄悄接近然后突然出现: *James loves sneaking up on his sister to frighten her.* 詹姆斯喜欢溜到妹妹身后吓她一大跳. ⇨Usage at PROWL 用法见PROWL.

▷ **sneak** *n* (*infml* 口) cowardly deceitful person (esp one who informs on others) 怯懦而惯于欺骗的人(尤指告密者).

sneak *adj* [attrib 作定语] acting or done without warning; secret and unexpected 出其不意的; 秘密而突如其来的: *a sneak attack* 偷袭 ○ *a sneak preview* 不公开试映 ○ *a sneak look at a letter* 偷看信.

sneak·ers *n* [pl] (*US*; *Brit infml* 口) = PLIMSOLLS: *He wore old jeans and a pair of sneakers.* 他穿着旧牛仔裤和胶底运动鞋.

sneak·ing *adj* [attrib 作定语] (esp of an unwanted feeling) secret and unexpressed (尤指不应有的情感)私下的, 暗地的: *have a sneaking respect, sympathy, etc for sb* 暗地里敬佩、同情…某人 ○ *I have a sneaking* (ie unproved and vague but possibly right) *suspicion that he stole my wallet.* 我心想准是他偷了我的钱包.

sneaky *adj* (**-ier**, **-iest**) (*infml derog* 口, 贬) done or acting in a secret or deceptive way 鬼鬼祟祟的; 偷偷摸摸的: *sneaky behaviour* 鬼鬼祟祟的举动 ○ *This sneaky girl was disliked by the rest of the class.* 全班同学都不喜欢这个鬼头鬼脑的女同学. **sneak·ily** *adv*. **sneaki·ness** *n* [U].

□ **'sneak-thief** *n* person who steals things without using force, eg through open doors and windows 小偷(不使用暴力的, 如经敞着的门窗入室行窃者).

sneer /snɪə(r); snɪr/ *v* [I, Ipr] **~ (at sb/sth)** smile with the upper lip curled, to show contempt (for sb/sth); laugh scornfully 嗤笑(某人[某事物]); 嘲笑; 讥笑: *sneer at one's supposed inferiors* 嘲笑自以为不如自己的人 ○ *I resent the way he sneers at our efforts.* 我们已十分努力而他却讥笑我们, 我很反感. ⇨Usage at SMIRK 用法见SMIRK.

▷ **sneer** *n* look, smile, word, phrase, etc that shows contempt 表示轻蔑的表情、微笑、词语等: *sneers of disbelief* 表示不相信的嘲笑 ○ *You can wipe that sneer off your face!* 你还是收起你讥笑人的嘴脸吧!

sneer·ingly /'snɪərɪŋlɪ; `snɪrɪŋlɪ/ *adv*.

sneeze /sni:z; sniz/ *n* sudden uncontrollable noisy outburst of air through the nose and mouth (usu caused by irritation in the nose from dust, etc or when one has a cold) 喷嚏; 嚏喷: *coughs and sneezes* 咳嗽和喷嚏 ○ *She let out a loud sneeze.* 她打了一个很响的喷嚏.

▷ **sneeze** *v* [I] **1** make a sneeze 打喷嚏: *With all that* *dust about, he couldn't stop sneezing.* 到处都是灰尘，他不停地打着喷嚏. ○ *Use a handkerchief when you sneeze.* 打喷嚏时，要用手帕遮住. **2** (idm 习语) **not to be 'sneezed at** (*infml esp joc* 口，尤作戏谑语) worth considering or having; not to be despised 值得考虑的；不可轻视的: *A prize of £50 is not to be sneezed at.* 50英镑的奖金可不是个小数.

snick /snɪk; snɪk/ *v* [Tn] make a small cut or notch in (sth) 在(某物)上划一道小口子或留下凹痕: *I snicked my finger on the sharp knife.* 那把锋利的刀把我的手指划了道小口子.

▷ **snick** *n* small cut or notch 小切口或凹痕: *a tiny snick in the dress material* 衣料上的一个小口子.

snicker /ˈsnɪkə(r); ˈsnɪkɚ/ *v* laugh in a suppressed, esp unpleasant, way; snigger 暗笑；窃笑: *snickering at obscene pictures* 看着春画偷偷地笑. ⇨Usage at GIGGLE 用法见GIGGLE.

▷ **snicker** *n* suppressed, esp unpleasant, laugh; snigger 暗笑；窃笑.

snide /snaɪd; snaɪd/ *adj* (*derog* 贬) critical in an indirect unpleasant way; sneering 挖苦的；嗤笑的；嘲笑的；讥笑的: *snide remarks about the chairman's wife* 挖苦主席夫人的话 ○ *He's always making snide comments about her appearance.* 他总是对她的外表冷嘲热讽. ▷ **snidely** *adv.* **snide·ness** *n* [U].

sniff /snɪf; snɪf/ *v* **1** [I] draw air in through the nose so that there is a sound 鼻子吸气发出声音: *sniffing and trying not to weep* 抽泣着而忍住不哭出声来 ○ *They all had colds and were sniffing and sneezing.* 他们都感冒了，鼻子吸气有声而且还打喷嚏. **2 (a)** [I, Ipr, Tn] **~ (at) sth** draw air in through the nose as one breathes, esp to discover or enjoy the smell of sth (呼吸时)用鼻吸气(尤指为闻出某气味或因爱闻某气味): *sniff the sea-air* 呼吸海上的空气 ○ *sniff (at) a rose* 闻闻玫瑰花香 ○ *The dog was sniffing (at) the lamp-post.* 那条狗在灯柱旁嗅来嗅去. **(b)** [Tn, Tn·p] **~ sth (up)** draw sth up through the nose 用鼻子吸入某物: *sniff snuff* 吸鼻烟 ○ *He sniffed the vapour up (through his nose).* 他(用鼻子)吸入蒸气. **(c)** [Tn] (*infml* 口) take (a dangerous drug) by breathing it in through the nose 用鼻子吸(毒品): *sniff glue* 吸胶毒. **3** [Tn] say (sth) in a self-pitying, complaining way 自己怜悯自己、抱怨地说(某事): *'Nobody understands me,' he sniffed.* '谁都不理解我,'他埋怨说. **4** (phr v) **sniff at sth** ignore or show contempt for sth 嗤之以鼻: (*infml* 口) *His generous offer is not to be sniffed at,* ie should be considered seriously. 他的慷慨厚意不可嗤之以鼻. **sniff sb out** (*infml* 口) discover sb; find sb out 发现某人；找出某人: *sniff out the culprit* 发现犯人 ○ *The police were determined to sniff out the ringleaders.* 警方决心要找到匪首.

▷ **sniff** *n* act or sound of sniffing; breath (of air, etc) 用鼻孔吸气(声)；呼吸；嗅；闻: *tearful sniffs* 含泪的抽泣 ○ *get a sniff of sea air* 呼吸一下海上的空气 ○ *One sniff of this is enough to kill you.* 此物闻一闻即足以致命. ○ *'I'm going,' she said with a sniff.* '我要走了,'她抽了一下鼻子说.

sniffle /ˈsnɪfl; ˈsnɪfl/ *v* [I] sniff slightly or repeatedly (esp because one is crying or has a cold) 抽鼻子(轻轻地或频频地发出吸气声，尤指因哭泣或感冒): *I wish you wouldn't keep sniffling.* 但愿你别总这么抽鼻子.

▷ **sniffle 1** *n* act or sound of sniffling 抽鼻子(声). **2** (idm 习语) **get/have the 'sniffles** (*infml* 口) get/have a slight cold 患轻感冒.

snif·ter /ˈsnɪftə(r); ˈsnɪftɚ/ *n* **1** (*infml* 口) small amount of an alcoholic drink, esp spirits 少量含酒精饮料(尤指烈酒): *have a quick snifter before the party* 在参加聚会前喝一点烈性酒. **2** glass shaped like a small bowl that narrows at the top (小口大肚矮脚的)酒杯: *a snifter of brandy* 一杯白兰地酒.

snig·ger /ˈsnɪgə(r); ˈsnɪgɚ/ *n* half-suppressed unpleasant laugh (esp at sth improper or at another's misfortune) 窃笑，暗笑(尤指笑某事物不当或他人不幸): *Her shabby appearance drew sniggers from the guests.* 她样子寒酸，客人不禁暗自发笑.

▷ **snig·ger** *v* [I, Ipr] **~ (at sb/sth)** laugh in this way 窃笑；暗笑: *superior people who sniggered at her foreign accent* 暗笑她有外国腔调的那些自以为比她强的人. ⇨ Usage at GIGGLE 用法见GIGGLE.

snip /snɪp; snɪp/ *v* **(-pp-) 1** [Ipr, Tn] **~ (at) sth** cut sth sharply (esp with scissors or shears) in short quick strokes 快速剪某物: *snip (at) a stray lock of hair* 剪一绺散开的头发. **2** (phr v) **snip sth off** remove sth with short quick strokes 快速剪掉某物: *snip off a few loose threads* 剪掉几条散开的线头 ○ *snip the corner off the carton of milk* 剪掉盛牛奶的纸盒的边角.

▷ **snip** *n* **1** cut made by snipping 剪口: *There's a snip in this cloth.* 这块布有一个剪口. **2** small piece cut off by snipping 剪下的小片: *snips of material scattered over the floor* 地板上到处都是从料子上剪下的碎片. **3** act of snipping 剪: *With a few quick snips of the shears he pruned the bush.* 他用大剪刀几下子就把灌木给修剪好了. **4** (*Brit infml* 口) surprisingly cheap article; bargain 极廉价的物品；便宜货: *It's a snip at only 50p!* 才50便士，真便宜!

snip·ping *n* small piece of material, etc snipped off a larger piece 从大块材料上剪下的小块材料: *a patchwork quilt made of snippings from old clothes* 用从旧衣物上剪下的碎料缝成的被子.

snipe[1] /snaɪp; snaɪp/ *n* (*pl* unchanged 复数不变) water-bird with a long straight bill that lives in marshes 沙锥(滨鸟，嘴细长，生活在沼泽区). ⇨illus at App 1 见附录1插图, page v.

snipe[2] /snaɪp; snaɪp/ *v* [I, Ipr] **~ (at sb/sth) 1** shoot from a hiding place (usu from a distance) 伏击，狙击(通常指远距离): *terrorists sniping at soldiers from well-concealed positions* 从十分隐蔽的位置伏击士兵的恐怖分子. **2** (*fig* 比喻) make unpleasant critical remarks attacking sb/sth 抨击某人[某事物]: *sniping at political opponents* 抨击政治对手 ○ *Film stars are often sniped at in the newspapers.* 报纸上经常抨击电影明星.

▷ **sniper** *n* person who snipes 狙击手: *shot by snipers* 遭狙击手伏击.

snip·pet /ˈsnɪpɪt; ˈsnɪpɪt/ *n* **1** small piece cut off 切下的小块或碎片. **2 ~ (of sth)** small piece or item (of information, news, etc); brief extract (消息、新闻等的)片段；简短摘录: *snippets of gossip* 闲言碎语 ○ *I've got a snippet of information that might interest you.* 我刚得到一点消息，是你可能感兴趣的.

snitch /snɪtʃ; snɪtʃ/ *v* (*Brit sl* 俚) **1** [Tn] steal (sth) by taking it quickly 迅速偷走(某物): *'Who's snitched my pen?'* '一转眼，谁把我的笔偷走了?' **2** [I, Ipr] **~ (on sb)** inform on sb; sneak 告发某人；告密: *Promise you won't snitch (on me)?* 答应我，一定不告发我行吗?

snivel /ˈsnɪvl; ˈsnɪvḷ/ *v* (**-ll-**; *US* also **-l-**) (*derog* 贬) [I] **(a)** cry and sniff in a miserable, usu self-pitying, way 伤心地啼哭和抽泣: *a tired snivelling baby* 哭累了的幼儿. **(b)** complain in a miserable whining way 哭诉: *She's always snivelling about her unhappy childhood.* 她总是伤心哭诉自己童年不幸.

▷ **sniv·el·ling** (*US* also **sniv·el·ing**) *adj* [attrib 作定语] (*derog* 贬) tending to whine and complain; weak 爱啼哭抱怨的；软弱的: *He's a snivelling idiot!* 他是个爱哭鼻子的傻瓜!

sniv·el·ler (*US* **sniv·eler**) *n* (*derog* 贬) person who snivels 哭泣的人；哭诉的人.

snob /snɒb; snab/ *n* (*derog* 贬) **(a)** person who pays too much respect to social position and wealth, or who despises people of a lower social position 势利小人: *snobs who despised their working-class son-in-law* 看不起女婿当工人的很势利的人. **(b)** person who feels he has superior tastes, knowledge, etc 自以为高雅、有学问等的人: *an intellectual snob* 自以为有学识的人 ○ *a wine snob who will only drink the best wines* 自命不凡非上等酒不喝的人.

▷ **snob·bery** /ˈsnɒbərɪ; ˈsnabərɪ/ *n* [U] (*derog* 贬) behaviour, language, etc characteristic of a snob 势利的行为、语言等: *They considered her behaviour a shameful piece of snobbery.* 他们认为她为人势利，行为可耻.

snob·bish *adj* (*derog* 贬) of or like a snob (似)势利的或自以为高人一等的: *a snobbish contempt for the poor* 蔑视穷人的势利眼 ○ *a snobbish attitude to pop music* 认为流行音乐不值一听的态度. **snob·bishly** *adv.* **snob·bish·ness** *n* [U].

□ **'snob appeal** (also **'snob value**) qualities that appeal to people's snobbishness 对势利眼或自视甚高的人有吸引力的特质: *This part of the town has a lot of snob appeal.* 该城的这一区很能吸引自视甚高的人. ○ *This car sells well because of its snob value.* 这种汽车很

有派头,因此很畅销.

SNOBOL (also **Snobol**) /ˈsnəʊbɒl; ˈsnobɔl/ *abbr* 缩写 = (*computing* 计) string-oriented symbolic language (a programming language, esp for handling symbols) 面向字符串的符号语言(一种计算机程序设计语言, 尤用于符号处理).

snog /snɒg; snɑg/ *v* **(-gg-)** [I, Ipr] **~ (with sb)** (*Brit infml* 口) kiss and cuddle 亲吻拥抱: *snog in the back row of the cinema* 在影院后排座位上拥抱接吻.

▷ **snog** *n* [sing] (*Brit infml* 口) act of snogging 亲吻拥抱: *have a bit of a snog* 拥抱亲吻一阵.

snog·ging *n* [U] (*Brit infml* 口) action of cuddling and kissing 拥抱亲吻.

snook /snu:k; snuk/ *n* (idm 习语) **cock a snook at sb/sth** ⇨ COCK[3].

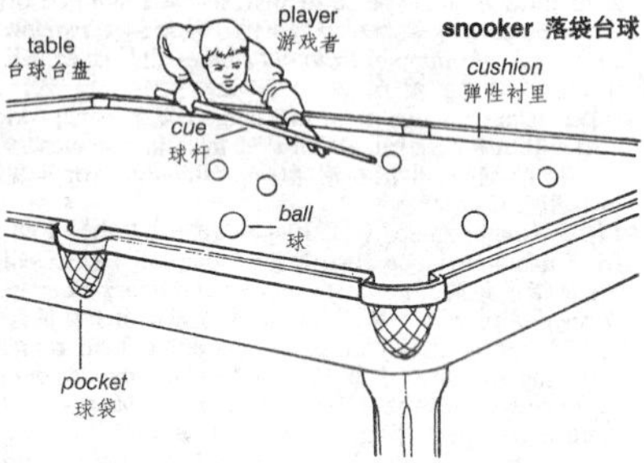

snooker 落袋台球

snooker /ˈsnu:kə(r); ˈsnukɚ/ *n* [U] game played with 15 red balls and 7 balls of other colours on a billiard-table 落袋台球(使用15个红色球和7个其他颜色球的游戏): [attrib 作定语] *a snooker match* 落袋台球比赛. ⇨ illus 见插图. Cf 参看 POOL[2] 4.

▷ **snooker** *v* [Tn esp passive 尤用于被动语态] **1** leave (an opponent) in a difficult position when playing snooker (玩落袋台球游戏时)使(对手)处于困境. **2** (*infml fig* 口, 比喻) place (sb) in a difficult position; trick or defeat (sb) 使(某人)处于困境; 欺骗或击败(某人): *You can't win; you've been completely snookered!* 你怎么做都没用, 你已经完全落入圈套了!

snoop /snu:p; snup/ *v* (*infml usu derog* 口, 通常作贬义) **1** [I, Ipr, Ip] **~ (about/around sth)**; **~ (about/around)** search or investigate (eg to find mistakes, signs that people are breaking rules, etc) in a persistent and secretive way 持续而秘密地寻找或调查(如找出错误、违章现象等): *snooping around at night* 夜晚四处窥探 ○ *snooping about the school entrance looking for late-comers* 在学校入口处窥视迟到的人. **2** [Ipr] **~ into sth** try to find out things that do not concern oneself; pry into 打听闲事.

▷ **snooper** *n* (*usu derog* 通常作贬义) person who snoops 窥探者; 打听闲事的人: *a government snooper* 政府的秘密调查员.

snooty /ˈsnu:tɪ; ˈsnutɪ/ *adj* **(-ier, -iest)** (*infml derog* 口, 贬) showing disapproval and contempt towards others 目中无人的; 妄自尊大的: *a snooty letter refusing the invitation* 一封拒绝邀请措词傲慢的信 ○ *She's so snooty; she never speaks to the neighbours.* 她很傲慢, 从不与邻居说话. ▷ **snoot·ily** /-ɪlɪ; -l̩ɪ/ *adv*. **snooti·ness** *n* [U].

snooze /snu:z; snuz/ *v* [I] (*infml* 口) take a short sleep (esp during the day); doze 小睡(尤指在白天); 打盹: *Dad was snoozing by the fire.* 爸爸正在炉火旁打盹.

▷ **snooze** *n* [sing] (*infml* 口) a short sleep; nap 小睡; 午睡: *I'm going to have a snooze after lunch.* 我午饭后要睡个午觉.

snore /snɔ:(r); snɔr/ *v* [I, Ip] breathe roughly and noisily while sleeping 打鼾; 打呼噜: *snoring noisily with his mouth open* (他)张着嘴大声打鼾 ○ *Does my snoring bother you?* 我打呼噜影响你吗?

▷ **snore** *n* act or sound of snoring 打鼾(声); 打呼噜(声): *Loud snores from the other room kept her awake.* 那边房间有人打鼾声音很大她无法入睡.

snorer /ˈsnɔ:rə(r); ˈsnɔrɚ/ *n* person who snores habitually 经常打鼾的人.

snor·kel /ˈsnɔ:kl; ˈsnɔrkl/ *n* **1** tube that allows a swimmer to take in air while under water 潜水通气管(潜水人用的). **2** device that allows a submarine to take in air while under water (潜水艇的)通气管.

▷ **snor·kel** *v* [I] **(-ll-**; *US* **-l-)** swim with a snorkel 戴潜水通气管潜泳. **snor·kel·ling** (US **-kel·ing**) /ˈsnɔ:kəlɪŋ; ˈsnɔrkəlɪŋ/ *n* [U] action or sport of swimming with a snorkel 戴潜水通气管潜泳(运动).

snort /snɔ:t; snɔrt/ *v* **1** [I] (usu of animals, esp horses) force air out through the nostrils with a loud noise (通常指动物, 尤指马)喷鼻息作声, 打响鼻. **2** [I, Ipr] **~ (at sb/sth)** (of people) do this to show impatience, contempt, disgust, amusement, etc (指人)发哼声(喷鼻息表示不耐烦、蔑视、厌恶、欢娱等): *snort with rage (at sb/sth)* (对某人[某事物])愤怒地哼了一声 ○ *snort with mirth at the suggestion* 对该建议高兴地哼了一声. **3** (*sl* 俚) sniff (drugs) 从鼻孔吸入(毒品): *snort cocaine* 从鼻孔吸入可卡因.

▷ **snort** *n* **1** act or sound of snorting 喷鼻息; 打响鼻; 发哼声; (从鼻孔)吸毒: *give a snort of contempt* 轻蔑地哼了一声 ○ *She could not conceal a snort of laughter.* 她忍不住扑哧一笑. **2** (*infml* 口) small drink of alcohol swallowed in one gulp (供一口喝下的)一小杯酒. **3** (*sl* 俚) small amount of a drug that is sniffed (用鼻孔吸入的)少量毒品: *a quick snort of cocaine* 用鼻孔匆匆吸些可卡因.

snorter *n* (esp *sing* 尤作单数) (*infml* 口) thing that is remarkably impressive, violent, difficult, etc 极感人、激烈、困难...的事物: *She sent me a real snorter of a letter.* 她给我寄来一封异乎寻常的信.

snot /snɒt; snɑt/ *n* [U] (*infml* 口) mucus of the nose 鼻涕: *snot running down the child's nose* 从这孩子的鼻子里流出的鼻涕.

▷ **snotty** *adj* **(-ier, -iest)** (*infml* 口) **1** running with or covered with snot 流着鼻涕的; 沾满鼻涕的: *a child with a snotty nose* 流着鼻涕的小孩 ○ *washing his snotty handkerchiefs* 洗着他的满是鼻涕的手帕. **2** (also **ˌsnotty-ˈnosed**) (*derog* 贬) superior; snooty 高傲的; 目中无人的: *He's such a ˌsnotty-nosed little ˈwimp.* 他是个高傲而懦弱的人.

snout /snaʊt; snaut/ *n* **1** [C] projecting nose and mouth of an animal (esp a pig) 动物突出的口鼻部(尤指猪的): *a sow with her snout in a trough of food* 用鼻子拱饲料槽中食物的大母猪. ⇨illus at App 1 见附录1插图, page iii. ⇨illus at PIG 见 PIG 插图. **2** [C] projecting front part of sth thought to resemble a snout 猪鼻状突出物: *the ugly snout of a revolver* 左轮手枪难看的枪管. **3** [C] (*Brit sl derog* 俚, 贬) person's nose (人的)鼻子: *a huge red snout* 大红鼻子 ○ *She's always poking her snout into everything*, ie interfering. 她总爱多管闲事. **4** [C] (*Brit sl* 俚) police informer 向警方告密者. **5** [U] (*Brit sl* 俚) tobacco 烟草; 烟叶: *Got any snout?* 有烟叶吗?

snow[1] /snəʊ; sno/ *n* **1** [U] frozen water vapour that falls to the ground from the sky in soft white flakes; mass of such flakes on the ground, etc 雪; 雪花; 雪片; 积雪: *a heavy fall of snow* 下大雪 ○ *roads deep in snow* 积雪很深的道路 ○ *Children were playing in the snow.* 孩子们在雪中玩耍. **2** [C usu *pl* 通常作复数] (*fml* 文) fall of snow 下雪; 降雪: *The snows came early that year.* 那年雪下得很早. **3** [U] (*sl* 俚) powdered cocaine (粉状的)可卡因. **4** (idm 习语) **pure as the driven snow** ⇨ PURE. **white as snow** ⇨ WHITE[1].

□ **ˈsnowball** *n* mass of snow pressed into a hard ball for throwing in play 雪球: *children throwing snowballs at each other* 打雪仗的儿童. — *v* [I] **1** throw snowballs 掷雪球; 打雪仗: *children snowballing in the park* 在公园打雪仗的儿童. **2** (*fig* 比喻) grow quickly in size, importance, etc (体积、重要性等)(像滚雪球般)迅速增大: *Opposition to the war snowballed.* 反战情绪急速增长.

ˈsnow-blind *adj* [usu pred 通常作表语] (temporarily) unable to see because the eyes are dazzled by the glare of the sun on snow 雪盲(眼睛受雪地反射的阳光刺激而暂时失明). **ˈsnow-blindness** *n* [U]: *skiers suffering from snow-blindness* 患雪盲的滑雪人.

ˈsnow-blower *n* (*esp US*) machine for blowing snow from roads, pathways, etc 吹雪机(用鼓风法清除路面积雪的机器).

ˈsnow-bound *adj* unable to travel, go out, etc because

of heavy falls of snow 受大雪困住的; 被大雪封闭的: *a snow-bound train* 被大雪阻住的火车 ○ *We were snow-bound in the cottage for two weeks.* 我们让大雪困在村舍里两个星期.

'snow-capped *adj* (*rhet* 修辞) (of mountains, etc) with the peak covered in snow (指山等)顶部有积雪的.

'snow-covered (also *rhet* 修辞 **'snow-clad**) *adj* covered with snow 被雪覆盖的: *snow-covered roofs* 有雪的屋顶 ○ *snow-clad fir trees* 有积雪的枞树.

'snow-drift *n* deep bank of snow heaped up by the wind (风刮成的)雪堆: *The train ran into a snow-drift.* 火车碰上了雪堆.

'snowdrop *n* type of small white flower growing from a bulb at the end of winter or early spring 雪花莲(冬末或初春时开小白花). ⇨illus at App 1 见附录1插图, page ii.

'snowfall *n* **1** [C] fall of snow on one occasion (一次的)降雪: *There was a heavy snowfall last week.* 上星期下了一场大雪. **2** [U] amount of snow that falls in a period of time (eg one winter or one year) in a certain place 某地一段时期(如一冬或一年)的降雪量: *The average snowfall here is 10cm a year.* 这里年平均降雪量为10 厘米.

'snow-field *n* permanent wide expanse of snow, eg on high mountains 雪原(终年积雪的大片地区, 如高山上).

'snowflake *n* any one of the soft small collections of ice crystals that fall as snow 雪花; 雪片: *snowflakes melting as they reached the ground* 落地融化的雪花.

'snow-goose *n* large white goose with black wing tips that lives in arctic areas 雪雁(体羽纯白, 翅尖黑色, 产于北极).

'snow job (*infml* 口 *esp US*) attempt at deception or persuasion by elaborate, often insincere, talk 花言巧语的欺骗或劝说: *They're claiming that he's not guilty but that's just a snow job.* 他们声称他无罪, 那只不过是遮人耳目而已.

'snow-leopard *n* type of large wild cat of the mountainous areas of central Asia, with pale brown or grey fur and black markings 雪豹(产于亚洲中部山区, 毛呈浅褐色或灰色, 有黑色斑纹).

'snow-line *n* level (in feet or metres) above which snow lies permanently at any one place 雪线(终年积雪的下界线, 用英尺或公尺丈量): *climb above the snow-line* 攀越雪线.

'snowman /-mæn; -ˌmæn/ *n* (*pl* **-men** /-men; -mɛn/) figure of a man made of snow, esp by children for fun 雪人(尤指儿童用雪堆成的).

'snow-plough (*US* **'snow-plow**) *n* device or vehicle for clearing snow from roads, railways, etc 雪犁, 除雪机(用以清除公路、铁路等的积雪的).

'snow-shed *n* (*esp US*) shelter with a long roof over a stretch of road or railway to prevent it being blocked by falling or sliding snow 防雪棚(防止因降雪或雪崩堵塞公路或铁路的建筑).

'snow-shoe *n* device with a frame and leather straps, attached to the bottom of a shoe to allow a person to walk on deep snow without sinking in 雪鞋(以革条穿在木框上制成, 装在鞋底上, 可在深雪处行走).

'snowstorm *n* heavy fall of snow, esp with a strong wind 暴风雪; 雪暴.

ˌsnow-'white *adj* pure bright white in colour 雪白的; 纯白色的: *ˌsnow-white 'shirts* 雪白的衬衫.

snow[2] /snəʊ; sno/ *v* **1** [I] (used with *it* 与 it 连用) come down from the sky as snow 下雪; 降雪: *It snowed all day.* 下了一整天雪. ○ *It was snowing when I woke up.* 我醒来时正在下雪. **2** [Tn] (*US infml* 口) attempt to deceive or persuade (sb) by elaborate but often insincere talk 用花言巧语欺骗或说服(某人). **3** (phr v) **snow sb in/up** (usu passive 通常用于被动语态) prevent sb from going out by snowing heavily 被大雪困住(不能外出): *We were snowed in for three days last winter by the blizzards.* 去年冬天, 一场暴风雪把我们困在家里三天没出门. **snow sb under (with sth)** (usu passive 通常用于被动语态) overwhelm sb 使某人不胜负荷: *I was snowed under with work.* 我工作忙得不可开交. ○ *snowed under with applications for the job* 求职申请书多得接应不暇.

▷ **snowy** *adj* (**-ier, -iest**) **1** covered with snow 被雪覆盖的: *snowy roofs* 有雪的屋顶. **2** with snow falling 下雪的: *snowy weather* 下雪的天气. **3** as white or fresh as newly fallen snow (像刚下的雪那样)洁白清新的: *a snowy (white) tablecloth* 洁白的桌布.

Snr *abbr* 缩写 = SEN 3.

snub[1] /snʌb; snʌb/ *v* (**-bb-**) [Tn esp passive 尤用于被动语态] treat (sb) coldly, rudely or with contempt, esp by paying no attention (to him) 冷落, 怠慢, (尤指)不理睬(某人): *She was repeatedly snubbed by her neighbours.* 她多次遭到邻居的冷遇. ○ *She snubbed them by not replying to their invitation.* 她没答复他们的邀请藉此冷落他们.

▷ **snub** *n* snubbing words or behaviour 冷落、怠慢的言辞或行为: *suffer a snub* 受到冷遇 ○ *hurt by the snubs of the other children* 受其他儿童冷落而伤心.

snub[2] /snʌb; snʌb/ *adj* (of a nose) short and turned up slightly at the end (指鼻子)短而略微上翘的.

□ **'snub-nosed** *adj*: *a snub-nosed little dog* 翘鼻小狗.

snuff[1] /snʌf; snʌf/ *n* [U] powdered tobacco taken into the nose by sniffing 鼻烟(粉末状烟叶, 用鼻孔吸入): *take a pinch of snuff* 吸一捏鼻烟.

□ **'snuff-box** *n* small, usu decorative, box for holding snuff 鼻烟盒(通常为有装饰的): *She collects snuff-boxes.* 她收集鼻烟盒.

snuff[2] /snʌf; snʌf/ *v* **1** [Tn] cut or pinch off the burnt black end of the wick of (a candle) 剪(蜡烛)的心. **2** (idm 习语) **'snuff it** (*Brit sl joc* 俚, 谑) die 吹灯, 吹灯拔蜡(死亡): *His dad snuffed it a couple of years ago.* 他爸爸两年前就吹灯了. **3** (phr v) **snuff sth out** (**a**) put out (a candle flame, etc); extinguish sth 熄灭(烛光等); 扑灭某事物. (**b**) put an end to sth; finish sth 消灭或结束某事物: *His hopes were nearly snuffed out.* 他的希望几乎破灭了.

snuffle /'snʌfl; 'snʌfl̩/ *v* [I, Ip] (**a**) make sniffing noises 用鼻子吸气发出声音; 抽鼻子: *The dog was snuffling around the roots of a tree.* 那条狗在树根处嗅来嗅去. (**b**) breathe noisily (as when the nose is partly blocked with catarrh) 呼吸发出声音(如因黏膜发炎): *a child snuffling with a bad cold* 因患重感冒鼻子呼呼有声的小孩.

▷ **snuffle** *n* act or sound of snuffling 抽鼻子(声); (鼻腔受阻的)呼吸(声): *speak in/with a snuffle*, ie with a blocked nose 抽着鼻子说话.

snug /snʌg; snʌg/ *adj* (**-gg-**) **1** sheltered from cold, wind, etc; warm and comfortable; cosy 不受风寒侵袭的; 温暖而舒适的: *a snug little house* 温暖舒适的房子 ○ *snug in bed* 在床上舒舒服服 ○ *The children are wrapped up snug by the fire.* 孩子们穿得暖暖和和的围在炉火旁. **2** (of clothes) fitting (too) tightly or closely (指衣服)(过于)贴身的, 紧身的: *a snug-fitting coat* 紧而合身的大衣 ○ *This jacket's a bit snug now.* 这件外衣有点瘦了. **3** (*infml* 口) enough to be comfortable 够舒适的: *a snug little income* 足够过舒适生活的收入. **4** (idm 习语) **(as) snug as a bug in a rug** (*joc infml* 谑, 口) very snug and cosy 非常舒适; 十分安逸.

▷ **snug** *n* (*Brit*) small warm room, esp in a pub, with seats for only a few people (只有少数座位的)温暖的小房间(尤指酒店的).

snugly *adv* **1** warmly and comfortably 温暖而舒适地: *They were curled up snugly in bed.* 他们舒适地在床上蜷着. **2** tidily and tightly 整齐而紧密地: *He fitted the map snugly into the bag.* 他把地图整齐地塞进包里.

snug·ness *n* [U].

snuggle /'snʌgl; 'snʌgl/ *v* [I, Ip] **~ (up to sb); ~ (up/down)** lie or get close (to sb) for warmth, comfort or affection 依偎, 挨近(某人)或蜷缩着以获得温暖、舒适或疼爱: *The child snuggled up to her mother.* 那孩子紧贴在母亲身边. ○ *They snuggled up (together) in bed.* 他们依偎着躺在床上. ○ *She snuggled down in bed.* 她蜷缩着躺在床上.

so[1] /səʊ; so/ *adv* (used before *adjs* and *advs* 用于形容词与副词之前) **1** to such an extent 到这种程度; 这么; 那么: *Last time I saw him he was so fat!* 我上次见到他时, 他那么胖! ○ *Don't look so angry* (ie as angry as you appear now)! 别这么生气! **2 not ~ + *adj/adv* (+ as ...)** not to the same extent (as) 不(像)...这么...; 不(像)...那么...: *It wasn't so bad as last time!* 这次不像上次那么坏! ○ *It didn't take so long as we expected.* 时间没像我们预料的那么久. ○ *I haven't enjoyed myself so much for a long time.* 我很长时间没有这么高兴过了.

3 ~ + *adj*/*adv* + (that) ... (indicating the result 表示结果): *He was so ill that we had to send for a doctor.* 他病得很重, 我们只好给他请医生了. ○ *She was so angry (that) she couldn't speak.* 她气得说不出话来. **4 ~ + *adj*/*adv* + as to do sth** to the extent that one does sth 到做某事的程度: *She was so kind as to phone for a taxi for me.* 她很热心, 为我打电话叫了计程车. ○ *How could you be so stupid as to believe him?* 你怎么这么笨竟相信他的话? ○ *Would you be so good as to lock the door when you leave?* 你离开时请把门锁上行吗? **5 ~ + *adj* + a/an + *n* (+ as sb/sth)** (used in making comparisons 用于做比较): *He was not so quick a learner as his brother.* 他没他弟弟学得快. ○ *He's not so good a player as his wife.* 他没他妻子演奏得好. ○ *Is this so unusual a case* (ie more unusual than most)? 这种情况那么不寻常吗? **6** very; extremely 很; 极: *I'm so glad to see you.* 见到你非常高兴. ○ *It was 'so kind of you to remember my birthday.* 你还记得我的生日, 十分感谢. ○ *We have 'so much to do.* 我们有很多事要做. ○ *She's feeling so much better today.* 她今天身体好多了. **7** (idm 习语) **not so much sth as sth** not one thing but rather sth else 不是...而是...: *She's not so much poor as careless with money.* 她倒不是穷而是太不在乎钱了. **so many/much** an unspecified number or amount 多少(表示不定的数量): *A recipe tells you that you need so many eggs, so much milk, etc.* 这个食谱上说需要多少鸡蛋、多少牛奶等等. ○ *Write on the form that you stayed so many nights at so much per night.* 把你住了几个晚上、每晚多少钱, 填在这个表上. **ˌso much 'sth** a great deal of (nonsense, etc) 大量的(废话等): *His promises were just so much meaningless talk.* 他许诺的都是空话. **ˌso much for 'sb/'sth** nothing further need be said or done about sb/sth 关于某人[某事物]要说的或要做的只有这些: *So much for our hopes of going abroad — we can forget it.* 我们出国的希望告一段落——不必再提了. **ˌso much 'so that** (/ðət; ðət/) to such an extent that 到这种程度以致: *We are very busy — so much so that we can't manage to take a holiday this year.* 我们很忙——忙得今年都没办法度假了. **with not/without so much as sth** with not even sth 甚至连某事物都没有: *Off he went, without so much as a 'goodbye'.* 他走了, 甚至连'再见'都没说.

so² /səʊ; so/ *adv* **1** in this or that way; thus 这样; 那样; 就这样: *Stand with your arms out, so.* 两臂伸开站着, 就这样. ○ *So it was that he had his first sight of snow.* 就那样, 他第一次见到了雪. **2** (used to avoid repetition, esp after *believe*, *hope*, *suppose*, *tell*, *say*, *do* 用以避免重复, 尤用于believe、hope、suppose、tell、say、do之后): *'Is he coming?' 'I believe so.'* '他来吗?' '我想他能来.' ○ *I'm not sure if I'll succeed, but I certainly hope so.* 我不知道我能不能成功, 当然我希望能成功了. ○ *'He's got the job?' 'So she said.'* '他得到那份工作了?' '她是这么说的.' ○ *They think she may try to phone. If so, someone must stay here.* 他们认为她可能来电话.要是这样的话, 就得有人守在这儿. **3** (used to express agreement 用以表示同意): *'You were invited to that party, weren't you?' 'So I was, I'd forgotten.'* '已经邀请你参加那个聚会了, 是吧?' '可不是吗, 我都忘了.' ○ *'They won the championship five years ago.' 'So they did.'* '他们五年前获得过冠军.' '可不是吗.' ○ *'There's a bird nesting in the garage.' 'So there is.'* '有只鸟正在车库里搭窝.' '可真是.' **4** also 也: *He is divorced and so am I.* 他离了婚, 我也离了婚. ○ *'I've been to Moscow.' 'So have I.'* '我去过莫斯科.' '我也去过.' **5** (idm 习语) **and 'so on (and 'so forth)** (used to show that a list or sequence continues in a similar way 用以表示列举未尽): *He talked about how much we owed to our parents, our duty to our country and so on and so forth.* 他谈到我们受到父母多少恩惠、我们对国家应尽的义务等等. **so as to do sth** with the intention of doing sth 为了做某事: *I left a message so as to be sure of contacting her.* 我留下了张条子以便与她取得联系. ○ *He disconnected the phone so as not to be disturbed.* 他为了不受打扰, 把电话线路关掉了. **so 'be it** (indicating an acceptance of events, facts, etc 表示对某情况、事情等认可、同意等): *If he doesn't want to be involved, then so be it.* 要是他不想参与这件事, 就随他便吧. **so that; so...that (a)** with the aim that; in order that 为的是; 以便: *She worked hard so that everything would be ready by 6 o'clock.* 她拼命干以便能到6点时把一切都准备好. ○ *He has so organized his life that his wife suspects nothing.* 他把生活安排得井井有条, 为的是不让妻子有任何怀疑. **(b)** with the result that; to the extent that 结果; 以致; 因此: *Nothing more was heard from him so that we began to wonder if he was dead.* 再也没听到他的消息, 因此我们有些怀疑他是否死了. ○ *He so adores his daughters that he keeps buying them expensive toys.* 他非常疼爱女儿, 经常给她们买贵重的玩具.

□ **'so-and-so** *n* (*pl* **so-and-so's**) (*infml* 口) **(a)** imaginary or unknown person; some person or other 某某; 某人: *Let's suppose a Mr So-and-so registers at the hotel.* 咱们打个比方吧, 有个某某先生来旅馆登记. **(b)** (*derog* 贬) person who is disliked 讨厌的人: *Some so-and-so has pinched my towel.* 谁那么讨厌把我的毛巾拿走了. ○ *Our neighbour's a bad-tempered old so-and-so.* 我们的邻居是个脾气很坏的傢伙.

ˌso-'called *adj* [usu attrib 通常作定语] (*often derog* 常作贬义) (used to suggest that the words used to describe sb/sth are not appropriate 用以指对描述某人[某事物]的词语含不承认意): *Where are your ˌso-called 'friends now?* 你那些所谓的朋友现在都到哪儿去了? ○ *Our ˌso-called 'villa by the sea was a small bungalow two miles from the coast.* 我们的所谓海滨别墅是离海岸两英里的一座小平房. ○ *This is the patio, so-called — it's really just the back yard.* 这就是所谓的院子——其实只是后院.

so³ /səʊ; so/ *conj* **1** (indicating result 表示结果) and that is why 因此; 所以: *The shops were closed so I didn't get any milk.* 商店都关门了, 所以我没买到牛奶. ○ *The manager was ill so I went in his place.* 经理病了, 所以我替他. ○ *These glasses are very expensive so please be careful with them.* 这些玻璃杯十分昂贵, 因此请小心些. **2** (*infml* 口) (indicating purpose 表示目的): *I gave you a map so you wouldn't get lost.* 我给你一张地图, 这样你就不会迷路了. ○ *She whispered to me so no one else would hear.* 她低声跟我说话以免别人听见. **3** (used to introduce the next part of the story 用以引出下文): *So now it's winter again and I'm still unemployed.* 瞧, 冬天又到了, 我还没找到工作呢. ○ *So after shouting and screaming for an hour she walked out in tears.* 就这样, 她连喊带叫一个钟头, 含着眼泪走出去了. **4** (used to introduce a statement on which one wishes to comment in a critical or contrasting way 用以引出一段话进行批评或对比): *So I've been in prison for three years. That doesn't mean I can't do a job.* 不错, 我是坐了三年牢. 这并不等于说我就不能工作了. ○ *So you've come back. What's your story this time?* 好哇, 你回来了. 这次你打算怎么说? **5** (idm 习语) **so what?** (*infml* 口) I admit this may be true but I am not concerned 我承认此事即使属实, 我也不在乎: *He's fifteen years younger than me. So ˌwhat if he 'is?* 他比我小十五岁. 即使如此, 又有什么了不起?

so⁴ = soh.

So *abbr* 缩写 = (*US*) South(ern).

soak /səʊk; sok/ *v* **1 (a)** [I, Ipr] **~ (in sth)** become thoroughly wet by being in liquid or by absorbing liquid 浸; 泡; 湿透: *The dirty clothes are soaking in soapy water.* 脏衣服都在肥皂水里泡着呢. ○ *Leave the dried beans to soak overnight.* 把这些干豆子泡一夜. **(b)** [Tn, Tn·pr] **~ sth (in sth)** cause sth to absorb as much liquid as possible 使某物尽量吸收液体; 使浸透: *soak bread in milk* 把面包泡在牛奶里 ○ *He soaked his stained shirt in hot water.* 他把脏衬衫浸在热水里了. ○ (*fig* 比喻) *He soaked himself in* (ie allowed himself to absorb) *the atmosphere of the place.* 他尽情沉浸在这种环境的气氛之中. **2** [Ipr, Ip] **~ into/through sth; ~ in** enter (and pass through) sth; penetrate 进入(并穿过)某物; 渗透: *The rain had soaked through his coat.* 雨把他的大衣淋透了. ○ *Clean up that wine before it soaks in(to the carpet).* 趁那酒还没渗进(地毯里)去, 快把它擦干净. **3** [Tn] (*infml* 口) extract money from (sb) by charging or taxing very heavily 向(某人)榨取金钱或征收重税: *Are you in favour of soaking the rich?* 你赞成向富人多征税吗? **4** (idm 习语) **soaked/wet to the skin** ⇨ SKIN. **5** (phr v) **soak sth off/out** remove sth by soaking in water 浸泡以除去某物: *soak out a stain from a shirt* 浸掉衬衫上的污迹 ○ *Soak a label off a jam jar.* 把果酱罐上的标签泡下去. **soak sb through** make a person and his clothes completely wet 使某人全身湿透: *Don't stand out there: you'll get soaked through.* 你别站在外边, 要不全身都要湿透了. **soak sth up** (**a**) take in (liquid); absorb sth 吸入(液体); 吸收某物: *Use a paper towel to soak up the cooking oil.* 用纸巾把食油吸干. (**b**) receive and absorb sth 接受并吸收某事物: *soaking up the sunshine* 晒太阳 ○ *soaking up the atmosphere of the Spanish villages* 沉浸在西班牙乡村的空气中 ○ *That child soaks up new facts like a sponge!* 那孩子吸收新知识像海绵似的!

▷ **soak** (also **soak·ing**) *n* **1** act of soaking 浸; 泡; 湿透: *Give the sheets a good soak.* 把床单好好泡一泡. **2** (*infml* 口) habitual drinker; alcoholic 酒徒; 酒鬼: *He's a dreadful old soak.* 他可真是大酒鬼.

soaked /səʊkt; sokt/ *adj* [pred 作表语] **1** completely wet 湿透: *You're soaked!* 你全都湿透了! **2 ~ in sth** (*fig* 比喻) full of sth; steeped in sth 充满某事物; 沉浸于某事物之中: *This house is soaked in memories.* 这所房子经历了许多可纪念的事情.

soak·ing /ˈsəʊkɪŋ; sokɪŋ/ *adj* (also ˌ**soaking ˈwet**) very wet 极湿的: *a soaking wet coat* 很湿的大衣.

soap /səʊp; sop/ *n* [U] **1** substance used for washing and cleaning, made of fat or oil combined with an alkali 肥皂: *a bar of soap* 一条肥皂 ○ *There's no soap in the bathroom!* 浴室里没有肥皂! ○ *Use plenty of soap and water.* 多用些肥皂和水. **2** [C] (*infml* 口) = SOAP OPERA: *Do you watch any of the soaps on TV?* 你看电视连续剧吗?

▷ **soap** *v* [Tn, Tn·p] apply soap to (sb/sth); rub with soap 将肥皂涂在(某人[某物])上; 用肥皂擦: *soap oneself down* 在身上打些肥皂 ○ *soap the car and then rinse it* 先在汽车上抹些肥皂再清洗.

soapy *adj* (**-ier, -iest**) **1** (**a**) of or like soap (似)肥皂的: *This bread has a soapy taste.* 这面包有肥皂味. (**b**) full of soap 有肥皂的: *soapy water* 肥皂水. **2** (*infml derog* 口, 贬) too anxious to please; ingratiating 很想讨好的; 谄媚的: *a soapy voice, manner, style* 很想讨好人的语调、态度、作风. **soapiness** *n* [U].

□ ˈ**soap-box** *n* improvised stand for a speaker (in a street, park, etc) (街头、公园等处的)临时讲演台: [attrib 作定语] *soap-box oratory* 街头演说 ○ (*fig* 比喻) *He gets on his soap-box at the first opportunity*, ie He is always ready to talk at length. 他一有机会就长篇大论讲个没完.

ˈ**soap-bubble** *n* ball of air surrounded by a film of soap that changes colour and bursts easily 肥皂泡: *children blowing soap-bubbles* 吹肥皂泡的儿童.

ˈ**soap-flakes** *n* [pl] thin flakes of soap, sold in a packet and used for washing clothes, etc 皂片: *use soap-flakes rather than a powder detergent* 用皂片而不用洗涤粉.

ˈ**soap opera** (also **soap**) (*sometimes derog* 有时作贬义) radio or TV serial drama dealing with the events and problems of the characters' daily lives, often in a sentimental way (电台或电视)连续剧: *a TV diet of soap opera* 冗长而乏味的电视连续剧.

ˈ**soap powder** powder made from soap and additives, used for washing clothes 肥皂粉.

ˈ**soapstone** *n* [U] type of soft stone that feels like soap, used for making ornaments, etc 皂石(一种质软岩石, 具有肥皂感, 用以制造装饰品等): [attrib 作定语] *a soapstone statue* 皂石雕像.

ˈ**soapsuds** *n* [pl] frothy lather of soap and water 肥皂泡沫: *He was up to his elbows in soapsuds, washing his shirts.* 他洗衬衫时, 连胳膊肘都弄上了肥皂泡沫.

soar /sɔː(r); sɔr/ *v* [I, Ipr] **1** (**a**) go up high in the air quickly 急速升入高空: *The jet soared into the air.* 那架喷气式飞机飞上了天空. ○ (*fig* 比喻) *Prices are soaring*, ie rising rapidly. 物价飞涨. ○ (*fig* 比喻) *soaring temperatures*, ie rapidly getting very hot 迅速增高的温度. (**b**) be very high or tall 高耸; 矗立: *cliffs soaring above the sea* 矗立在海上的峭壁 ○ *Skyscrapers soar above the horizon.* 摩天大楼拔地而起高耸入云. **2** hover in the air without moving the wings or using the engine; glide 翱翔; 滑翔: *seagulls soaring over the cliffs* 翱翔于悬崖峭壁之上的海鸥 ○ *a glider soaring above us* 从我们头顶飞过的滑翔机.

sob /sɒb; sɑb/ *v* (**-bb-**) **1** [I, Ipr] draw in breath noisily and irregularly from sorrow, pain, etc, esp while crying 啜泣; 抽噎: *We could hear the child sobbing in the other room.* 我们听到那间屋子里的小孩在抽抽搭搭地哭着. ○ *She sobbed into her handkerchief.* 她用手绢掩面啜泣. ⇨Usage at CRY[1] 用法见 CRY[1]. **2** (idm 习语) **cry/sob oneself to sleep** ⇨ SLEEP[1]. **sob one's ˈheart out** cry bitterly with great emotion 哭得极伤心. **3** (phr v) **sob sth out** tell sth while sobbing 抽噎地说; 哭诉: *She sobbed out the story of her son's violent death.* 她哭着诉说儿子横死的经过.

▷ **sob** *n* act or sound of sobbing 啜泣(声); 抽噎(声): *The child's sobs gradually died down.* 那孩子的啜泣声渐渐静了下来.

sob·bingly *adv*.

□ ˈ**sob-story** *n* (*infml usu derog* 口, 通常作贬义) story intended to arouse sympathy or sadness in the listener or reader 伤感的故事: *He told me a real sob-story of how his wife had gone off with his best friend.* 他告诉我他的妻子与他最好的朋友私奔这件伤心事.

ˈ**sob-stuff** *n* [U] (*infml often derog* 口, 常作贬义) sentimental writing or talking intended to arouse sympathy and sadness 伤感的文章; 伤心话: *The idea of all that sob-stuff was to get me to lend her money.* 她说那番伤心话的意思是为了让我借给她钱.

sober /ˈsəʊbə(r); ˈsobɚ/ *adj* **1** with one's actions and thoughts not affected by alcohol 未醉的: *Does he ever go to bed sober?* 他有过不醉着就寝的时候吗? ○ *He drinks a lot but always seems sober.* 他喝酒喝得很多但好像总是很清醒. **2** serious and thoughtful; solemn 认真的; 审慎的; 郑重的: *a very sober and hard-working young man* 认真而勤奋的年轻人 ○ *make a sober estimate of what is possible* 审慎地估计可能发生的情况 ○ *a sober analysis of the facts* 对事实的仔细分析 ○ *in sober truth*, ie in fact, contrasted with what is imagined or hoped for 在客观事实上(与想像的或希望出现的情况相对). **3** (of colour) not bright; dull (指颜色)不鲜艳的, 暗淡的: *a sober grey suit* 一套暗灰色的西服. **4** (idm 习语) **(as) sober as a judge** (**a**) not at all drunk 一点都不醉的. (**b**) very serious and solemn 极认真郑重的.

▷ **sober** *v* **1** [I, Tn] (cause sb to) become serious and thoughtful (使某人)认真而审慎: *The bad news had a sobering effect on all of us.* 对我们大家来说, 这个坏消息是发人深省的. **2** (phr v) **sober (sb) down** (cause sb to) become calm and serious (esp after a period of irresponsible or frivolous behaviour) (使某人)冷静而严肃认真(尤指有马大哈之类举动之后): *Please sober down a bit; I've got some important news for you.* 请严肃点, 我有重要消息要告诉你们. **sober (sb) up** (cause sb to) become sober (使某人)醒酒或清醒: *Put him to bed until he sobers up.* 把他放到床上去等他醒醒酒. ○ *Give her some black coffee — that'll help to sober her up.* 给她一些清咖啡 —— 让她清醒清醒.

soberly *adv*: *soberly dressed* 穿得很素淡.

□ ˌ**sober-ˈminded** *adj* serious and thoughtful 认真而审慎的.

sob·ri·ety /səˈbraɪətɪ; səˈbraɪətɪ/ *n* [U] quality or state of being sober(2) 认真; 审慎; 郑重: *a conscientious man noted for his sobriety* 以认真审慎著称的男子.

Soc *abbr* 缩写 = **1** Socialist. **2** Society: *Amateur Drama Soc* 业余剧团.

soc·cer /ˈsɒkə(r); ˈsɑkɚ/ *n* [U] (in Britain now used mainly in newspapers and on radio and TV; in US the usual word 在英国现主要用于报纸、电台与电视广播上; 在美国则为常用词) = ASSOCIATION FOOTBALL (ASSOCIATION): [attrib 作定语] *measures to curb soccer violence* 防止足球赛引起的暴力事件的措施 ○ *soccer hooligans*, ie football supporters who cause trouble before, after or during a match 足球迷小流氓.

so·ci·able /ˈsəʊʃəbl; ˈsoʃəbl/ *adj* fond of the company of other people; friendly 好交际的; 友好的; 合群的: *He has never really been the sociable type.* 他从不好交际. ○ *I'm not in a sociable mood.* 我没兴致与人交往. ▷ **so·ci·ab·il·ity** /ˌsəʊʃəˈbɪlətɪ; ˌsoʃəˈbɪlətɪ/ *n* [U]. **so·ci·ably** /-əblɪ; -əblɪ/ *adv*.

so·cial /ˈsəʊʃl; ˈsoʃəl/ *adj* **1** [esp attrib 尤作定语] concerning the organization of and relations between people and communities 社会的: *social problems* 社会问题 ○ *social customs, welfare, reforms* 社会习俗、福利、改革. **2** [attrib 作定语] of or in society; of or concerning rank and position within society 社会上的; 社会阶层的; 社会地位的: *one's social equals*, ie people of the same class as oneself in society 与自己社会地位相同的人 ○

S

social advancement, ie improvement of one's position in society 社会地位的提高 ○ (*derog* 贬) *a social climber*, ie sb who constantly strives to improve his social position 在社会地位上向上爬的人. **3** [attrib 作定语] (of animals, etc) living in groups, not separately (指动物等)群居的: *Most bees and wasps are social insects.* 大多数蜜蜂和黄蜂都是群居昆虫. ○ *Man is a social animal.* 人是群居的动物. **4** of or designed for companionship and recreation 社交的; 交谊的; 联谊的; 联欢的: *a social club* 联谊会 ○ *a social evening* 联欢晚会 ○ *a busy social life* 繁忙的社交生活. **5** sociable 好交际的; 友好的; 合群的: (*infml* 口) *He's not a very social person.* 他不很合群.

▷ **so·cial** (*US* also **so·ci·able** /ˈsəʊʃəbl; ˈsoʃəbl̩/) *n* informal meeting or party organized by a group or club 社交聚会; 联欢会: *a church social* 教友联谊会.

so·ci·ally /-ʃəlɪ; -ʃəlɪ/ *adv*: *I know him through work, but not socially.* 我是通过工作而不是在社交中认识他的.

□ **the ˌSocial and ˌLiberal ˈDemocrats** (*abbr* 缩写 **SLD**) former name of the British political party (now called 现称 **the Liberal Democrats**) formed in 1988 from the merging of the Social Democratic Party and the Liberal Party 社会自由民主党(英国政党, 由社会民主党与自由党于1988年合并成立).

ˌsocial ˈscience (also **ˌsocial ˈstudies**) group of subjects concerned with people within society and including economics, sociology, politics and geography 社会科学: *Social anthropology is one of the social sciences.* 社会人类学是社会科学的一门学科.

ˌsocial seˈcurity (*Brit*) (*US* **welfare**) government payments to people who are unemployed, ill, disabled, etc 社会福利: *Most of the families in our road are on social security*, ie receiving such help. 我们这条街多数家庭都享受社会福利.

ˌsocial ˈservices [pl] organized government service providing help and advice (eg in matters of health, housing, mental illness, child care, the law, etc) 社会福利事业(政府提供的援助, 如解决健康、房屋、精神疾患、幼儿看护、法律等方面的问题): *threatened cuts in social services* 提出可能要削减社会福利经费.

ˈsocial work profession of people who work in the social services 社会福利工作: *She wants to do social work when she finishes college.* 她打算毕业后从事社会福利工作. **ˈsocial worker** person who works in the social services 社会福利工作者: *Social workers claimed the children were being ill-treated.* 社会福利工作人员指出那些儿童正受到虐待. ○ *social workers visiting people just out of hospital* 正在访问刚出院康复病人的社会福利工作人员.

so·cial·ism /ˈsəʊʃəlɪzəm; ˈsoʃəlˌɪzəm/ *n* [U] (**a**) political and economic theory advocating that a country's land, transport, natural resources and chief industries should be owned and controlled by the whole community or by the State, and that wealth should be equally distributed 社会主义. (**b**) policy or practice based on this theory 社会主义的方针、政策或实践: *the struggle to build socialism* 建设社会主义的斗争 ○ *the best features of socialism* 社会主义最优秀的特点. Cf 参看 CAPITALISM.

▷ **so·cial·ist** /ˈsəʊʃəlɪst; ˈsoʃəlɪst/ (**a**) supporter of socialism 拥护社会主义的人; 社会主义者. (**b**) member of a socialist party or movement 社会主义政党党员; 社会主义运动的成员. — *adj* characterized by, supporting or relating to socialism 社会主义的; 拥护社会主义的; 有关社会主义的: *a Socialist Party* 社会党 ○ *socialist policies* 社会主义的政策.

so·cial·istic /ˌsəʊʃəˈlɪstɪk; ˌsoʃəˈlɪstɪk/ *adj* characterized by or supporting some of the features of socialism 有社会主义特点的; 拥护社会主义主张的: *Some of her views are rather socialistic.* 她的观点颇有一些社会主义倾向.

so·cial·ite /ˈsəʊʃəlaɪt; ˈsoʃəˌlaɪt/ *n* (*sometimes derog* 有时作贬义) person who is prominent in fashionable society, attending many parties, etc 上流社会的名人; 社会名流: *rich socialites moving from one fashionable resort to another* 常光顾高级游乐处所的有钱的社会名流.

so·cial·ize, -ise /ˈsəʊʃəlaɪz; ˈsoʃəˌlaɪz/ *v* **1** [I, Ipr] ~ **(with sb)** mix socially (with others) (同他人)来往, 交往, 交际: *an opportunity to socialize with new colleagues* 跟新同事交往的机会. **2** [Tn] adapt (sb) to society 使(某人)适应社会生活: *recent immigrants to the country who are not fully socialized* 尚未完全适应该国社会生活的新移民. ▷ **so·cial·iza·tion, -isation** /ˌsəʊʃəlaɪˈzeɪʃn; *US* -lɪˈz-; ˌsoʃəlɪˈzeʃən/ *n* [U].

so·ci·ety /səˈsaɪətɪ; səˈsaɪətɪ/ *n* **1** [U] system whereby people live together in organized communities; social way of living 社会; 社会体制; 群居: *a danger to society*, ie a person, an idea, etc that endangers the welfare of members of a community 社会的祸害 ○ *Society has a right to see law-breakers punished.* 社会有权要违法者受到惩罚. **2** [C, U] particular grouping of humanity with shared customs, laws, etc (具有共同的习俗、法律等的人群组成的)社会, 团体: *modern industrial societies* 现代工业社会 ○ *working class society* 工人阶级的社会团体 ○ *Islamic society* 伊斯兰教团体. **3** [U] (*fml* 文) company; companionship 相伴; 陪同; 交往: *spend an evening in the society of one's friends* 跟朋友聚会过一个晚上 ○ *avoid the society of other people* 避免与他人交往. **4** [U] class of people who are fashionable, wealthy, influential or of high rank in a place; the upper class 名人圈子; 上层社会: *high society*, ie rich and important people 富贵阶层 ○ *leaders of society* 上流社会的顶尖人物 ○ [attrib 作定语] *a society wedding* 名人嘉礼 ○ *society news*, ie as printed in some newspaper, etc 名流新闻. **5** [C] organization of people formed for a particular purpose; club; association (为某种目的组成的)会, 社, 团体, 协会: *the school debating society* 学校辩论协会 ○ *a co-operative society* 合作社 ○ *a drama society* 戏剧社. **6** (idm 习语) **the alternative society** ⇨ ALTERNATIVE. **a mutual admiration society** ⇨ MUTUAL.

socio- *comb form* 构词成分 of society; social 社会的: *sociology*.

so·ci·ology /ˌsəʊsɪˈɒlədʒɪ; ˌsosɪˈɑlədʒɪ/ *n* [U] scientific study of the nature and development of society and social behaviour 社会学: [attrib 作定语] *a sociology course* 社会学课程. Cf 参看 ANTHROPOLOGY, ETHNOLOGY.

▷ **so·ci·olo·gical** /ˌsəʊsɪəˈlɒdʒɪkl; ˌsosɪəˈlɑdʒɪkl̩/ *adj* of or concerning sociology 社会学的; 关于社会学的: *sociological theories, issues* 社会学的理论、问题.

so·ci·olo·gically /-klɪ; -klɪ/ *adv*.

so·ci·olo·gist /-dʒɪst; -dʒɪst/ *n* student of or expert in sociology 社会学研究者; 社会学家.

sock[1] /sɒk; sɑk/ *n* **1** short stocking (usu of wool, nylon or cotton) covering the ankle and lower part of the leg, usu well below the knee 短袜: *a pair of socks* 一双短袜. **2** (idm 习语) **pull one's ˈsocks up** (*Brit infml* 口) (make an effort to) improve one's performance (努力)改进自己的表现或成绩: *His teachers told him to pull his socks up, or he'd undoubtedly fail his exam.* 老师要他加把劲儿, 不然考试准不及格. **put a ˈsock in it** (*dated Brit infml* 旧, 口) be quiet; stop talking or making a noise 安静下来; 不再讲话; 不再弄出响声: *Can't you put a sock in it? I'm trying to work.* 别出声了好不好? 我要工作呢.

sock[2] /sɒk; sɑk/ *n* (*infml* 口) strong blow, esp one given with the fist 重击(尤指用拳): *Give him a sock on the jaw!* 给他下巴上来一拳!

▷ **sock** *v* **1** [Tn, Tn·pr] (*infml* 口) give (sb) such a blow 狠揍(某人)(尤指用拳): *Sock him on the jaw!* 揍他的下巴! **2** (idm 习语) **sock it to sb** (*dated infml* 旧, 口) attack sb forcefully; express oneself forcefully 猛力攻击某人; 有力地表达意见: *The speaker really socked it to them!* 发言的人给他们个迎头痛击!

socket 插座

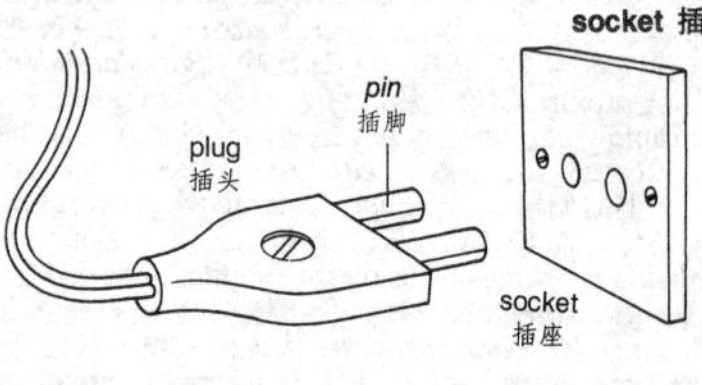

socket /ˈsɒkɪt; ˈsɑkɪt/ *n* natural or artificial hollow into which sth fits or in which sth turns (天然的或人造的)承物凹座, 窝(用以容纳某物或某物可在其中转动); 插口;

插座: *the eye socket*, ie the hollow in a human or an animal skull for the eye 眼窝 ○ *a socket for an electric light bulb* 电灯泡插座. ⇨ illus 见插图.

sod[1] /sɒd; sɑd/ *n* (*fml or rhet* 文或修辞) (**a**) [U] layer of earth with grass growing in it 草地. (**b**) [C] square or piece of this cut off; turf 草皮: *sods newly placed on a grave* 坟上新植的草皮.

sod[2] /sɒd; sɑd/ *n* (⚠ *Brit sl* 讳, 俚) **1** (**a**) (used as a term of abuse, showing annoyance and sudden anger) person, esp a man (咒骂语)人(尤指男性): *You stupid sod!* 你这个蠢蛋! ○ *The new boss is a mean sod!* 新来的上司是个大坏蛋! (**b**) (used as a term of pity or sympathy 用以表达怜悯或同情) person, esp a man 傢伙(尤指男性): *The poor old sod got the sack yesterday.* 那个可怜的傢伙昨天给辞退了. **2** thing that is difficult or causes problems 困难的或惹麻烦的事物: *What a sod this job is proving to be!* 这事儿可真棘手哇!

▷ **sod** *v* (**-dd-**) (⚠ *Brit sl* 讳, 俚) **1** (idm 习语) **sod (it)!** damn (it)! 该死! **2** (phr v) **sod off** (esp imperative 尤用于祈使句) go away 滚开.

sod·ding *adj* [attrib 作定语] (⚠ *Brit sl* 讳, 俚) (used in anger and annoyance to give emphasis 于发怒、烦恼时用以加强语气): *What a sodding mess!* 真他妈的乱七八糟! ○ *It's all your sodding fault!* 都他妈的怪你!

soda /ˈsəʊdə; ˋsodə/ *n* **1** [U] chemical substance in common use, a compound of sodium 苏打; 碳酸钠: *ˈwashing-soda*, ie sodium carbonate, used for softening water, etc 洗涤碱(用以使水软化等) ○ *ˈbaking soda/biˌcarbonate of ˈsoda*, ie sodium bicarbonate, used in cooking 小苏打 ○ *caustic soda*, ie sodium hydroxide, used in the manufacture of soap 苛性苏打(俗称烧碱, 用于制皂业). **2** [U, C] = SODA-WATER: *Add some soda to the whisky, please.* 请在威士忌中加点苏打水. ○ *A whisky and soda, please.* 请来杯搀苏打水的威士忌. **3** [U, C] (also **soda pop**) (*US infml* 口) fizzy drink made with flavoured soda-water (加调味剂的)苏打汽水: *a glass of cherry soda* 一杯樱桃苏打汽水 ○ *two lime sodas* 两杯酸橙苏打汽水. **4** (also ˌ**ice-cream** ˈ**soda**) (*US*) drink made from ice-cream, syrup and soda-water 冰激凌苏打冷饮: *three strawberry sodas* 三客草莓冰激凌苏打水.

□ ˈ**soda-fountain** *n* device for supplying soda-water; counter in a shop from which fizzy drinks, ice-cream sodas, etc are served 汽水龙头(供应汽水的装置); 冷饮部.

ˈ**soda siphon** = SIPHON.

ˈ**soda-water** *n* [U, C] water made fizzy by being filled with carbon dioxide under pressure 苏打水; 汽水: *I won't have any wine; I'll just have (a) soda water.* 我不喝酒, 给我来杯汽水吧.

sod·den /ˈsɒdn; ˋsɑdn̩/ *adj* **1** soaked through; very wet 浸透的; 湿透的: *My shoes are sodden from walking in the rain.* 我在雨里这么一跑, 鞋全湿了. **2** (in compounds 用以构成复合词): *drink-sodden*, ie stupid through drinking too much alcohol 因酗酒而痴呆的.

so·dium /ˈsəʊdɪəm; ˋsodɪəm/ *n* [U] chemical element, a silver-white metal that comes naturally only in compounds 钠. ⇨App 10 见附录10.

□ ˌ**sodium biˈcarbonate** (also **biˌcarbonate of ˈsoda**, ˈ**baking soda**) (also *infml* 口语作 **bicarb** /ˈbaɪkɑːb; ˋbaɪˌkɑrb/) white soluble compound in the form of crystals, used in fizzy drinks, baking-powder and medicines 碳酸氢钠; 小苏打.

ˌ**sodium ˈcarbonate** (also ˈ**washing soda**) white soluble compound in the form of crystals, used in making glass, soap and paper, and to soften water 碳酸钠.

ˌ**sodium ˈchloride** common table salt 氯化钠; 食盐.

ˌ**sodium hyˈdroxide** (also ˌ**caustic ˈsoda**) white corrosive solid used in making paper, aluminium and soap 氢氧化钠; 烧碱.

sod·omy /ˈsɒdəmɪ; ˋsɑdəmɪ/ *n* [U] anal sexual intercourse between a man and (esp) another man 鸡奸(尤指男性间的).

▷ **sod·om·ite** /ˈsɒdəmaɪt; ˋsɑdəmˌaɪt/ *n* (*dated fml* 旧, 文) person practising this 鸡奸者.

sofa /ˈsəʊfə; ˋsofə/ *n* large comfortable padded seat with raised arms and back, wide enough for two or more people 长沙发(可至少坐二人的): *He was lying on the sofa watching TV.* 他躺在沙发上看电视. ○ *The sofa converts into a bed.* 这张沙发可以改成床. ⇨illus at App 1 见附录1插图, page xvi.

soft /sɒft; *US* sɔːft; sɔft/ *adj* (**-er, -est**) **1** changing shape easily when pressed; not hard or firm to the touch 软的; 柔软的: *soft soil, ground, mud, etc* 软土、软土地面、软泥 ○ *Warm butter is soft.* 温的黄油是软的. ○ *She likes a soft pillow and a hard mattress.* 她喜欢软枕头、硬床垫. Cf 参看 HARD[1]. **2** (of surfaces) smooth and delicate to the touch (指物体的表面)光滑柔软的, 细腻的, 柔嫩的: *as soft as velvet* 像丝绒一般柔滑的 ○ *soft skin* 细嫩的皮肤 ○ *soft furnishings*, ie curtains, hangings, rugs, etc 软家具(帘幕、悬挂式陈设、小地毯等) ○ *Our cat has very soft fur.* 我们那只猫的毛非常柔滑. **3** [usu attrib 通常作定语] (of light, colours, etc) not bright or glaring (指光线、色彩等)柔和的, 不耀眼的: *a soft pink rather than a harsh red* 柔和的粉红色而不是刺眼的大红色 ○ *lampshades that give a soft light* 使光线柔和的灯罩 ○ *the soft glow of candlelight* 蜡烛发出的柔光. **4** (of outlines) not sharp or clear; indistinct (指轮廓)不清晰的, 模糊的. **5** (of winds, etc) mild and gentle (指风等)温和的, 微的, 细的: *soft summer winds* 夏日的轻风 ○ *a soft sea breeze* 温和的海风. **6** (of sounds) quiet and subdued; not loud (指声音)轻柔的; 低声的: *soft music* 轻柔的乐曲 ○ *in a soft voice* 轻声地 ○ *soft whispers* 低声细语. **7** (*infml* 口) (of words, answers, etc) not harsh or angry; gentle; mild (指言语、回答等)温和的, 柔和的, 不刺耳的: *His reply was soft and calm.* 他回答得平和从容. **8** **~ (on sth/with sb)** sympathetic and kind, sometimes to too great an extent (有时过分)有同情心的, 心肠软的: *have a soft heart* 有一副软心肠 ○ *That teacher is too soft with his class; they're out of his control.* 那位教师对学生太软了, 他们都不听他的. **9** (*infml derog* 口, 贬) weak and childish; lacking in determination, courage, etc 软弱娇气的; 不果断的; 缺乏勇气的: *Don't be so soft — there's nothing to be afraid of.* 别这么窝囊, 没什么可怕的嘛. **10** (*infml derog* 口, 贬) foolish or silly; mad 傻的; 蠢的; 疯狂的: *He's gone soft in the head.* 他傻头傻脑的. **11** **~ on/about sb** (*infml* 口) feeling attraction for sb; in love with sb 倾心于某人; 爱上某人. **12** (*infml derog* 口, 贬) not requiring hard work; without problems 不费力的; 不困难的; 轻松的: *a soft job*, ie an easy, well-paid job 轻松而待遇优厚的工作 ○ *He has a very soft life really.* 他日子过得实在是很悠闲. **13** (of consonants) not hard; not plosive (指辅音)软的, 不爆发的; (指辅音字母)发软音的: *C is soft in 'city' and hard in 'cat'.* c 字母在city一字中发软音而在cat一字中发硬音. ○ *G is soft in 'gin' and hard in 'get'.* g 字母在gin一字中发软音而在get一字中发硬音. **14** (of drink) not alcoholic (指饮料)软的(不含酒精的): *Would you like some wine or something soft?* 你是喝葡萄酒呢, 还是来点儿软饮料呢? ○ *I'd prefer a soft drink.* 我喜欢喝软饮料. **15** (of water) free from mineral salts and therefore good for washing (指水)软性的(不含矿盐, 适合洗涤用的): *Don't use much soap powder — the water here is very soft.* 肥皂粉别用得太多, 这儿的水很软. **16** (idm 习语) **an easy/a soft touch** ⇨ TOUCH[2]. **the hard/soft sell** ⇨ SELL *n*. **have a soft ˈspot for sb/sth** (*infml* 口) be specially fond of sb/sth 偏爱某人[某事物]: *I've always had a real soft spot for him.* 我一向对他挺有好感.

▷ **soft·ish** *adj* rather soft 相当软的: *softish ice-cream* 软软的冰激凌.

softly *adv* in a soft way 柔软地; 轻柔地; 柔和地: *speak softly* 轻声地说话 ○ *She pressed his hand softly.* 她轻轻捏了捏他的手. ○ *softly shining lights* 光线柔和的灯 ○ *music softly played* 轻轻奏出的乐曲 ○ *treating the children too softly* 过分惯着孩子.

soft·ness *n* [U].

softy (also **softie**) /ˈsɒftɪ; *US* ˈsɔːftɪ; ˋsɔftɪ/ *n* (*infml* 口) (**a**) (*derog* 贬) physically weak person 身体虚弱的人: *'You're a bunch of softies!' the sergeant shouted to the new recruits.* '你们这帮东西, 弱不禁风!'中士对新兵嚷道. (**b**) kind-hearted or (too) sentimental person 好心人; 过分心软的人: *He's a real softie at heart.* 他真是个好心人.

□ ˈ**softball** (*esp US*) game similar to baseball played on a smaller field with a larger soft ball 垒球(与棒球相似, 但球场较小, 球较大而软).

ˌ**soft-ˈboiled** *adj* (of eggs) boiled for a short time so that the yolk is still soft (指蛋)煮得半熟的, 煮成溏心儿的.

S

ˌ**soft 'currency** currency that is not convertible into gold or into certain other currencies which are more in demand 软通货; 软货币.

'**soft drug** drug not likely to cause addiction (eg marijuana) and less dangerous than a hard drug such as heroin 软性毒品(不易使人上瘾且危害性不及海洛因之类的硬性毒品者, 如大麻).

'**soft fruit** small fruits without stones, such as strawberries and currants 无核小果(如草莓、加仑子).

ˌ**soft-'hearted** *adj* sympathetic and kind, sometimes to too great an extent 有同情心的, 心肠软的(有时过分): *He's always lending her money; he's too soft-hearted.* 他老是把钱借给她, 心肠也太软了. ˌ**soft-'heartedness** *n* [U].

ˌ**soft 'landing** landing of a spacecraft (eg on the moon) that avoids damage or destruction 软着陆(航天器着陆而不受损, 如着陆于月球时).

ˌ**soft 'option** (*often derog* 常作贬义) alternative which is thought to involve less work, inconvenience, etc 避重就轻的选择: *Language courses are wrongly thought to be soft options.* 人们误以为选修语言课程较轻松.

ˌ**soft 'palate** back part of the roof of the mouth 软腭.

ˌ**soft-'pedal** *v* (**-ll-**; *US* **-l-**) [I, Tn] (*infml* 口) make (an issue, etc) seem less serious or important; play (sth) down 减弱(问题等)的严重性或重要性; 使(某事物)大事化小: *The government has been soft-pedalling (on) the question of teachers' pay.* 政府一直低调处理教师的工资问题.

ˌ**soft 'porn** pornography of a less explicit or violent type 软性色情作品(不太露骨的). Cf 参看 HARD PORN (HARD).

ˌ**soft 'shoulder** (also **verge**) soft edge at the side of a road that is not suitable for vehicles to drive on (不适宜车辆行驶的)软质路肩.

S

ˌ**soft 'soap** **1** semi-liquid soap 半液体皂; 软肥皂. **2** (*fig* 比喻) persuasion by flattery (用奉承话的)劝诱; 灌米汤的做法: *I'm tired of his soft soap!* 他老是说好话想打动我, 我都听腻了! ˌ**soft-'soap** *v* [Tn] (*infml* 口) persuade (sb) by flattery 以甜言蜜语打动(某人); 向(某人)灌米汤: *Don't try to soft-soap me; I'm not changing my mind.* 别给我灌米汤了, 反正我不改主意.

ˌ**soft-'spoken** *adj* having a gentle quiet voice 细声细气的: *a* ˌ*soft-spoken young 'woman* 说话斯文的年轻女子.

'**software** *n* [U] (*computing* 计) data, programmes, etc not forming part of a computer but used when operating it 软件. Cf 参看 HARDWARE (HARD[1]).

'**softwood** *n* [C, U] wood from coniferous trees such as pine that is cheap to produce and can be cut easily 软木料, 软材(成本低、易于切割的针叶木材, 如松木). Cf 参看 HARDWOOD (HARD[1]).

soften /'sɒfn; *US* 'sɔ:fn; ˋsɔfən/ *v* [I, Tn] **1** (cause sth to) become soft or softer (使某事物)软化, 变温和, 变柔和, 变软弱: *The butter will soften out of the fridge.* 黄油从冰箱中取出会变软. ○ *The lampshade will soften the light.* 这个灯罩能使光线柔和一些. **2** (phr v) **soften sb up** (**a**) weaken (an enemy's position) by shelling or bombing it heavily 用火力削弱(敌方阵地). (**b**) (*infml* 口) make sb unable or less able to resist an attack or persuasion to buy sth, etc 瓦解或削弱某人的抗拒力(以便进攻或劝其购买某物等): *Housewives were softened up with free gifts before the salesmen began the hard talking.* 推销员先用赠品打动家庭妇女的心, 接着就开始直截了当的兜售了.

▷ **softener** *n* [U, C] chemical substance used for softening hard water; device using this 硬水软化剂; 硬水软化器.

soggy /'sɒgɪ; ˋsɑgɪ/ *adj* (**-ier**, **-iest**) **1** very wet; heavy with water 湿透的: *The ground was soggy after heavy rain.* 下了一场大雨, 地面很湿. **2** (*usu derog* 通常作贬义) moist and unpleasantly heavy 潮湿而沉重的: *soggy bread* 潮乎乎的面包. ▷ **sog·gily** /-ɪlɪ; -ɪlɪ/ *adv*. **soggi·ness** *n* [U].

soh /səʊ; so/ (also **so**, **sol** /sɒl; sɑl/) *n* the fifth note in the musical octave 八度音阶中的第五音.

soigné /'swɑ:njeɪ; *US* swɑ:'njeɪ; ˌswɑˋnje/ *adj* (*fem* 阴性作 **soignée**) [usu pred 通常作表语] (*French* 法) (of a person's way of dressing, etc) carefully and fashionably arranged; elegant (指衣着等)考究入时, 高雅.

soil /sɔɪl; sɔɪl/ *n* [C, U] **1** upper layer of earth in which plants, trees, etc grow; ground 土壤; 泥土; 土地; 地面: *good, poor, sandy, etc soil* 良土、瘠土、沙土 ○ *heavy soil* 难耕的土地 ○ *clay soil* 黏土 ○ (*rhet* 修辞) *a man of the soil*, ie one who works on the land 庄稼人. ⇨Usage at EARTH 用法见 EARTH. **2** (*fml* 文) country; territory 国家; 国土; 领土: *one's native soil* 祖国 ○ *born on British soil* 在英国出生.

▷ **soil** *v* [I, Tn] (*fml* 文) (cause sth to) become dirty (使某物)变脏: *This material soils easily.* 这种料子不禁脏. ○ *a basket for soiled sheets*, ie used ones that are waiting to be washed 盛放待洗被单的篮子 ○ *He refused to soil his hands*, ie refused to do dirty work. 他不愿把手弄脏(即拒绝干脏活).

soirée /'swɑ:reɪ; *US* swɑ:'reɪ; swɑˋre/ *n* (*fml* 文) social gathering in the evening, esp for music, conversation, etc and often to help the aims of a club, society, etc 社交晚会(尤指可欣赏音乐者, 常用以推动某俱乐部、协会等的运作).

so·journ /'sɒdʒən; *US* səʊ'dʒɜ:rn; soˋdʒɝn/ *v* [I] (*fml* 文) stay (with sb) in a place for a time 在某处(某人家中)暂住: *He sojourned with a friend in Wales for two weeks.* 他在威尔士一个朋友那儿住了两个星期.

▷ **so·journ** *n* (*fml* 文) temporary stay (in a place) (在某处的)临时逗留, 小住: *a sojourn of two or three weeks in the mountains* 在山里为时两三个星期的小住.

sol = SOH.

sol·ace /'sɒlɪs; ˋsɑlɪs/ *n* [C, U] (*fml* 文) (thing that gives) comfort or relief (from pain, trouble, distress, etc) 安慰; 慰藉; 给予安慰的事物: *The sick man found solace in music.* 那男病人从音乐中获得了安慰. ○ *His work has been a real solace to him.* 他从工作中得到莫大的慰藉.

▷ **sol·ace** *v* [Tn, Tn·pr] **~ sb (with sth)** (*fml* 文) give solace to sb 安慰某人: *She was distracted with grief and refused to be solaced.* 她悲痛得精神恍惚, 怎么安慰也没用.

solar /'səʊlə(r); ˋsolɚ/ *adj* [attrib 作定语] **1** of, concerning or related to the sun 太阳的; 关于太阳的; 与太阳相关的: *solar energy* 太阳能 ○ *solar time* 太阳时. **2** using the sun's energy 利用太阳能的: *solar heating* 太阳能加热 ○ *solar-powered* 以太阳能为动力的.

□ **solar 'cell** device (as used in satellites) that converts the energy of sunlight into electric energy 太阳能电池.

solar 'plexus /'pleksəs; ˋplɛksəs/ *n* (**a**) system of nerves at the back of the stomach 腹腔丛. (**b**) (*infml* 口) stomach area below the ribs 上腹部; 胸口; 心口: *a painful punch in the solar plexus* 对心口击出的让对方叫痛的一拳.

the 'solar system the sun and the planets which move around it 太阳系.

the solar year the time it takes the earth to go round the sun once, approximately $365\frac{1}{4}$ days 太阳年(地球绕太阳旋转一周所需的时间, 约$365\frac{1}{4}$天).

sol·ar·ium /səʊ'leərɪəm; so'lɛrɪəm/ *n* (*pl* **~s** or, in formal or scientific use, **solaria** /səʊ'leərɪə; so'lɛrɪə/ 复数作 **solariums**, 作庄重语或科技用语时复数作 **solaria**) **1** place enclosed with glass, where sunlight can be enjoyed or used in treating patients 日光浴室; 日光治疗室. **2** bed equipped with special lights used for giving sb an artificial sun-tan or in treating certain medical conditions 日光浴床(设有特殊灯光, 用以晒黑皮肤或治疗某些疾病): *The new sports centre has saunas and solariums.* 新建的运动中心设有蒸汽浴室及日光浴床.

sold *pt, pp* of SELL.

sol·der /'sɒldə(r); *US* 'sɒdər; ˋsɑdɚ/ *n* [U] soft mixture of metals used, when melted, for joining harder metals, wires, etc together 焊料; 焊锡.

▷ **sol·der** *v* [Tn, Tn·pr, Tn·p] **~ sth (on/onto/to sth); ~ sth (up/on)** join or mend sth with solder 用焊料连接或修补某物; 焊接某物: *He soldered the wire back on.* 他把金属丝重新焊了上去. '**soldering-iron** *n* tool used, when heated, to solder things together (焊接用的)烙铁.

sol·dier /'səʊldʒə(r); ˋsoldʒɚ/ *n* **1** member (usu male) of an army, esp one who is not an officer 军人(通常指男性); (尤指)士兵: *two soldiers, a sailor and a civilian* 两名士兵、一名水手和一个平民 ○ *The children were playing at soldiers.* 孩子们玩着当军人的游戏. **2** (idm 习语) **a** ˌ**soldier of 'fortune** (*dated* 旧) person who will serve any country or person who will hire him as a soldier; mercenary 雇佣兵(可受雇为任何国家或个人作战的).

▷ **sol·dier** *v* (phr v) **soldier 'on** continue bravely with one's work, etc despite difficulties (不畏困难)勇往直前地工作等: *The walkers soldiered on although the weather was terrible.* 尽管天气恶劣, 但竞走运动员还是勇敢地继续前行. **sol·dier·ing** *n* [U] the life of a soldier 军人生活; 戎马生涯: *enjoy soldiering* 喜欢部队生活 ○ *peace-time soldiering* 和平时期的从军生活.

sol·dierly (also **soldier-like**) *adj* like a soldier; with the qualities of a soldier 像军人的; 有军人品质的: *a tall, soldierly man* 英武的大汉 ○ *a soldierly bearing* 军人的风度.

sol·diery /'səʊldʒərɪ; 'soldʒərɪ/ *n* [pl *v*] (*dated fml* 旧, 文) soldiers (of a specified, usu bad, type) as a class or group 军人, 当兵的(总称)(指某类型的, 通常指坏的): *the undisciplined soldiery* 纪律涣散的军队 ○ *brutal soldiery* 兽兵.

sole[1] /səʊl; sol/ *n* (*pl* unchanged or **~s** 复数或不变或作 **soles**) [C, U] flat sea-fish that is eaten as food 鳎; 鳎目鱼: *sole cooked in white sauce* 奶油沙司鳎目鱼 ○ *Would you like some more sole?* 再来点鳎目鱼好吗?

sole[2] /səʊl; sol/ *n* **1** bottom surface of the human foot, the part on which one walks and stands 脚掌. ⇨illus at FOOT 见 FOOT 插图. **2** part of a sock, shoe, etc covering this (usu not including the heel) 袜子、鞋等的底部(通常不包括后跟); 袜底; 鞋底: *holes in the soles of his socks* 他袜子底部的洞 ○ *leather soles* 皮制的鞋底 ○ *The soles of his boots needed repairing.* 他那双靴子的底该补了. ⇨illus at SHOE 见 SHOE 插图.

▷ **sole** *v* [Tn usu passive 通常用于被动语态] put a sole on (a shoe, etc) 给(鞋等)上底: *have a pair of shoes soled and heeled* 给一双鞋换底及打后掌.

-soled (forming compound *adjs* 用以构成复合形容词) with soles of the specified kind 有某类型的脚掌、袜底或鞋底的: *rubber-soled boots.*

sole[3] /səʊl; sol/ *adj* [attrib 作定语] **1** one and only; single 唯一的; 单独的: *the sole cause of the accident* 事故的唯一原因 ○ *the sole survivor of the crash* 那次车祸的唯一幸存者. **2** belonging to or restricted to one person or group; not shared 属于或限于一人或一组人的; 专有的; 独用的: *have sole responsibility* 单独负责 ○ *We have the sole right to sell this range of goods.* 我们有独家经销这类货物的权利.

▷ **solely** /'səʊllɪ; 'sollɪ/ *adv* alone; only 唯一地; 单独地; 只; 仅: *solely responsible* 单独负责的 ○ *solely because of you* 仅仅由于你的缘故.

sol·ecism /'sɒlɪsɪzəm; 'sɑlə,sɪzəm/ *n* (*fml* 文) **1** mistake in the use of language, esp one that shows sb to be foreign or of low social class 语言错误, 语病(尤指显示某人为外国人或社会阶层低下的). **2** offence against good manners or etiquette 失礼.

sol·emn /'sɒləm; 'sɑləm/ *adj* **1** not happy or smiling; looking very serious 不愉快的; 无笑容的; 表情严肃的: *solemn faces* 严肃的面孔 ○ *look as solemn as a judge* 像法官一样板着脸. **2** done, said, etc in a serious and committed way, after deep thought 庄重的; 郑重的; 深思熟虑的: *a solemn promise, undertaking, pledge, etc* 郑重的许诺、保证、誓言等. **3** performed with religious or other ceremony; formal 隆重的; 正式的; 庄严的: *a solemn funeral procession* 肃穆的送葬行列. ▷ **sol·emnly** *adv*: *'I have some distressing news for you,' he began solemnly.* '有件伤心事要告诉你,'他郑重其事地说道. **sol·emn·ness** *n* [U].

sol·em·nity /sə'lemnətɪ; sə'lɛmnətɪ/ *n* (*fml* 文) **1** [U] state or quality of being solemn; seriousness 庄严; 严肃: *the solemnity of the occasion, moment, procession* 那个场合、时刻、行列的庄严肃穆. **2** [U, C esp *pl* 作不可数名词或可数名词, 后者尤作复数] solemn ceremony 郑重的仪式; 典礼: *The Queen was crowned with all solemnity/with all the proper solemnities.* 女王在隆重之至的典礼中加冕.

sol·em·nize, -ise /'sɒləmnaɪz; 'sɑləm,naɪz/ *v* [Tn] (*fml* 文) perform (a religious ceremony, esp a wedding) 举行(宗教仪式, 尤指婚礼): *solemnize a marriage in church* 在教堂举行婚礼.

▷ **sol·em·niza·tion, -isation** /ˌsɒləmnaɪ'zeɪʃn; *US* -nɪ'z-; ˌsɑləmnə'zeʃən/ *n* [U] (*fml* 文) action of solemnizing 仪式的举行.

solen·oid /'səʊlənɔɪd; 'solə,nɔɪd/ *n* coil of wire that becomes magnetic when an electrical current is passed through it 螺线管: [attrib 作定语] *a solenoid switch* 电磁开关.

sol-fa /ˌsɒl'fɑ:; *US* ˌsəʊl-; sol'fɑ/ *n* (also ˌ**tonic sol-'fa**) (in teaching sb to sing) method of showing musical notes by syllables (eg do, re, mi, fa, so, la, etc) (声乐教学中的)阶名唱法, 首调唱法(以 do、re、mi、fa、so、la 等唱名唱出音符的方法).

so·li·cit /sə'lɪsɪt; sə'lɪsɪt/ *v* **1** [I, Ipr, Tn, Tn·pr] **~ (sb) (for sth); ~ (sth) (from sb)** (*fml* 文) ask (sb) for (eg money, help, votes) earnestly; try to obtain (sth) 恳求(某人)给予(钱、帮助等); 向(某人)拉(选票); 设法获得(某事物): *solicit (sb) for money/solicit money (from sb)* 向(某人)要钱[(向某人)要钱] ○ *solicit information about the new motorway* 探询新的高速公路的情况 ○ *Both candidates solicited my opinion.* 两位候选人都来向我征求意见. **2** [I, Tn] (of a prostitute) make a sexual offer (to sb), esp in a public place (指妓女)拉(客)(尤指在公共场所): *She was fined for soliciting.* 她因拉客而被罚款.

so·li·citor /sə'lɪsɪtə(r); sə'lɪsətɚ/ *n* **1** (*Brit*) lawyer who prepares legal documents (eg for the sale of land or buildings), advises clients on legal matters, and speaks for them in the lower courts 事务律师(其职责为处理如房地产买卖等法律文件、答复法律询问、在初级法院出庭辩护等). Cf 参看 ADVOCATE *n* 2, BARRISTER. **2** (*US*) law officer of a city, town, etc (城镇等的)法务官. **3** (*US*) person who solicits trade, support, etc, esp by going from door to door; canvasser (eg for votes) 兜生意者, 游说者(尤指逐门逐户进行的); 拉选票者.

□ **Soˌlicitor-'General** *n* (*pl* **Solicitors-General**) one of the chief law officers in the British Government, advising on legal matters (英国政府的)副检察长. Cf 参看 ATTORNEY-GENERAL (ATTORNEY).

so·li·cit·ous /sə'lɪsɪtəs; sə'lɪsɪtəs/ *adj* **~ (for/about sth/sb)** (*fml* 文) very concerned and anxious about (sb's welfare, comfort, etc) 为(某人的福利、安康等)操心的, 焦虑的: *a solicitous husband* 对妻子关怀备至的丈夫 ○ *solicitous enquiries about her health* 对她健康的关切的询问 ○ *He was very solicitous for her safe return.* 他心神不定, 祈望她平安归来.

▷ **so·li·cit·ously** *adv* (*fml* 文): *He always enquires most solicitously about your health.* 他总是极为关切地问起你的健康状况.

so·li·cit·ude /sə'lɪsɪtju:d; *US* -tu:d; sə'lɪsə,tud/ *n* [U] **~ (for/about sth/sb)** (*fml* 文) being solicitous; concern or anxiety 牵挂; 关心; 担心: *my deep solicitude for your welfare* 我对您的安康甚为挂念 ○ *the solicitude of a caring husband for his wife* 体贴的丈夫对妻子的关怀.

solid /'sɒlɪd; 'sɑlɪd/ *adj* **1** not in the form of a liquid or gas; keeping its shape; firm 固体的; 保持形状的; 密实的: *solid fuels*, eg coal, wood 固体燃料(如煤、木) ○ *solid food*, ie not liquid or slightly liquid 固体食物 ○ *When water freezes it becomes solid and we call it ice.* 水遇冷凝结, 称之为冰. ○ *This horse has good solid muscle on him.* 这匹马长得很结实. **2** without holes or spaces; not hollow 实心的; 无孔的; 无空隙的: *a solid sphere* 实心的球体 ○ *The word 'teapot' is a solid compound*, ie not hyphenated. teapot是个连写的复合词(即中间无连字符). ○ *The demonstrators stood in a solid line with linked arms.* 示威的人一字排开, 挽着手臂紧挨在一起. **3** (**a**) [attrib 作定语] of the same substance throughout; containing only one (specified) material 单一物质的; 纯的: *solid gold bath taps* 纯金的浴缸龙头 ○ *steps cut in the solid rock* 在整块岩石上凿出的台阶 ○ *solid silver cutlery* 纯银刀叉餐具. (**b**) of one (specified) colour only (某种)单一颜色的: *the solid blue sky of the painting* 那幅画上的一片蔚蓝的天空. **4** strong and firm in construction; able to support weight or resist pressure; substantial 坚固的; 结实的; 可支撑重物的; 耐压的; 实在的: *solid buildings* 坚固的建筑物 ○ *solid furniture* 结实的家具 ○ *built on solid foundations* 在坚实的地基上建造的 ○ *on solid ground* 在牢固的基础上. **5** that can be depended on; reputable and reliable 牢靠的; 有信誉的; 可靠的: *solid arguments* 有说服力的论点 ○ *a solid business firm*, ie one without financial or other problems 实力雄厚的公司 ○ *a woman of solid character* 为人可靠

S

的女子 ○ *a good solid worker* 工作出色、可靠的人. **6** in complete agreement; unanimous 一致的: *The miners were solid on this issue.* 矿工们在这件事上是一条心的. ○ *There was a solid vote in favour of the proposal.* 提案获全体一致通过. **7** [attrib or immediately following a *n* 作定语或用于名词之后] without a break or pause; continuous 无间断的; 连续的: *wait for a solid hour* 整整等上一个钟头 ○ *sleep ten solid hours/ten hours solid* 一觉睡十个小时. **8** (*geometry* 几) having length, breadth and thickness; three-dimensional 立体的: *a solid figure*, eg a cube 立体图形(如立方体) ○ *solid geometry*, ie study of solid, not flat figures 立体几何学. **9** (idm 习语) **firm/solid as a rock** ⇨ ROCK[1].

▷ **solid** *n* **1** substance or object that is solid, not a liquid or gas 固体: *Cheese is a solid; milk is a liquid.* 干酪是固体, 奶是液体. ○ *The baby is not yet taking solids*, ie solid foods. 那婴儿还不能吃固体食物. **2** (*geometry* 几) figure of three dimensions, having length, breadth and thickness 立体图形: *A cube is a solid.* 立方体是立体图形.

solid·ity /səˈlɪdətɪ; səˈlɪdətɪ/ (also **solid·ness**) *n* [U] quality or state of being solid 固态; 纯度; 可靠性; 坚固性: *the solidity of a building, argument, metal* 建筑物的坚固性、论据的可信性、金属的纯度.

solidly *adv* **1** firmly and substantially 坚固地; 结实地: *solidly-built foundations* 打得很坚固的基础 ○ *These cars are solidly constructed.* 这些汽车制造得很结实. **2** continuously 连续地: *It rained solidly for three hours.* 雨不停地下了三个小时. **3** agreeing completely; unanimously 一致地: *We are solidly united on this issue.* 我们在这个问题上是团结一致的.

□ ˌ**solid-ˈstate** *adj* [usu attrib 通常作定语] (of electronic devices) using only transistors, ie without valves (指电子装置)固态的, 全晶体管的: *a ˌsolid-state ˈamplifier* 固态放大器.

so·lid·ar·ity /ˌsɒlɪˈdærətɪ; ˌsɑləˈdærətɪ/ *n* [U] unity and agreement resulting from shared interests, feelings, actions, sympathies, etc 团结; 一致: *national solidarity in the face of danger* 危难当头举国团结一致 ○ *'We must show solidarity with the strikers,' declared the student leaders.* 学生领袖声称: '我们要申明与罢工工人团结一致.'

so·lid·ify /səˈlɪdɪfaɪ; səˈlɪdəˌfaɪ/ *v* (*pt, pp* **-fied**) [I, Ipr, Tn] **~ (into sth)** (cause sth to) become solid, hard or firm (使某物)变为固体, 变硬, 变得坚固: *The paint had solidified in the tin.* 罐子里的颜料已经干了. ○ *The mixture solidifies into toffee.* 这种混合物凝结之后就成了太妃糖. ○ (*fig* 比喻) *Vague objections to the system solidified into firm opposition.* 对该体制隐约的反感演变成了坚决的反抗. ▷ **so·lidi·fica·tion** /səˌlɪdɪfɪˈkeɪʃn; səˌlɪdəfəˈkeʃən/ *n* [U].

so·li·lo·quy /səˈlɪləkwɪ; səˈlɪləkwɪ/ *n* [C, U] (instance of) speaking one's thoughts aloud, esp in a play when a character does this without another character being present on stage 自言自语; (尤指戏剧中的)独白: *Hamlet's famous soliloquy* 哈姆雷特的一段著名的独白.

▷ **so·li·lo·quize, -ise** /səˈlɪləkwaɪz; səˈlɪləˌkwaɪz/ *v* [I] (*fml* 文) talk to oneself; say one's thoughts aloud, esp in a play 自言自语; (尤指戏剧中)用独白表达: (*joc* 谑) *soliloquizing in front of the bathroom mirror* 对着卫生间的镜子自言自语.

sol·ips·ism /ˈsɒlɪpsɪzəm; ˈsɑlɪpsɪzm/ *n* [U] (*philosophy* 哲) theory that one can have knowledge only of the self 唯我论(认为人的认识只限于自我).

so·lit·aire /ˌsɒlɪˈteə(r); *US* ˈsɒlɪteə(r); ˈsɑləˌtɛr/ *n* **1** [U] game for one person in which marbles, balls, pegs, etc are removed from their places on a special board after other pieces are moved over them, the object being to have only one piece left on the board 自娱棋(单人游戏, 用弹子、小球、栓棒等棋子在棋盘上跳越走棋, 移去被跳过的棋子, 直到只剩下一粒为止). **2** = PATIENCE 3. **3** [C] (piece of jewellery such as a ring or an ear-ring having a) single gem or jewel 独粒宝石; 镶有独粒宝石的饰物(如戒指或耳环): [attrib 作定语] *a solitaire diamond* 独粒钻石.

sol·it·ary /ˈsɒlɪtrɪ; *US* -terɪ; ˈsɑləˌtɛrɪ/ *adj* **1** (**a**) [usu attrib 通常作定语] (living) alone; without companions 单独的; 独居的; 独自的: *a solitary walk* 独自一人的散步 ○ *lead a solitary life* 过独居的生活 ○ *One solitary tree grew on the mountainside.* 山腰上孤零零地长着一棵树. (**b**) fond of being alone; used to being alone 喜欢独处的; 习惯于独处的: *a solitary kind of person* 喜欢离群索居的人. **2** not often visited; in a lonely remote place 人迹罕至的; 荒僻的: *a solitary valley* 荒僻的山谷 ○ *far-flung solitary villages* 偏远冷清的村落. ⇨Usage at ALONE 用法见 ALONE. **3** [usu attrib 通常作定语] (esp in negative sentences and questions 尤用于否定句和疑问句中) only one; single 唯一的; 仅有的: *There's not a solitary instance* (ie not even one) *of this having happened before.* 这样的事以前一次也没有发生过. ○ *She couldn't answer a solitary question correctly.* 她连一个问题都答不对.

▷ **sol·it·ar·ily** /ˈsɒlɪtrəlɪ; *US* ˌsɒlɪˈterəlɪ; ˌsɑləˈtɛrəlɪ/ *adv*.

sol·it·ary *n* **1** [U] (*infml* 口) = SOLITARY CONFINEMENT: *He's in solitary for the weekend.* 他周末遭单独禁闭. **2** [C] (*fml* 文) person who chooses to live completely alone; hermit 喜欢完全独居的人; 隐士.

□ ˌ**solitary conˈfinement** (also *infml* 口语作 **solitary**) prison punishment in which sb is kept alone in a separate cell 隔离监禁: *He has been put in solitary confinement for attacking another prisoner.* 他因伤害另一囚犯而被隔离监禁.

sol·it·ude /ˈsɒlɪtju:d; *US* -tu:d; ˈsɑləˌtud/ *n* [U] (state or quality of) being alone without companions; solitary state 孤单; 独居: *not fond of solitude* 不喜欢孤身一人 ○ *She enjoys the solitude of her own flat.* 她喜欢独自在自己的公寓里.

solo /ˈsəʊləʊ; ˈsolo/ *n* (*pl* **~s**) **1** [C] piece of music, dance, entertainment, etc performed by only one person 独唱歌曲; 独奏曲; 独舞; 单人表演: *a violin, piano, flute, etc solo* 小提琴、钢琴、长笛等的独奏 ○ *sing a solo* 唱一首独唱歌曲. **2** [C] flight in which the pilot flies alone without an instructor (飞行员无教练员相伴的)单独飞行: *The trainee pilot flew his first solo today.* 那个受训的飞行员今天首次单独飞行. **3** [U] type of whist (a card-game) in which one player opposes others 惠斯特纸牌戏中一人对三人的玩法.

▷ **solo** *adj* [attrib 作定语], *adv* **1** by oneself, without a companion, etc 独自(的); 单独(的): *a solo attempt* 独自进行的尝试 ○ *his first solo flight* 他的首次单独飞行 ○ *She wanted to fly solo across the Atlantic.* 她想单人驾驶飞机飞越大西洋. **2** of, concerning or performed as a solo(1) 单人表演(的): *a fine solo performance on the flute* 优美的长笛独奏 ○ *a piece for solo cello* 大提琴独奏曲 ○ *sing solo* 独唱.

so·lo·ist *n* person who performs a musical solo 独唱者; 独奏者.

sol·stice /ˈsɒlstɪs; ˈsɑlstɪs/ *n* either of the two times of the year at which the sun is furthest North or South of the equator 至日; 冬至或夏至: *summer solstice*, ie about 21 June in the Northern hemisphere 夏至 ○ *winter solstice*, ie about 22 December in the Northern hemisphere 冬至. Cf 参看 EQUINOX.

sol·uble /ˈsɒljʊbl; ˈsɑljəbl̩/ *adj* **1 ~ (in sth)** that can be dissolved 可溶的: *soluble aspirin* 溶解性阿司匹林 ○ *tablets soluble in water* 可溶于水的药片 ○ *water-soluble vitamins*, ie that can be dissolved in water 水溶维生素. **2** (*fml* 文) that can be solved or explained; solvable 可解决的; 可解释的; 可解答的: *problems that are not readily soluble* 不易解决的问题. ▷ **solu·bil·ity** /ˌsɒljʊˈbɪlətɪ; ˌsɑljəˈbɪlətɪ/ *n* [U].

so·lu·tion /səˈlu:ʃn; səˈluʃən/ *n* **1** [U, C] **~ (to sth)** (action or way of finding an) answer to a problem, question, difficulty, etc 解决; 解答; 解释; 答案; 解决方法: *problems that defy solution*, ie cannot be solved 无法解决的问题 ○ *the solution to a crossword puzzle* 纵横填字谜的谜底 ○ *She can find no solution to her financial troubles.* 她经济困难无法克服. ○ *Resorting to violence is not the best solution to an argument.* 使用武力不是解决争执的上策. **2** [C, U] liquid in which sth is dissolved; state of being dissolved 溶液; 溶解状态: *a solution of salt in water* 盐的水溶液 ○ *salt in solution* 溶解状态的盐. **3** [U] process of dissolving a solid or a gas in liquid 溶解过程: *the solution of sugar in tea* 糖在茶中的溶解.

solve /sɒlv; sɑlv/ *v* [Tn] **1** find an answer to (a problem, etc); explain or make clear (a mystery, etc) 解决, 解答(难题等); 解释, 揭示(秘密等): *solve a crossword puzzle* 解纵横填字谜 ○ *solve a mathematical equation* 解数学

方程式 ○ *solve a crime* 破案. **2** find a way of dealing with (a difficulty, etc) 解决(困难等): *Help me to solve my financial troubles.* 请帮我解决经济困难.

▷ **solv·able** *adj* that can be solved or explained; soluble(2) 可解决的; 可解释的; 可解答的: *problems that are not immediately solvable* 不能马上得到解决的问题.

solver *n* (in compounds 用以构成复合词) person who finds an answer or a solution 解答或解决问题者: *a crime-solver* 破案者 ○ *He's a good problem-solver.* 他解决难题很拿手.

solv·ent /ˈsɒlvənt; ˋsɑlvənt/ *adj* [usu pred 通常作表语] **1** having enough money to pay one's debts; not in debt 有偿付能力; 不负债: *He's never solvent.* 他总也还不清债. **2** (*fml* 文) that can dissolve another substance 有溶解力: *the solvent action of water* 水的溶解作用.

▷ **solv·ent** *n* (U, C] substance (esp a liquid) that can dissolve another substance 溶剂; 溶媒: *Petrol is a good grease solvent*, ie dissolves grease well. 汽油是一种有效的油脂溶剂.

solv·ency /-nsɪ; -nsɪ/ *n* [U] being solvent(1) 偿付能力.

sombre (*US* **som·ber**) /ˈsɒmbə(r); ˋsɑmbɚ/ *adj* **1** dark-coloured; dull and dismal 暗淡的; 阴沉的: *sombre clothes* 暗色的衣服 ○ *a sombre January day* 一月份中一个阴沉的日子. **2** sad and serious 忧郁的; 严峻的: *a sombre expression on his face* 他脸上忧郁的神情 ○ *a sombre picture of the future of the world* 世界未来的惨淡写照. ▷ **sombrely** *adv*: *sombrely dressed* 衣着素淡的. **sombre·ness** *n* [U].

som·brero /sɒmˈbreərəʊ; sɑmˋbrɛro/ *n* (*pl* **~s**) man's felt or straw hat with a very wide brim (as worn in Latin American countries, esp Mexico) 阔边毡帽, 阔边草帽 (如墨西哥等拉丁美洲国家男子所戴的).

some[1] /səm; səm/ *indef det* (used in affirmative sentences, or in questions expecting a positive reply; after *if/whether*, when the sentence has a positive emphasis; and in invitations and requests 用于肯定句或希望得到肯定回答的问句; 置于 if/whether 之后, 语义偏重于肯定; 用以表示邀请和请求) **1** (used with [U] *ns* 与不可数名词连用) an unspecified amount of 一些; 若干: *There's some ice in the fridge.* 冰箱里有些冰块儿. ○ *Some mail came for you this morning.* 今天上午有你的邮件. ○ *You left some money on the table.* 你把钱落在桌子上了. ○ *Would you like some milk in your tea?* 要不要在茶里加点儿牛奶? ○ *Isn't there some (more) wine in the cellar?* 酒窖里(还)有酒吗? ○ *If you save some money each week, we can go on holiday.* 要是你每星期能存点儿钱, 咱们就可以外出度假了. ○ *Please have some cake.* 请吃点儿蛋糕. **2** (used with *pl* [C] *ns*, usu referring to three or more 与复数可数名词连用, 通常指三个或三个以上) an unspecified number of 一些; 若干: *Some children were playing in the park.* 有些小孩儿在公园里玩儿. ○ *Why don't you give her some flowers?* 何不送给她一些花? (Cf 参看 *I suggest you give her some flowers.*) ○ *Didn't you borrow some records of mine?* 你没向我借过一些唱片吗? (Cf 参看 *You borrowed some records of mine, didn't you?*) ○ *If you put some pictures on the wall the room will look brighter.* 你要是在墙上挂几幅画, 这个房间就更有生气. Cf 参看 ANY[1].

some[2] /sʌm; sʌm/ *indef det* **1** (used with [C] and [U] *ns* 与可数和不可数名词连用) (**a**) a number or amount of sth that is less than the total being considered 部分; 有些: *Some people have naturally beautiful voices while others need to be trained.* 有些人生就一副好嗓子, 有些人则需要训练. ○ *Some modern music sounds harsh and tuneless.* 现代音乐中有一些又刺耳又不成调子. (**b**) a considerable number or amount of 相当多的; 好些: *We went some* (ie several) *miles out of our way.* 我们偏离原定路线走了好几英里. ○ *That is some help to us*, ie It helps to a certain extent. 那对我们很有用. ○ *I shall be gone (for) some time*, ie for quite a long time. 我将有好些日子不在这儿. ○ *The headmistress spoke at some* (ie considerable) *length.* (女)校长讲话讲了好一会儿. **2** (used with *sing* [C] *ns* 与单数可数名词连用) person, place or thing that is unknown or unspecified 未知的或未确指的人、地点或事物: *Some man at the door is asking to see you.* 门口有人要见你. ○ *She won a competition in some newspaper or other.* 她参加某报纸举办的比赛获胜. **3** (used with numbers 与数词连用) approximately 大约; 近于: *He spent some twelve years of his life in Africa.* 他在非洲度过了近十二个年头. ○ *Some thirty people attended the funeral.* 参加葬礼的约有三十人.

some[3] /sʌm; sʌm/ *indef pron* **1** an unspecified number or amount of people or things 一些人或事物. (**a**) (referring back 用以复指前文): *Some were at the meeting yesterday.* 有些人昨天出席了会议. ○ *You'll find some in the cupboard.* 柜橱里有一些. ○ *There's some (more) in the pot.* 锅里(还)有一些. ○ *I already have some but it's not enough for six.* 我有一些, 但不够六个人的. (**b**) (referring forward 用以预指后文): *Some of the chairs are broken.* 有些椅子坏了. ○ *Some of the money was stolen.* 有些钱给偷走了. **2** part of the whole number or amount being considered 其中的一部分. (**a**) (referring back 用以复指前文): *Thirty people came — some stayed until the end but many left early.* 来了三十人——有些人一直呆到最后, 但很多人先走了. (**b**) (referring forward 用以预指后文): *Some of the students had done their homework but most hadn't.* 有些学生做了作业, 但大多数都没做. ○ *Some of the letter was illegible.* 那封信有些字难以辨认. Cf 参看 ANY[2].

-some *suff* 后缀 **1** (with *ns* and *vs* forming *adjs* 与名词和动词构成形容词) producing; likely to 引起…的; 有…倾向的: *fearsome* ○ *quarrelsome* ○ *meddlesome*. **2** (with numbers forming *ns* 与数词构成名词) group of the specified number 某数目的一组: *threesome*.

some·body /ˈsʌmbədɪ; ˋsʌmbədɪ/ (also **some·one** /ˈsʌmwʌn; ˋsʌm,wʌn/) *indef pron* **1** some person 某人; 有人: *There's somebody at the door.* 门口有个人. ○ *Somebody from your office phoned.* 你的办公室有人来过电话. ○ *If you saw somebody drowning what would you do?* 假若看见有人快淹死了, 你怎么办呢? **2** an important person 重要人物: *He thinks he's really somebody.* 他自以为很了不起.

NOTE ON USAGE 用法: Indefinite pronouns such as **somebody, someone, everyone, no one,** etc are singular and, grammatically, should be followed by other singular pronouns (**he, she, his, her,** etc). ☆ **somebody**、**someone**、**everyone**、**no one** 等不定代词均为单数, 根据语法规则, 后面应该用其他单数代词(**he**、**she**、**his**、**her** 等). Traditionally, if the sex of the person is unknown, the masculine pronouns **he, him, his** have been used to refer to both females and males 按照传统用法, 若性别不详则男女两性均用阳性代词 **he**、**him**、**his** 表示: *Everybody has his own view of what happened.* 对于所发生的事情, 各人有各人的看法. ○ *Somebody has lost his car keys.* 有人把汽车钥匙丢了. ○ *Did anybody hurt himself?* 有人受伤了吗? Many people today consider this shows sexual bias and try to avoid it. 如今很多人认为这种用法有性别偏见之嫌, 因而尽量加以避免. The preferred way, especially in speech, is to use **they, them** or **their** with a singular neutral meaning 较为可取的方法是使用 **they**、**them** 或 **their**, 并赋以单数的中性含义, 尤用于口语: *Everyone said they would help.* 大家都表示要帮忙. ○ *Either John or Jane has to give up their job.* 不是约翰就是简, 总有一个得放弃工作. Another way, especially in writing, is to use **(s)he, he or she, him or her, his or her,** though some people find this clumsy 另一种方法尤见于书面形式, 是使用 **(s)he**、**he or she**、**him or her**、**his or her**, 但有些人认为过于累赘: *Somebody has lost his or her car keys.* 有人把汽车钥匙丢了. A third possibility is to rephrase the sentence to make the subject plural, thus avoiding the problem 第三种用法是修改句子, 使主语变为复数以避开这个问题: *Did any of you hurt yourselves?* 有人受伤了吗? See also note on usage at HE. 参见 HE 词条的用法说明.

some·day /ˈsʌmdeɪ; ˋsʌm,de/ *indef adv* (also **some day**) at some time in the future 将来有一天; 他日: *Someday we'll be together.* 我们总有一天能聚在一起. ○ *Some day he will be a king.* 有朝一日他能当上国王. Cf 参看 SOME[2] 2.

some·how /ˈsʌmhaʊ; ˋsʌm,haʊ/ (*US* also **some·way** /ˈsʌmweɪ; ˋsʌm,we/) *indef adv* **1** in some way; by some means 以某种方式; 通过某种途径: *We must stop him from seeing her somehow.* 我们得想个办法不能让他再

S

跟她来往. ○ *Somehow we must get to Glasgow.* 我们得设法到格拉斯哥去. **2** for a reason that is unknown or unspecified 由于未知的或未确指的原因: *Somehow, I don't feel I can trust him.* 不知什么缘故, 我觉得不能信任他. ○ *I always knew I'd get the job, somehow.* 也不知为什么, 我总是觉得我能得到那份工作.

some·one /ˈsʌmwʌn; ˈsʌm,wʌn/ *indef pron* = SOMEBODY.

some·place /ˈsʌmpleɪs; ˈsʌmples/ *indef adv* (*esp US*) = SOMEWHERE.

som·er·sault /ˈsʌməsɔ:lt; ˈsʌmɚ,sɔlt/ *n* acrobatic rolling movement in which a person turns his feet over his head on the ground or in the air (杂技中的)滚翻, 空翻, 跟头: *A gymnast on the trampoline was turning* (ie performing) *somersaults.* 有个体操运动员正在蹦床上做空翻.

▷ **som·er·sault** *v* [I, Ipr] perform a somersault or somersaults 做滚翻; 做空翻; 翻跟头: *The child somersaulted across the gymnasium.* 那孩子翻着跟头从体育馆这头翻到那头.

some·thing /ˈsʌmθɪŋ; ˈsʌmθɪŋ/ *indef pron* **1** some thing 某事物: *There's something under the table.* 桌子底下有个东西. ○ *I want something to eat.* 我想要点儿吃的. ○ *Have you got something I could read?* 你有什么可让我读读的吗? ○ *There's something interesting on the front page.* 头版上有些有意思的消息. **2** some thing thought to be significant 被视为有意义的事物: *There's something* (ie some truth, some fact or opinion worth considering) *in what she says.* 她说的有点道理. ○ *It's something* (ie a thing that one should feel happy about) *to have a job at all these days.* 这年头有一份工作就算不错了. ○ *He's something/He does something in* (ie He has a job connected with) *television.* 他是干电视这一行的. **3** (idm 习语) **or something** (*infml* 口) or another thing similar to that mentioned 或诸如此类的事物: *She's writing a dictionary or something.* 她在编写词典之类的书. ○ *He hit a tree or something.* 他撞上了一棵树或其他什么东西. ○ *She rescued three children from a fire or something.* 她从一起火灾之类的事故中救出了三个孩子. ˌ**something like** (**a**) ˈ**sb/sth** (**a**) partially similar to sb/sth 类似某人[某事物]: *A thesaurus is something like a dictionary.* 类语词典与普通词典相仿. ○ *The ceremony was something like a christening.* 那个典礼有点像洗礼仪式. ○ *The tune goes something like this.* 那曲调大致是这样的. (**b**) approximately sb/sth 近似于某人[某事物]: *He earns something like £35 000.* 他的收入在35 000英镑上下. **something** ˈ**like it** roughly what is required or desirable 大致符合要求或符合愿望的事物: *That's something like it*, ie That will be satisfactory. 那样就差不多了. **something of a sth** to some degree 达到某种程度: *She found herself something of a celebrity.* 她意识到自己已小有名气了. ○ *I'm something of an expert on antiques.* 我对古董略有研究.

some·time /ˈsʌmtaɪm; ˈsʌm,taɪm/ *indef adv* (also **some time**) at a particular but unspecified time 在某个时候: *I saw him sometime last summer.* 去年夏天的某个时候我曾经见过他. ○ *Phone me some time next week.* 下星期什么时候给我打个电话吧. Cf 参看 SOME² 2.

▷ **some·time** *adj* [attrib 作定语] (*fml* 文) formerly 从前的: *Thomas Atkins, sometime vicar of this parish* 托马斯·阿特金斯, 本牧区从前的牧师.

some·times /ˈsʌmtaɪmz; ˈsʌm,taɪmz/ *indef adv* at some times but not all the time; occasionally 有时候; 间或; 偶尔: *He sometimes writes to me.* 他间或给我写写信. ○ *Sometimes I go by car.* 有时我坐汽车去. ○ *Sometimes we went to the beach and at other times we sunbathed on the patio.* 我们有时去海滩, 有时在院子里做日光浴.

some·way /ˈsʌmweɪ; ˈsʌm,we/ *indef adv* (*infml* 口 *esp US*) = SOMEHOW.

some·what /ˈsʌmwɒt; *US* -hwɒt; ˈsʌm,hwɑt/ *indef adv* to some degree; rather 达到某种程度; 颇为: *I was somewhat surprised to see him.* 见到他我有点吃惊. ○ *He answered somewhat nervously.* 他回答时有些局促不安.

some·where /ˈsʌmweə(r); *US* -hweər; ˈsʌm,hwɛr/ (*US* also **some·place**) *indef adv* in, at or to some place 在某处; 到某处: *He lost it somewhere between here and the station.* 他在从这儿到车站的这段路上把它给丢了. ○ *I'm going somewhere else* (ie to a different place) *this evening.* 今晚我去另一个地方.

▷ **some·where** *indef pron* some place 某处: *I'll think of somewhere to stay.* 我要找个住处. ○ *I know somewhere (where) you can eat Japanese food.* 我认识个地方, 可以吃日本菜.

somn·am·bu·lism /sɒmˈnæmbjʊlɪzəm; sɑmˈnæmbjə,lɪzəm/ *n* [U] (*fml* 文) activity or habit of walking in one's sleep; sleep-walking 梦行(症); 梦游.

▷ **somn·am·bu·list** /-lɪst; -lɪst/ *n* (*fml* 文) person who does this; sleep-walker 梦行者; 梦游者.

som·no·lent /ˈsɒmnələnt; ˈsɑmnələnt/ *adj* (*fml* 文) **1** almost asleep; sleepy; drowsy 瞌睡的; 困的; 昏昏欲睡的: *feeling rather somnolent after a large lunch* 中午饱餐一顿后有些困. **2** causing or suggesting sleep 使人瞌睡的; 催眠的: *The noise of the stream had a pleasantly somnolent effect.* 小河潺潺的流水声有宜人的催眠效果.

▷ **som·no·lence** /-əns; -əns/ *n* [U] (*fml* 文) sleepiness; drowsiness 瞌睡; 困乏.

som·no·lently *adv.*

son /sʌn; sʌn/ *n* **1** [C] male child of a parent 儿子: *I have a son and two daughters.* 我有一个儿子和两个女儿. **2** [C esp *pl* 尤作复数] (*rhet* 修辞) male descendant; male member of a family, country, etc 男性后代; 子孙; 家庭、国家等的男性成员: *one of France's most famous sons* 最著名的法国男儿 ○ *sons of the tribe going out to hunt* 部落中外出打猎的男人 ○ (*fig* 比喻) *a son of the soil*, ie sb who follows his father in working on the land (继承父业的)农夫. **3** (form of address used by an older man to a young man or boy 年长者对年轻或年幼男子的称呼): *'What's the matter with you, son?' asked the doctor.* '孩子, 哪儿不舒服哇?' 医生问道. ○ *'What is it you want to tell me, my son?' asked the priest.* '年轻人, 你有什么话要对我说呢?' 教士问道. ○ (*derog* 贬) *Listen, son, don't start giving me orders.* 听着, 小伙子, 别来对我发号施令. **4 the Son** [sing] Jesus Christ 圣子; 耶稣基督: *the Father, the Son and the Holy Spirit* 圣父、圣子、圣灵. **5** (idm 习语) **like father, like son** ⇨ FATHER¹. **a** ˌ**son of a** ˈ**bitch** (⚠ *sl* 讳, 俚) unpleasant person; bastard 狗东西; 狗娘养的; 混蛋: *I'll kill that son of a bitch when I get my hands on him!* 等我抓到那狗东西就把他给宰了!

□ ˈ**son-in-law** *n* (*pl* ˈ**sons-in-law**) husband of one's daughter 女婿.

the ˌ**Son of** ˈ**God, the** ˌ**Son of** ˈ**Man** Jesus Christ 圣子; 耶稣基督.

sonar /ˈsəʊnɑ:(r); ˈsonɑr/ *n* [U] device or system for detecting and locating objects under water by means of reflected sound waves 声纳装置; 声纳系统. Cf 参看 RADAR.

son·ata /səˈnɑ:tə; səˈnɑtə/ *n* piece of music composed for one instrument (eg the piano), or two (eg piano and violin), usu with three or four movements 奏鸣曲: *Bach's cello sonatas* 巴赫的大提琴奏鸣曲.

son et lu·mi·ère /ˌsɒn eɪ lu:ˈmjeə(r); ˌsonelumˈjɛr/ (*French* 法) night-time entertainment at a famous building or place, where its history is told and acted with special lighting and sound effects 名胜掌故晚会(在著名的建筑物或场所就地举行, 以讲述和表演的形式再现该处历史, 并配以灯光和音响效果): *son et lumière in the grounds of a ruined abbey* 在一座大修道院的废墟上举行的该处名胜掌故晚会.

song /sɒŋ; *US* sɔ:ŋ; sɔŋ/ *n* **1** [C] (usu short) poem set to music and intended to be sung 歌; 歌曲; 歌词: *a popular song* 流行歌曲 ○ *a collection of folk-songs* 民歌集 ○ *a beautiful love-song* 优美的情歌. **2** [U] music for the voice; (activity of) singing 声乐; 歌唱: *burst into song*, ie suddenly begin singing 突然唱起歌来. **3** [U] musical call or sound(s) made by a bird 鸟鸣: *the song of the thrush* 鸫鸟的鸣唱 ○ *the song of the birds* 鸟的鸣声 ○ *birdsong* 鸟鸣. **4** (idm 习语) **for a** ˈ**song** (*infml* 口) at a very low price; cheaply 以很低的价钱; 便宜地: *This table was going for a song at the market.* 这张桌子正在市场上廉价出售. **(make) a song and** ˈ**dance (about sth)** (*infml derog* 口, 贬) (make) a great fuss (about sth), usu unnecessarily (对某事物)小题大作: *You may be a bit upset, but it's really nothing to make a song and dance about.* 你尽管有些苦恼, 但实在不必小题大作. **sing a different song/tune** ⇨ SING. **wine, women and song** ⇨ WINE.

▷ **song·ster** /-stə(r); -stɚ/ *n* (*dated or fml* 旧或文) singer; songbird 歌唱者; 歌手; 鸣禽: *merry songsters* *singing carols* 欢乐地唱着颂歌的歌手.

song·stress /-strɪs; -strɪs/ *n* (*dated or fml* 旧或文) female singer 女性歌唱者; 女歌手.

□ ˈ**songbird** *n* bird noted for its musical cry 鸣禽: *Blackbirds and thrushes are songbirds.* 黑鹂和鸫鸟都是鸣禽.

ˈ**song-book** *n* collection of songs (with both words and music) 歌曲集; 歌本: *a children's song-book* 儿歌集.

ˈ**songwriter** *n* person who composes (usu popular) songs as a profession 歌曲(通常指流行歌曲)作家.

sonic /ˈsɒnɪk; ˋsɑnɪk/ *adj* (usu in compounds 通常用以构成复合词) relating to sound, sound-waves or the speed of sound 声音的; 声波的; 声速的.

□ ˌ**sonic** ˈ**barrier** = SOUND BARRIER (SOUND).

ˌ**sonic** ˈ**boom** noise made when an aircraft exceeds the speed of sound 声震, 音爆(飞行器超过声速时发出的声音).

son·net /ˈsɒnɪt; ˋsɑnɪt/ *n* type of poem containing 14 lines, each of 10 syllables, and with a formal pattern of rhymes 十四行诗(每行十个音节、韵律规范的诗体): *Shakespeare's sonnets* 莎士比亚的十四行诗.

sonny /ˈsʌnɪ; ˋsʌnɪ/ *n* (*infml* 口) (familiar, sometimes patronizing, form of address used by an older person to a young boy or young man 用作长者对年幼或年轻男子的昵称, 有时含屈尊意): *Run along now, sonny; mummy wants to have a rest.* 乖乖, 走开吧; 妈妈想歇一会儿. ○ *Don't try to teach me my job, sonny.* 小伙子, 我的工作用不着你来指教.

son·or·ous /ˈsɒnərəs, *also* səˈnɔːrəs; ˋsɑnərəs, səˋnɔrəs/ *adj* (*fml* 文) **1** having a full deep sound (声音)圆润低沉的: *a sonorous voice* 圆润低沉的嗓音 ○ *the sonorous tones of the priest* 教士那圆润低沉的声调 ○ *a sonorous bell* 声音圆润低沉的钟. **2** (of language, words, etc) sounding impressive and important (指语言、文字等)感人的, 堂皇的: *a sonorous style of writing* 华丽的文体.

▷ **son·or·ity** /səˈnɒrətɪ; *US* -ˈnɔːr-; səˋnɔrətɪ/ *n* [U] (*fml* 文): *the sonority of the bass voices* 男低音部的低沉声音. **son·or·ously** *adv*.

soon /suːn; sun/ *adv* **1** (used in mid-position with the *v* or, esp with *too, quite, very,* in end position 与动词连用置于句中; 尤与 too、quite、very 连用置于句末) not long after the present time or the time mentioned; within a short time 不久: *We shall soon be home.* 我们快到家了. ○ *We soon got there.* 我们很快就到那儿了. ○ *We shall be home quite soon now.* 我们这就快到家了. ○ *He'll be here very soon.* 他马上就要到这儿了. ○ *It will soon be five years since we came to live in Cairo.* 我们来到开罗居住快五年了. **2** (often in the pattern *the sooner...the sooner...* 常用于 the sooner...the sooner... 的结构中) early; quickly 早; 很快地: *How soon can you be ready?* 你最快要多长时间才能准备好? ○ *Must you leave so soon?* 你真得这么早就走吗? ○ *She will be here sooner than you expect.* 她很快就到, 比你预料的要早. ○ *The sooner you begin the sooner you'll finish,* ie If you begin earlier you'll finish earlier. 早开始早结束. ○ *The sooner you leave the sooner you'll be home.* 早走早到家. **3** (idm 习语) **as** ˈ**soon as** (used as a *conj* 用作连词) at the moment that; not later than (the moment when) 一...就...; 不迟于: *He left as soon as he heard the news.* 他一听到这事儿就走了. ○ *I'll tell him as soon as I see him.* 我一见到他就告诉他. ○ *He didn't arrive as soon as we'd hoped.* 他到达的时间比我们预期的要迟. **(just) as soon do sth (as do sth)** with equal willingness or readiness (as) 同样乐于做某事(像做另一事一样): *I'd (just) as soon stay at home as go for a walk.* 我呆在家里也行, 出去散步也行. **least said soonest mended** ⇨ LEAST. **no** ˌ**sooner** ˌ**said than** ˈ**done** (of a promise, question, request, etc) done, fulfilled, etc immediately (指诺言、问题、要求等)说到立即做、履行、解决、满足等. **no sooner...than** immediately when or after 一...就...: *He had no sooner/No sooner had he arrived than he was asked to leave again.* 他刚到就被支走了. **soon after (sb/sth)** a short time after (sb/sth) 在(某人[某事物])之后不久: *He arrived* ˌ*soon after* ˈ*three.* 他是刚过三点的时候到的. ○ *They left* ˌ*soon after* ˈ*we did.* 我们走后不久他们也离开了. ○ *I rang for a taxi and it arrived soon* ˈ*after.* 我打电话叫了计程车, 不一会儿车就到了. **the** ˌ**sooner the** ˈ**better** as quickly as possible 越快越好: *'When should I ask him?' 'The sooner the better.'* '我什么时候问他好呢?' '越快越好.' ˌ**sooner or** ˈ**later** one day; eventually (whether soon or later on) 早晚; 迟早; 总有一天: *You should tell her, because she'll find out sooner or later.* 你还是告诉她吧, 因为她迟早会发觉的. **sooner do sth (than do sth)** (*fml* 文) rather do sth 宁愿做某事: *She would sooner resign than take part in such dishonest business deals.* 她宁可辞职也不愿参与这种不正当的买卖. ○ *Go back there? I'd sooner emigrate!* 回去? 我宁可移居海外也不回去! ○ *Will you tell him, or would you sooner* (ie prefer it if) *I did?* 是你去告诉他呢, 还是你愿意让我去告诉他呢? **speak too soon** ⇨ SPEAK.

soot /sʊt; sut/ *n* [U] black powder in the smoke of wood, coal, etc 炱; 烟中的黑灰: *sweep the soot out of the chimney* 把烟囱里的黑灰扫掉 ○ *One small fire in the kitchen covered the whole house in soot.* 厨房里只有一个小火炉就把整个房子都熏黑了.

▷ **soot** *v* (phr v) **soot sth up** (usu passive 通常用于被动语态) cover sth with soot 使某物蒙上黑烟灰: *The flue has become sooted up.* 烟道里都是黑灰.

sooty *adj* **1** covered with soot; black with soot 有黑烟灰的; 被烟炱熏黑的: *the chimney-sweep's sooty face* 烟囱清扫工满是黑灰的脸. **2** of the colour of soot; black 烟炱的颜色; 乌黑的: *a sooty cat* 黑猫.

soothe /suːð; suð/ *v* [Tn] **1** make (a person who is distressed, anxious, etc) quiet or calm; calm or comfort 使(悲伤、焦虑等的人)平静或镇定; 安慰; 抚慰: *soothe a crying baby* 哄啼哭的小孩儿. **2** make (pains, aches, etc) less severe or painful; ease 使(痛苦、疼痛等)变轻; 缓解: *soothe sb's toothache* 使某人牙痛减轻 ○ *This will help to soothe your sunburn.* 这有助于减轻你晒伤处的疼痛. ▷ **sooth·ing** *adj*: *soothing music* 令人舒畅的音乐 ○ *a soothing voice* 有安抚作用的嗓音 ○ *a soothing lotion* 润肤液. **sooth·ingly** *adv*: *'There, there,' he said soothingly, 'Don't distress yourself!'* '好了, 好了,' 他安慰道, '别伤心了!'

sooth·sayer /ˈsuːθseɪə(r); ˋsuθˌseɚ/ *n* (*arch* 古) fortune-teller; prophet 占卜者; 预言者: *the soothsayer in Shakespeare's 'Julius Caesar'* 莎士比亚的剧作《裘力斯·凯撒》中的预言家.

sop /sɒp; sɑp/ *n* **1** [sing] **~ (to sb/sth)** thing offered to a displeased or troublesome person to calm him or win his favour 用以慰藉或讨好某人的事物: *offered as a sop to his anger* 给他消气儿用的 ○ *The child was given a prize as a sop to her disappointed parents.* 给那孩子一个奖品是为了安慰她父母的失望心情. **2** [C] piece of bread, etc dipped in liquid (eg milk, soup) before being eaten or cooked 泡湿的面包片等(如浸过牛奶、汤等).

▷ **sop** *v* **(-pp-)** (*infml* 口) **1** [Tn] dip or soak (bread, etc) in liquid 将(面包等)在液体中蘸或浸泡: *sop bread in soup* 把面包浸在汤中. **2** (phr v) **sop sth up** take up (liquid, etc) with a sponge, cloth, etc 用海绵、布等吸起(液体等): *Sop up the water with a paper towel.* 用纸巾把水吸干.

sop·ping *adj, adv* very wet; drenched 很潮湿的; 湿透的: *Your clothes are sopping (wet)!* 你的衣服湿透了!

soph·ist /ˈsɒfɪst; ˋsɑfɪst/ *n* (*fml* 文) person who uses clever but false arguments intended to deceive 诡辩者: *Many politicians are cunning sophists.* 许多政客都是狡猾的诡辩家.

▷ **soph·ism** /ˈsɒfɪzəm; ˋsɑfɪzəm/ *n* [C, U] (*fml* 文) (use of) such arguments 诡辩; 诡辩之辞.

soph·ist·ic·ated /səˈfɪstɪkeɪtɪd; səˋfɪstɪˌketɪd/ *adj* **1** having or showing much worldly experience and knowledge of fashionable life (显得)世故的, 老练的, 高雅时髦的: *a sophisticated woman* 老于世故的女子 ○ *wearing sophisticated clothes* 穿着考究的衣服 ○ *sophisticated tastes* 高雅的口味. **2** complicated and refined; elaborate; subtle 复杂的; 精良的; 精细的; 尖端的: *sophisticated modern weapons* 精良的现代武器 ○ *sophisticated devices used in spacecraft* 航天器中的尖端装置 ○ *a sophisticated discussion, argument, etc* 缜密的讨论、论点等.

▷ **soph·ist·ic·ate** /səˈfɪstɪkeɪt; səˋfɪstɪˌket/ *n* (*often ironic* 常作反语) sophisticated person 老于世故的人: *The sophisticates in the office drink lemon tea; we have coffee.* 办公室里那些不同凡俗的人喝的是柠檬茶, 我们这些人喝咖啡.

soph·ist·ica·tion /səˌfɪstɪˈkeɪʃn; səˌfɪstɪˋkeʃən/ *n* [U] quality of being sophisticated 世故; 复杂性: *proud of her newly-acquired sophistication* 她因最近学得老成而自豪 ○ *the sophistication of modern aircraft* 现代飞行器的高精尖.

soph·istry /ˈsɒfɪstrɪ; ˋsɑfɪstrɪ/ *n* (*fml* 文) (**a**) [U] use of sophisms 诡辩术: *He won the argument by sophistry.* 他靠诡辩赢了那场争论. (**b**) [C] instance or example of this 诡辩: *the sophistries of the discussion* 讨论中的诡辩.

sopho·more /ˈsɒfəmɔ:(r); ˋsɑfm̩ˌɔr/ *n* (*US*) student in the second year of a course at a high school, college or university (中学、专科学校或大学的)二年级学生.

sop·or·ific /ˌsɒpəˈrɪfɪk; ˌsɑpəˋrɪfɪk/ *n, adj* (substance, medicine, drink, etc) causing sleep 催眠的(物质、药剂、饮料等): *a soporific drug* 安眠药 ○ (*fig* 比喻) *a soporific speech* 使听者欲睡的讲话. ▷ **sop·or·ific·ally** /-klɪ; -klɪ/ *adv*.

sop·ping ⇨ SOP.

soppy /ˈsɒpɪ; ˋsɑpɪ/ *adj* (*Brit infml derog* 口, 贬) foolishly sentimental 感情用事的; 庸俗伤感的: *a soppy film* 庸俗伤感的影片 ○ *'She's just a soppy girl,' said her youngest brother.* '她呀, 就是爱动感情,' 她小弟弟说道. ▷ **sop·pily** *adv*. **sop·pi·ness** *n* [U].

sop·rano /səˈprɑ:nəʊ; *US* -ˈpræn-; səˋpræno/ *n* (*pl* **~s** /-nəʊz; -noz/) **1** singing voice of the highest range for a woman or boy 女高音; 男童声最高音: [attrib 作定语] *a soprano voice* 女高音. **2** (**a**) singer with such a voice 女高音歌手; 高音部男童声歌手: *The sopranos sang beautifully.* 那些女高音歌手的歌声很美妙. (**b**) musical part written for such a voice 乐曲的高音部: [attrib 作定语] *a difficult soprano part* 难唱的高音部. **3** musical instrument with a range about that of a soprano 高音乐器.

▷ **sop·rano** *adv* with a soprano voice 以最高音: *She sings soprano.* 她唱高音.

sor·bet /ˈsɔ:beɪ, *also* ˈsɔ:bət; ˋsɔrbət/ (*US* **sherbet**) *n* type of dessert made from water, sugar and fruit-juice; water-ice 果汁雪糕; 雪糕: *blackcurrant sorbet* 黑醋栗雪糕.

sor·cerer /ˈsɔ:sərə(r); ˋsɔrsərɚ/ *n* (*fem* 阴性作 **sor·cer·ess** /ˈsɔ:sərɪs; ˋsɔrsərɪs/) person who is believed to practise magic, esp with the help of evil spirits; magician 方士(尤指运用妖术者); 施魔法者: *sorcerers in old-fashioned fairy-tales* 传统童话中的术士.

▷ **sor·cery** /ˈsɔ:sərɪ; ˋsɔrsərɪ/ *n* [U] art, use or practice of magic, esp with evil spirits; witchcraft 魔法; 妖术; 魔法的施用.

sor·did /ˈsɔ:dɪd; ˋsɔrdɪd/ *adj* (*derog* 贬) **1** (of conditions, places, etc) dirty and unpleasant; squalid (指状况、地方等)肮脏不堪的, 邋遢的: *a sordid slum* 污秽的贫民窟 ○ *living in sordid poverty* 过着潦倒的生活. **2** (of people, behaviour, etc) displaying selfishness, meanness, etc (指人、行为等)自私自利的, 卑污的, 龌龊的: *a sordid affair* 肮脏的勾当 ○ *sordid motives* 卑鄙的动机. ▷ **sor·didly** *adv*. **sor·did·ness** *n* [U]: *the sordidness of the men's living quarters* 男宿舍的邋遢状况.

sore /sɔ:(r); sɔr/ *adj* **1** (**a**) (of a part of the body) hurting when touched or used; tender and painful; aching (指身体局部)一触或一用就痛的, 易痛的, 疼痛的: *a sore knee, throat, etc* 膝痛、喉咙痛 ○ *My leg is still very sore.* 我的腿还是很疼. (**b**) [usu pred 通常作表语] feeling pain 感到疼痛: *She's still a bit sore after the accident.* 她出事后直到现在还觉得痛呢. **2** [usu pred 通常作表语] **~ (at sb)** (*infml* 口 *esp US*) hurt and angry (esp because one has been treated unfairly); irritated 气恼(尤指因受委屈); 被激怒: *She feels sore about not being invited to the party.* 因未邀请她参加聚会, 她很恼火. ○ *Is she still sore at* (ie angry with) *you?* 她还生你的气吗? **3** (*fml or dated* 文或旧) serious; severe 严重的; 剧烈的: *in sore distress* 悲痛万分 ○ *in sore need of help* 极需帮助 ○ *His mother is a sore trial to him,* ie causes him much distress. 他母亲让他伤透了脑筋. **4** (idm 习语) **like a bear with a sore head** ⇨ BEAR[1]. **a sight for sore eyes** ⇨ SIGHT[1]. **a ˌsore ˈpoint** issue or matter that makes sb feel hurt or angry whenever it is mentioned 使某人伤心或生气的话题或事情: *I wouldn't ask him about his job interview; it's rather a sore point with him at the moment.* 我不去问他求职面试的情况, 这是他现在的伤心事. **stand/stick out like a sore ˈthumb** be very obvious or conspicuous, and often unpleasing 很显眼(常含贬义); 扎眼: *The modern office block sticks out like a sore thumb among the old buildings in the area.* 那座现代的办公楼直挺挺地竖在那片旧建筑物群中十分扎眼.

▷ **sore** *n* painful place on the body (where the skin or flesh is injured) (肌肤的)痛处, 伤处: *treat a sore* 治疗伤处 ○ *Her hands are covered in sores.* 她双手有很多痛处.

sorely *adv* (*fml* 文) seriously; very greatly 严重地; 极度地: *be sorely tempted to interrupt* 极想插嘴 ○ *Your financial help is sorely needed.* 你的资助太要紧了. ○ *She was sorely missed at the reunion.* 大家团聚时她不在, 非常遗憾.

sore·ness *n* [U]: *the soreness of his skin* 他皮肤的疼痛.

sor·ghum /ˈsɔ:gəm; ˋsɔrgəm/ *n* [U] type of millet grown as food in warm climates 高粱.

sor·or·ity /səˈrɒrətɪ; *US* -ˈrɔ:r-; səˋrɔrətɪ/ *n* [CGp] (*US*) (members of a) women's social club in a college or university (学院或大学中的)女生联谊会, 女生联谊会会员. Cf 参看 FRATERNITY 3.

sor·rel[1] /ˈsɒrəl; *US* ˈsɔ:rəl; ˋsɔrəl/ *n* [U] type of herb with sour-tasting leaves used in cooking, in salads, etc 酸模(草本植物, 叶酸, 用于烹调、做色拉等): [attrib 作定语] *sorrel soup* 酸模汤.

sor·rel[2] /ˈsɒrəl; *US* ˈsɔ:rəl; ˋsɔrəl/ *n* (**a**) reddish-brown colour 红褐色; 栗色. (**b**) horse of this colour 栗色马: *The sorrel easily won the race.* 那匹栗色马轻易地赢了那场赛马.

▷ **sor·rel** *adj* of a reddish-brown colour 红褐色的: *a sorrel coat* 红褐色的大衣.

sor·row /ˈsɒrəʊ; ˋsɑro/ *n* **1** [U] **~ (at/for/over sth)** feeling of sadness or distress caused esp by loss, disappointment or regret; grief 悲伤; 悲痛; 懊丧; 悔恨: *express sorrow for having done wrong* 因做错了事而表示懊悔 ○ *to my great sorrow* 令我悲痛万分 ○ *to the sorrow of all those who were present* 使所有在场的人感到难过 ○ *sorrow at sb's death* 因某人去世而感到的悲伤 ○ *in sorrow and in joy*, ie when we are sad and also when we are happy 无论是在悲伤还是在快乐的时候. **2** [C] particular cause of this feeling; misfortune 悲伤的原因; 懊丧的原因; 不幸: *the sorrow(s) of war* 战争带来的灾祸 ○ *He has had many sorrows in his life.* 他生活中颇多不幸. ○ *Her death was a great sorrow to everyone.* 她死了, 大家万分悲痛. **3** (idm 习语) **drown one's sorrows** ⇨ DROWN. **more in ˌsorrow than in ˈanger** with more regret than anger for what was done, etc (对做过的事等)感到遗憾, 倒并不生气: *It was more in sorrow than in anger that he criticized his former colleague.* 他批评以前的同事, 并非出于气愤而是为他惋惜.

▷ **sor·row** *v* [I, Ipr] **~ (at/for/over sth)** (*fml* 文) feel, express or show sorrow; grieve 感到、表示或显得悲哀或懊悔; 悲叹; 惋惜: *sorrowing over his child's death* 因他孩子夭折而悲伤 ○ *sorrowing at his misfortune* 哀叹他的不幸.

sor·row·ful /-fl; -fəl/ *adj* (*esp fml* 尤作文雅语) feeling, showing or causing sorrow 感到、显得或引起悲哀或懊悔的: *a sorrowful occasion* 使人心酸的场合 ○ *Her face was anxious and sorrowful.* 她满面悲愁. **sor·row·fully** /-fəlɪ; -fəlɪ/ *adv*: *weeping sorrowfully* 伤心地落泪. **sor·row·ful·ness** *n* [U].

sorry /ˈsɒrɪ; ˋsɑrɪ/ *adj* **1** [pred 作表语] **~ (to do sth/that...)** feeling sadness or regret 感到悲伤或遗憾: *We're sorry to hear of your father's death.* 我们获悉令尊去世, 非常难过. ○ *I'm sorry to say that I won't be able to accept the job.* 很遗憾, 我不能接受这工作. ○ *I'd be sorry if you were to think that I disliked you.* 若是你认为我不喜欢你, 那我就太伤心了. **2** [pred 作表语] **~ (for/about sth)** full of shame and regret (esp about a past action); apologetic 惭愧; 懊悔; 自责; 表示歉意: *Aren't you sorry for/about what you've done?* 你难道不为自己做的事情感到惭愧吗? ○ *If you say you're sorry* (ie if you apologize) *we'll forget the incident.* 你要是道个歉, 我们就不追究这件事了. **3** (used to express mild regret, disagreement or refusal, and in making apologies and excuses 用以表示有些惋惜、不同意或拒绝, 用以表达歉意或借以搪塞): *'Can you lend me a pound?' 'I'm sorry, I can't.'* '能不能借给我一镑?' '很抱歉, 我无能为力.' ○ *I'm sorry, but I don't share your opinion.* 对不起, 您的意见我不能同意. ○ *I'm sorry I'm late.* 对不起, 我来

晚了. 4 [attrib 作定语] (**-ier, -iest**) (*usu derog* 通常作贬义) poor and shabby; pitiful 贫穷而残破的; 可怜的: *a sorry sight* 可怜的情景 ○ *The house was in a sorry state.* 那房子残破不堪. ○ (*dated* 旧) *a sorry excuse*, ie a worthless one 拙劣的借口. 5 (idm 习语) **be/feel sorry for sb** (**a**) feel sympathy for sb 同情某人: *I feel sorry for anyone who has to drive in this sort of weather.* 我很同情在这种天气还得开车的人. (**b**) feel pity for, or mild disapproval of, sb 怜悯某人; 对某人有些不赞成: *If he doesn't realize the consequences of his actions, I'm sorry for him.* 倘若他意识不到自己行为的后果, 那我就觉得他很可悲了. **better safe than sorry** ⇨ BETTER². **cut a sorry, etc figure** ⇨ FIGURE¹.

▷ **sorry** *interj* 1 (used for apologizing, making excuses, etc 用以表示歉意、搪塞等): *Sorry, did I knock your elbow?* 对不起, 我是不是撞到你的胳膊肘了? ○ *Sorry, I don't know where she lives.* 很抱歉, 我不知道她住在哪儿. 2 (*esp Brit*) (used when asking sb to repeat sth one has not heard properly 因未听清而请求对方再说一遍的用语) what did you say? 你说什么?: *'I'm hungry.' 'Sorry?' 'I said I'm hungry.'* '我饿了.' '你说什么?' '我说我饿了.' ⇨Usage at EXCUSE² 用法见 EXCUSE².

sort¹ /sɔ:t; sɔrt/ *n* 1 [C] group or class of people or things (which are alike in some way); type 类; 种类; 类型: *He's the sort of person I really dislike.* 他这种人我真不喜欢. ○ *What sort of paint are you using?* 你用的是哪种颜料? ○ *We can't approve of this sort of thing/these sorts of things/things of this sort.* 我们不能赞同这种事. 2 [C usu *sing* 通常作单数] (*infml* 口) type of character; person (某种)性格; 人: *a good/decent sort* 好人[正派的人] ○ *He's not a bad sort really.* 他其实并不坏. 3 (idm 习语) **it takes all sorts (to make a world)** (*saying* 谚) people vary very much in character and abilities (and this is a good thing) 什么人都有(才成其为世界); 人的性格、能力迥异(却是好事). **nothing of the kind/sort** ⇨ KIND². **of a ˈsort/of ˈsorts** (*infml derog* 口, 贬) of a poor or inferior type 差劲的; 劣等的: *They served coffee of a sort.* 他们供应的咖啡很差. ○ *It was a meal of sorts, but nobody enjoyed it.* 那勉强算是一顿饭, 谁都没吃好. **a sort of sth** (*infml* 口) vague, unexplained or unusual type of sth 说不清的、难以解释的或不寻常的某类事物: *I had a sort of feeling he wouldn't come.* 我隐约觉得他不会来. **out of ˈsorts** (*infml* 口) (**a**) feeling unwell 身体不适: *She's been out of sorts since the birth of her baby.* 她生了孩子以后身体一直不好. (**b**) in a bad temper; annoyed 脾气坏的; 恼怒的: *He's always out of sorts early in the morning.* 他大清早总是不痛快. **sort of** (*infml* 口) to some extent; in some way or other 达到某种程度; 有几分; 有点: *I sort of thought this might happen.* 我多少猜到了这件事会发生. ○ *You sort of twist the ends together.* 你怎么把顶端缠绕在一起了. ○ *I feel sort of queasy.* 我有些恶心. ⇨Usage at KIND² 用法见 KIND².

sort² /sɔ:t; sɔrt/ *v* 1 [Tn, Tn·pr, Tn·p] **~ sth (out) (into sth)**; **~ sth (out) from sth** arrange things in groups; separate things of one type, class, etc from things of other types, etc 将事物分类; 整理: *He was sorting his foreign stamps (into piles).* 他正在整理外国邮票(, 都分成一摞一摞的). ○ *We must sort out the good apples from the bad.* 咱们得把好苹果拣出来, 同坏的分开. 2 (idm 习语) **sort out the ˌmen from the ˈboys** show or prove which people are truly brave, skilful, competent, etc 表明或证明谁真正勇敢、有技巧、有才能等: *Climbing that mountain will certainly sort out the men from the boys.* 爬爬那座山就知道谁行谁不行了. 3 (phr v) **sort sth out** (**a**) separate sth from a larger group 将某物拣出: *sort out the smaller plants and throw them away* 把小棵的挑出来扔掉. (**b**) (*infml* 口) put sth in good order 整理某事物: *This room needs sorting out*, ie tidying. 这房间需要收拾一下. **sort sth/oneself out** find a solution to (a problem/one's problems, etc) 解决(某个[自己的]问题等): *I'll leave you to sort this problem out.* 我把这个问题交给你来处理. ○ *Let's leave them to sort themselves out*, ie clear up their problems, resolve their arguments etc. 他们的事儿让他们自己解决吧. ○ *I need to sort my life/myself out a bit, before I start looking for a new job.* 我需要先安顿一下, 然后再去找新的工作. **sort sb out** (*sl* 俚) deal with sb by punishing or attacking him 整治某人: *I'll soon sort him out. Just let me get my hands on him!* 我就要收拾他了, 等我捉到他时再说! **sort through sth** go through (a number of things), arranging them in groups 查看(某些事物)并加以分类整理: *sort through a pile of old photographs* 把一堆旧照片整理一下.

▷ **sorter** *n* person or machine that sorts and arranges letters, postcards, etc 拣信员; 拣信机: *Many workers in the sorting office lost their jobs when an automatic sorter was introduced.* 拣信室安装了自动拣信机之后, 许多拣信员都失业了.

sor·tie /ˈsɔ:ti:; ˈsɔrti/ *n* 1 attack made by soldiers coming out from a position of defence on those trying to capture it 突围反击. 2 flight made by one aircraft during military operations 军事行动中一架飞行器的出动次数; 架次: *The four planes each made two sorties yesterday.* 那四架飞机昨天各出动两次. 3 brief trip away from home, esp to an unfamiliar or unfriendly place 短暂的外出(尤指去陌生处或不便处): *a sortie into the city centre to do some shopping* 到市中心去买东西 ○ (*fig* 比喻) *His first sortie into* (ie attempt to enter) *politics was unsuccessful.* 他跻身政界的第一次尝试没有成功.

SOS /ˌes əʊ ˈes; ˌɛs o ˈɛs/ *n* [sing] (**a**) urgent message for help (sent by radio, etc, usu in code) from a ship, an aircraft, etc when in danger 紧急求救信号(船只、飞机等发出的, 通常为无线电代码): *send an SOS to the coastguard* 向海岸警卫队发出求救信号 ○ [attrib 作定语] *an SOS message* 紧急求救信号. (**b**) urgent appeal for help or response (eg a radio broadcast to find relatives of a seriously ill person) 紧急求助或寻人呼叫(如为重病人寻找亲属的无线电广播): *We heard the SOS about Bill's father on the car radio.* 我们从汽车收音机里听到了有关比尔父亲的紧急寻人广播. ○ (*joc* 谑) *Our daughter sent us an SOS for some more money.* 我们的女儿给我们发来了再要点钱的求救信号. Cf 参看 MAYDAY.

S

so-so /ˈsəʊ səʊ; ˈso ˌso/ *adj* [pred 作表语], *adv* (*infml* 口) not very good; not very well; reasonably good or well 不太好; 欠佳; 平平; 还好: *'How are you feeling today?' 'Oh, only so-so.'* '今天身体好吗?' '呃, 还可以.' ○ *'What was the exam like?' 'So-so!'* '考试考得怎样啊?' '还行!'

sot /sɒt; sɑt/ *n* (*dated derog* 旧, 贬) person who is in the habit of getting drunk very often, esp sb whose mind has become confused through drinking too much 酒徒, 酒鬼(尤指因贪杯而头脑迟钝者): *her drunken sot of a husband* 她的醉鬼丈夫.

▷ **sot·tish** /ˈsɒtɪʃ; ˈsɑtɪʃ/ *adj* (*dated derog* 旧, 贬) in the habit of being drunk and, for this reason, stupid and confused 常醉酒的; 因贪杯而愚蠢糊涂的.

sotto voce /ˌsɒtəʊ ˈvəʊtʃɪ; ˌsɑto ˈvotʃɪ/ *adj, adv* (*Italian fml or joc* 意, 文或谑) in a low voice, so as not to be heard by everyone 轻声(的); 低声(的): *a sotto voce remark* 轻声说出的话 ○ *The defendant leant forward and spoke to his barrister, sotto voce.* 被告探身跟讼务律师嘀咕了几句.

sou /su:; su/ *n* 1 former French coin of low value 苏(法国旧时低值硬币). 2 (*infml* 口) very small amount of money 极少的钱: *He hasn't a sou*, ie He's very poor. 他穷得连一个子儿也没有.

soufflé /ˈsu:fleɪ; *US* su:ˈfleɪ; suˈfle/ *n* [C, U] dish of eggs, milk and flour, flavoured (with cheese, etc), beaten to make it light, and baked 蛋奶酥: *a spinach soufflé* 菠菜蛋奶酥 ○ *Would you like some soufflé?* 你要来点蛋奶酥吗?

sough /sʌf; *US* saʊ; saʊ/ *v* [I] *n* (*arch or fml* 古或文) (make a) murmuring or whispering sound (as of wind in trees) (发出)细小的声音(如树间风声); (发出)瑟瑟声, 飒飒声: *the sough of the wind in the chimney* 烟囱里的风呼呼作响.

sought *pt, pp* of SEEK.

soul /səʊl; sol/ *n* 1 [C] spiritual or non-material part of a person, believed to exist after death 灵魂: *commend one's soul to God* 将灵魂付托给上帝 ○ *Do you believe in the immortality of the soul?* 你相信灵魂不朽吗? ○ *Christians believe that a person's soul survives the death of his body.* 基督徒相信人的灵魂在躯体死后依然存在. 2 [C, U] decency and honesty of feeling; emotional, moral and intellectual energy, eg as revealed in works of art 高

尚的情操; 精神; 精力; 魄力; 道义; 智力: *He is a man without a soul.* 他是个无情无义的人. ○ *a very polished performance, but without soul* 技巧精湛的表演, 但没有内涵 ○ *This music has no soul.* 这音乐没有气魄. **3** [sing] **the ~ of sth** perfect example or pattern (of some virtue or quality) (某种美德或品质的)完美典型, 化身: *He is the soul of honour/discretion.* 他是荣誉的化身[为人极为谨慎]. **4** [C] spirit of a dead person 鬼魂; 亡灵; 幽魂: *lost souls still walking the earth* 仍在大地上行走的迷惘的幽灵 ○ *All Souls' Day*, ie 2 November 万灵节(11月2日). **5** [C] (**a**) person 人: *There wasn't a soul to be seen*, ie No one was in sight. 一个人影儿都看不见. ○ *Don't tell a soul*, ie Don't tell anybody. 谁也别告诉. (**b**) (with *adjs*, indicating familiarity, pity, etc 与形容词连用, 表示亲密、怜悯等) person, child, etc 人; 傢伙: *a dear old soul* 可爱的人儿 ○ *She's a cheery little soul*, ie a cheerful girl, etc. 她是个活泼开朗的孩子. ○ *She's lost all her money, poor soul.* 她的钱全没了, 真可怜. **6** [U] (also **soul music**) type of popular modern Black American music, derived from gospel, blues and jazz, that expresses strong emotion 灵乐(美国现代黑人通俗音乐, 源自福音音乐、布鲁斯音乐和爵士乐, 表达浓烈的情感): *the sound of soul* 灵乐之韵 ○ [attrib 作定语] *a soul singer* 灵乐歌手. **7** [U] (*US infml* 口) Black American culture and racial identity; qualities enabling a person to be in harmony with himself and others 美国黑人文化及其种族特性; 开朗随和的性格特点. **8** (idm 习语) **bare one's heart/soul** ⇨ BARE[2]. **body and soul** ⇨ BODY. **heart and soul** ⇨ HEART. **keep body and soul together** ⇨ BODY. **the life and soul of sth** ⇨ LIFE. **sell one's soul** ⇨ SELL. **upon my soul!** (*dated* 旧) (used as an exclamation of shock or surprise 用以表示震惊或惊奇).

▷ **soul·ful** /-fl; -fl/ *adj* having, affecting or showing deep (usu sad) feeling 热情的; 深情的; (通常指)悲伤的: *a soulful expression* 伤感的表情 ○ *soulful music* 充满激情的音乐. **soul·fully** /-fəlɪ; -flɪ/ *adv*: *soulfully playing the guitar* 深情地弹奏着吉他. **soul·ful·ness** *n* [U].

soul·less /ˈsəʊllɪs; ˈsollɪs/ *adj* **1** (of a person) without higher or deeper feelings (指人)无高尚心灵的, 无深厚感情的. **2** (of life, a job, etc) boring and unimportant (指生活、工作等)枯燥而不重要的: *his soulless work in the factory* 他在工厂里干的枯燥无味的工作. **soul·lessly** *adv*.

□ ˈ**soul brother** (*fem* 阴性作 ˈ**soul sister**) (*infml* 口 *esp US*) (used esp by young Black Americans 尤为美国黑人青年用语) black person (esp one who thinks and feels in the same way as oneself) 黑人(尤指与自己意趣相投的).

ˈ**soul-destroying** *adj* (of work, etc) very repetitive and dull (指工作等)单调无味的, 无聊得折磨人的: *soul-destroying jobs in the factory* 工厂里极乏味的工作.

ˈ**soul food** (*US*) food traditionally associated with Black Americans in the southern US 美国南方黑人常吃的食物.

ˈ**soul mate** person with whom one has a deep lasting friendship and understanding 知己; 执友.

ˈ**soul music** = SOUL 6.

ˈ**soul-searching** *n* [U] deep examination of one's conscience and mind 深刻反省; 自省: *After days of soul-searching he finally came to the decision to leave home.* 他经过几天的反躬自问, 最终决定离家而去.

ˈ**soul-stirring** exciting, moving, etc 激动人心的; 感人至深的; 动人心魄的: *soul-stirring music* 动人心魄的音乐.

sound[1] /saʊnd; saund/ *adj* **1** in good condition; not hurt, diseased, injured or damaged 完好的; 健康的; 健全的; 无损伤的: *have sound teeth* 牙齿结实 ○ *have a sound mind*, ie not mentally ill 心智健全 ○ *a sound constitution* 强健的体质 ○ *a house built on sound foundations* 地基坚实的房子. **2** based on reason, sense or judgement; dependable 合理的; 明智的; 正确的; 稳妥的: *a sound argument, policy, etc* 正确的论据、政策等 ○ *sound advice* 忠告 ○ *a sound business firm* 信誉好的公司 ○ *Is he sound on state education?* ie Are his views well founded, officially acceptable, etc? 他对国家教育的见解有道理吗? **3** [usu attrib 通常作定语] (*esp fml* 尤作文雅语) full and complete; thorough 充分的; 彻底的: *a sound telling-off, thrashing, etc* 一顿痛骂、痛打等. **4** careful and accurate; competent 细心的; 严谨的; 有能力的; 稳健的: *a sound tennis player* 网球技巧娴熟的人 ○ *a sound piece of writing* 好文章. **5** [usu attrib 通常作定语] (of sleep or a sleeper) deep, peaceful and uninterrupted (指睡眠)酣的, 香甜的, 不中断的; (指睡觉的人)酣睡的: *be a sound sleeper* 睡得很沉 ○ *a sound night's sleep* 睡一夜好觉. **6** (idm 习语) **safe and sound** ⇨ SAFE[1]. **(as) sound as a bell** in perfect condition 健康的; 完好的: *The doctor said I was as sound as a bell.* 医生说我身体很好. ˌ**sound in** ˌ**wind and** ˈ**limb** (*dated or joc* 旧或谑) physically fit 体格强健的: *remarkably sound in wind and limb for his age* 就他的年纪而言, 身体十分硬朗.

▷ **sound** *adv* (idm 习语) **be/fall sound aˈsleep** be/become deeply and peacefully asleep 酣睡着[安然入睡].

soundly *adv* in a sound manner; thoroughly and fully 健全地; 充分地; 彻底地; 稳健地: *a soundly based argument* 有充分根据的论点 ○ *be soundly beaten at chess* 下棋一败涂地 ○ *sleep soundly* 酣睡. **sound·ness** *n* [U]: *the soundness of her advice* 她的劝告的正确性 ○ *the soundness of his performance* 他表演的娴熟.

sound[2] /saʊnd; saund/ *n* **1** [U] sensation detected by the ear, caused by the vibration of the air surrounding it 声; 声音: *an experiment to measure the speed at which sound travels* 测定声速的试验 ○ *Sound travels more slowly than light.* 声波比光波传播得慢. **2** [C, U] thing that produces such a sensation; thing that can be heard 声音; 声响: *the sound of the wind, sea, a car, voices, breaking glass* 风、大海、汽车、人们说话、打碎玻璃的声音 ○ *the sound of music* 音乐声 ○ *I heard a strange sound outside.* 我听到外面有一种奇怪的声音. ○ *He crept upstairs without a sound*, ie noiselessly. 他悄悄地上了楼. ○ ˈ*vowel sounds*, eg /uː, ʌ, ə/ 元音(如/uː/、/ʌ/、/ə/). **3** [sing] mental impression produced by a piece of news, a description, etc (对某消息、言语等的)印象, 感觉: *I don't like the sound of her husband!* 我对她丈夫没有好感! ○ *The news has a sinister sound*, ie seems to be sinister. 这消息听起来好像不妙. **4** [U] distance within which sth can be heard 可听见的范围: *A true Cockney is born within (the) sound of Bow Bells.* 一个人, 要是在他出生的地方能听得到伦敦鲍教堂的钟声, 那他才算得上是真正的伦敦人. **5** (idm 习语) **like, etc the** ˌ**sound of one's own** ˈ**voice** (*derog* 贬) talk a lot or too much (usu without wanting to hear what others have to say) 滔滔不绝地说话(通常指不想听别人说话): *She's much too fond of the sound of her own voice.* 她总是说个不停.

▷ **sound·less** *adj* without a sound; silent 没有声响的; 悄悄的; 寂静的: *soundless movements* 静悄悄的动作. **sound·lessly** *adv*.

□ ˌ**sound** ˈ**archives** (collection of) recordings on record or tape of broadcasts considered important enough to be preserved 录音资料; 录音档案: *the BBC sound archives* 英国广播公司的录音资料.

ˈ**sound barrier** (also ˌ**sonic** ˈ**barrier**) point at which an aircraft's speed equals that of sound waves, causing sonic booms 声障; 音障: *break the sound barrier*, ie move faster than the speed of sound 突破声障(即以超声速飞行).

ˈ**sound effect** (esp *pl* 尤作复数) sound other than speech or music used in a film, play, etc to produce an atmospheric effect 音响效果: *The sound effects of the fight were very good in that radio play.* 广播剧中那场战斗的音响效果很好.

ˈ**sound-proof** *adj* made or constructed so that sound(s) cannot pass through or in 隔音的: *sound-proof material* 隔音材料 ○ *a sound-proof studio* 隔音的演播室. — *v* [Tn] make (sth) sound-proof 使(某物)隔音: *I wish we could sound-proof the boys' bedroom!* 把男生的寝室能弄成隔音的才好呢!

ˈ**sound-recording** *n* [C, U] recording in sound only 录音.

ˈ**sound-track** *n* (**a**) (music, etc on a) track or band at the side of a cinema film which has the recorded sound on it (电影胶片边上的)声带; 声带上的音乐等. (**b**) recorded music from a film, musical play, etc (on a record, cassette, etc) (录在唱片、盒式磁带等上的)电影、音乐剧等中的音乐: *I've bought the sound-track of* *that film.* 我买到了那部电影的音乐录音唱片.

ˈ**sound-wave** *n* vibration made in the air or some other medium by which sound is carried 声波.

sound[3] /saʊnd; saʊnd/ *v* **1 (a)** [La, Ln] give a specific impression when heard 听起来; 似乎: *That music sounds beautiful.* 那音乐优美动听. ○ *His voice sounded hoarse.* 他说话声音嘶哑. ○ *His explanation sounds reasonable.* 他解释得听起来合情合理. ○ *His excuse sounds unconvincing.* 他说的理由好像不可信. ○ *She sounds just the person we need for the job.* 听起来她正是我们需要的人, 适合做这事儿. **(b)** ~ **(to sb) as if.../ as though...** (not in the continuous tenses 不用于进行时态) give the impression that... 给(某)人的印象是...: *I hope I don't sound as if I'm criticizing you.* 希望不要把我的话听成是含有批评你的意思. ○ *That cough sounds as if it's getting worse.* 患的咳嗽像是更重了. ○ *It sounds to me as if there's* (ie I think I can hear) *a tap running somewhere.* 听起来好像哪儿有水龙头在流水. ⇨Usage at FEEL[1] 用法见 FEEL[1]. **2 (a)** [Tn] produce a sound from (sth); make (esp a musical instrument) produce a sound 用(某物)发出声音; 使(尤指乐器)发出声音: *sound a trumpet* 吹喇叭 ○ *The bell is sounded every hour.* 那个钟每小时响一次. **(b)** [I] give out a sound 发出声音; 作响: *The trumpet sounded.* 喇叭吹响了. ○ *The A key on this piano won't sound*, ie No sound is produced when the key is struck. 这钢琴上的A键按下去不响. **3** [Tn] give (a signal) by making a sound; announce 用声音发(信号); 发布: *sound a note of alarm /danger/warning* 发出警报[危险信号/警告信号] ○ *sound the alarm*, eg by ringing a bell 发警报(如按响电铃) ○ *sound the retreat*, eg by blowing a bugle 发撤退信号(如吹撤退号). **4** [Tn esp passive 尤用于被动语态] (*fml* 文) pronounce (sth) 发出(某事物)的声音: *You don't sound the 'h' in 'hour'.* hour 中的h不发音. ○ *The 'b' in 'dumb' isn't sounded.* dumb 中的b不发音. **5** [Tn] (*fml* 文) test or examine (sth) by tapping or striking to produce a sound and listening carefully 以敲击听音的方式检测(某物); 对(某物)进行叩诊: *sound a person's chest*, ie by tapping it 对某人的胸部进行叩诊 ○ *sound the wheels of a train*, ie by striking them 敲击火车车轮进行检查. **6** (idm 习语) **strike/sound a false note** ⇨ FALSE. **strike/sound a note (of sth)** ⇨ NOTE[1]. **7** (phr v) **sound off (about sth)** (*infml derog* 口, 贬) talk noisily and boastfully (about sth) (对某事物)大声吹嘘: *He's always sounding off about how he would manage the firm.* 他总是大言不惭地说他能把公司经营好.

▷ **-sound·ing** (forming compound *adjs* 用以构成复合形容词) having a specified sound or giving a mental impression of a specified kind 有某种声音的; 使听者产生某种印象的: *loud-sounding pop music* 吵闹的流行音乐 ○ *a very grand-sounding name* 很响亮的名字.

□ ˈ**sounding-board** *n* **(a)** board or canopy placed over a platform, stage, etc to direct the speaker's voice towards the audience, so enabling him to be heard more clearly 增音板(装在讲台、舞台等上方增加音响洪亮度的板或顶篷). **(b)** means of causing an opinion, a plan, etc to be widely heard 宣扬意见、计划等的手段: *The magazine became a sounding-board for its editor's political beliefs.* 那杂志成了编辑宣扬其政治主张的传声筒.

sound[4] /saʊnd; saʊnd/ *v* **1** [I, Tn] **(a)** test or measure the depth of (the sea, etc) by using a weighted line (called a **sounding line**) 以测深索(**sounding line**)检查或测定(海等)的深度. **(b)** find the depth of water in a ship's hold (with a **sounding rod**) (以测深杆 **sounding rod**)测定船舱内的水深. **2** (phr v) **sound sb out (about/on sth)** try to discover sb's views, opinions, etc (on sth), esp in a cautious or reserved way 试探某人(对某事物)的意见、观点等(尤指审慎地): *Have you sounded him out* (ie found out his opinions) *yet about taking the job?* 你是否探听出他对接受这项工作的意见了? ○ *I'll try to sound out the manager on the question of holidays.* 关于放假的问题, 我要去探探经理的口风.

▷ **sound·ings** *n* [pl] **1** measurements obtained by sounding (sound[4] 1); depth measured 测深所得的数据; 测得的深度: *underwater soundings* 水下测得的深度. **2 (a)** [C, U] (action of) finding out sb's views in a cautious way (对某人意见的)试探: *take soundings* 试探一番 ○ *What results have your soundings turned up?* 你试探出什么名堂来了? **(b)** reactions obtained (调查意见得到的)反应: *Our soundings are displayed in the form of a graph.* 我们的调查结果已用图表列出.

sound[5] /saʊnd; saʊnd/ (also esp in place names **Sound** 又作 **Sound**, 尤用于地名) *n* narrow passage of water joining two larger areas of water; strait 海峡: ˌ*Plymouth* ˈ*Sound* 普利茅斯海峡.

soup[1] /suːp; sup/ *n* [U, C] **1** liquid food made by cooking vegetables, meat, etc in water 汤; 羹: *chicken, tomato, vegetable, etc soup* 鸡、蕃茄、蔬菜等汤 ○ *a range of tinned soups* 各种罐头汤 ○ *Will you have some soup before the meat course?* 吃荤菜前先来点汤好吗? **2** (idm 习语) **in the** ˈ**soup** (*infml* 口) in trouble or difficulties 处于困境; 出麻烦: *If your Mum finds out what you've done, you'll really be in the soup!* 要是你妈妈发觉你干的事, 你就要倒霉了!

□ ˈ**soup-kitchen** *n* place where soup and other food is supplied free to people with no money, esp after a disaster such as an earthquake or a flood 施粥所(尤指赈灾的).

ˈ**soup-plate** *n* large deep plate with a wide rim, used esp for soup (深盘状)汤碗.

soup[2] /suːp; sup/ *v* (phr v) **soup sth up** (esp passive 尤用于被动语态) (*infml* 口) increase the power of (a car, etc) by modifying the engine (通过改装发动机)增加(汽车等)的马力: *a souped-up old mini* 为加大马力改装的旧微型汽车 ○ (*fig* 比喻) *The 'new' film is just a souped-up version of the 1948 original.* 这部'新'电影只不过是在1948年的原版片中做些更动而已.

soup·çon /ˈsuːpsɒn; *US* suːpˈsɒn; supˈsɑn, supˈsõ/ *n* [sing] **~ (of sth)** (*sometimes joc* 有时作戏谑语) very small amount; trace 少量; 微量: *a soupçon of garlic in the salad* 色拉里的一丁点大蒜 ○ *a soupçon of malice in his remark* 他的话里的些微恶意.

sour /ˈsaʊə(r); ˈsaʊr/ *adj* **1 (a)** having a sharp taste (like that of vinegar, a lemon or unripe fruit) 有酸味的; 酸的: *sour gooseberries* 酸的醋栗 ○ *This apple is really sour!* 这苹果真酸哪! **(b)** tasting or smelling sharp and unpleasant from fermentation; not fresh 有酸臭味道或气味的; 馊的: *The milk's turned sour.* 牛奶变酸了. ○ *a sour smell* 馊味. **2** having or showing a bad temper; disagreeable in manner 坏脾气的; 别扭的; 乖戾的: *a sour and disillusioned man* 阴郁颓丧的人 ○ *What a sour face she has!* 她的脸色多难看! **3** (idm 习语) **go/turn** ˈ**sour** become unfavourable or unpleasant; turn out badly 变得令人不愉快; 变坏; 变糟: *Their relationship soon went sour.* 他们的关系不久就变坏了. ○ *His original enthusiasm has turned sour.* 他当初的积极性已淡下去了. **sour** ˈ**grapes** (*saying* 谚) (said when sb pretends that what he cannot have is of little or no value or importance 用以指某人因得不到某事物而佯称该事物不好): *He says he didn't want to marry her anyway, but that's just sour grapes.* 他说自己反正不想娶她, 那不过是吃不到葡萄反而说葡萄酸罢了.

▷ **sour** *v* [I, Tn] (cause sth/sb to) become sour (使某物)变酸, 变馊; (使某事)变糟; (使某人)阴郁或乖戾: *The hot weather soured the milk.* 天热牛奶酸了. ○ (*fig* 比喻) *His personality has soured.* 他品性变差了. ○ *The old man has been soured by poverty.* 那老人因贫困脾气都坏了.

sourly *adv*.

sour·ness *n* [U]: *the sourness of the fruit* 水果的酸味 ○ *the sourness of her expression* 她满脸不悦.

□ **sour** ˈ**cream** cream deliberately made sour by the addition of bacteria, used in various savoury dishes (加菌发酵致酸的)酸味奶油.

ˈ**sourdough** *n* (*US*) **1** [U] fermented dough mixture used in bread-making 面肥: [attrib 作定语] *sourdough bread* 用面肥发的面包. **2** person with long experience in pioneering or gold prospecting (in N Canada or Alaska) (加拿大北部或阿拉斯加的)垦荒老手, 探金矿的行家.

ˈ**sourpuss** *n* (*infml* 口) bad-tempered person 脾气坏的人: *She's an old sourpuss.* 她是个脾气坏的老太太.

source /sɔːs; sɔrs/ *n* **1** starting-point of a river 河流的源头; 发源地: *the sources of the Nile* 尼罗河的发源地 ○ *Where is the source of the Rhine?* 莱茵河发源于何处?

S

2 place from which sth comes or is obtained 来源; 出处: *news from a reliable source* 来源可靠的消息 ○ *a limited source of income* 有限的收入来源 ○ *Is that well the source of all the cases of infection?* 所有这些传染病病例都是由那口井引发的吗? **3** (esp *pl* 尤作复数) person or thing (esp a book, document, etc) supplying information, esp for study 提供资料的人, 原始资料(尤指书、文件等)(尤指供研究的资料): *He cited many sources for his book.* 他在书中引用了许多资料. ○ [attrib 作定语] *source material* 原始资料. **4** (idm 习语) **at 'source** at the point of origin or beginning 在源头; 在发源地; 在开端: *money taxed at source*, ie before it is given to the earner 扣除税金后发放的钱 ○ *Is the water polluted at source or further downstream?* 河水是在源头还是在流出之后受到污染的?

souse /saus; saus/ *v* **1** [Tn] (*infml* 口) plunge (sb/sth) into or soak in water; throw water on or over 将(某人[某物])投入或浸入水中; 将水泼在...上. **2** [Tn esp passive 尤用于被动语态] put (fish, etc) into salted water, vinegar, etc to preserve it 腌制(鱼等): *soused herrings* 腌鲱鱼.

▷ **soused** /saust; saust/ *adj* [pred 作表语] (*sl* 俚) drunk 醉.

south /saʊθ; saυθ/ *n* **1** [U] (*abbr* 缩写 **S,** *US* also **So**) one of the four main points of the compass, on the right of a person facing the rising sun 南; 南方: *South is opposite north on a compass.* 罗盘上南与北是相对的. Cf 参看 EAST, NORTH, WEST. **2** [U, sing] this direction, or any part of the earth lying in this direction 南面; 南边: *The window faces south.* 窗子朝南. ○ *The wind is in* (ie blowing from) *the south today.* 今天刮南风. ○ *The town is to the south of* (ie situated further south than) *London.* 那镇位于伦敦南面. **3 the South** [sing] (**a**) part of a country further south than the rest; southern part or region 国家的南方; 南部; 南部地区: *have a holiday in the South of France* 在法国南部度假 ○ *He came to the South to look for a job.* 他到南方来找工作. (**b**) south-eastern states of the US 美国的东南各州.

▷ **sou'** /saυ; saυ/ *n* (*esp nautical* 尤用于航海) (short form of *south* used in compounds 在复合词中south的缩略形式): *sou'-east* 东南 ○ *sou'-sou'-west* 西南南.

south (also **South**) *adj* [attrib 作定语] **1** in, near, towards or at the south 南方的; 在南方的; 近南部的; 向南的; 在南侧的: *South Wales* 南威尔士 ○ *South America* 南美洲 ○ *the South Pacific* 南太平洋 ○ *grow roses on a south wall* 贴着南墙种玫瑰 ○ *on the south coast* 在南岸. **2** (of a wind) coming from the south (指风)南来的: *a south wind* 南风.

south *adv* **1** to or towards the south 到南方; 向南: *go south out of town* 出城向南走 ○ *birds flying south for winter* 飞到南方过冬的鸟 ○ *The ship was sailing due south.* 船向正南方航行. **2** (idm 习语) **down 'south** (*infml* 口) to or in the south 到南方; 在南方: *go down south for a few days* 南下几天 ○ *They used to live in Scotland but they moved down south.* 他们以前住在苏格兰, 后来移居南方了.

□ ˌ**South 'African** of southern Africa or of the republic of South Africa; native or inhabitant of these countries 非洲南部的(人); 南非共和国的(人).

'**southbound** *adj* travelling towards the south 向南行进的: *a southbound train* 南行的列车 ○ *swallows southbound for the winter* 南飞过冬的燕子.

ˌ**south-'east** (also ˌ**South-'East**) *n* [sing], *adj*, *adv* (situated in, towards, coming from or in the direction of) the point on the compass midway between south and east (位于、向着、来自或对着)东南(的): *live in the South-East* 住在东南部 ○ *a* ˌ*south-east 'wind* 东南风 ○ *a house facing south-east* 向着东南的房子. ˌ**south'easter** *n* strong wind blowing from the south-east 东南强风. ˌ**south-'easterly** *adj* (**a**) (of a wind) from the south-east (指风)来自东南方向的: *a south-easterly air flow* 东南气流. (**b**) (of a direction) towards the south-east (指方向)朝东南的. ˌ**south-'eastern** /-'iːstən; -'istɚn/ *adj* of, from or situated in the south-east part (esp of a country) 有关、来自或位于(尤指国家的)东南部的: *the south-eastern states of the US* 美国的东南各州.

'**southpaw** *n* (*infml* 口) left-handed person (esp in sports such as boxing) 惯用左手者, 左撇子(尤用于拳击等运动中).

the ˌ**South 'Pole** southernmost point of the Earth 南极: *a journey to the South Pole* 南极之行. ⇨illus at GLOBE 见GLOBE插图.

southward(s) /'saυθwədz; 'saυθwɚdz/ *adv*, *adj* (travelling) towards the south 向南地; 向南的; 南行(的): *driving southwards along the motorway* 沿高速公路向南行驶. ⇨Usage at FORWARD[2] 用法见 FORWARD[2].

ˌ**south-'west** (also ˌ**South-'West**) *n* [sing], *adj*, *adv* (situated in, towards, coming from or in the direction of) the point on the compass midway between south and west (位于、向着、来自或对着)西南(的): *travel south-west* 向西南而行 ○ *stand facing south-west* 面向西南站立 ○ *a south-west wind* 西南风 ○ *live in the South-West (of a country)* 住在(某国的)西南部. ˌ**south'wester** *n* = SOU'WESTER 2. ˌ**south-'westerly** *adj* (**a**) (of a wind) from the south-west (指风)来自西南方向的. (**b**) (of a direction) towards the south-west (指方向)朝西南的: *travel in a south-westerly direction for 6 miles* 向西南方向走6英里. ˌ**south-'western** /-'westən; -'wɛstɚn/ *adj* of, from or situated in the south-west 有关、来自或位于西南的.

south·erly /'sʌðəlɪ; 'sʌðɚlɪ/ *adj*, *adv* **1** (of winds) blowing from the south (指风)从南方刮来(的): *southerly breezes* 从南方刮来的和风. **2** towards the south 向南方(的): *The plane flew off in a southerly direction.* 飞机向南飞去.

▷ **south·erly** *n* (esp *pl* 尤作复数) wind blowing from the south 南风: *warm southerlies* 和煦的南风.

south·ern /'sʌðən; 'sʌðɚn/ **southern** *adj* in or of the south 在南方的; 南方的: *southern Europe* 南欧 ○ *the Southern states of the USA* 美国南部各州 ○ *the Southern hemisphere*, ie the southern half of the globe 南半球.

▷ **south·erner** *n* person from the southern part of a country, eg from the South in the USA 南方人: *a southerner now living in the north of England* 现住在英格兰北部的南方人 ○ *You can tell southerners by their accent.* 听口音就能辨别出南方人.

□ ˌ**southern 'lights** = AURORA AUSTRALIS (AURORA 2).

southernmost /-məʊst; -ˌmost/ *adj* furthest south 最南端的: *the southernmost point of an island* 岛的南端.

sou·venir /ˌsuːvə'nɪə(r); *US* 'suːvənɪər; ˌsuvəˌnɪr/ *n* thing taken, bought or received as a gift, and kept to remind one of a person, a place or an event 纪念品; 纪念物: *a souvenir of my holiday* 我的假期的纪念品 ○ [attrib 作定语] *a souvenir shop for tourists* 旅游纪念品商店.

sou'wester /ˌsaυ'westə(r); ˌsaυ'wɛstɚ/ *n* **1** waterproof hat (usu of oilskin) with a wide flap at the back to protect the neck 护颈防水帽(通常用油布制成, 后侧宽可遮颈). **2** (also **southwester** /ˌsaυθ'w-; ˌsaυθ'w-/) strong wind blowing from the south-west 西南强风.

sov·er·eign /'sɒvrɪn; 'sαvrɪn/ *adj* (*fml* 文) **1** (of power) without limit; highest (指权力)无限的, 至高无上的: *Who holds sovereign power in the state?* 谁掌握国家的最高权力? **2** [attrib 作定语] (of a nation, state, ruler) fully independent and self-governing; having total power (指民族、国家、统治者)完全独立自主的, 有主权的: *become a sovereign state* 成为主权国家. **3** [attrib 作定语] (*fml* 文) very effective; excellent 有特效的; 极好的: *Is there a sovereign remedy for this condition?* 在这种情况下有没有万全之策?

▷ **sov·er·eign** *n* **1** (*fml* 文) ruler with sovereign power, eg a king, a queen or an emperor 最高统治者(如国王、皇帝). **2** former British gold coin, originally worth one pound 旧时英国金币, 面值一英镑.

sov·er·eignty /'sɒvrəntɪ; 'sαvrəntɪ/ *n* [U] (*fml* 文) **1** independent sovereign power 最高统治权; 君权. **2** quality of being a country with this power 国家的主权: *respect an island's sovereignty* 尊重一岛国的主权.

so·viet /'səυvɪət, 'sɒv-; 'sovɪət, 'sαv-/ *n* **1** [C] (formerly) any of the councils of workers, etc in any part of the USSR (the Union of Soviet Socialist Republics) (旧时)苏维埃(苏联各地的工人等的代表会议): *the Supreme Soviet*, ie the governing council of the whole of the USSR 最高苏维埃(苏联的全国权力机构). **2 the Soviets** [pl] (*esp US*) (formerly) the people of the USSR; their leaders (旧时)苏联人民, 苏联领导人.

▷ **So·viet** *adj* [usu attrib 通常作定语] (formerly) of or concerning the USSR and its people (旧时)苏联(人民)

的，有关苏联(人民)的：*Soviet Navy* 苏联海军 ○ *the Soviet Union* 苏联.

sow[1] /saʊ; saʊ/ *n* fully grown female pig (成熟的)母猪. ⇨illus at PIG 见 PIG 插图. Cf 参看 BOAR, HOG 1.

sow[2] /səʊ; so/ *v* (*pt* **sowed**, *pp* **sown** /səʊn; son/ or **sowed**) **1** [Tn, Tn·pr] **~ A (in/on B)/; ~ B (with A)** put or scatter (seed) in or on the ground; plant (land) with seed 播(种子)；在(田地)里播种：*sow grass* 种草 ○ *sow a plot of land with grass* 在一块地里播草种 ○ *sow cabbage seed in pots* 把洋白菜种子种在花盆里 ○ *sow a field with wheat* 在田里种植小麦. **2** [Tn, Tn·pr] **~ sth (in sth)** (*fig* 比喻) spread or introduce (feelings, ideas, etc) 传播，使产生(情感、想法等)：*sow doubt in sb's mind* 使某人起疑心 ○ *sow the seeds of hatred* 播下仇恨的种子. **3** (idm 习语) **sow one's wild 'oats** go through a period of irresponsible pleasure-seeking while young (年轻时)放荡，纵情玩乐：*He sowed all his wild oats before he married.* 他荒唐够了才结婚的.

▷ **sower** *n* person who sows 播种的人；传播的人：(*fig* 比喻) *a sower of discontent among the people* 挑拨人们不满情绪的人.

soya bean /'sɔɪə bi:n; 'sɔɪə ˌbin/ (also *esp US* **soy bean** /'sɔɪ bi:n; 'sɔɪ ˌbin/) *n* type of bean (originally from SE Asia) rich in protein, grown for food and used esp as a substitute for meat 大豆：*a casserole made with soya beans* 大豆焙盘 ○ [attrib 作定语] *soya oil*, ie extracted from soya beans 豆油 ○ *soya flour* 大豆粉 ○ *soya milk*, ie milk substitute made from processed soya beans 豆浆.

□ ˌ**soya 'sauce** (also ˌ**soy 'sauce**) dark brown sauce made by fermenting soya beans in salty water, used in oriental cooking 酱油：*adding soy sauce to the stir-fried vegetables* 炒蔬菜中加酱油.

sozzled /'sɒzld; 'sɑzəld/ *adj* (*infml* 口) very drunk 烂醉的：*He got absolutely sozzled at the Christmas party.* 他在圣诞节聚会上烂醉如泥.

sp *abbr* 缩写 = (esp on corrected written work 尤用于校正文字时) spelling.

spa /spɑ:; spɑ/ (also in place names 用于地名时作 **Spa**) *n* (place where there is a) spring of mineral water with medicinal properties 矿泉；有矿泉的地方：*Cheltenham Spa* 切尔滕纳姆矿泉 ○ [attrib 作定语] *spa water* 矿泉水.

space /speɪs; spes/ *n* **1** [C] unused or unfilled gap or area between two or more objects or points 空白；空隙；空地：*the spaces between words* 字与字之间的空隙 ○ *There's a space here for your signature.* 你可以在这空白处签字. ○ *Is there a space for the car in the firm's car park?* 公司停车场有没有这辆车的位子？ ○ *We were separated by a space of ten feet.* 我们相距十英尺. **2** [U] unoccupied area or place available for use; room 空地方；空处：*There isn't much space left for your luggage.* 剩下的地方不太够你放行李的. ○ *Have you enough space to work in?* 你做事的地方够大吗？ ○ *There isn't enough space in the classroom for thirty desks.* 教室里放不下三十张桌子. ⇨Usage 见所附用法. **3** [C, U] large area (esp of land not built on) 开阔地区，空旷处(尤指无建筑物的)：*open spaces for children to play on* 供儿童玩耍的空地 ○ *a country of wide open spaces* 土地辽阔的国家 ○ *the freedom and space of the countryside* 乡村的自由和广阔天地. **4** [U] continuous expanse in which all things exist and move 空间：*He was staring into space.* 他极目远眺. **5** [U] (also ˌ**outer 'space**) (often in compounds 常用以构成复合词) universe beyond the earth's atmosphere in which all other planets and stars exist 外层空间；太空：*travel through space to other planets* 穿越太空飞向其他行星 ○ *the exploration of outer space* 对外层空间的探索. **6** [C usu *sing* 通常作单数] interval of time 时间的持续；期间：*(with)in the space of two hours*, ie during a period not longer than two hours 两小时之内 ○ *a space of two weeks between appointments* 两次约会之间相隔的两星期. **7** (idm 习语) **cramped for room/space** ⇨ CRAMP[2]. ˌ**watch this 'space** (*catchphrase* 警语) (in a newspaper, etc) keep alert because sth interesting or surprising will appear here soon (见于报纸等)请留意此处(即将有不容错过的内容).

▷ **space** *v* [Tn, Tn·p] **~ sth (out)** set sth out with regular spaces between 将某事物均匀隔开：*space out the posts three metres apart* 把这些柱子间隔三米排开 ○ *space out* (ie spread) *payments for a house over twenty years* 房款分二十年付清 ○ *space the rows 10 inches apart* 排列成行距10英寸 ○ *The letter was well spaced*, ie typed, etc with a suitable amount of space between each line, etc. 信中的间隔距离处理得很整齐.

spa·cing *n* [U] amount of space left between objects, words, etc in laying or setting sth out (物体、字词等之间的)间隔，间距：*Be careful with your spacing or you won't get the heading on one line.* 注意间隔，否则这个标题一行排不下. ○ *Shall I use single or double spacing* (ie single or double spaces between the lines) *when I type this letter?* 我打这封信是用单行行距还是用双行行距？

□ **'space-age** *adj* [attrib 作定语] very modern and advanced 航天时代的；太空时代的：*space-age technology, equipment* 太空时代的技术、设备.

'space-bar *n* bar on a typewriter, tapped to make spaces between words (打字机的)空格键.

'spacecraft *n* (*pl* unchanged 复数不变) (also **'spaceship**) vehicle manned or unmanned for travelling in space 航天器；宇宙飞船；太空船：*spacecraft orbiting the earth* 绕地球运行的航天器.

'spaceman /-mæn; -mæn/ (*fem* 阴性作 **'spacewoman**) *n* (*pl* **-men**, **-women**) (also **astronaut**) person who travels in outer space 宇航员；太空人.

'space invaders (*propr* 专利名) popular computerized game in which players try to prevent creatures from space landing on earth 太空侵略者(阻止天外怪物入侵地球的流行的电脑游戏).

'space probe = PROBE 2.

'spaceship *n* = SPACECRAFT.

'space shuttle spacecraft designed for repeated use, eg between earth and a space station or the moon 航天飞机；太空穿梭机.

'space station large manned artificial satellite used as a base for operations in space(5), eg for scientific research, as a launching pad for spacecraft, etc 航天站；太空站.

'spacesuit *n* sealed suit covering the whole body and supplied with air, allowing the wearer to move about in space(5) 宇航服；太空服.

'spacewalk *n* act or time of moving about in space outside a spacecraft (在航天器舱外进行的)太空行走，太空行走的时间.

NOTE ON USAGE 用法：**Space, room, place** and **seat** all relate to an area in a room, building, vehicle, etc which can be occupied by a person or thing. ☆ **space**、**room**、**place**、**seat** 均指房间、建筑物、车辆等中可容纳人或物的范围. **Space** (countable and uncountable) and **room** (uncountable) are the most general and suggest an undefined area, big enough for something or for a purpose ☆ **space**(为可数和不可数名词)和 **room**(不可数名词)最通用，指不确定的范围，可容下某物或符合某目的：*The wardrobe takes up too much space/room.* 这衣橱太占地方了. **Place** and **seat** (both countable) are used for specific spaces, usually for people to sit ☆ **place** 和 **seat**(均为可数名词)指具体的空处，通常指座位：*We'll try to get places/seats at the front of the hall.* 我们要设法弄到大厅前面的座位. ○ *There are only two places/seats left for tonight.* 今晚只剩下两个座位了.

spa·cious /'speɪʃəs; 'speʃəs/ *adj* having or providing much space; roomy 宽敞的；宽广的：*a very spacious kitchen* 非常宽敞的厨房 ○ *the spacious back seat of a car* 汽车上宽舒的后座. ▷ **spa·ciously** *adv*. **spa·cious·ness** *n* [U].

spade[1] /speɪd; sped/ *n* **1** tool for digging, with a wooden handle and a broad metal blade 锹；铲：*a garden spade* 种花草用的锹. **2** (idm 习语) **call a spade a spade** ⇨ CALL[2].

▷ **spade·ful** /'speɪdfʊl; 'spedˌfʊl/ *n* amount (of earth, etc) carried on a spade 一锹的量：*three spadefuls of sand* 三锹沙子.

□ **'spadework** *n* [U] (*fig* 比喻) hard work done in preparation for sth 艰苦的准备工作：*She got the praise for the job but he did all the spadework.* 工作完成后她获得赞誉，但筹备期间的苦活儿全是他干的.

spade[2] /speɪd; sped/ *n* **(a) spades** [sing or pl *v*] suit of playing-cards marked with black figures shaped like pointed leaves with short stems (纸牌中的)黑桃：*the* *five of spades* 黑桃五 ○ *Spades is/are trumps.* 黑桃是王牌. (**b**) [C] card from this suit 黑桃牌: *I've only one spade left.* 我只剩一张黑桃了. ⇨illus at PLAYING-CARD 见 PLAYING-CARD 插图.

spade and shovel 锹、铲或锹

spa·ghetti /spəˈgetɪ; spəˈgetɪ/ *n* [U] Italian pasta made in long thin rods, cooked in boiling water until soft and usu served with a sauce 意大利面条.

spam /spæm; spæm/ *n* [U] (*propr* 专利名) type of tinned meat made from spiced and chopped cooked ham, usu eaten cold 香火腿(碎火腿加香料制成的罐头, 通常冷食): *spam and salad* 香火腿和色拉.

span[1] /spæn; spæn/ *n* **1** distance or part between the supports of an arch or a bridge 跨度, 跨径, 跨(拱或桥支撑物之间的距离或部分): *The arch has a span of 60 metres.* 那个拱的跨度为60米. ○ *The bridge crosses the river in a single span.* 河上那座桥是单跨桥. **2** length of time over which sth lasts or extends from beginning to end (某事物)自始至终的持续时间或期间: *the span of life* 一生的时间 ○ *a short span of time* 短暂的一段时间 ○ *over a span of six years* 六年期间 ○ *have a short concentration span*, ie be capable of concentrating for only a short period of time 不能长久集中注意力. **3** (*dated* 旧) distance from the tip of the thumb to the tip of the little finger when the hand is stretched out; about 23 centimetres (9 inches) 拃, 一拃宽(手掌张开时拇指尖与小指尖的距离, 约23厘米或9英寸).

▷ **span** (**-nn-**) *v* [Tn] **1** form a bridge or arch over (sth); extend across 建造跨越(某物)的桥或拱; 横跨: *The river Thames is spanned by many bridges.* 泰晤士河上有很多桥. **2** extend over or across (sth); stretch across 跨越, 穿越(某事物); 贯穿: (*fml* 文) *His knowledge spans many different areas.* 他的知识广博遍及许多领域. ○ *Her life spanned almost the whole of the 19th century.* 她的一生几乎经历了整个19世纪. **3** stretch one's hand across (sth) in one span 将手指作一拃状跨于(某物)上: *Can you span an octave on the piano?* 你一拃能按到钢琴的八个键吗?

span[2] /spæn; spæn/ *adj* (idm 习语) **spick and span** ⇨ SPICK.

spangle /ˈspæŋgl; ˋspæŋgl/ *n* tiny piece of shining metal or plastic used for decoration on a dress, etc, esp in large numbers 闪光饰片(装饰衣物等的金属或塑料片, 尤指大量的): *the spangles on the fairy's dress in the pantomime* 童话剧中仙女连衣裙上的闪光饰片.

▷ **spangle** *v* [esp passive 尤用于被动语态: Tn, Tn·pr] **~ sth (with sth)** cover or decorate sth with spangles or small bright objects like spangles 用闪光饰片等小物件布满或装饰某物: *a dress spangled with tiny silver sequins* 用闪光的圆形小银片儿装饰的连衣裙.

span·iel /ˈspænjəl; ˋspænjəl/ *n* breed of dog with large ears which hang down 西班牙猎狗(耳大下垂的一种狗): *a cocker spaniel* 西班牙猎鸡狗.

Span·ish /ˈspænɪʃ; ˋspænɪʃ/ *adj* of Spain; of the people of Spain or their language 西班牙的; 西班牙人的; 西班牙语的: *a Spanish dance* 西班牙舞 ○ *Spanish customs* 西班牙的风俗.

▷ **Span·ish** *n* [U] the language of Spain 西班牙语: *Do you speak Spanish?* 你会说西班牙语吗?

□ **the ˌSpanish ˈMain** (former name for the) NE coast of S America and the Caribbean Sea near this coast (旧称)南美东北沿岸及其附近的加勒比海海域.

spank /spæŋk; spæŋk/ *v* **1** [Tn] slap (esp a child) with a flat hand, esp on the buttocks, as a punishment 掴(尤指小孩)(尤指打屁股惩罚): *spank a child's bottom* 掴小孩的屁股. **2** (phr v) **~ along** (*dated infml* 旧, 口) (esp of a horse, ship or car) move along quickly (尤指马、船或汽车)快速向前行进, 疾驶: *fairly spanking along* 很快地行进.

▷ **spank** *n* slap with a flat hand, esp on the buttocks 掴(尤指打屁股): *a spank on the bottom* 打在屁股上的一巴掌.

spank·ing *n* series of spanks; process of spanking (打在屁股上的)一顿巴掌: *The boy got a sound spanking.* 那男孩的屁股着实挨了一顿巴掌. — *adj* [usu attrib 通常作定语] (*dated infml* 旧, 口) quick and energetic 快速而有力的: *go at a spanking pace* 很快地走着. — *adv* (*infml* 口) (used esp before *adjs* like *fine*, *new* 尤用于 fine、new 等形容词之前) outstandingly; very 非常; 十分: *a spanking new boat* 崭新的船 ○ *spanking white paint* 纯白的颜料.

spanner (*US* **wrench**)
扳子

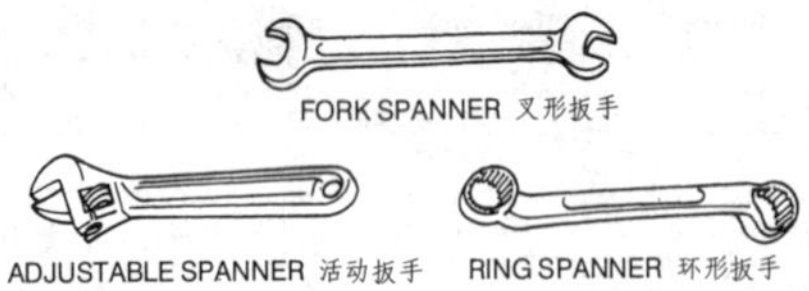

span·ner /ˈspænə(r); ˋspænɚ/ (*Brit*) (*US* **wrench**) *n* **1** tool for gripping and turning nuts on screws, bolts, etc 扳子; 扳手: *I'll need a spanner to change the back wheel.* 我需要一把扳手来换后轮. **2** (idm 习语) **(throw) a ˈspanner in the works** (*Brit infml* 口) (cause the) ruin or sabotage of a plan, scheme, etc 破坏一计划、方案等.

spar[1] /spɑ:(r); spɑr/ *n* strong wooden or metal pole used as a mast, yard, boom, etc on a ship 圆材(木质或金属质, 用作桅杆、帆桁等).

spar[2] /spɑ:(r); spɑr/ *v* (**-rr-**) [I, Ipr] **~ (with sb)** **1** box (sb) using light blows, usu for practice only 用拳轻击(某人)(通常仅作拳击练习). **2** argue or dispute (with sb), usu in a friendly way (与某人)争辩(通常指善意): *children sparring with each other* 争吵着的孩子.

□ **sparring-partner** /ˈspɑ:rɪŋ; ˋspɑrɪŋ/ *n* **1** person with whom a boxer spars as part of training 练拳的对手. **2** (*infml* 口) person with whom one enjoys frequent, usu friendly, arguments 经常斗嘴的对手: *They've been sparring-partners ever since they were at school together.* 他俩从一块儿读书起就没停过斗嘴.

spare[1] /speə(r); spɛr/ *adj* **1** in addition to what is usu needed or used; kept in reserve for use when needed 多余的; 剩余的; 备用的: *Do you carry a spare wheel in your car?* 你的汽车上有备用车轮吗? ○ *We have no spare room* (ie space) *for a table.* 我们没有放桌子的空地方. ○ *I wish we had a spare room,* ie an extra bedroom (eg for guests). 我们要是有一间富余的卧室就好了(如给客人用). ○ *I have no spare money this month.* 这个月我没有余钱. **2** (of time) for leisure; free; unoccupied (指时间)空闲的, 未占用的: *a busy woman with little spare time* 忙得没有空的女子 ○ *He paints in his spare time.* 他在空闲时绘画. **3** (*esp fml* 尤作文雅语) (of people) thin; lean (指人)瘦的: *a tall spare man* 又高又瘦的男子 ○ *a spare figure* 瘦削的身材 ○ *spare of build* 体格瘦削的. **4** [attrib 作定语] (*fml* 文) small in quantity 少量的: *a spare meal* 量小的一顿饭 ○ *on a spare diet* 在节食. **5** (idm 习语) **go ˈspare** (*Brit sl* 俚) become very annoyed or upset 烦恼; 难过: *Your mum will go spare if she finds out what you've done!* 要是你妈妈知道你干的事, 她会气坏的!

▷ **spare** *n* spare part (for a machine, car, etc), esp an extra wheel for a car (机器、汽车等的)备件; (尤指)汽

车备用车轮: *I've got a puncture and my spare is flat too!* 我的车胎扎破了, 备用的也瘪了! ○ *I'll show you where the spares are kept.* 我来指给你看放备件的地方.

□ ˌ**spare** ˈ**part** part (for a machine, car, etc) used to replace an identical part if it gets lost, damaged, etc 备用零件; 备件; 配件: *It's difficult to get spare parts for old washing-machines.* 旧洗衣机的配件已很难弄到.

ˌ**spare-**ˈ**rib** *n* rib of pork with most of the meat cut off (肉少的)猪排骨: *barbecued spare-ribs* 烤猪排骨.

ˌ**spare** ˈ**tyre** **1** extra wheel for a car, etc (汽车等的)备用车轮. **2** (*Brit infml joc* 口, 谑) roll of fat around the waist 腰部的一圈脂肪: *I'll have to exercise to get rid of my spare tyre.* 我得运动运动以减少腰部的脂肪.

spare[2] /speə(r); spɛr/ *v* **1** [Tn, Dn·n] refrain from hurting, harming or destroying (sb/sth); show mercy to 不伤害(某人[某事物]); 饶恕; 宽容: *Please spare (ie don't kill) me!* 请饶了我(一命)吧! ○ (*fml* 文) *spare a person his life*, ie not kill him 饶某人一命 ○ *if I am spared*, ie if I live 假若我幸而不死 ○ *They killed the men but spared the children.* 他们把男人都杀了, 但放过了孩子. ○ *The woodman spared* (ie did not cut down) *a few trees.* 伐木工人留下了几棵树没砍掉. **2** [Tn, Dn·n] refrain from using, giving, etc (sth); use as little as possible 节制使用或提供(某事物); 吝惜; 节约: *No trouble was spared to ensure our comfort.* 为了我们舒适, 已竭尽全力. ○ *Try to spare her as much distress as possible when you tell her.* 你告诉她的时候, 尽量不要让她伤心. ○ *He does not spare himself*, ie works, etc very hard indeed. 他不偷懒. ○ *Please spare me* (ie don't tell me) *the gruesome details.* 你可别给我讲那些可怕的细节. **3** [Tn, Tn·pr, Dn·n, Dn·pr] **~ sth (for sb/sth)** be able to afford to give (time, money, etc) (to sb for a purpose) (为某人或某目的)提供(时间、钱等); 拨出; 匀出; 分出: *I can't spare the time for a holiday at the moment.* 目前我抽不出时间去度假. ○ *Can you spare me a few minutes of your time?* 我能耽搁你几分钟吗? ○ *Can you spare me a few litres of petrol?* 你能匀给我几升汽油吗? ○ *Can you spare a cigarette for me?* 给我根烟行吗? **4** [Tn, Tn·pr] (*infml* 口) manage without (sb) 无(某人)也可以: *I can't spare him today — we need everybody here.* 我今天需要他——我们需要人人都到齐. ○ *I can't spare you for that job; you must finish this one first.* 我不能放你去做那件事; 你必须先把这件做完. **5** (idm 习语) **no expense spared** ⇨ EXPENSE. **spare sb's** ˈ**blushes** do not embarrass sb by praising him 不夸奖某人以免使之难为情. **spare sb's** ˈ**feelings** avoid hurting sb's feelings 避免伤害某人的感情; 不使某人难堪: *He spared her feelings by not criticizing her husband in front of her.* 他没当她的面说她丈夫的不是, 以免使她难堪. **spare no pains doing/to do sth** (*fml* 文) take as much trouble as is necessary to achieve sth 不遗余力地做某事: *The hotel staff spared no pains to ensure that our stay was as enjoyable as possible.* 旅馆工作人员对我们照顾得无微不至, 尽量让我们住得舒适. ˌ**spare the** ˌ**rod and** ˌ**spoil the** ˈ**child** (*saying* 谚) if you do not punish a child when he does wrong you will spoil his character 孩子不打不成器. **(and) to** ˈ**spare** more than is needed; left over 过剩; 有余; 剩余: *We have enough fruit and to spare.* 我们的水果充足有余. ○ *Do you have any sugar to spare?* 你的食糖有富余吗? ○ *There's no time to spare!* ie You must act, go, etc as quickly as possible. 没有多余的时间了!

▷ **spar·ing** /ˈspeərɪŋ; ˈspɛrɪŋ/ *adj* [pred 作表语] **~ with/of/in sth** (*fml* 文) economical or frugal with sth; not wasteful of sth 节约; 俭省; 不浪费: *be sparing with the sugar* 节约用糖 ○ *sparing of one's energy* 节省精力 ○ *not sparing in his advice to others* 他向别人提供意见时知无不言. **spar·ingly** *adv*: *Use the perfume sparingly!* 少用些香水!

spark /spɑːk; spɑrk/ *n* **1** [C] **(a)** tiny glowing particle thrown off from sth burning or produced when two hard substances (eg stone, metal, flint) are struck together 火花; 火星: *Sparks from the fire were flying up the chimney.* 火星沿着烟囱向上飘. ○ *The firework exploded in a shower of sparks.* 烟火炸开放出一阵火花. ○ *Rubbing stones together produces sparks to start a fire.* 用石头相擦可产生火花用来引火. **(b)** flash of light produced by the breaking of an electric current (切断电流而产生的)电火花: *a faulty light switch sending out sparks* 冒着火花的有故障的电灯开关. **2** [sing] **~ of sth** trace (of a particular quality) (某特质的)极微的量: *He hasn't a spark of generosity in him.* 他一点也不慷慨. ○ *without a spark of enthusiasm* 没有丝毫的积极性. **3** (idm 习语) **a bright spark** ⇨ BRIGHT. **make the fur/sparks fly** ⇨ FLY[2].

▷ **spark** *v* [I] **1** give out sparks (SPARK 1); produce sparks 发出火花; 冒火星: *The fire is sparking dangerously.* 那堆火迸出火星, 十分危险. **2** (phr v) **spark sth off** (*infml* 口) be the immediate cause of (usu sth bad); lead to sth 直接导致(尤指坏事); 引发某事: *His comment sparked off a quarrel between them.* 他提的意见引起了他们之间的争吵. ○ *The incident sparked off a whole chain of disasters.* 那件事惹出了一连串的灾祸.

sparks *n* [sing *v*] (*sl* 俚) electrician or radio operator (esp on a ship) 电工, 无线电操作员(尤指船上的).

□ ˈ**sparking-plug** (also ˈ**spark-plug**) *n* device producing an electrical spark which fires the petrol mixture in a petrol engine 火花塞: *The sparking-plugs need cleaning.* 火花塞要清理一下了. ⇨illus at App 1 见附录1插图, page xii.

sparkle /ˈspɑːkl; ˈspɑrkl̩/ *v* [I, Ipr] **~ (with sth)** **1** shine brightly with flashes of light 闪耀; 闪烁: *Her diamonds sparkled in the candle-light.* 她的钻石在烛光中闪闪发亮. ○ *pavements sparkling with frost* 冰霜闪耀的人行道 ○ *Her eyes sparkled with excitement.* 她目光闪烁显露出激动的神情. **2** be full of life and wit 活力和才智焕发; 活跃: *She was really sparkling (with happiness) at the wedding.* 在婚礼上她(幸福得)容光焕发. ○ *She always sparkles at parties.* 在聚会上她总是神采奕奕.

▷ **sparkle** *n* [U, C] effect made by sparkling (SPARKLE 1, 2); act of sparkling 光亮; 活力; 闪光: *the sparkle of sunlight on snow* 阳光照射在雪上的闪光 ○ *There was a sudden sparkle as the fireworks were lit.* 烟火点燃后火花迸发. ○ *a performance that lacked sparkle* 缺乏生气的表演.

spark·ler /ˈspɑːklə(r); ˈspɑrklɚ/ *n* **1** [C] type of small hand-held firework that sends off showers of sparks (手持的)喷火星的小烟火. **2** **sparklers** [pl] (*sl* 俚) diamonds 钻石.

spark·ling /ˈspɑːklɪŋ; ˈspɑrklɪŋ/ *adj* [attrib 作定语] **1** (of wine, etc) giving off tiny bubbles of gas (指酒等)起泡的: *sparkling white wine* 白葡萄汽酒 ○ *sparkling mineral water* 矿泉汽水. **2** lively and witty 活泼机智的: *sparkling conversation* 轻松愉快的交谈 ○ *a brilliant, sparkling young woman* 聪明活泼的年轻女子.

spar·row /ˈspærəʊ; ˈspæro/ *n* type of small brownish-grey bird common in many parts of the world 麻雀: *sparrows twittering in the roof-tops* 在屋顶上吱吱喳喳叫的麻雀. ⇨illus at App 1 见附录1插图, page iv.

□ ˈ**sparrow-hawk** *n* small hawk that eats smaller birds 雀鹰.

sparse /spɑːs; spɑrs/ *adj* not dense, thick or crowded; thinly scattered 稀少的; 稀疏的; 稀落的: *a sparse population* 稀少的人口 ○ *a sparse beard* 稀疏的胡须 ○ *The television coverage of the event was rather sparse.* 电视上对这件事报道得很少. ▷ **sparsely** *adv*: *a sparsely furnished room*, ie one with little furniture 陈设简陋的房间 ○ *sparsely spread financial resources* 分散的财力. **sparse·ness** (also **spars·ity** /ˈspɑːsətɪ; ˈspɑrsətɪ/) *n* [U]: *the sparseness of trees on the landscape* 景物中树木寥寥无几.

spar·tan /ˈspɑːtn; ˈspɑrtn̩/ *adj* (*fml* 文) (of conditions) simple and harsh; without luxury or comforts (指环境)简陋而艰苦的, 清苦的: *lead a spartan life in the mountains* 在山里过清苦的生活 ○ *a spartan meal*, ie a very simple one 一顿简单的饭.

spasm /ˈspæzəm; ˈspæzəm/ *n* [C, U] **1** strong, sudden and uncontrollable tightening of a muscle or muscles 痉挛; 抽搐; 发作: *an asthma spasm* 气喘发作 ○ *painful muscular spasms* 引起疼痛的痉挛 ○ *The muscles in the athlete's leg went into spasm*, ie tightened uncontrollably and painfully. 那运动员的腿抽筋了. **2** sudden short burst (of activity, emotion, etc) (活动、情感等的)突发, 发作: *a spasm of energy, excitement, pain, coughing* 一阵活力的爆发、兴奋、疼痛、咳嗽.

spas·modic /spæzˈmɒdɪk; spæzˈmɑdɪk/ *adj* **1** occurring or done at irregular intervals (usu for short periods at a time); not continuous or regular 一阵阵的; 时断时续的:

S

spasmodic efforts to clean the house 对房子时干时停的打扫 ○ *spasmodic periods of happiness followed by misery* 时而快乐，时而痛苦. **2** caused by or affected by spasms 痉挛的；痉挛性的：*spasmodic asthma* 支气管气喘. ▷ **spas·mod·ic·ally** /-klɪ; -klɪ/ *adv*: *spasmodically energetic* 表现出阵阵活力的.

spas·tic /ˈspæstɪk; ˈspæstɪk/ *n, adj* (person who is) physically disabled because of cerebral palsy, a condition in which there are faulty links between the brain and motor nerves causing jerky or uncontrollable movements 患大脑性麻痹的(人)：*a special school for spastics* 专为大脑性麻痹患者办的学校 ○ *spastic children* 大脑性麻痹患儿.

spat[1] *pt, pp* of SPIT[1].

spat[2] /spæt; spæt/ *n* (*US infml* 口) small or unimportant quarrel 小争吵：*a spat between brother and sister* 兄妹俩的小吵小闹.

spat[3] /spæt; spæt/ *n* (usu *pl* 通常作复数) cloth or leather covering for the ankle worn formerly by men over the shoe and fastened at the side (旧时男子用的)护踝鞋罩：*a pair of spats* 一双鞋罩.

spate /speɪt; spet/ *n* **1** [sing] sudden fast rush (of business, etc) (生意等的)突然增多：*a spate of orders* 突如其来的一大批订货单 ○ *a spate of new cars on the market* 突然上市的一批新汽车 ○ *a spate of (cases of) influenza in the winter* 冬天的一阵流感. **2** (idm 习语) **in ˈspate** (of a river, etc) flowing strongly at a much higher level than normal (指河水等)高涨：*After the storm all the rivers were in spate.* 暴雨过后河水都上涨了.

spa·tial /ˈspeɪʃl; ˈspeʃəl/ *adj* (*fml* 文) of, concerning or existing in space 空间的；有关空间的；存在于空间的：*the spatial qualities of the new concert hall* 新音乐厅的空间特性. ▷ **spa·tially** /-ʃəlɪ; -ʃəlɪ/ *adv*.

S

spat·ter /ˈspætə(r); ˈspætɚ/ *v* **1** [Tn, Tn·pr] **~ sth (on/over sb/sth); ~ sb/sth (with sth)** scatter, splash or sprinkle sth in drips (over sb/sth) 洒、溅或泼在(某人[某物])上：*spatter oil on one's clothes/spatter one's clothes with oil* 把油溅在衣服上 ○ *As the bus passed it spattered us with mud.* 公共汽车开过时，溅了我们一身泥. ⇨Usage at SPRAY[2] 用法见SPRAY[2]. **2** [I, Ipr, Ip] fall or rain down in drops 滴下；洒落：*We heard the rain spattering down on the roof of the hut.* 我们听到雨滴滴答答打在小屋的屋顶上. ○ *Bullets spattered around us.* 子弹像雨点般射在我们周围.

▷ **spat·ter** *n* [sing] **~ (of sth)** (**a**) sprinkling; small shower 溅；洒；泼；滴落：*a spatter of rain, bullets, etc* 一阵雨、弹雨. (**b**) sound of spattering 洒、溅、泼等的声音：*the spatter of rain on the tent* 雨落在帐篷上的滴沥声 ○ *a spatter of applause* 劈里啪拉的一阵掌声.

spat·ula /ˈspætʃʊlə; ˈspætʃələ/ *n* **1** tool with a wide flat blunt blade used for mixing and spreading, esp in cooking and painting (搅拌或涂敷用的)铲；(尤指)烹调用铲，漆工抹刀：*He scraped the mixture out of the bowl with a plastic spatula.* 他用塑料铲把盆里的混合料刮了出来. ○ *She levelled the surface of the cake mixture with a metal spatula.* 她用金属铲抹平了蛋糕配料. ⇨illus at KITCHEN 见KITCHEN插图. **2** strip of hard material (usu wood) used by a doctor for pressing the tongue down when examining the throat 压舌板.

spawn /spɔːn; spɔn/ *n* [U] (esp in compounds 尤用以构成复合词) **1** eggs of fish, shellfish and frogs, toads, etc (鱼、甲壳动物、蛙、蟾等的)卵：*ˈfrog-spawn* 蛙卵. **2** (*biology* 生) white fibrous matter from which mushrooms and other fungi grow 菌丝.

▷ **spawn** *v* [I, Tn] (**a**) (of fish, frogs, etc) produce (eggs) (指鱼、蛙等)产(卵)：*salmon spawning* 产卵的鲑鱼 ○ *Have the frogs spawned yet?* 那些蛙产卵了吗? (**b**) (*esp derog* 尤作贬义) appear or produce (sth) in great numbers 大批涌现；大量产生(某事物)：*departments which spawn committees and sub-committees* 派生出一大串委员会和附属委员会的部门 ○ *new housing estates spawning everywhere* 处处涌现出的新住宅区.

spay /speɪ; spe/ *v* [Tn] remove the ovaries of (a female animal) to prevent breeding 切除(动物的)卵巢；骟(雌性动物)：*Has your cat been spayed yet?* 你那只母猫骟了吗?

speak /spiːk; spik/ *v* (*pt* **spoke** /spəʊk; spok/, *pp* **spoken** /ˈspəʊkən; ˈspokən/) **1** [I] make use of words in an ordinary voice (not singing); utter words 说话；讲话：*He can't speak.* 他不会说话. ○ *Please speak more slowly.* 请慢点说. ○ *'May I speak to Susan?'* ie at the beginning of a telephone conversation. '可以请苏珊听电话吗?' ○ *'Speaking,'* ie this is Susan speaking (in reply to previous question). '我就是.'(对前一句的回答). **2** [Tn] (not in the continuous tenses 不用于进行时态) know and be able to use (a language) 会说(某语言)：*He speaks several languages.* 他会说好几种语言. ○ *She speaks a little Urdu.* 她会一点儿乌尔都语. ○ *Does anyone speak English here?* 这儿有人会说英语吗? **3** [Ipr] **~ (to/with sb) (about/of sb/sth)** have a conversation (with sb); express oneself in words; talk (与某人)交谈；用语言表达；谈话：*I was speaking to him only yesterday.* 昨天我还跟他说过话呢. ○ *Can we speak about plans for the holidays?* 我们谈谈假期的打算好吗? ○ *She was speaking about it for hours.* 那件事她谈了好几个钟头. ○ *She didn't speak of her husband at all.* 她完全没谈到她丈夫. **4** [I, Ipr] **~ (on/about sth)** make a speech (to an audience) 发言；讲话；演讲：*She spoke for forty minutes at the conference.* 她在会上讲了四十分钟. ○ *Are you good at speaking in public?* 你善于当众讲话吗? ○ *I told him to speak on any subject he wanted.* 我已告诉他想谈什么就谈什么. **5** [Tn] make (sth) known; say or express 表明(某事)；说出：*speak the truth* 说实话 ○ *He spoke only two words the whole evening.* 一晚上他只说了两个字. ⇨Usage at SAY 用法见SAY. **6** [I, Ipr] **~ (to/with sb)** (usu in negative sentences 通常用于否定句) (*infml* 口) be on friendly or polite terms (with sb) (与某人)礼尚往来：*They're not speaking (to each other) after their argument.* 他们争吵过后就互不理睬了. **7** (idm 习语) **actions speak louder than words** ⇨ ACTION. **be on ˈspeaking terms (with sb)** (**a**) know sb well enough to speak to him 与某人熟识到可交谈的程度：*I see him on the train every day but we're not on speaking terms.* 我每天都在火车上见到他，但彼此没说过话. (**b**) be on friendly or polite terms; be willing to talk (to sb) (esp after an argument) 礼尚往来；肯(对某人)说话(尤指争吵后)：*At last they're on speaking terms again!* 他们终于又互相说话了! ○ *They're not on speaking terms after their quarrel.* 他们那次吵过架后就互不理睬了. **the facts speak for themselves** ⇨ FACT. **in a manner of speaking** ⇨ MANNER. **nothing to ˈspeak of** nothing worth mentioning; not much 不值一提；不多：*She has saved a little money, but nothing to speak of.* 她存了一点钱，但少得不值一提. **not to speak of/no sth to speak of** not worth mentioning/no sth worth mentioning 谈不上[没有值得一提的事物]：*We've not had any summer to speak of.* 直到现在还没有像样的夏天. ○ *We've had no food to speak of today.* 谈不上今天吃过东西了. **roughly, generally, personally, etc speaking** in a rough, general, etc way; from a general, personal, etc point of view 大致上；一般来说；从一般、个人等角度来看：*Generally speaking, I don't like spicy food.* 我一般不爱吃辛辣的食物. ○ *Personally speaking, I prefer the second candidate.* 我本人喜欢第二个候选人. Cf 参看 STRICTLY SPEAKING (STRICT). **ˌso to ˈspeak** one could say; as it were 可以说；可谓：*The new procedures have been officially christened, so to speak.* 新措施可以说已经正式实施了. **speak for itˈself/themˈselves** need no explaining; be self-evident 无需说明；不言自喻：*The events of that evening speak for themselves.* 那天晚上发生的事情不用说也很清楚. **speak for oneˈself** express one's opinion, etc in one's own way 自己表达自己的意思：*I'm quite capable of speaking for myself, thank you!* 我还是有能力把话说清楚的，谢谢你吧! **speak for yourˈself** (*joc or derog catchphrase* 谑或贬，警语) don't think you are speaking on behalf of everyone 你只能代表你自己；你不能代表别人：*'We all played very badly.' 'Speak for yourself, I think I played quite well.'* '我们在场上表现得都很差劲.' '你只能说你自己，我觉得我表现得很不错.' **speak ill of sb** (*fml* 文) speak in an unkind or unfavourable way about sb 说某人坏话：*Don't speak ill of the dead.* 别说死者的坏话. ○ *I've never spoken ill of him in my life.* 我这辈子从来没说过他的坏话. **speak one's ˈmind** express one's views directly and frankly 直率地表达意见. **speak/talk of the devil** ⇨ DEVIL[1]. **speak the same ˈlanguage (as sb)** (*infml* 口) have similar tastes and ideas (as sb); have a common understanding (与某人)口味和意见相同; 有共同的想法: *As soon as I met Liz, it was obvious we spoke the same language.* 我和利兹一见面就明显觉得我们俩很说得来. **speak volumes for sb/sth** be strong evidence of sb/sth's merits, qualities, etc 充分证明某人[某事物]的优点、品质等: *These facts speak volumes for her honesty.* 这些事实都有力地证明了她为人诚实. **speak 'well for sb** be evidence in favour of sb 证明某人很好: *Her reputation as a good mother speaks well for her.* 大家都知道她是个好母亲, 这足以证明她人品好. **'spoken for** reserved, etc in advance 事先预订的: *I'm afraid you can't use those chairs — they're already spoken for.* 很抱歉, 你不能用这些椅子——有人预先说好了要用的. **the spoken/written word** ⇨ WORD. **8** (phr v) **speak for sb** (no passive 不用于被动语态) **(a)** state the wishes, views, etc, of sb; act as a spokesman for sb 表达某人的愿望、意见等; 代某人说话: *I'm afraid I can't speak for Geoff, but...* 很抱歉, 我不能代表杰夫说话, 但是.... **(b)** give evidence on behalf of sb 为某人作证; 为某人辩护: *Who is prepared to speak for the accused?* 谁来为被告辩护? **speak of sth** (*fml* 文) indicate sth; suggest sth 表明某事物; 意味着某事物: *Her behaviour speaks of suffering bravely borne.* 她的表现显示出她勇敢地承受着痛苦. **speak out (against sth)** say boldly and clearly what one thinks (in opposition to sth) 大胆明确地说出(反对某事物)的意见: *He was the only one to speak out against the closure of the hospital.* 只有他一人直言不讳地表示反对关闭医院. **speak to sb** (*euph* 婉) reprimand; tell off 责备; 训斥: *Your children are disturbing my wife; can you speak to them, please?* 你的孩子吵得我妻子不得安宁, 请说说他们好吗? **speak to sth** (*fml* 文) give information about (a subject), esp at a meeting 讲述(某事)(尤指在会上): *Will you speak to this item, David?* 戴维, 你来谈谈这个问题好吗? **speak up** speak louder 大点声说: *Please speak up; we can't hear you at the back.* 请大点儿声说, 我们在后面听不见. **speak up (for sb)** state clearly and freely what one thinks (on behalf of sb) (为某人)明确而坦率地说出想法: *It's time to speak up for those who are suffering injustice.* 现在该为蒙受不公正对待的人们大声疾呼了.

▷ **speaker** *n* **1** person who makes speeches; person who speaks or was speaking 发言者; 演讲者; 说(着)话的人: *May I introduce our speaker for this evening?* 我来介绍一下今晚演讲的人好吗? ○ *a good, poor, interesting, etc speaker* 演讲水平高的人、演讲能力差的人、发言有趣的人 ○ *I turned and saw the speaker at the back of the room.* 我转过脸看见说话的人是在屋子的最后面. **2** (*infml* 口) = LOUDSPEAKER (LOUD). **3** person who speaks a language 说某种语言的人: *French speakers/speakers of French* 说法语的人. **4 the Speaker** person who presides over business in the House of Commons and other legislative assemblies (英国下议院及其他议会的)议长: *'Order! Order!' shouted the Speaker.* '安静! 安静!' 议长大声说道. ○ *MP's trying to attract the attention of the Speaker* 尽力引起议长注意的下议院议员.

-spoken (forming compound *adjs* 用以构成复合形容词) speaking in a specified way 以某种方式说话的: *well-spoken* ○ *a soft-spoken man.*

□ **ˌspeaking 'clock** (*Brit infml* 口) telephone service that gives spoken statements of the time 电话报时服务.

'speak-easy *n* place where alcohol may be bought illegally (esp formerly in the US during Prohibition) 非法售酒处(尤指美国禁酒时期).

-speak *suff* 后缀 (forming *ns* 用以构成名词) (*infml often derog* 口, 常作贬义) language or jargon (esp of a particular group or organization) 语言, 术语, 行话(尤指某群体或机构的): *computerspeak* 计算机术语 ○ *newspeak* 新说法(模棱两可、互相矛盾的宣传用语).

spear /spɪə(r); spɪr/ *n* **1** weapon with a metal point on a long handle, used (esp formerly) for hunting and fighting 矛; 长枪; 标枪: *antelopes killed with spears* 用长枪刺死的羚羊. **2** long pointed leaf or stem (eg of grass or asparagus) growing directly out of the ground 长而尖的叶或茎(直接从地面生出的, 如草或芦荀): *spears of the snowdrop plant* 雪花莲的茎.

▷ **spear** *v* [Tn] strike, pierce or wound (sb/sth) with a spear; kill with a spear (用矛)刺穿, 刺伤, 刺死(某人[某物]): *They were standing in the river spearing fish.* 他们站在河里叉鱼. ○ *The warriors speared the man to death.* 武士们把那个男子戳死了.

□ **'spearhead** *n* (usu *sing* 通常作单数) person or group that begins or leads an attack 先锋; 前锋; 先头部队: *The new managing director will act as spearhead of the campaign.* 新上任的常务董事将在这场运动中挂帅. — *v* [Tn] act as a spearhead for (sth) 为(某事)作先锋; 带头做(某事): *The tanks spearheaded the offensive.* 坦克在那次进攻中打头阵.

spear·mint /ˈspɪəmɪnt; ˈspɪrˌmɪnt/ *n* [U] common variety of mint used for flavouring (esp chewing-gum) 留兰香: [attrib 作定语] *spearmint toffees* 留兰香太妃糖. Cf 参看 PEPPERMINT.

spec /spek; spɛk/ *n* (idm 习语) **on 'spec** (*infml* 口) as a speculation or gamble, without being sure of obtaining what one wants 碰运气: *I went to the concert on spec: I hadn't booked a seat.* 我去听音乐会是碰运气, 因为没预订座位.

spe·cial /ˈspeʃl; ˈspɛʃəl/ *adj* **1** [usu attrib 通常作定语] of a particular or certain type; not common, usual or general 特殊的; 特别的: *goods on special offer*, ie cheaper than usual 特价货 ○ *He did it as a special favour.* 他做这事算是特别照顾. ○ *What are your special interests?* 你有些什么特别爱好? ○ *She's a very special friend.* 她是个特殊的朋友. **2** [attrib 作定语] designed, reserved or arranged, etc for a particular purpose 专门的; 特设的: *a special train*, eg for a holiday excursion 专列(如为假日出游特设的) ○ *a special occasion* 特别安排的活动 ○ *You'll need a special tool to do that.* 干那个活儿要用专用工具. ○ *She has her own special way of doing things.* 她做事自有一套办法. ○ *Newspapers send special correspondents to places where important events take place.* 报社往往派遣特派记者到有重大事件的现场. **3** [attrib 作定语] exceptional in amount, degree, quality, etc 额外的; 格外的: *Take special care of it.* 对这东西要特别细心. ○ *Why should we give you special treatment?* 凭什么要我们对你特殊照顾? ○ *He takes no special trouble with his work.* 他在工作上不特别卖力. Cf 参看 ESPECIAL.

▷ **spe·cial** *n* **1** person or thing that is not of the usual or regular type, esp a special constable, train or edition (of a newspaper, etc) 特别的人或事物; (尤指)特种警察, 专列, 号外, 特刊: *an all night television special on the election* 电视上整夜的选举专题报道 ○ *Specials were brought in to help the regular police force.* 已增派特警部队协助常规警察. **2** (*US infml* 口) reduced price (in a shop) given prominence through advertising, etc (通过广告等宣传的)大减价: *There's a special on coffee this week.* 本周咖啡特价出售. ○ *Coffee is on special* (ie being sold at a lower price than usual) *this week.* 本周咖啡大减价.

spe·cial·ist /-ʃəlɪst; -ʃəlɪst/ *n* person who is an expert in a special branch of work or study, esp of medicine 专业工作者; 专家; (尤指)专科医生: *an 'eye specialist* 眼科医师 ○ *a specialist in plastic surgery* 整形外科医生.

spe·cially /-ʃəlɪ; -ʃəlɪ/ *adv* **1** for a particular purpose 特意地; 专门地: *I came here specially to see you.* 我是专程来看你的. ○ *I made this specially for your birthday.* 这是我特意为你生日而做的. **2** (also **especially**) exceptionally; particularly 格外地; 特别地; 特殊地: *I enjoyed the evening, but the meal wasn't specially good.* 整个晚上我过得很高兴, 但那顿饭不怎么样.

□ **'Special Branch** (*Brit*) department of the police force that deals with national security (警察部门的)政治保安处.

ˌspecial 'constable person trained to help the police force occasionally, esp in an emergency 特种警察.

'special 'delivery delivery of mail (a letter, parcel, etc) by a special messenger instead of by the usual postal service (信件、包裹等的)专递: *If you want the letter to arrive tomorrow send it (by) special delivery.* 要让这封信明天到, 就得用专递服务.

ˌspecial 'licence licence allowing a marriage to take place at a time or place not usu authorized 结婚特别许可(不限在通常规定的时间或地点举行婚礼).

ˌspecial 'pleading (*law* 律) persuasive but unfair reasoning that favours one side of an argument 偏向的诡辩.

'special school school for handicapped children 特殊学校(残疾儿童学校).

S

ˈ**special student** (*US*) student at an American university not on a degree course 美国大学中不就读学位课程的学生.

spe·ci·al·ity /ˌspeʃɪˈælətɪ; ˌspɛʃɪˈælətɪ/ (also *esp US* **spe·cialty** /ˈspeʃəltɪ; ˈspɛʃəltɪ/) *n* **1** interest, activity, skill, etc to which a person gives particular attention or in which he specializes 专业; 特长: *Her speciality is medieval history.* 她专修中世纪史. ○ *His speciality is barbecued steaks.* 烤牛排是他的拿手好菜. **2** service or product for which a person, place, firm, etc is well-known; particularly good product or service 招牌性的或优质的服务或产品; 特制品; 拳头产品: *Wood-carvings are a speciality of this village.* 木雕是这个村的特殊工艺品. ○ *Home-made ice-cream is one of our specialities.* 本店自制的冰激凌别具风味.

spe·cial·ize, -ise /ˈspeʃəlaɪz; ˈspɛʃəlˌaɪz/ *v* [I, Ipr] ~ **(in sth)** (**a**) be or become a specialist 成为专家; 专门从事; 专攻: *He specializes in oriental history.* 他专门研究东方史. (**b**) give particular attention to (a subject, product, etc); be well-known for 专注于(某项目、产品等); 以…闻名: *This shop specializes in chocolates.* 这个商店专门出售巧克力.

▷ **spe·cial·iza·tion, -isation** /ˌspeʃəlaɪˈzeɪʃn; *US* -lɪˈz-; ˌspɛʃəlɪˈzeʃən/ *n* [U].

spe·cial·ized, -ised *adj* **1** adapted or designed for a particular purpose (为适应某目的或为某目的而设计的)专门的: *specialized tools* 有专门用途的工具. **2** of or relating to a specialist 专业的; 专科的: *specialized knowledge* 专业知识 ○ *specialized work* 专业性的工作.

spe·cie /ˈspiːʃiː; ˈspiʃɪ/ *n* [U] (*fml* 文) money in the form of coins (contrasted with paper) 硬币(相对纸币而言): [attrib 作定语] *specie payments* 硬币支付 ○ *payment in specie* 以硬币支付.

S

spe·cies /ˈspiːʃiːz; ˈspiʃiz/ *n* (*pl* unchanged 复数不变) **1** group of animals or plants within a genus(1) differing only in minor details from the others, and able to breed with each other but not with other groups 物种; 种: *a species of antelope* 一种羚羊 ○ *various animal species* 各种动物 ○ *the human species*, ie mankind 人类. Cf 参看 PHYLUM, CLASS 7, ORDER[1] 9, FAMILY 4. **2** (*infml or joc* 口或谑) sort; type 种类; 类型: *an odd species of writer* 古怪的作家.

spe·cific /spəˈsɪfɪk; spɪˈsɪfɪk/ *adj* **1** detailed, precise and exact 详细而精确的; 确切的: *specific instructions* 明确的指示 ○ *What are your specific aims?* 你有确切的目标吗? **2** relating to one particular thing, etc; not general 特定的; 具体的: *The money is to be used for one specific purpose: the building of the new theatre.* 这笔钱有专门用途: 就是建造新剧院.

▷ **spe·cific** *n* **1** (*medical* 医) drug used to treat a particular disease or condition 特效药: *Quinine is a specific for malaria.* 奎宁是治疗疟疾的特效药. **2** particular aspect or precise detail 具体的方面; 详情; 细节: *moving from the general to the specific* 从泛泛而谈转向具体论述 ○ *We all agreed on our basic aims, but when we got down to specifics it became more complicated.* 关于基本目标, 大家的意见是一致的, 但谈到具体事情时, 情况就复杂了.

spe·cif·ic·ally /-klɪ; -klɪ/ *adv* in a specific manner 确切地; 具体地; 特别地: *You were specifically warned not to eat fish.* 已经特别叮嘱过你不要吃鱼. ○ *The houses are specifically designed for old people.* 这些房子是专为老年人设计的.

□ **speˌcific ˈgravity** mass of any substance in relation to an equal volume of water 比重.

spe·ci·fica·tion /ˌspesɪfɪˈkeɪʃn; ˌspɛsəfəˈkeʃən/ *n* **1** [C esp *pl* 尤作复数] details and instructions describing the design, materials, etc of sth to be made or done 规格; 规格说明: *specifications for (building) a garage* (建造)车房的规格说明 ○ *the technical specifications of a new car* 新汽车的技术规格. **2** [U] action of specifying 具体说明; 详述: *the specification of details* 细节的详述.

spe·cify /ˈspesɪfaɪ; ˈspɛsəˌfaɪ/ *v* (*pt, pp* **-fied**) [Tn, Tf, Tw] (*esp fml* 尤作文雅语) state or name clearly and definitely (details, materials, etc) 确切说明(细节、材料等); 明确规定; 详述: *The contract specifies red tiles, not slates, for the roof.* 合同中规定屋顶要用红瓦而不用石板瓦. ○ *The regulations specify that you may use a dictionary in the examination.* 规则中指明考试时可以用词典.

spe·ci·men /ˈspesɪmən; ˈspɛsəmən/ *n* **1** thing or part of a thing taken as an example of its group or class (esp for scientific research or for a collection) 样品, 标本(尤用于科研或作收藏品): *There were some fine specimens of rocks and ores in the museum.* 博物馆里有些很好的岩石和矿石标本. ○ [attrib 作定语] *a specimen signature* 签字样 ○ *a publisher's catalogue with specimen pages of a book* 附有某书样张的出版物目录. **2** sample (esp of urine) to be tested (usu for medical purposes) 标本; 样; (尤指)尿样: *supply specimens for laboratory analysis* 提供作实验分析的标本. **3** (*infml sometimes derog* 口, 有时作贬义) person of a specified sort, esp one who is unusual in some way 有某特点的人(尤指有些怪异的): *a fine specimen (of humanity)* 好人 ○ *That new librarian is an odd specimen, isn't he?* 新来的图书管理员挺古怪的, 是不是?

spe·cious /ˈspiːʃəs; ˈspiʃəs/ *adj* (*fml* 文) seeming right or true but actually wrong or false 似是而非的: *a specious argument* 似是而非的论点. ▷ **spe·ciously** *adv*: *speciously convincing* 貌似有理而让人信服. **spe·cious·ness** *n* [U].

speck /spek; spɛk/ *n* very small spot or stain; tiny particle (of dirt, etc) 小斑点; 小污点; (泥土等的)小颗粒: *a speck of soot on his shirt* 他衬衫上的黑炱斑 ○ *Do you ever see specks in front of your eyes?* 你是否有过眼前出现黑斑的现象? ○ *The ship was a mere speck on the horizon.* 那只船在天水交接处不过是一个小点儿.

speckle /ˈspekl; ˈspɛkl̩/ *n* small mark or spot, esp one of many, often occurring as natural markings on a different coloured background (on the skin, feathers, eggs, etc) (皮肤、羽毛、蛋壳等上的)斑点, 色斑, 色点: *brown speckles on a white egg* 白色蛋上的褐斑 ○ *speckles of red in a blue background* 蓝底红点儿.

▷ **speckled** *adj* marked with speckles 有斑点的; 有色斑的: *a speckled hen* 有花斑的母鸡 ○ *speckled eggs* 有色斑的蛋.

specs /speks; spɛks/ *n* [pl] (*infml* 口) = GLASSES (GLASS 5).

spec·tacle /ˈspektəkl; ˈspɛktəkl̩/ *n* **1** grand public display, procession, performance, etc 大场面(壮观的公开展示、队列、表演等): *The ceremonial opening of Parliament was a fine spectacle.* 该议会的开幕式场面隆重. **2** impressive, remarkable or interesting sight 精彩的、非凡的或有趣的情景: *The sunrise seen from high in the mountains was a tremendous spectacle.* 从山上居高远望, 日出景象蔚为奇观. **3** (*usu derog* 通常作贬义) object of attention, esp sb/sth unusual or ridiculous 注意的目标; (尤指)不同寻常的或滑稽的人[事物]: *The poor fellow was a sad spectacle.* 那可怜的傢伙看着就叫人难过. **4** (idm 习语) **make a ˈspectacle of oneself** draw attention to oneself by behaving, dressing, etc ridiculously, esp in public (因行为、穿着等)出丑, 出洋相: *make a spectacle of oneself by arguing with the waiter* 跟服务员争吵而出丑.

spec·tacles /ˈspektəklz; ˈspɛktəkl̩z/ *n* [pl] (*usu fml* 通常作文雅语) = GLASSES (GLASS 5): *I've lost a pair of spectacles.* 我丢了一副眼镜. ○ *Where are my spectacles?* 我的眼镜呢?

▷ **spec·tacled** /-kəld; -kl̩d/ *adj* wearing spectacles 戴眼镜的.

spec·tacu·lar /spekˈtækjʊlə(r); spɛkˈtækjələ˞/ *adj* (**a**) making a very fine display or show 壮观的; 精彩的: *a spectacular display of fireworks* 壮观的烟火会. (**b**) (attracting attention because) impressive or extraordinary 引人注目的; 出色的; 与众不同的: *a spectacular victory by the French athlete* 那个法国运动员的辉煌胜利.

▷ **spec·tacu·lar** *n* (supposedly) impressive show or performance; spectacle 精彩的节目或表演; 壮观的场面: *a Christmas TV spectacular* 圣诞节精彩的电视节目 ○ *an aerobatic spectacular at the air show* 航空表演中的特技飞行奇观. **spec·tacu·larly** *adv*: *a spectacularly daring performance* 扣人心弦的惊险表演.

spec·tator /spekˈteɪtə(r); *US* ˈspekteɪtər; ˈspɛktetə˞/ *n* person who watches (esp a show or game) 观看者; (尤指表演或比赛的)观众: *noisy spectators at a football match* 足球比赛中喧闹的观众.

□ **specˈtator sports** sports that attract many spectators, eg football 观众多的体育运动(如足球): *Many spectator sports are now televised.* 有许多体育项目因观众多现已

由电视转播.

spec·tral /ˈspektrəl; ˋspɛktrəl/ *adj* (*fml* 文) **1** of or like a spectre(1) (似)鬼的, 幽灵的: *spectral figures* 鬼影. **2** of the spectrum or spectra 谱的; 光谱的: *spectral colours* 谱色.

spectre (*US* **spec·ter**) /ˈspektə(r); ˋspɛktɚ/ *n* (*fml* 文) **1** ghost; phantom 鬼; 幽灵: *haunted by spectres from the past* 闹鬼的. **2** unpleasant and frightening mental image of possible future trouble (因可能出现困难而产生的)忧虑, 恐怖: *The spectre of unemployment was always on his mind.* 他心头一直萦绕着可能失业的恐惧感.

spectro- *comb form* 构词成分 of or concerned with a spectrum 谱的; 有关谱的: *spectrometer.*

spec·tro·meter /spekˈtrɒmɪtə(r); spɛkˋtrɑmətɚ/ *n* type of instrument that can be used for measuring spectra 分光计; 分光仪; 谱仪.

spec·tro·scope /ˈspektrəskəʊp; ˋspɛktrə,skop/ *n* instrument for producing and examining the spectra of a ray of light 分光镜.

▷ **spec·tro·scopic** /ˌspektrəˈskɒpɪk; ,spɛktrəˋskɑpɪk/ *adj* of or by means of a spectroscope 分光镜的; 藉分光镜的: *spectroscopic analysis* 光谱分析.

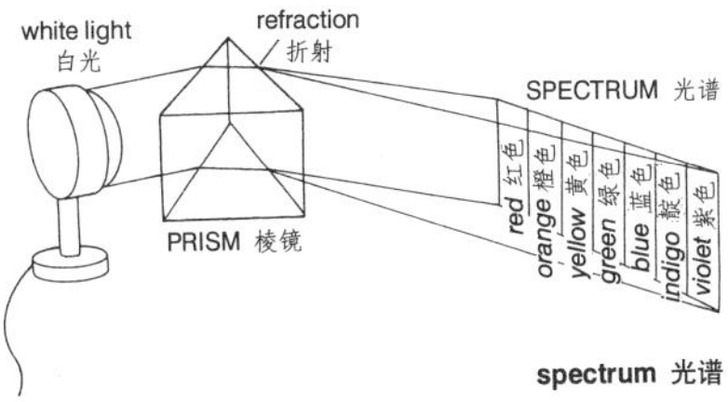

spectrum 光谱

spec·trum /ˈspektrəm; ˋspɛktrəm/ *n* (*pl* **spectra** /ˈspektrə; ˋspɛktrə/) (usu *sing* 通常作单数) **1** image of a band of colours as seen in a rainbow (and usu described as red, orange, yellow, green, blue, indigo and violet), formed by a ray of light that has passed through a prism 光谱. **2** similar series of bands of sound 声谱; 频谱: *the sound spectrum* 声谱. **3** (*fig* 比喻) full or wide range or sequence 范围; 系列: *covering the whole spectrum of ability* 涉及整个能力范围. ⇨Usage at DATA 用法见 DATA.

spec·ulate /ˈspekjʊleɪt; ˋspɛkjə,let/ *v* **1** [I, Ipr, Tf] **~ (about/on/upon sth)** form opinions without having definite or complete knowledge or evidence; guess 思考; 思索; 推断; 推测: *speculate about/upon the future* 对未来的推想 ○ *I wouldn't like to speculate on the reasons for her resignation.* 我不愿意猜测她辞职的原因. ○ *I can only speculate that he left willingly.* 我看他一定是自愿走的. **2** [I, Ipr] **~ (in sth)** buy and sell goods or stocks and shares in the hope of making a profit through changes in their value, but with the risk of losing money 投机; 做投机买卖: *speculate in oil shares* 做石油股票的投机买卖 ○ *speculating on the stock market* 进行证券投机.

▷ **specu·lator** *n* person who speculates (SPECULATE 2) 投机者; 投机商.

specu·la·tion /ˌspekjʊˈleɪʃn; ,spɛkjəˋleʃən/ *n* **1** (**a**) [U] **~ (over/about/upon/on sth)** action of speculating (SPECULATE 1) 思考; 思索; 推断; 推测: *much speculation over the cause of the air crash* 对飞机坠毁原因的多方推测. (**b**) [C] opinion reached in this way; guess 推测结论; 猜测: *My speculations proved totally wrong.* 我猜想的全错了. **2** (**a**) [U] **~ (in sth)** activity of speculating (SPECULATE 2) 投机活动: *speculation in oil* 在石油业中的投机活动 ○ *dishonest speculation in property development* 房地产开发中的欺诈性投机活动. (**b**) [C] business deal, transaction, etc involving this 投机买卖; 投机生意: *make some unprofitable speculations* 做些无利可图的投机生意 ○ *buy many shares as a speculation* 买入许多股票进行投机.

specu·lat·ive /ˈspekjʊlətɪv; *US also* ˈspekjəleɪtɪv; ˋspɛkjələtɪv, ˋspɛkjə,letɪv/ *adj* **1** concerned with or formed by speculation(1) 思考的; 思索的; 有关推断的; 推测出的: *speculative philosophy* 思辨哲学 ○ *His conclusions are purely speculative,* ie based on reasoning, not facts. 他做出的结论纯粹是推测而来的. **2** as a speculation(2) 投机的; 投机生意的: *speculative buying of grain* 投机购买谷物 ○ *speculative housing* 投机性营造房屋.

sped *pt, pp* of SPEED.

speech /spiːtʃ; spitʃ/ *n* **1** [U] (**a**) power or act of speaking 说话的能力; 说话: *Man is the only animal that has the faculty of speech.* 人类是唯一有说话能力的动物. ○ *We can express our thoughts by speech.* 我们能以说话的方式表达思想. ○ *His illness left him without the power of speech.* 他病后丧失了说话能力. ○ *freedom of speech,* ie freedom to say openly in public what one thinks, eg on social and political questions 言论自由. (**b**) manner or way of speaking 说话的方式: *His indistinct speech made it impossible to understand him.* 他口齿不清, 无法听懂他的意思. ○ *She's doing a study of children's speech.* 她正在研究儿童说话现象. ○ *His speech was slurred: he'd clearly been drinking.* 他说话含混不清, 显然喝了酒了. **2** [C] (**a**) **~ (on/about sth)** formal talk given to an audience 讲话; 发言; 演说: *make/deliver/give a speech* 发言 ○ *a speech on/about racism* 关于种族主义的讲话 ○ *He made a very boring after-dinner speech.* 他在宴会后的讲话很枯燥. (**b**) (usu long) group of lines to be spoken by an actor in a play (通常指长的)台词: *I've got some very long speeches to learn in Act 2.* 第2幕中我有些大段台词要记.

▷ **speech·less** *adj* (**a**) unable to speak, esp because of strong feeling 说不出话的(尤指因激动): *speechless with surprise* 惊讶得说不出话来 ○ *Anger left him speechless.* 他气得说不出话来. (**b**) that cannot be expressed in words 无法用言语表达的: *speechless rage* 无法用言语表达的愤怒. **speech·lessly** *adv*: *speechlessly furious* 气愤得说不出话来. **speech·less·ness** *n* [U].

□ ˈ**speech-day** *n* annual school celebration with speeches and distribution of certificates and prizes (学校一年一度的)毕业典礼日.

ˌ**speech** ˈ**therapy** special treatment to help people with speech problems to speak more clearly 言语治疗. ˌ**speech** ˈ**therapist** person trained to provide this 言语治疗专家.

speech·ify /ˈspiːtʃɪfaɪ; ˋspitʃə,faɪ/ *v* (*pt, pp* **-fied**) [I] (*infml usu derog* 口, 通常作贬义) make a speech or speeches pompously; talk as if making speeches 高谈阔论; 煞有介事地讲话: *town councillors speechifying at the opening of a new building* 在新大厦的启用典礼上放言高论的市镇议员.

speed /spiːd; spid/ *n* **1** [U] quickness of movements; swiftness 快; 迅速: *He moves with great speed.* 他动作很迅速. ○ *The tennis player's speed is his great asset.* 那个网球运动员动作迅速, 这是他的一大优势. **2** [C, U] rate at which sb/sth moves 速度; 速率: *at a speed of fifty kilometres an hour* 以每小时五十公里的速度 ○ *at (a) very slow speed* 以很慢的速度 ○ *at top speed* 以最高速度. **3** [C] (**a**) sensitivity of photographic film to light 感光度: *What's the speed of the film you're using?* 你用的胶卷感光度是多少? (**b**) time taken by a camera shutter to open and close 快门速度: *different shutter speeds* 不同的快门速度 ○ *a photograph taken at a speed of $\frac{1}{250}$ of a second* 用$\frac{1}{250}$秒的快门速度拍摄的照片. **4** [U] (*sl* 俚) amphetamine used as a drug to produce a sense of well-being and excitement 苯异丙胺, 安非他明(用以产生欣快感和兴奋感): *He's hooked on* (ie addicted to) *speed.* 他使用安非他明已成瘾. **5** [C] (esp in compounds 尤用以构成复合词) gear 排挡: *a ten-speed bicycle* 十速自行车. **6** (idm 习语) **at speed** at high speed; quickly 高速地; 快地: *It's dangerous to go round corners at speed.* 高速转弯很危险. **full pelt/tilt/speed** ⇨ FULL. **full speed/steam ahead** ⇨ FULL. **more haste, less speed** ⇨ HASTE. **pick up speed** ⇨ PICK[3]. **a turn of speed** ⇨ TURN[2]. **with all** ˈ**speed**/ˈ**haste** as quickly as possible 尽快地. **with lightning speed** ⇨ LIGHTNING[2].

▷ **speed** *v* (*pt, pp* **sped** /sped; spɛd/; in senses 2 and 3 用于下述第2义和第3义时作 **speeded**) **1** [Ipr] move along or go quickly 快速行进; 疾行: *cars speeding past the school* 从学校旁快速驶过的汽车 ○ *He sped down the street.* 他沿那条街快步走去. **2** [Tn, Tn·pr] cause

S

(sth) to move or go quickly 使(某事物)快速移动或行进: *This medicine will help speed her recovery.* 这药能加快她康复. **3** [I] (usu in the continous tenses 通常用于进行时态) drive or go faster than the speeds allowed by law 违章超速驾驶或行驶: *The police said he'd been speeding on the motorway.* 警察说他在高速公路上违章超速行驶. **4** (phr v) **speed (sth) up** (cause sth to) increase speed (使某事物)加速: *They've speeded up production of the new car.* 他们加快了新汽车的生产. ○ *The train soon speeded up.* 火车不久就加快了速度.

speed·ing *n* [U] traffic offence of travelling at an illegal or a dangerous speed 违章超速行驶: *fined £60 for speeding* 因超速而被罚款60英镑.

speedo·meter /spi:ˈdɒmɪtə(r); spiˈdɑmətɚ/ *n* instrument showing the speed of a motor vehicle, etc (机动车等的)速度计: *The speedometer is faulty.* 这个速度计有毛病. ➪illus at App 1 见附录1插图, page xii.

speedy *adj* (**-ier, -iest**) **1** (*often infml* 常作口语) moving quickly; fast 快速的; 迅速的: *a speedy business operator* 办事效率高的经营者. **2** coming, done or carried out, etc without delay 迅即的; 及早的: *wish sb a speedy recovery from illness* 祝某人早日康复. **speed·ily** *adv*. **speedi·ness** *n* [U]: *the speediness of his recovery from the accident* 他在事故后的迅速康复.

□ ˈ**speedboat** *n* motor-boat designed to go at high speeds 快艇.

ˈ**speed-indicator** *n* (*fml* 文) speedometer 速度计.

ˈ**speed limit** highest speed at which it is legal to travel (on a particular stretch of road) (某段道路的)速度限制: *What's the speed limit on the motorway?* 高速公路的速度限制是多少? ○ *The speed limit is 40 miles per hour.* 规定的最高时速为40英里.

S

ˈ**speed merchant** (*sl derog* 俚, 贬) person who drives a car or motor bike very fast 高速驾驶汽车或摩托车的人.

ˈ**speed trap** system used by the police to catch motorists, etc who are driving faster than the speed limit 车速监视路段.

ˈ**speedway** *n* (**a**) [C] track for fast driving and racing, esp by motor-bikes 赛车跑道(尤指摩托车的). (**b**) [U] sport of racing motor-bikes on such a track 摩托车赛: *Do you like speedway?* 你喜欢摩托车赛吗? (**c**) [C] (*US*) road on which fast driving is allowed 高速公路.

ˈ**speed-up** *n* (*infml* 口) increase in speed; acceleration 加速; 加快: *a speed-up in the rate of production* 生产速度的提高.

speed·well /ˈspi:dwel; ˈspidwɛl/ *n* type of small wild plant with bright blue flowers 婆婆纳(草本植物, 开鲜艳蓝花).

spe·le·ology (also **spe·lae·ology**) /ˌspi:lɪˈɒlədʒɪ; ˌspilɪˈɑlədʒɪ/ *n* [U] **1** scientific study and exploration of caves 洞穴学. **2** sport of walking in and exploring caves 洞穴探险(运动).

▷**spe·le·olo·gical** (also **spe·lae-**) /ˌspi:lɪəˈlɒdʒɪkl; ˌspilɪəˈlɑdʒɪkəl/ *adj*: *speleological exploration* 洞穴探索.

spe·le·olo·gist (also **spe·lae-**) /ˌspi:lɪˈɒlədʒɪst; ˌspilɪˈɑlədʒɪst/ *n* scientist who studies caves; expert in speleology 洞穴学学者; 洞穴探险家.

spell[1] /spel; spɛl/ *n* **1** (**a**) [C] words which when spoken are thought to have magical power; charm 咒语; 咒; 符咒: *a book of spells* 咒语集 ○ *The wizard recited a spell.* 那术士念了一咒. (**b**) [C usu *sing* 通常作单数] state or condition caused by the speaking of such words (used esp in the expressions shown) 被咒语镇住的状态, 中魔(尤用于以下示例): *be under a spell*, ie be in this state 被咒语镇住 ○ *cast/put a spell on sb* 对某人施魔咒. **2** [sing] great attraction, fascination, etc caused by a person or thing; strong influence 魅力; 魔力; 威势: *under the spell of her beauty* 被她的美艳迷住 ○ *the mysterious spell of music* 音乐的神奇魔力.

□ **spellbinder** /ˈspelbaɪndə(r); ˈspɛlˌbaɪndɚ/ person (esp a speaker) who can hold sb's attention completely (as if) by magic (似乎)以魔法吸引住他人注意力者; (尤指)使听者入迷的演讲者. **spellbinding** /-baɪndɪŋ; -baɪndɪŋ/ *adj* holding the attention in this way; entrancing 使人入迷的; 迷人的: *a spellbinding performance* 迷住人的表演. **spellbound** /-baʊnd; -ˌbaʊnd/ *adj* [usu pred 通常作表语] with the attention held by, or as if by, a magical spell; entranced 着魔; 入迷; 出神: *The magician held* (ie kept) *the children spellbound.* 魔术师把孩子都迷住了.

spell[2] /spel; spɛl/ *n* **1** period of time during which sth lasts (某事物持续的)一段时间: *a long spell of warm weather* 持续很久的温暖的天气 ○ *a cold spell in January* 一月份中一段寒冷的日子 ○ *rest for a short spell* 歇一会儿. **2** ~ (**at/on sth**) period of activity or duty (esp one which two or more people share); turn 活动的或工作的一段时间; (尤指)轮班的时间: *a spell at the wheel of the car*, eg when two people are sharing the driving 轮流驾驶汽车 ○ *a spell on the typewriter* 打一会儿字 ○ *We took spells at carrying the baby.* 我们轮流抱孩子.

spell[3] /spel; spɛl/ *v* (*pt, pp* **spelled** /speld; spɛld/ or **spelt** /spelt; spɛlt/) ➪Usage at DREAM[2] 用法见 DREAM[2]. **1** (**a**) [Tn, Tn·pr, Cn·n] name or write letters of (a word) in their correct order (用字母)拼(某字); 拼写: *How do you spell your name?* 你的名字怎么拼写? ○ *That word is spelt with a PH, not an F.* 那个字里的f音拼作PH而不是F. ○ *You spell his name P-A-U-L.* 他的名字拼作P-A-U-L. (**b**) [I, Tn] put the letters of (words) together in the correct or accepted order 正确地拼(字): *These children can't spell.* 这些孩子不会拼字. ○ *Why don't you learn to spell my name (correctly)?* 你怎么不花点工夫把我的名字拼对呢? **2** [Tn] (of letters) form (words) when put together in a particular order (指字母)拼成(字): *C-A-T spells cat.* C-A-T拼成cat. **3** [Tn] have (sth) as a result; mean 招致(某事物); 意味着: *The failure of their crops spelt disaster for the peasant farmers.* 作物歉收农民就要受灾. **4** (phr v) **spell sth out** (**a**) say aloud or write the letters of (a word) in their correct order 拼出(某字): *Could you spell that word out for me again?* 那个字你再拼一遍好吗? (**b**) make sth clear and easy to understand; explain sth in detail 讲清楚某事; 详细解释某事: *My instructions seem simple enough — do I have to spell them out again?* 我的要求算是够明白的了——还要我再讲清楚吗? ○ *She's so stupid that you have to spell everything out.* 她笨极了, 什么事都要给她解释得明明白白.

▷ **speller** *n* person who spells (usu in the way indicated by the *adj*) 拼字者(通常有形容词修饰): *She's a good/poor speller.* 她拼字的功底很好[差].

spell·ing *n* **1** [U] (**a**) ability of a person to spell 拼写的能力: *His spelling is terrible.* 他的拼字功底极差. ○ [attrib 作定语] *They were given a spelling test.* 对他们进行了拼写测验. (**b**) action or process of forming words correctly from letters 拼写. **2** [C] way a word is spelt 拼法: *Which is the better spelling: Tokio or Tokyo?* Tokio和Tokyo哪种拼法好呢? ○ *English and American spelling(s)* 英式拼法和美式拼法.

spelt[1] ➪ SPELL[3].

spend /spend; spɛnd/ *v* (*pt, pp* **spent** /spent; spɛnt/) **1** [I, Tn, Tn·pr] ~ **sth (on/sth)** give or pay out (money) for goods, services, etc 用(钱); 花(钱): *He spends as if he were a millionaire.* 他用起钱来像个百万富翁似的. ○ *She's spent all her money.* 她把钱都花光了. ○ *He spends too much (money) on clothes.* 他在衣着上花费太大. **2** [Tn, Tn·pr] ~ **sth (on sth/in doing sth)** (**a**) use (time, etc) for a purpose 花(时间等): *spend a lot of time on a project/(in) explaining a plan* 花很多时间进行某项目[解释某方案] ○ *spend one's energy cleaning the place up* 用力气把那地方打扫干净. (**b**) use sth up; exhaust sth 用完, 耗尽(某物): *The blizzard quickly spent itself*, ie used up all its force. 暴风雪很快就停了下来. ○ *They went on firing until they had spent all their ammunition.* 他们不停地射击, 耗尽了所有的弹药. ○ *I've spent all my energy on this.* 我对此事已呕尽心血. **3** [Tn, Tn·pr] pass (time) 度过, 消磨(时间): *How do you spend your spare time?* 你业余时间怎么打发? ○ *spend a weekend in Paris* 在巴黎过周末 ○ *spend summer holidays by the sea* 在海滨过暑假. **4** (idm 习语) **spend the ˈnight with sb** (*euph* 婉) sleep for a night in the same bed as and have sexual intercourse with sb to whom one is not married 跟某人过一夜(与非配偶同床并发生性行为). **spend a ˈpenny** (*infml euph* 口, 婉) go to the toilet; urinate 去厕所; 解小便: *I'm just going to spend a penny.* 我要去厕所.

▷ **spender** *n* person who spends money (usu in way indicated by the *adj*) 花钱者(通常有形容词修饰): *a big/an extravagant spender* 大手大脚的人[挥金如土的人] ○ *a miserly spender* 用钱很小气的人.

□ ˈ**spendthrift** *n* person who spends money extravagantly and wastefully 挥霍者; 败家子.

spent /spent; spɛnt/ *adj* (**a**) [usu attrib 通常作定语] having lost power or strength; used 失去效力的; 衰竭的; 用过的: *a spent match* 燃过的火柴 ○ *a spent cartridge/bullet* 空的弹壳[弹头]. (**b**) (*fml* 文) exhausted 筋疲力尽的: *He returned home spent, dirty and cold.* 他回到家时筋疲力尽, 又脏又冷.

sperm /spɜ:m; spɝm/ *n* **1** [C] (*pl* unchanged or **~s** 复数或不变或作 **sperms**) male reproductive cell able to fertilize a female ovum 精子: *He has a low sperm count,* ie He has few sperm cells and so is not very fertile. 他的精液中精子含量少. **2** [U] fertilizing fluid of a male animal containing these; semen 精液.

▷ **spermi·cide** /-ɪsaɪd; -ə,saɪd/ *n* substance that kills sperm 杀精子剂. **sperm·icidal** /ˌspɜ:mɪˈsaɪdl; ˌspɝmə-ˈsaɪdəl/ *adj* [attrib 作定语]: *spermicidal jelly* 杀精膏.

sper·ma·ceti /ˌspɜ:məˈsetɪ; ˌspɝməˈsɛtɪ/ *n* [U] white waxy fatty substance contained in solution in the heads of sperm whales, used (esp formerly) for ointments, candles, etc 鲸蜡; 鲸脑油.

sper·ma·to·zoon /ˌspɜ:mətəˈzəʊən; ˌspɝmətəˈzoən/ *n* (*pl* **-zoa** /-ˈzəʊə; -ˈzoə/) (*biology* 生) sperm 精子; 精液.

sperm whale /ˈspɜ:m weɪl; ˈspɝm ˌhwel/ *n* large whale producing spermaceti 抹香鲸.

spew /spju:; spju/ *v* **1** [I, Ip, Tn, Tn·p] **~ (sth) (out/up)** (*esp infml* 尤作口语) vomit 呕吐: *spewing up in the basin* 呕吐到盥洗盆里 ○ *She spewed up the entire meal.* 她把那顿饭全吐出来了. **2** [Ip, Tn, Tn·p] **~ out; ~ sth (out)** (cause sth to) send out in a stream (使某事物)喷出, 射出: *Water spewed out of the hole.* 水从孔中射出. ○ *The volcano spewed molten lava.* 火山喷出了熔岩.

sp gr *abbr* 缩写 = specific gravity.

sphag·num /ˈsfægnəm; ˈsfægnəm/ *n* (*pl* **~s** or **sphagna** /ˈsfægnə; ˈsfægnə/) type of moss that grows in wet areas, used esp for packing plants 泥炭藓(尤用于包裹植物).

sphere /sfɪə(r); sfɪr/ *n* **1** (**a**) solid figure that is entirely round (ie with every point on the surface at an equal distance from the centre) 球体; 球形. ⇨illus at CUBE 见CUBE 插图. (**b**) any object having approximately this shape (eg a ball, a globe) 球状物. **2** (**a**) range or extent (of sb's interests, activity, influence, etc) (某人的兴趣、活动、影响等的)范围: *a sphere of influence,* eg area over which a country, etc claims certain rights 势力范围(如一国的) ○ *Her sphere of interests is very limited.* 她的爱好很有限. (**b**) group in society; person's place in society 社会阶层; 社会地位: *It took him completely out of his sphere.* 这件事完全超出了他的生活范围了. ○ *distinguished in many different spheres,* eg in artistic, literary and political circles 在许多领域出众(如艺术、文学、政治等方面).

▷ **spher·ical** /ˈsferɪkl; ˈsfɛrɪkl/ *adj* shaped like a sphere 球形的; 球状的; 球面的: *a spherical object* 球状的物体.

spher·oid /ˈsfɪərɔɪd; ˈsfɪrɔɪd/ *n* solid object that is almost, but not perfectly, spherical 扁球体; 椭形球.

-sphere *comb form* 构词成分 (forming *ns* 用以构成名词) of or like a sphere 球体的; 球状的: *ionosphere* ○ *atmosphere*. ▷ **-spheric** (also **-spherical**) (forming *adjs* 用以构成形容词): *atmospheric*.

sphinc·ter /ˈsfɪŋktə(r); ˈsfɪŋktɚ/ *n* (*fml* 文) ring of muscle that surrounds an opening in the body and can contract to close it 括约肌: *the anal sphincter* 肛门括约肌.

sphinx /sfɪŋks; sfɪŋks/ *n* **1** (esp 尤作 **the Sphinx**) stone statue in Egypt with a lion's body and a man's or an animal's head 斯芬克斯(埃及的狮身人面或狮身兽面石像). **2** person who keeps his thoughts and feelings secret; enigmatic person 内心世界不外露的人; 谜一样的人: *I've always found her rather sphinx-like.* 我总觉得她像个谜一样, 难以捉摸.

spice /spaɪs; spaɪs/ *n* **1** (**a**) [C] any of various types of substance obtained from plants, with a strong taste and/or smell, used, esp in powder form, for flavouring food 香料(从植物中提取而得, 尤指粉状的): *Ginger, nutmeg, cinnamon, pepper and cloves are common spices.* 姜、肉豆蔻、肉桂、胡椒、丁香都是常用的香料. (**b**) [U] such substances considered as a group 香料(总称): *mixed spice* 混合香料 ○ *too much spice in the cake* 糕饼中香料太多 ○ [attrib 作定语] *a spice jar* 香料瓶. **2** [U] (*fig* 比喻) extra interest or excitement 额外的趣味或刺激性的事物: *a story that lacks spice* 乏味的故事 ○ *add a bit of spice to their marriage* 给他们的婚姻增添了些微情趣. Cf 参看 SALT 5.

▷ **spice** *v* [Tn, Tn·pr] **~ sth (with sth)** **1** add flavour to sth with spice 用香料给某物调味: *Have you spiced this cake?* 这蛋糕中加香料了吗? ○ *He spiced the biscuits with cinnamon.* 他在饼干里加了肉桂. **2** (usu passive 通常用于被动语态) add (humour, etc) to give interest, variety, etc 加入(幽默成分等)以增添趣味、新鲜感等: *a boring life spiced with moments of intrigue* 除了几件秘史点缀外枯燥无味的一生 ○ *His stories are spiced with humour.* 他的小说里有很多幽默风趣的片断.

spiced *adj* containing spice(1) or spices 含香料的: *heavily spiced curries* 味道浓的咖喱食品 ○ *spiced biscuits* 香味饼干.

spicy *adj* (**-ier, -iest**) **1** flavoured with spice; smelling or tasting of spice 用香料调味的; 有香料味的; 辛辣的: *Do you like spicy food?* 你喜欢吃辣的食物吗? **2** exciting or interesting (esp because slightly indecent or scandalous) 有刺激性的, 有趣味的(尤指有些猥亵或丑事成分的): *spicy details of a film star's love life* 某影星的桃色底蕴. **spi·ci·ness** *n* [U]: *the spiciness of Indian food* 印度菜的辛辣.

spick /spɪk; spɪk/ *adj* (idm 习语) ˌ**spick and** ˈ**span** [usu pred 通常作表语] neat, clean and tidy 整洁: *They always keep their kitchen spick and span.* 他们的厨房总是很整洁.

spider 蜘蛛

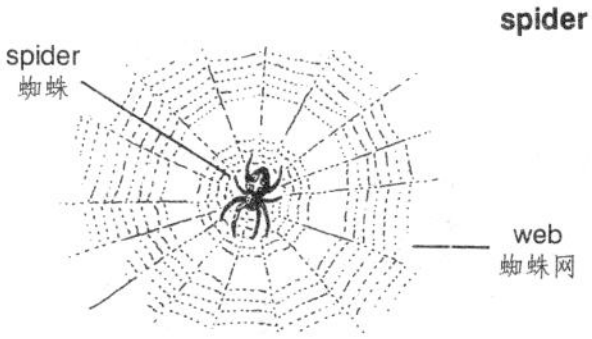

spider /ˈspaɪdə(r); ˈspaɪdɚ/ *n* any of several types of small creature with eight thin legs, many of which spin webs to trap insects as food 蜘蛛.

▷ **spidery** /ˈspaɪdərɪ; ˈspaɪdərɪ/ *adj* **1** (esp of handwriting) having thin angular lines like a spider's legs (尤指笔迹)细长而有棱角的: *written in her spidery scrawl* 她用细长而潦草的字体写的. **2** full of spiders 有很多蜘蛛的.

□ ˈ**spider-man** /-mæn; -mæn/ *n* (*pl* **-men** /-men; -mɛn/) man who works at a great height in constructing buildings 高空作业的建筑工人.

ˈ**spider plant** plant with thin leaves and long stems from which fresh young plants grow 醉蝶花属植物.

spied *pt, pp* of SPY.

spiel /ʃpi:l; *US* spi:l; spil/ *n* (*infml usu derog* 口, 通常作贬义) long or fast prepared speech (usu intended to persuade sb or as an excuse) 滔滔不绝的讲话(通常为说服某人或用作借口): *The salesman gave (us) a long spiel about why we should buy his product.* 推销员口若悬河, 说我们应该买他的东西.

spigot /ˈspɪgət; ˈspɪgət/ *n* (usu wooden) peg or plug used to stop the hole of a barrel, etc or to control the flow of liquid from a tap (通常为木质的)塞子.

spike /spaɪk; spaɪk/ *n* **1** [C] hard thin pointed piece of metal, wood, etc; sharp point (金属、木质等的)尖状物, 尖头: *sharp spikes on top of the railings in the park* 公园栏杆上的尖头. **2** (**a**) [C] any of a set of metal points attached to the sole of a shoe, etc to prevent the wearer slipping while running in sports, etc (鞋底的)防滑钉. (**b**) **spikes** [pl] running-shoes fitted with these 钉鞋: *a pair of spikes* 一双钉鞋. **3** [C] long metal nail or pin (金属的)长钉, 长针, 大钉. **4** [C] ear (of corn, etc) (玉米等的)穗: *spikes of barley* 大麦穗. **5** [C] long pointed group of flowers on a single stem 穗状花: *spikes of lavender* 薰衣草的穗状花.

▷ **spike** *v* [Tn] **1** (usu passive 通常用于被动语态) put spikes on (shoes, etc) 给(鞋等)装上钉: *spiked running shoes* 带钉的跑鞋. **2** pierce or injure with a spike 用尖

物刺或伤害. **3** (*esp US*) = LACE *v* 2. **4** (idm 习语) **spike sb's 'guns** spoil the plans of (an opponent) 破坏(对手)的计划.

spiky *adj* (**-ier, -iest**) **1** having sharp points or spikes 有尖刺的: *Your hairbrush is too spiky for me.* 你的发刷我觉得太尖了. **2** (*infml fig* 口, 比喻) (of people) easily offended and difficult to please; irritable (指人)难对付的, 难取悦的, 易怒的. **spi·ki·ness** *n* [U].

spill[1] /spɪl; spɪl/ *v* (*pt, pp* **spilt** /spɪlt; spɪlt/ or **spilled**) ⇨Usage at DREAM[2] 用法见DREAM[2]. **1** [I, Ipr, Ip, Tn, Tn·pr] **~ (sth) (from, out of, etc sth)**; **~ out** (allow or cause liquid, etc to) run or fall over the edge of a container 流出; 溢出; 洒出: *The ink spilt all over the desk.* 墨水洒了一桌子. ○ *He knocked the bucket over and all the water spilt out.* 他撞翻了水桶, 水全流出去了. ○ *Who has spilt/spilled the milk?* 谁把牛奶泼出来了? ⇨ illus at POUR 见POUR插图. **2** [Tn] (*infml* 口) reveal or make sth known 泄漏某事物: *Who spilt the news?* 是谁把这消息捅出去的? **3** (idm 习语) **cry over spilt milk** ⇨ CRY[1]. **spill the 'beans** (*infml* 口) reveal (esp secret) information, deliberately or unintentionally (故意地或无意地)泄露(尤指秘密的)信息. **spill 'blood** (*fml* 文) (cause people to) be injured or killed; shed blood (使人)受伤, 被杀, 流血: *Much innocent blood is spilt in war.* 许多无辜的人在战争中受伤或死亡. **4** (phr v) **spill over** overflow from sth that is full 从某物中溢出: *The meeting spilt over from the hall into the corridor.* 参加会议的人从大厅到走廊挤得水泄不通.

▷ **spill** *n* **1** fall from a horse, bicycle, etc (从马、自行车等上)跌下: *have a nasty spill* 重重地摔了下来. **2** (idm 习语) **thrills and spills** ⇨ THRILL *n*.

spill·age /'spɪlɪdʒ; ˋspɪlɪdʒ/ *n* (**a**) [U] action of spilling 溢出; 泼出; 洒出. (**b**) [C] amount spilt 溢出量; 洒出量: *spillages of drink* 饮料洒出的量.

□ **'spillway** *n* passage for surplus water from a reservoir, river, etc 溢洪道; 泄洪道.

spill[2] /spɪl; spɪl/ *n* thin strip of wood or twisted paper, used for lighting candles, pipes, fires, etc (点燃蜡烛、烟斗等用的)木片, 纸捻.

spin /spɪn; spɪn/ *v* (**-nn-**; *pt* **spun** /spʌn; spʌn/ or, in archaic use, 古语拼作 **span** /spæn; spæn/, *pp* **spun**) **1** (**a**) [Tn, Tn·p] **~ sth (round)** make sth turn round and round rapidly 使某物快速旋转: *spin the ball*, eg in cricket or tennis 打旋转球(如板球或网球中) ○ *spin a top* 转陀螺 ○ *He spun the wheel of his bicycle.* 他快速转动自行车的轮子. ○ *They spun a coin to decide who should start*, ie threw it spinning in the air to see which side was uppermost when it landed. 他们抛转硬币来决定谁开场. (**b**) [I, Ipr, Ip] move round and round rapidly 快速旋转: *The revolving sign was spinning round and round in the wind.* 旋转的标志牌在风中打着旋儿. ○ *The collision sent the car spinning across the road.* 汽车被撞得转着圈儿冲到路的另一边. ○ *The blow sent him spinning back against the wall.* 他被打得晕头转向, 撞在后面的墙上. ○ *She spun round to catch the ball.* 她飞快地转身接球. ○ (*fig* 比喻) *My head is spinning*, ie I feel dizzy. 我头晕. **2** (**a**) [I, Tn, Tn·pr] **~ (A into B)/(B from A)** form (thread) from wool, cotton, silk, etc by drawing out and twisting; make (yarn) from wool, etc in this way 纺(线); 纺(纱): *She spins goat's hair into wool/spins wool from goat's hair.* 她把山羊毛纺成毛线. (**b**) [I] engage in the occupation or pastime of spinning thread 纺纱(为业或消遣): *I enjoy spinning.* 我喜欢纺纱. **3** [Tn] (of a spider, silkworm, etc) produce (fine silk or silk-like material) from the body in order to make (a web, cocoon, etc) (指蜘蛛等)结(网); (指蚕等)吐丝做(茧): *spiders spinning their webs* 结网的蜘蛛 ○ *silkworms spinning cocoons* 做茧的蚕. **4** (idm 习语) **spin (sb) a 'yarn** tell a (usu long) story, often in order to deceive sb 讲故事(通常很长, 常用以蒙人): *The old sailor loves to spin yarns about his life at sea.* 那老水手爱信口开河地讲他的航海生涯. ○ *He spun us this unlikely yarn about being trapped for hours in a broken lift.* 他对我们胡诌在坏电梯中困了几个小时. **5** (phr v) **spin along (sth)** move along rapidly on wheels (车辆)疾驰: *The car was spinning merrily along (the road).* 汽车(沿路)轻快地奔驰着. **spin sth out** make sth last as long as possible 使某事物尽量延长或拖延: *spin out the time by talking* 靠说话来拖延时间 ○ *spin one's money out until the next pay-day* 省着花钱以维持到发工资那天.

▷ **spin** *n* **1** [U, C] turning or spinning movement 旋转: [attrib 作定语] *spin bowling* 投旋转球 ○ *The bowler gave (a) spin to the ball*, eg in cricket, baseball, etc. 投球手发了一个旋转球(如在板球、棒球等运动中). ○ *He gambled his money on one spin of the wheel*, eg at a game of roulette. 他把钱压在(轮盘赌等的)一局上. **2** [C usu *sing* 通常作单数] fast spinning movement of an aircraft during a diving descent (飞行器的)旋冲: *go/get into a spin* 进入旋冲状态 ○ *come/get out of a spin* 脱离旋冲状态. **3** [C] (*infml* 口) short ride for pleasure (in a car, on a bicycle, etc) (乘汽车、骑自行车等)兜风: *Let's go for a spin in my new car.* 坐我的新汽车兜一圈吧. **4** (idm 习语) **in a (flat) 'spin** in a state of panic or confusion 惊慌失措; 晕头转向: *I've been in a real spin all morning.* 我整个上午都晕头转向的.

spin·ner **1** person who makes thread, etc by spinning 纺纱者; 纺纱工: *spinners and weavers* 纺纱工和织布工. **2** (**a**) = SPIN BOWLER. (**b**) cricket ball bowled with a spinning movement (板球的)旋球.

spin·ning *n* [U] art, occupation or pastime of spinning wool, etc into yarn 纺纱: *Spinning is one of my hobbies.* 我很喜爱纺纱. ○ [attrib 作定语] *spinning wool/thread/yarn* 纺出的毛线[线/纱]. ˌ**spinning-'jenny** *n* early type of machine for spinning more than one thread at a time 詹妮纺纱机(初期的多轴纺纱机). **'spinning-wheel** *n* simple household machine for spinning thread continuously on a spindle turned by a large wheel, usu worked by a foot pedal 纺车(通常为脚踏的).

□ **'spin bowler** (also **spinner**) (in cricket) bowler who gives the ball a spinning movement (板球中)投出旋转球者.

ˌ**spin-'dry** *v* (*pt, pp* **-dried**) [Tn] dry (washed clothes) by spinning them in a rotating drum to remove excess water 给(洗好的衣物)用旋转式脱水机脱水; 甩干. ˌ**spin-'drier** *n* machine for doing this 旋转式脱水机; 甩干机.

'spin-off *n* benefit or product that is produced incidentally from a larger process, or while it is being developed 副产品; 派生物: *This new material is a spin-off from the space industry.* 这种新材料是航天工业的副产品.

spun 'glass glass made into threads by being spun while heated 玻璃纤维.

spun 'silk cheap material made from short threads and waste pieces of silk, often mixed with cotton 绢丝纺绸.

spun 'sugar sugar made into fluffy threads by being spun when in a thick liquid form 棉花糖. Cf 参看 CANDY-FLOSS (CANDY).

spina bif·ida /ˌspaɪnə 'bɪfɪdə; ˌspaɪnə ˋbɪfɪdə/ (*medical* 医) condition in which certain bones of the spine are not properly developed at birth and allow parts of the spinal cord to protrude (causing severe disability) 脊柱裂.

spin·ach /'spɪnɪdʒ; *US* -ɪtʃ; ˋspɪnɪtʃ/ *n* [U] type of common garden plant with wide dark-green leaves that are cooked and eaten as a vegetable 菠菜: [attrib 作定语] *spinach soup* 菠菜汤.

spinal /'spaɪnl; ˋspaɪnl/ *adj* [usu attrib 通常作定语] of or relating to the spine 脊柱的; 与脊柱相关的: *a spinal injury* 脊柱受伤.

□ ˌ**spinal 'column** backbone; spine 脊梁骨; 脊柱.

ˌ**spinal 'cord** mass of nerve fibres enclosed in the spine 脊髓.

spindle /'spɪndl; ˋspɪndl/ *n* **1** thin rod on which thread is twisted or wound by hand in spinning 纺锤; 锭子. **2** bar or pin which turns or on which sth (eg an axle or a shaft) turns 转杆; 轴; 心轴.

▷ **spindly** /'spɪndlɪ; ˋspɪndlɪ/ *adj* (*infml sometimes derog* 口, 有时作贬义) very long or tall and thin 细长的; 又高又瘦的: *a young foal with spindly legs* 细长腿的小驹子 ○ *a few spindly plants* 几棵细长的花草.

spine /spaɪn; spaɪn/ *n* **1** row of bones along the back of humans and some animals; backbone 脊柱; 脊椎: *He sustained an injury to his spine when he fell off his horse.* 他从马上摔下来, 伤了脊梁骨. ⇨illus at SKELETON 见SKELETON插图. **2** any of the sharp needle-like parts on some plants (eg cactuses) and animals (eg porcupines, hedgehogs) (仙人掌等的)刺; (豪猪、刺猬等的)刺毛.

⇨illus at App 1 见附录1插图, page iii. **3** back part of the cover of a book, where the pages are joined together (ie the part that is visible when it is in a row on a shelf, usu with the book's title on it) 书脊.

▷ **spine·less** *adj* **1** (of an animal, etc) having no spine(1); invertebrate (指动物等)无脊椎的. **2** (*fig derog* 比喻, 贬) (of people) weak, cowardly or easily frightened (指人)软弱的, 胆小的, 无骨气的. **spine·lessly** *adv*. **spine·less·ness** *n* [U].

spiny *adj* (**-ier**, **-iest**) full of or covered with spines (SPINE 2); prickly 长满刺的; 多刺的; 带刺的: *a spiny fish* 鳍上多刺的鱼.

□ ˈ**spine-chiller** *n* book, film, etc that is frightening in a thrilling way 令人毛骨悚然的书、电影等. ˈ**spine-chilling** *adj*: *a spine-chilling horror story* 令人毛骨悚然的恐怖小说.

spinet /spɪˈnet; *US* ˈspɪnɪt; ˋspɪnɪt/ *n* old type of musical instrument with a keyboard, similar to a harpsichord 古钢琴.

spin·naker /ˈspɪnəkə(r); ˋspɪnəkɚ/ *n* large triangular extra sail carried on the mainmast of a racing-yacht, used when sailing with the wind coming from behind the boat (赛艇的)大三角帆(顺风时用). ⇨illus at YACHT 见 YACHT 插图.

spin·ney /ˈspɪnɪ; ˋspɪnɪ/ *n* (*Brit*) small wood with thick undergrowth; thicket 矮树林; 灌木林.

spin·ster /ˈspɪnstə(r); ˋspɪnstɚ/ *n* (**a**) (*law or fml* 律或文) unmarried woman 未婚女子. (**b**) (*often derog* 常作贬义) woman who remains single after the usual age for marrying 老处女. Cf 参看 BACHELOR 1.

▷ **spin·ster·hood** /-hʊd; -ˌhʊd/ *n* [U] state of being a spinster 未婚女子身分; 老处女身分.

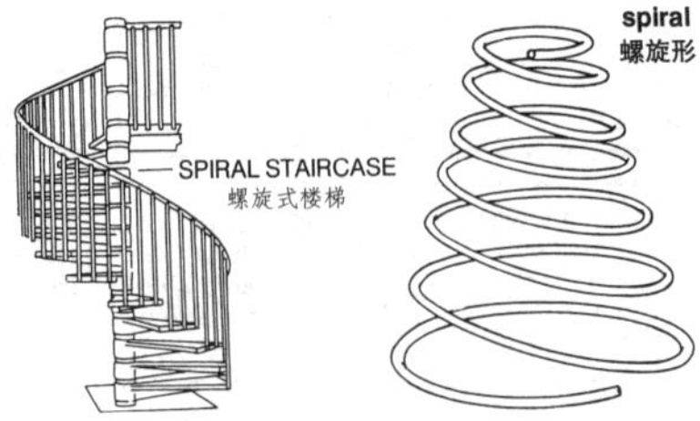

spiral /ˈspaɪərəl; ˋspaɪrəl/ *adj* advancing or ascending in a continuous curve that winds round a central point 螺旋形的; 盘旋的: *a spiral staircase* 螺旋式楼梯 ○ *A snail's shell is spiral in form.* 蜗牛壳是螺旋形的.

▷ **spiral** *n* **1** (**a**) spiral line 螺线. (**b**) object that has a spiral shape 螺旋状的物体. **2** continuous increase or decrease in two or more quantities alternately because each depends on the other(s) 互为前提的至少两个量之间的交替上升或下降: *an inflationary spiral* 螺旋式上升的通胀 ○ *the spiral of rising wages and prices* 工资和物价的交替上升. **3** (idm 习语) **a vicious spiral** ⇨ VICIOUS.

spiral *v* (**-ll-**; *US also* **-l-**) **1** [Ipr, Ip] move in a spiral course 螺旋形移动; 盘旋移动: *The falling leaf spiralled to the ground.* 落叶盘旋着飘到了地上. ○ *The smoke spiralled upwards.* 那股烟袅袅上升. **2** [I, Ip] increase or decrease continuously 连续增长或减少: *Prices are still spiralling*, ie increasing rapidly. 物价仍在急剧上涨.

spir·ally *adv*: *a spirally bound book*, ie with its pages held together by wire bent spirally 用螺旋丝装订的书.

spire /ˈspaɪə(r); ˋspaɪr/ *n* pointed structure in the form of a tall cone or pyramid, esp on a church tower (圆锥形或角锥形的)尖顶; (尤指)教堂塔尖: *a magnificent view of the spires of the city* 全城建筑物尖顶尽收眼底的美景. ⇨illus at App 1 见附录1插图, page viii.

spirit /ˈspɪrɪt; ˋspɪrɪt/ *n* **1** [U, C] person's mind or feelings as distinct from his body; soul 精神; 心灵: *He is troubled in spirit/His spirit is troubled.* 他内心苦恼. **2** [C] soul thought of as separate from the body; soul without a body; ghost 魂; 灵魂; 鬼魂; 鬼: *the spirits of the dead* 亡灵 ○ *raise spirits*, ie communicate with dead people 招魂 ○ *It was believed that people could be possessed by evil spirits.* 据说人能中邪. ○ [attrib 作定语] *the spirit world* 阴界. **3** [C] (*dated* 旧) supernatural creature; elf, fairy, etc 超自然的生物(精灵、仙子等). **4** [U, C] life and consciousness not associated with a body 神灵: *tribal beliefs that spirit is everywhere and in everything* 认为神灵无所不在、无事不有的部落信仰 ○ *God is pure spirit.* 上帝纯粹是灵. ○ *the Holy Spirit* 圣灵. **5** [C] (always with an *adj* 必须与形容词连用) person (of a specified type, emotion, temper, etc) (某类型的或有某种情感、脾气等的)人: *a brave, proud, generous, mean, etc spirit* 勇敢的、骄傲的、慷慨的、小气的…人 ○ *He was one of the leading spirits of the reform movement.* 他是改革运动的先行者. ○ *She's an independent spirit.* 她是有独立性的人. **6** [U] willingness to assert oneself; courage; liveliness 志气; 勇气; 活力; 精神: *He answered with spirit.* 他回答得很带劲儿. ○ *break sb's spirit*, ie destroy sb's will, sense of independence, etc 挫败某人的锐气 ○ *Although they lost, the team played with tremendous spirit.* 那队输是输了, 但却表现了极其顽强的精神. **7** [sing] state of mind or mood; attitude 心态; 心理; 态度: *do sth in a spirit of mischief* 以恶作剧的心理做某事 ○ *approach sth in the wrong/right spirit* 以错误的[正确的]态度对待某事物 ○ *Whether it was unwise or not depends upon the spirit in which it was done.* 这件事可取与否全在于做这件事的态度. ○ *The party was successful because everyone entered into the spirit of the thing.* 这次聚会因大家积极参与所以很成功. **8** (**a**) [sing] characteristic quality or mood of sth 某事物的特点或气氛: *the spirit of the times* 时代气息 ○ *the 16th-century spirit of exploration* 16世纪的探险风. (**b**) [U] real or intended meaning or purpose 实质的含义或宗旨: *obey the spirit, not the letter* (ie the apparent meaning of the words) *of the law* 遵循法律的宗旨, 而不拘泥其中的文字. **9** (**a**) [C usu *pl* 通常作复数] strong distilled alcoholic drink 烈酒: *I don't drink spirits.* 我不喝烈酒. ○ *Whisky, brandy, gin and rum are all spirits.* 威士忌、白兰地、杜松子酒、朗姆酒都是烈酒. (**b**) [U] distilled alcohol for industrial, etc use 酒精; 乙醇: *white spirit* 石油溶剂 ○ *surgical spirit* 消毒酒精 ○ *methylated spirit(s)* 甲基化酒精. **10 spirits** [pl] person's feelings or state of mind 精神状态; 情绪; 心境: *in high spirits*, ie cheerful 情绪高 ○ *in low/poor spirits*, ie depressed, gloomy 情绪低 ○ *raise sb's spirits*, ie make sb more cheerful 鼓舞某人的情绪 ○ *Have a glass of brandy to keep your spirits up.* 来杯白兰地提提神吧. **11** (idm 习语) **in spirit** in one's thoughts 在内心; 在精神上: *I shall be with you in spirit*, ie thinking about you though not with you physically. 我的心和你在一起. **a kindred spirit** ⇨ KINDRED. **the ˌspirit is ˈwilling (but the ˌflesh is ˈweak)** (*saying* 谚) one's intentions and wishes are good but laziness, love of pleasure, etc prevent one from acting according to them 心余力绌.

▷ **spirit** *v* (phr v) **spirit sb/sth away/off** take or carry sb/sth away quickly, secretly or mysteriously (as if magic) 迅速地、偷偷地或神秘地带走某人[某物]; 诱拐; 诱带: *The pop-star was spirited away at the end of the concert before her fans could get near her.* 音乐会一结束, 那位流行乐曲歌手没等歌迷接近她就没影儿了.

spir·ited /ˈspɪrɪtɪd; ˋspɪrɪtɪd/ *adj* [usu attrib 通常作定语] full of spirit(6); lively; forceful 精神饱满的; 活跃的; 猛烈的: *a spirited attack, reply, conversation* 猛烈的攻击、响亮的回答、活跃的交谈 ○ *a spirited horse* 勇猛的马.

spir·itedly *adv*.

-spir·ited (forming compound *adjs* 用以构成复合形容词) having the mood or state of mind specified 有某种情绪的; 处于某种心境的; 心地…的: *ˌmean-ˈspirited* ○ *ˌhigh-spirited ˈchildren*.

spir·it·less *adj* **1** without spirit(6); not having or showing liveliness or courage 没精打采的; 沉闷的; 胆小的. **2** depressed or unhappy 沮丧的; 不快活的: *The old man seemed dejected and spiritless.* 那老汉显出一副垂头丧气的潦倒相.

□ ˈ**spirit-lamp** *n* lamp that burns methylated spirit or a similar fuel 酒精灯.

ˈ**spirit-level** *n* glass tube partly filled with water or alcohol, with a bubble of air, used to test whether sth is horizontal by means of the position of the bubble 酒精水准仪.

spir·itual /ˈspɪrɪtʃʊəl; ˋspɪrɪtʃʊəl/ *adj* [usu attrib 通常作

定语] **1** of the human spirit(4) or soul; not of physical things 精神的; 心灵的; 非物质的: *concerned about sb's spiritual welfare* 关心某人精神上的幸福. Cf 参看 MATERIAL². **2** (**a**) of the Church or of religion 教会的; 宗教的: *The Pope is the spiritual leader of many Christians.* 教皇是众多基督徒的宗教领袖. (**b**) of or from God; divine 上帝的; 神的; 神授的; 天赐的. Cf 参看 TEMPORAL 1. **3** (idm 习语) **one's spiritual 'home** place where one is, or thinks one could be, happiest; country to which one feels more strongly attached than to one's own country 乐土; 心灵上的祖国.

▷ **spir·itual** *n* (also **Negro 'spiritual**) religious folk-song of the type originally sung by black slaves in America (原先由美国黑奴唱的)黑人圣歌.

spir·itu·al·ity /ˌspɪrɪtʃʊˈæləti; ˌspɪrɪtʃuˈæləti/ *n* [U] state or quality of being concerned with spiritual matters; devotion to spiritual things 精神性; 灵性; 信仰.

spir·itu·ally /-tʃʊli; -tʃʊli/ *adv*: *a spiritually impoverished culture* 精神枯竭的文化.

spir·itu·al·ism /ˈspɪrɪtʃʊəlɪzəm; ˈspɪrɪtʃʊəlˌɪzəm/ *n* [U] belief in the possibility of receiving messages from the spirits of the dead; practices based on this belief 唯灵论; 阴阳界相通论; 招魂术.

▷ **spir·itu·al·ist** /-ɪst; -ɪst/ *n* person who believes in or practises spiritualism 唯灵论者; 相信阴阳界相通者; 招魂术士; 关亡人; 巫师.

spir·itu·ous /ˈspɪrɪtʃʊəs; ˈspɪrɪtʃʊəs/ *adj* (of a drink) containing much alcohol (指饮料)酒精含量高的: *spirituous liquors*, ie those that are distilled and not only fermented 烈性酒.

spit¹ /spɪt; spɪt/ *v* (**-tt-**; *pt, pp* **spat** /spæt; spæt/; also *esp US* **spit**) **1** [Tn, Tn·pr, Tn·p] **~ sth (out) (at/on/onto sb/sth)** send (liquid, saliva, food, etc) out from the mouth 吐出(液体、唾液、食物等): *He was spitting blood after being hit in the mouth.* 他嘴上挨了打之后, 吐出血来. ○ *The baby spat its food (out) onto the table.* 婴儿把吃进去的东西吐在桌子上了. ○ *He took one sip of the wine and spat it out.* 他抿了一口酒, 又吐了出来. **2** [I, Ipr] (**a**) send saliva from the mouth 吐口水; 吐唾沫; 吐痰: *In many countries it is considered rude to spit in public.* 在许多国家, 当众吐痰属不雅行为. ○ *He's inclined to spit when he talks quickly.* 他说话说快了就爱喷唾沫星. ○ *The boys were spitting out of the train window.* 那些男孩子向火车窗外吐口水. (**b**) do this as a sign of contempt or anger 啐唾沫(以示鄙夷或愤怒): *She spat at him/in his face.* 她向他[他的脸上]啐了一口唾沫. **3** (**a**) [Tn, Tn·p] **~ sth (out)** utter sth violently or forcefully 厉声说出某事: *She spat (out) curses at me.* 她厉声咒骂我. (**b**) [I, Ipr] make a noise like spitting to show anger 发出啐唾沫的声音以示愤怒: *He walked off spitting with fury.* 他发出呸的声音生气地走了. ○ *The cat spat at the dog.* 那只猫朝着狗发出呼呼声. **4** [I] (of a fire, hot fat, etc) make a spitting noise; throw out sparks, etc violently and noisily (指火、熬热的油脂等)毕剥作响, 噼啪作响; (尤指猛烈、大声地)迸出火花: *fried bacon spitting in the pan* 在锅内噼啪作响的煎腌肉 ○ *The gun spat twice and he fell dead.* 乒乒两枪, 他应声扑地身亡. **5** [I] (*infml* 口) (used with *it,* in the continuous tenses 与 it 连用, 用于进行时态) rain lightly 下小雨: *It's not raining heavily any more, but it's still spitting a bit.* 大雨已经停了, 但是还在飘着小雨. **6** (idm 习语) **be the (very/spitting) image of sb/sth** ⇨ IMAGE. **spit it 'out** (*infml* 口) say what you want to say quickly and concisely 爽快地说出来: *'What exactly are you trying to tell me? Come on, spit it out!'* '你到底想跟我说什么? 你就爽快点说出来吧!'

▷ **spit** *n* **1** [U] liquid in the mouth; saliva 口水; 唾液. **2** [C usu *sing* 通常作单数] act of spitting 吐唾沫; 吐痰. **3** [U] white frothy liquid produced by some insects and found on plants, etc (某些昆虫留在植物等上的)白色泡沫状分泌物. **4** (idm 习语) **be the dead spit of sb** ⇨ DEAD. **spit and 'polish** thorough cleaning and polishing of equipment, esp by soldiers 对设备(尤指军用装备)彻底的擦洗.

□ **'spitfire** *n* person with a very fiery temper 烈性子的人.

spit² /spɪt; spɪt/ *n* **1** long thin metal spike pushed through meat, etc to hold and turn it while it is roasted over a fire or in an oven (烤肉等所用的)金属扦. **2** small narrow point of land that extends into the sea, a lake, etc 岬; 岬角.

▷ **spit** *v* (**-tt-**) [Tn] put a spit through (a piece of meat, a chicken, etc) 用烤肉扦刺穿(肉、鸡等): *a spitted whole lamb* 串在烤扦上的整只羔羊.

spit³ /spɪt; spɪt/ *n* depth of earth equal to the length of the blade of a spade 一锹的深度: *Dig the whole vegetable plot two spits deep.* 把整块菜地按两锹深翻挖一遍.

spite /spaɪt; spaɪt/ *n* **1** [U] desire to hurt, annoy or offend another person; ill will 恶意; 坏心: *I'm sure he only said it out of/from spite.* 我肯定他说这话完全是出于恶意. **2** (idm 习语) **in spite of** (used as a *prep* 用作介词) not being prevented by (sb/sth); regardless of; despite 不顾(某人[某事物]); 不管; 尽管: *They went out in spite of the rain.* 尽管下着雨, 他们还是出去了. ○ *In spite of all his efforts he failed.* 他已竭尽全力, 但仍然失败了.

▷ **spite** *v* **1** [Tn] (only used in the infinitive with *to* 仅用于带 to 的不定式中) injure, annoy or offend (sb) because of spite 恶意地伤害、惹怒或冒犯(某人): *The neighbours play their radio loudly every afternoon just to spite us.* 邻居每天下午把收音机的音量开得很大, 向我们泄愤. **2** (idm 习语) **cut off one's nose to spite one's face** ⇨ NOSE¹.

spite·ful /-fl; -fəl/ *adj* showing or caused by spite; full of spite 恶意的; 怀恨的: *a spiteful comment* 恶意的评论 ○ *He's just being spiteful.* 他心怀恶意. **spite·fully** /-fəli; -fəli/ *adv*. **spite·ful·ness** *n* [U].

spittle /ˈspɪtl; ˈspɪtl̩/ *n* [U] liquid that forms in the mouth; saliva 口水; 唾液; 痰.

spit·toon /spɪˈtuːn; spɪˈtun/ *n* container for spitting into, eg in a bar 痰盂.

spiv /spɪv; spɪv/ *n* (*Brit sl derog* 俚, 贬) flashily dressed man who has no regular job but makes money by (usu dishonest) business dealings 衣冠楚楚、无固定工作的人(通常做黑市买卖者). ▷ **spiv·ish** *adj*.

splash /splæʃ; splæʃ/ *v* **1** [Tn, Tn·pr, Tn·p] **~ sth (about) (on/onto/over sb/sth); ~ sb/sth (with sth)** cause (a liquid) to fly about in drops; make sb/sth wet in this way 使(液体)溅起; 溅湿某人[某物]: *Stop splashing me!* 别再溅我了! ○ *splash water on/over the floor* 把水洒在地板上 ○ *splash paint onto the canvas* 把颜料泼在画布上 ○ *splash the floor with water* 用水把地板泼湿 ○ *splash water about* 四处泼水 ○ *The children love splashing water over each other.* 儿童喜欢互相泼水. ⇨Usage at SPRAY² 用法见 SPRAY². **2** [I, Ipr, Ip] (of a liquid) fly about and fall in drops (指液体)溅落: *Water splashed into the bucket from the tap.* 水从龙头里喷溅着注入水桶中. ○ *The rain splashed down all day.* 雨噼里啪啦下了一整天. **3** [usu passive 通常用于被动语态: Tn, Tn·pr] **~ sth (with sth)** decorate sth with large or irregular patches of colour, paint, etc 以大片的或不规则的颜色等装饰某物: *a bath towel splashed with blue and green* 有绿色和蓝色大花的浴巾. **4** [Tn·pr, Tn·p] **~ sth (about) (across, on, etc sth)** (**a**) display (a news story, photograph, etc) prominently 显眼地展示(新闻报道、照片等): *The story was splashed across the front page of the newspaper.* 这篇报道刊登在报纸头版显著位置. (**b**) spend (money) freely and ostentatiously 大手大脚地花(钱): *He thinks he can win friends by splashing his money about.* 他以为花钱大方就可以赢得朋友. **5** (phr v) **splash about (in sth)** sit or stand in water and make it fly about with one's hands or feet (坐在或站在水里)用手或脚溅水: *children happily splashing about in the bath* 在浴缸里快活地溅着水玩的孩子. **splash across, along, away, through, etc** move across, etc with a splashing noise 带着泼溅声走过等: *We splashed (our way) across the stream.* 我们哗啦哗啦地蹚过小河. ○ *She splashed through the puddles.* 她哗哗地蹚过水坑. **splash down** (esp of a spacecraft) land in water with a splash (尤指宇宙飞船)溅落: *The spacecraft splashed down in the Pacific.* 那艘宇宙飞船溅落在太平洋中. **splash out (on sth)** (*infml* 口) spend money (on sth) in an impulsive or a carefree way 心血来潮地或随意地花钱(于某事物上): *She splashed out on a new pair of shoes.* 她心血来潮买了一双新鞋.

▷ **splash** *n* **1** (sound or act of) splashing 溅泼声; 溅泼: *He fell into the water with a splash.* 他扑通一声跌入水中. **2** mark, spot, etc made by splashing 溅上的斑点

等: *There are some splashes of mud on your trousers.* 你的裤子溅上泥点了. **3** amount of liquid splashed 溅泼的量: *splashes of water all over the floor* 溅得一地板的水. **4** bright patch of colour 鲜艳的色斑: *Her dog is brown with white splashes.* 她的狗是带白花的黄狗. **5** (*dated Brit infml* 旧, 口) small quantity of a liquid, esp of soda-water, added to a drink (搀入饮料中的)少量液体(尤指苏打水). **6** (idm 习语) **make, etc a 'splash** (*infml* 口) do sth or happen in such a way as to attract attention, create a sensation, etc 惹人注目; 引起轰动: *She has made quite a splash in literary circles with her first book.* 她的第一本书在文学界大为轰动. ○ *Their engagement created a terrific splash in the popular press.* 他俩订婚的事在广受欢迎的新闻界极为轰动.

□ **'splash-down** *n* landing of a spacecraft in the sea (航天器的)溅落: *Splash-down is scheduled for 5.30 am.* 航天器的预定溅落时间为上午5时30分.

splat·ter /'splætə(r); 'splætɚ/ *v* [I, Ipr, Ip, Tn, Tn·pr, Tn·p] (cause sth to) splash, esp with continuous or noisy action (使某物)溅泼(尤指连续地或发出声响): *rain splattering on the roof* 劈里啪啦打在屋顶上的雨点 ○ *overalls splattered with paint* 溅上了颜料的长罩衫. ⇨ Usage at SPRAY[2] 用法见SPRAY[2].

splay /spleɪ; sple/ *v* [I, Ip, Tn, Tn·p] **~ (sth) (out)** (cause sth to) open out and become wider at one end; (cause sth to) slant or slope (使某物)张开, 展开一端; (使某物)倾斜, 成斜面: *The pipe splays (out) at one end.* 管子一端呈喇叭形. ○ *The plumber splayed the end of the pipe before fitting it over the next section.* 铅管工把管口撑大后套在另一截管子上. ○ *splayed feet/fingers/elbows*, ie spread outwards 八字脚[张开的手指/向外撑的胳膊肘儿] ○ *a splayed window*, eg one in a thick wall with the opening on one side of the wall wider than that on the other 斜展形窗户(如开在厚墙上的, 窗口一面宽一面窄).

▷ **splay** *adj* [usu attrib 通常作定语] (esp of feet) broad, flat and turned outwards (尤指脚)扁平外翻的: *He has splay feet.* 他是外八字脚. **,splay-'footed** *adj* having splay feet 八字脚的; 外翻足的.

spleen /spli:n; splin/ *n* **1** [C] organ of the body situated at the left of the stomach, which regulates the quality of the blood 脾; 脾脏. ⇨illus at DIGESTIVE 见DIGESTIVE插图. **2** [U] (*fml or dated* 文或旧) bad temper; irritability or grumpiness 坏脾气; 怒气; 怨气: *a fit of spleen* 一阵怒气 ○ *vent one's spleen on sb* 对某人发脾气.

splen·did /'splendɪd; 'splɛndɪd/ *adj* **1** magnificent; displaying splendour 华丽的; 壮丽的; 堂皇的; 辉煌的: *a splendid sunset, house, victory* 壮观的日落景色、堂皇的房子、辉煌的胜利. **2** (*infml* 口) very fine; excellent 极好的; 绝妙的: *a splendid dinner* 美餐 ○ *a splendid idea, achievement, piece of writing* 极好的主意、成就、文章.

splen·di·fer·ous /splen'dɪfərəs; splɛn'dɪfərəs/ *adj* (*infml joc* 口, 谑) splendid 极好的; 了不起的.

splend·our (*US* **splendor**) /'splendə(r); 'splɛndɚ/ *n* (**a**) [U] state or quality of being splendid, magnificent, glorious, or grand 华丽; 壮观; 辉煌; 光辉: *the splendour of the stained glass windows* 彩色玻璃窗之华丽 ○ *Can the city recapture its former splendour?* 这座城市还能重现其往昔的光辉吗? (**b**) **splendours** [pl] splendid, magnificent, etc features or attributes of sth 华丽、壮观等的特质: *the spendours of Rome*, ie its fine monuments, buildings, sights, etc 罗马的壮观.

splen·etic /splɪ'netɪk; splɪ'nɛtɪk/ *adj* (*fml* 文) habitually grumpy and irritable 脾气坏的; 乖戾的; 易怒的.

splice /splaɪs; splaɪs/ *v* [Tn] **1** (*nautical* 海) join (two ends of rope) by weaving the strands of one into the strands of the other 捻接(绳头). **2** join (two pieces of wood, magnetic tape, film, etc) by fastening them at the ends 拼接(木片、磁带、胶片等). **3** (idm 习语) **get 'spliced** (*infml* 口) get married 结婚: *Have you heard? John's just got spliced.* 听说了吗? 约翰刚结了婚. **,splice the 'mainbrace** (*infml joc* 口, 谑) celebrate (esp the end of a hard day's work) by drinking or distributing strong alcoholic drink (尤指辛苦一天后)喝酒乐一乐, 分发酒让大家乐一乐.

▷ **splice** *n* join (in a film, tape, rope, etc) made by splicing (胶片、磁带、绳索等的)拼接, 捻接, 拼接处, 捻接处.

splicer *n* device for joining two pieces of magnetic tape, film, etc (磁带、胶片等的)接合器.

splint /splɪnt; splɪnt/ *n* piece of wood, metal, etc strapped to an injured arm, leg, etc to keep it in the right position while it heals (用以固定受伤肢体的)夹板: *put an arm in splints* 给胳膊上夹板.

splin·ter /'splɪntə(r); 'splɪntɚ/ *n* small thin sharp piece of wood, metal, glass, etc broken off a larger piece (木头、金属、玻璃等的)带尖儿的小碎片: *I've got a splinter in my finger.* 我手指扎了根刺.

▷ **splin·ter** *v* **1** [I, Ipr, Ip, Tn, Tn·pr, Tn·p] **~ (sth) (into/to sth); ~ (sth) off** (cause sth to) break into splinters (使某物)裂成碎片: *This wood splinters easily.* 这种木头容易裂成片. ○ *The windscreen cracked but did not splinter.* 挡风玻璃裂了, 但没碎. ○ *The waves smashed the boat against the rocks, splintering it to pieces.* 浪头把船冲向岩石, 撞成碎片. **2** [I, Ipr, Ip] **~ (off) (into sth)** (*fig* 比喻) separate off from a larger group; form a splinter group (从较大的团体中)分裂出来, 组成小派别.

□ **'splinter group** small group that has broken off from a larger one, esp in politics 分裂出来的小派别(尤指政界).

split /splɪt; splɪt/ *v* (**-tt-**, *pt, pp* **split**) **1** [I, Ipr, Ip, Tn, Tn·pr, Tn·p] **~ (sth/sb) (up) (into sth)** (**a**) (cause sth to) break or be broken (into two or more parts), esp from end to end (使某物)裂开, 碎裂: *Some types of wood split easily.* 有些木头容易劈. ○ *She was splitting logs with an axe.* 她正用斧子劈木头. ○ *A skilled person can split slate into layers.* 手巧的人能把板岩剖成片. (**b**) (cause people to) separate or divide into (often opposing) groups or parties (使人们)分裂成或分成(常为相对的)集体或派别: *The children split (up) into groups.* 孩子们分成了小组. ○ *an issue which has split the party (from top to bottom)* 导致该党(自上而下)分裂的问题. **2** [Tn, Tn·pr, Tn·p] **~ sth (up) (into sth)** break sth into parts; divide and share sth 将某事物分成若干部分; 分某事物: *split the cost of the meal* 分摊饭钱 ○ *split the atom*, ie by means of nuclear fission 使原子产生核裂变 ○ *Would you like to split a bottle with me?* 咱俩分一瓶喝好吗? ○ *They split (up) the money between them.* 他们把钱分了. ○ *For the purposes of the survey we've split the town into four areas.* 为了便于调查, 我们把这个镇划成四个区. **3** [La, I, Cn·a] **~ (sth) (open)** (cause sth to) break open by bursting (使某物)撑破, 绽裂, 裂开: *Suddenly the box split open and a puppy jumped out.* 箱子突然打开, 从里面蹦出只小狗. ○ *His coat had split at the seams.* 他的大衣开线了. ○ *She split open the coconut.* 她把椰子劈开了. **4** [I, Tn] (*sl* 俚 *esp US*) leave (a place) 离开(某处): *It's boring here — let's split.* 这儿没意思——咱们走吧. ○ *They've split the scene*, ie left the event, place, party, etc. 他们走了. **5** (idm 习语) **split the 'difference** (when making a bargain) settle on an amount half-way between two proposed amounts (讲价时)各让一步, 折中. **split 'hairs** (*derog* 贬) make very fine but unnecessary distinctions (in an argument, etc) (在争论等中)作不必要的过细区分. **split an in'finitive** (in speaking or writing) place an adverb between *to* and the infinitive (as in 'to quickly read a book') 分裂不定式(在to与动词之间插入副词, 如to quickly read a book). **split one's 'sides (laughing/with laughter)** laugh uncontrollably 控制不住地大笑; 捧腹(大笑). **6** (phr v) **split (sth) away/off (from sth)** separate or divide (sth) from a larger body or group (将某事物)分离出来: *The group have split away/off from the official union.* 这一部分人已从正式的联盟中分裂出来了. ○ *The storm has split the branch off from the main tree trunk.* 暴风雨把树枝从树干上刮了下来. **split on sb (to sb)** (*infml* 口) give away information about a person (usu an accomplice) that will get him into trouble 出卖或揭发某人(通常指共犯或同谋): *Billy's friend split on him to the teacher.* 比利的朋友向老师告了他一状. **split up (with sb)** end a friendship, relationship or marriage; separate 绝交; 断绝关系; 离婚; 分离: *Jenny and Joe have split up.* 珍妮和乔闹翻了. ○ *John has just split up with his girl-friend.* 约翰刚刚跟女朋友吹了.

▷ **split** *n* **1** [C] act or process of splitting or being split 分开; 劈开; 裂开; 分担. **2** [C] crack or tear made by splitting 裂口; 裂缝: *sew up a split in a seam* 缝好绽开的

S

线缝. **3** [C] division or separation resulting from splitting 分裂; 分离: *a split in the Labour Party* 工党的分裂. **4** [C] pudding made from fruit (esp a banana) cut in two lengthways with cream, ice-cream, etc on top (覆有奶油、冰激凌等的)水果条甜食; (尤指)奶油冰激凌香蕉条: *a banana split* 奶油冰激凌香蕉条. **5 the splits** [pl] acrobatic position in which the legs are stretched across the floor in opposite directions with the rest of the body upright 劈叉: *do the splits* 劈一字腿.

split·ting *adj* [attrib 作定语] (esp of a headache) very painful (尤指头痛)剧烈的, 剧痛的: *I've got a splitting headache.* 我头疼得要裂开似的.

□ ˌ**split inˈfinitive** (*grammar*) infinitive with an adverb placed between *to* and the verb 分裂不定式.

ˌ**split-ˈlevel** *adj* **1** (of a building) having sets of rooms at different levels between storeys in other parts of the building, eg when built on sloping ground (指建筑物)错层式的(如建于倾斜地面的). **2** (of a cooker) having the oven placed separately from the burners or hotplates, not below them (指炉灶)分立式的(烤箱分立而不置于炉灶下的).

ˌ**split ˈpeas** dried peas split into halves 干豌豆瓣儿.

ˌ**split persoˈnality** mental condition in which a person behaves sometimes with one set of emotions, actions, etc, and sometimes with another set; schizophrenia 人格分裂症; 精神分裂症.

ˌ**split ˈpin** metal pin with split ends which can be opened out to hold the pin in position 开尾销.

ˌ**split ˈring** ring with its ends not joined but closely overlapping, as used for keeping keys on 叠口环(如钥匙圈).

ˌ**split ˈsecond** very short moment of time 瞬间; 刹那. ˌ**split-second** *adj* [attrib 作定语] very rapid or accurate 极快的; 极精确的: *The plan depends on* ˌ*split-second ˈtiming.* 这计划要想成功就得分秒不差.

ˌ**split ˈshift** shift²(2) in which there are two or more periods of duty 分段班(在时间上分段进行的一个工作班次).

ˌ**split ˈticket** (*US politics* 政) ballot-paper marked with votes for candidates of more than one party 分裂票(同时选举不同党派候选人的选票).

splotch /splɒtʃ; splɑtʃ/ (*Brit* also **splodge** /splɒdʒ; splɑdʒ/) *n* dirty mark or spot (of ink, paint, etc); irregular patch (of colour, light, etc) (墨水、颜料等的)斑, 斑点, 污斑; (颜色、光等的)形状不规则的一片.

▷ **splotch** (*Brit* also **splodge**) *v* [Tn] mark (sth) with splotches 使(某物)有污斑、色斑或光斑.

splurge /splɜːdʒ; splɝdʒ/ *n* (*infml* 口) **1** act of spending money freely 挥霍: *I had a splurge and bought two new suits.* 我大手大脚花了一笔钱买了两套新衣服. **2** ostentatious display or effort (intended to attract attention) 夸示; 炫耀; 卖弄: *make a splurge* 炫耀一番.

▷ **splurge** *v* [I, Ipr, Tn, Tn·pr] **~ (sth) (on sth)** spend (money) freely or extravagantly 无节制地花(钱); 挥霍(金钱): *She won £100 and then splurged it all on new clothes.* 她赢了100英镑, 都挥霍在买新衣服上了.

splut·ter /ˈsplʌtə(r); ˋsplʌtɚ/ *v* **1** (also **sputter**) **(a)** [I, Ip] speak quickly and confusedly (from excitement, anger, etc) (因激动、气愤等)急促而语无伦次地说话. **(b)** [Tn, Tn·p] **~ sth (out)** say (words) quickly, confusedly or indistinctly 急促地、语无伦次地或含混不清地说(话): *splutter (out) a few words of apology* 语无伦次地道歉. **2** [I] make a series of spitting sounds; sputter 发劈啪声; 毕剥作响: *She dived into the water and came up coughing and spluttering.* 她扎入水中, 浮上来时呛得连咳嗽带喷水.

▷ **splut·ter** *n* spluttering sound 劈啪声; 毕剥声: *The candle gave a few faint splutters and then went out.* 蜡烛发出轻轻的毕剥声后就熄灭了.

spoil /spɔɪl; spɔɪl/ *v* (*pt, pp* **spoilt** /spɔɪlt; spɔɪlt/ or **spoiled** /spɔɪld; spɔɪld/) ⇨Usage at DREAM² 用法见 DREAM². **1** [Tn] make (sth) useless, valueless or unsatisfactory; ruin 毁掉, 损坏, 破坏, 糟蹋(某事物): *holidays spoilt by bad weather* 因天气坏而使人扫兴的假期 ○ *spoilt ballot papers*, ie made invalid because the voters have not marked them properly 废选票(因划票不符规定而失效) ○ *The new road has completely spoiled the character of the village.* 新修的路彻底毁掉了那个村庄的特色. ○ *The bad news has spoilt my day.* 这坏消息把我这一天给毁了. ○ *Don't spoil your appetite by eating sweets between meals.* 不要在两顿饭之间吃糖果, 以免吃不下饭. **2** [Tn] **(a)** harm the character of (esp a child) by lack of discipline or too much generosity, attention, praise, etc 娇惯, 宠坏, 溺爱(尤指儿童): *That little girl is terribly spoilt — her parents give her everything she asks for.* 那个小女孩真惯得不像话——父母对她是有求必应. **(b)** pay great or too much attention to the comfort and wishes of (sb); pamper 格外或过分关注(某人)的安适和愿望: *Everybody enjoys being spoiled from time to time.* 谁都喜欢偶尔让人宠一宠. **3** [I] (of food, etc) become bad or unfit to be used, eaten, etc (指食物等)变坏, 变质, 腐败: *Some kinds of food soon spoil.* 有些食物易变质. **4** (idm 习语) **be spoiling for sth** be very eager for (a fight, an argument, etc) 憋足了劲儿要(打架、争吵等): *He's spoiling for trouble.* 他憋足了劲儿要找麻烦. **be spoilt for choice** have so many possibilities to choose from that it is difficult to choose 因供选择的事物过多而无从下手. **spare the rod and spoil the child** ⇨ SPARE². **too many cooks spoil the broth** ⇨ COOK *n*.

▷ **spoil** *n* [U] = SPOILS.

spoil·age /ˈspɔɪlɪdʒ; ˋspɔɪlɪdʒ/ *n* [U] spoiling of food, etc by decay (食物等的)变坏, 变质, 腐败.

spoiler *n* **1** person or thing that spoils 把事物搞坏的人或事物; 宠坏他人的人或事物; 造成(食物等)腐败的东西. **2** **(a)** device on an aircraft to slow it down by interrupting the flow of air 扰流器(飞行器的). **(b)** similar device on a vehicle to prevent it being lifted off the road when travelling very fast 气流偏导器(车辆的).

spoils *n* [U] (also **spoils** [pl]) **1** **(a)** stolen goods 偷来的东西; 赃物: *The thieves divided up the spoils.* 窃贼把赃物分了. **(b)** things taken by a victorious army; plunder 战利品; 掠取之物. **2** profits, benefits, etc gained from political power 凭政治权力获取的利益等: *the spoils of office* 利用官职捞取的私利.

□ ˈ**spoil-sport** *n* person who spoils the enjoyment of others 扫人兴的人; 煞风景者: *Don't be such a spoil-sport!* 别这么扫人兴!

ˈ**spoils system** (*esp US*) system by which important public positions are given to supporters of the political party that wins power 政党分肥制(获胜政党将重要公职委派给支持者的制度).

spoke¹ /spəʊk; spok/ *n* **1** any of the bars or wire rods that connect the centre (*hub*) of a wheel to its outer edge (*rim*), eg on a bicycle 辐条. ⇨illus at App 1 见附录1插图, page xiii. **2** (idm 习语) **put a ˈspoke in sb's wheel** (*Brit*) prevent sb from carrying out his plans 阻挠某人的计划.

spoke² *pt* of SPEAK.

spoken *pp* of SPEAK.

spoke·shave /ˈspəʊkʃeɪv; ˋspok,ʃev/ *n* tool used for planing curved surfaces, esp of wood 辐刨.

spokes·man /ˈspəʊksmən; ˋspoksmən/ *n* (*pl* **-men** /-mən; -mən/) (*fem* 阴性作 **spokes·wo·man** /ˈspəʊkswʊmən; ˋspoks,wʊmən/, *pl* **-wo·men** /-wɪmɪn; -wɪmɪn/) person who speaks, or is chosen to speak, on behalf of a group 发言人. ⇨Usage at CHAIR 用法见 CHAIR.

spo·li·ation /ˌspəʊlɪˈeɪʃn; ˌspolɪˋeʃən/ *n* [U] (*fml* 文) activity of spoiling (SPOIL 1) or damaging, esp with force; pillaging or plundering 损坏, 破坏, 毁坏(尤指以武力进行者); 掠夺; 抢劫.

spon·dee /ˈspɒndiː; ˋspɑndi/ *n* metrical foot in poetry consisting of two long or stressed syllables 扬扬格(诗歌音步, 由两个长音节或重音节组成). ▷ **spon·daic** /spɒnˈdeɪɪk; spɑnˋdeɪk/ *adj*.

sponge /spʌndʒ; spʌndʒ/ *n* **1** [C] type of simple sea animal with a light elastic body-structure full of holes that can absorb water easily 海绵. **2** [C, U] (part of) one of these, or a substance of similar texture, used for washing, cleaning or padding (用作清洗工具或衬垫物的)海绵, 海绵状物: *a large bath sponge*, ie for washing one's body in the bath 洗澡用的大块海绵 ○ *filled with sponge* 内填海绵的 ○ [attrib 作定语] *sponge rubber* 泡沫橡胶. **3** [C] piece of absorbent material, eg gauze, used in surgery (外科用的)吸水物(如纱布). **4** [C esp *sing* 尤作单数] act of cleaning, wiping, etc with a sponge; sponging 用海绵或吸水物进行的清洗、擦拭等: *She gave the floor a vigorous sponge all over.* 她用海绵把地板

使劲儿擦了一遍. **5** [C, U] = SPONGE-CAKE: *Would you like some more sponge?* 你再来点海绵蛋糕好吗? **6** (idm 习语) **throw up the sponge** (*infml* 口) admit that one is defeated 认输.

▷ **sponge** *v* **1** [Tn, Tn·p] **~ sb/oneself/sth (down)** wipe, wash or clean sb/oneself/sth with a sponge 用海绵或海绵状物擦拭或清洗某人[自己/某物]: *sponge a wound* 用海绵擦洗伤口 ○ *He sponged down the car to remove the shampoo.* 他用海绵把汽车上的洗涤剂擦掉了. **2** [I, Tn, Tn·pr] **~ (sth) (from sb)** (*infml* 口) get (money, etc) from sb without giving or intending to give anything in return 白拿, 白得(钱等); 揩油: *sponge a dinner* 白吃一顿 ○ *sponge a fiver* (ie £5) *from an old friend* 向老朋友揩油硬要五英镑. **3** (phr v) **sponge sth off/out** remove sth by sponging 用海绵等清除某物: *sponge out a stain in the carpet* 用海绵把地毯上的污迹擦掉. **sponge on/off sb** (*infml usu derog* 口, 通常作贬义) live at another person's expense; get money, food, etc from sb without giving or intending to give anything in return 依赖他人为生; 当食客; 从某人那儿白得(钱、食物等); 揩油: *He always sponges off others.* 他总是揩别人的油. **sponge sth up** remove (liquid) with a sponge 用海绵等将(液体)吸掉. **sponger** *n* person who sponges (SPONGE *v* 2) 依赖他人生活者; 寄生虫; 吃白食的人; 揩油者. **spong·ing** *n* (usu *sing* 通常作单数) = SPONGE *n* 4: *give a child's face a good sponging* 用海绵给孩子好好洗洗脸.

spongy *adj* (**-ier, -iest**) soft, elastic and able to absorb water like a sponge 海绵似的(柔软而有弹性和吸水性的): *spongy moss* 湿软的苔藓. **spon·gi·ness** *n* [U].

□ ˈ**sponge-bag** *n* (*Brit*) waterproof bag for holding one's toothpaste, soap, toothbrush, etc, esp when one is travelling 盥洗用品袋(不透水, 尤用于旅行).

ˈ**sponge-cake** *n* [C, U] soft light cake made with eggs, sugar and flour 海绵蛋糕.

ˌ**sponge-ˈpudding** *n* [C, U] pudding like a sponge-cake 海绵布丁.

spon·sor /ˈspɒnsə(r); ˋspɑnsɚ/ *n* **1** person who makes himself responsible for another (eg sb who is training for sth) 担保人, 保人(如为求学者作担保者). **2** godparent 教父; 教母. **3** person who puts forward or guarantees a proposal (eg for a new law) 发起者; 倡议者; 提案人; (建议的)保证人. **4** person or firm that pays for a radio or TV programme, or for a musical, artistic or sporting event, usu in order to use them for advertising 赞助人; 赞助公司; 广告客户. **5** person who pays money to charity in return for a specified activity by another person 向慈善事业捐款以换取他人的某项活动者.

▷ **spon·sor** *v* [Tn] act as a sponsor for (sb/sth) 担保或赞助(某人[某事物]); 倡议(某事): *an athlete sponsored by a bank* 由某银行资助的运动员 ○ *a sponsored walk*, ie one over a fixed distance for which the walkers arrange sponsorship beforehand in aid of charity 募捐性步行 ○ *a government-sponsored cheap textbooks scheme* 政府资助的提供廉价教科书的方案 ○ *I'm doing a sponsored swim on Saturday — will you sponsor me?* 星期六我要参加慈善游泳——您愿意出钱赞助吗?

spon·sor·ship *n* [U]: *We're very grateful for his sponsorship.* 我们十分感激他慷慨资助.

spon·tan·eous /spɒnˈteɪnɪəs; spɑnˋtenɪəs/ *adj* (**a**) done, happening, said, etc because of a voluntary impulse from within, not caused or suggested by sth/sb outside 自发的; 主动的; 自动的: *a spontaneous offer of help* 主动提供的帮助 ○ *spontaneous applause* 自发的鼓掌. (**b**) natural, not forced 自然的; 非勉强的: *a spontaneous gaiety of manner* 天真愉快的神态.

▷ **spon·tan·eously** *adv*.

spon·tan·eous·ness (also **spon·tan·eity** /ˌspɒntəˈneɪətɪ; ˌspɑntəˋneətɪ/) *n* [U] quality of being spontaneous 自发性; (举止等的)自然.

□ **sponˌtaneous comˈbustion** burning caused by chemical changes, etc inside the material, not by the application of fire from outside 自燃.

spoof /spu:f; spuf/ *n* (*infml* 口) **1 ~ (of/on sth)** humorous imitation or parody 滑稽的模仿: [attrib 作定语] *a spoof horror film* 模拟恐怖片的滑稽影片. **2** trick; hoax 骗人的玩意儿; 鬼把戏.

▷ **spoof** *v* [Tn esp passive 尤用于被动语态] (*infml* 口) trick or swindle (sb) 愚弄, 哄骗(某人): *You've been spoofed.* 你上当了.

spook /spu:k; spuk/ *n* (*infml usu joc* 口, 通常作戏谑语) ghost 鬼: *Are you afraid of spooks?* 你怕不怕鬼?

▷ **spook** *v* [Tn] (*infml* 口 *esp US*) frighten; scare 吓; 吓唬: *Something in the bushes spooked her horse.* 矮树林里有东西惊了她的马.

spooky *adj* (**-ier, -iest**) (*infml* 口) suggesting spooks; frightening 使人想到鬼的; 吓人的: *a spooky old house* 阴森森的老房子. **spooki·ness** *n* [U].

spool /spu:l; spul/ *n* **1** = REEL[1] 1. **2** amount (of thread, etc) held on one of these (指线等)一轴上所绕的数量: *How many spools of thread did you use?* 你用了几轴线?

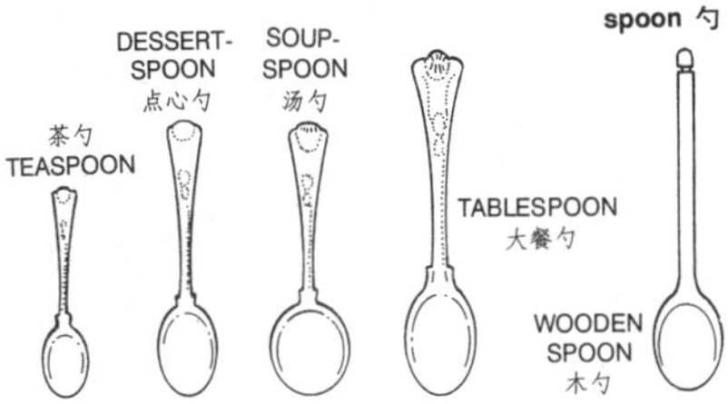

spoon /spu:n; spun/ *n* (often in compounds 常用以构成复合词) **1** utensil with a shallow oval or round bowl on a handle, used for stirring, serving and taking up food (esp puddings and soups) to the mouth 勺; 匙子; 羹匙: *a large wooden* ˈ*spoon* 大木勺 ○ *a* ˈ*tablespoon* 大餐匙 ○ *a* ˈ*soup-spoon* 汤匙 ○ *a* ˈ*teaspoon* 茶匙. **2** amount this can hold; spoonful 一勺的量: *Two spoons of sugar, please.* 请放两匙糖. **3** (idm 习语) **born with a silver spoon in one's mouth** ⇨ BORN.

▷ **spoon** *v* [Tn·pr, Tn·p] **1** lift and move (sth) with a spoon in the specified way or direction 用勺舀(某物): *spoon sugar from the packet into a bowl* 把食糖从袋子中舀到糖罐里 ○ *spoon up one's soup* 用勺舀汤 ○ *spoon out the peas* 用匙子舀取豌豆. **2 ~ sth (up)** hit (a ball) feebly upwards 轻轻向上击(球).

spoon·ful /-fʊl; -ˌfʊl/ *n* (*pl* **-fuls**) amount that a spoon can hold 一勺的量: *a heaped spoonful of sugar* 满满的一匙糖.

□ ˈ**spoon-feed** *v* (*pt, pp* **-fed**) [Tn] (**a**) feed (a baby, etc) with a spoon 用勺喂(小孩儿等). (**b**) (*fig esp derog* 比喻, 尤作贬义) give (sb) too much help or teaching in a way that does not allow him to think for himself 给(某人)过多的帮助或指教(使其无法独立思考): *Some teachers spoon-feed their students.* 有些教师教书如喂食, 使学生不会独立思考.

spoon·er·ism /ˈspu:nərɪzəm; ˋspunəˌrɪzəm/ *n* (often humorous) result of changing round, esp accidentally, the initial sounds of two or more words when speaking, eg *well-boiled icicle* for *well-oiled bicycle* (常产生滑稽效果的)首音误置(如将well-oiled bicycle 说成well-boiled icicle).

spoor /spɔ:(r); *US* spʊər; spʊr/ *n* [C] track or scent left by a wild animal (enabling it to be followed) (野生动物的)足迹, 臭迹.

spor·adic /spəˈrædɪk; spəˋrædɪk/ *adj* happening or seen only occasionally or in a few places; occurring irregularly 偶发的; 偶见的; 仅在少数地方发生或见到的: *sporadic showers* 阵雨 ○ *sporadic raids, gunfire, fighting* 零星的袭击、炮击、战斗. ▷ **spor·ad·ic·ally** /-klɪ; -klɪ/ *adv*.

spore /spɔ:(r); spor/ *n* (*botany* 植) any of the tiny seed-like reproductive cells of some plants such as ferns, mosses and fungi 孢子: *mushroom spores* 蘑菇孢子.

spor·ran /ˈspɒrən; ˋspɑrən/ *n* large pouch, usu made of leather or fur, that is worn by men in front of the kilt as part of the Scottish national dress (苏格兰男子系于短裙前的)毛皮袋.

sport /spɔ:t; spɔrt/ *n* **1** [U] physical activity done, esp outdoors, for exercise and amusement, usu played in a special area and according to fixed rules 文体活动(尤指户外的); 运动; 游戏: *She plays a lot of sport.* 她经常运动. ○ *He's very fond of sport.* 他非常喜欢文体活动.

S

2 (**a**) [C] particular form of such activity; particular game or pastime 文体活动; 某种游戏或消遣: *team sports* 队与队的竞赛 ○ *Hockey, volleyball, football and tennis are all sports.* 曲棍球、排球、足球、网球都是体育项目. ○ *Which sports do you like best?* 你最喜欢哪些运动? ○ *athletic sports*, eg running, jumping 田径运动(如跑和跳) ○ *country sports*, eg hunting, fishing, shooting, horse-racing 乡间户外运动(如打猎、钓鱼、射击、赛马) ○ [attrib 作定语] *sports coverage on TV* 电视上的体育新闻报道 ○ *a sports programme* 体育节目 ○ *a 'sports field* 运动场. (**b**) [U] such activities or pastimes collectively 文体活动(总称): *the world of sport* 体育界. ⇨Usage 见所附用法. **3 sports** [pl] meeting for athletic competitions 运动会: *the school sports* 学校运动会 ○ *inter-university sports* 大学校际运动会 ○ [attrib 作定语] *a 'sports day* 运动会日. **4** [U] amusement; fun 娱乐; 消遣; 玩笑; 戏谑: *do sth for sport* 为取乐而做某事 ○ *say sth in sport*, ie not seriously 说着玩儿. **5** [C] (*dated infml* 旧, 口) pleasant, cheerful and generous-minded person 随和、开朗、大度的人: *Come on, be a sport!* 好了, 随和点吧! ○ *a good/bad sport*, ie sb who behaves well/badly in sporting or similar activities 文体道德好[坏]的人. **6** [C] (*infml esp Austral* 口, 尤用于澳大利亚) (as a term of address 作称呼语) chap; fellow; friend 老兄; 哥儿们; 朋友: *How are you doing, sport!* 你好哇, 哥儿们! **7** [C] (*biology* 生) plant or animal that deviates in some unusual way from the normal type 变态的植物或动物. **8** (idm 习语) **make sport of sb** (*fml* 文) mock or joke about sb 嘲笑某人; 开某人的玩笑.

▷ **sport** *v* **1** [Tn] have or wear (sth) proudly for others to see 夸示(某物); 炫耀地穿戴(某物): *sport a moustache, a diamond ring, a flower in one's buttonhole* 神气地蓄着小胡子、戴着钻石戒指、在钮扣眼中插着花. **2** [I, Ip] (usu in the continuous tenses 通常用于进行时态) play about; amuse oneself; have fun 玩耍; 嬉戏: *seals sporting (about/around) in the water* 在水中嬉戏的海豹.

sporty *adj* (*infml* 口) **1** fond of or good at sport 爱好或擅长文体活动的: *She's very sporty.* 她非常爱好文体活动. **2** attractive and dashing 漂亮而时髦的: *a sporty new pullover* 漂亮的套头毛衣. **sport·ily** *adv*. **spor·ti·ness** *n* [U].

□ '**sports car** low (usu open) car designed for travelling at high speeds 跑车(车身较低, 通常为敞篷的汽车).

'**sportscast** *n* (*US*) TV or radio broadcast of sports news or a sports event (电视台或电台的)体育节目广播. '**sportscaster** *n* (*US*) person who introduces or commentates on such a programme (电视台或电台的)体育节目的播音员、主持人或解说员.

'**sports-editor** *n* newspaper editor responsible for reports of sports and games (报纸的)体育新闻编辑.

'**sports jacket** (*Brit*) man's jacket for informal wear (not part of a suit) (男子作便服的)外套. ⇨illus at JACKET 见JACKET插图.

'**sportsman** /-mən; -mən/ *n* (*pl* **-men** /-mən; -mən/) (*fem* 阴性作 '**sportswoman** /-wʊmən; -ˌwʊmən/, *pl* **-women** /-wɪmɪn; -ˌwɪmɪn/) **1** person who takes part in or is fond of sport 运动员; 爱好运动的人. **2** person who plays sport fairly, is willing to take risks, and doesn't become upset or bad-tempered if he loses 有文体道德的人. '**sportsmanlike** *adj* behaving fairly and generously 公正大度的: *a sportsmanlike attitude, gesture* 高姿态、风格高的做法. '**sportsmanship** *n* [U] sportsmanlike quality or spirit 公正大度的品质或精神.

'**sports writer** person (esp a journalist) who writes about sport 体育文章的作者; (尤指)体育记者.

NOTE ON USAGE 用法: **Sport** plays a big part in many people's lives. 文体活动(**sport**)是许多人生活中的重要内容. At school children can play football, netball and other **sports** and there are clubs for playing indoor **games** such as chess or snooker. 在学校里, 学生可以参加足球、无挡板篮球以及其他体育运动(**sports**), 也可以加入国际象棋、落袋台球等各种室内文娱(**games**)社团. After work, a lot of people enjoy a **game** of tennis or squash. 许多人工余喜欢打网球或壁球. On TV we can watch tennis and football **matches** throughout the year and horse **races** are broadcast almost every day. 人们整年都可以通过电视观看网球和足球比赛(**matches**), 赛马(**races**)节目则几乎每天都有. Events in which people compete against each other, often for prizes, are **competitions** or **contests** 具比赛性质的、常设有锦标的运动称作**competitions**或**contests**: *a dancing competition* 舞蹈比赛 ○ *an archery, angling, etc contest* 射箭、钓鱼等比赛. A **tournament** or **championship** is a series of contests ☆ **tournament**或**championship**指的是联赛或锦标赛: *a tennis tournament* 网球联赛 ○ *the European Football Championship* 欧洲足球锦标赛.

sport·ing /ˈspɔːtɪŋ; ˈsportɪŋ/ *adj* **1** [attrib 作定语] connected with or interested in sport 娱乐的; 运动的; 爱好文体活动的: *a sporting occasion* 一项体育活动 ○ *a sporting man* 爱好运动的男子. **2** showing fairness; generous; sportsmanlike 公正的; 大度的; 风格高的: *It's very sporting of you to give me an initial advantage.* 你开局先让我一步, 真是够大方的. ○ *He made me a sporting offer*, ie one that involved some risk of his losing. 他甘愿自己冒风险, 大方地向我开了一个价. **3** (idm 习语) **a sporting 'chance** a reasonable chance of being successful 公平的机会: *give sb a sporting chance* 给某人一个公平的机会 ○ *We've still got a sporting chance of winning.* 我们获胜的可能性还是有的.

sport·ive /ˈspɔːtɪv; ˈsportɪv/ *adj* playful 爱玩耍的; 顽皮的; 闹着玩儿的. ▷ **sport·ively** *adv*. **sport·ive·ness** *n* [U].

spot /spɒt; spɑt/ *n* **1** small (usu round) mark different in colour, texture, etc from the surface it is on 斑点(通常指圆的): *a white skirt with red spots* 白底红点儿的裙子 ○ *Which has spots, the leopard or the tiger?* 豹跟虎哪一个身上有斑点? **2** roundish mark or stain 圆形的斑点或污迹: *spots of mud on your trousers* 你裤子上的泥斑. **3** small red mark or blemish on the skin, caused by illness, etc; pimple (皮肤上由于疾病而起的)红斑, 红疙瘩; 丘疹: *a teenage boy worried about his spots*, ie acne 因出粉刺而烦恼的十几岁的男青年 ○ *She had chicken-pox and was covered in spots.* 她得了水痘, 出了一身丘疹. **4** (**a**) particular place or area 地点; 场所: *a nice picnic spot/spot for a picnic* 野餐的好去处 ○ *a well-known beauty spot*, ie a place well-known for its natural beauty 风景胜地 ○ *stand rooted to the spot*, ie not moving 站在原处不动 ○ *This is the (very) spot where he was murdered.* 他就是在这儿遭谋杀的. ○ *There are several weak spots in your argument.* 你的论点中有几处经不起推敲. (**b**) (*infml* 口) place of entertainment 娱乐场所: *a popular night spot* 很受欢迎的夜总会. **5** drop 滴: *Did you feel a few spots of rain?* 下了几滴雨, 你感觉到了吗? **6** place for an individual item of entertainment, esp a short regular one, in a television, radio or theatre show (插入电视、电台或戏院节目中的)节目档(尤指短小、固定的): *a ten-minute guest spot on a radio programme* 电台某节目中的十分钟特约贵宾固定栏目 ○ *She has a regular cabaret spot at a local night-club.* 她在当地一家夜总会有她固定的歌舞节目档. **7** (usu *sing* 通常作单数) **~ of sth** (*Brit infml* 口) small amount of sth 少量的某事物: *Are you ready for a spot of lunch?* 你想吃点儿午饭吗? ○ *What about doing a spot of work?* 做点儿事怎么样? ○ *You seem to be having a spot of bother with your car — can I help?* 看来你的汽车有点让你伤脑筋了——要我帮忙吗? **8** (*fig* 比喻) flaw in a person's character; moral blemish 性格上的缺陷; 品行上的污点: *There isn't a spot on her reputation.* 她的声誉没有半点瑕疵. **9** (*infml* 口) = SPOTLIGHT. **10** (*US infml* 口) playing-card or banknote of a particular (specified) value 某点数的纸牌; 某票面的钞票: *He passed me a ten spot.* 他出给了我一张十点的牌. **11** (idm 习语) **change one's spots** ⇨ CHANGE[1]. **have a soft spot for sb/sth** ⇨ SOFT. **a hot spot** ⇨ HOT. **in a (tight) 'spot** (*infml* 口) in a difficult position or situation 处在困难的地位或环境中: *I'm in a bit of a spot financially.* 我经济上有点困难. **knock spots off sb/sth** ⇨ KNOCK[2]. **on the 'spot** (**a**) immediately; without moving from that place; then and there 立即; 当场: *He was hit by a falling tree and killed on the spot.* 一棵树倒下来, 把他当场砸死了. (**b**) at the place where an event happened (esp when one is needed) 在现场, 到现场(尤指能提供帮助的人): *The police were on the spot within a few minutes of my telephone call.* 我打电话几分钟后警察就赶到了现场.

○ *Luckily there was a doctor on the spot.* 幸亏当时有位医生在场. **put sb on the ˈspot** put a person in a difficult position; force sb to take action or justify himself 置某人于困境; 使某人为难; 迫使某人采取行动或进行辩解: *You've put me on the spot here — I can't answer your question.* 这你可把我难住了——你这个问题我答不上来.

▷ **spot** *v* (**-tt-**) **1** [I, Tn, Tn·pr usu passive 通常用于被动语态] **~ sth (with sth)** (cause sth to) become marked with a spot or spots (使某事物)有斑点或污点: *material that spots easily* 容易沾上污斑的料子 ○ *a table spotted with ink* 墨迹斑斑的桌子. **2** [Tn, Tw, Tng, Cn·n/a] **~ sb/sth (as sth)** (not in the continuous tenses 不用于进行时态) pick out (one person or thing from many); catch sight of; recognize; discover (从许多人或事物中)找出, 辨出, 认出(某人或某事物); 瞥见; 发觉: *He finally spotted just the shirt he wanted.* 他最后找到了他想要的衬衫. ○ *She spotted her friend in the crowd.* 她在人群中认出了她的朋友. ○ *I can't spot the difference between them.* 我看不出两者的区别. ○ *Can you spot the flaw in their argument?* 你能指出他们论点中的谬误吗? ○ *spot the winner of a race*, ie pick out the winner before the race starts 预先料到赛跑的获胜者 ○ *I soon spotted what to do.* 我很快就知道该怎么办了. ○ *He was spotted by police boarding a plane for Paris.* 他登上飞往巴黎的飞机时被警方认出. ○ *She has been spotted as a likely tennis star of the future.* 她很有希望成为网球明星. **3** [I, Ipr] (*Brit infml* 口) (used with *it* 与it连用) rain slightly; spit 下小雨: *It's beginning to spot.* 开始下小雨了. ○ *It's spotting with rain.* 正在下小雨. **spot·ted** *adj* marked or covered with spots 有斑点的; 满是斑点的: *a spotted dog* 身上有花斑的狗 ○ *a spotted dress* 带花点儿的连衣裙. **spotted ˈdick** (*Brit*) suet pudding containing currants 葡萄干板油布丁.

spot·ter *n* (esp in compounds 尤用以构成复合词) person who looks for and writes down details of a specified type of thing or person, as a hobby or job 寻找某事物或某人并作记录的人(作为嗜好或职业): *an ˈaircraft spotter*, ie one who looks for and identifies different types of aircraft, esp in wartime 飞机观察员(寻找并辨认各类飞机的人, 尤指战时) ○ *a ˈtalent-spotter*, ie an agent who visits clubs, theatres, etc looking for new acts 星探(到俱乐部、剧院等处发掘新秀的人) ○ *He's an avid ˈtrain-spotter.* 他特别喜欢观察火车. ○ [attrib 作定语] *a spotter plane*, ie one used for observing enemy manoeuvres 侦察机.

spot·less *adj* **1** very clean and tidy 极清洁的: *He keeps his house spotless.* 他把家里收拾得很整洁. **2** (*fig fml* 比喻, 文) free from flaws; morally pure 无瑕疵的; 道德上纯洁的: *a spotless reputation* 清白的名声. **spot·lessly** *adv*. **spot·less·ness** *n* [U].

spotty *adj* (**-ier**, **-iest**) (*infml* 口) **1** (*esp derog* 尤作贬义) (of a person) having spots (SPOT 3), esp on the face (指人)长斑点的(尤指脸上): *spotty youths* 满脸粉刺的青少年 ○ *a spotty complexion* 带斑点的脸. **2** marked with spots (SPOT 2); spotted 带斑点的; 有污迹的: *a spotty table-cloth* 有污迹的桌布.

□ **spot ˈcash** (*commerce* 商) money paid immediately for goods when they are bought (购物时付的)现金.

spot ˈcheck check made suddenly and without warning on a person or thing chosen at random 突击抽查; 抽样检查: *The campaign against drinking and driving will include spot checks on motorists.* 在禁止酒后开车这一行动中要对司机突击检查.

ˈspot welding welding of small areas of metal that are in contact 点焊.

spot-ˈon *adj* [pred 作表语] (*infml* 口) exactly right; accurate 一点不错; 对极了; 准确: *His assessment of the situation was spot-on.* 他对形势判断得很正确. ○ *Your budget figures were spot-on this year.* 你做的本年度预算数字十分准确.

spot·light /ˈspɒtlaɪt; ˈspɑtˌlaɪt/ *n* **1** (also **spot**) [C] (lamp used for sending a) strong beam of light directed onto a particular place or person, eg on the stage of a theatre 聚光灯(的光)(如舞台上的). ⇨illus at App 1 见附录1插图, page ix. **2 the spotlight** [sing] (*fig* 比喻) full attention or publicity 大家的注意: *a sportsman who likes to be in the spotlight* 爱出风头的运动员 ○ *This week the spotlight is on the world of fashion.* 本周引人瞩目的是时装界.

▷ **spot·light** *v* (*pt, pp* **spotlit** /-lɪt; -ˌlɪt/ or, esp in sense 2, **spotlighted** 亦作 **spotlighted**, 尤用于下述第2义) [Tn] **1** direct a spotlight onto (sb/sth) 将聚光灯射向(某人[某物]): *a spotlit stage* 有聚光照明的舞台. **2** (*fig* 比喻) draw attention to (sth); make conspicuous or obvious 使注意(某事物); 使突出或显眼: *The report has spotlighted real deprivation in the inner cities.* 这篇报道披露了旧城区的贫困真相.

spouse /spaʊz; *US* spaʊs; spaʊs/ *n* (*arch or law or joc* 古或律或谑) husband or wife 配偶.

spout /spaʊt; spaʊt/ *n* [C] **1** projecting pipe or tube through or from which liquid pours, eg for carrying rain-water from a roof or tea from a teapot 供液体流出的凸起管状物(如落水管或茶壶嘴): *The spout is chipped so it doesn't pour very well.* 这壶嘴儿有个豁口, 倒起来不方便. **2** jet of liquid coming out with great force (喷出的)液体流, 液体柱. **3** (idm 习语) **up the ˈspout** (**a**) (*infml* 口) in a hopeless condition; broken, ruined, defeated, etc 没指望; 毁坏; 完蛋: *My holiday plans are completely up the spout.* 我的假期计划全吹了. (**b**) (*sl derog* 俚, 贬) pregnant 怀孕.

▷ **spout** *v* **1** (**a**) [I, Ipr, Ip] **~ (out of/from sth)/(out/up)** (of a liquid) come out with great force (指液体)喷出, 涌出: *blood spouting from a severed artery* 动脉割断后喷出的鲜血 ○ *water spouting (out) from a broken water-pipe* 从破裂的水管中喷出的水. (**b**) [Tn, Tn·p] **~ sth (out/up)** send out (a liquid) with great force 喷出, 涌出(液体): *a broken pipe spouting (out) water* 喷(出)水的坏管子 ○ *The wound spouted blood.* 伤口涌出血来. (**c**) [I] (of whales) send a jet of water up through a hole in the head (指鲸)喷水. **2** [I, Ipr, Tn, Tn·pr, Tn·p] (*infml usu derog* 口, 通常作贬义) recite (poetry, etc) or speak lengthily and loudly 没完没了地大声吟诵(诗歌等)或说话: *Children dislike being spouted at by pompous teachers.* 学生不喜欢听自命不凡的教师对他们夸夸其谈. ○ *spouting unwanted advice* 啰啰嗦嗦地说出没人想听的建议 ○ *He can spout Shakespeare for hours.* 他能滔滔不绝地朗朗背诵莎士比亚的作品.

sprain /spreɪn; spren/ *v* [Tn] injure (a joint in the body, esp a wrist or an ankle) by sudden twisting or wrenching so that there is pain and swelling 扭伤(关节, 尤指腕和踝): *sprain one's wrist* 扭伤手腕 ○ *suffering from a sprained ankle* 踝部扭伤.

▷ **sprain** *n* injury caused in this way 扭伤: *a bad sprain* 严重的扭伤.

sprang *pt* of SPRING[3].

sprat /spræt; spræt/ *n* **1** small edible European sea-fish of the herring family 西鲱(欧洲产的可食小海鱼). **2** (idm 习语) **a ˌsprat to catch a ˈmackerel** (*saying* 谚) relatively small or unimportant thing that is offered or sacrificed in the hope of getting sth much bigger or better 用小鱼钓大鱼; 吃小亏占大便宜.

sprawl /sprɔːl; sprɔl/ *v* (*esp derog* 尤作贬义) **1** (**a**) [I, Ipr, Ip] **~ (out/about/around) (across, in, on, etc sth)** sit, lie or fall with the arms and legs spread out loosely 四肢摊开着坐、卧或倒下: *He was sprawling in an armchair in front of the TV.* 他伸开手脚坐在电视机前的单座沙发上. ○ *be sent sprawling in the mud* 被打倒在污泥中 ○ *sprawling about on the sofa* 手脚摊开着躺在沙发上. (**b**) [usu passive 通常用于被动语态: Tn, Tn·pr, Tn·p] spread (oneself or one's limbs) out loosely in this way 伸展(身体或四肢): *They were sprawled out in front of the fire.* 他们摊开手脚烤着火. **2** [I, Ipr, Ip] spread out loosely and irregularly over much space 散乱地延伸: *sprawling handwriting* 潦草的字迹 ○ *suburbs that sprawl out into the countryside* 向野外散乱延展的市郊.

▷ **sprawl** *n* [U, C usu *sing* 作不可数名词或可数名词, 后者通常作单数] (*esp derog* 尤作贬义) **1** sprawling position or movement 四肢伸开的姿势或动作: *pick one's way through the sprawl of people sunbathing* 小心翼翼地穿过伸开四肢晒太阳的人群 ○ *He lay in a sprawl over the desk.* 他手脚摊开趴在书桌上. **2** widespread untidy area, esp of buildings 杂乱的大片地方(尤指建筑物): *London's suburban sprawl* 伦敦郊外无计划扩展的地区.

spray[1] /spreɪ; spre/ *n* **1** (**a**) small branch of a tree or plant, with its leaves and flowers (树或花草的)小枝(带叶和花的). (**b**) artificial ornament in a similar form (人

S

造的)枝状花饰: *a spray of diamonds* 镶钻石的枝状饰物. **2** bunch of cut flowers, etc arranged attractively, eg as a decoration on clothes 小花簇(如用作衣服上的饰物): *He had a spray in his buttonhole.* 他的钮孔中插着一簇花. ○ *She carried a spray of pink roses.* 她拿着一簇粉红色的玫瑰花.

spray 喷雾器

spray² /spreɪ; spre/ *n* **1** [U] liquid sent through the air in tiny drops (by the wind or through an apparatus) 雾状液体(藉风力或喷洒装置形成的); 水花; 浪花: ˈ*sea spray*, ie blown from waves 大海的浪花 ○ *the spray of a waterfall* 瀑布的水花. **2** (**a**) [C, U] (esp in compounds 尤用以构成复合词) liquid (eg perfume, disinfectant, insecticide) applied in the form of spray from a special device (eg an atomizer or aerosol) under pressure 喷雾液体(如香水、消毒剂、杀虫剂): ˈ*hair spray* 喷发定型剂 ○ ˈ*fly-spray* 灭蝇喷剂 ○ [attrib 作定语] *spray paint* 喷雾颜料. (**b**) [C] device (eg an atomizer or aerosol) used for applying such a liquid in this form 喷雾器(如外压式的或内压式的): *I've lost my throat spray.* 我的润喉剂喷筒丢了. ⇨illus 见插图.

S

▷ **spray** *v* **1** [Tn, Tn·pr] **~ sth (on/over sb/sth)**; **~ sb/sth (with sth)** send out (liquid) onto sb/sth in tiny drops; wet sb/sth with liquid in this way 向某人[某物]喷雾状的(液体): *spraying paint on her car* 给她的汽车喷上漆 ○ *a farmer spraying his crops with pesticide* 给作物喷杀虫剂的农夫 ○ (*fig* 比喻) *spray the target with bullets* 向目标扫射. **2** [Ipr, Ip] **~ (out) (over, across, etc sb/sth)** (of a liquid) be sent out in tiny drops (指液体)喷出(呈雾状): *Water sprayed out over the floor.* 水喷洒在地上. **sprayer** *n* (**a**) person who sprays (usu as part of a job) 喷雾者(通常指职业性的): *He's a paint sprayer in the local factory.* 他在当地工厂当喷漆工. (**b**) apparatus for spraying 喷雾器; 喷漆器; 喷洒器: *a crop sprayer* 作物喷雾器.

□ ˈ**spray-gun** *n* device using pressure to spray paint, etc over surfaces 喷枪.

NOTE ON USAGE 用法: Compare **spray, shower, spatter, splatter, splash** and **slosh.** 试比较**spray**、**shower**、**spatter**、**splatter**、**splash**、**slosh**的用法. These verbs indicate the spreading of liquid or powder in a variety of ways. 这些动词表示以不同方式喷洒液体或粉末. We **spray** small drops of paint, perfume, chemicals, etc, usually with an aerosol or a spray-gun, in order to cover an area completely ☆ **spray** 用以指喷洒颜料、香水、化学制品等借以完全遮住某处, 通常用内压式喷雾器或喷枪操作: *I had to get my car resprayed after the accident.* 出了事故以后, 我只好把汽车重新喷了一次漆. **Shower** usually suggests people being covered with drops of water, dust, etc by accident or against their will ☆ **shower** 通常指人意外地或无法防备地被洒上水滴、尘土等: *The shoppers were showered with broken glass from the explosion.* 炸碎的玻璃劈头盖脸地落到购物顾客的身上. **Spatter** suggests larger amounts of paint, mud, blood, etc being thrown at somebody and making him or her dirty ☆ **spatter** 指较多的颜料、泥、血等溅到某人身上造成污斑: *The bus spattered them with mud as it passed in the rain.* 公共汽车在雨中驶过, 溅了他们一身泥. Eggs, etc are **splattered** over the floor when they are dropped or thrown. 鸡蛋等掉在或摔在地上为**splatter**. ☆ We **splash** liquids when we spill them accidentally 不慎洒出液体为**splash**: *Don't let the acid splash on your hand.* 别让酸液溅到手上. We **slosh** large quantities of paint, water, etc by throwing it around carelessly 乱甩颜料、水等为**slosh**: *He sloshed the paint on without bothering to catch the drips.* 他把油漆胡乱往上一甩, 连滴下来的也懒得抹一抹.

spread /spred; sprɛd/ *v* (*pt, pp* **spread**) **1** (**a**) [Tn, Tn·pr, Tn·p] **~ sth (out) (on/over sth)** extend the surface area, width or length of sth by unfolding or unrolling it 展开; 铺开; 摊开: *The bird spread (out) its wings.* 那只鸟张开了翅膀. ○ *spread a cloth on the table* 把桌布铺在桌子上 ○ *spread out one's arms*, eg to welcome or embrace sb 张开两臂(如欢迎或拥抱某人) ○ *spread the map out on the floor* 在地板上摊开地图. (**b**) [Tn·pr] **~ sth with sth** cover sth with sth by doing this 将某物铺于某物上: *spread a table with a cloth* 把桌布铺在桌子上. **2** (**a**) [Tn·pr] **~ A on B** put (a substance) on (a surface) and extend its area by flattening, etc; apply sth as a layer on sth 在(某物表面)上涂(某物); 敷: *spread butter on bread* 把黄油涂在面包上 ○ *spread glue on paper* 把胶水涂在纸上. (**b**) [Tn·pr] **~ B with A** cover (a surface) with (a substance) by doing this 将(某物)涂在(某物表面)上: *spread bread with butter* 把黄油涂在面包上. (**c**) [I] be able to be spread in this way; be applied in a layer 能涂敷; 被涂开: *Butter spreads more easily when it's softer.* 黄油软一些就容易涂抹. ○ *margarine that spreads straight from the fridge*, ie does not go hard when cold 从冰箱中取出便可涂开的人造黄油. **3** [I, Ipr, Tn, Tn·pr] (**a**) (cause sth to) become (more) widely known, felt or suffered (使某事物)传播, 流传, 蔓延: *The disease is spreading fast.* 这种病正在迅速蔓延. ○ *Fear spread quickly through the village.* 全村不多久便人心惶惶了. ○ *The strike has already spread to other factories.* 这次罢工已在其他工厂产生连锁反应. ○ *The water spread over the floor.* 水流了一地. ○ *Flies spread disease.* 苍蝇能传播疾病. ○ *He spread the news around the town.* 他在镇上到处传播这一消息. (**b**) (cause sth to) become distributed (使某事物)散布, 散开: *Settlers soon spread inland.* 移居到发展中地区的人不久就迁徙到内地了. **4** [I, Ipr] extend in size, area, etc 扩大; 伸展; 扩展: *a desert spreading for hundreds of miles* 绵延上百英里的沙漠 ○ *The forest spreads as far as the river.* 这片森林一直延伸到河边. **5** [Tn, Tn·pr] **~ sth (over sth)** distribute sth over a period of time 将某事物分散于某段时间内: *spread the payments over three months* 分三个月付清 ○ *a course of studies spread over three years* 为期三年的课程. **6** [usu passive 通常用于被动语态: Tn, Tn·pr] **~ sth (with sth)** prepare (a table) for a meal 在(餐桌)上摆上饭菜: *The table was spread with cakes and sandwiches.* 桌上摆好了糕饼和三明治. **7** (idm 习语) **spread like** ˈ**wildfire** (esp of rumours, reports, disease) travel, spread, etc very fast (尤指谣言、传闻、疾病)飞速地传开、蔓延等: *The news spread like wildfire.* 这消息不胫而走. **spread one's** ˈ**net** prepare to catch sb or get sb in one's power or influence 布下罗网(以捉住某人或迫使某人就范). ˈ**spread oneself** (**a**) occupy much space (eg by lying out with limbs extended) 占用很多地方(如四肢摊开躺着): *Since there was no one else in the compartment I was able to spread myself.* 车厢间隔里没有别人, 我正好能伸胳膊伸腿舒坦一下. (**b**) talk or write at length (on a subject) (就某主题)滔滔不绝地说或长篇大论地写. (**c**) spend or provide things generously 大方地花费或提供物品. **spread one's** ˈ**wings** (have confidence to) extend one's activities and interests (有信心去)扩展活动和爱好: *We hope college life will help him to spread his wings a bit.* 我们希望大学生活有助于他扩展兴趣爱好. **8** (phr v) **spread (sb/oneself) out** move (sb/oneself) away from others in a group so as to cover a wider area 使(某人[自己])离开其他人或散开: *The search party spread out over the moor.* 搜索队在荒草地分散行动. ○ *Don't all sit together, spread yourselves out.* 别都挤在一块儿, 分开坐吧.

▷ **spread** *n* **1** (usu *sing* 通常作单数) (**a**) extent, width or expanse of sth 范围; 宽度; 宽阔度: *the spread of a bird's wings* 鸟的翼展 ○ *The survey revealed a wide spread of opinion.* 调查结果表明各种意见差别很大. (**b**) extent of space or time; stretch (空间的)范围; 连续的一段时间: *a spread of 100 years* 100年的时间. **2** [U] process or activity of spreading (SPREAD 3) or being spread; extension; diffusion 传播; 散布; 蔓延; 扩散: *the spread of disease, knowledge, education* 疾病的蔓延、知识的传播、教育的普及 ○ *the spread of crime* 犯罪活动的蔓延. **3** [C] newspaper or magazine article, advertisement, etc, esp one covering more than one printed column 报刊文

章或广告等(尤指跨栏的): *a double-page spread* 横贯两版篇幅的文章. **4** [C] (*infml* 口) (usu large) meal spread out on a table (通常指丰盛的)一桌饭菜: *What a spread!* 多丰盛的饭菜呀! **5** (usu in compounds 通常用以构成复合词) **(a)** [C] thing that is spread(1b), esp a cloth for covering sth 铺开之物; (尤指)用以铺盖某物的布: *a* '*bedspread* 床单. **(b)** [C, U] expansion 扩展: (*joc* 谑) *middle-aged spread*, ie increased size around the waist in middle age 中年发福(即腰围增大). **6** [U, C] sweet or savoury paste spread on bread, etc (涂抹面包等的)美味酱: *chocolate spread* 巧克力酱 ○ *cheese spreads* 干酪酱.

□ ˌ**spread** '**eagle** figure of an eagle with legs and wings extended, as an emblem on coins, etc 张足展翼的鹰像(如硬币上的). **spread-eagle** *v* [Tn] place (sb) in a position with the arms and legs spread out 使(某人)呈四肢张开状: *Sunbathers lay spread-eagled on the grass.* 做日光浴的人呈大字形躺在草地上. ○ *The blow spread-eagled him against the wall.* 那一记把他打得张开四肢撞到了墙上.

spread·sheet /'spredʃi:t; 'sprɛdˌʃit/ *n* (*computing* 计) program for displaying and manipulating rows of figures, used esp for accounting; display or print-out produced by this 空白表格程序(尤用于会计); (以这一程序显示或印出的)空白表格.

spree /spri:; spri/ *n* (*infml* 口) lively and enjoyable outing, usu with much spending of money 外出作乐, 游乐(通常指花很多钱的): *have a spree* 痛痛快快地出去乐一乐 ○ *a spending/buying/shopping spree* 大买特买 ○ *go out on a spree*, ie go out to enjoy a spree 出去狂欢一番.

sprig /sprɪg; sprɪg/ *n* **~ (of sth)** small twig (of a plant or bush) with leaves, etc (有叶等的)小枝: *a sprig of holly, parsley, heather, etc* 一根冬青、欧芹、石南等的小枝 ○ *a sprig of mistletoe for Christmas* 作圣诞节装饰用的槲寄生小枝.

sprightly /'spraɪtlɪ; 'spraɪtlɪ/ *adj* **(-ier, -iest)** lively and full of energy 活泼的; 精力充沛的: *He's surprisingly sprightly for an old man.* 他这把年纪了, 还这么精神, 真了不起. ▷ **spright·li·ness** *n* [U].

spring 弹簧

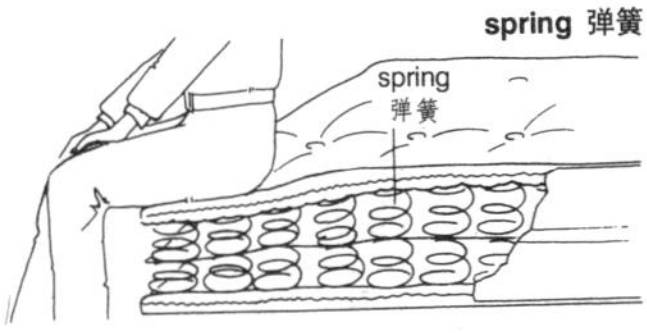

spring[1] /sprɪŋ; sprɪŋ/ *n* **1** [C] act of springing or jumping up; jump 跳; 跳跃: *With an easy spring the cat reached the branch.* 那猫轻轻一跃就够到了树枝. **2** [C] (place where there is) water coming up naturally from the ground; flow of this 泉; 泉水; 有泉水处; 泉水的流淌: *a* '*hot spring* 温泉 ○ *a* '*mineral spring* 矿泉 ○ [attrib 作定语] *spring water* 泉水. **3** [C] device of twisted, bent or coiled metal or wire that can be pushed, pulled or pressed but tends to return to its original shape or position when released (used to drive clockwork, make seats more comfortable, etc) 弹簧; 发条: *a watch spring* 表的发条 ○ *the springs in an armchair* 单座沙发内的弹簧 ○ [attrib 作定语] *a spring-*'*mattress*, ie one containing spiral springs in a rigid frame 弹簧床垫 ○ *Don't bounce on the bed — you'll break the springs!* 别在床上乱蹦——你要把弹簧弄断了! ⇨illus 见插图. **4** [U, sing] **(a)** elastic quality; elasticity 弹性; 弹力: *an old trampoline that has lost some of its spring* 失去一些弹性的旧蹦床. **(b)** (*fig* 比喻) lively, healthy quality 活力: *walk with a spring in one's step/heels* 脚步轻快地行走.

▷ **springy** *adj* **(-ier, -iest) 1** that can return to its original shape easily after being pushed, pulled, stretched, etc; elastic 有弹性的; 有弹力的: *a springy bed* 有弹性的床 ○ *The turf felt springy under their feet.* 他们走在草皮上, 觉得很松软. **2** having (a) spring[1](4b) 有活力的; 轻快的: *a youthful springy step* 富有青春活力的、轻快的脚步. **springi·ness** *n* [U].

□ ˌ**spring** '**balance** device that measures weight by the tension of a spring 弹簧秤.

'**springboard** *n* **1** strong flexible board from which a person can jump high before diving or performing a gymnastic feat (跳水运动的)跳板; (体操运动的)踏跳板. **2 ~ (to/for sth)** (*fig* 比喻) starting point that gives impetus to a future activity 发展事业的起点: *The college debating society was a natural springboard for her career in politics.* 大学里的辩论社自然成了她从政的垫脚石.

spring-'**tide** *n* tide with the greatest rise or fall, occurring soon after the new and full moon each month 大潮(朔望时潮差最大的潮汐). Cf 参看 NEAP-TIDE (NEAP).

spring[2] /sprɪŋ; sprɪŋ/ *n* **1** [U, C] the first season of the year (in which plants begin to grow), coming between winter and summer, ie from March to May in the northern hemisphere 春季; 春天: [attrib 作定语] *spring flowers, weather* 春季的花、天气 ○ *In (the) spring leaves begin to grow on the trees.* 树木在春天开始长出叶子. **2** (idm 习语) **full of the joys of spring** ⇨ FULL.

□ **spring** '**chicken 1** young chicken for eating 笋鸡. **2** (*fig joc* 比喻, 谑) young person 年轻人: *She's no spring chicken, is she?* 她已经不是黄毛丫头了, 对吧?

ˌ**spring-**'**clean** *v* [Tn] clean (a house, room, etc) thoroughly 彻底打扫(房屋等); 对...进行大扫除. **spring-clean** (also *esp US* ˌ**spring-**'**cleaning**) *n* (usu *sing* 通常作单数): *give the place a good spring-clean(ing)* 把这地方好好打扫一下.

spring '**greens** (*Brit*) tender young cabbage cooked and eaten as a vegetable 嫩洋白菜.

spring '**onion** (*US* **scallion**) small young onion with a thin white bulb and green stem, usu eaten raw 春葱.

'**springtide** *n* [U] (*arch* 古) = SPRINGTIME.

'**springtime** *n* [U] season of spring 春季; 春天: *The blossom on the trees looks lovely in (the) springtime.* 春天里树上开的花很漂亮.

spring[3] /sprɪŋ; sprɪŋ/ *v* (*pt* **sprang** /spræŋ; spræŋ/, *pp* **sprung** /sprʌŋ; sprʌŋ/) **1** [Ipr, Ip] jump quickly or suddenly, esp from the ground in a single movement; move suddenly (eg from a hiding-place or a position of relaxation) 蹦; 跃起; 跳出; 突然活动(如从隐藏处或松弛状态): *spring out of bed, into action, to one's feet* 一跃下床、立即投入行动、突然站起 ○ *A cat sprang out of the bushes.* 灌木丛中窜出一只猫来. ○ *sprang (up) from his seat* (他)从座位上一跃而起 ○ *He sprang forward to help me.* 他纵身上前帮我一把. ⇨Usage at JUMP[2] 用法见 JUMP[2]. **2** [I, Tn] (cause sth to) operate by means of a mechanism (使某物)藉机械装置操作: *spring a mine*, ie cause it to explode 触雷 ○ *spring a trap*, ie cause it to close suddenly 触发捕捉器 ○ *The box sprang open.* 盒子弹开了. **3** [Tn] **(a)** (*infml* 口) help (a prisoner, etc) to escape 帮助(囚犯等)逃跑: *spring a convict from gaol* 帮囚犯越狱. **(b)** cause (an animal) to leave a hiding-place 使(动物)离开躲藏处. **4** (idm 习语) **come/spring to mind** ⇨ MIND[1]. **spring a** '**leak** (of a boat, ship, container, etc) develop a hole so that water enters or leaks out (指船、容器等)破裂漏水. **spring to** '**life** suddenly become active 突然活跃起来: *On hearing his name called the sleeping dog sprang to life.* 那狗正在睡觉, 听到有人唤它, 猛地惊醒过来. **5** (phr v) **spring back** return suddenly to its previous or usual position, having been pushed, bent, etc (被推、折弯等后)弹回到原来的位置: *The branch sprang back and hit me in the face.* 树枝弹回来打在我脸上. **spring from sth/...** **(a)** have sth as a source or origin; originate from sth 发源于某事物; 来自某事物; 出身于: *He sprang from peasant stock.* 他是农民出身. ○ *Hatred often springs from fear.* 仇恨常常源于恐惧. **(b)** (*infml* 口) appear suddenly or unexpectedly from (a place) 从(某处)突然地或意外地出现: *Where on earth did you spring from?* 你是打哪儿冒出来的? **spring sth on sb** (*infml* 口) present, introduce or propose sth suddenly to sb as a surprise or without warning 向某人突然说出或提出某事物(令人惊奇或猝不及防): *spring bad news on sb* 单刀直入把坏消息告诉某人 ○ *spring a surprise on sb* 使某人感到惊奇 ○ *I hate to spring this on you at such short notice.* 很抱歉, 向你突如其来提出这件事. **spring up** appear, develop, grow, etc quickly or suddenly 迅速地或突然地出现、发展、生

长等: *weeds springing up everywhere* 很快长得到处都是的杂草 ○ *A breeze sprang up as we were returning.* 我们回来时突然起了一阵轻风. ○ *New houses were springing up all over the town.* 全镇各处很快盖起了新房子. ○ *Doubts have begun to spring up in my mind.* 我突然起了疑心.

spring·bok /ˈsprɪŋbɒk; ˋsprɪŋˌbɑk/ *n* small S African gazelle that can jump high into the air 跳羚(非洲南部的小羚羊, 善跳).

sprinkle /ˈsprɪŋkl; ˋsprɪŋkl/ *v* [Tn, Tn·pr] **~ A (on/onto/over B); ~ B (with A)** scatter or throw sth in small drops or particles; scatter a shower of small drops, etc on (a surface) 撒某物; 将某物洒在(另一物的表面)上: *sprinkle water on a dusty path/sprinkle a dusty path with water* 把水洒在尘土飞扬的小路上 ○ *sprinkle pepper on one's food* 把胡椒洒在食物上. ⇨Usage at SCATTER 用法见SCATTER.

▷ **sprinkle** *n* (usu *sing* 通常作单数) sprinkling 少量; 少数: *a sprinkle of sand* 一点沙子.

sprink·ler /ˈsprɪŋklə(r); ˋsprɪŋklɚ/ *n* device for sprinkling water (eg on a lawn) or as part of a fire-extinguishing system installed in a building 洒水装置; 洒水器; 消防喷嘴: [attrib 作定语] *a ˈsprinkler system*, ie set of sprinklers in a building that operate automatically when there is a rise in temperature caused by a fire 自动喷洒灭火设备. ⇨illus at App 1 见附录1插图, page vii.

sprink·ling /ˈsprɪŋklɪŋ; ˋsprɪŋklɪŋ/ *n* **~ (of sth/sb)** (usu *sing* 通常作单数) small amount or number 少量; 少数: *a sprinkling of rain* 小雨 ○ *a sprinkling of hooligans in the crowd* 夹在人群中的一小撮小流氓.

sprint /sprɪnt; sprɪnt/ *v* [I, Ipr, Ip, Tn] run a short distance at full speed 短距离全速奔跑: *He had to sprint to catch the bus.* 他得猛跑一阵才能赶上公共汽车. ○ *He sprinted past the other runners just before reaching the tape.* 他在到达终点之前全速冲刺, 超越了其他赛跑者. ○ *She sprinted off/away into the distance.* 她飞快地跑了. ○ *She sprinted the length of the road.* 她全速跑完了那条路的全长. ⇨Usage at RUN[1] 用法见RUN[1].

▷ **sprint** *n* **1** run of this type 短距离的全速奔跑; 短跑: *a 100m sprint* 100米短跑. **2** similar burst of speed in swimming, cycling, etc (游泳、自行车运动等的)冲刺.

sprinter *n* person who sprints 短距离全速奔跑者; 短跑者; 短跑运动员: *I'm a long-distance runner, not a sprinter.* 我是长跑运动员, 不是短跑运动员.

sprite /spraɪt; spraɪt/ *n* fairy, elf or goblin 小仙子; 小精灵; 小妖精; 小妖怪.

sprocket /ˈsprɒkɪt; ˋsprɑkɪt/ *n* **1** each of several teeth on a wheel that connect with the links of a chain or the holes in a film or in paper or magnetic tape 链轮齿. **2** (also ˈ**sprocket-wheel**) such a wheel, eg on a bicycle 链轮. ⇨illus at App 1 见附录1插图, page xiii.

sprout /spraʊt; spraʊt/ *v* **1** [I, Ipr, Ip] **~ (out/up) (from sth)** begin to grow or appear; put out leaves, shoots, etc 长出来; 出现; 发芽; 萌芽: *We can't use these potatoes; they've all sprouted.* 这些土豆儿不能吃了, 都出芽了. ○ *new buds sprouting on the trees* 树上长出的新芽 ○ *The onions are beginning to sprout (up).* 洋葱正在抽芽. ○ *Abundant hair sprouted from his broad chest.* 他宽阔的胸膛上长出许多毛. **2** [Tn] develop or produce (sth) 生出, 产生(某物): *When do deer first sprout horns?* 鹿在多大的时候开始生角? ○ *Tom has sprouted a beard since we saw him last.* 汤姆长胡子了, 我们上次见到他时还没长呢.

▷ **sprout** *n* **1** new shoot or bud of a plant 苗; 芽; 嫩枝: *bean sprouts* 豆芽. **2** = BRUSSELS SPROUT (BRUSSELS).

spruce[1] /spru:s; sprus/ *adj* tidy and clean in appearance; smart 外表整洁的; 漂亮的.

▷ **spruce** *v* (phr v) **spruce (oneself/sb) up** make (oneself/sb) tidy and clean; smarten up 使(自己[某人])整洁; 打扮: *He spruced (himself) up for the interview.* 他打扮了一下去参加面试. ○ *They were all spruced up for the party.* 他们都打扮得漂漂亮亮的去参加聚会.

sprucely *adv.*

spruce·ness *n* [U].

spruce[2] /spru:s; sprus/ *n* (**a**) [C] type of fir tree with dense foliage 云杉. (**b**) [U] its soft wood, used in paper-making 云杉木(质软, 用于造纸).

sprung[1] /sprʌŋ; sprʌŋ/ *pp* of SPRING[3].

sprung[2] /sprʌŋ; sprʌŋ/ *adj* fitted with springs (SPRING[1] 3) 装有弹簧的: *a sprung floor, mattress, seat* 弹簧地板、床垫、坐具.

spry /spraɪ; spraɪ/ *adj* (**-er**, **-est**) lively and active 活泼的; 活跃的: *still spry at eighty* 八十岁仍很矫健. ▷ **spryly** *adv.* **spry·ness** *n* [U].

spud /spʌd; spʌd/ *n* (*infml* 口) potato 土豆: *How many spuds do you want?* 你要多少土豆儿?

□ ˈ**spud-bashing** *n* [U] (*Brit army sl* 英军俚) peeling potatoes, esp as a punishment 削土豆皮(尤指惩罚性的).

spume /spju:m; spjum/ *n* [U] (*arch* 古) foam; froth 泡沫.

spun *pp* of SPIN.

spunk /spʌŋk; spʌŋk/ *n* [U] **1** (*dated infml* 旧, 口) courage; spirit 勇气; 胆量; 活力. **2** (*Brit sl* 俚) semen 精液; 屄.

▷ **spunky** *adj* (**-ier, -iest**) (*dated infml* 旧, 口) having spunk(1); plucky; spirited 有胆量的; 勇敢的; 劲头十足的.

spur /spɜ:(r); spɝ/ *n* **1** either of a pair of sharp-toothed wheels or projecting points, worn on the heels of a rider's boots and used to make a horse go faster 马刺: *a pair of spurs* 一副马刺. **2** (*fig* 比喻) **~ (to sth)** thing that urges a person on to greater activity; incentive 激励因素; 刺激; 鞭策: *the spur of poverty* 穷则思变 ○ *a spur to greater efficiency* 提高效率的刺激因素. **3** thing shaped like a spur, esp the sharp hard projection on the back of a cock's leg 马刺状物; (尤指)雄鸡腿上的距. **4** ridge extending from a mountain or hill 山嘴; 支脉; 横岭. **5** road or railway track that branches off the main road or line (公路或铁路的)支线: [attrib 作定语] *a ˈspur road* 岔道儿. **6** (idm 习语) **on the ˌspur of the ˈmoment** on a sudden impulse, without previous planning 一时冲动之下(未经仔细考虑): *She went to London on the spur of the moment.* 她一时兴起就到伦敦去了. ○ [attrib 作定语] *a ˌspur-of-the-moment iˈdea* 心血来潮的主意. **win one's ˈspurs** ⇨ WIN.

▷ **spur** *v* (**-rr-**) **1** [Tn, Tn·pr, Tn·p, Tnt] **~ sb/sth (on to sth/on)** (**a**) make (one's horse) go faster by pricking it with spurs 以马刺策(马)前进. (**b**) strongly encourage sb/sth to do better, achieve more, etc; incite or stimulate sb/sth 激励或刺激某人[某事物]: *The magnificent goal spurred the team on to victory.* 他们那一球进得漂亮, 鼓舞了全队的士气夺取胜利. ○ *He was spurred on by ambition.* 他胸怀大志. **2** [Ip] (*arch* 古) ride fast or hard 骑马疾驰; 驰驱: *The rider spurred on/forward to his destination.* 骑者向目的地疾驰而去. **spurred** *adj* [usu pred 通常作表语] having spurs; fitted with spurs 有马刺; 装有马刺: *booted and spurred* 穿着带马刺的靴子 ○ *spurred boots* 装有马刺的靴子.

spuri·ous /ˈspjʊərɪəs; ˋspjʊrɪəs/ *adj* not genuine or authentic; false or fake 假的; 伪造的: *spurious coins, credentials, documents, evidence* 伪造的硬币、证书、文件、证据 ○ *a spurious argument* 站不住脚的论据. ▷ **spuri·ously** *adv.* **spuri·ous·ness** *n* [U].

spurn /spɜ:n; spɝn/ *v* [Tn] reject or refuse (sb/sth) scornfully or contemptuously 傲慢地或轻蔑地拒绝(某人[某事物]); 唾弃: *a spurned lover* 被抛弃的情人 ○ *spurn sb's offer of help* 傲慢地拒绝某人提供的帮助 ○ *She spurned his advances.* 她轻蔑地拒绝了他的追求.

spurt /spɜ:t; spɝt/ *v* **1** (**a**) [I, Ipr, Ip] **~ (out) (from sth)** (of liquids, flame, etc) come out in a sudden burst; gush (指液体、火焰等)喷出, 迸出, 涌出: *water spurting from a broken pipe* 从破裂的管子中喷出的水 ○ *Blood spurted (out) from the wound.* 血从伤口涌出. (**b**) [Tn, Tn·p] **~ sth (out)** send out (liquids, flame, etc) in this way 喷出(液体、火焰等): *The wound was spurting blood.* 伤口淌着血. ○ *The volcano spurted (out) molten lava.* 火山喷出了熔岩. **2** [I] increase one's speed, effort, etc suddenly, esp in a race or other contest 突然加速、用力等; (尤指在赛跑等竞赛中)冲刺: *The runner spurted as he approached the line.* 那赛跑选手在接近终点线时加速冲刺.

▷ **spurt** *n* **1** sudden bursting out; gush 喷射; 涌出: *The water came out with a spurt.* 水喷了出来. **2** sudden burst of speed, effort, activity, etc 突然的加速; 劲头的迸发; 活跃程度的突然增大: *put on* (ie make) *a spurt* 突然加速 ○ *make a spurt for the line* 向终点线冲刺 ○ *a sudden spurt of energy, anger* 精力的迸发、突发的怒火 ○ *working in spurts* 一阵阵地拼命工作.

S

sput·nik /ˈspʊtnɪk; ˋspʊtnɪk/ *n* Russian artificial satellite orbiting the earth (俄国的)人造卫星.

sput·ter /ˈspʌtə(r); ˋspʌtɚ/ *v* [I] **1** make a series of spitting or popping sounds 发出劈劈啪啪声; 毕剥作响: *sausages sputtering in the frying-pan* 在煎锅中毕剥作响的香肠 ○ *The engine sputtered feebly for a while and then stopped.* 发动机发出一阵微弱的嗒嗒声后停了下来. **2** = SPLUTTER 1: *sputtering with embarrassment* 尴尬得语无伦次.

▷ **sput·ter** *n* sputtering sound or way of speaking 劈啪声; 慌乱的说话方式.

spu·tum /ˈspju:təm; ˋspjutəm/ *n* [U] (*fml or medical* 文或医) liquid and mucus coughed up from the throat or lungs (esp as used to diagnose some diseases); saliva or spittle 痰(尤指可作诊断依据的); 唾液; 口水.

spy /spaɪ; spaɪ/ *n* **1** person who tries to get secret information about military affairs, etc, esp one employed by a government to do this in another country 间谍: *suspected of being a spy* 有间谍嫌疑的 ○ [attrib 作定语] *a spy trial* 对间谍嫌疑犯的审讯. **2** person who secretly watches and reports on what others do, where they go, etc 秘密侦察他人行动者; 密探: *police spies*, ie people employed by the police to watch suspected criminals 警方的密探 ○ *industrial spies*, ie those employed to learn the secrets of business rivals, etc 工业间谍. Cf 参看 MOLE² 2.

▷ **spy** *v* (*pt, pp* **spied**) **1** [I, Ipr] **~ (on sb); ~ (on/into sth)** (**a**) keep watch secretly 暗中监视; 侦察; 窥探: *spy on the enemy's movements* 侦察敌方行动 ○ *spy into other people's affairs* 窥探他人的私事 ○ *I'm sure my neighbours spy on me.* 我肯定邻居暗中监视我. (**b**) be a spy; collect secret information 作间谍或窥探活动; 收集机密情报: *She was accused of spying for the enemy.* 她被指控为敌方间谍. **2** [Tn, Tng] (*fml or joc* 文或谑) (usu not in the continuous tenses 通常不用于进行时态) observe (sb/sth); see; notice 观察(某人[某事物]); 看见; 注意到: *We spied three figures in the distance.* 我们望见远处有三个人影儿. ○ *I spy someone coming up the garden path.* 我看到有人正沿着花园小径走来. **3** (idm 习语) ˌ**spy out the ˈland** assess the situation by making discreet inquiries, etc 摸清情况. **4** (phr v) **spy sth out** explore and discover (esp an illegal activity) without being observed 暗中查明(尤指非法活动).

□ ˈ**spyglass** *n* small telescope 小望远镜.

Sq *abbr* 缩写 = (in street names) Square (用于街道名)路, 街, 道: *6 Hanover Sq* 汉诺威道6号.

sq *abbr* 缩写 = square (measurement) 平方: *10 sq cm* 10平方厘米.

Sqn Ldr *abbr* 缩写 = Squadron Leader 空军少校: *Sqn Ldr (Philip) Jones* 皇家空军少校(菲利普·)琼斯.

squab /skwɒb; skwɑb/ *n* **1** young pigeon, esp when eaten as food 乳鸽. **2** soft seat or cushion, esp as part of a seat in a car 软座, 软坐垫(尤指汽车的).

squabble /ˈskwɒbl; ˋskwɑbl̩/ *v* [I, Ipr] **~ (with sb) (about/over sth)** quarrel noisily (as children do), esp over unimportant matters 大声争吵(尤指为琐事, 如儿童间的): *birds squabbling over bits of bread* 为争一些小面包屑叽叽喳喳叫的鸟 ○ *Tom keeps squabbling with his sister about who is going to use the bicycle.* 汤姆跟妹妹都争着要骑那辆自行车.

▷ **squabble** *n* noisy quarrel about sth unimportant 无谓的大声争吵.

squad /skwɒd; skwɑd/ *n* [CGp] (**a**) small group of soldiers working or being trained together (军队中的)班. (**b**) group of people, eg athletes or sportsmen, working as a team 小队, 小组(如由运动员组成的): *the Olympic squad*, ie the athletes chosen to represent their country at the Olympic Games 参加奥林匹克运动会的国家代表队.

▷ **squad·die** (also **squaddy**) *n* (*Brit sl* 俚) soldier, esp a young private; recruit 士兵(尤指年轻的列兵); 新兵: *a bunch of squaddies* 一帮新兵.

□ ˈ**squad car** police patrol car 巡逻警车.

squad·ron /ˈskwɒdrən; ˋskwɑdrən/ *n* [CGp] **1** group of military aircraft forming a unit in the Royal Air Force 英国皇家空军中队. **2** group of warships on special service 海军中队. **3** division of a cavalry or an armoured regiment 骑兵中队; 装甲连.

□ ˈ**squadron leader** (*abbr* 缩写 **Sqn Ldr**) officer commanding a squadron in the Royal Air Force (英国)皇家空军中队长, 皇家空军少校. ⇨App 9 见附录9.

squalid /ˈskwɒlɪd; ˋskwɑlɪd/ *adj* (*derog* 贬) **1** very dirty and unpleasant (esp because of neglect or poverty) 污秽的; 肮脏的; 邋遢的: *squalid housing* 肮脏的房屋 ○ *living in squalid conditions* 住在污秽的环境中. **2** morally degrading; sordid 道德败坏的; 卑鄙的: *a squalid tale of greed and corruption* 描述贪得无厌和腐败堕落等丑恶现象的故事. ▷ **squal·idly** *adv*.

squall /skwɔ:l; skwɔl/ *n* **1** sudden violent wind, often with rain or snow 飑(突起的狂风, 常夹有雨或雪). **2** loud cry or scream of pain or fear (esp from a baby) (因痛苦或恐惧而发出的)高声哭喊, 尖叫(尤指幼儿的).

▷ **squall** *v* [I] cry noisily 大声哭喊; 尖叫: *a squalling baby* 嚎哭的幼儿.

squally *adj* having squalls (SQUALL 1) 有狂风的: *a squally February day* 二月里狂风大作的一天 ○ *squally showers of rain or sleet* 狂风中的一阵阵雨或雨夹雪.

squalor /ˈskwɒlə(r); ˋskwɑlɚ/ *n* [U] squalid state 污秽; 卑劣: *the squalor of the slums* 贫民窟的污秽状况 ○ *live in abject squalor* 住在肮脏凄惨的环境中.

squan·der /ˈskwɒndə(r); ˋskwɑndɚ/ *v* [Tn, Tn·pr] **~ sth (on sb/sth)** waste (time, money, etc); use sth wastefully 浪费(时间、金钱等); 挥霍: *He's squandered all his savings on drink.* 他把存的钱全买酒喝了. ○ (*fig* 比喻) *Don't squander your affection on him — he'll never love you.* 别把感情耗在他身上了 —— 他永远不会爱你的. ▷ **squan·derer** *n*.

square¹ /skweə(r); skwɛr/ *adj* **1** having four equal sides and four right angles; having the shape of a square²(1) 正方形的; 四方的: *a square room, table, handkerchief* 正方形的房间、桌子、手帕. ⇨illus at QUADRILATERAL 见 QUADRILATERAL 插图. **2** having or forming (exactly or approximately) a right angle 成直角或近似直角的; 方的: *square corners* 方角 ○ *a square jaw/chin*, ie angular, not curved 棱角分明的下颌[下巴]. **3** of comparatively broad solid shape 宽阔结实的: *a woman of square frame/build* 健硕的女子. **4** [pred 作表语] properly arranged; tidy 妥当; 整洁: *We should get everything square before we leave.* 咱们应该把一切都安排妥当了再走. **5** [pred 作表语] (**a**) **~ (with sth)** level or parallel 水平; 平行: *tables arranged square with the wall* 沿墙壁平行排列的桌子. (**b**) settled; paid for; balanced 结清的; 已付的; 收支相抵的: *get one's accounts square* 把帐结清. **6** measuring a specified amount on all four sides, as a calculation of area 平方的: *one square metre*, ie an area equal to that of a square with sides that are each one metre in length 一平方米 ○ *A carpet six metres square* (ie having all four sides measuring 6 metres) *has an area of 36 square metres.* 六米见方的地毯面积是36平方米. **7** straightforward; uncompromising 干脆的; 坚决的: *a square refusal* 断然拒绝. **8** fair; honest 公平的; 公正的; 诚实的; 正当的: *a square deal* 公正的协议 ○ *square dealings*, eg in business 公平的交易 ○ *I want you to be square with me.* 我要求你对我以诚相待. **9** (*dated infml* 旧, 口) out of touch with new ideas, styles, etc; old-fashioned; conventional 不合时尚的; 守旧的; 传统的. **10** (in cricket) in a position approximately at right angles to the batsman (板球运动中)与击球员约成直角位置的: *a fielder standing square on the off side* 站在击球员头部方向与之成直角位置的守场员. **11** (idm 习语) **be (all) square (with sb)** (**a**) (in sport) have equal scores (文体活动中)比分相同的, 打平的, 平局的: *all square at the ninth hole*, ie in a golf match 在第九洞积分相等(指高尔夫球). (**b**) with neither person in debt to the other 彼此两不欠帐的: *Let's call it all square, shall we?* 咱们谁也不欠谁的了, 对吧? **a fair/square deal** ⇨ DEAL⁴. **a square ˈmeal** large and satisfying meal 丰盛的一顿饭: *He looks as though he hasn't had a square meal for months*, ie looks underfed. 瞧他那样子, 好像几个月没好好吃过一顿饭似的. **a square ˈpeg (in a round ˈhole)** person whose character or abilities make him unsuitable for or uncomfortable in his job or position (性格或能力)不适宜做某工作或任某职务的人.

▷ **square** *adv* **1** squarely; directly 正对着; 径直: *hit sb square on the jaw* 对准某人的下颌打. **2** (idm 习语) **fair and square** ⇨ FAIR².

squarely *adv* **1** so as to form a right angle; directly centred 成直角; 处于正中央位置: *Her hat was set squarely on her head.* 她把帽子戴得端端正正. **2** fairly; honestly 公平地; 公正地; 诚实地; 正当地: *act squarely* 行为正直. **3** directly opposite 正对着: *He faced me squarely across the table.* 他在桌子那边正对着我. **4** (idm 习语) **fairly and squarely** ⇨ FAIRLY.

square·ness *n* [U].

□ ˌ**square** ˈ**brackets** the marks [ ] 方括号[ ]. ⇨App 3 见附录3.

ˈ**square dance** (*US*) dance in which sets of four couples dance together, starting by facing inwards from four sides 方舞(每组四对男女共舞).

ˈ**square knot** (*US*) = REEF KNOT (REEF[1]).

ˌ**square** ˈ**leg** (in cricket) (position of a) fielder at some distance from the batsman's leg-side and nearly in line with the wicket (板球运动中)(在击球员后部与三柱门约成一线位置的)守场员(的位置).

ˌ**square** ˈ**measure** measurement of an area expressed in square metres, feet, etc 面积单位.

ˌ**square** ˈ**root** number greater than 0, which when multiplied by itself gives a particular specified number 平方根: *The square root of 16 is 4.* 16的平方根是4. ○ *What is the square root of 9?* 9的平方根是多少?

ˌ**square-**ˈ**shouldered** *adj* with the shoulders at right angles to the neck, not sloping 平肩的. Cf 参看 ROUND-SHOULDERED (ROUND[1]).

ˌ**square-**ˈ**toed** *adj* (of shoes) having a square toe-cap (指鞋)平头的, 方头的.

square[2] /skweə(r); skwɛr/ *n* **1** geometric figure with four equal sides and four right angles 正方形. ⇨App 5 见附录5. ⇨illus at QUADRILATERAL 见QUADRILATERAL 插图. **2** object having this shape, or approximately this shape 正方形物; 方形物: *the squares on a chess board* 棋盘上的方格 ○ *cut the paper into squares* 把纸裁成方形 ○ *soldiers drawn up in squares* 排成四方阵的士兵. **3** (**a**) four-sided open area, eg in a town, used as a garden or for recreation, or one enclosed by streets and buildings (方形)广场, 街心: *a market square* 集市广场 ○ *listen to the band playing in the square* 聆听广场上乐队的演奏. (**b**) **Square** (*abbr* 缩写 **Sq**) (in addresses) buildings and streets surrounding this (用作地址)广场四周的建筑及街道: *He lives at No 95 Russell Square/Sq.* 他住在罗素广场95号. **4** result when a number or quantity is multiplied by itself 平方: *The square of 7 is 49.* 7的平方是49. ○ *49 is a perfect square.* 49是完全平方. **5** L-shaped or (also **T-square**) T-shaped instrument for drawing or testing right angles 曲尺; 丁字尺. **6** (*dated infml* 旧, 口) person who is out of touch with new ideas, styles, etc; conventional or old-fashioned person 守旧的人; 老古板: *I'm basically a bit of a square.* 我是比较古板的. **7** (idm 习语) **back to square one** back to the starting-point in an enterprise, a task, etc with no progress made (事情、工作等因无进展)退回到起点: *That idea hasn't worked, so it's/we're back to square one.* 那主意行不通, 得从头再来. **on the** ˈ**square** (*infml* 口) fair(ly); honest(ly) 公平(地); 诚实(地); 正直(地): *Is their business on the square?* 他们做生意规矩吗? **out of square (with sth)** not at right angles (with sth) (与某物)不成直角.

□ ˈ**square-bashing** *n* [U] (*sl* 俚) military drill (esp marching, etc) 军事操练(尤指行军等).

square[3] /skweə(r); skwɛr/ *v* **1** [Tn] make (sth) right-angled; give a square shape to; make square 使(某物)成直角; 使成方形: *square timber*, ie give it rectangular edges 把木材加工成长方体 ○ *squared corners* 方角. **2** [Tn] make (sth) straight or level 使(某物)变直或变平: *square one's shoulders* 端起肩膀. **3** [Tn usu passive 通常用于被动语态] multiply (a number) by itself; get the square[2](4) of (a number) 使(某数)成平方; 求(某数)的平方: *3 squared is 9.* 3的平方是9. ○ $y^2 = y \times y$, ie y squared y的平方. **4** [Tn usu passive 通常用于被动语态] mark (sth) with squares; square off 在(某物)上做出方格: *squared paper* 方格纸. **5** [Tn, Cn·t] get the co-operation of (sb) by dishonest means; bribe 拉拢(某人); 贿赂; 收买: *All the officials had to be squared before they would help us.* 所有的官员都得给好处才肯帮助我们. ○ *He has been squared to say nothing.* 他已被收买, 什么也不说. **6** [Ipr, Tn·pr] **~ (sth) with sth** (*infml* 口) be or make (sth) consistent with sth; (cause sth to) agree with sth 使(某事物)与另一事物一致; (使某事物)与另一事物相符: *Your theory doesn't square with the known facts.* 你的说法跟已知的事实不符. ○ *You should square your practice with your principles.* 你的行为应该跟你的原则一致. **7** [Tn] cause (a total of points, wins, etc) to be even or level 使(总分、比赛成绩等)相等: *This victory has squared the series.* 赢了这一场, 把这组赛事的总分拉平了. **8** (idm 习语) **square one's ac**ˈ**count/square accounts with sb** (**a**) pay sb or be paid by him what is owed 与某人结帐. (**b**) get one's revenge on sb 向某人报复. **square the** ˈ**circle** (attempt to) do sth that is impossible (尽力)做不可能做到的事. **9** (phr v) **square sth off** (**a**) give sth a square or rectangular shape or outline 将某物弄成方形或矩形: *square off a piece of wood* 把一块木头加工成方形. (**b**) divide (a surface) into squares 在(某物表面)上分割成方格: *Square the page off with your ruler.* 用尺在这页纸上打上方格. **square up to sb/sth** (*infml* 口) (**a**) prepare to fight sb (ie by raising the fists like a boxer) 摆开格斗架势(准备跟某人厮打). (**b**) confront sb or sth (esp a difficult situation) with determination 坚定地对付某人或某事物(尤指困境): *He must square up to the reality of being out of work.* 他必须正视失业这一现实. **square up (with sb)** pay (sb) the money one owes (esp before leaving a restaurant, etc) 向(某人)付帐(尤指离开餐馆等处之前): *Can I leave you to square up with the waiter?* 我把跟服务员结帐的事交给你办行吗? ○ *It's time we squared up*, ie settled our accounts. 咱们该结帐了.

squar·ish /ˈskweərɪʃ; ˈskwɛrɪʃ/ *adj* approximately square 近似方形的; 方方的.

squash[1] /skwɒʃ; skwɑʃ/ *v* **1** (**a**) [Tn, Cn·a] press or squeeze (sb/sth) flat or into a pulp; crush 将(某人[某物])压扁, 压烂, 挤扁, 挤碎: *squashed tomatoes* 挤烂的蕃茄 ○ *The cat got run over by the lorry and squashed.* 那只猫被卡车碾死了. ○ *He sat on his hat and squashed it (flat).* 他把帽子坐扁了. (**b**) [I] become squashed or pressed out of shape 被压扁或压烂; 因挤压而变形: *Soft fruit squashes easily.* 无核的小水果容易压烂. **2** [Ipr, Ip, Tn·pr, Tn·p] force (sth/sb/oneself) in the specified direction by squeezing; crowd 将(某物[某人/自己])向某方向挤; 挤进去: *Don't all try to squash into the lift together.* 不要统统挤进电梯里去. ○ *They squashed through the gate into the football ground.* 他们挤过大门, 进入足球场. ○ *There's room for one more in the car if you squash in.* 汽车里还可以坐一个, 你挤进来吧. ○ *They managed to squash forty people into the bus.* 那辆公共汽车好不容易塞进了四十个人. ○ *She squashed her clothes down into the suitcase.* 她把衣服塞进箱子里了. **3** [Tn] (*infml* 口) silence or subdue (sb) rudely, esp with an unpleasant reply; snub 粗暴地使(某人)住嘴; 镇住(某人); (尤指)拿话噎(某人); 厉声呵斥: *I felt completely squashed by her sarcastic comment.* 她冷嘲热讽把我噎得一句话都说不出来. **4** [Tn] (**a**) defeat or subdue (a rebellion, etc); crush 平定(叛乱等); 镇压; 制服. (**b**) (*infml* 口) reject or dismiss (an idea, a proposal, etc) 拒绝接受(主意、提议等): *My plan was firmly squashed by the committee.* 委员会把我的计划全盘否定了. **5** (phr v) **squash (sb) up (against sb/sth)** (cause sb to) press tightly and uncomfortably (against another person or thing) (使某人)(跟他人或某物)挤在一起: *We had to squash up to make room for the others who wanted to use the lift.* 我们得挤出空位让其他想搭电梯的人进来. ○ *There were four of us squashed up against each other on the seat.* 我们四个人挤在座位上.

▷ **squash** *n* **1** (**a**) [C usu *sing* 通常作单数] crowd of people pressed together in a confined space 拥挤的人群: *What a squash!* 真拥挤呀! ○ *a violent squash at the gates* 在门口拼命猛挤的人群. (**b**) state of being pressed together in this way 拥挤: *It'll be a bit of a squash, but I think I can get you all in the car.* 挤是挤一点, 但我看可以把你们全弄上汽车. **2** [U, C] (*Brit*) soft drink made from fruit juice, sugar and water, usu sold in bottles and drunk with water added 果汁饮料(通常为瓶装, 饮用时加水): *some orange squash* 一些橙汁饮料 ○ *Two squashes, please.* 请来两客果汁饮料. **3** [U] (also *fml* 正规作 ˈ**squash rackets**) game played with rackets and a small softish hollow rubber ball, in a court

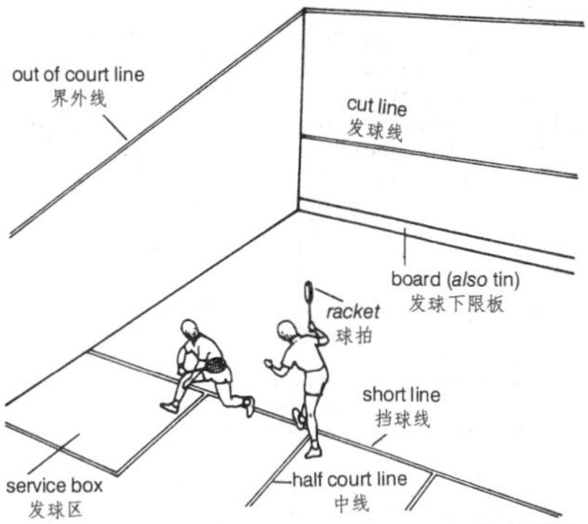

squash 墙网球

enclosed by walls and a roof (软式)墙网球; 壁球: [attrib 作定语] *a squash racket, ball, court, game* 墙网球的球拍、球、球场、比赛 ○ *Do you play squash?* 你会打墙网球吗? Cf 参看 RACKET[1] 2. ⇨illus 见插图.

squashy *adj* easily squashed; soft 易压扁的; 易压烂的; 软的: *a big squashy sofa* 柔软的大沙发 ○ *The fruit is rather squashy.* 这种水果怕压.

squash[2] /skwɒʃ; skwɑʃ/ *n* (*pl* unchanged or **~es** 复数或不变或作 **squashes**) [U, C] any of several types of large gourd common in the US and eaten as a vegetable 西葫芦; 美国南瓜.

squat[1] /skwɒt; skwɑt/ *v* (**-tt-**) **1** [I, Ipr, Ip] **~ (down)** (**a**) (of people) sit on one's heels or on the ground with the knees drawn up under or close to the body; crouch (指人)蹲, 收膝而坐, 伏下身子: *The old man squatted (down) by the fire.* 老人蹲在炉火旁. ⇨illus at KNEEL 见 KNEEL 插图. (**b**) (of animals) crouch with the body close to the ground (指动物)伏在地上. (**c**) (*infml* 口 *esp Brit*) sit 坐: *Can you find somewhere to squat?* 你找个地方坐下好吗? **2** [I] occupy an empty building or settle on unoccupied land, etc without permission 擅自占用空建筑; 擅自在空地上安家: *homeless people squatting in a derelict house* 擅自居住在破旧的空屋里的无家可归的人.

▷ **squat** *n* **1** [sing] squatting position 蹲; 收膝而坐. **2** [C] building occupied by squatters (SQUATTER 2) 被擅自占用的建筑物: *living in a squat* 住在私占的屋子里.

squat·ter *n* **1** person who sits in a squatting position 蹲着的人. **2** person who occupies a building or land without permission 擅自占用房屋或土地的人: *claim squatters' rights* 要求获得擅自占房者应得的权利. **3** (*Austral* 澳) sheep-farmer 牧羊场主.

squat[2] /skwɒt; skwɑt/ *adj* (**-tter, -ttest**) (*usu derog* 通常作贬义) short and thick; dumpy 矮胖的; 矮墩墩的: *a squat man* 矮胖的男子 ○ *a squat teapot* 扁而粗的茶壶.

squaw /skwɔ:; skwɔ/ *n* N American Indian woman or wife 北美印第安女子或妻子.

squawk /skwɔ:k; skwɔk/ *v* [I] **1** (esp of birds) utter a loud harsh cry (eg when hurt or frightened) (尤指鸟)发出响而粗的叫声(如受伤或受惊时): *The parrot squawked loudly.* 那鹦鹉嘎嘎大叫. **2** (*infml esp joc* 口, 尤作戏谑语) complain loudly 大声诉苦或抗议.

▷ **squawk** *n* **1** loud harsh cry 刺耳的大叫. **2** loud complaint 大声的诉苦或抗议.

squeak /skwi:k; skwik/ *n* **1** short high-pitched cry or sound 短促而尖利的叫声或响声: *the squeak of a mouse* 老鼠的吱吱叫声 ○ *The door opened with a squeak.* 门吱嘎一声打开了. **2** (idm 习语) **a narrow squeak** ⇨ NARROW.

▷ **squeak** *v* **1** [I] make a squeak 发出短促而尖利的声音: *Can you hear the mice squeaking?* 你听到老鼠吱吱叫吗? ○ *These new shoes squeak.* 穿上这双新鞋走起路来嘎吱嘎吱的. **2** [Tn, Tn·p] **~ sth (out)** say sth in a squeaking voice 以尖利的声音说话: *'Let go of me!' he squeaked nervously.* '放开我!'他紧张地尖声嚷道. ○ *squeak out a few frightened words* 惊恐地尖叫几声. **3** [I] (*sl* 俚) give secret information (esp to the police); become an informer 告密(尤指向警方); 充当告密者: *Somebody's squeaked!* 有人告密了! Cf 参看 SQUEAL *v*.

squeaker *n*.

squeaky *adj* (**-ier, -iest**) making a squeaking sound 发短促而尖利的声音的: *a squeaky floor* 走上去嘎吱作响的地板 ○ *in a squeaky voice* 尖利的嗓音 ○ *squeaky clean*, ie washed so clean that it squeaks 极其干净. **squeak·ily** *adv*. **squeaki·ness** *n* [U].

squeal /skwi:l; skwil/ *n* high-pitched cry or sound, longer and louder than a squeak (often indicating terror or pain) 长而尖的叫声或响声(常因惊恐或痛苦所致): *the squeal of brakes*, eg on lorries 刹车发出的嘎的一声 ○ *There were squeals of excitement from the children.* 孩子们兴奋得尖叫起来.

▷ **squeal** *v* **1** [I] make a squeal 发出长而尖的声音: *The pigs were squealing.* 猪在尖叫. ○ *He squealed like a pig.* 他像猪似的号叫着. **2** [Tn, Tn·p] **~ sth (out)** say sth in a squealing voice 尖声地说; 号叫着说: *He squealed the words out.* 他吼叫着说出那些话. **3** [I, Ipr] **~ (on sb) (to sb)** (*sl* 俚) give secret information (esp to the police about a partner or accomplice in crime); become an informer 告密(尤指向警方告发同伙或同谋); 充当告密者: *He squealed on his friends.* 他把朋友给告了. **squealer** *n* **1** animal that squeals 尖声号叫的动物. **2** (*sl* 俚) informer 告密者.

squeam·ish /ˈskwi:mɪʃ; ˋskwimɪʃ/ *adj* **1** (**a**) having a delicate stomach and easily made sick (因胃过敏)易恶心的. (**b**) easily disgusted, shocked or offended 易生厌的; 易受惊的; 易生气的; 神经质的: *an explicit and violent film, definitely not for the squeamish* 一部露骨的、渲染暴力的影片, 神经脆弱的人肯定受不了. **2** too scrupulous, modest or proper (about principles, morals, etc) (在原则、道德等方面)过分拘谨的、谦虚的或正经的. ▷ **squeam·ishly** *adv*. **squeam·ish·ness** *n* [U].

squee·gee /ˈskwi:dʒi:, ˌskwi:ˈdʒi:; ˋskwidʒi, skwiˋdʒi/ *n* **1** tool with a rubber edge on a long handle, used for removing water, etc from smooth surfaces 橡皮清洁刷(用于抹去光滑表面的水等): *use a squeegee to clean windows* 用橡皮清洁刷擦窗户. **2** similar tool with a small rubber roller on a short handle for pressing water from photographic prints (挤出相片水分的)橡皮磙子.

▷ **squee·gee** *v* (*pt, pp* **-geed**) [Tn] use a squeegee on (sth) 用此等工具擦或碾磙.

squeeze /skwi:z; skwiz/ *v* **1** (**a**) [Tn, Tn·p, Cn·a] press on (sth) from opposite sides or all sides 挤, 榨, 捏, 向内收紧(某物): *squeeze a sponge, a tube of toothpaste* 挤海绵、牙膏 ○ *squeeze sb's hand*, eg as a sign of affection, sympathy, etc 握着某人的手捏一捏(如表示爱意、同情等) ○ *a doll that squeaks when you squeeze it* 一捏会叫的玩具娃娃 ○ *squeeze the dish-cloth out* 把洗碗布挤干 ○ *squeeze a lemon dry* 把柠檬榨干 ○ (*fig* 比喻) *a company squeezed by* (ie under financial pressure because of) *reduced sales* 因销售量下降而处境困难的公司. (**b**) [Tn·pr] **~ sth into sth** change the shape, size, etc of sth into that specified by doing this 将某物挤成某形状、大小等: *squeeze paste into a ball* 把面团捏成球形. **2** (**a**) [Tn, Tn·pr, Tn·p] **~ sth (from/out of sth)**; **~ sth (out)** get (water, juice, etc) out of sth by pressing it hard 挤出, 榨出(水、汁等): *squeeze the juice out of a lemon* 榨柠檬汁 ○ *squeeze the water out (of the cloth)* 把(那块布中的)水挤出 ○ (*fig* 比喻) *squeezed out of the job market by younger men* 被年轻人挤出了就业市场 ○ *She felt as if every drop of emotion had been squeezed out of her.* 她感到自己的感情被榨得一滴不剩了. (**b**) [Tn·pr] cause sth to move from one place to another by squeezing 以挤压的方式使某物移动: *squeeze lemon-juice into a glass* 向玻璃杯中挤柠檬汁 ○ *squeeze toothpaste from the tube onto a toothbrush* 把牙膏挤到牙刷上. **3** [Ipr, Ip, Tn·pr, Tn·p] **~ (sb/sth) into, through, etc sth**; **~ (sb/sth) through, in, past, etc** force (oneself/sb/sth) into, through, etc a narrow gap or restricted space (使某人[某物])挤入, 挤过: *squeeze through a gap in the hedge/through a crowd* 由树篱的缺口挤过去[从人丛中挤过去] ○ *squeeze (one's way) onto a crowded bus* 挤上拥挤的公共汽车 ○ *There were already four people in the lift, but he managed to squeeze in.* 电梯里已经有四个人了, 但他还是挤进去了. ○ *Can you squeeze past/by?* 你能挤过去吗? ○ *She squeezed as many books onto the shelf as she could.* 她把书架塞得不能再满了. ○ (*fig* 比喻) *I've a busy morning but I could* *squeeze you in* (ie find time for you) *at 10.15.* 我上午没空，但10点15分时可以挤出点时间来给你. **4** (phr v) **squeeze sth out of sb** get sth from sb by applying pressure (eg threats of violence, force, harsh laws) 向某人榨取某事物; 勒索; 敲诈: *squeeze more money out of the taxpayer* 向纳税人再榨取一些钱 ○ *squeeze a promise out of sb* 逼某人作出保证. **squeeze (sb) up (against sb/sth)** (cause sb to) press tightly and uncomfortably (against another person or thing); move closer together (使某人)(跟他人或某物)挤在一起; 贴近: *There'll be enough room if we all squeeze up a bit.* 咱们大家挤一挤就够地方了. ○ *I had to sit squeezed up against the wall.* 我得紧贴着墙坐.

▷ **squeeze** *n* **1** [C] (**a**) act of squeezing 挤; 榨; 捏; 向内收紧的动作: *give the tube of toothpaste a squeeze* 把牙膏挤一挤. (**b**) affectionate hug or clasp 亲切的拥抱或握手: *a hug and a squeeze* 亲热的拥抱 ○ *She gave my hand a gentle squeeze.* 她握着我的手, 轻轻捏了捏. **2** [C] small amount of sth produced by squeezing 挤出来的少量事物: *a squeeze of lemon in your drink* 挤在你饮料中的少量柠檬汁. **3** [sing] state of being squeezed, as when many people or things are pressed tightly together 拥挤; 挤压: *It was a tight squeeze but we finally got all the clothes into the case.* 箱子已经很满了, 但我们还是把衣服全塞进去了. **4** [C usu *sing* 通常作单数] difficulty or hardship caused by shortage of money or time, etc 缺少钱或时间等所引致的困难或困苦; 拮据; 短缺: *She's just lost her job, so they're really feeling the squeeze.* 她刚失了业, 这下他们真正感到艰难了. **5** [C] (*infml* 口) restrictions on borrowing, etc during a financial crisis 银根紧缩: *a credit squeeze* 信贷紧缩. **6** (idm 习语) **put the squeeze on sb (to do sth)** (*infml* 口) put pressure on sb to act in a particular way 对某人施加压力(以迫使其做某事). **a tight squeeze** ⇨ TIGHT.

squeezer *n* (usu in compounds 通常用以构成复合词) device for squeezing out juice, etc 压榨器; 榨汁器: *a 'lemon-squeezer* 柠檬榨汁器.

squelch /skweltʃ; skwɛltʃ/ *v* **1** [I] make a sucking sound as when feet are lifted from thick sticky mud 发吧唧声或扑哧声(如脚从黏泥中拔出时): *water squelching in my boots* 我靴子里的水扑扑作响. **2** [Ipr, Ip] move in the specified direction making this sound 发出吧唧声或扑哧声行走: *cows squelching across the field* 发出吧唧声穿过牧场的母牛 ○ *squelching along (in the mud)* (在泥泞中)扑哧扑哧向前走.

▷ **squelch** *n* squelching sound 吧唧声; 扑哧声.

squib /skwɪb; skwɪb/ *n* **1** small firework that jumps around on the ground making a hissing sound before exploding 蹦蹦炮(先在地上发嗞嗞声蹦跳, 然后再爆炸的小爆竹). **2** (idm 习语) **a damp squib** ⇨ DAMP[1].

squid /skwɪd; skwɪd/ *n* (*pl* unchanged or **~s** 复数或不变或作 **squids**) [C, U] sea creature related to the cuttle-fish with ten arms round the mouth 枪乌贼; 鱿鱼: *Would you like some squid?* 你想来点儿鱿鱼吗? ⇨ illus at OCTOPUS 见 OCTOPUS 插图.

squidgy /ˈskwɪdʒɪ; ˋskwɪdʒɪ/ *adj* (*infml* 口 *esp Brit*) soft and moist; soggy 软而湿的; 很潮的: *a nice squidgy cream cake* 松软可口的奶油蛋糕.

squiffy /ˈskwɪfɪ; ˋskwɪfɪ/ *adj* (**-ier, -iest**) (*Brit infml* 口) slightly drunk 微醉的.

squiggle /ˈskwɪgl; ˋskwɪgl/ *n* short twisting or wavy line, esp in handwriting; scribble 歪扭的或波形的短线条(尤指笔画); 潦草的字迹: *Is this squiggle supposed to be a signature?* 这歪歪扭扭的玩意儿就算是签名吗? ▷ **squig·gly** /ˈskwɪglɪ; ˋskwɪglɪ/ *adj*.

squint /ˈskwɪnt; skwɪnt/ *v* **1** [I] have eyes that do not move together but look in different directions at once 患斜视. **2** [I, Ipr] **~ (at, through, up, etc sth)** look (at sth) with eyes half shut or turned sideways, or through a narrow opening 眯着眼睛, 也斜着眼睛(看某物); 瞟; 从小孔或缝隙里看, 窥看(某物): *squinting in the bright sunlight* 在很亮的阳光下眯起眼睛 ○ *squinting through the letter-box* 从投信口向信箱里面看.

▷ **squint** *n* **1** (abnormal condition causing the) squinting position of an eyeball or eyeballs 斜视; 斜视症: *He was born with a squint.* 他先天斜视. ○ *They both have squints.* 他俩都是斜视. **2** (*Brit infml* 口) look or glance 看; 瞥: *Have/Take a squint at this.* 你看看这个吧.

squint *adv, adj* [usu attrib 通常作定语] (*infml* 口) not straight; askew 不直(的); 歪斜(的): *The bottle-top has been screwed on squint.* 瓶盖儿没拧正.

squinty *adj*: *squinty eyes* 斜视眼.

squire /ˈskwaɪə(r); skwaɪr/ *n* **1** (in titles 称谓中作 **Squire**) (formerly) country gentleman, esp the chief landowner in a country district (旧时)乡绅(尤指乡区的大地主). **2** (formerly) young man who was a knight's attendant until he himself became a knight (旧时)骑士的年轻扈从(直至自己成为骑士时为止). **3** (*US*) justice of the peace or local judge 治安法官; 地方法官. **4** (*Brit infml or joc* 口或谑) (used as a friendly but respectful form of address by one man to another 用作男人间亲切而尊敬的称谓): *What can I get you, squire?* 您要点儿什么, 先生?

▷ **squire·archy** /ˈskwaɪərɑːkɪ; ˋskwaɪˌrɑrkɪ/ *n* [CGp] landowners as a class having political or social influence (esp formerly in England) 地主阶级, 乡绅阶层(尤指英格兰旧时的).

squirm /skwɜːm; skwɝm/ *v* **1** [I, Ipr, Ip] move by twisting the body about; wriggle; writhe 蠕动; 扭动: *He was squirming (around) on the floor in agony.* 他躺在地上痛苦地扭动着. **2** [I] feel embarrassment, discomfort, or shame 难为情; 不舒服; 羞愧: *It made him squirm to think how he'd messed up the interview.* 他想到面试时自己表现得那么差劲儿, 心里真不是滋味儿.

squir·rel /ˈskwɪrəl; *US* ˈskwɜːrəl; ˋskwɝəl/ *n* **1** [C] small tree-climbing animal with a bushy tail and red or grey fur 松鼠: *Red squirrels are now very rare in Britain.* 红色的松鼠在英国已十分罕见了. ⇨ illus at App 1 见附录1 插图, page iii. **2** [U] its fur 松鼠的毛皮: [attrib 作定语] *a squirrel hat* 松鼠皮帽.

squirt /skwɜːt; skwɝt/ *v* (**a**) [Tn, Tn·pr, Tn·p] **~ sth (out of/from sth)**; **~ sth (out)** force (liquid, powder, etc) out in a thin stream or jet 使(液体、粉末等)喷出: *squirt soda-water into a glass* 把苏打水倒进玻璃杯 ○ *squirt oil out (of a can) into a machine* 把油(从罐中)喷入机器内 ○ *Stop squirting water at me!* 别对我喷水了! (**b**) [I, Ipr, Ip] **~ (out of/from sth)**; **~ (out)** (of liquid, powder, etc) be forced out in this way (指液体、粉末等)喷出: *Water squirted (from the tap) all over me.* (龙头里的)水喷了我一身. ○ *I squeezed the bottle and the sauce squirted out.* 我把瓶子一捏, 沙司就挤出来了. (**c**) [Tn, Tn·pr] **~ sb/sth (with sth)** cover sb/sth with liquid, powder, etc forced out in this way 向某人[某物]喷液体或粉末等: *The little girl squirted us with (water from) her water-pistol.* 那小姑娘用水枪向我们射(水).

▷ **squirt** *n* **1** (**a**) thin stream or jet of liquid, powder, etc (液体、粉末等的)喷射. (**b**) small quantity produced by squirting 喷射出的少量液体或粉末等. **2** (*infml derog* 口, 贬) small or unimportant but self-assertive person 年轻或地位不高但很自负的人; 妄自尊大的人: *He's such a little squirt.* 他年纪不大, 傲气不小.

Sr *abbr* 缩写 = **1** SEN 3. **2** (*religion* 宗) Sister: *Sr Mary Francis* 玛丽·弗朗西斯修女.

SRC /ˌes ɑː ˈsiː; ˌɛs ɑr ˋsi/ *abbr* 缩写 = (*Brit*) Science Research Council 科学研究委员会: *SRC-funded projects* 科学研究委员会资助的项目.

SRN /ˌes ɑːr ˈen; ˌɛs ɑr ˋɛn/ *abbr* 缩写 = (*Brit*) State Registered Nurse (with 3 years' training) 国家注册护士(经3年培训者): *be an SRN* 为国家注册护士 ○ *Sally Ward SRN* 萨莉·沃德, 国家注册护士. Cf 参看 SEN.

SS *abbr* 缩写 = **1** Saints. **2** /ˌes ˈes; ˌɛs ˋɛs/ steamship: *SS Warwick Castle* 沃里克城堡号汽船.

St *abbr* 缩写 = **1** Saint: *St Peter* 圣彼得. Cf 参看 S 1. **2** Street: *Fleet St* 弗利特街(旧译舰队街).

st *abbr* 缩写 = (*Brit*) stone (weight) 吩(重量单位): *She weighs 10st.* 她体重10吩.

Sta *abbr* 缩写 = (esp on a map 尤作地图上的标记) Station: *Victoria Sta* 维多利亚站.

stab /stæb; stæb/ *v* (**-bb-**) **1** [Tn, Tn·pr] pierce (sth) or wound (sb) with a pointed tool or weapon; push (a knife, etc) into sb/sth 戳(某物); 刺伤(某人); 用(刀等)捅某人[某物]: *He was stabbed to death*, ie killed by being stabbed. 他被刺死了. ○ *She stabbed him in the leg with a kitchen knife.* 她拿菜刀捅伤了他的腿. ○ *He stabbed the meat with his fork/stabbed his fork into the meat.* 他用叉子扠肉. **2** (idm 习语) **stab sb in the 'back** (*infml* 口) attack sb's position, reputation, etc treacherously; betray sb 背地里中伤某人; 背叛某人.

3 (phr v) **stab at sb/sth** aim a blow at sb/sth with or as if with a pointed weapon 扎向某人[某物]: *He stabbed at the earth with his stick.* 他拿手杖戳着地. ○ *She stabbed at the air with her finger to emphasize what she was saying.* 她手指一戳一戳的, 强调她说的话. ⇨Usage at NUDGE 用法见 NUDGE.

▷ **stab** *n* **1 (a)** act of stabbing; blow made by stabbing 刺; 戳; 捅; 扎; 戳击: [attrib 作定语] *several stab wounds* 几处刺伤的地方. **(b)** wound made by stabbing 刺伤或捅伤的伤口: *a stab in the arm* 手臂上捅的伤口. **2** sudden sharp pain caused by, or as if by, stabbing 刺痛: *a stab of pain in the chest* 胸部的一阵刺痛 ○ *a stab of guilt* 强烈的内疚. **3** (idm 习语) **have a stab at sth/doing sth** (*infml* 口) attempt (to do) sth 尽力做某事: *You'll never mend your car like that — let me have a stab at it.* 你这样怎么能修好汽车 — 让我来试试吧. **a ˌstab in the ˈback** (*infml* 口) treacherous attack, eg on sb's reputation or position; betrayal 背后的中伤; 背叛行为.

stab·ber *n* person who stabs sb (用刀等)刺人的人.

stab·bing *adj* [usu attrib 通常作定语] (of pain, etc) very sharp and sudden as if caused by a stab (指疼痛等)突然而剧烈的, 似被刀刺的: *a stabbing pain in the chest* 胸部的一阵刺痛. — *n* instance of stabbing or being stabbed with a knife, etc 用利器伤人的事件: *The police are worried about the increase in the number of stabbings in the city.* 市内利器伤人案增多, 警方甚感忧虑.

stable[1] /ˈsteɪbl; ˋstebḷ/ *adj* **(a)** firmly established or fixed; not likely to move or change 稳定的; 稳固的; 牢固的; 安定的: *a stable relationship, job, government* 稳定的关系、工作、政府 ○ *a house built on stable foundations* 建在牢固基础上的房子 ○ *The patient's condition is stable.* 病人情况稳定. **(b)** (of a person or his character) not easily upset or disturbed; well-balanced; reliable (指人或性格)沉稳的, 持重的, 可靠的: *Mentally she's very stable.* 她情绪十分稳定. ○ *He's about the most stable person I know.* 我认识的人当中, 数他最稳重. **(c)** (of a substance) tending to stay in the same chemical or atomic state; not breaking down easily or naturally (指物质)稳定的(保持化学或原子状态的), 不易变化的: *an element forming stable compounds* 可形成稳定的化合物的元素.

▷ **sta·bil·ity** /stəˈbɪlətɪ; stəˋbɪlətɪ/ *n* [U] quality or state of being stable 稳定性; 稳定状态; 沉稳.

sta·bil·ize, -ise /ˈsteɪbəlaɪz; ˋstebḷˌaɪz/ *v* [I, Tn] (cause sth/sb to) become stable (使某事物)稳定; (使某人)变得沉稳: *His condition has now stabilized.* 他的情况稳定下来了. ○ *government measures to stabilize prices* 政府采取的稳定物价的措施. **sta·bil·iza·tion, -isation** /ˌsteɪbəlaɪˈzeɪʃn; *US* -lɪˈz-; ˌstebḷəˋzeʃən/ *n* [U]. **sta·bil·izer, -iser** /ˈsteɪbəlaɪzə(r); ˋstebəˌlaɪzɚ/ *n* substance or device that stabilizes, esp a device that prevents an aircraft or ship from rolling, or one that helps to keep a child's bicycle upright 稳定装置; 稳定器; 平衡器; (飞行器的)安定面: *He can now ride his bike without stabilizers.* 他现在骑自行车不需要平衡器了.

stably /ˈsteɪblɪ; ˋsteblɪ/ *adv:* in a stable manner 稳定地; 沉稳地.

stable[2] /ˈsteɪbl; ˋstebḷ/ *n* **1** building in which a horse or horses are kept and fed 马厩: [attrib 作定语] *a stable door* 马厩的门. **2** (often *pl* with *sing* meaning and sometimes *sing v* 常作复数, 但词义为单数, 有时动词亦用单数) establishment that specializes in keeping horses for a particular purpose; the horses kept in this 专用马房; 专用马房中的马: *Is there a riding stables near here?* 附近有专供骑用马的马房吗? ○ *He owns a racing stable(s),* ie a group of racehorses and the buildings they are kept in. 他是马房主. **3** (*fig* 比喻) place such as an athletics club, a school, a theatre, etc where a number of people have been trained in the same way 训练基地; 培训处; 学校: *actors from the same stable* 在同一处受训的演员. **4** (idm 习语) **lock, etc the stable door after the horse has bolted** try to prevent or avoid loss, damage, etc when it is already too late 亡马锁厩, 为时已晚; 贼去关门.

▷ **stable** *v* [Tn] put or keep (a horse) in a stable 将(马)置于厩中: *Where do you stable your pony?* 你那匹矮种马养在哪儿?

sta·bling /ˈsteɪblɪŋ; ˋsteblɪŋ/ *n* [U] accommodation for horses 马厩设备: *The house has stabling for 20 horses.* 这所房子有可容纳20匹马的设备.

□ **ˈstable-boy** (also **ˈstable-lad**) *n* (usu young) person (of either sex) who works in a stable (通常指年少的)马伕(男性或女性); 小马倌儿.

stac·cato /stəˈkɑːtəʊ; stəˋkɑto/ *adj, adv* (*music* 音) (to be played) with each successive note short, clear and detached; not smooth(ly) (应奏成)断音(的), 断奏(的), 不连贯(的): *staccato notes* 断音音符 ○ *Play this phrase staccato.* 这一乐句要奏成断音. ○ (*fig* 比喻) *He shouted a series of staccato orders.* 他一顿一顿地大声下了几道命令.

stack /stæk; stæk/ *n* **1** circular or rectangular pile of hay, straw, grain, etc, usu with a sloping top for storage in the open; rick (干草、麦秆、谷物等的)堆, 垛(通常为斜顶, 便于露天贮存): *a haystack* 干草垛. **2** pile or heap, usu neatly arranged 堆, 摞(通常指堆放得整齐的): *a wood stack* 木材堆 ○ *a stack of newspapers* 一摞报纸 ○ *They put the rifles into a stack.* 他们把步枪架在一起. **3** (esp *pl* 尤作复数) **~ of sth** (*infml* 口) large number or quantity 大量; 一大堆: *stacks of money* 大量的钞票 ○ *I've got stacks of work to do.* 我有一大堆工作要做. ○ *There's a whole stack of bills waiting to be paid.* 有一大堆帐要付呢. **4 (a)** tall chimney (esp on a factory) or funnel (on a ship) for carrying away smoke 大烟筒(尤指工厂的); (船上的)烟囱. **(b)** group of chimneys standing together 烟囱群. **5** (often *pl* 常作复数) rack with shelves for books in a library or bookshop (图书馆或书店的)书架. **6** number of aircraft circling at different heights while waiting for instructions to land at an airport 分层盘旋的待降机群. **7** (idm 习语) **blow one's stack** ⇨ BLOW[1].

▷ **stack** *v* **1** [Tn, Tn·pr, Tn·p] **~ sth (up)** make sth into a stack or stacks; pile sth up 将某物堆起或摞起: *Please stack your chairs before you leave.* 走之前请把椅子摞在一起. ○ *stack logs (into piles)* 把原木堆起来 ○ *stack (up) the dishes on the draining-board* 把碗盘摞起放在滴水板上. **2** [Tn, Tn·pr] **~ sth (with sth)** put heaps or piles of things on or in (a place) 把某物堆放于(某处): *The whole garden was stacked with bricks.* 园子里堆满了砖. **3** [Tn, Tn·pr] **~ sth (against sb)** arrange (playing-cards) unfairly 洗(纸牌)时作弊: (*US*) *stack the deck,* ie arrange a whole pack of cards in this way 洗牌时做手脚. **4 (a)** [I, Ip] **~ (up)** (of an aircraft) fly in a stack(6) while waiting to land (指飞行器)定高盘旋(以等待降落). **(b)** [Tn, Tn·p] **~ sth (up)** make (aircraft) fly in a stack; arrange (aircraft) in a stack 使(飞行器)分层盘旋待降; 指示(飞行器)分层盘旋待降. **5** (idm 习语) **have the cards/odds stacked aˈgainst one** be at a disadvantage or in a difficult situation, so that one seems unlikely to succeed 处于不利的地位或困境(因而难以成功). **6** (phr v) **stack up (against sth)** (*US infml* 口) compare (with sth); measure up (to sth) 能(与某事物)相比; 比得上(某事物): *How well do you think this washing powder stacks up against your usual brand?* 这种洗衣粉跟你常用的那种比怎么样?

sta·dium /ˈsteɪdɪəm; ˋstedɪəm/ *n* (*pl* **~s** or **-dia** /-dɪə; -dɪə/) enclosed area of land for games, athletic contests, etc, usu with seats for spectators 体育场, 运动场(通常有看台): *build a new stadium for the Olympic Games* 为奥林匹克运动会建造新的体育场.

staff /stɑːf; *US* stæf; stæf/ *n* **1** [C] strong stick or pole used as a support when walking or climbing, as a weapon, or as a symbol of authority or sign of office 手杖; 棍棒; 权杖: *The old man leant on a long wooden staff.* 老人拄着一根长长的木手杖. **2** [C usu *sing* 通常作单数, Gp] group of assistants working together in a business, etc responsible to a manager or person in authority 全体职工; 全体雇员: *the hotel staff* 旅馆的全体工作人员 ○ *We need more staff in the office.* 我们办公室需要增加人手. ○ *I have a staff of ten.* 我手下有十个职员. ○ *The staff in this shop are very helpful.* 这家店里的店员很热心. **3** [pl *v*] people in authority in an organization (contrasted with students, etc); those doing administrative work (as distinct from manual work) 当权的人员(相对于学生等而言); 行政人员(与体力劳动者相区分): *a head teacher and her staff* (女)校长及全体

S

教师 ○ *a new member of (the) staff* 新来的职员 ○ *The school staff are expected to supervise school meals.* 学校的教职员应监督学生的膳食. ○ [attrib 作定语] *a staff party, room, meeting* 职员的聚会、活动室、会议. **4** [C usu *sing* 通常作单数, Gp] group of senior army officers assisting a commanding officer (军队的)全体参谋人员: *the general's staff* 将军的参谋人员 ○ [attrib 作定语] *a ˈstaff officer* 参谋. **5** (also **stave** /steɪv; stev/) [C] (*music* 音) set of five horizontal parallel lines on which music is written 五线谱. ⇨illus at MUSIC 见MUSIC 插图. **6** (idm 习语) **the ˌstaff of ˈlife** (*arch or rhet* 古或修辞) bread 面包.

▷ **staff** *v* [Tn usu passive 通常用于被动语态] provide (sth) with staff(2); act as staff for 为(某部门)配备人员; 担任(某部门)的工作人员: *a well-staffed hotel* 工作人员齐全的旅馆 ○ *The school is staffed entirely by graduates.* 这个学校的教职员全是大学毕业生. ○ *There's nobody to staff the office today.* 今天这个办事处没有职员.

□ ˈ**staff nurse** hospital nurse ranking just below a sister(4) 医院护士(比护士长低一级).

ˈ**staff sergeant** (**a**) (*Brit*) senior sergeant in a non-infantry (eg cavalry) company (非步兵连的)陆军上士. (**b**) (*US*) non-commissioned officer ranking just above a sergeant 陆军上士; 海军上士; 空军上士.

stag /stæg; stæg/ *n* **1** fully-grown male deer (成年的)牡鹿. ⇨illus at DEER 见DEER 插图. Cf 参看 BUCK[1] 1, DOE, FAWN[1] 1, HART. **2** (*Brit*) person who buys newly issued stocks and shares hoping that the prices will rise and he will be able to make a quick profit 购买新上市股票的人(以期升值后售出迅速获利者).

▷ **stag** *adj* [attrib 作定语] for men only 只限男子参加的: *a stag night at the golf club* 高尔夫球俱乐部中只限男子参加的晚会.

□ ˈ**stag-beetle** *n* large beetle with projecting mouth-parts which resemble a stag's antlers 锹甲.

ˈ**stag-party** *n* party for men only, esp one for a man just before he gets married 雄鹿会(只限男子参加的聚会, 尤指为准新郎举行的). Cf 参看 HEN-PARTY (HEN).

stage /steɪdʒ; stedʒ/ *n* **1** [C] platform or area (usu in a theatre) on which plays are performed to an audience 舞台(通常指剧场中的): *He was on (the) stage for most of the play.* 他几乎整出戏都在台上. ⇨illus at App 1 见附录1插图, page ix. **2 the stage** [sing] the profession of actors and actresses; life and work in the theatre 演员的职业; 戏剧表演; 舞台生涯: *She advised her son not to choose the stage as a career.* 她劝儿子不要选择戏剧表演作职业. **3** [sing] (*fig* 比喻) scene of action; place where events occur 场所; (事件发生的)现场: *Geneva has become the stage for many meetings of world leaders.* 日内瓦已成为世界领袖经常召开会议的地方. **4** [C] point, period or step in the development, growth or progress of sth/sb 某事物[某人]的发展、成长或进步的程度、时期或阶段: *at an early stage in our history* 在我们历史发展的早期 ○ *At this stage it's impossible to know whether our plan will succeed.* 目前尚无法预见我们的计划能否实现. ○ *The baby has reached the talking stage*, ie is beginning to talk. 这婴儿已经会说话了. **5** [C] (**a**) distance between two stopping-places on a journey; part of a journey (行程中两站之间的)路程; 一段路: *travel by easy stages*, ie only for a short distance at a time 分段作短程舒适的旅行 ○ *She did the first stage of the trip by train.* 她行程的第一段是乘火车的. (**b**) (*Brit*) section of a bus route for which there is a fixed fare (有固定票价的)一段公共汽车路程: *travel two stages for 30p* 乘坐两段路程, 车费30便士. (**c**) stopping-place after such a part of a journey or bus-ride (一段路程终了的)站. **6** [C] section of a space-rocket with a separate engine, jettisoned when its fuel is used up (火箭的)级. **7** [C] (*infml* 口) = STAGE-COACH: *take the next stage out of town* 乘下一趟公共马车出镇. **8** (idm 习语) **be/go on the ˈstage** be/become an actor 当[成为]演员; 登台演出: *She's wanted to go on the stage from an early age.* 她从小就想当演员. **set the stage for sth** prepare for sth; make sth possible or easy 为某事作好准备或创造条件: *The president's recent death set the stage for a military coup.* 总统最近死后, 酝酿着一场军事政变. ˌ**up/ˌdown ˈstage** further from/nearer to the front of the stage when acting in a play, etc (演出时)在(向)舞台后部[前部].

▷ **stage** *v* [Tn] **1** present (a play, etc) on a stage; put (sth) before the public 将(戏剧等)搬上舞台; 上演: *stage a new production of 'King Lear'* 上演新编排的《李尔王》. **2** arrange for (sth) to take place; carry out 实行(某事); 进行; 举行: *stage a protest rally* 举行抗议大会 ○ *stage a ˈcome-back*, eg after retiring as a sportsman 复出.

□ ˈ**stage-coach** *n* (formerly) public vehicle pulled by horses carrying passengers (and often mail) along a regular route (旧时的)公共马车, 驿车.

ˈ**stage direction** note in the text of a play telling actors where to move, how to perform, etc on stage (剧本的)舞台指示.

ˌ**stage ˈdoor** entrance at the back of a theatre used by actors, theatre staff, etc 剧场后门(供演员、职员等进出的).

ˈ**stage fright** nervousness felt by an actor, etc in front of an audience (演员等的)怯场.

ˈ**stage-hand** *n* person employed to help move scenery, etc in a theatre 舞台工作人员(负责移动布景、道具等的).

ˌ**stage ˈleft** left side of a stage for an actor facing the audience (面对观众的)舞台左侧.

ˌ**stage-ˈmanage** *v* [Tn] organize (sth) as or like a stage-manager 担任(某剧)的舞台监督; 对(某事)进行幕后安排: *The demonstration had been carefully stage-managed to coincide with the Prime Minister's visit.* 这次示威活动事先作了精心安排, 正好在首相访问时进行.

ˌ**stage-ˈmanager** *n* person in charge of a theatre stage, equipment, scenery, etc during the rehearsals and performances of a play 舞台监督.

ˌ**stage ˈright** right side of a stage for an actor facing the audience (面对观众的)舞台右侧.

ˈ**stage-struck** *adj* (*often derog* 常作贬义) having a (too) great desire to become an actor (过分)渴望当演员的: *His ten-year old daughter is completely stage-struck.* 他那十岁的女儿想当演员都入迷了.

ˌ**stage ˈwhisper** loud whisper (on stage) that is intended to be heard by the audience 低声旁白(为让观众听见的舞台低语).

stag·fla·tion /ˌstægˈfleɪʃn; ˌstægˋfleʃən/ *n* [U] (*finance* 财) (formed from *stag*nation + in*flation* 由*stag*nation + in*flation* 二词构成) state of monetary inflation without a corresponding increase in demand and employment 滞胀.

stag·ger /ˈstægə(r); ˋstægɚ/ *v* **1** [I, Ipr, Ip] walk or move unsteadily as if about to fall (from carrying sth heavy, being weak or drunk, etc) 蹒跚; 踉跄; 摇晃着移动: *She staggered and fell.* 她踉跄了几步, 跌倒在地. ○ *stagger to one's feet, across the room, from side to side* 摇摇晃晃地站起来、走到房间的另一边、忽左忽右 ○ *staggering along, around, about, etc* 摇摇摆摆地走着、转来转去、四处走等. ⇨Usage at SHUFFLE 用法见SHUFFLE. **2** [Tn usu passive 通常用于被动语态] (of news, etc) shock (sb) deeply; cause (sb) astonishment, worry or confusion (指消息等)使(某人)震惊、担心或慌乱: *I was staggered to hear/on hearing/when I heard of his death.* 我听到他死的消息大吃一惊. **3** [Tn usu passive 通常用于被动语态] place (sth) in a zigzag or alternating arrangement 交错安排(某事物); 使(某事物)错开: *a staggered junction*, ie a cross-roads where the side-roads are not directly opposite each other 旁侧路口不相对的交叉处. **4** [Tn] arrange (the times of events) so that they do not occur together 错开(时间): *staggered office hours*, ie arranged so that employees are not all using buses, trains, etc at the same time 错开的办公时间(以减低使用交通工具的拥挤现象) ○ *stagger the annual holidays* 错开年假.

▷ **stag·ger** *n* unsteady staggering movement 蹒跚; 踉跄; 摇晃不稳的动作: *He picked up the heavy suitcase and set off with a stagger.* 他提起沉重的箱子, 打个趔趄就走了.

stag·ger·ing /ˈstægərɪŋ; ˋstægərɪŋ/ *adj* astonishing; shocking 令人吃惊的; 惊人的: *a staggering achievement* 惊人的成就 ○ *I find their decision simply staggering.* 我觉得他们的决定简直太惊人了. **stag·ger·ingly** *adv*: *She's staggeringly beautiful.* 她漂亮极了.

sta·ging /ˈsteɪdʒɪŋ; ˋstedʒɪŋ/ *n* [C, U] **1** (usu temporary) platform or support for people working, eg on a building site; scaffolding (通常指临时的)工作台, 工作架; 脚手架. **2** (way or method of) presenting a play on the stage of a theatre (戏剧的)上演, 演出; 演剧技巧: *an imaginative new staging of 'Macbeth'* 以表现出丰富的想像力的新手法上演的《麦克佩斯》.

□ **'staging post** regular stopping-place on a long journey, esp on an air route 中途站; (尤指飞机航线上的)中途机场.

stag·nant /ˈstægnənt; ˈstægnənt/ *adj* **1** (of water) not flowing and therefore dirty and smelling unpleasant; still and stale (指水)因不流动而污浊、腐臭的, 静止而不新鲜的: *water lying stagnant in ponds and ditches* 池塘和沟中的死水. **2** (*fig* 比喻) showing no activity (and therefore not developing or progressing); sluggish 停滞的; 不景气的: *Business was stagnant last month.* 上个月生意萧条. ▷ **stag·nancy** /-nənsɪ; -nənsɪ/ *n* [U].

stag·nate /stægˈneɪt; *US* ˈstægneɪt; ˈstægnet/ *v* [I] **1** be or become stagnant(1) 不流动; 成为死水. **2** (*fig* 比喻) be or become dull or unsuccessful because of lack of activity, development, opportunity, etc 停滞; 变迟钝; 不景气; 不发展: *a stagnating industry* 不景气的工业 ○ *I feel I'm stagnating in this job.* 我觉得我干这份工作没什么前途. ○ *His mind has stagnated since his retirement.* 他退休后头脑迟钝了. ▷ **stag·na·tion** /stægˈneɪʃn; stægˈneʃən/ *n* [U].

stagy /ˈsteɪdʒɪ; ˈstedʒɪ/ *adj* (**-ier**, **-iest**) (*usu derog* 通常作贬义) (too) theatrical in style, manner or behaviour; exaggerated for effect (太)戏剧化的; 演戏似的; 做作的: *The room was decorated with stagy opulence.* 那房间装饰得富丽堂皇, 像戏台似的. ▷ **sta·gily** /-ɪlɪ; -əlɪ/ *adv*. **sta·gi·ness** *n* [U].

staid /steɪd; sted/ *adj* (*sometimes derog* 有时作贬义) (of people, their appearance, behaviour, tastes, etc) serious, dull and old-fashioned; conservative (指人、外表、行为、爱好等)古板的, 保守的, 一本正经的: *I was surprised to see him at the jazz club; I always thought of him as a rather staid old gentleman.* 我在爵士舞俱乐部见到他时很感意外, 我还一直以为他是个挺古板的绅士呢. ▷ **staidly** *adv*. **staid·ness** *n* [U].

stain /steɪn; sten/ *v* **1** [esp passive 尤用于被动语态: Tn, Tn·pr, Cn·a] **~ sth (with sth)** change the colour of sth; leave or make coloured patches or dirty marks on sth, esp ones that are difficult to remove 改变某物的颜色; 染污, 沾污(某物)(尤指难以清除): *fingers stained with nicotine* 被尼古丁染黄的手指 ○ *blood-stained hands* 沾着血污的手 ○ *a tablecloth stained with gravy* 沾上肉汁的桌布 ○ *The blackberry juice stained their fingers (red).* 黑莓汁把他们的手指给染(红)了. **2** [I] become discoloured or marked in this way 被染污; 被沾污: *Our white carpet stains easily.* 我们的白地毯不耐脏. **3** [Tn, Tn·pr, Cn·a] colour (wood, fabric, etc) with a substance that penetrates the material; dye 给(木材、布等)染色或着色: *The biologist stained the specimen before looking at it through the microscope.* 那位生物学家先把标本染色, 然后再通过显微镜进行观察. ○ *He stained the wood dark brown.* 他把木头染成深褐色了. **4** [esp passive 尤用于被动语态: Tn, Tn·pr] (*fml fig* 文, 比喻) bring disgrace to or damage (sb's reputation, good name, etc); blemish 玷污, 败坏(某人的名声等): *The incident stained his career.* 那件小事给他的事业抹上了污斑.

▷ **stain** *n* **1** [U, C] liquid, etc used for staining wood, fabric, etc; dye 染色剂; 着色剂; 染料; 颜料: *How much stain should I buy for the table?* 给这张桌子上色, 我得买多少颜料? ○ *a range of wood stains* 木材着色剂系列. **2** [C] dirty mark or patch of colour caused by staining (STAIN *v* 1) 污点; 污斑; 污迹: *There's an ink stain on your shirt.* 你的衬衫上有一个墨水斑. ○ *I can't get these coffee stains out of the carpet.* 我弄不掉地毯上的咖啡污迹. [C] thing that causes disgrace (to a person's reputation, etc); moral blemish 玷污(某人名声等的)事物; 品德上的污点: *He left the court without a stain on his character.* 他经法庭一役, 人格丝毫无损.

stain·less *adj* free from stains or blemishes; spotless 无污点的; 无瑕疵的: *a stainless reputation* 清白的名声.

ˌ**stainless ˈsteel** type of steel alloy that does not rust or corrode 不锈钢: *knives made of stainless steel* 不锈钢刀 ○ [attrib 作定语] *a stainless steel sink* 不锈钢洗涤槽.

□ ˌ**stained ˈglass** glass coloured with transparent colouring while it is being made 彩色玻璃; 彩画玻璃: [attrib 作定语] *a* ˌ*stained glass* ˈ*window*, ie one made of pieces of glass of different colours, as seen in many churches 彩画玻璃窗(由各色玻璃拼成, 常见于教堂中). ⇨illus at App 1 见附录1插图, page viii.

stair /steə(r); stɛr/ *n* **1 stairs** [pl] series of fixed steps from one floor of a building to another, usu inside (楼层之间的)楼梯(通常在建筑物内): *climb a long/short flight of stairs* 上一大[小]段楼梯 ○ *She always runs up/down the stairs.* 她总是跑着上[下]楼梯. ○ *I passed her on the stairs.* 我在楼梯上遇见她了. ○ *The stairs need cleaning.* 楼梯该打扫一下了. ○ *at the foot/head of the stairs*, ie at the bottom/top of a set of stairs 在楼梯的下端[上端]. **2** [C] any one of these steps 梯级: *The child was sitting on the bottom stair.* 那孩子正坐在楼梯最下面的一级上. ○ *The top stair is broken.* 楼梯最上面的一级坏了. ⇨illus 见插图. **3** (idm 习语) **below 'stairs** (*dated* 旧) in the basement of a house (in large houses, formerly the part used by servants) 在地下室(指大房子中的, 旧时为仆人用的): *Their affairs were being discussed below stairs*, ie by the servants. 他们的仆人正在谈论他们的事情.

□ **'stair-carpet** *n* strip of carpet for laying on stairs 楼梯地毯.

staircase 楼梯

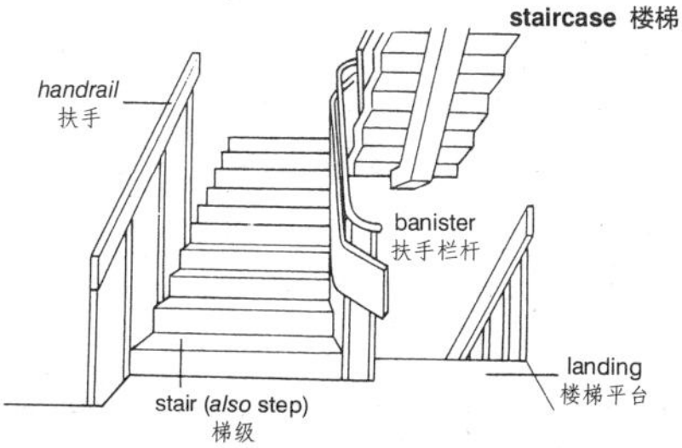

'staircase (also **'stairway**) *n* set of stairs (often with banisters) and its supporting structure, inside a building (建筑物内的)楼梯(常有栏杆): *a spiral staircase*, ie stairs winding round a central pillar 螺旋式楼梯. ⇨illus 见插图.

'stair-rod *n* metal or wooden rod fixed in the angle between two stairs to keep a stair-carpet in place 楼梯毯棍(两梯级间固定地毯用的).

'stairway *n* = STAIRCASE.

'stairwell *n* part of a building containing the staircase; space for the stairs 楼梯井(建筑物的楼梯占用的部分).

NOTE ON USAGE 用法: (Flights of) **stairs** are mostly found inside houses or other buildings where people live or work (eg an office block) ☆ (flights of) **stairs** 多见于房屋或其他供人居住或工作的建筑物(如办公楼)中: *He finds it difficult to climb the stairs with his bad leg.* 他的一条腿有毛病, 上楼梯很困难. ○ *vacuum the stairs* 用吸尘器打扫楼梯. A **staircase** is the part of the building including the stairs and banisters and sometimes the walls and ceilings surrounding them ☆ **staircase** 指建筑物内容纳楼梯及其栏杆的部分, 有时包括周围的墙壁和天花板: *We must redecorate the staircase.* 我们得把楼梯重新装饰一下. (Flights of) **steps** are usually made of stone or concrete and found outside or in an uninhabited building. ☆ (flights of) **steps** 通常为石料或混凝土制成的, 建于户外或非住房型的建筑物中. We also talk of individual **steps** which make up a staircase or a flight of steps ☆ **steps** 还可用以指构成楼梯或一段台阶的梯级: *I'll meet you on the steps of the museum.* 我在博物馆的台阶上和你相见. ○ *There are 150 steps to the top of the tower.* 到塔顶有150级台阶. ○ *sitting on the top/bottom step* 坐在最上[下]的梯级上.

stake /steɪk; stek/ *n* **1** [C] strong wood or metal stick, pointed at one end, that can be driven into the ground, eg to support a young tree, as a post for a fence, etc or as a marker 桩; 标桩. **2 the stake** [sing] (formerly) post to which a person was tied before being burnt to death as a punishment (旧时的)火刑柱: *be burnt at the stake* 以火刑处死 ○ *go to the stake*, ie be killed in this way 处以火刑. **3** [C usu *pl* 通常作复数] money, etc risked or gambled on the unknown result of a future event (eg a race, a card-game) 赌注: *playing for high stakes* 下大赌注. **4** money, etc invested by sb in an enterprise so that he has an interest or share in it 投资; 投放的本钱: *have a stake in a company* 在一家公司有股分 ○ *She has a stake in the future success of the business.* 她在这项生意上投了资以期将来获利. **5 stakes** (**a**) [pl] prize money, esp in a horse-race 奖金(尤指赛马的). (**b**) (usu 通常作 **Stakes**) [sing *v*] (esp in names) horse-race in which all the owners of the horses in the race contribute to the prize money (尤用于名称中)有奖赛马(参赛马的马主均须捐款用作奖金): *The Newmarket Stakes is always a popular race.* 纽马基特赛马总是吸引很多人. **6** (idm 习语) **at stake** to be won or lost; being risked, depending on the outcome of an event 在胜败关头; 冒风险: *This decision puts our lives at stake.* 这么一决定, 我们的生命就吉凶难卜了. ○ *Our children's education is at stake.* 我们孩子的教育好坏无法预料. **go to the stake over sth** maintain (an opinion, a principle, etc) at any cost 不惜一切代价地坚持(观点、原则等): *I think I'm right on this issue but I wouldn't go to the stake over it.* 我认为我在这个问题上是正确的, 但我并不想拼命坚持这一点.

▷ **stake** *v* **1** [Tn] support (sth) with a stake 用桩支撑(某物): *stake newly planted trees* 用桩支撑新栽的树. **2** [Tn, Tn·pr] **~ sth (on sth)** gamble or risk (money, one's hopes, one's life, etc) on sth 拿(金钱、希望、生命等)就某事物打赌或冒险: *stake £5 on the favourite*, eg in a horse-race 在那个大热门(如赛马中的某匹马)上压5英镑 ○ *I'd stake my life on it*, ie I'm very confident about it. 我敢拿性命来担保. **3** [Tn] (*US infml* 口) give financial or other support to (sb/sth) 资助, 支持(某人[某事物]): *stake a business* 资助一家公司. **4** (idm 习语) **stake (out) a/one's 'claim (to sb/sth)** (**a**) mark out (a piece of land, etc) as one's own (esp formerly when arriving in a new country or area) 划(一块土地等)归为己有(尤指旧时初到某国或某地时). (**b**) declare a special interest (in sb/sth); claim a right (to sb/sth) 声称(与某人[某事物])有特殊关联; 提出(对某人[某事物]的)所有权要求: *Several clubs have already staked a/their claim to this outstanding young footballer.* 有几个足球俱乐部均表示这个年轻的足球健将是他们的人. **5** (phr v) **stake sth out** (**a**) mark (an area) with stakes (esp formerly to claim ownership) 用桩标出(地)界(尤指旧时用以表明所有权). (**b**) declare a special interest in or right to (eg an area of study, a place) 声称对(研究领域、地方等)有特殊关联或所有权: *He's staked out this part of the house as his own.* 他说屋子的这一部分归他所有. (**c**) (*infml* 口 *esp US*) (of the police) watch (a place) continuously and secretly (指警方)持续监视(某处): *Detectives have been staking out the house for two days now.* 警方的侦查人员已对这座房子监视两天了.

□ **'stake-out** *n* (*infml* 口 *esp US*) (**a**) continuous secret watch by the police; surveillance (警方的)监视. (**b**) area or house being watched in this way 受警方监视的地方或房子.

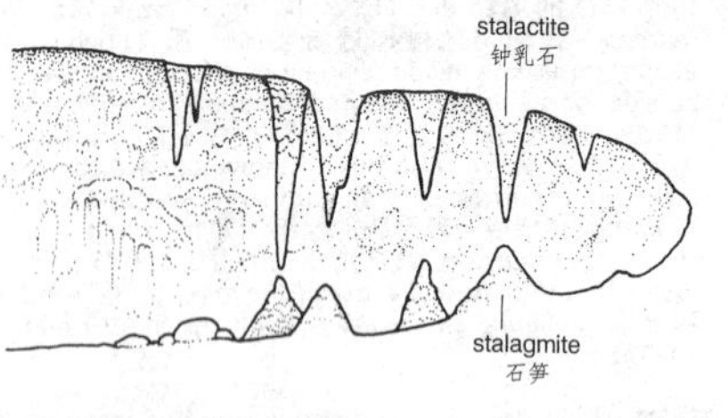

stal·ac·tite /ˈstæləktaɪt; *US* stəˈlæktaɪt; stəˈlæktaɪt/ *n* icicle-shaped formation of lime hanging from the roof of a cave, formed by the steady dripping of water containing minerals 钟乳石; 石钟乳; 石乳.

stal·ag·mite /ˈstæləgmaɪt; *US* stəˈlægmaɪt; stəˈlægmaɪt/ *n* formation of lime extending upwards like a pillar from the floor of a cave as water from a stalactite drips onto it 石笋. ⇨illus at STALACTITE 见 STALACTITE 插图.

stale /steɪl; stel/ *adj* **1** (esp of food) smelling or tasting unpleasant, mouldy or dry, because no longer fresh (尤指食物)不新鲜的, 走味的, 带霉味的, 干瘪的: *stale biscuits, bread, cake, beer* 不新鲜的饼干、面包、糕饼、啤酒 ○ *the smell of stale cigarette smoke* 陈旧香烟的烟味. **2** no longer interesting because heard, done, etc too often before; not new 因陈旧而乏味的; 过时的: *stale news, jokes, ideas* 老掉牙的消息、笑话、思想 ○ *Her performance has become stale.* 她的表演没有新意了. **3** (of athletes, musicians, performers, etc) no longer able to perform well because of too much training, playing, practice, etc (指运动员、音乐工作者、表演者等)(因训练、演奏、练习等过度)疲沓的.

▷ **stale** *v* [I] become stale 变得不新鲜; 走味; 失去新意; 变得疲沓: *The pleasure I get from listening to such music never stales.* 这种音乐我百听不厌.

stale·ness *n* [U].

stale·mate /ˈsteɪlmeɪt; ˈstelˌmet/ *n* [U, C usu *sing* 作不可数名词或可数名词, 后者通常作单数] **1** position of the pieces in the game of chess in which the player whose move it is cannot move without putting his king in check (国际象棋中的)僵局, 和棋(一方只能移动王棋以摆脱困境). **2** stage of a dispute, contest, etc at which further action or discussion by either side seems to be impossible; deadlock 僵持阶段; 僵局: *Negotiations have reached (a) stalemate.* 谈判陷入了僵局.

▷ **stale·mate** *v* [Tn usu passive 通常用于被动语态] bring (sb/sth) to a position of stalemate 使(某人[某事物])陷入僵局.

stalk[1] /stɔːk; stɔk/ *n* **1** main stem of a plant (not a tree) (植物的)茎, 秆: *daffodils with long stalks* 茎很长的水仙花. ⇨illus at App 1 见附录1插图, page ii. **2** stem that supports a leaf, flower or fruit and joins it to another part of the plant 叶柄; 花梗; 果实的柄: *Remove the stalks from the cherries before you eat them.* 吃樱桃前要先把梗儿去掉. **3** thin structure supporting a part or organ in some animals (某些动物的)肉柄, 肉茎. **4** (idm 习语) **have one's eyes on stalks** ⇨ EYE[1].

stalk[2] /stɔːk; stɔk/ *v* **1** (**a**) [Ipr, Ip] walk with slow stiff strides, esp in a proud, self-important or threatening way 踱着方步走(尤指显出高傲、自命不凡或盛气凌人的样子): *He stalked angrily out of the room.* 他悻悻然踱出了房间. ○ *stalk along (the road)* (在路上)得意地踱着方步. (**b**) [Ipr, Tn] (*fml or rhet* 文或修辞) (of an evil force, disease, etc) move silently and threateningly (through a place) (指邪恶势力、疾病等)悄悄而可怕地(在某地)蔓延: *Fear stalks (through) the town at night.* 入夜后, 镇上笼罩着恐怖的气氛. ○ *Ghosts are said to stalk the castle walls.* 据说有鬼魂在这座城堡的墙上出没. **2** [Tn] move quietly and slowly towards (wild animals, etc) in order to get near without being seen 偷偷接近, 潜近(野生动物等): *stalking deer* 偷偷接近鹿 ○ (*fig* 比喻) *a rapist stalking his victim* 悄悄逼近攻击对象的强奸者.

▷ **stalker** *n* person who stalks animals 用潜近法猎捕动物的人.

stall /stɔːl; stɔl/ *n* **1** [C] compartment, usu with three sides, for one animal in a stable or cattle shed 牲畜棚中的一栏(通常三面有墙). **2** [C] (often in compounds 常用以构成复合词) table, stand or small open-fronted shop from which things are sold in a market, on a street, in a railway station, etc 摊位; 铺子; 售货亭: *a 'bookstall at the station* 车站的书亭 ○ *a 'fruit stall in the market* 菜场里的水果摊儿 ○ *run a 'cake stall at the bazaar* 在市场中经营糕饼铺子. **3 stalls** [pl] (*Brit*) (set of seats in) the part of a theatre that is nearest to the stage (戏院的)正厅前排(座位): *two seats in the stalls* 两个前排座位 ○ *laughter from the stalls* 前排观众发出的笑声. ⇨ illus at App 1 见附录1插图, page ix. **4** [C] any of several fixed seats, usu with its back and sides enclosed, in the choir or chancel of a church (教堂内)唱诗班席位; (高坛上的)牧师座位: *the canon's 'stall* 牧师的座位 ○ *the 'choir stalls* 唱诗班席位. **5** [C] any small room or compartment, usu for one person 小房间, 小隔间(通常

指供单人使用的): *stalls for changing in at the swimming-pool* 游泳池的更衣间. **6** [C] (instance of the) stalling of an aircraft or engine; condition resulting from this (飞行器失速造成的)失控下降; (发动机的)熄火: *go into/get out of a stall* 进入[脱离]失控下降状态. **7** [C] = FINGER-STALL (FINGER).

▷ **stall** *v* **1** [Tn] place or keep (an animal) in a stall(1), esp for fattening 将(动物)关在栏内(尤指为了养肥). **2** (**a**) [I] (of an engine) stop suddenly because of insufficient power or speed (指发动机因力量或速度不够)熄火: *The car stalled at the roundabout.* 那辆汽车在环形交叉处抛锚了. (**b**) [I, Tn] (of a driver) cause (an engine) to do this (指司机)使(发动机)熄火: *Learner drivers often stall (their cars).* 见习司机常造成(汽车)熄火现象. **3** (**a**) [I] (of an aircraft) get out of control and start to drop because of loss of speed (指飞行器)(因失速)失控下降: *The plane stalled suddenly.* 那飞机突然失控下降. (**b**) [I, Tn] (of a pilot) cause (an aircraft) to do this (指飞行器驾驶员)造成(飞行器)失控下降. **4** (**a**) [I] avoid giving a definite answer or taking action (in order to get more time); delay 支吾, 拖延(以争取时间): *stall for time* 拖延时间 ○ *Stop stalling and give me an answer!* 别支支吾吾的了, 快回答我的问题! (**b**) [Tn] avoid answering (a person, request, etc) in this way 对(某人、某要求等)支吾或敷衍: *stall one's creditors* 敷衍债主.

□ ˈ**stall-holder** *n* person who rents or owns and runs a stall in a market, etc 摊主; 铺子的主人; 售货亭主人.

stal·lion /ˈstælɪən; ˋstæljən/ *n* fully grown male horse that has not been castrated, esp one used for breeding 牡马(尤指种马). Cf 参看 COLT 1, GELDING (GELD), MARE[1] 1.

stal·wart /ˈstɔːlwət; ˋstɔlwɚt/ *adj* **1** (*dated or fml* 旧或文) (of a person) strong and sturdy (指人)强壮的, 健壮的, 结实的: *a boxer of stalwart build* 体格强壮的拳击手. **2** [usu attrib 通常作定语] dependable, firm and loyal 坚定的; 忠实的: *one of the team's most stalwart supporters* 这支运动队最坚定的支持者之一 ○ *give the team stalwart support* 忠实地支持那支运动队.

▷ **stal·wart** *n* loyal supporter (of a political party, etc) (政党等的)忠实拥护者, 坚定分子: *rally the stalwarts of the party* 把这个党的坚定分子团结起来.

stal·wartly *adv*.

stal·wart·ness *n* [U].

sta·men /ˈsteɪmən; ˋstemən/ *n* (*botany* 植) any of the small thin male parts in the middle of a flower that produce pollen 雄蕊.

stam·ina /ˈstæmɪnə; ˋstæmənə/ *n* [U] ability to endure much physical or mental strain; long-lasting energy and resilience; staying-power 精力; 耐力; 韧劲: *Marathon runners need plenty of stamina.* 参加马拉松长跑要有耐力. ○ *He doesn't have the stamina to be a teacher.* 他没有当教师的精力.

stam·mer /ˈstæmə(r); ˋstæmɚ/ *v* **1** (also **stutter**) [I] speak with sudden pauses and a tendency to repeat rapidly the same sound or syllable (because of a speech defect or from fear, excitement, etc) 口吃; 结巴着说话: *'G-g-give me that b-b-book,' said Henry, unable to stop stammering.* '给、给、给我那本、本、本书,'亨利结结巴巴地说. **2** [Tn, Tn·p] ~ **sth (out)** say sth in this way 结巴着说某事: *'G-g-goodb-b-bye,' she stammered.* 她结结巴巴地说出: '再、再、再见、见、见.' ○ *stammer out a request* 结结巴巴地提出请求.

▷ **stam·mer** *n* (usu *sing* 通常作单数) (**a**) tendency to stammer 口吃; 结巴: *speak with a stammer* 说话结巴 ○ *He's always had a slight stammer.* 他一向有点儿口吃. (**b**) stammering speech 结巴的言语.

stam·merer /ˈstæmərə(r); ˋstæmərɚ/ *n* person who stammers 口吃的人; 结巴.

stam·mer·ingly /ˈstæmərɪŋlɪ; ˋstæmərɪŋlɪ/ *adv*.

stamp[1] /stæmp; stæmp/ *v* **1** [I, Tn, Tn·pr, Tn·p, Cn·a] ~ **sth (down)** put (one's foot) down heavily on (the ground, etc); flatten (sth) by doing this 重重地踩在(地面等)上; 跺; 踏平, 踩扁(某物): *He stamped (his foot) in anger.* 他气得直跺脚. ○ *stamping the ground to keep warm* 跺脚使身体暖和 ○ *She stamped the soil (flat/down) round the plant.* 她把那株植物周围的土踩(平[实])了. **2** [I, Ipr, Ip] walk with loud heavy steps 迈着很重的步子走; 踩着脚走: *Don't stamp, you'll wake everyone up.* 脚步别这么重, 会把大家都吵醒的. ○ *stamp about* 跺着脚到处走 ○ *stamp out of a room* 迈着沉重的步子走出房间 ○ *stamp upstairs* 脚步重重地走上楼. **3** [Tn, Tn·pr] ~ **A (on B)**; ~ **B (with A)** print (a design, the date, lettering, etc) on paper, cloth or some other surface; mark (paper, etc) with a design, an official seal, etc 在纸、布或其他物体表面印上(图案、日期、文字等); 在(纸等)的上面盖图案、公章等: *They didn't stamp my passport.* 我的护照上没盖章. ○ *The librarian forgot to stamp my library books*, ie with the date on which they should be returned. 图书管理员忘了在我借的书上盖日期了. ○ *stamp one's name and address on an envelope/stamp an envelope with one's name and address* 把自己的姓名地址盖在信封上 ○ *crates of oranges stamped with the exporter's trademark* 印有出口商牌子的装着橙子的板条箱. **4** [Tn esp passive 尤用于被动语态] stick a postage stamp or some other stamp on (a letter, etc) 在(信)上贴邮票; 贴其他的票于(某物): *I enclose a stamped addressed envelope for your reply.* 兹附上贴有邮票并写好地址的回邮信封. **5** [Tn, Tn·pr, Tn·p] ~ **sth (out) (from sth)** cut and shape (metal, etc) into pieces by striking it with a specially shaped tool or cutter 冲压(金属等): *a machine for stamping out engine parts* 冲压发动机部件的机器. **6** [Tn, Tn·pr] ~ **sth (on sb/sth)** (*fig* 比喻) impress or fix sth permanently 使某事物铭记或牢固附着: *stamp one's personality/authority on a game*, ie as an outstanding player 把自己的特长[权威性]带到某项运动中(因技艺超群) ○ *The date is stamped on her memory forever.* 那个日子她永志不忘. **7** [Cn·n/a] ~ **sb as sth** give a certain character to sb; mark sb out as sth 赋予某人以某特征; 表明某人为...: *This achievement stamps her as a genius.* 这一成就已足见她是个天才. **8** (phr v) **stamp sth off (sth)** remove sth by stamping with the foot 跺掉某物: *stamped the mud off their shoes* (他们)把鞋上的泥跺掉. **stamp on sth** (**a**) crush sth by bringing one's foot down heavily on it 将某物踩扁、踩碎或踩烂: *stamp on a spider* 踩死一只蜘蛛. (**b**) control or suppress sth, esp by force; quell sth 控制或压制某事物(尤指用武力); 镇压; 平息: *The rebellion was soon stamped on by the army.* 军队很快平息了叛乱. **stamp sth out** (**a**) extinguish (a fire, etc) by stamping 踩灭(火等): *stamp out the embers of the camp fire* 把篝火的余烬踏灭. (**b**) eliminate, destroy or suppress sth, esp by force or vigorous action 消除、毁灭或压制某事物(尤指用武力或积极行动): *stamp out terrorism, a rebellion, an epidemic disease* 剪除恐怖活动、镇压叛乱、消灭流行病.

□ ˈ**stamping-ground** *n* (*infml* 口) place where a particular person or animal may usually be found; favourite place or haunt (某人或某动物)常在的地方, 经常出没之处: *one of my old stamping-grounds* 我常去的一个老地方.

stamp[2] /stæmp; stæmp/ *n* **1** small piece of paper (usu rectangular, with perforated edges) with an official design on it, stuck on an envelope or a parcel or a document to show that postage or duty or some other fee has been paid 邮票; 印花: *an 18p stamp* 18便士的邮票 ○ *a book of (postage) stamps* 一本邮票 ○ *I'd like three first-class stamps, please.* 请给我三张第一类邮件的邮票. ○ *collecting stamps*, ie as a hobby 集邮 ○ [attrib 作定语] *a stamp collection* 收集的邮票. **2** (also ˈ**trading stamp**) similar piece of paper given to customers with purchases, exchangeable for various articles or goods 酬宾赠物票. **3** instrument with which a design, mark, etc is stamped on a surface 印章; 图章: *a rubber stamp*, ie one on which a design, words, etc are cut, used for printing dates, signatures, addresses, etc 橡皮图章. **4** design, word(s), etc made by stamping on a surface 印记; 戳记: *Have you got any stamps in your passport?* 你的护照盖印了吗? **5** act or sound of stamping with the foot 跺脚; 跺脚声: *give a stamp of impatience* 不耐烦地跺脚. **6** (usu *sing* 通常作单数) (*fml fig* 文, 比喻) characteristic mark or quality 特点; 特质; 烙印: *She bears the stamp of genius.* 她有天才的特质. ○ *His face bears the stamp of suffering.* 他的脸上有饱经苦难的烙印. ○ *Their story has the stamp of truth*, ie seems very likely to be true. 他们说的这事儿看来是真的. **7** (usu *sing* 通常作单数) (*fml fig* 文, 比喻) kind; class; sort 种类; 类型: *men of a different stamp* 另一类的人.

□ ˈ**stamp album** special book in which a stamp-collector keeps his stamps 集邮簿.

ˈ**stamp-collecting** *n* [U] collecting postage stamps as objects of interest or value 集邮. ˈ**stamp-collector** *n* person who does this 集邮的人.

ˈ**stamp-duty** *n* tax imposed on certain types of legal documents (on which an official stamp is put to show that the tax has been paid) 印花税.

stam·pede /stæmˈpi:d; stæmˋpid/ *n* **1** sudden rush of frightened animals (指动物的)惊逃, 乱窜. **2** sudden wild rush or mass movement of people (指人)突然的大规模移动, 蜂拥: *There was a stampede towards the stage when the singer appeared.* 歌手出现时观众向台前涌去. **3** (in Canada) form of entertainment in which cowboys display their skill at handling animals; rodeo (加拿大的)牧人竞技表演: *the Calgary Stampede* 卡尔加里牧人竞技会.

▷ **stam·pede** *v* **1** (**a**) [I] (of animals or people) take part in a stampede (指动物或人)惊逃, 蜂拥: *The cattle stampeded towards the farm.* 受惊的牛群向牧场涌去. (**b**) [Tn] cause (esp animals) to do this 使(尤指动物)惊逃. **2** [Tn·pr] **~ sb into sth/doing sth** cause sb to rush into rash or unreasonable action 使某人冲动行事或失去理智: *Don't be stampeded into buying the house.* 不要一时冲动买下这所房子.

stance /stæns *or, in British use,* 英式英语读作 stɑ:ns; stæns/ *n* (usu *sing* 通常作单数) **1** person's position or way of standing (esp in sports such as cricket, golf, etc when preparing to hit the ball); pose 站立姿势(尤指板球、高尔夫球等运动中准备击球的); 姿势. **2 ~ (on sth)** moral or intellectual attitude (to sth); standpoint (对某事物的)姿态, 态度; 观点; 立场: *He maintains a rigidly right-wing political stance.* 他坚持僵硬的右派政治立场. ○ *What is your stance on corporal punishment?* 你对体罚持什么态度? Cf 参看 POSTURE.

stanch /stɑ:ntʃ; *US* stæntʃ; stæntʃ/ (also **staunch** /stɔ:ntʃ; stɔntʃ/) *v* [Tn] (**a**) stop the flow of (esp blood) 止住(尤指血)的流出: *stanch the bleeding* 止血. (**b**) stop or control the flow of blood from (a wound) 止住或控制(受伤处)的流血: *stanch a cut* 止住伤口的血.

stan·chion /ˈstænʃən; *US* ˈstæntʃən; ˋstæntʃən/ *n* upright bar or post forming a support 支撑用的杆或柱; 支柱.

stand[1] /stænd; stænd/ *n* **1** [sing] stationary condition; halt or standstill 停止的状态; 中止; 停顿: *come to a stand* 停下来. **2** [sing] position taken up; act or instance of standing 立脚点; 站立: *He took his stand* (ie stood) *near the window.* 他站在窗旁. **3** [C] (period of time of) resistance to attack 抵抗; 抵御; 抵抗时期: *the rebels' last stand* 叛乱者的最后抵抗 ○ *a stand of sixty days* 六十天的抵抗. **4** [C] (often in compounds 常用以构成复合词) small piece of furniture (eg a rack, pedestal, frame, etc) on or in which sth may be placed (置物的)架, 座, 台: *a ˈhat/an umˈbrella/a ˈcoat stand* 帽[伞/衣]架 ○ *a ˈcake stand* 糕饼架 ○ *a ˈmusic-stand*, ie for supporting sheet music while it is being played 乐谱架. **5** [C] (**a**) structure (eg a table or kiosk) from which goods are sold; stall 货摊; 售货亭: *a ˈnews-stand* 报摊 ○ *a market stand* 集市的货摊. (**b**) area or structure where things are displayed, exhibited, advertised, etc 摊位(用于陈列、展览、宣传等目的的): *one of the stands at a book fair* 书展中的一个摊位. **6** [C] place where vehicles may stand in a line in a street, etc while waiting for passengers (街道等处的)车辆候客处: *a ˈtaxi-stand* 计程车站 ○ *a stand for six taxis* 有六个车位的计程车候客处. **7** [C often *pl* 常作复数] large, usu sloping, structure at a sports ground, racecourse etc, with rows of seats for spectators 看台: *A cheer rose from the south stand(s).* 南看台上响起一片欢呼声. ⇨illus at ASSOCIATION FOOTBALL (ASSOCIATION) 见 ASSOCIATION FOOTBALL (ASSOCIATION) 插图. Cf 参看 GRANDSTAND (GRAND). **8** [C] stop made for a performance by a touring theatrical company, pop group, etc (巡回演出的剧团、流行乐乐队等的)停留演出: *a series of ˌone-night ˈstands* 演一晚换一处的巡回演出. **9** [C usu *sing* 通常作单数] (*US*) witness-box (in a lawcourt) 证人席: *take the stand* 作证. **10** (idm 习语) **make a stand (against/for sth/sb)** be ready to resist, fight, argue, etc 准备抵抗、格斗、争论等: *make a stand against the enemy* 摆开架势迎击敌人 ○ *make a stand for one's principles* 准备为维护自己的原则而争斗. **take a/one's stand (on sth)** declare one's position, opinion, etc (on sth) 宣布(对某事物的)立场、意见等; 表明态度: *She took a firm stand on nuclear disarmament.* 她在核裁军的问题上态度很坚决.

stand[2] /stænd; stænd/ *v* (*pt, pp* **stood** /stʊd; stud/)

▸ UPRIGHT POSITION OR EXTENSION 直立的姿势或状态 **1** [I] have, take or keep an upright position 站立; 直立; 站着: *She was too weak to stand.* 她虚弱得站不起来. ○ *A chair will not stand on two legs.* 椅子只用两条腿着地是立不住的. ○ *Don't stand there arguing about it.* 不要站在那儿争论这件事. ○ *Stand still while I take your photograph.* 我给你拍照时, 站着不要动. ○ *After the bombing only a few houses were left standing.* 轰炸之后, 只剩下几所房子没倒塌. **2** [I, Ip] **~ (up)** rise to one's feet 起立; 站起来: *Everyone stood (up) when the Queen entered.* 女王进来时大家都站起来了. ○ *We stood (up) to see better.* 我们站了起来, 好看得清楚些. ○ *Stand up, please!* 请起立! **3** [Tn·pr, Tn·p] put (sth/sb) in an upright position; place 使(某物[某人])直立; 放置: *Don't stand cans of petrol near the fire.* 不要把汽油罐放在近火处. ○ *Stand the ladder* (*up/upright*) *against the wall.* 把梯子竖起来靠在墙上. ○ *I stood the child on a stool so that she could reach the shelf.* 我把孩子抱到凳子上, 她就能够到那架子了. **4** [In/pr] have a specified height 高度为…: *He stands six foot two.* 他身高六英尺二英寸. ○ *The tower stands fifty metres.* 这座塔高五十米.

▸ BEING OR REMAINING IN A PLACE OR CONDITION 处于某地方或某状况 **5** [I] be in a certain place; be situated 在某处; 位于: *a clock standing on the sideboard* 在餐具柜上的钟 ○ *A tall poplar tree once stood here.* 这儿曾经有过一棵高大的白杨树. ○ (*fig* 比喻) *Where do you stand* (ie What is your opinion) *on these issues?* 对这些问题你有什么看法? **6** [I] (of a vehicle, etc) remain in the same place (指车辆等)停着: *a train standing in the station* 停在车站里的火车 ○ *The car stood at the traffic lights for a few moments, then moved off.* 那辆汽车在交通灯前停了一会儿, 然后驶去了. **7** [I] remain unchanged; remain valid 维持原状; 保持效力: *Let the words stand.* 不要改动这些字. ○ *The agreement must stand*, ie cannot be altered or cancelled. 这合约决不能动. ○ *My offer still stands.* 我提出的愿效劳的想法仍然未变. **8** (**a**) [La, Ln, I] be in a certain condition or situation 处于某种状态或情形: *The house has stood empty for months.* 那所房子空了几个月了. ○ *The emergency services stand* (ie are) *ready to help if necessary.* 紧急救难处随时可以驰援. ○ *She stood convicted of fraud.* 她被判犯有诈骗罪. ○ *I stand corrected*, ie accept that I was mistaken and that the person who corrected me is right. 我接受指正. ○ *She stands high in the esteem of* (ie is greatly respected by) *her colleagues.* 她深受同事的尊敬. ○ (*fml* 文) *Will you stand* (ie be) *godmother to the child?* 你愿意做这个孩子的教母吗? ○ *As things stand, there is little chance of a settlement in the dispute.* 就目前情况看, 解决这一纠纷的希望不大. (**b**) [Ipr] **~ at sth** be at a certain level, point of a scale, etc 处于某水平; 指向某一点: *The clock stands at ten to four.* 那个钟上的时间是三点五十分. ○ *The fund stands at £500*, ie there is £500 in it. 这项基金有500英镑. **9** [It] be in a situation where one is likely to do sth 看情形很可能做某事: *stand to win, lose, gain, etc* 很可能赢、输、获利等 ○ *You stand to make a lot of money from this deal.* 你做这笔交易准能赚很多钱. **10** [I] (of a liquid, mixture, etc) remain still; not flow or be disturbed (指液体、混合料等)处于静止状态, 不流动: *standing pools of rainwater* 一汪汪下雨积的水 ○ *Mix the batter and let it stand for twenty minutes.* 和好面糊, 搁二十分钟.

▸ OTHER MEANINGS 其他意义 **11** [no passive 不用于被动语态: Tn, Tt, Tg, Tsg] (esp in negative sentences and in questions, with *can/could*; not in the continuous tenses 尤用于否定句和疑问句中, 与can/could连用, 不用于进行时态) endure sth/sb; bear 忍受某事物; 容忍某人的行为; 经受得起: *He can't stand hot weather.* 他受不住炎热的天气. ○ *My nerves won't stand the strain much longer.* 这么紧张, 我的神经快吃不消了. ○ *She says she will stand no nonsense*, ie will not put up with foolish behaviour. 她说她决不容忍荒唐的行为. ○ *I can't stand* (ie I strongly dislike) *him.* 我对他忍无可忍. ○ *She couldn't stand to be told what to do.* 她不容别人指使她. ○ *He can't stand being kept waiting.* 让他等着, 他可不干. ○ *I can't stand him interrupting all the time.* 他老是插嘴, 真让我受不了. **12** [Tn no passive 不用于被动语态, Dn·n] provide (sth) for sb at one's own expense 自己付钱向某人提供(某物): *stand drinks all round*, ie pay for drinks for everyone 请大家喝饮料 ○ *She was kind enough to stand us a meal.* 她慷慨地请我们吃了顿饭. **13** (*esp Brit*) (also *esp US* **run**) [I, Ipr] **~ (for sth)** be a candidate in an election 任候选人: *She stood unsuccessfully in the local elections.* 她在地方选举中落选了. ○ *stand for parliament* 为议会议员候选人 ○ *stand for President* 参加总统竞选. **14** [I, Ipr, Ip] (*nautical* 海) steer a specified course in a ship (船航行时)取某航向: *stand westward (for the island)* 向西(朝着那个岛)航行. **15** (idm 习语) **stand well, etc with sb** have a specified type of relationship with sb 与某人相处得...: *Do you stand well with your boss?* 你同上司相处得好吗? ○ *I don't know how I stand with her.* 我不知道她对我有什么看法. (For other idioms containing **stand**, see entries for *ns, adjs,* etc 查阅与 **stand** 搭配的其他习语见有关名词、形容词等的词条, 如 **stand trial (for sth)** ⇨ TRIAL; **stand fast** ⇨ FAST[2].) **16** (phr v) **stand a'side** (**a**) move to one side 站到一边去; 让开: *stand aside to let sb pass* 站在一边让某人通过. (**b**) take no part in events; do nothing 不参与; 不行动; 不做事: *Don't stand aside and let others do all the work.* 不要什么都不干, 事情都让别人做. (**c**) withdraw, eg as a candidate in an election 退出(如竞选中): *stand aside in favour of another applicant* 退出而有利于另一候选人.

stand 'back (from sth) (**a**) move back 退后; 向后站: *The policeman ordered us to stand back.* 警察命令我们向后退. (**b**) be situated away from sth 位于与某物有一段距离的地方: *The house stands back a little (from the road).* 那房子离公路有一段距离.

stand 'by (**a**) be present but not do anything 袖手旁观: *How can you stand by and let him treat his dog like that?* 他那样虐待他那只狗, 你怎么能袖手旁观呢? (**b**) be ready for action 准备行动: *The troops are standing by.* 部队正严阵以待. **stand by sb** support or help sb 支持或援助某人: *I'll stand by you whatever happens.* 无论如何, 我都支持你. **stand by sth** be faithful to (a promise, etc) 信守(承诺等); 遵守: *She still stands by every word she said.* 她仍然信守自己说的每一句话.

stand 'down (**a**) (of a witness) leave the witness-box in a lawcourt after giving evidence (指证人)(作证后)退出证人席. (**b**) withdraw (eg as a candidate in an election); resign from one's position 退出(如竞选中); 退职: *The President has stood down after five years in office.* 总统执政五年后已经引退. **stand (sb) 'down** (*military* 军) (order sb to) relax after an alert (命令某人)解除戒备状态: *The troops (were) stood down: it was a false alarm.* 部队解除了戒备状态, 原来是虚惊一场.

'stand for sth (**a**) (no passive 不用于被动语态) be an abbreviation of sth 为某事物的缩略形式: *What does 'T. G.' stand for in 'T. G. Smith'?* 在 T. G. Smith 中的 T. G. 是哪两个字的缩写? (**b**) (no passive 不用于被动语态) represent sth 代表某事物: *I condemn fascism and all it stands for.* 我谴责法西斯主义及其代表的一切. (**c**) (no passive 不用于被动语态) be in favour of sth; support sth 赞同、支持或主张某事物: *a party that stands for racial tolerance* 主张种族间互谅互让的政党. (**d**) (*infml* 口) tolerate 容忍; 忍受: *I won't stand for this insolence.* 我决不容忍这种傲慢无礼的行为.

stand 'in (for sb) take sb's place; deputize 代替某人; 代表: *My assistant will stand in for me while I'm away.* 我不在的时候我的助手将代表我处理事务. ○ *Another man stands in for the big star in the dangerous scenes.* 拍摄危险的场景时, 这位大明星有个替身.

stand 'out (from/against sth) be easily seen; be noticeable 突出; 显眼: *bright lettering that stands out well from/against a dark background* 由深色地衬托出很醒目的字. **stand 'out (from sb/sth)** be much better than sb/sth 远远超过某人[某事物]: *Her work stands out from the rest as easily the best.* 她的工作成绩远比其他人都好. **stand 'out (against sth)** continue to resist 坚持抵抗: *We managed to stand out against all attempts to close the company down.* 我们竭力顶住了要关闭公司的一切作法. **stand out for sth** (*infml* 口) delay reaching an agreement in order to get what one wants 拖延而暂不达成协议以期达到某目的: *The nurses have been offered an extra 5%, but they're standing out for a 7% pay rise.* 当局答应给护士增加5%的工资, 但她们坚持要得到7%的增幅.

stand over sb supervise or watch sb closely 严密监督或监视某人: *Don't stand over me while I am cooking.* 我做饭的时候别盯着我. ○ *I hate to have my boss standing over me.* 我不喜欢上司监督我.

stand (sb) 'to (order soldiers to) take up positions against an attack (命令士兵)进入阵地备战.

stand sb up (*infml* 口) fail to keep an appointment with sb 未如约与某人见面: *First she agreed to come out with me, then she stood me up.* 她先是同意跟我出去, 后来又爽约了. **stand up for sb/sth** speak, work, etc in favour of sb/sth; support sb/sth 为某人[某事物]说话、工作等; 支持某人[某事物]: *Always stand up for your friends.* 要永远维护朋友的利益. ○ *You must stand up for your rights.* 你一定要维护自己的权利. **stand 'up (to sth)** withstand (a test, etc) 经得起(考验等): *Your argument just won't stand up (to close scrutiny).* 你的论点经不起(仔细)推敲. **stand up to sb** resist sb 对抗某人: *It was brave of her to stand up to those bullies.* 她挺身反抗那些恃强欺弱的人, 真勇敢. **stand up to sth** (of materials, products, etc) remain in good condition in spite of (hard wear, etc) (指材料、产品等)经得起(磨损等): *Will this car stand up to winter conditions here?* 这汽车经得起这儿冬天的气候条件吗? ○ *This cloth is designed to stand up to a lot of wear and tear.* 这种布料十分耐用.

□ **'stand-by** *n* (*pl* **-bys**) **1** person or thing available as a substitute or in an emergency 后备人员; 备用的事物: *Aspirin is a good stand-by for headaches.* 阿司匹林是必备的头痛良药. ○ [attrib 作定语] *a stand-by ticket*, ie a cheaper type of airline ticket available when not all the tickets for a flight have been sold 剩余机票(因未事先售出而价廉). **2** (idm 习语) **on 'stand-by** in a state of readiness 待命状态: *The troops are on 24-hour stand-by*, ie ready to move within 24 hours of receiving the order. 部队待命 24 小时(接到命令后 24 小时内可行动).

'stand-in *n* person who acts as a deputy for or in place of sb else, esp one who takes the part of an actor in dangerous scenes 替代者; (尤指演员做危险动作的)替身.

ˌstand-off 'half (also **'fly-half**) one of the half-backs in Rugby football (英式橄榄球的)外侧前卫.

ˌstand-'offish *adj* cold and distant in behaviour; reserved; aloof 冷漠的; 冷淡的; 矜持的. **stand-offishly** *adv*. **stand-offishness** *n* [U].

'stand-up *adj* [attrib 作定语] **1** (of a meal) eaten while standing (指饭)站着吃的. **2** (of a comedian) giving a performance which consists of standing in front of an audience and telling a series of jokes (指喜剧演员)说单口相声的: *a stand-up comic* 单口相声演员. **3** (of a fight, disagreement, etc) direct and violent (指打斗、争吵等)直接而激烈的: *I had a stand-up row with my boss today.* 今天我跟上司大吵了一顿.

stand·ard /'stændəd; 'stændərd/ *n* **1** thing used as a test or measure for weights, lengths, quality, purity, etc 标准; 水准; 规格; 规范: *the standard of height required for recruits to the police force* 加入警察队伍的身高标准 ○ *an international standard of weight* 国际重量标准 ○ *the monetary standard*, ie the proportions of fine metal and alloy in gold and silver coins (金银币的)法定成分 ○ *People were very poor then, by today's standards*, ie compared with people today. 以今天的标准而言, 那时候的人很穷. **2** (often *pl* 常作复数) required, expected or accepted level of quality (要求的或认可的)水平, 水准: *a restaurant with a low standard of hygiene* 卫生水准低的餐馆 ○ *a high moral standard* 很高的道德水准 ○ *set low standards of behaviour* 定下很低的行为标准 ○ *conform to the standards of society*, ie live and behave in a way that is acceptable to others in society 符合社会的规范. **3** (**a**) average quality 平均质量: *The standard of her work is high.* 她的工作质量很高. (**b**) specified level of proficiency 熟练程度; 业务水平: *His work does not reach the standard required.* 他的工作成绩达不到要求.

4 (**a**) distinctive ceremonial flag, esp one to which loyalty is given (礼仪性的)旗, 旗帜(尤指效忠的对象): *the royal standard* 王旗. (**b**) carved figure, image, etc fixed to a pole and carried (esp formerly) by an army going into battle 军队(尤指旧时)作战时用的标竿(顶端有雕像等): *a Roman standard* 罗马军队的标竿. **5** upright pole or stand, esp one used as a support 直立的柱子或台座; (尤指)支柱, 基座. **6** tree or shrub that has been grafted on an upright stem (contrasted with a bush or climbing plant) 嫁接于直干上的树或无主茎灌木(与灌木丛或攀缘植物相对而言): [attrib 作定语] *standard roses* 嫁接在直干上的玫瑰. **7** (idm 习语) **be up to/below 'standard** be equal to/not so good as what is normal, required, etc 达到[未达到]标准: *Their work is not up to standard.* 他们的工作成绩不够标准.

▷ **stand·ard** *adj* [esp attrib 尤作定语] **1** serving as, used as or conforming to a standard(1) 标准的; 符合标准的: *standard sizes of paper, units of weight, etc* 纸的标准尺寸、标准重量单位. **2** average, normal or usual; not special or unusual 普通的; 正常的; 一般的: *the standard model of a car*, ie not the de luxe model, etc 普通型的汽车(非豪华型的) ○ *This procedure is standard.* 这一手续是正常的. **3** of generally recognized and accepted authority or merit 公认为权威的或优秀的: *This is the standard textbook on the subject.* 这是这一科的权威性课本. **4** (of spelling, pronunciation, grammar, etc) widely accepted as the usual form (指拼法、读音、语法等)规范的: *standard English* 规范的英语.

□ **'standard-bearer** *n* (**a**) person who carries a standard(4) 旗手; 掌旗者. (**b**) (*fig* 比喻) prominent leader in a cause, esp a political one 领导人; 先行者; (尤指政治上的)旗手: *a standard-bearer for women's rights* 争取妇女权利的旗手.

'standard lamp (*US* **'floor lamp**) household lamp on a tall support, with its base on the floor 落地灯.

,standard of 'living level of material comfort and wealth enjoyed by a person or group 生活水平: *They have/enjoy a high standard of living.* 他们生活水平很高. ○ *The standard of living in our country is lower than in yours.* 我国的生活水平低于贵国.

'standard time time officially adopted for a country or part of it 标准时间.

stand·ard·ize, -ise /'stændədaɪz; 'stændɚd,aɪz/ *v* [Tn] make (sth) conform to a fixed standard, shape, quality, type, etc 使(某事物)标准化或合乎规格: *an attempt to standardize spelling* 统一拼字法的设想 ○ *Car parts are usually standardized.* 汽车部件一般都是统一规格的.

▷ **stand·ard·iza·tion, -isation** /stændədaɪ'zeɪʃn; *US* -dɪ'z-; ,stændɚdə'zeʃən/ *n* [U] action or process of standardizing; making regular 标准化: *the problem of the standardization of the use of hyphens in compounds* 复合词中连字号使用法的规范化问题.

stand·ing /'stændɪŋ; 'stændɪŋ/ *n* [U] **1** (esp social) position or reputation; status; rank (尤指社会上的)地位, 名声, 身分, 等级: *a woman of some standing in the community* 在那个群体中颇有地位的女子 ○ *a scientist of good/high standing*, ie respected, eminent 有名望的科学家. **2** length of time that sth has existed; duration 持续时间: *a debt, dispute, friendship of long standing* 多时的欠债、纠纷、友谊.

▷ **stand·ing** *adj* [attrib 作定语] **1** (**a**) remaining in force or use; permanent and established 常备的; 永久的; 确立的: *a standing army* 常备军 ○ *a standing committee*, ie a permanent one that meets regularly 常务委员会. (**b**) continuing to be effective or valid 长期有效的: *We have a standing invitation to visit them when we're in the area.* 他们邀请我们将来到那里时去他们家做客. ○ *a standing joke*, ie sth that regularly causes amusement 永不乏味的笑料. **2** (*esp sport* 尤用于体育) performed without a run; done from a standing position 没有助跑的; 站着进行的: *a standing start/jump* 立定起跑[起跳]. **3** upright 直立的; 竖直的: *standing corn*, ie not yet cut 地里长着的谷物.

□ **,standing 'order** (**a**) (also **,banker's 'order**) customer's instruction to a bank to pay a certain amount at regular intervals (eg rent, mortgage repayments) (客户委托银行定期付款的)长期委托(如交租金、抵押物分期付款). (**b**) regular order that remains valid and does not have to be repeated 长期有效的订单: *a standing order for milk, newspapers, etc* 牛奶、报纸等的长期订单.

,standing o'vation enthusiastic expression of approval by people standing up from their seats to clap 起立鼓掌: *The singer got a ten-minute standing ovation.* 观众起立向那位歌手鼓掌达十分钟.

'standing-room *n* [U] space for people to stand in, esp in a theatre, sports ground, etc 站立的位置(尤指剧场、运动场等中的): *There was standing-room only left in the concert hall.* 音乐厅内只剩下站位了.

stand-pipe /'stændpaɪp; 'stænd,paɪp/ *n* vertical pipe connected to a main water supply and used to provide water outside or at a distance from buildings 竖管(向建筑物外供水用的).

stand·point /'stændpɔɪnt; 'stænd,pɔɪnt/ *n* position from which things are seen and opinions are formed; point of view 立场; 立脚点; 看问题的角度: *from the standpoint of the customer* 从顾客的角度来说.

stand·still /'stændstɪl; 'stænd,stɪl/ *n* [sing] halt; stop 停顿; 中止: *be at/come to/bring sth to a standstill* 处于停顿状态[使某事物陷入停顿状态] ○ *Work is grinding to a standstill.* 工作逐渐陷入停顿. ○ *Traffic in the city is at a complete standstill.* 城里的交通完全瘫痪了. ○ [attrib 作定语] *a standstill agreement*, ie one that agrees to no change, eg in rates of pay or hours of work 固定的协议(如对工资或工作时间不作变动的).

stank *pt* of STINK.

stanza /'stænzə; 'stænzə/ *n* group of (esp rhyming) lines forming a unit in some types of poem; verse of poetry (诗歌的)节, 段(尤指押韵的): *the second stanza* 诗的第二节.

staple[1] /'steɪpl; 'stepl̩/ *n* **1** small thin piece of bent wire that is driven into sheets of paper, etc and flattened to fasten them together 订书钉. **2** U-shaped piece of metal with pointed ends that is hammered into wood, etc to hold something (eg an electrical wire) in place U形钉(如固定电线用的).

▷ **staple** *v* [Tn] attach or secure (sth) with a staple or staples 用订书钉或U形钉钉住或固定(某物). **stapler** /'steɪplə(r); 'steplɚ/ *n* small hand-operated instrument for fastening papers, etc together with staples (小型手动的)订书机.

staple[2] /'steɪpl; 'stepl̩/ *adj* [attrib 作定语] main or principal; standard 主要的; 基本的; 标准的: *the staple product of a country* 一个国家的主要产品 ○ *Rice is the staple diet in many Asian countries.* 稻米是亚洲许多国家的主食. ○ *She seems to be the staple topic of conversation at the moment.* 看来她是此时的热门话题.

▷ **staple** *n* (often *pl* 常作复数) **1** main product that a country or district trades in (某国家或地区买卖的)主要产品: *Cotton is one of Egypt's staples.* 棉花是埃及的主要贸易项目之一. **2** main or principal item or element (esp of a diet) 主要成分; 主要内容; (尤指)主食: *Bread, potatoes and other staples continue to rise in price.* 面包、土豆及其他主食的价格继续上涨. ○ *The weather forms the staple of their conversation.* 天气状况是他们的主要话题.

star /stɑ:(r); stɑr/ *n* **1** [C] any one of the distant bodies appearing as a point of light in the sky at night 星: *a fixed star*, ie one which is not a planet 恒星 ○ *There are no stars out* (ie No stars can be seen) *tonight.* 今晚天上没有星星. **2** [C] (*astronomy* 天) any large ball in outer space that is made up of gases and gives out light, such as the sun 恒星. **3** [C] (**a**) figure, object, decoration, etc with radiating points, suggesting a star by its shape; asterisk (*) 星形图案; 星状物; 星号(即*). (**b**) mark of this shape used to indicate a category of excellence (表示质量等级的)星形符号: *This restaurant gets three stars in the guidebook.* 这家餐馆在旅游指南中标有三颗星. ○ [attrib 作定语] *a five-star hotel* 五星级旅馆. (**c**) metal badge in the shape of a star, worn on certain uniforms to indicate rank (表示职衔的)星章: *a sheriff's star* 行政司法长官的星章. **4** [C] famous or brilliant singer, performer, sportsman, etc 明星; 健将: *a tennis star* 网球明星 ○ *a film star* 电影明星 ○ *the stars of stage and screen* 舞台及影视明星 ○ *I can remember who directed the film but not who the stars* (ie leading performers) *were.* 我记得那部片子的导演, 但是谁主演的就忘了. ○ [attrib 作定语] *He's got the star role in the* *new film.* 他将主演这部新片子. ○ *an all-star cast*, ie one in which the leading players are all stars 全部为明星的阵容. **5** [C] (in astrology) planet or heavenly body believed to influence a person's life, luck, personality, etc (星象学中的)命星: *born under a lucky star*, ie successful and happy 生来福星高照. **6 stars** [pl] horoscope 星象: *What do my stars say?* 我的星象怎么样? ○ *It's written in the stars.* 这是命中注定的. **7** (idm 习语) **reach for the stars** ⇨ REACH. **see 'stars** (*infml* 口) have a feeling of seeing flashes of light, esp as a result of being hit on the head 眼冒金星(尤指因头部被击所致). **thank one's lucky stars** ⇨ THANK.

▷ **star** *v* (**-rr-**) **1** [Tn usu passive 通常用于被动语态] mark or decorate (sth) with, or as with, a star or stars, eg an asterisk to direct attention to sth on a list, etc 为(某物)标上星号; 以星形图案或星状物装饰(某物): *The starred dishes on the menu are suitable for vegetarians.* 菜单上标有星号的菜最宜食素者选用. **2 (a)** [I, Ipr] **~ (in sth)** be a star(4) (in a play, film, etc) (在戏剧、电影等中)担任主角, 主演: *taken many starring roles* 多次担任主角 ○ *She is to star in a new film.* 她将主演一部新影片. **(b)** [Tn, Tn·pr] **~ sb (in sth)** present sb as a star(4); feature sb 使某人担任主角; 由某人主演: *My favourite film stars Marilyn Monroe.* 我最喜欢的电影是玛丽莲·梦露主演的. ○ *The director wanted to star Michael Caine in his new film.* 这位导演想让迈克尔·凯恩主演他的新片子.

star·dom /'stɑ:dəm; 'stɑrdəm/ *n* [U] status of being a famous actor, performer, etc 明星的身分或地位: *He is being groomed* (ie prepared and trained) *for stardom.* 他正在接受培植, 以求他日成为明星.

star·less *adj* with no stars to be seen 无星光的: *a starless sky/night* 没有星星的天空[夜晚].

star·let /'stɑ:lɪt; 'stɑrlɪt/ *n* (*sometimes derog* 有时作贬义) young actress who hopes to become a film star but is not yet very well known 尚未如愿成名的年轻女演员; 准明星.

starry /'stɑ:rɪ; 'stɑrɪ/ *adj* (**-ier, -iest**) **(a)** lighted by stars 星光照耀的: *a starry night* 星光闪闪的夜晚. **(b)** shining like stars (像星一般)闪闪发光的: *starry eyes* 闪闪溜溜的眼睛. ˌ**starry-'eyed** *adj* (*infml often derog* 口, 常作贬义) romantically enthusiastic but impractical 热情而不切实际的: *He's completely starry-eyed about his new girl-friend.* 他对这个新的女朋友充满了美好的幻想. ○ *She's got some starry-eyed notion about reforming society.* 她对社会改革有些异想天开的想法.

□ **'star-dust** *n* [U] (imaginary twinkling dust-like substance causing a) dreamy, romantic or magic feeling 梦幻感; 浪漫的情感; 奇异的感觉; (想像中的可产生这些感觉的)虚无缥缈的物质.

'starfish *n* (*pl* unchanged 复数不变) flattish star-shaped sea animal with five arms 海星.

'star-gazer *n* (*infml often joc* 口, 常作戏谑语) person who studies the stars as an astronomer or astrologer 天文学家; 星象学家. **'star-gazing** *n* [U].

'starlight *n* [U] light from the stars 星光: *walk home by starlight* 借着星光走回家.

'starlit *adj* lighted by the stars 星光照耀的: *a starlit scene* 星光照耀的景色.

the ˌStars and 'Stripes the national flag of the US 星条旗(美国国旗).

'star sign (*infml* 口) any one of the 12 signs of the zodiac (黄道的)宫, 星宫: *What's your star sign?* 你是属什么星座的?

'star-studded *adj* featuring a lot of famous performers 明星荟萃的: *a star-studded cast* 明星云集的阵容.

ˌ**star 'turn** main item in an entertainment or a performance 主要节目: *The star turn in our show tonight will be a group of Chinese acrobats.* 我们今天晚上节目中最精彩的是中国杂技表演.

star·board /'stɑ:bəd; 'stɑrˌbord/ *n* [U] side of a ship or aircraft that is on the right when one is facing forward (船或飞行器的)右舷: *alter course to starboard* 转向右方航行 ○ [attrib 作定语] *the starboard side of a ship* 船的右侧. Cf 参看 PORT[3].

starch /stɑ:tʃ; stɑrtʃ/ *n* [U] **1 (a)** white tasteless carbohydrate food substance found in potatoes, flour, rice, etc 淀粉. **(b)** food containing this 含淀粉的食物: *You eat too much starch.* 你吃的含淀粉的食物太多了. **2** this substance prepared in powder or other forms and used for stiffening cotton clothes, etc 粉浆: *Spray starch on the shirt collars before ironing them.* 熨衬衫领要先喷些粉浆再熨.

▷ **starch** *v* [Tn] stiffen (clothes, etc) with starch 浆(衣服等): *starched white uniforms* 浆过的白制服.

starchy *adj* (**-ier, -iest**) **1 (a)** of or like starch (似)淀粉的. **(b)** containing a lot of starch 含大量淀粉的: *starchy food* 淀粉含量高的食物. **2** (*infml derog* 口, 贬) (too) formal, stiff or conventional in manner 刻板的; 拘谨的: *He's always been rather starchy.* 他一向非常刻板.

stare /steə(r); stɛr/ *v* **1** [I, Ipr, Ip] **~ (at sb/sth)** look (at sb/sth) with the eyes wide open in a fixed gaze (in astonishment, wonder, fear, etc) (对某人[某物])瞪着眼睛凝视, 盯着看: *It's rude to stare.* 盯着人看是没有礼貌的. ○ *They all stared in/with amazement.* 他们都惊讶得瞪大了眼睛. ○ *Do you like being stared at?* 你愿意人家盯着你看吗? ○ *She was staring into the distance/into space.* 她凝视着远方. ○ *He was staring out over the fields.* 他目不转睛地看着外面的田野. **2** [I, Ipr, Ip] **~ (at sb/sth)** (of the eyes) be wide open with a fixed gaze (指眼睛)睁大注视: *He gazed at the scene with staring eyes.* 他瞪大眼睛注视着这场面. ⇨Usage at LOOK[1] 用法见 LOOK[1]. **3** [Tn·pr] **~ sb into sth** bring or force sb into a specified condition by staring 瞪着某人使其做出某种反应: *She stared him into silence.* 她把他盯得不吭声了. **4** (idm 习语) **be staring sb in the 'face** be directly in front of sb; be obvious, easy or clear 就在某人眼前; 十分明显、容易或清楚: *The book I was looking for was staring me in the face.* 我找的书其实就在我面前. ○ *Defeat was staring them in the face*, ie seemed certain. 他们眼看着就要失败了. ○ *The answer to his problem was staring him in the face.* 他那个问题的答案是明摆着的. **make sb 'stare** surprise or astonish sb 使某人惊愕. **stark raving/staring mad** ⇨ STARK. **5** (phr v) **stare sb down/out** stare at sb until he feels forced to lower his eyes or turn away 逼视某人直至他不敢对视下去; 以目光镇慑某人: *The two children were having a competition to see who could stare the other out.* 两个孩子在较量, 看谁能把对方瞪得受不了.

▷ **stare** *n* long fixed gaze; staring look 凝视; 注视; 瞪; 盯: *give sb a rude stare* 不礼貌地瞪某人一眼 ○ *We received a number of curious stares from passers-by.* 过路人向我们投来好奇的目光. ○ *with a vacant stare*, ie suggesting an empty mind 茫然凝视着 ○ *with a glassy stare*, ie suggesting indifference 带着漠不关心的眼神.

stark /stɑ:k; stɑrk/ *adj* (**-er, -est**) **1 (a)** desolate and bare; grim; cheerless 荒凉的; 光秃秃的; 空落落的; 阴郁的: *stark prison conditions* 监狱中一无所有的状况 ○ *The landscape was grey and stark.* 景色灰暗荒凉. **(b)** [usu attrib 通常作定语] plain and unadorned 朴实的; 无装饰的: *the stark facts* 毫无遮掩的事实. **2** clearly obvious to the eye or the mind 显而易见的; 明摆着的; 鲜明的: *in stark contrast* 成鲜明对比. **3** [attrib 作定语] complete; utter; downright 完全的; 十足的: *stark madness* 彻底的疯狂.

▷ **stark** *adv* **1** completely; entirely 完全地; 十足地: *stark naked/crazy/mad* 赤裸裸的[荒唐之极的/彻底疯狂的]. **2** (idm 习语) ˌ**stark raving/staring 'mad** completely mad 完全疯的.

starkers /'stɑ:kəz; 'stɑrkɚz/ *adj* [pred 作表语] (*Brit infml esp joc* 口, 尤作戏谑语) completely naked 赤身裸体: *We saw him running down the road starkers.* 我们看见他一丝不挂地沿着街跑.

starkly *adv*: *It soon became starkly evident that...* 不久, 情况就完全明朗了, 原来... ○ *The black rocks stood out starkly against the sky.* 那些黑色的岩石在天空衬托下十分显眼.

stark·ness *n* [U]: *The starkness of their living conditions shocked him.* 他们的生活条件一无所有, 他感到十分震惊.

star·ling /'stɑ:lɪŋ; 'stɑrlɪŋ/ *n* type of small noisy bird with glossy black and brown-spotted feathers 椋鸟; 欧椋鸟. ⇨illus at App 1 见附录1插图, page iv.

starry ⇨ STAR.

start[1] /stɑ:t; stɑrt/ *n* **1 (a)** [C] beginning of a journey, an activity, a plan, a race, etc; process or act of starting 开始; 起始; 起程; 出发; 开端; 起始点: *make an early start (on a journey)* 早早动身 ○ *from start to finish* 自始至终

S

○ *We won't finish the job today but we'll have made a start.* 这工作我们今天是做不完的，但可以开个头. ○ *I've written one page of my essay: it's not much but it's a start.* 我的论文写了一页，这虽然不多，但算是开了个头了. ○ *He knew from the start the idea was hopeless.* 一开始他就知道这主意行不通. (**b**) **the start** [sing] place where a race begins 起跑线: *runners lined up at the start* 在起跑线上各就各位的运动员 ○ (*fig* 比喻) *We're only at the start in our house-hunting.* 我们找房子的事才刚刚开始. **2** [C] opportunity for, or help in, starting 开始的时机; 起推动作用的外力: *give sb a fresh start* 给某人一个重新开始的机会 ○ *The money gave him just the start he needed.* 这笔钱正是他起步所需要的. **3** [U, sing] (amount of) advantage gained or allowed in starting; advantageous position 起始时的领先(程度); 起始优势; 优势地位: *The smaller boys were given a start of 10 seconds in the race.* 在赛跑时让年龄小的男生提早了10秒钟起跑. ○ *They didn't give me much/any start.* 他们没给我什么[任何]优先权. ○ *He got a good start in business.* 他在生意上起步时占了很大的优势. **4** [C usu sing 通常作单数] sudden quick movement of surprise, fear, etc (因惊奇、恐惧等)震动: *He sat up/woke up with a start.* 他一惊，猛然坐了起来[猛然惊醒过来]. ○ *The news gave me quite a start,* ie surprised me. 这消息让我吃了一惊. **5** (idm 习语) **by/in fits and starts** ⇨ FIT[4]. **a false start** ⇨ FALSE. **for a 'start** (used in an argument 用于说理) as a first point 首先: *I'm not buying it — I can't afford it for a start.* 我不买——起码这个价钱我就付不起. **get off to a good, bad, etc 'start** start well, badly, etc 开始时很好、不好等: *Their marriage got off to rather a shaky start.* 他们的婚姻一开始就有些不稳固.

S **start**[2] /stɑːt; stɑrt/ *v* **1** [I, Ip] ~ **(out)** begin a journey; leave; set off 出发; 起程; 动身: *We started at six.* 我们是六点出发的. ○ *We must start (out) early.* 我们必须早些动身. **2** [It, Tn, Tg] begin (sth/to do sth) 开始(某事[做某事]); 着手: *It started to rain.* 下起雨来了. ○ *start work at 9 am* 上午9时开始工作 ○ *He's just started a new job.* 他刚开始一项新工作. ○ *start* (ie begin using) *a new tin of paint* 新开了一罐颜料 ○ *He started laughing.* 他笑了起来. **3** [Ipr, Tn, Tn·pr] ~ **(on) sth; ~ sb on sth** (cause sb to) make a beginning on sth; (cause sb to) begin doing (a job, an activity, a piece of work, etc) (使某人)开始进行某事; (使某人)着手做(某事): *start (on) one's journey home* 起程回家 ○ *Have you started (on)* (ie begun to read or write) *your next book yet?* 你开始看(或写)下一本书了吗? ○ *It's time to get/time we got started on* (ie began) *the washing up.* 我们该洗餐具了. ⇨Usage at BEGIN 用法见 BEGIN. **4** (**a**) [I] (of an engine, etc) begin running (指发动机等)启动: *The car won't start.* 这辆汽车发动不起来. (**b**) [Tn] cause (a machine, etc) to start working 使(机器等)开始运转: *I can't start the car.* 这辆汽车我发动不起来. **5** [Tn, Tn·pr, Cn·g] bring (sth) into existence; cause or enable (sb/sth) to begin or begin happening; establish; originate 产生; 使开始; 引发; 建立; 开创: *start a fire* 点火 ○ *He decided to start a newspaper.* 他决定创办一份报纸. ○ *His uncle started him in business,* ie helped him, eg by supplying money. 他的叔父帮他创办了事业(如资助他). ○ *The news started me thinking.* 我听了这消息便沉思起来. ○ *The smoke started her coughing.* 烟呛得她直咳嗽. **6** [I, Ip] ~ **(up)** (*fml* 文) (**a**) make a sudden movement or change of position (because of fear, surprise, pain, etc) (因恐惧、吃惊、痛苦等)突然移动、改换姿势或震动: *She started at the sound of my voice.* 她听到我的声音，吓了一跳. (**b**) jump (up) suddenly 猛然跳起: *He started (up) from his seat.* 他从座位上突然跳了起来. **7** [Ipr] (*fml* 文) move, rise or appear suddenly 突然活动、升起或出现: *Tears started to* (ie suddenly came into) *her eyes.* 她的眼睛里突然涌出了泪水. ○ *His eyes almost started out of his head,* ie suddenly opened wide (in surprise, etc). 他突然睁大了眼睛(因吃惊等). **8** [Tn] (*fml* 文) drive (an animal) from a hiding-place into the open 将(动物)从隐藏处赶到空旷处: *start a hare* 把野兔轰出来. **9** (idm 习语) **keep/start the ball rolling** ⇨ BALL[1]. **raise/start a hare** ⇨ HARE. **start a 'baby** (*infml* 口 *esp Brit*) become pregnant 怀孕. **start a 'family** begin to have children 开始生儿育女: *They want to start a family but can't afford it at the moment.* 他们想生个孩子，但暂时还养不起. **start (sth) from 'scratch** begin (sth) from the very beginning without advantage or preparation, esp when building or developing sth 从头开始进行(某事)(尤指建设或开发): *He lost all his money and had to start again completely from scratch.* 他损失了所有的钱，只好再从头做起. **start off on the right/wrong 'foot (with sb)** (*infml* 口) begin sth (esp a relationship) in the right/wrong way 开始做某事物时正确[不正确](尤指人际关系): *The new student started off on the wrong foot with the teacher by answering back rudely.* 那个新来的学生粗鲁地跟老师顶嘴，一开始就把关系搞僵了. **'start something** (*infml* 口) begin a fight, an argument, trouble, etc 惹事; 惹麻烦; 闯祸: *You shouldn't have spoken to him like that — you've really started something now.* 你不该那样跟他说话——这下你可闯了祸了. **to 'start with** (**a**) in the first place; as the first point 第一; 首先: *To start with we haven't enough money, and secondly we're too busy.* 一来我们的钱不够，二来我们没时间. (**b**) at the beginning; initially 起初; 开始时: *The club had only six members to start with.* 这个俱乐部最初只有六个成员. **10** (phr v) **start back** (**a**) begin to return 动身返回: *Isn't it time we started back? It's getting dark.* 咱们该回去了吧? 天快黑了. (**b**) jump or step back suddenly (in fear, shock, surprise, etc) (因恐惧、惊吓、吃惊等)往后一跳，突然向后退. **start for...** leave one place to go to another 动身前往: *What time do you start for work?* 你几点钟去上班? ○ *Let's start for home.* 咱们动身回家吧. **start in on sb (for sth)** (*infml* 口) begin to criticize, scold or shout at sb 对某人批评、责骂或嚷叫起来: *He started in on us again for poor work.* 因为我们干得不好，他又数落开了. **start in to do sth/on sth/on doing sth** (*infml* 口) begin to do sth 开始做某事: *We started in to discuss/on a discussion of/on discussing the idea.* 我们开始讨论那个意见. **start off** begin to move 开始活动: *The horse started off at a steady trot.* 那匹马快步稳健地跑了起来. **start (sb) off (on sth)** (cause sb to) begin working on, doing, saying, etc sth (使某人)开始(进行某事): *It's impossible to stop him talking once he starts off.* 他一打开话匣子就停不住了. ○ *What started him off on this crazy idea?* 他这个荒唐的主意是哪儿来的? ○ *Don't start her off on one of her boring stories.* 不要惹她说她那些乏味的故事. **start out (on sth); start out (to do sth)** (**a**) begin a journey 出发; 起程; 动身: *start out on a 20-mile walk* 开始走一段20英里长的路程 ○ *What time did you start out?* 你是几点钟动身的? (**b**) (*infml* 口) take the first steps; intend when starting 迈开最初的几步; 开始时打算; 本来想要: *start out in business* 开始做生意 ○ *start out on a new career* 在新的事业上起步 ○ *start out to write/with the intention of writing a novel* 动笔[想]写一部长篇小说. **start over** (*US*) begin again 重新开始: *She wasn't satisfied with our work and made us start (all) over.* 她不满意我们的工作，让我们(全部)返工. **start (sth) up** (cause sth to) begin or begin working, running, happening, etc (使某事物)启动，开始: *The engine started up suddenly.* 发动机突然发动起来了. ○ *start up a new bus company* 建立新的公共汽车公司 ○ *What started the argument up?* 这场争论是由什么引起的? ○ *We couldn't start the car up.* 那辆汽车我们发动不起来. **start (sb) up (in sth)** (cause sb to) begin a career, working life, etc (使某人)开始从事事业、工作等: *start up in business* 在事业上起步 ○ *He started his daughter up in the trade.* 他让女儿从事这一行业.

□ **'starting-block** *n* either one of two blocks fixed to the ground against which a runner braces his feet at the start of a race 起跑器.

'starting-gate *n* barrier that is raised at the start of a horse- or dog-race, allowing the animals to move off 起跑门(赛马或赛狗时用的).

'starting-point *n* place or point from which sth begins 起点: *We'll take this as the starting-point for our discussion.* 咱们就从这一点开始讨论吧.

'starting-post *n* place from which competitors start in a race 起跑点.

'starting-price *n* final odds just before the start of a horse-race, etc (赛马等的)临赛赔率.

starter /ˈstɑːtə(r); ˈstɑrtɚ/ *n* **1** person, horse, etc taking part in a race at the start 起跑的人、马或其他动物: *Of the five starters in the race only three finished.* 起跑时有五

个, 只有三个跑完全程. Cf 参看 NON-STARTER. **2** person who gives the signal for a race to start 起跑裁判员; 发令员: *waiting for the starter's gun to fire* 等待发令员的枪响. **3** (usu with an *adj* 通常与形容词连用) person who starts sth (esp in the way specified by the *adj*) 开始进行某事者(尤指以该形容词所描述的方式): *He's a fast starter.* 他做事起步很快. **4** device for starting a machine, esp an engine 启动装置(尤指发动机的). **5** (*infml* 口 *esp Brit*) (*US* also **appetizer**) first course of a meal (esp one with more than two courses) 第一道菜(尤指其后尚有至少两道菜): *What would you like as a starter?* 您第一道菜想来点什么? **6** (idm 习语) **for ˈstarters** (*infml* 口) first of all; to start with 首先; 作为开头. **under ˌstarter's ˈorders** (of horses, athletes, etc ready to start a race) waiting for the order or signal to start (指参赛的马、运动员等)等待起跑的口令或信号.

startle /ˈstɑːtl; ˋstɑrtḷ/ *v* [Tn] give a sudden shock or surprise to (a person or an animal); cause to move or jump suddenly (from surprise) 使(人或动物)惊吓或吓一跳: *You startled me — I didn't hear you come in.* 你吓了我一跳——我没听见你进来. ○ *I was startled to hear his news/by his news.* 我听到他的消息大吃一惊. ○ *The sudden noise in the bushes startled her horse.* 灌木丛中突如其来的响声把她的马吓惊了. ○ *He had a startled look on his face.* 他一脸吃惊的神情.

▷ **start·ling** /ˈstɑːtlɪŋ; ˋstɑrtlɪŋ/ *adj* very surprising; astonishing; remarkable 令人震惊的; 惊人的: *a startling result* 惊人的结果 ○ *What startling news!* 这消息多令人震惊啊! **start·lingly** *adv*: *startlingly beautiful* 漂亮得出奇.

starve /stɑːv; stɑrv/ *v* **1** [I, Ipr, Tn, Tn·pr] (cause a person or an animal to) suffer severely or die from hunger (使人或动物)挨饿, 饿死: *Thousands of cattle are starving.* 成千上万的牛正在挨饿. ○ *starve to death* 饿死 ○ (*infml* 口) *She's starving herself to try to lose weight.* 她正在用节食的办法减轻体重. **2** [Ipr, Tn·pr usu passive 通常用于被动语态] **~ for sth**; **~ sb of sth** (cause sb to) suffer or long for sth greatly needed or wanted; deprive sb of sth (使某人)得不到某事物而受苦或渴望获得某事物; 缺乏: *children starving for/starved of affection* 渴望受人疼爱的孩子 ○ (*fig* 比喻) *Industry is being starved of technical expertise.* 工业界技术力量匮乏. **3** [I] (*infml* 口) (used only in the continuous tenses 仅用于进行时态) feel very hungry 感觉很饿: *What's for dinner? I'm starving!* 晚饭吃什么? 我饿极了! **4** (phr v) **starve sb into sth/doing sth** force sb to do sth by not allowing him to get food 使某人挨饿以迫其做某事: *starved into surrender/surrendering* 饿得只好投降. **starve sb out (of sth)** force sb out of a hiding-place, etc by stopping supplies of food 将某人饿得从隐藏处出来: *It took 8 days to starve them out (of the building).* 用了8天时间才把他们饿得(从那座建筑物里)出来了.

▷ **star·va·tion** /stɑːˈveɪʃn; stɑrˋveʃən/ *n* [U] suffering or death caused by lack of food 挨饿; 饿死: *die of starvation* 饿死 ○ [attrib 作定语] *starvation wages*, ie too low to buy enough food 不够维持基本生活的工资 ○ *a starvation diet*, ie barely enough food to keep one alive 仅够存活的日常饮食.

stash /stæʃ; stæʃ/ *v* [Tn, Tn·pr, Tn·p] **~ sth (away)** (*infml* 口) store sth safely and secretly; hide sth 隐藏某物; 将某物藏起来: *He's got his life savings stashed (away) in an old suitcase.* 他把一辈子的积蓄保藏在一口旧箱子里.

▷ **stash** *n* (*infml* 口 *esp US*) **1** thing that is stored secretly 隐藏的东西. **2** place where sth is hidden; hiding-place 隐藏处: *a secret stash of stolen jewels* 隐藏偷来的珠宝的地方.

state[1] /steɪt; stet/ *n* **1** [C] condition in which a person or thing is (in circumstances, appearance, mind, health, etc); quality of circumstances, characteristics, etc 状态; 状况; 情况; 情形: *The house was in a dirty state.* 那房子很脏. ○ *These buildings are in a bad state of repair*, ie need to be repaired. 这些建筑物亟待修葺. ○ *a confused state of mind* 缭乱的心绪 ○ *a poor state of health* 健康欠佳 ○ *in a state of undress*, ie naked 赤身露体 ○ *not in a fit state to drive* 不适宜开车的身心状态 ○ *a state of emergency*, eg declared by a government because of war, natural disaster, etc 紧急状态(如政府宣布的) ○ *She was in a terrible state* (ie very upset, agitated, etc) *when we arrived.* 我们抵达时, 她情绪很不好. **2** (also **State**) [C] country considered as an organized political community controlled by one government; territory occupied by this 国; 国家; 领土: *the State of Israel* 以色列国 ○ *modern European states* 现代的欧洲国家. ⇨Usage at COUNTRY 用法见COUNTRY. **3** (also **State**) [C] organized political community forming part of a country that is a federation or republic (联邦或共和国的)州, 邦: *How many States are there in the United States of America?* 美国有多少州? ○ *Which state where you born in?* 你是在哪个州出生的? Cf 参看 COUNTY, PROVINCE 1. **4** (esp 尤作 **the State**) [U] civil government of a country 政府; 国家: *matters/affairs of state* 国家大事[事务] ○ *Church and State* 教会和政府 ○ *railways run by the state/state-run railways* 国营铁路 ○ *Many believe the State should provide schools, homes and hospitals for everyone.* 许多人认为国家应该为全民提供学校教育、住房以及医疗服务. **5** [U] ceremonial formality connected with high levels of government; pomp 国家级的礼仪; 盛观: *The Queen was in her robes of state.* 女王穿着御礼袍. ○ *The President was driven in state through the streets.* 总统在盛大的仪式中乘车从街上通过. **6 the States** [pl] (*infml* 口) the United States of America 美国: *I've never been to the States.* 我从来没去过美国. **7** (idm 习语) **in/into a ˈstate** (*infml* 口) (**a**) in/into an excited or agitated state of mind 处于[陷入]激动或焦躁的情绪中: *She got herself into a state about the exams.* 她对这次考试心里很慌. ○ *He was in a real state when I last saw him.* 我上次见到他时, 他很激动. (**b**) dirty, neglected, untidy, etc (according to the context) 肮脏的, 没有妥善照管的, 凌乱的(视上下文而定): *What a state this place is in!* 这地方真乱哪! **in a state of ˈnature** (*fml or joc* 文或谑) completely naked 赤身露体; 一丝不挂. **lie in state** ⇨ LIE[2]. **a state of afˈfairs** circumstances or conditions; situation 情况; 局势: *What a shocking state of affairs!* 局势真惊人哪! **the state of ˈplay** (**a**) score (esp in cricket) 分数(尤指板球运动中的). (**b**) how opposite sides in a dispute stand in relation to one another 争论中各方的对立情况: *What is the latest state of play in the disarmament talks?* 裁军谈判的最新情况怎么样?

▷ **state** (also **State**) *adj* [attrib 作定语] **1** of, for or concerned with the State(4) 政府的; 国家的; 关于国家的: *state ˈrailways* 国营铁路 ○ *ˈstate schools*, ie free schools run by public authorities 国立学校 ○ *state ˈsecrets* 国家机密 ○ *State Socialism advocates state control of industry.* 国家社会主义主张工业应由国家管理. **2** of, for or involving ceremony; used or done on ceremonial occasions 礼仪的; 礼仪上的; 礼节性的: *a state occasion* 国家的礼仪场合 ○ *the state apartments* 国家举行仪式用的厅堂 ○ *a state visit*, eg by a monarch to another country 国事访问 ○ *the state opening of Parliament* 议会的隆重开幕式.

state·less *adj* (of a person) not recognized as a citizen of any country; having no citizenship (指人)无国籍的, 无公民身分的. **state·less·ness** *n* [U].

□ **ˈstatecraft** *n* [U] skill in managing State affairs; statesmanship 治国才能; 政治才智.

the ˈState Department the US government department of foreign affairs (美国的)国务院.

ˌState Enrolled ˈNurse (*abbr* 缩写 **SEN**) (*Brit*) (title of a) person who has trained as a nurse and passed examinations that allow her or him to practise most areas of nursing (lower in rank than a State Registered Nurse) 国家登记护士(低于国家注册护士).

ˌstate of the ˈart current state of development of a subject, technique, etc (学科、技术等的)当前发展状况: [attrib 作定语] *a state-of-the-art computer program*, ie the most advanced one available 最先进的计算机程序.

ˌState Registered ˈNurse (*abbr* 缩写 **SRN**) (*Brit*) (title of a) person who has trained fully as a nurse and passed examinations that allow her or him to practise all areas of nursing 国家注册护士.

ˈstateroom *n* **1** apartment used by royalty, important government members, etc 王室或政府要人的宅邸. **2** private cabin or sleeping compartment on a ship (轮船的)特等客舱.

ˌState's ˈevidence (idm 习语) **ˌturn State's ˈevidence** (*US*) = TURN KING'S/QUEEN'S EVIDENCE (EVIDENCE).

ˈ**stateside** *adj, adv* (*US infml* 口) of, in or towards the US 美国的; 在美国; 向美国.

ˈ**statewide** *adj, adv* (*US*) throughout a state(2, 3) 全国(的).

state[2] /steɪt; stet/ *v* **1** [Tn, Tf, Tw] express (sth) in spoken or written words, esp carefully, fully and clearly 陈述或说明(某事)(尤指仔细、详尽而明确地): *state one's views* 说明自己的见解 ○ *state the obvious*, ie obvious facts, etc 陈述明显的事实 ○ *He stated positively that he had never seen the man.* 他肯定地说他从未见过那个男子. ○ *The document clearly states what is being planned.* 这份文件把计划内容交代得清清楚楚. **2** [Tn usu passive 通常用于被动语态] arrange, fix, or announce (sth) in advance; specify 预先安排、定下或宣布(某事); 规定; 确定: *at stated times/intervals* 在规定的时间[间隔时间] ○ *You must work the hours stated.* 你必须按规定的时间工作.

▷ **state·ment** *n* **1** [U] (*fml* 文) stating sth or expressing sth in words 陈述; 叙述; 说明: *Clearness of statement is more important than beauty of language.* 表述清晰比用辞优美更重要. **2** [C] thing that is stated 表达的内容: *The president made a statement of his aims.* 总统提出了他的目标. ○ (*fig* 比喻) *The artist regards his painting as a political statement.* 那个画家用作品表达自己的政治观点. **3** [C] formal account of facts, views, problems, etc; report 声明; 报告: *issue a statement* 发表声明 ○ *The police asked the man to make a statement*, ie a written account of facts concerning an alleged crime, used in court if legal action follows. 警方要那男子写一份供词. **4** [C] = BANK STATEMENT (BANK): *My bank sends me monthly statements.* 银行按月把结算单寄给我.

stately /ˈsteɪtlɪ; ˋstetlɪ/ *adj* (**-ier**, **-iest**) dignified; imposing; grand 威严的; 庄严的; 堂皇的; 宏伟的; 盛大的: *a stately old woman* 仪态高贵的老妇人 ○ *with stately grace* 庄重高雅地. ▷ **state·li·ness** *n* [U].

□ ˌ**stately** ˈ**home** (*Brit*) large and grand house, usu of historical interest, esp one that the public may visit 豪华宅第(通常指具有历史意义的, 尤指开放供人参观的).

states·man /ˈsteɪtsmən; ˋstetsmən/ *n* (*pl* **-men** /-mən; -mən/) (*fem* 阴性作 **states·woman** /-wʊmən; -ˌwʊmən/, *pl* **-women** /-wɪmɪn; -ˌwɪmɪn/) person who plays an important part in the management of State affairs, esp one who is skilled and fair; wise political leader 政治家(尤指贤明公正的).

▷ **states·man·like** *adj* having or showing the qualities and abilities of a wise statesman 有政治家的品质和才能的.

states·man·ship *n* [U] skill and wisdom in managing public affairs 政治才能; 治国之才.

static /ˈstætɪk; ˋstætɪk/ *adj* **1** not moving or changing; stationary 静止的; 稳定的; 静态的: *House prices, which have been static for several months, are now rising again.* 房价稳定了几个月, 现在又上涨了. ○ *static water*, eg in a tank, needing to be pumped 静止的水(如水箱中需要抽掉的) ○ *a rather static performance*, ie one in which there is little movement 动作较少的表演. **2** (*physics* 物) (of force) acting by weight without motion (指力)静止的, 静力的. Cf 参看 DYNAMIC 1.

▷ **static** *n* [U] **1** atmospheric conditions causing poor radio or television reception, marked by loud crackling noises; atmospherics 大气静电干扰; 天电: *There was too much static to hear their message clearly.* 天电干扰太大, 听不清他们的电讯. **2** (also ˌ**static elec**ˈ**tricity**) electricity that accumulates on or in an object which cannot conduct a current 静电: *Her hair was full of static.* 她的头发上静电很强.

stat·ics *n* [sing *v*] branch of physics that deals with bodies remaining at rest or with forces that balance one another 静力学.

sta·tion /ˈsteɪʃn; ˋsteʃən/ *n* **1** [C] place, building, etc where a service is organized and provided, or specialized (esp scientific) work is done (提供某种服务或从事科学研究等专业工作的)站, 所: *a po'lice, 'fire station* 派出所、消防站 ○ *a 'radar station* 雷达站 ○ *an agriˌcultural re'search station* 农业研究所 ○ *a nuclear 'power station* 核电站. **2** [C] company that broadcasts on radio or television; building from which this is done 电台; 电视台: *Which TV station is the programme on?* 这个节目在哪家电视台播放? ○ *a pirate radio station*, ie one using a frequency illegally 非法的广播电台. **3** [C] (**a**) place where trains stop on a railway line; the buildings (eg ticket office, waiting rooms) connected with this 火车站: *Which station are you going to?* 你要到哪个火车站? ○ [attrib 作定语] *the station platform, staff* 站台、火车站员工. (**b**) similar place where buses and coaches stop (公共汽车或长途汽车的)车站: *The bus leaves the bus station at 9.42 am.* 那公共汽车上午9时42分离站. **4** [C] (*dated or fml* 旧或文) social position; rank; status 社会地位; 等级; 身分: *people in all stations of life* 社会各阶层人士 ○ *He has ideas above his station.* 他的思想超越了自己的地位. **5** [C] (*Austral* 澳) (usu large) sheep or cattle ranch (通常指大的)牧羊场, 牧牛场. **6** [C, CGp] (people living in a) small military or naval base (陆军或海军)驻地, 驻地人员: *He's returning to his army station.* 他准备回驻地. **7** [U] position, or relative position, to be taken up or maintained by sb/sth 某人[某事物]应处的位置或相对位置; 岗位; 战位: *One of the warships was out of station*, ie not in its correct position relative to other ships. 有一艘军舰未在其编队位置. **8** (idm 习语) **panic stations** ⇨ PANIC.

▷ **sta·tion** *v* [esp passive 尤用于被动语态: Tn, Tn·pr] put (sb, oneself, an army, etc) at or in a certain place 置(某人、自己、部队等)于某处: *Their regiment is stationed in Cyprus.* 他们的团驻扎在塞浦路斯. ○ *The detective stationed himself* (ie hid) *among the bushes.* 那个侦探藏在灌木丛中.

□ ˈ**station-master** *n* person in charge of a railway station (铁路的)站长.

ˌ**Stations of the** ˈ**Cross** series of fourteen images or pictures telling the story of Christ's sufferings and death, at which prayers are said in certain Churches 苦路(十四幅耶稣受难像, 某些教会的教徒在这些圣像前作祈祷).

ˈ**station-wagon** *n* (*US*) = ESTATE CAR (ESTATE).

sta·tion·ary /ˈsteɪʃənrɪ; *US* -nerɪ; ˋsteʃənˌɛrɪ/ *adj* **1** (**a**) not moving 静止的: *remain stationary* 停着不动 ○ *collide with a stationary van* 撞上一辆停着的客货车. (**b**) that cannot be moved or is not intended to be moved 固定的; 不可移动的: *a stationary crane* 固定式起重机. Cf 参看 MOBILE 1. **2** not changing in condition or quantity 恒定的; 不变的; 无增减的.

sta·tioner /ˈsteɪʃnə(r); ˋsteʃənɚ/ *n* person who runs a shop that sells stationery 文具店店主: *Is there a good stationer's (shop) near here?* 附近有没有好的文具店?

▷ **sta·tion·ery** /ˈsteɪʃənrɪ; *US* -nerɪ; ˋsteʃənˌɛrɪ/ *n* [U] writing materials (eg paper, pens, envelopes, etc) 文具: [attrib 作定语] *a stationery cupboard*, eg in an office 文具柜.

stat·ist·ics /stəˈtɪstɪks; stəˋtɪstɪks/ *n* (**a**) [pl] collection of information shown in numbers (一组)数据, 统计数字, 统计资料: *Politicians love to use statistics to support their arguments.* 搞政治的喜欢用数据资料来印证自己的论点. ○ *Have you seen the latest statistics on crime?* 你看到最新的犯罪统计资料了吗? (**b**) [sing *v*] science of collecting, classifying and analysing such information 统计学: *She's studying statistics at university.* 她在大学学习统计学.

▷ **stat·istic** *n* item of information expressed in numbers 数据: *unearthed a fascinating statistic* 得到一个很可喜的数据.

stat·ist·ical /stəˈtɪstɪkl; stəˋtɪstɪkl/ *adj* of or shown by statistics 统计的; 统计学的; 以数据表示的: *statistical evidence* 以统计数字表明的证据. **stat·ist·ic·ally** /-klɪ; -klɪ/ *adv*: *It has been proved statistically that*... 有统计数字证明....

stat·isti·cian /ˌstætɪˈstɪʃn; ˌstætəˋstɪʃən/ *n* person who studies or works with statistics 统计学的研究者; 统计学家; 统计员.

statu·ary /ˈstætʃʊərɪ; *US* -ʊerɪ; ˋstætʃʊˌɛrɪ/ *n* [U] **1** statues 雕塑作品; 雕像; 塑像; 铸像: *a display of bronze statuary* 青铜雕塑作品展览. **2** art of making statues and sculptures 雕塑艺术.

statue /ˈstætʃuː; ˋstætʃu/ *n* figure of a person, an animal, etc in wood, stone, bronze, etc, usu life-size or larger 雕像, 塑像, 铸像(其大小通常等于或大于真人或实物): *erect a statue of the king on a horse* 树立一座国王骑着马的雕像.

▷ **sta·tu·esque** /ˌstætʃʊˈesk; ˌstætʃʊˋɛsk/ *adj* (*approv*

褒) (**a**) like a statue in size, dignity or stillness (在大小、端庄的神态或静止的状态方面)雕像般的, 塑像般的, 铸像般的. (**b**) (usu of a woman) tall, graceful and dignified (通常指女子)身材高大、仪态优雅端庄的: *her statuesque figure* 她那修长、优美的身材.

sta·tu·ette /ˌstætʃʊˈet; ˌstætʃʊˋɛt/ *n* small statue 小雕像; 小塑像; 小铸像: *A china statuette of a shepherdess stood on the table.* 桌上有一个牧羊女的小瓷像.

stat·ure /ˈstætʃə(r); ˋstætʃɚ/ *n* [U] **1** natural height of the body 身高: *short of stature* 身材矮小. **2** importance and reputation gained by ability or achievement (凭才能或成就而获得的)名望: *a scientist of international stature* 有国际声望的科学家.

sta·tus /ˈsteɪtəs; ˋstetəs/ *n* [U] **1** person's social, legal or professional position or rank in relation to others 地位; 身分; 职位: *Women have very little status in many countries.* 在许多国家, 妇女没有什么地位. ○ *What's your official status in the company?* 你在公司里的正式职位是什么? **2** high rank or social position 重要地位; 重要身分: *seek status and security* 追求社会地位和生活保障 ○ *He's very aware of his status.* 他很在意自己的重要身分.

□ ˈ**status symbol** possession that is thought to show sb's high social rank, wealth, etc 社会地位、身分、财富等的象征: *He only bought the yacht as a status symbol — he hates sailing.* 他买游艇只是为了显示身分 —— 其实他根本不喜欢玩游艇.

sta·tus quo /ˌsteɪtəs ˈkwəʊ; ˋstetəsˋkwo/ **the status quo** situation or state of affairs as it is now, or as it was before a recent change 现状; 原来的状况: *upset/restore/preserve the status quo* 打破现状[恢复原状/维持现状] ○ *conservatives who defend the status quo* 维护现状的保守派.

stat·ute /ˈstætʃuːt; ˋstætʃʊt/ *n* [C] **1** law passed by Parliament or a similar law-making body and written down formally 成文法; 法规; 法令: *decreed by statute* 按照法规限定的. **2** any of the rules of an institution 条例; 规则; 章程: *under the University's statutes* 根据该大学的章程.

▷ **stat·ut·ory** /ˈstætʃʊtrɪ; *US* -tɔːrɪ; ˋstætʃʊˌtorɪ/ *adj* [usu attrib 通常作定语] fixed, done or required by statute 法定的; 依法完成的; 法规要求的; 章程规定的: *one's statutory rights* 自己享有的法定权利 ○ *statutory control of prices and incomes* 物价与收入的法定管制. **stat·ut·or·ily** *adv*.

□ ˈ**statute-book** *n* collection of all the laws made by a government; book(s) in which these are recorded 成文法典; 法令全书; 法规汇编: *not on the statute book*, ie not included in statute law 成文法中没有规定的.

ˈ**statute law** all the statutes as a group 成文法. Cf 参看 CASE-LAW (CASE¹), COMMON LAW (COMMON¹).

staunch¹ /stɔːntʃ; stɔntʃ/ *adj* (**-er, -est**) firm, loyal and dependable in opinion and attitude 坚定而忠实可靠的: *a staunch Christian, Conservative, Republican, etc* 忠实的基督徒、保守党人、共和党人等 ○ *one of our staunchest allies* 我们最坚定的同盟者之一.

staunch² = STANCH.

stave¹ /steɪv; stev/ *n* **1** any of the curved pieces of wood forming the side of a barrel or tub 桶板, 桶材(用作木桶或木盆边的弧形木板). **2** (*music* 音) = STAFF 5.

stave² /steɪv; stev/ *v* (*pt, pp* **staved** or **stove** /stəʊv; stov/) (phr v) **stave sth in** break, smash, or make a hole in sth 打破、砸破或击穿某物; 在某物上凿孔: *The side of the boat was staved in by the collision.* 船侧撞穿了. ○ *The victim's skull had been stove in by a heavy instrument.* 遇害者的头颅是用重物击穿的. **stave sth off** (*pt, pp* **~d**) keep sth off or away; delay sth, esp temporarily 挡开或避开某事物; 延迟某事物(尤指暂时): *stave off disaster, danger, bankruptcy, the pangs of hunger* 避开灾难、躲过危险、防止破产、延迟饥饿的折磨.

stay¹ /steɪ; ste/ *v* **1** (**a**) [La, I, Ipr, Ip, It, In/pr] remain or continue in the same place (for a long or short time, permanently or temporarily, as specified by the context); not depart or change 停留; 留下; 住; 在某处呆一段时间: *stay (at) home*, ie not go out or to work 呆在家里 ○ *stay late at the office* 在办公室呆到很晚 ○ *I'm afraid I can't stay*, ie I must leave now. 很抱歉, 我得走了. ○ *stay in the house, in bed, in one's room, etc* 呆在房子里、床上、房间里等 ○ *stay in teaching, journalism, etc*, ie not change one's job 继续教书、从事新闻工作等 ○ *stay away from* (ie not go to) *school* 不上学 ○ *Stay on this road for two miles then turn left.* 沿这条路走两英里, 然后向左拐. ○ *Stay here until I come back.* 我回来之前你别走. ○ *We stayed to see what would happen.* 我们留下来看进一步的发展. ○ *I can only stay a few minutes.* 我只能呆上几分钟. ⇨ Usage at AND 用法见 AND. (**b**) [La, Ln] continue in a certain state 维持某状态: *stay awake* 不睡觉 ○ *stay single*, ie not marry 不结婚 ○ *He never stays sober for long.* 他不醉的时候不多. ○ *They stayed friends for years.* 他们的友谊维持了多年. **2** [I, Ipr, In/pr] remain or live somewhere temporarily, esp as a visitor or a guest 逗留, 暂住(尤指过访或作客时): *It's late — why don't you stay* (ie for the night)? 很晚了 —— 你就在这儿过夜好吗? ○ *stay in a hotel* 住在旅馆里 ○ *Why don't you come to stay with us next time you visit Durham?* 下次来达勒姆就住在我们这儿好吗? ○ *Jenny's staying in Dublin for a few days, but she now lives/is now living* (ie has her home) *in Belfast.* 珍妮目前在都柏林小住几日, 她的家是在贝尔法斯特. ○ *stay the night with sb*, ie sleep at sb's house for the night 在某人家过夜. **3** [Tn] (*fml* 文) stop, delay, postpone or check (sth) 停止, 延缓, 推迟, 控制(某事物): *stay* (ie delay) *punishment/judgement* 延缓惩罚[审判] ○ *stay the progress of a disease* 防止病情恶化 ○ *a little food to stay* (ie temporarily satisfy) *one's hunger* 暂且充饥的一点食物 ○ (*arch* 古) *stay one's hand*, ie refrain from doing sth 不去做某事. **4** [I] (*arch* 古) (usu imperative 通常用于祈使句) wait a moment; pause; stop 稍等; 稍停; 停下: *Stay! What is this I see?* 且慢! 这是什么? **5** (idm 习语) **be here to stay/have come to stay** (*infml* 口) be permanent and generally accepted 固定下来; 普遍认可; 成为风尚: *I hope that (the idea of) equality of opportunity for men and women has come to/is here to stay.* 我希望男女机会平等(的思想)能形成风气. **keep/stay/steer clear** ⇨ CLEAR². **stay the** ˈ**course** continue going to the end (of sth difficult, eg a race, a struggle) 坚持到底: *I don't think he's sufficiently dedicated to stay the course.* 我认为他不够坚定, 不会坚持到底的. **stay** ˈ**put** (*infml* 口) remain where one/it is or is placed 呆在原处; 留在原地; 固定不动: *The baby wouldn't stay put long enough for the photo to be taken.* 这孩子总动换, 拍不了照片. **6** (phr v) **stay away (from sb/sth)** keep a distance (from sb/sth); not interfere (with sb/sth) (与某人[某事物])保持距离; 不打扰(某人[某事物]): *Tell him to stay away from my sister!* 叫他离我妹妹远点儿!

stay behind remain at a place after others have left (esp to go home) (别人走后)在某处留下不走(尤指暂不回家): *They stayed behind after the party to help clear up.* 聚会结束之后, 他们留下来帮助收拾东西. ○ *The teacher told him to stay behind after class.* 老师要他下课后先别走. **stay down** (**a**) (of food) remain in the stomach (rather than be vomited) (指食物)留在胃里(不呕吐出来): *She's so ill that nothing will stay down, not even water.* 她病得很重, 吃什么都吐出来, 连喝水都吐. (**b**) remain in a lowered position 停留在较低的位置: *The switch on the kettle won't stay down.* 这个水壶上的开关按下时卡不住了.

stay for/to sth remain at a person's house for (a meal) 留在某人家(吃饭): *Won't you stay for/to supper?* 你吃了晚饭再走好吗?

stay in (**a**) not go outdoors 不出门; 呆在家里: *The doctor advised me to stay in for a few days.* 医生嘱我在家休息几天. (**b**) remain at school after others have left, esp as a punishment 课后留在学校(尤指作为惩罚).

stay on (**a**) remain in position on top of sth 留在某物上面: *My hat won't stay on properly.* 我这帽子总也戴不正. (**b**) remain alight, burning, running, etc 保持某种活动状态(亮着、烧着、运动着...): *The TV stays on all day at this place.* 这个地方的电视成天开着. **stay on (at...)** remain at (a place of study, employment, etc) after others have left (别人走后)留在(学习、工作等的地方): *He stayed on at university to do research.* 他留在大学里做研究工作.

stay out (**a**) remain out of the house or outdoors (esp after dark) 不回家, 呆在户外(尤指天黑后): *I don't like you staying out so late.* 我不喜欢你在外面呆到这么晚. (**b**) remain on strike 继续罢工: *The miners stayed out for* *a whole year.* 矿工罢工已整整一年了. **stay out of sth** remain at a point where one cannot be reached or affected by sb/sth 避开或躲开某人[某事物]: *His father told him to stay out of trouble.* 他父亲叫他避开是非之地.

stay up (**a**) remain awake; not go to bed 醒着; 不去睡: *She promised the children they could stay up for their favourite TV programme.* 她答应孩子们可以晚点儿睡, 看他们最喜爱的电视节目. (**b**) remain in a position where put, built, etc; not fall or sink or be removed 处于原位不动; 不倒; 不沉; 不被移走: *I'm surprised some of those cheap houses stay up at all.* 那些质量差的房子仍然原封未动, 我感到很惊奇. ○ *My trousers only stay up if I wear a belt.* 我这条裤子要是不系皮带就往下掉. ○ *The poster only stayed up a few hours, before it was stolen.* 那张海报贴上去没几个小时就让人给偷走了.

stay with sb (*infml* 口) continue to listen attentively to sb 继续留心地听某人说话: *Please stay with me a moment longer — I'm getting to the point of the story.* 请再听我往下说 —— 我这就说到关键内容了.

▷ **stay** *n* **1** period of staying; visit 停留; 逗留; 逗留时间: *an overnight stay in Karachi* 在卡拉奇过夜 ○ *a fortnight's stay with my uncle* 在叔叔家做客两星期. **2** (idm 习语) **a ˌstay of exeˈcution** (*esp law* 尤用于法律) (order permitting a) delay in the carrying out of a court judgement or a postponement of some (usu unpleasant) activity 缓期执行(的裁决); 推迟进行(的命令)(通常指延迟某项令人不快的活动): *They were due to start demolishing the old theatre today but there's been a last-minute stay of execution.* 原定今天把这座旧戏院拆掉, 但临时突然决定暂缓进行.

stayer *n* person or animal with endurance or stamina 有耐力的人或动物: *He's not a fast horse but he's certainly a stayer.* 这匹马跑得不快, 但很有耐力.

□ **ˈstay-at-home** *n* (*infml usu derog* 口, 通常作贬义) person who rarely leaves his home to go anywhere; unadventurous person 深居简出的人; 不爱闯荡的人.

ˈstaying-power *n* [U] ability to keep going; endurance; stamina 持久力; 耐力: *Long-distance runners need staying-power.* 长跑运动员耐力要强.

stay[2] /steɪ; ste/ *n* **1** [C] rope or wire supporting a mast, pole, etc (船桅、杆等的)支索. **2** [C] any prop or support 可倚靠的人或事物; 支撑物: (*fig* 比喻) *the stay of* (ie the person who helped him in) *his old age* 他晚年的倚靠. **3 stays** [pl] old-fashioned type of corset, stiffened with strips of bone or plastic 带撑条的旧式紧身内衣.

STD /ˌes tiː ˈdiː; ˌɛs ti ˈdi/ *abbr* 缩写 = (*Brit*) subscriber trunk dialling (by telephone) 用户直通长途电话: *The STD code for London is 071.* 伦敦的用户长途直通号码是 071.

stead /sted; stɛd/ *n* (idm 习语) **in sb's/sth's ˈstead** (*fml* 文) in sb's/sth's place; instead of sb/sth 代替某人[某事物]: *I can't attend the meeting but I'll send my assistant in my stead.* 这个会我来不了, 我让助手代我出席. **stand sb in good ˈstead** be useful or helpful to sb when needed 在需要时对某人有用或有帮助: *My anorak has stood me in good stead this winter.* 我这件皮猴儿今年冬天可帮了大忙了.

stead·fast /ˈstedfɑːst; *US* -fæst; ˈstɛdˌfæst/ *adj* **~ (in sth/to sb/sth)** (*fml usu approv* 文, 通常作褒义) firm and not changing or yielding; constant 坚定的; 不动摇的; 固定不动的: *a steadfast friend* 忠实的朋友 ○ *a steadfast gaze, refusal* 凝视、坚决的拒绝 ○ *steadfast in adversity* 在逆境中毫不动摇 ○ *be steadfast to one's principles* 坚持自己的原则. ▷ **stead·fastly** *adv.* **stead·fast·ness** *n* [U].

steady /ˈstedɪ; ˈstɛdɪ/ *adj* (**-ier**, **-iest**) **1** firmly fixed, supported or balanced; not shaking, rocking or likely to fall over 稳的; 平稳的; 牢固的; 不摇晃的: *hold the ladder steady* 把梯子扶稳 ○ *make a table steady*, eg by repairing a leg 使桌子不摇晃(如把一条桌腿儿修好) ○ *He's not very steady on his legs after his illness.* 他病愈后走路还不太稳. ○ *Such fine work requires a steady hand and a steady eye.* 做这样精细的工作, 手要稳、眼要准. ○ *She was trembling with excitement but her voice was steady.* 她激动得发抖, 但声音却很平稳. **2** done, happening, working, etc in an even and regular way; developing, etc gradually without interruptions 均匀而有规律的; 稳定的; 持续的; 不断的: *a steady wind* 匀速的风 ○ *a steady speed, flow, rate, pace, etc* 稳定的速度、流速、速率、步子等 ○ *steady progress, improvement, etc* 持续的进步、改善等. **3** regular in behaviour, habits, etc; sensible and dependable 稳重的; 理智而可靠的: *a steady young man* 稳重的年轻男子 ○ *a steady worker* 可靠的工作者. **4** constant; unchanging 固定的; 恒定的; 不变的; 坚定的: *a steady faith* 坚定的信仰 ○ *with a steady purpose* 目的始终如一 ○ *Have you got a steady boy-friend?* 你有关系固定的男朋友吗? ○ *The ship kept to a steady course.* 那艘船一直沿原航线航行. **5** (idm 习语) **steady (ˈon)!** (*infml* 口) (used as a warning 作提醒用) be careful; control yourself 当心; 注意; 镇定: *I say, steady on! You can't say things like that about someone you've never met.* 哎, 慢着! 你对素未谋面的人不能那样说人家.

▷ **stead·ily** /ˈstedɪlɪ; ˈstɛdəlɪ/ *adv*: *work steadily* 平稳地工作 ○ *Prices are rising steadily.* 物价正持续上涨. ○ *His health is getting steadily worse.* 他的健康逐渐恶化.

steadi·ness *n* [U].

steady *adv* (idm 习语) **go steady (with sb)** (*dated infml* 旧, 口) (of sb not engaged to marry) go out regularly with sb of the opposite sex; have a serious long-lasting relationship (指未订婚的人)与某异性朋友经常约会; (与某人)有固定的情侣关系: *Are Tony and Jane going steady?* 托尼跟简是正在谈恋爱吗?

steady *n* (*dated infml* 旧, 口) regular boy-friend or girl-friend 关系固定的男朋友或女朋友: *He's my steady.* 他是我的对象.

steady *v* (*pt, pp* **steadied**) [I, Tn] (cause sth to) become steady; keep steady (使某事物)稳固, 不摇晃, 保持平稳或稳定: *Prices are steadying.* 物价渐趋稳定. ○ *steady a boat* 使船保持平稳 ○ *He steadied himself by holding on to the rail*, eg on the deck of a rolling ship. 他抓住栏杆使自己站稳(如在颠簸的船甲板上).

steak /steɪk; stek/ *n* **1** [C, U] (thick slice of) meat (esp beef) or fish, cut for frying or grilling, etc 肉排; 鱼排; (尤指)牛排: *fillet/rump steak* (无骨)牛排[(臀部)肉排] ○ *two tuna steaks* 两片金枪鱼排 ○ [attrib 作定语] *a steak knife*, ie for cutting steak, etc when eating it 牛排餐刀. **2** [U] beef from the front of the animal, cut for stewing or braising (供焖或煨的)牛前部的肉.

□ **ˈsteak-house** *n* restaurant that specializes in serving meat steaks 肉排餐馆; (尤指)牛排餐馆.

steal /stiːl; stil/ *v* (*pt* **stole** /stəʊl; stol/, *pp* **stolen** /ˈstəʊlən; ˈstolən/) **1** [I, Ipr, Tn, Tn·pr] **~ (sth) (from sb/sth)** take (another person's property) secretly without permission or legal right; take (sth) dishonestly 偷(他人的财物); 窃取(某物): *It's wrong to steal.* 偷东西是不对的. ○ *He stole from the rich to give to the poor.* 他偷富人的东西去接济穷人. ○ *Someone has stolen my watch.* 有人把我的表偷走了. ○ *I have had my watch stolen.* 我的表让人偷走了. ○ *He stole a bun from the shop.* 他从店里偷了一个圆面包. ⇨Usage at ROB 用法见 ROB. **2** [Tn, Tn·pr] (*fml* 文) obtain (sth) quickly or stealthily, esp by a surprise or trick 快速地或偷偷地取得(某事物)(尤指出其不意或运用计策): *steal a few minutes' sleep* 偷闲睡上几分钟 ○ *steal a kiss from sb* 乘某人不备吻一下 ○ *steal a glance at sb in the mirror* 从镜中偷看某人一眼. **3** [Ipr, Ip] **~ in, out, away, etc** move in the specified direction secretly and quietly, or without being noticed 偷偷地移动: *He stole into the room.* 他潜入房间. ○ *A tear stole down her cheek.* 她脸上悄悄淌下了一滴眼泪. ○ *The morning light was stealing through the shutters.* 晨光悄悄穿过了百页窗. ⇨Usage at PROWL 用法见 PROWL. **4** (idm 习语) **steal a ˈmarch (on sb)** gain an advantage over sb by doing sth secretly or slyly, or by acting before he does 偷偷地抢在某人之前. **steal the ˈscene/ˈshow** attract the most attention and praise (esp unexpectedly) 抢风头(尤指出其不意): *Despite fine acting by several well-known stars it was a young newcomer who stole the show.* 尽管几位名角演出都很出色, 却未曾想竟让一名新秀抢尽风头. **steal sb's ˈthunder** spoil sb's attempt to impress by anticipating him, detracting from what he is saying, doing, etc 抢在某人之前或贬低某人的言行使之不受他人注意.

▷ **steal** *n* **1** (*US sl* 俚) instance of stealing; theft 偷; 盗窃. **2** (*infml* 口 *esp US*) good bargain; easy task 极便宜

的东西; 易做的事情: *'Ladies and gentlemen, it's a steal at only $50.'* '女士们、先生们, 这个只卖50美元, 太便宜啦.'

stealth /stelθ; stɛlθ/ *n* [U] acting or behaving in a quiet or secret way 悄悄的或秘密的行动: *Tracking wild animals requires great stealth.* 跟踪野生动物必须悄然无声. ○ *The burglars had entered the house by stealth.* 窃贼偷偷进了那座房子.

▷ **stealthy** *adj* (**-ier**, **-iest**) doing things, or done, with stealth 悄悄的; 偷偷的; 暗中进行的: *stealthy footsteps* 悄悄的脚步. **stealth·ily** /-ılı; -ılı/ *adv*. **stealthi·ness** *n* [U].

steam /sti:m; stim/ *n* [U] **1** (**a**) invisible gas into which water is changed by boiling 水蒸气; 蒸汽. (**b**) power obtained using this gas under pressure 加压蒸汽产生的动力: *a building heated by steam* 有暖气的建筑物 ○ [attrib 作定语] *a steam brake, whistle, winch, etc*, ie worked by steam 蒸汽制动器、汽笛、汽动绞车 ○ *steam cleaning*, ie done by steam 蒸汽洗涤. **2** visible mist that forms when steam condenses in the air 水汽: *steam coming out of a boiling kettle* 水烧开后从壶里冒出来的水汽 ○ *The laundry was full of steam.* 洗衣房里水汽腾腾. **3** (idm 习语) **full speed/steam ahead** ⇨ FULL. **blow off/let off 'steam** (*infml* 口) release surplus energy or emotion from being restrained 宣泄被压抑的过剩精力或情感: *The children were out in the playground letting off steam.* 那些孩子在操场上玩, 宣泄过剩的精力. **get up 'steam** (**a**) (of a vehicle or an engine) slowly increase speed (指汽车或发动机)慢慢加速. (**b**) (*infml* 口) (of a person) collect one's energy; gradually become excited or angry (指人)打起精神, 渐渐激动或愤怒. **ˌrun out of 'steam** (*infml* 口) become exhausted 失去动力; 筋疲力尽: *There is a danger of the housing programme running out of steam*, ie losing its impetus. 住宅兴建计划有半途而废之虞. **ˌunder one's own 'steam** without help from others; unaided 靠自己的力量.

▷ **steam** *v* **1** [I, Ip] give out steam or vapour 放出蒸汽; 冒水汽: *steaming hot coffee* 热气腾腾的咖啡 ○ *The kettle was steaming (away) on the stove.* 水壶在炉子上冒着热气. **2** [Tn, Cn·a] cook, soften or clean (sth), by the use of steam 用蒸汽处理(某物); 蒸; 蒸汽软化; 蒸汽洗涤: *steamed pudding* 蒸的布丁 ○ *Steam the fish for 10 minutes.* 把鱼蒸10分钟. ○ *steam open an envelope*, ie use steam to soften the glue on the flap 用蒸汽把信封口嘘开. ⇨Usage at COOK 用法见COOK. **3** (idm 习语) **be/get (all) steamed 'up (about/over sth)** (*infml* 口) become very enthusiastic, angry, excited, etc 变得很热心、愤怒、激动等: *Calm down — it's nothing to get steamed up about!* 冷静一点——没什么可激动的! **4** (phr v) **steam across, along, away, off, etc** move in the specified direction using the power of steam 藉蒸汽动力沿某方向移动: *a boat steaming up the Nile* 向尼罗河上游行驶的汽船 ○ *The train steamed into/out of the station.* 火车驶进[出]了车站. ○ *We were steaming along at 50 mph.* 我们靠蒸汽动力以每小时50英里的速度向前行驶. **steam sth off (sth)** remove (one piece of paper) from another using steam to melt the glue sticking them together 用蒸汽嘘(纸)(使之与粘贴物分开): *steam stamps off envelopes* 用蒸汽嘘邮票以便从信封上揭下. **steam (sth) up** (cause sth to) become covered with condensed steam (使某物)蒙上水汽: *The car windows steamed up.* 汽车窗户上有一层水汽.

steamer *n* **1** steamship 汽船; 汽艇. **2** metal container with small holes in it, in which food is cooked using steam 蒸锅.

steamy *adj* (**-ier**, **-iest**) **1** of, like or full of steam (似)蒸汽的; 充满水汽的: *a steamy jungle* 雾气弥漫的丛林. **2** (*infml* 口) erotic and passionate 色情而狂放的: *steamy love scenes* 狂放的性爱场面. **steami·ness** *n* [U].

□ **'steamboat** *n* boat powered by steam, used (esp formerly) on rivers and along coasts (沿河流或近岸海中行驶的)汽船, 汽艇(尤指旧时用的).

'steam-engine *n* locomotive or engine driven by steam 蒸汽机车; 蒸汽机.

'steam iron electric iron that can send out jets of steam from its flat surface 蒸汽电熨斗.

ˌsteam 'radio (*infml joc* 口, 谑) radio broadcasting considered as very old-fashioned by comparison with television 老掉牙的电台广播(与电视相比而言).

'steamroller *n* heavy slow-moving engine with a large roller, used in road-making 蒸汽压路机. — *v* **1** [Tn] crush or defeat (sb/sth) as with a steamroller (像用蒸汽压路机一般)压倒(某人), 碾平或碾碎(某事物): *steamrollering all opposition* 压倒一切反对力量. **2** (phr v) **steamroller sb into sth/doing sth** force sb into (a situation or course of action) 迫使某人就范.

'steamship *n* ship driven by steam 汽船; 汽艇.

'steam-shovel *n* (*esp US*) machine for excavating, originally worked by steam 汽铲; (汽动)挖掘机.

'steam train train pulled by a steam-engine 蒸汽机火车: [attrib 作定语] *a steam train enthusiast* 蒸汽机火车爱好者.

steed /sti:d; stid/ *n* (*arch or joc* 古或谑) horse 马: *my trusty steed* 我那匹得力的马.

steel /sti:l; stil/ *n* **1** [U] (**a**) strong hard alloy of iron and carbon, much used for making vehicles, tools, knives, machinery, etc 钢: *It's made of steel.* 这是钢制的. ○ [attrib 作定语] *steel knives* 钢刀. (**b**) industry that produces steel; production of steel 炼钢工业; 钢铁生产: [attrib 作定语] *the steel strike* 炼钢业的罢工 ○ *deserted steel mills* 废弃的炼钢厂 ○ *the steel areas of the north* 北方的钢铁工业区. **2** [C] thin roughened rod of steel, used for sharpening knives, etc 钢棒(用以磨刀等). **3** [C] (*arch* 古) weapon, esp a sword (contrasted with a gun, etc) 钢制武器, (尤指)刀, 剑(与枪炮等相对): *an enemy worthy of one's steel*, ie one who will fight well 值得与之较量的劲敌. **4** (idm 习语) **of steel** of great strength or hardness 钢铁般的; 强有力的; 坚硬的: *a man of steel* 钢铁般坚强的男子 ○ *nerves of steel* 巨大的勇气 ○ *a grip of steel* 强劲的紧握.

▷ **steel** *v* [Tn, Tn·pr, Cn·t] **~ oneself/sth (for/against sth)** make (oneself, one's heart, etc) hard or strong in preparation for sth 使(自己、自己的心理承受力等)坚强起来去应付某事: *I'm afraid I have bad news for you, so steel yourself.* 很抱歉, 有坏消息要告诉你, 你得坚强些. ○ *She had to steel her heart against pity.* 她须硬起心肠以顶住怜悯之情.

steely *adj* (**-ier**, **-iest**) like steel in colour, hardness, brightness or strength (在颜色、硬度、光泽或强度方面)似钢的: *a steely look* 冷冰冰的神情 ○ *with steely determination* 以钢铁般的决心. **steeli·ness** *n* [U].

□ **ˌsteel 'band** West Indian band of musicians with instruments made from empty oil drums (西印度群岛的)钢鼓乐队(用空油桶做的乐器演奏).

ˌsteel-'plated *adj* covered with steel plates; armoured 复以钢板的; 装甲的.

ˌsteel 'wool mass of fine steel shavings used for cleaning, scouring and polishing 钢丝绒(用以擦洗或磨光物件的). Cf 参看 WIRE WOOL (WIRE).

'steel worker person who works in the steel industry 炼钢工人.

'steelworks *n* (*pl* unchanged 复数不变) [sing or pl *v*] factory where steel is made 炼钢厂.

steel·yard /'sti:ljɑ:d *or, rarely,* 罕读作 'stıljəd; 'stilˌjɑrd, 'stıljəd/ *n* type of weighing-machine with two arms of unequal lengths, the longer one marked with a scale along which a weight is moved 杆秤.

steep[1] /sti:p; stip/ *adj* (**-er**, **-est**) **1** (of a slope, stairs, etc) rising or falling sharply, not gradually (指斜坡、楼梯等)陡的, 陡峭的, 陡直的: *a steep path, descent, hill, climb, gradient* 陡峭的小路、坡路、小山、攀登路、斜面 ○ *a steep roof* 斜的屋顶 ○ *I never cycle up that hill — it's too steep.* 我从来不骑车上那座山——太陡了. **2** (*infml* 口) (of a price or demand) too much; unreasonable; excessive (指价格或要求)过高的, 不合理的, 过分的: *She wants you to feed her cats for four weeks — that's a bit steep!* 她竟然要你替她喂猫喂四个星期——这可有点过分了! ○ *I wouldn't pay £300 for his old car — it's too steep.* 我才不花300英镑买他那辆旧汽车呢——这个价钱太高了.

▷ **steepen** /'sti:pən; 'stipən/ *v* [I, Tn] (cause sth to) become steep[1](1) or steeper (使某物)变陡, 变得更陡峭: *The path steepens as you climb the hillside.* 沿着山坡往上爬时, 那条小径越来越陡.

steep·ish *adj* quite steep 较陡的; 有点陡峭的.

steeply *adv*.

steep·ness *n* [U].

steep[2] /stiːp; stip/ *v* **1** [esp passive 尤用于被动语态: Tn, Tn·pr] **~ sth (in sth)** soak sth thoroughly in liquid (esp in order to soften, clean or flavour it) 浸泡某物(尤指为使之软、清洁或增味): *fruit steeped in brandy* 泡在白兰地中的水果 ○ *steep onions in vinegar*, ie to pickle them 把洋葱腌泡在醋里. **2** (phr v) **steep sb/oneself/sth in sth** (esp passive 尤用于被动语态) pervade or fill sth thoroughly with sth; give oneself/sb a thorough knowledge of sth 使某事物弥漫或充满某事物; 使自己[某人]精通某事物: *steeped in ignorance/prejudice* 极为无知[充满偏见] ○ *a city steeped in history* 历史悠久的城市 ○ *He steeped himself in the literature of ancient Greece and Rome.* 他精通古希腊和古罗马文学.

steeple /ˈstiːpl; ˋstipl/ *n* tall tower with a spire on top, rising above the roof of a church (教堂的)尖塔. ⇨illus at App 1 见附录1插图, page viii.

□ **ˈsteeplejack** *n* person who climbs steeples, tall chimneys, etc to repair or paint them 高空作业修建工(爬上尖塔、高烟囱等进行修缮或粉刷者).

steeple·chase /ˈstiːpltʃeɪs; ˋstipl,tʃes/ *n* **1** horse-race across country or on a course with various hedges and ditches to be jumped 越野赛马; 障碍赛马. Cf 参看 FLAT RACING (FLAT[2]). **2** race for athletes, across country or on a running track, with obstacles such as fences, hedges and ditches to be jumped 越野赛跑; 障碍赛跑.

▷ **steeple·chaser** *n* person or horse competing in steeplechases 参加越野(或障碍)赛跑的人; 越野(或障碍)赛马的参赛马.

steer[1] /stɪə(r); stɪr/ *v* **1** (**a**) [I, Ipr, Tn, Tn·pr] direct or control the course of (a boat, car, etc) 操纵(船、汽车等)的行驶方向; 驾驶: *You steer and I'll push.* 你来掌方向盘, 我来推. ○ *steer by the stars* 参照星星的方位来驾驶 ○ *steer a boat into (the) harbour* 把船驶进港 ○ (*fig* 比喻) *He managed to steer the discussion away from the subject of money.* 他设法把讨论内容从钱的话题上岔开了. ○ (*fig* 比喻) *She steered me towards a table in the corner.* 她要我到角落里的一张桌子那儿. (**b**) [I] (of a boat, car, etc) be able to be steered (指船、汽车等)可驾驶: *a car that steers well on corners* 转弯灵活的汽车. **2** [Tn] follow or keep to (a course) 向(某方向)行驶: *keep steering north/a northerly course* 向北行驶. **3** (idm 习语) **keep/stay/steer clear** ⇨ CLEAR[2].

▷ **steerer** /ˈstɪərə(r); ˋstɪrɚ/ *n* person who steers 驾驶者; 掌舵的人; 舵手.

steer·ing /ˈstɪərɪŋ; ˋstɪrɪŋ/ *n* [U] equipment or mechanism for steering a car, boat, etc (汽车、船等的)转向装置, 操舵装置: *power steering* 动力转向装置 ○ *There is something wrong with the steering.* 转向装置出毛病了.

steers·man /-zmən; -zmən/ *n* (*pl* **-men** /-mən; -mən/) person who steers a boat, ship, etc 掌舵的人; 舵手. Cf 参看 HELMSMAN (HELM).

□ **ˈsteering-column** *n* column-shaped part of a car, etc on which the steering-wheel is fitted 转向柱.

ˈsteering committee committee that decides the order of certain business activities and guides their general course 程序委员会.

ˈsteering lock mechanism in a vehicle's steering-column that allows the steering-wheel to be locked in a fixed position to prevent anyone stealing the vehicle 防盗方向盘锁.

ˈsteering-wheel *n* wheel for controlling the steering in a car, ship, etc 方向盘; 舵轮. ⇨illus at App 1 见附录1插图, page xii.

steer[2] /stɪə(r); stɪr/ *n* young (usu castrated) male animal of the ox family, raised for its meat (肉用的)小公牛(通常指阉过的). Cf 参看 BULL[1] 1, BULLOCK, OX 1.

steer·age /ˈstɪərɪdʒ; ˋstɪrɪdʒ/ *n* [U] **1** action of steering and its effects on a ship, vehicle, etc 驾驶; 操舵; 舵效. **2** section of a ship nearest the rudder, where accommodation was formerly provided for passengers travelling at the lowest fares (旧时)(客轮的)统舱(近舵处, 票价最廉): *travel steerage* 乘坐统舱 ○ [attrib 作定语] *steerage class* 统舱级.

□ **ˈsteerage-way** *n* [U] (*nautical* 海) forward movement needed by a ship, boat, etc to allow it to be steered or controlled properly 舵效航速.

stel·lar /ˈstelə(r); ˋstɛlɚ/ *adj* [esp attrib 尤作定语] (*fml* 文) of a star or stars 星的; 星球的: *stellar light* 星光. Cf 参看 INTERSTELLAR.

stem[1] /stem; stɛm/ *n* **1** (**a**) main central part of a plant, bush or tree coming up from the roots, from which the leaves or flowers grow (花草的)茎; (树木的)干. ⇨illus at FUNGUS 见 FUNGUS 插图. (**b**) part of a leaf, flower or fruit that joins it to the main stalk or twig (叶片、花朵或果实的)梗, 柄. ⇨illus at App 1 见附录1插图, page ii. **2** thin stem-shaped part of sth, esp the narrow part of a wineglass between the base and the bowl or the part of a tobacco pipe between the mouthpiece and the bowl 茎状部分; (尤指)高脚酒杯的颈, 烟斗柄. **3** (*grammar*) root or main part of a noun or verb from which other parts or words are made, eg by altering the endings 词干. **4** (*fml* 文) main line of descent of a family 血统. **5** (idm 习语) **from ˌstem to ˈstern** from the front to the back (esp of a ship) 从头到尾; (尤指)从船首到船尾: *The liner has been refitted from stem to stern.* 那艘班轮已经全面整修.

▷ **stem** *v* (**-mm-**) (phr v) **stem from sth** arise from sth; have sth as its origin or cause 来自或起源于某事物; 由某事物造成: *discontent stemming from low pay and poor working conditions* 因工资低、工作条件差而产生的不满情绪.

-ˈstemmed (forming compound *adjs* 用以构成复合形容词) having a stem or stems of the specified type 具有某种茎、干、梗或柄的: *ˌlong-/ˌshort-/ˌthick-stemmed ˈglasses* ○ *a ˌstraight-stemmed ˈflower.*

stem[2] /stem; stɛm/ *v* (**-mm-**) [Tn] restrain or stop (the flow of liquid, etc) 遏制, 阻止(液体流动等): *bandage a cut to stem the bleeding* 用绷带包扎伤口止血 ○ *stem the flow of water from a burst pipe* 止住破裂的水管中流出的水 ○ (*fig* 比喻) *The government are unable to stem the tide of popular indignation.* 政府压制不住公愤.

Sten /sten; stɛn/ *n* (also **ˈSten gun**) type of small machine-gun, usu fired from the hip 司登枪(冲锋枪).

stench /stentʃ; stɛntʃ/ *n* (usu *sing* 通常作单数) very unpleasant smell 恶臭; 臭气: *the stench of rotting meat* 腐肉的恶臭.

sten·cil /ˈstensl; ˋstɛnsl/ *n* [C] **1** thin sheet of metal, cardboard, etc with a design or letters cut out of it, used for putting this design, etc onto a surface when ink or paint is applied to it (镂有图案或文字供印刷用的)模版, 型版; 蜡版. **2** design, lettering, etc produced in this way 用模版印出的图案或文字: *decorate a wall with flower stencils* 用模版印花图案装饰墙壁. **3** waxed sheet from which a stencil is made by a typewriter 打字蜡纸: *cut a stencil* 在蜡纸上打字.

▷ **sten·cil** *v* (**-ll-**; *US* also **-l-**) [I, Tn, Tn·pr] **~ (A on B/B with A)** produce (a design, lettering, etc) by using a stencil; mark (a surface) with a stencil 用模版或蜡纸印刷(图案、文字等); 在(某物表面)印上模版图案或文字: *Do you know how to stencil?* 你会用模版印图吗? ○ *stencil a pattern on cloth/stencil cloth with a pattern* 把图案印在布上[给布印上图案].

steno /ˈstenəʊ; ˋstɛno/ *n* (*infml* 口 *esp US*) = STENOGRAPHER (STENOGRAPHY).

ste·no·graphy /stəˈnɒgrəfɪ; stəˋnɑgrəfɪ/ *n* [U] (*esp US*) = SHORTHAND.

▷ **ste·no·grapher** /-fə(r); -fɚ/ (*esp US*) (*Brit* **ˌshorthand-ˈtypist**) *n* person who can write shorthand or is employed to do this 会速记的人; 速记员.

sten·tor·ian /stenˈtɔːrɪən; stɛnˋtorɪən/ *adj* (*fml* 文) (of a voice) loud and powerful (指嗓音)洪亮的, 响亮的: *stentorian tones* 响亮的音调.

step[1] /step; stɛp/ *v* (**-pp-**) [Ipr, Ip] **1** lift and put down the foot, or one foot after the other, as in walking 踩; 踏; 跨步; (连续)迈步: *step on sb's foot* 踩着某人的脚 ○ *step in a puddle* 踏进水坑 ○ *step forwards/backwards* 向前迈步[向后退步]. **2** move a short distance in this way in the direction specified 向某方向走一小段距离: *step across a stream* 蹚过小溪 ○ *step into a boat* 登船 ○ *step onto/off the platform* 走上[下]讲台 ○ *'Kindly step this way* (ie come here, follow me), *please.'* '请往这边走.' ○ (*fig* 比喻) *step into a job*, ie get one without effort 轻易得到一份工作. **3** (idm 习语) **step into the ˈbreach** help to organize sth by filling the place of sb who is absent (某人不在时)代理某事. **step into sb's ˈshoes** take control of a responsible task or job from another person 接替某人. **ˈstep on it** (*US* also **step on the**

ˈ**gas**) (*infml* 口) go faster; increase speed (esp in a vehicle); hurry 快走; 加速(尤指开车时); 踩油门; 赶快: *You'll be late if you don't step on it.* 你要是不加快速度就要迟到了. ˌ**step out of** ˈ**line** behave or act differently from what is expected 出格; 越轨: *The teacher warned them that she would punish anyone who stepped out of line.* 老师警告他们说谁要不守规矩就罚谁.

4 (phr v) **step aside** allow another person to take one's place, position, job, etc 让开; 让位: *He stepped aside to let me pass.* 他站到一边让我过去. ○ *It's time for me to step aside and let a younger person become chairman.* 我该把主席的位子让给年轻的人了.

step down resign (usu from an important position, job, etc) to allow another person to take one's place 辞职(以让位给他人, 通常指重要职位、工作等).

step forward present oneself (eg to offer help or information); come forward 站出来(如提供帮助或信息); 自告奋勇: *The organizing committee is appealing for volunteers to step forward.* 组织委员会号召志愿者自告奋勇.

step in intervene (to help or hinder sb/sth) 干预(以帮助或阻止某人[某事物]); 介入: *If the police had not stepped in when they did there would have been serious violence.* 当时若警方迟一些干预就会发生严重的暴力事件了.

step out walk faster; move more quickly 加快脚步; 加速.

step up come forward 站出来; 自告奋勇. **step sth up** increase sth; improve sth 增加某事物; 促进某事物: *step up production* 增加生产 ○ *step up* (ie put more effort into) *the campaign for nuclear disarmament* 加强争取核裁军的运动.

□ ˈ**stepping-stone** *n* (**a**) flat stone (usu one of several) providing a place to step on when crossing a stream, river, etc on foot (过河等用的)踏脚石. (**b**) (*fig* 比喻) means or stage of progress towards achieving or attaining sth 借以达到目标的手段或阶段: *a first stepping-stone on the path to success* 通向成功的第一步.

step[2] /step; stɛp/ *n* **1** [C] act of stepping once (in walking, running, dancing, etc) (走、跑、跳舞等的)步, 脚步: *walk with slow steps* 慢步行走 ○ *The water was deeper at every step.* 每走一步水就更深一些. ○ *He took a step towards the door.* 他向门口迈了一步. **2** [C] distance covered by this 一步的距离: *retrace one's steps*, ie go back 原路折回 ○ *move a step closer to the fire* 向那火走近一步 ○ *It's only a few steps farther.* 只有几步远. ○ *He walked with us every step of the way.* 他跟我们走了一路. **3** [sing] short distance 短距离: *It's only a step to the park from here.* 公园离这儿很近. **4** (also ˈ**footstep**) [C] (**a**) sound of sb stepping or walking 脚步声; 走路的声音: *We heard steps outside.* 我们听到外面有脚步声. (**b**) way of stepping or walking (as seen or heard) 步态; 走路的姿势或声音: *with a light cheerful step* 以轻快的脚步 ○ *That's Lucy — I recognize her step.* 那是露西——我听得出她的脚步声. **5** [C] particular way of moving the feet in dancing (forming a pattern) 舞步: *I don't know the steps for this dance.* 我不会这种舞步. **6** [C] any one of a series of things done in some process or course of action or development (某过程中的)一步: *a step in the right direction* 方向正确的一步 ○ *This has been a great step forward*, ie Much progress has been made. 这是向前迈出的很大的一步. ○ *What's the next step?* ie What must we do next? 下一步该怎么办? **7** [C] level surface on which the foot is placed in going from one level to another 台阶; 梯级: *a flight of steps* 一段台阶 ○ *Mind the steps when you go down into the cellar.* 你走到地下室去时要当心台阶. ○ *They had to cut steps in the ice as they climbed.* 他们往上爬时得在冰上凿出踏脚处. ○ *The child was sitting on the top step.* 那孩子坐在最上一级台阶上. ⇨illus at STAIR 见STAIR插图. ⇨Usage at STAIR 用法见STAIR. **8 steps** [pl] = STEP-LADDER: *a pair of steps* 一副折梯 ○ *We need the steps to get into the loft.* 我们上阁楼要用折梯. **9** [C] rank, grade or stage in a series or on a scale; stage of promotion 级别; 等级; 阶段; 晋升的一级: *Our marketing methods put us several steps ahead of our main rivals.* 我们的销售方法得力, 超过主要对手几个等级. ○ *When do you get your next step up?* ie When will you be promoted? 你何时晋级? **10** (idm 习语) **break** ˈ**step** get out of step (when dancing or marching) 乱了步伐(跳舞或齐步走时). **change step** ⇨ CHANGE[1]. **a false step** ⇨ FALSE. **in/out of step (with sb/sth)** (**a**) (in marching or dancing) putting/not putting one's correct foot on the ground at the same time as others (齐步走或跳舞时)与他人步子一致[不一致]. (**b**) conforming/not conforming to what others are doing or thinking 与他人谐调[不谐调]: *He's out of step with modern ideas.* 他同现代思想不合拍. **keep step (with sb)** walk or (esp) march in step (with sb) (与某人)步伐一致地走(尤指齐步走). **mind/watch one's** ˈ**step** (**a**) walk carefully 小心地行走. (**b**) behave or act cautiously 谨慎地做事或行动: *You'll be in trouble if you don't watch your step.* 你要是不谨慎从事就要倒霉了. ˌ**step by** ˈ**step** proceeding steadily from one stage to the next; gradually 一步一步地; 逐步地; 逐渐地: [attrib 作定语] *a* ˌ*step-by-step in*ˈ*struction manual* 逐项解释的说明书. **take steps to do sth** take action in order to achieve a desired result 采取步骤以达到某目的: *The government is taking steps to control the rising crime rate.* 政府正采取措施, 控制不断上升的犯罪率.

□ ˈ**step-ladder** *n* portable folding ladder that can stand on its own, with steps rather than rungs and usu a small platform at the top 折梯. ⇨illus at LADDER 见LADDER插图.

step- *pref* 前缀 related as a result of one parent's remarrying, not by blood 父或母再婚而构成的亲缘关系, 但无血缘关系(参看 half-).

□ ˈ**stepbrother**, ˈ**stepsister** *ns* male/female child of one's stepmother or stepfather by an earlier marriage 继母与其前夫或继父与其前妻所生的儿子[女儿](参看 half-brother、half-sister).

ˈ**stepchild** *n* (*pl* **-children**) child of one's husband or wife by an earlier marriage 丈夫与其前妻或妻子与其前夫所生的孩子.

ˈ**stepfather**, ˈ**stepmother** *ns* husband of one's mother/wife of one's father by a later marriage 继父; 继母.

ˈ**step-parent** *n* later husband of one's mother or wife of one's father 继父或继母.

ˈ**stepson**, ˈ**stepdaughter** *ns* son/daughter of one's husband or wife by an earlier marriage 丈夫与其前妻或妻子与其前夫所生的儿子[女儿].

steppe /step; stɛp/ *n* (usu *pl* 通常作复数) flat grassy plain with few trees, esp in SE Europe and Siberia (树木稀少的)大草原; (尤指东南欧和西伯利亚的)干草原. Cf 参看 PAMPAS, PRAIRIE, SAVANNAH, VELD.

-ster *suff* 后缀 (with *ns* and *adjs* forming *ns* 与名词和形容词结合构成名词) person connected with or having the quality of 与…有关的人; 有…品性的人: *gangster* ○ *prankster* ○ *youngster*.

ste·reo /ˈsterɪəʊ; ˈstɛrɪo/ *n* (*pl* **~s**) **1** [U] stereophonic sound or recording 立体声; 立体声录音: *broadcast in stereo* 立体声广播 ○ [attrib 作定语] *a stereo recording, record, cassette, system* 立体声的录音、唱片、盒式磁带、音响设备. **2** stereophonic record-player, radio, etc 立体声音响器材(立体声唱机、收音机等): *Where's your stereo?* 你的立体声音响设备在哪儿呢? Cf 参看 MONO.

stereo- *comb form* 构词成分 having three dimensions; solid 三维空间的; 立体的; 固体的: *stereoscope*.

ste·reo·phonic /ˌsterɪəˈfɒnɪk; ˌstɛrɪəˈfɑnɪk/ *adj* **1** (of recorded or broadcast sound) giving the effect of naturally distributed sound, and requiring two loudspeakers placed separately (指录制的或广播的声音)有立体效果的, 立体声的: *a stereophonic recording* 立体声录音. **2** (of apparatus) designed for recording or reproducing sound in this way (指器材)立体声录音或放音的. Cf 参看 MONOPHONIC.

ste·reo·scope /ˈsterɪəskəʊp; ˈstɛrɪəˌskop/ *n* apparatus through which two photographs, taken from slightly different angles, can be seen as if united and with the effect of depth and solidity 体视镜(可观看两张拍摄角度稍异的照片, 产生立体感).

▷ **ste·reo·scopic** /ˌsterɪəˈskɒpɪk; ˌstɛrɪəˈskɑpɪk/ *adj* giving a three-dimensional effect 产生三维空间效果的; 有立体感的: *a stereoscopic image, photograph, etc* 有立体感的图像、照片等.

ste·reo·type /ˈsterɪətaɪp; ˈstɛrɪəˌtaɪp/ *n* [C] **1** image, idea, character, etc that has become fixed or standardized in a conventional form without individuality (and is therefore perhaps false) 模式化的形象、思想、人物等;

老一套: *He doesn't conform to the usual stereotype of the city businessman with a dark suit and rolled umbrella.* 他不像典型的城市商人那样, 穿一身深色的套服、带一把收好的雨伞. ○ [attrib 作定语] *a play full of stereotype characters* 充斥着公式化人物的话剧. **2** printing-plate made from a mould of a set piece of movable printing type 铅版.

▷ **ste·reo·typed** *adj* (*often derog* 常作贬义) (of images, ideas, characters, etc) fixed, unchanging or standardized; without individuality (指形象、思想、人物等)模式化的, 无个性的: *stereotyped images of women in advertisements* 广告中千篇一律的女性形象.

ste·reo·typ·ing *n* [U]: *sexual stereotyping* 性别的模式化.

ster·ile /ˈsteraɪl; *US* ˈsterəl; ˈstɛrəl/ *adj* **1** (of plants, animals or humans) not producing or not able to produce seeds, young or children (指植物、动物或人)不产生种子的, 不能生殖的, 不育的: *Medical tests showed that he was sterile.* 医学检查表明他没有生育能力. **2** (of land) that cannot produce crops; barren (指土地)不能长庄稼的, 不毛的, 荒瘠的. **3** (*fig* 比喻) (of discussion, communication, etc) producing no useful results; unproductive (指讨论、联系等)无结果的, 无效果的: *a sterile debate* 毫无结果的辩论. **4** free from germs, bacteria, etc 无菌的; 消过毒的: *sterile bandages* 无菌绷带 ○ *An operating theatre should be completely sterile.* 手术室应该完全无菌. Cf 参看 FERTILE.

▷ **ster·il·ity** /stəˈrɪlətɪ; stəˈrɪlətɪ/ *n* [U] state or quality of being sterile 不产生种子; 无生殖力; 荒瘠; 无结果; 无菌.

ster·il·ize, -ise /ˈsterəlaɪz; ˈstɛrə,laɪz/ *v* [Tn] **1** make (sth) sterile(4) or free from bacteria 为(某物)消毒或杀菌: *sterilized milk* 消毒牛奶 ○ *sterilized surgical instruments* 消过毒的外科手术器械. **2** make (a person or an animal) unable to produce young or children (esp by removal or obstruction of the reproductive organs) 使(人)绝育; 使(动物)失去生殖能力: *After her fourth child she decided to be/have herself sterilized.* 她生了第四个孩子后决定做绝育手术. **ster·il·iza·tion, -isation** /ˌsterəlaɪˈzeɪʃn; *US* -lɪˈz-; ˌstɛrələˈzeʃən/ *n* [U].

ster·ling /ˈstɜːlɪŋ; ˈstɝlɪŋ/ *adj* **1** (*abbr* 缩写 **stg**) (of coins or precious metal) of standard value and purity; genuine (指硬币或贵金属)标准纯度的, 真的: *sterling silver cutlery* 标准纯银的餐具. **2** [usu attrib 通常作定语] (*fig* 比喻) (of a person or his qualities, etc) admirable or excellent in quality (指人或其品质等)令人钦佩的, 优秀的: *her sterling qualities as an organizer* 她那高超的组织才能.

▷ **ster·ling** *n* [U] British money 英国货币: *the pound sterling*, ie the British £ 英镑 ○ *payable in sterling or American dollars* 可用英镑或美元支付. Cf 参看 POUND[1] 2.

□ **the ˈsterling area** group of countries that formerly kept their reserves in British sterling currency and between which money could easily be transferred 英镑区(旧时用英镑作准备金的各国).

stern[1] /stɜːn; stɝn/ *adj* (**-er, -est**) (**a**) serious and grim, not kind or cheerful; expecting to be obeyed 严肃的; 严厉的; 不苟言笑的; 要求别人服从的: *a stern taskmaster, teacher, parent, etc* 严厉的监工、教师、父亲(或母亲)等 ○ *a stern face, expression, look, etc* 严肃的面容、表情、神态等. (**b**) severe and strict 严厉的; 严格的; 严酷的; 严峻的; 苛刻的: *stern treatment for offenders* 对犯法者的严厉对待 ○ *Police are planning sterner measures to combat crime.* 警方正在制订更严厉的措施来打击犯罪活动. ▷ **sternly** *adj*. **stern·ness** *n* [U].

stern[2] /stɜːn; stɝn/ *n* [C] **1** back end of a ship or boat 船尾: *standing at/in the stern of the boat* 站在船尾 ○ *walk towards the stern of a ship* 向船尾走. ⇨illus at YACHT 见 YACHT 插图. **2** (*infml esp joc* 口, 尤作戏谑语) rear part of anything, esp a person's bottom 后部; 尾部; 末端; (尤指人的)屁股: *Move your stern, I want to sit down.* 你把屁股挪一挪, 我想坐下. **3** (idm 习语) **from stem to stern** ⇨ STEM[1].

sternum /ˈstɜːnəm; ˈstɝnəm/ *n* (*pl* **~s** or **sterna** /ˈstɜːnə; ˈstɝnə/) (*anatomy* 解) = BREASTBONE (BREAST).

ster·oid /ˈsterɔɪd, ˈstɪərɔɪd; ˈstɛrɔɪd, ˈstɪrɔɪd/ *n* (*chemistry* 化) any of a number of organic compounds naturally produced in the body, including certain hormones and vitamins 甾族化合物; 类固醇: *He's being treated with steroids for leukaemia.* 他因患白血病正在接受类固醇治疗.

ster·tor·ous /ˈstɜːtərəs; ˈstɝtərəs/ *adj* (*fml* 文) (of breathing or a person breathing) making a loud snoring noise (指呼吸或人呼吸时)发出呼噜声的, 打鼾的. ▷ **ster·tor·ously** *adv*.

stet /stet; stɛt/ *v* **1** [I] (used only in the form *stet* as an instruction to a printer, etc when written beside a word that has been crossed out or corrected by mistake 仅用原形stet, 作校对批注用语, 写于已删除或误改之文字旁) let it stay or remain as written or printed 不删; 不改; 保留原样. **2** (**-tt-**) [Tn] write 'stet' beside (sth); cancel the correction of 在(删改处)旁注上'保留'字样; 取消对…的删改: *The proof-reader had changed a word but I stetted it.* 校对员改动了一个词, 我批注不应改动, 恢复原状.

stetho·scope /ˈsteθəskəʊp; ˈstɛθə,skop/ *n* instrument used by doctors for listening to the beating of the heart, sounds of breathing, etc 听诊器.

stet·son /ˈstetsn; ˈstɛtsn̩/ *n* man's hat with a high crown and wide brim, worn esp by cowboys (男用)高顶阔边帽(尤指牧牛工戴的). ⇨illus at HAT 见 HAT 插图.

steve·dore /ˈstiːvədɔː(r); ˈstivə,dɔr/ *n* person whose work is loading and unloading ships; docker (船货)装卸工; 码头工人.

stew /stjuː; *US* stuː; stu/ *v* **1** [I, Tn] (cause sth to) cook slowly in water or juice in a closed dish, pan, etc (将某物)用文火煮, 炖, 煨, 焖: *The meat needs to stew for several hours.* 这肉得炖几个钟头. ○ *stewing steak*, ie beef suitable for stewing 宜作炖食的牛排 ○ *stewed chicken, fruit* 炖熟的鸡、水果 ○ *stewed apple and custard* 浇蛋奶汁的炖苹果. **2** [I] (*infml* 口) be very hot; swelter 很热; 热得难受: *Please open a window — we're stewing in here!* 请打开窗户吧 —— 我们热死了! **3** (idm 习语) **let sb ˈstew** (*infml* 口) leave sb to continue suffering from the unpleasant consequences of his own actions (without offering help, sympathy, etc) 让某人自讨苦吃(而不相助、不同情等). **stew in one's own ˈjuice** (*infml* 口) suffer from the unpleasant consequences of one's own actions 自作自受: *I don't see why I should help her — she can stew in her own juice for a bit.* 我干吗要帮她 —— 她自作自受得吃点苦头才好呢.

▷ **stew** *n* **1** [C, U] (dish of) stewed meat, vegetables, etc 炖菜: *make a stew* 做一道炖菜 ○ *have some more stew* 再吃点炖菜. **2** (idm 习语) **get (oneself) into/be in a ˈstew (about sth)** (*infml* 口) become/be nervous, anxious or agitated (about sth) (对某事物)不安, 担忧, 激动: *He's got himself into a complete stew about his exams.* 他对考试紧张得不得了.

stewed *adj* [usu pred 通常作表语] **1** (of tea) tasting unpleasantly strong and bitter from being left in the teapot too long (指茶)(因久泡)酽而苦. **2** (*sl* 俚) drunk 喝醉.

stew·ard /stjʊəd; *US* ˈstuːərd; ˈstuɚd/ *n* **1** person employed to manage another's property, esp a large house or estate (受雇管理他人财产的)管理员, 管家(尤指巨宅或地产的). **2** person whose job is to arrange for the supply of food to a college, club, etc (大学、俱乐部等的)膳食管理员. **3** (*fem* 阴性作 **stew·ard·ess** /ˌstjʊəˈdes; *US* ˈstuːərdəs; ˈstuɚdəs/) person who attends to the needs of passengers on a ship, an aircraft or a train (轮船、飞机或火车上的)服务员: *the baggage/cabin/deck steward* 负责行李[客舱/舱面]的服务员 ○ *an ˈair stewardess* 空中小姐. **4** official responsible for organizing a dance, race-meeting, show, public meeting, demonstration, etc (舞会、赛马大会、表演、公共集会、示威活动等的)组织者, 筹备人, 干事, 理事: *The stewards will inspect the course to see if racing is possible.* 那些干事将检视赛马场看是否适宜比赛.

▷ **stew·ard·ship** *n* [U] (*fml* 文) position and duties of a steward 管理员、服务员、筹备人的职位和职责.

Sth *abbr* 缩写 = South: *Sth Pole*, eg on a map 南极(如标于地图上的).

stick[1] /stɪk; stɪk/ *n* **1** [C] short thin piece of wood used as a support, as a weapon or as firewood (作支持物、武器或柴火的)棍, 棒, 柴枝: *collect dry sticks to make a fire* 拾些干柴生火 ○ *cut sticks to support peas in the garden* 砍些小树枝以支撑园子里的豌豆. **2** [C] = WALKING-STICK (WALK[1]): *The old man cannot walk without a stick.*

那位老先生离开手杖就走不了路. **3** [C] implement used to hit and direct the ball in hockey, polo, etc (曲棍球、马球等的)球棍. **4** [C] (often in compounds 常用以构成复合词) long thin rod-shaped piece of a substance 细长如棍之物; 棒状物; 条状物: *sticks of celery, chalk, charcoal, dynamite, rhubarb, wax* 一根根的芹菜、粉笔、木炭、炸药、食用大黄、蜡 ○ *brass candlesticks* 黄铜烛台. **5** [C] conductor's baton 指挥棒. **6** [C] set of bombs dropped one after the other so that they fall in a row 连续投下的一串炸弹. **7** [C usu *pl* 通常作复数] **~ (of sth)** (*infml* 口) piece (of furniture) (家具的)件: *These few sticks (of furniture) are all he has left.* 这几件(家具)就是他留下的全部物品了. **8** [C] (*infml* 口) person of the specified type, esp a dull or an unsociable one 某种类型的人; (尤指)呆头呆脑的人, 不善交际的人: *He's a rather boring old stick.* 他是个相当乏味的傢伙. **9 the sticks** [pl] (*infml* 口) rural areas far from cities 远离城市的边远地方: *live (out) in the sticks* 住在远离城市的边远地方. **10** (idm 习语) **be in a cleft stick** ⇨ CLEAVE[1]. **the big stick** ⇨ BIG. **the carrot and the stick** ⇨ CARROT. **get the wrong end of the stick** ⇨ WRONG. **get/take stick (from sb)** (*infml* 口) be punished or treated severely 受到严惩或严厉对待: *The government has taken a lot of stick from the press recently.* 政府近来受到新闻界猛烈抨击. **give sb 'stick** (*infml* 口) punish or treat sb severely 严惩或严厉对待某人. **a rod/stick to beat sb with** ⇨ BEAT[1]. **up sticks** ⇨ UP *v*.

□ **'stick insect** large insect with a body shaped like a twig 竹节虫.

'stickpin *n* (*US*) = TIE-PIN (TIE[1]).

'stick shift (*US*) way of operating the gears in a car by means of a gear-lever mounted on the floor (汽车)操纵变速杆(换挡的方法).

stick[2] /stɪk; stɪk/ *v* (*pt, pp* **stuck** /stʌk; stʌk/) **1 (a)** [Tn·pr, Tn·p] **~ sth in/into/through sth; ~ sth in/through** push or thrust (esp sth pointed) into, through, etc sth 插入或刺穿某物(尤指用尖物): *Stick the fork into the potato.* 用叉子插土豆. ○ *The cushion was stuck full of pins.* 针插上插满了针. **(b)** [Ipr, Ip] **~ in/into/through sth; ~ in/through** (of sth pointed) be pushed or thrust into or through sth and remain in position (指尖物)插入或穿入某物中: *The needle stuck in my finger.* 针扎进我的手指了. ○ *I found a nail sticking in the tyre.* 我发现轮胎上扎着一根钉子. ○ *Your umbrella is sticking into my back.* 你的伞戳着我的背了. **2** [I, Ipr, Ip, Tn, Tn·pr, Tn·p] (cause sth to) become fixed, joined or fastened with a sticky substance (将某物)粘牢, 粘住, 粘在一起: *This glue doesn't stick very well.* 这种胶水粘不住. ○ *The dough stuck to my fingers.* 生面团粘在我的手指上了. ○ *stick a stamp on a letter* 把邮票贴在信上 ○ *stick a broken cup (back) together* 把破了的杯子(重新)粘在一起. **3** [Tn·pr, Tn·p] (*infml* 口) put or fix (sth) in a position or place, esp quickly or carelessly 把(某物)放置在某处或固定在某位置上[尤指匆促地或粗心地]: *stick up a notice on the notice-board* 把布告贴在布告牌上 ○ *He stuck the pen behind his ear.* 他把笔夹在耳朵上. ○ *Stick the books on the table, will you?* 把书放在桌子上, 好吗? **4** [I, Ipr] **~ (in sth)** be or become fixed in one place and unable to move 卡在某处不能移动: *This drawer sticks badly.* 这个抽屉卡得死死的. ○ *The key stuck in the lock.* 钥匙在锁中卡住了. ○ *The bus stuck in the mud.* 公共汽车陷在泥里了. **5** [Tn] (*infml* 口) (in negative sentences and questions 用于否定句和疑问句) tolerate or bear (esp an unpleasant person or situation) 容忍, 忍受(尤指令人不快的行为或情况): *I don't know how you stuck that man for so long.* 我不知道你这么长时间是怎么忍受他这种行为的. ○ *I won't stick your rudeness any longer.* 我再也不能容忍你这种粗暴行为了. **6** [I] (*infml* 口) be or become established 建立; 确定: *They couldn't make the charges stick*, ie prove that they were true. 他们拿不出那些指控的依据来. ○ *He got the nickname 'Fatty' on his first day at school — and unfortunately the name stuck*, ie has been used ever since. 他第一天上学就得了一个绰号叫'胖子' —— 倒霉的是从此就叫开了. **7** (idm 习语) **cling/stick to sb like a leech** ⇨ LEECH. **mud sticks** ⇨ MUD. **poke/stick one's nose into sth** ⇨ NOSE[1]. **put/shove/stick one's oar in** ⇨ OAR. **stand/stick out like a sore thumb** ⇨ SORE. **stand/stick out a mile** ⇨ MILE. **stick/stop at 'nothing** be willing to do anything to get what one wants, even if it is immoral 为达目的不择手段. **stick 'em 'up!** (*infml* 口) (said by an armed robber telling sb to raise his hands above his head 持械劫匪令人高举双手的用语) **stick 'fast** be or become solidly fixed in one position and unable or unwilling to move 牢牢卡在某处不能或不愿移动: *His head was stuck fast in the railings.* 他的头卡在栅栏里动弹不得. ○ (*fig* 比喻) *He stuck fast to his theory*, ie maintained it firmly. 他坚持自己的看法. **stick in one's 'mind** (of a memory, image, etc) be remembered for a long time (指记忆、形象等)历久不忘: *The image of the dead child's face stuck in my mind for ages.* 那孩子已死去多时, 我对其面容仍记忆犹新. **stick in one's 'throat** (*infml* 口) **(a)** (also **stick in one's 'craw/'gizzard**) be difficult or impossible to accept 难以接受; 不可能接受: *It sticks in my throat to have to accept charity from them.* 我不得不接受他们的施舍, 此事教我耿耿于怀. **(b)** (of words) be difficult or impossible to say (指言词)难于启齿, 说不出口: *I wanted to tell her, but the words stuck in my throat.* 我想要告诉她, 只是有口难言. **stick one's 'neck out** (*infml* 口) do sth risky 做有风险的事: *I may be sticking my neck out* (ie in predicting sth uncertain), *but I think he's going to win.* 我这可谓孟浪之言, 但我仍认为他能获胜. **stick to one's 'guns** (*infml* 口) refuse to change one's opinions, actions, etc in spite of criticism 尽管受到抨击, 仍不改变言、行等; 坚持立场. **stick to one's last** not try to do things that one cannot do well 不做无把握的事.

8 (phr v) **stick around** (*infml* 口) stay in or near a place (waiting for sth to happen, sb to arrive, etc) 在某处或在附近(等候某事发生、某人到来等): *Stick around, we may need you.* 不要走远, 我们可能需要你.

stick at sth work persistently and continuously at sth; persevere 坚持做某事; 坚持不懈: *If we stick at it, we should finish the job today.* 我们要是接着干下去, 今天就能把这项工作做完.

stick by sb (*infml* 口) continue to support and be loyal to sb (esp through difficult times) 继续支持并忠于某人(尤指在逆境中): *Her husband stuck by her in good times and bad.* 无论境遇好坏她的丈夫都对她忠贞不渝.

stick sth down (a) fasten (the cover, flap, etc of sth) with glue, paste, etc (用胶水、糨糊等)粘住(封套、信封口等): *stick down (the flap of) an envelope* 粘住信封(的口盖). **(b)** (*infml* 口) put or place sth down 把某物放下或放置好: *Stick it down anywhere you like.* 把它放在哪儿都行. **(c)** (*infml* 口) write sth down 写下某事: *Stick down your names on the list.* 把你们的名字写在名单上.

stick sth in/into sth fix, fasten sth into a book, etc with glue, paste, etc (用胶水、糨糊等)把某物固定、粘贴在书本等内: *stick stamps into an album* 把邮票贴在集邮册里.

stick sth on (sth) fix, fasten sth (to a surface) with glue, paste, etc (用胶水、糨糊等)把某物固定、粘贴在(某物表面)上: *Stick a label on your suitcase.* 把标签粘贴在你的手提箱上.

stick (sth) out (cause sth to) project (使某物)突出, 伸出: *His ears stick out.* 他长着一对扇风耳. ○ *a girl sticking her tongue out at her brother* 向哥哥伸舌头的女孩儿 ○ *Don't stick your head out of the car window.* 不要把头伸出汽车窗外. **stick it/sth out** (*infml* 口) continue with sth to the end, despite difficulty or unpleasantness (虽然困难或不愉快)坚持到底, 一直忍下去: *He hates the job — but he's determined to stick it out because he needs the money.* 他讨厌那工作 —— 但因为需要钱, 只好横下心来干下去. **stick out for sth** (*infml* 口) refuse to give up until one gets sth one wants 坚持要求某事物; 不获得某事物绝不罢休: *They're sticking out for higher wages.* 他们坚持要求提高工资.

stick to sth (a) not abandon or change sth; keep to sth 不放弃或不改变某事物; 坚持或维持某事物: *'Would you like some wine?' 'No, I'll stick to beer, thanks.'* '你喝点葡萄酒吗?' '不, 谢谢你, 我还是喝啤酒吧.' ○ *We don't want to hear your opinions; stick to the facts!* 我们不想听你的想法, 只讲事实! ○ *That's my story and I'm sticking to it*, ie I shall maintain that it is true. 我说的就是这些, 句句实情. **(b)** continue doing sth (despite difficulties, etc) (尽管有困难等)继续做某事: *stick to a*

S

task until it is finished 坚持完成任务.
stick together (*infml* 口) (of people) remain friendly and loyal to one another; be united (指人)彼此忠诚友好, 团结一致: *If we keep calm and stick together, we'll be all right.* 我们保持镇定、同心协力就没有问题.
stick up project upwards; be upright 向上突出; 竖起: *The branch was sticking up out of the water.* 树枝直挺挺地伸出水面. **stick sth up** (*infml* 口) threaten the people in (a place) with a gun in order to rob it 用枪胁迫(某处)的人以便抢劫: *stick up a bank, post office, etc* 持枪抢劫银行、邮局等. **stick up for sb/oneself/sth** support or defend sb/oneself/sth 支持或维护某人[自己/某事物]: *Don't allow those big boys to bully you; stick up for yourself!* 别让那些大孩子欺负你, 要保护你自己! ○ *stick up for one's rights* 维护自己的权利.
stick with sb/sth (*infml* 口) continue to support or retain one's connection with sb/sth 继续支持某人[某事物]; 保持与某人[某事物]的联系: *I'm sticking with my original idea.* 我坚持我原来的主张. ○ *Stick with me and you'll be all right.* 有事你来找我就没问题了.

□ ˈ**stick-in-the-mud** *n* (*infml derog* 口, 贬) person who resists change 反对变革的人: [attrib 作定语] *stick-in-the-mud attitudes* 保守的态度.

ˈ**stick-on** *adj* [attrib 作定语] having glue, etc on the back; adhesive 背面涂有黏胶的; 可粘贴的: *stick-on labels* 背面涂有黏胶的标签.

ˈ**sticking-plaster** (also **plaster**) *n* [C, U] (*Brit*) (*US* **adhesive** ˈ**plaster**) (small strip of) fabric, plastic, etc that can be stuck to the skin to protect a small wound or cut 橡皮膏. Cf 参看 BAND-AID.

ˈ**stick-up** *n* (*infml* 口) robbery with a gun; hold-up 持枪抢劫; 抢劫: *Don't move — this is a stick-up!* 不许动——这是抢劫!

S

sticker /ˈstɪkə(r); ˋstɪkɚ/ *n* **1** sticky label with a picture or message on it (有黏胶的)图文标签: *The child had stickers all over his school books.* 那孩子把他的课本贴满了图文标签. **2** (*infml approv* 口, 褒) person who does not give up in spite of difficulties 坚持不懈的人; 锲而不舍的人.

stickle·back /ˈstɪklbæk; ˋstɪklˌbæk/ *n* small fish with sharp spikes on its back 刺鱼(背上有尖刺的小鱼).

stick·ler /ˈstɪklə(r); ˋstɪklɚ/ *n* **~ for sth** person who thinks that a certain goal is very important and tries to make other people aim at it 认为某事重要而竭力让别人做好的人: *a stickler for accuracy, punctuality, discipline, etc* 要求准确、准时、纪律严明...的人.

sticky /ˈstɪkɪ; ˋstɪkɪ/ *adj* (**-ier, -iest**) **1** that sticks or tends to stick to anything which touches it 黏的; 黏性的: *sticky fingers covered in jam* 沾满果酱的黏糊糊的手指 ○ *The floor's very sticky near the cooker.* 炉具旁边地面上黏黏糊糊的. **2** (*infml* 口) (of weather) unpleasantly hot and damp, causing one to sweat (指天气)湿热得难受的: *a sticky August afternoon* 八月里一个湿热得令人难受的下午. **3** (*infml* 口) unpleasant; difficult 不愉快的; 困难的: *His dismissal was rather a sticky business for all concerned.* 他遭解雇一事, 有关的人都很为难. ○ *Their marriage is going through a sticky patch*, ie an unpleasant period of time. 他们的婚姻关系如临深渊. **4** [usu pred 通常作表语] (*infml* 口) making or likely to make objections, be unhelpful, etc 持异议、不肯帮忙...: *The bank manager was a bit sticky about letting me have an overdraft.* 银行经理不太同意让我透支. **5** (idm 习语) **come to a bad/sticky end** ⇨ END[1]. **sticky** ˈ**fingers** (*euph* 婉) tendency to steal 手黏(好偷窃). **a sticky** ˈ**wicket** (*Brit*) (**a**) (in cricket) a wet wicket (playing-surface) which dries quickly in the sun and is difficult to bat on (板球)湿软的三柱门(场地)(湿后迅即晒干因而难以击球的). (**b**) (*fig* 比喻) situation that is hard to deal with 难以应付的情况: *We're on a sticky wicket with these negotiations — they could very well fail.* 我们在谈判中已陷入泥淖——很可能失败. ▷ **stick·ily** /-ɪlɪ; -əlɪ/ *adv*. **sticki·ness** *n* [U].

□ **sticky** ˈ**tape** long thin strip of plastic, etc which is sticky on one side, and is used for joining things together 黏胶带.

stiff /stɪf; stɪf/ *adj* (**-er, -est**) **1** not easily bent, folded, moved, changed in shape, etc 不易弯曲、打折、移动、变形等的; 坚硬的; 僵直的: *a sheet of stiff cardboard* 一块硬纸板 ○ *a stiff drawer* 很紧的抽屉 ○ *a stiff pair of shoes* 一双硬邦邦的鞋 ○ *have a stiff neck*, ie painful and difficult to move 颈部强直 ○ *feel stiff* (ie have stiff muscles and joints) *after a long walk* 走长路后感觉肢体发僵. **2** thick and hard to stir; not liquid 稠的; 难搅拌的; 非液态的: *Stir the flour and milk to a stiff paste.* 把面粉和牛奶搅成很稠的糊. **3** (**a**) hard to do; difficult 不好做的; 困难的: *a stiff climb* 吃力的攀登 ○ *a stiff exam* 难度大的考试. (**b**) severe; tough 严厉的; 激烈的: *The judge imposed a stiff sentence.* 法官做出了严厉的判决. ○ *Competition is stiff.* 竞争很激烈. **4** formal in manner, behaviour, etc; not friendly (态度、举止等)生硬的, 拘谨的, 不友好的: *Their manner was rather stiff.* 他们的态度很生硬. **5** (*infml* 口) (of a price) (too) high (指价格)(太)高: *pay a stiff membership fee* 缴纳很高的会费. **6** (of a breeze) blowing strongly (指风)强劲的, 猛烈的. **7** (of an alcoholic drink) strong and undiluted (指酒)烈性的, 未经稀释的: *That was a shock — I need a stiff drink!* 这可真吓人——我得喝点烈酒了! ○ *a stiff glass of rum* 一杯纯的朗姆酒. **8** (idm 习语) **stiff/straight as a ramrod** ⇨ RAMROD. **(keep) a stiff upper lip** (show) an ability to appear calm and unworried when in pain, trouble, etc (遇痛苦、困难等时)(表现)沉着而坚强的能力, 咬紧牙关.

▷ **stiff** *adv* (*infml* 口) to an extreme degree; very much 极度地; 非常: *worried/scared/frozen stiff* 非常担心[极其害怕/冻僵] ○ *The opera bored me stiff.* 这个歌剧真把我腻烦透了.

stiff *n* (*sl* 俚) dead body; corpse 死尸, 尸体(尤指人的).

stiffly *adv*: *He bent down stiffly.* 他直僵僵地弯下身子.

stiff·ness *n* [U].

□ ˌ**stiff-**ˈ**necked** *adj* (*fml derog* 文, 贬) obstinate and proud 顽固而傲慢的.

stiffen /ˈstɪfn; ˋstɪfən/ *v* [I, Ipr, Ip, Tn, Tn·pr, Tn·p] **~ (sth) (up) (with sth)** (cause sth to) become stiff or stiffer (使某物)变得(更加)坚硬、僵硬、困难、生硬、强烈等: *My back has stiffened (up) overnight.* 我的后背一夜之间强直了. ○ *He stiffened (with terror) at the horrific sight.* 他看到那恐怖的情景吓呆了. ○ *cotton stiffened with starch* 上浆后发挺的棉布 ○ (*fig* 比喻) *The promise of a reward might stiffen their resolve*, ie make them braver. 答应给他们奖励, 他们就可能更勇敢了.

▷ **stiff·ener** /ˈstɪfnə(r); ˋstɪfənɚ/ *n* thing used to stiffen 用以变硬或变强之物: *a collar stiffener* 衣领衬料.

stiff·ening /ˈstɪfnɪŋ; ˋstɪfənɪŋ/ *n* [U] material used to stiffen a piece of cloth or a garment 浆硬剂(使布或服装挺括的材料).

stifle /ˈstaɪfl; ˋstaɪfl/ *v* **1** [I, Tn] feel or make (sb) unable to breathe (easily) because of lack of fresh air; suffocate 感到窒息; 使(某人)不能(顺畅)呼吸: *We were stifling in that hot room with all the windows closed.* 我们在那间关着窗户的热屋子里, 简直透不过气来. ○ *a baby stifled by a pillow* 被枕头捂住无法呼吸的婴儿 ○ *The smoke filled the room and almost stifled the firemen.* 屋里浓烟弥漫呛得消防队员喘不过气来. **2** [Tn] extinguish (a fire); put out 熄灭(火); 扑灭: *stifle flames with a blanket* 用毯子扑灭火焰. **3** [Tn] suppress (sth); restrain 镇压(某事物); 遏制: *stifle a rebellion* 平息叛乱 ○ *stifle a yawn, laugh, cry, sob, etc* 忍住哈欠、笑、哭、抽泣等 ○ (*derog* 贬) *stifle ideas, initiative* 压制思想、主动性. ▷ **sti·fling** /ˈstaɪflɪŋ; ˋstaɪflɪŋ/ *adj*: *It's stifling in here; open a window!* 这里很闷, 打开窗户吧! ○ *the stifling atmosphere of the royal court, with all its petty restrictive rules* 宫廷里那令人窒息的气氛, 因为有各种繁文缛节. **sti·flingly** *adv*: *stiflingly hot* 闷热.

stigma /ˈstɪgmə; ˋstɪgmə/ *n* **1** [C, U] mark of shame or disgrace; shameful feeling or reputation 耻辱的标记; 羞耻之心; 污名: *There is less stigma attached to illegitimacy now than there used to be.* 私生子女已不像过去那样见不得人了. **2** [C] (*botany* 植) part that receives the pollen in the centre of a flower 柱头(花的中央接受花粉的部分).

stig·mata /ˈstɪgmətə; ˋstɪgmətə/ *n* [pl] marks resembling the wounds made by nails on the body of Christ when he was crucified, said to have appeared on the bodies of various saints and considered as a sign of holiness by some Christians 圣痕(与耶稣受难伤痕相应的瘢痕, 据称曾在许多圣徒身上出现, 有些基督徒视之为神圣的标志).

stig·mat·ize, -ise /ˈstɪgmətaɪz; ˋstɪgmə,taɪz/ *v* [Cn·n/a usu passive 通常用于被动语态] **~ sb/sth as sth** (*fml* 文) describe or consider sb/sth as sth disgraceful or shameful 将某人[某事物]形容为、视为可耻之物: *stigmatized as a coward and a liar* 被指责为胆小鬼和说谎的人.

stile /staɪl; staɪl/ *n* **1** set of steps enabling walkers to get over or through a fence, wall, etc in the country (乡村中供人穿越栅栏、围墙等的)台阶. **2** (idm 习语) **help a lame dog over a stile** ⇨ HELP[1].

stil·etto /stɪˈletəʊ; stɪˋlɛto/ *n* (*pl* **~s** /-təʊz; -toz/) **1** small dagger or tool with a narrow pointed blade 短剑; 匕首. **2** (usu *pl* 通常作复数) (*Brit infml* 口) woman's shoe with a stiletto heel 细高跟女鞋.

□ **sti,letto ˈheel** (*Brit*) high, very narrow heel on a woman's shoe (女鞋的)细高跟.

still[1] /stɪl; stɪl/ *adj* (**-er, -est**) **1** (**a**) (almost) without movement or sound; quiet and calm (几乎)不动或无声的; 静止的; 寂静的: *still water* 死水 ○ *absolutely/completely/perfectly still* 极其[十分/非常]宁静 ○ *Please keep/stay/hold/sit/stand still while I take your photograph.* 我给你拍照时请别动. (**b**) without wind 无风的: *a still day in August* 八月里无风的一天. ⇨Usage at QUIET 用法见 QUIET. **2** [attrib 作定语] (of drinks) not containing bubbles of gas; not sparkling or fizzy (指饮料)不含碳酸气的, 不起泡的: *still cider, orange, mineral water, etc* 无汽的苹果汁、橙子汁、矿泉水等. **3** (idm 习语) **the still small ˈvoice (of conscience)** (*rhet* 修辞) a person's sense of right and wrong 良心的呼唤; 是非感. **still waters run ˈdeep** (*saying* 谚) a quiet or apparently calm person can have strong emotions, much knowledge or wisdom, etc 静水流深(沉静或寡言者或有强烈情感、丰富知识或非凡智慧等).

▷ **still** *n* **1** single photograph of a scene from a cinema film (电影片中某一镜头的)剧照, 定格画面: *stills from a new film*, eg as used for advertising 新影片的剧照(如用作广告的). **2** (idm 习语) **the still of the ˈnight** (*rhet* 修辞) the calmness or silence of the night 夜间的寂静.

still *v* [I, Tn] (*fml* 文) (cause sth to) become calm or at rest (使某物)平静下来或静止: *The waves stilled.* 波浪平静下来了. ○ (*fig* 比喻) *She couldn't still her anxiety.* 她无法消除内心的不安.

still·ness *n* [U] quality of being still 静止; 寂静; 安静; 平静.

□ **ˈstill birth** (**a**) birth at which the baby is born dead 死产. (**b**) baby born dead 死产儿. Cf 参看 LIVE BIRTH (LIVE[1]).

ˈstillborn *adj* **1** (of a baby) dead when born (指婴儿)死产的. **2** (*rhet* 修辞) (of an idea or a plan) not developing further (指思想或计划)夭折的.

,still ˈlife (**a**) [U] representation of non-living objects (eg fruit, flowers, etc) in painting (绘画中的)静物(如水果、花等); 静物画: *I prefer landscape to still life.* 我喜欢风景画, 不喜欢静物画. (**b**) [C] (*pl* **still lifes**) picture of this type 静物画.

still[2] /stɪl; stɪl/ *adv* **1** (usu in the middle position, but sometimes occurring after a direct object 通常置于句子中部, 但有时用于直接宾语之后) up to and including the present time or the time mentioned 至目前或当时为止; 仍然; 依旧; 还是: *She's still busy.* 她仍然很忙. ○ *He still hopes/is still hoping for a letter from her.* 他仍盼望她能来信. ○ *Will you still be here when I get back?* 我回来的时候你还在这里吗? ○ *Do you still live in London?* 你还住在伦敦吗? ○ *I still can't do it.* 我还是不会做. ○ *We could still change our minds.* 我们还可以改变主意. ○ *I need you still; don't go yet.* 我还需要你, 先别走. **2** in spite of that; nevertheless; even so 尽管那样; 然而; 不过; 虽然如此: *He's treated you badly: still, he's your brother and you should help him.* 他待你很不好; 但他终归是你的兄弟, 你应该帮助他. ○ *Although she felt ill, she still went to work.* 她虽然觉得身体不舒服, 但仍然去上班了. **3** (**a**) (with a comparative 与比较级连用) in a greater amount or degree; even 更; 还要: *Tom is tall, but Mary is taller still/still taller.* 汤姆很高, 但是玛丽更高. ○ *That would be nicer still/still nicer.* 那就更好了. (**b**) in addition; besides; yet 加之; 此外; 还有: *He came up with still more stories.* 他写出的小说更多了. **4** (idm 习语) **,better/,worse ˈstill** even better/worse 还要好[坏].

still[3] /stɪl; stɪl/ *n* apparatus for making alcoholic liquor (eg brandy, whisky) by distilling 蒸馏器(制造如白兰地、威士忌等酒精饮料用的).

stilt /stɪlt; stɪlt/ *n* **1** either of a pair of poles, each with a support for the foot, on which a person can walk raised above the ground 高跷: *a pair of stilts* 一副高跷 ○ *walk on stilts* 踩高跷. **2** any one of a set of posts or poles on which a building, etc is supported above the ground (将建筑物等支离地面的)桩子, 支柱: *a house (up) on stilts* 用桩子支撑着的房子.

stil·ted /ˈstɪltɪd; ˋstɪltɪd/ *adj* (*derog* 贬) (of a manner of talking, writing, behaving, etc) stiff and unnatural; artificial (指言谈、文笔、举止等)生硬的, 不自然的, 矫揉造作的: *a rather stilted conversation* 颇为生硬的对话.

▷ **stil·tedly** *adv*.

Stil·ton /ˈstɪltən; ˋstɪltn̩/ *n* [U] white English cheese with green-blue lines of mould running through it and a strong flavour 斯蒂尔顿干酪(英国的一种白乳酪, 有蓝绿色霉纹, 味浓).

stimu·lant /ˈstɪmjʊlənt; ˋstɪmjələnt/ *n* **1** (drink containing a) drug that increases physical or mental activity and alertness 兴奋剂; 含兴奋剂的饮料: *Coffee and tea are mild stimulants.* 咖啡和茶都是平和的兴奋剂. ○ [attrib 作定语] *stimulant drugs* 兴奋剂. **2 ~ (to sth)** event, activity, etc that encourages greater or further activity 起刺激、激励作用的事情、活动等: *It is hoped the tax cuts will act as a stimulant to further economic growth.* 希望降低税率这一措施能刺激经济进一步增长.

stimu·late /ˈstɪmjʊleɪt; ˋstɪmjə,let/ *v* **1** [Tn, Tn·pr, Cn·t] **~ sb/sth (to sth)** make sb/sth more active or alert; arouse sb/sth 使某人[某事物]奋发起来; 刺激、激励某人[某事物]: *Praise always stimulates him to further efforts/to make greater efforts.* 一表扬他就能激励他更加努力. ○ *The exhibition stimulated interest in the artist's work.* 这次展览引起人们对这位艺术家的作品的兴趣. **2** [Tn, Cn·t] cause (sth) to work or function 促使(某事物)发挥作用: *a hormone that stimulates ovulation* 促进排卵的激素. **3** [Tn] arouse the interest and excitement of (sb) 激发(某人)的兴趣和热情: *a low level of conversation that failed to stimulate me* 不能引起我兴趣的程度很低的会话.

▷ **stimu·lat·ing** *adj* (**a**) tending to stimulate; arousing 刺激性的; 起激励作用的: *the stimulating effect of coffee* 咖啡的提神作用. (**b**) interesting or exciting 饶有兴味的; 使人兴奋的: *a stimulating discussion* 使人感兴趣的讨论 ○ *I find his work very stimulating.* 我觉得他的作品引人入胜.

stimu·la·tion /ˌstɪmjʊˈleɪʃn; ˌstɪmjəˋleʃən/ *n* [U]: *a working atmosphere lacking in stimulation* 死气沉沉的工作环境.

stimu·lus /ˈstɪmjʊləs; ˋstɪmjələs/ *n* (*pl* **-li** /-laɪ; -laɪ/) **~ (to sth/to do sth)** **1** thing that produces a reaction in living things 使生物体产生反应之物; 刺激物: *The nutrient in the soil acts as a stimulus to growth/to make the plants grow.* 土壤中的养分能促进植物生长. ○ *Does the child respond to auditory stimuli?* ie Does he react to the sounds around him? 那孩子对声音有反应吗? **2** (*fml* 文) thing that encourages or excites sb/sth to activity, greater effort, etc 起鼓舞或激励作用的事物; 促进因素: *the stimulus of fierce competition* 引起激烈竞争的事物 ○ *Her words of praise were a stimulus to work harder.* 她赞扬的话鼓舞人工作更努力.

sting[1] /stɪŋ; stɪŋ/ *n* **1** [C] sharp pointed organ of some insects (eg bees, wasps) and other animals, used for wounding and (usu) injecting poison (某些昆虫, 如蜜蜂、黄蜂, 及其他动物的)螫针, 螫刺, 毒刺: *The sting of a scorpion is in its tail.* 蝎子的毒钩在其尾部. **2** [C] sharp pointed hair on the surface of the leaf of some plants (eg nettles) that causes pain when touched (某些植物, 如荨麻, 叶子表面上的)螫毛. **3** [C] (**a**) (pain from) wounding by an animal's or a plant's sting (动物螫刺或植物螫毛造成的)螫痛, 刺痛: *That bee gave me a nasty sting.* 那只蜜蜂狠狠地蜇了我一下. ○ *The sting of a jellyfish is very painful.* 让水母刺着是很痛的. (**b**) place of a wound made by a sting 螫伤处; 蜇伤处: *Her face was covered in wasp stings.* 她脸上满是黄蜂蜇过的伤痕. **4** [C, U] any sharp pain of body or mind; wounding effect (身体上或精神上的)剧痛, 造成伤痛的作用力:

S

ointment to take the sting out of the burn 烧伤止痛药膏 ○ *the sting of the wind* 风刮的刺痛 ○ *the sting of remorse, jealousy, etc* 因悔恨、忌妒等而感到的剧烈痛苦 ○ *His tongue has a nasty sting*, ie He says hurtful things. 他的舌头能蜇人(说话伤人). **5** (idm 习语) **a ˌsting in the ˈtail** unpleasant feature which only becomes apparent at the end 直到最后才显现出来的坏处: *The announcement of the pay rise had a sting in its tail — we would have to work longer hours.* 宣布了提高工资有个倒霉事在后头——我们得延长工时.

□ **ˈsting-ray** *n* large wide flat fish that can cause severe wounds with its stinging tail 刺魟(体扁而宽的大鱼, 尾有毒刺具杀伤力).

sting[2] /stɪŋ; stɪŋ/ *v* (*pt, pp* **stung** /stʌŋ; stʌŋ/) **1** [I, Tn] prick or wound (sb) with or as if with a sting; have the ability to do this 蜇(伤), 刺(伤)(某人); 有蜇(伤)的能力: *Not all nettles sting.* 并非所有的荨麻接触后都有刺痛感. ○ *a stinging wind* 刺骨的风 ○ *A bee stung me on the cheek.* 一只蜜蜂蜇了我的脸. ○ *The smoke is stinging my eyes.* 烟把我的眼睛熏得很疼. ○ *The impact of the tennis ball really stung his leg.* 网球撞击在他的腿上, 真够疼的. ○ (*fig* 比喻) *His words certainly stung (her).* 他的话确实刺痛了(她). ○ *He was stung* (ie deeply upset) *by their insults.* 他因受到他们的侮辱而非常气愤. **2** [I] feel sharp pain 感到剧痛: *My eyes are stinging from the smoke.* 我的眼睛让烟熏得很疼. ○ *His knee stung from the graze.* 他的膝盖擦伤后十分疼痛. **3** [Tn, Tn·pr] **~ sb (to/into sth)** provoke sb by making him angry, upset or offended 激怒、惹恼或冒犯某人: *Their taunts stung him to action/into fighting.* 他们冷嘲热讽惹得他采取了行动[打了起来]. ○ *Her insult stung him into making a rude reply.* 她侮辱了他, 气得他粗鲁地反唇相讥. **4** [Tn, Tn·pr] **~ sb (for sth)** (*infml* 口) charge sb too much money (for sth); swindle sb (为某事物)向某人索取高价, 诈骗某人钱财: *He was stung for £5*, ie had to pay this amount. 他让人家敲了5英镑的竹杠. ○ *How much did they sting you for?* 他们骗了你多少钱?

▷ **stinger** *n* (*infml* 口) thing that stings, esp a painful blow 造成伤痛的事物; (尤指)使人疼痛的一击.

□ **ˈstinging-nettle** *n* = NETTLE 1.

stingy /ˈstɪndʒɪ; ˋstɪndʒɪ/ *adj* (*infml* 口) spending, using or giving unwillingly; mean 吝啬的; 吝惜的; 小气的: *Don't be so stingy with the sugar!* 别那么吝惜糖! ○ *He's very stingy about lending money.* 他非常吝啬, 不愿借钱给别人. ○ *a stingy portion of food* 量很少的一份食物. ▷ **stin·gily** /-ɪlɪ; -əlɪ/ *adv*. **stingi·ness** *n* [U].

stink /stɪŋk; stɪŋk/ *v* (*pt* **stank** /stæŋk; stæŋk/ or **stunk** /stʌŋk; stʌŋk/, *pp* **stunk**) (*infml* 口) **1** [I, Ipr] **~ (of sth)** have a very unpleasant and offensive smell 有臭味; 发臭: *That rotten fish stinks.* 那条鱼腐烂得发臭了. ○ *Her breath stank of garlic.* 她呼吸中有大蒜味. **2** [I, Ipr] **~ (of sth)** (*fig* 比喻) seem very unpleasant, bad or dishonest 似乎很让人讨厌、很糟糕或很不正当: *The whole business stinks (of corruption)!* 这件事从头到尾都散发着(贪污腐化的)臭味! ○ *What do I think of the film? It stinks* (ie is of very low quality)*!* 我认为这部影片怎么样? 简直糟透了! **3** (phr v) **stink sth out** fill a place with a very unpleasant smell 使某处充满臭味: *He stank the whole house out with his tobacco smoke.* 他吸烟把整所房子弄得难闻极了.

▷ **stink** *n* **1** [C] (*infml* 口) very unpleasant smell 非常难闻的气味; 臭味: *What a stink!* 真臭! **2** [sing] (*sl* 俚) trouble; fuss 麻烦; 忙乱: *The whole business caused quite a stink.* 整件事弄得乱七八糟. ○ *kick up/raise/make a ˈstink (about sth)* (在某事上)惹出麻烦. **3** (idm 习语) **like ˈstink** (*sl* 俚) intensely; very hard 紧张地; 十分努力: *working like stink* 干活十分卖力.

stinker *n* (*Brit*) **1** (*dated sl* 旧, 俚) very unpleasant person 讨厌的人. **2** (*infml* 口) thing that is very severe or difficult to do 非常棘手或困难的事情: *The biology paper* (ie in an examination) *was a real stinker.* 生物试卷真难答.

stink·ing *adj* [attrib 作定语] (*sl* 俚) very bad or unpleasant; horrible 极坏的; 很讨厌的; 糟透的: *I don't want your stinking money.* 我才不要你的臭钱呢. ○ *She'd got a stinking cold.* 她得了重感冒. — *adv* (*sl* 俚) extremely; very 极其; 非常: *stinking rich/drunk* 十分富有[烂醉如泥].

□ **ˈstink-bomb** *n* small container which when broken gives off a very unpleasant smell (as a practical joke) 臭弹(破碎时可发出恶臭, 作恶作剧用).

stint /stɪnt; stɪnt/ *v* [I, Ipr, Tn, Tn·pr] **~ on sth; ~ sb/oneself (of sth)** (usu in negative sentences 通常用于否定句) restrict, limit sb/oneself to a small amount of (esp food) 节制、限制某人[自己](尤指食物): *Don't stint (on) the cream!* 不要舍不得奶油! ○ *She stinted herself of food in order to let the children have enough.* 她自己省着吃, 好让孩子们吃饱. Cf 参看 UNSTINTING.

▷ **stint** *n* **1** person's fixed or allotted amount or period of work, etc (工作等)固定的或指定的量或期限; 定量; 定额; 任期: *Everybody must do a daily stint in the kitchen.* 每个人都应该每天在厨房里干点活儿. ○ *Then I had a stint as security officer in Hong Kong.* 我那时在香港做过一阵护卫员. **2** (idm 习语) **without ˈstint** (*fml* 文) without holding back; generously and in large amounts 毫无保留地; 慷慨地; 大量地: *She praised them without stint.* 她极力夸奖他们.

sti·pend /ˈstaɪpend; ˋstaɪpɛnd/ *n* official income (esp of a clergyman); salary 薪俸(尤指神职人员的); 薪金.

▷ **sti·pen·di·ary** /staɪˈpendɪərɪ; *US* -dɪerɪ; staɪˋpɛndɪˌɛrɪ/ *adj* receiving a stipend 有薪俸的; 受薪的: *a stipendiary magistrate*, ie a paid professional magistrate 受薪的地方法官. — *n* stipendiary magistrate 受薪的地方法官.

stipple /ˈstɪpl; ˋstɪpl̩/ *v* [Tn esp passive 尤用于被动语态] paint, draw or engrave (sth) in small dots (not in lines, etc) 用点画、点描或点刻法描绘或雕刻(某物)(不用线条等): *a stippled effect* 点画效果.

stipu·late /ˈstɪpjʊleɪt; ˋstɪpjəˌlet/ *v* [Tn, Tf] (*fml* 文) state (sth) clearly and firmly as a requirement 讲明, 规定(某要求): *I stipulated red paint, not black.* 我已讲明要红漆, 不要黑漆. ○ *It was stipulated that the goods should be delivered within three days.* 按规定货物须在三日内送交.

▷ **stipu·la·tion** /ˌstɪpjʊˈleɪʃn; ˌstɪpjəˋleʃən/ *n* (*fml* 文) **(a)** [U] action of stipulating 讲明; 规定. **(b)** [C] thing stipulated; condition 契约; 合同; 协定; 条件; 条款: *on the stipulation that...* 按规定… ○ *There are several stipulations.* 有几项条件.

stir[1] /stɜː(r); stɝ/ *v* (**-rr-**) **1 (a)** [Tn, Tn·pr] **~ sth (with sth)** move a spoon, etc round and round in (a liquid or some other substance) in order to mix it thoroughly 搅动, 搅和, 搅拌(液体等): *stir one's tea with a spoon* 用匙搅动茶 ○ *stir the porridge, cake mixture, sauce, etc* 搅动麦片粥、做蛋糕的混合料、沙司等. **(b)** [Tn·pr, Tn·p] **~ sth into sth; ~ sth in** add one substance to another in this way 用搅拌方法将某物搀入另一物中: *stir milk into a cake mixture* 把牛奶搅和到做蛋糕的混合料中 ○ *stir the nuts in (well)* 把果仁(均匀地)拌入. **2** [I, Tn] (cause sth to) move slightly (使某物)微动: *Not a leaf was stirring*, ie There was no wind to move the leaves. 树叶一动都不动(无风). ○ *A gentle breeze stirred the leaves.* 微风吹动了树叶. ○ *Nobody was stirring in the house*, ie Everybody was resting, sleeping, etc. 屋里没有动静(大家都在休息、睡觉等). ○ *She's not stirring/She hasn't stirred yet*, ie She is still in bed. 她还没起床. ○ *Stir yourself!* ie Get moving! Get busy! 动弹动弹(活动起来; 找点事干)! **3** [Tn, Tn·pr] **~ sb (to sth)** excite or arouse (a person or his feelings, etc) 激励, 鼓励(某人); 激发(某人的感情等): *The story stirred the boy's imagination.* 那故事引发了那男孩的幻想. ○ *Discontent stirred the men to mutiny.* 不满情绪酿成了兵变. **4** [I] (esp of a feeling) begin to be felt (尤指感情)引起, 激起, 挑起, 唤起: *Pity stirred in her heart.* 她油然产生恻隐之心. ○ *Old memories stirred as she looked at the photographs.* 她看到这些照片, 唤起了对往事的回忆. **5** [I] (*infml derog* 口, 贬) cause trouble between people (esp by telling untrue stories, gossiping, etc) 搬弄是非(尤指以不实之词、流言蜚语等): *Who's been stirring?* 是谁搬弄是非? **6** (idm 习语) **stir one's/the ˈblood** rouse sb to excitement or enthusiasm 使某人的血液沸腾; 使某人激动或兴奋: *The music really stirred my blood.* 这音乐的确使我非常激动. **stir one's ˈstumps** (*infml joc* 口, 谑) walk or move faster; hurry 快走; 赶紧; 赶快. **7** (phr v) **stir sb up** rouse sb to action 鼓动某人采取行动: *The men are being stirred up by outsiders.* 士兵受到了外人的煽动. ○ *He needs stirring up.* 他需要鼓励. **stir sth up** cause (trouble, etc) 惹起(麻烦等): *stir up trouble, unrest, discontent, etc among the workers*

在工人中挑起事端、煽起动乱、激起不满情绪等.

▷ **stir** *n* **1** [C] action of stirring (STIR[1] 1a) 搅动; 搅和; 搅拌: *Give the soup a stir.* 把汤搅拌一下. **2** [sing] excitement; fuss; disturbance 激动; 纷乱; 骚乱: *The news caused quite a stir in the village.* 那消息在村里引起了一片混乱.

stir·rer /ˈstɜːrə(r); ˈstɝɚ/ *n* (*infml derog* 口, 贬) person who habitually causes trouble between other people 经常搬弄是非的人; 捣乱分子.

stir·ring /ˈstɜːrɪŋ; ˈstɝɪŋ/ *adj* [usu attrib 通常作定语] very exciting 令人兴奋的; 激动人心的: *stirring adventure stories* 扣人心弦的冒险故事. **stir·ringly** *adv*.

□ ˈ**stir-fry** *v* (*pt, pp* **-fried**) [Tn] cook (vegetables, meat, etc) by frying them for a short time in very hot oil while stirring them (用旺火)快炒(蔬菜、肉等). — *n* oriental dish made in this way (东方式)炒菜.

stir[2] /stɜː(r); stɝ/ *n* (idm 习语) **in stir** (*sl* 俚) in prison 坐牢.

stir·rup /ˈstɪrəp; ˈstɪrəp/ *n* either of a pair of D-shaped metal or leather foot-supports hanging down from a horse's saddle 马镫: *a pair of stirrups* 一副马镫.

□ ˈ**stirrup-cup** *n* drink (of wine, etc) given to a rider on horseback before he begins a journey, esp formerly (给骑马登程者喝的)饯别酒等(尤指旧时).

ˈ**stirrup-pump** *n* small portable pump used for putting out small fires (手提式)小型灭火泵.

stitch /stɪtʃ; stɪtʃ/ *n* **1** [C] (**a**) single passing of a needle and thread into and out of cloth, etc in sewing, or into and out of skin tissue, etc in surgery (缝纫或外科缝合的)一针. ⇨illus at SEW 见SEW插图. (**b**) (in knitting or crochet) one complete turn of the wool, etc over the needle (编结或编织的)一针; (钩针编织的)一钩. **2** [C] (**a**) loop of thread, wool, etc made in this way 针脚: *make long, short, neat, etc stitches* 缝长、短、匀整...针脚 ○ *The cut in my hand needed five stitches.* 我手上的伤口需要缝五针. (**b**) piece of thread used to sew tissue together in surgery (外科的)缝线: *I'm having my stitches (taken) out today*, ie removed from a wound that has healed. 我的伤口今天拆线. **3** [C, U] (esp in compounds 尤用以构成复合词) particular pattern of stitches or way of stitching (in sewing, knitting or crochet) 缝法; 针法; 织法; 编结法: *chain-stitch* 链形缝法 ○ *knitting in purl stitch* 以反针编织. **4** [C usu *sing* 通常作单数] sudden sharp pain in the muscles at the side of the body (caused eg by running too hard) (胁部的)突然剧痛(如跑步过力所致): *Can we slow down and walk for a bit? I'm getting a stitch.* 咱们放慢速度步行一会儿好吗? 我觉得腰部突然一阵剧痛. **5** (idm 习语) **drop a stitch** ⇨ DROP[2]. **have not (got) a ˈstitch on/ not be wearing a ˈstitch** (*infml* 口) be naked 一丝不挂; 赤身露体. **in ˈstitches** (*infml* 口) laughing uncontrollably 大笑不止; 捧腹大笑: *The play had us in stitches.* 这出戏把我们笑得前仰后合. **a ˌstitch in ˌtime saves ˈnine** (*saying* 谚) if one takes action or does a piece of work immediately, it may save a lot of extra work later 一针及时, 可省九针(及时行动, 免得问题成堆).

▷ **stitch** *v* **1** (**a**) [I, Tn] put stitches in or on (sth); sew 缝, 缝合, 编结, 编织(某物); 缝纫: *stitching (a shirt) by candlelight* 点着蜡烛缝(衬衫). (**b**) [Tn·pr] join or fasten (sth) with stitches 将(某物)缝上: *stitch a button on a dress* 在连衣裙上钉个钮扣 ○ *stitch a zip into a skirt* 给裙子缝上拉链. **2** (phr v) **stitch sth up** join together or close sth by stitching 缝合、缝补某物: *stitch up a wound/a hole* 缝合伤口[缝补破洞] ○ *We'll soon have you* (ie your wound) *stitched up!* 我们很快就把你的伤口缝好!

stitch·ing *n* [U] (row, group, etc of) stitches 针脚(的一行、串等): *neat stitching* 匀整的针脚 ○ *The stitching has come undone.* 针脚开线了.

stoat /stəʊt; stot/ *n* ermine, esp when its fur is brown in the summer 扫雪, 短尾鼬, 白鼬(尤指夏季毛为褐色时). Cf 参看 WEASEL.

stock[1] /stɒk; stɑk/ *n* **1** [C, U] store of goods available for sale, distribution or use, in a shop, warehouse, etc (商店、货栈等的)库存物, 存货: *a good stock of shoes* 库存充足的鞋 ○ *Our new stock of winter clothes will arrive soon.* 我们的新冬装很快就到货. ○ *Your order can be supplied from stock.* 您订的货可从仓库中提取. **2** [C, U] **~ (of sth)** supply or amount of sth available for use, etc 供给; 供应; 贮备量: *a good stock of jokes* 很多的笑话 ○ *get in stocks of coal for the winter* 储存冬季用煤 ○ *Stocks of food are running low.* 存的食物越来越少了. ○ [attrib 作定语] *Stationery is kept in the stock cupboard.* 文具存放在贮物柜里. **3** (also ˈ**livestock**) [U] farm animals 家畜; 牲畜: *buy some more stock for breeding* 再买些牲畜来饲养. **4** [C, U] money lent to a government at a fixed rate of interest 公债: *government stock* 公债. **5** (**a**) [U] capital of a business company (公司的)资本. (**b**) [C usu *pl* 通常作复数] portion of this held by an investor (different from *shares* in that it is not issued in fixed amounts) 股分(不按固定数目发行的, 有别于 shares): *invest in stocks and shares* 投资于证券. **6** [U] person's line of ancestry; family line (of the type specified by the *adj*) 世系, 家世, 血统(以形容词表明所属类型): *a woman of Irish stock* 有爱尔兰血统的女子 ○ *born of farming stock*, ie in a family of farmers 农民家庭出身. **7** [U] (*fml* 文) person's standing or reputation in the opinion of others (别人的)评价; 名声: *His stock is high*, ie He is well thought of. 他的声望很高. **8** [U] raw material ready to be used in manufacturing sth 原料: ˈ*paper stock*, eg rags, wood, etc to be made into paper 造纸原料(如破布、木材等). **9** [C, U] liquid made by stewing bones, meat, fish, vegetables, etc in water, used as a basis for soups, gravy, etc (用骨头、肉、鱼、蔬菜等炖成的)汤汁, 高汤: *sauce made with chicken stock* 用鸡汤做的沙司. **10** [C] base, support or handle of an instrument, a tool, etc (仪器、工具等的)基座, 支座, 手柄: *the stock of a rifle/plough/ whip* 步枪枪托[犁具手柄/鞭子把手]. ⇨illus at GUN 见GUN插图. **11** [C] lower and thicker part of a tree trunk 树干下部的粗大部分. **12** [C] growing plant onto which a cutting is grafted 砧木. **13 stocks** [pl] framework supporting a ship while it is being built or repaired 船台(造船或修船的). **14 stocks** [pl] wooden framework with holes for the feet (and sometimes also the hands) in which wrongdoers were formerly locked, as a punishment 足枷(有时附手枷, 旧时刑具): *be put in the stocks* 被戴上足枷. Cf 参看 PILLORY. **15** [C] (**a**) wide band of stiff material formerly worn around the neck by men (旧时男子颈上围的)硬领. (**b**) type of cravat worn as part of a formal riding kit (作为正式骑马服装之配件的)领巾. (**c**) piece of black or purple fabric worn hanging from a clergyman's collar over the front of his shirt (牧师系的)黑领带或紫领带. **16** [C, U] type of garden plant with single or double brightly coloured and sweet-smelling flowers 紫罗兰. **17** (idm 习语) **(be) in/ out of ˈstock** available/not available (in a shop, etc) (商店等中)有[无]现货的: *The book is in/out of stock.* 该书有库存[已脱销]. ○ *Have you any grey pullovers in stock?* 你们有灰色套头毛衣的现货吗? **lock, stock and barrel** ⇨ LOCK[2]. **on the ˈstocks** being constructed or prepared 在建造中; 在准备中: *Our new model is already on the stocks and will be available in the autumn.* 我们正着手生产一种新的款式, 可望在秋季面世. **take stock (of sth)** examine and make a list of all the goods (in a shop, warehouse, etc) (商店、仓库等)盘点存货. **take stock (of sb/sth)** review, assess and form an opinion (about a situation, sb's abilities, etc) (对情况、某人的能力等)进行检查、评估和鉴定: *After a year in the job, she decided it was time to take stock (of her situation).* 她从事此工作一年之后, 决定(对自己的情况)检讨一番.

▷ **stock** *adj* [attrib 作定语] **1** usually kept in stock and regularly available 通常备有现货的; 常备的: *stock sizes* 常备尺码 ○ *one of our stock items* 本店常备商品之一. **2** commonly used; used too much (and therefore not interesting, effective, etc) 常用的; 陈腐的: *a stock argument* 陈腐的论点 ○ *stock questions/answers* 经常碰到的问题[老一套的回答] ○ *She's tired of her husband's stock jokes.* 她已听厌了丈夫说的那些老一套的俏皮话.

□ ˈ**stock-breeder** *n* farmer who raises or breeds livestock 牲畜饲养者; 畜牧业者.

ˈ**stockbroker** (also **broker**) *n* person who buys and sells stocks and shares for clients 证券经纪人; 股票经纪人. ˈ**stockbroking** *n* [U]: *He's in stockbroking.* 他从事股票经纪业务. ○ [attrib 作定语] *a stockbroking friend of mine* 我那干股票经纪的朋友.

S

ˈ**stock-car** *n* **1** ordinary car that has been specially strengthened for use in racing where deliberate bumping is allowed 经特别加固可在允许故意碰撞的比赛中使用的普通汽车. **2** (*US*) railway truck for carrying cattle 运牲口的火车车厢. ˈ**stock-car racing** racing of stock-cars(1) 普通型汽车赛.

ˈ**stock certificate** (*US*) certificate for the purchase of shares (SHARE[1] 3) 股票; 股分证书.

ˈ**stock company** **1** company of actors who have a repertoire of plays which they perform at a particular theatre 固定剧团(在固定剧场演出保留节目的专业剧团). **2** (also **joint-ˈstock company**) group of people who carry on a business with money contributed by all 股分公司.

ˈ**stock-cube** *n* cube of dried stock[1](9) used for making soup, etc 固体汤料: *beef stock-cubes* 固体牛肉汤料.

ˈ**stock exchange** place where stocks and shares are publicly bought and sold; (group of professional dealers engaged in) such business 股票交易所; 证券交易所: *The London Stock Exchange is in turmoil today.* 今天伦敦证券市场一片混乱. ○ *lose money on the stock exchange* 在股票交易中赔钱.

ˈ**stockholder** *n* (*esp US*) person who owns stocks and shares 股票持有人; 股东.

ˌ**stock-in-ˈtrade** *n* [U] **1** everything needed for a particular trade or occupation 干某行业所需的一切. **2** (*fig* 比喻) words, actions, behaviour, etc commonly used, displayed, etc by a particular person 某人惯用的言辞、手段、作法等: *Facetious remarks are part of his stock-in-trade.* 讲俏皮话是他的拿手好戏.

ˈ**stockjobber** *n* member of a stock exchange who buys and sells stocks and shares so as to take advantage of variations in their prices, dealing with stockbrokers but not with the general public 证券批销经纪(仅与证券经纪交易以赚取差价, 不直接与公众交易者).

ˈ**stockman** /-mən; -mən/ *n* (*pl* **-men** /-mən; -mən/) (*Austral* 澳) man in charge of livestock (男)畜牧工, 饲养员.

ˈ**stock-market** *n* stock exchange or the business conducted there 股票市场; 证券市场; 股票交易; 证券交易: *dealings on the stock-market* 股票市场的交易 ○ [attrib 作定语] *stock-market prices* 股市价格.

ˈ**stockpile** *n* large supply of goods, materials, etc collected and kept for future use (esp because they may become difficult to obtain, eg in a war) 物资贮备(尤指紧缺货物、材料等之储存, 如战时所为). — *v* [Tn] collect and keep (a supply of goods, etc) in this way 储备, 贮存(供应品等): *stockpiling nuclear weapons* 储备核武器.

ˈ**stock-pot** *n* pot in which stock[1](9) is made or kept (炖或存原汁汤用的)锅, 罐.

ˈ**stock-taking** *n* [U] **1** making a list of all the stock[1](1) in a shop, etc 清点存货; 盘存: *Next week we shall be closed for stock-taking.* 下星期我们暂停营业盘点存货. **2** review of one's situation, position, resources, etc (对自己的情况、地位、资源等的)估量, 评估.

ˈ**stockyard** *n* enclosure where cattle are kept temporarily or sorted, eg at a market, before being killed or sold or moved elsewhere (临时的或分种类的)牲畜栏(如市场上的、屠宰或出售前的或转运前的).

stock[2] /stɒk; stɑk/ *v* **1** [Tn] keep (goods) in stock; keep a supply of 储备, 贮存(货物); 保持...之供应: *Do you stock raincoats?* 你们有雨衣存货吗? ○ *They stock all sizes.* 他们各种尺码齐备. **2** [Tn, Tn·pr] **~ sth (with sth)** provide or equip sth with goods, livestock or a supply of sth (以货物、牲畜或供应品)供应某处: *stock a shop with goods* 向商店供货 ○ *a shop well stocked with the latest fashions* 备有各种最新款式的商店 ○ *a badly stocked library* 藏书不多的图书馆 ○ (*fig* 比喻) *He has a memory well stocked with facts.* 他记着很多事情. **3** (phr v) **stock up (on/with sth) (for sth)** collect and keep supplies (of sth for a particular occasion or purpose) (为某种需要或目的)储备(某物): *As soon as they heard about possible food shortages, they began to stock up.* 他们一听说食物可能短缺, 就立即储备起来. ○ *stock up on fuel for the winter* 贮存燃料以备过冬 ○ *stock up with food for Christmas* 为圣诞节购备食品.

▷ **stock·ist** /ˈstɒkɪst; ˈstɑkɪst/ *n* person or business firm that stocks certain goods for sale 有存货的商人或商号: *available from all good stockists* 从所有存货齐备的商店都可买到.

stock·ade /stɒˈkeɪd; stɑkˋed/ *n* line or wall of strong upright (esp wooden) posts, built as a defence (防御用的)栅栏(尤指木头的).

▷ **stock·ade** *v* [Tn usu passive 通常用于被动语态] defend (an area) with a stockade 用栅栏防御(某区域).

stock·inet (also **stock·inette**) /ˌstɒkɪˈnet; ˌstɑkɪnˋɛt/ *n* [U] fine elastic machine-knitted material, used for underwear, etc 弹力织物(用作内衣料等).

stock·ing /ˈstɒkɪŋ; ˋstɑkɪŋ/ *n* **1** either of a pair of tight-fitting coverings for the feet and legs, reaching to or above the knee 长筒袜: *a pair of nylon/silk/woollen/cotton stockings* 一双长筒的尼龙[丝/毛/棉]袜. Cf 参看 TIGHTS. **2** (idm 习语) **in one's stocking(ed) ˈfeet** wearing socks or stockings but not shoes 只穿袜不穿鞋的.

stock-still /ˌstɒk ˈstɪl; ˋstɑkˋstɪl/ *adv* motionlessly 静止地: *remain standing stock-still* 一动不动地站着.

stocky /ˈstɒkɪ; ˋstɑkɪ/ *adj* (**-ier, -iest**) (usu of people) short, strong and solid in appearance (通常指人)矮而强壮的: *stocky legs* 短而粗的腿 ○ *a stocky little man* 敦实的男子. ▷ **stock·ily** *adv*: *a stockily built man* 五短身材的壮汉. **stocki·ness** *n* [U].

stodge /stɒdʒ; stɑdʒ/ *n* [U] (*infml usu derog* 口, 通常作贬义) food that is heavy, solid and not easy to digest 水分少而不易消化的食物.

▷ **stodgy** /ˈstɒdʒɪ; ˋstɑdʒɪ/ *adj* (**-ier, -iest**) (*infml derog* 口, 贬) **1** (of food) heavy, solid and difficult to digest (指食物)水分少而难消化的: *stodgy school meals* 学校里吃的淀粉多而不好消化的饭菜. **2** (of a book, etc) written in a heavy uninteresting way (指书等)冗长乏味的. **3** (of a person) uninteresting; not lively; dull (指人)无趣的, 无生气的, 迟钝的. **stodgily** *adv*. **stodgi·ness** *n* [U].

stoic /ˈstəʊɪk; ˋsto·ɪk/ *n* (*fml* 文) person who has great self-control and who endures pain, discomfort or misfortune without complaining or showing signs of feeling it 斯多葛派人士(有高度自制力的人, 能忍受困苦或不幸而无怨言或仍泰然自若).

▷ **sto·ical** /-kl; -kḷ/ (also **stoic**) *adj* (*fml* 文) of or like a stoic; enduring pain, etc without complaint (似)斯多葛派的; 经受痛苦等而无怨言的: *a very stoical response to hardship* 经受苦难仍泰然自若. **sto·ic·ally** /-klɪ; -klɪ/ *adv*.

sto·icism /ˈstəʊɪsɪzəm; ˋsto·ɪˌsɪzəm/ *n* [U] (*fml* 文) behaving stoically 斯多葛哲学; 自制; 坚忍: *She showed great stoicism during her husband's final illness.* 她在丈夫患病临终期间表现出了坚强的毅力. ○ *They reacted to the appalling weather with typical British stoicism.* 他们忍受着恶劣天气的煎熬, 表现了英国人典型的坚忍不拔的精神.

stoke /stəʊk; stok/ *v* **1** [Tn, Tn·pr, Tn·p] **~ sth (up) (with sth)** put (coal or some other fuel) on the fire of a furnace, an engine, etc (给熔炉、机车等)添加(煤或其他燃料): *stoke the boiler with coal* 给锅炉加煤. **2** (phr v) **stoke up (with sth)** (**a**) stoke a fire, etc (往火里等)加煤, 加燃料: *The caretaker stokes up twice a day.* 管理员每天往火里加两次煤. (**b**) (*infml* 口) fill oneself with food; eat a lot 吃饱; 大吃: *You should stoke up now — you may not get another meal today.* 你现在得吃得饱饱的——你今天可能再没饭吃了.

▷ **stoker** *n* **1** person who stokes a furnace, etc, esp on a ship 司炉(尤指船上的). **2** mechanical device for doing this 加煤机; 加燃料机.

□ ˈ**stokehole** (also ˈ**stokehold**) *n* place where a ship's furnaces are stoked (轮船上的)锅炉舱.

STOL /ˌes tiː əʊ ˈel *or, in informal use,* 俗读作 stɒl; ˌɛs ti o ˋɛl, stol/ *abbr* 缩写 = (of aircraft) short take-off and landing (指飞机)短距起落: *a STOL plane* 短距起落飞机 ○ *flying STOLs* 短距起落飞行. Cf 参看 VTOL.

stole[1] /stəʊl; stol/ *n* **1** women's garment like a wide scarf, worn around the shoulders (女用)披肩. **2** strip of silk or other material worn (round the neck with the ends hanging down in front) by some Christian priests during services (某些基督教教士在举行仪式时佩的)圣带(用绸或其他料子制成, 佩在领部, 两端垂于前方).

stole[2] *pt, pp* of STEAL.

stolen *pp* of STEAL.

stolid /ˈstɒlɪd; ˈstɑlɪd/ *adj* (*usu derog* 通常作贬义) (of a person) not easily excited; showing little or no emotion or interest (指人)不易激动的, 不热情的, 冷漠的: *He conceals his feelings behind a rather stolid manner.* 他装作无动于衷的样子以掩盖自己的感情. ▷ **stol·idly** *adv.* **stol·id·ity** /stəˈlɪdətɪ; stəˈlɪdətɪ/ (also **stolid·ness**) *n* [U].

stom·ach /ˈstʌmək; ˈstʌmək/ *n* **1** [C] bag-like organ of the body into which food passes when swallowed and in which the first part of digestion occurs 胃: *It's unwise to swim on a full stomach*, ie when one has just eaten a meal. 刚吃完饭不宜游泳. ○ *I don't like going to work on an empty stomach*, ie without having eaten anything. 我不愿意空着肚子去上班. ○ *He felt an aching feeling in (the pit of) his stomach.* 他胃疼. ○ [attrib 作定语] *a stomach upset, disorder, etc* 反胃、胃不适. ⇨illus at DIGESTIVE 见 DIGESTIVE 插图. **2** [C] (*infml* 口) front part of the body between the chest and thighs; abdomen 肚子; 腹部: *He hit me in the stomach.* 他击中我的肚子. **3** [U] (**a**) appetite for food 食欲; 胃口: *have a very small stomach* 胃口很小. (**b**) **~ for sth** (*fig* 比喻) desire or eagerness for sth 对某事物的欲望或渴求: *I had no stomach for a fight.* 我不想打架. **4** (idm 习语) **sb's eyes are bigger than his stomach** ⇨ EYE[1]. **sick to one's stomach** ⇨ SICK. **a strong stomach** ⇨ STRONG. **turn one's ˈstomach** cause sb to be disgusted or revolted 使某人反胃或恶心: *The film about eye operations turned my stomach.* 这部眼科手术的影片看得我恶心极了.

▷ **stom·ach** *v* [Tn] (esp in negative sentences or questions 尤用于否定句或疑问句) **1** eat (sth) without feeling ill 吃(某物)而不感到难受: *I can't stomach seafood.* 我吃不惯海味. **2** endure (sth); tolerate 忍受(某事物); 容忍: *How could you stomach all the violence in the film?* 那部影片里的那些暴力场面, 你怎么竟看得下去呢?

□ ˈ**stomach-ache** *n* [C] pain in the stomach or the bowels 胃痛; 腹痛; 肚子痛.

ˈ**stomach-pump** *n* pump with a flexible tube, inserted into the stomach through the mouth and used to remove (esp poisonous) substances from the stomach or to force liquid into it 胃唧筒(洗胃器具).

stomp /stɒmp; stɑmp/ *v* [Ipr, Ip] **~ about, around, off, etc** (*infml* 口) move, walk, dance, etc with a heavy step (in the specified direction) 以重踏步方式(向某方向)移动、行进、跳舞等: *stomp about noisily* 脚步重重地踱来踱去 ○ *She slammed the door and stomped (off) out of the house.* 她砰的一声关上了门, 噔噔地走出了屋子. ⇨Usage at STUMP 用法见 STUMP.

stone /stəʊn; ston/ *n* **1** [U] (often used attributively or in compounds 常用作定语或用以构成复合词) hard solid mineral substance that is not metallic; (type of) rock 石; 石头; 岩石: *ˈsandstone* 沙岩 ○ *ˈlimestone* 石灰岩 ○ *a house built of grey ˈstone* 用灰色石料砌成的房子 ○ *stone walls, buildings, floors, statues*, ie made or built of stone 石墙、石楼、石板地面、石雕 ○ *What type of stone is this?* 这是什么石头? **2** [C] piece of rock of any shape, usu small in size, broken or cut off 石块; 石子; 碎石: *a pile of stones* 一堆石块 ○ *a road covered with stones* 碎石路 ○ *Small stones rolled down the hillside as they ran up.* 他们跑上山坡, 同时有些小石子滚了下来. ○ *She picked up the stone and threw it into the river.* 她捡起那块石头扔进河里了. **3** [C] (usu in compounds 通常用以构成复合词) piece of stone shaped for a particular purpose 加工成某形状作某用途的石块: *a ˈgravestone* 墓碑 ○ *ˈstepping-stones* 踏脚石 ○ *ˈpaving stones* 铺路石 ○ *ˈtombstones* 墓碑 ○ *ˈmillstones* 磨石. **4** (also **precious ˈstone**) [C] jewel or gem 宝石; 钻石: *a sapphire ring with six small stones* 镶有六颗小蓝宝石的戒指. **5** (also *esp US* **pit**) [C] (sometimes in compounds 有时用以构成复合词) hard shell containing the nut or seed inside some fruits (eg apricots, olives, plums, cherries, peaches) 核(如杏、橄榄、李子、樱桃、桃的): *a damson stone* 西洋李子的核. ⇨illus at FRUIT 见 FRUIT 插图. **6** [C] (esp in compounds 尤用以构成复合词) small hard object that has formed in the bladder or kidney and causes pain 结石(膀胱或肾脏中的): *an operation to remove ˈkidney stones* 取出肾结石的手术. Cf 参看 GALLSTONE (GALL). **7** [C] (*pl* unchanged 复数不变) (*abbr* 缩写 **st**) (*Brit*) unit of weight; 14 pounds 吃(重量单位, 等于14磅): *He weighs 10 stone.* 他体重10吃. ○ *two stones of potatoes* 两吃的土豆. ⇨App 5 见附录5. **8** (idm 习语) **blood out of/from a stone** ⇨ BLOOD[1]. **hard as nails/stone** ⇨ HARD[1]. **a heart of stone** ⇨ HEART. **kill two birds with one stone** ⇨ KILL. **leave no stone unturned** ⇨ LEAVE[1]. **people in glass houses shouldn't throw stones** ⇨ PEOPLE. **sink like a stone** ⇨ SINK[1]. **a ˈstone's throw** a very short distance 很短的距离: *We live a stone's throw from/within a stone's throw of here.* 我们住的地方离这里很近. **a rolling stone gathers no moss** ⇨ ROLL[2].

▷ **stone** *v* [Tn] **1** throw stones at (sb) (esp formerly as a punishment) 向(某人)扔石块; 用石头砸(某人)(尤指旧时作为惩罚手段): *stoned to death* 受以石击毙刑. **2** remove the stones (STONE 5) from (fruit) 去掉(水果)的核: *stoned dates* 去核的枣. **3** (idm 习语) ˌ**stone the ˈcrows** (*Brit sl* 俚) (used as an exclamation of surprise, shock, disgust, etc 用作感叹语, 表示惊讶、震惊、嫌恶等): *Well, stone the crows, he's done it again!* 哎呀, 好家伙, 他又干了一次! **stoned** *adj* [usu pred 通常作表语] (*sl* 俚) (**a**) very drunk 烂醉. (**b**) under the influence of (usu soft) drugs 在(通常为软性的)毒品刺激下.

ˈ**stone·less** *adj* without stones 无核的: *stoneless fruit* 无核的水果.

□ **the ˈStone Age** very early period of human history when tools and weapons were made of stone, not metal 石器时代: [attrib 作定语] *Stone Age settlements* 石器时代的居民点.

ˌ**stone-ˈcold** *adj* completely cold 完全凉的: *The body was stone-cold.* 尸体冰凉了. ○ *This soup is stone-cold.* 这汤全凉了. ˌ**stone-cold ˈsober** completely sober and not under the influence of alcoholic drinks 完全清醒的; 未醉的.

ˌ**stone-ˈdead** *adj* completely dead 完全死的.

ˌ**stone-ˈdeaf** *adj* completely deaf 完全聋的.

ˈ**stone-fruit** *n* [C, U] fruit of a type that contains stones (STONE 5) 核果.

ˈ**stonemason** *n* person who cuts and prepares stone or builds with stone 石工; 石匠.

ˈ**stoneware** *n* [U] pottery made from clay containing a small amount of flint 粗陶器: [attrib 作定语] *stoneware jugs* 粗陶的罐子.

ˈ**stonework** *n* [U] stone parts of a building, etc, esp when decoratively fashioned; masonry 建筑物等的石造部分(尤指装饰性的); 石工(技艺): *a church with beautiful stonework* 有精美石雕的教堂.

stone·wall /ˌstəʊnˈwɔːl; ˌstonˈwɔl/ *v* **1** [I, Tn] (*infml* 口 *esp Brit*) obstruct (a discussion, etc) by non-committal, evasive or very long replies (用含糊其辞或冗长的回答)阻碍(议事等): *a deliberate attempt to stonewall (the debate)* 蓄意设法阻碍(辩论). **2** [I] (in cricket) bat without trying to score runs (板球)守势击球(不拟跑动得分). ▷ **stone·waller** *n*. **stone·wall·ing** *n* [U].

stony /ˈstəʊnɪ; ˈstonɪ/ *adj* (**-ier, -iest**) **1** full of, covered in or having stones 多石的; 铺石的; 有石的: *a stony road* 碎石路 ○ *a river with a stony bottom* 河底有石子的河. **2** hard, cold, and unsympathetic 铁石心肠的; 冷酷的; 无同情心的: *a stony stare, glare, look, gaze, etc* 冷眼注视、怒视、观望、凝视等 ○ *maintaining a stony silence* 表现毫无同情心的冷漠 ○ ˌ*stony-ˈhearted* 铁石心肠的. **3** [pred 作表语] (*sl* 俚) completely without money; penniless 一文不名; 身无分文. **4** (idm 习语) **flat/stony broke** ⇨ BROKE[2].

▷ **sto·nily** /-ɪlɪ; -əlɪ/ *adv* in a stony(2) manner 冷酷地; 无情地: *stonily polite* 冷冰冰地表示有礼的 ○ *She stared stonily in front of her.* 她面无表情地注视着前方.

stood *pt, pp* of STAND.

stooge /stuːdʒ; studʒ/ *n* **1** (*theatre sl* 戏剧界俚语) comedian's assistant, used as the object of his jokes 滑稽演员的配角(作丑角打趣的对象). **2** (*infml derog* 口, 贬) (**a**) person used by another to do routine (usu unpleasant) work 受他人指使处理例行(通常指厌恶的)事务的人. (**b**) person whose actions are entirely controlled by another 完全受他人指使的人: *She's fed up with being her husband's stooge.* 她再也不愿意当丈夫的附属品了.

▷ **stooge** *v* [Ipr] **~ for sb** act as a stooge for (a comedian on stage) 给(台上滑稽演员)当配角.

stool /stu:l; stul/ *n* **1** (often in compounds 常用以构成复合词) seat without a back or arms, usu for one person 凳子(通常指单人的): *a* ˈ*bar stool* 酒吧间的高凳 ○ *a* ˈ*piano stool* 弹钢琴坐的凳子 ○ *sitting on stools around the table* 坐在桌子四周的凳子上. ⇨illus at App 1 见附录1插图, page xvi. **2** = FOOTSTOOL (FOOT[1]). **3** (usu *pl* 通常作复数) (*medical or fml* 医或文) (piece of) solid waste from the body; faeces 大便; 粪便. **4** (idm 习语) **fall between two** ˈ**stools** fail to be or take either of two satisfactory alternatives 两头落空: *The author seems uncertain whether he is writing a comedy or a tragedy, so the play falls between two stools.* 作者似乎拿不定主意是写喜剧还是写悲剧, 致使这个剧非驴非马.

□ ˈ**stool-pigeon** *n* (*infml* 口) person who acts as a decoy, esp to trap a criminal 诱人上圈套者; (尤指)用以诱捕罪犯的人.

stoop /stu:p; stup/ *v* **1** (**a**) [I, Ipr, Ip] ~ **(down)** bend forward and down 俯身; 弯腰: *She stooped low to look under the bed.* 她俯身查看床底. ○ *He stooped under the low beam.* 他在低矮的横梁下弯着腰. ○ *stoop (down) to pick sth up* 弯腰拾起某物. (**b**) [Tn] bend (a part of the body) forward and down 俯(身); 弯(腰): *stoop one's head to get into the car* 俯身进入轿车. **2** [I] have the head and shoulders habitually bent over (习惯性)弓背: *He's beginning to stoop with age*, ie as he gets older. 他年事渐高, 背也开始变驼了. **3** (idm 习语) **stoop so low (as to do sth)** lower one's moral standards so far (as to do sth) 降低自己的道德标准(以致做出某事): *He tried to make me accept a bribe — I hope I would never stoop so low.* 他想让我接受贿赂——我但愿我决不至于做出这种低级的事. **4** (phr v) **stoop to sth/doing sth** lower one's moral standards to do sth 降低自己的道德标准做某事: *He'd stoop to anything*, ie He has no moral standards. 他无论多么不道德的事都干得出来. ○ *I would never stoop to cheating.* 我可决不至于下贱到骗人的地步.

▷ **stoop** *n* (usu *sing* 通常作单数) stooping position of the body 俯身; 弯腰: *walk with a slight stoop* 弓着背行走.

S

stop[1] /stɒp; stɑp/ *v* (**-pp-**) **1** [Tn] put an end to (the movement, progress, operation, etc of a person or thing); cause to halt or pause 使(人或事物的活动、进展、操作等)停止; 使中止或暂停: *stop a car, train, bicycle, etc* 使汽车、火车、自行车等停下来 ○ *Rain stopped play*, eg in cricket. 赛事因雨暂停(如板球赛). ○ *He stopped the machine and left the room.* 他停了机器, 离开了房间. ○ *The earthquake stopped all the clocks.* 地震把所有的钟都震停了. **2** [Tn, Tg] cease or discontinue (sth); leave off 停止或不继续做(某事物); 中断: *stop work* 停止工作 ○ *Stop it!* ie Don't do that! 停下(住手)! ○ *He never stops talking.* 他总是说个没完. ○ *She's stopped smoking.* 她戒烟了. ○ *Will you stop making that horrible noise!* 你别再弄出那种讨厌的响声来行不行! ○ *Has it stopped raining yet?* 雨停了吗? ○ *Supplies have stopped reaching us.* 给我们的供应品中断了. **3** [Tn, Tn·pr, Tsg, Tng] **~sb/sth from doing sth** prevent sb from doing sth or sth from happening 阻止某人做某事; 阻碍某事物发生: *I'm sure he'll go, there's nothing to stop him.* 我肯定他要去的, 没法阻止他. ○ *You can't stop our going/us (from) going if we want to.* 假若我们要去, 你是阻止不了的. ○ *Can't you stop your son from getting into trouble?* 你能不能制止你儿子别惹上麻烦? ○ *I only just managed to stop myself from shouting at him.* 我极力控制住自己没对他喊叫起来. ○ *We bandaged his wound but couldn't stop it bleeding/stop the bleeding.* 我们给他包扎了伤口, 但止不住血. **4** (**a**) [I] refrain from continuing; cease working, moving, etc 不继续进行; 终止工作、活动等: *The rain has stopped.* 雨停了. ○ *The clock stopped.* 钟停了. ○ *His heart has stopped.* 他的心脏停止了跳动. (**b**) [I, Ipr] come to rest; halt or pause 停下; 中止; 暂停: *They stopped for a while to admire the scenery.* 他们停了一会儿来欣赏风景. ○ *Do the buses stop here?* 公共汽车在这里停吗? ○ *The train stopped at the station.* 火车在车站上停了下来. ⇨ Usage at AND 用法见 AND. **5** [Tn, Tn·pr, Tn·p] **~ sth (up) (with sth)** fill or close (a gap, hole, etc) by plugging or obstructing; block sth 堵塞, 阻塞(缝隙、洞孔等): *stop a leak in a pipe, a gap in a hedge* 堵住管子的漏洞、树篱的缺口 ○ *stop up a mouse hole* 堵塞老鼠洞 ○ *stop one's ears*, ie cover them with one's hands to avoid hearing sth 堵住自己的耳朵. **6** [Tn] fill a cavity in (a tooth) 填补(牙)洞. **7** [Tn, Tn·pr] **~ sth (out of/from sth)** refuse to give or allow (sth normally given); keep sth back 拒绝给予或允许(通常给予之事物); 扣留某物: *stop a cheque*, ie order a bank not to cash it 停止兑现支票(通知银行不予兑付) ○ *The cost was stopped out of* (ie deducted from) *my wages.* 那笔费用已从我的工资中扣除. **8** [I, Ipr] (*Brit infml* 口) stay (esp for a short time) 停留(尤指短时间); 逗留: *Are you stopping (for supper)?* 你留在这儿(吃晚饭)吗? ○ *I'm stopping (at) home tonight.* 我今晚待在家里. ○ *We stopped at a campsite for a week.* 我们在露营地呆了一个星期. **9** [Tn] (*music* 音) press down (a string or key) or block (a hole on a musical instrument) to produce the note wanted 按(乐器的弦、键或孔)(以演奏). **10** (idm 习语) **the buck stops here** ⇨ BUCK[4]. **stick/stop at nothing** ⇨ STICK[2]. **stop** ˈ**dead (in one's** ˈ**tracks)** stop very suddenly 突然停止. **stop short of sth/doing sth** be unwilling to go beyond a certain limit in one's actions 不愿超越行动上的某种界限; 不愿逾矩: *He can be ruthless in getting what he wants, but I believe he would stop short of blackmail.* 他这个人为达到目的是心黑手辣的, 但我认为他还不至于使用敲诈手段. **stop the** ˈ**show** receive so much attention, applause, etc from an audience that the performance, etc cannot continue (因观众或听众气氛热烈、掌声不断等)无法继续演出. **11** (phr v) **stop by** (also **stop round**) (*esp US*) make a short visit to sb's house, etc; call in 串门子; 串门儿: *Ask him to stop by for a chat.* 请他来坐坐, 聊聊天. **stop off (at/in ...)** make a short break in a journey (to do sth) 中途稍作停留(做某事): *stop off at the pub on the way home* 归途中在酒馆逗留片刻. **stop over (at/in ...)** break one's journey (esp when travelling by air) for a stay 中途停留(尤指乘飞机旅行时): *stop over in Rome for two days en route for the Middle East* 在飞往中东途中在罗马停留两天. **stop up** not go to bed until later than usual 晚睡觉; 熬夜: *stop up (late) to watch a film on TV* 熬夜看电视影片.

▷ **stop·page** /ˈstɒpɪdʒ; ˈstɑpɪdʒ/ *n* [C] **1** interruption of work in a factory, etc, esp because of a strike 停工(尤指因罢工): *another stoppage at the car plant* 汽车厂的又一次罢工. **2 stoppages** [pl] amount of money deducted by an employer from wages and salaries, for tax, national insurance, etc (工资薪金中用作纳税、购买国民保险等的)扣除款: *There's not much money left after stoppages.* 工资中扣除税款等费用后所剩无几. **3** act of cancelling or withholding (payment, holidays, etc) 停止或取消(付款、假期等): *stoppage of leave*, eg in the army as a punishment 取消休假(如军队中的惩罚). **4** state of being blocked; blockage or obstruction 堵塞; 阻塞: *a stoppage in a gas pipe* 煤气管道的堵塞.

stop·ping *n* filling for a hole in a tooth 牙洞的填充(料).

□ ˈ**stopcock** *n* valve or tap that can regulate the flow of liquid or gas through a pipe (调节管道流量的)阀门, 旋塞: *If a water-pipe bursts turn off the stopcock immediately.* 水管破裂时要立即关紧旋塞.

ˈ**stopgap** *n* person or thing that acts as a temporary substitute for another 临时替代的人或物: [attrib 作定语] *stopgap measures in an emergency* 紧急情况下的临时措施.

ˌ**stop-**ˈ**go** *n* [esp attrib 尤作定语] (*Brit*) deliberate alternating of periods of inflation and deflation 通货膨胀时期与通货紧缩时期的有计划的交替: *a government's* ˌ*stop-go eco*ˈ*nomic policy* 政府采取的使通货膨胀与通货紧缩交替进行的经济政策.

ˈ**stop-light** *n* (*US*) **1** = TRAFFIC LIGHT (TRAFFIC). **2** = BRAKE LIGHT (BRAKE).

ˈ**stopover** *n* (**a**) break in a journey (esp for one night) 中途停留; (尤指)途中过夜. (**b**) place where one does this 中途停留处; 途中过夜处.

ˈ**stopping train** train that stops at many stations between main stations (铁路的)慢车.

ˌ**stop-**ˈ**press** *n* [U] (*Brit*) late news inserted into a newspaper after printing has begun; space into which this is inserted 报纸开印后临时加插的最新消息; 加插最新消息的空栏: *read sth in the stop-press* 阅读报纸加插的最新消息 ○ [attrib 作定语] *a* ˈ*stop-press item* 报纸

开印后加插的一则最新消息.
ˈ**stop-watch** *n* watch with a hand that can be stopped and started by pressing buttons, used to time races, etc very accurately 秒表, 跑表(速度比赛等用的).

stop[2] /stɒp; stɑp/ *n* [C] **1** act of stopping or state of being stopped 停止; 中止; 停留; 逗留: *make a short stop on a journey* 在途中作短暂停留 ○ *The train came/was brought to a sudden stop.* 火车突然停了下来. ○ *The train goes from London to Leeds with only two stops.* 这列火车从伦敦开往利兹只停两站. ○ *Production at the factory has come to a complete/full stop.* 这家工厂的生产已完全停顿. **2** place where a bus, train, etc stops regularly (eg to allow passengers to get on or off) (公共汽车、火车等的)停车站: *Where is the nearest bus-stop?* 离这儿最近的公共汽车站在哪里? ○ *Which stop do I get off at?* 我在哪一站下车? ○ *Is this a request stop?* 这个站是招手停车的汽车站吗? **3** punctuation mark, esp a full stop (.) 标点符号; (尤指)句号. **4** (*music* 音) (**a**) row of pipes in an organ providing tones of one quality (风琴的)排列的管子. (**b**) knob or lever controlling these (球状或杆状)音栓(控制上述管子的). **5** (*music* 音) device for covering any of certain holes on a wind instrument (eg a flute) in order to change the pitch 管乐器(如长笛)的按孔(装置). **6** (in a camera) device for regulating the size of the aperture through which light reaches the lens (照相机的)光圈. **7** (*phonetics* 语音) consonant sound produced by the sudden release of air that has been held back (eg /p, b, k, g, t, d/); plosive 塞音(气流受阻后突然释放发出的辅音, 如/p/、/b/、/k/、/g/、/t/、/d/). **8** (esp in compounds 尤用以构成复合词) device or object that regulates or stops the movement of sth 调节或制止某物动作的装置或物体: *The door was held open by a doorstop.* 那门用了门碰头, 一直开着. **9** (idm 习语) **pull out all the stops** ⇨ PULL[2]. **put an end/a stop to sth** ⇨ END[1].

stop·per /ˈstɒpə(r); ˋstɑpɚ/ (*US* **plug**) *n* object that fits into and closes an opening, esp the top of a bottle or pipe 阻塞物; 堵塞物; (尤指)瓶塞, 管塞; 栓: *put the stopper back into a bottle* 把瓶塞再塞在瓶子上. ⇨illus at BOTTLE 见 BOTTLE 插图.
▷ **stop·per** *v* [Tn] close (sth) with a stopper (用塞子等)塞住(某物).

stor·age /ˈstɔːrɪdʒ; ˋstɔrɪdʒ/ *n* [U] **1** (**a**) storing of goods, etc (货物等的)贮存, 贮藏: [attrib 作定语] *storage space* 贮存场地 ○ *a loft with large storage capacity* 能储放大量物品的阁楼. (**b**) space used or available for this 贮存场地; 贮藏所; 仓库: *fish kept in cold* (ie refrigerated) *storage* 冷藏鱼 ○ *put furniture in storage* 把家具存放起来 ○ [attrib 作定语] *storage tanks*, eg for oil 储存容器(如储油罐). **2** cost of storing things 储存物品的费用; 保管费: *have to pay storage* 须缴纳保管费.
□ ˈ**storage heater** electric radiator that stores heat (accumulated during periods when electricity is cheaper) 蓄热电暖器(可在电费低廉时储存热能).

store /stɔː(r); stɔr/ *n* **1** [C] quantity or supply of sth kept for use as needed 贮存; 储藏; 储备: *lay in* (ie buy and keep) *stores of coal for the winter* 储存冬季用煤 ○ *have a good store of food in the house* 家里储备了大量食物. **2** [C usu *sing* 通常作单数] **~ (of sth)** large accumulated quantity or amount 累积而成的巨大数量: *a library with a store of rare books* 藏有大量珍本的图书馆 ○ *She keeps a store of amusing stories in her head.* 她头脑里有许多有趣的故事. **3 stores** [pl] (**a**) goods, etc of a particular type, or for a special purpose (某类或某用途的)货物、物品等: *military stores* 军需品 ○ *government stationery stores* 政府的文书用具. (**b**) supply of such goods or place where they are kept 储备品等的供应; 仓库; 储藏所: *available from stores* 有存货的. **4** [C] (*computing* 计) device in a computer for storing and retrieving information 存储器. **5** [C] (*esp US*) (often in compounds 常用以构成复合词) shop 商店: *the liquor store* 酒店 ○ *the drugstore* 药店. **6** [C] (esp large) shop selling many different types of goods (尤指大型的)百货商店: *a big department store* 大百货公司 ○ *a general store in the village* 乡村的百货商店. **7** (idm 习语) **in store (for sb/sth)** (**a**) kept ready for (future) use 储存着; 备有: *He always keeps several cases of wine in store.* 他总是备有几箱酒. (**b**) coming in the future; about to happen 必将到来; 快要发生: *I can see trouble in store.* 我预见到以后要有麻烦. ○ *There's a surprise in store for you.* 你一定要大吃一惊的. **set (great/little/no/not much) store by sth** consider sth to be of (great/little, etc) importance or value 认为某事物(非常[不太]等)重要或有价值: *I don't set (much) store by weather forecasts.* 我认为天气预报(有些)靠不住.
▷ **store** *v* **1** [Tn, Tn·pr, Tn·p] **~ sth (up/away)** collect and keep sth for future use 储备或储存某物: *a squirrel storing (up) food for the winter* 储存食物准备过冬的松鼠 ○ *I've stored my winter clothes (away) in the attic.* 我把冬天的衣服存放在阁楼里了. **2** [Tn] put (furniture, etc) in a warehouse, etc to be kept safe 将(家具等)保存在仓库等中: *They've stored their furniture while they go abroad.* 他们出国时把家具送到仓库保管起来. **3** [esp passive 尤用于被动语态: Tn, Tn·pr] **~ sth (with sth)** stock sth (with sth useful); supply or fill sth 装备某事物; 供应或装满某事物: *a gallery stored with fine paintings* 藏有珍品画的艺术馆 ○ *a mind well stored with facts* 博闻强记的头脑. **4** [Tn] hold (sth); contain 容纳(某物); 含有: *This cupboard can store enough food for a month.* 这个食橱能装下足够一个月之用的食物.
□ ˈ**storekeeper** *n* (*esp US*) = SHOPKEEPER (SHOP).
ˈ**storehouse** (**a**) building where things are stored 仓库; 货栈. (**b**) (*fig* 比喻) person, place or thing having or containing much information 知识渊博的人; 知识宝库: *This book is a storehouse of useful information.* 这本书里汇集了大量有用的资料.
ˈ**store-room** *n* room used for storing things, esp in a house 贮藏室(尤指住宅中的).

storey (*US* **story**) /ˈstɔːrɪ; ˋstɔrɪ/ *n* (*pl* **storeys**; *US* **stories**) **1** section of a building with rooms all at the same level; floor 楼层: *a house of two storeys* 两层的楼房 ○ *live on the third storey of a block of flats* 住在公寓楼的第四层楼上 ○ *a five-storey building* 五层楼的大厦 ○ *a multi-storey car-park* 多层停车场. **2** (idm 习语) **the top storey** ⇨ TOP[1].
▷ **-storeyed** (*US* **-storied**) /-ˈstɔːrɪd; -ˋstɔrɪd/ (forming compound *adjs* 用以构成复合形容词) having the number of storeys specified 有若干楼层的: *a six-storeyed building* 六层的大楼.

stork /stɔːk; stɔrk/ *n* large (usu white) water bird with a long beak, neck and legs, sometimes building its nest on the tops of high buildings 鹳; (通常指)白鹳.

storm /stɔːm; stɔrm/ *n* **1** [C] (often in compounds 常用以构成复合词) occasion of violent weather conditions, with strong winds and usu rain or snow or thunder, etc 风暴; 暴风雨; 暴风雪; 雷暴天气: *a ˈthunder-/ˈwind-/ˈrain-/ˈsnow-/ˈdust-/ˈsand-storm* 雷暴[风暴/雨暴/雪暴/尘暴/沙暴] ○ *A storm is brewing*, ie coming. 暴风雨要来了. ○ [attrib 作定语] *a storm warning* 风暴警报 ○ *cross the Channel in a storm* 在暴风雨中渡过英吉利海峡 ○ *The forecast says there will be storms.* 天气预报称将有暴风雨. **2** [C] **~ (of sth)** sudden violent outburst or display of strong feeling 感情的猛然爆发或激烈表现: *a storm of anger, weeping, cheering, abuse, criticism* 一阵愤怒、大哭、欢呼、辱骂、抨击 ○ *His proposal was met by a storm of protest.* 他的建议遭到激烈的反对. **3 storms** [pl] (*US infml* 口) storm-door or storm-window (防风暴的)外重门或外重窗. **4** (idm 习语) **any port in a storm** ⇨ PORT[1]. **the calm before the storm** ⇨ CALM *n.* **the eye of the storm** ⇨ EYE[1]. **ride out/weather the/a ˈstorm** (**a**) (*nautical* 海) endure and survive a storm (esp at sea) 战胜风暴(尤指在海上). (**b**) survive opposition, criticism, difficult circumstances, etc without being seriously affected 经受住反对、批评、困难的处境等; 渡过难关. **a storm in a ˈteacup** a lot of fuss, excitement, disturbance, etc about sth unimportant 茶杯里的风暴(小事惹起的轩然大波). **take sth/sb by ˈstorm** (**a**) capture sth by a violent and sudden attack (以猛烈袭击)攻占某处或袭取某事物: *take a city by storm* 以袭击攻克一城市. (**b**) (of a performer or performance) have great and rapid success with (people or a place); captivate sth/sb (指表演者或演出)在(观众中或某地)大获成功; 迷住某事物[某人]: *The play took the audience/Paris by storm.* 该剧一下子迷住了观众[轰动了巴黎].
▷ **storm** *v* **1** [I, Ipr, Tn] **~ (at sb)** express violent anger; shout angrily and loudly 大发雷霆; 愤怒地大声喊叫: *'Get out of here!' he stormed.* '滚出去!'他嚷道.

2 [Ipr, Ip] **~ about, around, off, etc** move or walk in a very angry or violent manner in the direction specified 怒气冲冲地或其势凶猛地向某方向移动或行走: *storming round the house* 围着房子乱闯 ○ *storm out of the room* 愤怒地冲出房间 ○ *After the argument she stormed off.* 经过争论之后她愤然离开. **3** [Ipr, Ip, Tn·pr, Tn·p] **~ (one's way) across, in, through, etc** attack violently and force a way across, etc (a place) 猛攻而强行穿越、经过…(某处): *Three soldiers stormed into the house.* 有三名士兵冲进了那所房子. ○ *They stormed (their way) in.* 他们闯了进去. **4** [Tn] capture (sth) by a sudden and violent attack 攻占, 袭取(某事物): *storm a castle, fort, building, etc* 攻占一城堡、要塞、建筑物等.

stormy *adj* (**-ier, -iest**) **1** marked by or having strong winds, heavy rain, snow, hail, etc 有暴风、大雨、雪、冰雹等的; 暴风雨的: *stormy weather* 狂暴的天气 ○ *a stormy night* 暴风雨之夜 ○ *The day was cold and stormy.* 那天很冷又有暴风雪. **2** full of strong feeling, violent outbursts, anger, etc 激情迸发的; 感情冲动的; 狂怒的: *a stormy discussion, meeting, etc* 激烈的讨论、会议等 ○ *stormy scenes during the debate* 辩论中的激烈场面. **storm·ily** *adv*. **'stormi·ness** *n* [U].

,stormy 'petrel **1** = STORM PETREL. **2** person whose presence seems to attract trouble 招惹是非的人; 带来麻烦的人.

□ **'storm-bound** *adj* prevented by storms from continuing or starting a journey, going out or receiving supplies (途中、起程或补给供应)为暴风雨等所阻的: *storm-bound ships in harbour* 被暴风雨困于港湾的船只 ○ *The island was storm-bound for a week.* 那个岛被暴风雨困了一周.

'storm-centre (**a**) area at the centre of a storm 风暴中心. (**b**) (*fig* 比喻) centre of a disturbance or trouble 骚乱的中心; 麻烦所在.

'storm-cloud *n* (**a**) large black cloud coming with a storm or indicating that a storm is likely to happen 暴风云(暴风雨时出现的或预示暴风雨将至的浓密的乌云). (**b**) (usu *pl* 通常作复数) (*fig* 比喻) sign of sth dangerous or threatening 危险的迹象; 凶兆: *storm-clouds of war gathering over Europe* 笼罩着欧洲上空的战争乌云.

'storm-door *n* (*esp US*) door fitted outside another to protect against cold, rain, wind, etc (防寒、防雨、防风等的)外重门.

'storm-lantern *n* = HURRICANE LAMP (HURRICANE).

,storm 'petrel (also **stormy petrel**) type of small black and white seabird of the N Atlantic and Mediterranean, said to be active before a storm 海燕(产于北大西洋及地中海, 据称暴风雨前很活跃).

'stormproof *adj* that can resist storms 防风暴的; 能抵御暴风雨的: *This house isn't exactly stormproof — the roof leaks!* 这所房子并不能防暴风雨——屋顶漏了!

'storm-tossed *adj* damaged or blown about by storms 遭暴风雨损坏的; 被风暴吹得飘摇不定的.

'storm-trooper *n* soldier specially trained for violent and ruthless attacks 突击队员.

'storm-window *n* (*esp US*) window fitted outside another to protect against cold, rain, wind, etc (防寒、防雨、防风等的)外重窗.

story[1] /'stɔːrɪ; 'stɔrɪ/ *n* **1 ~ (about/of sb/sth)** (**a**) account of past events, incidents, etc (实有的)故事; 记事; 史话: *the Christmas story* 圣诞的故事 ○ *the story of Martin Luther King* 马丁·路德·金的事迹 ○ *stories of ancient Greece* 古希腊史话. (**b**) account of invented or imagined events, etc (虚构的或编造的)故事; 小说; 传奇; 传说: *a 'fairy story* 童话 ○ *a 'ghost story* 鬼故事 ○ *an adventure story for children* 给儿童讲的冒险故事 ○ *My father always used to tell us bedtime stories.* 我父亲总在我们临睡前给我们讲故事. ○ *The play is really a love story.* 这出戏实际上是一个爱情故事. **2** (also **'story-line**) narrative or plot of a book, play, etc (书、戏剧等的)故事情节: *a spy novel with a strong story(-line)* 故事情节扣人心弦的间谍小说. **3** (*journalism* 新闻) (**a**) report of an item of news in a newspaper; article 新闻报道; 文章: *a front-page story* 头版新闻报道. (**b**) event, situation or material suitable for this 新闻报道的题材: *That'll make a good story.* 这件事可以成为新闻报道的好题材. **4** (*infml* 口) untrue statement, description, etc; lie 谎言; 假话: *Don't tell stories, Tom.* 汤姆, 不要撒谎. **5** (idm 习语) **a cock-and-bull story** ⇨ COCK[1]. **cut a long story short** ⇨ LONG[1]. **a hard-luck story** ⇨ HARD[1]. **a likely story** ⇨ LIKELY. **the same old story** ⇨ SAME[1]. **the story goes that.../so the 'story goes** people are saying (that...); so it is said 传说…; 据说如此. **a success story** ⇨ SUCCESS. **a tall story** ⇨ TALL. **that's the ,story of my 'life** (*infml* 口) (said by sb who has had an unfortunate experience and regards it as like many similar experiences he has had in the past 遭遇到很多不幸后, 又遇到类似不幸时, 说出此成语).

□ **'story-book** *n* book of fictional stories, usu for children 故事书(通常指为儿童编写的): [attrib 作定语] *Their love affair had a story-book ending*, ie ended happily, as most children's stories do. 他们的恋爱结局是皆大欢喜(有如大多数儿童故事的结尾).

'story-teller *n* **1** person who tells stories 讲故事的人. **2** (*infml* 口) person who makes untrue statements; liar 说假话的人; 说谎者.

story[2] (*US*) = STOREY.

stoup /stuːp; stup/ *n* stone basin for holy water on or in the wall of a church 圣水钵(教堂墙上或墙内的).

stout /staʊt; staʊt/ *adj* **1** [usu attrib 通常作定语] strong and thick 粗壮的; 结实的: *stout boots for climbing* 登山用的结实的靴子 ○ *a stout walking-stick* 粗大的手杖. **2** (*esp euph* 尤作委婉语) (of a person) rather fat; solidly built (指人)相当胖的, 强壮的: *She's growing rather stout.* 她渐渐富态了. ⇨Usage at FAT[1] 用法见FAT[1]. **3** [usu attrib 通常作定语] (*fml* 文) determined, brave and resolute 坚决的; 勇敢的; 不屈不挠的: *a stout heart* 勇气 ○ *offer stout resistance* 作顽强的抵抗.

▷ **stout** *n* (**a**) [U] type of strong dark beer (烈性的)黑啤酒. (**b**) [C] glass of this 一杯黑啤酒: *Three stouts, please.* 劳驾, 来三杯黑啤酒.

stoutly *adv*.

stout·ness *n* [U].

□ **,stout-'hearted** *adj* (*fml* 文) brave and resolute 勇敢的; 有决心的.

stove[1] /stəʊv; stov/ *n* [C] **1** apparatus containing one or more ovens, used for cooking (炊事用的)炉子: *put a pot on the stove* 把壶放在炉子上. Cf 参看 COOKER 1. **2** closed apparatus burning wood, coal, gas, oil or other fuel, used for heating rooms (以木柴、煤炭、煤气、石油等为燃料用来取暖的)炉子, 火炉: *a wood-burning stove* 烧木柴的火炉. Cf 参看 FIRE[1] 3, HEATER (HEAT[2]).

stove[2] ⇨ STAVE[2].

stow /stəʊ; sto/ *v* **1** [Tn, Tn·pr, Tn·p] **~ A with B; ~ B (away) in/into A** pack sth, esp carefully, neatly and out of sight 将某物装好收起(尤指细心地): *stow a trunk with clothes* 把衣服装在衣箱里 ○ *stow clothes (away) into a trunk* 把衣服装进衣箱里 ○ *stow cargo in a ship's hold* 把货物装进船舱 ○ *Passengers are requested to stow their hand-baggage in the lockers above the seats.* 旅客须将随身携带的行李放入座位上方的贮藏柜里. **2** (phr v) **stow away** hide oneself as a stowaway 无票偷乘(船或飞机): *stow away on a ship bound for New York* 偷乘一艘开往纽约的船.

▷ **stow·age** /'stəʊɪdʒ; 'stoɪdʒ/ *n* [U] **1** stowing or being stowed 装载. **2** space used or available for this 装载货物处.

□ **'stowaway** *n* person who hides himself in a ship or aircraft before its departure, in order to travel without paying or being seen 无票偷乘船或飞机的人.

Str *abbr* 缩写 = Strait: *Magellan Str*, eg on a map 麦哲伦海峡(如地图上的标记).

straddle /'strædl; 'strædl/ *v* **1** [I, Tn] sit or stand across (sth) with both legs wide apart 跨坐或跨立在(某物)上: *straddle a fence, ditch, horse* 跨在栅栏、沟、马上. **2** [Tn] fire shots or drop bombs, etc slightly in front of and behind (a target) 夹叉射击或轰炸(某目标).

strafe /strɑːf, streɪf; strɑf, stref/ *v* [Tn] attack (sth/sb) with gunfire; bombard 枪击(某物[某人]); 轰炸.

straggle /'strægl; 'strægl/ *v* **1** [I, Ipr] grow or spread in an irregular or untidy manner 无规则地或散乱地生长或散布: *a straggling village* 布局散乱的村子 ○ *vines straggling over the fences* 蔓生在篱笆上的藤蔓. **2** [I, Ipr, Ip] walk, march, etc too slowly to keep up with the rest of the group; drop behind 落伍; 掉队; 落后: *a few young children straggling along behind their parents* 跟不上父母步子的几个小孩儿.

▷ **strag·gler** /ˈstræɡlə(r); ˈstræɡlɚ/ *n* person who straggles (STRAGGLE 2) 落伍、掉队或落后的人: *The last stragglers are just finishing the race.* 跑在最后面的人刚刚到达终点.

strag·gly /ˈstræɡlɪ; ˈstræɡlɪ/ *adj* (**-ier**, **-iest**) straggling 蔓生的; 散乱的: *wet straggly hair* 乱蓬蓬的湿毛发.

straight[1] /streɪt; stret/ *adj* **1** without a bend or curve; extending or moving continuously in one direction only 直的; 向一个方向延伸或运动的: *a straight road, line, rod* 直的路、线、杆 ○ *straight hair*, ie not curly 直的毛发 ○ *a straight skirt*, ie not flared 直筒裙. **2** [usu pred 通常作表语] arranged in proper order; tidy; correct 井然有序; 整齐; 正确: *It took hours to get the house straight.* 用了很长时间才把房子收拾好. **3** [pred 作表语] properly positioned; parallel to sth else; level or upright 端正; 与他物平行; 水平; 竖直: *Put the picture straight.* 把这幅画放正. ○ *Is my tie straight?* 我的领带系得正不正? ○ *His hat isn't on straight.* 他的帽子没戴正. **4** (of a person, his behaviour, etc) honest; truthful (指人、其行为等)正直的, 诚实的: *give a straight answer to a straight question* 直率地回答直率的问题 ○ *I don't think you're being straight with me.* 我认为你对我不够坦诚. ○ *It's time for some straight talking*, ie some frank discussion. 现在该坦率地谈谈了. **5** [attrib 作定语] accurate and without additions; not modified or elaborate 准确的; 无渲染的; 无虚饰的: *tell a straight story* 实事求是地讲一件事 ○ *give sb a straight* (ie reliable and accurate) *tip* 给某人一个准确的内部消息. **6** [attrib 作定语] (of a play or theatrical style) of the ordinary type; serious (指戏剧或戏剧风格)一般的, 朴实无华的, 严肃的: *a straight actor* 演技朴实的男演员 ○ *a straight play*, ie not a musical or variety show 话剧. **7** [attrib 作定语] in continuous succession 接连的; 连续的: *ten straight wins in a row* 接连十次获胜. **8** (also **neat**) (of an alcoholic drink) without water, soda-water, etc added; undiluted (指酒精饮料)不搀水、苏打水等的, 纯的: *Two straight whiskies, please.* 请来两杯不加水的威士忌. ○ *I like my vodka straight.* 我喜欢喝纯的伏特加酒. **9** (*sl* 俚) (**a**) conventional and conservative 传统的; 保守的. (**b**) heterosexual 异性恋的: *straight men* 异性恋的男性. **10** (idm 习语) **get sth right/straight** ⇨ RIGHT[1]. **keep a straight ˈface** stop oneself from smiling and laughing 绷着脸; 忍住不笑: *He has such a strange voice that it's difficult to keep a straight face when he's talking.* 他的声音很古怪, 说起话来很难让人不笑. **put/set the record straight** ⇨ RECORD[1]. **put sb straight (about sth)** correct sb's mistake; make sure that sb knows the correct facts, etc 纠正某人的错误; 务必使某人了解事实等. **put sth straight** make sth tidy 将某物弄整齐: *Please put your desk straight before you leave the office.* 请你先把办公桌收拾好再离开办公室. **stiff/straight as a ramrod** ⇨ RAMROD. **(as) straight as an ˈarrow/ˈdie** (**a**) in a straight line or direction 成直线; 笔直; 径直. (**b**) (of a person) honest and straightforward (指人)诚实的, 正直的. **the ˌstraight and ˈnarrow** (*infml* 口) proper, honest and moral way of behaving 正当、诚实和正派: *He finds it difficult to stay on/stick to the straight and narrow for long.* 他觉得长期地坚持走正道很难. **(vote) the straight ˈticket** (*US*) (vote for a) political party's complete programme or list of candidates without any changes or modifications to it (投票支持)某一政党的全部纲领或候选人.

▷ **straight** *n* (*sl* 俚) (**a**) conventional person 恪守传统的人. (**b**) heterosexual person 异性恋者.

straighten /ˈstreɪtn; ˈstretn̩/ *v* **1** [I, Ip, Tn, Tn·p] ~ **(sth) (up/out)** (cause sth to) become straight (使某物)变直: *The road straightens (out) after a series of bends.* 这条路经过几个转弯之后就直了. ○ *straighten one's tie, skirt* 把领带、裙子弄平整 ○ *Straighten your back (up)!* 把背挺直! **2** (phr v) **straighten sth out** settle or resolve sth; remove difficulties from sth 解决某事物; 排除某事物存在的困难: *Let's try to straighten out this confusion.* 咱们努力收拾这个混乱的局面吧. **straighten sb out** (*infml* 口) remove the doubt or ignorance in sb's mind 使某人消除疑虑; 给某人解释清楚: *You're clearly rather muddled about office procedures but I'll soon straighten you out.* 你显然不大明白办事的手续, 我很快就给你解释清楚. **straighten (oneself) up** make one's body upright 把身子挺直.

straight·ness *n* [U].

□ ˈ**straight-edge** *n* strip of wood or metal with one edge straight, used for checking or marking straight lines (校正或绘制直线用的)直尺.

ˌ**straight ˈfight** (*esp politics* 尤用于政治) competition between only two people or parties 只有两人或两个政党参加的竞争.

ˈ**straight man** member of a comedy act who makes remarks or creates situations for the main performer to make jokes about 喜剧中的配角; 滑稽演员的搭档.

straight[2] /streɪt; stret/ *adv* **1** not in a curve or at an angle; in a straight line; directly 挺直地; 成直线地; 直接地: *sit up straight*, ie without bending one's back 坐直 ○ *Keep straight on for two miles.* 一直往前走两英里. ○ *Look straight ahead.* 一直往前看. ○ *The smoke rose straight up.* 那股烟直线上升. ○ *He was too drunk to walk straight.* 他酩酊大醉, 走起路来步子不稳. ○ *I can't shoot straight*, ie aim accurately. 我射击瞄不准. ○ (*fig* 比喻) *I can't think straight, ie logically.* 我的思维很乱(缺乏条理). **2** by a direct route; without delay or hesitation 径直; 立即; 不犹豫地: *Come straight home.* 直接回家. ○ *He went straight to Lagos, without stopping in Nairobi.* 他径直前往拉各斯, 未在内罗毕停留. ○ *She went straight from school to university.* 她中学一毕业就马上进了大学. ○ *I'll come straight to the point — your work isn't good enough.* 我要直截了当地说——你的工作做得不够好. **3** honestly and frankly; in a straightforward manner 坦诚地; 直截了当地: *I told him straight that I didn't like him.* 我坦率地对他说我不喜欢他. **4** (idm 习语) **go ˈstraight** live an honest life after leading a life of crime 改邪归正. **play ˈstraight (with sb)** be honest and fair in one's dealings (with sb) 诚实而公平; 老实无欺. **right/straight away/off** ⇨ RIGHT[2]. ˌ**straight from the ˈshoulder** (of criticism, etc) frankly and honestly stated (指批评等)坦诚的, 直言不讳的: *She gave it to me straight from the shoulder.* 她坦诚地批评我. **straight ˈout** without hesitation; frankly 不犹豫地; 直截了当地; 坦率地: *I told him straight out that I thought he was lying.* 我直率地对他说我认为他是在撒谎. ○ *She didn't hesitate for a moment but came straight out with her reply.* 她没有迟疑, 痛快地答复了. ˌ**straight ˈup** (*Brit sl* 俚) (used esp in asking and answering questions 尤用于问答中) honestly; really 的确; 真的.

straight[3] /streɪt; stret/ *n* **1** (usu *sing* 通常作单数) straight part of sth, esp the final part of a track or racecourse 直线部分; (尤指临近终点的)直线跑道: *on the home straight*, ie approaching the finishing line 临近终点 ○ *The two horses were level as they entered the final straight.* 这两匹马同时进入最后的直线跑道. **2** (in the card-game of poker) hand with five cards in sequence but from more than one suit (扑克牌戏)一手不同花色的顺子牌(共五张).

straight·for·ward /ˌstreɪtˈfɔːwəd; ˌstretˈfɔrwɚd/ *adj* **1** (of a person, his manner, etc) honest and frank, without evasion (指人、态度等)诚实的, 坦率的, 老实的, 坦白的: *straightforward in one's business dealings* 老老实实做生意. **2** easy to understand or do; without complications or difficulties 易懂的; 易做的; 简单的; 不难的: *a straightforward examination question* 容易回答的试题 ○ *written in straightforward language* 用浅易文字写成的 ○ *The procedure is quite straightforward.* 手续很简单. ▷ **straight·for·wardly** *adv*: *behave, speak straightforwardly* 老老实实地做人、说话. **straight·for·ward·ness** *n* [U]: *She admired his straightforwardness.* 她称赞他为人正直.

straight·way /ˌstreɪtˈweɪ; ˈstretˌwe/ *adv* (*arch* 古) at once; immediately 立刻; 马上.

strain[1] /streɪn; stren/ *v* **1** [Tn, Tn·pr] stretch (sth) tightly by pulling 拉紧, 绷紧(某物): *strain a rope (to breaking-point/until it breaks)* 把绳子拉紧(直到拉断). **2** [I, It, Tn, Tnt] make the greatest possible effort; use all one's power, energy, etc (to do sth) 竭力; 用全力(做某事): *wrestlers heaving and straining* 尽力拼搏的摔跤运动员 ○ *strain (one's ears) to hear a conversation* 聚精会神地听别人交谈 ○ *straining to understand what she meant* 努力弄懂她的意思 ○ *strain one's voice to shout* 扯着嗓门叫喊. **3** [Tn] injure or weaken (esp a part of the body) by stretching too much or trying too hard 因过度伸展或用力而损伤(尤指身体某部位): *strain a muscle, one's heart*

肌肉、心肌劳损 ○ *strain one's eyes*, eg by reading in a bad light 损害视力(如在微弱光线下阅读) ○ *strain one's voice*, ie by speaking or singing too long or too loudly 喊哑嗓子(因说话或唱歌时间过长或声音过大) ○ (*ironic* 反语) *I would welcome some help — but don't strain yourself!* 我倒是盼着有人来帮忙 —— 只是别累坏了你自己! **4** [Tn] (*fml fig* 文, 比喻) force (sth) beyond a limit of what is acceptable 竭力使(某事物)超过极限: *strain the credulity of one's listeners* 使听的人难以相信 ○ *strain one's authority, rights, power, etc*, ie go beyond what is allowed or reasonable 滥用权威、权利、权力等 ○ *Her prose strains language* (ie the meaning of words) *to the limits.* 她的散文在语言运用上已超越了规范的极限. **5** [Tn] pass (food, etc) through a sieve, cloth, etc when separating solids from liquids 过滤(食物等): *strain the soup, vegetables* 过滤汤、蔬菜 ○ *The tea hasn't been strained*, ie It is full of tea-leaves. 这茶未经过滤(未滤去茶叶). **6** (idm 习语) **strain after ef'fects/an ef'fect** try in a forced or unnatural way to make sth seem impressive 勉强地或造作地使某事物显得了不起. **strain at the 'leash** (*infml* 口) be eager to have the freedom to do what one wants 渴望挣脱束缚: *teenagers straining at the leash to escape parental control* 极力要摆脱父母控制的青少年. **strain every 'nerve (to do sth)** try as hard as one can 尽力(做某事). **7** (phr v) **strain at sth** make a strenuous effort by pulling at sth 用力拉、拖、拽、曳…某物: *rowers straining at the oars* 用力划桨的划船手 ○ *dogs straining at the lead* 用力拖曳牵狗皮带的狗. **strain sth off (from sth)** remove (eg liquid) from solid matter by using a sieve, etc 滤去(液体等): *strain off the water from the cabbage when it is cooked* 烹调洋白菜时把水分滤掉.

▷ **strained** *adj* **1** unnatural, forced and artificial; not easy or relaxed 不自然的; 勉强的; 造作的; 紧张的: *a strained laugh* 勉强的笑 ○ *strained relations*, ie unpleasant tension between people, groups or countries 紧张的关系(人际、团体或国家之间的). **2** overtired and anxious 过度疲劳和焦虑的; 心力交瘁的: *She looked very strained when I last saw her.* 我上次看见她时, 她显得非常憔悴.

strainer *n* (esp in compounds 尤用以构成复合词) device for straining (STRAIN[1] 5) liquids 过滤器; 滤网: *a 'tea-strainer* 滤茶器.

strain[2] /streɪn; stren/ *n* **1** [C, U] (**a**) condition of being stretched or pulled tightly 拉紧; 绷紧; 张紧: *The rope broke under the strain.* 绳子拉断了. (**b**) force causing this 拉力; 张力; 应变: *calculate the strains and stresses of a bridge* 计算桥梁的应变和应力 ○ *What is the breaking strain of this cable?* ie How much strain would break it? 这缆索的致断拉力是多少? **2** (**a**) [C, U] severe demand on one's mental or physical strength, resources, abilities, etc 对智力、体力、财力、能力等的严格要求; 负担; 压力: *be under severe strain* 处于极度紧张的状态 ○ *beginning to feel the strain* 开始感到有压力 ○ *the strain of modern life* 现代生活的压力 ○ *Paying all the bills is a strain on my resources.* 支付所有这些费用是我经济上的一大负担. ○ *He finds his new job a real strain.* 他觉得新的工作的确很紧张. ○ *How do you stand* (ie cope with) *the strain?* 你是怎样克服这种压力的? (**b**) [U] state of anxiety, tension or exhaustion caused by this 因有压力而产生的焦虑、紧张或心力交瘁: *suffering from mental/nervous strain* 精神[神经]极度紧张. **3** [C, U] injury to a part of the body caused by twisting a muscle, etc; sprain 劳损; 扭伤: *a painful strain* 使人疼痛的扭伤 ○ *a groin strain* 阴部受伤. **4** [C usu *pl* 通常作复数] (*fml* 文) part of a tune or piece of music being performed (演出的)音乐片段, 乐曲: *hear the strains of the church organ* 听到教堂风琴奏出的音乐 ○ *the angelic strains of choirboys singing* 唱诗班的男童唱出的优美动听的曲子. **5** [C usu *sing* 通常作单数] tone, style or manner of sth written or spoken 写作或说话的方式或风格; 笔调; 语调: *Her speech continued in the same dismal strain.* 她以悲伤的语调接着往下说.

strain[3] /streɪn; stren/ *n* **1** (usu *sing* 通常作单数) **~ (of sth)** tendency in a person's character 个性特点; 性格倾向; 气质; 性情: *There's a strain of madness in the family.* 那一家人都有点疯疯颠颠的. **2** breed or type (of animal, insect, plant, etc) (动物、昆虫、植物等的)系, 品系, 品种, 类型: *a new strain of wheat* 小麦的新品种 ○ *strains of mosquitoes that are resistant to insecticide* 对杀虫剂有抗药性的蚊虫.

strait /streɪt; stret/ *n* **1** [C often *pl* with *sing* meaning, esp in proper names 常以复数表示单数意义, 尤用于专有名称] narrow passage of water connecting two seas or two large areas of water 海峡; (联接两大水域之间的)狭窄水道: *the Straits of Gibraltar* 直布罗陀海峡 ○ *the Magellan Straits* 麦哲伦海峡. **2 straits** [pl] trouble; difficulty 困难: *be in (dire/desperate/serious) financial straits* 陷于(恶劣的[极度的/严重的])财务困境中.

straitened /'streɪtnd; 'stretn̩d/ *adj* (idm 习语) **in straitened 'circumstances** (*fml esp euph* 文, 尤作委婉语) having scarcely enough money to live on; in poverty 勉强餬口的; 穷困的.

strait-jacket /'streɪtdʒækɪt; 'stret,dʒækɪt/ *n* **1** strong jacket-like garment put on a violent person (esp one who is mentally ill) to stop him struggling by restricting the arms 约束衣(尤指束缚精神病患者手臂用的). **2** (*fig derog* 比喻, 贬) thing that stops growth or development 妨碍生长或发展的事物; 束缚; 约束; 限制: *the strait-jacket of repressive taxation* 苛捐杂税的桎梏.

▷ **strait-jacket** *v* [Tn] **1** put a strait-jacket on (sb) 给(某人)穿约束衣. **2** (*fig* 比喻) restrict the growth or development of (sth) 限制(某事物)的生长或发展; 束缚(某事物): *feel strait-jacketed by poverty* 感到受贫困掣肘 ○ *feel strait-jacketed by the lack of government subsidy* 因缺少政府补贴而感到捉襟见肘.

strait-laced /,streɪt 'leɪst; 'stret'lest/ *adj* (*derog* 贬) having or showing a very strict attitude to moral questions; prim and proper (在道德问题上)极拘谨的; 一本正经的; 古板的: *My old aunts are very strait-laced.* 我的老姨妈都很古板.

strand[1] /strænd; strænd/ *n* (*arch or rhet* 古或修辞) sandy shore of a lake, sea or river (多沙的)湖滨, 海滨, 海滩, 河岸.

▷ **strand** *v* [Tn esp passive 尤用于被动语态] cause (sth) to be left on the shore and unable to return to the sea; cause to go aground 使(某物)留在岸上无法返回海中; 使搁浅: *a ship stranded on a sandbank* 搁浅在沙滩上的船 ○ *a whale stranded by the high tide* 被大海潮冲到岸上的鲸鱼.

stranded *adj* left in difficulties, eg without money, friends or transport 陷于困境的(如无钱、无友或无交通工具): *stranded tourists* 受困无援的旅行者 ○ *be left stranded in a foreign country without one's passport* 在外国因无护照而陷入困境.

strand[2] /strænd; strænd/ *n* **1** (**a**) any of the threads, wires, etc twisted together to form a rope or cable (绳子、缆索的)股, 缕. (**b**) single thread of string or fibre 线; 纤维丝: *a strand of cotton hanging from the hem of a skirt* 从裙子边垂下的一条棉线. **2** lock of hair 一绺毛发. **3** (*fig* 比喻) line of development (in a story, etc) (故事等的)情节发展线索: *drawing together the strands of the narrative* 把该故事的几条线索联在一起.

strange /streɪndʒ; strendʒ/ *adj* (**-r**, **-st**) **1** not previously known, seen, felt, heard of, etc; not familiar or of one's own 前所未知、未见、未觉察、未听说过等的; 不熟悉的; 陌生的; 不属于自己的: *in a strange country, town, neighbourhood, etc* 在陌生的国度、城市、地方等 ○ *Never accept lifts from strange men.* 千万不要坐陌生人的顺路车. **2** unusual; surprising 不同寻常的; 奇特的; 奇异的; 奇怪的: *What strange clothes you're wearing!* 你穿的衣服真特别! ○ *It's strange we haven't heard from him.* 奇怪的是我们没有他的音信. ○ *She says she feels strange*, ie rather unwell, perhaps dizzy. 她说她觉得不大舒服. ○ *It feels strange to be visiting the place again after all these years.* 时隔多年, 旧地重访使人感到很新奇. **3** [pred 作表语] **~ to sth** fresh or unaccustomed to sth 对某事物感到陌生或不习惯: *He's strange to the work.* 他对这工作很外行. ○ *The village boy was strange to city life.* 那个农村男孩儿过不惯城市生活. **4** (idm 习语) **,strange to re'late/'say...** it is surprising that... 说也奇怪…: *Strange to say, he won!* 说来奇怪, 他赢了! ▷ **strangely** *adv*: *The house was strangely quiet.* 这所房子静得出奇. ○ *It turned out we'd been at school together, strangely enough.* 原来我们以前是同学, 多奇怪. **strange·ness** *n* [U].

stranger /'streɪndʒə(r); 'strendʒɚ/ *n* **1** person that one does not know 陌生人: *I'd met Anna before, but her friend was a complete/total stranger to me.* 我见过安娜，但从未见过她那位朋友。○ *Our dog barks at strangers.* 我们那只狗见了生人就汪汪叫. **2** person in a new or an unfamiliar place or with people that he does not know 外地人; 异乡人; 外人: *I'm a stranger in this town*, ie I do not know my way around it. 我在这个城镇里人地生疏. **3** (idm 习语) **be a/no stranger to sth** (*fml* 文) be unaccustomed/accustomed to a certain feeling, experience, condition, job, etc 不惯于[习惯于]某种感情、经历、状况、工作等: *He's no stranger to misfortune*, ie He has experienced it before. 他饱经忧患.

strangle /ˈstræŋgl; ˋstræŋgl/ *v* **1** [Tn] kill (sb) by squeezing or gripping the throat tightly; throttle 扼死, 勒死, 绞死, 掐死(某人); 使窒息: *He strangled her with her own scarf.* 他用她的围巾把她勒死了. ○ (*infml* 口) *I could cheerfully strangle you for getting me into this mess!* 你让我这样难堪, 我恨不得掐死你! ○ (*fig* 比喻) *This stiff collar is strangling me*, ie making it difficult for me to breathe. 这硬领把我的脖子卡得喘不过气来. **2 (a)** [Tn] restrict or prevent the proper growth, operation or development of (sth) 限制或阻止(某事物)的正常生长、操作或发展: *She felt her creativity was being strangled.* 她觉得她的创造力难以发挥. **(b)** [Tn usu passive 通常用于被动语态] restrict the utterance of (sth) 限制(某事物)的发声: *a strangled* (ie partly suppressed) *cry* 哽咽.

▷ **stran·gler** *n* person who strangles sb 扼死他人的人; 压制者.

□ ˈ**stranglehold** *n* **(a)** strangling grip 扼制; 压制; 束缚. **(b)** (usu *sing* 通常作单数) **~ (on sth)** (*fig* 比喻) firm control, making it impossible for sth to grow or develop properly 控制某事物; 使某事物不能正常成长或发展: *The new tariffs have put a stranglehold on trade.* 新的关税制对开展贸易极为不利.

stran·gu·late /ˈstræŋgjʊleɪt; ˋstræŋgjəˌlet/ *v* [Tn esp passive 尤用于被动语态] (*medical* 医) compress or tightly squeeze (a vein, an intestine, etc) so that nothing can pass through it 绞窄或挤压(静脉、肠等)(使其不通): *a strangulated hernia*, ie one from which the blood supply has been cut off 绞窄性疝.

▷ **stran·gu·la·tion** /ˌstræŋgjʊˈleɪʃn; ˌstræŋgjəˋleʃən/ *n* [U] **1** strangling or being strangled 扼杀; 勒死; 绞死; 掐死; 窒息; 抑制; 压制; 束缚. **2** strangulating or being strangulated 绞窄; 挤压.

strap /stræp; stræp/ *n* (esp in compounds 尤用以构成复合词) **1** [C] strip of leather, cloth or other flexible material, often with a buckle, used to fasten things together or to keep things in place or to support, hold or hang sth by 带子(用皮、布等做成的, 通常有扣): *a watch-strap* 表带 ○ *My camera strap has broken.* 我照相机上的皮带断了. ○ *A rucksack has straps that go over the shoulders.* 背包上有两条背带. **2** [C] narrow strip of material worn over the shoulders as part of a dress, etc (连衣裙等套在肩上的)挎带, 肩带, 背带: *bra-straps* 胸罩肩带 ○ *a summer dress with thin shoulder-straps* 有细肩带的夏季连衣裙. **3 the strap** [sing] (esp formerly) punishment by beating with a leather strap (尤指旧时)用皮鞭抽打的惩罚: *I got/was given the strap.* 我挨了一顿鞭打.

▷ **strap** *v* **1** [Tn·pr, Tn·p] hold, secure or fasten (sth/sb) with a strap or straps 用带子系、扎、捆、绑(某物[某人]): *strap sth in place* 用带子把某物固定住 ○ *They strapped their equipment on(to their backs).* 他们用带子把用品拴在背上. ○ *Make sure the passengers are strapped in(to their seats) before driving off.* 开车前请乘客务必系好安全带. ○ *The lorry's load had been securely strapped down.* 卡车上的货物已捆扎牢固了. **2** [Tn, Tn·p] **~ sth (up)** bind (a wound, limb, etc) with bandages (用绷带)包扎(伤口、肢体等): *His injured arm was tightly strapped (up).* 他受伤的手臂已妥善地包扎好了. **3** [Tn] beat (sb) with a strap 用皮鞭抽打(某人).

strap·less /ˈstræplɪs; ˋstræplɪs/ *adj* (esp of a dress or bra) without straps (STRAP 2) (尤指连衣裙或胸罩)无背带的, 无肩带的.

strapped *adj* [pred 作表语] **~ (for sth)** (*infml* 口) not having enough (of sth, esp money) 短缺(尤指钱): *I'm a bit strapped for cash.* 我现金有点不足.

strap·ping *adj* (*esp joc* 尤作戏谑语) big, tall and strong; robust 高大健壮的; 强健的: *She's a strapping lass.* 她是个身强体壮的姑娘.

□ **straphanger** /ˈstræphæŋə(r); ˋstræpˌhæŋɚ/ *n* (*often derog* 常作贬义) standing passenger in a bus, train, etc who supports himself by holding onto a strap attached to the ceiling; commuter (公共汽车、火车等上手拉吊带的)站立的乘客; 通勤者.

strata *pl* of STRATUM.

stra·ta·gem /ˈstrætədʒəm; ˋstrætədʒəm/ *n* (*fml* 文) trick, plan or scheme to deceive sb (esp an enemy) 蒙蔽他人(尤指敌人)的计谋、策略或花招: *a cunning stratagem* 诡计.

stra·tegic /strəˈtiːdʒɪk; strəˋtidʒɪk/ (also **stra·tegical**) *adj* [usu attrib 通常作定语] **1** of strategy; forming part of a plan or scheme 战略(上)的; 策略(上)的: *strategic(al) decisions* 战略决策. **2** giving an advantage; right for a particular purpose 有战略意义的; 战略上适合的: *a strategic position, move* 战略地位、行动 ○ *strategic bombing*, eg of industrial areas and communication centres 战略轰炸 ○ *strategic materials*, ie those that are necessary for war 战略物资. **3** (of weapons, esp nuclear missiles) directed against an enemy's country rather than used in a battle (指武器, 尤指核武器)战略性的. Cf 参看 TACTICAL (TACTIC). ▷ **stra·tegic·ally** /-klɪ; -klɪ/ *adv*: *a strategically placed microphone* 设在关键位置上的话筒.

strat·egy /ˈstrætədʒɪ; ˋstrætədʒɪ/ *n* **1** [U] (art of) planning and directing an operation in a war or campaign 战略(学): *military strategy* 军事部署 ○ *skilled in strategy* 善于制定战略. **2** [U] (skill in) planning or managing any affair well 策略; 谋略; 计划或管理: *By careful strategy she negotiated a substantial pay rise.* 她精心策划后, 谈妥了大幅增加工资的事. **3** [C] plan or policy designed for a particular purpose 针对性措施; 对策; 政策: *economic strategies* 经济政策 ○ *a new police strategy for crowd control* 警方为控制人群拥挤现象而采取的新措施. Cf 参看 TACTIC.

▷ **strat·egist** /-dʒɪst; -dʒɪst/ *n* person skilled in (esp military) strategy 善于谋划的人; (尤指)战略家.

strat·ify /ˈstrætɪfaɪ; ˋstrætəˌfaɪ/ *v* (*pt, pp* **-fied**) [Tn usu passive 通常用于被动语态] arrange (sth) in strata or grades, etc 使(某事物)分层或分等级等: *stratified rock* 成层岩 ○ *a highly stratified society*, ie having many different levels 有很多阶层的社会.

▷ **strati·fica·tion** /ˌstrætɪfɪˈkeɪʃn; ˌstrætəfəˋkeʃən/ *n* [U] arrangement in strata, etc; stratifying or being stratified 层次; 成层; 分层: *social stratification* 社会阶层.

stra·to·sphere /ˈstrætəsfɪə(r); ˋstrætəˌsfɪr/ *n* [sing] layer of the earth's atmosphere between about 10 and 60 kilometres above the surface of the earth 平流层, 同温层(距地表约10至60公里之间的大气层). Cf 参看 IONOSPHERE.

stratum /ˈstrɑːtəm; *US* ˈstreɪtəm; ˋstretəm/ *n* (*pl* **strata** /-tə; -tə/) **1** any of a series of horizontal layers, esp of rock in the earth's crust 层; (尤指)岩层. **2** level or class in society (社会的)阶层: *a gathering of people from a variety of social strata* 不同社会阶层的人的集会.

straw /strɔː; strɔ/ *n* **1** [U] cut and dried stalks of grain plants (eg wheat, barley) used as a material for thatching roofs, making hats, mats, etc and as bedding and food for animals (收割后干燥的)禾秆, 麦秆, 稻草: *a stable filled with straw* 堆满干草的马厩 ○ [attrib 作定语] *a straw mattress*, ie one filled with straw 草垫. **2** [C] single stalk or piece of this (一根)禾秆, 麦秆, 稻草: *There are a few straws in your hair.* 你的头发上有几根稻草. **3** [C] thin tube of paper or plastic through which a drink is sucked up (纸或塑料制的)饮料吸管: *drinking lemonade through a straw* 用吸管吸汽水 ○ *A packet of (drinking) straws, please.* 请给我一包吸管. **4 a straw** [sing] insignificant thing or amount (used esp in the expressions shown) 微不足道的事物或数量(尤用于以下示例): *not care a straw* 毫不在乎 ○ *be not worth a straw* 毫无价值. **5** (idm 习语) **clutch/grasp at a ˈstraw/ˈstraws** try to take some slight chance of escaping or being rescued from sth 抓救命稻草(竭力抓住微小的机会以求逃脱或获救). **the last/final straw (that breaks the camel's back)** additional event, act, task, etc that makes a situation finally intolerable (事情、行动、任务等)使人终于不胜负荷的最后的量.

S

make bricks without straw ⇨ BRICK. **a man of straw** ⇨ MAN[1]. **a straw in the 'wind** slight indication of how things may develop (显示事物动向的)征兆, 迹象, 苗头.

□ **'straw-coloured** *adj* light yellow 草黄色的; 浅黄色的.

straw poll (also **straw vote**) (*esp US*) unofficial survey of public opinion 非正式的民意调查.

straw·berry /'strɔ:brɪ; *US* -berɪ; 'strɔ,bɛrɪ/ *n* **(a)** [C] soft juicy red fruit with tiny yellow seeds on the surface 草莓: *fresh strawberries and cream* 鲜草莓拌奶油 ○ [attrib 作定语] *strawberry jam* 草莓酱 ○ *strawberry pink* 草莓般的粉红色. **(b)** low-growing plant on which this fruit grows 草莓(指植株).

□ **'strawberry-mark** *n* reddish birthmark on the skin 草莓状红斑(皮肤上的红色胎记).

stray /streɪ; stre/ *v* [I, Ipr, Ip] **1** move away from one's group, proper place, etc with no fixed destination or purpose; wander 离群, 走离(无固定去向或目的); 走失; 迷失; 闲逛: *Some of the cattle have strayed.* 有些牛走失了. ○ *stray into the path of an oncoming car* 偏离车道而误入逆向行驶的汽车道 ○ *Young children should not be allowed to stray from their parents.* 不要让儿童离开父母到处乱跑. ○ *He had strayed from home while still a boy.* 他小时候就离开家到处流浪了. **2** deviate from a direct course or leave a subject 偏离; 背离; 离题: *My mind kept straying from the discussion (to other things).* 我在讨论时总是走神(去想别的事情). ○ *Don't stray (away) from the point.* 不要离题.

▷ **stray** *adj* [attrib 作定语] **1** having strayed; lost 离群的; 走失的; 迷失的; 闲逛的; 偏离的: *a home for stray dogs* 走失的狗的收容处 ○ (*fig* 比喻) *Stray papers littered his desk.* 他的书桌上都是乱七八糟的纸. **2** occurring here and there, not as one of a group; isolated 零星的; 散乱的; 孤立的: *killed by a stray bullet*, ie by chance, not on purpose 被流弹击毙 ○ *The streets were empty except for a few stray passers-by.* 除了寥寥几个行人外, 街上空空如也.

stray *n* **(a)** person or domestic animal that has strayed 迷路的人; 流浪者; 走失的家畜: *This dog must be a stray.* 这只狗一定是找不着家了. Cf 参看 WAIF. **(b)** thing that is out of its proper place or separated from others of the same kind 不在原处的东西; 不与同类在一起的事物.

streak /stri:k; strik/ *n* **~ (of sth)** **1** long thin mark, line or band of a different substance or colour from its surroundings (与整体不同物质或颜色的)条纹, 线条, 斑纹: *streaks of grey in her hair* 她头发上夹杂着的缕缕白发 ○ *a streak* (ie flash) *of lightning* 一道闪电 ○ *streaks of fat in the meat* 这块肉中一层层的膘. **2** element or trace (in a person's character) (个性中的)些微特点或特征: *a streak of jealousy, vanity, cruelty, etc* 几分嫉妒、虚荣、残忍等 ○ *have a jealous streak* 有点儿嫉妒. **3** (esp in gambling) period of continuous success or failure (尤指赌博)连赢或连输的一段时间: *a streak of good luck* 一阵子好运气 ○ *hit* (ie have) *a winning/losing streak* 碰上连赢[输]的运气. **4** (idm 习语) **like a streak of lightning** ⇨ LIGHTNING[1]. **a yellow streak** ⇨ YELLOW.

▷ **streak** *v* **1** [esp passive 尤用于被动语态: Tn, Tn·pr] **~ sth (with sth)** mark sth with streaks 在某物上加条纹: *have one's hair streaked* 把头发染成一缕缕不同的颜色 ○ *white marble streaked with brown* 带褐色条纹的白色大理石. **2** [Ipr, Ip] (*infml* 口) move very fast (in the specified direction) 飞快地(向某方向)移动: *The children streaked off (down the street) as fast as they could.* 孩子们拼命地(沿街)飞跑. **3** [I] run through a public place with no clothes on, in order to shock or amuse people 裸跑(为使人震惊或发笑). **streaker** *n* person who streaks (STREAK *v* 3) 裸跑的人.

streaky *adj* (**-ier**, **-iest**) marked with, having or full of streaks (加)有(很多)条纹的: *streaky bacon*, ie with layers of fat and lean in it 五花腌猪肉(肉层肥瘦相间).

stream /stri:m; strim/ *n* **1** small river or large brook (小)河; (大)溪; 河沟: *a small stream running through the woods* 流过树林的小溪. **2 ~ (of sth/sb)** flow (of liquid, people, things, etc) (液体、人群、事物等的)流、流动或涌出: *a stream of blood* 一股血 ○ *a steady stream of abuse, complaints, etc* 一连串的辱骂、抱怨等 ○ *streams of shoppers, traffic* 购物者的人流、车辆的川流不息. **3** current or direction of sth flowing or moving (流动或移动的)水流、气流、趋势或趋向: *leaves moving with the stream* 顺流飘动的落叶. **4** (*esp Brit*) (in some schools) class or division of a class into which children of the same age and level of ability are placed (某些学校中同龄儿童按智力水平编成的)能力班或能力小组: *the A, B, C, etc stream* A、B、C...级能力小组. **5** (idm 习语) **go up/down stream** move up/down the river 溯流而上[顺流而下]. **go, swim, etc with/against the stream/tide** conform/not conform to accepted behaviour, opinions, etc; be/not be carried along by the course of events 顺应潮流[反潮流]; 随[不随]大溜: *Teenagers often go against the stream.* 青少年经常反潮流而动. **on stream** in active operation or production 在实际运转或生产中: *The new plant comes on stream in March.* 新工厂将于三月份投产.

▷ **stream** *v* **1** [I, Ipr] flow or move as a stream (像水流般)流, 流动: *Sweat streamed down his face.* 他脸上汗水直流. ○ *People were streaming out of the station.* 人们涌出了车站. **2 (a)** [Tn] emit a stream of (sth) 流出(某物): *The wound streamed blood.* 伤口流出了血. **(b)** [I, Ipr] **~ (with sth)** run with liquid 流淌: *a streaming cold*, ie with much liquid coming from the nose 伴有流鼻涕的感冒 ○ *His face was streaming with sweat.* 他脸上淌着汗. **3** [I, Ipr, Ip] float or wave at full length (esp in the wind) 飘扬, 招展(尤指在风中): *Her hair streamed (out) in the wind.* 她的头发迎风飘动着. **4** [Tn usu passive 通常用于被动语态] (*esp Brit*) place (schoolchildren) in streams (STREAM 4) 将(学童)按年龄和智力编班或分组: *Children are streamed according to ability.* 儿童按智力水平分成小组. **streamer** *n* **1** long narrow flag 狭长的旗子. **2** long narrow ribbon of coloured paper 狭长的彩色纸带: *a room decorated with balloons and streamers* 用气球和纸彩带装饰的房间. **3** = BANNER HEADLINE (BANNER). **stream·ing** *n* [U] (policy of) placing schoolchildren in streams (STREAM 4) 按学童智力水平编成班或组(的原则).

□ **stream of consciousness** (writing that seeks to express the) continuous flow of ideas, thoughts and feelings experienced by a person when conscious 意识流(个人有意识时所体验到的思想和情感的具有连续性的流动); 意识流创作(法).

stream·line /'stri:mlaɪn; 'strim,laɪn/ *v* [Tn] **1** give a streamlined form to (sth) 使(某物)成流线型. **2** make (sth) more efficient and effective, eg by improving or simplifying working methods 使(某事物)效率更高、作用更大(如藉改进或简化工作方法): *We must streamline our production procedures.* 我们必须精简生产程序以提高效率.

▷ **stream·lined** *adj* having a smooth even shape so as to be able to move quickly and easily through air, water, etc 流线型的: *modern streamlined cars* 现代的流线型汽车.

street /stri:t; strit/ *n* **1** (*abbr* 缩写 **St**) public road in a city, town or village with houses and buildings on one side or both sides 街; 街道: *cross the street* 穿越街道 ○ *meet a friend in the street* 在街上遇见一个朋友 ○ *gangs roaming the streets* 在街头游荡的流氓 ○ *His address is 155 Smith Street.* 他的地址是史密斯大街155号. ○ [attrib 作定语] *at street level*, ie on the ground floor 在与街道齐平的一层 ○ *a 'street map/plan of York* 约克城的街道地图[详图] ○ *street lighting* 路灯 ○ *street theatre*, ie plays, etc performed in the street, usu with a social or political theme 街头剧(在街头演出的, 通常为社会性或政治性的). ⇨Usage at ROAD 用法见 ROAD. **2** people who live or work in a particular street 在某一街道居住或工作的人们: *Our street puts on a carnival every year.* 我们这条街的居民每年举行一次狂欢会. **3** (idm 习语) **be in Queer Street** ⇨ QUEER. **be (out) on/walk the streets** (*infml* 口) **(a)** be homeless 流落街头; 无家可归. **(b)** (*euph* 婉) work as a prostitute 当娼妓. **go on the streets** (*euph* 婉) earn one's living as a prostitute 操皮肉生涯; 以卖淫为生. **the man in the street** ⇨ MAN. **not in the same street (as sb/sth)** (*infml* 口) not nearly so good; inferior (to sb/sth) 远不如; 比不上(某人[某事物]). **streets ahead (of sb/sth)** (*infml* 口) much better, more efficient, cleverer, etc (than sb/sth) (比某人[某事物])好、有效、聪明...得多.

(right) up one's street (*infml* 口) within one's area of knowledge, interest, activity, etc 在自己的知识、兴趣、活动等范围内: *This job seems right up your street.* 这项工作看来正适合你做.

□ ˈ**streetcar** *n* (*US*) = TRAM.

ˌ**street crediˈbility** (also ˌ**street ˈcred**) (*infml* 口) up-to-date image, style, etc that is acceptable to ordinary (esp young) people 为一般人(尤指年轻人)认同的最新形象、式样等.

ˈ**street-girl** (also ˈ**street-walker**) *n* prostitute who looks for customers on the streets 街头拉客的娼妓.

ˈ**street value** price for which sth illegal or illegally obtained can be sold (非法或非法获得之物品的)黑市价格: *Customs officers have seized drugs with a street value of over £1 million.* 海关人员查获了按黑市价格超过100万英镑的毒品.

ˈ**street-wise** *adj* (*infml* 口) knowledgeable about how ordinary people behave, survive, etc, esp in big cities 对一般人(尤指都市人)的行为、生存方式等十分了解的.

strength /streŋθ; strɛŋθ/ *n* **1** [U] quality of being strong; degree of intensity of this 力量; 力气; 强度; 浓度: *a man of great strength* 强壮的男子 ○ *strength of character, mind, will* 性格、思想、意志的坚强 ○ *regain one's strength after an illness* 病后恢复体力 ○ *the strength of a rope*, ie its ability to resist strain 绳子的强度 ○ *put on a show of strength*, ie show how strong one is 显示力量 ○ *For a small woman she has surprising strength.* 她个子虽小但力大惊人. ○ *The strength of feeling on this issue is considerable.* 在这个问题上表现出的情绪很强. ○ *How is the strength of alcoholic drinks measured?* 含酒精饮料的浓度是如何测定的? ⇨Usage 见所附用法. **2** [C, U] that which makes sb/sth strong; particular respect in which a person or thing is strong 力量的源泉; 强点; 长处: *the strengths and weaknesses of an argument* 一论据的长处和弱点 ○ *Tolerance is one of her many strengths.* 宽容是她的一个优点. ○ *His strength as a news-reader lies in his training as a journalist.* 他胜任新闻广播员的工作, 在于他有当过记者的锻炼. **3** [U] number of people present or available; full number 现有的或可召集到的人员; 人力; 实力: *What is the strength of the work-force?* 职工总数是多少? **4** (idm 习语) **be at full/be below strength** have the required/less than the required number of people 满员[未满员]. **bring sth/be up to (full) strength** make sth reach/be the required number 使某事物达到所需数量: *We must bring the police force up to (full) strength.* 我们必须让警察人数达到(全部)编制所需的数量. **from strength to strength** with ever-increasing success 不断进步: *Since her appointment the department has gone from strength to strength.* 自从她任职以来, 这个部门越办越好了. **in (full, great, etc) strength** in large numbers 大量(的): *The army paraded in (full) strength.* (全部)军队接受了检阅. **on the strength** (*infml* 口) included as an official member of an organization, armed force, etc 在编. **on the strength of sth** on the basis of sth; relying on (a fact, sb's advice, etc) 基于某事物; 根据(事实、某人的意见等): *I got the job on the strength of your recommendation.* 承蒙足下推荐, 我已获得这份工作. **outgrow one's strength** ⇨ OUTGROW. **a tower of strength** ⇨ TOWER.

▷ **strengthen** /ˈstreŋθn; ˈstrɛŋθən/ *v* [I, Tn] (cause sth/sb to) become stronger (使某物[某人])更强: *The current strengthened as we moved down the river.* 我们顺流而下时, 水流更急了. ○ *a special shampoo to strengthen your hair* 能保养头发的一种特效洗发剂 ○ *strengthen a garrison with extra troops* 增派部队以加强驻地的兵力 ○ *This latest development has further strengthened my determination to leave.* 最近事态的发展更增强了我离开的决心.

NOTE ON USAGE 用法: Compare **strength, power, force** and **vigour** (*US* **vigor**). 试比较**strength**、**power**、**force**、**vigour**(美式拼写作**vigor**). **Strength** and **power** indicate an internal quality of an object or person. ☆ **strength**和**power**表示物体或人的内在特性. The **strength** of a body, bridge or rope is its ability to hold great weight ☆ **strength**用于身体指力气, 用于桥梁指承重强度, 用于绳索指抗拉强度: *I haven't the strength to carry you.* 我抱不动你. The **power** in a person's body, in a machine or in the wind is the energy within it that can be applied ☆ **power**用于人体、机械或风时指可应用的能量: *We can harness the power of the wind to make electricity.* 我们可以利用风力发电. **Force** and **vigour** relate to the application of energy. ☆ **force**和**vigour**指能量的应用. The **force** of an explosion, a storm or a blow is the energy released and its impact on objects ☆ **force**用于爆炸、风暴或打击时, 指释放的能量及其对物体的冲击力: *The car was completely wrecked by the force of the collision.* 这辆汽车受到很大的撞击力而完全损坏. A person's **vigour** is the energy used, especially in work ☆ **vigour**用于人时, 指所用的体力、精力, 尤指工作活力或干劲: *She does her work with tremendous vigour.* 她工作起来干劲十足.

strenu·ous /ˈstrenjʊəs; ˈstrɛnjuəs/ *adj* **1** making great efforts; energetic 努力的; 精力充沛的: *strenuous workers* 干劲十足的工作人员 ○ *make a strenuous attempt to reach the top of the mountain* 力求登上山顶. **2** requiring great effort 必须努力的: *a strenuous itinerary* 艰难的旅行路线 ○ *strenuous work* 累人的工作 ○ *lead a strenuous life* 过艰苦的生活. ▷ **strenu·ously** *adv*: *She strenuously denies all the charges.* 她竭力否认一切指控.

strep·to·coc·cus /ˌstreptəˈkɒkəs; ˌstrɛptəˈkɑkəs/ *n* (*pl* **-cocci** /-ˈkɒkaɪ; -ˈkɑkaɪ/) (*medical* 医) any of a group of bacteria that cause serious infections and illnesses 链球菌. ▷ **strep·to·coc·cal** /-ˈkɒkl; -ˈkɑkəl/ *adj*.

strep·to·my·cin /ˌstreptəʊˈmaɪsɪn; ˌstrɛptəˈmaɪsɪn/ *n* [U] (*medical* 医) antibiotic drug used to treat infections, etc 链霉素.

stress /stres; strɛs/ *n* **1** [U, C] (pressure or worry resulting from) mental or physical distress, difficult circumstances, etc 精神上或肉体上的痛苦、困难的情况等(所造成的压力或忧虑): *be under/suffer from stress* 在压力下[受到压力] ○ *in times of stress*, ie difficulty, trouble, etc 在困难时期 ○ *the stresses and strains of modern life* 现代生活的压力和紧张. **2** [U] ~ **(on sth)** special emphasis or significance 强调; 重要性: *He feels that there is not enough stress on drama at the school.* 他觉得这所学校对戏剧不够重视. ○ *She lays great stress on punctuality*, ie regards it as very important. 她非常强调要遵守时刻. **3** [C, U] **(a)** (result of) extra force used in speaking a particular word or syllable 重读; 重音: *In 'strategic' the stress is/falls on the second syllable.* strategic 这个字的重音在第二个音节上. ○ *Stress and rhythm are important in speaking English.* 说英语时, 重音和节奏是很重要的. ○ *You must learn where to place the stresses.* 必须掌握在什么地方重读. Cf 参看 INFLECTION 2, INTONATION 2. **(b)** (result of) extra force used when making a sound in music (音乐中声音的)加强, 加强音: *Put a stress on the first note in each bar.* 每一小节的第一个音符要加强. **4** [C, U] ~ **(on sth)** (esp in mechanics) force that acts on a thing or between parts of a thing, and tends to pull or twist it out of shape; tension (尤指力学的)应力: *High winds put great stress on the structure.* 大风作用于该建筑物上而产生巨大的应力. ○ [attrib 作定语] *a stress fracture of a bone in the leg* 腿部的应力性骨折.

▷ **stress** *v* [Tn, Tf] put stress or emphasis on (sth) 着重, 强调(某事物); 重读(某音节); 加强(某音符): *You stress the first syllable in 'happiness'.* happiness一字的第一个音节要重读. ○ *He stressed the point that ....* 他强调这一点.... ○ *I must stress that what I say is confidential.* 我要强调我说的话是保密的.

stress·ful /-fl; -fəl/ *adj* causing stress(1) 有压力的: *She finds her new teaching job very stressful.* 她觉得新的教学工作非常紧张.

□ ˈ**stress mark** mark (as used in this dictionary) to indicate the stress(3a) on a syllable in a word 重音符号(表示字中某一音节须重读的符号, 如本词典所用的): *In the word 'sympathetic' /ˌsɪmpəˈθetɪk; ˌsɪmpəˈθɛtɪk/ the primary stress (ˈ) is on the third syllable, and the secondary stress (ˌ) is on the first syllable.* 在sympathetic一字中, 主重音符号(ˈ)是在第三个音节上, 次重音符号(ˌ)在第一个音节上.

stretch /stretʃ; strɛtʃ/ *v* **1** [Tn, Tn·pr, Tn·p, Cn·a] make (sth) longer, wider or tighter by pulling 拉长, 撑大, 拽紧(某物): *stretch a rope across a path* 把绳索拉到道路对面 ○ *stretch a pair of gloves/shoes*, eg to make them fit

S

better 把手套[鞋]撑大(如使之更合适) ○ *stretch a hat to fit one's head* 把帽子撑一撑以便戴着合适 ○ *stretch a rope tight* 把绳索拉紧. **2** [I] be able to become longer, wider, etc without breaking; be elastic; (be liable to) extend beyond the proper limit 能伸展; 能延伸; 有弹性; (可能)超过限度: *These socks stretch.* 这双短袜有弹性. ○ *The pullover stretched* (ie out of shape) *after I had worn it a few times.* 这件套头毛衣我穿了几次之后就撑大了(变形了). ○ (*fig* 比喻) *I'd love a holiday if our money will stretch that far.* 我们的钱省着花要是能富余出来, 我倒是很想去度假. **3** [I, Ipr, Ip, Tn, Tn·pr, Tn·p] extend or thrust out (a limb or part of the body) and tighten the muscles, esp after being relaxed or in order to reach sth 伸长或伸出(一肢或身体某部)并绷紧肌肉(尤指在放松后或为够着某物): *He woke up, yawned and stretched.* 他一觉醒来, 边打呵欠边伸懒腰. ○ *She stretched across the table for the butter.* 她探身去取放在餐桌对面的黄油. ○ *stretch one's arms, legs* 伸展双臂、双腿 ○ *He stretched out his arm to take the book.* 他伸出手臂去拿书. ○ *She stretched her neck up*, eg to see over the heads of people in a crowd. 她伸着脖子(如从人群头顶上看). **4** [I, Ipr, Ip] spread out over an area or a period of time; extend 绵延; 延续; 伸展: *forests stretching for hundreds of miles* 绵延数百英里的森林 ○ *The road stretched (out) across the desert into the distance.* 这条道路穿过沙漠伸向远方. ○ *The ocean stretched as far as they could see on all sides.* 海洋十分辽阔, 他们极目远眺无边无涯. ○ *The long summer holiday stretched ahead (of them).* 漫长的暑假就在(他们的)眼前. **5** [Tn] make great demands on (sb or sb's ability, strength, etc) 对(某人或某人的能力、体力等)提出高的要求: *The race really stretched him/his skill as a runner.* 这次赛跑对他这个参赛者[他的水平]来说, 确是勉为其难. ○ *She has not been sufficiently stretched at school this term.* 她本学期功课不太紧张. ○ *We can't take on any more work — we're fully stretched* (ie working to the utmost of our powers) *at the moment.* 我们不能再接受更多的工作了── 目前已经全力以赴了. **6** [Tn] strain or exert (sth) as far as possible or beyond a reasonable or an acceptable limit 尽力或过度使用(某事物): *stretch the truth*, ie exaggerate or lie 言过其实 ○ *stretch the meaning of a word* 过分引申某词义 ○ *You can't stretch the rules to suit yourself.* 你不能为你自己而牵强附会解释这些规章. **7** (idm 习语) **stretch one's legs** go for a walk as exercise 去散步: *She went out to stretch her legs after lunch.* 她午饭后出去散步了. **stretch a point** go beyond what is usually allowed; make a concession 超出一般所允许的范围; 做出让步: *She doesn't have all the qualifications but I think we should stretch a point in her favour.* 她并非全部合格, 但我认为我们可以为她放开一些限制. **8** (phr v) **stretch (sth) out** (make sth) last or be enough to cover one's needs (使某事物)延续或足够所需: *He couldn't stretch out his money to the end of the month.* 他的钱花不到月底. **stretch (oneself) out** relax by lying at full length 躺着舒展身体: *He stretched (himself) out in front of the fire and fell asleep.* 他舒展开身体躺在炉火旁边睡着了.

▷ **stretch** *n* **1** [C usu *sing* 通常作单数] act of stretching or state of being stretched 拉长; 撑大; 拽紧; 伸展; 延伸; 高要求; 过度使用: *With a stretch of his arm, he reached the shelf.* 他伸出手臂, 够着了那个架子. ○ *The dog woke up, had a good stretch and wandered off.* 那条狗醒过来, 舒舒服服地伸展了一下身子便走开了. **2** [U] ability to be stretched; elasticity 伸展的能力; 弹性; 伸缩性: *This material has a lot of stretch in it.* 这种材料很有弹性. ○ [attrib 作定语] *stretch jeans, seat-covers, underwear* 弹力牛仔裤、椅套、内衣. **3** [C] (**a**) **~ (of sth)** continuous expanse or extent (of sth) 扩展; 延伸; 连绵: *a beautiful stretch of countryside* 一片郊外美景 ○ *a long stretch of open road* 长长的郊野公路. (**b**) continuous or unbroken period of time 连续的一段时间: *a four-hour stretch* 连续四小时. **4** [C usu *sing* 通常作单数] (*sl* 俚) period of service or imprisonment 服役期间; 服刑期间: *do a stretch in the army* 在军队里服役 ○ *He did a long stretch for attempted murder.* 他因谋杀未遂罪坐了很长时间的牢. **5** [C usu *sing* 通常作单数] straight part of a track or racecourse 直线跑道: *the final/finishing/home stretch*, ie the last part of the course 临近终点的直线跑道. **6** (idm 习语) **at full stretch** ⇨ FULL. **at a stretch** without stopping; continuously 不停地; 连续地: *She worked for six hours at a stretch.* 她连续工作了六个小时. **not by any/by no stretch of the imagination** however hard one may try to believe or imagine sth 无论怎样想像: *By no stretch of the imagination could you call him ambitious.* 不管你怎么想, 也不能说他存有野心.

stretchy /ˈstretʃɪ; ˋstrɛtʃɪ/ *adj* (**-ier, -iest**) (*infml* 口) that can be stretched; tending to become stretched 能伸展的; 可延伸的; 有弹性的: *stretchy materials* 弹性材料. **stretchi·ness** *n* [U].

stretcher /ˈstretʃə(r); ˋstrɛtʃɚ/ *n* **1** framework of poles, canvas, etc for carrying a sick or injured person in a lying position 担架: *An ambulance officer brought a stretcher for the injured woman.* 救护车工作人员带来了一副担架抢救受伤女子. **2** any of various devices for stretching things or holding things in a stretched position 拉伸、扩展物品的器具; 扩展器; 延伸器; 撑具.

□ **stretcher-bearer** *n* person (usu one of two) who helps to carry a stretcher 抬担架的人.

strew /struː; stru/ *v* (*pt* **strewed**, *pp* **strewed** or **strewn** /struːn; strun/) **1** [Tn, Tn·pr] **~ A (on/over B); ~ B with A** scatter sth (over a surface); cover (a surface) with scattered things; sprinkle 撒某物(于某一表面); 以所撒之物覆盖(某一表面); 散播: *strew papers over the floor/strew the floor with papers* 把文件扔得满地都是. **2** [Tn] lie scattered on or over (a surface) 撒在(某一表面)上; 撒满: *a litter-strewn playground* 扔满废弃物品的操场 ○ *Papers strewed the floor.* 文件扔了一地. ⇨Usage at SCATTER 用法见SCATTER.

strewth /struːθ; struθ/ *interj* (*Brit sl becoming dated* 俚, 渐旧) (used to express surprise, annoyance, dismay, etc 用以表示惊讶、烦恼、愕然等): *Strewth, look at the time! We're late!* 哎呀, 瞧这时间! 咱们迟到了!

stri·ated /straɪˈeɪtɪd; *US* ˈstraɪeɪtɪd; ˋstraɪetɪd/ *adj* (*fml* 文) marked with stripes, lines or furrows 有道道条纹、线条或沟痕的.

▷ **stri·ation** /straɪˈeɪʃn; straɪˋeʃən/ *n* (*fml* 文) **1** [C] stripe, line or furrow 条纹; 线条; 沟痕. **2** [U] state of being striated 条纹图样.

stricken /ˈstrɪkən; ˋstrɪkən/ *adj* **~ (by/with sth)** (esp in compounds 尤用以构成复合词) affected or overcome (by sth unpleasant, eg illness, grief) 经受或不堪(某坏事, 如疾病、悲痛)之苦的: *stricken with malaria, cancer, fever, etc* 染疟疾、患癌症、发烧 ○ *stricken by poverty/ 'poverty-stricken* 贫困不堪的 ○ *'grief-/'panic-/'terror-stricken* 悲痛[惊恐/恐惧]已极的 ○ *Rescue teams raced to the stricken ship.* 救援队竞相前往抢救遇难轮船.

strict /strɪkt; strɪkt/ *adj* (**-er, -est**) **1** demanding total obedience or observance (of rules, ways of behaving, etc); severe; not lenient 要求完全服从或遵守的; 严厉的; 严格的: *a strict teacher* 严师 ○ *a strict upbringing* 严格的教养 ○ *a strict rule against smoking* 禁止吸烟的严格规定 ○ *She's very strict with her children.* 她待子女很严. **2** (**a**) clearly and exactly defined; precise 明确的; 严密的; 精确的: *in the strict sense of the word* 确如该词之义的 ○ *the strict truth* 确凿的事实 ○ *a strict understanding, interpretation* 明确的了解、解释. (**b**) complete; absolute 完全的; 绝对的: *give information in strictest confidence/in strict secrecy*, ie expecting complete secrecy 极秘密地提供情报.

▷ **strictly** *adv* **1** in a strict manner; completely 严厉地; 严格地; 严密地; 确切地; 完全地; 绝对地: *Smoking is strictly prohibited.* 严禁吸烟. **2** (idm 习语) **strictly speaking** if one uses words, applies rules, etc in their exact sense 严格说来: *Strictly speaking, he's not qualified for the job.* 严格说来, 他没有资格做这份工作.

strict·ness *n* [U].

stric·ture /ˈstrɪktʃə(r); ˋstrɪktʃɚ/ *n* **1** (usu *pl* 通常作复数) (*fml* 文) severe criticism or condemnation 严厉的批评或谴责: *pass strictures on sb* 严厉批评某人. **2** (*medical* 医) abnormal constriction or narrowing of a tube-shaped part of the body (身体某管状部分异常的)狭窄.

stride /straɪd; straɪd/ *v* (*pt* **strode**, *pp* rarely **stridden** /ˈstrɪdn; ˋstrɪdn̩/ 过去分词作 **stridden**, 罕用) **1** [Ipr, Ip] walk with long steps (in the specified direction) (朝某方向)大步行走: *stride along the road* 沿路大步行走 ○ *striding across the fields* 大步走过田地 ○ *She turned and*

S

strode off. 她转身迈着大步走了. ○ *striding out for* (ie walking determinedly towards) *the distant hills* 大步流星向远处的山冈走去. **2** [Ipr] **~ across/over sth** cross sth with one step 一步跨越某物: *stride over a ditch* 跨过一条沟.

▷ **stride** *n* **1** (distance covered by) one long step 大步; 跨一步(的距离): *I was three strides from the door.* 我距离那门有三大步远. **2** person's way of striding; gait (大步的)步法, 步态. **3** (idm 习语) **get into one's stride** settle into a fast, confident and steady pace (of doing sth) 开始加快速度、充满信心并稳健地(做某事): *She found the job difficult at first, but now she's really getting into her stride.* 起初她觉得这工作很难, 但现在已驾轻就熟了. **make great, rapid, etc strides** make good, fast, etc progress; improve quickly 进步很大、很快等: *Tom has made enormous strides in his maths this term.* 汤姆本学期数学大有进步. **take sth in one's stride** accept and deal with sth without special effort 不特别费力地认同并处理某事物: *Some people find retiring difficult, but he has taken it all in his stride.* 有的人觉得很难适应退休后的生活, 但他却能安之若素.

stri·dent /ˈstraɪdnt; ˋstraɪdn̩t/ *adj* (of a sound, esp a voice) loud and harsh; shrill (指声音, 尤指嗓音)粗厉的, 尖锐刺耳的: *strident protests* 尖利的抗议声 ○ *strident in their demands* 他们提出要求时声嘶力竭的.
▷ **stri·dency** /ˈstraɪdənsɪ; ˋstraɪdn̩sɪ/ *n* [U]. **stri·dently** *adv.*

stridu·late /ˈstrɪdjʊleɪt; *US* ˈstrɪdʒʊleɪt; ˋstrɪdʒəˌlet/ *v* [I] (of insects such as crickets) make high-pitched chirping sounds by rubbing together certain parts of the body (指昆虫, 如蟋蟀)发尖锐刺耳的唧唧声. ▷ **stridu·la·tion** /ˌstrɪdjʊˈleɪʃn; *US* -dʒ-; ˌstrɪdʒəˋleʃən/ *n* [U].

strife /straɪf; straɪf/ *n* [U] state of conflict; angry or violent disagreement; quarrelling 冲突; 争斗; 争吵: *industrial strife*, ie between employers and workers 劳资纠纷 ○ *a nation torn by political strife* 由于政治纷争而四分五裂的国家.

strike[1] /straɪk; straɪk/ *n* **1** organized stopping of work by employees because of a disagreement (eg over pay, conditions, etc); act or instance of striking (STRIKE[2] 10) 罢工: *a miners' strike* 矿业工人罢工 ○ *industrial strikes* 工业部门的罢工 ○ *a strike by bus drivers* 公共汽车司机的罢工 ○ *a general, an unofficial, a wildcat strike* 大罢工、未经工会同意的罢工、自发举行的罢工 ○ *call a strike* 号召举行罢工 ○ *break a strike* 破坏罢工 ○ [attrib 作定语] *take strike action* 进行罢工. **2** sudden discovery of gold, oil, etc in the earth (金矿、油田等的)突然发现: (*fig* 比喻) *a lucky strike*, ie a fortunate discovery 幸运的发现. **3** sudden attack (esp by aircraft or a missile) 袭击(尤指用飞机或导弹的): *an air strike* 空袭 ○ [attrib 作定语] *first strike capacity in a nuclear war*, ie the ability to attack an enemy before they can attack you 核战争中先发制人的能力 ○ *The footballer took a strike at the goal.* 那个足球队员飞脚射门. ○ *the strike of a hawk on its prey* 鹰向猎物之猛扑. **4** (idm 习语) **be/go on ˈstrike**; **be/come/go out on ˈstrike** be engaged in/start an industrial strike 举行[开始]罢工: *We are (going) on strike.* 我们正(要)进行罢工. ○ *The shipbuilders came/went out on strike for higher pay.* 造船工人为提高工资而举行了罢工.

□ **ˈstrikebound** *adj* unable to function because of an industrial strike 因罢工而停顿的: *The docks were strikebound for a week.* 码头因罢工而瘫痪了一个星期.

ˈstrike-breaker *n* person who continues to work while fellow employees are on strike, or who is employed in place of striking members 破坏罢工者(指罢工时继续上班的或受雇代替罢工者工作的人). Cf 参看 BLACKLEG.

ˈstrike-breaking *n* [U].

ˈstrike pay money paid by a trade union to striking members during a strike officially recognized by the union 罢工津贴(在工会正式组织的罢工期间由工会发给罢工者的).

strike[2] /straɪk; straɪk/ *v* (*pt, pp* **struck** /strʌk; strʌk/) **1** (**a**) [Tn, Tn·pr, Dn·n] subject (sb/sth) to an impact; hit (sb/sth) 使(某人[某物])遭受撞击; 打, 击, 敲(某人[某物]): *The stone struck me on the side of the head.* 石子打中了我头部的侧面. ○ *He struck the table a heavy blow with his fist.* 他用拳头猛击了一下桌子. ⇨Usage at HIT[1] 用法见 HIT[1]. (**b**) [I, Tn, Tn·pr] (cause sth to) come sharply into contact with sth (使某事物)突然遭遇到某事物: *There was a crash of thunder, then the storm struck.* 一声惊雷过后, 狂风暴雨突然袭来. ○ *People say that lightning never strikes twice in the same place.* 据说闪电从来不会在同一处重复出现. ○ *The ship struck a rock.* 船触礁了. ○ *The tree was struck by lightning.* 那棵树被雷电击中了. ○ *He struck his head on/against the beam.* 他的头撞到梁上了. ○ *He struck the beam with his head.* 他的头撞到梁上了. ○ (*fig* 比喻) *The family was struck by yet another tragedy.* 这个家庭又遭不幸了. (**c**) [Tn] give (a blow) 给予(一击): *Who struck the first blow* (ie started the fight)? 是谁先出手打人的? (**d**) [Ipr] **~ at sb/sth** aim a blow at sb/sth 向某人[某物]打去: *He struck at me repeatedly with a stick.* 他一再挥棍向我打来. (**e**) [Tn·pr, Tn·p] cause (sb/sth) to move or fall with a blow or stroke 将(某人[某物])打跑、打掉或打倒: *He struck her to the ground.* 他把她打倒在地. ○ *She struck the ball away.* 她把球打了出去. **2** (**a**) [I] attack, esp suddenly 攻击; (尤指)袭击: *Enemy troops struck just before dawn.* 敌军在拂晓前发起了进攻. ○ *The lioness crouched ready to strike.* 母狮低伏着身子准备攻击. (**b**) [I, Tn esp passive 尤用于被动语态] (of disaster, disease, etc) afflict (sb/sth) (指灾难、疾病等)侵袭, 折磨(某人[某事物]): *It was not long before tragedy struck again.* 没多久, 灾难又再次降临. ○ *The area was struck by an outbreak of cholera.* 该地区突然发生了霍乱. **3** (**a**) [Tn, Tn·pr] produce (a light, spark, etc) by friction 藉摩擦产生(亮光、火花等): *strike sparks from a flint* 用燧石打出火花. (**b**) [I, Tn] (cause sth to) ignite in this way (使某物)摩擦点燃: *These damp matches won't strike.* 这些潮湿的火柴划不着. ○ *strike a match* 划火柴. **4** (**a**) [Tn, Tn·pr] produce (a musical note, sound, etc) 发出(乐音、声音等): *strike a chord on the piano* 在钢琴上弹出和声 ○ (*fig* 比喻) *strike a note of* (ie give an impression of) *gloom, optimism, caution* 显得忧郁、乐观、谨慎. (**b**) [I, Tn] (of a clock) indicate (the time) by sounding a bell, etc (指时钟)敲响报(时): *The clock has just struck (three).* 钟刚敲过(三点). ○ *The clock strikes the hours.* 这钟能按小时打点. (**c**) [I] (of time) be indicated in this way (指时间)由时钟鸣报出: *Four o'clock had just struck on the church clock.* 教堂的时钟刚敲过四点. **5** [Tn] discover or reach (gold, minerals, oil, etc) by digging or drilling (经挖掘或钻探)发现或接触到(黄金、矿物、石油等): *strike a rich vein of ore* 发现丰富的矿脉. **6** [Tn] make (a coin, medal, etc) by stamping or punching metal 用冲压法制造(钱币、奖章等): *The Royal Mint will strike a commemorative gold coin.* 英国皇家造币厂将铸造一种纪念金币. **7** [Cn·a esp passive 尤用于被动语态] bring (sb) suddenly into a specified state (as if) by a single stroke 使(某人)(如同)受到一击而突然处于某状态: *be struck blind, dumb, silent, etc* 顿时看不见东西、说不出话来、哑口无言等. **8** [Tn, Dn·f, Dn·w] (not in the continuous tenses 不用于进行时态) occur to sb's mind 产生于某人的头脑中: *An awful thought has just struck me.* 我刚才产生了一种很坏的想法. ○ *What struck me was/I was struck by* (ie I noticed) *their enthusiasm for the work.* 使我深有感触的是他们的工作热情[他们的工作热情我深有体会]. ○ *It strikes me that nobody is in favour of the changes.* 我留意到谁也不喜欢这些改革. ○ *It suddenly struck me how we could improve the situation.* 我突然想到一个办法可以让我们改进这种局面. **9** [Tn, Tn·pr] **~ sb (as sth)** have an effect on sb; impress sb (in the way specified) 对某人产生某种效果; (以某种方式)给某人留下印象: *How does the idea strike you?* 这个主意你觉得怎么样? ○ *The plan strikes me as ridiculous.* 我觉得这个计划荒谬可笑. ○ *The house strikes you as welcoming when you go in.* 这所房子你一进去就感到很舒服. **10** [I, Ipr] **~ (for/against sth)** (of workers) stop work in protest about a grievance (指工人)罢工: *Striking workers picketed the factory.* 罢工工人在工厂周围设置了纠察队. ○ *The union has voted to strike for a pay increase of 10%.* 工会投票决定为要求提高工资10%而举行罢工. **11** [Tn] lower or take down (a sail, tent, etc) 降下或拆除(帆、帐篷等): *strike* (ie dismantle) *the set after the play is over* 戏演完后撤掉布景. Cf 参看 PITCH[2] 1. **12** [Tn] arrive at or achieve (an average) by reckoning 算出(平均数). **13** [Tn] come upon (a path, etc); find 偶然发现(路径等); 找到: *It was some time before we struck the track.* 我们用

S

了很长时间才找到了路. **14** [Tn] take (a cutting) from a plant and put it in the soil so that it grows new roots 插(条)(把某些植物的枝插入土壤中使其生根发芽); 进行插技、插穗. **15** (idm 习语) **be struck on sb/sth** (*infml* 口) be favourably impressed by sb/sth; like sb/sth very much 对某人[某事物]产生良好印象; 非常喜欢某人[某事物]: *He's very much struck on his new girl-friend.* 他非常喜欢这个新交的女朋友. **hit/strike home** ⇨ HOME[3]. **hit/strike the right/wrong note** ⇨ NOTE[1]. **lightning never strikes in the same place twice** ⇨ LIGHTNING[1]. **strike an 'attitude/a 'pose** hold or put the body in a certain way or use gestures to emphasize what one says or feels; speak or write about one's opinions, intentions or feelings in a dramatic or artificial way 摆姿势或做手势以强调自己的话语或感觉; 做作地说出或写出自己的观点、意图或感情; 装腔作势: *He struck an attitude of defiance with a typically hard-hitting speech.* 他以惯用的强硬言词做出违抗的姿态. **strike at the root of sth** ⇨ ROOT[1]. **strike a 'balance (between A and B)** find a sensible middle point between two demands, extremes, etc; compromise 找到折衷办法; 妥协: *It was difficult to strike the right balance between justice and expediency.* 在公正与私利之间很难两全. **strike a 'bargain (with sb)** come to an agreement (with sb) esp after much discussion and argument (与某人)达成协议(尤指经多次磋商和争论之后): *They struck a bargain with the landlord that they would look after the garden in return for being allowed to use it.* 他们与房东达成协议, 允许他们使用花园, 但须负责照管. **strike a blow for/against sth** perform an action on behalf of or in support of/against (a belief, cause, principle, etc) 为(信念、事业、原则等)而奋斗: *By their action, they struck a blow for democracy.* 他们以实际行动争取民主. **strike camp** take down and pack up one's tents, etc 拆除帐篷等; 拔营. **strike a 'chord (with sb)** say sth that other people sympathize or identify with 引起(某人)内心共鸣; 打动(某人): *The speaker had obviously struck a chord with his audience.* 那位演讲者显然打动了听众. **strike/sound a false note** ⇨ FALSE. **strike fear, etc into sb/sb's heart** cause sb to feel fear, etc 使某人感到恐惧等: *The news of the epidemic struck terror into the population.* 流行病蔓延的消息使居民感到恐慌. **strike 'gold/'oil** discover a rich source of information, wealth, happiness, etc 找到丰富的消息来源、财源、幸福源泉等: *She hasn't always been lucky with her boy-friends but she seems to have struck gold this time.* 她结交男朋友一直运气不佳, 而这一次似乎称心如意了. **strike a light!** (*dated Brit sl* 旧, 俚) (exclamation expressing astonishment or protest 表示惊讶或反对的感叹语). **strike (it) 'lucky** (*infml* 口) have good luck in a particular matter 在某问题上交好运: *We certainly struck (it) lucky with the weather.* 我们真幸运, 遇上了好天气. **strike/sound a note (of sth)** ⇨ NOTE[1]. **ˌstrike it 'rich** (*infml* 口) acquire a lot of money, esp suddenly or unexpectedly 获得大量金钱(尤指突然或意外地). **ˌstrike while the ˌiron is 'hot** (*saying* 谚) (often imperative 常用于祈使句) make use of an opportunity immediately; act while conditions are favourable 勿错失良机; 趁热打铁. **take/strike root** ⇨ ROOT[1]. **within 'striking-distance** near enough to be reached or attacked easily 在对方易达到或易攻击的距离内.

16 (phr v) **strike sb down (a)** (*fml* 文) hit sb so that he falls to the ground 把某人打倒在地. **(b)** (of a disease, etc) make sb unable to lead an active life; make sb seriously ill or kill sb (指疾病等)使某人生活不能自理, 使某人垂危或丧命: *He was struck down by cancer at the age of thirty.* 他三十岁时死于癌症.

strike sth off remove sth with a sharp blow; cut sth off 以猛击动作除去某物: *He struck off the rotten branches with an axe.* 他用斧头砍掉了朽烂的树枝. **strike sb/sth off (sth)** remove sb/sb's name from sth, esp from membership of a professional body 将某人[某人的名字]从...中除去(尤指从专业团体中除名): *Strike her name off the list.* 把她的名字从名单中除去. ○ *The doctor was struck off for incompetence.* 那医生因不称职而被除名.

strike on sth get or find sth suddenly or unexpectedly 突然或意外地获得或发现某事物: *strike on a brilliant new idea* 突然想出一个绝妙的新主意.

strike out (at sb/sth) aim vigorous blows or attacks (对准某人[某物])猛力打去, 猛烈攻击: *He lost his temper and struck out wildly.* 他大发脾气, 疯狂地出手打人. ○ (*fig* 比喻) *In a recent article she strikes out at her critics.* 她最近写了一篇文章对批评她的人予以猛烈回击. **strike sth out/through** remove sth by drawing a line through it; cross sth out 删去某物; 将某物划掉: *The editor struck out the whole paragraph.* 编辑把整段全删掉了. **strike out (for/towards sth)** move in a vigorous and determined way (towards sth) (朝某事物)奋力前进: *strike out on foot for the distant hills* 以坚定的步伐向远处的山冈走去 ○ *He struck out* (ie started swimming) *strongly for the shore.* 他开始拼命向岸边游去. ○ (*fig* 比喻) *strike out on one's own*, ie start an independent life, a new career, etc 开始独立的生活、新的生涯等.

strike (sth) up (of a band, an orchestra, etc) begin to play (a piece of music) (指乐队、管弦乐团等)开始演奏(某乐曲): *The band struck up (a waltz).* 乐队开始演奏(华尔兹舞曲). **strike up sth (with sb)** begin (a friendship, an acquaintance, a conversation, etc) esp casually (与某人)开始(交往、认识、交谈等)(尤指偶然): *He would often strike up conversations with complete strangers.* 他经常与陌生人搭讪.

striker /ˈstraɪkə(r); ˈstraɪkɚ/ *n* **1** worker who is on strike 罢工的人. **2** (*sport* 体) **(a)** (in football) attacking player whose most important role is to try to score goals (足球)前锋. ⇨illus at ASSOCIATION FOOTBALL (ASSOCIATION) 见ASSOCIATION FOOTBALL (ASSOCIATION)插图 Cf 参看 FORWARD[4]. **(b)** (in cricket) batsman who is facing the bowling (板球)击球手.

strik·ing /ˈstraɪkɪŋ; ˈstraɪkɪŋ/ *adj* **1 (a)** attracting attention or interest 引人注意的; 饶有兴趣的: *a striking display, effect* 饶有兴趣的展示、显著的效果 ○ *There is a striking contrast between the two interpretations.* 这两种解释截然不同. **(b)** attracting attention because of a good appearance; attractive (因相貌好)惹人注目的; 吸引人的: *his striking good looks* 他那堂堂仪表 ○ *a very striking young woman* 美貌动人的年轻女子. **2** (of a clock, etc) that strikes (指时钟等)鸣响报时的. ▷ **strik·ingly** *adv*: *a strikingly handsome man* 极英俊的男子.

string[1] /strɪŋ; strɪŋ/ *n* **1 (a)** [U] thin cord made of twisted threads; twine (细的)绳子; 合股的线: *a ball of string* 一团线 ○ *tie up a parcel with string* 用绳子把包裹捆起来 ○ *attach sth with a length/piece of string* 用一根绳子把某物系住. **(b)** [C] length of this or similar material used to fasten or pull sth, or interwoven in a frame to form the head of a racket 拴或拉某物的绳; (球拍的)绷绳: *a puppet on strings*, ie made to move by pulling strings attached to its joints 牵线木偶 ○ *The key is hanging on a string by the door.* 钥匙挂在门边的一根绳子上. ○ *She wore the medal on a string round her neck.* 她脖子上戴着一个用绳子穿着的奖牌. ○ *I have broken several strings in my tennis racket.* 我把我那网球拍上的几条绷绳给弄断了. **2** [C] tightly stretched piece of catgut or wire, eg in a violin, harp or guitar, which produces a musical note when it vibrates (琴)弦. ⇨illus at App 1 见附录1插图, page xi. **3 the strings** [pl] (players of) the stringed instruments (eg violins, cellos, etc) in an orchestra (管弦乐队的)弦乐器(如小提琴、大提琴等); 弦乐器演奏者. ⇨illus at App 1 见附录1插图, page xi. **4** [C] **(a)** set or series of things put together on a thread, cord, etc 穿在线、绳等上的一串东西: *a string of beads, pearls, etc* 一串珠子、珍珠等 ○ *a string of onions* 一串洋葱. **(b)** series or line of people or things 成列或成行的人; 一连串的事物: *a string of visitors* 一列参观者 ○ *a string of small lakes* 一个接一个的小湖 ○ *a string of abuse, curses, lies* 一连串的辱骂、诅咒、谎言 ○ *a string of wins* 一连串的胜利. **(c)** group of racehorses that are trained at one stable 在同一马房里训练的一群赛马. **5** [C] tough piece of fibrous substance that connects the two halves of a bean-pod, etc (豆荚等的)筋. **6** (idm 习语) **the first/second 'string** first/alternative person or thing (to be) relied on for achieving one's purpose 赖以实现目标的占首位的[可作替代的]人或事物. **have/keep sb on a 'string** have/keep sb under one's control 操纵或支配某人: *She's had us all on a string for too long.* 我们大家受她摆布已经很

长时间了. **have two strings/a second, etc string to one's bow** ⇨ BOW[1]. **one's mother's, etc apron strings** ⇨ APRON. **(with) no ˈstrings attached/without ˈstrings** (*infml* 口) with no special conditions or restrictions 不附带条件; 无任何限制: *a loan of £3 000 and no strings attached* 一笔3 000英镑的无条件贷款. **pull strings/wires** ⇨ PULL[2]. **pull the strings/wires** ⇨ PULL[2].

▷ **stringy** *adj* (**-ier**, **-iest**) **1** like string 像细绳的; 线状的: *lank stringy hair* 平直如线绳的头发. **2** (**a**) (of beans, etc) having a strip of tough fibre (指豆荚等)有韧性纤维的, 有筋的. (**b**) (of meat) tough (指肉)多筋的. **stringi·ness** *n* [U].

□ ˌ**string ˈband**, ˌ**string ˈorchestra** band or orchestra consisting only of stringed instruments 弦乐队; 弦乐团.

ˈ**string bean** = RUNNER BEAN (RUNNER).

ˌ**string quarˈtet** (music to be played by) four people playing stringed instruments 弦乐四重奏曲(演奏者).

ˌ**string ˈvest** (*esp Brit*) vest made of material with large meshes 网眼背心.

string[2] /strɪŋ; strɪŋ/ *v* (*pt*, *pp* **strung** /strʌŋ; strʌŋ/) **1** [Tn] put a string[1](3) or strings on (a bow, violin, tennis racket, etc) 给(弓、小提琴、网球拍等)装弦: *loosely/tightly strung* 装弦装得松[紧]. **2** [Tn] thread (pearls, beads, etc) on a string[1](1b) 用线或细绳将(珍珠、珠子等)穿起来. **3** [Tn·pr, Tn·p] **~ sth (up)** hang or tie (sth) in place with a string, rope, etc (用线、绳等)悬挂, 系住(某物): *Lanterns were strung in the trees around the pool.* 水池周围的树上悬挂着灯笼. ○ *Flags had been strung up across the street.* 用绳子穿着的旗子横悬在街道上. **4** [Tn] remove the tough fibrous strip from (beans) 除去(豆荚)的筋. **5** (phr v) **string sb along** deliberately mislead sb, esp about one's own intentions, beliefs, etc 蓄意误导某人(尤指对于自己的意图、信念等): *She has no intention of marrying him — she's just stringing him along.* 她并不想嫁给他——只是想钩住他不放. **string along (with sb)** stay with or accompany sb casually or as long as it is convenient; tag along 暂与某人相处或为伴; 跟随: *I don't want them stringing along as well!* 我也同样不愿意让他们跟着来! ○ *She decided to string along with the others as she had nothing else to do.* 她反正也无事可做, 所以就跟着大家去了. **string (sb/sth) out** (cause sb/sth to) be or become spread out at intervals in a line (使某人[某物])有间隔地成行展开: *The players were told to string out across the field.* 运动员们得到指示在场上按间隔距离站成一排. ○ *The horses were strung out towards the end of the race.* 比赛中的马临近终点时拉开了距离. ○ *Warning notices were strung out along the motorway.* 高速公路上隔一段距离就有一个示警牌. **string sth together** combine (words, phrases, etc) to form meaningful statements 将(词、词组等)连结成语句: *I can just manage to string a few words of French together.* 我只能勉强把法语的几个词拼凑在一起. ○ *He hadn't prepared a speech but he managed to string together a few remarks at the end of the meeting.* 他并没有准备讲话, 但在会议结束时现凑了几句. **string sb up** (*infml* 口) kill sb by hanging (esp not legally) 绞死或吊死某人(尤指非法地): *If the crowd catch him, they'll string him up on the nearest tree.* 那帮人要是抓住他, 准得找棵树把他吊死.

□ ˈ**stringed instrument** musical instrument with strings that are played by touching them with a bow or plectrum 弦乐器: *The viola is a stringed instrument.* 中提琴是一种弦乐器.

strin·gent /ˈstrɪndʒənt; ˋstrɪndʒənt/ *adj* **1** (of a law, rule, etc) that must be obeyed; strict or severe (指法律、规则等)必须遵守的, 严格的, 严厉的: *a stringent ban on smoking* 禁止吸烟的严格规定. **2** (of financial conditions) difficult because there is not enough money (指财务状况)因缺钱而困难的, 银根紧的: *a stringent economic climate* 窘迫的经济情势. ▷ **strin·gency** /-nsɪ; -nsɪ/ *n* [U]: *in these days of financial stringency* 在银根收缩的这段日子里. **strin·gently** *adv*: *The regulations must be stringently observed.* 这些规则必须严格遵守.

stringer /ˈstrɪŋə(r); ˋstrɪŋɚ/ *n* newspaper correspondent who is not on the regular staff 特约记者.

strip /strɪp; strɪp/ *v* (**-pp-**) **1** (**a**) [Tn, Tn·pr, Tn·p, Cn·a] **~ sth (from/off sth/sb)**; **~ sth/sb (of sth)**; **~ sth (off)** take off (clothes, coverings, parts, etc) from sb/sth 从某人[某物]处除去(衣物、覆盖物、零件等): *strip* (ie dismantle) *a machine* 拆卸机器 ○ *strip the bark off a tree/strip a tree of its bark* 剥去树皮 ○ *The bandits stripped him (naked)/stripped him of his clothes.* 强盗把他的衣服剥光了. ○ *The paint will be difficult to strip off.* 这层漆很难除掉. ○ *They stripped the house bare*, ie removed everything from it. 他们把房子里的东西都搬空了. (**b**) [I, Ipr, Ip] **~ (down) (to sth)**; **~ (off)** take off one's clothes 脱去衣服: *The doctor asked the patient to strip.* 医生让病人脱掉衣服. ○ *strip to* (ie remove all one's clothes except) *one's underwear* 脱到只剩内衣 ○ *strip to the waist*, ie remove clothes from the upper part of one's body 脱光上身衣服 ○ *They stripped off and ran into the water.* 他们脱掉衣服跑进水里. **2** [Tn·pr] **~ sb of sth** take away (property, honours, etc) from sb 剥夺某人的(财产、荣誉等): *He was stripped of all his possessions.* 剥夺了他的全部财产. ○ *The general was stripped of his rank.* 这位将军被免去了军阶. **3** [Tn] damage the thread of (a screw) or the teeth of (a gear), esp by misuse 损坏(螺钉等)的螺纹或(齿轮)的齿(尤因使用不当). **4** (idm 习语) **strip to the buff** (*infml* 口) take all one's clothes off; undress completely 脱光衣服. **5** (phr v) **strip sth down** remove all the detachable parts of (esp an engine) in order to clean or repair it 卸掉(尤指发动机)的所有零件进行清理或检修.

▷ **strip** *n* **1** act of stripping (STRIP 1b), esp in a strip-tease show 脱衣; (尤指)脱衣舞表演: *do a strip* 表演脱衣舞. **2** long narrow piece (of material, etc) or area (of land, etc) 狭长的一块(材料、土地等): *a strip of paper* 一张纸条 ○ *a strip of land suitable for a garden* 适合做园子的一块狭长土地 ○ *a landing-strip in the jungle* 丛林中的简易飞机跑道. **3** (*infml* 口) clothes of a particular colour or colours worn by the members of a football team (足球队员的)运动服(可为单色或彩色): *England are playing in the blue and white strip.* 英格兰队穿着蓝白色运动衣进行比赛. **4** (idm 习语) **tear sb off a strip/tear a strip off sb** ⇨ TEAR[2].

strip·per *n* **1** [C] person who performs in a strip-tease 脱衣舞表演者. **2** [C, U] device or solvent for removing paint, etc 清除油漆等的器具或溶剂; 剥离器; 清除剂.

□ ˈ**strip cartoon** (*Brit*) = COMIC STRIP (COMIC).

ˈ**strip club** (*US* also ˈ**strip joint**) club in which strip-tease is performed 脱衣舞夜总会.

ˈ**strip lighting**, ˈ**strip light** (method of lighting with a) long tubular fluorescent lamp (instead of a bulb) 荧光灯管(照明方法).

ˈ**strip-tease** *n* [C, U] entertainment (eg in a theatre, bar or nightclub) in which a performer slowly undresses in front of an audience 脱衣舞(剧场、酒吧或夜总会等中的一种节目, 表演者当众徐徐脱掉衣服).

stripe /straɪp; straɪp/ *n* **1** long narrow band (usu of the same width throughout its length) on a surface that is usu different from it in colour, material or texture 条纹, 线条(通常全长等宽, 而颜色、材料或质地通常异于底面): *a white table-cloth with red stripes* 有红色条纹的白桌布 ○ *the tiger's stripes* 老虎的斑纹 ○ *The plates have a blue stripe round the edge.* 这些盘子边缘上有一道蓝线. ⇨illus at PATTERN 见PATTERN插图. **2** badge (often in the shape of a V) that is worn on the uniform of a soldier, policeman, etc as a mark of rank; chevron (军警等制服上的)级别条纹(常呈V字形); V形臂章: *How many stripes are there on a sergeant's sleeve?* 中士的袖子上有几道V形条纹? ○ *She was awarded another stripe.* 她又升了一级. **3** (usu *pl* 通常作复数) (*arch* 古) blow with a whip; stroke 鞭打; 抽打.

▷ **striped** /straɪpt; ˋstraɪpt/ *adj* marked with or having stripes (STRIPE 1) 以条纹作标志的; 有条纹的: *striped material* 有条纹的料子 ○ *a striped shirt, suit, tie* 带条纹的衬衫、一套衣服、领带.

stripy /ˈstraɪpɪ; ˋstraɪpɪ/ *adj* (**-ier**, **-iest**) (*infml* 口) = STRIPED: *bright stripy cloth* 带条纹的鲜艳的布.

strip·ling /ˈstrɪplɪŋ; ˋstrɪplɪŋ/ *n* (*fml or joc* 文或谑) male person between boyhood and manhood; youth or lad 青年男子; 小伙子: *a young man, hardly more than stripling* 一个小伙子, 尚不及而立之年.

strive /straɪv; straɪv/ *v* (*pt* **strove** /strəʊv; strov/, *pp* **striven** /ˈstrɪvn; ˋstrɪvən/) (*fml* 文) **1** [Ipr, It] **~ (for/after sth)** try very hard (to obtain or achieve sth) (为获得或实现某事物)努力, 奋斗: *strive for success* 力争获得

成功 ○ *strive to improve one's performance* 努力提高演技. **2** [I, Ipr] **~ (against/with sb/sth)** carry on a conflict; struggle 进行斗争; 争斗: *strive against oppression, the enemy* 反抗压迫、抗击敌人.

stro·bo·scope /ˈstrəʊbəskəʊp; ˈstrobə,skop/ *n* instrument that produces a rapidly flashing bright light 频闪观测仪. ▷ **stro·bo·scopic** /ˌstrəʊbəˈskɒpɪk; ,strobəˈskɑpɪk/ *adj*. □ ˈ**strobe light** (also **strobe**) light that flashes rapidly on and off 频闪灯: *disco dancers lit by strobe lights* 在频闪灯照射下跳迪斯科舞的人.

strode *pt* of STRIDE.

stroke[1] /strəʊk; strok/ *n* **1** (**a**) act or process of striking; blow 击; 打; 打击: *kill sb with one stroke of a sword* 一剑劈死某人 ○ *20 strokes with a whip* 鞭打20下. (**b**) (*sport* 体) (in tennis, golf, etc) act of striking a ball; (in golf) this used as a unit of scoring (网球、高尔夫球等)击球动作; (高尔夫球)得分的一击: *a forehand stroke* 正手击球 ○ *a graceful stroke with the bat* 用拍击球的一个优美动作 ○ *She won by two strokes.* 她两次击球得分获胜. **2** (**a**) any of a series of repeated movements, esp in swimming or rowing 一连串反复动作中的一次; (尤指游泳或划船的)一次划水: *long powerful strokes* 有力的长划动作 ○ *a fast/slow stroke*, ie in rowing 快[慢]划(划船). (**b**) (esp in compounds 尤用以构成复合词) style of stroke in swimming 游泳姿势; 游法: *do (the) breast-stroke, back-stroke, etc* 进行蛙泳、仰泳等 ○ *Which stroke are you best at?* 你最擅长哪一种游法? **3** (in a rowing crew) oarsman who sits nearest the stern of a racing boat, and sets the speed of the strokes (划船者中的)尾桨手(位于船尾, 掌握划速). Cf 参看 BOW[3] 2. **4** **~ of sth** single successful or effective action or occurrence (of the specified kind) (某类型的)一次成功或有效的行动或事情: *Your idea was a stroke of genius!* 你的主意真了不起! ○ *It was a stroke of luck that I found you here.* 我在这里碰见你真是运气. ○ *Various strokes of misfortune led to his ruin.* 他遭诸多不幸而一蹶不振. **5** (mark made by a) single movement of a pen or brush (钢笔、毛笔等的)一笔, 笔画: *thin/thick strokes* 细[粗]笔画 ○ *with a stroke of the pen* 用笔一挥 ○ *put the finishing strokes to a painting* 画上最后几笔. **6** sound made by a bell or clock striking the hours (报时的)铃声或钟声: *on the stroke of three*, ie at three o'clock exactly 钟鸣三响(三时正). **7** (*medical* 医) sudden attack of illness in the brain that can cause loss of the power to move, speak clearly, etc 中风; 卒中: *The stroke left him paralysed on one side of his body.* 他因患中风而致半身不遂. Cf 参看 APOPLEXY. **8** (idm 习语) **at a/one ˈstroke** with a single immediate action 一下子; 一举: *They threatened to cancel the whole project at a stroke.* 他们扬言要一下子取消整个项目. **not do a stroke (of work)** not do any work 什么工作都不做: *We'll have to get rid of him — he never does a stroke.* 我们得把他弄走——他什么活儿都不干. **put sb off his ˈstroke** cause sb to falter, hesitate, etc in what he is doing 使某人行事动摇、犹豫等: *My speech went quite well until I was put off my stroke by the interruption.* 我起初讲得很顺利, 可是受到干扰后就结巴起来了.

▷ **stroke** *v* **1** [Tn] act as a stroke[1](3) to (a boat or crew) 当...的尾桨手. **2** [Tn·pr, Tn·p] strike (a ball) 击(球): *stroked the ball cleverly past her opponent* 她巧妙地一击把球打过对手.

stroke[2] /strəʊk; strok/ *v* [Tn] pass the hand gently over (a surface), usu again and again (用手)轻抚, 抚摩(某物表面)(通常指反复地): *stroke a cat, one's beard, sb's back* 抚摩猫、自己的胡须、某人的背.

▷ **stroke** *n* (usu *sing* 通常作单数) act of stroking; stroking movement 轻抚; 抚摩: *give her hair an affectionate stroke* 深情地抚摸她的头发.

stroll /strəʊl; strol/ *n* slow leisurely walk 散步; 漫步; 闲逛; 溜达: *go for/have a stroll* 去散步.

▷ **stroll** *v* [I, Ipr, Ip] walk in a slow leisurely way 散步; 漫步; 闲逛; 溜达: *strolling (around) in the park* 在公园(各处)溜达 ○ *He strolls in and out as he pleases.* 他随意地出来进去闲逛. **stroller** *n* **1** person who strolls 散步者; 闲逛者. **2** (*esp US*) = PUSH-CHAIR (PUSH[2]).

strong /strɒŋ; *US* strɔːŋ; strɔŋ/ *adj* (**-er** /-ŋɡə(r); -ŋɡɚ/, **-est** /-ŋɡɪst; -ŋɡɪst/) **1** (**a**) not easily broken, hurt, injured, captured, etc; solid and sturdy 不易破坏、损坏、伤害、捕获等的; 坚固的; 强壮的: *a strong stick, fort, structure* 结实的手杖、堡垒、构造 ○ *feel quite strong again*, ie in good health after an illness 觉得完全康复了 ○ *The chair wasn't strong enough and it broke when he sat on it.* 这把椅子不够结实, 他一坐上去就散架了. ○ *We need strong defences against the enemy.* 我们需要建立强大的防御力量以抗击敌人. ○ *We still have a strong chance of winning.* 我们仍很有希望获胜. (**b**) having great power, esp of the body 强有力的(尤指身体): *strong muscles* 强健的肌肉 ○ *a strong country*, ie one with a large army, etc 强国(拥有大量军队等的) ○ *an actor with a strong voice* 嗓音洪亮的男演员 ○ *strong enough to lift a piano alone* 力气大得能独自搬起钢琴. (**c**) done or happening with great power 用力的; 强劲的: *a strong push, blow* 有力的一推、一击 ○ *play a strong shot*, eg in tennis 用力一击(如网球赛中). **2** (**a**) (of emotions, opinions, etc) that can resist influence (指感情、观点等)能抵御外来影响的, 坚定的, 不动摇的: *strong will, belief, determination* 坚强的意志、信念、决心 ○ *have strong nerves*, ie be not easily frightened, worried, etc 有非凡的勇气. (**b**) that can exert great influence 能发挥巨大影响力的: *a strong conviction, protest* 坚定的信仰、强烈的抗议 ○ *a strong personality* 很强的个性 ○ *strong leadership* 坚强的领导 ○ *There is strong* (ie convincing) *evidence of her guilt.* 她的罪证确凿. (**c**) [attrib 作定语] (of a person) convinced; determined (指人)有坚定信仰的, 有决心的: *a strong believer, supporter* 坚定的信徒、支持者. **3** moving quickly 快速移动的: *a strong wind, current, etc* 强风、急流. **4** (**a**) (capable of) having a great effect on the senses; intense or powerful (能)产生强烈的感官效果的; 强烈的; 有力的: *a strong light, colour* 强光、浓重的颜色 ○ *a strong feeling of nausea* 很强烈的厌恶感 ○ *Her breath is rather strong*, ie has an unpleasant smell. 她口臭很重. (**b**) having a lot of flavour 味浓的: *strong tea, cheese, etc* 酽茶、味重的干酪 ○ *a strong taste of garlic* 强烈的蒜味. (**c**) (of a drink) containing much alcohol (指酒)酒精含量高的, 烈性的: *Whisky is stronger than beer.* 威士忌比啤酒度数大. **5** (of a person) effective; skilful; able (指人)工作效率高的, 有技巧的, 能干的: *a strong candidate for a job*, ie one who is likely to get it 极有可能被录用的人 ○ *a pupil who is strong in physics but weak in English* 物理好而英语差的学生. **6** (after numbers 用于数词之后) having the specified number 有某数量的: *an army 5 000 strong/a 5 000-strong army* 一支5 000人的军队. **7** (*commerce* 商) (**a**) rising steadily 稳步上升的: *strong prices, share values, etc* 坚挺的价格、股票价值等 ○ *The stock market is stronger now*, ie People are more willing to buy shares, etc. 股票行情现在看涨(买者踊跃). (**b**) (of a currency) having a high value in relation to other currencies (指某货币)较为坚挺的: *Is the pound strong or weak (against the yen) at the moment?* 目前英镑(对日元)是坚挺还是疲软? **8** [usu attrib 通常作定语] (*grammar*) (**a**) (of a verb) forming the past tense by a vowel change (eg *sing, sang*), not by adding *-d, -ed* or *-t* (指动词)强的, 不规则的(用元音变化而不用添加词尾d、ed或t的方法构成过去式的, 如sing、sang). (**b**) (of the pronunciation of some words) that is the version used when the word is stressed (指某些字的读音)强式的: *The strong form of 'and' is* /ænd; ænd/. ☆ and一字的强式读音为 /ænd/. **9** [pred 作表语] (*infml* 口 *esp Brit*) not to be tolerated, believed, etc 难以容忍、无法相信等: *It was a bit strong of him to call me a liar in front of the whole department.* 他当着全体同事的面说我撒谎, 未免太过分了. **10** (idm 习语) **be strong on sth** be good at sth or doing sth 擅长某事物的; 善于做某事的: *I'm not very strong on dates.* 我不善于和异性朋友约会. **one's best/strongest card** ⇨ CARD[1]. **going ˈstrong** (*infml* 口) continuing (a race, an activity, etc) vigorously; continuing to be healthy 精力充沛地继续(赛跑、活动等); 依然健壮: *She's 91 years old and still going strong.* 她已91岁了, 仍然很健康. ○ *The runner is still going strong on the last lap.* 那个赛跑运动员在跑最后一圈时仍然劲头很足. **(as) strong as a ˈhorse/an ˈox** having great physical strength; able to do heavy work 体壮如马的; 力大如牛的. **one's/sb's strong ˈpoint/ˈsuit** thing that one/sb does well 自己[某人]所擅长的事物: *Don't ask me to add up the bill: arithmetic isn't my strong point.* 别叫我算帐单, 我的算术可不怎么样. **a strong stomach** ability not to feel nausea 不感

到恶心: *You have to have a strong stomach to watch animals being slaughtered.* 要想看宰杀动物, 得看着不恶心才行. ▷ **strongly** *adv*: *strongly built* 体格健壮的 ○ *a light shining strongly* 很明亮的灯 ○ *a strongly-worded protest* 措辞激烈的抗议 ○ *She finished the race strongly.* 她很有毅力地跑完了全程. ○ *I feel strongly that...*, ie I firmly believe that... 我坚信....

□ **'strong-arm** *adj* [attrib 作定语] using violence 使用暴力的: *use strong-arm methods, tactics, etc* 采用强制方法、策略等.

'strong-box *n* sturdy box for keeping valuable things in 保险箱; 保险柜.

'stronghold *n* **1** fort 堡垒; 要塞. **2** (*fig* 比喻) place where there is much support for a cause, etc 某事业备受支持的地方; 据点; 根据地: *a stronghold of republicanism* 共和运动的据点.

,strong 'language (*euph* 婉) language containing curses and swearing 骂人的话.

,strong-'minded *adj* having a determined mind 意志坚强的; 有决心的.

'strong-room *n* room, eg in a bank, with thick walls and a sturdy door, where valuables are kept (银行等中放置贵重物品的)保险库.

stron·tium /'strɒntɪəm; *US* -nʃɪəm; 'strɑnʃɪəm/ *n* [U] chemical element, a soft silver-white metal 锶. ⇨App 10 见附录10.

□ **strontium '90** radioactive form of strontium found in the fall-out from nuclear explosions and extremely harmful to people and animals when taken into the body 锶90(锶的放射性同位素).

strop /strɒp; strɑp/ *n* leather strap on which a razor is sharpened, or a machine used for the same purpose 磨剃刀的皮带或机器.

▷ **strop** *v* (**-pp-**) [Tn] sharpen (a razor) on a strop 在皮带或打磨机上磨(剃刀).

stroppy /'strɒpɪ; 'strɑpɪ/ *adj* (**-ier, -iest**) (*Brit sl* 俚) (of a person) awkward to deal with; bad-tempered (指人)难对付的, 脾气坏的: *Don't get stroppy with me — it's not my fault!* 别对我发火——那不是我的错!

strove *pt* of STRIVE.

struck *pt, pp* of STRIKE.

struc·tur·al·ism /'strʌktʃərəlɪzəm; 'strʌktʃərə,lɪzəm/ *n* [U] method of analysing a subject (eg social sciences, psychology, language, literature), which concentrates on the structure of a system and the relations between its elements, rather than on the function of those elements 结构主义(社会科学、心理学、语言学、文学等学科采用的研究方法, 注重系统中的结构及其各成分间的关系而并非各成分的功能).

▷ **struc·tur·al·ist** /-rəlɪst; -rəlɪst/ *adj* [esp attrib 尤作定语]: *a structuralist approach, analysis* 结构主义的方法、分析法. — *n* person who uses structuralist methods 结构主义者.

struc·ture /'strʌktʃə(r); 'strʌktʃɚ/ *n* **1** [U, C] way in which sth is put together, organized, built, etc 结构; 构造: *the structure of the human body* 人体的构造 ○ *rules of sentence structure* 句子的结构规则 ○ *the company's management structure* 公司的管理机构 ○ *molecular structure* 分子的结构. **2** [C] anything made of many parts; any complex whole; building 有结构的事物; 复杂的整体; 建筑物: *The model is an odd-looking structure of balls and rods.* 这个模型是由球和杆组成的结构, 样子很奇特. ○ *The Parthenon is a magnificent structure.* 帕台农神庙是一座宏伟的建筑物.

▷ **struc·ture** *v* [Tn] give a structure to (sth); plan or organize 使(某事物)形成结构; 计划; 组织: *structure one's day, life, career* 安排自己的一天、生活、职业 ○ *an intelligently structured essay* 结构巧妙的文章.

struc·tural /'strʌktʃərəl; 'strʌktʃərəl/ *adj* [usu attrib 通常作定语] of a structure or the framework of a structure 结构(上)的; 构架(上)的: *structural alterations to a building*, eg removing internal walls to make rooms bigger 建筑物结构上的改变(如拆掉隔墙以加大房间面积). **struc·tur·ally** /-ərəlɪ; -ərəlɪ/ *adv*: *The building is structurally sound.* 这座建筑物结构很坚固.

stru·del /'stru:dl; 'strudḷ/ *n* [C, U] type of cake made of sweetened fruit, etc rolled up in thin pastry and baked 果馅卷饼: *a slice of apple strudel* 一块苹果馅卷饼.

struggle /'strʌgl; 'strʌgḷ/ *v* **1** (**a**) [I, Ipr, Ip] **~ (with sb)** fight (with sb) (与某人)争斗, 搏斗, 打斗: *two boys struggling (together)* (在一起)扭打着的两个男孩 ○ *The shopkeeper struggled with the thief.* 店主与那窃贼搏斗起来. (**b**) [I, Ipr, Ip, It] **~ (against/with sb/sth)** move one's body vigorously, eg trying to get free 挣扎: *The prisoner struggled (against his captors) but couldn't escape.* 那囚犯挣扎着(要摆脱那些逮他的人), 却未能逃脱. ○ *She struggled to get away from her attacker.* 她挣扎着想摆脱那个侵犯她的人. **2** [I, Ipr, It] **~ (against/with sb/sth) (for sth)** try to overcome difficulties, etc; make great efforts 斗争; 拼搏; 奋斗; 努力: *struggle with a problem, one's conscience* 同困难作斗争、与自己的良心搏斗 ○ *The two leaders are struggling for power.* 那两个领导人正在争夺权力. ○ *We must struggle against this prejudice for a more tolerant attitude to our beliefs.* 我们必须努力克服这种偏见, 从而在信仰上采取更为宽容的态度. ○ *I'm struggling to finish the huge helping you gave me.* 你给我添的这么多吃的, 我得尽力把它吃完. **3** [Ipr, Ip] make one's way with difficulty (in the specified direction) 艰难地(朝某方向)行进: *The chick finally broke through the shell and struggled out (of it).* 小鸡终于破开蛋壳, 挣扎着(从中)钻了出来. **4** (phr v) **struggle along/on** manage to survive in spite of great difficulties 勉强生存下去: *We're struggling along on a tiny income.* 我们依靠极少的收入过活.

▷ **struggle** *n* **1** fight 打斗; 格斗; 搏斗; 战斗; 斗争: *a fierce struggle between two wrestlers* 两名摔跤运动员之间的激烈搏斗 ○ *a power struggle* 权力斗争 ○ *the class struggle* 阶级斗争 ○ *We will not surrender without a struggle.* 我们绝不会不战而降. **2** (usu *sing* 通常作单数) great effort 努力; 奋斗: *After a long struggle, she gained control of the business.* 她经过长期的努力, 在业务上已能应付自如.

strum /strʌm; strʌm/ *v* (**-mm-**) [I, Ipr, Ip, Tn] **~ (on sth)** play (a stringed instrument), esp rather unskilfully or monotonously 演奏(弦乐器)(尤指不很熟练或单调乏味): *strumming (away) on my guitar* (我)胡乱拨弄着吉他 ○ *strum a tune on the banjo* 用班卓琴乱弹一曲.

strum·pet /'strʌmpɪt; 'strʌmpɪt/ *n* (*arch or joc derog* 古或谑, 贬) female prostitute 妓女; 婊子.

strung *pt, pp* of STRING[2].

□ **strung up** /,strʌŋ 'ʌp; ,strʌŋ 'ʌp/ nervously tense or excited 神经紧张的; 激动的: *I get very strung up before an exam.* 我临考试前紧张得不得了.

strut[1] /strʌt; strʌt/ *n* rod or bar placed in a framework to strengthen and brace it (框架的)支杆, 支柱, 支撑物.

strut[2] /strʌt; strʌt/ *v* (**-tt-**) [I, Ipr, Ip] (*often derog* 常作贬义) walk in an upright, proud way 趾高气扬地走; 高视阔步: *strutting peacocks* 大摇大摆的孔雀 ○ *She strutted past us, ignoring our greeting.* 她神气活现地从我们跟前走过, 我们打招呼她都不理.

▷ **strut** *n* (usu *sing* 通常作单数) such a way of walking 趾高气扬的步态; 高视阔步的样子.

strych·nine /'strɪkni:n; 'strɪknin/ *n* [U] poisonous substance used in very small doses to stimulate the nerves 士的宁, 马钱子碱(有毒, 微量可作兴奋剂).

stub /stʌb; stʌb/ *n* **1** short end piece or stump remaining from a pencil, cigarette or similarly-shaped object; butt (铅笔、香烟等物的)残段, 残端; 铅笔头; 烟蒂: *The crayon had been worn down to a stub.* 这枝蜡笔用得只剩一小段了. ○ *The dog only has a stub of a tail*, ie a very short one. 这条狗的尾巴很短. **2** counterfoil 票根; 存根: *fill in a cheque stub* 填写支票的存根.

▷ **stub** *v* (**-bb-**) **1** [Tn, Tn·pr] **~ sth (against/on sth)** strike (esp one's toe) accidentally against sth hard 使(尤指脚趾)碰到某物: *I've stubbed my toe on a rock.* 我的脚趾碰到石头上了. **2** (phr v) **stub sth out** extinguish (esp a cigarette) by pressing it against sth hard (在硬物上)碾灭(尤指香烟).

stub·ble /'stʌbl; 'stʌbḷ/ *n* [U] **1** short ends of grain stalks left in the ground after harvesting 作物收割后遗留在地里的残茎; 茬子. **2** short stiff hairs of a beard 短而硬的胡茬子: *three days' stubble on his chin* 他下巴上三天未刮的胡茬子.

▷ **stub·bly** /'stʌblɪ; 'stʌblɪ/ *adj* of or like stubble (似)茬子的: *a stubbly beard, chin* 短硬的胡茬子、长满胡茬子的下巴.

stub·born /'stʌbən; 'stʌbɚn/ *adj* **1** (*often derog* 常作贬义) determined not to give way; strong-willed; obstinate

S

不退让的; 倔强的; 固执的; 顽固的: *be too stubborn to apologize* 硬是不肯道歉 ○ *show stubborn resistance to change* 对改革采取顽抗态度. **2** difficult to move, remove, cure, etc 难以移动、去除、医治等的: *You'll have to push hard, that door is a bit stubborn.* 你得用力推才行, 那门不大好开. ○ *a stubborn cough that has lasted for weeks* 已持续几周难以治愈的咳嗽. **3** (idm 习语) **obstinate/stubborn as a mule** ⇨ MULE[1]. ▷ **stub·bornly** *adv*: *stubbornly refuse to do it* 顽固地拒绝做那件事. **stub·born·ness** *n* [U].

stubby /ˈstʌbɪ; ˋstʌbɪ/ *adj* (**-ier, -iest**) short and thick 短而粗的: *stubby fingers* 又短又粗的手指 ○ *a stubby tail* 短而粗的尾巴.

stucco /ˈstʌkəʊ; ˋstʌko/ *n* [U] plaster or cement used for covering or decorating walls or ceilings (涂饰墙壁或天花板用的)灰泥. ▷ **stuc·coed** *adj*.

stuck[1] *pt, pp* of STICK[2].

stuck[2] /stʌk; stʌk/ *adj* **1** [pred 作表语] not able to move or continue doing sth 不能动; 不能继续做某事: *Help! I'm stuck in the mud!* 救命啊! 我陷进泥里不能动了! ○ *We were stuck in a traffic jam for an hour.* 我们因交通堵塞而受阻一个小时. ○ *I'm stuck on* (ie unable to answer) *the second question.* 我在第二个问题上卡住了(不会回答). **2** [attrib 作定语] (of an animal) that has been stabbed or has had its throat cut (指动物)被刺的, 被割破咽喉的: *scream like a stuck pig* 像宰猪似的尖叫. **3** [pred 作表语] **~ on sb** (*infml* 口) very fond of sb 非常喜欢某人: *He's really stuck on his new girl-friend.* 他可真爱这个新交的女朋友. **4** [pred 作表语] **~ with sb/sth** (*infml* 口) having sb/sth one does not want 与不喜欢的某人[某事物]在一起: *I'm stuck with my sister for the whole day.* 我一整天都让妹妹给缠住了. ○ *Why am I always stuck with the washing-up?* 干吗总是要我洗餐具? **5** (idm 习语) **get stuck in(to sth)** (*infml* 口) start doing sth enthusiastically 积极地开始做某事: *Here's your food. Now get stuck in* (ie start eating it)*!* 这是给你吃的. 快吃吧! ○ *We got stuck into the job immediately.* 我们立刻动手干了起来.

stuck-up /ˌstʌk ˈʌp; ˋstʌkˋʌp/ *adj* (*infml* 口) conceited and unwilling to mix with others; snobbish 高傲的; 倨傲不群的; 自命不凡的.

stud[1] /stʌd; stʌd/ *n* **1** (**a**) small two-headed button-like device put through buttonholes to fasten a collar, shirt-front, etc (两端突起的)领扣, 饰钮(衬衫前面用的). (**b**) piece of jewellery (esp an ear-ring) consisting of a precious stone, etc attached to a small bar (镶有宝石等并有一条小棍连着的)首饰; (尤指)耳环: *diamond studs in her ears* 她耳朵上戴的钻石耳环. **2** (**a**) large-headed nail or knob (usu one of many) on the surface of sth (eg a gate or a shield) as an ornament 饰钉, 大头钉(如钉在门、盾等上的). (**b**) small round knob on the sole of a shoe or boot, to allow it to grip better 鞋钉(鞋靴底部的, 用以增加附着力): *the studs on a football boot* 足球靴的靴钉.

▷ **stud** *v* (**-dd-**) [Tn, Tn·pr usu passive 通常用于被动语态] **~ sth (with sth)** decorate (a surface) with many studs, precious stones, etc 用许多饰钮、饰钉、宝石等装饰(某物表面): *millions of stars studding the night sky* 布满夜空的繁星 ○ *a crown studded with jewels* 镶满宝石的皇冠 ○ *a sea studded with small islands* 有许多小岛的大海.

stud[2] /stʌd; stʌd/ *n* **1** (**a**) number of horses kept esp for breeding 一群马(尤指种马): [attrib 作定语] *a stud mare* 雌性种马. (**b**) (also ˈ**stud-farm**) place where such horses are kept 种马场. **2** (⚠ *infml* 讳, 口) young man, esp one who is thought to be very active sexually and is regarded as a good sexual partner 小伙子(尤指性欲旺盛堪为性伴侣的). **3** (idm 习语) **at ˈstud** (of a stallion) available for breeding on payment of a fee (指牡马)供配种以收取费用的. **put sth out to ˈstud** keep (a horse) for breeding 为配种而饲养(马).

□ ˈ**stud-book** *n* book containing the pedigrees of (esp) racehorses 马种系谱; (尤指)赛马血统登记簿.

stu·dent /ˈstjuːdnt; *US* ˈstuː-; ˋstudn̩t/ *n* **1** (**a**) person who is studying for a degree, diploma, etc at a university or some other place of higher education or technical training 大学生; 专科学校学生: *a BA student* 修读文学士学位的大学生 ○ *a medical student* 医科学生 ○ [attrib 作定语] *a student nurse, teacher, etc* 实习的护士、教师等 ○ *student politics* 大学生的政治活动. (**b**) (*esp US*) boy or girl at school 中学生; 小学生. **2 ~ of sth** (*fml* 文) person who is studying or has a particular interest in sth 研究者; 学者: *a student of politics, human nature, theology* 研究政治学、人性、神学的学者.

studied /ˈstʌdɪd; ˋstʌdɪd/ *adj* carefully considered; intentional; deliberate 审慎考虑的; 有意的; 蓄意的: *reply with studied indifference* 故作冷漠的回答 ○ *the studied slowness of his movements* 他那故意做出的慢吞吞的动作.

stu·dio /ˈstjuːdɪəʊ; *US* ˈstuː-; ˋstudɪˌo/ *n* (*pl* **~s**) **1** work-room of a painter, sculptor, photographer, etc (画家、雕塑家、摄影师等的)工作室, 画室, 雕塑室, 摄影室, 照相馆. **2** room from which radio or television programmes are regularly broadcast or in which recordings are made (电台或电视的)播音室, 演播室, 录制室: [attrib 作定语] *a studio audience*, ie an audience in a studio, to provide applause, laughter, etc 录制现场的观众(提供掌声、笑声等效果的). **3** (**a**) place where cinema films are acted and photographed (电影)摄影棚. (**b**) (usu *pl* 通常作复数) cinema company, including all its buildings, offices, etc 电影公司; 电影制片厂: [attrib 作定语] *a studio executive* 电影公司经理.

□ **studio ˈcouch** couch that can be converted into a bed (坐卧两用的)长沙发, 沙发床.

ˈ**studio flat** (*Brit*) (also *esp US* **studio aˈpartment**) small flat, usu having a main room for living and sleeping in, with a small kitchen and a bathroom 单间公寓(通常有一主要房间兼作起居室和卧室, 另加小厨房和浴室); 独单元住宅.

stu·di·ous /ˈstjuːdɪəs; *US* ˈstuː-; ˋstudɪəs/ *adj* **1** spending a lot of time studying 勤于学习的; 好学的; 用功的: *a studious pupil* 用功的学生. **2** [esp attrib 尤作定语] (*fml* 文) showing great carefulness; deliberate 仔细的; 用心的; 故意的: *the studious checking of details* 仔细查对细节 ○ *with studious politeness* 故作有礼. ▷ **stu·di·ously** *adv*. **stu·di·ous·ness** *n* [U].

study[1] /ˈstʌdɪ; ˋstʌdɪ/ *n* **1** [U] (also **studies** [pl]) process of gaining knowledge of a subject, esp from books 学习; (尤指)读书; 研究: *fond of study* 好学 ○ *give all one's spare time to study* 把业余时间全用于学习 ○ *My studies show that*... 我经研究得出结论... ○ [attrib 作定语] *study time* 学习时间. **2** [C] (**a**) (book, etc that is the result of an) investigation of a subject 研究; 研究成果; 作为研究成果的著作等: *make a study of the country's export trade* 研究该国的出口贸易 ○ *publish a study of Locke's philosophy* 发表研究洛克哲学思想的论述. (**b**) (usu *pl* 通常作复数) subject that is (to be) investigated 研究科目; 学科; 课题: *scientific, legal studies* 科学方面的、法律方面的研究课题. **3** [C] room, esp in sb's home, used for reading and writing 书房(尤指家中的). **4** [C] (**a**) drawing, etc done for practice, esp before doing a larger picture (绘画等)习作; (尤指绘制大幅图画之前的)试画. (**b**) (*music* 音) composition designed to give a player exercise in technical skills 练习曲. **5 a study** [sing] thing worth observing; unusual sight 值得注意的事物; 不寻常的景象: *His face was a study as he listened to their amazing news.* 他听到他们那令人吃惊的消息时, 脸上呈现异样的表情. **6** (idm 习语) **in a brown study** ⇨ BROWN.

study[2] /ˈstʌdɪ; ˋstʌdɪ/ *v* (*pt, pp* **studied**) **1** [I, Ipr, It, Tn, Tw] give one's time and attention to learning about (sth), esp by reading, attending a university, etc 学习(某事物)(尤指阅读、上大学等); 研读; 攻读; 研究: *studying (for a degree in) medicine* 攻读医科(的学位) ○ *studying to be a doctor* 读医科 ○ *It's hard finding time to study (the subject).* 很难找出时间来学习(这门学问). ○ *I'm studying how children learn to speak.* 我正在研究儿童是如何学说话的. **2** [Tn, Tn·pr] examine (sth) very carefully 仔细察看(某事物): *study the map, menu, programme* 细阅地图、菜单、节目单 ○ *Scientists are studying the photographs of Mars for signs of life.* 科学家在仔细察看火星照片, 看有没有生命的迹象.

stuff[1] /stʌf; stʌf/ *n* **1** [U] material of which sth is made 原料; 材料: *What stuff is this jacket made of?* 这件夹克是用什么料子做的? ○ *A kind of plastic stuff is used to make the plates.* 这些盘子是用一种塑料制造的. ○ (*fig* 比喻) *Real life is the stuff* (ie subject-matter) *of all good novels.* 现实生活是所有优秀小说的题材. ○ (*fig* 比喻)

We must find out what stuff he is made of, ie what sort of man he is, what his character is. 我们得弄清楚他为人怎样. **2** [U] (*sl* 俚) unnamed things, belongings, activities, subject-matter, etc 东西、财物、活动、题材等: *Leave your stuff in the hall.* 把你的东西放在门厅里. ○ *This book is really boring stuff.* 这本书真是枯燥无味. ○ *Do you call this stuff beer?* 你把这东西叫做啤酒吗? ○ *There has been some really good stuff on TV lately.* 近来电视上有些节目确实不错. **3** (idm 习语) **a bit of stuff** ⇨ BIT[1]. **do one's 'stuff** (*infml* 口) show what one can do, etc 显身手: *It's your turn to sing now, so do your stuff.* 现在轮到你唱了, 露一手吧. **hot stuff** ⇨ HOT. **know one's onions/stuff** ⇨ KNOW. **ˌstuff and 'nonsense** *interj* (*dated infml* 旧, 口) (used to dismiss sth that has been said 用以驳斥说过的话): *Stuff and nonsense! You don't know what you're talking about.* 胡说八道! 你说得太不像话了. **ˌthat's the 'stuff!** (*infml* 口) that is good or what is needed 这就对啦; 这才是需要的.

stuff[2] /stʌf; stʌf/ *v* **1** (**a**) [Tn, Tn·pr, Tn·p] **~ sth (up) (with sth)** fill sth tightly (with sth); cram sth (with sth) (用某物)塞满某物: *stuff a pillow (with feathers)* (用羽毛)填充枕头 ○ *stuff up a hole (with newspapers)* (用报纸)堵住洞 ○ *My nose is stuffed up*, ie full of mucus. 我的鼻子堵了(鼻涕多). ○ (*fig* 比喻) *Don't stuff him with silly ideas.* 别教他馊主意. (**b**) [Tn·pr, Tn·p] **~ sth into sth/in** cram sth tightly into sth 把某物塞入某物中: *stuff feathers into a pillow* 把羽毛填入枕头 ○ *She stuffed her clothes in and then tried to close the lid.* 她把衣服塞进去, 想盖上盖儿. **2** [Tn·pr, Tn·p] push (sth) quickly and carelessly (in the specified place or direction) 匆忙而胡乱地推或塞(某物): *She stuffed the coins into her pocket.* 她把硬币塞进口袋里. ○ *He stuffed the letter through (the door) and hurried away.* 他把信塞进门里就匆匆离开了. **3** [I, Tn, Tn·pr] **~ (sb/oneself) (with sth)** fill (sb/oneself) with food; eat greedily 让(某人[自己])吃饱; 狼吞虎咽地吃: *I'm stuffed* (ie full of food)! 我吃饱了! ○ *She sat stuffing herself with biscuits.* 她坐在那里吃饼干. **4** [Tn, Tn·pr] **~ sth (with sth)** put chopped and flavoured food into (a bird, etc) before cooking it 用剁碎的调味食品填入(禽等)(以备烹调): *stuffed veal* 加填料的牛犊肉 ○ *a turkey stuffed with parsley, thyme, chestnuts, etc* 加有欧芹、百里香、栗子等填料的火鸡. **5** [Tn esp passive 尤用于被动语态] fill the empty carcass of (a bird, an animal, etc) with enough material to restore it to its original shape, eg for exhibition in a museum 填充(鸟兽等)的掏空的躯体以保存(如陈列于博物馆中): *a stuffed tiger, owl, etc* 制成标本的老虎、猫头鹰等. **6** [Tn] (*sl* 俚) (used to express rejection of sth 用以表示摈弃某事物) dispose of (sth) as unwanted; do as one likes with (sth) 将不要的(某物)处理掉; 随意处理(某事物): *You can stuff the job, I don't want it.* 这工作你随意处理, 我不要. **7** [Tn] (⚠ *dated sl* 讳, 旧, 俚) have sexual intercourse with (a woman) 与(女子)性交. **8** (idm 习语) **get 'stuffed** (*Brit sl* 俚) (used to express contempt, rejection, etc 用以表示鄙夷、摈弃等): *He wanted to borrow some money from me but I told him to get stuffed.* 他想找我借点钱, 但我叫他滚开. **a stuffed 'shirt** (*infml* 口) pompous or pretentious person 妄自尊大的人; 自命不凡的人.

▷ **stuff·ing** *n* [U] **1** (*US* **dressing**) chopped and flavoured food used for stuffing (STUFF[2] 4) a bird, etc before it is cooked (禽等的)填料(烹制前填入内膛的经剁碎的调味食品). **2** padding used to stuff cushions, etc (垫子等的)填料. **3** (idm 习语) **knock the stuffing out of sb** ⇨ KNOCK[2].

stuffy /'stʌfɪ; 'stʌfɪ/ *adj* (**-ier, -iest**) **1** (of a room, etc) not having much fresh air (指房间等)通风不良的, 闷人的: *a smoky, stuffy pub* 烟雾弥漫、空气污浊的酒馆. **2** (*infml* 口) (of a person or thing) formal and dull; prim; staid (指人或事物)一本正经的, 古板的, 拘谨的: *a stuffy newspaper, club, legal practice* 沉闷乏味的报纸、俱乐部、司法工作 ○ *Only the stuffier members were shocked by her jokes.* 只有那些脑筋旧的人才认为她说的笑话令人吃惊. **3** (*infml* 口) (of the nose) blocked so that breathing is difficult; stuffed up (指鼻子)不通的, 堵塞的. ▷ **stuf·fily** /-ɪlɪ; -əlɪ/ *adv.* **stuf·fi·ness** *n* [U].

stul·tify /'stʌltɪfaɪ; 'stʌltəˌfaɪ/ *v* (*pt, pp* **-fied**) [Tn] (*fml* 文) **1** cause (sth) to be ineffective or seem absurd; negate 使(某事物)不起作用或显得荒谬; 使无效: *Their unhelpfulness has stultified our efforts to improve things.* 他们不管事, 我们为改进工作的用心也就白费了. **2** cause (sb) to feel dull, bored, etc 使(某人)感觉迟钝、厌烦等: *the stultifying effect of work that never varies* 毫无变化的工作使人产生的厌倦感. ▷ **stul·ti·fica·tion** /ˌstʌltɪfɪ'keɪʃn; ˌstʌltəfə'keʃən/ *n* [U].

stumble /'stʌmbl; 'stʌmbl/ *v* [I, Ipr] **1 ~ (over sth)** strike one's foot against sth and almost fall 绊脚: *stumble and fall* 绊倒 ○ *I stumbled over a tree root.* 树根绊了我的脚. **2 ~ (over sth); ~ through sth** make a mistake or mistakes as one speaks, plays music, etc (说话、演奏等)出错: *She stumbled briefly (over the unfamiliar word) but then continued.* 她(碰到不认识的字)愣了一下, 接着又往下念. ○ *The child stumbled through a piece by Chopin.* 那孩子演奏萧邦的曲子很不流畅. **3** (phr v) **stumble about, along, around, etc** move or walk unsteadily (in the specified direction) (朝某方向)摇摇晃晃地移动或步履蹒跚: *A drunk stumbled past us.* 有个喝醉的人跌跌撞撞地从我们身边走过. ○ *stumbling around in the dark* 在黑暗中瞎闯. ⇨Usage at SHUFFLE 用法见SHUFFLE. **stumble across/on sb/sth** find sb/sth unexpectedly or by chance 意外地或偶然地发现某人[某事物]: *Police investigating tax fraud stumbled across a drugs ring.* 警方在调查瞒税案件时意外地发现了一个贩毒集团.

▷ **stumble** *n* act of stumbling 绊脚; 出错.

□ **'stumbling-block** *n* thing that causes difficulty or hesitation; obstacle 造成困难或引起疑虑的事物; 障碍物; 绊脚石: *The failure to agree on manning levels is a major stumbling-block to progress in the talks.* 人员配备情况未能达成协议是会谈进行中的主要障碍.

stump /stʌmp; stʌmp/ *n* **1** part of a tree left in the ground after the rest has fallen or been cut down 树桩; 树墩. **2** (**a**) anything similar that remains after the main part has been cut or broken off, or worn down 残余部分; 残段; 残根: *the stump of a pencil, cigar, tooth* 铅笔头、雪茄烟蒂、牙的残根. (**b**) remaining part of an amputated limb 残肢. **3** (in cricket) any of the three short upright poles at which the ball is bowled (板球)三柱门的一柱: *the leg/middle/off stump* 三柱门的尾[中/头]柱. ⇨illus at CRICKET 见CRICKET插图. **4** (idm 习语) **draw stumps** ⇨ DRAW[2]. **stir one's stumps** ⇨ STIR[1].

▷ **stump** *v* **1** [Ipr, Ip] walk stiffly or noisily 僵直地行走; 跺步而行: *They stumped up the hill.* 他们举步困难地登上这座山. ○ *He stumped out in fury.* 他怒气冲冲地跺脚往外走. ⇨Usage 见所附用法. **2** [Tn esp passive 尤用于被动语态] (*infml* 口) be too difficult for (sb); puzzle 把(某人)难住; 使为难: *I'm stumped: I just don't know what to do.* 我很为难, 简直不知如何是好. ○ *Everybody was stumped by the problem.* 大家都被这个问题难住了. **3** [Tn] (*esp US*) go around (a region) making political speeches, eg before an election 在(某地区)作政治性巡回演说(如在选举前). **4** [Tn] (of a wicket-keeper in cricket) end the innings of (a batsman) by touching the stumps with the ball while he is out of his crease(3) (指板球赛的守门员)以球触三柱门的柱使(击球员)出局. **5** (phr v) **stump up (sth) (for sth)** (*infml* 口) pay (a sum of money) 付出(一笔钱): *I'm always being asked to stump up (extra cash) for school outings.* 总是要求我为学校郊游付(额外的)钱.

NOTE ON USAGE 用法: **Stump, stomp, plod, trudge** and **tramp** all indicate styles of walking with heavy steps. ☆ **stump**、**stomp**、**plod**、**trudge**、**tramp** 均指落脚很重的步行方式. **Stump** and **stomp** can both suggest making a noise while walking in order to show anger ☆ **stump**和**stomp**二者均可含有跺脚行走之意, 表示气愤: *He slammed the door and stumped/stomped upstairs.* 他砰的一声把门关上, 噔噔地上楼去了. Additionally, **stump** can indicate walking with stiff legs 此外, **stump**还可指两腿发僵地行走: *stumping up the garden path* 两腿发僵在花园小道上走着. **Stomp** can suggest clumsy and noisy walking or dancing ☆ **stomp**可指行走或跳舞时笨拙或发出响声: *He looked funny stomping round the dance floor.* 他在舞池里跺着舞步, 样子很可笑. **Plod** and **trudge** indicate a slow, weary walk towards a particular destination. ☆ **plod**和

trudge 指以缓慢、疲倦的步子向目的地走去. **Plod** suggests a steady pace and **trudge** suggests greater effort ☆ **plod** 有稳步行进之意, **trudge** 指举步更为艰难: *They had to plod wearily on up the hill.* 他们不得不迈着疲倦的步子登上山. ○ *We trudged home through deep snow.* 我们踏着很深的积雪, 吃力地走回家. **Tramp** indicates walking over long distances, possibly with no specified destination ☆ **tramp** 指走长路, 可能并无确定目的地: *They tramped the streets, looking for somewhere to stay the night.* 他们在街上不停地走着, 想找个过夜的地方.

stumpy /ˈstʌmpɪ; ˋstʌmpɪ/ *adj* (**-ier, -iest**) short and thick 短而粗的: *a stumpy little man* 敦实的男子 ○ *stumpy legs* 短而粗的腿. ▷ **stumpi·ness** *n* [U].

stun /stʌn; stʌn/ *v* **1** [Tn] (**-nn-**) make (a person or an animal) unconscious by a blow, esp to the head 将(人或动物)打昏(尤指打击头部): *The punch stunned me for a moment.* 那一拳把我打得昏了一阵. ○ *She sat stunned for a while, until she recovered.* 她一时昏迷, 坐下呆了一会才醒过来. **2** (*fig* 比喻) (**a**) [Tn] daze or shock (sb), eg with sth unexpected 使(某人)目瞪口呆或感到震惊: *I was stunned by the news of his death.* 我得知他的死讯十分震惊. (**b**) [Tn esp passive 尤用于被动语态] impress (sb) greatly 给(某人)以深刻的印象: *stunned by her beauty, cleverness, etc* 赞叹她美丽、聪明等.

▷ **stun·ner** *n* (*infml* 口) person, esp a woman, who is very attractive 极有魅力的人(尤指女子).

stun·ning *adj* (*infml* 口) (**a**) impressive; splendid 了不起的; 出色的: *You look stunning in your new suit.* 你穿着这套新衣服真漂亮. ○ *What a stunning idea!* 多好的主意呀! (**b**) surprising or shocking 令人惊奇的; 令人震惊的: *a stunning revelation* 惊人的新发现. **stun·ningly** *adv*.

S **stung** *pt, pp* of STING[2].

stunk *pp* of STINK[1].

stunt[1] /stʌnt; stʌnt/ *n* (*infml* 口) (**a**) thing done to attract attention 引人注意的举动: *a publicity stunt* 宣传噱头 ○ *pull* (ie perform) *a stunt* 做惊人之举. (**b**) dangerous or difficult thing done as entertainment 特技表演: *Her latest stunt is riding a motor cycle through a ring of flames.* 她的最新特技表演是骑摩托车钻火圈. ○ [attrib 作定语] *stunt flying*, ie aerobatics 特技飞行.

□ ˈ**stunt man** (*fem* 阴性作 ˈ**stunt woman**) person who does dangerous stunts in place of an actor in a film, etc (电影等中代替演员做危险动作的)替身演员.

stunt[2] /stʌnt; stʌnt/ *v* [Tn esp passive 尤用于被动语态] prevent (sth/sb) from growing or developing properly 阻碍(某事物[某人])的正常生长或发展: *stunted trees* 生长受到阻碍的矮小树木 ○ *Inadequate food can stunt a child's development.* 食物不足能影响儿童的发育.

stu·pefy /ˈstju:pɪfaɪ; *US* ˈstu:-; ˋstupəˏfaɪ/ *v* (*pt, pp* **-fied**) [esp passive 尤用于被动语态: Tn, Tn·pr] **~ sb (with sth)** **1** dull the mind or senses of (sb) 使(某人)神志不清或失去知觉: *stupefied with drink* 醉得迷迷糊糊 ○ (*fig* 比喻) *the stupefying boredom of this repetitive work* 这种重复性工作造成的昏沉乏味之感. **2** overcome (sb) with astonishment; amaze 使(某人)大为惊奇; 使目瞪口呆: *I was stupefied by what I read.* 我读到的内容把我惊呆了.

▷ **stu·pefac·tion** /ˌstju:pɪˈfækʃn; *US* ˌstu:-; ˏstupəˋfækʃən/ *n* [U] (*fml* 文) state of being stupefied 神志不清; 失去知觉; 大为惊奇; 目瞪口呆.

stu·pen·dous /stju:ˈpendəs; *US* stu:-; stuˋpɛndəs/ *adj* amazingly large, impressive, good, etc 极大的; 极感人的; 极好的: *a stupendous mistake, achievement* 极大的错误、成就 ○ *The opera was quite stupendous!* 这部歌剧很精彩! ▷ **stu·pen·dously** *adv*.

stu·pid /ˈstju:pɪd; *US* ˈstu:; ˋstupɪd/ *adj* (**-er, -est**) **1** (**a**) slow to learn or understand things; not intelligent or clever 笨的; 头脑迟钝的: *a stupid person, dog* 笨人、笨狗. (**b**) showing lack of good judgement; foolish 愚蠢的; 傻的: *a stupid plan, idea, remark* 愚蠢的计划、想法、言语 ○ *What a stupid thing to do!* 这事做得多蠢! (**c**) [attrib 作定语] (*infml* 口) (used dismissively or to show irritation 用以表示轻蔑或气恼): *I don't want to hear your stupid secret anyway!* 我根本不想听你那无聊的秘密. ○ *This stupid car won't start.* 这辆破汽车就是发动不起来. **2** [usu pred 通常作表语] **~ (with sth)** (*fml* 文) in a stupor 昏迷; 不省人事: *stupid with sleep* 睡得头昏脑胀.

▷ **stu·pid·ity** /stju:ˈpɪdətɪ; *US* stu:-; stuˋpɪdətɪ/ *n* **1** [U] state of being stupid 笨; 愚蠢. **2** [C usu *pl* 通常作复数] stupid act, remark, etc 愚蠢的行为、言语等: *the stupidities of schoolboy humour* 男学童调皮的愚蠢言行.

stu·pidly *adv*.

stu·por /ˈstju:pə(r); *US* ˈstu:-; ˋstupɚ/ *n* [U, C usu *sing* 作不可数名词或可数名词, 后者通常作单数] condition of being dazed or nearly unconscious caused by shock, drugs, alcohol, etc (震惊、药物、酒精等造成的)昏迷, 不省人事, 神志不清: *in a drunken stupor* 醉得昏迷不醒.

sturdy /ˈstɜ:dɪ; ˋstɝdɪ/ *adj* (**-ier, -iest**) **1** (**a**) strong and solid 强壮的; 结实的: *a sturdy chair, structure, car* 结实的椅子、结构、汽车. (**b**) fit and healthy 强健的; 健壮的: *a sturdy child, constitution* 健康的孩子、体格. **2** determined; firm; sound 坚决的; 坚强的; 坚定的; 健全的: *sturdy resistance to the plan* 对该计划的坚决抵制 ○ *sturdy common sense* 扎实的常识. ▷ **stur·dily** /-ɪlɪ; -ɪlɪ/ *adv*: *a sturdily built bicycle, man* 结构结实的自行车、体格强健的人. **stur·di·ness** *n* [U].

stur·geon /ˈstɜ:dʒən; ˋstɝdʒən/ *n* any of various types of large fish eaten as food, and from which caviare is obtained 鲟(体大, 可食用, 卵可制鱼子酱).

stut·ter /ˈstʌtə(r); ˋstʌtɚ/ *v* [I, Tn, Tn·p] = STAMMER.

▷ **stut·terer** /ˈstʌtərə(r); ˋstʌtərɚ/ *n* person who stutters 口吃的人; 说话结巴的人.

stut·ter·ingly /ˈstʌtərɪŋlɪ; ˋstʌtərɪŋlɪ/ *adv*.

sty[1] /staɪ; staɪ/ *n* = PIGSTY (PIG).

sty[2] (also **stye**) /staɪ; staɪ/ *n* (*pl* **sties** or **styes**) inflamed swelling on the edge of the eyelid 睑腺炎; 麦粒肿.

Stygian /ˈstɪdʒɪən; ˋstɪdʒɪən/ *adj* [usu attrib 通常作定语] (*fml* 文) very dark; gloomy 黑魆魆的; 阴森的: *the Stygian blackness of the night* 漆黑的夜晚.

style /staɪl; staɪl/ *n* **1** [C, U] (**a**) manner of writing or speaking, esp contrasted with what is actually written or said (语言或文字的)风格, 文风, 文体: *She's a very popular writer but I just don't like her style.* 她是很受欢迎的作家, 但我就是不喜欢她的文风. ○ *write in house style*, ie following the manner of spelling and punctuation, etc used by a particular publishing company 按出版社要求的格式写作(符合某出版社在拼写法及标点符号等方面的要求) ○ *a style of speech-making that is easy to listen to* 通俗易懂的演讲方式. (**b**) manner that is typical of a particular writer, artist, etc or of a particular literary, artistic, etc period (某作家、艺术家或某文艺时期的)独特风格: *a poem in classical style* 古典风格的诗歌 ○ *a building in Gothic, Romanesque, Tudor, etc style* 歌特、罗马、都铎...式建筑物 ○ *the architectural styles of ancient Greece* 古希腊的建筑风格. **2** [C, U] manner of doing anything 行为方式; 作风: *a typically British style of living* 典型的英国生活方式 ○ *a very unusual style of swimming* 非常独特的游泳姿式 ○ *American-style hamburgers* 美式汉堡包 ○ *I like your style*, ie the way you do things. 我喜欢你做事的方法. **3** [U] superior or fashionable quality of sb or sth; distinctiveness 风度; 格调; 气派: *She performs the songs with style and flair.* 她演唱歌曲既有风度又有才华. ○ *The piano gives the room a touch of style.* 这架钢琴把房间衬托得很有气派. **4** (**a**) [C, U] fashion in dress, etc (服装等的)款式, 流行式样: *the latest styles in trousers, hats, shoes, etc* 裤子、帽子、鞋等的最新式样 ○ *have a good sense of style* 很有格调. (**b**) [C] way in which sth is made, shaped, etc; design; type 样式; 花样; 型式: *a very short hair-style* 很短的发型 ○ *We have vases in various styles.* 我们有各种各样的花瓶. **5** [C] (*fml* 文) correct title for use when addressing sb 称谓; 称号: *Has he any right to use the style of Colonel?* 他有资格使用上校头衔吗? **6** [C] (*botany* 植) narrow extension of the seed-bearing part of a plant (植物的)花柱. **7** (idm 习语) **cramp sb's style** ⇨ CRAMP[2]. **in (great, grand, etc) style** in a grand or elegant way 有气派(的); 有风度(的): *dine in style* 很高雅地进餐 ○ *We arrived in fine style in a hired limousine.* 我们很气派地乘坐出租的豪华汽车到达那里. **(not/more) sb's style** what sb likes (非[较合乎])某人之所好: *Big cars are not my style.* 我不喜欢大的汽车. ○ *I don't like opera; chamber music is more my style.* 我不爱看歌剧, 喜欢听室内乐.

▷ **style** *v* **1** [Tn, Cn·a] design, shape or make (sth) in a particular (esp fashionable) style 将(某物)设计、塑

造或制作成某种(尤指时新的)式样: *style sb's hair (shorter)* 给某人设计(短)发型. **2** [Tn, Cn·n] (*fml* 文) give a style(5) to (sb/oneself) 以某称号称呼(某人[自己]): *How should we style her?* 我们应该怎样称呼她呢? ○ *Should he be styled 'Mr' or 'Reverend'?* 应该称呼他'先生'还是'牧师'?

styl·ing *n* [U] way in which sth is styled 款式; 式样: *the car's brand-new styling* 汽车的全新款式.

styl·ish *adj* having style(3); fashionable 有风度的; 有气派的; 有格调的: *stylish clothes, furniture* 时髦的服装、家具 ○ *a stylish skier, dancer, etc* 风度翩翩的滑雪的人、跳舞的人等. **styl·ishly** *adv*: *stylishly dressed* 穿着入时的. **styl·ish·ness** *n* [U].

styl·ist /ˈstaɪlɪst; ˋstaɪlɪst/ *n* **1** person, esp a writer, who has or tries to have a good or distinctive style 具有或追求优美或独特风格的人(尤指作家). **2** person who styles (STYLE *v* 1) things, eg clothes, hair 设计或制作时新款式或花样的人(如服装设计师、发型师): *a hair-stylist* 发型师.

▷ **styl·istic** /staɪˈlɪstɪk; staɪˋlɪstɪk/ *adj* [usu attrib 通常作定语] of or concerning literary or artistic style (文学或艺术)风格上的, 与风格有关的: *make a stylistic comparison of the two paintings* 对两幅画的风格进行比较. **styl·ist·ic·ally** /-klɪ; -klɪ/ *adv*. **styl·ist·ics** *n* [sing *v*] study of the style of spoken or written language and how it is used to create certain effects 风格学(对口语或书面语的风格及其运用技巧的研究).

styl·ize, -ise /ˈstaɪlaɪz; ˋstaɪlaɪz/ *v* [Tn esp passive 尤用于被动语态] treat (sth) in a fixed conventional style 按固定的传统风格处理(某事物).

▷ **styl·iza·tion, -isation** /ˌstaɪlaɪˈzeɪʃn; *US* -lɪˈz-; ˌstaɪlə-ˋzeʃən/ *n* [U].

styl·ized, -ised *adj* treated in a fixed conventional style 按固定的传统风格处理的: *the highly stylized form of acting in Japanese theatre* 日本戏剧中高度程式化的表演.

sty·lus /ˈstaɪləs; ˋstaɪləs/ *n* **1** sharp needle tipped with diamond or sapphire, used to reproduce sound by resting in the groove of a record as it turns on a record-player (唱机的)宝石唱针. **2** (esp in ancient times) pointed tool for drawing or writing (尤指古代的)尖笔.

sty·mie /ˈstaɪmɪ; ˋstaɪmɪ/ *n* **1** (in golf) situation on the green in which an opponent's ball is between one's own ball and the hole (高尔夫球)妨碍球, 阻碍球(自己的球与球穴之间有对方的球). **2** (*fig infml* 比喻, 口) awkward or difficult situation 尴尬或困难的处境.

▷ **sty·mie** *v* (*pt, pp* **stymied**, *pres p* **stymieing**) **1** [Tn] (in golf) put (sb, sb's ball or oneself) in a stymie (高尔夫球)使(某人、某人的球或自己)受对方球之阻碍. **2** [Tn esp passive 尤用于被动语态] (*fig infml* 比喻, 口) prevent (sb) from doing sth; obstruct 妨碍(某人)做某事; 阻碍: *I was completely stymied by her refusal to help.* 由于她拒不相助, 我完全陷入了困境.

styp·tic /ˈstɪptɪk; ˋstɪptɪk/ *n, adj* [usu attrib 通常作定语] (substance) checking the flow of blood 止血的; 止血剂: *a styptic pencil*, ie a stick of this, used eg on a cut made while shaving 止血笔(用止血剂制成的药棒, 如用于刮脸时划破之处).

suave /swɑːv; swɑv/ *adj* (*sometimes derog* 有时作贬义) (usu of a man) having self-confidence and smooth sophisticated manners (通常指男子)自信而老于世故的. ▷ **suavely** *adv*. **suave·ness**, **suav·ity** /-ətɪ; -ətɪ/ *ns* [U].

sub¹ /sʌb; sʌb/ *n* (*infml* 口) **1** submarine 潜水艇. **2** substitute, esp in football or cricket 代用品; 代替者; (尤指)(足球或板球)替补队员. **3** (usu *pl* 通常作复数) subscription to a club, etc (向俱乐部等交纳的)会员费. **4** sub-editor 审校员; 助理编辑.

sub² /sʌb; sʌb/ *v* (**-bb-**) (*infml* 口) **1** [I, Ipr] **~ (for sb)** act as a substitute 代替; 作替身; 作替补队员: *I had to sub for the referee, who was sick.* 裁判病了, 我得代为裁判. **2** [I, Tn] sub-edit (sth) 审校(文稿); 以助理编辑的身分编辑(稿件): *subbing on a local newspaper* 审校某份地方报纸.

sub- *pref* 前缀 **1** (with *ns* and *adjs* 与名词和形容词结合) under; below 在...之下; 低于...: *subway* ○ *subsoil* ○ *submarine*. **2** (with *ns* 与名词结合) lower in rank; inferior 级别较低的; 次于...的: *sub-lieutenant* ○ *subspecies*. **3** (with *adjs* 与形容词结合) not quite; almost 不完全的; 近似的: *subnormal* ○ *subtropical* ○ *substandard*. **4** (with *vs* and *ns* 与动词和名词结合) (form a) smaller or less important part of (形成)...之较小的或次要的部分: *subdivide* ○ *subcommittee* ○ *subset*. Cf 参看 UNDER-.

sub·al·tern /ˈsʌbltən; *US* səˈbɔːltərn; səbˋɔltɚn/ *n* (*Brit*) any officer in the army below the rank of captain 陆军中低于上尉的军官; 陆军中尉或少尉.

sub·arc·tic /ˌsʌbˈɑːktɪk; ˌsʌbˋɑrktɪk/ *adj* [usu attrib 通常作定语] of regions near the Arctic Circle 亚北极区的: *ˌsubarctic conˈditions, ˈtemperatures* 亚北极的环境、温度. Cf 参看 SUBTROPICAL.

sub·atomic /ˌsʌbəˈtɒmɪk; ˌsʌbəˋtɑmɪk/ *adj* [usu attrib 通常作定语] of or concerning particles that are smaller than atoms or occur in atoms 亚原子的; 与亚原子有关的; 原子内的: *subatomic theory, research* 亚原子理论、研究.

sub·com·mit·tee /ˈsʌbkəmɪtɪ; ˋsʌbkəˌmɪtɪ/ *n* committee formed for a special purpose from members of a main committee (由大委员会的委员组成的)小组委员会.

sub·con·scious /ˌsʌbˈkɒnʃəs; sʌbˋkɑnʃəs/ *adj* of or concerning the thoughts, instincts, fears, etc in the mind, of which one is not fully aware but which influence one's actions 下意识的; 潜意识的: *the subconscious self* 潜意识的自我 ○ *subconscious urges* 下意识的冲动. Cf 参看 UNCONSCIOUS.

▷ **the/one's sub·con·scious** *n* [sing] these thoughts, instincts, fears, etc 下意识; 潜意识.

sub·con·sciously *adv*: *I suppose that, subconsciously, I was reacting against my unhappy childhood.* 我认为我那是下意识地对我童年不幸的反动.

sub·con·tin·ent /ˌsʌbˈkɒntɪnənt; sʌbˋkɑntənənt/ *n* large land mass that forms part of a continent 次大陆: *the Indian subcontinent* 印度次大陆.

sub·con·tract /ˈsʌbkɒntrækt; sʌbˋkɑntrækt/ *n* contract to carry out a part or all of an existing contract 分包合同; 转包契约.

▷ **sub·con·tract** /ˌsʌbkənˈtrækt; *US* -ˈkɒntrækt; ˌsʌbˋkɑnˌtrækt/ *v* [Tn, Tn·pr] **~ sth (to sb)** give (a job of work) to sb as a subcontract 将(工作任务)分包或转包给某人: *subcontract the installation of the shower to a plumber* 把安装淋浴器的工作分包给水暖工. **sub·con·tractor** /ˌsʌbkənˈtræktə(r); *US* -ˈkɒntræk-; ˌsʌbˋkɑnˌtræktɚ/ *n* person, company, etc that accepts and carries out a subcontract 分包人; 分包公司.

sub·cul·ture /ˈsʌbkʌltʃə(r); ˋsʌbˌkʌltʃɚ/ *n* behaviour, practices, etc associated with a group within a society 亚文化(模式)(某社会内部一群体的行为、习俗等): *the teenage subculture* 青少年的亚文化模式.

sub·cu·ta·ne·ous /ˌsʌbkjuːˈteɪnɪəs; ˌsʌbkjuˋtenɪəs/ *adj* [usu attrib 通常作定语] under the skin 皮下的: *subcutaneous fat* 皮下脂肪 ○ *a subcutaneous injection* 皮下注射. ▷ **sub·cu·ta·ne·ously** *adv*.

sub·div·ide /ˌsʌbdɪˈvaɪd; ˌsʌbdəˋvaɪd/ *v* [I, Ipr, Tn, Tn·pr] **~ (sth) (into sth)** (cause sth to) be divided again into smaller divisions (将某物)进一步分成较小的部分: *Part of the building has been subdivided into offices.* 这座大楼的一部分隔开用作办公室了.

▷ **sub·di·vi·sion** /ˌsʌbdɪˈvɪʒn; ˌsʌbdəˋvɪʒən/ *n* **1** [U] action or process of subdividing 进一步细分. **2** [C] thing produced by subdividing 进一步分成的部分: *a subdivision of a postal area* 邮区属下的分区 ○ *This division of the chapter has several subdivisions.* 该章这一节里又分成几个小节.

sub·due /səbˈdjuː; *US* -ˈduː; səbˋdu/ *v* [Tn] **1** bring (sb/sth) under control by force; defeat 征服, 制伏(某人[某事物]); 击败: *subdue the rebels* 镇压反叛者. **2** calm (esp one's emotions) 克制(尤指情绪): *He managed to subdue his mounting anger.* 他极力克制郁积在心中的怒气.

▷ **sub·dued** /səbˈdjuːd; *US* -ˈduːd; səbˋdud/ *adj* **1** not very loud, intense, noticeable, etc 不太响亮、强烈、显著等的; 缓和的; 有节制的: *a subdued conversation* 细声的交谈 ○ *subdued lighting* 柔和的灯光 ○ *a note of subdued excitement in her voice* 她声音中流露出克制的兴奋之情. **2** not showing much excitement, interest, etc 不大兴奋、不甚感兴趣等的: *You're very subdued. What's wrong?* 你情绪很消沉. 怎么了?

sub-edit /sʌbˈedɪt; sʌbˋɛdɪt/ *v* [Tn] **1** check and correct (the text of a book, newspaper, etc) before it

S

is printed 审校(稿件等). **2** act as an assistant editor of (a newspaper, etc) 当(某报等)的助理编辑. ▷ **sub-editor** *n*.

sub·head·ing /ˈsʌbhedɪŋ; ˈsʌbˌhɛdɪŋ/ *n* heading over part of an article, etc, eg in a newspaper 副标题; 小标题.

sub·ject[1] /ˈsʌbdʒɪkt; ˈsʌbdʒɪkt/ *n* **1** (**a**) person or thing that is being discussed or described (in speech or writing), or represented, eg in a painting; topic; theme 主题; 对象: *an interesting subject of conversation* 有趣的话题 ○ *choose a subject for a poem, a picture, an essay, etc* 确定诗、画、文章等的主题 ○ (*fml* 文) *What did she say on the subject of* (ie about) *money?* 在钱的问题上她是怎么说的? (**b**) branch of knowledge studied in a school, etc 学科; 科目: *Physics and maths are my favourite subjects.* 物理和数学都是我喜欢的科目. **2** person or thing being treated in a certain way or being experimented on 以某种方式处理或实验的人或事物: *We need some male subjects for a psychology experiment.* 我们需要几个男子作心理学实验对象. **3** ~ **for sth** person or thing that causes a specified feeling or action 引起某种情感或行为的人或事物: *a subject for pity, ridicule, congratulation* 怜悯、取笑、祝贺的对象 ○ *His appearance was the subject for some critical comment.* 他的外表受到一些人的议论. **4** (*grammar*) (**a**) word(s) in a sentence naming who or what does or undergoes the action stated by the verb, eg *the book* in *The book fell off the table* 主语(动作的主体, 如在The book fell off the table一句中, the book是主语). Cf 参看 OBJECT[1] 5. (**b**) word(s) in a sentence about which sth is stated, eg *the house* in *The house is old* 主语(句子中陈述的对象, 如在The house is old一句中, the house 是主语). Cf 参看 PREDICATE[1]. **5** any member of a State apart from the supreme ruler 臣民; 国民: *I am French by birth and a British subject by marriage.* 我按出生是法国人, 因结婚而成为英国公民. ⇨Usage at CITIZEN 用法见CITIZEN. **6** (*music* 音) theme on which a piece of music is based 主题; 主旋律. **7** (idm 习语) **change the subject** ⇨ CHANGE[1].

□ ˈ**subject-matter** *n* [U] content of a book, speech, etc, esp as contrasted with the style (书、讲话等的)内容, 题材(尤与体裁相对): *Although the subject-matter (of her talk) was rather dull her witty delivery kept the audience interested.* 尽管(她讲的)内容有些枯燥, 但由于她善于表达, 大家仍听得津津有味.

sub·ject[2] /səbˈdʒekt; səbˈdʒɛkt/ *v* **1** [Tn, Tn·pr] ~ **sb/sth (to sth)** bring (a country, etc or a person) under one's control 使(国家等或人)臣服或顺从; 征服; 制伏: *Ancient Rome subjected most of Europe (to its rule).* 古罗马帝国征服了欧洲大部分. **2** [Tn·pr] ~ **sb/sth to sth** cause sb/sth to experience or undergo sth 使某人[某物]经历或遭受某事物: *subject sb to criticism, ridicule, abuse, etc* 使某人遭批评、取笑、辱骂等 ○ *She was repeatedly subjected to torture.* 她不断地受到折磨. ○ *As a test the metal was subjected to great heat.* 这种金属经过了高温试验.

▷ **sub·jec·tion** /səbˈdʒekʃn; səbˈdʒɛkʃən/ *n* [U] subjecting or being subjected 征服; 制伏; 臣服; 顺从: *the country's subjection of its neighbour* 该国对邻国的征服 ○ *The people were kept in subjection.* 这个民族已沦为附庸.

sub·ject[3] /ˈsʌbdʒɪkt; ˈsʌbdʒɪkt/ *adj* **1** [attrib 作定语] under the control of sb else; not politically independent 受人支配的; 政治上不独立的: *a subject province* 属地 ○ *subject peoples* 被统治的民族. **2** [pred 作表语] ~ **to sth/sb** obliged to obey sth/sb; under the authority of sth/sb 须服从某事物[某人]; 受某事物[某人]支配: *We are subject to the law of the land.* 我们须遵守当地的法律. ○ *Peasants used to be subject to the local landowner.* 农民过去受地主的压迫. **3** [pred 作表语] ~ **to sth** often having, suffering or undergoing sth; liable to sth 常有、常患或常遭某事物; 倾向某事物: *Are you subject to colds?* 你常患感冒吗? ○ *Trains are subject to delay(s) after the heavy snowfalls.* 一下大雪火车就往往误点. ○ *The timetable is subject to alteration.* 时刻表有可能更改. **4** [pred 作表语] ~ **to sth** depending on sth as a condition 以某事物为条件; 取决于某事物: *sold subject to contract*, ie provided that a contract is signed 依照合同出售 ○ *The plan is subject to the director's approval.* 该计划须经主管批准.

sub·ject·ive /səbˈdʒektɪv; səbˈdʒɛktɪv/ *adj* **1** (of ideas, feelings, etc) existing in the mind and not produced by things outside the mind (指思想、感情等)主观的(属于自我意识方面的): *a subjective impression, sensation, etc* 主观印象、感觉等 ○ *Our perception of things is often influenced by subjective factors, such as tiredness.* 我们对事物的感知能力常受到主观因素(如疲劳)的影响. **2** (*sometimes derog* 有时作贬义) based on personal taste, views, etc 主观的(以个人之好恶、观点等为依据的): *a very subjective judgement of the play* 对该剧极其主观的评判 ○ *A literary critic should not be too subjective in his approach.* 文学评论家的看法不应太主观. Cf 参看 OBJECTIVE.

▷ **sub·ject·ively** *adv* in a subjective way 主观地: *Don't judge her work too subjectively.* 评论她的作品不要过于主观.

sub·ject·iv·ity /ˌsʌbdʒekˈtɪvətɪ; ˌsʌbdʒɛkˈtɪvətɪ/ *n* [U].

sub·join /ˌsʌbˈdʒɔɪn; sʌbˈdʒɔɪn/ *v* [Tn, Tn·pr] ~ **sth (to sth)** (*fml* 文) add sth to the end of sth (在末尾)增补或添加某事物: *subjoin a postscript to a letter* 在信末加一附笔.

sub ju·dice /ˌsʌb ˈdʒu:dɪsɪ; sʌbˈdʒudɪsɪ/ (*Latin* 拉) (of a legal case) still being considered by a lawcourt (and therefore, in the UK, not to be commented on in a newspaper, etc) (指案件)正在审理(因此, 在英国, 不得在报刊等上发表评论).

sub·jug·ate /ˈsʌbdʒʊgeɪt; ˈsʌbdʒəˌget/ *v* [Tn] gain control of (a country, etc); subdue; conquer 征服(某国家等); 制伏; 降伏. ▷ **sub·juga·tion** /ˌsʌbdʒʊˈgeɪʃn; ˌsʌbdʒəˈgeʃən/ *n* [U].

sub·junct·ive /səbˈdʒʌŋktɪv; səbˈdʒʌŋktɪv/ *adj* (*grammar*) of the special form of a verb that expresses a wish, possibility, condition, etc (动词)虚拟式的, 虚拟语气的: *In the phrase 'if I were you', 'were' is subjunctive.* 在if I were you这一短语中, were是虚拟式的. Cf 参看 IMPERATIVE 3, INDICATIVE.

▷ **sub·junct·ive** *n* (*grammar*) **1 the subjunctive** [U] the whole group of subjunctive verb-forms; the subjunctive mood 虚拟式; 虚拟语气: *In 'I wish you were here', 'were' is in the subjunctive.* 在I wish you were here一句中, were表达的是虚拟语气. **2** [C] subjunctive verb 虚拟式动词.

sub·lease /ˌsʌbˈli:s; sʌbˈlis/ *v* [Tn, Tn·pr] ~ **sth (to sb)** lease (a house, land, etc leased to oneself) to another person; sublet sth 将(房屋、土地等)转租或分租给他人; 转租或分租某物: *The company subleases flats to students.* 公司把公寓分租给大学生.

▷ **sub·lease** *n* lease of this kind (房屋、土地等的)转租, 分租.

sub·let /ˌsʌbˈlet; sʌbˈlɛt/ *v* (**-tt-**; *pt, pp* **sublet**) [I, Tn, Tn·pr] ~ **sth (to sb)** rent (a house, flat, etc of which one is the tenant, or part of it) to sb else 将(房屋、其中部分等)转租或分租给他人: *sublet a room to a friend* 把一个房间转租给朋友.

sub-lieutenant /ˌsʌblefˈtenənt; *US* -lu:ˈt-; ˌsʌbluˈtɛnənt/ *n* naval officer next in rank below a lieutenant 海军中尉.

sub·lim·ate /ˈsʌblɪmeɪt; ˈsʌbləˌmet/ *v* [Tn] **1** (*psychology* 心) express (instinctual urges, esp sexual ones) in more socially acceptable ways 以较符合社会准则的方式表现(本能的冲动, 尤指性欲); 使升华: *sublimating one's sex drive by working hard* 把性的冲动转化成努力工作. **2** (*chemistry* 化) convert (a substance) from the solid state to vapour by heating it, then allowing it to cool and become solid again, in order to purify it 使(某物质)升华.

▷ **sub·lim·ate** *n* substance purified by sublimating (SUBLIMATE 2) 升华物.

sub·lima·tion /ˌsʌblɪˈmeɪʃn; ˌsʌbləˈmeʃən/ *n* [U].

sub·lime /səˈblaɪm; səˈblaɪm/ *adj* **1** of the greatest, most admirable kind; causing awe and reverence 伟大的; 崇高的; 令人赞叹的; 令人崇敬的: *sublime heroism, beauty, scenery* 令人叹为观止的英雄行为、美丽、景色 ○ *her sublime devotion to the cause* 她献身于事业的崇高精神 ○ (*infml* 口) *The food was absolutely sublime.* 这吃的东西棒极了. **2** [attrib 作定语] (*sometimes derog* 有时作贬义) extreme; suggesting a person who is not afraid of the consequences of his actions 极端的; 不顾后果的: *sublime conceit, indifference, impudence* 极其骄横、冷

淡、无耻 ○ *She approached the angry crowd with a sublime lack of concern for her own safety.* 她完全不顾自己的安全走近愤怒的人群. **3** (idm 习语) **from the sublime to the ridiculous** from sth great, admirable, etc to sth trivial, absurd, etc 由极好转到极无聊的事物上: *Interrupting an opera on television for a pet-food commercial is going from the sublime to the ridiculous.* 在电视播演歌剧时插播宠物食品广告真是煞风景. ▷ **sub·limely** *adv*: *play the piano sublimely* 钢琴弹得棒极了 ○ *She was sublimely unaware of how foolish she looked.* 她根本不知道她的样子多愚蠢. **sub·lim·ity** /sə'blɪmətɪ; sə'blɪmətɪ/ *n* [U].

sub·lim·inal /ˌsʌb'lɪmɪnl; sʌb'lɪmənl̩/ *adj* being perceived or affecting the mind without one being aware of it 下意识的; 潜意识的: *the subliminal message of the text*, ie one not explicitly stated 文中的言外之意 ○ *subliminal advertising*, eg by means of an image flashed onto a screen so briefly that it is noted only by the subconscious mind 潜意识广告(如影像在屏幕上一闪而过, 在观众潜意识中留下印象).

sub-machine-gun /sʌbmə'ʃi:ngʌn; ˌsʌbmə'ʃin,gʌn/ *n* lightweight machine-gun held in the hand for firing 冲锋枪; 手提轻机枪. ⇨ illus at GUN 见 GUN 插图.

sub·mar·ine /ˌsʌbmə'ri:n; *US* 'sʌbməri:n; 'sʌbmə,rin/ *n* **1** naval vessel that can operate underwater as well as on the surface 潜(水)艇: [attrib 作定语] *a submarine officer, crew* 潜艇军官、全体官兵. **2** (also ˌ**submarine 'sandwich**) (*esp US*) sandwich made from a long bread roll split lengthwise and filled with meat, cheese, salad, etc 潜艇三明治(长面包纵向切开, 夹肉、干酪、色拉等).

▷ **sub·mar·ine** *adj* [attrib 作定语] (existing or placed) under the surface of the sea (存在或置于)海面下的: *submarine plants* 海生植物 ○ *submarine exploration* 海中探测 ○ *a submarine cable* 海底电缆.

sub·mar·iner /sʌb'mærɪnə(r); *US* 'sʌbməri:nər; 'sʌbmə,rinɚ/ *n* member of a submarine's crew 潜艇人员.

sub·merge /səb'mɜ:dʒ; səb'mɝdʒ/ *v* **1** (**a**) [I] go under the surface of a liquid, the sea, etc 进入液面、海面等的下面: *The submarine submerged to avoid enemy ships.* 该潜艇潜入水下以躲避敌舰. (**b**) [Tn] cause (sth) to go under the surface of a liquid, the sea, etc; cover with a liquid 使(某物)进入液面、海面等之下; 淹没: *a wall submerged by flood water* 被洪水淹没的墙 ○ *The child submerged all her toys in the bath.* 那孩子把所有的玩具都泡在澡盆里. **2** [Tn usu passive 通常用于被动语态] (*fig* 比喻) completely cover (sb/sth); overwhelm 完全覆盖(某人[某事物]); 遮住: *be submerged by paperwork* 埋头于文牍工作 ○ *The main argument was submerged in a mass of tedious detail.* 大量单调乏味的细节掩盖了主要论点.

▷ **sub·merged** *adj* under the surface of the sea, etc 在海面等的下面的: *a partly-submerged wreck* 部分淹没的遇难船的残骸.

sub·mer·gence /səb'mɜ:dʒəns; səb'mɝdʒəns/, **sub·mer·sion** /səb'mɜ:ʃn; *US* -mɜ:rʒn; səb'mɝʒən/ *ns* [U].

sub·mers·ible /səb'mɜ:səbl; səb'mɝsəbl̩/ *n*, *adj* (ship or craft) that can be submerged 可潜入水中的(船只等): *exploring the sea bed in a submersible* 乘潜水器探测海底.

sub·mis·sion /səb'mɪʃn; səb'mɪʃən/ *n* **~ (to sb/sth)** **1** [U] (**a**) acceptance of another's power; submitting 归顺; 降服; 投降: *submission to sb's will* 屈从于某人的意志 ○ *starve the city into submission*, ie force it to submit by cutting off its food supplies 以饥饿迫使该城投降. (**b**) state in which one accepts the superior power of sb else 屈从; 服从; 顺从: *During the occupation, we had to live in total submission (to the invader).* 在沦陷时期, 我们得听凭(侵略者的)摆布. ○ *parents who want children to show complete submission to their wishes* 要孩子百依百顺的父母. **2** [C, U] (act of) presenting sth for consideration, a decision, etc 提交; 呈递: *the submission of a claim, a petition, an appeal, etc* 要求、请愿书、上诉书等的提交. **3** [C, U] (*law* 律) opinion or argument presented to a judge or jury 向法官或陪审团提出的意见或论据: *In my submission, the witness is lying.* 本人认为证人所言不实.

sub·mis·sive /səb'mɪsɪv; səb'mɪsɪv/ *adj* willing to yield to the authority of others; obedient 服从的; 顺从的: *a humble and submissive servant* 恭顺的仆人. ▷ **sub·mis·sively** *adv*. **sub·mis·sive·ness** *n* [U].

sub·mit /səb'mɪt; səb'mɪt/ *v* (**-tt-**) **1** [I, Ipr] **~ (to sb/sth)** accept the control, superior strength, etc (of sb/sth); yield (to sb/sth) 屈服或归顺于(某人[某事物]); 服从, 顺从(某人[某事物]): *I refuse to submit.* 我决不屈服. ○ *submit to discipline, superior force, etc* 遵守纪律、慑服于优势兵力 ○ *submit to the enemy, a tyrant, etc* 向敌人投降、向暴君低头. **2** [Tn, Tn·pr] **~ sth (to sb/sth)** give sth (to sb/sth) so that it may be considered, decided on, etc (向某人[某事物])提交或呈递某事物(以供考虑、裁决等): *submit an essay to one's tutor* 向指导教师呈交论文 ○ *submit plans to the council for approval* 向委员会提交计划呈请批准 ○ *submit an application, estimate, claim, etc* 提出一项申请、估价、要求等. **3** [Tf no passive 不用于被动语态] (*law* 律) suggest (sth); argue 建议(某事物); 认为: *Counsel for the defence submitted that his client was clearly innocent.* 被告的律师辩称其委托人显然是无辜的. ○ *The case, I would submit, is not proven.* 本人认为此案证据不足.

sub·nor·mal /ˌsʌb'nɔ:ml; sʌb'nɔrml̩/ *adj* **1** below normal; less than normal 低于正常的; 比正常少的: *subnormal temperatures* 低于正常的温度. **2** below the normal level of intelligence 智力低于正常标准的: *a subnormal child* 弱智儿童 ○ *educationally subnormal* 在教育方面认为智力低于正常标准的.

▷ **sub·nor·mal** *n* (*infml* 口) subnormal(2) person 智力逊常者; 弱智者.

sub·or·bital /ˌsʌb'ɔ:bɪtl; sʌb'ɔrbɪtl̩/ *adj* less than (or lasting less time than) one orbit of the earth, moon, etc (绕地球、月球等)不满一周的, 不足一周之时间的, 亚轨道的: *a suborbital space flight* 亚轨道宇宙飞行.

sub·or·din·ate /sə'bɔ:dɪnət; *US* -dənət; sə'bɔrdn̩ɪt/ *adj* (**a**) **~ (to sb)** lower in rank or position 级别或职位较低的; 下级的: *He was always friendly to his subordinate officers.* 他对下级官员一向和蔼可亲. (**b**) **~ (to sth)** of less importance 次要的; 附属的: *All the other issues are subordinate to this one.* 所有问题都要以这一问题为依归.

▷ **sub·or·din·ate** *n* person who is subordinate to sb else 下级; 部属: *the commanding officer and his subordinates* 指挥官及其部下.

sub·or·din·ate /sə'bɔ:dɪneɪt; *US* -dəneɪt; sə'bɔrdn̩,et/ *v* [Tn, Tn·pr] **~ sth (to sth)** treat sth as of lesser importance (than sth else) 将某事物置于次要地位: *In her book, she subordinates this issue to more general problems.* 在她的书中, 她把这个问题处理得不如一般问题重要. **sub·or·dina·tion** /səˌbɔ:dɪ'neɪʃn; *US* -dən'eɪʃn; səˌbɔrdn̩'eʃən/ *n* [U].

□ **suˌbordinate 'clause** (also **deˌpendent 'clause**) (*grammar*) clause, usu introduced by a conjunction, that functions like a noun, adjective or adverb, eg *when it rang* in *She answered the phone when it rang* 从句, 从属分句(通常以连词引导, 其作用相当于名词、形容词或副词, 如 She answered the phone when it rang 句中的 when it rang 即是). Cf 参看 CO-ORDINATE CLAUSE (CO-ORDINATE[1]).

sub·orn /sə'bɔ:n; sə'bɔrn/ *v* [Tn] (*fml* 文) use bribery or some other means to persuade (sb) to do sth illegal, esp tell lies in a court of law 以行贿或其他方法唆使(某人)做非法的事(尤指向法庭提供伪证): *suborn a witness* 收买证人. ▷ **sub·orna·tion** /ˌsʌbɔ:'neɪʃn; ˌsʌbɔr'neʃən/ *n* [U].

sub-plot /'sʌbplɒt; 'sʌb,plɑt/ *n* plot of a play, novel, etc that is separate from but linked to the main plot (戏剧、小说等的)次要情节, 从属情节.

sub·poena /sə'pi:nə; sə'pinə/ *n* (*law* 律) written order requiring a person to appear in a lawcourt (传唤出庭的)传票: *serve a subpoena on a witness* 向证人送达传票.

▷ **sub·poena** *v* [Tn, Cn·n/a, Cn·t] summon (sb) with a subpoena (用传票)传唤(某人): *subpoena a witness* 传唤证人 ○ *The court subpoenaed her (to appear) as a witness.* 法庭传她(到庭)作证.

sub·rout·ine /'sʌbru:ti:n; ˌsʌbru'tin/ *n* (*computing* 计) self-contained section of a computer program for performing a specific task 子程序; 子例行程序.

sub·scribe /səb'skraɪb; səb'skraɪb/ *v* **1** [I, Ipr, Tn, Tn·pr] **~ (sth) (to sth)** (agree to) contribute (a sum of money) 认捐, 捐助(一笔款项): *subscribe to a charity* 向慈善机构捐款 ○ *How much did you subscribe (to the disaster fund)?* 你(向赈灾基金)捐了多少钱? **2** [I, Ipr] **~ (to sth)** (agree to) buy (a newspaper, periodical, etc) regularly over a period of time 订阅, 订购(报刊等): *The magazine is trying to get more readers to subscribe.* 该杂志正大力发展新订户. ○ *Which journal(s) do you subscribe to?* 你订阅哪一种杂志? **3** [Tn, Tn·pr] **~ sth (to sth)** (*fml* 文) sign (esp one's name) at the foot of a document (在文件下面)签名, (尤指)签字, 签署: *subscribe one's name to a petition* 在请愿书上签名 ○ *subscribe a few remarks at the end of the essay* 在论文后面签注意见. **4** (phr v) **subscribe to sth** (*fml* 文) agree with (an opinion, a theory, etc) 同意, 赞成(某观点、理论等): *Do you subscribe to her pessimistic view of the state of the economy?* 你是否同意她对经济状况所持的悲观看法?

▷ **sub·scriber** *n* **1** person who subscribes(1,2) 认捐者; 捐助者; 订阅者; 订购者. **2** person who rents a telephone (电话)用户.

sub·scrip·tion /səbˈskrɪpʃn; səbˈskrɪpʃən/ *n* **1** [U] subscribing or being subscribed 认捐; 捐助; 订阅; 订购; 签字; 签署: *a monument paid for by public subscription* 由各界捐款建立的纪念碑. **2** [C] (**a**) sum of money subscribed 捐款; 订阅费; 订购款; 认捐额; 认购额: *a £5 subscription to charity* 向慈善事业提供的5英镑的捐款. (**b**) fee for membership of a club, etc (俱乐部等的)会员费: *renew one's annual subscription* 继续缴纳年度会费.

□ **subˌscriber ˈtrunk dialling** (abbr 缩写 **STD**) system of making long distance calls in which the caller is automatically connected (instead of using an operator) 用户长途电话直拨系统.

S

subˈscription concert concert where all tickets are paid for in advance 须预订票的音乐会.

sub·sec·tion /ˈsʌbsekʃn; ˈsʌbˌsɛkʃən/ *n* part of a section, esp in legal documents, etc 分段; 小节; (尤指法律文书等的)分款, 分项: *Please turn to section 5, subsection b.* 请翻到第5款, b项.

sub·sequent /ˈsʌbsɪkwənt; ˈsʌbsɪkwənt/ *adj* [attrib 作定语] later; following 后来的; 随后的: *Subsequent events proved me wrong.* 后来发生的事证明我错了. ○ *The first and all subsequent visits were kept secret.* 第一次以及随后的各次访问均严守秘密.

▷ **sub·sequently** *adv* afterwards 后来; 随后; 接着: *They subsequently heard he had left the country.* 他们后来听说他已出国.

□ **subsequent to** *prep* (*fml* 文) following (sth); after 继(某事物)之后; 在…之后: *Subsequent to its success as a play, it was made into a film.* 该剧在舞台上获得成功之后, 又摄制成了电影. ○ *He confessed to other crimes subsequent to the bank robbery.* 他供认抢劫银行案后, 又坦白了其他罪行.

sub·ser·vi·ent /səbˈsɜːvɪənt; səbˈsɝvɪənt/ *adj* **~ (to sb/sth)** **1** (*often derog* 常作贬义) giving too much respect, obedience, etc; submissive 必恭必敬的; 低声下气的; 恭顺的: *a subservient manner, attitude* 低三下四的样子、态度 ○ *Are priests too subservient to their bishops?* 牧师对主教是否过于恭顺? **2** less important; subordinate 次要的; 从属的: *People should not be regarded as subservient to the economic system.* 不应把人的因素看成是经济体制的附庸. ▷ **sub·ser·vi·ence** /-əns; -əns/ *n* [U]. **sub·ser·vi·ently** *adv*.

sub·side /səbˈsaɪd; səbˈsaɪd/ *v* **1** [I] sink to a lower or to the normal level 下降至较低或正常水平: *The flood waters gradually subsided.* 洪水逐渐退去. ○ *The boiling soup subsided when the pot was taken off the heat.* 把锅从炉子上端开时, 汤就不再沸腾了. **2** [I] (of land) sink, eg because of mining operations underneath (指土地)下陷(如因在地下采矿). **3** [I] (of buildings, etc) sink lower into the ground (指建筑物等)下陷: *Weak foundations caused the house to subside.* 由于地基不牢, 这所房子已下陷. **4** [I] become less violent, active, intense, etc 减弱; 减轻; 平静下来; 平息: *The storm began to subside.* 风暴渐渐平息了. ○ *He waited until the applause had subsided.* 他一直等到掌声平息下来, 才继续下去. ○ *I took an aspirin and the pain gradually subsided.* 我服用了阿斯匹林, 疼痛逐渐减轻. **5** [Ipr] (*infml joc* 口, 谑) let oneself drop into a chair, etc 一下子坐在椅子等上: *subsiding onto the sofa/into an armchair* 一屁股坐在长沙发[单座沙发]上.

▷ **sub·sid·ence** /səbˈsaɪdns, ˈsʌbsɪdns; səbˈsaɪdn̩s, ˈsʌbsədəns/ *n* **1** [U] process of subsiding (SUBSIDE 1) 下降; 回落; 回降: *the gradual subsidence of the river* 河水的逐渐回落. **2** [U, C] process or instance of subsiding (SUBSIDE 2, 3) (土地或建筑物等的)下陷: *a building damaged by subsidence* 因地基塌陷而毁坏的建筑物 ○ *The railway line was closed because of (a) subsidence.* 这条铁路因土地下陷而停止运营.

sub·si·di·ary /səbˈsɪdɪərɪ; *US* -dɪerɪ; səbˈsɪdɪˌɛrɪ/ *adj* **1** **~ (to sth)** connected to but smaller, of less importance, etc than sth else; subordinate 附属的; 从属的; 次要的: *a subsidiary stream flowing into the main river* 流入大河的支流 ○ *The question of finance is subsidiary to the question of whether the project will be approved.* 财务问题是这一项目是否获准的附带问题. **2** (of a business company) controlled by another (指业务机构)附属的, 附设的.

▷ **sub·si·di·ary** *n* subsidiary thing, esp a business company 附属事物; (尤指)附属公司.

sub·sidy /ˈsʌbsɪdɪ; ˈsʌbsədɪ/ *n* [C, U] money paid, esp by a government, to help an industry, to support the arts, to keep prices down, etc 补助金; (尤指政府为扶持工业、资助艺术事业、平抑物价等而发放的)津贴, 补贴: *food subsidies*, eg to reduce the price of basic foods 食品补贴(如用以降低基本食品的价格) ○ *increase/reduce the level of subsidy*, eg to the arts, farmers, etc 增加[减少]补贴(如对艺术界、农民等的).

▷ **sub·sid·ize, -ise** /ˈsʌbsɪdaɪz; ˈsʌbsəˌdaɪz/ *v* [Tn] give a subsidy to (sth/sb) 给(某事物[某人])津贴或补贴; 资助或补助(某人[某事物]): *subsidized industries* 受资助的工业. **sub·sid·iza·tion, -isation** /ˌsʌbsɪdaɪˈzeɪʃn; *US* -dɪˈz-; ˌsʌbsədəˈzeʃən/ *n* [U].

sub·sist /səbˈsɪst; səbˈsɪst/ *v* [I, Ipr] **~ (on sth)** (*fml* 文) (continue to) stay alive, esp with little food or money; exist (继续)存活, 活下去; (尤指藉微少的食物或金钱)维持生活; 生存: *How do they manage to subsist (on such a low wage)?* 他们(区区这点工资)怎样糊口? ○ *He subsisted mainly on vegetables and fruit.* 他主要依靠蔬菜和水果维持生命.

▷ **sub·sist·ence** /-təns; -təns/ *n* [U] (means of) subsisting 存活; 生存; 生计; 维生之道: *reduced to subsistence on bread and water* 降到以面包和水维持生活 ○ [attrib 作定语] *subsistence farming*, ie farming that produces only enough crops for the farmer and his family to live on, leaving no surplus which could be sold 自给农业(收成仅供自家食用, 无剩余出售者) ○ *a subsistence wage*, ie one that is only just enough to enable a worker to live 勉强糊口的工资.

□ **subˈsistence crop** crop grown to be eaten by the grower 自给作物(供种植者自身食用的). Cf 参看 CASH CROP (CASH).

subˈsistence level standard of living that is only just high enough to support life 勉强糊口的生活水平.

sub·soil /ˈsʌbsɔɪl; ˈsʌbˌsɔɪl/ *n* [U] layer of soil lying immediately beneath the surface layer 底土(层); 心土(层). Cf 参看 TOPSOIL (TOP[1]).

sub·sonic /ˌsʌbˈsɒnɪk; ˌsʌbˈsɑnɪk/ *adj* (flying at a speed) less than the speed of sound 亚音速(飞行)的: *a subsonic speed, aircraft, flight* 亚音速、亚音速飞机、亚音速飞行. Cf 参看 SUPERSONIC.

sub·stance /ˈsʌbstəns; ˈsʌbstəns/ *n* **1** [C] particular type of matter 物质: *a poisonous substance like cyanide* 类似氰化物的有毒物质 ○ *a substance that will prevent rust* 防锈物质 ○ *Water and ice are the same substance in different forms.* 水和冰是同一物质的不同状态. **2** [U] (**a**) real matter (contrasted with sth only seen, heard or imagined) 实物(与仅能看到、听到或想像之事物相对): *They maintained that ghosts had no substance.* 他们认为鬼魂不是实物. (**b**) firmness; solidity 坚固; 结实: *I like a meal that has some substance to it*, ie has nourishing food in it. 我喜欢吃富于营养的饭菜. ○ (*fig* 比喻) *an argument of little substance*, eg lacking specific details, etc 内容贫乏的议论. **3** [U] most important or essential part of sth; essential meaning 基本部分; 实质部分; 主旨; 要义: *the substance of the speech* 讲话的要旨 ○ *I agree with the substance of what you say/with what you say in substance, but differ on points of detail.* 我同意

你讲话的基本内容，不过在一些枝节问题上与你有分歧. **4** [U] (*fml* 文) money; property 金钱; 财物; 资产: *a man/woman of substance*, eg a property owner 有资产的男子[女子].

sub·stand·ard /ˌsʌbˈstændəd; sʌbˋstændɚd/ *adj* below the usual or required standard 低于标准的; 不够标准的: *substandard goods* 不合格的货物 ○ *She has written good essays before, but this one is substandard.* 她以前写的文章不错, 但这一篇却不怎么样.

sub·stan·tial /səbˈstænʃl; səbˋstænʃəl/ *adj* **1** large in amount; considerable 数目大的; 可观的: *a substantial improvement, decrease* 相当大的改善、缩减 ○ *Her contribution to the discussion was substantial.* 她在讨论中做了很多工作. ○ *obtain a substantial loan* 获得大笔贷款. **2** [usu attrib 通常作定语] solidly or strongly built or made 坚固的; 结实的: *a substantial padlock, chair, wall* 结实的挂锁、椅子、墙壁. **3** [usu attrib 通常作定语] owning much property; wealthy 有大量财产的; 富有的: *a substantial business, company* 殷实的商号、公司 ○ *substantial farmers* 富有的农民. **4** [attrib 作定语] concerning the most important part of sth; essential 实质的; 大体上的; 基本的: *We are in substantial agreement.* 我们的意见基本一致. **5** (*fml* 文) having physical existence, not merely seen or heard or imagined; real 实际存在的; 实物的; 真实的: *Was it something substantial that you saw, or was it a ghost?* 你见到的是实物, 还是鬼魂?

▷ **sub·stan·tially** /-ʃəlɪ; -ʃəlɪ/ *adv* **1** considerably; greatly 可观地; 大量地: *substantially improved* 大为改善 ○ *They contributed substantially to our success.* 他们对我们的成功做出了重大贡献. **2** concerning the substance (3) of sth; essentially 实质上; 大体上; 基本上: *Your assessment is substantially correct.* 你的估计基本正确.

sub·stan·ti·ate /səbˈstænʃɪeɪt; səbˋstænʃɪˌet/ *v* [Tn] give facts to support (a claim, statement, etc); prove 用事实支持(某主张、说法等); 证明; 证实: *Can you substantiate your accusations against him?* 你指责他, 能提出事实根据吗? ▷ **sub·stan·ti·ation** /səbˌstænʃɪˈeɪʃn; səbˌstænʃɪˋeʃən/ *n*.

sub·stant·ive[1] /ˈsʌbstəntɪv; ˋsʌbstəntɪv/ *adj* (*fml* 文) genuine or actual; real 真的; 真实的; 实在的; 实际的: *a discussion of substantive matters* 对实际问题的讨论 ○ *a guarantee of substantive progress* 取得实质性进展的保证.

▷ **sub·stant·ive** *n* (*dated* 旧 *grammar*) noun 名词.

sub·stant·ive[2] /səbˈstæntɪv; səbˋstæntɪv/ *adj* [attrib 作定语] (of military rank) permanent; not temporary (指军衔)永久的, 非临时的: *a substantive major* 在编的少校.

sub·sta·tion /ˈsʌbsteɪʃn; ˋsʌbˌsteʃən/ *n* place which relays electric current that has been generated elsewhere 变电所.

sub·sti·tute /ˈsʌbstɪtjuːt; *US* -tuːt; ˋsʌbstəˌtut/ *n* **~ (for sb/sth)** person or thing that replaces, acts for or serves as sb or sth else 代替、替换或代理的人或事物; 代替者; 代理人; 代用品: *The manager was unable to attend but sent his deputy as a substitute.* 经理不能出席, 派了个副手代表他. ○ *This type of vinyl is a poor substitute for leather.* 这种乙烯基材料代替皮革十分勉强. ○ [attrib 作定语] *a substitute player, horse, machine* 替换的队员、马、机器.

▷ **sub·sti·tute** *v* (**a**) [Tn, Tn·pr] **~ sb/sth (for sb/sth)** put or use sb/sth as a substitute (for sb/sth else) 用某人[某事物]代替(另外的人[事物]): *The understudy was substituted when the leading actor fell ill.* 主角演员患病, 由替角代替演出. ○ *We must substitute a new chair for the broken one.* 我们这把破损的椅子得换个新的. (**b**) [Ipr] **~ for sb/sth** act or serve as a substitute 代替; 替换; 代理; 取代: *Can you substitute for* (ie go instead of) *me at the meeting?* 你代我去开会好吗? ○ *Honey can substitute for sugar in this recipe.* 在这个食谱中, 可用蜂蜜代替食糖.

sub·sti·tu·tion /ˌsʌbstɪˈtjuːʃn; *US* -ˈtuːʃn; ˌsʌbstəˋtuʃən/ *n* **1** [U] substituting or being substituted 代替; 替换; 代理; 取代. **2** [C] act of substituting 代替; 替换; 代理; 取代: *Two substitutions* (ie of players) *were made during the match.* 在比赛中换了两次人.

sub·stratum /ˌsʌbˈstrɑːtəm; *US* ˈsʌbstreɪtəm; ˋsʌbˌstretəm/ *n* (*pl* **substrata** /ˌsʌbˈstrɑːtə; *US* ˈsʌbstreɪtə; ˋsʌbˌstretə/) **1** level lying below another 下面的一层; 底层: *a substratum of rock* 底层岩石. **2** (*fig* 比喻) foundation; basis 基础; 根基: *a substratum of truth in her story* 她叙述中的事实根据.

sub·struc·ture /ˈsʌbstrʌktʃə(r); ˋsʌbˌstrʌktʃɚ/ *n* underlying or supporting structure; base or foundation 下部结构; 支撑结构; 基础; 根基. Cf 参看 SUPERSTRUCTURE 1.

sub·sume /səbˈsjuːm; *US* -ˈsuːm; səbˋsum/ *v* [Tn, Tn·pr] **~ sth (in/under sth)** (*fml* 文) include sth in a particular group, class, etc or under a rule 将某事物归入某类型、类别等, 或纳入某规则中: *This creature can be subsumed in the class of reptiles.* 这种生物可以归入爬行动物一类.

sub·ten·ant /ˈsʌbtenənt; sʌbˋtɛnənt/ *n* person to whom a house, flat, etc (or part of it) is sublet by a tenant (房屋、公寓等的)转租承租人. ▷ **sub·ten·ancy** /-ənsɪ; -ənsɪ/ *n* [C, U].

subtend 对向

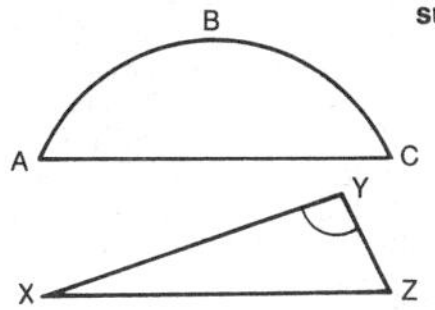

sub·tend /səbˈtend; səbˋtɛnd/ *v* [Tn] (*geometry* 几) (of a chord[2](1) or the side of a triangle) be opposite to (an arc(1) or angle) (指弦或三角形之边)对向(某弧或角): *The chord AC subtends the arc ABC. The side XZ subtends the angle XYZ.* AC弦对向ABC弧. XZ边对向XYZ角. ⇨ illus 见插图.

sub·ter·fuge /ˈsʌbtəfjuːdʒ; ˋsʌbtɚˌfjudʒ/ *n* (**a**) [C] trick or excuse, esp one used to avoid difficulties, blame, failure, etc 诡计; 花招; (尤指)(逃避困难、逃脱责备、避免失败等的)手段, 遁辞: *Her claim to be a journalist was simply a subterfuge to get into the theatre without paying.* 她自称是记者, 这只是个看戏不买票的花招而已. (**b**) [U] such trickery 诡计; 花招: *gain sth by subterfuge* 施诡计获得某事物.

sub·ter·ra·nean /ˌsʌbtəˈreɪnɪən; ˌsʌbtəˋrenɪən/ *adj* under the earth's surface; underground 地表下面的; 地下的: *a subterranean passage, river, tunnel* 地下通道、河流、隧道 ○ *subterranean digging* 在地下进行的采掘.

sub·title /ˈsʌbtaɪtl; ˋsʌbˌtaɪtḷ/ *n* **1** secondary title of a book, etc 副标题; 小标题. **2** (usu *pl* 通常作复数) (*esp cinema* 尤用于电影) words printed on a film that translate the dialogue of a foreign film, give those of a silent film or (on television) supply dialogue for deaf viewers 字幕.

▷ **sub·title** *v* [Tn usu passive 通常用于被动语态] give a subtitle or subtitles to (sth) 给(书等)加副标题或小标题; 给(影片等)加字幕: *a book subtitled 'A Study of Methodism'* 以《循道宗教义研究》为副标题的书.

subtle /ˈsʌtl; ˋsʌtḷ/ *adj* (**-r**, **-st**) (*esp approv* 尤作褒义) **1** not easy to detect or describe; fine; delicate 难以察觉或描述的; 细微的; 精细的: *a subtle charm, flavour, style* 难以形容的魅力、滋味、式样 ○ *subtle humour* 巧妙的幽默 ○ *a subtle distinction* 细微的差别 ○ *paint in subtle shades of pink* 粉红色度略微不同的颜料. **2** organized in a clever and complex way; ingenious; cunning 巧安排的; 巧妙的; 狡诈的: *a subtle argument, design, strategy* 巧妙的议论、设计、策略 ○ *a subtle analysis of the problem* 对该问题的精辟的分析. **3** able to see and describe fine and delicate differences; sensitive 敏锐的; 感觉灵敏的: *a subtle observer, critic, analyst, etc* 细心的观察者、评论者、分析者等 ○ *She has a very subtle mind.* 她头脑灵敏.

▷ **sub·tlety** /ˈsʌtltɪ; ˋsʌtḷtɪ/ *n* **1** [U] quality of being subtle 细微; 精细; 巧妙; 灵巧; 诡诈; 敏锐. **2** [C] subtle distinction, etc 细微的差别等.

subtly /ˈsʌtlɪ; ˋsʌtlɪ/ *adv*.

sub·to·pia /ˌsʌbˈtəʊpɪə; sʌbˋtopɪə/ *n* [C, U] unattractive suburbs spreading out into the countryside 难看的郊区(尤指城郊住宅区).

sub·to·tal /ˈsʌbtəʊtl; ˋsʌbˌtotḷ/ *n* total of a set of figures that are part of a larger group of figures 部分合计数; 小计.

sub·tract /səb'trækt; səb'trækt/ *v* [Tn, Tn·pr] **~ sth (from sth)** take (a number or quantity) away from (another number, etc) 从(某数等)中减去(某数或量): *subtract 6 from 9* 9减6 ○ *6 subtracted from 9 is 3*, ie 9－6＝3 9减6等于3. Cf 参看 ADD, DEDUCT.

▷ **sub·trac·tion** /səb'trækʃn; səb'trækʃən/ *n* **1** [U] process of subtracting 减; 减法. **2** [C] act of subtracting 减; 减法: *Two from five is a simple subtraction.* 五减二是简单的减法.

sub·trop·ical /ˌsʌb'trɒpɪkl; sʌb'trɑpɪkl/ *adj* of regions bordering on the tropics 亚热带的: *ˌsubtropical 'plants* 亚热带植物 ○ *a ˌsubtropical 'climate* 亚热带气候. Cf 参看 SUBARCTIC.

sub·urb /'sʌbɜ:b; 'sʌbɝb/ *n* (esp residential) district outside the central part of a town or city (城镇的)郊区; (尤指)城郊住宅区: *an industrial suburb* 城郊工业区 ○ *a suburb of Naples* 那不勒斯市郊 ○ *live in the suburbs*, ie in such a district 住在市郊 ○ *the inner/outer suburbs* 近[远]郊 ○ *a dormitory suburb*, ie one from which people travel elsewhere to work 市内工作者的郊外住宅区.

▷ **sub·urban** /sə'bɜ:bən; sə'bɝbən/ *adj* **1** of or in a suburb 城郊的; 在郊区的; 城郊住宅区的: *a suburban street, shop, newspaper* 郊区的街道、商店、报纸. **2** (*fig derog* 比喻, 贬) limited in outlook; dull or ordinary 见闻不广的; 乏味的; 平淡无奇的: *a rather suburban attitude to life* 闭目塞听的生活态度.

sub·urb·an·ite /sə'bɜ:bənaɪt; sə'bɝbəˌnaɪt/ *n* (*infml often derog* 口, 常作贬义) person who lives in the suburbs 郊区居民.

Sub·urbia /sə'bɜ:bɪə; sə'bɝbɪə/ *n* [U] (*esp derog* 尤作贬义) (type of life lived by or attitudes held by people who live in the) suburbs 郊区; 郊区人的生活方式或处世态度.

S

sub·ven·tion /səb'venʃn; səb'vɛnʃən/ *n* (*fml* 文) grant of money to support an industry, a theatre company, etc; subsidy (资助工业、戏剧团体等的)补助金, 补贴, 津贴.

sub·vers·ive /səb'vɜ:sɪv; səb'vɝsɪv/ *adj* **~ (of sth)** trying or likely to weaken or destroy a political system, an accepted belief, etc 为削弱或破坏某政治制度、公认的信仰等的; 颠覆性的: *subversive propaganda* 颠覆性的宣传 ○ *a subversive book, speaker, influence* 具有煽动性的书、演讲者、影响 ○ *Was her speech subversive (of law and order)?* 她讲的话是否(对法治)是破坏性的?

▷ **sub·vers·ive** *n* subversive person 颠覆分子.

sub·vers·ively *adv*.

sub·vers·ive·ness *n* [U].

sub·vert /sʌb'vɜ:t; səb'vɝt/ *v* [Tn] **1** destroy the authority of (a political system, religious faith, etc) 颠覆, 破坏(政治制度、宗教信仰等): *subvert the monarchy* 推翻君主政体 ○ *writings that subvert Christianity* 攻击基督教教义的文字. **2** corrupt the morals or loyalty of (sb) 使(某人)道德败坏或不忠: *a diplomat subverted by a foreign power* 受外国势力影响而变节的外交官. ▷ **sub·ver·sion** /səb'vɜ:ʃn; *US* -'vɜ:rʒn; səb'vɝʒən/ *n* [U].

sub·way /'sʌbweɪ; 'sʌbˌwe/ *n* **1** underground pedestrian tunnel, esp one beneath a road or railway 地下人行道(尤指公路或铁路下的): *Use the subway to cross the road.* 请用地下通道穿越马路. Cf 参看 UNDERPASS. **2** (*US*) underground railway in a city 市区地下铁道: *travel by subway* 乘地铁 ○ [attrib 作定语] *a subway train, station* 地铁列车、地铁站. Cf 参看 UNDERGROUND[2] *n*, TUBE 3, METRO.

sub·zero /ˌsʌb'zɪərəʊ; sʌb'zɪro/ *adj* (of temperatures) below zero (指温度)零度以下的: *the ˌsubzero 'temperatures of a Siberian winter* 西伯利亚冬季的零下气温.

suc·ceed /sək'si:d; sək'sid/ *v* **1** [I, Ipr] **~ (in sth/doing sth)** do what one is trying to do; achieve the desired end 成功; 做成; 达到目的: *The attack succeeded, and the fort was taken.* 这次袭击成功, 拿下了堡垒. ○ *She's absolutely determined to succeed (in life).* 她决心要实现自己的(人生)目的. ○ (*saying* 谚) *If at first you don't succeed, try, try again* 若一次不成功, 要再接再厉. ○ (*ironic* 反语) *I tried to clean the watch, but only succeeded in breaking it.* 我想把手表弄干净, 结果却弄坏了. Cf 参看 FAIL 1. **2** [Tn] come next after (sb/sth) and take his/its place 接替(某人[某事物]); 继任: *Who succeeded Churchill (as Prime Minister)?* 继邱吉尔出任(首相)的是谁? ○ *The silence was succeeded by the striking of a clock.* 时钟鸣响声打破了寂静. **3** [I, Ipr] **~ (to sth)** gain the right to (a title, property, etc) when sb dies 继承(头衔、财产等): *When the king died, his eldest son succeeded (to the throne).* 国王死后, 其长子继位. **4** (idm 习语) **ˌnothing sucˌceeds like suc'cess** (*saying* 谚) success often leads to further successes 一事成, 事事成: *I won the essay prize, then was offered a scholarship: nothing succeeds like success!* 我的作文得了奖, 接着就获得了奖学金, 真是一顺百顺!

suc·cess /sək'ses; sək'sɛs/ *n* **1** [U] achievement of a desired end, or of fame, wealth or social position; succeeding 成功; 成就; 成名; 发财; 胜利; 达到目的: *achieve great success in life* 在人生道路上大有成就 ○ *make a success of sth* 某事取得成功 ○ *The race ended in success for* (ie was won by) *the Irish horse.* 比赛的结果是爱尔兰马获胜. ○ *I haven't had much success in my applications for jobs.* 我那些求职信都没怎么达到目的. **2** [C] person or thing that succeeds 成功者; 达到目的的人或事物: *He wasn't a success as a teacher.* 他不是个好教师. ○ *Of her plays, three were successes and one was a failure.* 她的剧作有三部成功, 一部失败. **3** (idm 习语) **ˌnothing sucˌceeds like suc'cess** ⇨ SUCCEED. **a roaring success** ⇨ ROARING (ROAR). **a suc'cess story** person or thing that is very successful (esp unexpectedly or in the face of difficulties) 大获成功的人或事物(尤指意外地或面对困难时): *Her rapid rise to the top has been one of the film industry's most remarkable success stories.* 她迅速走红是电影界最杰出的一个事例.

▷ **suc·cess·ful** /-fl; -fəl/ *adj* having success 获得成功的; 取得成效的; 达到目的的: *a successful businesswoman, career, plan* 获得成功的女商人、事业、计划 ○ *My final attempt to fix it was successful.* 我最后这次到底把它修好了. **suc·cess·fully** /-fəlɪ; -fəlɪ/ *adv*.

suc·ces·sion /sək'seʃn; sək'sɛʃən/ *n* **1** [C] number of things or people coming one after the other in time or order; series 一连串的事物; 接二连三的人; 一系列: *a succession of wet days, defeats, poor leaders* 一个接一个的阴雨天、失败、不称职的领导人. **2** [U] the coming of one thing or person after another in time or order 连续; 接连: *the succession of the seasons* 四季的交替. **3** [U] (right of) succeeding to a title, the throne, property, etc (头衔、王位、财产等的)继承(权): *Who is first in succession to the throne?* 谁是王位的第一继承人? **4** (idm 习语) **in suc'cession** one after the other 连续(的); 一个接一个(的): *three victories in (quick) succession* 一连三次(迅速)获得的胜利.

suc·cess·ive /sək'sesɪv; sək'sɛsɪv/ *adj* [attrib 作定语] coming one after the other in an unbroken series 连续不断的; 接连的; 一连串的: *successive governments, victories, attempts* 一个接一个的政府、胜利、尝试 ○ *The school has won five successive games.* 该校已连胜五场比赛. ▷ **suc·cess·ively** *adv*.

suc·cessor /sək'sesə(r); sək'sɛsɚ/ *n* **~ (to sb/sth)** person or thing that comes after and takes the place of (sb/sth) 接替的人或事物; 后继者; 继任者; 继承人: *the successor to the throne* 王位的继承人 ○ *appoint a successor to the headmaster* 任命继任校长 ○ *This car is the successor to our popular hatchback model.* 这种汽车是我厂著名的带上掀式斜背小轿车的换代产品. Cf 参看 PREDECESSOR.

suc·cinct /sək'sɪŋkt; sək'sɪŋkt/ *adj* (*approv* 褒) expressed briefly and clearly; concise 简明的; 简洁的; 简要的: *a succinct summary of the argument* 论点的概要. ▷ **suc·cinctly** *adv*. **suc·cinct·ness** *n* [U].

suc·cour (*US* **suc·cor**) /'sʌkə(r); 'sʌkɚ/ *n* [U] (*fml* 文) help given to sb in need or in danger 援助; 援救: *bring succour to the sick and wounded* 援救伤病员.

▷ **suc·cour** *v* [Tn] (*fml* 文) give such help to (sb) 援助或援救(某人).

suc·cu·bus /'sʌkjʊbəs; 'sʌkjəbəs/ *n* (*pl* **succubi** /'sʌkjʊbaɪ; 'sʌkjəˌbaɪ/) female demon said to have sexual intercourse with sleeping males 传说中与熟睡的男子性交的女妖. Cf 参看 INCUBUS.

suc·cu·lent /'sʌkjʊlənt; 'sʌkjələnt/ *adj* **1** (*approv* 褒) (of fruit and meat) juicy and delicious (指水果及肉类)汁多味美的: *a succulent steak, pear, etc* 鲜美的牛排、梨等. **2** (of plants) having leaves and stems that are thick and contain a lot of water (指植物)茎叶肥厚含水分多的, 肉质的.

▷ **suc·cu·lence** /-əns; -əns/ *n* [U].
suc·cu·lent *n* succulent plant, eg a cactus 肉质植物(如仙人掌).

suc·cumb /səˈkʌm; səˈkʌm/ *v* [I, Ipr] **~ (to sth)** (*fml* 文) stop resisting (temptation, illness, attack, etc); yield 不再抵抗(诱惑、疾病、攻击等); 屈从: *The city succumbed after only a short siege.* 该城受围困仅很短时间就不再抵抗了. ○ *Several children have measles, and the others are bound to succumb (to it).* 有几个孩子患了麻疹, 其他孩子也必然传染上. ○ *The driver has succumbed to* (ie died of) *his injuries.* 司机已受伤不治.

such /sʌtʃ; sʌtʃ/ *det* **1 (a)** (referring back 用以复指前文) of the kind specified earlier 上述一类的; (像前面提及的)那样的, 这样的, 如此的: *He noticed her necklace. Such jewels must have cost thousands, he thought.* 他注意到了她的项链. 他想, 这样的首饰价值一定上千了. ○ *He told them about the job he had left. Such information was just what they needed.* 他告诉他们他刚辞去的工作的情况. 这些情况正是他们需要知道的. ○ *I've been invited to an Asian wedding. What happens on such occasions?* 我应邀参加亚洲人的婚礼. 这种婚礼是如何举行的? ○ *He said he hadn't got time or made some such excuse.* 他说他没有时间, 或是诸如此类的借口. ○ *This isn't the only story of starving children. Many such cases are reported every day.* 这并非饥饿儿童的唯一事例, 很多类似报道无日无之. **(b) ~ sth as/that...** (referring forward 用以预指后文) of the specified kind 下述一类的; (像后面提及的)那样的, 这样的, 如此的: *Such a disaster as her car being stolen had never happened before.* 有的祸事, 像她的汽车被盗之类, 以前从未发生过. ○ *Such poets as Keats and Shelley wrote Romantic poetry.* 有些诗人, 如济慈和雪莱, 写的是浪漫主义的诗歌. ○ *Such advice as* (ie The little advice that) *he was given proved almost worthless.* 给他提的那类建议简直毫无价值. ○ *The knot was fastened in such a way that it was impossible to undo.* 这个结系得那么紧, 根本解不开. **2 ~ sth (as/that...)** to the specified degree (of importance, worth, etc) (重要性、价值等)达到(后面提及的)那种程度的: *On an occasion such as this* (ie as important as this) *we are privileged to welcome...* 在这样重要的场合, 我们有幸能欢迎... ○ *He showed such concern that people took him to be a relative.* 他很关心别人, 因而大家都把他当作亲人. ○ *He's not such a fool as he looks.* 他并不像看上去的那样愚蠢. ○ *It was such a boring speech (that) I fell asleep.* 这讲演枯燥无味, 听得我都睡着了. ○ *I'm afraid I can't remember — it was such a long time ago.* 很抱歉, 我想不起来了 —— 那是很久以前的事了. ○ *Such is the influence of TV that it can make a person famous overnight.* 电视的影响力就是这么大, 可以让人转眼成名. **3** (as an intensifier 用以加强语气) so great; so very (much) 这么大的; 这样(极其): *She's got such talent.* 她有非凡的才能. ○ *We're having such a wonderful time.* 我们玩儿得真痛快. ○ *Baby giraffes seem to have such long legs.* 小长颈鹿的腿显得格外长. ○ *I've had such a shock.* 我震惊得不得了. ○ *Why are you in such a hurry?* 你为什么这样匆忙?

▷ **such** *pron* **1** person or thing of a specified kind 某类的人或事物. **(a)** (referring back 用以复指前文): *Cricket was boring. Such* (ie That) *was her opinion before meeting Ian.* 打板球没意思. 她在认识伊恩以前就是这种看法. ○ *She's a competent leader and has always been regarded as such by her colleagues.* 她是个很有能力的领导人, 她的同事一向都是这样认为的. **(b) ~ as to do sth; ~ that...** (referring forward 用以预指后文) *The pain in her foot wasn't such as to stop her walking.* 她脚疼, 但还不至于不能行走. ○ *The damage was such that it would cost too much money to repair.* 损坏得很严重, 要用很多钱才能修好. **2** (idm 习语) **as such** as the word is usually understood; in the strict sense of the word 按照某词通用的词义; 根据某词严格的词义: *The new job is not a promotion as such but it brings good prospects for the future.* 这一新的工作, 严格说来并不算提升, 不过以后很有发展前途. ○ *I can't call my book a best seller as such but it's very popular.* 我不敢说我的书是畅销书, 但可以说很受欢迎. **such as (a)** like; for example 像; 诸如; 例如: *Wild flowers such as orchids and primroses are becoming rare.* 兰花和报春花之类的野花越来越少了. **(b)** everything that 凡是: *Such as remains after tax will be yours when I die.* 我死以后全部财产除了交税以外都给你. **ˌsuch as it ˈis** (used to apologize for the poor quality of sth 用以对某物质量不好表示歉意): *You're welcome to join us for supper, such as it is — we're only having soup and bread.* 欢迎你和我们一起吃晚饭, 只是没什么好吃的 —— 只有汤和面包.

□ **ˈsuch-and-such** *pron, det* (thing) of a particular but unspecified type 某种未具体指明的(事物): *Always say at the start of an application that you're applying for such-and-such (a job) because...* 在求职信的开头一定要说明你要求某某工作, 理由是....

such·like /ˈsʌtʃlaɪk; ˈsʌtʃˌlaɪk/ *pron, det* (things) of the same kind 同类的(事物): *You can buy string, glue, paper-clips and suchlike (items) at the corner shop.* 在街角小店里可以买到细绳、胶水、回形针之类的东西.

suck /sʌk; sʌk/ *v* **1** [Tn, Tn·pr, Tn·p] **(a)** draw (liquid or air, etc) into the mouth by using the lip muscles (用嘴)吸(液体或气体等); 吮吸; 啜; 嘬: *suck the juice from an orange* 吸橙子的汁 ○ *suck the poison out (of a wound)* 吸出(伤口的)毒液 ○ *suck milk through a straw* 用吸管吸牛奶喝. ⇨illus at BLOW 见BLOW插图. **(b)** (of a pump, etc) draw (liquid or air, etc) out of sth (指泵等)抽出(液体或气体等): *The pump sucks air out (of the vessel) through this valve.* 这台泵通过这个阀门把(容器中的)空气抽出. ○ *plants that suck up moisture from the soil* 从土壤中吸收水分的植物. **2** [Tn, Cn·a] draw liquid from (sth) 从(某物)中吸出液体: *a baby sucking its mother's breast* 正在吃母乳的孩子 ○ *suck an orange dry* 把橙子吸干. **3** [I, Ipr, Ip] **~ (away) (at/on sth)** perform the action of sucking sth 吸食或吮吸某物: *The baby sucked (away) (at its bottle) contentedly.* 那婴儿舒适地嘬着(奶瓶). ○ *The old man was sucking at his pipe.* 那老汉正在吸着烟斗. ○ *Suck on the tube to draw up the water.* 用管子把水吸上来. **4** [Tn] squeeze or roll (sth) with the tongue while holding it in the mouth 将(某物)含在嘴里: *suck a toffee* 含着太妃糖 ○ *a child that sucks its thumb* 吮吸拇指的孩子. **5** (idm 习语) **milk/suck sb/sth dry** ⇨ DRY[1]. **teach one's grandmother to suck eggs** ⇨ TEACH. **6** (phr v) **suck sb in/into sth** (usu passive 通常用于被动语态) involve sb in (a scandal, an argument, etc), usu unwillingly 将某人卷入(丑闻、争论等)之中(通常为不情愿者): *I don't want to get sucked into the row about school reform.* 我不愿意牵扯到这场学制改革的争论之中. **suck sb/sth under, into, etc sth; suck sb/sth down, in, etc** pull sb/sth down, under, etc with great force of water or air (以水或气体的巨大吸力)把某人[某物]吞没: *The canoe was sucked (down) into the whirlpool.* 那独木舟卷进漩涡里了. ○ *Dangerous currents can suck swimmers under.* 险急的水流能把游泳的人吞没. **suck up (to sb)** (*derog sl* 贬, 俚) try to please sb by flattering, helping him, etc 奉承或巴结某人; 拍某人马屁: *She sucks up to him by agreeing with everything he says.* 她巴结他, 他说什么话她都同意.

▷ **suck** *n* act of sucking 吸; 吮吸; 啜; 咂: *have/take a suck (at sth)* 吮吸(某物).

□ **ˈsucking-pig** *n* young pig still taking its mother's milk 乳猪; 还在吃奶的小猪.

sucker /ˈsʌkə(r); ˈsʌkɚ/ *n* **1 (a)** organ of certain animals that enables them to stick to a surface by suction (某些动物的)吸盘: *An octopus has suckers on its tentacles* 章鱼的腕足上有吸盘. **(b)** concave (usu rubber) disc that sticks to a surface by suction, and is used eg to attach things to a wall 凹面吸盘(通常用橡胶制成, 可藉吸力附着于平面上, 如用以将物件固着于墙上). **2** shoot growing from the roots of a tree, shrub, etc 从树等的根部长出的新枝; 根出条. **3** (*infml* 口) person who is easily deceived 容易受骗的人: *all the suckers who bought these worthless shares* 购买这些不值钱的股票的那群外行. **4 ~ for sb/sth** (*infml* 口) person who cannot resist sb/sth or is very fond of sb/sth 抵挡不住某人[某事物]的人; 极喜爱某人[某事物]的人: *I've always been a sucker for romantic movies.* 我一向非常喜欢传奇性的影片.

suckle /ˈsʌkl; ˈsʌkl/ *v* [Tn] feed (a baby or young animal) with milk from the breast or udder 给(婴儿或小动物)喂奶 ⇨illus at COW 见COW插图. ▷ **suck·ling** /ˈsʌklɪŋ; ˈsʌklɪŋ/ *n* (idm 习语) **out of the mouths of babes and sucklings** ⇨ MOUTH[1].

suc·rose /ˈsuːkrəʊz, -rəʊs; ˈsukros/ *n* [U] sugar

S

obtained from sugar-cane and sugar-beet 蔗糖; 甜菜糖.

suc·tion /ˈsʌkʃn; ˋsʌkʃən/ *n* [U] removal of air to create a partial vacuum, used for making two surfaces stick together or for sucking in liquid, dust, etc by means of air pressure 吸; 抽吸: *Some pumps and all vacuum cleaners work by suction.* 有些泵和所有的真空吸尘器都是藉吸力工作的. ○ *Flies' feet stick to surfaces by suction.* 苍蝇的脚藉吸力可附着于物体表面上. ○ [attrib 作定语] *a suction pump, pad* 抽气泵、垫.

sud·den /ˈsʌdn; ˋsʌdn̩/ *adj* **1** happening, coming or done quickly and unexpectedly 迅速而意外地发生、出现或做出的; 突然的: *a sudden decision, arrival, increase* 突然的决定、到达、增加 ○ *a sudden turn in the road* 路上的急转弯 ○ *Your marriage was very sudden. Have you thought things over properly?* 你结婚太突然了. 都考虑好了吗? **2** (idm 习语) ˌ**all of a ˈsudden** unexpectedly 突然; 出乎意料地: *All of a sudden, the tyre burst.* 轮胎突然爆裂了. ˌ**sudden ˈdeath** deciding the result of a drawn or tied game by playing one more point or game (因胜负未决而延长比赛)加赛一分或一场以决胜负: [attrib 作定语] *a* ˌ*sudden-death* ˈ*play-off* 先得分者即为胜方的加时赛. ▷ **sud·denly** *adv*: *The end came quite suddenly.* 结局来得很突然. ○ *Suddenly, everyone started shouting and singing.* 突然间, 大家都喊起来、唱起来了. **sud·den·ness** *n* [U].

suds /sʌdz; sʌdz/ *n* [pl] **1** mass of tiny bubbles on soapy water (肥皂水上的)泡沫. **2** (*US infml* 口) beer 啤酒. ▷ **sudsy** *adj*: *sudsy water* 有肥皂泡沫的水.

sue /suː; *also, in British use,* 英式英语读作 sjuː; su/ *v* **1** [I, Ipr, Tn, Tn·pr] **~ (sb) (for sth)** make a legal claim (against sb) 控告(某人); (对某人)提起诉讼: *If you don't complete the work, I will sue you (for damages)*, ie for money to compensate for my loss. 你不把工作做完, 我就控告你(要你付损害赔偿金). **2** [Ipr] **~ for sth** (*fml* 文) formally ask for sth, often in a lawcourt 请求(常于法庭上): *sue for peace* 请求和解 ○ *a prisoner suing for mercy* 请求饶恕的囚犯 ○ *sue for a divorce* 要求离婚.

suede /sweɪd; swed/ *n* [U] type of soft leather with one side rubbed so that it has a soft roughened surface 绒面革; 仿麂皮: [attrib 作定语] *a suede coat, dress, etc* 绒面革的大衣、连衣裙等 ○ *suede shoes* 绒面革皮鞋.

suet /ˈsuːɪt; *also, in British use,* 英式英语读作 ˈsjuːɪt; ˋsuɪt/ [U] hard fat from round the kidneys of cattle and sheep, used in cooking (牛羊腰肾部的)硬脂肪油(烹调用): [attrib 作定语] *a suet pudding*, ie one made with flour and suet 牛羊脂肪油布丁. ▷ **su·ety** *adj* like or containing (much) suet 像牛羊脂肪油的; 含(大量)牛羊脂肪油的.

suf·fer /ˈsʌfə(r); ˋsʌfɚ/ *v* **1** [I, Ipr] **~ (from/with/for sth)** feel pain, discomfort, great sorrow, etc 感到疼痛、不适、悲伤等; 受苦; 吃苦头: *Do you suffer from* (ie often have) *headaches?* 你常头痛吗? ○ *She's suffering from loss of memory.* 她患有遗忘症. ○ *He suffers terribly with* (ie is pained by) *his feet.* 他的脚痛得不得了. ○ *He made a rash decision — now he's suffering for it.* 他做决定太仓促——现在可吃到苦头了. ○ *Think how much the parents of the kidnapped boy must have suffered.* 那个男孩儿给拐走了, 想想看他父母得多伤心哪. **2** [Tn] experience or undergo (sth unpleasant) 经历或遭受(不愉快之事): *suffer pain, torture, defeat* 遭受痛苦、折磨、失败 ○ *We suffered huge losses in the financial crisis.* 我们在金融危机中损失惨重. **3** [I] become worse; lose quality 变坏; 变差; 变糟: *Your studies will suffer if you play too much football.* 你要是总踢足球, 功课就糟了. ○ *Her business suffered* (eg made less profit) *when she was ill.* 她患病时, 生意受到了影响. **4** [Tn] (*fml* 文) tolerate (sth); stand 忍受, 容忍(某事物); 经得起: *How can you suffer such insolence?* 你怎能忍受这样的侮辱呢? **5** (idm 习语) **not/never suffer ˈfools gladly** not be patient with people whom one considers to be foolish 对自己认为很笨的人缺乏耐心: *an arrogant, impatient woman who doesn't suffer fools gladly* 不愿与笨人为伍的高傲而无耐性的女子.

▷ **suf·ferer** /ˈsʌfərə(r); ˋsʌfərɚ/ *n* person who suffers 受苦者; 受难者; 受害者; 患病者: *arthritis sufferers* 关节炎患者.

suf·fer·ing /ˈsʌfərɪŋ; ˋsʌfərɪŋ/ *n* **1** [U] pain of body or mind (肉体或内心的)痛苦: *There is so much suffering in this world.* 这个世界上多灾多难. **2 sufferings** [pl] feelings of pain, unhappiness, etc 痛苦、不幸等的感觉; 苦恼; 折磨: *the sufferings of the starving refugees* 饥饿中的难民所受的折磨.

suf·fer·ance /ˈsʌfərəns; ˋsʌfərəns/ *n* [U] (idm 习语) **on ˈsufferance** tolerated but not actually wanted 得到别人勉强地容忍: *He's here on sufferance.* 他是勉强获准留在此地的.

suf·fice /səˈfaɪs; səˋfaɪs/ *v* **1** [I, Ipr, It, Tn no passive 不用于被动语态] **~ (for sb/sth)** (not in the continuous tenses 不用于进行时态) (*fml* 文) be enough (for sb/sth); be adequate 能满足(某人[某事物])之需要的; 足够的: *Will £10 suffice for the trip?* 这趟行程10英镑够用吗? ○ *One warning sufficed to stop her doing it.* 给她一次警告就足以制止她做那件事了. ○ *A light lunch should suffice me.* 有一点儿午饭就够我吃了. **2** (idm 习语) **suffice it to say (that)...** (used to suggest that even though one could say more, what one does say should be enough to show what one means 用以指不必多说, 只须说...就够了): *I won't go into all the depressing details; suffice it to say that the whole affair was an utter disaster.* 我不必细说那些让人听了难受的事, 只说一句就够了, 整件事是个惨祸.

suf·fi·cient /səˈfɪʃnt; səˋfɪʃənt/ *adj* **~ (for sth/sb)** enough 足够的; 充足的: *sufficient money, time, fuel* 足够的钱、时间、燃料 ○ *Is £10 sufficient for your expenses?* 10英镑够你用的吗? ○ *Do we have sufficient (food) for ten people?* 我们有够十个人吃的(食物)吗?

▷ **suf·fi·ciency** /-nsɪ; -nsɪ/ *n* **~ of sth** [sing] (*fml* 文) sufficient quantity of sth 足量; 充足: *a sufficiency of fuel for the winter* 足够过冬的燃料.

suf·fi·ciently *adv*: *not sufficiently careful* 不够细心.

suf·fix /ˈsʌfɪks; ˋsʌfɪks/ *n* letter or group of letters added at the end of a word to make another word, eg *-y* added to *rust* to make *rusty*, or as an inflexion, eg *-en* in *oxen* 后缀, 词尾(加在词尾的字母, 用以构成新词, 如将y加在rust字后构成rusty, 或用作屈折成分, 如oxen字中的en). Cf 参看 PREFIX.

suf·foc·ate /ˈsʌfəkeɪt; ˋsʌfəˌket/ *v* **1** [I, Tn] (cause sb to) die as a result of not being able to breathe (使某人)窒息而死; (将某人)闷死: *Passengers suffocated in the burning aircraft.* 乘客在燃烧的飞机中窒息死亡. ○ *The fireman was suffocated by the fumes.* 那个消防队员让浓烟憋死了. **2** [I] have difficulty in breathing 呼吸困难; 窒息: *I'm suffocating in here; can't we open a few windows?* 我觉得这儿很憋气, 咱们开几扇窗户好吗?

▷ **suf·foc·at·ing** *adj* causing difficulty in breathing 使人呼吸困难的; 使人窒息的: *the suffocating heat of a tropical night* 热带地区晚间窒闷的炎热 ○ (*fig* 比喻) *a suffocating bureaucracy*, ie one which prevents freedom of action 压制自由的官僚政治.

suf·foca·tion /ˌsʌfəˈkeɪʃn; ˌsʌfəˋkeʃən/ *n* [U].

suf·fragan /ˈsʌfrəgən; ˋsʌfrəgən/ *adj* [attrib 作定语] (of a bishop) appointed to help another bishop by managing part of his diocese (指主教)被任命协助另一主教管理部分教区的; 副主教的; 副监督的.

▷ **suf·fragan** *n* suffragan bishop 副主教; 副监督.

suf·frage /ˈsʌfrɪdʒ; ˋsʌfrɪdʒ/ *n* [U] right to vote in political elections (政治性选举的)选举权, 投票权: *universal suffrage*, ie the right of all adults to vote 普选权(成年人均有的投票权) ○ *Women had to fight for their suffrage.* 妇女须为享有选举权而斗争.

▷ **suf·fra·gette** /ˌsʌfrəˈdʒet; ˌsʌfrəˋdʒɛt/ *n* member of a group of women who, in the early part of the 20th century, campaigned in Britain for women's suffrage ☆ 20世纪初英国为争取妇女选举权而开展斗争的妇女团体之成员.

suf·fuse /səˈfjuːz; səˋfjuz/ *v* [Tn, Tn·pr esp passive 尤用于被动语态] **~ sth (with sth)** (esp of colour or moisture) spread all over sth (尤指颜色或水气)弥漫于某物, 布满, 充满: *A blush suffused his cheeks.* 他瞬间满脸通红. ○ *The evening sky was suffused with crimson.* 黄昏时分天空红霞灿灿. ▷ **suf·fu·sion** /səˈfjuːʒn; səˋfjuʒən/ *n* [U].

sugar /ˈʃʊgə(r); ˋʃʊgɚ/ *n* **1** (a) [U] sweet substance obtained from the juices of various plants, used in cooking and for sweetening tea, coffee, etc 食糖: *Don't eat too much sugar.* 糖不要吃得太多. ○ *Do you take sugar?* ie Do you have it in your tea, etc? 你要放糖吗(你喝茶等加糖吗)? ○ [attrib 作定语] *a sugar plantation,* *refinery, bowl* 糖料作物种植园、炼糖厂、糖罐. (**b**) [C] cube or teaspoonful of sugar 一块方糖; 一茶匙糖: *Two sugars in my coffee, please!* 请在我的咖啡里放两块方糖! **2** (*infml* 口 *esp US*) (used as a form of address to sb one likes 用作亲热的称呼语): *Hello, sugar, nice to see you!* 喂, 亲爱的, 见到你真高兴!

▷ **sugar** *v* [Tn] **1** sweeten or coat (sth) with sugar 在(某物)中加糖; 给(某物)裹上糖衣: *Is this tea sugared?* 这茶放糖了吗? ○ *sugared almonds* 糖衣杏仁. **2** (idm 习语) ˌ**sugar**/ˌ**sweeten the** ˈ**pill** ⇨ PILL.

sug·ary /ˈʃʊɡərɪ; ˈʃʊɡərɪ/ *adj* **1** tasting of sugar; sweet 甜的; 含糖的: *sugary tea* 甜茶. **2** (*fig derog* 比喻, 贬) too sentimental or flattering 甜情蜜意的; 甜言蜜语的: *a sugary love scene in a film* 电影中柔情蜜意的爱情场面. **sug·ari·ness** *n* [U].

□ ˈ**sugar-beet** *n* [U] vegetable from whose large round roots sugar is made 甜菜; 糖萝卜.

ˈ**sugar-cane** *n* [U] tall tropical grass from which sugar is made 甘蔗.

ˌ**sugar-**ˈ**coated** *adj* **1** coated with sugar 有糖衣的; 裹糖的. **2** (*fig derog* 比喻, 贬) made to seem attractive 巧为粉饰的; 表面上吸引人的: *a* ˌ*sugar-coated* ˈ*promise* 甜言蜜语的许诺.

ˈ**sugar-daddy** *n* (*infml* 口) rich man who is generous to a younger woman, usu in return for sexual favours 对年轻女子慷慨的阔男子(通常为换取性方面的好处).

ˈ**sugar-lump** *n* small cube of sugar, used to sweeten tea, coffee, etc 方糖.

ˈ**sugar-maple** *n* N American maple tree, the sap of which is used to make sugar and syrup 糖槭(产于北美洲, 树汁可制糖和糖浆).

ˈ**sugar-tongs** *n* [pl] small tongs for picking up lumps of sugar at table (餐桌上用的)方糖夹子: *a pair of sugar-tongs* 一把方糖夹子.

sug·gest /səˈdʒest; *US* səɡˈdʒ-; səɡˈdʒɛst/ *v* **1** (**a**) [Tn, Tn·pr, Tf, Tw, Tg, Cn·n/a] **~ sb (for sth)**; **~ sb/sth (as sth)** put sth/sb forward for consideration 提出某事物[某人]供考虑; 提议; 建议: *I suggest a tour of the museum.* 我提议去参观博物馆. ○ *Whom would you suggest for the job?* 你建议由谁来做这工作? ○ *I wrote suggesting that he should come for the weekend.* 我写信请他来度周末. ○ *Can you suggest how we might tackle the problem?* 我们怎样处理这问题, 你能给出个主意吗? ○ *He suggested taking the children to the zoo.* 他提议带孩子们去动物园. ○ *I suggest Paris as a good place for a honeymoon.* 我提议去巴黎, 那是度蜜月的好去处. (**b**) [Dn·pr, Dpr·f, Dpr·w] **~ sth to sb** propose sth to sb 向某人提议某事物: *What did you suggest to the manager?* 你向经理提了什么建议? ○ *I suggested to him that we should tackle the problem another way.* 我向他建议我们用另一种方式处理这个问题. **2** [Tn, Tf, Dn·pr, Dpr·f] **~ sth (to sb)** put (an idea, etc) into sb's mind 使某人想到(某事物): *Which illness do these symptoms suggest (to you)?* 这些症状(照你看来)像是什么病? ○ *His cool response suggested that he didn't like the idea.* 他反应冷淡表明他并不喜欢这个主意. **3** [Tn, Tf] state (sth) indirectly; imply 间接表明(某事物); 暗示; 意味着: *'Are you suggesting that I'm not telling the truth?' 'I wouldn't suggest such a thing for a moment.'* '你的意思是不是说我没说实话?' '我没有那个意思.' **4** [Tn, Tn·pr] **~ itself (to sb)** come into sb's mind; occur to sb 出现在心头; 想到: *I tried to think what could have happened, but nothing suggested itself.* 我尽力回想到底出了什么事, 但什么也想不起来. ○ *An idea suggests itself to me.* 我想起一个主意来.

▷ **sug·gest·ible** /-əbl; -əbl̩/ *adj* easily influenced 易受影响的: *I did many stupid things when I was young and suggestible.* 我年轻时受外界的影响做过不少傻事. **sug·gest·ib·il·ity** /səˌdʒestəˈbɪlətɪ; *US* səɡˌdʒ-; səɡˌdʒɛstəˈbɪlətɪ/ *n* [U].

sug·gest·ive /-ɪv; -ɪv/ *adj* **1 ~ (of sth)** putting particular ideas or associations into sb's mind 提示的; 暗示的; 引起联想的: *an aroma suggestive of spring flowers* 使人想起春天的花朵的一种香气 ○ *a complex, suggestive poem* 意蕴很深的、予人以丰富联想的诗篇. **2** making sb think of improper (esp sexual) things 使人产生邪念(尤指淫乱思想)的: *He gave her a suggestive glance, and she blushed.* 他用挑逗的目光看了她一眼, 羞得她满脸通红. **sug·gest·ively** *adv*.

sug·ges·tion /səˈdʒestʃən; *US* səɡˈdʒ-; səɡˈdʒɛstʃən/ *n* **1** [U] suggesting (SUGGEST 1) or being suggested 提议; 建议: *On/At your suggestion* (ie Because you suggested it) *I bought the more expensive model.* 遵照你的建议, 我买了较贵的这种型号. **2** [C] **~ (that...)** idea, plan, etc or person that is suggested 提议或建议的内容(主意、计划、人选等): *I want suggestions about what to do today.* 今天做什么, 我想听听有何意见. ○ *Janet was my first suggestion as chairperson.* 珍妮特是我推荐可任主席的第一人选. ○ *There's no suggestion that she should resign,* ie That would be completely unthinkable. 没有任何迹象显示她要辞职. **3** [C usu *sing* 通常作单数] slight amount (of sth that can be detected) 微量; 征象: *speak English with the suggestion of a French accent* 说英语稍带法国口音. **4** [U] putting an idea, etc into sb's mind through linking it to other ideas, pictures, etc 暗示; 联想: *Most advertisements work through suggestion.* 广告多通过启发人的联想力而发挥作用.

sui·cide /ˈsuːɪsaɪd; *also, in British use,* 英式英语读作 ˈsjuː-; ˈsuəˌsaɪd/ *n* **1** (**a**) [U] killing oneself intentionally 自杀: *commit suicide* 自杀 ○ *four cases of suicide* 四起自杀案件. (**b**) [C] act of this 自杀行为: *three suicides in one week* 一周中的三起自杀事件. **2** [C] person who commits suicide 自杀者. **3** [U] (*fig* 比喻) any action that may have serious consequences for oneself 给自己带来严重后果的行为: *political suicide,* ie action by a politician that will ruin his career 政治上的自杀(政治家自毁前程) ○ *economic suicide,* eg adopting policies that will ruin the economy 经济上的自杀(如施行导致经济崩溃的政策).

▷ **sui·cidal** /ˌsuːɪˈsaɪdl; *also, in British use,* 英式英语读作 ˌsjuː-; ˌsuəˈsaɪdl̩/ *adj* **1** of suicide; likely to lead to suicide 自杀的; 可能导致自杀的: *suicidal tendencies* 自杀倾向 ○ *in a suicidal state* 处于可能自杀的状态. **2** (of a person) likely to commit suicide (指人)有自杀倾向的: *She's feeling suicidal today.* 她今天想自杀. **3** likely to lead to one's ruin 可能导致自我毁灭的: *a suicidal policy* 自取灭亡的政策. **sui·cid·ally** /-dəlɪ; -dlɪ/ *adv*: *suicidally depressed* 抑郁消沉得想自杀.

S

suit[1] /suːt; *also, in British use,* 英式英语读作 sjuːt; sut/ *n* **1** (**a**) set of outer garments of the same material, usu a jacket and trousers for a man and a jacket and skirt for a woman (同一料子的)一套外衣(通常指男子的短上衣和裤子, 或女子的短上衣和裙子): *a* ˈ*business suit* 一套西装 ○ *a* ˌ*pin-stripe* ˈ*lounge suit* 一套细条纹西装 ○ *a two-/*ˌ*three-piece* ˈ*suit,* ie of two/three garments 两[三]件式套装 ○ *a* ˈ*dress suit,* ie a man's formal evening suit 男子的晚礼服 ○ *a* ˈ*trouser-suit,* ie a woman's suit of jacket and trousers 长裤套装(包括短上衣和裤子的女装). (**b**) set of clothing for a particular activity (为某活动的)套装: *a* ˈ*spacesuit* 宇航服 ○ *a* ˈ*diving suit* 潜水服 ○ *an as*ˈ*bestos suit,* eg to protect sb from heat 石棉服(如用以隔热) ○ *a* ˌ*suit of* ˈ*armour* 一套盔甲. **2** any of the four sets (ie *spades, hearts, clubs, diamonds*) forming a pack of playing-cards (组成一副纸牌的)四种花色(即黑桃、红桃、梅花、方块)的牌中的任何一种. ⇨illus at PLAYING-CARD 见 PLAYING-CARD 插图. **3** (also ˈ**lawsuit**) case in a lawcourt; legal proceedings 诉讼案件; 法律程序: *file/bring a suit against sb* 对某人提起诉讼 ○ *a criminal/civil suit* 刑事[民事]诉讼 ○ *a divorce suit* 离婚诉讼. **4** (*fml* 文) request made to a person in authority, esp a ruler (向权威人物, 尤指当权者提的)请求, 恳求: *grant sb's suit* 答应某人的请求 ○ *press one's suit,* ie beg persistently 执意恳求. **5** (idm 习语) **follow suit** ⇨ FOLLOW. **in one's birthday suit** ⇨ BIRTHDAY. **one's/sb's strong suit** ⇨ STRONG.

▷ **-suited** (forming compound *adjs* 用以构成复合形容词) wearing a suit of the specified kind 穿着一套某类服装的: *sober-suited city businessmen.*

suit·ing *n* [U] material for making suits 套装衣料: *serge suiting* 哔叽套装衣料.

□ ˈ**suitcase** *n* case with flat sides, used for carrying clothes, etc when travelling 手提衣箱; 小提箱. ⇨illus at LUGGAGE 见 LUGGAGE 插图.

suit[2] /suːt; *also, in British use,* 英式英语读作 sjuːt; sut/ *v* **1** [Tn] (esp of clothes, hairstyles, etc) look attractive on (sb) (尤指衣服、发型等)适合于(某人): *Does this skirt suit me?* 这裙子我穿着好看吗? ○ *It doesn't suit you to have your hair cut short.* 你不适合剪短发. ○ *That colour* *doesn't suit your complexion.* 那颜色不适合你的肤色. **2** (**a**) [I, Tn] be convenient for or acceptable to (sb) 对(某人)方便; 合(某人)的心意: *Will Thursday suit (you)?* 星期四(对你)方便吗? ○ *The seven o'clock train will suit us very well.* 七点钟那一班火车对我们很合适. ○ *If you want to go by bus, that suits me fine.* 你要是想坐公共汽车去, 那对我很方便. ○ *Would it suit you to come at five?* 你五点钟来行吗? (**b**) [Tn] (usu in negative sentences 通常用于否定句) be right or beneficial for (sb/sth) 对(某人[某事物])合适或有利: *This climate doesn't suit me.* 这种气候对我很不相宜. ○ *Very spicy food doesn't suit my stomach,* ie makes me feel ill. 太辣的东西我吃了胃部不舒服. **3** [Tn] **~ oneˈself** (*infml* 口) act according to one's own wishes 随自己的意愿行事: *You don't want to join the club? Oh well, suit yourself.* 你不愿意参加俱乐部是吗? 那好, 随你的便吧. **4** [Tn·pr] **~ sth to sth/sb** make sth appropriate for sth/sb; adapt sth to sth/sb 使某事物适合于某事物[某人]: *suit the punishment to the crime* 使罚当其罪 ○ *suit the play to the audience* 使话剧迎合观众的口味. **5** (idm 习语) **suit one's/sb's book** (*infml* 口) be convenient or acceptable to sb 对某人方便; 合某人的心意: *It suits my book if I never have to go there again.* 若是我再也不用去那里了, 那真是求之不得呢. **suit sb ˌdown to the ˈground** (*infml* 口) be very convenient or appropriate for sb 对某人非常方便或合适: *I've found a job that suits me down to the ground.* 我找到了一份工作, 对我再合适不过了.

▷ **suited** *adj* [pred 作表语] **~ (for/to sb/sth)** suitable or appropriate (for sb/sth) 适合(于某人[某事物]): *He is better suited to a job with older pupils.* 他较适合教小学高年级学生. ○ *He and his wife are well suited (to each other).* 他和妻子十分般配.

S

suit·able /ˈsu:təbl; *also, in British use,* 英式英语读作 ˈsju:t-; ˋsutəbl/ *adj* **~ (for/to sth/sb)** right or appropriate for a purpose or an occasion 适合的; 适宜的; 恰当的: *a suitable room, book, proposal, date* 合适的房间、书、建议、日期 ○ *clothes suitable for cold weather* 适于冷天穿的衣服 ○ *a place suitable for a picnic* 适合野餐的地方 ○ *a suitable case for* (eg surgical, psychiatric, etc) *treatment* 适于(如外科、精神病等)治疗的病人 ○ *Would now be a suitable moment to show the slides?* 现在放幻灯片合适吗? ▷ **suit·ab·il·ity** /ˌsu:təˈbɪlətɪ; ˌsutəˋbɪlətɪ/, **suit·able·ness** *ns* [U].

suit·ably /-əblɪ; -əblɪ/ *adv*: *go to a party suitably dressed* 穿着得体去参加聚会.

suite /swi:t; swit/ *n* **1** set of matching pieces of furniture 一套家具: *a three-piece suite,* eg two armchairs and a sofa 三件一套的家具(如两张单座沙发和一张长沙发) ○ *a dining-room suite,* ie a table, chairs, and often a sideboard 一套饭厅用的家具(一张桌子, 几把椅子, 常包括餐具柜). **2** (**a**) set of rooms, eg (in a hotel) a bedroom, sitting-room and bathroom 一套房间, 套间(如旅馆的)(包括卧室、起居室和浴室等): *the honeymoon/bridal suite,* ie for a honeymoon couple in a hotel 蜜月[新婚]套间(旅馆中专为新婚夫妇设的). (**b**) (*US*) apartment; flat 一套公寓. **3** complete set of objects used together 一套物件: *a suite of programs for a computer* 计算机的一组程序. **4** (*music* 音) piece of music consisting of three or more related parts 组曲(由至少三个相关乐章组成的). **5** group of people attending an important person, eg a ruler; retinue (一批)随员, 随从, 侍从.

suitor /ˈsu:tə(r); *also, in British use,* 英式英语读作 ˈsju:-; ˋsutɚ/ *n* (*dated* 旧) man courting a woman 追求某女子的人: *She had rejected all her many suitors.* 她拒绝了所有追求她的人.

sulf·ate (*US*) = SULPHATE.

sulf·ide (*US*) = SULPHIDE.

sul·fur (*US*) = SULPHUR.

sulk /sʌlk; sʌlk/ *v* [I, Ipr] **~ (about/over sth)** (*derog* 贬) be silent or unsociable as a result of bad temper or resentment (因发脾气)不答理人; 生闷气: *He's been sulking for days about being left out of the team.* 他嗔怪队里没要他, 连日生着闷气.

▷ **the sulks** *n* [pl] (*infml* 口) fit of sulking 生闷气: *have (a fit of) the sulks* 生(一阵)闷气.

sulky *adj* (**-ier, -iest**) having or showing a tendency to sulk (爱)生闷气的: *a sulky person, look, mood* 生着闷气的人、样子、心情. **sulk·ily** /-ɪlɪ; -ɪlɪ/ *adv*. **sulki·ness** *n* [U].

sul·len /ˈsʌlən; ˋsʌlən/ *adj* (*derog* 贬) **1** silent, bad-tempered and gloomy 不答理人的; 脾气坏的; 闷闷不乐的: *a sullen person, look* 郁郁寡欢的人、样子 ○ *All my attempts to amuse the children were met with sullen scowls.* 我想尽办法哄这些孩子玩儿, 但是他们总是满脸不高兴. **2** (*esp rhet* 尤作修辞) dark and gloomy; dismal 阴沉的; 阴郁的: *a sullen sky* 阴沉的天空. ▷ **sul·lenly** *adv*. **sul·len·ness** *n* [U].

sully /ˈsʌlɪ; ˋsʌlɪ/ *v* (*pt, pp* **sullied**) [Tn] (*fml or rhet usu fig* 文或修辞, 通常作比喻) make (sth) dirty; stain; ruin or destroy (sb's reputation, etc) 弄脏(某物); 玷污或破坏(某人的名声等): *I wouldn't sully my hands by accepting a bribe.* 我决不接受贿赂, 一尘不染. ○ *sully sb's name, honour, etc* 玷污某人的名声、荣誉等.

sulpha drug (*US* **sulfa drug**) /ˈsʌlfə drʌg; ˋsʌlfəˌdrʌg/ = SULPHONAMIDE.

sulph·ate (*US* **sulf·ate**) /ˈsʌlfeɪt; ˋsʌlfet/ *n* [C, U] compound of sulphuric acid and another chemical 硫酸盐; 硫酸酯: *copper sulphate* 硫酸铜.

sulph·ide (*US* **sulf·ide**) /ˈsʌlfaɪd; ˋsʌlfaɪd/ *n* [C, U] compound of sulphur and another element 硫化物.

sul·phon·am·ide (*US* **sulfo-**, **sulpha drug**) /sʌlˈfɒnəmaɪd; sʌlˋfɑnəmaɪd/ *n* any of a group of chemical compounds which are used to kill bacteria 磺胺类药.

sul·phur (*US* **sul·fur**) /ˈsʌlfə(r); ˋsʌlfɚ/ *n* [U] chemical element, a light-yellow non-metallic solid that burns with a bright flame and a strong smell, used in medicine and industry 硫; 硫磺. ⇨App 10 见附录10.

▷ **sul·phur·et·ted** (*US* **sul·fur-**) /ˈsʌlfjʊretɪd; ˋsʌlfjʊˌretɪd/ *adj* [attrib 作定语] (of a compound) containing sulphur (指化合物)硫化的: *sulphuretted hydrogen,* ie hydrogen sulphide 硫化氢.

sul·phuric (*US* **sul·fu-**) /sʌlˈfjʊərɪk; sʌlˋfjʊrɪk/ *adj* containing a proportion of sulphur 含硫的. **sulphuric acid** type of very strong corrosive acid 硫酸.

sul·phur·ous (*US* **sul·fu-**) /ˈsʌlfərəs; ˋsʌlfərəs/ *adj* **1** of or like sulphur (似)硫的: *a sulphurous smell coming from the laboratory* 实验室散发出来的硫磺气味 ○ *the volcano's sulphurous fumes* 火山冒出的硫化蒸气. **2** containing a proportion of sulphur 含硫的.

sul·tan /ˈsʌltən; ˋsʌltn̩/ *n* sovereign ruler of certain Muslim countries 苏丹(某些穆斯林国家的最高统治者): *the Sultan of Brunei* 文莱国的苏丹.

▷ **sul·tan·ate** /ˈsʌltəneɪt; ˋsʌltn̩et/ *n* **1** position or period of rule of a sultan 苏丹的地位或统治期. **2** territory ruled by a sultan 苏丹统治的领土: *the Sultanate of Oman* 阿曼国苏丹统治的领土.

sul·tana /sʌlˈtɑ:nə; *US* -ænə; sʌlˋtænə/ *n* **1** small seedless raisin used in puddings and cakes 一种无子的小葡萄干(做布丁和糕饼用). **2** wife, mother, sister or daughter of a sultan 苏丹的女眷(妻室、母亲、姐妹或女儿).

sul·try /ˈsʌltrɪ; ˋsʌltrɪ/ *adj* (**-ier, -iest**) **1** (of the weather, air, etc) oppressively hot and humid (指天气、空气等)湿热难耐的, 闷热的: *a sultry summer afternoon* 夏天的一个闷热的下午. **2** (of a woman or her looks) darkly and sensually beautiful (指女子或其神态)隐现肉体美的: *a sultry smile* 迷人的微笑 ○ *a sultry Mexican beauty* 标致的墨西哥美人. ▷ **sul·trily** /-trəlɪ; -trɪlɪ/ *adv*. **sul·tri·ness** *n* [U].

sum /sʌm; sʌm/ *n* **1** [C often *pl* 常作复数] arithmetical calculation 算术: *do a sum in one's head* 做心算 ○ *be good at sums* 擅长算术. **2** [C] **~ (of sth)** amount of money 金额; 款项: *He was fined the sum of £200.* 他被处以200英镑罚金. ○ *Huge sums have been invested in this project.* 在这个项目中投入了大量资金. **3** (**a**) [C *usu sing* 通常作单数] **~ (of sth)** total obtained by adding together numbers, amounts or items 总数; 总和: *The sum of 5 and 3 is 8.* 5加3的和是8. (**b**) [sing] (*also* **ˌsum ˈtotal**) **the ~ of sth** all of sth, esp when it is considered as not being enough 总共, 全部(尤含数量不足之意): *Is that the sum of what you've done in the last two years?* 这就是你最近两年中完成的全部数量吗? **4** (idm 习语) **in ˈsum** (*dated* 旧) in a few words 简言之; 总而言之: *In sum, the plan failed.* 总之, 计划告吹了.

▷ **sum** *v* (**-mm-**) (phr v) **sum (sth) up** (**a**) give a brief summary (of sth) 总结, 概括(某事物): *Now sum*

up (your views) in a few words. 现在(把你的观点)用几句话来概括一下. (**b**) (of a judge) summarize the evidence or arguments in a legal case (指法官)归纳证词或双方论点. **sum sb/sth up** form an opinion of sb/sth 形成对某人[某事物]的看法: *I summed her up as a competent manager.* 我认为她是个很能干的经理. ○ *He summed up the situation at a glance*, ie realized at once what was happening. 他一眼就看清了当时的情况.
ˌsumming-ˈup *n* (*pl* **summings-up**) speech in which a judge sums up the evidence or arguments in a legal case (讼案中法官对证词或辩论情况做的)概述.
□ **ˌsum ˈtotal 1** final total, esp as formed by adding other totals together 总数, 总额(尤指各总数相加的). **2** = SUM 3b.

sum·mary /ˈsʌmərɪ; ˋsʌmərɪ/ *n* **1** brief statement of the main points of sth 总结; 摘要; 概要: *a two-page summary of a government report* 共两页的政府报告摘要 ○ *Here is a summary of the news/a news summary.* 以下是新闻摘要. **2** (idm 习语) **in ˈsummary** as a brief statement of the main point(s) 总的说来; 归纳起来: *And so I would say, in summary, that the campaign has been a great success.* 因此我认为, 总的看来, 这场运动成绩很大.
▷ **sum·mary** *adj* [usu attrib 通常作定语] **1** (*sometimes derog* 有时作贬义) done or given immediately, without attention to details or formal procedure 即刻作出或给予的(未顾及细节或正常程序): *summary justice, punishment, methods* 即决裁判、当场的处罚、简易的方法 ○ *Such an offence will lead to a summary fine.* 这类过错要当场予以罚款. **2** giving the main points only; brief 概括的; 扼要的; 简明的: *a summary account of a long debate* 对一长时的辩论的概述. **sum·mar·ily** /ˈsʌmərəlɪ; *US* səˈmerəlɪ; səˋmɛrəlɪ/ *adv*: *summarily dismissed* 立即开除.
sum·mar·ize, -ise /ˈsʌməraɪz; ˋsʌməˌraɪz/ *v* [I, Tn] be or make a summary of (sth) 总结, 概括(某事物): *a talk summarizing recent trends in philosophy* 概述当前哲学界动态的讲话.

sum·ma·tion /sʌˈmeɪʃn; sʌmˋeʃən/ *n* (*fml* 文) **1** summing-up; summary 总结; 概括: *begin a summation of the evidence presented* 对提供的证词进行总结. **2** addition 加(法): *do a rapid summation of the figures* 把数字很快加起来. **3** gathering together of different parts to form a representative whole (各部分聚集一起而形成的)有代表性的整体: *The exhibition was a summation of his life's work.* 这次展览汇集了他一生中典型的作品.

sum·mer /ˈsʌmə(r); ˋsʌmɚ/ *n* [U, C] **1** the second and warmest season of the year outside the tropics, coming between spring and autumn, ie from June to August in the northern hemisphere 夏; 夏天; 夏季: *In (the) summer we go on holiday.* 夏天我们常去度假. ○ *in the summer of 1979* 在1979年的夏季 ○ *this/next/last summer* 今年[明年/去年]夏天 ○ *a cool, hot, wet, etc summer* 凉爽的、炎热的、多雨的…夏天 ○ *a lovely summer's day* 夏日晴朗的一天 ○ (*rhet* 修辞) *a girl of ten summers*, ie ten years of age 十岁的女孩儿 ○ [attrib 作定语] *summer weather* 夏季的天气 ○ *the summer holidays* 暑假 ○ *a summer cottage*, ie for use during the summer 消夏的小屋舍. **2** (idm 习语) **an Indian summer** ⇨ INDIAN. **one swallow does not make a summer** ⇨ SWALLOW[2].
▷ **sum·mery** /ˈsʌmərɪ; ˋsʌmərɪ/ *adj* typical of or suitable for the summer 夏季的; 适合夏季的: *a summery day* 夏季的一天 ○ *a summery dress* 夏天穿的连衣裙.
□ **ˈsummer-house** *n* small hut with seats in a garden, park, etc, providing shade in the summer (花园、公园等的)凉亭.
ˌsummer ˈpudding (*Brit*) pudding of fruits such as raspberries and currants pressed into a case of bread 夏令布丁(用悬钩子和无子小葡萄干等做的点心).
ˈsummer school course of lectures, etc held in the summer vacation, esp at a university 暑期学校; (尤指大学开办的)暑期班.
ˈsummer-time *n* [U] season of summer 夏季: *It's beautiful here in (the) summer-time.* 夏天这里很美.
ˈsummer time (*Brit*) (*US* **ˈfast time**) time kept one hour in advance of the actual time during summer, giving long light evenings 夏令时间. Cf 参看 DAYLIGHT SAVING (DAYLIGHT).

sum·mit /ˈsʌmɪt; ˋsʌmɪt/ *n* **1** highest point; top, esp of a mountain 最高点; 顶点; (尤指)山顶: *climb to the summit* 登上山顶 ○ (*fig* 比喻) *the summit of her career, ambition, etc* 她事业的颠峰、最大的抱负等. ⇨illus at MOUNTAIN 见MOUNTAIN插图. **2** meeting between the heads of two or more governments, esp of the world's most powerful countries 最高级会议(政府首脑间的, 尤指强国的): *attend a summit in Washington* 出席在华盛顿召开的最高级会议 ○ [attrib 作定语] *a summit talk/meeting/conference* 最高级会谈[会晤/会议] ○ *the summit powers* 参加最高级会议的强国.

sum·mon /ˈsʌmən; ˋsʌmən/ *v* **1** (**a**) [Tn, Tn·pr, Tn·p, Dn·t] **~ sb (to sth)**; **~ sb (together)** send a message telling sb to come; call (people) together 召唤某人; 召集(大家): *I was summoned by my boss (to explain my actions).* 老板把我召去(要我对自己的行为做出解释). ○ *The shareholders were summoned to a general meeting.* 已召集了股东开全体大会. ○ *Summon the pupils together in the school hall.* 把学生召集到学校的礼堂里. (**b**) [Tn, Dn·t] order (sb) to attend a lawcourt; summons (sb) 传唤(某人)出庭; 召唤(某人): *The debtor was summoned (to appear before the magistrates).* (地方法官)已传唤债务人出庭. **2** [Tn] order a group of people to attend (a meeting, etc) 召开(会议等): *summon a conference* 召开会议 ○ *The Queen has summoned Parliament.* 女王已召集了议会开会. **3** [Tn, Tn·p] **~ sth (up)** force (a particular quality) to come as if from deep inside oneself, in an attempt to do sth 发挥出(某品性)来做某事: *summon (up) one's courage for the battle* 鼓起勇气进行战斗 ○ *I had to summon (up) all my nerve to face my boss.* 我得鼓足勇气去见上司. ○ *I can't summon up much enthusiasm for the project.* 这计划引不起我多大兴趣. **4** (phr v) **summon sth up** cause sth to come into the mind; evoke sth 使某事物浮现于脑际; 唤起某事物: *a smell which summons up memories of my childhood* 使我回忆起童年往事的一种气味.

S

sum·mons /ˈsʌmənz; ˋsʌmənz/ *n* (*pl* **~es**) **1** (**a**) order to attend a lawcourt, esp to answer a charge 传唤, 传讯(尤指对指控进行答辩): *issue a summons* 发出传讯命令. (**b**) document containing this (法院的)传票: *The summons was served by a bailiff.* 该传票已由法警送达. **2** order to do sth, esp to come to sb 命令(尤指来到某人处): *You must obey the king's summons.* 你必须奉诏觐见国王.
▷ **sum·mons** *v* [Tn, Tn·pr, Dn·t] **~ sb (for sth)** order sb to attend a lawcourt 传唤某人到庭; 传讯某人: *He was summonsed for speeding.* 他因超速行驶而被传讯出庭.

sump /sʌmp; sʌmp/ *n* **1** casing under an engine holding the lubricating oil (发动机下面的)润滑油箱. **2** cavity or hollow area into which waste liquid drains 污水坑; 聚水坑.

sump·tu·ous /ˈsʌmptʃʊəs; ˋsʌmptʃʊəs/ *adj* looking expensive and splendid 华贵的; 豪华的; 奢华的: *a sumptuous feast* 盛宴 ○ *sumptuous clothes* 华贵的服装.
▷ **sump·tu·ously** *adv*. **sump·tu·ous·ness** *n* [U].

sun /sʌn; sʌn/ *n* **1** (also **the sun**) [sing] the star around which the earth orbits and from which it receives light and warmth 太阳; 日: *the sun's rays* 太阳的光线 ○ *sending a space probe to the sun* 向太阳发射一个航天探测器 ○ *A watery sun shone through the rain-clouds.* 太阳透过雨云发出有雨意的光. **2** (also **the sun**) [sing, U] light and warmth from the sun; sunshine 太阳的光和热; 日光; 阳光: *sit in the sun* 坐在阳光下 ○ *have the sun in one's eyes* 阳光照眼 ○ *draw the curtains to shut out/let in the sun* 拉窗帘遮蔽[放进]阳光 ○ *I like lots of sun on holiday.* 我喜欢在假日里多晒太阳. **3** [C] any star, esp one around which planets orbit 星体; (尤指)恒星: *There are many suns larger than ours.* 有许多恒星比我们的太阳还要大. **4** (idm 习语) **catch the sun** ⇨ CATCH[1]. **make hay while the sun shines** ⇨ HAY. **a place in the sun** ⇨ PLACE[1]. **under the ˈsun** (anywhere) in the world 在世界上(任何地方): *the best wine under the sun* 世界上最好的酒 ○ *every country under the sun* 世界上每一个国家. **with the ˈsun** at dawn or sunset 在日出或日落时; 在黎明或傍晚时分: *get up/go to bed with the sun* 黎明即起[日落而息].
▷ **sun** *v* (**-nn-**) [Tn] **ˈ~ oneself** expose oneself to the rays of the sun 晒太阳: *He sat in a deck-chair ˈsunning himself.* 他坐在帆布躺椅上晒太阳.

sun·less *adj* without sunshine; receiving little or no sunlight 无阳光的；阳光不足的；晒不到太阳的：*a sunless day, room* 阴天、无阳光的房间.

sunny *adj* (**-ier**, **-iest**) **1** bright with sunlight; receiving much sunlight 阳光充足的；阳光很强的：*a sunny day, room, garden* 晴朗的一天、向阳的房间、阳光充足的花园. **2** (*fig* 比喻) cheerful 快活的；愉快的：*a sunny smile, disposition, welcome* 快活的微笑、性情、欢迎 ○ *She always looks on the sunny side*, ie is optimistic. 她总是看到光明的一面(即很乐观). **sun·nily** /-ɪlɪ; -ɪlɪ/ *adv*. **sun·ni·ness** *n* [U]. ˌ**sunny-side** ˈ**up** (*US*) (of an egg) fried on one side only (指蛋)只煎一面的.

□ ˈ**sun-baked** *adj* (**a**) made hard by the heat of the sun (太阳)晒硬或晒干的：*sun-baked mud, fields, etc* 晒硬的泥土、晒干的田地. (**b**) receiving much sunlight; very sunny 阳光充足的；阳光很强的：*sun-baked beaches* 烈日下的海滩.

ˈ**sunbathe** *v* [I] expose one's body to the sun, eg to become sun-tanned 晒太阳；沐日光浴.

ˈ**sunbeam** *n* ray of sunshine 日光；阳光.

ˈ**sun-blind** *n* curtain, awning, etc that stops sunlight coming through a window (阻止阳光进入窗内的)遮帘，遮篷，遮挡物.

ˈ**sunburn** *n* [U] reddening and blistering of the skin caused by being in the sun too much 晒伤的皮肤；晒斑. Cf 参看 SUN-TAN. **sunburned**, **sunburnt** /ˈsʌnbɜːnt; ˈsʌnˌbɝnt/ *adjs* (**a**) suffering from sunburn 皮肤晒伤的：*sunburnt shoulders* 晒伤的肩膀. (**b**) sun-tanned 晒黑的.

sundial 日晷

sundial /ˈsʌndaɪəl; ˈsʌnˌdaɪəl/ *n* device showing the time on a clock-like dial by means of a pointer whose shadow moves as the sun moves across the sky 日规；日晷(仪).

ˈ**sundown** *n* [U] (*esp US*) sunset 日落(时分).

ˈ**sundowner** *n* **1** (*Austral* 澳) tramp who usu arrives (at a sheep farm, etc) at sunset, looking for a place to sleep 通常于日落时分赶到(牧羊场等处)找地方过夜的流浪者. **2** (*Brit infml* 口) (usu alcoholic) drink taken at sunset (通常含酒精的)傍晚喝的饮料.

ˈ**sun-drenched** *adj* (*approv* 褒) receiving great heat and light from the sun 充满阳光的：*sun-drenched beaches along the Riviera* 里维埃拉一带阳光充足的海滩.

ˈ**sunfish** *n* large sea fish that is almost round, like a ball 太阳鱼(海中的一种大鱼，体圆如球).

ˈ**sunflower** *n* tall garden plant having large flowers with yellow petals round a dark centre 向日葵：[attrib 作定语] *sunflower seeds, oil* 葵花子、葵花子油.

ˈ**sun-glasses** *n* [pl] glasses with dark lenses to protect the wearer's eyes from bright sunlight 太阳眼镜；墨镜：*a pair of sun-glasses* 一副墨镜.

ˈ**sun-god** *n* the sun worshipped as a god 太阳神.

ˈ**sun-hat** *n* hat made to shade the head and neck from sunlight 太阳帽；遮阳帽.

ˈ**sun-lamp** *n* lamp producing ultra-violet light, with effects like those of sunlight, used eg for tanning the body 太阳灯(能产生紫外线的).

ˈ**sunlight** *n* [U] light of the sun 日光；太阳光.

ˈ**sunlit** *adj* [usu attrib 通常作定语] lighted by the sun 阳光照耀的；被阳光照射的：*a sunlit garden, scene, landscape* 阳光灿烂的花园、景象、景色.

ˈ**sun lounge** (*Brit*) (*US* ˈ**sun parlor**, ˈ**sun porch**) room, veranda, etc with glass sides, and situated so as to receive much sunlight 日光浴室、浴廊等(用玻璃做围墙，以吸收大量阳光).

ˈ**sun-ray** *n* ray of ultra-violet light as used on the body for tanning or for medical reasons (日光浴或医疗所用的)紫外线：[attrib 作定语] *a sun-ray lamp* 紫外线灯 ○ *sun-ray treatment* 紫外线疗法.

ˈ**sunrise** *n* [U] (time of the) rising of the sun; dawn 日出(时分)；黎明：*She got up at sunrise.* 她黎明即起.

ˈ**sunrise industry** new and expanding industry 新兴工业；发展中的工业.

ˈ**sun-roof** *n* (also ˌ**sunshine** ˈ**roof**) panel on the roof of a car that can be opened to let in air and sunshine (汽车的)天窗.

ˈ**sunset** *n* **1** [U] (time of the) setting of the sun 日落(时分)；傍晚：*finish work at sunset* 傍晚时做完工作. **2** [C] appearance of the sky at sunset 落日余辉；晚霞：*the beautiful sunsets in the desert* 沙漠里落日的美景.

ˈ**sunshade** *n* **1** umbrella for protecting sb from hot sunshine 阳伞. Cf 参看 PARASOL. **2** sun-blind 遮阳篷.

ˈ**sunshine** *n* [U] **1** light and heat of the sun 太阳的光和热；阳光：*sitting out in the bright/warm sunshine* 坐在室外灿烂［温暖］的阳光下. **2** (*fig infml* 比喻，口) cheerfulness 快活；愉快：*the loss of her closest friend which took the sunshine out of her life* 她那最亲密友伴的丧生，使她在生活中失去欢愉. **3** (*Brit infml* 口) (used for addressing sb, usu in a cheerful and friendly way 用作称呼语，通常表示快活和友好)：*Hello, sunshine!* 喂，你好! **4** (idm 习语) **a ray of sunshine** ⇨ RAY. ˌ**sunshine** ˈ**roof** = SUN-ROOF.

ˈ**sunspot** *n* **1** (*astronomy* 天) any of the dark patches that sometimes appear on the sun's surface, causing electrical disturbances and interfering with radio communications (太阳)黑子；日斑. **2** (*infml* 口) place that has a sunny climate (eg for holidays) 多阳光的地方(如度假胜地).

ˈ**sunstroke** *n* [U] illness caused by being exposed to the heat and light of the sun too much 日射病；中暑.

ˈ**sun-tan** *n* browning of the skin from exposing it to the sun (皮肤的)晒黑：*get a good sun-tan* 皮肤晒成健美的古铜色 ○ [attrib 作定语] *sun-tan oil, lotion, cream, etc* 防晒油、液、霜等. Cf 参看 SUNBURN. ˈ**sun-tanned** *adj*: *her sun-tanned legs* 她那晒得黑黑的腿.

ˈ**sun-trap** *n* warm sunny place that is sheltered from the wind 向阳避风处.

ˈ**sun-up** *n* [U] (*US infml* 口) sunrise 日出(时分)；黎明.

ˈ**sun-worship** *n* [U] **1** worship of the sun as a god 太阳崇拜(视太阳为神). **2** (*infml* 口) extreme fondness for sun-bathing 极爱日光浴. ˈ**sun-worshipper** *n*.

Sun *abbr* 缩写 = Sunday: *Sun 1 June* 6月1日，星期日.

sun·dae /ˈsʌndeɪ; *US* -diː; ˈsʌndɪ/ *n* dish of ice-cream with crushed fruit, fruit-juice, nuts, etc 三德冰激凌(加有压碎的水果、果汁、果仁等的)：*a peach sundae* 一份桃的三德冰激凌.

Sun·day /ˈsʌndɪ; ˈsʌndɪ/ *n* (*abbr* 缩写 **Sun**) **1** [C, U] the first day of the week (coming before Monday), a day of rest and worship for Christians 星期日；星期天；(基督教徒的)礼拜日. **2** [C usu *pl* 通常作复数] newspaper published on a Sunday 每逢星期日出版的报纸；星期日刊. **3** (idm 习语) **for/in a month of Sundays** ⇨ MONTH. **one's Sunday** ˈ**best** (*infml joc* 口，谑) one's best clothes (自己的衣服中)最好的衣服：*Go to the party in your Sunday best.* 穿上你最好的衣服去参加聚会.

□ ˈ**Sunday school** class held on Sundays at which children receive religious teaching 主日学校(于星期日授课，对儿童进行宗教知识教育).

For the uses of *Sunday* see the examples at *Monday*. 关于Sunday的用法见Monday词条中的示例.

sun·der /ˈsʌndə(r); ˈsʌndɚ/ *v* [Tn, Tn·pr] **~ sth/sb (from sth/sb)** (*fml or rhet* 文或修辞) separate sth/sb, esp by force or for ever 将某事物［某人］分开(尤指强制性地或永久性地).

sun·dry /ˈsʌndrɪ; ˈsʌndrɪ/ *adj* [attrib 作定语] **1** various 不同的；各种的：*on sundry occasions* 在各种场合 ○ *rice, flour and sundry other items of food* 米、面粉及其他各种食物. **2** (idm 习语) ˌ**all and** ˈ**sundry** (*infml* 口) everyone, without discrimination 每个人(一视同仁)：*She invited all and sundry to her party.* 她邀请所有的人都来参加聚会.

▷ **sun·dries** *n* [pl] various (esp small) items not separately named 杂物；杂项：*My expenses claim includes £15 for sundries.* 我的报销申请中包括15英镑杂项支出.

sung *pp* of SING.
sunk *pt, pp* of SINK[1].
sunken /ˈsʌŋkən; ˋsʌŋkən/ *adj* **1** [attrib 作定语] that has gone to the bottom of the sea 沉没海底的: *a sunken ship* 沉船 ○ *sunken treasure* 沉入海底的金银财宝. **2** (of cheeks, etc) hollow as a result of hunger, illness, etc (指面颊等)(因饥饿、疾病等)凹陷的: *the sunken eyes of the dying man* 那垂死男子的凹陷的眼睛. **3** [attrib 作定语] at a lower level than the surrounding area 比周围低的: *a sunken terrace at the bottom of the garden* 在园子尽头低洼处的梯田.
sup /sʌp; sʌp/ *v* **(-pp-)** **1** [Tn, Tn·p] **~ sth (up)** (*Brit dialect* 方) drink sth in small amounts 一点点地喝某物: *They sat supping their beer.* 他们坐着一小口一小口地喝着啤酒. ○ *Come on, sup up your tea.* 来, 把茶喝了吧. **2** [I, Ipr] **~ (on/off sth)** (*arch* 古) eat supper 吃晚饭: *We supped on cold roast beef.* 我们晚饭吃的是凉的烤牛肉.
▷ **sup** *n* (*Brit dialect* 方) small amount of liquid drunk (喝下的)少量饮料: *a sup of ale* 少量麦芽啤酒.
sup *abbr* 缩写 = above; earlier on (in a book, etc) (Latin *supra*) 在上, 在上文中(源自拉丁文 *supra*). Cf 参看 INF.
su·per[1] /ˈsu:pə(r); *also, in British use,* 英式英语读作 ˈsju:-; ˋsupɚ/ *adj* (*infml* 口) excellent; splendid 极好的; 了不起的; 棒的: *a super meal, book, dress* 极好的饭菜、书、连衣裙 ○ *You'll like her, she's super.* 你一定喜欢她, 她好极了.
su·per[2] /ˈsu:pə(r); *also, in British use,* 英式英语读作 ˈsju:-; ˋsupɚ/ (*Brit infml* 口) superintendent, esp in the police force 主管人; 负责人; (尤指)警务长: *the chief super* 警务总长.
super- *pref* 前缀 **1** (**a**) (with *ns* and *vs* 与名词和动词结合) above; over 在…之上; 超过: *superstructure* ○ *superimpose*. (**b**) (with *adjs* and *advs* 与形容词和副词结合) superior to; more than 优于; 超: *superhuman* ○ *supernaturally*. **2** (esp with *adjs* 尤与形容词结合) extremely; very 极端; 非常: *super-intelligent* ○ *super-chic*. **3** (esp with *ns* 尤与名词结合) larger, more efficient, etc than the standard sort 特大的; 特别有效的; 超级的: *superglue* ○ *super-lubricant*. Cf 参看 OVER-.
su·per·abund·ant /ˌsu:pərəˈbʌndənt; *also, in British use,* 英式英语读作 ˌsju:-; ˌsupərəˋbʌndənt/ (*fml* 文) very abundant; more than enough 极多的; 过剩的: *a superabundant harvest* 特大丰收.
▷ **su·per·abund·ance** /-əns; -əns/ *n* [U, sing] **~ (of sth)** (*fml* 文) amount that is more than enough 过多; 过剩: *food in superabundance* 过剩的食物 ○ *a superabundance of fuel* 燃料的过剩.
su·per·an·nu·ate /ˌsu:pəˈrænjʊeɪt; *also, in British use,* 英式英语读作 ˌsju:-; ˌsupɚˋænjʊˌet/ *v* [Tn] send (an employee) into retirement with a pension 使(雇员)退休(有养老金).
▷ **su·per·an·nu·ated** *adj* [usu attrib 通常作定语] (*infml esp joc* 口, 尤作戏谑语) old and barely fit for work or use 年老不适于工作的; 陈旧不宜使用的: *Are you still riding that superannuated old bike?* 你还骑那辆老掉牙的自行车吗?
su·per·an·nu·ation /ˌsu:pəˌrænjʊˈeɪʃn; *also, in British use,* 英式英语读作 ˌsju:-; ˌsupɚˌænjʊˋeʃən/ *n* [U] **1** superannuating 退休(有养老金). **2** (money paid towards a) pension that one gets when one retires 退休金.
su·perb /su:ˈpɜ:b; *also, in British use,* 英式英语读作 sju:-; sʊˋpɝb/ *adj* excellent; splendid 卓越的; 杰出的; 极好的: *a superb player, painting, view* 极好的运动员、画、景色 ○ *The sports facilities are superb.* 运动设施是第一流的.
▷ **su·perbly** *adv*.
su·per·charge /ˈsu:pətʃɑ:dʒ; *also, in British use,* 英式英语读作 ˈsju:-; ˌsupɚˋtʃardʒ/ *v* [Tn] increase the power of (an engine) by supplying air or fuel above the normal pressure 用增压法提高(发动机)的功率: *a supercharged racing-car (engine)* 提高功率的赛车(发动机).
▷ **su·per·char·ger** *n* device that supercharges an engine 增压器.
su·per·cili·ous /ˌsu:pəˈsɪlɪəs; *also, in British use,* 英式英语读作 ˌsju:-; ˌsupɚˋsɪlɪəs/ *adj* (*derog* 贬) thinking or showing that one thinks one is better than other people; arrogant and disdainful 自高自大的; 倨傲不逊的; 目空一切的: *a supercilious person, smile, attitude* 傲慢的人、微笑、态度 ○ *The shop assistant was very supercilious towards me when I asked for some help.* 我要买东西招呼售货员时, 那个售货员对我不屑一顾. ▷ **su·per·cili·ously** *adv*. **su·per·cili·ous·ness** *n* [U].
su·per·con·duct·iv·ity /ˌsu:pəˌkɒndʌkˈtɪvətɪ; *also, in British use,* 英式英语读作 ˌsju:-; ˌsupɚˌkɑndʌkˋtɪvətɪ/ *n* [U] (*physics* 物) property of certain metals, at temperatures near absolute zero, of having no electrical resistance, so that once a current is started it flows without a voltage to keep it going 超导电性.
▷ **su·per·con·ductor** /ˌsu:pəkənˈdʌktə(r); *also, in British use,* 英式英语读作 ˌsju:-; ˌsupɚkənˋdʌktɚ/ *n* metal that possesses superconductivity 超导体.
super-duper /ˌsu:pəˈdu:pə(r); ˋsupɚˋdupɚ/ *adj* (*infml* 口) excellent; splendid 极好的; 了不起的; 棒的: *I've got a super-duper new radio.* 我有一台特别好的新收音机.
super-ego /ˈsu:pəregəʊ; *also, in British use,* 英式英语读作 ˈsju:-; *US* -i:gəʊ; ˌsupɚˋigo/ *n* (*psychology* 心) part of a person's mind which contains a set of rules for right and wrong behaviour, acting as a conscience 超我. Cf 参看 EGO 1, ID.
su·per·fi·cial /ˌsu:pəˈfɪʃl; *also, in British use,* 英式英语读作 ˌsju:-; ˌsupɚˋfɪʃəl/ *adj* **1** of or on the surface only 表面的; 在表面上的: *a superficial wound* 表皮的损伤 ○ *Superficial scratches can be easily removed.* 表层的划痕很容易除掉. **2** apparent when looked at quickly or carelessly, but perhaps not real 表面的(乍看起来的, 未必真实): *a superficial similarity* 表面上的相似. **3** (**a**) not thorough or profound 肤浅的; 浅薄的: *a superficial book, mind* 立论肤浅的书、浅薄无知的头脑 ○ *have only a superficial knowledge of the subject* 对这个问题仅略知皮毛. (**b**) (*derog* 贬) having no depth of character, feeling or commitment (性格、感情或承诺方面)缺乏深度的, 停留在表面的: *You're too superficial to appreciate great literature like this.* 你没有钻劲, 无法欣赏这类文学巨著. ▷ **su·per·fi·ci·al·ity** /ˌsu:pəˌfɪʃɪˈælətɪ; *also, in British use,* 英式英语读作 ˌsju:-; ˌsupɚˌfɪʃɪˋælətɪ/ *n* [U]. **su·per·fi·cially** /-ʃəlɪ; -ʃəlɪ/ *adv*: *only superficially alike* 仅仅表面上相似.
su·per·fine /ˈsu:pəfaɪn; *also, in British use,* 英式英语读作 ˈsju:-; ˌsupɚˋfaɪn/ *adj* extremely or unusually fine in size, texture or quality (规格、质地或质量上)特级的, 最高档的, 精致的, 精制的: *superfine flour, grains* 精制的面粉、谷物 ○ *a superfine needle* 小号缝纫针 ○ *superfine silk* 高档丝绸.
su·per·flu·ous /su:ˈpɜ:flʊəs; *also, in British use,* 英式英语读作 sju:-; sʊˋpɝfluəs/ *adj* more than is needed or wanted 过多的; 过剩的; 多余的; 不必要的: *Repack all the superfluous cups in the box.* 把多余的杯子都重新装入箱中. ○ *The crowd was so well-behaved that the police presence was superfluous.* 群众秩序良好, 警方在场并无必要. ○ *That remark was superfluous*, ie It should not have been made, eg because it contributed nothing or was offensive. 那样的话多余说. ○ *They were only interested in each other, so I felt rather superfluous*, ie felt that I shouldn't be there. 他们只是意在对方, 所以我自觉多余在场.
▷ **su·per·flu·ity** /ˌsu:pəˈflʊətɪ; *also, in British use,* 英式英语读作 ˌsju:-; ˌsupɚˋfluətɪ/ *n* [U, sing] **~ (of sth)** (*fml* 文) superfluous amount 多余的量; 过剩的量: *have food in superfluity/a superfluity of food* 有过剩的食物.
su·per·flu·ously *adv*.
su·per·hu·man /ˌsu:pəˈhju:mən; *also, in British use,* 英式英语读作 ˌsju:-; ˌsupɚˋhjumən/ *adj* exceeding normal human power, size, knowledge, etc (力量、身材、知识等)超乎常人的: *It required superhuman effort to lift the huge boulder.* 要搬起这块大石头需要有超人的力量. ○ *Her intelligence seems almost superhuman.* 她很聪明, 可谓才智超人.
su·per·im·pose /ˌsu:pərɪmˈpəʊz; *also, in British use,* 英式英语读作 ˌsju:-; ˌsupərɪmˋpoz/ *v* [Tn, Tn·pr] **~ sth (on sth)** put sth on top of sth else, esp so that what is underneath can still be seen, heard, etc 将某物置于另一物上(尤指后者仍可见、可闻等): *a map of Great Britain superimposed on a map of Texas*, eg to show comparative size 放在得克萨斯地图上的英国地图(如用以比较大小) ○ *superimpose an English commentary on the original soundtrack* 把英语解说加录到原声带上. ▷ **su·per·im·posi·tion** /ˌsu:pəˌrɪmpəˈzɪʃn; *also, in*

S

British use, 英式英语读作 ˌsjuː-; ˌsupɚˌɪmpəˈzɪʃən/ *n* [U].

su·per·in·tend /ˌsuːpərɪnˈtend; *also, in British use,* 英式英语读作 ˌsjuː-; ˌsupərɪnˈtɛnd/ *v* [Tn] (*fml* 文) manage and control (workers, their work, etc); supervise 管理, 监督(工作人员、工作等); 主管: *appointed to superintend (the staff in) the toy department* 获任玩具部(全体员工)的负责人.

▷ **su·per·in·tend·ence** /-əns; -əns/ *n* [U] (*fml* 文) superintending 管理; 监督; 主管: *work done under the personal superintendence of the manager* 在经理亲自监管下做的工作.

su·per·in·tend·ent /-ənt; -ənt/ *n* **1** person who superintends 监管人; 主管人; 负责人: *the park superintendent* 公园管理员. **2** (in Britain) police officer next in rank above chief inspector (英国的)警务长.

su·per·ior /suːˈpɪərɪə(r); *also, in British use,* 英式英语读作 sjuː-; suˈpɪrɪɚ/ *adj* **1** (**a**) better than average 优于一般水平的; 优良的; 优秀的; 优等的: *a superior cloth, team, standard* 上等布、强队、高水平 ○ *a girl of superior intelligence* 智力出众的女孩子 ○ *This candidate is clearly superior.* 这个候选人显然比别的候选人强. (**b**) **~ (to sb/sth)** better, stronger, etc than sb/sth else (比某人[某事物])好的、强的等: *Which of the two methods is superior?* 这两种方法哪一种好? ○ *The match will show who is the superior player.* 这场比赛就能看出谁行谁不行. ○ *This cloth is superior to that.* 这种布比那种好. ○ *The enemy forces were superior in numbers.* 敌军在数量上占优势. ○ *Which side has the superior weapons?* 哪一方在武器上占优势? **2 ~ (to sb)** higher in rank or position 级别或地位较高的: *a superior court* 上级法院 ○ *A soldier must obey his superior officers.* 军人应服从上级军官. ○ *She works well with those superior to her in the firm.* 她与公司中的那些上级主管合作愉快. **3** (*derog* 贬) showing that one thinks one is better than others 有优越感的: *a superior smile, look, air, etc* 带优越感的微笑、样子、神态等 ○ *Don't be so superior!* 别自以为了不起! **4** [usu attrib 通常作定语] (*fml* 文) placed higher up; upper 位于较高处的; 上层的: *a superior stratum of rock* 上部岩石层. Cf 参看 INFERIOR.

▷ **su·per·ior** *n* **1** person of higher rank, position, etc 级别、地位...高的人; 上级; 长官: *obey one's superiors* 服从上级. **2** person or thing that is better 较好的人或事物; 优胜者: *She is my superior in knowledge*, ie knows more than I do. 她比我有知识. ○ *He has no superior as a Shakespearian actor.* 他演莎士比亚戏剧无出其右. **3** (in titles) head of a religious community (用作称谓)宗教团体的领导: *the Father Superior*, eg an abbot 男修道院院长.

su·peri·or·ity /suːˌpɪərɪˈɒrətɪ; *US* -ˈɔːr-; *also, in British use,* 英式英语读作 sjuː-; suˌpɪrɪˈɔrətɪ/ *n* [U] **~ (in sth)**; **~ (to/over sth/sb)** state of being superior 优秀; 优良; 优越; 优胜: *the superiority of one thing to another* 一事物之优于另一事物 ○ *her superiority in talent* 她才能之出众 ○ *They won the battle because of their massive superiority in numbers.* 他们人数远占优势而战斗获胜.

□ **superiˈority complex** (**a**) (*psychology* 心) state of mind that makes a person act as if he were better or more important than others although he actually feels that they are better, etc than him 优越情结(在自觉不如他人时, 反而故意表现出的优越感). (**b**) (*infml* 口) too great a belief that one is better or more important than others 过强的优越感. Cf 参看 INFERIORITY COMPLEX (INFERIOR).

su·per·lat·ive /suːˈpɜːlətɪv; *also, in British use,* 英式英语读作 sjuː-; suˈpɜlətɪv/ *adj* **1** of the highest degree or quality 最高级的; 最好的: *a superlative achievement, performance, meal* 最佳成就、表演、饭菜 ○ *This wine is quite superlative.* 这种酒相当好. **2** (*grammar*) of adjectives or adverbs expressing the highest or a very high degree, eg *best*, *worst*, *slowest*, *most difficult* (指形容词或副词)最高级的 (如best、worst、slowest、most difficult). Cf 参看 COMPARATIVE 3.

▷ **su·per·lat·ive** *n* superlative form of an adjective or adverb (形容词或副词的)最高级: *a book review full of superlatives*, ie expressions praising it highly 充满盛赞言辞的书评.

su·per·lat·ively *adv*: *She plays the mandolin superlatively well.* 她演奏曼陀林非常出色.

su·per·man /ˈsuːpəmæn; *also, in British use,* 英式英语读作 ˈsjuː-; ˈsupɚˌmæn/ *n* (*pl* **-men** /-men; -mɛn/) man with greater strength, ability, intelligence, etc than normal humans; superhuman man (力量、能力、才智等)超常的人; 超人: *He's a kind of intellectual superman.* 他是智力超常的人.

su·per·mar·ket /ˈsuːpəmɑːkɪt; *also, in British use,* 英式英语读作 ˈsjuː-; ˈsupɚˌmɑrkɪt/ *n* large shop selling food, household goods, etc which one takes from the shelves oneself and pays for at the exit 超级市场(开架出售食品、日用品等的商场).

su·per·nat·ural /ˌsuːpəˈnætʃrəl; *also, in British use,* 英式英语读作 ˌsjuː-; ˌsupɚˈnætʃrəl/ *adj* that cannot be explained by natural or physical laws; of the world of spirits, magic, etc 超自然的(自然或物理规律无法解释的); 神灵、幻术等的: *supernatural beings*, eg angels and devils 超自然体(如天使和魔鬼) ○ *witch-doctors believed to have supernatural powers* 据信有超自然力量的巫医.

▷ **the su·per·nat·ural** *n* [sing] supernatural beings, events, etc 超自然体; 超自然的事物: *an interest in the supernatural* 对超自然事物的兴趣.

su·per·nat·ur·ally /-ˈnætʃrəlɪ; -ˈnætʃrəlɪ/ *adv*.

su·per·nova /ˌsuːpəˈnəʊvə; *also, in British use,* 英式英语读作 ˌsjuː-; ˌsupɚˈnovə/ *n* (*pl* **-vae** /-viː; -vi/ or **~s**) (*astronomy* 天) star that suddenly becomes very much brighter as a result of an explosion 超新星(因爆炸而突然亮度大增的). Cf 参看 NOVA.

su·per·nu·mer·ary /ˌsuːpəˈnjuːmərərɪ; *US* -ˈnuːmərerɪ; *also, in British use,* 英式英语读作 ˌsjuː-; ˌsupɚˈnuməˌrɛrɪ/ *adj* (*fml* 文) in excess of the normal number; extra 超过正常数目的; 额外的; 多余的: *a supernumerary* (ie sixth) *finger* 多出的手指(六指儿的).

▷ **su·per·nu·mer·ary** *n* (*fml* 文) supernumerary person or thing 额外的或多余的人或事物.

su·per·phos·phate /ˌsuːpəˈfɒsfeɪt; *also, in British use,* 英式英语读作 ˌsjuː-; ˌsupɚˈfɑsfet/ *n* fertilizer containing soluble phosphates 过磷酸盐(用作化肥).

su·per·power /ˈsuːpəpaʊə(r); *also, in British use,* 英式英语读作 ˈsjuː-; ˌsupɚˈpaʊɚ/ *n* any of the most powerful nations in the world, esp the USA or former USSR 超级大国: [attrib 作定语] *a superpower summit* 超级大国最高级会议.

su·per·script /ˈsuːpəskrɪpt; *also, in British use,* 英式英语读作 ˈsjuː-; ˈsupɚˌskrɪpt/ *adj* [attrib 作定语] written or printed just above a word, figure or symbol 上角标的(写或印在字、数字或符号上面的); 标在上方的: *Different words with the same spelling are distinguished in this dictionary by superscript numbers.* 本词典在同形异义词的右上角标注数字以资区别.

su·per·sede /ˌsuːpəˈsiːd; *also, in British use,* 英式英语读作 ˌsjuː-; ˌsupɚˈsid/ *v* [Tn] take the place of (sth/sb that was present or used before); be introduced so as to be used instead of (sth/sb) 代替, 取代, 接替(某事物[某人]): *Motorways have largely superseded ordinary roads for long-distance travel.* 高速公路多已取代了普通公路. ○ *Will factory workers be entirely superseded by machines one day?* 工人将来能完全由机器取代吗?

su·per·sonic /ˌsuːpəˈsɒnɪk; *also, in British use,* 英式英语读作 ˌsjuː-; ˌsupɚˈsɑnɪk/ *adj* (that can travel) faster than the speed of sound 超音速的; 超声速的: *a supersonic aircraft* 超音速飞机 ○ *supersonic speeds* 超过声速的速度. Cf 参看 SUBSONIC.

su·per·star /ˈsuːpəstɑː(r); *also, in British use,* 英式英语读作 ˈsjuː-; ˌsupɚˌstɑr/ *n* (*infml* 口) very famous and admired entertainer (娱乐界的)超级明星, 巨星: *Hollywood superstars* 好莱坞超级明星 ○ [attrib 作定语] *superstar footballers* 超级足球明星.

su·per·sti·tion /ˌsuːpəˈstɪʃn; *also, in British use,* 英式英语读作 ˌsjuː-; ˌsupɚˈstɪʃən/ *n* [C, U] **1** (idea, practice, etc based on the) belief that certain events cannot be explained by human reason or physical laws; irrational fear of what is unknown or mysterious 迷信; 迷信的思想、行为等; (对未知的或神秘的事物的)盲目恐惧: *Ignorance and superstition prevent them from benefiting from modern medicine.* 由于无知和迷信, 他们无法得到现代医学的好处. **2** idea or belief held by many people for no good or logical reason 很多人持有的并无充分根据的说法: *It's just (a) superstition that you shouldn't walk* *under ladders.* 不应该在梯子下面穿过，人们都是这么说说罢了.

▷ **su·per·sti·tious** /-ˈstɪʃəs; -ˈstɪʃəs/ *adj* **1** of, based on or caused by superstition 迷信的；根据迷信的；由迷信引起的；无充分根据的说法的：*superstitious beliefs, ideas, practices* 迷信的说法、想法、做法. **2** believing in superstitions 受迷信思想支配的：*I always put my left shoe on first; I'm superstitious (about it).* 我穿鞋总是先左后右，我是很迷信(这件事)的. **su·per·sti·tiously** *adv.*

su·per·store /ˈsuːpəstɔː(r); *also, in British use,* 英式英语读作 ˈsjuː-; ˈsupɚˌstɔr/ *n* very large shop in which groceries and/or larger types of goods (eg furniture) are sold as in a supermarket 超级商场(出售食品杂货和[或]大件商品(如家具)者)：*a DIY superstore* 出售成套零件供顾客自行装配的超级商场.

su·per·struc·ture /ˈsuːpəstrʌktʃə(r); *also, in British use,* 英式英语读作 ˈsjuː-; ˈsupɚˌstrʌktʃɚ/ *n* **1** (**a**) structure built on top of sth else, eg the part of a building above the ground 上部结构，上层建筑物(如建筑物的地面部分). Cf 参看 SUBSTRUCTURE. (**b**) parts of a ship above the main deck 舰船主甲板上面的部分. **2** (esp in Marxist theory) institutions and culture that result from the economic system on which a society is based (尤指马克思理论中的)上层建筑.

su·per·tanker /ˈsuːpətæŋkə(r); *also, in British use,* 英式英语读作 ˈsjuː-; ˈsupɚˌtæŋkɚ/ *n* very large tanker ship 超级油轮.

sup·er·tax /ˈsuːpətæks; *also, in British use,* 英式英语读作 ˈsjuː-; ˈsupɚˌtæks/ *n* [U] additional tax on income, paid by those who earn a very large amount of money (对高收入者征收的)附加所得税.

su·per·vene /ˌsuːpəˈviːn; *also, in British use,* 英式英语读作 ˌsjuː-; ˌsupɚˈvin/ *v* [I] (*fml* 文) occur as an interruption or change 发生(因而干扰或变化)：*She was working well until illness supervened.* 她本来工作得很顺利，但生病后情况就不同了. ▷ **su·per·ven·tion** /-ˈvenʃn; -ˈvɛnʃən/ *n* [U].

su·per·vise /ˈsuːpəvaɪz; *also, in British use,* 英式英语读作 ˈsjuː-; ˌsupɚˈvaɪz/ *v* [I, Tn, Tng] watch or otherwise keep a check on (sb doing sth or sth being done) to make sure it is done properly 监督(某人做某事)；察看并指导(工作)：*The chief clerk supervises the work of the department.* 文书组长负责监督该部门的工作. ○ *I supervised the workers loading the lorry.* 我监督工人把货物装上卡车.

▷ **su·per·vi·sion** /ˌsuːpəˈvɪʒn; *also, in British use,* 英式英语读作 ˌsjuː-; ˌsupɚˈvɪʒən/ *n* [U] supervising or being supervised 监督；管理；指导：*Children should not be left to play without supervision.* 孩子玩儿的时候不能无人照看. ○ *This drug should only be taken under the supervision of* (ie as supervised by) *a doctor.* 此药须遵医嘱服用.

su·per·visor *n* person who supervises 监督人；监察员；管理人；指导者：*university students showing essays to their supervisor* 把文章交给指导教师审阅的大学生.

su·per·vis·ory /ˈsuːpəvaɪzərɪ; *also, in British use,* 英式英语读作 ˈsjuː-; *US* ˌsuːpəˈvaɪzərɪ; ˌsupɚˈvaɪzərɪ/ *adj* supervising 监督的；管理的；指导的：*supervisory duties* 监督的职责 ○ *a supervisory committee* 监察委员会.

su·pine /ˈsuːpaɪn; *also, in British use,* 英式英语读作 ˈsjuː-; suˈpaɪn/ *adj* (*fml* 文) **1** lying flat on the back, face upwards 仰卧的：*a supine figure on the bed* 仰卧在床上的人(绘画等中的). Cf 参看 PRONE 1, PROSTRATE 1. **2** (*fig derog* 比喻，贬) showing a weak or lazy unwillingness to act 消极的；懒散的；没精打采的：*accept unfair treatment in supine submission* 以消极的态度接受不公平的待遇. ▷ **su·pinely** *adv.*

sup·per /ˈsʌpə(r); ˈsʌpɚ/ *n* [C, U] last meal of the day, usu less large and less formal than dinner 晚饭；晚餐：*have cold meat for supper* 晚饭吃凉肉 ○ *have a late supper* 很晚才吃晚饭 ○ *eat very little supper* 晚饭吃得很少. ⇨Usage at DINNER 用法见 DINNER.

□ ˈ**supper-time** *n* [U] time at which supper is (usu) eaten 晚饭时间.

sup·plant /səˈplɑːnt; səˈplænt/ *v* [Tn] (*fml* 文) take the place of (sb/sth); replace 取代(某人[某事物])；代替：*Oil has supplanted coffee as our main export.* 我们的主要出口货已由原来的咖啡改为石油了. ○ *The party leader has been supplanted by his rival.* 那位党的领导人已被其对手取而代之. ○ *She has been supplanted by another in his affections,* ie He now loves sb else. 他爱上了另一个女人，不再爱她了.

supple /ˈsʌpl; ˈsʌpl/ *adj* (**-r**, **-st**) bent or bending easily; not stiff; flexible 易弯曲的；柔软的；灵活的：*the supple limbs of a child* 儿童的柔软四肢 ○ *Exercise keeps you supple.* 经常锻炼可使身体灵活. ○ *She has a supple mind,* ie is quick to respond to ideas. 她头脑灵活. ▷ **sup·plely** (also **supply**) /ˈsʌplɪ; ˈsʌplɪ/ *adv.* **sup·ple·ness** *n* [U].

sup·ple·ment /ˈsʌplɪmənt; ˈsʌpləmənt/ *n* **1** ~ **(to sth)** thing added to sth else to improve or complete it 增补的事物；补充：*The money I get from teaching the piano is a useful supplement to my ordinary income.* 我教钢琴挣的钱是一笔很管用的外快. **2** (**a**) ~ **(to sth)** book, section of a book, etc that gives further information, treats a special subject, etc (书等的)补编，补遗，附录：*the supplement to the Oxford English Dictionary*《牛津英语大辞典》补编. (**b**) additional section added to a newspaper (报纸的)增刊：*the colour supplements of the Sunday newspapers* 星期日报纸的彩色增刊. **3** extra amount of money paid for an additional service, item, etc (为增加的服务、项目等支付的)额外费用，附加费：*a £10 supplement for a single room with a shower* 带淋浴间的单人房间需付10英镑附加费.

▷ **sup·ple·ment** /ˈsʌplɪment; ˈsʌpləˌmɛnt/ *v* [Tn, Tn·pr] ~ **sth (with sth)** add to or complete sth with sth else 增加或补充某事物：*I supplement my grant by working in the evenings.* 我除享受助学金外还打夜工以增加收入. ○ *She supplements her diet with vitamin tablets.* 她服用维生素片剂以补充规定食谱中的营养.

sup·ple·ment·ary /ˌsʌplɪˈmentrɪ; *US* -terɪ; ˌsʌpləˈmɛntərɪ/ ~ **(to sth)** **1** additional; extra 增补的；补充的；附加的：*a supplementary payment, lecture, item* 额外的付款、讲座、项目. **2** (*mathematics* 数) (of an angle) making a total of 180° with another angle (指角)补角的.

□ ˌ**supplementary** ˈ**benefit** (in Britain) money paid regularly by the State to poor people (在英国)(政府定期发给穷人的)补助金：*a family (living) on supplementary benefit* 依靠补助金(生活)的家庭. Cf 参看 WELFARE 3.

sup·pli·ant /ˈsʌplɪənt; ˈsʌplɪənt/ *n, adj* (*fml* 文) (person) asking humbly for sth 恳求的(人)：*kneel as a suppliant at the altar,* ie praying to God for sth 跪在祭坛前祈求(向上帝祈祷) ○ *in a suppliant attitude* 以恳切的态度.

sup·plic·ate /ˈsʌplɪkeɪt; ˈsʌplɪˌket/ *v* [Ipr, Tn, Cn·t] ~ **(for) sth** (*fml* 文) ask (sb) humbly or pleadingly for sth 恳求，哀求，祈求，央求(某人)：*supplicate for pardon* 恳求原谅 ○ *supplicate sb's forgiveness,* ie ask sb to forgive one 乞求某人宽恕 ○ *supplicate sb to help* 向某人求助.

▷ **sup·plic·ant** /ˈsʌplɪkənt; ˈsʌplɪkənt/ *n* (*fml* 文) person who supplicates; suppliant 恳求的人.

sup·plica·tion /ˌsʌplɪˈkeɪʃn; ˌsʌplɪˈkeʃən/ *n* [C, U] (*fml* 文) (act of) supplicating 恳求；哀求；祈求；央求；祈祷：*He was deaf to my supplications.* 我恳求他，他连理都不理. ○ *kneel in supplication* 跪着祈祷.

sup·ply /səˈplaɪ; səˈplaɪ/ *v* (*pt, pp* **supplied**) **1** [Tn, Tn·pr] ~ **sth (to sb)**; ~ **sb (with sth)** give sb sth that is needed or useful; provide sb with sth 供给或供应某人所需或可用的物品；向某人提供某物：*a company supplying heating oil (to homes)* (向住户)供应燃油的公司 ○ *supply consumers with gas, electricity, etc* 向消费者提供煤气、电力等 ○ *He kept me well supplied with cups of coffee while I wrote the report.* 我写报告时，他一直不停地给我一杯杯续咖啡. **2** [Tn] provide enough (of sth) for (a need); fulfil 提供足够的(某物)以满足(需要)：*Will the new power-station be able to supply our cheap energy requirements?* 新建的发电厂能够满足我们对廉价能源的需求吗?

▷ **sup·ply** *n* **1** [U] supplying or being supplied 供给；供应；补给：*a contract for the supply of office stationery* 供应办公文具的合同 ○ *You promised us fuel, but can you guarantee its supply?* 你答应给我们提供燃料，但能保证供应吗? ○ *a reliable source of supply* 可靠的来源 ○ [attrib 作定语] *a supply train* 运送补给品的列车. **2** [C often *pl* 常作复数] thing that is supplied; stock or store of things provided or available 供给之物；供应品；补给品；贮备；存货；现货：*the water-supply* 供水 ○ *a supply of*

S

reading-matter for the journey 为旅途提供的读物 ○ *arms, food, fuel supplies* 武器、食物、燃料贮备 ○ *Have we got enough supplies of coal?* 我们贮存的煤够用吗? ○ *Helicopters dropped supplies* (ie of food, etc) *for the stranded villagers.* 直升飞机给受困的村民空投了物资. **3** (idm 习语) **in short supply** ⇨ SHORT[1]. **sup,ply and de'mand** (*esp economics* 尤用于经济) the amount of goods, etc available and the amount wanted by consumers, the relationship between which is regarded as controlling prices 供求关系.

sup·plier /səˈplaɪə(r); səˈplaɪɚ/ *n* person or firm supplying goods, etc 供应者(人或公司).

□ **sup'ply teacher** teacher employed to do the work of any other teacher who is absent through illness, etc 代课教师.

sup·port /səˈpɔːt; səˈpɔrt/ *v* **1** [Tn] bear the weight of (sth/sb); hold in position; carry 承受(某物[某人])的重量; 支撑; 扶持: *a beam supporting a roof* 支承屋顶的横梁 ○ *Is this bridge strong enough to support heavy lorries?* 这座桥禁得住重型卡车通行吗? ○ *He was weak with hunger, so I had to support him.* 他饿得没有力气, 我得搀着他. **2** (**a**) [Tn, Tn·pr] **~ sb/sth (in sth)** help sb/sth by one's approval or sympathy or by giving money (用表示赞同或同情或给钱)帮助某人[某事物]; 支持; 支援; 资助: *support a cause, political party, reform* 支持某事业、政党、改革 ○ *donate money to support a charity* 捐款赞助慈善事业 ○ *The directors were trying to get rid of her, but her staff all supported her.* 董事都想把她撤掉, 可是她那部门的人员全都支持她. ○ *The American public stopped supporting the war in Vietnam.* 美国公众不再支持美国在越南进行的战争了. ○ *Will you support me in my campaign for election?* 你支持我参加竞选吗? (**b**) [Tn] be a regular customer of or visitor to (sth); be a fan of (a team, etc) 经常光顾(某处); 为(某队等)捧场: *Support your local theatre: buy tickets regularly!* 请大力支持本地剧院, 欢迎经常光临! ○ *Which football team do you support?* 你是哪个足球队的球迷? **3** [Tn] help to show that (a theory, claim, etc) is true; confirm 支持(某理论、主张等); 证实; 肯定: *a theory that is not supported by the facts* 缺乏事实根据的理论 ○ *This evidence supports my argument that she is guilty.* 这一证据支持了我认为她有罪的推定. **4** [Tn] provide (sb) with the necessary money, etc to buy food, accommodation, etc 资助, 供养, 赡养(某人): *I was supported by my parents when I was studying.* 我求学期间由父母供养. **5** [Tn] provide enough food and water to keep (sb/sth) alive (提供食物和水)维持(某人[某物])的生命: *Such a barren desert can support very few creatures.* 在这样荒瘠的沙漠里, 很少生物能够存活.

▷ **sup·port** *n* **1** [U] **~ (for sth)** supporting or being supported 支撑; 扶持; 支持; 支援; 资助; 供养; 维持: *adequate support for the great weight of the crane* 对起重机巨大重量的足够的支承力 ○ *a proposal that received no, little, not much, etc support* 没有人、很少有人、没有多少人…支持的建议 ○ *I need some financial support for this venture.* 我需要一些财务赞助来兴办这一企业. ○ *Can I rely on your support* (ie Will you vote for me) *in this election?* 在此次选举中你能支持我吗? ○ *She is without any visible means of support,* ie has no work, income, etc. 她生活无着(无工作、收入等). **2** [C] thing that supports or bears the weight of sth 支撑物; 支柱; 支座; 支架: *wearing an athletic support* 穿着下体护身 ○ *supports holding up a collapsing wall* 支撑危墙的柱子. **3** [C] person who gives help, sympathy, etc 给予帮助、同情等的人: *Jim was a great support to us when father died.* 父亲死后, 吉姆给了我们巨大的帮助. **4** [U] people who support a political party, team, etc (政党、球队等的)支持者, 拥护者: *The theatre has had to close for lack of support.* 这家剧院光顾者寡只好关闭. **5** (idm 习语) **in sup'port** (eg of troops) in reserve; ready to give support (如指军队等)后备的, 准备给予支援的: *We have ten people to do the cooking, with several more in support.* 我们有十个人做饭, 还有几个人可随时来帮忙. **in support of sb/sth** supporting sb/sth; in favour of sb/sth 支持或支援某人[某事物]: *speak in support of a ban on arms supplies* 讲话支持武器禁运.

sup·port·able *adj* (*fml* 文) **1** that can be supported 禁得住的; 可承受的; 供养得起的. **2** (used in negative sentences 用于否定句中) that can be tolerated 可忍受的: *Such rudeness is scarcely supportable.* 这种粗暴的行为让人难以容忍.

sup·porter *n* person who supports a political party, team, etc (政党、球队等的)支持者, 拥护者: *The government's supporters welcomed the new law.* 拥护政府的人都欢迎新颁布的法规.

sup·port·ing *adj* [attrib 作定语] (in the theatre and cinema) of secondary importance (戏剧和电影中)次要的: *a supporting actor/cast/part/role* 配角演员 ○ *a supporting film*, eg one that is shown before the main film 电影加片.

sup·port·ive /səˈpɔːtɪv; səˈpɔrtɪv/ *adj* (*approv* 褒) giving help, encouragement or sympathy 给予帮助、鼓励或同情的; 支持的; 支援的; 赞助的: *She has been very supportive during my illness.* 我患病期间她帮了我很大忙.

sup·pose /səˈpəʊz; səˈpoz/ *v* **1** [Tf, Cn·a, Cn·t] accept as true or probable; believe; imagine; assume 认定; 认为; 以为; 猜想; 料想; 假定: *What do you suppose he wanted?* 你认为他想要什么? ○ *What makes you suppose (that) I'm against it?* 你根据什么认为我反对这件事? ○ *I don't suppose for a minute that he'll agree,* ie I'm sure that he won't. 我认为他决不同意. ○ *She'll be there today, I suppose.* 我想她今天能到那儿去. ○ *'Will he come?' 'Yes, I suppose so.'* '他来吗?' '对, 我想他能来.' ○ *I suppose you want to borrow money from me again?* ie showing annoyance 我猜你又要找我借钱了吧? ○ *I don't suppose you could help me* (ie Please help me) *with my homework.* 请你帮助我做家庭作业吧. ○ *It was generally supposed that it would not happen again.* 一般都认为此事不会再发生. ○ (*fml* 文) *Everyone supposes him (to be) poor, but he is really quite wealthy.* 大家都以为他穷, 实际上他很阔. ○ *It was widely supposed to have been lost during the war.* 普遍认为那东西在战争期间丢失了. **2** [Tn, Tf, Cn·t] pretend that (sth) is true; take (sth) as a fact 假定或假设(某事物)属实; 认定(某事物): *a theory which supposes the existence of other worlds besides our own* 假定除地球外还存在其他有生命的天体的理论 ○ *Suppose (that) the news is true: what then?* 假定这消息是真的, 那又怎样? ○ *Suppose you had a million pounds — how would you spend it?* 假如你有一百万镑——你怎么花呢? **3** [Tf] (used in the imperative, to make a suggestion 用于祈使句, 用以提出建议) consider as a proposal 作为建议来考虑: *Suppose we go* (ie Let's go) *for a swim!* 咱们去游泳吧! **4** [Tn] (*fml* 文) require (sth) as a condition 须以(某事物)为条件: *Creation supposes a creator.* 有了创造者, 才能有创造. **5** (idm 习语) **be supposed to do sth** (**a**) be expected or required to do sth (by rules, custom, etc) 被期望或被要求(按规则、惯例等)做某事: *Am I supposed to* (ie Should I) *clean all the rooms or just this one?* 我是应该打扫所有的房间, 还是只这一间? ○ *You're supposed to pay the bill by Friday.* 你最晚在星期五结清这笔帐. ○ *They were supposed to be here an hour ago.* 他们应该在一小时以前到达这里. (**b**) (*infml* 口) (used in negative sentences 用于否定句中) be allowed to do sth 获准做某事: *You're not supposed to play football in the classroom.* 在教室里是不准踢足球的.

▷ **sup·posed** /səˈpəʊzd; səˈpozd/ *adj* [attrib 作定语] wrongly believed or said to be the specified thing 误信的; 误传的; 信以为真的: *His supposed generosity is merely a form of self-interest.* 他貌似慷慨, 不过是变相的利己而已. ○ *The supposed beggar was really a police officer in disguise.* 那个众人眼中的乞丐, 其实是化了装的警察. **sup·pos·edly** /səˈpəʊzɪdlɪ; səˈpozɪdlɪ/ *adv* according to what is supposed (but not known for certain) 根据推测; 据认为; 据称; 大概; 可能: *This picture is supposedly worth more than a million pounds.* 这幅画大概值一百万镑以上.

sup·pos·ing *conj* (also **supposing that**) if we assume the fact or the possibility that; if 假定; 假设; 假如: *Supposing (that) it rains, can we play the match indoors?* 要是下雨的话, 我们在室内比赛行吗?

sup·posi·tion /ˌsʌpəˈzɪʃn; ˌsʌpəˈzɪʃən/ *n* **1** [U] supposing 假定; 猜想; 推测: *a newspaper article based on supposition*, ie only on what the writer supposes to be true, not on fact 根据臆想写出的报刊文章 ○ *We must not condemn her on pure supposition.* 我们不能单凭臆测而谴责她. **2** [C] **~ (that...)** thing supposed; guess 假

定的事物; 猜测: *Our suppositions were fully confirmed.* 我们猜测的事已全部证实. ○ *I am proceeding on the supposition that...*, ie by assuming it to be true that... 我假定....

sup·pos·it·ory /sə'pɒzɪtrɪ; *US* -tɔːrɪ; sə'pɑzə,torɪ/ *n* piece of a medicinal substance placed in the rectum or vagina to dissolve 栓剂(外用药, 置入直肠或阴道内使之溶化); 坐药.

sup·press /sə'pres; sə'prɛs/ *v* [Tn] **1** put an end to (sth), esp by force; crush 制止(尤指凭借武力); 镇压; 平定: *suppress an uprising, a revolt, etc* 镇压起义、叛乱等. **2** (**a**) (*usu derog* 通常作贬义) prevent (sth) from being known or seen 防止(某事物)被人知道或看到; 查禁或禁止发表(某事物): *suppress the truth about sth* 隐瞒某事物的真相 ○ *suppress a newspaper*, ie prevent it from being published 查禁一家报纸 ○ *Are the police suppressing some evidence?* 警方是否隐瞒了一些证据? ○ *The dictator tried to suppress all criticism of him.* 那独裁者竭力压制一切批评他的言论. (**b**) prevent (esp one's feelings) from being expressed 抑制, 压抑(尤指感情): *suppress one's anger, amusement, etc* 抑制愤怒、欢娱等心情而不形于色 ○ *He could scarcely suppress a laugh.* 他忍不住要笑出声来.

▷ **sup·press·ible** *adj* that can be suppressed 可制止的; 可禁止的; 可抑制住的: *anger that was barely suppressible* 难以抑制的愤怒.

sup·pres·sion /sə'preʃn; sə'prɛʃən/ *n* [U] suppressing or being suppressed 制止; 镇压; 查禁; 抑制: *the suppression of a revolt, the facts* 对叛乱的镇压、对事实的隐瞒 ○ *the suppression of one's anger, etc* 抑制愤怒.

sup·pressor *n* **1** person or thing that suppresses 制止者; 镇压者; 查禁者; 起抑制作用的事物. **2** device fitted to an electrical apparatus to stop it causing interference on radio or television sets 干扰抑制器(安装在用电器上, 可防止用电器对收音机或电视机产生干扰).

sup·pur·ate /'sʌpjʊreɪt; 'sʌpjə,ret/ *v* [I] (*fml* 文) (of a wound, etc) have a thick yellow liquid (*pus*) forming inside it because of infection (指伤口等)化脓: *a suppurating sore* 化脓的疮. ▷ **sup·pura·tion** /,sʌpjʊ'reɪʃn; ,sʌpjə'reʃən/ *n* [U].

supra- /'suːprə; 'suprə/ *pref* 前缀 above; beyond 在...之上; 超: *supranational*, ie going beyond national boundaries.

su·preme /suː'priːm; *also, in British use,* 英式英语读作 sjuː-; su'prim/ *adj* [usu attrib 通常作定语] **1** highest in authority, rank or degree (权力、级别或地位)最高的; 至高无上的: *the supreme ruler of a vast empire* 一个庞大帝国的最高统治者 ○ (*fig* 比喻) *After a year without defeat, the team now reigns supreme as the finest in the country.* 该队一年来所向无敌, 现已称雄全国. **2** most important; greatest 最重要的; 最大的: *make the supreme sacrifice*, eg die for what one believes in 做出最大的牺牲(如为信仰而捐躯) ○ *Winning an Olympic gold medal was, I suppose, the supreme moment of my life.* 我认为我荣获奥运会金牌时是我一生中最重要的时刻.

▷ **su·prem·acy** /suː'preməsɪ; *also, in British use,* 英式英语读作 sjuː-; su'prɛməsɪ/ *n* ~ **(over sb/sth)** [U] being supreme; position of the highest power, authority or status 至高无上; 最高权力; 最高权威; 最高地位: *achieve military supremacy over neighbouring countries* 获得超越邻国的军事优势 ○ *challenging Japan's supremacy in the field of electronics* 争夺日本在电子学领域中占据的领先地位 ○ *the dangerous notion of white supremacy*, ie that white races are better than others and should control them 白人至高无上的危险观念(认为白色人种优于其他人种因而应成为主宰者). **su·prem·acist** /suː'preməsɪst; *also, in British use,* 英式英语读作 sjuː-; su'prɛməsɪst/ *n*: *white supremacists* 白人至上主义者.

su·premely /suː'priːmlɪ; *also, in British use,* 英式英语读作 sjuː-; su'primlɪ/ *adv* in a supreme way; extremely 至高无上地; 极度地: *supremely happy* 极其快乐.

□ **the ,Supreme 'Being** (*fml* 文) God 上主; 上帝.

the Su,preme 'Court the highest court in a state of the US or in the whole of the US (美国各州或联邦)最高法院.

the Su,preme 'Soviet the law-making body of the former Soviet Union 最高苏维埃(前苏联的立法机构).

Supt *abbr* 缩写 = Superintendent (esp in the police force 尤用于警界): *Supt (George) Hill* (乔治·)希尔警务长.

sur·charge /'sɜːtʃɑːdʒ; 'sɝ,tʃɑrdʒ/ *n* **1** ~ **(on sth)** payment that is demanded in addition to the usual charge 增付的费用; 增收费; 附加费: *a 10% surcharge on the price of a holiday* 在度假费用之外增收的10% 附加费. **2** mark printed over a postage stamp, changing its value (加盖在邮票上的)改值印记.

▷ **sur·charge** /sɜː'tʃɑːdʒ; sɝ'tʃɑrdʒ/ *v* [Tn, Tn·pr, Dn·n] ~ **sb (on sth)** demand a surcharge from sb 向某人索取额外费用: *They've surcharged us 10% on the price of the holiday because of a rise in air fares.* 因飞机票涨价, 他们在度假费用中向我们增收了10% 附加费.

surd /sɜːd; sɝd/ *n* (*mathematics* 数) mathematical quantity, esp a root, that cannot be expressed as an ordinary number or quantity 不尽根: *The square root of 5 ($\sqrt{5}$) is a surd.* 5 的平方根($\sqrt{5}$)是不尽根.

sure /ʃɔː(r); *US* ʃʊər; ʃʊr/ *adj* (**-r**, **-st**) **1** [pred 作表语] ~ **(of/about sth)**; ~ **that...**; ~ **what, etc...** not doubting or seeming to doubt what one believes, knows, etc; confident that one is right 无疑; 确实; 自信; 有把握: *I think he's coming, but I'm not quite sure.* 我想他会来的, 但是不太有把握. ○ *I'm not sure when I saw her last.* 我不能确定上一次看见她是什么时候. ○ *Are you sure of your facts?* 你能肯定你的资料属实吗? ○ *If you're not sure how to do it, ask me.* 假若你拿不准怎样做, 就来问我好了. ○ *Can we be sure that she's honest?* 我们能相信她是诚实的吗? ○ *I think the answer's right but I'm not absolutely sure about it.* 我认为这答案是正确的, 但是没有绝对的把握. ○ *Jane is reliable, but I'm not so sure about Jim.* 简是信得过的, 至于吉姆, 我就不敢说了. ○ *She felt sure that she had done the right thing.* 她确信自己做得对. **2** [pred 作表语] ~ **of sth** certain to receive, win, etc sth 一定会获得、赢得...某事物: *You're sure of a warm welcome.* 你一定会受到热烈欢迎的. ○ *Can I be sure of a profit if I invest?* 我要是投资, 肯定能获利吗? ○ *You're sure of passing the exam if you work hard.* 只要用功, 就一定能考及格. **3** ~ **to do sth** definitely going to do sth; certain to do sth 肯定要做某事的; 一定做某事的: *It's sure to rain.* 肯定要下雨. ○ *You're sure to fail if you do it that way.* 你那样做一定失败. **4** undoubtedly true 无可置疑的; 千真万确的: *in the sure and certain knowledge of her guilt* 在确确实实知道她有罪的情况下 ○ *One thing is sure: we've won a great victory!* 有一点是确切无疑的: 我们已取得了巨大的胜利! ⇨Usage at CERTAIN 用法见CERTAIN. **5** (usu *attrib* 通常作定语) proven and reliable; trustworthy 经证明可靠的; 可信的: *no sure remedy for a cold* 没有包治感冒的灵丹妙药 ○ *There's only one sure way to do it.* 做此事只有一种万全之策. ○ *She has always been a sure friend.* 她一直就是靠得住的朋友. **6** not deviating or wavering; steady and confident 不偏离的; 不动摇的; 稳而有信心的: *She drew the outline with a sure hand.* 她笔力雄健地画出了轮廓. **7** (idm 习语) **be sure to do sth**; **be sure and do sth** don't fail to do sth 务必做某事: *Be sure (to write) and tell me all your news.* 务必(来信)把你的所有情况都告诉我. **for sure** (*infml* 口) without doubt 无疑: *I think he lives there but I couldn't say for sure.* 我想他是住在那里的, 但我不敢肯定. **make sure (of sth/that...)** (**a**) find out whether sth is definitely so 把某事物弄清楚; 核实或查明某事物: *I think the door's locked, but I'd better go and make sure (it is).* 我想门已经锁了, 但我最好还是去查看一下. (**b**) do sth to ensure that sth happens 设法确保出现某事物: *arrangements to make sure that the visit goes well* 为使参观得以顺利进行而做的安排. **sure of oneself** (*sometimes derog* 有时作贬义) (too) confident of one's own abilities, etc; self-confident (过于)自信: *You seem very sure of yourself, young man!* 小伙子, 你未免太自信了吧! **,sure 'thing** (*infml* 口 *esp US*) yes; of course 是的; 当然: *'Do you want to come too?' 'Sure thing!'* '你也想来吗?''当然了!' **to be 'sure** (*fml* 文) I cannot deny (that); admittedly 无可否认; 诚然: *He is clever, to be sure, but not very hard-working.* 他聪明是聪明, 但是不怎么勤奋.

▷ **sure** *adv* **1** (*infml* 口 *esp US*) certainly 的确; 当然: *It sure was cold!* 确实很冷! **2** (idm 习语) **(as) sure as eggs is 'eggs, as 'fate, as I'm standing 'here, etc** (*infml* 口) very certainly 的的确确; 千真万确: *He's dead, as sure as eggs is eggs.* 他确实死了. **,sure e'nough** (used to introduce a statement that confirms a previous prediction, etc 用以表示所说的与预料的相符): *I said it*

S

would happen, and sure enough it did. 我说过要有这样的事,果然如此.

sure·ness *n* [U] quality of being sure(4,6) 确切性; 真切; 沉稳: *a picture that shows the artist's sureness of touch* 显示出画家苍劲笔力的一幅画.

□ **'sure-fire** *adj* [attrib 作定语] certain to happen, be successful, etc 一定会发生、成功等的: *a ˌsure-fire suc'cess* 必定的胜利 ○ *This is a sure-fire way to get publicity.* 这样做就一定能引人注目.

ˌsure-'footed *adj* not likely to fall when walking or climbing 脚步稳的; 不会摔倒的. **sure-footedly** *adv.* **sure-footedness** *n* [U].

surely /'ʃɔ:lɪ; *US* 'ʃʊərlɪ; 'ʃʊrlɪ/ *adv* **1** without doubt; certainly 无疑; 当然: *He will surely fail.* 他必定失败. ○ *This will surely cause problems.* 这肯定会出问题的. **2** (used to show that the speaker is (almost) certain of what he is saying, or to express surprise at sth 用以表示说话者对所说的内容(几乎)确信无疑, 或表示对某事物感到惊奇): *This is surely her best play.* 这无疑是她最好的剧作. ○ *Surely I've met you before somewhere.* 我一定在什么地方和你见过面. ○ *Surely they won't refuse?* 难道他们不拒绝吗? ○ *Surely you're not going to eat that!* 好傢伙, 你不至于吃那种东西吧! ○ *He has refused to help? Surely not!* 他已拒绝给予援助了吗? 决不可能! ○ *'That's his wife.' 'His sister, surely?'* '那是他的妻子.' '是他妹妹吧?' **3** (*infml* 口 *esp US*) of course; yes 当然; 可以: *'Can I borrow your car?' 'Surely.'* '我用一下你的汽车可以吗?' '当然可以.' **4** (idm 习语) **slowly but surely** ⇨ SLOWLY (SLOW[1]).

surety /'ʃɔ:rətɪ; *US* 'ʃʊərtɪ; 'ʃʊrtɪ/ *n* [C, U] **1** (money, etc given as a) guarantee that sb will pay his debts, perform a duty, etc 担保; 保证; 保证金; 担保品: *offer £100 as (a) surety* 愿出100英镑作保证金. **2** person who makes himself responsible for the payment of debts, etc by sb else 担保人; 保证人: *stand* (ie act as a) *surety for sb* 做某人的担保人.

surfing 冲浪运动

surf /sɜ:f; sɝf/ *n* [U] (white foam on) waves breaking on the seashore 拍打在海岸上四处飞溅的波浪; 拍岸之白色浪花: *splashing about in the surf* 在拍岸的浪花中戏水.

▷ **surf** *v* [I] (usu 通常作 **go surfing**) stand or lie on a surfboard and allow the surf to carry one towards the shore, as a sport 作冲浪运动; 冲浪. **surfer** *n.*

□ **'surfboard** *n* long narrow board used for surfing 冲浪板. ⇨illus 见插图.

sur·face /'sɜ:fɪs; 'sɝfɪs/ *n* **1** [C] (**a**) outside of an object (物体的)表面: *the surface of a sphere, a ball, the earth* 球体、球、地球的表面 ○ [attrib 作定语] *the surface area of the brain* 大脑的表层. (**b**) any of the sides of an object (物体的)面: *A cube has six surfaces.* 立方体有六个面. (**c**) uppermost area or layer of sth 最上面的部分; 表层; 面层: *the rough surface of the wall* 那墙的粗糙表面 ○ *an asphalt road surface* 柏油路面 ○ *The insect's sting penetrates the surface of the skin.* 昆虫的螫针能够刺穿皮肤的表层. ○ *wipe all the surfaces in the kitchen*, ie the walls, the tops and sides of furniture, etc 把厨房的一切表面揩干净(墙及家具等的各面) ○ [attrib 作定语] *a surface layer* 表层 ○ *a surface wound*, ie not a deep one 轻度创伤 ○ *a surface worker*, ie a miner who works above ground 在井上工作的矿工 ○ *surface noise*, ie unwanted noise caused by dust, static electricity, etc on a record when it is being played (放唱片时由尘埃、静电等引起的)(唱针)划纹噪声, (唱片)纹噪声. **2** [C usu *sing* 通常作单数] top of a body of liquid, eg the sea 液面; 水面(如海面): *The submarine rose to the surface.* 潜艇露出了水面. ○ *the frozen surface of the lake* 结冰的湖面 ○ [attrib 作定语] *a surface vessel*, ie an ordinary ship, not a submarine 水面舰船(一般舰船, 与潜艇相对). **3** [sing] (*fig* 比喻) qualities of sb or sth that are easily seen, contrasted with deeper or hidden ones (人或事物的)表象, 外表, 外观: *Beneath her self-confident surface, she's quite unsure of herself.* 她看上去信心十足, 实际上很缺乏信心. ○ *You must not look only at the surface of things.* 看事物不能只看到表面现象. ○ [attrib 作定语] *surface politeness*, ie concealing anger, etc 勉强装出的礼貌(隐藏着愤怒等) ○ *surface impressions*, ie ones gained too quickly, without proper thought or observation 肤浅的印象. **4** (idm 习语) **on the 'surface** when not observed, thought about, etc deeply or thoroughly; superficially 在表面上; 在外表上: *The scheme seems on the surface to be quite practical.* 这方案表面上看来似乎很实际. ○ *On the surface, she's a charming, helpful person.* 从表面上看, 她又很动人又肯助人. **scratch the surface** ⇨ SCRATCH[1].

▷ **sur·face** *v* **1** [Tn, Tn·pr] **~ sth (with sth)** put a surface(1c) on sth 在某物上加表层: *surface a road (with tarmac)* (用柏油碎石)铺路面 ○ *a wall surfaced with plaster* 用灰泥饰面的墙. **2** [I] (of a submarine, skin-diver, etc) come up to the surface of a body of water (指潜艇、赤身潜水者等)浮到水面. **3** [I] (*infml* 口) (**a**) appear again after a period of remaining unseen, hidden, away from others, etc (隐蔽、隐藏、离开他人等一段时间后)重新出现: *After living abroad for years, she suddenly surfaced again in London.* 她在国外居住多年之后, 突然在伦敦重新露面了. ○ *Their old rivalry soon surfaced when they met again.* 他们重逢时, 昔日之明争暗斗旋即死灰复燃. (**b**) wake from sleep or unconsciousness 睡醒; 恢复知觉: *He finally surfaced at midday.* 他终于在中午时醒过来了.

□ **'surface mail** letters, etc carried by road, rail or sea, not by air 陆路邮件, 水路邮件(别于航空邮件).

ˌsurface 'tension property of liquids by which they form a film or layer at their surface and make its area as small as possible 表面张力.

ˌsurface-to-'air *adj* [attrib 作定语] (of missiles, etc) fired from the ground or from ships, aimed at aircraft (指导弹等)地对空的, 舰对空的.

sur·feit /'sɜ:fɪt; 'sɝfɪt/ *n* (usu *sing* 通常作单数) **~ (of sth)** too much of sth, esp of food and drink 过量, 过度(尤指饮食): *A surfeit of rich food is bad for you.* 多吃油腻食物对身体有害. ○ *There has been a surfeit of plays about divorce on the television recently.* 最近有关离婚的电视剧过多.

▷ **sur·feit** *v* [Tn, Tn·pr] **~ sb/oneself (with/on sth)** (*fml* 文) provide sb/oneself with too much of sth, esp food 向某人[自己]过多地提供某物(尤指食物): *surfeit oneself with fruit* 吃水果过多 ○ *be surfeited with pleasure* 作乐过度.

surge /sɜ:dʒ; sɝdʒ/ *v* **1** [I, Ipr, Ip] move forward in or like waves 在浪涛中或如同波浪般前进: *the surging tide* 汹涌的潮水 ○ *The floods surged along the valley.* 洪水沿着山谷滚滚流动. ○ *The crowd surged (past) into the stadium.* 观众涌入了体育场. **2** [I, Ip] **~ (up)** arise suddenly and intensely 急剧上升: *Anger surged (up) within him.* 他怒火中烧.

▷ **surge** *n* (usu *sing* 通常作单数) **~ (of/in sth)** **1** forward or upward movement 向前或向上的运动: *the surge of the sea* 大海的翻腾. **2** sudden occurrence or increase 突然发生; 激增: *a surge of anger, pity, etc* 一阵怒气、怜悯等 ○ *There's a surge in electricity demand at around 7 pm.* 晚上7点钟左右是用电高峰时间.

sur·geon /'sɜ:dʒən; 'sɝdʒən/ *n* doctor who performs surgical operations 外科医师: *a heart surgeon* 心脏外科医师. Cf 参看 PHYSICIAN.

sur·gery /'sɜ:dʒərɪ; 'sɝdʒərɪ/ *n* **1** [U] treatment of injuries or diseases by cutting or removing parts of the body 外科; 手术: *qualified in surgery and medicine* 内外

科合格的 ○ *prepare the patient for surgery* 给病人做术前准备 ○ *He underwent open-heart surgery.* 他接受了体外循环心脏手术. ○ *cosmetic surgery* 美容外科. **2** (*Brit*) (**a**) [C] place where a doctor, dentist, etc sees his patients (医师的)门诊处, 诊所. (**b**) [U] time during which a doctor, etc is available to see patients at his surgery 门诊时间: *Surgery lasts from 9 am to 10 am.* 门诊时间为上午9时至10时. ○ [attrib 作定语] ˈ*surgery hours* 门诊时间. **3** [C] (*Brit infml* 口) time when a Member of Parliament can be consulted by the people he represents (议员对选民的)接待时间: *She holds her surgery on Fridays at 6 pm.* 她星期五下午6时接待选民.

sur·gical /ˈsɜːdʒɪkl; ˋsɝdʒɪkl/ *adj* [attrib 作定语] of, by or for surgery 外科的; 外科手术的; 外科用的: *surgical instruments, treatment, skills* 外科器械、治疗、技术 ○ *a surgical ward*, ie for patients having operations 外科病房 ○ *a surgical stocking*, ie one specially designed to support an injured or diseased leg 外科治疗袜(用以支撑腿部的袜状物). ▷ **sur·gic·ally** /-klɪ; -klɪ/ *adv*: *a tumour removed surgically* 经手术切除的肿瘤.

□ ˌ**surgical** ˈ**spirit** (*Brit*) (*US* ˈ**rubbing alcohol**) clear liquid, consisting mainly of alcohol, used for cleaning wounds, etc 消毒用的酒精(用以清洗伤口等).

surly /ˈsɜːlɪ; ˋsɝlɪ/ *adj* (**-ier**, **-iest**) bad-tempered and unfriendly 脾气坏的; 乖戾的; 不友好的: *a surly person, look, refusal* 粗暴的人、样子、拒绝 ○ *Don't look so surly!* 别那么横眉立目的! ▷ **sur·li·ness** *n* [U].

sur·mise /səˈmaɪz; sɚˋmaɪz/ *v* [Tn, Tf, Tw] (*fml* 文) suppose (sth) without having evidence that makes it certain; guess 猜测(某事物); 猜想; 揣测: *With no news from the explorers we can only surmise their present position/where they are.* 我们没有探险者的消息, 只能猜测他们现在所处的位置. ○ *We surmised that he must have had an accident.* 我们猜想他一定出事了.

▷ **sur·mise** /ˈsɜːmaɪz; ˋsɝmaɪz/ *n* [C, U] (*fml* 文) guess(ing) 猜测; 猜想: *Your first surmise was right.* 你第一次猜得对. ○ *This is pure surmise.* 这纯属臆测.

sur·mount /səˈmaʊnt; sɚˋmaʊnt/ *v* **1** [Tn] deal with (a difficulty, etc); overcome 克服(困难等); 战胜: *We had many problems to surmount before we could start the project.* 我们得克服许多困难才能着手做这项工作. **2** [usu passive 通常用于被动语态: Tn, Tn·pr] be or be placed on top of (sth tall) 处于或置于(某高物)的顶端: *A weather-vane surmounts the spire/The spire is surmounted by a weather-vane.* 风向标装置在尖塔上[尖塔上装有风向标].

▷ **sur·mount·able** *adj* (of difficulties, etc) that can be overcome (指困难等)可克服的.

sur·name /ˈsɜːneɪm; ˋsɝˌnem/ *n* name shared by all the members of a family 姓; 姓氏: *Smith is a common English surname.* 史密斯是常见的英国姓. ⇨Usage at NAME[1] 用法见 NAME[1].

▷ **sur·named** *adj* [pred 作表语] having a specified surname 姓…的: *a boy surnamed Harris* 姓哈里斯的男孩.

sur·pass /səˈpɑːs; *US* -ˈpæs; sɚˋpæs/ *v* [Tn, Tn·pr] ~ **sb/sth (in sth)** (*fml* 文) do or be better than sb/sth; exceed sb/sth 优于或超过某人[某事物]: *surpass sb in speed, strength, skill* 在速度、力量、技术上超过某人 ○ *It will be hard to surpass this very high score.* 要超过这么高的分数是很难的. ○ *The beauty of the scenery surpassed all my expectations.* 我万万没想到风景那么漂亮.

▷ **sur·pass·ing** *adj* [attrib 作定语] (*fml* 文) of high quality or degree; exceptional 出色的; 卓越的; 格外的: *surpassing beauty* 绝色美人. **sur·pass·ingly** *adv*.

sur·plice /ˈsɜːplɪs; ˋsɝplɪs/ *n* loose (usu white) outer garment with wide sleeves worn by priests and singers in the choir during religious services (教士及唱诗班成员于举行仪式时穿的)罩衣(通常为白色).

sur·plus /ˈsɜːpləs; ˋsɝpləs/ *n* [C, U] **1** amount left over after one has used all that one needs; amount by which money received is greater than money spent 剩余(额); 过剩; 盈余; 顺差: *Surpluses of food can be sold for cash.* 多余的食物可卖钱. ○ *We have a trade surplus of £400 million.* 我们有4亿英镑的贸易顺差. ○ *a time of great surplus followed by a time of shortage* 物资大量过剩时期, 随之而来的物资短缺时期 ○ [attrib 作定语] *an army surplus store*, ie one selling clothes, equipment, etc no longer needed by the army 剩余军用物资商店(出售军服、装备品等的). Cf 参看 DEFICIT. **2** (idm 习语) **in** ˈ**surplus** having a surplus 有剩余; 有盈余: *Our trade is in surplus*, ie We are exporting more than we are importing. 我国贸易出现出超(出口量大于进口量).

▷ **sur·plus** *adj* ~ **(to sth)** more than is needed or used 剩余的; 过剩的: *surplus labour*, ie workers for whom there are no jobs 剩余劳动力 ○ *a sale of surplus stock* 剩余存货廉价出售 ○ *This food is surplus to requirements.* 这种食物供过于求.

sur·prise /səˈpraɪz; sɚˋpraɪz/ *n* **1** (**a**) [U] feeling caused by sth happening suddenly or unexpectedly 惊奇; 惊讶: *Their defeat caused little surprise*, ie was expected. 他们的失败不足为奇. ○ *To my surprise, the plan succeeded.* 我感到惊奇的是那计划竟然成功了. ○ *Imagine our surprise on seeing her there.* 你想想, 我们在那里看见她时, 是多么吃惊啊. ○ *She looked up in surprise when I shouted.* 我叫喊时, 她吃惊地抬起头来看. ○ *He expressed surprise that no one had offered to help.* 谁都不肯帮忙, 他感到诧异. (**b**) [C] event or thing that causes this feeling 令人吃惊的事物: *What a surprise!* 多么令人惊奇呀! ○ *We've had some unpleasant surprises.* 我们得到一些令人不快的意外消息. ○ *The gift came as a complete surprise (to me).* 这件礼物完全出乎(我的)意料. ○ *They sprang quite a surprise on me when they offered me that job.* 他们把那工作给了我, 我颇感意外. ○ [attrib 作定语] *a surprise visit, attack, party* 突然访问、袭击、料想不到的聚会. **2** (idm 习语) **take sb/sth by sur**ˈ**prise** attack, capture, etc sb/sth unexpectedly or without warning 出其不意或毫无预示而攻击、捕获…某人[某事物]: *The town was well defended so there was little chance of taking it by surprise.* 该城防守严密, 万难袭占. **take sb by sur**ˈ**prise** happen unexpectedly, so as to shock sb slightly 使某人吃一惊: *Her sudden resignation took us all by surprise.* 她突然辞职, 我们都为之愕然.

▷ **sur·prise** *v* **1** [Tn] cause (sb) to feel surprise 使(某人)吃惊: *She's over 80? You surprise me!* 她80多岁了? 真想不到! ○ *She was surprised by the boy's intelligence.* 那男孩的智力使她很吃惊. ○ *It wouldn't surprise me/I wouldn't be surprised if they lost*, ie I rather expect them to lose. 他们要是失败了也不足为奇. ○ *Would it surprise you to know that I'm thinking of resigning?* 我正考虑辞职, 你感到意外吗? **2** [Tn, Tng] attack, discover, etc (sb) suddenly and unexpectedly 突然而出人意料地攻击、发现…(某人): *surprise the opposition*, ie attack them when they are unprepared 袭击对方 ○ *We returned early and surprised the burglars searching through the cupboards.* 我们回来得早, 没想到正撞见有贼正在偷柜橱里的东西. **3** [Tn·pr] ~ **sb into sth/doing sth** cause sb to do sth through sudden unexpected action 以突然而出其不意的行动促使某人做某事: *By firing a few shots we can surprise them into revealing their positions.* 我们冷不防打几枪就能让他们暴露他们的位置.

sur·prised *adj* ~ **(at sth/sb)** experiencing or showing a feeling of surprise 惊奇的; 惊讶的; 吃惊的; 诧异的: *a surprised look, cry* 吃惊的样子、惊叫 ○ *We were surprised at the news.* 我们听到这消息很惊讶. ○ *I'm surprised at you, playing with dolls at your age!* 想不到你这年龄还玩玩具娃娃! ○ *I'm very surprised to see you here.* 我万万没想到能在这儿碰见你. ○ *I'm surprised that he didn't come.* 我很奇怪他竟没有来. ○ *It's nothing to be surprised about.* 没有什么值得大惊小怪的.

sur·pris·ing *adj* causing surprise 令人惊奇的; 使人吃惊的; 惊人的: *a surprising decision, defeat* 让人大吃一惊的决定、败北 ○ *It's surprising they lost.* 他们竟然失败了, 真没想到. **sur·pris·ingly** *adv*: *Surprisingly, no one came.* 真奇怪, 没有人来. ○ *She looked surprisingly well.* 她看上去身体好极了.

sur·real /səˈrɪəl; səˋriəl/ *adj* unlike reality, esp in having combinations or strange distortions of things, as in a dream; fantastic; bizarre 超现实的; 不现实的; 梦幻般的; 荒诞的; 离奇的: *Under the influence of the drug my mind was filled with surreal images.* 我受了麻醉药的刺激, 头脑里充满了稀奇古怪的幻觉. ○ *Meeting you here like this is positively surreal!* 像这样与你在此相逢真好比一场梦!

sur·real·ism /səˈrɪəlɪzəm; səˋriəlˌɪzəm/ *n* [U] 20th-century movement in art and literature that tries to express what is in the subconscious mind by showing objects and

S

events as seen in dreams, etc 超现实主义(20世纪的文艺潮流,藉表现梦境等以表达潜意识的内容).

▷ **sur·real·ist** /-lɪst; -lɪst/ *n, adj* [attrib 作定语] (artist, writer, etc) of surrealism 超现实主义的; 超现实主义者; 超现实主义流派的画家、作家等: *a surrealist painting, exhibition* 超现实主义的画、作品展览.

sur·real·istic /səˌrɪəˈlɪstɪk; səˌriəlˈɪstɪk/ *adj* **1** of surrealism 超现实主义的: *a surrealistic style* 超现实主义的风格. **2** surreal 超现实的; 梦幻般的; 离奇的.

sur·ren·der /səˈrendə(r); səˈrɛndɚ/ *v* **1** [I, Ipr, Tn, Tn·pr] **~ (oneself) (to sb)** stop resisting an enemy, etc; yield; give up 停止抵抗; 投降; 屈服; 放弃: *We shall never surrender.* 我们决不投降. ○ *The hijackers finally surrendered (themselves) to the police.* 劫机者终于向警方投降了. **2** [Tn, Tn·pr] **~ sth/sb (to sb)** (*fml* 文) give up possession of sth/sb when forced by others or by necessity; hand sth/sb over 被迫放弃对某物[某人]的控制权; 交出某事物[某人]: *We shall never surrender our liberty.* 我们决不放弃自由权. ○ *They surrendered their guns to the police.* 他们向警方交出枪枝. ○ *He surrendered his insurance policy*, ie gave up his rights under the policy in return for immediate payment 他中途退保(放弃保险以立即获得退保金). **3** (phr v) **surrender (oneself) to sth** (*fml or rhet usu derog* 文或修辞, 通常作贬义) allow (a habit, an emotion, an influence, etc) to control what one does 听任(某习惯、感情、影响等)摆布: *He surrendered (himself) to despair and eventually committed suicide.* 他陷于绝望, 终于自杀了.

▷ **sur·ren·der** *n* [U, C] surrendering or being surrendered 投降; 屈服; 放弃; 交出: *demand the surrender of the town* 要求该城投降 ○ *She accused the government of a cowardly surrender to big-business interests.* 她指责政府畏首畏尾屈从于大企业的利益. ○ [attrib 作定语] *What is the surrender value of these shares?* 这些股票的转让价额是多少?

sur·rep·ti·tious /ˌsʌrəpˈtɪʃəs; ˌsʌrəpˈtɪʃəs/ *adj* (*usu derog* 通常作贬义) done or acting secretly or stealthily 暗中进行的; 偷偷的: *a surreptitious glance* 偷偷的一瞥 ○ *She carried out a surreptitious search of his belongings.* 她暗地里搜查他的东西. ○ *I don't mind you smoking occasionally — there's no need to be so surreptitious about it!* 你偶尔吸烟我倒并不介意——何必这样躲躲闪闪!

▷ **sur·rep·ti·tiously** *adv*.

sur·rog·ate /ˈsʌrəgeɪt; ˈsʌrəˌget/ *n* **~ (for sb/sth)** (*fml* 文) person or thing that acts or is used instead of another; substitute 替代的人或事物; 替代者; 代理人; 替代物; 代用品: *Fiction is a poor surrogate for real experience.* 小说中的事远逊于实际体验. ○ [attrib 作定语] *a surrogate mother*, ie a woman who has a baby on behalf of another who is unable to have babies herself 代母(代不育女子生育的女子).

sur·round /səˈraʊnd; səˈraʊnd/ *v* [Tn, Tn·pr] **(a) ~ sb/sth (with sb/sth)** (cause sb/sth to) move into position all round sb/sth; encircle sb/sth, esp so as to prevent escape (使某人[某物])包围某人[某物]; 围住某人[某物](尤指使之无法脱逃): *Troops have surrounded the town.* 部队已将该城包围. ○ *They have surrounded the town with troops.* 他们出动军队包围了该城. ○ (*fig* 比喻) *He likes to surround himself with beautiful things.* 他喜欢生活在美的环境中. **(b) ~ sth/sb (by/with sth)** (esp passive 尤用于被动语态) be all round sth/sb 包围或环绕某物[某人]: *Trees surround the pond.* 树木围绕着池塘. ○ *The house was surrounded by high walls.* 房子的四周有高墙. ○ (*fig* 比喻) *The new plan is surrounded by much speculation*, ie Everyone is wondering about it. 新计划备受猜疑. ○ *She has always been surrounded with fashionable friends.* 她周围总有许多爱赶时髦的朋友.

▷ **sur·round** *n* (usu decorative) border around an object (通常指装饰性的)物体的边缘: *a fireplace with a tiled surround* 周围镶有瓷砖的壁炉.

sur·round·ing *adj* [attrib 作定语] that is around and nearby 周围附近的: *York and the surrounding countryside.* 约克城及其近郊. **sur·round·ings** *n* [pl] all the objects, conditions, etc that are around (and may affect) sb/sth; environment 周围的物体、条件等(可为有影响力的); 环境: *living in pleasant surroundings* 生活在舒适的环境中 ○ *Animals in zoos are not in their natural surroundings.* 动物园中的动物没有自然环境.

sur·tax /ˈsɜːtæks; ˈsɝˌtæks/ *n* [U] tax charged at a higher rate than the normal on income above a certain level 附加税(对超过限度的收入所征收的).

sur·veil·lance /sɜːˈveɪləns; sɚˈveləns/ *n* [U] careful watch kept on sb suspected of doing wrong (对涉嫌者的)监视: *The police are keeping the suspects under round-the-clock surveillance.* 警方对疑犯昼夜监视.

sur·vey /səˈveɪ; sɚˈve/ *v* [Tn] **1** look carefully at all of (sth/sb), esp from a distance 仔细全面地观察(某物[某人])(尤指自远处): *surveying the crowds from a balcony* 从阳台上观望人群 ○ *survey the countryside from the top of a hill* 从山顶上眺望郊野 ○ *She surveyed me haughtily over the top of her glasses.* 她傲慢地从眼镜的上方向我审视. **2** study (and describe) the general condition of (sth) 全面研究(及论述)(某事物): *a speech in which she surveyed the international situation* 她概括论述国际局势的讲话 ○ *In this book, the author surveys recent developments in linguistics.* 作者在本书中概述了语言学目前的发展情况. **3** find and record the area and features of (a piece of land) by measurement and/or calculation (eg using trigonometry) 测量, 勘察, 勘测(土地): *survey a plot of land for building* 勘测一建筑用地. **4** (*Brit*) examine (a building, etc) to make sure its structure is in good condition 检查(建筑物等)(鉴定其结构状况): *have a house surveyed before deciding to buy it* 买房子要先鉴定质量再决定购买与否. **5** investigate the behaviour, opinions, etc of (a group of people), usu by questioning them 调查(某部分人)的行为、意见等(通常以询问方式进行): *Of the five hundred householders surveyed, 40% had dishwashers.* 在接受调查的五百家住户中, 40%有洗碗机.

▷ **sur·vey** /ˈsɜːveɪ; ˈsɝve/ *n* **1** general view, examination or description 全面的观察、检查或论述; 审视; 概观; 概论: *A quick survey of the street showed that no one was about.* 扫视街道, 空无一人. ○ *a survey of the situation, subject* 对情况、问题的概括论述 ○ *a comprehensive survey of modern music* 现代音乐综述. **2** act of surveying (SURVEY *v* 3); map or record of this 测量; 勘测; 测量图; 勘测记录: *an aerial survey*, ie made by taking photographs from an aircraft 航空测量照片. **3** (*Brit*) examination of the condition of a house, etc (房屋等的)结构状况检查, 查勘, 鉴定. **4** act of surveying (SURVEY *v* 5); investigation (对部分人的行为、意见等的)调查: *a public oˈpinion survey* 民意调查 ○ *Surveys show that 75% of people approve of the new law.* 民意测验表明, 75%的人赞成新颁布的法规.

sur·veyor /səˈveɪə(r); sɚˈveɚ/ *n* **1** person who surveys (SURVEY *v* 4) and values buildings, etc (建筑物等的)鉴定估价人. **2** person who surveys (SURVEY *v* 3) land, etc (土地等的)测量员, 勘测员. **3** official appointed to check the accuracy, quality, etc of sth 检测官; 检验员: *surveyor of weights and measures* 度量衡检测官 ○ *the surveyor of highways* 公路视察员.

sur·vival /səˈvaɪvl; sɚˈvaɪvḷ/ *n* **1** [U] state of continuing to live or exist; surviving 继续生存或存在; 存活; 幸存: *the miraculous survival of some people in the air crash* 空难事件中有些人奇迹般大难不死 ○ *the survival of the fittest*, ie the continuing existence of those animals and plants which are best adapted to their surroundings, etc 适者生存(动植物最能适应环境等者得以存活) ○ [attrib 作定语] *a surˈvival kit*, ie a package of items needed by survivors of a disaster, eg at sea 救生包(装有维持生命之必需品, 如供海难等幸存者使用的). **2** [C] **~ (from sth)** person, thing, custom, belief, etc that has survived from an earlier time 过去时代留存下来的人、物、风俗、信仰等; 遗老; 遗习; 旧风俗; 旧思想: *a ceremony which is a survival from pre-Christian times* 从公元前沿袭下来的礼仪活动.

sur·vive /səˈvaɪv; sɚˈvaɪv/ *v* **1** [I, Ipr] **~ (from sth); ~ (on sth)** continue to live or exist 继续生存或存在: *the last surviving member of the family* 这家唯一活着的人 ○ *Of the six people in the plane that crashed, only one survived.* 在失事飞机上的六个人, 仅一人幸存. ○ *Many strange customs have survived from earlier times.* 有许多古怪的习俗源远流长. ○ *I can't survive on £30 a week*, ie It is not enough for my basic needs. 我每周收入30英镑难以活命. ○ (*fig* 比喻) *Life is hard at the moment, but we're surviving*, ie coping successfully with the difficulties.

目前生活很艰难，但我们正在挣扎求生. **2** [Tn] continue to live or exist in spite of nearly being killed or destroyed by (sth) 经历(某事物)幸存: *survive an earthquake, shipwreck, etc* 经历地震、沉船等而死里逃生 ○ *Few buildings survived the bombing raids intact.* 空袭过后幸存的建筑物绝无仅有. ○ *The plants may not survive the frost.* 这些植物不经冻. **3** [Tn] remain alive after (sb) 比(某人)长命: *The old lady has survived all her children.* 那老太太的子女都先她而去世了.

▷ **sur·vivor** *n* person who has survived 幸存者; 生还者: *send help to the survivors of the earthquake* 救助地震中的幸存者.

sus (also **suss**) /sʌs; sʌs/ *v* (**-ss-**) (*sl* 俚) **1** [Tn, Tn·p, Tf, Tw] **~ sb/sth (out)** discover sb/sth 发现、发觉或探明某人[某事物]: *I've got him/it sussed (out)*, ie I now understand him/it. 我现在已了解他[它]了. ○ *We've sussed (out) who did it.* 我们已弄清楚是谁干的了. **2** (phr v) **sus sth out** investigate sth carefully 仔细调查某事物: *I sent Joe along to sus out the possibility of doing a deal with them.* 我派乔去了解一下与他们做一笔交易的可能性.

sus·cept·ible /səˈseptəbl; səˋsɛptəbḷ/ *adj* **1 ~ to sth** [pred 作表语] easily influenced or harmed by sth 易受某事物影响或损害: *highly susceptible to flattery* 听几句好话就忘乎所以 ○ *plants that are not susceptible to disease* 不易受病害侵袭的植物. **2** easily influenced by feelings; impressionable 易受感情影响的; 易受影响的: *a naïve person with a susceptible nature* 幼稚而无主见的人 ○ *He's so susceptible that she easily gained his affection.* 他易受感情影响，所以她很轻易地就得到了他的爱. **3 ~ of sth** [pred 作表语] (*fml* 文) that can undergo sth; capable of sth 能经受某事物; 有某种能力: *Is your statement susceptible of proof?* 你的说法能加以证实吗?

▷ **sus·cept·ib·il·ity** /səˌseptəˈbɪlətɪ; səˌsɛptəˋbɪlətɪ/ *n* **1** [U] **~ (to sth)** state of being susceptible 易受影响或损害的状况: *take advantage of her susceptibility* 利用她在感情上的脆弱 ○ *susceptibility to persuasion* 容易被言词打动的特性. **2 susceptibilities** [pl] person's feelings, considered as being easily hurt 感情(之脆弱处): *Do nothing to offend her susceptibilities.* 不要伤害她的感情.

sus·pect /səˈspekt; səˋspɛkt/ *v* **1** [Tn, Tf, Tnt] have an idea of the existence, presence or truth of (sth); believe 有(某事物)存在或属实的想法; 相信: *He suspected an ambush.* 他感到有埋伏. ○ *I strongly suspect that they're trying to get rid of me.* 我强烈地感觉到他们要除掉我. ○ *Most people don't, I suspect, realize this.* 我想，大多数人是意识不到这一点的. ○ *What she said sounded convincing, but I suspect it to be a lie.* 她的话听起来像那么回事，但我认为那是谎话. **2** [Tn] feel doubt about (sth); mistrust 怀疑(某事物); 不信任: *suspect sb's motives* 怀疑某人的动机 ○ *I suspect the truth of her statement.* 我对她那番话的真实性表示怀疑. **3** [Tn, Tn·pr] **~ sb (of sth/doing sth)** feel that sb is guilty of sth, without certain proof 怀疑某人有某罪: *Who do the police suspect (of the crime)?* 警方怀疑谁(作的案)? ○ *What made you suspect her of having taken the money?* 你凭什么怀疑钱是她偷的?

▷ **sus·pect** /ˈsʌspekt; ˋsʌspɛkt/ *n* person suspected of a crime, etc 嫌疑犯; 可疑对象: *The police are interrogating two suspects.* 警方正在审讯两个嫌疑犯. ○ *He's a prime suspect in the murder case.* 他是这次谋杀案的主要怀疑对象.

sus·pect /ˈsʌspekt; ˋsʌspɛkt/ *adj* not to be relied on or trusted; possibly false 不可靠的; 不可信的; 可能有假的; 可疑的: *His statements are suspect.* 他的说法靠不住. ○ *The car has a suspect tyre*, eg one that is damaged and therefore dangerous. 这辆汽车的轮胎有问题(如已损坏故有危险).

sus·pend /səˈspend; səˋspɛnd/ *v* **1** [Tn, Tn·pr] **~ sth (from sth)** (*fml* 文) hang sth up 悬挂或吊起某物: *A lamp was suspended from the ceiling above us.* 我们头顶上的天花板上吊着一盏灯. **2** [Tn·pr usu passive 通常用于被动语态] not allow (sth) to fall or sink in air or liquid, etc 使(某物)悬浮: *a balloon suspended above the crowd* 悬浮在人群上方的气球 ○ *Smoke hung suspended in the still air.* 轻烟在静止的空气里悬浮着. ○ *particles suspended in water* 悬浮在水中的微粒. **3** [Tn] (**a**) prevent (sth) from being in effect for a time; stop (sth) temporarily 暂不实行(某事物); 使(某事物)暂停: *suspend a rule* 暂不实行一项规定 ○ *Rail services are suspended indefinitely because of the strike.* 铁路运输因罢工而无限期停运. ○ *During the crisis, the constitution was suspended*, ie people did not have their normal civil rights. 在危机期间，曾暂时停止实行宪法(人民不能正常地享有公民权利). (**b**) postpone (sth); delay 推迟(某事物); 延缓: *suspend introduction of the new scheme* 延缓实施新方案 ○ *suspend judgement*, ie delay forming or expressing an opinion 暂不决断 ○ *give a criminal a suspended sentence*, ie not send him to prison unless he commits a further offence 给一罪犯缓刑. **4** [Tn, Tn·pr] **~ sb (from sth)** prevent sb officially from holding his usual position, carrying out his usual duties, etc for a time 勒令某人暂时停职、停止履行职责等: *The policeman was suspended while the complaint was investigated.* 因该警察遭投诉，在调查期间已令其暂停职务. ○ *She was suspended from school for stealing.* 她因有偷窃行为遭勒令停学处分.

□ **suˌspended aniˈmation** state of being alive but not conscious 假死; 不省人事: (*fig* 比喻) *The whole project is in suspended animation while we wait for permission to proceed.* 我们整个项目暂时搁置以待审批.

sus·pender /səˈspendə(r); səˋspɛndɚ/ *n* **1** [C esp *pl* 尤作复数] (*Brit*) short elastic strap for holding up a sock or stocking by its top 吊带. **2 suspenders** [pl] (*US*) = BRACES.

□ **suˈspender belt** woman's belt-like undergarment, worn round the waist, with straps for holding up stockings (女用)吊带围腰.

sus·pense /səˈspens; səˋspɛns/ *n* [U] feeling of tenseness, worry, etc about what may happen (对可能发生之事的)紧张感，担心，挂虑: *We waited in great suspense for the doctor's opinion.* 我们焦急万分地等候医生做出诊断. ○ *Don't keep us in suspense any longer: tell us what happened!* 别再让我们着急了，快告诉我们出了什么事了!

sus·pen·sion /səˈspenʃn; səˋspɛnʃən/ *n* **1** [U] suspending or being suspended 悬挂; 悬浮; 暂停; 延缓; 停职: *the suspension of a rule, law, etc* 规则、法令等的暂停实施 ○ *the suspension of a pupil from school* 对一名学生的停学处分 ○ *She appealed against her suspension.* 她对被停职一事已进行上诉. **2** [U] system of parts (eg springs and shock absorbers) by which a vehicle is supported on its axles (车辆的)悬挂装置(如弹簧及减震器): *The poor suspension gives a rather bumpy ride.* 因悬挂装置性能差，行驶时很颠簸. ⇨illus at App 1 见附录1插图, page xii. **3** [C, U] (state of a) liquid containing tiny particles of solid matter floating in it 悬浮(液): *medicine in powder form held in suspension*, ie to be taken by drinking 药粉悬浮剂(口服用).

□ **suˈspension bridge** bridge suspended from steel cables supported by towers at each end 悬索桥; 吊桥. ⇨illus at BRIDGE 见BRIDGE插图.

sus·pi·cion /səˈspɪʃn; səˋspɪʃən/ *n* **1** (**a**) [U] suspecting or being suspected 怀疑; 涉嫌: *regard sb with suspicion* 怀疑某人 ○ *He was arrested on suspicion of having stolen the money.* 他因涉嫌偷那笔钱而被捕. ○ *Her behaviour aroused no suspicion.* 她的举动未受怀疑. ○ *After a crime, suspicion naturally falls on the person who has a motive for it.* 一罪案发生后，有作案动机的人自然受到怀疑. (**b**) [C] **~ (about sth/sb); ~ (that...)** belief or feeling that sth is wrong, that sb has done wrong, etc 疑心; 疑忌; 猜疑: *I have a suspicion that she is not telling me the truth.* 我疑心她没对我说实话. ○ *It appears to be genuine, but I have my suspicions (about it).* 这看来好像是真的，不过我(对此)有怀疑. **2** [sing] **~ (of sth)** slight taste or amount 些许味道; 少量; 一点儿: *a suspicion of garlic in the stew* 炖菜中的一点大蒜味 ○ *a suspicion of sadness in her voice* 她声音中的一丝悲伤. **3** (idm 习语) **aˌbove suˈspicion** too good, honest, etc to be suspected of wrongdoing 不受怀疑的: *Nobody who was near the scene of the crime is above suspicion.* 在犯罪现场附近的人无不受到怀疑. **under suˈspicion** suspected of wrongdoing 有嫌疑; 涉嫌.

sus·pi·cious /səˈspɪʃəs; səˋspɪʃəs/ *adj* **1 ~ (about/of sth/sb)** having or showing suspicion 有疑心的; 表示怀疑的: *a suspicious look, attitude* 怀疑的样子、态度 ○ *I'm very suspicious about her motives.* 我对她的动机甚为怀

疑. ○ *He is suspicious of* (ie does not trust) *strangers.* 他不信任陌生人. **2** causing suspicion 引起怀疑的; 可疑的: *a suspicious action, remark* 可疑的行动、言语 ○ *a suspicious character*, ie sb who may be dishonest 不可靠的人 ○ *It's very suspicious that she was in the house when the crime happened.* 案发时她在房子里, 此点非常可疑.
▷ **sus·pi·ciously** *adv*: *acting suspiciously* 形迹可疑 ○ *Everything was suspiciously quiet.* 一切静得离奇.

suss = SUS.

sus·tain /səˈsteɪn; səˈsten/ *v* [Tn] **1** (*fml* 文) bear (weight) without breaking or falling: support 承受住(重量); 支承; 支撑: *Will this shelf sustain the weight of all these books?* 这个书架承受得住这些书的重量吗? **2** (**a**) keep (sb/sth) alive or in existence 维持(某人[某物])的生命或存在: *You should eat good sustaining food*, ie food that gives strength. 你应该吃些能增强体力的食物. ○ *not enough oxygen to sustain life* 氧气稀少不足以维持生命 ○ *Only the hope that the rescuers were getting nearer sustained the trapped miners*, ie kept them cheerful and enabled them to stay alive. 遇难矿工盼望援救人员正在接近他们, 这是他们赖以坚持下去的唯一希望. (**b**) keep (a sound, an effort, etc) going; maintain 使(声音、努力等)持续下去; 保持: *The book's weakness is the author's inability to sustain an argument.* 该书的缺点在于作者未能把论证展开. ○ *sustain a note*, ie continue to play or sing it without interruption 继续演奏(或演唱)某一音符 ○ *make a sustained effort to finish off the work* 坚持不懈以完成该项工作 ○ *The clapping was sustained for several minutes.* 掌声持续了几分钟. **3** (*fml* 文) undergo (sth); suffer 经受(某事物); 遭受: *sustain a defeat, an injury, a loss* 遭受失败、伤害、损失 ○ *He sustained a severe blow on the head.* 他头部受到重击. **4** (*law* 律) decide that (a claim, etc) is valid; uphold 确认(某项要求等)正当有效; 认可; 准许: *The court sustained his claim that the contract was illegal.* 法庭确认他的要求正当, 宣布该合同不合法. ○ *Objection sustained!* 反对有效!

S

sus·ten·ance /ˈsʌstɪnəns; ˈsʌstənəns/ *n* [U] (nourishing quality of) food and drink; nourishment 食物; 营养; 养料: *There's not much sustenance in a glass of orange squash.* 一杯橙汁饮料没有什么营养. ○ *weak from lack of sustenance* 因缺乏营养而虚弱.

su·ture /ˈsuːtʃə(r); ˈsutʃɚ/ *n* (*medical* 医) stitch or stitches made in sewing up a wound, esp following an operation (伤口的)缝线, 缝术.
▷ **su·ture** *v* [Tn] (*medical* 医) sew up (a wound) 缝合(伤口).

su·zer·ain /ˈsuːzəreɪn; *US* -rɪn; ˈsuzərɪn/ *n* (*fml* 文) country or ruler that controls the foreign policy of another country but allows it to govern its own internal affairs 宗主国; 宗主国的统治者.
▷ **su·zer·ainty** /ˈsuːzərəntɪ; ˈsuzərɪntɪ/ *n* [U] (*fml* 文) authority or rule of a suzerain 宗主权; 宗主国的统治: *a country under the suzerainty of its powerful neighbour* 在强大邻国宗主权治下的国家.

svelte /svelt; svɛlt/ *adj* (*approv* 褒) (of a person) gracefully thin (指人)苗条的: *a svelte figure* 苗条的身材.

SW *abbr* 缩写 = **1** (*radio* 无) short wave. **2** South-West(ern): *SW Australia* 澳大利亚西南部 ○ *London SW15 6QX*, ie as a postal code 伦敦 SW15 6QX(如用作邮政编码).

swab /swɒb; swɑb/ *n* (**a**) piece of cotton wool, etc used in medicine for cleaning wounds, etc or for taking specimens, eg of mucus, for testing (医用的)拭子; 药签. (**b**) specimen taken in this way (用拭子取下的)化验标本: *take swabs from children suspected of having diphtheria* 取怀疑白喉患儿拭样供化验.
▷ **swab** *v* (**-bb-**) **1** [Tn, Tn·pr] clean or wipe (sth) with a swab 用拭子拭抹或擦净(某物): *swab the wound with cotton wool* 用药棉擦净伤口 ○ *swab the blood off her face* 用拭子揩掉她脸上的血迹. **2** [Tn, Tn·p] **~ sth (down)** clean sth with water using a mop, cloth, etc (用拖把、抹布等)擦洗(某物): *swab down the decks* 用拖把擦洗甲板.

swaddle /ˈswɒdl; ˈswɑdl/ *v* [Tn, Tn·pr] **~ sb (in sth)** **1** (*dated* 旧) wrap (a baby) in long narrow strips of cloth to stop it moving about 用长布条包裹(婴儿). **2** wrap sb/oneself in warm clothes, etc; swathe sb/oneself 用保暖的衣物等裹住某人[自己]的身体; 给某人[自己]包扎: *She sat by the fire, swaddled in a blanket.* 她用毯子裹住身子, 坐在火炉旁.
▷ **ˈswaddling-clothes** /ˈswɒdlɪŋ; ˈswɑdlɪŋ/ *n* [pl] (*dated* 旧) strips of cloth used for swaddling a baby 用作襁褓的长布条.

swag /swæg; swæg/ *n* **1** [C] carved ornament representing a hanging bunch of fruit and flowers 雕刻的有成簇下垂的水果及鲜花的装饰物. **2** [U] (*dated sl* 旧, 俚) stolen goods 赃物. **3** [C] (*Austral* 澳) bundle of belongings carried by a tramp 流浪者的行囊.
□ **ˈswagman** *n* (*pl* **-men**) (*Austral* 澳) tramp 流浪的人.

swag·ger /ˈswægə(r); ˈswægɚ/ *v* [I, Ipr, Ip] (*usu derog* 通常作贬义) walk or behave in a proud or boastful way 趾高气扬地行走或行事: *Don't swagger (around) just because you got the job.* 别因为得到了这份工作就得意忘形. ○ *He took his prize and swaggered back to his seat.* 他领奖后洋洋得意地回到自己的座位上.
▷ **swag·ger** *n* [sing] (*sometimes derog* 有时作贬义) swaggering movement or way of behaving 趾高气扬: *walk with a swagger* 大摇大摆地行走.
swag·ger·ingly *adv*.
□ **ˈswagger-stick** (also **ˈswagger-cane**) *n* (*Brit*) short stick carried by a military officer 军官用的短手杖.

swain /sweɪn; swen/ *n* **1** (*dated or joc* 旧或谑) young male lover; suitor 情郎; 求爱的男子. **2** (*arch* 古) young man from the country 乡村小伙子.

swal·low[1] /ˈswɒləʊ; ˈswɑlo/ *v* **1** (**a**) [I, Tn] cause or allow (esp food or drink) to go down the throat 吞下或咽下(尤指食物或饮料): *Taking pills is easy; just put them in your mouth and swallow.* 服用药片很容易, 只须放在口中咽下即可. ○ *Chew your food properly before swallowing it.* 食物嚼碎后再咽下. (**b**) [I] use the muscles of the throat as if doing this, eg in fear 做如同吞咽般的动作(如恐惧时): *She swallowed hard, and turned to face her accuser.* 她用力咽了一下唾液, 转身面对那个控告她的人. **2** [Tn] (*infml* 口) (**a**) accept (an insult, etc) without protest 忍受(侮辱等): *She called you a liar. Are you going to swallow that?* 她说你撒谎. 你打算忍受这种侮辱吗? ○ *He swallowed all the criticism without saying a thing.* 他默默地忍受一切责难. (**b**) believe (sth) too easily 轻信(某事物): *He flatters her outrageously, and she swallows it whole*, ie believes it entirely. 他极力奉承她, 而她竟以为完全是由衷之言. **3** [Tn, Tn·p] **~ sb/sth (up)** (**a**) take sb/sth into itself so that he/it can no longer be seen 吞没或掩盖某人[某事物]: *The jungle swallowed up the explorers.* 探险人员消失在密林里了. ○ *The aircraft was swallowed (up) in the clouds.* 飞机已没入云中. ○ (*fig* 比喻) *small firms being swallowed up by giant corporations*, ie taken over so that they disappear 被大公司兼并的小商行. (**b**) use sth up completely 用尽某事物: *The cost of the trial swallowed up all their savings.* 诉讼费用耗光了他们的全部积蓄. **4** [Tn] not express (a feeling, etc) openly 不流露(感情等): *She swallowed her anger and carried on.* 她忍气吞声地继续进行下去. ○ *I was forced to swallow my pride and ask for a loan.* 我无奈须忍辱告贷. **5** (idm 习语) **a bitter pill to swallow** ⇨ BITTER. **swallow the bait** accept sth that has been said, offered, etc to tempt one 上钩; 中圈套. **swallow/pocket one's pride** ⇨ PRIDE. **swallow one's words** admit that one has said sth wrong 承认说错了话: *He told me I wouldn't pass the test but I'm determined to make him swallow his words*, ie by passing. 他对我说我考不及格, 我一定让他将来承认说错了话.
▷ **swal·low** *n* (**a**) act of swallowing 吞; 咽. (**b**) amount swallowed at one time 一次吞咽的量: *take a swallow of beer* 喝一口啤酒.

swal·low[2] /ˈswɒləʊ; ˈswɑlo/ *n* **1** any of various types of small quick-flying insect-eating bird with a forked tail that migrate to northern countries (eg Britain) in summer 燕子. ⇨illus at App 1 见附录1插图, page iv. **2** (idm 习语) **ˌone swallow ˌdoes not make a ˈsummer** (*saying* 谚) a single fortunate or satisfactory incident, example, etc does not mean that all the others will be as good 一燕不成夏(仅有的一次幸运或好事等并不意味着一切都好).
□ **ˈswallow-dive** (*Brit*) (*US* **swan-dive**) *n* type of

dive with the arms spread out until one is close to the water (直体)向前跳水; 燕式跳水.

swam *pt* of SWIM.

swami /ˈswɑːmɪ; ˈswɑmɪ/ *n* Hindu religious teacher 印度教宗教导师.

swamp /swɒmp; swɑmp/ *n* [C, U] (area of) soft wet land; marsh 湿软土地; 沼泽; 沼泽区.

▷ **swamp** *v* **1** [Tn] flood or soak (sth) with water 淹没或浸泡(某物): *The sink overflowed and swamped the kitchen.* 洗涤槽的水溢出来了, 厨房里到处是水. ○ *A huge wave swamped the boat.* 一个巨浪淹没了那条船. **2** [esp passive 尤用于被动语态: Tn, Tn·pr] **~ sb/sth (with sth)** overwhelm sb/sth with a great quantity of things (以繁多的事物)压倒某人[某事物]: *We asked for applications and were swamped (with them).* 我们请大家提出申请, 因而(为此)应接不暇. ○ *I've been swamped with work this year.* 今年我工作忙得不可开交.

swampy *adj* (**-ier**, **-iest**): *swampy ground* 湿软的地面.

swan /swɒn; swɑn/ *n* **1** large graceful (usu white) water-bird with a long thin neck 天鹅. ⇨illus at App 1 见附录1插图, page v. **2** (idm 习语) **all sb's geese are swans** ⇨ GOOSE.

▷ **swan** *v* (**-nn-**) [Ipr, Ip] **~ off, around, etc** (*infml derog* 口, 贬) go off, around, etc in a leisurely but irresponsible manner 优游自在而不负责任地走开、闲逛等: *swanning around (the town) in her new sports car when she should have been at work* 在本该她工作的时间, 却开着她那辆新跑车(在城里)到处兜风 ○ *Are you swanning off on holiday again?* 你又是一走了之度假去了吗?

□ ˈ**swan-dive** *n* (*US*) = SWALLOW-DIVE (SWALLOW 2).

ˈ**swan-song** *n* person's last performance, achievement or composition 个人最后的演出、成就或作品: *His performance as King Lear was to be his swan-song before retiring.* 他扮演李尔王是他退休前的告别演出.

swank /swæŋk; swæŋk/ *v* [I] (*infml derog* 口, 贬) behave or talk in a boastful way; swagger 炫耀; 吹嘘; 趾高气扬: *She's swanking just because they said her essay was the best.* 皆因人称她的文章最好, 她就忘乎所以了.

▷ **swank** *n* (*infml derog* 口, 贬) **1** [U] behaviour or talk that is intended to impress people 炫耀; 吹嘘; 出风头: *wear an expensive watch just for swank* 仅为摆阔气而戴贵重的手表. **2** [C] person who swanks 炫耀者; 吹牛者; 出风头的人: *Don't be such a swank!* 别那么招摇!

swanky *adj* (**-ier**, **-iest**) (*infml derog* 口, 贬) **1** fashionable and expensive in a showy way 炫耀时髦的; 摆阔气的: *He stays in the swankiest hotels.* 他住最奢华的旅馆. **2** tending to swank 爱炫耀的: *Jill and her swanky friends.* 吉尔和她的那些爱出风头的朋友.

swap (also **swop**) /swɒp; swɑp/ *v* (**-pp-**) (*infml* 口) **1** [I, Ipr, Tn, Tn·pr, Tn·p, Dn·n] **~ (sth) (with sb)**; **~ (sb) sth for sth**; **~ sth (over/round)** give sth in exchange for sth else; substitute sth for sth else 以某物交换他物; 以此物代替彼物: *Your book looks more interesting than mine: do you want to swap (with me)?* 你的书好像比我的有意思, 你愿意(和我)交换吗? ○ *They swapped* (ie told each other) *stories about their army days.* 他们互相讲述了他们在军队中的经历. ○ *I'll swap (you) my Michael Jackson tape for your Bruce Springsteen album.* 我想用迈克尔·杰克逊的录音带交换你的布鲁斯·斯普林斯廷唱片专辑. ○ *She swapped our chairs (round), so I had hers and she had mine.* 她把我们俩的椅子对调了, 因此我坐的是她的, 她坐的是我的. ○ *I wouldn't swap places with him for anything,* ie would not wish to be in his situation. 我说什么也不愿意处于他的地位. **2** (idm 习语) **change/swap horses in mid-stream** ⇨ HORSE. **change/swap places** ⇨ PLACE[1].

▷ **swap** *n* **1** (usu *sing* 通常作单数) act of swapping; exchange 交换; 交易; 交流: *As you like my dress and I like yours, shall we do a swap?* 既然你喜欢我的连衣裙而我也喜欢你的, 咱们交换好吗? **2** thing swapped or suitable for swapping 交换之物; 适于交换之物.

sward /swɔːd; swɔrd/ *n* [U] (*dated or rhet* 旧或修辞) turf; grass 草皮; 草.

swarm[1] /swɔːm; swɔrm/ *n* **1** large number of insects, birds, etc moving around together, esp bees following a queen bee (昆虫、鸟类等移动中的)大群; (尤指跟随一蜂王的)蜂群: *a swarm of ants, starlings, locusts, etc* 一大群蚂蚁、椋鸟、蝗虫等. **2** (often *pl* 常作复数) (unpleasantly) large number of people; crowd (令人反感的)大群人; 人群: *swarms of children in the park* 公园里一帮一伙的儿童.

▷ **swarm** *v* **1** [I] (of bees) move around in a swarm, esp following a queen bee (指蜜蜂)成群飞行(尤指随一蜂王). **2** (**a**) [Ipr, Ip] move in large numbers (in the specified direction) 大群地(朝某方向)移动: *The guests swarmed round the tables where the food was set out.* 客人聚集到摆好饭菜的餐桌周围. ○ *The crowd was swarming out through the gates.* 人群一窝蜂地从出口涌出. (**b**) [I] be present in (unpleasantly) large numbers 聚集(而拥挤不堪): *crowds swarming in the streets* 街上拥挤不堪的人群. **3** (phr v) **swarm with sb/sth** (of a place) be (unpleasantly) crowded with or full of (people or things) (指地方)挤满或到处是(人或物): *The beach was swarming with bathers.* 海滩上挤满了游泳的人. ○ *The stables swarmed with flies.* 马厩里到处都是苍蝇.

swarm[2] /swɔːm; swɔrm/ *v* (phr v) **swarm down/up sth** climb down/up sth by holding on with the hands and feet 用手和脚附着某物往下[上]爬; 爬下[上]某物: *swarm down a rope, up a tree* 缘绳而下、爬上树.

swarthy /ˈswɔːðɪ; ˈswɔrðɪ/ *adj* (**-ier**, **-iest**) dark or dark-skinned 黝黑的; 黑皮肤的: *a swarthy skin, face, complexion, person* 黝黑的皮肤、面孔、肤色、人.

swash·buck·ling /ˈswɒʃbʌklɪŋ; ˈswɑʃˌbʌklɪŋ/ *adj* [usu attrib 通常作定语] typical of the exciting adventures and romantic appearance of pirates, soldiers of former times, etc, esp as shown in films (昔时海盗、武士等)惊险传奇式的(尤指影片中表现的): *swashbuckling heroes* 侠客 ○ *a swashbuckling tale of adventure on the high seas* 公海上惊心动魄的冒险故事.

swas·tika /ˈswɒstɪkə; ˈswɑstɪkə/ *n* symbol in the form of a cross with its ends bent at right angles, formerly used as a Nazi emblem 卐字(旧时用作纳粹党的党徽). ⇨ illus at CROSS 见 CROSS 插图.

swat /swɒt; swɑt/ *v* (**-tt-**) [Tn] hit (sth/sb) hard, esp with a flat object 猛击(某物[某人]); (尤指)重拍: *swat a fly* 拍苍蝇 ○ *She swatted him on the bottom with a rolled-up newspaper.* 她用卷着的报纸打他的屁股.

▷ **swat** *n* blow of this kind 猛击; 重拍: *Give that fly a swat.* 拍那只苍蝇.

swat·ter *n* instrument for swatting flies, etc, usu a flat piece of plastic or metal fixed to a handle 用作拍打的工具; 蝇拍.

swathe[1] /sweɪð; sweð/ (also **swath** /swɔːθ; swɔθ/) *n* **1** strip of grass or other plants cut by a mower, scythe, etc (用刈草机、长柄大镰刀等)割下的一行草或其他植物: (*fig* 比喻) *The storm cut a swathe through* (ie destroyed large areas of) *the forest.* 暴风雨把大片大片的森林夷为平地. **2** broad strip 长而宽的一条: *a swathe of daffodils across the lawn* 草坪上长而宽的一片黄水仙.

swathe[2] /sweɪð; sweð/ *v* [Tn, Tn·pr esp passive 尤用于被动语态] **~ sb/sth (in sth)** wrap sb/sth in several layers of bandages, warm clothes, etc (用绷带、保暖衣物等)缠绕或层层裹住某人[某物]: *thick bandages swathed his head* 他头上缠着的层层的绷带 ○ *They were swathed in scarves and sweaters.* 他们围着围巾, 穿着毛衣.

sway /sweɪ; swe/ *v* **1** [I, Tn] (cause sth to) move or lean slowly from side to side (使某物)摇晃, 摇摆, 摆动: *trees swaying in the wind* 在风中摇曳的树 ○ *He swayed slightly, as if about to fall.* 他身子一歪, 像要倒下. ○ *She swayed her hips seductively as she danced.* 她跳舞时诱人地摆动着臀部. **2** [Tn] influence or change the opinions or actions of (sb) 影响或改变(某人)的观点或行动: *a speech that swayed many voters* 影响众多选民的演说 ○ *Your arguments won't sway her: she's determined to leave.* 你讲的道理说服不了她, 她已下定决心离开.

▷ **sway** *n* [U] **1** swaying movement 摇晃; 摇摆; 摆动: *The sway of the ferry made him feel sick.* 渡船摇摇晃晃, 他感到恶心. **2** (*rhet* 修辞) rule or control 统治; 支配: *people under the sway of Rome,* ie ruled by Rome in ancient times 在罗马帝国统治下的人民. **3** (idm 习语) **hold ˈsway (over sb/sth)** (*dated or rhet* 旧或修辞) have the greatest power or influence; be dominant 有最大的权力或影响; 居于统治地位: *Among English playwrights, few would deny that Shakespeare holds sway.* 在英国的戏剧作家中鲜有人能否认莎士比亚文学泰斗的地位.

S

swear /sweə(r); swɛr/ *v* (*pt* **swore** /swɔ:(r); swɔr/, *pp* **sworn** /swɔ:n; swɔrn/) **1** [I, Ipr] **~ (at sb/sth)** use rude or blasphemous words in anger, surprise, etc; curse 咒骂, 诅咒: *She bumped her head in the doorway and swore loudly.* 她的头撞到门框上, 大骂了一声. ○ *The foreman is always swearing at the workers.* 那工头总是对工人骂骂咧咧. **2** [no passive 不用于被动语态: Tn, Tf, Tt] say or promise (sth) very seriously, definitely or solemnly 极其认真、明确或郑重地说或允诺(某事): *I've never seen him before, I swear it.* 我以前从未见过他, 我说的是实话. ○ *She swore that she'd never seen him.* 她肯定地说, 她从未见过他. ○ *I could have sworn* (ie I was certain) *I heard a knock at the door.* 我千真万确听到了敲门声. ○ *I swore not to tell anybody about it.* 我保证不把这事告诉任何人. **3** [I, Ipr, Tn, Tf, Tt no passive 不用于被动语态] (cause sb to) make a solemn promise or statement about (sth) (使某人)就(某事物)宣誓: *Witnesses have to swear on the bible (to tell the truth).* 证人须手按《圣经》宣誓(说实话). ○ *They have sworn (an oath of) allegiance to the crown.* 他们宣誓效忠君主. ○ *Has the jury been sworn* (ie officially appointed by taking an oath)? 陪审团宣誓了吗? ○ *Are you willing to swear in court that you saw him do it?* 你愿意在法庭上宣誓说你曾看见他做那件事了吗? **4** [Tn, Tn·pr] **~ sth (against sb)** make (a statement) promising officially that it is true 宣誓承认(某一陈述)属实: *swear an accusation/a charge against sb* 宣誓保证指控某人的内容属实. **5** (idm 习语) **swear 'blind** (*infml* 口) say definitely 一口咬定: *She swore blind that she had not taken the money.* 她一口咬定说她没有拿那笔钱. **swear like a 'trooper** use very obscene or blasphemous language 破口大骂. **swear sb to 'secrecy** make sb promise to keep a secret 使某人发誓保守秘密: *I swore her to secrecy about what I had told her.* 我要她起誓对我告诉她的事保守秘密. **6** (phr v) **swear by sb/sth** (**a**) name sb/sth as a guarantee of what one is promising 以某人[某事物]之名义起誓: *I swear by almighty God that I will tell the truth.* 我对全能的上帝起誓我一定说实话. (**b**) (*infml* 口) believe greatly in the usefulness or value of sth (and use it constantly) 极其信赖(并经常使用)某事物: *Many of my friends are using word processors but I still swear by my old typewriter.* 我有许多朋友都使用文字处理机, 可我还是爱用我的老式打字机. **swear sb in** (esp passive 尤用于被动语态) introduce sb officially or ceremonially to a new position, responsibility, etc by getting him to swear an oath 使某人宣誓就职: *The President has to be sworn in publicly.* 总统必须当众宣誓就职. ○ *Let the witness be sworn in.* 让证人宣誓作证. **swear off sth** (*infml* 口) declare that one will stop using sth 宣布停用某事物: *I've decided to swear off smoking.* 我已宣布戒烟了. **swear to sth** (*infml* 口) say definitely that sth is true 断言某事物为实; 肯定某事物: *I think I've met him before, but I wouldn't swear to it*, ie I'm not sure. 我好像见过他, 只是不敢肯定.

▷ **swearer** *n* person who swears (SWEAR 1) 咒骂者; 诅咒者.

□ **'swear-word** *n* rude or blasphemous word 骂人的话; 亵渎之辞.

sweat /swet; swɛt/ *n* **1** [U] natural moisture which comes through the skin when one is hot, ill, afraid, working hard, etc 汗: *wipe the sweat from one's forehead* 擦去额头上的汗水 ○ *a vest damp with sweat* 浸透了汗水的背心 ○ (*fig* 比喻) *They built it with the sweat of their brow*, ie by working hard. 他们辛辛苦苦地把它建成了. **2 a sweat** [sing] state of sweating or being covered with sweat 出汗; 流汗; 满身大汗: *be in/break out in a sweat* 出[发]汗 ○ *work up a good sweat by running* 跑出一身汗 ○ *They say a good sweat will cure a cold.* 据说好好发一身汗就能治好感冒. **3** [U] moisture that forms on any surface, eg by condensation (因冷凝作用等而形成于物体表面的)水汽, 水珠. **4** (*fig infml* 比喻, 口) (**a**) [U] hard work or effort 艰苦的工作或努力: *Making your own beer? It's not worth the sweat!* 你自己酿啤酒吗? 不值得费那个劲! (**b**) **a sweat** [sing] task, etc needing much effort 艰巨的任务等: *Climbing all these stairs is a real sweat.* 登上所有这些楼梯可真费力气. **5** (idm 习语) **all of a 'sweat** (*infml* 口) (**a**) wet with sweat 一身大汗. (**b**) anxious or frightened 焦急的; 害怕的: *I was all of a sweat before the exam.* 我临考前急得不得了. **no 'sweat** (*infml* 口) (used as a way of saying that sth will not be difficult or inconvenient 用作表示某事物并无困难或不便的用语): *'I'm sorry to give you so much extra work.' 'No sweat!'* ie It doesn't bother me. '很抱歉, 给你增加了这么多的工作.' '没什么!'

▷ **sweat** *v* **1** [I] produce sweat, eg when hot, ill, afraid, or working hard 出汗; 流汗; 发汗: *sweating heavily, profusely, etc* 流很多汗、出大汗 ○ *The long climb made us sweat.* 我们攀登了很长距离, 已大汗淋漓了. **2** [I] (*fig infml* 比喻, 口) be in a state of great anxiety 处于焦急万分的状态: *They all want to know my decision but I think I'll let them sweat a little*, ie by not telling them yet. 他们全都想知道我做出的决定, 但我想先让他们着一阵子急(先不告诉他们). **3** [I, Ipr] **~ (over sth)** work hard 辛苦工作: *I really sweated over my last essay.* 我写上一篇文章可费了劲了. **4** [Tn] (*Brit*) heat (meat, vegetables, etc) in a pan with fat or water, in order to extract the juices 将(肉、蔬菜等)加热(熬出汁液). **5** (idm 习语) **slog/sweat one's guts out** ⇨ GUT. **sweat 'blood** (*infml* 口) (**a**) work very hard 拼命工作. (**b**) be very afraid or worried 极害怕或担心: *I sweated blood for a while thinking I'd broken the TV.* 我想到自己弄坏了电视机, 十分着急. **6** (phr v) **sweat sth off** lose (weight) through strenuous exercise (通过努力锻炼)减轻(体重): *I sweated off ten pounds in a week by playing squash every day.* 我每天打壁球, 一个星期体重减轻了十磅. **sweat sth out** cure (a cold, fever, etc) by sweating 用发汗的办法医治(感冒、发烧等). **sweat it out** (*infml* 口) wait uncomfortably for sth to happen or end 不安地等待某事物发生或结束: *There was nothing more we could do, so we just had to sit and sweat it out until the result was announced.* 我们无能为力, 只好不安地坐着等候宣布结果.

sweaty *adj* (**-ier**, **-iest**) **1** covered or damp with sweat 有汗的; 汗淋淋的; 汗渍的: *sweaty armpits* 有汗的腋窝 ○ *a sweaty T-shirt* 汗渍的短袖汗衫 ○ *I'm all sweaty from running.* 我跑出了一身汗. **2** causing sb to sweat 使某人出汗的: *sweaty work* 让人出汗的工作 ○ *a hot sweaty day* 热得出汗的一天.

□ **'sweat-band** *n* band of absorbent cloth worn round the head or wrist, for soaking up or wiping away sweat (缠在头部或手腕上用以吸收或擦汗的)汗巾.

,sweated 'labour (*derog* 贬) (**a**) work done for low wages in bad conditions 劳动条件恶劣而工资低微的工作. (**b**) people forced to do such work 在恶劣的条件下工作的廉价劳工.

'sweat-gland *n* organ beneath the skin that produces sweat 汗腺.

'sweat-shirt *n* long-sleeved cotton sweater 长袖棉毛衫.

'sweat-shop *n* (*derog* 贬) place where people are forced to work for low wages in bad conditions 血汗工厂(工作条件恶劣而工资低的).

sweater /'swetə(r); 'swɛtɚ/ *n* = JERSEY 1.

swede /swi:d; swid/ (*US* also **rutabaga**) *n* [C, U] type of large yellow turnip 芜菁甘蓝. ⇨illus at TURNIP 见TURNIP插图.

sweep[1] /swi:p; swip/ *v* (*pt, pp* **swept** /swept; swɛpt/) **1** (**a**) [I, Tn, Tn·pr, Tn·p] **~ sth (from, off, into, etc sth); ~ sth (away, up, etc)** remove (dust, dirt, etc) with or as if with a broom or brush 扫, 掸, 打扫(灰尘、污垢等): *Have you swept in here?* 这里你打扫过了吗? ○ *sweep the dust from the carpets* 清扫地毯上的灰尘 ○ *sweep the crumbs under the carpet, off the table, into the dustpan* 清扫地毯下面的碎屑、抹去桌子上面的面包屑、把碎屑扫入簸箕里 ○ *sweep away bits of paper* 把碎纸片扫掉 ○ *sweep the dead leaves up* 扫除枯叶. (**b**) [Tn, Tn·p, Cn·a] **~ sth (out)** clean sth by doing this 扫、掸或打扫某物: *sweep the carpet, floor, yard* 打扫地毯、地板、院子 ○ *sweep out the porch* 把门廊打扫干净 ○ *sweep the chimney (free of soot)* 打扫烟囱(的煤炱) ○ *Have the stairs been swept clean?* 楼梯打扫干净了吗? **2** [Tn·pr, Tn·p] move or remove (sb/sth) powerfully and unstoppably by pushing, flowing, etc 藉推力、流动力等强劲而不停地带动或移走(某人[某物]): *The current swept the logs down the river.* 水流冲着原木沿河而下. ○ *We were almost swept off our feet by the waves.* 我们几乎让浪头给打倒了. ○ *She got swept along by the crowd.* 她被人群拥着向前走. ○ *Many bridges were swept away by the floods.*

洪水冲毁了许多桥梁. ○ (*fig* 比喻) *Old laws were swept away by the revolution.* 这场革命彻底摧毁了旧的法制. **3** [Ipr, Ip, Tn] move quickly over (an area) 扫过, 掠过(某地方): *A huge wave swept over the deck.* 一个巨浪掠过甲板. ○ *The fire swept rapidly across the wooded countryside.* 这场大火迅速烧遍树木茂密的郊野. ○ *Rumours swept through the town.* 城里谣言四起. ○ *Cold winds swept the plains.* 寒风掠过平原. ○ (*fig* 比喻) *The party swept the country,* ie won the election by a large majority. 该党在全国的选举中大获全胜. **4** [Ipr, Ip] move in a smooth or dignified way (in the direction specified) 平稳地或庄重地(向某方向)移动: *She swept out of the room.* 她大模大样地走出了房间. ○ *The big car swept up the drive to the front of the house.* 那辆大轿车稳稳地顺着车道驶到房子前面. **5** [Ipr, Ip] extend in an unbroken line, curve or slope (in the direction specified) 延伸; 蜿蜒; 伸展; 绵延: *The road sweeps round the lake.* 这条路环绕着湖往前蜿蜒. ○ *The coast sweeps (away) northwards in a wide curve.* 海岸呈一大弧形向北伸展. **6** [Tn] pass over (sth) in order to examine, search or survey it 扫视, 搜索(某物): *The searchlights swept the sky.* 探照灯搜寻着天空. ○ *Her eyes swept the room.* 她的眼睛扫视了一下那个房间. **7** [Tn] move over or along (sth) touching it lightly 轻轻擦过、掠过(某物): *His fingers swept the keys of the piano.* 他的手指在钢琴键盘上轻快地移动. ○ *Her dress swept the ground.* 她的连衣裙在地面上拖曳着. **8** (idm 习语) **sweep sth under the ˈcarpet** hide sth which might cause trouble or a scandal 掩盖某事(以免造成麻烦或丑闻): *sweep embarrassing evidence under the carpet* 把令人难堪的证据掩盖起来. **sweep the ˈboard** win all the prizes, money, games, etc 赢得所有的奖品、金钱、比赛等: *Switzerland swept the board in the skiing competition.* 瑞士在滑雪比赛中囊括了所有的奖项. **sweep sb off his feet** overwhelm sb with emotion, esp with love 使某人倾心(尤指因爱情): *I was swept off my feet by her wit and charm.* 她才貌双全, 我佩服得五体投地.

▷ **sweeper** *n* **1** (**a**) person who sweeps 清扫者; 清洁工: *a pavement sweeper* 打扫人行道的清洁工人. (**b**) thing that sweeps 清扫器: *a carpet sweeper* 地毯清扫器. **2** (in football) player positioned behind the defenders to tackle anyone who passes them (足球比赛的)自由中卫.

sweep·ings *n* [pl] dust, rubbish, scraps, etc collected by sweeping 扫集的尘土、垃圾、碎屑等.

□ ˌ**swept-ˈback** *adj* **1** (of aircraft wings) slanting towards the rear of the aircraft (指飞机机翼)后掠形的. **2** (of hair) brushed backwards from the face (指头发)向后梳的.

ˈ**swept-wing** *adj* [attrib 作定语] (of aircraft) having swept-back wings (指飞机)有后掠形机翼的.

sweep[2] /swiːp; swip/ *n* **1** (also ˈ**sweep-out**) [C usu *sing* 通常作单数] act of sweeping 扫; 撢; 打扫: *Give the room a good sweep.* 把这房间好好打扫一下. **2** [C] sweeping (SWEEP[1] 2) movement (藉推力、流动力等的)带动, 移走; 摆动; 挥动: *the sweep of a pendulum* 摆的摆动 ○ *with a sweep of his arm, scythe* 他用臂、镰刀一挥. **3** [C usu *sing* 通常作单数] long unbroken (often curved) stretch of road, river, coast, etc or of sloping land 延伸的(常指弯的)路、河、岸等; 绵延的坡地: *the broad sweep of white cliffs round the bay* 海湾周围一大片白色的峭壁. **4** [U] (*fig* 比喻) extent covered by sth; range 包括有某事物的一段; 范围: *the impressive sweep of a historical novel* 一部历史小说感人的内容. **5** [C] movement over an area in order to search, attack, etc 搜索、扫荡等行动: *a sweep over the bay by a rescue helicopter* 救援直升飞机在海湾进行的一次搜索活动 ○ *The police made a thorough sweep of the field where the dead child's body was found.* 警方在发现那孩子尸体的现场进行了仔细的搜查. **6** [C] = CHIMNEY-SWEEP (CHIMNEY). **7** [C] = SWEEPSTAKE. **8** (idm 习语) **a clean sweep** ⇨ CLEAN[1].

sweep·ing /ˈswiːpɪŋ; ˋswipɪŋ/ *adj* **1** (**a**) having an extremely wide effect; far reaching 有广泛影响的; 深远的: *sweeping reforms, changes, etc* 意义深远的改革、改变等 ○ *sweeping reductions in prices* 大幅度的降价. (**b**) [usu attrib 通常作定语] complete; decisive 全面的; 决定性的: *a sweeping victory* 全胜. **2** (*derog* 贬) (of statements, etc) without any exceptions; (too) general (指言语等)无例外的, (过于)笼统的: *make a sweeping generalization, accusation, etc* 做出笼统的推论、指责等.

sweep·stake /ˈswiːpsteɪk; ˋswipˌstek/ (also *infml* 口语作 **sweep**) *n* (**a**) type of gambling in which all the money bet on the result of a contest is divided among those who by chance have selected or been given tickets corresponding to the eventual winner(s) of the contest 赌金全赢制(胜者可获全部赌金者). (**b**) horse-race on which money is bet in this way 实行赌金全赢制的赛马.

sweet[1] /swiːt; swit/ *adj* (**-er**, **-est**) **1** tasting like sugar or honey; not sour, bitter or salty 甜的; 味甘的: *sweet apples, biscuits, drinks, etc* 甜的苹果、饼干、饮料等 ○ *sweet wine,* ie tasting sweet or fruity, not dry 甜酒(带甜味或水果味道的) ○ *Do you like your tea sweet?* 你喝茶喜欢放糖吗? ○ *This cake is much too sweet.* 这块糕太甜了. **2** smelling fragrant or perfumed 芬芳的; 芳香的: *Don't the roses smell sweet!* 这玫瑰花真香! ○ *gardens sweet with the scent of thyme* 散发着麝香草的芳香的花园. **3** pleasing to hear; melodious 悦耳的; 旋律优美的: *the sweet song of the blackbird* 黑鹂的悦耳歌声 ○ *The soprano's voice sounded clear and sweet.* 那女高音歌手的嗓音响亮而动听. **4** fresh and pure; wholesome 新鲜而纯净的; 有益于健康的: *sweet milk* 鲜奶 ○ *The spring water was sweet* (ie not salty, polluted, etc) *to the taste.* 这泉水纯净可口. ○ *the sweet air of the countryside* 郊野的清新空气. **5** giving satisfaction; gratifying 使人满意或满足的; 快意的: *the sweet feeling of freedom, success, etc* 自由、成功等的快感. **6** (**a**) (*infml* 口) attractive and charming 有吸引力的; 漂亮的; 可爱的: *a sweet face, smile, gesture* 讨人喜欢的脸、笑容、姿势 ○ *a sweet little poodle, baby, cottage* 招人爱的卷毛狗、幼儿、农舍 ○ *You look so sweet in that hat!* 你戴着那顶帽子真好看! (**b**) having or showing a pleasant nature; lovable 和蔼的; 温和的; 温柔的; 可亲的: *a sweet child, old lady, etc* 乖孩子、和蔼可亲的老太太 ○ *a sweet temper, nature, disposition, etc* 温顺的脾气、本性、性情等 ○ *It is sweet of you to have remembered us.* 你还惦记着我们, 真感谢你. ○ *such a sweet-tempered/sweet-natured girl* 如此温和的[温柔的]姑娘. **7** (idm 习语) **at one's ˌown sweet ˈwill**; **in one's ˌown sweet ˈtime**; **in one's ˌown sweet ˈway** just as one pleases, or taking as long as one pleases, often in spite of the orders or wishes of others 任凭自己的意愿(常指不顾他人): *It's no good telling him — leave him to find out in his own sweet time.* 跟他说也没用——他愿意怎么找就怎么找吧. **be sweet on sb** (*dated infml* 旧, 口) be fond of or in love with sb 喜欢或爱上某人. **have a sweet ˈtooth** (*infml* 口) like to eat sweet or sugary things 爱吃甜食. **keep sb sweet** (*infml* 口) be specially pleasant with sb in order to win favours 讨好某人: *I have to keep my boss sweet because I need to ask for a rise.* 我得跟老板套套近乎, 因为我惦着提升呢. **revenge is sweet** ⇨ REVENGE. **short and sweet** ⇨ SHORT[1]. **sweet ˈnothings** (*infml or joc* 口或谑) words of affection exchanged by lovers 情话: *She whispered sweet nothings into his ear.* 她对他悄悄地说情话.

▷ **sweet·ish** *adj* rather sweet 有甜味的; 惹人喜爱的.

sweetly *adv* in a sweet(2, 6) manner 芬芳地; 可爱地; 和蔼地; 温柔地: *sweetly perfumed flowers* 芬芳馥郁的花朵 ○ *singing, smiling sweetly* 唱得很动听、笑得很迷人.

sweet·ness *n* **1** [U] quality of being sweet 甜; 芳香; 悦耳; 新鲜; 可爱; 和蔼; 温柔. **2** (idm 习语) **(all) ˌsweetness and ˈlight** (*ironic* 反语) display of mildness and reason 温和而讲理: *She's all sweetness and light provided you're doing what she wants.* 只要顺着她, 她是又和蔼又讲理.

□ ˌ**sweet-and-ˈsour** *adj* [attrib 作定语] (of food) cooked in a sauce containing sugar and either vinegar or lemon (指食物)用糖和醋(或柠檬汁)作调味汁烹制的, 糖醋的, 酸甜的: ˌ*sweet-and-sour ˈpork,* ie a Chinese dish 咕噜肉(糖醋猪肉).

ˌ**sweet-ˈbriar** (also ˌ**sweet-ˈbrier**) *n* [U] = EGLANTINE.

ˈ**sweet corn** kind of maize with sweet grains 甜玉米.

ˈ**sweetheart** *n* **1** (*dated* 旧) one of a pair of lovers 恋人; 情人: *They were childhood sweethearts.* 他们原是青梅竹马的恋人. ○ *Mary has a sweetheart.* 玛丽有个心上人. **2** (used esp as a loving form of address, eg to a wife, husband, child, etc 尤用作爱称, 如称呼妻子、丈

夫、孩子等).

ˌ**sweet** ˈ**pea** climbing garden plant with brightly-coloured sweet-scented flowers 香豌豆(攀缘园艺植物, 花香而艳丽).

ˌ**sweet po**ˈ**tato** tropical climbing plant with thick edible roots, cooked as a vegetable 红薯, 山芋, 甘薯(指植物连同其块根). Cf 参看 YAM.

ˈ**sweet talk** (*US infml* 口) flattery 恭维的话; 甜言蜜语. ˈ**sweet-talk** *v* [Tn, Tn·pr] **~ sb (into sth/doing sth)** persuade sb by flattery, etc (to do sth) 用甜言蜜语劝诱某人(做某事): *You can't sweet-talk me into helping you!* 你别想用好话哄我帮助你!

ˌ**sweet-**ˈ**william** *n* garden plant with clustered sweet-scented flowers 美国石竹(园艺植物, 花簇生, 芳香).

sweet[2] /swi:t; swit/ *n* **1** [C often *pl* 常作复数] (*Brit*) (*US* **candy** [U, C]) small shaped piece of sweet substance, usu made with sugar and/or chocolate 糖果: *a packet of boiled sweets* 一袋硬糖 ○ [attrib 作定语] *a sweet shop* 糖果店. **2** [C, U] (*Brit*) = DESSERT: *What's for sweet?* 甜食吃什么? ○ *have some more sweet* 再吃点儿甜食. **3** **sweets** [pl] **the ~s of sth** satisfactions or pleasures 满意; 满足; 快乐; 乐趣: *taste the sweets of success, freedom, etc* 尝到成功、自由等的甜头 ○ *enjoy the sweets of life while one is young* 趁年轻时享受人生的欢乐. **4** (used as a loving form of address 用作爱称) darling 亲爱的: *Yes, my sweet.* 是的, 我亲爱的.

sweet·bread /ˈswi:tbred; ˋswitˌbrɛd/ *n* pancreas of a calf or lamb used as food (供食用的小牛或小羊的)胰脏.

sweeten /ˈswi:tn; ˋswitn̩/ *v* **1** [I, Tn] (cause sth to) become sweet or sweeter (使某事物)变甜或变得更甜、芳香、悦耳、新鲜、可爱、温和等: *Fruit sweetens as it ripens.* 水果成熟后就好吃了. ○ *I never sweeten my tea.* 我喝茶从来不加糖. ○ *sweeten (the air in) a room*, eg by opening a window 使房间里空气清新(如开窗). **2** [Tn, Tn·p] **~ sb (up)** (*infml* 口) make sb more agreeable, eg by offering gifts 使某人更随和(如向其送礼): *I'll sweeten her up a bit by inviting her to the party.* 我要邀请她参加聚会好让她随和一些. **3** (idm 习语) **sugar/sweeten the pill** ⇨ PILL.

▷ **sweet·ener** /ˈswi:tnə(r); ˋswitn̩ɚ/ *n* **1** [C, U] (piece of a) substance used to sweeten food or drink, esp as a substitute for sugar 使食物或饮料变甜的物质; (尤指)糖的代用品. **2** [C] (*infml* 口) attempt to persuade sb; bribe (对某人的)劝诱; 贿赂: *The firm offered her a generous bonus as a sweetener.* 公司提出给她一笔可观的花红借以拉拢她.

sweet·en·ing /ˈswi:tnɪŋ; ˋswitn̩ɪŋ/ *n* [C, U] substance, eg sugar, used to sweeten food or drink 甜味剂(如糖): [attrib 作定语] *sweetening agents* 甜味剂.

sweetie /ˈswi:tɪ; ˋswitɪ/ *n* (*infml* 口) **1** (*Brit*) (used esp by and to young children 尤作儿语) sweet[2](1) 糖果. **2** (*esp Brit*) kind or lovable person 好心人; 可爱的人: *Thanks for helping, you're a sweetie.* 谢谢你的帮助, 你真是好心肠. **3** (used as a loving form of address 用作爱称) darling 亲爱的.

swell /swel; swɛl/ *v* (*pt* **swelled** /sweld; swɛld/, *pp* **swollen** /ˈswəʊlən; ˋswolən/ or **swelled**) **1 (a)** [I, Ipr, Ip, Tn esp passive 尤用于被动语态, Tn·pr esp passive 尤用于被动语态, Tn·p esp passive 尤用于被动语态] **~ (to sth); ~ (sth) (up) (with sth)** (cause sth to) become larger or bulge outwards, eg because of pressure from inside (使某物)膨胀, 肿胀: *Wood often swells when wet.* 木材潮湿后往往会膨胀. ○ *My eyes swelled with tears.* 我的眼睛里含着泪. ○ *His face was swollen (up) with toothache.* 他的脸因牙痛而肿了起来. ○ *limping because of a swollen ankle* 因脚腕儿发肿而一瘸一拐地走. **(b)** [I, Ip, Tn, Tn·p] **~ (sth) (out)** (cause sth to) curve outwards; billow (使某物)凸出, 隆起; 鼓起: *The sails swelled (out) in the wind.* 船帆在风中鼓起. ○ *The wind swelled (out) the sails.* 风把船帆刮得鼓起来了. **2** [I, Ipr, Tn, Tn·pr esp passive 尤用于被动语态] **~ (into/to sth); ~ sth (to sth) (with sth)** (cause sth to) become greater in intensity, number, amount or volume (使某物)增强, 增多, 增大: *The group of onlookers soon swelled (in)to a crowd.* 旁观的人很快聚集起一大群. ○ *The murmur swelled into a roar.* 窃窃私语的声音变大形成一片喧哗. ○ *Small extra costs all swell the total.* 零星的额外费用积少成多使总数增大了. ○ *The river was swollen with flood water.* 洪水到来后河水上涨了. **3** [I, Ipr, Tn, Tn·pr] **~ (sth) (with sth)** (of a person, his heart, etc) feel like bursting with emotion (指人、内心等)感情迸发, 情绪高涨: *His breast/heart swelled with pride at his achievement.* 他有了成绩而沾沾自喜. **4** (idm 习语) **have a swelled/swollen** ˈ**head** (*infml* 口) be conceited, esp because of a sudden success 自负; (尤指因突然成功)冲昏头脑.

▷ **swell** *n* [U, sing] **1** slow heaving of the sea with waves that do not break 海面的缓慢起伏(有浪而无浪花): *feel seasick in the heavy swell* 在猛烈起伏的海面上感到晕船. **2** (*music* 音) gradual increase in the volume of sound (音量的)逐渐增强.

swell *adj* (*US infml* 口) **1** fashionable or smart 时髦的; 漂亮的: *You look swell in that dress!* 你穿着那件连衣裙真漂亮! **2** excellent; first-rate 极好的; 第一流的: *a swell vacation, player, guy* 极好的假期、选手、小伙子 ○ *That's swell!* 真棒!

swell·ing /ˈswelɪŋ; ˋswɛlɪŋ/ *n* **1** [U] condition of being swollen 膨胀; 肿胀; 凸出; 鼓起; 增强; 增多; 增大; (感情的)迸发: *reduce the swelling with ice-packs* 用冰袋消肿. **2** [C] abnormally swollen place on the body (身体上的)肿块: *He had a swelling on his knee.* 他膝盖上有个肿块.

swel·ter /ˈsweltə(r); ˋswɛltɚ/ *v* [I] (*infml* 口) be uncomfortably hot; suffer from the heat 热得难受: *lie sweltering on a beach* 躺在海滩上热得难受 ○ *a sweltering(-hot) day, summer, climate, room* 闷热的一天、夏天、气候、房间 ○ *We were sweltering in our winter clothes.* 我们穿着冬衣热得够呛.

swept *pt, pp* of SWEEP[1].

swerve /swɜ:v; swɝv/ *v* [I, Ipr, Ip] change direction suddenly 突然转向: *The lorry swerved sharply to avoid the child.* 卡车突然转向以免撞着那孩子. ○ *The ball swerved to the left.* 那球突然转向左方. ○ (*fml fig* 文, 比喻) *She never swerves from her determination to succeed.* 她争取胜利的决心决不动摇.

▷ **swerve** *n* swerving movement 突然的转向: *a wide, dangerous, sudden swerve* 大弧度的、危险的、突然的转向.

swift[1] /swɪft; swɪft/ *adj* (**-er, -est**) **1 ~ (to do sth/in doing sth)** quick or rapid; prompt 快的; 迅速的; 敏捷的: *a swift reply, reaction, revenge* 迅速的回答、反应、报复 ○ *He was swift to condemn the violence/in condemning the violence.* 他立即谴责了那种暴力行为. ○ (*fml* 文) *She is swift to anger*, ie She quickly becomes angry. 她爱生气. **2** (often in compounds 常用以构成复合词) that can move fast 能快速移动的: *a swift runner, horse* 跑得快的人、马 ○ *swift-flowing rivers* 湍急的河流 ○ *swift-footed greyhounds* 腿快的灵猩. ▷ **swiftly** *adv*. **swift·ness** *n* [U].

swift[2] /swɪft; swɪft/ *n* type of small fast-flying insect-eating bird with long narrow wings 雨燕(翅窄长, 飞行快速, 捕食昆虫).

swig /swɪg; swɪg/ *v* (**-gg-**) [Ipr, Tn, Tn·pr, Tn·p] **~ sth (down)** (*infml* 口) take a drink or drinks of (esp alcohol), usu in large gulps 喝(尤指酒)(通常指大口大口地): *swigging beer out of a bottle* 拿着瓶子大口大口地喝啤酒 ○ *swig down a glass of rum* 把一杯朗姆酒一饮而尽.

▷ **swig** *n* act of swigging; swallow 大喝; 吞咽: *taking long swigs (at a bottle) of beer* (对着瓶子)大喝啤酒.

swill /swɪl; swɪl/ *v* **1 (a)** [Tn, Tn·p] **~ sth (out/down)** (*esp Brit*) rinse or flush sth by pouring large amounts of water, etc into, over or through it 涮洗、冲洗或灌洗某物: *swill down the front steps* 冲洗屋前的台阶 ○ *He swilled his mouth out with antiseptic.* 他用杀菌剂漱口. **(b)** [Ipr, Ip] **~ around, over, through, etc** (of liquid) flow or pour in the specified direction (指液体)流动, 灌注: *Beer swilled around the bottom of the barrel.* 啤酒在桶底晃荡. ○ *Muddy water swilled over the planks.* 泥浆在木板上流过. **2** [Tn] (*infml derog* 口, 贬) drink (sth) in large quantities; guzzle 大喝(某物); 狂饮: *swill beer, tea, etc* 大喝啤酒、茶等.

▷ **swill** *n* **1** [sing] act of swilling; rinse 涮洗; 冲洗; 灌洗; 流动; 大喝: *give the bucket a swill (out)* 把桶冲洗一下. **2** (also ˈ**pigswill**) [U] left-over vegetable peelings, etc given to pigs as food (作猪饲料的)剩下的菜屑等; 猪食.

swim /swɪm; swɪm/ *v* (**-mm-**; *pt* **swam** /swæm; swæm/, *pp* **swum** /swʌm; swʌm/) **1** (**a**) [I, Ipr, Ip] move the body through water by using arms, legs, fins, tail, etc 游水; 游泳: *Fish swim.* 鱼会游水. ○ *Let's go swimming.* 咱们去游泳吧. ○ *swim on one's back* 仰泳 ○ *When the ship sank we had to swim for it*, ie save ourselves by swimming. 船沉时我们不得不游泳逃生. ○ *swim underwater, upstream, across, ashore* 潜泳、逆水而游、游泳横渡、游上岸. (**b**) [Tn] use particular movements to do this 用某姿势游泳: *swim breast-stroke, back-stroke, crawl, etc* 游蛙泳、仰泳、爬泳等. **2** (**a**) [Tn, Tn·pr] cover a distance by swimming 游(一段距离): *swim a mile, race, river* 游一英里、比赛游泳、游过河 ○ *swim two lengths of the pool* 在游泳池中游一个来回 ○ *swim the Channel* 泅渡英吉利海峡. (**b**) [no passive 不用于被动语态: Tn·pr, Tn·p] cause (an animal) to do this 使(动物)游水: *She swam her horse across (the river).* 她使马游水过河. **3** (usu in the continuous tenses 通常用于进行时态) (**a**) [I, Ipr] **~ (with sth)** be flooded or overflowing (with liquid) 被淹; 溢: *Her eyes were swimming (with tears).* 她泪眼汪汪. ○ *The bathroom floor was swimming with water.* 浴室的地面上都是水. (**b**) [Ipr] **~ in sth** be covered with liquid as if floating in it 浸于液体中; 泡: *meat swimming in gravy* 浸在浓汁中的肉. **4** (**a**) [I, Ipr] seem to be whirling 似在旋转: *The room swam before his eyes/around him.* 他感觉房间好像在他眼前[在他周围]旋转. (**b**) [I] have a dizzy feeling 感到眩晕; 发晕: *The whisky made his head swim.* 他喝了威士忌感到头晕目眩. ○ *My brain swam at the complexity of the calculations.* 这种复杂的计算搞得我头昏眼花. **5** (idm 习语) **sink or swim** ⇨ SINK[1].

▷ **swim** *n* **1** action or period of swimming 游泳: *go for a swim* 去游泳 ○ *I only had two swims last year.* 去年我只游泳两次. **2** (idm 习语) **in/out of the ˈswim** (*infml* 口) aware or involved/not aware or involved in what is going on 了解或介入[不了解或不介入]当前情况: *Although I'm retired, voluntary work keeps me in the swim (of things).* 我虽已退休, 但仍做些义务工作, 以便了解当前的情势.

swim·mer *n* person who swims (esp in the way specified by the *adj*) 游泳者(尤与修饰性形容词连用): *a strong, good, fast, etc swimmer* 强壮的、优秀的、速度快的...游泳运动员.

□ **ˈswimming-bath** *n* (esp *pl* 尤作复数) (*Brit*) indoor swimming-pool 室内游泳池.

ˈswimming-costume (also **ˈbathing-costume**) (*esp Brit*) (*US* also **ˈbathing-suit**) *n* one-piece garment worn for swimming 游泳衣.

ˈswimming-pool *n* artificial pool for swimming in (人工)游泳池.

ˈswim-suit *n* one-piece garment worn by women and girls for swimming 女式泳装.

ˈswimming-trunks *n* [pl] short pants or trousers worn by men and boys for swimming 男游泳裤: *a pair of swimming-trunks* 一条游泳裤.

swim·mingly /ˈswɪmɪŋlɪ; ˈswɪmɪŋlɪ/ *adv* (*infml* 口) pleasantly and smoothly 顺利地: *We're getting along swimmingly.* 我们进展顺利. ○ *Everything went swimmingly*, ie proceeded without difficulties. 一切都进行得很顺利.

swindle /ˈswɪndl; ˈswɪndl̩/ *v* (*infml* 口) [Tn, Tn·pr] (**a**) **~ sb/sth (out of sth)** cheat sb/sth, esp in a business transaction 诈骗某人[某事物](尤指在生意中): *swindle an insurance company* 诈骗保险公司 ○ *You're easily swindled!* 你很容易上当! ○ *I've been swindled out of £5.* 我让人骗了5英镑. (**b**) **~ sth (out of sb/sth)** get (money, etc) by fraud 诈取, 骗得(金钱等): *She swindled £1 000 out of the Social Security.* 她骗得了1 000英镑社会保险金.

▷ **swindle** *n* **1** act of swindling 诈骗行为: *victims of a tax, mortgage, etc swindle* 税款、抵押贷款等诈骗案的受害者. **2** person or thing that is presented wrongly in order to deceive people 冒名者; 冒充货; 骗人的东西: *That newspaper story's a complete swindle.* 报纸上那篇报道纯粹是骗人的鬼话.

swind·ler /ˈswɪndlə(r); ˈswɪndlɚ/ *n* person who swindles 诈骗者; 骗子.

swine /swaɪn; swaɪn/ *n* **1** [pl] (*arch or fml* 古或文) pigs 猪. **2** [C] (*infml derog* 口, 贬) obnoxious person or thing 令人不快的人或事物: *Take your hands off me, you filthy swine!* 把你的手放开, 别碰我, 你这个坏蛋! ○ *Those nails were real swines to get out.* 那些钉子真难拔. **3** (idm 习语) **cast pearls before swine** ⇨ CAST[1].

□ ˌ**swine-ˈfever** *n* [U] (*Brit*) virus disease affecting pigs 猪瘟.

swing[1] /swɪŋ; swɪŋ/ *v* (*pt, pp* **swung** /swʌŋ; swʌŋ/) **1** [I, Ipr, Ip, Tn, Tn·pr] (cause sb/sth to) move to and fro while hanging or supported (吊着或支着)摆动, 摇摆: *His arms swung/He swung his arms as he walked.* 他走路时摆动着手臂. ○ *The bucket swung from the end of a rope.* 水桶吊在绳上来回摇荡. ○ *The gymnast swung on the parallel bars.* 体操运动员在双杠上摆动身子. **2** [Ipr, Ip, Tn·pr, Tn·p] move (sb/oneself) from one place to another by gripping sth and leaping, etc 使(某人[自己])握住某物纵身一跃等: *The ape swung (along) from branch to branch.* 那只猿猴从一根树枝荡到另一根树枝上. ○ *He swung himself (up) into the saddle/into the driver's seat.* 他纵身跨上马鞍[坐到司机的座位上]. **3** [Ipr, Ip] walk or run with an easy rhythmical movement 轻快而有节奏地走或跑: *The band swung lightly down the street.* 那伙人踏着轻快的步伐沿街走去. ○ *A company of guardsmen swung past.* 一队卫兵整齐地跑过去. **4** [Ipr, Ip, Tn, Tn·pr, Tn·p, Cn·a] (cause sth to) move in a curve (使某物)转弯, 转向: *A car swung sharply round the corner.* 一辆汽车在街角急转弯. ○ *The boom swung over (the deck).* 帆杠在(甲板上)转动. ○ *She swung the rucksack (up) onto her back.* 她把帆布背包转到身后. ○ *swing a telescope through 180°* 把望远镜旋转180度 ○ *The gate (was) swung slowly to/shut.* 大门慢慢地关上了. **5** [Ipr, Ip] **~ around/round** turn suddenly to face the opposite way 突然转向相反方向: *She swung round (on him) angrily.* 她气愤地转过身来(朝向他). ○ *He swung round to confront his accusers.* 他突然转过身来面对着那些指控他的人. **6** [Ipr, Ip, Tn·pr, Tn·p] **~ (sb) (from sth) to sth** (cause sb to) change suddenly from one opinion or mood, etc to another (使某人)突然改变观点或情绪等: *Voters have/Voting has swung to the left.* 选民转而支持左派. ○ *He swings from wild optimism to total despair.* 他由极其乐观一变而为完全绝望. ○ *Can you swing them round to my point of view?* 你能让他们转而支持我的观点吗? **7** [I] have a rhythmic feeling or drive 有节奏感; 有节奏的力量: *He can write music that really swings.* 他能创作旋律优美的音乐作品. **8** [Tn] (*infml* 口) succeed in obtaining or achieving (sth), esp by devious means 获得或实现(某事物)(尤指用不当的手段): *Can you swing it for me so that I get the job?* 你能替我谋到那份工作吗? ○ *She managed to swing an interview with the Prince.* 她设法采访了亲王. **9** (idm 习语) **room to swing a cat** ⇨ ROOM. ˌ**swing into ˈaction** act swiftly 迅速采取行动: *The police swung into action against the gunmen.* 警方迅速采取行动制服了持枪歹徒. **swing the ˈlead** (*dated Brit infml* 旧, 口) (try to) avoid work or a duty, usu by pretending to be ill (竭力)逃避工作或责任(通常指装病). **10** (phr v) **swing for sb** (*sl or joc* 俚或谑) be executed by hanging for having killed sb 因杀某人而被绞死: *That wretched child — I'll swing for him one of these days!* 那个讨厌的孩子——早晚得把我逼死!

swing[2] /swɪŋ; swɪŋ/ *n* **1** [C] swinging movement or action or rhythm 摆动; 摇摆; 摇荡; 转向; 转变; 节奏: *The golfer took a swing at the ball.* 打高尔夫球的人挥棒击了一下球. ○ *the swing of a pendulum, pointer, needle, etc* 钟摆、指针、磁针等的摆动 ○ *the swing of her hips as she walked* 她行走时臀部扭来扭去. **2** [C] (**a**) seat for swinging on, hung from above on ropes or chains 秋千: *children riding on the swings* 打秋千的儿童. (**b**) action of swinging on this 打秋千: *have a swing* 打一会儿秋千 ○ *give the children a swing* 帮孩子们打秋千. **3** [U] (also **ˈswing music**) smooth rhythmic type of jazz played. esp by big dance bands in the 1930's 摇摆乐(三十年代流行的爵士乐, 多由大型舞蹈乐团演奏). **4** [U, sing] rhythmic feeling or drive 节奏感; 有节奏的力量: *music with a swing (to it)* 节奏鲜明的音乐. **5** [C] amount by which sth changes from one opinion, etc to another (改变观点等的)变动幅度: *Voting showed a 10% swing to the Opposition.* 投票结果表明有10%的人转而支持反对党. ○ *He is liable to abrupt swings in mood*, eg from happiness to despair. 他情绪极不稳定(如由高兴突然变为绝望). **6** (idm 习语) **get in the ˈswing (of sth)**

(*infml* 口) adapt to a routine, etc 适应情况: *I've only been at university for a week, so I haven't got into the swing of things yet.* 我上大学才一个星期, 还不熟悉情况. **go with a ˈswing** (*infml* 口) (**a**) (of music, poetry, etc) have a strong rhythm (指音乐、诗歌等)节奏强劲. (**b**) (of entertainment, etc) be lively and enjoyable (指娱乐活动等)活跃而精彩: *The party went with a swing.* 聚会搞得有声有色. **in full swing** ⇨ FULL. **ˌswings and ˈroundabouts** (*infml* 口 *esp Brit*) a matter of balancing profits against losses 有得有失的事: *Higher earnings mean more tax, so it's all swings and roundabouts.* 多挣钱就要多交税, 有得有失. ○ *What you gain on the swings you'll probably lose on the roundabouts.* 有所得也可能有所失. **the ˌswing of the ˈpendulum** the movement of public opinion from one extreme to the other 舆论的剧变(由一个极端转到另一个极端).

□ **ˈswing-boat** *n* boat-shaped swing at fairs, etc 船形秋千.

ˌswing ˈbridge bridge that can be swung aside to let ships pass 平旋桥; 平转桥.

ˌswing-ˈdoor *n* door that opens in either direction and closes itself when released 双开式弹簧门.

ˈswing shift (*US infml* 口) employees on the evening shift, usu from 4 pm to midnight (三班制的)午后班工人(通常指工作时间从下午4时至半夜).

ˌswing-ˈwing *n* (aircraft with a) type of wing that can be moved forward for landing, etc and backward for high-speed flying 可变后掠翼(飞机).

swinge·ing /ˈswɪndʒɪŋ; ˋswɪndʒɪŋ/ *adj* [attrib 作定语] (*esp Brit*) **1** (of a blow) hard or forcible (指打击)沉重的, 有力的. **2** large in amount or number or range 巨额的; 大量的; 大范围的: *swingeing fines, taxes, costs, etc* 巨额的罚款、税款、费用等 ○ *swingeing cuts in public services* 公用事业费用的大量削减.

S

swipe /swaɪp; swaɪp/ *v* (*infml* 口) **1** [Ipr, Tn, Tn·pr] ~ (**at**) **sth/sb** (try to) hit sth/sb with a swinging or reckless blow 重击或猛打某物[某人]: *He swiped at the dog with his stick, but missed.* 他用手杖向那条狗打去, 但没打中. ○ *He swiped the ball into the grandstand.* 他把球打到看台上去了. **2** [Tn] (*esp joc* 尤作戏谑语) steal (sth), esp by snatching 偷窃(某物); (尤指)抢走: *Who's swiped my calculator?* 谁把我的计算器偷走了?

▷ **swipe** *n* ~ (**at sb/sth**) (attempt at a) swinging or reckless blow 重击, 猛打, 猛击(的意图): *have/take a swipe at the ball* 重击球 ○ *make a sudden vicious swipe at sb* 冷不防地照着某人猛击.

swirl /swɜːl; swɝl/ *v* [I, Ipr, Ip, Tn·pr esp passive 尤用于被动语态, Tn·p esp passive 尤用于被动语态] (cause air, water, etc to) move or flow with twists and turns and with varying speed (使空气、水等)打旋, 旋动, 起旋涡: *dust swirling (around) in the streets* 在街道上盘旋飞扬的尘土 ○ *Smoke swirled up the chimney.* 烟气从烟囱里袅袅上升. ○ *The log was swirled away downstream by the current.* 水流载着原木盘旋而下.

▷ **swirl** *n* ~ (**of sth**) **1** swirling movement; eddy 打旋; 旋动; 旋涡; 涡流: *Dancers spun in a swirl of skirts.* 跳舞的人旋转着, 裙子也不停地打转. **2** swirled shape or twist 旋涡状; 螺旋形: *strawberries topped with a swirl of cream* 浇有旋涡状奶油的草莓果.

swish[1] /swɪʃ; swɪʃ/ *v* **1** (**a**) [Ipr, Ip, Tn, Tn·pr, Tn·p] (cause sth to) swing through the air with a hissing sound (使某物)摆动或挥动出声: *Scythes swished to and fro.* 长柄大镰刀嗖嗖地来回挥动. ○ *The horse swished its tail (about).* 那匹马刷刷地挥动尾巴. (**b**) [I, Ipr] move with or make this sound; rustle 在空中移动出声; 发出摩擦声: *We swished through the long grass.* 我们穿过深草地发出沙沙的响声. ○ *She swished across the floor in her long silk dress.* 她穿着丝绸长服窸窣作响地在房间里走过. **2** (phr v) **swish sth off** cut sth off by swinging a stick, etc at it 挥棍等打掉某物: *He swished off the tops of the nettles with his cane.* 他用藤杖抽断了荨麻的顶部.

▷ **swish** *n* [sing] hissing or rustling sound 物体迅速移动的声音; 摩擦的声音: *Her skirts gave a swish.* 她衣服的下摆发出沙沙声.

swish[2] /swɪʃ; swɪʃ/ *adj* (*infml* 口 *esp Brit*) smart, fashionable or expensive 漂亮的; 时髦的; 昂贵的: *swish hotels, resorts, cars* 豪华的旅馆、漂亮的游览胜地、昂贵的汽车.

Swiss /swɪs; swɪs/ *adj* of Switzerland, its people or its dialects 瑞士的; 瑞士人的; 瑞士方言的.

▷ **Swiss** *n* (*pl* unchanged 复数不变) native of Switzerland 瑞士人.

□ **ˌSwiss ˈroll** thin flat sponge-cake spread with jam, etc and rolled up 瑞士卷(夹有果酱等的蛋糕卷).

Swiss ˈchard = CHARD.

switch /swɪtʃ; swɪtʃ/ *n* **1** (**a**) device for completing or breaking an electric circuit (电路的)开关, 电门, 转换器, 闸: *a light switch* 灯的电门 ○ *press the on/off switch* 按开关通电[断电] ○ *a two-way switch*, eg at the top and bottom of a staircase 双路开关(如楼梯上下两端的). (**b**) device at the junction of railway tracks to allow trains to go from one track to another (铁路的)道岔, 转辙器. (**c**) (*US*) = POINTS (POINT[1] 18). **2** (also **ˈswitch-over**) (*infml* 口) (esp sudden) shift or change (尤指突然的)转变, 改变: *Polls showed a switch to Labour.* 民意测验表明形势转而对工党有利. ○ *a switch from gas to electric* 由使用煤气改为使用电气 ○ *make a switch from publishing to teaching* 由出版工作改做教学工作 ○ *a switch in method, policy, opinion* 方法、政策、观点的改变. **3** thin flexible twig or shoot cut from a tree; tapering rod like this used for urging a horse, etc forward (从树上砍下的)细软枝条; (策马等用的)枝条状的鞭子. **4** piece of real or false hair for making a woman's hair appear thicker or longer (女用)假发.

▷ **switch** *v* **1** [I, Ipr, Ip, Tn, Tn·pr, Tn·p] ~ (**sth**) (**over**) (**to sth**) (cause sth to) shift or change, esp suddenly (使某事物)转变或改变(尤指突然): *switch to modern methods* 改用现代方法 ○ *Many voters switched to Labour.* 许多选举人改投工党的票. ○ *Computers are everywhere now — our firm is switching over soon.* 计算机现已普及——我公司亦即将使用. ○ *switch the conversation to a different topic* 改变谈话的话题 ○ *Could you switch the TV over?* 请你改换电视频道好吗? **2** [I, Ipr, Ip, Tn, Tn·pr, Tn·p] ~ (**sth**) (**with sb/sth**); ~ (**sth**) **over/round** (cause sb/sth to) exchange positions; change over (使某人[某事物])交换位置; 转换: *Our glasses have been switched — this is mine.* 咱们的玻璃杯对调了——这个是我的. ○ *Husband and wife should switch roles (with each other) occasionally.* 夫妻间应该偶尔(彼此)对调充当的角色. ○ *You drive first and then we'll switch round/over.* 你先驾驶, 过一会儿咱们再换着开. **3** [Tn] whip or flick (a horse, etc) with a switch(3) 用鞭子等抽打(马等). **4** [Tn·pr] move (a train, etc) onto another track 将(列车等)转入另一轨道: *switch a train into a siding* 把一列火车转入支线轨道. **5** (phr v) **switch (sth) off** disconnect (electricity, etc) 切断(电流等): *Switch off the gas, power, etc at the mains* 切断煤气源、电源等 ○ *Don't switch (the TV) off yet.* 暂时不要关掉(电视机). **switch (sb) off** (*infml* 口) (cause sb to) become dull, bored, etc (使某人)感到乏味、厌烦等: *I switch off when he starts talking about cars.* 他一谈起汽车我就厌烦. ○ *Long lectures really switch me off.* 我觉得冗长的演讲很烦人. **switch (sth) on** connect (electricity, etc or an appliance) 接通(电流等); 开(用电器): *Switch on the light at the wall-socket.* 把电灯接通在墙上的电源插座上. ○ *Don't switch (the radio) on yet.* 暂时不要打开(收音机).

□ **ˈswitch-blade** *n* = FLICK-KNIFE (FLICK).

switchboard /ˈswɪtʃbɔːd; ˋswɪtʃˌbɔrd/ *n* (staff controlling a) central panel with a set of switches for making telephone connections or operating electrical circuits 电话交换台、总机或配电板(工作人员): *on duty at the switchboard* 在电话交换台值班 ○ *Protesting viewers jammed the BBC switchboard.* 观众抗议的电话使英国广播公司的总机应接不暇. ○ [attrib 作定语] *switchboard operators* 交换台接线员.

switched-ˈon *adj* (*dated infml* 旧, 口) aware of what is going on; up-to-date 了解当前情况的; 跟上时代的.

ˈswitch-man /-mən; -mən/ *n* (*pl* **-men** /-mən; -mən/) (*US*) = POINTSMAN (POINT[1]).

ˈswitch-over *n* = SWITCH 2.

ˈswitch-yard *n* (*US*) area where railway cars are switched between lines to make up trains (铁路的)编组站, 调车场.

switch·back /ˈswɪtʃbæk; ˋswɪtʃˌbæk/ *n* **1** (*esp Brit*) = ROLLER-COASTER (ROLLER). **2** zigzag railway or road for ascending or descending steep slopes (上下陡坡的)之字形铁路或公路.

swivel /'swɪvl; ˋswɪvl̩/ *n* (esp in compounds 尤用以构成复合词) link or pivot between two parts enabling one part to revolve without turning the other 转环; 转节; 旋转接头; 旋轴: *a swivel-chain, -hook* 转动链、转动钩 ○ *a swivel-chair*, ie one that rotates 转椅.

▷ **swivel** *v* (**-ll-**; *US* **-l-**) [I, Ip, Tn, Tn·p] **~ (sth) (round)** (cause sth to) turn on or as if on a swivel (使某物)(似)在旋轴上转动: *He swivelled (round) in his chair to face us.* 他把坐着的转椅转过来面向着我们. ○ *She swivelled the telescope (round).* 她用望远镜向四周看.

swizz /swɪz; swɪz/ (also **swizzle**) *n* (usu *sing* 通常作单数) (*Brit infml* 口) swindle or disappointment 骗局; 失望: *You didn't get a leaving present? What a swizz!* 你没有得到临别礼物吗? 真叫人失望!

swizzle /'swɪzl; ˋswɪzl̩/ *n* **1** any of various types of tall frothy mixed drink, usu made with rum 有高层泡沫的混合饮料(通常混有朗姆酒). **2** = SWIZZ.

□ **'swizzle-stick** *n* (**a**) long glass rod for stirring a swizzle(1) (调泡沫饮料用的)玻璃棒. (**b**) small stick for stirring or decorating cocktails (调鸡尾酒用的)搅拌棒(或作装饰用).

swol·len *pp* of SWELL.

swoon /swu:n; swun/ *v* (**a**) [I, Ipr, Ip] (*dated* 旧) lose consciousness; faint 失去知觉; 昏厥; 晕倒: *She swooned into his arms for joy.* 她喜极而昏倒在他的怀里. ○ *She swooned away.* 她失去了知觉. (**b**) [I, Ipr] **~ (over sb/sth)** (*fig esp joc* 比喻, 尤作戏谑语) be emotionally affected (by sb/sth) (因某人[某事物])动感情: *All the girls are swooning over the new maths teacher.* 所有的女同学都迷上了那位新来的数学教师. ▷ **swoon** *n* (*dated* 旧): *fall into a swoon* 昏厥; 昏倒.

swoop /swu:p; swup/ *v* **1** [I, Ipr, Ip] **~ (down) (on sb/sth)** come down suddenly with a rushing movement 突然下降; 向下猛冲; 猛扑: *The owl swooped down on the mouse.* 那只猫头鹰向着老鼠猛扑下来. ○ *Planes swooped (low) over the ship.* 飞机低飞着掠过那艘船. ○ (*fig* 比喻) *Detectives swooped (on the house) at dawn.* 侦缉人员于拂晓时(对那所房子)进行了突然搜查. **2** (phr v) **swoop sth away/up** (*infml* 口) seize or snatch the whole of sth in one movement 一下子抓住或抢走某物: *The robber swooped up the banknotes.* 劫匪把钞票一把抢走了.

▷ **swoop** *n* **1 ~ (on sth/sb)** (**a**) swooping movement 突降; 向下猛冲; 猛扑. (**b**) sudden and unexpected attack 袭击: *Police made a dawn swoop.* 警方于拂晓时发动了突袭. **2** (idm 习语) **at one fell swoop** ⇨ FELL².

swop = SWAP.

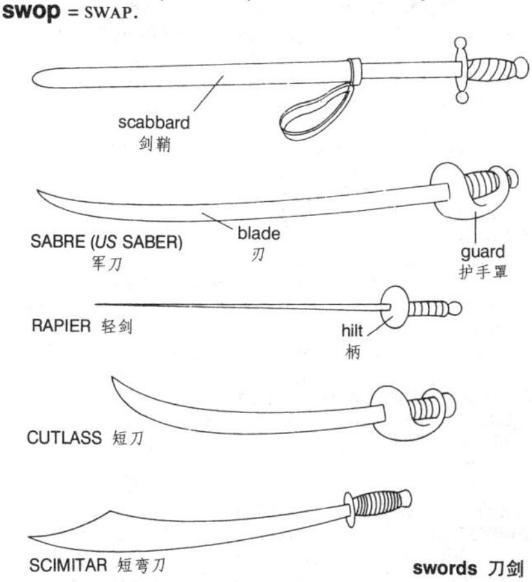

swords 刀剑

sword /sɔ:d; sɔrd/ *n* **1** weapon with a long thin metal blade and a protected handle (用作武器有防护手柄的)剑, 刀: *draw/sheathe one's sword*, ie take it out of/put it into its sheath 把剑拔出[插入鞘中]. **2** (idm 习语) **cross swords** ⇨ CROSS². **fire and sword** ⇨ FIRE¹. **the pen is mightier than the sword** ⇨ PEN¹. **put sb to the 'sword** (*dated or rhet* 旧或修辞) kill sb with a sword 用刀或剑杀死某人. **a sword of 'Damocles** /'dæməkli:z; ˋdæmə,kliz/ (*fml* 文) something unpleasant, dreadful, etc that seems to be about to happen to sb, and causes a feeling of apprehension and imminent danger 达摩克勒斯剑(比喻某人将有祸事临头): *The possibility of losing her job hung over her like a sword of Damocles all last year.* 去年她一直提心吊胆生怕失去工作.

□ **'sword-dance** *n* dance between and over swords placed on the ground, or one in which swords are waved or clashed 剑舞(在置于地上的剑之间起舞, 或舞剑或使其铿锵作声).

'swordfish *n* large sea-fish with an extremely long thin pointed upper jaw 剑鱼(大海鱼, 上颌突出如剑).

'sword-play *n* [U] fighting with swords 剑术.

'swordsman /-zmən; -zmən/ *n* (*pl* **-men**) man skilled in the use of a sword 剑客; 击剑运动员: *a good, poor, etc swordsman* 优秀的、差劲的...击剑运动员. **'swordsmanship** /-mənʃɪp; -mən,ʃɪp/ *n* [U].

'sword-stick *n* hollow walking-stick concealing a blade that can be used as a sword 二人夺(内藏刀剑的手杖).

swore *pt* of SWEAR.

sworn¹ *pp* of SWEAR.

sworn² /swɔ:n; swɔrn/ *adj* [attrib 作定语] **1** made under a solemn promise to tell the truth 保证说实话的; 宣过誓的: *a sworn statement* 宣过誓的陈述. **2** extreme in affection or dislike 感情极深的; 极端厌恶的: *sworn friends/enemies* 知己[不共戴天的敌人].

swot /swɒt; swɑt/ *v* (**-tt-**) [I, Ipr, Ip, Tn·p] **~ (up) (for/on sth)**; **~ sth up** (*Brit infml often derog* 口, 常作贬义) study sth very hard, esp in preparation for an exam 刻苦学习某事物(尤指为准备考试): *swotting for her exams* (她)为考试而用功 ○ *I'm swotting up my maths/swotting up on my history.* 我正在用功温习数学[历史].

▷ **swot** (also **swot·ter**) *n* person who swots 刻苦学习的人(尤指为准备考试).

swum *pp* of SWIM.

swung *pt, pp* of SWING.

sy·bar·ite /'sɪbəraɪt; ˋsɪbə,raɪt/ *n* (*fml* usu derog 文, 通常作贬义) person who is very fond of luxury and comfort 好享受图安逸的人.

▷ **sy·bar·itic** /,sɪbə'rɪtɪk; ,sɪbəˋrɪtɪk/ *adj* (*fml usu derog* 文, 通常作贬义) typical of a sybarite 好享受图安逸的; 穷奢极欲的: *sybaritic tastes, pleasures* 骄奢淫逸的爱好、乐趣.

sy·ca·more /'sɪkəmɔ:(r); ˋsɪkə,mɔr/ *n* **1** [C] (**a**) (*esp Brit*) large tree of the maple family 西克莫(一种大树). ⇨illus at App 1 见附录1插图, page i. (**b**) (*esp US*) type of plane tree 悬铃木. **2** [U] valuable hard wood of the sycamore 西克莫木材(材质坚硬而贵重): [attrib 作定语] *a sycamore desk, chair, etc* 西克莫木书桌、椅子等.

sy·co·phant /'sɪkəfænt; ˋsɪkəfənt/ *n* (*fml derog* 文, 贬) person who tries to gain people's favour by insincerely flattering them and always agreeing with them 谄媚者; 阿谀奉承者. ▷ **sy·co·phancy** /'sɪkəfənsɪ; ˋsɪkəfənsɪ/ *n* [U]. **sy·co·phantic** /,sɪkə'fæntɪk; ,sɪkəˋfæntɪk/ *adj*: *a sycophantic smile* 谄笑. **sy·co·phant·ic·ally** /-klɪ; -klɪ/ *adv*.

syl·lable /'sɪləbl; ˋsɪləbl̩/ *n* **1** any of the units into which a word may be divided, usu consisting of a vowel-sound with a consonant before or after 音节(通常由一个元音加上其前面或后面的辅音构成): *'Arithmetic' is a word of four syllables.* arithmetic 一字有四个音节. **2** (idm 习语) **in words of one syllable** ⇨ WORD.

▷ **syl·lab·ary** /'sɪləbərɪ; *US* -berɪ; ˋsɪlə,bɛrɪ/ *n* list of written or printed symbols (eg in Japanese) representing syllables 音节符号表; (日语的)假名表.

syl·labic /sɪ'læbɪk; sɪˋlæbɪk/ *adj* **1** of or in syllables 音节的; 分音节的; 拼音的. **2** (of a consonant) making a syllable on its own, without a vowel (指辅音)自成音节的. **syl·lab·ic·ally** /-bɪklɪ; -bɪklɪ/ *adv*.

syl·labify /sɪ'læbɪfaɪ; sɪˋlæbə,faɪ/ *v* (*pt, pp* **-fied**) [Tn] divide (a word or words) into syllables 将(词)划分音节. **syl·labi·fica·tion** /sɪ,læbɪfɪ'keɪʃn; sɪ,læbəfəˋkeʃən/ *n* [U] (system of) dividing into syllables 音节划分(法).

-syllabled (forming compound *adjs* 用以构成复合形容词) having the specified number of syllables 有...个音节的: *a two-, three-, four-, etc syllabled word.*

syl·la·bub (also **sil·la·bub**) /ˈsɪləbʌb; ˈsɪlə,bʌb/ *n* [C, U] dish of sweetened cream mixed vigorously to a froth with wine, etc 用甜奶油与葡萄酒等混合用力搅拌产生泡沫的甜食.

syl·labus /ˈsɪləbəs; ˈsɪləbəs/ *n* (*pl* **~es**) list of subjects, topics, texts, etc included in a course of study 教学大纲: *'Hamlet' is on this year's English literature syllabus.*《哈姆雷特》是本学年英国文学教学大纲中规定的作品. Cf 参看 CURRICULUM.

syl·lo·gism /ˈsɪlədʒɪzəm; ˈsɪlə,dʒɪzəm/ *n* form of reasoning in which a conclusion is drawn from two statements, eg *All men must die; I am a man; therefore I must die.* 三段论法(从两个前提得出结论的推理方法, 如'凡是人都必有一死; 我是人; 所以我必有一死.') Cf 参看 PREMISE 2.

▷ **syl·lo·gistic** /,sɪləˈdʒɪstɪk; ,sɪləˈdʒɪstɪk/ *adj* in the form of or being a syllogism 三段论式的; 三段论法的.

sylph /sɪlf; sɪlf/ *n* **1** (in ancient myth) one of a type of female nature spirits believed to inhabit the air (古代神话中的)气精(生活在空气中的女精灵). **2** (*fml approv* 文, 褒) slender and graceful girl or woman 苗条而优雅的女子; 窈窕淑女. Cf 参看 NYMPH.

▷ ˈ**sylph·like** *adj* (*approv or joc* 褒或谑) slender and graceful 苗条而优雅的; 窈窕的: *'You're not exactly sylphlike, are you?' she said to her fat friend.* '你并不算苗条, 对吧?' 她对她那胖胖的朋友说.

syl·van ⇨ SILVAN.

sym·bi·osis /,sɪmbɪˈəʊsɪs, -baɪ-; ,sɪmbɪˈosɪs, -baɪ-/ *n* [U] (*biology* 生) relationship between two species, organisms, etc that live close together and depend on each other in various ways 共生(关系): *the symbiosis between a plant and the insect that fertilizes it* 一植物与使其受精昆虫的共生关系. ▷ **sym·bi·otic** /-ˈɒtɪk; -ˈɑtɪk/ *adj*.

S

sym·bol /ˈsɪmbl; ˈsɪmbl̩/ *n* **1 ~ (of sth)** image, object, etc that suggests or refers to sth else; emblem 象征; 标志: *The cross is the symbol of Christianity.* 十字架是基督教的标志. ○ *The lion is the symbol of courage.* 狮子是勇武的象征. **2 ~ (for sth)** mark or sign with a particular meaning, eg plus and minus signs in mathematics, punctuation marks, musical notation, etc 符号, 记号(如数学中的加减号、标点符号、乐谱等): *On maps, a cross is the symbol for a church.* 在地图上, 十字符号代表教堂. ○ *Au is the chemical symbol for gold.* 'Au'是金的化学元素符号. ○ *algebraic signs and symbols* 代数符号.

▷ **sym·bolic** /sɪmˈbɒlɪk; sɪmˈbɑlɪk/, **sym·bol·ical** /-kl; -kl̩/ *adjs* **~ (of sth)** of, using or used as a symbol 符号的; 使用符号的; 用作符号的; 象征(性)的: *The cross is symbolic of Christianity.* 十字架是基督教的象征. ○ *The power of the monarchy in Britain today is more symbolical than real.* 今日英国君主的权力多为象征性的, 无甚实际意义. **sym·bol·ic·ally** /-klɪ; -klɪ/ *adv*.

sym·bol·ism /ˈsɪmbəlɪzəm; ˈsɪmbl̩,ɪzəm/ *n* [U] use of symbols to represent things, esp in art and literature; the symbols thus used 符号的使用; (尤指文艺中的)象征主义, 象征手法: *poetry full of religious symbolism* 用大量象征手法表现宗教色彩的诗篇. **sym·bol·ist** /ˈsɪmbəlɪst; ˈsɪmbəlɪst/ *n* artist, writer, etc who habitually uses symbols 象征主义者; 象征主义的艺术家、作家等.

sym·bol·ize, -ise /ˈsɪmbəlaɪz; ˈsɪmbl̩,aɪz/ *v* **1** [Tn] be a symbol of (sth) 作为(某事物)的符号或标志; 象征(某事物): *a picture of a red disc with rays coming from it, symbolizing the sun* 画着一个光芒四射的红色圆盘以代表太阳的一幅画. **2** [Tn, Tn·pr, Cn·n/a] **~ sth/sb (with/as sth)** represent sth/sb by means of a symbol 用符号代表某事物[某人]: *The poet has symbolized his lover with a flower.* 那诗人用花象征他的爱人.

sym·metry /ˈsɪmətrɪ; ˈsɪmɪtrɪ/ *n* [U] **1** exact match in size and shape between the two halves of sth 对称: *the perfect symmetry of the building* 这座建筑物完美的对称格局. **2** pleasingly regular way in which parts are arranged 匀称: *the symmetry of her features* 她的五官端正.

▷ **sym·met·ric** /sɪˈmetrɪk; sɪˈmɛtrɪk/, **sym·met·rical** /-rɪkl; rɪkl̩/ *adjs* (of a design, etc) having two halves which are the same in size and shape (指图案等)对称的: *The plan of the ground floor is completely symmetrical.* 一楼的平面图是完全对称的. ○ *the symmetrical arrangement of the gardens*, ie one that shows symmetry 花园中对称的布局. Cf 参看 ASYMMETRIC. **sym·met·ric·ally** /-klɪ; -klɪ/ *adv*.

sym·path·etic /,sɪmpəˈθetɪk; ,sɪmpəˈθɛtɪk/ *adj* **1 ~ (to/towards/with sb)** feeling, showing or resulting from sympathy 同情的; 表示同情的; 出于同情的: *a sympathetic look, smile, remark* 表示同情的目光、笑容、言语 ○ *feel sympathetic towards sb who is suffering* 对遭到不幸的某人十分同情 ○ *He was enormously sympathetic when my father died.* 我父亲去世时他深为同情. **2** likeable 可爱的; 讨人喜欢的: *a sympathetic character*, ie person 一个讨人喜欢的人 ○ *I don't find her very sympathetic.* 我觉得她不太讨人喜欢. **3** [pred 作表语] **~ (to sth/sb)** showing favour or approval 表示好感或赞同: *We asked for her support in the election, but she wasn't sympathetic (to our request).* 我们请求她在选举中给予支持, 但她(对我们的请求)无动于衷. ▷ **sym·path·et·ic·ally** /-klɪ; -klɪ/ *adv*.

sym·pathy /ˈsɪmpəθɪ; ˈsɪmpəθɪ/ *n* **1** [U] **~ (for/towards sb)** (capacity for) sharing the feelings of others; feeling of pity and sorrow (for sb) 同情; 同情心: *feel great sympathy for sb* 对某人深为同情 ○ *She never expressed any sympathy when I was injured.* 我受伤时她从未表示过同情. ○ *Out of sympathy for the homeless children he gave them shelter for the night.* 他怀着恻隐之心, 留那些无家可归的孩子过夜. **2 sympathies** [pl] feeling or expression of sorrow, approval, etc 哀悼; 慰问; (感情上的)支持, 赞同: *You have my deepest sympathies on the death of your wife.* 对于令夫人之去世, 谨向您表示最深切的慰问. ○ *My sympathies are with the workers in this dispute.* 在这场纠纷中, 我站在工人一方. **3** [U] **~ (between sb and sb)** liking for each other produced in people who have similar opinions or tastes 志同道合; 意气相投: *A bond of sympathy developed between members of the group.* 该组织成员间产生了志同道合的凝聚力. **4** (idm 习语) **in sympathy (with sb/sth)** showing support or approval for a cause, etc 对某事业等表示支持或赞同: *The steel workers came out in sympathy with the miners*, ie went on strike to show support for them. 钢铁工人为声援矿工举行了罢工. ○ *I'm sure she will be in sympathy with your proposal.* 我确信她一定赞成你的建议. **have no, some, etc sympathy with sb/sth** be unable/able to share sb's views, etc 不同意[同意]某人的观点等: *He's wrong — I have no sympathy with him.* 他错了——我不同意他的意见. ○ *I have some sympathy with that point of view.* 我比较赞成这种看法.

▷ **sym·path·ize, -ise** /ˈsɪmpəθaɪz; ˈsɪmpə,θaɪz/ *v* [I, Ipr] **~ (with sb/sth)** feel or express sympathy or support 同情; 表示同情; 赞同; 支持: *I sympathize with you; I've had a similar unhappy experience myself.* 我很同情你, 我自己也有过类似的不幸遭遇. ○ *We have long sympathized with the aims of the Green Party.* 我们长期以来一直支持绿党保护生态环境的目标. **sym·path·izer, -iser** *n* person who sympathizes, esp one who supports a cause or a political party 同情者; (尤指某事业或政党的)支持者, 拥护者: *Socialist sympathizers* 社会主义的支持者.

sym·phony /ˈsɪmfənɪ; ˈsɪmfənɪ/ *n* long complex musical composition, usu in three or four parts (*movements*) for a large orchestra 交响曲; 交响乐: [attrib 作定语] *a symphony orchestra*, ie a large orchestra that plays symphonies, etc 交响乐团.

▷ **sym·phonic** /sɪmˈfɒnɪk; sɪmˈfɑnɪk/ *adj* of or like a symphony (似)交响乐的.

sym·po·sium /sɪmˈpəʊzɪəm; sɪmˈpozɪəm/ *n* (*pl* **-sia** /-zɪə; -zɪə/) **1** small conference for discussion of a particular subject (专题)讨论会, 研讨会. **2** collection of essays by several people on a particular subject, published as a book 专题论文集: *contribute to a symposium on environmental issues* 为环境问题论文集撰稿.

symp·tom /ˈsɪmptəm; ˈsɪmptəm/ *n* **1** change in the body that indicates an illness 症状: *the rash that is a symptom of measles* 麻疹症状呈现的疹子. **2** sign of the existence of sth bad (坏事的)征兆, 征候: *This demonstration was a symptom of discontent among the students.* 这次示威表明学生中有不满情绪.

▷ **symp·to·matic** /,sɪmptəˈmætɪk; ,sɪmptəˈmætɪk/ *adj* [pred 作表语] **~ (of sth)** being a symptom 作为症状或征兆: *Chest pains may be symptomatic of heart disease.*

胸痛可能是心脏病的症状. ○ *Is inflation symptomatic of economic decline?* 通货膨胀是经济衰退的征兆吗?

syn·agogue /ˈsɪnəgɒg; ˈsɪnə,gɔg/ *n* building used by Jews for religious worship or teaching (犹太人进行宗教活动或学习的)会堂.

sync (also **synch**) /sɪŋk; sɪŋk/ *n* [U] (*infml* 口) = SYNCHRONIZATION (SYNCHRONIZE): *The film's sound-track is out of sync/not in sync with the picture.* 这部影片的声迹与图像不同步.

syn·chro·mesh /ˌsɪŋkrəʊˈmeʃ; ˈsɪŋkrə,mɛʃ/ *n* [U] device in a vehicle's gearbox that makes the parts turn at the same speed and thus allows gears to be changed smoothly (机动车齿轮箱中的)同步齿轮系.

syn·chron·ize, -ise /ˈsɪŋkrənaɪz; ˈsɪŋkrə,naɪz/ *v* [I, Ipr, Tn, Tn·pr] **~ (sth) (with sth)** (cause sth to) operate, move, turn, etc at the same time, speed, etc (使某物)以相同的时间、速度等运转、移动、转动等; (使某物)同步: *The wheels must synchronize as they revolve.* 这些轮子须同速转动. ○ *The sound on a film must synchronize with the action.* 影片中的声音必须与动作配合一致. ○ *Let's synchronize our watches,* ie set them to show the same time. 咱们把表校准吧. ▷ **syn·chron·iza·tion, -isation** /ˌsɪŋkrənaɪˈzeɪʃn; *US* -nɪˈz-; ˌsɪŋkrənɪˈzeʃən/ (also *infml* 口语作 **sync**) *n* [U].

syn·co·pate /ˈsɪŋkəpeɪt; ˈsɪŋkə,pet/ *v* [Tn usu passive 通常用于被动语态] change (the rhythm or beats) in a piece of music so that a strong beat becomes weak and a weak beat becomes strong 切分(音乐的节奏或节拍)(使强弱倒置): *The song has a syncopated rhythm in the jazz version.* 这首歌曲改编为爵士乐后采用了切分音节奏. ▷ **syn·co·pa·tion** /ˌsɪŋkəˈpeɪʃn; ˌsɪŋkəˈpeʃən/ *n* [U].

syn·cope /ˈsɪŋkəpɪ; ˈsɪŋkəpɪ/ *n* **1** [U, C] (*medical* 医) brief loss of consciousness; faint(ing) 晕厥. **2** [U] (*linguistics* 语言) shortening of a word by omitting one or more letters or syllables in the middle, eg 'bosun' for 'boatswain' 词中省音, 央字失落, 央音失落(省略词中的字母或音节, 如将 boatswain 略为 bosun).

syn·dic·al·ism /ˈsɪndɪkəlɪzəm; ˈsɪndɪkḷ,ɪzəm/ *n* [U] theory that factories, businesses, etc should be owned and managed by the workers employed in them 工团主义(主张工厂、企业等应归其员工所有并管理).
▷ **syn·dic·al·ist** /-kəlɪst; -kəlɪst/ *n* supporter of syndicalism 工团主义者.

syn·dic·ate /ˈsɪndɪkət; ˈsɪndɪkɪt/ *n* group of people or business companies combined to undertake a joint project 辛迪加(某些人或工商企业的联合组织).
▷ **syn·dic·ate** /ˈsɪndɪkeɪt; ˈsɪndɪ,ket/ *v* [Tn usu passive 通常用于被动语态] publish (an article, a strip cartoon, etc) in many different newspapers, magazines, etc by means of a central distributing agency (经报业辛迪加在多家报刊上)发表(文章、连环漫画等): *His column is syndicated throughout the world.* 他的专栏文章通过报业辛迪加在世界许多报刊上发表. **syn·dica·tion** /ˌsɪndɪˈkeɪʃn; ˌsɪndɪˈkeʃən/ *n* [U].

syn·drome /ˈsɪndrəʊm; ˈsɪndrom/ *n* **1** (*medical* 医) set of symptoms which together indicate a particular disease or abnormal condition 综合病征; 综合症状. **2** (*fig* 比喻) any set of opinions, events, actions, etc that are characteristic of a particular condition 在某条件下有共同特征的一系列言论、事件、行动等: *Unemployment, inflation, and low wages are all part of the same economic syndrome.* 失业、通货膨胀以及低工资等问题都是在同一经济状况下的现象.

synod /ˈsɪnəd; ˈsɪnəd/ *n* official assembly of church members to discuss and decide on matters of religious teaching, church policy and administration, etc (讨论和决定宗教教义、教会政策及管理等问题的)会议, 大会.

syn·onym /ˈsɪnənɪm; ˈsɪnə,nɪm/ *n* word or phrase with the same meaning as another in the same language, though perhaps with a different style, grammar or technical use 同义词; 同义词组; 同义语: *'Slay' and 'kill' are synonyms.* slay 和 kill 是同义词.
▷ **syn·onym·ous** /sɪˈnɒnɪməs; sɪˈnɑnəməs/ *adj* **~ (with sth)** having the same meaning 同义的: *'Slay' is synonymous with 'kill' (though it is more forceful and rather dated).* slay 与 kill 同义(但语气较重且较陈旧). ○ (*fig* 比喻) *Wealth is not necessarily synonymous with generosity,* ie Rich people are not always generous. 财富与慷慨未必同义(富人不见得都慷慨). Cf 参看 ANTONYM.

syn·op·sis /sɪˈnɒpsɪs; sɪˈnɑpsɪs/ *n* (*pl* **-opses** /-siːz; -siz/) summary or outline of a book, play, etc (书、剧本等的)大纲, 提要.
▷ **syn·op·tic** /sɪˈnɒptɪk; sɪˈnɑptɪk/ *adj* [attrib 作定语] of or forming a synopsis 提纲的; 概要的.
□ **the sy,noptic 'gospels** (in the Bible) the gospels of Matthew, Mark and Luke, which are very similar (whereas that of John is very different) (《圣经》中的)对观福音书(马太、马可、路加三福音书).

syn·tax /ˈsɪntæks; ˈsɪntæks/ *n* [U] (*linguistics* 语言) (rules for the) arrangement of words into phrases and phrases into sentences 句法; 语句结构.
▷ **syn·tactic** /sɪnˈtæktɪk; sɪnˈtæktɪk/ *adj* of syntax 句法的: *syntactic differences between English and French* 英语和法语句法上的差异. **syn·tact·ic·ally** /-klɪ; -klɪ/ *adv*: *a syntactically complex written style* 使用复杂语句的写作风格. Cf 参看 GRAMMAR 1, MORPHOLOGY 2.

syn·thesis /ˈsɪnθəsɪs; ˈsɪnθəsɪs/ *n* (*pl* **-theses** /-siːz; -,siz/) **1** (**a**) [U] combining of separate parts, elements, etc to form a complex whole 综合; 结合: *develop a new theory by the synthesis of several earlier theories* 综合以前的几种学说而创立的新学说. (**b**) [C] what is produced in this way 综合体: *a new method that is a synthesis of the best features of the old methods* 综合旧方法的长处而成的新方法 ○ *Her novels are an odd synthesis of English reserve and Welsh emotionalism.* 她的小说把英格兰人的拘谨和威尔士人的情感外露很独特地结合在一起. **2** [U] combining of substances into a compound, or the artificial production of a substance that occurs naturally in plants and animals 合成; 人造: *produce rubber from petroleum by synthesis* 以合成法用石油制取橡胶 ○ *the synthesis of insulin* 胰岛素的合成.
▷ **syn·thes·ize, -ise** /ˈsɪnθəsaɪz; ˈsɪnθə,saɪz/ *v* [Tn] **1** make (sth) by synthesis 用合成法制造(某物): *synthesize diamonds, rubber, fuel, etc* 用合成法制造钻石、橡胶、燃料等. **2** combine (parts) into a whole 将(各部分)结合成一整体; 合成: *The two elements are synthesized by a chemical process.* 这两种元素已经化学合成.
syn·thes·izer, -iser *n* electronic musical instrument producing a large number of different sounds, including imitations of other instruments (电子)音响合成器.
syn·thetic /sɪnˈθetɪk; sɪnˈθɛtɪk/ *adj* **1** made by synthesis(2); artificial 用合成法制造的; 人造的: *synthetic diamonds, rubber, etc* 人造钻石、合成橡胶. **2** [attrib 作定语] of synthesis(2) 合成的: *synthetic chemistry* 合成化学. **3** (*infml derog* 口, 贬) not genuine or natural; false 假的; 非天然的; 虚伪的: *the salesman's synthetic friendliness* 那男售货员的虚情假意 ○ *a synthetic blonde,* ie sb whose hair is dyed blonde 染成金发的人.
syn·thetic *n* synthetic substance or fibre 合成物; 合成纤维: *natural fibres and synthetics* 天然纤维和合成纤维.
syn·thet·ic·ally /-klɪ; -klɪ/ *adv*.

syph·ilis /ˈsɪfɪlɪs; ˈsɪfḷɪs/ *n* [U] (also **the pox**) infectious disease passed from one person to another by sexual contact 梅毒.
▷ **syph·il·itic** /ˌsɪfɪˈlɪtɪk; ˌsɪfḷˈɪtɪk/ *adj* of or suffering from syphilis 梅毒的; 患梅毒的. — *n* person affected with syphilis 梅毒患者.

syr·inga /sɪˈrɪŋgə; səˈrɪŋgə/ *n* [C, U] **1** shrub with strong-scented white flowers 山梅花(灌木, 开白花, 味香). **2** (*botany* 植) lilac 丁香花.

syr·inge /sɪˈrɪndʒ; ˈsɪrɪndʒ/ *n* **1** any of various types of device for taking liquid in and forcing it out again in a thin stream, used for spraying plants, washing wounds, etc 液体喷射器(如浇花用的喷水器、洗伤口用的冲洗器等): *a garden syringe* 浇花用的喷水器. **2** = HYPODERMIC SYRINGE (HYPODERMIC). ⇨illus at INJECTION 见 INJECTION 插图.
▷ **syr·inge** *v* [Tn] clean, spray, or inject liquid into (sth) with a syringe (用液体喷射器)冲洗, 喷洒, 注射(某物): *syringe a wound, plant* 冲洗伤口、喷浇植物.

syrup /ˈsɪrəp; ˈsɪrəp/ *n* [U] **1** water in which sugar is dissolved 糖浆; 糖水: *tinned peaches in (heavy) syrup* 罐装(浓)糖水桃 ○ *cough syrup,* ie syrup with medicine in it to cure coughs 止咳糖浆. **2** any thick sweet liquid, eg treacle 甜而稠的汁液(如糖饴).
▷ **syr·upy** *adj* **1** of or like syrup (似)糖浆的: *a drink that is too syrupy* 过甜的饮料. **2** (*fig derog* 比喻, 贬) too

S

sentimental; sugary (SUGAR 1) 过于多情的; 甜得发腻的: *a rather syrupy love-story* 颇为感伤的爱情故事.

sys·tem /ˈsɪstəm; ˋsɪstəm/ *n* **1** [C] group of things or parts working together as a whole 系统; 组合装置: *the nervous system* 神经系统 ○ *the digestive system* 消化系统 ○ *a railway system* 铁路系统 ○ *a stereo system*, eg a record-deck, an amplifier, loud-speakers, etc combined 立体声音响设备 ○ *The lifting device is a system of ropes and pulleys.* 这种起重装置是由缆索和滑轮组成的. **2** [C] person's or animal's body as a whole, including its internal organs and processes (人或动物的)身体: *The poison has passed into his system.* 毒物已进入他的体内. ○ *Alcohol is bad for your system.* 喝酒对身体有害. **3** [C] set of ideas, theories, principles, etc according to which sth is done (思想、理论、原则等的)体系, 体制, 方法, 方式: *a system of philosophy* 哲学体系 ○ *the democratic system of government* 民主政体 ○ *a good system of teaching languages* 教授语言的良好方法 ○ *a foolproof new system for winning at roulette* 轮盘赌必胜新法. **4** [U] orderly way of doing things; tidy arrangement 制度; 步骤; 条理: *You'll find little system in his method of work.* 他的工作方法无甚条理. ○ *We must introduce some system into our office routine.* 我们须在我们日常公务中建立一些制度. **5 the system** [sing] (*infml* 口) the traditional methods, practices and rules existing in a society, an institution, a business, etc (某社会、机构、企业等中)沿袭已久的方法、做法和规则: *You can't beat the system,* ie You must conform to it. 老规矩触动不得(必须照办). **6** (idm 习语) **get sth out of one's 'system** (*infml* 口) get rid of a strong feeling or desire by expressing it openly or trying to fulfil it 宣泄强烈的感情或满足强烈的愿望: *He desperately wants to be an actor, so you'll have to give him time to get it out of his system.* 他渴望当演员, 你就得容他时间让他施展自己的抱负.

▷ **sys·tem·atic** /ˌsɪstəˈmætɪk; ˌsɪstəˋmætɪk/ *adj* **1** done or acting according to a system or plan; methodical 有系统的; 有计划的; 有条理的: *the systematic arrangement of the chairs* 按照顺序排列的座椅 ○ *He's very systematic in all he does.* 他做一切事情都很有条理. **2** [attrib 作定语] (*derog* 贬) planned in advance and done with malicious thoroughness and exactness 有预谋的; 蓄意的: *a systematic attempt to ruin sb's reputation* 蓄谋破坏某人的名誉. **sys·tem·at·ic·ally** /-klɪ; -klɪ/ *adv*.

sys·tem·at·ize, -ise /ˈsɪstəmətaɪz; ˋsɪstəməˌtaɪz/ *v* [Tn] arrange (sth) according to a well-organized system 使(某事物)系统化或有条理; 使(某事物)成制度或成体系: *We must try to systematize the way we do the accounts.* 我们必须力求把记帐方法制度化. **sys·tem·at·iza·tion, -isation** /ˌsɪstəmətaɪˈzeɪʃn; *US* -tɪˈz-; ˌsɪstəmətɪˋzeʃən/ *n*.

sys·temic /sɪˈstemɪk, *also* sɪˈsti:mɪk; sɪsˋtɛmɪk/ *adj* **1** of or affecting the whole of the body 全身的; 影响全身的. **2** acting by entering the tissues of a plant and killing insects and other pests which try to feed on it 内吸收的, 内吸性的(通过渗入植物组织内以消灭以之为食的昆虫及其他有害生物的): *systemic fungicides* 内吸性杀真菌剂. **sys·tem·ic·ally** /-klɪ; -klɪ/ *adv*.

□ **'systems analysis** analysis of all the steps in an operation in order to decide how to perform it most efficiently, esp using a computer 系统分析(尤指用计算机). **'systems analyst** expert in systems analysis 系统分析专家.

S

T t

T, t /ti:; ti/ *n* (*pl* **T's, t's** /ti:z; tiz/) **1** the twentieth letter of the English alphabet 英语字母表的第二十个字母: *'Committee' is spelt with two t's.* ☆ committee 这个字中有两个t. **2** (idm 习语) **dot one's/the i's and cross one's/the t's** ⇨ DOT. **to a 'T/'tee** (*infml* 口) in every detail; exactly 至每一细节; 精确地; 恰到好处: *This new job suits me to a T.* 这项新工作对我来说处处称心如意.
□ **'T-bone** *n* T-shaped bone, esp one in a piece of beefsteak 丁字骨; (尤指)丁字骨牛排.
'T-junction *n* place where one road or pipe, etc joins another but does not cross it, thus forming the shape of a T 丁字路口; (管道等的)三通管, 丁字接头.
'T-shirt (also **tee-shirt**) *n* shirt with short sleeves that has the shape of a T when spread out flat 短袖汗衫.

t (*US* **tn**) *abbr* 缩写 = ton(s); tonne(s): *5t* (ie tonnes) *of wheat per acre* 每英亩5英吨小麦.

ta /tɑ:; tɑ/ *interj* (*Brit infml* 口) thank you 谢谢.

tab /tæb; tæb/ *n* **1** small projecting flap or strip of cloth, metal, paper, etc, esp one by which sth can be grasped, hung, fastened or identified 小片, 小条, 小带(尤指用以抓住、悬挂、固定或识别某物的): *To open, pull tab*, eg on a can of beer. 拉环开罐(如啤酒罐上的字样). ○ *a 'name-tab*, ie one sewn into clothes, etc 名字标签(缝在衣物等上的). **2** (*US*) bill[1](1) (used esp in the expression shown) 帐单(尤用于下列示例): *pick up* (ie pay) *the tab* 付款. **3** (idm 习语) **keep a tab/tabs on sth/sb** (*infml* 口) keep account of sth/sb; keep sth/sb under observation 记入某事物[某人]的帐; 监视某事物[某人]: *keep tabs on who's using the phone* 记录打电话的人名.

Ta·basco /tə'bæskəʊ; tə'bæsko/ *n* [U] (*propr* 专利名) spicy sauce made from peppers 塔巴斯哥辣沙司.

TAB (also **Tab**) /ˌti: eɪ 'bi:; ˌti e 'bi/ *abbr* 缩写 = typhoid-paratyphoid A and B vaccine 伤寒—副伤寒甲和乙菌苗: *have a Tab injection* 注射伤寒—副伤寒甲、乙预防针.

tabby /'tæbɪ; 'tæbɪ/ (also **'tabby-cat**) *n* cat with grey or brownish fur and dark stripes 斑猫.

tab·er·nacle /'tæbənækl; 'tæbɚˌnækḷ/ *n* **1 the tabernacle** [sing] (*Bible*《圣经》) the portable shrine used by the Israelites during their wanderings in the wilderness 会幕(以色列人在荒野流浪时便于移动的圣所). **2** [C] (in the Roman Catholic Church) receptacle containing consecrated elements of the Eucharist (天主教的)圣体盘. **3** [C] place of worship used by Nonconformists (eg Baptists) or Mormons (不信奉国教派教徒, 如浸礼会教徒, 或摩门教徒的)礼拜堂, 教堂.

table /'teɪbl; 'tebḷ/ *n* **1** [C] piece of furniture consisting of a flat top supported on one or more legs 桌子; 台子; 几: *a 'dining-table* 餐桌 ○ *a 'bedside-table* 床侧小几 ○ *a 'billiard-table* 台球台 ○ *lay/set the table*, ie prepare it for a meal with plates, cutlery, etc 摆餐具(准备用餐). ⇨ illus at App 1 见附录1插图, page xvi. **2** [sing] people seated at a table for a meal, etc (用餐等的)一桌人: *His jokes amused the whole table.* 他讲的笑话把满桌人都逗笑了. ○ *a table of card-players* 一桌玩纸牌的人. **3** [sing] food provided at table (摆上餐桌的)食物: *He keeps a good table*, ie provides good meals. 他常备佳肴. **4** [C] (also **'table·land** /-lænd; -lænd/) large area of high level land; plateau 台地; 高地; 高原. **5** [C] list of facts or figures systematically arranged, esp in columns 一览表; 目录; 表: *a table of contents*, ie a summary of what a book contains 目录 ○ *learn one's (multiplication) tables* 学会乘法表 ○ *Do you know your six times table?* 你会六的乘数表吗? ○ *log tables* 对数表. **6** (idm 习语) **at 'table** (while) having a meal 吃饭(时); 用餐(时): *Children must learn to behave at table.* 小孩吃饭时必须有规矩. ○ (*fml* 文) *They were at table when we called.* 我们去拜访时, 他们正在吃饭. **drink sb under the table** ⇨ DRINK[2]. **lay/put one's cards on the table** ⇨ CARD[1]. **the negotiating table** ⇨ NEGOTIATE. **on the 'table (a)** (*Brit*) offered for consideration or discussion 提交考虑或讨论: *Management have put several new proposals on the table.* 主管人员已将几项新建议提交讨论. **(b)** (*esp US*) (of a proposal, etc) left for discussion until some future date (指建议等)搁置, 留待日后讨论. **turn the 'tables (on sb)** reverse a situation so as to put oneself in a position of superiority 由劣势转为优势; 扭转形势. **under the 'table** (of money) paid secretly, esp as a bribe (指钱)私下付的(尤指作为贿赂). **wait at table** ⇨ WAIT[1].
▷ **table** *v* [Tn] **1** (*Brit*) submit (a motion or report in Parliament, etc) for discussion (在国会等)提出(动议或报告)供讨论: *The Opposition have tabled several amendments to the bill.* 反对党已对议案提出几项修正. **2** (*esp US*) leave (a proposal, etc) to be discussed at some future date 将(建议等)搁置, 留待日后讨论.
□ **'table-cloth** *n* cloth for covering a table, esp during meals 桌布, 台布(尤指吃饭时用的).
'table-knife *n* knife for use while eating 餐刀. ⇨illus at KNIFE 见 KNIFE 插图.
'table-linen *n* [U] table-cloths, napkins, etc 桌布、餐巾等.
'table manners proper behaviour while eating with others 进餐时的规矩.
'table-mat *n* mat placed under a hot dish, etc to protect the table 碗盘垫.
'tablespoon *n* **1** large spoon for serving food at table 餐匙. ⇨illus at SPOON 见 SPOON 插图. **2** (also **'tablespoonful** /-fʊl; -fʊl/) amount held by this 一餐匙的量: *add 2 tablespoons/tablespoonfuls of flour* 加2餐匙面粉.
'table-talk *n* [U] conversation during a meal 进餐时的谈话; 席间的谈话.
'table tennis = PING-PONG.
'table-turning *n* [U] movement of a table at which people are sitting during a seance, thought to be caused by some supernatural force 桌子的灵动(降神时认为超自然力所致).
'tableware *n* [U] plates, bowls, cutlery, etc used for meals 餐具.

tab·leau /'tæbləʊ; 'tæblo/ *n* (*pl* **~x** /-ləʊz; -loz/) **1** (also **tab·leau viv·ant** /ˌtæbləʊ 'vi:vɑ:n; *US* vi:'vɑ:n; ˌtæblo vi'vɑn/) (*pl* **~x vivants** /ˌtæbləʊ 'vi:vɑ:n; *US* -vi:'vɑ:n; ˌtæblo vi'vɑn/) representation of a picture or scene by a silent and motionless group of people, esp on stage (不作声不活动的)人构成的画面或场景; (尤指)舞台造型. **2** dramatic or picturesque scene 戏剧性的场面; 绚丽的场景.

table d'hôte /ˌtɑ:bl 'dəʊt; 'tæbḷ'dot/ (of a restaurant meal) consisting of a limited range of dishes served at a fixed inclusive price (指餐馆饮食)定餐, 分饭: *The table d'hôte menu offers good value.* 定餐菜单上列出的都很实惠. Cf 参看 À LA CARTE.

tab·let /'tæblɪt; 'tæblɪt/ *n* **1** slab or panel with words cut or written on it, esp one fixed to a wall as a memorial 碑, 牌, 匾额(尤指固定于墙上作纪念的). **2** small measured amount of medicine compressed into a solid form; pill 药片; 药丸: *Take two of the tablets three times daily before meals.* 每日三次, 每次两片, 饭前服用. **3** small flattish bar of soap, etc (肥皂等的)块.

tab·loid /'tæblɔɪd; 'tæblɔɪd/ *n* popular newspaper with pages that are half the size of those of larger newspapers 小型报纸; 小报: [attrib 作定语] *the tabloid press* 小报新闻界 ○ (*often derog* 常作贬义) *tabloid journalism* 小报业. Cf 参看 BROADSHEET 2.

ta·boo /tə'bu:; *US* tæ'bu:; tæ'bu/ *n* (*pl* **~s**) **1** [C, U] (in certain cultures) ban or prohibition on sth that is regarded for religious or other reasons as not to be done, touched, used, etc (某些文化的)禁忌, 忌讳. **2** [C] (*fig* 比喻) general agreement not to discuss or to do sth 不涉及某事物之一致作法: *There's a taboo on smoking in this office.* 在这个办公室里一向是都不吸烟的.

▷ **ta·boo** *adj* prohibited by a taboo 禁忌的; 忌讳的: *Questions and problems that were once taboo are now discussed openly.* 一度视为犯忌的许多问题现在可以公开谈论了. ○ *Sex is no longer the taboo subject it used to be.* 现在不再像过去那样把性的问题视为禁区. ○ *Any mention of politics is taboo in his house.* 在他家里一提政治就犯忌.

□ **ta'boo words** words likely to be considered offensive, shocking or indecent by certain people (though not necessarily by everyone), eg those marked ⚠ in this dictionary 禁忌语(某些人视为不雅的或下流的词语, 如本词典中标有 ⚠ 者).

tabu·lar /ˈtæbjʊlə(r); ˋtæbjəlɚ/ *adj* arranged or displayed in a table(5) or list 列成表的; 表格式的: *statistics presented in tabular form* 以表格表示的统计数字.

tabu·late /ˈtæbjʊleɪt; ˋtæbjəˌlet/ *v* [Tn] arrange (facts or figures) in the form of a table(5) or list 将(事实或数字)列成表.

▷ **tabu·la·tion** /ˌtæbjʊˈleɪʃn; ˌtæbjuˋleʃən/ *n* [U, C].

tabu·lator *n* **1** person or thing that tabulates 制表人; 制表之物; 制表机. **2** device on a typewriter for advancing to a series of set positions in tabular work (打字机的)制表键.

tacho·graph /ˈtækəgrɑːf; ˋtækəˌgræf/ *n* device in a motor vehicle which automatically records the speed of the vehicle during a journey and how far it has travelled (机动车的)里程表.

ta·cit /ˈtæsɪt; ˋtæsɪt/ *adj* [usu attrib 通常作定语] understood without being put into words; implied 心照不宣的; 暗含的: *give tacit consent, agreement, etc* 默许、默契. ▷ **ta·citly** *adv*.

ta·cit·urn /ˈtæsɪtɜːn; ˋtæsəˌtɝn/ *adj* (in the habit of) saying very little; uncommunicative 沉默寡言的; 不爱说话的. ▷ **ta·cit·urn·ity** /ˌtæsɪˈtɜːnətɪ; ˌtæsəˋtɝnətɪ/ *n* [U].

tack /tæk; tæk/ *n* **1** [C] small nail with a broad head 平头钉; 大头钉: *a 'carpet tack*, ie one used for securing a carpet to the floor 地毯钉 ○ *a 'tin-tack* 镀锡平头钉. **2** [C] long loose stitch used in fastening pieces of cloth together loosely or temporarily 绷; 假缝; 粗缝: *tailor's tacks*, ie ones used to mark the place for a seam, etc 绷线. **3** [C] (*nautical* 海) (of sailing vessels) oblique course sailed with the wind blowing towards one side of the ship (指帆船)抢风航程: *on the right/wrong tack* 航向正确[错误] ○ *on the port/starboard tack*, ie with the wind on the port/starboard side 左舷[右舷]抢风. **4** [U, sing] (*fig* 比喻) course of action; policy 方针; 政策: *It would be unwise to change tack now.* 现在改变方针是不明智的. ○ *try a different tack* 试行不同的政策 ○ *be on the right/wrong tack* 实行正确的[错误的]方针. **5** (idm 习语) **get down to brass tacks** ⇨ BRASS.

▷ **tack** *v* **1** [Tn, Tn·pr, Tn·p] nail (sth) with a tack(1) or tacks 用平头钉钉住(某物): *tack down the carpet* 用平头钉钉住地毯. **2** [Tn, Tn·pr, Tn·p] stitch (sth) with tacks (TACK 2) 绷上, 绷住(某物): *tack a ribbon onto a hat* 在帽子上绷一条饰带 ○ *tack (up) the hem of a dress* 绷上连衣裙的边 ○ *tack down a fold* 绷住衣褶 ○ *a tacking stitch* 绷的针脚. **3** (*nautical* 海) [I, Ipr, Ip] move from one tack(3) to another; sail a zigzag course in this way 抢风航行; 作Z字形航行: *tack to port/starboard* 左舷[右舷]抢风航行 ○ *tacking about* 作Z字形航行. **4** (phr v) **tack sth on(to sth)** (*infml* 口) add sth as an extra item 附加或增添某事物: *a cover charge tacked onto the bill* 帐单上的服务费.

tackle /ˈtækl; ˋtækḷ/ *n* **1** [U] set of ropes and pulleys for working a ship's sails or for lifting weights (操纵船帆或吊起重物用的)滑车, 滑轮, 滑轮组. **2** [U] equipment for a task or sport 用具; 器械: *'fishing-tackle* 鱼具. **3** [C] act of tackling in or as in football, etc (如橄榄球等中的)擒抱, 擒拿: *The policeman brought the thief to the ground with a flying tackle.* 警察飞身上前把盗贼扑倒在地上.

▷ **tackle** *v* **1** [Tn] deal with or overcome (an awkward problem, a difficult piece of work, etc) 应付, 对付, 处理(棘手的问题、困难的工作等): *It's time to tackle my homework.* 现在该对付我的家庭作业了. ○ *tackle a problem head-on*, ie boldly and vigorously 迎向困难着手解决. **2** [Tn·pr] **~ sb about/over sth** speak to sb about (an awkward matter) 向某人提起(尴尬之事): *When are you going to tackle your brother about that money he owes me?* 你打算什么时候跟你兄弟提他欠我钱的事? **3** [I, Tn] (**a**) (in football, hockey, etc) try to take the ball from (an opponent) by intercepting it (足球、曲棍球等)拦截(对方)抢球, 抢截: *no good at tackling* 不善于抢球 ○ *He was tackled just outside the penalty area.* 他恰在罚球区外让对方把球截过去了. (**b**) (in Rugby football) seize and stop (an opponent holding the ball) (橄榄球)擒抱(对方持球队员). **tack·ler** /ˈtæklə(r); ˋtæklɚ/ *n* player who tackles 抢球的队员; 擒抱的队员: *renowned as a fearless tackler* 以勇于拼抢而著名的队员.

tacky /ˈtækɪ; ˋtækɪ/ *adj* (**-ier, -iest**) **1** (of paint, glue, etc) slightly sticky; not quite dry (指油漆、胶水等)发黏的, 未干透的: *still tacky to the touch* 摸着还有些黏. **2** (*infml* 口 *esp US*) in poor taste; shabby or gaudy 俗气的; 破旧的; 花哨的. ▷ **tacki·ness** *n* [U].

tact /tækt; tækt/ *n* [U] skill at not offending people or at gaining goodwill by saying or doing the right thing 言行得体不得罪人或能赢得好感的技巧: *She showed great tact in dealing with a tricky situation.* 她处理棘手的局面表现得十分老练. ○ *You need a lot of tact to be an air hostess.* 当空中小姐言行需十分得体.

▷ **tact·ful** /-fl; -fəl/ *adj* having or showing tact 言行得体的; 不得罪人的; 能赢得好感的. **tact·fully** /-fəlɪ; -fəlɪ/ *adv*.

tact·less *adj* lacking tact 言行不得体的; 得罪人的. **tact·lessly** *adv*. **tact·less·ness** *n* [U].

tac·tic /ˈtæktɪk; ˋtæktɪk/ *n* **1** means of achieving sth; expedient 手段; 策略: *a brilliant tactic* 高招. **2 tactics** (**a**) [sing or pl *v*] art of placing or moving fighting forces in a battle 战术; 兵法. (**b**) [pl] (*fig* 比喻) procedure adopted in order to achieve sth 方法; 策略: *use surprise tactics* 采取出人意料的作法 ○ *These tactics are unlikely to help you.* 这种方法对你未必有用. Cf 参看 STRATEGY 1.

▷ **tac·tical** /-kl; -kḷ/ *adj* [usu attrib 通常作定语] **1** of tactics 战术上的; 兵法上的; 策略上的: *a tactical advantage, error* 战术上的优势、错误. **2** planning or planned skilfully 善于筹划的: *a tactical move* 有谋略的一步 ○ *tactical voting*, ie voting not for the candidate or party one prefers but for another that is more likely to defeat the candidate, etc one wishes to be defeated 策略投票(不投心目中的候选人或党派的票, 而投可击败某候选人等的票). **3** (of weapons, bombing, etc) used or carried out against enemy forces at short range (指武器、炸弹等)用于攻击近距离敌人的, 短程的, 战术的: *tactical missiles* 战术导弹. Cf 参看 STRATEGIC. **tac·tic·ally** /-klɪ; -klɪ/ *adv*: *vote tactically* 策略性投票.

tac·ti·cian /tækˈtɪʃn; tækˋtɪʃən/ *n* expert in tactics 战术家; 兵法家.

tact·ile /ˈtæktaɪl; *US* -təl; ˋtæktḷ/ *adj* (*fml* 文) of or using the sense of touch (用)触觉的: *a tactile reflex* 触觉反射 ○ *tactile organs* 触觉器官.

tad /tæd; tæd/ *n* (*US infml* 口) **1** small child, esp a young boy 小孩; (尤指)小男孩. **2** small bit 少量; 一点儿: *just a tad more milk* 只再加一点儿牛奶.

tad·pole /ˈtædpəʊl; ˋtædˌpol/ *n* form of a frog or toad at the stage when it lives under water and has gills and a tail 蝌蚪.

taf·feta /ˈtæfɪtə; ˋtæfɪtə/ *n* [U] shiny silk-like dress fabric 塔夫绸.

taff·rail /ˈtæfreɪl; ˋtæfˌrel/ *n* rail round the stern of a ship or boat 船尾栏杆.

Taffy /ˈtæfɪ; ˋtæfɪ/ *n* (*infml derog* 口, 贬) Welshman 威尔士人.

taffy (*US*) = TOFFEE.

tag /tæg; tæg/ *n* **1** [C] metal or plastic point at the end of a shoe-lace, etc (鞋带等末端的)金属或塑料包头. **2** [C] label fastened to or stuck into sth to identify it, show its price, etc 标签: *put a 'name-tag on it* 附上名字标签. **3** [C] any loose or ragged end or projection 任何松散不整的末端或突出物. **4** [C] (*linguistics* 语言) word or phrase that is added to a sentence to give emphasis, eg *that is* in *That's nice, that is* (为加强语气而附于句尾的)附加词语(如That's nice, that is一句中的that is): [attrib 作定语] *a tag question*, ie a tag in the form of a question, eg *isn't it?, won't you?, aren't they?* 附加疑问句(由附加在陈述句或祈使句后的简短的疑问句成分(如isn't it?或won't you?或aren't they?等)构成的疑问句) **5** [C] phrase, saying or quotation that is often used

(常用的)短语, 格言, 引语, 套语: *Latin tags* 常用的拉丁文短语. **6** (also **tig**) [U] game in which one child chases the others and tries to touch one of them (儿童的)捉人游戏.

▷ **tag** *v* **(-gg-)** **1** [Tn] label (sth) with a tag 给(某物)附上标签. **2** (phr v) **tag along (after/behind/with sb)** follow closely 尾随; 紧随: *children tagging along behind their mother* 紧跟在母亲后面的孩子 ○ *If you're going to the cinema, do you mind if I tag along (with you)?* 你要是去看电影, 我也(跟你)一起去行吗? **tag sth on (to sth)** add sth as an extra item; attach sth 附加某事物; 系某物于: *a postscript tagged on (to her letter) at the end* 加在(她的信)末尾的附言.

□ **'tag day** (*US*) = FLAG DAY (FLAG).

tail /teɪl; tel/ *n* **1** [C] movable part at the end of the body of a bird, an animal, a fish or a reptile 尾; 尾巴: *Dogs wag their tails when they are pleased.* 狗一高兴就摇尾巴. ⇨illus at App 1 见附录1插图, page iii. **2** [C] thing like a tail in its shape or position 尾状物; 似尾的部位; 尾部: *the tail of a comet, a kite, an aircraft, a procession* 彗星、风筝、飞机、行列的尾部. **3** [C] (*dated infml* 旧, 口) buttocks 屁股: *give sb a smack on the tail* 打某人屁股一下. **4** [C] (*infml* 口) person following or watching sb (usu without being seen by him) 尾巴(跟踪者): *put a tail on sb*, ie tell sb to follow him 给某人安个尾巴(派某人跟踪他). **5 tails** [pl] (also **'tail·coat** [C]) man's long coat, divided and tapered at the back, worn as part of formal dress at weddings, etc 燕尾服. Cf 参看 MORNING COAT (MORNING). **6 tails** [sing *v*] side of a coin without the head of a person on it, turned upwards after being tossed 文面(硬币没有人头像的一面). Cf 参看 HEADS (HEAD[1] 5). **7** (idm 习语) **have, etc one's tail between one's 'legs** (*infml* 口) be humiliated, dejected or defeated 夹着尾巴; 垂头丧气; 遭到失败. **heads I win, tails you lose** ⇨ HEAD[1]. **heads or tails?** ⇨ HEAD[1]. **make head or tail of sth** ⇨ HEAD[1]. **on sb's 'tail** following sb closely 紧跟某人. **a sting in the tail** ⇨ STING[1]. **the tail wagging the 'dog** situation in which a minor part of sth is controlling or determining the course of the whole 尾巴摇狗(次要部分支配或决定全局). **turn 'tail** run away from a fight, etc (从冲突等场合中)逃走, 逃跑: *As soon as they saw us coming they turned tail and ran.* 他们一看见我们来了, 掉头就跑.

▷ **tail** *v* **1** [Tn, Tn·pr] follow (sb) closely, esp to watch where he goes and what he does 跟踪(某人); 钉(某人)的梢: *He tailed the spy to his hotel.* 他跟踪那间谍到他住的旅馆. **2** [Tn] remove the stalks of (fruit, etc) 除去(水果等)的柄、梗、蒂或把儿: *top and tail gooseberries* 掐掉醋栗的尖儿和把儿. **3** (phr v) **tail away; tail off (a)** become smaller, fewer, weaker, etc 变小; 变少; 变弱: *The number of tourists starts to tail off in October.* 游客在十月份开始见少. ○ *The actor's voice tailed away as he forgot his lines.* 那演员忘了台词, 说话的声音越来越小了. **(b)** (of remarks, etc) end inconclusively (指言语等)不了了之: *His feeble excuses soon tailed off (into silence).* 他的借口站不住脚, 很快就没词儿了(不作声了). **(c)** fall behind in a straggling line 散落在后面.

-tailed (forming compound *adjs* 用以构成复合形容词) having a tail of the specified type 有某种尾巴的: *'long-tailed* ○ *'curly-tailed.*

tail·less *adj* having no tail 无尾的: *a tailless species* 无尾种类.

□ **'tailback** *n* long line of traffic extending back from an obstruction (车辆因受阻而排成的)长队.

'tail-board *n* = TAIL-GATE.

'tailcoat *n* [C] = TAILS (TAIL 5).

ˌtail-'end *n* (usu *sing* 通常作单数) **~ (of sth)** very last part 后部; 末尾; 末端: *the tail-end of the concert* 音乐会的结尾 ○ *I only heard the tail-end of their conversation.* 我只听到了他们谈话的末尾.

'tail-gate *n* door or flap at the back of a motor vehicle, used for loading or unloading (机动车的)尾门, 后拦板. — *v* [I, Tn] (*US*) drive too closely behind (another vehicle) 紧随(另一车辆)行驶; 尾随.

'tail-light (*US* **'tail-lamp**) *n* red light at the back of a motor vehicle, bicycle, train, etc (机动车、自行车、火车等的)尾灯. ⇨illus at App 1 见附录1插图, page xii.

'tailpiece *n* **1** (in a book, etc) decoration printed in the blank space at the end of a chapter, etc (印在书等章节后之空白处的)补白图案. **2** part added to the end of sth to lengthen or complete it 附加部分; 续补部分.

'tailpipe *n* exhaust-pipe of a motor vehicle (机动车的)排气管.

'tailplane *n* horizontal part or surface of the tail of an aircraft (飞机的)横尾翼, 水平安定面.

'tail-spin *n* spiral dive of an aircraft in which the tail makes wider circles than the front (飞机的)尾旋, 尾螺旋.

'tail wind wind blowing from behind a travelling vehicle, aircraft, etc 顺风. Cf 参看 HEAD WIND (HEAD[1]).

tailor /ˈteɪlə(r); ˋtelɚ/ *n* maker of men's clothes, esp one who makes coats, jackets, etc for individual customers (男装)裁缝, 成衣匠(尤指缝制定做的外衣者): *go to the tailor to be measured for a suit* 到裁缝店定做西装.

▷ **tailor** *v* **1** [Tn esp passive 尤用于被动语态] make (clothes) 做, 缝(衣服): *a well-tailored coat* 做工考究的大衣. **2** [Tn·pr esp passive 尤用于被动语态] **~ sth for/to sb/sth** make or adapt sth for a special purpose (为某目的)做某事物或适应某事物: *homes tailored to the needs of the elderly* 专为老人建立的养老院.

□ **ˌtailor-'made** *adj* **1** made by a tailor (衣物等)定做的: *a ˌtailor-made 'suit* 定做的西装. **2** [esp pred 尤作表语] **~ (for sb/sth)** (*fig* 比喻) perfectly suited 完全适合; 十分合适: *He seems tailor-made for the job.* 他好像是专门做这项工作的材料.

taint /teɪnt; tent/ *n* [C, U] trace of some bad quality or decay or infection (坏的、腐败的或感染的)迹象, 痕迹, 因素: *a taint of insanity in the family* 家族中有精神病遗传素质 ○ *meat free from taint* 新鲜的肉.

▷ **taint** *v* [esp passive 尤用于被动语态: Tn, Tn·pr] **~ sth (with sth)** affect sth with a taint (坏的因素)影响某事物: *tainted meat* 腐肉 ○ *His reputation was tainted by the scandal.* 那一丑闻玷污了他的名声.

taint·less *adj* without taint; pure 无污点的; 纯洁的.

take[1] /teɪk; tek/ *v* (*pt* **took** /tʊk; tuk/, *pp* **taken** /ˈteɪkən; ˋtekən/) **1** [Tn, Tn·pr, Tn·p, Cn·g, Dn·n, Dn·pr] **~ sb/sth (with one)**; **~ sth (to sb)** carry sb/sth or accompany sb from one place to another 携带、运载或伴随某人[某物]: *Don't forget to take your umbrella (with you) when you go.* 你走时别忘了带伞. ○ *It's your turn to take the dog for a walk.* 轮到你去遛狗了. ○ *She takes her children to school by car.* 她用汽车送孩子上学. ○ (*fig* 比喻) *Her energy and talent took her to the top of her profession.* 她精力充沛、天禀聪颖, 成就了她在事业上达到卓尔不群的顶峰. ○ *The accused was taken away in a police van.* 被告已用警车带走. ○ *I'm taking the children swimming/for a swim later.* 我要带孩子去游泳. ○ *She took him some flowers when she went to see him in hospital.* 她带着花去医院探望他. ○ *Take this glass of water (up) to your father/Take your father (up) this glass of water.* 把这杯水给你父亲送去. **2** [Tn, Tn·pr, Tn·p] get or lay hold of (sb/sth) with the hands, arms, etc or with an instrument (以手、臂等或工具)拿, 握, 抱, 夹: *I passed him the rope and he took it.* 我递给他绳子, 他接住了. ○ *take sb's hand/take sb by the hand* 握住某人的手 ○ *Would you mind taking* (ie holding) *the baby for a moment?* 你给抱一会儿孩子行吗? ○ *Take three eggs and beat them gently.* 拿三个鸡蛋, 轻轻打匀. ○ *She took a cigarette from the packet.* 她从烟盒里拿出一枝烟. ○ *He took her in his arms and kissed her.* 他拥抱着她亲吻. ○ *He took a book (down) from the top shelf.* 他从最上面的架子上拿(下)一本书. ○ *She opened the drawer and took out a pair of socks.* 她拉开抽屉, 拿出一双短袜. **3 (a)** [Tn] remove (sth) from its proper place without permission or by mistake 擅自取走, 错拿, 偷窃(某物): *Someone has taken my gloves.* 有人把我的手套拿走了. ○ *Who's taken my bicycle?* 谁把我的自行车骑走了? ○ *Did the burglars take* (ie steal) *anything of value?* 贼偷走什么值钱的东西没有? **(b)** [Tn·pr] **~ sth from sth** (not usu in the continuous tenses 通常不用于进行时态) remove or obtain sth from (a particular place or source) (从某处)拿去或得到某物: *Part of her article is taken (straight) from my book on the subject.* 她文章中的一部分是从我写的同一内容的书中(直接)搬来的. ○ *Today's lesson is taken from the St Mark's Gospel.* 今日的经文选自《马可福音》. ○ *The machine takes its name from its inventor.* 这机器的名字来自其发明者. **(c)** [Tn, Tn·pr] **~ sth (from sth)** (not in the continuous tenses 不用于进行时

T

态) subtract (a number) from another one (从一数中)减去(另一数): *If you take five from twelve, you're left with seven.* 十二减去五得七. **4** [Tn, Cn·n] (not usu in the continuous tenses 通常不用于进行时态) gain possession of (sth); capture or win (sth) 占有(某物); 夺得或赢得(某物): *take a fortress, garrison, town, etc*, ie in a war 占领堡垒、要塞、城镇等 ○ *The army took many prisoners.* 军队抓了很多俘虏. ○ *He took my bishop with his queen*, ie in a game of chess. 他用后吃了我的象(下国际象棋). ○ *Our bull took first prize at the agricultural show.* 我们的公牛在农业展览会上夺得头奖. ○ *The enemy took him prisoner/He was taken prisoner by the enemy.* 敌人把他俘虏了[他被敌人俘虏]. **5** [Tn] (not usu in the continuous tenses 通常不用于进行时态) accept or receive (sth) 接受、领受或收到(某物): *I'd like you to take this bracelet as a gift.* 我希望你把这手镯礼物收下. ○ *He took the blow* (ie The blow hit him) *on the chest.* 他胸部挨了一击. ○ *Will you take £2 000 for the car* (ie sell it for £2 000)? 你这辆汽车卖2 000英镑行吗? ○ *The shop took* (ie sold goods worth a total of) *£50 000 last week.* 这商店上星期做了50 000英镑的生意. ○ *She was accused of taking bribes.* 她被控受贿. ○ *Does the hotel take traveller's cheques?* 这旅馆收旅行支票吗? ○ *I'll take the (telephone) call in my office.* 我想在我的办公室里接这个电话. ○ *Why should I take the blame for somebody else's mistakes?* 我为什么要代人受过? ○ *If you take my advice, you'll have nothing more to do with him.* 你若接受我的劝告, 就不要再跟他来往了. ○ *I take your point* (ie accept the validity of your argument), *but my views on the matter remain the same.* 我认为你说的有道理, 但我对此事的看法仍然不变. ○ *The workers would never agree to take a cut in wages.* 工人们绝不会同意削减工资. **6** [Tn] (not usu in the continuous tenses 通常不用于进行时态) accept (sb) as a client, patient, tenant, etc 接纳或接受(某人)为委托人、病人、房客等: *She takes paying guests.* 她招房客. ○ *Dr Brown takes some private patients.* 布朗医生也接纳些私人病人. ○ *The school doesn't take girls*, ie only has boys as pupils. 该校不收女生. **7** [Tn] (not in the continuous tenses 不用于进行时态) have enough space for (sb/sth); hold or contain 容下(某人[某物]); 盛; 装; 容纳: *This bus takes 60 passengers.* 这公共汽车能容下60位乘客. ○ *The tank takes 12 gallons.* 这罐能盛12加仑. ○ *I don't think the shelf will take any more books.* 我看这架子摆不下更多的书了. **8** [Tn] (not usu in the continuous tenses 通常不用于进行时态) be able to endure (sth); bear 能忍受(某事); 承受; 受得了: *She can't take criticism/being criticized.* 她受不了批评. ○ *He can take a joke*, ie does not mind being laughed at. 他禁得起开玩笑(受取笑而不恼). ○ *I don't think I can take much more of your nagging.* 我再也受不了你的唠叨了. ○ *I'm not taking any more of your insults!* 我再也不能忍受你的侮辱了! ○ *I find his political views a little hard to take.* 我认为他的政治观点有点儿难以接受. **9** [Tn] (usu followed by an *adv* or used in questions after *how* 通常用于副词前或用于how之后的疑问句中) react to (sb/sth) in the specified way (以某方式)对待(某人[某事]); 应付: *She knows how to take him/his teasing.* 她知道怎样回敬他的取笑. ○ *'How did he take the news of her death?' 'He took it badly'*, ie He was very upset by it. '他对她的死讯反应如何?' '他万分悲痛.' ○ *Police are taking the terrorists' threats of a bombing campaign very seriously indeed.* 恐怖分子扬言要大搞爆炸, 警方正在认真对付. ○ *You take things too seriously; try to enjoy life a bit more!* 你对事情过于认真, 尽量多享受些人生乐趣吧! **10** [Cn·n/a, Cn·t] **~ sth as sth** (not in the continuous tenses 不用于进行时态) understand or interpret sth in a particular way (以某种方式)理解或解释某事: *She took what he said as a compliment.* 她把他的话看做是恭维话. ○ *What did you take his comments to mean?* 你明白他的评论是什么意思吗? ○ *How am I supposed to take that remark?* 我应该怎样理解这话的意思呢? **11** [Tn·pr, Cn·t] **~ sb/sth for sb/sth** (not in the continuous tenses 不用于进行时态) suppose, assume or consider sb/sth to be sb/sth 假定、以为或认为某人[某事物]为他人[他事物]: *Even the experts took the painting for a genuine Van Gogh.* 连行家都认为那幅画是凡高的真迹. ○ *Do you take me for a fool?* 你以为我是傻瓜吗? ○ *I took you to be an honest man.* 我原以为你是诚实的人. **12** [Tn] (not in the continuous tenses 不用于进行时态) understand (sth) 理解, 明白(某事): *I don't think she took my meaning.* 我想她不明白我的意思. **13** [Tn] rent (a house, etc) 租用(房屋等): *We're taking a cottage in Devon for a month.* 我们打算在德文郡租间农舍住一个月. ○ *He took lodgings in the East End of London.* 他在伦敦东区租用寄宿舍. **14** [Tn] choose or buy (sth) 挑选, 购买(某物): *I'll take the grey trousers, please.* 劳驾, 我买这条灰色的裤子. **15** [Tn] buy (sth, esp a newspaper) regularly 按时购买(某物); (尤指)订(报刊): *She takes 'The Guardian'.* 她订阅《卫报》. **16** [Tn] eat or drink (sth); consume 吃, 喝(某物); 食用; 饮用; 消费: *Do you take sugar* (ie in tea or coffee)? 你(往茶或咖啡里)放糖吗? ○ *The doctor has given her some pills to take for her cough.* 医生给了她一些治咳嗽的药片吃. ○ *He takes* (ie is addicted to) *drugs.* 他嗜毒成瘾. ○ *Have you ever taken cocaine?* 你用过可卡因吗? **17** [Tn no passive 不用于被动语态, Tg, Cn·n] (often with *it* 常与it连用) need or require (the specified time, quality, person or action) 需要, 要求(所示之时间、素质、人或行动): *The journey from London to Oxford takes about an hour and a half.* 从伦敦到牛津大约需要一个半小时. ○ *That cut is taking a long time to heal.* 那伤口要很长时间才能愈合. ○ *It'll take time* (ie a long time) *for her to recover from the illness.* 她的病要很长时间才能痊愈. ○ *It takes stamina to run a marathon.* 跑马拉松要有耐力. ○ *It would take a strong man to lift that weight.* 身强力壮的人才能举得起那么重的东西. ○ (*infml* 口) *She didn't take much persuading*, ie She was easily persuaded. 她不用人多费口舌(她很听人劝告). ○ *Shifting that wardrobe must have taken some doing!* 搬那个衣柜一定够费劲儿的! ○ *It took her three hours to mend her bicycle/It took three hours for her to mend her bicycle.* 她修理自行车用了三个小时. **18** [Tn no passive 不用于被动语态] (not in the continuous tenses 不用于进行时态) wear (a particular size in shoes or clothes) 穿用(某尺码的鞋或衣物): *What size shoes do you take?* 你穿多少号的鞋? ○ *He takes a 42-inch chest.* 他穿胸围42英寸的衣服. **19** [Tn] (not in the continuous tenses 不用于进行时态) (of a verb, etc) have or require (sth) as part of a grammatical construction (指动词等)有或要求(某成分)作语法结构的一部分: *The verb 'eat' takes a direct object.* 动词eat要求有直接宾语. **20** [Tn] do (an examination, a test, etc) in order to obtain a qualification 参加(考试、测验等)以取得资格: *She takes her finals next summer.* 她明年夏天要参加毕业考试. ○ *When are you taking your driving test?* 你什么时候参加驾驶执照考试? **21** [Tn] be awarded or obtain (a degree) 被授予, 获得(等级): *She took a first in English at Leeds.* 她在利兹时英语获得优等. **22** [Tn] study (an academic subject) 学习(某学科): *She plans to take a course in applied linguistics.* 她打算学习应用语言学课程. **23** [Tn, Tn·pr] **~ sb (for sth)** give sb lessons or instruction (in a particular subject); teach sb 给某人讲授(某学科的)课程; 给某人(某学科的)指导; 教某人: *Mrs Biggs is ill and will be unable to take you today.* 比格斯夫人病了, 今天不能给你们上课了. ○ *Who takes you for French?* 谁教你们法语? **24** [Tn] find out and record (sth); write down (sth) 找出并记录(某事); 写下, 记下(某事): *The policeman took my name and address.* 警察记下了我的姓名和住址. ○ *Did you take notes at the lecture?* 你听课时做笔记吗? ○ *She hates taking letters.* 她不喜欢记录口授信函. **25** [Tn] test or measure (sth) 测定, 量度(某事物): *take sb's pulse/temperature/blood pressure* 测量某人的脉搏[体温/血压] ○ *The tailor took my measurements for a new suit.* 裁缝给我量做新西装的尺寸. **26** [Tn] use (sth) as a means of transport; go by (sth) 使用, 搭乘(某种交通工具); 乘坐(某物): *take the coach, plane, train, etc* 用长途汽车、飞机、火车等运输 ○ *take a taxi* 乘计程车 ○ *'How do you get to work?' 'I take the bus.'* '你怎么去上班?' '我坐公共汽车去.' **27** [Tn] use (a road, path, etc) as a route to go to a place 取(某条路、小径等)作为到某地的路线: *I usually take the M6 when I go to Scotland.* 我到苏格兰去通常都取道6号高速公路. ○ *Take* (ie Turn into) *the second turning/road on the right after the station.* 过了车站在第二个路口向右拐. **28** [Tn] (usu followed by an *adv*; not in the continuous tenses 通常用于副词前, 不用于进行时态) go over or round (sth) 越过, 绕过(某物): *The horse* *took the first fence beautifully.* 那匹马跨越了第一道障碍, 动作十分漂亮. ○ *You took that corner much too fast.* 你拐的那个弯太快了. **29** [Tn] (not usu in the continuous tenses 通常不用于进行时态) hold or adopt (a view, an attitude, etc) 持(某种观点); 采取(某种态度): *He takes the view that people should be responsible for their own actions.* 他的观点是人应对自己的行为负责. ○ *The government is taking a tough line on drug abuse.* 政府对滥用麻醉药品采取强硬方针. **30** [Tn] (usu imperative 通常用于祈使句) consider (sb/sth) as an example 将(某人[某事物])作为例证; 以(某人[某事物])为例: *A lot of women manage to bring up families and go out to work at the same time — take Angela, for example.* 很多女子既能料理家务同时又外出工作——譬如安杰拉, 就是个例子. **31** [Tn] (not in the continuous tenses 不用于进行时态) sit down or be seated in (a chair, etc) 坐在(椅子等)上: *take a chair, seat, stool, etc* 坐在椅子、座位、凳子等上. **32** [Tn] make (sth) by photography; photograph (sb/sth) 摄制(某物); 拍摄(某人[某物]): *take a photograph/picture/snapshot of sb/sth* 给某人[某物]照相[拍照/照快相] ○ *have one's picture taken* 为自己拍照. **33** [Tn] officiate at (sth); conduct 主持(某事); 领导; 指导: *Mr Perkins will take the evening service.* 珀金斯先生将主持晚礼拜. **34** [I] (esp of a drug or dye) have the desired effect (尤指药物或染料)产生预期效果: *The inoculation did not take.* 预防接种没起作用. ○ *The dye won't take* (ie won't colour things) *in cold water.* 那染料在冷水中染不上色. **35** [I, Tn] (of fish) bite (the hook on a fisherman's line) (指鱼)咬(钓钩); 上钩: *The fish don't seem to be taking today.* 看起来今天鱼不上钩. ○ (*fig* 比喻) *take the bait*, ie be deceived by a trick 上钩(中计). **36** [Tn] (of a man) have sexual intercourse with (a woman) (指男人)与(女人)性交: *He took her on the sofa.* 他与她在沙发上交欢. **37** [Tn] (used with *ns* to show that the specified action is being carried out or performed 与名词连用表示开始某行动或进行某动作): *take* (ie have) *a break, a holiday, a rest, etc* 暂停一下、度假、休息一下 ○ *take* (ie have) *a bath, a shower, a wash, etc* 洗澡、淋浴、梳洗一下 ○ *take a look, a walk, a deep breath* 看看、散步、深呼吸. **38** (idm 习语) **take sb/sth as he/it 'comes** accept or tolerate sb/sth without wishing him/it to be different 安于或忍受某人[某事物]的现状: *She takes life as it comes.* 她安于生活现状. **take it (that...)** assume or suppose (that...) 假定...; 假设...; 认为...: *I take it you won't be coming to Sophie's party.* 我想你不会去参加索菲家的聚会. ○ *Are we to take it that you refuse to co-operate?* 我们是否可以认为你拒绝合作? **take it from 'me (that...)** (*infml* 口) you can believe me absolutely (when I say...) 你可以绝对相信我(的话...): *Take it from me — he'll be managing director of this company by the time he's 30.* 你就记住我这句话——他到30岁时准能当上本公司的总经理. **take it on/upon oneself to do sth** decide to do sth without asking for permission 擅自决定做某事: *You can't take it upon yourself to make important decisions like that.* 你不能擅自做出那样的重要决定. **take it/a lot 'out of sb** make sb physically or mentally tired 使某人疲乏或厌倦: *Her job takes a lot out of her.* 她的工作使她疲惫不堪. **take some/a lot of 'doing** (*infml* 口) be very difficult to do 难做; 难办; 费力; 费事: *Did you move all this furniture on your own? That must have taken some doing!* 是你自己搬的这些家具吗? 那一定够费劲儿的! **you can/can't take sb 'anywhere** the specified person can/cannot be trusted to behave well in any situation 某人在任何场合都能[不能]举止得当; 拿得[不]出去: *His manners are appalling — you can't take him anywhere!* 他没有正形——到哪儿都拿不出去! (For other idioms containing **take**, see entries for *ns, adjs, etc* 习语中有**take**者, 见有关名词、形容词等词条, 如 **take the biscuit** ⇨ BISCUIT; **take sb unawares** ⇨ UNAWARES.)

39 (phr v) **take sb a'back** (esp passive 尤用于被动语态) shock or surprise sb 使某人震惊或惊奇: *I was taken aback by his rudeness.* 他那样粗鲁无礼使我大吃一惊.

take after sb (no passive 不用于被动语态) resemble (one's mother or father) in appearance or character (在长相或性格方面)像(其母亲或父亲): *Your daughter doesn't take after you at all.* 你女儿一点儿都不像你.

take against sb/sth begin to dislike sb/sth 开始不喜欢某人[某事物]: *Why have you suddenly taken against her?* 你怎么突然又不喜欢她了?

take sb/sth apart (*infml* 口) (**a**) (in sport) defeat sb easily (运动)轻易击败某人: *Becker took Connors apart in the third set*, ie in tennis. 贝克尔在第三盘轻而易举战胜了康纳斯(网球赛). ○ *We were simply taken apart by the opposition.* 对方很容易就把我们打败了. (**b**) criticize sb/sth severely 严厉地批评某人[某事]: *Her second novel was taken apart by the critics.* 她的第二部小说受到评论家的严厉批评. **take sth apart** separate (esp a machine) into its component parts; dismantle sth 将(尤指机器)拆开, 拆卸; 拆散某物: *Let's take the radio apart and see what's wrong with it.* 咱们把收音机拆开看看有什么毛病.

take sth away (**a**) (*US* **take sth out**) buy (a cooked dish) at a restaurant and carry it away to eat at home 在餐馆买(饭菜)带回家吃; 外卖; 带走: *Two chicken curries and rice to take away, please.* 劳驾, 要两份外卖的咖喱鸡饭. (**b**) cause (a feeling, sensation, etc) to disappear 使(感情、感觉等)消失: *The doctor has given her some tablets to take away the pain.* 医生给了她一些止疼药片. ○ *Nothing can take away the anguish of losing a child.* 什么都不能解除失去孩子的巨大悲痛. ○ *Anxiety has taken away his appetite.* 他愁得吃不下饭. **take sb/sth away (from sb/sth)** remove sb/sth (from sb/sth) (从某人[某物]处)移去, 移开, 除掉某人[某物]: *What takes you away* (ie Why are you leaving) *so early?* 你为什么这么早就要走? ○ *These books must not be taken away from the library.* 这些书不准携出图书馆. ○ *The child was taken away from its parents on the recommendation of social workers.* 根据社会工作者的建议把那孩子与其父母隔离了. **take sth away (from sth)** subtract (one number) (from another) (从一数中)减去(另一数): *If you take four away from ten, that leaves six/Ten take away four is/leaves six.* 十减去四得[剩下]六. **take away from sth** weaken, lessen or diminish the effect or value of sth; detract from sth 减弱; 减少; 减小; 降低: *The scandal took away greatly from his public image.* 那丑闻极大地损害了他的形象.

take sth back (**a**) (of a shop) agree to accept or receive back (goods previously bought there) (指商店)同意(顾客)退货: *We only take goods back if customers can produce the receipt.* 顾客如能出示收据, 我们才能予以退货. (**b**) admit that sth one said was wrong or that one should not have said it; retract or withdraw sth 承认说了错话或不该说的话; 撤回或收回某言语: *I take back what I said (about you being selfish).* 我承认我不该说你(自私). **take sb back (to...)** cause sb's thoughts to return to a past time 使某人回想(起...): *The smell of seaweed took him back to his childhood.* 海草的气味使他回想起童年时代. ○ *Hearing those old songs takes me back a bit.* 我听到那些旧歌曲就有些怀旧.

take sb before sth/sb make sb appear in a court, before sb in authority, etc to explain his actions or be punished 使某人到法庭、见当权者、主事者等(解释其行为或受处罚): *He was taken before the headmaster and made to confess.* 他被带到校长面前认错.

take sth down (**a**) remove sth from a high level 将某物从高处取下: *Will you help me take the curtains down?* 你能帮我把帘幕取下来吗? (**b**) lower (a garment worn below the waist) without actually removing it 褪下(衣物至腰部以下): *take down one's skirt, trousers, underpants, etc* 把裙子、长裤、内裤等褪到腰部以下. (**c**) remove (a structure) by separating it into pieces; dismantle sth 拆除(构造物); 拆掉某物: *take down a tent, gate, fence* 拆掉帐篷、大门、篱笆 ○ *Workmen arrived to take down the scaffolding.* 工人们已去拆除脚手架. (**d**) write sth down in order to make a record of it 记下某事: *The reporters took down the speech.* 记者把讲话记录下来了. ○ *Anything you say may be taken down and used as evidence against you.* 你说的每句话都可能记录下来用作指控你的证据.

take sb in (**a**) allow sb to stay in one's home, sometimes for payment 允许某人寄宿家中: *She takes in lodgers.* 她招收寄宿者. ○ *He was homeless, so we took him in.* 他无家可归, 我们就收留了他. (**b**) (often passive 常用于被动语态) deceive, delude or fool sb 欺骗、蒙蔽或愚弄某人: *She took me in completely with her story.* 她用谎话把我完全蒙蔽了. ○ *You won't take me in that*

T

easily! 你别以为我那么容易上当! ○ *Don't be taken in by his charming manner; he's completely ruthless.* 不要被他那副讨人喜欢的外表所迷惑, 其实他冷酷无情. **take sth in** (**a**) absorb sth into the body by breathing or swallowing it 将某物吸入或吞入(体内); 摄取: *Fish take in oxygen through their gills.* 鱼通过鳃摄取氧气. (**b**) make (a garment) narrower or tighter by altering its seams 将(衣服)改瘦: *This dress needs to be taken in at the waist.* 这件连衣裙的腰身需要改瘦. (**c**) accept (work to do in one's home) for payment (为赚钱)承揽(在家中做的工作): *She supplements her pension by taking in washing.* 她在家里替人洗衣服以贴补养老金之不足. (**d**) include or cover sth 包括; 包含; 包罗: *The United Kingdom takes in England, Wales, Scotland and Northern Ireland.* 联合王国包括英格兰、威尔士、苏格兰、北爱尔兰. ○ *The tour took in six European capitals.* 那次观光包括欧洲六个国家的首都. ○ *Her lecture took in all the recent developments in the subject.* 她的讲座将该学科的新发展全部包罗在内. (**e**) go to see or visit (a film, museum, etc) when one is in a place for a different purpose 顺便看(电影)或参观(博物馆等): *I generally try to take in a show when I'm in New York on business.* 我到纽约公干时常顺便看场演出. (**f**) note sth with the eyes; observe sth 注视或观察某事物: *He took in every detail of her appearance.* 他端详了她一番. ○ *He took in the scene at a glance.* 他看了一眼那里的景色. ○ *The children took in the spectacle open-mouthed.* 孩子们张着嘴注视精彩表演. (**g**) understand or absorb sth that one hears or reads 理解或吸收(听到或阅读的)某事: *I hope you're taking in what I'm saying.* 我希望你能听得进去我说的话. ○ *Half-way through the chapter I realized I hadn't taken anything in.* 这一章我看到一半才意识到我根本没看懂.

take 'off (**a**) (of an aeroplane, a helicopter, etc) leave the ground and begin to fly (指飞机等)起飞: *The plane took off despite the fog.* 尽管有雾, 飞机仍照常起飞. (**b**) (*infml* 口) leave hurriedly or suddenly 匆忙离去; 突然离去: *He took off for the station at a run.* 他匆忙向车站跑去. ○ *When he saw the police coming he took off in the opposite direction.* 他一看见警察来了, 转身就溜了. (**c**) (*infml* 口) (of an idea, a product, etc) suddenly become successful or popular; (of sales of a product) rise very quickly (指观念、产品等)突然大受欢迎; (指产品的销售量)急升: *The new dictionary has really taken off.* 这部新词典极受欢迎. ○ *Sales of home computers have taken off in recent years.* 家庭电脑的销售量近年来上升很快. **take oneself off (to...)** (*infml* 口) leave a place (in order to reach the specified destination) 离开某地(去某处): *It's time I took myself off.* 现在我该走了. ○ *She's taken herself off to the country for a quiet weekend.* 她到乡村去过个清静的周末. **take sb off** imitate or mimic sb in an amusing or satirical way (以诙谐或嘲讽的方式)模仿或假扮某人: *She takes off the Prime Minister to perfection.* 她模仿首相的样子惟妙惟肖. **take sth off** (**a**) remove (an item of clothing) from one's body (从身上)除掉, 脱下(衣物等): *take off one's coat, hat, shoes, skirt, trousers, etc* 脱大衣、帽、鞋、裙子、裤子等 ○ *I wish you'd take* (ie shave) *off that beard!* 我希望你把胡子剃掉! (**b**) amputate (a part of the body) 切除(身体的一部分): *His leg had to be taken off above the knee.* 他的一条腿从膝盖以上截去了. (**c**) no longer perform (a play, etc); withdraw sth 不再上演(戏剧等); 收回或撤销某物: *The show had to be taken off because of poor audiences.* 因观众太少而取消演出. (**d**) (often passive 常用于被动语态) remove or withdraw (a bus, train, etc) from service 取消(公共汽车、火车等)的服务: *The 7 am express to Bristol will be taken off next month.* 上午7时开往布里斯托尔的快车将于下月停驶. (**e**) have (the specified period of time) as a holiday or break from work (某段时间)休假, 休息: *take the day/morning/afternoon off* 休息一天[一上午/一下午] ○ *I'm taking next week off (work).* 我下周要休假. **take sb off (sth)** (**a**) rescue sb from (a ship) 将某人从(船)上救出: *The crew were taken off (the wrecked vessel) by helicopter.* 船员被直升飞机(从遇难的船中)救出. (**b**) (often passive 常用于被动语态) remove sb from (a job, position, etc) 使某人离开(工作、职位等); 调离: *The officer leading the inquiry has been taken off the case.* 主持调查该事的官员已被调离. **take sth off (sth)** (**a**) remove or detach sth from (a surface or an edge) 使某物离开或脱离(一表面或边缘): *Would you mind taking your foot off my hand?* 你踩着我的手了, 请你把脚抬一下行吗? ○ *take the lid off a jar* 打开广口瓶的盖 ○ *The heat has taken the paint off the doors.* 门上的油漆受热而剥落. (**b**) remove (an item) from a menu (从菜单上)删除(一项): *The mixed grill has been taken off (the menu).* 烤杂拌这道菜已(从菜单上)取消了. **take sth off sth** (**a**) deduct (an amount of money) from sth (从某事物中)减去(一笔钱): *take 10 pence a gallon off the price of petrol* 汽油的价格每加仑减去10便士. (**b**) cause (a product) to be no longer on sale 使(产品)停止销售: *Doctors recommended that the drug should be taken off the market.* 医生建议市面上应停止出售该类药物.

take 'on (**a**) (*infml* 口) become fashionable or popular 流行; 时髦; 受欢迎: *The idea never really took on.* 这一观念一向不太得人心. (**b**) (used with an *adv* 与副词连用) (*dated infml* 旧, 口) become upset or agitated 烦乱; 不安; 烦恼; 激动: *Don't take on so!* 别这么激动! **take on sth** (no passive 不用于被动语态) begin to have (a particular quality, appearance, etc); assume sth 呈现(某种性质、样子等); 装成某事物: *He's taken on some irritating mannerisms.* 他新添了些讨人嫌的怪毛病. ○ *The chameleon can take on the colours of its background.* 避役可将身体颜色变得与周围环境相同. ○ *Her eyes took on a hurt expression.* 她的眼里流露出受委屈的神情. **take sb on** (**a**) employ sb; engage sb 雇用某人; 聘用某人: *take on new staff* 雇用新员工 ○ *She was taken on as a graduate trainee.* 她应聘为新毕业的实习生. (**b**) accept sb as one's opponent in a game, etc; tackle sb 同意与某人比赛; 对付某人: *take sb on at snooker, squash, tennis, etc* 与某人比赛彩色台球、壁球、网球等 ○ *Ajax will take on Juventus in this year's European Cup Final.* 在今年的欧洲杯足球决赛中阿贾克斯队将与尤文图斯队比赛. **take sb/sth on** (of a bus, plane, ship, etc) allow sb/sth to enter; take sb/sth on board (指公共汽车、飞机、轮船等)许可某人搭乘, 许可装载某物: *The bus stopped to take on more passengers.* 公共汽车停下让乘客上车. ○ *The ship took on more fuel at Freetown.* 轮船在弗里敦加燃料. **take sth on** decide to do sth; undertake sth 决定做某事; 承担某事: *take on extra work* 承担额外工作 ○ *She took on greater responsibilities when she was promoted.* 她得到提升, 担负了更大的责任. ○ *Don't take on more than you can cope with.* 要量力而行.

take sb out escort or accompany sb to the theatre, a restaurant, etc 伴随或陪伴某人(去剧院、饭店等): *Have you taken her out yet?* 你带她出去过吗? ○ *He took his wife out to dinner/for a meal on her birthday.* 他在妻子过生日时请她出去吃晚饭. **take sb/sth out** (*infml* 口) kill sb or destroy sth; put sb/sth out of action 杀死某人; 毁坏某物; 使某人[某物]不能活动或失去作用: *Enemy missiles took out two of our fighters.* 敌人的导弹炸毁我们两架战斗机. **take sth out** (**a**) (*US*) = TAKE STH AWAY. (**b**) remove or extract (a part of the body) 除去, 切除, 拔除(身体的一部分): *She's gone into hospital to have her appendix taken out.* 她已住院去切除阑尾. ○ *How many teeth did the dentist take out?* 牙科医生给患者拔了几颗牙? (**c**) obtain (an official document or a service) 获得(官方文件或处理): *take out an insurance policy, a mortgage, a patent* 领到保险单、抵押单据、专利证书. **take sth out (against sb)** issue (a document that requires sb to appear in court) 发出(传票): *The police have taken out a summons against the drivers of both cars involved in the accident.* 警方已向肇事的双方驾驶人发出传票. **take sth out (of sth)** (**a**) remove sth from sth 将某物从另一物处移开: *Take your hands out of your pockets.* 把你的手从衣袋里拿出来. (**b**) withdraw (money) from a bank account (从银行户头中)提(款): *How much do you need to take out (of the bank)?* 你需要(从银行)取多少钱? (**c**) deduct (an amount of money from sth) (从总额中)减去(一笔钱): *Monthly contributions to the pension scheme will be taken out of your salary.* 养老金制度中每月的公积金要从薪金中扣除. (**d**) cause sth to disappear from sth 使某物消失; 除掉某物: *Cold water should take that stain out of your skirt.* 用凉水可洗去你裙子上的污迹. **take it/sth out on sb** behave in an unpleasant way towards sb because one feels angry, disappointed, etc (因生气、失望等)向某人发泄: *I know you've had a bad day — but*

there's no need to take it out on me! 我知道你不痛快——可是也用不着拿我撒气呀! ○ *He took out his anger on the cat*, eg by kicking it. 他拿自己的猫出气(如踢它). **take sb 'out of himself** make sb forget his worries and become less concerned with himself, his thoughts, etc 使某人摆脱苦恼: *A holiday would help to take her out of herself.* 她要是去度假就能散散心.
take (sth) 'over gain control of (a country, political party, etc) 控制, 管理(国家、政党等): *The army is/are threatening to take over if civil unrest continues.* 军方声称如内乱不平息将实行军管. ○ *Has the party been taken over by extremists?* 该党是否已被极端分子控制? **take sth over** acquire or gain control of (a business company), esp by obtaining the support of a majority of its shareholders 接收, 接管(公司)(尤指依靠多数股东支持): *The firm has been taken over by an American conglomerate.* 该公司已被美国一企业集团接管. **take (sth) 'over (from sb)** take control of or responsibility for sth, esp in place of sb else 接手; 接替; 接任: *Peter will take over as managing director when Bill retires.* 比尔退休时将由彼得接任总经理一职. ○ *When she fell ill her daughter took over the business from her.* 她患病期间生意曾由她女儿代管. ○ *George is taking over the running of our American operation.* 乔治准备接手经营我们的美国企业. ○ *Would you like me to take over (the driving) for a while?* 你愿意让我接替你(开)一会儿(车)吗?
take to... go away to (a place), esp to escape from an enemy; take refuge in (a place) 离去而到(某处)(尤指为躲避敌人); 逃入(某处): *take to the forest, woods, jungle, etc* 逃进森林、树林、丛林等 ○ *The crew took to the lifeboats when the ship was torpedoed.* 船被鱼雷击中, 船员逃上救生艇. **take to sb/sth** develop a liking for sb/sth; develop an ability for sth 对某人[某事物]产生好感; 培养从事某事的能力: *I didn't take to her husband at all.* 我对她丈夫毫无好感. ○ *I took to her the moment I met her.* 我一见到她就立刻对她产生了好感. ○ *He hasn't taken to his new school.* 他对这所新学校还不感兴趣. **take to sth/doing sth** begin to do sth as a habit 逐渐惯于做某事: *take to smoking a pipe, sleeping late, going on solitary walks* 对吸烟斗、晚睡、独自散步逐渐习惯 ○ *She's taken to drink*, ie has started to drink a lot of alcoholic drinks. 她喝酒已喝上瘾了. ○ *He took to gardening in his retirement.* 他退休后就搞起了园艺.
take up continue 继续: *This chapter takes up where the last one left off.* 本章接续上一章谈到的内容. **take up sth** fill or occupy (the specified space or time) 填满, 占据(某空间或时间): *This table takes up too much room.* 这张桌子太占地方. ○ *Her time is fully taken up with writing.* 她的时间都用于写作了. **take sb up (a)** adopt sb as a protégé; help sb 提携某人; 扶掖某人: *The young soprano was taken up by a famous conductor.* 那年轻的女高音歌手受到一著名指挥家的提携. **(b)** interrupt sb in order to contradict or criticize him 打断某人的话(以反驳或批评): *She took me up sharply when I suggested that the job was only suitable for a man.* 我提出那工作只适合男人做, 她不容我说完就把我斥责一番. **take sth up (a)** lift sth up; raise sth 拿起; 举起; 抬起; 提起: *take up one's pen*, ie in order to write 拿起笔(写字) ○ *The carpets had to be taken up when the house was rewired.* 这房子重新安装电线时, 把地毯都掀了起来. **(b)** absorb (a liquid) 吸收(液体): *Blotting-paper takes up ink.* 吸墨纸能吸墨水. **(c)** make (a garment, curtains, etc) shorter 将(衣服、帘幕等)改短: *This skirt will need taking up*, ie to be taken up. 这条裙子需要改短. **(d)** adopt sth as a hobby or pastime 以某事作为爱好或消遣: *take up gardening, golf, yoga* 以园艺、打高尔夫球、瑜伽作消遣 ○ *She has taken up* (ie has begun to learn to play) *the oboe.* 她学起双簧管来了. **(e)** start or begin sth, esp a job 开始从事某事(尤指职业): *She has taken up a job as a teacher.* 她当上教师了. ○ *She takes up her duties/responsibilities next week.* 她下周开始履行职责. **(f)** add one's voice to sth; join in sth 一起说、唱或喊; 参加某事: *The whole crowd took up the cry: 'Long live the King!'* 人们齐声欢呼: '国王万岁!' ○ *take up a chorus, refrain, song, etc* 一起合唱、唱副歌、唱歌等. **(g)** continue (a story) that has been interrupted, or left unfinished by sb else 接续讲(中断的或他人未讲完的故事): *She took up the narrative where John had left off.* 她接着讲约翰未讲完的故事. **(h)** adopt or assume (an attitude, a position, etc) 采取(某种态度); 占据(某位置): *Our troops took up defensive positions on high ground overlooking the river.* 我部队在临河高地上占据了防御阵地. **(i)** accept sth 接受某事物: *take up a challenge* 接受挑战 ○ *She took up his offer of a drink.* 他邀请她喝酒, 她也就接受了. **(j)** mention sth in order that it may be discussed 提出某事(以期商讨): *I'd like to take up the point you raised earlier.* 我想把你曾提过的问题提出来讨论一下. **take sb up (on sth)** question or challenge sb (about sth); argue with sb (about sth) 询问或质问某人(某事); 与某人争论(某事): *I must take you up on that point.* 我一定要就那个问题和你辩论. ○ *I'd like to take you up on what you said about unemployment.* 对于你谈过的失业情况, 我想向你提出问题. **take up with sb** (*infml* 口) begin to be friendly with or spend a lot of time with sb (esp sb unpleasant or disreputable) 开始与某人(尤指不好的人)交往: *She's taken up with an unemployed actor.* 她跟一个失业的男演员混得很熟了. **take sb up on sth** (*infml* 口) accept (a challenge, a bet, an offer, etc) from sb 接受(某人的挑战、提出之事、提供之物); 同意与某人打赌: *'I bet I can run faster than you.' 'I'll take you up on that.'* '我跟你打赌我跑得比你快.' '我同意跟你打赌.' ○ *Thanks for the invitation; we may take you up on it some time.* 多谢邀请, 我们改日一定应邀. **take sth up with sb** speak or write to sb about sth; raise sth with sb (口头或书面)向某人谈及某事; 向某人提出某事: *I'm thinking of taking the matter up with my MP.* 我要向下议院议员提出此事. **be taken up with sb/sth** have much of one's time and energies occupied by sb/sth 时间和精力多用于某人[某事物]上: *She's very taken up with voluntary work at the moment.* 她目前大部分时间和精力都用在志愿工作上了.
be taken with sb/sth find sb/sth attractive or interesting 被某人[某事物]吸引; 对某人[某事物]感兴趣: *We were all very taken with her.* 我们都被她吸引住了. ○ *I think he's rather taken with the idea.* 我认为他对那个想法挺感兴趣.

□ **'take-away** (*US* **'take-out**) *adj* [attrib 作定语] (of food) bought at a restaurant for eating elsewhere (指食物)外卖的, 带走的: *a take-away hamburger, pizza, curry* 外卖的汉堡包、意大利饼、咖喱食品. — *n* **1** restaurant selling such food 外卖餐馆: *I'm too tired to cook — let's get something from the Chinese take-away.* 我累得做不了饭了——咱们从中国外卖餐馆买些东西来吃吧. **2** meal bought at such a restaurant 在外卖餐馆买的饭菜: *I fancy an Indian take-away.* 我想吃外卖的印度饭菜.
'take-home pay amount of one's wages or salary remaining after taxes, etc have been deducted 实得工资(扣除税等后净剩者).
'take-off *n* **1** place at which the feet leave the ground in jumping 起跳处; 起跳点. **2** (of an aeroplane) act of leaving the ground and rising (指飞机)起飞: *a smooth take-off* 平稳的起飞 ○ *The crash occurred only three minutes after take-off.* 飞机起飞后才三分钟就坠毁了. **3 ~ (of sb)** humorous imitation of sb (对某人)滑稽的模仿: *She does a brilliant take-off of the boss.* 她学老板的样子学得可笑极了.
'take-over *n* **1** act of taking control of a company by buying most of its shares (以收购大部分股票的方式对某公司的)接收: [attrib 作定语] *a take-over bid* 接收出价. **2** act of taking over a country, etc (对国家等的)接管: *a military take-over* 军事管制.
'take-up spool (on a cine-projector, tape-recorder, etc) spool onto which film, tape, etc is wound after use (电影放映机、录音机等上的)收片卷轴, 收带卷轴.

NOTE ON USAGE 用法: Both **last** and **take** are concerned with duration. ☆ **last** 和 **take** 都涉及时间的延续. **1 Take** indicates that a certain amount of time is needed in order to complete a task, journey, etc. ☆ **take** 指做一件事、走一段路等所需的时间. **Take** must be used with an expression of time ☆ **take** 必须与表示时间的词语连用: *How long will the job take?* 做这项工作需要多长时间? ○ *It takes a long time to get there.* 要用很长时间才能到达那里. ○ *It took (me) four hours to write the essay.* (我)写那篇文章用了四小时. ○ *I'll clear up — you take too long.* 我来清理吧——你用的时间太长. **2 Last** indicates that an event will continue for a period of time or that there is enough of something for the

T

required purpose. ☆ **last** 指一件事所持续的时间或为达到某目的有充足的条件. The time expression is not obligatory 不一定要有表示时间的词语: *His illness has lasted a long time.* 他已病了很长时间. ○ *I hope this fine weather lasts.* 我希望这样的好天气能持续下去. ○ *Do you think that paint will last (out)?* 你看那油漆能耐久吗? **3** Notice the difference between 请注意下面两句话的区别: *It takes (me) ten minutes to smoke a cigarette* and *A cigarette lasts (me) ten minutes.* '(我)吸一枝烟用十分钟'及'一枝烟(我)可吸十分钟'. **4** A journey can be seen as either a task or an event 走一段路程既可以看作是一项工作也可以看作是一件事: *The journey takes/lasts two hours.* 走这段路用两小时.

take[2] /teɪk; tek/ *n* **1** (usu *sing* 通常作单数) (**a**) amount of fish, game[1](6), etc caught (捕鱼、鸟兽等的)捕获量. (**b**) amount of money, taken or received, eg in return for tickets sold 收入额(如售票所得). **2** (*cinema* 影) sequence of film photographed at one time without stopping the camera (一次拍摄的连续)镜头: *shoot the scene in a single take* 不停机一次连续拍摄那场面.

taker /ˈteɪkə(r); ˋtekɚ/ *n* person who accepts an offer or takes a bet 收取者; 接受者; 同意打赌的人: *There's still some cake left — any takers?* ie Does anyone want some? 还剩下些蛋糕——有人想吃吗? ○ *The bookies were offering odds of 3 to 1, but there were no takers.* 赌马经纪人提出3比1的赔率, 但无人下注.

tak·ing /ˈteɪkɪŋ; ˋtekɪŋ/ *adj* (*dated* 旧) attractive; charming 吸引人的; 迷人的.

▷ **tak·ings** *n* [pl] amount of money that a shop, theatre, etc gets from selling goods, tickets, etc; receipts (商店、剧场等的)营业所得, 收入: *the day's takings* 一日的营业额.

talc /tælk; tælk/ (also **tal·cum** /ˈtælkəm; ˋtælkəm/) *n* [U] **1** smooth soft mineral that is powdered for use as a lubricant 滑石. **2** talcum powder 滑石粉; 扑粉; 爽身粉.

□ ˈ**talcum powder** talc, powdered and usu perfumed, put on the skin to make it feel smooth and dry 扑粉; 爽身粉.

T

tale /teɪl; tel/ *n* **1** narrative or story 故事: ˈ*fairy tales* 神话 ○ *tales of adventure* 冒险故事. **2** report spread by gossip, often false or invented 传言; 传闻; 流言蜚语: *I've heard some odd tales about her.* 我听到些关于她的怪事. ○ *You hear all sorts of tales.* 各种流言蜚语满天飞. **3** (idm 习语) **dead men tell no tales** ⇨ DEAD. **live, etc to tell the tale** ⇨ TELL. **an old wives' tale** ⇨ OLD. **tell its own tale** ⇨ TELL. **tell tales** ⇨ TELL. **thereby hangs a tale** ⇨ HANG[1].

□ ˈ**talebearer**, ˈ**taleteller** *ns* person who spreads gossip or reports what is meant to be secret 爱传播流言或秘密的人.

tal·ent /ˈtælənt; ˋtælənt/ *n* **1** [C, U] **~ (for sth)** (instance of) special or very great ability 特殊的能力; 才能; 才干; 天才: *Her talents are well known.* 人人都知道她很有才干. ○ *possess a remarkable talent for music* 具有非凡的音乐天才 ○ *a painter of great talent* 天才的画家. **2** [U] people who have this 有才能的人; 天才; 人才: *We're always looking for new/fresh talent.* 我们总是不断寻找新的天才. ○ *an exhibition of local talent*, eg of works by local amateur artists 当地人才作品展(如当地业余艺术家的作品展) ○ [attrib 作定语] *a television talent show,* ie one featuring talented young performers 电视新秀展播. **3** [U] (*sl* 俚) sexually attractive people 性感的人: *eyeing up the local talent* 盯着看当地的漂亮人. **4** [C] unit of money or measure of weight used in ancient times in certain countries 泰伦(古代某些国家使用的货币或重量单位).

▷ **tal·en·ted** *adj* having talent; gifted 有才能的; 有才干的; 天才的: *a talented musician* 天才的音乐家.

tal·ent·less *adj* without talent; not talented 无才能的; 无才干的; 平庸的.

□ ˈ**talent-scout** *n* person whose job is to find talented performers for the entertainment industry, sports teams, etc 星探(为娱乐业、运动队等寻找人才者).

tal·is·man /ˈtælɪzmən, *also* ˈtælɪs-; ˋtælɪzmən, ˋtælɪs-/ *n* (*pl* **~s**) [C] object that is thought to bring good luck, eg a ring or locket 认为可带来好运之物(如戒指或盒式项链坠); 辟邪物.

talk[1] /tɔːk; tɔk/ *n* **1** [C] conversation; discussion 交谈; 商谈; 谈论; 会谈: *I had a long talk with the headmaster about my son.* 关于我儿子的问题我与校长谈了很长时间. ○ *hold disarmament talks* 举行裁军会谈 ○ *The latest round of pay talks has broken down,* ie failed to reach an agreement. 最近一轮的工资谈判已经破裂. **2** [U] (**a**) talking, esp without action or result 谈话; (尤指)空谈: *There's too much talk and not enough work being done.* 说得太多而做得太少. (**b**) rumour or gossip 谣言; 闲话: *There's (some) talk of a general election.* 谣传要进行大选. **3** [C] informal lecture or speech 非正式的演讲或讲话: *She gave a talk on her visit to China.* 她就访华情况发表了非官方的讲话. **4** [U] (esp in compounds 尤用以构成复合词) way of speaking 说话的方式: *baby-talk.* **5** (idm 习语) **be all ˈtalk (and no action)** make empty promises, claims, etc 说空话; 空许愿. **fighting talk/words** ⇨ WORD. **the talk of sth** the main subject of conversation in (a place) (某地)谈论的主要话题; 街谈巷议的话题: *Their engagement is the talk of the town.* 他们订婚的事成了镇上谈论的话题.

NOTE ON USAGE 用法: **1 Talk** as an uncountable noun is a general word indicating the activity of speaking ☆ **talk** 作不可数名词时, 是泛指说话这一活动的词: *In politics there is too much talk and not enough action.* 在政治方面向来是说得多做得少. ○ *Talk is very important in a child's development.* 儿童的语言表达能力在其发育过程中是很重要的. **Talk** can also be a countable noun referring to a (usually) short informal speech to a small audience, or, when used in the plural, to formal occasions of serious talking, often between politicians ☆ **talk** 还可作可数名词, (通常)指在普通场合对少数人发表的简短讲话; 而作复数时则常指政治家之间在庄重的场合中进行的严肃谈话: *She gave the society an illustrated talk on her travels in India.* 她在协会中借助图片讲述其印度之行. ○ *The two sides in the war have agreed to hold peace talks.* 交战双方同意举行和谈. **2 Discussion** indicates (a) talk with a serious purpose. ☆ **discussion** 指有重要目的之谈话. It is often a formal exchange of words in which speakers argue about and examine different aspects of a subject 这一词常指发言者就某问题的各个方面交换意见及进行辩论: *The problem was solved only after several lengthy discussions.* 那个问题几经长时间的讨论才得以解决. ○ *a panel discussion on the radio on the future of the Health Service* 无线电广播的展望公共医疗卫生服务的专题小组讨论会. **3 Conversation** is usually social and friendly, often for the exchange of ideas or information ☆ **conversation** 通常指亲切的交谈, 常以交流思想或情况为目的: *Television has killed the art of conversation.* 电视扼杀了交谈的艺术. ○ *We had an interesting conversation about schools at lunch-time.* 我们吃午饭时兴致勃勃地谈论各学校的情况. **4 Chat** is (a) friendly talk, usually to exchange personal news, etc ☆ **chat** 是亲切的交谈, 通常为交流个人的情况等: *I hadn't seen him for years and we had a long chat about old times.* 我几年没见他了, 我们聊过去的事聊了很长时间. **5 Gossip** is derogatory and refers to talk about the private lives of other people, often of a critical kind. ☆ **gossip** 是贬义词, 指议论他人的私生活, 常有挑剔性质. A **gossip** is a person who gossips ☆ **gossip** 是爱说闲话的人: *People always gossip a lot in a small village like this.* 在这样的小村子里人们总是相互说长道短. ○ *He's a terrible gossip.* 他专爱说人闲话.

talk[2] /tɔːk; tɔk/ *v* **1** [I, Ipr] **~ (to/with sb) (about/of sth/sb)** say things; speak to give information, discuss sth, etc 说话; 谈话: *We talked* (ie to each other) *for almost an hour.* 我们谈了近一小时. ○ *He was talking to/with a friend.* 他在和朋友谈话. ○ *What are they talking about?* 他们说什么呢? ○ *She talked of applying for another job.* 她谈到要另申请一份工作. ○ *Are they talking in Spanish or Portuguese?* 他们说的是西班牙语还是葡萄牙语? **2** [I] have the power of speech 有说话的能力: *The child is learning to talk.* 那孩子正在学说话. **3** [Tn] (**a**) discuss (sth) 讨论(某事); 谈论; 洽谈: *talk business, politics, cricket* 谈论生意、政治、板球. (**b**) express (sth) in words 用语言表达(某事); 说(某事): *talk sense/nonsense* 说得有理[无理] ○ *You're talking rubbish.* 你胡说. **4** [Tn] use (a particular language) when speaking 用(某种语言)说; 说(某种语言): *talk French* 说法语. **5** [Cn·a] bring (oneself) into a certain condition by talking 说话说得(自己)(呈某种状态): *talk oneself hoarse* 说话说得声音嘶哑. **6** [I] gossip 说闲话: *We must stop meeting like this — people are beginning to talk!* 我们绝不能再这样约会了 —— 人们已经说起闲话来了! **7** [I] give information 提供情况; 招供: *The police persuaded the suspect to talk.* 警方劝嫌疑犯招供. **8** [I] imitate the sounds of speech 模仿说话的声音: *You can teach some parrots to talk.* 可以教某些鹦鹉说话. ⇨ Usage at SAY 用法见SAY. **9** (idm 习语) **be/get oneself 'talked about** be/become the subject of gossip 成为闲谈的话题; 成为话柄: *Be more discreet or you'll get yourself talked about.* 要更谨慎些 —— 否则你就会成为人们的话柄. **know what one is talking about** ⇨ KNOW. **look who's 'talking** (*infml* 口) you shouldn't say such things about others since you are just as bad yourself 你还说别人(你自己也那样). **money talks** ⇨ MONEY. **now you're talking** (*infml* 口) I welcome that offer or suggestion 这才像话; 这才合我的心意: *Take the day off? Now you're talking!* 休息一天怎么样? 这就好了! **speak/talk of the devil** ⇨ DEVIL[1]. **talk 'big** boast 吹牛; 说大话: *He talks big but doesn't actually do anything.* 他光吹牛, 什么实际的事都不干. **talk dirty** use obscene language 说脏话; 说下流话. **talk, etc nineteen to the dozen** ⇨ DOZEN. **talk one's 'head off** talk too much 说得太多. **talk sb's 'head off** weary sb by talking too much 说话太多而令某人生厌. **talk the hind legs off a donkey** (*infml* 口) (be able to) talk endlessly (能)说个没完. **talk sense** talk sensibly; say sth that is correct, acceptable, etc 说得有理; 说得对. **talk 'shop** (*usu derog* 通常作贬义) discuss one's work with colleagues, esp when with other people 与同事谈论自己的工作(尤指当着别人的面). **talk through one's 'hat** talk nonsense 胡说; 乱说. **talk (to sb) like a Dutch 'uncle** lecture sb severely but kindly 严厉而善意地教训某人. **talk 'turkey** (*infml* 口 *esp US*) talk frankly and bluntly 说话坦率. **talk one's way out of sth/doing sth** avoid sth by clever talking 靠口才避开某事: *I'd like to see him talk his way out of this one,* ie this trouble he has got into. 我倒要看看他能说会道过得去这一关. **talking of sb/sth** while on the subject of sb/sth 说到或提到某人[某事物]: *Talking of Jim, have you heard that he's getting married?* 说到吉姆, 你听说他要结婚了吗? **'you can/can't talk** (*infml* 口) = LOOK WHO'S TALKING.

10 (phr v) **talk at sb** speak to sb without listening to his replies 对某人说话而不听其反应: *I don't like being talked at.* 我可不愿意听着一味冲着我讲的话.

talk back (to sb) reply defiantly to a reprimand, etc 回嘴; 顶嘴.

talk sb down stop sb speaking by talking loudly or persistently 以高声或连续讲话来制止某人说话. **talk sb/sth down** bring (a pilot or an aircraft) to a landing by radio instructions from the ground (在地面通过无线电指挥)引导(飞行员或飞机)着陆. **talk down to sb** speak to sb in condescendingly simple language 以简单语言屈高就下与某人谈话.

talk sb into/out of doing sth persuade sb to do/not to do sth 说服某人做[不做]某事: *He talked his father into lending him the car.* 他说服父亲把汽车借给他了. ○ *I tried to talk her out of coming.* 我尽量劝她不要来.

talk sth out (**a**) resolve (a problem, etc) by discussion 通过商谈解决(问题等). (**b**) (*Brit*) prevent (a bill) being approved by Parliament by discussing it for so long that a vote cannot be taken (以拖长讨论时间)阻止议会通过(议案).

talk sb over/round (to sth) persuade sb to accept or agree to sth 说服某人接受或同意某事: *We finally managed to talk them over/round (to our way of thinking).* 我们终于设法说服他们接受了(我们的想法). **talk sth over (with sb)** discuss sth 讨论某事.

talk round sth discuss sth without coming to the point 不着边际地谈论某事: *waste an hour talking round the real problem* 围绕实质问题兜圈子谈论浪费一个小时.

talk sb/sth up (*US*) speak in favour of sb/sth; praise sb/sth 说某人[某事物]的好话; 称赞某人[某事物].

▷ **talk·at·ive** /ˈtɔ:kətɪv; ˋtɔkətɪv/ *adj* fond of talking 爱说话的; 多话的: *a very talkative child* 爱说话的孩子. **talk·at·ive·ness** *n* [U].

talker *n* **1** (esp with an *adj* 尤与形容词连用) person who talks (in the specified way) (以某种方式)谈话的人: *a good/poor talker* 健谈[不健谈]的人 ○ *She's a great talker,* ie She talks a lot. 她很能说. ○ *He's a fast talker,* ie able to get out of trouble by talking cleverly. 他是个能言善辩的人. **2** person who talks a lot but does not act 空谈者; 讲空话的人: *Don't rely on him to do anything — he's just a talker.* 什么事都不要依靠他 —— 他光会说空话.

□ **'talking-point** *n* topic that is likely to be discussed or argued about (易引起谈论或争论的)话题.

'talking-to *n* (*pl* **-tos**) (*esp sing* 尤作单数) reproof; scolding 训斥; 责骂: *That child needs a good talking-to.* 那孩子得说他一顿.

tall /tɔ:l; tɔl/ *adj* **(-er, -est) 1** (of people or objects) of more than average height; of objects whose height is greater than their width; higher than surrounding objects (指人或物)高的; (指物)长的, 高于周围物体的: *She's taller than me.* 她比我高. ○ *a tall tree, chimney, spire, mast* 高大的树、烟囱、塔尖、船桅. Cf 参看 SHORT[1] 1. **2** of a specified height 有所示之高度的: *Tom is six feet tall.* 汤姆身高六英尺. ⇨Usage at HEIGHT 用法见 HEIGHT. **3** (idm 习语) **a tall 'order** (*infml* 口) difficult task or unreasonable request 困难的任务; 无理的要求. **a tall 'story** (*infml* 口) story that is difficult to believe 荒诞不经的故事; 难以置信的事. **ten feet tall** ⇨ FOOT[1]. **walk tall** ⇨ WALK[1]. ▷ **tall·ness** *n* [U].

□ **'tallboy** (*Brit*) (*US* **'highboy**) *n* tall chest with drawers for clothes, etc (带抽屉的)高衣柜.

tal·low /ˈtæləʊ; ˋtælo/ *n* [U] animal fat used for making candles, soap, lubricants, etc (用以制造蜡烛、肥皂、润滑剂等的)动物脂.

tally /ˈtælɪ; ˋtælɪ/ *n* **1** score; reckoning 计分; 计算: *Keep a tally of how much you spend.* 把你的花费都记录下来. **2** label or ticket used for identification (用以核对的)标签, 票据.

▷ **tally** *v* (*pt, pp* **tallied**) [I, Ipr] **~ (with sth)** (of stories, amounts, etc) correspond; agree (指叙事、故事、数量等)符合, 一致: *His account of the accident tallies with yours.* 他对该事故的说法跟你说的一样. ○ *The two lists do not tally.* 这两张单子不相符.

Tal·mud /ˈtælmʊd; *US* ˈtɑ:l-; ˋtælməd/ *n* collection of ancient writings on Jewish law and tradition 塔木德(犹太法典).

talon /ˈtælən; ˋtælən/ *n* (usu *pl* 通常作复数) claw, esp of a bird of prey 爪(尤指猛禽的).

tam·ar·ind /ˈtæmərɪnd; ˋtæmə,rɪnd/ *n* (edible fruit of a) tropical tree 罗望子树(热带树木); 罗望子果(可食).

tam·ar·isk /ˈtæmərɪsk; ˋtæmə,rɪsk/ *n* evergreen shrub with feathery branches and spikes of pink or white flowers 柽柳(常绿灌木, 枝条柔软, 穗状花呈粉红色或白色).

tam·bour /ˈtæmbʊə(r); ˋtæmbʊr/ *n* **1** rolling top or front for a desk, cabinet, etc, made of narrow strips of wood glued to canvas (书桌的)滑动罩盖, (柜子的)拉门(用许多细木条粘在帆布上制成的). **2** small circular frame for holding fabric taut while it is being embroidered (刺绣用的圆形的)绷子.

tam·bour·ine /ˌtæmbəˈri:n; ˌtæmbəˋrin/ *n* (*music* 音) percussion instrument that consists of a small shallow drum with jingling metal discs set in the rim, and is played by shaking or hitting with the hand 铃鼓(四周有金属圆片, 摇动或用手拍打发声).

tame /teɪm; tem/ *adj* (**-r, -st**) **1** (of animals) gentle and unafraid of human beings; not wild or fierce (指动物)驯服的, 不怕人的, 不凶猛的: *a tame monkey* 驯服的猴子 ○ *The pigeons are so tame they will sit on your shoulder.* 这些鸽子不怕人能落在人的肩膀上. **2** [attrib 作定语] (*joc* 谑) (of people) available and willing to be told what to do; submissive (指人)听使唤的, 温顺的: *I've got a tame mechanic who keeps my car in order.* 我有个随和的汽车修理工, 他把我的车保养得很好. **3** dull or unadventurous 沉闷的; 无奇的; 平淡的: *I quite enjoyed the book but found the ending rather tame.* 我很爱看那本书, 只是结尾颇觉逊色. ○ *The scenery around here is a little tame.* 这周围的风景没什么特色. ○ *a tame attempt to reform the system* 对改革体制浅尝辄止.

▷ **tame** *v* [Tn] make (sth) tame or manageable 使(某

物)驯服或顺从: *tame wild birds* 调教野鸟 ○ *man's attempts to tame the elements* 人类控制自然力的尝试. **tame·able** *adj* that can be tamed 可驯服的. **tamer** *n* (usu in compounds 通常用以构成复合词) person who tames and trains wild animals 驯养者; 驯兽师: *a 'lion-tamer* 驯狮者.
tamely *adv*.
tame·ness *n* [U].

tam-o'-shanter /ˌtæm ə ˈʃæntə(r); ˌtæmə'ʃæntɚ/ (also **tammy** /ˈtæmɪ; ˈtæmɪ/) *n* round Scottish woollen cap with a soft full top (苏格兰人的)呢子圆帽.

tamp /tæmp; tæmp/ *v* (phr v) **tamp sth down** tap or ram sth down tightly 拍紧或捣实某物: *tamp down the tobacco in a pipe* 把烟斗中的烟丝压实.

tam·per /ˈtæmpə(r); ˈtæmpɚ/ *v* [Ipr] **~ with sth** meddle or interfere with sth; alter sth without authority 干预或干涉某事; 乱弄某物; 擅自改动某事物: *Someone has been tampering with the lock.* 有人乱动过这把锁. ○ *The records of the meeting had been tampered with.* 会议记录已被人擅自改动. ○ (*fig* 比喻) *tamper with* (ie bribe) *a jury* 贿赂陪审团.

tam·pon /ˈtæmpɒn; ˈtæmpɑn/ *n* plug of cotton wool or other absorbent material inserted into a woman's vagina to absorb blood during menstruation (女子使用的)月经棉塞, 卫生栓.

tan[1] /tæn; tæn/ *v* (**-nn-**) **1** [Tn] convert (animal skin) into leather by treating it with tannic acid, etc 硝(皮); 制(革); 鞣(革). **2** [I, Tn] (cause sth to) become brown by exposure to the sun (使某物)晒成褐色, 晒黑: *My skin tans easily.* 我的皮肤一晒就黑. ○ *I want to tan my back a bit more.* 我想把后背晒得再黑点儿. ○ *You look very tanned — have you been on holiday?* 你晒得挺黑的——是度假去了吗? **3** [Tn] (*infml* 口) beat (sb/sth); thrash 打(某人[某物]); 痛打. **4** (idm 习语) **tan sb's 'hide** (*infml* 口) beat sb hard 痛打某人.
▷ **tan** *n* **1** [U] yellowish-brown colour 黄褐色. **2** [C] brown colour of the skin after exposure to the sun 晒黑的肤色: *get a good tan* 晒得很黑 ○ *My tan's beginning to fade.* 我晒黑的肤色逐渐变浅了. — *adj* yellowish-brown 黄褐色的: *tan leather gloves* 黄褐色的皮手套.
tan·ner *n* person who tans skins to make leather 制革工人; 硝皮匠.
tan·nery /ˈtænərɪ; ˈtænərɪ/ *n* place where skins are tanned to make leather 制革厂; 硝皮厂.

tan[2] /tæn; tæn/ *abbr* 缩写 = (*mathematics* 数) tangent.

T and AVR (also **TAVR**) *abbr* 缩写 = (*Brit*) Territorial and Army Volunteer Reserve 本土军暨陆军志愿后备队.

tan·dem /ˈtændəm; ˈtændəm/ *n* **1** bicycle with seats and pedals for two or more people, one behind another (双人或多人骑的)串联式自行车. **2** (idm 习语) **in tandem** one behind another 一前一后地; 排成纵列: *drive/ride in tandem* 一前一后地驾车[骑车] ○ *horses harnessed in tandem* 前后串套着的马 ○ (*fig* 比喻) *The two systems are designed to work in tandem*, ie alongside each other, together. 这两套系统是为同步工作而设计的. ○ *He and his wife run the business in tandem*, ie as partners. 他和妻子共同经营这生意.

tan·doori /tænˈdʊərɪ; tɑnˈdʊrɪ/ *n* [U] type of Indian food cooked over charcoal in a clay oven 唐杜里(印度食品, 在泥炉中的炭火上烹调而成): [attrib 作定语] *tandoori chicken* 唐杜里鸡.

tang /tæŋ; tæŋ/ *n* (usu *sing* 通常作单数) sharp taste, flavour or smell, esp one that is characteristic of sth 强烈的味道或气味(尤指某物特有的): *with a tang of lemon* 带柠檬味的 ○ *There's a tang of autumn in the air.* 空气中有秋天的气息. ▷ **tangy** /ˈtæŋɪ; ˈtæŋɪ/ *adj* (**-ier, -iest**): *a tangy aroma* 浓烈的香味.

tan·gent /ˈtændʒənt; ˈtændʒənt/ *n* **1** (*geometry* 几) straight line that touches the outside of a curve but does not cross it 切线. ⇨illus at CIRCLE 见CIRCLE插图. **2** (*abbr* 缩写 **tan**) (*mathematics* 数) (in a right-angled triangle) ratio of the sides opposite and adjacent to a given angle 正切. Cf 参看 COSINE, SINE. **3** (idm 习语) **go/fly off at a 'tangent** change suddenly from one line of thought, action, etc to another 突然改变思想、行动等.

tan·ger·ine /ˌtændʒəˈriːn; *US* ˈtændʒəriːn; ˈtændʒəˌrin/ *n* **1** [C] type of small sweet loose-skinned orange 橘子. **2** [U] its deep orange-yellow colour 橘红色.

tan·gible /ˈtændʒəbl; ˈtændʒəbl/ *adj* **1** (*fml* 文) that can be perceived by touch 可触知的. **2** [usu attrib 通常作定语] clear and definite; real 明确的; 确切的; 真实的: *tangible advantages* 真正的优势 ○ *tangible proof* 确凿的证据 ○ *the company's tangible assets*, eg its buildings, machinery, etc, but not its reputation, etc 公司的有形资产(如其建筑物、机器等, 但不包括其信誉). ▷
tan·gib·il·ity /ˌtændʒəˈbɪlətɪ; ˌtændʒəˈbɪlətɪ/ *n* [U].
tan·gibly /-əblɪ; -əblɪ/ *n* [U].

tangle /ˈtæŋgl; ˈtæŋgl/ *n* [C] **1** confused mass (of string, hair, etc) (绳子、毛发等的)乱团: *brush the tangles out of a dog's fur* 刷顺狗毛 ○ *The wool got in a fearful tangle.* 毛线乱成了一团. **2** confused condition 混乱: *His financial affairs are in such a tangle.* 他的钱财是糊涂帐.
▷ **tangle** *v* **1** [I, Ip, Tn, Tn·p] **~ (sth) (up)** (cause sth to) become twisted into a confused mass (使某物)乱作一团, 绞在一起: *Her hair got all tangled up in the barbed wire fence.* 她的头发让刺钢丝篱笆都给挂住了. **2** [Ipr] **~ with sb/sth** become involved in a quarrel or fight with sb/sth 与某人吵嘴或打架; 与某事有纠葛: *I shouldn't tangle with Peter — he's bigger than you.* 我不该与彼得纠缠——他比你块头大. **tan·gled** *adj*: *tangled hair, wire, undergrowth* 乱毛发、金属丝、灌木丛.
tangly *adj* tangled 混乱的; 乱作一团的.

tango /ˈtæŋgəʊ; ˈtæŋgo/ *n* (*pl* **~s** /-gəʊz; -goz/) (music for a) ballroom dance with gliding steps and a strongly marked rhythm 探戈舞; 探戈舞曲: *dance/do the tango* 跳探戈舞.
▷ **tango** *v* (*pt, pp* **-goed**, *pres p* **-going**) [I] dance the tango 跳探戈舞.

tangy ⇨ TANG.

tank 坦克

tank /tæŋk; tæŋk/ *n* **1** (**a**) large container, usu for liquid or gas 大容器(通常盛液体或气体); 大桶; 箱; 罐; 槽: *the 'petrol-tank of a car* 汽车的油箱 ○ *keep tropical fish in a glass tank* 在玻璃缸中养热带鱼 ○ *Water is stored in tanks under the roof.* 水贮存于屋顶下的水箱中. (**b**) (also **tank·ful** /-fʊl; -fʊl/) contents of this 大桶、箱、罐、槽等所盛之物或量: *We drove there and back on one tank of petrol.* 我们开车到那里来回用了一油箱汽油. **2** armoured fighting vehicle with guns which moves on Caterpillar tracks 坦克车; 坦克: [attrib 作定语] *a tank commander* 坦克指挥官. **3** (in India, Pakistan, etc) large artificial reservoir for storing water (印度、巴基斯坦等)人工大水库.
▷ **tank** *v* (phr v) **tank up** fill the tank of a vehicle, etc 将车辆等的油箱加满油. **be/get tanked up** (*sl* 俚) be/become drunk 喝醉: *We got really tanked up on whisky and beer.* 我们喝威士忌和啤酒喝醉了.
tanker *n* (**a**) ship or aircraft for carrying petroleum, etc in bulk 运送石油等的轮船或飞机: *an oil tanker* 油轮. (**b**) (*US* also **'tank truck**) heavy road vehicle with a large cylindrical tank for carrying oil, milk, etc in bulk (陆上运送油、奶等的)卡车, 罐车.

tank·ard /ˈtæŋkəd; ˈtæŋkɚd/ *n* large (usu metal) drinking mug with a handle, esp one for beer (通常为金属的)有把手的大缸子; (尤指)啤酒杯. ⇨illus at CUP 见CUP插图.

tan·ner, tan·nery ⇨ TAN[1].

tan·nic /ˈtænɪk; ˈtænɪk/ *adj* of tannin 鞣酸的; 单宁酸的.
□ **tannic 'acid** tannin 鞣酸; 单宁; 单宁酸.

tan·nin /ˈtænɪn; ˈtænɪn/ *n* [U] any of various compounds obtained from the bark of oak and other trees and used in tanning, dyeing, etc 鞣酸; 单宁; 单宁酸.

Tan·noy /ˈtænɔɪ; ˈtænɔɪ/ *n* (*propr* 专利名) type of public-address system 坦诺扩音系统: *an announcement* *made over/on the Tannoy* 经坦诺扩音系统发布的通告.

tan·tal·ize, -ise /ˈtæntəlaɪz; ˋtæntḷ,aɪz/ *v* [Tn] tease or torment (a person or an animal) by the sight of sth that is desired but cannot be reached (以可望而不可即之物)逗引或招惹(人或动物): *Give the dog the bone — don't tantalize him.* 把那块骨头给那条狗吧 —— 别让它干着急了. ○ *He was tantalized by visions of power and wealth.* 他追求不到可望而不可即的权力和财富, 受尽了折磨. ▷ **tan·tal·iz·ing, -ising** *adj*: *a tantalizing smell of food* 诱人的食物气味. **tan·tal·iz·ingly, -isingly** *adv*: *tantalizingly near* 近得使人跃跃欲试.

tan·ta·mount /ˈtæntəmaʊnt; ˋtæntə,maʊnt/ *adj* [pred 作表语] **~ to sth** equal in effect to sth; as good as sth 与某事物效果相等; 与某事物相同: *The King's request was tantamount to a command.* 国王的要求就相当于命令. ○ *Her statement is tantamount to a confession of guilt.* 她的供述等于认罪.

tan·trum /ˈtæntrəm; ˋtæntrəm/ *n* outburst of bad temper, esp in a child 脾气发作(尤指儿童): *have/throw a tantrum* 发脾气 ○ *be in/get in(to) a tantrum* 在发脾气.

tap[1] /tæp; tæp/ *n* **1** (*US* **fau·cet**) device for controlling the flow of liquid or gas out of a pipe or container (控制液体或气体流出的)龙头, 旋塞: *hot and cold taps*, eg on a basin, bath, etc 冷水和热水的龙头 ○ *turn the tap on/off* 打开[关上]龙头 ○ *Don't leave the taps running*, ie Turn them off. 要把龙头关上. Cf 参看 VALVE 1. **2** act of tapping a telephone or connection for doing this 电话窃听(接线): *put a tap on sb's phone* 给某人的电话接通窃听器. **3** (idm 习语) **on tap** (**a**) (of beer, etc) in a barrel with a tap; on draught (指啤酒等)装在有龙头的桶里的, 散装的. (**b**) (*fig* 比喻) available when needed 现成的; 随时可获得的.

▷ **tap** *v* (**-pp-**) **1** (**a**) [Tn] draw liquid from (sth) 从(某物)中放出液体: *tap a cask of cider* 从桶中放出苹果酒. (**b**) [Tn, Tn·pr, Tn·p] **~ sth (off) (from sth)** draw (liquid) through the tap of a barrel 打开桶的龙头放出(液体): *tap off some cider* 打开龙头放出些苹果酒 ○ *tap cider from a cask* 打开桶的龙头放出苹果酒. **2** (**a**) [Tn] cut the bark of (a tree) in order to collect the sap 割开(树)的皮(以收取汁液): *tap rubber-trees* 割胶. (**b**) [Tn, Tn·pr, Tn·p] **~ sth (off)** collect (sap) in this way (割开树皮)收取(汁液). **3** [Tn, Tn·pr] **~ sth/sb (for sth)** extract or obtain (sth) from sth/sb 自某物[某人]处引出或获取(某物): *vast mineral wealth waiting to be tapped* 待开采的大量矿产 ○ *new ways of tapping the skills of young people* 使青年人发挥技能的新途径 ○ (*infml* 口) *tap sb for a loan* 向某人借钱. **4** [Tn] fit a listening device to (a telephone line) 在(电话线路)上装窃听器: *I think my phone is being tapped.* 我想现在有人窃听我的电话.

□ ˈ**tap-root** *n* chief root of a plant, growing straight downwards (植物的)主根.

ˈ**tap-water** *n* [U] water supplied through pipes to taps in a building, esp contrasted with types of bottled water 自来水.

tap[2] /tæp; tæp/ *n* **1** [C] (sound of a) quick light blow 轻快的敲击(声): *They heard a tap at the door.* 他们听见轻轻的敲门声. ○ *He felt a tap on his shoulder.* 他觉得有人轻拍他的肩膀. ○ *She gave the lid a few gentle taps to loosen it.* 她把盖子轻拍了几下使它松动. **2 taps** [sing *v*] (*US*) (in the armed forces) last bugle call of the day, the signal for lights to be put out (军队)熄灯号.

▷ **tap** *v* (**-pp-**) **1** (**a**) [Tn, Tn·pr] **~ sb/sth (with sth)** knock gently on sb/sth 轻拍某人; 轻敲某物: *tab sb on the shoulder* 轻拍某人肩膀 ○ *He tapped the box with a stick.* 他用小棒敲打盒子. (**b**) [Tn, Tn·pr] **~ sth (against/on sth)** strike (sth) lightly with sth 以某物轻击(某物): *tapping her fingers on the table* 用她的手指轻敲着桌子. **2** [I, Ipr] **~ (at/on sth)** give a tap or taps 轻敲; 轻拍; 轻击; 轻踏: *Who's that tapping at the window?* 谁在敲窗户?

□ ˈ**tap-dance** *n* dance in which an elaborate rhythm is tapped with the feet 踢跶舞. — *v* [I] perform this dance 跳踢跶舞. ˈ**tap-dancer** *n*. ˈ**tap-dancing** *n* [U].

tape /teɪp; tep/ *n* **1** [C, U] (piece of a) narrow strip of material used for tying, fastening or labelling things (用以捆、系物品或作标记的)带子, 线带: *three yards of linen tape* 三码亚麻带 ○ *a parcel tied up with tape* 用带子捆着的包裹 ○ *The seat covers are held in place by tapes.* 椅套用带子系在椅子上. **2** [C] piece of this stretched across a race-track at the finishing-line (拉在跑道终点的)终点线: *He breasted/broke the tape* (ie finished the race) *half a second ahead of his rival.* 他比对手早半秒钟撞线(到达终点). **3** [U] strip of paper or other flexible material coated with adhesive for fastening packages, etc (粘贴包裹等的)胶带, 胶条: *sticky tape* 胶粘带 ○ *insulating tape* 绝缘胶带. **4** [U] narrow continuous strip of paper on which a teleprinter prints a message (电传打印机的)收报纸带. **5** [C, U] (reel of) magnetic tape; recording made on this 磁带; 录像(带); 录音(带): *The police seized various books and tapes.* 警方查获了各种书和磁带. ○ *make a tape of sb's conversation* 录下某人的谈话 ○ *listening to a tape of the Beatles* 听披头士乐队的录音带 ○ *I've got all the Beethoven symphonies on tape.* 我有贝多芬交响乐全部的录音带. **6** [C] = TAPE-MEASURE.

▷ **tape** *v* **1** [Tn, Tn·p] **~ sth (up)** tie or fasten sth with tape 用带子捆或系某物. **2** [Tn] record (sb/sth) on magnetic tape 将(某人[某事物])录在录像带上; 给(某人[某事物])录音: *taped a concert off/from the radio* 录下音乐会的无线电广播. **3** (idm 习语) **have (got) sb/sth taped** (*infml* 口 *esp Brit*) understand sb/sth fully; be able to manage, influence or control sb/sth 全面了解某人[某事物]; 能管理、影响或控制某人[某事物]: *It took me a while to learn the rules of the game but I think I've got them taped now.* 我用了些时间学习游戏规则, 大概现在已经掌握了.

□ ˈ**tape deck** tape recorder as one component in a hi-fi system (高保真度的音响装置中的)录音座.

ˈ**tape-measure** *n* (also **tape**, ˈ**measuring tape**) strip of tape or flexible metal marked in inches or centimetres, etc for measuring length 卷尺; 皮尺.

ˈ**tape-recorder** *n* apparatus for recording sounds on magnetic tape and playing back the recording 录音机.

ˈ**tape-recording** *n* recording made on magnetic tape (录在磁带上的)录音, 录像.

ˈ**tapeworm** *n* tape-like worm that lives as a parasite in the intestines of man and other animals 绦虫.

taper[1] /ˈteɪpə(r); ˋtepɚ/ *n* length of wax-covered thread like a very thin candle burned to give light or to light other candles, etc 蜡捻子, 细蜡烛(点燃后用以照明或引火): *put a taper to the fire* 用蜡捻儿引火.

taper[2] /ˈteɪpə(r); ˋtepɚ/ *v* **1** [I, Ipr, Ip, Tn, Tn·pr, Tn·p] **~ (sth) (off) (to sth)** become or make (sth) gradually narrower 逐渐变窄; 使(某物)逐渐变窄: *tapering at the ends* 末端渐窄 ○ *a blade that tapers off to a fine point* 缩窄成细尖的叶片 ○ *The trouser legs are slightly tapered.* 裤腿逐渐向里收窄了一些. Cf 参看 FLARE[2]. **2** [Ip, Tn·p] **~ (sth) off** (cause sth to) become less in amount, etc or to cease gradually (使某物)变少, 变小; (使某物)逐渐终止: *The number of applicants for the course has been tapering off recently.* 申请上该课程的人近来已逐渐减少. ○ *taper off production* 逐渐停产.

▷ **taper** *n* (usu *sing* 通常作单数) gradual narrowing of a long object (长形物体的)逐渐变窄: *trousers with a slight taper* 裤脚稍瘦进一些的长裤.

tap·es·try /ˈtæpəstrɪ; ˋtæpɪstrɪ/ *n* [C, U] (piece of) cloth into which threads of coloured wool are woven or embroidered by hand to make pictures or designs, used for covering walls and furniture 绣帷; 织花帷; 壁毯; 挂毯.

▷ **tap·es·tried** *adj* hung or decorated with tapestries 挂绣帷或挂毯的; 以绣帷或挂毯装饰的: *tapestried walls* 挂有绣帷的墙.

ta·pi·oca /ˌtæpɪˈəʊkə; ˌtæpɪˋokə/ *n* [U] starchy food in hard white grains, obtained from the cassava plant 木薯淀粉.

ta·pir /ˈteɪpə(r); ˋtepɚ/ *n* small pig-like animal of tropical America and Malaysia, with a long flexible nose 貘(产于马来西亚和美洲热带地区).

tap·pet /ˈtæpɪt; ˋtæpɪt/ *n* projection in a piece of machinery that causes a certain movement by tapping against sth, used eg to open and close a valve 挺杆.

taps ⇨ TAP[2] 2.

tar[1] /tɑː(r); tɑr/ *n* [U] **1** thick black sticky liquid, hard when cold, obtained from coal, etc and used in making roads, to preserve timber, etc 焦油; 焦油沥青; 柏油. **2** similar substance formed by burning tobacco (烟草燃

T

烧产生的)烟碱，尼古丁: [attrib 作定语] *low-/middle-/high-tar cigarettes* 尼古丁含量低[中/高]的香烟.

▷ **tar** *v* (**-rr-**) **1** [Tn] cover (sth) with tar 以焦油或沥青覆盖或涂抹(某物); 铺以柏油: *a tarred road, rope, roof* 铺柏油的路、涂焦油的绳子、涂沥青的屋顶. Cf 参看 TARMAC. **2** (idm 习语) **tar and 'feather sb** put tar on sb and then cover him with feathers, as a punishment 将某人涂以沥青然后覆以羽毛(作为处罚). **tarred with the same 'brush (as sb)** having the same faults (as sb) (与某人)有同样的缺点.

tar² /tɑ:(r); tɑr/ *n* (also **Jack tar**) (*dated infml* 旧, 口) sailor 水手; 水兵.

tara·diddle /ˈtærədɪdl; *US* ˌtærəˈdɪdl; ˌtærəˈdɪdl̩/ *n* (*dated infml* 旧, 口) **1** [C] petty lie; fib 小谎. **2** [U] nonsense 胡说; 瞎说: *That's all taradiddle!* 那都是胡说八道!

ta·ra·ma·sa·la·ta /ˌtærəməsəˈlɑ:tə; ˌtærəməsəˋlɑtə/ *n* [U] edible (usu pink) paste made from the smoked roe of mullet or cod (以鲻鱼子或鳕鱼子熏制的)鱼子酱(通常呈粉红色).

ta·ran·tella /ˌtærənˈtelə; ˌtærənˋtɛlə/ *n* (music for a) fast whirling Italian dance 塔兰台拉舞; 塔兰台拉舞曲.

ta·ran·tula /təˈræntjʊlə; *US* -tʃələ; təˋræntʃələ/ *n* any of several types of large spider, many of them hairy and some of them poisonous 大蜘蛛(多有毛, 有的有毒).

tar·boosh /tɑ:ˈbu:ʃ; tɑrˋbuʃ/ *n* brimless felt cap like a fez, worn by Muslim men in certain countries 塔布什帽(某些国家穆斯林男子戴的无沿毡帽).

tardy /ˈtɑ:dɪ; ˋtɑrdɪ/ *adj* (**-ier, -iest**) (*fml* 文) **1** slow to act, move or happen 行动缓慢的; 缓缓移动的; 迟缓的; 拖拉的: *tardy in offering help* 提供帮助不及时 ○ *tardy progress, repentance, recognition* 缓慢的进步、事过后悔、缓慢的认识. **2** (of actions, etc; *US* also of people) late (指行动等; 美式英语亦用于指人)晚的, 迟的: *a tardy arrival, return, departure, etc* 迟到、迟归、迟动身 ○ *be tardy for/to school* 上学迟到. ▷ **tard·ily** /-ɪlɪ; -ɪlɪ/ *adv*. **tar·di·ness** *n* [U].

T

tare /teə(r); tɛr/ *n* **1** weight of the container in which goods are packed, or of the vehicle carrying them 皮重(包装货物的容器重量); 包装重量; 车身重(载货车辆的重量); 车皮重. **2** allowance made for this when the goods are weighed together with their container or vehicle 皮重的扣除.

tar·get /ˈtɑ:gɪt; ˋtɑrgɪt/ *n* **1** object or mark that a person tries to hit in shooting, etc; disc marked with concentric circles for this purpose in archery 目标; 靶. ⇨illus at ARCHERY 见 ARCHERY 插图. **2** person or thing against which criticism, etc is directed 受批评等的人或事物; 批评的目标、对象: *become the target of scorn, derision, spite, etc* 成为受轻蔑、嘲笑、怨恨等的对象. **3** result aimed at; objective 目的; 目标: *meet one's export targets* 达到出口指标 ○ *Production so far this year is on/off target.* 今年到目前为止生产已达到[未达到]指标. ○ *The embassy is an obvious target for terrorist attacks.* 大使馆是恐怖分子攻击的明显目标. ○ [attrib 作定语] *a target date*, ie one set for completion of a project, etc 预定日期(为完成计划等订立的).

▷ **tar·get** *v* [usu passive 通常用于被动语态: Tn, Tn·pr] **~ sth (at/on sth/sb)** aim sth 瞄准某物: *missiles targeted on Britain* 瞄准英国的导弹 ○ *a sales campaign targeted at the youth market* 面向青年人市场的大推销.

tar·iff /ˈtærɪf; ˋtærɪf/ *n* **1** list of fixed charges, esp for rooms, meals, etc at a hotel 价目表(尤指旅馆的房间、餐食等的). **2** duty to be paid on imports or (less often) exports 进出口货物(较少指出口货物)关税: [attrib 作定语] *raise tariff barriers against foreign goods* 提高进口税. Cf 参看 TAX 1.

Tar·mac /ˈtɑ:mæk; ˋtɑr,mæk/ *n* [U] (**a**) (*propr* 专利名) (also **tar mac·adam**) material for surfacing roads, etc, consisting of broken stone mixed with tar (铺设路面的)碎石和沥青的混合材料. (**b**) **tarmac** area surfaced with this, esp on an airfield 柏油碎石路面(尤指飞机场的): *The plane taxied along the tarmac.* 飞机沿跑道滑行. Cf 参看 MACADAM.

▷ **tar·mac** *v* (*pt, pp* **tar·macked**, *pres p* **tar·mack·ing**) [Tn] surface (sth) with Tarmac 以碎石沥青铺盖(某物)表面: *I'm going to tarmac the front drive.* 我要把前面的汽车道铺上碎石沥青.

tarn /tɑ:n; tɑrn/ *n* (often in names) small mountain lake (常用于名字)山中的小湖.

tar·nish /ˈtɑ:nɪʃ; ˋtɑrnɪʃ/ *v* **1** [I, Tn] (cause sth to) lose its brightness by being exposed to air or damp (因暴露于空气或潮气)(使某物)失去光泽: *mirrors that have tarnished with age* 因年深月久而失去光泽的镜子 ○ *The brasswork needs polishing — it's badly tarnished.* 那黄铜制品该擦了——黑糊糊的. **2** [Tn] stain or blemish (a reputation, etc) 玷污, 损害(名誉等): *The firm's good name was badly tarnished by the scandal.* 这件丑事玷污了公司的好名声.

▷ **tar·nish** *n* [C, U] loss of brightness; stain or blemish 晦暗; 污点; 瑕疵: *remove the tarnish from silver* 除去银子上的污点.

taro /ˈtɑ:rəʊ; ˋtɑro/ *n* (*pl* **~s**) any of various types of tropical plant with a starchy root used as food, esp in the Pacific islands 芋; 芋头.

tarot /ˈtærəʊ; ˋtæro/ *n* (**a**) [C] any one of a special pack of cards used mainly for fortune-telling 塔罗特纸牌(主要用于占卜). (**b**) [sing] game played with these 塔罗特纸牌戏: *playing the tarot* 玩塔罗特纸牌 ○ [attrib 作定语] *tarot cards* 塔罗特纸牌.

tar·paulin /tɑ:ˈpɔ:lɪn; tɑrˋpɔlɪn/ *n* [C, U] (sheet or covering of) canvas made waterproof, esp by being treated with tar 防水帆布; 防水帆布罩; (尤指)柏油帆布: *goods on a lorry covered by a tarpaulin* 卡车上苫着雨布的货物.

tar·ra·gon /ˈtærəgən; *US* -gɒn; ˋtærə,gɑn/ *n* [U] (herb with) leaves that are used for flavouring salads and vinegar 龙蒿; 龙蒿叶(用以为色拉和醋调味): *add a sprinkling of dried tarragon* 放点儿干的龙蒿叶.

tarry¹ /ˈtærɪ; ˋtærɪ/ *v* (*pt, pp* **tarried**) [I, Ipr] (*arch or rhet* 古或修辞) delay in coming to or going from a place; linger 耽搁; 逗留; 徘徊: *Tarry awhile at this charming country inn.* 在这个可爱的乡村小酒馆里呆一会儿吧.

tarry² /ˈtɑ:rɪ; ˋtɑrɪ/ *adj* (**-ier, -iest**) of, like or covered with tar 沥青的; 柏油的; 如沥青的; 涂有沥青的.

tarsal /ˈtɑ:sl; ˋtɑrsl̩/ *adj* (*anatomy* 解) of the bones in the ankle 跗骨的.

▷ **tarsal** *n* (*anatomy* 解) one of the bones in the ankle 跗骨(之一块). ⇨illus at SKELETON 见 SKELETON 插图.

tar·sus /ˈtɑ:səs; ˋtɑrsəs/ *n* (*pl* **tarsi** /-saɪ; -saɪ/) (*anatomy* 解) group of seven small bones in the ankle 跗骨(由踝部七块小骨组成).

tart¹ /tɑ:t; tɑrt/ *adj* **1** sharp-tasting; acid 辛辣的; 酸的: *This fruit tastes rather tart.* 这水果吃着有些酸. **2** [usu attrib 通常作定语] (*fig* 比喻) sharp in manner; cutting or sarcastic 尖酸的; 尖刻的; 伤害的; 讽刺的: *a tart remark, reply, tone* 尖酸的言语、回答、语调 ○ *He can be quite tart.* 他有时很刻薄. ▷ **tartly** *adv*. **tart·ness** *n* [U].

tart² /tɑ:t; tɑrt/ *n* **1** (*esp Brit*) pie containing fruit or other sweet filling, often without a covering of pastry 果馅饼(以水果或其他甜料作馅, 常无上面的饼皮). **2** small circle of pastry cooked with jam, etc on it (上面有果酱等的)小圆饼. Cf 参看 FLAN.

tart³ /tɑ:t; tɑrt/ *n* (*sl* 俚) **1** prostitute 妓女. **2** (*derog* 贬) girl or woman, esp one regarded as being sexually immoral 小妞儿; 娘儿们; (尤指)破鞋.

▷ **tart** *v* (phr v) **~ sb/sth up** (*infml* 口) dress or decorate sb/sth in a gaudy way; smarten sb/sth up, esp cheaply or superficially 将某人打扮得妖艳; 将某物装饰得俗气; (尤指以廉价的服饰或从外表上)打扮某人, 装饰某物: *tarting herself up for the disco* 把她自己打扮得花枝招展去跳迪斯科 ○ *They've tarted up the restaurant but the food hasn't improved.* 他们已将饭店装修了一番, 但饭菜并无改进.

tar·tan /ˈtɑ:tn; ˋtɑrtn̩/ *n* **1** [C, U] pattern of coloured stripes crossing at right angles, esp one associated with a Scottish clan 花格图案(尤指与苏格兰家族有关的). **2** [U] woollen fabric woven in such a pattern 彩色格呢; 苏格兰格呢: [attrib 作定语] *a tartan skirt* 彩色格呢裙.

tar·tar¹ /ˈtɑ:tə(r); ˋtɑrtɚ/ *n* [U] **1** hard chalky deposit that forms on the teeth 牙垢; 牙石. Cf 参看 PLAQUE². **2** reddish deposit that forms on the inside of a cask in which wine is fermented 酒石(形成于酒的发酵桶内侧者).

▷ **tar·taric** /tɑ:ˈtærɪk; tɑrˋtærɪk/ *adj* of or derived from tartar 酒石的; 由酒石生成的.

□ **tar,taric 'acid** acid of tartar, found in many plants

and the juice of fruit, and used in making baking powder, etc 酒石酸，果酸（存在于许多植物和果汁中，用以制发酵粉等）.

tar·tar² /ˈtɑ:tə(r); ˋtɑrtɚ/ *n* person who has a violent temper or is difficult to deal with 脾气暴躁的人；难对付的人.

tar·tar sauce /ˌtɑ:tə(r) ˈsɔ:s; *US* ˈtɑ:rtər sɔ:s; ˋtɑrtɚˌsɔs/ cold sauce of mayonnaise with chopped onions, herbs, capers, gherkins, etc, eaten esp with fish 塔塔沙司（用蛋黄酱加碎洋葱、香料、续随子及小黄瓜制成，尤用以佐鱼）.

task /tɑ:sk; *US* tæsk; tæsk/ *n* **1** piece of (esp hard or unpleasant) work that has to be done 必须做的工作（尤指困难的或讨厌的）；任务：*holiday tasks* 假期作业 ○ *I set myself the task of chopping up the firewood.* 我给自己安排了劈柴的任务. ○ *perform the gruesome task of identifying the dead bodies* 执行辨认尸体这一可怕的任务 ○ *Becoming fluent in a foreign language is no easy task*, ie is difficult. 熟练地掌握一门外语是一项艰苦的工作. ⇨Usage at WORK¹ 用法见 WORK¹. **2** (idm 习语) **take sb to task (about/for/over sth)** rebuke or criticize sb 指责或批评某人：*I was taken to task for arriving late.* 我因迟到而受批评. ○ *She took the government to task over its economic record.* 她批评政府的经济劣迹.

▷ **task** *v* [Tn·pr esp passive 尤用于被动语态] **~ sb with sth** give sth to sb as a task 将某事作为任务交与某人：*tasked with the design of a new shopping centre* 被派给设计新购物中心的任务.

□ ˈ**task force** group of people and resources specially organized for a particular (esp military) task 特派组；特遣部队.

ˈ**taskmaster** (*fem* 阴性作 ˈ**taskmistress**) *n* person who is strict in making others work hard 监工：*a hard taskmaster* 严厉的监工.

TASS /tæs; tæs/ *abbr* 缩写 = official news agency of the former USSR (Russian *Telegrafnoye Agenstvo Sovietskovo Soyuza*) 塔斯社（前苏联官方通讯社）（源自俄文 *Telegrafnoye Agenstvo Sovietskovo Soyuza*）.

tassel 穗

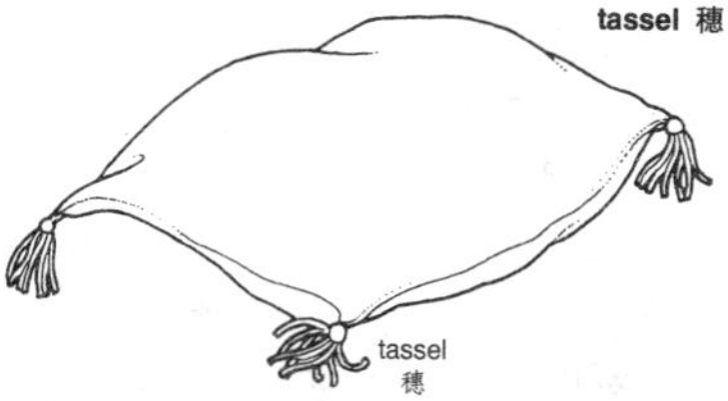

tas·sel /ˈtæsl; ˋtæsl̩/ *n* bunch of threads tied at one end and hanging (from a cushion, tablecloth, hat, etc) as an ornament（垫子、台布、帽子等垂下的）穗，缨，流苏.

▷ **tas·selled** (*US* **tas·seled**) *adj* ornamented with a tassel or tassels 饰有穗、缨或流苏的.

taste¹ /teɪst; test/ *n* **1** [C, U] sensation caused in the tongue by things placed on it 味道：*Sugar has a sweet taste.* 糖有甜味. ○ *a strong taste of garlic* 很浓的蒜味 ○ *I don't like the taste of this cheese.* 我不喜欢这乳酪的味道. ○ *a wine that has no/very little/not much taste* 没味的［味淡的/没什么味的］酒. **2** [U] sense by which flavour is known 味觉：*I've got a cold and so I have no taste/have lost my sense of taste.* 我伤风了，尝不出味道. ○ *bitter to the taste* 苦味. **3** [C usu *sing* 通常作单数] **~ (of sth)** (**a**) small quantity of food or drink taken as a sample（品尝的）少量食物或饮料：*Just have a taste of this cheese!* 尝一点儿这种乳酪吧！(**b**) (*fig* 比喻) first/early experience of sth 首次的［最初的］经历或体验；尝试：*her first taste of life in a big city* 她对大城市生活初次的体验 ○ *Although we didn't know it, this incident was a taste of things to come.* 我们当时并不了解，这件事就是后来这类事的发端. **4** [C, U] **~ (for sth)** liking or preference 爱好；嗜好：*She has a taste for foreign travel.* 她有到国外旅行的爱好. ○ *have expensive tastes in clothes* 喜欢昂贵的衣服 ○ *Modern art is not (to) everyone's taste*, ie Many people dislike it. 现代艺术不见得合所有人的口味（很多人不喜欢）. **5** [U] ability to perceive and enjoy what is beautiful or harmonious, or to behave in an appropriate and a pleasing way 判断力；鉴赏力；审美力；欣赏力；适度而得体的举止：*have excellent taste in clothes, art, music, etc* 对服装、艺术、音乐等很有鉴赏力 ○ *He's got more money than taste*, ie is rich but unrefined. 他有钱却无修养. ○ *a room furnished in/with perfect taste* 布置得相当雅致的房间 ○ *It would be bad taste to refuse their invitation.* 拒绝他们的邀请是不礼貌的. **6** (idm 习语) **an acquired taste** ⇨ ACQUIRE. **(be) in good, bad, poor, the best of, the worst of, etc** ˈ**taste** (of sb's behaviour, etc) appropriate and pleasing/unsuitable and offensive（指某人的举止等）适度而得体［失当而粗俗］：*She always dresses in the best possible taste.* 她总是穿得很雅致. ○ *I thought his jokes were in very poor taste.* 我认为他讲的笑话太粗俗了. **leave a bad/nasty taste in the mouth** ⇨ LEAVE¹. **there's no accounting for taste** ⇨ ACCOUNT². **to** ˈ**taste** (esp in recipes) in the amount preferred（尤用于食谱中）适量：*Add salt to taste.* 按口味放盐.

▷ **taste·ful** /-fl; -fəl/ *adj* showing good taste¹(5) 有良好判断力、鉴赏力等的；举止得体的. **taste·fully** /-fəlɪ; -fəlɪ/ *adv*: *tastefully decorated* 装饰得高雅的. **taste·ful·ness** *n* [U].

taste·less *adj* **1** having no flavour 无味的. **2** showing poor taste¹(5) 无判断力、鉴赏力等的；举止粗俗的：*tasteless jokes* 粗俗的笑话. **taste·lessly** *adv*. **taste·less·ness** *n* [U].

tasty *adj* (**-ier**, **-iest**) having a strong and pleasant flavour; appetizing 美味的；引起食欲的：*a tasty dish* 一道好吃的菜. **tas·tily** /-ɪlɪ; -ɪlɪ/ *adv*. **tas·ti·ness** *n* [U].

□ ˈ**taste-bud** *n* (usu *pl* 通常作复数) any of the small projections on the tongue by which flavours are perceived 味蕾.

taste² /teɪst; test/ *v* **1** [I, Tn] (not used in the continuous tenses; often with *can* 不用于进行时态；常与 can 连用) be able to perceive (flavours) 能辨别（味道）；尝出；品出：*I can't taste, I've got a bad cold.* 我得了重感冒，尝不出味道来. ○ *Can you taste the garlic in this stew?* 你尝得出炖肉里有大蒜味儿吗？ **2** [La, Ipr] **~ (of sth)** have a certain (specified) flavour 有某种（所指的）味道：*taste sour, bitter, sweet, etc* 有酸、苦、甜等味 ○ *It tastes strongly of mint.* 这有挺冲的薄荷味儿. **3** [Tn] test the flavour of (sth) 尝（某物）的味道；品：*He tasted the soup to see if he had put enough salt in it.* 他尝尝汤，看是否够咸. ⇨Usage at FEEL¹ 用法见 FEEL¹. **4** [Tn] eat or drink (food or liquid) 吃（食物）；喝（液体）：*They hadn't tasted hot food for over a week.* 他们已有一个多星期没吃上热东西了. ○ *That's the best wine I've ever tasted.* 那是我喝过的最好的酒. **5** [Tn] (*fig* 比喻) experience (sth) 体验，领略（某事）：*taste power, freedom, failure, defeat, etc* 尝到权力、自由、失败、挫败等的滋味.

▷ **taster** *n* person whose job is to judge the quality of wine, tea, etc by tasting it 品尝员；品酒师；品茶师.

tast·ing *n* event at which sth is tasted 品尝会：*go to a wine/cheese tasting* 去参加酒类［乳酪］品尝会.

-tasting (forming compound *adjs* 用以构成复合形容词) having the specified flavour or taste 有某种风味或滋味的：*sweet-tasting* ○ *fresh-tasting*.

tat¹ /tæt; tæt/ *v* (**-tt-**) (**a**) [I] do tatting 梭织. (**b**) [Tn] make (sth) by tatting 用梭织法编织（某物）.

tat² /tæt; tæt/ *n* [U] (*Brit infml* 口) tatty things; shoddy or shabby goods 不整洁之物；劣质的或破旧的货物：*a shop selling dreadful old tat* 出售破烂旧物的铺子.

tat³ /tæt; tæt/ *n* (idm 习语) **tit for tat** ⇨ TIT².

ta-ta /tə ˈtɑ:; ˋtɑˌtɑ/ *interj* (*Brit infml* 口) goodbye 再见.

tat·ters /ˈtætəz; ˋtætɚz/ *n* [pl] **1** irregularly torn pieces of cloth, etc; rags 碎布；破旧的衣服：*a poor beggar dressed in rags and tatters* 衣衫褴褛的、可怜的乞丐 ○ *His clothes hung in tatters.* 他的衣服破成了条儿耷拉着. **2** (idm 习语) **in tatters** destroyed; ruined 破坏的；毁坏的；毁灭的：*left his reputation, life, career, etc in tatters* 使他的名誉、生活、事业等受损害 ○ *She replied to my points so convincingly that my argument was soon in tatters.* 她反驳我提出的各点都很有说服力，很快就将我的论点驳倒.

▷ **tat·tered** *adj* ragged 破烂的；褴褛的.

tat·ting /ˈtætɪŋ; ˋtætɪŋ/ *n* [U] (**a**) type of lace that is made by hand and used for trimming（用于装饰的）手工花边. (**b**) process of making this 编织手工花边.

tattle /ˈtætl; ˋtætl̩/ *v* [I] chatter or gossip idly; reveal information by doing this 闲谈; 闲聊; (聊天中)透露消息: *Who's been tattling?* 谁在说闲话呢?

▷ **tattle** *n* [U] idle chatter or gossip 闲谈; 闲聊.

tat·tler /ˈtætlə(r); ˋtætlɚ/ (*US* ˈ**tattle-tale**) *n* person who tattles 爱闲聊的人; 爱透露消息的人.

tat·too[1] /təˈtu:; *US* tæˈtu:; tæˋtu/ *n* (*pl* **~s**) **1** [sing] evening drum or bugle signal calling soldiers back to their quarters 归营鼓; 归营号: *beat/sound the tattoo* 敲归营鼓[吹归营号]. **2** [C] elaborate version of this with music and marching, performed as a public entertainment 归营游行(配有军乐的表演): *a torchlight tattoo* 火炬游行. **3** [C] drumming or tapping 敲鼓; 轻击: *beating a tattoo on the table with his fingers* 以手指在桌子上轻击鼓点.

tat·too[2] /təˈtu:; *US* tæˈtu:; tæˋtu/ *v* [Tn, Tn·pr] (**a**) mark (sb's skin) with a permanent picture or pattern by pricking it and inserting a dye 给(某人的皮肤)刺染图案. (**b**) put (a picture or pattern) on the skin in this way 刺染(图案)于皮肤上: *had a ship tattooed on his arm* 在他的臂上刺一只船.

▷ **tat·too** *n* (*pl* **~s**) tattooed picture or pattern 刺在皮肤上的图案; 文身: *His chest was covered in tattoos.* 他的胸部刺满了花纹. ○ [attrib 作定语] *a tattoo artist* 文身的艺术家.

tatty /ˈtætɪ; ˋtætɪ/ *adj* (**-ier, -iest**) (*infml* 口) **1** shabby and untidy; ragged 不整洁的; 邋遢的; 破烂的: *tatty old clothes* 破烂的旧衣服. **2** cheap and tawdry 廉价而艳丽的; 俗丽的. ▷ **tat·tily** /-ɪlɪ; -ɪlɪ/ *adv*. **tat·ti·ness** *n* [U].

taught *pt, pp* of TEACH.

taunt /tɔ:nt; tɔnt/ *v* [Tn, Tn·pr] **~ sb (with sth)** try to provoke sb with scornful or critical remarks; jeer at sb 试图以嘲笑或批评惹恼某人; 嘲弄某人: *They taunted him with cowardice/with being a coward.* 他们讥笑他胆怯[是胆小鬼].

▷ **taunt** *n* (often *pl* 常作复数) taunting remark 嘲弄的言语; 嘲笑; 讥讽: *ignoring the taunts of the opposition* 不理睬对方的嘲笑.

taunt·ingly *adv*.

T

Taurus /ˈtɔ:rəs; ˋtɔrəs/ *n* **1** [U] the second sign of the zodiac, the Bull 金牛宫(黄道第二宫). ⇨illus at ZODIAC 见 ZODIAC 插图. **2** [C] person born under the influence of this sign 属金牛宫星座的人. ▷ **Taur·ean** *n, adj* ⇨ Usage at ZODIAC 用法见 ZODIAC.

taut /tɔ:t; tɔt/ *adj* **1** (of rope, wire, cloth, etc) tightly stretched; not slack (指绳索、金属线、布等)拉紧的, 不松弛的. **2** (of muscles or nerves) tense (指肌肉或神经)紧张的. ▷ **tautly** *adv*. **taut·ness** *n* [U].

tauten /ˈtɔ:tn; ˋtɔtn̩/ *v* [I, Tn] (cause sth to) become taut (使某物)变紧, 紧张.

tau·to·logy /tɔ:ˈtɒlədʒɪ; tɔˋtɑlədʒɪ/ *n* (**a**) [U] saying the same thing more than once in different ways without making one's meaning clearer or more forceful; needless repetition 无谓的重复; 赘述. (**b**) [C] instance of this 重复的话; 赘言. Cf 参看 PLEONASM. ▷ **tau·to·lo·gical** /ˌtɔ:təˈlɒdʒɪkl; ˌtɔtl̩ˋɑdʒɪkl̩/, **tau·to·log·ous** /tɔ:ˈtɒləgəs; tɔˋtɑləgəs/ *adjs*.

tav·ern /ˈtævən; ˋtævɚn/ *n* (*arch or rhet* 古或修辞) inn or public house 客栈; 酒店; 酒馆.

TAVR *abbr* 缩写 = T AND AVR.

taw·dry /ˈtɔ:drɪ; ˋtɔdrɪ/ *adj* (**-ier, -iest**) showy or gaudy but without real value 俗丽的; 华而不实的: *tawdry jewellery, furnishings* 俗丽的珠宝、家具. ▷ **taw·drily** /-əlɪ; -əlɪ/ *adv*. **taw·dri·ness** *n* [U].

tawny /ˈtɔ:nɪ; ˋtɔnɪ/ *adj* brownish-yellow 黄褐色: *the lion's tawny mane* 狮子的黄褐色鬃毛.

tax /tæks; tæks/ *n* **1** [C, U] (sum of) money to be paid by people or businesses to a government for public purposes 税; 税额: *income/property/sales tax* 所得[物业/营业]税 ○ *value-added tax* 增值税 ○ *levy a tax on sth* 对某物征税 ○ *direct/indirect taxes* 直接[间接]税 ○ *paid over £1 000 in taxes last year* 去年交纳1 000多英镑的税 ○ [attrib 作定语] *tax evasion* 逃税. Cf 参看 DUTY 3, TARIFF 2. **2** (idm 习语) **a tax on sth** a burden or strain on sth 某物的负担或重负: *a tax on one's health, patience, strength, etc* 对健康、耐力、体力等的影响.

▷ **tax** *v* [Tn] **1** impose a tax on (sb/sth); require (sb) to pay tax 对(某人[某事物])征税; 要求(某人)纳税: *tax luxuries* 征奢侈品税 ○ *tax rich and poor alike* 对贫富一律征税 ○ *My income is taxed at source*, ie Tax is deducted from it before it is paid to me. 我的收入已先行扣除了所得税. **2** make heavy demands on (sth); strain 造成(某事物)的重负; 使超过极限: *His constant requests for help taxed our goodwill.* 他不断要求我们帮助他, 过分利用了我们对他的好意. ○ *All these questions are beginning to tax my patience.* 所有这些问题逐渐使我不胜其烦. **3** pay tax on (sth) 给(某物)纳税; 上税: *The car is taxed until July.* 这辆汽车七月前已上税. **4** (idm 习语) **tax one's/sb's brain(s)** set sb/oneself a difficult mental task 给某人[自己]安排伤脑筋的工作: *This crossword will really tax your brain.* 这纵横字谜真能让人大伤脑筋. **5** (phr v) **tax sb with sth** (*fml* 文) accuse sb of sth 指控某人某事: *She was taxed with negligence/with having been negligent.* 她被指控疏忽职守. **tax·able** *adj* that can be or is liable to be taxed 应纳税的; 可能需纳税的: *taxable earnings* 应纳税的收入. **tax·ing** *adj* tiring or demanding 累人的; 烦人的; 繁重的: *a taxing job* 烦人的工作.

taxa·tion /tækˈseɪʃn; tæksˋeʃən/ *n* [U] (system of) raising money by taxes; taxes to be paid 征税; 课税; 税制; 税款; 税金: *direct/indirect taxation*, ie on incomes/expenditure 直接[间接]税 ○ *reduce/increase taxation* 减[增]税.

□ ˌ**tax-deˈductible** *adj* (of expenses) that may be deducted from income before the amount of tax to be paid is calculated (指费用)计算所得税时可扣除的.

ˌ**tax-ˈfree** *adj* on which tax need not be paid 免税的: *a ˌtax-free ˈbonus* 免税红利.

ˈ**tax haven** country where income tax, etc is low 所得税等项税额低的国家.

ˈ**taxman** /-mæn; -mæn/ *n* (*pl* **-men** /-men; -mɛn/) **1** [C] person whose job is to collect taxes 税务员; 收税员. **2 the taxman** [sing] (*infml* 口) government department that is responsible for collecting taxes 税务部门; 税务机关: *He had been cheating the taxman for years.* 他多年来一直欺骗税务部门.

ˈ**taxpayer** *n* person who pays taxes (esp income tax) 纳税人.

ˈ**tax return** statement of personal income, etc, used for calculating the amount of tax to be paid 纳税申报表.

taxi /ˈtæksɪ; ˋtæksɪ/ (also ˈ**taxi-cab**, *esp US* **cab**) *n* car that may be hired for journeys, esp one with a meter that records the fare to be paid 计程车; 出租汽车: *call/hail/hire/take a taxi* 叫[招呼/雇/坐]计程车.

▷ **taxi** *v* [I, Ipr, Ip] (of an aircraft) move along on the ground or on water under its own power, esp before or after flying (指飞机)在地面或水面滑行(尤指起飞前或降落后): *The plane taxied/was taxiing along the runway.* 飞机在跑道上滑行.

□ ˈ**taxi rank** (also ˈ**taxi stand**, *US* ˈ**cabstand**) place where taxis park while waiting to be hired 计程车站.

taxi·dermy /ˈtæksɪdɜ:mɪ; ˋtæksəˌdɝmɪ/ *n* [U] art of preparing and stuffing the skins of dead animals, birds and fish so that they look like living ones (动物标本)剥制术.

▷ **taxi·derm·ist** /-ɪst; -ɪst/ *n* person who practises taxidermy 剥制动物标本的人; 标本剥制家.

tax·onomy /tækˈsɒnəmɪ; tæksˋɑnəmɪ/ *n* (**a**) [U] scientific process of classifying living things 生物分类学. (**b**) [C] instance of this 生物分类. ▷ **taxo·nom·ical** /ˌtæksəˈnɒmɪkl; ˌtæksəˋnɑmɪkəl/ *adj*. **taxo·nom·ically** /-klɪ; -klɪ/ *adv*. **tax·on·om·ist** /tækˈsɒnəmɪst; tæksˋɑnəmɪst/ *n*.

TB /ˌti: ˈbi:; ˌti ˋbi/ *abbr* 缩写 = tuberculosis: *be vaccinated against TB* 接受抗结核病预防接种.

tbsp (*pl* **tbsps**) *abbr* 缩写 = tablespoonful: *Add 3 tbsps salt.* 加3餐匙盐.

tea /ti:; ti/ *n* **1** [U] (dried leaves of an) evergreen shrub grown in China, India, etc 茶叶; 茶树: *a pound of tea* 一磅茶叶. **2** (**a**) [U] drink make by pouring boiling water on these leaves 茶: *a cup/mug/pot of tea* 一杯[茶缸子/壶]茶 ○ *China, lemon, iced tea* 中国茶、柠檬茶、加冰的茶 ○ *Shall I make (the) tea?* 我沏点儿茶好吗? (**b**) [C] cup of this 一杯茶: *Two teas, please.* 劳驾, 要两杯茶. **3** [U] drink made by pouring boiling water on the leaves of other plants 代茶(用其他植物的叶子沏的饮料): *camomile, mint, herb tea* 菊花、薄荷、药草茶. **4** [C, U] (light meal served at an) occasion when tea is drunk, esp in the late afternoon 茶(点); (尤指)下午茶点: *The waitress has served twenty teas since 4 o'clock.* 这女服务

员从4点钟开始已供应了20份茶点. ○ *We usually have tea at half-past four.* 我们一般在四点半喝下午茶. ○ *When is tea?* 什么时候有茶点? ⇨Usage at DINNER 用法见DINNER. **5** (idm 习语) **sb's cup of tea** ⇨ CUP[1]. **not for all the tea in 'China** no matter how great the reward 无论报酬多高; 无论得到多大好处: *I wouldn't marry him for all the tea in China.* 有天大好处我也不嫁给他.

□ **'tea-bag** *n* small paper bag holding enough tea for one person (供一人饮用的)袋茶.

'tea-break *n* (*Brit*) (in an office, a factory, etc) short period of time when work is stopped and tea, etc may be taken (办公室、工厂等处的)喝茶时间, 工间休息时间.

'tea-caddy (also **caddy**) *n* box in which tea is kept for daily use 茶叶盒; 茶叶罐.

'teacake *n* (*Brit*) small flat cake, usu eaten hot with butter at tea 茶点饼(扁平的小饼, 通常在饮茶时加黄油热食): *toasted teacakes* 再烤的茶点饼.

'tea-chest *n* light wooden box lined with metal, in which tea is exported 茶箱(装茶叶出口的大木箱).

'tea-cloth *n* **1** cloth for a tea-table or tea-tray 茶几布; 茶盘布. **2** (*Brit*) = TEA-TOWEL.

'tea-cosy *n* cover placed over a teapot to keep the tea inside it warm 茶壶保温套; 茶壶暖罩.

'teacup *n* **1** cup in which tea is served 茶杯. **2** (idm 习语) **a storm in a teacup** ⇨ STORM.

'tea-leaf *n* (*pl* **-leaves**) leaf of tea, esp after tea has been made (泡过的)陈茶叶, 茶叶渣: *throw away the old tea-leaves* 倒掉陈茶叶 ○ *tell sb's fortune from the tea-leaves in his cup* 藉察看某人杯中的陈茶叶为其占卜.

'tea-party *n* social occasion at which tea is served, esp in the late afternoon 茶会(尤指午后的).

'teapot *n* **1** container with a spout, in which tea is made and from which it is poured into cups, etc 茶壶. ⇨illus at POT 见POT插图. **2** (idm 习语) **a tempest in a teapot** ⇨ TEMPEST.

'tea-room (also **'tea-shop**) *n* (usu small) restaurant in which tea and light meals are served 茶馆; 茶室.

'tea-service (also **'tea-set**) *n* set of cups, plates, etc for serving tea 一套茶具.

'teaspoon *n* **1** small spoon for stirring tea, etc 茶匙. ⇨illus at SPOON 见SPOON插图. **2** amount that this can hold 茶匙的量. **'teaspoonful** /-fʊl; -fʊl/ *n* amount that a teaspoon can hold 一茶匙的量: *two teaspoonfuls of sugar* 两茶匙的糖.

'tea-strainer *n* device for holding back tea-leaves when pouring tea into a cup, etc 滤茶器.

'tea-table *n* (usu small) table at which tea is served 茶几; 茶桌: [attrib 作定语] *tea-table conversation* 茶话.

'tea-things *n* [pl] (*infml* 口) = TEA-SERVICE.

'tea-time *n* [U] time at or during which tea is taken in the afternoon 用(下午)茶点的时间.

'tea-towel *n* (also **tea-cloth**, *US* **'dish towel**) towel for drying washed crockery, cutlery, etc 擦餐具等的抹布.

'tea-tray *n* small tray suitable for carrying a tea-set, etc 茶盘.

'tea-trolley (also **'tea-wagon**) *n* small table on wheels, used for serving tea 茶具车. ⇨illus at TROLLEY 见TROLLEY插图.

'tea-urn *n* container in which water is boiled for making a large quantity of tea, eg in a café (泡大量茶用的)大茶罐. ⇨illus at URN 见URN插图.

teach /ti:tʃ; titʃ/ *v* (*pt*, *pp* **taught** /tɔ:t; tɔt/) **1** (**a**) [I, Tn, Dn·w, Dn·t] give instruction to (sb); cause (sb) to know or be able to do sth 教(某人); 使(某人)明白或会做某事: *She teaches well.* 她教得好. ○ *teach children* 教小孩儿 ○ *He taught me (how) to drive.* 他教我开汽车. (**b**) [Tn, Dn·n, Dn·pr] **~ sth (to sb/sth)** communicate (knowledge, skill, etc) 传授(知识、技能等); 教授: *teach French, history, judo, etc* 教法语、历史、柔道等 ○ *She teaches advanced students English/teaches English to advanced students.* 她教高水平的学生英语. ○ *He's taught his dog some clever tricks.* 他已经训练他的狗耍些灵巧的把戏. **2** [I, Tn] do this for a living 以教书为生: *She teaches at our local school.* 她在我们这地区的学校教书. ○ *He taught mathematics for many years.* 他教数学已很多年了. ⇨Usage 见所附用法. **3** [Tn, Tf, Dn·n, Dn·f, Dn·t] put (sth) forward as a fact or as a principle; advocate 提出(某事)作为事实或原则; 倡导; 提倡: *Christ taught forgiveness*, ie that we should forgive our enemies, etc. 基督倡导宽恕(应宽恕敌人等). ○ *He taught that the earth revolves around the sun.* 他指出地球是围绕太阳转的. ○ *My parents taught me never to tell lies.* 我父母告诫我千万不要说谎. **4** [no passive 不用于被动语态: Tn, Dn·n, Dn·t] (*infml* 口) persuade (sb) to do or not to do sth by punishment or as a result of experience 教育、教导(某人)做某事; 告诫、训诫(某人)不做某事: *So you lost all your money? That'll teach you (to gamble).* 这么说, 你把钱都输光了? 这就是(赌博)给你的教训. ○ *It taught him a lesson he never forgot.* 这给了他一个终生难忘的教训. ○ *I'll teach you to call me a liar!* ie punish you for doing so. 你说我说谎, 我就要教训你! **5** (idm 习语) **know/learn/teach sb the ropes** ⇨ ROPE. **teach one's grandmother to suck 'eggs** tell or show sb how to do sth that he can already do perfectly well, and probably better than oneself 教比自己强的人做某事. **(you can't) teach an old dog new 'tricks** (*saying* 谚) (one can't) successfully get old people who are set in their ways to change their ideas, methods of work, etc (无法)改变老人的想法、做法等. **teach 'school** (*US*) be a schoolteacher 当老师; 任教师.

▷ **teach·able** *adj* **1** (of a subject) that can be taught (指学科)可教的. **2** (of a person) able to learn by being taught (指人)能学习的, 可教育的.

teacher *n* person who teaches, esp in a school 教师(尤指中小学的): *my English teacher* 我的英语老师.

teach·ing *n* **1** [U] work of a teacher; instruction 教师的工作; 教学工作; 教授; 教导; 指导: *Teaching is a demanding profession.* 教学工作是个要求很高的工作. **2** [U, C often *pl* 作不可数名词或可数名词, 后者常作复数] that which is taught; doctrine 所教的东西; 教义; 主义: *the teaching(s) of the Church* 教会的教义.

□ **'teach-in** *n* (*dated infml* 旧, 口) lecture and discussion, or a series of these, on a subject of topical interest 研讨会.

NOTE ON USAGE 用法: **1 Educate** refers to the overall development of (especially children's) knowledge and intellect, usually through the formal **education** system of schools and universities ☆ **educate** 指对(尤指儿童的)知识和智力进行全面的培养, 通常是由学校进行系统的正规教育: *He was educated at the local comprehensive school.* 他曾在地区的综合中学受教育. ○ *The country needs an educated population.* 该国需要受过教育的国民. **2 Teach** has the widest use in formal and informal situations and at all levels. ☆ **teach** 一词使用范围最广, 可用于庄重的和一般的场合, 可用于各种教育程度. It can refer to an academic subject or a practical skill 这一词既可指某一学科也可指某种技能: *She teaches history at a secondary school/to undergraduates.* 她在中学教历史[教大学生历史课]. ○ *My father taught me how to swim.* 我父亲教过我游泳. **3 Coach** is used of non-formal teaching, either of an academic subject (especially for an examination) or of a sport ☆ **coach** 一词表示非正规的教导, 既可指对某一学科(尤指为考试)进行辅导, 也可指对体育运动的指导: *I'm coaching their children in A level maths in the evenings.* 我晚上辅导他们的孩子准备数学的高级考试. ○ *She coaches the tennis team at the weekend.* 她在周末指导网球队. **4 Train** means producing a desired result in behaviour, standard of skill or physical ability. ☆ **train** 的意思是使在行为、技能或体能上达到要求. It is sometimes contrasted with **educate**. 这一词与 **educate** 相比有时有差别. It can be used of people or animals 它可用以指人或动物: *It's hard to train children to behave well at the table.* 培养儿童用餐时举止得体是很困难的. ○ *He's training the horse for the Grand National.* 他为参加英国大赛马而训练那匹马. ○ *The swimming team's in training for the Olympics.* 该游泳队正在为参加奥林匹克运动会而进行训练. **5 Instruct** means giving practical information or knowledge, especially to groups of trainees (eg soldiers or nurses) ☆ **instruct** 指传授实践知识, 特别是针对集体受训者(如士兵或护士): *She instructed the trainee nurses in giving injections.* 她指导实习护士练习注射.

teak /ti:k; tik/ *n* (**a**) [U] strong hard wood of a tall evergreen Asian tree, used for making furniture, in shipbuilding, etc 柚木(用以制造家具、船等). **(b)** [C] this tree 柚木(树).

teal /ti:l; til/ *n* (*pl* unchanged 复数不变) small wild duck living near rivers or lakes 水鸭(栖于河湖附近的小野鸭).

team /ti:m; tim/ *n* [CGp] **1** group of players forming one side in certain games and sports (某些游戏及运动的)队: *Which team do you play for?* 你在哪个队效力? ○ *Leeds was/were the better team.* 利兹队是个好队. **2** group of people working together 在一起工作的人; 队; 组: *a sales team* 推销小组 ○ [attrib 作定语] *He's a good team worker*, ie He works well with others. 他是个好搭档. **3** two or more animals pulling a cart, plough, etc together (一起拉车、犁等的)牲畜.

▷ **team** *v* [Ipr, Ip] **~ up (with sb)** work together (with sb), esp for a common purpose (与某人)一起工作(尤指为一共同目标); 合作: *The two companies have teamed up to develop a new racing car.* 那两个公司已合作研制新型赛车.

team·ster /ˈti:mstə(r); ˈtimstɚ/ *n* (*US*) lorry driver 卡车司机.

□ ˌ**team ˈspirit** (*approv* 褒) willingness to act for the good of one's team rather than one's individual advantage, etc 集体精神.

ˈ**team-work** *n* [U] organized co-operation; combined effort 有组织的合作; 协力工作: *The success of the project was largely the result of good team-work.* 这一项目能获得成功主要是大家通力合作的结果.

tear[1] /tɪə(r); tɪr/ *n* **1** [C usu *pl* 通常作复数] drop of salty water coming from the eye, esp as the result of grief, irritation by fumes, etc 泪; 泪水; 泪珠: *A tear rolled down his cheek.* 一滴泪珠沿着他的面颊流下来. ○ *a tear-stained face* 带着泪痕的脸 ○ *Her eyes filled with tears.* 她眼泪汪汪的. ○ *a story that moved/reduced us to tears*, ie made us cry 使我们感动得落泪的故事 ○ *shed/weep bitter tears* 流出痛苦的泪水 ○ *He burst into tears*, ie began to cry. 他哭了起来. ○ *The memory of his dead mother brought tears to his eyes.* 他忆起去世的母亲便热泪盈眶. **2** (idm 习语) **bore sb to death/tears** ⇨ BORE. **crocodile tears** ⇨ CROCODILE. **in ˈtears** crying 哭泣: *She was in tears over the death of her puppy.* 她因小狗死去而哭泣.

T

▷ **tear·ful** /-fl; fl/ *adj* crying or ready to cry 哭泣的; 要哭的: *her tearful face* 她那挂着泪珠的脸 ○ *a crowd of tearful mourners* 一群哭泣着的送葬者. **tear·fully** /-fəlɪ; -flɪ/ *adv*.

□ ˈ**tear-drop** *n* single tear 泪珠.

ˈ**tear-gas** *n* [U] gas that causes severe irritation and watering of the eyes, used to disperse crowds, etc 催泪瓦斯.

ˈ**tear-jerker** *n* (*infml sometimes derog* 口, 有时作贬义) story, film, etc designed to make people cry in sympathy, etc 催人泪下的故事、电影等.

tear[2] /teə(r); tɛr/ *v* (*pt* **tore** /tɔ:(r); tɔr/, *pp* **torn** /tɔ:n; tɔrn/) **1 (a)** [Tn, Tn·pr, Tn·p, Cn·a] pull (sth) forcibly apart or away or to pieces 将(某物)撕开、扯下或撕碎: *tear a sheet of paper in two* 把一张纸撕成两半 ○ *a torn handkerchief* 撕破的手帕 ○ *He tore his shirt on a nail.* 他的衬衣让钉子挂破了. ○ *tear a parcel open* 把包裹撕开. **(b)** [Tn·pr] **~ sth (in sth)** make (a hole or split) in sth in this way (在某物上)撕, 扯, 划, 刺(洞或裂口): *The explosion tore a hole in the wall.* 墙炸开一个洞. **2 (a)** [Tn, Tn·pr, Tn·p] cause (sth) to be out of place by pulling sharply 撕下, 撕掉, 扯下, 扯掉(某物): *tear a page out of a book, a notice down from a wall, the leaves off a tree* 撕下一页书、从墙上撕下布告、从树上揪下树叶. **(b)** [Tn·pr] **~ sb from sb/sth** remove sb from sb/sth by force 强行使某人离开某人[某物]; 夺去; 揪走: *The child was torn from its mother's arms.* 把孩子从母亲怀抱中夺走了. ⇨Usage at CUT[1] 用法见CUT[1]. **3** [I] become torn 撕碎; 撕裂; 撕破: *This cloth tears easily.* 这布料容易撕破. ○ *Don't pull the pages so hard or they will tear.* 别那么使劲扯书页, 那会撕破的. **4** [Tn, Tn·pr esp passive 尤用于被动语态] destroy the peace of (sth) 破坏(某物)的安宁; 扰乱: *a country torn by war* 战乱不安的国家 ○ *Her heart was torn by grief.* 她肝肠寸断. **5** [Ipr, Ip] move (in the specified direction) very quickly or excitedly 飞跑; 飞奔; 冲(向某方向): *cars tearing past* 飞驶而过的汽车 ○ *She tore downstairs and out of the house shouting 'Fire!'* 她奔下楼梯, 冲出房门高喊'着火了!' **6** (idm 习语) **tear sth aˈpart, to ˈshreds, to ˈbits, etc** destroy or defeat sth completely; criticize sth harshly 彻底毁灭或击败某事物; 严厉地批评某事物: *tore his hopes to shreds* 使他的希望彻底破灭 ○ *The critics tore her new play to pieces.* 剧评家们将她的新戏批评得一无是处. **tear one's ˈhair (out)** (*infml* 口) show great sorrow, anger, etc 表示极大的悲伤、愤怒等: *My boss is tearing his hair out about the delay in the schedule.* 我们老板因进度拖延而气得七窍生烟. **(be in) a tearing ˈhurry, ˈrush, etc** (show) extreme or violent haste (显得)匆忙, 慌忙: *There's no need to be in such a tearing hurry — we've got plenty of time.* 用不着这样匆忙 —— 我们有的是时间. **tear sb ˌlimb from ˈlimb** (*often joc* 常作戏谑语) attack sb very violently 猛击某人. **tear sb ˈoff a strip**; **tear a ˈstrip off sb** (*infml* 口) scold sb severely 痛骂某人. ˌ**that's ˈtorn it** (*infml* 口) that has spoilt our plans 那打乱了我们的计划; 那就糟了. **wear and tear** ⇨ WEAR[1]. **7** (phr v) **tear at sth (with sth)** attack sth violently, esp by cutting or ripping 撕扯或撕开某物: *tore at the meat with his bare hands* 用他的手撕肉. **tear oneself away (from sb/sth)** leave sb/sth reluctantly 舍不得离开某人[某事物]: *Do tear yourself away from the television and come out for a walk.* 你别舍不得离开电视了, 出去散散步吧. **be torn between A and B** have to make a painful choice between two things or people (在两个事物或人之间)作痛苦的抉择: *torn between love and duty* 在爱情和职责间作痛苦的抉择. **tear sth down** bring sth to the ground by pulling sharply; demolish sth 弄倒某物; 拆除某物: *They're tearing down these old houses to build a new office block.* 他们正拆除这些旧房子以便建一座新办公楼. **tear into sb/sth** attack sb/sth physically or with words 攻击或抨击某人[某事物]. **tear sth up** destroy (a document, etc) by tearing 撕毁(文件等): *She tore up all the letters he had sent her.* 她把他写来的信都撕了. ○ (*fig* 比喻) *He accused the government of tearing up* (ie repudiating) *the negotiated agreement.* 他控告政府撕毁(不履行)协议.

▷ **tear** *n* hole or split caused by tearing (撕破的)洞或裂缝: *This fabric has a tear in it.* 这织物上有个破洞.

□ ˈ**tearaway** /ˈteərəweɪ; ˈtɛrə,we/ *n* (*infml* 口) impetuous and irresponsible person 鲁莽而不可靠的人: *Her son's a bit of a tearaway.* 她儿子有些莽撞.

tease /ti:z; tiz/ *v* **1** [I, Tn, Tn·pr] make fun of (sb) in a playful or unkind way; try to provoke (sb) with questions or petty annoyances 取笑, 嘲弄(某人); 逗弄, 招惹(某人): *Don't take what she said seriously — she was only teasing.* 别拿她的话当真 —— 她不过是逗弄人. ○ *The other boys used to tease him because of/about his accent.* 别的男孩子常拿他的口音取笑他. ○ *Stop teasing the cat*, eg by pulling its tail. 别逗猫(如揪猫尾巴). **2** [Tn] **(a)** pick (wool) into separate strands 梳理(羊毛等). **(b)** brush up the surface of (cloth) to make it fluffy 使(布)的表面起毛. **3** [Tn] (*esp US*) = BACKCOMB (BACK[3]).

▷ **tease** *n* person who is fond of teasing others 爱嘲弄他人的人: *What a tease she is!* 她可真爱取笑别人!

teaser *n* (*infml* 口) problem that is difficult to solve 难以解决的问题: *This one's a real teaser.* 这可真是个难题.

teas·ingly *adv* in a teasing manner; in order to tease 嘲笑地; 嘲弄地.

tea·sel (also **tea·zel, tea·zle**) /ˈti:zl; ˈtizl̩/ *n* plant with prickly flowers formerly used (when dried) for teasing cloth, etc 川续断(旧时用以使布等表面起毛的植物).

teat /ti:t; tit/ *n* **1** animal's nipple (动物的)乳头, 奶头. ⇨illus at cow 见cow插图. **2** (also **nipple**) rubber mouthpiece on a child's feeding-bottle, through which the contents are sucked 橡胶奶嘴.

tech /tek; tɛk/ *n* (usu *sing* 通常作单数) (*infml* 口) technical college or school 技术学院或学校: *doing an engineering course at the local tech* 在地区技术学校学工程学.

tech·nical /ˈteknɪkl; ˈtɛknɪkl̩/ *adj* **1** [usu attrib 通常作定语] of or involving the mechanical arts and applied sciences 技术的; 应用科学的: *a technical school* 技术学校 ○ *a technical education* 技术教育. **2** [usu attrib 通常作定语] of a particular subject, art or craft, or its techniques 专科的; 艺术的; 工艺的; 技艺的; 技巧的: *the technical terms of chemistry* 化学专业术语 ○ *the technical* *difficulties of colour printing* 彩色印刷的技术难题 ○ *a musician with great technical skill but not much feeling* 技巧娴熟但缺少情感的音乐家. **3** (of a book, etc) requiring specialized knowledge; using technical terms (指书等)要求有专门知识的, 使用术语的, 专业的: *The article is rather technical in places.* 这篇论文中有些地方相当专业化. **4** [attrib 作定语] in a strict legal sense 严格按法律意义的: *technical assault* 法律上成立的人身攻击.

▷ **tech·nic·al·ity** /ˌteknɪˈkæləti; ˌtɛknɪˋkælətɪ/ *n* **1** technical term or point 术语; 专业上的细节: *The book is full of scientific technicalities.* 这本书里尽是科学术语. ○ *The lawyer explained the legal technicalities to his client.* 律师给委托人解释法律上的要点. **2** detail of no real importance 不重要的细节: *a mere technicality* 无足轻重的细节.

tech·nic·ally /-klɪ; -klɪ/ *adv* **1** with reference to the technique displayed 技术上; 技巧上; 专门地: *Technically the building is a masterpiece, but few people like it.* 就技术而言那座建筑物是杰作, 但却没人喜欢. **2** according to a precise interpretation of the laws, meaning of words, etc; strictly 准确地按照法律、词义等的解释; 严格地: *Although technically (speaking) you may not have lied, you certainly haven't told us the whole truth.* 尽管严格来说你没算撒谎, 但肯定你并没把实情都告诉我们.

□ ˈ**technical college** (*Brit*) college offering students further education in technical and other subjects after they have left school 技术学院.

ˌ**technical** ˈ**hitch** breakdown caused by a mechanical fault 技术故障.

tech·ni·cian /tekˈnɪʃn; tɛkˋnɪʃən/ *n* **1** expert in the techniques of a particular subject, art or craft 技术员; 技师; 工艺师. **2** skilled mechanic 巧匠.

Tech·ni·color /ˈteknɪkʌlə(r); ˋtɛknɪˌkʌlɚ/ *n* [U] **1** (*propr* 专利名) process of colour photography used for cinema films (电影片的)彩色印片法. **2** (also **technicolour**) (*infml* 口) vivid or artificially brilliant colour 鲜明的色彩; 人工的鲜艳色彩: [attrib 作定语] *The fashion show was a technicolour extravaganza.* 那时装表演是艳丽色彩的大汇展.

tech·nique /tekˈni:k; tɛkˋnik/ *n* (**a**) [C] method of doing or performing sth, esp in the arts or sciences 技术; 方法; 手段; (尤指艺术或科学方面的)技法, 手法, 技巧: *applying modern techniques to a traditional craft* 将现代技术用于传统手工业. (**b**) [U] skill in this 技能: *displayed (a) flawless technique* 显示出精湛的技艺.

techno- *comb form* 构词成分 of the applied sciences 技术的; 工艺的; 技巧的: *technology* ○ *technocrat*.

tech·no·cracy /tekˈnɒkrəsɪ; tɛkˋnɑkrəsɪ/ *n* (**a**) [U] control or management of a country's industrial resources by technical experts 专家政治(由技术专家对国家工业资源的治理). (**b**) [C] country where this occurs 实行专家政治的国家: *Is Britain becoming a technocracy?* 英国是否要成为实行专家政治的国家?

▷ **tech·no·crat** /ˈteknəkræt; ˋtɛknəˌkræt/ *n* expert in science, engineering, etc, esp one who favours technocracy 技术专家; (尤指)专家政治论者. **tech·no·cratic** /ˌteknəˈkrætɪk; ˌtɛknəˋkrætɪk/ *adj*.

tech·no·logy /tekˈnɒlədʒɪ; tɛkˋnɑlədʒɪ/ *n* [U] **1** scientific study and use of mechanical arts and applied sciences, eg engineering 科技; 工艺及应用科学(如工程技术); 工艺学; 工程学. **2** application of this to practical tasks in industry, etc (工业等方面的)技术应用: *recent advances in medical technology* 医疗技术的新进展 ○ *the technology of computers* 计算机的工业技术.

▷ **tech·no·lo·gical** /ˌteknəˈlɒdʒɪkl; ˌtɛknəˋlɑdʒɪkl/ *adj*: *a major technological breakthrough* 主要的技术性突破 ○ *technological changes, problems* 技术上的改变、问题. **tech·no·lo·gic·ally** /-klɪ; -klɪ/ *adv*: *technologically advanced* 技术上先进的.

tech·no·lo·gist /tekˈnɒlədʒɪst; tɛkˋnɑlədʒɪst/ *n* expert in technology 技术、工艺、工程等的专家.

teddy bear /ˈtedɪ beə(r); ˋtɛdɪ ˌbɛr/ soft furry toy bear (软毛)玩具熊.

Teddy boy /ˈtedɪ bɔɪ; ˋtɛdɪ ˌbɔɪ/ (also **ted** /ted; tɛd/) *n* (*Brit infml* 口) (in the 1950's) young man who expressed rebellion by wearing clothes similar to those of the Edwardian period (1901-10), and sometimes behaved violently (五十年代的)不良少年(穿着类似爱德华时代——1901-1910——的服装, 行为有时粗野以示叛逆).

te·di·ous /ˈti:dɪəs; ˋtidɪəs/ *adj* tiresome because of being too long, slow or dull; boring (因过长、过慢或单调)令人厌倦的; 烦人的: *The work is tedious.* 这工作令人厌倦. ○ *We had to sit through several tedious speeches.* 我们只得坐在那里听着几个乏味的讲演. ▷ **te·di·ously** *adv*: *tediously long* 冗长得令人厌烦. **te·di·ous·ness** *n* [U].

te·dium /ˈti:dɪəm; ˋtidɪəm/ *n* [U] tediousness; boredom 厌倦; 厌烦; 乏味: *two hours of unrelieved tedium* 烦闷难解的两小时.

tee /ti:; ti/ *n* **1** (**a**) (in golf) flat area from which a player strikes the ball when beginning to play each hole (高尔夫球运动的)开球处. (**b**) small spiked stand of wood, plastic, etc on which a player places his golf ball before striking it at the start of each hole 球座(高尔夫球运动中发球时放置球的小台). **2** mark aimed at in certain games, eg quoits, bowls, curling (掷环、滚木球、冰上溜石游戏的)目标. **3** (idm 习语) **to a T/tee** ⇨ T.

▷ **tee** *v* (*pt, pp* **teed**) **1** [Tn] place (a golf ball) on a tee 将(高尔夫球)置于球座上. **2** (phr v) **tee off** play the ball from the tee 自球座击球. **tee sb off** (*US sl* 俚) make sb angry or annoyed 使某人生气或烦恼. **tee (sth) up** prepare to play (a golf ball) by placing it on a tee (将高尔夫球置于球座上)准备击球.

teem[1] /ti:m; tim/ *v* **1** [Ipr] **~ with sth** have sth in great numbers 有很多、大量的某事物: *The river was teeming with fish.* 河里的鱼很多. ○ (*fig* 比喻) *His mind is teeming with bright ideas.* 他心里有很多好主意. **2** [I] be present in great numbers 大量出现; 有很多: *Fish teem in these waters.* 这些湖里有很多鱼.

teem[2] /ti:m; tim/ *v* [I, Ipr, Ip] **~ (with sth)/(down)** (esp in the continuous tenses 尤用于进行时态) (of water, rain, etc) fall heavily; pour (指水、雨等)暴降, 倾注: *a teeming wet day* 大雨倾盆的日子 ○ *It was teeming with rain.* 天降暴雨. ○ *The rain was teeming down.* 大雨滂沱.

teens /ti:nz; tinz/ *n* [pl] years of a person's age from 13 to 19 13至19岁的年龄; 十几岁: *be in one's teens* 十几岁 ○ *She is not yet out of her teens*, ie is under 20. 她还不到20岁.

□ **teen·age** /ˈti:neɪdʒ; ˋtiˌnedʒ/ *adj* [attrib 作定语] of or for teenagers 青少年的: *teenage fashions, problems, children* 青少年的风尚、青少年的问题、少年儿童. **teen·aged** *adj* in one's teens 十几岁的. **teen·ager** /ˈti:neɪdʒə(r); ˋtinˌedʒɚ/ (also *infml esp US* **teen** /ti:n; tin/ 口语作 **teen**, 尤用于美式英语) *n* person in his or her teens 少年男女; 青少年: *a club for teenagers* 青少年俱乐部.

teeny /ˈti:nɪ; ˋtinɪ/ (also **teeny-weeny** /ˌti:nɪ ˈwi:nɪ; ˌtinɪ ˋwinɪ/, **teensy** /ti:nzɪ; ˋtinzɪ/, **teensy-weensy** /ˌti:nzɪ ˈwi:nzɪ; ˌtinzɪ ˋwinzɪ/) *adj* (**-ier, -iest**) (*infml* 口) tiny 极小的.

teeny-bopper /ˈti:nɪ bɒpə(r); ˋtinɪˌbɑpɚ/ *n* (*infml usu derog* 口, 通常作贬义) young teenager, esp a girl, who eagerly follows current fashions in clothes, pop music, etc 时髦青少年(尤指追求时髦衣服、流行音乐等的少女).

tee-shirt = T-SHIRT (T).

tee·ter /ˈti:tə(r); ˋtitɚ/ *v* [I, Ipr, Ip] stand or move unsteadily 摇晃地站立或移动: *The drunken man teetered on the edge of the pavement.* 那醉汉在人行道边上东倒西歪的. ○ *She was teetering along/about/around in very high-heeled shoes.* 她穿着高跟鞋摇摇晃晃地走着[四处走]. ○ (*fig* 比喻) *teetering on the brink/edge of disaster* 在灾难边缘摇摇欲坠.

teeth *pl* of TOOTH.

teethe /ti:ð; tið/ *v* [I] (usu in the continuous tenses, or as a gerund or present participle 通常用于进行时态或用作动名词或现在分词) (of a baby) have its first teeth starting to grow through the gums (指幼儿)长牙, 出牙: *Babies like to chew something when they're teething.* 幼儿长牙时爱咬东西.

□ ˈ**teething troubles** (*fig* 比喻) minor problems occurring in the early stages of an enterprise 创业初期遇到的小问题.

tee·to·tal /ti:ˈtəʊtl; *US* ˈti:təʊtl; tiˋtotl/ *adj* (in favour of) never drinking alcoholic drinks (赞成)不饮酒的, 滴酒不沾的.

▷ **tee·to·tal·ism** *n* [U].

tee·to·tal·ler (*US* also **tee·to·taler**) /-tlə(r); -tlɚ/ *n* person who is teetotal 不饮酒者; 滴酒不沾者.

TEFL /ˌtiː iː ef ˈel *or, in informal use,* 俗读作 ˈtefl; ˌti i ɛf ˈɛl, ˋtɛfl/ *abbr* 缩写 = Teaching English as a Foreign Language 作为外语的英语教学. Cf 参看 TESL.

tel *abbr* 缩写 = **1** telegraph(ic). **2** telephone (number): *tel 0865-56767* 电话 0865-56767.

tel(e)- *comb form* 构词成分 **1** over a long distance; far 远距离的; 远的: *telepathy* ○ *telescopic*. **2** of television 电视的: *teleprompter* ○ *teletext*.

tele·com·mu·ni·ca·tions /ˌtelɪkəˌmjuːnɪˈkeɪʃnz; ˌtɛləkəˌmjunəˋkeʃənz/ *n* [pl] communications by satellite, cable, telegraph, telephone, radio or TV 电信.

tele·gram /ˈtelɪgræm; ˋtɛləˌgræm/ *n* message sent by telegraph and then delivered in written or printed form 电报: *send/receive a telegram (of congratulations, condolence, etc)* 发[收](祝贺、吊唁等)电报. Cf 参看 CABLE 4.

tele·graph /ˈtelɪgrɑːf; *US* -græf; ˋtɛləˌgræf/ *n* (**a**) [U] means of sending messages by the use of electric current along wires 打电报. (**b**) [C] apparatus for doing this 电报机.

▷ **tele·graph** *v* (**a**) [I, Ipr, Tn, Tn·pr] send (a message) by telegraph 打电报传达(消息); 电告. (**b**) [Dn·t] send instructions to (sb) by telegraph 打电报向(某人)发指令、命令; 电令.

tele·graph·ese /ˌtelɪgrəˈfiːz; ˌtɛləgræˋfiz/ *n* [U] shortened style of language used in telegrams, leaving out all unnecessary words 电报文体(省略非必要字句者).

tele·graphic /ˌtelɪˈgræfɪk; ˌtɛləˋgræfɪk/ *adj* suitable for or sent by telegraphy 适于打电报的; 打电报发送的. **tele·graph·ic·ally** /-klɪ; -klɪ/ *adv*. **telegraphic adˈdress** shortened or registered address for use in telegrams 用于电报的简略地址.

tele·graph·ist /tɪˈlegrəfɪst; təˋlɛgrəfɪst/ (also **tele·grapher** /tɪˈlegrəfə(r); təˋlɛgrəfɚ/) *n* person whose job is to send and receive messages by telegraph 电报员; 报务员.

tele·graphy /tɪˈlegrəfɪ; təˋlɛgrəfɪ/ *n* [U] process of communication by telegraph 电报通讯术: *wireless telegraphy* 无线电报通讯.

□ ˈ**telegraph-line** (also **-wire**) *n* wire along which telegraph or telephone messages travel 电报或电话线路.

ˈ**telegraph-pole** (also **-post**) *n* pole supporting telegraph-lines (电报线路的)电线杆.

tele·metry /tɪˈlemətrɪ; təˋlɛmətrɪ/ *n* [U] process of automatically recording the readings of an instrument and transmitting them over a distance, usu by radio (无线电)遥测术.

tele·ology /ˌtelɪˈɒlədʒɪ, ˌtiːlɪ-; ˌtɛlɪˋɑlədʒɪ, ˌtilɪ-/ *n* [U] theory that events and developments are meant to fulfil a purpose and happen because of that 目的论(认为事情的发生和发展都是为达到某目的).

▷ **tele·olo·gical** /ˌtelɪəˈlɒdʒɪkl, ˌtiːlɪə-; ˌtɛlɪəˋlɑdʒɪkl, ˌtilɪə-/ *adj*.

tele·olo·gist /ˌtelɪˈɒlədʒɪst, ˌtiːlɪ-; ˌtɛlɪˋɑlədʒɪst, ˌtilɪ-/ *n* person who believes in teleology 目的论者.

tele·pathy /tɪˈlepəθɪ; təˋlɛpəθɪ/ *n* [U] **1** communication of thoughts or ideas from one mind to another without the normal use of the senses 传心术; 心灵感应. **2** (*infml* 口) ability to be aware of the thoughts and feelings of others 解心能力(对旁人的思想及感情的理解能力).

▷ **tele·path** /ˈtelɪpæθ; ˋtɛləˌpæθ/ *n* telepathic person 用传心术的人; 有解心能力的人; 能理解他人思想感情的人.

tele·pathic /ˌtelɪˈpæθɪk; ˌtɛləˋpæθɪk/ *adj* (**a**) of or using telepathy 用传心术的; 心灵感应的. (**b**) (of a person) able to communicate by telepathy (指人)会传心术的, 有心灵感应的: *How did you know what I was thinking? You must be telepathic.* 我心里想的事情你是怎么知道的? 你准是有心灵感应. **tele·path·ic·ally** /-klɪ; -klɪ/ *adv*.

tele·phone /ˈtelɪfəʊn; ˋtɛləˌfon/ (also **phone**) *n* **1** [U] system of transmitting the human voice to a distance by wire or radio 电话: *You can always reach* (ie contact) *me by telephone.* 你打电话随时都能找到我. **2** [C] instrument used for this, with a receiver and mouthpiece 电话机: *answer the telephone*, ie pick up the receiver to receive an incoming call 接电话. **3** (idm 习语) **on the ˈtelephone** (**a**) connected to the telephone system 接上电话; 接通电话: *They've just moved and they're not on the telephone yet.* 他们刚搬的家, 还没接通电话. (**b**) using the telephone 在打电话: *She's on the telephone at the moment.* 她正在打电话. ○ *You're wanted* (ie Somebody wants to speak to you) *on the telephone.* 你的电话(有人打电话找你).

▷ **tele·phone** (also **phone**) *v* [I, Tn, Tn·pr] send (a message) or speak to (sb) by telephone 以电话传送(消息); 给(某人)打电话: *Will you write or telephone?* 你写信还是打电话? ○ *We must telephone our congratulations (to the happy couple).* 我们得(给那对幸福的夫妇)打个电话表示祝贺. ○ *He telephoned (his wife) to say he'd be late.* 他(给妻子)打电话说他要晚到.

tele·phonic /ˌtelɪˈfɒnɪk; ˌtɛləˋfɑnɪk/ *adj*.

tele·phon·ist /tɪˈlefənɪst; təˋlɛfənɪst/ *n* = TELEPHONE OPERATOR.

tele·phony /tɪˈlefənɪ; təˋlɛfənɪ/ *n* [U] process of transmitting sound by telephone 电话通讯; 电话技术.

□ ˈ**telephone box** (also ˈ**phone box**, ˈ**telephone booth**, ˈ**phone booth**, ˈ**call-box**) small covered or enclosed structure containing a telephone for use by the public 公用电话亭.

ˈ**telephone directory** (also ˈ**telephone book**, ˈ**phone book**) book listing the names, addresses and telephone numbers of people in a particular area who have a telephone 电话号码簿; 电话簿.

ˈ**telephone exchange** (also **exchange**) place where telephone connections are made 电话局; 电话交换台; 总机.

ˈ**telephone number** (also ˈ**phone number**) number assigned to a particular telephone and used in dialling a call to it 电话号码. ⇨App 4 见附录 4.

ˈ**telephone operator** person whose job is to connect calls in a telephone exchange 话务员; 接线员.

tele·photo /ˌtelɪˈfəʊtəʊ; ˌtɛləˋfoto/ *adj* = TELEPHOTOGRAPHIC.

□ ˌ**telephoto** ˈ**lens** lens that produces a large image of a distant object that is being photographed 摄远镜头.

tele·pho·to·graphy /ˌtelɪfəˈtɒgrəfɪ; ˌtɛləfoˋtɑgrəfɪ/ *n* [U] process of photographing distant objects using a telephoto lens 摄远摄影术.

▷ **tele·pho·to·graphic** /ˌtelɪfəʊtəˈgræfɪk; ˌtɛləˌfotəˋgræfɪk/ *adj* of or for or using telephotography 摄远摄影术的; 为或用摄远摄影术的.

tele·printer /ˈtelɪprɪntə(r); ˋtɛləˌprɪntɚ/ (*US* **tele·type·writer**) *n* device for automatically typing and sending messages by telegraph, and for receiving and typing messages similarly 电传打印机.

tele·prompter /ˈtelɪprɒmptə(r); ˋtɛləˌprɑmptɚ/ *n* device by which a speaker on television can read the text of his script from a screen in front of him that cannot be seen by his audience 讲词提示器(将电视播音者的讲稿显示其面前的屏幕上之装置). Cf 参看 AUTOCUE.

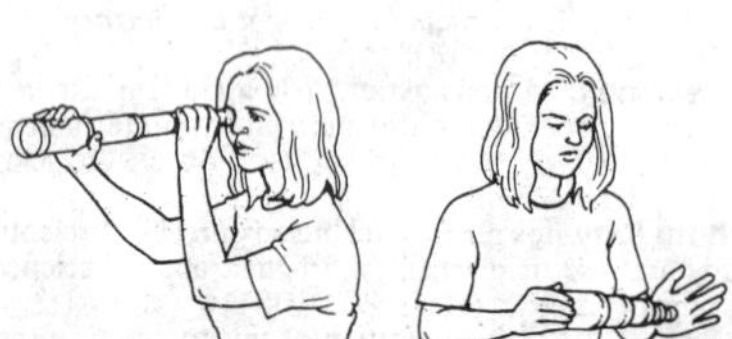

telescope 望远镜

tele·scope /ˈtelɪskəʊp; ˋtɛləˌskop/ *n* optical instrument shaped like a tube, with lenses to make distant objects appear larger and nearer 望远镜.

▷ **tele·scope** *v* **1** [I, Tn] (cause sth to) become shorter by sliding overlapping sections inside one another (使某物)变短(叠缩在一起). ⇨illus 见插图. **2** [I, Tn] (cause sth to) become compressed forcibly (使某物)叠缩, 嵌入: *The first two carriages of the train (were) telescoped in the crash.* 火车撞车时前两节车箱叠嵌在一起了. **3** [Tn, Tn·pr] **~ sth (into sth)** condense sth so that it occupies less space or time 压缩某物使其少占空间或时间: *Three episodes have been telescoped into a single programme.* 把三集的内容压缩成了一个节目.

tele·scopic /ˌtelɪˈskɒpɪk; ˌtɛləˋskɑpɪk/ *adj* **1** of a telescope; magnifying like a telescope 望远镜的; 如望远

镜般放大的; 望远的: *a telescopic sight*, eg on a rifle, to magnify the target 望远瞄准器(如装于步枪上放大目标者). **2** (that can be) seen through a telescope (能)从望远镜中见到的: *a telescopic view of the moon* 从望远镜中见到的月亮 ○ *telescopic stars*, ie those that are invisible to the naked eye 用望远镜才能看到的星星. **3** having sections which slide one within another 伸缩的; 套叠的; 叠缩的: *a telescopic aerial, stand, umbrella* 伸缩式天线、伸缩式支架、折叠伞. **tele·scop·ic·ally** /-klɪ; -klɪ/ *adv*.

tele·text /ˈtelɪtekst; ˋtɛlə,tɛkst/ *n* [U] computerized service providing news and other information on the television screens of subscribers 电视电报(可在用户的电视接收机上显示的信息).

tele·type·writer /ˌtelɪˈtaɪpraɪtə(r); ˌtɛləˋtaɪp,raɪtɚ/ *n* (*US*) = TELEPRINTER

tele·vi·sion /ˈtelɪvɪʒn; ˋtɛlə,vɪʒən/ (also *Brit infml* 英式口语作 **telly**) *n* (*abbr* 缩写 **TV**) **1** [U] process of transmitting and reproducing on a screen events, scenes, plays, etc in pictures and sound, using radio signals 电视. **2** [U] programmes broadcast in this way 电视(播放的)节目: *spent the evening watching television* 看电视节目度过夜晚 ○ [attrib 作定语] *a television documentary* 电视播放的记实节目. **3** [C] (also ˈ**television set**) apparatus with a screen and loudspeaker for receiving television broadcasts 电视接收机; 电视机: *a colour/black-and-white television* 彩色[黑白]电视机. **4** [U] organization producing and transmitting television programmes 电视行业; 电视台: *She works in television.* 她在电视台工作. ○ [attrib 作定语] *a television announcer* 电视节目主持人. **5** (idm 习语) **on (the) ˈtelevision** broadcasting or being broadcast by television 电视播放的: *The Prime Minister, speaking on television, denied reports that...* 首相在电视讲话中否认传说的... ○ *Is there anything good on (the) television tonight?* 今晚的电视有好节目吗?

▷ **tele·vise** /ˈtelɪvaɪz; ˋtɛlə,vaɪz/ *v* [Tn] broadcast (sth) by television 以电视播放(某事): *The BBC plans to televise all Shakespeare's plays.* 英国广播公司计划播放莎士比亚的全部戏剧. ○ *The Olympic Games are always televised.* 奥林匹克运动会一向经电视播放.

telex /ˈteleks; ˋtɛlɛks/ *n* **1** [U] system of communication using teleprinters 用户电报, 电传系统(使用电传打印机的传送系统). **2** [C] message sent or received by this system 经用户电报发或收的消息; 电传: *Several telexes arrived this morning.* 今天上午收到几份电传. **3** [C] (*infml* 口) apparatus for sending and receiving messages by telex 电传收发机; 电传机: *We've installed a new telex in the office.* 我们在办公室里装了一台新电传机.

▷ **telex** *v* [Tn, Tn·pr, Dn·f] send (a message) or communicate with (sb) by telex 以电传发出(消息)或与(某人)联系.

tell /tel; tɛl/ *v* (*pt, pp* **told** /təʊld; told/) **1** [Tn, Dn·n, Dn·pr, Dn·f, Dn·w] **~ sth (to sb)** make sth known, esp in spoken or written words (用言语或文字)告知, 告诉, 讲述某事: *tell jokes/stories* 讲笑话[故事] ○ *I could tell you a thing or two about him.* 我可以给你讲他的一两件事. ○ *He told the news to everybody in the village.* 他把那消息告诉了全村的人. ○ *Did she tell you her name?* 她告诉你姓名了吗? ○ *They've told us (that) they're not coming.* 他们已跟我们说过不来了. ○ *Tell me where you live.* 把你的住处告诉我. ○ *I can't tell you* (ie I can't find words to express) *how happy I am.* 我真不知道怎么表达我的快乐. ○ *So I've been told*, ie That is what I've been told. 那就是我听说的事. **2** [Dn·n, Dn·f, Dn·w, Dn·t] give information to (sb) 向(某人)提供情况或信息: *a book which will tell you all you need to know about personal taxation* 说明个人纳税须知的书 ○ *This gauge tells you the amount of petrol you have left/how much petrol you have left.* 这计量表可指示还剩多少汽油. **3** [Tn] express (sth) in words; utter 说(某事); 讲; 述: *tell the truth/lies/a lie* 说实话[谎/谎话] ○ (*dated* 旧) *tell* (ie reveal) *one's love* 泄露个人的情人. ⇨Usage at SAY 用法见SAY. **4** [I] reveal a secret 泄露秘密: *Promise you won't tell.* 你要保证不泄密. ○ (*infml* 口) *kiss and tell*, ie reveal one's love affairs 吐露个人的风流韵事. **5** **(a)** [I, Tf, Tw] decide or determine; know definitely 决定; 决心; 肯定; 确定: *It may rain or it may not. It's hard to tell.* 天也许下雨, 也许不下. 说不准. ○ *You can tell (that) he's angry when he starts shouting a lot.* 他什么时候一大喊大叫, 肯定是生气了. ○ *How do you tell when to change gear?* 你怎么确定何时换挡? ○ *The only way to tell if you like something is by trying it.* 要确定是否喜欢某事物, 唯一的办法是试一下. **(b)** [Tn, Tn·pr, Tw] **~ A from B** (esp with *can/could/be able to* 尤与can/could/be able to连用) distinguish A from B 辨认A和B; 辨别; 识别: *I can't tell the difference between margarine and butter*, ie can't identify them by their tastes. 我尝不出人造黄油和黄油有什么区别. ○ *Can you tell Tom from his twin brother?* 你能分辨出汤姆和他的孪生兄弟吗? ○ *These kittens look exactly alike — how can you tell which is which?* 这些小猫看上去一模一样 —— 你怎么能分出哪个是哪个? **6** [I, Ipr] **~ (on sb)** produce a noticeable effect 产生能觉察出的效果; 起明显作用: *Every blow told.* 每一击都打中了. ○ *The government's policies are beginning to tell.* 政府的政策开始发挥作用了. ○ *All this hard work is telling on him*, ie is affecting his health, etc. 这些繁重的工作他已吃不消了(影响着他的健康等). ○ *Her lack of experience told against her*, ie was a disadvantage to her. 她缺乏经验, 这对她很不利. **7** [Dn·t, Dn·w] order or direct (sb) 吩咐, 命令(某人): *Tell him to wait.* 叫他等一等. ○ *Do what I tell you.* 照我的吩咐做. ○ *Children must do as they're told.* 孩子必须听话. ○ *You won't be told* (ie won't obey orders or listen to advice), *will you?* 你不听话(不服从命令或不听从劝告), 是不是? ⇨Usage at ORDER[2] 用法见ORDER[2]. **8** [Tn] (*arch* 古) count the number of (sth) 数(某物)的数目; 计算: *tell one's beads*, ie say prayers while counting the beads on a rosary 边数念珠边祈祷. **9** (idm 习语) **all told** with all people, items, etc counted and included 将所有的人、项目等都计算在内; 总共: *There are 23 guests coming, all told.* 总共来了23位客人. **dead men tell no tales** ⇨ DEAD. **hear tell of sb/sth** ⇨ HEAR. **I/I'll ˌtell you ˈwhat** (*infml* 口) (used to introduce a suggestion 用以提出建议): *I'll tell you what — let's ask Fred to lend us his car.* 我说 —— 咱们去找弗雷德借汽车吧. **I ˈtold you (so)** (*infml* 口) I warned you that this would happen 我提醒过你要出事; 我早就跟你说过: *He loves to say 'I told you so!' when things go wrong.* 只要一出事他就爱说'我早就跟你说过吧!' **ˌlive, etc to ˌtell the ˈtale** survive a difficult or dangerous experience so that one can tell others what really happened 脱离困境或险境后向他人讲述事情的原委. **tell/know A and B apart** ⇨ APART. **tell me aˈnother!** (*infml* 口) I don't believe you 我不相信. **tell/see sth a mile off** ⇨ MILE. **tell its own tale** explain itself, without need of further explanation or comment 本身即可说明问题: *The many crashes on the icy roads told their own tale.* 路上结冰发生多起撞车事故, 路面情况已不言而喻. **tell ˈtales (about sb)** make known another person's secrets, misdeeds, faults, etc 揭人隐密; 揭人之短: *Someone's been telling tales about me, haven't they?* 有人总在揭我的短处, 是不是? **tell ˈthat to the marines!** (*sl* 俚) I don't believe you 我不相信. **tell the ˈtime** (*US* **tell ˈtime**) read the time from a clock, etc 说出钟表等指示的时间: *She's only five — she can't tell the time yet.* 她才五岁 —— 还不会看表. **tell sb ˌwhere to get ˈoff/ˌwhere he gets ˈoff** (*infml* 口) warn sb that his behaviour is unacceptable and will no longer be tolerated 警告某人其行为已令人无法忍受. **ˌtell the ˈworld** announce sth publicly 将某事公之于世. **there is ˌno ˈtelling** it is impossible to know 不可能知道: *There's no telling what may happen.* 不可能知道会发生什么事. ○ *As to his plans, there's simply no telling.* 至于他的计划, 根本就无法得知. **to ˌtell (you) the ˈtruth** (used to introduce a confession or an admission 用以引出自白或承认的话): *To tell the truth, I fell asleep in the middle.* 老实说, 我在中间睡着了. **you can ˌnever ˈtell; you ˌnever can ˈtell** you can never be sure, eg because appearances are often deceptive 谁也不知道(如因外表常靠不住). **you're telling ˈme!** (*infml* 口) I completely agree with you 这还用你说; 我早就知道. **10** (phr v) **tell sb off (for sth/doing sth)** (*infml* 口) scold or reprimand sb 斥责或责骂某人: *You'll get told off if you're caught doing that.* 要是发现你做那种事, 你就得挨骂. ○ *I told the boys off for making so much noise.* 那些男孩子很吵闹, 我把他们骂了一顿. **tell sb off for sth/to do sth** (*fml* 文) assign (a task or duty) to sb 给某人指定(任务或差事): *Six* *men were told off to collect fuel.* 派了六个人去收集燃料. **tell on sb** (*infml* 口) reveal sb's activities, esp to a person in authority 揭发某人的活动(尤指向负责人报告): *John caught his sister smoking and told on her.* 约翰发现他姐姐吸烟就给告了一状.

▷ **tell·ing** *adj* have a noticeable effect; impressive 有明显效果的; 显著的: *a telling argument* 有力的论据 ○ *His punches to his opponent's body proved especially telling.* 他打在对手身上的重拳显然非常有力. **tell·ingly** *adv*.

□ ˌ**telling-ˈoff** *n* (usu *sing* 通常作单数) reprimand; scolding 斥责; 责骂: *give sb a telling-off for sth* 为某事而斥责某人.

ˈ**tell-tale** *n* **1** person who reports another's secrets, misdeeds, etc 泄密者; 告发者: *Don't be such a tell-tale!* 别去告密! **2** mechanical device that serves as an indicator 指示器. — *adj* [attrib 作定语] revealing or indicating sth 泄露或显示某事的: *a tell-tale blush* 泄露真情而呈现的面色绯红 ○ *the tell-tale smell of cigarette smoke*, ie revealing that sb has been smoking 明显的香烟气味(可见有人吸过香烟).

teller /ˈtelə(r); ˈtɛlɚ/ *n* **1** person who receives and pays out money in a bank (银行的)出纳员. **2** person appointed to count votes, eg in the House of Commons (投票时的)计票员(如下议院中者). **3** (esp in compounds 尤用以构成复合词) person who tells stories, etc 讲故事等的人; 讲述者: *a story-teller* 讲故事的人 ○ *a marvellous teller of jokes* 笑话讲得很精彩的人.

telly /ˈtelɪ; ˈtɛlɪ/ *n* [U, C] (*Brit infml* 口) = TELEVISION.

te·mer·ity /tɪˈmerətɪ; təˈmɛrətɪ/ *n* [U] (*fml* 文) audacity; rashness 鲁莽; 冒失: *He had the temerity to call me a liar.* 他竟胆敢说我撒谎.

temp /temp; tɛmp/ *n* (*infml* 口) temporary employee, esp a secretary 临时雇员(尤指秘书).

▷ **temp** *v* [I] (*infml* 口) do temporary work 做临时工作: *He's been temping for over a year now and wants a permanent job.* 他做临时工作已一年多了, 想找个固定的工作.

temp *abbr* 缩写 = temperature: *temp 65°F* 65华氏度.

T

tem·per[1] /ˈtempə(r); ˈtɛmpɚ/ *n* **1** **(a)** [C] state of the mind as regards anger or calmness 心情; 心境; 脾气; 性情: *in a bad/good temper*, ie angry/amiable 心情坏[好]. **(b)** [C, U] tendency to become angry easily 脾气; 容易发怒的性情: *learn to control one's temper* 学会忍住脾气 ○ *have a (short/quick/nasty) temper* 脾气急[暴/坏] ○ *fly into a temper* 发怒 ○ *a fit of temper* 发脾气. **2** [U] degree of hardness and elasticity of a tempered metal (金属回火后的)硬度和弹性. **3** (idm 习语) **in a (bad, foul, rotten, etc) ˈtemper** angry 发怒; 发脾气. **keep/lose one's ˈtemper** succeed/fail in controlling one's anger 忍住[发]脾气.

▷ **-tempered** /-tempəd; -tɛmpɚd/ (forming compound adjs 用以构成复合形容词) having or showing the specified type of temper 有或显出某种性情、脾气的: ˌ*good-*/ˌ*bad-ˈtempered* ○ *a* ˌ*hot-tempered ˈman* ○ *a* ˌ*sweet-tempered ˈchild*.

tem·per[2] /ˈtempə(r); ˈtɛmpɚ/ *v* **1** [Tn] bring (metal) to the required degree of hardness and elasticity by heating and then cooling 使(金属)回火: *tempered steel* 回火钢. **2** [Tn, Tn·pr] **~ sth (with sth)** moderate or soften the effects of sth; mitigate sth 调和或减轻某事物的作用; 使某事缓和: *temper justice with mercy*, ie be merciful when punishing sb justly 法外施恩(惩罚某人时公正而仁慈).

tem·pera /ˈtempərə; ˈtɛmpərə/ *n* [U] **1** paint consisting of pigment mixed with yolk or white of egg and water 蛋彩画颜料(用颜料与蛋黄或蛋清及水调成). **2** method of painting on canvas or plaster using this 蛋彩画法.

tem·pera·ment /ˈtemprəmənt; ˈtɛmprəmənt/ *n* [C, U] person's nature as it affects the way he thinks, feels and behaves 气质; 性情; 禀性: *I've got a very nervous temperament.* 我很神经质. ○ *a man with an artistic temperament* 有艺术家气质的男子 ○ *The two brothers have entirely different temperaments.* 他们兄弟俩的性情完全不同. ○ *To be a champion, skill is not enough — you have to have the right temperament.* 要当冠军, 光有技巧还不够——还必须有相应的禀赋. ○ *Opera singers often display a lot of temperament*, ie are moody or excitable. 歌剧演员的性情常常不稳定(情绪多变或爱激动).

▷ **tem·pera·mental** /ˌtemprəˈmentl; ˌtɛmprəˈmɛntl̩/ *adj* **1** caused by a person's temperament 由人的气质引起的; 生来的: *a temperamental aversion to hard work* 生性厌恶艰苦的工作. **2** (*often derog* 常作贬义) having or showing fits of excitable or moody behaviour; not calm or consistent 神经质的; 不冷静的; 变化无常的: *He's a very temperamental player*, ie plays well or badly according to his mood. 他是个情绪波动的演员(演得好坏由心情而定). ○ (*joc* 谑) *My car is a bit temperamental*, ie is likely to break down, fail to start, etc. 我的汽车没准脾气(可能出毛病、发动不起来等). **tem·pera·ment·ally** /-təlɪ; -tlɪ/ *adv*: *temperamentally unsuited for the job* 气质上不适合那项工作.

tem·per·ance /ˈtempərəns; ˈtɛmpərəns/ *n* [U] **1** moderation and self-restraint in one's behaviour or in eating and drinking (在行为或饮食上)节制, 自制, 克己. **2** drinking no (or almost no) alcoholic drinks (近于)滴酒不沾, 戒酒, 禁酒: [attrib 作定语] *a temperance society*, ie one promoting temperance 戒酒协会(提倡戒酒者) ○ *a temperance hotel*, ie one that does not serve alcoholic drinks 禁酒饭店(不供应酒者).

tem·per·ate /ˈtempərət; ˈtɛmpərɪt/ *adj* **1** behaving with temperance(1); showing self-control (行为)有节制的; 克制的: *Please be more temperate in your language.* 在言语上请再克制一些. **2** (of climate or climatic regions) having a mild temperature without extremes of heat or cold (指气候或有某种气候的地区)温和的: *temperate zones* 温带. ▷ **tem·per·ately** *adv*.

tem·per·at·ure /ˈtemprətʃə(r); *US* ˈtempərtʃʊər; ˈtɛmprəˌtʃɚ/ *n* **1** [C, U] degree of heat or cold (in a body, room, country, etc) 温度; 体温; 室温; 气温: *keep the house at an even temperature* 保持房内恒温 ○ *heat the oven to a temperature of 200°C* 使烤箱的温度升至200摄氏度 ○ *Some places have had temperatures in the 90's*, ie over 90° Fahrenheit. 有些地方的温度超过90华氏度. ○ *a climate without extremes of temperature* 气温不特别高也不特别低的气候. ⇨App 4, 5 见附录4、5. **2** (idm 习语) **get/have/run a ˈtemperature** get/have an abnormally high temperature of the body 体温过高; 发烧. **raise the temperature** ⇨ RAISE. **take sb's ˈtemperature** measure the temperature of sb's body with a thermometer (以温度计)量某人的体温; 试体温: *The nurse took the temperatures of all the patients.* 那位护士为所有的病人量了体温.

tem·pest /ˈtempɪst; ˈtɛmpɪst/ *n* **1** violent storm 暴风雨; 风暴. **2** (idm 习语) **a tempest in a teapot** (*US*) = A STORM IN A TEACUP (STORM).

▷ **tem·pes·tu·ous** /temˈpestʃʊəs; tɛmˈpɛstʃʊəs/ *adj* stormy; violently agitated; turbulent 有暴风雨的; 激烈的; 剧烈的; 骚动的; 动乱的: *a tempestuous sea* 波涛汹涌的海洋 ○ *a tempestuous political debate* 激烈的政治辩论. **tem·pes·tu·ously** *adv*. **tem·pes·tu·ous·ness** *n* [U].

tem·plate /ˈtempleɪt; ˈtɛmplɪt/ *n* pattern or gauge, usu of thin board or metal, used as a guide for cutting or drilling metal, stone, wood, etc or for cutting fabric (切割或钻穿金属、石料、木材等或剪裁织物的)样板, 模板, 型板.

temple[1] /ˈtempl; ˈtɛmpl̩/ *n* building used for the worship of a god or gods, esp in non-Christian religions 庙; 寺; 神殿(尤指非基督教者): *a Greek, Roman, Hindu, Buddhist, etc temple* 希腊、罗马、印度教、佛教等的庙宇.

temple[2] /ˈtempl; ˈtɛmpl̩/ *n* flat part at each side of the forehead 太阳穴(前额两侧); 颞. ⇨illus at HEAD 见HEAD插图.

tempo /ˈtempəʊ; ˈtɛmpo/ *n* (*pl* **~s** or, in music, 音乐术语复数作 **tempi** /ˈtempi:; ˈtɛmpi/) **1** speed or rhythm of a piece of music 乐曲的速度或拍子: *Your tempo is too slow.* 你演奏的速度太慢了. ○ *in waltz tempo* 以华尔兹的拍子. **2** (*fig* 比喻) pace of any movement or activity (运动或活动的)速度, 进度: *the exhausting tempo of city life* 令人精疲力竭的城市生活节奏 ○ *upset the even tempo of one's existence* 打乱生活规律.

tem·poral /ˈtempərəl; ˈtɛmpərəl/ *adj* **1** of worldly affairs, ie not spiritual; secular 世俗的(即非宗教的); 现世的: *the temporal power of the Pope*, ie as head of the Vatican State 教皇在世俗方面的权力 ○ *the lords temporal*, ie British peers of the realm 世俗议员(英国上议院中非主教的贵族议员). Cf 参看 SPIRITUAL 2. **2** (*grammar*) of or denoting time 时间的; 表示时间的:

temporal conjunctions, eg *when*, *while* 表示时间的连词(如when、while). **3** of the temple(s) of the head 太阳穴的; 颞部的; 颞的: *the temporal artery* 颞动脉.

tem·por·ary /ˈtemprərɪ; *US* -pərerɪ; ˌtɛmpəˈrɛrɪ/ *adj* lasting or meant to last for a limited time only; not permanent 暂时的; 临时的; 一时的; 非永久的: *temporary employment* 临时工作 ○ *a temporary bridge* 临时桥 ○ *This arrangement is only temporary.* 这只是暂时的安排. Cf 参看 IMPERMANENT. ▷ **tem·por·ar·ily** /ˈtemprərəlɪ; *US* ˌtempəˈrerəlɪ; ˌtɛmpəˈrɛrəlɪ/ *adv*. **tem·por·ari·ness** *n* [U].

tem·por·ize, -ise /ˈtempəraɪz; ˈtɛmpəˌraɪz/ *v* [I] (*fml* 文) delay making a decision, giving a definite answer or stating one's purpose, in order to gain time 拖延(暂不作决定、作答复或说明目的以争取时间); 敷衍: *a temporizing move* 一步缓棋.

tempt /tempt; tɛmpt/ *v* [Tn, Tn·pr, Cn·t] **~ sb (into sth/doing sth)** **1** persuade or try to persuade sb to do sth, esp sth wrong or unwise 劝说或鼓动某人做某事(尤指错事、傻事); 怂恿: *He was tempted into a life of crime by greed and laziness.* 他受贪婪和懒惰的驱使步入了罪恶的一生. ○ *They tried to tempt her (into staying) with offers of promotion.* 他们提出给她晋级来劝说她(留下). ○ *Nothing would tempt me to join the army.* 什么也不能引诱我参军. **2** arouse a desire in sb; attract sb 引起某人的欲望; 吸引某人: *The warm weather tempted us into going for a swim.* 暖和的天气诱使我们去游泳. ○ *I am tempted*(ie feel inclined) *to take the day off.* 我打算休一天假. **3** (idm 习语) **tempt ˈfate/ˈprovidence** act rashly; take a risk 鲁莽; 冒险.

▷ **tempter** *n* **1** [C] person who tempts 引诱者; 诱惑者. **2 the Tempter** [sing] the Devil; Satan 魔鬼; 撒旦.

tempt·ing *adj* attractive; inviting 吸引人的; 诱人的; 有诱惑力的; 动人的: *a tempting offer* 诱人的提议 ○ *That cake looks very tempting.* 那蛋糕的样子很吸引人. **tempt·ingly** *adv*.

temp·tress /ˈtemptrɪs; ˈtɛmptrɪs/ *n* (*usu joc* 通常作戏谑语) woman who tempts, esp sexually 引诱人的女子(尤指性方面).

temp·ta·tion /tempˈteɪʃn; tɛmpˈteʃən/ *n* **1** [U] tempting or tempted 劝诱; 诱惑: *the temptation of easy profits* 容易获利的诱惑 ○ *yield/give way to temptation* 经不住诱惑 ○ *put temptation in sb's way*, ie tempt him 引诱某人. **2** [C] thing that tempts or attracts 有诱惑力或吸引力之物: *The bag of sweets on the table was too strong a temptation for the child to resist.* 桌上那包糖果对那孩子是个难以抗拒的诱惑. ○ *Clever advertisements are just temptations to spend money.* 巧妙的广告诱使人花钱.

ten /ten; tɛn/ *pron, det* **1** 10; one more than nine 10, 十(个). ⇨App 4 见附录4. **2** (idm 习语) ˌ**ten to ˈone** very probably 十之八九; 非常可能地: *Ten to one he'll be late.* 十之八九他会迟到.

▷ **ten** *n* the number 10 ☆ 10; 十.

ten- (in compounds 用以构成复合词) having ten of the thing specified 有十个...的: *a ten-gallon drum* 容量为十加仑的桶.

tenth /tenθ; tɛnθ/ *pron, det* 10th; next after ninth 第10, 第十(个). — *n* one of ten equal parts of sth $\frac{1}{10}$; 十分之一. **tenthly** *adv* in the tenth position of place 在第十位; 占第十位.

□ **tenfold** /ˈtenfəʊld; ˈtɛnˌfold/ *adj, adv* **1** ten times as many or as much 十倍(的). **2** having ten parts 有十部分(的).

ˌ**ten ˈpence** (also **10p** /ˌten ˈpiː; ˌtɛn ˈpi/) *n* (*Brit*) (coin worth) ten new pence (面值)十便士(的硬币).

For the uses of *ten* and *tenth* see the examples at *five* and *fifth*. 关于ten和tenth的用法见five和fifth词条中的示例.

ten·able /ˈtenəbl; ˈtɛnəbḷ/ *adj* **1** that can be defended successfully against opposition or attack 可防守的; 守得住的; 可维护或防护的: *a tenable position* 可防守的位置 ○ *The view that the earth is flat is no longer tenable.* 认为地球是平的这一观点站不住脚了. **2** [pred 作表语] **~ (for...)** (of an office or postion) that can be held (for a certain time) (指职务或职位)可保有, 可维持(一定时间): *The lectureship is tenable for a period of three years.* 讲师这一职位任期三年. ▷ **ten·ab·il·ity** /ˌtenəˈbɪlətɪ; ˌtɛnəˈbɪlətɪ/ *n* [U].

ten·acious /tɪˈneɪʃəs; tɪˈneʃəs/ *adj* **1** sticking or clinging firmly together or to an object 粘牢的; 粘住的; 抓牢的; 抓紧的: *The eagle seized its prey in a tenacious grip.* 鹰将捕获物紧紧抓住. **2** keeping a firm hold on property, principles, life, etc; resolute 紧握的; 不放松的; 坚决的: *a tenacious adversary* 紧逼不放的对手 ○ *She is tenacious in defence of her rights.* 她坚决维护自己的权利. **3** (of memory) retentive; not forgetting things (指记忆力)持久的, 强的; 记性好的. ▷ **ten·aciously** *adv*: *Though seriously ill, he still clings tenaciously to life.* 他虽病得很重, 但仍顽强地活下去. **ten·acity** /tɪˈnæsətɪ; tɪˈnæsətɪ/ *n* [U].

ten·ant /ˈtenənt; ˈtɛnənt/ *n* **1** person who pays rent to a landlord for the use of a room, a building, land, etc 房客; 租户; 佃户: *evict tenants for non-payment of rent* 赶出未付房租的房客 ○ [attrib 作定语] *a tenant farmer*, ie one who farms land which he does not own 佃农. **2** (*law* 律) person who occupies or owns a particular building or piece of land (建筑物或土地的)占用者, 占有者.

▷ **ten·ancy** /-ənsɪ; -ənsɪ/ (**a**) [U] use of land or buildings as a tenant(1) 租用; 租赁: *during his tenancy of the farm* 在他租用该农场期间. (**b**) [C] period of this 租用或租赁期: *hold a life tenancy of a house* 终生租用某所房子.

ten·antry /ˈtenəntrɪ; ˈtɛnəntrɪ/ *n* [Gp] all the tenants occupying land or buildings on one estate (某一地产或房产的)全体佃户或房客.

NOTE ON USAGE 用法: A **tenant** occupies a flat, a building, a farm, etc but does not own it. ☆ **tenant**(房客或佃户)占用公寓、建筑物、农场等, 但并非所有者. He or she pays money **(rent)** regularly for its use to the **landlord**, who is the owner 房客或佃户定期付给**landlord**(房主或地主)租金(**rent**): *Are you an owner-occupier or a tenant?* 你住自己的房子还是租房住? ○ *He's a tenant farmer.* 他是佃农. ○ *His landlord owns 5 000 acres.* 他的地主有5 000英亩土地. A similar relationship exists between a **lessee** and a **lessor,** which are legal terms. 表示上述两者关系的词还有**lessee**(承租人)和**lessor**(出租人), 是法律用语. They both sign a **lease** (a written legal agreement defining the terms of the **tenancy**) 双方共同签订**lease**(合同)——规定**tenancy**(租赁)条款的法律性书面协议: *The lessor can evict the lessee for failure to pay rent.* 出租人可驱逐不付租金的承租人.

T

tench /tentʃ; tɛntʃ/ *n* (*pl* unchanged 复数不变) European freshwater fish of the carp family 丁鲹(欧洲产鲤鱼科淡水鱼).

tend[1] /tend; tɛnd/ *v* [Tn] **1** take care of or look after (sb/sth) 照料, 照管(某人[某事物]): *nurses tending (the wounds of) the injured* 照料受伤者的护士 ○ *shepherds tending their sheep* 照管羊的牧人. **2** (*US*) serve customers in (a shop, bar, etc) 在(店铺、酒吧等)中接待顾客: *tend the store* 照看店铺.

tend[2] /tend; tɛnd/ *v* **1** [It] be likely to behave in a certain way or to have a certain characteristic or influence 倾向; 趋向; 趋于: *I tend to go to bed earlier during the winter.* 我在冬天常睡得较早. ○ *Women tend to live longer than men.* 女人多比男人长寿. ○ *Recent laws have tended to restrict the freedom of the press.* 新法例有限制新闻自由的趋势. ○ *It tends to rain here a lot in summer.* 这里夏天较为多雨. **2** [I, Ipr] **~ to/towards sth** take a certain direction 朝某方向: *The track tends upwards.* 这痕迹是朝着上方的. ○ (*fig* 比喻) *He tends towards extreme views.* 他的观点趋于偏激.

▷ **tend·ency** /ˈtendənsɪ; ˈtɛndənsɪ/ *n* **1 ~ (to/towards sth)/(to do sth)** way a person or thing tends to be or behave (人或物呈现的)倾向, 趋势: *a tendency to fat/towards fatness/to get fat* 发胖的趋势 ○ *homicidal tendencies* 有杀人的可能. **2** direction in which sth moves or changes; trend (事物运动或变化的)趋向, 倾向, 趋势: *Prices continue to show an upward tendency*, ie to increase. 物价呈持续上升的趋势.

ten·den·tious /tenˈdenʃəs; tɛnˈdɛnʃəs/ *adj* (*derog* 贬) (of a speech, a piece of writing, etc) aimed at helping a cause; not impartial (指演说、文章等)宣传性的, 不公平的, 有倾向性的: *Such tendentious statements are likely to provoke strong opposition.* 这种有倾向性

的说法可能招致强烈的反对. ▷ **ten·den·tiously** *adv*. **ten·den·tious·ness** *n* [U].

ten·der[1] /ˈtendə(r); ˋtɛndɚ/ *adj* **1** easily damaged or hurt; delicate 易受伤害的; 脆弱的; 纤弱的: *tender blossoms, plants, shoots, etc*, eg that can be harmed by frost 娇嫩的花、树木、幼芽等(如易遭霜冻). **2** painful when touched; sensitive 有触痛的; 敏感的: *My leg is still very tender where it was bruised.* 我腿上碰伤的部位仍有触痛. ○ *That's a rather tender subject*, ie one that must be dealt with carefully to avoid hurting people's feelings. 那是个相当敏感的问题(须小心处理以免伤人感情者). **3** easily moved to pity or sympathy; kind 心肠软的; 善良的: *a tender heart* 软心肠. **4** loving; gentle 亲切的; 温和的; 文雅的: *tender looks* 温和的表情 ○ *tender loving care* 悉心、亲切的照顾 ○ *be a tender parent* 做慈母 ○ *bid sb a tender farewell* 与某人亲切地道别. **5** (of meat) easy to chew; not tough (指肉)嫩的, 易咀嚼的, 柔软的. **6** (idm 习语) **at a tender ˈage/of tender ˈage** young and immature 年幼而未成熟的.

▷ **ten·der·ize, -ise** /ˈtendəraɪz; ˋtɛndə,raɪz/ *v* [Tn] make (meat) more tender (eg by beating it) 使(肉)变软(如经捶打): *tenderized steak* 捶软的肉排.

ten·derly *adv*.

ten·der·ness *n* [U].

□ **ˈtenderfoot** *n* (*pl* **-foots**) newcomer who is unused to hardships; inexperienced person 尚未习惯于吃苦的新来者; 无经验者; 生手.

ˌtender-ˈhearted *adj* having a kind and gentle nature; tender(4) 生性善良的; 仁慈的.

ˈtenderloin *n* [U] (also **ˌtenderloin ˈsteak**) (*esp US*) most tender middle part of a loin of beef or pork (牛或猪的腰部中间的)嫩腰肉, 里脊. Cf 参看 UNDERCUT[1].

ten·der[2] /ˈtendə(r); ˋtɛndɚ/ *n* **1** (esp in compounds 尤用以构成复合词) person who looks after or tends sth 照管、照料或照看某事物者: *a ˈbartender* 酒吧服务员. **2** small ship used for carrying freight or passengers to or from a larger ship 勤务船(为大船运送货物或旅客者); 供应船. **3** truck attached to a steam locomotive, carrying fuel and water 煤水车(挂于蒸汽机车之后).

ten·der[3] /ˈtendə(r); ˋtɛndɚ/ *v* **1** [Tn, Dn·pr] **~ sth (to sb)** (*fml* 文) offer or present sth formally 正式提供或提出某事: *tender money in payment of a debt* 交付金钱偿还债务 ○ *May I tender my services?* 我可以效劳吗? ○ *He tendered his resignation to the Prime Minister.* 他向首相递了辞呈. **2** [I, Ipr] **~ (for sth)** make an offer (to carry out work, supply goods, etc) at a stated price 投标: *Firms were invited to tender for the construction of the new motorway.* 各公司应邀投标承建新高速公路.

▷ **ten·der** (also *esp US* **bid**) *n* formal offer to supply goods or carry out work at a stated price 投标: *put work out to tender*, ie ask for such offers 招标 ○ *put in/make/submit a tender for sth* 参加某项投标 ○ *accept the lowest tender* 接受最低价格的投标.

ten·don /ˈtendən; ˋtɛndən/ *n* strong band or cord of tissue that joins muscle to bone; sinew 腱: *strain a tendon* 扭伤腱.

ten·dril /ˈtendrəl; ˋtɛndrəl/ *n* thread-like part of a climbing plant (eg ivy) by which it clings to a support (攀缘植物如常春藤的)卷须.

tene·ment /ˈtenəmənt; ˋtɛnəmənt/ *n* **1** apartment or room let for living in (出租的)公寓, 房间. **2** (*US* also **ˈtenement-house**) large building with apartments or rooms let to a number of families at low rents 廉租公寓(多户合租, 租金低廉的大楼). **3** (*law* 律) land or other permanent property held by a tenant (承租者的)保有物, 占有物, 享有物.

tenet /ˈtenɪt; ˋtɛnɪt/ *n* principle; belief; doctrine 原则; 信条; 教义; 教条: *one of the basic tenets of the Christian faith* 基督教信仰的基本信条之一.

ten·ner /ˈtenə(r); ˋtɛnɚ/ *n* (*Brit infml* 口) (note worth) ten pounds sterling; £10 十英镑(的纸币); 10英镑: *I'll give you a tenner for your old bike.* 我出十英镑买你的旧自行车.

ten·nis /ˈtenɪs; ˋtɛnɪs/ *n* [U] (also **ˌlawn ˈtennis**) game for two or four players, who hit a ball backwards and forwards across a net with rackets 网球. ⇨App 4 见附录4. Cf 参看 REAL TENNIS (REAL).

□ **ˈtennis court** marked area on which tennis is played 网球场.

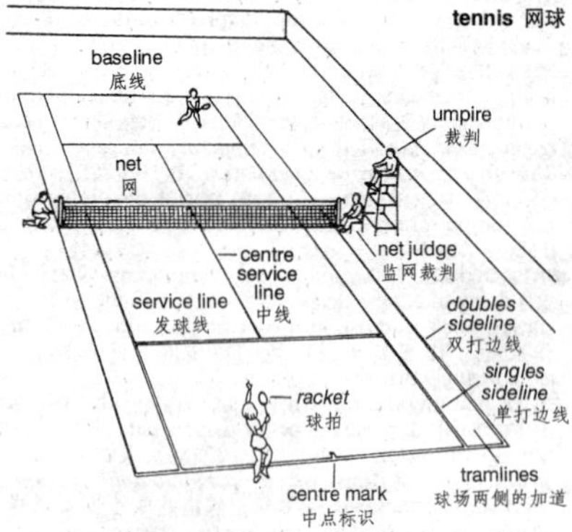

TENNIS COURT 网球场

ˌtennis ˈelbow painful swelling of the elbow caused by playing tennis, etc 网球肘(因打网球等引起的肘部肿痛).

tenon /ˈtenən; ˋtɛnən/ *n* projecting end of a piece of wood shaped to fit into a mortise to make a joint 榫; 榫头; 榫子.

tenor[1] /ˈtenə(r); ˋtɛnɚ/ *n* [U] **the ~ of sth** **1** general routine or course of sth (某事的)常规, 进展方向: *disrupting the even tenor of her life* 打乱她的生活规律. **2** general meaning or drift of sth (某事的)要旨, 大意: *know enough of the language to grasp the tenor of what is being said* 懂得该种语言足以了解对方谈话的大意.

tenor[2] /ˈtenə(r); ˋtɛnɚ/ *n* (*music* 音) **1** (**a**) highest normal adult male voice 男高音. (**b**) singer with such a voice 男高音歌手. (**c**) part written for such a voice (乐谱中的)男高音部. **2** [esp attrib 尤作定语] instrument with a range about that of a tenor voice 音域相当于次中音的乐器: *a tenor saxophone* 次中音萨克管.

ten·pin bowl·ing /ˌtenpɪn ˈbəʊlɪŋ; ˌtɛnpɪn ˋbolɪŋ/ (*US* also **ten·pins** /ˈtenpɪnz; ˋtɛn,pɪnz/ [pl]) game like ninepins, but with an extra skittle 十柱保龄球戏. Cf 参看 SKITTLE.

tense[1] /tens; tɛns/ *adj* (**-r, -st**) **1** stretched tightly; taut 拉紧的; 紧张的. **2** with muscles tight in anticipation of what may happen (因预料要出事)肌肉绷紧的: *faces tense with anxiety* 因焦急而显得紧张的面孔. **3** unable to relax; edgy 不能松弛的; 神经紧张的; 易怒的: *He's a very tense person*. 他是个神经紧张的人. **4** causing tenseness 引起紧张的; 令人紧张的: *a tense moment, atmosphere, meeting* 令人感到紧张的时刻、气氛、会议 ○ *The game is getting tenser all the time.* 比赛自始至终越来越紧张.

▷ **tense** *v* **1** [Tn] **2** (cause sb/sth to) become tense(2) (使某人[某事物])变得紧张: *She tensed, hearing the noise again.* 她再次听到那个声音就紧张起来. ○ *with muscles tensed, waiting for the race to start* 肌肉紧绷着, 等待起跑. **3** (idm 习语) **be/get tensed ˈup** be/become tense(3) 变得神经紧张: *Players get very tensed up before a match.* 运动员在比赛前都感到神经紧张.

tensely *adv*.

tense·ness *n* [U].

tense[2] /tens; tɛns/ *n* (*grammar*) any of the forms of a verb that may be used to indicate the time of the action or state expressed by the verb (动词的)时态: *the present, past, future, etc tense* 现在、过去、将来等时态.

tens·ile /ˈtensaɪl; *US* ˈtensl; ˋtɛnsḷ/ *adj* **1** [attrib 作定语] of tension 拉力的; 张力的; 紧张的: *the tensile strength of wire, rope, etc*, ie the load it will support without breaking 金属线、绳索等的抗拉强度. **2** that can be stretched 可延展的; 可伸长的; 可伸延的.

ten·sion /ˈtenʃn; ˋtɛnʃən/ *n* **1** [U] state or degree of stretching or being stretched 拉力; 张力; 紧张的状态或程度: *adjust the tension of a violin string, a tennis racket, etc* 调小提琴弦、网球拍等的松紧 ○ *Massage helps relieve the tension in one's muscles.* 按摩可使僵硬的肌肉松弛. **2** [U] mental, emotional or nervous strain; tenseness 心理、情绪或神经方面的紧张: *suffer from* *(nervous) tension* 感到(神经)紧张 ○ *Tension is a major cause of heart disease.* 精神紧张是引起心脏病的主要原因. **3** [U, C usu *pl* 作不可数名词或可数名词, 后者通常作复数] condition when feelings are tense or relations between people, groups, etc are strained 心情紧张的状态; (人、团体等间)关系紧张的状态: *racial/political/social tension(s)* 种族间的[政治上的/社会生活中的]紧张状态 ○ *The incident has further increased the tension between the two countries.* 该事件导致两国关系更趋紧张. **4** [U] voltage 电压: *high-tension cables* 高压电缆.

tent /tent; tɛnt/ *n* (usu portable) shelter or dwelling made of canvas, etc supported by poles and ropes attached to pegs driven into the ground (通常指便携式的)帐篷, 帐棚: *camping in tents* 在帐篷中露营.

□ **'tent-peg** *n* wooden or metal peg used to fasten a rope supporting a tent, etc to the ground 帐篷桩(用以把帐篷等的绳索固定于地上者). ⇨illus at PEG 见 PEG 插图.

tent·acle /'tentəkl; 'tɛntəkl̩/ *n* slender flexible part extending from the body of certain animals (eg snails, octopuses), used for feeling or grasping things or for moving 触须; 触角; 触手.

tent·at·ive /'tentətɪv; 'tɛntətɪv/ *adj* done, said, etc to test sth; hesitant or exploratory; not definite or decisive 试验性质的; 踌躇的; 试探性的; 不确定的; 非决定性的: *make a tentative suggestion, proposal, plan, etc* 提出试探性的建议、提案、计划等 ○ *reach a tentative conclusion* 得出暂时的结论. ▷ **tent·at·ively** *adv*: *played rather too tentatively* 演奏得太不果断. **tent·at·ive·ness** *n* [U].

ten·ter·hooks /'tentəhʊks; 'tɛntɚ,hʊks/ *n* (idm 习语) **(be) on 'tenterhooks** in a state of anxious suspense or uncertainty 忧虑不安; 不确定: *We were kept on tenterhooks for hours while the judges were deciding the winners.* 我们在等待裁判员裁决出优胜者, 几个小时如坐针毡.

tenth ⇨ TEN.

tenu·ous /'tenjʊəs; 'tɛnjuəs/ *adj* **1** thin; slender 薄的; 细的: *the tenuous threads of a spider's web* 蜘蛛网的细丝. **2** having little substance or significance; very slight 空洞无物的; 无关紧要的; 细微的: *tenuous distinctions* 细微的区别 ○ *preserve tenuous links with one's former friends* 与过去的朋友维持不即不离的联系 ○ *The difference, if it exists, is extremely tenuous.* 这种差别即使存在也是微不足道的. ▷ **tenu·ously** *adv*. **tenu·ous·ness** (also *fml* 庄重语作 **tenu·ity** /tɪ'nju:ətɪ; *US* te'nu:-; tɛn-'uətɪ/) *n* [U].

ten·ure /'tenjʊə(r); *US* -jər; 'tɛnjɚ/ *n* [U] **1** holding of (eg political) office or land or other property, etc (职位, 如政治地位, 土地或其他资产等的)保有. **2** period or manner of this (上述事物的)保有期, 保有状况, 保有权, 保有条件: *The tenure of the US Presidency is four years.* 美国总统的任期是四年. ○ *freehold/leasehold tenure* 无限期完全保有的[租赁保有的]状况 ○ *security of tenure*, ie the right to remain as a tenant 承租人使用权的保障. **3** (*esp US*) permanent appointment as a teacher, etc in a university or some other institution (大学或其他机构中教师等的)长期聘用: *granted tenure after six years* 六年之后受长期聘用.

te·pee /'ti:pi:; 'tipi/ *n* cone-shaped tent made of skins or bark on a frame of poles, used (esp formerly) by American Indians (兽皮或树皮制的)圆锥帐篷(尤指旧时美洲印第安人使用的). Cf 参看 WIGWAM.

tepid /'tepɪd; 'tɛpɪd/ *adj* lukewarm 温的; 不冷不热的: *The water was tepid.* 那水是温的. ○ (*fig* 比喻) *tepid applause* 稀稀拉拉的掌声. ▷ **tepidly** *adv*. **tepid·ness** (also **tep·id·ity** /tɪ'pɪdətɪ; tɪ'pɪdətɪ/) *n* [U].

te·quila /tə'ki:lə; tə'kilə/ *n* **(a)** [U] strong alcoholic drink distilled from a tropical plant, chiefly in Mexico 龙舌兰酒(主要产于墨西哥). **(b)** [C] glass of this 一杯龙舌兰酒.

ter·cen·ten·ary /,tɜ:sen'ti:nərɪ; *US* tɜ:'sentənerɪ; tɝ'sɛntə,nɛrɪ/ (also **ter·cent·en·nial** /,tɜ:sen'tenɪəl; ,tɝsɛn'tɛnɪəl/) *n* 300th anniversary 300 周年纪念: *the tercentenary of the school's foundation* 建校三百周年纪念 ○ [attrib 作定语] *tercentenary celebrations* 三百周年庆典.

▷ **ter·cent·en·nial** *adj* [usu attrib 通常作定语] of a tercentenary 三百周年的.

term /tɜ:m; tɝm/ *n* **1** period of time for which sth lasts; fixed or limited time 期间; 期限: *a long term of imprisonment* 长期监禁 ○ *during the President's first term of office* 在该总统的首届任期. **2** (*fml* 文) end or completion of such a period of time 期间或期限的终止或完结; 到期; 期满: *a pregnancy approaching its term* 妊娠期满 ○ *His life had reached its natural term.* 他已尽其天年. **3** any of the three or four periods in the year during which classes are held in schools, universities, etc (学校的)学期: *the autumn/spring/summer term* 秋[春/夏]季学期 ○ *end-of-term examinations* 期终考试 ○ *during/in term(-time)* 在学期当中. Cf 参看 SEMESTER. **4** (*law* 律) period of time during which a lawcourt holds sessions 法庭的开庭期. **5** word or phrase used as the name or symbol of sth (用作某事物名称或象征的)词或词组, 术语, 说法: *'The nick' is a slang term for 'prison'.* the nick 一词是俚语, 意为'班房'. ○ *technical, legal, scientific, etc terms* 技术、法律、科学等的术语. **6** (*mathematics* 数) each of the quantities or expressions in a series, ratio, etc (数列、比例等的)项. **7** (idm 习语) **a contradiction in terms** ⇨ CONTRADICTION (CONTRADICT). **in the 'long/'short term** in the distant/near future 长[短]期: *We must aim for world peace in the long term.* 我们要争取持久的世界和平.

▷ **term** *v* [Cn·a, Cn·n] (*fml* 文) call (sth/sb) by a certain term(5); name 用某词语称(某事物[某人]); 将(某事物[某人])称做: *term an offer unacceptable* 把一提议称做是难以接受的 ○ *a type of music that is termed plainsong* 称为素歌的一种音乐.

ter·mag·ant /'tɜ:məgənt; 'tɝməgənt/ *n* bad-tempered bullying woman 泼妇; 悍妇.

ter·min·able /'tɜ:mɪnəbl; 'tɝmɪnəbl̩/ *adj* (*fml* 文) that can be terminated 可终止的; 有期限的: *a contract terminable at a month's notice* 可在通知后一个月终止的合同.

ter·minal /'tɜ:mɪnl; 'tɝmənl̩/ *adj* **1** of the last stage in a fatal disease (致命疾病的)晚期的, 末期的: *His illness is terminal*, ie cannot be cured. 他的病已到末期. ○ *terminal cancer* 晚期癌症 ○ *the 'terminal ward*, ie in a hospital, for patients who are dying 末期病人病房 ○ *a terminal case*, ie a patient who is terminally ill 病危患者. **2** of or taking place each term(3) (每)学期的: *terminal examinations, inspections, accounts* 期终考试、检查、报告. **3** of, forming or situated at the end or boundary of sth 末端的; 终点的; 分界处的: *a terminal marker* 终点的标志.

▷ **ter·minal** *n* **1** (building at the) end of a railway line, bus route, etc (铁路、公共汽车等的)终点, 终点站. Cf 参看 TERMINUS. **2** building at an airport or in a town where air passengers arrive and depart (机场或城市中的)航空集散站. **3** point of connection in an electric circuit (电路的)接头: *the positive/negative terminals*, eg of a battery 正[负]极(如电池的). **4** (*computing* 计) apparatus, usu consisting of a keyboard and screen, for communicating with the central processor in a computing system (计算机系统的)终端机.

ter·min·ally /-nəlɪ; -nl̩ɪ/ *adv*: *a hospice for the terminally ill* 收治垂危患者的医院.

ter·min·ate /'tɜ:mɪneɪt; 'tɝmə,net/ *v* [I, Tn] (*fml* 文) come to an end or bring (sth) to an end 结束; 使(某事)终止, 终结: *The meeting terminated in disorder.* 会议在混乱中结束. ○ *terminate sb's contract* 终止某人的合同 ○ *terminate a pregnancy*, eg by means of an abortion 终止妊娠(堕胎).

ter·mina·tion /,tɜ:mɪ'neɪʃn; ,tɝmə'neʃən/ *n* **1 (a)** [C, U] point at which or way in which sth ends 终点; 结局; 终止; 结束: *the termination of one's contract* 合同的终止. **(b)** [C] (*medical* 医) ending of a pregnancy with the death of the unborn child; abortion 终止妊娠; 堕胎. **2** [C] final part or letter of a word, eg in an inflexion or derivation 词尾, 词的末一字母(如词尾变化或派生词中者).

ter·mino·logy /,tɜ:mɪ'nɒlədʒɪ; ,tɝmə'nɑlədʒɪ/ *n* **1** [U, C] technical terms of a particular subject (某学科的)专门用语, 术语: *a word not used except in medical terminology* 仅用于医学的专业词 ○ *various scientific terminologies* 科学方面的各种术语. **2** [U] proper use of words as names or symbols 术语的正确使用; 术语用法: *problems, differences of terminology* 术语用法上的问题、不同之处. ▷ **ter·mino·lo·gical** /,tɜ:mɪnə'lɒdʒɪkl; ,tɝmɪnə'lɑdʒɪkl̩/ *adj*. **ter·mino·lo·gic·ally** *adv*: *terminologically incorrect* 术语方面的错误.

T

ter·minus /ˈtɜːmɪnəs; ˋtɝmənəs/ *n* (*pl* **-ni** /ˈtɜːmɪnaɪ; ˋtɝmɪˌnaɪ/ or **~es** /-nəsɪz; -nəsɪz/) **(a)** station at the end of a railway line (铁路的)终点站. **(b)** last stop on a bus route, etc (公共汽车等的)终点站. Cf 参看 TERMINAL *n* 1.

ter·mite /ˈtɜːmaɪt; ˋtɝmaɪt/ *n* small insect, found chiefly in tropical areas, that is very destructive to timber (popularly called *white ant*, but not of the ant family) 白蚁.

terms /tɜːmz; tɝmz/ *n* [pl] **1 (a)** conditions offered or accepted (提出的或接受的)条件: *peace terms* 和平条件 ○ *according to the terms of the contract* 按照合同的条件. **(b)** payment offered or asked (付出的或索要的)报酬, 代价: *hire-purchase on easy terms* 优惠的分期付款 ○ *enquire about terms for renting a house* 询问租房子的价钱. **2** way of expressing oneself 表达方式; 措辞; 说法: *protest in the strongest terms* 以最强硬的措词抗议 ○ *He referred to your work in terms of high praise/in flattering terms.* 他对你的工作大加赞扬[大捧特捧]. **3** (idm 习语) **be on good, friendly, bad, etc ˈterms (with sb)** have a good, etc relationship 关系好、密切、不好等: *I didn't know you and she were on such intimate terms*, ie were such close friends. 我不知道你和她关系这么密切. **be on speaking terms** ⇨ SPEAK. **come to terms (with sb)** reach an agreement 达成协议. **come to terms with sth** reconcile oneself to sth; learn to accept sth 使自己顺从某事物; 设法忍受某事物: *come to terms with her handicap* 安于她自己的困难处境 ○ *You'll just have to come to terms with the fact that*... 你不得不接受的现实情况是.... **in no uncertain terms** ⇨ UNCERTAIN. **in terms of sth; in sth terms** as regards sth; expressed as sth 在某事物方面; 以某说法来表达: *Think of it in terms of an investment.* 从投资的角度来考虑那件事. ○ *The figures are expressed in terms of a percentage/in percentage terms.* 那些数字是以百分数表示的. **on equal terms** ⇨ EQUAL. **on one's own/sb's terms** on conditions that one/sb else decides 按个人[他人]决定的条件.

□ ˌ**terms of ˈreference** scope or range of an inquiry, etc 询问、调查等的范围或界限: *The committee decided that the matter lay outside/within its terms of reference*, ie that it could not/could consider it. 委员会决定对该事不予[加以]考虑.

tern /tɜːn; tɝn/ *n* sea-bird with long pointed wings and a forked tail 燕鸥.

ter·race /ˈterəs; ˋtɛrəs/ *n* **1** raised level area of ground or a series of these into which a hillside is shaped so that it can be cultivated 台地; 梯田. **2** flight of wide shallow steps, eg for spectators at a sports ground (梯级宽且矮的)台阶(如运动场之看台). **3** paved area beside a house (房侧的)铺砌地面. Cf 参看 PATIO. **4** continuous row of similarly designed houses in one block 排房(设计相同的一排房屋): *6 Olympic Terrace*, ie in a postal address 奥林匹克排房 6 号(通信地址) ○ [attrib 作定语] *a terrace-house*, ie one of those in such a row 一所排房(上述排房中的一所). ⇨illus at App 1 见附录1插图, page vi.

▷ **ter·race** *v* [Tn esp passive 尤用于被动语态] form (sth) into a terrace or terraces 使(某物)成梯田形或台阶形: *a terraced hillside* 阶梯状的山坡.

ter·ra·cotta /ˌterəˈkɒtə; ˌtɛrəˋkɑtə/ *n* [U] **1** unglazed reddish-brown pottery 无釉赤陶: [attrib 作定语] *a terracotta vase* 赤陶花瓶. **2** its colour 赤褐色; 土红色.

terra firma /ˌterə ˈfɜːmə; ˋtɛrəˋfɝmə/ dry land; the ground (contrasted with water or air) 陆地, 大地(与水或空中相对): *glad to be on terra firma again*, eg after a trip by boat or aeroplane 又回到陆地上, 很高兴(如下船或下飞机时).

ter·rain /təˈreɪn *or, in British use,* 英式英语读作 ˈtereɪn; tɛˋren/ *n* [C, U] stretch of land, with regard to its natural features 地形; 地貌; 地势; 地带: *difficult terrain for cycling* 骑自行车难以行走的地带 ○ [attrib 作定语] *an all-terrain vehicle* 全地形式的车.

ter·ra·pin /ˈterəpɪn; ˋtɛrəpɪn/ *n* any of various types of edible freshwater tortoise of N America 水龟(产于北美淡水中, 可食).

ter·rest·ri·al /təˈrestrɪəl; təˋrɛstrɪəl/ *adj* **1** of or living on land 陆地的; 陆生的; 陆栖的: *the terrestrial parts of the world* 地球的陆地部分 ○ *terrestrial species* 陆栖种类. **2** of the planet earth 地球的. Cf 参看 CELESTIAL. ▷ **ter·rest·ri·ally** /-trɪəlɪ; -trɪəlɪ/ *adv*.

ter·rible /ˈterəbl; ˋtɛrəbl/ *adj* **1** causing great fear or distress; appalling 可怕的; 使人苦恼的; 骇人的: *a terrible war, accident, murder* 可怕的战争、事故、谋杀案. **2** hard to bear; extreme 难以忍受的; 极端的: *terrible toothache* 难以忍受的牙疼 ○ *The heat was terrible.* 热得受不了. **3** (*infml* 口) very bad 极坏的; 很糟的: *I'm terrible at tennis.* 我打网球打得很不好. ○ *What a terrible meal!* 这顿饭糟透了! ○ *He's a terrible bore.* 他这人讨厌极了.

▷ **ter·ribly** /-əblɪ; -əblɪ/ *adv* **1** very badly 很糟糕: *She suffered terribly when her son was killed.* 她儿子被杀, 她痛苦已极. **2** (*infml* 口) very 很; 非常: *not a terribly good film* 不特别好的影片 ○ *I'm terribly sorry.* 我非常抱歉.

ter·rier /ˈterɪə(r); ˋtɛrɪɚ/ *n* any of various types of small active dog (某些种类的)活泼的小狗: *a fox terrier*, ie one used for hunting foxes 猎狐狗.

ter·rific /təˈrɪfɪk; təˋrɪfɪk/ *adj* (*infml* 口) **1** very great; extreme 很大的; 极端的: *a terrific storm* 狂风暴雨 ○ *driving at a terrific speed* 以极高的速度驾驶. **2** excellent; wonderful 极好的; 了不起的: *doing a terrific job* 干得很棒 ○ *The view was terrific.* 景色美极了.

▷ **ter·rif·ic·ally** /-klɪ; -klɪ/ *adv* (*infml* 口) extremely 极度地: *terrifically clever, generous, rich* 非常聪明、大方、富有.

ter·rify /ˈterɪfaɪ; ˋtɛrəˌfaɪ/ *v* (*pt, pp* **-fied**) [Tn] fill (sb) with terror; make very frightened 使(某人)感到恐怖; 使害怕: *terrified his children with ghost stories* 讲鬼故事吓坏了他的孩子 ○ *a terrifying experience* 可怕的经历.

▷ **ter·ri·fied** *adj* **~ (of sb/sth)/(at sth)** feeling terror; very afraid (对某人[某事物])感到恐惧的, 很害怕的: *terrified of spiders, heights, the dark* 惧怕蜘蛛、登高、黑暗 ○ *I'm terrifed at the prospect of being alone in the house.* 我要是自己呆在一所房子里就很害怕.

ter·rine /teˈriːn; tɛˋrin/ *n* [U, C] paste made of cooked meat; pâté (熟的)肉糜; 肉酱.

ter·rit·or·ial /ˌterəˈtɔːrɪəl; ˌtɛrəˋtɔrɪəl/ *adj* of a country's territory 领土的: *territorial possessions* 领土 ○ *have territorial claims against another country*, ie claim part of its territory 向另一国提出领土要求(要求该国部分领土).

▷ **Ter·rit·or·ial** *n* (*Brit*) member of the Territorial Army 国防义勇军士兵.

□ ˌ**Territorial ˈArmy** (*Brit*) military force of part-time volunteers trained for the defence of Great Britain (英国)国防义勇军.

ˌ**territorial ˈwaters** the sea near a country's coast and under its control 领海: *fishing illegally in foreign territorial waters* 在他国领海非法捕鱼.

ter·rit·ory /ˈterətrɪ; *US* -tɔːrɪ; ˋtɛrəˌtorɪ/ *n* **1** [C, U] (area of) land under the control of a ruler, country, city, etc 领土(的范围): *Turkish territory in Europe* 土耳其在欧洲部分的领土 ○ *occupying enemy territory* 占领敌方的土地 ○ *new territories* 新的领土. **2 Territory** [C] country or area forming part of the US, Australia or Canada but not ranking as a state or province (美国、澳大利亚或加拿大的)未列为州或省的地方: *North West Territory* 西北地区. **3** [C, U] (extent of the) area for which sb has responsibility or over which a salesman, etc operates (某人负责的)地区(范围); (推销员等的)营业地区: *Our representatives travel over a very large territory.* 我们的推销员活动地区很广. ○ *How much territory does this medical practice cover?* 这一医疗服务包括的地区有多大? **4** [C, U] (extent of the) area claimed or dominated by one person, group or animal and defended against others (个人、团体或动物占据的)领域: *He seems to regard that end of the office as his territory*, ie He resents anyone else using it. 他把办公室的那一头看成是他的地盘. ○ *Mating blackbirds will defend their territory against intruders.* 黑鹂交配时不容许地盘受到外来的滋扰. **5** [C] area of knowledge or activity (知识或活动的)范围, 领域: *Legal problems are very much Andrew's territory*, ie He handles them. 法律方面的问题主要是由安德鲁负责处理.

ter·ror /ˈterə(r); ˋtɛrɚ/ *n* **1 (a)** [U] extreme fear 恐怖; 惊骇: *run away in terror* 惊慌地跑开 ○ *scream with terror* 吓得尖叫起来 ○ *be in terror of one's life*, ie afraid of being killed 为自己的生命安全担惊受怕 ○ *strike terror into* (ie terrify) *sb* 使某人胆战心惊. **(b)** [C] instance of this 恐怖的事: *have a terror of heights* 害怕登高 ○ *The terrors of the night were past.* 夜间的那些恐怖事都已成过去. **2** [C] terrifying person or thing 可怕的人或事物: *hooligans who are a terror to/the terror of the entire town* 使全城人都恐惧的流氓 ○ *Death holds no terrors for* (ie does not frighten) *me.* 死神吓不倒我. **3** [C] (*infml* 口) formidable or troublesome person or thing 令人惧怕或讨厌的人或事物: *My aunt can be a bit of a terror.* 我姑姑有时候还真有点讨人厌. ○ *That puppy is an absolute terror,* ie a great nuisance. 那只小狗讨厌极了. **4** (idm 习语) **a holy terror** ➪ HOLY.

▷ **ter·ror·ism** /ˈterərɪzəm; ˋtɛrə,rɪzəm/ *n* [U] use of violence and threats of violence, esp for political purposes 恐怖主义, 恐怖手段(尤指有政治目的者). **ter·ror·ist** /ˈterərɪst; ˋtɛrə,rɪst/ *n* person who supports or participates in terrorism 恐怖主义者; 恐怖分子: *The terrorists are threatening to blow up the hijacked airliner.* 恐怖分子扬言要炸毁劫持的客机. ○ [attrib 作定语] *terrorist attacks* 恐怖分子的攻击.

ter·ror·ize, -ise /ˈterəraɪz; ˋtɛrə,raɪz/ *v* (**a**) [Tn] fill (sb/sth) with terror 使(某人[某事物])畏惧: *local gangs terrorizing the neighbourhood* 使附近地区人心惶惶的地痞. (**b**) [Tn·pr] **~ sb into sth/doing sth** force sb to do sth by threats of violence, etc 胁迫某人做某事: *villagers terrorized into leaving their homes* 被逼离乡别井的村民. **ter·ror·iza·tion, -isation** /ˌterəraɪˈzeɪʃn; *US* -rɪˈz-; ˌtɛrərəˋzeʃən/ *n* [U].

□ ˈ**terror-stricken** (also ˈ**terror-struck**) *adj* filled with terror 胆战心惊的; 人心惶惶的.

terry /ˈterɪ; ˋtɛrɪ/ *n* [U] cotton fabric used for towels, etc, with raised loops of thread left uncut 毛圈棉织物(用以做毛巾等的).

terse /tɜːs; tɝs/ *adj* (*sometimes derog* 有时作贬义) using few words; concise; curt 用词简练的; 洗练的; 简短的: *written in a terse style* 以简练的文笔写成的 ○ *a terse reply, comment, remark, etc* 简短的答复、评论、言语等 ○ *a terse speaker* 语言精练的演说者. ▷ **tersely** *adv*. **terse·ness** *n* [U].

ter·tiary /ˈtɜːʃərɪ; *US* -ʃɪerɪ; ˋtɝʃɪ,ɛrɪ/ *adj* third in order, rank, importance, etc; next after secondary 第三等的; 第三位的; 第三的: *the Tertiary period*, ie (in geology) the third stage in the formation of rocks (地质学上岩石形成的)第三纪 ○ *tertiary education*, ie at university or college level 高等教育 ○ *tertiary* (ie very severe) *burns* 三度烧伤(极严重的).

Tery·lene /ˈterəliːn; ˋtɛrəlin/ (*US* **Dacron**) *n* [U] (*propr* 专利名) (fabric made from a) type of synthetic fibre 涤纶(人造纤维); 涤纶织物.

TESL /ˌtiː iː es ˈel *or, in informal use,* 俗读作 ˈtesl; ˌti i ɛs ˋɛl, ˋtɛsl/ *abbr* 缩写 = Teaching English as a Second Language 作为第二语言的英语教学. Cf 参看 TEFL.

tes·sel·lated /ˈtesəleɪtɪd; ˋtɛsl̩,etɪd/ *adj* (of a pavement) made from small flat pieces of stone of various colours arranged in a pattern (指人行道)用彩色小石块镶嵌成图案的.

test /test; tɛst/ *n* **1** (**a**) examination or trial of the qualities, etc of a person or thing (对人或事物的)测验, 试验, 考验: *an enˈdurance test*, eg for a new engine, soldiers in training, etc 耐力试验(如对新发动机、受训的士兵等的) ○ [attrib 作定语] *a ˈtest bore*, ie a hole bored into the ground to discover whether it contains mineral, oil, etc 勘察钻孔(为探测矿藏、石油等的) ○ (*fig* 比喻) *She left her purse on the table as a test of the child's honesty.* 她把钱包留在桌子上来考验那孩子是否诚实. ○ *The long separation was a test of their love.* 长期分离对他们的爱情是个考验. (**b**) such an examination conducted for medical purposes (医疗上的)试验, 检验, 化验: *an ˈeye test* 眼睛检查 ○ *a ˈblood/ˈurine test* 验血[尿]. **2** examination of a person's knowledge or ability in a particular area (对人在某方面的知识或能力的)测验, 测试, 考查: *give the pupils a test in arithmetic* 对小学生进行算术测验 ○ *an IˈQ/inˈtelligence test* 智商[智力]测验 ○ *aˈdriving-test*, ie to obtain a driving licence 驾驶执照考试. **3** means or procedure for testing 试验或检验的手段或程序: *a ˈlitmus test* 石蕊试验 ○ [attrib 作定语] *a ˈtest circuit*, ie one for testing motor vehicles, etc 机动车试验环路 ○ *a test for AIDS, cancer, tetanus, etc* 艾滋病、癌、破伤风…试验 ○ *a ˈpregnancy test* 妊娠试验. **4** (*infml* 口) = TEST MATCH. **5** (idm 习语) **the acid test** ➪ ACID[1]. **put sb/sth to the proof/test** ➪ PROOF[1]. **stand the test of ˈtime, etc** prove to be durable, reliable or of lasting value over a long period 经得起长时间的考验: *fine old buildings that have stood the test of centuries* 经历了数世纪的美观的建筑物.

▷ **test** *v* **1** [I, Ipr, Tn, Tn·pr] **~ (sb/sth) (for sth); ~ sth (on sb/sth)** examine and measure the qualities, etc of (sb/sth) 检验和衡量(某人[某物])的品质、质量等; 试验; 考验: *testing for pollution in the water/testing the water for pollution* 检验水的污染情况 ○ *a well-tested remedy* 经试验证实有效的医疗法 ○ *testing nuclear weapons under the sea* 海底核武器试验 ○ *have one's eyesight/hearing tested* 视力[听力]检查 ○ *The long climb tested our powers of endurance.* 那次长距离爬山考验了我们的耐力. ○ *Many people are against new drugs being tested on animals.* 很多人都反对用动物做新药试验. **2** [Tn, Tn·pr] **~ sb (on sth)** test sb's knowledge or ability (in a particular area) 测验某人(在某方面的知识或能力): *She tested the whole class on irregular verbs.* 她对全班学生进行不规则动词测验.

□ ˈ**test case** lawsuit or other procedure that provides a decision which is expected to be used in settling similar cases in the future 判例案件(诉讼案件或其他程序的先例, 可供以后比照类似案件之判例): *The outcome of these wage talks is seen as a test case for future pay negotiations.* 这一系列工资谈判的结果可视为今后薪酬谈判的先例.

ˈ**test drive** drive taken to judge the performance, etc of a car one is thinking of buying 试车(对欲购之汽车作驾驶测试). ˈ**test-drive** *v* (*pt* **-drove**, *pp* **-driven**) [Tn] take a test drive in (a car) 对(某汽车)作试车驾驶.

ˈ**test match** (also *infml* 口语作 **test**) cricket or Rugby match between teams of certain countries, usu one of a series during a tour (板球或英式橄榄球的)国际间的比赛(通常包括若干赛次).

ˈ**test pilot** pilot whose job is to fly newly designed aircraft to test their performance (新型飞机的)试飞员.

test-tube 试管

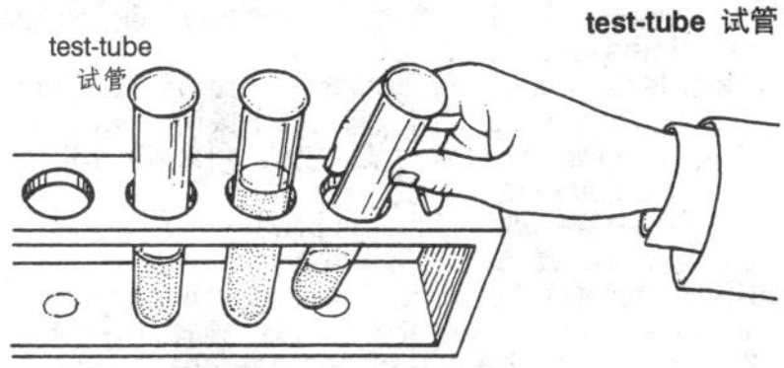

ˈ**test-tube** *n* slender glass tube, closed at one end, used in chemical experiments 试管. ˈ**test-tube baby** baby that is conceived by artificial insemination, or that develops elsewhere than in a mother's body 试管婴儿.

testa·ment /ˈtestəmənt; ˋtɛstəmənt/ *n* (*fml* 文) **1** (usu *sing* 通常作单数) **~ (to sth)** thing that provides clear proof of sth (某事物的)确实证明: *a testament to sb's beliefs* 对某人信仰的证明 ○ *The new model is a testament to the skill and dedication of the work-force.* 从这个新产品可以看出全体职工的技术水平和工作态度. **2** = WILL[4] 4.

▷ **testa·ment·ary** /ˌtestəˈmentrɪ; ˌtɛstəˋmɛntərɪ/ *adj* (*fml* 文) of or given in a person's will 遗嘱的; 由遗嘱中遗赠的: *a testamentary bequest* 遗赠的遗产.

test·ate /ˈtesteɪt; ˋtɛstet/ *adj* (*law* 律) having left a valid will at one's death 留下有效遗嘱的.

▷ **test·ator** /teˈsteɪtə(r); *US* ˈtesteɪtər; ˋtɛstetɚ/ (*fem* 阴性作 **test·at·rix** /teˈsteɪtrɪks; tɛsˋtetrɪks/) *n* person who has made a will[4](4) 立有遗嘱的人.

testes *pl* of TESTIS.

test·icle /ˈtestɪkl; ˋtɛstɪkl̩/ *n* either of the two glands of the male sex organ in which sperm-bearing fluid is produced 睾丸. ➪illus at MALE 见 MALE 插图.

test·ify /ˈtestɪfaɪ; ˋtɛstə,faɪ/ *v* (*pt, pp* **-fied**) **1** [I, Ipr, Tf] **~ (to sth); ~ (against/in favour of sb)** give evidence; declare as a witness, esp in court 提供证据; 作证(尤指出庭): *summoned to testify in court* 被传出庭作证 ○ *The teacher testified to the boy's honesty.* 老师证明那男孩很诚实. ○ *Two witnesses testified against her and one in her favour.* 有两个证人的证词对她不利, 另一个人的对她

有利. ○ *He testified under oath that he had not been at the scene of the crime.* 他宣誓称自己当时不在犯罪现场. **2** [Ipr, Tn] **~ (to) sth** (*fml* 文) be evidence of sth 作为某事的证据; 证明: *tears that testified (to) her grief* 可见她悲伤的眼泪.

tes·ti·mo·nial /ˌtestɪˈməʊnɪəl; ˌtɛstəˈmonɪəl/ *n* **1** written statement testifying to a person's character, abilities or qualifications (人品、能力、资格的)证明书, 鉴定书, 推荐书: *She sent a testimonial from her former employer when applying for the post.* 她申请那职位时寄去了前雇主的推荐书. Cf 参看 REFERENCE 4. **2** thing given to sb, eg by his colleagues, to show appreciation of his services or achievements (为感谢某人的贡献或成就而赠予的)奖品, 纪念品(如同事赠送的): [attrib 作定语] *a testimonial match, game, etc*, ie to honour a distinguished sportsman 纪念比赛等(以褒扬优秀运动员).

testi·mony /ˈtestɪmənɪ; *US* -məʊnɪ; ˈtɛstəˌmonɪ/ *n* **1** [U, C] written or spoken statement declaring that sth is true, esp one made under oath (书面或口头的)证词(尤指发誓后作出的): *According to the witness's testimony, you were present when the crime was committed.* 根据证人证词所示, 案发时你在犯罪现场. **2** [U, sing] **~ (to sth)** evidence in support of sth (对某事物的)见证或证明: *The pyramids are (a) testimony to the Ancient Egyptians' engineering skills.* 金字塔是古埃及人工程技术精湛的丰碑.

testis /ˈtestɪs; ˈtɛstɪs/ *n* (*pl* **-tes** /-tiːz; -tiz/) (*anatomy* 解) testicle 睾丸.

testy /ˈtestɪ; ˈtɛstɪ/ *adj* (**-ier, -iest**) easily annoyed; irritable 易被激怒的; 急躁的: *a testy person, reply* 性急的人、急忙做出的答复. ▷ **test·ily** /-ɪlɪ; -ɪlɪ/ *adv*. **testi·ness** *n* [U].

tet·anus /ˈtetənəs; ˈtɛtn̩əs/ *n* [U] disease in which the muscles contract and stiffen, caused by bacteria entering the body 破伤风. Cf 参看 LOCKJAW (LOCK[2]).

tetchy /ˈtetʃɪ; ˈtɛtʃɪ/ *adj* (**-ier, -iest**) peevish; irritable 易怒的; 暴躁的: *a tetchy person, mood, remark* 急躁的人、情绪、言语 ○ *There's no need to be so tetchy (with me)!* 何必(跟我)那么着急! ▷ **tetch·ily** /-ɪlɪ; -əlɪ/ *adv*. **tetchi·ness** *n* [U].

tête-à-tête /ˌteɪt ɑː ˈteɪt; ˈtetəˈtet/ *n* private conversation between two people 两人间的私下谈话: *have regular tête-à-têtes with sb* 经常与某人密谈 ○ [attrib 作定语] *a tête-à-tête dinner* 两人共餐.

▷ **tête-à-tête** *adv* together in private 私下在一起: *dine tête-à-tête with sb* 单独与某人共餐.

tether /ˈteðə(r); ˈtɛðɚ/ *n* **1** rope or chain by which an animal is fastened while it is grazing (拴牲畜的)绳或链. **2** (idm 习语) **at the end of one's tether** ⇨ END[1].

▷ **tether** *v* [Tn, Tn·pr] **~ sth (to sth)** fasten (an animal) with a tether 用绳或链拴住(牲畜): *He tethered his horse to a tree.* 他用绳子把马拴在树上.

tetr(a)- *comb form* 构词成分 four 四: *tetrasyllable*, ie a word with four syllables 四音节词.

Teut·onic /tjuːˈtɒnɪk; *US* tuː-; tuˈtɑnɪk/ *adj* **1** of the Germanic (ie Anglo-Saxon, Dutch, German and Scandinavian) peoples or their languages 条顿人的, 条顿语的(即盎格鲁撒克逊人、荷兰人、德国人及斯堪的那维亚人的). **2** [usu attrib 通常作定语] showing qualities thought to be typical of German people 有德意志民族特点的; 有德国人风格的: *Teutonic thoroughness* 德国人做事的彻底精神.

text /tekst; tɛkst/ *n* **1** [U] main written or printed part of a book or page (contrasted with notes, diagrams, illustrations, etc) (书或书页的)正文, 本文(与注释、图表、插图等相对): *too much text and not enough pictures* 文字太多而插图太少 ○ *The index refers the reader to pages in the text.* 书的索引为读者列出了正文中的页数. **2** [C] original words of an author, document, etc (contrasted with later revisions, shortened versions, etc) (作者、文件等的)原文: *the full text of the Prime Minister's speech* 首相讲话的全文 ○ *the problems of establishing the text of 'King Lear'* 考证《李尔王》原文所遇到的问题 ○ *a corrupt text*, eg one altered by mistakes in copying 异文(如因抄写错误而造成的). **3** [C] sentence or short passage from the Bible, etc used as the subject of a sermon or discussion (引自《圣经》等的)文句(用作讲道的或讨论的题目): *I take as my text*… 我要讲的经文是…. **4** [C] book, play, etc prescribed for study or as part of a syllabus (指定要学的或定为教学大纲内容的)书、戏剧等: *'Hamlet' is a set text for A level this year.* 《哈姆雷特》是今年高级程度考试中指定的必读书.

▷ **tex·tual** /ˈtekstʃʊəl; ˈtɛkstʃʊəl/ *adj* [usu attrib 通常作定语] of or in a text 正文的; 本文的; 原文的; 在正文、原文等中的: *textual criticism* 原文校勘 ○ *textual errors* 原文的错误. **tex·tu·ally** /-ʊəlɪ; -ʊəlɪ/ *adv*.

□ **textbook** /ˈteksbʊk; ˈtɛkstˌbʊk/ *n* book giving instruction in a subject 教科书; 课本: *an algebra textbook* 代数课本 ○ [attrib 作定语] *a textbook example of how the game should be played*, ie worth copying, exemplary 这一比赛的范例(值得效仿、学习的).

tex·tile /ˈtekstaɪl; ˈtɛkstaɪl/ *n* (esp *pl* 尤作复数) woven or machine-knitted fabric 织物; 纺织品: *factories producing a range of textiles* 生产各种纺织品的工厂 ○ *get a job in textiles* 得到在纺织业中的一份工作 ○ [attrib 作定语] *the textile industry* 纺织工业.

tex·ture /ˈtekstʃə(r); ˈtɛkstʃɚ/ *n* **1** [C, U] way a surface, substance or fabric looks or feels to the touch, ie its thickness, firmness, roughness, etc (一物体表面、物质或织物的)质地, 外观, 手感(如厚薄、软硬、粗细等): *the delicate texture of her skin* 她细嫩的皮肤 ○ *cement with a fine/coarse texture* 光滑的[粗糙的]水泥面 ○ *The cake has a nice light texture.* 这蛋糕松软可口. **2** arrangement of the threads in a fabric (织物的)疏密, 松紧: *cloth with a loose/close texture* 质地疏松[紧密]的布.

▷ **tex·tured** *adj* (esp in compounds 尤用以构成复合词) having a distinct or specified texture 有独特或所示之外观或质地的: *textured* (ie not smooth) *wallpaper* 起纹的壁纸 ○ *The walls have a textured finish.* 墙壁上有织纹状饰面. ○ *ˌcoarse-ˈtextured* 质地粗糙的.

-th *suff* 后缀 **1** (with a few *vs* and *adjs* forming *ns* 与少数动词及形容词结合构成名词): *growth* ○ *width*. **2** (with simple numbers except *one*, *two* and *three* forming ordinal numbers 与除 one、two 和 three 以外的基数词构成序数词): *sixth* ○ *fifteenth* ○ *hundredth*.

tha·lid·om·ide /θəˈlɪdəmaɪd; θəˈlɪdəˌmaɪd/ *n* [U] sedative drug formerly given to pregnant women until it was found that some of them gave birth to babies with deformed limbs 酞胺哌啶酮, 反应停(镇静药, 旧时孕妇服用后曾产肢体畸形儿, 已禁用): [attrib 作定语] *a thalidomide child*, ie one born deformed in this way 酞胺哌啶酮畸形儿.

than /ðən; ðən; *rare strong form* 罕、强读式 ðæn; ðæn/ *conj* (used after a comparative *adj* or *adv* to introduce a clause or phrase in which a comparison is expressed 用于形容词或副词的比较级之后, 引导表示比较关系的从句或短语): *He's never more annoying than when he's trying to help.* 他要是想帮忙就更让人讨厌他. ○ *She's a better player than (she was) last year.* 她演得比去年好. ○ *He loves me more than you do.* 他比你更爱我. ○ *She should know better than to poke the animal with her umbrella.* 她应当知道不该用伞去捅动物.

▷ **than** *prep* **1** (used before a *n* or *pron* to express a comparison 用于名词或代词前表示比较关系): *You gave me less than him*, ie less than you gave him or (*infml*) less than he gave me. 你给我的比给他的少(在口语中: 你给我的比他给的少). ○ *I'm older than her.* 我比她年岁大. ○ *Nobody understands the situation better than you.* 谁也不如你了解情况. ○ *There was more whisky in it than soda.* 那里面的威士忌比苏打水多. **2** (used after *more* or *less* and before an expression of time, distance, etc to indicate how long sth takes, how far it is, etc 用于 more 或 less 之后和表示时间、距离等的词语之前, 表明做某事所用的时间、与某物的距离等): *It cost me more than £100.* 这个花了我 100 多英镑. ○ *It never takes more than an hour.* 所用的时间从不超过一小时. ○ *He can't be more than fifteen.* 他不超过十五岁. ○ *It's less than a mile to the beach.* 离海滨不到一英里.

thank /θæŋk; θæŋk/ *v* **1** [Tn, Tn·pr] **~ sb (for sth/doing sth)** express gratitude to sb 谢谢或感谢某人; 向某人道谢: *There's no need to thank me — I was only doing my job.* 不用谢——这是我应做的工作. ○ *We thanked them for all their help.* 我们感谢他们鼎力相助. ○ (*ironic* 反语) *He won't thank you* (ie He'll be annoyed with you) *for leaving him all the washing-up to do.* 你把刷锅洗碗的活儿都留给他干, 他不会感谢你(他会生你的气). **2** (idm 习语) **have oneself/sb to thank (for**

sth) (*ironic* 反语) be responsible/hold sb responsible (for sth) (对某事)负有责任; 使某人(对某事)负责: *She only has herself to thank for what happened.* 出了事只能怪她自己. ○ *Who do we have to thank for this fiasco?* 我们遭此惨败怨谁呢? **I'll thank you for sth/to do sth** (used in making politely formal requests or commands 用作提出请求或要求的礼貌用语): *I'll thank you for* (ie Please give me) *that book.* 请您把那本书送给我吧. ○ *I'll thank you to mind your business.* 请您少管闲事. ˌ**no, 'thank you** (used to decline an offer, a proposal, etc politely 用以表示婉拒他人的好意、提议等). **thank 'God/'goodness/'heaven(s)** (used to express relief 用以表示松心或宽慰): *Thank God you're safe!* 谢天谢地, 你平安无事! **thank one's lucky stars** be or feel especially fortunate 吉星高照; 感到非常幸运: *You can thank your lucky stars (that) you don't have to go to this dreary reception.* 你真走运, 不用出席那死气沉沉的招待会. **'thank you** (used to express gratitude or to accept an offer, a proposal, etc 用以表示感谢或接受他人的好意、提议等): *Thank you for giving me a lift.* 谢谢你开车送我一程. ○ *Thank you very much indeed.* 真是太感谢你了.

▷ **thank·ful** /-fl; -fəl/ *adj* **1** grateful 感谢的; 感激的; 欣慰的: *You should be thankful to have escaped/that you have escaped with only minor injuries.* 你仅受轻伤而脱险, 应感到欣慰. **2** (idm 习语) **be grateful/thankful for small mercies** ⇨ SMALL. **thank·fully** /-fəlɪ; -fəlɪ/ *adv* **1** in a thankful way 感激地; 欣慰地. **2** (*infml* 口) I/we are glad; luckily 我[我们]很高兴; 幸运地: *Thankfully, it's at last stopped raining.* 谢天谢地, 雨总算停了. ⇨ Usage at HOPEFUL 用法见HOPEFUL. **thank·ful·ness** *n* [U].

thank·less *adj* **1** not feeling or expressing gratitude 不感谢的; 不领情的; 忘恩的. **2** (of an action) not likely to win thanks, appreciation or reward for the person performing it (指行为)不可能得到感谢、感激或报偿的: *a thankless role, task* 受累不讨好的角色、工作. **thank·lessly** *adv*. **thank·less·ness** *n* [U].

thanks *n* [pl] **1** expressions of gratitude 感谢的表示; 谢意; 谢忱: *Thanks are due to all those who helped.* 向所有帮过忙的人表示感谢. ○ *My heartfelt thanks to you all.* 我谨向各位表示衷心的感谢. ○ *give thanks to God* 感谢上帝. **2** (idm 习语) **no thanks to sb/sth** despite sb/sth 并非某人[某事物]之功: *It's no thanks to you (that) we arrived on time — your short cuts weren't short cuts at all!* 我们及时赶到可并没叨你的光——你说的近路一点儿也不近! **thanks to sb/sth** (*sometimes ironic* 有时作反语) because of sb/sth 由于或因为某人[某事物]: *The play succeeded thanks to fine acting by all the cast.* 由于全体演员的出色表演, 那出戏才获得成功. ○ *Thanks to the bad weather, the match had been cancelled.* 多亏这个倒霉天气, 挺好的比赛取消了. **a vote of thanks** ⇨ VOTE. — *interj* (*infml* 口) thank you 谢谢你; 谢谢: *'Would you like some more cake?' 'No, thanks.'* '再要点蛋糕吗?' '不要了, 谢谢.'

□ **'thanksgiving** *n* [C, U] **1** expression of gratitude, esp to God 感谢(尤指对上帝); 感恩. **2 Thanksgiving (Day)** holiday in the USA (on the fourth Thursday in November) and Canada (on the second Monday in October), originally set apart for giving thanks to God 感恩节(在美国为十一月的第四个星期四, 在加拿大为十月的第二个星期一).

'thank-you *n* expression of thanks 感谢; 致谢: *Have you said your thank-yous to Mrs Brown for the party?* 你参加布朗太太举办的聚会后向她道谢了吗? ○ *She walked away without so much as a thank-you.* 她走时连句感谢话都没说. ○ [attrib 作定语] *thank-you letters* 感谢信.

that[1] /ðæt; ðæt/ *det* (*pl* **those** /ðəʊz; ðoz/) **1** (used to make a person or thing specific, esp when he/it is seen as distant in space or time from the speaker/writer 用以指人或事物, 尤指在空间或时间上较远的): *Look at that man standing there.* 瞧站在那儿的那个男子. ○ *That box is bigger than this.* 那个盒子比这个大. ○ *How much are those apples at the back?* 后边那些苹果多少钱? ○ *Where did that noise come from?* 那响声从哪儿来的? ○ *Have you read that book about China?* 你读过那本关于中国的书吗? ○ *I was still living with my parents at that time/in those days*, ie at that particular time in the past. 我那时还跟父母住在一起. Cf 参看 THIS. **2** (**a**) (used to specify a person or thing that is indicated or mentioned 用以指要表明的或要提及的人或事物): *Did you see that boy?* 你看见那个男孩儿了吗? ○ *He began by writing a thriller. That book sold a million copies.* 他是写惊险小说起家的. 那本书卖了一百万册. (**b**) (used with a *n* followed by a possessive 与名词连用, 后接物主代词): *Did you meet that friend of his?* 你见过他的那个朋友吗? ○ *That dress of hers is too short.* 她那件连衣裙太短了. **3** (used in front of the antecedent of a relative clause 用于关系从句的先行词前): *Have you forgotten about that money I lent you last week?* 你忘了上星期我借给你的钱了吧? ○ *Those students who failed the exam will have to take it again.* 考试不及格的学生需补考. ○ *Who was that man you were talking to?* 刚才你正和一个人说话, 他是谁?

▷ **that** *adv* to that degree; so 达到那样的程度; 如此; 这般: *I can't walk that far*, ie as far as that. 我可走不了那么远. ○ *They've spent that much*, ie as much as is indicated. 他们花了那些钱. ○ *It's about that long*, ie as long as that. 那个东西大约有那么长. ○ *It isn't all that cold*, ie not as cold as you are suggesting or not extremely cold. 还没冷到那种程度(不像你说的那么冷或极冷).

that[2] /ðæt; ðæt/ *pron* (*pl* **those** /ðəʊz; ðoz/) **1** (**a**) (used to make a thing specific, esp one more distant in space or time than another 用以表示所指的事物, 尤指在空间或时间上较另一事物远的): *Those look juicier than these.* 那些显得比这些汁液多. ○ *That's a nice hat.* 那顶帽子很好. (**b**) (referring to people, only with the verb *be* 用以指人, 只能与动词be连用): *That's Peter at the bus-stop.* 在公共汽车站那儿的那个人是彼得. ○ *Who's that?* 那是谁? **2** (used to specify a thing, an event, an idea, etc that is indicated or mentioned 用以指要表明的或要提及的事物、想法等): *Look at that!* 看那个! ○ *Do you remember going to Norway? That was a good holiday.* 你还记得去挪威的情景吗? 那个假期真好. ○ *Send her some flowers — that's the easiest thing to do.* 给她送些花儿去——那是最好办的事. **3** (used as the antecedent of a relative clause 用作关系从句的先行词): *Is that what you really think?* 你真的那样想吗? ○ *That's what he told me.* 他就是那么跟我说的. ○ *Those who expect the worst are less likely to be disappointed.* 把事情想得坏的人, 不容易失望. ○ *Those present were in favour of a change.* 出席的人都赞成改一改. ○ *There are those who say* (ie Some people say) *she should never have been appointed.* 有人说根本就不应该委派她. **4** (idm 习语) **'that is (to say)** (**a**) which means 就是; 即: *He's a local government administrator, that is to say a Civil Servant.* 他是地方行政官员, 也就是说是文官. (**b**) to be specific 确切地: *She's a housewife — when she's not teaching English, that is.* 她是个家庭主妇——是指她不教英语的时候. ˌ**that's 'that** (used to indicate the end of a discussion, search, development, etc 用以表示谈论、调查、进展等的结束): *I take it that's that — we've heard your final offer?* 我看就这样了——我们已经了解到你们出的最高价了吧? ○ *So that's that. At last we're all agreed.* 就这样了. 我们终于取得了一致的意见.

that[3] /ðət; ðət; *rare strong form* 罕、强读式 ðæt; ðæt/ *conj* **1** (used to introduce a clause that is the subject or object of a *v* 用以引导主语从句或宾语从句): *That the attempt to save her had failed soon became widely known.* 想救她而未救成, 此事不久已尽人皆知. ○ *She said that the book was based on a true story.* 她说那本书取材于一件真事. ○ *I thought that 13 May would be the date of the election.* 我以为5月13日是选举的日子. ○ *It's possible that he hasn't received the letter.* 可能他还没收到那封信呢. **2** (*rhet* 修辞) (used to express wishes and regrets 用以表示愿望和遗憾): *Oh that I could see him again!* 我真希望能再见到他! ○ *That I should see a child of mine arrested for selling drugs!* 我竟然看见自己的孩子因贩毒而被捕!

that[4] /ðət; ðət; *rare strong form* 罕、强读式 ðæt; ðæt/ *rel pron* 关系代词 **1** (used to introduce a defining clause after a *n*, esp referring to things 用以引导名词之后的限定从句, 尤指表示事物的) (**a**) (as the subject of the *v* in the clause 在从句中作主语): *The letter that came this morning is from my father.* 今天早晨收到的那封信是我父亲寄来的. ○ *The clothes that are on the floor are dirty.* 地板上的那些衣物是脏的. ○ *The woman that spoke to* *me in the shop used to live next door.* 在商店里跟我说话的那个女人从前就住隔壁. ○ *Who was it that won the World Cup in 1982?* 谁赢得了1982年的世界杯? (**b**) (as the object of the *v* in the clause, but usu omitted in this position 在从句中作宾语, 但通常省略此字): *The watch (that) you gave me keeps perfect time.* 你给我的那个表走得很准. ○ *Here are the books (that) I borrowed from you a week ago.* 这些是我一周前向你借的书. ○ *The person (that) I have to phone lives in India.* 我要打电话找的那个人住在印度. (**c**) (as the object of a *prep* in the clause, but usu omitted in this position 在从句中作介词宾语, 但通常省略此字): *The photographs (that) you're looking at were taken by my brother.* 你看的那些相片是我哥哥拍的. ○ *The man (that) I was talking to had just arrived from Canada.* 我与之谈话的那个人刚从加拿大来. ○ *These are the children (that) I looked after last summer.* 这都是去年夏天我照看的孩子. **2** (used to introduce a clause following superlatives, *the only*, *all*, etc 用以引导形容词最高级以及the only、all等之后的从句): *Shakespeare is the greatest English writer that ever lived.* 莎士比亚是有史以来最伟大的英国作家. ○ *This is the most expensive watch (that) I've ever owned.* 在我所有的表当中, 这个最贵. ○ *The only part of the meal (that) I really liked was the dessert.* 这顿饭只有甜食是我爱吃的. ○ *All that I have is yours.* 凡我所有都是你的. **3** (used after an expression of time instead of *when* 用于表示时间的词语之后, 代替when): *the year that my father died* 我父亲去世的那年 ○ *the day that war broke out* 战争爆发的那天.

thatch /θætʃ; θætʃ/ *n* **1** [C, U] (roof or roof-covering made of) dried straw, reeds, etc 茅草; 干稻草; 芦苇; 茅草屋顶. **2** [sing] (*infml* 口) thick growth of hair on the head 浓密的头发.

▷ **thatch** *v* [Tn] cover (a roof) or roof (a house, etc) with thatch 用茅草盖(屋顶); 用茅草做(房屋等的)顶: *a village hut thatched with palm leaves* 用棕榈叶作顶的乡村小屋 ○ *a thatched cottage* 用茅草作屋顶的小屋.

that·cher *n* person who puts thatch on a house, etc 用茅草盖屋顶等的人.

T

thaw /θɔː; θɔ/ *v* **1** (**a**) [I, Ip, Tn, Tn·p] **~ (sth) (out)** (cause sth to) pass into an unfrozen or a liquid state after being frozen (使某物)解冻, 融化, 融解: *All the snow has thawed.* 雪都融化了. ○ *leave frozen food to thaw before cooking it* 先让冷冻食物解冻再烹调 ○ *thaw out (the ice in) the pipes* 使管道(中的冰)化冻. (**b**) [I] (used only with *it* 仅与it连用) (of the weather) become warm enough to melt snow and ice (指天气)(暖和得使冰雪)化冻, 解冻: *It's starting to thaw.* 天暖得化冻了. ⇨Usage at WATER[1] 用法见WATER[1]. **2** [I, Ip] **~ (out)** (of people, their behaviour, etc) become less cool or formal in manner (指人、态度、行为等)变得温和、不甚拘礼: *After a few drinks the party atmosphere began to thaw (out).* 喝过几杯酒之后, 聚会的气氛变得轻松自然了.

▷ **thaw** *n* (usu *sing* 通常作单数) (weather that causes) thawing 融化; 融解; 使江河、土地等解冻的天气: *go skating before the thaw* 趁着没解冻去溜冰 ○ *A thaw is setting in.* 江河渐渐解冻了. ○ (*fig* 比喻) *a thaw in East-West relations* 东西方关系的缓和.

the /ðə, ðɪ; ðə, ðɪ; *strong form* 强读式 ðiː; ði/ ⇨Detailed Guide 6.2 见词条使用详细说明6.2. ⇨Usage at A[2] 用法见A[2]. *def art* (used to make the following *n* refer to a specific person, thing, event or group 用于名词前, 表示为特指的人、物、事或群体) **1** (when it has already been mentioned or implied 指已提到过的或已知所指的人、物、事或群体): *A boy and a girl were sitting on a bench. The boy was smiling but the girl looked angry.* 一个男孩和一个女孩坐在长凳上. 那男孩在微笑, 那女孩像在生气. ○ *There was an accident here yesterday. A car hit a tree. The driver was killed.* 昨天这里出事了. 有一辆汽车撞在树上了. 司机死了. **2** (when a *n* is followed by a phrase that restricts its meaning 用于后接限定性短语的名词): *the centre of town* 市中心 ○ *the topic of conversation* 谈话的主题 ○ *the man of her dreams* 她梦想的男子 ○ *the house that Jack built* 杰克盖的房子. **3** (**a**) (when it has unique reference 用以指独一无二的人或事物): *the sun* 太阳 ○ *the moon* 月亮 ○ *the stars* 星星. (**b**) (used with some parts of the natural world without a preceding *adj* 与表示自然界某部分之名词连用, 该名词前须无形容词): *The sky was blue.* 天空是蓝的. (Cf 参看 *There was a blue sky.*) ○ *The sea is rough.* 海上波涛汹涌. (Cf 参看 *There's a rough sea.*) ○ *The atmosphere was stuffy.* 空气不流通. (Cf 参看 *There was a stuffy atmosphere.*) **4** (when the person or thing that is referred to is obvious within the situation 用以指不言而喻的人或事物): *The milkman was late this morning.* 送牛奶的人今晨来晚了. ○ *Have you seen the paper?* 你看见报纸了吗? ○ *The children are in the garden.* 孩子都在花园里呢. ○ *Would you pass the salt, please?* 劳驾把盐递给我. **5** (used with superlative *adjs*, *first*, *last*, *next*, etc 与形容词最高级, 以及first、last、next等连用): *the best day of your life* 你一生中最美好的一天 ○ *the hottest day of the holiday* 假日中最热的一天 ○ *What was the last thing I said?* 我最后说的是什么? **6** (used with an *adj* to refer to all members of a class or nationality 与形容词连用, 表示某类或某国的全体分子或成员): *trying to do the impossible* 试图做做不到的事 ○ *The rich get richer and the poor get poorer.* 富的越富, 穷的越穷. ○ *The French are famous for their cooking.* 法国人以善烹调著称. **7** (used with a *singular* [C] *n* to mean the whole class 与可数名词的单数连用, 指这一类的全体): *The chimpanzee is an endangered species.* 黑猩猩是濒于灭种的动物. ○ *The poodle is a popular house pet.* 卷毛狗是很多人都喜爱的宠物. **8** (used for inventions in general 用以泛指发明的东西): *Who invented the zip-fastener?* 是谁发明的拉链? ○ *The motor car has been with us for almost a century.* 汽车问世已近百年了. ○ *Let's not waste time re-inventing the wheel*, ie working to develop sth that has already been produced. 我们别浪费时间再去发明别人已经做出来的东西了. **9** (used in front of a unit of measure to mean 'every' 用于量度单位前, 表示'每一'): *My car does forty miles to the gallon.* 我的汽车每加仑汽油跑四十英里. ○ *I work free-lance and am paid by the hour.* 我是自由职业者, 按小时计酬. ○ *The price is 50p the dozen.* 价格是每打50便士. **10** (used to indicate that the person or thing referred to is well-known or important 用以表明所指的人或事物是出名的或重要的): *Michael Crawford? Not 'the Michael Crawford?* 迈克尔·克劳福德? 莫不是那个迈克尔·克劳福德? ○ *The royal wedding was 'the social event of the year.* 皇室婚礼是当年社会生活中的大事. **11** (idm 习语) **the more, less, etc ... the more, less, etc ...** (used to show that the increase/decrease in one amount or degree of sth continues at the same rate as another 用以表示某事物与另一事物在数量或程度方面以相同的比例增加[减少]): *The more she thought about it, the more depressed she became.* 她越想越别扭. ○ *The more beautiful the hat, the more expensive it usually is.* 帽子越好看, 一般来说价钱就越贵. ○ *I want you out of here, and the sooner the better.* 你给我走开, 越快越好. ○ *The less said about the whole affair, the happier I'll be.* 对整件事谈得越少我越高兴.

theatre (*US* **theater**) /ˈθɪətə(r); ˈθɪətɚ/ *n* **1** [C] building or outdoor area for the performance of plays and similar entertainments 戏院; 剧院; 露天剧场: *West End theatres* 伦敦西区的戏院 ○ *an open-air theatre* 露天剧场 ○ *use the school gymnasium as a theatre* 用学校的体育馆作剧场. ⇨illus at App 1 见附录1插图, page ix. **2** [C] (**a**) room or hall for lectures, etc with seats in rows rising one behind another (供演讲等用的)阶梯教室或礼堂. (**b**) (also **ˈoperating-theatre**) room in a hospital, etc where surgical operations are performed (医院等处的)手术室: *The patient is on her way to (the) theatre.* 那个女病人马上就到手术室. ○ [attrib 作定语] *a theatre sister*, ie a nurse assisting during operations 手术室护士. **3** [C] **~ of sth** (*rhet* 修辞) scene of important events (esp of war) 重大事件发生的场所; (尤指)战场, 战区: *the latest theatre of internal conflict* 内战的最新战场. **4** (**a**) [U] dramatic literature or art; the writing, acting and producing of plays 戏剧; 戏剧文学或艺术; 剧本的写作、演出及上演: *a study of Greek theatre* 对希腊戏剧的研究 ○ *Do you often go to the theatre* (ie go to see a play)? 你常去看戏吗? ○ *The play is well written but it is not/does not make good theatre*, ie is not effective when performed. 这个剧本写得很好, 但演出效果不好. (**b**) **the theatre** [sing] the theatrical world as a profession or way of life 戏剧界; 戏剧业: *She wants to go into the theatre*, eg become an actress. 她想入戏剧界(如当演员).

▷ **the·at·rical** /θɪˈætrɪkl; θɪˋætrɪkḷ/ *adj* **1** [usu attrib 通常作定语] of or for the theatre 戏院的; 剧场的; 戏剧的; 为演出的: *theatrical scenery, performances, reviews* 戏剧布景、演出、评论 ○ *a theatrical company* 剧团. **2** (of behaviour) exaggerated in order to create an effect; unnaturally showy; histrionic (指行为)为产生某种效果而夸张的, 做作的, 演戏般的: *theatrical gestures* 做作的姿势. **the·at·ric·ally** /-klɪ; -kḷɪ/ *adv*.
the·at·ric·als *n* [pl] theatrical performances 戏剧演出: *amateur theatricals* 业余戏剧演出.
□ ˈ**theatre-goer** *n* person who frequently goes to see plays, etc 经常看戏等的人.
theatre-in-the-ˈround *n* [U] form of dramatic performance with the audience seated around a central stage 圆环形剧场; 圆形舞台; 中心舞台; 岛屿式舞台.
theatre ˈweapons weapons that are of intermediate range, between tactical and strategic weapons 中程武器.

thee /ðiː; ði/ *pron* (*arch or dialect* 古或方) (object form of *thou*) 你(thou 的宾格).

theft /θeft; θɛft/ *n* [C, U] (act or instance of) stealing 偷; 行窃; 偷窃: *A number of thefts have been reported recently.* 近来有些偷窃案的报道. ○ *guilty of theft* 偷窃罪.

their /ðeə(r); ðɛr/ *possess det* of or belonging to them 他们的; 她们的; 它们的: *Their parties are always fun.* 他们的聚会总是很有趣. ○ *Their own car is being mended — this one is hired.* 他们自己的汽车正在修理——这辆是租的. ○ *Their fame rests entirely on one record.* 他们完全是靠着一张唱片出的名.
▷ **theirs** /ðeəz; ðɛrz/ *possess pron* of or belonging to them 他们的, 她们的, 它们的(所有物): *Theirs are the children with very fair hair.* 那些长着金黄头发的是他们的孩子. ○ *It's a favourite place of theirs.* 这是他们喜欢的地方.

the·ism /ˈθiːɪzəm; ˋθiɪzəm/ *n* [U] belief in the existence of a God or gods, esp a God revealed to man as the creator and ruler of the universe 有神论. Cf 参看 DEISM.
▷ **the·ist** /ˈθiːɪst; ˋθiɪst/ *n* believer in theism 有神论者. **the·istic** /θiːˈɪstɪk; θiˋɪstɪk/, **the·ist·ical** (/-kl; -kḷ/) *adjs*.

them /ðəm; ðəm; *strong form* 强读式 ðem; ðɛm/ *pers pron* 人称代词 **1** (used as the object of a *v* or of a *prep*; also used independently or after *be* 用作动词或介词的宾语, 也可单独使用或用于be之后): *Tell them the news.* 把那消息告诉他们. ○ *Give them to me.* 把那些东西给我. ○ *Did you eat all of them?* 你是否都吃光了? ○ *Oh, them! We needn't worry about them.* 哦, 他们哪! 我们用不着为他们担心. **2** (used informally instead of *him* or *her* 在口语中用以代替 him 或 her): *If a customer comes in before I get back ask them to wait.* 我回来之前若有顾客来, 就请他等一会儿. **3** (idm 习语) ˌ**them and ˈus** rich or powerful people contrasted with ordinary people like the speaker(s) 有钱或有势的人与寻常百姓(如说此话者)之对比: *We should try to get away from a 'them and us' attitude in industrial relations.* 我们应该努力摆脱劳资关系中'那群人和我们'这种对立的态度. Cf 参看 THEY.

them·atic /θɪˈmætɪk; θiˋmætɪk/ *adj* of or related to a theme(1) 主题的; 题目的; 与主题或题目有关的. ▷ **them·at·ic·ally** /-klɪ; -kḷɪ/ *adv*.

theme /θiːm; θim/ *n* [C] **1** subject of a talk, a piece of writing or a person's thoughts; topic (谈话或写作的)主题; (某人观念的)核心; 题目: *The theme of our discussion was 'Europe in the 1980's'.* 我们讨论的题目是'八十年代的欧洲'. **2** (*music* 音) melody that is repeated, developed, etc in a composition, or on which variations are composed (乐曲的)主题, 主旋律. **3** (*US*) (subject set for a) student's essay or exercise 学生的作文或练习(题目).
□ ˈ**theme park** amusement park in which the entertainments are based on a single idea or group of ideas 专题乐园(有专题娱乐活动的公园).
ˈ**theme song** (also ˈ**theme tune**) (**a**) melody that is often repeated in a musical play, film, etc (音乐剧、电影等中的)主题曲, 主题歌. (**b**) = SIGNATURE TUNE (SIGNATURE).

them·selves /ðəmˈselvz; ðəmˋsɛlvz/ *reflex, emph pron* 反身、强调代词 (only taking the main stress in sentences when used emphatically 在句中仅于加强语气时方重读) **1** (*reflex* 反身) (used when the people or animals performing an action are also affected by it 用以指人或动物所施的动作返回到本身): *The children can look 'after them'selves for a couple of hours.* 孩子们能照顾自己几个小时. **2** (*emph* 强调) (used to emphasize *they* or *them* 用以强调 they 或 them): *They them'selves had had a similar experience.* 他们自己就曾有过相似的经历. ○ *Denise and Martin paid for it them'selves.* 丹妮斯和马丁他们自己付的钱. ○ *The teachers were them'selves too surprised to comment.* 老师们自己惊奇得不知该说什么好. **3** (idm 习语) **by themˈselves** (**a**) alone 独自地; 单独地. (**b**) without help 独力地.

then /ðen; ðɛn/ *adv* **1** (referring to past or future time 指过去或将来) (**a**) at that time 当时; 那时; 其时; 届时: *We were living in Wales then.* 我们那时住在威尔士. ○ *I was still married to my first husband then.* 我那时还是跟第一个丈夫保持着婚姻关系. ○ *See you on Thursday — we'll be able to discuss it then.* 我们星期四见——到时就可以商量一下了. ○ *Jackie Kennedy, as she then was, was still only in her twenties.* 杰基·肯尼迪, 她当时叫这个名字, 还只不过二十多岁. ○ [attrib 作定语] *The then Prime Minister took her husband with her on all her travels.* 当时的首相每次外出都与夫偕行. (**b**) next; after that; afterwards 其后; 然后; 以后; 继之: *I'll have soup first and then the chicken.* 我想先喝汤再吃鸡. ○ *The liquid turned green and then brown.* 那液体先变成绿色, 又变成棕色了. ○ *We had a week in Rome and then went to Vienna.* 我们在罗马呆了一个星期, 然后去的维也纳. (**c**) (used after a *prep* 用于介词之后) that time 那时: *From then on he refused to talk about it.* 从那以后他就不再谈这件事了. ○ *We'll have to manage without a TV until then.* 我们现在没有电视也得将就着, 到时候就好了. ○ *She'll have retired by then.* 她到那时就要退休了. Cf 参看 NOW. **2** and also 还有; 而且: *There are the vegetables to peel and the soup to heat. Then there's the table to lay and the wine to cool.* 菜要择, 汤要加热. 还得摆上餐具, 把酒冰镇一下. ○ *I've sent cards to all my family. Then there's your family and the neighbours.* 我已给我全家人都寄去了请帖. 还要给你家的人及邻居们寄. **3** in that case; therefore 那么; 因此: *If it's not on the table then it will be in the drawer.* 要是不在桌子上, 那就在抽屉里. ○ *Offer to take him out for lunch, then* (ie as a result of this) *he'll feel in a better mood.* 请他出去吃午饭, 那样他心情就会好些. ○ *He'll be looking for a new secretary then?* 那么, 他就要找个新秘书了? **4** (idm 习语) **(but) then aˈgain** (used to introduce a contrasting piece of information 用以谈起另一方面的情况): *He's clumsy and untidy but then again he's always willing to help.* 他笨手笨脚的又邋遢; 可是话说回来, 他总是乐于助人. **then and there** ⇨ THERE AND THEN (THERE).

thence /ðens; ðɛns/ *adv* (*arch or fml* 古或文) from there 由彼处; 从那里: *They travelled by rail to the coast and thence by boat to America.* 他们乘火车到海岸, 再从那里乘船去美国.

the(o)- *comb form* 构词成分 of God or a god 上帝的; 神的: *theology* ○ *theocratic*.

theo·cracy /θɪˈɒkrəsɪ; θiˋɑkrəsɪ/ *n* (country with a) system of government by priests or a priestly class in which the laws of the State are believed to be the laws of God 僧侣政治, 僧侣统治, 神权政治(的国家). ▷ **theo·cratic** /ˌθɪəˈkrætɪk; ˌθiəˋkrætɪk/ *adj*.

theo·dol·ite /θɪˈɒdəlaɪt; θiˋɑdḷˌaɪt/ *n* instrument used by surveyors for measuring horizontal and vertical angles 经纬仪.

theo·logy /θɪˈɒlədʒɪ; θiˋɑlədʒɪ/ *n* **1** [U] formal study of the nature of God and of the foundations of religious belief 神学; 宗教学; 宗教信仰学: [attrib 作定语] *a theology student* 研究神学的人. **2** [C] set of religious beliefs; theological system 宗教信仰的理论; 宗教信仰的制度: *rival theologies* 敌对的宗教信仰理论.
▷ **theo·lo·gian** /ˌθɪəˈləʊdʒən; ˌθiəˋlodʒən/ *n* expert in or student of theology 神学家; 神学研究者.
theo·lo·gical /ˌθɪəˈlɒdʒɪkl; ˌθiəˋlɑdʒɪkl/ *adj*: *theological argument* 神学上的争论 ○ *a theological college* 神学院. **theo·lo·gic·ally** /-klɪ; -kḷɪ/ *adv*.

the·orem /ˈθɪərəm; ˋθiərəm/ *n* **1** rule in algebra, etc, esp one expressed as a formula (代数等的)定理(尤指以公式表示的). **2** mathematical statement to be proved by a chain of reasoning (数学的)命题.

the·or·et·ical /ˌθɪəˈretɪkl; ˌθiəˋrɛtɪkḷ/ *adj* **1** concerned with the theory of a subject 理论的; 理论上的: *a* *theoretical physicist* 理论物理学家 ○ *This book is too theoretical; I need a practical guide.* 这本书理论性太强, 我需要一本实用手册. Cf 参看 PRACTICAL 1. **2** supposed but not necessarily true 假设的: *Lendl's strength on clay gives him a theoretical advantage.* 兰德尔体格健壮, 按说他占些优势. ▷ **the·or·et·ic·ally** /-klɪ; -klɪ/ *adv*: *Theoretically we could still win, but it's very unlikely.* 按道理讲我们还能赢, 但可能性很小.

the·ory /ˈθɪərɪ; ˋθɪərɪ/ *n* **1** [C] set of reasoned ideas intended to explain facts or events 学说; 理论: *Darwin's theory of evolution* 达尔文的进化论. **2** [C] opinion or supposition, not necessarily based on reasoning 意见, 揣测(未必基于推理的): *He has a theory that wearing hats makes men go bald.* 他有个看法是男人戴帽子就会秃顶. **3** [U] ideas or suppositions in general (contrasted with *practice*) 想法, 设想(与实践相对): *It sounds fine in theory, but will it work?* 道理是不错, 但能否行得通? ○ *In theory, three things could happen*, ie there are three possibilities. 推测起来, 有三种可能性. **4** [C, U] (statement of the) principles on which a subject is based 原理; 原则; 论述: *studying music theory* 学习乐理.
▷ **the·or·ist** /ˈθɪərɪst; ˋθiə,rɪst/ *n* person who forms theories 理论家.
the·or·ize, -ise /ˈθɪəraɪz; ˋθiə,raɪz/ *v* [I, Ipr] **~ (about sth)** form theories 建立理论; 理论化.

theo·sophy /θiːˈɒsəfɪ; θiˋɑsəfɪ/ *n* [U] (*philosophy* 哲) any of several systems that aim at a direct knowledge of God by means of meditation, prayer, etc 通神学, 通神论(认为可藉冥想、祈祷等直接认识神).
▷ **theo·soph·ical** /ˌθiːəˈsɒfɪkl; ˌθiəˋsɑfɪkḷ/ *adj*.
theo·soph·ist /θiːˈɒsəfɪst; θiˋɑsəfɪst/ *n* believer in theosophy 通神论者.

thera·peutic /ˌθerəˈpjuːtɪk; ˌθɛrəˋpjutɪk/ *adj* of the art of healing or the curing of disease 治疗术的; 治疗学的; 治病的: *therapeutic exercises*, eg after a surgical operation 治疗性的锻炼(如外科手术之后) ○ *the therapeutic effects of sea air* 海洋空气的疗效.
▷ **thera·peut·ic·ally** /-klɪ; -klɪ/ *adv*.
thera·peutics *n* [*sing v*] branch of medicine concerned with curing disease 治疗学.

ther·apy /ˈθerəpɪ; ˋθɛrəpɪ/ *n* [U] **1** any treatment designed to relieve or cure an illness or a disability 治疗; 疗法: *have/undergo therapy* 接受治疗 ○ *radio-therapy* 放射治疗 ○ *occupational therapy* 职业治疗法. **2** physiotherapy 物理疗法. **3** psychotherapy 心理疗法.
▷ **ther·ap·ist** /ˈθerəpɪst; ˋθɛrəpɪst/ *n* specialist in a particular type of therapy (某疗法的)治疗专家: *a speech therapist* 语言治疗专家.

there[1] /ðeə(r); ðɛr/ *adv* **1** (**a**) in, at or to that place 在那里; 往那里: *We shall soon be there.* 我们很快就到那里. ○ *We are nearly there*, ie have nearly arrived. 我们快到了. ○ *If John sits here, Mary can sit there.* 约翰要是坐在这儿, 玛丽可以坐在那儿. ○ *We liked the hotel so much that we're going there again this year.* 我们很喜欢那个旅馆, 所以今年还要住在那里. (**b**) (used after a *prep* 用于介词之后) that place or thing 那里; 那个: *Put the keys under there.* 把钥匙放在那下面. ○ *They fit in there.* 他们在那里很合适. ○ *Go to the church and ask again — it's near there.* 先去教堂再问一下 —— 就在那儿附近. Cf 参看 HERE. **2** at or with reference to that point (in a story, a series of actions, an argument, etc) (在叙述、行动、辩论等中)在那一点上, 关于那一点: *Don't stop there. What did you do then?* 别说到那儿就不说了. 后来你怎么办了? ○ *There I have to disagree with you, I'm afraid.* 很抱歉, 在那一点上我不能同意你的意见. **3** (used for emphasis before some *vs*, eg *go, stand, lie,* to show the location of sb/sth, with the subject following the *v* if it is not a *pron* 用于某些动词如 go、stand、lie 之前, 以加强语气, 表示某人[某物]的位置, 若句子的主语不是代词, 则置于动词之后): *There goes the last bus.* 最后一班公共汽车开走了. ○ *There it goes.* 它走了. ○ *There it is: just to the right of the church.* 就在那儿: 在教堂的右侧. ○ *There you are. I've been waiting for over an hour.* 你可来了. 我等了你一个多小时了. **4** (used to call attention to sth 用以引起对某事物的注意): *There's the school bell — I must run.* 听, 上课铃响了 —— 我得赶紧走了. ○ (*ironic* 反语) *There's gratitude for you*, ie Look how ungrateful he/she is. 瞧, 就这样感激你(看他[她]多不领情). **5** (**a**) (used after *that* + a *n* for emphasis 用于 that + 名词之后以加强语气): *That woman there is 103.* 在那儿的那个女人都103岁了. (**b**) (used to emphasize a call or greeting 在招唤或寒暄时用以加强语气): *You there! Come back!* 说你呢! 回来! ○ *Hello there! Lovely to see you again!* 嘿! 又见到你了, 真高兴! **6** (idm 习语) ˌ**there and** ˈ**back** to and from a place 往返; 来回: *Can I go there and back in a day?* 我一天内能打来回吗? ˌ**there and** ˈ**then**; ˌ**then and** ˈ**there** at that time and place 当场立即; 当时当地: *I took one look at the car and offered to buy it there and then.* 我看了一眼那辆汽车当时就出价买了下来. ˌ**there you** ˈ**are** (**a**) (used when giving sb a thing he wants or has requested 用于将某人所要的东西给他时): *There you are. I've brought your newspaper.* 给你. 我把你要的报纸带来了. (**b**) (used to give reassurance when explaining, demonstrating or commenting on sth 于解释、示范或说明某事时, 用以加强对方信心): *You switch on, wait until the screen turns green, push in the disk and there you are!* 你打开开关, 等屏幕变成绿色, 把磁盘推进去就行了! ○ *There you are! I told you it was easy.* 就是这样! 我早就说过很容易. ˌ**there you** ˈ**go/go a**ˈ**gain** (used to comment, usu critically, on a typical example of sb's behaviour 用以褒贬某人一贯的行为): *There you go again — jumping to conclusions on the slightest evidence.* 你又来这一套了 —— 仅凭一点点证据就匆忙下结论.
▷ **there** *interj* **1** (used to express triumph, dismay, encouragement, etc 用以表示胜利、沮丧、鼓励等): *There (now)! What did I tell you?* ie You can see that I was right. 瞧! 我怎么跟你说的? (这回你知道我对了吧.) ○ *There! You've (gone and) woken the baby!* 看! 你(一去)把孩子吵醒了! ○ *There! That didn't hurt too much, did it?* 哎哟! 不太疼吧? **2** (idm 习语) ˌ**there,** ˈ**there!** (used to comfort a small child 用以安慰幼儿): *There, there! Never mind, you'll soon feel better.* 好啦, 好啦! 不要紧, 你呆一会儿就好了.

there[2] /ðə(r); ðɚ; *strong form* 强读式 ðeə(r); ðɛr/ *adv* **1** (used in place of a subject with *be, seem, appear,* etc, esp when referring to sb/sth for the first time 与be、seem、appear等动词连用代替主语, 尤在首次提及某人[某事物]时使用): *There's a man at the bus-stop.* 公共汽车站上有一个男人. (Cf 参看 *The man is at the bus-stop.*) ○ *There's no reason to go.* 没有理由去. ○ *There seems (to be) no doubt about it.* 此事似乎确切无疑. ○ *There appeared to be nobody willing to help.* 看来没人愿意帮忙. ○ *There can be no going back.* 不可能返回. ○ *I don't want there to be any misunderstanding.* 我可不希望有任何误解. ○ *There comes a time* (Cf 参看 *The time comes*) *when dying seems preferable to staying alive.* 有的时候觉得死了似乎比活着好. ○ *There once lived a poor farmer who had four sons.* 从前有一个穷苦的农夫, 他有四个儿子. **2** (idm 习语) ˈ**there's a good boy, girl, dog, etc** (used to praise or encourage small children or animals 用以夸奖或鼓励幼儿或小动物): *Finish your tea, there's a good boy.* 把茶喝完了吧, 乖孩子.

there·abouts /ˈðeərəbaʊts; ˋðɛrə,baʊts/ (also *US* **there·about** /ˈðeərəbaʊt; ˋðɛrə,baʊt/) *adv* (usu after *or* 通常用于 or 之后) **1** somewhere near there 在附近的某地: *The factory is in Leeds or somewhere thereabouts.* 那工厂在利兹, 也许在利兹附近. **2** near that number, quantity, time, etc 近于(某数目、数量、时间等); 大约; 左右: *I'll be home at 8 o'clock or thereabouts.* 我8点钟回家, 8点左右吧.

there·af·ter /ˌðeərˈɑːftə(r); *US* -ˈæf-; ðɛrˋæftɚ/ *adv* (*fml* 文) after that 此后; 其后: *You will be accompanied as far as the border; thereafter you must find your own way.* 有人送你到边境, 然后你就得自己走了.

thereby /ˌðeəˈbaɪ; ðɛrˋbaɪ/ *adv* (*fml* 文) by that means 借以; 从而; 由此: *They paid cash, thereby avoiding interest charges.* 他们付的是现金, 以免付利息.

there·fore /ˈðeəfɔː(r); ˋðɛr,fɔr/ *adv* for that reason 为此; 因此; 所以.

therein /ˌðeərˈɪn; ðɛrˋɪn/ *adv* (*fml or law* 文或律) (**a**) in that place 在那里; 在其中: *the house and all the possessions therein* 那所房子及其中一切财产. (**b**) in that respect 在那方面; 在那一点上: *Therein lies the crux of the matter.* 问题的关键就在那里.

there·in·after /ˌðeərɪnˈɑːftə(r); *US* -ˈæf-; ˌðɛrɪnˋæftɚ/ *adv* (*law* 律) in that part (of a document, etc) that follows 在(文件等的)下部分; 在下文中.

thereof /ˌðeər'ɒv; ðɛr'ɑv/ *adv* (*fml or law* 文或律) of that; of it 由是; 由此; 它的; 其.

thereto /ˌðeə'tu:; ðɛr'tu/ *adv* (*fml or law* 文或律) to that; to it 附之; 随附: *the agreement and the documents appended thereto* 协议及附件.

there·under /ˌðeər'ʌndə(r); ðɛr'ʌndɚ/ *adv* (*fml or law* 文或律) under that part (esp of a document, etc) 在那部分(尤指文件等的)之后; 在其下.

there·upon /ˌðeərə'pɒn; ˌðɛrə'pɑn/ *adv* (*fml* 文) **1** as the result of that 于是; 因此. **2** immediately after that 随即.

therm /θɜ:m; θɝm/ *n* unit of heat, used esp in measuring a gas supply (= 1 000 000 British thermal units) 撤姆(热量单位, 等于1 000 000英国热量单位, 尤用以计算煤气供应量).

ther·mal /'θɜ:ml; 'θɝml/ *adj* [esp attrib 尤作定语] **1** of heat 热的; 热量的: *thermal insulation* 热绝缘 ○ *a ˌthermal 'power station*, ie one using heat to generate electricity 热电站 ○ *thermal units*, ie for measuring heat 热量单位. **2** warm or hot 温暖的; 热的: *thermal springs* 温泉. **3** (of clothes) designed to keep the wearer warm in cold weather (指衣物)保暖的, 防寒的: *thermal underwear* 保暖的内衣.

▷ **ther·mal** *n* rising current of warm air (as used by a glider to gain height) 热气流(如滑翔机借以上升的).

□ **ˌthermal ca'pacity** (*physics* 物) number of units of heat needed to raise the temperature of a body by one degree 热容量.

ther·mi·onic /ˌθɜ:mɪ'ɒnɪk; ˌθɝmɪ'ɑnɪk/ *adj* of that branch of physics that deals with the emission of electrons at high temperatures 热离子学的.

□ **ˌthermionic 'valve** (*US* **ˌthermionic 'tube**) vacuum tube in which a flow of electrons is emitted by heated electrodes, used in the receiving of radio signals, etc 热离子管.

therm(o)- *comb form* 构词成分 of heat 热的: *thermonuclear* ○ *thermometer*.

ther·mo·couple /'θɜ:məʊkʌpl; 'θɝmoˌkʌpl/ *n* device for measuring temperatures by means of the thermoelectric voltage developing between two pieces of wire of different metals joined to each other at each end 热电偶; 温差电偶.

ther·mo·dyn·amics /ˌθɜ:məʊdaɪ'næmɪks; ˌθɝmodaɪ'næmɪks/ *n* [sing *v*] branch of physics dealing with the relations between heat and other forms of energy 热力学. ⇨App 11 见附录11.

ther·mo·elec·tric /ˌθɜ:məʊɪ'lektrɪk; ˌθɝmoɪ'lɛktrɪk/ *adj* producing electricity by difference of temperature 热电的; 温差电的.

ther·mo·meter /θə'mɒmɪtə(r); θə'mɑmətɚ/ *n* instrument for measuring temperature 温度计; 寒暑表; 体温表. ⇨ illus at BULB 见 BULB 插图.

ther·mo·nuc·lear /ˌθɜ:məʊ'nju:klɪə(r); *US* -'nu:klɪər; ˌθɝmo'nuklɪɚ/ *adj* of nuclear reactions that occur only at very high temperatures 热核反应的; 热核的: *a thermonuclear bomb, missile, warhead, etc*, ie one using such reactions 热核炸弹、导弹、弹头等.

ther·mo·plas·tic /ˌθɜ:məʊ'plæstɪk; ˌθɝmo'plæstɪk/ *n, adj* (plastic substance) that becomes soft and easy to bend when heated and hardens when cooled 热塑性的; 热塑性物质; 热塑塑料.

Ther·mos /'θɜ:məs; 'θɝməs/ *n* (also **'Thermos flask**, *US* **'Thermos bottle**) (*propr* 专利名) type of vacuum flask 保温瓶; 暖水瓶; 冰瓶.

ther·mo·set·ting /ˌθɜ:məʊ'setɪŋ; 'θɝmoˌsɛtɪŋ/ *adj* (of plastics) becoming permanently hard when heated (指塑料)热固的, 热硬性的.

ther·mo·stat /'θɜ:məstæt; 'θɝməˌstæt/ *n* device for automatically regulating temperature by cutting off or restoring a supply of heat (eg in a centrally-heated building, an oven, etc) 恒温器(如中央供暖的建筑物、烤箱等中的). ▷ **ther·mo·static** /ˌθɜ:mə'stætɪk; ˌθɝmə'stætɪk/ *adv*: *thermostatic control* 恒温控制. **ther·mo·stat·ic·ally** /-klɪ; -klɪ/ *adv*: *thermostatically controlled* 恒温控制的.

the·saurus /θɪ'sɔ:rəs; θɪ'sɔrəs/ *n* (*pl* **~es** /-rəsɪz; -rəsɪz/ or **thesauri** /θɪ'sɔ:raɪ; θɪ'sɔraɪ/) **1** book containing lists of words and phrases grouped according to their meanings 同类语词汇编; 同义语词汇编. **2** dictionary containing words of a certain type 同类词词典; 分类词典: *a thesaurus of slang* 俚语词典.

these ⇨ THIS.

thesis /'θi:sɪs; 'θisɪs/ *n* (*pl* **theses** /'θi:si:z; 'θisiz/) **1** statement or theory put forward and supported by arguments 论题; 论文. **2** long written essay submitted by a candidate for a university degree; dissertation 毕业论文; 学位论文.

Thes·pian (also **thespian**) /'θespɪən; 'θɛspɪən/ *adj* (*joc or rhet* 谑或修辞) of acting or the theatre 表演的; 演出的; 戏剧的.

▷ **Thes·pian** *n* (also **thespian**) (*joc or rhet* 谑或修辞) actor or actress 演员.

they /ðeɪ; ðe/ *pers pron* 人称代词 (used as the subject of a *v* 用作动词的主体) **1** people, animals or things mentioned earlier or being observed now (已经提到过的或正涉及到的)人、动物或事物; 他们; 她们; 它们: *'Where are John and Mary?' 'They went for a walk.'* '约翰和玛丽呢?' '他们散步去了.' ○ *I've got two sisters. They're both doctors.* 我有两个姐姐. 她们都是医生. ○ *They* (eg The things you are carrying) *go on the bottom shelf.* 这些东西(如你拿着的)放在架子的底层上. **2** (used informally instead of *he or she* 在口语中用以代替 he 或 she): *If anyone arrives late they'll have to wait outside.* 谁要是迟到, 他就得在外面等着. ⇨Usage at HE 用法见 HE. **3** people in general 人们: *They say we're going to have a hot summer.* 人家说今年夏天很热. ○ *They've* (ie The people in authority have) *sent us another form to fill in.* 上面(负责人)又送来一个表格让我们填写. Cf 参看 THEM.

they'd /ðeɪd; ðed/ *contracted form* 缩约式 **1** they had ⇨ HAVE. **2** they would ⇨ WILL[1], WOULD[2].

they'll /ðeɪl; ðel/ *contracted form* 缩约式 they will ⇨ WILL[1].

they're /ðeə(r); ðer/ *contracted form* 缩约式 they are ⇨ BE.

they've /ðeɪv; ðev/ *contracted form* 缩约式 they have ⇨ HAVE.

thick /θɪk; θɪk/ *adj* (**-er**, **-est**) **1** of relatively great distance or of a specified distance between opposite surfaces or sides 厚的; 粗的: *a thick slice of bread* 厚厚的一片面包 ○ *a thick line* 一条粗线 ○ *ice three inches thick* 三英寸厚的冰 ○ *a thick coat, pullover, etc*, ie made of thick material 厚大衣、套头毛衣等. **2** having a large number of units close together 稠密的; 密集的; 茂密的: *a thick forest* 密林 ○ *thick hair* 浓密的头发 ○ *in the thickest part of the crowd* 人群中最稠密之处. **3** (of a liquid or paste) relatively stiff in consistency; not flowing easily (指液体或糊状物)浓的, 黏稠的: *thick soup, paint, glue* 浓汤、稠油漆、黏胶. **4** (of a vapour or the atmosphere) not clear; dense (指汽、烟、雾或空气)不清澈的, 混浊的, 浓的: *thick fog, mist, cloud* 浓雾、重雾、密云 ○ *thick darkness* 昏暗. **5** (**a**) (of the voice) unclear, eg because one has a cold; indistinct (指嗓音)不清楚的(如因伤风所致). (**b**) (of an accent) very noticeable; strong (指口音)很明显的, 重的: *speak with/in a thick brogue* 说话带很重的土腔. **6** (*infml* 口) stupid; dull 愚笨的; 迟钝的. **7 ~ (with sb)** (*infml* 口) intimate 亲密的: *John is very thick with Anne.* 约翰和安很亲近. **8** (idm 习语) **a bit thick** ⇨ BIT[1]. **blood is thicker than water** ⇨ BLOOD[1]. **give sb/get a thick 'ear** (*sl* 俚) punish sb/be punished with a blow, esp on the ear (causing it to swell) 打耳光惩罚某人[受惩罚而吃耳光](尤指打肿耳朵). **have, etc a thick 'head** (*infml* 口) (**a**) be dull or stupid 迟钝的; 愚笨的. (**b**) be suffering from a headache, hangover, etc 头疼、过量饮酒后的不适等: *I woke up with a very thick head this morning.* 我早晨醒来觉得头昏昏沉沉的. **have a thin/thick skin** ⇨ SKIN. **(as) thick as 'thieves** (*infml* 口) (of two or more people) very friendly (指人与人)非常亲密, 要好. **(as) thick as two short 'planks** (*sl* 俚) very stupid 非常愚笨. **(have) a thick 'skull** (*infml* 口) (show) a lack of intelligence 笨头笨脑: *How can I get it into your thick skull* (ie make you understand) *that we can't afford a car?* 我怎么才能让你木头脑瓜开窍, 明白我们买不起汽车呢? **(be) thick with sth/sb** densely covered or filled with things or people 布满或充满某物; 挤满人: *a garden thick with flowers* 鲜花繁茂的花园 ○ *The building was thick with reporters.* 大楼里挤满了记者.

▷ **thick** *adv* **1** thickly 厚厚地; 密密地; 浓浓地: *Don't*

T

spread the butter too thick. 别把黄油涂得太厚. ○ *snow lying thick on the ground* 地上厚厚的积雪. **2** (idm 习语) **lay it on ˈthick/with a ˈtrowel** (*infml* 口) make sth seem bigger, worse, etc than it really is; exaggerate 使某事物似比原来的大、坏等; 夸大. **ˌthick and ˈfast** rapidly and in great numbers 又快又多: *Offers of help are coming in thick and fast.* 四面八方立即伸出援助之手.

thick *n* [U] **1** (idm 习语) **in the thick of sth** in the busiest or most crowded part of sth 某事物最繁忙的或最拥挤的部分: *He's always in the thick of it/things.* 他总是哪里最忙就在哪里. ○ *We were in the thick of the fight.* 我们那时正在酣战. **2 through ˌthick and ˈthin** in spite of all the difficulties 不顾艰难: *He remained loyal to me through thick and thin.* 他历尽艰辛始终都忠实于我.

thicken /ˈθɪkən; ˋθɪkən/ *v* [I, Tn] **1** (cause sth to) become thicker (使某物)变得厚、密、浓、混浊不清等: *when the sauce thickens* 沙司变浓时 ○ *The fog is thickening.* 雾渐渐重了. ○ *Use flour to thicken the gravy.* 加面粉使肉汁浓稠. ○ *Several drinks had thickened his voice.* 他喝了几杯酒以后嗓音变得沙哑了. **2** (idm 习语) **the plot thickens** ⇨ PLOT[2]. **thick·en·ing** /ˈθɪkənɪŋ; ˋθɪkənɪŋ/ *n* [U] material or substance used to thicken sth 使某物变浓的材料或物质; 增稠剂.

thickly *adv*.

thick·ness *n* **1** [U] quality or degree of being thick 厚、密、浓、混浊等(的程度): *4cm in thickness/a thickness of 4cm* 厚4厘米[4厘米的厚度]. **2** [C] layer 层: *one thickness of cotton wool and two thicknesses of felt* 一层棉絮及两层毛毡. **3** [C] part (of sth) that is thick or between two opposite surfaces (某物的)较厚的或夹在两层中间的部分: *steps cut into the thickness of the wall* 在墙的横断面凿出的台阶.

□ **ˌthick-ˈheaded** *adj* stupid 愚笨的.

ˌthickˈset *adj* (**a**) having a short stout body; solidly built 矮胖的; 身体结实的. (**b**) (of a hedge) with the bushes growing closely together (指树篱)茂密的.

ˌthick-ˈskinned *adj* not sensitive to criticism or insults 脸皮厚的; 对批评或侮辱感觉迟钝的.

T

thicket /ˈθɪkɪt; ˋθɪkɪt/ *n* mass of shrubs and small trees, etc growing close together 灌木丛.

thief /θi:f; θif/ *n* (*pl* **thieves** /θi:vz; θivz/) **1** person who steals, esp secretly and without violence 贼; 小偷; 窃贼. Cf 参看 BURGLAR, ROBBER (ROB). **2** (idm 习语) **honour among thieves** ⇨ HONOUR[1]. **like a thief in the night** without being seen or expected; furtively 偷偷摸摸的; 鬼鬼祟祟的. **procrastination is the thief of time** ⇨ PROCRASTINATION (PROCRASTINATE). **ˌset a ˌthief to ˈcatch a thief** (*saying* 谚) a person who has been a criminal is the best person to catch or prevent another person of the same type 用贼捉贼; 以毒攻毒. **thick as thieves** ⇨ THICK.

▷ **thieve** /θi:v; θiv/ *v* (**a**) [I] be a thief 做贼; 当小偷: *a life of thieving* 终生行窃 ○ (*joc* 谑) *Take your thieving hands off my radio!* 你那双贼手别碰我的收音机! (**b**) [Tn] steal (sth) 偷窃(某物).

thiev·ery /ˈθi:vərɪ; ˋθivərɪ/ *n* [U] stealing; theft 偷窃; 做贼.

thiev·ish *adj* having the character or habits of a thief 有偷窃行为或习惯的. **thiev·ishly** *adv*.

thigh /θaɪ; θaɪ/ *n* (**a**) part of the human leg between the knee and the hip (人的)股, 大腿. ⇨illus at HUMAN 见HUMAN插图. (**b**) corresponding part of the hind legs of other animals 动物后腿的相应部分.

□ **ˈthigh-bone** *n* bone of this part of the leg; femur 股骨.

thimble /ˈθɪmbl; ˋθɪmbl̩/ *n* small cap of metal, plastic, etc worn on the end of the finger to protect it and push the needle in sewing 顶针.

□ **thim·ble·ful** /-fʊl; -ˌfʊl/ *n* very small quantity, esp of liquid to drink 微量(尤指饮料的): *Just a thimbleful of sherry, please.* 劳驾, 来一点点雪利酒.

thin /θɪn; θɪn/ *adj* (**-nner** /ˈθɪnə(r); ˋθɪnɚ/, **-nnest** /ˈθɪnɪst; ˋθɪnɪst/) **1** having opposite surfaces relatively close together; of small diameter 薄的; 细的: *a thin sheet of metal* 一张薄金属板 ○ *That ice is too thin to stand on.* 那冰很薄, 经不住踩. ○ *a thin wire* 细的金属丝 ○ *a thin layer of glue* 薄薄的一层胶 ○ *The rope was wearing thin in one place.* 那条绳子上有一处磨细了. ○ *a thin cotton dress*, ie one made out of thin material 薄棉布连衣裙. **2** not having much flesh; lean 肉少的; 瘦的: *He's tall and rather thin.* 他个子高而且很瘦. ○ *Her illness had left her looking pale and thin.* 她病后显得苍白、清瘦. Cf 参看 FAT[1] 2. ⇨Usage 见所附用法. **3** lacking density 稀薄的: *a thin mist, haze, etc* 薄雾、霾等. **4** having units that are not closely packed together or numerous 稀疏的; 稀少的: *His hair's/He's getting rather thin on top*, ie He is starting to go bald. 他渐渐歇顶了(他头顶的头发逐渐稀少). ○ *The population is thin in this part of the country.* 该国的那一地区人口稀少. ○ *a thin audience* 寥寥可数的观众. **5** (of a liquid or paste) lacking substance; watery (指液体或糊状物)稀薄的, 多水的: *thin soup, stew, gravy, etc* 稀汤、稀汁炖肉、稀肉汁. **6** (*fig* 比喻) of poor quality or lacking some important ingredient; feeble 质量差的; 缺乏某些重要成分的; 弱的; 无力的: *thin humour* 肤浅的幽默 ○ *a thin* (ie unconvincing) *excuse* 站不住脚的借口 ○ *a thin disguise*, ie one that is easily seen through 易为人识破的伪装 ○ *The critics found her latest novel rather thin.* 书评家认为她最近写的那部小说没什么意思. **7** (idm 习语) **be skating on thin ice** ⇨ SKATE[1]. **have a thin/thick skin** ⇨ SKIN. **have a thin ˈtime (of it)** (*infml* 口) be uncomfortable or disappointed 不舒服的; 不好受的; 失望的; 受挫的: *The team's been having a thin time (of it) recently — not a single win in two months.* 那个队近来日子不好过 —— 两个月里一场都没赢. **the thin end of the ˈwedge** event, action, demand, etc that seems unimportant but is likely to lead to others that are much more important, serious, etc 可能引起重大、严重等结果的小事、小的行动、小的要求等: *Unions regard the government's intention to ban overtime as the thin end of the wedge.* 工会认为政府禁止加班的用意是老鼠拉木锨, 大头在后边. **(be) thin on the ˈground** not numerous; scarce 不多的; 少的. **through thick and thin** ⇨ THICK. **vanish, etc into thin ˈair** disappear completely 完全消失. **wear thin** ⇨ WEAR[2].

▷ **thin** *adv* thinly 薄; 细; 瘦; 稀疏: *The bread is cut too thin.* 那面包切得太薄了.

thin *v* (**-nn-**) **1** [I, Ip, Tn, Tn·p] **~ (sth) (out)** (cause sth to) become less dense or fewer in number (使某事物)变得稀或少: *wait until the fog thins (out)* 等到雾变薄些 ○ *The traffic was thinning out.* 来往车辆渐渐稀少了. ○ *War and disease had thinned the population.* 战争和疾病已使人口减少. ○ *thin out seedlings*, ie remove some to improve the growth of the rest 间苗. **2** (phr v) **thin down** become slimmer 变瘦; 变苗条: *He's thinned down a lot since he went on a diet.* 他自从节制饮食以来已经瘦了不少. **thin sth down** make sth thinner 使某物变薄、细、稀等: *thin down paint with white spirit* 用石油溶剂稀释油漆.

thinly *adv* in a thin manner 薄; 细; 瘦; 稀疏: *Spread the butter thinly.* 薄薄地涂一层黄油. ○ *thinly-sliced ham* 切成薄片的火腿.

thin·ner /ˈθɪnə(r); ˋθɪnɚ/ (also **thin·ners**) *n* [U] substance for diluting paint, etc 稀释剂; 稀料.

thin·ness /ˈθɪnnɪs; ˋθɪnnɪs/ *n* [U]

NOTE ON USAGE 用法: Compare **thin**, **skinny**, **underweight**, **slim**, etc. 试比较 **thin**、**skinny**、**underweight**、**slim** 等词的用法. When describing people whose weight is below normal, **thin** is the most general word. 指人的体重低于标准时, **thin** 是最常用的词. It may be negative, suggesting weakness or lack of health 该词可含贬义, 指虚弱或不健康: *She's gone terribly thin since her operation.* 她动过手术以后瘦得很厉害. **Bony** is often applied to parts of the body such as hands or face. ☆ **bony** 一词常用来修饰人体的某部分, 如手或脸. **Skinny** and **scrawny** are negative and can suggest lack of strength ☆ **skinny** 和 **scrawny** 都是贬义词, 表示无力: *He looks much too skinny/scrawny to be a weight-lifter.* 他瘦骨嶙峋的, 当不了举重运动员. **Underweight** is the most neutral ☆ **underweight** 最无褒贬含义: *The doctor says I'm underweight.* 医生说我的体重低于标准. **Emaciated** indicates a serious condition resulting from starvation. ☆ **emaciated** 指因饥饿造成的严重状况. It is often thought desirable to be **slim** or **slender**, **slim** being used especially of those who have reduced their weight by diet or exercise ☆ **slim** 或 **slender** 常为心向

往之的，**slim** 一词尤用于描述经节食或锻炼来减轻体重的人：*I wish I was as slim as you.* 但愿我能像你一样苗条。○ *You have a beautifully slender figure.* 你的体形十分苗条。

thine /ðaɪn; ðaɪn/ *possess pron* (*arch* 古) the thing(s) belonging to you 你的(所有物)。

▷ **thine** *possess det* (*arch* 古) (form of *thy* before a vowel or an *h* ☆ thy 的另一形式，用于元音字母前或以h开始的字母前) of or belonging to you; your 你的。

thing /θɪŋ; θɪŋ/ *n* **1** [C] any unnamed object 东西；物：*What's that thing on the table?* 桌子上的那个东西是什么？○ *There wasn't a thing* (ie There was nothing) *to eat.* 没有可吃的东西。○ *She's very fond of sweet things*, ie sweet kinds of food. 她很爱吃甜食。○ *I haven't a thing to wear*, ie I have no suitable clothes. 我没有可穿的衣服。**2 things** [pl] (**a**) personal belongings, clothing, etc 个人的所有物、衣物等：*Don't forget your swimming things*, ie swim-suit, towel, etc. 别忘了带游泳用品。○ *Have you packed your things for the journey?* 你收拾好旅行用的东西了吗？○ *Put your things* (eg coat, hat) *on and let's go.* 你把衣帽穿戴起来，咱们走吧。(**b**) tools, implements, etc 工具、器具等：*my painting things* 我的绘画用具 ○ *wash up the tea-things*, eg plates, cups, cutlery 清洗茶具(如杯碟、刀叉)。(**c**) circumstances or conditions 形势；情况：*Things are going from bad to worse.* 事态越来越糟了。○ *Think things over before you decide.* 你要先把一切考虑好再做决定。○ *You mustn't take things so seriously.* 你不要把情况看得那么严重。(**d**) (with an *adj* following 后接形容词) all that can be so described (所使用的形容词所描述的)一切事物：*interested in things Japanese* 对日本的一切事物都感兴趣。(**e**) (*law* 律) property 财产。**3** [C] (**a**) task, course of action, etc 任务、工作、做法等：*a difficult thing to do* 难做的事 ○ *The general, common, usual, established, etc thing is to*... 一般的、普通的、通常的、传统的等做法是....(**b**) fact, subject, etc 事实、事情、题目、主题等：*The main thing to remember is*... 要记住的主要事实是....○ *There's another thing I want to ask you about.* 我想再问你一件事。○ *I find the whole thing very boring.* 我觉得整个事情让人烦透了。**4** [C] (used of a person or an animal, expressing affection, pity, contempt, etc 用于指人或动物，表示可爱、怜悯、轻视等)：*What a sweet little thing your daughter is!* 你女儿真是个可爱的小姑娘！○ *My cat's been very ill, poor old thing.* 我的猫病得挺厉害，真可怜。○ *You stupid thing!* 你这蠢货！**5 the thing** [sing] what is appropriate, suitable or most important 适当的、合适的或很重要的事物：*A holiday will be just the thing for you.* 你现在需要的就是放假。○ *The thing is not to interrupt him while he's talking.* 要紧的是他说话的时候不要打断他的话。○ *say the right/wrong thing* 说话得体[不得体] ○ *The main thing is to get more orders.* 关键问题是要多弄到些定单。○ *The thing about her is that she is completely honest.* 她这个人最重要一点就是十分诚实。**6** (idm 习语) ˌ**all things conˈsidered** when one considers every aspect of a problem, situation, etc 考虑到问题、情况等的各个方面：*All things considered, we're doing quite well.* 从各方面的情况看，我们目前干得挺好。**as things ˈstand** in the present set of circumstances 就目前情况看：*As things stand, we won't finish the job on time.* 据目前情况看，我们不能按时完成任务了。**be a good thing (that)...** be fortunate that... 幸运的是...：*It's a good thing we brought the umbrella.* 幸亏我们带伞了。**be on to a good ˈthing** (*infml* 口) have found a job or style of life that is pleasant, well paid, etc 找到了挣钱多的工作或愉快的生活方式等。**be ˈseeing things** (*infml* 口) have hallucinations 产生幻觉：*Am I seeing things or is that Bill over there? I thought he was dead.* 是我看花眼了呢，还是在那儿的人是比尔呢？我以为他死了。**a close/near ˈthing** a fine balance between success and failure, life and death, doing or not doing sth, etc (成败、生死、做与不做某事等)险些非此即彼：*We just managed to win, but it was a close thing.* 我们好不容易才获胜，真险哪。**do one's own ˈthing** (*infml* 口) follow one's own interests and inclinations; be independent 照个人的爱好和意愿行事；独立自主；不受约束。**first/last ˈthing** early in the morning/late in the evening 一早[夜晚最后](做的事)：*I always take the dog for a short walk last thing before going to bed.* 我总是在晚上就寝以前带狗去散散步。**first things first** ➪ FIRST[1]. **for ˈone thing** (used to introduce a reason for sth 用以引出某事的理由)：*For one thing, I've no money; and for another I'm too busy.* 一来我没钱，二来我太忙。**have a thing about sb/sth** (*infml* 口) (**a**) be obsessed by sb/sth 对某人[某事物]耿耿于怀。(**b**) have a prejudice against sb/sth 对某人[某事物]有偏见：*I've got a thing about men with beards.* 我腻味留胡子的人。**know a thing or two** ➪ KNOW. **make a ˈthing of sth** (*infml* 口) make a fuss about sth 对某事物小题大做：*I don't want to make a (big) thing of it but you have been late for work three times this week.* 我并非想小题大做，但你本星期上班已迟到三次了。**not know the first thing about sth** ➪ KNOW. **(just) ˌone of those ˈthings** an unfortunate event, experience, etc that one must accept as unavoidable 难免的倒霉事、经历等。**one (damned, etc) thing after aˈnother** a succession of unpleasant or unwelcome happenings 不愉快的或讨厌的事情连续发生。**other things being ˈequal** provided that circumstances elsewhere remain the same 假若其他情况相同。**sure thing** ➪ SURE. **take it/things easy** ➪ EASY[2]. **taking ˌone thing with aˈnother** considering every aspect of the situation 考虑情况的各个方面。**the ˌthing ˈis** the question to be considered is 要考虑的问题是：*The thing is, can we afford a holiday?* 问题在于我们能否付得起度假的费用？**a ˌthing of the ˈpast** thing that is old-fashioned or out of date 老式的或过时的事物：*The art of writing letters seems to be a thing of the past.* 讲求写信的技巧似已过时。ˌ**things that go ˌbump in the ˈnight** (*joc* 谑) strange or frightening noises, etc 奇怪的或可怕的声音等。**what with ˌone thing and aˈnother** (*infml* 口) because of various duties, commitments, happenings, etc 因为各种任务、承诺、事情等：*What with one thing and another, I forgot to tell you we couldn't come.* 因为事情很多，弄得我忘记告诉你我们不能来了。

thing·ummy /ˈθɪŋəmɪ; ˈθɪŋəmɪ/ (also **thing·uma·jig** /ˈθɪŋəmədʒɪg; ˈθɪŋəməˌdʒɪg/, **thing·uma·bob** /ˈθɪŋəməbɒb; ˈθɪŋəməˌbɑb/, **thingy** /ˈθɪŋɪ; ˈθɪŋɪ/) *n* (*infml* 口) person or thing whose name one does not know or has forgotten or does not wish to mention 某人，某物(其名不详或已忘记或不愿提及)。

think[1] /θɪŋk; θɪŋk/ *v* (*pt, pp* **thought** /θɔːt; θɔt/) **1** [I, Ipr] **~ (about sth)** use the mind in an active way to form connected ideas 想；思索；思考：*Are animals able to think?* 动物能思考吗？○ *Think before you act*, ie Do not act hastily or rashly. 先思而后行。○ *Let me think a moment*, ie Give me time to think before I answer. 让我考虑一下。○ *He may not say much but he thinks a lot.* 别看他说得不多，但他想得很多。○ *Do you think in English or translate mentally from your own language?* 你是用英语思考呢，还是在头脑中把自己的语言翻译过来呢？○ *You're very quiet — what are you thinking (about)?* 你静静的不出声，想什么呢？**2** [Tf, Tw no passive 不用于被动语态, Cn·t esp passive 尤用于被动语态, Cn·a, Cn·n] have as an idea or opinion; consider 认为；以为：*'Do you think (that) it's going to rain?' 'Yes, I think so.'* '你认为会下雨吗？''我想可能下。' ○ *'It's going to rain, I think.' 'Oh, I don't think so.'* '我看快要下雨了。''嗳，我看下不了。' ○ *I think you're very brave.* 我认为你很勇敢。○ *I think this is their house but I'm not sure.* 我想这是他们家，但不敢肯定。○ *Do you think it likely/that it is likely?* 你认为这事可能吗？○ *I thought I heard a scream.* 我好像听到了一声尖叫。○ *What do you think she'll do now?* 现在你认为她要干什么？○ *Who do you think you are?* ie Why are you behaving in this overbearing, etc way? 你以为你很了不起吗？○ *a species long thought to be extinct* 早就认为已经灭绝的种类 ○ *He's thought to be one of the richest men in Europe.* 人们认为他是欧洲最大的富翁之一。○ *You must think me very silly.* 你准认为我很蠢。○ *Some people think him a possible future champion.* 有些人认为他可能是未来的冠军。**3** [Tf] have or form as an intention or plan 有意；打算；计划：*I think I'll go for a swim.* 我想游泳去。○ *It is thought that the Prime Minister will visit Moscow next month.* 据估计首相于下月访问莫斯科。**4** [Tw no passive 不用于被动语态] (used in negative sentences with *can/could* 用于否定句，与can/could连用) form an idea of; imagine 料想；想像：*I can't think what you mean.* 我想像不出你是什么意思。○ *We*

T

couldn't think where she'd gone to. 我们想不出来她到哪里去了. ○ *You can't 'think how glad I am to see you!* 你无法想像我见到你有多高兴! **5** [Tw no passive 不用于被动语态] take into consideration; reflect 考虑; 深思; 细想: *Think how nice it would be to see them again.* 想想能再次见到他们该有多好哇. ○ *I was just thinking (to myself) what a long way it is.* 我刚才还在琢磨着这条路多长啊. **6** [Tn, Tf, Tt] expect (sth) 预料到, 料想到(某事): *Who'd have thought it?* eg of a surprising event 谁能料到有这样的事呢? ○ *I never thought (that) I'd see her again.* 我从未想到还能见到她. ○ *Who would have thought to find you here?* 谁能料到你在这儿呢? **7** [I, Tn] (*infml* 口 *esp US*) direct one's thoughts in a certain manner or to (a subject) 朝某一方面想; 专想(某件事): *Let's think positive.* 我们往好的方面想想吧. ○ *If you want to make money you've got to think money.* 你要是想赚钱, 脑子里就得想着钱. **8** (idm 习语) **I 'thought as much** that is what I expected or suspected 我就是这么想的; 果然不出我所料. **see/think fit** ⇨ FIT[1]. **ˌthink a'gain** reconsider the situation and change one's idea or intention 重新考虑情况并改变想法或意图: *If you think I'm going to lend you my car you can think again!* 你要是以为我能把汽车借给你, 你还是另打主意吧! **think a'loud** express one's thoughts as they occur 边想边说出声来; 自言自语. **think better of (doing) sth** decide against (doing) sth after thinking further about it (深思后)决定不采纳某事物或不做某事. **think (all) the better of sb** have a higher opinion of sb 对某人有更高的评价. **think nothing 'of it** (used as a polite response to apologies, thanks, etc 用作回应道歉、感谢等的客气话). **think nothing of sth/doing sth** consider (doing) sth to be normal and not particularly unusual 认为(做)某事很平常、不特殊: *She thinks nothing of walking thirty miles a day.* 她觉得一天走三十英里无所谓. **think twice about sth/doing sth** think carefully before deciding to do sth 认真考虑后再决定做某事: *You should think twice about employing someone you've never met.* 你要雇用素未谋面的人应三思而行. **think the world, highly, a lot, not much, poorly, little, etc of sb/sth** (not used in the continuous tenses 不用于进行时态) have a good, poor, etc opinion of sb/sth 对某人[某事物]评价高、不高等: *His work is highly thought of by the critics.* 他的作品深受评论家推崇. ○ *I don't think much of my new teacher.* 我认为我们的新老师不怎么样.

9 (phr v) **think about sb/sth** (**a**) reflect upon sb/sth; recall sb/sth 回想或想起某人[某事]: *Do you ever think about your childhood?* 你是否回忆过童年的事? (**b**) take sb/sth into account; consider sb/sth 考虑到某人[某事物]: *Don't you ever think about other people?* 你从来就不考虑考虑别人吗? ○ *All he ever thinks about is money.* 他想的只是钱. **think about sth/doing sth** consider or examine sth to see if it is desirable, practicable, etc 考虑或盘算某事(看是否可取、可行等): *I'll think about it and let you know tomorrow.* 我要把这事仔细想想, 明天再给你回话. ○ *She's thinking about changing her job.* 她正考虑要换个工作.

think ahead (to sth) cast one's mind forward; anticipate (an event, a situation, etc) 预想, 预见(某事、某情况等).

think back (to sth) recall and reconsider sth in the past 想起并重新考虑(过去的)某事; 反思.

think for oneself form one's opinions, make decisions, etc independently 独立思考(形成看法、做出决定等).

think of sth/doing sth (**a**) take sth into account; consider sth 考虑到某事物: *There are so many things to think of before we decide.* 我们要考虑到许多方面然后才能做决定. ○ *You can't expect me to think of everything!* 你不能指望我把什么事都想到了! (**b**) contemplate the possibility of sth (without reaching a decision or taking action) 考虑某事的可能性(未做出决定亦未采取行动): *They're thinking of moving to America.* 他们有意移居美国. ○ *I did think of resigning, but I decided not to.* 我原来确实打算辞职, 但后来打消了这个念头. (**c**) imagine sth 想像某事物: *Just think of the expense!* 想想这笔开销吧! ○ *To think of his not knowing* (ie How surprising that he didn't know) *about it!* 想想看, 他对此事竟一无所知! (**d**) have the idea of sth 对某事物有见解 (often used with *could*, *would*, *should*, and *not* or *never* 常与could、would、should及not、never连用): *I couldn't think of letting you take the blame.* 我没想到过能让你承担责任. ○ *She would never think of marrying someone so old.* 她从未想过嫁给年纪这么大的人. (**e**) call sth to mind; remember sth 想起或记得某事物: *I can't think of his name at the moment.* 我一时想不起他的名字了. (**f**) put sth forward; suggest sth 提出或建议某事: *Can anybody think of a way to raise money?* 有人能想出筹款的办法吗? ○ *Who first thought of the idea?* 是谁先出的这个主意?

think sth out consider sth carefully; produce (an idea, etc) by thinking 仔细思考某事; 想出(主意等): *Think out your answer before you start writing.* 要想好答案再动笔. ○ *a well-thought out plan* 考虑周详的计划.

think sth over reflect upon sth (esp before reaching a decision) 慎重思考某事(尤指做出决定之前): *Please think over what I've said.* 请仔细考虑我说的话. ○ *I'd like more time to think things over.* 我要多用些时间把事情好好想想.

think sth through consider (a problem, etc) fully 全面地考虑(问题等).

think sth up (*infml* 口) produce sth by thought; invent or devise sth 想出、发明出或设计出某事物: *There's no telling what he'll think up next.* 谁也不知道他下次会想出什么花样. ○ *Can't you think up a better excuse than that?* 难道你想不出比这个借口更像样的了吗?

□ **'think-tank** *n* [CGp] organization or group of experts providing advice and ideas on national or commercial problems (国家的或商业的)智囊团, 专家小组.

think[2] /θɪŋk; θɪŋk/ *n* (*infml* 口) **1** [sing] act of thinking 思索; 思考; 考虑: *I'd better have a think before I decide.* 我最好还是先想想再做决定. **2** (idm 习语) **have (got) another think coming** must revise one's opinions, plans, etc; be forced to think again 必须修改个人的意见、计划等; 不得不重新考虑: *If you think I'm going to pay all your bills you've got another think coming.* 你要是以为我会替你付清帐单, 你还是再琢磨琢磨去吧.

thinkable /'θɪŋkəbl; 'θɪŋkəbl/ *adj* [pred 作表语] (usu with a negative 通常与否定词连用) that can be imagined; conceivable 可想像出来; 可想像: *Unemployment has reached a level that would not have been thinkable ten years ago.* 失业问题已达到严重地步, 在十年前是难以想像的.

thinker /'θɪŋkə(r); 'θɪŋkɚ/ *n* (usu with an *adj* 通常与形容词连用) person who thinks deeply or in a specified way 深思的人; 用某方式思维的人; 思想家: *a great, an original, an important, etc thinker* 伟大的、有创见的、卓越的...思想家.

think·ing /'θɪŋkɪŋ; 'θɪŋkɪŋ/ *adj* [attrib 作定语] intelligent; rational; thoughtful 思想的; 理性的; 有思考力的: *All thinking people must hate violence.* 凡是有理智的人都憎恶暴力行为.

▷ **think·ing** *n* **1** [U] thought; reasoning 思想; 思考: *do some hard thinking,* ie think deeply 深思 ○ *What's your thinking on* (ie What do you think about) *this question?* 你对这个问题有什么想法? **2** (idm 习语) **to 'my way of thinking** ⇨ WAY[1]; Cf 参看 WISHFUL THINKING (WISH).

□ **'thinking-cap** *n* (idm 习语) **put one's 'thinking-cap on** (*infml* 口) try to solve a problem by thinking about it 经思考而努力去解决问题.

third /θɜːd; θɝd/ *pron, det* 3rd; next after second 第3, 第三(个). ⇨App 4 见附录4.

▷ **third** *n* **1** one of three equal parts of sth 三分之一. **2 ~ (in sth)** (*Brit*) third class of university degree 大学的三级荣誉学位: *get a third in biology at Durham* 获达勒姆大学生物系三级荣誉学位.

thirdly *adv* in the third position or place 第三位; 第三点. ⇨Usage at FIRST[2] 用法见FIRST[2].

□ **ˌthird de'gree** long and severe questioning; use of torture to make sb confess or give information 疲劳讯问; 刑讯; 逼供.

ˌthird degree 'burn very serious burn on the skin 三度烧伤.

the ˌthird di'mension the dimension of height 第三维(指高度).

ˌthird 'party another person besides the two main people involved 第三者. **ˌthird-party in'surance** insurance that gives protection against damage or injury caused by the insured person to other people 第三者责任保险.

ˌthird-ˈrate *adj* of very poor quality 三流的; 三等的; 劣质的: *a ˌthird-rate ˈfilm* 差劲的电影.

the ˌThird ˈWorld the developing countries of Africa, Asia and Latin America, esp those not politically aligned with Communist or Western nations 第三世界: [attrib 作定语] *ˌthird-world ˈcountries* 第三世界国家.

For the uses of *third* see the examples at *fifth.* 关于 third 的用法见 fifth 词条中的示例.

thirst /θɜːst; θɝst/ *n* **1 (a)** [U, sing] feeling caused by a desire or need to drink 渴: *quench* (ie satisfy) *one's thirst with a long drink of water* 喝很多水来解渴 ○ *Working in the sun soon gave us a (powerful) thirst.* 我们在烈日下干活儿, 很快就觉得渴(极)了. **(b)** [U] suffering caused by this 渴: *They lost their way in the desert and died of thirst.* 他们在沙漠中迷路而渴死了. **2** [sing] **~ (for sth)** (*fig* 比喻) strong desire; craving 热望; 渴望; 渴求: *a/the thirst for knowledge, fame, revenge* 渴求知识、渴望成名、决心复仇.

▷ **thirst** *v* **1** [I] (*arch* 古) feel a need to drink 渴. **2** (phr v) **thirst for sth** be eager for sth 渴求某事物: *thirsting for revenge* 一定要报仇.

thirsty *adj* (**-ier**, **-iest**) **1 ~ (for sth)** feeling thirst 渴的: *be/feel thirsty* 感到渴 ○ *Salty food makes you thirsty.* 吃了咸的就觉得渴. ○ (*fig* 比喻) *The team is thirsty for success.* 该队渴望获得成功. **2 ~ (for sth)** (of land) in need of water (指土地)缺水的, 干旱的: *fields thirsty for rain* 干旱缺雨的田地. **3** (*infml* 口) causing thirst 使人渴的: *thirsty work* 让人觉得渴的工作. **thirs·tily** /-ɪlɪ; -ɪlɪ/ *adv*: *They drank thirstily.* 他们渴得大喝一阵.

thir·teen /ˌθɜːˈtiːn; θɝˈtin/ *pron, det* 13; one more than twelve 13, 十三(个). ⇨App 4 见附录 4.

▷ **thir·teen** *n* the number 13 ☆ 13; 十三.

thir·teenth /ˌθɜːˈtiːnθ; θɝˈtinθ/ *pron, det* 13th; next after twelfth 第13, 第十三(个). — *n* one of thirteen equal parts of sth 十三分之一.

For the uses of *thirteen* and *thirteenth* see *five* and *fifth.* 关于 thirteen 和 thirteenth 的用法见 five 和 fifth 词条中的示例.

thirty /ˈθɜːtɪ; ˈθɝtɪ/ *pron, det* 30; one more than twenty-nine 30, 三十(个). ⇨App 4 见附录 4.

▷ **thir·tieth** /ˈθɜːtɪəθ; ˈθɝtɪɪθ/ *pron, det* 30th; next after twenty-ninth 第30, 第三十(个). — *n* one of thirty equal parts of sth 三十分之一.

thirty *n* **1** [C] the number 30 ☆ 30; 三十. **2 the thirties** *n* [pl] numbers, years or temperature from 30 to 39 从 30 到 39 的数目、年数或温度. **3** (idm 习语) **in one's thirties** between the ages of 30 and 40 在 30 岁到 40 岁之间.

For the uses of *thirty* and *thirtieth* see the examples at *fifty*, *five* and *fifth*. 关于 thirty 和 thirtieth 的用法见 fifty、five 和 fifth 词条中的示例.

this /ðɪs; ðɪs/ *det, pron* (*pl* **these** /ðiːz; ðiz/) **1** (used to refer to a person, a thing, a place or an event that is close to the speaker/writer, esp when compared with another 用以指较近的人、物、地方或事情, 尤用于与他者比较时): *Come here and look at this picture.* 过来看看这幅画. ○ *These shoes are more comfortable than those.* 这双鞋比那双穿着舒服. ○ *Is this the book you mean?* 这是你说的那本书吗? ○ *Would you give her these?* 你要把这些给她吗? ○ *What's all this noise about?* 这些响声是怎么回事? ○ *What's this I hear about your getting married?* 我听说你结婚了, 这是怎么回事? ○ *This is my husband.* 这是我丈夫. **2** (used to refer to sb/sth previously mentioned 用以指前面提到过的某人[某事物]): *Jane wrote a letter to a newspaper. This letter contained some startling allegations.* 简给报社写了封信. 这封信里有些极其严重的指责. **3** (used to introduce sth 用以引出某事物): *Listen to this: a boy in London has died of rabies.* 你听听这件事: 伦敦有一个男孩儿得狂犬病死了. ○ *Do it like this*, ie in this way. 照这样去做. **4** (used with days or periods of time related to the present 与包括现在的日子或一段时间的词语连用): *this* (ie the current) *week, month, year, etc* 本周、月、年等 ○ *this morning*, ie today in the morning 今晨 ○ *this Tuesday*, ie Tuesday of this week 这个星期二 ○ *this minute*, ie now 现在 ○ *these days*, ie currently; recently 近来. ⇨Usage at LAST[1] 用法见 LAST[1]. **5** (*infml* 口) (used in front of a *n* followed by a possessive 用于后接属有格的名词之前): *When are we going to see this car of yours?* 我们什么时候去看你这辆汽车? ○ *These jeans of mine are dirty.* 我的这条牛仔裤脏了. ○ *This friend of hers is said to be very rich.* 她的这个朋友据说很有钱. **6** (*infml* 口) (used to refer to people and things in a narrative 用以指叙述中的人或事物) a certain 某一个: *There was this peculiar man sitting opposite me in the train.* 在火车上有个挺特别的男人坐在我对面. **7** (idm 习语) **ˌthis and ˈthat**; **ˌthis, that and the ˈother** various things, activities, etc 各种各样的事物、活动等: *'What did you talk about?' 'Oh, this and that.'* '你刚才谈什么来着?' '噢, 东一件事西一件事什么都谈.'

▷ **this** *adv* to this degree; so 到此程度; 如此: *It's about this high.* 大约有这么高. ○ *I didn't think we'd get this far*, ie as far as this. 我没想到我们会走这么远. ○ *Can you afford this much* (ie as much as this)? 你花得起这么多钱吗? Cf 参看 THAT[1, 2].

thistle /ˈθɪsl; ˈθɪsl̩/ *n* any of various types of wild plant with prickly leaves and purple, white or yellow flowers (the national emblem of Scotland) 蓟(野生, 叶有刺, 花呈紫色、白色或黄色, 为苏格兰的民族象征). ⇨illus at App 1 见附录 1 插图, page ii.

□ **ˈthistledown** *n* [U] light fluff that contains thistle seeds and is blown from thistle plants by the wind 蓟种子冠毛: *as light as thistledown* 轻如蓟的冠毛.

thither /ˈðɪðə(r); ˈðɪðɚ/ *adv* **1** (*arch* 古) to or towards that place 到那里; 向那里. **2** (idm 习语) **hither and thither** ⇨ HITHER.

tho' ⇨ THOUGH.

thole /θəʊl; θol/ (also **ˈthole-pin**) *n* peg set in the gunwale of a boat to keep an oar secure 桨叉; 桨耳. Cf 参看 ROWLOCK.

thong /θɒŋ; *US* θɔːŋ; θɔŋ/ *n* **1** narrow strip of leather used as a fastening, whip, etc (用以系物、作鞭子等的)窄长的皮带. **2** (*US*) = FLIP-FLOP.

thorax /ˈθɔːræks; ˈθoræks/ *n* (*pl* **~es** or **thor·aces** /θɔːˈreɪsiːz; ˈθorəˌsiz/) **1** part of the body between the neck and the abdomen (eg, in man, the chest) 胸(如人的). **2** middle of the three main sections of an insect (bearing the legs and wings) (昆虫的)胸部. ⇨illus at INSECT 见 INSECT 插图.

thorn /θɔːn; θɔrn/ *n* **1** [C] sharp pointed growth on the stem of a plant (植物的)刺, 棘刺: *The thorns on the roses scratched her hands.* 玫瑰上的刺把她的手划了. ⇨ illus at App 1 见附录 1 插图, page ii. **2** [C, U] (usu in compounds 通常用以构成复合词) thorny tree or shrub 带刺的树; 荆棘: *ˈhawthorn* 山楂 ○ *ˈblackthorn* 黑刺李 ○ [attrib 作定语] *a thorn hedge* 荆刺树篱. **3** (idm 习语) **a thorn in one's flesh/side** person or thing that continually annoys or hinders one 不断惹人烦恼或造成妨碍的人或事物: *He's been a thorn in my side ever since he joined this department.* 他自从到了这个部门就总让我不得安生.

▷ **thorny** *adj* (**-ier**, **-iest**) **1** having thorns 有刺的; 多刺的. **2** (*fig* 比喻) causing difficulty or disagreement 造成困难的; 引起不合的: *a thorny problem, subject, issue, etc* 棘手的问题.

thor·ough /ˈθʌrə; *US* ˈθʌrəʊ; ˈθʌro/ *adj* **1 (a)** [usu attrib 通常作定语] done completely and with great attention to detail; not superficial 彻底的; 完全的; 细致的; 深入的: *aim to provide a thorough training in all aspects of the work* 旨在为这项工作提供各方面的严格训练 ○ *give the room a thorough cleaning* 把房间彻底打扫一番. **(b)** doing things in this way 做事彻底的、全面的、细致的或深入的: *He's a slow worker but very thorough.* 他做事慢, 但非常仔细. **2** [attrib 作定语] (*derog* 贬) utter; complete 十足的; 彻头彻尾的: *That woman is a thorough nuisance.* 那个女人讨厌透了. ▷ **thor·oughly** *adv*: *The work had not been done very thoroughly.* 这工作做得不太彻底. ○ *He's a thoroughly nice person.* 他是个大好人. ○ *I'm thoroughly fed up with you.* 我觉得你烦透了. **thor·ough·ness** *n* [U].

□ **ˈthoroughgoing** *adj* [attrib 作定语] thorough(1a, 2) 做事彻底的、全面的、细致的或深入的: *a thoroughgoing revision* 认真仔细的校订 ○ *It was all a thoroughgoing waste of time.* 那完全是浪费时间.

thor·ough·bred /ˈθʌrəbred; ˈθʌrəˌbrɛd/ (also **ˈpure-bred**) *n, adj* (animal, esp a horse) of pure or pedigree stock 纯种的; 纯种动物(尤指马): *breeding thoroughbred racehorses* 饲养纯种赛马.

thor·ough·fare /ˈθʌrəfeə(r); ˋθɝo,fɛr/ *n* public road or street that is open at both ends, esp for traffic 大道; 大街; 通衢: *The Strand is one of London's busiest thoroughfares.* 斯特兰德大街是伦敦最热闹的要道之一. ○ *No thoroughfare*, ie on a sign, indicating that a road is private or that there is no way through 此路不通(告示字样, 指为私人的或无法通过的路).

those ⇨ THAT[1,2].

thou /ðaʊ; ðaʊ/ *pers pron* 人称代词 (*arch* 古) (used as the second person singular subject of a *v* 用作第二人称单数动词的主体) you 汝; 你: *Who art thou?* 汝何人也?

though (also **tho'**) /ðəʊ; ðo/ *conj* **1** (more formal when used at the beginning of the sentence 用于句首时较为庄重) despite the fact that; although 虽然; 虽则; 尽管: *She won first prize, though none of us had expected it.* 她得了头奖, 虽然这件事我们都没想到. ○ *Strange though it may seem*..., ie Although it seems strange... 尽管这事似乎很奇怪... ○ *Though they lack official support they continue their struggle.* 他们虽然没有得到官方的支持, 但仍继续奋斗. **2** (used to introduce a clause at the end of a sentence 用以引出位于句末的从句) all the same; but 然而; 但是; 可是; 不过: *I'll try to come, though I doubt if I'll be there on time.* 我尽量来, 但不敢说能准时到. ○ *He'll probably say no, though it's worth trying.* 他很可能不同意, 但不妨去试探一下. ⇨Usage at ALTHOUGH 用法见 ALTHOUGH.

▷ **though** *adv* (*infml* 口) in spite of this; however 虽然如此; 然而; 但是; 可是; 不过: *I expect you're right — I'll ask him, though.* 我认为你说得对——我去问问他也好. ○ *She promised to phone. I heard nothing, though.* 她答应要打电话来. 可我没听到回信儿.

thought[1] *pt, pp* of THINK[1].

thought[2] /θɔːt; θɔt/ *n* **1** [U, C] (act, power or process of) thinking 思索; 思考; 思维能力; 思考的过程: *He spent several minutes in thought before deciding.* 他考虑了几分钟才做决定. ○ *deep/lost in thought*, ie concentrating so much on one's thoughts that one is unaware of one's surroundings 沉思 ○ *a thought-provoking book*, ie one that makes one think seriously about what is in it 发人深思的书 ○ *Her thoughts turned/She turned her thoughts to* (ie She started to think about) *what the children were doing.* 她的思维转到孩子们正在做的事情上. **2** [U] way of thinking that is characteristic of a particular period, class, nation, etc (某一时期、阶级、国家等的)思想, 思潮: *modern, scientific, Greek thought* 现代、科学、希腊思想. **3** [U, C] **~ (for sb/sth)** consideration; care 考虑; 顾虑; 关注: *He acted without thought.* 他行事欠思量. ○ *I've read your proposal and given it some serious thought.* 我看了你的建议也认真考虑过了. ○ *Spare a thought for those less fortunate than you.* 关心一下比你困苦的人. ○ *I don't need your help, thank you, but it was a kind thought.* 我倒并不需要你帮忙, 但你的好意我心领了. **4** [C often *pl* 常作复数] idea or opinion produced by thinking 看法; 想法; 意见: *an article full of striking thoughts* 有许多卓越见解的文章 ○ *That boy hasn't a thought in his head*, ie is stupid. 那孩子没脑子(很笨). ○ *Let me have your thoughts on* (ie Tell what you think about) *the subject.* 让我听听你对这个问题的看法. ○ *He keeps his thoughts to himself*, ie does not reveal what he is thinking. 他把自己的想法闷在心里. ○ *It's not difficult to read your thoughts*, ie to know what you're thinking. 不难看出你的意思. ○ *'How will we find the house if we don't know the address?' 'That's a thought.'* '我们要是不知道地址, 怎么能找到那座房子呢?' '这倒是个事儿.' **5** [U] **~ (of doing sth)** intention 意向; 意图: *I had no thought of hurting your feelings.* 我无意伤你的感情. ○ *You can give up all/any thought of marrying Tom.* 你一定要断了嫁给汤姆的念头. ○ *Didn't you have some thought of going to Spain this summer?* 你想过今年夏天去西班牙吗? ○ *The thought of resigning never crossed my mind*, ie never occurred to me. 我从来没想过要辞职. **6 a thought** [sing] a little; rather 一点儿; 有点儿; 稍微: *You might be a thought more considerate of other people.* 你该多想着点儿别人. **7** (idm 习语) **food for thought** ⇨ FOOD. **a penny for your thoughts** ⇨ PENNY. **perish the thought** ⇨ PERISH. **read sb's mind/thoughts** ⇨ READ[5]. **second 'thoughts** (*US* **second 'thought**) change of opinion after reconsidering (经重新考虑后)改变的想法: *We had second thoughts about buying the house when we discovered the price.* 我们知道了房价以后, 对买这所房子一事又另有想法了. ○ *On second thoughts I think I'd better go now.* 我又一想, 认为最好是立刻就走. **a school of thought** ⇨ SCHOOL[1]. **the wish is father to the thought** ⇨ WISH *n*.

▷ **thought·ful** /-fl; -fəl/ *adj* **1** thinking deeply; absorbed in thought 深思的; 思考的: *thoughtful looks* 沉思的表情. **2** (of a book, writer, remark, etc) showing signs of careful thought (指书、作家、言语等)经缜密思考的. **3** showing thought[2](3) for the needs of others; considerate 顾及他人需要的; 体谅的; 体贴的; 关切的: *It was very thoughtful of you to send flowers.* 你送花来, 想得真周到. **thought·fully** /-fəlɪ; -fəlɪ/ *adv*. **thought·ful·ness** *n* [U].

thought·less *adj* **1** not aware of the possible effects or consequences of one's actions, etc; careless 考虑不周的; 粗心大意的. **2** inconsiderate of others; selfish 不顾及他人的; 自私的. **thought·lessly** *adv*. **thought·less·ness** *n* [U].

□ **'thought-reader** *n* person who claims or seems to know what people are thinking without these thoughts being expressed in words (自称)能揣摩别人思想的人; 似能解人心思的人.

thou·sand /ˈθaʊznd; ˋθaʊzn̩d/ *pron, det* **1** (after *a* or *one*, an indication of quantity; no *pl* form 用于 a 或 one 之后表示数量, 无复数形式) 1000; ten hundred 1000, 千(个): (*infml* 口) *I've got a thousand and one* (ie many) *things to do.* 我有许多事要做. ⇨App 4 见附录4. **2** (idm 习语) **one, etc in a thousand** = ONE, ETC IN A MILLION (MILLION).

▷ **thou·sand** *n* (*sing* after *a* or *one*, but often *pl* 用于 a 或 one 之后时作单数, 但常用其复数形式) the number 1000 ☆ 1000; 千.

thou·sand·fold /-fəʊld; -,fold/ *adj, adv* one thousand times as much or as many 千倍的; 成千倍.

thou·sandth /ˈθaʊznθ; ˋθaʊzn̩θ/ *pron, det* 1000th; next after nine hundred and ninety-ninth 第1000, 第一千(个). — *n* one of one thousand equal parts of sth 千分之一.

□ ,**Thousand Island 'dressing** salad dressing made of mayonnaise with ketchup and chopped pickles, etc 千岛色拉酱(用蛋黄酱、番茄酱、碎泡菜等配制的).

For the uses of *thousand* and *thousandth* see the examples at *hundred* and *hundredth*. 关于 thousand 和 thousandth 的用法见 hundred 和 hundredth 词条中的示例.

thrash /θræʃ; θræʃ/ *v* **1** [Tn] beat (a person or an animal) with a stick or whip, esp as a punishment (用棍或鞭)打或抽(人或动物)(尤指惩罚). **2** [Tn] hit (sth) with repeated blows 连续击打(某物): *The whale thrashed the water with its tail.* 那条鲸鱼不住地用尾巴击水. **3** [Tn] defeat (sb) thoroughly in a contest (在比赛中)彻底击败(某人): *Chelsea were thrashed 6-1 by Leeds.* 切尔西队被利兹队以6比1打得一败涂地. **4** [I, Ip] **~ (about/around)** make violent or convulsive movements 激烈地运动或活动: *Swimmers are thrashing about in the water.* 游泳的人在水中用力打水. **5** [Tn] = THRESH. **6** (phr v) **thrash sth out (a)** discuss sth thoroughly and frankly 深入而坦率地商讨某事: *call a meeting to thrash out the problem* 召集会议深入讨论该问题. **(b)** produce sth by discussion of this kind 藉深入而坦率的商讨产生某事物: *After much argument we thrashed out a plan.* 我们经充分地讨论制定出一个计划.

▷ **thrash·ing** *n* **1** beating 打; 殴打: *give sb/get a good thrashing* 痛打某人[挨狠打]. **2** severe defeat 大败; 惨败: *Leeds celebrated their 6-1 thrashing of Chelsea.* 利兹队欢庆以6比1大胜切尔西队.

thread /θred; θrɛd/ *n* **1** [C, U] (length of) spun cotton, wool, silk, etc; thin strand of nylon, etc (一段)棉、毛、丝等线; 细股尼龙等: *loose threads* 未捻紧的线 ○ *a needle and thread*, ie for sewing 针线(用于缝纫的) ○ *a robe embroidered with gold thread* 用金线绣的长袍. **2** [C] **~ (of sth)** (*fig* 比喻) very thin thing resembling a thread 细如线状的东西: *fine threads of red in the marble* 大理石上的红色线状花纹 ○ *A thread of light emerged from the keyhole.* 从钥匙孔透出一线亮光. **3** [C] (*fig* 比喻) line of thought connecting parts of a story, etc (贯穿故事等各部分的)线索, 脉络: *pick/take up the thread(s)*, ie continue after an interruption 接上

线(中断后的联系) ○ *The chairman gathered up the threads of the debate*, ie summarized what had been said. 主席把辩论中的各种意见概括了一下. **4** [C] spiral ridge of a screw or bolt 螺纹. ⇨illus at SCREW 见SCREW 插图. **5 threads** [pl] (*US sl* 俚) clothes 衣物; 衣服. **6** (idm 习语) **hang by a hair/a single thread** ⇨ HANG[1]. **lose the thread** ⇨ LOSE.

▷ **thread** *v* **1** [Tn, Tn·pr] (**a**) pass thread, string, etc through (sth) 将线、细绳、带子等穿过(某物); 纫: *thread a needle (with cotton)* (用线)纫针. (**b**) put (beads, etc) on a thread, etc 将(珠子等)穿在线等上: *threading pearls (on a string) to make a necklace* 把珍珠穿(在绳)上做项链. **2** [Tn, Tn·pr, Tn·p] pass (film, tape, string, etc) through sth and into the required position for use 将(影片、带子、绳子等)穿过某物置于备用位置: *thread film in(to a projector)* 把影片装进(放映机里)去 ○ *thread the wire through (the pulley)* 把金属丝穿进(滑轮)去. **3** (idm 习语) **thread one's way through (sth)** go carefully or with difficulty through (sth) 小心地穿过或挤过(某物): *threading my way through the crowded streets* (我)小心地穿过拥挤的街道.

ˈ**thread·like** *adj* resembling a thread; long and slender 如线般的; 细长的: *threadlike strands of glass fibre* 线一般细的玻璃纤维.

□ ˈ**threadbare** /-beə(r); -ˌbɛr/ *adj* **1** (of cloth, clothing, etc) worn thin; shabby (指织物、衣服等)磨薄的, 破旧的: *a threadbare carpet, coat* 破烂的地毯、大衣. **2** (*fig* 比喻) too often used or too well known to be effective; hackneyed 因经常使用或尽人皆知而无效力的; 陈腐的: *a threadbare argument, joke, plot* 陈旧的论点、笑话、情节.

threat /θret; θrɛt/ *n* **1** [C, U] expression of one's intention to punish or harm sb, esp if he does not obey 恐吓; 威胁: *make/utter threats (against sb)* (对某人)恐吓 ○ *carry out a threat (to do sth)* 威胁(要做某事) ○ *an empty threat*, ie one that cannot be put into effect 虚张声势的威胁 ○ *He is impervious to threat(s)*. 他不怕恐吓. **2** [C usu *sing*, U 作可数名词时通常作单数, 亦作不可数名词] **~ (to sb/sth) (of sth)** indication or warning of future danger, trouble, etc (对险阻等的)前兆, 预兆: *This constitutes a threat to national security.* 这对国家安全是不祥之兆. ○ *a country living under the constant threat of famine* 生活在饥馑之灾长期笼罩下的国家 ○ *some threat of rain* 有雨的某些征兆 ○ *The railway is under threat of closure.* 那条铁路有停止运营的迹象. **3** [C usu *sing* 通常作单数] person or thing regarded as likely to cause danger or ruin 可能造成危险或损害的人或事物: *Terrorism is a threat to the whole country.* 恐怖主义是整个国家的祸根.

threaten /ˈθretn; ˈθrɛtn̩/ *v* **1** [Tn, Tn·pr] **~ sb (with sth)** make a threat or threats against sb; try to influence sb by threats 恐吓或威胁某人: *threaten an employee with dismissal* 以开除要挟雇员 ○ *My attacker threatened me with a gun.* 攻击我的人用枪威胁我. **2** [Tn, Tt] use (sth) as a threat 用(某事)相要挟: *He threatened legal action.* 他以起诉相要挟. ○ *The hijackers threatened to kill all the passengers if their demands were not met.* 劫机者扬言若不满足他们的要求, 就把乘客都杀死. **3** (**a**) [It, Tn] give warning of (sth) 预示(某事): *It keeps threatening to snow*, ie Snow seems likely all the time. 天总像是要下雪. ○ *The clouds threatened rain.* 有乌云预示要下雨. (**b**) [I, It] seem likely to occur or to do sth undesirable 似将发生; 似将做出令人不快的事: *under a threatening sky* 在阴沉的天空下 ○ *If a gale threatens, do not go to sea.* 假若要起风, 就不要出海. ○ *a mistake that threatens to be costly* 可能造成重大损失的错误. **4** [Tn] be a threat to (sb/sth) 对(某人[某事])构成威胁: *the dangers that threaten us* 威胁着我们的种种危险 ○ *a species threatened by/with extinction* 有灭绝之虞的物种.

▷ **threaten·ingly** *adv*: *The dog growled at me threateningly.* 那条狗对着我狂吠, 很吓人.

three /θri:; θri/ *pron, det* **1** 3; one more than two 3, 三(个). ⇨App 4 见附录4. **2** (idm 习语) **by/in twos and threes** ⇨ TWO.

▷ **three** *n* the number 3 ☆ 3; 三.

three- (in compounds 用以构成复合词) having three of the thing specified 具有三个所示之事物: *a ˌthree-cornered ˈhat* 三角帽 ○ *a ˌthree-day eˈvent* 三日赛(全面马术测验竞赛).

□ ˌ**three-ˈdecker** *n* **1** (formerly) sailing-ship with three decks (旧时)三层甲板船. **2** anything with three layers, esp a sandwich or a cake 任何三层之物(尤指三明治或蛋糕).

ˌ**three-diˈmensional** (also **three-D**, **3-D** /ˌθri:ˈdi:; ˌθri ˈdi/) *adj* having the three dimensions of length, breadth and depth 有三度空间的; 立体的; 三维的: *a ˌthree-dimensional ˈobject* 立体物体.

ˈ**threefold** *adj, adv* three times as much or as many 三重(的); 三倍(的).

three-legged race /ˌθri:legɪd ˈreɪs; ˌθriˈlɛgɪd ˈres/ race in which competitors run in pairs, the right leg of one runner being tied to the left leg of the other 三足赛跑(参赛者两人一组, 将一人左腿与另一人右腿绑在一起跑).

ˌ**three-line ˈwhip** (*Brit*) written notice to Members of Parliament from their party leader insisting that they attend a debate and vote in a particular way (政党领袖要求本党议员出席辩论并按指示投票的)书面通知.

threepence /ˌθri:ˈpens, *formerly* 旧时读作 ˈθrepns; ˈθrɪpəns, ˈθrɛpəns/ *n* [U] (*Brit*) (esp formerly) sum of three pence (尤指旧时)三便士.

ˈ**threepenny** /ˈθrepənɪ, ˈθrʌpənɪ; ˈθripənɪ/ [attrib 作定语] (*Brit*) costing or worth three pence 三便士的.

threepenny bit /ˌθrepnɪ ˈbɪt; ˌθriˌpənɪ ˈbɪt/ former British coin worth three pence (英国旧时的)三便士硬币.

ˈ**three-piece** *adj* consisting of three separate pieces 三件一套的: *a ˌthree-piece ˈsuit*, ie a set of clothes consisting of a skirt or trousers, a blouse and a jacket for a woman, or trousers, a waistcoat and a jacket for a man 三件式套服(女服为裙或裤加衬衫和外套, 男服为西装衣裤加西装背心) ○ *a ˌthree-piece ˈsuite*, ie a set of three pieces of furniture (usu a sofa and two armchairs) 三件一套的家具(通常指一个长沙发和两个单座沙发). ⇨illus at App 1 见附录1插图, page xvi.

ˌ**three-point ˈturn** method of turning a car, etc in a small space by driving forwards, then backwards, then forwards again 三点掉头(汽车等窄路掉头法, 先向前、再退后、再向前而成).

ˈ**three-ply** *adj* (of wool, wood, etc) having three strands or thicknesses (指毛线、木材等)三股的, 三层的.

ˌ**three-ˈquarter** *adj* [attrib 作定语] consisting of three quarters of a whole 四分之三的: *a three-quarter length coat* 短大衣. — *n* (in Rugby football) player with a position between the half-backs and the full-back (英式橄榄球)中卫.

the three ˈRs ⇨ R *n*.

ˈ**threescore** *det* (*arch* 古) sixty 六十.

threesome /ˈθri:səm; ˈθrisəm/ *n* **1** group of three people; trio 三人一组; 三个一组. **2** game played by three people 三人玩的游戏或比赛.

For the uses of *three* see the examples at *five*. 关于three的用法见five词条中的示例.

thresh /θreʃ; θrɛʃ/ *v* [I, Tn] beat out or separate (grain) from husks of wheat, etc using a machine or (esp formerly) an implement held in the hand (用机器)脱粒; (尤指旧时以手持工具)打麦等.

▷ **thresher** *n* person or machine that threshes 打谷者; 脱粒机.

thresh·old /ˈθreʃhəʊld; ˈθrɛʃhold/ *n* **1** piece of wood or stone forming the bottom of a doorway 门槛. **2** entrance of a house, etc (房屋等的)门口: *cross the threshold*, ie enter 跨过门槛(进入). **3** (usu *sing* 通常作单数) (*fig* 比喻) point of entering or beginning sth 入门; 起点; 开端: *He was on the threshold of his career.* 他的事业刚刚起步. ○ *at the threshold of a new era in medicine* 医学领域新时代的开端. **4** (*medical or psychology* 医或心) limit below which a person does not react to a stimulus 阈: *above/below the threshold of consciousness* 阈上[下]知觉 ○ *have a high/low pain threshold*, ie be able to endure much/little pain, eg during illness 有很高[低]的痛觉阈.

threw *pt* of THROW[1].

thrift /θrɪft; θrɪft/ *n* [U] **1** careful or economical use of money or resources 节俭; 节约. **2** (also **sea-pink**) seashore or alpine plant with bright pink flowers 海石竹(沿海或高山植物, 开鲜艳的粉红色花).

▷ **thrifty** *adj* (**-ier**, **-iest**) showing thrift; economical 节

T

俭的；节约的. **thrift·ily** /-ılı; -ılı/ *adv*. **thrif·ti·ness** *n* [U].

thrill /θrıl; θrıl/ *n* **1 (a)** wave of excited feeling; nervous tremor 兴奋；激动；紧张；震颤：*a thrill of joy, fear, horror, etc* 一阵欢乐、害怕、恐怖等 ○ *He gets his thrills from rock-climbing.* 他从攀岩运动中得到兴奋、刺激的感受. ○ *With a thrill I realized that I had won.* 我意识到自己获得了胜利，心里一阵激动. **(b)** experience causing this 引起激动等的经历：*It was a real thrill to meet the Queen.* 能见到女王的确是令人兴奋的事. ○ *the thrill of a lifetime* 一生中最令人激动的经历. **2** (idm 习语) **(the) thrills and spills** excitement caused by taking part in or watching dangerous sports or entertainments（参加或观看危险的文体活动或表演所感受的）紧张和刺激.

▷ **thrill** *v* **1** [Tn, Tnt esp passive 尤用于被动语态] cause (sb) to feel a thrill or thrills 使（某人）感到兴奋或激动：*a thrilling experience* 令人激动的经历 ○ *The film thrilled the audience.* 那部电影对观众很有刺激性. ○ *I was thrilled by her beauty.* 她花容月貌教我一见倾心. ○ *We were thrilled to hear your wonderful news.* 我们听到你的好消息非常兴奋. **2** [I, Ipr] **~ (with sth)** feel a thrill or thrills 感到兴奋或激动：*a film to make you thrill with excitement* 使人兴奋已极的电影. **3** (idm 习语) **(be) thrilled to 'bits** (*infml* 口) (be) extremely pleased 非常愉快：*The children were thrilled to bits by their presents.* 孩子们得到礼物高兴极了. **thriller** *n* novel, play or film with an exciting and gripping plot, esp one involving crime 情节扣人心弦的小说、戏剧或电影（尤指关于罪案的）：[attrib 作定语] *a thriller writer* 写惊险故事的作家.

thrive /θraıv; θraıv/ *v* (*pt* **thrived** or **throve** /θrəʊv; θrov/, *pp* **thrived** or, in archaic use, 古语拼作 **thriven** /ˈθrıvn; ˈθrıvən/) [I, Ipr] **~ (on sth)** grow or develop well and vigorously; prosper 茁壮成长；蓬勃发展；繁荣：*a thriving industry* 蓬勃发展的工业 ○ *A business cannot thrive without investment.* 企业缺少了投资就不会兴旺. ○ *He thrives on criticism.* 他接受批评而不断进步.

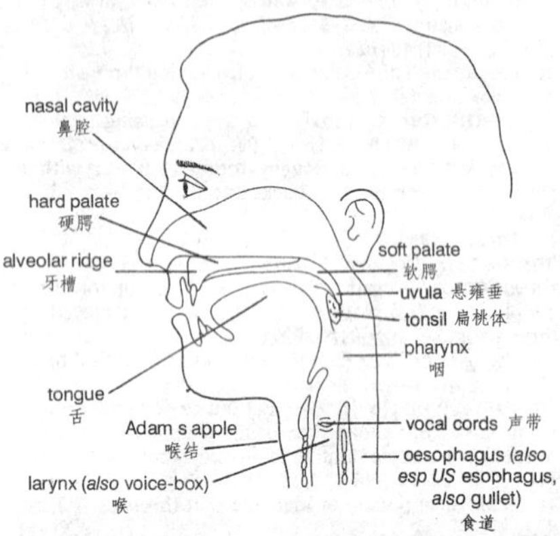

the throat 咽

throat /θrəʊt; θrot/ *n* **1** front part of the neck 颈（脖子的前面部分）：*grab sb by the throat* 掐住某人的颈部. **2** passage in the neck through which food passes to the stomach and air passes to the lungs 咽；咽头；咽喉；喉咙；嗓子：*clear one's throat*, ie by coughing, to remove phlegm or hoarseness 清清嗓子 ○ *A fish bone has stuck in my throat.* 一根鱼刺卡在我嗓子里了. ○ *The victim's throat had been cut.* 遇害者喉咙被割断了. ⇨illus 见插图. **3** (idm 习语) **cut one's own 'throat** (*infml* 口) act in such a way as to harm oneself or one's interests, by being foolish, stubborn, etc（因愚蠢、顽固等）做损害自己或自己利益的事，卡自己的脖子. **force, thrust, ram, etc sth down sb's 'throat** (*infml* 口) try to make sb accept or listen to (one's views, beliefs, etc) 勉强某人接受或听取（观点、信仰等）：*I do dislike having her extremist ideas rammed down my throat.* 我十分厌恶她强加于我的那些偏激观念. **have, etc a frog in one's throat** ⇨ FROG. **have, etc a lump in one's/the throat** ⇨ LUMP[1]. **jump down sb's throat** ⇨ JUMP[2]. **lie in/through one's teeth/throat** ⇨ LIE[1]. **stick in one's throat** ⇨ STICK[2].

▷ **-throated** (forming compound *adjs* 用以构成复合形容词) having a throat of the specified type or colour 有某种特点的嗓音；有某种颜色的颈部：*a deep-throated roar* 低沉的吼叫 ○ *a red-throated bird* 红颈的鸟.

throaty *adj* (**-ier, -iest**) **(a)** uttered deep in the throat; guttural 喉音的；发自喉部的：*a throaty laugh* 低沉的笑声. **(b)** sounding hoarse 声音嘶哑的：*a throaty cough* 沙哑的咳嗽声. **throat·ily** /-ılı; -ılı/ *adv*. **throati·ness** *n* [U].

throb /θrɒb; θrab/ *v* (**-bb-**) [I, Ipr] **~ (with sth)** **1** (of the heart, pulse, etc) beat, esp faster or stronger than usual（指心脏、脉搏等）跳动（尤指跳动较快或较强）；悸动；搏动：*His head throbbed*, ie He had a bad headache. 他头痛得很厉害. ○ *Her heart was throbbing with excitement.* 她兴奋得心直跳. **2** vibrate or sound with a persistent rhythm（有规律地）跳动、震颤或发出声响：*a throbbing wound*, ie one that gives steadily pulsating pain 阵阵疼痛的伤口 ○ *The ship's engines throbbed quietly.* 船上的发动机发出轻微的震动. ○ *a voice throbbing with emotion* 激动得声音颤抖.

▷ **throb** *n* steady continuous beat 平稳而连续的跳动或震颤：*throbs of joy, pain, pleasure, etc* 阵阵的欢乐、疼痛、愉快等 ○ *the throb of distant drums* 远处阵阵的鼓声.

throes /θrəʊz; θroz/ *n* [pl] **1** severe pains 剧痛：*the throes of childbirth* 分娩时的阵痛 ○ *death throes* 临终的痛苦. **2** (idm 习语) **in the throes of sth/of doing sth** (*infml* 口) struggling with the task of sth/of doing sth 为完成某事而拼搏；苦干：*in the throes of moving house* 为搬家而辛劳.

throm·bosis /θrɒmˈbəʊsıs; θramˈbosıs/ *n* (*pl* **-boses** /-ˈbəʊsi:z; -ˈbosiz/) [C, U] formation of a clot of blood in a blood-vessel or in the heart 血栓形成：*coronary thrombosis* 冠状动脉血栓形成.

throne /θrəʊn; θron/ *n* **1** [C] special chair or seat used by a king, queen, bishop, etc during ceremonies（国王、君主、主教等的）宝座，御座. **2 the throne** [sing] royal authority or power 王权；王位；帝位：*Queen Elizabeth II succeeded to the throne in 1952.* 伊丽莎白二世女王于1952年即位. ○ *Albania lost its throne* (ie ceased to be a monarchy) *after the war.* 阿尔巴尼亚于战后废除了君主制. ○ *come to/ascend/mount the throne*, ie become king or queen 即位 ○ *be on the throne*, ie be king or queen 在位. **3** (idm 习语) **the power behind the throne** ⇨ POWER.

throng /θrɒŋ; *US* θrɔ:ŋ; θrɔŋ/ *n* crowded mass of people or things 拥挤的人群；繁多的事物：*a throng of fans waiting to see the star* 等着看球星的大群球迷 ○ *throngs of flies filled the air* 空中的蝇群.

▷ **throng** *v* **1** [Ipr, Ip, It] move or press in a crowd 群集；拥塞：*The students thronged forward as the exam results were announced.* 公布考试结果时学生们都拥上前去. ○ *People are thronging to (see) his new play.* 人们成群结队地去看他那出新戏. **2** [Tn, Tn·pr esp passive 尤用于被动语态] **~ sth (with sb/sth)** fill (a place) with a crowd（人群）挤满（某处）：*Crowds thronged the main square of the city.* 城里的大广场上挤满了人群. ○ *The airport was thronged with holiday-makers.* 飞机场挤满了去度假的人.

throttle /ˈθrɒtl; ˈθratl/ *v* **1** [Tn] seize (sb) by the throat and stop him breathing; choke; strangle 扼（某人）的颈部；使窒息；勒死：*throttled the guard before robbing the safe* 勒死警卫然后抢保险箱 ○ (*fig* 比喻) *accused the government of throttling the freedom of the press* 谴责政府扼杀新闻自由. **2** (phr v) **throttle (sth) back/down** control the supply of fuel, steam, etc in order to reduce the speed of (an engine or a vehicle) 控制燃料、蒸汽等的供给以降低（发动机或车）的速度.

▷ **throttle** *n* valve controlling the supply of fuel, steam, etc to an engine; lever or pedal operating this 节流阀；节气门；风门；（油门或气门的）节流杆或踏板：*open (out)/close the throttle* 开[关]节气门 ○ *at full/half throttle*, ie with the throttle completely/half open 以全[半]速 ○ *take one's foot off the throttle*, ie off the accelerator, in a car 脚离开（汽车的）油门踏板.

through (*US* also **thru**) /θru:; θru/ *prep* (For special uses with many *vs*, eg *get through sth, see through sb/sth,* see the *v* entries. 可与许多动词连用, 如get through sth、see through sb/sth, 其释义见各动词词条.) **1 (a)** from one end or side of (a channel, passage, etc) to the other 从(水、陆通道等)的一端至另一端; 穿过; 贯穿; 经过: *The River Thames flows through London.* 泰晤士河流经伦敦. ○ *The burglar got in through the window.* 窃贼是从窗户进来的. ○ *Air pressure forces the water through the pipe.* 空气压力使水通过管道. **(b)** from one side of (a surface or screen) to the other 从(物体表面或屏、幕)的一边至另一边; 透过; 穿过: *You can see through glass.* 可以透过玻璃看过去. ○ *He could see three people through the mist.* 他透过雾能看见三个人. ○ *She drained the water out through a sieve.* 她用漏勺把水控出去. ○ *Cars are not allowed to go through the city centre.* 禁止汽车从市中心穿行. ○ *We had to wade through the river to the opposite bank.* 我们只好涉水过河到对岸. **(c)** passing from one side to the other of (sth hard or resistant) 从(坚硬的或有阻力的某物)的一边到另一边; 穿透: *His knees have gone through* (ie made holes in) *his jeans again.* 他的膝盖又把牛仔裤给磨破了. ○ *You need a sharp knife to cut through the knot.* 你需用快刀才能把结切断. ○ *The bullet went straight through him.* 子弹把他穿透了. ○ *The blood soaked through his shirt and stained his jacket.* 他的血透过衬衫染污了上衣. ○ *I can't feel anything through these gloves.* 我戴着手套什么都摸不出来. **(d)** (moving) from one side to the other of (sth which has height and may obstruct movement) 从(较高的或妨碍运动的某物)的一边到另一边: *He was running through the streets.* 他跑着穿过条条街道. ○ *The dog rushed straight through the flower-bed.* 那条狗直蹿过花坛. ○ *The path led through the trees to the river.* 那条小路穿过树林通向河边. ○ *The doctor pushed through the crowd to get to the injured man.* 医生挤过人群来到受伤的男子面前. ○ *She made her way through the traffic to the other side of the road.* 她穿过来往的车辆走到路的对面. Cf 参看 ACROSS[2]. **2** from the beginning to the end of (sth) 从(某事)的开始至结束; 自始至终; 从头到尾: *He will not live through the night,* ie He will die before morning. 他活不过今天夜里了. ○ *The children are too young to sit through a long concert.* 这些孩子太小, 音乐会时间长他们就坐不住了. ○ *She nursed me through my long illness.* 我病了很长时间, 她都一直护理着我. ○ *I'm half-way through (reading) his second novel.* 他写的第二本小说我正看了一半儿. **3** (*US*) up to and including; until 一直到并包括; 直至: *stay in London Tuesday thru Friday* 从星期二到星期五一直呆在伦敦. **4 (a)** (indicating the agent or means 表示作用物或方法): *I heard of the job through a newspaper advertisement.* 我从报上的广告中知道了这个工作. ○ *It was through you* (ie as a result of your help) *that we were able to meet again.* 全仗你的帮助我们才能重聚. **(b)** (indicating the cause or reason 表示原因或理由): *We missed the plane through being held up on the motorway.* 由于高速公路上交通阻塞, 我们误了班机. ○ *The accident happened through no fault of mine.* 出了这一事故并非我的过错. ○ *The vase was broken through carelessness.* 由于不小心打破了花瓶. **5** past (a barrier) or avoiding (a control imposed by law) 通过(障碍); 避开(法律的约束): *How did you manage to get all that wine through Customs?* 你是怎样使那些酒都通过海关检查的? ○ *He drove through a red light* (ie passed it without stopping) *and a policeman saw him.* 他开车闯红灯让警察看见了.

▷ **through** (*US* also **thru**) *adv part* (For special uses with many *vs,* eg *go through with sth, pull through,* see the *v* entries. 可与许多动词连用, 如go through with sth、pull through, 其释义见各动词词条.) **1** from one side of sth to the other 从某物的一边到另一边: *Put the coffee in the filter and let the water run through.* 把咖啡倒入滤器里让水流过. ○ *The tyre's flat — the nail has gone right through.* 轮胎瘪了——钉子把它扎透了. ○ *We're coming to a farmyard — I suppose we can just walk through.* 我们来到一个农家场院——我看我们可以径直走着穿过去. ○ *It's a bit crowded in here — can you get through?* 这里有些挤——你过得去吗? ○ *The flood was too deep to drive through.* 水太深汽车开不过去. **2** from the beginning to the end of sth 某事的自始至终; 从头到尾: *Don't tell me how it ends — I haven't read all the way through yet.* 先别告诉我书的结尾——我还没看完呢. ○ *We had an awful storm last night but the baby slept right through.* 昨夜我们这里风雨很大, 这孩子却一直睡着没醒. **3** past a barrier or avoiding a control imposed by law 通过障碍; 逃避法律的约束: *The light was red but the ambulance drove straight through.* 红灯亮着, 但救护车闯了过去. **4** all the way into and out of a place 一直进入或离开某地: *This train goes straight through,* ie without stopping. 这是直通车. ○ [attrib 作定语] *two 'through trains a day* 每天有两次直达列车 ○ *'through traffic* 联运 ○ *No 'through road,* ie The road is closed at one end. 此路不通. **5 (a)** (*Brit*) connected by telephone 接通电话: *Ask to be put through to me personally.* 你告诉接电话的人, 要求和我本人通电话. ○ *I tried to ring you but I couldn't get through,* eg because the line was engaged or faulty. 我给你打过电话, 但没打通(如因占线或线路故障). ○ *You're through now,* ie You can begin to speak. 您的电话接通了. **(b)** (*US*) ready to end a telephone call (准备)结束电话通话: *How soon will you be through?* 您要用多长时间打完电话? **6** (idm 习语) **ˌthrough and 'through** completely 完全; 彻底: *He's an Englishman through and through,* ie He has many typically English characteristics. 他是地地道道的英国人. ○ *We've been friends so long I know you through and through.* 咱们是多年的朋友, 我对你十分了解. **7** (phr v) **be through (with sb/sth)** (indicating that a friendship, practice, etc is ended 表示友谊、习惯等终止) have finished 已结束: *Keith and I are through.* 基思和我已不来往了. ○ *She's through with her new boy-friend.* 她跟新交的男朋友吹了. ○ *I'm finally through with* (ie I have stopped taking) *drugs.* 我终于戒毒了.

□ **'throughput** *n* [U] amount of material put through a process, esp in a specified period of time 生产量, 吞吐量, 处理量(尤指一定时期的).

'throughway *n* (*US*) = EXPRESSWAY (EXPRESS[1]).

through·out /θru:ˈaʊt; θruˋaut/ *adv* **1** in every part 各处; 各方面: *The house was painted green throughout.* 那房子整个涂成绿色的了. ○ *Certain names in the book were underlined throughout.* 书中在某些名字下面都划了线. **2** during the whole duration of sth 在某事的整个期间: *I watched the film and cried throughout.* 我看那个电影时从头哭到尾.

▷ **through·out** *prep* **1** in or into every part of (sth) 在或至(某物)的各部分: *News spread throughout the country.* 这消息传遍了全国. ○ *References to pain occur throughout the poem.* 诗中字里行间流露出痛苦之情. **2** during the whole duration of (sth) 在(某事)的整个期间: *Food was scarce throughout the war.* 在战争期间食物匮乏. ○ *Throughout his life he had always kept bees.* 他有生之年一直养蜂. ○ *Throughout their marriage he had only once seen her cry.* 在他们婚后的日子里, 他只看到她哭过一次.

throve ⇨ THRIVE.

throw[1] /θrəʊ; θro/ *v* (*pt* **threw** /θru:; θru/, *pp* **thrown** /θrəʊn; θron/) **1** [I, In/pr, Tn, Tn·pr, Tn·p, Dn·n] send (sth) through the air with some force, esp by moving the arm 投, 抛, 掷, 扔(某物): *He throws well.* 他投掷很好. ○ *How far can you throw?* 你能扔多远? ○ *Stop throwing stones at that dog!* 别再向那条狗扔石子了! ○ *Throw the ball to your sister.* 把球扔给你妹妹. ○ *She threw the ball up and caught it again.* 她把球抛起又接住. ○ *Please throw me that towel.* 请把那条毛巾给我扔过来. ○ (*fig* 比喻) *She threw me an angry look,* ie glanced angrily at me. 她生气地瞪了我一眼. **2** [Tn·pr, Tn·p] **~ sth around/over sb/sth; ~ sth on/off** put (clothes, etc) on or off quickly or carelessly 匆忙或随随便便穿、脱、戴、摘、披(衣物等): *He threw a blanket over the injured man.* 他急忙给受伤的人披上条毯子. ○ *threw on his uniform* (他)匆匆穿上制服 ○ *threw off her coat* (她)随手脱下大衣. **3** [Tn·pr, Tn·p] turn or move (a part of the body) quickly or violently in the specified direction 快速或猛烈地(向所示之方向)转动或移动(身体的某部分): *Throw your arms out in front of you as you dive.* 跳水时手臂迅速前伸. ○ *The sergeant threw his shoulders back and his chest out.* 那巡佐用力挺着胸. ○ *He threw back his head and roared with laughter.* 他仰着头哈哈大笑. ○ *She threw up her hands in horror at the idea.* 她听到那个主意吓得把手都举了起来. **4** [Tn, Tn·pr] hurl (sb) to the ground or the floor 用力将(某人)摔在地上: *Two jockeys were thrown in the second race.* 有两个骑师在第二场赛马时摔了下来. ○ *The wrestler succeeded in*

T

throwing his opponent (to the canvas). 那摔跤手把对方摔倒(在地)了. **5** [Tn] **(a)** cause (dice) to fall to the table after shaking them 掷(色子). **(b)** obtain (a number) by doing this 掷出(色子的点数): *He threw three sixes in a row.* 他掷出一连三个六点. **6** [Tn] shape (pottery) on a potter's wheel (在陶钧上)制(陶坯): *a hand-thrown vase* 手工拉制的陶瓶. **7** [Tn] (*infml* 口) disturb (sb); disconcert 惊扰(某人); 使不安; 使慌乱: *The news of her death really threw me.* 她的死讯真让我伤心. ○ *The speaker was completely thrown by the interruption.* 演讲的人因受到干扰而心烦意乱. **8** [Tn·pr esp passive 尤用于被动语态] cause (sb) to be in a certain state 使(某人)处于某种状态: *Hundreds were thrown out of work.* 数以百计的人失去了工作. ○ *We were thrown into confusion by the news.* 我们让那消息给弄糊涂了. **9** **(a)** [Tn·pr] cause (sth) to extend 使(某物)伸展或延长: *throw a bridge across a river* 在河上架一座桥. **(b)** [Tn, Tn·pr] project or cast (light, shade, etc); cause to be 投射(光线、影子等); 使成为: *The trees threw long shadows across the lawn.* 树在草坪上都投下长长的影子. **(c)** [Tn] deliver (a punch) 挥, 出(拳): *In the struggle several punches were thrown.* 在搏斗中打出了几拳. **10** [Tn] move (a switch, lever, etc) so as to operate it 按动, 扳动, 推动(开关、操纵杆等). **11** [Tn] (*US infml* 口) lose (a game or contest) deliberately 故意输掉(比赛或竞赛). **12** [Tn] have or display (a fit, etc) 表现出(发作等): *She regularly throws tantrums.* 她经常大发脾气. **13** [Tn] (*infml* 口) give (a party) 举行(聚会). **14** (For idioms containing **throw**, see entries for *ns*, *adjs*, etc 习语中有 **throw** 者, 见有关名词、形容词等的词条, 如 **throw the book at sb** ⇨ BOOK[1]; **throw cold water on sth** ⇨ COLD[1].)

15 (phr v) **throw sth about/around** scatter sth 乱抛某物: *Don't throw litter about like that.* 不要乱扔杂物.

throw oneself at sth/sb **(a)** rush violently at sth/sb 冲向某物[某人]. **(b)** (*infml* 口) (of a woman) make over-eager advances to (a man) (指女子)热切亲近(男子): *Everyone can see she's just throwing herself at him.* 谁都看得出来她跟他套近乎.

throw sth away **(a)** discard sth as useless or unwanted 丢弃某物(因无用或不需要): *That's rubbish — you can throw it away.* 那东西没用 —— 你把它扔了吧. **(b)** fail to make use of sth 未能利用某事物: *throw away an opportunity, advantage, etc* 失去机会、优势等 ○ *My advice was thrown away* (ie wasted) *on him.* 我对他的劝告都白费了. **(c)** (of actors, etc) speak (words) in a deliberately casual way (指演员等)有意淡淡地说出(台词): *This speech is meant to be thrown away.* 这段话要漫不经心地说出来.

throw sb back on sth (usu passive 通常用于被动语态) force sb to rely on sth (because nothing else is available) 迫使某人依靠某事物(因别无他物): *The television broke down so we were thrown back on our own resources*, ie had to entertain ourselves. 电视机坏了, 我们只好自作消遣了.

throw sth in **(a)** include sth with what one is selling or offering, without increasing the price (出售或出价时)额外赠送某物: *You can have the piano for £60, and I'll throw in the stool as well.* 这架钢琴可以卖给你60英镑, 琴凳我奉送. **(b)** make (a remark, etc) casually 随口说出(话语等).

throw oneself into sth begin to do sth energetically 积极地做起某事来: *throwing themselves into their work* (他们)精力充沛地工作起来.

throw sth off produce or compose sth in a casual way, without apparent effort 轻易做成某事物: *threw off a few lines of verse* 随笔写出几行诗. **throw sth/sb off** manage to get rid of sth/sb 摆脱某事物[某人]: *throw off a cold, a troublesome acquaintance, one's pursuers* 治好伤风、摆脱一个讨厌的认识的人、甩掉紧追不放的人.

throw oneself on sb/sth (*fml* 文) rely entirely on sb/sth; entrust oneself to sb/sth 完全依赖某人[某事物]; 将自己托付给某人[某事物]: *He was clearly guilty and could only throw himself on the mercy of the court.* 他显然有罪, 只好听凭法庭处置.

throw sb out **(a)** force (a trouble-maker, etc) to leave 赶走, 轰走(闹事的人等): *The drunk was thrown out (of the pub).* 那醉鬼(从酒馆)给赶了出去. **(b)** distract or confuse sb; cause sb to make a mistake 使某人分心、糊涂或出差错: *Do keep quiet or you'll throw me out in my calculations.* 你可得安静点儿了, 要不然我没法计算了. **throw sth out** **(a)** utter sth in a casual or spontaneous way 漫不经心地或随口说出某事: *throw out a hint, a suggestion, an idea, etc* 漫不经心地吐露口风、提出建议、说出想法等. **(b)** reject (a proposal, an idea, etc) 拒不接受(建议、主意等). **(c)** = THROW STH AWAY (a): *It's time we threw that old chair out — it's completely broken.* 咱们得把那个旧椅子扔了 —— 已经散架子了.

throw sb over desert or abandon sb 背弃或抛弃某人: *When he became rich he threw over all his old friends.* 他发财之后把老朋友都抛弃了.

throw sb together bring (people) into contact with each other, often casually 使(人与人)相遇或相聚(常指不期而遇): *Fate had thrown them together.* 命运把他们聚在一起了. ○ *As the only English speakers, we were rather thrown together.* 因为只有我们是说英语的, 所以我们是这么凑到一起的. **throw sth together** make or produce sth hastily 仓促做出或制出某物: *I'll just throw together a quick supper.* 我马上做一顿简便的晚餐吧.

throw sth up **(a)** vomit (food) 呕出(食物). **(b)** resign from sth 辞去某事: *throw up one's job* 辞职 ○ *You've thrown up a very promising career.* 你放弃了一个很有前途的职业. **(c)** bring sth to notice 使某事物引起注意: *Her research has thrown up some interesting facts.* 她在研究中有些发现令人很感兴趣. **(d)** build sth suddenly or hastily 突然或匆匆建造某物.

□ ˈ**throw-away** *adj* [attrib 作定语] **(a)** intended to be discarded after use 使用后丢弃的; 一次性使用的: *throw-away cups, tissues, razors* 一次性杯子、纸巾、剃刀. **(b)** spoken in a deliberately casual way; not emphasized 故意脱口而出的; 漫不经心说出的: *a throw-away remark* 脱口而出的话.

ˈ**throw-back** *n* animal, etc that shows characteristics of an ancestor earlier than its parents 有返祖现象的动物等. Cf 参看 ATAVISM.

ˈ**throw-in** *n* (in football) throwing in of the ball after it has gone outside the area of play (足球的)掷界外球, 掷边线球.

throw[2] /θrəʊ; θro/ *n* **1** act of throwing 投; 掷; 抛; 扔: *a well-aimed throw* 准确的投掷 ○ *It's your throw*, eg your turn to throw the dice. 该你掷了(如该你掷色子). **2** distance to which sth is or may be thrown 投掷的距离: *a throw of 70 metres* 70米远的投掷 ○ *a record throw of the discus* 创铁饼投掷纪录的距离. **3** (*US*) piece of cloth used to cover a chair, sofa, etc (盖于椅子、沙发等上的)罩, 套. **4** (idm 习语) **a stone's throw** ⇨ STONE.

thru (*US*) = THROUGH.

thrush[1] /θrʌʃ; θrʌʃ/ *n* any of various types of songbird, esp one with a brownish back and speckled breast (the *song-thrush*) 鸫科鸣禽的任何一种(尤指棕色背、胸部有斑点的). ⇨illus at App 1 见附录1插图, page iv.

thrush[2] /θrʌʃ; θrʌʃ/ *n* [U] **(a)** infectious disease producing white patches in the mouth and throat, esp in children 鹅口疮, 真菌性口炎(患者多为幼儿). **(b)** similar disease affecting the vagina 念珠菌阴道炎.

thrust /θrʌst; θrʌst/ *v* (*pt, pp* **thrust**) **1** [I, Ipr, Ip, Tn, Tn·pr, Tn·p] push (sth/sb/oneself) suddenly or violently 猛然或用力推(某物[某人]); (自己)向前挤: *a thrusting* (ie aggressive) *young salesman* 有闯劲的年轻推销员 ○ *He thrust (his way) through the crowd.* 他从人群中挤了过去. ○ *thrust a tip into the waiter's hand* 把小费塞在服务员手里 ○ (*fig* 比喻) *My objections were thrust aside*, ie dismissed. 我提出的异议被置之一旁. ○ *She tends to thrust herself forward too much*, ie to be too self-assertive or ambitious. 她这个人太好强. **2** [Ipr, Tn·pr] **~ at sb (with sth)/~ sth at sb** make a forward stroke at sb with (a sword, etc) 用(剑等)向某人刺去: *The mugger thrust at his victim with a knife.* 抢劫者用刀子向受害人刺去. ○ *thrust one's bayonet at the enemy* 用刺刀刺敌人. **3** (phr v) **thrust sth/sb on/upon sb** force sb to accept sth/sb or to undertake sth 迫使某人同意(做)某事、接受某物或接待某人: *Some men have greatness thrust upon them*, ie become famous without wishing or trying to be. 有些人成名是环境造就的. ○ *She is rather annoyed at having three extra guests suddenly thrust on her.* 因为突然多来了三个不速之客要接待, 她心里直冒火.

▷ **thrust** *n* **1** [C] **(a)** act or movement of thrusting 推;

插; 挤; 刺; 戳: *killed by a bayonet thrust* 被刺刀刺死. **(b)** strong attack in war or in a contest (战争或比赛中的)猛攻: *a deep thrust into the opponent's territory* 深入对手范围内的猛攻. **(c)** (*fig* 比喻) hostile remark aimed at sb 对某人的抨击: *a speech full of thrusts at the government* 对政府大加挞伐的演说. **2** [U] forward force produced by a propeller, jet engine, rocket, etc (推进器、喷气发动机、火箭等的)推力. **3** [U] (*architecture* 建) stress or pressure between neighbouring parts of a structure (eg an arch) 压力; 推力. **4** [U] **~ (of sth)** main point or theme (of remarks, etc); gist (言语、评论等的)要点, 主题, 要旨: *What was the thrust of his argument?* 他的论据的要点是什么? **5** (idm 习语) **cut and thrust** ⇨ CUT².

thruster *n* person who thrusts himself forward (to win an advantage, etc) 抢先的人(为赢得优势等).

thud /θʌd; θʌd/ *n* low dull sound like that of a blow on sth soft 沉闷的声响(似撞击软物的声音): *The car hit the child with a sickening thud.* 汽车把那个孩子撞了, 发出一声可怕的闷响.

▷ **thud** *v* (**-dd-**) [Ipr, Ip] move, fall or hit sth with a thud 砰然移动、落下或打击某物: *the sound of branches thudding against the walls of the hut* 树枝碰击木屋墙壁发出的声音 ○ *I could hear him thudding about upstairs in his heavy boots.* 我听见他穿着沉重的靴子在楼上咯咯地走来走去.

thug /θʌg; θʌg/ *n* violent criminal or hooligan 暴徒; 流氓; 恶棍. ▷ **thug·gery** /ˈθʌgərɪ; ˋθʌgərɪ/ *n* [U].

thumb /θʌm; θʌm/ *n* **1** short thick finger set apart from the other four 拇指. ⇨illus at HAND 见HAND插图. **2** part of a glove covering this (手套的)拇指部分. **3** (idm 习语) **be all (fingers and) ˈthumbs** be very clumsy, esp when handling things 十分笨拙; (尤指)笨手笨脚. **a rule of thumb** ⇨ RULE. **stand/stick out like a sore thumb** ⇨ SORE. **thumbs ˈup/ˈdown** (phrase or gesture used to indicate success or approval/failure or rejection 表示成功或赞许[失败或拒绝]的用语或手势): *give sb/sth the thumbs up* 称赞某人[某事物] ○ *I'm afraid it's thumbs down for your new proposal.* 我看你的新建议是行不通了. **twiddle one's thumbs** ⇨ TWIDDLE. **under sb's ˈthumb** completely under sb's influence or control 完全受某人的影响或支配: *She's got him under her thumb.* 她把他管住了.

▷ **thumb** *v* **1** [Ipr, Tn] **~ (through) sth** turn over the pages of (a book); make (a book, pages) worn or dirty by doing this 翻(书)页; 将(书、书页)翻坏或弄脏: *thumbing through the dictionary* 翻查词典 ○ *a well-thumbed copy* 翻旧了的一本书. **2** (idm 习语) **thumb a ˈlift** (try to) get a free ride in a motor vehicle by signalling with one's thumb; hitch-hike 向路过的机动车竖起拇指表示要求免费搭车. **thumb one's nose at sb/sth** make a rude gesture at sb/sth by putting one's thumb against the end of one's nose 将拇指放在鼻尖上作为对某人[某事物]表示轻蔑的手势.

□ **ˈthumb-index** *n* set of lettered notches cut in the edge of a book, used to identify the position of the various sections in it (eg the words beginning with a certain letter in a dictionary) 拇指页标(书边切割的缺口, 一般按字母顺序排列, 用以标示各字母所在书中的位置, 如某些字典中的).

ˈthumb-nail *n* nail at the tip of the thumb 拇指的指甲. — *adj* [attrib 作定语] briefly written 文字简洁的: *a thumb-nail sketch/portrait/description of sb/sth* 对某人[某事物]的简略描述.

ˈthumbscrew *n* former instrument of torture that squeezed the thumb 拇指夹(旧时的刑具).

ˈthumb-stall *n* sheath to cover an injured thumb 拇指套(保护受伤拇指的).

ˈthumb-tack *n* (*US*) = DRAWING-PIN (DRAWING).

thump /θʌmp; θʌmp/ *v* [I, Ipr, Ip, Tn, Tn·pr, Tn·p, Cn·a] beat or strike or knock heavily, esp with the fist 狠打, 重击, 猛捶(尤指用拳): *My heart was thumping (with excitement).* 我(激动得)心砰砰跳. ○ *Someone thumped (on) the door.* 有人使劲敲门. ○ *two boys thumping each other (on the head)* 挥拳互打(头部)的两个男孩 ○ (*fig* 比喻) *He thumped out a tune* (ie played it loudly) *on the piano.* 他用力在钢琴上弹奏一支曲子. ○ *She thumped the cushion flat.* 她把垫子捶平了.

▷ **thump** *n* **(a)** heavy blow 重击: *gave him a thump* 狠打他一拳. **(b)** noise made by this 重击声: *The sack of cement hit the ground with a thump.* 水泥袋砰的一声落在地上.

thump·ing (also **thundering**) *adj* [attrib 作定语] (*infml* 口) big 大的: *a thumping lie* 大瞎话 ○ *win by a thumping majority* 以绝对多数获胜. — *adv* (*infml* 口) extremely 极; 非常: *lives in a thumping great house in the country* 住在乡间一座特别大的房子里.

thun·der /ˈθʌndə(r); ˋθʌndɚ/ *n* [U] **1** loud noise that follows a flash of lightning 雷; 雷声: *a crash/peal/roll of thunder* 雷声大作 ○ *There's thunder in the air*, ie Thunder is likely. 好像要打雷了. ○ *We haven't had much thunder this summer.* 今年夏天我们没怎么听见打雷. **2** any similar noise 似雷的声音: *the thunder of the guns, jets, drums* 大炮、喷气飞机、鼓的隆隆声 ○ *a/the thunder of applause* 掌声如雷. **3** (idm 习语) **blood and thunder** ⇨ BLOOD¹. **steal sb's thunder** ⇨ STEAL.

▷ **thun·der** *v* **1** [I, In/pr] (used with *it* 与it连用) sound with thunder 打雷: *It thundered all night.* 夜间一直在打雷. **2** **(a)** [Ipr] make a noise like thunder; sound loudly 发出雷鸣般的声音; 响声大作: *A voice thundered in my ear.* 我耳边响起雷鸣般的讲话声. ○ *Someone was thundering at the door*, ie beating it. 有人使劲地敲着门. **(b)** [Ipr, Ip] move in the specified direction making a loud noise 轰隆隆地向某方向移动: *The train thundered through the station.* 火车隆隆地驶过车站. ○ *heavy lorries thundering along, by, past, etc* 隆隆驶过的重型卡车. **3** **(a)** [Ipr] **~ against sth/at sb** utter loud threats, etc against sth/sb 大声说反对某事或威胁某人的话: *reformers thundering against corruption* 高呼反腐败的改革者 ○ *What right have you to thunder at me like that?* 你有什么权力大嚷大叫地威胁我? **(b)** [Tn] utter (threats, etc) loudly 喊出(威胁的话等): *'How dare you speak to me like that?' he thundered.* '你竟敢这样跟我说话?'他喝道. **thun·derer** /ˈθʌndərə(r); ˋθʌndərɚ/ *n*. **thun·der·ing** /-dərɪŋ; -dərɪŋ/ *adj*, *adv* = THUMPING (THUMP): *a thundering (great) nuisance* 极讨厌的东西.

thun·der·ous /-dərəs; -dərəs/ *adj* like thunder; very loud 雷鸣般的; 声音很大的: *thunderous applause* 掌声雷动. **thun·der·ously** *adv*.

thundery /-dərɪ; -dərɪ/ *adj* (of weather) giving signs of thunder (指天气)似要打雷的: *a thundery day* 雷雨欲来的一天.

□ **ˈthunderbolt** *n* **1** flash of lightning with a crash of thunder 雷电; 霹雳. **2** (*fig* 比喻) startling or terrible event or statement 突然的或可怕的事情或言语: *The unexpected defeat came as a thunderbolt.* 这意外的失败犹如晴天霹雳. ○ *He unleashed a thunderbolt by announcing his resignation.* 他宣布辞职好似晴天炸雷一般.

ˈthunderclap *n* **1** crash of thunder 雷声; 霹雳. **2** sudden terrible event or piece of news; thunderbolt(2) 突然而可怕的事情或消息.

ˈthunder-cloud *n* large dark cloud that can produce lightning and thunder 雷雨云.

ˈthunderstorm *n* storm with thunder and lightning and usu heavy rain 雷雨; 雷暴.

ˈthunderstruck *adj* [esp pred 尤作表语] amazed 大吃一惊.

Thur (also **Thurs**) *abbr* 缩写 = Thursday: *Thurs 26 June* 6月26日星期四.

Thurs·day /ˈθɜːzdɪ; ˋθɝzdɪ/ *n* [C, U] (*abbrs* 缩写 **Thur, Thurs**) the fifth day of the week, next after Wednesday 星期四.

For the uses of *Thursday* see the examples at *Monday.* 关于Thursday的用法见Monday词条中的示例.

thus /ðʌs; ðʌs/ *adv* (*fml* 文) **1** in this way; like this 以此方式; 如此; 这样: *calculate the area of the triangle thus formed* 计算这样形成的三角形的面积 ○ *Hold the wheel in both hands, thus.* 用双手握住方向盘, 像这样. **2** as a result of this; accordingly 其结果是; 因此; 于是; 所以: *He is the eldest son and thus heir to the title.* 他是长子, 因此是头衔的继承人. **3** to this extent 到如此程度: *Having come thus far do you wish to continue?* 已经走了这么远了, 你还想走吗?

thwart¹ /θwɔːt; θwɔrt/ *v* [Tn] prevent (sb) doing what he intends; oppose (a plan, etc) successfully 阻挠(某人)成事; 阻止(计划等)实现: *He was thwarted (in his aims) by bad luck.* 他运气不好, 未能达到目的. ○ *thwarted ambitions* 受挫折无法实现的抱负.

thwart² /θwɔːt; θwɔrt/ *n* seat across a rowing-boat for an

T

oarsman（划艇上桨手的）坐板.

thyme /taɪm; taɪm/ *n* [U] (**a**) any of various types of herb with fragrant leaves 百里香属植物. (**b**) leaves of this plant used in cookery 百里香叶（用于烹调）.

thyr·oid /ˈθaɪrɔɪd; ˋθaɪrɔɪd/ *n* (also **thyroid ˈgland**) large gland at the front of the neck, producing a hormone which controls the body's growth and development 甲状腺.

ti /tiː; ti/ *n* (*music* 音) the seventh note in the sol-fa scale（首调唱法的）任何大音阶的第七音.

ti·ara /tɪˈɑːrə; tɪˋɑrə/ *n* **1** woman's crescent-shaped head-dress, usu ornamented with jewels and worn on ceremonial occasions（女用）冕状头饰（通常镶有宝石，礼仪场合戴用）. **2** triple crown worn by the Pope 三重冕（天主教教皇戴的）.

tibia /ˈtɪbɪə; ˋtɪbɪə/ *n* (*pl* **~e** /-bɪiː; -bɪ,i/) (*anatomy* 解) = SHIN-BONE (SHIN). ⇨illus at SKELETON 见 SKELETON 插图.

tic /tɪk; tɪk/ *n* occasional involuntary twitching of the muscles, esp of the face 抽搐;（尤指）面肌抽搐: *have a nervous tic* 患神经性面肌抽搐.

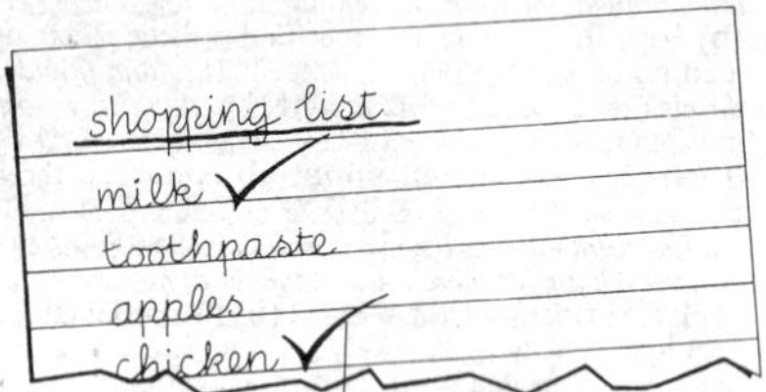

tick (*US* **check**) 对号

tick[1] /tɪk; tɪk/ *n* **1** light and regularly repeated sound, esp that of a clock or watch 滴答声（尤指钟表的）. **2** (*infml* 口) moment 一会儿: *Just wait a tick!* 等一下儿! ○ *I'll be down in half a tick/in two ticks.* 我马上就下来. **3** (*US* **check**) mark put beside an item in a list to show that it has been checked or done or is correct（画于表册上的项目旁边，表示已核对、已做或正确无误的）记号，对号. ⇨illus 见插图.

▷ **tick** *v* **1** [I, Ip] **~ (away)** (of a clock, etc) make a series of ticks (TICK[1] 1)（指钟等）发出滴答声: *My watch doesn't tick because it's electric.* 我的表是电动的，不滴答响. ○ *listened to the clock ticking/the ticking of the clock* 听钟滴答作响 ○ *While we waited the taxi's meter kept ticking away.* 我们等候时，计程车里的计程表一直在滴答地响着. **2** [Tn, Tn·p] **~ sth (off)** put a tick[1](3) beside (an item, etc) 在（项目等）旁边做核对记号: *tick (off) the names of those present* 在出席者的姓名旁做记号 ○ *The jobs that are done have been ticked off.* 做完的工作都标上了记号. **3** (idm 习语) **what makes sb ˈtick** (*infml* 口) what makes sb behave in the way he does 某人这样做的原因是什么: *I've never really understood what makes her tick.* 我实在弄不明白她为什么这样. **4** (phr v) **tick away/by** (of time) pass（指时间）过去: *Meanwhile the minutes kept ticking away.* 其时，时间一分一分地过去. **tick sth away** (of a clock, etc) mark the passage of time（指钟等）表示时间过去: *The station clock ticked away the minutes.* 车站的钟显示时间一分一分地过去. **tick sb off** (*infml* 口) rebuke or scold sb 责骂或斥责某人: *get ticked off for careless work* 因工作不细心而挨骂. **tick over** (**a**) (of an engine) idle（指发动机）空转，慢转: *I stopped the car but left the motor ticking over.* 我停住汽车，让发动机空转. (**b**) (of activities) continue in a routine way（指活动）照常进行: *Just try and keep things ticking over while I'm away.* 在我离开的期间，尽量使事情照常进行.

□ ˌ**ticking-ˈoff** *n* (*pl* **tickings-off**) (*infml* 口) rebuke or reprimand 责骂; 斥责: *give sb a good ticking-off* 把某人狠狠骂一顿.

ˈ**tick-tack** *n* [U] (*Brit*) system of signalling by moving the hands, used by bookmakers on racecourses（赛马场上以接受赛马赌注为业者使用的）手势信号.

ˌ**tick-tack-ˈtoe** *n* [U] (*US*) = NOUGHTS AND CROSSES (NOUGHT).

ˌ**tick-ˈtock** *n* (usu *sing* 通常作单数) ticking sound of a large clock（大时钟的）滴答声.

tick[2] /tɪk; tɪk/ *n* **1** any of various types of small parasitic insect that suck blood 蜱. **2** (*Brit sl* 俚) unpleasant or contemptible person 讨厌的或可鄙的人.

tick[3] /tɪk; tɪk/ *n* **1** [C] case of a mattress or pillow, in which the filling is contained 褥套; 枕心套. **2** [U] = TICKING.

tick[4] /tɪk; tɪk/ *n* [U] (*infml* 口 *esp Brit*) credit 赊欠: *get tick* 赊帐 ○ *buy goods on tick* 赊帐购物.

ticker /ˈtɪkə(r); ˋtɪkɚ/ *n* (*infml* 口) **1** heart 心脏: *His ticker's not very strong,* ie He has a weak heart. 他心脏衰弱. **2** (*dated* 旧) watch 表.

□ ˈ**ticker-tape** *n* [U] (*esp US*) (**a**) paper tape from a teleprinter, etc（电传打字机等的）纸带: *reading the stock market prices off the ticker-tape* 阅读电传打字机纸带上显示的股市行情. (**b**) this or similar material thrown from windows to greet a celebrity（为欢迎名人而从窗口抛下的）纸带: [attrib 作定语] *a ticker-tape parade* 抛纸带迎宾式 ○ *get a ticker-tape reception* 受到抛纸带的盛大欢迎.

ticket /ˈtɪkɪt; ˋtɪkɪt/ *n* **1** [C] written or printed piece of card or paper that gives the holder a certain right (eg to travel by plane, train, bus, etc or to a seat in a cinema) 票（如机票、车票、电影票或入场券等）: *Do you want a single or a return ticket?* 你要单程票还是往返票? ○ *I've got two tickets for the Cup Final.* 我弄到两张优胜杯决赛的票. ○ *You must present your library ticket every time you borrow books.* 你每次借书都必须出示借书证. ○ *Admission by ticket only,* eg as a notice outside a hall, etc. 凭票入场. **2** [C] label attached to sth, giving details of its price, size, etc（附于某物上标明价格、尺码等的）标签. **3** [C usu *sing* 通常作单数] (*esp US*) list of the candidates put forward by one party in an election（党派推荐的）候选人名单: *run for office on the Republican ticket* 作为共和党的候选人参加竞选. **4** [C] official notice of an offence against traffic regulations（交通违章）通知单，罚款单: *get a parking/speeding ticket* 接到违章停车[超速驾驶]罚款单. **5** [C] (*infml* 口) certificate issued to a qualified ship's master, aircraft pilot, etc（发给船长、飞行器驾驶员等的）资格证明书. **6 the ticket** [sing] (*dated infml* 旧，口) the correct or desirable thing 正确、恰好的事; 所需之物: *All packed up and ready to go? That's the ticket.* 行李都收拾好了，可以走了吧? 对了. **7** (idm 习语) **the straight ticket** ⇨ STRAIGHT[1].

▷ **ticket** *v* [Tn esp passive 尤用于被动语态] put a ticket on (an article for sale, etc) 在（待出售等的物品）上加标签.

tick·ing /ˈtɪkɪŋ; ˋtɪkɪŋ/ (also **tick**) *n* [U] strong material for covering mattresses and pillows（做褥套、枕心套的）结实布料.

tickle /ˈtɪkl; ˋtɪkl/ *v* **1** [I, Tn, Tn·pr] touch or stroke (sb) lightly, esp at sensitive parts, so as to cause a slight tingling sensation, often with twitching movements and laughter 轻触或抚摸（某人）使发痒: *This blanket tickles (me).* 这毯子扎得我痒痒. ○ *tickle sb in the ribs* 搔某人的肋部使之发痒 ○ *She tickled my nose with a feather.* 她拿羽毛弄得我鼻子发痒. **2** [I] feel such a sensation 发痒: *My nose tickles.* 我鼻子痒痒. **3** [Tn] please (sb's vanity, sense of humour, etc); amuse 满足（某人的虚荣心、幽默感等）; 使高兴: *The story tickled her fancy/curiosity.* 这个故事满足了她的好奇心. ○ *I was highly tickled by the idea.* 这主意让我高兴极了. **4** (idm 习语) **(be) tickled ˈpink/to ˈdeath** (*infml* 口) extremely pleased or amused 感到非常满足或高兴: *I'm tickled pink that my essay won the prize.* 我的文章获奖了，我高兴得要命. **tickle sb's ribs** (*infml* 口) amuse sb 逗某人发笑. Cf 参看 RIB-TICKLING (RIB).

▷ **tickle** *n* **1** act or sensation of tickling 抓搔使痒; 痒感: *I've got this tickle in my throat — I think I may be getting a cold.* 我嗓子发痒——大概是感冒了. **2** (idm 习语) **slap and tickle** ⇨ SLAP *n*.

tick·ler /ˈtɪklə(r); ˋtɪklɚ/ *n* (*dated infml* 旧，口 *esp Brit*) puzzle; problem 难题; 问题: *an awkward little tickler to solve* 需要解决的小难题.

tick·lish /ˈtɪklɪʃ; ˋtɪklɪʃ/ *adj* **1** (of a person) sensitive to tickling（指人）易痒的，怕痒的: *I'm terribly ticklish.* 我特别怕痒. **2** (*infml* 口) (of a problem) requiring careful handling; difficult（指问题）需小心处理的，难解决的: *a* *ticklish question* 棘手的问题 ○ *in a ticklish situation* 处于难以应付的局面. **tick·lish·ness** *n* [U].

ticky-tacky /ˈtɪkɪ tækɪ; ˌtɪkɪˈtækɪ/ *adj, n* [U] (*US infml* 口) (made of) shoddy ugly buildings or materials 质量低劣又难看的建筑物; 劣质材料(制成的): *suburbs full of ticky-tacky* 遍布劣等建筑物的郊区.

tidal /ˈtaɪdl; ˈtaɪdḷ/ *adj* of or affected by a tide or tides 潮的; 有潮的; 受潮汐影响的: *a tidal river, estuary, harbour, etc* 感潮河道、感潮河口、潮港.

□ **tidal ˈwave** **1** great ocean wave, eg one caused by an earthquake 潮波; 海啸. **2 ~ (of sth)** (*fig* 比喻) great wave of popular enthusiasm, indignation, etc 公众热情、愤恨等的浪潮; 热潮; 怒潮: *carried along on a tidal wave of hysteria* 受歇斯底里般狂热的裹挟.

tid·bit (*US*) = TITBIT.

tid·dler /ˈtɪdlə(r); ˈtɪdlɚ/ *n* (*infml* 口) **1** very small fish, esp a stickleback or minnow 小鱼; (尤指)刺鱼, 米诺鱼. **2** unusually small thing or child 异常小的东西或孩子.

tiddly /ˈtɪdlɪ; ˈtɪdlɪ/ *adj* (**-ier, -iest**) (*infml* 口) **1** (*esp Brit*) slightly drunk; tipsy 微醉的; 有醉意的: *feeling a bit tiddly* 觉得稍有醉意. **2** (*Brit*) very small; negligible 很小的; 微不足道的: *Two tiddly biscuits with cheese on? You can't call that a proper meal!* 两块小饼干抹上点奶酪? 这不能算正经饭吧?

tiddly-winks /ˈtɪdlɪ wɪŋks; ˈtɪdlɪˌwɪŋks/ *n* [U] game in which players try to make small plastic discs jump into a cup by pressing them on the edge with a larger disc 挑圆片游戏(用一圆片压小塑料圆片的边缘使之弹入杯形容器).

tide /taɪd; taɪd/ *n* **1** (**a**) [C, U] regular rise and fall in the level of the sea, caused by the attraction of the moon and sun 潮; 潮汐: *spring/neap* (ie maximum/minimum) *tides* 大[小]潮 ○ *at high/low tide* 在高[低]潮时. (**b**) [C] water moved by this 潮水: *We were cut off by the tide.* 我们让潮水截住了. ○ *The tide is (coming) in/(going) out.* 正在涨[落]潮. ○ *driftwood washed up by the tide(s)* 被潮水冲上来的浮木 ○ *Swimmers should beware of strong tides.* 游泳的人要提防汹涌的潮水. **2** [C usu *sing* 通常作单数] direction in which opinion, events, luck, etc seem to move; trend (舆论、事件、运气等的)潮流, 趋势, 动向: *a rising tide of discontent* 不满情绪的不断增涨 ○ *The tide turned in our favour.* 形势变得对我们有利. **3** [U] (*arch* 古) (in compounds 用以构成复合词) season 季; 时: *ˈyule-tide* ○ *ˈWhitsuntide.* **4** (idm 习语) **go, swim, etc with/against the stream/tide** ⇨ STREAM. **time and tide wait for no man** ⇨ TIME[1].

▷ **tide** *v* (phr v) **tide sb over (sth)** help sb through (a difficult period) by providing what he needs (通过提供所需)帮助某人渡过(困难时期): *Will you lend me some money to tide me over until I get my pay cheque?* 你能否借给我点儿钱, 帮我维持到发薪时?

□ **ˈtide-mark** *n* **1** mark made by the tide water at its highest point on a beach, etc (沙滩等处潮水留下的)高潮痕. **2** (*joc* 谑) (**a**) line between washed and unwashed parts of sb's body (身上洗到的和没洗到的部位之间的)垢痕. (**b**) line left on a bath by the dirty water (污水留在浴盆上的)垢痕.

ˈtide-table *n* list showing the times of high tide at a place 潮汐表.

ˈtideway *n* (**a**) channel where a tide runs 潮汐水道; 潮路. (**b**) tidal part of a river (河流的)感潮段.

tid·ings /ˈtaɪdɪŋz; ˈtaɪdɪŋz/ *n* [pl] (*arch or joc* 古或谑) news 消息; 音信: *Have you heard the glad tidings?* 你听到那个好消息了吗?

tidy /ˈtaɪdɪ; ˈtaɪdɪ/ *adj* (**-ier, -iest**) **1** (**a**) arranged neatly and in order 安排或排列整齐的: *a tidy room, desk, garden* 整整齐齐的房间、书桌、花园 ○ *keeps her house very tidy* 保持她住宅整整齐齐. (**b**) having the habit of keeping things neat and orderly 爱整齐的; 有整齐习惯的: *a tidy boy* 有整齐习惯的男孩 ○ *tidy habits* 爱整齐的习惯 ○ *have a tidy mind*, ie be able to think clearly and sensibly 思维有条理. **2** [attrib 作定语] (*infml* 口) (esp of a sum of money) fairly large; considerable (尤指一笔钱)相当大的, 可观的: *She left a tidy fortune when she died.* 她死时留下大笔财产. ○ *It must have cost a tidy penny*, ie quite a lot of money. 这准花了好多钱.

▷ **ti·dily** *adv*.

ti·di·ness *n* [U].

tidy *n* receptacle for odds and ends 盛零星物件的容器: *a ˈdesk tidy*, ie for pens, paper-clips, etc 书桌上盛钢笔、曲别针等的容器 ○ *a ˈsink tidy*, ie for bits of kitchen waste (厨房洗涤槽的)残渣过滤器.

tidy *v* (*pt, pp* **tidied**) **1** [I, Ip, Tn, Tn·p] **~ (sth/sb/oneself) (up)** make (sth/sb/oneself) tidy 使(某物[某人/自己])整齐: *Who's been tidying in here?* 是谁一直在收拾这地方? ○ *spent all morning tidying up* 用一上午的时间整理 ○ *You'd better tidy this room (up) before the guests arrive.* 你最好在客人到来之前把屋子整理好. ○ *I must tidy myself up*, ie make myself look tidy. 我得梳理一下. **2** (phr v) **tidy sth away** put sth in a certain place (esp out of sight) so that a room, etc appears tidy 将某物收起(尤指见不到处)使房间等显得整齐: *Tidy away your toys when you've finished playing.* 你玩儿过玩具之后要收起来. **tidy sth out** remove unnecessary or unwanted items from sth and arrange the rest neatly 移去不要之物而将余下物品整理好; 清理: *tidy out one's drawers, a cupboard, etc* 清理抽屉、柜橱等.

tie[1] /taɪ; taɪ/ *n* **1** (also **ˈnecktie**) strip of decorative material worn round the neck under the collar and knotted in front 领带. ⇨illus at JACKET 见JACKET插图. **2** piece of cord, wire, etc used for fastening or tying sth (系物、捆扎用的)带、绳、线等: *ties for sealing plastic bags* 封塑料袋用的捆扎条. **3** (**a**) rod or beam holding parts of a structure together (连接结构物各部的)系杆, 系梁. (**b**) (*US*) = SLEEPER 2. **4** (usu *pl* 通常作复数) (*fig* 比喻) thing that unites people; bond 使人结合在一起的事物; 连接物: *the ties of friendship* 友谊的纽带 ○ *family ties* 家族关系 ○ *The firm has ties with an American corporation.* 该商行与美国一家公司有关系. **5** (*fig* 比喻) thing that limits a person's freedom of action 限制人行动自由的事物; 束缚: *He doesn't want any ties; that's why he never married.* 他不愿受束缚, 所以不结婚. ○ *Pets can be a tie when you want to go away on holiday.* 要想外出度假时, 宠物会成为牵累. **6** equal score in a game or competition (比赛或竞争中)得分相同, 不分胜负, 平手: *Each team scored twice and the game ended in a tie.* 每个队都有两次得分, 比赛不分胜负. **7** sports match between two or a group of competing teams or players 淘汰赛: *the first leg of the Cup tie between Aberdeen and Barcelona* 阿伯丁队和巴塞罗那队在优胜杯淘汰赛中的第一轮比赛. **8** (*music* 音) curved line in a score over two notes of the same pitch that are to be played or sung as one 连结线. ⇨illus at MUSIC 见MUSIC插图.

□ **ˈtie-beam** *n* horizontal beam connecting rafters 系梁.

ˈtie-breaker (also **ˈtie-break**) *n* means of deciding the winner when competitors have tied (TIE[2] 5) 平局决胜制: *The first set* (ie of a tennis match) *was won on the tie-break.* 这次网球比赛的第一盘是以平局决胜制获胜的.

ˈtie-pin (*US* **ˈstickpin**, **ˈtie-tack**) *n* ornamental pin for holding a tie[1](1) together or in place 领带别针.

tie[2] /taɪ; taɪ/ *v* (*pt, pp* **tied**, *pres p* **tying**) **1** [Tn, Tn·pr, Tn·p] fasten or bind (sth) with rope, string, etc (用绳、带等)系, 结, 缚, 绑, 扎, 捆, 拴(某物): *Shall I tie the parcel or use sticky tape?* 我把包裹捆上还是用胶带粘上? ○ *The prisoner's hands were securely tied.* 那犯人的双手给牢牢捆住了. ○ *tie a dog to a lamp-post* 把狗拴在灯柱上 ○ *tie sb's feet together* 把某人的双脚捆住 ○ *tie a branch down* 把树枝绑住. **2** [Tn, Tn·pr, Tn·p] **~ sth (on)** attach sth by means of its strings, etc (用某物的带子等将其)系上, 系牢: *Could you tie this apron round me?* 你受累把围裙给我系上行吗? ○ *tie on a label* 系上标签. **3** (**a**) [Tn, Tn·pr, Tn·p] arrange (ribbon, string, etc) to form a knot or bow 将(丝带、细绳等)打成结或打成蝴蝶结: *tie a ribbon, scarf, tie, cravat, etc* 系丝带、头巾、领带、围巾等 ○ *She tied her hair in(to) a bun.* 她把头发挽成个髻. ○ *tie (up) one's shoe-laces* 系(上)鞋带. (**b**) [Tn, Tn·pr] make (a knot or bow) in this way 打(结或蝴蝶结): *tie a knot in a piece of rope* 在绳子上打结. **4** [I, Ipr, Ip] be fastened 系上; 打结: *This rope won't tie properly.* 这绳子打不好结. ○ *Does this sash tie in front or at the back?* 这腰带是在前面打结还是在后面? **5** [I, Ipr, Tn usu passive 通常用于被动语态, Tn·pr usu passive 通常用于被动语态] **~ (sb) (with sb) (for sth)** make the same score as (another competitor) 与(另一参赛者)得分相同: *The two teams tied (with each other).* 那两队不分胜负. ○ *Britain are tied with Italy for*

T

second place. 英国队和意大利队并列第二. **6** [Tn] (*music* 音) unite (notes) with a tie[1](8) 用连结线连接(音符): *tied crotchets* 用连结线连接的四分音符. **7** (idm 习语) **bind/tie sb hand and foot** ⇨ HAND[1]. **have one's hands free/tied** ⇨ HAND[1]. **tie oneself into/(up) in ˈknots** get very confused 大惑不解. **tie the knot** (*infml* 口) get married 结婚. **8** (phr v) **tie sb/oneself down (to sth)** restrict sb/oneself (to certain conditions, a fixed occupation or place, etc) 使某人[自己]受(某环境、固定的职业或地点等的)约束: *Children do tie you down, don't they?* 孩子简直把你拖累住了吧? ○ *refuse to be tied down by petty restrictions* 不理会琐细规章的限制. **tie in (with sth)** (of information, facts, etc) agree or be connected (指资料、事实等)一致或有联系: *This evidence ties in with what we already know.* 这证据与我们已掌握的情况相符. **tie (sth) up** moor (sth) or be moored 系住, 拴住(船等); 停泊: *We tied (the boat) up alongside the quay.* 我们把船停泊在码头处. **tie sb up** (**a**) bind sb with rope, etc so that he cannot move or escape 捆绑某人: *The thieves left the night-watchman tied up and gagged.* 窃贼把夜班守卫员捆住, 把他的嘴也堵住了. (**b**) (usu passive 通常用于被动语态) occupy sb so that he has no time for other things 缠住某人使之无暇顾及他事: *I'm tied up in a meeting until 3 pm.* 我开会直到下午三点钟方可脱身. **tie sth up** (**a**) bind sth with cord, rope, etc 系、拴、捆、绑或扎某物. (**b**) (often passive 常用于被动语态) invest (capital) so that it is not easily available for use 将(金钱)用于投资致使难以动用: *Most of his money's tied up in property.* 他大部分钱都投资在房地产上无法动用. (**c**) make conditions restricting the use or sale of (property, etc) 制定条款限制(财产等)的使用或出售. (**d**) bring (work, progress, etc) to a halt; obstruct sth 使(工作、进展等)停顿; 阻碍某事: *The strike tied up production for a week.* 这次罢工造成停产一周.

▷ **tied** *adj* [attrib 作定语] (of a house) rented to sb on condition that he works for the owners (指房子)只租给为房东工作的人的: *a ˌtied ˈcottage* 农场主租给其雇工的农舍 ○ *a job with tied accommodation* 提供住所的工作. **ˈtied house** (*Brit*) public house that is owned or controlled by a particular brewery 某啤酒厂开设的或特约经营的酒店. Cf 参看 FREE HOUSE (FREE[1]).

□ **ˈtie-dye** *v* [Tn] produce dyed patterns on (fabric) by tying parts of it so that they are protected from the dye 扎染(织物). **ˈtie-dyeing** *n* [U].

ˈtie-on *adj* [attrib 作定语] (of a label, etc) that may be attached by tying (指标签等)可系上的, 可拴上的.

ˈtie-up *n* **1 ~ (with sb/sth)** link; merger; partnership 联系; 联合; 协作. **2** (*esp US*) halt in work, progress, etc; standstill (工作、进展等的)停顿; 停滞不前: *a traffic tie-up* 交通阻塞.

tier /tɪə(r); tɪr/ *n* any of a series of rows (esp of seats) or parts of a structure placed one above the other 一排(尤指座位); (阶梯式的)一层: *a box in the first tier*, ie in a theatre (剧院中的)第一排的一个包厢 ○ *a wedding-cake with three tiers*/*a three-tier wedding-cake* 有三层的结婚蛋糕. ⇨illus at LAYER 见 LAYER 插图.

▷ **tiered** *adj* arranged in tiers 成排的; 分层的: *tiered seating* 成排的座位.

-tiered (forming compound *adjs* 用以构成复合形容词) having the specified number of tiers 有所示之排数或层数的: *a three-tiered cake* 三层的蛋糕 ○ *a two-tiered system*, ie one with two distinct levels 双重系统(有两个层次的).

tiff /tɪf; tɪf/ *n* slight quarrel between friends or acquaintances (朋友或相识的人之间的)争吵, 拌嘴, 口角: *She's had a tiff with her boy-friend.* 她和男朋友吵嘴了.

tig /tɪg; tɪg/ *n* [U] = TAG 6.

ti·ger /ˈtaɪgə(r); ˈtaɪgɚ/ *n* **1** large fierce animal of the cat family, with yellowish and black stripes, found in Asia 虎, 老虎(产于亚洲). ⇨illus at CAT 见 CAT 插图. **2** (idm 习语) **fight like a tiger** ⇨ FIGHT[1]. **a paper tiger** ⇨ PAPER.

▷ **ti·ger·ish** /ˈtaɪgərɪʃ; ˈtaɪgərɪʃ/ *adj* like a tiger, esp (of a person) fiercely energetic 似虎的; (尤指人)生龙活虎的.

tig·ress /ˈtaɪgrɪs; ˈtaɪgrɪs/ *n* female tiger 雌虎.

□ **ˈtiger-lily** *n* tall garden lily having orange flowers spotted with black or purple 卷丹(高株园艺植物, 花呈橘红色, 上有紫黑色斑点).

ˈtiger-moth *n* moth with wings striped like a tiger's skin 灯蛾.

tight /taɪt; taɪt/ *adj* (**-er, -est**) **1** fixed, fastened or drawn together firmly; hard to move or undo 牢的; 紧的; 不松动的; 难解开的: *a tight knot* 系紧的结 ○ *I can't get the cork out of the bottle — it's too tight.* 我无法把瓶塞拔出来——太紧了. ○ *The drawer is so tight I can't open it.* 这抽屉太紧了, 我打不开. ○ *keep a tight hold on the rope* 紧紧抓住绳子. **2** (**a**) fitting closely 紧密相合的: *a tight joint* 紧密的接合处 ○ *These shoes are too tight for me.* 这双鞋我穿着太紧. ○ *a tight ship*, ie one that does not leak 不漏水的船 ○ *tight* (ie strict) *controls* 严密的控制. (**b**) (in compound *adjs* 用以构成复合形容词) made so that a specified thing cannot get in or out 不漏的; 不透的: *ˈairtight* ○ *ˈwatertight*. **3** (**a**) with things or people arranged closely 紧密的; 密集的: *a tight mass of fibres* 很紧的一团纤维 ○ *a tight schedule*, ie leaving little time to spare 紧凑的日程安排. (**b**) (of a game, etc) evenly contested (指比赛等)势均力敌的: *a tight race, match, contest, etc* 旗鼓相当的赛跑、比赛、竞争等. **4** fully stretched; taut 绷紧的; 拉紧的: *a tight rope, belt, rein, etc* 拉紧的绳子、带子、缰绳等 ○ *My chest feels rather tight*, eg because of asthma. 我觉得胸闷憋气(如因哮喘所致). **5** [usu pred 通常作表语] (*infml* 口) drunk 喝醉酒: *got a bit tight at the party* 在聚会上喝得有些醉. **6** (*finance* 财) (**a**) (of money) not easy to obtain, eg on loan from banks (指钱)难得到的(如银行贷款). (**b**) (of the money market) in which credit is severely restricted (指金融市场)银根紧的. **7** (*infml* 口) stingy; miserly 小气的; 抠搜的; 吝啬的: *She's tight with her money.* 她在钱上特别抠唆. **8** (idm 习语) **keep a tight ˈrein on sb/sth** allow little freedom to sb/sth 对某人[某事物]严加约束. **a ˌtight ˈsqueeze** cramped or crowded situation 密集; 拥挤: *We managed to get all the luggage into the car but it was a tight squeeze.* 我们总算把行李都塞进汽车里了, 不过挤得要命.

▷ **tight** *adv* **1** tightly 紧; 紧紧地; 牢牢地 (not used before a past participle: *packed tight* but *tightly packed* 过去分词之前不用 tight 而用 tightly: packed tight 及 tightly packed): *Hold tight!* 抓紧了! **2** (idm 习语) **sit tight** ⇨ SIT. **sleep tight** ⇨ SLEEP[2].

tighten /ˈtaɪtn; ˈtaɪtn̩/ *v* **1** [I, Ipr, Ip, Tn, Tn·pr, Tn·p] **~ (sth) (up)** (**a**) (cause sth to) become tight or tighter (使某物)变紧: *This screw needs tightening.* 这螺钉需再拧紧些. ○ *tighten (up) the ropes* 拉紧绳子 ○ *He tightened his grip on her arm.* 他紧抓住她的手臂. (**b**) (cause sth to) become stricter (使某事)变得更严格: *Controls have gradually tightened.* 控制逐渐加强. ○ *tighten up security* 使安全措施更严密. **2** (idm 习语) **loosen/tighten the purse-strings** ⇨ PURSE. **tighten one's ˈbelt** eat less food, spend less money, etc because there is little available 勒紧腰带(省吃俭用): *The management warned of the need for further belt-tightening*, ie economy. 资方提醒有必要进一步节约. **3** (phr v) **tighten up (on sth)** become more careful, vigilant or strict 变得更小心、警惕或严格: *The police are tightening up on drunken driving.* 警方目前采取严厉手段对付醉酒驾车行为.

tightly *adv* in a tight manner 紧紧地; 紧密地: *squeeze sb tightly* 紧紧地拥抱某人 ○ *tightly sealed* 密封的.

tight·ness *n* [U].

□ **ˌtight-ˈfisted** *adj* stingy; miserly 吝啬的; 小气的.

ˌtight-ˈlipped *adj* keeping the lips pressed firmly together, esp to restrain one's emotion or to keep silent; grim-looking 双唇紧闭的(尤指克制感情或保持沉默); 表情冷酷的.

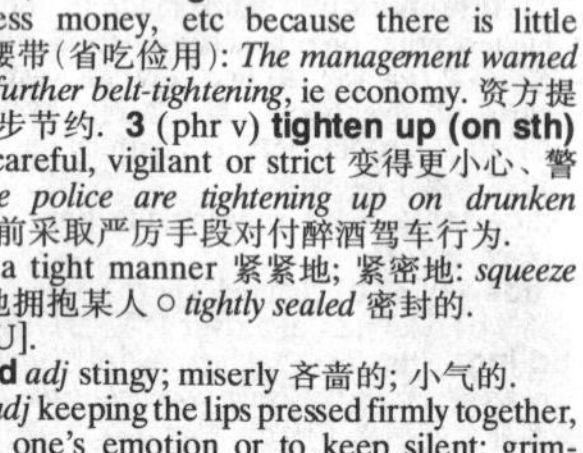

tightrope 钢丝

tight·rope /ˈtaɪtrəʊp; ˈtaɪtˌrop/ *n* **1** rope stretched tightly high above the ground, on which acrobats perform (供杂技演员表演用的)绷紧的绳索或钢丝: [attrib 作定语] *a tightrope walker* 走钢丝的演员. **2** (idm 习语) **tread/walk a 'tightrope** have to act in a situation which allows little scope for manoeuvre and in which an exact balance must be preserved 无甚回旋余地需小心权衡行事.

tights /taɪts; taɪts/ *n* [pl] **1** (also **pantihose, pantyhose**) close-fitting garment covering the hips, legs and feet, worn by girls and women 裤袜(臀部、腿部、足部连成一件的女用紧身下装): *a pair of cotton tights* 一条棉织裤袜. Cf 参看 STOCKING. **2** similar garment covering the legs and body, worn by acrobats, dancers, etc (杂技、芭蕾舞等演员穿的)紧身衣.

tike = TYKE.

tilde /'tɪldə, *in sense 2* 用于下述第2义时读作 tɪld; 'tɪldə/ *n* **1** mark (˜) placed over the Spanish *n* when it is pronounced *ny* /nj; nj/ (as in *cañon*), or the Portuguese *a* or *o* when it is nasalized (as in *São Paolo*) 波形号, 腭化符号(˜)(用以表示鼻音化的附加符号, 如西班牙语的*cañon*或葡萄牙语的*São Paolo*). **2** mark (~) used in this dictionary to replace the headword in certain parts of an entry 代字号(~)(在本词典的词条项内代替某些首词的符号).

tile /taɪl; taɪl/ *n* **1** slab of baked clay or other material used in rows for covering roofs, walls, floors, etc (盖屋顶、贴墙、铺地等用的)瓦, 瓷砖, 板, 片: *covered the wall in cork tiles* 用软木板贴墙 ○ *insulated the ceiling with expanded polystyrene tiles* 用多孔聚苯乙烯板使天花板保温 ○ *carpet tiles*, ie carpet sold in small squares for laying in rows 小方地毯. ⇨illus at App 1 见附录1插图, page vii. **2** any of the small flat pieces used in certain board games (某些用棋盘进行之游戏的)棋子. **3** (idm 习语) **on the 'tiles** (*sl* 俚) enjoying oneself away from home in a wild or drunken way 在外狂欢或纵酒作乐.

▷ **tile** *v* [Tn] cover (a surface) with tiles 用瓦、瓷砖等覆盖(某物表面): *a tiled bathroom* 铺瓷砖的浴室.

till[1] ⇨ UNTIL.

till[2] /tɪl; tɪl/ *n* **1** drawer in which money is kept behind the counter in a shop, bank, etc or in a cash register (店铺、银行等的)放钱的抽屉. **2** (idm 习语) **have, etc one's fingers in the till** ⇨ FINGER.

till[3] /tɪl; tɪl/ *v* [Tn] prepare and use (land) for growing crops 耕(地).

▷ **till·age** /'tɪlɪdʒ; 'tɪlɪdʒ/ *n* [U] **1** action or process of tilling 耕种; 耕作. **2** tilled land 耕过的田地.

til·ler *n* person who tills 耕种者; 农夫.

til·ler /'tɪlə(r); 'tɪlɚ/ *n* horizontal bar used to turn the rudder of a small sailing-boat (小帆船的)舵柄. ⇨illus at YACHT 见 YACHT 插图. Cf 参看 HELM.

tilt /tɪlt; tɪlt/ *v* **1** [I, Ipr, Ip, Tn, Tn·pr, Tn·p] (cause sth to) move into a sloping position (使某物)倾斜, 倾侧: *This table tends to tilt (to one side/over).* 这桌子歪(向一边[倒])了. ○ *Popular opinion has tilted* (ie shifted) *in favour of the Socialists.* 公众舆论已倒向社会党人一边. ○ *She sat listening, with her head tilted slightly to one side.* 她坐着, 侧耳倾听. ○ *Don't tilt your chair or you'll fall over!* 别翘椅子, 不然你就摔倒了! ○ *Tilt the barrel forward to empty it.* 把桶向前倾, 倒出里面的东西. **2** [I, Ipr] **~ (at sb/sth)** run or thrust with a lance in jousting 骑马持长矛跑或刺杀. **3** (idm 习语) **tilt at 'windmills** fight imaginary enemies 攻击想像中的敌人. **4** (phr v) **tilt at sb/sth** attack sb/sth in speech or writing 用言语或文字攻击某人[某事]; 抨击: *a satirical magazine tilting at public figures* 攻击社会名流的讽刺性杂志.

▷ **tilt** *n* **1** (usu *sing* 通常作单数) tilting; sloping position 倾斜; 倾斜的位置: *with a tilt of his head* 他的头侧着 ○ *The table is on/at a slight tilt.* 这张桌子没放平, 有点儿歪. **2** act of tilting with a lance 骑马用长矛刺杀. **3** (idm 习语) **full pelt/speed/tilt** ⇨ FULL. **have a tilt at sb** attack sb in a friendly way during a debate, conversation, etc (在辩论、交谈等中)善意抨击某人.

tilth /tɪlθ; tɪlθ/ *n* [U] depth of soil affected by cultivation 耕作深度: *rake a seed-bed to a good tilth*, ie until there is a depth of fine crumbly soil 把苗床耙至适当深度.

tim·ber /'tɪmbə(r); 'tɪmbɚ/ *n* **1** (*US* **lumber**) [U] wood prepared for use in building or carpentry (建筑或木工用的)木材, 木料: *dressed timber*, ie sawn, shaped and planed ready for use 刨好的木材 ○ [attrib 作定语] *a 'timber-merchant* 木材商 ○ *a 'timber-yard*, ie where timber is stored, bought and sold, etc 木材场. **2** [U] trees suitable for this 用材林: *standing* (ie growing) *timber* 未伐的树木 ○ *cut down/fell timber* 伐木 ○ *put a hundred acres of land under timber*, ie plant it with trees 种植一百英亩用材林. **3** [C] piece of wood, esp a beam, used in constructing a house or ship (造房屋或船用的)木料, (尤指)大梁: *roof/floor timbers* 房檩[地板龙骨].

▷ **tim·ber** *interj* (used as a warning that a tree is about to fall after being cut 伐木工在树木将倒时示警的呼喊声).

tim·bered /'tɪmbəd; 'tɪmbɚd/ *adj* **1** (of buildings) built of wooden beams or with a framework of these (指建筑物)木造的, 木结构的. **2** (of land) planted with trees; wooded (指土地)生长着树木的, 有林木的.

□ **'timber-line** *n* [sing] = TREE-LINE (TREE).

'timber-wolf *n* large grey wolf of N America (北美产的)大灰狼.

timbre /'tæmbrə, 'tɪmbə(r); 'tæmbɚ, 'tɪmbɚ/ *n* characteristic quality of sound produced by a particular voice or instrument 音色; 音质; 音品.

time[1] /taɪm; taɪm/ *n* **1** [U] all the years of the past, present and future 时间: *past/present/future time* 过去的[现在的/将来的]时间 ○ *The world exists in space and time.* 世界存在于空间与时间之中. **2** [U] passing of these taken as a whole 时间流逝: *Time has not been kind to her looks*, ie She is no longer as beautiful as she was. 岁月无情, 她已失去昔日的美貌. ○ *(old) Father Time*, ie this process personified 时间老人(拟人化用法). **3** [U] indefinite period in the future 未来的某段时间: *Time heals all wounds.* 时间能医好一切创伤. **4** [U] portion or measure of time 一段时间: *That will take time*, ie cannot be done quickly. 那要花费些时间. ○ *I don't have (much) time to read these days.* 我这些日子没(什么)时间读书. ○ *We have no time to lose*, ie We must hurry. 我们不能耽误时间了(要抓紧). ○ *What a waste of time!* 太浪费时间了! ○ *I spent most of my time (in) sightseeing.* 我大部分时间都用在观光游览上了. ○ *I'm rather pressed for time*, ie in rather a hurry. 我的时间很紧. ○ *What a (long) time you've been!* 你花费那么长的时间了! ○ *I had a most unpleasant time at the dentist's.* 我在牙医那里受了大罪. **5** [U] point of time stated in hours and minutes of the day 一天中以时、分表达的时间的某一点: *What time is it?/What is the time?* 几点钟了? ○ *Do you have the time (on you)?* 你知道现在几点了吗? ○ *My youngest daughter has just learnt to tell the time.* 我最小的女儿刚学会看表. ⇨App 4, 5 见附录4、5. **6** [U, C] period of time measured in units (years, months, hours, etc) 以(年、月、小时等)单位计量的时间: *The winner's time was 11.6 seconds.* 获胜者用的时间是11.6秒. ○ *He ran the mile in record time*, ie faster than any previous runner. 他跑一英里的时间已创记录. ○ *Although she came second their times were only a tenth of a second apart.* 她虽然得第二名, 但与第一名仅差十分之一秒. ⇨App 4, 5, 11 见附录4、5、11. **7** [U] measured time spent in work, etc 用于工作等的时间: *be on short time*, ie a reduced working week 论星期开工时间不足 ○ *paid time and a half/double time*, ie paid one and a half times/twice the usual rate 付予一倍半[双倍]工资. **8** [U] point or period of time used, available or suitable for sth (用于、有或适于)做某事的时间: *at the time you're speaking of* 在你所说的时间 ○ *by the time we reached home* 到我们回到家的时候 ○ *last time I was there* 我上次在那儿的时候 ○ *every time I see her* 每次我见到她的时候 ○ *'lunch-time* 午餐时间 ○ *This is not the time to bring up that subject.* 现在不是提那事的时候. ○ *Now's your time*, ie opportunity. 你的机会来了. ○ *It's time we were going/time for us to go*, ie We should leave now. 我们现在该走了. ○ *Time is up*, ie The time allowed for sth is ended. 时间到了(规定的时间). ○ *Time, please!* ie warning that a pub is about to close. 请注意, 时间到了(酒馆营业时间结束的提醒语). **9** [C] occasion; instance 次数; 次; 回: *this, that, another, next, last, etc time* 这、那、另一、下、上...次 ○ *the time before last* 上上次 ○ *for the first, second, last, etc time* 第一回、第二回、最后一回 ○ *He failed his driving test five times.* 他考驾驶执照五次都没及格. ○ *told sb umpteen, a dozen, countless, etc times* (ie repeatedly) *not to do sth* 一再告诉某人别那样做. **10** [C often *pl* 常作复数] **(a)** period of time associated with certain events, people, etc 时代; 时期: *in*

T

'*Stuart times/the time(s) of the 'Stuarts*, ie when the Stuart kings ruled 在斯图亚特王朝时代 ○ *in 'ancient, prehis'toric, 'recent, etc times* 在古代、史前期、近代 ○ *Mr Curtis was the manager in 'my time*, ie when I was working there. 我在那儿工作时，柯蒂斯先生是经理. ○ *The house is old but it will last 'my time*, ie will serve me for the rest of my life. 这房子旧是旧了，但在我有生之年尚可居住. **(b)** period of time associated with certain conditions, experiences, etc (与某情况、经历等有关的)时期: *University was a good time for me.* 我的大学时期十分愉快. ○ *Times are hard for the unemployed.* 失业者的日子很难熬. ○ *in time(s) of danger, hardship, prosperity, etc* 在危险、艰苦、繁荣等时期. **11** [U] (*music* 音) **(a)** type of rhythm 拍子: '*common time*, ie two or four beats in each bar 普通拍子(每小节两拍或四拍) ○ *three 'eight time*, ie three quavers to the bar 八分之三拍 ○ *in 'waltz/ 'march time* 以华尔兹[进行曲]的拍子 ○ *beating time to the music* 随乐曲打拍子. **(b)** rate at which a piece of music is to be played; tempo (乐曲演奏的)速度: *quick time* 快速. **12** (idm 习语) **(and) about 'time ('too)** (*infml* 口) and this is sth that should have happened some time ago 早该发生的事; 早该如此: *I hear old Fred got promoted last week — and about time too, I'd say.* 我听说弗雷德上星期升职了 —— 我看早就该升了. **ahead of 'time** earlier than expected 提前. **ahead of one's 'time** having ideas that are too advanced or enlightened for the period in which one lives 具有超前意识; 思想超越同时代的人. **all the 'time (a)** during the whole of the time in question (在该段时间内)一直: *That letter I was searching for was in my pocket all the time*, ie while I was searching for it. 我找的那封信其实一直就在我口袋里. **(b)** always 向来; 一向: *He's a business man all the time*, ie He has no other interest. 他一向是做生意的. **at 'all times** always 随时; 永远: *I'm at your service at all times.* 我随时为您效劳. **(even) at the best of times** ➪ BEST[3]. **at 'one time** at some period in the past; formerly 一度; 从前: *At one time I used to go skiing every winter.* 我有一度每到冬季就去滑雪. **at 'other times** on other occasions 在其他时候; 也有时候: *Sometimes he's fun to be with; at other times he can be very moody.* 有时候他很有风趣，可也有时候脾气一上来就喜怒无常. **at the same time** ➪ SAME. **at a 'time** in sequence; separately 依次; 逐一; 每次: *Don't try to do everything at once; take it a bit at a time.* 不要什么事情都一块儿干，要一次做一点儿. ○ *Take the pills two at a time.* 每次服两粒. **at the 'time** at a certain moment or period in the past 在那时; 在那段时间: *I agreed at the time but later changed my mind.* 我当时同意了，但后来又变了主意. ○ *We were living in London at the time.* 我们那阵儿住在伦敦. **at 'my, 'your, 'his, etc time of life** at my, your, his, etc age 在我、你、他...这样的年纪: *He shouldn't be playing football at his time of life*, ie He is too old for it. 在他这把年纪可不该踢足球了. **at 'times** sometimes 有时; 间或. **before one's 'time** before the period one can remember or the point at which one became involved 在本人记事之前; 在与本人有关的时刻之前: *The Beatles were a bit before my time.* 披头士乐队风靡的时候我还不记事儿呢. ○ *The headquarters used to be in Bristol, but that was before my time*, ie before I worked there. 总部当时设在布里斯托尔，但那时我还没到总部工作. **behind 'time** late 迟; 晚: *The plane was an hour behind time.* 班机误点一小时. ○ *He's always behind time with the rent.* 他总晚交租金. **behind the 'times** no longer fashionable or modern in one's ideas, methods, etc 思想、方法等陈旧的; 过时的; 落伍的. **better luck next time** ➪ BETTER[1]. **bide one's time** ➪ BIDE. **the big time** ➪ BIG. **born before one's time** ➪ BORN. **borrowed time** ➪ BORROW. **buy time** ➪ BUY. **do 'time** (*sl* 俚) serve a prison sentence 服刑: *He's done time for armed robbery.* 他曾因持械抢劫罪而服刑. **every time** whenever possible; whenever a choice can be made 无论何时; 任何时候: *Different people like different sorts of holiday, but give me the seaside every time.* 各人有各人的度假方式，我总是喜欢去海边. **for old times' sake** ➪ OLD. **for a 'time** for a short period 短时间内; 暂时. **for the time 'being** until some other arrangement is made 暂且: *You'll have your own office soon but for the time being you'll have to share one.* 你很快就有自己的办公室了，不过暂时还得和别人合用一间. **from/since ˌtime imme'morial** (*saying* 谚) from/since longer ago than anyone can remember 自古以来. **from ˌtime to 'time** now and then; occasionally 不时; 偶尔; 间或. **gain time** ➪ GAIN[2]. **give sb/have a rough, hard, etc 'time (of it)** (cause sb to) suffer, esp from harassment, overwork, etc (使某人)受折磨, 吃苦(尤指因烦扰、过劳等). **(in) half the time (a)** (in) a much shorter time than expected (以)远较预期短的时间: *If you'd given the job to me I could have done it in half the time.* 你要是把这活儿交给我，我早就做完了. **(b)** a considerable time; too long a time 相当长的时间; 过长的时间: *I'm not surprised he didn't complete the exam: he spent half the time looking out of the window.* 他没答完试卷，我并不感到奇怪: 他朝着窗外看了半天了. **have an easy time** ➪ EASY. **have, etc a good 'time** enjoy oneself, generally or on a particular occasion 过得很愉快; 玩儿得很痛快. **have/give sb a high old time** ➪ HIGH[1]. **have a lot of time for sb/sth** (*infml* 口) be enthusiastic about sb/sth 对某人[某事物]极感兴趣. **have no time for sb/sth** be unable or unwilling to spend time on sb/sth; dislike sb/sth 不能或不愿为某人[某事]花费时间; 不喜欢某人[某事物]: *I've no time for lazy people/laziness.* 我讨厌懒人[懒惰行为]. **have a thin time** ➪ THIN. **have the ˌtime of one's 'life** (*infml* 口) be exceptionally happy or excited 异常高兴或兴奋: *The children had the time of their lives at the circus.* 孩子们看马戏时别提多高兴了. **have time on one's hands/time to kill** (*infml* 口) have nothing to do 没事可做. **have a whale of a time** ➪ WHALE. **(it is) 'high/a'bout time** the time is long overdue when sth should happen or be done 早就该有某事或做某事了: *It's high time you stopped fooling around and started looking for a job.* 你可别再游手好闲了，也该找份工作了吧. **in course of time** ➪ COURSE[1]. **in the fullness of time** ➪ FULLNESS (FULL). **in good time** early 早: *There wasn't much traffic so we got there in very good time.* 路上车不多，所以我们早早就到那儿了. **(all) in good 'time** after a reasonable or appropriate space of time, but not immediately 不消多久(但并非立刻): *'Can we have lunch now — I'm hungry.' 'All in good time.'* '咱们现在能吃午饭了吗 —— 我饿了.' '很快就好了.' **in the nick of time** ➪ NICK[1]. **in (less than) 'no time** very quickly 极快; 立即; 马上. **in one's own good 'time** at the time or rate that one decides oneself 以自己定的时间和速度: *There's no point getting impatient with her; she'll finish the job in her own good time.* 不必跟她着急，她自己能找时间完成工作的. **in one's own time** in one's free time; outside working hours 在闲暇时; 业余时间. **in one's own sweet time** ➪ SWEET[1]. **in one's 'time** at a previous period or on a previous occasion in one's life 在自己一生中一度: *I've seen some slow workers in my time but this lot are the slowest by far.* 我以前倒也见过一些笨工人，但是这群人可算是最笨的了. **in 'time** sooner or later; eventually 迟早; 最后: *You'll learn how to do it in time.* 你早晚能学会做这件事的. **in time (for sth/to do sth)** not late 及时; 不迟: *Will I be in time for the train/to catch the train?* 我赶得上那趟火车吗? **in/out of 'time** (*music* 音) in/not in the correct time[1](11) 合[不合]节拍: *tapping one's fingers in time to/with the music* 用手指合着音乐的拍子轻轻敲. **it's only a matter of time** ➪ MATTER[1]. **keep 'time (a)** (of a clock or watch) show the correct time (指钟表)走得准: *My watch always keeps excellent time.* 我的表非常准. **(b)** sing or dance in time[1](11) 按节拍唱歌或跳舞. **keep up, move, etc with the 'times** change one's attitudes, behaviour, etc in accordance with what is now usual 随着潮流改变态度、行为等. **kill time** ➪ KILL. **long time no see** ➪ LONG[1]. **lose/waste no time (in doing sth)** do sth quickly and without delay 赶紧做某事. **make good, etc 'time** complete a journey quickly 路上花的时间很短. **make up for lost time** ➪ LOST[2]. **'many's the time (that)**; **'many a time** many times; frequently 多次; 常常: *Many's the time (that) I've visited Rome.* 我曾多次到罗马游览. ○ *I've visited Rome many a time.* 我到罗马去游览过很多次. **mark time** ➪ MARK[2]. **near her 'time** (of a pregnant woman) about to give birth (指孕妇)临产. **ˌnine times out of 'ten**; **ˌninety-nine times out of a 'hundred** almost always 十之八九; 几乎总是. **(there is) no time like the**

T

present (*saying* 谚) now is the best time to do sth 现在是做某事的最佳时机. **once upon a time** ⇨ ONCE. **on 'time** neither late nor early; punctually 按时; 准时: *The train arrived (right/bang) on time.* 火车正点到达. **pass the time of day** ⇨ PASS². **play for 'time** try to gain time by delaying (以拖延的手段)争取时间. **procrastination is the thief of time** ⇨ PROCRASTINATION (PROCRASTINATE). **a race against time** ⇨ RACE¹. **quite some time** ⇨ QUITE. **a sign of the times** ⇨ SIGN¹. **a stitch in time saves nine** ⇨ STITCH. **take one's 'time (over sth/to do sth/doing sth)** (**a**) use as much time as one needs; not hurry 要用多少时间就用多少; 不着急: *Take your time — there's no rush.* 你用多长时间都行——不着急. (**b**) (*ironic* 反语) be unreasonably late or slow 晚得或慢得离谱: *You certainly took your time getting here!* 你来得这么晚, 也太不像话了! **tell the time** ⇨ TELL. **ˌtime after 'time; ˌtime and (time) a'gain; ˌtimes without 'number** on many occasions; repeatedly 无数次; 屡次; 一再. **time and tide wait for 'no man** (*saying* 谚) no one can delay the passing of time (so one should not put off a favourable opportunity to do sth) 岁月不待人(机不可失). **time 'flies** (*saying* 谚) time passes quickly, esp more quickly than one realizes 光阴似箭: *Oh dear — hasn't time flown!* 天哪——时间如白驹过隙呀! **time hangs/lies heavy on one's 'hands** time passes too slowly (esp because one has nothing to do) 时间过得太慢(尤指因无所事事). **time is on sb's 'side** sb can afford to wait before doing or achieving sth 某人有充足的时间等待做某事: *Although she failed the exam she has time on her side: she'll still be young enough to take it in her next year.* 她虽然没考及格但时间有的是, 她还年轻可以明年再考. **the time is ripe for sth/sb to do sth** it is the right moment for (doing) sth (做)某事的时机成熟. **the time of 'day** the hour as shown by a clock (钟表指示的)时刻, 时间. **time presses** we must not delay 时间紧迫. **time 'was (when)...** there has been a time when... 曾经有那么个时候...: *Time was you could get a good three-course meal for less than a pound.* 那年头吃一顿三道菜的好饭还花不了一英镑. **time (alone) will 'tell, etc** it will become obvious with the passing of time 时间能证明: *Time will show which of us is right.* 时间能证明咱们谁对谁错. **watch the time** ⇨ WATCH². **work, etc against 'time** work, etc as fast as possible so as to finish by a specified time 尽快工作以按时完成; 赶任务.

□ **'time bomb** bomb that can be set to explode after a certain period of time 定时炸弹.

'time-card (also **'time-sheet**) *n* record of the number of hours sb works 考勤卡; 工作时间记录卡.

'time-consuming *adj* taking or needing much time 耗费时间的: *Some of the more time-consuming jobs can now be done by machines.* 有些更费时间的工作现在可以用机器做了.

'time exposure photographic exposure in which the shutter is left open for longer than the briefest time (ie usu more than a second or two) 长时间曝光(即通常指一两秒钟以上的).

'time-fuse *n* fuse designed to burn for or explode after a given time 定时引信.

'time-honoured (*US* **-honored**) *adj* (esp of a custom, etc) respected because of long tradition (尤指习俗等)因有悠久传统而受尊重的.

'timekeeper *n* **1** person or device that records time spent at work 工作时间记录员或记录器. **2** (preceded by an *adj* 用于形容词之后) watch or clock 表; 时钟: *a good/bad* (ie accurate/inaccurate) *timekeeper* 走得准的[不准的]时计.

'time-lag *n* interval of time between two connected events (两件相关事情的)时间间隔; 时滞: *the time-lag between a flash of lightning and the thunder* 闪电和打雷相隔的时间 ○ *the time-lag between research and development* 研究与开发之间相隔的时间.

'time-limit *n* limit of time within or by which sth must be done 时限; 期限: *set a time-limit for the completion of a job* 为一项工作规定完成的期限.

'timepiece *n* (*fml* 文) clock or watch 钟; 表; 时计.

'time-scale *n* period of time in which a sequence of events takes place; successive stages of a process, an operation, etc (一系列事件发生的)一段时间; (过程、操作等的)连续阶段.

'time-server *n* (*derog* 贬) person who adopts fashionable opinions or those held by people in power, esp for selfish purposes 随波逐流者, 趋炎附势者(尤指为达到个人目的).

'time-serving *adj* [esp attrib 尤作定语] behaving like a time-server 随波逐流的; 趋炎附势的: *time-serving politicians* 趋炎附势的政客.

'time-sharing *n* [U] **1** use of a computer for different operations by two or more people at the same time 分时(计算机使用方法, 可使至少两用户同时操作各自的程序). **2** arrangement in which a holiday home is owned jointly by several people who agree to use it each at different times of the year 几人分时使用度假住房的方法.

'time-sheet *n* = TIME-CARD.

'time-signal *n* sound or sounds indicating the exact time of day 报时信号.

'time-switch *n* switch that can be set to operate automatically at a certain time (自动)定时开关: *The central heating is on a time-switch.* 集中供热设备是定时开关的.

'timetable (also *esp US* **schedule**) *n* list showing the time at which certain events will take place 时间表; 时刻表: *a school timetable*, ie showing the time of each class 课程表 ○ *a train, bus, ferry, etc timetable* 火车、公共汽车、渡轮等的时刻表 ○ *I've got a very busy timetable this week*, ie a lot of appointments, etc. 我这星期的时间安排很紧.

'time warp (in science fiction) distortion of time so that the past or the future becomes the present (科幻小说中的)时间错位(过去或将来的时间均出现于现在).

'time-worn *adj* worn or damaged by age 用久而磨损或毁坏的: *a time-worn* (ie hackneyed) *expression* 陈词滥调.

'time zone region (between two parallels of longitude) where a common standard time is used 时区(地球两平行经线范围内共用标准时间的区域).

PREPOSITIONS OF TIME 时间介词

介词	使用范围	示例
in (the)	parts of the day (not night) 一天的部分时间(但 night 除外)	*in the morning(s), etc* 在早晨、上午等
	months 月份	*in February* 在二月份
	seasons 季节	in (the) summer 在夏天
	years 年份	in 1987 在 1987 年
	decades 年代	*in the 1920's* 在 20 世纪 20 年代
	centuries 世纪	*in the 20th century* 在 20 世纪
on (the)	days of the week 星期	*on Saturday(s)* 在星期六
	dates 日期	*on (the) 20th (of) February* 在 2 月 20 日
	specific days 某日	*on Good Friday* 在耶稣受难日 *on New Year's Day* 在元旦 *on my birthday* 在我生日这天 *on the following day* 在次日
at (the)	clock time 钟点	*at 5 o'clock* 在 5 点钟, *at 7.45 pm* 在晚上 7 时 45 分
	night 夜晚	*at night* 在夜晚
	holiday periods 假期	at Christmas 在圣诞节 at the weekend 在周末

time² /taɪm; taɪm/ *v* **1** [Tn, Tn·pr, Cn·t esp passive 尤用于被动语态] choose the time or moment for (sth); arrange the time of 选择(某事)的时机; 安排...的时间: *You've timed your holiday cleverly — the weather's at its best.* 你真会选度假时间——正是天气最好的时候. ○ *His remark was well/badly timed*, ie made at a suitable/an unsuitable moment. 他说的话正合[不合]时宜. ○ *Kick-off is timed for 2.30.* 足球开赛时间定于下午 2 时

30分. ○ *The train is timed to connect with the ferry.* 火车时刻编排得可与渡轮运行时刻衔接. ○ *The bomb was timed to explode during the rush-hour.* 炸弹已经校准在人最多的时候爆炸. **2** [Tn] (*sport* 体) make (a stroke) or strike (the ball) at a certain moment (在某一时刻)发出(一击)或击(球): *He timed that shot beautifully.* 他这一击时间恰到好处. **3** [Tn, Tw] measure the time taken by (a runner, etc) or for (a race, process, etc) (为跑者、赛跑、某过程等)计时: *This egg is hard — you didn't time it properly.* 这鸡蛋煮老了——你没掌握好火候. ○ *Time me while I do/Time how long it takes me to do two lengths of the pool.* 给我记一下我游一个来回的时间.

▷ **timer** *n* (often in compounds 常用以构成复合词) person or device that times sth 记时员; 记时器: *an 'egg-timer* 煮蛋计时器.

tim·ing *n* [U] (**a**) determining or regulating the time when an action or event occurs 定时; 调整时间: [attrib 作定语] *a 'timing device* 定时装置 ○ *The timing of the announcement was rather unexpected.* 选择那个时间公布, 真出人意料. ○ *valve timing*, ie the time at which valves in a motor engine open and close 阀定时. (**b**) skill in this, as a way of achieving the desired result 时间的选择; 时机的掌握: *He's not playing his shots well — his timing is faulty.* 他没打好——时间掌握不当. ○ *A good actor must learn the art of timing*, ie when to deliver a line most effectively. 要想当个好演员就要学会掌握道白的时间分寸.

time·less /ˈtaɪmlɪs; ˋtaɪmlɪs/ *adj* (*fml or rhet* 文或修辞) **1** not appearing to be affected by the passing of time 不受时间影响的: *her timeless beauty* 她那永不衰退的姿色 ○ *a landscape with a timeless quality* 价值永存的风景画. **2** unending; permanent 永远的; 永久的: *the timeless laws of nature* 永恒的自然法则. ▷ **time·lessly** *adv*. **time·less·ness** *n* [U].

timely /ˈtaɪmlɪ; ˋtaɪmlɪ/ *adj* (**-ier, -iest**) occurring at just the right time; opportune 及时的; 适时的; 合时宜的: *thanks to your timely intervention* 多亏你及时调停 ○ *This has been a timely reminder of the need for constant care.* 这件事适时地提起我们注意要时时谨慎. ▷ **time·li·ness** *n* [U].

T

times /taɪmz; taɪmz/ *prep* multiplied by 乘以: *Five times two is/equals ten*, ie 5 × 2 = 10. 5乘以2等于10.

▷ **times** *n* [pl] (used to express multiplication 用以表示倍数): *This book is three times as long as/three times longer than/three times the length of that one.* 这本书是那本书篇幅的三倍[比那本书长两倍/篇幅为那本书的三倍].

timid /ˈtɪmɪd; ˋtɪmɪd/ *adj* easily frightened; shy 胆怯的; 羞怯的: *as timid as a rabbit* 胆小如兔. ▷ **tim·id·ity** /tɪˈmɪdətɪ; tɪˋmɪdətɪ/, **tim·id·ness** *ns* [U]. **tim·idly** *adv*.

tim·or·ous /ˈtɪmərəs; ˋtɪmərəs/ *adj* (*fml* 文) timid 胆怯的; 羞怯的. ▷ **tim·or·ously** *adv*. **tim·or·ous·ness** *n* [U].

tim·pani /ˈtɪmpənɪ; ˋtɪmpənɪ/ *n* [sing or pl *v*] set of kettledrums in an orchestra (交响乐团中的)定音鼓.

▷ **tim·pan·ist** /ˈtɪmpənɪst; ˋtɪmpənɪst/ *n* person who plays the timpani 定音鼓手.

tin /tɪn; tɪn/ *n* **1** [U] chemical element, a soft white metal used in alloys and for coating iron and steel to prevent corrosion 锡: [attrib 作定语] *tin cans* 镀锡白铁罐 ○ *a tin whistle* 锡哨. ⇨App 10 见附录10. **2** (also *esp US* **can**) [C] (**a**) container made of tin plate, esp one in which food is sealed to preserve it 马口铁容器; (尤指)罐头盒: *open a tin of beans* 开一听豆子罐头. ⇨illus at CAN 见CAN插图. (**b**) contents of this 罐头所盛之物: *He ate a whole tin of stew.* 他吃了整整一听炖肉. **3** (idm 习语) **a (little) tin 'god** (*infml* 口) person or thing that is greatly respected or worshipped for no good reason 受到不应得的崇敬之人或物.

▷ **tin** *v* (**-nn-**) [Tn esp passive 尤用于被动语态] (*US* **can**) seal (food) in a tin(2a) to preserve it 将(食物)制成罐头: *tinned sardines, peas, peaches* 罐头沙丁鱼、豌豆、桃.

tinny *adj* (**-ier, -iest**) (*derog* 贬) **1** (of metal objects) not strong or solid (指金属制品)不结实的: *a cheap tinny radio* 廉价的劣质收音机. **2** having a thin metallic sound 发出薄的金属声的: *a tinny piano* 发洋铁罐声的钢琴.

□ **tin 'foil** very thin sheets of tin or aluminium alloy used for wrapping and packing things (包装物品用的)锡纸: *a roll of tin foil* 一卷锡纸.

tin 'hat (*army sl* 军俚) soldier's steel helmet (士兵的)钢盔.

'tin-opener *n* device or tool for opening tins of food 开罐器; 罐头刀.

'tin plate iron or steel sheets coated with tin 镀锡铁皮; 马口铁.

'tinpot *adj* [attrib 作定语] (*derog* 贬) inferior or worthless 劣质的; 不值钱的: *a tinpot little dictator* 无足轻重的独裁者.

'tinsmith *n* person who makes things out of tin or tin plate 锡匠; 白铁匠.

'tin-tack *n* short nail made of iron coated with tin 镀锡平头铁钉.

tin 'whistle (also **penny whistle**) simple musical instrument, played by blowing, with six holes for the different notes 六孔小笛.

tinc·ture /ˈtɪŋktʃə(r); ˋtɪŋktʃɚ/ *n* **~ (of sth)** **1** [C, U] medical substance dissolved in alcohol 酊; 酊剂: *a/some tincture of iodine, quinine, etc* 一些碘酊、奎宁酊等. **2** [sing] (*fml* 文) slight trace or flavour (of a thing or quality) (事物或性质的)些微迹象或特色: *a tincture of heresy* 稍有异端意味.

▷ **tinc·ture** *v* [Tn, Tn·pr esp passive 尤用于被动语态] **~ sth (with sth)** (*fml* 文) tinge or flavour sth; affect sth slightly (with a quality) 使某物染色、着色、有气味或稍受(某种性质)影响.

tin·der /ˈtɪndə(r); ˋtɪndɚ/ *n* [U] any dry substance that catches fire easily 干燥易燃之物.

□ **'tinder-box** *n* box containing tinder with a flint and steel, formerly used for lighting a fire 火绒盒: (*fig* 比喻) *There is much racial unrest in the community and the whole place is a tinder-box*, ie violence could easily break out. 该社区存在种族骚乱, 整个地区随时都能酿出大祸.

tine /taɪn; taɪn/ *n* (**a**) any of the points or prongs of a fork, harrow, etc (叉、耙等的)尖, 齿. (**b**) branch of a deer's antler 鹿角的分叉.

ting /tɪŋ; tɪŋ/ *n* clear ringing sound 丁零声.

▷ **ting** *v* [I, Tn] (cause sth to) make such a sound (使某物)发丁零声.

□ **ˌting-a-'ling** *n* series of tings, made eg by a small bell 一连串丁零声(如小铃发出的). — *adv*: *The bell went ting-a-ling.* 铃铛丁零零地响.

tinge /tɪndʒ; tɪndʒ/ *v* [Tn, Tn·pr esp passive 尤用于被动语态] **~ sth (with sth)** **1** colour sth slightly 使某物稍染颜色: *hair tinged with grey* 有些花白的头发. **2** affect sth slightly 使某事物略受影响: *admiration tinged with envy* 稍含妒意的赞美.

▷ **tinge** *n* (esp *sing* 尤作单数) **~ (of sth)** slight colouring or trace 淡淡的色调或痕迹: *There was a tinge of sadness in her voice.* 她的声音中有几分伤感. ○ *Do I detect a tinge of irony?* 我觉得这话有点儿像反话吧?

tingle /ˈtɪŋgl; ˋtɪŋgl/ *v* (**a**) [I, Ipr] **~ (with sth)** have a slight pricking, stinging or throbbing feeling in the skin 皮肤感到轻微的刺痛: *The slap she gave him made his cheek tingle.* 他挨了她一个嘴巴, 脸上热辣辣的. ○ *fingers tingling with cold* 手指冻得发疼. (**b**) [Ipr] **~ with sth** (*fig* 比喻) be affected by (an emotion) 受(某种情绪)的影响: *tingling with excitement, indignation, shock, etc* 感到兴奋、愤慨、吃惊等.

▷ **tingle** *n* (usu *sing* 通常作单数) tingling feeling 刺痛之感: *have a tingle in one's fingertips* 指尖感到刺痛 ○ *feel a tingle of anticipation* 因有预感觉得痛苦.

tin·ker /ˈtɪŋkə(r); ˋtɪŋkɚ/ *n* **1** [C] person who travels from place to place repairing kettles, pans, etc (走街串巷的)小炉匠儿. **2** [sing] **~ (at/with sth)** act of tinkering (随便的或胡乱的)做事, (尤指)修补, 修理, 改进: *I had a tinker at your radio, but I can't mend it.* 我把你的收音机修了一下, 但没修好.

▷ **tin·ker** *v* [I, Ipr, Ip] **~ (at/with sth)** work in a casual or inexpert way, esp trying to repair or improve sth 随便地或以外行方式做(尤指试着修理或改进某物): *tinker (away) at a broken clock* 胡乱修理(着)出毛病的钟 ○ *He likes tinkering with computers.* 他爱乱改进计算机. ○ *Who's been tinkering (around) with the wiring?* 谁总瞎改动电线线路?

tinkle /ˈtɪŋkl; ˋtɪŋkl/ *n* (esp *sing* 尤作单数) **1** series of short light ringing sounds 一连串的丁零声: *the tinkle of* *a bell, of breaking glass, of ice being stirred in a drink* 铃、玻璃破碎、冰块在饮料中搅动的丁零声. **2** (*Brit infml* 口) telephone call 电话通话: *Give me a tinkle when you get home.* 你一到家就给我打个电话.

▷ **tinkle** *v* [I, Tn] (cause sth to) make a tinkle (使某物)发丁零声.

tinny ⇨ TIN.

tin-pan alley /ˌtɪn pæn ˈælɪ; ˌtɪn pæn ˋælɪ/ (*infml sometimes derog* 口, 有时作贬义) composers, performers and publishers of popular music and the type of life they live 流行音乐作曲家、表演者、出版商及其生活方式: *He's been in tin-pan alley for twenty years.* 他二十年来一直演奏流行乐曲.

tin·sel /ˈtɪnsl; ˋtɪnsḷ/ *n* [U] **1** glittering metallic substance used in strips or threads as a decoration (装饰用的)光片, 金属线: *decorate a Christmas tree with tinsel* 用光亮金属片装饰圣诞树 ○ *a dress trimmed with tinsel* 饰有光片的连衣裙. **2** (*derog* 贬) superficial brilliance or glamour 表面的光彩或魅力.

▷ **tin·selled** /-sld; -səld/, **tin·selly** /-səlɪ; -slɪ/ *adjs* **1** decorated with tinsel 饰有光片或金属线的. **2** (*derog* 贬) superficially brilliant or glamorous 外表有光彩或有魅力的.

tint /tɪnt; tɪnt/ *n* **1** shade or variety of a colour 色度; 颜色的浓淡: *tints of green in the sky at dawn* 黎明时天空中浓淡不同的青色 ○ *an artist who excels at flesh tints*, ie painting the colours of the human body 善于画人体颜色的画家 ○ *red with a bluish tint* 发蓝的红色. **2** (**a**) weak dye for colouring the hair 染发剂. (**b**) act of colouring the hair in this way 染发: *She had a tint.* 她染头发了.

▷ **tint** *v* [Tn, Cn·a] apply or give a tint to (sth); tinge 在(某物)上着色; 稍染: *leaves tinted in autumn colours* 秋色点染的树叶 ○ *blue-tinted hair* 染蓝的头发 ○ (*fig* 比喻) *His comments were tinted with sarcasm.* 他的评论带有讽刺的味道.

tiny /ˈtaɪnɪ; ˋtaɪnɪ/ *adj* (**-ier**, **-iest**) **1** very small 极小的; 微小的: *a tiny baby* 小小的婴儿 ○ *living in a tiny cottage* 住在小村舍里 ○ *I feel a tiny bit better today.* 我今天觉得稍好一点儿. **2** (idm 习语) **the patter of tiny feet** ⇨ PATTER².

-tion ⇨ -ION.

tip¹ /tɪp; tɪp/ *n* **1** pointed or thin end of sth 尖端; 尖儿: *the tips of one's fingers/one's fingertips* 手指尖 ○ *the tip of one's nose* 鼻尖 ○ *walking on the tips of her toes* (她)踮着脚走 ○ *the northern tip of the island* 岛的北端. **2** small part or piece fitted to the end of sth (装在某物顶端的)小部分或小物件: *shoes with metal tips* 带金属包头的鞋 ○ *a cane with a rubber tip* 带橡皮头的手杖. **3** (idm 习语) **(have sth) on the tip of one's ˈtongue** just about to be spoken or remembered 话到嘴边或几乎想起: *His name's on the tip of my tongue, but I just can't think of it.* 他的名字就在嘴边上, 可我就是想不起来. **the tip of the ˈiceberg** small but evident part of a much larger concealed situation, problem, etc 重要情况、重大问题等显露出的小部分: *Over 100 burglaries are reported every month, and that's just the tip of the iceberg*, ie many more occur but are not reported. 每月报案的入室盗窃案超过百起, 而这只不过是已知的一小部分.

▷ **tip** *v* (**-pp-**) [Tn, Tn·pr] **~ sth (with sth)** fit a tip to sth; put on the tip of sth 给某物装上尖头; 置于某物顶端: *filter-tipped cigarettes* 带过滤嘴的香烟 ○ *The legs of the table were tipped with rubber.* 桌子腿装上了橡皮头. ○ *The native warriors tipped their spears with poison.* 土著斗士把毒药涂在长矛尖上.

tip² /tɪp; tɪp/ *v* (**-pp-**) **1** [I, Ip, Tn, Tn·p] (**a**) **~ (sth) (up)** (cause sth to) rise, lean or tilt on one side or at one end (使某物)侧边提高, 倾斜, 翻倒: *Don't lean on the table or it'll tip up.* 别倚桌子, 不然就倚倒了. ○ *Tip the box up and empty it.* 把那盒子翻过来倒空. (**b**) **~ (sth) (over)** (cause sth to) turn or fall over (使某物)翻转, 倾覆: *Careful! You'll tip the boat over.* 当心! 你要把船弄翻了. **2** [Tn, Tn·pr, Tn·p] (*Brit*) cause (the contents of sth) to pour out by tilting 将(所盛之物)倒出: *No rubbish to be tipped here/No tipping*, eg on a notice warning people not to dump rubbish. 此处禁倒垃圾. ○ *Tip the dirty water out of the bowl and into the sink.* 把盆里的脏水倒入洗涤槽里. ○ *My neighbour has been tipping dead leaves over the wall into my garden.* 我的邻居把落叶从墙头上倒进我的花园里了. ○ *The train stopped abruptly, nearly tipping me out of my bunk.* 火车突然停住, 我差点儿从铺位上摔下来. **3** (idm 习语) **tip the ˈbalance/ˈscale** be the deciding factor for or against sth 成为同意或反对某事物的决定因素: *Her greater experience tipped the balance in her favour and she got the job.* 她经验更丰富, 这是她得到那份工作的决定性因素. **tip/turn the scale at sth** ⇨ SCALE³.

▷ **tip** *n* **1** place where rubbish may be tipped (TIP² 2) 垃圾弃置场: *the municipal ˈrefuse tip* 市政局管理的垃圾弃置场 ○ *take a broken old refrigerator to the tip* 把废冰箱送到垃圾弃置场. Cf 参看 DUMP *n* 1. **2** (*infml* 口) dirty or untidy place 脏的或乱的地方: *Their house is an absolute tip.* 他们家简直是个垃圾堆.

□ **ˈtipper lorry** (also **ˈtipper truck**) lorry whose body can be raised at one end to tip out the contents 翻斗卡车; 自倾卸货卡车.

ˈtip-up *adj* [attrib 作定语] (of seats) that can be raised to allow people to pass easily, eg in a cinema (指座位)可翻起的(如戏院中的).

tip³ /tɪp; tɪp/ *v* (**-pp-**) **1** (**a**) [Tn] touch or strike (sth) lightly 轻触, 轻打, 轻敲(某物): *The ball just tipped the edge of his racket.* 球仅仅碰到他球拍的边儿. (**b**) [Tn·pr, Tn·p] cause (sth) to move in the specified direction by doing this 将(某物)轻击向某方向: *She just tipped the ball over the net.* 她刚好把球击过网. **2** [Tn] give a small sum of money to (a waiter, taxi-driver, etc) 给(服务员、计程车司机等)小费: *tip the porter 50p* 给搬运工50便士小费. **3** [Tn, Cn·n/a, Cn·t esp passive 尤用于被动语态] **~ sb/sth (as sth/to do sth)** give advice or an opinion about sb/sth 就某人[某事物]提出建议或意见: *tip the winner*, ie name the winner of a race, etc before it takes place 事先指出获胜者(比赛等的) ○ *He has been widely tipped as the President's successor/to succeed the President.* 很多人认为他将继任总统. **4** (idm 习语) **tip sb the ˈwink** (*infml* 口) give sb private information; warn sb secretly 向某人透露秘密消息; 暗中警告某人. **5** (phr v) **tip sb off** (*infml* 口) give sb an advance warning or hint 事先给某人警告或暗示: *Someone tipped off the police about the robbery.* 有人事先向警方报告了要有抢劫的消息.

▷ **tip** *n* **1** small sum of money given to a waiter, taxi-driver, etc as a personal reward for their services (给服务员、计程车司机等的)小费, 小帐: *He left a tip under his plate.* 他把小费放在盘子下面了. **2** (**a**) small but useful piece of practical advice 有用的小建议; 实用的小提示: *Here's a handy tip for removing stains from clothing.* 有个除掉衣服上污点的窍门儿. (**b**) private or special piece of information, esp about horse-races, the stock-market, etc 私下的或特别的情报(尤指有关赛马、股市等的): *a hot* (ie very good) *tip for the Derby* 有关德比大赛马的极好的信息 ○ *Take my tip/Take a tip from me and buy these shares now.* 听我的, 立即买下这些股分.

□ **ˈtip-off** *n* hint or warning 暗示; 警告: *Acting on a tip-off, the police arrested the drug smugglers.* 警方根据密报逮捕了毒品走私者.

tip·pet /ˈtɪpɪt; ˋtɪpɪt/ *n* (**a**) long piece of fur, etc worn by a woman round the neck and shoulders, with the ends hanging down in front (女用)披肩. (**b**) similar article of clothing worn by judges, clergy, etc (法官等的)披肩; (教士的)圣带.

tipple /ˈtɪpl; ˋtɪpḷ/ *v* [I] be in the habit of drinking alcoholic drinks, esp too often or too much 酗酒: *He started tippling when his wife left him.* 他自妻子离去之后便开始酗酒.

▷ **tipple** *n* (usu *sing* 通常作单数) (*infml* 口) alcoholic drink 烈酒: *What's your tipple?* ie What would you like to drink? 你想喝什么酒? ○ *His favourite tipple is whisky.* 他爱喝的烈酒是威士忌.

tip·pler /ˈtɪplə(r); ˋtɪplɚ/ *n*.

tip·ster /ˈtɪpstə(r); ˋtɪpstɚ/ *n* person who gives tips (TIP³ *n* 2b), usu in return for money 提供赛马或股票等情报的人(通常指贩卖情报的).

tipsy /ˈtɪpsɪ; ˋtɪpsɪ/ *adj* (**-ier**, **-iest**) (*infml* 口) slightly drunk 微醉的. ▷ **tip·sily** *adv*. **tip·si·ness** *n* [U].

tip·toe /ˈtɪptəʊ; ˋtɪpˌto/ *n* (idm 习语) **on ˈtiptoe** on the tips of one's toes; with one's heels not touching the ground 踮着脚: *stand on tiptoe to see over the crowd* 踮

T

着脚隔着人群看 ○ *creep around on tiptoe to avoid making a noise* 踮着脚走以免弄出声音.

▷ **tip·toe** *v* [I, Ipr, Ip] walk quietly and carefully on tiptoe 踮着脚悄悄地走: *She tiptoed (across) to the bed where the child lay asleep.* 孩子睡着了, 她踮着脚走到他床前. ⇨Usage at PROWL 用法见 PROWL.

tip·top /ˌtɪpˈtɒp; ˈtɪpˈtɑp/ *adj* (*infml* 口) excellent; first-rate 极好的; 头等的; 一流的: *tiptop quality* 一流的质量 ○ *That meal was tiptop.* 那顿饭棒极了.

TIR /ˌti: aɪ ˈɑ:(r); ˌti aɪ ˈɑr/ *abbr* 缩写 = (esp on lorries in Europe) international road transport (French *Transport International Routier*) (尤指欧洲载货卡车上的标记)国际陆路货运(源自法文 *Transport International Routier*).

tir·ade /taɪˈreɪd; *US* ˈtaɪreɪd; ˈtaɪred/ *n* long angry speech of criticism or accusation 长篇的批评性或谴责性讲话.

tire[1] /ˈtaɪə(r); taɪr/ *v* **1** [I, Tn, Tn·p] (cause a person or an animal to) become weary or in need of rest (使人或动物)疲劳, 疲倦: *She's got so much energy — she never seems to tire.* 她精力充沛——似乎从不感到疲倦. ○ *Old people tire easily.* 老年人容易疲倦. ○ *The long walk tired me (out).* 我长途步行之后很累. **2** [Ipr] **~ of sth/doing sth** become uninterested in (doing) sth 对(做)某事感到厌倦: *After a week I tired of eating fish.* 我吃鱼吃了一个星期之后就腻了. ○ *He never tires of the sound of his own voice*, ie He talks too much. 他的话太多.

▷ **tired** /ˈtaɪəd; taɪrd/ *adj* **1** feeling that one would like to sleep or rest 困倦的; 疲倦的: *He was a tired man when he got back from that long climb.* 他长途爬山回来感到疲倦了. ○ *I'm dead* (ie extremely) *tired.* 我累得要死. **2** (*derog* 贬) over-familiar; hackneyed 陈旧的; 陈腐的: *The film had a rather tired plot.* 那电影的情节是老掉牙的. ○ *see the same tired old faces at every party* 每次聚会都看到这些熟悉的面孔. **3** (idm 习语) **be (sick and) tired of sb/sth/doing sth** have had enough of sb/sth/doing sth; be impatient or bored with sb/sth/doing sth 对某人[某事/做某事]不耐烦或感到厌烦: *I'm tired of (listening to) your criticisms.* 我听腻了你的批评. ˌ**tired ˈout** completely exhausted 筋疲力尽. **tired·ness** *n* [U].

T

tire·less *adj* not tiring easily; energetic 不易疲倦的; 精力充沛的: *a tireless worker* 不倦的工作者 ○ *thanks to your tireless efforts on our behalf* 多亏你为我们所做的不懈努力. **tire·lessly** *adv*.

tire·some /ˈtaɪəsəm; ˈtaɪrsəm/ *adj* troublesome, tedious or annoying 令人厌倦的; 讨厌的; 烦人的: *Selling your house can be a tiresome business.* 卖房子有时候是很麻烦的事. ○ *The children were being rather tiresome.* 孩子们那时很讨人厌. **tire·somely** *adv*.

tir·ing /ˈtaɪərɪŋ; ˈtaɪrɪŋ/ *adj*: *a tiring journey* 令人疲倦的旅行 ○ *The work is very tiring.* 这个工作很累人.

tire[2] (*US*) = TYRE.

tiro (also **tyro**) /ˈtaɪərəʊ; ˈtaɪro/ *n* (*pl* **~s**) person with little or no experience; beginner or novice 缺乏经验的人; 新手; 生手.

tis·sue /ˈtɪʃu:; ˈtɪʃʊ/ *n* **1** [U, C] mass of cells forming the body of an animal or a plant (动植物的)组织: *muscular, nervous, connective, etc tissue* 肌肉、神经、结缔等组织 ○ *The tissues have been destroyed and a scar has formed.* 那些组织受到破坏, 结了疤. **2** [C] piece of soft absorbent paper that is thrown away after use (as a handkerchief, etc) (用作手帕等的)纸巾: *a box of tissues* 一盒纸巾 ○ *ˈface/ˈfacial tissues*, ie for removing make-up, etc 面纸巾(用以清除脸部化妆物等的). **3** (also **ˈtissue-paper**) [U] very thin soft paper used for wrapping and packing things (包装物品用的)薄纸, 绵纸. **4** [C, U] (any type of) fine thin woven fabric (任何种类的)薄织物. **5** [C] **~ (of sth)** (*fig* 比喻) connected or interwoven series (相关的或交织的)一套, 一系列: *His story is a tissue of lies.* 他的话是一派谎言. ○ *the complex tissue of myth and fact* 虚实交错的复杂情况.

tit[1] /tɪt; tɪt/ *n* any of various types of small bird, often with a dark top to the head (任何一种)山雀: *titmouse* 山雀 ○ *tomtit* 山雀 ○ *blue tit* 蓝山雀.

tit[2] /tɪt; tɪt/ *n* (idm 习语) ˌ**tit for ˈtat** blow, injury, insult, etc given in return for one received 还击: *He hit me so I hit him back — it was tit for tat.* 他打我, 我也打他——以牙还牙.

tit[3] /tɪt; tɪt/ *n* **1** (⚠ *sl* 讳, 俚) (**a**) (esp *pl* 尤作复数) woman's breast (女子的)乳房. (**b**) nipple 乳头; 奶头. **2** (*Brit sl* 俚) (used as a vulgar term of abuse 用作辱骂的粗俗词): *He's a stupid little tit!* 他这个蠢货!

Ti·tan /ˈtaɪtn; ˈtaɪtn̩/ *n* (also **titan**) person of great size, strength, intellect, importance, etc 高大、强壮、智力高、重要...的人.

▷ **ti·tanic** /taɪˈtænɪk; taɪˈtænɪk/ *adj* gigantic; immense 巨大的; 极大的: *The two of them are locked in a titanic struggle for control of the company.* 他们俩为争夺对公司的控制权打得不可开交.

tit·bit /ˈtɪtbɪt; ˈtɪtˌbɪt/ (*US* **tid·bit** /ˈtɪdbɪt; ˈtɪdˌbɪt/) *n* (**a**) specially attractive bit of food 味美的少量食品: *She always keeps some titbits to give to her cat.* 她总留点儿特别好吃的东西喂猫. (**b**) **~ (of sth)** small but interesting piece of news, gossip, etc 趣闻; 轶闻: *titbits of scandal* 丑闻.

tithe /taɪð; taɪð/ *n* one tenth of the annual produce of a farm, etc formerly paid as a tax to support the clergy and the church 什一税(旧时付给圣职人员和教会的农产品).

□ ˈ**tithe barn** barn built to store tithes 什一税农产品储存库.

tit·il·late /ˈtɪtɪleɪt; ˈtɪtl̩ˌet/ *v* [Tn] stimulate or excite (sb), esp sexually 刺激(某人)(尤指性欲): *The book has no artistic merit — its sole aim is to titillate (the reader).* 那书毫无艺术价值, 只是撩拨(读者)情欲. ▷ **tit·il·lat·ing** *adj*: *a mildly titillating film* 稍有性刺激的影片. **tit·il·la·tion** /ˌtɪtɪˈleɪʃn; ˌtɪtl̩ˈeʃən/ *n* [U].

tit·iv·ate /ˈtɪtɪveɪt; ˈtɪtəˌvet/ *v* [I, Tn] (*infml* 口) make (esp oneself) smart or attractive 修饰, 打扮(尤指自己): *She spent an hour titivating (herself) before going out.* 她打扮了一个小时才出门儿. ▷ **tit·iva·tion** /ˌtɪtɪˈveɪʃn; ˌtɪtəˈveʃən/ *n* [U].

title /ˈtaɪtl; ˈtaɪtl̩/ *n* **1** [C] name of a book, poem, picture, etc (书、诗歌、图画等的)名称, 题目, 标题. **2** [C] word used to show a person's rank, occupation, etc (eg *King, mayor, captain*) or used in speaking to or about him (eg *Lord, Doctor, Mrs*) 称号; 头衔(如国王、市长、船长); 称谓(如勋爵、博士、夫人): *She has a title*, ie is a member of the nobility. 她有贵族头衔. **3** [U, C] **~ (to sth/to do sth)** (*law* 律) right or claim, esp to the ownership of property 权益; 权利; (尤指)财产所有权: *Has he any title to the land?* 他有这块土地的所有权吗? ○ *disputing the country's title to the islands* 争论该国对那些岛是否有主权. **4** [C] (*sport* 体) championship 冠军: *win the world heavyweight title* 获重量级世界拳击冠军 ○ [attrib 作定语] *a title fight* 冠军争夺战.

▷ **titled** /ˈtaɪtld; ˈtaɪtl̩d/ *adj* having a title of nobility 有爵位的; 有贵族头衔的: *a titled lady*, eg a duchess 有爵位的女士(如女公爵).

□ ˈ**title-deed** *n* legal document proving sb's title to a property 房地产所有权契据.

ˈ**title-holder** *n* (*sport* 体) champion 冠军: *the British 800-metres title-holder* 英国的800米冠军 ○ *Liverpool are the current title-holders.* 利物浦是目前的冠军.

ˈ**title-page** *n* page at the front of a book giving the title, author's name, etc 书名页; 扉页.

ˈ**title-role** *n* part in a play, etc that is used as the title (戏剧、电影等中的)剧名角色, 片名角色: *She has sung the title-role in 'Carmen'*, ie sung the role of Carmen in that opera. 她在歌剧《卡门》中演唱卡门一角.

tit·mouse /ˈtɪtmaʊs; ˈtɪtˌmaʊs/ *n* (*pl* **titmice** /-maɪs; -ˌmaɪs/) type of tit[1] 山雀.

tit·ter /ˈtɪtə(r); ˈtɪtɚ/ *n* short nervous laugh 短促而神经质的笑.

▷ **tit·ter** *v* [I] give a titter 发出短促而神经质的笑声: *The audience tittered politely.* 听众很有礼貌地吃吃地笑了笑.

tittle-tattle /ˈtɪtl tætl; ˈtɪtl̩ˌtætl̩/ *n* [U] silly or trivial talk; petty gossip 闲谈; 聊天.

▷ **tittle-tattle** *v* [I] talk about unimportant things; gossip 闲谈; 聊天.

titu·lar /ˈtɪtjʊlə(r); *US* -tʃʊ-; ˈtɪtʃələ/ *adj* [attrib 作定语] (*fml* 文) **1** having a certain title(2) or position but no real authority 名义上的; 有名无实的: *the titular Head of State* 名义上的国家元首 ○ *titular sovereignty* 有名无实的统治权. **2** held as the result of having a title(2) 由有称号或头衔的人持有的: *titular sovereignty* 因有头衔而持有的统治权.

tizzy /ˈtɪzɪ; ˈtɪzɪ/ *n* (usu *sing* 通常作单数) (*infml* 口) state of nervous excitement or confusion 紧张; 慌乱: *be in/get in(to) a tizzy* 处于紧张状态[慌张起来].

T-junction ⇨T, T.

TM *abbr* 缩写 = trademark.

tn *abbr* 缩写 = (*US*) ton(s); tonne(s).

TNT /ˌti: en ˈti:; ˋtiˌɛnˋti/ *abbr* 缩写 = trinitrotoluene (a powerful explosive) 三硝基甲苯(黄色炸药).

to[1] /*before consonants* tə; tə; *before vowels* tʊ; tu *or* tu:; tə; *strong form* tu:; tu 辅音前读作 tə, 元音前读作 tʊ 或 tu:; 强读式为 tu:/ *prep* **1** (**a**) in the direction of (sth); towards 向, 朝, 对着(某方向或某处): *walk to the office* 朝办公室走去 ○ *I'm going to the shops.* 我正要去商店. ○ *fall to the ground* 落到地上 ○ *on the way to the station* 在去火车站的路上 ○ *point to sth* 指向某物 ○ *hold it (up) to the light* 把它拿起来对着光 ○ *turn to the left/right* 向左[右]转 ○ *travelling from town to town, place to place, etc* 从一城到另一城、从一地到另一地 ○ *go to Majorca for one's holidays* 去马霍卡岛度假 ○ *He was taken to hospital for treatment.* 把他送到医院治疗去了. (**b**) **~ the sth (of sth)** located in a specified direction (from sth) 位于(某物的)某一方向: *There are mountains to the north/south/east/west of here.* 这儿的北[南/东/西]面有山. ○ *Pisa is to the west (of Florence).* 比萨在(佛罗伦萨的)西边. ○ *The shed is to the side of the house.* 小棚屋在房子的一边. **2** towards (a condition, state, quality, etc); reaching the state of (sth) 趋于, 倾向(某种情况、状态、性质等); 至(某种)状态: *a move to the left*, eg in politics 转向左(如政治上) ○ *stir sb to action* 鼓动某人采取行动 ○ *bring/reduce/move sb to tears* 把某人感动得落泪 ○ *rise to power* 上台掌权 ○ *He tore the letter to pieces.* 他把那封信撕碎了. ○ *The mother sang her baby to sleep.* 母亲唱歌哄孩子睡觉. ○ *Wait until the traffic lights change from red to green.* 要等到交通灯由红变绿再走. **3** (**a**) as far as (sth); reaching 到(某处); 达: *The garden extends to the river bank.* 这个花园直伸展到河岸. ○ *Her dress reached down to her ankles.* 她的连衣裙垂至脚踝. (**b**) (esp after *from sth* 尤用于from sth 之后) until and including (sth) 直到并包括(某事物): *from beginning to end* 自始至终 ○ *from first to last* 从头到尾 ○ *faithful to the end/last* 忠实到底 ○ *wet, soaked, drenched, etc to the skin* 浑身湿透 ○ *cooked to perfection* 烹调火候恰到好处 ○ *count (from 1) to 10* (从1)数到10 ○ *all the colours from red to violet* 从红到紫的各种颜色 ○ *from Monday to Friday* 从星期一到星期五 ○ *from morning to night* 从早到晚 ○ *How long is it to lunch?* ie How much time is there until lunch? 离吃午饭还有多长时间? **4** (of time) before (sth) (指时间)在(某时间)之前: *a quarter to six* 差一刻六点 ○ *ten (minutes) to two* 一点五十(分). Cf 参看 PAST[2] 1. **5** (used to introduce the indirect object of *vs* marked Dn·pr, Dpr·f, Dpr·t, Dpr·w 用以引导标有 Dn·pr、Dpr·f、Dpr·t、Dpr·w 符号之动词的间接宾语): *He gave it to his sister.* 他把那个给他妹妹了. ○ (*fml* 文) *To whom did she send the book?* 她把书送到谁那儿去了? ○ (*infml* 口) *Who did she send the book to?* 她把书送到谁那儿了? ○ *She said to us that she was surprised.* 她跟我们说她很惊讶. ○ *I'll explain to you where everything goes.* 我要向你解释每一项的去向. ○ *He shouted to his friend to remember the wine.* 他大声提醒他朋友别忘了酒. **6** belonging to (sb/sth); for 属于(某人[某物]); 为: *the key to the door* 开这个门的钥匙 ○ *be secretary to the managing director* 做总经理的秘书 ○ *the words to a tune* 为一首曲子作的词. **7** (indicating a comparison or ratio 表示相比或比率): *I prefer walking to climbing.* 我喜欢步行不喜欢爬山. ○ *We won by six goals to three.* 我们以六比三获胜. ○ *This is inferior/superior to that.* 这个不如[胜过]那个. ○ *Compared to me, he's rich.* 跟我比起来, 他算有钱. ○ *odds of 100 to 1* 以100比1的赔率赌. **8** making (sth); adding up to 构成(某数); 加起来等于: *There are 100 pence to the pound*, ie £1 = 100p. 1英镑等于100便士. ○ *There are 100 centimetres to the metre.* 100厘米是1米. **9** (indicating a rate 表示比率): *do 30 miles to the gallon* 每加仑可行驶30英里 ○ *get 10 francs to the pound* 1英镑可换10法郎. Cf 参看 PER. **10** (indicating a possible range 表示可能的范围): *20 to 30 years of age* 20到30岁 ○ *3 to 4 centimetres long* 3到4厘米长. **11** in honour of (sb/sth) 向(某人[某事物])表示敬意: *drink to sb/to sb's health* 为某人[某人的健康]干杯 ○ *a toast to the cook* 向厨师敬酒 ○ *a monument to (the memory of) the soldiers who died in the war* 阵亡将士纪念碑. **12** close enough to be touching (sb/sth); facing 接近得触到(某人[某物]); 紧靠着; 面对着: *dance cheek to cheek* 脸贴脸跳舞 ○ *with an ear to the door* 把耳朵贴着门 ○ *sit back to back* 背靠背坐着 ○ *cars queueing bumper to bumper on the motorway* 高速公路上首尾相接排成长队的汽车. **13** (used after *vs* of motion eg *come, go, rush* 用于动作动词之后, 如 come、go、rush 等动词) with the intention of giving (sth) 有提供(某物)的意图: *come to our aid/help/assistance/rescue* 前来帮助我们. **14** concerning (sth) 与(某事物)有关: *a right to the throne* 王位的继承权 ○ *a solution to a problem* 解决问题的方法 ○ *She's devoted to her family.* 她一心为了自己的家庭. **15** causing (sth) 引起(某事): *To my surprise, delight, annoyance, etc the Labour Party won the election*, ie Their winning caused me surprise, delight, etc. 工党在选举中获胜, 真让我吃惊、高兴、烦恼等. ○ *To my shame, I forgot* (ie I am ashamed that I forgot) *his birthday.* 我把他的生日忘了, 真不好意思. **16** (used after *vs* of perception, eg *seem, appear, feel, look, smell* 用于表示感觉的动词之后, 如 seem、appear、feel、look、smell 等动词) in the opinion of (sb); according to 按(某人)的看法; 根据(某人)的意见: *It feels like velvet to me.* 我摸起来像天鹅绒. ○ *Does it look to you like gold?* 你看那个像金子吗? ○ *It sounded like crying to him.* 他听着那像是哭声. **17** satisfying (sb/sth) 适合(某人[某事]): *not really to my liking* 并非真正符合我的心意 ○ *quite nice, but not to her taste* 好是好, 但不合她的口味.

to[2] /*before consonants* tə; tə, *before vowels* tʊ; tu *or* tu:; tə; *strong form* tu:; tu 辅音前读作 tə, 元音前读作 tʊ 或 tu:; 强读式为 tu:/ (Used immediately before the simple (root) form of a *v* to form the infinitive. 置于动词原形(词根)之前, 构成不定式. The following are only a few uses of the infinitive; others are given in *n, adj,* and *v* entries. 下面仅是动词不定式的几种用法; 其他用法见各名词、形容词和动词的词条.) **1** (used as the object of many *vs*, esp those labelled Tt, Tn·t, Cn·t, Dpr·t, Dn·t 用作许多动词的宾语, 尤其是标有 Tt、Tn·t、Cn·t、Dpr·t、Dn·t 的动词): *He wants to go.* 他想去. ○ *We had hoped to finish by four o'clock.* 我们原希望四点钟前能完成. ○ *She asked me to go.* 她要求我去. ○ *She persuaded him to tell the truth.* 她劝他说实话. **2** (expressing purpose or result in an *adv* clause 在状语成分中表示目的或结果): *They came (in order) to help me.* 他们来(为的是)帮助我. ○ *She's working hard to earn money.* 她为了挣钱而努力工作. ○ *We make our goods to last*, ie so that they will last. 我们制造的货物经久耐用. ○ *They went there to cause trouble.* 他们到那里惹麻烦去了. ○ *She ran to the station only to find that the train had left.* 她跑到火车站, 但火车却开走了. **3** (used alone to avoid repetition of the whole infinitive 单独使用, 以避免重复整个动词不定式): *I'd like to do it but I don't know how to.* 我倒是愿意做, 但不知怎么做. ○ *I intended to go but forgot to.* 我原来想去, 可是忘了去了. ○ *He often does things you wouldn't expect him to.* 他常做出谁也料不到的事.

T

to[3] /tu:; tu/ *adv part* (For special uses with *vs* and in compounds, eg *bring sb to, come to, set-to, lean-to*, see the *v* entries 可与动词连用及构成复合词, 如 bring sb to、come to、set-to、lean-to, 其释义见各动词词条.) **1** (usu of a door) in or into a closed position; shut (通常指门)在或到关闭的位置, 关闭: *Push the door to.* 把门关上. ○ *Leave it to.* 让它关着吧. **2** (idm 习语) ˌ**to and ˈfro** backwards and forwards 来回地; 往复地: *walking to and fro* 走来走去 ○ *journeys to and fro between London and Paris* 伦敦与巴黎之间的往返旅程.

toad /təʊd; tod/ *n* **1** frog-like animal that lives on land except when breeding 蟾蜍; 癞蛤蟆. ⇨illus at FROG 见 FROG 插图. **2** (used esp as a term of abuse 尤作辱骂用词) disgusting or disliked person 可憎的或讨厌的人: *You repulsive little toad!* 你这个讨厌的癞蛤蟆!

□ ˌ**toad-in-the-ˈhole** *n* [U] (*Brit*) dish consisting of sausages baked in batter 裹上面糊烤的香肠.

toad·stool /ˈtəʊdstu:l; ˋtodˌstul/ *n* any of various types of umbrella-shaped fungus, esp a poisonous one 伞菌科的菌; (尤指)毒蕈. ⇨illus at FUNGUS 见 FUNGUS 插图. Cf 参看 MUSHROOM.

toady /ˈtəʊdɪ; ˋtodɪ/ *n* (*derog* 贬) person who flatters another or treats him with excessive respect in the hope of gain or advantage 谄媚者; 马屁精.

▷ **toady** *v* (*pt, pp* **toadied**) [I, Ipr] **~ (to sb)** (*derog* 贬) behave in this way 谄媚; 奉承; 拍马: *toadying to the boss* 拍老板马屁.

toast[1] /təʊst; tost/ *n* [U] **1** sliced bread made brown and crisp by heating under a grill, in a toaster, etc 烤面包片(面包切成片后放在烤架下、面包片加热器等中烤黄、烤脆): *make some toast for breakfast* 把面包片烤热作早餐 ○ *a poached egg on toast* 烤面包片加荷包蛋 ○ *two slices of buttered toast* 两片涂黄油的烤面包片. **2** (idm 习语) **have sb on 'toast** (*infml* 口) have sb completely at one's mercy 任意摆布某人. **warm as toast** ⇨ WARM[1].

▷ **toast** *v* [I, Tn] become or make brown and crisp by heating 烤黄; 烤脆: *a toasted (cheese) sandwich* 烤过的(干酪)三明治 ○ (*fig* 比喻) *toasting oneself/one's feet in front of the fire* 烤火[烤烤脚]. **toaster** *n* electrical device for toasting slices of bread (电的)面包片加热器.

□ **'toasting-fork** *n* fork with a long handle used for toasting bread, etc in front of a fire 烤面包片叉(将面包片在明火上加热的长柄叉).

'toast-rack *n* rack for holding slices of toast at the table 面包片架(餐桌上放置烤热的面包片用的). ⇨illus at RACK 见 RACK 插图.

toast[2] /təʊst; tost/ *v* [Tn] wish happiness, success, etc to (sb/sth) by drinking wine, etc 为(某人[某事物])幸福、成功等祝酒: *toast the bride and groom* 为新娘和新郎祝酒 ○ *toast the success of a new company* 为新公司获得成功而干杯.

▷ **toast** *n* **1** act of toasting 祝酒; 敬酒: *propose a loyal toast to the Queen* 提议向女王敬酒 ○ *drink a toast* 干杯 ○ *reply/respond to the toast*, ie (of the person toasted) make a speech in reply (接受敬酒的人)致答词. **2** person, etc toasted 受敬酒的人等: *be the toast of* (ie praised and congratulated by) *the whole neighbourhood* 受到邻里交口称赞和祝贺的人.

□ **'toast-master** *n* person who announces the toasts at a formal banquet 宴会上宣布祝酒的人.

T

to·bacco /tə'bækəʊ; tə'bæko/ *n* (*pl* **~s**) **1** [C, U] (type of) leaves that are dried, cured and used for smoking (in pipes, cigarettes and cigars) or chewing, or as snuff 烟叶. **2** [U] plant from which these leaves are obtained 烟草.

▷ **to·bac·con·ist** /tə'bækənɪst; tə'bækənɪst/ *n* shopkeeper who sells cigarettes, cigars and pipe-tobacco 烟草店老板.

to·bog·gan /tə'bɒgən; tə'bɑgən/ *n* long light narrow sledge, often curved upwards at the front, used for sliding downhill on snow 长雪橇.

▷ **to·bog·gan** *v* [I] use a toboggan 乘长雪橇滑行: *go tobogganing* 去滑雪橇.

toby jug /'təʊbɪ dʒʌg; 'tobɪ,dʒʌg/ mug or jug (formerly for beer) in the form of an old man with a three-cornered hat 人形缸子或罐(呈头戴三角帽的老人形, 旧时盛啤酒用的).

toc·cata /tə'kɑːtə; tə'kɑtə/ *n* (*music* 音) composition for a keyboard instrument (esp the organ or harpsichord) in a free style, designed to show the performer's technique 托卡塔(用键盘乐器演奏的乐曲, 尤指用风琴或拨弦键琴演奏的).

toc·sin /'tɒksɪn; 'tɑksɪn/ *n* (*dated or fml* 旧或文) **1** (bell rung as a) signal of alarm 警钟; 警铃; 警戒信号; 警报. **2** (*fig* 比喻) warning of danger 危险警报.

tod /tɒd; tɑd/ *n* (idm 习语) **on one's 'tod** (*Brit infml* 口) on one's own; alone 独自; 单独: *I spent the evening on my tod again.* 我又单独度过了这一晚. ○ *You mean you did it all on your tod* (ie without help)? 你是说这都是你独自一人做的?

to·day /tə'deɪ; tə'de/ *adv, n* [U] **1** (on) this day 今天; 今日; 本日: *What are we doing today?* 今天我们做什么? ○ *We're leaving today week/a week (from) today*, ie in a week's time. 我们于下周的今天动身. ○ *Today is my birthday.* 今天是我的生日. ○ *Have you seen today's paper?* 你看见今天的报纸了吗? **2** (at) the present period or age 当今; 现代; 当世: *Women today no longer accept such treatment.* 如今女子再也不接受此种待遇了. ○ *the young people of today* 现代青年.

toddle /'tɒdl; 'tɑdl/ *v* [I, Ipr, Ip] **1** (esp of a young child) walk with short unsteady steps (尤指幼儿)摇摇摆摆地走: *Her two-year-old son toddled into the room.* 她的两岁的儿子摇摇摆摆地走进屋里. **2** (*infml* 口) walk 步行; 走: *toddle round to see a friend* 走着去看朋友 ○ *I think we should be toddling along/off*, ie should leave. 我看我们该走了.

▷ **tod·dler** /'tɒdlə(r); 'tɑdlɚ/ *n* child who has only recently learnt to walk 刚学会走路的孩子.

toddy /'tɒdɪ; 'tɑdɪ/ *n* [C, U] (glass of) alcoholic drink made of spirits, sugar and hot water (一杯)加糖加热水的烈酒.

to-do /tə'duː; tə'du/ *n* (*pl* **~s**) (usu *sing* 通常作单数) fuss; commotion 纷扰; 喧闹: *What's all the to-do about?* 这么吵吵嚷嚷的是怎么回事? ○ *She made a great to-do about his forgetting her birthday.* 他把她的生日给忘了, 她大吵大闹了一场.

toe /təʊ; to/ *n* **1** (**a**) each of the five divisions of the front part of the human foot (人的)脚趾. ⇨illus at FOOT 见 FOOT 插图. (**b**) similar part of an animal's foot (动物的)足趾. **2** part of a sock, shoe, etc that covers the toes (袜、鞋等的)足尖部. ⇨illus at SHOE 见 SHOE 插图. **3** (idm 习语) **dig one's heels/toes in** ⇨ DIG[1]. **from head to foot/toe** ⇨ HEAD[1]. **from top to toe** ⇨ TOP[1]. **on one's 'toes** ready for action; alert 准备行动的; 警觉的: *The constant threat of danger kept us all on our toes.* 我们因随时都会发生危险而保持警觉. **tread on sb's corns/toes** ⇨ TREAD.

▷ **toe** *v* (*pt, pp* **toed**, *pres p* **toeing**) (idm 习语) **toe the (party) 'line**; *US* also **toe the 'mark** obey the orders of one's group or party; conform 服从团体或党的命令; 遵从.

□ **'toe-cap** *n* outer covering of the toe of a shoe or boot (鞋或靴尖的)包头.

'toe-hold *n* slight foothold (eg in mountain climbing) 小的立足点(如登山途中的): (*fig* 比喻) *Thanks to this contract the firm gained a toe-hold in the European market.* 有了这个合同, 该公司在欧洲的市场才有立足之地.

'toe-nail *n* nail of a human toe (人的)趾甲. ⇨illus at FOOT 见 FOOT 插图.

toff /tɒf; tɑf/ *n* (*dated Brit sl* 旧, 俚) rich or well-dressed person of high social class 上流社会有钱的或衣着讲究的人.

tof·fee /'tɒfɪ; *US* 'tɔːfɪ; 'tɔfɪ/ (*US* also **taffy** /'tæfɪ; 'tæfɪ/) *n* [C, U] **1** (piece of) hard sticky sweet made by heating sugar, butter, etc (一块)太妃糖(用食糖与黄油等加热后制成的黏性硬糖果). **2** (idm 习语) **can't do sth for 'toffee** (*infml* 口) lack the skill or ability needed to do sth 没本事做某事; 不能胜任某事: *She can't sing for toffee!* 她根本不会唱歌!

□ **'toffee-apple** *n* (*Brit*) apple coated with a thin layer of toffee and fixed on a stick (插在签子上的)敷太妃糖衣的苹果.

'toffee-nosed *adj* (*Brit sl* 俚) snobbish; snooty 势利的; 目空一切的.

tog /tɒg; tɑg/ *v* (**-gg-**) (phr v) **tog oneself out/up (in sth)** (*infml* 口) put on smart clothes; dress up 穿上漂亮衣服; 穿上盛装: *children togged out in their Sunday best* 穿着漂亮衣服的儿童.

▷ **togs** *n* [pl] (*infml* 口) clothes 衣物; 衣服: *games togs* 运动服 ○ *summer togs* 夏季衣服.

toga /'təʊgə; 'togə/ *n* loose outer garment worn by men in ancient Rome 托加袍(古罗马男子穿的宽松罩袍).

to·gether /tə'geðə(r); tə'gɛðɚ/ *adv* **1** in or into company; with or towards each other 在一起; 到一起; 共同: *Let's go for a walk together.* 咱们一起去散步吧. ○ *I hear they're living together*, ie in the same house. 我听说他们住在一起. ○ *Get all the ingredients together before you start cooking.* 把所有材料都放在一起再动手烹饪. **2** so as to be in contact or united 致使相接触或相结合: *glue, nail, tie, etc two boards together* 把两块木板粘、钉、捆等在一起 ○ *Mix the sand and cement together, then add water.* 把沙子和水泥混在一起再加水. ○ (*fig* 比喻) *He's got more money than the rest of us (put) together.* 他的钱比我们大家的加在一起的总数还多. **3** in or into agreement or harmony 一致; 协调; 变得一致或协调: *negotiations aimed at bringing the two sides in the dispute closer together* 使辩论双方意见趋于一致的谈判 ○ *The party is absolutely together on this issue.* 该党在这一问题上意见完全一致. **4** at the same time; simultaneously 同时; 一起: *All my troubles seem to come together.* 我的各种问题似乎同时出现了. ○ *They were all talking together* *and I couldn't understand a word.* 他们一起说话, 我一个字都听不清. **5** without interruption; in continuous succession 不间断地; 连续地: *It rained for three days together.* 一连下了三天雨. ○ *She can sit reading for hours together.* 她能连续几个小时坐在那儿看书. **6** (idm 习语) **get sth/it toˈgether** (*sl* 俚) get sth/it organized or under control 使某事物有组织或受控制: *She would be a very good player if only she could get it together.* 她若能控制得当就能成为很好的选手. **together with** as well as; and also 和; 连同: *These new facts, together with the other evidence, prove the prisoner's innocence.* 这些新的事实连同其他证据已证明在押者无罪.

▷ **to·gether** *adj* (*sl approv* 俚, 褒 *esp US*) organized; capable 有组织的; 有能力的: *He's incredibly together for someone so young.* 他这么年轻, 能力真了不起. ○ *a really together organization* 很严密的组织.

to·gether·ness *n* [U] feeling of unity, friendship or love 团结; 友爱.

toggle /ˈtɒgl; ˈtɑgḷ/ *n* fastening consisting of a short piece of wood, etc that is passed through a loop or hole (eg instead of a button on a coat) 套索钉; 棒形纽扣(如大衣上的).

□ **ˈtoggle-switch** *n* electrical switch operated by a short lever which is moved (usu) up and down 扳钮开关; 肘节开关.

toil /tɔɪl; tɔɪl/ *v* (*fml or rhet* 文或修辞) **1** [I, Ipr, Ip, It] **~ away (at/over sth)** work long or hard 长时间或辛苦工作: *students toiling over their homework* 辛辛苦苦做功课的学生 ○ *We toiled away all afternoon to get the house ready for our guests.* 我们忙了一下午收拾房子准备迎接宾客. **2** [Ipr, Ip] move slowly and with difficulty in the specified direction 缓慢而艰难地向某方向移动: *The bus toiled up the steep hill.* 公共汽车艰难地爬上陡峭的山岗. ○ *The ground was muddy and uneven, but we toiled on.* 地面泥泞不平, 我们仍吃力地向前走.

▷ **toil** *n* [U] (*fml or rhet* 文或修辞) hard or lengthy work 辛苦的或长时间的工作: *after years of toil* 辛苦地工作了多年之后. ⇨Usage at WORK[1] 用法见 WORK[1].

toiler *n*.

toi·let /ˈtɔɪlɪt; ˈtɔɪlɪt/ *n* **1** [C] (room containing a) lavatory 厕所; 卫生间; 盥洗室; 恭桶: *Can you tell me where the toilets are?* 您能告诉我洗手间在哪儿吗? ⇨Usage 见所附用法. **2** [U] (*dated* 旧) process of washing and dressing oneself, arranging one's hair, etc 化妆; 梳洗; 打扮: [attrib 作定语] *a ˈtoilet set* 一套梳妆用具 ○ *ˈtoilet articles*, ie hairbrushes, combs, hand-mirrors, etc 梳妆用具(发刷、梳子、手镜等).

▷ **toi·let·ries** /ˈtɔɪlɪtrɪz; ˈtɔɪlətrɪz/ *n* [pl] (in shops) articles or products used in washing, dressing, etc (商店中的)化妆用品.

□ **ˈtoilet-paper** *n* [U] paper for use in a lavatory 卫生纸; 手纸.

ˈtoilet-roll *n* roll of toilet-paper 卫生纸卷; 手纸卷.

ˈtoilet-train *v* [Tn esp passive 尤用于被动语态] train (a child) to control its urination and defecation and to use a lavatory 训练(孩子)控制大小便和上厕所: *She isn't toilet-trained yet.* 她还没学过用厕所. **ˈtoilet-training** *n* [U].

ˈtoilet water scented water for use on the skin, esp after washing 花露水.

NOTE ON USAGE 用法: In British English **the toilet** in private houses is called **the lavatory**, **toilet**, **WC** (dated), or **loo** (informal). 在英式英语中, 私人住宅中的厕所称为**the lavatory**、**toilet**、**WC**(已陈旧)或**loo**(用于口语). In public places it is called **the Gents/the Ladies** or **public conveniences.** 公共场所的厕所称为**the Gents/the Ladies**或**public conveniences**. In US English it is called **the lavatory, toilet** or **bathroom** in private houses and **the washroom** or **rest-room** in public buildings. 在美式英语中私人住宅中的厕所称为**the lavatory**、**toilet**或**bathroom**, 在公共建筑物中的称为**the washroom**或**rest-room**.

toils /tɔɪlz; tɔɪlz/ *n* [pl] (*fml usu fig* 文, 通常作比喻) nets; traps 罗网; 陷阱: *caught in the toils of the law* 落入法网.

to·ing /ˈtu:ɪŋ; ˈtuɪŋ/ *n* (idm 习语) **ˌtoing and ˈfroing** movement backwards and forwards 前前后后的运动: *After much toing and froing we got all the children back to their homes.* 我们来来往往很多次把孩子们都送回家了.

token /ˈtəʊkən; ˈtokən/ *n* **1** sign, symbol or evidence of sth 表征; 标志; 证据: *A white flag is used as a token of surrender.* 白旗是用作投降的信号. ○ *These flowers are a small token of my gratitude.* 谨以此花聊表谢忱. **2** disc like a coin used to operate certain machines or as a form of payment (用以启动某些机器或用作付款形式的)代币, 专用辅币: *Tokens for the cigarette machine are available at the bar.* 在柜台可以买到供自动售烟机使用的代币. ○ *milk tokens*, ie (in Britain) bought from the milkman and left on the doorstep to pay for the milk delivered 牛奶票(送奶人出售的票证, 购者用以付送奶费, 可置于门外). **3** (esp in compounds 尤用以构成复合词) voucher or coupon, usu attached to a greetings card, which can be exchanged for goods of the value shown 赠券; 礼券: *a £10 ˈbook/ˈrecord/ˈgift token* 金额10英镑的书券[唱片券/礼券]. **4** (idm 习语) **by the same token** ⇨ SAME[1]. **in token of sth** as evidence of sth 作为某事的证据: *Please accept this gift in token of our affection for you.* 请接受这一礼物, 这是我们微薄的情意.

▷ **token** *adj* [attrib 作定语] **1** serving as a sign or pledge of sth 象征性的; 作为对某事的保证的: *a token payment*, ie payment of a small part of what is owed, as an acknowledgement of the debt 象征性的偿付(偿付小部分欠款, 作为承认该债务的象征) ○ *a token strike*, ie a short strike serving as a warning that a longer one may follow 象征性罢工(短期罢工, 以警告对方可能发动长期罢工). **2** done, existing, etc on a small scale as a gesture of sth that is not seriously or sincerely meant; superficial or perfunctory 装样子的; 敷衍的; 表面的: *Our troops encountered only token resistance.* 我们的部队仅受到表面上的抵抗. ○ *a token attempt, effort, offer, etc* 装样子的尝试、努力、好意等 ○ *the token woman on the committee*, ie included to avoid charges of sexual discrimination 委员会中做装点的女性(以免遭性别歧视的指责).

told *pt, pp* of TELL.

tol·er·ate /ˈtɒləreɪt; ˈtɑləˌret/ *v* **1** [Tn, Tsg] allow (sth that one dislikes or disagrees with) without interfering 容忍(不喜欢或不赞成的某事物): *a government which refuses to tolerate opposition* 不容有人反对的政府 ○ *I won't tolerate such behaviour/your behaving in this way.* 我不能容忍这种行为[你这样做]. **2** [Tn] endure (sb/sth) without protesting 忍受(某人[某事]): *How can you tolerate that awful woman?* 你怎么能忍得了那可恶的女人? ○ *tolerate heat, noise, pain, etc well* 很能忍受炎热、吵闹、痛苦等. **3** [Tn] (*medical* 医) be able to take (a drug, etc) or undergo (a treatment) without harm 能服用(药等); 能经受(治疗): *The body cannot tolerate such large amounts of radiation.* 身体经不住那么大剂量的放射线.

▷ **tol·er·able** /ˈtɒlərəbl; ˈtɑlərəbḷ/ *adj* **1** that can be tolerated; endurable 可容忍的; 可忍受的: *The heat was tolerable at night but suffocating during the day.* 这种炎热的天气在夜间尚能忍受, 但白天就令人感到呼吸困难. **2** fairly good; passable 尚好的; 还可以的: *tolerable weather* 还算好的天气 ○ *in tolerable health* 尚算健康 ○ *We had a very tolerable* (ie excellent) *lunch.* 我们吃了顿很不错的午饭. **tol·er·ably** /-əblɪ; -əblɪ/ *adv* in a moderate degree; fairly well 相当地; 尚好: *feel tolerably* (ie almost completely) *certain about sth* 觉得对某事相当有把握 ○ *He plays the piano tolerably well.* 他弹钢琴弹得还不错.

tol·er·ance /ˈtɒlərəns; ˈtɑlərəns/ *n* **1** [U] willingness or ability to tolerate sb/sth 容忍; 忍受; 宽容: *religious/racial tolerance* 宗教[种族]上的宽容 ○ *As the addict's tolerance increases, he requires ever larger doses of the drug.* 嗜毒者由于对药物的耐受性增加了, 因而需要更大剂量的毒品. **2** [C, U] (*engineering* 工) amount by which the size, weight, etc of a part can vary without causing problems 容许偏差; 公差; 容限: *working to a tolerance of 0.0001 of an inch/to very fine tolerances* 加工至公差0.0001英寸[极小].

tol·er·ant /-rənt; -rənt/ *adj* **~ (of/towards sb/sth)** having or showing tolerance 容忍的; 忍受的; 宽容的: *I'm a tolerant man but your behaviour is more than I can bear.* 我是个能忍的人, 但你的行为我已忍无可忍. ○ *Her own mistakes made her very tolerant of/towards (the* *faults of) others.* 她因自己有错误, 对别人(的错误)就概不计较了. **tol·er·antly** *adv.*

tol·era·tion /ˌtɒləˈreɪʃn; ˌtaləˈreʃən/ *n* [U] action or practice of tolerating (TOLERATE 1, 2) 容忍; 忍受; 宽容.

toll[1] /təʊl; tol/ *n* **1** money paid for the use of a road, bridge, harbour, etc (道路、桥梁、港口等的)使用费, 通行费, 停泊费. **2** loss or damage caused by sth 某事造成的损失或毁坏: *the death-toll in the earthquake, on the roads, after the massacre*, ie the number of people killed 地震、交通事故、大屠杀的死亡人数. **3** (idm 习语) **take a heavy toll/take its toll (of sth)** cause loss, damage, etc 造成损失、毁坏等: *The war took a heavy toll of human life.* 这次战争夺去了许多人的生命. ○ *Every year at Christmas drunken driving takes its toll.* 每年的圣诞节都有醉酒驾车的伤亡事故.

□ ˈ**toll-bridge** *n* bridge at which a toll is charged 收费桥.

ˈ**toll-gate** *n* gate across a road to prevent anyone passing until the toll has been paid (收费路上的)收费门.

ˈ**toll-house** *n* house occupied by the person who collects tolls on a road, etc 收费亭; 收费所; 收费处.

toll[2] /təʊl; tol/ *v* **1** [Tn, Tn·pr] **~ (for sb/sth)** ring (a bell) with slow regular strokes, esp for a death or funeral 缓慢而有规律地敲(钟); (尤指)敲(丧钟). **2** [Ipr] **~ (for sb/sth)** (of a bell) sound in this way (指钟)缓慢而有规律地鸣响.

▷ **toll** *n* [sing] sound of a tolling bell 缓慢而有规律的钟声.

Tom /tɒm; tam/ *n* (idm 习语) **(any/every) ˌTom, Dick and ˈHarry** (*usu derog* 通常作贬义) anybody at all; people at random 任何人; (泛指的)人: *We don't want any (old) Tom, Dick and Harry using the club bar.* 我们不能让随便什么人都来用俱乐部的酒吧.

tom /tɒm; tam/ *n* = TOM-CAT.

toma·hawk /ˈtɒməhɔːk; ˈtaməˌhɔk/ *n* light axe used as a tool or weapon by N American Indians 印第安战斧(北美印第安人用作工具或武器的).

to·mato /təˈmɑːtəʊ; *US* təˈmeɪtəʊ; təˈmeto/ *n* (*pl* **~es**) (**a**) soft juicy red or yellow fruit eaten raw or cooked as a vegetable 番茄; 西红柿: [attrib 作定语] *tomato juice, sauce, soup, ketchup* 番茄汁、沙司、汤、酱. ⇨illus at SALAD 见SALAD 插图. (**b**) plant on which this fruit grows 番茄(植物).

tomb /tuːm; tum/ *n* hole dug in the ground, etc for a dead body, esp one with a stone monument over it 坟, 墓(尤指有石碑的).

□ ˈ**tombstone** *n* memorial stone set up over a tomb 墓碑.

tom·bola /tɒmˈbəʊlə; ˈtambolə/ *n* [C, U] (*Brit*) type of lottery with prizes for the holders of tickets picked out of a revolving drum 一种摇彩抽奖.

tom·boy /ˈtɒmbɔɪ; ˈtamˌbɔɪ/ *n* girl who enjoys rough noisy games 爱打打闹闹的女孩儿. ▷ **tom·boy·ish** *adj.*

tom-cat /ˈtɒm kæt; ˈtamˌkæt/ (also **tom**) *n* male cat 郎猫(雄猫).

tome /təʊm; tom/ *n* large heavy book, esp a scholarly or serious one 大部头书, 大本书(尤指学术性的或理论性的).

tom·fool /ˌtɒmˈfuːl; ˈtamˈful/ *adj* very foolish; stupid 极傻的; 愚蠢的: *a tomfool thing to do* 干蠢事.

▷ **tom·fool·ery** /-ərɪ; -ərɪ/ *n* [U, C usu *pl* 作不可数名词或可数名词, 后者通常作复数] foolish behaviour or act 愚蠢的举动.

tommy-gun /ˈtɒmɪ gʌn; ˈtamɪ ˌgʌn/ *n* type of sub-machine-gun (汤姆式)冲锋枪.

tommy-rot /ˌtɒmɪ ˈrɒt; ˈtamɪˌrat/ *n* [U] (*infml* 口) absurd statement; nonsense 荒唐的话; 胡扯; 废话: *Don't talk such tommy-rot!* 别胡说八道!

to·mor·row /təˈmɒrəʊ; təˈmɔro/ *n* [U] **1** the day after today 明天: *Today is Tuesday so tomorrow is Wednesday.* 今天是星期二, 那么明天就是星期三. ○ *Tomorrow is going to be fine according to the forecast.* 据天气预报报道, 明天晴. ○ *The announcement will appear in tomorrow's newspapers.* 该通告将于明日见报. ○ [attrib 作定语] *tomorrow morning/afternoon/evening/night* 明天上午[下午/晚上/夜里]. **2** the near future 不久的将来: *Who knows what changes tomorrow may bring?* 谁知道将来有什么变化? ○ *tomorrow's world* 明日世界. **3** (idm 习语) **the day after tomorrow** ⇨ DAY.

▷ **to·mor·row** *adv* on the day after today 在明天: *She's getting married tomorrow.* 她明天结婚. ○ *See you this time tomorrow, then.* 那么, 我们明天此时见面.

tom·tit /ˈtɒmtɪt; ˈtamˌtɪt/ *n* type of tit(1), esp the blue tit 山雀(尤指蓝山雀).

tom-tom /ˈtɒm tɒm; ˈtamˌtam/ *n* **1** long narrow African or Asian drum played with the hands (非洲或亚洲的)长手鼓. **2** similar drum used in jazz bands, etc (爵士乐队等的)长鼓.

ton /tʌn; tʌn/ *n* **1** [C] measure of weight, in Britain 2 240 lb (*long ton*) and in the US 2 000 lb (*short ton*) 吨(英国为2 240磅, 即长吨; 美国为2 000磅, 即短吨). ⇨App 5 见附录5. Cf 参看 TONNE. **2** [C] measure of capacity for various materials, esp 40 cubic feet of timber 容积吨(尤指容纳40立方英尺木材的). **3** [C] (*nautical* 海) (**a**) measure of the size of a ship (1 ton = 100 cubic feet) (船的)吨位(1吨=100立方英尺). (**b**) measure of the amount of cargo a ship can carry (1 ton = 40 cubic feet) (船的)装载吨, 载货吨(1吨=40立方英尺). **4 tons** [pl] **~s (of sth)** (*infml* 口) a lot 大量; 很多: *They've got tons of money.* 他们有很多钱. ○ *I've still got tons (of work) to do.* 我还有许多事要做. **5** (idm 习语) **do a/the ˈton** (*sl* 俚) drive at a speed of 100 mph or more 以每小时至少100英里的速度开车: *got caught doing a ton on the motorway* 在高速公路上以100英里时速开车而被抓住. **(come down on sb) like a ton of ˈbricks** (*infml* 口) (criticize or punish sb) with great force or violence 严厉地(斥责或惩罚某人). **weigh a ton** ⇨ WEIGH.

□ **ton-ˈup** *adj* [attrib 作定语] (*dated sl* 旧, 俚) (of a driver) driving at a speed of 100 mph or more (指驾车者)以每小时至少100英里的速度开车的: *one of the ton-up boys* 以每小时100英里速度开车的一个男孩儿.

tonal /ˈtəʊnl; ˈtonḷ/ *adj* **1** of (a) tone or tones 声音的; 音调的. **2** (*music* 音) of tonality 调性的.

▷ **ton·al·ity** /təʊˈnælətɪ; toˈnælətɪ/ *n* [U, C] (*music* 音) (use of a particular) key, esp as the basis of a melody or composition 调性, 调(的运用)(尤指作为某旋律或乐曲的基调).

tone[1] /təʊn; ton/ *n* **1** [C] sound, esp with reference to its pitch, quality, strength, etc 声音; 音调; 音质: *the ringing tones of an orator's voice* 演说者宏亮的声音 ○ *the alarm bell's harsh tone* 刺耳的警钟的声音. **2** [C] manner of expression in speaking 语气; 口气; 腔调: *speak in an angry, impatient, entreating, etc tone* 以愤怒、不耐烦、恳求等的语气说话 ○ *a tone of command, reproach, regret, etc* 命令、责备、抱歉等的口气 ○ *Don't speak to me in that tone (of voice)*, ie in that unpleasant, insolent, critical, etc way. 别用那种腔调跟我说话. **3** [C, U] quality or character of sound produced by a musical instrument (乐器的)音质, 音色: *a violin with (an) excellent tone* 音色优美的小提琴. **4** [sing] general spirit or character of sth 某事物的格调或特性: *Overall, the tone of the book is satirical/the book is satirical in tone.* 总的说来, 这本书是讽刺性的. ○ *set the tone for/of the meeting with a conciliatory speech* 以表示和解的讲话为会议定调子 ○ *lower/raise the tone of a conversation, an occasion, an organization*, ie make it worse/better 使谈话不投机[投机]、冲淡[增加]一场合的气氛、减弱[增强]一组织的声势. **5** [C] (*music* 音) any one of the five larger intervals between one note and the next that (together with two semitones) make up an octave 全音. **6** [C] (**a**) tint or shade (of a colour); degree (of light) 色度; 光度: *a carpet in tones of brown and orange* 有棕色和橙色交织的一块地毯. (**b**) general effect of colour, light and shade 色调、明暗、影调的总体效果: *a picture in warm, dull, bright, etc tones* 暖色调的、暗淡的、明亮的...画儿 ○ *an artist's fine painting of skin tones* 画家将肤色明暗处理得很好的画. **7** [U] proper firmness of the body 身体强壮: *good muscular tone* 肌肉结实. **8** [C] audible signal on a telephone line (打电话时听到的)信号: *the dialling/ringing tone* 表示可以拨号的嗡声[对方电话的振铃声] ○ *That tone means that the number is engaged.* 那种声音表示该号电话占线. ○ *Please speak after the tone*, eg as an instruction on an answering machine. 听到信号后请讲话(如应答机的提示). **9** [C] (*linguistics* 语言) pitch aspect of a syllable; rise or fall of pitch in speaking 音调; 声调: *In 'Are you ill?' there is*

usually a rising tone on 'ill' , while in 'He's ill' there is usually a falling tone on 'ill'. 在 'Are you ill?' 一句中, ill 一词通常用升调, 在 'He's ill' 一句中, ill 一词通常用降调.
▷ **-toned** (forming compound *adjs* 用以构成复合形容词) having the specified type of tone[1](3) 有某种音质的: *silver-toned trumpets* 声音清脆的小号.
tone·less *adj* lacking colour, spirit, expression, etc; dull 无色调的; 无生气的; 无表情的; 沉闷的; 呆板的: *answer in a toneless voice* 以平淡的声调回答. **tone·lessly** *adv*.
□ ˌ**tone-ˈdeaf** *adj* unable to distinguish accurately between different musical notes 不能辨别不同音高的.
ˈ**tone language** (*linguistics* 语言) language in which the meaning of a word depends on the pitch at which it is uttered (eg Chinese) 声调语言(如汉语).
ˈ**tone-poem** *n* (*music* 音) orchestral composition written to illustrate a poetic idea, legend, place, etc musically 交响诗.

tone[2] /təʊn; ton/ *v* **1** [Tn] give a particular tone of sound or colour to (sth) 使(某物)具有某种声调或色调; 给(某物)定调子或色调. **2** (phr v) **tone (sth) down** (cause sth to) become less intense (使某事)变得缓和: *Their enthusiasm has toned down since they discovered the cost.* 他们知道了价钱之后心气儿就低了. ○ *You'd better tone down the more offensive remarks in your article.* 你最好把你文章里的攻击性词句写得含蓄些. **tone in (with sth)** harmonize in colour (在颜色方面)调和, 相配合: *The new curtains tone in beautifully with the carpet.* 新帘幕与地毯的颜色非常协调. **tone (sth) up** (cause sth to) become brighter, intenser, or more vigorous (使某事物)强化, 加强, 有力: *Exercise tones up the muscles.* 运动能使肌肉结实.

tongs 夹子

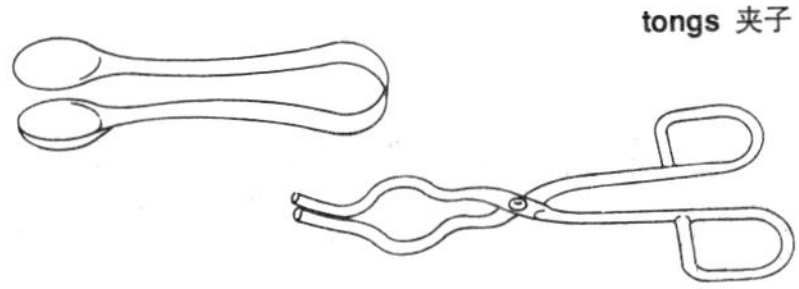

tongs /tɒŋz; tɔŋz/ *n* [pl] **1** instrument with two movable arms joined at one end, used for picking up and holding things 钳; 夹剪: *a pair of tongs* 一把夹剪 ○ *ˈsugar/ˈcoal/ˈice tongs* 糖[煤/冰块]夹子. **2** (idm 习语) **be/go at it/each other hammer and tongs** ⇨ HAMMER[1].

tongue /tʌŋ; tʌŋ/ *n* **1** [C] movable organ in the mouth, used in tasting, licking, swallowing and (in man) speaking 舌; 舌头. ⇨illus at THROAT 见 THROAT 插图. ⇨ Usage at BODY 用法见 BODY. **2** [C, U] tongue of an ox, etc as food 口条: *ham and tongue sandwiches* 火腿加口条三明治. **3** [C] (*fml or rhet* 文或修辞) language 语言: *He speaks English, but his native tongue is German.* 他会说英语, 但他的母语是德语. Cf 参看 MOTHER TONGUE (MOTHER). **4** [C] (**a**) projecting strap or flap 突出的带或盖; 舌状物: *the tongue of a shoe*, ie the strip of leather under the laces 鞋舌 ○ *the tongue* (ie clapper) *of a bell* 铃舌 ○ *a narrow tongue of land* (ie promontory) *jutting out into the sea* 突入海中的尖形陆地(岬角). (**b**) tapering jet of flame 火苗; 火舌: *tongues of flame lapping the edges of the bonfire* 舔着火堆边缘的火舌. **5** (idm 习语) **bite one's tongue** ⇨ BITE[1]. **an evil tongue** ⇨ EVIL. **find/lose one's voice/tongue** ⇨ FIND[1]. **get one's ˈtongue round/around sth** manage to pronounce (a difficult word or name) correctly 尽力将(难读的单词或名称)读正确. **give sb/get the edge of one's/sb's tongue** ⇨ EDGE[1]. **have a loose tongue** ⇨ LOOSE[1]. **hold one's peace/tongue** ⇨ PEACE. **loosen sb's tongue** ⇨ LOOSEN. **on the tip of one's tongue** ⇨ TIP[1]. **put/stick one's ˈtongue out** show one's tongue outside one's lips, eg to a doctor or as a rude gesture 伸舌头, 吐舌头(如让医生看或作为粗俗的动作): *Don't you dare stick your tongue out at me!* 你竟敢冲我吐舌头! **a silver tongue** ⇨ SILVER. **tongues wag** (*infml* 口) there is gossip or rumour 说闲话; 造谣: *Their scandalous affair has really set tongues wagging.* 他们的风流事可招来了不少闲话. **a slip of the pen/tongue** ⇨ SLIP[1]. **with (one's) tongue in (one's) ˈcheek** not intending to be taken seriously; with irony or humour 并非让人信以为真; 带有反话或幽默意味: *Don't be fooled by all his complimentary remarks — they were all said with tongue in cheek.* 别让他的恭维话给糊弄住 —— 那些话可当不得真. **with one's ˈtongue hanging out** (**a**) extremely thirsty 非常渴. (**b**) eagerly expecting sth 渴望某事物.
▷ **-tongued** (forming compound *adjs* 用以构成复合形容词) having the specified manner of speaking 有某种说话方式的: *sharp-tongued* 言语尖苛的.
□ ˌ**tongue-in-ˈcheek** *adj* not intended seriously; ironical or joking 并非当真的; 有反话意味的; 开玩笑的: *tongue-in-cheek remarks* 说说而已的话.
ˈ**tongue-lashing** *n* severe rebuke or scolding 严厉的指责或叱责.
ˈ**tongue-tied** *adj* silent because of shyness or embarrassment (因羞怯或尴尬)张口结舌的.
ˈ**tongue-twister** *n* word or phrase that is difficult to pronounce correctly or quickly, eg *She sells sea shells on the sea-shore* 绕口令.

tonic /ˈtɒnɪk; ˈtɑnɪk/ *n* **1** [C, U] medicine that gives strength or energy, taken after illness or when tired 补药; 滋补品. **2** [C usu *sing* 通常作单数] (*fig* 比喻) anything that makes people feel healthier or happier 使人感到健康或快乐的事物: *Praise can be a fine tonic.* 赞美的话有时真让人感到美滋滋的. ○ *The good news acted as a tonic on us all.* 那个好消息使我们大家欢欣鼓舞. ○ [attrib 作定语] *the tonic effects of sea air* 海上空气的保健作用. **3** [C, U] = TONIC WATER. **4** [C] (*music* 音) keynote 主音.
□ ˈ**tonic water** (also **tonic**) mineral water flavoured with quinine 汤尼水(以奎宁调味的含矿物质的饮料): *a bottle of tonic water* 一瓶汤尼汽水 ○ *a gin and tonic* 杜松子酒加汤尼水 ○ *Two tonic waters/tonics, please.* 请来两份汤尼汽水.

to·night /təˈnaɪt; təˈnaɪt/ *n* [U] (**a**) the present evening or night (此时的)晚间, 夜里: *Here are tonight's football results.* 现在报告晚间足球赛的结果. (**b**) the evening or night of today 今晚; 今夜: *Tonight will be cloudy.* 今天夜间多云.
▷ **to·night** *adv* on the present evening or night or that of today 在今晚; 在今夜: *See you at nine o'clock tonight, then.* 那么, 咱们晚上九点见吧. ○ *Are you doing anything tonight?* 你今天晚上有事吗?

ton·nage /ˈtʌnɪdʒ; ˈtʌnɪdʒ/ *n* [U, C] **1** (*nautical* 海) (**a**) size of a ship, expressed in tons (TON 1) (船的)吨位. (**b**) amount of cargo a ship can carry, expressed in tons (TON 3b) (船的货运的)吨位. (**c**) size of a country's merchant fleet, expressed in tons (TON 3a) (一国商船船队的)吨位. **2** (*commerce* 商) charge per ton for carrying cargo or freight 每吨货物的运费.

tonne /tʌn; tʌn/ *n* metric ton, 1000 kilograms 吨, 公吨 (1000 公斤). ⇨App 5 见附录 5. Cf 参看 TON 1.

ton·sil /ˈtɒnsl; ˈtɑnsl/ *n* either of two small organs at the sides of the throat near the root of the tongue 扁桃体: *have one's tonsils out*, ie have them removed by a surgeon 切除扁桃体. ⇨illus at THROAT 见 THROAT 插图.
▷ **ton·sil·litis** /ˌtɒnsɪˈlaɪtɪs; ˌtɑnslˈaɪtɪs/ *n* [U] inflammation of the tonsils 扁桃体炎.

ton·sure /ˈtɒnʃə(r); ˈtɑnʃɚ/ *n* **1** [U] shaving the top or all of the head of a person about to become a priest or monk (做僧侣时的)削发. **2** [C] part of the head shaved in this way (僧侣的)头顶剃光部位. ▷ **ton·sured** *adj*.

too /tuː; tu/ *adv* **1** (usu placed at the end; in speech, with stress on *too* and on the word it modifies 通常置于句末; 说话时, too 及其修饰的词重读) in addition; also 也; 又; 还: *ˈI've been to Paris ˈtoo*, ie in addition to other people. 我也去过巴黎(除别人外). ○ *I've been to ˈParis, ˈtoo*, ie in addition to other places. 我还去过巴黎(除其他地方外). ○ *He plays the guitar and ˈsings ˈtoo.* 他会弹吉他, 也会唱歌. ⇨Usage at ALSO 用法见 ALSO. **2** (used before *adjs* and *advs* 用于形容词和副词之前) to a higher degree than is allowed, desirable or possible 过于; 过度; 太: *drive too fast*, ie faster than the permitted speed limit or than is sensible 开车过快(超过限定速度或快得不当) ○ *These shoes are much too small for me.* 我穿这双鞋太小. ○ *It's too cold to go in the sea yet.* 天太冷还不能下海. ○ *This is too difficult a text for them/This text is too difficult for them.* 这篇课文对他们来说太难了. ○ *We can't ski because there's too little snow.* 因为雪下得太少,

T

我们不能滑雪. ○ *It's too long a journey to make in one day.* 路程太远, 一天之内到不了. ○ (*fml* 文) *Her work has been too much ignored for too long.* 她的工作长期以来太不受重视了. **3** (indicating surprise and usu displeasure 表示惊讶, 通常为不愉快的): *I had flu last week. And I was on holiday ˈtoo!* 我上星期得了流感. 我当时还正度假呢! ○ *I've lost an ear-ring. It was an expensive one ˈtoo.* 我丢了一只耳环. 还是个挺贵的. **4** very 很; 非常: *I'm not too sure if this is right.* 这是否正确, 我没有把握. **5** (idm 习语) **be too much for sb** (**a**) (require one to) be superior in skill, strength, etc to sb else (要求自己)在技巧、力量等方面超过他人; 非某人力所能及: *The Cambridge team were too much for the Oxford team in the quiz.* 在智力竞赛中, 剑桥队远胜牛津队. ○ *A cycling holiday would be too much for an unfit person like me.* 像我这种身体, 骑自行车度假力不从心. (**b**) be more than can be tolerated 忍无可忍: *All that giggling and whispering was too much for me — I had to leave the room.* 我受不了那些咯咯的笑声和交头接耳的样子——只好离开了那间屋子.

took *pt* of TAKE[1].

tool /tu:l; tul/ *n* **1** instrument held in the hand and used for working on sth 工具: *A screwdriver and a hammer are the only tools you need.* 你需用的工具只是改锥和锤子. ○ *garden tools*, eg spade, rake, etc 园艺工具(如锹、耙等). **2** anything used to do or achieve sth 用具; 器具: *The computer is now an indispensable tool in many businesses.* 目前计算机是很多公司不可或缺的用具. ⇨ Usage at MACHINE 用法见 MACHINE. **3** person used or exploited by another, esp for selfish or dishonest purposes 受人利用的人(尤指被利用为他人谋私利或做坏事的人): *The prime minister was a mere tool in the hands of the country's president.* 那个总理只不过是该国总统的马前卒. **4** (⚠ *sl* 讳, 俚) penis 鸡巴; 阴茎. **5** (idm 习语) **down tools** ⇨ DOWN[3].

▷ **tool** *v* **1** [Tn esp passive 尤用于被动语态] make a design on (the cover or binding of a book) by pressing with a heated tool(1) 用压印器在(书的封面或封底)上压印图案: *hand-tooled leather* 用手工压印的皮封面 ○ *The spine is tooled in gold.* 那书脊是烫金的. **2** (phr v) **tool along** (*infml* 口) drive in a casual and relaxed way 悠闲自在地开车. **tool sth up** equip (a factory) with the necessary machine tools 用所需的机械设备装备(工厂).

toot /tu:t; tut/ *n* [C] short sound from a horn, whistle, etc (号角、笛等发出的)短鸣, 嘟嘟声.

▷ **toot** *v* [I, Tn] (cause sth to) make a toot (使某物)发嘟嘟声: *The driver tooted his horn as he approached the bend.* 开车的人在快要转弯时按响了喇叭.

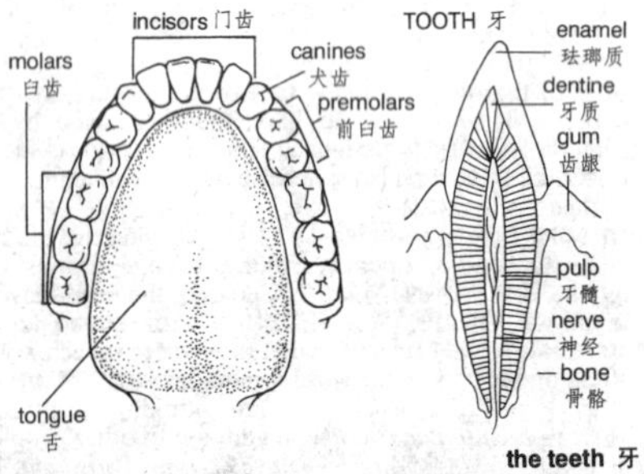

the teeth 牙

tooth /tu:θ; tuθ/ *n* (*pl* **teeth** /ti:θ; tiθ/) **1** [C] each of the hard white bony structures rooted in the gums, used for biting and chewing 牙; 齿: *The baby's first front teeth are just coming through.* 那孩子的门牙刚长出来. ○ *have a tooth out*, ie extracted by a dentist 拔一颗牙 ○ *She still has all her own teeth*, ie no false ones. 她满口牙还很好. **2** [C] tooth-like part, eg on a comb, saw or gear 齿状部分(如梳子、锯或齿轮的). **3 teeth** [pl] (*infml* 口) effective force 有效的力量: *The law must be given more teeth if crime is to be properly controlled.* 要想有效控制住犯罪活动, 就得加强法制的威力. **4** (idm 习语) **armed to the teeth** ⇨ ARM[3]. **bare its teeth** ⇨ BARE[2]. **by the skin of one's teeth** ⇨ SKIN. **cast, fling, throw, etc sth in sb's ˈteeth** reproach sb with sth 以某事责备某人. **cut a ˈtooth** have a tooth that is just pushing out through the gum 长出牙齿. **cut one's ˈteeth on sth** gain experience from sth 从某事中获得经验. **draw sb's/sth's teeth/fangs** ⇨ DRAW[2]. **fight, etc tooth and ˈnail** fight, etc very fiercely or persistently 猛烈或顽强地斗争等. **get/take the bit between one's/the teeth** ⇨ BIT[2]. **get one's teeth into sth** deal with or concentrate on sth 处理某事; 专心于某事: *Now you know what the job involves here's something to get your teeth into.* 你既然对这项工作已有所了解, 有些事就由你去处理吧. **grit one's teeth** ⇨ GRIT *v*. **have a sweet tooth** ⇨ SWEET[1]. **in the teeth of sth** (**a**) in spite of sth; in opposition to sth 不顾某事; 反对某事: *The new policy was adopted in the teeth of fierce criticism.* 那项新政策尽管受到强烈抨击却硬是采用了. (**b**) directly against (the wind, etc) 顶着, 迎着(风等). **a kick in the teeth** ⇨ KICK[2]. **lie in/through one's teeth/throat** ⇨ LIE[1]. **long in the tooth** ⇨ LONG[1]. **set sb's ˈteeth on edge** (esp of a sharp sound or taste) annoy or displease sb (尤指刺耳的声音或强烈的味道)恼人的, 使人难受的. **show one's teeth** ⇨ SHOW[2].

▷ **toothed** /tu:θt; tuθt/ *adj* [attrib 作定语] **1** having teeth 有齿的. **2** (in compounds 用以构成复合词) having teeth of the specified type 有某种齿的: *a saw-toothed wheel* 锯齿的.

tooth·less *adj* without teeth 无牙的; 无齿的.

toothy (**-ier**, **-iest**) *adj* having many, large or noticeable teeth 多齿的; 有巨齿的; 露齿的: *a toothy grin* 露齿一笑. **tooth·ily** *adv*.

□ **ˈtoothache** *n* [C, U] pain in a tooth or teeth 牙痛: *I've got (a/the) toothache.* 我牙疼.

ˈtoothbrush *n* brush for cleaning the teeth 牙刷. ⇨ illus at BRUSH 见 BRUSH 插图.

ˈtoothpaste *n* [U] paste for cleaning the teeth 牙膏.

ˈtooth-powder *n* [U, C] powder for cleaning the teeth 牙粉.

ˈtoothpick *n* short pointed piece of wood, etc for removing bits of food from between the teeth 牙签.

tooth·some /ˈtu:θsəm; ˈtuθsəm/ *adj* (*fml* 文) (of food) tasting pleasant (指食物)美味的, 可口的.

tootle /ˈtu:tl; ˈtutl/ *v* **1** [I, Ipr] **~ (on sth)** toot gently or repeatedly 发轻柔或连续的嘟嘟声. **2** [Ipr, Ip] (*infml* 口) go in a casual or leisurely way 悠闲自得地走: *tootling into town* 溜溜达达地进城去 ○ *tootle around on one's bike* 骑自行车闲逛.

top[1] /tɒp; tɑp/ *n* **1** [C] highest part or point 顶; 顶部; 上部; 上端: *at the top of the hill* 在山顶 ○ *the surrounding hilltops* 四周的山顶 ○ *five lines from the top of the page* 该页上端五行 ○ *My office is at the top of the building.* 我的办公室在楼的顶层. **2** [C] upper surface 上面; 上边: *polish the top of the table/the ˈtable-top* 把桌面磨光 ○ *put the luggage on top of the car*, eg on a roof-rack 把行李放在汽车顶上(如顶部行李架上). **3** [sing] **~ (of sth)** highest or most important rank or position 最高的或最重要的级别或位置: *come to/rise to/reach the top*, ie achieve fame, success, etc 登峰造极(成名、成功等) ○ *Liverpool finished the season (at the) top of the football league.* 利物浦队在该赛季足球联赛中独占鳌头. ○ *He's at the top of his profession.* 他在同行中首屈一指. ○ *We've got a lot of things to do, but packing is top of the list.* 我们有许多事情要做, 但最重要的是先收拾行李. ○ *the top of the table*, ie the upper end, where eg the most distinguished people sit 上座(如最尊的坐位). **4** [C] (**a**) thing forming or covering the upper part of sth 构成或罩在上部之物: *the top of the milk*, ie the layer of cream floating on it 浮在牛奶上的奶皮儿 ○ *Put the top back on that felt-tip pen or it will dry out.* 给毡头笔套上笔帽, 不然就干了. ○ *She took off the top of her bikini.* 她脱去了比基尼泳装的上部. (**b**) lid or stopper 盖子; 塞子: *Where's the top of this paint can?* 这油漆罐的盖儿在哪儿呢? ○ *a bottle with a screw-top* 带螺口盖儿的瓶子. (**c**) (esp woman's) garment covering the upper part of the body (尤指女用的)上衣: *I need a top to go with these slacks.* 我需要一件上衣来配这条宽松裤. **5** [U] = TOP GEAR: *You shouldn't be in top.* 你不应该使用高速挡. **6** [C usu *pl* 通常作复数] leaves of a plant grown chiefly for its root (根菜作物的)叶子: ˈ*turnip tops* 芜菁的叶子. **7** (idm 习语) **at the top of the ˈtree** in the highest position or rank in a profession, career, etc 居于行业、事业等的最高地位或级别. **at the top of one's ˈvoice** as loudly as one can 以最大的嗓音: *cheering, shouting, screaming, etc at the top(s) of their voices* 可着嗓子欢呼、喊叫、尖叫等. **blow one's top** ⇨ BLOW[1]. **from ˌtop to ˈbottom** completely 从上到下; 完全地; 全部地: *We searched the house from top to bottom.* 我们把那所房子彻底搜寻了一遍. **from ˌtop to ˈtoe** from head to foot 从头到脚. **in the first/top flight** ⇨ FLIGHT[1]. **off the ˌtop of one's ˈhead** (*infml* 口) (of sth said) without previous thought or preparation (指说出的话)未经考虑或准备的: *I can't tell you the answer off the top of my head.* 我不经考虑无法告诉你答案. **on ˈtop** (**a**) above 在上边: *The green book is at the bottom of the pile and the red one is on top.* 绿皮的书在那一摞的底下, 红皮的在上边. (**b**) in a superior position; in control 处于优势; 在控制之中: *Lendl was on top throughout the match.* 伦德尔在比赛中始终占优势. **on top of sth/sb** (**a**) over or above sth/sb 在某物[某人]的上方或上边: *Put this record on top of the others.* 把这张唱片放在其他唱片上面. ○ *Many people were crushed when the building collapsed on top of them.* 那座大楼倒塌时把下面的很多人都砸死了. (**b**) in addition to sth 加在某事物上: *He gets commission on top of his salary.* 他除了薪水之外还得到佣金. ○ *On top of borrowing £50, he asked me to lend him my car.* 他向我借了50英镑, 此外还向我借汽车. (**c**) (*infml* 口) very close to sth 紧接着某事; 紧靠着某物: *There is no privacy when houses are built on top of each other like that.* 像那样房子挨着房子, 也就无所谓私生活了. **(be/feel) on ˌtop of the ˈworld** very happy or proud, esp because of success or good fortune 非常愉快或自豪(尤指因获成功或好运). **ˌover the ˈtop** (*infml* 口 *esp Brit*) to an exaggerated or excessive degree 过火; 过头: *The film's violent ending is completely over the top.* 影片结尾的暴力场面太过分了. ○ *an actor who tends to go over the top*, ie to overact 表演得过火的演员. **(the) top ˈbrass** (*sl* 俚) senior officers or officials 高级军官或官员: *Plenty of top brass attended the ceremony.* 有很多大官儿出席了典礼. **(be) top ˈdog** (*sl* 俚) person, group, country, etc having superiority or advantages over others 有优势的人、团体、国家等. **the top ˈstorey** (*joc* 谑) the brain (of a person) (人的)头脑: *He's a bit weak in the top storey*, ie not very intelligent. 他的脑筋差点事儿.

▷ **top** *adj* [usu attrib 通常作定语] highest in position, rank or degree (位置、地位、级别或程度)最高的: *a room on the top floor* 位于顶层的房间 ○ *one of Britain's top scientists* 英国最杰出的科学家之一 ○ *top jobs, people* 要职、要人 ○ *travelling at top* (ie maximum) *speed* 以最快的速度行进.

top·less *adj* (**a**) (of a woman) having the breasts and upper part of the body bare (指女子)上身裸露的, 无上装的: *a topless waitress* 无上装女服务员. (**b**) (of a woman's garment) exposing the breasts (指女装)露乳房的: *a topless dress* 露乳房的连衣裙. — *adv* with the breasts bare 露着乳房: *sunbathe topless* 露着乳房作日光浴.

□ **ˈtop-boot** *n* boot reaching to just below the knee 高筒靴.

ˈtopcoat *n* **1** last of several coats of paint applied to a surface (几道涂料的)最外涂层. Cf 参看 UNDERCOAT 1. **2** (*dated* 旧) = OVERCOAT.

ˌtop ˈdrawer the highest social position 社会的最高地位: *She's out of the top drawer/She's very top drawer.* 她出身上层社会[她社会地位极高].

ˌtop-ˈdress *v* [Tn] apply manure, etc to the surface of (soil or land) without ploughing or digging it in 在(土地)的表层施肥等. **ˌtop-ˈdressing** *n* [C, U] (substance used for) this process (在土地表层)施肥的过程或肥料.

ˌtop-ˈflight *adj* in the highest rank of achievement 成就的最高级别的; 造诣最高的: ˌ*top-flight comˈputer scientists* 最优秀的计算机科学家.

ˌtop ˈgear highest gear (usu fourth), allowing the fastest speeds 最高挡(通常为第四挡): *If you try to start off in top gear you'll stall.* 要是刚一发动就用最高挡, 那就会熄火.

ˌtop ˈhat (also **topper**) man's tall black or grey hat, worn with formal dress (男用黑色或灰色的)高顶礼帽. ⇨ illus at HAT 见HAT插图.

ˌtop-ˈheavy *adj* too heavy at the top and therefore in danger of falling over 上部过重的; 头重脚轻的.

ˈtopknot *n* knot or tuft of hair, usu ornamented with ribbon, feathers, etc, worn or grown on top of the head, esp by women 顶髻, 顶部发束(尤指女子的).

ˈtopmost /-məʊst; -ˌmost/ *adj* [attrib 作定语] highest 最高的: *on the topmost shelf* 在最高的架子上.

ˌtop-ˈnotch *adj* (*infml* 口) excellent; first-rate 最好的; 一流的: *a* ˌ*top-notch* ˈ*lawyer* 最棒的律师.

ˌtop-ˈranking *adj* [attrib 作定语] of the highest rank or importance; leading 最高级的; 最重要的; 主要的.

ˌtop ˈsecret of the highest category of secrecy 最高机密的; 绝密的: *a file of top secret information* 一份绝密资料.

ˈtopside *n* [U] **1** (*Brit*) joint of beef cut from the upper part of the leg (割下的)牛大腿肉. **2** side of a ship above the water-line (船的)水上舷侧.

ˈtopsoil *n* [U] (layer of) soil near the surface 表土; 表土层. Cf 参看 SUBSOIL.

ˌtop ˈten, ˌtop ˈtwenty ten/twenty best-selling pop records 流行乐曲十[二十]大畅销唱片: *She's a popular singer, but her records never make* (ie get into) *the top ten.* 她是流行曲歌手, 但她的唱片从未打入十大畅销唱片之中.

top[2] /tɒp; tɑp/ *v* (**-pp-**) **1** [Tn, Tn·pr esp passive 尤用于被动语态] provide or be a top for (sth) 为(某物)加顶; 作为(某物)之顶端: *a church topped by/with a steeple* 有尖塔顶的教堂 ○ *ice-cream topped with chocolate sauce* 浇上巧克力汁的冰激凌. **2** [Tn] reach the top of (sth) 达到(某物)的顶端: *When we finally topped the hill we had a fine view.* 我们爬到山顶时, 看到了优美的景色. **3** [Tn] (**a**) be higher than (sth); surpass 比(某事物)高; 超越: *Exports have topped the £80 million mark.* 出口额已超过8 000万英镑. (**b**) come first in (a poll, etc) 获(投票、评选等)第一名: *a chart-topping record* 每周最畅销流行音乐唱片名列榜首的唱片. **4** [Tn] remove the top of (a plant, fruit, etc) 除去(植物、水果等的)顶端: *top and tail* (ie remove the ends from) *gooseberries* 掐掉醋栗的尖儿和把儿. **5** [Tn] (esp in golf) mishit (a ball) by striking it above the centre (尤指高尔夫球)误击(球)的上部. **6** [Tn] (*sl* 俚) execute (sb) by hanging 将(某人)处以绞刑. **7** (idm 习语) **head/top the bill** ⇨ BILL[1]. **8** (phr v) **top (sth) out** complete (a building) by adding the highest stone, etc (用石块等)给(建筑物)封顶. **top (sth) up** fill up (a partly empty container) 将(未满的容器)装满: *top up with petrol/oil* 加满汽油[机油] ○ *top up a car battery*, ie by adding distilled water 往汽车蓄电池里加满蒸馏水 ○ (*infml* 口) *Let me top you up*, ie refill your glass. 我给你满上这杯.

▷ **top·ping** *n* [C, U] cream, etc on top of a cake, pudding, etc (蛋糕、布丁等上面的)奶油等: *a range of fruit-flavoured toppings* 蛋糕上的各种果味配料.

□ **ˈtop-up** *n* refill 再装满: *Who's ready for a top-up* (ie for another drink)? 谁要添酒?

top[3] /tɒp; tɑp/ *n* **1** toy that spins on a point when it is set in motion by hand or by a string, etc 陀螺. **2** (idm 习语) **sleep like a log/top** ⇨ SLEEP[2].

to·paz /ˈtəʊpæz; ˈtopæz/ *n* (**a**) [U] transparent yellow mineral 黄玉(矿物). (**b**) [C] semi-precious gem cut from this 黄玉; 黄宝石.

topi /ˈtəʊpɪ; *US* təʊˈpiː; toˈpi/ *n* sun-helmet, esp one worn in tropical countries 遮阳帽(尤指在热带国家戴的).

to·pi·ary /ˈtəʊpɪərɪ; *US* -ɪerɪ; ˈtopɪˌɛrɪ/ *n* [U] art of clipping shrubs, etc into ornamental shapes such as birds and animals 树木整形术(将灌木等修剪成装饰形状, 如鸟、兽等者): [attrib 作定语] *topiary work* 树木整形工作.

topic /ˈtɒpɪk; ˈtɑpɪk/ *n* subject of a discussion, talk, programme, written work, etc 论题; 话题; 题目: *a topic of conversation* 交谈的话题 ○ *Is drug abuse a suitable topic for a school debate?* 把滥用麻醉药品问题当作学校辩论的题目是否合适?

▷ **top·ical** /-kl; -kl/ *adj* of current interest or relevance 目前受到注意的; 与当前有关的: *a play full of topical allusions to well-known people* 处处影射名人目前言行的一出戏. **top·ic·al·ity** /ˌtɒpɪˈkælətɪ; ˌtɑpɪˈkælətɪ/ *n* [U]. **top·ic·ally** /-klɪ; -klɪ/ *adv*.

T

to·po·graphy /tə'pɒgrəfɪ; tə'pɑgrəfɪ/ *n* [U] (description of the) features of a place or district, esp the position of its rivers, mountains, roads, buildings, etc 地形; 地志; 地形学. ▷ **to·po·graph·ical** /ˌtɒpə'græfɪkl; ˌtɑpə'græfɪkl/ *adj*: *a topographical map* 地形图. **to·po·graph·ic·ally** /-klɪ; -klɪ/ *adv*.

top·per /'tɒpə(r); 'tɑpɚ/ *n* (*infml* 口) = TOP HAT (TOP[1]).

top·ping[1] /'tɒpɪŋ; 'tɑpɪŋ/ *n* ⇨ TOP[2].

top·ping[2] /'tɒpɪŋ; 'tɑpɪŋ/ *adj* (*dated Brit infml* 旧, 口) excellent 极好的.

topple /'tɒpl; 'tɑpl̩/ *v* **1** (**a**) [I, Ipr, Ip] **~ (over)** be unsteady and fall 不稳而倒下: *The pile of books toppled over onto the floor.* 那一摞书倒在地板上了. (**b**) [Tn, Tn·pr] cause (sth) to do this 使(某物)倒下: *The explosion toppled the old chimney.* 这次爆炸把那个旧烟囱给炸倒了. **2** [Tn, Tn·pr] (*fig* 比喻) cause (sb/sth) to fall from power or authority; overthrow 将(某人[某事物])推翻; 打倒: *a crisis which threatens to topple the government (from power)* 使政府有垮台之虞的危机.

tops /tɒps; tɑps/ *n* [pl] (usu 通常作 **the tops**) (*infml* 口) the very best 最好的人或事物: *I like most cities, but for me New York is (the) tops.* 一般的城市我都很喜欢, 但最喜欢纽约.

topsy-turvy /ˌtɒpsɪ 'tɜ:vɪ; 'tɑpsɪ'tɝvɪ/ *adv*, *adj* **1** in or into a state of disordered confusion 乱七八糟(的): *This sudden development turned all our plans topsy-turvy.* 这一情况出现得很突然, 把我们的计划都打乱了. **2** upside-down 颠倒(的).

tor /tɔ:(r); tɔr/ *n* small hill or rocky peak, esp in parts of SW England 小山, 突岩(尤指英格兰西南部的).

torch /tɔ:tʃ; tɔrtʃ/ *n* **1** (*US* '**flash·light**) small hand-held electric lamp powered by a battery 手电筒; 电棒. **2** (*US*) = BLOWLAMP (BLOW[1]). **3** piece of wood, esp one wrapped in cloth and soaked in oil, etc, which is lit and held in the hand to give light 火炬; 火把. **4** (idm 习语) **carry a torch for sb** ⇨ CARRY.
□ '**torchlight** *n* [U] light of a torch or torches 手电筒的或火炬的光: *put up the tent by torchlight* 用手电筒照着搭帐篷 ○ [attrib 作定语] *a torchlight procession*, ie one in which burning torches are carried 持火炬游行.

tore *pt* of TEAR[2].

tor·eador /'tɒrɪədɔ:(r); *US* 'tɔ:r-; 'tɔrɪəˌdɔr/ *n* (in Spain) bullfighter, esp one on horseback (西班牙)斗牛士(尤指骑马的).

tor·ment /'tɔ:ment; 'tɔrmɛnt/ *n* (**a**) [U, C usu *pl* 作不可数名词或可数名词, 后者通常作复数] severe physical or mental suffering (肉体或精神上的)折磨, 痛苦: *be in great torment* 备受折磨 ○ *suffer torment(s) from toothache* 牙疼得难受. (**b**) [C] thing or person that causes this 造成痛苦的事物或人: *His shyness made public speaking a torment to him.* 他很腼腆, 当众讲话简直是受罪. ○ *What a little torment that child is!* ie because it is noisy, demanding, etc. 这孩子真烦人!
▷ **tor·ment** /tɔ:'ment; tɔr'mɛnt/ *v* [Tn] **1** cause severe suffering to (sb) 使(某人)备受折磨或痛苦: *tormented by hunger, anxiety, mosquitoes* 饿得、愁得、蚊子咬得十分难受. **2** tease or annoy (sb) 戏弄或烦扰(某人): *Stop tormenting your sister.* 别再耍弄你姐姐了. ○ *tormenting their teacher with silly questions* 用愚蠢的问题烦扰老师. **tor·mentor** /tɔ:'mentə(r); tɔr'mɛntɚ/ *n*: *turn on* (ie fight back against) *one's tormentors* 反抗折磨自己的人.

torn *pp* of TEAR[2].

tor·nado /tɔ:'neɪdəʊ; tɔr'nedo/ *n* (*pl* **~es**) violent and destructive storm over a small area; whirlwind 龙卷; 旋风: *The town was hit by a tornado.* 那个城镇遭龙卷风袭击.

tor·pedo /tɔ:'pi:dəʊ; tɔr'pido/ *n* (*pl* **~es**) tube-shaped explosive underwater missile launched against ships by submarines, aircraft or surface ships 鱼雷.
▷ **tor·pedo** *v* (*pt*, *pp* **torpedoed**, *pres p* **torpedoing**) [Tn] **1** attack or sink (a ship) with a torpedo or torpedoes 用鱼雷袭击或击沉(船). **2** (*fig* 比喻) wreck or ruin (a policy, an event, an institution, etc) 破坏(政策、事情、制度等): *accused the union of torpedoing the negotiations* 谴责工会破坏谈判.
□ **tor'pedo-boat** *n* small fast warship armed with torpedoes 鱼雷快艇.

tor·pid /'tɔ:pɪd; 'tɔrpɪd/ *adj* (*fml* 文) dull and slow; inactive; sluggish 迟钝的; 不活动的; 行动缓慢的.
▷ **tor·pid·ity** /tɔ:'pɪdətɪ; tɔr'pɪdətɪ/ *n* [U] (*fml* 文) torpid condition 迟钝; 呆滞; 迟缓. **tor·pidly** *adv*.

tor·por /'tɔ:pə(r); 'tɔrpɚ/ *n* [U] (*fml* 文) torpid condition 迟钝; 呆滞; 迟缓: *a state of torpor induced by the tropical heat* 热带的炎热气候引起的懒散.

torque /tɔ:k; tɔrk/ *n* [U] twisting force causing rotation in machinery (使机器旋转的)扭转力.

tor·rent /'tɒrənt; *US* 'tɔ:r-; 'tɔrənt/ *n* **1** violently rushing stream of water, lava, etc (水、熔岩等的)急流, 湍流: *mountain torrents* 山洪 ○ *torrents of rain* 瓢泼大雨 ○ *rain falling in torrents* 大雨滂沱. **2** (*fig* 比喻) violent outburst 爆发; 迸发: *a torrent of abuse, insults, questions, etc* 滔滔不绝的谩骂、凌辱、问题等.
▷ **tor·ren·tial** /tə'renʃl; tə'rɛnʃəl/ *adj* like a torrent 似急流的: *torrential rain* 暴雨.

tor·rid /'tɒrɪd; *US* 'tɔ:r-; 'tɔrɪd/ *adj* **1** (of a climate or country) very hot and dry (指气候或国家)炎热而干燥的: *the 'torrid zone*, ie the part of the earth's surface between the tropics 热带. **2** passionate; erotic 热情的; 色情的; 引起性欲的: *torrid love-scenes* 撩人情欲的爱情场面.

tor·sion /'tɔ:ʃn; 'tɔrʃən/ *n* [U] **1** twisting, esp of one end of sth while the other end is held fixed 扭转(尤指一端固定而扭转另一端). **2** state of being twisted in a spiral 被旋转成的螺旋形.

torso /'tɔ:səʊ; 'tɔrso/ *n* (*pl* **~s**) **1** main part of the human body, not including the head, arms and legs; trunk (人体的)躯干. **2** statue of this part of the body only (人体的)躯干雕塑像.

tort /tɔ:t; tɔrt/ *n* (*law* 律) private or civil wrong (other than breach of contract) for which the wronged person may claim damages 侵权行为(受害者可要求获得损害赔偿).

tor·tilla /tɔ:'ti:jə; tɔr'tijə/ *n* round thin cake of maize flour, usu eaten hot with a filling of meat, etc, esp in Mexico 玉米粉圆饼(通常有肉馅, 热食, 尤指墨西哥的).

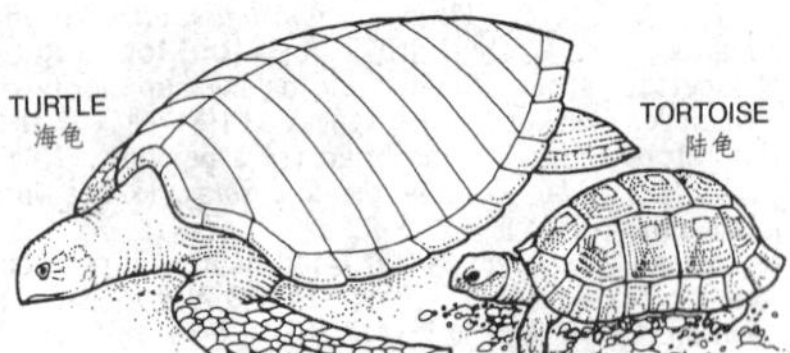

tor·toise /'tɔ:təs; 'tɔrtəs/ *n* slow-moving four-footed reptile with a hard shell 陆龟; 龟.
□ '**tortoiseshell** /'tɔ:təʃel; 'tɔrtəsˌʃɛl/ *n* **1** [U] hard shell of certain turtles, esp the type with yellow and brown markings, used to make combs, etc 玳瑁壳: [attrib 作定语] *a hairbrush with a tortoiseshell back* 背面镶玳瑁的发刷. **2** [C] cat with yellowish-brown markings 有黄棕色花纹的猫. **3** [C] type of butterfly with brownish markings 一种有棕色花纹的蝴蝶.

tor·tu·ous /'tɔ:tʃʊəs; 'tɔrtʃʊəs/ *adj* **1** full of twists and turns 弯弯曲曲的: *followed a tortuous road down the mountainside* 顺着蜿蜒的路下山. **2** (*fig usu derog* 比喻, 通常作贬义) (of a policy, etc) not straightforward; devious (指政策等)不直接阐明的, 含混不清的: *a tortuous argument* 含糊其辞的论据 ○ *tortuous logic* 费解的逻辑. ▷ **tor·tu·os·ity** /ˌtɔ:tʃʊ'ɒsətɪ; ˌtɔrtʃʊ'ɑsətɪ/ [U]. **tor·tu·ously** *adv*.

tor·ture /'tɔ:tʃə(r); 'tɔrtʃɚ/ *n* [C, U] **1** (method of) deliberately inflicting severe pain, as a punishment or in order to force sb to say or do sth 刑法; 刑讯; 严刑逼迫: *barbaric tortures* 野蛮的刑法 ○ *the widespread use of torture* 遍施酷刑 ○ *She died under torture.* 她受严刑拷打致死. ○ [attrib 作定语] *torture instruments* 刑具. **2** (*fig* 比喻) (instance of) great physical or mental suffering 对肉体或精神的折磨: *the tortures of suspense, fear, jealousy, etc* 疑虑、恐惧、忌妒等的煎熬 ○ *This tooth of mine is sheer torture!* 我这颗牙真折磨人!
▷ **tor·ture** *v* [Tn] **1** inflict severe pain on (sb) 使(某

人)极其痛苦; 折磨: *accused the regime of torturing its political opponents* 谴责该政权迫害政敌. **2** (*fig* 比喻) cause (sb) great physical or mental suffering 造成(某人)肉体或精神上的巨大痛苦: *tortured by anxiety* 受焦虑的煎熬. **tor·turer** /ˈtɔːtʃərə(r); ˋtɔrtʃərɚ/ *n*.

Tory /ˈtɔːrɪ; ˋtɔrɪ/ *n, adj* (member) of the British Conservative Party 英国保守党的(党员): *the Tory Party conference* 英国保守党会议 ○ *Tory policies* 英国保守党的政策. ▷ **Tory·ism** *n* [U].

toss /tɒs; *US* tɔːs; tɔs/ *v* **1** (**a**) [Tn, Tn·pr, Tn·p, Dn·n, Dn·pr] **~ sth (to sb)** throw sth lightly or carelessly or easily 扔; 抛; 掷: *He tossed the book down on the table.* 他把书扔在桌子上. ○ *toss sth aside/away/out* 把某物丢在一边[丢开/丢掉] ○ *They were tossing a ball about.* 他们把球扔来扔去. ○ *He tossed the beggar a coin/tossed a coin to the beggar.* 他把一枚硬币扔给乞丐. (**b**) [Tn, Tn·pr, Tn·p] (of a bull, etc) throw (sb) up with the horns (指公牛等)以角挑起(某人). **2** [Tn, Tn·p] jerk (one's head, etc), esp in contempt or indifference 猛然扭(头等)(尤指以示轻视或冷漠). **3** [I, Ipr, Ip, Tn, Tn·pr, Tn·p] (cause sb/sth to) move restlessly from side to side or up and down (使某人[某物])摇荡, 摇摆, 颠簸: *branches tossing in the wind* 迎风摇摆的树枝 ○ *I couldn't sleep, but kept tossing and turning/tossing about in bed all night.* 我整夜在床上翻来覆去睡不着. ○ *The ship was tossed back and forth by the waves.* 那船随波涛颠簸. **4** [Tn, Tn·pr] coat (food) by shaking or turning it in dressing, etc 将(食品)拌上调料等: *toss the salad in oil and vinegar* 把油和醋拌入色拉. **5** [I, Ipr, Ip, Tn, Tn·pr, Tn·p] **~ (up) (sth)**; **~ (sb) for sth** send (a coin) spinning up into the air in order to decide sth by chance, according to which side is uppermost when it falls 掷(硬币)作决定: *Have the two captains tossed yet* (eg to decide which team will start the match)*?* 那两个队的队长掷硬币了吗(如决定哪队开球)? ○ *Who's going to cook tonight? Let's toss up.* 今晚谁做饭? 咱们掷硬币决定吧. ○ *There's only one pillow — I'll toss you for it.* 只有一个枕头——我跟你掷硬币决定谁用吧. **6** (phr v) **toss (oneself) off** (⚠ *Brit sl* 讳, 俚) masturbate 手淫. **toss sth off** (**a**) drink sth straight down 一饮而尽. (**b**) produce sth quickly and without much thought or effort 迅速而不费力地做成某事物: *I can toss off my article for the local newspaper in half an hour.* 我给本地的报纸写文章只用半小时就可一挥而就.

▷ **toss** *n* **1** tossing action or movement 扔; 抛; 掷; 摇荡; 颠簸: *The decision depended on the toss of a coin.* 那项决定是靠掷硬币的方法做出的. ○ *take a toss*, ie be thrown from a horse 从马上摔下 ○ *a contemptuous, disdainful, scornful, etc toss of the head* 轻蔑地把头一扬. **2** (idm 习语) **argue the toss** ⇨ ARGUE. **not give a ˈtoss (about sb/sth)** (*sl* 俚) not care at all 毫不在乎. **win/lose the ˈtoss** guess correctly/incorrectly when a coin is tossed up which way it will fall (esp to decide which team will start a match) 猜中[猜错]掷硬币的结果(尤指决定哪一队开球).

□ **ˈtoss-up** *n* **1** act of tossing a coin 掷硬币. **2** (*infml* 口) even chance 机会相等: *Both players are equally good so it's a toss-up* (ie impossible to predict) *who will win.* 那两个运动员不相上下, 谁能取胜还很难说.

tot¹ /tɒt; tɑt/ *n* **1** small child 幼儿: *a TV programme for tiny tots* 为幼儿看的电视节目. **2** small glass of alcoholic drink, esp spirits 小杯的酒(尤指烈酒).

tot² /tɒt; tɑt/ *v* (**-tt-**) (phr v) **tot (sth) up** (*infml* 口) add up 把某数加起来: *It's surprising how the bills tot up.* 这帐是怎么加在一起的, 真奇怪. ○ *Let's tot up our expenses.* 咱们把费用加起来吧. **tot up to sth** (*infml* 口) add up to sth; equal sth 总计达到某数; 等于某数: *The bill totted up to almost £40.* 那帐单合计近 40 英镑.

total /ˈtəʊtl; ˋtotl/ *adj* [usu attrib 通常作定语] complete; entire 完全的; 全部的: *total silence* 寂静无声 ○ *the total number of casualties* 伤亡者总数 ○ *live in total ignorance (of sth)* 全然不知(某事) ○ *That's total nonsense!* 那是一派胡言! ○ *The firm made a total profit of £200 000.* 该公司的利润总额达 200 000 英镑. ○ *total war*, ie war waged with the full resources of a country 总体战 ○ *a total eclipse of the sun/moon*, ie one in which the sun/moon is completely obscured 日[月]全食 ○ *a total waste of time* 纯粹浪费时间.

▷ **total** *n* **1** total number or amount 总数; 总额: *What does the total come to?* 总数是多少? ○ *England scored a total of 436 runs.* 英格兰板球队获总分 436 分. **2** (idm 习语) **in ˈtotal** altogether 总共: *That will cost you £7.50 in total.* 你总共要花 7.50 英镑.

total *v* (**-ll-**; *US* also **-l-**) [Tn] **1** count the total of (sb/sth) 计算(人[事物])的总和: *The takings haven't been totalled yet.* 总营业额还未算出. **2** amount to (sth) 总数达(若干): *He has debts totalling more than £200.* 他负债总数超过 200 英镑. **3** (*US sl* 俚) wreck (esp a car) completely; destroy 彻底毁坏(尤指汽车); 毁灭.

to·tal·ity /təʊˈtælətɪ; toˋtælətɪ/ *n* **1** [U] state of being total 整个; 全部; 全体. **2** [C] total number or amount 总数; 总额.

tot·ally /ˈtəʊtəlɪ; ˋtotḷɪ/ *adv* completely; utterly 完全; 全部地; 整个地: *totally blind* 全盲的 ○ *I'm afraid I totally forgot about it.* 很抱歉, 我把这件事忘得干干净净了.

to·tal·it·arian /ˌtəʊtælɪˈteərɪən; toˌtæləˋtɛrɪən/ *adj* of a system of government in which there is only one political party and no rival parties or loyalties are allowed, usu demanding that the individual submit totally to the requirements of the State 极权主义的. ▷ **to·tal·it·arian·ism** /-ɪzəm; -ˌɪzəm/ *n* [U].

to·tal·iz·ator, -is·ator /ˈtəʊtəlaɪzeɪtə(r); *US* -lɪz-; ˋtotḷəˌzetɚ/ (also *infml* 口语作 **tote**) *n* (*fml* 文) device automatically registering the bets staked on horses, etc, so that the total amount can be divided among those who bet on the winner (赛马等的)赌金计算器.

tote¹ /təʊt; tot/ *n* (*infml* 口) = TOTALIZATOR: *betting on the tote* 通过赌金计算器下赌注.

tote² /təʊt; tot/ *v* [Tn, Tn·pr, Tn·p] (*US infml* 口) carry (sth) 携带(某物): *I've been toting this bag round all day.* 我一整天都带着这个提包.

totem /ˈtəʊtəm; ˋtotəm/ *n* (image of a) natural object, esp an animal, considered by N American Indians as the emblem of a clan or family 图腾; 图腾形象.

□ **ˈtotem-pole** *n* tall wooden pole carved or painted with a series of totems 图腾柱.

tot·ter /ˈtɒtə(r); ˋtɑtɚ/ *v* [I, Ipr, Ip] **1** walk or move unsteadily; stagger 走得或动得不稳; 踉跄; 蹒跚: *The child tottered across the room.* 那孩子跌跌撞撞走到房间那一边. ○ *She tottered to her feet.* 她摇晃着站起来. **2** rock or shake as if about to fall 摇摇欲坠: *The tall chimney tottered (to and fro) and then collapsed.* 那座高烟囱摇摇晃晃地倒了下来. ▷ **tot·tery** /ˈtɒtərɪ; ˋtɑtərɪ/ *adj*: *feel faint and tottery* 觉得头晕脚步不稳.

T

tou·can /ˈtuːkæn, -kən; *US also* tuˈkɑːn; ˋtukæn, tuˋkɑn/ *n* tropical American bird with brightly coloured feathers and a very large beak 鹞鸮(产于美洲热带地区的鸟, 羽色鲜明, 喙极大).

touch¹ /tʌtʃ; tʌtʃ/ *v* **1** [I, Tn] be or come together with (sth else) so that there is no space between 触, 接触, 触及(他物): *The two wires were touching.* 那两条金属线搭在一起了. ○ *One of the branches was just touching the water.* 有一个树枝刚碰着水面. ○ *The two properties touch (each other)*, ie share a boundary. 这两块地产相毗邻. **2** [Tn] press or strike (sth/sb) lightly, esp with the hand 轻触, 轻碰(某物[某人])(尤指用手碰): *Don't touch that dish — it's very hot!* 别摸那个盘子——烫极了! ○ *Can you touch the top of the door* (ie reach it with your hand)*?* 你够得着门的上边吗? ○ *He touched me on the arm*, eg to attract my attention. 他碰碰我胳膊(如让我注意). ○ *Don't let your coat touch the wall — the paint's still wet.* 你的大衣别蹭着墙——涂料还没干呢. **3** [Tn] move or interfere with (sb/sth); harm 移动, 妨碍(某人[某物]); 损坏: *I told you not to touch my things!* 我告诉过你, 别动我的东西! ○ *The valuable paintings were not touched by the fire.* 那场火并未波及这些名画. ○ *What he did was perfectly legal — the police can't touch* (ie arrest) *him for it.* 他做的事完全合法, 警方不能碰他. **4** [Tn] (usu in negative sentences 通常用于否定句) eat or drink even a little of (sth) 仅吃或喝少量(某物): *You've hardly touched your steak.* 这块牛排你没怎么动啊. **5** [Tn, Tn·pr] (**a**) **~ sb/sth (with sth)** make (sb/sb's feelings) sympathetic or sad 感动(某人); 触动(某人[某人的感情]); 使(某人)怜悯或悲哀: *Her tragic story touched us all deeply/touched our hearts with sorrow.* 她的经历很悲惨, 我们都深受感动[我们都很伤心]. ○ *He never seems to have been touched with the slightest remorse for his crimes.* 他似乎从来没有丝毫悔罪之意.

(**b**) [Tn, Tn·pr] **~ sb/sth (on sth)** cause (sb/sb's feelings) to be hurt or offended 伤害(某人[某人的感情]); 触犯(某人): *Her sarcasm touched his self-esteem.* 她讥讽的言语伤了他的自尊心. ○ *You've touched me on a tender spot*, ie mentioned sth I find painful or unpleasant. 你触到了我的痛处(提及使我痛苦或不快的事). **6** [Tn] (usu in negative sentences 通常用于否定句) be associated or connected with (sth) 与(某事)有联系或有关系: *Your objections do not touch the point at issue.* 你提的反对意见与问题的实质无关. ○ *I wouldn't touch anything illegal.* 我与违法的事沾不上边儿. ○ *She never touches* (ie drinks) *alcohol.* 她向来滴酒不沾. **7** [Tn] (usu in negative sentences 通常用于否定句) equal (sb/sth) in excellence; rival 与(某人[某事物])媲美或匹敌; 抵得上: *No one can touch him* (ie He is the best) *as a comedian/in comedy.* 他这个喜剧演员[演喜剧]没人能比得上. ○ *There's nothing to touch mountain air for giving you an appetite.* 再也没有比山间清新的空气更能促进食欲的了. **8** [Tn] reach (a certain level, etc) 达到(某一水平等): *The speedometer was touching 120 mph.* 速度计显示时速达120英里. ○ *After touching 143, the price* (ie of shares on the stock-market) *fell back to 108 by the close of trading.* 股票价格攀上143点后, 收市时回落到108点. ○ *touch the depths of despair* 达到绝望的深渊. **9** (idm 习语) **hit/touch a nerve** ⇨ NERVE. **not touch sb/sth with a 'barge-pole** (*Brit infml* 口) not wish to have or be associated with sb/sth 但愿从未或决不与某人[某事物]有任何关系: *I don't know why she's marrying that appalling man; I wouldn't touch him with a barge-pole.* 我不明白她为什么要嫁给那个糟糕透顶的人, 我连理都不愿意理他. **touch 'bottom** (**a**) reach and touch the ground at the bottom of a body of water 触到水底: *The ship has touched bottom — the estuary must be shallower than we thought.* 船搁浅了——这河口的水比我们想像的要浅. (**b**) (*fig* 比喻) reach the worst possible state or condition 达到最坏的境况: *When he was forced to beg from his friends he felt he had touched bottom and could sink no lower.* 等到他被迫向朋友乞讨时, 他觉得自己的境况已糟到无以复加的地步了. **touch sb on the 'raw** hurt sb's feelings by mentioning sth about which he is sensitive 触某人的痛处(提及某人敏感的事而伤害某人的感情); 揭某人的疮疤. **touch the right 'chord** appeal cleverly to sb's feelings 巧妙地触动某人的感情. **touch 'wood** (*catchphrase* 警语) (expression used, often while touching sth made of wood, in the superstitious or humorous hope of avoiding bad luck 迷信的或诙谐的避邪用语, 常边说此语边触木制物品): *I've been driving for 20 years and never had an accident — touch wood!* 我开车开了20年从来没出过车祸——摸摸木头避邪! **10** (phr v) **touch at sth** (no passive 不用于被动语态) (of a ship) stop for a period at (a place); call at sth (指船)在(某地)停一段时间, 停于某处: *Our ship touched at Naples.* 我们的船曾在那不勒斯停靠. **touch down** (**a**) (of an aircraft) land (指飞行器)着陆, 接地. (**b**) (in Rugby) score a try by putting the ball on the ground behind the other team's goal line (英式橄榄球)底线得分, 触地球(在对方球门线后以球触地). **touch sb for sth** (*sl* 俚) get sb to give one money (as a loan or by begging) 让某人给些钱(或借或讨): *He tried to touch me for a fiver.* 他想让我给他五英镑. **touch sth off** (**a**) cause sth to explode or catch fire 使某物爆炸或着火. (**b**) (*fig* 比喻) cause sth to start 触发或引起某事: *His arrest touched off a riot.* 他被捕后引起了骚乱. **touch on/upon sth** mention or deal with (a subject) briefly 提及或涉及(某问题): *The matter was hardly touched on.* 那件事几乎没涉及到. **touch sb up** (*sl* 俚) touch sb in a sexually improper or suggestive way (猥亵地或为挑逗性欲)触摸某人. **touch sth up** improve sth by making small changes 稍作修改以改进某事物: *I'm going to touch up those scratches with a bit of paint.* 我要用点儿颜料修补那些划痕.

□ **'touchdown** *n* **1** (of an aircraft) landing (指飞行器)着陆, 接地. **2** (in American football) score made by taking the ball across the other team's goal line (美式橄榄球)持球触地(持球越对方门线得分).

touch[2] /tʌtʃ; tʌtʃ/ *n* **1** [C usu *sing* 通常作单数] act or fact of touching 触; 接触: *I felt a touch on my arm.* 我觉得有人摸了我胳膊一下. ○ *A bubble will burst at the slightest touch.* 气泡稍微一碰就破. ○ *He managed to get a touch to the ball.* 他尽力触到了球. **2** [U] faculty of perceiving things or their qualities by touching them 触觉: *Blind people rely a lot on touch.* 盲人在很大程度上依靠触觉. ○ *a highly developed sense of touch* 高度发达的触觉. **3** [sing] way sth feels when touched 触摸时的感觉: *soft to the touch* 摸起来很柔软 ○ *The material has a warm, velvety touch.* 这料子摸着如天鹅绒般温暖柔软. ○ *the cold touch of marble* 触摸大理石的冰冷感觉. **4** [C] small detail (细节中)微小之处: *put the finishing touches to a piece of work* 给一个作品作最后加工 ○ *humorous touches* 幽默的细微之处 ○ *That was a clever touch.* 那是巧妙的装点. **5** [sing] **a ~ (of sth)** slight quantity; trace 少许; 微量: *This dish needs a touch more garlic.* 这菜里要再加点儿蒜. ○ *'Do you take sugar?' 'Just a touch.'* '你要糖吗?' '只要一点儿.' ○ *There's a touch of frost in the air.* 空气中略有寒意. ○ *I've got a touch of flu.* 我有点儿感冒. ○ *have a touch of the sun*, ie slight sunstroke 轻微中暑. **6** [sing] manner or style of workmanship, performance, etc (技艺、表演等的)手法, 风格: *the touch of a master*, ie expert style, eg in painting 大师风范(如绘画中的) ○ *play the piano with a light, heavy, firm, delicate, etc touch* 以轻快的、有力的、稳健的、灵巧的...指法弹钢琴 ○ *His work lacks that professional touch.* 他的作品缺乏专业技巧. **7** [sing] person's special skill 个人的特殊能力; 技能: *I can't do the crossword today — I must be losing my touch.* 我今天填不出这纵横字谜了——一定是本事不济了. ○ *Has he regained his old touch?* 他恢复以前的能力了吗? ○ *another adventure film with that inimitable Steven Spielberg touch* 具有独树一帜的史蒂文·斯皮尔伯格技巧的另一部冒险影片. **8** [U] (in football and Rugby) part of the pitch outside the sidelines (足球及英式橄榄球)边线以外区域: *The ball is out of/in touch.* 球已出[在]边线外区域. ○ *kick the ball into touch* 把球踢出边线外. **9** (idm 习语) **at a 'touch** if touched, however lightly 一触即: *The machine stops and starts at a touch.* 这机器一触即可停止或开动. **the common touch** ⇨ COMMON[1]. **an easy/a soft 'touch** (*sl* 俚) person who readily gives or lends money if asked (一经要求)愿意给人钱或借给人钱的人. **in/out of 'touch (with sb)** in/not in communication 有[无]联系: *Let's keep in touch.* 咱们保持联系. ○ *Do get in touch soon*, eg by phone. 一定要尽早联系(如打电话). ○ *Our head office can put you in touch with a branch in your area.* 我们总公司可安排您与当地分公司取得联系. ○ *I'll be in touch again towards the end of the week.* 我到周末时再联系. ○ *We've been out of touch with Roger for years now.* 我们至今已有数年未与罗杰来往了. **in/out of touch with sth** having/not having information about sth 了解[不了解]某事的信息: *I try to keep in touch with current events by reading the newspapers.* 我经常读报来尽量了解时事. **lose touch** ⇨ LOSE. **a touch** (with an *adj* or *adv* 与形容词或副词连用) slightly 少许: *It's a touch colder today.* 今天有点儿冷. ○ *She hit the ball a touch too hard.* 她击球的力量大了点儿.

□ **,touch-and-'go** *adj* [usu pred 通常作表语] (*infml* 口) uncertain as to the result 无法确定结果; 无把握: *It was touch-and-go whether we would get to the airport in time.* 我们是否能按时到机场还很难说. ○ *The patient is out of danger now, but it was touch-and-go* (ie uncertain whether he would survive) *for a while.* 病人现已脱离危险, 但曾有一度吉凶未卜.

'touch-judge *n* linesman in Rugby football (英式橄榄球)巡边员, 边线裁判员.

'touch-line *n* line marking the side of a football field (足球场的)边线.

'touch-type *v* [I] type without looking at the keys (不看打字机键盘)按指法打字.

tou·ché /'tu:ʃeɪ; *US* tu:'ʃeɪ; tu'ʃe/ *interj* (expression used to acknowledge that one's opponent has made a good or effective point in an argument, a discussion, etc 在辩论、讨论等中用以承认对方言之成理的词语).

touched /tʌtʃt; tʌtʃt/ *adj* [pred 作表语] **1** made to feel warm sympathy or gratitude 受感动; 感激: *I was very touched by/to receive your kind letter.* 我收到你的来信, 十分感激. **2** (*infml* 口) slightly mad 精神有些失常; 轻微疯癫.

touch·ing /'tʌtʃɪŋ; 'tʌtʃɪŋ/ *adj* arousing pity or sympathy 引起怜悯或同情的: *a touching sight, story, scene* 使人产生恻隐之心的情景、经历、场面 ○ (*ironic* 反语) *She* *showed a touching* (ie perhaps mistaken) *faith in her own invincibility.* 她坚信自己无往不利，这念头未免太可怜了.

▷ **touch·ing** *prep* (*fml* 文) having an effect on (sth); concerning 对(某事物)有影响; 关于: *measures touching our interests* 关系到我们的利益的措施.

touch·ingly *adv*.

touchy /ˈtʌtʃɪ; ˋtʌtʃɪ/ *adj* (**-ier, -iest**) **1** easily offended 易生气的: *Don't be so touchy!* 别动不动就生气! **2** (of a subject, situation, etc) requiring careful handling because of potential controversy or offence (指问题、情况等)需小心处理的(因可能引起争议或不悦): *Racism remains a touchy issue.* 种族主义可是个要小心处理的问题. ▷ **touch·ily** /-ɪlɪ; -ılı/ *adv*. **touchi·ness** *n* [U].

tough /tʌf; tʌf/ *adj* (**-er, -est**) **1** not easily cut, broken, or worn out 坚韧的; 不易切开、打破或磨损的: *as tough as leather* 坚韧如皮革 ○ *Tough glass is needed for windscreens.* 挡风玻璃需要用不易碎的玻璃. ○ *a tough pair of walking boots* 一双结实的步行靴. **2** able to endure hardship; not easily defeated or injured 能耐劳苦的; 不易击败的; 不易伤害的: *You need to be tough to survive in the jungle.* 要在丛林中活下来就要有坚忍不拔的意志. ○ *Coal-miners are a tough breed.* 煤矿工人都是能吃苦耐劳的. **3** (*esp US*) rough; violent 粗暴的; 凶恶的: *one of the toughest areas of the city* 该市治安最坏的一个地区. ○ *a tough criminal* 凶暴的罪犯. **4** (*derog* 贬) (of meat) hard to cut or chew (指肉)切不动的, 咬不动的, 硬的, 老的: *a tough steak* 咬不动的牛排. **5** severe; unyielding 严厉的; 不屈的; 强硬的: *tough measures to deal with terrorism* 对付恐怖主义的严厉措施 ○ *take a tough line with offenders* 对犯罪分子采取强硬方针. **6** difficult 困难的: *It's tough finding a job these days.* 近来很难找到工作. ○ *a tough game, assignment, problem, journey* 艰苦的比赛、困难的任务、难题、艰辛的旅程. **7** ~ **(on sb)** (*infml* 口) unfortunate 不幸的; 倒霉的: *That's tough!* ie Bad luck! 真倒霉! ○ *It's rather tough on him falling ill just as he's about to go on holiday.* 他正要去度假却生病了, 真倒霉. ○ *Oh, tough luck!* 嗨, 真不走运! **8** (idm 习语) **be/get tough (with sb)** adopt a firm attitude; take severe measures 采取坚决态度; 采用强硬手段: *It's time to get tough with football hooligans.* 现在该对足球迷小流氓采取强硬措施了. ○ [attrib 作定语] *a get-tough policy* 强硬的方针. **a hard/tough nut** ⇨ NUT. **(as) tough as old ˈboots** (*infml* 口) (esp of meat) very tough; difficult to chew (尤指肉)很硬的, 很老的, 咬不动的. **a ˌtough ˈcustomer** (*infml* 口) person who is difficult to control, overcome, satisfy, etc 难对付的人.

▷ **tough** (also **toughie** /ˈtʌfɪ; ˋtʌfı/) *n* (*infml* 口) rough and violent person 粗暴的人: *a gang of young toughs* 一帮年轻的恶棍.

tough *v* (phr v) **tough sth out** (*infml* 口) endure (a difficult situation) with determination 坚决忍受着(困难的情况).

toughen /ˈtʌfn; ˋtʌfn̩/ *v* [I, Ip, Tn, Tn·p] ~ **(sth/sb) (up)** (cause sth/sb to) become tough or tougher (使某事物[某人])(更)坚韧, 坚强, 强硬: *The law needs toughening (up).* 需要加强法制的威力. ○ *toughened glass* 钢化玻璃.

tough·ness *n* [U].

tou·pee /ˈtu:peɪ; *US* tu:ˈpeɪ; tuˋpe/ *n* patch of false hair worn to cover a bald spot; small wig (遮掩秃斑的)小撮假发; 小型假发.

tour /tʊə(r); *also, in British use,* 英式英语读作 tɔ:(r); tʊr/ *n* **1** journey for pleasure during which various places of interest are visited 旅行; 旅游: *a round-the-world tour* 环球旅行 ○ *a coach tour of* (ie around) *France* 乘长途汽车周游法国 ○ *a cycling/walking tour* 骑自行车[徒步]旅游 ○ [attrib 作定语] *tour operators* 旅行社经营者. **2** brief visit to or through a place 参观; 游览: *go on/make/do a tour of the palace, museum, ruins, etc* 参观宫殿、博物馆、废墟等 ○ *a conducted/guided tour,* ie made by a group led by a guide 有导游的旅行. ⇨Usage at JOURNEY 用法见 JOURNEY. **3** official series of visits for the purpose of playing matches, giving performances, etc 巡回比赛、演出等: *the Australian cricket team's forthcoming tour of England* 澳大利亚板球队即将来英国进行的巡回比赛 ○ *The orchestra is currently on tour in Germany.* 该管弦乐团目前正在德国巡回演出. ○ *The Director leaves tomorrow for a tour of overseas branches,* ie to inspect them. 董事长明天动身去视察海外分支机构. **4** period of duty abroad 海外任职期间: *a tour of three years as a lecturer in Nigeria* 在尼日利亚当讲师的三年任期.

▷ **tour** *v* [I, Ipr, Tn] ~ **(in sth)** make a tour of or in (a place) 在(某地)旅行、旅游或巡回: *They're touring (in) India.* 他们正在印度游历. ○ *The play will tour the provinces next month.* 该剧将于下月在各地巡回演出.

tour·ism /ˈtʊərɪzəm; *also, in British use,* 英式英语读作 ˈtɔ:r-; ˋtʊrˌɪzəm/ *n* [U] business of providing accommodation and services for tourists 旅游业: *The country's economy is dependent on tourism.* 该国经济依赖于旅游业.

tour·ist /ˈtʊərɪst; *also, in British use,* 英式英语读作 tɔ:r-; ˋtʊrɪst/ *n* **1** person who is travelling or visiting a place for pleasure 旅行者; 旅游者; 观光客: *London is full of tourists in the summer.* 在夏季伦敦有很多游客. ○ [attrib 作定语] *a ˈtourist agency* 旅行社. **2** (*sport* 体) member of a team on tour(3) 巡回比赛运动队队员: *the Australian tourists* 澳大利亚巡回比赛运动队队员. **tour·isty** *adj* (*infml derog* 口, 贬) full of tourists; designed to attract tourists 游客很多的; 吸引游客的: *The coast is terribly touristy now.* 海滨区现在到处都是游客.

□ **ˈtourist class** (on aircraft and ships) second class (飞机或轮船上的)二等舱, 经济舱.

ˈtourist trap (*infml* 口) place that exploits tourists (by overcharging, etc) 敲旅客竹杠的地方.

tour de force /ˌtʊə də ˈfɔ:s; ˌtʊrdəˋfɔrs/ (*pl* **tours de force**/ˌtʊə də ˈfɔ:s; ˌtʊrdəˋfɔrs/) (*French* 法) outstandingly skilful performance or achievement 绝技; 壮举; 杰作.

tour·na·ment /ˈtɔ:nəmənt; *US* ˈtɜ:rn-; ˋtɝnəmənt/ *n* **1** series of contests of skill between a number of competitors, often on a knock-out basis 联赛, 比赛, 竞赛, 锦标赛(常为淘汰制): *a tennis, chess, snooker, etc tournament* 网球、国际象棋、落袋台球等比赛. ⇨Usage at SPORT 用法见 SPORT. **2** (formerly) contest between knights on horseback armed with blunted weapons, esp lances (旧时)武士骑马比武(用钝武器, 尤指长矛).

tour·ni·quet /ˈtʊənɪkeɪ; *US* ˈtɜ:rnɪkət; ˋtɝnɪˌkɛt/ *n* device for stopping the flow of blood through an artery by twisting sth tightly around a limb 止血带; 压脉器: *applying a tourniquet to the wounded man's arm* 给受伤者的臂上扎止血带.

tousle /ˈtaʊzl; ˋtaʊzl̩/ *v* [Tn] make (hair, etc) untidy by pulling or rubbing it about 弄乱(头发等): *a girl with tousled hair* 头发蓬乱的女孩儿.

tout /taʊt; taʊt/ *v* **1** [I, Ipr, Tn] ~ **(for sth)** try to get people to buy (one's goods or services), esp in an annoyingly insistent way 兜售(货物); 招揽(生意): *touting for custom* 招揽生意 ○ *touting one's wares* 兜售商品. **2** [Tn] (*Brit*) sell (tickets to sports events, concerts, etc) at a price higher than the official one 卖高价票(体育比赛、音乐会等的); 卖黑市票.

▷ **tout** *n* person who touts things 兜售者; 招揽生意的人; 卖高价票的人: *a ˈticket tout* 票贩子.

tow[1] /təʊ; to/ *v* [Tn, Tn·pr, Tn·p] pull (sth) along with a rope, chain, etc (用绳、链等)拖, 拉, 拽, 曳(某物): *tow a damaged ship into port* 把损坏的船拖进港 ○ *If you park your car here the police may tow it away.* 你要是把汽车停在这里, 警察就会把它拖走. ⇨Usage at PULL[2] 用法见 PULL[2].

▷ **tow** *n* **1** (esp *sing* 尤作单数) act of towing sth 拖; 拉; 拽; 曳: *My car won't start — can you give me a tow?* 我的汽车发动不起来了——你能帮我拖一下吗? **2** (idm 习语) **in tow** **(a)** (*infml* 口) accompanying or following behind 伴随; 跟随: *He had his family in tow,* ie with him. 他拖家带口. **(b)** = ON TOW: *The damaged freighter was taken in tow.* 那损坏的货轮被拖着走. **on tow** being towed 被拖、拉、拽或曳: *The lorry was on tow.* 那货车被拖着走.

□ **ˈtow-bar** *n* bar fitted to the back of a car for towing a caravan, etc (用以牵引拖车等的)牵引杆.

ˈtow-line, ˈtow-rope *ns* line or rope used for towing 拖索; 拖缆; 纤绳.

ˈtow-path *n* path along the bank of a river or canal, formerly used by horses towing barges, etc 纤道, 纤路(沿河岸的道路, 旧时马拖船走的).

tow[2] /təʊ; to/ *n* [U] short coarse fibres of flax or hemp, used for making rope, etc 粗麻屑(用以制绳索).

to·wards /tə'wɔ:dz; *US* tɔ:rdz; tɔrdz/ (also **to·ward** /tə'wɔ:d; *US* tɔ:rd; tɔrd/) *prep* **1** in the direction of (sb/sth) 向, 朝, 对着(某人[某事物])的方向: *walk towards the river* 朝着河走去 ○ *look out towards the sea* 向外面的大海看 ○ *The child came running towards me.* 那孩子向我跑来. ○ *She turned her back towards the sun.* 她转过身背对着太阳. **2** moving closer to achieving (sth) 趋于达成(某事): *The meeting is seen as the first step towards greater unity between the parties.* 这一会议可视为两党走向进一步联合的第一步. ○ *We have made some progress towards reaching an agreement.* 我们在达成协议方面已取得些进展. **3** in relation to (sb/sth) 对于或关于(某人[某事]): *The local people are always very friendly towards tourists.* 当地人对游客一向十分热情. ○ *He behaved very affectionately towards her children.* 他非常疼爱她的孩子. ○ *As you get older your attitude towards death changes.* 人随着年龄的增长, 对死亡的看法也会有所改变. **4** with the aim of acquiring or contributing to (sth) 为得到或用于(某物): *The money will go towards (the cost of) building a new school.* 此款项将用于建设新学校(的开销). ○ *£30 a month goes towards a pension fund.* 每月交30英镑用作退职基金. **5** near (a point in time) 接近(某一时间): *Food shortages will probably get worse towards the end of the century.* 食物短缺的情况到本世纪末可能更加严重. ○ *Now he's getting towards retirement age he's started playing golf.* 他因接近退休年龄, 就打起高尔夫球来了.

towel /'taʊəl; 'taʊəl/ *n* **1** piece of absorbent cloth or paper for drying oneself or wiping things dry 毛巾; 手巾; 抹布; 纸巾: *a 'hand-/'bath-towel* 手[浴]巾 ○ *a paper 'towel* 纸巾. **2** (idm 习语) **throw in the 'towel** (*infml* 口) admit that one is defeated 承认失败; 认输. Cf 参看 THROW UP THE SPONGE (SPONGE).

▷ **towel** *v* (**-ll-**; *US* **-l-**) [Tn, Tn·pr, Tn·p] **~ oneself/sb (down) (with sth)** dry oneself/sb with a towel 用毛巾擦干自己[某人].

tow·el·ling (*US* **tow·el·ing**) *n* [U] thick soft absorbent cloth (of a type) used for making towels 毛巾布.

□ **'towel-rail** *n* rail for hanging towels on 毛巾架.

tower /'taʊə(r); 'taʊə/ *n* **1** tall narrow structure, usu square or circular, either standing alone (eg as a fort) or forming part of a church or a castle or some other large building 塔: *the Tower of London* 伦敦塔 ○ *the church's bell tower* 教堂的钟楼. ⇨illus at App 1 见附录1插图, page viii. **2** (idm 习语) **an ivory tower** ⇨ IVORY. **3 a ˌtower of 'strength** person who can be relied upon for protection, strength or comfort in time of trouble (危难时)可依赖的人, 靠山.

▷ **tower** *v* (phr v) **tower above/over sb/sth 1** be of much greater height than others nearby 远高于周围的人或物: *the skyscrapers that tower over New York* 高耸于纽约市的摩天大楼 ○ *At six feet, he towers over his mother.* 他身高六英尺, 比他母亲高得多. **2** (*fig* 比喻) greatly surpass others in ability, quality, fame, etc (在能力、品德、名声等方面)远超过他人: *Shakespeare towers above all other Elizabethan dramatists.* 莎士比亚远超过伊丽莎白时代所有的剧作家.

tower·ing /'taʊərɪŋ; 'taʊərɪŋ/ *adj* [attrib 作定语] **1** extremely or impressively tall or high 极高的; 高大的: *the towering dome of the cathedral* 大教堂高大的圆顶. **2** (of rage, etc) intense; extreme (指发怒等)强烈的, 极度的. **3** (*approv* 褒) outstanding 杰出的: *Einstein, one of the towering intellects of the age* 爱因斯坦, 一位当世俊彦.

□ **'tower block** (*Brit*) very tall block of flats or offices 高层建筑; 公寓大楼; 办公大楼.

town /taʊn; taʊn/ *n* **1** (**a**) [C] centre of population that is larger than a village but smaller than a city 镇; 集镇; 市镇: *drove through several large industrial towns* 开车穿过几座大的工业市镇 ○ *the historic town of Cambridge* 历史名城剑桥. (**b**) [CGp] its inhabitants 城镇居民: *The whole town turned out to welcome the team home.* 镇上居民全体出动迎接该队归来. **2** [U] towns or cities, esp as contrasted with the country 镇, 城市(尤与乡村相对): *Do you live in town or in the country?* 你住在城里还是住在乡下? ○ [attrib 作定语] *town life* 城市生活. **3** [U] (preceded by a *prep* and without *the* or *a* 用于介词之后, 不加冠词 the 或 a) (**a**) main business and commercial area of a neighbourhood (一地区的)商业区: *I'm going into town this morning — do you want me to get you anything?* 我今天上午要到商业区去 —— 你想让我给你捎什么东西来吗? (**b**) chief town or city of an area; (in England) London (一地区的主要的)镇或城市; (在英格兰指)伦敦: *Mr Green is not in town/is out of town.* 格林先生不在城里. ○ *He went up to town this morning.* 他今天早晨进城了. ○ *She's spending the weekend in town.* 她正在伦敦度周末. **4** (idm 习语) **go to 'town (on sth)** (*infml* 口) do sth with great vigour or enthusiasm, esp by spending a lot of money 以极大的精力或热情做某事(尤指花很多钱): *When they give parties they really go to town.* 他们每次搞聚会都不惜钱财. ○ *The critics really went to town on his latest film,* ie discussed it at length, esp unfavourably. 影评界把他最新的电影数落个够. **a man about town** ⇨ MAN. **(out) on the 'town** visiting places of entertainment (eg night-clubs, theatres) in a town or city, esp at night 去城里的娱乐场所(如夜总会、剧院)(尤指夜间): *For a birthday treat they took him out on the town.* 他们为庆贺他的生日请他去城里娱乐场所玩. **paint the town red** ⇨ PAINT².

□ **ˌtown 'centre** (*esp Brit*) main business and commercial area of a town 镇上的主要商业区. Cf 参看 DOWNTOWN.

ˌtown 'clerk official in charge of the records of a town or city 镇执事, 镇书记(掌管案卷者).

ˌtown 'council (*Brit*) governing body of a town 镇政务会. **ˌtown 'councillor** member of this 镇政务会委员.

ˌtown 'crier (esp formerly) person employed to make official announcements in public places (尤指旧时)街头公告员(受雇在公共场所宣读公告的人).

ˌtown 'hall building containing local government offices and usu a hall for public meetings, concerts, etc 镇公所; 市政厅; 市镇集会所.

'town house 1 house in town owned by sb who also has one in the country (兼有城乡住宅者的)市内住宅. **2** modern house built as part of a planned group or row of houses (规划住宅群中的)新式住宅.

ˌtown 'planning control of the growth and development of a town, its buildings, roads, etc, esp by a local authority 市镇规划.

'townsfolk, **'townspeople** *ns* [pl] people of a town 镇民.

'townsman /-mən; -mən/ *n* (*pl* **-men**) man who lives in a town 住在镇里的人.

townee /taʊ'ni:; taʊ'ni/ (also **townie, towny** /'taʊnɪ; 'taʊnɪ/) *n* (*derog* 贬) person who lives in a town or city and is ignorant of country life (不了解乡村生活的)城里人.

town·ship /'taʊnʃɪp; 'taʊnʃɪp/ *n* **1** (community living in a) small town 小镇(的居民). **2** (in S Africa) town or suburb designated for use by non-whites (南非)有色人种居住的镇或郊区. **3** (in US, Canada) division of a county; district six miles square (美国、加拿大的)镇区, 六平方英里的地区.

tox·aemia (also **tox·emia**) /tɒk'si:mɪə; tɑks'imɪə/ *n* [U] (*medical* 医) = BLOOD-POISONING (BLOOD¹).

toxic /'tɒksɪk; 'tɑksɪk/ *adj* poisonous 有毒的: *toxic drugs* 毒药 ○ *the toxic effects of alcohol* 酒精的毒性.

▷ **tox·icity** /tɒk'sɪsətɪ; tɑks'ɪsətɪ/ *n* [U] quality or degree of being toxic 毒性; 毒力: *the comparative toxicity of different insecticides* 不同杀虫剂的相对的毒性.

tox·ico·logy /ˌtɒksɪ'kɒlədʒɪ; ˌtɑksɪ'kɑlədʒɪ/ *n* scientific study of poisons 毒理学; 毒物学. **tox·ico·lo·gist** /-dʒɪst; -dʒɪst/ *n* student of or expert in toxicology 研究毒理或毒物的人; 毒理或毒物学家.

toxin /'tɒksɪn; 'tɑksɪn/ *n* poisonous substance, esp one formed by bacteria in plants and animals and causing a particular disease 毒素(尤指细菌导致动植物疾病的).

toy /tɔɪ; tɔɪ/ *n* **1** thing to play with, esp for a child 玩具(尤指儿童的). **2** (*usu derog* 通常作贬义) thing intended for amusement rather than for serious use 为玩耍的而并非为使用的东西: *His latest toy is a personal computer.* 他的最新玩物是个人计算机. ○ *executive toys* 行政人员的小玩物.

▷ **toy** *adj* [attrib 作定语] **1** made in imitation of the specified thing and used for playing with 作玩具的: *a toy car, gun, telephone* 玩具汽车、枪、电话 ○ *toy* (ie model) *soldiers* 玩具士兵. **2** (of a dog) of a small breed or variety, kept as a pet (指狗)体型小的(作宠物的): *a toy spaniel* 西班牙种的小猎鸡狗.

toy *v* (phr v) **toy with sth** 1 consider sth idly or without serious intent 漫不经心地考虑某事: *I've been toying with the idea of moving abroad.* 我一直胡乱想着移居国外好不好. 2 handle or move sth carelessly or absent-mindedly 粗心地或心不在焉地摆弄或移动某物: *toying with a pencil* 摆弄着铅笔 ○ *She was just toying with her food, as if she wasn't really hungry.* 她把饭拨弄着玩儿, 好像并不饿.

□ **'toyshop** *n* shop where toys are sold 玩具店.

trace[1] /treɪs; tres/ *n* 1 [C, U] mark, track, sign, etc showing what has existed or happened 踪迹; 痕迹; 形迹: *traces of prehistoric habitation* 史前居民的遗迹 ○ *The police have been unable to find any trace of the gang.* 警方一直未能找到那团伙的任何踪迹. ○ *We've lost all trace of him*, ie We no longer know where he is. 我们现在不知道他的下落了. ○ *The ship had vanished without trace.* 那船消失得无影无踪. 2 [C] very small amount 极微的量: *The post-mortem revealed traces of poison in his stomach.* 验尸发现他胃中有微量毒物. ○ *He spoke without a trace of emotion.* 他说话时毫不动感情.

□ **'trace element** substance occurring or needed only in extremely small amounts (esp in the soil, for the proper growth of plants) 微量元素, 痕量元素(尤指土壤中的, 植物正常生长所需要的).

trace[2] /treɪs; tres/ *v* 1 (a) [Tn, Tn·pr] **~ sb/sth (to sth)** follow or discover sb/sth by finding and noticing marks, tracks or other evidence 追踪; 跟踪; 追溯; 探索; 查出: *I cannot trace the letter to which you refer.* 我查不到你提到的那封信. ○ *Archaeologists have traced many Roman roads in Britain.* 考古学家在英国发现了许多古罗马的道路. ○ *The criminal was traced to Glasgow.* 追踪那个罪犯直追到格拉斯哥. (b) [Tn] describe the development of (sth) 描述(某事)的发展过程: *a book which traces the decline of the Roman empire* 叙述罗马帝国衰亡的书. 2 [Tn, Tn·pr, Tn·p] **~ sth (back) (to sth)** find the origin of sth 找出某事的根源: *He traces his descent back to an old Norman family.* 他追踪自己的世系上溯至一个古老的诺曼家族. ○ *Her fear of water can be traced back to a childhood accident.* 她很怕水, 起因可归于儿时的一次事故. ○ *The cause of the fire was traced to a faulty fuse-box.* 起火的原因已查出是因保险丝盒中有短路. 3 [Tn, Tn·p] **~ sth (out)** (a) sketch or indicate the outline of sth 画出或描绘出某物的轮廓: *We traced out our route on the map.* 我们在地图上画出我们的路线. ○ (*fig* 比喻) *Those who came later followed the policies he had traced out.* 后来的人都按他制定的方针政策行事. (b) form letters, etc slowly and with difficulty 缓慢而费力地写字等: *He traced his signature laboriously.* 他吃力地签上自己的名字. 4 [Tn] copy (a map, drawing, etc) on transparent paper placed over it (将透明纸置于地图、图画等上)复制, 描摹.

▷ **tracer** *n* 1 person or thing that traces 追踪者; 追踪装置; 描摹者; 描摹工具. 2 bullet or shell whose course is made visible by a line of smoke, etc left behind it 曳光弹: [attrib 作定语] *tracer bullets* 曳光弹. 3 radioactive substance whose course through the human body, etc can be traced by the radiation it produces, used for investigating a chemical or biological process 示踪物.

tra·cing *n* copy of a map, drawing, etc made by tracing (TRACE[2] 4) it 摹图; 描图.

□ **'tracing-paper** *n* [U] strong transparent paper for making tracings 描图纸.

trace[3] /treɪs; tres/ *n* 1 (usu *pl* 通常作复数) either of the two straps, chains or ropes by which a horse is attached to and pulls a wagon, carriage, etc 挽绳; 挽缰. ⇨illus at HARNESS 见 HARNESS 插图. 2 (idm 习语) **kick over the traces** ⇨ KICK[1].

tracery /'treɪsərɪ; 'tresərɪ/ *n* [U, C] 1 ornamental pattern of stonework in a church window, etc (教堂窗户等上的)石制花饰. ⇨illus at App 1 见附录1插图, page viii. 2 decorative pattern resembling this 类似石制花饰的图案: *the delicate traceries of frost on the window-pane* 结在窗户玻璃上的精美的霜花.

tra·chea /trə'kɪə; US 'treɪkɪə; 'trekɪə/ *n* (*pl* 复数作 **~s** *or, in scientific use,* 科技用语复数作 **~e** /-kɪi:; -'ki·i/) (*anatomy* 解) windpipe 气管. ⇨illus at RESPIRE 见 RESPIRE 插图.

tra·che·otomy /ˌtrækɪ'ɒtəmɪ; ˌtrekɪ'ɑtəmɪ/ *n* (*medical* 医) operation to cut a hole in the trachea, esp to help breathing 气管切开术.

trach·oma /trə'kəʊmə; trə'komə/ *n* [U] (*medical* 医) contagious disease of the eye causing inflammation of the inner surface of the eyelids 沙眼.

track /træk; træk/ *n* 1 (usu *pl* 通常作复数) line or series of marks left by a moving vehicle, person, animal, etc (车辆、人、动物等行走时留下的)踪迹, 足迹, 痕迹: *'tyre tracks in the mud* 泥地上的车胎印 ○ *We followed his tracks through the snow.* 我们循着雪地上他留下的脚印走. ○ *fresh 'bear tracks* 熊的新足迹. 2 course taken by sth/sb (whether it can be seen or not) 某事物的进程; 某事物[某人]的路径或路线: *the track of a storm, comet, satellite* 风暴、彗星、卫星的路线 ○ *following in the track of earlier explorers* 沿着先前探险者的路径前进. 3 path or rough road, esp one made by vehicles, people or animals 路, 小径(尤指车辆、人或动物造成的): *a muddy track through the forest* 穿过森林的泥泞小路 ○ *'sheep tracks across the moor* 羊群踏出的穿越高沼地的小径. 4 (a) set of rails for trains (火车的)轨道: *a single/double track*, ie one pair/two pairs of rails 单[双]轨 ○ *The train left the track*, ie was derailed. 火车出轨了. (b) (*US*) railway platform (火车站的)站台: *The train for Chicago is on track 9.* 开往芝加哥的列车停靠在第9站台. 5 prepared course or circuit for racing (比赛用的)跑道: *a 'cycling/'running/'greyhound/'motor-racing track* 自行车赛[赛跑/赛狗/汽车赛]的跑道 ○ [attrib 作定语] *'track racing* 径赛. ⇨Usage at PATH 用法见 PATH. 6 (a) section of a gramophone record 唱片的一段录音: *Her new album has two great tracks* (eg songs) *on it.* 她的新唱片集里有两段(如歌曲)特别棒. (b) channel of a recording tape (录音磁带上的)声道: [attrib 作定语] *a sixteen-track tape recorder* 十六声道录音机. (c) (*computing* 计) section of a disk, etc in which information is stored (磁盘等的)道(储存信息用的). 7 continuous belt round the wheels of a bulldozer, tank, etc, on which it moves (推土机、坦克等的)履带. 8 rail along which sth (eg a curtain or a cupboard door) is moved (物件, 如帘幕、橱门等的)滑道, 滑轨. 9 (idm 习语) **cover one's tracks** ⇨ COVER[1]. **from/on the wrong side of the tracks** ⇨ WRONG. **hot on sb's tracks/trail** ⇨ HOT. **in one's 'tracks** (*infml* 口) where one is; suddenly 就地; 当场; 突然: *He fell dead in his tracks.* 他当场死去. ○ *Your question stopped him in his tracks*, ie disconcerted him. 你提的问题让他当场下不来台. **jump the rails/track** ⇨ JUMP[2]. **keep/lose track of sb/sth** keep/fail to keep informed about sb/sth 与某人[某事]保持[失去]联系: *It's hard to keep track of* (ie maintain contact with) *all one's old school friends.* 与中学时的所有老校友都保持联系是很困难的. ○ *lose track of time*, ie forget what time it is 说不准现在的确切时间. **make 'tracks (for...)** (*infml* 口) leave (for a place) 离去(向某地): *It's time we made tracks (for home).* 我们该(家)走了. **off the beaten track** ⇨ BEAT[1]. **on the right/wrong 'track** thinking or acting in a correct/incorrect way 想法或做法对[不对]: *We haven't found the solution yet, but I'm sure we're on the right track.* 我们还没有找到解决办法, 但我肯定我们的思路是对的. **on sb's track** pursuing sb 追踪某人: *The police are on the track of the gang.* 警方正在追踪那帮团伙.

▷ **track** *v* 1 [Tn, Tn·pr] **~ sb/sth (to sth)** follow the track of sb/sth 追踪某人[某物]: *track a satellite, missile, etc using radar* 用雷达追踪卫星、导弹等 ○ *The police tracked the terrorists to their hide-out.* 警方追踪恐怖分子至其藏匿处. ○ *track an animal to its lair* 追踪一动物至其窝穴. 2 [I, Ipr, Ip] (*cinema* 影) (of a camera) move along while filming (指摄影机)移动摄影: *a tracking shot* 跟踪摄影. 3 (phr v) **track sb/sth down** find sb/sth by searching 经追踪或搜索而发现某人[某物]: *track down an animal (to its lair)* 追踪(至窝穴)发现一动物 ○ *I finally tracked down the reference in a dictionary of quotations.* 我终于在引语词典中查到了那段引文.

tracker *n* person who tracks wild animals, etc 追踪野兽等的人. **'tracker dog** dog used for tracking criminals, etc 用以追踪犯罪分子等的犬.

tracked *adj* having tracks (TRACK 7) 有履带的: *tracked vehicles* 履带车.

□ **ˌtrack and 'field** (*esp US*) sports performed on a track or on a field, usu one surrounded by a track; athletics 田径运动; 体育运动(尤指跑和跳).

T

ˈ**track events** (*sport* 体) athletic events involving the running of races (eg sprinting, hurdles, steeplechase) 径赛项目(如短跑、跨栏、障碍赛跑). Cf 参看 FIELD EVENTS (FIELD[1]).

ˈ**tracking station** place from which the movements of satellites, missiles, etc are tracked by radar or radio (用雷达或无线电追踪卫星、导弹等的)跟踪站.

ˈ**track record** past achievements of a person, an organization, etc (个人、组织等)过去的成绩或成就: *He has an excellent track record* (ie has been very successful) *as a salesman.* 他当推销员一向十分出色. ○ *a company with a poor track record* 一向无效益的公司.

ˈ**track suit** warm loose-fitting trousers and jacket worn for athletic practice, as casual clothes, etc (运动练习时或作便服穿的)宽松而暖的衣裤.

tract[1] /trækt; trækt/ *n* **1** large stretch or area of land 大片土地; 地带: *huge tracts of forest, desert, farmland, etc* 大片森林、沙漠、耕地等. **2** (*anatomy* 解) system of connected tube-like parts along which sth passes 道; 束: *the diˈgestive/reˈspiratory/ˈurinary tract* 消化[呼吸/尿]道.

tract[2] /trækt; trækt/ *n* pamphlet containing a short essay, esp on a religious or political subject 小册子(尤指宗教或政治内容的).

tract·able /ˈtræktəbl; ˋtræktəbḷ/ *adj* (*fml* 文) easily guided, handled or controlled; docile 易于引导的; 易处理的; 易驾御的; 温顺的. ▷ **tract·ab·il·ity** /ˌtræktəˈbɪlətɪ; ˌtræktəˋbɪlətɪ/ *n* [U].

trac·tion /ˈtrækʃn; ˋtrækʃən/ *n* [U] **1** (power used in) pulling sth along a surface (在物体平面上的)牵引, 拖拉, 牵引力, 拉力: *electric/steam traction* 电力[蒸汽]牵引. **2** (*medical* 医) treatment involving a continuous pull on a limb, etc (对肢体等的)牵引: *She's injured her back and is in traction for a month.* 她背部受伤, 正在作一个月的牵引治疗. **3** ability of a tyre or wheel to grip the ground without sliding (轮胎或车轮对地面的)附着摩擦力: *Winter tyres give increased traction in mud or snow.* 使用冬季专用车胎在泥地或雪地上可增加附着摩擦力.

T

□ ˈ**traction-engine** *n* vehicle, powered by steam or diesel, formerly used for pulling heavy loads (以蒸汽或柴油为动力的)牵引车(旧时用以拖重物的).

trac·tor /ˈtræktə(r); ˋtræktɚ/ *n* **1** powerful motor vehicle used for pulling farm machinery or other heavy equipment 拖拉机; 牵引机. ⇨illus at PLOUGH 见 PLOUGH 插图. **2** (*US*) part of a tractor-trailer in which the driver sits (铰接车的)驾驶室.

□ ˈ**tractor-trailer** *n* (*US*) = ARTICULATED LORRY (ARTICULATE 2).

trad /træd; træd/ *n* [U] (*infml* 口) traditional jazz (ie in the style of the 1920's, with fixed rhythms and harmonies and much improvisation) 传统爵士乐(二十年代风格的, 有固定的节奏、和声及很多即兴发挥).

trade[1] /treɪd; tred/ *n* **1 (a)** [U] **~ (with sb/sth)** exchange of goods or services for money or other goods; buying and selling 交易; 贸易; 商业; 买卖: *Since joining the Common Market, Britain's trade with Europe has greatly increased.* 英国自从加入共同市场以来, 与欧洲的贸易大增. ○ *Trade is always good* (ie Many goods are sold) *over the Christmas period.* 圣诞节期间生意一向很好. ○ [attrib 作定语] *a trade agreement* 贸易协定. **(b)** [C] **~ (in sth)** business of a particular kind (某种)行业, 生意: *be in the ˈcotton, ˈfurniture, ˈbook trade*, ie sell or make cotton, furniture, etc 以棉花、家具、书籍生意为业 ○ *The country earns most of its income from the tourist trade.* 这个国家的大部分收入来自旅游业. ○ *The new shop has been doing a brisk trade in cut-price clothes.* 那新商店做减价服装生意一直很兴隆. **2 (a)** [U, C] way of making a living, esp a job that involves making sth; occupation 谋生之道(尤指以制造某物为业); 手艺; 职业: *be a butcher, carpenter, tailor, etc by trade* 做肉商、木匠、裁缝等 ○ *Basket-weaving is a dying* (ie declining) *trade.* 编篮子这一行已逐渐衰落. ○ *The college offers courses in a variety of trades.* 该学院开设多种职业课程. **(b) the trade** [Gp] people or firm engaged in a particular business (做某种生意的)同行的人或商行: *We sell cars to the trade, not to the general public.* 我们向经销商出售汽车, 不卖给一般人. ○ *offer discounts to the trade* 对同行的人给予优惠. ⇨Usage 见所附用法. **3** (idm 习语) **do a roaring trade** ⇨ ROARING (ROAR). **a jack of all trades** ⇨ JACK[1]. **ply one's trade** ⇨ PLY[2]. **the tricks of the trade** ⇨ TRICK.

□ ˈ**trade gap** difference between the value of what a country imports and what it exports 贸易差额.

ˈ**trade mark** **1** registered design or name used to identify a manufacturer's goods (注册的)商标. **2** (*fig* 比喻) distinctive characteristic 明显的特征: *a startling use of line and colour that is this artist's special trade mark* 使用线条和色彩的惊人笔法, 构成这位画家的明显特征.

ˈ**trade name** **1** name given by a manufacturer to a widely available product to identify a particular brand 商品名; 商标名: *Aspirin in various forms is sold under a wide range of trade names.* 阿司匹林以各种商标出售, 五花八门、各式各样. **2** name taken and used by a person or firm for business purposes (商人或商店用的)字号, 商号, 牌号.

ˈ**trade price** price charged by a manufacturer or wholesaler to a retailer 同业售价; 批发价格.

ˌ**trade ˈsecret** **1** device or technique used by a firm in manufacturing its products, etc and kept secret from other firms or the general public 行业秘密. **2** (*fig infml* 比喻, 口) fact, etc that one is not willing to reveal (个人不愿透露的)秘密.

ˈ**tradesman** /-zmən; -zmən/ *n* (*pl* **-men** /-mən; -mən/) **1** person who comes to people's homes to deliver goods 送货人: *the tradesmen's entrance*, ie the side entrance to a large house 送货人入口(大住宅的旁门). **2** shopkeeper 店主; 商人.

ˌ**trade ˈunion** (also ˌ**trades ˈunion**, **union**, *US* ˈ**labor union**) organized association of employees engaged in a particular type of work, formed to protect their interests, improve conditions of work, etc 工会. ˌ**trade-ˈunionism** *n* [U] this system of association 工会制度; 工会主义. ˌ**trade-ˈunionist** *n* member of a trade union 工会会员. ˌ**Trades ˌUnion ˈCongress** (*abbr* 缩写 **TUC**) association of representatives of British trade unions 英国职工大会.

ˈ**trade wind** strong wind continually blowing towards the equator from the SE or the NE 信风; 贸易风.

NOTE ON USAGE 用法: **1 Employment** is formal and official. ☆ **employment** 是庄重的公文用词. It indicates the state of having paid work 这个词指有可获报酬的工作: *The national employment figures are published every month.* 全国就业人数按月公布. ○ *Are you in gainful employment?* ie Do you have a paid job? 你有有报酬的工作吗? ○ *Employment agencies help people to find work.* 职业介绍所可帮助人寻找工作. **2 Occupation** and **job** indicate a particular type of paid work. ☆ **occupation** 和 **job** 指有报酬的某种工作. **Occupation** is more formal and is used additionally of work which may not provide a regular income ☆ **occupation** 一词较文, 还可指不一定有固定收入的工作: *'What's his job?' 'He's a lorry driver, teacher, etc.'* '他做什么工作?' '他是卡车司机、教师等.' ○ *Occupation: Artist*, eg when filling in a form 职业: 画家(如填表格的字样) ○ *Do you get any job satisfaction?* 你能从工作中得到乐趣吗? **3** A **profession** is an occupation which requires higher education and specific training. ☆ **profession** 指需要受过较高深教育和专门训练才能从事的职业. A **trade** requires training and skill with the hands ☆ **trade** 指需要受过训练有手艺的职业: *She's a lawyer by profession.* 她的职业是律师. ○ *He's a carpenter by trade.* 他的职业是木匠.

trade[2] /treɪd; tred/ *v* **1** [I, Ipr] **~ (in sth) (with sb)** engage in trade; buy and sell 做生意; 做买卖: *The firm is trading* (ie doing business) *at a profit/loss.* 这个公司做买卖赚钱[赔钱]. ○ *a company which has ceased trading*, ie gone out of business 已停业的公司 ○ *Britain's trading partners in Europe* 英国在欧洲的贸易伙伴 ○ *a firm which trades in arms, textiles, grain* 经营军火、纺织品、谷物的公司 ○ *ships trading between London and the Far East* 往来于伦敦和远东进行贸易的商船 ○ *an increase in the number of firms trading with Japan* 同日本贸易的公司数目增加. **2** [Ipr] **~ at sth** (*US*) buy goods at (a particular shop) 在(某商店)买东西: *Which store do you trade at?* 你常在哪个商店买东西? **3** [Tn·pr, Dn·n] **~**

(sb) sth for sth exchange sth for sth else; barter sth for sth 用一物交换另一物; 以物易物: *She traded her roller-skates for Billy's portable radio.* 她拿旱冰鞋换了比利的手提收音机. ○ *I'll trade you my stamp collection for your model boat.* 我想用我搜集的邮票换你的模型船. ○ *I wouldn't trade my job for anything*, ie because I enjoy it so much. 我这个工作给我什么都不换. **4** (phr v) **trade sth in (for sth)** give (a used article) to a seller as part of the payment for a new article 用(旧物)贴换新物: *He traded in his car for a new model.* 他把旧汽车折价添钱买了辆新型号的. **trade sth off (against sth)** give sth up (in exchange for sth else) as a compromise 放弃某物作为让步(以换取他物): *The company is prepared to trade off its up-market image against a stronger appeal to teenage buyers.* 该公司拟改变只售高档商品的形象, 以吸引青少年顾客. **trade on sth** (*esp derog* 尤作贬义) make use of sth for one's own advantage 利用某事谋取私利: *You shouldn't trade on her sympathy.* 你不应该利用她的同情心. ○ *He trades on his father's reputation.* 他用他父亲的名誉牟利.

▷ **trader** *n* person who trades; merchant 买卖人; 商人. ⇨Usage at DEALER 用法见 DEALER.

trad·ing *n* [U] doing business; buying and selling 经商; 做买卖; 做生意: *Trading was brisk on the Stock Exchange today.* 今日证券交易所交投活跃.

□ **'trade-in** *n* used article given as part of the payment for a new article (充当部分购货款的)用以折价贴换的旧物: [attrib 作定语] *an old cooker's trade-in value* 一个旧炉具的作价价值.

'trade-off *n* **~ (between sth and sth)** balancing of various factors in order to achieve the best combination; compromise (为获得最佳组合, 对各种因素的)权衡, 协调: *a trade-off between efficiency in use and elegance of design* 使用效能和设计优美两方面的协调一致.

'trading estate (*Brit*) area designed to be occupied by a number of industrial and commercial firms (按规划使用的)工商业区. Cf 参看 INDUSTRIAL ESTATE (INDUSTRIAL).

'trading post = POST[2] 4.

'trading stamp stamp that is given by certain shops, etc to their customers and may be exchanged for goods or cash 交易券(商店等给顾客的赠券, 可换物品或现金).

tra·di·tion /trəˈdɪʃn; trəˋdɪʃən/ *n* **(a)** [U] passing of beliefs or customs from one generation to the next, esp without writing 信仰或风俗的世代相传(尤指无文字记载的); 传统: *By tradition, people play practical jokes on 1 April.* 按照传统风俗, 4月1日可以开恶作剧的玩笑. ○ *They decided to break with* (ie not observe) *tradition.* 他们决定要打破传统. **(b)** [C] belief or custom passed on in this way; any long-established method, practice, etc 传统的信仰和风俗; 长期以来形成的方法、做法等: *It's a tradition to sing 'Auld Lang Syne' on New Year's Eve.* 在除夕唱'美好的往日'是传统风俗. ○ *James Joyce's 'Ulysses' challenged the literary traditions of his day.* 詹姆斯·乔伊斯写的《尤利西斯》打破了他那一时代的文学传统.

▷ **tra·di·tional** /-ʃənl; -ʃənḷ/ *adj* according to or being tradition 按照传统的; 传统的: *It's traditional in England to eat turkey on Christmas Day.* 圣诞节时吃火鸡是英格兰的传统. ○ *country people in their traditional costumes*, ie of a type worn for many centuries 穿着传统服装的乡村居民. **tra·di·tion·al·ism** /-ʃənəlɪzəm; -ʃənḷˌɪzəm/ *n* [U] respect or support for tradition, esp as contrasted with modern or new practices 传统主义(尤指与现代的或新的做法相对). **tra·di·tion·al·ist** /-ʃənəlɪst; -ʃənḷɪst/ *n* person who follows or supports tradition 传统主义者. **tra·di·tion·ally** /-ʃənəlɪ; -ʃənḷɪ/ *adv*: *In England, turkey is traditionally eaten on Christmas Day.* 在英格兰, 圣诞节时按传统要吃火鸡.

tra·duce /trəˈdjuːs; *US* -ˈduːs; trəˋdus/ *v* [Tn] (*fml* 文) say damaging untrue things about (sb/sth); slander or defame 诽谤(某人[某事物]); 诋毁; 中伤. ▷ **tra·ducer** *n*.

traf·fic /ˈtræfɪk; ˋtræfɪk/ *n* [U] **1** vehicles moving along a road or street 往来于街道的车辆; 交通: *heavy/light traffic* 往来车辆很多[不多] ○ *There's usually a lot of traffic at this time of day.* 每天在这段时间往来车辆都很多. ○ *Traffic was brought to a standstill by the accident.* 出了事故以后, 交通陷于停顿. ○ *London-bound traffic is being diverted via Slough.* 开往伦敦的车辆现绕道经过斯劳. ○ [attrib 作定语] *a traffic accident* 交通事故. **2** movement of ships or aircraft along a route (船只或飞机沿航线的)航行: *cross-channel traffic*, ie ships crossing the English Channel 横渡英吉利海峡的船只 ○ [attrib 作定语] *a threatened strike by air-traffic controllers* 航空调度员扬言要进行的罢工. **3** number of people or amount of goods moved from one place to another by road, rail, sea or air (公路、铁路、海上或空中人员或货物的)流量: *an increase in freight/goods/passenger traffic* 货运[货运/客运]量的增加 ○ *the profitable North Atlantic traffic* 有利可图的北大西洋运输业务. **4 ~ (in sth)** illegal or immoral trading 非法的或不道德的买卖: *the traffic in drugs/arms/stolen goods* 毒品[武器/赃物]的非法交易 ○ *the ˌwhite 'slave traffic* 将妇女卖为娼妓的勾当.

▷ **traf·fic** *v* (-ck-) [I, Ipr] **~ (in sth)** trade, esp illegally or immorally 买卖(尤指在非法的或不道德的事物方面): *drug trafficking* 毒品买卖 ○ *He trafficked in illicit liquor.* 他做过买卖私酒的生意. **traf·ficker** *n*.

□ **'traffic circle** (*US*) = ROUNDABOUT.

'traffic indicator = TRAFFICATOR.

'traffic island (also **island**, **refuge**, **safety island**, *US* **safety zone**) raised area in the middle of a road dividing two streams of traffic, esp for use by pedestrians when crossing the road 交通岛, 安全岛(道路中间分隔两股车辆的平台, 尤为行人过路用的).

'traffic jam situation in which vehicles cannot move freely and traffic comes to a standstill 交通阻塞.

'traffic-light (also **'stoplight**) *n* (usu *pl* 通常作复数) automatic signal that controls road traffic, esp at junctions, by means of red, yellow and green lights 交通信号灯.

'traffic warden official whose job is to make sure that people do not park their vehicles illegally, and to report on those who do (处理违章停车的)交通管理员.

traf·fic·ator /ˈtræfɪkeɪtə(r); ˋtræfɪˌketɚ/ *n* (also **'traffic indicator**) flashing light or other device on a vehicle, used to show the direction in which it is about to turn (车辆上的)方向灯, 方向指示器.

tra·gedy /ˈtrædʒədɪ; ˋtrædʒədɪ/ *n* **1** [C, U] terrible event that causes great sadness 悲惨的事: *Investigators are searching the wreckage of the plane to try and find the cause of the tragedy.* 调查人员在飞机残骸中搜索, 希望找出造成这一悲惨事件的原因. ○ *a life blighted by tragedy* 饱经惨事折磨的一生 ○ (*fig* 比喻) *It's a tragedy* (ie extremely regrettable) *for this country that he never became prime minister.* 他从未当上首相, 这是国家的极大不幸. **2 (a)** [C] serious play with a sad ending 悲剧: *Shakespeare's tragedies and comedies* 莎士比亚的悲剧和喜剧. **(b)** [U] branch of drama that consists of such plays 悲剧艺术: *classical French tragedy* 法国的古典悲剧艺术. Cf 参看 COMEDY.

▷ **tra·gedian** /trəˈdʒiːdɪən; trəˋdʒidɪən/ *n* **1** writer of tragedies 悲剧作家. **2** actor in tragedy 悲剧演员.

tra·gedi·enne /trəˌdʒiːdɪˈen; trəˌdʒidɪˋɛn/ *n* actress in tragedy 悲剧女演员.

tra·gic /ˈtrædʒɪk; ˋtrædʒɪk/ *adj* **1** causing great sadness, esp because extremely unfortunate or having terrible consequences 悲惨的; 悲痛的; 可悲的: *a tragic accident, mistake, loss* 可悲的事故、错误、损失 ○ *Hers is a tragic story.* 她的经历十分悲惨. ○ *The effect of the pollution on the beaches is absolutely tragic.* 污染海滩后果可悲. ○ *It's tragic that he died so young.* 他英年早逝令人悲哀. **2** [attrib 作定语] of or in the style of tragedy 悲剧的; 悲剧风格的: *one of our finest tragic actors* 我们的最优秀的一个悲剧演员. ▷ **tra·gic·ally** /-klɪ; -klɪ/ *adv*: *her tragically short life* 她短暂得可悲的一生.

tra·gi·com·edy /ˌtrædʒɪˈkɒmədɪ; ˌtrædʒɪˋkɑmədɪ/ *n* [C, U] (type of) play with both tragic and comic elements 悲喜剧(体裁). ▷ **tra·gi·comic** /-ˈkɒmɪk; -ˋkɑmɪk/ *adj*.

trail /treɪl; trel/ *n* **1** mark or sign in the form of a long line left by sth or sb passing by 痕迹; 足迹; 踪迹: *vapour trails*, eg those left in the sky by high-flying aircraft 蒸汽尾迹(如飞机在高空飞行留下的) ○ *The hurricane left a trail of destruction behind it.* 飓风过后满目疮痍. ○ *tourists who leave a trail of litter everywhere they go* 一路走一路乱扔垃圾的游客. **2** path, esp through rough country 小路(尤指穿过不平坦的郊野的): *a trail through the forest* 穿过森林的小路 ○ *a 'nature trail* 穿过郊野的小路. **3** track or scent followed in hunting (打猎或追踪时搜寻的)痕迹, 臭迹: *The police are on the escaped*

T

convict's trail, ie are pursuing him. 警方正在追捕逃犯. **4** (idm 习语) **blaze a trail** ⇨ BLAZE[3]. **hit the trail** ⇨ HIT[1]. **hot on sb's tracks/trail**; **hot on the trail** ⇨ HOT.

▷ **trail** *v* **1** [I, Ipr, Ip, Tn, Tn·pr, Tn·p] (cause sth to) be dragged behind (使某物)被拖在后面: *Her long skirt was trailing along/on the floor.* 她的长裙拖在地板上. ○ *a bird trailing a broken wing* 耷拉着一个断翅的鸟 ○ *I trailed my hand in the water as the boat drifted along.* 小船漂流向前, 我把手伸进水里让它拖着走. ⇨Usage at PULL[2] 用法见PULL[2]. **2** [Ipr, Ip] **~ along behind (sb/sth), etc** walk or move wearily, esp behind or later than others 疲惫地走或磨蹭(尤指跟在或落在后面): *The tired children trailed along behind their parents.* 孩子们累了, 没精打采地跟在父母后面. ○ *The horse I had backed trailed in last.* 我下赌注的那匹马落在后面, 跑了个倒数第一. ○ (*fig* 比喻) *This country is still trailing far behind (others) in computer research.* 这个国家的计算机研究工作远远落后(他国). **3** [I, Ipr] **~ (by/in sth)** (usu in the continuous tenses 通常用于进行时态) be losing a game or some other contest (在比赛、竞赛等中)输, 失败, 失利: *trailing by two goals to one at half-time* 上半场以二比一落后 ○ *The party is trailing badly in the opinion polls.* 该党在民意测验中大大失利. **4** [Ipr] (of plants) grow randomly over a surface, downwards or along the ground with long winding stems (指植物)蔓生, 蔓延: *roses trailing over the walls* 蔓生在墙上的蔷薇. **5** [Tn, Tn·pr] **~ sb/sth (to sth)** follow the trail of sb/sth; track sb/sth 追踪或尾随某人[某事物]: *trail a criminal, a wild animal* 追踪罪犯、野兽. **6** (phr v) **trail away/off** (of sb's speech) gradually become quieter and then stop, esp because of shyness, confusion, etc (指某人说话)声音逐渐减弱到不出声(尤指因害羞、慌乱等所致).

□ **'trail-blazer** *n* person who does sth new or original; pioneer 创新者; 创始人; 先驱. **'trail-blazing** *adj* [usu attrib 通常作定语] (*approv* 褒) pioneering 先驱的; 首创的: *a trail-blazing scientific discovery* 创新的科学发现.

T

trailer /ˈtreɪlə(r); ˋtrelɚ/ *n* **1 (a)** truck or other wheeled container pulled by another vehicle 拖车; 挂车: *They packed the food and camping equipment in the trailer.* 他们把食物和野营用具都装上拖车上了. **(b)** (*esp US*) = CARAVAN. **2** series of short extracts from a film or TV programme, shown in advance to advertise it (电影或电视节目的)预告片.

train[1] /treɪn; tren/ *n* **1** railway engine with several carriages or trucks linked to and pulled by it 列车; 火车: *a ˈpassenger/ˈgoods/ˈfreight train* 一列客车[货车] ○ *ˈexpress/ˈstopping trains* 快[慢]车 ○ *I normally catch/take/get the 7.15 train to London.* 我一般乘7点15分的火车去伦敦. ○ *get on/off a train* 上[下]火车 ○ *You have to change trains at Didcot.* 你需在迪德科特倒车. ○ *If you miss the train there's another an hour later.* 你要是赶不上这趟火车, 一小时后还有一趟. ○ *Travelling by train is more relaxing than driving.* 乘火车旅行比开汽车轻松得多. ○ [attrib 作定语] *a ˈtrain driver* 火车司机. **2** number of people or animals, etc moving in a line 鱼贯而行的人、动物等: *a ˈcamel train* 骆驼队 ○ *the ˈbaggage train*, ie people and animals transporting luggage 运输行李的人和役畜的队伍. **3** group of people who follow sb around; retinue 追随某人的人群; 随员: *The pop star was followed by a train of admirers.* 那位流行歌曲歌星周围蜂拥着许多歌迷. **4** (usu *sing* 通常作单数) **~ (of sth)** sequence of connected events, thoughts, etc 一系列相关的事情、想法等: *His telephone call interrupted my train of thought.* 他的电话打断了我的思路. ○ *The military coup brought dire consequences in its train*, ie as a result of it. 这次军事政变后患无穷. **5** part of a long dress or robe that trails on the ground behind the wearer 长的衣、袍、裙等拖在地上的部分. **6** (idm 习语) **in train** (*fml* 文) being prepared 准备妥当: *Arrangements for the ceremony have been put in train.* 典礼的各项安排都已就绪.

□ **'train-bearer** *n* attendant who holds up the train[1](5) of sb's dress or robe 为他人挽着衣、袍、裙等拖地部分的人.

'trainman /-mən; -mən/ *n* (*pl* **-men** /-mən; -mən/) (*US*) member of the crew operating a railway train 列车员.

'train set toy consisting of a model train which runs on a model track 模型铁路(包括铁轨、列车在内的成套玩具).

'train-spotter *n* person who collects the numbers of railway locomotives he has seen, as a hobby 搜集自己见过的机车号码的人(作为爱好).

train[2] /treɪn; tren/ *v* **1 (a)** [Tn, Tn·pr, Cn·n/a, Cn·t] **~ sb (as sth/in sth)** bring (a person or an animal) to a desired standard of efficiency, behaviour, etc by instruction and practice 培养, 训练(某人或某动物): *There is a shortage of trained nurses.* 受过正规训练的护士十分缺乏. ○ *He was trained as an engineer/in engineering.* 他受过担任工程师的[工程学方面的]培训. ○ *I've trained my dog to fetch my slippers.* 我把狗训练得能给我叼拖鞋. ⇨Usage at TEACH 用法见 TEACH. **(b)** [I, Ipr, It] **~ (as sth/in sth)** undergo such a process 受训练或培养: *She trained for a year as a secretary.* 她受过一年做秘书的培训. ○ *He trained to be a lawyer.* 他受过做律师的训练. **2** [I, Ipr, Tn, Tn·pr] **~ (sb/sth) (for sth)** (cause a person or an animal to) become physically fit by exercise and diet (使人或动物通过锻炼及调理饮食)身体健康: *The challenger has been training hard for the big fight.* 这位健将为参加拳击大赛夺魁而进行坚苦的锻炼. ○ *train a horse for a race* 训练马参加比赛. **3** [Tn·pr] **~ sth on sb/sth** point or aim (a gun, camera, etc) at sb/sth 将(枪、照相机等)对准或瞄准某人[某物]: *He trained his binoculars on the distant figures.* 他把双筒望远镜对准远处的景物. **4** [Tn, Tn·pr] cause (a plant) to grow in a required direction 使(植物)朝某方向生长; 整枝: *train roses against/along/over/up a wall* 使蔷薇靠着[沿着/爬过/爬上]墙生长.

▷ **trainee** /treɪˈniː; trenˋi/ *n* person being trained for a job, etc 接受训练的人: [attrib 作定语] *a trainee salesman* 实习售货员.

trainer *n* **1** person who trains (esp athletes, sportsmen, racehorses, circus animals, etc) 训练人或动物的人; (尤指)教练员、驯马师、驯兽师等. **2** aircraft (or device that behaves like an aircraft) used for training pilots 教练机; 飞行练习器. **3** (usu *pl* 通常作复数) (also **'training shoe**) soft rubber-soled shoe worn by athletes while exercising, or as casual footwear (运动员训练时或平时穿的)软胶底鞋, 运动鞋: *a pair of trainers* 一双运动鞋.

train·ing *n* [U] process of preparing or being prepared for a sport or job 训练; 受训: *He mustn't drink beer; he's in strict training for his next fight.* 他不能喝啤酒, 他正在为下次比赛进行严格训练. **'training-college** *n* (*Brit*) college that trains people for a trade or profession 专科学校; 职业学院.

traipse /treɪps; treps/ *v* [Ipr, Ip] (*infml* 口) walk wearily; trudge 疲惫地走; 拖着脚步走: *We spent the afternoon traipsing from one shop to another.* 我们用了一下午的时间逛商店, 疲惫不堪地逛了一家又一家.

trait /treɪt; *also, in British use,* 英式英语读作 treɪ; tret/ *n* element in sb's personality; distinguishing characteristic 人的个性; 显著的特点; 特征: *One of his less attractive traits is criticizing his wife in public.* 他有个不大讨人喜欢的特点, 就是爱当众责备妻子.

traitor /ˈtreɪtə(r); ˋtretɚ/ *n* **~ (to sb/sth)** **1** person who betrays a friend, his country, a cause, etc 背叛者; 卖国贼; 叛徒: *He's a traitor to himself*, ie has acted against his own principles. 他背叛了自己的信条. **2** (idm 习语) ˌ**turn ˈtraitor** become a traitor 成为叛徒.

▷ **trait·or·ous** /ˈtreɪtərəs; ˋtretərəs/ *adj* (*fml* 文) of or like a traitor; treacherous (似)叛徒的; 背叛的: *traitorous conduct* 背叛行为.

tra·ject·ory /trəˈdʒektərɪ; trəˈdʒɛktərɪ/ *n* curved path of sth that has been fired, hit or thrown into the air, eg a missile (抛射体, 如导弹的)弹道, 轨迹, 轨道: *a bullet's trajectory* 子弹的弹道.

tram /træm; træm/ (also **tram·car** /ˈtræmkɑː(r); ˋtræmˌkɑr/, *US* **'streetcar, trolley**) *n* public passenger vehicle, usu driven by electricity, running on rails laid along the streets of a town (有轨的)电车.

□ **'tramlines** *n* [pl] **1** rails for a tram 电车轨道. **2** (*infml* 口) pair of parallel lines on a tennis court marking the additional area used when playing doubles (网球双打时)球场两侧的加线. ⇨illus at TENNIS 见 TENNIS 插图.

tram·mel /ˈtræml; ˋtræml̩/ *v* (**-ll-**; *US* **-l-**) [Tn esp passive

尤用于被动语态] (*fml or rhet* 文或修辞) take away the freedom of action of (sb); hamper; impede 限制(某人)行动自由; 束缚; 阻碍; 妨碍: *No longer trammelled by his responsibilities as chairman, he could say what he wished.* 他不当董事长就不受职务约束了, 想说什么就说什么.

▷ **tram·mels** *n* [pl] (*fml or rhet* 文或修辞) things that limit or impede one's freedom to move, act, etc 形成阻碍或束缚的事物: *the trammels of routine, convention, superstition* 常规、惯例、迷信的束缚.

tramp /træmp; træmp/ *v* **1** [Ipr, Ip] walk with heavy or noisy steps 重踏步行走; 跺着脚行走: *We could hear him tramping about upstairs* 我们可以听见他在楼上噔噔地走来走去. ○ *They came tramping through the kitchen leaving dirty footmarks.* 他们重踏着脚步穿过厨房走来, 留下了肮脏的脚印. **2** [Ipr, Ip, In/pr, Tn] travel across (an area) on foot, esp for a long distance and often wearily 步行经过(一地区)(尤指长途且疲惫不堪): *tramping over the moors* 徒步越过高沼地 ○ *We tramped (for) miles and miles without finding anywhere to stay.* 我们走啊走啊, 始终找不到个栖身之处. ○ *tramp the streets looking for work* 在街上来回奔走寻找工作. ⇨Usage at STUMP 用法见STUMP.

▷ **tramp** *n* **1** [C] person with no fixed home or occupation who wanders from place to place; vagrant 无家无业到处流浪的人; 流浪者. **2** [C usu *sing* 通常作单数] long walk 长途步行: *go for a solitary tramp in the country* 独自在郊野远足. **3** [sing] **the ~ of sb/sth** sound of heavy footsteps 沉重的脚步声: *the tramp of marching soldiers/of soldiers' marching feet* 行军士兵的[士兵行军的]重踏步声. **4** [C] (also 'tramp steamer) cargo ship that does not travel on a regular route but carries cargo between many different ports 航线不定但停靠许多港口的货船. **5** [C] (*dated sl derog* 旧, 俚, 贬) sexually immoral woman 婊子; 荡妇.

trample /'træmpl; 'træmpl̩/ *v* **1** [Tn, Tn·pr, Tn·p] **~ sth/sb (down)** tread heavily on sth/sb so as to cause damage or destruction 踩坏或踩伤某物[某人]: *The campers had trampled the corn (down).* 野营的人踩坏了庄稼. ○ *The crowd panicked and ten people were trampled to death.* 人群惊慌失措, 踩死了十个人. **2** [Ipr] **~ on sth/sb** (**a**) crush or harm sth by treading on it 踩碎、踩坏或踩伤某物: *trample on sb's toes* 踩着某人的脚趾. (**b**) (*fig* 比喻) disregard sb unfeelingly or contemptuously 无视或蔑视某人: *trample on sb's feelings/rights* 伤害某人的感情[侵犯某人的权利] ○ *I refuse to be trampled on any longer!* 别人要再小看我那可不行! **3** [Ipr, Ip] walk with heavy or crushing steps 重踏步行走或踩过: *I don't want all those people trampling about all over my flower beds.* 我可不能让那些人都在我的花坛里到处乱踩.

tram·po·line /'træmpəli:n; 'træmpəlin/ *n* sheet of strong fabric attached by springs to a frame, used by gymnasts for jumping high into the air to do somersaults, etc 蹦床, 弹床(体操器械).

▷ **tram·po·line** *v* [I] use a trampoline 在蹦床上弹跳: *enjoy trampolining* 玩跳蹦床游戏.

trance /trɑ:ns; *US* træns; træns/ *n* **1** sleep-like state, caused eg by being hypnotized 昏睡状态; 催眠状态: *go/fall into a trance* 进入[陷入]昏睡状态 ○ *put/send sb into a trance* 使某人进入昏睡状态 ○ *come out of a trance* 从昏睡状态中醒来. **2** dreamy state in which one concentrates on one's thoughts and does not notice what is happening around one 出神; 发呆: *She's been in a trance all day — I think she's in love.* 她整天发愣 —— 我看她是陷入情网了.

tran·quil /'træŋkwɪl; 'træŋkwɪl/ *adj* calm, quiet and undisturbed 平静的; 安静的; 安宁的: *lead a tranquil life in the country* 在乡间过着宁静的生活.

▷ **tran·quil·lity** (*US* also **tran·quil·ity**) /træŋ'kwɪlətɪ; træŋ'kwɪlətɪ/ *n* [U] tranquil condition 平静; 安静; 安宁.

tran·quil·lize (*US* also **tran·quil·ize**), **-ise** /-aɪz; -aɪz/ *v* [Tn] make (a person or an animal) calmer or sleepy, esp by means of a drug 使(人或动物)安静或入睡(尤指用药物): *The game wardens tranquillized the rhinoceros with a drugged dart.* 猎物保护区管理员用麻醉射器让犀牛静了下来. ○ *the tranqullizing effect of gentle music* 轻柔的音乐具有的安眠作用. **tran·quil·lizer** (*US* also **tran·quil·izer**), **-iser** *n* drug for making an anxious person feel calm; sedative 安定药; 镇静剂: *She's on* (ie is taking) *tranquillizers.* 她经常使用镇静剂.

tran·quilly *adv*.

trans *abbr* 缩写 = translated (by).

trans- *pref* 前缀 **1** (with *adjs* 与形容词连用) across; beyond 横穿; 通过; 超越: *transatlantic* ○ *trans-Siberian*. **2** (with *vs* 与动词连用) into another place or state 进入另一处或另一状态: *transplant* ○ *transform*.

trans·act /træn'zækt; trænz'ækt/ *v* [Tn, Tn·pr] **~ sth (with sb)** (*fml* 文) conduct or carry out (business), esp between two people 办理或处理(事务)(尤指在两人之间): *This sort of business can only be transacted in private.* 这种事情只能私下处理.

trans·ac·tion /træn'zækʃn; trænz'ækʃən/ *n* **1** [U] **~ (of sth)** transacting 办理; 处理: *the transaction of business* 处理事务. **2** [C] piece of business transacted 业务; 交易: *Payments by cheque easily outnumber cash transactions.* 用支票付款在数量上大大超过现金交易. ○ *transactions on the Stock Exchange* 证券交易所的业务. **3 transactions** [pl] (record of the) lectures and discussions held at the meetings of an academic society (学术团体的)报告会, 讨论会, 会议记录, 公报: *the transactions of the Kent Archaeological Society* 肯特考古学会的会刊.

trans·at·lantic /ˌtrænzət'læntɪk; ˌtrænzət'læntɪk/ *adj* [esp attrib 尤作定语] **1** on or from the other side of the Atlantic 在(或来自)大西洋彼岸的: *The President affirmed America's commitment to its transatlantic* (ie European) *allies.* 总统申明美国履行对其欧洲盟国承担的义务. ○ *Two years in New York have left him with a transatlantic* (ie American) *accent.* 他在纽约住了两年就带上了美国口音. **2** crossing the Atlantic 横越大西洋的: *a transatlantic flight, voyage, telephone call* 横越大西洋的飞行、横渡大西洋的航行、大西洋的越洋电话. **3** concerning countries on both sides of the Atlantic 涉及大西洋两岸国家的: *a transatlantic trade agreement* 大西洋两岸国家的贸易协定.

tran·scend /træn'send; træn'sɛnd/ *v* (*fml* 文) **1** [Tn] be or go beyond the range of (human experience, belief, powers of description, etc) 超出或超越(经验、信念、描写能力等)的范围: *Such matters transcend man's knowledge*, ie We cannot know about them. 这些问题人类是无法了解的. **2** [Tn, Tn·pr] **~ sb/sth (in sth)** be much better or greater than sb/sth; surpass 优于或胜过某人[某事物]: *She far transcends the others in beauty and intelligence.* 她才貌出众.

tran·scend·ent /træn'sendənt; træn'sɛndənt/ *adj* [usu attrib 通常作定语] (*fml approv* 文, 褒) extremely great; supreme 卓越的; 至高无上的: *a writer of transcendent genius* 杰出的天才作家. ▷ **tran·scend·ence** /-dəns; -dəns/, **tran·scend·ency** /-dənsɪ; -dənsɪ/ *ns* [U].

tran·scend·ental /ˌtrænsen'dentl; ˌtrænsɛn'dɛntl̩/ *adj* [usu attrib 通常作定语] going beyond the limits of human knowledge, experience or reason, esp in a mystical or religious way 超出人类知识、经验或理性的(尤指有神秘或宗教色彩的); 玄奥的; 先验的: *Gazing at that majestic painting was for me an almost transcendental experience.* 我凝视着那幅气势磅礴的画, 一种堪称超凡的感受油然而生. Cf 参看 EMPIRICAL.

▷ **tran·scend·ent·al·ism** /ˌtrænsen'dentəlɪzəm; ˌtrænsɛn'dɛntl̩ˌɪzəm/ *n* [U] philosophy that stresses belief in transcendental things and the importance of spiritual rather than material existence 先验论(一种哲学观点, 相信超凡的事物, 认为精神存在比物质存在更重要). **tran·scend·ent·al·ist** /-təlɪst; -tl̩ɪst/ *n* believer in transcendentalism 先验论者.

tran·scend·ent·ally /-təlɪ; -tl̩ɪ/ *adv*.

□ ˌ**transcendental medi'tation** technique of meditation and relaxation that originates in Hinduism and involves repeating a special phrase to oneself over and over again 超在禅定法(念诵梵文真言松心缓性法, 源于印度教).

trans·con·tin·ental /ˌtrænzkɒntɪ'nentl; ˌtrænskɑntə'nɛntl̩/ *adj* crossing a continent 横贯大陆的: *a transcontinental highway, flight, journey* 穿越大陆的公路、飞行、旅行.

tran·scribe /træn'skraɪb; træn'skraɪb/ *v* **1** [Tn, Tn·pr] **~ sth (into sth)** copy sth in writing 抄写、誊写或用打字机打印某物: *She jotted down a few notes, and later transcribed them into an exercise book.* 她草草做了些笔记, 然后誊写在练习本上. **2** [Tn, Cn·n, Cn·n/a] **~sth (as sth)** represent (a sound) by means of a phonetic symbol 用音标标出(声音): *In this dictionary, the last vowel of 'transcendent' is transcribed (as)* /ə; ə/. 在本词典中, transcendent一词最后一个元音标作/ə/. **3** [Tn, Tn·pr] **~ sth (for sth)** rewrite (music) so that it can be played on a different instrument, sung by a different voice, etc 改编(乐曲)(以适应他种乐器或声部): *a piano piece transcribed for the guitar* 改编成用吉他演奏的钢琴曲. **4** [Tn, Tn·pr] **~ sth (on/onto sth)** copy recorded sound using a different recording medium (用不同的录音手段)转录, 复制: *a performance now transcribed onto compact disc* 现已制成激光唱片的一次演出.

▷ **tran·script** /ˈtrænskrɪpt; ˋtræn,skrɪpt/ *n* **1** written or recorded copy of what has been said or written 抄本; 誊本; 打字本; 副本: *a transcript of the trial* 审讯记录的文字本. **2** (*US*) copy of an official record of a student's work, showing courses taken and grades achieved 学生成绩报告单.

tran·scrip·tion /trænˈskrɪpʃn; trænˋskrɪpʃən/ *n* **1** [U] action or process of transcribing 抄写; 誊写; (打字机的)打印: *errors made in transcription* 抄写中的错误. **2** [C] (**a**) transcript 抄本; 誊本; 打字本; 副本. (**b**) representation of speech sounds in writing 语音的标注; 注音; 音标: *a phonetic transcription of what they said* 用音标写出的他们谈话的内容. **3** [U] recording of radio or TV programmes for later broadcast (广播或电视节目的)预制(以备到时播放): [attrib 作定语] *the BBC transcription service* 英国广播公司录音节目的播放.

tran·sept /ˈtrænsept; ˋtrænsɛpt/ *n* (*architecture* 建) (either end of the) part of a cross-shaped church which is built at right angles to the main central part (the *nave*) (十字形平面式教堂的)耳堂: *the north/south transept of the cathedral* 大教堂的北[南]耳堂. ⇨illus at App 1 见附录1插图, page viii.

trans·fer[1] /trænsˈfɜː(r); trænsˋfɝ/ *v* (**-rr-**) **1** [Tn, Tn·pr] **~ sth/sb (from ...) (to ...)** move sth/sb from one place to another 将某物[某人]由一处转移到另一处: *The head office has been transferred from London to Cardiff.* 总部已由伦敦迁至加的夫. ○ *She's being transferred to our Paris branch.* 她已调到我们在巴黎的分部. ○ (*fig* 比喻) *transfer one's affections/one's allegiance*, ie become fond of/loyal to sb else 转移爱心[忠诚](至另一对象). **2** [Tn, Tn·pr] **~ sth (from sb) (to sb)** hand over the possession of (property, etc) 转让(财产等): *transfer rights to sb* 把权利让与某人. **3** [Tn, Tn·pr] **~ sth (from sth) (to sth)** copy (recorded material) using a different recording or storage medium (用不同的录制或存储手段)转录或转存(资料): *transfer computer data from disk to tape* 把计算机资料由磁盘转录到磁带上. **4** [I, Ipr] **~ (from ...) (to ...)** (**a**) change to another place, group, occupation, etc 调动; 调任: *He has transferred from the warehouse to the accounts office.* 他已由仓库调到会计室任职. (**b**) change to another route, means of transport, etc during a journey (旅途中)改变路线、交通工具等; 转乘; 换乘: *We had to transfer from Gatwick to Heathrow to catch a plane to Belfast.* 我们得从盖特威克机场转到希思罗机场好赶上飞往贝尔法斯特的班机.

▷ **trans·fer·able** /-ˈfɜːrəbl; -ˋfɝəbl̩/ *adj* that can be transferred 可转移的; 可转让的; 可转录的; 可调动的; 可中转的: *This ticket is not transferable*, ie may only be used by the person to whom it is issued. 此票不得转让.

trans·fer·ab·il·ity /ˌtrænsˌfɜːrəˈbɪlətɪ; ˌtrænsfɝəˋbɪlətɪ/ *n* [U].

trans·fer·ence /ˈtrænsfərəns; *US* trænsˈfɜːrəns; trænsˋfɝəns/, **trans·fer·ral** (*US* also **trans·feral**) /trænsˈfɜːrəl; trænsˋfɝəl/ *ns* [U] transferring or being transferred 转移; 迁移; 转让; 转录; 调动; 中转: *the transference of heat from one body to another* 热量由一个物体到另一个物体的传导 ○ *the transferral of power to a civilian government* 权力向文官政府的移交.

trans·fer[2] /ˈtrænsfɜː(r); ˋtrænsfɝ/ *n* **1** [C, U] (instance of) transferring or being transferred 转移; 转让; 转录; 调动: *The club's goalkeeper isn't happy here, and has asked for a transfer (to another club).* 该足球俱乐部的守门员在此不愉快, 已要求转到其他俱乐部. ○ *the transfer of currency from one country to another* 货币由一国向另一国的汇兑. **2** (**a**) [U] changing to a different vehicle, route, etc during a journey (旅途中的)中转, 换乘, 改变路线: [attrib 作定语] *Would all transfer passengers please report to the airport transfer desk.* 凡需中转的旅客请到机场的中转服务台办理手续. (**b**) [C] (*esp US*) ticket that allows a passenger to continue his journey on another bus, etc 换乘票(可中途换乘另一公共汽车等的票). **3** [C] (*esp Brit*) decorative picture or design that is or can be removed from (usu) a piece of paper and stuck onto another surface by being pressed, heated, etc 移印图案(供转印的装饰画或图案, 通常附于纸上, 可用加压、加热等方法转印到他物上).

□ ˈ**transfer fee** amount of money paid for a transfer, esp of a professional footballer to another club 转让费; (尤指职业足球运动员的)转会费.

ˈ**transfer list** list of professional footballers who are available for transfer to other clubs 可以转会的职业足球运动员名单.

trans·fig·ure /trænsˈfɪgə(r); *US* -gjər; trænsˋfɪgjɚ/ *v* [Tn] (*fml* 文) change the appearance of (sb/sth), esp so as to make him/it nobler or more beautiful 改变(某人[某物])的外表(尤指改好): *Her face was transfigured by happiness.* 她高兴得容光焕发.

▷ **trans·fig·ura·tion** /ˌtrænsfɪgəˈreɪʃn; *US* -gjəˈr-; ˌtrænsfɪgjəˋreʃən/ *n* **1** [U, C] (*fml* 文) change of this sort 变形; 改观. **2 the Transfiguration** [sing] Christian festival (6 August) commemorating the moment when Christ appeared before three of his disciples in a mystically changed form 主显圣容节(基督教节日, 在8月6日, 纪念基督在三个门徒前面貌的改变).

trans·fix /trænsˈfɪks; trænsˋfɪks/ *v* (*fml* 文) **1** [esp passive 尤用于被动语态: Tn, Tn·pr] **~ sth/sb (with/on sth)** stick sth pointed completely through sth/sb 用某物刺穿某物[某人]: *a fish transfixed with a harpoon* 用鱼叉叉穿的鱼. **2** [usu passive 通常用于被动语态: Tn, Tn·pr] **~ sb (with sth)** make sb unable to move, think or speak because of fear, astonishment, etc 使某人(因恐惧、惊愕等)不能动弹、思想或说话: *He stood staring at the ghost, transfixed with terror.* 他站在那里看着那个鬼, 吓得不能动弹.

trans·form /trænsˈfɔːm; trænsˋfɔrm/ *v* [Tn, Tn·pr] **~ sth/sb (from sth) (into sth)** completely change the appearance or character of sth/sb 完全改变某事物[某人]的外观或特性: *A fresh coat of paint can transform a room.* 房间重新粉刷一遍可大为改观. ○ *She used to be terribly shy, but a year abroad has completely transformed her*, ie so that she is no longer shy. 她过去十分腼腆, 但在国外呆了一年以后完全变了. ○ *a complete change of climate which transformed the area from a desert into a swamp* 使该地区由沙漠变为沼泽的气候的彻底改变 ○ *the process by which caterpillars are transformed into butterflies* 毛虫变为蝴蝶的过程.

▷ **trans·form·able** /-əbl; -əbl̩/ *adj* that can be transformed 可改变外观或性质的.

trans·forma·tion /ˌtrænsfəˈmeɪʃn; ˌtrænsfɚˋmeʃən/ *n* [C, U] (instance of) transforming or being transformed (外观或性质的)改变, 改观, 转变: *His character seems to have undergone a complete transformation since his marriage.* 他结婚之后性格判若两人.

trans·former *n* apparatus for increasing or reducing the voltage of an electric power supply, to allow a particular piece of electrical equipment to be used 变压器.

trans·fu·sion /trænsˈfjuːʒn; trænsˋfjuʒən/ *n* [C, U] act or process of putting one person's blood into another person's body 输血: *The injured man had lost a lot of blood and had to be given a transfusion.* 那个受伤的男子失血过多, 必须进行输血.

trans·gress /trænzˈgres; trænzˋgrɛs/ *v* **1** [Tn] (*fml* 文) go beyond (the limit of what is morally or legally acceptable) 超出(道德或法律的限度); 违反(法律); 违背(道德): *transgress the bounds of decency* 逾矩. **2** [I, Ipr] **~ (against sth)** (*dated* 旧) offend against a moral principle; sin 违反道德准则; 违犯戒律.

▷ **trans·gres·sion** /trænzˈgreʃn; trænzˋgrɛʃən/ *n* (*fml* 文) (**a**) [U] transgressing 违法; 违反道德; 违犯戒律. (**b**) [C] instance of this; sin 违法; 违反道德; 违犯戒律.

trans·gres·sor *n* (*fml* 文) person who transgresses; sinner 违法的人; 违反道德或违犯戒律的人.

tran·si·ent /ˈtrænzɪənt; *US* ˈtrænʃnt; ˋtrænʃənt/ *adj* lasting for only a short time; brief; fleeting 短暂的; 片刻的; 转瞬即逝的: *transient success* 一时的成功 ○ *Their happiness was to be sadly transient.* 他们的幸福可惜是短

暂的. Cf 参看 TRANSITORY.
▷ **tran·si·ence** /-əns; -əns/, **tran·si·ency** /-nsɪ; -nsɪ/ *ns* [U]: *the transience of human life* 人生之短暂.
tran·si·ent *n* person who stays or works in a place for a short time only, before moving on 仅短暂在某地停留或工作的人: [attrib 作定语] *a transient population* 流动人口.

tran·sis·tor /træn'zɪstə(r), -'sɪst-; træn'zɪstə˞, -'sɪst-/ *n* **1** small electronic device used in radios, televisions, etc for controlling an electrical signal as it passes along a circuit 晶体管. **2** (also ˌ**transistor 'radio**) portable radio with transistors 晶体管收音机.
▷ **tran·sist·or·ized, -ised** /-təraɪzd; -təˌraɪzd/ *adj* equipped with transistors 装有晶体管的.

transit /'trænzɪt, -sɪt; 'trænzɪt, -sɪt/ *n* **1** [U] process of going or being taken or transported from one place to another 搬运; 载运; 运输: *goods delayed or lost in transit* 在运输中延误或遗失的货物 ○ [attrib 作定语] *an urban rapid-transit system* 城市高速运输系统. **2** [C, U] (*astronomy* 天) movement of one object in space (eg a planet) between another and an observer, so that the first seems to pass across the surface of the second 宇宙中一天体(如一行星)运行到另一天体与观察者之间, 使前者如同经过后者之表面; 凌日: *observe the transit of Venus*, eg across the sun 观测金星之凌日.
□ **'transit camp** camp providing temporary accommodation for refugees, soldiers, etc (难民、士兵等的)临时宿营地.
'transit visa visa allowing a person to pass through a country but not to stay there 过境签证(允许过境而不许停留).

trans·ition /træn'zɪʃn; træn'zɪʃən/ *n* [C, U] **~ (from sth) (to sth)** (instance of) changing from one state or condition to another 过渡; 转变; 变迁: *the transition from childhood to adult life* 从童年到成年的过渡阶段 ○ *a period of transition* 过渡时期 ○ *His attitude underwent an abrupt transition*, ie changed suddenly. 他的态度突然改变了. ▷ **trans·itional** /-ʃənl; -ʃənḷ/ *adj*: *a transitional stage* 过渡阶段 ○ *a transitional government*, ie one holding power temporarily during a period of change 过渡政府. **trans·ition·ally** /-ʃənəlɪ; -ʃənḷɪ/ *adv*.

trans·it·ive /'trænsətɪv; 'trænsətɪv/ *adj* (*grammar*) (of a verb) that is used with a direct object either expressed or understood (指动词)及物的. Cf 参看 INTRANSITIVE.
▷ **trans·it·ively** *adv*.

trans·it·ory /'trænsɪtrɪ; *US* -tɔːrɪ; 'trænsəˌtɔrɪ/ *adj* lasting for only a short time; transient 短暂的; 片刻的; 转瞬即逝的: *a transitory feeling of well-being* 片刻的安逸. ▷ **trans·it·ori·ness** *n* [U].

trans·late /trænz'leɪt; trænz'let/ *v* **1** [I, Ipr, Tn, Tn·pr] **~ (sth) (from sth) (into sth)** express (sth spoken or esp written) in another language or in simpler words 翻译(某言语, 尤指文字); 用简易的语言表达(某事): *He doesn't understand Greek, so I offered to translate.* 他不懂希腊文, 我主动给他翻译. ○ *translate an article into Dutch* 把一篇文章译成荷兰文 ○ *'War and Peace', newly translated from the original Russian* 从俄语原文重新翻译的《战争与和平》○ *Can someone translate this legal jargon into plain English for me?* 谁能把这一法律术语用简单易懂的英语给我说一遍? **2** [I] be capable of being translated in another language 能被翻译: *Most poetry doesn't translate well.* 诗歌大多翻译不好. **3** [Tn·pr] **~ sth into sth** express (ideas, feelings, etc) in a different (esp a more concrete) form 把(思想、情感等)用另一种(尤指更具体的)形式表现出来: *It's time to translate our ideas into action.* 我们该把思想变为行动了. **4** [Cn·n/a] **~ sth as sth** judge or guess that sth has the specified meaning or intention; interpret sth as sth 断定或猜想某事物的意义或意图; 解释某事物: *I translated her silence as assent.* 我认为她沉默不语就是同意了. Cf 参看 INTERPRET.
▷ **trans·lat·able** /-əbl; -əbḷ/ *adj* that can be translated 可翻译的.
trans·la·tion /-'leɪʃn; -'leʃən/ *n* **1** [U] translating 翻译; 用简易语言或另一种形式的表达; 认为; 解释: *errors in translation* 翻译中的错误 ○ *the translation of theories into practice* 理论到实践的转变. **2** [C] thing that is translated 译作; 译文: *make/do a translation* 做翻译 ○ *a rough, literal, exact, etc translation* 粗率的、逐字的、准确的...翻译 ○ *the available translations of Dante* 现有的但丁译本. **3** (idm 习语) **in translation** translated into another language; not in the original language 翻译成另一种语言的; 非原来语言的: *read Cervantes in translation* 阅读塞万提斯的译本.
trans·lator *n* person who translates (esp sth written) 译者(尤指笔译的). Cf 参看 INTERPRETER (INTERPRET).

trans·lit·er·ate /trænz'lɪtəreɪt; trænz'lɪtəˌret/ *v* [Tn, Tn·pr, Cn·n/a] **~ sth (into/as sth)** write words or letters in or as the letters of a different alphabet 将词或字母用另一字母体系中的字母写出: *transliterate Greek place-names into Roman letters* 把希腊文地名用罗马字母写出. ▷ **trans·lit·era·tion** /ˌtrænzlɪtə'reɪʃn; ˌtrænzlɪtə'reʃən/ *n* [C, U].

trans·lu·cent /trænz'luːsnt; trænz'lusṇt/ *adj* allowing light to pass through but not transparent 半透明的: *lavatory windows made of translucent glass* 用半透明玻璃做的厕所窗户. ▷ **trans·lu·cence** /-sns; -sṇs/, **trans·lu·cency** /-snsɪ; -sṇsɪ/ *ns* [U]: *the shimmering translucency of her fine silk gown* 她那闪光的半透明丝制华贵长袍.

trans·mi·gra·tion /ˌtrænzmaɪ'greɪʃn; ˌtrænzmaɪ'greʃən/ *n* [U] **(a)** passing of a person's soul after death into another body (死后灵魂的)转生, 转世. **(b)** = MIGRATION (MIGRATE).

trans·mis·sion /trænz'mɪʃn; trænz'mɪʃən/ *n* **1** [U] action or process of transmitting or being transmitted 传送; 传播; 传递; 传达; 传染: *the transmission of disease by mosquitoes* 由蚊子引起的疾病传染 ○ *a break in transmission* (ie of a radio or TV broadcast) *due to a technical fault* 由于技术故障造成的(广播或电视)播送中断. **2** [C] radio or TV broadcast (无线电或电视的)播送: *a live transmission from Washington* 来自华盛顿的实况转播. **3** [C, U] connected set of parts (clutch, gears, etc) by which power is passed from the engine to the axle in a motor vehicle (机动车的)传动装置, 变速器: *a car fitted with (a) manual/(an) automatic transmission* 装有手动[自动]变速器的汽车.

trans·mit /trænz'mɪt; trænz'mɪt/ *v* (**-tt-**) **1** [usu passive 通常用于被动语态: Tn, Tn·pr] **~ sth (from...) (to...)** send out (a signal, programme, etc) electronically by radio waves, along a telegraph wire, etc (藉无线电波、沿电报线路等)传输, 传播(信号、节目等): *The World Cup final is being transmitted live to over fifty countries.* 世界杯决赛现正向五十多个国家作实况转播. **2** [Tn, Tn·pr] **~ sth/itself (from...) (to...)** send or pass on sth/itself from one person, place or thing to another 将某事物传送、传递、传达或传染给对方: *sexually transmitted diseases* 由性生活传染的疾病 ○ *transmit knowledge from one generation to another* 把知识由一代人传给另一代人 ○ *The tension soon transmitted itself to all the members of the crowd.* 这种紧张情绪很快感染了人群中所有的人. **3** [Tn] allow (sth) to pass through or along 传导(某事物): *Iron transmits heat.* 铁能传热.
▷ **trans·mit·ter** *n* **1** device or equipment for transmitting radio or other electronic signals 发射机; 发报机; 发射台; 发报台. **2** person or creature or thing that transmits 起传送或传播作用的人或生物或事物: *The mosquito is a transmitter of disease.* 蚊子能传染疾病.

trans·mog·rify /trænz'mɒgrɪfaɪ; trænz'mɑgrəˌfaɪ/ *v* (*pt, pp* **-fied**) [Tn] (*joc* 谑) completely change the appearance or character of (sb/sth), esp in a magical or a surprising way 完全改变(某人[某事物])的外表或特性(尤指藉魔法或出乎意料). ▷ **trans·mog·ri·fica·tion** /ˌtrænzmɒgrɪfɪ'keɪʃn; trænzˌmɑgrəfɪ'keʃən/ *n* [C, U].

trans·mute /trænz'mjuːt; trænz'mjut/ *v* [Tn, Tn·pr] **~ sth (into sth)** change sth (into sth completely different) 将某事物改变(为完全不同的事物): *In former times it was thought that ordinary metal could be transmuted into gold.* 古时认为一般金属能变成黄金.
▷ **trans·mut·able** /-əbl; -əbḷ/ *adj* that can be transmuted 可改变的.
trans·mu·ta·tion /ˌtrænzmjuː'teɪʃn; ˌtrænzmju'teʃən/ *n* [C, U].

trans·oceanic /ˌtrænzˌəʊʃɪ'ænɪk; ˌtrænzoʃɪ'ænɪk/ *adj* [esp attrib 尤作定语] beyond or crossing an ocean 在海洋彼岸的; 横越海洋的: *transoceanic colonies* 海外殖民地 ○ *the transoceanic migration of birds* 鸟类的越洋迁徙.

tran·som /'trænsəm; 'trænsəm/ *n* **1** horizontal bar of

T

wood, stone, etc across the top of a door or window (门窗上端的)横楣, 横档. ⇨illus at App 1 见附录1插图, page viii. **2** (*esp US*) window above the transom of a door or of a larger window; fanlight (门或大窗户横楣上方的)气窗, 顶窗, 扇形窗.

trans·par·ent /træns'pærənt; træns'pɛrənt/ *adj* **1** allowing light to pass through so that objects behind can be seen clearly 透明的: *a type of plastic that is as transparent as glass but stronger* 一种透明如玻璃且比玻璃坚固的塑料 ○ *a box with a transparent lid* 带有透明盖儿的盒子. **2** about which there can be no doubt; unmistakable 明显的; 无疑的; 无错误的: *a transparent lie* 易识破的谎言 ○ *a man of transparent sincerity, honesty, etc* 绝对忠诚、诚实等的人. **3** (*approv* 褒) easily understood; clear 易懂的; 清楚的: *a transparent style of writing* 简明的文体.

▷ **trans·par·ency** /-rənsɪ; -rənsɪ/ *n* **1** [U] state of being transparent 透明; 明显; 清楚. **2** [C] photograph printed on transparent plastic, so that it can be viewed by shining a light through it; slide[1](4a) 幻灯片; 透明正片.

trans·par·ently *adv*: *transparently honest* 很老实的.

tran·spire /træn'spaɪə(r); træn'spaɪr/ *v* **1** [I] (used with *it* and a *that*-clause; usu not in the continuous tenses 与it和that从句结合使用; 通常不用于进行时态) (of an event, a secret, etc) become known (指事情、秘密等)公开, 为人所知: *This, it later transpired, was untrue.* 此事后来得知不属实. ○ *It transpired that the gang had had a contact inside the bank.* 据报这伙匪徒在银行里有内应. **2** [I] (*infml* 口) happen 发生: *You're meeting him tomorrow? Let me know what transpires.* 你是明天见他吗? 把见面后的情况告诉我. **3** [I, Tn] (of plants) give off (watery vapour) from the surface of leaves, etc (指植物)(从叶面等)散发(水汽).

▷ **tran·spira·tion** /ˌtrænspɪ'reɪʃn; ˌtrænspə'reʃən/ *n* [U] process of transpiring (TRANSPIRE 3) (叶面等水汽的)散发, 蒸发.

trans·plant /træns'plɑːnt; *US* -'plænt; træns'plænt/ *v* **1** [Tn, Tn·pr] **~ sth (from...) (to...)**; **~ sth (in/into sth)** remove (a growing plant) with its roots and replant it elsewhere 移栽, 移种(植物): *Transplant the seedlings into peaty soil.* 把幼苗移栽到含泥炭的土壤里. **2** [Tn, Tn·pr] **~ sth (from sb/sth) (to sb/sth)** take (tissue or an organ) from one person, animal or part of the body and put it into another 移植(组织或器官): *transplant a kidney from one twin to another* 把孪生儿之一的肾脏移植到另一人身上. **3** [Tn, Tn·pr] **~ sb/sth (from...) (to...)** (*fig* 比喻) move (a person, an animal, etc) from one place to another 使(人、动物等)迁移: *He hated being transplanted from his home in the country to the noise and bustle of life in the city.* 他很不喜欢从乡间的居所迁居到了喧闹的城市里. **4** [I, Ipr] **~ (from...) (to...)** be able to be transplanted 能被移植; 能被迁移: *an old custom that does not transplant easily to the modern world* 不易融入现代社会的旧习俗.

▷ **trans·plant** /'trænsplɑːnt; *US* -plænt; 'trænsplænt/ *n* instance of transplanting (TRANSPLANT 2) (组织或器官的)移植: *have a bone-marrow transplant* 接受骨髓移植 ○ [attrib 作定语] *a heart transplant operation* 心脏移植手术.

trans·planta·tion /ˌtrænsplɑː'nteɪʃn; *US* -plæn-; ˌtrænsplæn'teʃən/ *n* [U].

trans·po·lar /trænz'pəʊlə(r); træns'polɚ/ *adj* [esp attrib 尤作定语] across the polar regions 穿越极区的: *transpolar flights from London to Tokyo* 由伦敦至东京穿越极地的航班.

trans·port[1] /træn'spɔːt; træns'pɔrt/ *v* [Tn, Tn·pr] **~ sth/sb (from...) (to...)** **1** take sth/sb from one place to another in a vehicle 运送, 运输(某物[某人]): *transport goods by lorry* 用卡车运载货物. **2** (esp formerly) send a criminal to a distant place as a punishment (尤指旧时)流放: *transported to Australia for life* 终身流放至澳大利亚.

▷ **trans·portable** /-əbl; -əbl̩/ *adj* that can be transported 可运输的; 可流放的.

trans·porta·tion /ˌtrænspɔː'teɪʃn; ˌtrænspɚ'teʃən/ *n* [U] **1** (*esp US*) = TRANSPORT: [attrib 作定语] *transportation costs* 运费. **2** transporting or being transported 运送; 运输; 流放: *sentenced to transportation* 判处流刑.

trans·ported *adj* [pred 作表语] **~ (with sth)** (*rhet* 修辞) overcome by emotion 情不自禁: *Listening to her recent performance I felt totally transported.* 我听着她最近演出的作品, 喜不自胜. ○ *transported with joy, anger, fear, etc* 乐不可支、怒不可遏、惊恐万状.

trans·porter /træn'spɔːtə (r); træns'pɔrtɚ/ *n* large vehicle used for carrying cars, etc (大型的)运输车(用于装运汽车等的).

trans·port[2] /'trænspɔːt; 'trænspɔrt/ *n* **1** [U] (**a**) (also *esp US* **transportation**) transporting or being transported 运送; 运输; 流放: *road and rail transport* 公路及铁路运输 ○ *the transport of goods by air* 空运货物 ○ [attrib 作定语] *London's transport system* 伦敦的运输系统 ○ *transport charges* 运费. (**b**) means of transport; vehicle or vehicles 运输工具: *My car is being repaired so I'm without transport at the moment.* 我的汽车正在修理, 所以我现在没有代步工具了. ○ *I normally travel by public transport.* 我出门通常乘坐公共交通工具. **2** [C] ship or aircraft for carrying troops or supplies (运送部队或补给品的)运输船, 运输机. **3** (idm 习语) **in transports of sth** (*rhet* 修辞) overcome by emotion 情不自禁: *in transports of rage, delight, terror, etc* 怒不可遏、喜不自胜、惊恐万状.

□ **'transport café** café, esp for the use of long-distance lorry drivers 路边小餐馆(尤指供长途卡车司机用餐的).

trans·pose /træn'spəʊz; træns'poz/ *v* **1** [Tn] cause (two or more things) to change places 使(物体)互换位置: *Two letters were accidentally transposed, and 'hand' got printed as 'hnad'.* 有两个字母颠倒了, hand印成了hnad. **2** [Tn, Tn·pr, Tn·p] **~ sth (up/down) (from sth) (into/to sth)** (*music* 音) rewrite or play (a piece of music) in a different key 使(乐曲)变调: *transposing the song down to D minor* 把这首歌曲降为D小调.

▷ **trans·posi·tion** /ˌtrænspə'zɪʃn; ˌtrænspə'zɪʃən/ *n* [C, U] (instance of) transposing or being transposed (位置的)互换; 变调.

trans·sexual /trænz'sekʃʊəl; trænz'sɛkʃʊəl/ *n* **1** person who emotionally feels himself or herself to be a member of the opposite sex 有异性转化欲的人. **2** person who has had his or her external sexual organs changed surgically in order to resemble the other sex (经外科手术)改变性别的人; 变性人.

trans·ship (also **tran·ship**) /træn'ʃɪp; træns'ʃɪp/ *v* (**-pp-**) [Tn] transfer (cargo) from one ship, carrier, etc to another 将(货物)由一运载工具转到另一运载工具; 转运(货物). ▷ **trans·ship·ment** (also **tran·ship-**) *n* [U].

tran·sub·stan·ti·ation /ˌtrænsəbˌstænʃɪ'eɪʃn; ˌtrænsəbˌstænʃɪ'eʃən/ *n* [U] (*religion* 宗) doctrine that the bread and wine in the Eucharist are changed by consecration into the body and blood of Christ, though their appearance does not change 变体(圣体礼所用的饼和葡萄酒在礼仪过程中变成基督的身体和血, 但外观并无变化).

trans·verse /'trænzvɜːs; trænz'vɝs/ *adj* [usu attrib 通常作定语] lying or acting in a crosswise direction 横的; 横向的; 横断的: *a transverse engine*, ie one placed parallel to the axles of a car, instead of at right angles to them 横向发动机(与车轴平行装置的). ▷ **trans·versely** *adv*.

trans·vest·ism /trænz'vestɪzəm; trænz'vɛstɪzəm/ *n* [U] dressing in the clothing of the opposite sex, as a sexual tendency 异性装扮癖(穿着异性衣物的癖好).

▷ **trans·vest·ite** /trænz'vestaɪt; trænz'vɛstaɪt/ *n* person who does this 有异性装扮癖的人.

trap /træp; træp/ *n* **1** device for catching animals, etc 捕动物等的器具; 陷阱: *a 'mouse-trap* 老鼠夹 ○ *a 'fly-trap* 捕蝇器 ○ *lay/set a trap (for rabbits)* 设置(捉兔子的)器具 ○ *caught in a trap* 落入陷阱. **2** (*fig* 比喻) (**a**) plan for capturing or detecting sb (为擒拿或侦获某人的)计策: *The thieves were caught in a police trap.* 窃贼遭警方用计擒获. (**b**) trick or device to make sb betray himself, reveal a secret, etc (诱人暴露自己、泄露秘密等的)圈套, 诡计: *You fell right into my trap.* 你恰恰中了我的计. ○ *Is this question a trap?* 这个问题是不是个圈套? (**c**) unpleasant situation from which it is hard to escape (难以摆脱的)困境: *For some women marriage is a trap.* 对有的妇女来说, 婚姻就是一种羁绊. **3** U-shaped or S-shaped section of a drain-pipe that holds liquid and so prevents unpleasant gases entering from the drain 存水

弯(排水管道中的U形或S形弯管，用以阻止臭气外溢). **4** light two-wheeled carriage drawn by a horse or pony 轻便双轮马车. **5** (**a**) compartment from which a greyhound is released at the start of a race 赛狗开始时把狗放出的隔栏. (**b**) device for sending clay pigeons, balls, etc into the air to be shot at 抛靶器(可将泥鸽、球等弹射至空中作为活靶). **6** = TRAPDOOR. **7** (*sl* 俚) mouth 嘴: *Shut your trap!* 住嘴!

▷ **trap** *v* (**-pp-**) **1** [Tn, Tn·pr, Tn·p] keep (sb) in a place from which he wants to move but cannot 使(某人)陷入困境: *Help! I'm trapped — open the door!* 救命啊! 我出不来了——快开门! ○ *They were trapped in the burning hotel.* 他们被困在发生火灾的旅馆里. ○ *The lift broke down and we were trapped inside (it).* 电梯出故障了，我们困在里面出不来. **2** [Tn] keep (sth) in a particular place, usu so that it can be easily removed, used later, etc 使(某物)留在某处(通常为易于除去、以待使用等): *A filter traps dust from the air.* 过滤网可存住空气中的尘埃. ○ *a special fabric that traps body heat* 对体温有良好保暖性能的织物. **3** [Tn, Tn·pr] **~ sb (into sth/doing sth)** catch sb by a trick 用计捕捉某人或使某人上当: *trapped into an unhappy marriage* 陷入不幸的婚姻中 ○ *I was trapped into telling the police all I knew.* 我中计了，把所知道的一切全都告诉了警方. **4** [Tn] catch (a creature) in a trap 用捕捉器捕捉(动物): *It's cruel to trap birds.* 诱捕鸟是很残忍的. **trap·per** *n* person who traps animals, esp for their fur (用捕捉器)捕捉动物的人(尤指为获得毛皮).

□ ˌ**trap'door** (also **trap**) *n* door in a floor, ceiling or roof (地板、天花板或房顶上的)活板门，地板门，活动天窗.

'**trap-shooting** *n* [U] sport of shooting at objects released into the air from a trap(5b) 飞靶射击; 多向飞碟射击.

tra·peze /trə'pi:z; *US* træ-; træ'piz/ *n* horizontal bar hung from ropes, used as a swing by acrobats and gymnasts 吊杠(杂技演员和体操运动员用的).

tra·pez·ium /trə'pi:zɪəm; trə'pizɪəm/ *n* (*pl* **~s**) (*geometry* 几) **1** (*Brit*) (*US* **trapezoid**) four-sided figure with one pair of opposite sides parallel and the other pair not 梯形. ⇨illus at QUADRILATERAL 见 QUADRILATERAL 插图. **2** (*US*) = TRAPEZOID.

trap·ezoid /'træpɪzɔɪd; 'træpəˌzɔɪd/ *n* (*geometry* 几) **1** (*Brit*) (*US* **trapezium**) four-sided figure in which no sides are parallel 不规则四边形. ⇨illus at QUADRILATERAL 见 QUADRILATERAL 插图. **2** (*US*) = TRAPEZIUM.

trap·pings /'træpɪŋz; 'træpɪŋz/ *n* [pl] outward signs of prestige, wealth, etc (威望、财富等的)外部标志: *a big car, a country house, and all the other trappings of success* 豪华汽车、乡村别墅以及所有其他标志事业有成之物 ○ *He had the trappings of high office but no real power.* 他空有高官的派头却并无实权.

Trap·pist /'træpɪst; 'træpɪst/ *n, adj* (member) of an order of monks who live a very austere life and vow never to speak 特拉普派的，苦修会的(修道士)(实行苦修，坚守缄默).

trash /træʃ; træʃ/ *n* [U] **1** material, writing, etc of poor quality 拙劣的材料、作品等: *He thinks most modern art is trash.* 他认为现代艺术大都是糟粕. **2** (*US*) household or other waste; refuse 垃圾; 废物: *put out the trash* 把垃圾拿出去. **3** (*US infml derog* 口, 贬) people that one does not respect 没出息的人: *white trash*, ie poor or deprived white people 贫贱的白人.

▷ **trashy** *adj* of poor quality 拙劣的: *trashy novels* 无聊的小说.

□ '**trashcan** *n* (*US*) = DUSTBIN (DUST[1]).

trauma /'trɔ:mə; *US* 'traumə; 'traumə/ *n* (*pl* **~s**) [U, C] **1** (**a**) (*psychology* 心) emotional shock producing a lasting harmful effect (精神上的)创伤. (**b**) (*infml* 口) any distressing or unpleasant experience 痛苦; 不幸: *going through the traumas of divorce* 经受离婚的痛苦. **2** (*medical* 医) wound or injury 创伤; 外伤; 损伤.

▷ **trau·matic** /trɔ:'mætɪk; *US* trau-; trau'mætɪk/ *adj* **1** (*psychology or medical* 心或医) of or causing trauma (精神上或肉体上)创伤的, 造成创伤的; 外伤的. **2** (*infml* 口) (of an experience) distressing or unpleasant (指经历)痛苦的，不愉快的: *Our journey home was pretty traumatic.* 我们归途中不太顺心. **trau·mat·ic·ally** /-klɪ; -klɪ/ *adv*.

trav·ail /'træveɪl; *US* trə'veɪl; trə'vel/ *n* [U] **1** (*arch or rhet* 古或修辞) painful effort 艰辛的努力. **2** (*arch* 古) pains of giving birth to a child (分娩的)阵痛.

travel /'trævl; 'trævl/ *v* (**-ll-**; *US* **-l-**) **1** (**a**) [I, Ipr, Ip, In/pr] make a journey 行走; 行驶; 旅行; 游历: *I love (to go) travelling.* 我喜欢旅行. ○ *We travelled all over the country.* 我们游遍全国各地. ○ *She travels to work by bike.* 她骑自行车去上班. ○ *We travelled over by car.* 我们是坐汽车去的. ○ *We had been travelling (for) over a week.* 那时我们已经走了一个多星期了. (**b**) [Tn, Tn·pr] cover (a distance) in travelling; journey through, around, etc (an area) 行走、行驶、旅行或游历(一段距离); 走过、绕过...(某地区): *He's travelled the whole world.* 他游遍了世界各地. ○ *travel forty miles to work each day* 每天走四十英里去上班. ⇨Usage 见所附用法. **2** [I, Ipr, Ip] move; go 移动; 走: *Light travels faster than sound.* 光比声音速度快. ○ *News travels quickly these days.* 近来消息传播得很快. ○ *The billiard ball travelled gently across the table.* 台球慢慢地滚过台面. ○ (*fig* 比喻) *His mind travelled back to his youth.* 他回想起自己青年时代. **3** [Ipr] **~ (in sth) (for sb)** go from place to place as a salesman 巡回推销; 四处兜售: *He travels in carpets for a big London firm.* 他为伦敦的一家大公司到处推销地毯. **4** [I] (of wine, etc) not be spoilt by long journeys (指葡萄酒等)经长途运输不变质的: *Lighter wines often travel badly.* 低度葡萄酒往往经不起长途运输. **5** [I] (*infml* 口) move very fast 快速移动: *I don't know the car's exact speed, but it was certainly travelling.* 我不知道那辆汽车的准确速度，但确实非常快. **6** (idm 习语) **travel 'light** (**a**) travel with as little luggage as possible 轻装上路. (**b**) (*fig* 比喻) try to avoid responsibilities, problems, etc 极力回避责任、问题等.

▷ **travel** *n* **1** [U] travelling, esp abroad 行走，行驶，旅行(尤指出国): *the cost of travel* 旅费 ○ *Travel in the mountains can be slow and dangerous.* 走山路有时候又慢又危险. ○ [attrib 作定语] '*travel books* 游记. **2 travels** [pl] journeys, esp abroad 旅游; (尤指)出国旅游: *write an account of one's travels* 写一部游记 ○ (*joc* 谑) *If you see John on your travels* (eg about town), *tell him to ring me.* 你在城里游逛时要是遇到约翰，告诉他给我打个电话. ⇨ Usage at JOURNEY 用法见 JOURNEY. **3** [U] extent, rate or type of movement of a mechanical part (机件的)行程，冲程: *There's too much travel on the brake, it needs tightening.* 制动器太松了，需要调紧.

trav·elled (*US* **trav·eled**) *adj* (usu in compounds 通常用以构成复合词) **1** (of a person) having travelled to many places (指人)到过许多地方的: *a well-/much-/widely-travelled journalist* 见多识广的新闻工作者. **2** (of a road, etc) used by travellers (指道路等)旅行者使用的: *The route was once much travelled but has fallen into disuse.* 这条路线旅行的人以前常走，但是现在已不用了.

trav·el·ler (*US* **trav·eler**) /'trævlə(r); 'trævlɚ/ *n* **1** person who is travelling or who often travels (常)出远门的人; 旅行者; 旅游者: *an experienced traveller* 富有旅行经验的人. **2** travelling salesman 巡回推销员: *a commercial traveller* 巡回推销员. **3** (*Brit*) gypsy or other itinerant person 吉卜赛人; 浪迹天涯的人. **4** (idm 习语) ˌ**traveller's 'tales** stories, esp about places and people far away, which are fascinating but hard to believe 引人入胜但难以置信的故事; (尤指)海外奇谈. '**traveller's cheque** (*US* '**traveler's check**) cheque for a fixed amount, sold by a bank, etc and easily cashed in foreign countries 旅行支票.

trav·el·ling (*US* **trav·el·ing**) *adj* [attrib 作定语]: *a travelling circus* 巡回演出马戏团 ○ *a travelling clock*, ie one in a case, for use when travelling 旅行钟 ○ '*travelling expenses* 旅行费用. ˌ**travelling 'salesman** representative of a business firm who visits shops, etc to show products and get orders 巡回推销员.

trav·elogue (*US* also **trav·elog**) /'trævəlɒg; *US* -lɔ:g; 'trævlˌɔg/ *n* film or lecture about travel 旅行记录影片; 旅行见闻讲座.

□ '**travel agent** person whose job is making arrangements for people wishing to travel, eg buying tickets, making hotel reservations, etc 旅行代理人: *I booked my holiday through my local travel agent.* 我是由本地的旅游代理人预先安排的度假事宜. '**travel agency** (also '**travel bureau**) firm or office of travel agents 旅行社.

T

ˈ**travel-sick** *adj* feeling sick because of the movement of the vehicle in which one is travelling 晕车的; 晕船的; 晕机的. ˈ**travel-sickness** *n* [U]

NOTE ON USAGE 用法: The person who **drives** a car, bus or train is the person in control of it. 开汽车、公共汽车或火车要用 **drive** 这个词. Similarly we **ride** a bicycle or horse, **sail** a boat or a ship (whether it sails or has an engine), and **fly** a plane. 骑自行车或骑马用 **ride**, 驾船(或用帆或用发动机)用 **sail**, 开飞机用 **fly**. ☆ We **steer** a car, bicycle or ship when we turn it in a particular direction. 改变汽车、自行车或船的方向用 **steer**. ☆ When travelling as a passenger we **ride in** a car, bus or train, **sail in** a ship, and **fly in** a plane. 作为乘客, 坐汽车、公共汽车或火车用 **ride in**, 坐船用 **sail in**, 坐飞机用 **fly in**. When talking about means of transport we can use **go by** (car, boat/ship/sea, plane/air, bicycle, etc) 谈到交通工具, 用 **go by** (car、boat/ship/sea、plane/air、bicycle 等): *Are you going by sea or by air?* 你打算坐船去还是坐飞机去? ○ *He always comes to work by bus.* 他总是坐公共汽车来上班.

tra·verse /trəˈvɜːs; trəˈvɝs/ *v* [Tn] travel, lie or extend across (an area) 走过、横贯或穿越(某地区): *searchlights traversing the sky* 扫过天空的探照灯灯光 ○ *skiers traversing the slopes* 穿越斜坡的滑雪者 ○ *The road traverses a wild and mountainous region.* 这条公路穿过荒芜的山区.

▷ **tra·verse** *n* **1** part of a structure that lies across another (一结构中)横贯一物体的部件; 横梁; 横臂. **2** sideways movement across sth, esp (in mountaineering) across a rock face, etc; place where this is necessary to continue the ascent or descent (横越某物的)侧向运动(尤指爬山时的); 需侧向行进之处.

trav·esty /ˈtrævəstɪ; ˋtrævəstɪ/ *n* **~ (of sth)** absurd imitation of or inferior substitute for sth 荒谬的模仿或拙劣的替代物: *The trial was a travesty of justice.* 这次审判嘲弄了法律的公正性.

▷ **trav·esty** *v* (*pt, pp* **-tied**) [Tn] make or be a travesty of (sth) 荒谬地或拙劣地模仿或替代(某事物): *travestying sb's style of writing* 拙劣地模仿某人的文笔.

trawl /trɔːl; trɔl/ *n* **1** (also ˈ**trawl-net**) large net with a wide opening, dragged along the bottom of the sea by a boat (渔船用的)拖网. **2** (also ˈ**trawl line**, ˈ**setline**) (*US*) long fishing line, used at sea, to which many short lines with hooks are attached (海上捕鱼用的)排钩.

▷ **trawl** *v* **1** (**a**) [I, Ipr] **~ (for sth)** fish with a trawl 用拖网或排钩捕鱼. (**b**) [Tn] fish (an area of water) in this way 在(某水域)用拖网或排钩捕鱼. **2** [Ipr, Tn] **~ (through) sth (for sth)** (*fig* 比喻) search through (records, etc) 查阅(档案等): *The police are trawling (through) their files for similar cases.* 警方正在查阅类似案件的档案. **trawler** *n* boat used in trawling 拖网渔船.

tray /treɪ; tre/ *n* **1** flat piece of wood, metal, plastic, etc with raised edges, used for carrying or holding things, esp food 盘; 托盘: *a* ˈ*tea-tray* 茶盘 ○ *Take her some breakfast on a tray.* 用托盘给她送些早餐. ⇨illus at App 1 见附录1插图, page xvi. **2** shallow open receptacle for holding a person's papers, etc in an office (办公室用的)文件盘: *Letters were piled high in the tray on his desk.* 他办公桌上的文件盘里有很多信.

treach·er·ous /ˈtretʃərəs; ˋtrɛtʃərəs/ *adj* **1** behaving with or showing treachery 背叛的; 不忠的. **2** dangerous, esp when seeming to be safe 危险的(尤指貌似安全的): *That ice is treacherous*, ie not as strong or thick as it looks. 那冰并不像看上去的那么结实. ○ *treacherous currents* 貌似和缓的湍流.

▷ **treach·er·ously** *adv*.

treach·ery /ˈtretʃərɪ; ˋtrɛtʃərɪ/ *n* [C, U] (act of) betraying a person or cause, esp secretly 背叛, 不忠(尤指秘密的): *underhand treachery* 暗地的背叛行为.

treacle /ˈtriːkl; ˋtrikl/ (*US* **molasses**) *n* [U] thick sticky dark liquid produced when sugar is refined 糖饴. Cf 参看 SYRUP.

▷ **treacly** /ˈtriːklɪ; ˋtriklɪ/ *adj* **1** like treacle 似糖饴的. **2** (*fig derog* 比喻, 贬) unpleasantly sentimental; cloying 过分多情的; 甜得发腻的: *the treacly clichés of romantic fiction* 传奇小说中令人腻烦的陈词滥调.

tread /tred; trɛd/ *v* (*pt* **trod** /trɒd; trɑd/, *pp* **trodden** /ˈtrɒdn; ˋtrɑdn̩/ or **trod**) **1** [I, Ipr] **~ (on, etc sth/sb)** (**a**) set one's foot down; walk or step 踩; 行走; 踏: *She trod lightly so as not to wake the baby.* 她步子很轻, 以免惊醒孩子. ○ *explorers going where no man had trod* (ie been) *before* 前往杳无人迹之处的勘探者 ○ *tread on sb's toe* 踩在某人的脚趾上 ○ *Mind you don't tread in that puddle.* 小心, 别踩着那水坑. ○ (*fig* 比喻) *It is a sensitive issue so we must tread* (ie speak, proceed) *carefully.* 这是个敏感的问题, 绝不可掉以轻心. (**b**) (of a foot) be set down (指脚)踩下, 踏下. **2** [Tn, Tn·pr, Tn·p] **~ sth (in/down/out)** press or crush sth with the feet 踩紧或踩碎某物: *tread grapes*, ie to make wine 踩碎葡萄(制酒) ○ *Don't tread your ash into my carpet!* 别把你的烟灰踩到我的地毯里! ○ *tread the earth down around the roots* 把根部周围的泥土踩实 ○ *tread out fire in the grass* 把草地上的火踩灭. **3** [Tn, Tn·pr] make (a path, etc) by walking 踩出(一条路等): *The cattle had trodden a path to the pond.* 牛群踩出了一条通往池塘的小径. **4** (idm 习语) ˌ**tread the** ˈ**boards** (*rhet or joc* 修辞或谑) be an actor 当演员. ˌ**tread on** ˈ**air** feel very happy 欢天喜地. ˌ**tread on sb's** ˈ**corns**/ˈ**toes** (*infml* 口) offend or annoy sb 冒犯或得罪某人: *I don't want to tread on anybody's toes so I won't say what I think.* 我谁也不想得罪, 所以我不把想法说出来. ˌ**tread on sb's** ˈ**heels** follow sb closely 紧跟某人. ˌ**tread**/ˌ**walk a** ˈ**tightrope** ⇨ TIGHTROPE. ˌ**tread** ˈ**water** keep oneself upright in deep water by making treading movements with the legs 踩水(游泳动作).

▷ **tread** *n* **1** [sing] manner or sound of walking 步法; 步态; 脚步声: *walk with a heavy tread* 脚步沉重地行走. **2** [C] upper surface of a step or stair (台阶或楼梯的)踏面, 梯面. **3** [C, U] outer grooved surface of a tyre that is in contact with the road (轮胎的)踏面, 胎面: *Driving with worn tread(s) can be dangerous.* 轮胎胎面磨损的汽车开着有危险.

□ ˈ**treadmill** *n* **1** mill-wheel turned by the weight of people or animals treading on steps round its inside edge (formerly worked by prisoners as a punishment) (人力或畜力的)踏车(旧时用以惩治囚犯). **2** (*fig* 比喻) tiring or monotonous routine work; drudgery 累人的或单调的例行工作; 繁重乏味的工作: *I can't get off the office treadmill.* 我无法摆脱单调的坐班工作.

treadle /ˈtredl; ˋtrɛdl̩/ *n* lever worked by the foot to drive a machine, eg a lathe or sewing-machine (车床或缝纫机等的)踏板.

treas *abbr* 缩写 = treasurer.

treason /ˈtriːzn; ˋtrizn̩/ *n* [U] treachery to one's country (eg by helping its enemies in wartime) or its ruler (eg by plotting to kill him) 叛国(如战时通敌); 背叛, 叛逆(如阴谋弑逆). ▷ **treas·on·able** /ˈtriːzənəbl; ˋtriznn̩əbl/ *adj*: *a treasonable offence*, ie one that can be punished as treason 叛国罪. **treas·on·ably** /-əblɪ; -əblɪ/ *adv*.

treas·ure /ˈtreʒə(r); ˋtrɛʒɚ/ *n* **1** [C, U] (store of) gold, silver, jewels, etc 金银财宝; 财富: *buried treasure* 埋藏的财宝. **2** [C esp *pl* 尤作复数] highly valued object 宝物; 珍宝; 珍品: ˈ*art treasures* 艺术珍品. **3** [C] person who is much loved or valued 极爱的人; 极有价值的人: *My dearest treasure!* 我的宝贝儿! ○ *Our new secretary is a perfect treasure.* 我们新来的秘书十分能干.

▷ **treas·ure** *v* **1** [Tn] value (sth) highly 珍重, 珍爱(某事物): *treasure sb's friendship* 珍视某人的情谊 ○ *He treasures your letters.* 他把你的信看得非常宝贵. **2** [Tn, Tn·p] **~ sth (up)** keep sth as precious or greatly loved 珍藏某事物: *I shall always treasure the memory of our meetings.* 我将永远记住我们相聚的情景. ○ *treasure sth up in one's heart* 将某事物铭记于心. **treas·urer** /ˈtreʒərə(r); ˋtrɛʒərɚ/ *n* person responsible for the money, bills, etc of a club or society (俱乐部或会社的)财务主管, 司库, 会计, 出纳.

□ ˈ**treasure-house** *n* building where treasure is stored 存放金银财宝的建筑物.

ˈ**treasure-hunt** *n* (**a**) search for treasure 寻宝. (**b**) game in which players try to find a hidden object 寻宝游戏.

ˈ**treasure trove** /trəʊv; trov/ **1** treasure that is found hidden and whose owner is unknown 发现的无主财宝. **2** (*fig* 比喻) place, book, etc containing many useful or beautiful things 视为宝库的处所、书等: *The gallery is a treasure trove of medieval art.* 这个画廊是中世纪艺术的

宝库.

treas·ury /ˈtreʒərɪ; ˋtrɛʒərɪ/ *n* **1 the Treasury** [Gp] (in Britain and some other countries) government department that controls public revenue (英国及其他一些国家的)财政部. **2** [C] place where treasure is stored 金银财宝存放处. **3** [C] (*fig* 比喻) book, etc containing items of great value or interest 内容极有价值或有意义的书等: *a treasury of poetic gems* 诗歌精选.

□ ˈ**Treasury bill 1** (*Brit*) bill of exchange issued by the government to raise money for temporary needs 国库券. **2** (*US*) investment issued by the government, valid for up to one year and bearing no interest 国库券.

treat /triːt; trit/ *v* **1** [Tn, Tn·pr, Cn·n/a] **~ sb (as/like sth)** act or behave in a certain way towards sb 对待某人: *They treat their children very badly.* 他们对待子女很不好. ○ *You should treat them with more consideration.* 你应该多体谅他们一点. ○ *Don't treat me as (if I were) an idiot.* 别把我当傻瓜. **2** [Cn·n/a] **~ sth as sth** consider sth in a certain way 把某事物看作; 视某事物为: *I decided to treat his remark as a joke*, eg instead of being offended by it. 我把他的话当作玩笑话(如不为此生气). **3** (**a**) [Tn, Tn·pr] deal with or discuss (a subject) 探讨, 讨论(问题): *The problem has been better treated in other books.* 这问题在其他书里说得更清楚. ○ *The documentary treated the question in some detail.* 这部记录片探讨这个问题有些深度. (**b**) [Ipr] **~ of sth** (*dated or fml* 旧或文) (of a book, lecture, etc) be about sth (指书、讲座等)论及某事物: *an essay treating of philosophical doubt* 涉及哲学上有关怀疑的论文. **4** [Tn, Tn·pr] **~ sb/sth; ~ sb (for sth)** give medical or surgical care to (a person or a condition) 医治(人或疾病): *a new drug to treat rheumatism* 治疗风湿病的新药 ○ *Last year the hospital treated over forty cases of malaria.* 去年这所医院医治了四十余例疟疾病人. ○ *She was treated for sunstroke.* 她因中暑接受治疗. **5** [Tn, Tn·pr] **~ sth (with sth)** apply a process or a substance to sth to protect it, preserve it, etc (用防护措施或物质)处理某物: *wood treated with creosote* 用杂酚油处理过的木材 ○ *treat crops with insecticide* 用杀虫剂处理作物. **6** [Tn, Tn·pr] **~ sb/oneself (to sth)** give sb/oneself sth enjoyable, eg special food or entertainment, at one's own expense 以某事物(如食物或娱乐)款待某人或使自己获得享受: *She treated each of the children to an ice-cream.* 她请孩子每人吃个冰激凌. ○ *I decided to treat myself to a taxi*, eg instead of walking. 我决定坐他一次计程车. ○ *We were treated to the unusual sight of the Prime Minister singing on TV.* 我们有幸目睹首相上电视一展歌喉的难得场面. **7** [Ipr] **~ with sb** (*dated or fml* 旧或文) negotiate with sb 与某人谈判: *The government refuses to treat with terrorists.* 当局拒绝与恐怖分子谈判. **8** (idm 习语) **treat sb like** ˈ**dirt/a** ˈ**dog** (*infml* 口) treat sb with no respect at all 视某人如草芥: *They treat their workers like dirt.* 他们把工人看得粪土不如.

▷ **treat** *n* **1** thing that gives great pleasure, esp sth unexpected or not always available 乐事, 乐趣(尤指意想不到的或难得的): *Smoked salmon — what a treat!* 吃熏大马哈鱼——那可太棒了! ○ *Her son's visits are a great treat for her.* 她儿子来看望她, 她心里喜滋滋的. **2** act of treating (TREAT 6) sb to sth 款待; 招待; 请客: *This is my treat*, ie I'll pay. 这次我请客. **3** (idm 习语) **a Dutch treat** ⇨ DUTCH. **trick or treat** ⇨ TRICK *n*.

treat·able *adj*: *a treatable cancer* 能治疗的癌症.

treat·ise /ˈtriːtɪz, -tɪs; ˋtritɪs/ *n* **~ (on sth)** long written work dealing systematically with one subject (专题)论文.

treat·ment /ˈtriːtmənt; ˋtritmənt/ *n* **1** [U] process or manner of treating sb or sth 对待的方法或态度; 待遇; 处理; 治疗: *undergoing medical treatment* 接受治疗 ○ *protesting against the brutal treatment of political prisoners* 抗议对政治犯的残酷虐待 ○ *Shakespeare's treatment of madness in 'King Lear'* 莎士比亚在《李尔王》中对疯癫的处理手法. **2** [C] thing done to relieve or cure an illness or a defect, etc 疗法; 处理方法: *a new treatment for cancer* 癌症的新疗法 ○ *an effective treatment for dry rot* 防止干腐病的有效方法. **3** (idm 习语) **give sb/get preferential treatment** ⇨ PREFERENTIAL.

treaty /ˈtriːtɪ; ˋtritɪ/ *n* **1** [C] formal agreement between two or more countries (国家之间的)条约, 协定: *the Treaty of Rome* 罗马条约 ○ *make/sign a* ˈ*peace treaty with a neighbouring country* 与邻国签订和平条约. **2** [U] formal agreement between people, esp for the purchase of property (人与人之间的)协议, 协商: *sell a house by private treaty*, ie instead of by public auction, etc 私下商议出售房子(不经公开拍卖等方式).

treble[1] /ˈtrebl; ˋtrɛbl/ *adj*, *n* three times as much or as many 三倍的; 三重的: *a treble portion of ice-cream*, ie three times as big as the normal one 三倍分量的冰激凌 ○ *He earns treble my salary.* 他挣的钱是我的三倍.

▷ **treble** *v* [I, Tn] (cause sth to) become three times as much or as many (使某事物)增加到三倍或增加两倍: *He's trebled his earnings in two years.* 他两年间收入已增加两倍. ○ *The newspaper's circulation has trebled since last year.* 去年以来该报的发行量已增加到原来的三倍.

□ ˌ**treble** ˈ**chance** (*Brit*) football pool competition in which people try to predict whether certain matches will be draws or wins for the home team or wins for the away team 三重彩(足球普尔赌博法, 赌某些比赛中的平局数或主队赢数或客队赢数).

treble[2] /ˈtrebl; ˋtrɛbl/ *n* (**a**) highest voice in choral singing, esp the unbroken male voice (合唱中的)最高音(尤指连续的男声): *a choir of trebles* 最高音合唱. (**b**) child with such a voice 唱最高音的儿童. (**c**) part for such a voice 最高声部: *He sings treble.* 他唱最高声部.

▷ **treble** *adj* [attrib 作定语] high-pitched in tone 声调高的; 高音的; 尖声的: *a treble voice* 尖利的嗓音 ○ *a treble recorder* 高音竖笛 ○ *the treble clef*, ie the symbol in music showing that the notes following it are high in pitch 高音谱号. Cf 参看 BASS.

tree /triː; tri/ *n* **1** large (usu tall) long-lasting type of plant, having a thick central wooden stem (the *trunk*) from which wooden branches grow, usu bearing leaves 树; 乔木: *an oak, ash, elm, etc tree* 栎树、梣树、榆树 ○ *We sheltered under the trees.* 我们躲在树下. ⇨illus at App 1 见附录1插图, page i. Cf 参看 BUSH, SHRUB. **2** (esp in compounds 尤用以构成复合词) piece of wood or other material for certain purposes 有某用途的成块木头或其他材料: *a* ˈ*shoe-tree* 鞋楦. **3** (idm 习语) **at the top of the tree** ⇨ TOP[1]. **bark up the wrong tree** ⇨ BARK[2]. **not grow on trees** ⇨ GROW. **not see the wood for the trees** ⇨ WOOD.

▷ **tree** *v* (*pt, pp* **treed**) [Tn usu passive 通常用于被动语态] force (a person or an animal) to climb up a tree for safety 迫使(人或动物)上树躲避.

tree·less *adj* without trees 无树的: *a treeless plain* 没有树的平原.

□ ˈ**tree-fern** *n* large fern with an upright woody stem 桫椤(高大的蕨类植物, 茎部挺直).

ˈ**tree-house** *n* structure built in the branches of a tree, usu for children to play in or on 树上的小屋(建在树枝之间的, 通常供儿童游戏用).

ˈ**tree-line** (also ˈ**timber-line**) *n* level of land, eg on a mountain, above which trees will not grow 林木线(树木生长的上限, 如山上的).

ˈ**tree-top** *n* (esp *pl* 尤作复数) branches at the very top of a tree 树梢: *birds nesting in the tree-tops* 在树梢上筑巢的鸟儿.

tre·foil /ˈtrefɔɪl; ˋtrifɔɪl/ *n* **1** any of various types of plant with three leaves on each stem (eg clover) 三叶草(如车轴草). **2** ornament or design shaped like such a leaf 三叶形装饰或图案.

trek /trek; trɛk/ *n* long hard journey, esp on foot 艰辛的路程(尤指徒步的).

▷ **trek** *v* (**-kk-**) [I, Ipr, Ip] make such a journey 艰难地行走: *trekking for days across the desert* 行走数日穿过沙漠.

trel·lis /ˈtrelɪs; ˋtrɛlɪs/ *n* [C, U] light framework of crossing strips of wood, plastic, etc used esp to support climbing plants and often fastened to a wall 格子棚架(用木头、塑料等搭成, 尤用于支撑攀缘植物, 通常固定在墙上). ⇨illus at App 1 见附录1插图, page vii.

tremble /ˈtrembl; ˋtrɛmbl/ *v* **1** (**a**) [I, Ipr] **~ (with sth)** shake involuntarily (from fear, cold, weakness, etc); quiver (因恐惧、寒冷、虚弱等)颤抖, 战栗, 哆嗦: *trembling hands* 颤抖的手 ○ *His voice trembled with rage.* 他气得声音都颤抖了. ○ *We were trembling with excitement.* 我们兴奋得颤抖起来. (**b**) [I] shake slightly 轻轻摇晃; 颤动: *leaves trembling in the breeze* 在微风中摇晃的叶子 ○ *The bridge trembled as the train sped across it.* 火车过桥

T

时速度很快，震得桥身直颤. **2** [I, Ipr, It] be very anxious or agitated 焦虑; 担心; 不安: *I tremble at the thought of what may happen.* 我想到可能出现的情况就不寒而栗. ○ *She trembled to think what might have happened to him.* 她想到他可能遇到的情况就十分担心. **3** (idm 习语) **in fear and trembling** ⇨ FEAR[1].

▷ **tremble** *n* feeling, movement or sound of trembling; tremor 内心的战栗; 颤抖的动作或声音; 震颤: *There was a tremble in his voice.* 他的声音有点颤抖. ○ (*infml* 口) *She was all of a tremble*, ie trembling all over. 她浑身哆嗦.

trem·bler /ˈtremblə(r); ˋtrɛmblɚ/ *n* spring that makes an electrical contact when shaken (继电器的)振颤片.

trem·bly /ˈtremblɪ; ˋtrɛmblɪ/ *adj* (*infml* 口) trembling 颤抖的; 战栗的; 哆嗦的: *I felt all trembly.* 我浑身哆嗦.

tre·mend·ous /trɪˈmendəs; trɪˋmɛndəs/ *adj* **1** very great; immense 极大的; 巨大的: *a tremendous explosion* 极大的爆炸声 ○ *travelling at a tremendous speed* 高速行进 ○ *It makes a tremendous difference to me.* 这对我来说差别极大. ○ *They had the most tremendous row.* 他们吵得天翻地覆. **2** (*infml* 口) very good; extraordinary 极好的; 不平常的; 格外的: *a tremendous film, pianist, experience* 了不起的影片、钢琴家、经历 ○ *He's a tremendous walker*, ie He walks a lot. 他很能走路. ▷ **tre·mend·ously** *adv*: *tremendously pleased* 极其高兴.

trem·olo /ˈtreməlәʊ; ˋtrɛməˌlo/ *n* (*pl* **~s**) (*music* 音) trembling or vibrating sound made by playing a stringed instrument or singing in a special way (弦乐器的或歌唱的)颤音. Cf 参看 VIBRATO.

tremor /ˈtremə(r); ˋtrɛmɚ/ *n* **1** slight shaking or trembling 轻轻摇晃; 颤动; 颤抖: *There was a tremor in her voice.* 她的声音有点颤抖. ○ ˈ*earth tremors*, eg during an earthquake 地面颤动(如地震时). **2** thrill 发抖; 激动; 兴奋: *tremors of fear, delight, anxiety, etc* 阵阵恐惧、喜悦、焦虑等.

tremu·lous /ˈtremjʊləs; ˋtrɛmjələs/ *adj* (*fml* 文) **1** trembling from nervousness or weakness (因紧张或体弱)颤抖的, 震颤的, 战栗的, 哆嗦的: *in a tremulous voice* 以颤抖的声音 ○ *with a tremulous hand* 用颤抖的手. **2** timid or uncertain 胆怯的; 不确定的: *a tremulous look* 怯生生的样子. ▷ **tremu·lously** *adv*.

trench /trentʃ; trɛntʃ/ *n* ditch dug in the ground, eg for drainage or to give troops shelter from enemy fire 沟; 渠; 堑壕; 战壕: *irrigation trenches* 灌溉渠 ○ *The workmen dug a trench for the new water-pipe.* 工人挖了一条沟敷设新水管. ○ [attrib 作定语] *trench warfare* 堑壕战.

▷ **trench** *v* [Tn] dig a trench or trenches in (the ground) 在(地)上开沟或挖战壕.

□ ˈ**trench coat** belted coat or raincoat with pockets and flaps in the style of a military coat (军装式)大衣, 雨衣(有腰带、口袋及口袋盖).

trench·ant /ˈtrentʃənt; ˋtrɛntʃənt/ *adj* (of comments, arguments, etc) strongly and effectively expressed; penetrating (指言论、论据等)有力的, 有效的, 尖锐的: *trenchant wit, criticism* 犀利的机智言词、批评. ▷ **trench·antly** *adv*.

trencher /ˈtrentʃə(r); ˋtrɛntʃɚ/ *n* (*arch* 古) (formerly) large wooden plate on which food was served or carved (旧时)(盛食物或切食物用的)大木盘.

▷ **trench·er·man** /-mən; -mən/ *n* (*pl* **-men** /-mən; -mən/) (idm 习语) **a good, etc trencherman** (*joc* 谑) person who usually eats a lot 胃口大的人.

trend /trend; trɛnd/ *n* **1** general tendency or direction 趋势; 趋向; 动向: *The trend of prices is still upwards.* 物价仍有上涨趋势. ○ *a growing trend towards smaller families* 家庭日益小型化的趋势 ○ *contemporary trends in psychiatry* 当今精神病学的动态 ○ *following the latest trends in fashion* 追求最新的流行款式. **2** (idm 习语) ˌ**set a/the** ˈ**trend** start a style, practice, fashion, etc that others copy 开风气之先; 带领新潮流.

▷ **trend** *v* [Ipr, Ip] show a particular tendency 显示某种趋向: *house prices trending upwards* 有上涨趋势的房价.

trendy *adj* (**-ier, -iest**) (*infml* 口) showing or following the latest trends of fashion 时髦的; 赶时髦的: *trendy clothes* 时髦衣物 ○ (*derog* 贬) *trendy intellectuals*, ie ones who do not examine new ideas carefully 赶浪头的知识分子(盲目追求新思潮者). — *n* (*Brit infml esp derog* 口, 尤作贬义) trendy person 赶时髦的人: *middle-aged trendies* 赶时髦的中年人. **trend·ily** *adv*. **trendi·ness** *n* [U].

□ ˈ**trend-setter** *n* person who leads the way in fashion, etc 新潮倡导人. ˈ**trend-setting** *adj* [attrib 作定语]: *a trend-setting film* 带领新潮流的影片.

tre·pan /trɪˈpæn; trɪˋpæn/ *v* (**-nn-**) [Tn] (*medical* 医) = TREPHINE.

▷ **tre·pan** *n* **1** (*medical* 医) early form of trephine (早期的)环钻, 环锯. **2** (*engineering* 工) bore for drilling a mine shaft 钻井机.

tre·phine /trɪˈfi:n; *US* -ˈfaɪn; trɪˋfaɪn/ *v* [Tn] (*medical* 医) (also **trepan**) cut a (small hole) in sb's skull or the cornea of the eye 在人的颅骨或眼睛角膜上开(小孔).

▷ **tre·phine** *n* (*medical* 医) surgeon's cylindrical saw used for this (做以上手术用的)环钻, 环锯.

trep·ida·tion /ˌtrepɪˈdeɪʃn; ˌtrɛpəˋdeʃən/ *n* [U] great worry or fear about sth unpleasant that may happen (担心可能出事的)惊恐, 恐慌: *The threat of an epidemic caused great alarm and trepidation.* 流行病猖獗因而人心惶惶.

tres·pass /ˈtrespəs; ˋtrɛspəs/ *v* **1** [I, Ipr] **~ (on sth)** enter sb's land or property without his permission or other authority 非法侵入某人地界: *He accused me of trespassing on his estate.* 他控告我擅自进入他的庄园. ○ *No trespassing*, ie as a warning sign. 严禁擅自进入(告示用语). **2** [Ipr] **~ on sth** (*fml* 文) take advantage of sth in a selfish way; use sth unreasonably 侵占或无理使用某事物: *trespass on sb's time/hospitality/privacy* 占用某人的时间[利用某人的好客之情/侵扰某人的个人自由]. **3** [I, Ipr] **~ (against sb)** (*arch or Bible* 古或《圣经》) do wrong; sin 犯过失; (在宗教或道德方面)犯罪.

▷ **tres·pass** *n* **1** (**a**) [U] trespassing 非法侵入: *the law of trespass* 有关非法侵入的法律. (**b**) [C] act or instance of this 非法侵入的行为: *an accidental trespass* 并非有意的非法侵入. **2** [C] (*arch or Bible* 古或《圣经》) sin; wrongdoing 罪过; 过失.

tres·passer *n* person who trespasses 非法侵入的人: *Trespassers will be prosecuted*, eg on a notice. 闲人莫入, 违者必究(告示用语).

tress /tres; trɛs/ *n* (*fml* 文) **1** [C] lock of a person's hair 一绺头发. **2 tresses** [pl] long hair, esp of a woman 长发(尤指女子的): *combing her dark tresses* 梳理着她那长长的黑发.

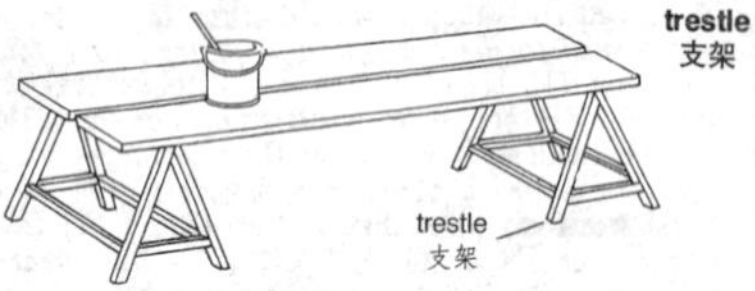

trestle /ˈtresl; ˋtrɛsl/ *n* structure of wood, metal, etc with legs, used in pairs to support planks, a table-top, a bench, etc (放置木板、桌面、坐板等的)支架, 条凳(成对使用).

□ ˌ**trestle-**ˈ**table** *n* table supported on trestles 用支架支撑的桌子.

trews /tru:z; truz/ *n* [pl] close-fitting tartan trousers 格子呢紧身裤: *a pair of trews* 一条格子呢紧身裤.

tri- *pref* 前缀 (with *ns* and *adjs* 与名词和形容词结合) three; triple 三; 三倍; 三重: *triangle* ○ *tricolour* ○ *trilingual*. Cf 参看 BI-, DI-.

triad /ˈtraɪæd; ˋtraɪæd/ *n* **1** group or set of three related people or things 三人或三物的组合. **2** (also **Triad**) Chinese secret organization involved in criminal activities 三合会.

trial /ˈtraɪəl; ˋtraɪəl/ *n* **1** [C, U] examination of evidence in a lawcourt, by a judge and often a jury, to decide if sb accused of a crime is innocent or guilty 审问; 审讯; 审理; 审判: *The trial lasted a week.* 审讯持续了一个星期. ○ *trial by jury* 陪审 ○ *commit sb for trial*, ie send sb to prison, for later trial 将某人拘押候审 ○ *The defendant claimed that he had not had a fair trial.* 被告声称未获公正审讯. ○ *The case comes to trial/comes up for trial* (ie will be tried) *next month.* 该案将于下月开庭审理. **2** [C, U] (act or process of) testing the ability, quality, performance, etc of sb or sth (对能力、质量、性能等

的)测试, 试验, 考验: *give job applicants a trial* 对求职者进行测试 ○ *put a car through safety trials* 对汽车进行安全性能试验 ○ *a trial of strength*, ie a contest to see who is stronger 力气的较量 ○ *The new drug has undergone extensive medical trials.* 这种新药已做了大量的医学试验. ○ [attrib 作定语] *for trial purposes* 为了试验的目的 ○ *employ sb for a trial period* 雇用某人试用一段时间 ○ *a trial separation*, ie of a couple whose marriage is in difficulties 试验性分居(婚姻关系出现裂痕时的). **3** [C] sports match to test the ability of players who may be selected for an important team (挑选运动员的)预赛, 选拔赛. **4** [C] **~ (to sb)** troublesome or irritating person or thing that one must endure (不得不容忍的)讨厌的人或事物: *Her child is a trial to his teachers.* 她的孩子让老师很伤脑筋. ○ *life's trials* 生活中的磨难. **5** (idm 习语) **go on 'trial/stand 'trial (for sth)** be tried in a lawcourt 受审判: *She went on/stood trial for murder.* 她因涉及谋杀罪而受审. **on 'trial** being examined and tested 在试验中; 在测试中: *Take the machine on trial for a week.* 把这机器试验一星期. ○ (*fig* 比喻) *Democracy itself is on trial as the country prepares for its first free elections.* 这个国家准备进行首次自由选举, 民主制度本身正面临考验. **put sb/be on 'trial (for sth)** (cause sb to) be accused and examined in a lawcourt (使某人)被控告并受审: *She was put on trial for fraud.* 她因涉及诈骗罪而受审. ○ *He's on trial for his life.* 他正在受决定他生死的审判. **ˌtrial and 'error** process of solving a problem by trying various solutions and learning from one's failures 反复试验, 从失败中找出解决办法: *learn by trial and error* 通过反复试验学习 ○ [attrib 作定语] *trial-and-error methods* 反复试验法. **ˌtrials and 'tribulations** irritations and troubles 烦躁和苦恼.

□ **ˌtrial 'run** preliminary test of the quality, effectiveness, ability, etc of sth or sb (对质量、性能、能力等的)初步测试: *Take the car for a trial run to see if you like it.* 试试那辆汽车, 看看你是否满意. ○ *The programme was given a trial run to gauge viewers' reactions.* 该节目进行了试演以了解观众的反应. ○ *She's taking the exam a year early, just as a trial run (for the real thing).* 她提前一年参加考试, 算是(正式考试的)试考.

triangle 三角形

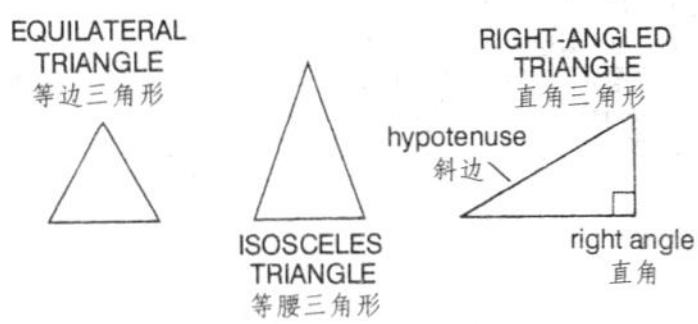

tri·angle /ˈtraɪæŋgl; ˋtraɪˌæŋgl/ *n* **1** geometric figure with three straight sides and three angles 三角形. **2** thing shaped like this 三角形的物体: *a scarf made of a triangle of blue silk* 用蓝绸子做的三角形围巾 ○ *a triangle of grass beside the path* 路边的三角形草地 ○ *benches arranged in a triangle* 排成三角形的长凳. **3** (*music* 音) percussion instrument consisting of a steel rod bent in the shape of a triangle and struck with another steel rod 三角铁(一种打击乐器). ⇨illus at App 1 见附录1插图, page xi. **4** situation involving three people, ideas, opinions, etc 含有三个(人、主意、想法等)的情况: *a love triangle* 三角恋爱. **5** (idm 习语) **the eternal triangle** ⇨ ETERNAL.

▷ **tri·an·gu·lar** /traɪˈæŋgjʊlə(r); traɪˋæŋgjələ˞/ *adj* **1** shaped like a triangle 似三角形的. **2** involving three people 涉及三人的: *a triangular contest in an election*, ie one with three candidates 竞选中三位候选人的角逐.

tribal /ˈtraɪbl; ˋtraɪbl̩/ *adj* [usu attrib 通常作定语] of a tribe or tribes 部落的: *tribal loyalties, dances, gods, wars* 对部落的效忠、部落的舞蹈、部落崇拜的神祇、部落之间的战争.

▷ **tri·bal·ism** /ˈtraɪbəlɪzəm; ˋtraɪbl̩ɪzm̩/ *n* [U] **1** state of being organized in a tribe or tribes 部落制度. **2** behaviour and attitudes that result from belonging to a tribe 部落人的习性.

tribe /traɪb; traɪb/ *n* **1** racial group (esp in a primitive or nomadic culture) united by language, religion, customs, etc and living as a community under one or more chiefs 部落: *Zulu tribes* 祖鲁人的部落 ○ *the twelve tribes of ancient Israel* 早期以色列人十二支族. **2** group of related animals or plants (动植物的)族. **3** (often *pl* 常作复数) (*infml esp joc* 口, 尤作戏谑语) large number of people 大帮(人): *tribes of holiday-makers* 大群的度假的人 ○ *What a tribe* (ie large family) *they've got!* 他们这一家人口真多! **4** (*usu derog* 通常作贬义) set or class of people 一伙(人); 一类(人): *I hate the whole tribe of politicians.* 我很不喜欢政客.

□ **'tribesman** /-zmən; -zmən/ *n* (*pl* **-men** /-mən; -mən/) member of a tribe(1) 部落成员.

tri·bu·la·tion /ˌtrɪbjʊˈleɪʃn; ˌtrɪbjəˋleʃən/ *n* **1** [C, U] (*rhet* 修辞) (sad event, accident, illness, etc that causes) great trouble or suffering 忧患; 苦难; 带来极大困难或痛苦的伤心事、事故、病痛等: *He bore his tribulations bravely.* 他勇敢地忍受着困苦. ○ *a time of great tribulation* 极苦难的时期. **2** (idm 习语) **trials and tribulations** ⇨ TRIAL.

tri·bu·nal /traɪˈbju:nl; traɪˋbjunl̩/ *n* [CGp] group of officials with the authority to settle certain types of dispute (被授权解决某种纠纷的)审理团; 特别法庭: *a rent tribunal*, ie one hearing appeals against high rents 租务裁判处(受理对高租金提起的申诉) ○ (*fig* 比喻) *the tribunal of public opinion* 舆论的公断.

tri·bu·tary /ˈtrɪbjʊtrɪ; *US* -terɪ; ˋtrɪbjəˌtɛrɪ/ *n* river or stream that flows into a larger one or into a lake (河川或湖泊的)支流: *The Avon is a tributary of the Severn.* 埃文河是塞文河的支流.

▷ **tri·bu·tary** *adj* **1 ~ (to sth)** (of a river or stream) flowing in this way (指河川)支流的: *rivers tributary to the Thames* 泰晤士河的支流. **2** [attrib 作定语] (of a country or ruler) paying tribute(3) to another (指国家或统治者)纳贡的, 进贡的.

trib·ute /ˈtrɪbju:t; ˋtrɪbjut/ *n* **1** [C, U] action, statement or gift that is meant to show one's respect or admiration 表示敬意或称赞的行动、言语或礼物: *floral tributes*, ie gifts of flowers 献礼的花 ○ *Tributes to the dead leader have been received from all around the world.* 世界各地的人们向已故领袖表示哀悼. ○ *The mourners stood in silent tribute as the coffin was laid to rest.* 灵柩下葬时, 送葬者默立致哀. **2** [sing] **a ~ (to sth)** indication of the effectiveness of sth 有效性的标示: *His recovery is a tribute to the doctors' skill.* 他能够康复充分说明该医师医术高超. **3** [C, U] (esp formerly) payment made by one country or ruler to another, esp to avoid war (尤指旧时)(一国向他国交纳的)贡品, 贡金, 贡(尤指为避免战争). **4** (idm 习语) **pay tribute to sb/sth** ⇨ PAY².

trice /traɪs; traɪs/ *n* (idm 习语) **in a trice** very quickly or suddenly 立即; 瞬息间; 突然间: *I'll be with you in a trice.* 我马上就来. ○ *In a trice, he was gone.* 一转眼他就走了.

tri·ceps /ˈtraɪseps; ˋtraɪsɛps/ *n* (*pl* unchanged 复数不变) large muscle at the back of the upper arm 三头肌. Cf 参看 BICEPS.

trick /trɪk; trɪk/ *n* **1** thing done in order to deceive or outwit sb 诡计; 计谋; 花招; 骗术: *play a trick on sb* 对某人施用诡计 ○ *We need a trick to get past the guards.* 我们需要用计骗过岗哨. ○ *You can't fool me with that old trick!* 你玩弄那种老花招骗不了我! ○ (*fig* 比喻) *a trick of the light*, ie that makes one see sth that is not there 光线引起的幻觉 ○ [attrib 作定语] *a 'trick question* 骗人的问题 ○ *'trick photography* 特技摄影. **2** exact or best way of doing sth; particular technique 诀窍; 技巧; 技艺: *The trick is to hold your breath while you aim.* 窍门就在于瞄准时须屏住呼吸. ○ *I can't open the box — is there a trick to it?* 这箱子我打不开——有什么好办法吗? ○ *before artists had mastered the tricks of perspective* 在画画的人掌握透视画法以前 ○ *I've never learnt the trick of making friends easily.* 我一向不擅长轻易交上朋友. **3** skilful act performed for entertainment, esp one involving illusion 戏法; 把戏; (尤指)魔术手法: *conjuring tricks* 变戏法 ○ *Let me show you some card tricks.* 我来给你表演一些纸牌戏法. ○ *She had trained her dog to do tricks*, eg to stand on its hind legs. 她把狗训练得能表演杂技动作(如用后腿站立). **4** characteristic habit; mannerism 特殊习惯; 习性; 毛病: *He has an annoying trick of saying 'You know?' after every sentence.* 他有个讨厌的口头语, 每句话后面都要来个'你知道吗?' ○ *My car has*

T

developed a trick of stalling on steep hills. 我的汽车出了个毛病, 一上山坡就熄火. **5** (cards played in) one round of a card-game (纸牌游戏的)一圈, 一墩, 一圈所打的牌, 一墩牌: *take/win a trick*, ie win a round 赢一墩牌 ○ *How many tricks did we lose?* 我们输了几墩了? **6** (idm 习语) **be up to one's (old) 'tricks** (*infml* 口) be acting in a characteristic way that sb disapproves of 施展让某人不悦的惯技: *Half my money's gone — you've been up to your tricks again, haven't you?* 我的钱少了一半——又是你干的, 对不对? **do the job/trick** ⇨ JOB. **every/any trick in the 'book** every/any trick that can be used to achieve what one wants 每一种[各种]着数或计谋: *I tried every trick in the book but I still couldn't persuade them.* 我使尽了浑身解数也劝不动他们. ○ *He'll use any trick in the book to stop you.* 他一定千方百计阻止你. **have a 'trick up one's sleeve** have an idea, plan, etc that can be used if it becomes necessary 必要时可用的主意、计划等; 袖里玄机; 袖里的鬼招儿. **how's 'tricks?** (*sl* 俚) how are you? 你好吗? **not/never miss a trick** ⇨ MISS[3]. **teach an old dog new tricks** ⇨ TEACH. **,trick or 'treat** (*esp US*) (phrase said by children who call at houses on Hallowe'en to receive sweets, etc and threaten mischief if they do not receive any 万圣节前夕儿童挨家索要糖果等的用语, 谓若不给则搞恶作剧). **the ,tricks of the 'trade** (**a**) clever ways of doing things, known to and used by experts (内行人的)诀窍, 窍门. (**b**) ways of attracting customers, gaining advantages over rivals, etc 吸引顾客、在竞争中取胜等的手段; 生意经: *She's only been with us a month so she's still learning the tricks of the trade.* 她到我们这里才一个月, 还正在学习行内乾坤. **the whole bag of tricks** ⇨ WHOLE.

▷ **trick** *v* **1** [Tn, Tn·pr] deceive (sb) 欺骗, 欺诈(某人): *You've been tricked.* 你受骗了. **2** [Tn·pr] (**a**) **~ sb into sth/doing sth** cause sb to do sth by means of a trick 用计诱使某人做某事: *She tricked him into marriage/into marrying her.* 她施了个巧计诱他娶她为妻. (**b**) **~ sb out of sth** cause sb to lose sth by means of a trick; swindle 骗走某人的某物; 诈骗: *Her partner tried to trick her out of her share.* 她的合伙人企图骗走她的股分. **3** (phr v) **trick sb/sth out/up (in/with sth)** decorate or ornament sb/sth 打扮或装饰某人[某物]: *tricked herself out in all her finery* 把她自己竭尽所能打扮起来.

trick·ery /-ərɪ; -ərɪ/ *n* [U] deception; cheating 欺骗; 欺诈; 施诡计; 耍花招.

trick·ster /-stə(r); -stɚ/ *n* person who tricks or cheats people; swindler 耍花招的人; 骗子.

tricky *adj* (**-ier, -iest**) (**a**) (of work, etc) requiring skill or tact (指工作等)需要技巧或智谋的: *a tricky situation, problem, decision* 需慎重对待的情况、需慎重处理的问题、需慎重做出的决定. (**b**) (of people or their actions) crafty; deceptive (指人及人的行为)诡计多端的, 欺骗的: *He's a tricky fellow to do business with.* 他诡计多端难以共事. **trick·ily** *adv.* **tricki·ness** *n* [U].

trickle /ˈtrɪkl; ˋtrɪkḷ/ *v* **1** [I, Ipr, Ip, Tn·pr, Tn·p] (cause sth to) flow in a thin stream (使某物)成小股流动: *Blood trickled from the wound.* 血液从伤口中流出. ○ *tears trickling down her cheeks* 顺着她的面颊流下的泪水 ○ *trickle oil into the mixture bit by bit* 把油一点点地注入混合物中. **2** [Ipr, Ip] come or go somewhere slowly or gradually 慢慢地或渐渐地来或去: *people trickling into the hall* 缓缓进入大厅的人们 ○ *The ball trickled into the hole.* 那球慢慢地滚进洞内. ○ *News is starting to trickle out.* 消息逐渐传出.

▷ **trickle** *n* **1** thin flow of liquid 小股水流; 涓涓细流: *The stream is reduced to a mere trickle in summer.* 夏天那小河水量减少, 成了涓涓细流. **2** (usu *sing* 通常作单数) **~ (of sth)** small amount coming or going slowly 缓慢来的或离去的少量事物: *a trickle of information* 一点一点来的少量信息.

□ **'trickle charger** device for the slow continuous charging of an accumulator 涓流充电器(使蓄电池缓慢而连续充电的装置).

tri·col·our (*US* **tri·co·lor**) /ˈtrɪkələ(r); *US* ˈtraɪkʌlər; ˋtraɪ,kʌlɚ/ *n* **1** [C] flag with three colours in stripes 三色旗. **2 the Tricolour** [sing] the French national flag, with vertical blue, white and red stripes 法国国旗.

tri·cycle /ˈtraɪsɪkl; ˋtraɪsɪkḷ/ (also *infml* 口语作 **trike**) *n* vehicle like a bicycle but with one wheel at the front and two at the back 三轮脚踏车.

tri·dent /ˈtraɪdnt; ˋtraɪdṇt/ *n* spear with three points (carried by Neptune and Britannia as a symbol of power over the sea) 三叉戟(尼普顿海神及不列颠女神所执, 为海权象征).

tried *pt, pp* of TRY[1].

tri·en·nial /traɪˈenɪəl; traɪˋɛnɪəl/ *adj* lasting for or happening every three years 持续三年的; 每三年一次的. ▷ **tri·en·ni·ally** /-nɪəlɪ; -nɪəlɪ/ *adv*: *The games occur triennially.* 运动会每三年举行一次.

trier ⇨ TRY[1].

trifle /ˈtraɪfl; ˋtraɪfl/ *n* **1** [C] thing, question or activity that has little value or importance 无多大价值或重要性的事物、问题或活动: *I bought a few trifles as souvenirs.* 我买了些零碎的纪念品. ○ *It's silly to quarrel over trifles.* 为鸡毛蒜皮的小事争吵真不值得. ○ *He spends all his time on crosswords and other trifles.* 他把所有的时间都用在做纵横填字游戏和其他无聊的活动上. **2** [C] small amount of money 少量的钱: *It cost a mere trifle.* 值不了多少钱. **3** [C, U] sweet dish made of sponge-cake and sometimes fruit, usu soaked in wine or jelly, and topped with custard and cream 松糕点心(用蛋糕做成的甜食, 有时带水果, 通常浸于酒中或果冻中, 上浇蛋奶沙司和奶油). **4** (idm 习语) **a trifle** slightly; rather 稍微; 有点儿: *This dress is a trifle short.* 这件连衣裙稍短了点. ○ *Isn't the meat a trifle tough?* 这肉有点老吧? ○ *Try turning the key a trifle (more).* 你试试把钥匙再(多)转一点儿.

▷ **trifle** *v* [Ipr] **~ with sb/sth** treat sb/sth lightly or casually; toy with sb/sth 轻视或随便对待某人[某事物]; 心不在焉地考虑或处理某人[某事物]: *He's not a man to be trifled with*, ie He must be treated with respect. 他这人可小看不得. ○ (*fml* 文) *Its wrong of you to trifle with her affections*, ie make her think you love her when you don't. 你玩弄她的感情是不对的. **tri·fling** /ˈtraɪflɪŋ; ˋtraɪflɪŋ/ *adj* unimportant; trivial 不重要的; 琐碎的: *a few trifling errors* 一些小错误 ○ *This is no trifling matter*, ie It is serious. 这可不是小事. **tri·fler** /ˈtraɪflə(r); ˋtraɪflɚ/ *n* person who trifles 轻视或随便对待某人[某事物]的人.

trig·ger /ˈtrɪgə(r); ˋtrɪgɚ/ *n* lever that releases a spring, esp so as to fire a gun (释放弹簧的)扳柄; (尤指枪的)扳机: *squeeze the trigger* 扣扳机 ○ *have one's finger on the trigger*, ie be ready to shoot 手指触及扳机(准备射击). ⇨illus at GUN 见GUN插图.

▷ **trig·ger** *v* [Tn, Tn·p] **~ sth (off)** be the cause of a sudden (often) violent reaction; set an action or a process in motion 成为突然发生的(常为激烈的)反应的原因; 发动; 引发: *The riots were triggered (off) by a series of police arrests.* 警方一连串的逮捕行动激发了暴乱. ○ *The smoke triggered off the alarm.* 这些烟把警报器触响了.

□ **'trigger-happy** *adj* (*infml derog* 口, 贬) ready to react violently, esp by shooting, even when only slightly provoked 爱做出激烈反应的; (尤指)动辄开枪的.

tri·go·no·metry /,trɪgəˈnɒmətrɪ; ,trɪgəˋnɑmətrɪ/ *n* [U] branch of mathematics dealing with the relationship between the sides and angles of triangles, etc 三角学.
▷ **tri·go·no·met·ric, -met·rical** /,trɪgənəˈmetrɪk, -kl; ,trɪgənəˋmɛtrɪk, -kl/ *adjs*. **tri·go·no·met·ric·ally** /-klɪ; -klɪ/ *adv*.

trike /traɪk; traɪk/ *n* (*infml* 口) = TRICYCLE.

tri·lat·eral /,traɪˈlætərəl; traɪˋlætərəl/ *adj* [usu attrib 通常作定语] involving three sides, groups, countries, etc 涉及三个方面、团体、国家等的; 三边的: *,trilateral di'scussions* 三方之间的商讨 ○ *a ,trilateral a'greement* 三边协定. ▷ **tri·lat·erally** *adv*.

trilby /ˈtrɪlbɪ; ˋtrɪlbɪ/ *n* man's soft felt hat with a narrow brim and the top part hollowed from front to back (男用)软毡帽.

tri·lin·gual /,traɪˈlɪŋgwəl; traɪˋlɪŋgwəl/ *adj* speaking or using three languages 能说三种语言的; 使用三种语言的.

trill /trɪl; trɪl/ *n* **1** vibrating sound made by the voice or in bird song (人或鸟发出的)颤动声. **2** (*music* 音) (sound of) two notes a tone or a semitone apart being played or sung several times one after the other (音的)颤动; 颤音. **3** speech sound made by pronouncing 'r' while vibrating the tongue (舌的)颤音, 颤动辅音.

▷ **trill** *v* [I, Ip, Tn] **1** sound or sing (a musical note) with a trill 用颤音发声; 用颤音唱(某乐音): *The canary was trilling away in its cage.* 那只金丝雀在笼中鸣啭. **2** pronounce (a letter) with a trill 用颤音发(某字母)的音; 发某字母的颤音.

tril·lion /ˈtrɪlɪən; ˋtrɪljən/ *n, pron, det* **1** (*Brit*) (the number) 1 000 000 000 000 000 000; one million million million 一百亿亿(个). ⇨App 4 见附录4. **2** (*US*) (the number) 1 000 000 000 000; one million million 一万亿(个). ⇨ App 4 见附录4. ▷ **tril·lionth** /ˈtrɪlɪənθ; ˋtrɪljənθ/ *n, pron, det.*

For the use of *trillion* and *trillionth* see the examples at *hundred* and *hundredth.* 关于trillion和trillionth的用法见hundred和hundredth词条中的示例.

tri·lob·ite /ˈtraɪləbaɪt; ˋtraɪlə,baɪt/ *n* extinct sea animal found as a fossil 三叶虫(已绝灭的海洋动物, 仅存化石).

tri·logy /ˈtrɪlədʒɪ; ˋtrɪlədʒɪ/ *n* group of three related works, esp three novels or operas 三部曲(尤指小说或歌剧).

trim[1] /trɪm; trɪm/ *adj* **(-mmer, -mmest)** (*approv* 褒) **1** in a good order; neat and tidy 整然有序的; 整齐的: *a trim ship* 整齐的船 ○ *He keeps his garden trim.* 他把花园整理得井然有序. **2** slim or elegant 修长的; 苗条的; 优雅的: *a trim waistline, figure, etc* 苗条的腰身、身材等. ▷ **trimly** *adv.* **trimness** *n* [U].

trim[2] /trɪm; trɪm/ *v* **(-mm-)** **1 (a)** [Tn, Tn·p] make (sth) neat or smooth by cutting away irregular parts (藉切除不规则的部分)使(某物)整齐或光滑; 整修, 修剪(某物): *trim the top of a hedge* 修剪树篱 ○ *trim one's beard (back)* 修胡子. **(b)** [Tn, Tn·pr, Tn·p] **~ sth (off sth/off)** remove sth or reduce sth by cutting (用切、割、剪、砍等方式)除去或削减某物: *The article's too long. Can you trim it (by a quarter)?* 这篇文章太长. 你能删减(四分之一)吗? ○ *Please trim the excess fat off (the meat).* 请把过多的肥膘(从肉上)切掉. ○ *I trimmed an inch off the hem of this skirt* 我把这条裙子的下摆剪短了一英寸. ○ *We had to trim a lot off our travel budget.* 我们当时只好大量削减旅行预算. ⇨Usage at CLIP[2] 用法见CLIP[2]. **2** [Tn, Tn·pr] **~ sth (with sth)** decorate or ornament sth 装饰某物: *trim a dress with lace* 用花边装饰连衣裙 ○ *a hat trimmed with flowers* 用花装饰的帽子. **3** [Tn] make (a boat, a ship or an aircraft) evenly balanced by arranging the position of the cargo or passengers 调整货物或乘客的位置使(船或飞机)平稳. **4** [Tn] set (sails) to suit the wind 调整(船帆)以适应风向.

▷ **trim** *n* **1** [C usu *sing* 通常作单数] trimming of hair, etc 修剪毛发等: *The lawn needs a trim.* 草坪得修剪了. **2** [C, U] decorations or fittings for clothes, furniture, etc (衣物、家具等的)饰物或配件: *a yard of gold trim* 一码的金色边饰 ○ *The car is available with black or red trim,* ie upholstery, etc. 这种汽车的装修(即坐具等)有黑色的也有红色的. **3** (idm 习语) **be in/get into ˈtrim** be/get ready or fit 准备好; 健康适宜: *in good, proper, excellent, etc trim* 身体好、健康、极佳等 ○ *She's got a month to get into trim for the race.* 她参加径赛前有一个月的准备时间.

trim·mer *n* person or thing that trims 做修剪或装饰等工作的人或工具: *an electric hedge trimmer* 电动树篱修剪机.

trim·ming *n* **1** [U, C] material, eg lace or tinsel, used to decorate sth 装饰材料(如花边或金属箔). **2 trimmings** [pl] **(a)** pieces cut off when sth is trimmed 修剪下来的东西: *pastry trimmings* 切下的油酥面团的多余部分. **(b)** usual accompaniments of sth; extras 通常的伴随物或附加物; 额外的事物: *roast turkey and all the trimmings,* ie vegetables, stuffing, sauces, etc 烤火鸡及各种配料(蔬菜、填料、沙司等).

tri·maran /ˈtraɪməræn; ˋtraɪmə,ræn/ *n* boat built like a catamaran but with three parallel hulls instead of two 三体船(有三个平行的船身).

tri·nit·ro·tolu·ene /ˌtraɪˌnaɪtrəʊˈtɒljʊiːn; traɪ,naɪtroˋtɑlju,in/ *n* [U] ⇨ TNT.

trin·ity /ˈtrɪnətɪ; ˋtrɪnətɪ/ *n* **1** (*fml* 文) group of three things or people; trio 三个事物或三个人的一组; 三件的一套; 三人小组; 三合一. **2 the Trinity** (in Christianity) the union of Father, Son and Holy Spirit as one God (基督教教义中的)三位一体(圣父、圣子及圣灵合为上帝).

□ ˌ**Trinity ˈSunday** Sunday after Whit Sunday 三一节(圣灵降临节后的第一个星期日).

trin·ket /ˈtrɪŋkɪt; ˋtrɪŋkɪt/ *n* small ornament, piece of jewellery, etc of little value 廉价的小装饰品、首饰等.

trio /ˈtriːəʊ; ˋtrio/ *n* (*pl* **~s**) **1** [CGp] group of three people or things 三个人或三个事物的一组; 三人小组; 三件一套; 三合一. **2** [C, CGp] (*music* 音) (composition for a) group of three players or singers 三重奏小组; 三重唱小组; 三重奏曲; 三重唱曲: *a piano trio,* eg for piano, violin and cello 钢琴三重奏(如由钢琴、小提琴及大提琴组成的).

trip /trɪp; trɪp/ *v* **(-pp-)** **1 (a)** [I, Ipr, Ip] **~ (over/up)** catch one's foot on sth and stumble or fall 绊; 绊倒: *She tripped (over the cat) and fell.* 她(让猫)绊了一跤. ○ *Be careful you don't trip (up) on the mat.* 小心别在地席上绊倒了. ○ *I tripped over, dropping the tray I was carrying.* 我绊了一下, 手中的托盘掉在地上了. **(b)** [Tn, Tn·p] **~ sb (up)** cause sb to do this 使某人绊跤; 绊倒某人: *He tried to trip me up.* 他想把我绊倒. **2** [I, Ipr, Ip] walk, run or dance with quick light steps 轻快地行走、奔跑或跳舞: *She came tripping down the garden path.* 她轻快地沿着花园小路跑来. ○ (*fig* 比喻) *a melody with a light tripping rhythm* 节奏轻快的曲调. **3** [Tn] release (a switch or catch); operate (a mechanism) by doing this 松开(开关); (松开开关)开动(机器): *trip the shutter,* ie of a camera 按动快门 ○ *If anyone tampers with this door it trips the alarm.* 要是有人撬这扇门, 就会触响警报器. **4** [I, Ip] **~ (out)** (*dated sl* 旧, 俚) have a trip(*n* 1) (通常指短途)行走, 行驶, 旅行(尤指娱乐). **5** (phr v) **trip (sb) up** (cause sb to) make a mistake, reveal a secret, etc (使某人)犯错误、泄漏秘密等: *The lawyer was trying to trip the witnesses up,* ie make them contradict themselves. 那律师竭力想让证人互相矛盾. ○ *I tripped up in the interview and said something rather silly.* 我在面试中不慎说了一些蠢话.

▷ **trip** *n* **1** (usu short) journey, esp for pleasure (通常指短途的)行走, 行驶, 旅行(尤指娱乐性的): *a trip to the seaside* 海滨之行 ○ *during my last trip to London* 在我上次去伦敦的行程中 ○ *a honeymoon trip to Venice* 前往威尼斯的蜜月旅行. ⇨Usage at JOURNEY 用法见JOURNEY. **2** (*sl* 俚) experience, esp one caused by taking a hallucinating drug 体验; (尤指服用致幻剂后的)幻觉体验: *an acid* (ie LSD) *trip* 迷幻药产生的幻觉 ○ *a good/bad trip* 舒服的[不舒服的]迷幻感受. **3** act of tripping (TRIP *v* 1) or being tripped; fall or stumble 绊; 绊倒. **4** device for tripping (TRIP *v* 3) a mechanism 松开机械开关的装置.

trip·per *n* person making a short journey for pleasure 作短程旅游的人: *The beach was packed with day trippers.* 海滩上到处都是当日远足的人.

trip·ping *adj* [esp attrib 尤作定语] (of movements, rhythms, etc) quick and light (指运动、节奏等)快而轻的. **trip·pingly** *adv.*

□ ˈ**trip-wire** *n* wire stretched close to the ground, which works a trap or warning device, etc when a person or an animal trips against it (陷阱或报警装置的)绊索, 绊网.

tri·part·ite /ˌtraɪˈpɑːtaɪt; traɪˋpɑrtaɪt/ *adj* [usu attrib 通常作定语] (*fml* 文) having three parts or involving three people, groups, etc 有三部分的; 涉及三人、三团体等的: *a triˌpartite diˈvision* 包括三部分的划分 ○ *triˌpartite diˈscussions* 三方的磋商 ○ *a triˌpartite aˈgreement* 三者间的协议.

tripe /traɪp; traɪp/ *n* [U] **1** stomach of a cow, etc used as food 肚儿(用做食物的牛羊等的胃): *boiled tripe and onions* 洋葱炖牛肚. **2** (*sl* 俚) **(a)** nonsense 废话; 胡说: *Don't talk tripe!* 别说废话! **(b)** writing, music, etc of low quality 拙劣的文章、音乐等: *I don't read that tripe.* 我才不看那种无聊的东西呢.

triple /ˈtrɪpl; ˋtrɪpl/ *adj* [usu attrib 通常作定语] **1** having three parts or involving three people, groups, etc 有三部分的; 涉及三人、三团体等的: *The plan has a triple purpose,* ie three purposes. 这个计划有三个目的. ○ *triple time,* ie rhythm with three beats to the bar 三拍子(每节有三拍的节奏) ○ *a triple alliance,* ie between three countries 三国同盟. **2** three times as much or as many 三倍的; 三重的: *travelling at triple the speed* 以三倍的速度前进 ○ *a triple whisky,* ie a glass containing three times the usual quantity 一杯含三倍分量的威士忌酒 ○ *a triple murderer,* ie one who has killed three people 谋杀三个

T

人的人.

▷ **triple** *v* [I, Tn] (cause sth to) become three times as much or as many (使某物)增至三倍, 成三倍: *Output has tripled.* 产量已增加到三倍.

triply *adv.*

□ **the triple ˈjump** athletic contest of jumping as far forward as possible with three leaps, the first two landing on alternate feet, the third on both feet 三级跳远.

trip·let /ˈtrɪplɪt; ˋtrɪplɪt/ *n* **1** (usu *pl* 通常作复数) any of three children or animals born at one time 三胞胎中的一个: *His wife gave birth to triplets.* 他妻子生了三胞胎. **2** set of three things 三个的一组; 三件之一套. **3** (*music* 音) group of three equal notes to be performed in the time usually taken to perform two of the same kind 三连音符.

trip·lic·ate /ˈtrɪplɪkət; ˋtrɪpləkɪt/ *n* (idm 习语) **in triplicate** consisting of three identical copies, of which one is the original 一式三份(其中一份为正本): *submit an application in triplicate* 提交一式三份的申请书.

▷ **trip·lic·ate** /ˈtrɪplɪkeɪt; ˋtrɪplə,ket/ *v* [Tn] copy (sth) so that there are three copies including the original 把(某物)制成一式三份(包括正本).

tri·pod /ˈtraɪpɒd; ˋtraɪpɑd/ *n* support with three legs for a camera, telescope, etc (照相机、望远镜等的)三脚架.

trip·per ⇨ TRIP.

trip·tych /ˈtrɪptɪk; ˋtrɪptɪk/ *n* picture or carving on three panels fixed side by side, esp one placed over an altar in a church 三幅相联的图画或雕刻(尤指置于教堂圣坛上方的).

tri·sect /traɪˈsekt; traɪˋsɛkt/ *v* [Tn] divide (a line, an angle, etc) into three equal parts 将(一线、角等)分成三等份. ▷ **tri·sec·tion** /traɪˈsekʃn; traɪˋsɛkʃən/ *n* [U].

trite /traɪt; traɪt/ *adj* (of a phrase, an opinion, etc) not new or original, because often used; hackneyed; commonplace (指词语、意见等)陈腐的, 老一套的, 平淡无奇的.

tri·umph /ˈtraɪʌmf; ˋtraɪəmf/ *n* **1** [U] (joy or satisfaction at) being successful or victorious 成功或胜利(的喜悦或满足): *shouts of triumph* 胜利的欢呼声 ○ *The winning team returned home in triumph.* 获胜的队奏凯而归. **2** [C] great achievement or success 巨大的成就或成功: *one of the triumphs of modern science* 现代科学的一项重大成就 ○ *She scored a resounding triumph over her rival.* 她击败对手大获全胜.

▷ **tri·umph** *v* [I, Ipr] **~ (over sb/sth)** be successful or victorious 获得成功或胜利: *Common sense triumphed in the end.* 人的理智终于战胜了一切. ○ *triumph over one's difficulties*, ie overcome them 战胜困难.

tri·umphal /traɪˈʌmfl; traɪˋʌmfḷ/ *adj* [usu attrib 通常作定语] **1** of or for a triumph 胜利的; 成功的; 庆祝胜利的: *a triumphal arch*, ie one built to honour a victory in war 凯旋门(为纪念战争胜利而建). **2** expressing triumph 表现成功或胜利的: *a triumphal chorus* 凯歌大合唱.

triumphant /traɪˈʌmfnt; traɪˋʌmfənt/ *adj* (rejoicing at) having triumphed 成功的; 获胜的; (因成功或胜利)欢欣鼓舞的: *a triumphant cheer* 胜利的欢呼声. **tri·umph·antly** *adv.*

tri·um·vir·ate /traɪˈʌmvɪrət; traɪˋʌmvərɪt/ *n* ruling group of three people 三人统治集团; 三人领导小组: *The company is run jointly by a triumvirate of directors.* 这家公司是由三人组成的董事会经管的.

trivet /ˈtrɪvɪt; ˋtrɪvɪt/ *n* **1** metal stand, usu with three legs, for holding hot pans, etc, or formerly for kettles or pots placed over a fire (垫热锅盆等用的)金属架(通常有三脚, 旧时放在火上坐壶、锅等). **2** (idm 习语) **right as a trivet** ⇨ RIGHT[1].

trivia /ˈtrɪvɪə; ˋtrɪvɪə/ *n* [pl] (*usu derog* 通常作贬义) unimportant things, details or pieces of information 无关紧要的事物、细节或信息.

triv·ial /ˈtrɪvɪəl; ˋtrɪvɪəl/ *adj* (*often derog* 常作贬义) that has little importance 不重要的; 琐碎的: *a trivial mistake, loss, offence* 小小的错误、损失、罪过 ○ *raise trivial objections to sth* 对某事物提出小小不言的反对意见 ○ (*fml* 文) *a trivial young man*, ie one who is only concerned with trivial things 浅薄的年轻男子.

▷ **tri·vi·al·ity** /ˌtrɪvɪˈælətɪ; ˌtrɪvɪˋælətɪ/ *n* (*derog* 贬) **1** [U] state of being trivial 无足轻重. **2** [C] trivial thing 琐碎的事物: *waste time on trivialities* 把时间浪费在琐碎的小事上.

trivi·al·ize, -ise /ˈtrɪvɪəlaɪz; ˋtrɪvɪəl,aɪz/ *v* [Tn] (*derog* 贬) make (a subject, problem, etc) seem trivial 使(某事情、问题等)显得不重要、琐碎等: *Too many films trivialize violence.* 有许许多多影片把暴力行为描述成是鸡毛蒜皮的事. **trivi·al·iza·tion, -isation** /ˌtrɪvɪəlaɪˈzeɪʃn; *US* -lɪˈz-; ˌtrɪvɪələˋzeʃən/ *n* [U, C].

trivi·ally /-ɪəlɪ; -ɪəlɪ/ *adv.*

trod *pt* of TREAD.

trod·den *pp* of TREAD.

trog·lo·dyte /ˈtrɒglədaɪt; ˋtrɑglə,daɪt/ *n* person living in a cave, esp in prehistoric times 穴居人(尤指史前时期的).

troika /ˈtrɔɪkə; ˋtrɔɪkə/ *n* **1** small Russian carriage pulled by three horses (俄国的)三驾马车. **2** group of three people working together, esp as political leaders of a country 三人工作小组; (尤指国家的)三人领导班子, 三头政治.

Tro·jan /ˈtrəʊdʒən; ˋtrodʒən/ *n, adj* **1** (inhabitant) of Troy, an ancient city in Asia Minor (小亚细亚古城)特洛伊的, 特洛伊人: *the Trojan war*, ie between the Greeks and the Trojans, as described by Homer 特洛伊战争(古希腊人与特洛伊人之战, 荷马史诗曾述其事). **2** (idm 习语) **work like a ˈblack/ˈTrojan** ⇨ BLACK[2].

□ ˌ**Trojan ˈhorse** person or thing used to harm an enemy or opponent, who wrongly believes he is being helped 特洛伊木马(用以使敌方或对手上当误以为于己有益的破坏性的人或事物).

troll[1] /trəʊl; trol/ *v* [I, Ipr] **~ (for sth)** fish with a rod and line by pulling bait through the water behind a boat (在船后用杆和绳)拖饵钓鱼: *trolling for pike* 拖钓狗鱼.

troll[2] /trəʊl; trol/ *n* (in Scandinavian myths) evil giant or mischievous but friendly dwarf (斯堪的那维亚神话中的)山精(邪恶的巨怪或顽皮的侏儒).

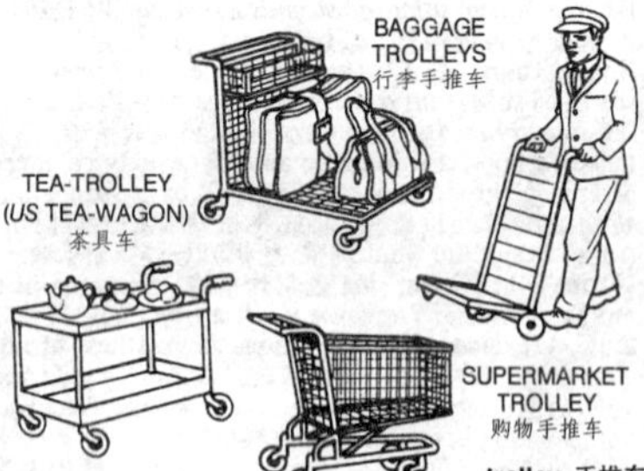

trolley 手推车

trol·ley /ˈtrɒlɪ; ˋtrɑlɪ/ *n* (*pl* **~s**) **1** cart on wheels that can be pushed or pulled along and is used for moving goods 手推车; 手拉车: *a ˈluggage trolley* 运送行李的手推车 ○ *a ˈshopping trolley*, eg in a supermarket 购物手推车(如超级市场中的). **2** small table on wheels for transporting or serving food, etc (运或送食物等用的)脚轮车, 台车: *a ˈtea-trolley* 茶具车. ⇨illus at App 1 见附录1插图, page xvi. **3** small low truck running on rails, used eg by workmen repairing tracks 在铁轨上行驶的小车(如查道车). **4** (also ˈ**trolley-wheel**) small wheel or other device making contact between an electrically powered vehicle and an overhead cable (电动车辆与架空电缆接触的)触轮或其他设备. **5** (*US*) = TRAM.

□ ˈ**trolley bus** *n* bus powered by electricity from an overhead cable 无轨电车.

trol·lop /ˈtrɒləp; ˋtrɑləp/ *n* (*dated derog* 旧, 贬) untidy or sexually immoral woman; slut 邋遢女人; 荡妇.

trom·bone /trɒmˈbəʊn; trɑmˋbon/ *n* large brass musical instrument with a sliding tube used to raise or lower the note 长号(装有可伸缩套管的). ⇨illus at App 1 见附录1插图, page x.

▷ **trom·bon·ist** /trɒmˈbəʊnɪst; trɑmˋbonɪst/ *n* person who plays a trombone 吹长号的人.

troop /tru:p; trup/ *n* **1** [C] large group of people or animals, esp when moving (人或动物的)大群(尤指移动中的): *a troop of schoolchildren* 一群小学生 ○ *troops* *of deer* 成群的鹿. **2 troops** [pl] soldiers 军队; 部队: *demand the withdrawal of foreign troops* 要求撤出外国军队. **3** [C] unit of armoured vehicles or artillery or cavalry 装甲或炮兵部队的连队; 骑兵队; 骑兵连. **4** [C] local group of Scouts 童子军队.

▷ **troop** *v* **1** [I, Ipr, Ip] (with a *pl* subject 与复数主语配合) come or go together as a troop or in large numbers 成群结队而行: *children trooping out of school* 成队离开学校的儿童. **2** (idm 习语) **ˌtrooping the ˈcolour** (*Brit*) ceremony of carrying a regiment's flag along ranks of soldiers, esp on the birthday of the king or queen 军旗敬礼分列式(尤指于国君诞辰日举行的).

trooper *n* **1** soldier in an armoured unit or a cavalry unit 装甲兵; 骑兵. **2** (*US*) member of a State police force 州警察. **3** (idm 习语) **swear like a trooper** ⇨ SWEAR.

□ ˈ**troop-ship** *n* ship for transporting soldiers 运兵船.

trope /trəʊp; trop/ *n* (*fml* 文) figurative use of a word or phrase 辞格; 修辞格.

trophy /ˈtrəʊfɪ; ˈtrofɪ/ *n* **1** object awarded as a prize, esp for winning a sports tournament 奖品(尤指体育比赛的): *the Wimbledon ˈtennis trophy* 温布尔登网球赛奖杯. **2** object taken or kept as a souvenir of success in hunting, war, etc (狩猎、战争等中获得的)纪念品, 战利品: *a set of antlers and other trophies* 一对鹿角及其他狩猎纪念物.

tropic /ˈtrɒpɪk; ˈtrɑpɪk/ *n* **1** [C usu *sing* 通常作单数] line of latitude 23°27′ north (*the tropic of Cancer*) or south (*the tropic of Capricorn*) of the equator 回归线(北纬23°27′之北回归线称 the tropic of Cancer, 南纬 23°27′之南回归线称 the tropic of Capricorn). ⇨ illus at GLOBE 见 GLOBE 插图. **2 the tropics** [pl] region between these two latitudes, with a hot climate 热带(地区).

▷ **trop·ical** /-kl; -kḷ/ *adj* of, like or found in the tropics (似)热带(地区)的; 见于热带地区的: *tropical fruit* 热带水果 ○ *a tropical climate* 热带气候 ○ *August was almost tropical* (ie very hot) *this year.* 今年的八月十分炎热.

trop·ic·ally /-klɪ; -klɪ/ *adv*.

tro·po·sphere /ˈtrɒpəsfɪə(r); *US* ˈtrəʊp-; ˈtropəˌsfɪr/ *n* [sing] (usu 通常作 **the troposphere**) layer of the atmosphere that extends about seven miles upwards from the earth's surface 对流层(距地表约七英里).

Trot /trɒt; trɑt/ *n* (*sl usu derog* 俚, 通常作贬义) Trotskyist 托洛茨基分子; 托派分子.

trot /trɒt; trɑt/ *v* (**-tt-**) **1** (**a**) [I, Ipr, Ip] (of a horse or its rider) move at a pace faster than a walk but slower than a gallop (指马或骑马者)小跑. (**b**) [Tn, Tn·pr, Tn·p] ride (a horse) at such a pace 骑(马)小跑. **2** [I, Ipr, Ip] (**a**) (of a person) run with short steps (指人)小步快跑: *The child was trotting along beside its parents.* 那孩子小跑着跟在父母身边. (**b**) (*infml* 口) walk or go (usu at a normal pace) 步行, 走(通常指正常速度): *I'm just trotting round to the pub.* 我现在要到酒店那儿去. ⇨Usage at RUN[1] 用法见 RUN[1]. **3** (phr v) **trot sth out** (*infml derog* 口, 贬) produce (esp information, explanations, etc often given before) for sb to hear or see 让某人听或看(尤指信息、解说性的事物等, 常指提供过的): *He always trots out the same old excuses for being late.* 他每次迟到总是重复那一套借口.

▷ **trot** *n* **1** [sing] trotting pace 小跑; 小步快跑: *go at a steady trot* 一路小跑. **2** [C] period of trotting 小跑的一段时间: *go for a trot* 去小跑一阵. **3 the trots** [pl] (*sl* 俚) diarrhoea 腹泻: *get the trots* 拉肚子. **4** (idm 习语) **on the ˈtrot** (*infml* 口) (**a**) one after the other 一个接一个; 接连: *for eight hours on the trot* 一连八个小时. (**b**) continually busy 忙忙碌碌: *I've been on the trot all day.* 我忙了一整天. ○ *Her new job certainly keeps her on the trot.* 她的新工作把她忙得不可开交.

trot·ter *n* **1** horse bred and trained for trotting-races (为作快步马赛训练的)快步马. **2** (usu *pl* 通常作复数) pig's or sheep's foot, esp as food 猪蹄, 羊蹄(尤指作食物的).

troth /trəʊθ; *US* trɔːθ; troθ/ *n* (*arch* 古) (idm 习语) **plight one's troth** ⇨ PLIGHT[2].

Trot·sky·ism /ˈtrɒtskɪɪzəm; ˈtrɑtskɪˌɪzəm/ *n* [U] political or economic ideas of Leon Trotsky, esp the principle of world-wide socialist revolution 托洛茨基主义(利昂·托洛茨基的政治或经济思想, 尤指世界范围的社会主义革命学说).

▷ **Trot·sky·ist** /ˈtrɒtskɪɪst; ˈtrɑtskɪɪst/ (also **Trot·sky·ite** /ˈtrɒtskɪaɪt; ˈtrɑtskiˌaɪt/) *n*, *adj* (supporter) of Trotskyism 托洛茨基主义的; 托洛茨基分子.

trou·ba·dour /ˈtruːbədɔː(r); *US* -dʊər; ˈtrubəˌdʊr/ *n* French travelling poet and singer in the 11th-13th centuries (11-13 世纪法国的)游吟诗人.

trouble /ˈtrʌbl; ˈtrʌbḷ/ *n* **1** [C, U] (situation causing) worry, pain, difficulty, danger, etc 忧虑、苦恼、痛苦、困难、危险等(产生的环境): *We're having trouble with our new car.* 我们的新汽车很让人伤脑筋. ○ *My teeth are giving* (ie causing) *me trouble.* 我牙疼得难受. ○ *If we're late, there'll be/it'll mean trouble*, ie unpleasantness, perhaps involving punishment. 我们要是迟到就倒霉了. ○ *family trouble(s)*, eg disagreements between parents and children 家庭纠纷(如父母与子女不合) ○ *Our troubles are not over yet.* 我们的烦恼还没完呢. ○ *The idea soon ran into trouble.* 那种想法不久就捅出娄子了. ○ *The trouble* (ie problem) *(with you) is...* (你的)问题在于... ○ *What's the trouble?* ie What's wrong? 出什么事了? **2** (**a**) [U] **~ (to sb)** inconvenience; bother 不便; 麻烦; 烦扰: *I don't want to be any trouble (to you).* 我不想打扰(你). ○ *Were the children much trouble?* 这些孩子很烦人吗? ○ *I can come back tomorrow, it's no trouble.* 我可以明天回来, 没问题. ○ *Repairing it is more trouble than it's worth.* 这东西修理起来很麻烦, 不值得修. ○ *I'm sorry to have to put you to so much trouble.* 很抱歉, 给您添了这么多麻烦. (**b**) [sing] (*fml* 文) thing that causes inconvenience or difficulty 造成不便或困难的事物: *This dish is delicious but rather a trouble to prepare.* 这种菜好吃不好做. ○ *I find getting up early a great trouble.* 我觉得早起床可不容易. **3** [C, U] disputes, fighting, etc; unrest 纠纷、纷争等; 不宁; 动乱: *the recent trouble(s) in South Africa* 南非近日的动乱 ○ *The firm's been hit by a lot of labour trouble*, eg strikes. 这个公司劳资纠纷(如罢工)频仍而严重受挫. **4** [U] (**a**) illness 疾病: *stomach, heart, liver, etc trouble* 胃病、心脏病、肝病 ○ *a history of mental trouble* 精神病病史. (**b**) faulty operation, eg of a machine or vehicle 故障(如机器或车辆的): *My car's got engine trouble.* 我的汽车发动机出毛病了. **5** (idm 习语) **ask for trouble/it** ⇨ ASK. **ˌget into ˈtrouble** cause trouble for oneself, eg by making a mistake 惹上麻烦(如因犯错所致): *Even an experienced climber can get into trouble.* 哪怕是个有经验的登山者也能陷入困境. ○ *He got into trouble with the police*, eg was arrested. 他惹事落到了警方手里(如被捕了). **get sb into ˈtrouble** (**a**) cause trouble for sb 给某人惹上麻烦: *Don't mention my name or you'll get me into trouble.* 别提我的名字, 免得给我惹麻烦. (**b**) (*infml* 口) make (an unmarried woman) pregnant 使(未婚女子)怀孕: *He got his girl-friend into trouble.* 他使女朋友怀孕了. **give (sb) (some, no, any, etc) ˈtrouble** cause trouble 造成苦恼、困难、麻烦等: *The new computer's been giving (us) a lot of trouble*, ie not working properly. 这台新计算机(给我们)添了许多麻烦(运转不正常). **go to a lot of, considerable, etc trouble (to do sth)** do sth even though it involves effort, inconvenience, etc 不辞劳苦、不怕费事做某事: *Thank you for going to so much trouble to find what I was looking for.* 多谢你这么费心找到了我要找的东西. **in trouble** (**a**) in a situation that involves danger, punishment, pain, worry, etc 在危险、受罚、痛苦、忧虑等的处境中: *If we can't keep to the schedule, we'll be in (a lot of) trouble.* 我们不按时完成计划就要倒(大)霉了. ○ *I'm in trouble with the police over drugs.* 我因毒品事落入警方手中. (**b**) (*infml* 口) (of an unmarried woman) pregnant (指未婚女子)怀孕. **ˈlook for trouble** (*infml* 口) behave in a way that suggests that one is hoping for unpleasantness, a violent reaction, etc 自找麻烦; 自寻烦恼; 自找苦吃: *drunken youths roaming the streets looking for trouble* 在街头游荡惹事生非的醉酒青年. **make trouble (for sb)** (eg of an enemy) cause trouble (如指仇敌)制造麻烦, 捣乱: *If I say no, the boss will only make trouble for me.* 我要是说个'不'字, 老板准跟我过不去. **take trouble over sth/with sth/to do sth/doing sth** use much care and effort in doing sth 尽心尽力地做某事: *They took a lot of trouble to find the right person for the job.* 他们费尽心血找适合做这项工作的人. **take the trouble to do sth** do sth even though it involves effort or difficulty 不怕费事或困难尽力做某事: *Decent journalists should take the* *trouble to check their facts.* 责任心强的新闻工作者应该不厌其烦地核实报道内容.

▷ **trouble** *v* **1** [Tn] cause worry, pain or inconvenience to (sb); bother 使(某人)忧虑、苦恼、痛苦或不便; 打扰: *be troubled by illness, doubt, bad news* 因疾病、疑虑、坏消息而苦恼 ○ *My back's been troubling me.* 我一直背疼难受. ○ *a troubled look* 忧虑的样子 ○ *What troubles me is that*… 使我感到苦恼的是… ○ *I'm sorry to trouble you, but*… 对不起打扰您一下, …. **2** [Tn·pr, Cn·t] **~ sb for sth** (**a**) (*fml* 文) (used with *may* or *might* in polite requests 与may或might连用表示客气的请求): *May I trouble you for the salt?* 麻烦您把盐递给我行吗? ○ *Might I trouble you to give me a lift to the station?* 劳驾让我顺便坐您的汽车到车站去可以吗? (**b**) (*dated* 旧) (used with *I'll* or *I must* in ironic or sarcastic requests 与I'll或I must连用, 表示带揶揄性或讽刺性的请求): *I'll trouble you to watch your manners.* 请您注意风度. **3** [I, Ipr, It] **~ (about sth)** (*fml* 文) (used esp in questions and negative sentences 尤用于疑问句和否定句中) let oneself be worried or concerned about sth 费神; 费心; 费劲: *'Do you want me to post it for you?' 'No, don't trouble (about it), thank you.'* '要我给您寄出去吗?' '不必费心了, 谢谢你.' ○ *Why should I trouble to explain it all?* 为什么我得费事都解释一遍呢? **4** (idm 习语) **fish in troubled waters** ⇨ FISH². **pour oil on troubled waters** ⇨ POUR.

'trouble·some /-səm; -səm/ *adj* giving trouble; causing annoyance, pain, etc 带来麻烦的; 造成烦恼、痛苦等的: *a troublesome child, problem, headache* 让人心烦的孩子、问题、头痛 ○ *My cough is rather troublesome today.* 我今天咳嗽得很难受.

□ **'trouble-maker** *n* person who often causes trouble, esp by upsetting others 常惹麻烦的人; 惹事生非的人; (尤指)惹人烦恼的人.

'trouble-shooter *n* person who helps to settle disputes (eg in industrial relations), or who traces and corrects faults in machinery, etc 调解人, 调停人(如劳资关系的); (机器等的)检修人员.

T

'trouble-spot *n* place where trouble frequently occurs, esp a country where there is a war 经常出事的地方; (尤指)战乱频仍的国家: *the world's major trouble-spots* 世界上主要的不安定地区.

trough /trɒf; *US* trɔːf; trɔf/ *n* **1** long narrow open box for animals to feed or drink from 饲料槽; 饮水槽. ⇨ illus at PIG 见PIG插图. **2** shallow channel that allows water, etc to drain away 排水沟. **3** low area between two waves or ridges 波谷; 低谷. ⇨illus at SURF 见SURF插图. **4** (in meteorology) long narrow region of low atmospheric pressure between two regions of higher pressure (气象)低压槽. Cf 参看 RIDGE 3.

trounce /traʊns; traʊns/ *v* [Tn] **1** defeat (sb) heavily 将(某人)打得大败: *Wales were trounced 5-0 by Poland.* 威尔士队让波兰队以5比0打得一败涂地. **2** (*dated* 旧) punish (sb) severely; thrash 严惩(某人); 痛打.

troupe /truːp; trup/ *n* [CGp] group of performing artists, esp those of a circus or ballet (演出的)班子, 团, 队; (尤指)马戏团, 芭蕾舞团: *a 'dance troupe* 舞蹈队.

▷ **trouper** *n* **1** (*dated* 旧) member of a theatrical troupe 剧团团员. **2** (*infml approv* 口, 褒) loyal dependable person 忠实可靠的人: *Thanks for helping, you're a real trouper.* 谢谢你的帮助, 你真是信得过的人.

trousers /'traʊzəz; 'traʊzɚz/ *n* [pl] **1** outer garment covering both legs and reaching from the waist to the ankles 裤子: *a pair of grey trousers* 一条灰裤子. **2** (idm 习语) **catch sb with his pants/trousers down** ⇨ CATCH¹. **wear the pants/trousers** ⇨ WEAR².

▷ **trouser** *adj* [attrib 作定语] of or for trousers 裤子的; 为裤子用的: *trouser buttons, legs, pockets* 裤子扣、裤腿、裤子口袋 ○ *a trouser press* 裤子压平器.

'trouser-suit *n* woman's suit of jacket and trousers (女子的)衣裤套装.

trous·seau /'truːsəʊ; 'truso/ *n* (*pl* **~s** or **~x** /-səʊz; -soz/) (esp formerly) clothes and other possessions, collected by a bride to begin married life with (尤指旧时的)嫁妆, 妆奁.

trout /traʊt; traʊt/ *n* (*pl* unchanged 复数不变) **1** (**a**) [C] any of various types of freshwater fish that are good to eat and fished for by anglers 鳟鱼. (**b**) [U] flesh of such fish as food (供食用的)鳟鱼肉: *a piece of smoked trout* 一块熏鳟鱼. **2** (idm 习语) **an old trout** ⇨ OLD.

trowel /'traʊəl; 'traʊəl/ *n* **1** small tool with a flat blade, used for spreading mortar on bricks or stone, plaster on walls, etc 镘刀, 抹子(抹砂浆、灰泥用的). **2** small gardening tool with a curved blade for lifting plants, digging holes, etc (园艺用的)小铲子. **3** (idm 习语) **lay it on thick/with a trowel** ⇨ THICK *adv*.

troy weight /'trɔɪ weɪt; 'trɔɪ ,wet/ British system of weights used for gold, silver and jewels, in which 1 pound = 12 ounces or 5 760 grains (英国的)金衡, 金衡制(金、银、珠宝的衡量制, 每金衡磅等于12金衡盎司或5 760金衡格令).

tru·ant /'truːənt; 'truənt/ *n* **1** child who stays away from school without permission 逃学的儿童; 旷课的小学生. **2** person who avoids doing his work or duty; idler 逃避工作或责任的人; 游手好闲的人. **3** (idm 习语) **play 'truant** (*US* **play 'hooky** /'hʊkɪ; 'hʊkɪ/) stay away from school as a truant 逃学; 旷课.

▷ **tru·ancy** /-ənsɪ; -ənsɪ/ *n* [C, U] (instance of) playing truant 逃学; 旷课.

truce /truːs; trus/ *n* (**a**) agreement between enemies or opponents to stop fighting for a certain time 休战, 停战(协定): *declare/negotiate/break a truce* 宣布[谈判/破坏]休战协定. (**b**) time that such an agreement lasts 休战期; 停战期: *a three-day truce* 休战三天.

truck¹ /trʌk; trʌk/ *n* **1** (*Brit*) open railway wagon for carrying goods (铁路上的)敞篷货车. **2** (*esp US*) = LORRY. **3** vehicle for carrying goods that is pushed or pulled by hand; handcart or barrow (运送货物的)手推车, 手拉车, 两轮小车.

▷ **trucker** *n* (*esp US*) person whose job is driving a lorry 卡车司机.

truck·ing *n* [U] (*US*) business or process of carrying goods by road 公路货运(业).

truck² /trʌk; trʌk/ *n* [U] **1** (*US*) fresh vegetables, fruit, etc grown for the market (为出售而种植的)新鲜蔬菜、水果等. **2** (idm 习语) **have no truck with sb/sth** refuse to deal or associate with sb; refuse to tolerate or consider sth 拒不与某人打交道; 不容忍或不考虑某事物: *I'll have no truck with extremists/extremism.* 我绝不同极端分子来往[与极端主义格格不入].

□ **'truck farm** (*US*) = MARKET GARDEN (MARKET¹). **'truck farmer, 'truck farming.**

truckle /'trʌkl; 'trʌkl/ *v* (phr v) **truckle to sb** accept sb's orders or authority in a timid or cowardly way (怯懦地)屈从或顺从某人: *refusing to truckle to bullies* 不甘受人欺负.

truckle-bed /'trʌkl bed; 'trʌkl ,bɛd/ (*US* **'trundle-bed**) *n* low bed on wheels that can be pushed under another when not being used 装有脚轮的矮床(不用时可推入另一床下).

truc·ulent /'trʌkjʊlənt; 'trʌkjələnt/ *adj* (*derog* 贬) defiant and aggressive 寻衅的; 好斗的: *truculent behaviour* 挑衅行为 ○ *He became very truculent and started arguing with me angrily.* 他当时盛气凌人, 气冲冲地同我吵了起来.

▷ **truc·ulence** /-ləns; -ləns/ *n* [U]. **truc·ulently** *adv*.

trudge /trʌdʒ; trʌdʒ/ *v* [I, Ipr, Ip, In/pr] walk slowly or with difficulty because one is tired, on a long journey, etc (因疲惫、走长路等)缓慢或吃力地走: *trudging (along) through the deep snow* 在深雪中慢慢地走 ○ *He trudged 20 miles.* 他吃力地走了20英里. ⇨Usage at STUMP 用法见STUMP.

▷ **trudge** *n* (usu *sing* 通常作单数) long tiring walk 疲累的长途步行; 长途跋涉.

true /truː; tru/ *adj* (**-r, -st**) **1** corresponding to known facts 合于事实的; 真的; 真实的; 确实的: *Is it true you're getting married?* 你要结婚是真的吗? ○ *a true story* 真实的故事 ○ *The food is good and the same is true of the service,* ie that is good too. 吃的东西很好, 服务质量也不错. ○ *'We've always found somewhere to stay here before.' 'True, but we may not always be so lucky.'* '我们已往在这里总能找到个落脚的地方.' '话倒是这么说, 可我们不一定总那么运气呀.' ○ *Unfortunately what you say is only too true.* 遗憾的是, 你说的都是实实在在的事. **2** [esp attrib 尤作定语] (**a**) agreeing with correct principles or accepted standards 合乎正确的原则或公认的标准的: *a true judgement, assessment, analysis, etc* 正确的判断、评估、分析等. (**b**) rightly called what one/it is called; genuine 名副其实的; 真正的: *true love* 真正

的爱 ○ *The frog is not a true reptile.* 青蛙并非真正的爬行动物. ○ *claimed to be the true heir* 提出本人为合法继承人这一要求. **3** [esp attrib 尤作定语] exact; accurate 准确的; 精确的: *a true copy of a document* 文件的准确副本 ○ *a true pair of scales* 精确的天平. **4** [esp pred 尤作表语] fitted or placed in its proper (esp upright) position (安装或放置)正, 准, (尤指)垂直: *Is the wheel true?* 轮子安正了吗? ○ *Make sure the post is true before the concrete sets.* 在混凝土凝固以前, 一定要把柱子竖直了. **5 ~ (to sth)** loyal; faithful 忠实的; 忠诚的: *a true patriot* 忠贞的爱国者 ○ *remain true to one's principles* 坚持自己的原则 ○ *be true to one's word/promise*, ie do as one has promised 信守诺言. **6** (idm 习语) **come ˈtrue** (of a hope, prediction, etc) really happen; become fact (指希望、预言等)实现, 成为事实: *It's like a dream come* (ie that has come) *true.* 这有如梦想变成了现实. **one's true ˈcolours** (*often derog* 常作贬义) one's true character; what one is really like 本性; 真面目: *Once he achieved power he showed (himself in) his true colours.* 他一掌了权就露出了本来面目. **true to sth** being or acting as one would expect from sth 符合某事物; 忠实反映某事物: *True to form* (ie As usual), *he arrived late.* 跟往常一样, 他来晚了. ○ *The film is very true to life*, ie realistic. 这部影片非常现实. ○ *Plants grown from seed are not always true to type*, ie exactly like the plant that gave the seed. 植物由种子发育成熟并不见得与该植物原型一模一样.

▷ **true** *adv* **1** truly 真实地; 确实地: *She spoke truer than she knew.* 她说的比她了解的更接近事实. **2** accurately 准确地; 精确地: *The arrow flew straight and true to its mark.* 那箭不偏不斜地直朝目标飞去.

true *n* (idm 习语) ˌ**out of ˈtrue** not in its proper or accurate position 位置不正: *The door is out of true.* 这扇门位置不正.

□ ˌ**true-ˈblue** *n, adj* (person who is) completely faithful and loyal, esp to traditional principles 忠心耿耿的(人); (尤指)坚持传统原则的(人): *a true-blue Tory of the old school* 一个老派的坚定的保守党人.

ˌ**true-ˈhearted** *adj* loyal 忠实的; 忠诚的.

ˌ**true-ˈlife** *adj* [attrib 作定语] that really happened 实有其事的; 真实的: *a* ˌ*true-life adˈventure* 真实的奇遇.

ˈ**true-love** *n* person who loves or is loved genuinely and deeply; sweetheart 真心爱的或被爱的人; 爱人.

ˌ**true ˈnorth** north according to the earth's axis, not magnetic north 真北(以地轴北极为正北的, 非磁极之北).

truffle /ˈtrʌfl; ˋtrʌfl/ *n* **1** type of edible fungus that grows underground and is enjoyed for its rich flavour 块菌(可食, 味美). **2** soft sweet made of a chocolate mixture 一种巧克力软糖.

trug /trʌg; trʌg/ *n* shallow basket used by gardeners to carry tools, plants, etc (园丁盛放工具、秧苗等的)浅筐.

tru·ism /ˈtru:ɪzəm; ˋtruɪzəm/ *n* statement that is obviously true, esp one that does not say anything important, eg *Nothing lasts for ever* 不言而喻的道理(尤指无重要意义的, 如'没有一成不变的事物').

truly /ˈtru:lɪ; ˋtrulɪ/ *adv* **1** truthfully 真实地; 如实地: *Tell me truly what you think.* 实话告诉我你是怎么想的. **2** sincerely 真诚地; 诚恳地: *I'm truly grateful.* 我由衷地感激. **3** genuinely; really 真正地; 确实地: *a truly generous act* 的确很慷慨的举动 ○ *Her last novel was truly awful.* 她最近的这部小说真糟糕. **4** (idm 习语) **well and truly** ⇨ WELL[3]. ⇨Usage at YOUR 用法见 YOUR.

trump[1] /trʌmp; trʌmp/ *n* **1** (in card-games such as whist or bridge) card of a suit that temporarily has a higher value than the other three suits (惠斯特或桥牌等牌戏的)王牌, 主牌, 将牌: *Hearts are trumps.* 红桃是王牌. ○ *He took my ace with a low trump.* 他用一张小的王牌吃了我的A牌. ○ *We played the game in no trumps*, ie with no suit chosen as trumps. 我们打的是无主的牌. **2** (*infml dated* 口, 旧) person who is generous, loyal, helpful, etc 慷慨、忠诚、乐于助人等的人. **3** (idm 习语) ˌ**come/** ˌ**turn up ˈtrumps** (*infml* 口) (**a**) be especially helpful or generous 大有帮助; 格外慷慨: *Nobody else in the family gave anything for the jumble sale, but my sister came up trumps.* 家里人谁也没拿出东西来捐助这次义卖活动, 只有我妹妹慷慨相助. (**b**) do or happen better than expected 结果比预期的要好: *The team turned up trumps on the day.* 那个队这一天的成绩好得出乎意料. **declare trumps** ⇨ DECLARE. **draw trumps** ⇨ DRAW[2].

▷ **trump** *v* **1** [Tn, Tn·pr] **~ sth (with sth)** take (a card or trick) with a trump 出王牌吃掉(一牌或一墩牌): *trumped my ace (with a six)* 用(六点的)王牌吃掉了我的A牌. **2** (phr v) **trump sth up** (usu passive 通常用于被动语态) invent (a false excuse, accusation, etc) in order to harm sb 编造(谎言、罪名等)加害某人: *arrested on a trumped-up charge* 根据罗织的罪名被捕.

□ ˈ**trump-card** *n* (**a**) card of the suit that is trumps 王牌; 将牌; 主牌. (**b**) (*fig* 比喻) way of gaining what one wants, esp after trying other ways; most valuable resource 为达到目的采取的方法(尤指已试过其他方法); 最有效的一招: *Finally she played her trump-card and threatened to resign.* 最后她使出了绝招, 扬言要辞职.

trump[2] /trʌmp; trʌmp/ *n* (*arch* 古) sound made by a trumpet 喇叭声; 号声.

trump·ery /ˈtrʌmpərɪ; ˋtrʌmpərɪ/ *adj* [attrib 作定语] (*dated derog* 旧, 贬) showy but of little value 花哨而无价值的: *trumpery ornaments* 不值钱的花哨饰物.

trum·pet /ˈtrʌmpɪt; ˋtrʌmpɪt/ *n* **1** brass musical instrument with a bright ringing tone 小号; 喇叭: *hear a distant trumpet*, ie its sound 听到远处的小号声. ⇨illus at App 1 见附录1插图, page x. **2** thing shaped like a trumpet, esp the open flower of a daffodil 喇叭形物; (尤指)绽开的水仙花. ⇨illus at App 1 见附录1插图, page ii. **3** (idm 习语) **blow one's own trumpet** ⇨ BLOW[1].

▷ **trum·pet** *v* **1** [I, Tn] proclaim (sth) loudly and forcibly 大声宣告或鼓吹(某事物): *He's always trumpeting his own opinions.* 他总是不遗余力地宣扬自己的观点. **2** [I] (of an elephant) make a loud blaring noise like a trumpet (指象)吼叫. **trum·peter** *n* person who plays a trumpet, esp a cavalry soldier giving signals 吹号的人; (尤指骑兵的)号兵: *Trumpeter, sound the charge!* 号兵, 吹冲锋号!

trun·cate /trʌŋˈkeɪt; *US* ˈtrʌŋkeɪt; ˋtrʌŋket/ *v* [Tn esp passive 尤用于被动语态] shorten (sth) by cutting off the top or end 截去(某物)的顶端或末端; 将(某物)截短: *a truncated cone, pyramid, etc* 截锥、截角锥 ○ *published her article in truncated form* 以节录形式发表她的文章.

trun·cheon /ˈtrʌntʃən; ˋtrʌntʃən/ (also **baton**) *n* short thick stick carried as a weapon, esp by police officers (作为武器携带的)粗短的棍子; (尤指)警棍.

trundle /ˈtrʌndl; ˋtrʌndl/ *v* [I, Ipr, Ip, Tn, Tn·pr, Tn·p] (cause sth to) roll or move heavily (使某物)沉重地滚动或移动: *A goods train trundled past.* 一列货运列车隆隆地驶过. ○ *trundling a wheelbarrow down the path* 推着手推车沿路走去.

□ ˈ**trundle-bed** *n* (*US*) = TRUCKLE-BED (TRUCKLE).

trunk /trʌŋk; trʌŋk/ *n* **1** [C] main stem of a tree, from which the branches grow 树干. ⇨illus at App 1 见附录1插图, page i. **2** [C usu *sing* 通常作单数] body apart from the head, arms and legs 躯干. ⇨illus at HUMAN 见HUMAN插图. Cf 参看 TORSO. **3** [C] large box with a hinged lid for storing or transporting clothes or other items 大衣箱; 大旅行箱. ⇨illus at LUGGAGE 见LUGGAGE插图. **4** [C] long nose of an elephant 象鼻. ⇨illus at ELEPHANT 见ELEPHANT插图. **5 trunks** [pl] shorts worn by men or boys for swimming, boxing, etc (男子游泳、拳击等时穿的)短裤. **6** [C] (*US*) boot of a car (汽车后部的)行李箱. ⇨illus at App 1 见附录1插图, page xii.

□ ˈ**trunk-call** *n* (*Brit dated* 旧) (*US* **long-ˈdistance call**) telephone call to a distant place in the same country (国内)长途电话.

ˈ**trunk-road** *n* important main road 公路干线; 干道.

truss /trʌs; trʌs/ *n* **1** padded belt worn by a person suffering from a hernia 疝带(疝病患者用的). **2** framework supporting a roof, bridge, etc (支撑屋顶、桥梁等的)构架, 桁架. **3** (*Brit*) bundle of hay or straw (干草或稻草的)捆, 束.

▷ **truss** *v* **1** [Tn, Tn·pr, Tn·p] **~ sth/sb (up) (with sth)** tie or bind sth/sb securely 将某物[某人]捆好、缚紧或系牢: *truss a chicken*, ie fasten its legs and wings securely before cooking 把鸡扎紧(扎紧腿和翅膀以便烹调) ○ *The thieves had trussed the guard up with rope.* 盗贼用绳子把警卫捆了起来. **2** [Tn esp passive 尤用于

被动语态] support (a roof, bridge, etc) with trusses (TRUSS 2) 用构架支撑(屋顶、桥梁等).

trust[1] /trʌst; trʌst/ *n* **1** [U] **~ (in sb/sth)** belief or willingness to believe that one can rely on the goodness, strength, ability, etc of sb/sth 信任; 信赖; 相信: *A good marriage is based on trust.* 美满的婚姻是建立在互相信任的基础上的. ○ *I have absolute trust in the (skill of) doctors.* 我绝对相信医生(的医术). ○ *I put my trust in you.* 我信任你. ○ *You've betrayed my trust,* eg told a secret or not kept a promise. 你辜负了我对你的信任(如泄露秘密或违背诺言). **2** [U] responsibility 责任: *a position of great trust* 责任重大的职位. **3** (*law* 律) **(a)** [C] money or property given to a person or people (*trustees*) who must take care of it and use it for another person's benefit or for a specified purpose 信托财产: *In his will he created trusts for his children.* 他在遗嘱里为子女安排好了信托财产. ○ *The project is financed by a charitable trust.* 这项工程是由慈善基金机构赞助的. **(b)** [U] responsibility assumed by trustees; trusteeship 受信托人的职责. **4** [C] association of business firms formed to reduce competition, control prices, etc 托拉斯(为减少竞争、垄断价格等而成立的企业联合组织): *anti-trust laws* 反托拉斯法. **5** [C] organization founded to encourage or preserve sth, eg historic buildings or cultural activities (为促进或保护某事物而设的)信托基金机构(如为保护历史建筑或促进文化活动等而设的): *a wildfowl trust* 保护野禽信托基金机构. **6** (idm 习语) **in trust** kept as a trust[1](3a) 受托保管财产: *The money is being held in trust for him until he is twenty-one.* 这笔钱委托他人代管, 到他二十一岁才能使用. **on trust (a)** without proof or investigation 不经证明或调查: *You'll just have to take what I say on trust.* 你只管相信我说的话就是了. **(b)** on credit 以赊欠方式: *supply goods on trust* 赊给货物.

▷ **trust·ful** /-fl; -fəl/, **trust·ing** *adjs* showing trust; not suspicious 表示信任的; 无疑心的. **trust·fully** /-fəlɪ; -fəlɪ/, **trust·ingly** *advs.* **trust·ful·ness** *n* [U].

ˈ**trust·worthy** *adj* worthy of trust; reliable 值得信任的; 可信赖的; 可靠的. ˈ**trust·wor·thi·ness** *n* [U].

trusty *adj* **(-ier, -iest)** (*arch or joc* 古或谑) trustworthy 可信任的; 可信赖的; 可靠的: *mounted his trusty steed* 骑上他那匹得力的马 ○ *my trusty old bicycle* 我那忠心耿耿的自行车. — *n* prisoner who is given special privileges or responsibilities because of good behaviour 模范犯人(因表现好而获优待或担负责任的).

□ ˈ**trust company** (*esp US*) firm that manages trusts, investments, etc 信托公司; 信托投资公司; 信托银行.

ˈ**trust fund** money that is held in trust for sb 信托基金: *set up a trust fund* 设立信托基金.

trust[2] /trʌst; trʌst/ *v* **1** [Tn] have or place trust[1](1) in (sb/sth); treat (sb/sth) as reliable 信任, 信赖, 相信(某人[某事物]): *They're not to be trusted/not people I would trust.* 他们不可靠[不是我信赖的人]. ○ *I trust you implicitly.* 我绝对信任你. ○ *You can't trust what the papers say.* 报纸上的话不可信. **2** [Tn·pr, Cn·t] depend on (sb) to do sth, use sth, look after sth, etc properly or safely 依靠、有赖于或信得过(某人)能做好某事: *I can't trust that boy out of my sight.* 我一看不见那个男孩儿就不放心. ○ *I'd trust him with my life.* 我把命交给他都放心. ○ *Can I trust you to post this letter?* 我托你把这封信寄走行吗? ○ (*ironic* 反语) *Trust you* (ie It is typical of you) *to forget my birthday!* 你管保把我的生日给忘了! **3** [It, Tf] (*fml* 文) hope 希望: *We trust to receive a cheque at your earliest convenience.* 我们希望早日收到你的支票. ○ *I trust (that) she's not seriously ill.* 但愿她病情不严重. ○ *You've no objection, I trust.* 我希望你不反对吧. **4** (phr v) **trust in sb/sth** have confidence in sb/sth 信任、信赖或相信某人[某事物]: *trust in providence* 相信天命 ○ *You must trust in your own judgement.* 你得相信自己的判断力. **trust to sth** leave the result or progress of events to be decided by (chance, etc) 依靠(运气等); 任凭自然发展: *trust to luck, fate, fortune, etc* 靠运气、命运、幸运等 ○ *At such times you have to trust to instinct.* 在这种情况下就只能凭直觉办事了.

trustee /trʌˈstiː; trʌsˈti/ *n* **1** person who is responsible for managing a trust[1](3a) 受信托人(受信托管理财产的人). **2** member of a group of people managing the business affairs of an institution (机构的)管理班子成员.

▷ **trust·ee·ship** /-ʃɪp; -ʃɪp/ *n* **1** [U, C] position of a trustee 受信托人的职责. **2** [U] responsibility for the administration of a territory granted to a country by the United Nations Organization 托管(联合国委托某一国家管理某一地区).

truth /truːθ; truθ/ *n* (*pl* **~s** /truːðz; truðz/) **1** [U] quality or state of being true 真实(性): *There's no truth/not a word of truth in what he says.* 他说的毫不属实. **2 (a)** [U] that which is true 真相; 实情; 真实情况; 事实: *the whole truth* 全部事实 ○ *the search for (the) truth* 调查事实真相 ○ *tell the truth,* ie speak truthfully, not lie 说实话 ○ *We found out the truth about him.* 我们了解到了有关他的事实. ○ *The (plain) truth is, I forgot about it.* 老实说, 我忘了. **(b)** [C] fact, belief, etc that is accepted as true 真理; 原理: *one of the fundamental truths of modern science* 现代科学的一项基本原理. **3** (idm 习语) **a home truth** ⇨ HOME[1]. **in truth** (*fml* 文) truly; really 的确; 事实上: *It was in truth a miracle.* 这确实是个奇迹. **the moment of truth** ⇨ MOMENT. **the naked truth** ⇨ NAKED 2. **to tell the truth** ⇨ TELL.

▷ **truth·ful** /-fl; -fəl/ *adj* **1** (of a person) honest in what he says; never lying (指人)诚实的, 从不说谎的. **2** (of statements) true (指陈述)真确的, 如实的. **truth·fully** /-fəlɪ; -fəlɪ/ *adv.* **truth·ful·ness** *n* [U].

try[1] /traɪ; traɪ/ *v* (*pt, pp* **tried**) **1** [I, It] (In informal use, *try to* + infinitive is often replaced by *try and* + infinitive, esp in the imperative, and *don't/didn't try to* by *don't/didn't try and.* 在口语中, 'try to +动词不定式'这种结构常改为'try and +动词不定式', 尤以祈使句为然, 否定形式'don't/didn't try to'则改为'don't/didn't try and'.) make an attempt 试; 尝试; 打算; 努力做: *I don't know if I can come, but I'll try.* 我不知道是否能来, 但是我尽可能来. ○ *I tried till I was tired.* 我试着做, 一直试到累了才停下来. ○ *Try to/and be here on time.* 请尽量按时到这儿来. ○ *He's trying his best/hardest/utmost,* ie as much as he can. 他尽了最大的努力. ○ *I tried hard not to laugh.* 我极力忍住不笑. ○ *You haven't even tried to lift it.* 你连试着举一下都没试过. ○ *Don't try to/and swim across the river.* 别打算游过那条河. ⇨Usage at AND 用法见AND. **2** [Tn, Tn·pr, Tg] use, do or test (sth) to see whether it is satisfactory, effective, enjoyable, etc 试用, 试做, 试验(某物): *I've tried this new detergent with excellent results.* 我试用了这种新型洗涤剂, 效果很好. ○ *'Would you like to try some raw fish?' 'Why not, I'll try anything once.'* '你想尝点儿生鱼吗?' '好哇, 我什么都愿意尝一点儿.' ○ *Have you ever tried windsurfing?* 你做过风帆冲浪运动吗? ○ *Try that door,* ie Try opening it to see if it is locked or to find what is on the other side. 推一推那扇门(看看是否锁上了或门的那一面有什么). ○ *Don't try any funny stuff with me!* 别想跟我耍鬼花招! ○ *Let's try the table in a different position.* 咱们把桌子换个位置试试看. ○ *I think we should try her for the job.* 我认为我们应该让她试试这个工作. ○ *Try phoning his home number.* 给他家里打个电话试试. **3 (a)** [Tn esp passive 尤用于被动语态] examine and decide (a case) in a lawcourt 审讯, 审判(案件): *The case was tried before a jury.* 此案是有陪审团参加审理的. **(b)** [Tn, Tn·pr] **~ sb (for sth)** hold a trial of (sb) 审问, 审判(某人): *He was tried for murder.* 他以谋杀罪名受审. **4** [Tn] be very tiring or difficult to bear for (sb/sth); be a strain on (sb/sth) 使(某人[某物])忍受极度劳累或艰难困苦: *Small print tries the eyes.* 印刷字体太小伤眼睛. ○ *Don't try my patience!* 别逼得我忍无可忍! ○ *His courage was severely tried by his ordeal.* 他的勇气在艰难困苦中经受了严峻的考验. **5** (idm 习语) **do/try one's damnedest** ⇨ DAMNEDEST (DAMNED). **try one's hand (at sth)** attempt (eg a skill or sport) for the first time 初试身手(如技艺或运动): *I'd like to try my hand at computing.* 我想试试我的计算机运算技术. **try one's luck (at sth)** try to do or get sth, hoping to succeed 碰碰运气(试做某事或争取获得某事物, 希望能成功): *I think I'll try my luck at roulette.* 我想玩玩轮盘赌碰碰运气. **6** (phr v) **try for sth** make an attempt to get or win sth 力图获得或赢得某事物: *try for a scholarship, an Olympic medal, a job in the Civil Service* 力图获得奖学金、奥运会奖牌、公务员的工作. **try sth on (a)** put on (clothing, etc) to see if it fits and how it looks 试穿(衣物等): *Try on the shoes before you buy them.* 买鞋要先穿上试试再买. **(b)** (*infml* 口) do sth (eg ask too high a price for sth or behave badly) that one expects not to be allowed to do, while hoping that sb will not object 做明知不准做的事，希望某人无异议（如索取高价或为非作歹）: *Don't try anything on with me, kid, or you'll be sorry.* 小毛孩子，别跟我来这一套，要不然有你后悔的. **try out (for sth)** (*US*) take a test, a trial, an audition, etc 测试；试验；试演等: *You won't make the team if you don't try out.* 不参加选拔就不能加入这个队. ○ *She's trying out for the part of Cleopatra.* 她正在试演克娄巴特拉这个角色. **try sb/sth out (on sb)** test sb/sth by using him/it 试用某人［某物］: *try out a young quarter-back* 试用一名年轻的四分卫 ○ *The drug has not been tried out on humans yet.* 这种药尚未经过人体试验.

▷ **tried** *adj* [attrib 作定语] that has been proved to be effective, reliable, etc 经证明有效、可靠等的: *a tried (and tested) remedy* 经（试验）证明有效的疗法 ○ *a tried and true friend* 经过考验的真正的朋友.

trier *n* person who tries hard and always does his best 经受磨练始终尽力的人: *He's not very good but he's a real trier.* 他不十分出色，却是个勤勤恳恳的人.

try·ing *adj* that strains one's temper or patience; annoying 磨练脾气或耐性的；使人厌烦的: *a trying person to deal with* 难对付的人 ○ *have a trying day* 度过难熬的一天.

□ **'try-on** *n* (*infml* 口) doing sth that one does not expect to be allowed to do, while hoping sb will not object 做明知不准做的事（希望某人无异议）.

'try-out *n* test of the qualities or performance of a person or thing （对人或事物的质量或表现的）测试；试用；试演: *give sb/sth a try-out* 测试某人［某物］.

try[2] /traɪ; traɪ/ *n* **1 ~ (at sth/doing sth)** attempt 尝试；努力: *I'll give it a try/It's worth a try.* 我要试一试［这值得一试］. ○ *He had three tries at mending the lock and gave up.* 他把那个锁试着修了三次以后，放弃不修了. **2** (in Rugby football) action by a player of touching down the ball behind the opponents' goal-line, which also entitles his side to a kick at goal （英式橄榄球）在对方球门线后以球触地（并获得由己方队员踢定位球射门之权利）. Cf 参看 CONVERT[1] 3.

tsar (also **tzar**, **czar**) /zɑː(r); tsɑr/ *n* (title of the) emperor of Russia (before 1917) 沙皇(1917年以前俄罗斯皇帝或其称号).

▷ **tsar·ina** (also **tzar·ina**, **czar·ina**) /zɑː'riːnə; tsɑ'rinə/ *n* (title of the) empress of Russia or of the wife of the tsar （俄国的）女皇或皇后.

tsetse /'tsetsɪ; 'tsɛtsɪ/ *n* (also **'tsetse fly**) tropical African fly that carries and transmits disease, esp sleeping sickness, to humans and animals by its bite 舌蝇，采采蝇（热带非洲蝇科昆虫，叮咬人及大动物传播疾病）.

T-shirt ⇨ T, T.

tsp (*pl* **tsps**) *abbr* 缩写 = teaspoonful: *Add 2 tsps sugar* 加两茶匙的糖.

T-square ⇨ SQUARE[2] 5.

TT /ˌtiː 'tiː; ˌti 'ti/ *abbr* 缩写 = **1** teetotal(ler). **2** (*Brit*) Tourist Trophy 旅游杯: *the TT motorcycle races on the Isle of Man* 在马恩岛上举行的旅游杯摩托车比赛. **3** (of milk) tuberculin-tested （指牛奶）经结核菌素试验的.

tub /tʌb; tʌb/ *n* **1** (**a**) (often in compounds 常用以构成复合词) open flat-bottomed (usu round) container used for washing clothes, holding liquids, growing plants, etc （洗衣物、盛液体、栽培植物等用的）盆，桶: *wash-tubs* 洗涤盆 ○ *wooden plant-tubs* 栽培植物的木桶. ⇨illus at BUCKET 见 BUCKET 插图. (**b**) similar small container of plastic, etc used for food, etc （用塑料等做的）盛食物等的小容器: *a tub of ice-cream, cottage cheese, margarine, etc* 一盒冰激凌、农家乳酪、人造黄油等. (**c**) (also **tub·ful** /-fʊl; -fʊl/) amount held by a tub 一盆或一桶的容量. **2** (**a**) = BATH-TUB (BATH). (**b**) = BATH 1: *have a cold tub before breakfast* 早餐前洗个冷水澡. **3** (*infml esp joc* 口，尤作戏谑语) slow clumsy boat 行驶缓慢的笨重的船: *a leaky old tub* 破漏的老爷船.

□ **'tub-thumper** *n* (*infml derog* 口，贬) public speaker with a loud, violent or ranting manner 声嘶力竭的演讲者. **'tub-thumping** *n*, *adj*.

tuba /'tjuːbə; US 'tuː-; 'tubə/ *n* long brass musical instrument of low pitch 大号（发音低沉的铜管乐器）. ⇨ illus at App 1 见附录1插图, page x.

tubby /'tʌbɪ; 'tʌbɪ/ *adj* (**-ier**, **-iest**) (*infml* 口) short and fat 矮胖的: *a tubby little man* （男的）胖墩儿. ⇨Usage at FAT[1] 用法见 FAT[1].

tube /tjuːb; US tuːb; tub/ *n* **1** [C] long hollow cylinder of metal, glass, rubber, etc for holding or conveying liquids, gases, etc （金属、玻璃、橡胶等材料的）管，管子，筒子: *laboratory test-tubes* 实验室的试管 ○ *an inner tube*, eg of a bicycle or car tyre 内胎 ○ *Blood flowed along the tube into the bottle.* 血液沿管子流入瓶中. **2** [C] **~ (of sth)** container made of thin flexible metal or plastic with a screw cap, used for holding pastes, etc ready for use （金属或塑料的）软管（有螺旋盖，盛膏装物用的）: *tubes of glue, mayonnaise* 管装的胶水、蛋黄酱 ○ *squeeze toothpaste from/out of a tube* 挤出管子里的牙膏. **3 the tube** (also **the underground**) [U, sing] (*Brit infml* 口) the underground railway system in London 伦敦的地下铁道: *travel to work by tube/on the tube* 乘伦敦地铁上班 ○ *take a/the tube to Victoria* 乘地铁到维多利亚站 ○ [attrib 作定语] *tube trains, tickets, etc* 地铁列车、车票等. Cf 参看 SUBWAY. **4** [C] = CATHODE RAY TUBE (CATHODE). **5** [C usu *pl* 通常作复数] hollow tube-shaped organ in the body （身体内的）管状器官: *bronchial, Fallopian, Eustachian tubes* 支气管、输卵管、耳咽管.

▷ **tube·less** *adj* [usu attrib 通常作定语] (of a tyre) having no inner tube （指轮胎）无内胎的.

tub·ing *n* [U] length of tube; tubes 管子材料；管子: *two metres of copper, plastic, etc tubing* 两米铜管、塑料管等.

tu·bu·lar /'tjuːbjʊlə(r); US 'tuː-; 'tubjələ˞/ *adj* **1** tube-shaped 管状的: *a tubular container* 管状容器. **2** having or consisting of tubes; made of tube-shaped pieces 有管的；由管构成的；管式的: *tubular scaffolding* 由管子搭成的脚手架 ○ *tubular furniture* 用管料制造的家具.

tuber /'tjuːbə(r); US 'tuː-; 'tubə˞/ *n* short thick rounded part of an underground stem (eg of a potato) or root (eg of a dahlia) which stores food and produces buds from which new plants will grow 块茎.

▷ **tuber·ous** /'tjuːbərəs; US 'tuː-; 'tubərəs/ *adj* **1** of or like a tuber （似）块茎的. **2** having or producing tubers 有块茎的；生长块茎的.

tuber·cu·losis /tjuːˌbɜːkjʊ'ləʊsɪs; US tuː-; tuˌbɝkjə'losɪs/ *n* [U] (*abbr* 缩写 **TB**) infectious wasting disease in which growths appear on body tissue, esp the lungs 结核病；（尤指）肺结核.

▷ **tuber·cu·lar** /tjuː'bɜːkjʊlə(r); US tuː-; tu'bɝkjələ˞/ *adj* of, causing or affected with tuberculosis 结核病的；引致结核病的；感染结核病的: *a tubercular infection, lung* 结核病之传染、感染结核病的肺部.

TUC /ˌtiː juː 'siː; ˌti ju 'si/ *abbr* 缩写 = (*Brit*) Trades Union Congress 英国职工大会.

tuck[1] /tʌk; tʌk/ *n* **1** [C] flat fold stitched into a garment, etc to make it smaller or for ornament （衣服等的）褶，裥: *put in/take out a tuck in a dress* 在连衣裙上加上［去掉］一个褶. **2** [U] (*Brit infml esp dated* 口，尤作旧) food, esp sweets, cakes, pastry, etc that children enjoy 儿童喜爱的食物（尤指糖果、糕饼、香酥点心等）: [attrib 作定语] *a school tuck-shop* 校内食品小卖部.

tuck[2] /tʌk; tʌk/ *v* **1** [Tn·pr, Tn·p] (**a**) **~ sth into sth; ~ sth in/up** push or fold or turn the ends or edges (of cloth, paper, etc) so that they are hidden or held in place 将（布、纸等）的端部或边缘掖好、叠拢或卷起（使之看不见或固定住）: *tuck your trousers into your boots* 把你的裤脚塞进靴子里 ○ *tuck your shirt in*, ie into your trousers, shorts, etc 把你的衬衣下摆塞进裤子里去 ○ *He tucked up his shirt-sleeves.* 他捋起了衬衫袖子. ○ *The sheets were tucked in neatly*, ie under the mattress. 床单的边缘整整齐齐地掖在褥垫下面. ○ *tuck the flap of an envelope in* 把信封的口盖折进信封里. (**b**) draw (sth) together into a small space 将（某物）缩拢起来塞入狭小空间: *The nurse tucked her hair (up) under her cap.* 那护士把头发聚拢起来塞进帽子里. ○ *He sat with his legs tucked (up) under him.* 他盘着腿坐着. **2** [Tn·pr] put sth round (sb/sth) snugly and comfortably 用某物舒适地裹住（某人［某物］）: *tuck a blanket round sb's knees/legs* 用毯子好好地盖住某人的膝部［腿部］. **3** [Tn·pr] put (sth) away compactly or tidily 将（某物）收拢或收好: *The hen tucked her head under her wing.* 那母鸡把头缩在翅膀下. ○ *tucked the map under his arm, into the glove compartment* 把地图夹在腋下、收藏在汽车仪表板下的贮物箱里. **4** (idm 习语) **nip and tuck** ⇨ NIP. **5** (phr v) **tuck sth away** (*infml* 口 *esp Brit*) eat (a lot of food) 吃（大量食物）. **tuck sth/oneself away** (*infml* 口) store

T

or hide sth/oneself 将某物存起来或藏起来; 躲藏: *He's got a fortune tucked away in a Swiss bank account.* 他把一大笔钱存在瑞士银行里了. ○ *The farm was tucked away in the hills.* 那个农场隐蔽在群山之中. **tuck into sth/in** (*infml* 口 *esp Brit*) eat (sth) heartily 痛快地吃某物: *He tucked into the ham hungrily.* 他狼吞虎咽地大吃火腿. ○ *Come on, tuck in, everybody!* 来呀, 大家尽量吃吧! **tuck sb up** cover sb snugly with bedclothes 给某人盖好被子: *tuck the children up in bed* 给孩子们盖好被子.

□ **'tuck-in** *n* (usu *sing* 通常作单数) (*Brit infml* 口) large meal 大餐: *have a good tuck-in* 大吃一顿.

tucker /'tʌkə(r); 'tʌkɚ/ *n* (idm 习语) **one's best bib and tucker** ⇨ BEST[1].

▷ **tucker** *v* [usu passive 通常用于被动语态: Tn, Tn·p] **~ sb (out)** (*US infml* 口) tire or exhaust (sb) 使(某人)劳累或筋疲力尽: *I'm fair tuckered out.* 我累坏了.

Tue (also **Tues**) *abbr* 缩写 = Tuesday: *Tues 9 March* 3月9日, 星期二.

Tues·day /'tju:zdɪ; *US* 'tu:-; 'tuzdɪ/ *n* [U, C] (*abbrs* 缩写 **Tue, Tues**) the third day of the week, next after Monday 星期二.

For the uses of *Tuesday* see the examples at *Monday*. 关于 Tuesday 的用法见 Monday 词条中的示例.

tuft /tʌft; tʌft/ *n* bunch of hair, feathers, grass, etc, growing or held together at the base (在底部丛生的或聚集的)一束毛发、一簇羽毛或一丛草等.

▷ **tufted** *adj* having, or growing in, a tuft or tufts 成束的; 簇生的; 丛生的: *a tufted carpet* 簇绒地毯.

tug /tʌg; tʌg/ *v* (**-gg-**) (**a**) [I, Ipr, Tn, Tn·pr] **~ (at sth)** pull (sth) hard or violently 用力拉或拖(某物): *We tugged so hard that the rope broke.* 我们一用力把绳子给拉断了. ○ *tug at sb's elbow/sleeve*, eg to attract attention 拽某人的肘部[袖子](如为引起注意). (**b**) [Tn, Tn·p] pull (sth/sb) in a particular direction (沿某方向)拉或拖(某物[某人]): *The wind nearly tugged my umbrella out of my hand.* 大风险些把我手中的伞给刮跑了. ○ *It is difficult tugging the children round the shops with me*, ie because they resist. 让我拉着孩子逛商店可真不易(因为拉不住他们).

T

▷ **tug** *n* **1** sudden hard pull (突然的)猛拉, 猛拽: *I felt a tug at my sleeve.* 我觉得有人拽了一下我的袖子. ○ *Tom gave his sister's hair a hard tug.* 汤姆使劲地扯了一下他姐姐的头发. ○ (*fig* 比喻) *She felt a sharp tug at her heart-strings* (ie pang of sorrow) *as he left.* 他离去的时候, 她非常伤心. **2** (also **'tug·boat**) small powerful boat for towing ships, esp into harbour or up rivers 拖船.

□ **,tug of 'love** (*Brit infml* 口) dispute over the custody of a child, esp between separated or divorced parents 对监护权的争夺(尤指分居或离婚时争夺子女监护权): [attrib 作定语] *a tug-of-love drama* 争夺监护权的戏剧性事件.

,tug of 'war contest in which two teams pull at opposite ends of a rope until one drags the other over a central line 拔河比赛.

tu·ition /tju:'ɪʃn; *US* tu:-; tu'ɪʃən/ *n* [U] (**a**) (*esp fml* 尤作文雅语) teaching or instruction, esp that given to individuals or small groups 教学, 讲授(尤指对个人或小组的): *have private tuition in French* 私人教授法语. (**b**) fee paid for this, esp in colleges and universities 学费(尤指大专院校的).

tu·lip /'tju:lɪp; *US* 'tu:-; 'tulɪp/ *n* garden plant growing from a bulb in spring, with a large brightly-coloured cup-shaped flower on a tall stem 郁金香. ⇨illus at App 1 见附录1插图, page ii.

tulle /tju:l; *US* tu:l; tul/ *n* [U] soft fine silky net-like material used esp for veils and dresses 绢网, 丝网眼纱(尤用以制面纱及连衣裙).

tumble /'tʌmbl; 'tʌmbḷ/ *v* **1** (**a**) [I, Ipr, Ip, Tn·pr, Tn·p] (cause sb/sth to) fall, esp helplessly or violently, but usu without serious injury (使某人[某物])倒下, 坠落(尤指身不由己或猛劲儿, 但通常并无重伤): *tumble down the stairs, off a bicycle, out of a tree, over a step, etc* 从楼梯上滚下、从自行车上摔下、从树上掉下、绊倒在台阶上 ○ *Toddlers keep tumbling over.* 学步的儿童老是摔跤. ○ *The children tumbled* (ie pushed) *each other (over) in the snow.* 孩子们互相推来推去倒在雪地上了. (**b**) [I] fall rapidly in value or amount (价格或数量)急遽下降: *Share prices tumbled on the stock-market.* 股市上股票价格暴跌. **2** [I, Ipr, Ip] roll to and fro or over and over or up and down in a restless and disorderly way 打滚; (不安地和胡乱地)翻滚: *The puppies were tumbling about on the floor.* 小狗在地板上打着滚. ○ *The stream tumbled over the rocks.* 溪水滚滚流过岩石. ○ *The breakers came tumbling onto the shore.* 浪涛滚滚而来拍打着岸边. **3** [Ipr, Ip] **~ into/out of sth; ~ in/out** move or rush in the specified direction in a headlong or blundering way 急促地或胡乱地朝某方向移动或猛冲: *I threw off my clothes and tumbled into bed.* 我脱掉衣服倒在床上便睡了. ○ *The children tumbled into/out of the car.* 孩子们一窝蜂上了[下了]汽车. ○ *My shopping bag broke and everything tumbled out.* 我的购物袋破了, 东西纷纷都掉了出来. **4** [Tn, Tn·p] rumple or disarrange (sth) 弄乱, 搅乱(某物): *The wind tumbled her hair.* 风把她的头发吹乱了. ○ *The bedclothes were tumbled (about) as though the bed had been slept in.* 床上的被褥都弄乱了, 好像有人睡过觉. **5** (phr v) **tumble down** fall into ruin; collapse 已残破不堪; 倒塌; 垮掉: *The old barn we bought to convert into flats was practically tumbling down.* 那个旧谷仓我们买下想改建住房的, 实际上已经快塌了. **tumble to sb/sth** (*infml* 口) realize the true character of sb or grasp a hidden meaning, etc 看穿某人或了解到隐含的意义等: *I tumbled to him/to what he was up to when I found some of his letters to Jane.* 我发现了他写给简的一些信, 赫然了解了他的为人[他居心何在].

▷ **tumble** *n* **1** [C] helpless or violent fall (身不由己的或猛力的)倒下; 摔倒; 跌跤; 坠落; 倒塌: *have/take a nasty tumble* 重重跌一跤. **2** [sing] untidy or confused state 混乱; 杂乱: *bedclothes in a tumble on the floor* 散乱在地上的被褥.

□ **'tumbledown** *adj* [attrib 作定语] falling or fallen into ruin; dilapidated 倒塌的; 残破的; 摇摇欲坠的: *a tumbledown old shack* 破旧的棚屋.

'tumble-drier (also **'tumbler-drier**) *n* machine for drying washed clothes, etc in a heated drum that rotates 滚筒式干衣机.

'tumbleweed *n* [U] bush-like plant growing in desert areas of N America, which withers in autumn, breaks off and is rolled about by the wind 风滚草(生长于北美洲沙漠地区, 秋季干枯, 枝叶断落, 随风滚动).

tum·bler /'tʌmblə(r); 'tʌmblɚ/ *n* **1** (**a**) flat-bottomed straight-sided drinking-glass with no handle or stem (无柄、无脚、平底、直壁的)玻璃杯. ⇨illus at GLASS 见 GLASS 插图. (**b**) (also **tum·bler·ful** /-fʊl; -ful/) amount held by a tumbler 一玻璃杯的容量: *a tumbler of milk* 一玻璃杯牛奶. **2** part of a lock that holds the bolt until lifted by a key (锁的)制栓(用钥匙开启锁栓的部件). **3** acrobat who turns somersaults, esp on the ground 翻筋斗的杂技演员(尤指在地面上的).

□ **tumbler-drier** *n* = TUMBLE-DRIER (TUMBLE).

tum·brel (also **tum·bril**) /'tʌmbrəl; 'tʌmbrəl/ *n* open cart, esp of the kind used to carry condemned people to the guillotine during the French Revolution 倾卸式两轮马车; (尤指法国大革命期间押送囚犯去断头台的)死囚车: *tumbrels rolling through the streets* 辘辘驶过街道的死囚车.

tu·mes·cent /tju:'mesnt; *US* tu:-; tu'mɛsṇt/ *adj* (*fml* 文) (of parts of the body) swelling or swollen, eg in response to sexual stimulation (指身体部位)肿胀的, 肿大的(如因受性刺激的反应). ▷ **tu·mes·cence** /-sns; -sṇs/ *n* [U].

tu·mid /'tju:mɪd; *US* 'tu:-; 'tumɪd/ *adj* (*fml* 文) (of parts of the body) swollen (指身体部位)肿大的, 肿起的. ▷ **tu·mid·ity** /tju:'mɪdətɪ; *US* tu:-; tu'mɪdətɪ/ *n* [U].

tummy /'tʌmɪ; 'tʌmɪ/ *n* (used esp by or to children 尤作儿语) stomach 肚子; 胃: *have a tummy-ache* 肚子痛 ○ *one's tummy-button*, ie navel 肚脐.

tu·mour (*US* **tu·mor**) /'tju:mə(r); *US* 'tu:-; 'tumɚ/ *n* abnormal mass of new tissue growing in or on part of the body (肿)瘤; 肿块: *cancerous tumours* 癌样肿瘤 ○ *benign/malignant tumours* 良性[恶性]瘤 ○ *a 'lung tumour* 肺部肿瘤. Cf 参看 GROWTH 4. ▷ **tu·mor·ous** *adj*.

tu·mult /'tju:mʌlt; *US* 'tu:-; 'tumʌlt/ *n* [U, sing] (*fml* 文) **1** (**a**) disturbance or confusion, esp of a large mass of people 混乱; (尤指大群人的)骚乱: *The demonstration broke up in tumult.* 示威集会在纷乱中解散了. ○ *the* *tumult of battle* 战斗的混乱. (**b**) din or uproar produced by this 喧闹声; 嘈杂声: *One had to shout to be heard above the tumult.* 声音嘈杂, 得大喊大叫别人才听得见. ○ *Her speech threw the House* (ie of Commons) *into a tumult (of protest).* 她的讲话在众议院激起一片抗议声. **2** disturbed or agitated state of mind; turmoil (思想上的)波动, 烦乱: *Her mind was/Her thoughts were in a tumult.* 她心烦意乱. ○ *a tumult of passion, jealousy, excitement, etc* 一阵激情、忌妒、激动等 ○ *When the tumult within him subsided...* 他激动的心情平静下来的时候....

▷ **tu·mul·tu·ous** /tjuːˈmʌltʃʊəs; *US* tuː-; tuˈmʌltʃʊəs/ *adj* **1** disorderly or confused; violent 无秩序的; 混乱的; 狂暴的: *tumultuous crowds, upheavals, passions* 混乱的人群、狂暴的动乱、缭乱的心绪. **2** noisy 嘈杂的; 喧闹的: *tumultuous applause, support, protest* 喧嚣的欢呼、支持、抗议 ○ *give sb a tumultuous welcome* 热烈地欢迎某人.

tu·mu·lus /ˈtjuːmjʊləs; *US* ˈtuː-; ˈtumjələs/ *n* (*pl* **-li** /-laɪ; -ˌlaɪ/) mound of earth over an ancient burial site (古坟的)坟头. Cf 参看 BARROW².

tun /tʌn; tʌn/ *n* **1** large cask for beer, wine, etc (装啤酒、葡萄酒等的)大酒桶. **2** measure of capacity (216 gallons of beer or 252 gallons of wine) 容量单位(指啤酒为216加仑; 指葡萄酒为252加仑).

tuna /ˈtjuːnə; *US* ˈtuːnə; ˈtunə/ *n* (*pl* unchanged or **~s** 复数或不变或作**tunas**) (**a**) (also **tunny**) [C] large sea-fish, eaten as food 金枪鱼(大海鱼, 可食). (**b**) (also **ˈtuna-fish**) [U] its flesh as food (食用的)金枪鱼肉.

tun·dra /ˈtʌndrə; ˈtʌndrə/ *n* [U, C] vast flat treeless Arctic regions of Europe, Asia and N America where the subsoil is permanently frozen 冻原, 苔原(欧、亚、北美辽阔平坦的北极地带, 不生树木, 土壤下层常年冰冻): [attrib 作定语] *tundra vegetation* 冻原植物.

tune /tjuːn; *US* tuːn; tun/ *n* **1** [C, U] (series of notes with or without harmony forming a) melody, esp a well-marked one 曲调, 曲子(尤指有明显旋律的): *whistle a catchy tune* 用口哨吹一支很顺口的曲子 ○ *hymn tunes* 赞美诗曲调 ○ *He gave us a tune on his fiddle.* 他用小提琴给我们奏了一个曲子. ○ *Modern music has no tune to it.* 现代音乐毫无旋律可言. **2** (idm 习语) **call the shots/the tune** ⇨ CALL². **change one's tune** ⇨ CHANGE¹. **dance to sb's tune** ⇨ DANCE². **he who pays the piper calls the tune** ⇨ PAY². **ˌin/ˌout of ˈtune (with sb/sth)** (**a**) at/not at the correct musical pitch 音高或调子正确[不正确]: *The violin is not quite in tune with the piano.* 这小提琴跟钢琴的调子不太和谐. ○ *The choir was (singing) distinctly out of tune in places.* 合唱团有些地方明显(唱)走调了. (**b**) (*fig* 比喻) in/not in agreement or emotional harmony 协调[不协调]; 融洽[不融洽]: *feel out of tune with one's surroundings, companions* 感到与环境、同伴格格不入. **sing a different song/tune** ⇨ SING. **to the tune of sth** (**a**) using the melody of sth 用某曲调: *We sang these lines to the tune of Yankee Doodle.* 我们用扬基歌的曲调唱这几句歌词. (**b**) (*infml* 口) to the (esp considerable) sum or amount of sth 达到某一(尤指可观的)总数: *He was fined for speeding to the tune of £200.* 他因超速行车被罚款达200英镑.

▷ **tune** *v* **1** [Tn] adjust (a musical instrument or note) to the correct pitch 为(乐器)调音; 调(音): *tune a guitar* 为吉他调弦. **2** [Tn] adjust (an engine, etc) so that it runs smoothly and efficiently 调整(发动机等)(使之运转正常). **3** (idm 习语) **(be) tuned (in) to sth** (of a radio, etc) adjusted to receive a certain programme (指收音机等)调整频率等以接收某一节目: *Stay tuned to us for the latest sports results.* 请继续收听我们播放的最新比赛结果. ○ *You're not properly tuned in.* 你没有把收音机调准. **4** (phr v) **tune in (to sth)** adjust the controls of a radio, TV, etc so that it receives a certain programme (调整收音机、电视机等的频率、频道等)收听或收看某一节目: *tune in to the BBC World Service* 收看英国广播公司的对外广播节目 ○ *Tune in next week at the same time!* 请在下周同一时间继续收听! **tune sb in to sth** (usu passive 通常用于被动语态) make sb sympathetically aware of (other people's thoughts and feelings, etc) 使某人理解或体谅(他人的思想及感情等): *Voters always elect the candidate most tuned in to their needs.* 选民总是选那些最能体察其疾苦的候选人. **tune (sth) up** adjust (musical instruments) so that they can play together in tune 调整(乐器)使合调: *The orchestra were tuning up as we entered the hall.* 我们进入大厅时, 管弦乐队正在调音.

tune·ful /-fl; -fəl/ *adj* having a pleasing tune; melodious 音调优美的; 悦耳的. **tune·fully** /-fəlɪ; -fəlɪ/ *adv*. **tune·ful·ness** *n* [U].

tune·less *adj* (*usu derog* 通常作贬义) without a tune; not melodious 不合调的; 不悦耳的. **tune·lessly** *adv*. **tune·less·ness** *n* [U].

□ **ˈtune-up** *n* act of tuning (TUNE *v* 2) the engine of a motor-vehicle (对机动车辆发动机的)调整: *My car needs a tune-up.* 我的汽车的发动机得调一调了.

ˈtuning-fork *n* small steel device like a two-pronged fork that produces a note of fixed pitch (usu middle C) when struck 音叉.

tuner /ˈtjuːnə(r); *US* ˈtuː-; ˈtunɚ/ *n* **1** (esp in compounds 尤用以构成复合词) person who tunes musical instruments, esp pianos 为乐器调音的人; (尤指)钢琴调音师. **2** part of a radio, TV, etc that selects signals (收音机、电视机等的)调谐器.

tung·sten /ˈtʌŋstən; ˈtʌŋstən/ (also **wolfram**) *n* [U] chemical element, a hard grey metal used in making steel alloys and the filaments of electric light bulbs 钨. ⇨App 10 见附录10.

tu·nic /ˈtjuːnɪk; *US* ˈtuː-; ˈtunɪk/ *n* **1** close-fitting jacket worn as part of a uniform by police officers, soldiers, etc (警察、士兵等的)紧身短上衣. **2** (**a**) loose (usu sleeveless) outer garment reaching to the knees and sometimes gathered at the waist with a belt, as worn by ancient Greeks and Romans 短袍(长至膝, 通常无袖, 有时束腰, 古代希腊人及罗马人穿用). (**b**) similar hip-length garment with open sleeves worn over trousers or a skirt by women or girls (女用)短上衣(长至臀部, 敞袖, 有时束腰, 罩于裤或裙外).

tun·nel /ˈtʌnl; ˈtʌnl̩/ *n* **1** (**a**) underground passage, eg for a road or railway through a hill or under a river or the sea 地下通道; 隧道; 地道: *the Channel Tunnel*, ie between England and France 海峡隧道(英法之间的). (**b**) similar underground passage made by a burrowing animal (穴居动物的)洞穴通道: *Moles dug tunnels under the lawn.* 鼹鼠在草地下面打洞. **2** (idm 习语) **light at the end of the tunnel** ⇨ LIGHT¹.

▷ **tun·nel** *v* (**-ll-**; *US* **-l-**) **1** [I, Ipr, Ip] **~ (into, through, under, etc)** dig a tunnel (in the specified direction) 掘地道; 开隧道: *The prisoners had escaped by tunnelling.* 犯人挖地道逃跑了. ○ *They tunnelled along under the walls and up into the woods beyond.* 他们在围墙下面挖地道通向远处林中. **2** [Tn, Tn·pr, Tn·p] **~ one's way into/through/under sth** make (a way through sth) by digging a tunnel 挖地道开辟(通过某物的道路): *The rescuers tunnelled their way (in) to the pot-holers.* 救援人员挖地道通向那些探察洞穴的人. ○ *tunnel a hole, shaft, passage, etc* 挖掘洞穴、矿井、通道等.

□ **ˈtunnel vision** **1** condition in which sight is poor or lost altogether at the edges of the normal field of vision 视野狭窄; 管状视. **2** (*derog* 贬) inability to grasp the wider implications of a situation, an argument, etc 不能领会深广的意义; 井蛙之见.

tunny /ˈtʌnɪ; ˈtʌnɪ/ *n* [C] = TUNA 1.

tup /tʌp; tʌp/ *n* (*esp Brit*) uncastrated male sheep; ram(1). (未去势的)公羊. Cf 参看 EWE.

tup·pence /ˈtʌpəns; ˈtʌpəns/ *n* (*Brit infml* 口) **1** = TWOPENCE (TWO). **2** (idm 习语) **not care/give ˈtuppence for sb/sth** consider sb/sth worthless or unimportant 认为某人[某事物]无价值或不重要. ▷ **tup·penny** /ˈtʌpənɪ; ˈtʌpənɪ/ *adj* [attrib 作定语] = TWOPENNY (TWO): *a tuppenny stamp* 两便士的邮票.

tur·ban /ˈtɜːbən; ˈtɝbən/ *n* (**a**) men's head-dress (worn esp by Muslims and Sikhs) made by winding a length of cloth tightly round the head (男用)头巾(尤指穆斯林和锡克教徒用的). (**b**) woman's close-fitting hat resembling this (女用)头巾帽.

▷ **tur·baned** *adj* wearing a turban 包着头巾的; 戴着头巾帽的: *a turbaned Sikh* 包着头巾的锡克教徒.

tur·bid /ˈtɜːbɪd; ˈtɝbɪd/ *adj* (*fml* 文) **1** (of liquids) opaque or muddy; not clear (指液体)浑浊的, 不清的: *the turbid floodwaters of the river* 泛滥的浑浊的河水.

T

2 (*fig* 比喻) disordered or confused 紊乱的; 混乱的: *a turbid imagination* 紊乱的想像 ○ *turbid thoughts* 杂乱的思绪. ▷ **tur·bid·ity** /tɜːˈbɪdətɪ; tɝˈbɪdətɪ/, **tur·bid·ness** *ns* [U].

tur·bine /ˈtɜːbaɪn; ˈtɝbaɪn/ *n* machine or motor driven by a wheel which is turned by a current of water, steam, air or gas 涡轮机; 透平机.

turbo-jet /ˌtɜːbəʊˈdʒet; ˈtɝboˌdʒɛt/ *n* (propellerless aircraft driven by a) turbine engine that delivers its propulsive power in the form of a jet of hot exhaust gases 涡轮喷气发动机; 涡轮喷气式飞机.

turbo-prop /ˌtɜːbəʊˈprɒp; ˈtɝboˌprɑp/ (also **prop-jet**) *n* (aircraft driven by a) turbine used as a turbo-jet and also to drive a propeller 涡轮螺旋桨发动机; 涡轮螺旋桨式飞机.

tur·bot /ˈtɜːbət; ˈtɝbət/ *n* (*pl* unchanged 复数不变) (**a**) [C] large European seawater flat-fish 大菱鲆(扁平的大海鱼, 产于欧洲). (**b**) [U] its flesh, highly valued as food 大菱鲆肉(为珍贵食品).

tur·bu·lent /ˈtɜːbjʊlənt; ˈtɝbjələnt/ *adj* **1** (of air or water) moving violently and unevenly (指空气或水)流动得猛烈而不稳定的: *turbulent waves* 汹涌的波浪 ○ *turbulent weather conditions* 恶劣多变的天气状况. **2** (**a**) in a state of commotion or unrest; disturbed 混乱的; 不宁的; 动荡的: *turbulent mobs, crowds, factions, etc* 混乱的暴民、人群、派系等 ○ *a city with a turbulent past* 经历过动乱的城市. (**b**) restless or uncontrolled 不安的; 失控的: *turbulent moods, passions, thoughts* 忐忑不安的心情、控制不住的激情、纷乱起伏的思绪.

▷ **tur·bu·lence** /-ləns; -ləns/ *n* [U] **1** unrest or disturbance 动荡; 混乱; 骚乱: *political, social, religious, etc turbulence* 政治的、社会的、宗教的...骚乱 ○ (*fig* 比喻) *emotions in a state of turbulence* 纷乱的情绪. **2** violent or uneven movement of air or water 猛烈的或不稳定的气流或水流: *We experienced some slight turbulence flying over the Atlantic.* 我们飞越大西洋时, 遇到一点不稳定的气流.

tur·bu·lently *adv*.

T

turd /tɜːd; tɝd/ *n* (*sl* 俚) **1** ball or lump of (usu animal) excrement 粪块, 粪团(通常指动物的): *dog turds* 狗屎. **2** (⚠ 讳) contemptible or unpleasant person 可鄙的人; 讨厌的人: *You turd!* 你这个臭狗屎!

tur·een /təˈriːn; tuˈrin/ *n* deep dish with a lid from which soup, vegetables, etc are served at table (盛汤、菜等的)有盖海碗.

turf /tɜːf; tɝf/ *n* (*pl* **turfs** or **turves** /tɜːvz; tɝvz/) **1** (**a**) [U] short grass and the surface layer of soil bound together by its roots 草皮: *clipped, springy, rolled, etc turf* 修剪过的、松软的、碾轧过的...草皮 ○ *lay turf*, eg to make a lawn 铺草皮(如造草坪). (**b**) [C] piece of this, usu square or rectangular, cut from the ground 草皮块(通常为正方形或长方形). **2** [C, U] (in Ireland) (slab of) peat for fuel (爱尔兰的)(用作燃料的)泥炭(块), 泥煤(块). **3 the turf** [sing] the racecourse; horse-racing 跑马场; 赛马. **4** [U] (*infml* 口 *esp US*) one's own neighbourhood or territory (自己的)地盘, 领域: *on my own turf* 在我自己的地盘内.

▷ **turf** *v* **1** [Tn] lay (ground) with turf 用草皮铺(地): *a newly-turfed lawn* 新铺上草皮的草坪. **2** (phr v) **turf sb/sth out (of sth)** (*Brit infml* 口) forcibly remove sb/sth; dispose of sth 赶走某人[某物]; 去掉、扔掉或处理掉某物: *Turf the cat out if you want to sit in the chair.* 你要想坐那把椅子, 就把猫赶走. ○ *You'd have more room in your wardrobe if you turfed out all your old clothes.* 你把所有的旧衣服都处理掉, 衣柜里地方就大了.

□ ˈ**turf accountant** (*Brit fml* 文) bookmaker (赛马等的)赌注经纪人.

tur·gid /ˈtɜːdʒɪd; ˈtɝdʒɪd/ *adj* **1** (*derog* 贬) (of language, style, etc) pompous and difficult to follow; boring (指语言、风格等)浮夸而晦涩的, 索然无味的: *a turgid article on medieval law* 论中世纪法律的艰涩文章. **2** swollen; bloated 肿胀的; 膨胀的. ▷ **tur·gid·ity** /tɜːˈdʒɪdətɪ; tɝˈdʒɪdətɪ/ *n* [U]. **tur·gidly** *adv*.

tur·key /ˈtɜːkɪ; ˈtɝkɪ/ *n* (*pl* **~s**) **1** (**a**) [C] large bird reared to be eaten, esp at Christmas 吐绶鸡; 火鸡. ⇨ illus at App 1 见附录1插图, page v. (**b**) [U] its flesh as food (食用的)火鸡肉: *a slice of roast turkey* 一片烤火鸡肉. **2** [C] (*US sl* 俚) failure; flop 失败; 失败的人或事物: *His last movie was a real turkey.* 他最后的那部影片一塌糊涂. **3** (idm 习语) **cold turkey** ⇨ COLD[1]. **talk turkey** ⇨ TALK[2].

Turk·ish /ˈtɜːkɪʃ; ˈtɝkɪʃ/ *adj* of Turkey, its people or its language 土耳其的; 土耳其人的; 土耳其语的.

▷ **Turk·ish** *n* [U] language of Turkey 土耳其语.

□ ˌ**Turkish** ˈ**bath** type of bath in which the body is made to sweat in hot air or steam, followed by washing, massage, etc 土耳其浴; 蒸汽浴.

ˌ**Turkish** ˈ**coffee** very strong, usu very sweet, black coffee 土耳其咖啡(浓烈的清咖啡, 通常很甜).

ˌ**Turkish deˈlight** sweet consisting of lumps of flavoured gelatine coated with powdered sugar 土耳其软糖(一种覆有糖粉的胶质糖果).

tur·meric /ˈtɜːmərɪk; ˈtɝmərɪk/ *n* [U] (**a**) E Indian plant of the ginger family 姜黄(产于东印度). (**b**) its root, powdered and used to colour or flavour food, eg in curry powder 姜黄根(磨成粉可作染料或调味料, 如用以制咖喱粉的).

tur·moil /ˈtɜːmɔɪl; ˈtɝmɔɪl/ *n* [C usu *sing*, U 作可数名词时通常作单数, 亦作不可数名词] (instance of) great disturbance, agitation or confusion 骚动; 混乱; 动乱: *The country was in (a) turmoil during the strike.* 这个国家在罢工期间陷于一片混乱.

turn[1] /tɜːn; tɝn/ *v*

▸ MOVEMENT AROUND A CENTRAL POINT 围绕一中心转动 **1** [I, Ipr, Tn, Tn·pr] (cause sth to) move round a point or an axis (使某物)转动, 旋转: *The hands of a clock turn very slowly.* 时钟的指针走得很慢. ○ *The earth turns* (ie rotates) *on its axis once every 24 hours.* 地球每24小时自转一圈. ○ *The wheels of the car began to turn.* 汽车的轮子开始转动. ○ *This tap turns easily/It's easy to turn this tap.* 这水龙头好拧. ○ *She turned the handle but the door wouldn't open.* 他旋动把手, 但门就是打不开. ○ *He turned the key in the lock.* 他转动钥匙开锁. ○ *She turned the steering-wheel sharply to the left to avoid a cyclist.* 她猛然向左转动方向盘避开一个骑车的人. **2** [I, Ip, Tn, Tn·p] **~ (sb/sth) (over)** (cause sb/sth to) move so that a different side faces outwards or upwards (使某人[某物])翻转, 翻过来: *If you turn over you might find it easier to get to sleep.* 你翻翻身, 就容易睡着了. ○ *Brown the meat on one side, then turn it (over) and brown the other side.* 先把肉的一面烤好, 然后翻过来烤另一面. ○ *He sat there idly turning the pages of a book.* 他无聊地坐在那儿翻着书. ○ *She turned the chair on its side to repair it.* 她把椅子翻转过来修理. ○ *You've turned your jumper inside out.* 你的套头毛衣里外穿反了. ○ *Turn the record over and put on* (ie start to play) *the other side.* 把唱片翻过来放另一面. **3** (**a**) [I, Ipr, Ip, Tn, Tn·pr, Tn·p] (cause sb/sth to) change position or direction so as to face or start moving in the specified direction (使某人[某物])改换方向, 转弯: *About/Left/Right turn!* ie as military commands 向后[左/右]转! ○ *It's time we turned and went back home.* 我们该返回家去了. ○ *She turned to look at me.* 她转过身来看着我. ○ *He turned towards her.* 他转向她. ○ *We turned off the motorway at Lancaster.* 我们在兰开斯特转弯离开了高速公路. ○ (*fig* 比喻) *Her thoughts turned to* (ie She began to think about) *her dead husband.* 她转而想起死去的丈夫. ○ *He turned his back to the wall.* 他转过身去背对着墙. ○ *She turned (her face) away in embarrassment.* 她不好意思地扭过脸去. (**b**) [I] (of the tide) start to come in or go out (指潮水)开始涨或落: *The tide is turning; we'd better get back.* 涨潮了, 咱们最好回去吧. **4** [Tn·pr] aim or point (sth) in the specified direction 瞄准或指向(某物): *Police turned water-cannon on the rioters*, ie to disperse them. 警察用高压水龙头对准闹事的人(驱散他们). ○ *They turned their dogs on us.* 他们放狗咬我们. ○ *She turned her eyes towards him.* 她的眼睛朝他看. ○ (*fig* 比喻) *It's time to turn our attention to the question of money.* 咱们该考虑钱的问题了.

▸ POINTING OR SENDING SOMETHING IN A PARTICULAR DIRECTION 朝着某方向(送某事物) **5** [Tn·pr, Tn·p, Cn·a] cause (sb/sth) to go in the specified direction 使(某人[某物])向某方向走: *turn a horse into a field* 把马放进一片地里 ○ *turn a boat adrift* 让船漂流 ○ *It would be irresponsible to turn such a man loose on society.* 把这样的人放在社会上不加管束是不负责任的. **6** [Tn·p] fold (sth) in the specified way 折起,

翻转(某物): *She turned down the blankets and climbed into bed.* 她掀起毯子上床去了. ○ *He turned up the collar of his coat and hurried out into the rain.* 他竖起大衣领子, 匆匆冒雨出去了.

▸ CHANGING DIRECTION 改变方向 **7** [Ipr, Tn] **~ (round) sth** go round sth 绕过某物: *The car turned (round) the corner and disappeared from sight.* 那辆汽车一转弯就不见了. ○ *She waved to me as she turned the corner.* 她拐弯时向我挥了挥手. **8** [Ln, Ipr] (of a river, road, etc) curve in the specified direction (指河流、道路等)朝某方向转弯: *The river turns north at this point.* 这条河从这里转向北方. ○ *Just before the trees the path turns sharply right.* 这条小路就在那片树前向右急转. ○ *The road turns to the left after the church.* 这条路在经过教堂之后向左转弯. **9** [Tn no passive 不用于被动语态] perform (the specified movement) by moving one's body in a circle 表演(旋转动作): *turn cartwheels/somersaults* 作侧手翻[翻筋斗] ○ *She turned a pirouette on the ice.* 她在冰上做了个单足旋转动作.

▸ CHANGING STATE OR FORM 改变状态或形式 **10 (a)** [La, Ln, Cn·a] (cause sb/sth to) become (使某人[某事物])变成, 成为: *The milk turned sour in the heat/The heat turned the milk sour.* 牛奶在高温下变酸了. ○ *He turned nasty when we refused to give him the money.* 我们不给他钱, 他就凶相毕露了. ○ *Leaves turn brown in autumn.* 叶子一到秋天就黄了. ○ *The weather has turned cold and windy.* 天气变得寒冷而多风. ○ *She turned a deathly shade of white when she heard the news.* 她听到这消息时吓得面无人色. ○ *He's a clergyman turned politician*, ie He was formerly a clergyman but is now a politician. 他以前是个教士, 现在成了政治家了. ⇨ Usage at BECOME 用法见 BECOME. **(b)** [Tn] (not in the continuous tenses 不用于进行时态) reach or pass (the specified age or time) 达到或超过(某年龄或时间): *She turned forty last June.* 她在刚过去的六月份满四十岁. ○ *It's turned midnight.* 已经午夜了. **11** [Ipr, Tn·pr] **~ (sb/sth) (from A) to/into B** (cause sb/sth to) pass from one condition or state to another one (使某人[某事物])由一种状况转为另一种状况: *Caterpillars turn into butterflies.* 毛虫能变成蝴蝶. ○ *Water turns into ice when it freezes.* 天气极冷时水能结成冰. ○ *His expression turned from bewilderment to horror as he realized what had happened.* 他初时一愣, 等他明白过来就害怕了. ○ *The experience has turned him into a sad and embittered man.* 他经此一役变成了一个凄苦而忧伤的人. ○ *The witch turned the prince into a frog.* 女巫把王子变成了青蛙. ○ *The novel was turned into a successful Hollywood film.* 那部小说搬上好莱坞银幕后十分成功. **12** [Tn] shape (sth) on a lathe 用车床加工(某物); 车削(某物): *turn a chair leg* 在车床上车椅子的腿. **13** [I, Tn] (cause sth to) become sour (使某物)变酸: *The thundery weather has turned the milk.* 在雷雨欲来的天气牛奶变酸了. **14** [I, Tn] (of the stomach) have a sick feeling; cause (the stomach) to have a sick feeling (指胃)不适, 作呕, 恶心; 使(胃)不适: *The sight of the greasy stew made his stomach turn/turned his stomach.* 他一看见油腻的炖肉就恶心. **15** (idm 习语) **as it/things turned 'out** as was shown or proved by later events 正如事后表明或证实的那样; 果然如此: *I didn't need my umbrella, as it turned out*, ie because it didn't rain. 我原本就不必带伞的, 果不其然(并未下雨). **be well, badly, etc turned 'out** be well, badly, etc dressed 穿装打扮得好、不好等: *Her children are always smartly turned out.* 她的孩子都总是穿得漂漂亮亮的. **turn round and do sth** (*infml* 口) say or do sth that displeases sb 说的或做的令人不快: *How could she turn round and say that, after all I've done for her.* 我为她辛辛苦苦, 她怎么竟说出那样的话来. (For other idioms containing **turn**, see entries for *ns*, *adjs*, etc 与 **turn** 搭配的其他习语见有关名词、形容词等的词条, 如 **not turn a hair** ⇨ HAIR; **turn a deaf ear** ⇨ DEAF.)

16 (phr v) ˌ**turn a'bout** (often used in the form *aˌbout 'turn* as a military command 常用 about turn 这一形式作为军事口令) (esp of soldiers) move so as to face in the opposite direction (尤指军人)向后转: *The colonel ordered the troops to turn about.* 上校命令部队向后转. ○ *'About turn!' barked the sergeant-major.* '向后转!'军士长厉声喊道.

turn (sb) against sb (cause sb to) become unfriendly or hostile towards sb (使某人)与某人反目或为敌: *She turned against her old friend.* 她与老朋友反目成仇了. ○ *After the divorce he tried to turn the children against their mother.* 他离婚后竭力教唆子女对抗他们的母亲.

turn around = TURN ROUND.

turn a'way (from sb/sth) stop facing or looking at sb/sth 转过脸不面对或不再看着某人[某物]: *She turned away in horror at the sight of so much blood.* 她一看见这么多血就立刻吓得转过脸去. **turn sb away (from sth)** refuse to allow sb to enter a place; refuse to give help or support to sb 不准某人进入某处; 拒绝帮助或支持某人: *Hundreds of people had to be turned away from the stadium*, eg because it was full. 数以百计的人被体育场拒之门外(如因满座). ○ *turn away a beggar*, ie refuse to give him money 不给乞丐钱 ○ *A doctor cannot turn away a dying man.* 医生是不能见死不救的.

turn (sb/sth) 'back (cause sb/sth to) return the way he/it has come (使某人[某物])循原路折返, 往回走: *The weather became so bad that they had to turn back.* 天气变得很坏, 他们只好原路而归了. ○ (*fig* 比喻) *The project must go ahead; there can be no turning back.* 这计划必须坚持下去, 不能打退堂鼓. ○ *Our car was turned back at the frontier.* 我们的汽车在边境处被勒令折返.

turn sb/sth 'down reject or refuse to consider (an offer, a proposal, etc or the person who makes it) 顶回或拒不理会(好意、建议等或提议的人): *He tried to join the army but was turned down (flat) because of poor health.* 他想参军, 但因身体不好被断然拒绝. ○ *He asked Jane to marry him but she turned him down/turned down his proposal.* 他请求简嫁给他, 但她拒绝了. **turn sth down** adjust (a cooker, radio, etc) in order to reduce the heat, noise, etc 调节(炉具、收音机等)使热度、音量等降低: *Don't forget to turn down the gas after an hour or so.* 别忘了过一小时左右把煤气关小点儿. ○ *Turn that record-player down — I'm trying to get some sleep.* 把电唱机的声音调低些——我想睡一会儿.

turn 'in (a) face or curve inwards 面朝内; 向内弯: *Her feet turn in as she walks.* 她走路时两脚呈内八字. **(b)** (*infml* 口) go to bed 去睡觉: *It's late; I think I'll turn in.* 不早了, 我该睡觉去了. **turn sb in** (*infml* 口) hand sb over to the police to be arrested 将某人交给警方拘押: *She threatened to turn him in.* 她威胁说要向警方告发他. **turn sth in (a)** give back sth that one no longer needs; return sth 交还或退还某物: *You must turn in your kit* (ie uniform, etc) *before you leave the army.* 退伍时应将装备(制服等)缴回. **(b)** stop doing sth; abandon sth 停止做某事; 放弃某事物: *The job was damaging his health so he had to turn it in.* 那工作危害他的健康, 所以他只好放弃了. **(c)** record or achieve (a score, performance, etc) 取得(分数等); 完成(表演等): *Thompson turned in a superb performance to win the decathlon.* 汤普森在十项全能比赛中表现十分出色. **turn 'in on oneself** become preoccupied with one's own problems and stop communicating with others 埋头于自己的事务而不与他人联系: *She's really turned in on herself since Peter left her.* 彼得离开她以后, 她就闭门杜绝人事了.

turn sth inside out make the inside face outwards 把里面翻作外面: *The wind turned my umbrella inside out.* 大风把我的伞吹得翻了过去. ○ *She turned all her pockets inside out looking for her keys.* 她把衣服口袋都翻出来找她的钥匙.

turn 'off leave one road in order to travel on another 离开一条路而走上另一条路: *Is this where we turn off/where the road turns off for Hull?* 这儿就是我们要转往赫尔市方向的路吗? **turn sb 'off** (*infml* 口) cause sb to be bored or disgusted by sth or not sexually attracted to sb 使某人厌烦或厌恶; 使某人在性的方面不喜爱对方: *All that talk about abattoirs turned me right off!* 关于屠宰场的那些话让我十分恶心! ○ *Bad breath is guaranteed to turn a woman off!* 有口臭管保让女子兴趣顿失! **turn sth off (a)** stop the flow of (electricity, gas, water, etc) by turning a knob, tap, etc 截断(电流、煤气、水等); 关掉; 关上: *turn off the light, oven, tap* 关上灯、烤箱、龙头 ○ *They've turned off the water while they mend a burst pipe.* 他们修理爆裂的水管时, 关上了水门. **(b)** stop (a radio, television, etc) by pressing a button, moving a switch, etc 关上(收音机、电视机等): *Let's turn the*

T

television off, I'd sooner read a book. 咱们把电视机关上吧，我宁愿看本书.
turn on sb attack sb suddenly and unexpectedly 突然出其不意地攻击某人: *His normally placid dog turned on him and bit him in the leg.* 他那条狗平日很温顺，这次突然发作咬了他的腿. ○ *Why are you all turning on me* (ie criticizing or blaming me)? 你们为什么都突然冲我来了(批评或责备我)? **turn on sth** have sth as its main topic 以某事物为主要议题: *The discussion turned on the need for better public health care.* 讨论的主要议题是必须改善大众保健服务. **turn on sth/doing sth** depend on sth 依某事物而定: *The success of a picnic usually turns on the weather.* 参加野餐是否尽兴，通常要看天气好坏. **turn sb 'on** (*infml* 口) excite or stimulate sb, esp sexually 使某人激动或兴奋(尤指性欲方面): *Jazz has never really turned me on.* 我从未对爵士乐真正产生过兴趣. ○ *She's often turned on by men with beards.* 有胡子的男子每每引起她的性欲. **turn sth on** cause (an oven, a radio, etc) to start functioning by moving a switch, knob, etc 扭开(烤箱、收音机等): *turn on the light, television, central heating* 打开电灯、电视机、集中供热设备 ○ *Turn on the gas and light the oven.* 转动煤气开关点燃烤箱. ○ *Could you turn on the bath* (ie cause the water to start flowing) *for me while you're upstairs?* 你在楼上替我打开浴缸的水龙头行吗?
turn 'out (a) be present at an event; appear, assemble or attend 在场; 露面; 集合; 出席: *A vast crowd turned out to watch the match.* 大群的观众到场观看比赛. ○ *The whole village turned out to welcome the pope.* 全村的人都出来欢迎教皇. ○ *Not many men turned out for duty.* 出勤人数不太多. **(b)** (used with an *adv* or *adj*, or in questions after *how* 与副词或形容词连用，或用于以how引导的疑问句中) take place or happen in the specified way; prove to be 以某方式发生; 证明为: *If the day turns out wet we may have to change our plans.* 万一下雨的话，我们也许得改变计划. ○ *'How did the party turn out?' 'It turned out very well, thanks.'* '宴会举行得怎么样?' '非常成功，谢谢.' ○ *I hope all turns out well for you.* 我希望你一切顺利. **turn (sth) 'out** (cause sth to) point outwards (使某物)向外: *Her toes turn out.* 她的脚趾向外撇. ○ *She turned her toes out.* 她把脚趾向外弯. **turn sb/sth out** produce sb/sth 培养出某人; 生产或制造某物: *The factory turns out 900 cars a week.* 该厂每周生产900辆汽车. ○ *The school has turned out some first-rate scholars.* 这所学校培养出了一些第一流的学者. **turn sth out (a)** switch (a light or fire) off; extinguish sth 关掉(灯或炉火); 熄灭: *Remember to turn out the lights before you go to bed.* 临睡前别忘了关灯. **(b)** remove the contents of sth; empty sth 将某物中的东西除掉; 弄空: *turn out the attic, one's drawers* 把阁楼、抽屉腾空 ○ *The teacher ordered him to turn out his pockets.* 老师叫他把衣袋里的东西全拿出来. **turn sb out (of/from sth)** force sb to leave a place 赶走某人: *My landlord is turning me out at the end of the month.* 我的房东让我月底搬走. ○ *She got pregnant and was turned out of the house by her parents.* 她怀孕了，父母把她赶出了家门. **turn out to be sb/sth; turn out that ...** prove to be sb/sth; came to be known that ... 证明是某人[某事物]; 原来是...: *She turned out to be a friend of my sister/It turned out that she was a friend of my sister.* 她原来是我妹妹的朋友. ○ *The job turned out to be harder than we thought.* 这工作结果比我们想的要难.
turn (sb/sth) over (cause sb/sth to) face in another direction by rolling (使某人[某物])翻身或翻转: *She turned over and went to sleep.* 她转过身就睡着了. ○ *The car skidded, turned over and burst into flames.* 那汽车一打滑，翻倒后起火了. ○ *The nurse turned the old man over to wash his back.* 护士给老人翻个身擦洗后背. **turn sth over (a)** do business worth (the specified amount) 做值(某数额)的生意; 营业额达...: *The company turns over £150 million a year.* 该公司每年的营业额达1.5亿英镑. **(b)** (of a shop) sell out and replace its stock (指商店)销货和进货, 周转: *A supermarket turns over its stock very rapidly.* 超级市场货物周转得非常快. **turn sb over to sb** deliver sb to (the authorities, the police, etc) 把某人交给(负责人、警方等): *Customs officials turned the man over to the police.* 海关人员把那男子送交警方处理. **turn sth over to sb** give the control or management of sth to sb 把某事物的控制权或管理权交给某人: *He turned the business over to his daughter.* 他把生意移交给女儿管理.
turn 'round (also **turn a'round**) **(a)** (of a ship or aircraft) unload at the end of one journey and reload for the next one (指船或飞机)在一航程终点卸货并为下一航程装货: *These cruise ships can turn round in two days.* 这些游船可用两天的时间装卸完毕. **(b)** (*commerce* 商) (of shares, the stock-market, etc) begin to show an opposite trend or movement (指股票、证券市场等)开始显示相反的动向: *The American market turned round sharply a week ago.* 美国证券市场于一周前急遽反转. **turn (sb/sth) 'round** (cause sb/sth to) face in a different direction (使某人[某物])面向另一方向: *Turn round and let me look at your back.* 转过去，让我看看你的后背. ○ *Turn your chair round to the fire.* 把你的椅子转向炉火一边.
turn to begin to work hard or energetically 开始努力地或热情地工作: *We turned to and got the whole house cleaned in an afternoon.* 我们起劲地干了起来，一个下午就把整所房子打扫干净了. **turn to sb/sth** go to sb/sth for help, advice, etc 向某人[某事物]寻求帮助、指教等: *She has nobody she can turn to.* 她求助无门. ○ *The parish priest is someone to whom people can turn in difficult times.* 牧区牧师是人们在困难时可以求助的人. ○ *The more depressed he got, the more he turned to drink.* 他情绪越低落越是借酒浇愁. ○ *The child turned to its mother for comfort.* 那孩子向母亲寻求安慰.
turn 'up (a) (*commerce* 商) (of shares, the stock-market, etc) rise; increase; improve (指股票、股市等)上扬, 反弹, 升值: *Investment is turning up sharply.* 投资额急遽增长. **(b)** make one's appearance; arrive 露面; 来到: *We arranged to meet at the cinema at 7.30, but he failed to turn up.* 我们约定7点30分在电影院见面，但他没来. ○ *We invited her to dinner but she didn't even bother to turn up.* 我们请她吃饭她都不露面. **(c)** be found (esp by chance) after being lost (失去后)被发现或找到(尤指偶然地): *I'm sure your watch will turn up one of these days.* 我担保你的手表准有一天能找到. **(d)** (of an opportunity) present itself; happen (指机会)出现, 到来: *He's still hoping something* (eg a job or a piece of good luck) *will turn up.* 他仍在期待机会出现(如得到工作或好运). **turn sth up (a)** cause sth to face or point upwards 使某物面朝上或指向上方: *He turned up his coat collar against the chill wind.* 他竖起大衣领抵御寒风. **(b)** shorten (a garment) by folding it up at the bottom 折起衣边改短(衣服): *These trousers are too long; they'll need turning up/to be turned up.* 这条裤子太长，需要改短些. **(c)** discover sth by digging; expose sth 挖掘而发现某物; 暴露出某物: *The farmer turned up a human skull while ploughing the field.* 那农民犁地时挖出一个人类的头颅骨. ○ *The soil had been turned up by the plough.* 那片地是用犁翻的. **(d)** increase the loudness of (a radio, television, etc) 开大(收音机、电视机等)的音量: *I can't hear the radio very well; could you turn it up a bit?* 收音机我听不太清楚，你把声音开大点行吗?

□ **'turn-about** *n* act of turning in a different or the opposite direction 转方向; 向后转: (*fig* 比喻) *The government's sudden turn-about* (ie change of policy) *on taxation surprised political commentators.* 政府在税收政策上突然改变，政评家非常吃惊.
'turn-around (also **'turn-round**) *n* (usu *sing* 通常作单数) complete change, eg from a very bad situation to a very good one 彻底的改变(如由极坏到极好): *The change of leader led to a turn-around in the fortunes of the Labour Party.* 工党领导人更换后全党时来运转.
'turn-off *n* **1** road that leads away from a larger or more important one 支路; 岔道: *This is the turn-off for Bath.* 这是通往巴斯市的岔道. **2** (usu *sing* 通常作单数) (*infml* 口) person or thing that bores or disgusts sb, or causes sb not to feel sexually attracted 某人厌烦或反感的人或事物; 使某人在性的方面不喜爱的人或事物: *Smelly feet are definitely a turn-off as far as I'm concerned.* 脚要是有味可真恶心人，这是我的看法.
'turn-on *n* (usu *sing* 通常作单数) (*infml* 口) person or thing that excites or stimulates sb, esp sexually 使人激动或兴奋的人或事物(尤指性欲方面): *She thinks hairy chests are a turn-on!* 她觉得胸部有毛很让人兴奋!
'turn-out *n* (usu *sing* 通常作单数) **1** number of people

who attend a match, meeting, etc; attendance（比赛、会议等的）全部参与人(数): *There was a good turn-out at yesterday's meeting.* 出席昨日会议的人很多. **2** act of emptying a drawer, a room, etc 清除抽屉、房间等中之物: *These drawers are full of rubbish; it's time I had a good turn-out.* 这些抽屉里净是没用的东西, 我得好好清理一下了. **3** way in which sb is dressed 某人的穿着打扮: *The headmaster praised the boys for their neat turn-out.* 校长表扬男同学服装整齐.

ˈturnover *n* **1** [sing] amount of business done by a company within a certain period of time（一定时期的）营业额: *The firm has an annual turnover of £75 million.* 这家公司的年营业额为7 500万英镑. ○ *make a profit of £2 000 on a turnover of £20 000* 从20 000英镑营业额中获利2 000英镑. **2** [sing] rate at which goods are sold and replaced in a shop（商店的）货物周转率: *We aim for a quick turnover of stock in our stores.* 我们的目的是要加速本百货店的库存周转. **3** [sing] rate at which workers leave a factory, company, etc and are replaced 人事变动率: *Why does your company have such a rapid turnover of staff?* 贵公司人员变动为什么这么快? **4** [C] type of small pie made by folding a piece of pastry round a filling of fruit, jam, etc（用水果、果酱等作馅的）油酥饺: *an apple turnover* 苹果油酥饺.

ˈturn-round *n* **1** (also **ˈturn-around**) (usu *sing* 通常作单数) (of a ship or an aircraft) process of being unloaded at the end of one journey and reloaded for the next one（指船或飞机）在一航程终点卸货并为下一航程装货的作业. **2** = TURN-AROUND.

ˈturnstile *n* revolving gate that allows one person at a time to enter or leave a stadium or sports ground（体育馆、场中只容一人进或出的）旋转栅门.

ˈturntable *n* **1** flat round revolving surface on which gramophone records are played（唱机上的）唱盘. **2** flat round platform onto which a locomotive runs to be turned round（铁路上的）转车台.

ˈturn-up *n* **1** (usu *pl* 通常作复数) turned-up end of a trouser leg（裤脚的）卷边: *Turn-ups are becoming fashionable again.* 裤脚留卷边又时兴起来了. **2** (idm 习语) **a ˈturn-up (for the book)** (*infml* 口) unusual or unexpected happening or event 极不寻常的事; 意想不到的事: *The champion beaten in the first round? That's a turn-up for the book!* 那冠军在第一回合中就败了? 真想不到哇!

turn[2] /tɜːn; tɝn/ *n* **1** [C] act of turning sth/sb round; turning movement 转动; 旋转: *give the handle a few turns* 将那把手转动几下. **2** [C] change of direction; point at which this occurs 方向的改变; 转折; 转折点: *He took a sudden turn to the left.* 他突然向左转. **3** [C] bend or corner in a road（道路的）转弯处: *a lane full of twists and turns* 弯弯曲曲的胡同 ○ *Don't take the turn too fast.* 转弯时不要太快. **4** [C] development or new tendency in sth 发展变化; 新的趋势: *an alarming turn in international relations* 国际关系中令人震惊的新情况 ○ *an unfortunate turn of events* 事态的不利变化 ○ *Matters have taken an unexpected turn.* 事情发生了意想不到的变化. ○ *Business has taken a turn for the better/worse.* 生意转好[坏]了. **5** [C usu *sing* 通常作单数] time when each one of a group must or may do sth（轮到的）机会: *Please wait (until it is/for) your turn to be served.* 请等一等就轮到为您服务了. ○ *Whose turn is it to do the washing-up?* 轮到谁刷锅洗碗了? ○ *I'll take a turn at the steering-wheel.* 该轮到我来驾驶了. **6** [C] short walk; stroll 短时间行走; 散步; 溜达: *I think I'll take a turn round the garden.* 我想到花园去转转. **7** [C] short performance by a comedian, singer, etc（喜剧演员、歌手等的）短小节目: *a comedy, song-and-dance, variety, etc turn* 喜剧、歌舞、杂耍等节目 ○ *The star turn* (ie main performance) *was a young rock group.* 主要的节目是一个青年摇滚乐队的表演. **8** (*infml* 口) (**a**) [sing] nervous shock 惊吓; 震惊: *You gave me quite a turn, bursting in like that!* 你那样闯进来, 吓了我一跳. (**b**) [C] feeling of illness 疾病的发作; 不适: *She's had one of her turns.* 她的病犯了. **9** (idm 习语) **at every ˈturn** everywhere or all the time 处处; 次次: *I keep meeting him at every turn.* 我每次都遇见他. ○ *She found her plans frustrated at every turn.* 她觉得她的计划到处碰壁. **by ˈturns** (of people or their actions) one after the other; in rotation（指人或人的动作）轮流地, 逐个地: *We did the work by turns.* 我们是轮流做这项工作的. ○ *He gets cheerful and depressed by turns.* 他的情绪高一阵低一阵. **do sb a good/bad ˈturn** be helpful/unhelpful to sb 对某人有好处[坏处]. **done, etc to a ˈturn** (of meat, etc) cooked for exactly the right length of time（指肉等）火候恰当. **have, etc an enquiring, etc turn of ˈmind** have, etc a particular way of thinking about things, tackling a problem, etc（对事情、处理问题等）有独特的思想方法: *She's always shown an academic turn of mind.* 她总是表现出学究式的思想方法. **in ˈturn** one after the other; in succession 依次; 逐个地: *The girls called out their names in turn.* 那些女孩儿逐一报出自己的名字. **not do a hand's turn** ⇨ HAND[1]. **on the ˈturn** about to change or go a different way 即将改变或另走一条路: *His luck is on the turn.* 他时来运转了. ○ *This milk is on the turn*, ie about to become sour. 这牛奶快要变酸了. **ˌone good ˌturn deserves aˈnother** (*saying* 谚) one should help or be kind to others who have been kind to one in the past 要以德报德. **ˌout of ˈturn** (**a**) before or after one's turn[2](5) 在轮到自己之前或之后. (**b**) not at the correct or permitted time 不合时宜; 未按规定时间: *speak out of turn*, ie in a tactless or foolish way 讲话不策略. **serve one's/sb's turn** ⇨ SERVE. **take ˈturns (at sth)** do sth one after the other 轮流做某事: *You can't both use the bike at once — you'll have to take turns.* 你们不能两人同时用这辆自行车——得轮流使用. **(do sth) ˌturn and ˌturn aˈbout** one after another; in succession 交替; 轮流. **a/the turn of events** change or development in circumstance, often unexpected or beyond one's control 情况的改变或发展（常指未料到的或无法控制的）. **a ˌturn of ˈphrase** way of expressing or describing sth 表达方式; 描述方式; 措辞: *She has an apt turn of phrase for summing up a situation.* 她很善于总结情况. **a ˌturn of the ˈscrew** extra amount of pressure, cruelty, etc added to a situation that is already difficult to bear or understand 在已不堪忍受的情况下增加的压力或残酷做法. **a ˌturn of ˈspeed** (ability to achieve) a sudden increase in one's speed or rate of progress（达到）速度或进度的突然加快(的能力): *She put on an impressive turn of speed to overtake the others.* 她突然奋勇加速力图超过别人. **the ˌturn of the ˈyear/ˈcentury** the time when a new year/century starts 年度[世纪]的新旧交替时期; 一年之始; 世纪之初.

turn·coat /ˈtɜːnkəʊt; ˋtɝnˌkot/ *n* (*derog* 贬) person who changes from one side, party, etc to another 变节者; 叛徒.

turner /ˈtɜːnə(r); ˋtɝnɚ/ *n* person who operates a lathe 车床工人: *a ˈmetal-/ˈwood-turner*, ie person who turns metal/wood on a lathe 金工[木工]车床工人. Cf 参看 TURN[1] 12.

turn·ing /ˈtɜːnɪŋ; ˋtɝnɪŋ/ *n* place where one road leads off from another（道路的）转弯处, 岔路口: *take the wrong turning* 拐错弯 ○ *Take the second turning on/to the left.* 在第二个拐弯处向左转.

□ **ˈturning-circle** *n* smallest possible circle in which a vehicle can turn（车辆的）回转圆.

ˈturning-point *n* time when a decisive change or development takes place 转折点; 转捩点; 转机: *The meeting proved to be a turning-point in her life.* 那次会见是她一生的转折点. ○ *The discovery of a vaccine was the turning-point in the fight against smallpox.* 牛痘苗的发现是根治天花的关键.

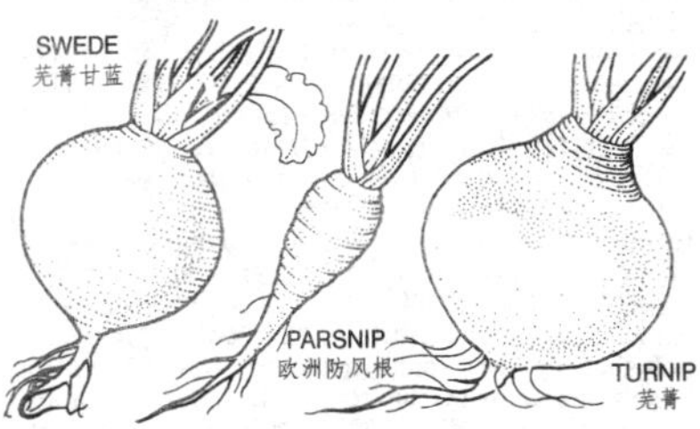

tur·nip /ˈtɜːnɪp; ˋtɝnɪp/ *n* **1** [C] (**a**) plant with a round white, or white and purple, root 芜菁. (**b**) plant with a brownish purple root; swede 芜菁. **2** [C, U] root of either of these used as a vegetable or as food for cattle 芜菁, 蔓菁, 大头菜(用作蔬菜或牛饲料): *mashed turnip* 大头菜泥 ○ [attrib 作定语] *turnip soup* 蔓菁汤.

turn·key /ˈtɜ:nki:; ˈtɝn,ki/ *adj* [attrib 作定语] built and handed over ready for use, occupation, etc 建成并已交付使用、入住等的: *a turnkey plant, apartment, etc* 已建成即可使用的工厂、成套房间等.

turn·pike /ˈtɜ:npaɪk; ˈtɝn,paɪk/ *n* **1** (*US*) road for fast-moving traffic which drivers must pay to drive on (收费的)高速公路: *the New Jersey turnpike* 新泽西州高速公路. **2** (*Brit* **pike**) (formerly) gate on a road that was opened when a traveller paid some money (旧时)(公路上的)收税栅门, 收税卡.

tur·pen·tine /ˈtɜ:pəntaɪn; ˈtɝpən,taɪn/ (also *infml* 口语作 **turps** /tɜ:ps; tɝps/) *n* [U] strong-smelling colourless liquid obtained from the resin of certain trees, used esp for thinning paint and as a solvent 松脂; 松节油.

tur·pi·tude /ˈtɜ:pɪtju:d; *US* -tu:d; ˈtɝpə,tud/ *n* [U] (*fml* 文) state or quality of being wicked; depravity 邪恶; 恶劣; 堕落; 腐化.

tur·quoise /ˈtɜ:kwɔɪz; ˈtɝkwɔɪz/ *n* **1** [C, U] type of greenish-blue precious stone 绿松石: [attrib 作定语] *a turquoise brooch* 绿松石的胸针. **2** [U] greenish-blue colour 青绿色: *pale turquoise* 浅淡的青绿色.

□ **tur·quoise** *adj* of this colour 青绿色的: *a turquoise dress* 青绿色的连衣裙.

tur·ret /ˈtʌrɪt; ˈtɝɪt/ *n* **1** small tower on top of a larger tower or at the corner of a building or defensive wall 塔楼; 角楼. **2** (on a ship, an aircraft, a fort or a tank) low flat (often revolving) steel structure where the guns are fixed and which protects the gunners (舰船、飞机、要塞或坦克上的)炮塔(通常可旋转): *a warship armed with twin turrets* 装备着双炮塔的战舰.

▷ **tur·reted** *adj* having a turret(1) or turrets 有塔楼或角楼的.

T

turtle /ˈtɜ:tl; ˈtɝtl̩/ *n* **1** large reptile that lives in the sea and has flippers and a large horny shell 海龟. **2** (*US*) any of various types of reptile with a large shell, eg a tortoise, terrapin, etc (任何种类的)龟(如陆龟、水龟等). ⇨illus at TORTOISE 见 TORTOISE 插图. **3** (idm 习语) **turn ˈturtle** (*infml* 口) (of a boat) turn upside down; capsize (指船)倾覆, 翻.

□ **ˈturtle-dove** *n* type of wild dove noted for its soft cooing and its affectionate behaviour towards its mate and young 斑鸠.

ˈturtle-neck *n* (garment, esp a sweater, with a) close-fitting neckband that is higher than a crew neck but does not turn over like a polo-neck 高而紧的(但不翻转的)领口; 有这种领口的衣服(尤指毛衣). **ˈturtle-necked** *adj*: *a turtle-necked sweater* 高领毛衣. ⇨illus at NECK 见 NECK 插图.

turves *pl* of TURF.

tusk /tʌsk; tʌsk/ *n* either of a pair of very long pointed teeth that project from the mouth of certain animals, eg the elephant, walrus and wild boar (象、海象、野猪等的)长牙. ⇨illus at ELEPHANT 见 ELEPHANT 插图. Cf 参看 IVORY.

tussle /ˈtʌsl; ˈtʌsl̩/ *n* (*infml* 口) struggle or fight, esp to take sth away from sb 争斗, 扭打(尤指为抢走物品): *I had a tussle to get the knife off him.* 我与他扭打一阵才把刀子夺下. ○ (*fig* 比喻) *We have a tussle every year about where to go on holiday.* 我们每年都要为前往何处度假而争论一番.

▷ **tussle** *v* [I, Ipr] **~ (with sb) (about/for/over sth)** struggle or fight to obtain sth; wrestle 争斗; 扭打: *They began to tussle with each other for the coins.* 他们为争夺硬币扭打起来. ○ (*fig* 比喻) *He tussled all night with the figures, but couldn't balance the account.* 他绞尽脑汁算了一夜也没把帐算清.

tus·sock /ˈtʌsək; ˈtʌsək/ *n* tuft or clump of grass that is thicker or higher than the grass growing round it (比周围的草长得密或高的)草丛.

tut /tʌt; tʌt/ (also **tut-tut** /ˌtʌt ˈtʌt; ˈtʌtˈtʌt/) *interj, n* (way of showing the) sound made by touching the top of one's mouth with the tongue to express disapproval, annoyance, etc (表示不赞成、烦恼等的)咂嘴(声): *Tut-tut, the boy's late again!* 咳, 这孩子又迟到了! ○ *a tut of disapproval* 表示不赞成的咂嘴动作.

▷ **tut** (also **tut-tut**) *v* (**-tt-**) [I] express disapproval, impatience, etc in this way 咂嘴表示不赞成、不耐烦等: *His wife tut-tutted with annoyance.* 他妻子不耐烦地咂着嘴.

tu·tel·age /ˈtju:tɪlɪdʒ; *US* ˈtu:-; ˈtutl̩ɪdʒ/ *n* [U] (*fml* 文) **1** (**a**) protection of and authority over a person, country, etc; guardianship (对人、国家等的)保护, 监护, 守护: *a child in tutelage* 受监护的孩子 ○ *royal, Papal, princely tutelage* 王室的、教皇的、王侯的监护. (**b**) state or period of being under the authority and protection of a guardian 保护或监护的状况或期间. **2** instruction; tuition 指导; 辅导; 教导: *under the tutelage of a master craftsman* 在工艺大师的指导下.

tu·tel·ary /ˈtju:tɪlərɪ; *US* ˈtu:təlerɪ; ˈtutl̩,ɛrɪ/ *adj* (*fml* 文) (**a**) acting as a guardian or protector 保护的; 监护的; 守护的. (**b**) of a guardian 保护人的; 监护人的; 守护者的: *tutelary authority* 监护人的职权.

tu·tor /ˈtju:tə(r); *US* ˈtu:-; ˈtutɚ/ *n* **1** private teacher, esp one who teaches a single pupil or a very small group 私人教师; 家庭教师: *There is a tutor to teach the children while they're in hospital.* 在孩子们住院期间, 有个私人教师给他们上课. **2** (**a**) (*Brit*) university teacher who supervises the studies of a student (大学中指导一个学生的)导师: *Her tutor says she is making good progress.* 她的导师说她进步很大. (**b**) (*US*) assistant lecturer in a college (大专院校的)助教. **3** book of instruction in a particular subject, esp music (某学科的)课本; (尤指)音乐课本: *a violin tutor* 小提琴课本.

▷ **tu·tor** *v* **1** (**a**) [Tn, Tn·pr] **~ sb (in sth)** act as a tutor(*n* 1, 2) to (sb); teach (任私人教师或大学导师)教(某人): *tutor sb for an examination* 任私人教师辅导某人准备考试 ○ *tutor sb in mathematics* 任导师教某人数学. (**b**) [I] work as a tutor 当私人教师; 当导师: *Her work was divided between tutoring and research.* 她兼做导师工作和研究工作. **2** [Tn, Cn·t] (*fml* 文) control (oneself or one's feelings) 控制, 约束(自己或感情): *tutor one's passions* 抑制强烈的感情 ○ *tutor oneself to be patient* 培养耐性.

tu·tor·ial /tju:ˈtɔ:rɪəl; *US* tu:-; tuˈtorɪəl/ *adj* of a tutor(*n* 1, 2) 私人教师的; 导师的: *tutorial classes, duties, responsibilities* 家庭教师的课、私人教师的工作、导师的责任 ○ *in a tutorial capacity* 以导师的身分. — *n* period of instruction given by a tutor in a university, esp to one or two students 指导课(尤指大学导师指导一两个学生的): *attend, give, miss a tutorial* 上、教、误了一节指导课.

tutti-frutti /ˌtu:tɪ ˈfru:tɪ; ˈtutɪˈfrutɪ/ *n* (also ˌ**tutti-frutti ice-ˈcream**) [U, C] (portion of) ice-cream that contains various types of fruit and sometimes nuts 什锦水果冰激凌(有时含坚果).

tutu /ˈtu:tu:; ˈtutu/ *n* ballet dancer's short skirt made of many layers of stiffened net 芭蕾舞裙.

tux·edo /tʌkˈsi:dəʊ; tʌkˈsido/ *n* (*pl* **~s** /-dəʊz; -doz/) (also *infml* 口语作 **tux** /tʌks; tʌks/) (*US*) = DINNER-JACKET (DINNER).

TV /ˌti: ˈvi:; ,ti ˈvi/ *abbr* 缩写 = television (set): *What's on TV tonight?* 今晚电视有什么节目? ○ *We're getting a new colour TV.* 我们要买个新的彩色电视机了.

twaddle /ˈtwɒdl; ˈtwɑdl̩/ *n* [U] nonsense or writing of low quality 胡言乱语; 拙劣的文字: *I've never heard such utter twaddle!* 我还从来没听过这么愚蠢透顶的话! ○ *The novel is sentimental twaddle.* 这部小说纯粹是无病呻吟.

twang /twæŋ; twæŋ/ *n* **1** sound made when a tight string is pulled and released, esp when the string or bow of a musical instrument is plucked 拨弦声; (尤指)弦乐器弹拨声. **2** nasal quality or tone in speech 鼻音: *speak with a twang* 说话带鼻音 ○ *a distinctive Texan twang* 特有的得克萨斯鼻音.

▷ **twang** *v* [I, Tn] (cause sth to) make a twang(1) (使某物)发拨弦声: *The bow twanged and the arrow whistled through the air.* 那张弓发出'嘣'的一声, 箭随之呼啸而去. ○ *Someone was twanging a guitar in the next room.* 隔壁有人弹着吉他.

twat /twɒt; twɑt/ *n* (⚠ *infml* 讳, 口) **1** female genitals 屄; 阴门. **2** (*derog* 贬) unpleasant or stupid person 讨厌鬼; 笨蛋.

tweak /twi:k; twik/ *v* [Tn] pinch and twist (sth) sharply

拧，扭(某物): *She tweaked his ear playfully.* 她拧他的耳朵玩儿.
▷ **tweak** *n* sharp pinch, twist or pull 拧; 扭; 拉: *He gave the boy's ear a painful tweak.* 他用力拧了一下那男孩的耳朵.

twee /twi:; twi/ *adj* (*Brit infml derog* 口，贬) attractive to those with sentimental or poor taste 情感柔懦的人或趣味低级的人所喜爱的: *I can't stand those twee little frills.* 我看不惯那些花哨的零碎儿. ○ *She has a rather twee manner that I find irritating.* 她娇里娇气，我觉得很讨厌.

tweed /twi:d; twid/ *n* **1** [U] woollen cloth with a rough surface, often woven with mixed colours 粗花呢(常为杂色的): *Scottish tweed* 苏格兰花呢 ○ [attrib 作定语] *a tweed coat* 花呢大衣. **2 tweeds** [pl] clothes made of tweed 花呢服装: *He is usually dressed in tweeds.* 他常穿花呢服装.
▷ **tweedy** *adj* (**a**) (*infml* 口) often dressed in tweeds 常穿花呢服装的: *The pub was full of tweedy farmers.* 小酒店里净是身穿花呢衣服的农民. (**b**) (*joc often derog* 谑，常作贬义) behaving in a hearty way associated with rich country people in Britain 有英国富裕乡下人的派头的; 粗豪的: *a rather tweedy golf partner* 粗豪的高尔夫球搭档.

tweet /twi:t; twit/ *n* chirp of a small bird (小鸟的)啁啁声，啾啾声.
▷ **tweet** *v* [I] (of a bird) make this sound (指鸟)啁啾而鸣.

tweeter /ˈtwi:tə(r); ˈtwitɚ/ *n* small loudspeaker for reproducing high notes 小型高频扬声器. Cf 参看 WOOFER.

tweezers /ˈtwi:zəz; ˈtwizɚz/ *n* [pl] small pincers for picking up or pulling out very small things, eg hairs from the eyebrows 镊子; 小钳子: *a pair of tweezers* 一把镊子 ○ *You'll need tweezers to hold up the specimen.* 你要用镊子来夹这标本.

twelve /twelv; twɛlv/ *pron*, *det* 12; one more than eleven 12, 十二(个). ⇨App 4 见附录 4.
▷**twelfth** /twelfθ; twɛlfθ/ *pron*, *det* 12th; next after eleventh 第12, 第十二(个). ˌ**twelfth ˈman** (in cricket) reserve player (板球的)预备队员，替补队员. ˌ**Twelfth ˈNight** night before the feast of the Epiphany, formerly celebrated with festivities 显现节的前夕(旧时有庆祝活动). — *n* one of twelve equal parts of sth 十二分之一.

twelve *n* **1** [C] the number 12 ☆ 12; 十二. **2 the Twelve** [pl] the twelve apostles of Jesus 耶稣的十二使徒.

twelve- (forming compound *adjs* 用以构成复合形容词) having twelve of the thing specified 有十二个...的: *a twelve-man expedition* 一支十二人的考察队.
□ ˈ**twelvemonth** *n* (*dated* 旧) year 一年.
For the uses of *twelve* and *twelfth*, see the examples at *five* and *fifth*. 关于 twelve 和 twelfth 的用法见 five 和 fifth 词条中的示例.

twenty /ˈtwentɪ; ˈtwɛntɪ/ *pron*, *det* 20; one more than nineteen 20, 二十(个). ⇨App 4 见附录 4.
▷ **twen·ti·eth** /ˈtwentɪəθ; ˈtwɛntɪɪθ/ *pron*, *det* 20th; next after nineteen 第 20, 第二十(个). — *n* one of twenty equal parts of sth 二十分之一.

twenty *n* **1** the number 20 ☆ 20; 二十. **2 the twenties** [pl] numbers, years or degrees of temperature from 20 to 29 从 20 到 29 的数目、年数或温度.

twenty- (forming compound *adjs* 用以构成复合形容词) having twenty of the thing specified 有二十个...的: *a twenty-volume dictionary* 一部有二十卷的词典.
For the use of *twenty* and *twentieth*, see the examples at *five* and *fifth*. 关于 twenty 和 twentieth 的用法见 five 和 fifth 词条中的示例.
□ ˌ**twenty-ˈone** *n* [U] = PONTOON[2].
ˌ**twenty ˈpence** (also ˌ**twenty ˈp, 20p**) (*Brit*) (coin worth) twenty new pence (新币)二十便士(的硬币).

twerp /twɜ:p; twɝp/ *n* (*infml* 口) stupid, irritating or contemptible person 笨蛋; 讨厌家伙; 卑鄙的人: *You twerp!* 你这个笨蛋! ○ *What a twerp he is!* 他这个人真讨厌!

twice /twaɪs; twaɪs/ *adv* **1** two times 两次: *I have seen the film twice.* 这部影片我看过两遍了. ○ *He has twice lied to us.* 他对我们撒过两次谎. **2** double in quantity, rate, etc 两倍: *The car's performance is twice as good since the engine's been tuned.* 这辆汽车调了发动机以后性能好了一倍. ○ *She did twice as much work as her brother.* 她干的工作比她弟弟干的多一倍. **3** (idm 习语) **be ˈtwice the man/woman (that sb is)** be much better, stronger, etc 好、强...得多: *How dare you criticize him? He's twice the man (that) you are!* 你怎么竟敢说他? 他比你强多了! **lightning never strikes in the same place twice** ⇨ LIGHTNING[1]. **once bitten, twice shy** ⇨ ONCE. **once or twice** ⇨ ONCE. **think twice about sth/doing sth** ⇨ THINK[1]. ˌ**twice ˈover** not just once but twice 不只一次，而是两次: *You've bought enough paint to paint the house twice over!* 你买的颜料足够把这所房子粉刷两次用的!

twiddle /ˈtwɪdl; ˈtwɪdḷ/ *v* **1** [Ipr, Tn] **~ with sth** twist or turn (sth), esp idly or aimlessly 旋弄，捻弄(某物)(尤指无聊地或无目的地): *He twiddled with the controls of the radio until he found the station.* 他旋弄了一阵收音机的旋钮才找到了那个电台. ○ *She sat twiddling the ring on her finger.* 她坐在那儿捻弄手指上的戒指. **2** (idm 习语) **twiddle one's thumbs** move one's thumbs round each other with one's fingers or waste one's time doing nothing 旋弄两手的大拇指; 无所事事: *I sat twiddling my thumbs waiting for him to finish using the phone.* 我坐着无聊地旋弄拇指，等候他用完电话. ○ *You're not being paid to twiddle your thumbs all day, you know!* 给你工钱不是让你整天游手好闲，明白吗!
▷ **twiddle** *n* (**a**) slight twist or turn; twirl 轻轻的拧或转; 转动. (**b**) twirled mark or sign 旋转的标志或符号.
twid·dly /ˈtwɪdlɪ; ˈtwɪdḷɪ/ *adj* (*infml* 口) awkward to handle, play, etc 不好处理、演奏等的; 棘手的: *the twiddly bits at the end of the sonata* 奏鸣曲结尾部难奏之处.

twig[1] /twɪg; twɪg/ *n* small thin branch that grows out of a larger branch on a shrub or tree 细枝; 嫩枝: *They used dry twigs to start the fire.* 他们用干燥的细树枝来引火. ⇨ illus at App 1 见附录 1 插图, page i.
▷ **twiggy** *adj* having many twigs 多细枝的; 多嫩枝的: *twiggy sticks* 有很多细枝的枝条.

twig[2] /twɪg; twɪg/ *v* (**-gg-**) [I, Tn, Tw] (*Brit infml* 口) realize or understand (sth) 意识到，明白，理解(某事物): *I gave him another clue, but he still didn't twig (the answer).* 我又提示他一次，他还是不理解(那答案). ○ *I soon twigged who had told them.* 我很快就明白了是谁告诉他们的.

twi·light /ˈtwaɪlaɪt; ˈtwaɪˌlaɪt/ *n* [U] **1** (**a**) faint light after sunset or before sunrise 日落后或日出前的微光; 曙光; 暮色: *I couldn't see their faces clearly in the twilight.* 我在曙色朦胧中看不清他们的脸. (**b**) period of this 黎明或薄暮时分: *farmers walking home at twilight* 黄昏时走回家的农民 ○ *Twilight is a dangerous time for drivers.* 黎明或黄昏是司机容易出事的时间. **2 the ~ (of sth)** (*rhet* 修辞) period of decreasing importance or strength; decline 衰落时期; 没落: *the twilight of his career* 他事业的衰退时期 ○ [attrib 作定语] *his twilight years* 他的暮年.
▷ **twi·lit** /ˈtwaɪlɪt; ˈtwaɪˌlɪt/ *adj* dimly lit (by the twilight) (曙色或暮色)微明的，昏暗的: *in the twilit gloom* 在黎明或黄昏的昏暗中.
□ ˈ**twilight zone** (**a**) inner city area where the buildings are dilapidated (建筑物破旧的)内城区. (**b**) uncertain area or condition between others that are more clearly defined (介于界限分明的两者之间的)过渡区域，模糊状态: *Wrestling is in a twilight zone between sport and entertainment.* 摔跤是介于运动和娱乐两者之间的活动.

twill /twɪl; twɪl/ *n* [U] type of strong woven fabric with diagonal lines across its surface 斜纹织物; 斜纹布; 哔叽: *cotton/wool twill* 斜纹布[毛哔叽] ○ [attrib 作定语] *a twill skirt* 哔叽裙子.

twin /twɪn; twɪn/ *n* **1** [C] either of a pair of children or young animals born of the same mother at the same time 双胞胎之一; 孪生儿之一: *She is expecting twins.* 她怀着双胞胎. ○ *One ewe has produced twins.* 一只母羊一胎生了两只小羊. ○ [attrib 作定语] *my twin brother/sister* 我的孪生兄弟[姐妹] ○ *twin lambs* 一胎生的两只小羊羔. **2** [C] either of a pair of similar, usu matching, things 一对相似的(通常相匹配的)事物之一: *The plate was one of a pair, but I broke its twin.* 这盘子原来有一对，我打坏了一个. ○ [attrib 作定语] *There are twin holes on each side of the instrument.* 这器械的两边有一对眼

T

孔. ○ *a ship with twin* (ie two identical) *propellers* 双推进器的船. **3 the Twins** [pl] = GEMINI.

▷ **twin** *v* (**-nn-**) [esp passive 尤用于被动语态: Tn, Tn·pr] **~ sth (with sth)** (**a**) join (two people or things) closely together; pair 将(两人或两事物)结合在一起; 匹配. (**b**) set up a special relationship between (two towns in different countries), eg by organizing social or sporting visits 在(两国各一城市)之间建立关系(如开展社交或体育互访活动): *Oxford is twinned with Bonn.* 牛津与波恩结成了友好城市.

□ ˌ**twin ˈbed** either of a pair of single beds in a room for two people 成对的单人床之一.

ˌ**twin-ˈengined** *adj* (of an aeroplane) having two engines (指飞机)双发动机的.

ˈ**twin set** (*Brit*) woman's matching jumper and long-sleeved cardigan (女用)套装毛衣(一件套头的和一件长袖开襟的).

ˌ**twin ˈtown** either of a pair of towns, usu in different countries, that have established special links with each other 建立关系的两城市之一(通常为两国间的): *Oxford and Bonn are twin towns.* 牛津和波恩是友好城市. ○ *Oxford's twin town in France is Léon.* 牛津在法国的友好城市是里昂.

twine /twaɪn; twaɪn/ *n* [U] strong thread or string made by twisting two or more strands of hemp, cotton, etc together (麻、棉等制成的)二股或多股的线或细绳: *a ball of twine* 一团合股线. ▷ **twine** *v* [Ipr, Tn·pr] **~ (sth) round sth** (cause sth to) twist, coil or wind round sth (使某物)盘绕、缠绕或卷绕某物: *vines that twine round a tree* 缠绕在树上的藤蔓 ○ *The weed had twined itself round the branches.* 杂草盘绕着树枝. ○ *She twined her arms around my neck.* 她用双臂搂着我的脖子.

twinge /twɪndʒ; twɪndʒ/ *n* **1** short sudden spasm of pain (一阵)剧痛, 刺痛: *an occasional twinge of rheumatism* 一阵突发的风湿痛. **2** short sharp (usu unpleasant) thought or feeling; pang 一阵思绪(通常指不快的); 痛苦: *a twinge of conscience, fear, guilt, regret, remorse, etc* 良心、恐惧、内疚、后悔、悔恨等的一阵难受.

T

twinkle /ˈtwɪŋkl; ˋtwɪŋkl/ *v* **1** (**a**) [I] shine with a light that changes constantly from bright to faint 闪烁; 闪耀: *stars twinkling in the sky* 在天空中闪烁的星星 ○ *the lights of the town twinkling in the distance* 在远处闪耀的万家灯火. (**b**) [I, Ipr] **~ (with sth)** (of a person's eyes) look bright or sparkle, esp because one is amused (指人的眼睛)发亮, 闪光(尤指因愉快): *Her eyes twinkled with mischief.* 她眼睛里闪烁着调皮的光辉. **2** [I] (esp of a person's feet) move rapidly to and fro (尤指人的双脚)迅速地来回移动: *The tune set our toes twinkling.* 这个曲调一响起, 我们的足趾也跟着摆动起来.

▷ **twinkle** *n* [sing] (**a**) twinkling light 闪光: *We could see the distant twinkle of the harbour lights.* 我们可以看见港湾的灯光在远处闪烁. (**b**) sparkle or gleam in the eyes 目光的闪烁或发亮: *She has an amused twinkle in her eye(s).* 她高兴得双目熠熠发亮. (**c**) rapid movement 迅速的移动: *the twinkle of the dancers' feet* 跳舞的人双脚的轻快移动.

twink·ling /ˈtwɪŋklɪŋ; ˋtwɪŋklɪŋ/ *n* (idm 习语) **in the ˌtwinkling of an ˈeye** very quickly; instantaneously 转眼; 瞬间; 一刹那: *The mood of the crowd can change in the twinkling of an eye.* 群众情绪转眼就能发生变化.

twirl /twɜːl; twɝl/ *v* **1** [Tn, Tn·pr] turn (sth) quickly and lightly round and round; spin 使(某物)轻快地转动; 使旋转: *He walked along briskly, twirling his cane in the air.* 他一边轻快地走着, 一边用手杖在空中旋转. ○ *She sat twirling the stem of the glass in her fingers.* 她坐在那里用手指捻着玻璃杯的杯颈. **2** [I, Ipr, Ip] move quickly round and round; spin 快速转动; 旋转: *I watched the dancers twirling (across the floor).* 我注视着跳舞的人(在舞池中)旋转. **3** [I, Tn, Tn·pr] (cause sth to) twist or curl (使某物)盘绕, 缠绕, 卷曲: *She twirled a strand of hair round her finger.* 她把一绺头发卷绕在手指上.

▷ **twirl** *n* **1** rapid circular movement; spin 快速的圆周运动; 转动; 旋转: *She did a twirl in front of the mirror.* 她对着镜子转了一圈. **2** twirled mark or sign; twiddle 旋转的标志或符号.

twist[1] /twɪst; twɪst/ *v* **1** (**a**) [Tn, Tn·pr, Tn·p] **~ sth (round sth/round)** coil or wind sth round sth else 使某物缠绕或盘绕另一物: *I twisted the bandage round her knee.* 我用绷带缠住了她的膝盖. ○ *The telephone wire has got twisted*, ie tangled. 电话线缠绕在一起了. (**b**) [Ipr, Ip] move or grow by winding round sth 以缠绕或盘绕方式运动或生长: *The snake twisted round my arm.* 那条蛇盘绕在我的手臂上. ○ *The sweet peas are twisting up the canes.* 香豌豆沿藤向上蔓生. **2** (**a**) [Tn, Tn·pr] **~ sth (into sth)** turn or wind (threads, etc) to make them into a rope, etc 把(线等)捻或搓成绳等: *We twisted the bed sheets into a rope and escaped by climbing down it.* 我们把床单搓成绳子, 援绳下坠逃跑了. (**b**) [Tn, Tn·pr] **~ sth (from sth)** make (a rope, etc) by doing this 捻成或搓成(绳子等): *twist a cord from/out of silk threads* 把丝线搓成绳子. **3** (**a**) [Tn, Tn·pr] bend or crush (sth) so as to spoil its natural shape 扭曲或挤压(某物)使之变形: *His face was twisted with pain.* 他疼得龇牙咧嘴. ○ *The car was now just a pile of twisted metal.* 那辆汽车已经成了一堆压缩的废铁了. ○ (*fig* 比喻) *Failure left her bitter and twisted.* 她失败后痛苦不堪, 失去常态. (**b**) [I, Ipr] be bent or crushed in this way 扭曲或挤压变形: *The metal frame tends to twist under pressure.* 这种金属框受压后容易变形. **4** (**a**) [Tn, Tn·pr, Tn·p] turn (sth) round; revolve 转动(某物); 旋转: *Twist the knob to the right setting.* 把旋钮拧到适当的定位挡上. ○ *I twisted my head round to reverse the car.* 我扭过头去把汽车向后倒. (**b**) [I, Ipr, Ip] turn round; revolve 转动; 旋转: *I twisted round in my seat to speak to her.* 我坐在位子上转过身来跟她说话. ○ *She was still twisting about in pain.* 她疼得一个劲儿地打滚. **5** [I, Ipr, Ip] (eg of a road) change its direction often; wind (道路等)曲折, 盘旋: *Downstream the river twists and turns a lot.* 这条河的下游弯弯曲曲. ○ *The path twisted down (the hillside).* 那条小路(沿山坡)蜿蜒而下. **6** [Tn] injure (eg one's wrist) by turning it too far; sprain 扭伤(腕部等); 崴: *a twisted ankle* 扭伤的踝关节. **7** [Tn, Tn·pr] deliberately give a false meaning to (words, etc) (故意)歪曲或曲解(词等)的意义: *The papers twisted everything I said.* 报纸把我的话全都歪曲了. ○ *The police tried to twist his statement into an admission of guilt.* 警方企图把他的话歪曲成承认有罪. **8** [I, Tn] (in billiards) (cause a ball to) move in a curved path while spinning (台球)(使球)侧旋前进. **9** (idm 习语) ˌ**twist sb's ˈarm** (*infml* 口) persuade or force sb to do sth 说服或强迫某人做某事: *She'll let you borrow the car if you twist her arm.* 你要是硬要她把汽车借给你, 她就借给你. **twist sb round one's little ˈfinger** (*infml* 口) (know how to) get sb to do anything that one wants (知道怎样)任意摆布某人: *Jane has always been able to twist her parents round her little finger.* 简总是能够让父母顺着她. **10** (phr v) **twist (sth) off (sth)** (cause sth to) come or break off with a twisting movement (将某物)拧开, 扭断: *The cap should twist off easily.* 这个帽儿应该容易拧开. ○ *I can't twist off the lid.* 我拧不开这个盖子.

▷ **twister** *n* (*infml* 口) **1** dishonest person; liar or cheat 不诚实的人; 说谎的人; 骗子: *What a twister!* 真是个骗子! **2** difficult puzzle or problem 棘手的事; 难题: *That's a real twister.* 这事真难办. **3** (*US*) tornado; whirlwind 龙卷; 旋风.

twist[2] /twɪst; twɪst/ *n* **1** [C] act of twisting sth (TWIST[1] 2, 4, 6); twisting movement 搓; 转; 扭; 拧; 旋转; 扭伤: *He gave my arm a twist.* 他扭了一下我的手臂. ○ *With a violent twist, he wrenched off the handle.* 他猛力一拧, 将那把手拧了下来. ○ *Give the rope a few more twists.* 把那绳子再搓几下. **2** [C] (**a**) thing formed by twisting 搓捻而成之物: *a rope full of twists*, ie kinks or coils 有很多扭结的绳子 ○ *a twist of paper*, ie a small paper packet with screwed-up ends 末端拧紧的小纸袋. (**b**) coiled shape 螺旋状: *a twist of smoke* 缭绕的烟 ○ *a shell with a spiral twist* 螺旋状贝壳. (**c**) place where a path, etc turns (道路等的)弯曲处, 曲折处: *a twist in the road* 道路的转弯处 ○ *the twists and turns of the river* 这条河弯弯曲曲的地方. **3** [C] change or development 转折; 转变; 发展: *the twists and turns in the economy, market, policy* 经济、市场、政策的转变 ○ *a strange twist of fate* 命运的奇异改变 ○ *The story had an odd twist at the end.* 那个故事煞尾处奇峰突出. **4** [sing] peculiar tendency in a person's mind and character 怪癖; 偏执: *the criminal twist in his personality* 他个性中的犯罪癖. **5** [U, sing] spinning motion given to a ball to make it move in a curved path (加之于球上的)弧圈运动. **6** (idm 习语) **get one's knickers in a twist** ⇨ KNICKERS. **round the bend/**

twist ⇨ BEND[2].

▷ **twisty** *adj* (**-ier**, **-iest**) full of twists (TWIST[2] 2c) 多曲折的; 弯弯曲曲的: *a twisty path, river, track, etc* 弯弯曲曲的小路、河、车辙等.

twit[1] /twɪt; twɪt/ *n* (*Brit infml often joc* 口, 常作戏谑语) stupid or annoying person 傻瓜; 笨蛋; 讨厌的家伙: *He's an arrogant little twit!* 他是个自高自大的笨蛋! ○ *Stop messing around, you silly twit!* 别胡闹了, 你这个蠢货!

twit[2] /twɪt; twɪt/ *v* (**-tt-**) [Tn, Tn·pr] **~ sb (about/with sth)** (*dated* 旧) make fun of sb, esp in a friendly way 取笑或挖苦某人(尤指善意地): *His unmarried friends twitted him about his wedding plans.* 他那些没结婚的朋友都奚落他的婚礼计划.

twitch /twɪtʃ; twɪtʃ/ *n* **1** sudden rapid (usu involuntary) movement of a muscle, etc 抽搐; 抽动; 痉挛: *I thought the mouse was dead, but then it gave a slight twitch.* 我以为那只老鼠死了, 这时候它却微微地抽动了一下. **2** sudden pull or jerk 突然的拉或晃动: *I felt a twitch at my sleeve.* 我觉得有人扯了一下我的袖子.

▷ **twitch** *v* **1** [I, Tn] (cause sb/sth to) move with a twitch or twitches (使某人[某物])抽动或抽搐: *The dog's nose twitched as it smelt the meat.* 那狗一闻到肉味, 鼻子直抽动. ○ *Her face twitched with pain.* 她的脸疼得抽搐起来. **2** [Ipr, Tn, Tn·pr] **~ at sth** pull sth sharply with a light jerk 猛然轻拉某物: *He twitched nervously at his tie.* 他紧张地拽了拽领带. ○ *She twitched the corner of the rug to straighten it.* 她拉了拉小地毯的一角, 把它弄正. ○ *The wind twitched the paper out of my hand.* 一阵风把我手中的报纸刮跑了.

twitchy *adj* (**-ier**, **-iest**) (*infml* 口) worried or frightened; nervous 忧虑的; 害怕的; 神经紧张的: *People are beginning to get twitchy about all these rumours.* 大家听到这些谣言都惊慌起来. **twitch·ily** *adv.* **twitchi·ness** *n* [U].

twit·ter /ˈtwɪtə(r); ˋtwɪtɚ/ *v* **1** [I, Ip] (of birds) make a series of light short sounds; chirp (指鸟)吱吱叫, 啁啾. **2** (*infml* 口) (**a**) [I, Ipr, Ip] **~ (on) (about sth)** talk rapidly in an excited or a nervous way (激动地或紧张地)唧唧喳喳地说话: *Stop twittering!* 别再唧唧喳喳地说了! ○ *What is he twittering (on) about?* 他唧唧喳喳地说什么呢? (**b**) [Tn] say (sth) in an excited or nervous way 激动地或紧张地说(某事): *'It's so marvellous to see you!' she twittered.* '见到你可太好啦!' 她兴奋地说.

▷ **twit·ter** *n* [sing] **1** sound of chirping 吱吱的叫声; 啁啾声: *the twitter of sparrows* 麻雀的叫声. **2** (*infml* 口) state of nervous excitement 激动; 兴奋; 紧张: *a twitter of suspense and anticipation* 又担心又期望的纷乱心情. **3** (idm 习语) **ˌall of a ˈtwitter** (*infml joc* 口, 谑) nervous and excited 紧张而兴奋的: *We were all of a twitter on the wedding day.* 举行婚礼的那一天, 我们都兴奋极了.

twit·tery /ˈtwɪtərɪ; ˋtwɪtərɪ/ *adj* (*infml* 口) nervous 神经紧张的.

two /tu:; tu/ *pron, det* **1** 2; one more than one 2, 二, 两(个). ⇨App 4 见附录4. Cf 参看 SECOND[1]. **2** (idm 习语) **by/in ˌtwos and ˈthrees** two or three at a time 三三两两地: *Applications for the job are coming in slowly in twos and threes.* 申请这份工作的信件三三两两来得很慢. **a ˈday, ˈmoment, ˈpound, etc or two** one or a few days, moments, pounds, etc 一两天、一会儿、一两镑等: *May I borrow the book for a day or two?* 这本书我可以借一两天吗? **in two** in or into two pieces or halves 成两块; 成两半; 成两部分: *The vase fell and broke into two.* 花瓶掉下来摔成两半了. ○ *She cut the cake in two and gave me half.* 她把蛋糕切成两半, 给了我一块. **it takes two to do sth** (*saying* 谚) one person cannot be entirely responsible for (making a happy or an unhappy marriage, a quarrel, a truce, etc) 双方均有责任(婚姻关系、争吵、休战等). **put ˌtwo and ˌtwo ˈtogether** guess the truth from what one sees, hears, etc 根据所见、所闻等推测出真相: (*joc* 谑) *He is rather inclined to put two and two together and make five,* ie imagine that things are worse, more exciting, etc than they really are 他一推测就出圈儿(把事情想像得比实际糟或有趣等). **that makes ˈtwo of us** (*infml* 口) I am in the same position or hold the same opinion 我也如此; 我也这么看: *'I'm finding this party extremely dull.' 'That makes two of us!'* '我觉得这个聚会沉闷极了.' '我也有同感!'

▷ **two** *n* the number 2 ☆ 2; 二.

two- (in compounds 用以构成复合词) having two of the thing specified 有两个…的: *blue and white two-tone shoes* 蓝白双色的鞋 ○ *a two-room flat* 两间一套的房子.

□ **ˌtwo ˈbits** (*US infml* 口) twenty-five cents 二角五分.

ˈtwo-bit *adj* (*US infml* 口) not very good, important, interesting, etc 不太好的; 不太重要的; 没什么意思的.

ˌtwo-diˈmensional *adj* having or appearing to have length and breadth but no depth 二度空间的; 二维的; 二向的; 平面的: *a ˌtwo-dimensional ˈimage* 平面图像 ○ (*fig* 比喻) *a ˌtwo-dimensional ˈcharacter*, ie sb who is not very interesting 无深度的人(无趣的人).

ˌtwo-ˈedged *adj* (**a**) (of a knife, sword, etc) having two cutting-edges (指刀、剑等)双刃的, 双锋的. (**b**) (*fig* 比喻) having two possible (and contradictory) meanings or effects at the same time 有双重(矛盾的)含义或作用的: *a ˌtwo-edged reˈmark* 一语双关的话 ○ *Publicity is a ˌtwo-edged ˈweapon.* 出了名有利也有弊.

ˌtwo-ˈfaced *adj* deceitful or insincere 两面派的; 虚伪的.

ˈtwofold *adj, adv* **1** twice as much or as many 两倍(的); 双重(的): *a twofold increase* 增加至两倍 ○ *Her original investment had increased twofold.* 她原先的投资额已增至两倍. **2** consisting of two parts 由两部分组成的: *a twofold development plan* 有两部分的发展计划.

ˌtwo-ˈhanded *adj* (**a**) (of a sword, etc) (to be) held with both hands (指剑等)双手握持的. (**b**) (of a saw, etc) (to be) used by two people, one at each end (指锯等)两人各持一端操作的, 双人的.

ˌtwo ˈpence (also **ˌtwo ˈp, 2p**) (*Brit*) (coin worth) two new pence (新币)两便士(的硬币).

twopence /ˈtʌpəns; *US* ˈtu:pens; ˋtʌpəns/ (also **tuppence**) *n* **1** (esp formerly) sum of two pence (尤指旧时)两便士(金额). **2** even the smallest amount 甚至最小的数量: *I don't give twopence for/care twopence what they think.* 我才不管他们怎么想呢. ○ *It's not worth twopence.* 这个分文不值.

twopenny /ˈtʌpənɪ; *US* ˈtu:penɪ; ˋtuˌpɛnɪ/ (also **tuppenny**) *adj* (**a**) costing or worth two pence 值两便士的: *a ˌtwopenny ˈstamp* 一张两便士的邮票. (**b**) of little or no value; cheap or worthless 没什么价值的; 便宜的; 不值钱的. **twopenny-halfpenny** /ˌtʌpnɪ ˈheɪpnɪ; *US* ˌtu:penɪ ˈhæfpenɪ; ˋtuˌpɛnɪˈhepnɪ/ *adj* (*infml* 口) insignificant, contemptible or worthless 无意义的; 可鄙的; 无价值的: *some twopenny-halfpenny little reporter* 某个微不足道的记者.

ˌtwo-a-ˈpenny *adj* [pred 作表语] easily obtained; cheap 易得到; 便宜: *Qualified staff are two-a-penny at the moment.* 合格的工作人员现在大有人在.

ˌtwo-ˈpiece *n* set of two matching garments, eg a skirt and a jacket or trousers and a jacket 两件一套的衣服(如裙子和上衣或裤子和上衣): [attrib 作定语] *a ˌtwo-piece ˈsuit, ˈbathing-costume, etc* 两件式套装、泳装等.

ˈtwo-ply *adj* (of wool, wood etc) having two strands or thicknesses (指毛线、木料等)双股的, 双层的.

ˌtwo-ˈseater *n* car, aircraft, etc with seats for two people 双座的汽车、飞机等.

ˈtwosome /-səm; -səm/ *n* **1** group of two people; pair; couple (两人的)一组, 一对, 一双. **2** game played by two people 两人游戏; 两人比赛.

ˈtwo-time *v* [I, Tn] (*infml* 口) deceive (esp a lover by being unfaithful); double-cross (sb) 欺骗(尤指所爱的人, 对之不忠); 背叛(某人): *a two-timing rogue* 欺骗对方的坏蛋 ○ *He'd been two-timing me for months!* 他另有所爱, 多少月一直瞒着我! **ˈtwo-timer** *n.*

ˈtwo-tone *adj* [attrib 作定语] having two colours or sounds 有两种颜色或声音的.

ˌtwo-ˈway *adj* [usu attrib 通常作定语] (**a**) (of a switch) allowing electric current to be turned on or off from either of two points (指开关)双路的, 双向的. (**b**) (of a road or street) in which traffic travels in both directions (指道路)双行的, 双向的. (**c**) (of traffic) in lanes travelling in both directions (指交通)双向流动的. (**d**) (of radio equipment, etc) for sending and receiving signals (指无线电设备等)收发两用的. (**e**) (of communication between people, etc) operating in both directions (指人等之间的交流)双向进行的, 有来有往的: *a ˌtwo-way ˈprocess* 双向交往.

For the uses of *two* see the examples at *five.* 关于 two 的

用法见 five 词条中的示例.

ty·coon /taɪˈkuːn; taɪˋkun/ *n* (*infml* 口) wealthy and powerful businessman or industrialist; magnate (企业界的)巨头, 大亨: *an ˈoil tycoon* 石油大亨 ○ *a ˈnewspaper tycoon* 报业巨子.

ty·ing ⇨ TIE[2].

tyke (also **tike**) /taɪk; taɪk/ *n* (*infml* 口) **1** (used as a term of abuse 用作辱骂语) worthless person 废物. **2** (*esp US*) small child, esp one who is naughty 小孩子(尤指顽皮的); 小淘气. **3** dog of mixed breed; cur 杂种狗.

tym·panum /ˈtɪmpənəm; ˋtɪmpənəm/ *n* (*pl* **~s** or **-na** /-nə; -nə/) (*anatomy* 解) **1** ear-drum 鼓膜; 耳膜. **2** middle ear 鼓室; 中耳.

type[1] /taɪp; taɪp/ *n* **1 ~ (of sth)** class or group of people or things that have characteristics in common; kind 类型; 种类: *different racial types* 不同人种 ○ *Which type of tea do you prefer?* 你喜欢哪种茶? ○ *all types of jobs/jobs of all types* 各种各样的工作 ○ *A bungalow is/Bungalows are a type of house.* 小平房是房子中的一种类型. ○ *wines of the Burgundy type/Burgundy-type wines* 勃艮第类型的葡萄酒. **2 ~ (of sth)** person, thing, event, etc considered as a representative example of a class or group 有代表性的人、物、事等; 典型: *I don't think she's the artistic type.* 我认为她不属艺术家那类的人. ○ *not the type of party I enjoy* 不是我喜欢的那种聚会 ○ *the old-fashioned type of English gentleman* 旧式的英国绅士 ○ *just the type of situation to avoid* 就是要防止这种情况. *He's true to type*, ie behaves as sb of his class, group, etc may be expected to behave. 他就是他那类人的典型. **3** (*infml* 口) person of a specified character 某种类型的人: *a brainy type* 聪明的人 ○ *He's not my type (of person)*, ie We have little in common. 他跟我不是一个类型的人. **4** (idm 习语) **revert to type** ⇨ REVERT.

▷ **type** *v* [Tn] classify (sth/sb) according to its type 将(某事物[某人])按类型划分: *patients typed by age and blood group* 按年龄和血型分类的病人.

□ **type-cast** /ˈtaɪpkɑːst; *US* -kæst; ˋtaɪp͵kæst/ *v* (*pt, pp* **type-cast**) [esp passive 尤用于被动语态: Tn, Cn·n/a] give (an actor) the kind of role which he has often played successfully before or which seems to fit his personality 让(演员)担任其擅长的或适合其个性的角色: *avoid being type-cast as a gangster* 避免常演歹徒角色.

type[2] /taɪp; taɪp/ *n* (**a**) [C] small block, esp of metal, with a raised letter or figure, etc on it, for use in printing (印刷用的)铅字, 活字. (**b**) [U] set, supply, kind or size of these 活字的宽度、储备、字体或字号等: *set sth in bold, roman, italic, etc type* 将某文稿排成黑体字、正体字、斜体字等.

▷ **type** *v* [I, Ip, Tn, Tn·p] **~ sth (out/up)** write sth using a typewriter or word processor 用打字机或文字处理机打印某文稿: *typing (away) with four fingers* 用四个手指打(着)字 ○ *This will need to be typed (out) again.* 这篇文稿要重新打一遍. **typ·ing** (also ˈ**type·writ·ing**) *n* [U] **1** (skill at) using a typewriter or word processor (使用打字机或文字处理机的)打字(技术): *practise typing* 练习打字 ○ [attrib 作定语] *a typing pool*, ie a group of typists who share a firm's typing work 打字小组(承担一部门打字工作的). **2** writing produced on a typewriter or word processor (用打字机或文字处理机打出的)文稿: *two pages of typing* 打出的两页文稿. **typ·ist** /ˈtaɪpɪst; ˋtaɪpɪst/ *n* person who types, esp one employed to do so 打字者; (尤指)打字员: *fast accurate typists required* 招聘打字快速、准确的打字员 ○ *copy, shorthand, etc typists* 依照原稿、速记等打字的打字员.

□ ˈ**type-face** (also **face**) *n* set of types in a particular design (活字的)字体: *headings printed in a different type-face from the text* 与正文字体不同的标题.

ˈ**typescript** *n* [C, U] typewritten text or document (打印出的)文稿, 文件: *We receive several new typescripts a day.* 我们一天收到几份打出的文稿. ○ *The poems arrived in (fifty pages of) typescript.* 送来的诗歌是(五十页)打字稿.

ˈ**typesetter** *n* person or machine that sets type for printing 排字工人; 排字机.

ˈ**typewriter** *n* machine for producing characters similar to those of print by pressing keys which cause raised metal letters, etc to strike the paper, usu through inked ribbon 打字机: *an electric typewriter* 电动打字机 ○ [attrib 作定语] *a typewriter ribbon, keyboard* 打字机色带、键盘. Cf 参看 WORD PROCESSOR (WORD).

ˈ**typewritten** *adj* written using a typewriter or word processor (使用打字机或文字处理机)打印的: *typewritten pages, letters, manuscripts* 打印的页数、信件、手稿.

typh·oid /ˈtaɪfɔɪd; ˋtaɪfɔɪd/ *n* [U] (also ͵**typhoid** ˈ**fever**) serious infectious feverish disease that attacks the intestines, caused by bacteria taken into the body in food or drink 伤寒: [attrib 作定语] *a typhoid epidemic* 伤寒的流行.

ty·phoon /taɪˈfuːn; taɪˋfun/ *n* violent tropical hurricane that occurs in the western Pacific 台风. Cf 参看 HURRICANE, CYCLONE.

typhus /ˈtaɪfəs; ˋtaɪfəs/ *n* [U] infectious disease with fever, great weakness and purple spots on the body 斑疹伤寒.

typ·ical /ˈtɪpɪkl; ˋtɪpɪkḷ/ *adj* **~ (of sb/sth)** **1** having the distinctive qualities of a particular type of person or thing; representative 典型的; 有代表性的: *a typical Scot, teacher, gentleman* 典型的苏格兰人、教师、绅士 ○ *a typical British pub* 典型的英式小酒店 ○ *a typical cross-section of the population* 有代表性的人口实例调查. **2** characteristic of a particular person or thing (某人或某事物)特有的, 独特的: *It was typical of her to forget.* 她这人就是爱忘事. ○ *He answered with typical curtness.* 他像往常一样, 回答时唐突无礼. ○ *On a typical* (ie normal, average) *day we receive about fifty letters.* 我们通常一天收到约五十封信. ○ *Such decoration was a typical feature of the baroque period.* 这种装饰是巴罗克时期的特征. ○ (*infml* 口) *The train's late again — typical!* 火车又晚点了——一贯如此!

▷ **typ·ic·ally** /-klɪ; -klɪ/ *adv* **1** representing a particular type of person or thing 典型地; 有代表性地: *typically American hospitality* 美国人特有的殷勤好客. **2** characteristic of a particular person or thing (某人或某事物)特有地, 独特地: *Typically, she had forgotten her keys again.* 她就是这样, 又忘了带钥匙.

typ·ify /ˈtɪpɪfaɪ; ˋtɪpə͵faɪ/ *v* (*pt, pp* **-fied**) [Tn] (usu not in the continuous tenses 通常不用于进行时态) be a representative example of (sb/sth) 作为(某人[某事物])的典型: *Now a millionaire, he typifies the self-made man.* 他成了百万富翁, 可以说是白手起家的典型. ○ *The nurses' strike typifies public concern about our hospitals.* 这次护士罢工集中地反映出公众对医疗事业的关心.

typ·ist ⇨ TYPE[2].

ty·po·graphy /taɪˈpɒgrəfɪ; taɪˋpɑgrəfɪ/ *n* [U] **1** art or practice of printing 印刷(术). **2** style or appearance of printed matter 印刷版面式样: *set to a high standard of typography* 排出高质量的版面.

▷ **ty·po·grapher** /taɪˈpɒgrəfə(r); taɪˋpɑgrəfɚ/ *n* person skilled in typography 印刷工人.

ty·po·graph·ical /͵taɪpəˈgræfɪkl; ͵taɪpəˋgræfɪkḷ/ *adj*.

ty·po·graph·ic·ally /-klɪ; -klɪ/ *adv*.

tyr·an·nical /tɪˈrænɪkl; tɪˋrænɪkḷ/ (also *fml* 文作 **tyr·an·nous** /ˈtɪrənəs; ˋtɪrənəs/) *adj* of or like a tyrant; obtaining obedience by force or threats (似)暴君的; 专横的: *a tyrannical regime* 专制政体 ○ *She works for a tyrannical new boss.* 她在一个专横的新上司手下工作.

▷ **tyr·an·nic·ally** /-klɪ; -klɪ/ *adv*.

tyr·an·nize, -ise /ˈtɪrənaɪz; ˋtɪrə͵naɪz/ *v* [Ipr, Tn] **~ (over) sb/sth** rule sb/sth as a tyrant; treat sb cruelly and unjustly 暴虐统治; 横暴对待某人: *tyrannize over the weak* 欺压弱小 ○ *He tyrannizes his family.* 他在家里称王称霸.

tyr·anny /ˈtɪrənɪ; ˋtɪrənɪ/ *n* **1** (**a**) [U] cruel, unjust or oppressive use of power or authority 暴虐; 残暴; 专横; 专制: *a lifelong hatred of tyranny* 终生对暴政疾恶如仇 ○ *the tyranny of military rule* 军事统治的残暴 ○ (*fig* 比喻) *submit to the tyranny of inflexible office hours* 屈从于硬性规定的办公时间. (**b**) [C esp *pl* 尤作复数] instance of this; tyrannical act 暴虐; 专横; 暴行: *the petty tyrannies of domestic routine* 内部惯常的专横做法. **2** [C, U] (country under the) rule of a tyrant 暴君统治(的国家).

tyr·ant /ˈtaɪərənt; ˋtaɪrənt/ *n* cruel, unjust or oppressive ruler, esp one who has obtained complete power by force; despot 暴虐的统治者(尤指凭武力夺取大权者); 专制君主; 暴君.

tyre (*US* **tire**) /ˈtaɪə(r); taɪr/ *n* covering fitted round the rim of a wheel to absorb shocks, usu of reinforced

T

rubber filled with air or covering a pneumatic inner tube 轮胎: *a bicycle tyre* 自行车胎 ○ *a spare tyre* 备用轮胎 ○ *a burst/flat/punctured tyre* 爆了的[瘪了的/穿了孔的]轮胎 ○ *Your tyres are badly worn.* 你的轮胎磨损得很厉害. ○ [attrib 作定语] *tyre pressure* 轮胎气压. ⇨ illus at App 1 见附录1插图, pages xii, xiii.

tyro = TIRO.

tzar, tzar·ina ⇨ TSAR.

T

U u

U, u[1] /juː; ju/ *n* (*pl* **U's, u's** /juːz; juz/) the twenty-first letter of the English alphabet 英语字母表的第二十一个字母: *'Ursula' begins with (a) U/'U'.* Ursula一字以U字母开始.
□ 'U-turn *n* **1** turn of 180° (by a car, etc) so as to face in the opposite direction without reversing (汽车等的) 180°转弯, 向后转, 掉头: *No U-turns,* ie as a sign on motorways, etc. 禁止后转弯(高速公路等的标牌用语). **2** (idm 习语) **do a 'U-turn** (*infml* 口) reverse one's policy 彻底改变政策: *The government has done a U-turn on its economic policy.* 政府的经济政策已经完全改变了.

U[2] /juː; ju/ *adj* (*infml approv or joc* 口, 褒或谑) thought to be characteristic of the upper class 视为上等阶层的; 有上流社会特征的: *very U behaviour* 极具上流社会特征的表现.

U /juː; ju/ *abbr* 缩写 = (*Brit*) (of films) universal, ie suitable for anyone, including children (指电影)适合所有观众观看的(包括儿童): *a U film* 老少皆宜的影片 ○ *a U certificate* 准予向所有观众放映的证明书.

UAE /ˌjuː eɪ ˈiː; ˌju e ˋi/ *abbr* 缩写 = United Arab Emirates 阿拉伯联合酋长国.

UAR /ˌjuː eɪ ˈɑː(r); ˌju e ˋɑr/ *abbr* 缩写 = United Arab Republic 阿拉伯联合共和国.

ubi·quit·ous /juːˈbɪkwɪtəs; juˋbɪkwətəs/ *adj* [esp attrib 尤作定语] (*fml or joc* 文或谑) (seeming to be) present everywhere or in several places at the same time (似乎)普遍存在的, 无处不有的: *Is there no escape from the ubiquitous cigarette smoke in restaurants?* 餐厅里吸烟的烟雾就没有地方躲得过去吗? ○ *ubiquitous traffic wardens* 到处都是管违章停车的交通管理员.
▷ **ubi·quity** /juːˈbɪkwətɪ; juˋbɪkwətɪ/ *n* [U] quality of being ubiquitous 普遍存在; 无处不有.

U-boat /ˈjuːbəʊt; ˋjuˌbot/ *n* (esp in World War II) German submarine (尤指第二次世界大战中的)德国潜艇.

UCCA /ˈʌkə; ˋʌkə/ *abbr* 缩写 = (*Brit*) Universities Central Council on Admissions 大学统一招生委员会: *fill in an UCCA form,* ie with the subjects and universities chosen 填写大学统一招生委员会表格(选择专业及学校).

UDA /ˌjuː diː ˈeɪ; ˌju di ˋe/ *abbr* 缩写 = Ulster Defence Association 北爱尔兰防务协会.

ud·der /ˈʌdə(r); ˋʌdɚ/ *n* bag-like organ of a cow, female goat, etc, with two or more teats, which produces milk (母牛、母羊等的)乳房. ⇨illus at cow 见 cow 插图.

UDI /ˌjuː diː ˈaɪ; ˌju di ˋaɪ/ *abbr* 缩写 = unilateral declaration of independence 单方面宣告独立.

UDR /ˌjuː diː ˈɑː(r); ˌju di ˋɑr/ *abbr* 缩写 = Ulster Defence Regiment 北爱尔兰防卫军.

UEFA /juːˈiːfə; juˋifə/ *abbr* 缩写 = Union of European Football Associations 欧洲足球协会联合会: *the UEFA cup* 欧洲足联杯.

UFO (also **ufo**) /ˌjuː ef ˈəʊ *or, in informal use,* 俗读作 ˈjuːfəʊ; ˌju ɛf ˋo, ˋjuˌfo/ *abbr* 缩写 = (*pl* **~s**) unidentified flying object (esp a flying saucer) 不明飞行物(尤指飞碟).

ugh (usu suggesting a sound like /ɜː; ɜ/ made with the lips either spread or rounded very strongly 通常指类似/ɜː/的声音, 发音时双唇呈扁或圆形) *interj* (used to indicate disgust or horror, and usu accompanied by an appropriate facial expression 用以表示厌恶或恐惧, 通常伴有相应的面部表情): *Ugh! You're eating snails!* 喔唷, 你吃蜗牛啊!

ugli /ˈʌglɪ; ˋʌglɪ/ *n* (*pl* **~s** or **~es**) (also ˈ**ugli fruit**) mottled green and yellow W Indian citrus fruit, a hybrid of a grapefruit and a tangerine 丑橘(产于西印度群岛的黄绿杂色柑橘, 系葡萄柚与橘的杂交品种).

ugly /ˈʌglɪ; ˋʌglɪ/ *adj* (**-ier, -iest**) **1** unpleasant to look at or to hear 难看的; 难听的; 丑陋的: *an ugly face, child, building* 难看的脸、小孩、建筑物 ○ *an ugly wound, gash, scar, etc* 丑陋的伤口、刀伤、伤痕等 ○ *the ugly screeching of parrots* 鹦鹉那难听的尖叫声. **2** hostile or menacing; ominous 有敌意的; 阴险的; 不祥的: *ugly threats, rumours, insinuations, etc* 居心叵测的威胁、谣言、旁敲侧击等 ○ *an ugly laugh, look, wink, etc* 奸险的笑声、表情、眨眼等 ○ *The situation in the streets was turning/growing ugly.* 街上的情形越发不妙了. ○ *The crowd was in an ugly mood.* 群众已人心汹汹. ○ *An ugly storm is brewing.* 一场可怕的风暴即将来临. **3** (idm 习语) **miserable/ugly as sin** ⇨ SIN. **an ˌugly ˈcustomer** (*infml* 口) person who is difficult, dangerous or unpleasant to deal with 难对付的人; 危险的人; 讨厌的人. **an ˌugly ˈduckling** person who at first seems unpromising but who later becomes much admired, very able, etc 丑小鸭(初时似无甚出息而后出人头地的人). ▷ **ug·li·ness** *n* [U].

UHF /ˌjuː eɪtʃ ˈef; ˌju etʃ ˋɛf/ *abbr* 缩写 = (*radio* 无) ultra-high frequency 超高频. Cf 参看 VHF.

UHT /ˌjuː eɪtʃ ˈtiː; ˌju etʃ ˋti/ *abbr* 缩写 = (of dairy products) ultra heat treated (for longer life) (指乳制品)经高温处理的: *UHT milk* 经高温消毒的牛奶.

UK /ˌjuː ˈkeɪ; ˌju ˋke/ *abbr* 缩写 = (esp in addresses) United Kingdom (of Great Britain and Northern Ireland) (尤用于通讯地址)(大不列颠及北爱尔兰)联合王国(即英国): *a UK citizen* 英国公民. ⇨Usage at GREAT 用法见 GREAT.

uku·lele /ˌjuːkəˈleɪlɪ; ˌjukəˋlelɪ/ *n* small four-stringed Hawaiian guitar similar to a banjo 尤克莱利琴(一种小型夏威夷四弦吉他, 形似班卓琴): *strumming tunes on his ukulele* (他)用尤克莱利琴随便弹奏曲调.

ul·cer /ˈʌlsə(r); ˋʌlsɚ/ *n* open sore containing poisonous matter on the outside of the body or on the surface of an internal organ 溃疡: *leg ulcers* 腿部溃疡 ○ *gastric ulcers* 胃溃疡 ○ *My mouth has an ulcer.* 我的口腔出现了溃疡.
▷ **ul·cer·ate** /ˈʌlsəreɪt; ˋʌlsəˌret/ *v* [I, Tn] (cause sth to) become affected with an ulcer or ulcers (使某物)形成溃疡: *Aspirin can ulcerate the stomach lining.* 阿司匹林能造成胃壁溃疡. **ul·cera·tion** /ˌʌlsəˈreɪʃn; ˌʌlsəˋreʃən/ *n*: *severe ulceration of the legs* 腿部的严重溃烂.
ul·cer·ous /ˈʌlsərəs; ˋʌlsərəs/ *adj* affected with or producing ulcers 溃疡的; 形成溃疡的.

ulna /ˈʌlnə; ˋʌlnə/ *n* (*pl* **-nae** /-niː; -ni/) (*anatomy* 解) inner and thinner of the two bones of the forearm in man; corresponding bone in an animal's foreleg or bird's wing 尺骨. ⇨illus at SKELETON 见 SKELETON 插图. Cf 参看 RADIUS.

ul·ter·ior /ʌlˈtɪərɪə(r); ʌlˋtɪrɪɚ/ *adj* [attrib 作定语] (*fml* 文) beyond what is obvious or admitted 隐秘的; 别有用心的: *This lever must serve some ulterior purpose.* 这撬棒准是用于不可告人的目的的. ○ *Jim had ulterior motives in buying me a drink — he wants to borrow my van.* 吉姆请我喝酒是另有所图 —— 他想借用我的客货车.

ul·ti·mate /ˈʌltɪmət; ˋʌltəmɪt/ *adj* [attrib 作定语] **1** beyond which no other exists or is possible; last or final 达到极限的; 最后的; 终极的: *the ultimate outcome, result, conclusion, etc* 最终的结局、结果、结论等 ○ *Management must take ultimate responsibility for the strike.* 资方对此次罢工该负完全的责任. ○ *Nuclear weapons are the ultimate deterrent.* 核武器是终极的威慑力量. **2** from which everything else is derived; basic or fundamental 基本的; 根本的; 首要的: *ultimate principles, questions, causes* 基本原理、问题、原因 ○ *the ultimate truths of philosophy and science* 哲学和科学的基本原则. **3** (*infml* 口) that cannot be surpassed or improved upon; greatest 无法超越的; 极好的; 最大的: *The ultimate luxury of the trip was flying in Concorde.* 这一行程中最大的享受就是乘坐协和式飞机.
▷ **ul·ti·mate** *n* [sing] **the ~ (in sth)** (*infml* 口) the greatest, most advanced, etc of its kind 最大的或最先进的事物: *These ceramic tiles are the ultimate in modern kitchen design.* 这种瓷砖是现代厨房装修中的极品.
ul·ti·mately *adv* **1** in the end; finally 最后; 终于: *Ultimately, all the colonies will become independent.* 所有的殖民地最终均将独立. **2** at the most basic level; fundamentally 根本; 基本上: *All matter ultimately consists of atoms.* 一切物质从根本上说都是由原子组成的.

ul·ti·matum /ˌʌltɪˈmeɪtəm; ˌʌltəˈmetəm/ *n* (*pl* **~s** or **-ta** /-tə; -tə/) final demand or statement of terms to be accepted without discussion, eg one sent to a foreign government and threatening war if the conditions are not accepted 最后通牒; 哀的美敦书: *accept, reject, issue, deliver an ultimatum* 接受、拒绝、发出、送交最后通牒.

ultra- *pref* 前缀 (used fairly freely with *adjs* 可用作较多形容词的前缀) **1** extremely; to excess 极端; 过分: *ultra-conservative* ○ *ultra-fashionable*. **2** beyond a specified limit, extent, etc 超过某一限度、范围等: *ultraviolet* ○ *ultra-high*. Cf 参看 INFRA-.

ul·tra·mar·ine /ˌʌltrəməˈriːn; ˌʌltrəməˈrin/ *adj, n* [U] (of a) brilliant pure blue 佛青色(的).

ul·tra·sonic /ˌʌltrəˈsɒnɪk; ˌʌltrəˈsɑnɪk/ *adj* (of sound waves) pitched above the upper limit of human hearing (指声波)超声(波)的.

ul·tra·sound /ˈʌltrəsaʊnd; ˈʌltrəˌsaʊnd/ *n* [U] sound with an ultrasonic frequency; ultrasonic waves 超声(波): [attrib 作定语] *an ultrasound scan*, eg to detect abnormality in a foetus 超声波扫描检查(如可用以检查胎儿是否畸形).

ul·tra·vi·olet /ˌʌltrəˈvaɪələt; ˌʌltrəˈvaɪəlɪt/ *adj* [usu attrib 通常作定语] **1** (*physics* 物) (of radiation) with a wavelength that is just beyond the violet end of the visible spectrum (指辐射)紫外的: *ultraviolet rays*, ie causing sun-tanning 紫外线. **2** of or using such radiation 紫外线的; 利用紫外线的: *an ultraviolet lamp* 紫外线灯 ○ *ultraviolet treatment*, ie for skin diseases 紫外线疗法(用以治疗皮肤病). Cf 参看 INFRA-RED (INFRA).

ulu·late /ˈjuːljʊleɪt; ˈjuljəˌlet/ *v* [I] (*fml* 文) howl or wail 嚎叫; 哀号. ▷ **ulu·la·tion** /-leɪʃn; -leʃən/ *n* [U, C]: *the ululations of the mourning women* 女子哀悼中的恸哭.

um·ber /ˈʌmbə(r); ˈʌmbɚ/ *n* [U] natural colouring-matter similar to ochre but darker and browner 棕土, 赭土(一种深棕色天然颜料): *burnt umber*, ie reddish-brown pigment 烧棕土(一种红棕色颜料).

▷ **um·ber** *adj* yellowish or reddish-brown 黄棕色的; 红棕色的.

um·bil·icus /ʌmˈbɪlɪkəs; *also, in medical use*, 作医学用语时读作 ˌʌmbɪˈlaɪkəs; ʌmˈbɪlɪkəs, ˌʌmbɪˈlaɪkəs/ *n* (*anatomy* 解) navel 脐.

▷ **um·bil·ical** /ʌmˈbɪlɪkl; *also, in medical use*, 作医学用语时读作 ˌʌmbɪˈlaɪkl; ʌmˈbɪlɪkl/ *adj* of, near or concerning the umbilicus 脐的; 近脐的; 与脐相关的.

□ **umˌbilical ˈcord** flexible tube of tissue connecting the placenta to the navel of the foetus and carrying nourishment to it before birth 脐带: (*fig* 比喻) *By leaving my parents' home, I cut/broke the umbilical cord.* 我离开父母开始自立.

um·bra /ˈʌmbrə; ˈʌmbrə/ *n* (*pl* **-rae** /-riː; -ri/ or **~s**) (*astronomy* 天) dark central part of the shadow cast by the earth or the moon in an eclipse, or of a sunspot 本影. Cf 参看 PENUMBRA.

um·brage /ˈʌmbrɪdʒ; ˈʌmbrɪdʒ/ *n* (idm 习语) **give ˈumbrage; take ˈumbrage (at sth)** (*fml or joc* 文或谑) (make sb) feel offended or slighted (使某人)感到受到了冒犯或怠慢: *I invited her because I was afraid of giving umbrage.* 我邀请了她, 因为我怕得罪她. ○ *He took umbrage at my remarks and left.* 他觉得我的话伤了他的感情, 便离开了.

um·brella /ʌmˈbrelə; ʌmˈbrɛlə/ *n* **1** folding frame of spokes attached to a stick and handle and covered with fabric, used to shelter a person from rain 伞; 雨伞: *put up/take down an umbrella* 把伞张开[合起]. Cf 参看 PARASOL, SUNSHADE (SUN). **2** (*fig* 比喻) any kind of general protecting force or influence 起保护作用的力量或势力: *sheltering under the American nuclear umbrella* 在美国核保护伞的庇护下 ○ *Police operated under the umbrella of the security forces.* 警方在保安部队的掩护下采取了行动. **3** [esp attrib 尤作定语] (*fig* 比喻) central controlling agency for a group of related companies: 企业集团的中央管理机构 ○ *an umbrella organization, group, project* 作为中央管理机构的组织、作为中央管理机构的团体、总项目.

um·laut /ˈʊmlaʊt; ˈʊmlaʊt/ *n* (**a**) [U] (in Germanic languages) vowel change in related forms of a word, shown by two dots over the vowel in one of them, eg *der Mann/die Männer* (= the man/the men) in German (日耳曼语系中的)元音变化(在元音上加两点作为标志, 如德语中的*der Mann/die Männer*). (**b**) [C] sign (consisting of two dots) that shows this 变音符(标示上述元音变化的两点). Cf 参看 DIAERESIS.

um·pire /ˈʌmpaɪə(r); ˈʌmpaɪr/ *n* (**a**) (in tennis, cricket, etc) person appointed to see that the rules are observed and to settle disputes (网球、板球等的)裁判员. ⇨ illus at BASEBALL, CRICKET, TENNIS 见 BASEBALL、CRICKET、TENNIS 插图. (**b**) person chosen to act as a judge between two parties who disagree 仲裁人; 公断人. Cf 参看 REFEREE.

▷ **um·pire** *v* [I, Tn] act as umpire in (a game, etc) 在(比赛等中)当裁判、仲裁人或公断人: *umpire a match, competition, dispute* 在比赛中当裁判、在竞争中当公断人、在争端中当仲裁人.

ump·teen /ˈʌmptiːn; ˈʌmpˈtin/ *pron, det* (*infml* 口) too many to count; numerous 数不清的; 无数的: *Umpteen of them left.* 他们许多人都走了. ○ *have umpteen reasons for being late* 迟到有许多理由. ▷ **ump·teenth** /ˈʌmptiːnθ; ˈʌmpˈtinθ/ *pron, det*: *For the umpteenth time, I tell you I don't know!* 我告诉你多少次了, 我不知道!

'un /ən; ən/ *pron* (*infml* 口) one 人; 事物: *That's a good 'un!* eg a good photograph, joke, excuse. 那个可真好! (如照片、玩笑、借口等) ○ *He went fishing and caught a big 'un.* 他去钓鱼, 钓到一条大的.

un- *pref* 前缀 **1** (with *adjs*, *advs* and *ns* 与形容词、副词和名词结合) not 不; 非: *unable* ○ *unconsciously* ○ *untruth*. **2** (**a**) (with *vs* forming *vs* 与动词结合构成动词) reverse or opposite of 相反; 对立: *unlock* ○ *undo*. (**b**) (with *ns* forming *vs* 与名词结合构成动词) remove from or deprive of 移走; 免去: *unearth* ○ *unmask* ○ *unhorse*.

NOTE ON USAGE 用法: Compare the negative prefixes **non-**, **un-**, **dis-** and **a-**. 试比较含否定意义的前缀**non-**、**un-**、**dis-**、**a-**. **1 Non-** and **un-** are the most freely added prefixes. ☆ **non-**和**un-**在使用上最为自由. **Non-** is used with nouns, adjectives and adverbs and indicates an absence of something ☆ **non-**附加在名词、形容词、副词前, 表示没有或不存在某事物: *a non-drinker* 不喝酒的人 ○ *a non-stick pan* 不粘底的锅 ○ *speaking non-stop* 说个不停. **Un-** is added to adjectives and indicates the opposite quality from the simple word ☆ **un-**附加在形容词前, 表示与原词相反的意义: *unexpected* = 'surprising' (没有料到的) ○ *unwise* = 'foolish' (愚蠢的). Compare *non-British* ('of a nationality which is not British') and *un-British* ('being disloyal to Britain'). 试比较non-British (非英国籍的)和un-British(不忠于英国的). **2 In-** is used with fewer words than **un-**, also to form opposites. ☆ **in-**也用以构成反义词, 但能与之结合的词较**un-**少些. There are variant spellings 这一前缀有几种拼写形式: **il-** before l (*illogical*); **im-** before b, m, p (*imbalance*, *immaterial*, *impossible*) and **ir-** before r (*irresponsible*). ☆ **il-**用于l之前(illogical); **im-**用于b、m、p之前(imbalance、immaterial、impossible); **ir-**用于r之前(irresponsible). **3 Dis-** is also used with verbs, adjectives and nouns to form opposites ☆ **dis-**亦用于动词、形容词、名词之前, 构成反义词: *dislike* 不喜欢 ○ *disobedient* 不服从的 ○ *distrust* 不信任. **4 A-** is mostly used in formal or technical words to indicate 'lacking in' or 'lack of' ☆ **a-**主要用在较文的词或科技词之前, 表示'缺乏'或'无': *amorphous* ('lacking in shape') 无定形的 ○ *anarchy* ('lack of rule') 无政府状态. **5** It is not possible to predict whether **un-**, **in-** or **dis-** is used with a particular word and the correct form must be noted and learned 一个词的前缀究竟是用**un-**、**in-**还是**dis-**是没有固定规律可循的, 只好留心逐一记住.

UN /ˌjuː ˈen; ˌju ˈɛn/ *abbr* 缩写 = United Nations 联合国: *the UN Secretary General* 联合国秘书长.

un·abashed /ˌʌnəˈbæʃt; ˌʌnəˈbæʃt/ *adj* (*fml or joc* 文或谑) not ashamed, embarrassed or awed, esp when there is reason for being so 不害羞的, 不难为情的, 无敬畏之心的(尤指有原因令人害羞、难为情等时): *Tim appeared unabashed by all the media attention.* 蒂姆成了传播媒介的焦点, 却也满不在乎.

un·abated /ˌʌnəˈbeɪtɪd; ˌʌnəˈbetɪd/ *adj* [usu pred 通常作表语] (of a storm, an argument, a crisis, etc) as strong, violent, serious, etc as before (指风暴、论争、危机等)仍然强烈、猛烈、严重等, 并未消减: *The gales continued unabated.* 风势毫未稍减. ○ *Our enthusiasm remained unabated.* 我们的热情一如既往.

un·able /ʌn'eɪbl; ʌn'ebl̩/ *adj* [pred 作表语] **~ to do sth** (*esp fml* 尤作文雅语) not having the ability, opportunity or authority to do sth 没有做某事的能力、机会或权力: *She is unable to walk.* 她不能行走. ○ *I tried to contact him but was unable to.* 我竭力想与他联系, 但是没联系上.

un·abridged /ˌʌnə'brɪdʒd; ˌʌnə'brɪdʒd/ *adj* (of a novel, play, speech, etc) published, performed, etc without being shortened in any way (指小说、戏剧、讲话等)未删节的, 完整的: *unabridged editions/versions of 'War and Peace'*《战争与和平》的全文版本.

un·ac·ceptable /ˌʌnək'septəbl; ˌʌnək'sɛptəbl̩/ *adj* that cannot be accepted, approved or forgiven 不能接受的; 不能赞同的; 不能原谅的: *unacceptable terms, suggestions, arguments, solutions* 不能接受的条件、建议、论点、解决办法 ○ *Imprisonment without trial is totally unacceptable in a democracy.* 在民主政体中, 不经审讯而监禁是不允许的.
▷ **un·ac·ceptably** /-blɪ; -blɪ/ *adv*: *unacceptably low standards* 无法接受的低标准.

un·ac·com·pan·ied /ˌʌnə'kʌmpənɪd; ˌʌnə'kʌmpənɪd/ *adj* **1** (*fml* 文) without a companion; unescorted 无伴的; 无陪伴的: *Children unaccompanied by an adult will not be admitted.* 儿童无成人带领不得入内. ○ *unaccompanied luggage/baggage*, ie travelling separately from its owner 托运的行李. **2** (*music* 音) performed without an accompaniment 无伴奏的: *sing unaccompanied* 无伴奏演唱.

un·ac·count·able /ˌʌnə'kaʊntəbl; ˌʌnə'kaʊntəbl̩/ *adj* **1** that cannot be explained or accounted for 无法解释的; 难以说明的: *an unaccountable increase in cot deaths*, ie of babies 难以解释的婴儿猝死数量上升的现象 ○ *For some unaccountable reason, the letter never arrived.* 不知何故, 那封信始终未收到. **2 ~ (to sb/sth)** (*fml* 文) not answerable for one's actions, etc; not accountable (对自己的行为等)不必负责任的, 无责任的.
▷ **un·ac·count·ably** /-əblɪ; -əblɪ/ *adv* inexplicably 难以说明地; 莫名其妙地: *unaccountably absent from the meeting* 无缘由未到会.

un·ac·coun·ted /ˌʌnə'kaʊntɪd; ˌʌnə'kaʊntɪd/ *adj* [pred 作表语] **~ for** (**a**) not included in an account, a tally, etc 未包括在某数目、帐目等中: *One passenger is still unaccounted for.* 仍有一个旅客未在其中. (**b**) not explained 未予解释的; 未加说明的: *His disappearance is unaccounted for.* 他失踪原因不明.

U

un·ac·cus·tomed /ˌʌnə'kʌstəmd; ˌʌnə'kʌstəmd/ *adj* **1 ~ to sth** not in the habit of doing sth; not used to sth 不习惯的; 不适应的: *Unaccustomed as I am to public speaking...* 本人并不习惯于当众讲话.... **2** uncharacteristic or unusual 不寻常的; 不一般的: *his unaccustomed silence* 他那罕有的沉默 ○ *the unaccustomed luxury of cheap foreign travel* 廉价国外旅游中难得的享受.

un·ac·know·ledged /ˌʌnək'nɒlɪdʒd; ˌʌnək'nɑlədʒd/ *adj* not fully recognized or appreciated 未得到充分认可、赏识或感谢的: *an unacknowledged master of his craft* 在他这行手艺中未受到赏识的大师 ○ *Her contribution to the research went largely unacknowledged.* 她在这项研究中的贡献大都没有获得承认.

un·adop·ted /ˌʌnə'dɒptɪd; ˌʌnə'dɑptɪd/ *adj* (*Brit*) (of a road) not taken over for maintenance by a local authority (指道路)未经地方当局承担保养的.

un·adul·ter·ated /ˌʌnə'dʌltəreɪtɪd; ˌʌnə'dʌltəˌretɪd/ *adj* **1** (esp of food) not mixed with other substances; pure (尤指食物)不掺其他物质的, 纯的. **2** [usu attrib 通常作定语] (*infml* 口) complete or utter 完全的; 十足的: *talking pure unadulterated nonsense* 纯粹胡说八道 ○ *unadulterated bliss* 极幸福.

un·af·fected /ˌʌnə'fektɪd; ˌʌnə'fɛktɪd/ *adj* **1 ~ (by sth)** not changed or affected (by sth) 无变化的; 不受影响的: *rights unaffected by the new laws* 不受新法规影响的权利 ○ *The children seem unaffected emotionally by their parents' divorce.* 孩子在情绪上似乎未受到父母离婚的影响. **2** free from affectation; sincere 不矫揉造作的; 真挚的: *welcome sb with unaffected pleasure* 以发自内心的喜悦欢迎某人.

un·al·loyed /ˌʌnə'lɔɪd; ˌʌnə'lɔɪd/ *adj* (*fml* 文) not mixed, eg with negative feelings; pure 不混杂的(如无不快的感情等); 纯粹的: *ˌunalloyed 'joy, en'thusiasm, ex'citement, etc* 真正的欢乐、热情、兴奋等.

un-American /ˌʌnə'merɪkən; ˌʌnə'mɛrəkən/ *adj* **1** against what are thought to be normal American customs or values 非美国的; 不合美国风俗习惯或价值观念的: *State control is a very un-American notion.* 实行国家控制是根本违背美国观念的. **2** against the political interests of the USA 违反美国政治利益的; 反美的; 非美的: *un-American activities*, eg spying 非美活动(如针对美国的间谍活动).

un·an·im·ous /ju:'nænɪməs; ju'nænəməs/ *adj* (**a**) **~ (in sth)** all agreeing on a decision or an opinion 一致同意的: *The villagers are unanimous in their opposition to the building of a bypass.* 村民一致反对修建旁道. (**b**) (of a decision, an opinion, etc) given or held by everybody (指决定、意见等)一致做出的, 一致通过的: *He was elected by a unanimous vote.* 他以全票当选. ○ *The proposal was accepted with unanimous approval.* 全体一致通过了那项建议.
▷ **un·an·im·ity** /ˌju:nə'nɪmətɪ; ˌjunə'nɪmətɪ/ *n* [U] complete agreement or unity 一致同意; 全体一致.
un·an·im·ously *adv*.

un·an·nounced /ˌʌnə'naʊnst; ˌʌnə'naʊnst/ *adj* without prior warning or notification; unexpected 未事先宣布的; 未通知的; 突如其来的: *make unannounced safety checks on equipment* 对设备进行突然的安全检查 ○ *He arrived unannounced.* 他未事先通知而来到.

un·an·swer·able /ˌʌn'ɑ:nsərəbl; *US* ˌʌn'æn-; ʌn'ænsərəbl̩/ *adj* that cannot be answered or refuted by a good argument to the contrary 无法回答的; 无可辩驳的: *His case/defence is unanswerable.* 他的辩解无懈可击.

un·ap·proach·able /ˌʌnə'prəʊtʃəbl; ˌʌnə'protʃəbl̩/ *adj* (of a person) difficult to talk to (because too stiff, formal, etc) (指人)(因太古板、拘谨等)难以接近的, 不易与之谈话的.

un·armed /ˌʌn'ɑ:md; ʌn'ɑrmd/ *adj* (**a**) without weapons 无武器的; 未武装的: *Britain is proud of its unarmed police force*, ie that does not carry guns. 英国引以自豪的是警察不携带武器. ○ *He walked into the camp unarmed.* 他走进战俘营中, 身上未带任何武器. (**b**) not using weapons 不使用武器的: *soldiers trained in unarmed combat* 受过徒手格斗训练的士兵.

un·ashamed /ˌʌnə'ʃeɪmd; ˌʌnə'ʃemd/ *adj* feeling or showing no guilt or embarrassment 无羞耻心的; 不觉难堪的: *They kissed each other with unashamed delight.* 他们愉快地相吻, 并不觉得难为情. ▷ **un·ashamedly** /ˌʌnə'ʃeɪmɪdlɪ; ˌʌnə'ʃemɪdlɪ/ *adv*: *unashamedly pursuing her own interests* 厚着脸皮追求她自己的利益.

un·asked /ˌʌn'ɑ:skt; *US* ˌʌn'æskt; ʌn'æskt/ *adj* without being asked or invited 未被问及的; 未经邀请的: *The meeting ended and the all-important question remained unasked.* 会议结束了, 重要的问题都未提出来. ○ *She came to the party unasked.* 她未经邀请而来参加聚会.
□ **unasked for** without being asked for or requested 未经要求的; 未经请求的; 主动的: [attrib 作定语] *unasked-for* (ie voluntary) *contributions to the fund* 为筹集基金的主动捐赠.

un·as·sail·able /ˌʌnə'seɪləbl; ˌʌnə'seləbl̩/ *adj* (**a**) that cannot be attacked or conquered 攻不破的; 不可征服的: *an unassailable stronghold, fortress, etc* 攻不破的堡垒、要塞等 ○ *Liverpool have (built up) an unassailable lead at the top of the First Division.* 利物浦队高居甲级队之首, 所向无敌. (**b**) (*fig* 比喻) that cannot be questioned or refuted 不容置疑的; 无可辩驳的: *Her position/argument is unassailable.* 她的立场[论点]是无懈可击的.

un·as·sum·ing /ˌʌnə'sju:mɪŋ; *US* ˌʌnə'su:-; ˌʌnə'sumɪŋ/ *adj* not drawing attention to oneself or to one's merits or rank; modest 不爱表现自己的; 不爱显示或夸耀的; 谦逊的: *a gentle, quiet and unassuming manner* 高雅、文静而谦逊的态度. ▷ **un·as·sum·ingly** *adv*.

un·at·tached /ˌʌnə'tætʃt; ˌʌnə'tætʃt/ *adj* **1** not connected with or belonging to a particular body, group, etc (与某团体、组织等)无关系的, 非附属的: *people unattached to any political organization* 同任何政治组织无联系的人们. **2** not married or engaged; without a regular companion 未结婚的; 未订婚的; 无固定伴侣的.

un·at·ten·ded /ˌʌnə'tendɪd; ˌʌnə'tɛndɪd/ *adj* **1** with its owner not present 物主不在场的: *unattended vehicles, suitcases, etc causing suspicion* 无主车辆、手提箱等令人生疑. **2 ~ (to)** not supervised or given care or attention 无人看管的; 无人照料的: *leave the shop-counter, telephone, etc unattended* 柜台、电话等无人照管 ○ *They left the baby at home unattended all evening.* 他们把那婴儿留在家里, 整晚无人照料. ○ *old correspondence still unattended to* 仍未答复的旧信件.

un·avail·ing /ˌʌnəˈveɪlɪŋ; ˌʌnəˋvelɪŋ/ *adj* without effect or success; futile 徒劳的; 无效的; 白费的: *unavailing efforts/attempts to stop smoking* 戒烟而未戒成 ○ *All our protests were unavailing.* 我们所有的反对意见都毫无作用.

un·avoid·able /ˌʌnəˈvɔɪdəbl; ˌʌnəˋvɔɪdəbl̩/ *adj* that cannot be avoided 不可免除的: *unavoidable duties* 不可推卸的责任. ▷ **un·avoid·ably** /-əblɪ; -əblɪ/ *adv*: *unavoidably absent/delayed* 不得已而缺席[耽搁].

un·aware /ˌʌnəˈweə(r); ˌʌnəˋwɛr/ *adj* [pred 作表语] ~ **(of sth/that...)** ignorant or not conscious of sth 不知道; 未觉察: *be socially, politically, etc unaware* 对社会、政治等问题不了解 ○ *He was unaware of my presence/that I was present.* 他不知道我在场. ○ (*fml* 文) *I am not unaware of the problem.* 我并非不了解这一问题.

▷ **un·awares** /-ˈweəz; -ˋwɛrz/ *adv* **1** by surprise; unexpectedly 吃惊地; 未料到地: *She came upon him unawares as he was searching her room.* 她撞见他正在搜查她的房间. **2** without being aware; unconsciously 不知不觉地; 无意地: *I must have dropped my keys unawares.* 我准是不留神把钥匙丢了. **3** (idm 习语) **catch/take sb unaˈwares** surprise or startle sb 使某人吃惊; 把某人吓一跳: *You caught us unawares by coming so early.* 你来得这么早, 我们都很惊讶.

un·bal·ance /ˌʌnˈbæləns; ʌnˋbæləns/ *v* [I, Tn] upset the balance of (sb/sth) 使(某人[某事物])失去平衡; 使(某人)精神紊乱: *Her death had an unbalancing effect on Joe*, ie on his mind. 她一死, 乔在精神上打击很大. ○ *Over-production is seriously unbalancing the EEC economy.* 因生产过剩, 欧洲共同体经济严重失衡.

▷ **un·bal·anced** *adj* **1** [esp pred 尤作表语] (of a person, his mind, etc) insane, abnormal or eccentric (指人、精神等)发狂、不正常或古怪: *mentally unbalanced* 精神错乱 ○ *He shot her while temporarily unbalanced.* 他一时精神失常向她开了枪. **2** [esp attrib 尤作定语] (of opinions, etc) giving too much or too little emphasis to a particular idea, etc; biased (指见解等)失去分寸的, 片面的, 偏颇的: *the unbalanced reporting of the popular tabloids* 通俗小报上片面的报道.

un·bar /ˌʌnˈbɑ:(r); ʌnˋbɑr/ *v* (**-rr-**) [Tn] remove bars from (a door, gate, etc) to allow entry 拉开(门等)的闩: (*fig* 比喻) *unbar the way to a nuclear-free world* 扫除通向无核世界的障碍.

un·bear·able /ʌnˈbeərəbl; ʌnˋbɛrəbl̩/ *adj* that cannot be tolerated or endured 难以忍受的; 不能容忍的: *I find his rudeness unbearable.* 我觉得他粗暴无礼难以忍受. ▷ **un·bear·ably** /-əblɪ; -əblɪ/ *adv*: *unbearably hot, painful, selfish* 热得、痛得、自私得叫人受不了.

un·beat·able /ˌʌnˈbi:təbl; ˌʌnˋbitəbl̩/ *adj* that cannot be defeated or surpassed 不可战胜的; 难以超越的: *The Brazilian team is regarded as unbeatable.* 巴西队可以说是不可战胜的. ○ *unbeatable prices, discounts, offers, etc* 竞争不过的价格、折扣、出价等 ○ *unbeatable value* 无与伦比的价值.

un·beaten /ˌʌnˈbi:tn; ʌnˋbitn̩/ *adj* not having been beaten, defeated or surpassed 未被打破、击败或超过的: *an unbeaten team* 战无不胜的队 ○ *an unbeaten record for the high jump* 未打破的跳高记录 ○ *His time of 3 min 2 sec remains unbeaten.* 他那3分2秒的记录仍未打破.

un·be·com·ing /ˌʌnbɪˈkʌmɪŋ; ˌʌnbɪˋkʌmɪŋ/ *adj* (*fml* 文) **1** not suited to the wearer 不适合穿用者的; 不合身的: *an unbecoming dress, style, colour* 不合适的连衣裙、样式、颜色. **2** ~ **(to/for sb)** not appropriate or seemly; improper 不适当的; 不得体的: *conduct unbecoming to an officer and a gentleman* 与官员和绅士身分不相称的行为 ○ *It was thought unbecoming for young ladies to smoke.* 年轻女子吸烟被认为有欠斯文.

un·be·lief /ˌʌnbɪˈli:f; ˌʌnbɪˋlif/ *n* [U] (*fml* 文) lack of belief or state of not believing, esp in God, religion, etc 无信仰; 不信; (尤指)不信上帝、宗教等. Cf 参看 DISBELIEF (DISBELIEVE).

▷ **un·be·liev·able** /ˌʌnbɪˈli:vəbl; ˌʌnbɪˋlivəbl̩/ *adj* that cannot be believed; astonishing 不可信的; 难以置信的; 惊人的: *unbelievable expense, skill, luck* 惊人的费用、技艺、幸运. Cf 参看 INCREDIBLE. **un·be·liev·ably** /-əblɪ; -əblɪ/ *adv*: *unbelievably hot, cheap, stupid* 热得、便宜得、愚蠢得难以置信.

un·be·liever *n* person who does not believe, esp in God, religion, etc 无信仰者; 不信者; (尤指)不信上帝、宗教等的人.

un·be·liev·ing *adj* not believing; doubting 不信的; 怀疑的: *She stared at me with unbelieving eyes.* 她以怀疑的眼光注视着我. Cf 参看 INCREDULOUS.

un·bend /ˌʌnˈbend; ʌnˋbɛnd/ *v* (*pt, pp* **unbent** /ˌʌnˈbent; ʌnˋbɛnt/) **1** [I, Tn] (cause sth/sb to) become changed from a bent position; straighten (使某物[某人])由弯变直, 弄直, 挺直. **2** [I] (*fig* 比喻) become relaxed and informal in behaviour 变得轻松和随便: *Most professors unbend outside the lecture theatre.* 教授在课下大都很随便.

▷ **un·bend·ing** *adj* (*esp derog* 尤作贬义) refusing to alter one's demands, decisions, etc; inflexible 不改变初衷、决定等的; 顽固的: *the government's unbending attitude towards the strikers* 政府对待罢工的人的顽固态度.

un·bid·den /ˌʌnˈbɪdn; ʌnˋbɪdn̩/ *adv* (*fml* 文) **1** not requested, invited or ordered 未被要求; 未经邀请; 非受命: *walk in, help unbidden* 擅自进入[主动帮助]. **2** (*fig* 比喻) voluntary or spontaneous 自愿的; 自发的: *memories, images, names, etc coming unbidden to one's mind* 不由自主地呈现于脑际的往事、形象、名字等.

un·blush·ing /ˌʌnˈblʌʃɪŋ; ʌnˋblʌʃɪŋ/ *adj* (*fml* 文) shameless 不知羞耻的; 无耻的: *an unblushing admission of guilt* 厚颜无耻的认罪. ▷ **un·blush·ingly** *adv*.

un·born /ˌʌnˈbɔ:n; ʌnˋbɔrn/ *adj* [esp attrib 尤作定语] not yet born; of the future 未出生的; 未来的: *unborn children, calves* 未出生的孩子、小牛 ○ *generations as yet unborn* 未来的世代.

un·boun·ded /ʌnˈbaʊndɪd; ʌnˋbaʊndɪd/ *adj* without limits; boundless 无限的; 无边际的: *unbounded ambition, curiosity, luxury* 极大的抱负、好奇心、奢侈.

un·bowed /ˌʌnˈbaʊd; ʌnˋbaʊd/ *adj* not conquered or subdued 不屈服的: *He remains bloody but unbowed*, ie He has suffered but not submitted. 他血流不止, 但就是不屈服.

un·break·able /ˌʌnˈbreɪkəbl; ˌʌnˋbrekəbl̩/ *adj* that cannot be broken 打不破的; 不破碎的: *unbreakable plastics, toys* 不碎的塑料制品、玩具 ○ (*fig* 比喻) *the unbreakable spirit of the resistance* 不屈不挠的抵抗精神.

un·bridled /ˌʌnˈbraɪdld; ʌnˋbraɪdl̩d/ *adj* [esp attrib 尤作定语] not controlled or checked 不受控制的; 不加约束的: *unbridled passion, enthusiasm, jealousy, etc* 抑制不住的激情、热情、忌妒心等 ○ (*dated* 旧) *speak with an unbridled tongue*, ie passionately, insolently or indiscreetly 信口开河. Cf 参看 BRIDLE *v* 2.

un·broken /ˌʌnˈbrəʊkən; ʌnˋbrokən/ *adj* **1** not interrupted or disturbed 未间断的; 未受打扰的: *ten hours of unbroken sleep* 连续十小时的睡眠 ○ *the unbroken silence of the woods* 林中无边的静寂. **2** (of records in sport, etc) not beaten or surpassed (指体育运动记录等)未被打破的, 未超过的. **3** (of a horse, etc) not tamed or subdued (指马等)未驯化的, 不驯服的.

un·buckle /ˌʌnˈbʌkl; ʌnˋbʌkl̩/ *v* [Tn] loosen or undo the buckle(s) of (a belt, etc) 松开或解开(带子等)的搭扣.

un·bur·den /ˌʌnˈbɜ:dn; ʌnˋbɝdn̩/ *v* [Tn, Tn·pr] ~ **oneself/sth (of sth) (to sb)** (*fml fig* 文, 比喻) relieve (oneself, one's mind, etc) of worry, etc, eg by talking about one's troubles to a friend 解除(自己、内心等)的烦恼等(如向友人诉说苦衷): *unburden one's heart, conscience, etc* 解除心灵上、良心上...的负担 ○ *unburden oneself of a secret* 说出秘密以放下压在心头的包袱.

un·busi·ness·like /ˌʌnˈbɪznɪslaɪk; ˌʌnˋbɪznɪsˌlaɪk/ *adj* unsystematic or lacking professionalism, esp in business matters 无条理的, 无章法的(尤指业务方面): *unbusinesslike methods, transactions, attitudes* 不守业务规矩的方法、交易、态度 ○ *It is unbusinesslike to arrive late for meetings.* 开会迟到不是办正事的态度.

un·but·ton /ˌʌnˈbʌtn; ʌnˋbʌtn̩/ *v* [Tn] undo the buttons of (a jacket, etc) 解开(上衣等)的钮扣.

▷ **un·but·toned** *adj* (*fig* 比喻) (feeling) free from formality; relaxed 无拘束(感)的; 松弛的: *her unbuttoned style of management* 她放开手的管理方式.

uncalled-for /ʌnˈkɔ:ld fɔ:(r); ʌnˋkɔld,fɔr/ *adj* unjustified; unnecessary 无理由的; 不必要的: *uncalled-for impertinence* 没来由的无礼举动 ○ *Your comments were quite uncalled-for.* 你提的意见很无道理.

un·canny /ʌnˈkænɪ; ʌnˋkænɪ/ *adj* (**-ier**, **-iest**) (**a**) unnatural 异乎寻常的: *The silence was uncanny.* 静得出奇. ○ *I had an uncanny feeling of being watched.* 我有一种奇怪的感觉, 好像有人监视我. (**b**) beyond what is normal or expected; extraordinary 超常的; 出乎意料的; 非凡的: *an uncanny coincidence, resemblance, etc* 意料不到的巧合、相似等. ▷ **un·can·nily** /-ɪlɪ; -ɪlɪ/ *adv*: *an uncannily accurate prediction* 异常准确的预言.

uncared-for /ˌʌnˈkeəd fɔ:(r); ʌnˋkɛrd,fɔr/ *adj* not looked after; neglected 无人照顾的; 被忽视的: *uncared-for children, gardens, pets* 没人照料的孩子、花园、宠物.

un·ceas·ing /ʌnˈsi:sɪŋ; ʌnˋsisɪŋ/ *adj* going on all the time; incessant 不停的; 不断的; 持续的: *unceasing efforts, protests, campaigns* 持续不断的努力、抗议、运动 ○ *nursing him with unceasing devotion* 时时刻刻地精心照料他. ▷ **un·ceas·ingly** *adv*.

un·ce·re·mo·ni·ous /ˌʌnˌserɪˈməʊnɪəs; ˌʌnsɛrəˋmonɪəs/ *adj* **1** (**a**) without proper formality or dignity 无正规形式的; 不很庄重的: *Their divorce was an unceremonious affair.* 他们离婚没有庄重的形式. (**b**) without ceremony; informal 不拘礼节的; 非正式的; 随便的: *The dinner was a relaxed, unceremonious occasion.* 那次宴会很轻松, 随随便便. **2** lacking in courtesy or politeness; rudely abrupt 不客气的; 无礼貌的; 粗鲁的; 唐突的: *his unceremonious departure, dismissal, removal, etc* 他唐突离去、遭解雇、遭免职等. ▷ **un·ce·re·mo·ni·ously** *adv* (*derog* 贬): *I was escorted unceremoniously to the door.* 很无礼地把我逐出门外.

un·cer·tain /ʌnˈsɜ:tn; ʌnˋsɝtn̩/ *adj* **1** (**a**) [usu pred 通常作表语] **~ (about/of sth)** not knowing definitely 知道得不确切; 无把握: *be/feel uncertain (about) what to do* 对要做什么事拿不定主意 ○ *uncertain about/of one's legal rights* 不明确自己的合法权利. (**b**) not known definitely 未被确切了解: *The outcome is still uncertain.* 结果仍不明朗. **2** not to be depended on; unreliable 靠不住; 不可信赖: *His aim is uncertain.* 他的目标不明确. **3** likely to vary; changeable 可能改变; 常变化: *uncertain weather* 变幻莫测的天气 ○ *a man of uncertain temper* 喜怒无常的人. **4** hesitant or tentative 犹豫; 迟疑不决: *an uncertain voice, smile* 吞吞吐吐的说话声、似笑非笑 ○ *the baby's first uncertain steps* 婴儿初学行走时不稳的脚步. **5** (idm 习语) **in ˌno unˌcertain ˈterms** clearly and forcefully 清楚而有力地: *I told him what I thought of him in no uncertain terms!* 我毫不含糊地把我对他的看法告诉了他!

▷ **un·cer·tainly** *adv* hesitantly 犹豫地; 迟疑地: *speak, wait uncertainly* 吞吞吐吐地说、左右为难地等候.

un·cer·tainty /ʌnˈsɜ:tntɪ; ʌnˋsɝtn̩tɪ/ *n* (**a**) [U] state of being uncertain 无把握; 不确定; 变化不定; 犹豫: *The uncertainty is unbearable!* 事情定不下来难以忍受! (**b**) [C esp *pl* 尤作复数] thing which is uncertain 无把握、不确定或变化不定的事物: *the uncertainties of life on the dole*, ie as an unemployed person 依靠救济金生活的不安定.

un·char·it·able /ˌʌnˈtʃærɪtəbl; ʌnˋtʃærətəbl̩/ *adj* severe or harsh, esp in judging (the conduct of) others 无慈悲心的, 严厉的, 苛刻的(尤指评判他人行为时): *uncharitable remarks, thoughts, etc* 不厚道的话、想法等 ○ *I don't want to be uncharitable, but she's not a terribly good cook.* 我并不想苛求别人, 但她烹调的手艺也实在不敢恭维. ▷ **un·char·it·ably** /-əblɪ; -əblɪ/ *adv*.

un·charted /ˌʌnˈtʃɑ:tɪd; ʌnˋtʃartɪd/ *adj* **1** not marked on a map or chart 图上未标明的: *an uncharted island* 地图上没有标明的岛. **2** not explored or mapped 未经勘测的; 未绘制成图的: *an uncharted area, zone, etc* 未经勘探的地区、地带等 ○ (*fig* 比喻) *the uncharted depths of human emotions* 未经探究的人的感情深处 ○ *Our research is sailing into uncharted waters/seas*, ie investigating fields that have not been researched before. 我们的研究工作正深入到从未涉及过的领域.

un·checked /ˌʌnˈtʃekt; ʌnˋtʃɛkt/ *adj* (*derog* 贬) not resisted or restrained 不受抑制的; 未加约束的: *the enemy's unchecked advance* 敌军未受阻遏向前推进 ○ *rumours spreading unchecked* 广为流传而未受制止的谣言 ○ *The use of credit continues/grows unchecked.* 信用贷款不断增加而未受限制.

un·chris·tian /ˌʌnˈkrɪstʃən; ʌnˋkrɪstʃən/ *adj* contrary to Christian teachings or principles; uncharitable 违反基督教教义或信条的; 无慈悲心的: *unchristian behaviour* 有悖基督教教义的行为 ○ *an unchristian attitude* 不仁厚的态度.

un·civil /ˌʌnˈsɪvl; ʌnˋsɪvl̩/ *adj* ill-mannered; rude 不文明的; 失礼的; 粗鲁的: *be uncivil to the neighbours* 对邻居不礼貌 ○ *It was uncivil of you to say that.* 你说那种话很失礼. Cf 参看 INCIVILITY 1.

uncle /ˈʌŋkl; ˋʌŋkl̩/ *n* **1** (**a**) brother of one's father or mother; husband of one's aunt 伯父; 叔父; 舅父; 姑父; 姨父: *my uncle Jim* 我的吉姆叔叔. ⇨App 8 见附录8. (**b**) man whose brother or sister has a child 当叔父、伯父、舅父、姑父或姨父的人: *Now you're an uncle.* 现在你当上叔叔了. **2** (*infml* 口) (used by children, esp in front of a first name 用作儿语, 尤用于名前) unrelated adult male friend, esp of one's parents 无亲戚关系的成年男姓朋友(尤指父母的朋友); 叔叔; 伯伯. **3** (idm 习语) **bob's your uncle** ⇨ BOB[4]. **talk like a Dutch uncle** ⇨ TALK[2].

□ ˌ**Uncle ˈSam** (*infml* 口) (people or Government of) the United States 山姆大叔; 美国; 美国人; 美国政府: *fighting for Uncle Sam* 为美国而战.

ˌ**Uncle ˈTom** (*US infml derog* 口, 贬) black person who associates with and is eager to please white people 汤姆大伯(与白人交往并竭力讨白人欢心的黑人).

un·clean /ˌʌnˈkli:n; ʌnˋklin/ *adj* (**a**) (of food) that cannot be eaten; forbidden as spiritually impure (指食物)不宜食用的, 按教规认为不洁净而禁止食用的. (**b**) lacking spiritual purity; unchaste (精神上)不纯的, 不纯洁的: ˌ*unclean* ˈ*minds*, ˈ*hearts*, ˈ*thoughts* 不纯洁的头脑、心灵、思想.

un·coil /ˌʌnˈkɔɪl; ʌnˋkɔɪl/ *v* [I, Tn] (cause sth/oneself to) become straightened from a coiled position; unwind (使某物[自己])由卷绕状而伸直, 展开: *The snake uncoiled (itself).* 那蛇伸开了盘着的身体. ○ *uncoil electric flex, a hose-pipe* 展开盘着的电线、水龙带.

un·col·oured (*US* **un·col·ored**) /ˌʌnˈkʌləd; ʌnˋkʌlɚd/ *adj* **~ (by sth)** (*fig* 比喻) not affected or influenced by sth 不受影响的: *an uncoloured description of events* 对事件的客观描述 ○ *His judgement was uncoloured by personal prejudice.* 他的判断并不带有个人成见.

un·com·fort·able /ʌnˈkʌmftəbl; *US* -fərt-; ʌnˋkʌmfɚtəbl̩/ *adj* **1** not comfortable 不舒服的; 不舒适的: *uncomfortable chairs, shoes, rooms* 不舒适的椅子、鞋、房间 ○ *lie in an uncomfortable position* 以一种不舒服的姿势躺着. **2** feeling or causing anxiety or unease 感到或引起不安的; 不自在的: *Children make some people feel uncomfortable.* 孩子常使一些人感到不舒服. ○ *The letter was an uncomfortable reminder of my debts.* 那封信是催促还债的通知, 让我很不痛快.

▷ **un·com·fort·ably** /-əblɪ; -əblɪ/ *adv* **1** not comfortably 不舒服地; 难受地: *uncomfortably cramped* 挤得难受. **2** in a way that causes disquiet or unease 使人不安地或不自在地: *The exams are getting uncomfortably close.* 快考试了, 真让人心神不安.

un·com·mit·ted /ˌʌnkəˈmɪtɪd; ˌʌnkəˋmɪtɪd/ *adj* **~ (to sth/sb)** not bound or pledged to (a particular policy, course of action, group, etc) 不受(某政策、做法、团体等)的约束的; 未做承诺的: *Some workers remain uncommitted to the project.* 有些工人仍未对该计划做出承诺. ○ *parties appealing to uncommitted voters* 向无党派人士拉选票的政党. Cf 参看 COMMITTED (COMMIT).

un·com·mon /ʌnˈkɒmən; ʌnˋkɑmən/ *adj* **1** not common; unusual 不普通的; 不寻常的: *an uncommon sight, occurrence, etc* 不平常的景象、事情等 ○ *Hurricanes are uncommon in England.* 飓风在英国非常罕见. **2** (*fml* 文) remarkably close; excessive 非常接近的; 极度的: *There was an uncommon likeness between the two boys.* 这两个男孩儿长得像极了.

▷ **un·com·monly** *adv* (*fml* 文) remarkably 显著地; 极其: *uncommonly intelligent, stupid, difficult* 极其聪明、愚蠢、困难.

un·com·prom·ising /ʌnˈkɒmprəmaɪzɪŋ; ʌnˋkɑmprəˌmaɪzɪŋ/ *adj* not ready to make any compromise; firm or unyielding 不妥协的; 坚定的; 不让步的: *an uncompromising negotiator, attitude, position* 不妥协的谈判者、态度、立场 ○ *attack the government's uncompromising stand on* *education cuts* 抨击政府在削减教育经费问题上的僵硬态度. ▷ **un·com·prom·isingly** *adv*.

un·con·cern /ˌʌnkənˈsɜːn; ˌʌnkənˋsɝn/ *n* [U] lack of care or interest 不关心; 不感兴趣; 冷漠: *She heard the news of his death with apparent unconcern.* 她听到他的死讯无动于衷.

un·con·cerned /ˌʌnkənˈsɜːnd; ˌʌnkənˋsɝnd/ *adj* **1** ~ **(with sth/sb)** not feeling or showing concern; uninterested 不关心的; 不感兴趣的; 冷漠的: *unconcerned with questions of religion or morality* 对宗教问题或道德问题不感兴趣. **2** ~ **(at/by sth)** free from anxiety; untroubled 无忧虑的; 不烦恼的: *Most tourists were unconcerned at the poor weather.* 那些游客大多没把坏天气放在心上. ▷ **un·con·cernedly** /ˌʌnkənˈsɜːnɪdlɪ; ˌʌnkənˋsɝnɪdlɪ/ *adv*.

un·con·di·tional /ˌʌnkənˈdɪʃənl; ˌʌnkənˋdɪʃənḷ/ *adj* not subject to conditions; absolute 无条件的; 绝对的: *an ˌunconditional surˈrender, reˈfusal, ˈoffer* 无条件投降、毫无商量余地的拒绝、无保留的提供. ▷ **un·con·di·tion·ally** /-ʃənəlɪ; -ʃənəlɪ/ *adv*.

un·con·di·tioned /ˌʌnkənˈdɪʃnd; ˌʌnkənˋdɪʃənd/ *adj* (esp of a reflex) not learned; instinctive (尤指反射)无条件的, 先天的. Cf 参看 CONDITIONED REFLEX (CONDITION[2]).

un·con·firmed /ˌʌnkənˈfɜːmd; ˌʌnkənˋfɝmd/ *adj* (of facts, etc) not proved to be true; not confirmed (指事实等)未经证实的, 未予确认的: *ˌunconfirmed reˈports, ˈrumours, etc of a coup* 有关政变的未经证实的报道、谣传等.

un·con·scion·able /ʌnˈkɒnʃənəbl; ʌnˋkɑnʃənəbḷ/ *adj* [attrib 作定语] (*fml or joc* 文或谑) unreasonable or excessive 昧着良心的; 不合理的; 过分的: *You take an unconscionable time getting dressed!* 你穿衣服用的时间未免太长了! ▷ **un·con·scion·ably** /-əblɪ; -əblɪ/ *adv*: *an unconscionably shy young man* 过于腼腆的年轻男子.

un·con·scious /ʌnˈkɒnʃəs; ʌnˋkɑnʃəs/ *adj* **1** (**a**) not conscious; insensible 失去知觉的: *knock sb unconscious* 把某人打得不省人事. (**b**) ~ **of sb/sth** not aware 不知道的; 未察觉的: *be unconscious of any change* 未察觉出任何变化. **2** done or spoken, etc without conscious intention 无意地做出或说出的: *an unconscious slight* 无意的冒犯 ○ *unconscious humour, resentment* 无形中产生的幽默、怨恨.

▷ **the un·con·scious** *n* (*psychology* 心) that part of one's mental activity of which one is unaware, but which can be detected and understood through the skilled analysis of dreams, behaviour, etc 潜意识. Cf 参看 SUBCONSCIOUS.

un·con·sciously *adv*: *He unconsciously imitated his father.* 他在不知不觉中仿效他的父亲.

un·con·scious·ness *n* [U] **1** being unconscious; lack of consciousness; insensibility 无知觉; 无意识: *lapse, fall, etc into unconsciousness* 昏了过去. **2** lack of awareness of what one is doing, saying, etc 神志不清; 不知不觉.

un·con·sidered /ˌʌnkənˈsɪdəd; ˌʌnkənˋsɪdɚd/ *adj* **1** (of words, remarks, etc) spoken or made without proper consideration or thought (指词语、话语等)未经充分思考的, 脱口而出的. **2** disregarded, as if of little value or worth 不值得考虑的; 被忽视的.

un·co·op·er·at·ive /ˌʌnkəʊˈɒpərətɪv; ˌʌnkoˋɑpəˌretɪv/ *adj* not willing to co-operate with others 不愿合作的; 不愿配合的: *uncooperative witnesses, patients, pupils, etc* 不愿配合的证人、病人、学生等.

un·couple /ˌʌnˈkʌpl; ʌnˋkʌpḷ/ *v* [Tn, Tn·pr] ~ **sth (from sth)** disconnect (railway carriages, etc) 使(列车车厢等)脱钩或分离.

un·couth /ʌnˈkuːθ; ʌnˋkuθ/ *adj* (of people, their appearance, behaviour, etc) rough, awkward or ill-mannered; not refined (指人、人的外表、行为等)粗野的, 笨拙的, 无礼貌的, 无教养的. ▷ **un·couth·ness** *n* [U].

un·cover /ʌnˈkʌvə(r); ʌnˋkʌvɚ/ *v* [Tn] **1** remove a cover or covering from (sth) 移去(某物)的覆盖物; 揭开(某物)的盖子. **2** (*fig* 比喻) make known or disclose (sth); discover 揭露或暴露(某事物); 发现: *Agents have uncovered a plot against the President.* 特工人员发现了一个反对总统的阴谋.

un·crit·ical /ˌʌnˈkrɪtɪkl; ʌnˋkrɪtɪkḷ/ *adj* ~ **(of sth/sb)** (*esp derog* 尤作贬义) unwilling or unable to criticize 不愿批评的; 无批评能力的: *an uncritical attitude, view, etc* 不愿批评的态度、观点等 ○ *uncritical supporters of the government* 不加批评而支持政府的人 ○ *The review is uncritical of the violence in the film.* 这篇评论对影片宣扬暴力方面未作批判. ▷ **un·crit·ic·ally** /-ɪklɪ; -ɪklɪ/ *adv*.

un·crossed /ˌʌnˈkrɒst; *US* -ˈkrɔːst; ʌnˋkrɔst/ *adj* (*Brit*) (of a cheque) not crossed (CROSS[2] 4) (指支票)未划线的.

un·crowned /ˌʌnˈkraʊnd; ʌnˋkraʊnd/ *adj* **1** (of a king, etc) not yet crowned (指国王等)尚未加冕的. **2** (idm 习语) **the ˌuncrowned ˈking/ˈqueen (of sth)** person considered to be the most talented or successful in a certain group or field 某类人或某领域中最有才华或成就的人: *the uncrowned king of chess players/chess/the chessboard* 国际象棋棋王.

UNCTAD /ˈʌŋktæd; ˋʌŋˌktæd/ *abbr* 缩写 = United Nations Conference on Trade and Development 联合国贸易和发展会议.

unc·tion /ˈʌŋkʃn; ˋʌŋkʃən/ *n* [U] **1** action of anointing with oil as a religious rite (作为宗教仪式的)涂油, 傅油礼. **2** (*fml derog* 文, 贬) = UNCTUOUSNESS.

unc·tu·ous /ˈʌŋktjʊəs; ˋʌŋktʃʊəs/ *adj* (*derog* 贬) insincerely earnest or flattering, esp in an oily way 虚情假意的, 谄媚的(尤指油腔滑调的): *speak in unctuous tones* 油腔滑调地说 ○ *unctuous assurances* 虚情假意的承诺. ▷ **unc·tu·ously** *adv*. **unc·tu·ous·ness** (also **unction**) *n* [U].

un·curl /ˌʌnˈkɜːl; ʌnˋkɝl/ *v* [I, Tn] ~ **(sth/oneself)** (cause sth/oneself to) become straightened from a curled position (使某物[自己])由弯变直, 伸直: *The cat uncurled (itself) sensuously.* 那猫舒舒服服地伸了个懒腰. ○ *She uncurled her legs from under her.* 她把盘着的腿伸直了.

un·cut /ˌʌnˈkʌt; ʌnˋkʌt/ *adj* **1** (of a book) with the outer folds of the pages not trimmed or cut open (指书)书页未切齐或未切开的, 毛边的. **2** (of a book, film, etc) not abridged or censored (指书、影片等)未删节的, 未删改的: *ˌuncut ˈversions, eˈditions, ˈshowings* 全译本、全版本、全片放映. **3** (of a gem) not shaped by cutting (指宝石)未雕琢的.

un·daun·ted /ˌʌnˈdɔːntɪd; ʌnˋdɔntɪd/ *adj* [usu pred 通常作表语] (*rhet* 修辞) not discouraged or intimidated; fearless 顽强; 不惧怕; 无畏: *He continued the climb, undaunted by his fall.* 他跌下来也并未气馁, 继续攀登.

un·de·ceive /ˌʌndɪˈsiːv; ˌʌndɪˋsiv/ *v* [Tn] (*fml* 文) free (sb) from an illusion or a deception 使(某人)不再抱幻想或不再受骗; 使(某人)醒悟: *His behaviour soon undeceived her as to his true intentions.* 他的行为很快就使她明白了他的真实意图.

un·de·cided /ˌʌndɪˈsaɪdɪd; ˌʌndɪˋsaɪdɪd/ *adj* [pred 作表语] **1** not settled or certain 未解决; 未确定: *The issue/matter remains undecided.* 这个问题仍然悬而未决. ○ *The (outcome of the) match is still undecided.* 比赛(的结果)尚未见分晓. **2** ~ **(about sth/sb)** not having made up one's mind; irresolute 尚未拿定主意; 犹豫不定: *I'm still undecided (about) who to vote for.* 我尚未决定投谁的票.

un·declared /ˌʌndɪˈkleəd; ˌʌndɪˋklɛrd/ *adj* (of goods liable to duty) not declared or shown to the Customs officers (指应纳税的货物)未向海关申报的, 未报关的.

un·demon·strat·ive /ˌʌndɪˈmɒnstrətɪv; ˌʌndɪˋmɑnstrətɪv/ *adj* not in the habit of showing strong feelings; reserved 不习惯表露强烈感情的; 喜怒不形于色的.

un·deni·able /ˌʌndɪˈnaɪəbl; ˌʌndɪˋnaɪəbḷ/ *adj* that cannot be disputed or denied; undoubtedly true 无可争辩的; 不可否认的; 确定无疑的: *undeniable facts* 无可否认的事实 ○ *gems of undeniable worth/value* 确实值钱的宝石 ○ *His charm is undeniable, but I still mistrust him.* 他有魅力无庸置疑, 但我仍对他没有信心. ▷ **un·deni·ably** /-əblɪ; -əblɪ/ *adv*: *undeniably difficult* 确实困难 ○ *Undeniably, the final stage is crucial.* 的确, 最后阶段是关键.

un·der /ˈʌndə(r); ˋʌndɚ/ *prep* **1** in, to or through a position directly below (sth) 在(某物)下面; 到(某物)下面; 通过(某物)下面: *The cat was under the table.* 那猫在桌子下面. ○ *Have you looked under the bed?* 你看过床底下了吗? ○ *Let's shelter under the trees.* 咱们在树下避一避吧. ○ *He threw himself under a bus.* 他扑到一辆公共汽车底下去了. ○ *The water flows under the bridge.* 水在桥下流过. ○ (*fig* 比喻) *What sign of the Zodiac were you born under?* 你是属什么星座的? Cf 参看 OVER[2] 1, 2. **2** below the surface of (sth); covered by 低于(某物)的

表面; 被(某物)遮蔽着: *Most of the iceberg is under the water.* 冰山的大部分在水面以下. ○ *Under the mountain there is a network of caves.* 这座山里有许多相通的洞穴. ○ *She crept in beside him under the bedclothes.* 她钻进被窝, 躺在他身旁. ○ *She pushed all her hair under a headscarf.* 她把头发都让头巾罩住. **3** in or to a position next to and lower than (sth) 在(某物)下方; 到(某物)下方: *under the castle wall* 在城墙下 ○ *a village under the hill* 山脚下的村庄. **4 (a)** younger than (a specified age) 比(某年龄)小; 在(某年龄)以下: *Many children under 5 go to nursery school.* 5岁以下的许多儿童都上幼儿园. ○ *It's forbidden to sell tobacco to children under 16.* 禁止向16岁以下的儿童出售烟草. ○ *If you are under 26 you can buy cheap rail tickets.* 未满26岁者可购买廉价火车票. **(b)** less than (a specified amount, distance or time) 少于(某一数目、距离或时间): *Anyone with an annual income of under £5 000 may be eligible to apply.* 凡年收入在5 000英镑以下者均可申请. ○ *It's under a mile from here to the post office.* 此处距邮局不足一英里. ○ *It took us under an hour.* 我们用了不到一个小时. Cf 参看 OVER[2] 5. **5 (a)** lower in rank than (sb); responsible to the authority of 级别低于(某人); 隶属于...; 听命于...: *No one under the rank of captain may enter the room.* 级别低于上尉者禁止入内. ○ *She has a staff of 19 working under her.* 她手下有19名工作人员. **(b)** governed or led by (sb) 在(某人)统治或领导下: *Britain under Cromwell, Thatcher, the monarchy* 在克伦威尔、撒切尔、君主制治下的英国 ○ *Under its new conductor, the orchestra has established an international reputation.* 这个管弦乐队在新指挥的领导下蜚声国际. **(c)** according to the terms of (an agreement, a law or a system) 根据(协议、法律或制度)的规定: *Six suspects are being held under the Prevention of Terrorism Act.* 根据防止恐怖活动法案, 拘留了六名疑犯. ○ *Under the terms of the lease you had no right to sublet the property.* 根据租约规定, 你无权转租物业. **6** carrying (a specified burden) 承受(某种负荷): *She was struggling under the weight of three suitcases.* 她提着三个箱子, 步履维艰. ○ (*fml* 文) *It was difficult to behave naturally under the burden of knowing the truth.* 了解了真相, 在此压力下自难行之若素. **7 (a)** being in a state of (sth) 在(某事物)的状况中: *buildings under repair/construction*, ie being repaired/built 在修缮[建造]中的建筑物 ○ *matters under consideration, discussion, etc* 正在考虑、讨论等中的问题. **(b)** being affected by (sb/sth) 在(某人[某事物])影响下: *He's very much under the influence of the older boys.* 那些比他大的男孩对他影响很大. ○ *You'll be under (an) anaesthetic, so you won't feel a thing.* 给你施麻醉后, 你就什么也感觉不到了. **8 (a)** using (a particular name) 使用(某名称): *open a bank account under a false name* 用假名字在银行开户 ○ *write a novel under the pseudonym of Colin Kettle* 用笔名科林·凯特尔写小说. **(b)** classified as (sth) 被分类为(某事物): *If it's not under sport, try looking under biography.* 要是在运动类中查不到, 可以查查传记类. **9** being planted with (sth) 种植着(某物): *fields under wheat* 种着小麦的田地.

▷ **under** *adv* **1** under water 在水下: *If you take a deep breath you can stay under for more than a minute.* 只要深吸一口气就能在水里待上一分多钟. ○ *The ship went under* (ie sank) *on its first voyage.* 那条船在首次航行时就沉没了. **2** without consciousness 无知觉; 失去知觉: *She felt herself going under.* 她感到渐渐失去了知觉.

under *adj* [attrib 作定语] lower; situated underneath 较低的; 在下面的: *the under layers* 下层 ○ *under surface* 底面.

under- *pref* 前缀 **1** (with *ns* 与名词结合) **(a)** below 在...下面; 在...之下: *undergrowth* ○ *undercurrent*. **(b)** lower in rank; subordinate 级别低于; 隶属于: *under-secretary* ○ *undergraduate*. **2** (with *adjs, vs* and their related forms 与形容词、动词及其相关形式结合) not enough 不足: *underripe* ○ *underestimate* ○ *underdeveloped*. Cf 参看 SUB-.

un·der·achieve /ˌʌndərəˈtʃiːv; ˌʌndərəˈtʃiv/ *v* [I] (*euph* 婉) do less well than was expected, esp in school work 成绩未如理想(尤指功课). ▷ **un·der·achiever** *n.*

un·der·act /ˌʌndərˈækt; ˈʌndɚˈækt/ *v* [I, Tn] act (a part) with less spirit, force, etc than expected 表演(角色)不够尽心、尽力等: *He underacted the title-role to considerable effect.* 他演剧名角色演得很不带劲. Cf 参看 OVERACT.

un·der·arm /ˈʌndərɑːm; ˈʌndɚˌɑrm/ **1** *adj* [attrib 作定语] in, of or for the armpit 腋下的; 为腋下的: *underarm hair, perspiration, deodorant* 腋毛、腋下出的汗、腋下除臭剂. **2** *adj, adv* (also **underhand**) (in cricket, etc) with the hand kept below the level of the shoulder (板球等)低手式地(投球时手低于肩): *underarm bowling* 低手投球 ○ *bowl, serve, throw, etc underarm* 低手投. Cf 参看 OVERARM.

un·der·belly /ˈʌndəbelɪ; ˈʌndɚˌbɛlɪ/ *n* [sing] **1** under surface of an animal's body, eg as a cut of meat, esp pork (动物的)下腹部(如切下的一块, 尤指猪肉). **2** (*fig* 比喻) area, region, etc that is vulnerable to attack 易受攻击的部位、区域等: *The stock-market crisis struck at the soft underbelly of the US economy*, eg its trade deficit. 股市危机打击了美国经济的薄弱环节(如贸易逆差).

un·der·bid /ˌʌndəˈbɪd; ˌʌndɚˈbɪd/ *v* (**-dd-**; *pt, pp* **underbid**) **1** [Tn] make a lower bid than (sb else), eg at an auction 出价低于(他人)(如拍卖时). **2** [I, Tn] (in bridge, etc) bid less on (a hand of cards) than its strength suggests (桥牌等中)叫牌低于(手中牌)的实力. Cf 参看 OVERBID.

un·der·brush /ˈʌndəbrʌʃ; ˈʌndɚˌbrʌʃ/ *n* [U] (*US*) = UNDERGROWTH.

un·der·car·riage /ˈʌndəkærɪdʒ; ˈʌndɚˌkærɪdʒ/ (also **ˈlanding-gear**) *n* aircraft's landing wheels and their supports (飞行器的)起落架: *raise/lower the undercarriage* 收起[放下]起落架. ⇨illus at AIRCRAFT 见 AIRCRAFT 插图.

un·der·charge /ˌʌndəˈtʃɑːdʒ; ˈʌndɚˈtʃɑrdʒ/ *v* [I, Ipr, Tn, Tn·pr, Dn·n] **~ (sb) (for sth)** charge (sb) too low a price (for sth) 向(某人)少收(某物的)价款: *He undercharged me £1 for the book/for the book by £1.* 我买这本书他少收了我一英镑. Cf 参看 OVERCHARGE 1.

un·der·clothes /ˈʌndəkləʊðz; ˈʌndɚˌkloðz/ *n* [pl] (also *fml* 文雅语作 **un·der·cloth·ing** /-kləʊðɪŋ; -kloðɪŋ/ [U]) = UNDERWEAR.

un·der·coat /ˈʌndəkəʊt; ˈʌndɚˌkot/ *n* **1** [U, C] (paint used for making a) layer of paint under a finishing coat 底层(涂料). Cf 参看 TOPCOAT (TOP[1]). **2** [U] (*US*) = UNDERSEAL.

un·der·cover /ˌʌndəˈkʌvə(r); ˌʌndɚˈkʌvɚ/ *adj* [esp attrib 尤作定语] **1** doing things secretly or done secretly; surreptitious 暗中进行的; 秘密做出的; 私下的: *ˌundercover ˈpayments*, eg bribes 暗中付的款(如贿赂). **2** engaged in spying on people while appearing to work normally among them 做密探工作的: *ˌundercover ˈagents, acˈtivities, organiˈzations* 密探、秘密活动、进行秘密活动的组织 ○ *detectives working undercover* 掩人耳目行事的侦探.

un·der·cur·rent /ˈʌndəkʌrənt; ˈʌndɚˌkʌrənt/ *n* **1** current of water flowing below the surface or below another current 潜流; 暗流: *strong, fierce, fast, dangerous, etc undercurrents* 强劲的、激烈的、湍急的、危险的...潜流. **2 ~ (of sth)** (*fig* 比喻) underlying feeling or influence or trend, esp one opposite to the apparent one 潜在的感情、影响或倾向(尤指与其表象相反的): *There was an undercurrent of resentment in their acceptance of the plan.* 他们接受该计划时心怀不满.

un·der·cut[1] /ˈʌndəkʌt; ˈʌndɚˌkʌt/ *n* [U] (*Brit*) (meat cut from the) underside of sirloin (牛的)腰部肉, 里脊. Cf 参看 TENDERLOIN (TENDER[1]).

un·der·cut[2] /ˌʌndəˈkʌt; ˌʌndɚˈkʌt/ *v* (**-tt-**; *pt, pp* **undercut**) [Tn] offer goods or services at a lower price than (one's competitors) 以低于(竞争者)的价码出售货物或提供服务: *They're undercutting us by 20p a packet.* 他们以每小包比我们的便宜20便士的价格跟我们抢生意.

un·der·developed /ˌʌndədɪˈveləpt; ˌʌndɚdɪˈvɛləpt/ *adj* **1** not fully grown or developed 未充分发育或发展的: *underdeveloped muscles* 不发达的肌肉. **2** (of a country, etc) not having achieved its potential in economic development (指国家等)经济不发达的.

un·der·dog /ˈʌndədɒg; *US* -dɔːg; ˈʌndɚˌdɔg/ *n* (esp 尤作 **the underdog**) person or country, thought to be in a weaker position, and therefore unlikely to win a contest, struggle, etc 处于劣势的人或国家(不易在竞争、斗争等中获胜的): *crowds supporting the underdog* 为处于劣势的一方鼓劲的人群.

un·der·done /ˌʌndəˈdʌn; ˈʌndɚˈdʌn/ *adj* not thoroughly done, esp lightly or insufficiently cooked 未充分做好的;

(尤指烹饪)未熟透的: *nicely underdone vegetables* 半生不熟恰到好处的蔬菜 ○ *The beef was underdone and quite uneatable.* 这牛肉未熟透, 简直不能吃.

un·der·es·tim·ate /ˌʌndərˈestɪmeɪt; ˋʌndɚˋɛstəˌmet/ *v* [Tn] make too low an estimate of (sb/sth) 过分低估(某人[某事物]): *underestimate the cost, danger, difficulty, etc of the expedition* 对此次考察的费用、危险、困难等估计不足 ○ *I underestimated the time we needed by 30%.* 我把我们需要的时间低估了30%. ○ *Never underestimate your opponent*, ie think that you will beat him easily. 千万不要低估对手. Cf 参看 OVERESTIMATE, UNDERRATE.

▷ **un·der·es·tim·ate** /-mət; -mɪt/ *n* estimate that is too low 低估: *a serious underestimate of losses on the Stock Exchange* 对在证券交易所中遭到的损失严重估计不足. Cf 参看 OVERESTIMATE.

un·der·ex·pose /ˌʌndərɪkˈspəʊz; ˋʌndərɪkˋspoz/ *v* [Tn esp passive 尤用于被动语态] expose (a film, etc) for too short a time or in too poor a light 使(底片等)曝光不足. Cf 参看 OVEREXPOSE. ▷ **un·der·ex·pos·ure** /-ɪkˈspəʊʒə(r); -ɪkˋspoʒɚ/ *n* [U].

un·der·fed /ˌʌndəˈfed; ˋʌndɚˋfɛd/ *adj* having had too little food 喂食太少的; 没吃饱的: *underfed cattle, troops, children* 没吃饱的牛、部队、儿童.

un·der·felt /ˈʌndəfelt; ˋʌndɚˌfɛlt/ *n* [U, C] felt for laying under a carpet 地毯垫毡. Cf 参看 UNDERLAY.

un·der·floor /ˌʌndəˈflɔː(r); ˌʌndɚˋflɔr/ *adj* [attrib 作定语] situated beneath the floor 在地板下的: *ˌunderfloor (eˌlectric) ˈwiring* 在地板下的电线线路 ○ *ˌunderfloor ˈheating*, eg using warm air 在地板下的供热系统.

un·der·foot /ˌʌndəˈfʊt; ˌʌndɚˋfʊt/ *adv* under one's feet; on the ground 在脚下; 在地上: *The snow underfoot was soft and deep.* 脚下的雪又软又厚. ○ *It's muddy underfoot.* 地上很泥泞. ○ *Fallen riders were trampled underfoot by the charging horses.* 摔下来的骑手遭飞奔马群践踏.

un·der·gar·ment /ˈʌndəgɑːmənt; ˋʌndɚˌgɑrmənt/ *n* (*dated or fml* 旧或文) article of underclothing 内衣.

un·der·go /ˌʌndəˈgəʊ; ˌʌndɚˋgo/ *v* (*pt* **underwent** /-ˈwent; -ˋwɛnt/, *pp* **undergone** /-ˈgɒn; *US* -ˈgɔːn; -ˋgɔn/) [Tn] **1** experience or endure (sth unpleasant or painful) 经历, 经受(不愉快的或痛苦的某事物): *undergo great hardship, suffering, privation, etc* 遭受极度的艰难、困苦、贫困等. **2** be subjected to (a process, etc) 接受, 承受(某过程等): *undergo major surgery, reform, repair* 接受大手术、经过大改革、接受大检修 ○ *The ship successfully underwent sea trials in coastal waters.* 那条船在近海水域试航成功. ○ *Our agenda underwent a rapid change after the chairman's resignation.* 主席辞职后, 我们的议事项目迅即做出变动.

un·der·gradu·ate /ˌʌndəˈgrædʒʊət; ˌʌndɚˋgrædʒʊɪt/ *n* university or college student who has not yet taken his first or bachelor's degree (尚未获学士学位的)大学生; 大学肄业生: *Cambridge undergraduates* 剑桥大学学生 ○ [attrib 作定语] *undergraduate courses, grants, students* 大学学士学位课程、给予大学生的助学金、大学生. Cf 参看 GRADUATE[1], POSTGRADUATE.

un·der·ground[1] /ˌʌndəˈgraʊnd; ˌʌndɚˋgraʊnd/ *adv* **1** under the surface of the ground 在地面下; 在地下. **2** (*fig* 比喻) in or into secrecy or hiding 秘密地; 暗中地: *He went underground to avoid the police.* 他藏了起来以免被警方发现.

un·der·ground[2] /ˈʌndəgraʊnd; ˋʌndɚˋgraʊnd/ *adj* [attrib 作定语] **1** under the surface of the ground 在地面下的; 地下的: *underground passages, caves, etc* 地下通道、洞穴等 ○ *an underground car-park* 地下停车场. **2** (*fig* 比喻) secret, esp of an illegal political organization 秘密的; (尤指)非法政治组织的: *the underground resistance movement*, ie of the French opposing the German occupation of France during World War II 地下抵抗运动(第二次世界大战期间法国反对德国占领的运动) ○ *the underground press* 地下刊物.

▷ **un·der·ground** *n* **the underground 1** [sing] (also *Brit infml* 英式口语作 **the tube**, *US* **subway**) underground railway 地下铁路; 地铁: *travel by underground* 乘坐地铁 ○ *fares on the London Underground* 伦敦地铁的车费 ○ [attrib 作定语] *underground stations* 地铁车站. **2** [CGp] secret (esp political) organization or activity 秘密的(尤指政治的)组织或活动: *work for, join, contact the underground* 为地下组织工作、参加地下组织、与地下组织取得联系.

un·der·growth /ˈʌndəgrəʊθ; ˋʌndɚˌgroθ/ (*US* **underbrush**) *n* [U] mass of shrubs, bushes, etc growing closely on the ground, esp under trees 灌木丛(尤指大树下的): *clear a path through the undergrowth* 从灌木丛中开辟一条小路.

un·der·hand /ˌʌndəˈhænd; ˋʌndɚˋhænd/ **1** *adj* (also **un·der·hand·ed** /ˌʌndəˈhændɪd; ˌʌndɚˋhændɪd/) done or doing things in a sly or secret way; deceitful 暗中或秘密进行的; 诡诈的: *ˌunderhand ˈtricks, ˈmethods, ˈmeans* 骗人的花招、方法、手段. **2** *adj, adv* = UNDERARM 2.

un·der·lay /ˈʌndəleɪ; ˋʌndɚˌle/ *n* [U, C] layer of felt, foam, rubber, etc laid (esp under a carpet) for support and insulation (毛毡、泡沫塑料、橡胶等做的)衬垫; (尤指)地毯垫. Cf 参看 UNDERFELT.

un·der·lie /ˌʌndəˈlaɪ; ˌʌndɚˋlaɪ/ *v* (*pt* **underlay** /ˌʌndəˈleɪ; ˌʌndɚˋle/, *pp* **underlain** /-ˈleɪn; -ˋlen/) **1** [I, Tn] lie or exist beneath (sth) 位于或存在于(某物)之下: *the underlying clay, rock, etc* 处于下层的黏土、岩石等. **2** [Tn no passive 不用于被动语态] (*fig* 比喻) form the basis of (sb's actions, a theory, etc); account for 构成(某人行动、理论等)的基础; 作(某事物)的说明或解释: *A deep faith underlies her work among refugees.* 她在难民中工作是因为她有很深的信念. ○ *the underlying reason for her refusal* 她拒绝的内在原因.

un·der·line /ˌʌndəˈlaɪn; ˌʌndɚˋlaɪn/ (also **underscore**) *v* [Tn] **1** draw a line under (a word, etc) 在(词等)下面画线. **2** (*fig* 比喻) reinforce (an attitude, a situation, etc); emphasize 强化(态度、形势等); 加强; 强调: *Strikes by prison officers underline the need for reform in our gaols.* 监狱工作人员罢工一事, 突出地表明我们的监狱制度亟须改革.

un·der·ling /ˈʌndəlɪŋ; ˋʌndɚlɪŋ/ *n* (*derog* 贬) person in a subordinate and inferior position 职位低的人; 下属: *hired underlings of a gangster boss* 流氓头子雇用的喽罗.

un·der·manned /ˌʌndəˈmænd; ˋʌndɚˋmænd/ *adj* (of a ship, factory, etc) having too few people to function properly (指轮船、工厂等)人员不足的: *complaints that our hospitals are seriously undermanned* 对我们的一些医院严重缺员的投诉. Cf 参看 UNDERSTAFFED, OVERMANNED.

un·der·men·tioned /ˌʌndəˈmenʃnd; ˋʌndɚˋmɛnʃənd/ *adj* [usu attrib 通常作定语] (*Brit fml* 文) mentioned below or at a later place (in a letter, etc) 下面提到的; 下述的. ▷ **the un·der·men·tioned** *n* (*pl* unchanged 复数不变): *The undermentioned is witness to this contract.* 以下为本合同之见证人. Cf 参看 ABOVE-MENTIONED (ABOVE[1]).

un·der·mine /ˌʌndəˈmaɪn; ˌʌndɚˋmaɪn/ *v* [Tn] **1** make a hollow or tunnel beneath (sth); weaken at the base 在(某物)下挖洞或挖通道; 从根基处损害: *Badgers had undermined the foundations of the church.* 獾在这座教堂的地基处打了洞. ○ *cliffs undermined by the sea* 底部被海水毁坏了的峭壁. **2** (*fig* 比喻) weaken (sth/sb) gradually or insidiously 逐渐削弱或暗中破坏(某事物[某人]): *undermine sb's position, reputation, authority, etc*, eg by spreading scandalous rumours 暗中损害某人的地位、声誉、威信等(如藉散播诽谤性的谣言) ○ *self-confidence undermined by repeated failures* 因屡遭挫折而逐渐削弱的自信心.

un·der·neath /ˌʌndəˈniːθ; ˌʌndɚˋniθ/ *prep* beneath (sth); below 在(某物)的底下或下面: *The coin rolled underneath the piano.* 硬币滚到钢琴下面去了. ○ *She found a lot of dust underneath the carpet.* 她发觉地毯下面有许多尘土. ○ *What does a Scotsman wear underneath his kilt?* 苏格兰男子在短裙下面穿着什么? ○ *Caving means exploring the passages underneath the hills.* 洞穴探险运动是指探察山中的通道而进行的活动.

▷ **un·der·neath** *adv* beneath; below 在底下; 在下面; 向下: *There's a pile of newspapers in the corner — have you looked underneath?* 角落里有一堆报纸——那底下你找过了吗? ○ *When they cleaned up the painting they discovered a Holbein underneath.* 他们擦这幅画时发现下面有一幅霍尔拜因的作品. ○ (*fig* 比喻) *He seems bad-tempered but he's very soft-hearted underneath.* 他似乎脾气很坏, 其实心底里很善良.

un·der·neath *n* [sing] lower surface or part of sth 物体下部的面; 底面; 底部; 下部: *the underneath of a car, shelf, sofa* 汽车、搁架、长沙发的底部.

un·der·nour·ished /ˌʌndəˈnʌrɪʃt; ˋʌndɚˋnɝɪʃt/ *adj* not provided with sufficient food of the right kind for good health and normal growth 营养不良的: *badly,*

U

severely, seriously undernourished 严重缺乏营养. Cf 参看 MALNOURISHED. ▷ **un·der·nour·ish·ment** /-ˈnʌrɪʃmənt; -ˋnɝɪʃmənt/ *n* [U].

un·der·pants /ˈʌndəpænts; ˋʌndɚˌpænts/ (also *infml* 口语作 **pants**) *n* [pl] short undergarment worn by men and boys covering the lower part of the body (男用)内裤, 衬裤: *put on some/a pair of clean underpants* 穿上一条干净的内裤 ○ *He stood there in his underpants*, ie not wearing anything else. 他只穿着内裤站在那儿. Cf 参看 KNICKERS.

un·der·pass /ˈʌndəpɑːs; *US* -pæs; ˋʌndɚˌpæs/ *n* (**a**) (section of a) road that goes under another road or a railway 高架桥下通道或路段(从另一条公路或铁路下方穿过的). Cf 参看 OVERPASS. (**b**) underground passage for pedestrians to cross below a road or railway 地下通道(供行人穿越道路或铁路的). Cf 参看 SUBWAY 1.

un·der·pay /ˌʌndəˈpeɪ; ˋʌndɚˋpe/ *v* (*pt, pp* **underpaid** /-ˈpeɪd; -ˋped/) [Tn, Tn·pr] **~ sb (for sth)** pay (an employee, etc) too little money 付给(雇员等)报酬过低: *Nurses are overworked and underpaid.* 护士的工作过重而报酬过低. ○ *He underpaid me for the work (by £10).* 我做这工作他少给了我(10英镑)工资. Cf 参看 OVERPAY.

un·der·pin /ˌʌndəˈpɪn; ˌʌndɚˋpɪn/ *v* (**-nn-**) [Tn] **1** support (a wall, etc) from below with masonry, etc 用砖石结构等从下面支撑(墙等); 加固(墙等)的基础. **2** (*fig* 比喻) form the basis for (an argument, a claim, etc); strengthen 为(论据、主张等)打下基础; 加强; 巩固: *The evidence underpinning his case was sound.* 有利于他的证据是确凿的. ○ *These developments are underpinned by solid progress in heavy industry.* 重工业的稳固发展为这些进展打下了基础.

un·der·play /ˌʌndəˈpleɪ; ˌʌndɚˋple/ *v* [Tn] give too little importance to (sth) 对(某事物)不够重视: *underplay certain aspects, factors, elements, etc* 对某些方面、因素、成分等不够重视. Cf 参看 OVERPLAY.

un·der·priv·ileged /ˌʌndəˈprɪvəlɪdʒd; ˋʌndɚˋprɪvəlɪdʒd/ *adj* (*euph* 婉) not having the standard of living or rights enjoyed by others in a society; deprived 生活水平或享有的权利比别人低的; 贫困的: *socially underprivileged families, groups, etc* 社会地位低下的家庭、阶层等. ▷ **the un·der·priv·ileged** *n* [pl *v*]: *The underprivileged need special support.* 贫困者需要特殊的帮助.

U

un·der·rate /ˌʌndəˈreɪt; ˋʌndɚˋret/ *v* [Tn] have too low an opinion of (sb/sth) 对(某人[某事物])评价过低: *underrate an opponent, achievement* 对对手、成就评价过低 ○ *an underrated play, actor* 受到贬抑的戏剧、演员 ○ *As an actor, he's seriously underrated.* 他这个演员受到的评价过低. Cf 参看 OVERRATE, UNDERESTIMATE.

un·der·score /ˌʌndəˈskɔː(r); ˌʌndɚˋskɔr/ *v* [Tn] = UNDERLINE.

un·der·sea /ˈʌndəsiː; ˋʌndɚˋsi/ *adj* [attrib 作定语] below the surface of the sea 海面下的: *undersea exploration* 海下探测.

un·der·seal /ˈʌndəsiːl; ˋʌndɚˌsil/ (*Brit*) (*US* **undercoat**) *n* [U] tar-like or rubber-like substance used to protect the under-side of a motor vehicle against rust, etc (机动车底部的)防蚀涂层.

▷ **un·der·seal** *v* [Tn] coat the under-side of (a motor vehicle, etc) with a protective seal 用防蚀涂层涂(机动车等)的底部.

under-secretary /ˌʌndəˈsekrətrɪ; *US* -terɪ; ˌʌndɚˋsɛkrəˌtɛrɪ/ *n* **1** person who is directly subordinate to a government official who has the title of 'secretary' 副大臣; 副部长; 次长; 副国务卿. **2** (*Brit*) senior civil servant in charge of a government department 次官(政府部长的副职): *be Parliamentary under-secretary to the Treasury* 当财政部政务次官.

un·der·sell /ˌʌndəˈsel; ˌʌndɚˋsɛl/ *v* (**-ll-**; *pt, pp* **undersold** /-ˈsəʊld; -ˋsold/) [Tn] sell (goods) at a lower price than (one's competitors) 以低于(竞争者)的价格出售(货物): *Our goods cannot be undersold*, ie Our prices are the lowest. 本公司货物价格别家无法竞争(我们的价格最低). ○ *They're underselling us.* 他们正在压价与我们竞争.

under-sexed /ˌʌndəˈsekst; ˌʌndɚˋsɛkst/ *adj* having less sexual desire or potency than normal 性欲不强的; 性功能低下的. Cf 参看 OVER-SEXED.

un·der·shirt /ˈʌndəʃɜːt; ˋʌndɚˌʃɝt/ *n* (*US*) = VEST[1] 1.

under-side /ˈʌndəsaɪd; ˋʌndɚˌsaɪd/ *n* [sing] side or surface that is underneath; bottom 下侧; 下部表面; 底面; 底部: *His shot hit the under-side of the bar*, ie the one across the goal-posts. 他射门击中了横梁的下侧.

un·der·signed /ˌʌndəˈsaɪnd; ˌʌndɚˋsaɪnd/ *adj* (*fml* 文) who has or have signed at the bottom of a document 在文件下端签字的. ▷ **the un·der·signed** *n* (*pl* unchanged 复数不变): *We, the undersigned* (ie We whose signatures appear below), *declare that*... 我们, 本文件之签署人声名如下....

un·der·sized /ˌʌndəˈsaɪzd; ˋʌndɚˋsaɪzd/ *adj* (*usu derog* 通常作贬义) of less than the usual size 较一般为小的: *ˌundersized ˈportions, ˈhelpings*, ie of food 小份的(食物) ○ *The cubs were sickly and undersized.* 那些幼兽又弱又矮小.

un·der·slung /ˌʌndəˈslʌŋ; ˌʌndɚˋslʌŋ/ *adj* **1** supported from above 下悬式的. **2** (of a vehicle chassis) hanging lower than the axles (指机动车底盘)下置车架的.

un·der·sold *pt, pp* of UNDERSELL.

un·der·staffed /ˌʌndəˈstɑːft; *US* -ˈstæft; ˌʌndɚˋstæft/ *adj* (of a school, a hospital, an office, etc) having too few people to function properly (指学校、医院、办公室等)人员不足的: *The school is badly understaffed.* 这所学校教职员工严重不足. Cf 参看 OVERSTAFFED, UNDERMANNED.

un·der·stand /ˌʌndəˈstænd; ˌʌndɚˋstænd/ *v* (*pt, pp* **understood** /-ˈstʊd; -ˋstʊd/) (not used in the continuous tenses 不用于进行时态) **1** (**a**) [I, Tn, Tw] grasp the meaning of (words, a language, a person, etc) 懂、理解或领会(语词、语言、某人等)的意思: *I'm not sure that I fully understand (you).* 我不敢说我已完全听懂了(你的话). ○ *understand the instructions, rules, conditions, etc* 了解指示、规则、情况等 ○ *I can understand French perfectly.* 法语我完全懂. ○ *I don't understand (a word of) what you're saying*, eg because you're speaking too quickly. 你的话我(一个字也)听不懂(因为你说得太快). (**b**) [Tn, Tw, Tsg] perceive the significance or importance of (sth); perceive the explanation for or cause of 了解(某事物)的意义或重要性; 认识到...的道理或原因: *Do you understand the difficulty of my position?* 你了解我处境的困难吗? ○ *I don't understand why he came/what the problem is.* 我不明白他为什么来[这是什么问题]. ○ *I just can't understand him/his taking the money.* 我真无法理解他[他为什么要偷钱]. **2** [I, Tn, Tf, Tw, Tsg] be sympathetically aware of (sb/sth); know how to deal with (sb/sth) 了解, 理解, 谅解, 同情(某人[某事物]); 善于与(某人[某事物])打交道: *understand children, machinery, modern music* 了解儿童、机器的性能、现代音乐 ○ *We thoroughly understand each other/one another, even if we don't always agree.* 我们彼此非常了解, 虽然有时候也有一些分歧. ○ *I quite understand that you need a change/your needing a change.* 你需要换换环境, 这一点我完全理解. ○ *He understands how hard things have been for you.* 他很同情你的艰难处境. **3** (*usu fml* 通常作文雅语) (**a**) [Tf, Cn·t] be aware from information received (that...); gather 得知; 获悉; 推断: *I understand she is in Paris.* 我听说她现在巴黎. ○ *Am I to understand that you refuse?* 看意思你是拒绝了? ○ *The situation, as I understand it, is very dangerous.* 情况据我看十分危险. ○ *I understood him to say/as saying that he would co-operate.* 我认为他愿意合作. (**b**) [Tf usu passive 通常用于被动语态] take (sth) for granted 认为(某事物)当然如此: *Your expenses will be paid, that's understood.* 你的费用给你付清, 当然了. **4** [Tn esp passive 尤用于被动语态] supply or insert (an omitted word or phrase) mentally 凭意会理解(省略的词语): *In the sentence 'I can't drive', the object 'a car' is understood.* 在'我不会驾驶'这句话中, 宾语'汽车'是不言而喻的. **5** (idm 习语) **give sb to understand (that)...** (*fml* 文) cause sb to believe or have the idea that... 使某人理解、相信或认为...: *We were given to understand that the accommodation was free.* 给我们的感觉是住宿是免费的. **ˌmake oneself underˈstood** make one's meaning clear 将自己的意思表达清楚: *He doesn't speak much English but he can make himself understood.* 他不大会说英语, 但能把自己的意思说清楚.

▷ **un·der·stand·able** /-əbl; -əbl̩/ *adj* that can be understood or sympathized with 能懂的; 可理解的; 可同情的: *The instructions were not readily/easily understandable.*

这份说明书不容易懂. ○ *understandable delays, objections, motives* 可以理解的延误、异议、动机. **un·der·stand·ably** /-əblɪ; -əblɪ/ *adv*: *She was understandably annoyed.* 她很生气, 这是可理解的.

un·der·stand·ing /ˌʌndəˈstændɪŋ; ˌʌndɚˋstændɪŋ/ *n* **1** [U] power of clear thought; intelligence 理解力; 洞察力; 智力; 智慧: *mysteries beyond human understanding* 人类无法理解的奥秘. **2** [U, sing] **~ (of sth)** knowledge of the meaning, importance or cause (of sth) 对(某事物的)意思、重要性或原因的了解: *I have only a limited understanding of French.* 我懂的法语很有限. **3** [U, sing] ability to show insight or tolerance; sympathetic awareness 体谅; 谅解; 通情达理: *no real understanding between husband and wife* 夫妻之间没有真正的相互体谅 ○ *our improved understanding of Soviet life* 我们对过去的苏联人的生活的进一步了解 ○ *work for a better understanding between world religions* 为促进世界上各宗教之间的互相谅解而努力. **4** (**a**) [U] **~ (of sth)** (*usu fml* 通常作文雅语) interpretation of information received 对信息的解释或理解: *My understanding was that we would meet here.* 根据我的理解, 我们将在这儿见面. (**b**) [C usu *sing* 通常作单数] preliminary or informal agreement (初步的或非正式的)协议, 协定, 谅解: *come to/reach an understanding with management about pay* 与资方就工资问题达成协议 ○ *We have an understanding that/There is an understanding between us that we will not sell to each other's customers.* 我们双方有个默契, 就是不把货物卖给对方的顾客. **5** (idm 习语) **on the understanding that...; on this understanding** on condition that...; on this condition 在...条件下; 以此为条件: *I lent him £5 on the understanding that he would repay me today.* 我借给他5英镑, 条件是他今天得还给我.

▷ **un·der·stand·ing** *adj* able to show tolerance of or sympathy towards others' feelings and views 体谅的; 谅解的; 通情达理的: *an understanding approach, smile, parent* 体谅的态度、微笑、父亲(或母亲).

un·der·state /ˌʌndəˈsteɪt; ˋʌndɚˋstet/ *v* [Tn] **1** state or express (sth) in a very controlled way 很有节制地陈述或表达(某事物): *understate one's views, feelings, reactions, etc* 轻描淡写地表达自己的观点、感情、反应等 ○ *She gave a beautifully understated performance as Ophelia.* 她扮演奥菲利亚这一角色用低调处理, 恰如其分. **2** state that (a number, etc) is less than it really is 少说, 少报(某数目等): *understate one's losses*, eg of money, troops 少报损失(如金钱、兵员的损失).

▷ **un·der·state·ment** /ˈʌndəsteɪtmənt; ˋʌndɚˏstetmənt/ *n* (**a**) [U] (action or practice of) understating 有节制的陈述或表达; 少说; 少报: *a clever use of understatement*, eg for effect 巧妙地轻描淡写(如为获得某种效果). (**b**) [C] statement that expresses an idea, etc too weakly 重事轻说; 轻描淡写: *To say that he was displeased is an understatement*, ie He was furious. 说他不高兴是重事轻说(他已怒不可遏).

un·der·study /ˈʌndəstʌdɪ; ˋʌndɚˏstʌdɪ/ *n* **~ (to sb)** person who learns the part of another in a play, etc in order to be able to take his place at short notice if necessary 候补演员; 替手: (*fig* 比喻) *The Vice-President acts as understudy to the President.* 副总统是总统的替手.

▷ **un·der·study** *v* (*pt, pp* **-died**) [Tn] learn (eg a part in a play) as understudy; act as understudy to (sb) 排练(如剧中角色)充当候补演员; 当(某人)的替手: *understudy (the role of) Ophelia* 排练奥菲利亚(一角)当候补演员 ○ *She understudied Judi Dench.* 她充当朱迪·登奇的替手.

un·der·take /ˌʌndəˈteɪk; ˏʌndɚˋtek/ *v* (*pt* **undertook** /-ˈtʊk; -ˋtʊk/, *pp* **undertaken** /-ˈteɪkən; -ˋtekən/) (*fml* 文) **1** [Tn] (start to) make oneself responsible for (sth) 承担(某事物); 负起(某事物)的责任: *undertake a mission, task, project, etc* 承担使命、任务、工程项目等 ○ *She undertook the organization of the whole scheme.* 她负责整个计划的组织工作. **2** [Tf, Tt] agree or promise to do sth 同意或答应做某事: *He undertook to finish the job by Friday.* 他答应在星期五以前完成那工作.

▷ **un·der·tak·ing** /ˌʌndəˈteɪkɪŋ; ˏʌndɚˋtekɪŋ/ *n* **1** [sing] work, etc that one has undertaken; task or enterprise 任务; 事业; 企业: *a commercial, financial, etc undertaking* 商业、金融等企业 ○ *Small businesses are a risky undertaking.* 小型企业要担很大的风险. ○ *Getting married is a serious undertaking.* 结婚是件大事. **2 ~ (that.../to do sth)** (*fml* 文) promise or guarantee 答应; 许诺; 保证; 担保: *an undertaking that the loan would be repaid* 一项偿还贷款的担保 ○ *She gave a solemn undertaking to respect their decision.* 她郑重地保证尊重他们的决定.

un·der·taker /ˈʌndəteɪkə(r); ˏʌndɚˋtekɚ/ (*US* also **mortician**) *n* person whose business is to prepare the dead for burial or cremation and arrange funerals 殡仪业人员.

▷ **un·der·tak·ing** /ˈʌndəteɪkɪŋ; ˏʌndɚˋtekɪŋ/ *n* [U] business of an undertaker 殡仪业.

un·der·tone /ˈʌndətəʊn; ˋʌndɚˏton/ *n* **1** (often *pl* 常作复数) low, quiet or subdued tone 低调; 低声; 低音: *speak, murmur, etc in an undertone* 低声说话、低语 ○ *threatening, sympathetic, sibilant undertones* 威胁的、同情的、咝咝的低声调. **2 ~ (of sth)** underlying feeling, quality, implication, etc; undercurrent 潜在的感情、特质、意义等; 暗流: *There were undertones of relief as the visitors left.* 客人走后大家都暗暗松了口气. Cf 参看 OVERTONE. **3** thin or subdued colour 淡色; 浅色; 柔和的色调: *pink with an undertone of mauve* 略带淡紫色的粉红.

un·der·tow /ˈʌndətəʊ; ˋʌndɚˏto/ *n* [sing] current below the surface of the sea, moving in the opposite direction to the surface current, esp the current caused by the backward flow of a wave breaking on a beach (海面下与海面水流呈反向流动的)回流(尤指浪拍岸退回形成的): *caught in an undertow* 碰上回流 ○ *The pull of the undertow can drag swimmers out to sea.* 近岸回流的冲力能把游泳的人涌到海里.

un·der·value /ˌʌndəˈvæljuː; ˋʌndɚˋvælju/ *v* [Tn, Cn·n/a] **~ sb/sth (as sth)** put too low a value on sb/sth 对某人[某事物]评价过低; 低估某人[某事物]: *We had undervalued the flat by £5 000.* 我们对这套公寓的估价少了5 000英镑. ○ *Don't undervalue Jim's contribution to the research.* 不要低估了吉姆在研究工作中的贡献. ○ *We clearly undervalued him as a member of our team.* 我们显然低估了他这个队员在我们队中的作用.

un·der·wa·ter /ˌʌndəˈwɔːtə(r); ˋʌndɚˏwɔtɚ/ *adj* situated or used or done below the surface of the water 水面下的; 水下使用的; 水下行动的: *ˌunderwater ˈcaves, ˈcameras* 水下洞穴、摄影机 ○ *underwater archaeology*, eg of wrecks 水下考古学(如有关失事船的). ▷ **un·der·wa·ter** *adv*: *The duck disappeared underwater.* 鸭子潜入水中了.

un·der·wear /ˈʌndəweə(r); ˋʌndɚˏwɛr/ *n* [U] (also **underclothes** [pl], *fml* 文雅语作 **underclothing** [U]) clothes worn under a shirt, dress, etc next to the skin 内衣物: *thermal underwear* 保暖内衣 ○ *She packed one change of underwear*, eg a bra, pants, tights. 她打点好一套替换的内衣物(如乳罩、内裤、裤袜).

un·der·weight /ˌʌndəˈweɪt; ˋʌndɚˋwet/ *adj* below the usual, legal or stated weight 低于一般重量的; 未达标准或规定之重量的; 重量不足的: *You are only slightly underweight for* (ie in relation to) *your height.* 按你的身高来说, 你体重仅稍轻一点儿. ○ *The coal is six pounds underweight/underweight by six pounds.* 这些煤的重量少了六磅. ⇨Usage at THIN 用法见THIN. Cf 参看 OVERWEIGHT.

un·der·went /ˌʌndəˈwent; ˏʌndɚˋwɛnt/ *pt* of UNDERGO.

un·der·world /ˈʌndəwɜːld; ˋʌndɚˏwɝld/ *n* **the underworld** [sing] **1** (in mythology) place under the earth inhabited by the departed spirits of the dead (神话中的)阴间, 阴曹. **2** part of society that lives by vice and crime 下流社会; 黑社会: *police contacts in the London underworld* 伦敦黑社会中的警方眼线 ○ [attrib 作定语] *leading underworld figures*, ie notorious criminals 黑社会的头面人物(劣迹昭彰的罪犯).

un·der·write /ˌʌndəˈraɪt; ˏʌndɚˋraɪt/ *v* (*pt* **underwrote** /-ˈrəʊt; -ˋrot/, *pp* **underwritten** /-ˈrɪtn; -ˋrɪtn/) [Tn] **1** sign and accept liability under (an insurance policy, esp for ships), thus guaranteeing payment in the event of loss or damage 在(保险单, 尤指船舶保险单)下方签署并承担责任(承保损失或损坏之责). **2** (*finance* 财) undertake to buy, at an agreed price, all stock in (a company) that is not bought by the public (按商定的价格)认购(某公司)的全部剩余证券; 包销(证券): *The shares were underwritten by the Bank of England.* 这些股票由英格兰银行包销. **3** undertake to finance (an enterprise) 同意资助(某事业): *The government underwrote the initial costs of the operation.* 政府为该项活动提供了开办时所需的费用.

▷ ˈ**un·der·writer** *n* person or organization that underwrites insurance policies, esp for ships 保险业者, 保险公司(尤指船只的): *an underwriter at Lloyd's* 劳埃德保险社承保人.

un·deserved /ˌʌndɪˈzɜːvd; ˌʌndɪˈzɝvd/ *adj* not fair or just 不恰当的; 不应得的: *an undeserved punishment, rebuke, reward* 不该受的惩罚、责备、报偿 ○ *His reputation as a Romeo is quite undeserved.* 他有罗密欧之称是名不副实的. ▷ **un·deservedly** /-dɪˈzɜːvɪdlɪ; -dɪˈzɝvɪdlɪ/ *adv*.

un·desir·able /ˌʌndɪˈzaɪərəbl; ˌʌndɪˈzaɪrəbl/ *adj* **1** likely to cause trouble or inconvenience; unwanted 可能招致麻烦或不便的; 不想要的: *The drug has no undesirable side-effects.* 这种药没有什么不良的副作用. ○ *Military intervention is highly undesirable.* 军事干涉极不相宜. **2** (of a person, his habits, etc) of a kind not to be welcomed in society; objectionable (指人、人的习惯等)不受大家欢迎的, 令人不快的, 讨厌的: *She's a most undesirable influence.* 她是个专门不起好作用的人.

▷ **un·desir·able** *n* undesirable person 不受欢迎的人; 讨厌的人: *drunks, vagrants and other undesirables* 醉鬼、无业游民等讨厌的人 ○ (*joc* 谑) *The club hires a bouncer to keep out undesirables.* 这个俱乐部雇用了一个保镖来驱逐捣乱分子.

un·desir·ably /-əblɪ; -əblɪ/ *adv*.

un·deterred /ˌʌndɪˈtɜːd; ˌʌndɪˈtɝd/ *adj* not deterred or discouraged 未被吓住的; 不气馁的: *undeterred by failure* 不因失败而气馁 ○ *It was raining heavily but he set out undeterred.* 雨下得很大, 他仍不顾一切出发了.

un·developed /ˌʌndɪˈveləpt; ˌʌndɪˈvɛləpt/ *adj* **1** not fully grown or developed 未充分发育的; 未发展的; 不发达的: *undeveloped fruit, muscles, organs* 未成熟的水果、不发达的肌肉、发育不良的器官. **2** not yet used for agriculture, industry, building, etc 尚未用于农业、工业、建筑业等的; 未开发的: *undeveloped land* 未开发的土地 ○ *undeveloped resources, sites* 未开发的资源、地点.

un·did /ʌnˈdɪd; ʌnˈdɪd/ *pt* of UNDO.

und·ies /ˈʌndɪz; ˈʌndɪz/ *n* [pl] (*infml* 口) (esp women's) underclothes (尤指女用的)内衣: *She appeared in her undies.* 她穿着内衣出来了.

un·dig·ni·fied /ʌnˈdɪgnɪfaɪd; ʌnˈdɪgnəˌfaɪd/ *adj* not showing proper dignity; clumsy 不庄重的; 不像样子的: *an undignified retreat, collapse, failure, etc* 不光彩的退却、倒台、失败等 ○ *His skis crossed and he sat down in a most undignified manner.* 他的滑雪板交叉在一起坐下时, 姿势很不雅观.

un·dis·charged /ˌʌndɪsˈtʃɑːdʒd; ˌʌndɪsˈtʃardʒd/ *adj* (*finance* 财) **1** (of a debt) not paid (指债务)未偿清的. **2** (esp of a bankrupt person or firm) still legally obliged to pay money owing to creditors (尤指破产的个人或公司)仍须清偿债务的. Cf 参看 DISCHARGE.

un·dis·puted /ˌʌndɪˈspjuːtɪd; ˌʌndɪˈspjutɪd/ *adj* **1** that cannot be doubted or questioned 无可置疑的; 毫无疑问的: *undisputed facts, talents, rights* 无可怀疑的事实、才干、权利. **2** accepted without dispute; unchallenged 无可争辩的; 无异议的: *the undisputed champion, winner, etc* 无可争辩的冠军、优胜者等 ○ *the undisputed market leader* 在市场上无与匹敌的产品(或公司).

un·dis·tin·guished /ˌʌndɪˈstɪŋgwɪʃt; ˌʌndɪˈstɪŋgwɪʃt/ *adj* lacking any outstanding feature; mediocre or poor 无特征的; 无特色的; 普普通通的; 平庸的: *an undistinguished career, appearance* 平淡无奇的事业、外表 ○ *be undistinguished as a diplomat* 当个平庸的外交官.

un·di·vided /ˌʌndɪˈvaɪdɪd; ˌʌndəˈvaɪdɪd/ *adj* (idm 习语) **give one's undivided attention (to sth/sb); get/have sb's undivided attention** concentrate fully (on sth/sb); be the one thing or person that sb attends to 全神贯注(于某事物[某人]); 为某人关注的对象: *You have my (full and) undivided attention.* 你是我一心(一意)注意的人. ○ *Tom seldom got his mother's undivided attention.* 汤姆很少受到母亲全心的关怀.

undo /ʌnˈduː; ʌnˈdu/ *v* (*pt* **undid** /ʌnˈdɪd; ʌnˈdɪd/, *pp* **undone** /ʌnˈdʌn; ʌnˈdʌn/) [Tn] **1** untie or unfasten (knots, buttons, etc); open (a parcel, an envelope, etc) 解开, 松开(结、钮扣等); 打开, 拆开(包裹、信封等): *My zip has come undone.* 我的拉锁开了. ○ *I can't undo my shoelaces.* 我解不开鞋带. ○ *undo* (ie unravel) *some knitting* 拆开编结物. Cf 参看 DO UP (DO[2]), DO STH UP. **2** destroy the effect of (sth); cancel 使(某事物)无效; 取消; 废除: *He undid most of the good work of his predecessor.* 他把前任的大部分业绩毁掉了. ○ *What is done cannot be undone.* 已做的事是既成事实.

▷ **un·do·ing** /ʌnˈduːɪŋ; ʌnˈduɪŋ/ *n* [sing] (*fml* 文) cause of sb's ruin or downfall 造成某人毁灭或垮台的原因: *Drink was his undoing.* 他酗酒是堕落的根源. ○ *lead, contribute to sb's undoing* 导致、促使某人毁灭.

un·done *adj* [pred 作表语] **1** untied, unfastened or opened 已解开; 已松开; 已拆开; 已打开: *Your buttons are all undone.* 你的钮扣全解开了. **2** not done; unfinished 未做的; 未完成的: *The work was left/remained undone.* 工作还没做完.

un·doubted /ʌnˈdaʊtɪd; ʌnˈdaʊtɪd/ *adj* [attrib 作定语] not doubted or questioned; indisputable 无疑的; 肯定的; 毋庸置疑的: *her undoubted skill, class, ability, etc as an athlete* 她身为运动员的无可置疑技术、水平、能力等 ○ *an undoubted improvement in my health* 我的身体确实的好转 ○ *an undoubted authority on the subject* 这学科毫无疑义的权威. ▷ **un·doubtedly** *adv*: *The painting is undoubtedly genuine.* 这幅画无疑是真品. ○ *undoubtedly so* 确实如此.

undreamed-of /ʌnˈdriːmd ɒv; ʌnˈdrimdɑv/ (also **undreamt-of** /ʌnˈdremt ɒv; ʌnˈdrɛmtɑv/) *adj* not thought to be possible; not (even) imagined 梦想不到的; 难以想像的: *undreamed-of wealth, success* 意想不到的财富、成功 ○ *We now travel round the world in a way previously undreamt-of.* 我们现今能周游世界, 以前简直做梦也想不到.

un·dress /ˌʌnˈdres; ʌnˈdrɛs/ *v* **1** [I] take off one's clothes 脱去衣物: *undress and get into bed* 脱掉衣服上床睡觉. **2** [Tn] remove the clothes of (sb/sth) 脱去(某人[某物])的衣物: *undress a child, doll* 脱掉孩子、玩具娃娃的衣服.

▷ **un·dressed** *adj* [usu pred 通常作表语] with one's clothes off; naked 已脱掉衣物; 裸露: *Are you undressed yet?* 你已经脱了衣服了吗? ○ *It's time the children got undressed.* 孩子都该脱衣服了.

un·drink·able /ˌʌnˈdrɪŋkəbl; ʌnˈdrɪŋkəbl/ *adj* not fit to be drunk, because of impurity or poor quality (因有杂质或质量低劣而)不能喝的, 不宜饮用的: *This wine is quite undrinkable.* 这种酒根本不能喝.

un·due /ˌʌnˈdjuː; *US* -ˈduː; ʌnˈdu/ *adj* [attrib 作定语] (*fml* 文) more than is right or proper; excessive 不当的; 过分的; 过度的: *with ˌundue ˈhaste* 过于仓促 ○ *show undue concern over sb/sth* 对某人[某事物]表现过分关心 ○ *apply undue pressure to make sb change his mind* 施加不适当的压力迫使某人改变想法.

un·du·late /ˈʌndjʊleɪt; *US* -dʒʊ-; ˈʌndjəˌlet/ *v* [I] have a wave-like movement or appearance 波动; 起伏; 呈波浪形: *(a field of) wheat undulating in the breeze* 在微风中起伏的(一片)麦浪 ○ *undulating hills, fields, etc* 起伏的山冈、田野等.

▷ **un·du·la·tion** /ˌʌndjʊˈleɪʃn; *US* -dʒʊ-; ˌʌndʒəˈleʃən/ *n* **(a)** [U] wave-like movement or appearance 波动; 起伏. **(b)** [C] one of a number of wave-like curves or slopes 波状的弯曲或斜坡: *The downs fell in gentle undulations to the sea.* 这块丘陵地略带倾斜伸向大海.

un·duly /ˌʌnˈdjuːlɪ; *US* -ˈduːlɪ; ʌnˈdulɪ/ *adv* (*fml* 文) more than is right or proper; excessively 不当地; 过分地; 过度地: *without being unduly pessimistic, suspicious, etc* 并不过于悲观、猜疑等 ○ *not unduly influenced/not influenced unduly by the media* 并未过分受传播媒介的影响.

un·dy·ing /ˌʌnˈdaɪɪŋ; ʌnˈdaɪɪŋ/ *adj* [attrib 作定语] everlasting or never-ending 不死的; 不朽的; 永恒的: *undying love, hatred, fame* 永恒的爱、永久的恨、不朽的名声.

un·earned /ˌʌnˈɜːnd; ʌnˈɝnd/ *adj* **1** not gained by working 非劳动所得的; 不劳而获的: *ˌunearned ˈincome*, eg from interest on investments 非劳动收入(如投资利润所得). **2** not deserved 不应得的: *ˌunearned ˈpraise* 不该受到的赞扬.

un·earth /ʌnˈɜːθ; ʌnˈɝθ/ *v* [Tn, Tn·pr] **~ sth (from sth) 1** uncover or obtain sth from the ground by digging 发掘或挖出某物: *unearth buried treasure* 发掘埋在地下的宝藏 ○ *The dog has unearthed some bones.* 那条狗刨出了一些骨头. **2** (*fig* 比喻) find sth by searching; discover and make known 搜寻到某事物; 发现并披露: *I unearthed the portrait from the attic.* 我从阁楼上搜出这幅画像. ○ *unearth new facts about Shakespeare* 发现有关莎士比亚的新资料.

un·earthly /ʌnˈɜːθlɪ; ʌnˋɝθlɪ/ *adj* **1** supernatural or mysterious or frightening 超自然的; 神秘的; 可怕的: *unearthly visions, screams* 怪异的幻象、尖叫声 ○ *The silence was unearthly.* 静得可怕. **2** [attrib 作定语] (*infml* 口) absurdly early or inconvenient 早得或不便得离谱的: *Why should I get up at this unearthly hour?* 为什么我得这么早起床? ○ *the unearthly time of 2.30 am* 凌晨两点三十分这么个不方便的时间.

un·easy /ʌnˈiːzɪ; ʌnˋizɪ/ *adj* (**-ier**, **-iest**) **1 ~ (about/at sth)** troubled or anxious 不安的; 忧虑的: *have an uneasy conscience*, ie feel guilty 良心不安(感到内疚) ○ *I'm uneasy in my mind about the future.* 我为前途担忧. **2** fitful or uncomfortable 一阵阵的; 不舒服的: *an uneasy truce, silence* 一阵一阵的休战、沉默 ○ *pass an uneasy night*, ie sleep badly 一夜没睡好觉. **3** disturbing or worrying 令人不安的; 使人担忧的: *They had an uneasy suspicion that all was not well.* 他们十分不安, 怀疑并非一切顺利.

▷ **un·ease** /ʌnˈiːz; ʌnˋiz/, **un·easi·ness** *ns* [U] apprehension 忧虑; 担心: *I waited with growing unease for her return.* 我等着她回来, 心里越来越不安.

un·eas·ily /ʌnˈiːzɪlɪ; ʌnˋizɪlɪ/ *adv*: *He moved uneasily in his chair.* 他坐在椅子上动来动去十分不安.

un·eat·able /ˌʌnˈiːtəbl; ʌnˋitəbl̩/ *adj* (of food, etc) not fit to be eaten, esp because of its poor condition (指食物等)不适于食用的, 不能吃的(尤因处理不善或变质). Cf 参看 INEDIBLE.

un·eco·nomic /ˌʌnˌiːkəˈnɒmɪk, ˌʌnˌek-; ˏʌnikəˋnɑmɪk, ˏʌnˏɛk-/ *adj* not likely to be profitable; not economic 不大可能赢利的; 不经济的: ˌ*uneconomic* ˈ*factories*, ˈ*industries*, ˈ*businesses, etc* 不太可能赚钱的工厂、工业、企业等 ○ *the closure of uneconomic pits*, ie coal-mines 不赢利煤矿之关闭.

un·eco·nom·ical /ˌʌnˌiːkəˈnɒmɪkl, ˌʌnˌek-; ˏʌnikəˋnɑmɪkəl, ˏʌnɛk-/ *adj* wasteful or inefficient; not thrifty 浪费的; 效率低的; 不节约的: *an uneconomical method of housekeeping* 缺乏精打细算的持家方法. ▷ **un·eco·nom·ic·ally** /-klɪ; -klɪ/ *adv*.

un·edu·cated /ʌnˈedʒʊkeɪtɪd; ʌnˋɛdʒʊˏketɪd/ *adj* **1** suggesting lack of the type of education, social background or good manners considered desirable 未受良好教育的; 缺乏教养的: *uneducated speech, handwriting* 缺乏修养的言语、书法 ○ *uneducated tastes* 庸俗的趣味. **2** having received little or no formal education at a school, etc 未受过正规教育的; 没上过学的; 文盲的.

un·em·ployed /ˌʌnɪmˈplɔɪd; ˏʌnɪmˋplɔɪd/ *adj* **1** temporarily without a paid job 未被雇用的; 失业的. **2** not in use 不在使用中的; 未用的: (*finance* 财) *unemployed capital*, ie capital that is not invested 游资(未用于投资的资金).

▷ **the un·em·ployed** *n* [pl *v*] people who are (temporarily) without work 失业的人.

un·em·ploy·ment /ˌʌnɪmˈplɔɪmənt; ˏʌnɪmˋplɔɪmənt/ *n* [U] (**a**) state of being unemployed 失业; 失业状况: *300 workers face unemployment* 300名工人面临失业 ○ *throughout the period of your unemployment* 在你失业的整个期间. (**b**) amount of unused labour 失业人数: *reduce unemployment*, eg by creating jobs 减少失业人数(如藉创造就业机会) ○ *the rising level of unemployment* 不断增长的失业率 ○ [attrib 作定语] *the monthly unemployment figures* 每月的失业人数.

□ **unemˈployment benefit** (*US* **unemployment compenˈsation**) [U] money paid to a worker who cannot find employment 失业津贴; 失业救济金.

un·end·ing /ʌnˈendɪŋ; ʌnˋɛndɪŋ/ *adj* **1** everlasting or unceasing 无止境的; 不停的: *the unending struggle between good and evil* 善与恶之间永无休止的斗争. **2** (*infml* 口) frequently repeated 不断重复的: *I'm tired of your unending complaints.* 我厌倦了你那没完没了的牢骚.

un·equal /ˌʌnˈiːkwəl; ʌnˋikwəl/ *adj* **1 ~ (in sth)** different (in size, amount, etc) (在大小、数量等方面)不同的, 不相等的: *The twins are unequal in height.* 这一对孪生儿高矮不一样. **2** not at the same level of strength, ability, etc (力量、能力等)不平等的, 不相称的: *an unequal bargain, contest, struggle* 不等价的交易、不平等的竞争、力量悬殊的斗争 ○ *unequal pay and conditions*, eg for women 不平等的工资和劳动条件(如对妇女的). **3** [pred 作表语] **~ to sth** (*fml* 文) not strong, clever, etc enough to do sth (对做某事)无力, 无才, 不胜任: *I feel unequal to the task.* 我觉得难以胜任这项工作. ▷ **un·equally** /-kwəlɪ; -kwəlɪ/ *adv*.

un·equalled /ˌʌnˈiːkwəld; ʌnˋikwəld/ *adj* superior to all others; unmatched 无比的; 无匹的; 无双的: *His record as a show-jumper is unequalled.* 他超越障碍赛马的记录无出其右. ○ *The husky is unequalled for stamina and endurance.* 爱斯基摩狗的体力和耐性是无双的.

un·equi·vocal /ˌʌnɪˈkwɪvəkl; ˏʌnɪˋkwɪvəkl̩/ *adj* (*fml* 文) having only one possible meaning; clear and unmistakeable 只有一种含义的; 清楚明白的: *an unequivocal attitude, position, demand* 明确的态度、立场、要求. ▷ **un·equi·voc·ally** /-kəlɪ; -kəlɪ/ *adv*: *state one's intentions unequivocally* 明确地说出自己的打算.

un·err·ing /ˌʌnˈɜːrɪŋ; ʌnˋɝɪŋ/ *adj* not making mistakes or failing or missing the mark; consistently accurate 不犯错误的; 万无一失的; 一贯准确的: *his unerring taste in clothes, instinct for a bargain, sense of direction* 他那万无一失的衣物审美观点、讨价还价的本能、方向感 ○ *He has an unerring knack of saying the wrong thing.* 他有个出言必失的本事. ○ *His aim was unerring.* 他百发百中. ▷ **un·err·ingly** *adv*.

UNESCO (also **Unesco**) /juːˈneskəʊ; juˋnɛsko/ *abbr* 缩写 = United Nations Educational, Scientific and Cultural Organization 联合国教育、科学及文化组织.

un·eth·ical /ˌʌnˈeθɪkl; ʌnˋɛθɪkl̩/ *adj* without principles, esp in business or professional conduct 无原则的(尤指业务或职业道德方面): *unethical decisions, practices* 无原则的决定、做法. ▷ **un·eth·ic·ally** /-klɪ; -klɪ/ *adv*.

un·even /ˌʌnˈiːvn; ʌnˋivən/ *adj* **1** not level or smooth or regular 不平坦的; 不平滑的; 不规则的: *an uneven hemline*, ie of a skirt 凹凸的底边线(裙子的) ○ *an uneven pavement, floor* 高低不平的人行道、地板. **2** not uniform or equal; varying 不一致的; 不相等的; 有差异的: *have an uneven pulse, heartbeat* 脉搏、心律紊乱 ○ *Emotion made his voice uneven.* 他激动得声音都变了. ○ *work of uneven quality* 质量不稳定的工作. **3** (of a contest, match, etc) unequal (指竞争、比赛等)不对等的, 不势均力敌的. ▷ **un·evenly** *adv*. **un·even·ness** *n* [U].

un·ex·cep·tion·able /ˌʌnɪkˈsepʃənəbl; ˏʌnɪkˋsɛpʃənəbl̩/ *adj* (*fml* 文) that cannot be criticized; entirely satisfactory 无可挑剔的; 无懈可击的: *her unexceptionable behaviour, conduct, etc* 她那无可指摘的行为、品行等. ▷ **un·ex·cep·tion·ably** /-əblɪ; -əblɪ/ *adv*.

un·ex·cep·tional /ˌʌnɪkˈsepʃənl; ˏʌnɪkˋsɛpʃənəl/ *adv* not outstanding or unusual; quite ordinary 不突出的; 平常的; 普通的. ▷ **un·ex·cep·tion·ally** /-ʃənəlɪ; -ʃənəlɪ/ *adv*.

un·ex·pec·ted /ˌʌnɪkˈspektɪd; ˏʌnɪkˋspɛktɪd/ *adj* causing surprise because not expected 未料到的; 意外的; 突如其来的: ˌ*unexpected* ˈ*guests*, ˈ*questions*, ˈ*gifts* 不速之客、突如其来的问题、料想不到的礼物 ○ ˌ*unexpected deˈvelopments*, ˈ*changes*, *reˈsults* 未料到的发展、变化、结果 ○ *His reaction was quite unexpected.* 他的反应完全出乎大家意料之外.

▷ **the un·ex·pec·ted** *n* [sing] event, etc that is unexpected 意外的事情: *be prepared for the unexpected (to happen)* 为意外情况(之发生)做好准备.

un·ex·pec·tedly *adv*.

un·ex·pec·ted·ness *n* [U].

un·fail·ing /ʌnˈfeɪlɪŋ; ʌnˋfelɪŋ/ *adj* (*approv* 褒) **1** never coming to an end; constant 永恒的; 无穷的: *an unfailing source of inspiration* 用之不竭的灵感的源泉 ○ *their unfailing efforts for peace* 他们为争取和平的不懈努力 ○ *his unfailing patience, good humour, devotion, etc* 他那始终如一的耐性、好脾气、奉献精神等. **2** [usu attrib 通常作定语] that can be relied on; certain 可靠的; 确实的: *her unfailing cooperation, support, etc* 她给予的可靠的合作、支持等.

▷ **un·fail·ingly** *adv* at all times 永远; 始终; 一贯: *unfailingly courteous* 一贯谦恭有礼.

un·fair /ˌʌnˈfeə(r); ʌnˋfɛr/ *adj* **1 ~ (on/to sb)** not right or just 不公正的; 不公平的: ˌ*unfair* ˈ*treatment, compeˈtition* 不公平的待遇、竞争 ○ *an* ˌ*unfair deˈcision, comˈparison, adˈvantage* 不公允的裁决、比较、有利地位 ○ *If some athletes use drugs, it is unfair on/to the others.* 有的运动员若使用兴奋剂, 其他运动员就要吃亏. ○ *She sued her* *employer for unfair dismissal.* 她控告雇主无理解雇工人. **2** not following normal rules or principles 违反规则或准则的: *ˌunfair ˈtactics* 不正当的手段 ○ *ˌunfair ˈplay*, eg at a football match 犯规动作(如足球比赛中的) ○ (*commerce* 商) *ˌunfair ˈtrading* 违例交易. ▷ **un·fairly** *adv*. **un·fair·ness** *n* [U].

un·faith·ful /ˌʌnˈfeɪθfl; ʌnˈfeθfəl/ *adj* **~ (to sb/sth) 1** having committed adultery 有通奸行为的; 不忠的: *Her husband is unfaithful (to her).* 她丈夫(对她)不忠. **2** (*dated* 旧) not loyal; treacherous 不忠实的; 背叛的; 变节的: *an unfaithful servant, subject, etc* 不忠实的仆人、臣民等. ▷ **un·faith·fully** /-fəlɪ; -fəlɪ/ *adv*. **un·faith·ful·ness** *n* [U].

un·fa·mil·iar /ˌʌnfəˈmɪlɪə(r); ˌʌnfəˈmɪljɚ/ *adj* **1 ~ (to sb)** not well known 不熟悉的: *His face was unfamiliar to me.* 我觉得他很面生. ○ *working in new and unfamiliar surroundings* 在不熟悉的新环境中工作. **2** [pred 作表语] **~ with sth** (*fml* 文) not having knowledge of sth; not acquainted with sth 对某事物不了解或不熟悉: *I'm unfamiliar with this type of computer.* 我不熟悉这种类型的计算机. ▷ **un·fa·mi·li·ar·ity** /ˌʌnfəˌmɪlɪˈærətɪ; ˌʌnfəˌmɪlɪˈærətɪ/ *n* [U].

un·fath·om·able /ʌnˈfæðəməbl; ʌnˈfæðəməbḷ/ *adj* (*fml* 文) **1** so deep that the bottom cannot be reached 深得无法到达底部的: *the ocean's unfathomable depths* 海洋中无法到达的深处. **2** (*fig* 比喻) too strange or difficult to be understood 莫测高深的; 难以了解的: *unfathomable motives, mysteries* 难以理解的动机、奥秘.

un·feel·ing /ʌnˈfiːlɪŋ; ʌnˈfilɪŋ/ *adj* hard-hearted or unsympathetic 无情的; 硬心肠的; 无同情心的: *unfeeling behaviour* 无情的行为 ○ *an unfeeling person, remark, attitude, reaction* 无同情心的人、言语、态度、反应. ▷ **un·feel·ingly** *adv*.

un·feigned /ʌnˈfeɪnd; ʌnˈfend/ *adj* not pretended; genuine or sincere 不虚伪的; 真正的; 真诚的: *greet sb with unfeigned pleasure, delight, sympathy, etc* 真正高兴地、喜悦地、同情地…招呼某人. ▷ **un·feignedly** /ˌʌnfeɪnɪdlɪ; ʌnˈfenɪdlɪ/ *adv*.

un·fit /ˌʌnˈfɪt; ʌnˈfɪt/ *adj* **1 ~ (for sth/to do sth) (a)** not of the required standard; unsuitable 不合格的; 不适宜的: *food unfit for human consumption* 人不能吃的食物 ○ *houses unfit for people to live in* 不适合居住的房屋. **(b)** lacking the ability needed; incapable 不胜任的; 无能力的: *She is unfit for such a senior position.* 她不胜任这种高级职务. ○ *He is unfit to drive in his present state*, eg because he is drunk. 他现在这样不能开车(如因喝醉了酒). **2** not perfectly healthy and fit 不太健康的; 不太健壮的: *The army rejected him as medically unfit.* 他因体检不合格而未能入伍.

un·flag·ging /ˌʌnˈflægɪŋ; ʌnˈflægɪŋ/ *adj* not showing signs of tiredness; untiring 毫无倦容的; 不疲倦的: *unflagging energy, zeal, devotion, etc* 充沛的精力、不衰的热情、不懈的奉献精神 ○ *listen with unflagging attention, interest, concentration, etc* 全神贯注地、兴趣昂然地、聚精会神地…听着. ▷ **un·flag·gingly** *adv*.

un·flap·pable /ˌʌnˈflæpəbl; ʌnˈflæpəbḷ/ *adj* (*infml* 口 *esp Brit*) remaining calm in a crisis; imperturbable 临危不乱的; 镇定自若的: *A busy manager needs a completely unflappable secretary.* 经理工作忙就需要一个头脑十分冷静的秘书. ▷ **un·flap·pab·il·ity** /ˌʌnflæpəˈbɪlətɪ; ʌnˌflæpəˈbɪlətɪ/ *n* [U].

un·flinch·ing /ʌnˈflɪntʃɪŋ; ʌnˈflɪntʃɪŋ/ *adj* not showing fear or shrinking in the face of danger, difficulty, etc 临危不惧的; 知难而上的: *unflinching courage, determination, resoluteness, etc* 临危不惧的勇气、知难而上的决心、百折不挠的毅力. ▷ **un·flinch·ingly** *adv*: *He held out his hand unflinchingly for the cane.* 他毫不畏缩地伸出手去挨藤条打.

un·fold /ʌnˈfəʊld; ʌnˈfold/ *v* **1** [I, Tn] (cause sth to) open or spread out from a folded state (使某物)展开, 打开: *The garden chair unfolds to make a camp-bed.* 花园中这把椅子可以打开当行军床用. ○ *unfold a map, tablecloth, etc* 展开地图、桌布等 ○ *The eagle unfolded its wings.* 那鹰伸展开了翅膀. **2** [I, Tn, Dn·pr] **~ sth (to sb)** (*fig* 比喻) (cause sth to) be revealed or made known (使某事物)显露, 展现: *The landscape unfolded before us.* 那景色展现在我们面前. ○ *as the story, scene, enquiry unfolds (itself)* 如故事、场景、调查所显示的那样 ○ *She unfolded her plans to me.* 她向我透露了她的计划.

un·fore·seen /ˌʌnfɔːˈsiːn; ˌʌnfɔrˈsin/ *adj* not known in advance; unexpected 未预见到的; 意料之外的: *ˌunforeseen ˈcircumstances, deˈvelopments, ˈdifficulties* 未预见到的情况、发展、困难.

un·for·get·table /ˌʌnfəˈgetəbl; ˌʌnfɚˈgɛtəbḷ/ *adj* (*esp approv* 尤作褒义) that cannot be easily forgotten; memorable 难忘的; 永远记得的: *an unforgettable experience, moment, scene* 难忘的经历、瞬间、场面.

un·formed /ˌʌnˈfɔːmd; ʌnˈfɔrmd/ *adj* not (yet) having developed fully; immature (尚)未充分发展的; 未成熟的: *her ˌunformed ˈhandwriting* 她那没有功底的书法 ○ *The child's character is as yet unformed.* 那孩子的性格尚未定型.

un·for·tu·nate /ʌnˈfɔːtʃənɪt; ʌnˈfɔrtʃənɪt/ *adj* **1** having or causing bad luck; unlucky 不幸的; 倒霉的: *I was unfortunate enough to lose my keys.* 我把钥匙丢了, 真倒霉. ○ *an unfortunate expedition* 运气不佳的探险 ○ *an unfortunate start to our holiday* 我们度假之出行不利. **2** unsuitable or regrettable 不合适的; 不恰当的; 令人遗憾的; 可惜的: *an unfortunate remark, coincidence, mishap* 不得体的话、令人遗憾的巧合、可悲的事故 ○ *a most unfortunate choice of words* 极不恰当的措辞 ○ *It is unfortunate that you missed the meeting.* 真可惜, 你没参加那次会议.

▷ **un·for·tu·nate** *n* (esp *pl* 尤作复数) unfortunate or wretched person 不幸的人; 可怜人: *Unlike many other poor unfortunates, I do have a job.* 我同许多不幸的人不一样, 我是有工作的.

un·for·tu·nately *adv* **~ (for sb)** regrettably; unluckily 遗憾地; 不幸地: *The notice is most unfortunately phrased.* 这份通知用语很不得当. ○ *I can't come, unfortunately.* 很遗憾, 我来不了. ○ *Unfortunately for him, he was wrong.* 很遗憾, 他错了.

un·foun·ded /ˌʌnˈfaʊndɪd; ʌnˈfaʊndɪd/ *adj* with no basis in fact; groundless 无事实根据的; 无基础的: *unfounded rumours, suspicions, hopes* 毫无根据的谣言、无端的猜疑、虚幻的希望.

un·freeze /ˌʌnˈfriːz; ʌnˈfriz/ *v* (*pt* **unfroze** /-ˈfrəʊz; -ˈfroz/, *pp* **unfrozen** /-ˈfrəʊzn; -ˈfrozən/) **1** [I, Tn] (cause sth to) thaw (使某物)解冻: *unfreeze some chops* 把一些冻排骨化开. Cf 参看 DEFROST. **2** [Tn] (*finance* 财) remove official controls on (the economy, etc) 解除对(经济等)的控制; 放开(经济等): *unfreeze wages, prices, etc* 解除对工资、价格等的冻结 ○ *unfreeze trade restrictions* 取消贸易限制.

un·friendly /ˌʌnˈfrendlɪ; ʌnˈfrɛndlɪ/ *adj* (**-ier, -iest**) **~ (to/towards sb)** hostile or unsympathetic 不友好的; 有敌意的; 冷漠的: *an unfriendly look, gesture, attitude* 不友好的神情、姿态、态度 ○ *He was distinctly unfriendly towards me.* 他对我很冷淡.

un·frock /ˌʌnˈfrɒk; ʌnˈfrɑk/ (also **defrock**) *v* [Tn esp passive 尤用于被动语态] dismiss (a priest guilty of bad conduct) from the priesthood 免去(行为不检的牧师)之圣职.

un·furl /ˌʌnˈfɜːl; ʌnˈfɝl/ *v* [I, Tn] unroll, unfold or spread out (sth) 展开, 张开, 铺开(某物): *unfurl a flag, banner, sail, etc* 展开旗子、旗帜、风帆等.

un·gainly /ʌnˈgeɪnlɪ; ʌnˈgenlɪ/ *adj* clumsy or awkward; not graceful 笨拙的; 难看的; 不雅的: *the ungainly movements of ducks out of water* 鸭子出水的笨拙动作 ○ *He walked in long ungainly strides.* 他迈着笨拙的大步子行走. ▷ **un·gain·li·ness** *n* [U].

unget-at-able /ˌʌngetˈætəbl; ˌʌngɛtˈætəbḷ/ *adj* (*infml* 口) (in a place that is) not easy to reach; inaccessible 难到达的; 在难到达之处的; 不易接近的.

un·godly /ˌʌnˈgɒdlɪ; ʌnˈgɑdlɪ/ *adj* **1** (*dated or fml* 旧或文) not giving reverence to God; sinful or wicked 不敬上帝的; 违反宗教或道德准则的; 邪恶的: *lead an ungodly life* 过着不道德的生活. **2** [attrib 作定语] (*infml* 口) very inconvenient 很不方便的: *Why are you phoning at this ungodly hour (of the night)?* 你为什么在(夜里)这个时候打电话来?

un·gov·ern·able /ˌʌnˈgʌvənəbl; ʌnˈgʌvɚnəbḷ/ *adj* (*fml* 文) impossible or difficult to control; violent 无法或难以控制的; 剧烈的: *fly into an ungovernable rage, temper, etc* 勃然大怒、大发雷霆 ○ *a man of ungovernable passions* 难以控制感情的人.

un·gra·cious /ˌʌnˈgreɪʃəs; ʌnˈgreʃəs/ *adj* grudging or

resentful; impolite 勉强的；忿恨的；不礼貌的：*her ungracious acceptance of my offer* 她接受我的提议时那种勉强的态度 ○ *It was ungracious of me not to acknowledge your help.* 你大力帮助而我尚未表示谢意，十分失礼. ▷ **un·gra·ciously** *adv*.

un·gram·mat·ical /ˌʌŋɡrəˈmætɪkl; ˌʌŋɡrəˈmætɪkl/ *adj* contrary to the rules of grammar 不符合语法的；违反语法规则的：*ungrammatical sentences, constructions, etc* 不合乎语法的句子、结构形式等. ▷ **un·gram·mat·ic·ally** /-klɪ; -klɪ/ *adv*.

un·grate·ful /ʌnˈɡreɪtfl; ʌnˋɡretfəl/ *adj* **~ (to sb) (for sth)** not recognizing a kindness, service, etc; not grateful 不感激的；不领情的；忘恩负义的：*You ungrateful wretch!* 你这忘恩负义的傢伙！ ▷ **un·grate·fully** /-fəlɪ; -fəlɪ/ *adv*.

un·guarded /ˌʌnˈɡɑːdɪd; ʌnˋɡɑrdɪd/ *adj* **1** not guarded 无防卫的；无人守护的：*The prisoner was left unguarded.* 那犯人无人看守. ○ *Never leave your luggage unguarded*, ie unattended. 千万注意看好自己的行李. **2** (esp of a person and what he says) careless or indiscreet（尤指人及言语）粗心的，不留神的，不谨慎的：*unguarded comments, criticisms, etc* 轻率的评语、批评等 ○ *catch sb in an unguarded moment* 乘某人不备将其抓住.

un·happy /ʌnˈhæpɪ; ʌnˋhæpɪ/ *adj* **(-ier, -iest)** **1** **(a)** sad or miserable; not happy 悲伤的；难过的；不幸福的；不愉快的：*look, sound, etc unhappy* 看上去、听起来…很不高兴 ○ *an unhappy occasion, atmosphere, face* 不愉快的场合、气氛、脸色. **(b)** **~ (about/at sth)** anxious or dissatisfied 忧虑的；发愁的；不满意的：*Investors were unhappy about the risk.* 投资者为这一风险而担心. **2** unfortunate or unlucky; regrettable 不幸的；不走运的；令人遗憾的：*an unhappy coincidence, chance, etc* 不幸的巧合、偶然事故等 ○ *What has led to this unhappy state of affairs?* 事情弄到这步田地是什么原因造成的？ **3** [usu attrib 通常作定语] (*fml* 文) not suitable or appropriate 不合适的；不恰当的：*an unhappy comment, decision, choice* 不恰当的评语、决定、选择.

▷ **un·hap·pily** /-ɪlɪ; -ɪlɪ/ *adv* **1** sadly 可悲地；难过地. **2** unfortunately 不幸地；不走运地；遗憾地：*Unhappily, she is not here today.* 真遗憾，她今天不在这儿.

un·hap·pi·ness *n* [U].

un·healthy /ʌnˈhelθɪ; ʌnˋhɛlθɪ/ *adj* **(-ier, -iest)** **1** not having or not showing good health 不健康的：*an unhealthy pallor, complexion, cough* 不健康的苍白、面容、咳嗽声 ○ (*fig* 比喻) *the unhealthy state of the economy* 不景气的经济状况. **2** harmful to health 有害于健康的；不卫生的：*an unhealthy climate, diet, life-style* 不利于健康的气候、固定饮食、生活方式 ○ *living in damp unhealthy conditions* 在有害于健康的潮湿环境中生活. **3** unwholesome or morbid 有害身心健康的；病态的：*show an unhealthy interest in/curiosity about murder* 对凶杀案表现出病态的兴趣[好奇心]. **4** (*infml* 口) dangerous to life 有生命危险的：*Terrorist attacks made our position very unhealthy.* 在恐怖分子的袭击下我们面临生命危险. ▷ **un·health·ily** /-ɪlɪ; -ɪlɪ/ *adv*. **un·healthi·ness** *n* [U].

un·heard /ˌʌnˈhɜːd; ʌnˋhɝd/ *adj* [usu pred 通常作表语] having nobody willing to pay attention; unheeded 无人理会；未引起注意：*Her case was/went unheard by the authorities.* 她的问题当局不予考虑.

□ **unheard-of** /ʌnˈhɜːd ɒv; ʌnˋhɝdˌɑv/ *adj* not previously known of or done; unprecedented 前所未闻的；无先例的；空前的：*Radiation reached unheard-of levels.* 辐射作用已达到前所未有的程度. ○ *It was unheard-of for anyone to complain.* 从未听说过有人投诉的事.

un·hinge /ʌnˈhɪndʒ; ʌnˋhɪndʒ/ *v* [Tn esp passive 尤用于被动语态] cause (sb) to become mentally unbalanced 使（某人）精神失常或错乱：*The shock unhinged his mind.* 他经这一打击精神失常了. ○ *Unhinged by her death, he fell ill.* 她死后他精神错乱而病倒了.

un·holy /ʌnˈhəʊlɪ; ʌnˋholɪ/ *adj* **(-ier, -iest)** [attrib 作定语] **1** wicked or sinful 亵渎神明的；违反宗教或道德准则的；邪恶的；罪恶的：*an unholy alliance between some Mafiosi and Fascists* 某些黑手党分子和法西斯分子之间罪恶的联盟. **2** (*infml* 口) (used as an intensifier 用以加强语气) outrageous or excessive 令人不能容忍的；极端的；过分的：*leave things in an unholy muddle/mess* 把事情弄得乱七八糟 ○ *making an unholy row/din/racket* 吵得受不了. ▷ **un·ho·li·ness** *n* [U].

unhoped-for /ʌnˈhəʊpt fɔː(r); ʌnˋhopt,fɔr/ *adj* not hoped for or expected 未曾料到的；意外的：*an unhoped-for piece of good luck* 出乎意料的好运.

uni- *comb form* 构词成分 having or consisting of one 单；一：*unilateral* ○ *unisex*.

UNICEF /ˈjuːnɪsef; ˋjunɪsɛf/ *abbr* 缩写 = United Nations Children's (formerly International Children's Emergency) Fund 联合国儿童基金会.

uni·cel·lu·lar /ˌjuːnɪˈseljʊlə(r); ˌjunɪˋsɛljələ˞/ *adj* (*biology* 生) (of an organism) consisting of a single cell（指有机体）单细胞组成的.

uni·corn /ˈjuːnɪkɔːn; ˋjunɪˌkɔrn/ *n* mythical animal resembling a horse with a single straight horn projecting from its forehead（神话中似马的）独角兽. ⇨illus at COAT OF ARMS (COAT) 见 COAT OF ARMS (COAT) 插图.

un·iden·ti·fied /ˌʌnaɪˈdentɪfaɪd; ˌʌnaɪˋdɛntɪˌfaɪd/ *adj* that cannot be identified 不能辨认的；无法识别的：*an unidentified species, submarine, caller* 辨别不出的种类、潜艇、来客 ○ *information from unidentified sources* 来源不明的信息.

□ ˌ**unidentified** ˌ**flying** ˈ**object** (*abbr* 缩写 **UFO**) = FLYING SAUCER (FLYING).

uni·form[1] /ˈjuːnɪfɔːm; ˋjunəˌfɔrm/ *adj* not changing in form or character; unvarying（形式或特征）无变化的；一律的：*of uniform length, size, shape, colour, etc* 长度、大小、形状、颜色等一样的 ○ *The rows of houses were uniform in appearance.* 这一排排的房子外观相同. ○ *be kept at a uniform temperature* 保持恒温 ○ *uniform distribution of weight* 重量的均匀分布. ▷ **uni·form·ity** /ˌjuːnɪˈfɔːmətɪ; ˌjunəˋfɔrmətɪ/ *n* (*esp derog* 尤作贬义) [U]: *a depressing uniformity of taste* 趣味方面使人感到沉闷的千篇一律. **uni·formly** *adv*: *Reaction to the cuts was uniformly negative.* 对削减经费一事一律持反对态度.

uni·form[2] /ˈjuːnɪfɔːm; ˋjunəˌfɔrm/ *n* **1** [C, U] distinctive clothing worn by all members of an organization or group, eg the police, the armed forces, nurses 制服（如警察、军人、护士穿的）：*children wearing school uniform(s)* 穿校服的儿童. **2** (idm 习语) **in uniform** **(a)** wearing such clothing 穿着制服：*officers in full dress uniform* 穿全套军装的军官. **(b)** belonging to the armed forces 属于军队：*How long was he in uniform?* 他在军队里服役多久了？

▷ **uni·formed** *adj* wearing uniform 穿着制服的：*uniformed staff*, eg at a hotel 穿着制服的工作人员（如旅馆服务员）○ *the uniformed branch of the police*, ie as contrasted with detectives, who wear plain clothes 穿制服的警察（以别于便衣警察）.

unify /ˈjuːnɪfaɪ; ˋjunəˌfaɪ/ *v* (*pt, pp* **-fied**) [Tn] form (sth) into a single unit or make uniform 使（某物）成为一体；使统一；使一致：*Germany was unified in 1871.* 德国于1871年统一了. ○ *the unifying effect of the nurses' strike* 护士罢工产生的团结效应 ○ *England and Scotland do not have a unified legal system.* 英格兰和苏格兰法制不统一. ▷ **uni·fica·tion** /ˌjuːnɪfɪˈkeɪʃn; ˌjunəfəˋkeʃən/ *n* [U]: *seeking the unification of Christian churches* 谋求基督教教派的统一.

uni·lat·eral /ˌjuːnɪˈlætrəl; ˌjunɪˋlætərəl/ *adj* [usu attrib 通常作定语] done by or affecting one person, group, country, etc and not another; one-sided 单方面做出的；仅影响一方的；单方面的；单边的：*unilateral decisions, agreements, declarations, etc* 单方面的决定、协议、宣布等 ○ *unilateral (nuclear) disarmament*, ie voluntary removal or dismantling by a country of its (nuclear) weapons 单方面（核）裁军. Cf 参看 BILATERAL, MULTILATERAL. ▷ **uni·lat·er·ally** /-rəlɪ; -rəlɪ/ *adv*.

un·im·peach·able /ˌʌnɪmˈpiːtʃəbl; ˌʌnɪmˋpitʃəbl/ *adj* (*fml approv* 文，褒) that cannot be doubted or questioned; trustworthy 无可怀疑的；无可指摘的；可靠的：*unimpeachable honesty, behaviour* 无可怀疑的诚实、行为 ○ *evidence from an unimpeachable source* 来源可靠的证据. ▷ **un·im·peach·ably** /-əblɪ; -əblɪ/ *adv*.

un·in·formed /ˌʌnɪnˈfɔːmd; ˌʌnɪnˋfɔrmd/ *adj* **1** not having or showing sufficient information 信息不足的；情况不明的：*an uninformed estimate, opinion, criticism* 情况不明的估计、看法、批评 ○ *Her colleagues had deliberately kept her uninformed.* 她那些同事故意不让她知道. **2** uneducated or ignorant 未受教育的；无知的：

U

the uninformed political discussion you hear in pubs 在酒馆里可听到的对于政治十分无知的谈论 ○ (*fml or joc* 文或谑) *Quercus, or, to the uninformed layman, the oak*... 栎属乔木, 亦即外行人所谓的橡树....

un·in·spired /ˌʌnɪnˈspaɪəd; ˌʌnɪnˋspaɪrd/ *adj* without imagination or inspiration; dull 无想像力的; 无灵感的; 枯燥的: *an uninspired speech, performance, painting, etc* 枯燥无味的讲话、表演、图画等.

un·in·spir·ing /ˌʌnɪnˈspaɪərɪŋ; ˌʌnɪnˋspaɪrɪŋ/ *adj* not producing interest or excitement; unpromising 引不起兴趣的; 无鼓舞作用的; 无指望的: *The book is fascinating, despite its uninspiring title.* 这本书很有意思, 虽然书名并不吸引人.

un·in·tel·li·gible /ˌʌnɪnˈtelɪdʒəbl; ˌʌnɪnˋtelɪdʒəbl/ *adj* impossible to understand 不可能理解的; 难懂的: *unintelligible handwriting, jargon* 看不懂的笔迹、莫名其妙的行话 ○ *speak in an almost unintelligible whisper* 用几乎听不清的低声说话. ▷ **un·in·tel·li·gibly** /-əblɪ; -əblɪ/ *adv*.

un·in·ter·ested /ʌnˈɪntrəstɪd; ʌnˋɪntrɪstɪd/ *adj* ~ **(in sb/sth)** having or showing no interest or concern; indifferent 不感兴趣的; 不关心的; 淡漠的. ⇨Usage at INTEREST[2] 用法见 INTEREST[2].

un·in·vit·ing /ˌʌnɪnˈvaɪtɪŋ; ˌʌnɪnˋvaɪtɪŋ/ *adv* not attractive; repellent 不吸引人的; 令人反感的: *an uninviting meal of cold fish and chips* 凉鱼和炸土豆条这样一顿不起眼的饭食 ○ *The hotel room was bare and uninviting.* 这个旅馆房间光秃秃的, 很不好看.

union /ˈjuːnɪən; ˋjunjən/ *n* **1** [U, sing] ~ **(of A with B/between A and B)** (act or instance of) uniting or being united 结合; 联合; 合并: *the union of three towns into one* 三个市镇之合而为一 ○ *support the union between our two parties/the union of our party with yours* 赞成我们两党的联合[我党同贵党的联合]. **2** [C] **(a)** (esp political) whole formed by uniting parts, states, etc (尤指政治上的)联盟、联邦等: *the Union of Soviet Socialist Republics* 苏维埃社会主义共和国联盟. **(b)** association or club formed by uniting people or groups 会社; 协会; 俱乐部: *the National Union of Working Men's Clubs* 全国劳工组织联合会 ○ *members of the Students' Union*, ie a general social and debating society at some universities and colleges 学生会成员(某些大专院校的) ○ *join the Mothers' Union* 加入母亲联合会. **(c)** = TRADE UNION (TRADE[1]). **3** (*fml or joc* 文或谑) **(a)** [U] state of being in agreement or harmony 一致; 和睦: *live together in perfect union* 十分和睦地在一起生活. **(b)** [C] instance of this, esp a marriage 一致, 和睦(尤指婚姻): *a happy union, blessed with six children* 有六个子女的美满婚姻. **4** [C] coupling for rods or pipes (棒或管的)连接(器).

▷ **uni·on·ize, -ise** /-aɪz; -aɪz/ *v* [I, Tn] organize (people) into a trade union 成立或组织工会: *unionize a firm's employees* 把公司的雇员组织成工会 ○ *a unionized work-force* 加入工会的职工总数. **uni·on·iza·tion, -isation** /ˌjuːnɪənaɪˈzeɪʃn; *US* -nɪˈz-; ˌjunjənəˋzeʃən/ *n* [U].

□ **the Union ˈJack** (also **the Union ˈflag**) the national flag of the United Kingdom 联合王国国旗; 英国国旗.

uni·on·ist /ˈjuːnɪənɪst; ˋjunjənɪst/ *n* **(a)** member of a trade union or supporter of trade unions 工会会员; 拥护工会的人. **(b) Unionist** person favouring political union, esp between Britain and Northern Ireland 拥护实行政治联合的人; (尤指)主张不列颠及北爱尔兰实行联合的人. ▷ **uni·on·ism** /ˈjuːnɪənɪzəm; ˋjunjəˌnɪzəm/ *n* [U].

unique /juːˈniːk; juˋnik/ *adj* **1 (a)** being the only one of its type 独一无二的; 仅有的; 唯一的: *a unique work of art* 独一无二的艺术作品. **(b)** having no like or equal; unparalleled 独特的; 无比的; 无双的: *a unique opportunity* 难得的机会 ○ *a unique ability* 独有的能力. **2** [pred 作表语] ~ **to sb/sth** concerning or related to one person or group or thing only 仅与一个人或一个群体或一件事物有关: *special difficulties unique to blind people* 盲人遇到的特殊困难. **3** (*infml* 口) unusual; remarkable 不寻常的; 突出的: *a rather unique little restaurant* 别具一格的餐馆. ▷ **uniquely** *adv*: *She is uniquely suited to the job.* 她是唯一适于做此工作的人. **unique·ness** *n* [U].

uni·sex /ˈjuːnɪseks; ˋjunɪsɛks/ *adj* designed to be suitable for both sexes in style or function (式样或用途)不分性别的, 男女皆宜的: *unisex fashions* 男女通用的时装 ○ *a unisex hairdressing salon* 男女美发厅.

uni·son /ˈjuːnɪsn, ˈjuːnɪzn; ˋjunəsn̩, ˋjunəzn̩/ *n* (idm 习语) **in unison (with sb/sth) (a)** sounding or singing together the same musical note (or the same note in different octaves) (同音或八度同音的)齐奏, 齐唱: *The last verse will be sung in unison.* 歌词的最后部分要齐唱. **(b)** (*fig fml* 比喻, 文) acting together in close association or agreement 一致的或协调的行动: *The banks have acted in unison with the building societies in lowering interest rates.* 银行降低了利率来配合房屋建筑协会的行动.

unit /ˈjuːnɪt; ˋjunɪt/ *n* **1** individual thing, person or group regarded for purposes of calculation, etc as single and complete, or as part of a complex whole (作为计算单位等的单个的事物、人或群体或构成复杂整体的)单位, 单元: *the family as the unit of society* 作为社会基本单位的家庭 ○ *The course book has twenty units.* 这个课本有二十个单元. **2** quantity chosen as a standard in terms of which other quantities may be expressed, or for which a stated charge is made (作为计量的)单位: *The metre is a unit of length.* 米是长度单位. ○ *The monetary unit of Great Britain is the pound.* 英国的货币单位是镑. ○ *SI units* 国际标准单位 ○ *a bill for fifty units of electricity* 一张用电五十度的帐单. **3** (esp in compounds 尤用以构成复合词) **(a)** part with a special function within a large or complex machine (机器的)部件, 元件, 构件: *a ˈfilter unit* 过滤装置 ○ *the central ˈprocessing unit in a computer* 计算机的中央处理机. **(b)** group with a special function within a large or complex organization (组织的)单位: *a unit of highly-trained soldiers* 经过高度训练的士兵小分队 ○ *a bomb-disposal unit* 未爆炸弹处理小组. **4** piece of furniture, equipment, etc designed to fit with others that are similar or complementary (组合家具、成套设备等的)组合件: *matching kitchen units* 配套的厨房设备 ○ *storage units* 存储设备. **5 (a)** smallest whole number; the number 1 最小整数; 1: *The number 34 consists of three tens and four units.* 34这个数含有三个十和四个一. **(b)** any whole number from 0 to 9 从0到9的任何一个整数: *a column for the tens and a column for the units* 十位数列和个位数列.

□ ˌ**unit ˈprice** price charged for each single item of goods of the same type 单价.

ˌ**unit ˈtrust** (*Brit*) (*US* ˈ**mutual fund**) investment company that invests the combined contributions of its members in various securities and pays them a dividend (calculated on the average return from these securities) in proportion to their holdings 单位信托投资公司(将信托者的资金集中投资于各种证券, 其收益按比例分与信托者).

Unit·arian /ˌjuːnɪˈteərɪən; ˌjunəˋtɛrɪən/ *n, adj* (member) of the Christian religious sect which rejects the doctrine of the Trinity and believes that God is one person 一位论派的(信徒)(认为上帝只有一位, 反对三位一体的教义): *the Unitarian Church* 一位论派教会. ▷ **Unit·ari·an·ism** /-ɪzəm; -ˌɪzəm/ *n* [U].

unite /juːˈnaɪt; juˋnaɪt/ *v* **1** [I, Ipr, Tn, Tn·pr] ~ **(sb/sth) (with sb/sth)** (cause people or things to) become one; come or bring together; join (使人或事物)合为一体, 联合, 合并, 统一, 团结: *The two parties have united to form a coalition.* 这两个党已结成联盟. ○ *After three years in prison he was again united with his wife and family.* 他在狱中关了三年之后, 又与妻子和家里人团圆了. ○ *the common interests that unite our two countries* 使我们两国联合起来的共同利益 ○ *The threat of war has united the country behind* (ie in support of) *its leaders.* 国难当头全国人民都团结在领袖的周围. **2** [I, Ipr] ~ **(in sth/doing sth)** act or work together 联合; 统一; 联合行动; 一齐工作: *We should unite in fighting/unite to fight poverty and disease.* 我们应该团结起来为消除贫穷和疾病而斗争.

▷ **united** *adj* **1** joined together by love or sympathy (由爱或同情)结合在一起的; 和睦的: *a very united family* 很和睦的家庭. **2** resulting from people joining together for a common purpose (为共同目标)团结的, 联合的: *make a united effort* 一致努力 ○ *present a united front to the enemy* 成立联合阵线共同对敌. **3** joined politically (政治上)统一的, 结盟的: *the campaign for a* *united Ireland* 争取爱尔兰统一的运动. **unitedly** *adv*.

□ **the U,nited 'Kingdom** (*abbr* 缩写 **(the) UK**) Great Britain and Northern Ireland (大不列颠及北爱尔兰)联合王国; 英国. ⇨Usage at GREAT 用法见 GREAT.

the U,nited 'Nations (*abbr* 缩写 **(the) UN**) international organization of many countries working for peace throughout the world 联合国.

the U,nited 'States (of A'merica) (*abbrs* 缩写 **(the) US, USA**) large country in N America consisting of 50 States and the District of Columbia (美利坚)合众国; 美国.

unity /'ju:nətɪ; 'junətɪ/ *n* **1** (**a**) [U] state of being one or a unit; oneness 单一; 唯一; 统一; 一体: *The figure on the left spoils the unity of the painting.* 画中左边的人物破坏了全幅画的整体性. (**b**) [C] thing consisting of parts that form a whole 统一的事物; 统一体; 整体. **2** [U] (*mathematics* 数) the number 1 (数字)1. **3** [U] harmony or agreement (in aims, ideas, feelings, etc) (目标、思想、情感等的)和谐, 协调, 和睦, 团结, 一致: *live together in unity* 和睦地在一起生活 ○ *Christian unity* 基督教的合一 ○ *political unity* 政治上的一致 ○ *National unity is essential in wartime.* 战时举国团结一致十分重要.

Univ *abbr* 缩写 = University: *London Univ* 伦敦大学 ○ *Univ of Salford* 索尔福德大学.

uni·ver·sal /,ju:nɪ'vɜ:sl; ,junə'vɝsl/ *adj* [esp attrib 尤作定语] of, belonging to, affecting or done by all people or things in the world or in a particular group 全体的; 影响全体的; 全体做的; 共同的: *Television provides universal entertainment.* 电视提供的是大众的娱乐. ○ *War causes universal misery.* 战争给所有的人带来苦难. ○ *universal suffrage*, ie the right of all members of a community to vote 普选权 ○ *There is universal agreement on this issue.* 在这个问题上, 大家观点一致. ○ *Their proposal met with almost universal condemnation.* 他们的提议遭到了几乎所有人的反对.

▷ **uni·ver·sal·ity** /,ju:nɪvɜ:'sælətɪ; ,junəvɝ'sælətɪ/ *n* [U].

uni·ver·sally /-sәlɪ; -slɪ/ *adv* by everyone or in every case 普遍地; 人人; 在所有情况下: *It is universally acknowledged that...* 普遍认为... ○ *The rules do not apply universally.* 这些规则并非放诸四海而皆准.

□ **,universal 'joint** (also **,universal 'coupling**) joint that connects two shafts in such a way that they can be at any angle to each other 万向接头.

uni·verse /'ju:nɪvɜ:s; 'junə,vɝs/ *n* **1 the universe** [sing] all existing things, including the earth and its creatures and all the stars, planets, etc in space 宇宙; 世界; 天地万物. **2** [C] system of galaxies 星系; 银河系: *Are there other universes outside our own?* 在我们的银河系之外还有别的星系吗?

uni·ver·sity /,ju:nɪ'vɜ:sətɪ; ,junə'vɝsətɪ/ *n* (**a**) [C] (colleges, buildings, etc of an) institution that teaches and examines students in many branches of advanced learning, awarding degrees and providing facilities for academic research 大学, 综合性高等学府(的学院、建筑物等): *She hopes to go to university next year.* 她希望明年能上大学. ○ [attrib 作定语] *a university student, lecturer, professor, etc* 大学生、讲师、教授. (**b**) [CGp] members of such an institution collectively 大学师生员工. ⇨Usage at SCHOOL[1] 用法见 SCHOOL[1].

un·just /,ʌn'dʒʌst; ʌn'dʒʌst/ *adj* not just; not fair or deserved 非正义的; 不公正的; 不公平的; 不该受的: *an unjust accusation* 不公正的指控. ▷ **un·justly** *adv*: *She was unjustly imprisoned without trial.* 她未经审讯而入狱是不公正的.

un·jus·ti·fi·able /ʌn'dʒʌstɪfaɪəbl; ʌn'dʒʌstə,faɪəbl/ *adj* that cannot be justified or excused 无法证明为正当的; 无可辩解的; 不可原谅的: *His behaviour was quite unjustifiable.* 他的行为毫无道理. ▷ **un·jus·ti·fi·ably** /-əblɪ; -əblɪ/ *adv*.

un·kempt /,ʌn'kempt; ʌn'kɛmpt/ *adj* not kept tidy; looking dishevelled or neglected 不整洁的; 凌乱的; 疏于整理的: *unkempt hair* 蓬乱的头发 ○ *He had an unkempt appearance.* 他仪容不整. ○ *The garden looks very unkempt.* 花园显得凌乱不堪.

un·kind /,ʌn'kaɪnd; ʌn'kaɪnd/ *adj* not having or showing kindness; cruel or harsh 不亲切的; 不和蔼的; 不厚道的; 不仁慈的; 残忍的; 苛刻的: *an unkind remark* 刻薄的言语 ○ *Don't be so unkind to your brother.* 别对你弟弟那么凶.

▷ **un·kindly** *adv* in an unkind manner 不亲切地; 不和蔼地; 不厚道地; 不仁慈地; 残忍地; 苛刻地: *Please don't take my remarks unkindly*, ie think I intend to be unkind in saying this. 请不要把我的话往坏处想.

un·kind·ness *n* [U, C].

un·know·ing /ʌn'nəʊɪŋ; ʌn'noɪŋ/ *adj* [usu attrib 通常作定语] not knowing; unaware; unwitting 不知道的; 未意识到的; 未察觉的: *He was the unknowing cause of all the misunderstanding.* 这一切误会都是他在无意中造成的.

▷ **un·know·ingly** *adv*: *All unknowingly, she had been waiting for hours in the wrong place.* 她记错了地方, 在那儿等了半天一直未发觉.

un·known /,ʌn'nəʊn; ʌn'non/ *adj* **~ (to sb)** **1** not known or identified 未知的; 不详的; 未被认识的; 未认出的: *The side-effects of the drug are as yet unknown (to scientists).* 这种药的副作用(科学家)尚未发现. ○ *Unknown forces were at work to overthrow the government.* 有些尚未查明的势力正在活动图谋推翻政府. **2** not famous or well known; unfamiliar 不出名的; 不闻名的; 不熟悉的; 陌生的: *The star of the film is a previously unknown actor.* 这部电影里的明星以前是个默默无闻的演员. **3** (idm 习语) **an ,unknown 'quantity** person or thing that one has no experience of and whose nature, significance, etc one therefore cannot predict 不了解的人或事物(因而无法估量其特点、重要性等): *The new sales director is still a bit of an unknown quantity.* 新来的销售部主任大家还不大了解. **unknown to sb** without the knowledge of sb 不为某人所知: *Quite unknown to me, she'd gone ahead and booked the holiday.* 在我完全不了解的情况下, 她已先行办好了度假的预订手续.

▷ **un·known** *n* (**a**) (usu 通常作 **the unknown**) [sing] thing, place, etc that is unknown 未知的或不了解的事物、地方等: *a journey into the unknown* 前往陌生地方之行 ○ *fear of the unknown* 对不了解的事物的恐惧. (**b**) [C] person who is not well known 不出名的人: *The leading role is played by a complete unknown.* 演主角的是一个毫无名气的演员. (**c**) [C] (*mathematics* 数) quantity that is not yet determined 未知元; 未知数; 未知量: *x and y are unknowns.* x 和 y 代表两个未知数.

un·lace /ʌn'leɪs; ʌn'les/ *v* [Tn] undo the laces of (esp shoes); unfasten or loosen (sth) by slackening its laces 解开(尤指鞋)的带子; 解开带子以放开或松开(某物).

un·laden /,ʌn'leɪdn; ʌn'ledn/ *adj* not loaded 未装载的: *,unladen 'weight*, ie the weight of a vehicle with nothing loaded into or onto it 无载重, 空车重(未装货的车的重量).

un·law·ful /,ʌn'lɔ:fl; ʌn'lɔfəl/ *adj* (*fml* 文) against the law; illegal 不合法的; 非法的: *unlawful assembly* 非法集会 ○ *a verdict of unlawful killing* 做出的不合法杀害的裁决. ▷ **un·law·fully** /-fəlɪ; -fəlɪ/ *adv*.

un·learn /,ʌn'lɜ:n; ʌn'lɝn/ *v* [Tn] cause (sth) to be no longer in one's knowledge or memory 从观念或记忆中清除(某事物): *You must start by unlearning all the bad habits your previous piano teacher taught you!* 你得先改掉以前钢琴老师教给你的一切坏习惯!

un·leash /ʌn'li:ʃ; ʌn'liʃ/ *v* [Tn, Tn·pr] **~ sth (against/on sb/sth)** (**a**) set sth free from a leash or restraint 解开带子或去掉限制以放开(某事物): *unleash the guard dogs* 解开带子放出警卫犬. (**b**) (*fig* 比喻) set sth free from control; release sth in a powerful attack (on sb/sth) 使某物不受控制; 放出某物对(某人[某物])进行强有力的攻击: *unleash the forces of nuclear power* 发出核动力的攻击力 ○ *He unleashed a torrent of abuse against the unfortunate shop assistant.* 他对那倒霉的店员骂不绝口.

un·leavened /,ʌn'levnd; ʌn'lɛvənd/ *adj* (of bread) made without yeast or other raising agent (指面包)未使用酵母或其他发酵剂的, 未经发酵的.

un·less /ən'les; ən'lɛs/ *conj* if...not; except if or except when 如果不; 除非; 除非在...的时候: *You'll fail in French unless you work harder.* 你要是不再加把劲儿, 法语就考不及格了. ○ *Unless England improve their game they're going to lose the match.* 英格兰队如果不改进打法, 就会输掉这场比赛. ○ *I wouldn't be saying this unless I were sure of the facts.* 要是我对这些事情没有把握, 我就不说这话了. ○ *Come at 8 o'clock unless I phone*, eg to tell you a different time. 请8点钟来, 如果我不打电话

U

的话. ○ *I sleep with the window open unless it's really cold.* 我总是开着窗户睡觉, 除非天气非常冷才关上窗户.

NOTE ON USAGE 用法: **Unless** and **if...not** can often be used in the same way ☆ **unless** 和 **if...not** 的用法常常是相同的: *Follow the green signs unless you have goods to declare/if you haven't any goods to declare.* 未携须申报货物者, 沿绿色标记通行. **Unless** cannot be used when referring to the result of something not happening and is, therefore, not used in 'imaginary' conditional sentences ☆ **unless** 不可用以指尚未发生的事情之结果, 因而不可用于'假想的'条件句中: *We would have had a lovely holiday if it hadn't rained* (NOT *unless it had rained*) *every day.* 要不是天天下雨的话, 我们的假日就过得痛快了. (本句中不可用 unless it had rained.) ○ *I'll be sorry if she doesn't come* (NOT *unless she comes*) *to the party.* 万一她不来参加聚会, 我就感到太遗憾了. (本句中不可用 unless she comes.) **Unless** (*not* **if...not**) is often used to introduce an afterthought, ie something added to the main statement ☆ **unless**(并非 **if...not**) 常用以引导出补充前言的话, 即是对刚说过的话想到要加些补充: *She hasn't got any hobbies — unless you call watching TV a hobby.* 她没有任何嗜好—— 除非把看电视也算作嗜好的话. ○ *Have a cup of tea — unless you'd prefer a cold drink.* 喝一杯茶吧 —— 除非你想喝冷饮.

un·let·tered /ˌʌnˈletəd; ʌnˈlɛtɚd/ *adj* (*fml* 文) unable to read; uneducated 文盲的; 未受教育的; 没有文化的. Cf 参看 ILLITERATE.

un·like /ʌnˈlaɪk; ʌnˈlaɪk/ *adj* [pred 作表语] dissimilar; different 不相似; 不同: *They are so unlike nobody would believe they were sisters.* 她们毫无相似之处, 谁也不相信她们是姐妹.

▷ **un·like** *prep* **1** different from (sth); not like 与(某事物)不同; 不像...: *Her latest novel is quite unlike her earlier work.* 她最近的小说与她以前的作品截然不同. ○ *The scenery was unlike anything I'd seen before.* 这风景跟我过去见到过的都不一样. ○ *Their celebrations at Christmas are not unlike our own.* 他们的圣诞节庆祝活动跟我们自己的并无不同. **2** uncharacteristic of (sb/sth) 无(某人[某事物])的特性: *It's very unlike him to be so abrupt.* 他这么粗鲁可不像他平时的样子. **3** in contrast to (sb) 与(某人)相反: *Unlike me, my husband likes to stay in bed.* 我丈夫与我相反, 喜欢睡懒觉. ○ *I was very interested in the lecture, unlike many of the students.* 我跟许多同学不同, 我很喜欢听这个课. ○ *He managed to finish the race, unlike more than half of the competitors.* 他在比赛中坚持跑完了全程, 不像大部分选手那样半途而废.

U

un·likely /ʌnˈlaɪklɪ; ʌnˈlaɪklɪ/ *adj* (**-ier, -iest**) (**a**) not likely or expected to happen 不大可能发生的; 未必会发生的: *It is unlikely to rain/that it will rain.* 不太可能下雨. ○ *There is unlikely to be rain.* 不太可能有雨. ○ *His condition is unlikely to improve.* 他的境况不大可能好转. ○ *In the unlikely event of a strike, production would be badly affected.* 罢工未必能发生, 若一旦发生, 生产势必受到严重影响. (**b**) [attrib 作定语] not likely to be true; improbable 不大可能是真实的; 不大可能的: *an unlikely tale, excuse, explanation, etc* 不太像真实的说法、托词、解释等. (**c**) not expected to succeed 未必会成功的: *the most unlikely candidate* 最不大可能当选的候选人 ○ *an unlikely couple,* ie two people who do not seem to be well suited to each other 不大般配的二人.

un·lim·ited /ˌʌnˈlɪmɪtɪd; ʌnˈlɪmɪtɪd/ *adj* not limited; very great in number or quantity 无限的; (数或量)极大的: *If only one had an unlimited supply of money!* 要是财源不断就好了!

un·lined /ˌʌnˈlaɪnd; ʌnˈlaɪnd/ *adj* **1** without a lining 无衬里的: *a ˌcheap ˌunlined ˈcoat* 无衬里的廉价大衣 ○ *The box was rough and unlined.* 这个盒子很粗糙又没有衬里. **2** not marked with lines 无线条的; 无皱纹的: *ˌunlined ˈpaper* 无条格的纸 ○ *a ˌsmooth ˌunlined comˈplexion* 光滑而无皱纹的面部皮肤.

un·lis·ted /ˌʌnˈlɪstɪd; ʌnˈlɪstɪd/ *adj* (**a**) not in a published list (esp of Stock Exchange prices) 未列表公布的(尤指证券价格); (证券)不上市的, 未上市的: *an unlisted company* 未上市的公司. (**b**) (*US*) = EX-DIRECTORY: *He/His number is unlisted.* 他[他的电话号码]未列入电话簿.

un·load /ˌʌnˈləʊd; ʌnˈlod/ *v* **1** (**a**) [I, Tn, Tn·pr] **~ sth (from sth)** remove a load from (sth); remove (a load) from sth 从(某物)上卸下货物; 从某物上卸下(货物): *Dockers started unloading (the ship).* 码头工人开始卸船. ○ *unload shopping from a car* 从汽车上卸下采购的物品. (**b**) [Tn] remove the charge from (a gun, etc) or the film from (a camera) 从(枪、炮等)中退出弹药; 从(照相机)中取出胶卷. **2** [I, Tn] (of vehicles, vessels etc) have (a load) removed (指车辆、船舶等)卸下(负载): *Lorries may only park here when loading or unloading.* 卡车非装卸货物时不得在此停车. **3** [Tn, Tn·pr] **~ sb/sth (on/onto sb)** (*infml* 口) pass sb/sth unwanted (to sb else); get rid of sb/sth 把不想要的某人[某物]交给(他人); 摆脱某人[某事物]: *Do you mind if I unload the children onto you this afternoon?* 今天下午我把孩子托付给你, 你不介意吧? Cf 参看 OFFLOAD.

un·lock /ˌʌnˈlɒk; ʌnˈlɑk/ *v* [Tn] **1** unfasten the lock of (a door, etc) using a key (用钥匙)开(门等)的锁: *unlock the gate* 打开大门的锁. **2** release (sth) by, or as if by, unlocking 开锁或似开锁般释放(某事物): *exploration to unlock the secrets of the ocean bed* 揭开大洋底部秘密的探险.

unlooked-for /ʌnˈlʊkt fɔː(r); ʌnˈlʊkt,fɔr/ *adj* (*fml* 文) not expected; unforeseen 未预料的; 未预见到的: *unlooked-for compliments, difficulties* 出乎意外的赞扬、困难.

un·loose /ˌʌnˈluːs; ʌnˈlus/ (also **un·loosen** /ʌnˈluːsn; ʌnˈlusən/) *v* [Tn] make (sth) loose; untie 放松, 放开(某物); 解开: *unloose the rope around one's waist* 解开系在腰上的绳子 ○ *He unloosened his collar.* 他把领口敞开了. ⇨Usage at LOOSE[1] 用法见 LOOSE[1].

un·lucky /ʌnˈlʌkɪ; ʌnˈlʌkɪ/ *adj* not lucky; having or bringing bad luck; unfortunate 不幸的; 倒霉的; 运气不好的: *I always seem to be unlucky at cards.* 我玩纸牌似乎总是手气不好. ○ *He was unlucky enough to lose his keys.* 他把钥匙丢了, 真够倒霉的. ○ *The number thirteen is often considered unlucky.* 十三这个数字常常认为是个不吉利的数字. ○ *an unlucky attempt,* ie one that did not succeed 一次运气不佳的尝试(未成功).

▷ **un·luck·ily** *adv* unfortunately 不幸地; 不吉利地; 遗憾地: *Unluckily (for Peter) he did not get the job.* (彼得)他可真不走运, 没能获得那份工作.

un·made /ˌʌnˈmeɪd; ʌnˈmed/ *adj* (of a bed) with the bedclothes not neatly arranged for sleeping in (指床)未铺好的: *She rushed off to work leaving her bed unmade.* 她匆忙去上班连床都没铺好.

un·man /ˌʌnˈmæn; ʌnˈmæn/ *v* (**-nn-**) [Tn] (*arch or rhet* 古或修辞) weaken the self-control or courage of (a man) 削弱(某男子)的自制力或勇气: *Unmanned by grief he broke down and wept.* 他悲伤得不像个男子汉不禁哭了起来.

un·manly /ʌnˈmænlɪ; ʌnˈmænlɪ/ *adj* (of behaviour) uncharacteristic of or inappropriate for men (指行为)无男子特性的, 不适于男子的: *It was once thought unmanly not to drink and smoke.* 身为男子不抽烟不喝酒曾视为无男子气概.

un·manned[1] *pt, pp* of UNMAN.

un·manned[2] /ˌʌnˈmænd; ʌnˈmænd/ *adj* not manned; operated automatically or without a crew 无人的; 无人操纵的; 自动的: *ˌunmanned ˈrailway signals* 自动控制的铁路信号 ○ *send an unmanned spacecraft to Mars* 把无人驾驶的宇宙飞船发射到火星上去.

un·man·nerly /ʌnˈmænəlɪ; ʌnˈmænɚlɪ/ *adj* (*fml derog* 文, 贬) without good manners; ill-mannered 没有礼貌的; 粗野的: *unmannnerly conduct* 无礼的行为.

un·mar·ried /ˌʌnˈmærɪd; ʌnˈmærɪd/ *adj* not married; single 未婚的; 独身的: *an ˌunmarried ˈmother, ˈcouple* 未婚的母亲、一对情侣.

un·mask /ˌʌnˈmɑːsk; *US* -ˈmæsk; ʌnˈmæsk/ *v* **1** [I, Tn] remove a mask from (sb) 除去(某人)的面具: *The revellers unmasked* (ie took off their masks) *at midnight.* 狂欢的人在午夜摘下了面具. **2** [Tn] reveal the true character of (sb/sth); expose 使(某人[某事物])露出真相; 揭露; 暴露: *unmask the culprit* 揭露罪犯的真面目 ○ *unmask a plot* 揭露阴谋.

un·matched /ˌʌnˈmætʃt; ʌnˈmætʃt/ *adj* that cannot be matched; without an equal; matchless 不相配的; 无双的; 无比的: *an achievement that remains unmatched to* *this day* 迄今无可匹敌的成就.

un·men·tion·able /ʌnˈmenʃənəbl; ʌnˋmɛnʃənəbl/ *adj* [usu attrib 通常作定语] too shocking or embarrassing to be mentioned or spoken about 说不出口的, 不堪提起的(因说出来会令人震惊或难堪): *an unmentionable disease*, eg venereal disease 难以明说的疾病(如性病). ▷ **un·men·tion·ables** *n* [pl] (*arch euph or joc* 古, 婉或谑) unmentionable people or things (esp underwear) 不宜提到的人或事物; (尤指)内衣.

un·mind·ful /ʌnˈmaɪndfl; ʌnˋmaɪndfəl/ *adj* [pred 作表语] **~ of sb/sth** (*fml* 文) not considering sb/sth; forgetting sb/sth 对某人[某事物]不加考虑或不理会: *He worked on, unmindful of the time.* 他一直工作, 没理会时间.

un·mis·tak·able /ˌʌnmɪˈsteɪkəbl; ˌʌnməˋstekəbl/ *adj* clearly recognizable or obvious; impossible to mistake for sb/sth else 明显的; 明白无误的; 不会弄错的: *the unmistakable sound of an approaching train* 清清楚楚的火车驶近的声音. ▷ **un·mis·tak·ably** /-əblɪ; -əblɪ/ *adv*.

un·mit·ig·ated /ʌnˈmɪtɪgeɪtɪd; ʌnˋmɪtəˌgetɪd/ *adj* [usu attrib 通常作定语] (of sth/sb bad) having no accompanying advantages whatever; complete; absolute (指坏事物[坏人])一无是处的, 十足的, 绝对的: *an unmitigated disaster, scoundrel* 十足的灾难、坏蛋.

un·moved /ˌʌnˈmuːvd; ʌnˋmuvd/ *adj* [pred 作表语] not affected by feelings of pity, sympathy, etc 不为怜悯、同情等感情所打动; 不受感动: *It's impossible to remain unmoved by the reports of the famine.* 了解到报道的饥荒情况不可能无动于衷.

un·nat·ural /ʌnˈnætʃrəl; ʌnˋnætʃrəl/ *adj* **1** not natural or normal; differing from what is the usual or expected 不自然的; 不正常的; 反常的; 出乎意料的: *His face turned an unnatural shade of purple.* 他气得脸色发紫, 十分难看. ○ *It was unnatural for the room to be so tidy.* 房间竟然这样整洁, 真出乎所料. **2** (*derog* 贬) (**a**) contrary to usual and generally accepted behaviour 行为反常而不合情理的: *unnatural sexual desires* 变态的性欲. (**b**) extremely cruel or wicked 极残酷的; 极邪恶的: *the unnatural murder of his own father* (他)丧尽天良的弑父. **3** not sincere; affected or forced 虚假的; 做作的; 勉强的: *an unnatural high-pitched laugh* 装出的尖声大笑. ▷ **un·nat·ur·ally** /-rəlɪ; -rəlɪ/ *adv*: *Not unnaturally, she was greatly upset by her father's sudden death.* 她父亲突然去世她悲痛不已, 这也是人之常情. ○ *an unnaturally jovial manner* 强颜欢笑.

un·ne·ces·sary /ʌnˈnesəsrɪ; *US* -serɪ; ʌnˋnɛsəˌsɛrɪ/ *adj* (**a**) [usu pred 通常作表语] not necessary or desirable; superfluous 不需要; 不必要; 多余: *It's unnecessary to cook a big meal tonight.* 今晚不必做很多饭. (**b**) [usu attrib 通常作定语] more than necessary; excessive 超过需要的; 过度的: *unnecessary expense* 多余的开销. (**c**) (of remarks, etc) not required in a situation and likely to be offensive; gratuitous (指言语等)无必要而可能得罪人的, 没来由的: *an unnecessary reference to his criminal past* 何必提到他的前科. ▷ **un·ne·ces·sar·ily** /ˌʌnˈnesəsrəlɪ; *US* ˌʌnˌnesəˈserəlɪ; ˌʌnnɛsəˋsɛrəlɪ/ *adv*.

un·nerve /ˌʌnˈnɜːv; ʌnˋnɝv/ *v* [Tn] cause (sb) to lose self-control, confidence or courage 使(某人)失去自制力、信心或勇气: *His encounter with the guard dog had completely unnerved him.* 他遇上了警卫犬, 把他吓坏了. ▷ **un·nerv·ing** *adj*: *She found the whole interview rather unnerving.* 她觉得整个面试都让人气馁.

un·no·ticed /ˌʌnˈnəʊtɪst; ʌnˋnotɪst/ *adj* [usu pred 通常作表语] not observed or noticed 未被察觉到; 未被注意到: *The event passed unnoticed.* 那件事谁也没注意到. ○ *I can't let this act of kindness go unnoticed.* 我不能让这种好人好事湮没无闻.

un·numbered /ˌʌnˈnʌmbəd; ʌnˋnʌmbɚd/ *adj* **1** having no number(s) 无号数的; 未编号的: *unnumbered tickets/seats*, eg at a concert hall or theatre 不对号的票[座位](如音乐会或戏院的). **2** (*arch or rhet* 古或修辞) more than can be counted; countless 不可胜数的; 数不清的; 无数的: *the unnumbered stars* 繁星.

UNO /ˈjuːnəʊ; ˋjuno/ *abbr* 缩写 = United Nations Organization 联合国组织.

un·ob·trus·ive /ˌʌnəbˈtruːsɪv; ˌʌnəbˋtrusɪv/ *adj* (*usu approv* 通常作褒义) not too obvious or easily noticeable; not drawing attention to itself or himself; discreet 不太显著的; 不引人注目的; 不招摇的; 谨慎的: *an unobtrusive but pleasing design* 悦目而不扎眼的图案 ○ *He was so quiet and unobtrusive that you would hardly know he was there!* 他很文静, 简直注意不到他在那儿! ▷ **un·ob·trus·ively** *adv*: *She slipped away from the party unobtrusively.* 她从聚会上悄悄地溜走了.

un·oc·cu·pied /ˌʌnˈɒkjʊpaɪd; ʌnˋɑkjəˌpaɪd/ *adj* **1** not occupied; empty; vacant 未被占用的; 空的; 无人住的: *find an unoccupied table* 找一张无人占用的桌子 ○ *The house had been left unoccupied for several years.* 这所房子已经几年无人居住了. **2** (of a region or country) not under the control of foreign troops (指地区或国家)未被敌军占领的, 未沦陷的: *unoccupied territory* 未沦陷的领土. **3** not busy; idle 不忙碌的; 空闲的: *in one of her rare unoccupied moments* 在她难得的一段空闲时间.

un·of·fi·cial /ˌʌnəˈfɪʃl; ˌʌnəˋfɪʃəl/ *adj* not official 非官方的; 非正式的: *an ˌunofficial ˈstrike*, ie one not authorized by the union 非正式的罢工(未经工会认可的) ○ *an ˌunofficial ˈstatement*, ie one not authorized for release to the public 非官方的声明(未经批准而向公众发布的声明) ○ *ˌunofficial ˈnews*, ie not confirmed by official sources or authorities 非官方新闻(未经官方证实的). ▷ **un·of·fi·cially** /-ʃəlɪ; -ʃəlɪ/ *adv*.

un·or·tho·dox /ˌʌnˈɔːθədɒks; ʌnˋɔrθəˌdɑks/ *adj* not in accordance with what is orthodox, conventional or traditional 非正统的; 非正规的; 非传统的: *unorthodox beliefs, opinions, etc* 非正统的信仰、见解等 ○ *unorthodox teaching methods* 非传统的教学法 ○ *She has an unorthodox technique, but is an excellent player.* 她不是科班出身, 但却身手不凡. Cf 参看 HETERODOX.

un·pack /ˌʌnˈpæk; ʌnˋpæk/ *v* (**a**) [I, Tn] take packed things out of (sth) 由(某物)中取出所包装之物; 打开(包装)取出某物: *Let's unpack before we go to bed.* 咱们打开行李再睡觉吧. ○ *a half-unpacked suitcase* 已取出一半衣物的手提箱. (**b**) [Tn, Tn·pr] **~ sth (from sth)** take out (things packed) 取出(包装之物): *unpack the books from the box* 从箱子里把书拿出来.

un·paid /ˌʌnˈpeɪd; ʌnˋped/ *adj* **1** (**a**) not yet paid 未支付的; 未缴纳的: *an ˌunpaid ˈbill/ˈdebt* 未付讫的帐单[未偿还的债款]. (**b**) **~ for** not paid for 未付款的; 未清帐的: *The car is three years old and still unpaid for.* 这汽车用了三年还没付购车款呢. **2** (**a**) (of people) not receiving payment for work done (指人)不得到报酬的, 无偿工作的: *an ˌunpaid ˈbaby-sitter* 无报酬的临时保姆. (**b**) (of work) done without payment to the worker(s) (指工作)无报酬的, 无偿的: *ˌunpaid ˈlabour* 无偿的劳动.

un·pal·at·able /ʌnˈpælətəbl; ʌnˋpælətəbl/ *adj* (*fml* 文) **1** not palatable; unpleasant to taste 不好吃的; 不可口的; 味道不好的: *The fish was particularly unpalatable.* 这鱼特别难吃. **2** (*fig* 比喻) unpleasant or unacceptable to the mind 使人不快的; 无法认同的: *His views on capital punishment are unpalatable to many.* 他对死刑存废的见解许多人都不以为然. ▷ **un·pal·at·ably** /-əblɪ; -əblɪ/ *adv*.

un·par·alleled /ʌnˈpærəleld; ʌnˋpærəˌlɛld/ *adj* having no parallel or equal; unmatched 无比的; 无双的; 无匹的: *an economic crisis unparalleled in modern times* 现代无两的经济危机.

un·par·lia·ment·ary /ˌʌnˌpɑːləˈmentrɪ; ˌʌnpɑrləˋmɛntrɪ/ *adj* (*derog* 贬) contrary to the accepted rules of behaviour in Parliament (because abusive or disorderly) 违反议会行为准则的(因出言不逊或扰乱秩序): *unparliamentary language, conduct* 违反议会惯例的语言、行为.

un·pick /ˌʌnˈpɪk; ʌnˋpɪk/ *v* (**a**) [Tn, Tn·pr] **~ sth (from sth)** take out (the stitches) 拆开(缝线): *unpick the stitches from a curtain* 拆开窗帘的缝线. (**b**) [Tn] take out the stitches from (sth) 拆去(某物)的缝线: *unpick a hem, seam, etc* 拆去布边、接缝处等的缝线.

un·placed /ˌʌnˈpleɪst; ʌnˋplest/ *adj* not one of the first three to finish in a race or contest (比赛)未获前三名的.

un·play·able /ˌʌnˈpleɪəbl; ʌnˋpleəbl/ *adj* **1** (in games, of a ball) that cannot be played (比赛等, 指球)无法打的. **2** (of ground) not fit to be played on (指场地)不适宜比赛的. **3** (of music) too difficult to be played (指音乐)难以演奏的.

un·pleas·ant /ʌnˈpleznt; ʌnˋplɛznt/ *adj* not pleasant; disagreeable 使人不愉快的; 不合意的: *unpleasant smells, weather* 讨厌的气味、天气 ○ *an unpleasant surprise* 使人

不愉快的意外事 ○ *I found his manner extremely unpleasant.* 我觉得他的态度讨厌极了.

▷ **un·pleas·antly** *adv*.

un·pleas·ant·ness *n* [C, U] (instance of) bad feeling or quarrelling between people 恶感; 争执; 不和: *I want to avoid any unpleasantness with the neighbours.* 我要避免与邻居有任何不快.

un·plug /ˌʌnˈplʌg; ʌnˈplʌg/ *v* **(-gg-)** [Tn] **1** disconnect (an electrical appliance) by removing its plug from the socket 拔出(电器)的电源插头: *Please unplug the TV before you go to bed.* 临睡前请拔下电视机的插头. **2** remove an obstruction from (sth) 除去(某物)的障碍物: *The drain is blocked and needs unplugging.* 排水管堵塞了, 得疏通一下.

un·popu·lar /ˌʌnˈpɒpjʊlə(r); ʌnˈpɑpjələ˞/ *adj* **~ (with sb)** not popular; not liked or enjoyed by a person, a group or people in general 不得人心的; 不受欢迎的: *an unpopular decision* 不得人心的决议 ○ *She's rather unpopular with her boss at the moment.* 老板现在不太待见她. ▷ **un·popu·lar·ity** /ˌʌnˌpɒpjʊˈlærətɪ; ʌnˌpɑpjəˈlærətɪ/ *n* [U].

un·prac·tised /ʌnˈpræktɪst; ʌnˈpræktɪst/ *adj* having little experience; inexpert; unskilled 无经验的; 不内行的; 不熟练的.

un·pre·ced·en·ted /ʌnˈpresɪdentɪd; ʌnˈprɛsəˌdɛntɪd/ *adj* without precedent; never having happened, been done or been known before 无前例的; 前所未有的; 空前的: *unprecedented levels of unemployment* 失业率达到的前所未有的严重程度 ○ *a situation unprecedented in the history of the school* 该校自有校史以来未曾出现过的情况.

un·pre·dict·able /ˌʌnprɪˈdɪktəbl; ˌʌnprɪˈdɪktəbl̩/ *adj* **(a)** that cannot be predicted 无法预料的; 不可预知的: *an unpredictable result* 难以预料的结果. **(b)** (of a person) whose behaviour cannot be predicted; changeable; unstable (指人)行为难以预知的, 易变的, 不稳定的: *You never know how she'll react: she's so unpredictable.* 谁也不知道她反应如何, 她这个人反复无常.

un·pre·ju·diced /ˌʌnˈpredʒʊdɪst; ʌnˈprɛdʒədɪst/ *adj* free from prejudice; not biased 无偏见的; 无成见的; 公正的.

un·pre·med·it·ated /ˌʌnpri:ˈmedɪteɪtɪd; ˌʌnprɪˈmɛdəˌtetɪd/ *adj* not previously and deliberately considered or planned; spontaneous 未经事先慎重考虑或计划的; 自发的: *an unpremeditated attack* 非预谋的攻击.

un·pre·pos·sess·ing /ˌʌnˌpri:pəˈzesɪŋ; ˌʌnpripəˈzɛsɪŋ/ *adj* (*fml* 文) not attractive or appealing in appearance (外表)不吸引人的, 不讨人喜欢的: *Though unprepossessing to look at he is highly intelligent.* 他虽然相貌平平, 但却很有才气.

un·pre·ten·tious /ˌʌnprɪˈtenʃəs; ˌʌnprɪˈtɛnʃəs/ *adj* (*approv* 褒) not showy or pompous; modest 不炫耀的; 不夸大的; 谦逊的: *an unpretentious little book but one that tells a simple story well* 把一个简单的故事讲得很生动的朴实无华的书.

un·prin·cipled /ʌnˈprɪnsəpld; ʌnˈprɪnsəpl̩d/ *adj* (*fml* 文) without moral principles; unscrupulous; dishonest 不道德的; 肆无忌惮的; 不诚实的: *unprincipled behaviour* 不道德的行为 ○ *an unprincipled rogue* 无耻的恶棍.

un·print·able /ʌnˈprɪntəbl; ʌnˈprɪntəbl̩/ *adj* (of words, articles, etc) too offensive or indecent to be printed (指词语、文章等)(因有攻击性或下流)不宜印出的: *I'm afraid that my views on their private life are unprintable!* 我自忖我对他们私生活的看法不印出也罢!

un·pro·fes·sional /ˌʌnprəˈfeʃənl; ˌʌnprəˈfɛʃənl/ *adj* (*derog* 贬) **1** (esp of conduct) contrary to the standards expected in a particular profession (尤指行为)违反职业准则的: *The board considers your behaviour highly unprofessional.* 董事会认为你的行为严重违反职业道德. **2** (of a piece of work, etc) not done with the skill or care of a trained professional (指一件工作等)未按专业水平做的: *He made a very unprofessional job of putting up the garden shed for us.* 他给我们搭的花园棚屋很没水平. ▷ **un·pro·fes·sion·ally** /-ʃənəlɪ; -ʃənlɪ/ *adv*.

un·promp·ted /ˌʌnˈprɒmptɪd; ʌnˈprɑmptɪd/ *adj* (of an answer or action) not said or done, etc as the result of a hint, suggestion, etc; spontaneous (指回答或行动)未经提示做出的, 自发的: *an unprompted offer of help* 主动的提出帮助.

un·pro·nounce·able /ˌʌnprəˈnaʊnsəbl; ˌʌnprəˈnaʊnsəbl̩/ *adj* (of a word, esp a name) too difficult to pronounce (指字, 尤指名字)难得发不成音的.

un·pro·vided /ˌʌnprəˈvaɪdɪd; ˌʌnprəˈvaɪdɪd/ *adj* (*fml* 文) **~ for** without provision having been made for 无供给的; 无生活来源的: *The widow was left unprovided for,* ie No money, etc had been left for her on her husband's death. 她成了寡妇而失去了生计.

un·pro·voked /ˌʌnprəˈvəʊkt; ˌʌnprəˈvokt/ *adj* (esp of verbal or physical violence) without provocation; not caused by previous action (尤指暴力言行)未受招惹而自发的, 无缘无故的: *ˌunprovoked agˈgression/atˈtacks* 无端的侵犯[攻击].

un·pun·ished /ˌʌnˈpʌnɪʃt; ʌnˈpʌnɪʃt/ *adj* [pred 作表语] not punished 未受惩罚: *Such a serious crime must not go unpunished.* 这种严重罪行不可不受惩罚.

un·put·down·able /ˌʌnpʊtˈdaʊnəbl; ˌʌnpʊtˈdaʊnəbl̩/ *adj* (*infml* 口) (of a book, etc) so interesting or absorbing that the reader is reluctant to stop reading until he has finished it (指书等)爱不忍释的, 不忍释手的.

un·quali·fied /ʌnˈkwɒlɪfaɪd; ʌnˈkwɑləˌfaɪd/ *adj* **1 (a) ~ (as sth/for sth/to do sth)** without legal or official qualifications for doing sth 无资格的; 不合格的: *an unqualified instructor* 不合格的教师 ○ *unqualified as a teacher/for teaching* 无资格当教师[任教]. **(b)** [pred 作表语] **~ to do sth** (*infml* 口) not competent or knowledgeable enough to do sth 不能胜任; 学识不够: *I feel unqualified to speak on the subject.* 我自觉无资格就此问题发言. **2** [usu attrib 通常作定语] not limited or restricted; absolute 无限制的; 无束缚的; 绝对的: *unqualified praise* 称赞不已 ○ *an unqualified success* 完全的胜利.

un·ques·tion·able /ʌnˈkwestʃənəbl; ʌnˈkwɛstʃənəbl̩/ *adj* beyond doubt; certain; indisputable 无疑的; 确实的; 无可争辩的: *His honesty is unquestionable.* 他很诚实, 这是毫无疑问的. ▷ **un·ques·tion·ably** /-əblɪ; -əblɪ/ *adv*.

un·ques·tioned /ʌnˈkwestʃənd; ʌnˈkwɛstʃənd/ *adj* not disputed or doubted 无争议的; 不容置疑的: *an unquestioned fact* 无可怀疑的事实 ○ *Her authority is unquestioned.* 她的权威是公认的.

un·ques·tion·ing /ʌnˈkwestʃənɪŋ; ʌnˈkwɛstʃənɪŋ/ *adj* done, etc without asking questions, expressing doubt, etc 不提出疑问的; 不表示怀疑的; 无异议的: *He demands unquestioning obedience from his followers.* 他要求追随者对他绝对服从. ▷ **un·ques·tion·ingly** *adv*.

un·quiet /ʌnˈkwaɪət; ʌnˈkwaɪət/ *adj* [usu attrib 通常作定语] (*fml* 文) restless; uneasy; disturbed 不安的; 不宁的; 烦扰的: *all the signs of an unquiet mind* 心烦意乱的表现.

un·quote /ʌnˈkwəʊt; ʌnˈkwot/ *n* (idm 习语) **quote (... unquote)** ⇨QUOTE *n*.

un·ravel /ʌnˈrævl; ʌnˈrævl̩/ *v* **(-ll-**; *US* **-l-)** [I, Tn] **1** (cause sth woven, knotted or tangled to) separate into strands (使编织、编结或纠结之物)解开, 拆开: *My knitting has unravelled.* 我编织的东西散开了. ○ *unravel a cardigan, a ball of string* 把对襟毛衣、一团细绳拆开. Cf 参看 RAVEL. **2** (*fig* 比喻) (cause sth to) become clear or solved (使某事物)变清楚或获解决: *The mystery unravels slowly.* 那件神秘的事渐渐明朗了. ○ *unravel a plot, puzzle, etc* 揭露阴谋、解决难题.

un·read /ˌʌnˈred; ʌnˈrɛd/ *adj* **1** (of a book) that has not been read (指书)未经阅读的, 尚未审阅的: *a pile of ˌunread ˈnovels* 一堆未看过的小说. **2** (of a person) not having read many books, etc (指人)读书不多的, 不学无术的: *She knows so much that she makes me feel very unread.* 她懂的事情很多, 相形之下我觉得自己很无知.

un·read·able /ˌʌnˈri:dəbl; ʌnˈridəbl̩/ *adj* **1** (*derog* 贬) too dull or too difficult to be worth reading (因枯燥或艰涩)不值一读的. **2** = ILLEGIBLE.

un·real /ˌʌnˈrɪəl; ʌnˈrɪəl/ *adj* (of an experience) not seeming real; imaginary; illusory (指经历)不真实的, 想像的, 虚幻的: *The whole evening seemed strangely unreal.* 整个晚上的事似乎如梦幻般令人生奇. ▷ **un·real·ity** /ˌʌnrɪˈælətɪ; ˌʌnrɪˈælətɪ/ *n* [U].

un·reas·on·able /ʌnˈri:znəbl; ʌnˈriznəbl̩/ *adj* **1** (of people) not reasonable in attitude, etc (指人)不讲道理的. **2** going beyond the limits of what is reasonable or just; excessive 超越情理的; 不合理的; 过分的: *make unreasonable demands on sb* 对某人提出无理的要求. ▷

un·reas·on·ably /-əblɪ; -əblɪ/ *adv*.

un·reas·on·ing /ʌnˈri:zənɪŋ; ʌnˈriznɪŋ/ *adj* (*fml* 文) (of a person or of attitudes, beliefs, etc) not using or guided by reason (指人或指态度、信仰等)不凭理智的, 无理性的: *an unreasoning fear of foreigners* 对外国人无缘由的恐惧.

un·reel /ˌʌnˈri:l; ʌnˈril/ *v* [I, Tn] (cause sth to) unwind from a reel (使某物)(从卷轴中)转开, 展开: *Unreel the hose fully before use.* 把水龙完全展开再使用.

un·re·lent·ing /ˌʌnrɪˈlentɪŋ; ˌʌnrɪˈlɛntɪŋ/ *adv* (**a**) not reducing in intensity, etc; continuous; relentless (强度等)未降低的; 持续的; 不间断的: *unrelenting pressure* 持续的压力. (**b**) (of a person) merciless; unwilling to relent (指人)冷酷的, 不愿宽容的: *a cruel and unrelenting master* 残酷无情的主人. ▷ **un·re·lent·ingly** *adv*: *The rain continued unrelentingly.* 雨一个劲儿地下个不停.

un·re·mit·ting /ˌʌnrɪˈmɪtɪŋ; ˌʌnrɪˈmɪtɪŋ/ *adj* never relaxing or ceasing; incessant; persistent 不放松的; 不停止的; 不间断的; 坚持的: *unremitting care, boredom, drudgery* 无休止的操心、厌倦感、繁重工作.

un·re·peat·able /ˌʌnrɪˈpi:təbl; ˌʌnrɪˈpitəbl/ *adj* **1** that cannot be repeated or done again 不可重复的; 不可再做的: *unrepeatable bargains/offers*, ie at specially low prices 仅此一次的大减价. **2** too indecent or offensive to be said again (因下流或有攻击性)不宜重述说出的: *His remarks were quite shocking — unrepeatable, in fact.* 他说的话太让人难堪——真无法再说出口.

un·re·quited /ˌʌnrɪˈkwaɪtɪd; ˌʌnrɪˈkwaɪtɪd/ *adj* (*fml* 文) (esp of love) not returned or rewarded (尤指爱情)得不到回应或报答的: *unrequited passion* 单相思.

un·re·served /ˌʌnrɪˈzɜ:vd; ˌʌnrɪˈzɝvd/ *adj* **1** (of seats, etc) not reserved for or allocated to a particular person in advance (指座位等)未被预订的, 未保留的: *We always keep a few unreserved tables.* 我们总留几张桌子不预订出去. **2** (*fml* 文) without any holding back; complete 无保留的; 完全的: *Do I have your unreserved attention?* 你是完全听着我说话呢吗?
▷ **un·re·servedly** /ˌʌnrɪˈzɜ:vɪdlɪ; ˌʌnrɪˈzɝvɪdlɪ/ *adv* without reservation or restriction; openly 无保留地; 无限制地; 公开地: *apologize unreservedly* 坦诚地道歉.

un·rest /ʌnˈrest; ʌnˈrɛst/ *n* [U] (state of) restlessness or dissatisfaction; disturbance 不安; 不满意; 动荡: *civil/industrial/political/social unrest* 国内的[工业的/政治的/社会的]动乱.

un·res·trained /ˌʌnrɪˈstreɪnd; ˌʌnrɪˈstrend/ *adj* not restrained; not held back or controlled; unchecked 不受抑制的; 无拘束的; 不受控制的; 未加制止的: *unrestrained anger, temper, violence, etc* 未受控制的愤怒、脾气、暴力等 ○ *the unrestrained use of military force* 对军队的滥用.

un·ripe /ˌʌnˈraɪp; ʌnˈraɪp/ *adj* not yet ripe 未成熟的: *ˌunripe baˈnanas* 未熟的香蕉.

un·ri·valled (*US* **un·rivaled**) /ʌnˈraɪvld; ʌnˈraɪvld/ *adj* **~ (in sth)** having no rival; unequalled 无对手的; 无双的: *have an unrivalled reputation* 无与伦比的声誉 ○ *unrivalled in courage* 英勇无比.

un·roll /ˌʌnˈrəʊl; ʌnˈrol/ *v* [I, Tn] (cause sth to) open out from a rolled position by rolling (使某物)(由卷曲状态)展开: *unroll a carpet, map, sleeping-bag* 把卷着的地毯、地图、睡袋展开. Cf 参看 ROLL[2] 3.

un·ruffled /ˌʌnˈrʌfld; ʌnˈrʌfld/ *adj* not upset or agitated; imperturbable 平静的; 镇定的; 沉着的: *She spoke with unruffled calm.* 她从容不迫地讲话. ○ *He remained unruffled by the charges.* 他受到这些指控仍处之泰然.

un·ruly /ʌnˈru:lɪ; ʌnˈrulɪ/ *adj* not easy to control or discipline; disorderly 不易控制或管教的; 不守规矩的: *unruly behaviour* 不守规矩的行为 ○ *an unruly mob, crowd, demonstration, etc* 难以控制的暴民、群众、示威集会等 ○ (*fig* 比喻) *unruly hair*, ie hard to manage 难以梳理的乱发. ▷ **un·ru·li·ness** *n* [U].

UNRWA /ˈʌnrə; ˈʌnrə/ *abbr* 缩写 = United Nations Relief and Works Agency 联合国难民救济及工程处.

un·said /ˌʌnˈsed; ʌnˈsɛd/ *adj* (*fml* 文) **1** [pred 作表语] not expressed; unspoken 未表达; 未说出: *Some things are better left unsaid.* 有些事情还是不说出来为好. **2** *pt*, *pp* of UNSAY.

un·sat·ur·ated /ʌnˈsætʃəreɪtɪd; ʌnˈsætʃəˌretɪd/ *adj* **1** not saturated 未浸透的; 未充满的. **2** (*chemistry* 化) (esp of an organic compound) that can combine with hydrogen, to form a third substance by the joining of molecules (尤指有机化合物)不饱和的, 未饱和的. Cf 参看 POLYUNSATURATED.

un·sa·voury (*US* **un·sa·vory**) /ˌʌnˈseɪvərɪ; ʌnˈsevərɪ/ *adj* **1** unpleasant to the taste or smell; disgusting 味道不好的; 气味难闻的; 令人厌恶的: *an unsavoury mixture of cold pasta and curry* 难吃的冷的意大利面食和咖喱食品. **2** (*fml or joc* 文或谑) morally unpleasant or offensive; disreputable (道德上)令人不快或厌恶的; 声名狼藉的: *unsavoury rumours, details, habits* 令人厌恶的谣言、细节、习惯 ○ *an unsavoury character, reputation* 缺德的人、坏的名声. Cf 参看 SAVOURY.

un·say /ˌʌnˈseɪ; ʌnˈse/ *v* (*pt*, *pp* **unsaid** /-ˈsed; -ˈsɛd/) [Tn esp passive 尤用于被动语态] (*fml* 文) take back (sth that has been said); retract 取消, 收回(说过的话); 撤回: *What is said cannot be unsaid.* 话已出口, 无法收回.

un·scathed /ˌʌnˈskeɪðd; ʌnˈskeðd/ *adj* [pred 作表语] not injured or hurt; unharmed 未受损伤; 未遭伤害: *The hostages emerged from their ordeal unscathed.* 人质经受磨难而平安生还.

un·scramble /ˌʌnˈskræmbl; ʌnˈskræmbl/ *v* [Tn] **1** restore (a scrambled message) to a form that can be understood 将(杂乱的信息)加以整理(以便理解). **2** (*infml* 口) restore (sth) to order from a confused state 整理或整顿(某事物): *After a few seconds to unscramble my thoughts, I replied…* 我稍微整理了一下思路, 然后回答说….

un·screw /ˌʌnˈskru:; ʌnˈskru/ *v* (**a**) [Tn] loosen (a screw, nut, etc) by turning it; unfasten (sth) by removing screws 旋松(螺丝、螺母等); 旋下螺丝以松开(某物): *unscrew the door-handle* 松开门拉手上的螺丝. (**b**) [I, Tn] (make sth) come undone by twisting (将某物)拧开: *The lid of this jam pot won't unscrew.* 这果酱罐的盖子拧不开.

un·scrip·ted /ʌnˈskrɪptɪd; ʌnˈskrɪptɪd/ *adj* (of a speech, broadcast, etc) made without a prepared script (指讲话、广播等)无讲稿的: *a language course based on natural unscripted dialogues, conversations, etc* 以无讲稿的自然对话、交谈等为基本教学方式的语言课.

un·scru·pu·lous /ʌnˈskru:pjʊləs; ʌnˈskrupjələs/ *adj* without moral principles 无道德原则的; 不讲道德的: *unscrupulous methods, behaviour* 不道德的方法、行为 ○ *He was utterly unscrupulous in his dealings with rival firms.* 他与对立公司竞争完全不讲道德. ▷ **un·scru·pu·lously** *adv*. **un·scru·pu·lous·ness** *n* [U].

un·seat /ˌʌnˈsi:t; ʌnˈsit/ *v* [Tn] **1** throw (sb) off a horse, bicycle, etc 使(某人)从马、自行车等上摔下. **2** remove (sb) from office, esp from a seat in parliament 免除(某人)的职务; (尤指)罢免(议员): *a move to unseat Labour militants* 为罢免工党激进分子而采取的行动.

un·seemly /ʌnˈsi:mlɪ; ʌnˈsimlɪ/ *adj* (*fml* 文) (of behaviour, etc) not proper or seemly; unbecoming (指行为等)不适当的, 不适宜的, 不得体的: *an unseemly rush to leave work* 为赶着下班的猴急相 ○ *make unseemly suggestions* 提出不恰当的建议 ○ *His language was most unseemly*, ie abusive. 他的话很不得当(出言不逊). ▷ **un·seem·li·ness** *n* [U].

un·seen /ʌnˈsi:n; ʌnˈsin/ *adj* **1** not seen; invisible 未被看见的; 看不见的: *I slipped from the room unseen*, ie unnoticed. 我悄悄地溜出房间, 无人察觉. **2** (of a translation) done without previous preparation (指翻译)事先无准备的. **3** (idm 习语) **sight unseen** ⇨ SIGHT[1].
▷ **un·seen** *n* (*Brit*) passage for translation from a foreign language into one's own language without previous preparation 不经准备需译成本族语的一段外文: *German unseens* 需当场翻译的几段德文.

un·ser·vice·able /ˌʌnˈsɜ:vɪsəbl; ʌnˈsɝvɪsəbl/ *adj* (*abbrs* 缩写 **US, u/s**) (*fml or joc* 文或谑) that cannot be used because worn out, broken, etc (因破旧、损坏等)不能使用的: *an unserviceable bicycle, telephone, tin-opener, etc* 已不能用的自行车、电话机、开罐器等.

un·settle /ˌʌnˈsetl; ʌnˈsɛtl/ *v* [Tn] (**a**) disturb the normal calm state of (sth/sb); upset 打扰(某事物[某人]); 使不安宁: *Our move* (ie to another house) *unsettled the children.* 我们搬家弄得孩子们不得安宁. ○ *Seafood unsettles my stomach.* 我一吃海鲜胃就不舒服. (**b**) make (sb) uneasy or anxious; disturb 使(某人)不安或担忧;

扰乱: *Living alone unsettled his nerves.* 他独自生活，情绪很不稳定.

▷ **un·settled** *adj* (**a**) unstable or upset or disturbed 不稳定的; 不安宁的; 扰乱的: *Conditions on the stock-market were unsettled.* 证券市场的行情不稳定. ○ *an unsettled stomach* 胃部不舒服 ○ *feel unsettled in one's new surroundings* 在新的环境里感到不安. (**b**) changeable or unpredictable 易变的; 多变的; 无法预料的: *unsettled weather* 变幻莫测的天气 ○ *Our future plans are still unsettled.* 我们将来的计划尚难逆料. (**c**) (of an argument, etc) open to further discussion (指争论等)需进一步讨论的, 未解决的. (**d**) (of a bill, etc) unpaid (指帐单等)未付款的.

un·shake·able /ʌnˈʃeɪkəbl; ʌnˈʃekəbḷ/ *adj* (of a belief, etc) that cannot be changed; absolutely firm (指信仰等)不可改变的, 坚定不移的: *an unshakeable conviction, resolve, faith, etc* 坚定不移的信念、决心、信仰等.

un·sightly /ʌnˈsaɪtlɪ; ʌnˈsaɪtlɪ/ *adj* not pleasant to look at; ugly 难看的; 不雅观的; 丑陋的: *unsightly facial hair,* eg on women 难看的面部汗毛(如女子的) ○ *London's unsightly suburban sprawl* 伦敦郊外不雅观的无计划扩展的地区. ▷ **un·sight·li·ness** *n* [U].

un·skilled /ˌʌnˈskɪld; ʌnˈskɪld/ *adj* not having or requiring special skill or training 无特殊技能的; 无需专门训练的: *ˌunskilled ˈworkers* 无特殊技能的工人 ○ *ˌunskilled ˈlabour* 非技术性的工人.

un·so·ci·able /ʌnˈsəʊʃəbl; ʌnˈsoʃəbḷ/ *adj* disliking the company of others; not sociable 不好交际的; 不合群的. Cf 参看 ANTISOCIAL.

un·so·cial /ʌnˈsəʊʃl; ʌnˈsoʃəl/ *adj* **1** unsociable 不好交际的; 不合群的. **2** not conforming to standard working times 不符合标准工作时间的: *unsocial hours,* eg on night shifts 非正常工作时间(如夜班).

un·so·li·cited /ˌʌnsəˈlɪsɪtɪd; ˌʌnsəˈlɪsɪtɪd/ *adj* given or sent voluntarily; not asked for 主动提供或送出的; 未经请求的: *ˌunsolicited ˈhelp, adˈvice, etc* 主动给予的帮助、劝告等 ○ *ˌunsolicited ˈcomments, ˈcriticisms, etc* 未经征求而做出的评语、批评等 ○ *ˌunsolicited (junk) ˈmail,* ie usu for advertising purposes 未经索要而寄来的(杂类)邮件(通常为宣传品).

un·soph·ist·ic·ated /ˌʌnsəˈfɪstɪkeɪtɪd; ˌʌnsəˈfɪstɪˌketɪd/ *adj* (*sometimes derog* 有时作贬义) **1** simple and natural 简单而自然的: *unsophisticated tastes, attitudes, looks* 简单的爱好、憨直的态度、自然的神情 ○ *To the unsophisticated* (ie naive) *mind of the average viewer...* 对于一般观众的单纯心理.... **2** not complex or refined; basic 不复杂的; 不精细的; 基本的: *unsophisticated tools, methods, designs* 简单的工具、方法、设计.

un·sound /ˌʌnˈsaʊnd; ʌnˈsaʊnd/ *adj* **1** in poor condition; weak 不健全的; 情况不佳的; 虚弱的: *The house roof was (structurally) unsound.* 这屋顶(结构)不牢固. ○ *His lungs were unsound.* 他的肺部不健康. **2** not free from defects or mistakes; flawed 有缺点的; 有错误的; 有缺陷的; 有瑕疵的: *unsound reasoning, judgement, advice* 不当的推理、判断、劝告 ○ *The findings of the research seem unsound.* 研究的结果似乎不确. **3** (idm 习语) **of ˌunsound ˈmind** (*law* 律) insane 精神错乱的.

un·spar·ing /ʌnˈspeərɪŋ; ʌnˈspɛrɪŋ/ *adj* **~ (in sth)** **1** giving freely and generously 慷慨的; 大方的: *be unsparing in one's efforts* 不遗余力. **2** severe or merciless 严厉的; 不留情的: *Nijinsky was unsparing in his demands for perfection.* 尼任斯基对演技精益求精一丝不苟.

▷ **un·spar·ingly** *adv* **1** generously 慷慨地; 大方地: *give unsparingly of one's time and money* 舍得花时间和金钱. **2** mercilessly 无情地; 残忍地: *He drove himself unsparingly.* 他强迫自己拼命干.

un·speak·able /ʌnˈspiːkəbl; ʌnˈspikəbḷ/ *adj* (*usu derog* 通常作贬义) that cannot be expressed in words; indescribable 不能以言语表达的; 难以言传的; 无法形容的: *unspeakable cruelty, behaviour, embarrassment* 难以形容的残忍、行为、尴尬 ○ *unspeakable joy, delight, etc* 说不出的快乐、喜悦等. ▷ **un·speak·ably** /-əblɪ; -əblɪ/ *adv*: *an unspeakably vile habit* 不可言状的坏习惯.

un·stable /ˌʌnˈsteɪbl; ʌnˈstebḷ/ *adj* **1** likely to move or fall; not firm 很可能移动或跌落的; 不稳的; 不坚固的: *an unstable load,* eg on a lorry 装得不稳的货物(如卡车上的) ○ *an unstable pile of chairs* 一堆放得不牢靠的椅子. **2** likely to change suddenly; unpredictable 很可能突然改变的; 难以预料的: *unstable share prices* 变化莫测的股票价格 ○ *The political situation is highly unstable.* 政局动荡得很厉害. **3** mentally or emotionally unbalanced (精神或情绪)不平衡的, 波动的: *His personality is a little unstable.* 他这个人有点反复无常.

un·steady /ˌʌnˈstedɪ; ʌnˈstɛdɪ/ *adj* (**-ier, -iest**) **1** not firm or secure 不坚固的; 不牢靠的; 不稳的: *Six whiskies made him unsteady on his feet.* 他喝了六杯威士忌就脚下不稳了. ○ *an unsteady hand, voice* 颤抖的手、声音 ○ *have an unsteady footing on the ladder* 在梯子上站得不稳. **2** not uniform or regular 不一贯的; 不一致的; 不规则的: *the candle's unsteady flame* 蜡烛的闪烁不定的火焰 ○ *His heartbeat/pulse was unsteady.* 他的心跳[脉搏]不规则. ▷ **un·stead·ily** /-ɪlɪ; -ɪlɪ/ *adv*: *wobble, tilt, rock, sway, etc unsteadily* 不稳定地摆动、倾倒、摇动、摇摆等. **un·steadi·ness** *n* [U].

un·stint·ing /ʌnˈstɪntɪŋ; ʌnˈstɪntɪŋ/ *adj* **~ (in sth)** giving freely and generously 慷慨的; 大方的: *unstinting generosity, support, praise* 无比的慷慨、大力的支持、高度的赞扬 ○ *She was unstinting in her efforts to help.* 她不遗余力地提供援助. **un·stint·ingly** *adj.*

un·stop /ˌʌnˈstɒp; ʌnˈstɑp/ *v* (**-pp-**) [Tn] remove a blockage from (a waste-pipe) 除去(污水管)的障碍: *unstop a sink, toilet, drain, etc* 疏通洗涤槽、抽水马桶、下水道等.

un·stop·pable /ʌnˈstɒpəbl; ʌnˈstɑpəbḷ/ *adj* (*esp infml* 尤作口语) that cannot be stopped or prevented 无法停止的; 不能防止的: *The Tories in their third term will be unstoppable.* 保守党势必接连第三届执政.

un·stuck /ˌʌnˈstʌk; ʌnˈstʌk/ *adj* **1** not stuck or glued on or together; detached 未粘住的; 未附着的; 松开的: *The (flap of the) envelope was unstuck.* 信封(的封口)没粘住. **2** (idm 习语) **ˌcome unˈstuck** (*infml* 口) be unsuccessful; fail 不成功; 失败: *His plan to escape came badly unstuck.* 他想逃走的打算完全吹了.

un·stud·ied /ˌʌnˈstʌdɪd; ʌnˈstʌdɪd/ *adj* natural and unaffected 自然而不做作的: *with ˌunstudied ˈelegance, ˈgrace, ˈcharm, etc* 以自然的文雅、优雅、魅力等.

un·sung /ˌʌnˈsʌŋ; ʌnˈsʌŋ/ *adj* (*fml* 文) not celebrated in poetry or song; unrecognized (在诗或歌中)未赞颂的; 未获承认的: *ˌunsung ˈheroes* 未受到颂扬的英雄 ○ *His exploits went unsung.* 他的英勇行为无人赏识.

un·sure /ˌʌnˈʃɔː(r); *US* -ˈʃʊər; ʌnˈʃʊr/ *adj* [pred 作表语] **1 ~ (of oneself)** having little self-confidence 缺乏自信心: *He's rather unsure of himself.* 他对自己没有什么信心. **2 ~ (about/of sth)** not having certain knowledge (about sth) (对某事)不确知, 无把握: *I'm unsure of the facts.* 我不能肯定事实是否如此. ○ *We were unsure (about) who was to blame.* 我们说不清该责怪谁.

un·sus·pect·ing /ˌʌnsəˈspektɪŋ; ˌʌnsəˈspɛktɪŋ/ *adj* feeling no suspicion; trusting 不怀疑的; 无猜疑的; 可信任的: *The murderer crept up on his unsuspecting victim.* 那个杀人凶手悄悄逼近毫无戒备之心的受害者.

un·swerv·ing /ʌnˈswɜːvɪŋ; ʌnˈswɝvɪŋ/ *adj* **~ (in sth)** steady or constant; unchanging 坚定的; 不改变的: *unswerving loyalty, devotion, belief, etc* 始终不渝的忠诚、奉献、信念等 ○ *He is unswerving in pursuit of his aims.* 他坚定地追求自己的目标.

un·tangle /ˌʌnˈtæŋgl; ʌnˈtæŋgḷ/ *v* [Tn, Tn·pr] free (sth) from knots, complexities, etc 解开(某物)的结; 使不再打结、不再紊乱等: *untangle knitting wool, electric flex* 解开缠结的毛线、电线 ○ *She untangled her hair from the hair-drier.* 她把搅在吹风机上的头发松开了. ○ (*fig* 比喻) *untangle a plot* 理出头绪 ○ *I can't untangle these accounts/figures.* 我算不清这些帐目[数字].

un·tapped /ˌʌnˈtæpt; ʌnˈtæpt/ *adj* not yet used or exploited 未使用的; 未开发的: *an untapped source of wealth, talent, inspiration* 未利用的财源、聪明才智、灵感 ○ *draw on untapped reserves of strength* 动用未曾用过的后备力量.

un·ten·able /ˌʌnˈtenəbl; ʌnˈtɛnəbḷ/ *adj* (of a theory, etc) that cannot be defended (指理论等)站不住脚的, 不堪一击的: *untenable arguments, claims, propositions, etc* 站不住脚的论据、要求、主张等 ○ *the untenable position of the Flat Earth Society* '地球平面说学会'的不堪一击的立论.

un·think·able /ˌʌnˈθɪŋkəbl; ʌnˈθɪŋkəbḷ/ *adj* too unlikely or undesirable to be considered; inconceivable (因绝少可能或极不可取)不必考虑的; 难以想像的; 不可思议的: *It is unthinkable that we should allow a nuclear* *holocaust to occur.* 我们若竟让核武器大屠杀的惨剧发生,简直是匪夷所思.

un·think·ing /ˌʌnˈθɪŋkɪŋ; ʌnˈθɪŋkɪŋ/ *adj* said, done, etc without proper consideration; thoughtless 考虑不周的; 未经思考的: *unthinking remarks, criticisms* 失慎的言语、批评 ○ *Unthinking, he threw his lighted match into the waste-paper basket.* 他想也没想就把燃着的火柴扔进了废纸篓里了. ▷ **un·think·ingly** *adv.*

un·tidy /ʌnˈtaɪdɪ; ʌnˈtaɪdɪ/ *adj* (**-ier, -iest**) not neat or orderly 不整齐的; 凌乱的: *an untidy desk, kitchen, cupboard, etc* 凌乱的书桌、厨房、橱柜等 ○ *untidy hair, writing* 蓬乱的头发、潦草的字迹 ○ *He's an untidy worker; he leaves his tools everywhere.* 他干活儿毫无条理, 工具随处乱扔. ▷ **un·ti·dily** /-ɪlɪ; -ɪlɪ/ *adv.* **un·ti·di·ness** *n* [U].

un·til /ənˈtɪl; ənˈtɪl/ (also **till**) (*till* more informal; *until* usu preferred in initial position ☆ till多用于口语; until通常用于句首) *conj* up to the time when 直到...时(为止): *Wait until the rain stops.* 等到雨停了再说吧. ○ *Don't leave till I arrive.* 我不来你不要离开. ○ *Continue in this direction until you see a sign.* 一直朝着这个方向走就看见指示牌了. ○ *Until she spoke I hadn't realized she was foreign.* 她要不说话我还一直不知道她是外国人. ○ *I won't stop shouting until you let me go.* 你不放我走我就一直喊叫. ○ *No names are being released until* (ie before) *the relatives have been told.* 只有在通知这些人的亲属以后才可透露其姓名.

▷ **un·til** (also **till**) *prep* (**a**) up to (a specified time) 直到(某一时刻): *wait until tomorrow* 等到明天 ○ *It may last till Friday.* 这可能要延续到星期五. ○ *Nothing happened until* (ie before) *5 o'clock.* 五点钟以前没有出现任何迹象. ○ *The street is full of traffic from morning till night.* 这条街从早到晚行人车辆很多. ○ *Until now I have always lived alone.* 我一直独自生活至今. ○ *I'd like to stay here up until Christmas.* 我想在这儿呆到圣诞节. (**b**) up to the time of (a specified event) 直到(发生某事): *The secret was never told until after the old man's death.* 这个秘密在老人去世后才说出来. ○ *Don't open it till your birthday.* 等到你过生日那天再打开. ○ *She was a bank clerk until the war, when she trained as a nurse.* 她战前是个银行职员, 战时受训当了护士.

un·timely /ʌnˈtaɪmlɪ; ʌnˈtaɪmlɪ/ *adj* **1** happening at an unsuitable time 不适时的; 不合时宜的: *an untimely arrival, remark, intervention* 不合时宜的到达、言语、干涉. **2** happening too soon or sooner than normal 过早的; 比正常情况早的: *her untimely death at 25* 她25岁时英年早逝. ▷ **un·time·li·ness** *n* [U].

un·tir·ing /ʌnˈtaɪərɪŋ; ʌnˈtaɪrɪŋ/ *adj* ~ (**in sth**) (*approv* 褒) continuing to work, etc at the same rate without showing tiredness 不知疲倦的; 坚持不懈的: *untiring campaigners for peace* 为争取和平不懈努力的人 ○ *She is untiring in her efforts to help the homeless.* 她帮助无家可归的人从不言倦. ▷ **un·tir·ingly** *adv.*

un·told /ˌʌnˈtəʊld; ʌnˈtold/ *adj* **1** not told 未说过的; 未叙述过的; 未透露的: *Her secret remains untold to this day.* 她的秘密至今仍未透露. **2** [attrib 作定语] (*esp derog* 尤作贬义) too many or too much to be counted, measured, etc 多得数不清或算不清的; 无数的; 无限的: *ˌuntold ˈsuffering, ˈdamage, ˈcruelty* 罄竹难书的苦难、损害、残忍 ○ *a man of ˌuntold ˈwealth* 腰缠万贯的男子 ○ *ˌuntold ˈthousands, ˈmillions, etc*, ie of pounds 数不清的以千、百万等计的(英镑).

un·touch·able /ʌnˈtʌtʃəbl; ʌnˈtʌtʃəbl/ *n, adj* (in India) (member) of a Hindu social class (caste) whose touch is regarded as defiling to other higher classes (印度的)不可接触的, 不可接触者(种姓制度中最低层的人).

un·to·ward /ˌʌntəˈwɔːd; *US* ʌnˈtɔːrd; ʌnˈtɔrd/ *adj* (*fml* 文) inconvenient or unfortunate; awkward 不便的; 不幸的; 造成困难的: *untoward incidents, developments, discoveries* 不妙的事情、变化状况、发现 ○ *I'll come if nothing untoward happens.* 我要是没有特殊情况一定来.

un·tram·melled (*US* also **-meled**) /ʌnˈtræmld; ʌnˈtræmḷd/ *adj* (*fml* 文) not hampered 不受阻碍的; 不受束缚的: *a life untrammelled by responsibilities* 无责任而一身轻的生活.

un·tried /ˌʌnˈtraɪd; ʌnˈtraɪd/ *adj* not yet tried or tested 未曾尝试的; 未经试验或检验的: *ˌuntried ˈproducts, ˈsystems, ˈmethods* 未经检验的产品、装置、方法.

un·true /ˌʌnˈtruː; ʌnˈtru/ *adj* **1** not true; contrary to fact 不真实的; 违反事实的; 假的. **2** ~ (**to sb/sth**) (*fml* 文) not loyal 不忠诚的; 不忠实的: *She was untrue* (ie unfaithful) *to him.* 她对他不忠实.

un·truth /ˌʌnˈtruːθ; ʌnˈtruθ/ *n* **1** [C] (*pl* **~s** /-ˈtruːðz; -ˈtruðz/) (*fml euph* 文, 婉) untrue statement; lie 谎言; 假话: *tell patent* (ie obvious) *untruths* 显然说谎. **2** [U] lack of truth 不真实; 虚假. ▷ **un·truth·ful** /ʌnˈtruːθfl; ʌnˈtruθfəl/ *adj.* **un·truth·fully** /-fəlɪ; -fəlɪ/ *adv.*

un·turned /ˌʌnˈtɜːnd; ʌnˈtɝnd/ *adj* (idm 习语) **leave no stone unturned** ⇨ LEAVE[1].

un·tutored /ˌʌnˈtjuːtəd; *US* -ˈtuː-; ʌnˈtutɚd/ *adj* (*fml or joc* 文或谑) untaught or untrained; unsophisticated 未受教导的; 未经训练的; 简单而自然的: *To my untutored ear, your voice sounds almost professional.* 照我这外行人听来, 你的嗓音差不多够专业水平了.

un·used[1] /ˌʌnˈjuːzd; ʌnˈjuzd/ *adj* never having been used 未曾使用过的: *an unused envelope, postage stamp* 未用过的信封、邮票.

un·used[2] /ˌʌnˈjuːst; ʌnˈjust/ *adj* [pred 作表语] **~ to sth/sb** unaccustomed to or unfamiliar with (sth/sb) 不习惯; 不熟悉: *The children are unused to city life/to living in a city.* 这些孩子不习惯城市生活.

un·usual /ʌnˈjuːʒl; ʌnˈjuʒəl/ *adj* **1** rare or exceptional 罕有的; 异乎寻常的: *This bird is an unusual winter visitor to Britain.* 这种鸟很少冬季到英国来. ○ *It's unusual for him to refuse a drink.* 给他酒他不喝, 这事可新鲜. **2** (*esp approv* 尤作褒义) remarkable because different; distinctive 独特的; 与众不同的: *The Lloyds building is nothing if not* (ie is very) *unusual.* 劳埃德大楼别具一格. ▷ **un·usu·ally** /-ʒəlɪ; -ʒəlɪ/ *adv* exceptionally or extremely 异常地; 极端地: *an unusually high rainfall for January* 一月份异常高的降雨量 ○ *Unusually for him, he wore a tie.* 他系了一条领带, 这可真少见.

un·ut·ter·able /ʌnˈʌtərəbl; ʌnˈʌtərəbḷ/ *adj* [attrib 作定语] (*fml* 文) too great, intense, etc to be expressed in words (因过大、过强烈等)无法用言语表达的: *unutterable pain, delight, boredom, relief, etc* 不可言状的痛苦、欢愉、厌倦、宽慰等 ○ *He's an unutterable bore.* 他这个人讨厌透了. ▷ **un·ut·ter·ably** /-əblɪ; -əblɪ/ *adv:* *unutterably foolish* 愚蠢透顶.

un·var·nished /ʌnˈvɑːnɪʃt; ʌnˈvɑrnɪʃt/ *adj* [attrib 作定语] **1** not varnished 未涂清漆的. **2** (*fig* 比喻) (of a statement, etc) basic or straightforward (指陈述等)不加修饰的, 基本的, 直率的: *the plain unvarnished truth* 直言无隐的实情 ○ *give an unvarnished account of what happened* 如实叙述发生的事.

un·veil /ˌʌnˈveɪl; ʌnˈvel/ *v* **1** [I, Tn] remove one's veil; remove a veil from (sth/sb) 除去面纱; 揭去(某物[某人])的面纱或遮盖物. **2** [Tn] (**a**) remove a cloth, etc from (sth), esp as part of a public ceremony 除去(某物)的幕布等; (尤指)为(某事物)揭幕: *unveil a statue, monument, plaque, portrait, etc* 揭去雕像、纪念碑、牌匾、肖像等的幕布. (**b**) show or announce (sth) publicly for the first time 首次公开、揭露或展示(某事物): *unveil new models at the Motor Show* 在汽车展览会上首次展出若干新型汽车 ○ *She unveiled her plans for reform.* 她首次公开了她的改革计划.

un·versed /ˌʌnˈvɜːst; ʌnˈvɝst/ *adj* **~ in sth** (*fml* 文) not experienced or skilled in sth 无经验的; 无技能的; 不熟练的: *foreigners unversed in the British way of life* 不熟悉英国生活方式的外国人 ○ *unversed in social etiquette* 不谙社交礼仪.

un·voiced /ˌʌnˈvɔɪst; ʌnˈvɔɪst/ *adj* (of thoughts, etc) not expressed or uttered (指想法等)未表达的, 未说出的: *an ˌunvoiced ˈprotest, ˈdoubt, suˈspicion* 内心的抗议、疑问、怀疑.

un·waged /ˌʌnˈweɪdʒd; ʌnˈwedʒd/ *adj* (*Brit euph* 婉) having no regular paid employment 无工资收入的; 无固定报酬的: *Unwaged members pay a lower entrance fee.* 无固定收入的人入场费从优. ▷ **the un·waged** *n* [pl v]: *half-price tickets for the unwaged* (无工资收入者用的)半价票.

un·wanted /ˌʌnˈwɒntɪd; ʌnˈwɑntɪd/ *adj* not wanted 不想要的; 无人要的; 不该有的: *an ˌunwanted ˈpregnancy* 不希望有的怀孕 ○ *feel unwanted* 觉得成为多余者.

un·war·rant·able /ʌnˈwɒrəntəbl; *US* -ˈwɔːr-; ʌnˈwɔrəntəbḷ/ *adj* (*fml* 文) unjustifiable 无正当理由的; 无法证明为正当的: *Their intrusion into our private lives is unwarrantable.* 他们侵扰我们的私生活是毫无道理的.

▷ **un·war·ran·ted** /ʌn'wɒrəntɪd; *US* -'wɔ:r-; ʌn'wɔrəntɪd/ *adj* unjustified or unauthorized 未证实为正当的; 未经授权的: *unwarranted fears, doubts, misgivings, etc* 不合情理的恐惧、怀疑、担忧等.

un·wary /ʌn'weərɪ; ʌn'wɛrɪ/ *adj* not cautious or aware of possible danger, etc; not vigilant 无警惕的; 不警觉的: *Pot-holes can be lethal for the unwary cyclist.* 路上的坑坑洼洼骑车的人一不小心就有致命危险. ▷ **the un·wary** *n* [pl *v*]: *Small print in documents can contain traps for the unwary.* 文件中的小号印刷字体可能藏有给粗心人设下的陷阱. **un·war·ily** /-ɪlɪ; -ɪlɪ/ *adv*. **un·wari·ness** *n* [U].

un·whole·some /ˌʌn'həʊlsəm; ʌn'holsəm/ *adj* **1** harmful to health or to moral well-being 不卫生的; 有害身心健康的: *an unwholesome climate* 有害健康的气候 ○ *unwholesome food* 不卫生的食物 ○ *unwholesome reading for a child* 对儿童身心健康有害的读物. **2** unhealthy-looking 看上去不健康的: *an unwholesome complexion* 不健康的面色.

un·wieldy /ʌn'wi:ldɪ; ʌn'wildɪ/ *adj* awkward to move or control because of its shape, size or weight (因形状、大小或重量的关系)不便移动或操纵的, 笨拙的, 不灵便的: *long, unwieldy punt poles* 长的、使用不便的撑船篙 ○ (*fig* 比喻) *the unwieldy bureaucracy of centralized government* 中央集权政府动转不灵的官僚体制. ▷ **un·wiel·di·ness** *n* [U].

un·will·ing /ʌn'wɪlɪŋ; ʌn'wɪlɪŋ/ *adj* not willing or inclined to do sth; reluctant 不愿意的; 不情愿的; 勉强的: *unwilling volunteers, victims, accomplices* 迫不得已的志愿者、牺牲者、从犯 ○ *my unwilling participation in the scheme* 我不得已参加这个计划 ○ *I was unwilling to co-operate without having more information.* 我不想在了解不足的情况下参与合作. ▷ **un·will·ingly** *adv*: *agree unwillingly to a request* 勉强答应一个要求.

un·wind /ˌʌn'waɪnd; ʌn'waɪnd/ *v* (*pt, pp* **unwound** /-'waʊnd; -'waund/) **1** [I, Tn, Tn·pr] **~ sth (from sth)** (cause sth to) become drawn out from a roll, ball, etc (使某物)从卷状或团状等展开; 解开(卷绕之物): *unwind a ball of string, a reel of thread, a roll of bandage, etc* 解开一团细绳、一卷线、一卷绷带等 ○ *He unwound the scarf from his neck.* 他从脖子上解下围巾. **2** [I] (*infml* 口) relax after a period of work or tension (工作或紧张之后)放松, 松弛: *Reading is a good way to unwind.* 阅读是休息的好方式. ○ *After a few drinks, he began to unwind,* ie to talk more freely. 他喝了几杯酒, 话就多起来了.

un·wise /ˌʌn'waɪz; ʌn'waɪz/ *adj* not wise; foolish 不聪明的; 不明智的; 愚蠢的: *an ˌunwise deˈcision, ˈmove, ˈstep, etc* 不智的决定、行动、步骤等 ○ *It was unwise (of you) to reject his offer.* (你)回绝他的好意, 这事办的可不聪明. ▷ **un·wisely** *adv*.

un·wit·ting /ʌn'wɪtɪŋ; ʌn'wɪtɪŋ/ *adj* [attrib 作定语] (*fml* 文) **1** not knowing or aware 不知道的; 未察觉的; 未意识到的: *an unwitting carrier of stolen goods* 不知就里而携赃物的人. **2** not intentional 无意的; 非故意的; 不知不觉的: *my unwitting interruption of their private conversation* 我无意中打断他们的私下谈话. ▷ **un·wit·tingly** *adv*: *If I offended you it was unwittingly.* 要是我冒犯了您, 也是无心之失.

un·wonted /ʌn'wəʊntɪd; ʌn'wontɪd/ *adj* (*fml* 文) not customary or usual 非惯常的; 不寻常的; 异常的; 罕见的: *an unwonted intrusion, interruption* 异乎寻常的闯入、打扰.

un·work·able /ˌʌn'wɜ:kəbl; ʌn'wɝkəbl/ *adj* not practical or feasible 不实用的; 不可行的; 行不通的: *an unworkable plan, proposal, scheme, etc* 不切实际的计划、建议、方案等.

un·worldly /ˌʌn'wɜ:ldlɪ; ʌn'wɝldlɪ/ *adj* spiritually-minded; not worldly 着重精神生活的; 非世俗的; 非尘世的; 超凡的: *an unworldly man, outlook, idealism* 超凡脱俗的男子、观点、理想主义. ▷ **un·world·li·ness** *n* [U].

un·worthy /ʌn'wɜ:ðɪ; ʌn'wɝðɪ/ *adj* **1** lacking worth or merit 无价值的; 没有优点的: *fighting for an unworthy cause* 为不值得的事而争斗. **2 ~ (of sth)** not deserving 不值得的; 不应得的: *trivia unworthy of your attention* 不值得您费心的琐事 ○ *I am unworthy of such an honour.* 我不配获得这样的荣誉. **3 ~ (of sb/sth)** not befitting the character of sb/sth 不适宜的; 不相称的: *conduct unworthy of a decent citizen* 正直的公民不应有的行为. ▷ **un·wor·thily** /-ɪlɪ; -ɪlɪ/ *adv*. **un·wor·thi·ness** *n* [U].

un·wound *pt, pp* of UNWIND.

un·writ·ten /ˌʌn'rɪtn; ʌn'rɪtn/ *adj* not written down 未写下的; 不成文的.

□ **an ˌunwritten ˈlaw/ˈrule** law/rule that is based on custom and practice, but is not written down 不成文法[规定].

un·yield·ing /ʌn'ji:ldɪŋ; ʌn'jildɪŋ/ *adj* **~ (in sth)** not giving way to pressure or influence, etc; firm (在压力和影响下)不弯曲或不让步的; 坚固的: *The mattress was hard and unyielding.* 这床垫很硬, 没有弹性. ○ (*fig* 比喻) *unyielding in her opposition to the plan* 她对该计划之坚决反对.

up /ʌp; ʌp/ *adv part* (For special uses with many *vs*, eg *pick sth up, wind sth up, screw sth up,* see the *v* entries 可与许多动词连用, 如 pick sth up、wind sth up、screw sth up, 其释义见各动词词条.) **1 (a)** to or in an upright position (esp one suggesting readiness for activity) 趋于或处于直立的姿势或位置(尤含准备活动之意): *I stood up to ask a question.* 我站起来提一个问题. ○ *He jumped up* (ie to a standing position) *from his chair.* 他突然从椅子上站了起来. Cf 参看 DOWN[1] 1. **(b)** not in bed 不在床上: *Is Peter up* (ie Has he got out of bed) *yet?* 彼得起床了吗? ○ *I was up late* (ie didn't go to bed until late) *last night.* 我昨天很晚才睡. ○ *It's time to get up!* 该起床了! ○ *I was up all night with a sick child.* 我陪伴着生病的孩子彻夜未眠. **2** to or in a higher place, position, condition, degree, etc 趋于或处于较高的地方、位置、条件、程度等: *Lift your head up.* 把头抬起来. ○ *Pull your socks up.* 加把劲儿. ○ *He lives three floors up.* 他住在往上数第三层楼. ○ *Prices are still going up,* ie rising. 物价仍在上涨. ○ *Put the packet up on the top shelf.* 把这个包放到架子顶格上去. ○ *The sun was coming up* (ie rising) *as we left.* 我们离开时, 太阳正在升起. ○ *We were two goals up* (ie ahead of the other team) *at half-time.* 我们在上半场赢了(领先于对方)两个球. Cf 参看 DOWN[1] 2. **3 ~ (to sb/sth)** so as to be close (to a specified person or thing) 靠近(某人或某物): *He came up (to me) and asked the time.* 他走到我跟前问我什么时间了. ○ *She went straight up to the door and knocked loudly.* 她径直走到门口重重地敲门. ○ *A car drove up and he got in.* 一辆汽车开来, 他上了车. **4 (a)** to or in an important place (esp a large city) 朝着重要地方或在重要地方(尤指大城市): *go up to London for the day* 今天上伦敦去 ○ *They're up in London.* 他们在伦敦. ○ [attrib 作定语] *The up train* (ie The train to London) *leaves every hour.* 上行火车(开往伦敦的火车)每小时一班. **(b)** (*Brit*) to or in a university (esp Oxford or Cambridge) 朝着大学或在大学(尤指牛津或剑桥): *She is going up to Oxford in October.* 她在十月份要上牛津大学. ○ *He's up at Cambridge.* 他在剑桥大学. **(c)** to or in the north of the country 朝着一国的北部; 在一国的北部: *We're going up to Edinburgh soon.* 我们不久就要到爱丁堡去了. ○ *They've moved up north,* ie to the north of England. 他们迁往北方(英格兰的北部)去了. ○ *She lives up in the Lake District.* 她住在北方的湖区. Cf 参看 DOWN[1] 3. **5** into pieces; apart 成碎片; 分离: *She tore the paper up.* 她把纸撕碎了. ○ *The road is up,* ie with the surface broken or removed while being repaired. 路面开了(修路时路面破开或除去). **6** (in phrasal verbs 用以构成短语动词) **(a)** completely 完全地; 彻底地: *We ate all the food up.* 我们把所有的东西都吃光了. ○ *The stream has dried up,* ie has become completely dry. 溪水已干涸. **(b)** securely 安全地; 稳妥地: *lock, fasten, stick, nail, etc sth up* 把某物锁住、系好、粘紧、钉牢等. **7** (*infml* 口) happening; going on (esp of sth unusual or unpleasant) 发生; 进行(尤指不寻常的或不愉快的事): *I heard a lot of shouting — what's up?* 我听见很多喊声 —— 出什么事了? ○ *I could tell something was up by the look on their faces.* 我一看他们的脸色就知道有事. **8** (idm 习语) **be on the ˌup-and-ˈup** (*infml* 口) **(a)** (*Brit*) be steadily improving, becoming more successful, etc 越来越好、越成功等; 蒸蒸日上: *Business is on the up-and-up.* 生意越做越大. **(b)** (*US*) be honest 诚实. **be up to sb (a)** be required as a duty or obligation from sb 是某人的职责或义务: *It's up to us to help those in need.* 我们有责任帮助那些有困难的人. ○ *It's not up to you to tell me how to do my job.* 我怎样干我的工作不用你来多嘴. **(b)** be left to sb to decide 由某人决定: *An Indian or a Chinese* *meal? It's up to you.* 吃印度饭菜还是吃中国饭菜? 由你决定吧. **be up with sb** be a source of discomfort, etc or a cause of illness, etc 是不舒适等的根源或疾病等的原因: *He's very pale. What's up with him?* 他脸色很苍白. 究竟怎么了? **not be 'up to much** not be worth much; not be very good 值不了多少; 不太好: *His work isn't up to much.* 他的作品不怎么样. **up against sth (a)** in close contact with sth; close to 与某物密切接触; 接近于: *The ladder is leaning up against the wall.* 那个梯子靠着墙呢. **(b)** (*infml* 口) faced with (problems, difficulties, etc) 面临(问题、困难等): *He came up against the local police.* 他跟地方警察惹上麻烦了. ○ *She's really up against it,* ie in great difficulties. 她现在非常困难. **ˌup and aˈbout; ˌup and ˈdoing** out of bed and active again (esp after illness) 下床恢复活动(尤指病愈后). **ˌup and ˈdown (a)** backwards and forwards; to and fro 上上下下; 前前后后: *walking up and down outside our house* 在我们的房子外面走来走去. **(b)** so as to rise and fall 起伏: *The boat bobbed up and down on/in the water.* 那小船在水面[水中]颠簸. **up before sb/sth** appearing in court (in front of a magistrate, etc) 上法庭(接受法官等审讯): *He was/came up before the magistrate for speeding.* 他因超速行车而出庭受审. ○ *His case was brought up before the court.* 他的案子已送交法庭审理. **up for sth (a)** being tried (for an offence, etc) (因某项过失等)受审: *up for speeding* 因超速行车而受审. **(b)** being considered for sth; on offer for sth 正被考虑; 提出供...: *The contract is up for renewal.* 该合同正考虑续订. ○ *The house is up for auction/sale.* 这所房子现供拍卖[出售]. **up to sth (a)** as a maximum number or amount 作为最大数量; 多达: *I can take up to four people in my car.* 我的汽车最多能坐四个人. ○ *count up to twenty slowly* 慢慢数到二十. **(b)** (also **up until sth**) not further or later than sth; as far as sth 不多于; 不迟于; 直到: *Read up to page 100.* 读到第100页. ○ *Up to now he's been quiet.* 他直到此刻仍保持沉默. ○ *Up until the war she had never lived alone.* 她在战争爆发前从未独自生活过. **(c)** comparable with sth 可与某事物相比: *It's not up to his usual standard.* 这次没达到他平时的水平. **(d)** capable of sth 有某种能力的; 能胜任: *He's not up to the part of Othello.* 他演不了奥赛罗这个角色. ○ *I don't feel up to going to work today.* 我今天不舒服, 不能上班. **(e)** (*infml* 口) occupied or busy with sth 正在做着或忙于某事物: *What's he up to?* 他忙什么呢? ○ *He's up to no good,* ie doing sth bad. 他现在没干好事. ○ *What tricks has she been up to* (ie playing)? 她搞什么鬼呢?

▷ **up** *prep* **1** to or in a higher position on (sth) 向着或在(某物)的较高处: *run up the stairs* 跑上楼 ○ *further up the valley* 向山谷高处 ○ *walk up* (ie along) *the road* 沿着路走 ○ *sail up a river,* ie against the current 向上游航行(逆流行驶). **2** (idm 习语) **up and down sth** backwards and forwards on sth 在某物上面来来去去: *walking up and down the platform* 在站台上走来走去. **ˌup ˈyours!** (*Brit* ⚠ *sl* 讳, 俚) (used to express extreme anger, disgust, annoyance, etc towards a person 用以表示对某人极端愤怒、厌恶、气恼等).

up *v* **(-pp-)** **1** [I] (*infml or joc* 口或谑) (followed by *and* and another *v* 后接and及另一动词) get or jump up; rouse oneself 起来; 跳起; 奋起: *She upped and left without a word.* 她一言不发站起来就走了. **2** [Tn] (*infml* 口) increase (sth) 增加(某事物): *up the price* 涨价 ○ *up an offer* 提高出价. **3** (idm 习语) **ˌup ˈsticks** move with all one's possessions to live and work in another place 携全部财产迁往另一处生活和工作.

up *n* **1** [sing] part of a ball's path in which it is still moving upwards after bouncing on the ground (球着地后的)弹起: *Try to hit the ball on the up.* 要在球弹起时击球. **2** (idm 习语) **ˌups and ˈdowns** alternate good and bad luck 幸运与不幸的交替: *He stuck by her through all life's ups and downs.* 他对她始终不渝, 同甘共苦.

□ **ˌup-and-ˈcoming** *adj* (*infml* 口) (of a person) making good progress; likely to succeed (esp in a career) (指人)进步很大的, 很可能成功的(尤指在事业上): *an ˌup-and-coming young ˈbarrister* 年轻有为的讼务律师.

up- *pref* 前缀 (with *ns, vs* and their related forms 与名词、动词及其相关形式结合) higher 更高: *upheaval* ○ *upland* ○ *upgrade.*

up·beat /ˈʌpbiːt; ˋʌpˌbit/ *n* (*music* 音) unaccented beat, esp at the end of a bar, shown by the conductor's baton moving upwards 上拍; 弱拍. Cf 参看 DOWNBEAT.

▷ **up·beat** *adj* (*fig* 比喻) optimistic or cheerful 乐观的; 快乐的.

up·braid /ˌʌpˈbreɪd; ʌpˋbred/ *v* [Tn, Tn·pr] **~ sb (for sth)** (*dated or fml* 旧或文) scold or reproach sb 责骂或申责某人: *upbraid sb for wrongdoing, incompetence, etc* 申斥某人干了坏事、不称职等.

up·bring·ing /ˈʌpbrɪŋɪŋ; ˋʌpˌbrɪŋɪŋ/ *n* (usu *sing* 通常作单数) treatment and education during childhood 儿童期的教养; 抚育; 养育: *a strict religious upbringing* 幼年时严格的宗教教育 ○ *The twins had different upbringings.* 这一对孪生儿幼时受的教育不同. ○ *Her country upbringing explains her love of nature.* 她是在乡村长大的, 所以非常热爱大自然.

up-country /ˌʌpˈkʌntrɪ; ˋʌpˋkʌntrɪ/ *adj, adv* (esp in large thinly-populated countries) in or towards the interior (尤指地广人稀的地区)在内地(的), 向内地(的): *ˌup-country ˈdistricts* 内陆区域 ○ *travel up-country* 往内地之行.

up·date /ˌʌpˈdeɪt; ʌpˋdet/ *v* **1** [Tn] bring (sth) up to date; modernize 更新(某事物); 使现代化: *update a dictionary, file, law* 修订词典、档案、法律 ○ *update production methods, computer systems* 更新生产方法、计算机设备. **2** [Tn, Tn·pr] **~ sb (on sth)** give sb the latest information (about sth) 向某人提供最新信息: *I updated the committee on our progress.* 我向委员会报告了我们的进展情况.

▷ **up·date** /ˈʌpdeɪt; ˋʌpdet/ *n* act of updating 更新; 现代化; 提供最新信息: *Maps need regular updates.* 地图需要经常修订. ○ *an update on the political situation* 对政局新的认识.

up-end /ˌʌpˈend; ʌpˋɛnd/ *v* [I, Tn] rise or set (sth) up on its end 上下颠倒着放(某物); 使(某物)倒立: *I up-ended the crate and sat on it.* 我把板条箱倒过来坐.

up·grade /ˌʌpˈɡreɪd; ˌʌpˋɡred/ *v* [Tn, Tn·pr] **~ sb/sth (to sb/sth)** raise sb/sth to a higher grade or rank 提高某人[某事物]的级别或等级: *She was upgraded to (the post of) sales director.* 她已提升为销售部主任. ○ *The consulate was upgraded to embassy status.* 该领事馆已升格为大使馆. Cf 参看 DOWNGRADE.

▷ **up·grade** /ˈʌpɡreɪd; ˋʌpˌɡred/ *n* (*US*) upward slope 向上的斜坡.

up·heaval /ʌpˈhiːvl; ʌpˋhivl̩/ *n* **(a)** sudden violent upward movement (突然而猛烈的)向上的运动: *volcanic upheavals* 火山的爆发. **(b)** (*fig* 比喻) sudden violent change or disturbance 激变; 剧变; 动乱: *political, social upheavals* 政治的、社会的动乱 ○ *Moving house causes such an upheaval.* 搬家引起了这么大的变化.

up·hill /ˌʌpˈhɪl; ˋʌpˋhɪl/ *adj* **1** sloping upwards; ascending 上坡的; 向上的: *an ˌuphill ˈroad, ˈclimb* 上坡路、向上的攀登 ○ *The last mile is all uphill.* 最后一英里全是上坡路. **2** [attrib 作定语] (*fig* 比喻) needing effort; difficult 费力的; 艰难的: *It's uphill work learning to ride.* 学骑马是件难事. ○ *an ˌuphill ˈtask/ˈstruggle* 艰巨的任务[斗争].

▷ **up·hill** *adv* up a slope 上坡: *walk uphill* 走上坡路.

up·hold /ˌʌpˈhəʊld; ʌpˋhold/ *v* (*pt, pp* **upheld** /-ˈheld; -ˋhɛld/) [Tn] **1** support (a decision, etc) against attack 维护, 支持(决定等): *uphold a verdict, policy, principle* 支持某项裁决、政策、原则. **2** maintain (a custom, etc) 维持, 保持(习俗等): *uphold ancient traditions* 保持古老的传统.

up·hol·ster /ˌʌpˈhəʊlstə(r); ʌpˋholstɚ/ *v* [Tn, Tn·pr] **~ sth (in/with sth)** provide (an armchair, etc) with padding, springs, fabric covering, etc 给(单座沙发等)装上垫子、弹簧、布面等: *upholster a sofa in leather* 给长沙发装上皮革面 ○ *upholstered in/with velvet* 装上天鹅绒面的.

▷ **up·hol·sterer** /-stərə(r); -stərɚ/ *n* person whose trade is to upholster furniture 家具装饰用品商.

up·hol·stery /-stərɪ; -stərɪ/ *n* [U] **1** trade of an upholsterer 家具装饰用品业. **2** materials used in this trade 家具装饰材料.

UPI /ˌjuː piː ˈaɪ; ˌju pi ˋaɪ/ *abbr* 缩写 = United Press International 合众国际社.

up·keep /ˈʌpkiːp; ˋʌpˌkip/ *n* [U] (cost or means of) keeping sth in good condition and repair; maintenance 保养; 维修; 养护; 维护费; 维修方法: *I can't afford the* *upkeep of a large house and garden.* 我负担不起带花园的大房子的维护费.

up·land /ˈʌplənd; ˋʌplənd/ *n* (often *pl* 常作复数) higher or inland parts of a country (一国的)高地, 内陆地区: *the barren upland(s) of central Spain* 西班牙中部的贫瘠高地 ○ [attrib 作定语] *an upland region* 高地区域.

up·lift /ˌʌpˈlɪft; ʌpˈlɪft/ *v* [Tn] (*usu fig* 通常作比喻) raise (sb/sth), esp spiritually, morally or emotionally 提高、抬高或鼓舞(某人[某事物])(尤指在精神、道德或情绪方面): *with uplifted hands* 双手高举着 ○ *an uplifting sermon* 鼓动人心的讲道.

▷ **up·lift** /ˈʌplɪft; ˋʌpˌlɪft/ *n* [U] spiritual, moral or emotionally elevating influence (精神、道德或情绪方面的)振作、振奋或提高: *Her encouragement gave me a great sense of uplift.* 她鼓励我激发了我的上进心.

up-market /ˌʌpˈmɑːkɪt; ˌʌpˋmɑrkət/ *adj* (of products, services, etc) designed to appeal to or satisfy people in the upper social classes (指商品、服务等)高级的, 高档的. Cf 参看 DOWN-MARKET.

upon /əˈpɒn; əˋpɑn/ *prep* **1** (*fml* 文) = ON[2] 1, 4b, 9, 10, 13. **2** (idm 习语) **once upon a time** ⇨ ONCE. **(almost) uˈpon him, them, us, etc** (of a time in the future) rapidly approaching (指将来的某一时刻)迅速接近: *Christmas is almost upon us again.* 圣诞节又快到了.

up·per /ˈʌpə(r); ˋʌpɚ/ *adj* [attrib 作定语] **1** higher in place or position; situated above another (esp similar) part (位置或地位)较高的; 位于另一(尤指相似的)部分之上的: *the upper lip, arm, jaw* 上唇、上臂、上颌 ○ *one of the upper rooms, floors, windows* 楼上的一个房间、上面的一层楼、上方的一个窗户 ○ *temperatures in the upper sixties*, ie between 65°F and 70°F 介于华氏65度至70度之间的温度. **2** situated on higher ground or to the north or far inland 位于高地的; 靠北的或深入内陆的: *Upper Egypt*, ie the part furthest from the Nile delta 上埃及地区(距尼罗河三角洲最远的部分) ○ *the upper (reaches of the) Thames* 泰晤士河的上游. **3** higher in rank or wealth 级别较高的; 较富有的: *the upper classes*, ie of society (社会的)上层阶级 ○ *salaries/people in the upper income bracket* 属高收入等级的薪金[人们]. Cf 参看 LOW[1] 3. **4** (idm 习语) **gain, get, etc the upper ˈhand (over sb)** get the advantage (over sb); control sb (较某人)处于有利地位; 占(某人的)上风; 控制某人: *Our team gained/had the upper hand in the second half.* 我们队在下半场占了上风. ○ *Don't let your feelings get the upper hand over you.* 不要感情用事. **a stiff upper lip** ⇨ STIFF. **the upper crust** (*infml or joc* 口或谑) the highest social class 社会的最高阶层: *belong to the upper crust* 属于上流社会.

▷ **up·per** *n* **1** part of a shoe or boot above the sole 鞋面; 靴面; 鞋帮. **2** (*infml* 口) drug that gives an exaggerated feeling of cheerfulness 兴奋剂. Cf 参看 DOWNER. **3** (idm 习语) **be on one's ˈuppers** (*infml* 口) have very little money 十分贫困.

□ ˌ**upper ˈcase** capital letters, esp in printing-type 大写字母(尤指印刷体): *titles set in upper case* 以大写字母排版的标题 ○ [attrib 作定语] ˌ*upper-case ˈtitles* 大写字母的标题.

the ˌUpper ˈChamber (also **the ˌUpper ˈHouse**) (in the British Parliament) the House of Lords (英国议会的)上议院.

ˈ**upper-cut** *n* (in boxing) punch delivered upwards with the arm bent (拳击中的)上钩拳.

up·per·most /ˈʌpəməʊst; ˋʌpɚˌmost/ *adj* highest in place or position or importance (位置或地位)最高的, 最上面的; 最重要的.

▷ **up·per·most** *adv* on or to the highest or most important position 向着或在最高或最重要的位置: *Store this side uppermost*, eg as a notice on a container. 此面朝上存放(如容器的标示用语). ○ *The children's future is always uppermost in my mind.* 孩子们的前途一向是我心中最重要的事.

up·pish /ˈʌpɪʃ; ˋʌpɪʃ/ *adj* (*infml* 口 *esp Brit*) (also *esp US* **uppity** /ˈʌpətɪ; ˋʌpətɪ/) self-assertive or arrogant 盛气凌人的; 傲慢的: *Don't get uppish with me, young lady!* 小姐, 别对我这么傲慢!

up·right /ˈʌpraɪt; ˋʌpˌraɪt/ *adj* **1** in a vertical position; erect 垂直的; 直立的; 竖直的: *his upright bearing/posture/stance* 他的笔直的姿势. **2** strictly honest or honourable 诚实的; 规矩的; 正直的: *an upright citizen* 正直的公民 ○ *be upright in one's business dealings* 规规矩矩地做生意. **3** (idm 习语) **bolt upright** ⇨ BOLT[3].

▷ **up·right** *adv* in or into an upright position (趋于)垂直地, 直立地: *sit, stand, hold oneself upright* 危坐、笔直地站着、保持直立姿势 ○ *pull the tent-pole upright* 把帐篷杆拉正.

up·right *n* **1** post or rod placed upright, esp as a support 垂直的柱子或杆子(尤指作支撑物的): *The ball bounced off the left upright of the goal.* 球碰到左侧球门柱后弹开. **2** = UPRIGHT PIANO.

up·right·ness *n* [U].

□ ˌ**upright piˈano** (also **upright**) piano with the strings arranged vertically 竖式钢琴. ⇨illus at App 1 见附录1插图, page xi.

up·ris·ing /ˈʌpraɪzɪŋ; ˋʌpˌraɪzɪŋ/ *n* revolt against those in power; rebellion 起义; 暴动: *an armed uprising* 武装起义.

up·roar /ˈʌprɔː(r); ˋʌpˌrɔr/ *n* [U, sing] (outburst of) noise and excitement or anger; tumult 喧嚣; 骚动; 吵闹: *The meeting ended in (an) uproar.* 会议以大吵大闹收场. ○ *There was (an) uproar over the tax increases.* 税款增加引起了鼓噪. ▷ **up·roari·ous** /ʌpˈrɔːrɪəs; ʌpˋrɔrɪəs/ *adj* [esp attrib 尤作定语] **(a)** very noisy or high-spirited 喧嚣的; 骚动的; 热闹的: *an uproarious welcome, evening, debate* 热烈的欢迎、晚会、辩论 ○ *They burst into uproarious laughter.* 他们哄然大笑. **(b)** very funny 非常有趣的: *uproarious jokes, disguises, mistakes* 令人捧腹的笑话、化装、错误. **up·roari·ously** *adv*: *shout uproariously* 大声地呼喊 ○ *uproariously funny* 极其滑稽.

up·root /ˌʌpˈruːt; ʌpˋrut/ *v* **1** [Tn esp passive 尤用于被动语态] pull (a tree, plant, etc) out of the ground together with its roots 将(树、花草等)连根拔起. **2** [Tn, Tn·pr] **~ sb/oneself (from sth/...)** (*fig* 比喻) force sb/oneself to leave a place where he/one was born or has become settled 迫使某人[自己]离开出生地或定居处: *She uprooted herself from the farm and moved to London.* 她别井离乡从农场搬到伦敦.

up·set /ˌʌpˈset; ʌpˋsɛt/ *v* (**-tt-** *pt, pp* **upset**) **1** [I, Tn] (cause sth to) become overturned or spilt, esp accidentally 打翻, 弄翻(某物)(尤指无意地): *upset one's cup, the milk, a plate of biscuits* 弄翻了自己的杯子、牛奶、一盘饼干 ○ *A large wave upset the boat.* 一个巨浪打翻了船. **2** [Tn] disrupt (a plan, etc) 打乱, 扰乱(计划等): *upset the balance of trade* 打破贸易平衡 ○ *Our arrangements for the weekend were upset by her visit.* 她一来把我们周末的安排给打乱了. ○ *Fog upset the train timetable.* 这场大雾搅乱了火车的班次. **3** [Tn] **(a)** distress the mind or feelings of (sb) 使(某人)苦恼或心烦: *be emotionally upset* 心烦意乱 ○ *Don't upset yourself — no harm has been done.* 不要难过——并没有造成伤害. ○ *The sight of physical suffering always upsets me.* 我看到身体受折磨的情形总是心惊肉跳. ○ *He was upset at not being invited.* 人家没邀请他, 他很不痛快. **(b)** cause (sb) to feel ill by disturbing his digestion 使(某人)感到肠胃不适: *Cheese often upsets her/her stomach.* 她吃乳酪后常常感到不舒服[肠胃不适]. **4** (idm 习语) **upset the/sb's ˈapplecart (a)** spoil a plan or disrupt an arrangement 打乱计划或安排: *Her refusal to help quite upset the applecart.* 她不肯帮忙, 计划也就落空了. **(b)** disprove a theory 推翻一理论或说法. ▷ **up·set** /ˈʌpset; ˋʌpˌsɛt/ *n* **1** [U, C] upsetting or being upset 翻倒; 扰乱; 不安: *Last-minute changes caused a great deal of upset.* 出现的临时变动造成一片混乱. ○ *She had a major emotional upset.* 她情绪上受到了沉重的打击. **2** [C] stomach disorder 肠胃不适: (*infml* 口) *in bed with a tummy upset* 因肠胃不适而卧床. **3** (in sport) unexpected result (运动)出乎意料的结局或成绩.

up·shot /ˈʌpʃɒt; ˋʌpˌʃɑt/ *n* [sing] **the ~ (of sth)** the final result or outcome 最后结果; 结局: *The upshot of it all was that he resigned.* 结果他辞职了.

upside-down /ˌʌpsaɪd ˈdaʊn; ˋʌpˌsaɪdˋdaʊn/ *adj, adv* **1** with the upper part underneath instead of on top 上下翻转过来(的): *That picture is upside-down.* 那幅画上下颠倒了. ○ *hold a book upside-down* 倒拿着书. **2** (*infml fig* 口, 比喻) in or into total disorder or confusion 乱七八糟(的); 毫无条理(的): *He has an upside-down way of doing things*, eg he deals with priorities last. 他做事毫无条理. ○ *Burglars had turned the house upside-down.* 窃贼

把房子翻得乱七八糟.

up·stage /ˌʌpˈsteɪdʒ; ˋʌpˋstedʒ/ *adj, adv* **1** at or towards the back of a theatre stage 在或向舞台后部(的): *an ˌupstage ˈdoor* 舞台后门 ○ *move upstage* 向舞台后部移动. **2** (*infml* 口) snobbish(ly) 势利(的); 谄上欺下(的): *They're much too upstage for us these days.* 他们近来对我们太势利了.

▷ **up·stage** *v* [Tn] **1** cause (an actor) to face away from the audience by moving nearer the back of the stage than him (自己向舞台后部移动)使(另一演员)无法面向观众. **2** (*fig* 比喻) divert attention from (sb) towards oneself; put at a disadvantage 将他人注意力从(某人)引向自己; 使处于不利地位: *He upstaged the other speakers by illustrating his talk with slides.* 他演讲中配上幻灯片, 比其他演讲人更吸引听众.

up·stairs /ˌʌpˈsteəz; ˋʌpˋstɛrz/ *adv* **1** up the stairs; to or on an upper floor 向楼上; 往楼上; 在楼上: *walk, leap, sleep upstairs* 走上楼、蹦跳着上楼、在楼上睡觉 ○ *I was upstairs when it happened.* 这件事发生时我正在楼上. Cf 参看 DOWNSTAIRS. **2** (idm 习语) **kick sb upstairs** ⇨ KICK[1].

▷ **up·stairs** *adj* situated on, living on or belonging to an upper floor 位于楼上的; 住在楼上的; 属于楼上的: *an ˌupstairs ˈroom, ˈwindow* 楼上的房间、窗户 ○ *the families upstairs/the ˌupstairs ˈfamilies* 楼上的住户.

up·stairs *n* [sing] (*infml* 口) upper floor of a house, etc 房屋等的上层; 楼上: *A bungalow does not have an upstairs.* 平房没有上层.

up·stand·ing /ˌʌpˈstændɪŋ; ʌpˋstændɪŋ/ *adj* [attrib 作定语] (*fml or rhet* 文或修辞) **1** strong, healthy and vigorous 强健而有活力的: *a fine upstanding figure of a man* 一个男子的强健、匀称的体格. **2** decent and honest 正派而诚实的: *upstanding members of the city council* 市议会的正派而诚实的议员们.

up·start /ˈʌpstɑːt; ˋʌpˌstɑrt/ *n* (*derog* 贬) person who has suddenly risen to wealth or a high position, esp one who behaves arrogantly and causes resentment 突然发迹者, 新贵, 暴发户(尤指傲慢令人反感者): *You can't marry that young upstart!* 你可不能嫁给那个年轻的暴发户! ○ [attrib 作定语] *upstart bureaucrats, financiers, officials, etc* 突然发迹的官僚、金融家、官员等.

up·stream /ˌʌpˈstriːm; ˋʌpˋstrim/ *adv, adj* in the direction from which a river, etc flows; against the current 向上游(的); 逆流(的): *row, swim, walk upstream* 往上游划、游、行走 ○ *Factories upstream (from us) are polluting the water.* 在(我们)上游的工厂污染了河水. Cf 参看 DOWNSTREAM.

up·surge /ˈʌpsɜːdʒ; ˋʌpˌsɝdʒ/ *n* (usu *sing* 通常作单数) **(a)** ~ **(in sth)** sudden increase in sth; rise 急剧增长; 上升: *an upsurge in sales, costs, investments* 销售额、费用、投资额的猛增. **(b)** ~ **(of sth)** sudden rush, esp of feeling 激发; (尤指感情的)突发: *an upsurge of anger, enthusiasm, violence* 愤怒、热情、暴力行为的爆发 ○ *an upsurge of interest in the environment* 对环境问题突然发生的兴趣.

up·swing /ˈʌpswɪŋ; ˋʌpˌswɪŋ/ *n* ~ **(in sth)** (esp sudden) upward movement or trend; improvement (尤指突然的)向上的运动或倾向; 上涨; 改进: *This policy led to an upswing in the party's popularity.* 这一政策使该党深得人心. Cf 参看 UPTURN.

up·take /ˈʌpteɪk; ˋʌpˌtek/ *n* (idm 习语) **ˌquick/ˌslow on the ˈuptake** quick/slow to understand what is meant 理解力强[弱]; 领会快[慢]: *You'll have to explain it to me carefully — I'm not very quick on the uptake.* 你得给我仔细解释一下 — 我理解力差.

up·tight /ˌʌpˈtaɪt; ˌʌpˈtaɪt/ *adj* ~ **(about sth)** (*infml* 口) **1** nervously tense 精神紧张的: *get uptight about exams, interviews, etc* 对考试、面试等十分紧张. **2** annoyed or hostile 恼怒的; 有敌意的: *Offers of help just make him uptight.* 主动帮助他反而惹他生气. **3** (*US*) rigidly conventional 因循守旧的.

up-to-date /ˌʌp tə ˈdeɪt; ˋʌptəˋdet/ *adj* [attrib 作定语] **1** modern or fashionable 现代的; 新式的: *ˌup-to-date ˈclothes, iˈdeas, ˈbooks* 新潮衣物、新思想、最新图书. **2** having or including the most recent information 包含最新信息的: *an ˌup-to-date ˈdictionary, reˈport* 最新的词典、报告.

up-to-the-minute /ˌʌp tə ðə ˈmɪnɪt; ˌʌptəðəˋmɪnɪt/ *adj* [attrib 作定语] **1** very modern or fashionable; very up-to-date 最现代化的; 最新式的. **2** having or including the most recent information possible 包含最新信息的: *an ˌup-to-the-minute acˌcount of the ˈriots* 关于骚乱的最新报道.

up·town /ˌʌpˈtaʊn; ˋʌpˋtaʊn/ *adj, adv* (*US*) in or to the outer residential districts of a town 位于或向着市镇外围住宅区(的): *uptown New York* 纽约的城外住宅区 ○ *go, drive, stay uptown* 往、开车去、呆在城外住宅区. Cf 参看 DOWNTOWN.

up·turn /ˈʌptɜːn; ˋʌpˌtɝn/ *n* ~ **(in sth)** upward trend in business, fortune, etc; improvement (生意、运气等)好转; 改进: *an upturn in the sales figures* 销售额的增长 ○ *Her luck seems to have taken an upturn/to be on the upturn.* 她似乎时来运转了. Cf 参看 UPSWING.

▷ **up·turned** /ˌʌpˈtɜːnd; ˌʌpˋtɝnd/ *adj* turned upwards or upside-down 向上翘的; 上下翻转过来的: *a slightly ˌupturned ˈnose* 稍微朝上翘的鼻子 ○ *She felt drops of rain on her ˌupturned ˈface.* 她感到有雨点落在她仰着的脸上. ○ *sitting on an ˌupturned ˈcrate* 坐在翻转过来的板条箱上.

up·ward /ˈʌpwəd; ˋʌpwɚd/ *adj* [usu attrib 通常作定语] moving, leading or pointing to what is higher, more important, etc 移向、引向或指向较高、较重要等之处的; 上升的; 向上的: *an upward glance, climb* 向上的一瞥、攀登 ○ *the upward trend in prices* 物价的上涨趋势.

▷ **up·ward** (also **up·wards** /-wədz; -wɚdz/) *adv* towards what is higher 向上地; 上升地: *The missile rose upward into the sky.* 导弹已升入天空. ○ *The boat floated bottom upwards,* ie upside-down. 那船底朝天漂着. ⇨ Usage at FORWARD[2] 用法见 FORWARD[2].

up·wards of *prep* more than (a number) 超过(某数): *Upwards of a hundred people came to the meeting.* 有一百多人来参加会议.

□ **ˌupward moˈbility** movement into a higher and wealthier social class 向较高和较富有的社会阶层的流动. **ˌupwardly ˈmobile** ready and able to move in this way 能向较高社会地位和经济地位流动的: *upwardly mobile young executives* 能升迁的年轻行政人员.

up·wind /ˌʌpˈwɪnd; ʌpˋwɪnd/ *adj, adv* ~ **(of sb/sth)** in the direction from which the wind is blowing 上风向的; 逆风的; 顶风的: *If we're upwind of the animal it may smell our scent.* 要是我们处于那动物的上风位置, 它就能闻到我们的气味.

ur·anium /jʊˈreɪnɪəm; jʊˋrenɪəm/ *n* [U] chemical element, a heavy grey radioactive metal used as a source of nuclear energy 铀. ⇨ App 10 见附录 10.

urban /ˈɜːbən; ˋɝbən/ *adj* [usu attrib 通常作定语] of, situated in or living in a city or town 市镇的; 位于市镇的; 住在市镇的: *urban areas* 市区 ○ *the urban population* 城市人口 ○ *urban renewal,* ie the renovation of old buildings, etc 城市更新(旧建筑物等的整修) ○ *urban guerrillas,* ie terrorists operating in urban areas by kidnapping, etc 城市游击队员(进行绑架等的). Cf 参看 RURAL.

▷ **urb·an·ize, -ise** /-aɪz; -ˌaɪz/ [Tn esp passive 尤用于被动语态] change (esp a rural place) into a town-like area 使(尤指农村地区)城市化. **urb·an·iza·tion, -isation** /ˌɜːbənaɪˈzeɪʃn; *US* -nɪˈz-; ˌɝbənɪˋzeʃən/ *n* [U].

ur·bane /ɜːˈbeɪn; ɝˋben/ *adj* (*fml sometimes derog* 文, 有时作贬义) having or showing refined manners, smooth elegance and sophistication 有礼貌的; 温文尔雅的; 老于世故的: *an urbane man, wit, smile, conversation* 彬彬有礼的男子、风趣的人、微笑、交谈. ▷ **ur·banely** *adv.* **ur·ban·ity** /ɜːˈbænətɪ; ɝˋbænətɪ/ *n* [U, C].

ur·chin /ˈɜːtʃɪn; ˋɝtʃɪn/ *n* **1 (a)** (*esp dated* 尤作旧) mischievous or naughty child, esp a boy 顽童, 淘气鬼(尤指男孩): *You little urchin!* 你这个小淘气! **(b)** (also **ˈstreet-urchin**) ragged or dirty child who is homeless and lives in poverty 街头流浪儿. **2** = SEA-URCHIN (SEA).

Urdu /ˈʊəduː; ˋʊrdu/ *adj, n* [U] (of the) language related to Hindi but with many Persian words, used esp in Pakistan 乌尔都语(与印地语有共同处, 但含许多波斯语词, 尤使用于巴基斯坦).

-ure *suff* 后缀 **1** (with *vs* forming *ns* 与动词结合构成名词) action or process of ...的动作或过程: *closure* ○ *failure* ○ *seizure.* **2** (with *vs* or *ns* forming *ns* 与动词或名词结合构成名词) group or thing having a specific function 有某功能的团体或事物: *legislature* ○ *prefecture.*

urea /jʊəˈrɪə; *US* ˈjʊrɪə; ˋjʊrɪə/ *n* [U] white soluble

U

crystalline compound contained esp in the urine of mammals 脲; 尿素.

ureter /jʊəˈriːtə(r); juˋritɚ/ *n* either of the two tubes by which urine passes from the kidneys to the bladder 输尿管.

ur·ethra /jʊəˈriːθrə; juˋriθrə/ *n* (*pl* 复数作 **~s** or, in scientific use, 科技用语复数作 **-rae** /-riː; -ri/) (*anatomy* 解) tube by which urine passes from the bladder out of the body 尿道. ⇨illus at MALE 见 MALE 插图.

urge /ɜːdʒ; ɝdʒ/ *v* **1** [Tn·pr, Tn·p, Cn·t] drive forcibly or hurry (a horse, etc) in a certain direction 驱赶, 驱策(马等): *urge a pony into a canter, up a slope* 驱策小马慢跑、上斜坡 ○ *urge one's mount on, forward, north* 策马继续前进、向前、朝北走 ○ *She urged her mare to jump the fence.* 她策马跳过障碍物. **2** [Tn, Tf, Tg, Tsg, Cn·t] try earnestly or persistently to persuade (sb) 诚恳地或持续地催促(某人): *'Don't give in now,' she urged.* '先别认输,' 她鼓励道. ○ *He urged that we should go/urged (our) going/urged us to go.* 他催我们走. **3** [Tn, Tn·pr, Cn·t] **~ sth (on/upon sb/sth)** recommend sth strongly with reasoning or entreaty 竭力推荐或力陈某事物: *We urged caution.* 我们特别提出要小心谨慎. ○ *The government urged on industry the importance of low pay settlements.* 政府向工商业界强调解决低工资问题的重要性. ○ *Motoring organizations are urging drivers not to travel by road if possible.* 机动车协会劝告开车的人暂时不要使用公路. **4** (phr v) **urge sb on** encourage or stimulate sb to do sth 鼓励或激励某人做某事: *The manager urged his staff on (to greater efforts).* 经理督促职员更加努力. ○ *Urged on by his colleagues, he stood for election.* 他受到同事的鼓励而参加竞选. ○ *The need to find a solution urged him on.* 亟须找出解决方法, 这是鞭策他的动力.
▷ **urge** *n* strong desire or impulse 强烈的欲望或冲动: *sexual urges* 性欲冲动 ○ *get, have, feel, give in to a sudden urge to travel* 心血来潮去旅行.

ur·gent /ˈɜːdʒənt; ˋɝdʒənt/ *adj* **1** needing immediate attention, action or decision 需立即注意、行动或决定的; 紧急的; 迫切的: *an urgent message, case, cry for help* 紧急的消息、情况、呼救 ○ *It is most urgent that we operate.* 咱们得马上动手术. ○ *My car is in urgent need of repair.* 我的汽车急需修理. **2** showing that sth is urgent; persistent in one's demands 催促的; 坚持要求的: *speak in an urgent whisper* 低声催促. ▷ **ur·gency** /-dʒənsɪ; -dʒənsɪ/ *n* [U]: *a matter of great urgency* 紧急的事 ○ *I detected a note of urgency in her voice.* 我从她声音中察觉到情况紧急. **ur·gently** *adv*: *Ambulance drivers are urgently needed.* 急需救护车司机.

uric /ˈjʊərɪk; ˋjʊrɪk/ *adj* [attrib 作定语] of urine 尿的: *uric acid* 尿酸.

ur·ine /ˈjʊərɪn; ˋjʊrɪn/ *n* [U] waste liquid that collects in the bladder and is passed from the body 尿.
▷ **ur·inal** /ˈjʊərɪnl *or, in British use,* 英式英语读作 jʊəˈraɪnl; ˋjʊrənl̩/ *n* building, place or receptacle for (esp) men and boys to urinate in (尤指男子用的)小便处, 小便器, 尿壶.
ur·in·ary /ˈjʊərɪnərɪ; *US* -nerɪ; ˋjʊrə,nɛrɪ/ *adj* [usu attrib 通常作定语] of urine or the parts of the body through which it passes 尿的; 泌尿的; 泌尿器的: *urinary infections, organs* 泌尿器感染、泌尿器.
ur·in·ate /ˈjʊərɪneɪt; ˋjʊrə,net/ *v* [I] pass urine from the body 排尿; 撒尿.

urn 瓮

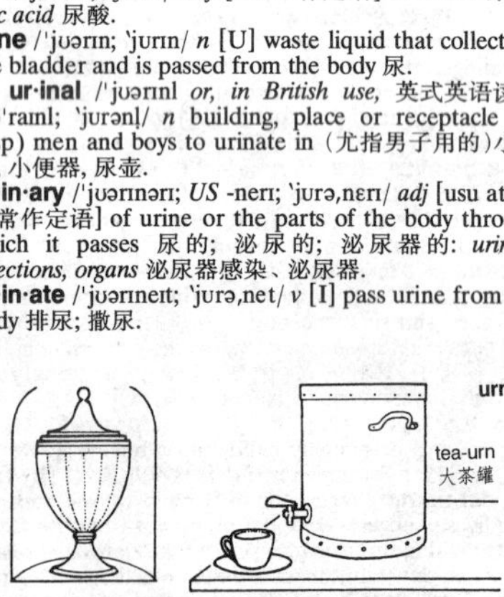

urn /ɜːn; ɝn/ *n* **1** tall vase, usu with a stem and a base, esp one used for holding the ashes of a cremated person 瓮; (尤指)骨灰瓮. **2** (esp in compounds 尤用以构成复合词) large metal container with a tap, in which tea, coffee, etc is made or from which it is served, eg in cafés or canteens (供应茶、咖啡等的)有龙头的金属容器(如小餐馆或食堂中的): *a tea urn* 茶桶. ⇨illus 见插图.

us /əs; əs *strong form* 强读式 ʌs; ʌs/ *pers pron* (used as the object of a *v* or of a *prep*; also used independently and after *be* 用作动词或介词的宾语; 亦可单独使用, 用于be之后) me and another or others; me and you 我们; 咱们: *She gave us a washing-machine.* 她送给我们一台洗衣机. ○ *We'll take the dog with us.* 我们要带着那条狗去. ○ *Hello, it's us back again!* 喂, 是我们回来了! Cf 参看 WE.

US /ˌjuː ˈes; ˌju ˋɛs/ *abbr* 缩写 = **1** United States (of America): *a US citizen* 美国公民. **2** (also **u/s**) (*infml* 口) unserviceable (ie useless): *This pen's US. Give me one that writes.* 这枝钢笔不能用了. 给我一枝能写的.

USA /ˌjuː es ˈeɪ; ˌju ɛs ˋe/ *abbr* 缩写 = **1** (*US*) United States Army 美国陆军. **2** (esp in addresses) United States of America (尤用于地址)美利坚合众国.

USAF /ˌjuː es eɪ ˈef; ˌju ɛs e ˋɛf/ *abbr* 缩写 = United States Air Force 美国空军.

us·age /ˈjuːsɪdʒ, ˈjuːzɪdʒ; ˋjusɪdʒ, ˋjuzɪdʒ/ *n* **1** [U] manner of using sth; treatment 用法; 处理; 对待: *The tractor had been damaged by rough usage.* 这辆拖拉机因使用不经心而损坏了. **2** [U, C] habitual or customary practice, esp in the way words are used 习惯; 惯例; (尤指)词语惯用法: *English grammar and usage* 英语的语法和惯用法 ○ *Languages develop continually through usage.* 语言在使用中不断发展. ○ *It's not a word in common usage.* 这个词不是个普通常用词. ○ *A dictionary helps one to distinguish correct and incorrect usages.* 词典可用以辨识遣词造句的正误.

use[1] /juːz; juz/ *v* (*pt, pp* **used** /juːzd; juzd/) **1** [Tn, Tn·pr, Tnt, Cn·n/a] **~ sth (for sth/doing sth)**; **~ sth (as sth)** employ sth for a purpose; bring sth into service 用; 使用; 运用; 利用: *Do you know how to use a lathe?* 你会使用车床吗? ○ *Use your common sense!* 用用你的常识吧! ○ *If you don't use* (ie practise) *your English you'll forget it.* 英语不用就容易忘. ○ *May I use your phone?* 我用一下您的电话行吗? ○ *A hammer is used for driving in nails.* 锤子是用来钉钉子的. ○ *She uses her unmarried name for professional purposes.* 她处理业务时使用娘家姓氏. ○ *I use my bike for (going) shopping.* 我买东西时骑自行车去. ○ *We used the money to set up an irrigation project.* 我们把钱用在兴建灌溉工程上了. ○ *They used force to persuade him.* 他们用武力逼他就范. ○ *May I use your name as a reference?* ie May I quote it, eg when I apply for a job? 我可以请您作我的荐举人吗? (我可否在求职信中把您的名字列入其中?) **2** [Tn] (*fml* 文) treat (sb) in a specified way; behave towards (以某种方式)对待(某人): *use one's friends well* 善待朋友 ○ *He has used her shamefully.* 他待她之坏, 人所不齿. ○ *He thinks himself ill-used*, ie considers that he is badly treated. 他认为遭到虐待. **3** [Tn, Cn·n/a] **~ sb/sth (as sth)** exploit sb/sth selfishly 自私地利用某人[某事物]: *He felt used by her.* 他觉得受她利用了. ○ *She simply used us for her own ends/to get what she wanted.* 她完全是为了自己的目的而利用我们. ○ *He used the bad weather as an excuse for not coming.* 他拿天气不好作不来的借口. **4** [Tn, Tn·pr] consume (sth) 消耗, 消费(某物): *Use the milk sparingly, there's not much left.* 少用些牛奶, 剩下的不多了. ○ *The car used a gallon of petrol for the journey.* 汽车在路上消耗了一加仑汽油. **5** [Tn] (*infml* 口) **(a)** take (drugs) 服(药). **(b)** (*US*) smoke (cigarettes, etc) 吸(烟等). **6** (idm 习语) **I, etc could use a ˈdrink, etc** (*infml* 口) I, etc would very much like a drink, etc 我…很想喝酒、做某事: *Boy, could I use a hot bath!* 啊, 我真想洗个热水澡! **use one's loaf** (*infml* 口) think effectively; use one's intelligence 好好想想; 动动脑筋. **7** (phr v) **use sth up (a)** use (material, etc) until no more is left; find a use for (remaining material or time) 用尽(材料等); 设法利用(剩余的材料或时间): *I've used up all the glue.* 我把胶水全用光了. ○ *She used up the chicken bones to make soup.* 她把鸡骨头全用来熬汤了. **(b)** exhaust or tire sth out 耗尽某事物; 使某事物衰竭: *use up all one's strength, energy, etc* 耗尽了体力、精力等.
▷ **us·able** /ˈjuːzəbl; ˋjuzəbl̩/ *adj* [pred 作表语] that can be used; that is fit to be used 可使用; 合用; 适用: *This tyre is so worn that it is no longer usable.* 这条轮胎磨损得很厉害, 不能再用了.

use[2] /juːs; jus/ *n* **1** [U, sing] **~ (of sth)** using or being used 用；使用；运用；利用：*the use of electricity for heating* 利用电力供热 ○ *learn the use of a lathe* 学习使用车床 ○ *an ingenious use of wind power* 巧妙利用风力 ○ *the use of force, terrorism, blackmail, etc* 使用武力、恐怖手段、敲诈伎俩等 ○ *keep sth for one's own use* 保留某物以自用 ○ *funds for use in emergencies* 应急基金 ○ *The ointment is for external use only*, eg It must not be swallowed. 此药膏仅供外用. ○ *bought for use, not for ornament* 为使用购买，非为装饰用途 ○ *The lock has broken through constant use.* 这把锁经常使用已经坏了. **2** [C, U] purpose for which sth is used; work that a person or thing is able to do 用途；功能：*a tool with many uses* 有多种用途的工具 ○ *find a (new) use for sth* 研究出某物的(新)用途. **3** [U] **~ (of sth) (a)** right to use sth 使用权：*allow a tenant the use of the garden* 准许房客使用花园 ○ *I have the use of the car this week.* 这辆汽车本星期归我使用. **(b)** power of using sth 使用的能力：*have full use of one's faculties* 充分发挥才能 ○ *lose the use of one's legs*, ie become unable to walk 失去腿部功能. **4** [U] value or advantage; usefulness 价值；益处；效用：*What's the use of worrying about it?* 着急有什么用呢？○ *It's no use pretending you didn't know.* 你装糊涂是无济于事的. ○ *You're no use in the choir — you can't sing a note!* 你对合唱团毫无益处——你简直唱不成调！○ *Recycled materials are mostly of limited use.* 再生材料大多用途有限. **5** [U] (*fml* 文) custom, practice or habit; usage(2) 习惯；惯例；词语的惯用法：*Long use has accustomed me to it.* 我对此已习惯成自然. **6** (idm 习语) **ˌcome into/ˌgo out of ˈuse** start/stop being used 开始[停止]被使用：*When did this word come into common use?* 这个词是什么时候用起来的？○ *The present phone boxes will go out of use next year.* 现有的公共电话亭明年就不再使用了. **have no use for sb** refuse to tolerate sb; dislike 不容忍某人；不喜欢；厌恶：*I've no use for people who don't try.* 我讨厌那些不想努力的人. **have no use for sth** have no purpose for which sth can be used 不需要或用不着某物：*I've no further use for this typewriter, so you can have it.* 我用不着这台打字机了，你拿去用吧. **in ˈuse** being used 被使用；在使用中. **make the best use of sth** ⇨ BEST[1]. **make use of sth/sb** use or benefit from sth/sb 使用或利用某事物[某人]：*Make full use of every chance you have to speak English.* 要充分利用一切机会说英语. ○ *We will make good use of her talents.* 我们要很好地发挥她的才能. **no earthly use** ⇨ EARTHLY. **of use** serving a purpose; useful 作某目的的；有用的：*These maps might be of (some) use to you on your trip.* 这些地图你在旅途中也许有(些)用. **put sth to good ˈuse** derive profit from sth 从某事物中获益：*He'll be able to put his experience to good use in the new job.* 他能在新的工作中把他的经验派上用场了.

used[1] /juːzd; juzd/ *adj* [usu attrib 通常作定语] (of clothes, cars, etc) having been worn, used, etc before; second-hand (指衣物、汽车等)用旧了的，使用过的，二手的.

used[2] /juːst; just/ *adj* **~ to sth/doing sth** having learned to accept sth; accustomed to sth (对某事物)已适应，已习惯：*be quite used to hard work/working hard* 很习惯做艰苦的工作 ○ *After three weeks she had got used to the extreme heat.* 三个星期以后她就适应酷热的环境了. ○ *The food in England is strange at first but you'll soon get used to it.* 英国食物乍一吃很不习惯，但不久就能适应了.

used to /ˈjuːs tə; ˈjustə; *before vowels and finally* 在元音前及末尾读作 ˈjuːs tuː; ˈjustu/ *modal v* (*neg* 否定式 **used not to**, *contracted form* 缩约式 **usedn't to, usen't to** /ˈjuːsnt tə; ˈjusn̩t tə; *before vowels and finally* 在元音前及末尾读作 ˈjuːsnt tuː; ˈjusn̩t tu/) (expressing a frequent or continuous action in the past; in questions and negative sentences usu with *did* 表达过去经常的或持续的行为，在疑问句和否定句中通常与did连用)：*I used to live in London.* 我过去一直住在伦敦. ○ *Life here is much easier than it used to be.* 如今在此地生活比起从前可舒服多了. ○ *You used to smoke a pipe, didn't you?* 你过去一向是抽烟斗的，对不对？

NOTE ON USAGE 用法：The following negative and question patterns are old-fashioned or very formal 以下的否定形式和疑问形式是古雅的或者是正统的形式：*I usedn't to like her.* 我未尝喜欢过她. ○ *Used you to go there?* 您昔时可常去那里？○ *There used to be a cinema here, use(d)n't there?* 往日此处曾有一影院，不知是与不是？Most people now use patterns with **did**, especially when speaking or writing informally 现在大多数人使用与**did**连用的形式，特别是在口语中或不拘谨的书面语中：*I didn't use to like her.* 我一向不喜欢她. ○ *Did you use to go there?* 你以前常到那儿去吗？○ *There used to be a cinema here, didn't there?* 从前这里有一家电影院，是不是？

use·ful /ˈjuːsfl; ˈjusfəl/ *adj* **1** that can be used for some practical purpose; serviceable or helpful 实用的；适用的；有用的；有益的；有帮助的：*a useful gadget, book, hint, acquaintance* 有用的小机械、书、线索、熟人 ○ *do sth useful with one's life* 尽自己毕生精力做些有益的事 ○ *Videos are useful things to have in the classroom.* 教室里有录像设备是很有助益的. **2** (*infml* 口) competent or capable 能干的；有能力的：*He's a useful member of the team.* 他是该队的主力队员. **3** (idm 习语) **come in handy/useful** ⇨ HANDY. **ˌmake oneself ˈuseful** help by performing useful tasks 做些有用的事来帮忙：*My nephews tried to make themselves useful about the house.* 我的侄子都想帮我收拾收拾房子. ▷ **use·fully** /-fəlɪ; -fəlɪ/ *adv*: *Is there anything I can usefully do here?* 这里有没有我能帮忙做的事情？**use·ful·ness** /-fəlnɪs; -fəlnɪs/ *n* [U]: *The old car has outlived its usefulness*, ie is no longer useful or worth keeping. 这辆旧汽车已经不能用了.

use·less /ˈjuːslɪs; ˈjuslɪs/ *adj* **1** not serving a useful purpose; not producing good results 无用的；无效的；无益的：*A car is useless without petrol.* 汽车没有汽油就不能使用. ○ *It's useless arguing/to argue with them.* 跟他们争论是徒劳无益的. ○ *All our efforts were useless.* 我们的一切努力都白费了. **2** (*infml* 口) weak or incompetent 差劲的；不怎么样的：*He's a useless player.* 他技艺很差. ○ *I'm useless at maths.* 我数学可不行. ▷ **use·lessly** *adv*. **use·less·ness** *n* [U].

user /ˈjuːzə(r); ˈjuzɚ/ *n* (esp in compounds 尤用以构成复合词) person or thing that uses 使用者；用户：*ˈdrug-users, ˈroad-users* 使用药的人、使用道路的人 ○ *I'm a great user of public transport.* 我经常使用公共交通工具. ○ *The steel industry is one of Britain's greatest users of coal.* 英国煤炭的最大用户是钢铁工业.

▷ **user-friendly** /ˌjuːzə ˈfrendlɪ; ˌjuzɚˈfrɛndlɪ/ *adj* (esp of computers, their software, etc) easy for non-experts to use; not difficult or intimidating (尤指计算机及其软件等)便于非专业者使用的，不难用的，不可怕的：*a ˌuser-friendly ˈkeyboard* 简便的键盘 ○ *Dictionaries should be as user-friendly as possible.* 词典应尽可能便于使用.

usher /ˈʌʃə(r); ˈʌʃɚ/ *n* **1** person who shows people to their seats in a cinema, church, public hall, etc or into sb's presence (电影院、教堂、公共大厅等的)引座员；(将客人领到某人面前的)招待员，迎宾员. **2** door-keeper in a lawcourt, etc (法院等处的)门房，传达员.

▷ **usher** *v* **1** [Tn·pr, Tn·p] lead (sb) in the specified direction; escort as an usher 引导(某人)；担任引座员、招待员、迎宾员、门房：*The girl ushered me along the aisle to my seat.* 引座小姐带领我沿着通道到我的座位上去. ○ *I was ushered in, and stood before the Queen.* 迎宾员把我带进去，站在女王的面前. **2** (phr v) **usher sth in** (*fig* 比喻) mark the start of sth; herald sth 开创、开始或引进某事物；预报；预示：*The new government ushered in a period of prosperity.* 新政府的成立带来了一个繁荣的时期.

ush·er·ette /ˌʌʃəˈret; ˌʌʃɚˈɛt/ *n* girl or woman who ushers people to their seats, esp in a cinema or theatre 女引座员(尤指电影院或戏院的).

USN /ˌjuː es ˈen; ˌju ɛs ˈɛn/ *abbr* 缩写 = United States Navy 美国海军.

USS /ˌjuː es ˈes; ˌju ɛs ˈɛs/ *abbr* 缩写 = United States Ship 美国船：*USS Oklahoma* 美国船俄克拉何马号. Cf 参看 HMS.

USSR /ˌjuː es es ˈɑː(r); ˌju ɛs ɛs ˈɑr/ *abbr* 缩写 = Union of Soviet Socialist Republics 苏联.

usual /ˈjuːʒl; ˈjuʒəl/ *adj* **1** such as happens or is done or used, etc in many or most instances; customary 通常的；平常的；惯常的：*make all the usual excuses* 用尽司空见惯的借口 ○ *She arrived later than usual.* 她到得比平常

晚. ○ *As is usual with children, they soon got tired.* 孩子们一贯如此，他们很快就厌倦了. ○ *When the accident happened, the usual crowd gathered.* 事故发生时，照例有许多人围观. ○ *He wasn't his usual self.* 他失去了常态. ○ (*infml* 口) *I'll have my usual, please,* ie my usual drink, etc. 请给我来一份我通常要的(我常要的饮料等). **2** (idm 习语) **as usual** as is usual 像往常一样: *You're late, as usual.* 你像平常一样又迟到了. ○ *As usual, there weren't many people at the meeting.* 像往常一样，来开会的人不多. **business as usual** ⇨ BUSINESS.

▷ **usu·ally** /ˈjuːʒəlɪ; ˋjuʒəlɪ/ *adv* in the way that is usual; most often 通常地; 惯常地: *What do you usually do on Sundays?* 你星期天通常做什么? ○ *He's usually early.* 他通常到得早. ○ *The canteen is more than usually busy today.* 今天食堂比往常忙得多.

us·urer /ˈjuːʒərə(r); ˋjuʒərɚ/ *n* (*dated usu derog* 旧，通常作贬义) person who lends money at excessively high interest 放高利贷的人.

usurp /juːˈzɜːp; juˋzɝp/ *v* [Tn] (*fml* 文) take (sb's power, right, position) wrongfully or by force 篡夺或武力夺取(某人的权力、权利、地位): *usurp the throne* 篡夺王位 ○ *usurp the role of leader* 夺取领导者的地位. ▷ **usurpa·tion** /ˌjuːzɜːˈpeɪʃn; ˌjuzɚˋpeʃən/ *n* [U]. **usurper** *n*.

us·ury /ˈjuːʒərɪ; ˋjuʒərɪ/ *n* [U] (*dated usu derog* 旧，通常作贬义) (lending of money at) excessively high interest 高利贷; 高利.

uten·sil /juːˈtensl; juˋtɛnsḷ/ *n* implement or container, esp for everyday use in the home 用具，器皿(尤指家庭日用的): ˈ*writing utensils,* eg pencils, pens, ink 书写用具(如铅笔、钢笔、墨水) ○ ˈ*cooking/*ˈ*kitchen utensils,* eg pots, pans 烹调[厨房]用具(如罐、锅).

uterus /ˈjuːtərəs; ˋjutərəs/ *n* (*pl* 复数作 **~es** or, in scientific use, 科技用语复数作 **uteri** /-raɪ; -raɪ/) (*anatomy* 解) womb 子宫. ⇨illus at FEMALE 见 FEMALE 插图.

▷ **uter·ine** /ˈjuːtəraɪn; ˋjutəraɪn/ *adj* of the uterus 子宫的.

util·it·arian /ˌjuːtɪlɪˈteərɪən; ˌjutɪləˋtɛrɪən/ *adj* **1** (*sometimes derog* 有时作贬义) designed to be useful rather than luxurious or decorative, etc; severely practical 实用的(非奢华的或装饰的); 功利的: *The student accommodation is strictly utilitarian.* 为学生提供的住宿极其实惠. **2** based on or supporting the belief that actions are good if they are useful or benefit the greatest number of people 功利主义的.

util·ity /juːˈtɪlətɪ; juˋtɪlətɪ/ *n* **1** [U] quality of being useful 有用; 实用; 效用; 功用: [attrib 作定语] *a utility vehicle,* ie one that can be used for various purposes 多用途车辆 ○ *the utility value of a dishwasher* 洗碟机的实用价值. **2** [C] = PUBLIC UTILITY (PUBLIC).

□ **uˈtility room** room, esp in a private house, containing one or more large fixed domestic appliances, eg a washing-machine 杂用间(放置大件家用电器如洗衣机的房间，尤指私人住宅的).

util·ize, -ise /ˈjuːtəlaɪz; ˋjutḷˌaɪz/ *v* [Tn] (*fml* 文) make use of (sth); find a use for 利用或应用(某事物): *utilize the available tools, resources* 利用现有的工具、资源 ○ *utilize solar power as a source of energy* 利用太阳能作为能源. ▷ **util·iza·tion, -isation** /ˌjuːtəlaɪˈzeɪʃn; *US* -lɪˈz-; ˌjutḷəˋzeʃən/ *n* [U].

ut·most /ˈʌtməʊst; ˋʌtˌmost/ (also **uttermost** /ˈʌtəməʊst; ˋʌtɚˌmost/) *adj* [attrib 作定语] greatest; furthest; most extreme 最大的; 最远的; 极度的: *in the utmost danger* 在极端的危险中 ○ *of the utmost importance* 极重要的 ○ *with the utmost care* 极其小心 ○ *pushed to the utmost limits of endurance* 逼到忍无可忍的程度.

▷ **the ut·most** (also **the uttermost**) *n* [sing] **1** the greatest, furthest or most extreme degree or point, etc that is possible 最大限度; 极限: *enjoy oneself to the utmost* 尽情享乐 ○ *Our endurance was tested to the utmost.* 我们已忍无可忍了. **2** (idm 习语) **do/try one's ˈutmost (to do sth)** do or try as much as one can 竭力; 竭尽所能: *I did my utmost to stop them.* 我已竭尽全力制止他们.

Uto·pia /juːˈtəʊpɪə; juˋtopɪə/ *n* [C, U] imaginary place or state of things in which everything is perfect 乌托邦: *create a political Utopia* 创造政治的乌托邦.

▷ **Uto·pian** /-pɪən; -pɪən/ *adj* (*usu derog* 通常作贬义) having or aiming for the perfection of Utopia but impossible to achieve; idealistic 乌托邦的; 空想的; 理想主义的: *Utopian ideals* 不切实际的理想.

ut·ter[1] /ˈʌtə(r); ˋʌtɚ/ *adj* [attrib 作定语] (used to give extra emphasis to a *n* 用以加强名词的词义) complete; total; absolute 完全的; 彻底的; 绝对的: *utter darkness, bliss, nonsense* 漆黑、极乐、纯粹的废话 ○ *an utter lie, disaster* 极大的谎言、灾难 ○ *to my utter delight, astonishment, etc* 使我十分高兴、吃惊等 ○ *She's an utter stranger to me.* 我根本不认识她. ▷ **ut·terly** *adv*: *She utterly despises him.* 她非常瞧不起他. ○ *We failed utterly to convince them.* 我们根本说服不了他们.

ut·ter[2] /ˈʌtə(r); ˋʌtɚ/ *v* [Tn] (**a**) make (a sound or sounds) with the mouth or voice (以口)发出(声音): *utter a sigh, cry of pain, etc* 发出叹息声、痛苦的叫喊声等. (**b**) say or speak 说; 讲: *utter threats, slanders, etc* 说出威胁、毁谤等的话 ○ *He never uttered a word of protest.* 他从来没说一句反对的话.

▷ **ut·ter·ance** /ˈʌtərəns; ˋʌtərəns/ *n* (*fml* 文) **1** [U] action of uttering or expressing things in words 用言语表达: *give utterance to one's feelings, thoughts, views, etc* 以言语表达感情、思想、观点等 ○ *The speaker had great powers of utterance.* 那个演讲人很有口才. **2** [C] spoken word or words; thing said 话语; 言语: *private/public utterances* 私下的[公开的]话.

ut·ter·most = UTMOST.

uvula /ˈjuːvjʊlə; ˋjuvjələ/ *n* (*pl* 复数作 **~s** or, in scientific use, 科技用语复数作 **-lae** /-liː; -ˌli/) (*anatomy* 解) small piece of flesh that hangs from the back of the roof of the mouth above the throat 悬雍垂; 小舌. ⇨ illus at THROAT 见 THROAT 插图.

uxori·ous /ʌkˈsɔːrɪəs; ʌkˋsorɪəs/ *adj* (*fml or joc* 文或谑) excessively fond of one's wife 宠爱妻子的.

V v

V, v /vi:; vi/ *n* (*pl* **V's, v's** /vi:z; viz/) **1** the twenty-second letter of the English alphabet 英语字母表的第二十二个字母: *Vivienne begins with (a) V/'V'.* Vivienne一字以V字母开始. **2** V-shaped thing V形物: *The geese were flying in a V.* 雁排成了V形飞行. ○ [attrib 作定语] *flying in (a) V formation* 排成V字队形飞行.

V *abbr* 缩写 = **1** victory: *give/make a V-sign*, ie with the first and second fingers spread to form a V, showing victory (with palm outwards), or vulgar derision (with palm inwards) 打出V形手势(伸出食指和中指作V形, 手掌向外时表示胜利, 手掌向内时表示粗俗的嘲弄之意). **2** volt(s): *240V*, eg on a light bulb 240V(如电灯泡上的字样). Cf 参看 W *abbr* 缩写 1.

V (also **v**) *symb* 符号 Roman numeral for 5 (罗马数字)5.

v *abbr* 缩写 = **1** (*pl* **vv**) verse: *St Luke ch 12 vv 4-10*《路加福音》第12章第4-10节. **2** verso. **3** (also **vs**) (esp in sporting contests) versus (ie against): *England v West Indies* 英格兰队对西印度群岛队. **4** (*infml* 口) very: *I was v pleased to get your letter.* 来信收到, 十分高兴. **5** see; refer to (Latin *vide*) 参看, 见(源自拉丁文 *vide*).

vac /væk; væk/ *n* (*Brit infml* 口) **1** = VACATION. **2** = VACUUM CLEANER (VACUUM).

va·cancy /'veɪkənsɪ; 'vekənsɪ/ *n* **1** [C] unoccupied accommodation (未被占用的)空余住处: *No vacancies*, eg on a hotel sign. 客满(如旅店告示牌的字样). **2** [C] unfilled position or post 空处; 空位; 空职; 空缺: *We have vacancies for typists/in the typing pool.* 我们缺少打字员[我们的打字组缺员]. **3** [U] lack of ideas or intelligence; emptiness of mind 无主意或智慧; 头脑空虚: *the vacancy of his stare, expression* 他那茫然若失的目光、表情.

va·cant /'veɪkənt; 'vekənt/ *adj* **1** not filled or occupied; empty 未占满的; 未占用的; 空着的: *Is the lavatory vacant?* 厕所里没有人吧? ○ *a vacant situation, post, hotel room* 空着的职务、空缺的职位、旅店的空房间. ⇨Usage at EMPTY[1] 用法见 EMPTY[1]. **2** (**a**) showing no sign of thought or intelligence; blank 无思想或智慧的; 木然的: *a vacant stare, look, etc* 茫然的凝视、目光等. (**b**) empty of thought (思想)空虚的: *a vacant mind* 空荡荡的头脑. ▷ **va·cantly** *adv*: *stare, look, gaze, etc vacantly into space* 木然地注视、观望、凝视...着空间.
□ ˌ**vacant pos'session** (used in house advertisements, etc 房屋出售等的广告用语) state of being empty of occupants and available for the buyer to occupy immediately 空房出售.

va·cate /və'keɪt; *US* 'veɪkeɪt; 'veket/ *v* [Tn] (*fml* 文) cease to occupy (a place or position) 停止占用, 腾出, 搬出, 空出(地方或场所); 不再担任(某职位): *vacate a house, hotel room* 腾出房子、搬出旅馆房间 ○ *vacate one's seat, post* 空出自己的座位、辞去职位 ○ *The squatters were ordered to vacate the premises.* 擅自占房者被勒令迁出.

va·ca·tion /və'keɪʃn; *US* veɪ-; ve'keʃən/ *n* **1** [C] (also **recess**, *Brit infml* 英式口语作 **vac**) any of the intervals between terms in universities and lawcourts (大学的)假期; (法庭的)休庭期: *the Christmas, Easter vacation* 圣诞节、复活节假期 ○ *the long vacation*, ie in the summer 暑假 ○ [attrib 作定语] *vacation work* 大学生的假期工作. **2** [C] (*esp US*) = HOLIDAY 1b: *take a vacation* 休假. **3** [U] (*fml* 文) action of vacating 停止占用; 腾出; 搬出; 空出: *Immediate vacation of the house is essential.* 立即腾出这所房子是当务之急. **4** (idm 习语) **on vacation** (*esp US*) on holiday 在度假. ⇨Usage at HOLIDAY 用法见 HOLIDAY.
▷ **va·ca·tion** *v* [I, Ipr] **~ (at/in...)** (*US*) have a holiday at/in (a place) 在(某处)度假.

vac·cin·ate /'væksɪneɪt; 'væksn̩ˌet/ *v* [Tn, Tn·pr] **~ sb/sth (against sth)** protect sb/sth (against a disease) by injecting vaccine 给某人[某物]接种疫苗: *have your dog vaccinated against rabies* 给你的狗注射疫苗以预防狂犬病. Cf 参看 IMMUNIZE (IMMUNE), INOCULATE.
▷ **vac·cina·tion** /ˌvæksɪ'neɪʃn; ˌvæksn̩'eʃən/ *n* [C, U] (instance of) vaccinating or being vaccinated 接种疫苗.

vac·cine /'væksi:n; *US* væk'si:n; 'væksin/ *n* [U, C] substance that is injected into the bloodstream and protects the body by making it have a mild form of the disease 疫苗; 菌苗: *develop a smallpox, polio, rabies, etc vaccine* 培养天花、小儿麻痹症、狂犬病等的疫苗. Cf 参看 SERUM 2.

va·cil·late /'væsəleɪt; 'væsl̩ˌet/ *v* [I, Ipr] **~ (between sth and sth)** (*fml usu derog* 文, 通常作贬义) keep changing one's mind; move backwards and forwards between two emotions (思想)动摇不定; 犹豫; (在两种情绪之间)变化不定: *She vacillated between hope and fear.* 她时而抱有希望, 时而心存恐惧. Cf 参看 OSCILLATE.
▷ **va·cil·la·tion** /ˌvæsə'leɪʃn; ˌvæsl̩'eʃən/ *n* [C, U] (*fml usu derog* 文, 通常作贬义) (instance of) vacillating (思想的)动摇; 犹豫; (情绪的)波动: *eternal, continual, constant, etc vacillations* 心里总是动摇不定.

va·cu·ity /və'kju:ətɪ; və'kjuətɪ/ *n* (*fml* 文) **1** [U] lack of purpose, meaning or intelligence (目的、意义或智慧的)缺乏; 空虚; 茫然; 愚蠢: *the total vacuity of his thoughts, statements* 他思想上的一片茫然、言语的空洞无物. **2** [C usu *pl* 通常作复数] inane remarks, acts, etc 无意义的言行.

va·cu·ous /'vækjʊəs; 'vækjʊəs/ *adj* (*fml* 文) showing or suggesting absence of thought or intelligence; inane 无思想的; 无智慧的; 空洞的; 无意义的: *a vacuous stare, remark, laugh, expression* 呆视、空洞的话、傻笑、茫然的表情. ▷ **va·cu·ously** *adv*. **va·cu·ous·ness** *n* [U].

va·cuum /'vækjʊəm; 'vækjʊəm/ *n* (*pl* 复数作 **~s** or, in scientific use, 科技用语复数作 **vacua** /-jʊə; -jʊə/) **1** (**a**) space that is completely empty of all matter or gas(es) 真空. (**b**) space in a container from which the air has been completely or partly pumped out (容器的)真空状态: *create a perfect vacuum* 形成完全的真空状态. **2** (usu *sing* 通常作单数) (*fig* 比喻) situation or environment characterized by emptiness (情况或环境的)空洞状态: *There has been a vacuum in his life since his wife died.* 他妻子去世后他的生活很空虚. **3** (*infml* 口) = VACUUM CLEANER. **4** (idm 习语) **in a 'vacuum** isolated from other people, facts, events, etc 与其他的人、事等脱离或隔绝: *live, work, etc in a vacuum* 在与外界隔绝的环境中生活、工作等.
▷ **va·cuum** *v* [I, Tn, Tn·p] **~ sth (out)** (*infml* 口) clean (sth) with a vacuum cleaner 用真空吸尘器清扫(某物): *vacuum the stairs, carpet* 用吸尘器清扫楼梯、地毯等 ○ *vacuum (out) the car* 用吸尘器打扫汽车.
□ '**vacuum cleaner** electrical appliance that takes up dust, dirt, etc by suction 真空吸尘器.
'**vacuum flask** (also **flask**, *US* '**vacuum bottle**) container with a double wall that encloses a vacuum, used for keeping the contents hot or cold 保温瓶. Cf 参看 THERMOS.
'**vacuum-packed** *adj* (esp of perishable foods) sealed in a pack from which most of the air has been removed (尤指易腐败的食物)真空包装的.
'**vacuum pump** pump that creates a partial vacuum in a vessel 真空泵.
'**vacuum tube** (*US*) (*Brit* **radio valve**) sealed glass tube with an almost perfect vacuum to enable an electric charge to pass through, formerly used in radios, televisions, etc 真空管; 电子管.

vade-mecum /ˌvɑ:dɪ'meɪkum, ˌveɪdɪ'mi:kəm; ˌvɑdɪ'mekəm, ˌvedɪ'mikəm/ *n* handbook or other small useful work of reference 手册; 便览: *The spelling dictionary is a vade-mecum for all secretaries.* 拼法字典是秘书必备的手册.

vaga·bond /'vægəbɒnd; 'vægəˌbɑnd/ *n* wanderer or vagrant, esp an idle or dishonest one 流浪者; 漂泊者; (尤指)无业游民, 无赖: [attrib 作定语] *lead a vagabond life* 过流浪生活.

vag·ary /'veɪgərɪ; 'vegərɪ/ *n* (usu *pl* 通常作复数) strange, unusual or capricious change; whim 怪异多变; 奇想: *the vagaries of fashion, the weather, the postal service* 时髦样

式、天气、邮政服务措施的变幻莫测.

va·gina /vəˈdʒaɪnə; vəˈdʒaɪnə/ *n* (*pl* 复数作 **~s** or, in scientific use, 科技用语复数作 **-nae** /-niː; -ni/ (*anatomy* 解) passage (in a female mammal) from the external genital organs to the womb 阴道. ⇨illus at FEMALE 见 FEMALE 插图. ▷ **va·ginal** /vəˈdʒaɪnl; vəˈdʒaɪnl/ *adj*.

vag·rant /ˈveɪgrənt; ˈvegrənt/ *n* (*fml or law* 文或律) person without a settled home or regular work; tramp 居无定所或无固定工作的人; 流浪者: *vagrant tribes* 游荡部落 ○ *lead a vagrant life* 过流浪生活.

▷ **vag·rancy** /ˈveɪgrənsɪ; ˈvegrənsɪ/ *n* [U] (offence of) being a vagrant 游荡(罪): *drunks arrested for vagrancy* 因游荡罪遭逮捕的喝醉的人.

vague /veɪg; veg/ *adj* (**-r, -st**) **1** not clearly expressed or perceived (表达或感知)含糊的, 不明确的, 不清楚的: *a vague answer, demand, rumour* 含糊其辞的回答、要求、传闻 ○ *vague memories, hopes, fears* 模糊的记忆、渺茫的希望、莫名的恐惧 ○ *I haven't the vaguest* (ie slightest) *idea/notion what you mean.* 我一点都不明白你的意思. **2** not specific or exact; imprecise 不具体的; 不确切的; 不精确的: *a vague estimate of the cost* 对费用的大致估计 ○ *The terms of the agreement were deliberately vague.* 协议的条款故意含糊其词. ○ *She can only give a vague description of her attacker.* 她只能粗略地描述了一下那个袭击她的人. **3** (**a**) (of persons) undecided or uncertain (about needs, intentions, etc) (指人)(有关需要、意图等)未决定的, 犹豫不决的, 不确定的: *be vague in/about one's plans* 对计划举棋不定 ○ *I'm still vague about what you want.* 我还是不清楚你想要什么. (**b**) (of a person's looks or behaviour) suggesting unclear thinking or absent-mindedness (指人的神情或行为)茫然的, 心不在焉的: *a vague smile, gesture* 用意不明的微笑、手势. **4** not clearly identified; indistinct 不清晰的; 模糊的: *the vague outline of a ship in the fog* 船在雾中的模糊的轮廓.

▷ **vaguely** *adv* **1** in a way one cannot specify 含糊地; 不明确地: *Her face is vaguely familiar.* 她有些面熟. **2** roughly; approximately 大致上; 近似地: *He pointed vaguely in my direction.* 他粗略地朝我的方向指了指. ○ *Italy vaguely resembles a boot.* 意大利国的形状像只靴子. **3** absent-mindedly 心不在焉地: *smile, gesture vaguely* 心不在焉地微笑、打个手势.

vague·ness *n* [U].

vain /veɪn; ven/ *adj* (**-er, -est**) **1** having too high an opinion of one's looks, abilities, etc; conceited (对自己的才、貌等)自视过高的; 自负的. **2** [attrib 作定语] (*esp rhet* 尤作修辞) having no value or significance 无价值的; 无意义的: *vain promises, triumphs, pleasures* 空头的许诺、虚无的胜利、空欢喜. **3** [usu attrib 通常作定语] useless or futile 无用的; 无益的; 无效的; 徒劳的: *a vain attempt* 劳而无功的努力 ○ *in the vain hope of persuading him* 指望说服他而徒费口舌. **4** (idm 习语) **in ˈvain** (**a**) with no result; uselessly 无结果地; 徒然: *try in vain to sleep* 怎么也睡不着. (**b**) fruitless or useless 无效果的; 无用的: *All our work was in vain.* 我们的工作全都白干了. **take sb's name in vain** ⇨ NAME[1].

▷ **vainly** *adv* **1** in a conceited manner 自负地. **2** uselessly or futilely 无用地; 无益地; 无效地; 徒劳地.

vain·ness *n* [U].

vain·glory /ˌveɪnˈglɔːrɪ; venˈglorɪ/ *n* [U] (*dated or fml* 旧或文) extreme vanity or pride in oneself; boastfulness 极度的虚荣; 自负; 自夸.

▷ **vain·glori·ous** /-ˈglɔːrɪəs; -ˈglorɪəs/ *adj* full of vainglory; conceited and boastful 虚荣心重的; 自负的; 自夸的.

val·ance /ˈvæləns; ˈvæləns/ *n* (**a**) short curtain or frill hung around the frame of a bed (床架四周的)短帷幔, 挂布. (**b**) (*esp US*) = PELMET.

vale /veɪl; vel/ *n* (*arch* except in place names 古, 现仅用于地名) valley 谷; 山谷: *the Vale of the White Horse* 怀特霍斯山谷.

va·le·dic·tion /ˌvælɪˈdɪkʃn; ˌvæləˈdɪkʃən/ *n* [C, U] (*fml* 文) (words used in) saying farewell, esp on serious occasions 告别; 告辞; 告别辞: *utter a valediction* 致告别辞 ○ *bow in valediction* 鞠躬告别.

▷ **va·le·dict·ory** /-tərɪ; -tərɪ/ *adj* [usu attrib 通常作定语] (*fml* 文) serving as or accompanying a farewell 告别的; 告辞的: *a valedictory speech, message, gift* 临别的演说、言语、礼物.

va·le·dict·ory *n* (*US*) farewell speech given by a top graduating student at a school or college 毕业生代表的告别演说. **va·le·dict·orian** /-ˈtɔːrɪən; -ˈtorɪən/ *n* (*US*) student giving a valedictory 致告别辞的毕业生代表.

val·ence /ˈveɪləns; ˈveləns/ *n* (*chemistry* 化) **1** [U] capacity of an atom to combine with, or be replaced by, another or others as compared with that of the hydrogen atom 化合价; 原子价: *Carbon has a valence of four.* 碳的化合价是四价. **2** [C] (*US*) = VALENCY.

valency /ˈveɪlənsɪ; ˈvelənsɪ/ (*US* **valence**) *n* (*chemistry* 化) unit of the combining-power of atoms (原子的)(化合)价: *Carbon has 4 valencies.* 碳的化合价是四价.

val·en·tine /ˈvæləntaɪn; ˈvælənˌtaɪn/ *n* (**a**) (also **valentine card**) sentimental or comic greetings card sent, usu anonymously, on St Valentine's Day (14 February) to a sweetheart 在圣瓦伦廷节(2月14日)寄给情人的贺卡(通常匿名). (**b**) sweetheart to whom one sends such a card 收受此类贺卡的情人: *Will you be my valentine?* 你愿意做我的情人吗?

va·lerian /væˈlɪərɪən; vəˈlɪrɪən/ *n* [U] any of various types of small herb with strong-smelling pink or white flowers 缬草(花呈粉红色或白色, 气味浓郁).

valet /ˈvæleɪ, ˈvælɪt; ˈvæle, ˈvælɪt/ *n* (**a**) man's personal male servant who looks after his clothes, serves his meals, etc (为男主人照料衣食等事务的)男仆. (**b**) hotel employee with similar duties (旅馆中负责该类事务的)服务员.

▷ **valet** /ˈvælɪt; ˈvælɪt/ *v* **1** [Tn] clean, brush and repair (eg clothes, chair-covers, car fittings) 洗刷及修补(如衣物、椅套、汽车坐具等): *a valeting service*, eg at a dry-cleaner's or garage 洗刷修补服务(如干洗店或汽车维修站的). **2** [I, Tn] act as valet to (sb) 为(某人)照料衣食.

va·le·tu·din·arian /ˌvælɪtjuːdɪˈneərɪən; ˌvæləˌtjudnˈɛrɪən/ *n* (*fml* 文) person who pays excessive attention to preserving his health 过分关心自己健康的人. Cf 参看 HYPOCHONDRIAC (HYPOCHONDRIA).

vali·ant /ˈvælɪənt; ˈvæljənt/ *adj* (*rhet* 修辞) brave or determined 勇敢的; 英勇的; 坚定的: *valiant resistance, efforts* 顽强的抵抗、努力 ○ *She made a valiant attempt to laugh.* 她放大了胆笑了起来. ▷ **va·li·antly** *adv*: *Tom tried valiantly to rescue the drowning man.* 汤姆勇敢地抢救那个溺水的男子.

valid /ˈvælɪd; ˈvælɪd/ *adj* **1** (**a**) legally effective because made or done with the correct formalities (因符合正当手续)有法律效力的: *a valid claim, contract* 在法律上有效的要求、合同 ○ *The marriage was held to be valid.* 这一婚姻关系是有效的. (**b**) legally usable or acceptable (法律上)有效的, 得到认可的: *a bus pass valid for one week, for ten journeys* 有效期为一周、为十趟旅程的公共汽车乘车券 ○ *A cheque card is not a valid proof of identity.* 银行发的支票保付卡并非有效的身分证明文件. **2** (of arguments, reasons, etc) well based or logical; sound (指论据、理由等)有充分根据的, 符合逻辑的, 确凿的: *raise valid objections to a plan* 对某项计划提出有力的反对 ○ *Her excuse was not valid.* 她的借口靠不住.

▷ **va·lid·ity** /vəˈlɪdətɪ; vəˈlɪdətɪ/ *n* [U] **1** state of being legally acceptable (法律上)有效; 合法(性): *test the validity of a decision* 验证某决定是否合法. **2** state of being logical 合逻辑; 正确(性): *question the validity of an argument, assumption* 对某一论据、假定的论点的正确性提出疑问.

val·id·ate /ˈvælɪdeɪt; ˈvæləˌdet/ *v* [Tn] **1** make (sth) legally valid; ratify 使(某事物)具有法律效力; 批准; 认可: *validate a contract, marriage, passport* 使合同生效、使婚姻具有合法性、签准护照. **2** make (sth) logical or justifiable 证实, 确证(某事物): *validate a theory, an argument, a thesis, etc* 证实某理论、论据、命题等. ▷ **val·ida·tion** /ˌvælɪˈdeɪʃn; ˌvæləˈdeʃən/ *n* [U].

va·lise /vəˈliːz; *US* vəˈliːs; vəˈlis/ *n* (*dated* 旧) small leather bag for clothes, etc during a journey (装衣物等的)皮制小旅行包.

Va·lium /ˈvælɪəm; ˈvælɪəm/ *n* (*propr* 专利名) (**a**) [U] drug used to reduce stress and nervous tension 安定(镇静药). (**b**) [C] (*pl* unchanged or **~s** 复数或不变或作 **Valiums**) tablet of this 安定药片.

val·ley /ˈvælɪ; ˈvælɪ/ *n* **1** stretch of land between hills or mountains, often with a river flowing through it 谷, 山谷(中间多有溪流). ⇨illus at MOUNTAIN 见 MOUNTAIN 插

V

图. **2** region drained by a river 流域: *the Nile valley* 尼罗河流域.

val·our (*US* **val·or**) /ˈvælə(r); ˈvælɚ/ *n* **1** [U] (*rhet* 修辞) bravery, esp in war 勇武, 英勇(尤指战时的): *display great valour* 显示出极大的勇气 ○ *soldiers decorated* (ie given awards) *for valour* 因勇敢而受奖的军人. **2** (idm 习语) **discretion is the better part of valour** ⇨ DISCRETION.

valu·able /ˈvæljʊəbl; ˈvæljʊəbl/ *adj* **1** worth a lot of money 贵重的; 值钱的: *a valuable collection of paintings* 一批很有价值的画儿. **2** very useful or worthwhile or important 很有用的; 很有价值的; 很重要的: *valuable advice, help, information, etc* 宝贵的意见、帮助、信息等 ○ *wasting valuable time and effort* 浪费宝贵的时间和精力 ○ *The jawbone was our most valuable find/discovery.* 这块颌骨是我们最重要的发现. ⇨Usage at INVALUABLE 用法见 INVALUABLE.

▷ **valu·ables** *n* [pl] valuable things, esp small personal possessions, jewellery, etc 贵重物品(尤指个人的小件物品、珠宝等): *recover stolen valuables* 起获失窃的贵重物品.

valu·ation /ˌvæljʊˈeɪʃn; ˌvæljuˈeʃən/ *n* **1** (**a**) [C, U] (act of) estimating, esp professionally, the financial value of sth 估计; (尤指专业人员的)估价: *property, land, stock, etc valuation* 对房地产、土地、存货等的估价 ○ *Surveyors carried out a valuation on/of our house.* 测量员对我们的房子做出了估价. (**b**) [C] financial value that is estimated in this way 估定的价值; 估值: *have a valuation made of one's jewellery* 请人给珠宝估价 ○ *Experts put/set a high valuation on the painting.* 专家对这幅画估价很高. **2** [U] (*fig* 比喻) estimation of a person's merit (对人的)评价: *take/accept sb at his own valuation*, ie according to his own opinion of himself 同意某人对他自己的评价.

value /ˈvælju:; ˈvælju/ *n* **1** (**a**) [C, U] worth of sth in terms of money or other goods for which it can be exchanged 价值: *a decline in the value of the dollar, pound, etc* 美元、英镑等价值的下跌 ○ *pay above/below the market value for sth* 付出高于[低于]市价购买某物 ○ *rising share, land, property values* 上涨的股票、土地、房地产的价值 ○ *gain, appreciate, go up, etc in value* 增值 ○ *drop, fall, go down, etc in value* 贬值 ○ *order software to the value of £700* 定购价值为700英镑的软件. (**b**) [U] worth of sth compared with the price paid for it 值(价值抵得上); 上算: *This tea is good value at 39p a packet.* 这种茶39便士一包, 很实惠. ○ *Charter flights give/offer the best value for (your) money.* 乘坐包机最合算. **2** [U] quality of being useful or worthwhile or important 实用性; 有价值; 重要性: *the value of regular exercise* 经常练习的好处 ○ *be of great, little, some, no, etc value to sb* 对某人有很大、没什么、有一些、毫无…帮助 ○ *have a high novelty, street, entertainment value* 在创新方面、黑市上、娱乐性上有很高价值 ○ *have a high energy, nutritional value* 有很高的能量、营养价值 ○ *the news value of a royal romance* 皇室春情的新闻价值. **3 values** [pl] moral or professional standards of behaviour; principles 价值观念; 道德观念; 职业道德; 行为标准; 准则: *artistic, legal, scientific values* 艺术、法律、科学标准 ○ *a return to Victorian values* 恢复到维多利亚时代的标准 ○ *the values of justice and democracy* 正义和民主的价值观 ○ *hold, respect, adopt, etc a set of values* 遵循、尊重、奉行…一套准则. **4** (**a**) [C] (*mathematics* 数) number or quantity represented by a letter 值; 数值: *find the value of x* 求x的值. (**b**) [C] (*music* 音) full time indicated by a note 时值: *Give the semibreve its full value.* 奏出该全音符的全音长. (**c**) [U] (in language) meaning; effect (语言的)意义, 作用: *use a word with all its poetic value* 充分发挥一词的诗意色彩. (**d**) [C] (in art) relation of light and shade (绘画的)明暗关系: *tone values in a painting* 画中的色调值. Cf 参看 FACE VALUE (FACE[1]).

▷ **value** *v* **1** [Tn, Tn·pr] **~ sth (at sth)** estimate the money value of sth 估计某物的价值; 给某物估价: *He valued the house for me at £80 000.* 那所房子他给我估价80 000英镑. **2** [Tn, Cn·n/a] **~ sth/sb (as sth)** (not used in the continuous tenses 不用于进行时态) have a high opinion of sth/sb 重视某事物[某人]: *value sb's advice* 重视某人的劝告 ○ *value truth above all else* 把真理看得比什么都重要 ○ *a valued client, customer, etc* 重要的主顾、顾客等 ○ *Do you value her as a friend?* 你把她当好朋友吗? **valuer** *n* person whose profession is to estimate the money value of property, land, etc (房地产等的)估价人.

value·less *adj* without value or effect; worthless 无价值的; 无效果的; 没用的. ⇨Usage at INVALUABLE 用法见 INVALUABLE.

□ ˌ**value** ˈ**added tax** (*abbr* 缩写 **VAT**) tax on the rise in value of a product at each stage of its manufacture 增值税(随产品在各生产阶段增加价值而加征的税款).

ˈ**value judgement** (*derog* 贬) estimate of moral, artistic, etc worth based on personal assessment rather than objective fact 价值判断(对道德、艺术等价值所作的主观评价): *make value judgements* 作价值判断.

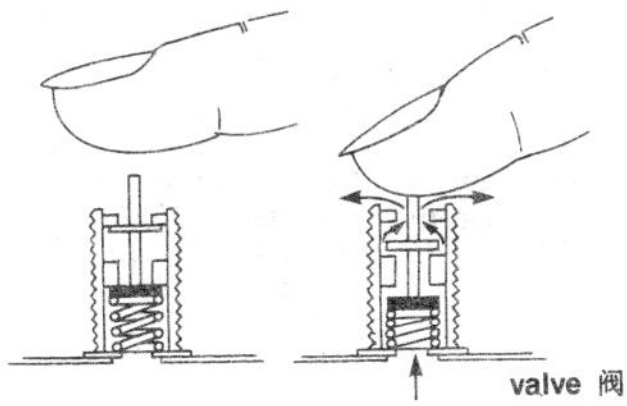

valve 阀

valve /vælv; vælv/ *n* **1** mechanical device for controlling the flow of air, liquid or gas in one direction only 阀; 阀门; 活门: *the inlet/outlet valves of a petrol or steam engine* 汽油发动机或蒸汽机的进给[排放]阀 ○ *the valve of a bicycle tyre* 自行车胎的气嘴 ○ *a safety, exhaust valve* 安全阀、排气阀. ⇨illus at App 1 见附录1插图, page xiii. Cf 参看 TAP[1] 1. **2** structure in the heart or in a blood-vessel allowing the blood to flow in one direction only (心脏或血管的)瓣膜. **3** device in certain brass musical instruments, eg cornets, for changing the pitch by changing the length of the column of air (管乐器的)活塞. ⇨illus at App 1 见附录1插图, page x. **4** (*biology* 生) each half of the hinged shell of oysters, mussels, etc 贝壳瓣. Cf 参看 BIVALVE. **5** = VACUUM TUBE.

▷ **valv·ular** /ˈvælvjʊlə(r); ˈvælvjəlɚ/ *adj* of valves, esp those regulating the flow of blood 阀的; (尤指)(心脏或血管)瓣(膜)的: *a valvular disease of the heart* 心脏瓣膜疾病.

va·moose /vəˈmu:s; væˈmus/ *v* [I] (*dated US infml* 旧, 口) (often imperative 常用于祈使语气) go away quickly 快走开.

vamp[1] /væmp; væmp/ *n* upper front part of a boot or shoe 靴面或鞋面的前部.

vamp[2] /væmp; væmp/ *v* **1** [I, Tn] (*esp derog* 尤作贬义) improvise (a basic tune or accompaniment), esp on the piano 即席奏出(基本曲调或伴奏曲)(尤指用钢琴). **2** (phr v) **vamp sth up** (*infml* 口) make sth new from old or existing material (用旧的或现有的材料)做出新的东西: *vamp up some lectures out of/from old notes* 用旧笔记中的材料拼凑成几篇讲演稿.

vamp[3] /væmp; væmp/ *n* (*dated infml* 旧, 口) (esp in the 1920's and 1930's) seductive woman using her attractions to exploit men (尤指二十世纪二十到三十年代)以色相勾引并利用男子的女子.

▷ **vamp** *v* [I, Tn] exploit or flirt with (a man) unscrupulously 不道德地利用(男子)或与之调情.

vam·pire /ˈvæmpaɪə(r); ˈvæmpaɪr/ *n* **1** reanimated corpse believed by some to leave its grave at night and suck the blood of living people 吸血鬼(传说在夜间离开坟墓去吸人血的). **2** ruthless person who preys on others 残酷剥削他人的人. **3** (also ˈ**vampire bat**) any of various types of bloodsucking bat from Central and S America 吸血蝠(产于中南美洲).

van[1] /væn; væn/ *n* **1** covered vehicle, with no side windows, for transporting goods or people (有篷盖的)客货车: *the ˈbaker's van* 装载面包的货车 ○ *a ˈfurniture/reˈmoval van* 搬运家具的[搬迁用的]货车 ○ *a poˈlice van*, ie for transporting police or prisoners 警车 ○ [attrib 作定语] *a ˈvan driver* 客货车司机. **2** (*Brit*) closed railway carriage for luggage, mail or goods, or for the use of the guard (铁路上运送行李、邮件或货物的)厢式货车, 守车: *the ˈluggage van* 装运行李的车厢 ○ *the ˈguard's van* 守车.

V

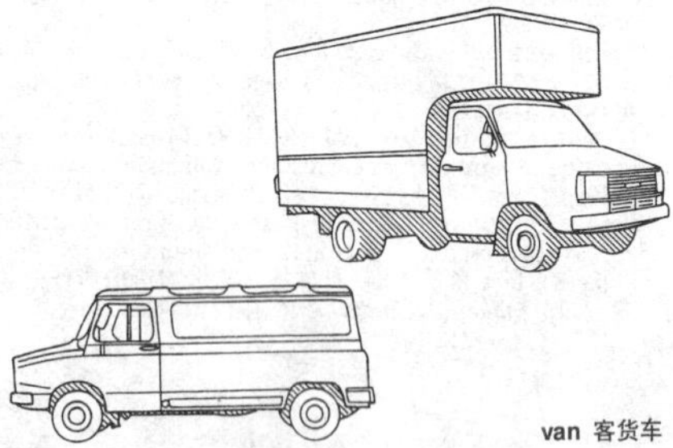

van 客货车

van[2] /væn; væn/ *n* **the van** [sing] (*dated* 旧) vanguard or forefront of an army or fleet (部队或舰队的)前锋, 先锋: *positioned in the van* 处于前锋位置.

va·na·dium /ˌvəˈneɪdɪəm; vəˈnedɪəm/ *n* [U] chemical element, a hard whitish metal sometimes used in steel alloys 钒. ⇨App 10 见附录10.

V and A /ˌvi: ən ˈeɪ; ˌvi ən ˈe/ *abbr* 缩写 = (*Brit infml* 口) Victoria and Albert Museum (in London) (伦敦)维多利亚和阿伯特博物馆.

van·dal /ˈvændl; ˈvændl̩/ *n* person who wilfully destroys or damages works of art, public and private property, the beauties of nature, etc 恣意破坏艺术品、公物、私人财产、自然美景等的人: *telephone vandals*, ie vandals who damage public phone boxes 破坏公用电话亭的流氓.

▷ **van·dal·ism** /-dəlɪzəm; -dl̩ˌɪzəm/ *n* [U] behaviour characteristic of vandals 恣意破坏公物等的行为.

van·dal·ize, **-ise** /-dəlaɪz; -dl̩ˌaɪz/ *v* [Tn esp passive 尤用于被动语态] wilfully destroy or damage (eg public property) 恣意破坏(公物等): *vandalize a train compartment, public convenience, lift* 故意毁坏列车车厢、公共厕所、电梯 ○ *The ground-floor flats had been badly vandalized.* 一楼公寓受到严重恶意破坏.

vane /veɪn; ven/ *n* **1** arrow or pointer on the top of a building, turned by the wind so as to show its direction 风向标; 风信旗. **2** blade of a propeller, sail of a windmill, or a similar device with a flat surface acted on or moved by wind or water (螺旋桨、风车、轮机等的)翼, 叶片.

van·guard /ˈvængɑ:d; ˈvænˌgɑrd/ *n* **the vanguard** [sing] **1** leading part of an advancing army or fleet 先头部队; 先头舰队; 前锋; 先锋. **2** (*fig* 比喻) leaders of a movement or fashion (运动或时尚的)先驱, 先锋, 领导者: *researchers in the vanguard of scientific progress* 在科学进步前列的研究人员. Cf 参看 REARGUARD (REAR[1]).

V

va·nilla /vəˈnɪlə; vəˈnɪlə/ *n* **1** [C] tropical orchid with sweet-smelling flowers 香子兰(热带兰科植物, 花味香醇). **2** [U] flavouring obtained from vanilla pods or a synthetic product resembling this 香草醛(自香子兰荚中提取或由人工合成的香精): [attrib 作定语] *vanilla ice-cream, essence* 香草冰激凌、香精.

van·ish /ˈvænɪʃ; ˈvænɪʃ/ *v* [I] (**a**) disappear completely and suddenly 突然完全消失: *The thief vanished into the crowd.* 那小偷消失在人群中. ○ *vanish into thin air*, ie completely 消失得无影无踪. (**b**) (*fig* 比喻) cease to exist or fade away 不复存在; 消逝: *My prospects/hopes of success have vanished.* 我的成功前景[希望]已破灭.

□ ˈ**vanishing-point** *n* [sing] (in perspective) point at which all parallel lines in the same plane appear to meet (透视法的)灭点, 消失点: (*fig* 比喻) *Our morale had almost reached vanishing-point*, ie disappeared. 我们的士气已丧失殆尽.

van·ity /ˈvænətɪ; ˈvænətɪ/ *n* **1** [U] having too high an opinion of one's looks, abilities, etc; conceit 自负; 虚荣; 虚荣心: *not a trace of vanity in her behaviour* 在她的举止中毫无虚荣表现 ○ *tickle sb's vanity*, ie do or say sth that flatters him 迎合某人的虚荣心 ○ *injured vanity*, ie resentment caused by some slight or humiliation 受到伤害的虚荣心. **2** (*fml* 文) (**a**) [U] quality of being unsatisfying or futile; worthlessness 不满意的或无益的境况; 无价值: *the vanity of human achievements* 人类成就之徒劳无益. (**b**) **vanities** [pl] vain, worthless thing or act 无意义、无价值的事物或行为.

□ ˈ**vanity bag**, ˈ**vanity case** woman's small bag or case for carrying cosmetics, toilet articles, etc (女子放梳妆用品等的)小手提包, 小梳妆盒.

van·quish /ˈvæŋkwɪʃ; ˈvæŋkwɪʃ/ *v* [Tn, Tn·pr] **~ sb (at/in sth)** (*fml* 文) defeat (an opponent, etc) 征服, 战胜(对手等): *vanquish the enemy in battle* 在战斗中打败敌人 ○ (*fig* 比喻) *vanquish one's rival at chess, tennis, etc* 在国际象棋、网球等比赛中击败对手.

vant·age /ˈvɑ:ntɪdʒ; *US* ˈvæn-; ˈvæntɪdʒ/ *n* **1** [U] position, etc that gives sb superiority or advantage 优势; 有利地位: *a point of vantage* 有利之处. **2** [C] (in tennis) first point scored after deuce (网球)平分后获得的第一分.

□ ˈ**vantage-point** *n* position from which one has a good or advantageous view of sth (观看某事物的)有利地点: *From their vantage-point on the cliff, they could watch the ships coming and going.* 他们在悬崖上居高临下, 能看到来来往往的船. ○ (*fig* 比喻) *the war, seen from the vantage-point of the 1980's* 以二十世纪八十年代的进步观点来看待这场战争.

vapid /ˈvæpɪd; ˈvæpɪd/ *adj* (*fml* 文) dull or uninteresting 乏味的; 无趣味的: *vapid utterances, remarks, comments, etc* 枯燥无味的话语、言语、评语等 ○ *His conversation was vapid in the extreme.* 他谈话乏味已极.

▷ **va·pid·ity** /vəˈpɪdətɪ; vəˈpɪdətɪ/ *n* (*fml* 文) (**a**) [U] state of being vapid 乏味; 枯燥. (**b**) [C] vapid remark 枯燥无味的言语.

va·por·ize, -ise /ˈveɪpəraɪz; ˈvepəˌraɪz/ *v* [I, Tn] (cause sth to) become vapour (使某物)汽化, 蒸发.

▷ **va·por·iza·tion, -isation** /ˌveɪpəraɪˈzeɪʃn; *US* -rɪˈz-; ˌvepərəˈzeʃən/ *n* [U].

va·por·izer, -iser *n* pressurized container for sending out liquid in the form of a vapour 汽化器; 喷雾器; 蒸馏器.

va·por·ous /ˈveɪpərəs; ˈvepərəs/ *adj* (*fml* 文) full of or like vapour 多蒸气的; 似蒸气的: *vaporous clouds of mist, smoke, steam* 雾、烟、蒸汽的弥漫.

va·pour (*US* **va·por**) /ˈveɪpə(r); ˈvepɚ/ *n* **1** [C, U] moisture or other substance spread about or hanging in the air 潮气; 水汽: *the steamy vapours of a Turkish bath* 土耳其浴的水蒸气. **2** [U] gaseous form into which certain liquid or solid substances can be converted by heating 蒸气: ˈ*water vapour* 水蒸气. **3 the vapours** [pl] (*arch or joc* 古或谑) sudden feeling of faintness 突然的眩晕感: *have/get (an attack of) the vapours* 突然(一阵)头昏眼花.

□ ˈ**vapour trail** (also ˌ**condenˈsation trail**) trail of condensed water left in the sky by a high-flying aircraft 雾化尾迹(飞机在高空飞行时留下的).

vari·able /ˈveərɪəbl; ˈvɛrɪəbl̩/ *adj* **1** varying; changeable 变化的; 可变的; 易变的: *variable pressure, rainfall, weather, speed* 变化不定的压力、降雨量、天气、速度 ○ *Winds are mainly light and variable.* 风力多微弱, 风向多变. ○ *His mood/temper is variable.* 他的情绪[脾气]反复无常. ○ *The quality of the hotel food is distinctly variable.* 这个旅馆的饭菜有时很好有时很差. **2** (*astronomy* 天) (of a star) periodically varying in brightness (指星)亮度周期变化的.

▷ **vari·able** *n* (often *pl* 常作复数) variable thing or quantity 可变的事物; 可变的量: *With so many variables, the exact cost is difficult to estimate.* 由于有许多可变因素, 很难准确地估算出成本. ○ *Temperature was a variable in the experiment.* 在该实验中温度是一个变量. Cf 参看 CONSTANT *n*.

vari·ab·il·ity /ˌveərɪəˈbɪlətɪ; ˌvɛrɪəˈbɪlətɪ/ *n* [U] quality of being variable; tendency to vary 可变性; 易变性.

vari·ably /-əblɪ; -əblɪ/ *adv*.

vari·ance /ˈveərɪəns; ˈvɛrɪəns/ *n* (idm 习语) **at variance (with sb/sth)** (*fml* 文) disagreeing or having a difference of opinion (with sb); in conflict (with sth) (与某人)意见不一, 有分歧; (与某事物)冲突, 矛盾: *Jill and Sue are at variance (with each other) over/about their lodger.* 吉尔和休在对待房客的问题上(彼此)意见不和. ○ *set people at variance (among themselves)*, ie make them quarrel 使大家不睦 ○ *This theory is at variance with the known facts.* 这种理论与已知事实不符.

vari·ant /ˈveərɪənt; ˈvɛrɪənt/ *n* thing that differs from other things or from a standard 变体; 变种; 变型: *The* *story has many variants.* 这个故事有很多说法. ○ [attrib 作定语] *forty variant types of pigeon* 四十种变种鸽子 ○ *variant spelling, pronunciation* 不同的拼法、发音.

vari·ation /ˌveərɪˈeɪʃn; ˌvɛrɪˈeʃən/ *n* **1** [C, U] **~ (in/of sth)** (degree of) varying or being variant 变化, 变动, 变异(的程度): *Prices have not shown much variation this year.* 今年物价没显出多大变化. ○ *Currency exchange rates are always subject to variation.* 货币兑换率是经常变的. ○ *The dial records very slight variations in pressure.* 刻度盘显示出压力有微小变化. **2** [C] **~ (on sth)** (*music* 音) repetition of a simple melody in a different (and usu more complicated) form 变奏; 变奏曲: *a set of variations on a theme by Mozart* 以莫扎特某一乐曲为主题的一组变奏曲 ○ *piano, orchestral, etc variations* 钢琴、管弦乐等变奏曲 ○ (*fig* 比喻) *His numerous complaints are all variations on a theme*, ie about the same thing. 他的牢骚说来道去都是一回事儿. **3** (**a**) [U] (*biology* 生) change in structure or form caused by new conditions, environment, etc 变异; 变种. (**b**) [U] (*mathematics* 数) change in a function, etc due to small changes in the values of constants 变分; 变差. (**c**) [C] instance of such change 变异; 变种; 变分; 变差.

var·ic·ose /ˈværɪkəʊs; ˈværɪˌkos/ *adj* [esp attrib 尤作定语] (of a vein, esp in the leg) permanently swollen or enlarged and therefore painful (指静脉, 尤指腿部的) 曲张的: *varicose ulcers*, ie caused by the condition of the veins 静脉曲张性溃疡.

var·ied /ˈveərɪd; ˈvɛrɪd/ *adj* **1** of different sorts; diverse 各种各样的; 不同的: *varied opinions, scenes, menus* 各种不同的意见、景象、菜单 ○ *Holiday jobs are many and varied.* 假期的工作又多又杂. **2** showing changes or variety 多变的; 多样的: *lead a full and varied life* 过丰富多彩的生活 ○ *My experience is not sufficiently varied.* 我的阅历不够广.

varie·gated /ˈveərɪgeɪtɪd; ˈvɛrɪˌgetɪd/ *adj* marked irregularly with differently coloured patches, streaks, spots, etc 杂色的; 斑驳的: *variegated geranium leaves, pansy flowers, etc* 杂色的天竺葵叶、三色堇花等 ○ *This specimen is richly variegated in colour.* 这件标本上有很多颜色.

▷ **varie·ga·tion** /ˌveərɪˈgeɪʃn; ˌvɛrɪˈgeʃən/ *n* [U] such irregular colouring or marking 杂色; 斑驳.

vari·ety /vəˈraɪətɪ; vəˈraɪətɪ/ *n* **1** [U] quality of not being the same, or not being the same at all times 变化; 多变(性); 多样(化): *offer, show, lack variety* 提供、显示出、缺乏多样化的事物 ○ *a life full of change and variety* 丰富多彩的生活 ○ *We all need variety in our diet.* 我们都需要饮食多样化. **2** [sing] **~ (of sth)** number or range of different things; assortment 若干不同的事物(的混合): *He left for a variety of reasons.* 他由于种种原因而离开了. ○ *a large/wide variety of patterns to choose from* 可供选择的种类繁多的花样. **3** [C] **~ (of sth)** (**a**) (member of a) class of things that differ from others in the same general group 同类中的分类事物: *collect rare varieties of stamps* 搜集邮票珍品. (**b**) (*biology* 生) subdivision of a species 变种: *several varieties of lettuce, mosquito, deer* 莴苣、蚊子、鹿的几个变种. **4** (*Brit*) (*US* **vaudeville**) [U] light entertainment consisting of a series of acts, eg singing, dancing, juggling, comedy, as performed on TV, at a theatre, or (esp formerly) in a music-hall 综艺节目(包括一系列演出, 如歌、舞、杂耍、滑稽剧等): [attrib 作定语] *a vaˈriety show, theatre, artist* 综艺表演、剧场、演员.

□ **vaˈriety store** (*US*) shop selling a wide range of small inexpensive items 杂货铺.

vari·ous /ˈveərɪəs; ˈvɛrɪəs/ *adj* **1** of several kinds, unlike one another 不同种类的; 各种各样的: *tents in various (different) shapes and sizes* 各种(不同)形状及大小的帐篷 ○ *Their hobbies are many and various.* 他们的业余爱好五花八门. **2** [attrib 作定语] more than one; individual and separate 不止一个的; 各个的; 各别的: *for various reasons* 由于种种原因 ○ *at various times* 多次 ○ *write under various names* 使用许多笔名写作.

▷ **vari·ously** *adv* (*fml* 文) differently according to the particular case, time, place, etc (情况、时间、处所等) 不同地: *He was variously described as a hero, a genius and a fool.* 把他说成是英雄、天才、笨蛋, 不一而足.

var·nish /ˈvɑːnɪʃ; ˈvɑrnɪʃ/ *n* [U, C] **1** (**a**) hard shiny transparent coating applied to the surface of esp woodwork or metalwork 清漆的面(尤指木器或金属制品上的): *a cover, coat, film, etc of varnish* 一层清漆 ○ *scratch, chip, scrape, etc the varnish on a table* 划伤、碰坏、刮掉...桌子上的清漆. (**b**) (particular type of) liquid used to give such a coating 清漆; 罩光漆; 凡立水: *a natural, a gloss, an oak, a polyurethane varnish* 天然的、发亮的、栎树、聚氨酯清漆. Cf 参看 LACQUER 1. **2** (*esp Brit*) = NAIL VARNISH (NAIL).

▷ **var·nish** *v* [Tn] put varnish on (sth) 在(某物)上涂清漆: *a highly varnished table-top* 涂了一层厚厚的清漆的桌面 ○ *sand and varnish a chair* 用砂纸把椅子打磨光再涂上清漆 ○ *varnish an oil-painting* 给一幅油画上光 ○ *Some women varnish their toe-nails.* 有些女子在脚趾甲上涂指甲油.

var·sity /ˈvɑːsətɪ; ˈvɑrsətɪ/ *n* **1** (*dated Brit infml* 旧, 口) (not used in names 不用于名称) university, esp Oxford or Cambridge 大学(尤指牛津或剑桥): [attrib 作定语] *a varsity tie, match, dinner* 大学的领带、体育比赛、宴会. **2** (*US*) team representing a university, college or school, esp in sports competitions (学校的)代表队, 校队(尤指体育的).

vary /ˈveərɪ; ˈvɛrɪ/ *v* (*pt, pp* **varied**) **1** [I, Ipr] **~ (in sth)** be different in size, volume, strength, etc (体积、容积、力量等)呈现不同: *These fish vary in weight from 3 lb to 5 lb.* 这些鱼的重量从3磅到5磅不等. ○ *Opinions vary on this point.* 对这一点看法各异. ○ *The results of the experiment varied wildly.* 实验结果差异很大. **2** [I, Ipr] **~ (with sth)**; **~ (from sth to sth)** change, esp according to some factor 改变, 变动, 变化(尤指伴随某种因素而产生): *Our routine never varies.* 我们的常规从无变化. ○ *Prices vary with the seasons.* 物价随季节而变动. ○ *Her mood varied from optimism to extreme depression.* 她的情绪由乐观一变而为极度消沉. ○ *work with varying degrees of enthusiasm* 工作积极性有所不同. ⇨Usage at CHANGE[1] 用法见 CHANGE[1]. **3** [Tn] make sth different by introducing changes 使某事物有变化; 改变某事物: *vary a programme, route* 更改程序、路线 ○ *varying the pace/speed at which you work* 改变你的工作节奏[速度].

vas·cu·lar /ˈvæskjʊlə(r); ˈvæskjələ/ *adj* of or containing vessels or ducts through which blood or lymph flows in animals or sap in plants 血管的; 维管的: *vascular tissue* 维管组织.

vase /vɑːz; *US* veɪs, *also* veɪz; ves, vez/ *n* vessel without handles, usu made of glass, china, etc and used for holding cut flowers or as an ornament 花瓶; 装饰瓶.

vas·ec·tomy /vəˈsektəmɪ; vəsˈɛktəmɪ/ *n* surgical removal of part of each of the ducts through which semen passes from the testicles, esp as a method of birth control 输精管切除术.

Vas·el·ine /ˈvæsəliːn; ˈvæsl̩ˌin/ *n* [U] (*propr* 专利名) yellowish petroleum jelly used as an ointment or a lubricant 凡士林; 矿脂.

vas·sal /ˈvæsl; ˈvæsl̩/ *n* **1** (in the Middle Ages) man promising to fight for and be loyal to a king or lord in return for the right to hold land (中世纪的)封臣, 家臣(为国君或领主效忠可受封土地者). **2** (*fig* 比喻) person or nation dependent on another 附庸; 下属; 属国: [attrib 作定语] *vassal states, kingdoms, etc* 附庸国、王国等. ▷ **vas·sal·age** /ˈvæsəlɪdʒ; ˈvæsl̩ɪdʒ/ *n* [U]: *reduce a dukedom to vassalage* 将一公爵降为封臣.

vast /vɑːst; *US* væst; væst/ *adj* [usu attrib 通常作定语] **1** very large in area, size, quantity or degree; immense (面积、体积、数量或程度)巨大的: *a vast expanse of desert, water, snow, etc* 浩瀚的沙漠、浩淼的水域、茫茫的积雪 ○ *His business empire was truly vast.* 他的企业规模极大. ○ *a vast crowd, throng, gathering, etc* 大群的人. **2** (*infml* 口) very great 极大的: *a vast fortune, expense, profit, sum of money, etc* 大量的财产、花费、利润、金钱等 ○ *a vast difference* 极大的差异.

▷ **vastly** *adv* (*esp infml* 尤作口语) very greatly 极大地: *a vastly superior intellect* 智慧超群的人 ○ *be vastly amused, suspicious* 非常逗人、可疑.

vast·ness *n* [U, C]: *lost in the vastness(es) of space* 消失在广阔无垠的太空.

vat /væt; væt/ *n* tank or large container for holding liquids, esp in distilling, brewing, dyeing and tanning 大桶、大盆等巨大容器(尤指蒸馏、酿造、染色及鞣革用的).

VAT (also **Vat**) /ˌviː eɪ ˈtiː, *also* væt; ˌvi e ˈti, væt/ *abbr* 缩写 = value added tax 增值税: *Prices include 15% VAT.*

V

价格中含有15%增值税.

Vat·ican /ˈvætɪkən; ˋvætɪkən/ *n* **the Vatican** (**a**) [sing] the Pope's residence in Rome 梵蒂冈(罗马教皇的驻在地). (**b**) [Gp] papal government 罗马教廷; 教皇权力.

vaude·ville /ˈvɔ:dəvɪl; ˋvɔdə,vɪl/ *n* [U] (*US*) = VARIETY 4.

vault 拱顶

vault[1] /vɔ:lt; vɔlt/ *n* **1** arched roof; series of arches forming a roof 拱券; 拱顶: *fan vaulting*, ie vaults where the arches have ribs, like a fan 扇形拱券. ⇨illus at App 1 见附录1插图, page viii. **2** (**a**) cellar or underground room used for storing things at a cool temperature 地窖; 地下室: ˈ*wine-vaults* 酒窖. (**b**) similar room beneath a church or in a cemetery, used for burials (教堂或坟场的)地下墓室: *in the family vault* 在家族的地下墓室中. **3** similar room, esp in a bank and protected by locks, alarms, thick walls, etc, used for keeping valuables safe (设于地下的)金库, 保险库(尤指银行的). **4** covering like an arched roof 拱券状覆盖物: (*rhet* 修辞) *the vault of heaven*, ie the sky 苍穹(天空).

▷ **vaul·ted** *adj* having a vault or vaults; built in the form of a vault 有拱券的; 建成拱状的: *a vaulted roof, chamber, etc* 拱形屋顶、有拱券的会堂等.

vault 撑物跳跃

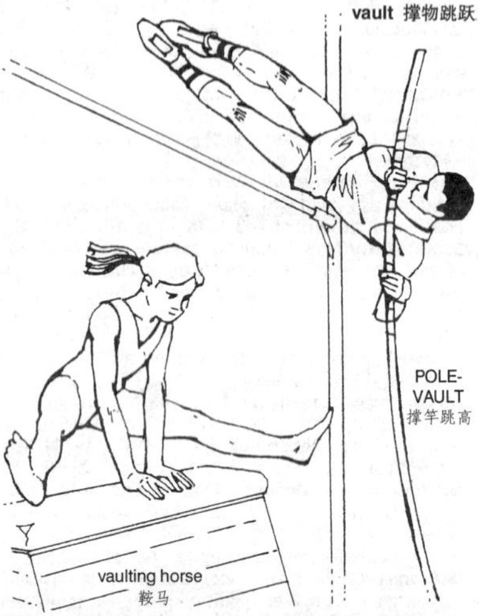

vault[2] /vɔ:lt; vɔlt/ *v* [I, Ipr] **~ (over sth)** jump in a single movement over or onto an object with the hand(s) resting on it or with the help of a pole (用手或竿支撑)跳跃: *vault (over) a fence* 用手支撑跳过篱笆墙 ○ *The jockey vaulted lightly into the saddle.* 那骑师用手一按马背轻身跃上了马鞍. ○ (*fig fml* 比喻, 文) *vaulting* (ie boundless, overreaching) *ambition* 奢想.

▷ **vault** *n* jump made in this way 撑物跳跃; 撑竿跳.

vaul·ter *n* (esp in compounds 尤用以构成复合词) person who vaults 撑物跳跃的人: *a pole-vaulter* 撑竿跳高运动员.

□ ˈ**vaulting horse** wooden apparatus for practice in vaulting (练习跳跃用的)鞍马. ⇨illus 见插图.

vaunt /vɔ:nt; vɔnt/ *v* [Tn] (*fml derog* 文, 贬) boast about (sth); draw attention to (sth) in a conceited way 吹嘘, 夸耀(某事物): *The bank's much-vaunted security system failed completely.* 这家银行大肆吹嘘的保安设施完全无济于事. ○ *vaunting her charm, success, wealth for all to see* 向大家炫示她的魅力、成就、财富. ▷ **vaunt·ingly** *adv*.

VC /ˌvi: ˈsi:; ˌvi ˋsi/ *abbr* 缩写 = **1** Vice-Chairman. **2** Vice-Chancellor. **3** Vice-Consul. **4** (*Brit*) Victoria Cross: *be awarded the VC* 获得维多利亚十字勋章 ○ *Col James Blunt VC* 维多利亚十字勋章获得者詹姆斯·勃朗特上校. Cf 参看 GC.

VCR /ˌvi: si: ˈɑ:(r); ˌvi si ˋɑr/ *abbr* 缩写 = video cassette recorder.

VD /ˌvi: ˈdi:; ˌvi ˋdi/ *abbr* 缩写 = venereal disease.

VDU /ˌvi: di: ˈju:; ˌvi di ˋju/ *abbr* 缩写 = (*computing* 计) visual display unit: *check a file on the VDU* 用视频显示器检验文件 ○ *a VDU operator* 视频显示器操作员. ⇨ illus at COMPUTER 见COMPUTER插图.

veal /vi:l; vil/ *n* [U] flesh of a calf used as meat (食用的)小牛肉: [attrib 作定语] *veal cutlets* 小牛肉的肉块.

vec·tor /ˈvektə(r); ˋvɛktɚ/ *n* **1** (*mathematics* 数) quantity that has both magnitude and direction, eg velocity 矢量; 向量. Cf 参看 SCALAR. **2** (*biology* 生) organism (esp an insect) that transmits a particular disease or infection (传播疾病的)媒介生物, (尤指)媒介昆虫. Cf 参看 CARRIER 4.

veer /vɪə(r); vɪr/ *v* **1** (**a**) [I, Ipr, Ip] (esp of a vehicle) change direction or course (尤指交通工具)改变方向或路线: *The plane veered wildly.* 那架飞机乱改航线. ○ *The car suddenly veered off the road.* 那辆汽车突然驶离了公路路面. ○ *The wind has veered round.* 风向相反了. (**b**) [Ipr] (*fig* 比喻) (of a conversation, sb's behaviour or opinion) change suddenly or very noticeably (指谈话内容、人的行为或观点)突然改变, 明显转变: *The discussion veered away from religion and round to politics.* 这场讨论从宗教问题一下子转到了政治问题上. **2** [I, Ipr, Ip] (of the wind) change gradually in a clockwise direction in the N Hemisphere and an anti-clockwise direction in the S Hemisphere (指风)(在北半球按顺时针方向、在南半球按反时针方向)逐渐转向: *The wind veered (round to the) north.* 近日风向已转北了. Cf 参看 BACK[4] 7.

veg /vedʒ; vɛdʒ/ *n* [U, C] (*pl* unchanged 复数不变) (*Brit infml* 口) vegetable(s) 蔬菜: *meat and two veg* 肉和两样蔬菜.

ve·gan /ˈvi:gən; ˋvigən/ *n* strict vegetarian who neither eats nor uses any animal products, eg eggs, silk, leather 纯素主义者(既不吃也不用任何动物产品, 如蛋、丝绸、皮革): [attrib 作定语] *a vegan diet, restaurant, fruit-cake* 纯素食谱、餐厅、水果糕点.

ve·get·able /ˈvedʒtəbl; ˋvɛdʒtəbḷ/ *n* **1** (part of various types of) plant eaten as food, eg potatoes, beans, onions 蔬菜: *green vegetables*, ie cabbage, lettuce, Brussels sprouts, etc 绿色蔬菜(卷心菜、莴苣、汤菜等) ○ *a salad of raw vegetables* 生菜色拉 ○ [attrib 作定语] *a vegetable curry, garden, knife* 咖喱素菜、菜园、蔬菜用刀 ○ *vegetable oils*, eg in margarine 植物油. Cf 参看 ANIMAL, MINERAL. **2** (*fig* 比喻) (**a**) person who is physically alive but mentally inactive because of injury, illness or abnormality 植物人(因伤、病或异常情况而丧失思维能力但仍有生命的人): *Severe brain damage turned him into a vegetable.* 他因脑部重伤而成了植物人. ○ [attrib 作定语] *lead a vegetable existence* 处于植物人的状态. (**b**) person who has a dull monotonous life 生活单调的人: *Stuck at home like this, she felt like a vegetable.* 像这样闷在家里, 她觉得生活太单调.

□ ˌ**vegetable** ˈ**marrow** (*fml* 文) = MARROW.

ve·get·arian /ˌvedʒɪˈteərɪən; ˌvɛdʒəˋtɛrɪən/ *n* person who, for humane, religious or health reasons, eats no meat 吃素的人: [attrib 作定语] *a vegetarian meal, diet, restaurant* 素食饭菜、食谱、餐馆. Cf 参看 VEGAN.

▷ **ve·get·ari·an·ism** /-ɪzəm; -ɪzəm/ *n* [U] practice or philosophy of being a vegetarian 素食; 素食主义.

ve·get·ate /ˈvedʒɪteɪt; ˋvɛdʒə,tet/ *v* [I] (*fig* 比喻) live a dull life with little activity or interest 过枯燥的生活(无甚活动或趣味): *the unemployed vegetating at home* 在家百无聊赖的失业者.

ve·geta·tion /ˌvedʒɪˈteɪʃn; ˌvɛdʒəˋteʃən/ *n* [U] plants in general; those found in a particular environment 植物(总称); 草木: *There is little vegetation in the desert.* 沙漠里植物稀少. ○ *the luxuriant vegetation of tropical rain forests* 热带雨林中繁茂的植物.

ve·he·ment /ˈviːəmənt; ˋviəmənt/ *adj* showing or caused by strong feeling; passionate 感情强烈的; 热情的: *a vehement objection, protest, denial, attack, etc* 强烈的反对、抗议、否认、攻击等 ○ *a vehement urge, impulse, desire, etc* 强烈的欲望、冲动、愿望等 ○ *He slammed the door with a vehement* (ie furious) *gesture.* 他愤怒地用力把门关上. ▷ **ve·he·mence** /-məns; -məns/ *n* [U]. **ve·he·mently** *adv*: *The charge was vehemently denied.* 那一指控遭断然否认.

vehicle /ˈvɪəkl; *US* ˈviːhɪkl; ˋvihɪkl̩/ *n* **1** (*esp fml* 尤作文雅语) conveyance such as a car, lorry or cart used for transporting goods or passengers on land 陆上交通工具; 车: *motor vehicles*, ie cars, buses, motor cycles, etc 机动车辆 ○ [attrib 作定语] *vehicle licensing laws*, eg for motor vehicles 机动车驾驶执照法 ○ *a space vehicle*, ie for carrying people into space 宇宙飞船. **2 ~ (for sth)** (*fig* 比喻) means by which thought, feeling, etc can be expressed 表达思想、感情等的工具或手段: *Art may be used as a vehicle for propaganda.* 艺术可用作宣传工具. ○ *The play was an excellent vehicle for the actress's talents.* 那出戏给了那位女演员一个大好机会一展才华.
▷ **vehicu·lar** /vɪˈhɪkjʊlə(r); viˋhɪkjələ˞/ *adj* (*fml* 文) intended for or consisting of vehicles 供车辆使用的; 车辆的: *vehicular access* 车辆驶入口 ○ *The road is closed to vehicular traffic.* 此路不准车辆通行.

veil /veɪl; vel/ *n* **1** [C] (**a**) covering of fine net or other (usu transparent) material worn, esp by women, to protect or hide the face, or as part of a head-dress 面纱, 面罩(尤指女用的): *a bridal veil* 新娘的面纱 ○ *She raised/lowered her veil.* 她撩起[放下]面罩. (**b**) piece of linen, etc covering the head and sometimes the shoulders, esp of nuns 头巾(尤指修女的). **2** [sing] (*fig* 比喻) thing that hides or disguises 遮盖物; 掩饰物: *a veil of mist over the hills* 笼罩小山上的薄雾 ○ *plot under the veil of secrecy, innocence* 在秘密、正经事物掩盖下搞的阴谋. **3** (idm 习语) **draw a curtain/veil over sth** ⇨ DRAW[2]. **take the ˈveil** become a nun 当修女.
▷ **veil** *v* [Tn] **1** put a veil over (sb/sth) 给(某人[某物])带面纱或面罩: *a veiled Muslim woman* 戴着面纱的穆斯林女子. **2** (*fig* 比喻) hide or disguise (sth) 遮掩, 掩饰(某事物): *a thinly veiled threat, insult, hint, etc* 含沙射影的威胁、侮辱、暗示等 ○ *He could hardly veil his contempt at my ignorance.* 他掩盖不住对我无知的轻蔑之情.

vein /veɪn; ven/ *n* **1** [C] any of the tubes carrying blood from all parts of the body to the heart 静脉: *Royal blood ran in his veins.* 他有王族血统. Cf 参看 ARTERY. **2** [C] any of the thread-like lines forming the framework of a leaf or of an insect's wing 叶脉; 翅脉. **3** [C] narrow strip or streak of a different colour in some kinds of stone, eg marble, or in some cheeses (大理石等或某些干酪的)纹理, 纹路. **4** [C] crack or fissure in rock, filled with mineral or ore; seam 矿脉; 岩脉; 矿层: *a vein of gold* 金矿脉. **5** [sing] **~ (of sth)** (*fig* 比喻) distinctive feature or quality; streak 特征; 气质; 性情: *have a vein of melancholy in one's character* 性格中含有忧郁的成分 ○ *Her stories struck/revealed a rich vein of humour.* 她的小说饶有风趣. **6** [sing] manner or style; mood 方式; 风格; 心情; 情绪: *in a sad, comic, creative, etc vein* 以忧伤的心情、喜剧的风格、富于创造性的方式等 ○ *The complaints continued in the same vein.* 总是那一类的牢骚话, 没完没了.
▷ **veined** /veɪnd; vend/, **veiny** /ˈveɪnɪ; ˋvenɪ/ *adjs* marked with or having veins 有静脉的; 有叶脉的; 有翅脉的; 有纹理的; 有矿脉的: *a veined hand* 显露青筋的手 ○ *veined marble* 有纹理的大理石 ○ *blue-veined cheese*, eg Stilton 有蓝色条纹的干酪(如斯第尔顿奶酪).

ve·lar /ˈviːlə(r); ˋvilə˞/ *adj* (*phonetics* 语音) (of a speech sound) made by placing the back of the tongue against or near the soft palate (指语音)软腭音的.
▷ **ve·lar** *n* velar speech sound (eg /k/, /g/) 软腭音(如/k/、/g/).

vel·cro (also **Velcro**) /ˈvelkrəʊ; ˋvɛlkro/ *n* [U] (*propr* 专利名) fastener for clothes, etc consisting of two nylon strips, one rough and one smooth, which stick together when pressed 尼龙搭扣(用于衣物等, 由两条尼龙带组成, 按压而粘合一起).

veld (also **veldt**) /velt; vɛlt/ *n* [U] flat treeless open grassland of the S African plateau (南非高原上的)草原. Cf 参看 PAMPAS, PRAIRIE, SAVANNAH, STEPPE.

vel·lum /ˈveləm; ˋvɛləm/ *n* [U] **1** fine parchment or bookbinding material made from calf, kid or lamb skin (用小牛皮或小羊皮制的)精制皮纸, 犊皮纸, 羊皮纸. **2** smooth fine-quality writing-paper 质优而光滑的书写用纸.

ve·lo·city /vɪˈlɒsətɪ; vəˋlɑsətɪ/ *n* **1** [U, C] (*esp physics* 尤用于物理学) (usu of inanimate things 通常用以指无生命之物) speed, esp in a given direction 速度(尤指沿已知方向的): *gain/lose velocity* 增加[降低]速度 ○ *the velocity of a projectile* 一个抛射体的速度. **2** [U] (*fml* 文) quickness or swiftness 迅速; 快速: *Gazelles can move with astonishing velocity.* 羚羊跑起来有时速度惊人.

ve·lour (also **ve·lours**) /vəˈlʊə(r); vəˋlʊr/ *n* [U] woven fabric like velvet or felt 丝绒: [attrib 作定语] *velour chair-covers, coats, hats* 丝绒椅罩、大衣、帽子.

vel·vet /ˈvelvɪt; ˋvɛlvɪt/ *n* [U] **1** woven fabric, esp of silk or nylon, with a thick soft nap on one side 立绒; 天鹅绒: [attrib 作定语] *a velvet jacket, curtain* 天鹅绒短上衣、帘子. **2** (idm 习语) **an iron fist/hand in a velvet glove** ⇨ IRON[1]. **smooth as velvet** ⇨ SMOOTH[1].
▷ **vel·vety** *adj* (*approv* 褒) soft like velvet 天鹅绒般柔软的: *a horse's velvety nose* 柔软的马鼻子 ○ *her velvety brown eyes* 她那柔和的棕色眼睛.

vel·vet·een /ˌvelvɪˈtiːn; ˌvɛlvəˋtin/ *n* [U] cotton fabric with a nap like velvet 平绒.

ve·nal /ˈviːnl; ˋvinl̩/ *adj* (*fml* 文) **1** ready to accept money for doing sth dishonest 贪财而行不义的: *venal judges, politicians, etc* 贪赃枉法的法官、政客等. **2** (of conduct) influenced by or done for bribery (指行为)因受贿而为的: *venal practices* 受贿而做的事.
▷ **ve·nal·ity** /viːˈnælətɪ; viˋnælətɪ/ *n* [U] quality of being venal 受贿做坏事; 贪赃枉法.
ve·nally /-nəlɪ; -nl̩ɪ/ *adv*.

vend /vend; vɛnd/ *v* [Tn] (*esp law* 尤用于法律) offer (esp small articles) for sale 出售(尤指小物件). ⇨Usage at SELL 用法见 SELL.
▷ **vendee** /venˈdiː; vɛnˋdi/ *n* (*law* 律) person to whom sth is sold 买主; 买方.
vendor /-də(r); -də˞/ *n* **1** (esp in compounds 尤用以构成复合词) person who sells food or other small items from a stall in the open air 摊贩; 小贩: ˈ*street vendors* 街头小贩 ○ ˈ*news-vendors*, ie newspaper sellers 报贩. **2** (*law* 律) seller of a house or other property (房屋等的)卖主, 卖方. Cf 参看 PURCHASER (PURCHASE[2]).
□ ˈ**vending-machine** *n* coin-operated slot machine for the sale of small items, eg cigarettes, drinks, sandwiches (投币式)自动售货机(出售小件商品的, 如香烟、饮料、三明治等).

ven·detta /venˈdetə; vɛnˋdɛtə/ *n* **1** hereditary feud between families in which murders are committed in revenge for previous murders 家族世仇; 族间仇杀. **2** bitter long-standing quarrel 长期争斗; 积怨: (*joc* 谑) *wage a personal vendetta against the Post Office* 个人向邮局进行的长期斗争.

ven·eer /vəˈnɪə(r); vəˋnɪr/ *n* **1** [C, U] (thin layer of) decorative wood or plastic glued to the surface of cheaper wood (for furniture, etc) 薄片镶饰(粘在廉价木料上的木质或塑料薄层, 如家具等上的). **2** [sing] **~ (of sth)** (*fig usu derog* 比喻, 通常作贬义) superficial appearance (of politeness, etc) covering or disguising the true nature of sb/sth 虚假的外表; 虚饰: *a thin veneer of Western civilization* 西方文明之金玉其外. Cf 参看 GLOSS[1] 2.
▷ **ven·eer** *v* [Tn, Tn·pr] **~ sth (with sth)** put a veneer on (a surface) 在(某物表面)上加薄片镶饰: *veneer a deal desk with walnut* 给松木书桌镶上胡桃木薄板.

ven·er·able /ˈvenərəbl; ˋvɛnərəbl̩/ *adj* **1** [usu attrib 通常作定语] (*fml* 文) deserving respect because of age, character, associations, etc (因年岁、品格、有某种关联等)值得敬重的, 受敬佩的: *a venerable scholar* 德高望重的学者 ○ *the venerable ruins of the abbey* 大寺院令人肃然起敬的遗迹. **2** (*religion* 宗) (**a**) (in the Church of England) title of an archdeacon (英国国教的)副主教的称号. (**b**) (in the Roman Catholic Church) title of sb thought to be very holy but not yet made a saint (天主教)备受敬仰但尚未被列入圣徒者的称号. ▷ **ven·er·ab·il·ity** /ˌvenərəˈbɪlətɪ; ˌvɛnərəˋbɪlətɪ/ *n* [U].

ven·er·ate /ˈvenəreɪt; ˋvɛnə,ret/ *v* [Tn] (*fml* 文) respect (sb/sth) deeply; regard as sacred 敬重(某人[某事物]); 崇敬: *venerate the memory, name, spirit, etc of Mozart* 怀着崇敬之情纪念莫扎特、景仰莫扎特的大名、崇敬莫扎特的精神. ▷ **ven·era·tion** /ˌvenəˈreɪʃn; ˌvɛnəˋreʃən/ *n* [U]: *The relics were objects of veneration/were held in veneration.* 这些遗物是备受崇敬之物.

ve·ner·eal dis·ease /vəˌnɪərɪəl dɪˈzi:z; və,nɪrɪəl dɪˋziz/ [C, U] (*abbr* 缩写 **VD**) disease communicated by sexual contact, eg gonorrhea, syphilis 性病.

ve·ne·tian blind /vəˌni:ʃn ˈblaɪnd; və,niʃən ˋblaɪnd/ window screen made of horizontal wooden or plastic slats that can be adjusted to let in light and air as desired 百叶窗帘.

ven·geance /ˈvendʒəns; ˋvɛndʒəns/ *n* **1** [U] **~ (on/upon sb)** paying back of an injury that one has suffered; revenge 报复; 报仇; 复仇: *take/seek/swear vengeance for the bombing* 因遭轰炸而进行[伺机/发誓]报复. **2** (idm 习语) **with a ˈvengeance** (*infml* 口) to a greater degree than is normal, expected or desired (比正常的、预期的或想要的)程度更深或更甚: *set to work with a vengeance* 加倍努力地干起活来 ○ *The rain came down with a vengeance.* 雨下得大极了.

venge·ful /ˈvendʒfl; ˋvɛndʒfəl/ *adj* (*fml* 文) showing a desire for revenge; vindictive 报复心驱使的; 图谋报复的; 复仇的. ▷ **venge·fully** /-fəlɪ; -fəlɪ/ *adv*.

ve·nial /ˈvi:nɪəl; ˋvinɪəl/ *adj* [esp attrib 尤作定语] (of a sin or fault) not serious; excusable (指罪过或过错)不严重的, 可原谅的.

ven·ison /ˈvenɪzn, ˈvenɪsn; ˋvɛnəzn̩, ˋvɛnəsn̩/ *n* [U] flesh of a deer used as meat (食用的)鹿肉: *roast venison* 烤鹿肉.

venom /ˈvenəm; ˋvɛnəm/ *n* [U] **1** poisonous fluid of certain snakes, scorpions, etc, injected by a bite or sting (某些蛇、蝎子等分泌的)毒液. **2** (*fig* 比喻) strong bitter feeling or language; hatred 愤恨的感情或言语; 怨恨: *'You liar!' he said, with venom in his voice.* '你撒谎!'他说道, 声音中含着怨恨.

▷ **ven·om·ous** /ˈvenəməs; ˋvɛnəməs/ *adj* **1** (of a snake, etc) secreting venom (指蛇等)分泌毒液的, 有毒的. **2** (*fig* 比喻) full of bitter or spiteful feeling 充满恶意的; 恶毒的: *a venomous look, remark, insult, etc* 恶狠狠的样子、言语、侮辱等. **ven·om·ously** *adv*.

ven·ous /ˈvi:nəs; ˋvinəs/ *adj* **1** (*anatomy* 解) of or contained in the veins 静脉的; 静脉中的: *venous blood* 静脉血. **2** (*botany* 植) having veins 有脉的: *a venous leaf* 有脉的叶子.

vent[1] /vent; vɛnt/ *n* **1** opening that allows air, gas, liquid, etc to pass out of or into a confined space (气体、液体等进出的)孔, 口. **2** anus of a bird, fish, reptile or small mammal (鸟、鱼、爬行动物或小哺乳动物的)肛门. **3** (idm 习语) **give (full) vent to sth** express sth freely (任意地)表达某事: *He gave vent to his feelings in an impassioned speech.* 他慷慨陈词抒发感情.

▷ **vent** *v* [Tn, Tn·pr] **~ sth (on sb)** find or provide an outlet for (an emotion) 发泄(情感): *He vented his anger on his long-suffering wife.* 他拿一贯受气的妻子出气.

vent[2] /vent; vɛnt/ *n* slit at the bottom of the back or side seam of a coat or jacket (大衣或上衣背部或侧面下端的)开口, 开衩.

vent·il·ate /ˈventɪleɪt; *US* -təleɪt; ˋvɛntl̩,et/ *v* [Tn] **1** cause air to enter and move freely through (a room, building, etc) 使空气进入(房间、建筑物等); 使空气流通: *ventilate the galleries of a coal-mine* 使煤矿坑道通风 ○ *My office is well-/poorly-ventilated.* 我的办公室通风良好[不良]. **2** (*fml fig* 文, 比喻) make (a question, grievance, etc) widely known and cause it to be discussed 将(问题、不满的意见等)公开并引起讨论: *These issues have been very well ventilated.* 这些问题已经过充分讨论.

▷ **vent·ila·tion** /ˌventɪˈleɪʃn; *US* -təˈleɪʃn; ˌvɛntl̩ˋeʃən/ *n* [U] **1** ventilating or being ventilated 空气流通: *increase ventilation by opening the top centre part of the carriage window* 把车厢窗户上面的中央部分打开以增进空气的流通 ○ [attrib 作定语] *the ventilation shaft of a coal-mine* 煤矿的通风竖井. **2** system or method by which a room, building, etc is ventilated 通风设备; 通风方法: *The ventilation isn't working.* 这个通风设备出故障了.

vent·il·ator /ˈventɪleɪtə(r); *US* -təl-; ˋvɛntl̩,etɚ/ *n* device or opening for ventilating a room, etc 通风设备; 通风口.

vent·ral /ˈventrəl; ˋvɛntrəl/ *adj* (*biology* 生) of or on the abdomen 腹的; 腹部的; 腹面的: *a fish's ventral fins* 鱼的腹鳍. ▷ **vent·rally** /-trəlɪ; -trəlɪ/ *adv*. Cf 参看 DORSAL.

vent·ricle /ˈventrɪkl; ˋvɛntrɪkl̩/ *n* (*anatomy* 解) **1** one of the chambers in the heart, whose function is to pump blood into the arteries 心室. Cf 参看 AURICLE 2. **2** any of various cavities in the body, esp the four in the brain (体内的)室, 腔, (尤指)脑室.

vent·ri·lo·quism /venˈtrɪləkwɪzəm; vɛnˋtrɪlə,kwɪzəm/ *n* [U] art of producing voice-sounds so that they seem to come from a person or place at a distance from the speaker 口技(使人听起来好像声音来自远方或另一人的发声技巧).

▷ **vent·ri·lo·quist** /-kwɪst; -kwɪst/ *n* person skilled in this 会口技的人: *a ventriloquist's dummy* 表演口技用的假人.

ven·ture /ˈventʃə(r); ˋvɛntʃɚ/ *n* **1** project or undertaking, esp a commercial one where there is a risk of failure 工作项目或事业; (尤指有风险的)商业, 企业: *embark on a risky, doubtful, etc venture* 从事一项冒险的、成败未卜的...企业项目 ○ *The car-hire firm is their latest (joint) business venture.* 这个出租汽车公司是他们最新的大胆的(合资)经营项目. ○ [attrib 作定语] *venture capital*, ie money invested in a new enterprise, esp a risky one 风险资本, 创业基金(投资于新企业的, 尤指有风险的). Cf 参看 ENTERPRISE 1. **2** (idm 习语) **at a ˈventure** (*fml* 文) at random; by chance 随便地; 碰运气地.

▷ **ven·ture** *v* (*fml* 文) **1** [Ipr, Ip] dare to go (somewhere dangerous or unpleasant) 敢于去(危险的或令人厌恶的地方): *venture into the water, over the wall* 敢于入水、越过墙头 ○ *venture too near the edge of a cliff* 敢于十分接近悬崖的边缘 ○ *The mouse never ventured far from its hole.* 老鼠从来不敢离开窝太远. ○ *I'm not venturing out in this rain.* 我不敢冒这样的雨外出. **2** [Tn, Tt] **(a)** dare to say or utter (sth) 敢说(某话): *venture an opinion, objection, explanation* 敢于亮明观点、表示异议、进行辩解 ○ *May I venture to suggest a change?* 我可以冒昧提个更动意见吗? ○ *I venture to disagree.* 恕我不敢苟同. **(b)** dare to do (sth dangerous or unpleasant) 敢做(危险的或令人厌恶的事): *venture a visit to the doctor/to visit the doctor* 硬着头皮去看病. **3** [Tn, Tn·pr] **~ sth (on sth)** take the risk of losing or failing in sth 冒着受损失或失败的风险: *I ventured a small bet on the horse.* 我在那匹马上下了一小笔赌注. **4** (idm 习语) **nothing ˈventure, nothing ˈgain/ˈwin** (*saying* 谚) one cannot expect to achieve anything if one risks nothing 不敢冒险就一事无成; 不入虎穴, 焉得虎子. **5** (phr v) **venture on/upon sth** dare to attempt sth 敢于尝试做某事: *venture on a trip up the Amazon* 敢于溯亚马逊河而上旅行.

ven·ture·some /-səm; -səm/ *adj* (*fml* 文) **(a)** (of people) ready to take risks; daring (指人)好冒险的, 大胆的: *be of a venturesome spirit* 有冒险精神. **(b)** (of acts or behaviour) involving danger; risky (指行动或行为)有危险的, 冒险的.

venue /ˈvenju:; ˋvɛnju/ *n* place where people agree to meet, esp for a sports contest or match 聚集地点; 会场; (尤指)体育比赛场所: *a last-minute change of venue* 事到临头更改的地点.

Venus /ˈvi:nəs; ˋvinəs/ *n* (*astronomy* 天) the planet second in order from the sun, next to the Earth 金星; 太白星.

ve·ra·cious /vəˈreɪʃəs; vəˋreʃəs/ *adj* (*fml* 文) **(a)** (of a person) truthful (指人)诚实的. **(b)** (of a statement, etc) true (指陈述等)真实的.

▷ **ve·ra·ciously** *adv*.

ve·ra·city /vəˈræsətɪ; vəˋræsətɪ/ *n* [U] (*fml* 文) truthfulness; truth 诚实; 真实: *I don't doubt the veracity of your report.* 我毫不怀疑你报告中的真实性.

ver·anda (also **ver·andah**) /vəˈrændə; vəˋrændə/ (*US* also **porch**) *n* roofed open-fronted terrace or platform which extends from the front, back or side(s) of a house, sports pavilion, etc (半敞的)走廊: *sitting on the veranda* 坐在走廊处. Cf 参看 PATIO 1.

verb /vɜ:b; vɝb/ *n* word or phrase indicating an action, an event or a state, eg *bring, happen, exist* 动词.

verbal /ˈvɜ:bl; ˋvɝbl̩/ *adj* **1** of or in words 词语的; 言语的; 文字的; 用言语的; 用文字的: *verbal skills*, ie reading

V

and writing 阅读和书写的技能 ○ *non-verbal communication*, ie gestures, facial expressions, etc 非言语交际(手势、面部表情等). **2** spoken, not written 口头的(非书面的): *a verbal explanation, agreement, warning, reminder, etc* 口头解释、协议、警告、提示等. **3** word for word; literal 逐字的; 一字不差的: *a verbal translation* 逐字的翻译. **4** (*grammar*) of verbs 动词的: *a noun performing a verbal function* 起动词作用的名词.

▷ **verb·ally** /ˈvɜːbəlɪ; ˋvɝblɪ/ *adv* in spoken words, not in writing 口头上(非书面形式).

□ **verbal ˈnoun** (also **gerund**) noun derived from a verb, eg *swimming* in the sentence *Swimming is a good form of exercise* 动名词(如在 Swimming is a good form of exercise 句中的 swimming).

veranda(h) (*US* also **porch**) 走廊

verb·al·ize, -ise /ˈvɜːbəlaɪz; ˋvɝblˌaɪz/ *v* [I, Tn] (*fml* 文) put (ideas or feelings) into words 用言语表达(思想或感情): *find it difficult to verbalize* 感到很难用言语表达.

ver·ba·tim /vɜːˈbeɪtɪm; vɝˋbetɪm/ *adj, adv* exactly as spoken or written; word for word 一字不差(的); 逐字(的): *a verbatim report* 一字不差的报告 ○ *report a speech verbatim* 逐字报道一篇讲话.

ver·bena /vɜːˈbiːnə; vɝˋbinə/ *n* type of herbaceous plant whose garden varieties have flowers of many colours 马鞭草.

ver·bi·age /ˈvɜːbɪɪdʒ; ˋvɝbɪɪdʒ/ *n* [U] (*fml derog* 文, 贬) (use of) too many words, or unnecessarily difficult words, to express an idea, etc 冗词, 艰涩词语(的使用): *The speaker lost himself in verbiage.* 那个人演讲叠床架屋兴头十足. ○ *plough through the verbiage of an official report*, ie read it with difficulty 吃力地阅读晦涩的官方报告.

verb·ose /vɜːˈbəʊs; vɝˋbos/ *adj* (*fml* 文) using or containing more words than are needed 冗长的: *a verbose speaker, speech, style* 言词冗赘的演讲者、讲话、文体.

▷ **verb·osely** *adv*.

verb·os·ity /vɜːˈbɒsətɪ; vɝˋbɑsətɪ/ *n* [U] (*fml* 文) state or quality of being verbose 冗长.

verd·ant /ˈvɜːdnt; ˋvɝdṇt/ *adj* (*fml or rhet* 文或修辞) (of grass, vegetation, fields, etc) fresh and green (指草、田野等)嫩绿的, 青翠的: *verdant lawns* 绿油油的草地 ○ *trees verdant with young leaves* 嫩叶青青的树木. ▷ **verd·ancy** /-dnsɪ; -dṇsɪ/ *n* [U].

ver·dict /ˈvɜːdɪkt; ˋvɝdɪkt/ *n* **1** decision reached by a jury on a question of fact in a law case (陪审团的)裁断, 裁决, 裁定: *question/dispute a verdict* 对裁断提出疑义[异议] ○ *The jury returned/announced/brought in their verdict.* 陪审团做出了裁断. ○ *a verdict of guilty/not guilty* 有罪[无罪]的裁断 ○ *a majority verdict of 8 to 4* 以8票对4票的多数通过的裁断. **2** (*fig* 比喻) decision or opinion given after testing, examining or experiencing sth (经过试验、检验或体验发表的)决定, 意见: *the verdict of the electors* 选举人的决定 ○ (*infml* 口) *My wife's verdict on my cooking was very favourable.* 我妻子认为我做的饭菜极好.

ver·di·gris /ˈvɜːdɪgrɪs, -griːs; ˋvɝdɪˌgrɪs, -gris/ *n* [U] greenish-blue substance that forms on copper, brass and bronze surfaces (as rust forms on iron surfaces) 铜绿.

verge /vɜːdʒ; vɝdʒ/ *n* **1** (**a**) = SOFT SHOULDER (SOFT): *Heavy lorries have damaged the grass verge.* 重型卡车把长草的软质路肩轧坏了. (**b**) grass edging along a path or round a flower-bed, etc (道路、花坛等的)长着草的边缘. **2** (idm 习语) **on/to the verge of sth** at or close to the point where sth new begins or takes place 在某事即将发生之际; 接近出现某事物之点: *on the verge of war, success, bankruptcy* 在接近战争爆发、成功、破产之际 ○ *Her misery brought her to the verge of tears.* 她难过得快要哭了.

▷ **verge** *v* (phr v) **verge on sth** be very close or similar to sth; be approaching sth 极接近某事物: *a situation verging on the ridiculous, tragic, chaotic, etc* 迹近可笑的、悲惨的、混乱的…地步 ○ *He's verging on 80 now and needs constant attention.* 他已近80岁, 需要侍候左右.

ver·ger /ˈvɜːdʒə(r); ˋvɝdʒɚ/ *n* **1** Church of England official who acts as a caretaker and attendant in a church (英国国教的)教堂司事. **2** (*Brit*) official who carries a mace, etc before a bishop or other dignitary (为主教或其他要人)持权杖等的人.

verify /ˈverɪfaɪ; ˋvɛrəˌfaɪ/ *v* (*pt, pp* **-fied**) **1** [Tn, Tf, Tw] make sure that (sth) is true or accurate; check 证实, 核对(某事物); 检查: *verify statements, allegations, conditions, facts, etc* 证实某些言论、说法、情况、资料等属实 ○ *verify the figures, details, etc of a report* 核实报告中的数字、细节等 ○ *The computer verified that/whether the data was loaded correctly.* 计算机已查实数据输入[是否]正确. **2** [Tn, Tf] show that (sb's fears, suspicions, etc) are justified; confirm 证明(某人之恐惧、怀疑等)有道理; 确定.

▷ **veri·fi·able** /ˈverɪfaɪəbl; ˋvɛrəˌfaɪəbḷ/ *adj* that can be verified 可证实的; 可核实的: *verifiable truths, facts, assets* 可核实的真相、事实、资产.

ve·ri·fica·tion /ˌverɪfɪˈkeɪʃn; ˌvɛrɪfɪˋkeʃən/ *n* [U, C] **1** verifying or being verified 证实; 核实: *Verification (eg Checking that weapons have been removed) could be an obstacle to an arms agreement.* 裁减军备协议难以达成, 症结在于如何证实(如检查武器确已销毁). **2** proof or evidence 证明; 证据.

ve·ri·si·mil·it·ude /ˌverɪsɪˈmɪlɪtjuːd; *US* -tuːd; ˌvɛrəsəˋmɪləˌtud/ *n* [U] (*fml* 文) appearance or semblance of being true or real 逼真; 貌似真实: *These flower illustrations show the artist's concern for verisimilitude.* 这些花卉插图表明这个画家很注重写实.

ver·it·able /ˈverɪtəbl; ˋvɛrətəbḷ/ *adj* [attrib 作定语] (*fml or joc* 文或谑) rightly named or called; real 名副其实的; 真正的: *a veritable villain* 不折不扣的坏蛋 ○ *The rain turned our holiday into a veritable disaster.* 这场雨把我们的假日完全毁了.

ver·ity /ˈverətɪ; ˋvɛrətɪ/ *n* **1** [U] (*arch* 古) truth (of a statement, etc) (陈述等的)真实性. **2** [C usu *pl* 通常作复数] (*fml* 文) idea, principle, etc generally thought to be true; fundamental fact 真理; 基本事实: *universal, scientific, moral, etc verities* 普遍的真理、科学的真谛、道德的准则. **3** (idm 习语) **the eternal verities** ⇨ ETERNAL.

ver·mi·celli /ˌvɜːmɪˈselɪ, -ˈtʃelɪ; ˌvɝməˋsɛlɪ, -ˋtʃɛlɪ/ *n* [U] pasta made into long slender threads, like spaghetti but much thinner, and often added to soups 细面条; 线面.

ver·mi·form /ˈvɜːmɪfɔːm; ˋvɝməˌfɔrm/ *adj* (*anatomy* 解) worm-like in shape 蠕虫样的: *the vermiform appendix* 阑尾. ⇨illus at DIGESTIVE 见 DIGESTIVE 插图.

ver·mil·ion /vəˈmɪlɪən; vɝˋmɪljən/ *adj, n* [U] (of a) bright red 朱红色(的); 鲜红(的): *a vermilion sash* 朱红色的腰带.

ver·min /ˈvɜːmɪn; ˋvɝmɪn/ *n* [U, usu pl *v* 通常与复数动词连用] **1** certain wild animals and birds (eg rats, foxes, moles, owls) which are harmful to crops and farmyard animals and birds 害兽及害鸟(为害庄稼及家畜家禽的, 如鼠、狐、鼹、鸮): *put down (exterminate) vermin* 消灭害兽和害鸟. Cf 参看 PEST 2. **2** insects (eg lice) sometimes found on the bodies of human beings and other animals 害虫(如虱): *a room alive/crawling with vermin* 有害虫的房间. **3** human beings who are harmful to society or who prey on others 为害社会或他人的人; 蠢贼; 害人虫.

▷ **ver·min·ous** /-əs; -əs/ *adj* **1** infested with fleas, lice, etc 有(蚤、虱等)害虫的: *verminous children* 长着虱子的儿童. **2** of the nature of or caused by vermin (1) 属害兽及害鸟一类的; 由害兽及害鸟引起的: *verminous diseases* 由害兽及害鸟引起的疾病.

ver·mouth /ˈvɜːməθ; *US* vərˈmuːθ; vɝˋmuθ/ *n* (**a**) [U] strong white wine flavoured with herbs, drunk as an aperitif (often in strong cocktails) 味美思酒(用作开胃酒, 常调入鸡尾酒中). (**b**) [C] glass or drink of this 一杯或一份味美思酒.

ver·na·cu·lar /vəˈnækjʊlə(r); vɝˋnækjəlɚ/ *n* [C] language

V

or dialect spoken in a particular country or region, as compared with a formal or written language 本地话; 土语; 本国语: *Arabic vernaculars*, ie as compared with classical Arabic 阿拉伯土语 ○ [attrib 作定语] *Vernacular literature quickly replaced Latin.* 用本国语创作的文学作品很快取代了拉丁文学. ○ *a vernacular poet*, ie one who writes in dialect 使用本地话写作的诗人.

ver·nal /ˈvɜ:nl; ˈvɝnl/ *adj* [attrib 作定语] (*fml or rhet* 文或修辞) of, in or appropriate to the season of spring 春季的; 在春季的; 适合春季的: *vernal breezes, flowers* 春风、春天的花.

Ver·onal /ˈverənl; ˈvɛrənəl/ *n* [U] (*propr* 专利名) type of sedative drug 佛罗那(镇静药).

ver·on·ica /vəˈrɒnɪkə; vəˈrɑnɪkə/ *n* [U, C] any of various types of herb, often with blue flowers; speedwell 婆婆纳(草本植物, 花多为蓝色).

ver·ruca /vəˈru:kə; vəˈrukə/ *n* (*pl* 复数作 **~s** or, in medical use, 医学用语复数作 **-cae** /-ki:; -ki/) small hard infectious growth on the skin (usu on the bottom of the feet); wart 疣(通常生于足底); 肉赘; 瘊子.

ver·sat·ile /ˈvɜ:sətaɪl; *US* -tl; ˈvɝsətl/ *adj* (*approv* 褒) **1** turning easily or readily from one subject, skill or occupation to another 有多种学问、技能或职业的; 多才多艺的: *a versatile cook, writer, athlete* 多才多艺的厨师、作家、运动员 ○ *a versatile mind* 多面手. **2** (of a tool, machine, etc) having various uses (指工具、机器等)多用途的, 多功能的: *a versatile drill, truck, etc* 万用钻、多用途卡车. ▷ **ver·sat·il·ity** /ˌvɜ:səˈtɪlətɪ; ˌvɝsəˈtɪlətɪ/ *n* [U].

verse /vɜ:s; vɝs/ *n* **1** [U] (form of) writing arranged in lines, often with a regular rhythm or rhyme scheme; poetry 韵文; 诗; 诗句; 诗体: *Most of the scene is written in verse, but some is in prose.* 这场戏大部分内容是用韵文写成的, 但也有一些是散文形式的. ○ *blank verse*, ie without rhymes at the end of the lines 无韵诗 ○ [attrib 作定语] *a verse translation of Homer's 'Iliad'* 荷马《伊利亚特》的诗体翻译. Cf 参看 PROSE. **2** [C] group of lines forming a unit in a poem or song (诗或歌的)句, 节: *a hymn of/with six verses* 一首有六节的赞美诗. **3 verses** [pl] (*dated* 旧) poetry 诗: *a book of humorous verses* 一本幽默诗集. **4** [C] any one of the short numbered divisions of a chapter in the Bible (《圣经》的)节. **5** (idm 习语) **chapter and verse** ⇨ CHAPTER.

versed /vɜ:st; vɝst/ *adj* [pred 作表语] **~ in sth** knowledgeable about or skilled in sth 精通某事物; 对某事物熟练: *well versed in mathematics, the arts, etc* 精通数学、文科等 ○ *well versed in the ways of journalists* 熟悉新闻工作.

vers·icle /ˈvɜ:sɪkl; ˈvɝsɪkl/ *n* each of the short sentences in the liturgy said or sung by the clergyman and answered by the congregation (做礼拜时, 牧师领读或领唱, 会众相随的)短句; (启应文中的)启文. Cf 参看 RESPONSE 3.

ver·sify /ˈvɜ:sɪfaɪ; ˈvɝsəˌfaɪ/ *v* (*pt, pp* **-fied**) (*fml* 文) **1** [I] compose verse 写韵文; 作诗. **2** [Tn] put (prose) into verse 将(散文)改写成韵文: *versify an old legend* 把一个古老的传说改写成韵文.

▷ **ver·si·fica·tion** /ˌvɜ:sɪfɪˈkeɪʃn; ˌvɝsəfəˈkeʃən/ *n* [U] (*fml* 文) (**a**) art of composing verse 诗格; 诗律. (**b**) style in which verse is composed; metre 诗体; 韵律.

ver·si·fier *n* (*sometimes derog* 有时作贬义) maker of verses 写韵文的人; 把散文改写成韵文的人; 平庸诗人: *amateur versifiers* 业余诗人.

ver·sion /ˈvɜ:ʃn; *US* -ʒn; ˈvɝʒən/ *n* **1** account of an event, etc from the point of view of one person (个人对一件事的)说法: *There were contradictory versions of what happened/of what the President said.* 对于发生的事情[对于总统说的话]说法相互矛盾. **2** (**a**) special or variant form of sth made (某制造物的具体的或改变的)种, 类: *the standard/de luxe version of this car* 这种汽车的标准的[豪华的]型号 ○ *the original/final version of the play* 这个话剧的最初的[最后的]形式. (**b**) special adaptation of a book, piece of music, etc (书、乐曲等的)某种版本或改编本: *the radio, film, etc version of 'Jane Eyre'* 根据《简·爱》改编的广播、电影等 ○ *an orchestral version of a suite for strings* 由弦乐组曲改编的管弦乐曲 ○ *a bilingual, an illustrated, etc version of the poems* 这些诗的双语的、插图的...版本. **3** translation into another language 译本; 译文: *the Authorized/Revised Version of the Bible* 《圣经》钦定英译本[钦定本的修订本].

verso /ˈvɜ:səʊ; ˈvɝso/ *n* (*pl* **~s**) any left-hand page of a book having an even number of pages (书的)左页; 偶数书页. Cf 参看 RECTO.

ver·sus /ˈvɜ:səs; ˈvɝsəs/ *prep* (*abbrs* 缩写 **v, vs**) (*Latin* 拉) against (sb/sth) 对, 对抗(某人[某事物]): *the advantage of better job opportunities versus the inconvenience of moving house and leaving one's friends* 较好的求职机会之利与搬家及远离朋友之弊 ○ *Kent v(ersus) Surrey*, eg in cricket 肯特对萨里(如板球比赛) ○ (*law* 律) *Rex v(ersus) Crippen* 雷克斯对克里平案.

ver·tebra /ˈvɜ:tɪbrə; ˈvɝtəbrə/ *n* (*pl* **-rae** /-ri:; -ri/) any one of the segments of the backbone 椎骨; 脊椎. ⇨ illus at SKELETON 见 SKELETON 插图.

▷ **ver·teb·ral** /-rəl; -rəl/ *adj*: *the vertebral column*, ie the backbone 脊柱.

ver·teb·rate /ˈvɜ:tɪbreɪt; ˈvɝtəˌbret/ *n, adj* (animal, bird, etc) having a backbone (鸟兽等)有脊柱的; 脊椎动物.

ver·tex /ˈvɜ:teks; ˈvɝtɛks/ *n* (*pl* **-tices** /-tɪsi:z; -təˌsiz/) **1** (*fml* 文) highest point or top; apex 最高点; 顶点: (*anatomy* 解) *the vertex of the skull* 颅骨顶. **2** (*mathematics* 数) (**a**) point of a triangle, cone, etc opposite the base (三角形、圆锥体等与底相对的)顶. (**b**) meeting point of lines that form an angle, eg any point of a triangle, polygon, etc (三角形、多角形等的)角的顶点.

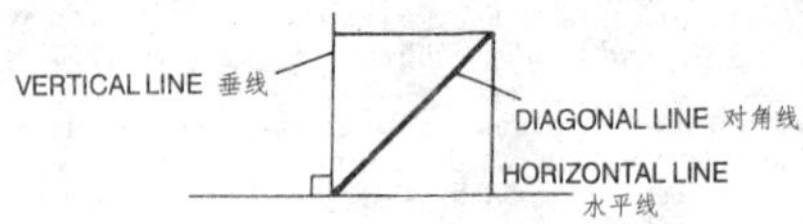

ver·tical /ˈvɜ:tɪkl; ˈvɝtɪkl/ *adj* **1** at a right angle to another line or plane, or to the earth's surface (相对于另一线或平面, 或相对于地面)垂直的, 竖的, 直立的: *the vertical axis of a graph* 图表的纵轴线 ○ *The cliff was almost vertical.* 那个悬崖近乎直上直下. ○ *a vertical take-off aircraft*, ie one that rises straight up into the air without needing a runway 垂直起飞的飞机. **2** in the direction from top to bottom of a picture, etc (图等上的方向)从上到下的, 纵向的: *the vertical clues of a crossword* 纵横字谜的纵行提示词语.

▷ **ver·tical** *n* vertical line, part or position 垂直线; 垂直部分; 垂直位置: *out of the vertical*, ie not vertical 不垂直的.

ver·tic·ally /-klɪ; -klɪ/ *adv*.

ver·ti·ces *pl* of VERTEX.

ver·tigo /ˈvɜ:tɪgəʊ; ˈvɝtɪˌgo/ *n* [U] feeling of losing one's balance, caused esp by looking down from a great height; dizziness 眩晕; (尤指)高处俯视性眩晕; 头晕: *suffer from (an attack of) vertigo* 感到(一阵)眩晕.

▷ **ver·ti·gin·ous** /vɜ:ˈtɪdʒɪnəs; vɝˈtɪdʒənəs/ *adj* of or causing vertigo 眩晕的; 引起眩晕的: *a vertiginous drop, descent, etc* 令人眩晕的下落、下降等.

verve /vɜ:v; vɝv/ *n* [U] enthusiasm, spirit or vigour, esp in artistic or literary work (尤指在艺术或文学工作中的)热忱, 精神, 活力: *write, sing, act, etc with verve* 积极地写作、歌唱、表演等 ○ *The performance lacked verve.* 这次表演缺乏生气.

very[1] /ˈverɪ; ˈvɛrɪ/ *adv* **1** (used as an intensifier before *adjs, advs* and *dets* 用于形容词、副词、限定词前以加强语气) in a high degree; extremely 很; 非常; 十分; 极: *very small, hot, useful* 很小、热、有用 ○ *very quickly, soon, far* 极快、早、远 ○ *very much, few, etc* 非常多、少等 ○ *'Are you busy?' 'Not very.'* '你忙吗?' '不太忙.' **2** (before a superlative *adj* or *own* 用于形容词最高级或 own 之前) in the fullest sense 十足; 完全: *the very best quality* 最好的质量 ○ *the very first to arrive* 最先到达者 ○ *six o'clock at the very latest* 最迟 6 点钟 ○ *your very own cheque-book* 你自己的那本支票簿. **3** exactly 正是: *sitting in the very same seat* 就坐在同一个座位上.

□ ˌ**very high** ˈ**frequency** (*abbr* 缩写 **VHF**) radio frequency of 30 to 300 megahertz 甚高频(30 到 300 兆赫的无线电频率).

NOTE ON USAGE 用法: **1 Very much** is used to modify verbs ☆ **very much** 用以修饰动词: *She likes*

Beethoven very much. 她很喜欢贝多芬的作品. ○ *We have enjoyed staying with you very much.* 我们很喜欢和你在一起. **2 Much** or **very much** can modify past participles ☆ **much** 或 **very much** 可用以修饰过去分词: *She is (very) much loved by everyone.* 她深受大家喜爱. **3 Very** is used to modify adjectives and past participles used as adjectives ☆ **very** 用以修饰形容词和作形容词用的过去分词: *She is very talented.* 她很有才华. ○ *I am very tired.* 我很累. ○ *They were very interested.* 他们很感兴趣.

very[2] /'verɪ; 'vɛrɪ/ *adj* [attrib 作定语] **1** itself, himself, etc and no other; actual; truly such 正是的; 实在的; 真正的: *This is the very book I want!* 这正是我想要的书! ○ *At that very moment the phone rang.* 正好在那个时候电话铃响了. ○ *You're the very man I want to see.* 你就是我想见的人. ○ *These pills are the very thing for your cold.* 这些药丸才是治你感冒的药. **2** extreme 极端的: *at the very end/beginning* 最终[最初]. **3** (used to emphasize a *n* 用以加强名词的语气): *He knows our very thoughts*, ie our thoughts themselves, even our innermost thoughts. 他了解我们内心深处的想法. ○ *The very idea* (ie The idea alone, quite apart from the reality) *of going abroad delighted him.* 他想到出国一事就很欢喜. ○ *The very idea/thought!* ie That is an impractical or improper suggestion. 真是个馊主意! (不切实际或不恰当.) ○ *Sardine tins can be the very devil* (ie very difficult) *to open.* 沙丁鱼罐头有时候还真难打开. **4** (idm 习语) **under/before one's very eyes** ⇨ EYE[1].

Very light /'verɪ laɪt; 'vɛrɪ ˌlaɪt/ coloured signal flare fired at night, eg as a sign of distress from a ship 维里信号弹(有彩色光, 夜间发射, 如用作船的遇难信号).

ves·icle /'vesɪkl; 'vɛsɪkḷ/ *n* (*anatomy or biology* 解或生) **1** small hollow bladder or cavity in the body of a plant or an animal (动植物体内的)囊, 泡. **2** blister 水疱.
▷ **ve·si·cu·lar** /və'sɪkjʊlə(r); və'sɪkjələ/ *adj* [usu attrib 通常作定语] of or characterized by the formation of vesicles 囊的; 泡的; 水疱的: *swine vesicular disease* 猪水疱病.

ves·pers /'vespəz; 'vɛspəz/ *n* [pl] church service or prayers in the evening; evensong (天主教及基督教某些教派的)晚课; (英国国教的)晚祷. Cf 参看 MATINS.

ves·sel /'vesl; 'vɛsḷ/ *n* **1** (*fml* 文) ship or boat, esp a large one 船(尤指大船); 舰: *ocean-going vessels* 远洋轮船 ○ *cargo vessels* 货轮. Cf 参看 CRAFT 2. **2** (*fml* 文) any hollow container, esp one used for holding liquids, eg a cask, bowl, bottle or cup 容器, 器皿(尤指盛液体的, 如桶、碗、瓶、杯). **3** tube-like structure in the body of an animal or a plant, conveying or holding blood or other fluid (动植物体内用以输送血液或其他液体的)管状结构; 血管; 脉管; 导管: *blood-vessels* 血管.

vest[1] /vest; vɛst/ *n* **1** (**a**) (*Brit*) (*US* **undershirt**) garment worn under a shirt, etc next to the skin 内衣; 汗衫; (贴身穿的)背心: *thermal, cotton, string, etc vests* 保暖汗衫、棉汗衫、网眼背心. (**b**) special (usu sleeveless) garment covering the upper part of the body 坎肩; (穿在外面的)背心: *a bullet-proof vest* 防弹背心. **2** (*US*) = WAISTCOAT(WAIST).
□ ˌ**vest-'pocket** *adj* [attrib 作定语] (*esp US*) small enough to fit in a waistcoat pocket 可放入坎肩口袋里的; 袖珍的: *a ˌvest-pocket 'camera* 袖珍照相机.

vest[2] /vest; vɛst/ *v* **1** [Tn·pr usu passive 通常用于被动语态] **~ sth in sb/sth; ~ sb/sth with sth** (*fml* 文) give sth as a firm or legal right to sb/sth; confer sth on sb/sth 给予或赋予某人[某事物](合法权力); 授予: *the powers vested in a priest* 赋予牧师的权力 ○ *Authority is vested in the people.* 权力属于人民. ○ *vest sb with authority, rights in an estate, etc* 授予某人权力、产权等 ○ *Parliament is vested with the power of making laws.* 国会有立法权. **2** [Tn] (*arch or religion* 古或宗) put on (ceremonial garments) 穿上(祭服). **3** (idm 习语) **have a vested interest (in sth)** expect to benefit (from sth) 期望(从某事物中)受益: *You have a vested interest in Tim's resignation*, eg because you may get his job. 蒂姆辞职可能对你有好处(如因你可能得到他那份工作).

ves·ti·bule /'vestɪbju:l; 'vɛstəˌbjul/ *n* **1** (*fml* 文) lobby or entrance hall, eg where hats and coats may be left 前厅, 门厅(如可放衣帽处): *the vestibule of a theatre, hotel, etc* 戏院、旅馆等的前厅. **2** (*US*) enclosed space between passenger coaches on a train 连廊, 通廊(列车两车厢相连处): [attrib 作定语] *vestibule train* 连廊列车.

vest·ige /'vestɪdʒ; 'vɛstɪdʒ/ *n* **1** small remaining part of what once existed; trace 残余部分; 遗迹; 痕迹: *Not a vestige of the abbey remains.* 那修道院的遗迹已荡然无存. **2** (esp in negative sentences 尤用于否定句) not even a small amount 毫无; 一点也不: *not a vestige of truth/common sense in the report* 该报告中之毫无真实性[常识]. **3** (*anatomy* 解) organ, or part of one, that is a survival of sth that once existed 退化的器官; 退化器官的痕迹: *man's vestige of a tail* 人的尾巴的痕迹.
▷ **ves·ti·gial** /ve'stɪdʒɪəl; vɛs'tɪdʒɪəl/ *adj* remaining as a vestige 残留的; 退化的.

vest·ment /'vestmənt; 'vɛstmənt/ *n* (esp *pl* 尤作复数) ceremonial garment, esp one worn by a priest in church 礼仪服装; (尤指牧师的)法衣, 圣衣, 祭服.

vestry /'vestrɪ; 'vɛstrɪ/ *n* room or building attached to a church, where vestments are kept and where clergy and choir can put them on (教堂的)法衣室, 法衣更衣处. ⇨ illus at App 1 见附录1插图, page viii.

vet[1] /vet; vɛt/ *n* (*infml* 口) = VETERINARY SURGEON (VETERINARY).

vet[2] /vet; vɛt/ *v* (**-tt-**) [Tn, Tn·pr] **~ sth/sb (for sth)** (*Brit*) examine (sb's past record, qualifications, etc) closely and critically 审查(某人过去的记录、资格等): *All staff are vetted for links with extremist groups before being employed.* 所有职员录用前均须审查是否与极端分子团体有关. ○ *be positively vetted for a government post*, ie be found to be trustworthy 已通过政府部门任职审查.

vet[3] /vet; vɛt/ *n* (*US infml* 口) = VETERAN 2.

vetch /vetʃ; vɛtʃ/ *n* plant of the pea family, used as fodder for cattle 巢菜, 大巢菜, 野豌豆(用作牲畜饲料).

vet·eran /'vetərən; 'vɛtərən/ *n* **1** person with much or long experience, esp as a soldier 经验丰富的人; 老手; (尤指)老军人, 老兵: *war veterans* 经历过战争的老战士 ○ *veterans of two World Wars* 经历过两次世界大战的老兵 ○ *veterans of the civil rights campaign* 民权运动的老战士 ○ [attrib 作定语] *a veteran politician, golfer* 资深的政治家、高尔夫球老手. **2** (also *infml* 口语作 **vet**) (*US*) any ex-serviceman 退伍军人: *'Veterans Day*, ie 11 November, commemorating the armistice (1918) in World War I 停战纪念日, 退伍军人节(11月11日, 为纪念1918年第一次世界大战停战日).
□ ˌ**veteran 'car** (*Brit*) car made before 1916, esp before 1905 老爷车(1916年以前的, 尤指1905年以前生产的): *a veteran Rolls Royce* 一辆劳斯莱斯老爷车. Cf 参看 VINTAGE 2.

vet·er·in·ary /'vetrɪnrɪ; *US* 'vetərɪnerɪ; 'vɛtərəˌnɛrɪ/ *adj* [attrib 作定语] of or for the diseases and injuries of (esp farm and domestic) animals (为医治)动物(尤指家畜家禽)疾病的; 兽医的: *veterinary medicine, studies* 兽医学、动物疾病研究.
□ ˌ**veterinary 'surgeon** (also *infml* 口语作 **vet**, *US* **ve·ter·in·arian** /ˌvetərɪ'neərɪən; ˌvɛtərə'nɛrɪən/) (*fml* 文) person who is skilled in the treatment of animal diseases and injuries 兽医.

veto /'vi:təʊ; 'vito/ *n* (*pl* **~es**) (**a**) [C, U] constitutional right to reject or forbid a legislative proposal or action 否决权: *the ministerial veto* 内阁的否决权 ○ *exercise the power/right of veto* 行使否决权 ○ *Permanent members of the United Nations Security Council have a veto over any proposal.* 联合国安全理事会常任理事国对一切提案均有否决权. ○ *Japan used her veto to block the resolution.* 日本使用了否决权反对该项决议. (**b**) [C] statement that rejects or forbids sth 否决或禁止某事物的声明.
▷ **veto** *v* (*pres p* **vetoing**) [Tn] reject or forbid (sth) authoritatively 否决或禁止(某事物): *The President vetoed the tax cuts.* 总统否决了削减税收的议案. ○ (*joc* 谑) *John's parents vetoed his plan to buy a motor bike.* 约翰的父母不同意他买摩托车.

vex /veks; vɛks/ *v* (*dated or fml* 旧或文) **1** [Tn] anger or annoy (sb), esp with trivial matters 使(某人)生气或恼怒(尤指因琐事): *His silly chatter would vex a saint.* 他说的话很无聊, 多有涵养的人也得气得发火. ○ *She was vexed that I was late.* 她嗔怪我来晚了. **2** [Tn esp passive 尤用于被动语态] worry or distress (sb) 使(某人)忧虑或悲哀: *He was vexed at his failure.* 他失败后垂

头丧气. **3** (idm 习语) **a vexed 'question** difficult problem that causes much discussion 引起很多争论的问题: *the vexed question of who pays for the damage* 应由谁赔偿损失, 这个争论不休的问题.

▷ **vexa·tion** /vek'seɪʃn; vɛks'eʃən/ *n* **1** [U] state of being annoyed or worried 烦恼; 忧虑. **2** [C esp *pl* 尤作复数] thing causing annoyance or worry 使人恼怒或忧虑的事物: *life's little vexations* 生活中恼人的琐事.

vexa·tious /vek'seɪʃəs; vɛks'eʃəs/ *adj* (*dated or fml* 旧或文) annoying or worrying 使人恼怒或忧虑的: *vexatious rules and regulations* 烦人的规章制度.

vg *abbr* 缩写 = (esp on corrected written work) very good (尤用以批改作业)很好.

VHF /ˌvi: eɪtʃ 'ef; ˌvi etʃ 'ɛf/ *abbr* 缩写 = (*radio* 无) very high frequency: *programmes broadcast on VHF* 以甚高频播出的节目 ○ *a VHF radio* 甚高频收音机. Cf 参看 UHF.

via /'vaɪə; 'vaɪə/ *prep* by way of (sth); through 经由(某事物); 通过: *go from London to Washington via New York* 从伦敦经纽约到华盛顿 ○ *I can send him a note via the internal mail system.* 我可以通过内部通讯系统给他发个通知.

vi·able /'vaɪəbl; 'vaɪəbl/ *adj* **1** sound and workable; feasible 切实可行的; 可实施的: *a viable plan, proposition, proposal, etc* 切实可行的计划、提议、建议等 ○ *scientifically, politically, economically viable* 科学上、政治上、经济上可行的. **2** (*biology* 生) capable of developing and surviving independently 能自行生长发育的: *viable eggs, seeds, foetuses* 能孵化的蛋、能萌发的种子、能成活的胎儿. ▷ **vi·ab·il·ity** /ˌvaɪə'bɪlətɪ; ˌvaɪə'bɪlətɪ/ *n* [U]: *test the commercial viability of solar power* 试验将太阳能商品化的可行性.

via·duct /'vaɪədʌkt; 'vaɪəˌdʌkt/ *n* long bridge, usu with many arches, carrying a road or railway across a valley or dip in the ground (跨越山谷或洼地以连通公路或铁路的)高架桥(通常有多孔).

vial /'vaɪəl; 'vaɪəl/ *n* = PHIAL.

vibes /vaɪbz; vaɪbz/ *n* **1** [sing or pl *v*] (*infml* 口) vibraphone 电颤琴: [attrib 作定语] *a vibes player*, eg in a jazz band 演奏电颤琴的人(如爵士乐队中的). **2** [pl] (*sl* 俚) = VIBRATIONS (VIBRATION 3): *get good, bad, weird, etc vibes from sth* 受某事物影响而产生的好的、不好的、奇怪的…情绪.

vi·brant /'vaɪbrənt; 'vaɪbrənt/ *adj* **1** vibrating strongly; resonant 振动的; 颤动的; 响亮的: *the vibrant notes of a cello, contralto, canary* 大提琴、女低音、金丝雀的颤音. **2** (*fig* 比喻) full of life and energy; exciting 充满生气的; 精力充沛的; 兴奋的: *a vibrant atmosphere, personality, performance* 活跃的气氛、活泼的个性、有活力的表演 ○ *She was vibrant with health and enthusiasm.* 她健康活泼生气勃勃. **3** (esp of colours) bright and striking (尤指颜色)鲜明的, 醒目的: *vibrant blues and yellows* 鲜明的蓝色和黄色. ▷ **vi·brancy** /-brənsɪ; -brənsɪ/ *n* [U].

V

vi·bra·phone /'vaɪbrəfəʊn; 'vaɪbrəˌfon/ *n* musical instrument like a xylophone but with electric resonators under the metal bars giving a vibrating effect 电颤琴(类似木琴, 在金属棒下有电子共鸣器可产生颤音效果).

vi·brate /vaɪ'breɪt; *US* 'vaɪbreɪt; 'vaɪbret/ *v* [I, Tn] **1** (cause sth to) move rapidly and continuously backwards and forwards; shake (使某物)振动, 颤动, 摇摆: *The whole house vibrates whenever a heavy lorry passes.* 重型卡车一经过, 整所房子都震. **2** (cause sth to) resound or quiver with rapid slight variations of pitch (使某物)振动出声或发颤音: *The strings of a piano vibrate when the keys are struck.* 钢琴的琴键一弹琴弦就振动出声. ○ *His voice vibrated with passion.* 他激动得声音发颤. ○ *The trilled 'r' is produced by vibrating the tongue against the upper teeth.* 发带颤音的 r, 舌抬向上齿颤动而成.

▷ **vi·brator** /-tə(r); -tɚ/ *n* device that vibrates or causes vibrations, esp one used in massage 振动装置; 震动器; (尤指)颤动按摩器.

vi·brat·ory /-tərɪ; *US* -tɔ:rɪ; -tɔrɪ/ *adj* [attrib 作定语] (*fml* 文) vibrating or causing vibrations 振动的; 颤动的; 产生振动的: *a vibratory massage* 颤动按摩.

vi·bra·tion /vaɪ'breɪʃn; vaɪ'breʃən/ *n* **1** [U, C] vibrating movement or sensation 振动; 颤动: *Even at full speed the ship's engines cause very little vibration.* 这条船即使全速前进, 发动机的震动也很小. **2** [C] (*physics* 物) single movement to and fro when equilibrium has been disturbed (偏离平衡位置的)一次往复振动: *Middle C is equivalent to 256 vibrations per second.* 中央C音相当于每秒钟振动256次. **3 vibrations** (*infml* 口) (also *sl* 俚语作 **vibes**) [pl] mood or mental influence produced by a particular person, thing, place, etc (由某人、事物、地方等引起的)感触, 感受.

vi·brato /vɪ'brɑ:təʊ; vɪ'brɑto/ *n* [U, C] (*pl* **~s**) (*music* 音) throbbing or tremulous effect in singing or on a stringed or wind instrument, consisting of rapid slight variations in pitch (演唱的或管弦乐器演奏产生的)颤音效果, 颤音. Cf 参看 TREMOLO.

vi·burnum /vaɪ'bɜ:nəm; vaɪ'bɝnəm/ *n* any of various types of shrub, usu with white flowers 荚蒾属(灌木, 通常开白花).

vicar /'vɪkə(r); 'vɪkɚ/ *n* (in the Church of England) clergyman in charge of a parish where tithes formerly belonged to another person or an institution (英国国教的)牧区牧师. Cf 参看 CURATE, MINISTER[1] 3, PRIEST, RECTOR.

▷ **vic·ar·age** /'vɪkərɪdʒ; 'vɪkərɪdʒ/ *n* house of a vicar 牧区牧师的住宅.

□ ˌ**Vicar of 'Christ** title sometimes given to the Pope 有时作教皇的称号.

vi·cari·ous /vɪ'keərɪəs; *US* vaɪ'k-; vaɪ'kɛrɪəs/ *adj* [esp attrib 尤作定语] **1** felt or experienced indirectly, by sharing imaginatively in the feelings, activities, etc of another person 设身处地的; 间接感受到的; 有同感的: *vicarious pleasure, satisfaction, etc* 间接得到的乐趣、满足感等 ○ *He got a vicarious thrill out of watching his son score the winning goal.* 他看着儿子射入一球获胜, 也感到同样兴奋. **2** done, felt or experienced by one person on behalf of another 代别人做的、感受的或经历的: *vicarious punishment, suffering, etc* 代人受的惩罚、苦难等. ▷ **vi·cari·ously** *adv*.

vice[1] /vaɪs; vaɪs/ *n* **1** (**a**) [U] evil or unprincipled conduct; wickedness 邪恶; 恶劣行径; 缺德行为: *vice and corruption in the Secret Service* 特工部门的邪恶与腐败现象. (**b**) [C] particular form of this 邪恶的或不道德的行为或现象: *Greed is a terrible vice.* 贪得无厌是可鄙的行为. Cf 参看 VIRTUE 1. **2** [C] (*infml or joc* 口或谑) fault or bad habit; weakness 缺点; 坏习惯; 坏毛病: *Sherry is one of my little vices!* 我有个毛病, 就是好喝雪利酒! **3** [U] criminal or immoral behaviour, eg gambling, drug-trafficking, pornography, prostitution 罪恶行径, 不道德的行为(如赌博、贩毒、色情勾当、卖淫): [attrib 作定语] *'vice squads*, ie groups of police who try to prevent this 警方取缔赌博、贩毒、色情活动的行动队 ○ *Detectives smash London vice ring*, eg in a newspaper headline. 警探侦破伦敦黄赌毒团伙(如报刊标题). **4** (idm 习语) **a den of iniquity/vice** ⇨ DEN.

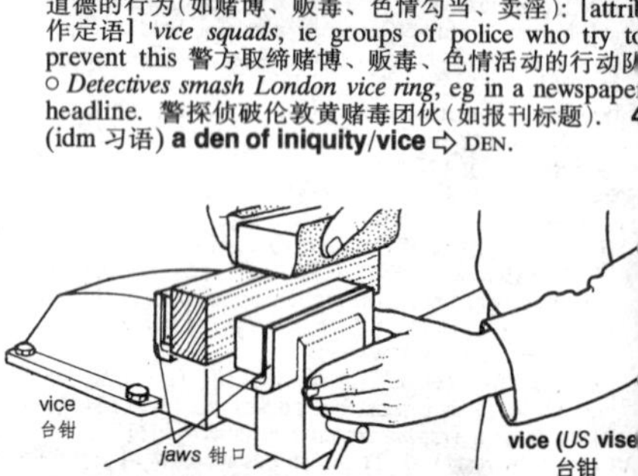

vice (*US* vise)
台钳

vice[2] (*US* **vise**) /vaɪs; vaɪs/ *n* metal tool, used in woodwork, etc, with a pair of jaws that hold a thing securely while work is done on it 台钳; (老)虎钳: (*fig* 比喻) *He held my arm in a vice-like* (ie very firm) *grip.* 他的手像虎钳一样紧紧抓住了我的手臂.

vice- *comb form* 构词成分 **1** acting as substitute or deputy for 代理; 副: *vice-president* ○ *vice-chancellor*. **2** next in rank to 级别低于: *vice-admiral*. ⇨App 9 见附录 9.

vice·roy /'vaɪsrɔɪ; 'vaɪsrɔɪ/ *n* person governing a colony, province, etc as the deputy of a sovereign (国王任命统治殖民地、自治领等的)总督.

▷ **vice·regal** /vaɪs'ri:gl; vaɪs'rigl/ *adj* of a viceroy 总督的.

vice·reine /'vaɪsreɪn; 'vaɪsren/ *n* wife of a viceroy; female viceroy 总督夫人; 女总督.

vice versa /ˌvaɪsɪ ˈvɜːsə; ˌvaɪsɪ ˈvɝsə/ the other way round; with the terms or conditions reversed 反之亦然; 反过来情况也一样: ˌ*We gossip about* ˈ*them and* ˌ*vice* ˈ*versa*, ie they gossip about us. 我们议论他们, 他们也议论我们.

vi·cin·ity /vɪˈsɪnətɪ; vəˈsɪnətɪ/ *n* (idm 习语) **in the vicinity (of sth)** (*fml* 文) in the surrounding district; in the neighbourhood 在周围地区; 在附近: *There isn't a good school in the (immediate) vicinity.* 附近没有好学校. ○ *crowds gathering in the vicinity of Trafalgar Square* 聚集在特拉法尔加广场周围的人群 ○ (*fig* 比喻) *a population in the vicinity of* (ie of approximately) *100 000* 10万左右的人口.

vi·cious /ˈvɪʃəs; ˈvɪʃəs/ *adj* **1** acting or done with evil intentions; spiteful 有恶意的; 恶毒的: *Vicious thugs attacked an elderly man.* 歹徒们袭击了一个老大爷. ○ *a vicious kick, look, remark* 恶狠狠的一踢、样子、言语. **2** given up to vice[1](3); depraved 邪恶的; 为非作歹的; 道德败坏的; 堕落的: *a vicious life* 堕落的生活 ○ *vicious practices, habits, etc* 恶行、恶习. **3** (of animals) savage and dangerous (指动物)凶猛而危险的. **4** (*infml* 口) violent or severe 剧烈的; 严重的: *a vicious wind, headache, flu-virus* 极厉害的大风、头痛、流感病毒. **5** (idm 习语) **a vicious ˈcircle** state of affairs in which a cause produces an effect which itself produces the original cause, so continuing the whole process 恶性循环: *I need experience to get a job but without a job I can't get experience — it's a vicious circle.* 我得有经验才能找到工作, 可是没有工作我就无法获得经验——这真是个恶性循环. **a vicious ˈspiral** continuous rise in one thing (eg prices) caused by a continuous rise in sth else (eg wages) 恶性螺旋形上升(如工资不断增加, 造成物价不断上涨). ▷ **vi·ciously** *adv*. **vi·cious·ness** *n* [U].

vi·cis·si·tude /vɪˈsɪsɪtjuːd; *US* -tuːd; vəˈsɪsəˌtud/ *n* (usu *pl* 通常作复数) (*fml* 文) change in one's circumstances, esp for the worse (个人境况的)改变, (尤指)变坏: *battling against the vicissitudes of life* 在每况愈下的生活中奋斗.

vic·tim /ˈvɪktɪm; ˈvɪktɪm/ *n* **1** person, animal or thing that is injured, killed or destroyed as the result of carelessness, crime or misfortune 被伤害、杀害或毁灭的人、动物或事物: *Many pets are victims of overfeeding.* 有许多宠物因喂食过量而遭殃. ○ *murder, rape victims* 谋杀案、强奸案的受害人 ○ *earthquake, accident, strike victims* 地震、事故、罢工事件的受难者 ○ (*fig* 比喻) *He is the victim of his own success*, eg because overwork has made him ill. 他成了自己成就的牺牲品(如积劳成疾). **2** (*fig* 比喻) person who is tricked or fooled 受骗者; 遭愚弄的人: *the victim of a hoax, practical joke, conspiracy, etc* 在骗局、恶作剧、阴谋等中上当的人. **3** living creature killed and offered as a religious sacrifice 为祭祀而宰杀的动物; 牺牲: *a sacrificial victim* 动物祭品. **4** (idm 习语) **fall victim (to sth)** be overcome (by sth); succumb (to sth) 被(某事物)降伏; 屈服(于某事物): *He soon fell victim to her charms.* 他很快就让她的魅力给迷住了.

vic·tim·ize, -ise /ˈvɪktɪmaɪz; ˈvɪktɪmˌaɪz/ *v* [Tn, Tn·pr] **~ sb (for sth)** **1** blame or punish sb unfairly for actions that others have carried out 责怪或处罚某人不当(使之受冤或代人受过): *Union leaders claimed that some members had been victimized* (eg by being dismissed) *for taking part in the strike.* 工会领袖声称有些会员参加罢工竟遭资方惩处(如遭解雇). **2** harm sb or make sb suffer unfairly; bully sb 不正当地使某人受损害或受苦难; 欺侮某人: *The fat boy was victimized by his classmates.* 那个胖小子挨同学欺侮了. ▷ **vic·tim·iza·tion, -isation** /ˌvɪktɪmaɪˈzeɪʃn; *US* -mɪˈz-; ˌvɪktɪməˈzeʃən/ *n* [U]: *The strikers agreed to return to work provided there would be no victimization of their leaders.* 罢工工人同意复工, 条件是不得惩处他们的领导人.

vic·tor /ˈvɪktə(r); ˈvɪktɚ/ *n* (*fml* 文) winner of a battle, contest, game, etc 胜利者; 获胜者: *emerge the victors* 产生胜利者.

Vic·toria Cross /vɪkˌtɔːrɪə ˈkrɒs; *US* ˈkrɔːs; vɪkˌtɔrɪə ˈkrɔs/ (*abbr* 缩写 **VC**) (*Brit*) the highest military award for bravery 维多利亚十字勋章: *Private Jones was awarded the Victoria Cross (for his gallantry).* 二等兵琼斯(因勇敢)被授予维多利亚十字勋章.

Vic·tor·ian /vɪkˈtɔːrɪən; vɪkˈtɔrɪən/ *adj* **1** of, living in or dating from the reign of Queen Victoria (1837-1901) 维多利亚女王时代(1837-1901)的; 生活于维多利亚时代的; 始于维多利亚时代的: *Victorian novels, poets, houses* 维多利亚女王时代的小说、诗人、房屋. **2** having the qualities and outlook attributed to middle-class people in Britain in the nineteenth century 有十九世纪英国中产阶级的品性及观点的: *Victorian attitudes to sexual morality*, ie ones stressing self-control, family loyalty, etc 维多利亚时代的性道德观(强调克己、忠于家庭等) ○ *Victorian values*, eg thrift, sobriety, hard work 维多利亚时代的价值观念和社会准则(如节俭、自制、勤勉).

▷ **Vic·tor·ian** *n* person living in the reign of Queen Victoria 维多利亚时代的人.

vic·tory /ˈvɪktərɪ; ˈvɪktərɪ/ *n* (**a**) [U] success in a war, contest, game, etc 胜利; 成功: *lead the troops to victory* 率领部队走向胜利 ○ [attrib 作定语] *victory parades, processions, celebrations, etc* 胜利的大游行、队伍、庆祝活动等. (**b**) [C] instance or occasion of this 胜利; 成功: *a narrow, decisive, resounding victory* 险胜、决定性的胜利、大胜 ○ *gain, win, score, etc a victory over one's rivals* 战胜对手 ○ *Labour did not have an easy election victory in East Oxford.* 工党在牛津东区选举中的胜利来之不易. ○ (*fig* 比喻) *The verdict of the court was a victory for common sense.* 法庭的这一裁断是情理的胜利.

▷ **vic·tori·ous** /vɪkˈtɔːrɪəs; vɪkˈtɔrɪəs/ *adj* **~ (in sth)**; **~ (over sb/sth)** having gained a victory; triumphant 获胜的; 胜利的: *the victorious players, team, etc* 获胜的选手、队等 ○ *The police are not always victorious in their fight against crime.* 警方与犯罪行为进行斗争并非百战百胜. **vic·tori·ously** *adv*.

victual /ˈvɪtl; ˈvɪtl̩/ *v* (**-ll-**; *US* also **-l-**) [Tn] supply (sth) with food and stores 给(某部门)供应食物及储备: *victual a ship* 给一艘船供应食物及储备.

▷ **victual·ler** (*US* also **victual·er**) /ˈvɪtlə(r); ˈvɪtl̩ɚ/ *n* trader or business supplying food and stores 食物及补给品的供应商或业务: (*Brit fml* 文) *a licensed victualler*, ie a public house keeper who sells food, spirits, beer, etc to be consumed on the premises 领有执照的酒店店主(出售食品、烈酒、啤酒等供顾客在店堂内享用).

victuals *n* [pl] (*dated* 旧) food and drink; provisions 食物及饮料; 粮食.

vi·cuna /vɪˈkjuːnə; *US* vaɪˈkuːnjə; vaɪˈkunjə/ *n* **1** [C] S American animal, related to the llama, with fine silky wool 骆马(产于南美, 与亚美利加驼有亲缘关系, 毛细而有光). **2** [U] (cloth made from the) wool of this animal 骆马毛绒(的料子): [attrib 作定语] *vicuna jackets* 骆马绒短上衣.

vide /ˈvɪdeɪ, ˈvaɪdiː; ˈviˌde, ˈvaɪdɪ/ *v* [Tn] (*Latin fml* 拉, 文) (used only in the imperative 仅用于祈使句) see or refer to (a passage in a book, etc) 见, 参看(书等的某段落). Cf 参看 INFRA.

video /ˈvɪdɪəʊ; ˈvɪdɪˌo/ *n* (*pl* **~s**) **1** [U] recording or broadcasting of moving pictures, as distinct from sound, by using television 电视; 电视录像; 电视广播: *video in schools*, ie as a teaching aid 教学用电视 ○ *amateur, commercial video* 业余、商业电视 ○ *The bank robbery was recorded on video.* 抢劫银行的情况有录像记录. ○ [attrib 作定语] *video frequencies* 视频 ○ *The satellite provides a video link between the White House and the Kremlin.* 该卫星提供了在白宫和克里姆林宫之间进行电视通讯联系的渠道. **2** [C] (**a**) (cassette or disc containing a) recording or broadcast made by using video 录像; 录像带; 录像盘: *watching, making, showing, etc videos* 观看、制作、放映…录像 ○ *The firm produced a short promotional video.* 这家公司制作了短小的广告录像带. ○ [attrib 作定语] *video shops, libraries* 录像带商店、资料室. (**b**) [C] = VIDEO CASSETTE RECORDER.

▷ **video** *v* (*pres p* **videoing**) [Tn] record (moving pictures) on videotape or videodisc 录制(影像): *video a TV programme* 录下电视节目.

□ ˌ**video caˈssette recorder** (also **video**, ˈ**video recorder**) (*abbr* 缩写 **VCR**) device which, when linked to a television, can record and show programmes, etc on videotape or videodisc 录像机.

ˈ**videodisc** *n* [U, C] plastic disc used, like videotape, to record moving pictures and sound 录像盘; 影碟.

ˈ**video game** game played using a home computer, etc in which the player controls images on a TV screen 电视游戏.

ˌ**video** ˈ**nasty** (*infml* 口) video film showing offensive scenes of sex and violence 表现性行为和暴力场面的不

堪入目的电视片.

'**videotape** *n* [U, C] magnetic tape used for recording moving pictures and sound 录像(磁)带. '**videotape** *v* [Tn] = VIDEO *v*.

vie /vaɪ; vaɪ/ *v* (*pt, pp* **vied** /vaɪd; vaɪd/, *pres p* **vying** /'vaɪɪŋ; 'vaɪɪŋ/) [Ipr] **~ with sb (for sth/to do sth); ~ for sth** (*fml* 文) compete keenly with sb (for sth); rival sb for sth 与某人(为某事物)激烈竞争; 与某人争夺某事物: *old rivals vying (with each other) for first place* (彼此)争夺第一名的老对手 ○ *Businesses vied with each other to attract customers.* 各商行互相竞争以招揽顾客.

view[1] /vju:; vju/ *n* **1** [U] state of seeing or being seen from a particular place; field of vision 观看; 看; 视野; 视场; 眼界: *The lake came into view/We came in view of the lake as we turned the corner.* 我们转过弯就看见那个湖了. ○ *The sun disappeared from view behind a cloud./A cloud hid the sun from view.* 太阳被云遮住看不见了. [浮云遮住了太阳.] ○ *She was soon lost from view among the crowd.* 她很快就在人群中消失了. ○ *The man in front was obstructing my view of the pitch.* 有前面那个人挡着, 我看不见球赛. **2** [C] what can be seen from a particular place, esp fine natural scenery 从某处看到的东西; (尤指)自然美景, 风景: *enjoying the magnificent views from the summit, over the mountains* 在群山之颠欣赏那壮丽的景色 ○ *10 different views of London*, eg on picture postcards 伦敦十景(如明信片上印的) ○ [sing] *You'll get a better view of the pianist if you stand up.* 你站起来, 就能更清楚地看到那位钢琴家. **3** (also **view·ing**) [C] (opportunity for a) special visual inspection of eg a film or an art exhibition (一次)观看(如影片或展览): *We had a private view of the jewels before the public auction.* 那些珠宝公开拍卖以前我们私下看了预展. **4** [C esp *pl* 尤作复数] **~ (about/on sth)** personal opinion or attitude; thought or observation (on a subject) (个人的)意见, 态度; (对某问题的)想法, 见解: *have, hold, express, air strong political views* 有、持、表达、发表强硬的政治观点 ○ *oppose, support sb's extreme views* 反对、支持某人过激的看法 ○ *What are your views on her resignation?* 你对她辞职有什么想法? ○ *We fell in with* (ie agreed with) *the committee's views.* 我们同意委员会的意见. **5** [sing] way of understanding or interpreting a subject, series of events, etc; mental impression (理解或解释某问题的)方式, 方法; 印象: *The scientific, legal, medical, etc view is that...* 科学的、法律上的、医学上的...解释是... ○ *a highly controversial view of modern art* 对现代艺术极有争议的理解方法 ○ *take a realistic, favourable, pessimistic, etc view of the problem* 对该问题有实际的、好的、悲观的...印象 ○ *This book gives readers an inside view of* (ie an insight into) *MI5.* 这本书向读者揭示了英国安全局的内幕. **6** (idm 习语) **a bird's eye view** ⇨ BIRD. **have, etc sth in 'view** (*fml* 文) have, etc sth as a clear idea, intention, plan, etc in the mind 头脑中对某事物有清楚的概念、打算、计划等: *What the President has in view is a world without nuclear weapons.* 总统考虑的是要建立一个没有核武器的世界. ○ *Keep your career aims constantly in view.* 要时刻牢记自己在事业上的奋斗目标. **in full view** ⇨ FULL. **in 'my, etc view** (*fml* 文) in my, etc opinion 依我...之见. **in view of sth** taking sth into account; considering sth 鉴于; 由于; 考虑到: *In view of the weather, we will cancel the outing.* 因天气关系, 我们要取消此次郊游. **on 'view** being shown or exhibited 陈列着; 展览着: *Our entire range of cars is now on view at your local showroom.* 我们各种型号的汽车现正在贵区陈列室里展出. **a point of view** ⇨ POINT[1]. **take a dim, poor, serious, etc 'view of sb/sth** regard sb/sth unfavourably, seriously, etc 不喜欢、重视...某人[某事物]: (*infml* 口) *He took a dim view of me/my suggestion.* 他认为我[我的建议]很蠢. **take the long view** ⇨ LONG[1]. **with a view to doing sth** (*fml* 文) with the intention or hope of doing sth 有做某事的打算或希望: *He is decorating the house with a view to selling it.* 他正在装修这所房子, 想把它卖了.

□ '**viewfinder** *n* device on a camera showing the area that will be photographed through the lens (照相机的)取景器. ⇨illus at CAMERA 见 CAMERA 插图.

'**viewpoint** *n* = POINT OF VIEW (POINT).

view[2] /vju:; vju/ *v* (*fml* 文) **1** [Tn, Tn·pr, Cn·n/a] **~ sth (as sth)** consider sth in the mind; regard sth (as sth) 考虑或认为某事物: *How do you view your chances of success?* 你认为你获得成功有多大把握? ○ *Future developments will be viewed with interest.* 未来的情况令人向往. ○ *Has the matter been viewed from the taxpayers' standpoint?* 这个问题是否从纳税人的立场上考虑过? ○ *Viewed from the outside, the company seemed genuine.* 从外表上看, 这家公司倒像是真的. ○ *The attack on the ship was viewed as an act of war.* 攻击了那条船已视作战争行为. **2** [Tn] look at or watch (sth) carefully 仔细察看或注视(某事物): *view a battle through binoculars from the top of a hill* 从山顶上用双筒望远镜观察战斗情况 ○ *The film hasn't been viewed by the censor.* 这部影片尚未经审查. **3** [Tn] inspect (a house, property, etc) with the idea of buying it 查看(房子、地产等)(以考虑购买): *open for viewing between 10.00 and 12.00* 10时至12时可供查看. **4** [I] watch television 看电视: *the viewing public* 电视观众. **5** (idm 习语) **an order to view** ⇨ ORDER[1].

▷ **viewer** /'vju:ə(r); 'vjuɚ/ *n* **1** person who views sth 观看者; 观察者: *viewers of the current political scene* 观察当前政治形势的人. **2** person watching a TV programme 电视观众: *regular viewers of 'Panorama'* '综合节目'的固定观众. **3** device for viewing photographic transparencies 摄影透明正片观看器: *a slide viewer* 幻灯式摄影正片观看器.

vi·gil /'vɪdʒɪl; 'vɪdʒəl/ *n* **1** [U, C] (action or period of) staying awake, esp at night, to keep watch or to pray 保持清醒(尤指夜间); 不眠(时刻); 守夜; 夜间祷告: *tired out by long nightly vigils at her son's bedside* (她)夜里长时间守护在儿子床前而疲惫不堪 ○ *hold a candle-light vigil for peace* 为和平而举行烛光祈祷. **2** eve of a religious festival, esp one observed by fasting 宗教节日的前夕(尤指斋戒的): *the Easter vigil* 复活节前夕.

vi·gil·ant /'vɪdʒɪlənt; 'vɪdʒələnt/ *adj* (*fml* 文) looking out for possible danger, trouble, etc; watchful or alert 警惕的; 警戒的; 警觉的: *under the vigilant eye of the examiner* 在检查员警惕的目光下. ▷ **vi·gil·ance** /-əns; -əns/ *n* [U]: *exercise constant, perpetual, etc vigilance* 时刻、永远...保持警惕 ○ *Police vigilance was eventually rewarded*, eg when an arrest was made. 警方时时警戒终有所获(如逮捕了罪犯). **vi·gil·antly** *adv*.

vi·gil·ante /ˌvɪdʒɪ'læntɪ; ˌvɪdʒə'læntɪ/ *n* (*esp derog* 尤作贬义) member of a self-appointed group of people who try to prevent crime and disorder in a community (自发组织的)治安团体的成员.

vign·ette /vɪ'njet; vɪn'jɛt/ *n* **1** **(a)** illustration, esp on the title-page of a book, but not in a definite border (无框线的)小插图(尤指书籍扉页上的). **(b)** photograph or drawing, esp of a person's head and shoulders, with the background gradually shaded off 晕映照, 晕映画像(尤指半身的). **2** (*fig* 比喻) short written description of sth, a person's character, etc (描述某事物、某人品性的)短文, 简介: *charming vignettes of Edwardian life* 描写爱德华时代生活的精妙短文.

vig·our (*US* **vig·or**) /'vɪgə(r); 'vɪgɚ/ *n* [U] **(a)** physical strength or energy; vitality 体力; 精力; 活力: *At 40, he was in his prime and full of vigour.* 他40岁时正年富力强. ○ *work with renewed vigour and enthusiasm* 以更加充沛的精力和热情工作. **(b)** forcefulness of thought, language, style, etc (思想、语言、风格等的)力量, 气势: *withstand the vigour of her protest, defence, attack, etc* 抵挡住她进行抗议、抗辩、攻击等的气势 ○ *music, poetry, etc of tremendous vigour* 气势磅礴的音乐、诗歌等. ⇨ Usage at STRENGTH 用法见 STRENGTH.

▷ **vig·or·ous** /'vɪgərəs; 'vɪgərəs/ *adj* **(a)** strong, active or energetic 强壮的; 积极的; 有力的: *avoid vigorous exercise, exertion, etc* 避免强度大的锻炼、劳动等 ○ *vigorous supporters of human rights* 积极拥护人权运动的人. **(b)** using forceful language, etc 语言犀利的: *vigorous debate, criticism, opposition, etc* 有力的争辩、批评、反对等 ○ *the poem's vigorous rhythms* 这首诗铿锵的韵律. **vig·or·ously** *adv*: *shake sb's hand vigorously* 用力握某人的手 ○ *argue vigorously in support of sth* 为某事物奋力争辩.

Vi·king /'vaɪkɪŋ; 'vaɪkɪŋ/ *n* (in the 8th to 10th centuries) Scandinavian warrior and pirate who settled in parts of N and W Europe, including Britain (8至10世纪的)北欧海盗(斯堪的那维亚武士, 活动于北欧与西欧部分地区, 包括英国): [attrib 作定语] *Viking raiders* 北欧海盗船.

vile /vaɪl; vaɪl/ *adj* (**-r, -st**) **1** extremely disgusting 非常

V

讨厌的; 可憎的: *a vile smell, taste, etc* 令人厌恶的气味、味道等 ○ *use vile language* 使用卑劣的语言. **2** despicable on moral grounds; corrupt 卑鄙的; 可耻的; 邪恶的; 不道德的: *vile deceits, accusations, slanders, etc* 可耻的欺骗、指控、诽谤等 ○ *Bribery is a vile practice.* 贿赂是卑鄙的行径. **3** (*infml* 口) extremely bad 极坏的: *vile weather* 恶劣的天气 ○ *be in a vile temper, mood, humour, etc* 脾气、心情、情绪等很坏. ▷ **vilely** /ˈvaɪllɪ; ˋvaɪllɪ/ *adv*. **vile·ness** *n* [U].

vil·ify /ˈvɪlɪfaɪ; ˋvɪlə,faɪ/ *v* (*pt, pp* **-fied**) [Tn] (*fml* 文) say evil or insulting things about (sb); slander 污蔑, 诋毁, 中伤(某人); 诽谤: *She was vilified by the press for her controversial views.* 因她持有异议, 新闻界对她横加挞伐. ▷ **vi·li·fica·tion** /ˌvɪlɪfɪˈkeɪʃn; ˌvɪləfəˋkeʃən/ *n* [U, C].

villa /ˈvɪlə; ˋvɪlə/ *n* **1** (*Brit*) (usu as part of an address 通常作住址的一部分) large detached or semi-detached house in a suburban or residential district (城郊或住宅区的)单独的或部分相连的住宅, 别墅: *No 3 Albert Villas* 艾伯特别墅3号. **2** house for holiday-makers at the seaside, in the countryside, etc (海滨、郊野等的)度假居所, 假日别墅: *rented villas in Spain* 在西班牙的出租的度假别墅. **3** country house with a large garden, esp in S Europe 乡村有大花园的住宅(尤指欧洲南部的): *the Villa d'Este*, ie in Italy 代斯泰花园住宅(意大利的). **4** (in Roman times) country house or farm with an estate attached to it (古罗马时代的)附有地产的乡间宅第或庄园.

vil·lage /ˈvɪlɪdʒ; ˋvɪlɪdʒ/ *n* **1** (**a**) [C] group of houses, shops, etc, usu with a church and situated in a country district 村庄, 乡村(通常设有教堂): [attrib 作定语] *the village school, fête, church* 乡村学校、义卖会、教堂. (**b**) [Gp] community of people who live there 村民(总称): *The whole village knew about the scandal.* 全村人都知道那件丑事了. Cf 参看 HAMLET, TOWN. **2** [C] (*US*) smallest unit of local government 村(最小的地方行政单位).
▷ **vil·la·ger** /ˈvɪlɪdʒə(r); ˋvɪlɪdʒɚ/ *n* person who lives in a village 在乡村住的人.

vil·lain /ˈvɪlən; ˋvɪlən/ *n* **1** (**a**) person guilty or capable of great wickedness 恶棍; 歹徒; 坏人. (**b**) (*Brit sl* 俚) (used esp by the police 尤为警方用语) criminal 罪犯. (**c**) (*infml* 口) mischievous rogue or rascal 淘气鬼; 坏蛋: *Get off my bike, you little villain!* 别动我的自行车, 你这个小淘气! **2** (in a story, play, etc) character whose evil actions or motives are important to the plot (小说、戏剧等中的)反面人物, 反派角色, 坏人. Cf 参看 HERO. **3** (idm 习语) **the ˈvillain of the piece** (*esp joc* 尤作戏谑语) person or thing responsible for some trouble, damage, etc 惹祸的、为害的...人或事物: *A faulty fuse was the villain of the piece.* 毛病就出在保险丝上.
▷ **vil·lain·ous** /ˈvɪlənəs; ˋvɪlənəs/ *adj* **1** characteristic of a villain; wicked 恶棍似的; 邪恶的: *a villainous plot, smile* 邪恶的阴谋、狰狞的笑. **2** (*infml* 口) extremely bad 极坏的: *villainous handwriting, weather* 糟糕的笔迹、天气. **vil·lain·ously** *adv*.
vil·lainy *n* [U, C] (*fml* 文) (act of) wickedness 邪恶(行为): *capable of great villainy/villainies* 能干出极坏的事.

vil·lein /ˈvɪleɪn; ˋvɪlɪn/ *n* (in medieval Europe) feudal tenant of land who was entirely subject to his lord (欧洲中世纪的)农奴(完全附属于封建领主的).
▷ **vil·lein·age** /ˈvɪlɪnɪdʒ; ˋvɪlənɪdʒ/ *n* [U] state of being a villein 农奴的身分或地位.

vim /vɪm; vɪm/ *n* [U] (*dated infml* 旧, 口) energy or vigour 力量; 活力; 精力: *full of vim* 精力充沛 ○ *Put more vim into your acting!* 你演出时要活泼些!

vi·nai·grette /ˌvɪnɪˈgret; ˌvɪnəˋgrɛt/ *n* [U, C] (also ˌ**vinaigrette ˈsauce**) salad dressing made from vinegar and oil, flavoured with herbs 香醋沙司(由醋和油制成、以香料调味的色拉调料).

vin·dic·ate /ˈvɪndɪkeɪt; ˋvɪndə,ket/ *v* [Tn] (*fml* 文) **1** clear (sb/sth) of blame or suspicion 澄清(某人[某事物])受到的责难或嫌疑: *The report fully vindicated the unions.* 这份报告充分说明工会是正确的. ○ *I consider that I've been completely vindicated.* 我认为已经证实了我完全无辜. **2** show or prove the truth, justice, validity, etc (of sth that has been disputed) 表明或证明(所争辩的事物)属实、正当、有效等: *Subsequent events vindicated his suspicions.* 后来的事实表明他的怀疑有道理. ○ *Her claim to the title was vindicated by historians.* 她说她有权得到这一头衔, 历史学家证明此事属实.
▷ **vin·dica·tion** /ˌvɪndɪˈkeɪʃn; ˌvɪndəˋkeʃən/ *n* (*fml* 文) (**a**) [U] vindicating or being vindicated (对所受到的责难或嫌疑的)澄清; 证实: *speak in vindication of one's conduct* 澄清自己的行为所受到的怀疑 ○ *the vindication of her claim* 她称有权得到的事物之业经证实. (**b**) [C] instance of this (对所受到的责难或嫌疑的)澄清; 证实: *The result was a vindication of all our efforts.* 这一结果表明我们的一切努力是必要的.

vin·dict·ive /vɪnˈdɪktɪv; vɪnˋdɪktɪv/ *adj* having or showing a desire for revenge; unforgiving 怀有或显示报复心的; 不宽恕的: *vindictive people, acts, urges, comments* 企图报复的人们、行为、心情、评语. ▷ **vin·dict·ively** *adv*. **vin·dict·ive·ness** *n* [U]: *He withheld the letter out of sheer vindictiveness.* 他扣下那封信纯粹是出于报复心理.

vine /vaɪn; vaɪn/ *n* **1** climbing or trailing plant with a woody stem whose fruit is the grape 葡萄藤: [attrib 作定语] ˈ*vine-grower* 种葡萄的人 ○ ˈ*vine leaves* 葡萄叶. **2** any plant with slender stems that trails (eg melons) or climbs (eg peas or hops) 蔓生植物(如瓜藤); 攀缘植物(如豌豆、蛇麻草).

vin·egar /ˈvɪnɪgə(r); ˋvɪnɪgɚ/ *n* [U] sour liquid made from malt, wine, cider, etc by fermentation and used for flavouring food and for pickling 醋.
▷ **vin·eg·ary** /ˈvɪnɪgərɪ; ˋvɪnɪgərɪ/ *adj* **1** of or like vinegar in smell or taste 醋的; 酸的; 有醋的气味或味道的. **2** (*fig* 比喻) sour-tempered; peevish 尖酸的; 刻薄的; 乖戾的.

vine·yard /ˈvɪnjəd; ˋvɪnjəd/ *n* plantation of grape-vines, esp for wine-making 葡萄园(尤指为酿酒而种植的).

vingt·et·un /ˌvænteɪˈɜːn; ˌvæn,teˋɑ̃n/ *n* [U] (*French* 法) = PONTOON[2].

vino /ˈviːnəʊ; ˋvino/ *n* [U] (*infml joc* 口, 谑) wine 葡萄酒; 果酒.

vin·ous /ˈvaɪnəs; ˋvaɪnəs/ *adj* (*fml or joc* 文或谑) of, like or due to wine (似)葡萄酒的; (似)果酒的; 由葡萄酒或其他果酒引起的: *a vinous flavour* 葡萄酒的味 ○ *sunk in a vinous stupor* 酩酊大醉.

vin·tage /ˈvɪntɪdʒ; ˋvɪntɪdʒ/ *n* **1** (**a**) [C usu *sing* 通常作单数] (period or season of) gathering grapes for wine-making 收获葡萄酿酒(的期间或季节): *The vintage was later than usual.* 那次葡萄采收期比平常年份晚. (**b**) [C, U] (wine made from the) season's harvest of grapes 一个收获季节采得的葡萄(所酿制的酒): *The claret was (of) a rare vintage*, ie (of) a year when the grapes produced a claret of high quality. 这一年份的法国波尔多红葡萄酒是稀有的好酒(为所收葡萄质量好的年份酿造的). ○ *1959 was an excellent vintage.* 1959年产的葡萄酒质量好. ○ *What vintage* (ie year) *is this wine?* 这种酒是哪一年酿造的? ○ [attrib 作定语] *vintage claret, port, etc* 某年酿制的法国波尔多葡萄酒、葡萄牙波尔图葡萄酒等 ○ *a vintage year for champagne* 酿制香槟酒的好年成. **2** [attrib 作定语] (**a**) (*fig* 比喻) characteristic of a period in the past; classic 有过去某一时期特征的; 经典的; 优秀的; 第一流的: *vintage jokes* 传统的笑话 ○ *vintage science fiction of the 1950's* 典型的20世纪50年代的科幻小说. (**b**) (*Brit*) (of a car) made between 1917 and 1930 (指汽车)1917年到1930年之间制造的: *vintage Fords* 1917年到1930年制造的福特汽车. Cf 参看 VETERAN CAR (VETERAN). **3** [attrib 作定语] (*infml* 口) (used before proper nouns 用于专有名词前) representing the best work of (a particular person); typical (某人)的最佳代表作的; 典型的: *This film is vintage Chaplin.* 这部影片是卓别麟的最佳代表作.

vint·ner /ˈvɪntnə(r); ˋvɪntnɚ/ *n* (*dated* 旧) wine-merchant 葡萄酒商.

vi·nyl /ˈvaɪnl; ˋvaɪnl̩/ *n* [U, C] (any of various types of) tough flexible plastic, esp PVC, used for making raincoats, records, book covers, etc 乙烯基塑料(尤指聚氯乙烯).

vi·ola[1] /vɪˈəʊlə; vɪˋolə/ *n* stringed musical instrument played with a bow, of larger size than a violin 中提琴. ⇨ illus at App 1 见附录1插图, page xi.

vi·ola[2] /ˈvaɪələ; ˋvaɪələ/ *n* any of various types of plant, including pansies and violets 堇菜目(包括三色堇和紫罗兰).

vi·ol·ate /ˈvaɪəleɪt; ˋvaɪə,let/ *v* [Tn] **1** break or be contrary to (a rule, principle, treaty, etc) 违反, 违背(规则、原则、条约等): *violate an agreement, oath, etc* 违背

协议、誓言等 ○ *These findings appear to violate the laws of physics.* 这些研究结果似乎有违物理定律. **2** treat (a sacred place) with irreverence or disrespect 亵渎(神圣的场所): *violate a tomb, shrine, etc* 亵渎陵墓、圣地等. **3** (*fig* 比喻) disturb or interfere with (personal freedom, etc) 干扰, 侵犯(个人自由等): *violate the peace*, eg by making a noise 扰乱宁静的环境(如弄出噪声) ○ *violate sb's privacy, right to free speech, etc* 侵犯某人的私生活、言论自由等. **4** (*fml or euph* 文或婉) rape (a woman or girl) 强奸(某女子).

▷ **vi·ola·tion** /ˌvaɪəˈleɪʃn; ˌvaɪəˈleʃən/ *n* (**a**) [U] violating or being violated 违反; 违背; 亵渎; 干扰; 侵犯; 强奸: *act in open/flagrant violation of a treaty* 公然地[明目张胆地]违反条约. (**b**) [C] instance of this 违反; 违背; 亵渎; 干扰; 侵犯; 强奸: *gross violations of human rights* 对人权的严重侵犯.

vi·ol·ator *n*.

vi·ol·ent /ˈvaɪələnt; ˋvaɪələnt/ *adj* **1** (**a**) using, showing or caused by strong (esp unlawful) physical force 使用暴力的, 显示暴力的, 暴力引起的(尤指非法的): *violent criminals, demonstrators, activists, etc* 使用暴力的罪犯、示威者、激进分子等 ○ *a violent attack, protest, struggle, etc* 猛烈的攻击、强烈的抗议、激烈的斗争 ○ *Students were involved in violent clashes with the police.* 学生与警方发生了暴力冲突. ○ *meet with/die a violent death*, eg be murdered 暴力致死(如被谋杀). (**b**) using, showing or caused by intense emotion 带有强烈感情的; 由强烈感情引起的: *violent passions, rages, fits, etc* 狂热的激情、暴怒、感情的迸发 ○ *violent language, abuse, etc* 激烈的言语、辱骂等 ○ *in a state of violent shock* 在万分震惊中 ○ *He has a violent dislike of school.* 他很讨厌上学. **2** severe or extreme 厉害的; 极度的: *violent winds, storms, earthquakes, etc* 强烈的风、风暴、地震等 ○ *violent toothache, pain, etc* 剧烈的牙痛、疼痛等 ○ *a violent contrast, change, etc* 强烈的对比、巨大的变化.

▷ **vi·ol·ence** /-əns; -əns/ *n* [U] **1** (**a**) violent conduct, esp of an unlawful kind 暴力行为(尤指非法的); 暴行: *crimes, acts, outbreaks, etc of violence* 暴力犯罪、暴力行为、暴力突发 ○ *the use of violence against one's attackers* 用暴力还击袭击者 ○ *TV violence/violence on TV* 电视中的暴力场面. (**b**) great emotional intensity; violent feeling 狂热; 激情; 强烈的感情: *We expressed our views with some violence.* 我们激动地亮明了观点. **2** severity or harshness 激烈; 猛烈; 厉害: *the violence of the gale, collision, outrage* 大风、碰撞、暴行之厉害程度. **3** (idm 习语) **do violence to sth** (*fml* 文) be contrary to sth; outrage sth 违背或违反某事物: *It would do violence to his principles to eat meat.* 吃肉与他的原则相违.

vi·ol·ently *adv*: *attack, disagree, react violently* 攻击、反对、反应十分强烈 ○ *The door slammed violently.* 门砰的一声关上了. ○ *He fell violently in love with her.* 他深深地爱上了她.

vi·olet /ˈvaɪələt; ˋvaɪəlɪt/ *n* **1** [C] small wild or garden plant, usu with sweet-smelling purple or white flowers 紫罗兰. ⇨illus at App 1 见附录1插图, page ii. **2** [U] colour of wild violets; bluish-purple 野生紫罗兰的颜色; 蓝紫色. ⇨illus at SPECTRUM 见 SPECTRUM 插图. **3** (idm 习语) **a shrinking violet** ⇨ SHRINK.

▷ **vi·olet** *adj* having the bluish-purple colour of wild violets 野生紫罗兰色的; 蓝紫色的: *violet eyes* 紫罗兰色的眼睛.

vi·olin /ˌvaɪəˈlɪn; ˌvaɪəˈlɪn/ *n* stringed musical instrument held under the chin and played with a bow 小提琴. ⇨ illus at App 1 见附录1插图, page xi. ▷ **vi·ol·in·ist** *n*.

VIP /ˌviː aɪ ˈpiː; ˌvi aɪ ˋpi/ *abbr* 缩写 = (*infml* 口) very important person 要人; 重要人物: *give sb/get (the) VIP treatment*, ie special favours and privileges 给予某人[享受]重要人物的待遇 ○ *the VIP lounge*, eg at an airport, for interviews with famous people, etc 贵宾厅(如机场中的、会见著名人士用的等).

vi·per /ˈvaɪpə(r); ˋvaɪpɚ/ *n* **1** any of various types of poisonous snake found in Africa, Asia and Europe 蝰蛇(有毒, 产于非洲、亚洲、欧洲). **2** (*fig* 比喻) spiteful and treacherous person 恶毒而奸诈的人. ▷ **vi·per·ish** /ˈvaɪpərɪʃ; ˋvaɪpərɪʃ/ *adj* (*fig* 比喻): *have a viperish* (ie malicious) *tongue* 用语恶毒.

vi·rago /vɪˈrɑːɡəʊ; vəˈreɡo/ *n* (*pl* **~s**) (*fml* 文) violent and bad-tempered woman who scolds and shouts 泼妇; 悍妇.

viral ⇨ VIRUS.

vir·gin /ˈvɜːdʒɪn; ˋvɝdʒɪn/ *n* **1** [C] person, esp a girl or woman, who has never had sexual intercourse 未发生过性行为的人; (尤指)处女. **2 the (Blessed) Virgin** [sing] the Virgin Mary, mother of Christ 童贞女马利亚(耶稣之母): [attrib 作定语] *the virgin ˈbirth*, ie the doctrine that Jesus was miraculously conceived by the Virgin Mary 童贞女之子(谓耶稣由童贞女马利亚从圣灵感孕而生的信条).

▷ **vir·gin** *adj* [usu attrib 通常作定语] (*esp approv* 尤作褒义) in an original or natural condition; untouched 原始的或天然的状态的; 未经触动的: *virgin snow* 洁白的雪 ○ *a jumper of pure new virgin wool* 用纯新羊毛制的套头毛衣 ○ *virgin forest, soil*, ie where cultivation has never been attempted 处女林、处女地(未经采伐、开垦的).

vir·gin·ity /vəˈdʒɪnətɪ; vɚˋdʒɪnətɪ/ *n* [U] state of being a virgin; virgin condition 童贞; 处女状态; 原始状况: *keep/lose one's virginity* 保持[失去]童贞.

vir·ginal /ˈvɜːdʒɪnl; ˋvɝdʒɪnl̩/ *adj* (*approv* 褒) of or suitable for a virgin 童贞的; 处女的; 适于处女的: *virginal innocence* 贞洁.

vir·gin·als /ˈvɜːdʒɪnəlz; ˋvɝdʒənəlz/ *n* [pl] square keyboard instrument without legs used in the 16th and 17th centuries 维金纳琴(方形, 有键盘, 无腿, 见于16和17世纪).

Vir·ginia /vəˈdʒɪnɪə; vɚˋdʒɪnɪə/ *n* [U] type of tobacco originally produced in the state of Virginia, USA 弗吉尼亚烟叶(原产于美国弗吉尼亚州): *Golden Virginia* 金牌弗吉尼亚烟 ○ [attrib 作定语] *Virginia cigarettes* 弗吉尼亚烟叶制成的香烟.

Vir·ginia ˈcreeper /vəˌdʒɪnɪə ˈkriːpə(r); vɚˌdʒɪnɪə ˋkripɚ/ [U, C] (*US* also **woodbine**) ornamental vine often grown on walls, with large leaves which turn scarlet in the autumn 弗吉尼亚爬山虎, 苦壁藤, 五叶爬山虎(常蔓生于墙上作为装饰, 叶大, 于秋天变成猩红色).

Virgo /ˈvɜːɡəʊ; ˋvɝɡo/ *n* **1** [U] the sixth sign of the zodiac, the Virgin 室女宫(黄道第六宫). ⇨illus at ZODIAC 见 ZODIAC 插图. **2** [C] (*pl* **~s**) person born under the influence of this sign 属室女宫星座的人. ▷ **Vir·goan** *n, adj*. ⇨Usage at ZODIAC 用法见 ZODIAC.

vir·ile /ˈvɪraɪl; *US* ˈvɪrəl; ˋvɪrəl/ *adj* (*usu approv* 通常作褒义) **1** (of men) having procreative power; sexually potent (指男子)有生殖力的, 性机能强的: *virile young males* 有生殖能力的年轻男子. **2** having or showing typically masculine strength or energy 具有或显示刚强气概的: *virile pursuits such as rowing and mountaineering* 划船和登山这类富刚强气概的活动 ○ *a virile performance of Othello* 奥塞罗这一角色刚强的表现.

▷ **vir·il·ity** /vɪˈrɪlətɪ; vəˋrɪlətɪ/ *n* [U] **1** (of men) sexual potency (男性的)生殖力, 性机能: *a need to prove, assert, etc one's virility* 需证明、表明...自己有生殖能力. **2** typically masculine strength or energy 刚强的气概.

viro·logy /vaɪəˈrɒlədʒɪ; vaɪˋrɑlədʒɪ/ *n* [U] scientific study of viruses and virus diseases 病毒学. ▷ **viro·lo·gical** /ˌvaɪərəˈlɒdʒɪkl; ˌvaɪrəˋlɑdʒɪkəl/ *adj*. **viro·logist** /vaɪəˈrɒlədʒɪst; vaɪˋrɑlədʒɪst/ *n*.

vir·tual /ˈvɜːtʃʊəl; ˋvɝtʃʊəl/ *adj* [attrib 作定语] being or acting as what is described, but not accepted as such in name or officially 事实上的, 实际上的, 实质上的(但未在名义上或正式获承认): *Our deputy manager is the virtual head of the business.* 我们的副经理是公司的实际负责人. ○ *A virtual state of war exists between the two countries.* 这两国间实际上处于战争状态.

▷ **vir·tu·ally** /-tʃʊəlɪ; -tʃʊəlɪ/ *adv* in every important respect; almost 在各重要方面; 事实上; 实际上; 几乎: *be virtually certain, impossible, fixed, agreed* 实际上已肯定、不可能、已固定、已同意 ○ *He virtually promised me the job*, ie but did not actually do so. 他已算答应把那工作交给我了(但事实上尚未这样做). ○ *There's virtually none left.* 实际上一个都没剩.

vir·tue /ˈvɜːtʃuː; ˋvɝtʃu/ *n* **1** (**a**) [U] moral goodness or excellence 美德; 道德上的优良品性: *lead a life of virtue* 过高尚的生活 ○ (*esp joc* 尤作戏谑语) *a paragon of virtue* 美德的典范. (**b**) [C] particular form of this; good habit 美德; 良好的习惯: (*saying* 谚) *Patience is a virtue.* 忍耐是一种美德. ○ *extol, praise, etc the virtues of thrift* 颂扬、赞美...节俭的好习惯. Cf 参看 VICE[1] 1. **2** [C, U] **the ~ (of sth/being sth/doing sth)** attractive or useful quality; advantage 优点; 长处: *This seat has the virtue of being adjustable.* 这种座位的好处是可以调节. ○ *The great virtue of camping is its cheapness/is that it is cheap.* 野营的一大优点是省钱. ○ *learn the virtue(s) of keeping one's mouth shut*, ie of not always saying what one thinks 要有慎言的优点. **3** [U] (*fml or joc* 文或谑) chastity, esp of a woman 操守; (尤指女子的)贞操, 贞节: *lose/preserve one's virtue* 失去[保持]贞洁. **4** (idm 习语) **by virtue of sth** (*fml* 文) on account of or because of sth 由于或因为某事物: *He was exempt from charges by virtue of his youth/of being so young/of the fact that he was so young.* 他因年幼而获得免费. **make a ˌvirtue of neˈcessity** do sth with a good grace because one has to do it anyway 做非做不可的事就痛痛快快地做: *Being short of money, I made a virtue of necessity and gave up smoking.* 我因缺钱, 倒也乐得把烟戒了. **a woman of easy virtue** ⇨ WOMAN. **virtue is its own reward** (*saying* 谚) behaving virtuously should give one enough satisfaction for one not to expect any further reward 做好事即乐在其中.

▷ **vir·tu·ous** /ˈvɜːtʃʊəs; ˈvɝtʃʊəs/ *adj* **1** having or showing moral virtue 有道德的; 品性好的; 品德高的. **2** (*derog or joc* 贬或谑) claiming to have or show better behaviour or higher moral principles than others; self-righteous 自命高尚的; 自以为是的: *feel virtuous at/about having done the washing-up* 因为刷洗了碗碟感到情操高尚. **vir·tu·ously** *adv.* **vir·tu·ous·ness** *n* [U].

vir·tu·oso /ˌvɜːtʃʊˈəʊzəʊ, -ˈəʊsəʊ; ˌvɝtʃʊˈozo, -ˈoso/ *n* (*pl* **~s** or **-si** /-ziː, -siː; -zi, -si/) **1** person who is exceptionally skilled in the techniques of a fine art, esp playing a musical instrument or singing (在某艺术方面)技艺超群的人; (尤指)演奏家, 歌唱家: *a cello, trumpet, etc virtuoso* 大提琴、小号等演奏家 ○ *a jazz virtuoso* 爵士乐演奏家 ○ *great virtuosos of the keyboard* 钢琴大师 ○ [attrib 作定语] *virtuoso players* 演奏大师. **2** [attrib 作定语] (*fig* 比喻) showing exceptional skill 表现卓越技巧的: *His handling of the meeting was quite a virtuoso performance.* 他掌握会议可真有一套.

▷ **vir·tu·os·ity** /ˌvɜːtʃʊˈɒsətɪ; ˌvɝtʃʊˈɑsətɪ/ *n* [U] skill of a virtuoso (艺术方面的)卓越技巧: *feats, displays, etc of virtuosity* 高超的技艺、卓越技巧的展示.

viru·lent /ˈvɪrʊlənt; ˈvɪrulənt/ *adj* **1** [esp attrib 尤作定语] (of a disease or poison) extremely harmful or deadly (指疾病或毒物)致命的, 剧毒的: *a virulent strain of flu* 一种致命的流感. **2** (*fml* 文) strongly and bitterly hostile 恶意的; 仇恨的: *virulent abuse* 衔恨的辱骂 ○ *make a virulent attack on the press* 恶意抨击新闻界 ○ *a particularly virulent form of racism* 不共戴天的种族主义表现. ▷ **viru·lence** /-ləns; -ləns/ *n* [U]. **viru·lently** *adv.*

virus /ˈvaɪərəs; ˈvaɪrəs/ *n* (*pl* **viruses**) (**a**) simple organism, smaller than bacteria, and causing infectious disease 病毒; 滤过性病毒: *the flu, rabies, AIDS, etc virus* 流感、狂犬病、艾滋病等病毒 ○ [attrib 作定语] *attacked by, suffering from, etc a virus infection* 受病毒感染. Cf 参看 MICROBE. (**b**) (*infml* 口) disease caused by one of these 病毒性疾病; 病毒病: *There's a/some virus going round the office*, ie making people ill. 办公室里流行着一种[某种]病毒性疾病.

▷ **viral** /ˈvaɪərəl; ˈvaɪrəl/ *adj* of, like or caused by a virus (似)病毒的; 病毒引起的.

Vis (also **Visc**) *abbr* 缩写 = Viscount(ess).

visa /ˈviːzə; ˈvizə/ *n* stamp or mark put on a passport by officials of a foreign country to show that the holder may enter, pass through or leave their country (护照的)签证: *entry/transit/exit visas* 入境[过境/出境]签证 ○ *get a Polish visa/a visa for Poland* 获得波兰的签证[去波兰的签证] ○ *renew/extend a visa*, ie before it expires 续签[延长]签证.

▷ **visa** *v* (*pt, pp* **visaed** /ˈviːzəd; ˈvizəd/) [Tn] mark (a passport) with a visa 在(护照上)办理签证.

vis·age /ˈvɪzɪdʒ; ˈvɪzɪdʒ/ *n* (*joc or rhet* 谑或修辞) person's face (人的)脸, 面容: *the funeral director's gloomy visage* 殡仪员的悲戚面容.

vis-à-vis /ˌviːzɑːˈviː; ˌvizəˈvi/ *prep* (*French* 法) **1** in relation to (sth) 关于(某事物): *discuss plans for the company vis-à-vis a possible merger* 洽谈公司可能合并的事宜. **2** in comparison with (sth) 和(某事物)相比: *Women's salaries are low vis-à-vis what men earn for the same work.* 女子的薪水比同工种的男子低. ○ *His salary vis-à-vis the national average is extremely high.* 他的薪水比起全国平均水平高出很多.

vis·cera /ˈvɪsərə; ˈvɪsərə/ *n* [pl] (usu 通常作 **the viscera**) (*anatomy* 解) large internal organs of the body, eg the heart, the liver and esp the intestines 内脏(如心、肝); (尤指)肠.

▷ **vis·ceral** /ˈvɪsərəl; ˈvɪsərəl/ *adj* **1** (*anatomy* 解) of the viscera 内脏的. **2** (*fig fml* 比喻, 文) (of feelings, etc) not rational; instinctive (指情感等)非理性的, 出于本能的: *a visceral mistrust of their peace moves* 对于他们争取和平的举措怀有直觉的不信任.

vis·cose /ˈvɪskəʊz, -əʊs; ˈvɪsˌkos/ *n* [U] (**a**) cellulose in a viscous state, used in the manufacture of rayon, etc 黏胶液. (**b**) fabric made of this 黏胶纤维织物.

vis·count /ˈvaɪkaʊnt; ˈvaɪkaunt/ *n* **1** (in Britain) nobleman ranking higher than a baron but lower than an earl (英国的)子爵(高于男爵而低于伯爵). **2** courtesy title of an earl's eldest son (对伯爵长子的尊称)子爵: *Viscount Linley* 林利子爵.

▷ **vis·countcy** /-tsɪ; -tsɪ/ *n* title or rank of a viscount 子爵的头衔或爵位.

vis·count·ess /ˈvaɪkaʊntɪs; ˈvaɪkaʊntɪs/ *n* **1** viscount's wife or widow 子爵夫人或遗孀. **2** female viscount 女子爵.

vis·cous /ˈvɪskəs; ˈvɪskəs/ *adj* (of a liquid) not pouring easily; thick and sticky (指液体)稠的, 黏的: *viscous pools of blood, oil, mud* 一滩滩黏稠的血、油、泥. ▷ **vis·cos·ity** /vɪˈskɒsətɪ; vɪsˈkɑsətɪ/ *n* [U].

vise (*US*) = VICE[2].

vis·ible /ˈvɪzəbl; ˈvɪzəbḷ/ *adj* **~ (to sb/sth)** **1** that can be seen; in sight 可见的; 看得见的: *The hills were barely visible through the mist.* 小山隐没在薄雾中难以看清. ○ *This star is not visible to the naked eye.* 这颗星肉眼看不见. **2** (*fig* 比喻) that can be noticed or ascertained; apparent 能注意到的; 能确定的; 明显的: *visible improvements, differences, changes, etc* 明显的改善、区别、变化等 ○ *speak with visible contempt, dismay, impatience, etc* 说话中流露出轻蔑、气馁、不耐烦...之意.

▷ **vis·ib·il·ity** /ˌvɪzəˈbɪlətɪ; ˌvɪzəˈbɪlətɪ/ *n* [U] **1** fact or state of being visible 可见性; 明显性. **2** condition of the light or weather for seeing things at a distance 可见度; 能见度: *Visibility was down to 100 metres in the fog.* 大雾中能见距离已降至100米. ○ *planes grounded because of poor/low/bad visibility* 因能见度太差[低/坏]而停飞的飞机.

vis·ibly /-əblɪ; -əblɪ/ *adv* noticeably 能注意到地; 明显地: *visibly offended, ill, in love* 看得出受到冒犯、生病、在恋爱.

vi·sion /ˈvɪʒn; ˈvɪʒən/ *n* **1** [U] (**a**) power of seeing; sight 视力; 视觉: *have perfect, poor, blurred, etc vision* 视力极好、不好、模糊等 ○ *The blow on the head impaired* (ie damaged) *his vision.* 他头部受击后损害了视力. ○ *within/outside my field of vision*, ie that I can/cannot see from a certain point 在我的视野以内[以外]. (**b**) (*fig* 比喻) ability to view a subject, problem, etc imaginatively; foresight and wisdom in planning 观察力; 想像力; 远见; 洞察力: *a statesman of (great breadth of) vision* (很)有远见的政治家. **2** [C] (**a**) dream or similar trance-like state, often associated with a religious experience 梦幻, 幻象, 幻觉, 异象(常带有宗教色彩): *Jesus came to Paul in a vision.* 耶稣在异象中向保罗显现. ○ *I had/saw a vision of the end of the world.* 我在梦幻中见到了世界末日. (**b**) (esp *pl* 尤作复数) thing seen vividly in the imagination 想像中的活生生的事物; 幻想: *the romantic visions of youth* 青年人浪漫的幻想 ○ *conjure up visions of married bliss* 悬想婚姻生活的幸福情景 ○ *I had visions of us going on strike.* 我想像我们正进行罢工. **3** [C] **~ of sth** (*rhet* 修辞) person or sight of unusual beauty 异常漂亮的人或景象: *She was a vision of loveliness.* 她是个可爱的美人儿. **4** [U] what is seen on a television or cinema screen; picture 电视或电影上的画面; 图像: *We get good vision but poor sound on this set.* 这台电视机图像清晰, 但声音不好.

vi·sion·ary /ˈvɪʒənrɪ; *US* -ʒənerɪ; ˈvɪʒənˌɛrɪ/ *adj* **1** (*approv* 褒) having or showing foresight or wisdom 具有或显示出远见或智慧的: *visionary leaders, writers, paintings, ideals* 表现出真知灼见的领袖、作家、画、理想. **2** having or showing too much imagination or fancy to be practical 空想的; 不切实际的.

▷ **vi·sion·ary** *n* (*usu approv* 通常作褒义) person who has visionary(1) ideas 有远见的人; 有智慧的人: *True visionaries are often misunderstood by their own generation.* 真正有远见卓识的人往往招致同时代人的误解.

visit /ˈvɪzɪt; ˋvɪzɪt/ *v* **1** [I, Tn] (**a**) go or come to see (a person, place, etc) either socially or on business or for some other purpose 去或来看(某人、某处等)(可为社交或公事或其他目的): *No answer — they must be out visiting.* 没有人接电话——他们准是出门了. ○ ˈ*visiting hours* (ie when relatives and friends can see patients) *at a hospital* 医院里探望病人的时间 ○ *visit a friend, dentist, fortune-teller, etc* 访友、去看牙病、去算命 ○ *Most tourists in London visit the British Museum.* 去伦敦的游客多半要去参观不列颠博物馆. (**b**) go or come to see (a place, an institution, etc) in order to make an official examination or check 去或来看(某地、某机构)(为视察或检查): *The school inspector is visiting next week.* 督学下周要来视察. ○ *The restaurant is visited regularly by public health officers.* 这个餐馆有公共卫生部门官员定期前来检查. **2** [I, Tn] stay temporarily at (a place) or with (a person) 在(某地或某人处)逗留: *We don't live here, we're just visiting.* 我们不住在这里, 只是短期停留. ○ *Owls visited the barn to rest.* 猫头鹰飞落在谷仓处. ○ *I'm going to visit my aunt for a few days.* 我打算去姑妈家住几天. **3** [Ipr] **~ with sb** (*US infml* 口) visit sb, esp for an informal talk or chat 去某人处(尤指为闲谈或聊天): *Please stay and visit with me for a while.* 请呆上一会儿跟我聊聊. ⇨Usage 见所附用法. **4** [Tn·pr] **~ sth on/upon sb/sth** (*arch* 古) inflict punishment, etc on sb/sth 对某人[某事物]进行惩罚等: *visit the sins of the fathers upon the children*, ie make the children suffer for their parents' failings 使子女因父母之过错而受惩罚.

▷ **visit** *n* **1 ~ (to sb/sth) (from sb/sth)** act or period of visiting; temporary stay 来或去见某人或到某处访问; 参观; 游览; 逗留: *It was his first visit to his wife's parents.* 那是他第一次去看望岳父和岳母. ○ *pay a visit to a friend, a doctor, a prospective customer, etc* 访友、去看病、去见客户洽谈生意 ○ *be, come, go on a visit to the seaside* 在、来、去海滨游玩 ○ *the Queen's state visit* (ie made for official or political reasons) *to China* 女王对中国的国事访问 ○ *regular visits from the landlord* 房东经常登门. **2** (*US infml* 口) chat or talk 聊天; 谈话: *We had a nice visit on the phone.* 我们在电话里谈得很高兴.

□ ˈ**visiting card** (*US* ˈ**calling card**) small card with one's name, address, company, etc printed on it, which one leaves with clients or social acquaintances 名片; 名刺.

ˌ**visiting proˈfessor** professor who teaches for a fixed period at another (esp foreign) university or college 客座教授(在本校外的, 尤指国外的, 大专院校任教一固定阶段的教授).

V

NOTE ON USAGE 用法: We can **visit** (*US* **visit with**) or **go to see** someone at home or at work. 去见在家中的或在工作处的某人可以说**visit**(用美式英语则说**visit with**), 也可说**go to see.** ☆ **Come/Go and stay** is used in informal English for a longer visit at somebody's house ☆ **come/go and stay**是口语说法, 指到某人家里呆上一段时间: *Come and stay with us soon.* 快来我们这里住些日子吧. ○ *I'm hoping to go and stay with my cousin Tom over Christmas.* 我希望到我表哥汤姆那儿去过圣诞节. We **call on** someone for an official purpose 因公事去见某人可以说**call on**: *A representative of the company will call on you to assess the damage.* 公司的代表将前往贵处评估受损失的状况. We **call in on** a friend for a short time, often when we are on our way to somewhere else ☆ **call in on**常指在前往某处的途中顺便到友人处短暂停留: *We could call in on Patrick on the way to your mother's.* 我们到你母亲家去, 不妨顺路到帕特里克家串个门儿. More informally, we **drop by** at somebody's (house), **drop in on** somebody or (in US English) **visit with** somebody when we make a casual visit to friends or relations ☆ **drop by**、**drop in on**或(在美式英语中作)**visit with**, 这些词组更多用于口语, 指随便到亲友家作客: *Let's drop in on Nick when we're in Bristol, shall we?* 咱们在布里斯托尔的时候, 去看看尼克, 好吗?

vis·ita·tion /ˌvɪzɪˈteɪʃn; ˌvɪzəˋteʃən/ *n* **1 ~ (of sb/sth)** (*fml* 文) official visit, esp of inspection 正式访问; (尤指)视察, 巡视: *a visitation of the sick*, ie made by a clergyman as part of his duties 对病人的探视(尽牧师之职). **2 ~ (from sb/sth)** (*infml* 口) visit, esp a prolonged or an unwelcome one 来访(尤指久呆不走或不受欢迎的): *We had sundry visitations from the Tax Inspector.* 税务检查员常来我们这里, 不胜其烦. **3 ~ (of sth)** (*fml* 文) trouble or disaster considered as a punishment from God (视为上帝惩罚的)灾祸, 灾难: *The famine was a visitation of God for their sins.* 那次饥荒算是上帝对他们罪孽的惩罚.

vis·itor /ˈvɪzɪtə(r); ˋvɪzɪtɚ/ *n* **~ (to sb/sth) (from sb/sth)** **1** (**a**) one who visits a person or place 来或去见某人或到某处的人; 访问者; 参观者: *The old lady never has/gets any visitors.* 从来没有人来探望这个老太太. ○ *She was a frequent visitor to the gallery.* 她经常参观这个美术馆. ○ *visitors from the insurance company* 从保险公司来的人. (**b**) person who stays temporarily at a place or with a person 游客; 宾客: *Rome welcomes millions of visitors each year.* 罗马每年要接待数以百万计的游客. **2** migratory bird that lives in an area temporarily or at a certain season 候鸟: *summer/winter visitors to British shores* 夏季[冬季]飞到英国海岸的候鸟.

□ ˈ**visitors' book** book in which visitors write their names, addresses and sometimes comments, eg at a hotel or place of public interest 来客登记簿; 来宾留言簿.

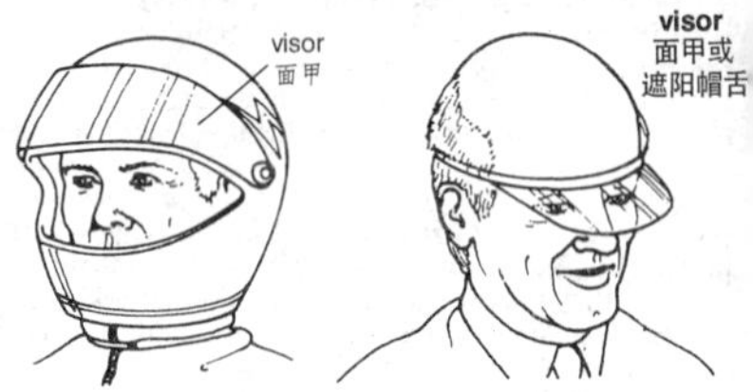

visor /ˈvaɪzə(r); ˋvaɪzɚ/ *n* **1** moving part of a helmet, used to cover and protect the face (头盔的)面甲, 面罩: *The motor-cyclist raised/lowered his visor.* 那个骑摩托车的人把面甲往上托[向下拉]. **2** (**a**) projecting piece of plastic, stiffened cloth, etc worn above the eyes to shield them from the sun 遮阳帽舌. (**b**) similar object forming the projecting front part of a cap; peak 帽舌. ⇨illus 见插图.

vista /ˈvɪstə; ˋvɪstə/ *n* (*fml* 文) **1** view as seen between long rows of trees, buildings, etc 从长长的两排树木、建筑物等中间望过去的景色: *This street offers a fine vista of the cathedral.* 这条街的尽头是个大教堂, 远远望去非常好看. **2** (*fig* 比喻) long series of scenes, events, etc that one can look back on or forward to 回顾或展望的一连串情景、事情等: *This discovery opens up new vistas of research for biologists.* 这一发现为生物学家展示了新的研究前景.

visual /ˈvɪʒʊəl; ˋvɪʒʊəl/ *adj* concerned with or used in seeing 视觉的; 用于视觉的: *visual images, effects, etc* 视觉图像、效果等 ○ *the visual arts*, ie painting, cinema, theatre, etc 视觉艺术(绘画、电影、戏剧等) ○ *visual humour*, ie humour that depends on actions rather than words for its effect 视觉幽默(依靠动作而不依靠言语产生幽默效果) ○ *Her designs have a strong visual appeal.* 她的设计在视觉上很有感染力. ○ *a good visual memory*, ie ability to remember what one sees 良好的视觉记忆力.

▷ **visu·al·ize, -ise** /-aɪz; -ˌaɪz/ *v* [Tn, Tsg, Cn·n/a] **~ sb/sth (as sth)** form a mental picture of sb/sth 想像或设想某人[某事物]: *I remember meeting him but I just can't visualize him.* 我记得我见过他, 可就是想不起他的样子了. ○ *I can't visualize myself ever getting married.* 我不能想像我有朝一日能结婚. ○ *Tom visualized the house as a romantic ruin.* 汤姆把那所房子想像成有传奇色彩的废墟. **visu·al·iza·tion, -isation** /ˌvɪʒʊəlaɪˈzeɪʃn; *US* -lɪˈz-; ˌvɪʒʊəlɪˋzeʃən/ *n* [U]: *powers of visualization* 想像力.

visu·ally /ˈvɪʒʊəlɪ; ˋvɪʒʊəlɪ/ *adv* **1** in seeing 在视觉上: *visually handicapped*, ie blind or nearly blind 有视觉障碍的(瞎的或几乎瞎的). **2** in appearance 外观上; 表面

上: *Visually, the decor was very striking.* 这个房间的装饰看上去非常醒目.

□ **ˌvisual ˈaid** (esp *pl* 尤作复数) picture, film, video, etc used as a teaching aid 直观教具.

ˌvisual diˈsplay unit (*abbr* 缩写 **VDU**) device resembling a TV screen, connected to a computer, etc, on which data can be displayed from the computer or fed in, eg by a keyboard or light pen (计算机等的)视频显示器.

vi·tal /ˈvaɪtl; ˋvaɪtḷ/ *adj* **1** [attrib 作定语] connected with or essential to life 与生命有关的; 维持生命所必需的: *The heart performs a vital bodily function.* 心脏起着维持生命的重要作用. ○ *He was wounded in a vital part of his anatomy,* eg the lungs, brain. 他身体的要害部分受了伤(如肺部、大脑). ○ (*fig* 比喻) *The vital spark that would have brought the play to life was missing.* 那出戏缺少的是可使之画龙点睛的生气. **2 ~ (to/for sth)** essential to the existence, success, or operation of sth (对某事物的存在、成功或运作)极重要的, 必不可少的: *vital information, research, legislation* 极其重要的信息、研究、法规 ○ *a vital clue to the killer's identity* 有关杀人犯身分的重大线索 ○ *The police perform a vital role in our society.* 警察在我们的社会中起着极其重要的作用. ○ *It is absolutely vital that the matter is kept secret.* 这件事要保密, 这是至关重要的. **3** (*approv* 褒) energetic or lively; dynamic 精力充沛的; 有活力的; 生气勃勃的: *She's a very vital sort of person.* 她是个精力旺盛的人.

▷ **vi·tally** /ˈvaɪtəlɪ; ˋvaɪtḷɪ/ *adv* extremely 极端地: *vitally important, necessary, etc* 极其重要、必要等 ○ *We are vitally concerned to win public support.* 我们对赢得公众的支持极为关注.

the vi·tals *n* [pl] (*dated or joc* 旧或谑) important organs of the body 身体的重要器官: *Fear gripped (at) my vitals.* 我内心极为恐惧. ○ *She kneed her attacker in the vitals* (ie in the genitals) *and ran away.* 她用膝盖撞那个袭击者的要害部位(生殖器), 然后跑掉了.

□ **ˌvital staˈtistics** **1** statistics relating to population figures or births, marriages and deaths 生命统计, 人口动态统计(人口数字或出生、婚姻、死亡的统计). **2** (*Brit infml* 口) measurements of a woman's bust, waist and hips 女子三围尺寸(胸围、腰围、臀围).

vi·tal·ity /vaɪˈtælətɪ; vaɪˋtælətɪ/ *n* [U] **1** persistent energy; liveliness or vigour 活力; 精力; 元气: *The dog was bouncing with health and vitality.* 那条狗又壮实又活跃, 欢蹦乱跳的. ○ *The ballet sparkled with vitality.* 那场芭蕾舞演得生动活泼. **2** (*fig* 比喻) (of institutions, etc) ability to endure or continue functioning (指机构等)维持生存或继续发挥作用的能力, 生命力: *The vitality of the movement is threatened.* 这个运动的生命力岌岌可危.

vit·amin /ˈvɪtəmɪn; *US* ˈvaɪt-; ˋvaɪtəmɪn/ *n* any of a number of organic substances which are present in certain foods and are essential to the health of humans and other animals 维生素: *vitamin A, B, C, etc* 维生素A、B、C等 ○ *Pork is rich in vitamin B1.* 猪肉里含有丰富的维生素B1. ○ [attrib 作定语] ˈ*vitamin pills* 维生素丸 ○ *one's daily vitamin requirements* 每日所需之维生素 ○ *Vitamin deficiency can cause illnesses,* eg scurvy, rickets. 缺乏维生素能引起疾病(如坏血病、佝偻病).

▷ **vit·am·in·ize, -ise** /ˈvɪtəmɪnaɪz; *US* ˈvaɪt-; ˋvaɪtəmə-ˌnaɪz/ *v* [Tn] add vitamins to (a food) 将维生素加入(食物)中.

viti·ate /ˈvɪʃɪeɪt; ˋvɪʃɪˌet/ *v* [Tn] (*fml* 文) **1** weaken or spoil the quality or efficiency of (sth) 削弱或损害(某事物)的性质或效能; 使(某物)变质; 败坏(某物): *the vitiated atmosphere of our polluted inner cities* 我们市中心区受到污染的恶浊的空气 ○ *The serum is vitiated by exposure to the air.* 血清暴露在空气中已变质. **2** weaken the force of (sth); make ineffective 削弱(某事物)的力量; 使无效: *vitiate a claim, contract, theory* 使权利要求、合同、理论无效. ▷ **viti·ation** /ˌvɪʃɪˈeɪʃn; ˌvɪʃɪˋeʃən/ *n* [U].

viti·cul·ture /ˈvɪtɪkʌltʃə(r), ˈvaɪt-; ˋvɪtɪˌkʌltʃɚ, ˋvaɪt-/ *n* [U] (science or practice of the) growing of grapes, esp for use in wine-making 葡萄栽培(尤指为酿酒的); 葡萄栽培学; 葡萄栽培术.

vit·re·ous /ˈvɪtrɪəs; ˋvɪtrɪəs/ *adj* (**a**) having a glass-like texture or finish 有玻璃般的质地或表层的; 玻璃状的; 玻璃质的: *vitreous enamel, china, porcelain, etc* 玻化搪瓷、瓷、瓷料等. (**b**) (of rocks) hard and shiny like glass (指岩石)如玻璃般坚硬光亮的.

vit·rify /ˈvɪtrɪfaɪ; ˋvɪtrəˌfaɪ/ *v* (*pt, pp* **-fied**) [I, Tn esp passive 尤用于被动语态] (cause sth to) be changed into a glass-like substance, esp by heat (使某物)呈玻璃状(尤指通过加热): *vitrified glazes,* eg on ceramics 呈玻璃状的釉料(如制陶工艺的). ▷ **vit·ri·fac·tion** /ˌvɪtrɪˈfækʃn; ˌvɪtrəˋfækʃən/, **vit·ri·fica·tion** /ˌvɪtrɪfɪˈkeɪʃn; ˌvɪtrəfəˋkeʃən/ *ns* [U].

vit·riol /ˈvɪtrɪəl; ˋvɪtrɪəl/ *n* [U] **1** (*dated* 旧) sulphuric acid or any of its salts 硫酸; 硫酸盐; 矾: *blue vitriol,* ie copper sulphate 胆矾(五水硫酸铜). **2** (*fig* 比喻) savagely hostile comments or criticism 深怀敌意的评语或批评: *His attack on the government was pure vitriol.* 他纯粹出于恶意抨击政府.

▷ **vit·ri·olic** /ˌvɪtrɪˈɒlɪk; ˌvɪtrɪˋɑlɪk/ *adj* savagely and bitterly hostile 深怀敌意的; 恶意的: *vitriolic criticism, attacks, etc* 恶意的批评、攻击等 ○ *We deplore the vitriolic nature of his remarks.* 他言语中敌意昭彰, 我们深感遗憾.

vitro ⇨ IN VITRO.

vi·tu·per·ate /vɪˈtjuːpəreɪt; *US* vaɪˈtuː-; vaɪˋtupəˌret/ *v* [I, Ipr] **~ (against sb/sth)** (*fml* 文) use abusive language or bitter criticism; revile sb/sth 责骂; 斥责; 辱骂某人[某事物]: *The prince vituperated against the developers for ruining London's skyline.* 王子斥责土地开发商破坏了伦敦市建筑物映在空中的轮廓线之美.

▷ **vi·tu·pera·tion** /vɪˌtjuːpəˈreɪʃn; *US* vaɪˌtuː-; vaɪˌtupəˋreʃən/ *n* [U] (*fml* 文) abusive language or bitter criticism 责骂; 斥责; 辱骂.

vi·tu·per·at·ive /vɪˈtjuːpərətɪv; *US* vaɪˈtuːpəreɪtɪv; vaɪˋtupəˌretɪv/ *adj*: *vituperative debate, criticism, etc* 辱骂式的辩论、批评等.

viva /ˈvaɪvə; ˋvaɪvə/ *n* (*Brit infml* 口) = VIVA VOCE.

vi·vace /vɪˈvɑːtʃɪ; vɪˋvɑtʃɪ/ *adv* (*music* 音) (to be played, sung, etc) in a brisk lively manner (演奏、歌唱等)轻快活泼地.

vi·va·cious /vɪˈveɪʃəs; vaɪˋveʃəs/ *adj* (*approv* 褒) (esp of a woman) lively or high-spirited (尤指女子)活泼的, 快活的: *bubbly and vivacious blonde seeks fun-loving gent,* eg as an advertisement in a 'lonely hearts' column 热情活泼金发女郎征求喜爱娱乐的男子(如报刊上征求异性朋友专栏字样) ○ *She gave a vivacious laugh.* 她爽朗地笑了起来. ▷ **vi·va·ciously** *adv*. **vi·va·city** /vɪˈvæsətɪ; vaɪˋvæsətɪ/ (also **vi·va·cious·ness**) *n* [U].

viva voce /ˌvaɪvə ˈvəʊsɪ, ˈvəʊtʃɪ; ˋvaɪvəˋvosɪ/ (also *Brit infml* 英式口语作 **viva**) *n* oral examination, esp in universities 口试(尤指大学的): *have, get, take, etc a viva (voce)* 参加口试.

▷ **viva voce** *adj, adv* of a viva voce examination; oral(ly) 口试(的); 口头(的).

vivid /ˈvɪvɪd; ˋvɪvɪd/ *adj* **1** (of light or colour) strong and bright; intense (指光线或颜色)鲜明的, 鲜艳的, 强烈的: *a vivid flash of lightning* 耀眼的闪电 ○ *vivid green trousers* 鲜绿色的裤子. **2** (of a mental faculty) creating ideas, etc in a lively or an active way (指头脑)活跃的, 富有创造性的: *a vivid memory, imagination, etc* 犹新的记忆、活跃的想像力. **3** producing strong clear pictures in the mind 在头脑中产生清晰图像的: *a vivid description, recollection, dream* 生动的描述、清晰的回忆、清楚的梦 ○ *The incident left a vivid impression on me.* 那件事给我留下了深刻的印象. ▷ **vividly** *adv*. **vivid·ness** *n* [U].

vi·vi·par·ous /vɪˈvɪpərəs; *US* vaɪ-; vaɪˋvɪpərəs/ *adj* (*biology* 生) (of most mammals) having offspring that develop within the mother's body, ie that do not hatch from eggs (指大多哺乳类动物)胎生的.

vi·vi·sec·tion /ˌvɪvɪˈsekʃn; ˌvɪvəˋsɛkʃən/ *n* (**a**) [U] practice of performing surgical experiments on live animals for scientific research 活体解剖: [attrib 作定语] *the anti-vivisection lobby* 为反对活体解剖而游说议员的团体. (**b**) [C] act or instance of this 活体解剖.

▷ **vi·vi·sec·tion·ist** /-ʃənɪst; -ʃənɪst/ *n* (**a**) person who performs vivisections 作活体解剖者. (**b**) person who considers vivisection is justifiable 主张活体解剖的人.

vixen /ˈvɪksn; ˋvɪksṇ/ *n* **1** female fox 雌狐. **2** (*esp dated* 尤作旧) bad-tempered quarrelsome woman 泼妇: *a real little vixen* 一个不折不扣的泼妇. ▷ **vixen·ish** /ˈvɪksənɪʃ; ˋvɪksṇɪʃ/ *adj*: *her nasty, vixenish ways* 她那泼妇般的凶相.

viz /vɪz; vɪz/ *abbr* 缩写 = (often read out as *namely* 通常读作 namely) that is to say; in other words (Latin

V

videlicet) 即，就是(源自拉丁文 *videlicet*): *these three persons, viz landlord, lessee and tenant*... 上述三人，即房东、承租人、房客....

NOTE ON USAGE 用法: The abbreviations **viz**, **ie** and **eg** are mostly used in formal or technical English. ☆ **viz**、**ie**、**eg** 这三个缩略词多用于较郑重的或科技的文体中. In speech and when reading a written text aloud we usually say **namely**, **that is (to say)** and **for example** respectively 在讲话或读文稿时，这三个词分别读作 **namely**、**that is (to say)**、**for example**. ☆ **Viz** (or **namely**) is used to expand or specify what has already been said ☆ **viz**(或 **namely**)用以补充或具体说明前面已经提到的事物: *There are three major advantages of the design, viz/namely cheapness, simplicity and availability.* 这种设计有三大优点，即价廉、简便、实用. ○ *I want to talk today about a major threat facing our society, namely AIDS.* 我今天要讲的是我们社会面临的一大危害，就是艾滋病. We use **ie** (or **that is**) to explain an unclear statement or word by rephrasing it ☆ **ie**(或 **that is**)的用法是通过重新措辞来解释一个不清楚的说法或词语: *He admitted being 'economical with the truth' (ie lying).* 他承认他'简化了事实真相'(即说了谎). In this dictionary we often use **ie** and **eg** after examples to give further explanation of the meaning of those examples. 在本词典中，常在示例后用 **ie** 和 **eg** 进一步解释示例的含义.

viz·ier /vɪ'zɪə(r); vɪ'zɪr/ *n* (esp formerly) high-ranking officials in some Muslim countries (尤指旧时)维齐(某些穆斯林国家的高级官员): *the grand vizier*, eg of the old Turkish empire 大维齐(旧时土耳其帝国的).

vo·cabu·lary /və'kæbjʊlərɪ; *US* -lerɪ; və'kæbjə,lerɪ/ *n* **1** [C] total number of words that make up a language (一种语言的)词汇，字汇. Cf 参看 LEXICON. **2** [C, U] (body of) words known to a person or used in a particular book, subject, etc; lexis (某人掌握的或某书、某学科等中使用的)词汇，词汇层: *a wide, limited, colourful, etc vocabulary* 宽泛的、有限的、丰富多彩的...词汇 ○ *Tim has an average (level of) vocabulary for a 3-year-old.* 蒂姆掌握了相当于3岁孩子的平均词汇(量). ○ *an active vocabulary*, ie words one recognizes and can use 积极词汇(个人认识并能使用的全部的词) ○ *a passive vocabulary*, ie words one recognizes only 消极词汇(个人认识但不会使用的全部的词) ○ *enrich, increase, extend, etc one's vocabulary* 丰富、增加、扩大...自己的词汇量. **3** (also *infml* 口语作 **vocab** /'vəʊkæb; 'vokæb/) [U, C] list of words with their meanings, esp one which accompanies a textbook in a foreign language (注有释义的)词汇表(尤指外语教科书所附的). Cf 参看 GLOSSARY.

V

vocal /'vəʊkl; 'vokl̩/ *adj* **1** [usu attrib 通常作定语] of, for or uttered by the voice 嗓音的; 适于嗓音的; 用口语表达的: *the vocal organs*, ie the tongue, lips, vocal cords, etc 发音器官(舌、唇、声带等) ○ *The cantata has a difficult vocal score.* 这个康塔塔有个难度很大的声乐总谱. ○ *Callas's vocal range was astonishing.* 卡拉斯的音域宽得惊人. **2** expressing one's opinions or feelings freely in speech; outspoken 用言语自由表达意见或感情的; 直言的: *vocal criticism, support* 坦率的批评、支持 ○ *We were very vocal about our rights.* 我们直言不讳表达了我们应有的权利. ○ *The protesters are a small but vocal minority.* 抗议的人虽然人数少，但却是直言的少数.

▷ **vocal** *n* (often *pl* 常作复数) sung part of a piece of jazz or pop music (爵士乐或流行音乐的)歌唱部分: *Who was on/sang lead vocal(s) on the group's last record?* 在这个乐队新出的唱片中，领唱的是谁?

vo·cal·ist /'vəʊkəlɪst; 'voklɪst/ *n* singer, esp in a jazz or pop group 歌手(尤指爵士乐队或流行音乐乐队的). Cf 参看 INSTRUMENTALIST (INSTRUMENTAL).

vo·cally /'vəʊkəlɪ; 'voklɪ/ *adv* **1** in a way that uses the voice 用嗓音; 口头地. **2** freely or outspokenly 自由地; 直言地: *protest vocally* 直言不讳提出抗议.

□ ,**vocal 'cords** voice-producing part of the larynx 声带. ⇨ illus at THROAT 见 THROAT 插图.

vo·cal·ize, -ise /'vəʊkəlaɪz; 'vokl̩,aɪz/ *v* [Tn] (*fml* 文) say or sing (sounds or words); utter 说(话); 唱(歌); 发声.

vo·ca·tion /vəʊ'keɪʃn; vo'keʃən/ *n* **1** [C] **~ (for/to sth)** feeling that one is called to (and qualified for) a certain kind of work, esp social or religious (认为自己合于做某事的)使命感(尤指社会上的或宗教上的): *vocations to the priesthood, ministry, etc* 任牧师等的使命感 ○ *have/follow one's vocation to become a nun* 奉神召当修女 ○ *Nursing is a vocation as well as a profession.* 护理工作既是职业也是救死扶伤的责任. **2** [U] **~ (for sth)** natural liking or aptitude for a certain type of work (对某种工作的)天生的爱好或才能: *He has little vocation for teaching.* 他不是教书的材料. **3** [C usu *sing* 通常作单数] (*fml* 文) person's trade or profession 行业; 职业: *find one's true vocation (in life)* 找到了(一生中)真正的职业 ○ *You should be an actor — you've missed your vocation*, ie you are following the wrong career. 你应该当演员——你入错行了.

▷ **vo·ca·tional** /-ʃənl; -ʃənl̩/ *adj* of or concerning the qualifications, etc needed for a trade or profession (关于)某职业所需的资格的: *vocational guidance, training, etc*, eg for students about to leave school 就业指导、职业训练(如为应届中学毕业生的).

voc·at·ive /'vɒkətɪv; 'vɑkətɪv/ *n* (*grammar*) special form of a noun, a pronoun or an adjective used (in some inflected languages) when addressing or invoking a person or thing (某些屈折语中的)呼格; (用作呼格的)名词、代词或形容词.

▷ **voc·at·ive** *adj* of or in the vocative 呼格的; 呼格形式的.

vo·ci·fer·ate /və'sɪfəreɪt; *US* vəʊ-; vo'sɪfə,ret/ *v* [I, Tn] (*fml* 文) say (sth) loudly or noisily; shout 大声地或吵嚷地说(话); 叫喊.

▷ **vo·ci·fer·ous** /və'sɪfərəs; *US* vəʊ-; vo'sɪfərəs/ *adj* loud or noisy; expressing one's views forcibly and insistently 大声的; 嘈杂的; 强行或坚持表达自己观点的: *vociferous complaints, protests, etc* 大声疾呼的抱怨、抗议等 ○ *a vociferous group of demonstrators* 一批喧嚣的示威者. **vo·ci·fer·ously** *adv*.

vodka /'vɒdkə; 'vɑdkə/ *n* **(a)** [U] strong alcoholic drink distilled from rye and other vegetable products, made esp in Russia 伏特加(烈酒，尤指俄国产的). **(b)** [C] glass or drink of this 一杯或一份伏特加: *a vodka and lime* 一杯酸橙伏特加.

vogue /vəʊg; vog/ *n* [C esp *sing* 尤作单数] **1 ~ (for sth)** current or prevailing fashion 流行的或盛行的式样: *a new vogue for low-heeled shoes* 低跟鞋新潮流. **2** popular favour or acceptance 风行; 流行: *His novels had a great vogue ten years ago.* 他的小说十年前风靡一时. **3** (idm 习语) **be ,all the 'vogue** (*infml* 口) be fashionable or popular everywhere 到处流行或受欢迎. **be in/come into 'vogue** be/become fashionable or popular 流行[流行起来]: *Short hair came back into vogue about ten years ago.* 大约十年前短发又开始流行起来了.

□ **'vogue-word** *n* word that is currently fashionable 时髦的词: *'Accountability' is the current vogue-word in politics.* '有解释责任'是当前政治上的流行词. Cf 参看 BUZZ-WORD (BUZZ).

voice /vɔɪs; vɔɪs/ *n* **1 (a)** [C] sounds formed in the larynx and uttered through the mouth, esp by a person speaking or singing 嗓音; (尤指)说话声，歌唱声: *I can hear voices through the wall.* 我听见隔着墙有说话的声音. ○ *Keep your voice down*, ie Don't speak loudly. 说话声音放低些. ○ *recognize sb's voice* 听出某人的声音 ○ *speak in a loud, rough, husky, gentle, etc voice* 大声地、粗声地、声音嘶哑地、柔声地...说话 ○ *He has a good singing voice*, ie can sing well. 他唱起歌来声音很好听. ○ *raise/lower one's voice*, ie speak more loudly/softly 提高[降低]嗓门 ○ *His voice has broken*, ie become deep like a man's. 他的嗓音变粗了(变低沉，像成年人的了). ○ *Her voice shook/trembled with emotion.* 她激动得声音发颤. **(b)** [U] ability to produce such sounds (人嗓子的)发声能力: *commands given in a firm tone of voice* 用坚定的语调下达的命令. **2** (*fig* 比喻) **(a)** [U, sing] **~ (in sth)** (right to express one's) opinion, etc in spoken or written words; influence (口头的或书面的)意见等; 发言权; 发表意见的权利; 影响: *have little, some, no, a voice in the matter* 对这件事没有什么、有一些、没有、有意见 ○ *The workers want a voice in management decisions.* 工人要求在管理决策上有发言权. **(b)** [sing] means by which such an opinion, etc is expressed 表达意见等的方式或手段: *listen to the voice of reason, experience, dissent*

听取理由、经历、不同政见 ○ *Our newspaper represents the voice of the people.* 我们的报纸代表着人民的心声. **3** [sing] (*grammar*) contrast between a sentence in which the doer of the action is subject (*active*) and one in which the person or thing affected is subject (*passive*) (动词的)语态: *in the active/passive voice* 用主动[被动]语态. **4** [U] (*phonetics* 语音) sound produced by vibration of the vocal cords and not with breath alone, used in the pronunciation of vowel sounds and certain consonants, eg /b, d, z/ 浊音, 有声音(发音时声带震动的, 如元音及某些辅音如/b/、/d/、/z/). **5** (idm 习语) **at the top of one's voice** ⇨ TOP[1]. **find/lose one's voice/tongue** ⇨ FIND[1]. **give voice to sth** (*fml* 文) express (feelings, worries, etc) 表露(感情、忧虑等): *give voice to one's indignation, dismay, concern, etc* 表现出愤慨、沮丧、关心等. **have, etc an edge to one's voice** ⇨ EDGE[1]. **in good, poor, etc 'voice** singing or speaking as well as usual, worse than usual, etc (唱歌或说话时)声音和平时一样好、不如平时等: *The bass soloist was in excellent voice.* 这个男低音独唱演员这次唱出了高水平. **like, etc the sound of one's own voice** ⇨ SOUND[2]. **make one's 'voice heard** express one's feelings, opinions, etc in such a way that they are noticed or acted on (为使他人注意或采取行动)表达感情、意见等: *This programme gives ordinary viewers a chance to make their voice(s) heard.* 这个节目给普通观众提供了一个发表意见的机会. **raise one's voice against sb/sth** ⇨ RAISE. **the still small voice** ⇨ STILL[1]. **with ˌone 'voice** (*fml* 文) unanimously 异口同声地; 一致地: *With one voice, the workers voted to strike.* 工人投票一致要求罢工.

▷ **voice** *v* [Tn] **1** express (feelings, etc) in words 用言语表达(情感等): *A spokesman voiced the workers' dissatisfaction.* 发言人表示了工人的不满情绪. **2** (*phonetics* 语音) utter (a sound) with voice (4) 发(浊音): *voiced consonants*, eg /d, v, z/ 浊辅音(如/d/、/v/、/z/).

-voiced (forming compound *adjs* 用以构成复合形容词) having a voice of the specified kind 有某种嗓音的: *loud-voiced* 嗓门大的 ○ *gruff-voiced* 声音粗哑的.

voice·less *adj* (*phonetics* 语音) (of a sound) uttered without voice(4) (指语音)清音的: *The consonants t, f and s are voiceless.* t、f、s这三个辅音是清辅音.

□ **'voice-box** *n* = LARYNX.

'voice-over *n* narration (eg in a film) by a speaker who is not seen 解说, 画外音(如电影的).

void /vɔɪd; vɔɪd/ *n* (usu *sing* 通常作单数) (*fml or rhet* 文或修辞) empty space; vacuum 空间; 真空: *the blue void we call the sky* 我们称之为天空的蔚蓝色空间 ○ (*fig* 比喻) *an aching void left by the death of her child* 她孩子死后留下的痛苦的空虚感.

▷ **void** *adj* (*fml* 文) **1** empty; vacant 空的; 空着的; 空虚的. **2** [pred 作表语] **~ of sth** without sth; lacking sth 没有某事物; 缺乏某事物: *Her face was void of all interest.* 她面部表情显得对什么都不感兴趣. Cf 参看 DEVOID. **3** (idm 习语) **null and void** ⇨ NULL.

void *v* [Tn] **1** (*law* 律) make (sth) not legally binding 使(某物)无效的. **2** (*fml* 文) empty the contents of (one's bowels or bladder) 排泄, 排放(大便或小便).

voile /vɔɪl; vɔɪl/ *n* [U] thin semi-transparent material of cotton, wool or silk 巴里纱(由棉、毛或丝织成, 半透明).

vol *abbr* 缩写 = **1** (*pl* **vols**) volume: *an edition in 3 vols* 三卷本的版本 ○ *Complete Works of Byron Vol 2*《拜伦全集》第2卷. **2** volume: *vol 125ml*, eg on a container 容量125毫升(如容器上的标记).

vol·at·ile /ˈvɒlətaɪl; *US* -tl; ˋvɑlətḷ/ *adj* **1** (of a liquid) changing rapidly into vapour (指液体)易挥发的. **2** (*esp derog* 尤作贬义) (of a person) changing quickly from one mood or interest to another; fickle (指人)情绪或兴趣多变的, 无常性的: *a highly volatile personality, disposition, nature, etc* 反复无常的个性、性情、天性等. **3** (of trading conditions, etc) likely to change suddenly or sharply; unstable (指商情等)很可能急剧波动的, 不稳定的: *volatile stock-markets, exchange rates* 不稳定的股市、汇率 ○ *a volatile political situation*, eg one that could lead to a change of government 动荡不定的政局. ▷ **vol·at·il·ity** /ˌvɒləˈtɪlətɪ; ˌvɑləˋtɪlətɪ/ *n* [U].

vol-au-vent /ˈvɒləvɑːŋ; ˌvɔloˋvɑŋ/ *n* small light case of puff pastry filled with meat, fish, etc in a rich sauce 酥皮合子(用肉、鱼等加浓汁作馅的糕点).

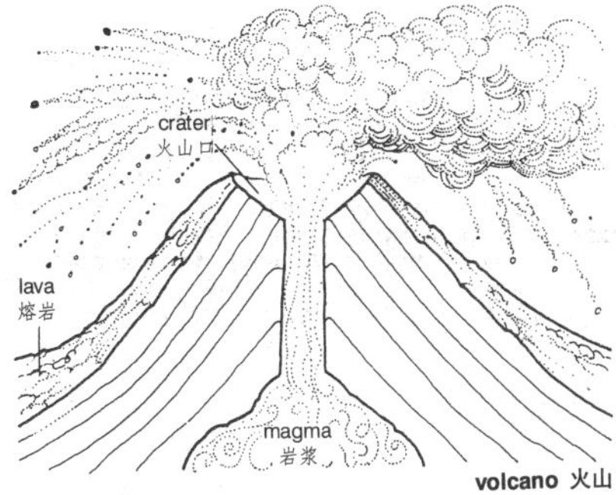

volcano 火山

vol·cano /vɒlˈkeɪnəʊ; vɑlˋkeno/ *n* (*pl* **~es**) mountain or hill with an opening or openings through which lava, cinders, gases, etc come up from below the earth's surface (*an active volcano*), may come up after an interval (*a dormant volcano*), or have ceased to come up (*an extinct volcano*) 火山(an active volcano为活火山, a dormant volcano为休眠火山, an extinct volcano为死火山). ⇨illus 见插图.

▷ **vol·canic** /vɒlˈkænɪk; vɑlˋkænɪk/ *adj* [esp attrib 尤作定语] of, from or like a volcano (似)火山的; 来自火山的: *volcanic eruptions, gases, etc* 火山的喷发、气体等 ○ (*fig* 比喻) *The French Revolution was a volcanic upheaval in European history.* 法国大革命是欧洲历史上的火山爆发.

vole /vəʊl; vol/ *n* small animal resembling a rat or mouse and living in hedgerows, river-banks, etc 田鼠: *a 'water-vole*, ie a large water-rat 水鼠. ⇨illus at App 1 见附录1插图, page iii.

vo·li·tion /vəˈlɪʃn; *US* vəʊ-; voˋlɪʃən/ *n* (*fml* 文) **1** [U] act of using one's will in choosing, making a decision, etc (按自己的意愿做出的)选择、决定等. **2** (idm 习语) **of one's own voˈlition** without being forced; voluntarily 出于本人意愿; 自愿地: *She left entirely of her own volition.* 她完全是自愿离开的. ▷ **vo·li·tional** /-ʃənl; -ʃənḷ/ *adj*: *a volitional act* 自愿的行动.

vol·ley /ˈvɒlɪ; ˋvɑlɪ/ *n* **1** (**a**) simultaneous throwing or firing of a number of stones, bullets, etc (石块、子弹等的)齐投, 齐射: *Police fired a volley* (ie of plastic bullets) *over the heads of the crowd.* 警察朝人群上方射出一排(塑料)子弹. (**b**) stones, bullets, etc thrown or fired in this way (齐投或齐射出的)石块、子弹等: *He was hit by a volley of snowballs.* 他让一齐投来的雪球给击中了. Cf 参看 SALVO. **2** (*fig* 比喻) number of questions, insults, etc directed at sb together or in quick succession (质问、辱骂等的)齐发, 连发: *He let out a volley of oaths.* 他像发连珠炮似的破口大骂. **3** (in tennis, football, etc) shot or stroke in which the ball is hit before it touches the ground (网球、足球等的)截击空中球, 凌空对打, 空中传(踢): *a forehand/backhand/overhead volley*, ie in tennis 正手[反手/头顶]截击(网球的) ○ *play, return, miss, etc an opponent's volley* 打、回击、没接住...对手截击过来的球 ○ *kick a ball on the volley* 踢凌空球.

▷ **vol·ley** *v* **1** [I] fire (guns) in a volley (枪或炮)齐发. **2** [I, Ipr, Tn, Tn·pr] (in tennis, football, etc) hit (a ball) before it touches the ground (网球等)截击(空中球); (足球)截踢(凌空球): *He volleyed (the ball) into the net/across the court.* 他凌空一脚把球踢入球门[把球截击到球场的另一边].

□ **'volley-ball** *n* game in which opposing teams of players hit a ball backwards and forwards over a high net with their hands without letting it touch the ground on their own side 排球运动; 排球(赛).

volt /vəʊlt; volt/ *n* (*abbr* 缩写 **v**) unit of electrical force, defined as the force needed to carry one ampere of current against one ohm of resistance 伏(特)(电压单位).

▷ **volt·age** /ˈvəʊltɪdʒ; ˋvoltɪdʒ/ *n* [U, C] electrical force measured in volts 电压; 伏特数: *high/low voltage* 高[低]压 ○ *check the voltage of an appliance against the supply*,

V

ie before connecting it 检查电器的额定电压与电源是否相符(然后再接通).

volte-face /ˌvɒlt ˈfɑːs; ˋvɑltˌfɑs/ *n* (usu *sing* 通常作单数) (*esp fml* 尤作文雅语) complete change or reversal of one's attitude towards sth (态度的)完全改变, 大转变: *Her latest speech represents a complete volte-face in government thinking.* 她最近的讲话表明政府观点完全改变了.

vol·uble /ˈvɒljʊbl; ˋvɑljəbl/ *adj* (*fml esp derog* 文, 尤作贬义) **(a)** (of a person) speaking a lot; talkative (指人)喋喋不休的, 爱说话的. **(b)** (of speech) quick, easy or fluent; glib (指说话)快的, 流畅的, 流利的: *voluble protests, excuses, etc* 振振有词的抗议、辩解等. ▷ **vo·lu·bil·ity** /ˌvɒljʊˈbɪlətɪ; ˌvɑljəˋbɪlətɪ/ *n* [U]. **vol·ubly** /ˈvɒljʊblɪ; ˋvɑljəblɪ/ *adv*.

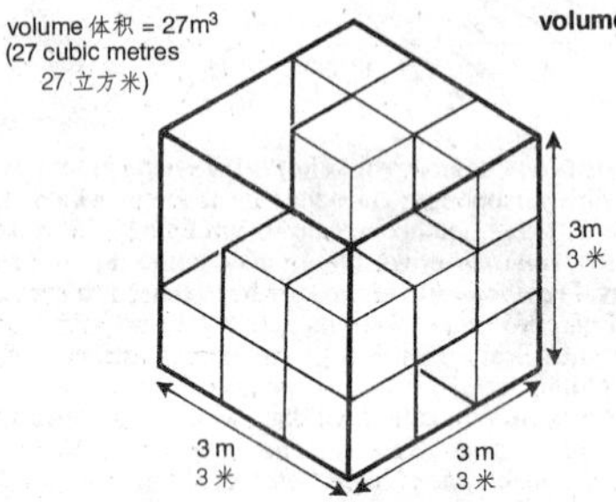

volume 体积

vol·ume /ˈvɒljuːm; *US* -jəm; ˋvɑljəm/ *n* **1** [C] book, esp one of a matching set or a series 书; (尤指一套或丛书中的)册, 本, 卷, 集: *an encyclopedia in 20 volumes* 一套有20册的百科全书 ○ *Volume 2 of Shaw's Complete Works is missing.* 《萧伯纳全集》的第2卷不见了. ○ (*fml* 文) *a library of over 12 000 volumes* 藏书超过12 000册的图书馆. **2** [U, C] amount of space (often expressed in cubic units) that a substance occupies; cubic capacity of a container 体积; 容积; 容量: *The liquid was 5 litres in volume.* 该液体的体积为5升. ○ *The jars hold different volumes of liquid/have different volumes.* 这些罐子可盛的液体多少不等[容量不同]. ⇨App 4 见附录4. ⇨illus 见插图. Cf 参看 AREA 1. **3 (a)** [U] large amount or quantity of sth 大量; 许多; 数量: *the sheer volume of business, work, mail, etc* 大量的业务、工作、邮件等 ○ *The volume of protest rose/fell.* 抗议事件已增加[减少]. **(b)** [C usu *pl* 通常作复数] rounded mass of steam, etc (蒸气等的)圆团: *Volumes of black smoke poured from the chimney.* 烟囱里冒出来团团黑烟. **4** [U] **(a)** strength or power of sound 音量; 响度: *The TV was on at full volume.* 电视机音量已开到了最大了. ○ *The music doubled in volume.* 音乐的声音加大了一倍. ○ [attrib 作定语] *a volume control* 音量控制装置. **(b)** switch on a radio, etc for adjusting this 音量调节器: *turn the volume up/down* 把音量调大[小]. **5** (idm 习语) **speak volumes** ⇨ SPEAK.

vo·lu·min·ous /vəˈluːmɪnəs; vəˋlumənəs/ *adj* (*fml or joc* 文或谑) **1** (of clothing etc) using much material; loose-fitting or ample (指衣物)用料多的, 宽松的, 肥大的: *wrapped in the voluminous folds of a blanket* 裹在大毯子的折层里 ○ *voluminous skirts, petticoats, etc*, eg as worn by a Victorian lady 宽松的裙子、衬裙等(如维多利亚时代女士穿的). **2** (of writing) great in quantity; abundant (指文字)大量的, 浩瀚的: *voluminous correspondence* 大量的信件 ○ *the voluminous works of Dickens*, ie filling many books 狄更斯的卷帙浩繁的著作. ▷ **vo·lu·min·ously** *adv*: *writing voluminously in one's diary* 记了大量日记.

vol·un·tary[1] /ˈvɒləntrɪ; *US* -terɪ; ˋvɑlənˌtɛrɪ/ *adj* **1** acting, done or given willingly 自愿的; 自动的; 主动的: *The prisoner made a voluntary statement.* 那个犯人主动地做了供述. ○ *Attendance is purely voluntary.* 这次出席纯粹是自愿的. ○ *Charities rely on voluntary donations/contributions.* 慈善事业依靠自愿捐赠. ○ *The firm went into voluntary liquidation.* 那家商号自动停业清算债务. **2** working, done or maintained without payment 志愿的; 无偿的; 义务的: *voluntary helpers*, eg at a fête, bazaar, etc 志愿的帮手(如在义卖会、义卖场等) ○ *She does voluntary social work.* 她从事义务社会工作. ○ *The organization is run on a voluntary basis.* 这个组织是由志愿人员管理的. ○ *a voluntary service, institution, centre, etc* 义务性的服务、机构、中心等. **3** (of bodily or muscular movements) controlled by the will (指身体活动或肌肉运动)由意志控制的, 随意的. Cf 参看 INVOLUNTARY.

▷ **vol·un·tar·ily** /ˈvɒləntrəlɪ; *US* ˌvɒlənˈterəlɪ; ˌvɑlənˋtɛrəlɪ/ *adv* **1** without compulsion; willingly 自愿地; 自动地; 主动地. **2** without payment; free of charge 志愿地; 无偿地; 义务地.

vol·un·tary[2] /ˈvɒləntrɪ; *US* -terɪ; ˋvɑlənˌtɛrɪ/ *n* solo played on a musical instrument before, during or after a church service (教堂礼拜仪式前后或进行期间的)乐器独奏: *organ, trumpet voluntaries* 风琴、小号独奏.

vo·lun·teer /ˌvɒlənˈtɪə(r); ˌvɑlənˋtɪr/ *n* **1 ~ (for sth/to do sth)** person who offers to do sth without being compelled or paid 自愿的或无偿的效劳的人; 志愿者: *volunteers for the post of treasurer* 自愿任财务工作的人 ○ *volunteers to run the Christmas show* 自愿操办圣诞节表演的人 ○ *Few volunteers came forward.* 没什么人自告奋勇的人. ○ [attrib 作定语] *volunteer social workers* 志愿的社会工作人员 ○ *volunteer groups* 志愿小组. **2** person who joins the armed forces voluntarily 志愿兵; 义勇兵: [attrib 作定语] *volunteer troops, forces, etc* 志愿部队、志愿军. Cf 参看 CONSCRIPT *n*.

▷ **vo·lun·teer** *v* **1** [I, Ipr, Tn, Tn·pr, Tt] **~ (sth) (for sth)** give or offer (one's help, a suggestion, etc) willingly or without being paid 自愿地或无偿地给予或提供(帮助、建议等): *She volunteered (her services) for relief work.* 她自愿参加救济工作. ○ *'Tim's busy but I'll come,' he volunteered.* '蒂姆很忙, 我来吧,' 他主动说道. ○ *volunteer information, advice, financial support* 自愿提供情况、意见、资助 ○ *I volunteered to act as chauffeur.* 我自愿充当汽车司机. **2** [I, Ipr, It] **~ (for sth)** join the forces as a volunteer 当志愿兵: *volunteer for military service/to join the army* 自愿服役[参军].

vo·lup·tu·ary /vəˈlʌptʃʊərɪ; *US* -ʊerɪ; vəˋlʌptʃʊˌɛrɪ/ *n* (*fml esp derog* 文, 尤作贬义) person who seeks and enjoys luxury and sensual pleasure 骄奢淫逸的人.

vo·lup·tu·ous /vəˈlʌptʃʊəs; vəˋlʌptʃʊəs/ *adj* **1 (a)** giving a feeling of luxury or sensual pleasure 给人奢华或感官享受的: *voluptuous thoughts, caresses, smiles* 刺激感官的想法、抚摸、微笑 ○ *the voluptuous enjoyment of a hot bath* 热水浴的舒适享受. **(b)** (*esp derog* 尤作贬义) devoted to such pleasure 耽于奢华或感官享受的: *voluptuous tastes, indulgences, urges, etc* 骄奢淫逸的兴味、放纵、欲望等. **2** (*approv* 褒) (of a woman) having a full and sexually desirable figure (指女子)体态丰满的: *voluptuous breasts, hips, curves* 丰满的乳房、臀部、曲线 ○ *Renoir's voluptuous nudes* 雷诺阿作的体态丰满的裸体画. ▷ **vo·lup·tu·ously** *adv*. **vo·lup·tu·ous·ness** *n* [U].

vo·lute /vəˈluːt; vəˋlut/ *n* **1** (*architecture* 建) spiral scroll-shaped ornamentation, esp at the top of Ionic columns 螺旋饰; 涡卷饰物; (尤指爱奥尼亚式柱头上的)盘蜗. **2** (*biology* 生) (any of the curves on a) spirally-coiled shell 涡螺壳; (螺壳上的)螺环.

▷ **vo·luted** *adj* decorated with or having volutes 有螺旋饰的; 螺旋形的; 有盘蜗的: *a voluted sea-shell* 螺旋形的海贝.

vomit /ˈvɒmɪt; ˋvɑmɪt/ *v* **1** [I, Tn, Tn·p] **~ sth (up)** eject (food, etc from the stomach) through the mouth; be sick 呕吐(食物等): *the noise of vomiting* 呕吐声 ○ *The mixture of drinks made me vomit.* 我喝了混合饮料后呕吐起来. ○ *vomit blood* 吐血 ○ *He vomited (up) all he had eaten.* 他把吃下去的东西全吐了出来. ⇨Usage at SICK 用法见SICK. **2** [Tn, Tn·p] **~ sth (out/forth)** (*fig* 比喻) (of a volcano, etc) eject sth violently (指火山等)喷出某物: *factory chimneys vomiting (forth) smoke* 正在冒烟的工厂烟囱.

▷ **vomit** *n* [U] food, etc from the stomach that has been vomited 从胃中吐出的食物等: *choke to death on one's own vomit* 呕吐的东西堵在喉咙里憋得要死.

voo·doo /ˈvuːduː; ˋvudu/ (also **voo·doo·ism**) *n* [U] form of religion based on belief in witchcraft and magical rites, practised by blacks in the W Indies, esp in Haiti 伏都教(西印度群岛黑人中的宗教, 崇奉巫术及魔法, 尤指海地的).

vo·ra·cious /vəˈreɪʃəs; vəˋreʃəs/ *adj* **1** very greedy in eating; ravenous 贪吃的; 极饿的: *a voracious eater* 贪吃的人 ○ *a voracious appetite, hunger* 极大的胃口、极饿. **2** (*fig* 比喻) very eager for knowledge, information, etc (对知识、信息等)渴求的: *a voracious reader* 求知欲强的读者 ○ *voracious seekers after truth* 如饥似渴探求真理的人. ▷ **vo·ra·ciously** *adv*. **vo·ra·city** /vəˈræsətɪ; vəˋræsətɪ/ *n* [U].

vor·tex /ˈvɔːteks; ˋvɔrtɛks/ *n* (*pl* 复数作 **~es** or, in scientific use, 科技用语复数作 **-tices** /-tɪsiːz; -tɪˏsiz/) **1** [C] whirling mass of water, air, etc, as in a whirlpool or whirlwind (水、空气等的)涡流, 涡旋, 旋涡, 旋风. **2** [sing] (*fig* 比喻) social group, profession, etc seen as sth that swallows those who approach it; whirl of activity 可将周围的人卷入的社会集团、职业等; 活动的旋涡: *drawn helplessly into the vortex of society, party politics, etc* 不由自主卷入社会、党派斗争等的旋涡里.

vo·tary /ˈvəʊtərɪ; ˋvotərɪ/ *n* **~ (of sb/sth)** (*fml* 文) person who dedicates himself to sth, esp religious work and service 献身者(尤指对宗教事务的): *votaries of peace, disarmament, etc* 致力于和平、裁军等的人 ○ (*joc* 谑) *votaries of golf* 高尔夫球迷.

vote /vəʊt; vot/ *n* **1** [C] **~ (for/against sb/sth); ~ (on sth)** formal expression of one's opinion or choice eg by ballot or show of hands 表决(如投票或举手表决): *cast/record one's vote* 投票 ○ *take/hold a vote on the motion* 对这项动议进行表决 ○ *settle, decide, resolve, etc the matter by a vote* 以表决方式解决、决定、解决...此事 ○ *a majority/minority vote* 多数[少数]票 ○ *counting, sorting, checking the votes*, ie papers on which votes are recorded 计算、整理、核对选票 ○ *postal votes* 邮寄的选票 ○ *The Tory candidate received/polled 8 000 votes.* 保守党候选人获8 000选票. ○ *The measure was passed/defeated by 9 votes to 6.* 该议案以9票赞成6票反对获得通过[以9票反对6票赞成被否定]. ○ *The vote went against him/against accepting the plan.* 经过表决他失败了[该方案否决了]. ○ *a vote of confidence/censure*, ie one showing the support/lack of support of the majority of voters 信任票[不信任票]. **2 the vote** [sing] votes given by or for a certain group, eg at a political election 投票总数, 得票总数(如政治性选举): *attempts to win the teenage, immigrant, Scottish, etc vote* 争取青少年的、移民的、苏格兰人的...选票的努力 ○ *increase/decrease the Tory vote by 5%* 使保守党票数增加[减少]5% ○ *split the vote*, eg between rival opposition parties so that the government is re-elected 拉平选票(如在敌对党之间以致重选政府) ○ *The Socialists got 35% of the vote.* 社会党人获得35%的选票. **3 the vote** [sing] right to vote, esp in political elections; franchise 投票权, 选举权(尤指政治选举中的); 公民权: *UK nationals get the vote at 18.* 英国国民18岁始有选举权. **4** (idm 习语) **put sth to the ˈvote** decide (an issue, etc) by asking for votes 将(问题等)付诸表决. **a ˌvote of ˈthanks** speech asking an audience to show their appreciation, esp by clapping 要求大家表示感谢的讲话(尤指请大家鼓掌): *propose a vote of thanks* 提议鼓掌致谢.

▷ **vote** *v* **1** [I, Ipr, Tn, Tt] **~ (for/against sb/sth); ~ (on sth)** formally express an opinion or choice by vote 以表决方式表明观点或选择: *vote by ballot, proxy, post* 无记名、由代理人、以邮寄方式投票 ○ *20 delegates voted for/against the motion.* 有20名代表投票赞成[反对]这个动议. ○ *If we cannot agree, let's vote on it.* 咱们意见要是不一致就表决吧. ○ *Vote (for) Smith/Labour on polling day!* 请在投票日投史密斯[工党]的票! ○ *I voted 'No' in the referendum.* 我在全民投票时投了反对票. ○ *We voted to continue the strike.* 我们投票决定继续罢工. **2** [Cn·n] elect (sb) to a position of authority by a majority of votes 选出(某人)(担任某职): *I was voted chairman.* 我当选为主席. **3** [Dn·n] grant (a sum of money, etc) by voting 表决通过拨给(款项等): *MPs have just voted themselves a pay rise.* 下议院议员刚投票决定为他们自己增加薪水. ○ *The hospital was voted £100 000 for research.* 经表决拨给该医院100 000英镑研究经费. **4** [esp passive 尤用于被动语态: Cn·a, Cn·n] (*infml* 口) declare (sth) to be good, bad, etc by general consent (根据大家的意见)认为(某事物)好、不好等: *The show was voted a success.* 大家一致认为表演很成功. **5** [Tf no passive 不用于被动语态] (*infml* 口) suggest or propose (sth) 建议, 提议(某事物): *I vote (that) we stay here.* 我建议我们留在这里. **6** (phr v) **vote sb/sth down** reject or defeat sb/sth by voting 投票击败某人[某事物]; 否决某事物. **vote sb in/out/on/off; vote sb into/out of/onto/off sth** elect sb to, or reject sb from, a position of authority 选出某人任某职[免去某人某职]: *vote the Liberals in* 投票选出自由党人任职 ○ *She was voted out of office/off the board.* 经投票免去她的职务[董事职务]. **vote sth through** approve or bring into force (a proposal, etc) by voting 表决通过(提案等): *Parliament voted the bill through without a debate.* 国会未经辩论就投票通过了这项法案. **voter** *n* person who votes or has the right to vote, esp in a political election 投票人, 选举人, 表决者(尤指政治性选举的): *floating, marginal, tactical, etc voters* 无党派的、意向不明的、有策略的...投票人.

vo·tive /ˈvəʊtɪv; ˋvotɪv/ *adj* [usu attrib 通常作定语] presented (esp in church) to fulfil a promise made to God 向上帝还愿的(尤指在教堂内): *votive offerings, candles, etc* 还愿的奉献物、蜡烛等.

vouch /vaʊtʃ; vaʊtʃ/ *v* [Ipr] **1 ~ for sb/sth** take responsibility for or express confidence in (a person, his behaviour, etc); guarantee 为(某人、其行为等)担保或作证; 保证: *I can vouch for him/his honesty.* 我可以为他[他的诚实]作担保. **2 ~ for sth** confirm (a claim, etc) by producing evidence or drawing on one's own experience (提供证据或现身说法)确定(某权利要求等): *Experts vouch for the painting's authenticity.* 由专家确认该画是否为真迹.

voucher /ˈvaʊtʃə(r); ˋvaʊtʃɚ/ *n* **1** (*Brit*) document, showing that money has been paid or promised, which can be exchanged for certain goods or services (代替现金的)凭单, 凭证, 代金券: *ˈgift vouchers*, ie offered as presents and later exchanged at the store for goods 礼券 ○ *special discount vouchers* 优惠券 ○ *luncheon vouchers*, ie tokens supplied by some employers, exchangeable for food at restaurants which have agreed to accept them 午餐代用券. **2** document showing that money has been paid for goods, etc received; receipt 收据; 收条.

vouch·safe /vaʊtʃˈseɪf; vaʊtʃˋsef/ *v* [Tn, Dn·n, Dn·pr] **~ sth (to sb)** (*dated or fml* 旧或文) grant sth (to sb) as a gift or privilege 将某事物赐予或给予(某人)(作为礼物或特权): *be vouchsafed a vision of the future* 有先见之明 ○ *vouchsafe to him certain official secrets* 让他知悉官方某些秘密.

vow /vaʊ; vaʊ/ *n* solemn promise or undertaking, esp of a religious nature 誓, 誓约, 誓言(尤指宗教的): *recite/pronounce/renew one's ˈmarriage vows* 念[发出/重复]自己的婚誓 ○ *keep/break a solemn vow* 履行[违反]庄严的誓约 ○ *take a vow of silence, secrecy, etc* 立誓保持沉默、保守秘密等 ○ *Nuns are under vows of poverty, chastity and obedience.* 修女须立誓保持清贫、贞洁、顺从.

▷ **vow** *v* [Tn, Tf, Tt] make a vow about (sth); swear, promise or declare solemnly 就(某事物)起誓; 立誓; 发誓: *They vowed revenge on their enemies.* 他们发誓要向敌人报仇. ○ *He vowed (that) he would lose weight.* 他立誓要减轻体重. ○ *She vowed never to speak to him again.* 她发誓再也不跟他说话了.

vowel /ˈvaʊəl; ˋvaʊəl/ *n* **(a)** speech-sound made without audible stopping of the breath by the tongue, lips, etc 元音: [attrib 作定语] *a vowel system* 元音系统. **(b)** letter or letters used to represent such a sound, eg a, e, i, o, u, ee, oa 元音字母. Cf 参看 CONSONANT[1].

vox pop·uli /ˌvɒks ˈpɒpjʊlaɪ; ˏvaks ˋpapjəlaɪ/ (*Latin* 拉) (also *infml* 口语作 **vox pop** /ˌvɒks ˈpɒp; ˏvaks ˋpap/) public opinion or popular belief, esp as expressed in short media interviews with ordinary people on matters of interest 舆论(尤指经传媒片断表达的).

voy·age /ˈvɔɪɪdʒ; ˋvɔɪ·ɪdʒ/ *n* long journey, esp by sea or in space 航行; (尤指)航海, 航天: *on the outward/homeward voyage* 在出航[返航]途中 ○ *make a voyage across the Atlantic* 作横越大西洋的航行 ○ *go on a voyage from Mombasa to Goa* 由蒙巴萨航行前往果阿 ○ *the voyages of Sinbad the Sailor* 水手辛伯达的几次航行. ⇨Usage at JOURNEY 用法见 JOURNEY.

▷ **voy·age** *v* [I, Ipr] (*fml* 文) go on a voyage; travel 航行; 航海; 航天飞行: *voyaging across the Indian Ocean, through space* 作穿越印度洋的航行、航天飞行. **voy·ager** /ˈvɔɪɪdʒə(r); ˋvɔɪ·ɪdʒɚ/ *n* (*dated* 旧) person making a voyage, esp to unknown parts of the world by sea 航行

者; 航海者; 航天者; (尤指)航海探险家: [attrib 作定语] *the Voyager 2 spacecraft* 旅行者 2 号宇宙飞船.

voy·eur /vɔɪˈɜː(r); vɔɪˈɝ/ *n* person who gets pleasure from watching in secret others undressing or engaging in sexual activities 窥阴癖者(秘密窥视他人脱衣或性行为而获快感的人).

▷ **voy·eur·ism** /vɔɪˈɜːrɪzəm; vɔɪˈɝrɪzəm/ *n* [U] state or practice of being a voyeur 窥阴癖. **voy·eur·istic** /ˌvwɑːjəˈrɪstɪk; ˌvwɑjərˋɪstɪk/ *adj*: *voyeuristic pleasures, pursuits, etc* 窥阴者的乐趣、嗜好等.

VP (also **V Pres**) *abbr* 缩写 = Vice-President.

vs *abbr* 缩写 = versus.

VS *abbr* 缩写 = Veterinary Surgeon.

VSO /ˌviː es ˈəʊ; ˌvi ɛs ˋo/ *abbr* 缩写 = (*Brit*) Voluntary Service Overseas (a scheme for people to work in developing countries) 海外志愿服务(为在发展中国家志愿工作的人员制定的计划): *do VSO* 从事海外志愿服务工作.

VTOL /ˌviː tiː əʊ ˈel *or, in informal use,* 俗读作 ˈviːtɒl; ˌvi ti o ˋɛl, ˋvi ˌtɔl/ *abbr* 缩写 = (of aircraft) vertical take-off and landing (指飞机)垂直起降: *a VTOL jet* 垂直起降喷气机 ○ *fly VTOLs* 驾驶垂直起降飞机. Cf 参看 STOL.

vul·can·ite /ˈvʌlkənaɪt; ˋvʌlkənˌaɪt/ *n* [U] hard black vulcanized rubber 硬质橡胶; 硬橡皮.

▷ **vul·can·ize**, **-ise** /ˈvʌlkənaɪz; ˋvʌlkənˌaɪz/ *v* [Tn] treat (rubber, etc) with sulphur, etc at great heat to make it stronger and more elastic 硫化(橡胶等). **vul·can·iza·tion**, **-isation** /ˌvʌlkənaɪˈzeɪʃn; *US* -nɪˈz-; ˌvʌlkənəˋzeʃən/ *n* [U].

vulgar /ˈvʌlgə(r); ˋvʌlgɚ/ *adj* **1** lacking in good taste or refinement 粗俗的; 庸俗的: *a vulgar display of wealth* 对财富庸俗的炫耀 ○ *dressed in cheap and vulgar finery* 穿着廉价而俗气的华丽衣服 ○ *a loud and vulgar laugh* 粗俗的大笑. **2** likely to offend many people; rude or obscene 易触犯众人的; 粗野的; 下流的: *a vulgar gesture, suggestion, joke* 下流的手势、示意、笑话.

▷ **vul·gar·ism** /ˈvʌlgərɪzəm; ˋvʌlgɚˌɪzəm/ *n* rude or obscene word or phrase 粗俗的词语: *'Arse' is a vulgarism for the buttocks.* arse 是用以指臀部的粗俗词.

vul·gar·ity /vʌlˈgærətɪ; vʌlˋgærətɪ/ *n* (**a**) [C usu *pl* 通常作复数] rude or obscene act or expression 粗鄙下流的举动; 粗话; 下流话. (**b**) [U] state of being vulgar 粗俗; 庸俗; 下流: *the vulgarity of his tastes, clothes, manners* 他情趣的低级、服装之俗不可耐、举止之粗俗.

vul·gar·ize, **-ise** /ˈvʌlgəraɪz; ˋvʌlgəˌraɪz/ *v* [Tn] **1** cause (a person, his manners, etc) to become vulgar 使(某人、举止等)粗俗或俗气. **2** spoil (sth) by making it too ordinary or well known; popularize 使(某事物)俗气、庸俗化或通俗化; 普及. **vul·gar·iza·tion**, **-isation** /ˌvʌlgəraɪˈzeɪʃn; *US* -rɪˈz-; ˌvʌlgərəˋzeʃən/ *n* [U, C].

vul·garly *adv* **1** in a tasteless, unrefined or offensive manner 庸俗地; 粗俗地; 无礼地. **2** (*dated or fml* 旧或文) commonly or popularly 一般地; 通俗地: *The Devil is vulgarly referred to as 'Old Nick'.* 魔鬼俗称 Old Nick.

□ ˌ**vulgar** ˈ**fraction** (also **simple fraction**) fraction represented by numbers above and below a line (eg $\frac{3}{4}$, $\frac{5}{8}$) 普通分数. ⇨App 4 见附录 4. Cf 参看 DECIMAL *n.*

Vul·gate /ˈvʌlgeɪt; ˋvʌlget/ *n* **the Vulgate** [sing] Latin version of the Bible made in the 4th century and preferred by the RC Church 拉丁通行本《圣经》(第 4 世纪译成的天主教会钦定文本).

vul·ner·able /ˈvʌlnərəbl; ˋvʌlnərəbḷ/ *adj* **~ (to sth/sb)** **1** that can be hurt, wounded or injured 能受伤害的: *Young birds are very vulnerable to predators.* 幼小的鸟易受食肉动物伤害. ○ *Cyclists are more vulnerable than motorists.* 骑自行车的人比开汽车的人容易受伤. ○ (*fig* 比喻) *His wife's death left him feeling vulnerable and depressed.* 他妻子去世后他感到六神无主十分消沉. **2** (*fig* 比喻) exposed to danger or attack; unprotected 暴露于危险面前的; 易受攻击的; 无防御的: *vulnerable to abuse, blackmail, criticism* 易受凌辱、敲诈、批评 ○ *a vulnerable point in NATO's defences* 北大西洋公约组织防御中的薄弱之处 ○ *The election defeat puts the party leader in a vulnerable position.* 该党落选后其领导人的地位岌岌可危. ▷ **vul·ner·ab·il·ity** /ˌvʌlnərəˈbɪlətɪ; ˌvʌlnərəˋbɪlətɪ/ *n* [U]. **vul·ner·ably** /-əblɪ; -əblɪ/ *adv*.

vulp·ine /ˈvʌlpaɪn; ˋvʌlpaɪn/ *adj* (*fml* 文) of or like a fox (似)狐狸的: *vulpine cunning, stealth, etc* 狐狸般的狡猾、鬼祟等 ○ *sharp vulpine features* 很像狐狸般的长相.

vul·ture /ˈvʌltʃə(r); ˋvʌltʃɚ/ *n* **1** large bird, usu with head and neck almost bare of feathers, that lives on the flesh of dead animals 秃鹫. **2** (*fig* 比喻) greedy person seeking profits from the misfortunes of others 乘他人之危谋利的人: *vultures round the bedside of the dying millionaire* 围拢在垂危的百万富翁床边的贪心人.

vulva /ˈvʌlvə; ˋvʌlvə/ *n* (*pl* 复数作 **~s** or, in scientific use, 科技用语复数作 **vulvae** /ˈvʌlviː; ˋvʌlvi/) (*anatomy* 解) external opening of the female genitals 外阴; 女阴.

vv *abbr* 缩写 = verses.

vy·ing *pres p* of VIE.

W w

W, w /ˈdʌbljuː; ˋdʌbljʊ/ *n* (*pl* **W's, w's** /ˈdʌbljuːz; ˋdʌbljʊz/) the twenty-third letter of the English alphabet 英语字母表的第二十三个字母.

W *abbr* 缩写 = **1** watt(s): *a 60W light bulb* 60瓦的电灯泡. Cf 参看 V *abbr* 缩写 2. **2** west(ern): *W Yorkshire* 西约克郡 ○ *London W5 5HY*, ie as a postal code 伦敦W5 5HY(用作邮政编码). **3** (esp on clothing) women's (size) (尤用于衣物标签)女用的(尺码).

WAC (also **Wac**) /ˌdʌbljuː eɪ ˈsiː: *or, in informal use,* 俗读作 wæk; ˌdʌbljʊ e ˋsi, wæk/ *abbr* 缩写 = (*US*) Women's Army Corps 陆军妇女队: *join the Wacs* 参加陆军妇女队.

wacky /ˈwækɪ; ˋwækɪ/ *adj* (**-ier, -iest**) (*infml* 口 *esp US*) eccentric or crazy; zany 古怪的; 疯癫的; 滑稽可笑的: *a wacky comedian* 滑稽的喜剧演员.

wad /wɒd; wɑd/ *n* **1** lump or bundle of soft material used for keeping things apart or in place, or to block a hole, etc 块状软物, 填料(作隔离、固定或填塞等用的): *The noise was so loud that she put wads of cotton wool in her ears.* 噪声很大, 她用棉花团把耳朵堵上了. **2** quantity of documents or banknotes folded, rolled or held together (文件或钞票的)卷, 沓, 捆: *He pulled a wad of £10 notes out of his pocket.* 他从衣袋里掏出一沓面额10英镑的钱. **3** (*Brit sl* 俚) bun or sandwich 圆面包; 三明治: *a cup of tea and a wad* 一杯茶和一个圆面包.

▷ **wad** *v* (**-dd-**) [Tn] **1** (**a**) fix (sth) in place with a wad, esp to protect it (用软物)固定(某物)(尤指为起保护作用的). (**b**) stuff (sth) with a wad (用软物)填塞(某物). **2** line (a garment, etc) with soft material (esp cotton or wool) 用软物(尤指棉或毛)絮(衣服等): *a wadded dressing-gown, jacket, quilt* 棉的晨袍、棉上衣、棉被. **wad·ding** /ˈwɒdɪŋ; ˋwɑdɪŋ/ *n* [U] soft material, usu cotton or wool, used for padding or lining garments, etc or protecting things when packing them 软物, 填料(通常指棉或毛, 用以絮衣物或作包装衬物).

waddle /ˈwɒdl; ˋwɑdl/ *v* [I, Ipr, Ip] (*often derog* 常作贬义) walk with short steps and a swaying movement, as a duck does 摇摆地行走(如鸭子般): *A short plump woman came waddling along the pavement.* 有个矮胖女子一摇一摆地沿人行道走来. ⇨Usage at SHUFFLE 用法见SHUFFLE.

▷ **waddle** *n* [sing] waddling way of walking 摇摇摆摆的行走; 蹒跚的步态: *walk with a waddle* 一摇一摆地走路.

wade /weɪd; wed/ *v* **1** (**a**) [I, Ipr, Ip] walk with an effort (through water, mud or anything that makes walking difficult) 费力地走、涉或蹚(过水、泥地等): *I can't wade in these boots.* 我穿着这双靴子没法蹚水. ○ *There's no bridge; we'll have to wade across (the stream).* 没有桥, 我们得蹚过(小河)去. ○ *The angler waded (out) into the middle of the river.* 钓鱼的人蹚水到河中央去了. ○ *They had to wade knee-deep through mud and debris to reach the victims.* 他们须通过齐膝的烂泥和堆积物, 磕磕绊绊来到遇难者身旁. Cf 参看 PADDLE[2] 1. (**b**) [Tn] cross (a stream, etc) by wading 蹚过(小河等): *Can we wade the brook?* 我们能蹚过这条小河吗? **2** (phr v) **wade in** (*infml* 口) start doing sth (esp sth difficult) with energy and determination 坚决努力着手做某事(尤指困难的事): *The job has to be done, so let's wade in immediately.* 这件工作非做不可, 咱们说干就干吧. **wade into sb/sth** attack sb/sth vigorously 猛烈攻击某人[某事物]: *She waded straight into her critics with her opening remarks.* 她在开场白里单刀直入抨击了批评她的人. **wade through sth** read sth that is long or difficult to read, without interest or enjoyment 费力地阅读冗长或艰深的材料(无兴致或乐趣): *wading through page after page of boring statistics* 吃力地一页页看着乏味的统计数字.

▷ **wader** *n* **1** [C] = WADING BIRD. **2 waders** [pl] angler's high waterproof boots worn when wading (钓鱼人涉水时穿的)长筒防水靴: *a pair of waders* 一双长筒防水靴.

□ ˈ**wading bird** any of several types of long-legged water-bird that wade (contrasted with web-footed birds that swim) 涉禽.

wadi /ˈwɒdɪ; ˋwɑdɪ/ *n* (in the Middle East and N Africa) rocky watercourse that is dry except after heavy rain (中东和北非的)多岩石的干涸河床(仅大雨后有水).

WAF (also **Waf**) /ˌdʌbljuː eɪ ˈef *or, in informal use,* 俗读作 wæf; ˌdʌbljʊ e ˋɛf, wæf/ *abbr* 缩写 = (*US*) Women in the Air Force 空军妇女队: *join the Wafs* 参加空军妇女队.

wafer /ˈweɪfə(r); ˋwefɚ/ *n* **1** very thin crisp sweet biscuit 威佛饼干(薄而脆的甜饼干): *an ice-cream wafer*, ie for eating with ice-cream 冰激凌威佛饼干(与冰激凌同吃的). **2** small round piece of unleavened bread used in Holy Communion 圣饼(用作圣餐的小圆饼). **3** small round piece of red paper stuck on the back of a document instead of a seal, to show that it is official 封缄纸(红色圆纸片, 贴在文件背面代替封印).

□ ˌ**wafer-ˈthin** *adj* very thin 极薄的: ˌ*wafer-thin* ˈ*sandwiches* 极薄的三明治 ○ *a* ˌ*wafer-thin majority* 微弱的多数.

waffle[1] /ˈwɒfl; ˋwɑfl/ *n* small crisp cake made of cooked batter with a pattern of squares on it, often eaten with syrup 瓦夫饼(蛋奶小脆饼, 上有方形图案, 常与糖浆同吃).

□ ˈ**waffle-iron** *n* utensil with two shallow metal pans, usu hinged together, in which waffles are cooked 烘瓦夫饼的铁模.

waffle[2] /ˈwɒfl; ˋwɑfl/ *v* [I, Ipr, Ip] (*Brit infml derog* 口, 贬) talk or write, esp at great length, without saying anything very important or sensible (胡乱地)说或写(尤指没完没了地): *What is she waffling about now?* 她又在那儿瞎写什么呢? ○ *He waffled on for hours but no one was listening.* 他絮叨了半天, 谁也没听进去.

▷ **waffle** *n* [U] vague, wordy and often meaningless talk or writing (含糊、冗长而常无内容的)谈话或文字: *The report looks impressive but it's really nothing but waffle.* 这篇报告貌似冠冕堂皇, 实际上空洞无物.

waft /wɒft; *US* wæft; wæft/ *v* [Ipr, Ip, Tn·pr, Tn·p] (cause sth to) be carried lightly and smoothly (as if) through the air (使某物)(似)在空中飘流、飘浮或飘荡: *The sound of their voices wafted across the lake to us.* 他们的声音飘过湖面传到我们这里. ○ *Delicious smells wafted up from the kitchen.* 厨房里飘出了香味. ○ *The scent of the flowers was wafted along by the breeze.* 微风送来了花香.

▷ **waft** *n* smell carried through the air; whiff (空气传播的)香味; 气味: *a waft of perfume* 香水的味 ○ *wafts of cigar smoke* 阵阵雪茄烟味.

wag[1] /wæg; wæg/ *v* (**-gg-**) **1** [I, Ipr, Ip, Tn, Tn·pr, Tn·p] (cause sth to) move quickly from side to side or up and down (使某物)来回或上下迅速摇摆: *The dog's tail wagged.* 那条狗尾巴摆了摆. ○ *The dog wagged its tail excitedly.* 那条狗兴奋地直摇尾巴. ○ *wag one's finger at sb*, ie as a way of showing one's disapproval of him 向某人摇手指(表示不赞成). Cf 参看 WAGGLE, WIGGLE. **2** (idm 习语) **the tail wagging the dog** ⇨ TAIL. **tongues wag** ⇨ TONGUE.

▷ **wag** *n* wagging movement 摇摆: *The dog gave a wag of its tail.* 那条狗摆了摆尾巴.

wag[2] /wæg; wæg/ *n* (*dated* 旧) person who is fond of making jokes; amusing or facetious person 爱开玩笑的人; 诙谐滑稽的人: *He's a bit of a wag.* 他爱开点玩笑.

▷ **wag·gish** /ˈwægɪʃ; ˋwægɪʃ/ *adj* (*dated* 旧) of, like, done or made by a wag (似)爱开玩笑的; 诙谐的人做的: *waggish remarks, tricks, youngsters* 诙谐的言语、花招、年轻人. **wag·gishly** *adv*. **wag·gish·ness** *n* [U].

wage[1] /weɪdʒ; wedʒ/ *n* (usu *pl* except in certain phrases and when used attributively 通常作复数, 但用于某些词组或作定语时除外) regular (usu weekly) payment made or received for work or services 工资(通常指按周的): *wages of £200 a week/a weekly wage of £200* 一星期200英镑的工资 ○ *Wages are paid on Fridays.* 每星期五

发工资. ○ *Tax and insurance are deducted from your wages.* 所得税和保险费从工资扣除. ○ *We expect a fair day's wage for a fair day's work.* 我们做好一天的工作, 就希望得到一天应得的工资. ○ *The workers are demanding to be paid a living wage*, ie one that enables them to live without hunger or hardship. 工人要求得到能够维持生活的工资. ○ *a minimum wage*, ie guaranteed basic pay in a particular industry or country 最低工资(某行业或某国的工资底线) ○ [attrib 作定语] *a wage increase/rise of £10 a week* 每星期的工资额增加10英镑. ⇨Usage at INCOME 用法见 INCOME.

□ **'wage-claim** *n* increase in wages demanded from an employer for workers by their union 增加工资的要求(工会向雇主提出的).

'wage-earner *n* **(a)** person who works for wages 挣工资的人(通常指按周领取工资的工人): *Are you a wage-earner or salaried?* 你是工人还是职员? **(b)** member of a family who earns money 家庭中挣钱的人: *There are two wage-earners in the family.* 这家有两个人挣钱.

'wage freeze legal ban on or control of increases in wages 工资冻结(合法禁止或控制工资的增长).

wage[2] /weɪdʒ; wedʒ/ *v* [Tn, Tn·pr] **~ sth (against/on sth)** begin and carry on (a war, campaign, etc) 开始, 进行(战争、运动等): *No country wants to wage a nuclear war.* 哪个国家也不想打核战争. ○ *The government is waging a campaign against sex discrimination in industry.* 政府正在展开反对工业界性别歧视的运动.

wager /'weɪdʒə(r); 'wedʒɚ/ *v* [I, Tn, Tn·pr, Tf, Dn·n, Dn·f] **~ sth (on sth)** (*dated or fml* 旧或文) stake (money) on the result of (sth); bet sth 在(某事物)上赌(钱); 打赌: *You won't find better goods anywhere else, I'll wager.* 你到哪儿也找不到比这个好的货, 我敢打赌. ○ *wager £5 (on a horse)* (在一匹马上)押注5英镑 ○ *I'll wager (you) (any money you like) he won't come.* 我(和你)打赌, (随便赌多少钱,)他不会来.

▷ **wager** *n* (*dated or fml* 旧或文) bet 赌博: *lay/make a wager* 打赌 ○ *take up* (ie accept) *a wager* 同意打赌.

waggle /'wægl; 'wægl/ *v* [I, Tn] (*infml* 口) (cause sth to) move with short movements from side to side or up and down (使某物)来回或上下小幅度摇摆: *His bottom waggles in a funny way when he walks.* 他走路时臀部扭来扭去, 很可笑. ○ *She can waggle her ears.* 她能让耳朵来回动. Cf 参看 WAG[1], WIGGLE. ▷ **waggle** *n*.

wagon (*Brit* also **wag·gon**) /'wægən; 'wægən/ *n* **1** four-wheeled vehicle for carrying heavy loads, usu pulled by horses or oxen (四轮的)货车(通常为牛马拉的). Cf 参看 CART. **2** (*US* **freight car**) open railway truck (eg for carrying coal) (铁路的)敞篷货车(如运煤的): *a train with passenger coaches and goods wagons* 挂有客车和货车的列车. **3** trolley used for carrying food, esp tea, etc (送食物的)小手推车(尤指送茶点的). **4** (idm 习语) **on the 'wagon** (*infml* 口) no longer drinking alcoholic drinks; teetotal 戒酒: *be/go on the wagon* 戒酒.

▷ **wag·oner** (*Brit* also **wag·goner**) *n* person in charge of a wagon(1) and its horses (四轮货车的)马车夫.

wagon-lit /ˌvægɒn 'li:; vagõ'li/ *n* (*pl* **wagons-lits** /ˌvægɒn 'li:; vagõ'li/) sleeping-car (on Continental railways) (欧洲铁路的)卧车.

W

wag·tail /'wægteɪl; 'wægˌtel/ *n* any of various types of small bird with a long tail that moves constantly up and down when the bird is standing or walking 鹡鸰(体小, 尾长而不停上下摆动).

waif /weɪf; wef/ *n* **1** homeless person, esp an abandoned child 无家可归的人; (尤指)流浪儿: *a home for waifs and strays*, ie homeless and neglected children 流浪儿童收容所 ○ *They looked thin, waif-like and half starved.* 他们瘦骨伶仃, 像流浪儿似的饿得半死. **2** object or animal with no owner 无主的东西或动物.

wail /weɪl; wel/ *v* **1 (a)** [I, Ipr] **~ (about/over sth)** cry or complain (about sth) in a loud (usu shrill) voice (大声)哭, 诉苦(通常指尖声地): *wail with grief* 恸哭 ○ *The sick child was wailing miserably.* 那个患儿难受得连哭带喊. ○ *There's no use wailing about/over mistakes made in the past.* 为过去的错误痛哭是没有用的. **(b)** [I] (*fig* 比喻) make a sound similar to that of a person wailing 发出似哭号的尖声: *ambulances racing along with sirens wailing* 高声鸣笛疾驶的救护车 ○ *You can hear the wind wailing in the chimney.* 可以听到风穿过烟囱发出的尖声. **(c)** [Tn, Tf] say (sth) in a wailing way 哭着说(某事): *'I've lost all my money!' she wailed.* 她哭着说: '我的钱都丢了!' ○ *The child was wailing loudly that she had hurt her foot.* 那个女孩儿大声哭着说她的脚受伤了. **2** [Ipr] **~ for sb** express one's grief at the loss or death of sb; mourn sb 为某人死亡而悲痛; 哀悼某人: *She was wailing for her lost child.* 她为死去的孩子伤心悲痛. ⇨Usage at CRY 用法见 CRY.

▷ **wail** *n* **(a)** shrill cry, esp of pain or grief 尖叫; (尤指)痛哭: *The child burst into loud wails.* 那个孩子突然大哭起来. ○ *She uttered a wail of grief.* 她悲痛地大声尖叫. **(b)** sound similar to this 尖叫声; (尤指)痛哭声: *the wail of sirens* 警报器的呼啸声.

wains·cot /'weɪnskət; 'wenskət/ *n* wooden covering, esp panelling on (usu the lower half of) the walls of a room 护板; (尤指)护墙板, 内壁板(通常指室内墙壁下半部的).

▷ **wains·coted** *adj* (of a room) having a wainscot (指房间)有护墙板的.

wains·cot·ing *n* [U] (material used for a) wainscot 护板, 护墙板(材料).

waist /weɪst; west/ *n* **1** part of the body between the ribs and the hips, usu narrower than the rest of the trunk 腰; 腰部; 腰围: *She wore a wide belt round her waist.* 她束了一条宽腰带. ○ *She has a 26-inch waist.* 她的腰围是26英寸. ○ *He measures 30 inches round the waist.* 他的腰围是30英寸. ○ *The workmen were stripped to* (ie wearing nothing above) *the waist.* 工人们光着上身. ○ [attrib 作定语] *waist measurements* 腰围的尺寸. **2 (a)** part of a garment that goes round the waist (衣服的)腰部: *If the skirt is too big, we can take in the waist.* 要是裙子太大了, 我们可以把腰部收紧一些. ○ *The waist is too tight for me.* 这件衣服我穿腰部太瘦. ○ *trousers with a 30-inch waist* 腰围30英寸的裤子. **(b)** garment, or part of a garment, that covers the body from the shoulders to the waist (衣服的)上身(或上身的部分). Cf 参看 SHIRTWAIST (SHIRT). **3 (a)** narrow part in the middle of sth (物体的)中间细的部分: *the waist of an hourglass, a violin, a wasp* 沙漏的中部、小提琴中间凹处、黄蜂的腰部. **(b)** part of a ship between the forecastle and the quarterdeck (轮船的)腰部.

▷ **waisted** *adj* (of a garment) becoming narrower at the waist (指衣服)腰部狭窄的: *a waisted coat* 腰部狭窄的大衣.

-waisted (forming compound *adjs* 用以构成复合形容词) having the type of waist specified 有某种腰身的: *ˌnarrow-'waisted* ○ *ˌwasp-'waisted* ○ *a ˌhigh-waisted 'garment*, ie one with its waist above the waist of the person wearing it.

□ **'waistband** *n* strip of cloth that forms the waist of a garment, esp at the top of trousers or a skirt 腰带; (尤指)裤带, 裙带.

waistcoat /'weɪskəʊt; *US* 'weskət; 'wɛskət/ (*US* also **vest**) *n* close-fitting sleeveless garment, buttoned down the front, usu worn under a jacket or coat and often forming part of a man's suit (西服的)背心.

ˌwaist-'deep *adv, adj* up to the waist 上至腰部的; 齐腰深的: *The water was waist-deep.* 水深及腰部. ○ *They were ˌwaist-deep in 'water.* 他们在齐腰深的水中. ○ *wade ˌwaist-deep into a 'stream* 到小河齐腰深的地方.

ˌwaist-'high *adj, adv* high enough to reach the waist 高至腰部的: *The grass had grown waist-high.* 草已长得齐腰高了.

'waistline *n* **1** measurement of the body round the waist 腰围的尺寸; 腰肥: *a narrow/slim waistline* 纤细的[苗条的]腰身. **2** narrow part of a garment that fits at or just above or below the waist 衣服腰部(或近腰处)狭窄的部分: *a dress with a high waistline* 腰部高的连衣裙.

wait[1] /weɪt; wet/ *v* **1 (a)** [I, Ipr, It] **~ (for sb/sth)** stay where one is, delay acting, etc for a specified time or until sb or sth comes or until sth happens 等候; 等待: *'Have you been waiting long?' 'Yes, I've been waiting (for) twenty minutes.'* '你等了很久了吗?' '是啊, 等了20分钟了.' ○ *Tell him I can't see him now, he'll have to wait.* 告诉他我现在无法见他, 他得等一等. ○ *Wait for me, please.* 请等我一会儿. ○ *We are waiting for the rain to stop.* 我们正在等着雨停下了. ○ *You'll have to wait until the end of the month before I can pay you.* 你得等到月底我才能付给你钱. ○ (*infml* 口) *I was just waiting for* (ie expecting) *that (to happen).* 我正盼着这件事(发生)呢.

○ *The chairman is waiting to begin (the meeting).* 主席正在等着宣布开会. ○ *I am waiting to hear the result.* 我正在等着听结果. ○ *I can't wait* (ie am impatient) *to read his latest novel.* 我巴不得要看他的新小说. **(b)** [Tn] wait and watch for (sth); await 等候, 等待(某事): *wait one's opportunity/chance to do sth* 等待时机[机会]做某事 ○ *You will just have to wait your turn*, ie wait until your turn comes. 你得等到轮到你才行. ⇨Usage 见所附用法. **(c)** [I] not be dealt with immediately; be postponed 暂缓处理; 推迟: *The matter can wait until the next meeting; it's not urgent.* 这件事可以等到下次会议处理, 不是急事. **2** [Tn, Dn·pr] **~ sth (for sb)** postpone (a meal) until sb arrives (为等候某人)推迟开(饭): *I shall be home late tonight, so don't wait dinner (for me).* 今晚我回来得晚, 别等我吃饭. **3** [I] stop a vehicle at the side of the road for a short time (机动车在路边)暂停: *No Waiting*, ie as a warning that vehicles must not stop at the side of the road even for a short time. 禁止停车. **4** (idm 习语) **keep sb 'waiting** cause sb to wait or be delayed, eg because one is unpunctual 使某人等候或耽搁某人(如因对方不准时): *I'm sorry to have kept you waiting.* 对不起, 让您久等了. ○ *He kept us waiting for ages while he packed his luggage.* 他收拾行李, 让我们等了好半天. **ready and waiting** ⇨ READY. **time and tide wait for no man** ⇨ TIME[1]. **ˌwait and 'see** wait and find out what will happen before taking action; be patient 等等看; 耐心等待: *We shall just have to wait and see; there's nothing we can do at the moment.* 我们只好等等看, 现在无能为力. **wait at 'table** (*US* **wait on 'table**) (of a waiter or a servant in a private house) serve food and drink to people, clear away dishes, etc (指服务员或用人)招待进餐. **wait for the 'cat to jump/to see 'which way the 'cat jumps** (*infml* 口) delay taking action or a decision until it becomes clear how events will turn out 待情况明朗后再采取行动或做出决定. **'wait for it** (*infml* 口) (used as a warning to sb not to act, speak, etc before the proper time to do so has come 用以警告某人时机未到时别采取行动或别说话等). **(play) a 'waiting game** (cause) a deliberate delay in taking action so that one may act more effectively later (实行)待机而动的策略. **wait on sb hand and 'foot** serve sb by attending to all his needs 无微不至地照顾某人: *He seemed to expect to be waited on hand and foot.* 他像是想要人尽心尽力伺候他. **what are we 'waiting for?** (*infml* 口) let us go ahead and do sth, esp sth that has been planned or discussed 咱们干吧, 还等什么呢? (尤指已计划的或商议过的事). **what are you 'waiting for?** (*infml ironic* 口, 反语) why don't you get on with the job, work, etc? 你还等什么呢? (怎么还不着手干活儿、工作等?) **(just) you 'wait** (used when threatening sb that one will punish him or get one's revenge on him later 用以威胁以后要惩罚或报复某人). **5** (phr v) **wait about/around** stay in a place (usu idly or impatiently, eg because sb who is expected has not arrived) 在某处等候(通常指无聊地或不耐烦地, 如应到者未到). **wait behind** stay after other people have gone, esp to speak to sb privately 待到他人走后留下来(尤指为与某人私下谈话): *Please wait behind after class today.* 今天课后请你留下. **wait in** stay at home, esp because sb is expected 在家等候(尤指等某人来到): *I waited in all day but they didn't arrive.* 我在家等了一天, 他们却没来. **wait on sb (a)** act as a servant for sb, esp by serving food and drink at a meal 照料或伺候某人(尤指进餐时). **(b)** (*dated fml* 旧, 文) make a formal visit to sb to show respect 拜访或探望某人. **wait up (for sb)** not go to bed (until sb comes home); stay up (为等候某人)不睡觉; 熬夜: *I shall be home very late tonight, so don't wait up (for me).* 我今天晚上很晚才回家, 不必熬夜等着我.

▷ **waiter** (*fem* 阴性作 **wait·ress** /ˈweɪtrɪs; ˋwetrɪs/) *n* person employed to take customers' orders, bring food, etc in a restaurant, hotel dining-room, etc (饭店、旅馆餐厅等的)服务员.

□ **'waiting-list** *n* list of people who are waiting for service, treatment, etc that is not available now and who will receive it when it becomes available 等候者名单(等候接受服务、治疗等的人的): *put sb on a waiting-list for theatre tickets* 把某人列入等候购戏票者的名单 ○ *a hospital waiting-list*, eg for operations 等候治疗者的名单(如等待做手术的).

'waiting-room *n* **(a)** room in a station where people can sit while they are waiting for trains 候车室. **(b)** room (eg in a doctor's or dentist's surgery) where people wait until they can be attended to 等候室(如候诊室).

NOTE ON USAGE 用法: Compare **wait for** and **expect.** 试比较 **wait for** 和 **expect.** ☆ *I'm expecting him to arrive soon* means that I'm sure that he will. ☆ I'm expecting him to arrive soon 意为我肯定他很快就来到. *I'm waiting for him to arrive* means that I thought he would come earlier but he is late. ☆ I'm waiting for him to arrive 意为我以为他到得比现在早, 但他晚了. **Waiting** (for something) can be seen as an action ☆ **waiting** (for something) 可视为动作: *I'll wait here until it's time to go.* 我就在这儿等着, 一直等到该走的时候. ○ *I'm too nervous to read when I'm waiting to see the dentist.* 我等候看牙的时候, 紧张得都看不了书. **Expecting** can suggest that nothing can be done to change an event in the future ☆ **expecting** 可指对将来的某事无能为力: *I'm expecting to fail my exams.* 我料想我考不及格. ○ *The fall in profits had been expected.* 利润下降未出所料.

wait[2] /weɪt; wet/ *n* **1 ~ (for sth/sb)** act or time of waiting 等候; 等待; 等候或等待的时间: *I was prepared for a wait.* 我有所准备要等候一阵. ○ *We had a long wait for the bus.* 我们等公共汽车等了很久. **2** (idm 习语) **lie in wait** ⇨ LIE[2].

waive /weɪv; wev/ *v* [Tn] (*fml* 文) not insist on (sth) in a particular case; forego 不坚持要求(某事物); 放弃: *waive a claim, privilege, right, rule* 放弃一要求、特权、权利、规定 ○ *We have decided to waive the age-limit for applicants in your case.* 针对你的情况, 我们决定免除申请人年龄限制.

▷ **waiver** /ˈweɪvə(r); ˋwevɚ/ *n* (*law* 律) (document that records the) waiving of a legal right, etc 弃权(书): *They were persuaded to sign a waiver of claims against the landlord.* 经劝说, 他们签署了放弃向房东索赔的权利.

wake[1] /weɪk; wek/ *v* (*pt* **woke** /wəʊk; wok/ *or, in archaic use,* 古语拼作 **waked**, *pp* **woken** /ˈwəʊkən; ˋwokən/ *or, in archaic use,* 古语拼作 **waked**) **1 (a)** [I, Ip, It] **~ (up)** stop sleeping 醒; 醒来: *What time do you usually wake (up) in the morning?* 你平常早晨几点钟醒? ○ *She had just woken from a deep sleep.* 她刚从熟睡中醒来. ○ *I woke early this morning.* 我今天早上醒得很早. ○ *Wake up! It's eight o'clock.* 醒醒吧! 已经八点钟了. ○ *I woke up in the night feeling cold.* 半夜把我冻醒了. ○ *She woke up with a start when the door slammed.* 关门声把她惊醒了. ○ *He woke (up) to find himself alone in the house.* 他一觉醒来发现房子里只剩下他一个人了. **(b)** [Tn, Tn·p] **~ sb (up)** cause sb to stop sleeping 唤醒或弄醒某人: *Try not to wake the baby (up).* 别把孩子吵醒了. ○ *I was woken (up) by a noise in the room.* 屋子里的声音把我吵醒了. Cf 参看 AWAKE[1], AWAKEN. **2** [Tn, Tn·p] **~ sb/sth (up)** cause sb/sth to become active, alert, attentive, etc 使某人[某事物]活跃、警觉、注意等: *A cold shower will soon wake you up.* 你洗个冷水澡, 马上就清醒了. ○ *The incident woke memories of his past sufferings.* 这件事唤起了他对过去苦难经历的回忆. ○ *The audience needs waking up.* 应该让观众的气氛活跃起来. **3** [Tn] (*fml* 文) cause (sth) to re-echo; disturb with noise 使(某物)反复回响; 以噪声搅扰: *His echoing cry woke the mountain valley.* 他叫喊的回声震荡着山谷. **4** (idm 习语) **wake the 'dead** (of a noise) be unpleasantly loud (指噪声)大得烦人: *They were making enough noise to wake the dead.* 他们喧闹的声音让人心烦. **one's 'waking hours** time when one is awake 醒着的时候: *She spends all her waking hours worrying about her job.* 她只要醒着就一直为工作发愁. **5** (phr v) **wake up to sth** become aware of sth; realize sth 意识到或认识到某事物: *It's time you woke up to the fact that you're not very popular.* 你早就该明白你没什么人缘儿. ○ *He hasn't yet woken up to the seriousness of the situation.* 他还没意识到情况的严重性.

▷ **wake·ful** /-fl; -fəl/ *adj* **(a)** unable to sleep 睡不着的; 失眠的. **(b)** alert; vigilant 警惕的; 警觉的. **(c)** (of a night) with little or no sleep; sleepless (指夜晚)没怎么睡的, 不眠的: *a wakeful night spent in prayer* 整夜祈祷. **wake·fully** /-fəlɪ; -fəlɪ/ *adv*. **wake·ful·ness** *n* [U].

waken /ˈweɪkən; ˋwekən/ *v* [I, Tn] (cause sb to) wake from sleep; awaken (使某人)醒; 唤醒.

wake[2] /weɪk; wek/ *n* (**a**) night spent keeping watch by a dead person's body before it is buried 守夜(在殡葬前夜在死者遗体旁守候). (**b**) (esp in Ireland) gathering of people for this purpose, with food and drink provided for the mourners by the dead person's family (尤指爱尔兰的)守夜的人群(由死者家属供饮食).

wake[3] /weɪk; wek/ *n* **1** track left on the surface of the water behind a moving ship (行船在水面留下的)水流, 船迹, 航迹: *the foaming white wake of the liner* 班轮驶过留下的白沫翻腾的航迹. **2** (idm 习语) **in the wake of sth** coming after or following sth 随某事物之后到来: *Outbreaks of disease occurred in the wake of the drought.* 那场旱灾过后疾病丛生. ○ *The war brought many social changes in its wake.* 经过这场战争, 社会发生了很多变化.

walk[1] /wɔːk; wɔk/ *v* **1** [I, Ipr, Ip, In/pr] (**a**) (of a person) move along at a moderate pace by lifting up and putting down each foot in turn, so that one foot is on the ground while the other is being lifted (指人)行走: *How old was the baby when she started to walk?* 这个女孩几岁开始走路的? ○ *We walked slowly home.* 我们慢慢走回家. ○ *He walked into the room.* 他走进了房间. ○ *walking up and down* 走来走去 ○ *They walked along the river.* 他们沿着河边走. ○ *I've walked ten miles today.* 我今天走了10英里路. Cf 参看 RUN[1], TROT 2. (**b**) travel in this way and not ride, drive, be driven, etc 步行: *'How did you get here?' 'I walked.'* '你是怎么来的?' '我走来的.' ○ *I missed the bus and had to walk home.* 我没赶上公共汽车, 只好走回家. (**c**) (often 常作 **go walking**) travel in this way for exercise or pleasure (为锻炼或娱乐)步行, 散步: *I like walking.* 我喜欢散步. ○ *We are going walking in the Alps this summer.* 今年夏天我们要到阿尔卑斯山去徒步旅行. (**d**) (of four-footed animals) move at the slowest pace, always having at least two feet on the ground (指四足动物)慢步走. Cf 参看 GALLOP, TROT 1. **2** [Tn, Tn·pr, Tn·p] cause (sb/sth) to walk, esp by accompanying him/it 使(某人[某物])行走(尤指与之同行): *Horses should be walked for a while after a race.* 马在比赛后应该遛一遛. ○ *He's out walking the dog.* 他出去遛狗去了. ○ *He walked the horse up the hill.* 他牵着马上山去了. ○ *He walked her to her car.* 他陪她走到她的汽车那儿. ○ *He put his arm round me and walked me away.* 他伸出手臂搂着我, 带我走开了. ○ *I'll walk you home.* 我陪你走回家去. **3** [Tn] go along or over (sth) on foot 步行沿(某处)走或走过(某处): *walk the fields looking for wild flowers* 走过田野寻找着野花. **4** [I] (*dated* 旧) (of a ghost, etc) be seen moving about; appear (指鬼魂等)出动, 出现: *It was the sort of night when phantoms might walk.* 这种夜晚正是幽灵出没的时候. **5** (idm 习语) **be on/walk the streets** ⇨ STREET. **run before one can walk** tackle difficult tasks before one has learnt the basic skills 不会走就想跑(未学会基本技能就想处理困难事物): *Don't try to run before you can walk.* 别不会走路就想跑. **walk before one can ˈrun** learn the basic skills before trying to tackle more difficult tasks 先学会了走再跑(学会基本技能后再处理困难事物). **a walking ˈdictionary, encycloˈpedia, etc** person who has a wide vocabulary or who seems to be very knowledgeable about a particular subject 活字典、活百科全书等: *She's a walking textbook of medicine.* 她是活的医学教科书. **walk one's legs off** (*infml* 口) walk until one is exhausted 走得筋疲力尽. **walk sb off his ˈfeet** (*infml* 口) tire sb by making him walk too far or too fast (走得太远或太快)把某人累得疲惫不堪. **walk the ˈplank** be sent to one's death by pirates by being forced to walk along a plank and to fall into the sea 被海盗逼着走上木板掉海淹死. **walk ˈtall** feel proud and confident 感到骄傲而自信. **walk/tread a tightrope** ⇨ TIGHTROPE (TIGHT). **6** (phr v) **walk away from sb/sth** beat (an opponent) easily in a contest (在比赛中)轻易击败(对手). **walk away/off with sth** (*infml* 口) (**a**) win (a prize) easily 轻易赢得(奖品): *She walked away with two first prizes.* 她轻而易举地赢了两项头等奖. (**b**) steal sth 偷走某物: *Somebody has walked off with my pen.* 有人把我的钢笔偷走了.

walk into sth (*infml* 口) (**a**) become caught in sth that one is not expecting, esp because one is not careful 出乎意料陷入某境地(尤指因不慎): *They set a trap for him and he walked right into it.* 他们设下圈套, 他果然落入其中. (**b**) be appointed to (a job) without having to make an effort 轻易获得(一份工作): *She simply walked into a job at the bank as soon as she graduated.* 她大学一毕业就轻易获得一份在银行中的工作. **walk into sth/sb** strike against sth/sb while walking 走路时撞上某物[某人]: *She wasn't looking where she was going and walked straight into me.* 她走路不看路, 一头撞在我身上.

walk out (*infml* 口) (of workers) go on strike suddenly (指工人)突然罢工. **walk out (of sth)** leave (a meeting, etc) suddenly and angrily 愤而当即退出(会场等). **walk out (with sb)** (*dated infml* 旧, 口) have a relationship with sb 与某人有某种关系: *They were walking out for years before they got married.* 他们恋爱多年才结婚.

walk out on sb (*infml* 口) abandon or desert sb 遗弃某人: *He had a row with his wife and just walked out on her.* 他和妻子吵架后就把她抛弃了.

walk over sb (*infml* 口) (**a**) thoroughly defeat sb in a competition (在比赛中)彻底打败某人: *The visiting team was too strong — they walked all over us.* 客队实力太强了——把我们打得一败涂地. (**b**) treat sb badly or unkindly 刻薄地或恶意地对待某人: *You mustn't let him walk over you like that.* 你不能让他那么欺负你.

walk up (usu imperative 通常用于祈使句) come and see (a circus, show, etc) 来看(马戏、表演等): *Walk up! Walk up! The performance is about to begin.* 快来看! 快来看! 马上开演了. **walk up (to sb/sth)** approach sb/sth 走近某人[某物]: *A stranger walked up to me and shook my hand.* 有个陌生人向我走来跟我握手. ○ *She walked up to the desk and asked to see the manager.* 她走到办公桌前要求见经理.

▷ **walker** *n* **1** person who walks, esp for exercise or enjoyment 行走的人(尤指为锻炼或散步). **2** framework that is used as a support by sb who cannot walk without one, eg a baby or a disabled person 助行架(如幼儿或伤残者用的).

□ ˈ**walkabout** *n* **1** (in Australia) period of wandering in the bush by an Aboriginal (澳洲的)土著在灌木丛中游荡的时间: *go walkabout* 到灌木丛中闲逛. **2** informal stroll among a crowd by an important visitor, esp a royal person (来访的要人)在人群中漫步(尤指皇室人员): *go on a walkabout* 到老百姓中间走走.

ˈ**walk-in** *adj* [attrib 作定语] **1** (*esp US*) (of a cupboard, wardrobe, etc) large enough to walk into (指壁橱、衣柜等)宽敞得可走进去的: *a walk-in closet* 小储藏室. **2** (*US*) (of a flat) having its own entrance (指单元房)有独自人口的: *a walk-in apartment* 有独自出入口的公寓.

ˈ**walking papers** (*US*) dismissal from a job 解雇(通知书): *be given one's walking papers* 遭解雇.

ˈ**walking rein** = LEADING-REIN (LEADING).

ˈ**walking-stick** *n* (also **stick**) stick carried or used as a support when walking 手杖.

ˈ**walking-tour** *n* holiday spent walking from place to place 徒步旅行度假.

ˈ**Walkman** *n* (*pl* **~s**) (*propr* 专利名) small cassette player with earphones that can be worn by sb walking about (可随身携带使用耳机的)小型放音机.

ˌ**walk-ˈon** *adj* [usu attrib 通常作定语] (of a part in a play) very small and without any words to say (指戏剧角色)无台词的小角色的.

ˈ**walk-out** *n* sudden strike by workers 突然的罢工.

ˈ**walk-over** *n* easy victory 轻易获得的胜利: *The match was a walk-over for the visiting team.* 比赛中客队轻易获胜.

ˈ**walk-up** *adj* [attrib 作定语] (*US*) (of a flat or block of flats) without a lift (指公寓或公寓楼)无电梯的. — *n* building or flat without a lift 无电梯的大楼或公寓.

ˈ**walkway** *n* passage or path for walking along 人行通道.

walk[2] /wɔːk; wɔk/ *n* **1** (**a**) [C] journey on foot, esp for pleasure or exercise 行走, 步行(尤指为散步或锻炼的): *go for a walk* 去散步 ○ *have a pleasant walk across the fields* 愉快地漫步走过田野 ○ *She took the dog for a walk.* 她带着狗去散步. (**b**) [sing] distance of this 步行的距离: *The station is ten minutes' walk from my house.* 车站离我家要步行十分钟. ○ *It's a short walk to the* *beach.* 步行没多远就可到海滩. **2** [sing] (**a**) manner or style of walking; gait 步态: *I recognized him at once by his walk.* 我一看那走路的样子就知道是他. (**b**) walking pace 步行的速度: *The horse slowed to a walk after its long gallop.* 那匹马跑了一大阵后慢下来缓步而行. ○ *After running for ten minutes, he dropped into a walk*, ie began to walk. 他跑了十分钟后就改成步行了. **3** [C] path or route for walking 步行的路径或路线: *The path through the forest is one of my favourite walks.* 我最喜欢散步的小路就是穿过树林的那条. ○ *Some of the walks in this area are only possible in dry weather.* 这一带的一些小路只有晴天才能走. ○ *The garden is well laid out, with many pleasant walks.* 这个花园布局很好, 有许多宜人小径. **4** (idm 习语) **cock of the walk** ⇨ COCK[1]. **a walk of ˈlife** person's occupation, profession or rank 行业; 职业; 阶层: *They interview people from all walks of life.* 他们采访各行各业的人.

walkie-talkie /ˌwɔːkɪ ˈtɔːkɪ; ˌwɔkɪˋtɔkɪ/ *n* (*infml* 口) small portable radio transmitter and receiver 步话机.

wall /wɔːl; wɔl/ *n* **1** (**a**) continuous upright solid structure of stone, brick, concrete, etc used to enclose, divide or protect sth (eg an area of land) 围墙; 城墙: *The old town on the hill had a wall right round it.* 小山上的古城四周有城墙. ○ *The fields were divided by stone walls.* 这片地都有石墙相隔. ○ *The fruit trees grew against the garden wall.* 那些果树都长在花园的墙边. (**b**) one of the vertical sides of a building or room 墙壁: *The castle walls were very thick.* 那座城堡的墙很厚. ○ *Hang the picture on the wall opposite the window.* 把画挂在窗户对面的墙上. ○ [attrib 作定语] *a wall light* 壁灯. ⇨illus at App 1 见附录1插图, page vi. **2** (*fig* 比喻) thing similar to a wall in its appearance or effect (样子或作用)似墙之物: *The mountain rose up in a steep wall of rock.* 这座山高而陡, 形成一道岩石屏障. ○ *The investigators were confronted by a wall of silence.* 调查人员碰了壁, 谁也不回答他们的问题. ○ *The tidal wave formed a terrifying wall of water.* 海啸形成一堵骇人的水墙. **3** outer layer of a hollow structure, esp an organ or a cell of an animal or a plant 外壁(尤指动植物器官或细胞的): *the abdominal wall* 腹腔壁 ○ *the wall of an artery, a blood-vessel, etc* 动脉、血管等的壁. **4** (idm 习语) **bang, etc one's head against a brick wall** ⇨ HEAD[1]. **a fly on the wall** ⇨ FLY[1]. **have one's back to the wall** ⇨ BACK[1]. **a hole in the wall** ⇨ HOLE. **to the ˈwall** to a difficult or desperate situation 陷于困境或绝境: *Several firms have gone to the wall* (ie been ruined) *recently.* 最近有几家公司倒闭了. ○ *drive/push sb to the wall*, ie defeat him 逼得某人走投无路. **up the ˈwall** (*infml* 口) furious or crazy 愤怒; 发狂: *That noise is driving/sending me up the wall.* 这种噪声快要把我逼疯了. ○ *I'll go up the wall if it doesn't stop soon.* 要是不赶快停下来就要把我气死了. ˌ**walls have ˈears** (*saying* 谚) beware of eavesdroppers 隔墙有耳: *Be careful what you say; even the walls have ears!* 说话要小心, 隔墙有耳啊! **the writing on the wall** ⇨ WRITING.

▷ **wall** *v* **1** [Tn esp passive 尤用于被动语态] surround (sth) with a wall or walls 用墙围住(某物): *a walled city, garden, town* 有围墙的城市、花园、小镇. **2** (phr v) **wall sth in/off** separate (and enclose) sth with a wall 用墙隔开(并围住)某物: *Part of the yard had been walled off.* 院子有一部分用墙隔开了. **wall sth up** block up sth with a wall or bricks 用墙或砖堵住某物: *a walled-up door, fireplace, passage* 用砖堵住的门、壁炉、通道.

□ ˈ**wallflower** *n* **1** common garden plant that has sweet-smelling (usu orange or brownish-red) flowers in spring 墙头花, 桂竹香(欧洲常见园艺植物, 春季开花, 味香, 通常呈橙色或赭色). **2** (*infml* 口) person (esp a woman) who has no dancing partners at a dance and has to sit or stand around while others dance 在舞会中因无舞伴而在一旁或坐或站者(尤指女子).

ˈ**wall-painting** *n* picture painted directly on the surface of a wall; fresco or mural 壁画.

ˈ**wallpaper** *n* [U] paper, usu with a coloured design, for covering the walls of a room 壁纸; 墙纸. — *v* [I, Tn] put wallpaper on (the walls of a room) 在(室内墙壁)上糊壁纸.

ˌ**wall-to-ˈwall** *adj, adv* (of a floor-covering) that covers the whole floor of a room (指室内地面覆盖物)覆盖全部地面(的): *a* ˌ*wall-to-wall* ˈ*carpet* 铺满全部地面的地毯 ○ *a room carpeted wall-to-wall* 全部地面铺有地毯的房间.

wal·laby /ˈwɒləbɪ; ˋwɑləbɪ/ *n* any of various types of small kangaroo 沙袋鼠.

wal·lah /ˈwɒlə; ˋwɑlə/ *n* (*infml* 口) (in India) person connected with a specified occupation or task (印度的)与某种职业或任务有关系的人: *bank wallahs* 银行界的人.

wal·let /ˈwɒlɪt; ˋwɑlɪt/ (*US* also ˈ**billfold**, ˈ**pocket-book**) *n* small flat folding case, usu made of leather, carried in the pocket and used esp for holding banknotes, documents, etc 钱包, 皮夹(尤用以放纸币、证件等的). Cf 参看 PURSE[1] 1.

wall-eyed /ˌwɔːl ˈaɪd; ˋwɔlˌaɪd/ *adj* having eyes that show an abnormal amount of white, esp because the irises turn outwards 患角膜白斑的; 患外斜视的.

wal·lop /ˈwɒləp; ˋwɑləp/ *v* [Tn, Tn·pr] (*infml* 口) **1** hit (sb/sth) hard; thrash 痛打(某人[某物]); 猛击: *If I ever catch the rascal I'll really wallop him!* 我要是逮住这个流氓, 非狠狠揍他一顿不可! ○ *She walloped the ball (for) miles.* 她把球打出很远很远. **2** (in a contest, match, etc) defeat (sb) thoroughly (在比赛中)彻底击败(某人): *I walloped him at darts.* 我在掷镖游戏中远远胜过了他.

▷ **wal·lop** *n* **1** [C] (*infml* 口) heavy resounding blow 重击: *He crashed down on the floor with a wallop.* 他砰的一声倒在地板上了. **2** [U] (*Brit sl* 俚) beer 啤酒.

wal·lop·ing *adj* [attrib 作定语] (*infml* 口) very big 极大的: *He had to pay a walloping (great) fine.* 他得付一(大)笔罚款. — *n* (*infml* 口) (**a**) thrashing 痛打: *She threatened the children with a walloping.* 她吓唬孩子说要狠狠打他们一顿. (**b**) thorough defeat 彻底失败: *Our team got a terrible walloping yesterday.* 我们队昨天吃了个大败仗.

wal·low /ˈwɒləʊ; ˋwɑlo/ *v* [I, Ipr, Ip] **~ (about/around) (in sth)** **1** lie and roll about in mud, water, etc (在泥、水等中)打滚: *The children enjoyed watching the hippopotamus wallowing (about) in the mud.* 孩子们真喜观看河马在泥中打滚. ○ *The ship wallowed in* (ie was tossed about by) *the rough sea.* 船在汹涌的海上颠簸. **2** take pleasure (in sth); indulge oneself (在某事物中)享乐; 放纵自己: *wallow in a hot bath* 舒服地洗个热水澡 ○ *wallowing in luxury* 耽于豪华的享乐之中 ○ *They're absolutely wallowing in money*, ie very rich. 他们家资广有(很富有). ○ *She seemed to be wallowing in her grief, instead of trying to recover from the disaster.* 她似乎缠绵悱恻无力自拔.

▷ **wal·low** *n* **1** act of wallowing 打滚; 享乐; 放纵. **2** place where animals go to wallow (动物常去打滚的)泥坑, 水坑.

Wall Street /ˈwɔːl striːt; ˋwɔlˌstrit/ (*infml* 口) the American money-market 华尔街; 美国金融市场: *Share prices fell on Wall Street today.* 今日华尔街股价下跌. ○ *Wall Street responded quickly to the news.* 美国金融界对这一消息反应迅速. ○ [attrib 作定语] *the Wall Street Journal* 《华尔街日报》.

wally /ˈwɒlɪ; ˋwɑlɪ/ *n* (*Brit infml* 口) stupid or foolish person; twit 笨蛋; 傻瓜; 白痴: *Don't be such a wally!* 别发傻了!

wal·nut /ˈwɔːlnʌt; ˋwɔlˌnʌt/ *n* **1** [C] nut containing an edible kernel with a wrinkled surface in a pair of boat-shaped shells 胡桃. ⇨illus at NUT 见NUT插图. **2** (**a**) [C] (also ˈ**walnut tree**) tree on which this nut grows 胡桃树. (**b**) [U] wood of this tree, used (esp as a veneer) in making furniture 胡桃木(用以制家具, 尤用作饰面).

wal·rus /ˈwɔːlrəs; ˋwɔlrəs/ *n* large sea-animal living in the Arctic regions, similar to a seal but having two long tusks 海象.

□ ˌ**walrus mouˈstache** (*infml* 口) long thick moustache that hangs down on each side of the mouth (嘴角两侧的)粗长胡子.

waltz /wɔːls; *US* wɔːlts; wɔlts/ *n* (**a**) ballroom dance for couples, with a graceful flowing melody in triple time 华尔兹舞. (**b**) music for this 华尔兹舞曲.

▷ **waltz** *v* **1** [I, Tn·pr] (cause sb to) dance a waltz (使某人)跳华尔兹舞: *She waltzes beautifully.* 她华尔兹舞跳得很美. ○ *He waltzed her round the room.* 他带着她满屋跳华尔兹舞. **2** [Ipr, Ip] (*infml* 口) move in the specified direction gaily or casually or by dancing 轻

快地或随便地或跳着舞走: *She waltzed up to us and announced that she was leaving.* 她蹦蹦跳跳地来到我们面前说她要走了. ○ *He waltzes in and out as if the house belongs to him.* 他大摇大摆地出来进去, 好像这所房子是他的一样. **3** (phr v) **waltz off with sth** (*infml* 口) (**a**) steal sth 偷走某物: *He's just waltzed off with my cigarette lighter!* 他刚才把我的打火机偷走了! (**b**) win sth easily 轻易赢得某事物: *She waltzed off with the school prizes for maths and science.* 她轻而易举赢得了全校数学奖和理科奖.

wam·pum /ˈwɒmpəm; ˋwɑmpəm/ *n* [U] ornaments made of shells threaded on a string like beads, used formerly by N American Indians as money 贝壳串珠(装饰品, 旧时北美印第安人用作货币).

wan /wɒn; wɑn/ *adj* (**-nner, -nnest**) (of a person, his appearance, etc) pale and looking ill or tired; pallid (指人、面色等)苍白憔悴的, 倦怠的, 带病容的: *a wan smile*, ie a slight one from sb who is ill or tired or unhappy 勉强的微笑(因病或倦怠或不悦) ○ (*fig* 比喻) *the wan light of a winter's morning* 冬日黯淡的晨光. ▷ **wanly** *adv*: *smile wanly* 虚弱地微笑. **wan·ness** /ˈwɒnnɪs; ˋwɑnnɪs/ *n* [U].

wand /wɒnd; wɑnd/ *n* **1** slender stick or rod held in the hand, esp by a conjuror, fairy or magician when performing magic 棍; 棒; 杖; (尤指小仙子或魔术师用的)魔杖: *The fairy godmother waved her (magic) wand.* 助人仙女挥动她的魔杖. **2** = LIGHT PEN (LIGHT[1]).

wan·der /ˈwɒndə(r); ˋwɑndɚ/ *v* **1** [I, Ipr, Ip] (**a**) move around in an area or go from place to place without any special purpose or destination; roam 游荡; 漫游; 闲逛; 流浪: *wander through the countryside* 在野外闲逛 ○ *enjoy wandering in a strange town* 喜欢逛陌生的小镇 ○ *She was wandering aimlessly up and down the road.* 她在路上信步来回溜达. ○ *We wandered around for hours looking for the house.* 我们为找那所房子转了半天. ○ (*fig* 比喻) *She was so weak that her pen kept wandering over the page as she wrote.* 她很虚弱, 写字时钢笔在纸上直打滑. (**b**) go slowly or aimlessly in the specified direction (沿某方向)慢走或漫步: *They wandered back to work an hour later.* 一小时后他们溜达着回去工作. ○ *He wandered in to see me as if he had nothing else to do.* 他溜溜达达进来看我, 好像无事可做的样子. ○ *They wandered out into the darkness.* 他们漫步走出去, 消失在黑暗中. ○ (*fig* 比喻) *Her thoughts wandered back to her youth.* 她思绪联翩, 回想到青春岁月. **2** [Tn] move aimlessly around in (a place); roam 漫步(某地); 漫游: *I've spent two years wandering the world.* 我用了两年时间周游世界. ○ *The child was found wandering the streets alone.* 人们看见那个孩子独自在街上瞎转. **3** [I, Ipr, Ip] (of a road or river) follow a winding path or course; meander (指道路或河流)蜿蜒, 迂回曲折: *The road wanders (along) through the range of hills.* 这条路在山丘间绕来绕去. **4** [I, Ipr, Ip] **~ (from/off sth)**; **~ (away/off)** (of a person or an animal) leave the right place or way; stray from one's group (指人或动物)离开原处或正道, 离群, 失散: *The shepherd set out to look for the sheep that had wandered (away).* 牧羊人出发去找走失的羊. ○ *We seem to have wandered from the path.* 我们好像已经偏离了原路. ○ *The child wandered off and got lost.* 那个孩子自己走开而迷了路. ○ (*fig* 比喻) *Don't wander from the subject: stick to the point*, ie Don't digress. 不要离题, 要针对这一问题谈. **5** [I] (of a person, his mind, etc) be inattentive, confused or delirious (指人、思想等)走神, 胡思乱想, 神志昏乱: *He realized his audience's attention was beginning to wander.* 他意识到听众精神已不太集中了. ○ *Her mind seemed to be wandering and she didn't recognize us.* 她好像精神恍惚, 没认出我们来.

▷ **wan·der** *n* (*infml* 口) act of wandering 游荡; 漫游; 闲逛; 流浪; 离群; 失散: *She went for a little wander round the park.* 她到公园去溜达溜达.

wan·derer /ˈwɒndərə(r); ˋwɑndərɚ/ *n* person or animal that wanders (WANDER 1) 游荡、漫游或闲逛的人; 各处走动的动物.

wan·der·ings /ˈwɒndərɪŋz; ˋwɑndərɪŋz/ *n* [pl] **1** journeys made from place to place 漫游之行: *After five years, he returned from his wanderings.* 他在外游逛五年后又回来了. **2** confused speech during illness (esp a high fever) (病中的)胡言乱语(尤指发烧时的).

wan·der·lust /ˈwɒndəlʌst; ˋwɑndɚˌlʌst/ *n* [U] strong desire to travel 想去漫游的强烈愿望.

W

wane /weɪn; wen/ *v* [I] **1** (of the moon) show a gradually decreasing area of brightness after being full (指月亮)亏, 缺. Cf 参看 WAX[2] 1. **2** gradually lose power or importance; become smaller or weaker or less impressive 衰败; 衰落; 变小; 变弱; 变差: *The power of the landowners waned during this period.* 这一时期地主的势力削弱了. ○ *Her enthusiasm for the expedition was waning rapidly.* 她对这次出行的热劲迅速减低. **3** (idm 习语) **wax and wane** ⇨ WAX[2].

▷ **wane** *n* (idm 习语) **on the ˈwane** gradually decreasing; waning 逐渐减弱; 衰败; 衰落.

wangle /ˈwæŋgl; ˋwæŋgl/ *v* (*infml* 口) **1** [Tn, Tn·pr, Dn·n] **~ sth (out of sb)** get or arrange sth that one wants by using trickery or clever persuasion 用巧计或花言巧语获得或安排某事物: *I'd love to go to the match tomorrow — do you think you can wangle it?* 我很想去看明天的比赛 —— 你能找个词儿安排一下吗? ○ *She managed to wangle an invitation to the reception.* 她设法弄到了招待会的请帖. ○ *He was trying to wangle his way onto the committee.* 他千方百计想钻人委员会中. ○ *I'll try to wangle a contribution out of him.* 我要设法让他出把力. ○ *She's wangled an extra week's holiday for herself.* 她多弄到一星期的假. **2** (phr v) **wangle out of sth/doing sth** avoid having to do sth by scheming 用计谋避免做某事: *It's bound to be a boring party — let's try to wangle out of it/going.* 这次聚会一定没意思 —— 咱们想个法子别去了.

▷ **wangle** *n* act of wangling 使用巧计或花言巧语: *get sth by a wangle* 要手腕儿得到某事物.

wank /wæŋk; wæŋk/ *v* [I] (△ *Brit sl* 讳, 俚) masturbate 手淫.

▷ **wank** *n* (△ *Brit sl* 讳, 俚) act of masturbating 手淫.

wanker (△ *Brit sl* 讳, 俚) **1** (*derog* 贬) inefficient, lazy or stupid person 无能的、懒惰的或愚蠢的人. **2** person who masturbates 手淫的人.

wanna /ˈwɒnə; ˋwɑnə/ *contracted form* 缩约式 (*infml* 口 *esp US*) **1** want to 想要(做): *I wanna hold your hand.* 我想握住你的手. **2** want a 想要(个): *You wanna cigarette?* 你想要支香烟吗?

want[1] /wɒnt; *US* wɔːnt; wɔnt/ *v* **1** [Tn, Tt, Tnt, Tsg, Cn·n/a] have a desire for (sth); wish for 要, 想要(某事物); 希望: *They want a bigger flat.* 他们想要一套大些的单元房. ○ *Have you decided what you want?* 你决定要什么了吗? ○ *The staff want a pay rise.* 全体职员希望增加工资. ○ *She wants to go to Italy.* 她要去意大利. ○ *She wants me to go with her.* 她想让我跟她一起去. ○ *I didn't want that to happen.* 我并不希望发生这样的事. ○ *I want it (to be) done as quickly as possible.* 我希望这件事尽快做好. ○ *I don't want you arriving late.* 我希望你不要迟到. ○ *The people want him as their leader.* 大家都想让他当领袖. ⇨ Usage 见所附用法. **2** [Tn, Tg] require or need (sth) 要, 要求, 需要(某事物): *We shall want more staff for the new office.* 我们的新办公室需要多增加些职员. ○ *Let me know how many copies you want.* 告诉我你要多少份. ○ (*infml* 口) *What that boy wants* (ie deserves) *is a good smack!* 那个男孩子就是欠揍! ○ *The plants want watering/want to be watered daily.* 这些花草得天天浇水. ○ *I'm sure you don't want reminding of the need for discretion.* 我知道无需提醒你一切需谨慎行事. **3** [Tt] (*infml* 口) should or ought to (do sth) 应该(做某事): *You want to be more careful.* 你应该再细心些. ○ *They want to remember who they're speaking to!* 应该让他们明白是跟谁说话呢! **4** [Tn] (*fml* 文) not have enough of (sth); lack 缺乏(某事物); 无: *He wants the courage to speak the truth.* 他缺乏说实话的勇气. ○ *After the disaster there were many who wanted food and shelter.* 这场灾难过后, 许多人既没有食物又没有住处. **5** [Tn usu passive 通常用于被动语态] require (sb) to be present; need (sb) 要求(某人)在场; 需要(某人): *You will not be wanted this afternoon.* 今天下午用不着你了. ○ *You are wanted immediately in the director's office.* 主任让你立刻到他的办公室去. ○ *He is wanted (for questioning) by the police*, eg because he is suspected of committing a crime. 警方要找他(问话)(如因涉嫌某罪案). **6** [Tn] feel sexual desire for (sb) 对(某人)有性欲. **7** [Tn] (used with *it* 与 it 连用) fall short by (sth) 缺少(某量): *It still wants half an hour till midnight.* 还差半小时才到午夜. **8** (idm 习语) **have/want it/things both ways** ⇨ BOTH[1]. **not**

not want to 'know (about sth) deliberately avoid contact with or information about sb/sth which may cause inconvenience, trouble, etc; not care 故意不接触或不了解某人[某事物](以免造成不便或麻烦); 不理会: *He was desperately in need of help but nobody seemed to want to know.* 他极需帮助, 可是似乎谁也不愿理会. **waste not, want not** ➪ WASTE². **9** (phr v) **want for sth** (esp in questions or negative sentences 尤用于疑问句或否定句) suffer because of a lack of sth 因缺少某事物而受苦: *Those children want for nothing/never want for anything,* ie have everything they need. 那些孩子什么也不缺(应有尽有). ○ *She didn't want for help from her friends.* 她从未感到在需要时没有朋友帮忙. **want 'in/'out** (*infml* 口) want to come in/go out 想进来[出去]: *I think the dog wants in — I can hear it scratching at the door.* 我看那条狗想进来——我听见它抓门的声音. **want 'out/out of sth** (*infml* 口 *esp US*) no longer want to be involved in (a plan, project, etc) 想退出(一计划、项目等).

NOTE ON USAGE 用法: When expressing an offer or issuing an invitation, **like** is the most usual verb 表达提议或邀请时, 最常用的动词是 **like**: *Would you like a cup of coffee?* 您想要杯咖啡吗? ○ *Would you like to come to dinner with us next week?* 您下星期来和我们一起吃饭好吗? **Care (for)** is more formal 用 **care (for)** 较为郑重: *Would you care for another piece of cake?* 您再来一块蛋糕好吗? ○ *Would you care to come for a walk with me?* 您来和我一起散散步好吗? **Want** is the most direct and informal ☆ **want** 一词最直接也最通俗: *Do you want a piece of chocolate?* 你想来块巧克力吗? ○ *We're going to the cinema tonight. Do you want to come with us?* 我们今天晚上去看电影. 你想和我们一起去吗?

want² /wɒnt; *US* wɔːnt; wɔnt/ *n* **1** [C usu *pl* 通常作复数] (**a**) desire for sth; requirement 欲望; 需要: *He is a man of few wants.* 他是个没什么欲望的人. ○ *This book meets a long-felt want,* ie has been needed for a long time. 这本书满足了盼望已久的需要(长久以来就需要有这样的书). (**b**) thing desired 想望的事物: *All their wants were provided by their host.* 他们得到主人应有尽有的照顾. **2** [U, sing] **~ of sth** lack or insufficiency of sth (某事物的)缺乏或不足: *The refugees are suffering for want of food and medical supplies.* 难民苦于缺少食物和医药用品. ○ *The plants died from want of water.* 这些植物因缺水而枯死了. ○ *She decided to accept the offer for want of anything better.* 她决定接受这一提议, 因为没有更好一些的. ○ *She couldn't find anywhere to live, though not for want of trying,* ie not because she hadn't tried. 她找不到个住处, 倒是找过不少. **3** [U] state of being poor or in need; poverty 贫穷; 匮乏; 贫困: *live in want* 生活在贫困中 ○ *Their health had suffered from years of want.* 他们长年贫困影响了身体健康. ○ *a policy aimed at fighting want and deprivation* 旨在改变民穷财尽状况的政策. **4** (idm 习语) **in want of sth** needing sth 需要某事物: *The house is in want of repair.* 这所房子该修了.

□ **'want ads** (*infml* 口 *esp US*) = CLASSIFIED ADVERTISEMENTS (CLASSIFY).

want·ing /'wɒntɪŋ; *US* 'wɔːn-; 'wɔntɪŋ/ *adj* [pred 作表语] **1 ~ (in sth)** (*fml* 文) lacking in quality or quantity; deficient (在质量或数量上)欠缺, 不足: *His behaviour was wanting in courtesy,* ie discourteous, rude. 他举止没有礼貌. **2** (idm 习语) **be found wanting** ➪ FIND¹.

wan·ton /'wɒntən; *US* 'wɔːn-; 'wantən/ *adj* **1** [esp attrib 尤作定语] (of an action) done deliberately for no good reason; wilful (指行动)不怀好意的, 恶意的, 恣意的: *wanton cruelty, damage, waste* 肆意的暴虐行为、破坏、浪费 ○ *the wanton destruction of a historic building* 对一座古建筑物的故意毁坏. **2** (*fml* 文) playful or capricious 顽皮的; 反复无常的: *a wanton breeze* 风向不定的微风 ○ *in a wanton mood* 以闹着玩的心情. **3** (of growth, etc) very abundant; luxuriant or wild (指生长物等)茂盛的, 繁密的, 滋生的: *The weeds grew in wanton profusion.* 遍地野草丛生. **4** (*dated fml* 旧, 文) not modest or chaste; licentious or immoral 不正派的; 不贞的; 放荡的; 不道德的: *a wanton creature* 放荡的傢伙 ○ *wanton behaviour* 不道德的行为.

▷ **wan·ton** *n* (*dated* 旧) licentious or immoral person (esp a woman) 放荡的人, 不道德的人(尤指女子).

wan·tonly *adv*: *wantonly destructive* 恣意毁坏的.

wan·ton·ness *n* [U].

wap·iti /'wɒpɪtɪ; 'wɑpətɪ/ *n* N American elk 美洲赤鹿.

war /wɔː(r); wɔr/ *n* **1** (**a**) [U] (state of) fighting between nations or groups within a nation using military force 战争(状态): *the horrors of war* 战争的恐怖 ○ *the outbreak* (ie beginning) *of war* 战争的爆发 ○ *The border incident led to war between the two countries.* 这一边境事件导致了两国交战. ○ *the art* (ie tactics and strategy) *of war* 兵法(战略和战术) ○ *the fortunes of* (ie what may happen in) *war* 战争中可能发生的事 ○ *The government wanted to avoid war at all costs.* 政府拟不惜一切代价避免战争. ○ *civil war* 内战. (**b**) [C] instance or period of such fighting 战争(期间): *during the Second World War* 在第二次世界大战期间 ○ *He had fought in two wars.* 他参加过两次战争. ○ *If a war breaks out, many other countries will be affected.* 一旦战争爆发, 许多国家都要受到波及. **2** (**a**) [C, U] competition, conflict or hostility between people, groups, etc 竞争; 冲突; 对抗: *the class war* 阶级斗争 ○ *a trade war* 贸易战 ○ *There was a state of war between the rivals.* 竞争对手间已处于敌对状态. (**b**) [sing] **~ (against sb/sth)** efforts made to eliminate disease, crime, etc (为消灭疾病、犯罪现象等的)斗争: *a major step in the war against cancer* 在战胜癌症方面迈出的一大步 ○ *Little progress has been made in the war against drug traffickers.* 打击贩毒分子的斗争无甚进展. **3** (idm 习语) **at war** in a state of war 处于交战状态: *The country has been at war with its neighbour for two years.* 这个国家与邻国已打了两年仗了. **carry the war into the enemy's camp** ➪ CARRY. **declare war** ➪ DECLARE. **go to war (against sb/sth)** start fighting a war (against sb/sth) (向某人[某事物])开战. **have been in the 'wars** (*infml or joc* 口或谑) show signs of being injured or badly treated 受过伤; 受过虐待; 吃过苦. **make/wage war on sb/sth** (**a**) fight sb/sth with weapons 用武器与某人[某事物]作战. (**b**) try to eliminate sth 努力消灭某事物: *wage war on crime, disease, poverty, etc* 与犯罪现象、疾病、贫困等作斗争. **a war of 'nerves** attempt to defeat an opponent by gradually destroying his morale, using threats, psychological pressures, etc 神经战. **a war of 'words** (campaign of) verbal abuse 舌战; 笔战; 论战: *As the election approaches the war of words between the main political parties becomes increasingly intense.* 大选在即, 主要政党间的论战愈演愈烈.

▷ **war** *v* (**-rr-**) [I] (*arch* 古) engage in a war or conflict 进行战争; 交战; 作战: *warring tribes* 交战的部落.

□ **'war bonnet** feathered head-dress worn by the warriors of certain N American Indian tribes (北美印第安某些部落战士戴的)羽毛头饰.

'war chest (*US*) fund of money collected to pay for a war or some other campaign (为战争或某些活动筹集的)专用基金.

'war-cry *n* (**a**) word or phrase shouted as a signal in battle 战斗口号. (**b**) catchword used in a contest (eg by a political party); slogan 竞争(如政党间的)口号; 标语.

'war-dance *n* dance performed by the warriors of a tribe, eg before going into battle or to celebrate a victory 战舞(部落战士跳的, 如作战前或庆祝凯旋的).

warfare /'wɔːfeə(r); 'wɔr,fɛr/ *n* [U] (**a**) (fighting a) war (作)战; 战争: *guerrilla, modern, nuclear warfare* 游击战、现代战争、核战. (**b**) (esp violent) conflict or struggle (尤指激烈的)冲突, 斗争: *There is open warfare between the opponents of the plan and its supporters.* 支持与反对这一计划的双方已公开论战.

'war-game *n* (**a**) game in which models representing troops, ships, etc are moved about on maps, in order to test the players' tactical skill 战争游戏. (**b**) mock battle used as a training exercise 作战演习.

'warhead *n* explosive head of a missile or torpedo (导弹或鱼雷的)弹头: *equipped with a nuclear warhead* 装有核弹头.

'war-horse *n* **1** (esp formerly) horse used in battle (尤指旧时)战马, 军马. **2** (*fig* 比喻) soldier, politician, etc who has fought in many campaigns 久经争战的士兵、政客等.

warlike /'wɔːlaɪk; 'wɔr,laɪk/ *adj* fond of or skilled in fighting; aggressive 好战的; 善战的; 侵略的; 好争斗的: *a warlike people* 好战的民族 ○ *a warlike appearance, mood, state* 好斗的模样、情绪、状态.

ˈ**war-lord** *n* (*dated or fml* 旧或文) (chief) military commander (大)将军; 军阀.

ˈ**war memorial** monument built to honour people who have died in a war 战争纪念碑(纪念阵亡将士的).

ˈ**warmonger** *n* (*derog* 贬) person who tries to cause a war or who favours war 战争贩子.

ˈ**war-paint** *n* [U] (**a**) paint put on the body before battle, eg by N American Indian warriors 出战前涂于身上的颜料(如北美印第安战士用的). (**b**) (*infml joc* 口, 谑) cosmetic make-up 化妆品: *She never goes out to a party without putting her war-paint on!* 她每逢参加聚会都非化妆不可!

ˈ**war-path** *n* (idm 习语) **(be/go) on the ˈwar-path** (*infml* 口) ready for a fight or a quarrel; hostile or angry 准备作战或打架; 敌对; 发怒: *Look out — the boss is on the war-path again!* 当心点——老板又发火了!

ˈ**warship** *n* ship for use in war 军舰.

ˈ**wartime** *n* [U] period of time when there is a war 战时: *Special regulations were introduced in wartime.* 战时实施了特殊规定. ○ [attrib 作定语] *wartime rationing* 战时的定量配给 ○ *the shortages of wartime Britain* 战时英国物资之匮乏.

warble /ˈwɔːbl; ˈwɔrbḷ/ *v* (**a**) [I] (esp of a bird) sing in a continuous gentle trilling way (尤指鸟)叫出柔和的颤音: *larks warbling in the sky* 在天空婉转叫着的百灵鸟. (**b**) [Tn] sing (a note, song, etc) in this way 用柔和的颤音唱(某音、歌等).

▷ **warble** *n* (usu *sing* 通常作单数) warbling sound 柔和的颤音: *the blackbird's warble* 黑鹂婉转的叫声.

warb·ler /ˈwɔːblə(r); ˈwɔrblɚ/ *n* any of various types of bird that warble (能叫出柔和颤音的)鸣禽.

ward /wɔːd; wɔrd/ *n* **1** separate part or room in a hospital for a particular group of patients 病房: *a children's, maternity, surgical ward* 儿科、产科、外科病房 ○ *a public/private ward* 普通[单人]病房. **2** division of a city, etc that elects and is represented by a councillor in local government (城市的)区(可选出一名地方议员的): *There are three candidates standing for election in this ward.* 这一区里有三名候选人参加竞选. **3** person, esp a child, who is under the care of a guardian or the protection of a lawcourt 由监护人或法院保护的人(尤指儿童): *She invested the money on behalf of her ward.* 她代表受她监护的人投资. ○ *The child was made a ward of court.* 那个孩子由法院监护. **4** (usu *pl* 通常作复数) any one of the notches or projections in a key or lock (designed to prevent the lock being opened by any key except the right one) (钥匙或锁中的)一个凹处或凸处. **5** (idm 习语) **a ˌward in ˈchancery** (in Britain) person, usu a child, whose affairs are looked after by the Lord Chancellor (eg because of the death of the ward's parents) (英国)由大法官监护的人(尤指儿童, 如因其父母去世).

▷ **ward** *v* (phr v) **ward sb/sth off** keep away (sb/sth that is dangerous or unpleasant); fend sb/sth off 避开(危险的或讨厌的人[事物]); 挡开某人[某事物]: *ward off blows, disease, danger, intruders* 避开打击、疾病、危险、闯入者.

-ward *suff* 后缀 (with *advs* forming *adjs* 与副词结合构成形容词) in the direction of 向着; 朝着; 对着: *backward* ○ *eastward* ○ *homeward.* ▷ **-wards** (also *esp US* **-ward**) (forming *advs* or *preps* 用以构成副词或介词): *onward* ○ *towards.*

war·den /ˈwɔːdn; ˈwɔrdṇ/ *n* **1** person responsible for supervising sth 负责监督、监护或监管的人: *a game warden* 猎物繁殖与保护区的管理员 ○ *a traffic warden* 处理违章停车的交通管理员 ○ *the warden of a youth hostel* 青年招待所管理员. **2** title of the heads of certain colleges and other institutions 某些学院及其他机构负责人的称谓: *the Warden of Merton College, Oxford* 牛津大学默顿学院院长. **3** (*US*) governor of a prison 监狱长.

warder /ˈwɔːdə(r); ˈwɔrdɚ/ *n* (*fem* 阴性作 **ward·ress** /ˈwɔːdrɪs; ˈwɔrdrɪs/) (*Brit*) person who works as a guard in a prison; jailer (监狱的)看守人.

ward·robe /ˈwɔːdrəub; ˈwɔrd,rob/ *n* **1** place where clothes are stored, usu a large cupboard with shelves and a rail for hanging things on 衣柜: *a built-in wardrobe*, ie one that forms part of the wall of a room 壁橱. ⇨illus at App 1 见附录1插图, page xvi. **2** (usu *sing* 通常作单数) person's stock of clothes (个人的)全部衣物: *an extensive wardrobe of elegant dresses* 个人所有的大批华美的连衣裙 ○ *buy a new winter wardrobe* 购买个人全部新冬装. **3** stock of costumes worn by actors in a theatrical company (剧团的)全部戏装.

□ ˈ**wardrobe master**, ˈ**wardrobe mistress** person responsible for looking after the costumes in a theatrical company 剧团服装保管员.

ward·room /ˈwɔːdrum, -ruːm; ˈwɔrd,rum, -,rum/ *n* place in a warship where all the commissioned officers except the commanding officer live and eat; mess-room (军舰上除舰长以外的军官的)起居室和餐厅, 食堂.

ware /weə(r); wɛr/ *n* **1** [U] (esp in compounds 尤用以构成复合词) (**a**) manufactured goods (of the specified type) (某类)制造品: ˈ*ironware* 铁器 ○ ˈ*hardware* 五金制品 ○ ˈ*silverware* 银器. (**b**) pottery or porcelain of a particular type or made for a particular purpose (为某用途的)陶器, 瓷器: ˈ*earthenware* 陶器 ○ ˈ*ovenware* 烤箱用器皿. **2 wares** [pl] (*dated* 旧) articles offered for sale (often not in a shop) 商品(常指不在商店中的): *advertise, display, sell, peddle one's wares* 为自己的货物做广告、陈列货物、出售货物、兜售货物.

□ **warehouse** /ˈweəhaus; ˈwɛr,haus/ *n* (**a**) building where goods are stored before being sent to shops 货仓. (**b**) building where furniture is stored for its owners (存放家具的)栈房. — *v* [Tn] store (sth) in a warehouse 将(某物)存入货仓或栈房: *the cost of warehousing goods* 仓储费.

war·fare ⇨ WAR.

war·ily, wari·ness ⇨ WARY.

warm[1] /wɔːm; wɔrm/ *adj* (**-er**, **-est**) **1** (**a**) of or at a fairly high temperature, between cool and hot 温暖的; 暖和的: *The weather is a bit warmer today.* 今天暖和一点儿了. ○ *gusts of warm air* 一阵阵温暖的空气 ○ *Food for a baby should be warm, not hot.* 给婴儿吃的东西应该是温的, 不能是烫的. (**b**) (of a person) having the normal body temperature, or a raised skin temperature (because of exercise, air temperature or excitement) (指人)体温正常的; (因运动、气温或激动)皮肤发热的: *The patient must be kept warm.* 这个病人须保持正常体温. ○ *Come and get warm by the fire.* 来烤烤火暖和暖和. ○ *I'm much too warm in here — please open the window.* 我觉得这儿太热了——请把窗户打开. ○ *have warm hands and feet* 手脚都很热. (**c**) (of clothing) that keeps the body from becoming cold (指衣物)保暖的: *a warm pullover* 暖和的套头毛衣 ○ *Put on your warmest clothes before you go out in the snow.* 下雪天外出要穿上最暖和的衣服. (**d**) (of work, exercise, etc) causing a feeling of heat (指工作、运动等)使人感到热的: *Sawing logs is warm work.* 锯原木这工作干起来浑身发热. ○ *It was a warm climb to the summit.* 向顶峰攀登时身上都热起来了. Cf 参看 COLD[1], HOT. **2** showing enthusiasm; hearty 热情的; 热心的: *warm applause, congratulations, thanks* 热诚的掌声、祝贺、感谢 ○ *a warm recommendation* 热情的推荐 ○ *give sb a warm welcome* 热烈欢迎某人 ○ *a warm invitation to stay with sb* 热情邀请与某人同住 ○ *get a warm* (ie strongly welcoming or hostile) *reception* 受到怀着激情的对待(热烈欢迎或强烈敌意). **3** sympathetic or affectionate 同情的; 示爱的: *She is a warm kindly person.* 她是个和蔼可亲的人. ○ *He has a warm heart.* 他心肠热. ○ *warm feelings of love and gratitude* 热爱与感激之情. **4** (of colours, sounds, etc) pleasantly suggesting warmth (指颜色、声音等)暖调的: *The room was furnished in warm reds and browns.* 这个房间是用红色和棕色装饰的暖色调. ○ *The orchestra had a distinctively warm and mellow sound.* 这个管弦乐队演奏的特色是声音优美柔和. **5** (**a**) (of a scent in hunting) recently made and easily followed by the hounds; fresh (指猎物的气味)不久前留下的(猎犬容易跟踪的), 新鲜的. (**b**) [pred 作表语] (in a guessing game or game of hide-and-seek) near to the object, word, etc that is being looked for (在猜谜或捉迷藏游戏中)将要猜中, 接近目标: *You're getting warm.* 你猜得差不多了. ○ *Am I getting warmer?* 我是不是离要找的目标更近了? **6** (idm 习语) **keep sb's ˈseat, etc warm (for him)** (*infml* 口) occupy a seat, post, etc temporarily so that it is available for sb later 为某人占坐位、暂留职位等. **make it/things warm for sb** (*infml* 口) make things unpleasant or make trouble for sb; punish sb 刁

难某人; 找某人的麻烦; 整某人; 惩罚某人. **(as) warm as 'toast** (*infml* 口) very warm; pleasantly warm 十分温暖; 暖洋洋: *We lit the fire and were soon as warm as toast.* 我们生起了火, 很快就觉得暖烘烘的了.

▷ **warmly** *adv* in a warm manner 温暖地; 暖和地; 热情地; 热烈地: *warmly dressed* 穿得很暖和 ○ *He thanked us all warmly.* 他衷心地感谢我们大家. ○ *I can warmly recommend it.* 我诚心诚意推荐它.

warmth /wɔːmθ; wɔrmθ/ *n* [U] **(a)** (also **warm·ness**) state of being warm 温暖; 暖和: *the warmth of the climate* 气候之温暖. **(b)** moderate heat 适当的热度: *Warmth is needed for the seeds to germinate.* 种子发芽需要适当的温度. **(c)** strength of feeling 感情的强度: *He was touched by the warmth of their welcome.* 他受到他们热情欢迎, 十分感动. ○ *She denied the accusation with some warmth*, ie strenuously, forcefully. 她有些激动, 竭力否认这一指责.

□ ˌ**warm-'blooded** *adj* **(a)** (of animals) having a constant blood temperature (in the range 36°C-42°C); not cold-blooded like snakes, etc (指动物)温血的(在36°C-42°C之间, 与蛇类等冷血动物不同的). **(b)** (of a person) having feelings, passions, etc that are easily roused; ardent (指人)容易动感情的, 热心的, 热情的.

ˌ**warm-'hearted** *adj* kind and sympathetic 热心肠的. ˌ**warm-'heartedness** *n* [U].

warm[2] /wɔːm; wɔrm/ *v* **1** [I, Ip, Tn, Tn·p] **~ (sth/sb) (up)** (cause sth/sb to) become warm or warmer (使某物[某人])温暖, 暖和: *a warming drink* 使人暖和的饮料 ○ *The milk is warming (up) on the stove.* 牛奶在炉子上热着呢. ○ *Please warm (up) the milk.* 请把牛奶热一热. ○ *warm oneself/one's hands by the fire* 烤火[手]. **2** (idm 习语) **warm the 'cockles (of sb's 'heart)** make sb feel pleased or happy 使某人愉快或高兴. **3** (phr v) **warm sth over** (*US*) **(a)** reheat (food); warm sth up 熥(食物); 将某物加热. **(b)** bring out (old ideas, etc) without adding anything new 重提(旧意见等); 炒冷饭; 旧调重弹. **warm to/towards sb** begin to like sb 喜欢上某人: *I warmed to her immediately.* 我立即喜欢上她了. ○ *He's not somebody one warms to easily.* 他不是容易讨人喜欢的人. **warm to/towards sth** become more interested in or enthusiastic about (a job, subject, task, etc); like sth more 对(某工作、问题、任务等)更有兴趣或更热心; 更加喜欢某事物. **warm up** **(a)** prepare for athletic exercise, dancing, playing the piano, etc by practising gently beforehand (运动、跳舞、弹琴等之前)做准备活动. **(b)** (of a machine, engine, etc) run for a short time in order to reach the temperature at which it will operate efficiently (指机器、发动机等)预热. **warm (sb/sth) up** (cause sb/sth to) become more lively (使某人[某事物])更活跃: *warm up an audience with a few jokes* 说几个笑话使观众活跃起来 ○ *The party soon warmed up.* 这个聚会的气氛很快就活跃起来了. **warm sth up** reheat (previously cooked food) 熥(食物): *warmed-up stew* 熥好了的炖菜.

▷ **warmer** *n* (esp in compounds 尤用以构成复合词) thing that warms 加热器: *a foot-warmer* 暖脚器.

□ '**warming-pan** *n* round metal pan with a lid and a long handle, formerly filled with hot coals and used to warm a bed 暖床器(有盖长柄金属火盆, 旧时盛热煤炭暖床用).

'**warm-up** *n* act or period of preparing for a game, performance, etc by practising gently (比赛、表演等前的)准备练习.

warm[3] /wɔːm; wɔrm/ *n* [sing] **1 the warm** warm atmosphere 温暖的空气: *Come out of the cold street into the warm.* 街上寒冷, 进来暖和暖和. **2** act of warming 加热: *She gave the sheets a warm by the fire before putting them on the bed.* 她把被褥烤暖后再铺到床上.

warn /wɔːn; wɔrn/ *v* **1 (a)** [Tn, Tn·pr, Dn·f, Dn·w] **~ sb (of sth)** give sb notice of sth, esp possible danger or unpleasant consequences; inform sb in advance of what may happen 提醒某人(尤指可能有危险的或有不良后果的事); 预先通知某人; 警告: *'Mind the step,' she warned.* '小心脚底下,'她提醒道. ○ *I tried to warn him, but he wouldn't listen.* 我事先跟他说过, 可他就是不听. ○ *She has been warned of the danger of driving the car in that state.* 已经告诉过她, 汽车这个样子开起来有危险. ○ *The police are warning (motorists) of possible delays.* 警方通知(驾驶汽车的人)交通可能受阻. ○ *If you warn me in advance, I will have your order ready for you.* 你若预先通知我, 我就能给您准备好了. ○ *They warned her that if she did it again she would be sent to prison.* 他们警告她说她再这么干就把她关进监狱. ○ *I had been warned what to expect.* 事先已经告诉过我要出这种事. **(b)** [Tn·pr] **~ sb about/against sb/sth; ~ sb against doing sth** put sb on his guard against sb/sth 让某人警惕或提防某人[某事物]: *He warned us against pickpockets.* 他告诉我们要小心扒手. ○ *The police have warned shopkeepers about the forged banknotes.* 警方已通知各店主留意伪钞. ○ *The doctor warned us against overtiring the patient.* 医生让我们注意病人不可过劳. **(c)** [Dn·t] advise sb (not) to do sth 建议或劝告某人(不要)做某事: *They were warned not to climb the mountain in such bad weather.* 已经劝过他们天气这么坏不要攀登那座山. ○ *She warned them to be careful.* 她告诉他们务必小心. **2** (phr v) **warn sb off (sth/doing sth)** give sb notice that he must go or stay away, eg from private property 通知某人离开或不要接触(如私人的地方): *I had been warned off visiting her while she was still unwell.* 已经告诉我她还没好不要去看她.

▷ **warn·ing** *n* **1** [C] statement, event, etc that warns 提醒或警告的言语或事情: *She has received a written warning about her conduct.* 她已接获对她操行的书面警告. ○ *Her warnings were ignored.* 她提出的警告没有引起注意. ○ *a gale warning to shipping* 向船只发出的大风警告 ○ *Let that be a warning to you*, ie Let that (accident, misfortune, etc) teach you to be more careful in future. 你要把这件事引为鉴戒. ○ *a warning of future difficulties* 将有重重困难的先兆 ○ [attrib 作定语] *warning lights, shots* 示警的灯、枪声. **2** [U] act of warning or state of being warned 提醒; 警告: *The attack occurred without (advance) warning*, ie unexpectedly. 没有(预先)警告就发动了攻击. ○ *You should take warning from* (ie be warned by) *what happened to me.* 你应以我的事情引为鉴戒. ○ *The speaker sounded a note of warning*, ie spoke of possible danger. 那个演讲的人提出有可能发生危险.

warp[1] /wɔːp; wɔrp/ *v* [I, Tn] **1** (cause sth to) become bent or twisted from the usual or natural shape, esp because of uneven shrinkage or expansion (使某物)弯曲, 翘棱(尤指因收缩或伸展不均所致): *The damp wood began to warp.* 这块潮湿的木材有些翘棱了. ○ *The hot sun had warped the cover of the book.* 太阳把这本书的书皮晒弯了. **2** (*fig* 比喻) (cause sb/sth to) become biased, distorted or perverted (使某人[某事物])有偏见, 受曲解, 反常: *His judgement was warped by self-interest.* 他受私心影响判断不确. ○ *a warped mind, sense of humour* 反常的想法、幽默感.

▷ **warp** *n* (usu *sing* 通常作单数) warped condition 弯曲; 翘棱; 偏见; 曲解; 反常: *a warp in his character* 他个性中的偏狭 ○ *a time warp* (科幻小说中的)时间错位.

warp[2] /wɔːp; wɔrp/ *n* **the warp** [sing] (in weaving) the threads on a loom over and under which other threads (the *weft* or *woof*) are passed to make cloth (纺织中的)经纱. ⇨illus at WEAVE 见 WEAVE 插图.

war·rant /ˈwɒrənt; *US* ˈwɔːr-; ˈwɔrənt/ *n* **1** [C] **~ (for sth)** **(a)** written order giving authority to do sth 授权命令: *issue a warrant for sb's arrest* 发出逮捕某人的逮捕状 ○ *a death-/search-warrant* 死刑执行令[搜查证] ○ *A warrant is out for his arrest/against him.* 已经发出了可逮捕他的逮捕证. **(b)** voucher that entitles the holder to receive goods, money, services, etc (可得到货物、钱、服务等的)凭证, 证件: *a travel warrant* 通行证 ○ *a warrant for dividends on shares* 股息单. **2 ~ for sth/doing sth** [U] (*fml* 文) justification or authorization for (an action, etc) 正当理由; 根据: *He had no warrant for doing that/what he did.* 他那样做毫无道理.

▷ **war·rant** *v* **1** [Tn] (*fml* 文) be a warrant(2) for (sth); justify or deserve 证明(某事物)正当、有理或恰当: *Nothing can warrant such severe punishment.* 这样严厉的惩罚毫无根据. ○ *Her interference was not warranted.* 她干涉得毫无道理. ○ *The crisis warrants special measures.* 大难当头有必要采取特别措施. **2** [usu passive 通常用于被动语态: Tn, Cn·a, Cn·n, Cn·t] guarantee (sth) as genuine 保证(某物)为真品或正品: *This material is warranted (to be) pure silk.* 这种料子保证是纯丝的. **3** (idm 习语) **I('ll) warrant (you)** (*dated* 旧) I assure or promise you 我(向你)保证: *The trouble isn't over yet, I'll warrant you.* 麻烦事并没有完, 我可以给你打包票.

W

war·rantee /ˌwɒrənˈtiː; *US* ˌwɔːr-; ˌwɔrənˈti/ *n* person to whom a warranty(1) is made 被保证人; 被担保人.

war·rantor /ˈwɒrəntɔː(r); *US* ˈwɔːr-; ˈwɔrənˌtɔr/ *n* person who makes a warranty(1) 保证人; 担保人.

war·ranty /ˈwɒrəntɪ; *US* ˈwɔːr-; ˈwɔrəntɪ/ *n* **1** [C, U] (written or printed) guarantee, esp one given to the buyer of an article, promising to repair or replace it if necessary (商品的)保证书, 保单, 保证: *It is foolish to buy a car without a warranty.* 购买没有保单的汽车是愚蠢的. ○ *The machine is still under warranty.* 这台机器仍在保修期内. **2** [U] (*fml* 文) authority 权威; 根据: *What warranty have you for doing this?* 你这样做有什么根据?

□ ˈ**warrant-officer** *n* (**a**) (*Brit*) non-commissioned officer of the highest grade in the army, air force or marines (陆军、空军或海军陆战队的)准尉. ⇨App 9 见附录9. (**b**) (*US*) non-commissioned officer of the highest grade in the army, air force, navy or marine corps (陆军、空军、海军或海军陆战队的)准尉. ⇨App 9 见附录9.

war·ren /ˈwɒrən; *US* ˈwɔːrən; ˈwɔrən/ *n* **1** area of land with many burrows in which rabbits live and breed 兔子繁殖场; 养兔场. **2** (*fig* 比喻) (usu over-populated) building or district with many narrow passages, where it is difficult to find one's way (通常为过分拥挤的)多狭窄通道易迷路的建筑或地区: *lost in a warren of narrow streets* 在纵横交错的狭窄街道上迷了路.

war·rior /ˈwɒrɪə(r); *US* ˈwɔːr-; ˈwɔrɪɚ/ *n* **1** (*fml* 文) (esp formerly) person who fights in battle; soldier (尤指旧时)武士, 勇士, 战士: [attrib 作定语] *a warrior nation*, ie fond of or skilled in fighting 善战的民族. **2** member of a tribe who fights for his tribe 部落的武士: *a Zulu warrior* 祖鲁人的武士.

wart /wɔːt; wɔrt/ *n* **1** (**a**) small hard dry growth on the skin 疣; 瘊子. (**b**) similar growth on a plant 树瘤. **2** (idm 习语) ˌ**warts and** ˈ**all** (*infml* 口) without concealing blemishes or unattractive features 不隐瞒缺点: *You agreed to marry me, warts and all!* 是你同意和我结婚的, 我又没掩饰缺陷.

▷ **warty** *adj* covered in warts 有疣的; 长着瘊子的; 有树瘤的.

□ ˈ**wart-hog** *n* any of several types of African wild pig with two large tusks and wart-like growths on the face 疣猪(产于非洲, 有一对獠牙, 脸部有肉疣).

wary /ˈweərɪ; ˈwɛrɪ/ *adj* (**-ier**, **-iest**) **~ (of sb/sth)** looking out for possible danger or difficulty; cautious (对可能发生的危险或困难)留意的, 小心的, 警惕的: *keep a wary eye on sb* 密切注意某人 ○ *She was wary of strangers.* 她很警惕陌生人. ○ *be wary of giving offence* 唯恐冒犯他人. ▷ **war·ily** /-rəlɪ; -rəlɪ/ *adv*: *They approached the stranger warily.* 他们小心翼翼地和那个陌生人接触. **wari·ness** *n* [U].

was ⇨ BE.

wash[1] /wɒʃ; wɔʃ/ *n* **1** [C usu *sing* 通常作单数] act of cleaning or being cleaned with water 洗; 洗涤: *He looks as if he needs a good* (ie thorough) *wash.* 他看样子得好好洗洗了. ○ *have a wash (and brush up)*, ie wash oneself (and make oneself tidy, brush one's hair, etc) (梳)洗一下 ○ *Please give the car a wash.* 请把汽车冲洗一下. ○ *The colour has faded after only two washes.* 这个颜色只洗两水就退色了. ○ *a cold wash*, ie a wash in cold water 用冷水洗. **2** (**a**) **the wash** [sing] process of laundering clothes 洗熨衣物: *All my shirts are in/have gone to the wash*, ie are being laundered. 我所有的衬衣都洗着呢. (**b**) [C usu *sing* 通常作单数] quantity of clothes, sheets, etc (to be) washed (要)洗的衣物的数量: *There is a large wash this week.* 本星期有很多衣物要洗. ○ *When does the wash come back from the laundry?* 送到洗衣店的衣服什么时候取回来? **3** [sing] (sound made by) disturbed water or air, eg behind a moving ship, aircraft, etc 搅动的水或空气(的声音)(如航行中的船、飞机等后面的): *the wash of the waves against the side of the boat* 波浪拍打船舷的声音 ○ *the wash made by the steamer's propellers* 汽船螺旋桨搅动的水. **4** [C] thin layer of water-colour painted on a surface (水彩的)薄涂层. **5** [U] waste scraps of food mixed in liquid and given to pigs to eat; swill (剩汤菜混合的)猪饲料. **6** (idm 习语) **come out in the** ˈ**wash** (*infml* 口) (of mistakes, etc) come right or be put right eventually, without any harm being done (指错误等)最后完全正确或得以纠正(未造成损失).

□ ˈ**washboard** *n* board with ridges on it used (esp formerly) for rubbing clothes on when washing them 搓板.

ˈ**wash-day** *n* (*dated* 旧) day on which clothes are washed 洗衣日.

ˈ**wash-drawing** *n* drawing done with a brush in a black or neutral water-colour 水墨画.

wash[2] /wɒʃ; *US* wɔːʃ; wɔʃ/ *v* **1** (**a**) [Tn, Cn·a] make (sb/sth) clean in water or some other liquid 洗(某人[某物]): *These clothes will have to be washed.* 这些衣服该洗了. ○ *Go and wash yourself.* 你洗个澡吧. ○ *Have these glasses been washed?* 这些玻璃杯洗过了吗? ○ *The beach had been washed clean by the tide.* 潮水把海滩冲刷得非常干净. (**b**) [I] make oneself, clothes, one's face and hands, etc clean with water 洗澡、洗衣物、洗脸、洗手等: *I had to wash and dress in a hurry.* 我得匆匆洗个澡穿好衣服. ○ *They had to wash in cold water.* 他们只好用冷水洗. (**c**) [I] (of clothes, fabrics, etc) be able to be washed without losing colour, shrinking, etc (指衣物、织物等)洗后不退色、不缩水等: *This sweater washes well.* 这件套头毛衣耐洗. ○ *If a garment won't wash, it must be dry-cleaned.* 用水洗就退色或缩水的衣服得干洗. **2** [Tn] (of the sea, a river, etc) flow past or against (sth) (指海水、河水等)流过或冲击(某物): *The sea washes the base of the cliffs.* 海水拍打着悬崖的底部. ○ *The garden wall is being washed by the flood water.* 大水冲刷着花园的围墙. **3** (**a**) [Ipr, Ip] (of water) flow in the specified direction (指水)(向某方向)流动: *waves washing against the side of a boat* 流经船舷的波浪 ○ *Water washed over the deck.* 水从甲板上流过. (**b**) [Tn·pr, Tn·p esp passive 尤用于被动语态] (of water) move (sb/sth) by flowing in the specified direction (指水)冲走(某人[某物]): *debris washed along by the flood* 洪水冲走的破烂东西 ○ *The body was washed out to sea.* 那具尸体已冲到海里. ○ *Pieces of the wreckage were washed ashore.* 遇难船只的残骸碎物已冲到了岸上. ○ *He was washed overboard in the storm.* 在暴风雨中他被从船上冲到水里. **4** [Tn, Tn·p] **~ sth (out)** (of water) form sth by flowing; scoop sth out (指水)冲成, 冲出: *The stream had washed (out) a channel in the sand.* 小河在沙地上冲出了一条沟. **5** [Tn] pour water through gravel, etc in order to find (gold, etc) 用水冲沙砾等以选出(沙金等): *washing ore* 淘洗矿石. **6** [Tn] cover (a surface) with a thin layer of water-paint 用水溶性颜料涂饰(物体表面). **7** [I, Ipr] (only in questions or negative sentences 只用于疑问句或否定句) **~ (with sb)** (*infml* 口) be accepted or believed (by sb) (被某人)接受或相信: *That excuse simply won't wash (with me).* 这种借口(让我)实在无法相信. **8** (idm 习语) **wash one's dirty linen in** ˈ**public** discuss one's personal (esp unpleasant) affairs or quarrels in public 公开谈论个人的(尤指坏的)事情或争吵的事; 家丑外扬. **wash one's hands of sb/sth** refuse to be responsible for sb/sth (any longer) 对某人[某事物]不(再)负责; 洗手不干: *I've washed my hands of the whole sordid business.* 我已经彻底洗手不干那种肮脏的勾当了.

9 (phr v) **wash sb/sth away** (of water) remove or carry sb/sth away to another place (指水)将某人[某物]冲掉或冲至另一处: *Her child was washed away in the flood.* 她的孩子让洪水给冲走了. ○ *footprints washed away by the rain* 被雨水冲掉的脚印 ○ *The cliffs are being gradually washed away by the sea.* 这处悬崖逐渐让海水冲刷剥蚀了.

wash sth down (with sth) (**a**) clean sth by using a stream or jet of water 用水喷射冲洗某物: *wash down the decks* 冲洗甲板 ○ *wash down a car with a hose* 用水龙冲洗汽车. (**b**) drink sth after, or at the same time as, eating (food) 用饮料将吃的(食物)送下: *I had bread and cheese for lunch, washed down with beer.* 我午餐吃的是面包和奶酪, 喝的是啤酒.

wash (sth) off (cause sth to) be removed from the surface of a material, etc by washing (使某物)被冲洗掉: *Those grease stains won't wash off.* 这些油迹洗不掉. ○ *Please wash that mud off (your boots) before you come in.* 请你先把(靴子上的)泥洗掉再进来.

wash out (of a dirty mark) be removed from a fabric by washing (指污迹)从织物上洗掉: *These ink stains* *won't wash out.* 这些墨迹洗不掉. **wash sth out (a)** wash sth or the inside of sth in order to remove dirt, etc 将某物或某物的内部洗净: *wash out the empty bottles* 把空瓶子洗干净 ○ *If I wash your sports kit out now, it'll be dry by tomorrow morning.* 要是我现在把你的运动用品洗了, 明天上午就能干了. **(b)** (of rain, etc) bring (a game) to an end or prevent it from starting (指雨等)迫使(比赛)结束或无法开始: *The match was completely washed out.* 这场比赛遇雨而完全停止了. ○ *Torrential rain washed out most of the weekend's events.* 这场雨很大, 周末比赛项目多数无法进行了.

wash over sb (*infml* 口) occur all around sb, or be expressed, without greatly affecting him 周围发生的一切事情对某人无多大影响: *The recent criticism she's had seems to have washed right over her.* 她最近受到批评不过是水过地皮湿无大影响.

wash up (a) (*Brit*) wash the dishes, cutlery, etc after a meal 饭后刷洗碗碟刀叉等餐具. **(b)** (*US*) wash one's face and hands 洗脸洗手. **wash sth up** (*Brit*) wash (dishes, cutlery, etc) after a meal; carry sth to shore 饭后刷洗(碗碟刀叉等餐具); 将某物冲到岸边: *The tide had washed up cargo from the wrecked ship.* 潮水把遇难船上的货物冲到了岸边.

▷ **wash·able** /-əbl; -əbl̩/ *adj* that can be washed without being spoiled 可洗而不致毁坏的; 耐洗的: *washable clothes, fabrics, paint, surfaces* 耐洗的衣物、织物、涂料、表面.

□ ˈ**wash-basin** (also ˈ**wash-hand-basin**, **basin**, *US* ˈ**wash-bowl**) *n* large bowl (usually fixed to a wall and fitted with taps) for washing one's hands, etc in 洗脸池(通常安装在墙上的, 有水龙头).

ˈ**wash-cloth** *n* (*US*) = FACE-CLOTH (FACE[1]).

ˌ**washed** ˈ**out (a)** (of fabric or colour) faded by washing (指织物或颜色)洗后退色的: *ˌwashed out blue ˈoveralls* 洗后退色的蓝色长罩衣 ○ *a ˌwashed out ˌcotton ˈdress* 洗后退色的棉质连衣裙. **(b)** (of a person, his appearance, etc) pale and tired; exhausted (指人、面色等)苍白怠倦的, 疲惫的: *She looks washed out after her illness.* 她病后气色很难看.

ˌ**washed** ˈ**up** (*infml* 口) ruined or defeated, having failed 毁灭的; 失败的: *Their marriage was washed up long before they separated.* 他们分居前婚姻早已破裂了.

ˌ**washing-**ˈ**up** *n* [U] **(a)** task of washing dishes, etc after a meal 饭后刷洗碗碟等的工作: *do the washing-up* 刷洗餐具. **(b)** dishes, cutlery, glasses, etc to be washed up 待刷洗的碗碟、刀叉、玻璃杯等: *The washing-up had been left in the sink.* 要洗的餐具都在洗涤槽里呢. **washing-**ˈ**up liquid** liquid detergent for washing dishes, etc (刷洗餐具用的)洗涤液.

ˈ**wash-leather** *n* [C, U] (piece of) chamois leather, used for cleaning and polishing windows, etc 擦拭皮(用于擦窗户等的软皮).

ˈ**wash-out** *n* (*infml* 口) person, event, etc that is a complete failure 完全失败的人、事情等: *The new manager is a wash-out.* 新经理没什么本事. ○ *The party was a total wash-out.* 这次聚会十分糟糕.

ˈ**washroom** *n* (*US euph* 婉) lavatory (esp in a public building) 厕所(尤指公共建筑物中的). ⇨Usage at TOILET 用法见 TOILET.

ˈ**wash-stand** *n* (esp formerly, in houses without a piped supply of water to a bathroom or bedroom) special table that holds a basin and jug, for washing oneself in a bedroom (尤指旧时无自来水时卧室内的)盥洗台.

ˈ**wash-tub** *n* large wooden tub used (esp formerly) for washing clothes 大木盆(尤指旧时洗衣用的).

washer /ˈwɒʃə(r); *US* ˈwɔː-; ˈwɔʃɚ/ *n* **1** small flat ring made of rubber, metal, plastic, etc placed between two surfaces (eg under a nut) to make a screw or joint tight, prevent leakage, etc 垫圈(橡胶、金属、塑料等的小扁环, 垫在被连接件如螺母下使之更紧、防漏等). ⇨illus at BOLT 见 BOLT 插图. **2** (*infml* 口) automatic machine for washing clothes 洗衣机.

wash·ing /ˈwɒʃɪŋ; *US* ˈwɔː-; ˈwɔʃɪŋ/ *n* **1** [C, U] (act of) washing or being washed 洗; 洗涤: *The sweater had shrunk after repeated washing(s).* 这件套头毛衣洗过多次已缩水了. ○ *Washing is a chore.* 洗衣服是烦人的事. **2** [U] clothes being washed or to be washed (正在洗的或待洗的)衣物: *hang the washing on the line to dry* 把洗好的衣物晾在绳子上 ○ *put a load of washing in the washing-machine* 把要洗的衣物放到洗衣机里 ○ *Send one's (dirty) washing to the laundry.* 把要洗的(脏)衣物送到洗衣店去.

□ ˈ**washing-machine** *n* electric machine for washing clothes 洗衣机.

ˈ**washing-powder** *n* [U] soap or detergent in the form of powder for washing clothes 洗衣粉.

ˈ**washing-soda** *n* [U] = SODIUM CARBONATE (SODIUM).

washy /ˈwɒʃɪ; *US* ˈwɔː-; ˈwɔʃɪ/ *adj* (*derog* 贬) **1** (of colours) pale (指颜色)苍白的. **2** (of liquids) (too) watery; thin or weak (指液体)(过于)稀薄的, 淡的: *washy coffee* 很淡的咖啡. **3** lacking force, vigour or clarity 无力的; 无活力的; 不清晰的: *washy encouragement, ideas, plans* 不起作用的鼓励、主意、计划. Cf 参看 WISHY-WASHY.

wasn't ⇨ BE.

wasp /wɒsp; wɑsp/ *n* any of several types of flying insect, the most common of which has black and yellow stripes, a narrow waist and a powerful sting in its tail 黄蜂.

▷ **wasp·ish** *adj* (*derog* 贬) making sharp comments or replies; irritable or snappish 尖刻的; 易怒的; 暴躁的: *waspish remarks* 刻薄的言语. **wasp·ishly** *adv*. **wasp·ish·ness** *n* [U].

□ ˌ**wasp-**ˈ**waisted** *adj* (*dated* 旧) (esp of a woman) having a very slender waist (尤指女子)细腰的.

WASP (also **Wasp**) /wɒsp; wɑsp/ *abbr* 缩写 = (*esp US usu derog* 通常作贬义) White Anglo-Saxon Protestant 盎格鲁撒克逊裔的白人新教徒: *a typically Wasp attitude* 典型的白人新教徒的态度.

was·sail /ˈwɒseɪl; ˈwɑsel/ *n* [U] (*arch* 古) merry-making (esp at Christmas) with eating and drinking 饮宴取乐(尤指圣诞节时). ▷ **was·sail** *v* [I]: *go wassailing* 去饮酒取乐.

wast·age /ˈweɪstɪdʒ; ˈwestɪdʒ/ *n* [U] **(a)** amount that is wasted 损耗量: *You must allow for five per cent wastage in transit.* 在运输中要允许有百分之五的损耗量. **(b)** loss caused by waste 损耗; 耗损: *The retailer has to absorb the cost of wastage.* 零售商须承受耗损的费用. ○ *natural wastage*, ie loss of employees because they retire or move to other jobs and not through redundancy 自然减员(因雇员退休或离职造成的, 并非人为裁减).

waste[1] /weɪst; west/ *adj* [usu attrib 通常作定语] **1** (of land) that is not (fit to be) used; not inhabited or cultivated (指土地)不(能)使用的, 无人烟的, 未开垦的: *an area of waste ground* 一片荒地. **2** no longer useful and to be thrown away 因无用而可抛弃的: *waste matter produced by the manufacturing process* 生产过程中产生的废料. **3** (idm 习语) **lay sth** ˈ**waste** (*fml* 文) destroy crops in (land, etc), esp during a war; ravage sth 毁坏(地里的)作物(尤指战时); 使某处荒芜: *fields laid waste by the invading army* 被侵略军糟蹋而荒芜的土地.

□ ˈ**wasteland** *n* **(a)** area of land that is not or cannot be used; barren or desolate land 未使用的或不能使用的土地; 不毛之地; 荒地: *an industrial wasteland*, ie an area that has been spoilt by industrial development and is no longer used 工业发展造成的废地. **(b)** (*fig* 比喻) situation or life that is culturally or spiritually unproductive 文化上或精神上贫乏的环境或生活.

ˌ**waste-**ˈ**paper** *n* [U] paper that is thought to be spoilt or no longer useful; scrap paper 废纸. ˌ**waste-**ˈ**paper basket** (*Brit*) (*US* ˈ**waste-basket**, ˈ**waste-bin**) basket or other container for paper, etc that is to be thrown away 废纸篓; 废物箱.

ˈ**waste product** useless by-product of a physical or industrial process 排泄物; (生产中的)无用的副产品.

waste[2] /weɪst; west/ *v* **1 (a)** [Tn, Tn·pr] **~ sth (on sb/ sth)** use sth extravagantly, needlessly or without an adequate result 浪费; 滥用: *Hurry up, we're wasting time.* 快点儿吧, 我们别再浪费时间了. ○ *A dripping tap wastes water.* 水龙头关不紧就浪费水. ○ *Don't waste food.* 不要浪费食物. ○ *All our efforts were wasted.* 我们全部的努力都白费了. ○ *I'm sorry you've had a wasted* (ie unnecessary, fruitless) *journey.* 很遗憾你白跑了一趟. ○ *I'm not going to waste any more words on the subject.* 在这个问题上我不想多费唇舌了. ○ *She has wasted her money on things she doesn't need.* 她花了冤枉钱, 买的是她自己并不需要的东西. ○ (*fig* 比喻) *The humour is wasted on them*, ie They do not appreciate it. 这种幽默他们并不欣赏. **(b)** [Tn usu passive 通常用于被动语态] not make full use of (a person or his abilities) 未充分使用(某人或某

W

人的能力): *She's wasted in her present job.* 她做现在的工作屈才. **2** [Tn esp passive 尤用于被动语态] cause (sb/sth) to become weaker and thinner 使(某人[某物])瘦弱: *His body was wasted by long illness.* 他久病体弱. ○ *a wasting disease* 使人瘦弱的疾病 ○ *limbs wasted by hunger* 饿得四肢瘦弱. **3** (idm 习语) **lose/waste no time in doing sth** ⇨ TIME[1]. **waste one's 'breath (on sb/sth)** speak (about sb/sth) but not have any effect (对某人[某事物])白费唇舌: *They won't listen, so don't waste your breath telling them.* 他们听不进去, 不必和他们白费唇舌了. **ˌwaste not, 'want not** (*saying* 谚) if you never waste anything (esp food or money), you will always have it when you need it 不浪费就不缺乏(尤指食物或钱). **4** (phr v) **waste away** (of a person) grow unhealthily thin or weak (指人)消瘦, 衰弱.

▷ **waster** *n* (*derog* 贬) (**a**) wasteful person 挥霍浪费的人. (**b**) = WASTREL.

waste[3] /weɪst; west/ *n* **1** [U, sing] (act of) wasting (WASTE[2] 1a) or being wasted 浪费; 滥用: *a policy aimed at reducing waste* 旨在减少浪费的政策 ○ *The waste of public money on the project was criticized.* 在这个项目上浪费公帑遭到批评. ○ *It's a waste of time* (ie It's not worth) *doing that.* 做那种事是浪费时间. ○ *In his opinion, holidays are a waste of time and money.* 他认为度假浪费时间和金钱. **2** [U] material, food, etc that is no longer needed and is (to be) thrown away; refuse 因无用而可抛弃的材料、食物等; 废料; 废物; 垃圾: *Dustbins are used for household waste.* 垃圾箱是盛扔掉的破烂东西的. ○ *regulations controlling the disposal of industrial waste* 处理工业废物的规章 ○ *radioactive waste from nuclear power stations* 核电站的放射性废物. **3** [C] (**a**) (usu *pl* 通常作复数) large area of land that is not or cannot be inhabited or cultivated; desert 无人烟的或不能住人的地区; 荒地; 荒漠: *the icy wastes of the Antarctic* 南极地区的冰原 ○ *the arid wastes of the Sahara* 撒哈拉干旱的沙漠. (**b**) dreary scene 凄凉的景象: *the derelict waste of disused factories* 工厂被弃置的凄凉景象. **4** (idm 习语) **go/run to 'waste** be wasted 被浪费: *What a pity to see all that food go to waste.* 那么多食物都浪费了, 看着觉得可惜.

▷ **waste·ful** /-fl; -fəl/ *adj* (**a**) causing waste 造成浪费的: *wasteful habits, methods, processes* 造成浪费的习惯、方法、程序. (**b**) using more than is needed; extravagant 浪费的; 挥霍的: *wasteful luxury, expenditure, housekeeping* 挥霍浪费的奢华、支出、持家之道. **waste·fully** /-fəlɪ; -fəlɪ/ *adv*. **waste·ful·ness** *n* [U].

□ **'waste-basket** (also **'waste-bin**) *n* (*US*) = WASTE-PAPER BASKET (WASTE[1]).

'waste-pipe *n* pipe that carries away water which has been used or is not needed, eg dirty water from a sink, bath, etc 污水管; 废水管.

wast·rel /'weɪstrəl; 'westrəl/ (also **waster**) *n* (*fml* 文) lazy good-for-nothing person 懒惰而无用的人.

watch[1] /wɒtʃ; wɑtʃ/ *n* **1** [C] (**a**) (in a ship) period of duty (usu four hours) for part of the crew (船上的)部分船员值班时间(通常为四小时): *the middle watch*, ie midnight to 4 am 午夜值勤(午夜至凌晨4时) ○ *the 'dog watches*, ie 4 pm to 6 pm and 6 pm to 8 pm 二时班(下午4时至6时和6时至8时各一班). (**b**) part (usu half) of a ship's crew on duty during such a period 值班船员(通常为全体船员的半数). **2** [sing] (**a**) **the watch** (formerly) body of men employed to go through the streets, esp at night, in order to protect people and their property (旧时)受雇的街道巡逻队(尤指夜间的): *the constables of the watch* 街道巡逻队队员 ○ *call out the watch* 召唤巡逻人员. (**b**) person or group of people employed to watch sb/sth (受雇的)看守人: *The police put a watch on the suspect's house.* 警方派人监视那个可疑人的住宅. **3** [C usu *pl* 通常作复数] (*arch or fml* 古或文) period of time when one is awake during the night 夜里醒着的时间: *in the long watches of the night* 夜里不眠的漫长时间. **4** (idm 习语) **keep 'watch (for sb/sth)** stay watching (for sb/sth) (为某人[某事物])注视或监视: *post a guard to keep 'watch while the others sleep* 派一个警卫在大家睡觉时放哨. **keep a close eye/watch on sb/sth** ⇨ CLOSE[1]. **on 'watch** on duty, eg as a member of a ship's crew or as a guard 值班(如船员或警卫人员). **(be) on (the) 'watch (for sb/sth)** (be) watching for sb/sth, esp possible danger 注意, 提防(尤指可能发生的危险): *Be on the watch for a sudden change in the patient's condition.* 要密切注意病人病情可能突然变化. ○ *The police warned people to be on the watch for intruders.* 警方预先通知大家防备有外人闯入.

▷ **watch·ful** /-fl; -fəl/ *adj* watching or observing closely; alert 密切注意的; 警惕的: *keep a watchful eye on sth* 密切注意某事物. **watch·fully** /-fəlɪ; -fəlɪ/ *adv*. **watch·ful·ness** *n* [U].

□ **'watch-dog** *n* (**a**) dog that is kept to guard property, esp a house 看门狗. (**b**) (*fig* 比喻) person, group, etc that acts as a guardian of people's rights, etc (监护人们权利等的)监察人, 监察组织: [attrib 作定语] *a watch-dog committee* 监察委员会.

'watchman /-mən; -mən/ *n* (*pl* **-men** /-mən; -mən/) person employed to guard a building (eg a bank, an office building or a factory), esp at night (受雇看守建筑物, 如银行、办公楼或工厂的)警卫员, 看守人(尤指夜间的).

'watch-night service religious service that takes place on the last night of the year (除夕举行的)守岁礼拜.

'watch-tower *n* high tower from which guards keep watch, eg in a forest to look for forest fires, or a fortified observation post 瞭望台.

watch[2] /wɒtʃ; wɑtʃ/ *v* **1** (**a**) [I, Tn, Tw no passive 不用于被动语态, Tng, Tni no passive 不用于被动语态] look at (sb/sth); observe 看(某人[某物]); 观察: *The students watched as the surgeon performed the operation.* 学生观看外科医生做手术. ○ *He watched to see* (ie in order to see) *what would happen.* 他注视着要发生的事情. ○ *Watch me carefully.* 仔细看着我. ○ *Watch what I do and how I do it.* 注意看我的动作和方法. ○ *She had a feeling that she was being watched*, ie spied on. 她觉得有人监视她. ○ *She watched the children crossing/as they crossed the road*, ie observed them as they did it (but not necessarily from start to finish). 她看着孩子们横过马路(但不一定注视全过程). ○ *She watched the children cross the road*, ie observed the action from start to finish. 她看着孩子们横过了马路(注视着全过程). (**b**) [Tn] look at (television, sport, etc) as an entertainment 观看(电视、体育运动等): *Are you going to play or will you just watch?* 你是参加比赛还是观看比赛? ○ *Do you watch football on television?* 你常看电视的足球比赛节目吗? ○ *The match was watched by over twenty thousand people.* 这场比赛有两万多人观看. **2** [Ipr, Tn] **~ (over) sb/sth** guard or protect sb/sth; keep an eye on sb/sth 守卫或保护某人[某物]; 留心; 注视: *Could you watch (over) my clothes while I have a swim?* 我游泳时你看着我的衣物行吗? ○ *He felt that God was watching over him.* 他感觉到上帝保佑着他. ○ *We'll have to watch the children in case they get too tired.* 我们得照看着孩子, 别让他们太累了. **3** [Ipr] **~ for sth** look or wait attentively for sth 盼望或等待某事物: *They are watching for further developments.* 他们等待着进一步的发展. ○ *You'll have to watch for the right moment.* 你得等候适当时机. **4** [Tn] (*infml* 口) be careful about (sb/sth), esp in order to keep him/it under control 小心或当心(某人[某事物])(尤指应加以控制): *watch one's language, manners, tongue, etc* 注意自己的语言、举止、言语等 ○ *Watch yourself!* ie Be careful what you do or say, or you will be punished. 当心你的言行! ○ *watch every penny*, ie be very careful about what one spends 花钱仔细 ○ *Watch what you say about the project, they don't like criticism!* 对这个计划说话要小心, 人家不喜欢听批评意见! **5** [I, Ipr] **~ (at sth)** (*esp arch* 尤作古语) remain awake 不睡: *watch all night at the bedside of a sick child* 守在患儿床边彻夜不眠. **6** (idm 习语) **mind/watch one's step** ⇨ STEP[2]. **'watch it** (*infml* 口) (esp imperative 尤用于祈使句) be careful 当心; 小心; 留神. **watch the 'clock** (*infml derog* 口, 贬) be careful not to work longer than the required time; think more about when one's work will finish than about the work itself 盯着钟表(盼着下班无心工作). **watch this 'space** (*infml catchphrase* 口, 警语) wait for further developments to be announced 等待发表进一步的消息. **watch the 'time** remain aware of what time it is (eg to avoid being late for sth) 留意时间(如以免误事). **watch the 'world go by** observe what is happening around one 注视周围发生的事情. **7** (phr v) **watch 'out** be on one's guard; keep looking out for possible trouble, etc 戒备, 提防(可能发生麻烦

等): *Watch out! There's a car coming.* 小心! 汽车来了. **watch out for sb/sth** be alert so that one notices sb/sth; look out for sb/sth 警惕或注意某人[某事物]: *The staff were asked to watch out for forged banknotes.* 已经要求职员留意伪钞.

▷ **watcher** *n* person who looks at sth; observer 观看的人; 观察的人.

□ ˌ**watching** ˈ**brief** brief of a lawyer who is present in court during a case in which his client is not directly concerned, in order to advise him and protect his interests 律师的案情摘要(律师出庭旁听与委托人无直接关系的案件, 向委托人提供建议).

watch[3] /wɒtʃ; wɑtʃ/ *n* small instrument showing the time, worn on the wrist or (esp formerly) carried in a pocket 表; 手表; (尤指旧时的)怀表: *a pocket-watch* 怀表 ○ *a wrist-watch* 手表 ○ *What time is it by your watch?/What does your watch say?* 你的表几点钟了? Cf 参看 CLOCK[1] 1.

□ ˈ**watchmaker** *n* person who makes and repairs watches and clocks 制造并修理钟表的人; 钟表匠.

ˈ**watch-strap** (*Brit*) (*US* ˈ**watch-band**) *n* strap for fastening a wrist-watch on one's wrist 手表带.

watch·word /ˈwɒtʃwɜːd; ˈwɑtʃˌwɝd/ *n* **1** word or phrase that expresses briefly the principles of a party or group; slogan or catchphrase 口号; 标语: *Our watchword is: 'Evolution, not revolution'.* 我们的口号是: '要循序渐进, 不要剧烈变革.' **2** = PASSWORD (PASS[1]).

wa·ter[1] /ˈwɔːtə(r); ˈwɔtɚ/ *n* **1** (**a**) [U] liquid without colour, smell or taste that falls as rain, is in lakes, rivers and seas, and is used for drinking, washing, etc 水: *Water is changed into steam by heat and into ice by cold.* 水加热变蒸汽, 冷却后结冰. ○ *Fish live in (the) water.* 鱼在水中生活. ○ ˈ*drinking water* 饮用水 ○ ˈ*mineral water* 矿泉水. (**b**) [U] this liquid as supplied to homes, factories, etc in pipes 自来水: *The water was turned off for several hours a day during the drought.* 在干旱时, 每天有几小时停止供应自来水. ○ *The houses in this village are without water.* 这个村子里家家户户都没有自来水. ○ *hot and cold running water*, ie a supply of hot and cold water piped to taps 热的和凉的自来水 ○ [attrib 作定语] *water rationing, shortages* 自来水定量供应、短缺. (**c**) [sing] mass of this liquid, esp a lake, river or sea 大片的水; (尤指)湖, 河, 海: *She fell in the water and drowned.* 她落水淹死了. ○ *The flood water covered the whole area.* 洪水把整个地区都淹没了. (**d**) [sing] surface of a lake, river, sea, etc (湖、河、海等的)水面: *float on the water* 漂浮在水面上 ○ *swim under the water* 潜泳 ○ *We could see fishes under the water.* 我们看见水面下有各种鱼. **2** [U] (esp in compounds 尤用以构成复合词) preparation containing water or sth similar to water 含水的或似水的制剂: ˈ*rose-water* 玫瑰香水 ○ ˈ*lavender-water* 薰衣草香水 ○ ˈ*soda-water* 苏打水. **3 waters** [pl] (**a**) mass of water (in a lake, river, etc) (湖、河等的)水域: *the (ˈhead-)waters of the Nile*, ie the lake from which it flows 尼罗河的源头 ○ *The waters of the lake flow out over a large waterfall.* 这个湖的水流出后形成一个大瀑布. ○ *the stormy waters of the Atlantic* 大西洋多暴风雨的海域. (**b**) sea near a particular country (某国附近的)海域: *British (territorial) waters* 英国的海域 ○ *in home/foreign waters* 在本国的[他国的]领海. **4** [U] state or level of the tide 潮水; 潮水的水位: *(at) high/low water* (处于)高[低]潮. **5** (idm 习语) **be in/get into hot water** ⇨ HOT. **blood is thicker than water** ⇨ BLOOD[1]. **bread and water** ⇨ BREAD. **by water** by boat, ship, barge, etc 由水路; 乘船: *transported by water* 经水运 ○ *You can reach the house by water.* 可乘船抵达那所房子那里. **cast one's bread upon the waters** ⇨ CAST[1]. **hell or high water** ⇨ HELL. **take the** ˈ**waters** visit a spa in order to drink or bathe in the spring water there to improve one's health 到矿泉疗养地(喝矿泉水或以矿泉水沐浴促进健康). **fish in troubled waters** ⇨ FISH[2]. **a fish out of water** ⇨ FISH[1]. **go through fire and water** ⇨ FIRE[1]. **hold** ˈ**water** (*infml* 口) (of an argument, an excuse, a theory, etc) be capable of standing up to examination or testing; be valid (指辩论、借口、理论等)经得起检验的, 站得住脚的. **in deep water** ⇨ DEEP[1]. **in smooth water** ⇨ SMOOTH[1]. **keep one's head above water** ⇨ HEAD[1]. **like a duck to water** ⇨ DUCK[1]. **like** ˈ**water** (*infml* 口) in great quantity; lavishly or recklessly 大量的; 无节制的; 不顾后果的: *spend money like water* 挥金如土 ○ *The wine flowed like water at the party.* 在宴会上大家开怀畅饮, 酒似流水. **a lot of/much water has flowed, etc under the** ˈ**bridge** many things have happened (since an event, etc) and the situation is different now (自从某件事以来)已发生了很多事, 情况不同了. **make** ˈ**water** (of a ship) have a leak (指船)漏水: *We're making water* (ie Water is coming into the ship) *fast.* 我们的船漏水漏得很厉害. **make/pass** ˈ**water** (*fml* 文) urinate 排泄尿; 撒尿. **milk and water** ⇨ MILK[1]. **muddy the waters** ⇨ MUDDY (MUD). **of the first water** ⇨ FIRST[1]. **pour/throw cold water on sth** ⇨ COLD[1]. **pour oil on troubled waters** ⇨ POUR. **still waters run deep** ⇨ STILL[1]. **throw out the baby with the bath water** ⇨ BABY. **tread water** ⇨ TREAD. **under** ˈ**water** (**a**) in and covered by water 在水中并被水没过: *swimming under water* 潜泳. (**b**) flooded 被水淹没: *Several fields are under water after the heavy rain.* 大雨过后有几片耕地被淹. **(like) water off a** ˈ**duck's** ˈ**back** (esp of criticisms, etc) without any effect (on sb) (尤指批评等)(对某人)不起作用: *Their hints about his behaviour were (like) water off a duck's back.* 他们示意他举止不当, 如同对牛弹琴. **water under the** ˈ**bridge** event, mistake, etc that has already occurred and cannot be altered, so there is no point in worrying about it 已经发生的事情、错误等无法更改, 犯不上烦恼: *Last year's dispute is (all) water under the bridge now.* 去年的争论(都)已是覆水难收了. **you can take a horse to water, but you can't make it drink** ⇨ HORSE.

▷ **wa·ter·less** *adj* (esp of an area of land) without water (尤指一地区)无水的: *waterless deserts* 无水的沙漠.

□ ˈ**water-bed** *n* mattress for sleeping on, made of rubber or plastic and filled with water 水床(橡胶或塑料制的充水床垫).

ˈ**water-bird** *n* any of several types of bird that swim or wade in (esp fresh) water 水鸟, 水禽(尤指淡水中的). ⇨illus at App 1 见附录1插图, page v.

ˈ**water-biscuit** *n* thin crisp unsweetened biscuit, usu eaten with butter and cheese 一种薄而脆的不甜的饼干(通常与黄油和奶酪一起食用).

ˈ**water-borne** *adj* (**a**) (of goods) carried by water (指货物)水运的. (**b**) (of diseases) spread by the use of contaminated water (指疾病)由污染的水传染的.

ˈ**water-bottle** *n* (**a**) glass container for drinking-water, eg at table or in a bedroom 玻璃水瓶(如桌上或卧室中用的). (**b**) (*US* **canteen**) metal flask for carrying drinking-water, used by a soldier, scout, etc 携带式金属水壶(士兵或童子军等用的).

ˈ**water-buffalo** *n* (*pl* unchanged or **~es** 复数或不变或作 **water-buffaloes**) common domestic Indian buffalo 水牛.

ˈ**water-butt** *n* = BUTT[1] 2.

ˈ**water-cannon** *n* machine that produces a powerful jet of water, used eg to disperse a crowd of rioters 水炮(强力喷水器, 如用以驱散暴乱人群的).

ˈ**water-closet** *n* (*abbr* 缩写 **WC**) (*dated* 旧) = LAVATORY.

ˈ**water-colour** (*US* **-color**) *n* **1** ˈ**water-colours** [pl] paints (to be) mixed with water and not oil 水彩(颜料). **2** [C] picture painted with such paints 水彩画.

ˈ**water-cooled** *adj* cooled by water circulating round it 用循环水冷却的; 水冷的: *a water-cooled engine, nuclear reactor* 水冷式发动机、核反应堆.

ˈ**watercourse** *n* (channel of a) stream, brook or man-made waterway 河道; 水道; 渠道.

ˈ**watercress** *n* [U] type of cress that grows in streams and pools, with strong-tasting peppery leaves used in salads 水田芥(生长于溪流和水塘中的植物, 叶辛辣, 用以制色拉).

ˈ**water-diviner** *n* = DIVINER (DIVINE 2).

ˈ**waterfall** *n* stream or river that falls from a height, eg over rocks or a cliff 瀑布.

ˈ**water-fowl** *n* (*pl* unchanged 复数不变) (usu *pl* 通常作复数) bird that swims and lives near or on water, esp one of the types that are hunted for sport 水鸟, 水禽(尤指视为猎物的).

ˈ**waterfront** *n* street, part of a town, etc that is next to water (eg a harbour or the sea) 滨水路, 滨水区(如港口或海边的).

ˈ**water-hammer** *n* [U] knocking noise in a pipe when water is turned on or off 水锤现象, 水击作用(水龙头开或关时水管发出的打击声).

ˈ**water-hole** *n* shallow depression in which water collects (esp in the bed of a river that is otherwise dry and to which animals go to drink) 水坑(尤指河床干涸时的积水部分, 为动物饮水处).

ˈ**water-ice** *n* [C, U] (portion of) frozen water flavoured with fruit juice and sugar, served as a dessert 雪糕(水加果汁和糖冷冻的甜食).

ˈ**water-jump** *n* (in show-jumping, steeplechases, etc) place where a horse has to jump over water, eg a ditch or a fence with water beside it (超越障碍赛马等的)水沟障碍.

ˈ**water-level** *n* (**a**) surface of water in a reservoir, etc (水库等的)水平面: *below the water-level* 在水平面以下. (**b**) height of this 水位; 水准; 水平: *raise the water-level* 提高水位.

ˈ**water-lily** *n* any of several types of plant that grow in water, and have broad floating leaves and white, yellow, blue or red flowers 睡莲.

ˈ**water-line** *n* line along which the surface of the water touches a ship's side (船的)吃水线, 水线: *the load water-line*, ie the water-line when the ship is loaded 载重水线(船载重后的) ○ *the light water-line*, ie the water-line when the ship is empty of cargo 空载水线(船未载重的).

ˈ**waterlogged** /-lɒgd; *US* -lɔːgd; -ˌlɔgd/ *adj* (**a**) (of timber) so saturated with water or (of a ship) so full of water that it will barely float (指木材)浸透水的, (指船)浸满水的(失去浮力的). (**b**) (of land) so saturated with water that it cannot hold any more; thoroughly soaked (指土地)水浸的: *The match had to be abandoned because the pitch was waterlogged.* 那场比赛因场地汪水只好取消.

ˈ**water-main** *n* main pipe in a water-supply system 总水管.

ˈ**waterman** /-mən; -mən/ *n* (*pl* **-men** /-mən; -mən/) boatman who ferries people or hires out his boat 船夫; 船工; 船东.

ˈ**watermark** *n* **1** manufacturer's design in some types of paper, which can be seen when the paper is held against the light (某些种类的纸上印制的)水印. **2** mark that shows how high water (eg the tide or a river) has risen or how low it has fallen 水位标志(如潮水或河流的).

ˈ**water-meadow** *n* meadow that is fertile because it is periodically flooded by a stream 常浸水因而肥沃的草地.

ˈ**water-melon** *n* [C, U] large smooth-skinned melon with juicy pink or red flesh and black seeds 西瓜: *eating a slice of water-melon* 吃一块西瓜.

ˈ**water-mill** *n* mill with machinery that is operated by water-power 水磨.

ˈ**water-pistol** *n* toy gun that shoots a jet of water 玩具水枪.

ˈ**water polo** game played by two teams of swimmers who try to throw a ball into a goal 水球运动.

W

ˈ**water-power** *n* [U] power obtained from flowing or falling water, used to drive machinery or generate electric current 水力.

ˈ**waterproof** *adj* that cannot be penetrated by water 不透水的; 防水的: *waterproof fabric* 防水织物. — *n* garment made from waterproof fabric, esp a raincoat 用防水织物制成的衣服; (尤指)雨衣. — *v* [Tn] make (sth) waterproof 使(某物)防水.

ˈ**water-rat** *n* rat-like animal that swims in water and lives in a hole beside a river, lake, etc 水鼠.

ˈ**water-rate** *n* (*Brit*) charge made for the use of water from a public water-supply (自来)水费.

ˈ**watershed** *n* (**a**) line of high land where streams on one side flow into one river or sea and streams on the other side flow into a different river or sea 分水线; 分水岭. (**b**) (*fig* 比喻) turning-point in a course of events 事情发展中的转折点: *Her visit to India proved to be a watershed in her life.* 她的印度之行成了她一生的转折点.

ˈ**waterside** *n* [sing] edge of a river, lake or sea 河边; 湖畔; 海滨: *stroll along the waterside* 沿水边散步 ○ [attrib 作定语] *a waterside housing development* 沿海滨兴建新住宅.

ˈ**water-ski** *n* (*pl* **-skis**) (usu *pl* 通常作复数) either of a pair of flat boards on which a person stands in order to ski on water 滑水橇: *a pair of water-skis* 一副滑水橇.

ˈ**water-skiing** *n* [U] sport of skiing on water while being towed along at speed by a fast motor boat 水橇运动(由摩托艇牵引运动员在水面上踏橇滑行的运动).

ˈ**water-softener** *n* [C, U] device or substance that softens hard water 硬水软化器; 软水剂.

ˈ**waterspout** *n* funnel-shaped column of water between the sea and the clouds, formed when a whirlwind draws up a whirling mass of water 水龙卷.

ˈ**water-supply** *n* (usu *sing* 通常作单数) (**a**) system of providing and storing water 给水(系统). (**b**) amount of water stored for a town, district, building, etc (城镇、地区、建筑物等的)存水量.

ˈ**water-table** *n* level below which the ground is saturated with water 地下水位: *The water-table has been lowered by drought.* 地下水位因干旱已降低.

ˈ**watertight** *adj* **1** made or fastened so that water cannot get in or out 防止水进入或流出的; 水密的: *a watertight compartment, joint, seal* 水密室、水密接合、水密封. **2** (*fig* 比喻) (**a**) (of an excuse or alibi) impossible to disprove (指借口或不在犯罪现场的申辩)无懈可击的. (**b**) (of an agreement) drawn up so that there is no chance of anyone misunderstanding or avoiding any part of it (指协议)严密的, 无漏洞的.

ˈ**water-tower** *n* tower that holds a water-tank at a height that ensures enough pressure for distributing a water-supply (自来)水塔.

ˈ**waterway** *n* route for travel by water (eg a canal or channel in a river where the water is deep enough for ships) 水路; 航道.

ˈ**water-wheel** *n* wheel turned by a flow of water, used to work machinery 水轮.

ˈ**water-wings** *n* [pl] pair of floats worn on the shoulders by a person who is learning to swim 水翼(学游泳的人套在双肩上的浮袋).

ˈ**waterworks** *n* **1** [sing or pl *v*] building with pumping machinery, etc for supplying water to a district 自来水厂. **2** [pl] (*infml euph* 口, 婉) (functioning of) the body's urinary system 人体泌尿系统(的功能): *Are your waterworks all right?* 你泌尿系统正常吗? **3** (idm 习语) **turn on the ˈwaterworks** (*infml derog* 口, 贬) (start to) cry 哭起来.

NOTE ON USAGE 用法: When water is **heated** to 100 degrees Celsius, it **boils** and becomes **steam**. 水加热(**heat**)到100摄氏度时, 沸腾(**boil**)变成水蒸气(**steam**). ☆ When steam touches a cold surface, it **condenses** and becomes water again. 水蒸气接触到冷的物体表面时, 凝结(**condense**)又变成水. When water is **cooled** below 0 degrees Celsius, it **freezes** and becomes **ice**. 水冷却(**cool**)到0摄氏度以下时, 冻结(**freeze**)成冰(**ice**). ☆ If the temperature increases, the ice **melts**. 温度上升时, 冰就融化(**melt**). ☆ When talking about **frozen** food or **icy** weather becoming warmer, we say it **thaws**. 冷冻的(**frozen**)食物或冰冷的(**icy**)天气变暖时, 称为解冻(**thaw**). ☆ Frozen food **thaws** or **defrosts** when we take it out of the freezer. 冷冻的食物从冷藏室取出解冻, 用 **thaw** 或 **defrost** 均可.

water[2] /ˈwɔːtə(r); ˈwɔtɚ/ *v* **1** [Tn] pour or sprinkle water on (sth) 在(某物)上浇水或洒水: *water a flowerbed, lawn, plant* 用水浇花坛、草地、植物. **2** [Tn] give water to (an animal) to drink 给(动物)水喝: *water the horses* 饮马. **3** [Tn] add water to (a drink) to dilute it 在(饮料)中加水冲淡: *The owner of the pub was accused of watering the beer.* 有人指责酒店老板在啤酒里搀水. **4** [I] (of the eyes) become full of tears or (of the mouth) produce saliva (指眼睛)充满眼泪; (指嘴)流口水: *The smoke made my eyes water.* 烟熏得我眼睛直流泪. ○ *The delicious smell from the kitchen made our mouths water.* 我们闻到厨房里的香味直流口水. **5** [Tn usu passive 通常用于被动语态] (esp of rivers) flow through (an area of land) and provide it with water (尤指河流)流经(某地区)(供水或灌溉): *a country watered by numerous rivers* 有众多河流水源充足的国家. **6** (phr v) **water sth down** (**a**) make (a liquid) weaker by adding water; dilute sth 加水冲淡(某液体); 稀释: *The milk had been* *watered down.* 那牛奶已经搀过水了. ○ *You have to water down the medicine before drinking it.* 你得把这种药加水稀释后再服用. (**b**) weaken the effect of sth, eg by making the details less vivid 减弱某事物的作用: *The criticisms had been watered down so as not to offend anybody.* 这些批评意见已修改得缓和些以免得罪人. ○ *They gave the press a watered-down version of what really happened.* 他们向新闻界提供的情况是经过删减的.

□ ˌ**watered** ˈ**silk** silk fabric that has a glossy surface with irregular wavy markings on it 波纹绸.

watering-can /ˈwɔːtərɪŋ kæn; ˈwɔtərɪŋ ˌkæn/ *n* container with a long spout, used for watering plants 喷壶; 洒水壶.

watering-place /ˈwɔːtərɪŋ pleɪs; ˈwɔtərɪŋ ˌples/ *n* (**a**) pool where animals go to drink; water-hole 动物饮水的水池; 水坑. (**b**) (*dated* 旧 *esp Brit*) spa or seaside resort 矿泉疗养地; 海滨度假胜地: *one of the favourite watering-places of the Victorians* 维多利亚时代的人最喜欢去的一个矿泉疗养地.

Wa·ter·loo /ˌwɔːtəˈluː; ˌwɔtɚˈlu/ *n* (idm 习语) **meet one's Waterloo** ⇨ MEET[1].

wa·tery /ˈwɔːtərɪ; ˈwɔtərɪ/ *adj* **1** (**a**) of or like water (似)水的: *a watery consistency* 稀薄似水的浓度 ○ (*fig* 比喻) *a watery grave*, ie death by drowning 溺毙. (**b**) (*usu derog* 通常作贬义) containing or cooked in too much water 含水过多的; (烹饪时)加水过多的: *watery coffee, soup, cabbage* 加水过多的咖啡、汤、洋白菜. **2** (of colours) pale (指颜色)淡的. **3** (**a**) full of moisture 潮湿的; 湿润的: *watery eyes* 水汪汪的眼睛 ○ *a watery* (ie weak and tearful) *smile* 含泪的微笑. (**b**) suggesting that there will be rain 有雨意的; 预兆下雨的: *a watery moon, sun, sky* 预兆要下雨的月光、阳光、天空.

watt /wɒt; wɑt/ *n* unit of electrical power 瓦, 瓦特(电功率单位): [attrib 作定语] *a 60-watt light-bulb* 60瓦的灯泡.

▷ **watt·age** /ˈwɒtɪdʒ; ˈwɑtɪdʒ/ *n* [U] amount of electrical power, expressed in watts 瓦特数; 瓦数: *a heater that runs on a very low wattage* 瓦数很低的加热器.

wattle[1] /ˈwɒtl; ˈwɑtl̩/ *n* **1** [U] structure of sticks or twigs woven under and over thicker upright sticks, used for fences, walls, etc 编条结构(用作篱笆、围墙等). **2** [C, U] any of several types of Australian acacia with long pliant branches and golden flowers (澳洲产的)金合欢树.

□ ˌ**wattle and** ˈ**daub** wattle[1](1) covered with mud or clay and used, esp formerly, as a building-material for walls and roofs 泥笆墙(尤指旧时的).

wattle[2] /ˈwɒtl; ˈwɑtl̩/ *n* red fleshy fold of skin that hangs down from the head or throat of a bird, eg a turkey (禽类, 如火鸡的)(头部的)皮瘤, (喉部的)肉垂.

wave[1] /weɪv; wev/ *v* **1** [I] (of a fixed object) move regularly and loosely to and fro or up and down (指固定的物体)往复或上下摆动或摇动: *a flag waving in the breeze* 在微风中飘扬的旗子 ○ *branches waving in the wind* 随风摇动的树枝 ○ *a field of waving corn* 起伏的麦浪. **2** (**a**) [I, Ipr] ~ (**at/to sb**) (of a person) move one's hand to and fro or up and down, eg in order to attract sb's attention (指人)挥手, 招手, 摆手: *He waved (to us) when he saw us.* 他看见我们时(向我们)挥了挥手. ○ *They waved at us from across the room.* 他们从房间那一头向我们招手. (**b**) [Tn, Tn·pr, Tn·p, Dpr·t] ~ **sth (at sb)**; ~ **sth about** cause (one's hand or sth held in one's hand) to move up and down or to and fro, eg in order to make a signal or give a greeting 挥动(手或手中物)(如为示意或致意): *wave a magic wand* 挥动魔杖 ○ *wave a hand, a flag, an umbrella (at sb)* (向某人)招手、摇旗子、挥动伞 ○ *He came out waving the document at the crowd.* 他出来时向人群挥舞着文件. ○ *wave one's arms (about) (in the air)* 挥舞着双臂 ○ *They waved to us to stay where we were.* 他们向我们挥手, 要我们停在原地. (**c**) [Tn, Dn·n, Dn·pr] ~ **sth (to sb)** give (a greeting) (to sb) by waving one's hand 挥手(向某人)(致意): *They waved farewell.* 他们挥手告别. ○ *wave sb goodbye/wave goodbye to sb* 向某人挥手告别. **3** [I, Tn] (cause sth to) form a series of curves (使某物)呈波形: *Her hair waves beautifully.* 她的鬈发很漂亮. ○ *She has had her hair waved.* 她烫发了. **4** (idm 习语) **fly/show/wave the** ˈ**flag** ⇨ FLAG[1]. **5** (phr v) **wave sb/sth along, away, on, etc** show that (a person or vehicle) should move in the specified direction, by waving one's hand 向(某人或车)挥手示意向某方向移动: *She waved them away impatiently.* 她不耐烦地挥手让他们走开. ○ *The policeman waved us on*, ie indicated that we should continue. 警察挥手让我们继续前进. **wave sth aside** dismiss (an objection, etc) as unimportant or irrelevant 不理会(反对意见等): *Their criticisms were waved aside.* 他们提出的批评意见没人理会. **wave sth/sb down** signal to (a vehicle or its driver) to stop, by waving one's hand 挥手示意让(车或司机)停下来.

wave[2] /weɪv; wev/ *n* **1** [C] (**a**) ridge of water, esp on the sea, between two hollows (波浪, 尤指海浪的)浪头: *The storm whipped up huge waves.* 暴风雨掀起了巨浪. (**b**) long ridge of water in the sea, etc that rises up in an arch and breaks on the shore (海面涌起的拍岸的)大波浪, 波涛: *waves crashing onto the beach* 拍打着海滩的大浪. ⇨illus at SURF 见SURF插图. (**c**) thing that is similar to this in appearance or movement, eg an advancing group of attackers 形状或运动像波浪的事物(如向前推进的进攻者): *the next wave of assault troops* 进攻部队像另一个浪头般涌来 ○ *It was not long before their peace was disturbed by the next wave of visitors.* 他们还没消停多久就又来了一批来访者. **2 the waves** [pl] (*fml* 文) the sea 海. **3** [C] act or gesture of waving 挥手; 招手; 摆手: *He greeted them with a wave.* 他挥手向他们致意. ○ *The magician made the rabbit disappear with a wave of his wand.* 魔术师把魔杖一挥, 兔子就不见了. **4** [C] (**a**) curve or arrangement of curves, like a wave or waves in the sea, eg in a line or in hair 波纹(如波状线或拳曲的毛发): *The child's hair grew in pretty waves.* 那个孩子长着的鬈发很好看. ○ *Her hair has a natural wave.* 她天生鬈发. (**b**) special treatment of the hair to give it these curves 烫发: *a permanent wave* 烫成的拳曲的头发. **5** [C] sudden, usu temporary, increase (and spread) of sth 突然的(通常指短暂的)增加(和传播): *a wave of anger, enthusiasm, hysteria, sympathy, etc* 突然表现出的愤怒、热情、歇斯底里、同情心等 ○ *a* ˈ*crime wave* 罪案的激增 ○ *a* ˈ*heatwave* 热浪. **6** [C] (**a**) wave-like motion by which heat, light, sound, magnetism, electricity, etc is spread or carried (热、光、声、磁、电等的)波状运动: *radio waves* 无线电波. (**b**) single curve in the course of this (波状运动中的)波. **7** [C] (*physics* 物) variation of an electromagnetic field as radiation is propagated through a medium or vacuum 电磁波. **8** (idm 习语) **in** ˈ**waves** in groups or at regular intervals 一批一批; 一阵一阵: *The disturbances seem to occur in waves.* 这种骚扰似乎是一阵一阵的. ○ *Invaders entered the country in waves.* 入侵者一批又一批地侵入这个国家. **on the crest of a wave** ⇨ CREST.

▷ **wave·let** /ˈweɪvlɪt; ˈwevlɪt/ *n* small wave of water 小波浪; 涟漪.

wavy *adj* (**-ier, -iest**) having curves like the waves of the sea 波状的; 波浪形的; 波纹的: *a wavy line* 波状线 ○ *wavy hair* 鬈发. **wa·vily** *adv*. **wa·vi·ness** *n* [U].

wave·band /ˈweɪvbænd; ˈwevbænd/ *n* = BAND 4.

wave·length /ˈweɪvleŋθ; ˈwevˌlɛŋθ/ *n* **1** distance between the corresponding points in a sound wave or an electromagnetic wave 波长. **2** length of the radio wave that a particular radio station uses to broadcast its programmes 波段. **3** (idm 习语) **on the same wavelength** ⇨ SAME[1].

waver /ˈweɪvə(r); ˈwevɚ/ *v* **1** [I] be or become weak or unsteady; falter 减弱; 动摇; 犹豫: *His courage never wavered.* 他的勇气从未减弱. ○ *Her steady gaze did not waver.* 她目不转睛地注视着. ○ *They did not waver in their support for him.* 他们毫不动摇地支持他. **2** [I, Ipr] ~ (**between sth and sth**) hesitate, esp about making a decision or choice; dither 犹豫不决; 踌躇: *While we were wavering, somebody else bought the house.* 就在我们犹豫不决的时候, 别人把那所房子买下了. ○ *waver between two points of view* 在两种观点之间摇摆不定. **3** [I] (esp of light) move unsteadily; flicker (尤指光线)摇曳, 闪烁. ▷ **wa·verer** /ˈweɪvərə(r); ˈwevərɚ/ *n*: *The strength of his argument convinced the last few waverers.* 他用有力的论点把剩下的几个犹豫不决的人也说服了. **wa·ver·ingly** /ˈweɪvərɪŋlɪ; ˈwevərɪŋlɪ/ *adv*.

wax[1] /wæks; wæks/ *n* [U] **1** (also ˈ**beeswax**) (**a**) soft sticky yellow substance produced by bees and used by them for making honeycombs 蜂蜡. (**b**) this substance

W

used, after being bleached and purified, for making candles, modelling, etc (从蜂蜡提纯的)蜡(用以制蜡烛、蜡像等). **2** any of various soft sticky or oily substances that melt easily (obtained eg from petroleum), used for making candles, polish, etc (从其他物质, 如石油提炼的)蜡(用以制蜡烛、上光剂等): *paraffin wax* 石蜡 ○ *sealing wax* 封蜡 ○ [attrib 作定语] *a wax candle* 蜡烛 ○ *wax polish* 上光蜡. **3** yellow substance like wax that is secreted in the ears 耳垢; 耵聍; 耳屎.

▷ **wax** *v* [Tn] **(a)** polish (sth) with wax 给(某物)上蜡: *waxed floors, linoleum, wood* 打过蜡的地板、油地毡、木头. **(b)** coat (sth) with wax 用蜡涂(某物): *waxed paper, thread* 上过蜡的纸、线.

waxen /ˈwæksn; ˋwæksn/ *adj* (*fml* 文) smooth or pale like wax 像蜡般光滑的或苍白的: *a waxen complexion* 蜡白的脸色.

waxy *adj* having a surface or texture like wax 表面或质地似蜡的: *waxy skin* 光滑如蜡的皮肤 ○ *waxy potatoes* 光洁如蜡的土豆. **waxi·ness** *n* [U].

□ ˈ**waxwork** *n* **(a)** [C] object modelled in wax, esp the form of a human being with face and hands in wax, coloured and clothed to look lifelike 蜡制雕塑品; (尤指)蜡人, 蜡像. **(b)** ˈ**waxworks** [sing or pl *v*] place where lifelike wax models of famous people are shown to the public 蜡像馆: *take the children to the waxworks* 带孩子去参观蜡像馆.

wax[2] /wæks; wæks/ *v* **1** [I] (of the moon) show a large bright area that gradually increases until the moon is full (指月亮)渐圆, 渐满. Cf 参看 WANE 1. **2** [La] (*dated or rhet* 旧或修辞) become; grow (逐渐)变成: *wax eloquent, lyrical, etc on the subject* 对这个问题畅谈起来、兴趣大增等. **3** (idm 习语) ˌ**wax and** ˈ**wane** increase and then decrease in strength or importance (力量或重要性)兴衰, 盛衰: *Throughout history empires have waxed and waned.* 历史上各个帝国革故鼎新均有兴衰.

way[1] /weɪ; we/ *n* **1** [C] (often in compounds 常用以构成复合词) **(a)** place for walking, travelling, etc along; path, road, street, etc 路; 道; 街; 径: *a way across the fields* 穿过田地的路 ○ *a covered* (ie roofed) *way* 有顶盖的路 ○ *across/over the way*, ie across/over the road 穿过这条路 ○ *a* ˈ*highway* 公路 ○ *the* ˈ*highways and* ˈ*byways*, ie main and minor roads 大路和小路 ○ *a* ˈ*waterway* 水路 ○ *a* ˈ*railway* 铁路. **(b) Way** name of certain roads or streets 路或街道的名称: *the Appian Way* 阿皮安路. **2** [C usu *sing* 通常作单数] **(a) ~ (from…) (to…)** route, road, etc (to be) taken in order to reach a place 路线: *the best, quickest, right,* ˈ*shortest, etc way from A to B* 从A地到B地的最好的、最快的、正确的、最近的…路线 ○ *Which way do you usually go to town?* 你进城一般走哪条路线? ○ *find one's way home* 找到回家的路 ○ *tell sb the way* 为某人指路 ○ *He asked me the way* (ie the best way) *to London.* 他问我去伦敦走哪条路最好. ○ *the way down, in, out, up, etc* 下去的、进去的、出去的、上去的…路 ○ (*fig* 比喻) *find a way out of one's difficulty* 找出摆脱困境之路 ○ (*fig* 比喻) *argue, bluff, talk, trick, etc one's way into, out of, etc sth*, ie enter, escape, etc by arguing, etc 用争论、吓唬、谈话、哄骗等方法进入或逃出 ○ (*fig* 比喻) *fight, force, shoot, etc one's way across, into, etc sth*, ie cross, enter, etc sth by fighting, etc 用打斗、武力、射击等手段穿过、进入…某处. **(b)** route along which sb/sth is moving or would move if there was space 行进的路线或通路: *cut a way through the undergrowth* 在下层灌丛中开出一条路来 ○ *We had to pick our way along the muddy track.* 我们须在泥泞小道上择路而行. ○ *There was a lorry blocking the way.* 有一辆卡车挡住了路. ○ *Get out of my way!* 别挡着我的路! **(c)** (in phrases after *which, this, that,* etc 用于which、this、that等之后, 构成短语) (in a specified) direction (沿某)方向: *'Which way did he go?' 'He went that way.'* '他往哪边去了?' '他往那边去了.' ○ *Look this way, please.* 请往这边看. ○ *Kindly step this way, ladies and gentlemen.* 女士们、先生们, 请往这边走. ○ *Look both ways* (ie to right and left) *before crossing the road.* 过马路前先要向两边看一看. ○ *They weren't looking our way*, ie towards us. 他们没朝我们这边看. ○ *Make sure that the sign's the right way up.* 一定要把符号的上下弄对. ○ *The arrow is pointing the wrong way.* 这个箭头指错了方向. ○ *If the tree falls that way, it will destroy the house.* 这棵树向那边倒下就会把那所房子压坏. ○ (*fig* 比喻) *Which way* (ie For which party) *will you vote?* 你投哪边(哪个党)的票? **3** [C] **(a)** (usu *sing* 通常作单数) method, style or manner of doing sth (做某事的)方法, 方式, 手段: *What is the best way to clean this?* 用什么办法能把这个弄干净? ○ *She showed them the way to do it.* 她向他们示范做这件事的方法. ○ *the best, right, wrong, etc way to do sth* 做某事的最好的、正确的、错误的…方法 ○ *I like the way you've done your hair.* 我喜欢你头发的样式. ○ *There are several ways of doing it.* 做这件事有好几种方法. ○ *a new way of storing information* 储存信息的新方法 ○ *You can see the way his mind works when you read his books.* 看他写的书就能了解他的思想方法. ○ *She spoke in a kindly way.* 她说话态度很和蔼. **(b)** (after *my, his, her,* etc 用于my、his、her等之后) course of action desired or chosen by sb (按照)某人想要的或选择的方式方法: *She'll do it* ˈ*her way whatever you suggest.* 你说出大天来她有她一定之规. ○ *We all have our favourite ways of doing certain things.* 我们做某些事都有自己爱用的办法. ○ *I still think* ˈ*my way is better!* 我仍然认为我的方法好! ○ *Try to find your* ˈ*own way to express the idea.* 尽量用你自己的语言来表达这个意见. **(c)** chosen, desired or habitual behaviour; custom or manner 独异的、喜爱的或习惯的行为; 习俗; 作风: *He has some rather odd ways.* 他有些怪招. ○ *Don't be offended, it's only his* ˈ*way*, ie manner of behaving that has no special significance. 不要介意, 他就是这么个人. ○ *It is not her* ˈ*way to be selfish*, ie She is not selfish by nature. 她并不是个自私的人. ○ *I don't like the way* (ie manner in which) *he looks at me.* 我不喜欢他那种样子看着我. ○ *It's disgraceful the way he treats his mother.* 他那样对待他母亲太不像话了. ○ *a fashionable way of dressing* 穿着时髦 ○ *They admired the way she dealt with the crisis.* 他们很佩服她处理这场危机的手法. **4** [sing] (esp after *long, little,* etc 尤用于long、little等之后) distance (to be travelled) between two points 两点间的距离: *It's a long way to London.* 从这里到伦敦很远. ○ *We are a long way from the coast.* 我们距离海边很远. ○ *There is quite a way still to go.* 还要走很长的路. ○ *The roots go a long way down.* 这些根扎得很深. ○ (*fig* 比喻) *December is a long way off/away*, ie in the future, from now. 现在离十二月份还有很长的时间. ○ *Success is still a long way off.* 离成功还远着呢. ○ *better by a long way*, ie much better 好得多了. **5** [sing] (*infml* 口) area near a place; neighbourhood 附近; 周围: *He lives somewhere* ˈ*Lincoln way.* 他住在林肯市附近. ○ *The crops are doing well down* ˈ*our way*, ie in our part of the country. 我们这一带的作物长势良好. ○ *Please visit us next time you're over this way.* 你下次到这一带来时请到我们家作客. **6** [C] particular aspect of sth; respect (某事物的)某方面: *Can I help you in any way?* 我能帮你点儿忙吗? ○ *She is in no way* (ie not at all) *to blame.* 根本不应该怪她. ○ *The changes are beneficial in some ways but not in others.* 这些变革有的方面有好处, 有的方面没好处. ○ *She helped us in every possible way.* 她帮助我们无微不至. **7** (idm 习语) ˌ**all the** ˈ**way** the whole distance 一路上. ˈ**be/be** ˈ**born/be** ˈ**made that way** (*infml* 口) (of a person) be as one is because of innate characteristics (指人)性格天生如此: *I'm afraid that's just the way he* ˈ*is.* 没法子, 他天生就是这么一种人. **be** ˌ**set in one's** ˈ**ways** be inflexible in one's habits, attitudes, etc (习惯、态度等)固定而不变通. **both** ˈ**ways/each** ˈ**way** (of money bet on a horse, race, etc) so that one will win money back if the horse, etc either wins or gains second or third place (指赛马等下的赌注)该马等获第一名或二三名均可赢钱: *have £5 each way on the favourite* 在大热门上投注5英镑压它赢前三名 ○ *back the favourite both ways* 压大热门赢前三名. **by the** ˈ**way (a)** by the roadside during a journey 在途中的路边上: *stopped for a picnic by the way* 在途中停在路边野餐. **(b)** (used to introduce a comment or question that is only indirectly related, if at all, to the main subject of conversation 在主要话题或交谈中用以插入题外的话或问题): *Oh, by the way, there is a telephone message for you.* 噢, 对了, 有你一个电话口信. ○ *What did you say your name was, by the way?* 顺便问一句, 您说您的名字叫什么来着? **by way of (a)** (*fml* 文) by a route that includes (the place mentioned); via 路经(某处); 途经: *They are travelling to France by way of London.* 他们经伦敦去法国. **(b)** as a type of (sth) or serving as (sth) 作为; 当作: *Let's eat out*

W

tonight, by way of a change. 咱们今天晚上到外面去吃饭吧，换换口味. ○ *What are you thinking of doing by way of a holiday this year?* 今年的假期你打算怎么过？○ *By way of an introduction, I shall explain some of the historical background.* 作为开场白，我来解释一下历史背景. (c) with the intention of or for the purpose of (doing sth) 意在或为了(做某事): *make enquiries by way of learning the facts of the case* 为了解实情作调查. **change one's ways** ⇨ CHANGE. **come one's 'way** occur or present itself to one 发生于或来到某人处: *An opportunity like that doesn't often come my way.* 这样的机会可不常落在我头上. **cut both/two 'ways** (of an action, argument, etc) have an effect both for and against sth (指行动、论点等)有利也有弊. **divide, split, etc, sth two, three, etc 'ways** share sth among two, three, etc people 在两个、三个…人之间分配. **each way** ⇨ BOTH WAYS. **the error of one's/sb's ways** ⇨ ERROR. **feel one's way** ⇨ FEEL[1]. **find one's way; find its way to ...** ⇨ FIND[1]. **get into/out of the way of (doing) sth** acquire/lose the habit of doing sth 培养[失去]做某事的习惯. **get/have one's own 'way** get or do what one wants, often in spite of opposition 为所欲为(常指不顾反对意见): *She always gets her own way in the end.* 到头来总是她想怎样就怎样. **give 'way** break or collapse 断裂；倒塌: *The bridge gave way under the weight of the lorry.* 卡车过重把这座桥压坏了. ○ *Her legs suddenly gave way and she fell to the floor.* 她两腿突然支持不住摔倒在地板上了. **give way (to sb/sth)** (a) allow sb/sth to be first; yield 让某人[某事物]在先；让出；放弃: *Give way to traffic coming from the right.* 让右方驶来的车辆先行. (b) let oneself be overcome (by sth) 被(某事物)制服: *give way to despair* 陷于绝望. (c) make concessions (to sb/sth) (向某人[某事物])让步，妥协: *We must not give way to their demands.* 我们决不能对他们的要求让步. **give way to sth** be replaced by sth 被某事物代替: *The storm gave way to bright sunshine.* 暴风雨过后出现了灿烂的阳光. **go far/a long way** ⇨ FAR[2]. **go far/a long way to do sth/towards sth** ⇨ FAR[2]. **go out of one's 'way (to do sth)** take particular care and trouble to do sth 特意不怕麻烦做某事: *The shop assistant went out of his way to find what we needed.* 那个店员不厌其烦地满足我们的需要. **go one's own 'way** act independently or as one chooses, esp against the advice of others 独立地或按自己的意愿行事(尤指不听人劝): *Whatever you suggest, she will always go her own way.* 无论怎样劝说，她也总是我行我素. **go one's way** (*dated* 旧) depart 离开；出发. **go sb's way** (a) travel in the same direction as sb 与某人同路: *I'm going your way so I can give you a lift.* 我和你同路，可以顺便开车送你. (b) (of events, etc) be favourable to sb (指事情等)对某人有利: *Things certainly seem to be going our way.* 看来事情确实对我们有利. **go the way of all 'flesh** (*saying* 谚) (live and) die as other people do; suffer the same changes, dangers, etc as other people 像别人一样(生与)死；和他人一样经受变革、危险等. **the hard way** ⇨ HARD[1]. **have come a long way** ⇨ LONG[1]. **have/want it/things 'both ways** ⇨ BOTH[1]. **have it/things/everything one's 'own way** have what one wants, esp by imposing one's will on others 为所欲为(尤指把自己的意愿强加于人): *All right, have it your own way — I'm tired of arguing.* 好了，随你的便吧——我懒得和你争了. **have a 'way with one** have the power to attract or persuade others 有吸引人或说服人的能力. **have a way with sb/sth** have a particular talent for dealing with sb/sth 专门善于同某人[某事物]打交道: *have a way with difficult children* 专门能对付不听话的孩子 ○ *have a way with motor bikes* 很会修理摩托车. **in a bad 'way** (a) very ill or in serious trouble 病得很重；情形很糟. (b) (*infml* 口) obviously drunk 烂醉如泥. **in a 'big/'small way** on a large/small scale 大[小]规模: *He's got himself into trouble in a big way.* 他可惹了大麻烦了. ○ *She collects antiques in a small way.* 她收集少许古玩. **in a fair way to do sth** ⇨ FAIR[1]. **in the family way** ⇨ FAMILY. **ˌin more ways than 'one** (used to draw attention to the fact that the statement made has more than one meaning 用以指出所说的事实尚有其他含义): *He's a big man — in more ways than one.* 他是个了不起的人——在很多方面. **in a 'way; in 'one way; in 'some ways** to a certain extent but not entirely 在某种程度上: *The changes are an improvement in one way.* 这些变从某种意义上说是一种进步. **in the ordinary way** ⇨ ORDINARY. **in one's own sweet way** ⇨ SWEET[1]. **in the 'way** causing inconvenience or an obstruction 造成不便或阻碍: *I'm afraid your car is in the way.* 看来你的汽车挡着道了. ○ *I left them alone, as I felt I was in the way.* 我躲开了他们，因为我觉得我碍他们的事. **know one's way around** ⇨ KNOW. **lead the way** ⇨ LEAD[3]. **look the other 'way** avoid seeing sb/sth, deliberately or by chance (避而)不看某人[某物]: *The usherette looked the other way so that the children could get into the cinema without paying.* 那个女检票员扭过脸去好让那些孩子不买票就进电影院里. **lose one's way** ⇨ LOSE. **make one's way (to/towards sth)** go 走；行走；前进: *I'll make my way home now.* 我现在要回家了. ○ *make one's way* (ie succeed) *in life* 在生活中有所成就. **make 'way (for sb/sth)** allow (sb/sth) to pass 让(某人[某事物])通过；给(某人[某事物])让路. **mend one's ways** ⇨ MEND. **not know where/which way to look** ⇨ KNOW. **(there are) no two ways a'bout it** (*saying* 谚) there is only one correct or suitable way to act, speak or think with regard to sth 对于某事物只有一种正确的或合适的方法来做、说或思考；别无他途. **ˌno 'way** (*infml* 口) under no circumstances or by no means (will sth happen/be done) 决不: *Give up our tea break? No way!* 让我们放弃工间休息时间？没门儿！○ *No way will I go on working for that man.* 我不再给那个人工作了. **ˌone way and aˈnother** considering various aspects of the matter together 考虑到各个方面: *She's been very successful, one way and another.* 无论从哪方面看，她都是很有成就的. **ˌone way or aˈnother** by some means, methods, etc 用某种方式、方法等: *We must finish the job this week one way or another.* 我们无论如何必须在本周做完这项工作. **on one's/the 'way** in the process of going or coming 在来或去的行进中；在路上: *I had better be on my way* (ie leave) *soon.* 我最好早点走. ○ *I'll buy some bread on the/my way home.* 我要在回家的路上买些面包. **on the 'way** (*infml* 口) (of a baby) conceived but not yet born (指婴儿)已成胎但尚未出生: *She has two children with another one on the way.* 她有两个孩子，现在还怀着一个. **on the way 'out** (a) in the process of leaving 正在离开: *I bumped into him on the way out.* 我正出门的时候碰上他了. (b) (*fig* 比喻) going out of fashion or favour; becoming obsolete 即将不流行或不受喜爱；渐渐过时或淘汰. **the ˌother way 'round** (a) reversed or inverted 颠倒；相反；反过来. (b) the opposite of what is expected or supposed 与料想的或以为的相反: *I was accused of stealing money from her but in fact it was the other way round.* 说我偷了她的钱，其实正相反是她偷了我的钱. **out of harm's way** ⇨ HARM *n*. **ˌout of the 'way** (a) far from a town or city; remote 远离城镇；偏远: [attrib 作定语] *a tiny ˌout-of-the-way 'village in Cornwall* 康沃尔郡的一个偏僻的小村庄. (b) exceptional; uncommon 异常的；罕见的；不普通的: *He has done nothing out of the way yet.* 他倒还没干出离谱的事. **a/the parting of the ways** ⇨ PARTING. **pave the way for sth** ⇨ PAVE. **pay one's/its way** ⇨ PAY[2]. **point the way** ⇨ POINT[2]. **put sb in the way of (doing) sth** make it possible for sb to do sth or give sb an opportunity to do sth 使某人有可能做某事；给某人做某事的机会. **rub sb up the wrong way** ⇨ RUB[1]. **see one's way (clear) to doing sth** find that it is possible or convenient to do sth 觉得可能或便于做某事: *I can't see my way clear to finishing the work this year.* 我看我今年做不完这项工作. ○ *Could you see your way to lending me £10 for a couple of days?* 你能不能借给我10英镑过两天还你？**see which way the wind is blowing** see what is likely to happen 观察将要发生什么事情. **show the way** ⇨ SHOW[2]. **(not) stand in sb's 'way** (not) prevent sb from doing sth (不)阻止某人做某事: *If you want to study medicine, we won't stand in your way.* 你要是想学医我们决不拦你. **take the easy way out** ⇨ EASY[1]. **ˌthat's the ˌway the ˌcookie 'crumbles** (*infml* 口 *esp US*) that is the state of things and nothing can be done about it 事情就是这样，没有别的办法. **to 'my way of thinking** in my opinion 我认为；依我看. **under 'way** having started and making progress 已经开始并进行着: *The project is now well under way.* 这一项目现正顺利进行. ○ *be/get under way*, ie (esp of a ship) move/start to move through the water (尤指船)在航行中[启航]. **wait for the cat to jump/to see which way the cat jumps** ⇨ WAIT[1]. **a/sb's way of ˈlife** normal pattern of social or working life of a person or group (某人的或某些人的)生活方式: *She adapted easily to the French way of life.* 她很容易就适应了法国人的生活方式. **the ˌway of the ˈworld** what many people do, how they behave, etc 大家都(这样)做的事. **ˌways and ˈmeans** methods and resources for doing sth, esp providing money (做某事的)方法和资源; (尤指)财源. **where there's a will, there's a way** ⇨ WILL[4]. **ˌwork one's ˈway (through college, etc)** have a paid job while one is a student 边挣钱边求学; 半工半读: *She had to work her way through law school.* 她须半工半读学习法律. **work one's way through sth** read or do sth from beginning to end 从头到尾阅读或做某事: *The board are still working their way through the application forms.* 委员会仍在审阅全部申请表. **ˌwork one's way ˈup** be promoted from a low grade to a high one 获提升; 晋级: *He has worked his way up from junior clerk to managing director.* 他已从初级职员升到总经理.

□ **ˈway-bill** *n* list of goods or passengers carried by a vehicle, with their destinations 运货单, 乘客名单(附到达地点).

ˈwayfarer /-feərə(r); -ˌferɚ/ *n* (*fml* 文) traveller, esp on foot 行路的人(尤指徒步的). **ˈwayfaring** /-feərɪŋ; -ˌferɪŋ/ *adj* [attrib 作定语] (*fml* 文) travelling 行路的: *a wayfaring man* 行路的男子.

ˈwayside *n* (usu *sing* 通常作单数) **1** (land at the) side of a road or path 路旁(的地方): [attrib 作定语] *wayside flowers* 路旁的花. **2** (idm 习语) **fall by the ˈwayside** (*euph* 婉) fail to make progress in life; slip into dishonest ways 未能在生活中取得成就; 步入歧途.

way[2] /weɪ; we/ *adv* (*infml* 口) **1** (used with a *prep* or an *adv* and usu not negatively 与介词或副词连用, 通常不用于否定句) very far 很远: *She finished the race way ahead of the other runners.* 她第一个跑到终点, 远远领先于其他选手. ○ *The shot was way off target.* 这次射得远离目标. ○ *The price is way above what we can afford.* 价格高得我们绝对付不起. ○ *The initial estimate was way out*, ie very inaccurate. 最初的估计差得很远. **2** (idm 习语) **ˈway back** a long time ago 很久以前: *I first met him way back in the ˈfifties.* 我和他初次见面是早在一九五几年的事.

□ **ˌway-ˈout** *adj* (*infml* 口) exaggeratedly unusual or strange in style; eccentric or exotic (风格或式样)极不寻常的, 离奇的; 古怪的; 奇特的: *ˌway-out ˈclothes, ˈfashions, iˈdeas, ˈmusic, ˈpoetry* 稀奇古怪的衣物、样式、想法、音乐、诗歌.

way·lay /ˌweɪˈleɪ; ˌweˈle/ *v* (*pt, pp* **waylaid** /-ˈleɪd; -ˈled/) [Tn] wait for and stop (sb who is passing), esp in order to rob him or to ask him for sth 等着拦截(经过的某人)(尤指为抢劫或要求某事物): *The patrol was waylaid by bandits.* 巡逻队遭到土匪伏击. ○ *He waylaid me with a request for a loan.* 他等我经过时拦住我向我借钱.

-ways *suff* 后缀 (with *ns* forming *adjs* and *advs* 与名词结合构成形容词和副词) in the specified direction 沿某方向: *lengthways* ○ *sideways*.

way·ward /ˈweɪwəd; ˈwewɚd/ *adj* not easily controlled or guided; childishly headstrong or capricious 不易管教的; 不听话的; 像孩子般任性的: *a wayward child* 任性的孩子 ○ *a wayward disposition* 倔强的性格. ▷ **way·ward·ness** *n* [U].

WC /ˌdʌblju: ˈsi:; ˌdʌbljʊ ˈsi/ *abbr* 缩写 = **1** water-closet 厕所. ⇨Usage at TOILET 用法见 TOILET. **2** West Central 西中央区: *London WC2B 4PH*, eg as a postal code 伦敦 WC2B 4PH(如作邮政编码).

WCC /ˌdʌblju: si: ˈsi:; ˌdʌbljʊ si ˈsi/ *abbr* 缩写 = World Council of Churches 世界基督教协进会.

W/Cdr *abbr* 缩写 = Wing Commander 空军中校: *W/Cdr (Bob)Hunt* (鲍勃·)亨特空军中校.

we /wi:; wi/ ⇨Detailed Guide 6.2 见词条使用详细说明 6.2. *pers pron* 人称代词 (used as the subject of a *v* 用作动词的主体) **1** I and another or others; I and you 我们; 咱们: *We've moved to London.* 我们已经搬到伦敦来了. ○ *We'd like to offer you a job.* 我们想聘请您做一项工作. ○ *Why don't we go and see it?* 咱们去看看好不好? **2** (*fml* 文) (used instead of *I* by a king, queen or pope or by the writer of an editorial article in a newspaper, etc 帝王或教皇或报刊编者用以自称). Cf 参看 THE ROYAL WE (ROYAL). **3** (used when speaking to children, sick people, etc to indicate kindly superiority 用以对儿童、病人等说话, 表示关怀): *Now what are we doing over here?* 你在这儿干什么呢? ○ *And how are we feeling today?* 您今天身体怎么样? Cf 参看 US.

WEA /ˌdʌblju: i: ˈeɪ; ˌdʌbljʊ i ˈe/ *abbr* 缩写 = (*Brit*) Workers' Educational Association 工人教育协会.

weak /wi:k; wik/ *adj* (**-er, -est**) **1** (**a**) lacking strength or power; easily broken, bent or defeated 弱的; 无气力的; 无势力的; 易毁坏的; 易弯的; 容易被击败的: *She was still weak after her illness.* 她病后仍很虚弱. ○ *too weak to walk far* 身体很虚弱不能走远道 ○ *Her legs felt weak/She felt weak in the legs.* 她感到双腿无力. ○ *The supports were too weak for the weight of the load.* 所载的分量很重已经禁不住了. ○ *a weak barrier, defence, team* 不结实的挡板、无力的防御、弱队 ○ *a weak chin/mouth*, ie suggesting or showing weakness of character 软弱的性格 ○ *identify the weak points in an argument*, ie those which may be attacked most easily 找出论据中的弱点. (**b**) (*commerce* 商) not financially sound or successful 疲软的; 萧条的: *a weak currency, economy, market* 疲软的货币、经济、市场. **2** not functioning properly; deficient 功能不佳的; 疲弱的: *weak eyes/sight* 视力弱的眼睛[不佳的视力] ○ *a weak heart* 衰弱的心脏 ○ *a weak stomach*, ie one that is easily upset by food 易引起恶心的胃. **3** not convincing or forceful 无说服力的; 无力的: *weak arguments, evidence* 无说服力的论据、证据. **4** not easily perceived; feeble or faint 不易察觉的; 微弱的: *a weak light, signal, sound* 微弱的光线、信号、声音 ○ *a weak smile* 微微的一笑. **5** (of liquids) containing a high proportion of water; dilute (指液体)稀的, 稀释的: *weak tea* 淡茶 ○ *a weak solution of salt and water* 稀释的盐水溶液. **6 ~ (at/in/on sth)** not achieving a high standard; deficient 未达高标准的; 有缺欠的: *Her school report shows that she is weak at/in arithmetic and biology.* 从她的学习成绩单可看出她算术和生物成绩差. ○ *The book is weak on* (ie in its treatment of) *the medieval period.* 这本书对中世纪时期论述不足. **7** (*grammar*) (of verbs) forming the past tense, etc by the addition of a suffix (eg *walk, walked* or *waste, wasted*) and not by a change of vowel (eg *run, ran* or *come, came*) (指动词)弱的, 规则的(构成过去时态需添加词尾的, 如walk、walked或waste、wasted, 并非改变元音的, 如run、ran或come、came). **8** (idm 习语) **ˌweak at the ˈknees** (*infml* 口) temporarily hardly able to stand because of emotion, fear, illness, etc 一时两腿发软站立不住(因激动、惧怕、疾病等所致): *The shock made me go all weak at the knees.* 这件事把我吓得两腿发软. **the weaker ˈsex** (*dated sexist* 旧, 性别偏见) women in general 女性. **ˌweak in the ˈhead** (*infml* 口) stupid 愚蠢的: *You must be weak in the head if you believe that.* 你相信那件事可就太傻了. **a weak ˈmoment** time when one is unusually easily persuaded or tempted 易被说服或诱惑的时刻: *In a weak moment, I agreed to pay for her holiday.* 我一时心软同意了支付她度假的费用.

▷ **the ˈweak** *n* [pl *v*] people who are poor, sick or powerless and are therefore easily exploited, infected, etc 弱者, 穷人, 病人, 无权势的人(因而易受剥削、欺压、影响的): *He argued that it was the role of governments to protect the weak.* 他的论点是政府有责任保护无告的百姓. ○ *the struggle of the weak against their oppressors* 被压迫者与压迫者之间的斗争.

weaken /ˈwi:kən; ˈwikən/ *v* **1** [I, Tn] (cause sb/sth to) become weak or weaker (使某人[某事物])变弱: *They watched her gradually weaken as the disease progressed.* 他们观察到她随着病情变化身体也渐渐衰弱下去. ○ *The dollar has weakened in international currency trading.* 美元在国际货币交易中已趋疲软. ○ *Hunger and disease had weakened his constitution.* 他饥饿与疾病交加, 体质已削弱. **2** [I] become less determined or certain about sth; waver (对某事物的决心或肯定程度)减弱, 动摇, 犹豫: *They have not yet agreed to our requests but they are clearly weakening.* 他们还没有同意我们的要求, 但态度已明显软化.

weak·ling /ˈwi:klɪŋ; ˈwiklɪŋ/ *n* (*derog* 贬) weak or feeble person or animal 软弱的人或动物: *Don't be such a weakling!* 别那么软弱!

weakly *adv* in a weak manner 软弱地; 无力地; 疲软地;

疲弱地; 微弱地: *smile weakly* 微微一笑.

weak·ness *n* **1** [U] state of being weak 弱; 软弱; 虚弱; 薄弱: *the weakness of a country's defences* 国家防御力量的薄弱 ○ *weakness of character* 性格之懦弱 ○ *New evidence revealed the weakness of the prosecution's case.* 这一新的证据表明原告理由不充足. **2** [C] defect or fault, esp in a person's character 弱点, 缺点(尤指性格的): *We all have our weaknesses.* 我们大家都有不足之处. **3** [C usu *sing* 通常作单数] **~ for sth/sb** special or foolish liking for sth/sb (对某事物[某人]的)特殊的或痴心的爱好: *have a weakness for peanut butter, fast cars, tall women* 偏爱花生酱、跑车、高个儿女子.

□ ˈ**weak form** (*phonetics* 语音) way of pronouncing certain common words in an unstressed position, with a shorter syllable and a different vowel sound, or by omitting a vowel sound or a consonant (eg /ən; ən/ or /n; n/ for *and*, as in *bread and butter* /ˌbred n ˈbʌtə(r); ˈbrɛd n̩ ˈbʌtɚ/) 弱读式(英语某些常用词在非重读位置上的读法, 为缩短音节、替换元音或省略元音或辅音, 如在bread and butter 词组中的and读作/ən/或/n/, 即/ˌbred n ˈbʌtə(r)/).

ˌ**weak-ˈkneed** *adj* (*fig* 比喻) (of a person) lacking determination or courage (指人)无决心的, 无勇气的.

ˌ**weak-ˈminded** *adj* (a) lacking determination or resolution 无决心的; 不果断的. (b) mentally deficient 心智不健全的. **weak-mindedly** *adv*. **weak-mindedness** *n* [U].

weal /wiːl; wil/ *n* raised mark on the skin made by hitting it with a stick, whip, etc (皮肤上的)隆起的伤痕(用棍、鞭等抽打所致的).

wealth /welθ; wɛlθ/ *n* **1** [U] (possession of a) large amount of money, property, etc; riches 财产(的占有); 财富: *a man of great wealth* 大富翁 ○ *Nobody knew how she had acquired her wealth.* 谁也不知道她的财产是怎么来的. ○ *Wealth had not brought them happiness.* 他们的财富并没给他们带来幸福. ○ *The country's wealth is based on trade.* 这个国家的财源主要来自贸易方面. **2** [sing] **~ of sth** large amount or number of sth; abundance of sth (某物的)大量, 众多, 丰富: *a book with a wealth of illustrations* 有大量插图的书 ○ *a wealth of opportunity* 很多的机会.

▷ **wealthy** *adj* (**-ier**, **-iest**) having wealth; rich 有财产的; 有财富的; 富有的. **wealth·ily** /-ɪlɪ; -əlɪ/ *adv*.

wean /wiːn; win/ *v* **1** [Tn, Tn·pr] **~ sb/sth (off sth) (on to sth)** gradually stop feeding (a baby or young animal) with its mother's milk and start feeding it with solid food 使(婴儿或幼小动物)断奶. **2** (phr v) **wean sb (away) from sth/doing sth** cause sb to stop doing sth, esp gradually 使某人不继续做某事(尤指逐渐地): *wean sb (away) from drugs, drinking, gambling, etc* 使某人渐渐戒毒、戒酒、戒赌等.

weapon /ˈwepən; ˈwɛpən/ *n* **1** thing designed or used for causing physical harm (eg a bomb, gun, knife, sword, etc) 武器, 兵器(如炸弹、枪、炮、刀、剑等): *They were carrying weapons.* 他们携带着武器. ○ *armed with weapons* 用武器武装的 ○ *a deadly weapon* 致命的武器. **2** action or procedure used to defend oneself or get the better of sb in a struggle or contest (在斗争中或竞争中)自卫的或克敌制胜的行动或手段: *Their ultimate weapon was the threat of an all-out strike.* 他们最后的杀手锏是威胁举行大罢工. ○ *Humour was his only weapon against their hostility.* 他有幽默感, 这是他对付他们的敌对行动的唯一手段.

▷ **weap·onry** /-rɪ; -rɪ/ *n* [U] weapons 武器; 兵器: *an arsenal of sophisticated weaponry* 尖端武器军械场.

wear[1] /weə(r); wɛr/ *n* [U] **1** wearing or being worn as clothing 穿着; 戴着; 佩带着: *a suit for everyday wear* 一套日常穿的衣服 ○ *Cotton is suitable for wear in summer.* 棉制品适于夏季穿用. **2** (esp in compounds 尤用以构成复合词) things for wearing; clothing 穿戴的衣物: *ˈchildren's/ˈladies' wear* 儿童的[女用的]衣物 ○ *ˈmenswear* 男装 ○ *ˈunderwear* 内衣 ○ *ˈfootwear* 鞋袜 ○ *ˈsportswear* 运动服装. **3** (damage or loss of quality caused by) use 使用; 用损; 用坏: *These shoes are showing (signs of) wear.* 这双鞋(看样子)穿坏了. ○ *The carpet gets very heavy wear.* 这块地毯已严重磨损. **4** capacity for continuing to be used 耐用性: *There is still a lot of wear left in that old coat.* 那件旧大衣还可以穿很久. **5** (idm 习语) ˌ**wear and ˈtear** damage, deterioration, strain, etc caused by ordinary use (正常使用造成的)损坏, 损耗, 用坏: *The insurance policy does not cover damage caused by normal wear and tear.* 保险单内容不包括正常使用所导致的损坏. **the worse for wear** ⇨ WORSE.

wear[2] /weə(r); wɛr/ *v* (*pt* **wore** /wɔː(r); wɔr/, *pp* **worn** /wɔːn; wɔrn/) **1** [Tn, Tn·pr, Cn·a] have (sth) on one's body, esp as clothing, as an ornament, etc 穿戴, 佩带(衣物等); 留, 蓄(毛发等): *wear a beard, coat, hat, ring, watch* 留胡须、穿大衣、戴帽子、戴戒指、戴手表 ○ *Bowler hats are not often worn nowadays.* 现在戴常礼帽的已不多见了. ○ *She was wearing sun-glasses.* 她戴着墨镜. ○ *She never wears green*, ie green clothes. 她从不穿绿色的衣服. ○ *He wore a gold chain round his neck.* 他戴着金项链. ○ *She wears her hair long*, ie has long hair. 她留着长发. ⇨Usage 见所附用法. **2** [Tn] have (a certain look) on one's face (脸上)流露(某种神态): *He/His face wore a puzzled frown.* 他皱着眉显出不解的样子. ○ (*fig* 比喻) *The house wore a neglected look.* 这所房子像是无人照管的样子. **3** [Tn] (*infml* 口) (esp in questions and negative sentences 尤用于疑问句和否定句) accept or tolerate (sth, esp sth that one does not approve of) 同意或容忍(尤指不赞成的事物): *He wanted to sail the boat alone but his parents wouldn't wear it.* 他要独自驾驶船航行, 但他父母不让. **4** [La, I, Tn, Tn·pr, Cn·a] (cause sth to) become damaged, useless or reduced by being used, rubbed, etc (使某物)用损, 用坏, 磨损, 消耗: *The sheets have worn thin in the middle.* 床单的中间部分磨薄了. ○ *The carpets are starting to wear.* 地毯渐渐磨坏了. ○ *That coat is starting to look worn.* 那件大衣已显得旧了. ○ *The lettering on the gravestone was badly worn and almost illegible.* 墓碑上的文字已严重磨损难以辨认. ○ *I have worn my socks into holes.* 我的袜子穿破了. ○ *The stones had been worn smooth by the constant flow of water.* 这些石头不断经流水冲刷已很光滑. **5** [Tn·pr] make (a hole, groove, path, etc) in sth by constant rubbing, dripping, etc (某物因不断磨擦、受水滴侵蚀等)造成(洞、沟、道等): *I've worn holes in my socks.* 我的袜子穿破了. ○ *Look at the holes that have been worn in this rug.* 瞧瞧这块小地毯上磨出的洞. ○ *The children have worn a path across the field where they walk each day to school.* 这些孩子每天上学穿过田地踩出了一条路. ○ *The water had worn a channel in the rock.* 水把岩石冲出了一条沟. **6** [I] endure or be capable of enduring continued use 耐用: *You should choose a fabric that will wear well*, ie last a long time. 你应该挑选耐穿的料子. ○ (*fig* 比喻) *Despite her age she had worn well*, ie still looked quite young. 别看她岁数大, 可长得少相. **7** (idm 习语) **wear one's ˌheart on one's ˈsleeve** allow one's emotions, esp one's love for sb, to be seen 流露出感情; (尤指)对某人示爱. **wear ˈthin** begin to fail 逐渐失去作用或消失: *My patience is beginning to wear very thin.* 我有些不耐烦了. ○ *Don't you think that joke's wearing a bit thin* (ie because we've heard it so many times)? 你不觉得那个笑话已经没什么意思了吗? **wear the ˈpants/ˈtrousers** (*often derog* 常作贬义) (usu of a woman) be the dominant person in a relationship, esp a marriage (通常指女子)作主, 当家, 掌权(尤指婚姻关系): *It's quite clear who wears the trousers in that house!* 很清楚那家谁说了算! **8** (phr v) **wear (sth) away** (cause sth to) become thin, damaged, weak, etc by constant use (使某物)用薄、用细、用坏或用旧等: *The inscription on the coin had worn away.* 铸造在硬币上的文字已经磨损. ○ *The steps had been worn away by the feet of thousands of visitors.* 参观的人成千上万, 把台阶踩得不像样子了. **wear (sth) down** (cause sth to) become gradually smaller, thinner, etc (使某物)逐渐变小、变细、变薄等: *The tread on the tyres has (been) worn down to a dangerous level.* 轮胎胎面花纹已经磨损得到了能发生危险的地步了. **wear sb/sth down** weaken sb/sth by constant attack, nervous strain, etc (因不断攻击、精神紧张等)使某人[某事物]衰弱: *She was worn down by overwork.* 她因过度劳累而垮了下来. ○ *The strategy was designed to wear down the enemy's resistance.* 这一策略旨在逐步削弱敌人的抵抗力. **wear (sth) off** (cause sth to) disappear or be removed gradually (使某事物)逐渐消失或除去: *The dishwasher has worn the glaze off the china.* 这些瓷器经常用洗碗机清洗, 光泽都消失了. ○ *The novelty will soon wear off*, ie It is only attractive because it is new. 这种新奇的感觉很快就会消失. ○ *The pain is slowly wearing off.* 疼痛的感觉正在

慢慢消退. **wear on** (of time) pass, esp tediously (指时间)过去(尤指觉得沉闷): *As the evening wore on, she became more and more nervous.* 当晚的时间过得很慢, 她越来越紧张了. ○ *His life was wearing on towards its close.* 他的生命即将完结. **wear (sth) out** (cause sth to) become useless, threadbare or exhausted through use (使某事物)用得不能再用、用坏或耗尽: *I wore out two pairs of boots on the walking tour.* 我徒步旅行穿坏了两双靴子. ○ *Her patience had/was at last worn out.* 她终于忍无可忍了. **wear sb out** cause sb to become exhausted; tire sb out 使某人精疲力竭或厌烦: *They were worn out after a long day spent working in the fields.* 他们在地里干了一整天的活儿, 累得疲惫不堪. ○ *Just listening to his silly chatter wears me out.* 我听着他无聊的话把我烦透了.

▷ **wear·able** /ˈweərəbl; ˋwɛrəbḷ/ *adj* that can be, or is fit to be, worn 可穿戴的; 适合穿戴的: *a wardrobe full of clothes that are no longer wearable* 充斥着不能再穿的衣物的衣柜.

wearer /ˈweərə(r); ˋwɛrɚ/ *n* person who is wearing sth 穿戴某物的人; 留着某类毛发的人: *These shoes will damage the wearer's feet.* 穿这种鞋脚会受伤.

wear·ing /ˈweərɪŋ; ˋwɛrɪŋ/ *adj* tiring 令人疲倦的; 令人厌烦的: *I've had a wearing day.* 我这一天很累. ○ *The old lady finds shopping very wearing.* 这个老太太觉得买东西很烦人.

NOTE ON USAGE 用法: We **wear** clothes, including gloves and scarves, also belts, spectacles, even perfume on our bodies ☆ **wear** 这个动词用以表示穿衣物, 包括戴手套、围巾, 还用于系腰带、戴眼镜, 甚至喷洒香水: *Do you have to wear a suit at work?* 你们上班得穿西装吗? ○ *She was wearing her mother's coat.* 她穿着她母亲的大衣. ○ *Are you wearing aftershave?* 你刮完胡子搽润肤液吗? We **carry** objects when we take them with us, especially in our hands or arms ☆ **carry** 这个动词用以表示随身携带东西, 尤指用手或手臂: *He wasn't wearing his raincoat, he was carrying it over his arm.* 他没穿着雨衣而是把它搭在胳膊上. ○ *She always carries an umbrella in her briefcase.* 她总是在公事包里带着一把伞.

weary /ˈwɪərɪ; ˋwɪrɪ/ *adj* (**-ier**, **-iest**) **1 (a)** very tired, esp as a result of effort or endurance; exhausted 疲倦的, 疲劳的(尤指因费力或持久所致); 精疲力竭: *weary in body and mind* 身心疲惫 ○ *They felt weary after all their hard work.* 他们把所有的累活儿都干完后感到筋疲力尽. **(b)** ~ **of sth** no longer interested in or enthusiastic about sth; tired of sth 对某事物再无兴趣或热情; 厌倦某事物: *The people are growing weary of the war.* 人民对这场战争越来越厌倦了. ○ *I am weary of hearing about your problems.* 我听腻了你那些麻烦事. **2** causing tiredness or boredom 令人疲倦的; 令人厌烦的: *a weary journey, wait* 令人厌倦的旅程、等待 ○ *the last weary mile of their climb* 他们攀登的令人疲惫的最后一英里路. **3** showing tiredness 显得疲倦或厌倦的: *a weary sigh, smile* 疲倦的叹息、笑容.

W

▷ **wear·ily** /ˈwɪərəlɪ; ˋwɪrəlɪ/ *adv.*

weari·ness *n* [U].

weari·some /ˈwɪərɪsəm; ˋwɪrɪsəm/ *adj* causing one to feel tired or bored 使人感到疲倦或厌倦的: *wearisome complaints, duties, tasks* 令人厌烦的抱怨、职责、任务.

weary *v* **1** [Tn, Tn·pr] **~ sb (with sth)** make sb feel annoyed or impatient 使某人感到烦恼或不耐烦: *It wearies me to have to explain everything in such detail.* 让我把一切都得解释得那么详细, 可真烦人. ○ *She was wearied by the constant noise.* 她很厌烦那些没完没了的噪杂声. ○ *weary sb with requests* 一再要求使某人生厌. **2** [Ip] **~ of sb/sth** (*fml* 文) become dissatisfied with sb/sth 对某人[某事物]不满: *She began to weary of her companions.* 她逐渐对同伴心怀不满. ○ *You will soon weary of living abroad.* 你在国外生活不消多久就不满意了.

weasel /ˈwi:zl; ˋwizḷ/ *n* small fierce animal with reddish-brown fur, that lives on rats, rabbits, birds' eggs, etc 鼬; 黄鼠狼. ⇨illus at App 1 见附录1插图, page iii. Cf 参看 ERMINE, FERRET, STOAT.

▷ **weasel** *v* (phr v) **weasel out (of sth)** (*infml derog* 口, 贬 *esp US*) avoid fulfilling a promise, doing a duty, etc 逃避已做出的承诺、承担的责任等.

□ ˈ**weasel word** (*infml* 口 *esp US*) word or expression that reduces the force of what one is saying, used when one wishes to avoid committing oneself to a definite statement 含糊其辞的推脱话.

weather[1] /ˈweðə(r); ˋwɛðɚ/ *n* **1** [U] condition of the atmosphere at a certain place and time, with reference to temperature and the presence of rain, sunshine, wind, etc 天气; 气象: *cold, sunny, warm, wet, windy, etc weather* 寒冷的、有阳光的、温暖的、下雨的、刮风的…天气 ○ *We had good weather on our holiday.* 我们度假时天气很好. ○ *The weather is very changeable.* 天气变化无常. ○ *The success of the crop depends on the weather.* 要收成好全得靠天气. ○ *if the weather breaks/holds,* ie if the present good weather changes/continues 要是天气变坏[还这么好] ○ *We shall play the match tomorrow, weather permitting,* ie if the weather is fine. 明天假设天气好, 我们就进行比赛. Cf 参看 CLIMATE 1. **2** (idm 习语) **in all weathers** in all kinds of weather, both good and bad 无论天气好坏. **keep a ˈweather eye open** be watchful and alert in order to avoid trouble 留意并警惕以避免麻烦. **make heavy weather of sth** ⇨ HEAVY. **under the ˈweather** (*infml* 口) feeling unwell or depressed 感到不舒服或消沉: *be/feel/look under the weather* 有些[感到/显得]情绪低落 ○ *She's been a bit under the weather recently.* 她近来身体不太好.

▷ **weather** *adj* [attrib 作定语] windward 上风的: *on the weather side* 在上风侧.

□ ˈ**weather-beaten** *adj* (esp of sb's skin) tanned, damaged, roughened, etc as a result of being exposed to the sun and wind (尤指人的皮肤)(因风吹日晒)变黑的、受损的、粗糙的等: *the weather-beaten face of an old sailor* 一个老水手的饱经风霜的脸.

ˈ**weather-board** *n* sloping board for keeping out rain and wind, esp one attached to the bottom of a door 风雨板(尤指安装在门底部的). ˈ**weather-boarding** (*US* ˈ**clapboard**) *n* [U] series of weather-boards with each one overlapping the one below, fixed to the outside wall of a building in order to protect it 封檐板.

ˈ**weather-bound** *adj* unable to make or continue a journey because of bad weather 因天气恶劣不能出行或不能继续前行的; 被天气所阻的.

ˈ**weather-chart**, ˈ**weather-map** *ns* diagram that shows details of the weather over a wide area 天气图.

ˈ**weathercock** *n* weather-vane, often in the shape of a cockerel 风向标; 风信鸡. ⇨illus at App 1 见附录1插图, page viii.

ˈ**weather forecast** forecast of the weather for the next day or few days, esp one broadcast on radio or television 天气预报(尤指电台或电视广播的).

ˈ**weatherman** /-mæn; -ˌmæn/ *n* (*pl* **-men** /-men; -mɛn/) (*infml* 口) person who reports and forecasts the weather; meteorologist 气象报告员或预报员; 气象学家.

ˈ**weatherproof** *adj* that can withstand exposure to the weather and keep out rain, snow, wind, etc 不受气候影响的; 防雨、雪、风等的; 全天候的: *a weatherproof shelter* 防恶劣天气的处所.

ˈ**weather-vane** *n* revolving pointer that can turn easily in the wind and is put in a high place, esp on top of a building, in order to show the direction of the wind 风向标.

weather[2] /ˈweðə(r); ˋwɛðɚ/ *v* **1** [Tn] dry or season (wood) by leaving it in the open air 晾干或风干(木材). **2** [I, Tn] (cause sth to) change shape or colour because of the action of the sun, rain, wind, etc (使某物)(受日晒、风吹、雨打等)变形或变色: *Teak weathers to a greyish colour.* 柚木经日晒、风吹、雨打颜色发灰了. ○ *rocks weathered by wind and water* 受风化和水蚀的岩石. **3** [Tn] come safely through (sth); survive 平安渡过(危难); 经历(危难)而存活: *weather a crisis, a storm, an upheaval* 经历危机、暴风雨、动乱而幸存. **4** [Tn] (in sailing) pass on the windward side of (sth) (船航行时)逆风经过(某处): *The ship weathered the cape.* 那艘船顶着风经过海角.

weave /wi:v; wiv/ *v* (*pt* **wove** /wəʊv; wov/ or in sense 4 用于下述第4义时作 **weaved**, *pp* **woven** /ˈwəʊvn; ˋwovən/ or in sense 4 用于下述第4义时作 **weaved**) **1 (a)** [Tn, Tn·pr] **~ sth (from sth)** make (fabric, etc) by passing threads or strips crosswise over and under lengthwise ones, by hand or on a machine (用手工或机

weave 编织

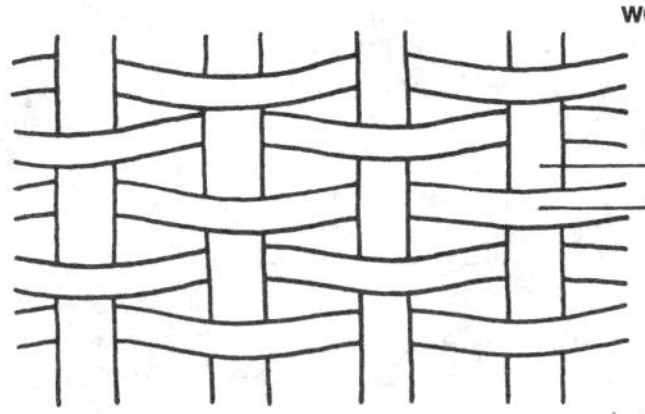

器)编, 织(织物等): *a tightly woven piece of cloth* 织得很密的布 ○ *cloth woven from silk and wool* 用丝与毛混纺的料子 ○ *weave a metre of tweed cloth* 织一米花呢 ○ *weave a basket from strips of willow* 用柳条编个篮子. **(b)** [I] work at a loom, making fabric, etc 纺织; 编织: *She had been taught to weave as a child.* 她从小就学会了织布. ○ *The women earn their living by weaving.* 这些女子以纺织为生. **(c)** [Tn, Tn·pr, Tn·p] **~ sth (into sth)** form fabric, etc out of (threads) by weaving 用(线)织成织物: *weave woollen yarn into cloth* 用毛纱织成呢 ○ *weave threads together* 用线织成. **2 (a)** [Tn·pr, Tn·p] **~ sth (into sth)** twist (flowers, twigs, etc) together to make a garland, wreath, etc 用(花、枝条等)编成花环、花圈等. **(b)** [Tn, Tn·pr] **~ sth (out of/from sth)** make sth by twisting flowers, etc in this way 用花等编成某物: *weave a garland out of primroses* 用报春花编成花环. **3** [Tn, Tn·pr] **~ sth (into sth)** (*fig* 比喻) put (facts, events, etc) together into a story or a connected whole; compose 将(素材、事情等)编成(故事或篇章); 编造: *weave a plot, a magic spell* 编造情节、符篆 ○ *weave one's ideas into a story* 把自己的构思编成故事. **4** [Ipr, Ip, Tn·pr, Tn·p] move along by twisting and turning to avoid obstructions, etc 迂回行进(以避开障碍等): *weave (one's way) through a crowd* 在人群中迂回前行 ○ *The road weaves through the range of hills.* 这条路在群山中绕来绕去. ○ *weave in and out through the traffic* 在来往车辆中穿插而行. **5** (idm 习语) **get 'weaving (on sth)** (*Brit infml* 口) start working (at sth) energetically or hurriedly 精力充沛地或匆忙地开始做(某物): *The work must be finished this week, so we'd better get weaving!* 这项工作本星期必须做完, 咱们最好动手干吧!

▷ **weave** *n* way in which material is woven; style of weaving 编法; 织法; 编织式样: *a coarse, fine, loose, tight, etc weave* 粗织、细织、松织、密织 ○ *a diagonal weave* 斜纹.

weaver *n* **1** person whose job is weaving cloth 织布工. **2** (also **'weaver-bird**) tropical bird that makes its nest by tightly weaving together leaves, grass, twigs, etc 织布鸟(产于热带).

web /web; wɛb/ *n* **1** network of fine threads spun by a spider or some other spinning creature (蜘蛛等动物结的)网: *a spider's web* 蜘蛛网. ➪illus at SPIDER 见 SPIDER 插图. Cf 参看 COBWEB. **2** (*usu fig* 通常作比喻) complex series or network 错综复杂的事物或网络: *a web of deceit, lies, intrigue, etc* 一整套骗术、谎话、诡计等. **3** piece of skin joining together the toes of some birds and animals that swim, eg ducks, geese, frogs, etc 蹼(如鸭、鹅、蛙等的). **4** large roll of paper for printing on 卷筒纸.

▷ **webbed** *adj* (of the foot of a bird or an animal) having the toes joined by webs (指鸟兽的足)有蹼的.

□ **ˌweb-'footed, ˌweb-'toed** *adjs* (of a bird or an animal) having the toes joined by webs (指鸟兽)有蹼的.

web·bing /'webɪŋ; 'wɛbɪŋ/ *n* [U] strong bands of woven fabric used in upholstery, for binding the edges of carpets and for making belts, etc 结实的带状织物(用作家具装饰、地毯边、带子等).

wed /wed; wɛd/ *v* (*pt, pp* **wedded** or **wed**) [I, Tn] (*dated or journalism* 旧或新闻) (not in the continuous tenses 不用于进行时态) marry 结婚; 娶; 嫁: *Rock star to wed top model*, eg as a headline 摇滚乐名星与名模儿联姻(如标题字样).

▷ **wed·ded** *adj* [pred 作表语] **~ to sth** (*fml* 文) **1** united or combined with sth 与某事物结合: *beauty wedded to simplicity* 朴素的美. **2** unable to give sth up; devoted to sth 不能放弃某事物; 致力于某事物: *He is wedded to his work.* 他专心致志于工作. ○ *She is wedded to her opinions and nothing will change her.* 她坚持己见决不动摇.

Wed (also **Weds**) *abbr* 缩写 = Wednesday: *Wed 4 May* 5月4日星期三.

we'd /wi:d; wid/ *contracted form* 缩约式 **1** we had ➪ HAVE. **2** we would ➪ WILL[1], WOULD[2].

wed·ding /'wedɪŋ; 'wɛdɪŋ/ *n* **1** marriage ceremony (and the party which usually follows it) 婚礼; 结婚庆典: *There will be a wedding in the village church on Saturday.* 星期六村里教堂将举行婚礼. ○ *We have been invited to their daughter's wedding.* 他们邀请我们参加他们女儿的婚礼. ○ [attrib 作定语] *a wedding anniversary, dress, guest, invitation, present* 结婚周年纪念、婚礼女用长服、婚礼宾客、婚礼请帖、结婚礼品. **2** (idm 习语) **a shotgun wedding** ➪ SHOTGUN (SHOT[1]).

□ **'wedding breakfast** special meal for the bride and bridegroom and their relatives, friends, etc after a marriage ceremony 婚宴.

'wedding-cake *n* [C, U] iced cake, often with several tiers, that is cut up and eaten at a wedding, with pieces also being sent to absent friends 结婚蛋糕.

'wedding-ring *n* ring that is placed on the bride's (and sometimes the groom's) finger during a marriage ceremony and worn afterwards to show that the wearer is married 结婚戒指: *In Britain, wedding-rings are worn on the third finger of the left hand.* 在英国, 结婚戒指戴在左手无名指上.

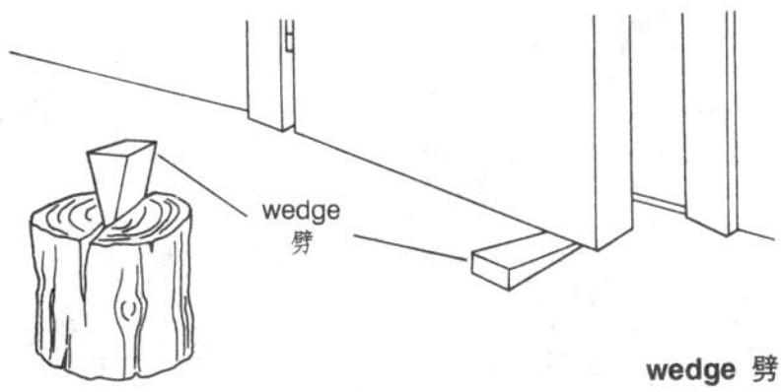

wedge 劈

wedge /wedʒ; wɛdʒ/ *n* **1 (a)** piece of wood or metal that is thick at one end and narrows at the other to a sharp edge, used eg to split wood or rock, to widen an opening or to keep things apart 劈; 尖劈; 楔子. **(b)** thing shaped like or used as a wedge 形状或用途似尖劈之物: *a wedge of cake, cheese, etc*, ie a piece cut from a large round cake, cheese, etc 一角蛋糕、干酪等. **2** (idm 习语) **drive a wedge between A and B** ➪ DRIVE[1]. **the thin end of the wedge** ➪ THIN.

▷ **wedge** *v* **1** [Tn, Cn·a] fix (sth) firmly or force (sth) apart using a wedge 用楔子揳牢; 用尖劈劈开: *The window doesn't stay closed unless you wedge it.* 这扇窗户关不严, 得用楔子揳上了. ○ *wedge a door open* 用楔子抵住门让门敞开. **2** [Tn·pr, Tn·p] pack or thrust (sth/sb/oneself) tightly into a space 将(某物[某人])塞入或插入某空间: *wedge packing material into the spaces round the vase* 用填料把花瓶周围楦好 ○ *I was so tightly wedged between two other passengers, I couldn't get off the bus.* 我紧紧夹在两个乘客中间下不了公共汽车了.

wed·lock /'wedlɒk; 'wɛdlɑk/ *n* [U] (*fml or law* 文或律) state of being married 已婚状况: *born out of wedlock*, ie illegitimate 非婚生的.

Wed·nes·day /'wenzdɪ; 'wɛnzdɪ/ *n* [U, C] (*abbrs* 缩写 **Wed, Weds**) the fourth day of the week, next after Tuesday 星期三.

For the uses of *Wednesday* see the examples at *Monday*. 关于 Wednesday 的用法见 Monday 词条中的示例.

wee[1] /wi:; wi/ *adj* **1** (*esp Scot* 尤用于苏格兰) little 小的: *the poor wee fellow* 可怜的小傢伙. **2** (*infml* 口) very small; tiny 很小的; 极小的: *I'll have a wee drop of cream in my coffee.* 我要在咖啡里放一丁点儿奶油. ○ *I'm a wee bit worried about him.* 我对他有些担心. ○ *We'll be a wee bit late, I'm afraid.* 我看我们有点儿晚了.

wee[2] /wi:; wi/ (also **wee-wee** /'wi:wi:; 'wiwi/) *n* [C, U] (*infml* 口) (used by or when talking to young children 儿语) urine; urinating 尿; 撒尿: *do (a) wee-wee* 尿尿.

▷ **wee** (also **wee-wee**) *v* (*pt* **(wee-)weed**) [I] urinate 撒尿.

W

weed /wi:d; wid/ *n* **1** (**a**) [C] wild plant growing where it is not wanted, esp among crops or garden plants 野草, 杂草(尤指庄稼地里的或园中的): *The garden is overgrown with weeds.* 这个园子里长了许多野草. ○ *She spent the afternoon pulling up the weeds in the flowerbeds.* 她用整个下午的时间拔除花坛中的杂草. (**b**) [U] any of several plants without flowers that grow in water and form a green, floating mass 水草: *The pond is full of weed.* 这个池塘里长满了水草. **2** [C] (*infml derog* 口, 贬) (**a**) thin weak-looking person 瘦弱的人. (**b**) person who has a weak character 懦弱的人: *Don't be such a weed!* 别这么懦弱! **3** (*infml* 口) (**a**) [sing] (usu 通常作 **the weed**) (*dated or joc* 旧或谑) tobacco or cigarettes 烟草; 香烟: *I wish I could give up the weed*, ie stop smoking. 但愿我能把烟戒掉. (**b**) [U] marijuana 大麻烟.

▷ **weed** *v* **1** [I, Tn] take out weeds from (the ground) 除去(地面)的杂草: *I've been busy weeding (in) the garden.* 我一直在园子里忙着除杂草. **2** (phr v) **weed sth/sb out** remove or get rid of (people or things that are not wanted) from amongst others that are valuable 除去, 剔除, 淘汰(不需要的人或物): *weed out the weakest saplings* 摘除最差的树苗 ○ *weed out the herd*, ie get rid of inferior animals 剔除兽群中的不好的 ○ *The new conductor started by weeding out the weaker players in the orchestra.* 管弦乐队新来的指挥一上任就先把较差的演奏人员清除出去了.

weedy *adj* (**-ier, -iest**) (**a**) full of or overgrown with weeds (WEED 1a) 多杂草的; 长满野草的. (**b**) (*infml derog* 口, 贬) thin and weak-looking 瘦弱的: *a weedy young man* 瘦弱的年轻男子.

□ ˈ**weed-killer** *n* [C, U] substance that destroys weeds 除草剂; 除莠剂: *a systematic weed-killer* 分类除草剂.

weeds /wi:dz; widz/ *n* [pl] black clothes worn (esp by a widow) to show that one is mourning sb who has died (黑色的)丧服(尤指寡妇穿的).

week /wi:k; wik/ *n* **1** (**a**) period of seven days, usu reckoned from midnight on Saturday 星期, 周(通常从星期六午夜算起): *last, next, this, etc week* 上、下、本... 星期 ○ *What day of the week was 2 July last year?* 去年7月2日是星期几? ○ *early next week* 下周初 ○ *at the end of last week* 上周末 ○ *Sunday is the first day of the week.* 星期日是一个星期的第一天. ○ *He comes to see us once a week.* 他每星期来看我们一次. (**b**) any period of seven days 七天的时间: *a six weeks' holiday* 六周的假期 ○ *a week ago today*, ie seven days ago 一星期前的今天 ○ *three weeks ago yesterday*, ie twenty-two days ago 三周前的昨天 ○ *They are going on holiday for two weeks.* 他们要度假两周. ○ *I shall be away for no more than a week.* 我离开不超过一个星期. **2** (**a**) the six days apart from Sunday (除星期日以外的)六天: *During the week, the road is very busy but there is very little traffic on Sundays.* 从星期一到星期六, 这条路一直川流不息, 但是星期日没什么车辆来往. (**b**) the five days other than Saturday and Sunday (除星期六和星期日以外的)五天: *They live in London during the week and go to the country at the weekend.* 他们从星期一到星期五都住在伦敦, 周末到郊外去. ○ *They never have time to go to the cinema during the week.* 他们从星期一到星期五从来都没有时间去看电影. (**c**) period in a week when one works 一星期工作的时间: *a 35-hour week* 35小时的工作周 ○ *The government is introducing a shorter working week.* 政府新采用减少每周工作时间的制度. ○ *How many lessons are there in the school week?* 学校里每星期有多少节课? **3** (idm 习语) **this day week** ⇨ DAY. **today, tomorrow, Monday, etc** ˈ**week** seven days after today, tomorrow, Monday, etc 一个星期后的今天、明天、那个星期一...; 即将到来的星期x之后的那个星期x: *Monday week* 下下星期一 ○ *Friday week* 下星期五. ˌ**week after** ˈ**week** (*infml* 口) continuously for many weeks 一个星期又一个星期; 一连数周: *Week after week the drought continued.* 干旱持续了许多星期. **week** ˌ**in, week** ˈ**out** every week without exception 每个星期(都); 每周均无例外: *Every Sunday, week in, week out, she writes to her parents.* 她每个星期日都给她父母写信. **a** ˌ**week last** ˈ**Monday,** ˈ**yesterday, etc** seven days before last Monday, yesterday, etc 一个星期前的那个星期一、昨天...: *It was a week yesterday (that) we heard the news.* 我们是在八天前听到这个消息的.

▷ **weekly** *adj, adv* (occurring, payable, published, etc) once a week or every week 每星期(的); 每周(发生、支付、出版等)一次(的): *weekly payments* 每星期支付的款项 ○ *a weekly wage of £100* 周薪100英镑 ○ *a weekly shopping trip* 每周一次购物之行 ○ *Wages are paid weekly.* 工资每星期支付一次. ○ *The machine must be checked weekly.* 这机器必须每星期检查一次. — *n* newspaper or magazine that is published once a week 周报; 周刊.

□ ˈ**weekday** /-deɪ; -ˌde/ *n* any day except Sunday (除星期日以外的)任何一天: *The library is open on weekdays only.* 这个图书馆星期一至星期六都开放. ○ *Weekdays are always busy here.* 这里除星期天以外每天都很忙. ○ [attrib 作定语] *weekday opening times* 除星期日以外的每日开放时间.

ˌ**week**ˈ**end** (*US* ˈ**weekend**) *n* (**a**) Saturday and Sunday 星期六和星期日: *The office is closed at the weekend.* 这个办事处星期六和星期日不办公. ○ *He has to work (at) weekends.* 他须在星期六和星期日工作. (**b**) Saturday and Sunday or a slightly longer period as a holiday or rest 星期六和星期日或稍长些的时间(作为假日或休息时间): *a weekend in the country* 在乡村度过的星期五晚上至星期一早晨 ○ *spend the weekend at home* 在家中度过星期六和星期日 ○ [attrib 作定语] *a weekend house, visit* 星期六和星期日的度假用房、访问. — *v* [Ipr, Ip] (esp in the continuous tenses 尤用于进行时态) make a weekend holiday or visit 星期六和星期日度假或访问、做客等: *They're weekending at the seaside.* 他们从星期五晚上至星期一早晨都在海滨. **weekender** *n* person who spends the weekend away from home; weekend visitor 离家度过星期六和星期日的人; 星期六和星期日的客人: *Many of the cottages in the village are now owned by weekenders.* 现在这个村里许多农舍其房主都是专来度过星期六和星期日的人.

weeny /ˈwi:nɪ; ˋwinɪ/ *adj* (**-ier, -iest**) (*infml* 口) tiny 极小的. Cf 参看 TEENY.

weep /wi:p; wip/ *v* (*pt, pp* **wept** /wept; wɛpt/) (*fml* 文) **1** (**a**) [I, Ipr, It] **~ (for/over sb/sth)** shed tears; cry 流泪; 哭泣: *The sight made me want to weep.* 我见到这种情形真想痛哭一场. ○ *weep for joy* 喜极而泣 ○ *a mother weeping over the death of her child* 为孩子之死而哭泣的妇女 ○ *She wept to see him in such a state.* 她一见他那种情形簌簌泪下. (**b**) [Tn] shed (tears) 流(泪): *weep tears of joy* 流出喜悦的眼泪. ⇨Usage at CRY[1] 用法见 CRY[1]. **2** [I] (esp of a wound) shed or ooze moisture, esp pus (尤指伤口)流出或渗出液体(尤指脓): *The cut is no longer weeping and is starting to heal.* 伤口已不流脓, 渐渐愈合了.

▷ **weep** *n* [sing] period of weeping 一阵哭泣: *A good weep would probably make you feel better.* 你痛痛快快哭上一阵也许就好受些了.

weep·ing *adj* [attrib 作定语] (of certain trees) having branches that droop (指某些树)有下垂枝条的: *a weeping birch, willow, etc* 枝条下垂的桦树、垂柳.

weepy *adj* (**-ier, -iest**) (**a**) inclined to weep; tearful 要哭的; 动不动就哭的; 含泪的: *She is still feeling weepy.* 她仍觉得想哭. (**b**) (of a film, story, etc) tending to make one weep; sentimental (指影片、故事等)催人泪下的, 伤感的: *a weepy ending* 使人落泪的结局.

wee·vil /ˈwi:vl; ˋwivḷ/ *n* type of small beetle with a hard shell that feeds on grain, nuts and other seeds, and destroys crops 象甲(小甲虫, 吃谷物、坚果等, 为害作物).

wef /ˌdʌblju: i: ˈef; ˌdʌblju i ˋɛf/ *abbr* 缩写 = (*esp commerce* 尤用于商业) with effect from 自...起生效: *wef 1 May 1986* 自1986年5月1日起生效.

weft /weft; wɛft/ *n* **the weft** [sing] (in weaving) threads taken crosswise over and under the lengthwise threads of the warp (纺织)纬纱, 纬线. ⇨illus at WEAVE 见 WEAVE 插图.

weigh /weɪ; we/ *v* **1** [Tn] measure how heavy (sth) is by means of scales, a balance, etc 称(某物)的重量: *He weighed himself on the bathroom scales.* 他在浴室的磅秤上称体重. ○ *The load must be weighed before it is put in the washing-machine.* 要洗的衣物须称过重量再放入洗衣机中. ○ *He weighed the stone in his hand*, ie estimated how heavy it was by holding it. 他用手掂了掂这块石头的重量. **2** [Ln] show a certain measure when put on scales, etc 测出重量: *She weighs 60 kilos.* 她体重为60公斤. ○ *How much do you weigh?* ie How heavy are you? 你体重多少? ○ *This piece of meat weighs four pounds.* 这

块肉重四磅. **3 (a)** [Tn, Tn·pr] **~ sth (with/against sth)** consider carefully the relative value or importance of sth 仔细考虑某事物的相对价值或重要性等; 权衡; 斟酌: *weigh one plan against another* 比较一计划与另一计划的优劣 ○ *weighing the pros and cons* 权衡正反两方面的意见 ○ *weigh the advantages of the operation against the risks involved* 仔细考虑做这种手术的好处与危险. **(b)** [Tn, Tn·p] **~ sth (up)** consider sth carefully 仔细考虑某事物: *weigh (up) the consequences of an action* 慎重考虑一行动的后果 ○ *weigh up one's chances of success* 琢磨成功的可能性. **4** [Ipr] **~ (with sb) (against sb/sth)** be considered important (by sb) when sb/sth is being judged (评定某人[某事物]时)被(某人)认为重要: *His criminal record weighed heavily against him (with the jury).* (陪审团)认为他的前科关系重大. ○ *Her past achievements weighed in her favour as a candidate.* 她已往的成就对她这个候选人很有利. **5** (idm 习语) **weigh 'anchor** raise the anchor of a ship at the start of a voyage, etc 起锚. **weigh the 'evidence** consider the relative value of the evidence for and against sb/sth 考虑一证据对某人[某事物]的相对价值. **weigh a 'ton** (*infml* 口) be very heavy 非常沉重: *These cases weigh a ton — what have you got in them?* 这些箱子非常重——你在里面放了什么了? **weigh one's 'words** choose carefully words that express exactly what one means 斟酌词句; 推敲: *I must weigh my words to avoid any misunderstanding.* 我须字斟句酌免生误解. **6** (phr v) **weigh sb down** make sb feel anxious or depressed 使某人感到忧虑或沮丧: *weighed down by worry and overwork* 因焦虑和过度劳累而情绪低落 ○ *The responsibilities of the job are weighing her down.* 她工作责任很重把她压得无精打采. **weigh sb/sth down** make sb/sth bend or sag 将某人[某物]压弯或压下: *The porter was weighed down by all the luggage.* 搬运工扛着这些行李压得直不起腰来. ○ *The branches were weighed down with ripe apples.* 苹果成熟了把树枝都压弯了. **weigh in (at sth)** (of a jockey, boxer, etc) be weighed before a race, boxing match, etc (指骑手、拳击手等)赛前测体重: *He weighed in at several pounds below the limit.* 他赛前量体重比规定限度少几磅. **weigh in (with sth)** (*infml* 口) join in a discussion, an argument, etc by saying sth important or convincing; contribute confidently (在讨论、辩论等时)提出重要的或令人信服的意见; 自信地提出看法: *At that point, the chairman weighed in with a strong defence of company policy.* 这时, 主席发言有理有据地维护了公司的政策. **weigh on sb/sth** make (sb/sb's mind, etc) anxious 使(某人[某人的精神]等)忧虑: *The responsibilities weigh (heavily) on him.* 他责任重大感到心情沉重. ○ *It's been weighing on my mind for days whether to tell her or not.* 我这几天心烦意乱, 不知道应该不应该告诉她. **weigh sth out** measure a quantity of sth by weight 称出指定重量的某物: *weigh out a kilo of tomatoes* 称出一公斤西红柿 ○ *Weigh out all the ingredients before you start making the cake.* 在动手做蛋糕之前先要把配料都量好.

□ **'weighbridge** *n* weighing-machine with a platform set into the road, onto which vehicles can be driven to be weighed 地秤; 地磅.

'weigh-in *n* (*pl* **-ins**) (usu *sing* 通常作单数) check on the weight of a boxer, jockey, etc, made just before a fight, race, etc (拳赛、赛马等之前, 对拳击手、骑手的)量体重.

'weighing-machine *n* machine for weighing people or things that are too heavy to be weighed on a simple balance 称量机.

'weighing-scale *n* balance used for weighing 秤; 台秤; 秤盘; 天平.

weight[1] /weɪt; wet/ *n* **1** [U] degree of heaviness of a thing, esp as measured on a balance, weighing-machine, etc and expressed according to a particular system of measuring (eg kilos, tons, etc) 重量; 分量: *Bananas are usually sold by weight.* 香蕉通常按重量卖. ○ *That man is twice my weight*, ie is twice as heavy as I am. 那个男子的体重比我重一倍. ○ *Her weight has increased to 70 kilos.* 她的体重增加到了 70 公斤. ○ *The two boys are (of) the same weight.* 那两个男孩体重相同. ○ *He has grown both in height and weight.* 他身高和体重都增加了. ⇨App 4, 5 见附录4、5. **2** [U] quality of being heavy 重(的特性): *Lead is often used because of its weight.* 铅因其重而常派上用场. ○ *The weight of the overcoat made it uncomfortable to wear.* 这件大衣很重, 穿着不舒服. **3** [U] (*physics* 物) amount of force with which a body is drawn downwards by gravity 重力; 地心引力. **4** [C, U] unit or system of units by which weight is measured and expressed 重量单位: *tables of weights and measures* 度量衡表 ○ *avoirdupois/troy weight* 常衡[金衡]制. ⇨ App 5 见附录5. **5** [C] **(a)** piece of metal of a known heaviness, used with scales for weighing things 砝码; 秤锤; 秤砣: *a 2lb weight* 两磅重的砝码. **(b)** heavy object, esp one used to bring or keep sth down 重物(尤指用以压住或坠住他物的): *a clock worked by weights* 靠钟锤走动的钟 ○ *a 'paperweight*, ie for keeping papers in place 镇纸 ○ *The dressmaker put small weights in the hem of the dress.* 那裁缝把小块重物缝进连衣裙的下摆里. ○ *The doctor said he must not lift heavy weights.* 医生说他切不可抬重物. **6** [sing] **~ (of sth)** **(a)** load to be supported (需支撑的)负荷: *The pillars have to support the weight of the roof.* 这些柱子须承受屋顶的重量. ○ *The weight of the water from the burst pipe caused the ceiling to collapse.* 水管破裂流出很多水把天花板压塌了. **(b)** (*fig* 比喻) burden of responsibility or worry 责任的重担; 思想负担: *The full weight of decision-making falls on her.* 决策的重任全落在她的肩上了. **7** [U] (degree of) importance, seriousness or influence 重要性、严重性或影响力(的程度): *arguments of great weight* 事关重大的争论 ○ *Recent events give added weight to their campaign.* 最近发生的事情更增加了他们那运动的影响力. ○ *The jury were convinced by the weight of the evidence against her.* 陪审团认为指控她有罪的证据很充分. **8** (idm 习语) **be/take a load/weight off sb's mind** ⇨ MIND. **carry weight** ⇨ CARRY. **lose/take off 'weight** (of a person) become less heavy; slim (指人)减轻体重, 变苗条. **ˌover/ˌunder 'weight** too heavy/not heavy enough 过重[过轻]. **pull one's weight** ⇨ PULL[2]. **put on weight** (of a person) become heavier; grow fat (指人)增加体重, 长胖: *He's put on a lot of weight since he gave up smoking.* 他戒烟后体重增加了许多. **take the 'weight off one's feet** (*infml* 口) sit down 坐下. **throw one's weight about/around** (*infml* 口) behave in an aggressively arrogant way 盛气凌人; 逞威风. **weight of 'numbers** combined weight, strength, influence, etc of a group which is larger than another 集体的重量、力量、影响等结合起来可敌得过对方: *They won the argument by sheer weight of numbers.* 他们纯靠人多势众在争论中获胜. **worth one's/its weight in gold** ⇨ WORTH.

▷ **weight·less** *adj* having no weight, or with no weight relative to one's/its surroundings because of the absence of gravity 无重量的; 失重的. **weight·less·ness** *n* [U]: *become accustomed to weightlessness in a spacecraft* 已适应宇宙飞船中的失重状态.

weighty *adj* **(-ier, -iest) 1 (a)** having great weight; heavy 重的; 沉重的. **(b)** burdensome 繁重的. **2** showing or requiring serious thought; important or influential 慎重的; 需认真考虑的; 重要的; 有影响的: *weighty arguments, decisions, matters* 重要的论据、决定、事情. **weight·ily** /-ɪlɪ; -əlɪ/ *adv*. **weighti·ness** *n* [U].

□ **'weight-lifting** *n* [U] lifting heavy objects as a sport or as exercise 举重. **'weight-lifter** *n* person who does weight-lifting 举重运动员.

weight[2] /weɪt; wet/ *v* **1 (a)** [Tn] attach a weight to (sth) 在(某物)上加重量. **(b)** [Tn, Tn·pr, Tn·p] **~ sth (down) (with sth)** hold sth down with a weight[1](5b) or weights 在某物上加重物使之向下: *The net is weighted to keep it below the surface of the water.* 这个网加了坠因而可没入水面以下. **(c)** [Tn, Tn·pr] **~ sth (with sth)** make sth heavier 使某物重些: *The stick had been weighted with lead.* 这条棍子灌了铅增加了分量. **2** [Tn] treat (a fabric) with a mineral substance to make it heavier 用矿物质处理(织物)(使之加重): *weighted silk* 经加重处理的丝绸. **3** [Tn·pr esp passive 尤用于被动语态] plan or organize (sth) in a way that favours a particular person or group; bias 计划或组织(某事物)使之偏向某人或某集体; 偏袒: *a law weighted against/towards/in favour of those owning land* 对土地持有者不利的[有利的/偏袒的]法规. **4** (phr v) **weight sb down (with sth)** burden sb 给某人加负担; 使某人负重: *She was weighted down with parcels.* 她携带着沉重的包裹.

W

▷ **weight·ing** *n* [U] (*esp Brit*) extra pay or allowances given in special cases, eg to people working in cities because of the higher cost of living there (在特殊情况下的)额外补贴或津贴(如发给在生活费用高的城市工作的人的): [attrib 作定语] *a London weighting allowance* 给在伦敦工作的人的额外津贴.

weir /wɪə(r); wɪr/ *n* **1** wall or barrier built across a river in order to control or divert the flow of water 堰; 拦河坝. **2** fence made of stakes or branches put across a stream in order to make a pool where fish may be caught 鱼簖.

weird /wɪəd; wɪrd/ *adj* (**-er, -est**) **1** (frightening because it is) unnatural, uncanny or strange 不自然的、怪异的或奇怪的(因而可怕的): *Weird shrieks were heard in the darkness.* 在黑暗中听见离奇的尖叫声. **2** (*infml often derog* 口, 常作贬义) unconventional, unusual or bizarre 非传统的; 不寻常的; 古怪的: *weird clothes, hairstyles, taste* 古怪的衣物、发型、口味 ○ *I found some of her poems a bit weird.* 我觉得她的诗有的有点儿怪.

▷ **weirdly** *adv*.

weird·ness *n* [U].

weirdo /ˈwɪədəʊ; ˋwɪrdo/ (*pl* **~s** /-əʊz; -oz/) (also **weirdie** /ˈwɪədɪ; ˋwɪrdɪ/) *n* (*infml usu derog* 口, 通常作贬义) person who behaves, dresses, etc in a bizarre or an unconventional way; eccentric person (行为、衣着等)奇怪的人, 古怪的人.

wel·come /ˈwelkəm; ˋwɛlkəm/ *adj* **1** received with or giving pleasure 受欢迎的; 令人愉快的: *a welcome change, relief, rest, sight, visitor* 可喜的变化、及时的救助、巴不得的休息、悦目的景象、受欢迎的客人 ○ *welcome news* 好消息 ○ *Your offer of a loan is extremely welcome just now.* 你提供这笔贷款是解救燃眉之急. ○ *We had the feeling that we were not welcome at the meeting.* 我们感到人家不欢迎我们到会. **2** [pred 作表语] **~ to sth/to do sth** (**a**) freely permitted to take sth or to do sth 可随意取用某物或做某事: *You are welcome to use/to the use of my car any time.* 你不必客气可随时用我的汽车. ○ *She's welcome to stay here whenever she likes.* 欢迎她随时到这里来住. ○ *You are welcome to any books you would like to borrow.* 你想借什么书就随便借好了. (**b**) (*ironic* 反语) freely permitted to have sth or to do sth because the speaker does not want to have it or to do it 可随意取用某物或做某事(因是说话的人不想要的或不想做的): *If anyone thinks he can do this job any better, he's welcome to it/to try!* ie I'll gladly let him do it. 谁要是能把这件事做得更好, 谁就来做[试试]! (我乐不得别人来做呢.) ○ *As far as I'm concerned, if it's my desk she wants, she's welcome to it!* 假若她想要的是我的办公桌, 她尽管拿走, 我还求之不得呢! **3** (idm 习语) **make sb ˈwelcome** make sb feel that he is welcome; receive sb hospitably 使某人感到受欢迎; 款待某人. **you're ˈwelcome** (used as a polite reply to thanks 用作答谢的客套话) there is no need to thank me 不用谢; 别客气.

▷ **wel·come** *interj* (greeting used by a person who is already in a place to one who is arriving 迎接时用的招呼语): *Welcome! Come in and meet my parents.* 欢迎、欢迎! 进来见见我的父母. ○ *Welcome back/home!* 欢迎归来! ○ *Welcome on board!* 欢迎各位乘坐本次航班! ○ *Welcome to England!* 欢迎您来到英国!

W

wel·come *n* **1** greeting or reception, esp a kind or glad one; saying 'welcome' 招呼, 接待, 招待(尤指亲切的或热情的); 说'欢迎': *an enthusiastic, a hearty, a warm, etc welcome* 热情的、衷心的、热烈的…欢迎 ○ *The victorious team were given a tumultuous welcome when they arrived home.* 凯旋的队受到热烈的欢迎. ○ *She was touched by the warmth of their welcome.* 他们热情欢迎她, 她深受感动. **2** (idm 习语) **outstay/overstay one's ˈwelcome** stay too long as a guest, causing inconvenience or annoyance to one's host 做客时间过久使主人不便或烦恼.

wel·come *v* **1** [Tn, Tn·pr, Tn·p] greet (sb) on his arrival 欢迎, 迎接(某人): *a welcoming smile* 欢迎的微笑 ○ *We were welcomed at the door by the children.* 我们一到门口, 孩子就都来欢迎我们. ○ *She welcomed the visitors warmly.* 她热情地迎接客人. ○ *It is a pleasure to welcome you (back) on the show.* 热烈欢迎您(回)来演出. **2** [Tn] (**a**) show or feel pleasure or satisfaction at (sth) 对(某事物)表示或感到愉快或满意: *The changes were welcomed by everybody.* 这些变动皆大欢喜. ○ *We welcome the opportunity to express our gratitude.* 我们能有机会表示谢意十分高兴. (**b**) react to (sth) in the specified manner 对(某事物)做出某种反应: *welcome the news with amazement, indifference, enthusiasm, etc* 对这一消息表示惊奇、无动于衷、很感兴趣等 ○ *welcome a suggestion coldly, enthusiastically, warmly, etc* 冷淡地、热情地、热心地…对待一项建议.

weld /weld; wɛld/ *v* **1** (**a**) [Tn, Tn·pr] **~ A and B (together); ~ A (on) to B** join (pieces of metal) by hammering or pressing (usu when the metal is softened by heat) or fuse them by using an oxy-acetylene flame or an electric arc 锻焊, 焊接(金属物): *weld the pieces of a broken axle* 焊接断轴 ○ *weld parts together* 把零件锻焊在一起 ○ *The car has had a new wing welded on.* 这辆汽车焊上了一个新的翼子板. (**b**) [Tn] make (sth) by joining pieces of metal in this way 用锻焊法或焊接法制造(某物). (**c**) [I] (of iron, etc) be capable of being welded (指铁等)能被锻焊或焊接: *Some metals weld better than others.* 有的金属容易焊, 有的不容易焊. **2** [Tn·pr] **~ sb/sth into sth** (*fig* 比喻) unite (people or things) into an effective whole 将(人或事物)结合起来: *weld a bunch of untrained recruits into an efficient fighting force* 把未经训练的一群新兵组织成有战斗力的部队. Cf 参看 FORGE² 1.

▷ **weld** *n* joint made by welding 锻焊处; 焊接点.

welder *n* person whose job is making welded joints (eg in a car factory) 焊工.

wel·fare /ˈwelfeə(r); ˋwɛl,fɛr/ *n* [U] **1** good health, happiness, prosperity, etc of a person or group (个人或集体的)健康、幸福、繁荣等: *Parents are responsible for the welfare of their children.* 父母要对子女的幸福负责. ○ *the welfare of the nation* 国家的繁荣昌盛 ○ *We are concerned about his welfare.* 我们关心他的健康. **2** care for the health, safety, etc of a particular group (对某群体的健康、安全等的)关心, 照顾, 福利: *child/infant welfare* 儿童[幼儿]福利 ○ [attrib 作定语] *a child welfare clinic* 儿童保健医院. **3** (*US*) (*Brit* **social security**) money paid by the State to those in need, eg because they are unemployed, disabled, etc (政府发放的)福利救济金(如对失业、伤残人士的). Cf 参看 SUPPLEMENTARY BENEFIT (SUPPLEMENTARY).

□ **ˌwelfare ˈstate** (often 常作 **the ˌWelfare ˈState**) (country that has a) system of ensuring the welfare of its citizens by means of social services (eg pensions, family allowances, free medical care, etc) provided by the State 福利国家, 福利制度(如政府向公民提供养老金、家庭津贴、公费医疗等).

ˈwelfare work (**a**) organized efforts to ensure the welfare of a group of people (eg employees in a factory, the poor, the disabled, etc) 福利工作(如为工厂职工、穷人、伤残人士等服务的). (**b**) (*US*) social work 社会福利工作. **ˈwelfare worker**.

well¹ /wel; wɛl/ *n* **1** (**a**) shaft dug in the ground, usu lined with brick or stone, for obtaining water from an underground source 井; 水井: *dig/drive/sink a well* 挖[凿/掘]井 ○ *The villagers get their water from a well.* 该村村民吃井水. ○ [attrib 作定语] *well water* 井水. (**b**) = OIL WELL (OIL). **2** enclosed space like the shaft of a well, eg one in a building from roof to basement that contains a staircase or lift 似井的空间(如建筑物中的楼梯或电梯通道). **3** (**a**) (*dated except in place-names* 旧, 现仅用于地名) spring or fountain 泉: *Tunbridge Wells* 坦布里奇韦尔斯. (**b**) **~ of sth** (*dated fml fig* 旧, 文, 比喻) source of sth 某事物的源泉或来源: *a well of information* 信息的来源. **4** (*Brit*) (in a lawcourt) space in front of the judge where lawyers sit, separated from the rest of the court by a railing (法庭中的)律师席(位于法官对面, 有栏杆与其他部分相隔).

▷ **well** *v* **1** [Ipr, Ip] **~ (out/up)** flow or rise like water from a well (像泉水般)流出, 涌出, 喷出: *Blood was welling (out) from the wound.* 鲜血从伤口中流出. ○ *Tears welled up in her eyes.* 她泪盈于睫. ○ *Anger was welling up in him.* 他怒火中烧. **2** (phr v) **well over** overflow 流出; 泛滥.

□ **ˈwell-head** (also **ˈwell-spring**) *n* source of a spring or fountain 泉源.

well² /wel; wɛl/ *adj* (*compar* **better** /ˈbetə(r); ˋbɛtɚ/, *superl* **best** /best; bɛst/) **1** [usu pred 通常作表语] in good health 健康: *be, feel, get, look, etc well* 身体好、觉得身体好、康复、气色好 ○ *Are you quite well?* 你身体很

好吧? ○ *Is she well enough to travel?* 她身体康复, 能够旅行了吗? ○ *I'm better now, thank you.* 我现在好些了, 多谢您关心. ○ *He's not a well man.* 他身体不好. ⇨ Usage at HEALTHY 用法见 HEALTHY. **2** [pred 作表语] in a satisfactory state or position 满意; 满足: (*saying* 谚) *All's well that ends well.* 结局好就算一切都好. ○ *We're very well where we are.* 我们处境很好. ○ *It seems that all is not well at home.* 看来家中并非事事如意. **3** [pred 作表语] advisable or desirable 可取; 相宜: *It would be well to start early.* 最好早点儿动身. **4** (idm 习语) ˌ**all very** ˈ**well (for sb)...** (*infml ironic* 口, 反语) (used to indicate that one is not happy, satisfied or in agreement with what sb has said or done 用以表示不悦、不满或不同意): *It's all very well (for* ˈ*you) to suggest a skiing holiday, but I'm the one who will have to pay for it.* 你提议假日滑雪倒是不错, 可付钱的却是我. ˌ**all well and** ˈ**good** (*infml* 口) satisfactory (though other things may not be satisfactory) 好倒是好(但也有不如意处): *The job's done — that's all well and good — but what about the bonus we were promised?* 工作完成了——好倒是好——但是答应给我们的奖金给不给? **(just) as** ˈ**well (to do sth)** prudent or appropriate 倒也不错; 也相宜: *It would be (just) as well to phone and say we will be late.* 还是打个电话说我们得迟到比较好.

well³ /wel; wɛl/ *adv* (*compar* **better** /ˈbetə(r); ˈbɛtɚ/, *superl* **best** /best; bɛst/) **1** (usu placed after the *v*, and after the direct object if the *v* is transitive 通常置于动词之后, 若是及物动词则置于直接宾语之后) **(a)** in a good, right or satisfactory manner 好; 对; 满意地: *The children behaved well/were well-behaved.* 孩子都表现得很好. ○ *She speaks English very well.* 她英语说得很好. ○ *The conference was organized very well.* 大会组织得很好. ○ *I can read well enough without glasses.* 我不戴眼镜也能看得很清楚. ○ *Well done, played, run, etc!* ie cries expressing admiration, congratulations, etc 干得、演得、跑得...好! ○ *I hope everything is going well* (ie is satisfactory) *with you.* 愿你事事如意. ○ *Things didn't go well for us at first, but everything is fine now.* 我们起初不很顺利, 现一切都好了. ○ *Do these colours go well together* (ie harmonize with each other)? 这些颜色配在一起协调吗? ○ *The plan didn't work out very well.* 这一计划实行起来不大满意. ○ *Investing in industry is money well spent.* 钱投资在工业上是正确的. Cf 参看 ILL¹ 1. **(b)** in a kind manner 和蔼地; 友好地: *They treated me very well.* 他们待我很好. Cf 参看 ILL¹ 2. **(c)** thoroughly, completely or carefully 彻底地; 完全地; 仔细地: *Shake the mixture well.* 把这个混合物充分摇匀. ○ *Read the document well before you sign it.* 仔细审阅文件后方可签字. ○ *The pan must be dried well before you put it away.* 这个锅用后要彻底擦干方可收起. ○ *His shoes were always well polished.* 他的鞋总是擦得干干净净. ○ *She doesn't know him very well.* 她不十分了解他. ○ *I'm well* (ie fully) *able to manage on my own.* 我完全能够独自处理. **2** with praise or approval 夸奖地; 称赞地: *speak/think well of sb* 称赞[钦佩]某人. **3** (after *can, could, may, might* 用于 can、could、may、might 之后) justifiably, reasonably or probably 有理由地; 合理地; 可能地: *You may well be right.* 很可能是你对. ○ *I might well consider it later.* 我也可能以后再考虑考虑. ○ *I can't very well leave now.* 我现在离开不大合适. ○ *I couldn't very well refuse to help them, could I?* 我不帮助他们说不过去吧, 是不是? ○ *'They've split up, you know.' 'I can well believe it.'* '你知道吗, 他们闹翻了.' '我看这是情理之中的事.' ○ *It may well be that the train is delayed.* 很有可能火车晚点了. **4** to a considerable extent or degree 到相当的程度: *I don't know how old he is, but he looks well over/past forty.* 我不知道他多少岁, 但是他看上去有四十多岁了. ○ *She was driving at well over the speed limit.* 她开车的速度远远超过了速度限制. ○ *lean well forward/back in one's chair* 坐在椅子上身体很向前[后]靠 ○ *It was well worth waiting for.* 这件事倒是很值得等待. ○ *Temperatures are well up in the forties.* 温度足有四十多度了. **5** (idm 习语) **as well (as sb/sth)** in addition (to sb/sth/doing sth) (除某人[某事物/做某事]外)也, 还, 而且: *Are they coming as well?* 他们也来吗? ○ *He grows flowers as well as vegetables.* 他既种菜也种花. ○ *She is a talented musician as well as being a photographer.* 她不但是摄影师还是个天才的音乐家. ⇨Usage at ALSO 用法见 ALSO. **augur well/ill for sb/sth** ⇨ AUGUR. **be** ˌ**well** ˈ**out of sth** (*infml* 口) be fortunate that one is not involved in sth 幸亏没牵涉在某事中. **be well up in sth** be well informed about sth 对某事物消息灵通或非常熟悉: *He's well up in all the latest developments in the industry.* 他很熟悉这个行业中所有的最新情况. **bloody well** ⇨ BLOODY². **bode well/ill** ⇨ BODE. **deserve well/ill of sb** ⇨ DESERVE. **do oneself well** provide oneself with comforts, luxuries, etc 生活优裕. **do** ˈ**well (a)** be successful; prosper 成功; 兴旺: *Simon is doing very well at school.* 西蒙的学习成绩很好. ○ *The business is doing well.* 生意十分兴隆. **(b)** (only in the continuous tenses 仅用于进行时态) be making a good recovery from an illness, etc 康复等情况良好: *The patient is doing well.* 病人身体恢复很好. ○ *Mother and baby are doing well.* 母子均平安. **do well by sb** treat sb generously 慷慨对待某人. **do** ˈ**well for oneself** become successful or prosperous (个人)成功, 富裕. **do well out of sb/sth** make a profit out of or obtain money from sb/sth 从某人[某事物]处获得利益或金钱. **do well to do sth** (esp as a warning) act wisely or prudently in doing sth (尤指提醒或警告)做某事时聪明或谨慎: *You would do well to remember who is paying the bill.* 你最好记住是谁付的帐. ○ *They would do well to concentrate more on their work.* 他们最好认真工作. ○ *You did well to sell when the price was high.* 你趁价高卖出做得聪明. **fucking well** ⇨ FUCK. **jolly well** ⇨ JOLLY. **leave/let well a**ˈ**lone** not interfere with sth that is satisfactory or adequate 对感到满意或满足的事物不再触动; 维持原状: *Any changes would be very difficult to make so it's better to leave well alone.* 做任何改动都很困难, 还是见好就收吧. **may/might (just) as well do sth** in the circumstances, no harm will come from doing sth 做某事倒也无妨: *Since nobody else wants the job, we might as well let him have it.* 既然谁也不要这份工作, 咱们不妨让他去做吧. **one may/might as well be hanged/hung for a sheep as a lamb** ⇨ HANG¹. **mean well** ⇨ MEAN¹. **mean well by sb** ⇨ MEAN¹. **pretty much/nearly/well** ⇨ PRETTY. **promise well** ⇨ PROMISE². **speak well for sb/sth** ⇨ SPEAK. **stand well with sb** be in sb's favour 受某人喜爱. ˌ**very** ˈ**well** (used to indicate that one agrees or obeys, esp after sb else has persuaded, ordered or requested one to do sth 用以表示同意或服从(尤指经劝说、命令或要求后)): *Very well, doctor, I'll try to take more exercise.* 好吧, 大夫, 那我就尽量多锻炼锻炼吧. ○ *Oh, very well, if you insist.* 噢, 好啦, 你一定要这样就听你的吧. ˌ**well and** ˈ**truly** (*infml* 口) completely; decisively 完全地; 果断地: *By that time we were well and truly lost.* 到那时, 我们完全迷路了. **well aware of sth/that...** fully informed or conscious 充分了解或意识到: *I'm well aware of the risks.* 我清楚知道其中的风险. ˈ**well away (a)** having made good progress 已很有进展: *By the end of the month, we'll be well away.* 到本月底我们就很有成绩了. **(b)** (*infml* 口) (beginning to be) drunk or hilarious (逐渐)醉或欢闹起来. **well in (with sb)** (*infml* 口) regarded as a close friend (by sb); accepted (被某人)视为密友; 被当作自己人: *She seems to be well in with the right people.* 她和她应该相处的人看来十分融洽. **well** ˈ**off** in a good position, esp financially 境况良好; (尤指)富裕: *His family is not very well off.* 他家不太富裕. ○ *You don't need to look for another job — you're well off where you are.* 你用不着另找工作——你现在的境况很不错了. **well off for sth** having plenty of sth 有很多: *We're well off for storage space in the new flat.* 我们的新公寓里有很多储藏东西的地方. **wish sb/sth well/ill** ⇨ WISH.

□ (Compound *adjs* formed from *well-* + past participles are usu hyphenated when attributive but not hyphenated when predicative, except when the *adj* has acquired a restricted sense. 由 well- + 过去分词构成的复合形容词, 用作定语时通常中间有连字符, 用作表语时中间无连字符, 但这类形容词的词义有限定时仍需用连接号.)

ˌ**well-ad**ˈ**vised** *adj* sensible; prudent 有见识的; 审慎的: *You would be well advised to* (ie You ought to) *reconsider your decision.* 你应该把你的决定再重新考虑一下才好. ○ *a* ˌ*well-advised* ˈ*move* 高招.

ˌ**well-ap**ˈ**pointed** *adj* having all the necessary equipment, furniture, etc 备有所需设备、家具等的: *a* ˌ*well-appointed a*ˈ*partment, ho*ˈ*tel,* ˈ*office, etc* 设备完善的公寓、旅馆、办公室等.

ˌ**well-**ˈ**balanced** *adj* (of a person) sensible and emotionally stable（指人）神智清醒、情绪稳定的：*healthy, ˌwell-balanced ˈchildren* 身心健康、情绪稳定的儿童 ○ *You need to be very well balanced to cope with the stress of a job like that.* 做这种工作压力那么大，情绪非得十分稳定不可.

ˈwell-being *n* [U] state of being healthy, happy, etc 健康、幸福等的状况：*have a sense of (physical/spiritual) well-being* 有（身体[精神]）健康的感觉.

ˌwell-ˈborn *adj* of an aristocratic or a socially superior family 贵族出身的；出身高贵的.

ˌwell-ˈbred *adj* having or showing good manners 有教养的；有礼貌的：*She was too well bred to show her disappointment.* 她很有涵养，遇到失望的事亦不形于色. Cf 参看 ILL-BRED (ILL[1]).

ˌwell-ˈbuilt *adj* (*usu approv* 通常作褒义)(of a person) strong and muscular（指人）身强力壮的，结实的.

ˌwell-conˈnected *adj* friendly with or related to rich, influential or socially superior people 与有钱、有势或有社会地位的人有亲友关系的.

ˌwell-disˈposed *adj* **~ (towards sb/sth)** (**a**) sympathetic or friendly to (sb) 对（某人）同情的或友好的：*She seemed well disposed towards us.* 她看来对我们颇有好感. (**b**) approving (a plan, etc); ready to help 对（计划等）赞成的；乐于帮助的：*The committee are well disposed towards the idea.* 委员会同意这一意见. Cf 参看 ILL-DISPOSED (ILL[1]).

ˌwell-ˈdone *adj* (of food, esp meat) cooked thoroughly or for a long time（指食物，尤指肉）熟透的，烹调久的：*He prefers his steak well-done.* 他喜欢吃煎得熟透的牛排.

ˌwell-eˈstablished *adj* existing (and operating successfully) for a long time 存在已久（且切实可行）的；确立的：*a ˌwell-established ˈfirm* 地位稳固的老公司 ○ *ˌwell-established proˈcedures* 行之有效的老办法.

ˌwell-ˈfed *adj* having good meals regularly 经常吃得好的：*The cat looked very sleek and well fed.* 这只猫毛很光滑，看来喂得很好.

ˌwell-ˈfounded *adj* based on facts; substantiated 有事实依据的；有根据的：*ˌwell-founded susˈpicions* 有根据的怀疑.

ˌwell-ˈheeled *adj* (*infml* 口) rich 有钱的：*a restaurant with many ˌwell-heeled ˈcustomers* 有很多阔顾客光顾的饭馆.

ˌwell-inˈformed *adj* having (access to) knowledge or information 有见识的；消息灵通的：*ˌwell-informed oˈpinion, ˈquarters, ˈsources* 有见识的看法、消息灵通方面、消息灵通人士.

ˌwell-inˈtentioned *adj* intended or intending to be helpful, useful, etc 出于好心的；善意的：*She reacted angrily to my ˌwell-intentioned reˈmarks.* 我一番好话反而惹她生了一肚子气. ○ *He's well-intentioned but not very good at getting things done.* 他常常是好心办不出好事.

ˌwell-ˈknown *adj* known to many people; familiar or famous 众所周知的；熟知的；著名的.

ˌwell-ˈmeaning *adj* acting with good intentions (but often not having the desired effect) 好心的，善意的（但常指效果未如愿）.

W

ˌwell-ˈmeant *adj* done, said, etc with good intentions but not having the desired effect 好心好意的（但效果未如愿）.

ˌwell-ˈoiled *adj* (*sl* 俚) drunk 喝醉的.

ˌwell-preˈserved *adj* (**a**) (of an old person) not showing many signs of old age; young-looking（指老人）不显老的，显得年轻的，少相的. (**b**) (of old things) in good condition（指旧物）保存得好的：*a well-preserved Greek temple* 保存得很好的希腊庙宇.

ˌwell-ˈread *adj* having read many books, and therefore very knowledgeable 书看得多的；博学的.

ˌwell-ˈrounded *adj* (**a**) (of a person's body) pleasantly plump（指人的身体）丰满的. (**b**) [usu attrib 通常作定语] wide and varied 广泛的；面面俱到的：*a ˌwell-rounded eduˈcation* 全面教育.

ˌwell-ˈspoken *adj* speaking correctly or in a refined way 说得对的；善于辞令的.

ˌwell-ˈthought-of *adj* (of a person) respected, admired and liked（指人）受人尊敬、钦佩、喜爱的：*He is well-thought-of in government circles.* 他在政府各部门中很受敬重.

ˌwell-ˈthumbed *adj* (of a book, etc) having its pages marked or worn, because it has been read so often（指书等）（因常翻阅）书页上有记号、污斑或破损处的.

ˌwell-ˈtimed *adj* done, said, etc at the right time or at a suitable time 时间正好的；适时的：*Your remarks were certainly well timed.* 你的话说得正是时候. ○ *a ˌwell-timed interˈvention* 及时的介入. Cf 参看 ILL-TIMED (ILL[1]).

ˌwell-to-ˈdo *adj* prosperous; wealthy 富裕的；富有的.

ˌwell-ˈtried *adj* often used and therefore known to be reliable 常使用而知其可靠的：*a ˌwell-tried ˈmethod, ˈremedy, etc* 屡试不爽的方法、疗法等.

ˌwell-ˈturned *adj* (*fml* 文) expressed elegantly 措辞高雅的：*a ˌwell-turned ˈcompliment, ˈphrase, etc* 措辞优美的赞扬、词语等.

ˌwell-ˈversed *adj* [pred 作表语] **~ (in sth)** knowing a lot (about sth); experienced 精通；有经验：*well-versed in the art of flattery* 善于阿谀奉承.

ˈwell-wisher *n* person who hopes that another will be happy, successful, healthy, etc 希望别人幸福、成功、健康等的人：*They received many letters of sympathy from well-wishers.* 他们收到许多来信，寄信人向他们表示同情和祝福.

ˌwell-ˈworn *adj* (**a**) (of a phrase, etc) over-used (and therefore commonplace or trite)（指词语等）滥用的（因而陈腐的）. (**b**) very worn as a result of much use（因使用频繁）破旧的：*a ˌwell-worn old ˈcoat* 穿得已破旧的大衣.

well[4] /wel; wɛl/ *interj* (esp in spoken English 尤用于口语) **1** (used to express astonishment 用以表示惊讶)：*Well, who would have thought it?* 嗳，谁想得到是这样啊？○ *Well, well (— I should never have guessed it)!* 呦，呦（——那我可决猜不着）！○ *Well, you ˈdo surprise me!* 哟，你真吓了我一跳！ **2** (used to express relief 用以表示宽慰)：*Well, thank goodness that's over!* 嗳，谢天谢地，这件事总算过去了！○ *Well, here we are at last!* 好啦，我们终于到了！ **3** (also **oh well**) (used to express resignation 用以表示无可奈何)：*Oh well, there's nothing we can do about it.* 唉，这件事我们无能为力了. ○ *Well, it can't be helped.* 唉，没有办法. **4** (also **very well**) (used to express agreement or understanding 用以表示同意或理解)：*Very well, then, I'll accept your offer.* 好吧，那我就接受你的好意. **5** (used when conceding a point in an argument, etc 在争论等中，用以对某一点表示让步)：*Well, you may be right.* 好了，也许你说得对. **6** (used when resuming a conversation, etc or changing the subject after a pause 在交谈的停顿后，用以接续或改换话题)：*Well, as I was saying,...* 唉，我刚才说的... ○ *Well, the next day...* 对了，第二天... ○ *Well, let's move on to the next item.* 好了，咱们谈下一个问题吧. **7** (used to express hesitation, doubt, etc 用以表示犹豫、怀疑等)：*'Do you want to come?' 'Well — I'm not sure.'* '你想来吗？''嗯——我还说不好.' **8** (idm 习语) **well I ˈnever (ˈdid)!** (*infml* 口) (used as an exclamation of pleased or annoyed astonishment 用作喜悦的或恼怒的惊叹语).

we'll /wi:l; wil/ *contracted form* 缩约式 **1** we shall ⇨ SHALL. **2** we will ⇨ WILL[1].

wel·ling·ton /ˈwelɪŋtən; ˈwɛlɪŋtən/ *n* (also **ˌwellington ˈboot**, *infml* 口语作 **welly**) (*esp Brit*) waterproof rubber boot, usu reaching almost to the knee 威灵顿长筒靴（通常为及膝的橡胶雨靴）：*a pair of wellingtons/wellington boots* 一双威灵顿长筒靴. ⇨illus at BOOT 见 BOOT 插图.

well·nigh /ˈwelnaɪ; ˋwɛlˋnaɪ/ *adv* (*fml or rhet* 文或修辞) almost 几乎；差不多：*The task is ˌwellnigh imˈpossible.* 这项任务几乎无法完成. ○ *The party was wellnigh over by the time we arrived.* 我们到达时，聚会差不多快结束了.

welly /ˈwelɪ; ˋwɛlɪ/ *n* (*Brit infml* 口) = WELLINGTON：*a new pair of green wellies* 一双新的绿色的威灵顿长筒靴.

Welsh /welʃ; wɛlʃ/ *adj* of Wales, its people or its language 威尔士的；威尔士人的；威尔士语的：*the Welsh coastline* 威尔士海岸 ○ *Welsh poetry* 威尔士诗歌.

▷ **Welsh** *n* **1** [U] Celtic language of Wales 威尔士的凯尔特语. **2 the Welsh** [pl] the people of Wales 威尔士人民.

□ **ˌWelsh ˈdresser** type of sideboard with cupboards and drawers in the lower part and shelves in the upper part 威尔士式餐具柜（柜橱与抽屉在下，上有架子）. ⇨ illus at App 1 见附录1插图，page xvi.

Welshman /ˈwelʃmən; ˋwɛlʃmən/ (*pl* **-men** /-mən; -mən/, *fem* 阴性作 **Welshwoman** /-wʊmən; -ˌwʊmən/, *pl* **-women** /-wɪmɪn; -ˌwɪmɪn/) *n* native of Wales 威尔士人.

ˌ**Welsh** ˈ**rarebit** (also **rarebit,** ˌ**Welsh** ˈ**rabbit**) dish of melted cheese on toast 威尔士小吃(面包片烤热, 上有融化奶酪).

welsh /welʃ; wɛlʃ/ *v* (*derog* 贬) **1** [I, Ipr] **~ (on sth)** avoid paying money owed, esp at gambling 赖帐; (尤指)赌博赖帐: *welsh on one's debts* 赖帐. **2** [Ipr] **~ on sb/sth** break one's promise to sb 对某人食言或失信: *She welshed on (the bargain she made with) us.* 她与我们洽谈成交后又翻悔了. ▷ **welsher** *n*.

welt /welt; wɛlt/ *n* **1** strip of leather round the edge of the upper(*n* 1) of a shoe, to which the sole is stitched 沿条(鞋面与鞋底相缝的皮条). **2** mark left on the skin by a heavy blow, esp with a whip; weal (皮肤上的)伤痕, (尤指)鞭痕.

wel·ter /ˈweltə(r); ˈwɛltɚ/ *n* [sing] **~ of sth/sb** disorderly mixture of things or people; general confusion (人或物的)混杂; 混乱: *a welter of unrelated facts* 互不相关的事情混在一起 ○ *carried forward by the welter of surging bodies* 被滔滔流水冲走.

wel·ter·weight /ˈweltəweɪt; ˈwɛltɚˌwet/ *n* boxer weighing between 61 and 67 kilograms, next above lightweight 次中量级拳击手(体重在61至67公斤之间者): *Throughout his career, he fought as a welterweight/at welterweight.* 他在整个拳击生涯中都是以次中量级参赛. ○ [attrib 作定语] *a welterweight contest* 次中量级拳击赛.

wen /wen; wɛn/ *n* harmless, usu permanent, tumour on the skin, esp on the head 表皮囊肿, 皮脂囊肿, 粉瘤(尤指头部的).

wench /wentʃ; wɛntʃ/ *n* (*arch or joc* 古或谑) mature girl or young woman (成年的)姑娘, 少女; 少妇.

wend /wend; wɛnd/ *v* (idm 习语) **wend one's way** (*arch or joc* 古或谑) go; leave 去; 走; 离开: *It's time we were wending our way*, ie We must go. 我们该走了.

went *pt* of GO[1].

wept *pt, pp* of WEEP.

were ⇨ BE.

we're /wɪə(r); wɪr/ *contracted form* 缩约式 we are ⇨ BE.

weren't ⇨ BE.

were·wolf /ˈwɪəwʊlf; ˈwɪrˌwʊlf/ *n* (*pl* **-wolves** /-wʊlvz; -ˌwʊlvz/) (in stories) person who changes, or is capable of changing, into a wolf, esp at the time of the full moon (故事中的)可变成狼的人(尤指在月圆时).

Wes·leyan /ˈwezlɪən; ˈwɛslɪən/ *n, adj* (member) of the Methodist Church founded by John Wesley 卫斯理宗的(教徒); 循道宗的(教徒).

west /west; wɛst/ *n* [sing] (*abbr* 缩写 **W**) **1 the west** point on the horizon where the sun sets; one of the four main points of the compass 西; 西方: *The rain is coming from the west.* 这场雨是从西面来的. ○ *Bristol is in the west of England.* 布里斯托尔位于英格兰的西部. ○ *She lives to the west of* (ie further west than) *Glasgow.* 她住在格拉斯哥以西的地方. Cf 参看 EAST, NORTH, SOUTH. **2 the West** (**a**) the non-Communist countries of Europe and America 西方国家(欧美非共产党执政的国家). (**b**) Europe, contrasted with Oriental countries 西方(欧洲, 与东方国家相对照). **3 the West** the western side of the USA 美国西部: *She's lived in the West* (eg California) *for ten years now.* 她在西部(如加利福尼亚州)到现在已住了十年了. **4** (idm 习语) **go** ˈ**west** (*dated sl* 旧, 俚) be destroyed, used up, ruined, etc 完蛋; 用光; 毁灭; 归西; 上西天: *There was a fire, and five years of research work went west.* 失了一场火, 五年的研究工作毁于一旦.

▷ **west** *adj* [attrib 作定语] **1** in or towards the west 在西方的; 向西方的; 朝西的: *the west side of London* 伦敦的西部. **2** (of winds) blowing from the west (指风)来自西方的. Cf 参看 WESTERLY.

west *adv* towards the west 向西方: *travel west* 向西方行进 ○ *three miles west of here* 从这里向西三英里 ○ *The building faces west.* 这座建筑物面朝西.

west·ward /ˈwestwəd; ˈwɛstwɚd/ *adj* towards the west 向西的: *a westward journey* 向西之行.

west·wards (also **west·ward**) *adv*: *travel westward(s)* 向西行进. ⇨Usage at FORWARD[2] 用法见 FORWARD[2].

□ **westbound** /ˈwestbaʊnd; ˈwɛstˌbaʊnd/ *adj* travelling or leading towards the west 西行的: *westbound traffic* 西行车辆 ○ *the westbound carriageway of the motorway* 高速公路的西行车道.

the ˈ**West Country** (*Brit*) the south-west region of Britain (英国的)西南地区: [attrib 作定语] *a West-Country village* 英国西南地区的一个村庄.

the ˌ**West** ˈ**End** (*Brit*) the area of London that includes most theatres, fashionable and expensive shops, etc 伦敦西区(伦敦多数剧院、时髦及豪华商店等的所在地): [attrib 作定语] *a* ˌ*West-End* ˈ*cinema* 伦敦西区的一家电影院. Cf 参看 THE EAST END (EAST).

west·erly /ˈwestəlɪ; ˈwɛstɚlɪ/ *adj* **1** [attrib 作定语] in or towards the west 在西方的; 向西方的; 朝西的: *westerly shores* 西岸 ○ *in a westerly direction* 朝西的方向. **2** [usu attrib 通常作定语] (of winds) blowing from the west (指风)来自西方的.

▷ **west·erly** *n* wind blowing from the west 西风: *a gale-force westerly* 蒲福风级达8级的西风. — *adv* towards the west 向西: *travel westerly* 向西方行进.

west·ern /ˈwestən; ˈwɛstɚn/ *adj* **1** [attrib 作定语] of or in the west 西方的; 西部的; 在西方的; 在西部的: *western regions of the British Isles* 不列颠群岛的西部地区 ○ *the western United States* 美国的西部. **2** (also **Western**) [usu attrib 通常作定语] (characteristic) of the West 欧美的、欧洲的、美国西部的或有这类西方特征的: *the Western way of life* 西方国家的生活方式 ○ *western attitudes, clothes, nations, philosophy* 西方国家的态度、衣物、民族、哲学.

▷ **west·ern** *n* film or book about the life of cowboys in the western part of the USA, esp during the time of the wars with the American Indians 西部的电影或小说(描写美国西部牛仔生活的, 尤指与美洲印第安人战争时期的).

west·erner *n* (**a**) native or inhabitant of the West 欧美人、欧洲人或美国西部的人: *a country in Asia visited by few westerners* 几乎没有西方人到过的亚洲的一个国家. (**b**) native or inhabitant of the western part of a country, esp the USA 住在一个国家西部的人; (尤指)美国西部的人.

west·ern·ize, -ise /-aɪz; ˌnaɪz/ *v* [Tn] make (an Eastern country, person, etc) more like one in the West, esp in ways of living and thinking, institutions, etc 使(东方的国家、人等)西方化(尤指生活、思想、风俗、制度等方面): *The island became fully westernized after the war.* 这个岛战后已全盘西化了. **west·ern·ization, -isation** /ˌwestənaɪˈzeɪʃn; *US* -nɪˈz-; ˌwɛstɚnəˈzeʃən/ *n* [U].

west·ern·most /-məʊst; -ˌmost/ *adj* farthest west 最西的; 极西的: *the westernmost tip of the island* 岛的最西端.

wet /wet; wɛt/ *adj* (**-tter**, **-ttest**) **1** covered, soaked or moistened with liquid, esp water 有液体的; (尤指)湿的, 浸透的, 潮湿的: *wet clothes, grass, roads* 湿的衣物、草、道路 ○ *Her cheeks were wet with tears.* 她泪流满面. ○ *Did you get wet* (eg in the rain)? 你淋湿了吗? ○ *dripping/soaking/wringing* (ie thoroughly) *wet* 湿透的. **2** (of weather, etc) rainy (指天气等)有雨的, 下雨的, 多雨的: *a wet day* 下雨天 ○ *the wet season* 雨季 ○ *It was the wettest October for many years.* 多年来十月份从来没下过这么多雨. **3** (of ink, paint, plaster, etc) recently applied and not yet dry or set (指墨水、油墨、油漆、灰泥等)尚未干的, 尚未凝固的: *Be careful — the paint is still wet.* 小心——油漆还没干呢. ○ *Don't walk on the wet cement.* 水泥未干时不要在上面行走. **4** (*Brit infml derog* 口, 贬) (of a person) lacking purpose or spirit; ineffectual, indecisive or dull (指人)无目的的, 无精神的, 不能胜任的, 不果断的, 迟钝的: *It was rather wet of you to say nothing when you had the chance.* 你有机会说却什么也没说, 真笨. **5** (idm 习语) **like a wet** ˈ**rag** tired and bedraggled 又累又湿又脏. **soaked/wet to the skin** ⇨ SKIN. **(still)** ˌ**wet behind the** ˈ**ears** (*infml derog* 口, 贬) immature or inexperienced; naïve 无经验的; 幼稚的; 乳臭未干的. **a** ˌ**wet** ˈ**blanket** (*infml* 口) person who spoils other people's pleasure because he is gloomy, dull, pessimistic, etc (因自己消沉、沉闷、悲观等)使别人兴致低落的人, 扫兴的人: *He was such a wet blanket at the party that they never invited him again.* 他在那次聚会中异常扫兴, 人家再也不邀请他了. ˌ**wet** ˈ**through** thoroughly soaked 湿透: *We got wet through.* 我们都湿透了. ○ *My overcoat is wet through.* 我的大衣完全湿透了.

▷ **wet** *n* **1 the wet** [sing] wet weather; rain 雨天; 雨: *Come in out of the wet.* 快进来免得淋着. **2** [U] moisture 潮湿; 水气. **3** [C] (*Brit derog* 贬) (**a**) dull or feeble person 迟钝的或软弱的人. (**b**) politician who favours moderate rather than extreme policies 稳健而不激进的政治家: *Tory wets* 保守党中的温和派.

wet *v* (**-tt-**; *pt, pp* **wet** or **wetted**) **1** [Tn] make (sth) wet; moisten (sth) 使(某物)湿; 弄湿(某物): *Wet the clay a bit more before you start to mould it.* 把泥再弄湿点再动手塑造. **2** (idm 习语) **wet the/one's 'bed** (not passive; past tense usu *wet* 不用于被动语态; 过去时态通常作wet) urinate when in bed (and asleep) (睡眠中)尿床. **wet one's 'whistle** (*dated infml* 旧, 口) have a drink, esp an alcoholic one 喝饮料(尤指酒). **wet·ting** *n* (usu *sing* 通常作单数) instance of becoming or being made wet 弄湿: *get a wetting in the heavy rain* 在大雨中淋湿.

wetly *adv*: *The leaves glistened wetly in the rain.* 叶子在雨中湿淋淋的闪闪生光.

wet·ness *n* [U].

□ ˌ**wet 'dock** dock filled with water so that a ship can float in it 湿船坞; 有闸港池.

ˌ**wet 'dream** erotic dream that causes an emission of semen (梦中)遗精.

'**wet fish** fresh uncooked fish for sale in a shop, etc (商店等出售的)鲜鱼.

'**wetlands** *n* [pl] marshy areas 沼泽地: *birds of the wetlands* 沼泽地区的鸟 ○ [attrib 作定语] *wetland birds* 沼泽地区的鸟.

'**wet-nurse** *n* (esp formerly) woman employed to breast-feed another woman's baby (尤指旧时的)乳母, 奶妈.

'**wet suit** porous rubber garment worn by underwater swimmers, etc to keep warm (保暖的)潜水服.

wether /ˈweðə(r); ˈwɛðɚ/ *n* castrated ram 去势的羊.

we've /wi:v; wiv/ *contracted form* 缩约式 we have ⇨ HAVE.

whack /wæk; *US* hwæk; hwæk/ *v* [Tn] (*infml* 口) strike or beat (sb/sth) vigorously 猛打(某人[某物]).

▷ **whack** *n* **1** (sound of a) heavy blow 重击(的声音): *heard a sudden whack* 突然听到重击声 ○ *I'll give you such a whack!* 我得狠狠打你一顿! **2** (*infml* 口) **~ (at sth)** attempt 尝试: *I'm prepared to have a whack at it.* 我准备试一试. **3** (*infml* 口) share 分儿: *Have you all had a fair whack?* 你们是不是都得到了公平的一份了? ○ *Some people are not doing their whack.* 有的人没有尽力.

whacked *adj* [usu pred 通常作表语] (*infml* 口) (of a person) tired out; exhausted (指人)累垮, 精疲力竭: *I'm absolutely whacked!* 我可真累坏了!

whack·ing *n* (*infml* 口) beating 殴打: *That child deserves a whacking.* 那个孩子欠揍. — *adj* (*infml* 口) big of its kind (在同类中)大的: *a whacking lie* 大瞎话. — *adv* (*infml* 口) very 非常: *a whacking great bruise* 很大的一块青肿.

whale 鲸

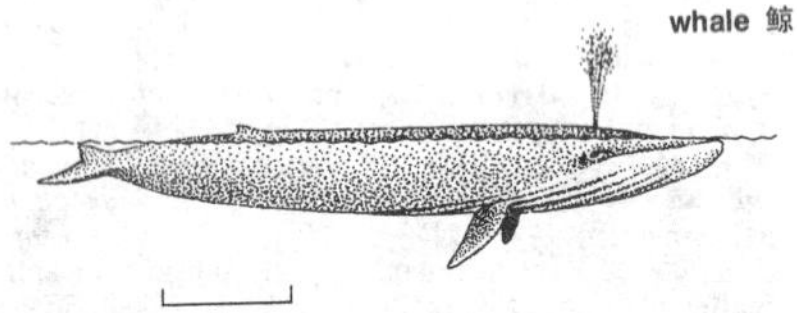

5 m
5米

whale /weɪl; *US* hweɪl; hwel/ *n* **1** any of several types of very large mammal that live in the sea, some of which are hunted for their oil and flesh 鲸. **2** (idm 习语) **have a 'whale of a time** (*infml* 口) enjoy oneself very much; have a very good time 玩得非常痛快; 过得非常愉快: *The children had a whale of a time at the funfair.* 孩子们在游乐场玩得很高兴.

▷ **whale** *v* [I] (usu in the continuous tenses 通常用于进行时态) hunt whales (and produce oil, etc from their carcasses) 捕鲸(并提取鲸油). **whaler** *n* (**a**) ship used for hunting whales 捕鲸船. (**b**) person who hunts whales 捕鲸的人. **whal·ing** *n* [U] hunting whales 捕鲸: [attrib 作定语] *the whaling fleet* 捕鲸船队.

□ '**whalebone** *n* [U] thin hard springy substance found in the upper jaw of some types of whale, used (esp formerly) for stiffening garments, eg corsets 鲸须, 须板(某些鲸类种群上颌的角质薄片, 用以支撑服装, 尤指旧时用的, 如紧身内衣中的).

wham /wæm; *US* hwæm; hwæm/ *interj, n* (*infml* 口) (imitation of the) sound of a sudden heavy blow 突然的重击声(的象声词): *Wham! The car hit the wall.* 砰! 汽车撞到墙上了. ○ *The door struck him in the face with a terrific wham.* 门砰的一声巨响, 把他的脸撞了.

▷ **wham** *v* (**-mm-**) (*infml* 口) (**a**) [Ipr, Ip] strike sth/sb violently 猛打某物[某人]: *It whammed into the wall.* 那东西猛然撞到墙上. (**b**) [Tn, Tn·pr, Tn·p] strike (sth/sb) violently; move (sth) quickly, noisily or forcefully 猛打(某物[某人]); 移动(某物)(迅速地、同时发出声响或有力地): *He whammed the ball into the back of the net.* 他一用力把球打到球网的后面去了.

wharf /wɔ:f; *US* hwɔ:rf; hwɔrf/ *n* (*pl* **~s** or **-ves** /wɔ:vz; *US* hwɔ:rvz; hwɔrvz/) structure made of wood or stone at the water's edge, where ships may moor to load or unload cargo 码头.

what[1] /wɒt; *US* hwɒt; hwɑt/ *interrog det* (used to ask sb to specify one or more things, places, people, etc from an indefinite number 用以要求某人在未限定的数量中指明某事物、地方、人等): *What books have you got to read on the subject?* 你研究这个问题要看什么书? ○ *What time/date is it?* 现在几点钟了[今天几号了]? (Cf 参看 *Tell me what time it is.*) ○ *What experience has she had?* 她有什么体验? (Cf 参看 *Ask her what experience she has had.*) ○ *What woman are you thinking of?* 你想的是哪个女人? ○ *Guess what famous person said this?* 你猜猜是哪个名人说过这句话? ⇨Usage at WHICH 用法见WHICH.

▷ **what** *interrog pron* **1** (used to ask sb to specify one or more things, etc from an indefinite number 用以要求某人在未限定的数量中指明某事物等): *What did you say?* 你说什么? ○ *What* (ie What job) *does he do?* 他是做什么工作的? ○ *What are you reading, sewing, thinking, etc?* 你正在读、缝、想...什么呢? ○ *What's the time/date?* 现在几点钟了[今天几号了]? ○ *What does it mean?* 这是什么意思? **2** (idm 习语) **and 'what not** (*infml* 口) and other things of the same type 以及同类的其他事物: *tools, machines and what not* 工具、机器等等. **get/give sb what 'for** (*infml* 口) be punished/punish sb severely 受到严惩[严惩某人]: *I'll give her what for if she does that again.* 她要是再这样干我就收拾她. **what for** for what purpose 为什么目的: *What is this tool for?* 这个工具是干什么用的? ○ (*infml* 口) *What did you do that for?* ie Why did you do that? 你为什么做这件事呢? **what if?** what would happen if? 要是...又怎样?: *What if it rains when we can't get under shelter?* 假若下起雨来, 我们又没处避雨可怎么办? ○ *What if the rumour is true?* 万一谣传真有其事呢? **what 'of it?**; **so 'what?** (*infml* 口) (used to admit that sth is true, but to question whether it is important or whether sb is going to do anything about it 用以承认某事属实, 进而提问其重要性或是否某人要有何行动): *Yes, I wrote it. What of it?* 不错, 是我写的. 那又怎么样呢? **what's 'what** (*infml* 口) what things are useful, important, etc 什么事物有用、重要等: *She certainly knows what's what.* 她可知道都是怎么回事. **what with sth** (used to list various causes 用以列举各种原因): *What with the weather and my bad leg, I haven't been out for weeks.* 由于天气不好, 我的腿又不方便, 我已经好几个星期没出门了.

□ '**what-d'you-call-him/-her/-it/-them** (also '**what's-his/-her/-its/-their-name**) *n* (used instead of a name that one cannot remember 用以代替想不起来的名字): *She's just gone out with old what-d'you-call-him.* 她刚和那个他叫什么来着一起出去了.

'**whatnot** *n* **1** trivial, unknown or unspecified thing 琐碎的、未知的或未指明的事物: *She'd put these whatnots in her hair as decoration.* 她把那些也不知道是什么的东西弄到头发上当饰物. **2** piece of furniture with shelves for small objects 珍品架(陈列小摆设用的).

what[2] /wɒt; *US* hwɒt; hwɑt/ *det* the (thing(s) or people) that ...的(事物或人): *What money I have will be yours when I die.* 我一死我的钱就都给你. ○ *I spent what little time I had with my family.* 我仅有的那一点时间都与家人在一起度过了. ○ *What family and friends I still have live abroad.* 我现在所有的家人和朋友都住在国外.

▷ **what** *pron* the thing(s) that ...的事物: *What you say may well be true.* 你说的很可能是事实. ○ *No one knows what will happen next.* 谁也不知道下一步有什么事.

what[3] /wɒt; *US* hwɒt; hwɑt/ *det, adv* (used in exclamations 用于感叹句中): *What (awful) weather we're having!* 天气(可)太坏了! ○ *What a lovely view!* 景色真美呀! ○ *What a terrible noise!* 多讨厌的噪声啊! ○ *What big feet you've got!* 你的脚可真大!

▷ **what** *interj* **1** (used to show disbelief or surprise 用以表示不相信或惊奇): *'I've won a holiday in New York.' 'What?'* '我中了奖可以到纽约度假.''有这种事?' ○ *'It will cost £500.' 'What?'* '这可要用500英镑.''真的?' **2** (*infml* 口) (used when one has not heard what sb has said 用于未听清对方说的话时): *What? Can you say that again?* 什么? 你能再说一遍吗?

what·ever /wɒt'evə(r); *US* hwɒt-; hwɑt'ɛvɚ/ *det, pron* **1** any or every (thing) 任何(事物); 每样(事物): *We will be grateful for whatever amount you can afford.* 你买得起多少, 我们都欢迎. ○ *You can eat whatever you like.* 你愿意吃什么就吃什么. ○ *Whatever I have is yours.* 我的东西都是你的. **2** regardless of what 无论什么; 不管什么: *Whatever nonsense the papers print, some people always believe it.* 不管报纸胡说什么都有人信. ○ *You are right, whatever opinions may be held by others.* 你做得对, 别人怎么看不必理会. ○ *Keep calm, whatever happens.* 不论出什么事都要保持镇静. **3** (idm 习语) **or what'ever** (*infml* 口) or any other(s) of a similar type 或其他类似的事物: *Take any sport — basketball, ice hockey, swimming or whatever.* 要参加体育活动 — 篮球、冰球、游泳之类的活动.

▷ **what·ever** *interrog pron* (expressing surprise or bewilderment 用以表示惊讶或困惑) what (究竟是)什么: *Whatever do you mean?* 你究竟是什么意思? ○ *Whatever can it be?* 这到底是什么呢? ○ *You're going to keep snakes! Whatever next?* 你打算养蛇! 下一步还想干什么?

what·ever (also **what·so·ever**) *adv* (used after *no* + *n*, *nothing*, *none*, etc for emphasis 用于no + 名词、nothing、none等之后, 以加强语气): *There can be no doubt whatever about it.* 这件事毫无疑问. ○ *'Are there any signs of improvement?' 'None whatsoever.'* '有改进的迹象吗?''一点儿都没有.'

wheat /wi:t; *US* hwi:t; hwit/ *n* [U] **1** (**a**) grain from which flour (for bread, etc) is made 小麦(子实): *a tonne of wheat* 一吨小麦 ○ [attrib 作定语] *wheat loaves* 白面的面包. (**b**) plant that produces this 小麦(草本植物): *a field of wheat* 麦田 ○ [attrib 作定语] *wheat farming* 种植小麦. ⇨illus at CEREAL 见CEREAL插图. **2** (idm 习语) **separate the wheat from the chaff** ⇨ SEPARATE[2].

▷ **wheaten** /'wi:tn; *US* 'hwi:-; 'hwitn̩/ *adj* [usu attrib 通常作定语] made from wheat 小麦做的: *wheaten bread, cakes, flour* 小麦制的面包、蛋糕、面粉.

□ **'wheatcake** *n* (*US*) pancake made with whole wheat flour 全麦粉做的饼.

'wheat germ centre of the wheat grain, extracted during milling, which is a rich source of vitamins 小麦胚芽(磨麦时提取的, 含丰富维生素).

'wheatmeal *n* [U] wholemeal flour made from wheat 全麦面粉.

wheedle /'wi:dl; *US* 'hwi:-; 'hwidl̩/ *v* (*derog* 贬) (**a**) [I, Tn, Tn·pr] **~ sth (out of sb)** obtain sth by being pleasant to or flattering sb (用讨好或奉承某人的手法)获得某事物: *a wheedling tone of voice* 哄骗的腔调 ○ *She wheedled the money out of her father.* 她哄她父亲给她些钱. ○ *He wheedled his way into the building*, ie got into it by wheedling. 他靠花言巧语混进了那所楼房. (**b**) [Tn·pr] **~ sb into doing sth** persuade sb to do sth by being pleasant to or flattering him 用讨好或奉承的手法劝诱某人做某事: *The children wheedled me into letting them go to the film.* 孩子们把我哄得同意让他们去看电影了.

wheel /wi:l; *US* hwi:l; hwil/ *n* **1** (**a**) disc or circular frame that turns on an axle, as on carts, cars, bicycles, etc or as part of a machine, etc 轮; 车轮; 机轮. ⇨illus at App 1 见附录1插图, page xiii. (**b**) (esp in compounds 尤用以构成复合词) any of several types of machine of which a wheel is an essential part 以轮子为主要部件的机器: *a potter's 'wheel* 陶钧 ○ *a 'spinning-wheel* 纺车. **2** (usu *sing* 通常作单数) = STEERING-WHEEL (STEER[1]): *The driver sat patiently behind the wheel.* 司机在方向盘前耐心地坐着. ○ *He took* (ie grasped) *the wheel and steered the ship into port.* 他掌稳舵轮把船驶进了港口. **3** circular movement, esp that of a line of soldiers pivoting on one end 旋转运动; (尤指横排士兵以一端为中心的)旋转: *a left/right wheel* 向左[右]转. **4** (idm 习语) **at/behind the 'wheel (of sth)** (**a**) steering (a vehicle or a ship) 驾驶(车或船): *Who was at the wheel when the car crashed?* 汽车碰撞时开车的是谁? (**b**) (*fig* 比喻) in control (of sth) 控制(某事物): *With her at the wheel, the company began to prosper.* 有了她当主管, 公司开始兴旺起来. **oil the wheels** ⇨ OIL *v*. **put one's shoulder to the wheel** ⇨ SHOULDER. **put a spoke in sb's wheel** ⇨ SPOKE[1]. **ˌwheels within 'wheels** situation in which a complicated or secret network of influences, motives, etc exists, making it difficult to understand fully 错综复杂的或秘密的势力、动机等交织在一起难以了解的情况.

▷ **wheel** *v* **1** [Tn, Tn·pr, Tn·p] (**a**) push or pull (a vehicle with wheels) 推或拉(车): *wheel a barrow (along the street)* (在街上)推手推车. (**b**) carry (sb/sth) in a vehicle with wheels 用车运载(某人[某物]): *wheel sb to the operating theatre on a trolley* 用担架车把某人送到手术室. **2** (**a**) [I, Ipr, Ip] move in a curve or circle 转动; 旋转: *birds wheeling (about) in the sky above us* 在我们上空盘旋的鸟. (**b**) [I, Ip] **~ (round/around)** turn round and face the other way 转身: *Left/Right wheel!* ie as an order given to soldiers 向左[右]转! ○ *They wheeled round in amazement.* 他们惊奇地转过身来. **3** (idm 习语) **ˌwheel and 'deal** (*infml* 口 *esp US*) negotiate or bargain in a clever, often dishonest, way (用精明的, 常指欺骗的方法)洽谈、商量或讨价还价: *There will be a lot of wheeling and dealing before an agreement is reached.* 还要有一番讨价还价才能达成协议.

-wheeled (forming compound *adjs* 用以构成复合形容词) having the specified number of wheels 有某数量的轮子的: *a ˌsixteen-wheeled 'lorry* 一辆十六轮大卡车.

-wheeler (forming compound *ns* 用以构成复合名词) vehicle with the specified number of wheels 有某数量轮子的车: *a ˌthree-'wheeler* 三轮机动车.

wheelie *n* (*sl* 俚) act of riding a bicycle or motor cycle balancing on the back wheel, with the front wheel off the ground 骑自行车或摩托车时抬起前轮用后轮保持平衡的动作: *do a wheelie* 做抬起前轮只用后轮保持平衡的动作.

wheelbarrow
(*also* barrow)
独轮车

□ **'wheelbarrow** (also **barrow**) *n* open container for moving small loads in, with a wheel at one end, and two legs and two handles at the other 独轮车; 手推车.

'wheelbase *n* (usu *sing* 通常作单数) distance between the front and rear axles of a motor vehicle (机动车的)轴距.

'wheelchair *n* chair with wheels, in which sb who is unable to walk can move himself or be pushed along 轮椅: *She had polio as a child and spent the rest of her life in a wheelchair.* 她小时候得了小儿麻痹症, 终生没离开过轮椅.

'wheel-house *n* small enclosed cabin on a ship where the pilot, etc stands at the wheel to steer (船上的)驾驶室.

'wheelwright *n* person who makes and repairs (esp wooden) wheels for carts, wagons, etc 制造与修理(尤指木制的)车轮的人.

wheeler-dealer /ˌwi:lə 'di:lə(r); *US* ˌhwi:-; ˌhwilɚ'dilɚ/ *n* (*infml* 口 *esp US*) person who is skilled at bargaining, often dishonestly 善于讨价还价的人(常指不正直的).

wheeze /wi:z; *US* hwi:z; hwiz/ *v* **1** [I] (**a**) breathe noisily, esp with a whistling sound in the chest (eg when suffering from asthma, bronchitis, etc) 呼吸时有声响

(尤指胸部发出的哨声, 如因患哮喘、支气管炎等). **(b)** (of a machine, pump, etc) make a similar sound (指机器、泵等)发出类似上述的声响. **2** [Tn] say, sing, etc (sth) while breathing noisily or with difficulty (呼吸时有声响或呼吸困难情况下)说, 唱(某词语): *'I've got a sore throat,' he wheezed.* '我嗓子疼,'他吃力地说.

▷ **wheeze** *n* **1** sound of wheezing 有声响的呼吸声; 机器等发出的类似声响: *He has a slight wheeze in his chest.* 他呼吸时胸部发出轻微的响声. **2** (*dated Brit infml* 旧, 口) good idea, esp a joke or trick 好主意; (尤指)玩笑, 花招.

wheezy *adj* (**-ier**, **-iest**) making a wheezing sound 呼吸时发出响声的; 发出类似响声的: *a wheezy old man, pump* 呼吸时发出响声的老人、发出呼呼响声的泵 ○ *My cold's a lot better but I'm still a bit wheezy.* 我的感冒好多了, 就是呼吸时还有点声音. **wheez·ily** /-ɪlɪ; -əlɪ/ *adv.* **wheezi·ness** *n* [U].

whelk /welk; *US* hwelk; hwɛlk/ *n* any of several types of snail-like sea-animal with a spiral shell, esp one used as food 蛾螺(尤指食用的).

whelp /welp; *US* hwelp; hwɛlp/ *n* **1** young animal of the dog family; puppy or cub 犬科的幼兽; 幼犬或幼小的狐、熊、狮、虎等. **2** (*dated derog* 旧, 贬) badly-behaved child or young man 行为不良的儿童或年轻男子.

▷ **whelp** *v* [I] (*fml* 文) (of a female dog, wolf, etc) give birth (指母狗、母狼等)产(崽).

when /wen; *US* hwen; hwɛn/ *interrog adv* at what time; on what occasion 什么时候; 什么场合: *When can you come?* 您什么时候能来? ○ *When did he die?* 他是什么时候死的? ○ *I don't know when he died.* 我不知道他是什么时候死的. ○ *When were you living in Spain?* 您是什么时候住在西班牙的? ○ *Since when has he been missing?* 他是从什么时候失踪的?

▷ **when** *rel adv* 关系副词 **1** (used after *time*, *day*, *month*, etc 用于time、day、month等之后) at or on which 在那时; 其时: *Sunday is the day when very few people go to work.* 星期日是没什么人上班的日子. ○ *There are times when I wonder why I do this job.* 有时候我也不明白我为什么要做这个工作. ○ *It was the sort of morning when everything goes wrong.* 那天上午就是那样, 事事不顺心. **2** at which time; on which occasion 在那时; 当时; 当场: *The Queen's last visit was in May, when she opened the new hospital.* 女王上次来访是在五月份, 她那时主持了这座医院的落成典礼.

when *conj* **1** at or during the time that 在...时; 当...时: *It was raining when we arrived.* 我们到的时候正在下雨. ○ *When he saw her, he waved.* 他一看见她就摆了摆手. ○ *When visiting London I like to travel by bus.* 我游览伦敦时喜欢坐公共汽车. **2** since; considering that 既然; 考虑到: *How can they learn anything when they spend all their spare time watching television?* 他们把所有的空闲时间都用来看电视了, 还能学什么东西呢?

whence /wens; *US* hwens; hwɛns/ *adv* (*arch or fml* 古或文) from where 从该处; 从那里: *They have returned whence they came.* 他们从哪儿来的已经回哪儿去了.

when·ever /wen'evə(r); *US* hwen-; hwɛn'ɛvɚ/ *conj* **1** at any time, regardless of when 在任何时候; 无论何时: *I'll discuss it with you whenever you like.* 你愿意什么时候我就什么时候和你商量这件事. **2** every time that; as often as 每次; 每当: *Whenever she comes, she brings a friend.* 她每次来都带个朋友. ○ *The roof leaks whenever it rains.* 每逢下雨屋顶就漏雨. **3** (idm 习语) **or when'ever** (*infml* 口) or at any time 或者任何时间: *It's not urgent — we can do it next week or whenever.* 不是急事——我们可以下星期做或其他时候做.

▷ **when·ever** *interrog adv* (expressing surprise 用以表示惊讶) when (究竟在)什么时候, 什么场合: *Whenever did you find time to do all that cooking?* 你怎么能有时间做了这么多吃的东西?

where /weə(r); *US* hweə(r); hwɛr/ *interrog adv* in or to what place or position 在哪里; 到哪里; 在什么位置: *Where does he live?* 他住在哪儿? ○ *Where does she come from?* 她是哪儿的人? ○ *I wonder where she comes from.* 我不知道她是哪儿的人. ○ *Where* (ie At what point) *did I go wrong in my calculation?* 我在计算中什么地方出了差错? ○ *Where are you going for your holidays?* 你打算到哪儿去度假? ○ *Where is all this leading?* ie What is the conclusion of what you are saying? 你说这话到底是什么意思?

▷ **where** *rel adv* 关系副词 **1** (used after words or phrases that refer to a place 用于表示地点的词语之后) at, in, or to which (place) 在那(地方); 到那(地方); 该处: *the place where you last saw it* 你上次看到该事物之处 ○ *one of the few countries where people drive on the left* 少数沿左侧开车的国家之一. **2** at which place 在那个地方; 在该处: *We then moved to Paris, where we lived for six years.* 我们后来搬到巴黎, 在那里住了六年.

where *conj* (in) the place in which (在)...的地方: *Put it where we can all see it.* 把它放在我们都看得见的地方. ○ *Where food is hard to find, few birds remain throughout the year.* 在很难找到食物的地方就没有什么鸟能长年栖息. ○ (*fig* 比喻) *That's where you're wrong.* 你错就错在这儿.

□ '**whereabouts** *interrog adv* in or near what place; where 在什么地方; 靠近什么地方; 哪里: *Whereabouts did you find it?* 你在哪儿找到它的? ○ *She won't tell me whereabouts she put it.* 她不告诉我她把它放在哪儿了. — *n* [sing or pl *v*] place where sb/sth is 某人[某物]所在的地方; 下落; 行踪: *a person whose whereabouts is/are unknown* 一个下落不明的人.

where'by *rel adv* 关系副词 (*fml* 文) by which 靠那个; 凭那个; 借以: *She devised a plan whereby they might escape.* 她想出了一个他们可用以逃跑的计划.

where'in *rel adv* 关系副词 (*fml* 文) in which; in what; in what respect 其中; 在那里; 在哪方面: *a dark forest wherein dangers lurk* 潜伏着危险的黑暗的森林.

whereu'pon *conj* after which; and then 在这以后; 然后; 于是: *She laughed at him, whereupon he walked out.* 她嘲笑他, 他随之离去.

whereas /ˌweər'æz; *US* ˌhweər'æz; hwɛr'æz/ *conj* **1** (*esp law* 尤用于法律) taking into consideration the fact that 考虑到...; 鉴于. **2** (*fml* 文) but in contrast; while 然而; 而: *He earns £8 000 a year whereas she gets at least £20 000.* 他一年挣8 000英镑而她至少可获20 000英镑.

wher·ever /ˌweər'evə(r); *US* ˌhweər-; hwɛr'ɛvɚ/ *conj* **1** in any place, regardless of where 在无论什么地方: *Sit wherever you like.* 您愿意坐在哪儿都行. ○ *I'll find him, wherever he is.* 不管他在哪儿我都要把他找到. ○ *He comes from Boula, wherever that may be,* ie and I don't know where that is. 他原籍是布拉, 也不用管它在什么地方吧. **2** in all places that; everywhere 在...的各个地方; 各处; 处处: *Wherever she goes, there are crowds of people waiting to see her.* 她所到之处都有成群的人等着见她. ○ *Wherever there is injustice, we try to help.* 凡有不公正的地方, 我们都竭力相助匡正. **3** (idm 习语) **or wher'ever** (*infml* 口) or any (other) place 或者任何(其他的)地方: *many foreign tourists from Spain, France or wherever* 来自西班牙、法国或其他国家的许多游客.

▷ **wher·ever** *interrog adv* (expressing surprise 用以表示惊讶) where (究竟)在哪儿: *Wherever did you get that funny hat?* 你到底从哪儿弄来这么一顶怪帽子?

where·withal /'weəwɪðɔ:l; *US* 'hweər-; ˋhwɛrwɪðˏɔl/ *n* **the wherewithal** [sing] (*rhet or joc* 修辞或谑) the money needed for sth 为做某事而需要的钱: *I'd like a new stereo, but I haven't got the wherewithal (to buy it).* 我倒是想要一套新的立体声音响器材, 可是没这笔钱(买).

whet /wet; *US* hwet; hwɛt/ *v* (**-tt-**) [Tn] **1** (*fml* 文) sharpen (the blade of a knife, an axe, etc), esp by rubbing with a stone 磨(刀、斧等)(尤指用石头磨). **2** excite or stimulate (one's appetite, desire, interest, etc) 引起, 刺激(食欲、欲望、兴趣等): *Reading travel brochures whets one's appetite for a holiday.* 看了旅游手册就巴不得去度假.

□ '**whetstone** *n* shaped stone used for sharpening tools, eg chisels, scythes, etc 磨石; 磨刀石; 油石.

whether /'weðə(r); *US* 'hweðər; 'hwɛðɚ/ *conj* **1** (used before a clause or an infinitive expressing or implying alternatives 用于从句或不定式之前以表达或意含两者之间的选择) **(a)** (used as the object of *vs* like *know*, *doubt*, *wonder*, etc 用作know、doubt、wonder等动词的宾语): *I don't know whether I will be able to come.* 我不知道我是否能来. ○ *We'll be told tomorrow whether we should take the exam or not.* 我们明天才知道是不是应该参加考试. ○ *I asked him whether he had done all the work himself or whether he had had any assistance.* 我问他这些工作都是他自己做的还是别人帮他做的. (Note that when there are two alternative clauses separated by *or, whether* is repeated. 注意: 在两个供选择的从句之间若用or字, 则须重复whether一字.) ○ *We were wondering whether to go today or tomorrow.* 我们弄不清是今天走还是明天走. Cf 参看 IF. **(b)** (after *adjs* and *preps* 用于形容词或介词之后): *She was undecided (about) whether she should accept his offer.* 她拿不定主意应该不应该接受他的好意. ○ *He hesitated about whether to drive or take the train.* 他开车去还是坐火车去, 犹豫不决. ○ *It all depends on whether she likes the boss or not.* 一切都取决于她喜欢还是不喜欢这个老板. **(c)** (used as the subject or complement of a sentence 用作句子的主语或补语): *It's doubtful whether there'll be any seats left.* 说不上还有没有空座位了. ○ *The question is whether to go to Munich or Vienna.* 问题是去慕尼黑还是去维也纳. **2** (idm 习语) **whether or not** (used to introduce two alternative possibilities 用以引导出两种非此即彼的可能性): *Whether or not it rains/Whether it rains or not, we're playing football on Saturday.* 无论下不下雨, 我们星期六一定踢足球. ○ *Tell me whether or not you're interested.* 告诉我你有没有兴趣. ○ *They'll find out who did it, whether you tell them or not.* 你告诉不告诉他们, 他们都能查出是谁干的. ⇨Usage at IF 用法见 IF.

whew (also **phew**) /fjuː; fju/ *interj* (used as the written form of any of various sounds made by breathing out strongly or whistling to express amazement, relief, exhaustion or dismay 用作有声响的呼气声或口哨声之书面语象声词, 表示惊讶、宽慰、疲劳或沮丧均可): *Whew! That car was going fast!* 嘿! 那辆汽车可真快! ○ *Whew! That was a lucky escape!* 嘿! 这可是侥幸脱险哪!

whey /weɪ; US hweɪ; hwe/ *n* [U] watery liquid that remains after sour milk has formed curds 乳清(牛奶变酸凝结后产生的含水成分).

which /wɪtʃ; US hwɪtʃ; hwɪtʃ/ *interrog det* (used to ask sb to specify one or more people or things from a limited number 用以要求某人在有限数量中指明某人或某事物): *Which way is quicker — by bus or by train?* 怎么去更快——坐公共汽车还是坐火车? ○ *Which Mr Smith do you mean — the one who teaches history or the one who teaches music?* 你说的是哪个史密司先生——是教历史的那个还是教音乐的? ○ *Which languages did you study at school?* 你上学时学的都是哪些语言? ○ *Ask him which platform the London train leaves from.* 问问他到伦敦去的列车从哪个站台开出? Cf 参看 WHAT[1]. ⇨Usage 见所附用法.

▷ **which** *interrog pron* which person or thing (from a limited number) (有限数量中的)哪个人或哪个事物: *Which is your favourite subject?* 你最喜欢哪个科目? ○ *Which of the boys is tallest?* 这些男孩儿哪个最高? ○ *Here are the chairs. Tell me which are worth buying.* 就是这些椅子. 告诉我买哪儿把好. ○ *The twins are so much alike that I can't tell which is which,* ie can't distinguish one from the other. 这对双胞胎长得可真像, 我都分不出谁是谁了.

which *rel det* 关系限定词 (*fml* 文) (used to refer back to the preceding *n* or statement 用以复指前文的名词或内容): *The questions were all on opera, about which subject I know nothing.* 那些问题都是关于歌剧的, 我对歌剧一无所知. ○ *The postman comes at 6.30 in the morning, at which time* (ie when) *I am usually fast asleep.* 邮递员早晨6点30分来, 这个时候我通常还睡着大觉呢.

which *rel pron* 关系代词 (used to refer to sth previously mentioned 用以指提到过的事物): *Take the book which is lying on the table.* 把桌子上的那本书拿走. ○ *A house which overlooks the park will cost more.* 面向公园的房子贵些. ○ *Read the passage to which I referred in my talk.* 读一读我在讲话中提到的那段文章. ○ *His best film, which won several awards, was about the life of Gandhi.* 他的最佳影片, 就是荣获几项奖的那部, 是关于甘地生平的. ○ *His new car, for which he paid £7 000, has already had to be repaired.* 他那辆新汽车, 花了7 000英镑买的, 已经得修理去了.

NOTE ON USAGE 用法: Compare the use of **which** and **what** as determiners and pronouns in questions. 试比较**which**和**what**用作限定词和代词时, 在疑问句中的用法. **Which** refers to one or more members of a limited group ☆ **which**指在有限数量中的一个或一些: *Which car is yours/Which is your car? The Ford or the Volvo?* 哪辆汽车是你的[哪辆是你的汽车]? 是'福特'牌的还是'富豪'牌的? **What** is used when the group is not so limited 若所指的并非在有限的数量中, 要用**what**: *What are your favourite books?* 你最喜欢什么书? When we are referring to people, we often use **which** even if the choice is not restricted 指人时, 即使所在范围不受限制, 也往往用**which**: *Which/What actors do you admire most?* 你最喜爱哪些演员?

which·ever /wɪtʃˈevə(r); US hwɪtʃ-; hwɪtʃˈevɚ/ *det, pron* **1** the person or thing which ... 的那个人或事物: *Take whichever hat suits you best.* 挑个最适合你戴的帽子. ○ *We'll eat at whichever restaurant has a free table.* 哪个饭馆有空桌我们就在哪儿吃吧. ○ *Whichever of you comes first will receive a prize.* 你们谁第一谁就能得奖. **2** regardless of which 无论哪个或哪些: *Whichever you buy, there is a six-month guarantee.* 不管买哪个都有六个月的保用期. ○ *It takes three hours, whichever route you take.* 不论走哪条路都要三小时.

▷ **which·ever** *interrog det, interrog pron* (expressing surprise 用以表示惊讶) which (究竟)哪个, 哪些: *Whichever of these children is yours?* 这些孩子哪个是你的?

whiff /wɪf; US hwɪf; hwɪf/ *n* **~ (of sth)** **(a)** faint smell or puff of air or smoke 些微的气味、空气或烟: *catch a whiff of perfume, of cigar smoke* 闻到一股香水味、雪茄烟味 ○ *have a whiff of fresh air* 吸一点儿新鲜空气 ○ (*fig* 比喻) *a whiff* (ie a trace or hint) *of danger, scandal, suspicion* 有点危险、丑事、怀疑. **(b)** small amount breathed in (呼吸时)吸入少量的某物: *a whiff of anaesthetic* 吸入一点麻醉剂 ○ *He took a few whiffs,* ie of a cigar, pipe, etc. 他吸了几口(雪茄、烟斗等). **(c)** (*infml euph* 口, 婉) bad smell 难闻的气味: *There is an awful whiff coming from the dustbin.* 垃圾箱里冒出很臭的味.

while[1] /waɪl; US hwaɪl; hwaɪl/ *n* [sing] **1** (period of) time (一段)时间: *She worked in a bank for a while before studying law.* 她学法律之前在银行工作过一段时间. ○ *For a long while we had no news of him.* 很长一段时间我们没有他的消息. ○ *I'll be back in a little while,* ie soon. 我一会儿就回来. ○ *It took quite a while* (ie a long time) *to find a hotel.* 很长时间才找到一家旅馆. ○ *We waited for three hours, all the while hoping that someone would come and fetch us.* 我们等候了三个小时, 一直希望能有人来接我们. **2** (idm 习语) **once in a while** ⇨ ONCE. **worth sb's while** ⇨ WORTH.

▷ **while** *v* (phr v) **while sth away** pass (a period of time) in a leisurely way 逍遥自在地度过(一段时间): *We whiled away the time at the airport reading magazines.* 我们在机场阅读杂志消磨时间. ○ *It's easy to while a few hours away in a museum.* 在博物馆里很容易打发掉几个小时.

while[2] /waɪl; US hwaɪl; hwaɪl/ (also **whilst** /waɪlst; US hwaɪlst; hwaɪlst/) *conj* **1** **(a)** during the time that; when 在...期间; 当...的时候: *He fell asleep while (he was) doing his homework.* 他做着做着功课就睡着了. ○ *While I was in Madrid there was a carnival.* 我在马德里的时候正赶上狂欢节. ○ *While (locked up) in prison, she wrote her first novel.* 她在狱中写出了第一部小说. **(b)** at the same time as 与...同时: *While Mary was writing a letter, the children were playing outside.* 玛丽写信时孩子都在外面玩儿. ○ *He listens to the radio while driving to work.* 他去上班一边开着车一边听音乐. ○ *I lived in a hostel while I was a student.* 我求学期间住在青年招待所里. **2** (used to show a contrast 用以表示对比或相反的情况): *I drink black coffee while he prefers it with cream.* 我爱喝清咖啡而他喜欢加奶油的. ○ *English is understood all over the world while Turkish is spoken by only a few people outside Turkey itself.* 英语世界通行, 但土耳其语离开本国就很少有人说了. **3** (*fml* 文) although 虽然: *While I admit that there are problems, I don't agree that they cannot be solved.* 尽管我承认有问题存在, 但我不同意说这些问题不能解决.

whim /wɪm; US hwɪm; hwɪm/ *n* sudden desire or idea, esp an unusual or unreasonable one; caprice 一时的兴致; 突然的念头; (尤指)突发奇想, 异想天开; 心血来潮: *It's only a passing whim,* ie one that will soon be forgotten. 这只不过是一闪之念. ○ *They seem ready to indulge* (ie satisfy) *his every whim.* 他们简直惯着他随心所欲.

whim·per /ˈwɪmpə(r); *US* ˈhwɪ-; ˋhwɪmpɚ/ *v* **1** [I] (of a dog, person, etc) whine or cry softly, esp with fear or pain (指狗、人等)发出长而高音的或微弱的哭声或叫声,(尤指因恐惧或痛苦)呜咽,啜泣. **2** [Tn] say (sth) in this way 呜咽或啜泣着说(某事): *'Please don't leave me alone,' he whimpered.* '请不要丢下我不管,'他抽抽搭搭地说. ⇨Usage at CRY[1] 用法见CRY[1].

▷ **whim·per** *n* whimpering cry; low sobbing sound 呜咽声;啜泣声.

whimsy /ˈwɪmzɪ; *US* ˈhwɪ-; ˋhwɪmzɪ/ *n* **1** [U] odd or playful behaviour or humour 希奇的或耍笑的举动或幽默: *His speech was full of whimsy.* 他妙语如珠. ○ *'Why did you do it?' 'I don't know, pure whimsy.'* '你怎样做出这种事来?''我也不知道,纯粹是闹着玩儿.' **2** [C] fanciful idea or desire; whim 奇异的念头或兴致;奇想: *one of her bizarre whimsies* 她的一个古怪的念头.

▷ **whim·sical** /ˈwɪmzɪkl; *US* ˈhwɪ-; ˋhwɪmzɪkl/ *adj* full of whimsy; fanciful, playful or capricious 有很多希奇的或耍笑的举动或幽默的;异想天开的;闹着玩儿的;突发奇想的: *a whimsical sense of humour* 离奇的幽默感 ○ *a whimsical story for children* 希奇古怪的儿童故事. **whim·sic·al·ity** /ˌwɪmzɪˈkæləti; *US* ˌhwɪ-; ˌhwɪmzəˋkælətɪ/ *n* [U]. **whim·sic·ally** /-klɪ; -klɪ/ *adv*.

whin /wɪn; *US* hwɪn; hwɪn/ *n* [U] = GORSE.

whine /waɪn; *US* hwaɪn; hwaɪn/ *n* (usu *sing* 通常作单数) (**a**) long high-pitched complaining cry, esp one made by a dog or child 长而高音的哭声或叫声(尤指狗或儿童发出的). (**b**) similar high-pitched (esp irritating) sound made by a siren, motor-cycle engine, etc (警笛、摩托车发动机等发出的)长而高音的响声(尤指烦人的): *the steady whine of a mechanical saw* 机械锯发出的吱吱的声音.

▷ **whine** *v* **1** [I, It] make a whine 发出长而高音的呜咽声或其他响声: *a whining voice* 呜咽的声音 ○ *The dog sat outside the door whining (to be let in).* 那条狗坐在门外猜猜叫着(要进来). **2** (**a**) [I, Ipr] (*derog* 贬) complain, esp about trivial things 抱怨,埋怨(尤指为琐事): *Do stop whining!* 别再埋怨了! ○ *What is that child whining about now?* 那个孩子现在又抱怨什么呢? (**b**) [Tn] (*derog* 贬) say (sth) in a pleading or complaining voice 以哀求的或抱怨的声音说(某事): *'I want to go home,' he whined.* '我要回家,'他哀求着说. **whiner** *n* animal or person that whines 发出呜咽声的动物或人.

whinny /ˈwɪnɪ; *US* ˈhwɪ-; ˋhwɪnɪ/ *n* gentle neighing sound (轻微的)马嘶声.

▷ **whinny** *v* (*pt*, *pp* **whinnied**) [I, Ipr] make this sound 发出轻微的马嘶声: *The horse whinnied with pleasure.* 那匹马舒服地嘶叫着.

whip 鞭子

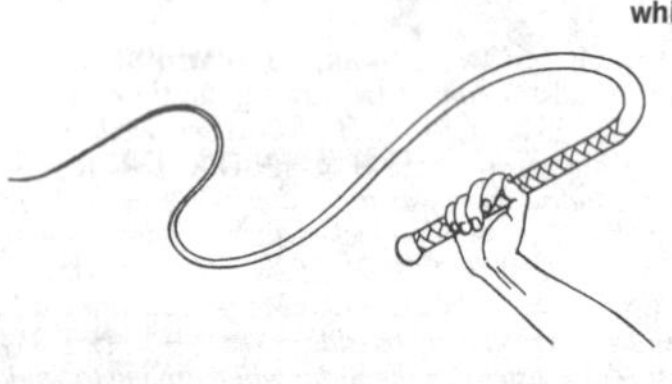

whip[1] /wɪp; *US* hwɪp; hwɪp/ *n* **1** [C] length of cord or strip of leather fastened to a handle, used esp for urging on an animal (esp a horse) or for striking a person or an animal as a punishment 鞭子. Cf 参看 HORSEWHIP (HORSE). **2** [C] (**a**) (in Britain and the US) official of a political party who has the authority to maintain discipline among its members, esp to make them attend and vote in important government debates (英国和美国的)政党的纪律委员(尤指敦促党员出席政府重要辩论会进行投票者). (**b**) instructions given by this official 党纪委员发出的指令: *a ˌthree-line* (ie very urgent) *ˈwhip* 要求本党议员出席辩论并按指示投票的紧急书面通知. **3** [C] = WHIPPER-IN. **4** [C, U] dish of whipped cream, eggs, etc with fruit or other flavouring 搅拌的奶油、蛋等加水果或其他调料制成的甜食: *caramel, chocolate, strawberry, etc whip* 焦糖、巧克力、草莓…奶油甜品. **5** (idm 习语) **a fair crack of the whip** ⇨ FAIR[1]. **get, have, hold, etc the ˈwhip hand (over sb)** be in a position where one has power or control (over sb) 位居控制(某人)的地位: *Their opponents had the whip hand and it was useless to resist.* 他们因对手权柄在握,反抗也没用.

▷ **whippy** *adj* flexible; springy 易弯曲的;有弹性的: *a whippy cane* 有弹力的藤条.

□ ˈ**whipcord** *n* [U] **1** type of strong, tightly twisted cord used for making whips, etc 鞭绳. **2** type of hard-wearing worsted fabric 马裤呢.

ˈ**whiplash** *n* lash of a whip 鞭打. ˈ**whiplash injury** injury to the neck caused by a sudden jerk of the head (as in a collision) 鞭子式损伤,颈椎过度屈伸损伤(如撞车事故造成的).

whip[2] /wɪp; *US* hwɪp; hwɪp/ *v* (**-pp-**) **1** [Tn] strike (a person or an animal) with a whip, esp as a punishment 鞭打(人或动物)(尤指作为惩罚);鞭笞: *The culprit will be whipped when he is found.* 那个罪犯找到后就要挨鞭子抽打. **2** [Tn, Tn·pr, Tn·p] **~ sth (up) (into sth)** stir (eggs, cream, etc) rapidly with a fork or some other instrument in order to make a stiff light mass 搅打(蛋、奶油等): *coffee with whipped cream* 加入搅打奶油的咖啡 ○ *Whip the ingredients (up) into a smooth paste.* 把配料搅打成均匀的糊状. **3** [Tn] (*Brit infml* 口) steal (sth) 偷(某物): *Who's whipped my umbrella?* 谁把我的伞偷走了? **4** [Ipr, Ip, Tn·pr, Tn·p] (cause sb/sth to) move rapidly or suddenly in the direction specified (使某人[某物])沿某方向快速或突然移动: *The thief whipped round the corner and out of sight.* 那个贼一溜烟儿转过街角就看不见了. ○ *She whipped round just as he was about to attack her from behind.* 他正要从她后面袭击她,她一下子转过身来. ○ *The branch whipped back and hit me in the face.* 那树枝突然弹回打在我的脸上. ○ *The intruder whipped out a knife (from his pocket).* 闯进来的人突然(从他的衣袋里)掏出一把刀来. ○ *The wind whipped several slates off (the roof).* 那阵风(从屋顶上)刮下几块瓦来. ○ *The star was whipped into a fast car and driven off.* 那个明星迅速上了一辆汽车疾驶而去. **5** [Tn] (**a**) sew (a seam, piece of cloth, etc) with stitches that pass over the edge, esp in order to prevent fraying 锁缝(布等的边)(尤指为防止脱线). (**b**) bind (a stitch, the end of a rope, etc) with a close tight covering of thread or string (用线或绳)将(缝线、绳索末端等)缠紧. **6** (phr v) **whip sb/sth on** drive sb to go faster, work harder, etc; make (an animal) go faster by striking it with a whip 鞭策、驱使或督促某人快走、努力等;用鞭子抽打(动物)使之快走. **whip sth/sb up** (**a**) create (excitement, enthusiasm, etc) in people or cause (people) to be enthusiastic, etc; arouse 激发(情绪、热情等);激励(人们);唤起: *They're trying to whip up support for their candidate.* 他们竭力激励大家支持他们的候选人. ○ *The people were whipped up into a frenzy by the speaker.* 人们听了演说人的话群情激奋. (**b**) (*infml* 口) prepare (a meal, etc) very quickly 匆匆做(饭等): *I can easily whip you up some scrambled eggs.* 我马上就能给你炒点鸡蛋.

▷ **whip·ping** *n* [C, U] (instance of) being beaten with a whip as a punishment 鞭打(作为惩罚). ˈ**whipping-boy** *n* person who is regularly made to take the blame and punishment for the faults of others; scapegoat 经常代人受过的人;替罪羊: *I am tired of being used as the whipping-boy for all the mistakes that are made in the office.* 办公室里一出差错就让我背黑锅,我已经忍无可忍了. ˈ**whipping cream** cream that is suitable for whipping (WHIP 2) 可供搅打的奶油.

□ ˈ**whip-round** *n* (*Brit infml* 口) appeal for contributions from a group of people 募捐;凑份子: *a whip-round for (a Christmas present for) the office cleaners* 为办公室清洁工凑份子(买圣诞礼物).

whipper-in /ˌwɪpər ˈɪn; *US* hw-; ˌhwɪpɚˋɪn/ *n* (*pl* **~s-in**) (also **whip**) person responsible for controlling the hounds during a hunt (打猎时)管猎狗的人.

whipper-snapper /ˈwɪpə snæpə(r); *US* ˈhwɪ-; ˋhwɪpɚˌsnæpɚ/ *n* (*dated infml derog* 旧,口,贬) young and unimportant person who behaves in a cheeky or over-confident way 厚颜无耻的或妄自尊大的年轻人.

whip·pet /ˈwɪpɪt; *US* ˈhw-; ˋhwɪpɪt/ *n* small thin dog similar to a greyhound, often used for racing 小灵狗(常用作赛狗).

whirl /wɜːl; *US* hw-; hwɝl/ *v* **1** [I, Ipr, Ip, Tn, Tn·pr,

Tn·p] (cause sb/sth to) move quickly round and round (使某人[某物])旋转,打转,回旋: *the whirling blades of the fan* 旋转着的风扇叶片 ○ *The leaves whirled (round) as they fell.* 树叶打着转飘落下来. ○ *The wind whirled (up) the fallen leaves.* 一阵风把落叶刮得旋转起来. ○ *She whirled the rope round and round (her head).* 她(在头上)一圈一圈地旋转着绳带. ○ *He whirled his partner round the dance floor.* 他带着舞伴环绕舞池旋转. **2** [Ipr, Ip, Tn·pr, Tn·p] (cause sb/sth to) move or travel rapidly (in the specified direction) (使某人[某物])(沿某方向)迅速移动或行进: *The houses whirled past us as the train gathered speed.* 火车越开越快,周围的房子在我们旁边一闪而过. ○ *He whirled them away/off in his new sports car.* 他开着他的新跑车载着他们疾驶而去. **3** [I] (of the brain, senses, etc) seem to go round and round, so that one feels confused or excited; reel (指头脑、知觉等)混乱不清,异常兴奋;头晕目眩: *I couldn't sleep: my mind was still whirling from all I had seen and heard.* 我睡不着觉,所见所闻仍在头脑中转来转去.

▷ **whirl** *n* [sing] **1** whirling movement 旋转;回旋: *the whirl of the propeller blades* 螺旋桨叶片的旋转. **2** rapid succession of activities 一个紧接一个的活动: *an endless whirl of parties* 接连的无尽无休的聚会 ○ *the social whirl* 一连串的社交活动. **3** state of confusion 混乱: *My mind is in a whirl.* 我心里很乱. **4** (idm 习语) **give sth a 'whirl** (*infml* 口) try sth as an experiment, to see if it is suitable, pleasant, etc 试试某事物(看是否恰当、合意等): *The job doesn't sound very exciting but I'll give it a whirl.* 这个工作听起来没什么意思,可是我还是要去试一试.

□ **'whirlpool** *n* place in a river or the sea where there are whirling currents; circular eddy (河水或海水的)旋涡.

'whirlwind *n* **1** funnel-shaped column of swiftly circulating air 旋风: [attrib 作定语] (*fig* 比喻) *a whirlwind* (ie very rapid) *affair/courtship/romance* 仓促间的暧昧关系[求婚/风流韵事]. **2** (idm 习语) **reap the whirlwind** ⇨ REAP.

whir·li·gig /ˈwɜːlɪɡɪɡ; *US* ˈhw-; ˈhwɜˈlɪˌɡɪɡ/ *n* **1** any of several types of spinning or whirling toy, esp a top 旋转式玩具;(尤指)陀螺. **2** = ROUNDABOUT 1.

whirr (also *esp US* **whir**) /wɜː(r); *US* hw-; hwɜ˞/ *n* (usu *sing* 通常作单数) continuous rapid buzzing or vibrating sound 连续而迅速的嗡嗡声或震动声: *the whirr of a fan, motor, propeller* 风扇、发动机、螺旋桨的呼呼声.

▷ **whirr** (also *esp US* **whir**) *v* [I] make this sound 发出嗡嗡声或震动声: *The bird flew past, its wings whirring.* 那只鸟飞了过去,翅膀发出呼呼的声音.

whisk /wɪsk; *US* hw-; hwɪsk/ *n* **1** device (usu made of coiled wire) for whipping eggs, cream, etc (搅打蛋、奶油等的)搅拌器,打蛋器(通常为金属圈制成的). ⇨illus at KITCHEN 见 KITCHEN 插图. **2** small brush made from a bunch of grass, twigs, bristles, etc tied to a handle (用干草、细枝、鬃毛等制的)小扫帚: *a 'fly-whisk* 蝇拂. **3** quick light brushing movement (eg of a horse's tail) 掸,拂(如马尾的摆动).

▷ **whisk** *v* **1** [Tn] move (sth) quickly through the air with a light sweeping movement 挥,甩(某物): *The horse whisked its tail angrily.* 那匹马发着怒甩动着尾巴. **2** [Tn] beat (eggs, etc) into a froth; whip 搅打(鸡蛋等). **3** (phr v) **whisk sth away/off** brush sth quickly and lightly away as if with a whisk 刷去或扫掉某物: *whisk the flies away* 轰走苍蝇. **whisk (sb/sth) away, off, etc** go or take (sb/sth) away quickly and suddenly 突然匆匆走开或将(某人[某物])带走: *The waiter whisked away the food before we had finished.* 服务员没等我们吃完就把饭菜都拿走了. ○ *She (was) whisked up to the top floor in the lift.* 她乘电梯迅速到达顶层.

whis·ker /ˈwɪskə(r); *US* ˈhwɪ-; ˈhwɪskɚ/ *n* **1 whiskers** [pl] long hair growing on a man's face 络腮胡子;连鬓胡子. Cf 参看 BEARD[1] a, MOUSTACHE 1. **2** [C] any of the long stiff hairs that grow near the mouth of a cat, rat, etc (猫、鼠等的)须. ⇨illus at App 1 见附录1插图, page iii. **3** (idm 习语) **be the cat's whiskers/pyjamas** ⇨ CAT[1]. **by a 'whisker** by a very small amount or margin 差一点儿: *She missed the first prize by a whisker.* 她只差一点儿就能得到头奖了.

▷ **whis·kered** /ˈwɪskəd; *US* ˈhw-; ˈhwɪskɚd/, **whis·kery** /ˈwɪskərɪ; *US* ˈhw-; ˈhwɪskərɪ/ *adjs* having whiskers 有络腮胡子的;(猫、鼠等)有须的.

whisky (*Brit*) (*US or Irish* 美式或爱尔兰式英语作 **whis·key**) /ˈwɪskɪ; *US* ˈhwɪ-; ˈhwɪskɪ/ *n* (**a**) [U] strong alcoholic drink distilled from malted grain (esp barley or rye) 威士忌: *a bottle of whisky* 一瓶威士忌. (**b**) [C] type of this 威士忌: *This is a very good whisky.* 这种威士忌非常好. (**c**) [C] glass of this 一杯威士忌: *Two whiskies, please.* 请来两杯威士忌.

whis·per /ˈwɪspə(r); *US* ˈhwɪ-; ˈhwɪspɚ/ *v* **1** (**a**) [I] speak softly, using the breath but without vibrating the vocal cords 声带不振动而用呼吸声说话;低语;小声说: *Why are you whispering?* 你为什么低声说话? (**b**) [I, Ipr, Tn, Tn·pr, Tf, Dn·pr, Dpr·f, Dpr·t] **~ (about sb/sth); ~ sth (to sb)** talk or say sth in this way, esp privately or secretly 小声说某事(尤指私事或秘密事): *Don't you know it's rude to whisper?* 你难道不知道窃窃私语是不礼貌的吗? ○ *He whispered a word in my ear.* 他对我附耳说了一句话. ○ *'I feel very afraid,' she whispered.* '我觉得很害怕,'她低声说. ○ *She whispered (to me) that she felt very afraid.* 她小声(对我)说她觉得很害怕. ○ *It is whispered* (ie There is a rumour) *that he is heavily in debt.* 据说他负债累累. **2** [I] (of leaves, the wind, etc) make soft sounds; rustle (指叶子、风等)发沙沙声,发飒飒声: *The wind was whispering in the trees.* 一阵风穿过树林沙沙作响.

▷ **whis·per** *n* **1** whispering sound, speech or remark 低语;小声说的话: *He spoke in a whisper.* 他低声说话. **2** rumour 传言;谣言: *I've heard whispers that the firm is likely to go bankrupt.* 我听到传闻说公司很可能要破产.

□ **'whispering campaign** attack on sb's reputation made by passing malicious statements about him from person to person 散布流言诽谤某人.

whist /wɪst; *US* hwɪst; hwɪst/ *n* [U] card-game for two pairs of players, similar to bridge[2] 惠斯特(纸牌游戏,由两对游戏者参加,类似桥牌).

□ **'whist drive** series of games of whist played by several sets of partners at different tables, with certain players moving after each round to the next table 惠斯特组合赛(由几对参赛者在各桌进行,某些参赛者一局后换至下一桌).

whistle /ˈwɪsl; *US* ˈhwɪ-; ˈhwɪsl̩/ *n* **1** (**a**) clear shrill sound made by forcing breath through a small hole between partly closed lips 口哨声: (*fig* 比喻) *the whistle of a steam engine* 蒸汽发动机的汽笛声. (**b**) similar tuneful sound made by a bird 鸟发出的类似口哨的声音: *the blackbird's whistle* 黑鹂的鸣叫声. **2** instrument used to produce a clear shrill sound, esp as a signal 哨子;汽笛;警笛: *The referee blew his whistle.* 裁判吹响了哨子. **3** (idm 习语) **blow the whistle on sb/sth** ⇨ BLOW[1]. **clean as a whistle** ⇨ CLEAN[1]. **wet one's whistle** ⇨ WET *v*.

▷ **whistle** *v* **1** (**a**) [I, Ipr, Ip] make the sound of a whistle 发出哨子或汽笛等的声音: *The boy was whistling (away) cheerfully.* 那个男孩愉快地(一直)吹着口哨. ○ *A train whistled in the distance.* 一列火车在远处鸣响了汽笛. ○ *The wind whistled through a crack in the door.* 风从门的裂缝中呼呼地刮了进来. (**b**) [Tn] produce (a tune) in this way 用口哨吹出(曲调): *He whistled a happy tune as he walked along.* 他边走边用口哨吹着快乐的曲子. (**c**) [Ipr, Tn·pr, Tn·p, Dn·pr, Dpr·t] make a signal to (sb/sth) in this way 用口哨或汽笛等向(某人[某物])发信号: *She whistled her dog back.* 她一吹口哨就把她的狗唤了回来. ○ *She whistled for her dog.* 她吹口哨唤她的狗来. ○ *He whistled to his friend to keep hidden.* 他吹口哨通知朋友继续隐蔽. **2** [I, Ipr, Ip] move swiftly with a noise like a whistle 发出似口哨声迅速移动: *A bullet whistled past his head.* 一颗子弹嗖的一声从他头上经过. **3** (idm 习语) **whistle in the 'dark** try to overcome one's fear in a frightening or dangerous situation 在惊险情况下尽力给自己壮胆. **4** (phr v) **whistle for sth** (*infml* 口) wish for or expect sth in vain 徒然希望或指望某事物: *If he wants his money now he'll have to whistle for it, I'm afraid.* 要是他现在想要他的钱,我看他是吹了.

□ **'whistle-stop** *n* (**a**) (*US*) small railway station where trains stop only when signalled to do so (仅于发出停车信号才停的)小火车站. (**b**) (*fig* 比喻) short stop made by a politician during an election campaign (竞选活动中政客的)短暂停留: [attrib 作定语] *on a whistle-*

W

stop tour of the country 在全国各地作短暂停留的竞选旅行.

whit /wɪt; *US* hwɪt; hwɪt/ *n* [sing] (usu in negative sentences 通常用于否定句中) the smallest amount 极少的量;一点儿: *I don't care a whit* (ie in the least) *whether she stays or not.* 我毫不在乎她的去留. ○ *I've read the report but I'm no whit the wiser*, ie I don't understand it at all. 我看了这份报告, 一点都不明白.

Whit /wɪt; *US* hwɪt; hwɪt/ *n* [U, often attrib 常作定语] = WHITSUN: *the Whit weekend* 圣灵降临节的周末.

□ ˌ**Whit** ˈ**Sunday** the seventh Sunday after Easter; Pentecost 圣灵降临节(复活节后的第七个星期日).

white¹ /waɪt; *US* hwaɪt; hwaɪt/ *adj* (**-r, -st**) **1** of the very palest colour, like fresh snow, common salt or milk 白的; 白色的: *walls painted white* 已刷成白色的墙壁 ○ *strong white teeth* 健康洁白的牙齿 ○ *Her hair has turned white*, eg with age. 她的头发已经白了(如上了年纪). ○ *I like my coffee white*, ie with milk or cream in it. 我喜欢加牛奶或奶油的咖啡. Cf 参看 BLACK¹. **2** of a pale-skinned race 白种人的. **3** ~ **(with sth)** (of a person) pale as a result of emotion or illness (指人)(因情绪变化或生病)脸色苍白的: *He was white with fury.* 他气得脸色煞白. **4** (idm 习语) **(in) black and white** ⇨ BLACK². **bleed sb white** ⇨ BLEED. **show the white feather** ⇨ SHOW². **(as) ˌwhite as a ˈsheet** very pale, esp as a result of fear or shock 苍白的(尤指因恐惧或震惊所致): *She went as white as a sheet when she heard the news.* 她听到这个消息顿时脸色苍白. **(as) white as ˈsnow** very white 雪白的; 极白的: *an old man with hair as white as snow* 一个白发苍苍的老先生. **a white elephant** possession that is useless and often expensive to maintain 无用的而常指保管昂贵的东西.

▷ **white** *v* [Tn] (idm 习语) **a whited ˈsepulchre** (*fml* 文) person who seems to be good, but is really evil; hypocrite 伪君子.

whiten /ˈwaɪtn; *US* ˈhwaɪ-; ˈhwaɪtn/ *v* [I, Tn] (cause sth to) become white or whiter (使某物)变白或更白: *whiten one's tennis shoes* 刷白自己的网球鞋.

white·ness *n* [U].

whit·ish *adj* tending towards white; fairly white 发白的; 稍白的: *a whitish blue* 略白的蓝色 ○ *a whitish dress* 发白的连衣裙.

□ ˈ**white ant** = TERMITE.

ˈ**whitebait** *n* [U] young herrings, sprats or other small silvery white fish that are eaten whole as food 鲱、西鲱的幼鱼或其他银白色小鱼(可整条食用).

ˈ**white cell**, ˌ**white** ˈ**corpuscle** any of the cells in the blood that fight infection; leucocyte 白血球. Cf 参看 RED CORPUSCLE (RED¹).

ˌ**white** ˈ**coffee** coffee with milk or cream added 加牛奶或奶油的咖啡.

ˌ**white-**ˈ**collar** *adj* [usu attrib 通常作定语] (of a job, worker, etc) not manual (指工作、工作者等)白领的(不使用体力的). Cf 参看 BLUE-COLLAR (BLUE¹).

ˌ**white** ˈ**dwarf** small, very dense, faint star 白矮星. Cf 参看 RED GIANT (RED¹).

W

ˌ**white** ˈ**ensign** flag flown by ships of the British navy 英国皇家海军军旗. Cf 参看 RED ENSIGN (RED¹).

ˌ**white** ˈ**flag** symbol of surrender 白旗(投降的标志).

ˌ**white** ˈ**heat** high temperature at which metal looks white 白热; 白炽.

ˌ**white** ˈ**horses** waves in the sea with white crests on them 白浪.

ˌ**white** ˈ**hope** (*infml* 口) person who is expected to bring success to a team, group, etc 可望给一队、一集体等带来成功的人: *He was once the great white hope of the Labour Party.* 他一度是工党中深孚众望的人.

ˌ**white-**ˈ**hot** *adj* at white heat; extremely hot 白热的; 炽热的.

the ˈ**White House** (**a**) the official residence (in Washington DC) of the President of the USA 白宫(美国总统府, 位于美国首都华盛顿). (**b**) the US President and his advisers 白宫; 美国总统及其顾问: *The White House has denied the report.* 白宫已否认这一报道.

ˌ**white** ˈ**lead** poisonous compound of lead carbonate, used as a pigment 白铅(碳酸铅, 有毒, 用作颜料).

white ˈ**lie** harmless or trivial lie, esp one told in order to avoid hurting sb 无害的或无关紧要的谎话(尤指为避免伤及某人而说的).

ˈ**white man** (*fem* 阴性作 ˈ**white woman**) member of a pale-skinned race; Caucasian 白人; 白种人: *remote areas where no white man had ever been* 白种人没到过的偏远地区.

ˈ**white meat** (**a**) poultry, veal or pork 白色肉(家禽肉、小牛肉或猪肉). (**b**) meat from the breast of a cooked chicken or other bird (烹调的鸡肉或其他禽肉的)胸脯肉. Cf 参看 RED MEAT (RED²).

ˌ**white** ˈ**noise** noise that contains many frequencies with approximately equal energies 白噪声; 白噪音.

ˌ**White** ˈ**Paper** (*Brit*) report published by the government about its policy on a matter that is to be considered by Parliament 白皮书. Cf 参看 GREEN PAPER (GREEN¹).

ˌ**white** ˈ**pepper** pepper made by grinding peppercorns after the husks have been removed 白胡椒.

ˌ**white** ˈ**sauce** sauce made from butter, flour and milk 白沙司(用黄油、面粉、牛奶制成的调味汁): *Add cheese to the white sauce.* 在白沙司里加上奶酪.

ˌ**white** ˈ**slave** woman forced into becoming a prostitute, esp in a foreign country 被迫为娼的女子(尤指在国外): [attrib 作定语] *the white-ˈslave trade/traffic* 迫良为娼的买卖. ˌ**white** ˈ**slavery**.

ˌ**white** ˈ**spirit** (*esp Brit*) light petroleum used as a paint solvent or cleaning substance 石油溶剂: *remove paint from the brushes with white spirit* 用石油溶剂除去刷子上的油漆.

ˌ**white** ˈ**tie** (man's white bow-tie worn as part of) full formal evening dress (男用)全套正式晚礼服(配用的白领结): [attrib 作定语] *Is it a white-tie affair?* 参加这个聚会是不是得穿全套晚礼服?

ˈ**whitewash** *n* **1** [U] powdered lime or chalk mixed with water, used for painting (粉刷用的)石灰水. **2** [C, U] (*fig* 比喻) (process of) hiding sb's errors, faults, etc 粉饰; 掩饰: *The opposition dismissed the report as a whitewash.* 反对党认为这份报告文过饰非不予理会. — *v* [Tn] **1** put whitewash on (a wall, etc) 粉刷(墙壁等): *whitewash the outside of the cottage* 粉刷农舍的外墙. **2** try to make (sb, sb's reputation, etc) appear blameless by hiding errors, faults, etc 为(某人、某人的名誉等)涂脂抹粉.

ˌ**white** ˈ**wedding** wedding at which the bride wears a white dress, esp one that takes place in a church 新娘穿白色礼服的婚礼(尤指在教堂举行的).

ˌ**white** ˈ**wine** wine that is very pale yellow, amber or golden 白葡萄酒; 浅色果酒. Cf 参看 RED WINE (RED¹), ROSÉ.

white² /waɪt; *US* hwaɪt; hwaɪt/ *n* **1** [U] white colour or pigment 白色; 白的颜料: *Mix some more white in to make the paint paler.* 再搀些白颜料使涂料浅些. **2** (**a**) [U] white clothes or material 白色的衣物或材料: *dressed all in white* 穿着一身白色衣服. (**b**) **whites** [pl] white clothes, esp as worn for sports 白色衣物(尤指运动时穿戴的): *tennis whites* 白色网球运动服 ○ *It's unwise to wash whites with coloureds*, ie coloured clothes. 白色衣服不应该和有颜色的衣服一起洗. **3** [C, U] transparent substance that surrounds the yolk of an egg and becomes white when cooked 蛋清; 蛋白: *Use the whites of two eggs/two egg whites.* 用两个鸡蛋的蛋白. ⇨illus at EGG 见EGG 插图. **4** [C] white-skinned person; Caucasian 白种人. **5** [C] white part of the eye-ball 白眼珠: *The whites of her eyes are bloodshot.* 她的白眼珠充血了. **6** (idm 习语) **black and white** ⇨ BLACK *n*.

White·hall /ˈwaɪthɔ:l; *US* ˈhwaɪ-; ˈhwaɪtˋhɔl/ *n* (**a**) [U] street in London where there are many Government offices 怀特霍尔(伦敦一街道, 政府机关所在地): *Rumours are circulating in Whitehall.* 怀特霍尔街上流传着谣言. (**b**) [Gp] the British Government 白厅; 英国政府: *Whitehall is/are refusing to confirm the reports.* 英国政府对这些报道不予证实.

whither /ˈwɪðə(r); *US* ˈhwɪ-; ˋhwɪðɚ/ *adv* (*arch or rhet* 古或修辞) to what place or state 向何处; 到何种情况: *Whither goest thou?* 汝欲何往? ○ *Whither* (ie What is the likely future of) *the shipping industry?* 航运业何去何从?

whit·ing¹ /ˈwaɪtɪŋ; *US* ˈhwaɪ-; ˋhwaɪtɪŋ/ *n* (*pl* unchanged 复数不变) any of several types of small silvery-grey sea-fish 牙鳕(多种银灰色小海鱼).

whit·ing² /ˈwaɪtɪŋ; *US* ˈhwaɪ-; ˋhwaɪtɪŋ/ (also **whiten·ing** /ˈwaɪtnɪŋ; *US* ˈhwaɪ-; ˋhwaɪtnɪŋ/) *n* [U] powdered white chalk used for making whitewash, silver polish, etc (用

于粉刷、擦亮银器等的）白垩粉.

whit·low /ˈwɪtləʊ; *US* ˈhwɪ-; ˋhwɪtlo/ *n* small painfully inflamed place on a finger or toe, esp near a nail 瘭疽; 化脓性指头炎.

Whit·sun /ˈwɪtsn; *US* ˈhwɪ-; ˋhwɪtsn̩/ (also **Whit** /wɪt; *US* hwɪt; hwɪt/) *n* Whit Sunday and the days close to it 圣灵降临节及其前后几天.
□ ˈ**Whit·sun·tide** /-taɪd; -ˌtaɪd/ *n* = WHITSUN.

whittle /ˈwɪtl; *US* ˈhwɪ-; ˋhwɪtl̩/ *v* **1** (**a**) [Ipr, Tn] **~ (at) sth** cut thin slices or strips off (wood, etc) 削(木头等). (**b**) [Tn, Tn·pr] **~ A (from B)**; **~ B (into A)** make or shape (sth) by doing this 削成(某物): *whittling a tent-peg from a branch/a branch into a tent-peg* 把树枝削成帐篷钉. **2** (phr v) **whittle sth away** gradually remove or decrease sth 逐渐削减某事物: *Inflation has whittled away their savings.* 通货膨胀蚕食了他们的积蓄. **whittle sth down** (**a**) make sth thinner by cutting off fine slices with a knife 用刀将某物削薄. (**b**) reduce the size of sth gradually 逐渐减少某事物: *The number of employees is being whittled down in order to reduce costs.* 为节省开支现正逐渐裁员.

whiz /wɪz; *US* hwɪz; hwɪz/ *v* (**-zz-**) [I, Ipr, Ip] (**a**) make a sound like that of an object moving very fast through the air 发出如物体急速穿过空气的声音: *A bullet whizzed past my ear.* 一颗子弹嗖的一声从我耳边飞过. (**b**) (*infml* 口) move very fast 高速移动: *whizzing along (the motorway)* (在高速公路上)飞速行驶.

NOTE ON USAGE 用法: Compare **zoom, whiz, zip, shoot, dart,** and **nip.** 试比较**zoom**、**whiz**、**zip**、**shoot**、**dart**、**nip**这几个动词. **Zoom** and **whiz** are both informal and indicate the rapid noisy movement of a vehicle, etc. ☆ **zoom**与**whiz**均为口语用词, 指车等快速行驶同时发出声响. **Zoom** suggests a low engine noise; **whiz** suggests a high whistling sound ☆ **zoom**指发动机的低声, **whiz**指似口哨或汽笛的高声: *The jet zoomed low over the houses, frightening everyone.* 那架喷气式飞机低飞掠过房顶, 隆隆声把大家吓了一跳. ○ *A bullet whizzed past my ear.* 一颗子弹嗖的一声从我耳边飞过. **Zip** also describes a vehicle moving fast but does not suggest noise. ☆ **zip**也指车快速行驶, 但不含发出声响之意. It can refer to people getting through a task or a process quickly 这个词还可指人迅速完成一任务或经过一过程: *These new trains really zip along.* 这些新列车行驶得可真快. ○ *We were lucky — we just zipped through customs.* 我们很运气——一下子就过了海关. **Shoot** and **dart** indicate the sudden rapid movement of a person, an animal or a thing ☆ **shoot**和**dart**指人、动物或东西突然快速移动: *A car suddenly shot out of a side road and nearly hit me.* 有一辆汽车冷不防从岔道上冲出, 险些撞着我. ○ *The boy suddenly darted across the road in front of the bus.* 那个男孩突然从公共汽车前面冲过马路. **Nip** is informal, indicating someone hurrying somewhere for a short time and for a particular purpose ☆ **nip**是口语用词, 指某人为某目的匆匆去一下某处: *I must nip round to the shops for some milk.* 我得赶快到商店转一圈买点儿牛奶.

whiz-kid /ˈwɪzkɪd; *US* ˈhwɪz-; ˋhwɪzˌkɪd/ *n* (*infml sometimes derog* 口, 有时作贬义) person who becomes successful very quickly 迅速获得成功的人: *The new manager is a real whiz-kid.* 新经理是个平地青云的人.

who /hu:; hu/ *interrog pron* **1** (used as the subject of a *v* to ask about the name, identity or function of one or more people 用作动词的主体, 用以询问人的姓名、身分或职位): *Who is the woman in the black hat?* 戴黑帽子的那个女的是谁? ○ *I wonder who phoned this morning.* 我不知道今天上午谁打来过电话. ○ *Who are the men in white coats?* 穿着白大衣的那些男的是什么人? ○ *Do you know who broke the window?* 你知道是谁把窗户打破的吗? **2** (*infml* 口) (used as the object of a *v* or *prep* 用作动词或介词的宾语): *Who did you see at church?* 你做礼拜时看见谁了? ○ *Who are you phoning?* 你给谁打电话呢? ○ *Who shall I give it to?* 我把这个给谁? ○ *Who is the money for?* 这钱是给谁的? **3** (idm 习语) **who am ˈI, are ˈyou, is ˈshe, etc, to do sth?** what right, authority, etc have I, etc to do sth 我、你、她等有什么权利、资格等做某事: *Who are you to tell me I can't leave my bicycle here? It's not your house.* 你凭什么不让我把自行车放在这儿? 这又不是你们家. **(know, learn, etc) who's ˈwho** (be informed about) people's names, jobs, status, etc (知道)人的名字、工作、身分等; (了解)谁是谁: *You'll soon find out who's who in this department.* 你很快就能弄清楚这个部门每个人的情况.
▷ **who** *rel pron* 关系代词 **1** (**a**) (in clauses which define the preceding *n* 用于限定先行名词的从句中): *the man/men who wanted to meet you* 想要见你的人 ○ *The people who called yesterday want to buy the house.* 昨天打来电话的人想买这所房子. (**b**) (in clauses which do not define the preceding *n* 用于不限定先行名词的从句中): *My wife, who is out at the moment, will phone you when she gets back.* 我的太太现在出去了, 等她回来给你去电话. ○ *Mrs Smith, who has a lot of teaching experience, will be joining us in the spring.* 史密斯夫人很有教学经验, 她将在春天来和我们一道工作. **2** (used as the object of a *v* or *prep* 用作动词或介词的宾语) (**a**) (in a defining clause, where it can be omitted 用于限定性从句中, 此时who字可省去不用): *The couple (who) we met on holiday have sent us a card.* 我们度假时遇到的那对夫妇给我们寄来一张明信片. ○ *The boy (who) I spoke to a moment ago is the son of my employer.* 那个男孩, 就是我刚才和他说话的那个, 是我们雇主的儿子. (**b**) (in a non-defining clause 用于非限定性从句中): *Mary, who we were talking about earlier, has just walked in.* 玛丽, 我们刚才还说她来着, 已经进来了. ⇨Usage at WHOM 用法见 WHOM.

WHO /ˌdʌblju: eɪtʃ ˈəʊ; ˌdʌblju etʃ ˋo/ *abbr* 缩写 = World Health Organization 世界卫生组织.

whoa /wəʊ; wo/ *interj* (used as a command to a horse, etc to stop or stand still 用以叫马停下来或站住不动的口令).

who'd /hu:d; hud/ *contracted form* 缩约式 **1** who had ⇨ HAVE. **2** who would ⇨ WILL[1], WOULD[2].

who·dunit (also **who·dunnit**) /ˌhu:ˈdʌnɪt; huˋdʌnɪt/ *n* (*infml* 口) detective story or play in which the person who does the crime is only revealed at the end (在故事情节中作案罪犯在结局时才揭示出来的)侦探小说或戏剧: *her latest whodunit* 她最新的一部悬疑侦探小说.

who·ever /hu:ˈevə(r); huˋɛvɚ/ *pron* **1** the person who ...的那个人: *Whoever says that is a liar.* 说那话的人是个骗子. ○ *You're responsible to whoever is in charge of sales.* 你要向主管销售的人负责. **2** regardless of who 无论谁: *Whoever wants to speak to me on the phone, tell them I'm busy.* 不管谁要我接电话, 就说我现在正忙着呢. ○ *Tell whoever you like — it makes no difference to me.* 你愿意告诉谁就告诉谁——对我来说都无所谓.
▷ **who·ever** *interrog pron* (expressing surprise 用以表示惊讶) who (究竟)谁: *Whoever heard of such a thing!* 谁听说过这种事!

whole /həʊl; hol/ *adj* **1** [attrib 作定语] entire; complete 完全的; 整体的; 全部的: *three whole days* 三整天 ○ *We drank a whole bottle each.* 我们每人都喝了整整一瓶. ○ *The whole town was destroyed by the earthquake.* 整个小镇已遭地震摧毁. ○ (*infml* 口) *The whole country* (ie All the people in it) *mourned the death of the queen.* 举国哀悼女王晏驾. ○ *I've sold the whole lot*, ie everything. 我把所有东西都卖了. ○ *Let's forget the whole affair/matter/thing.* 咱们完全不要再想这件事了. ○ *Tell me the whole truth.* 把实情一五一十都告诉我. ⇨Usage at HALF[1] 用法见 HALF[1]. **2** not broken, damaged or injured; intact 完整的; 无损伤的: *After the party, there wasn't a glass left whole.* 这场聚会结束时, 玻璃杯连一个完整的也没剩下. ○ *cook sth whole*, ie without cutting it up 烹治整个儿的某物(不切开) ○ *swallow sth whole*, ie without chewing it 把某物囫囵吞下(不咀嚼) ○ (*fml* 文) *make sb whole*, ie well again (after injury or illness) 使某人痊愈. **3** (idm 习语) **go the whole hog** (*infml* 口) do sth thoroughly or completely 彻底地或完全地做某事: *They painted the kitchen and then decided to go the whole hog and redecorate the other rooms as well.* 他们粉刷了厨房, 后来又决心干到底, 把其他房间也都修饰了一番. **the whole bag of ˈtricks/caˈboodle/sheˈbang/ˈshooting match** (*infml* 口) the whole collection of facts or things 全部事物: *I just threw the whole caboodle in the back of the car.* 我把所有东西都扔到汽车后座上去了. ○ *They bought the house, the land, the stables — the whole shooting match.* 他们买下了那所房子、那片土地、那个马厩——所有东西都一齐买下了. **a whole lot (of sth)** (*infml*

口) a large number or amount 大量: *a whole lot of reasons for not doing it* 不做这件事的许许多多理由 ○ *a whole lot of trouble* 很多麻烦. **with all one's heart/one's whole heart** ⇨ HEART.

▷ **whole** *n* **1** [C] thing that is complete in itself 自成完整的事物; 整体; 整个; 全体: *Four quarters make a whole.* 四个四分之一可构成一个整体. ○ *A whole is greater than any of its parts.* 整体大于其组成部分. ⇨Usage at HALF[1] 用法见HALF[1]. **2** [sing] **~ of sth** all that there is of sth 某事物的全部: *She spent the whole of the year in hospital.* 她住院住了整整一年了. **3** (idm 习语) **as a ˈwhole** (**a**) as one thing or piece and not as separate parts 作为整体: *Is the collection going to be divided up or sold as a whole?* 这批收藏品是零卖还是一起卖? (**b**) in general 普遍说来; 一般地说: *The population as a whole is/are in favour of the reform.* 全体人民普遍拥护改革. **on the whole** considering everything 总的说来; 一切都考虑在内: *On the whole, I'm in favour of the proposal.* 总的说来, 我赞成这个提议.

whole·ness *n* [U].

wholly /ˈhəʊllɪ; ˈholɪ/ *adv* completely; entirely 完全地; 全部地: *not a wholly successful book* 并不十分成功的书 ○ *I'm not wholly convinced by your argument.* 您的论证我尚未尽以为然.

□ ˈ**whole food,** ˈ**whole foods** food that has not been processed or refined and is free from artificial substances 全部原食物(未经加工或精炼而无人造物质食物): [attrib 作定语] *a whole-food restaurant* 全部原食物餐厅.

ˌ**whole-ˈhearted** *adj* without doubts or hesitation 全心全意的: *give ˌwholehearted supˈport* 给予全心全意的支持. ˌ**whole-ˈheartedly** *adv*: *wholeheartedly in favour of the scheme* 全心全意赞成这项计划.

ˌ**whole ˈholiday** single whole day taken as a holiday, esp at a school 一整天的假(尤指学校的).

ˈ**wholemeal** *n* [U] flour that is made from the whole grain of wheat, etc including the husk 全麦面粉: [attrib 作定语] *wholemeal bread* 全麦面包.

ˌ**whole ˈnote** (*US*) = SEMIBREVE.

ˌ**whole ˈnumber** (*mathematics* 数) number that consists of one or more units, with no fractions; integer 整数.

whole·sale /ˈhəʊlseɪl; ˈhol,sel/ *n* [U, usu attrib 通常作定语] selling of goods (esp in large quantities) to shopkeepers for resale to the public 批发; 趸批出卖: *the wholesale trade* 批发业 ○ *wholesale prices* 批发价格. Cf 参看 RETAIL.

▷ **whole·sale** *adj, adv* (**a**) of, involving or engaged in wholesale as a method of trading 批发(的); 趸批出卖(的): *We buy our supplies wholesale.* 我们以批发交易方式进货. (**b**) (*often derog* 常作贬义) on a large scale 大规模(的): *the wholesale slaughter of innocent people* 大批屠杀无辜百姓.

whole·sale *v* [Tn] sell (goods) wholesale 批发(货物).

whole·saler *n*.

whole·some /ˈhəʊlsəm; ˈholsəm/ *adj* (**a**) good for one's health or well-being 有益于健康的: *plain but wholesome meals* 清淡却有益于健康的饭菜 ○ (*fig* 比喻) *wholesome advice* 有益的劝告. (**b**) suggesting a healthy condition 显示健康的: *have a wholesome appearance* 显出健康的样子. ▷ **whole·some·ness** *n* [U].

who'll /hu:l; hul/ *contracted form* 缩约式 who will ⇨ WILL[1].

wholly ⇨ WHOLE.

whom /hu:m; hum/ *interrog pron* (*fml* 文) (used as the object of a *v* or *prep* 用作动词或介词的宾语) which person or people 谁: *Whom did they invite?* 他们邀请谁了? ○ *To whom should I refer the matter?* 我应该找谁办这件事? ○ *By whom was the order executed?* 这项命令是谁执行的?

▷ **whom** *rel pron* 关系代词 (*fml* 文) **1** (used as the object of a *v* or *prep* introducing a clause that describes a person 用作动词或介词的宾语, 以引导出修饰人的从句): *The author whom you criticized in your review has written a letter in reply.* 您在评论中批评的那个作者已经写了一封回信. ○ *The person to whom this letter was addressed died three years ago.* 这封信的收信人三年前就去世了. **2** (used esp in formal written English as the object of a *v* or *prep* in a non-defining clause 尤用于庄重的书面语中, 作动词或介词的宾语以引导出非限定从句): *My parents, whom I'm sure you remember, passed away within a week of one another.* 我的父母, 您一定还记得他们的, 已于一周内相继去世. ○ *Her elder daughter, in whom she placed the greatest trust, failed to match her expectations.* 她的长女, 她对之无比信任, 却辜负了她的期望.

NOTE ON USAGE 用法: **Whom** is rarely used in everyday language. 在日常使用的语言中很少用到 **whom** 这个词. **Who** is more common as the object form, especially in questions 与之相比, **who** 倒常用作宾语, 尤用于疑问句中: *Who did you see at the party?* 你在聚会中看见谁了? **Whom** is necessary after prepositions 在介词后面必须用 **whom**: *With whom did you go?* 您是同何人一道去的? This use of preposition + **whom** is very formal and occurs especially in writing. 这种'介词 + **whom**'的用法极为庄重且特别用于书面语中. In informal language we say 在口语中应说: *Who did you go with?* 您是跟谁一起去的? In defining relative clauses **whom** is also unusual. 在限定性关系从句中也很少用 **whom** 这个词. The object pronoun is often omitted or replaced by **who** or **that** 在这种从句中, 宾格代词 **whom** 往往省去不用, 或用 **who** 或 **that** 代之: *The students (whom/who/that) we examined last week were excellent.* 我们上星期考的学生都好极了. In non-defining relative clauses **whom** or **who** (not **that**) is used and the pronoun cannot be omitted 在非限定性关系从句中, 要用 **whom** 或 **who** (不可用 **that**) 而且不可省略: *Our doctor, whom/who we all like very much, is leaving.* 常给我们看病的那个医生, 我们都非常喜欢他, 他要走了. This construction is uncommon in spoken English. 这种结构很少用于口语中.

whoop /hu:p, wu:p; *US* hwu:p; hwup/ *n* **1** loud cry, esp one expressing joy or excitement 大叫, 呼喊(尤指表达喜悦或兴奋的): *They opened the parcel with whoops of delight.* 他们打开包裹, 高兴地叫喊起来. **2** harsh gasping sound made by sb with whooping cough (百日咳患者的)咳嗽和哮喘声.

▷ **whoop** *v* [I] **1** utter a loud (joyful or excited) cry 发出(喜悦的或激动的)叫喊声: *whoop with joy* 欢呼. **2** cough with a whoop(2) 发出咳嗽和哮喘声. **3** (idm 习语) ˌ**whoop it ˈup** /wu:p; *US* hwʊp; hwup/ (*infml* 口) take part in noisy celebrations 欢闹; 狂欢庆祝: *After their victory they were whooping it up all night long.* 他们获胜后通宵狂欢庆祝.

□ ˈ**whooping cough** infectious disease, esp of children, with gasping coughs and long rasping intakes of breath 百日咳.

ˌ**whooping ˈcrane** large N American bird that makes a whooping sound (WHOOP 2) 高鸣鹤(产于北美).

whoo·pee /ˈwʊpi:; *US* ˈhwʊ-; ˈhwʊpi/ *interj* (expressing joy 表示喜悦的呼喊).

▷ **whoo·pee** *n* (idm 习语) **make ˈwhoopee** (*dated infml* 旧, 口) rejoice or celebrate noisily 欢闹; 狂欢庆祝.

whoops /wʊps; wups/ *interj* (*infml* 口) (**a**) (used when one has almost had an accident, broken sth, etc 用于险些出事故、打破某物等时): *Whoops! I nearly dropped the tray.* 哎哟! 我差点儿把托盘弄掉了. (**b**) (used to express apology or regret when one has said something tactless, revealed a secret, etc 说了唐突的话、泄露了秘密等时, 用以表示歉意或悔意).

whop /wɒp; *US* hwɒp; hwɑp/ *v* (**-pp-**) [Tn] (*infml* 口 *esp US*) thrash or defeat (sb) 痛打, 打败(某人).

▷ **whop·per** *n* (*infml* 口) (**a**) thing that is very big of its kind (同类中的)极大的事物: *The fisherman had caught a whopper.* 那个打鱼的捕到一条特大的鱼. (**b**) big lie 弥天大谎: *If she said that, she was telling a real whopper.* 要是她那么说的, 她就是说了个大瞎话.

whop·ping (*infml* 口) *adj* very big 极大的: *a whopping lie* 大瞎话. — *adv* (*infml* 口) very 非常: *a whopping big hole in the ground* 地上的一个极大的洞.

whore /hɔ:(r); hɔr/ *n* (*dated or derog* 旧或贬) (**a**) prostitute 妓女; 男妓. (**b**) sexually immoral woman 性关系不道德的女子.

□ ˈ**whore-house** *n* (*dated or derog* 旧或贬) brothel 妓院.

who're /ˈhu:ə(r); ˈhuɚ/ *contracted form* 缩约式 who are ⇨ BE.

whorl /wɜ:l; *US* hw-; hwɝl/ *n* **1** one turn of a spiral (—

圈)螺纹. **2** complete circle formed by the ridges of a fingerprint (指纹的)涡. **3** ring of leaves, petals, etc round the stem of a plant 轮生体(环生于植物茎部的叶、花瓣等).

whor·tle·berry /ˈwɜːtlberɪ; *US* ˈhwɜːrtlberɪ; ˈhwɝtl͵bɛrɪ/ *n* = BILBERRY.

who's /huːz; huz/ *contracted form* 缩约式 **1** who is ⇨ BE. **2** who has ⇨ HAVE.

whose /huːz; huz/ *interrog pron, interrog det* of whom 谁的: *Whose (house) is that?* 那是谁的(房子)? ○ *I wonder whose (book) this is.* 我不知道这是谁的(书).

▷ **whose** *rel det* 关系限定词 of whom; (less commonly) of which 谁的; 哪个的(不常用): *the boy whose father is in prison* 他父亲正在坐牢的那个男孩儿 ○ *the people whose house was broken into last week* 上星期闹贼的那家人 ○ *the house whose door has a glass panel*, ie instead of *the house with a door with a glass panel* 门上镶着玻璃的那所房子.

who've /huːv; huv/ *contracted form* 缩约式 who have ⇨ HAVE.

why /waɪ; *US* hwaɪ; hwaɪ/ *interrog adv* **1** for what reason or purpose 为什么原因或目的: *Why were you late?* 你为什么迟到? ○ *Why did you buy a spade?* 你买铁锨干什么? ○ *Tell me why you did it.* 告诉我你为什么干那件事? ○ *Do you know why the door is locked?* 你知道不知道门为什么锁上了? **2** (used in front of a *v* to suggest that sth is unacceptable or unnecessary 用于动词前表示某事不可取或不必要): *Why get upset just because you got a bad mark?* 何必因为得的分数差就想不开? ○ *Why bother to write? We'll see him tomorrow.* 还写信干什么? 我们明天就见到他了. **3** (idm 习语) **why ever** (used to express surprise 用以表示惊讶) why (究竟)为什么, 怎么: *Why ever didn't you tell us before?* 你怎么不早告诉我们呢? **why not** (used to make or agree to a suggestion 用以提出一建议或对一建议表示同意): *Why not go now?* 现在就去好不好? ○ *'Let's go to the cinema.' 'Why not?'* '咱们去看电影吧.' '好哇.'

▷ **why** *rel adv* 关系副词 (used esp after *reason* 尤用于reason一词之后) for which (reason) 因此(原因): *the reason why he left her* 他离开她的原因 ○ *That is (the reason) why I came early.* 这就是我来早了的原因.

why *interj* (expressing surprise, impatience, etc 用以表示惊讶、不耐烦等): *Why, it's you!* 呦, 是你呀! ○ *Why, it's easy — a child could do it!* 欸, 这很容易 —— 连孩子都会!

why *n* (idm 习语) **the whys and (the) wherefores** the reasons 原因; 缘故; 理由: *I don't need to hear all the whys and the wherefores, I just want to know what happened.* 我无需听那些大道理, 我只想知道是怎么了.

WI *abbr* 缩写 = **1** (esp in addresses) West Indies (尤用作地址上的字样)西印度群岛. **2** /͵dʌbljuː ˈaɪ; ͵dʌblju ˈaɪ/ (*Brit infml* 口) Women's Institute 妇女协会.

wick /wɪk; wɪk/ *n* **1** (**a**) length of thread in the centre of a candle, the top end of which is lit and burns as the wax melts 蜡烛心. ⇨illus at CANDLE 见CANDLE插图. (**b**) flat or rounded length of woven material by which oil is drawn up to be burnt, in oil-lamps, oil-stoves and some types of cigarette lighter 灯心; (某些类型的打火机的)油绳: *trim the wick of a lamp* 修剪灯心. **2** (idm 习语) **get on sb's ˈwick** (*Brit infml* 口) irritate sb continually 不断招惹某人.

wicked /ˈwɪkɪd; ˈwɪkɪd/ *adj* (**-er, -est**) **1** (of a person or his actions) morally bad; sinful or evil (指人或人的行为)不道德的, 缺德的, 邪恶的: *That was very wicked of you.* 你干的事可真缺德. ○ *a wicked deed, lie, plot* 邪恶的行为、谎言、阴谋 ○ (*fig* 比喻) *wicked* (ie very high) *prices* 邪乎的(极高的)价格 ○ *wicked* (ie very bad or unpleasant) *weather* 糟糕的天气. **2** intended to harm or capable of harming 意欲伤害的; 有伤害能力的: *a wicked blow* 意欲打伤的一击 ○ *a wicked-looking knife* 杀气腾腾的刀. **3** mischievous 淘气的; 顽皮的: *a wicked sense of humour* 恶作剧的幽默感.

▷ **the wicked** *n* [pl *v*] **1** wicked people 恶人. **2** (idm 习语) **(there's) no peace, rest, etc for the ˈwicked** (*saying usu joc* 谚, 通常作戏谑语) wrongdoers have (and must expect) a life full of fear, worry, etc 恶人永无宁日.

wickedly *adv*: *The knife gleamed wickedly in the moonlight.* 那把刀在月光下闪着凶光.

wicked·ness *n* [U].

wicker /ˈwɪkə(r); ˈwɪkɚ/ *n* [U] twigs or canes woven together, esp to make baskets or furniture 编结的树枝或藤条(尤指为制作篮、筐或家具用的): [attrib 作定语] *a wicker chair* 藤椅.

□ **ˈwickerwork** *n* [U] baskets, furniture, etc made of wicker (用枝条制作的)篮、筐、家具等: [attrib 作定语] *wickerwork chairs* 藤椅.

wicket /ˈwɪkɪt; ˈwɪkɪt/ *n* **1** small door or gate, esp one at the side of (or part of) a larger one 小门(尤指大门旁的或大门上的). **2** (**a**) (in cricket) either of the two sets of three stumps (with cross-pieces called *bails* on), at which the ball is bowled and which is defended by the batsman (板球)三柱门: *take a wicket*, ie dismiss a batsman 把一击球员杀出局 ○ *Surrey are four wickets down/have lost four wickets*, ie Four of their batsmen are out. 萨里队有四名击球员出局. ○ *We won by six wickets*, ie won with seven of our batsman not out. 我们队以七名击球员未出局而获胜. ⇨illus at CRICKET 见CRICKET插图. (**b**) stretch of ground between the two wickets 两座三柱门之间的场地: *a fast/slow wicket*, ie one on which the ball bounces at a quick/slow pace when bowled 球弹起快[慢]的场地 ○ (*fig infml* 比喻, 口) *be on an easy, good, soft, sticky, etc wicket*, ie be in circumstances, a job, etc of the type specified 处于舒适的、良好的、轻松的、困难的等环境. **3** (idm 习语) **keep ˈwicket** act as a wicket-keeper 防守三柱门. **leg before wicket** ⇨ LEG. **pitch wickets** ⇨ PITCH[2].

□ **ˈwicket-keeper** *n* (in cricket) player who stands behind the wicket in order to stop balls that the batsman misses, to catch balls that the batsman hits, etc (板球)三柱门守门员. ⇨illus at CRICKET 见CRICKET插图.

wide /waɪd; waɪd/ *adj* (**-r, -st**) **1** (**a**) measuring much from side to side; not narrow 宽的; 宽阔的: *a wide river* 宽阔的河 ○ *The gap in the fence was just wide enough for the sheep to get through.* 篱笆上的豁口宽度刚好能让羊钻过去. ○ (*fig* 比喻) *a wide* (ie large) *selection* 广泛的可供选择的范围. Cf 参看 BROAD[1] 1. (**b**) having the specified width 有某宽度的: *The garden is thirty feet wide.* 这个花园三十英尺宽. ○ *a two-inch-wide ribbon* 两英寸宽的带子. **2** extending over a large area 广大的; 宽广的: *the whole wide world* 整个大世界 ○ *a manager with wide experience of industry* 在工业方面有丰富经验的经理 ○ *The affair raises wider issues of national interest.* 此事向全民提出了广为关注的问题. **3** fully open 完全张开的: *She stared at him with eyes wide.* 她睁大了眼睛注视着他. **4** far from the point aimed at 远离目标的: *Her shot was wide (of the target).* 她射的离目标很远. **5** (idm 习语) **be/fall wide of the ˈmark** be inaccurate or far from the point aimed at 不准确的; 离目的远的: *His guesses were all very wide of the mark.* 他猜得都很离谱. **give sb/sth a wide ˈberth** remain at a safe distance from sb/sth 与某人[某事物]保持安全距离: *He's so boring that I always try to give him a wide berth at parties.* 他这个人很没意思, 在聚会上我总是对他退避三舍.

▷ **wide** *adv* **1** to the full extent; fully 充分地; 完全地: *wide awake* 完全清醒 ○ *with legs wide apart* 两腿劈开很大 ○ *Open your mouth wide.* 把嘴张大. **2** (idm 习语) **cast one's net wide** ⇨ CAST[1]. **far and near/wide** ⇨ FAR. **wide ˈopen** (of a contest) with no competitor who is a certain winner (指竞赛)没有一个参赛者有必胜把握的. **3 wide open (to sth)** exposed (to attack, etc) (对于外来的攻击等)敞开着的, 暴露着的, 可以受到的: *wide open to criticism* 尽可受到批评. **͵widea ˈwake** *adj* (*infml approv* 口, 褒) alert 警觉的; 警惕的: *a ͵wideawake young ˈwoman*, ie one who realizes what is going on, etc and is not easily deceived 机敏的年轻女子. **ˈwidespread** *adj* found or distributed over a large area 遍布的; 大面积的: *widespread damage, confusion* 大面积的损坏、各处呈现的混乱.

wide *n* (in cricket) ball that is judged by the umpire to be bowled outside the batsman's reach (板球)(裁判认为投的球为)坏球.

-wide (forming *adjs* and *advs* 用以构成形容词和副词) extending to the whole of sth 达到某处全部范围: *a nationwide search* ○ *travelled worldwide.*

widely *adv* **1** to a large extent or degree 达到大的范围或程度: *differing widely in their opinions* 他们的意见分歧很大. **2** over a large area 广泛地; 遍布: *widely*

W

scattered 遍及各处 ○ *It is widely known that...* 众所周知....

widen /ˈwaɪdn; ˋwaɪdn̩/ *v* [I, Tn] (cause sth to) become wider (使某物)变宽; 加宽; 放宽: *The road is being widened.* 这条路正在拓宽. ○ *He wants to widen his knowledge of the industry.* 他想扩充自己在这一行业的知识.

□ ˌ**wide-angle** ˈ**lens** camera lens that can give a wider field of vision than a standard lens 广角透镜.

ˈ**wide boy** (*dated Brit infml derog* 旧, 口, 贬) person who is shrewd, unscrupulous and often dishonest, esp in business 刁滑的、肆行无忌的且常为不诚实的人(尤指做生意时).

ˌ**wide-ˈeyed** *adj* with eyes open widely in amazement or innocent surprise 睁大眼睛的, 目瞪口呆的(因惊奇或少见多怪).

ˌ**wide-ˈranging** *adj* covering a large area or many subjects 范围或内容广泛的: ˌ*wide-ranging investiˈgations* 范围广泛的调查.

widgeon /ˈwɪdʒən; ˋwɪdʒən/ *n* (*pl* unchanged or **~s** 复数或不变或作 **widgeons**) any of several types of wild duck 凫; 野鸭.

widow /ˈwɪdəʊ; ˋwɪdo/ *n* woman whose husband has died and who has not married again 寡妇; 孀妇: *She has been a widow for ten years.* 她守寡十年了. ○ *He married his brother's widow.* 他娶了他哥哥的遗孀.

▷ **widow** *v* [Tn esp passive 尤用于被动语态] cause (sb) to become a widow or widower 使(某人)成寡妇或鳏夫: *She was widowed at an early age.* 她年轻时就成了寡妇. ○ *Many people were widowed by the war.* 很多人因战乱丧偶.

ˈ**widow·hood** *n* [U] state or time of being a widow 守寡; 孀居.

wid·ower /ˈwɪdəʊə(r); ˋwɪdəwɚ/ *n* man whose wife has died and who has not married again 鳏夫.

width /wɪdθ, wɪtθ; wɪdθ, wɪtθ/ *n* **1** (**a**) [U, C] measurement from side to side 宽度: *10 metres in width* 10米宽 ○ *measure the width of the floor* 测量地板的宽度 ○ *The carpet is available in various widths.* 地毯现货尺寸齐全. ⇨illus at DIMENSION 见 DIMENSION 插图. (**b**) [C] piece of material of a certain width 呈某宽度的材料: *Two widths of cloth were joined to make the curtain.* 是用两幅布料拼成的这个帘子. **2** [U] quality or state of being wide; wideness 宽; 广: *The river can be used by many ships because of its width.* 这条河很宽可容许多船航行. ○ (*fig* 比喻) *width of experience, knowledge, mind* 经验之丰富、知识之广博、心胸之宽阔. **3** [C] distance between the sides of a swimming-pool 游泳池横向两边之间的距离: *She can swim two widths now.* 她现在能在游泳池里横向游一个来回了.

□ ˈ**widthways** *adv* along the width and not the length 沿宽边(非沿长边): *The fabric was folded widthways.* 这块织物是沿宽边折起的.

wield /wiːld; wild/ *v* [Tn] hold in one's hand(s) and use (a weapon, tool, etc) 手持着使用(武器、工具等): *wield an axe, a sword, a tennis racket* 使用斧头、剑、网球拍 ○ (*fig* 比喻) *wield authority, control, power, etc* 运用权力、控制手段、权势等.

W

wiener /ˈwiːnə(r); ˋwinɚ/ *n* (*US*) =FRANKFURTER.

wife /waɪf; waɪf/ *n* (*pl* **wives** /waɪvz; waɪvz/) **1** married woman, esp when considered in relation to her husband 已婚女子; 妻: *the doctor's wife* 那个医生的妻子 ○ *She was a good wife and mother.* 她是贤妻良母. **2** (idm 习语) **husband and wife** ⇨ HUSBAND. **an old wives' tale** ⇨ OLD. **all the world and his wife** ⇨ WORLD.

▷ **wifely** *adj* of, like or expected of a wife (似)妻子的; 为妻(应有)的: *wifely duties, support, virtues* 做妻子的责任、支持、美德.

wig /wɪg; wɪg/ *n* covering for the head made of real or artificial hair, worn to hide baldness, or in a lawcourt by barristers and judges, or by actors as part of a costume 假发: *She disguised herself with a blonde wig and dark glasses.* 她乔装打扮戴着金色假发和墨镜. Cf 参看 TOUPEE.

wig·ging /ˈwɪgɪŋ; ˋwɪgɪŋ/ *n* (usu *sing* 通常作单数) (*dated Brit infml* 旧, 口) lengthy rebuke; scolding 痛骂; 责骂: *get/give sb a good wigging* 挨一顿大骂[把某人痛骂一顿].

wiggle /ˈwɪgl; ˋwɪgl/ *v* [I, Tn] (*infml* 口) (cause sth to) move from side to side with rapid short movements (使某物)摆动, 摇动, 扭动: *Stop wiggling and sit still!* 不要摇摇晃晃的, 坐着别动! ○ *The baby was wiggling its toes.* 那幼儿扭动着脚趾. Cf 参看 WAG, WAGGLE.

▷ **wiggle** *n* (*infml* 口) wiggling movement 摆动; 摇动; 扭动.

wiggly /ˈwɪglɪ; ˋwɪglɪ/ *adj* (*infml* 口) (**a**) moving with a wiggle 摆动的; 摇动的; 扭动的: *a wiggly worm* 扭动的虫子. (**b**) not straight; wavy 弯曲的; 波状的: *a wiggly line* 波浪形线.

wig·wam /ˈwɪgwæm; *US* -wɑːm; ˋwɪgwɑm/ *n* hut or tent made by fastening mats or animal skins over a framework of poles, esp as used formerly by N American Indians (用席或兽皮等制作的)棚屋(尤指旧时北美印第安人使用的). Cf 参看 TEPEE.

wilco /ˈwɪlkəʊ; ˋwɪlko/ *interj* (used in signalling, etc to confirm that a message has been received and orders will be carried out 用作信号语, 证实信息收悉并照办).

wild /waɪld; waɪld/ *adj* (**-er**, **-est**) **1** [usu attrib 通常作定语] (**a**) (of animals, birds, etc) that normally live in natural conditions; not tame or domesticated (指动物)野生的, 野的, 未驯化的: *a wild cat, giraffe, duck* 野猫、野生的长颈鹿、野鸭 ○ *filming wild animals* 拍摄野生动物. (**b**) (of plants) growing in natural conditions; not cultivated (指植物)野生的, 非栽培的: *wild flowers* 野花 ○ *wild roses, strawberries* 野生的玫瑰、草莓. **2** [usu attrib 通常作定语] (of a person, tribe, etc) not civilized; savage (指人、部落等)未开化的, 野蛮的. **3** (of scenery, an area of land, etc) not populated or cultivated; looking desolate (指风景、地区等)无居民的, 荒凉的: *a wild mountain region* 荒无人烟的山区. **4** tempestuous; stormy 暴风雨的; 暴风雪的: *a wild night* 有狂风暴雨的夜晚. **5** out of control; undisciplined 失去控制的; 不守规矩的: *wild disorder* 乱七八糟 ○ *He led a wild life in his youth.* 他年轻时放荡不羁. **6** full of strong unrestrained feeling; very angry, excited, passionate, etc 感情奔放的; 非常气愤、兴奋、热情等的: *wild laughter* 哈哈大笑 ○ *The crowd went wild with delight.* 群众欣喜若狂. ○ *It makes me wild* (ie very angry) *to see such cruelty.* 我见到这种残酷现象怒不可遏. ○ *She had a wild look on her face.* 她怒容可掬. **7** [pred 作表语] **~ (about sth/sb)** (*infml* 口) extremely enthusiastic (about sth/sb) (对某事物[某人])极热心或热爱: *The children are wild about the new computer.* 孩子们都特别喜欢这个新计算机. ○ *I can't say I'm wild about her new husband.* 我很难说我非常喜欢她的新婚丈夫. **8** not carefully aimed or planned; foolish or unreasonable 目标或计划不精确的; 愚蠢的; 不合理的: *a wild aim, guess, shot* 胡乱的瞄准、猜测、射击 ○ *a wild scheme* 盲目的计划. **9** (idm 习语) **beyond one's wildest** ˈ**dreams** far more than one could ever have imagined or hoped for 远远超出想像或希望的. **run** ˈ**wild** (of an animal, plant, person, etc) grow or stray freely without any control (指人、动植物等)自由生长的, 不受控制的: *Those boys have been allowed to run wild.* 那些男孩子无人管教肆无忌惮. **sow one's wild oats** ⇨ SOW[2].

▷ **wild** *n* (**a**) **the wild** [sing] natural state or habitat 自然的状态或生存环境: *animals living in the wild* 在自然状态下生活的动物. (**b**) **the wilds** [pl] (*sometimes derog* 有时作贬义) remote (usu uncultivated) area where few people live 人烟稀少的边远地区(通常指未开垦的): *the wilds of Australia* 澳洲的荒地 ○ *live out in the wilds*, ie far from towns, etc 住在边远地区.

wildly *adv* (**a**) in a wild manner 处于野生的或失控的状态; 野蛮地; 狂暴地; 激烈地: *rushing wildly from room to room* 闯入各个房间 ○ *talk wildly*, ie in an exaggerated or a very emotional way 说话言过其实(或感情用事). (**b**) extremely 极; 非常: *a wildly exaggerated account* 极为夸张的叙述.

wild·ness *n* [U].

□ ˈ**wild card** (in card-games) playing-card that has been given the value of certain other cards (纸牌戏中的)百搭牌.

ˈ**wildcat** *adj* [attrib 作定语] (esp in business and finance) reckless or risky (尤指在商业和财务上)鲁莽的, 冒险的: *a wildcat scheme* 冒险的计划. ˌ**wildcat** ˈ**strike** sudden and unofficial strike by workers 未经工会允许的突然罢工.

ˈ**wildfire** *n* (idm 习语) **spread like wildfire** ⇨ SPREAD.

ˈ**wildfowl** *n* (*pl* unchanged 复数不变) any of the types

of bird that are shot or hunted as game, eg ducks, geese, pheasants, quail, etc (视为猎物的)野禽(如野鸭、雁、雉、鹑等).

ˌ**wild-ˈgoose chase** foolish or hopeless search, eg for sth or sb that does not exist or can only be found elsewhere 愚蠢的或毫无希望的追寻(如寻找的事物或人并不存在或在他处者): *The hoaxer had sent the police on a wild-goose chase.* 那个捣蛋的人让警方白白搜索了一番.

ˈ**wildlife** *n* [U] wild animals, birds, etc 野生的鸟兽等: *the conservation of wildlife* 对野生生物的保护 ○ [attrib 作定语] *a wildlife sanctuary* 野生动物保护区.

the ˌWild ˈWest the western States of the USA during the period when they were being settled by Europeans and there was much lawlessness 蛮荒的西部(欧洲人移入时的美国西部各州, 多无法无天事): *films about the Wild West* 关于美国蛮荒的西部的影片.

wil·de·beest /ˈwɪldɪbi:st; ˈwɪldəˌbist/ *n* (*pl* unchanged or **~s** 复数或不变或作 **wildebeests**) = GNU.

wil·der·ness /ˈwɪldənɪs; ˈwɪldənɪs/ *n* (usu *sing* 通常作单数) **1** area of wild uncultivated land; desert 未开垦的荒地; 荒漠; 沙漠: *the Arctic wilderness* 北极的荒原. **2** **~ (of sth)** area where plants, esp weeds, grow in an uncontrolled way 植物(尤指杂草)丛生的地方: *The garden is turning into a wilderness.* 这个园子逐渐变成杂草丛生之处. ○ (*fig* 比喻) *a wilderness of old abandoned cars* 旧汽车的弃置地. **3** (idm 习语) **in the ˈwilderness** no longer in an important or influential (esp political) position 不再处于重要的或有影响的地位(尤指政治上): *After a few years in the wilderness he was reappointed to the Cabinet.* 他消沉了几年之后, 又获任命进入了内阁.

wiles /waɪlz; waɪlz/ *n* [pl] trickery intended to deceive or attract sb (旨在欺骗或吸引人的)诡计, 花招: *All her wiles were not enough to persuade them to sell the property.* 她花言巧语也未能打动他们卖掉物业.

wil·ful (*US* also **will·ful**) /ˈwɪlfl; ˈwɪlfəl/ *adj* [usu attrib 通常作定语] (*derog* 贬) **1** (of sth bad) done deliberately; intentional (指坏事)故意做的, 特意的: *wilful disobedience, negligence, murder, waste* 故意的不服从、不理会、杀人、浪费. **2** (of a person) determined to do as one wishes; headstrong or obstinate (指人)任性的, 倔强的, 固执的: *a wilful child* 任性的孩子. ▷ **wil·fully** /-fəlɪ; -fəlɪ/ *adv*. **wil·ful·ness** *n* [U].

will[1] /wɪl; wɪl/ *modal v* (*contracted form* 缩约式 **'ll** /l; l/; *neg* 否定式 **will not**, *contracted form* 缩约式 **won't** /wəunt; wont/; *pt* **would** /wəd;wəd; *strong form* 强读式 wud; wud/, *contracted form* 缩约式 **'d** /d; d/; *neg* 否定式 **would not**, *contracted form* 缩约式 **wouldn't** /ˈwudnt; ˈwudn̩t/) **1 (a)** (indicating future predictions 用以表示对未来事物的预料): *Next year will be the centenary of this firm.* 明年是这家公司成立的一百周年. ○ *He'll start school soon, won't he?* 他很快就要上学了, 对吧? ○ *You'll be in time if you hurry.* 你要是快一点儿就能来得及. ○ *How long will you be staying in Paris?* 你在巴黎要呆多久? ○ *Fred said he'd soon be leaving.* 弗雷德说他很快就要走了. ○ *If you phoned my secretary she'd give you an appointment.* 你给我秘书打个电话, 她就会给你约定个时间. ⇨Usage 1 at SHALL 见 SHALL 所附用法第1项. **(b)** (indicating present predictions 用以表示对目前事物的预料): *That'll be the postman now!* 这准是邮递员来了! ○ *They'll be home by this time.* 他们现在一定到家了. **2 (a)** (indicating willingness or unwillingness 用以表示愿意或不愿意): *He'll take you home — you only have to ask.* 他愿意送你回家—— 你跟他一说就行. ○ *I'll check this letter for you, if you want.* 你要想让我给你查查这封信, 我就给你查查. ○ *We won't lend you any more money.* 我们不再借给你钱了. ○ *She wouldn't come to the zoo — she was frightened of the animals.* 她不愿意到动物园来—— 她害怕动物. ○ *We said we would keep them.* 我们说过我们愿意保留它们. ⇨Usage 2 at SHALL 见 SHALL 所附用法第2项. **(b)** (indicating requests 用以表示请求): *Will you post this letter for me, please?* 请您把这封信给我寄出去行吗? ○ *Will you (please) come in?* 您(请)进来好吗? ○ *You'll water the plants while I'm away, won't you?* 我不在的时候, 你给这些植物浇浇水行吗? ○ *I asked him if he wouldn't mind calling later.* 我问他等一会儿再打电话来行不行. **3** (giving an order 用于发出命令或指示时): *You will carry out these instructions and report back this afternoon.* 你要执行这些指示并于今日下午报告执行情况. ○ *Will you be quiet!* 安静点儿! ⇨Usage 3 at SHALL 见 SHALL 所附用法第3项. **4 (a)** (describing general truths 用于叙述真理时): *Oil will float on water.* 油能浮在水面上. ○ *Engines won't run without lubricants.* 没有润滑剂发动机就不能运转. **(b)** (describing habits in the present or past 用于叙述目前的或过去的习惯时): *She will listen to records, alone in her room, for hours.* 她独自一人在屋里听唱片, 每每一听就是半天. ○ *He would spend hours in the bathroom or on the telephone.* 他以前一进洗澡间或是一打电话, 往往就是半天. **5** (insistence on the part of the subject 用以表示施事者执意要做的事): *He ˈwill comb his hair at the table, even though he knows I don't like it.* 他偏偏要在饭桌那儿梳头, 还明明知道我腻味这事儿. ○ *He ˈwould keep telling those dreadful stories.* 他专门爱讲那些讨厌的故事.

will[2] /wɪl; wɪl/ *v* [I] (only used in the simple present tense; *3rd pers sing* **will** 仅用于一般现在时态; 第三人称单数作 **will**) **1** (*dated or fml* 旧或文) wish 希望; 愿意: *Call it what you will, it's still a problem.* 不管怎么说, 这仍旧是个问题. ○ *You're free to travel where you will in the country.* 在这个国家里, 你想上哪儿去就可以上哪儿去. **2** (idm 习语) **if you ˈwill** (*fml* 文) if you prefer to express it in these terms 你若愿意这样说也行: *He became her senior adviser — her deputy, if you will.* 他成了她的高级顾问—— 你要说是她的副手也未尝不可.

will[3] /wɪl; wɪl/ *v* **1** [Tn, Tnt] try to make (sth) happen or to make (sb) do sth by using one's mental powers 用意志的力量使(某事)发生或使(某人)做某事: *As a child he thought that his grandmother's death had happened because he had willed it.* 他小小年纪以为祖母死了是因为他曾经想过让她死. ○ *The crowd were cheering their favourite on, willing her to win.* 大家都在给他们心目中的热门参赛者加油, 暗使劲儿使之获胜. **2** [Tn, Tf] (*fml* 文) intend (sth); desire 想要(某事); 愿望: *This happened because God willed it.* 发生了这件事是上帝的旨意. ○ *God wills that man should be happy.* 上帝愿人类幸福. **3** [Dn·n, Dn·pr] **~ sth (to sb)** (*fml* 文) leave (property, etc) to sb by means of a will and testament 将(财产等)遗赠某人: *Father willed me the house and my sister the income from the investments.* 父亲把房子遗赠给我了, 把投资收入遗赠给了妹妹. ○ *He willed most of his money to charities.* 他把钱大多遗赠给慈善机构了.

will[4] /wɪl; wɪl/ *n* **1** [U, sing] mental power by which a person can direct his thoughts and actions or influence those of others 意志: *the freedom of the will* 意志上的自由 ○ *Man has (a) free will.* 人类有自由的意志. **2 (a)** [U, sing] (also ˈ**will-power** [U]) control that one can use over one's own impulses 意志力; 自制力; 主见: *have a strong/weak will* 有坚强的意志力[意志力薄弱] ○ *He has no will of his own.* 他没有主见. ○ *She shows great strength of will.* 她表现出了坚强的意志力. **(b)** [U, C] strong desire; determination 强烈的愿望; 决心; 毅力: *Despite her injuries, she hasn't lost the will to live.* 她尽管受了伤却没有失去生存的毅力. ○ *There was a clash of wills among committee members.* 委员们意愿不一, 发生了冲突. **3** [U] that which is desired (by sb) (某人的)旨意: *try to do God's will* 要按照上帝的旨意行事 ○ *It is the will of Allah.* 这是安拉的旨意. **4** (also **testament**) [C] legal document in which a person states how he wants his property and money to be disposed of after his death 遗嘱: *one's last will and testament* 自己最后的遗嘱. **5** (idm 习语) **against one's ˈwill** not according to one's wishes 违背自己的意愿: *I was forced to sign the agreement against my will.* 我被迫违心地在协议上签了字. **at one's own sweet will** ⇨ SWEET. **at ˈwill** wherever, whenever, etc one wishes 随意; 任意: *The animals are allowed to wander at will in the park.* 这些动物可以在公园里随意走动. **of one's own free will** ⇨ FREE. **where there's a ˌwill there's a ˈway** (*saying* 谚) a person with determination will find a way of doing sth 有志者事竟成. **with the best will in the world** ⇨ BEST[1]. **with a ˈwill** willingly and enthusiastically 愿意地; 乐意地; 热情地: *She started digging the garden with a will.* 她在园子里起劲地翻起土来.

▷ **-willed** (forming compound *adjs* 用以构成复合形容词) with a will of a specified kind 有某种意志的: *strong-willed* ○ *weak-willed*.

□ ˈ**will-power** *n* [U] = WILL 2a.

wil·lies /ˈwɪlɪz; ˋwɪlɪz/ *n* **the willies** [pl] (*infml* 口) uneasy or nervous feeling 不自在的或紧张的感觉: *Being alone in that gloomy house gave me the willies.* 我一个人在那所阴暗的房子心里就发毛.

will·ing /ˈwɪlɪŋ; ˋwɪlɪŋ/ *adj* **1 (a)** ready or eager to help 愿意或乐于相助的: *willing assistants* 主动帮忙的人. **(b)** [pred 作表语] **~ (to do sth)** having no objection (to doing sth); prepared 不反对(做某事); 愿意: *Are you willing to accept responsibility?* 你愿意承担责任吗? **2** [attrib 作定语] done, given, etc readily or gladly 愿意或喜欢做的、给的等: *willing co-operation, help, support, etc* 自愿的合作、帮助、支持等. **3** (idm 习语) **God willing** ⇨ GOD. **show willing** ⇨ SHOW². **the spirit is willing** ⇨ SPIRIT. **a willing ˈhorse** person who works willingly (contrasted with sb who complains or resists) 积极工作的人(有别于常发牢骚或不满的人): *She's the willing horse in the office and so gets given most of the work to do.* 她是办公室里埋头苦干的人, 大部分的工作都交给她去做. ▷ **will·ingly** *adv*. **will·ing·ness** *n* [U, sing]: *show (a) willingness to please* 表现出愿意讨好别人.

will-o'-the-wisp /ˌwɪl ə ðə ˈwɪsp; ˏwɪləðəˋwɪsp/ *n* **1** bluish moving light that may be seen at night on marshy ground 磷火; 鬼火. **2** person or thing that is impossible to catch or reach 捉不到或接触不到的人或事物: *You shouldn't hope to find perfect happiness — it's just a will-o'-the-wisp.* 不要指望能找到十全十美的幸福——那只不过是镜花水月.

wil·low /ˈwɪləʊ; ˋwɪlo/ *n* **(a)** (also ˈ**willow-tree**) [C] any of various types of tree and shrub with thin flexible branches and long narrow leaves, usu growing near water 柳; 柳树: *a weeping willow* 垂柳. ⇨illus at App 1 见附录1插图, page i. **(b)** [U] its wood, used esp for making cricket bats 柳木(尤用以制作板球棒).

▷ **willowy** *adj* (of a person) tall, lithe and slender (指人体)修长而柔软的, 苗条的: *a willowy young actress* 一个苗条的年轻女演员.

□ ˈ**willow-pattern** *n* [U] traditional blue and white Chinese design that includes a picture of a willow-tree and a river, used esp on china plates, etc 柳景图案(中国传统蓝白二色图案, 有小河垂柳, 尤见于瓷盘等上): [attrib 作定语] *a willow-pattern dinner service* 一套柳景图案的餐具.

willy /ˈwɪlɪ; ˋwɪlɪ/ *n* (*Brit infml* 口) (used esp by or when speaking to young children 儿语) penis 小鸡鸡(阴茎).

willy-nilly /ˌwɪlɪ ˈnɪlɪ; ˏwɪlɪˋnɪlɪ/ *adv* whether one wants it or not; willingly or unwillingly 无论想要不想要; 不管愿意不愿意: *They all had to take part, willy-nilly.* 他们都得参加, 不论他们愿意不愿意.

wilt /wɪlt; wɪlt/ *v* **(a)** [I] (of a plant or flower) droop and wither (指花草)凋谢, 枯萎, 蔫: *The leaves are beginning to wilt.* 这些叶子有些蔫了. ○ (*fig* 比喻) *spectators wilting* (ie becoming tired and weak) *in the heat* 因天热而发蔫的观众(又累又乏). **(b)** [Tn] cause (a plant or flower) to droop (使花草)凋谢, 枯萎, 蔫: *The plants were wilted by the heat.* 天气很热, 花草都蔫了.

W **wily** /ˈwaɪlɪ; ˋwaɪlɪ/ *adj* **(-ier, -iest)** crafty or cunning; full of wiles 狡诈的; 狡猾的; 诡计多端的: *as wily as a fox* 像狐狸一样狡猾 ○ (*infml* 口) *a wily old bird*, ie a cunning person 大滑头. ▷ **wi·li·ness** *n* [U].

wimp /wɪmp; wɪmp/ *n* (*infml derog* 口, 贬) weak and timid person, esp a man 懦弱的人(尤指男的): *Don't be such a wimp!* 别那么窝囊!

▷ **wimp·ish** *adj* (*infml derog* 口, 贬) (behaving) like a wimp (表现)懦弱的.

wimple /ˈwɪmpl; ˋwɪmpl/ *n* **(a)** head-dress made of linen or silk folded round the head and neck, worn by women in the Middle Ages 温帕尔头巾(中世纪女子戴的). **(b)** similar linen head-dress worn by certain nuns 某些修女用的头巾.

win /wɪn; wɪn/ *v* **(-nn-**; *pt, pp* **won** /wʌn; wʌn/) **1** [I, Tn] be victorious in (a battle, contest, race, etc); do best 在(战斗、比赛等)中赢; 获胜: *Which team won?* 哪个队赢了? ○ *She was determined to win (the race).* 她决心要赢(这项径赛). ○ *win a bet/wager* 赢一赌注. **2** [Tn, Tn·pr] **~ sth (from sb)** obtain or achieve sth as the result of a bet, competition, race, etc (在赌博、竞争、径赛等中)赢得或获得某事物: *She won first prize (in the raffle).* 她获得了(慈善抽奖)头奖. ○ *The Conservatives won the seat* (ie in Parliament) *from Labour at the last election.* 保守党在上次议会选举中从工党手里夺得这个议席. **3 (a)** [Tn] obtain or reach (sth), esp as a result of hard work or perseverance 赢得或达到(某事物)(尤指因努力或坚持): *They are trying to win support for their proposal.* 他们竭力争取群众支持他们的建议. **(b)** [Dn·n, Dn·pr] **~ sth (for sb/sth)** cause (sb) to obtain or achieve sth 使(某人)获得或取得某事物: *Her performance won her much critical acclaim.* 她的表演大获评论界赞颂. **4** (idm 习语) **carry/win the day** ⇨ DAY. **gain/win sb's hand** ⇨ HAND. **gain/win one's laurels** ⇨ LAUREL. **heads I win, tails you lose** ⇨ HEAD¹. **lose/win by a neck** ⇨ NECK. **nothing venture, nothing gain/win** ⇨ VENTURE *v*. **win free** free oneself from a difficult position, etc by effort (通过努力)摆脱困境. **win (sth) ˌhands ˈdown** (*infml* 口) win easily, by a large margin 轻易大胜; 垂手赢得: *The local team won (the match) hands down.* 主队以悬殊比分垂手赢得(这场比赛的)胜利. **win one's ˈspurs** (*fml* 文) achieve distinction or fame 获得荣誉或名声. ˌ**win or ˈlose** whether one succeeds or fails 无论胜负; 不管输赢; 不论成败: *Win or lose, it should be a very good match.* 姑不论胜负, 这场比赛想必十分精彩. **win/lose the toss** ⇨ TOSS *n*. **you, one, etc ˌcan't ˈwin** (*infml* 口) there is no way of achieving success or of pleasing people 无论怎样做都不能成功或都不讨好. **5** (phr v) **win sth/sb back** regain sth/sb after a struggle 经过奋斗重新获得某事物[某人]: *The party must try to win back the support it has lost.* 该党须设法重获人心. ○ *He hoped to win her love back.* 他希望努力重新获得她的爱. **win sb over/round (to sth)** gain sb's support or favour, esp by persuasion 获得某人的支持或好感(尤指通过劝说): *She's against the idea, but I'm sure I can win her over.* 她反对这个意见, 但我准能说服她改变主意. **win out/through** (*infml* 口) come successfully through a difficult period; achieve success eventually 摆脱困境; 终获成功: *We are faced with a lot of problems but we'll win through in the end.* 我们面临许多问题, 但终将获得成功.

▷ **win** *n* victory in a game, contest, etc (游戏、比赛等中的)胜, 赢: *Our team has had five wins and no losses this season.* 我队今年赛季赢五场而未输过.

win·ner *n* **1** person, horse, etc that wins 获胜的人、马等: *The winner was presented with a trophy.* 获胜者得到了奖品. **2** (*infml* 口) thing, idea, etc that is successful 成功的东西、想法等: *Their latest model is certain to be a winner.* 他们最新型号的产品一定很成功. **3** (idm 习语) **pick a winner** ⇨ PICK³.

win·ning *adj* **1** [attrib 作定语] that wins or has won 胜利的; 获胜的: *the winning horse, number, ticket* 获胜的马、中奖的号码、中奖的彩票. **2** [usu attrib 通常作定语] attractive or persuasive 吸引人的; 有说服力的: *a winning smile* 动人的微笑 ○ *She has a winning way with her.* 她有令人折服的本领. ˈ**winning-post** *n* post that marks the end of a race (马场上的)终点标柱: *Her horse was first past the winning-post.* 她的马第一个冲过终点标柱.

win·nings /ˈwɪnɪŋz; ˋwɪnɪŋz/ *n* [pl] money that is won, esp by betting, gambling, etc 赢得的钱(尤指打赌或赌博赢的): *collect one's winnings* 收取赢得的钱.

wince /wɪns; wɪns/ *v* [I, Ipr] **~ (at sth)** show pain, distress or embarrassment by a slight involuntary movement, esp of the muscles in the face 表示痛苦、沮丧或尴尬(以不由自主的轻微动作表现, 尤指面部肌肉): *He winced as she stood on his injured foot.* 她踩着他受伤的脚, 他疼得龇牙咧嘴. ○ *I still wince at the memory of the stupid things I did.* 我一想起自己做过的蠢事就不由得摇头叹气. ▷ **wince** *n* (usu *sing* 通常作单数).

win·cey·ette /ˌwɪnsɪˈet; ˏwɪnsɪˋɛt/ *n* [U] soft fabric made from cotton, or from cotton and wool, used esp for making pyjamas, night-dresses, etc 色织棉法兰绒(尤用以做睡衣等).

winch /wɪntʃ; wɪntʃ/ *n* machine for hoisting or pulling heavy objects by means of a rope or chain wound round a drum; windlass 卷扬机; 绞车; 辘轳.

▷ **winch** *v* [Tn, Tn·pr, Tn·p] move (sb/sth) by using a winch 用卷扬机移动(某人[某物]): *winch a glider off the ground*, ie pull it along by means of a winch until it rises into the air 用绞车把滑翔机拉起升空 ○ *The helicopter winched the survivor up* (eg out of the sea) *to*

winch 卷扬机

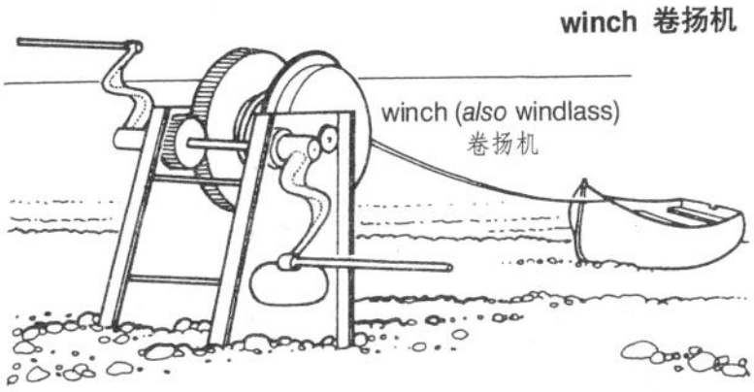

safety. 直升机把幸存者吊起送到安全的地方(如救援海中遇难者).

wind[1] /wɪnd; wɪnd/ *n* **1** [C, U] (also **the wind**) (used with *a* or in the plural when referring to the type of wind or its direction, etc; used with *much, little*, etc when referring to its strength, etc 指风的种类或方向等时, 与不定冠词a连用或用复数形式; 指风的强度时与much、little等连用) air moving as a result of natural forces 风; 气流: *A gust of wind blew my hat off.* 一阵风把我的帽子刮掉了. ○ *The day was very still, without a breath of wind.* 天空十分平静, 一点风都没有. ○ *a north wind*, ie one that blows from the north 北风 ○ *warm southerly winds* 温暖的南风 ○ *The wind has dropped* (ie is less strong) *now.* 风势现已减弱. **2** [U] smell carried by the wind (空气传送的)气味: *The deer have got our wind.* 鹿已闻到我们的气味了. **3** [U] breath, esp as needed for continuous exercise or for sounding a musical instrument 呼吸(尤指运动时的或吹奏乐器时的): *The runner had to stop and regain her wind*, ie wait until she could breathe more easily. 那个女的跑着半截停下来喘大气. **4** [U] air that has been swallowed with food or drink, or gas that forms in the stomach or intestines and causes discomfort; flatulence (肠胃中的)气: *get a baby's wind up*, ie cause it to belch by stroking or patting its back 让婴儿胃里的气出来(拍抚其后背使之打嗝). **5** [U] useless or boastful talk 无用的或吹嘘的话; 空话: *He's just full of wind, the pompous fool!* 他空话连篇, 是个自负的蠢材! **6 the wind** [Gp, sing] (players of the) wind instruments in an orchestra (管弦乐队的)管乐器(吹奏者): [attrib 作定语] *the wind section* 管乐组. **7** (idm 习语) **break 'wind** (*euph* 婉) expel air from the intestines through the anus 放屁. **the eye of the wind/wind's eye** ⇨ EYE[1]. **get one's second 'wind** feel strong again after getting very tired 极疲倦后重新感到有精力: *I often feel sleepy after supper and then I get my second wind later in the evening.* 我吃完晚饭常感到困, 一到晚上就又精神了. **get wind of sth** hear a rumour that sth is happening; hear about sth secret 听到某事的风声; 听到秘密消息: *Our competitors must not be allowed to get wind of our plans.* 千万别让我们的竞争对手听到有关我们计划的事. **get/have the 'wind up (about sth)** (*infml* 口) become/be frightened 受惊; 害怕. **in the 'wind** about to happen 即将发生: *They sensed that there was something in the wind.* 他们察觉出要有事了. **it's an ill wind** ⇨ ILL[2]. **like the 'wind** very fast 极快; 像一阵风似的: *She goes like the wind on her new bicycle.* 她飞快地骑着新自行车. **put the wind up sb** (*infml* 口) cause sb to be frightened; alarm sb 使某人害怕; 惊吓某人. **run/sail before the 'wind** (*nautical* 海) sail with the wind behind the ship 顺风航行. **sail close/near to the wind** ⇨ SAIL[2]. **see which way the wind is blowing** ⇨ WAY[1]. **sound in wind and limb** ⇨ SOUND[1]. **a straw in the wind** ⇨ STRAW. **take the 'wind out of sb's sails** (*infml* 口) cause sb to lose his confidence or pride 使某人气馁或泄气: *Being beaten by a newcomer has really taken the wind out of his sails.* 一个新来的人就比他强, 他觉得很窝囊. **throw, etc caution to the winds** ⇨ CAUTION. **to the four winds** (*rhet* 修辞) (blown, scattered, etc) in all directions (刮得、撒得…)四面八方. **a wind of 'change** influence that causes change; tendency to change 产生变化的影响或趋势: *There is a wind of change in the attitude of voters.* 选民的态度有改变的趋向.

▷ **wind·less** *adj* without wind 无风的: *a windless day* 无风的一天.

wind·ward /-wəd; -wəd/ *adj, adv* on or to the side from which the wind is blowing 上风(的); 向风(的); 顶风(的): *the windward side of the boat* 那条船迎风的一侧. Cf 参看 LEE, LEEWARD. — *n* [U] side or direction from which the wind is blowing 上风面; 上风方向: *sail to windward* 逆风航行 ○ *get to windward of sth*, ie place oneself on the windward side of sth, eg in order to avoid a bad smell! 到某物的上风处(如避免难闻的气味).

windy *adj* (**-ier, -iest**) **1** (**a**) with much wind 多风的: *a windy day* 刮风的一天. (**b**) exposed to (esp strong) winds 受风吹的; (尤指)遭大风刮的: *a windy hillside* 迎风的山坡. **2** (*dated Brit infml* 旧, 口) nervous or frightened 心情紧张的; 害怕的: *a bit windy about staying alone in the house* 独自一人呆在这所房子里有些害怕. **wind·ily** /-ɪlɪ; -əlɪ/ *adv.* **windi·ness** *n* [U].

□ **'windbag** *n* (*infml derog* 口, 贬) person who talks a lot but says nothing important 言语空洞无物的人.

'wind-break *n* row of trees or a hedge, fence, etc that gives protection from the wind 有防风作用的树木、篱笆等.

'wind-cheater (*US* **'wind-breaker**) *n* close-fitting jacket designed to protect the wearer from the wind 防风的紧身甲克.

'windfall *n* **1** fruit, esp an apple, that has been blown off a tree by the wind 风吹落的果实(尤指苹果). **2** (*fig* 比喻) unexpected piece of good fortune, esp a legacy 意外的好运; (尤指)意外获得的遗产.

'wind-gauge *n* = ANEMOMETER.

'wind instrument musical instrument (eg a flute or trumpet) in which sound is produced by a current of air, esp by the player's breath 管乐器; 吹奏乐器.

windmill 风车

'windmill *n* **1** mill worked by the action of wind on long projecting arms (*sails*) that turn on a central shaft 风车. **2** (idm 习语) **tilt at windmills** ⇨ TILT.

'windpipe *n* passage from the throat to the bronchial tubes, through which air reaches the lungs 气管. ⇨illus at RESPIRE 见 RESPIRE 插图.

'windscreen (*Brit*) (*US* **'windshield**) *n* glass window in the front of a motor vehicle (机动车前面的)挡风玻璃窗. ⇨illus at App 1 见附录1插图, page xii. **'windscreen wiper** (*Brit*) (*US* **'windshield wiper**) electrically operated blade with a rubber edge that wipes a windscreen clear of rain, snow, etc (机动车挡风玻璃上的)刮水器, 风挡雨雪刷. ⇨illus at App 1 见附录1插图, page xii.

'windshield *n* (**a**) (*US*) = WINDSCREEN. (**b**) glass or plastic screen that provides protection from the wind, eg at the front of a motorcycle 挡风玻璃, (塑料的)挡风罩(如摩托车前面的).

'wind-sock (also **'wind-sleeve**) *n* canvas tube, open at both ends, that is flown at the top of a pole (eg on an airfield) to show the direction of the wind 风向袋(如机场上的).

'windsurfer *n* (*propr* 专利名) **1** board, similar to a surfboard, with a sail 帆板. **2** person who surfs on a windsurfer 帆板运动员. **'windsurf** *v* [I] (usu 通常作 **go 'windsurfing**) surf on a windsurfer 做帆板运动. **windsurfing** *n* [U] sport of surfing on a windsurfer 帆板运动.

'wind-swept *adj* (**a**) (of a place) exposed to strong winds (指地方)受强风吹的: *a wind-swept hillside* 受强风吹袭的山坡. (**b**) (of a person's appearance) untidy after being blown about by the wind (指人的外表)被风刮得不整洁的: *wind-swept hair* 被吹乱的头发.

wind[2] /wɪnd; wɪnd/ *v* [Tn] **1** cause (sb) to be out of breath 使(某人)气急: *We were winded by the steep climb.*

我们爬那个陡坡累得上气不接下气. ○ *The punch in the stomach completely winded me.* 我肚子上挨了一拳一时完全喘不过气来. **2** help (a baby) to expel wind[1](4) from its stomach by patting or stroking its back 帮助(婴儿)打出嗝来(拍抚其后背). **3** detect the presence of (sb/sth) by smelling 嗅出(某人[某物])的存在: *The hounds had winded the fox.* 猎狗闻出了有狐狸的气味.

windsurfing 帆板运动

wind[3] /waɪnd; waɪnd/ *v* (*pt, pp* **wound** /waʊnd; waʊnd/) **1** [I, Ipr, Ip, Tn·pr, Tn·p] (cause sth to) follow a curving, twisting or spiral course (使某物)沿弧形的、弯曲的或旋转的路线前进: *a winding road* 盘旋的路 ○ *The river winds down to the sea.* 这条河蜿蜒流向大海. ○ *The staircase winds upwards round a central pillar.* 这座楼梯绕着中间的柱子向上呈螺旋状. ○ *She wound her way through the crowds.* 她绕来绕去穿过了人群. **2** [Tn, Tn·pr, Tn·p] twist or coil (string, wool, yarn, etc) round and round on itself so that it forms a ball, or onto a reel, etc 将(绳、毛线、纱等)缠绕成球或缠绕在轴上: *wind wool (up) into a ball* 把毛线缠成团 ○ *wind sewing thread onto a reel* 把缝纫用的线缠绕在线轴上. **3** [Tn·pr] (**a**) **~ sth round sb/sth; ~ sb/sth in sth** fold sth round sb/sth closely; wrap sb/sth in sth 将某物紧紧缠绕住某人[某物]; 将某人[某物]包在某物中: *wind a bandage round one's finger* 用绷带包住手指 ○ *wind a shawl round the baby/the baby in a shawl* 用围巾裹住幼儿. (**b**) **~ itself round sb/sth** become twisted or entangled round sb/sth 绕住或缠住某人[某物]: *The film flew off the spool and wound itself round the projector.* 电影胶片从卷轴滑出缠绕在放映机上了. **4** [Tn] turn (a handle, windlass, etc) 转动(把手、绞车等): *You operate the mechanism by winding this handle.* 操纵这台机器要转动这个把手. **5** [Tn, Tn·p] **~ sth (up)** cause a mechanism (esp a clock or watch) to operate, eg by turning a key to tighten the spring 上(尤指钟表)发条: *Have you wound your watch?* 你的表上发条了吗? **6** (phr v) **wind sth back, down, forward, in, off, on, up, etc** cause sth to move in the specified direction by turning a handle, spool, etc (转动把手或卷轴等)使某物沿某方向移动: *wind a tape back/forward/on* 把带子向后[向前/继续]卷绕 ○ *wind a car window down/up* 把汽车窗摇下去[上来] ○ *wind a fishing line in* 把钓鱼线摇起收回. **wind down** (**a**) (of a clock or watch) go slow and then stop (指钟表)慢下来后停住. (**b**) (of a person) relax, esp after a period of stress or excitement (指人)松弛下来, 放松(尤指经过一段紧张或兴奋阶段): *This year has been frantically busy for us — I need a holiday just to wind down.* 今年我们忙得要命——我需要有一段假期放松一下. **wind up** (*infml* 口) (of a person) arrive finally in a place; end up (指人)终于到达某处, 安顿: *We eventually wound up (staying) in a super little hotel by the sea.* 我们最终在一个很棒的海滨旅馆落脚(住下来). ○ *I always said he would wind up in jail.* 我常说他到头来非进监狱不可. **wind (sth) up** finish (a speech, etc) 结束(讲话等): *Before I wind up, there are two more things to be said.* 在我结束讲话之前, 还有两件事要说. ○ *If we all agree, let's wind up the discussion.* 要是大家都同意的话, 咱们这次讨论就到此结束. **wind sb up** cause sb to reach a high level of excitement or agitation 使某人高度兴奋或激动: *He gets so wound up when he's arguing.* 他一辩论起来就十分激动. ○ (*infml* 口) *Are you deliberately winding me up* (ie annoying me)? 你是想故意气我吧? **wind sth up** settle the affairs of and finally close (a business, company, etc) 清理业务并最后关闭(企业、公司等): *wind up one's affairs* 清理并结束自己的事务.

▷ **wind** *n* (**a**) bend or turn in a course, path, etc (道路等的)弯曲处, 转弯处. (**b**) single turn made in winding (WIND[3] 5) (钟表的)上一圈发条: *Give the clock another couple of winds.* 给这座钟再上两圈发条.

winder *n* lever or other instrument for winding (esp a clock, watch, etc) (上发条的)旋杆或旋柄(尤指钟表上的).

□ '**winding-sheet** *n* = SHROUD.

'**wind-up** *n* (*infml* 口) deliberate attempt to annoy or provoke sb 故意激怒或招惹某人: [attrib 作定语] *a wind-up artist/merchant*, ie sb who does this 存心气人的艺术家[商人].

wind·lass /'wɪndləs; 'wɪndləs/ *n* device for pulling or lifting things (eg a bucket of water from a well) by means of a rope or chain that winds round a horizontal axle; winch 绞车; 辘轳; 卷扬机.

win·dow /'wɪndəʊ; 'wɪndo/ *n* **1** (**a**) opening in the wall or roof of a building, car, etc to let in light (and often air), usu filled with glass in a frame 窗户: *Please open the window.* 请把窗户打开. ○ *I saw them through the window.* 我透过窗户看见他们了. ○ *He prefers to travel in a seat near the window.* 他坐车、船、飞机都喜欢坐靠窗户的座位. ⇨illus at App 1 见附录1插图, pages vi, xii. (**b**) opening that resembles this 窗状开口: *There is a little window in the cassette case so that you can see the tape.* 盒式音像带上有个小窗,能看见里面的磁带. ○ *the window of an envelope*, ie the transparent part in which an address can be read 信封上的透明窗(有的信封上的透明部分, 可露出信纸上的收信人地址). (**c**) piece of glass in the frame of a window 窗玻璃: *The ball smashed a window.* 那个球把一块窗玻璃打碎了. (**d**) space behind the window of a shop where goods are displayed for sale (商店的)橱窗: *I saw the vase in the window of an antique shop.* 我在一家古玩店的橱窗里看见了那个花瓶. ○ [attrib 作定语] *a window display* 橱窗陈列. **2** (*computing* 计) screen of a visual display unit regarded as a means of displaying part of a drawing, etc stored in a computer; part of a drawing, etc chosen for display 视窗(视频显示器的荧屏, 用以显示储存在计算机中的部分图像等); 显示出的部分图像等. **3** (idm 习语) **fly/go out of the 'window** (*infml* 口) be no longer considered; disappear 不再被考虑; 消失: *With the failure of the peace talks all hopes of a swift end to the war have flown out of the window.* 和谈失败后, 迅速结束战争的希望都已化为乌有. **a window on the 'world** means of observing and learning about people, esp those of other countries 世界之窗(观察和了解人民, 尤指他国人民的手段): *International news broadcasts provide a window on the world.* 国际新闻广播节目给大家提供了一个了解他国人民的世界之窗.

□ '**window-box** *n* long narrow box fixed outside a window, in which plants are grown 窗口花坛(固定于窗外的长条形的栽花容器).

'**window-dressing** *n* [U] (**a**) art or skill of arranging goods attractively in shop windows 橱窗装饰术. (**b**) (*usu derog* 通常作贬义) presentation of facts, etc in a way that creates a good (and often false) impression 给人良好印象的展示手法(常指虚伪的): *The company's support of scientific research is just window-dressing.* 这个公司支持科学研究只不过是摆样子给人看的.

'**window-pane** *n* pane of glass for or in a (section of a) window 窗玻璃. ⇨illus at App 1 见附录1插图, page vi.

'**window shade** (*US*) = BLIND[3].

'**window-shopping** *n* [U] looking at goods displayed in shop windows (usu without intending to buy anything) 浏览橱窗(通常指无意购物者): *go window-shopping* 去逛大街浏览橱窗.

'**window-sill** (also '**window-ledge**) *n* ledge at the base of a window, either inside or outside 窗台. ⇨illus at App 1 见附录1插图, page vi.

windy ⇨ WIND[1].

wine /waɪn; waɪn/ *n* **1** [U, C] alcoholic drink made from the fermented juice of grapes 葡萄酒: *red/rosé/white wine* 红葡萄酒[玫瑰红葡萄酒/白葡萄酒] ○ *dry/sweet wine* 干葡萄酒[甜葡萄酒] ○ *a barrel/bottle/carafe/glass of wine* 一桶[瓶/饮料瓶/杯]葡萄酒 ○ *a wine from a famous vineyard* 由著名葡萄园酿造的葡萄酒. **2** [U, C] alcoholic drink made from plants or fruits other than grapes (除葡萄以外的花草或水果酿造的)果酒: *apple, cowslip, parsnip wine* 苹果酒、黄花九轮草酒、欧洲防风酒. **3** [U] dark purplish red colour similar to that of red wine 紫红色: [attrib 作定语] *a wine velvet evening dress* 紫红色的立绒晚礼服. **4** (idm 习语) **ˌwine, ˌwomen and ˈsong** drinking, dancing, etc and enjoying oneself 饮酒、跳舞等作乐.

▷ **wine** *v* (idm 习语) **ˌwine and ˈdine (sb)** entertain (sb) or be entertained with food and drink, esp lavishly 用酒宴招待(某人)或受到酒宴招待(尤指款待): *Our hosts wined and dined us very well.* 主人设酒宴盛情款待我们. ○ *Too much wining and dining is making him fat.* 他酒宴过多而身体发胖.

□ **ˈwine bar** place where a variety of wines is sold and drunk, sometimes with food (供应各种果酒的)酒吧, 酒馆(有时供应佐酒食物).

ˈwine-cellar *n* **(a)** underground room where wine is stored (储存果酒的)酒窖. **(b)** (also **cellar**) wine stored in this 藏于地窖中的果酒: *He has an excellent wine-cellar.* 他有窖藏佳酿.

ˈwineglass *n* glass for drinking wine from (饮果酒用的)酒杯. ⇨illus at GLASS 见 GLASS 插图.

ˈwinepress *n* press[1](2) in which grapes are crushed for making wine 葡萄压榨器(制酒用的).

wing /wɪŋ; wɪŋ/ *n* **1** [C] **(a)** either of the pair of feathered limbs that a bird uses to fly (鸟的)翅膀, 翼. ⇨illus at App 1 见附录1插图, page iv. **(b)** either of the similar projecting parts that an insect or a bat uses to fly (昆虫或蝙蝠的)翅膀, 翼. ⇨illus at BUTTERFLY 见 BUTTERFLY 插图. **(c)** thing that is similar to this, eg the thin projection on the seeds of maple or sycamore trees 翼状物(如槭树或西克莫树的翅果). **2** [C] part that projects from the side of an aircraft and supports it in the air (飞行器的)翅膀, 机翼. ⇨illus at AIRCRAFT 见 AIRCRAFT 插图. **3** [C] part of a building that projects from the main part 建筑物突出的侧面部分; 侧厅; 耳房: *the east/west wing of a house* 一所房子的东[西]耳房 ○ *build a new wing of a hospital* 建一座与一医院一侧相连的楼房. **4** [C] (*Brit*) (*US* **fender**) projecting part of the bodywork of a motor vehicle above the wheel 翼子板: *The nearside wing was damaged in the collision.* 汽车碰撞时左侧的翼子板撞坏了. ○ [attrib 作定语] *a wing mirror* 装在翼子板上的后视镜. ⇨illus at App 1 见附录1插图, page xii. **5** [C] either of the flanks of an army lined up for battle (军队作战阵势的)翼, 侧翼. **6** [C usu *sing* 通常作单数] part of an organization, esp a political party that holds certain views or has a particular function (组织中的)派, 翼(尤指党派中持某观点或起某作用的): *the radical wing of the Labour Party* 工党中的激进派. Cf 参看 LEFT-WING (LEFT[2]), RIGHT-WING (RIGHT[5]). **7** [C] **(a)** side part of the playing area in football, hockey, etc (足球、曲棍球等场地的)边侧: *playing on the wing* 踢边锋 ○ *kick the ball out to the wing* 把球踢到场地边侧. **(b)** (also **winger**) (in football, hockey, etc) either of the forward players whose place is at the extreme end of the forward line (足球、曲棍球等的)边锋队员: *the team's new left wing* 这个球队新的左边锋. **8** (*Brit*) **(a)** [C] (in the Royal Air Force) unit of two or more squadrons (英国皇家空军的)联队. **(b)** **wings** [pl] (in the Royal Air Force) pilot's badge (英国皇家空军的)飞行徽章: *get one's wings* 获得飞行徽章. **9 the wings** [pl] (in a theatre) area to the right and left of the stage that is hidden from the audience by curtains, scenery, etc 舞台上观众看不到的侧面: *She stood watching the performance from the wings.* 她站在舞台上的侧面观看演出. ⇨illus at App 1 见附录1插图, page ix. **10** (idm 习语) **clip sb's wings** ⇨ CLIP[2]. **(wait, etc) in the ˈwings** ready to do sth or to take over from sb 准备做某事或接替某人: *He retires as chairman next year; his successor is already waiting in the wings.* 他明年从主席职位上退下, 继任人已做好接任准备. **on the ˈwing** (while it is) flying 在飞行中: *photograph a bird on the wing* 拍摄飞着的鸟. **spread one's wings** ⇨ SPREAD. **take ˈwing** fly away 飞走. **under sb's/one's ˈwing** under sb's/one's protection 在某人的[自己的]保护下: *She immediately took the new arrivals under her wing*, ie looked after them. 她立刻去照看那些新来的.

▷ **wing** *v* **1** [Ipr, Ip, Tn·pr, Tn·p] travel on wings; fly 飞行: *planes winging (their way) across the sky* 飞过天空的飞机. **2** [Tn] **(a)** wound (a bird) in the wing 弄伤(鸟)的翅膀. **(b)** wound (sb) slightly, esp in an arm 微伤(某人)(尤指手臂). **winged** *adj* (often forming compound *adjs* 常用以构成复合形容词) having wings, esp of the specified number or type 有翅膀的(尤指有某数目或某类型的): *winged insects* 有翅膀的昆虫 ○ *delta-winged aircraft* 三角翼飞机.

winger *n* **1** (in football, hockey, etc) player who plays on the wing(7a) (足球、曲棍球等的)边锋队员. **2 -winger** (forming compound *ns* 用以构成复合名词) **(a)** person who plays on the wing 边锋队员: *a ˌleft-/ˌright-ˈwinger* 左[右]边锋. **(b)** person on the left or right wing in politics or a political party (政治上的或政党内的)左翼或右翼分子: *She was active as a left-winger in the party.* 她是党内积极的左翼分子.

wingless *adj* (esp of insects) without wings (尤指昆虫)无翼的.

□ **ˈwing-chair** *n* armchair with a high back that has projecting pieces at each side 有翼单座沙发(高靠背两侧连接有向前伸出的宽边).

ˈwing commander officer in the Royal Air Force between the ranks of squadron leader and group captain (英国皇家空军的)空军中校. ⇨App 9 见附录9.

ˈwing-nut *n* nut with projections so that it can be turned by a thumb and a finger on a screw or bolt 蝶形螺帽; 元宝螺母. ⇨illus at BOLT 见 BOLT 插图.

ˈwing-span *n* distance between the end of one wing and the end of the other when the wings are fully stretched out 翼展: *a bird with a two-foot wing-span* 翼展为两英尺的鸟.

wing·ding /ˈwɪŋdɪŋ; ˋwɪŋˌdɪŋ/ *n* (*US infml* 口) wild festive party 狂欢的聚会.

wink /wɪŋk; wɪŋk/ *v* **1** [I, Ipr] **~ (at sb)** close one eye very briefly, esp as a private signal to sb 眨一只眼(尤指向某人使眼色): *He winked at me to show that he was playing a joke on the others.* 他向我眨了眨一只眼, 意思是他正在开别人的玩笑. **2** [I] (of a light, star, etc) shine with a light that flickers or flashes quickly on and off (指光、星等)闪烁: *We could see the lighthouse winking in the distance.* 我们看见远处灯塔一闪一闪地发光. ○ *The car in front is winking — it's going to turn right.* 前面汽车指示灯闪着光——示意要向右转. **3** (idm 习语) **easy as winking** ⇨ EASY. **4** (phr v) **wink at sth** (*dated* 旧) pretend that one does not notice (bad behaviour, etc) 假装没注意到(坏的举动等): *His wife has winked at his infidelity for years.* 他多年来对妻子不忠, 妻子也只装作不知情.

▷ **wink** *n* **1** act of winking, esp as a signal 眨一只眼(尤指使眼色): *give sb a meaningful wink* 向某人眨一只眼示意. **2** (idm 习语) **(have/take) forty ˈwinks** short sleep, esp during the daytime 盹(尤指于白天). **a nod is as good as a wink** ⇨ NOD *n*. **not get/have a ˈwink of sleep; not sleep a ˈwink** not sleep at all 完全没睡觉: *The neighbours were having a party and we didn't get a wink of sleep all night.* 邻居举行晚会, 吵得我们一夜都没合眼. **tip sb the wink** ⇨ TIP[3].

winker *n* (*Brit*) small light on a motor vehicle that flashes in order to indicate that it is going to change direction; indicator (机动车的频闪式的)指示灯.

winkle /ˈwɪŋkl; ˋwɪŋkl/ *n* = PERIWINKLE 2.

▷ **winkle** *v* (phr v) **winkle sb/sth out (of sth)** (*infml* 口) get sb/sth out (of a place) slowly and with difficulty 缓慢而费力地把某人[某物](从某处)弄出: *The children were finally all winkled out of their hiding places.* 最后总算把孩子从躲藏的地方都找了出来. **winkle sth out (of sb)** (*infml* 口) obtain information, etc from sb with difficulty 费力地从某人处得到信息: *She's very clever at winkling secrets out of people.* 她很会从别人那里探听到秘密.

□ **ˈwinkle-picker** *n* (usu *pl* 通常作复数) (*dated sl* 旧, 俚) shoe with a long pointed toe 尖头皮鞋: *a pair of winkle-pickers* 一双尖头皮鞋.

win·ner, win·ning ⇨ WIN.

win·now /ˈwɪnəʊ; ˋwɪno/ *v* **(a)** [Tn] blow a current of air through (grain) in order to remove (the chaff) 风选(谷物)(以除去皮壳). **(b)** [Tn·pr, Tn·p] **~ sth away/out; ~ sth from sth** remove (the chaff) from grain in this

W

way (用风选法)除去(皮壳): *winnow the husks from the corn* 用风选法除去谷物的壳 ○ (*fig* 比喻) *winnow the truth from the mass of conflicting evidence* 从大量相互矛盾的证据中去伪存真.

wino /ˈwaɪnəʊ; ˈwaɪno/ *n* (*pl* **~s**) (*infml* 口) person who is addicted to alcohol, esp to cheap wine; an alcoholic 酒鬼(尤指饮廉价果酒的).

win·some /ˈwɪnsəm; ˈwɪnsəm/ *adj* (*fml* 文) attractive and pleasant 吸引人的; 讨人喜欢的: *a winsome smile* 动人的微笑 ○ *She was a winsome creature.* 她十分可爱. ▷ **win·somely** *adv*. **win·some·ness** *n* [U].

win·ter /ˈwɪntə(r); ˈwɪntɚ/ *n* [U, C] **1** the last and coldest season of the year, coming between autumn and spring, ie from December to February in the Northern hemisphere 冬, 冬天, 冬季(在北半球为十二月至二月): *Many trees lose their leaves in winter.* 有许多树在冬季落叶. ○ *The plants have survived the winter.* 这些植物经过冬天没有冻死. ○ *They worked on the building all through the winter.* 他们一冬都在建这座楼. ○ *They spend the winter(s) in a warmer climate.* 他们在气候较暖的地方过冬. ○ *She lived alone in the house for a whole winter.* 她独自一人在这所房子里过了一冬. ○ *He is going to retire next winter.* 他打算到冬天就退休了. ○ *on a dark winter's night* 在冬天一个漆黑的夜晚 ○ [attrib 作定语] *winter quarters*, ie (esp formerly) place where an army spends the winter during a campaign (尤指旧时)冬季兵营. **2** (idm 习语) **in the dead of winter** ⇨ DEAD *n*.

▷ **win·ter** *v* [I] (*fml* 文) spend the winter 过冬: *It became fashionable for the rich to winter in the sun.* 在阳光充足的地方过冬成了富人的时尚. ○ *birds wintering in the south* 在南方过冬的鸟.

win·ter·ize, -ise /ˈwɪntəraɪz; ˈwɪntəˌraɪz/ *v* [Tn] (*esp US*) prepare (a house, car, etc) for winter weather 为过冬收拾(房子、汽车等).

wintry /ˈwɪntrɪ; ˈwɪntrɪ/ *adj* (**-ier, -iest**) of or like winter; cold, snowy, etc (似)冬天的; 寒冷的; 多雪的: *a wintry landscape* 冬天的景色 ○ *wintry light, weather* 冬季的阳光、天气 ○ (*fig* 比喻) *a wintry smile*, ie lacking warmth, unfriendly 冷若冰霜的微笑. **wint·ri·ness** *n* [U].

□ ˌ**winter** ˈ**sports** sports that take place on snow or ice, eg skiing and skating 冬季运动.

ˈ**winter-time** *n* [U] period or season of winter 冬季: *The days are shorter in (the) winter-time.* 冬季白天较短.

wipe /waɪp; waɪp/ *v* **1 (a)** [Tn, Tn·pr, Tn·p, Cn·a] **~ sth (on sth); ~ sth (down/over)** clean or dry sth by rubbing its surface with a cloth, piece of paper, etc 擦、拭或揩某物: *wipe the dishes*, ie dry them after they have been washed 把碟子擦干 ○ *wipe the table* 擦桌子 ○ *Please wipe your feet*, ie remove the dirt from your shoes by wiping them on the doormat. 请把鞋在蹭鞋垫上擦一擦. ○ *wipe one's eyes*, ie to remove the tears 擦干眼泪 ○ *wipe one's nose*, ie with a handkerchief 擦鼻子 ○ *wipe* (ie remove what has been recorded on) *a magnetic tape* 抹掉磁带上的内容 ○ *wipe one's hands on a towel* 用毛巾擦手 ○ *wipe down the kitchen cupboards*, ie clean them with a cloth, etc from top to bottom 把碗柜从上到下擦干净 ○ *wipe sth clean/dry* 把某物擦干净[干]. **(b)** [Tn·pr] rub (a cloth, etc) over a surface 用(布等)擦: *wipe a damp sponge across one's face* 用湿海绵擦脸. **(c)** [Tn·pr] put (a substance) onto a surface by rubbing 搽(某物质): *Wipe the lotion onto your face.* 你在脸上搽些护肤液. **2** [Tn·pr, Tn·p] **~ sth from/off sth; ~ sth away/off/up** clear or remove sth by wiping 擦净或擦掉某物: *wipe (away) the tears from one's eyes* 擦(掉)眼泪 ○ *wipe the writing from the blackboard* 把黑板上的字擦掉 ○ *wipe (up) the spilt milk off the floor* 把洒在地板上的牛奶擦干净 ○ *wipe a recording off (a tape)* 抹掉磁带上录制的内容 ○ (*fig infml* 比喻, 口) *Wipe that smile/grin/expression off your face!* ie Stop smiling, etc. 别笑[咧着嘴笑/做出那种表情]! **3** (idm 习语) **wipe the** ˈ**floor with sb** (*infml* 口) defeat sb decisively in an argument, a competition, etc (在辩论、竞赛等中)把某人打得一败涂地. **wipe sth off the** ˌ**face of the** ˈ**earth/off the** ˈ**map** utterly destroy sth 彻底消除某事物. **wipe the** ˈ**slate clean** forget past faults or offences; make a fresh start 勾销过去的错误或过失; 重新开始. **4** (phr v) **wipe sth out (a)** clean the inside of (a bowl, etc) by rubbing it with a cloth 擦拭(盆、碗等)的内部: *This vase wasn't wiped out properly before it was put away.* 这个花瓶没擦干净就收起来了. **(b)** remove or cancel sth 除去或取消某事物: *wipe out one's debts*, ie by repaying them 还清债务 ○ *This year's losses have wiped out* (ie reduced to nothing) *last year's profits.* 今年亏损把去年的赢利都赔光了. **(c)** destroy sth completely 彻底消灭或摧毁某事物: *Whole villages were wiped out in the bombing raids.* 整座整座的村庄都在轰炸中摧毁了. ○ *The government is trying to wipe out drug trafficking.* 政府竭力清除毒品买卖活动.

▷ **wipe** *n* act of wiping 擦; 拭; 揩; 抹; 搽: *Please give the table mats a quick wipe.* 请把桌上的盘碗垫擦一下.

wiper *n* **(a)** thing that wipes or is used for wiping 擦拭用的东西. **(b)** = WINDSCREEN WIPER (WIND[1]).

wire /ˈwaɪə(r); waɪr/ *n* **1 (a)** [C, U] (piece or length of) metal that has been formed into a thin flexible thread-like rod 金属丝; 金属线: *a (coil of) copper wire* (一卷)铜丝 ○ *barbed* ˈ*wire* 刺钢丝. **(b)** [C, U] (piece or length of) wire used to carry electric current or signals 电线; 导线: ˈ*fuse wire* 保险丝 ○ ˈ*telephone wires* 电话线. **(c)** [U, sing] barrier, framework, fence, etc made from wire 金属丝制成的障碍物、构架、栅栏等: *The hamster had got through the wire at the front of its cage.* 仓鼠从其笼子前部的栅栏处钻出去了. **2** [C] (*infml* 口 *esp US*) telegram 电报: *send sb a wire* 给某人发电报. **3** (idm 习语) **get one's** ˈ**wires crossed** (*infml* 口) be mistaken or confused about what sb is saying or has said 误解或弄不清某人说的话: *We seem to have got our wires crossed. I thought you were coming yesterday.* 我们大概误会了. 我还以为你昨天来呢. **a live wire** ⇨ LIVE[1]. **pull (the) strings/wires** ⇨ PULL[2].

▷ **wire** *v* **1 (a)** [Tn·pr, Tn·p] **~ A (on) to B; ~ A and B together** fasten or join one thing to another with wire 用金属丝将一物与另一物连结在一起: *A handle had been wired (on) to the box.* 已经用金属丝把一个把手绑在箱子上了. ○ *The two pieces of wood were wired together.* 这两块木头已用金属丝捆在一起了. **(b)** [Tn esp passive 尤用于被动语态] put wire(s) in or on (sth), eg to strengthen it 在(某物)的里面或上面加上金属丝(如用以加固): *The fabric was displayed on a wired stand.* 那种织物陈列在金属制的架子上. **2** [Tn, Tn·pr, Tn·p] **~ sth (up); ~ sth (for sth)** connect sth to a supply of electricity by means of wires 用导线将某物与电源接通: *The house is not wired for electricity yet.* 这所房子还没有铺设好电线. ○ *The studio is being wired for sound.* 这个播音室正在安装音响设备用的电线. ○ *As soon as the equipment is wired up, you can use it.* 这个设备一接通电源你就能用了. **3 (a)** [Tn, Tf, Dn·f, Dpr·f, Dn·t, Dpr·t] (*infml* 口 *esp US*) send (sb) a message by telegram 给(某人)发电报: *He wired (to) his brother to send some money.* 他给他哥哥打了个电报要求寄些钱来. ○ *She wired (us) that she would be delayed.* 她给我们打来电报说她得晚到. **(b)** [Dn·n, Dn·pr] **~ sth to sb** (*infml* 口 *esp US*) send sth to sb by means of a telegram 用电报将某物传送给某人: *wire money to sb*, ie instruct a bank by telegram to give money to sb 给某人电汇. **wir·ing** /ˈwaɪərɪŋ; ˈwaɪrɪŋ/ *n* [U] system of wires, esp for supplying electricity to a building 电线线路、设备或系统(尤指为建筑物供电的): *The wiring is faulty and needs to be replaced.* 线路上有短路需要换线.

wiry /ˈwaɪərɪ; ˈwaɪrɪ/ *adj* (**-ier, -iest**) **(a)** (of a person) lean but strong (指人)瘦而结实的. **(b)** tough and flexible, like wire 硬而韧的; 像金属丝的: *wiry* (ie coarse and curly) *hair* 粗而拳曲的头发. **wiri·ness** *n* [U].

□ ˈ**wire-cutter** *n* (esp *pl* 尤作复数) tool for cutting wire 切割金属丝的工具: *a pair of wire-cutters* 一把克丝钳子.

ˌ**wire-**ˈ**haired** *adj* (esp of a dog) having stiff or wiry hair (尤指狗)毛硬而韧的: *a* ˌ*wire-haired* ˈ*terrier* 毛硬而韧的小狗.

ˌ**wire** ˈ**netting** [U] netting made by weaving wires into a mesh, used for fences, etc 金属丝网(用作篱笆等的).

ˈ**wire-tapping** *n* [U] practice of listening to other people's telephone conversations by making a secret connection to the telephone line (用秘密接线方法)窃听电话.

ˌ**wire** ˈ**wool** mass of fine wires, used for cleaning and polishing, often in the form of a small pad 金属丝团(用作洗刷工具). Cf 参看 STEEL WOOL (STEEL).

ˈ**wire-worm** *n* any of several types of worm-like larva that destroy plants by eating them 金针虫(叩甲的幼虫).

W

wire·less /ˈwaɪələs; ˋwaɪrlɪs/ *n* (*dated* 旧) **1** [U] radio communications 无线电: *broadcast by wireless* 无线电广播. **2** [C] (**a**) radio receiver or transmitter 无线电接收机或发射机. (**b**) [C] = RADIO 2b.

wis·dom /ˈwɪzdəm; ˋwɪzdəm/ *n* [U] **1** (**a**) experience and knowledge (shown in making decisions and judgements); quality of being wise (在做决定或判断时表现出的)经验和知识; 智慧: *She had acquired much wisdom during her long life.* 她经年累月造就了很高的智慧. (**b**) good judgement; advisability; common sense 正确的判断; 明智; 常识: *I question the wisdom of giving the child so much money.* 我怀疑给这个孩子这么多钱是好事还是坏事. ○ *Events were to prove the wisdom of their decision.* 这些事情都可证明他们的决定是正确的. **2** (*fml* 文) wise thoughts, sayings, etc 有见识的想法、说法等: *the wisdom of the ancients* 古人的至理名言 ○ *the conventional/received wisdom*, ie the generally accepted view 公认的看法. **3** (idm 习语) **wit and wisdom** ⇨ WIT.
□ ˈ**wisdom tooth** any of the four molars at the back of the mouth that appear when one is about 20 years old 智牙.

wise /waɪz; waɪz/ *adj* (**-r, -st**) **1** (**a**) having or showing good judgement 有判断力的; 聪明的: *a wise choice, decision, precaution, friend* 高明的选择、决定、预防方法、朋友 ○ *It was not very wise of you to sell the property.* 你把物业卖了可不是办法. ○ *I'm sure you're wise to wait a few days.* 我知道你很聪明一定等候几天. ○ *a wise nod of the head*, ie suggesting that one is wise 聪明地点点头. (**b**) having knowledge 有知识的: *a wise old man* 博学多识的老先生. **2** (idm 习语) **be ˌwise after the eˈvent** be able to explain sth after it has happened but without having foreseen it 事后聪明: *We don't pay our financial analysts to be wise after the event!* 我们花钱请财务分析家不是让他们当事后诸葛亮! **be/get wise to sth/sb** (*infml* 口 *esp US*) be/become aware of sth or of sb's qualities or behaviour 了解某事物或某人的品行: *He thought he could fool me but I got wise to him.* 他以为他能骗得了我, 其实我知道他是怎么回事. **no/none the/not any the ˈwiser** knowing no more than before 还是不知道; 并不比以前明白: *Even after listening to his explanation I'm none the wiser.* 我即便听了他的解释, 仍然不明白. **penny wise pound foolish** ⇨ PENNY. **put sb ˈwise (to sth)** (*infml* 口 *esp US*) inform sb about sth 把某事告诉某人. **sadder but wiser** ⇨ SAD. **(as) ˌwise as an ˈowl** very wise 非常聪明. **a word to the wise** ⇨ WORD.
▷ **wise** *v* (phr v) **wise (sb) up (to sth)** (*infml* 口 *esp US*) (cause sb to) become aware or informed of sth (使某人)明白或知道某事物: *It's about time he wised up to the fact that people think his behaviour is ridiculous.* 他早就该明白大家都认为他很荒唐.
wisely *adv.*
□ ˈ**wiseacre** *n* (*dated* 旧) person who pretends to be wise; know-all 自作聪明的人; 万事通.
ˈ**wisecrack** *n* (*infml* 口) smart or clever (often unkind) saying or remark 俏皮话; (常指)风凉话. — *v* [I] make wisecracks 说俏皮话; 说风凉话.
ˈ**wise guy** (*infml derog* 口, 贬) person who speaks or behaves as if he knows more than other people 自以为多知多懂的人; 能耐梗.

-wise *suff* 后缀 (with *ns* forming *adjs* and *advs* 与名词结合构成形容词和副词) **1** in the manner or direction of 以某方式、方法或沿某方向: *likewise* ○ *clockwise* ○ *anti-clockwise* ○ *lengthwise*. **2** (*infml* 口) with reference to; as far as sth is concerned 关于; 在某方面: *businesswise* ○ *weatherwise* ○ *profitwise*.

wish /wɪʃ; wɪʃ/ *v* **1** (**a**) [Ipr] **~ for sth/sb** have or express a desire for sth/sb (esp sth/sb that is likely to be achieved or obtained only by good fortune) 想要某事物[某人](尤指靠运气方可得者): *It's no use wishing for things you can't have.* 想要得不到的事物是徒劳的. ○ *His wife is everything a man could wish for.* 他的妻子具有男人想要的一切优秀品质. ○ *What more could one wish for?* ie Everything is perfect. 夫复何求? (一切已尽善尽美.) (**b**) [Tf, Cn·a] (with *that* often omitted and the *that*-clause usu in the past tense 与that从句连用, 但常省去that, 从句通常用过去时态) have as a desire that is unfulfilled or unlikely to be fulfilled 怀着(未实现的或不大可能实现的)愿望: *I wish you hadn't told me all this.* 我倒希望你当初别把这一切都告诉我. ○ *She wished she had* (ie was sorry she had not) *stayed at home.* 她懊悔的是她当时要是在家就好了. ○ *I wish I knew what was going to happen.* 但愿我能知道要发生什么事. ○ *I wish he wouldn't go out every night.* 他要不是每天晚上都出去就好了. ○ *I wish I were rich.* 我恨不得我很富有. ○ *She began to wish the whole business finished.* 她这时巴不得整个事情都结束才好. ○ *He's dead and it's no use wishing him alive again.* 他已经死了, 希望他再活过来的想法也是枉然. (**c**) [Tn, Tt, Cn·t] (*fml* 文) demand or want (sth) 要求或想要(某事物): *I'll do it if that's what you wish.* 要是您要求这样做, 我一定照办. ○ *I wish to leave my property to my children.* 我想把财产留给子女. ○ *She wishes to be alone.* 她希望别打扰她. ○ *I wish it to be clear that the decision is final.* 我希望明确一下儿, 这个决定是不可更改的. ○ *Do you wish me to serve dinner now?* 您想让我现在开饭吗? ⇨Usage at HOPE 用法见HOPE. **2** [Dn·n] (**a**) say that one hopes sb will have sth 祝愿某人有某事物: *They wished us a pleasant journey.* 他们祝我们旅途愉快. ○ *His colleagues wished him happiness on his retirement.* 他的同事祝他退休后幸福安乐. ○ *Wish me luck!* 祝我走运吧! (**b**) say (sth) as a greeting 说(某话语)(表示问候或用以打招呼): *wish sb good morning, goodbye, happy birthday, welcome, etc* 向某人说早上好、再见、生日快乐、欢迎等. **3** [I] formulate (and express) a desire 怀着(并表达)某愿望: *Do you wish when you see a shooting star?* 你看见流星时提出愿望吗? **4** (idm 习语) **(just) as you ˈwish** I am prepared to agree with you or to do what you want 随你的便: *We can meet at my house or yours, just as you wish.* 我们可以在我家见面也可在你家, 随你的便. **wish sb/sth ˈwell/ˈill** hope that sb/sth does/does not have good fortune 希望某人[某事物]走运[倒霉]: *I wish him well in his new job.* 我希望他在新的工作中万事如意. ○ *She said she wished nobody ill.* 她说她希望谁也别遭殃. **5** (phr v) **wish sth away** try to get rid of something by wishing it did not exist 希望某事物并不存在借以竭力摆脱之: *These problems can't be wished away, you know.* 你要知道, 这些问题并不是你希望它不存在它就不存在. **wish sb/sth on sb** (*infml* 口) pass (an unwanted or unpleasant task, visitor, etc) on to sb 把(不喜欢的任务、来访者等)转给某人: *It's not a job I'd wish on anybody.* 这项工作并不是我不喜欢而想把它推给别人. ○ *I don't think we can wish the children on your parents while we're away.* 我认为咱们不在家时不能把孩子都硬塞给你父母看管.
▷ **wish** *n* **1** (**a**) [C] **~ (to do sth); ~ (for sth)** (expression of a) desire or longing 愿望; 希望: *She expressed a wish to be alone.* 她表示希望不要打搅她. ○ *He had no wish to intrude on their privacy.* 他原本就不想触犯他们私人活动的自由. ○ *If you had three wishes what would you choose?* 假设你有三个愿望, 这三个愿望都是什么呢? ○ *Her wish came true*, ie She got what she wished for. 她的愿望实现了. ○ *You have deliberately acted against my wishes.* 你故意和我的想法对着干. (**b**) **wishes** [pl] **~es (for sth)** (expression of) hopes for sb's happiness or welfare 祝愿; 祝福: *with best wishes*, eg at the end of a letter 祝好(如信中结尾语) ○ *We all send our best wishes (for your recovery).* 我们都祝你早日康复. **2** [U] that which is wished for 希望得到的事物: *You will get your wish.* 你将如愿以偿. **3** (idm 习语) **the ˌwish is ˌfather to the ˈthought** (*saying fml* 谚, 文) one thinks that sth is true or likely because one wants it to be so 有什么心愿就有什么想法. **your wish is my comˈmand** (*fml or joc* 文或谑) I am ready to do whatever you ask 我唯阁下之命是从.

wish·ful /-fl; -fəl/ *adj* (*fml* 文) having or expressing a wish 怀有希望的; 表达愿望的: *wishful statements* 表达愿望的言语. ˌ**wishful ˈthinking** belief based on wishes and not on facts 不根据事实而仅基于愿望的想法: *I think her condition is improving but it may just be wishful thinking on my part.* 我认为她的情况正在改善, 但这也许是我一厢情愿的想法.
□ ˈ**wishbone** *n* forked bone between the neck and the breast of a fowl (often pulled apart by two people, with the one who gets the larger part being allowed to make a wish) (鸡的颈和胸之间的)叉骨(常由二人相拉, 获大端者可实现一心愿).

wishy-washy /ˈwɪʃɪ ˌwɒʃɪ; *US* wɔːʃɪ; ˋwɪʃɪ,wɔʃɪ/ *adj* (*usu*

W

derog 通常作贬义) weak or feeble in colour, characteristics, quality, etc (颜色、特征、性质等)浅的, 淡的, 弱的: *a wishy-washy blue* 淡淡的蓝色 ○ *a wishy-washy liberal*, ie one whose ideas are not clearly defined 一个稀里糊涂的自由主义者.

wisp /wɪsp; wɪsp/ *n* **~ (of sth)** **1 (a)** small separate bunch, bundle or twist (of sth) (某物的)小束, 小捆, 小绺, 小缕: *a wisp of hair/hay/straw/grass* 一束头发[干草/稻草/青草]. **(b)** small streak or ribbon 小的条或带: *a wisp of smoke* 一缕烟. **2** small thin person 瘦小的人: *a wisp of a girl* 瘦小的女孩儿.

▷ **wispy** *adj* **(-ier, -iest)** like a wisp or in wisps; slight or straggly 似一束的; 成捆的; 稀疏的: *wispy hair, clouds* 成缕的头发、云彩 ○ *a wispy white beard* 一绺白胡子.

wis·taria (also **wis·teria**) /wɪˈsteərɪə; wɪsˋtɛrɪə/ *n* [U] any of several types of climbing plant with a woody stem and long drooping clusters of pale purple or white flowers 紫藤.

wist·ful /ˈwɪstfl; ˋwɪstfəl/ *adj* full of or expressing sad or vague longing (esp for sth that is past or unobtainable) 发愁的, 渴望的(尤指过去的或不可得的事物): *wistful eyes* 露出渴求目光的眼睛 ○ *a wistful mood* 愁苦的心情.

▷ **wist·fully** /-fəlɪ; -fəlɪ/ *adv*: *sighing wistfully* 发愁的叹息 ○ *'If only I had known you then,' he said wistfully.* '要是我那时候认识你就好了,'他伤感地说. **wist·ful·ness** *n* [U].

wit /wɪt; wɪt/ *n* **1 (a)** [U] ability to combine words, ideas, etc so as to produce a clever type of humour 用措辞、构想等产生巧妙幽默的能力: *have a ready wit* 随时能说俏皮话的 ○ *a journalist much admired for her wit* 因机智幽默而备受敬重的女新闻工作者 ○ *a literary style full of elegance and wit* 涉笔典雅风趣的文学风格. **(b)** [C] person who has or is famous for this; witty person 才思敏捷言语诙谐的人; 机智幽默的人: *a well-known wit and raconteur* 一个有名的妙语如珠会讲故事的人. **2** [U] (also **wits** [pl]) quick understanding; intelligence 悟性; 智慧; 理解力; 智力: *He hadn't the wits/wit enough to realize the danger.* 他悟性差, 没有意识到存在的危险. **3** (idm 习语) **at one's wits' ˈend** not knowing what to do or say because of worry or desperation 智尽能索; 张皇失措: *I'm at my wits' end worrying about how to pay the bills.* 我怎样付清这些帐, 完全没有主意. **a battle of wits** ⇨ BATTLE. **collect/gather one's ˈwits** become calm again after an unexpected shock, etc so that one can think clearly 镇定下来, 恢复理智: *I needed time to gather my wits before seeing him again.* 我需要先镇定一下才能再次见他. **frighten/scare sb out of his ˈwits** ⇨ FRIGHTEN. **have/keep one's ˈwits about one** be/remain alert and ready to act 时刻警惕; 随机应变: *You need to keep your wits about you when you're dealing with a man like that.* 同那种人打交道得随机应变. **live by one's wits** ⇨ LIVE². **sharpen sb's wits** ⇨ SHARPEN (SHARP). **to ˈwit** (*dated fml* 旧, 文) that is to say; namely 也就是说; 即: *He will leave at the end of term, to wit 30 July.* 他要在期末离开, 也就是7月30日. ˌ**wit and ˈwisdom** combination of quick intelligence, good judgement and learning, esp in a writer or speaker 才思(尤指作家或演说家的).

▷ **wit·less** *adj* unintelligent or foolish; out of one's mind 无智慧的; 愚蠢的; 精神错乱的: *scare sb witless*, ie out of his wits 把某人吓得发傻.

-witted (forming compound *adjs* 用以构成复合形容词) having a certain type of intelligence 有某种智力的: ˌ*dim-ˈwitted* ○ ˌ*quick-ˈwitted* ○ ˌ*slow-ˈwitted*.

witty *adj* **(-ier, -iest)** full of clever humour 诙谐的; 风趣的: *a witty speaker* 言语幽默的人 ○ *witty comments* 诙谐的评语. **wit·ti·cism** /ˈwɪtɪsɪzəm; ˋwɪtəˌsɪzəm/ *n* witty remark 诙谐的言语. **wit·tily** /-ɪlɪ; -ɪlɪ/ *adv*. **wit·ti·ness** *n* [U].

witch /wɪtʃ; wɪtʃ/ *n* **(a)** (esp formerly) woman thought to have evil magic powers (often portrayed in fairy stories wearing a black cloak and pointed hat and flying on a broomstick); sorceress (尤指旧时)女巫(在童话中常描述成身着黑色斗篷和尖帽乘扫帚飞行者); 女魔法师. **(b)** (*fig* 比喻) fascinating or bewitching woman 迷人的女子. **(c)** (*derog* 贬) ugly old woman; hag 丑老太婆.

▷ **witch·ery** /ˈwɪtʃərɪ; ˋwɪtʃərɪ/ *n* [U] (*fml* 文) **1** witchcraft 巫术; 魔法. **2** bewitching power of beauty, eloquence, etc (美貌、谈吐等的)迷惑力.

witch·ing *adj* [attrib 作定语] (*dated fml* 旧, 文) bewitching 行使巫术的; 迷人的: *the witching hour*, ie midnight, the time when witches are active 午夜(女巫活跃的时刻).

□ ˈ**witchcraft** *n* [U] use of magic powers, esp evil ones; sorcery 巫术; (尤指)妖术; 魔法.

ˈ**witch-doctor** (also **medicine-man**) *n* (esp formerly in Africa) tribal doctor with supposed magic powers (尤指旧时非洲的)巫医.

ˈ**witch-hazel** (also ˈ**wych-hazel**) *n* **1** [C] type of Asian or N American tree with yellow flowers 金缕梅(亚洲或北美产乔木, 开黄花). **2** [U] liquid obtained from the bark of this tree, used to treat bruises or sores on the skin 得自金缕树皮的汁液, 用以医治痛伤.

ˈ**witch-hunt** *n* **(a)** search to find and destroy people thought to be witches 搜捕女巫. **(b)** (*fig usu derog* 比喻, 通常作贬义) investigation made in order to persecute people who hold unorthodox or unpopular views 为迫害持非正统观点者而进行的调查: *The crusade for sexual morality is turning into a witch-hunt.* 捍卫性道德的运动正在转化成对持异议人士的迫害.

with /wɪð, wɪθ; wɪð, wɪθ/ *prep* **1 (a)** in the company or presence of (sb/sth) 和(某人[某事物])在一起: *live with one's parents* 与父母住在一起 ○ *go on holiday with a friend* 和朋友一起去度假 ○ *spend time with the children* 跟孩子在一起度时光 ○ *discuss the plans with an expert* 同专家研究计划 ○ *I've got a client with me at the moment.* 我现在有个委托人. ○ *Put the dolls away with your other toys.* 把这些玩具娃娃和你的其他玩具放在一起. ○ *If you mix blue with yellow you get green.* 把蓝色和黄色混合在一起就成了绿色. ○ *Can I wear this tie with my blue shirt?* 我穿蓝衬衫能系这条领带吗? ○ *The money is on the table with the shopping-list.* 钱在桌子上跟购物单在一起呢. **(b)** in the care, charge or possession of (sb) 由(某人)照看、管理或持有: *I leave the baby with my mother every day.* 我每天都把婴儿交给我母亲照料. ○ *I left a message for you with your secretary.* 我给你留了个信儿交给你秘书了. ○ *The keys are with reception.* 钥匙都在接待处呢. **2** having or carrying (sth) 有或带着(某物): *a girl with* (ie who has) *red hair* 红头发的女孩儿 ○ *the man with the scar* 带伤疤的男子 ○ *a person with a knowledge of European markets* 熟悉欧洲市场的人 ○ *a coat with a belt* 有腰带的大衣 ○ *a house with a swimming-pool* 带游泳池的房子 ○ *the man with a wooden leg* 有一条木腿的男子 ○ *the boy with a camera* 带着照相机的男孩儿 ○ *He looked at her with a hurt expression.* 他带着受伤害的神情看着她. **3 (a)** (indicating the tool or instrument used 用以表示使用的工具或器具): *cut it with a knife* 用刀把它切开 ○ *You can see it with a microscope.* 用显微镜就能看见. ○ *He hit it with a hammer.* 他用锤子砸. ○ *feed the baby with a spoon* 用勺喂小孩儿 ○ *sew with cotton thread* 用棉线缝 ○ *hold the door open with a stone* 用石头顶着门让它开着 ○ *I can only move it with your help.* 只有靠你帮忙我才能移动它. ○ *It was easy to translate with a dictionary.* 借助词典进行翻译就很容易. **(b)** (indicating the material or item used 用以表示使用的材料或物件): *fill the bowl with water* 把这个盆装满水 ○ *sprinkle the dish with salt* 在这盘菜上撒点盐 ○ *The lorry was loaded with timber.* 这辆卡车上装的是木材. ○ *The bag was stuffed with dirty clothes.* 这个袋子里塞满了脏衣服. **4 (a)** agreeing with or supporting (sb/sth) 与(某人[某事物])一致; 支持(某人[某事物]): *We've got all the nurses with us in our fight to stop closures.* 我们竭力反对停业, 获得全体护士的支持. ○ *She's going along with management on this issue.* 她在这个问题上同意资方的意见. ○ *I'm with you all the way!* 我始终和你的意见一致! **(b)** in opposition to (sth); against (sth) 与(某事物)对立; 反对(某事物): *fight, argue, quarrel, etc with sb* 与某人打斗、争论、吵架等 ○ *I had a row with Jane.* 我跟简吵了一架. ○ *in competition with our rivals* 同我们的对手竞争 ○ *play tennis with sb* 同某人打网球 ○ *at war with a neighbouring country* 同邻国交战. **5** because of (sth); on account of (sth) 因为或由于(某事物): *blush with embarrassment* 因难为情而脸红 ○ *tremble with fear* 吓得发抖 ○ *shaking with laughter* 笑得浑身直颤 ○ *Her fingers were numb with cold.* 她手指冻木了. **6** (indicating the manner, circumstances or condition in which sth is done or takes place 用以表示方式、情况、环境或条件): *I'll do it with pleasure.* 我很高兴做这件事. ○ *I can lift 50 kilos with an effort.* 我用力能举起50公斤的重量.

○ *She performed a somersault with ease*, ie easily. 她一下子就翻了一个跟头. ○ *He acted with discretion*, ie discreetly. 他做得很谨慎. ○ *She sleeps with the light on.* 她爱开着灯睡觉. ○ *He welcomed her with open arms.* 他热情地欢迎她. ○ *Don't stand with your hands in your pockets.* 站着的时候不要把手插在口袋里. ○ *With your permission, sir, I'd like to speak.* 先生, 若您允许, 我想发言. **7** in the same direction as (sth) 与(某物)方向一致: *sail with the wind* 顺风驶船 ○ *swim with the tide* 顺着潮流游泳 ○ *drift with the current* 顺水飘浮 ○ *The shadow moves with the sun.* 这个影子跟着太阳移动. **8** because of and at the same rate as (sth) 随着(某事物): *The shadows lengthened with the approach of sunset.* 随着太阳下落, 影子也逐渐伸长. ○ *Skill comes with experience.* 经验越多, 技巧越熟练. ○ *Good wine will improve with age.* 佳酿越陈越醇. **9** in regard to, towards or concerning (sb/sth) 对于或关于(某人[某事物]): *careful with the glasses* 当心这些玻璃杯 ○ *patient with your aunt* 对你姑姑耐心些 ○ *angry with my children* 生我孩子的气 ○ *pleased with the result* 对结果满意 ○ *inconsistent with an earlier statement* 与前述不一致 ○ *a problem with accommodation* 关于住宿的问题 ○ *What can he want with me?* 他能要我做什么呢? ○ *What can one do with half a chess set?* 只有半副棋有什么办法呢? **10** in the case of (sb/sth); as regards (sb/sth) 对(某人[某事物])来说; 至于(某人[某事物]): *With Italians it's pronunciation that's the problem.* 对意大利人来说, 发音是个问题. ○ *It's a very busy time with us at the moment.* 我们现在非常忙. **11** and also (sth); including (sth) 连…带…; 包括(某事物): *The meal with wine came to £12 each.* 那顿饭连酒每人12英镑. ○ *With preparation and marking a teacher works 12 hours a day.* 一个教师连备课带改作业每天工作12小时. ○ *The week cost us over £500 but that was with skiing lessons.* 那个星期我们花了500多英镑, 但其中包括滑雪课的学费. **12** (as) an employee or client of (an organization) (作为)(一组织)的雇员或委托人: *I hear he's with ICI now.* 我听说他现在在帝国化学工业公司工作. ○ *She acted with a repertory company for three years.* 她在一个轮演剧目剧团里演出三年. ○ *We're with the same bank.* 我们是同一个银行的客户. **13** (indicating separation from sth/sb 用以表示与某事物[某人]分离): *I could never part with this ring.* 我永远戴着这个戒指. ○ *Can we dispense with the formalities?* 咱们能免去这些礼节吗? **14** considering (one fact in relation to another) 考虑到(一事与另一事的关系): *With only two days to go we can't afford to relax.* 只有两天时间了, 我们可不能松懈. ○ *With no hope of a holiday life's very depressing.* 度假无望, 日子自然过得很沉闷. ○ *She won't be able to help us, with all her family commitments.* 她帮不了我们, 她家里的事还多着呢. **15** in spite of (sth); despite 尽管; 虽然: *With all her faults he still liked her.* 尽管她有那么多缺点, 可他还是喜欢她. **16** (idm 习语) **be with sb** (*infml* 口) be able to follow what sb is saying 能明白某人说的话: *I'm afraid I'm not quite with you.* 很抱歉, 我不太懂您的意思. **ˈwith it** (*dated sl* 旧, 俚) **(a)** knowledgeable about current fashions and ideas; alert 了解时代潮流和意识; 敏感的: *Come on — get with it!* 好啦——时髦点儿吧! ○ *He's not very with it today.* 他今天有点迟钝. **(b)** (of clothes and their wearers) fashionable (指衣物和穿着者)时髦的: *She's more with it now than she was 20 years ago.* 她比20年前时髦了. **with ˈthat** immediately after that 紧接着; 随即: *He muttered a few words of apology and with that he left.* 他支支吾吾地道个歉就马上走了.

with·draw /wɪðˈdrɔː, *also* wɪθˈd-; wɪðˈdrɔ, wɪθˈd-/ *v* (*pt* **withdrew** /-ˈdruː; -ˈdru/, *pp* **withdrawn** /-ˈdrɔːn; -ˈdrɔn/) **1** [Tn, Tn·pr] **~ sb/sth (from sth) (a)** pull or take sb/sth back or away 收回、取回、撤回或撤走某人[某事物]: *The general refused to withdraw his troops.* 那个将军拒不撤回部队. ○ *The old coins have been withdrawn from circulation.* 旧硬币已经收回不再流通了. ○ *The workers have threatened to withdraw their labour*, ie go on strike. 工人扬言要罢工. **(b)** remove (money) from a bank account, etc 从银行帐户等提(款); 取(钱): *She withdrew all her savings and left the country.* 她把全部存款取出后离开了那个国家. **2** [Tn] (*fml* 文) take back (a promise, an offer, a statement, etc); retract 撤回或撤消(诺言、提议、言论等): *Unless the contract is signed immediately, I shall withdraw my offer.* 若不立即签署合同我就撤回我提出的条件. ○ *I insist that you withdraw your offensive remarks immediately.* 我要求你必须立刻收回那些过头的话. **3** [I, Ipr] **~ (from sth)** go away from a place or from other people 离开或脱离某处或某些人: *He talked to us for an hour and then withdrew.* 他跟我们谈了一小时的话就走了. ○ *withdraw into oneself*, ie become unresponsive or unsociable 离群索居 ○ *The troops had to withdraw to a less exposed position.* 部队已经撤到不易受攻击的地点.

▷ **with·drawal** /-ˈdrɔːəl; -ˈdrɔəl/ *n* **1 (a)** [U] withdrawing or being withdrawn 收回; 取回; 撤回; 撤走: *the withdrawal of supplies, support, troops* 撤消供应、不再支持、撤回部队 ○ *the withdrawal of a product from the market* 从市场上收回一种产品 ○ (*psychology* 心) *She is showing signs of withdrawal* (ie not wanting to communicate with other people) *and depression.* 她表现出孤僻与消沉的现象. **(b)** [C] instance of this 收回; 取回; 撤回; 撤走: *You are allowed to make two withdrawals a month from the account.* 允许你每月从帐户中提取两次存款. **2** [U] process of ceasing to take an addictive drug, often accompanied by unpleasant reactions 戒除毒瘾的过程(常有不适反应): [attrib 作定语] *withdrawal symptoms* 戒毒过程中出现的症状.

with·drawn *adj* (of a person) uncommunicative or unsociable (指人)不交际的, 离群索居的: *He's become increasingly withdrawn since his wife's death.* 他从妻子死后越来越孤僻了.

wither /ˈwɪðə(r); ˈwɪðɚ/ *v* **1** [I, Ip, Tn, Tn·p] **~ (away); ~ (sth) (up)** (cause sth to) become dry, shrivelled or dead (使某物)枯萎, 凋谢: *The flowers will wither if you don't put them in water.* 这些花不放在水里就要枯死了. ○ (*fig* 比喻) *Their hopes gradually withered away.* 他们的希望逐渐破灭了. ○ *limbs withered by disease and starvation* 因疾病和饥饿而造成的四肢萎缩. **2** [Tn] subdue or overwhelm (sb) with scorn, etc 以鄙视等态度降服或震慑(某人): *She withered him with a glance.* 她瞟了他一眼把他镇住了.

▷ **with·er·ing** /ˈwɪðərɪŋ; ˈwɪðərɪŋ/ *adj* (of a look, remark, etc) scornful or contemptuous (指神情、言语等)表示轻蔑的或鄙夷的: *withering sarcasm* 轻蔑的讽刺. **with·er·ingly** *adv*.

with·ers /ˈwɪðəz; ˈwɪðɚz/ *n* [pl] highest part of the back of a horse, between the shoulder-blades 马肩隆(马的两肩骨间的隆起部分). ⇨illus at HORSE 见 HORSE 插图.

with·hold /wɪðˈhəʊld, *also* wɪθˈh-; wɪðˈhold, wɪθˈh-/ *v* (*pt, pp* **withheld** /-ˈheld; -ˈhɛld/) (*fml* 文) **(a)** [Tn, Tn·pr] **~ sth (from sb/sth)** (*fml* 文) refuse to give sth; keep sth back 拒绝给某事物; 保留某事物: *withhold one's consent/permission* 拒不同意[准许] ○ *withhold information* 保留住信息 ○ *The board has decided to withhold part of their grant money from certain students.* 委员会决定不发给某些学生的部分助学金. **(b)** [Tn] hold (sth) back; restrain 抑制(某事物); 制止: *We couldn't withhold our laughter.* 我们忍不住大笑起来.

within /wɪˈðɪn; wɪðˈɪn/ *prep* **1 (a)** after not more than (the specified period of time) 不超过(某段时间); 在(某段时间)之内: *She returned within an hour.* 她不到一小时就回来了. ○ *If you don't hear anything within seven days, phone again.* 你要是在七天之内听不到任何消息就再打个电话. **(b) ~ sth (of sth)** not further than (the specified distance) (from sth) 不超过(某段距离); 在(某段距离)之内: *a house within a mile of the station* 距火车站不到一英里的一所房子 ○ *The village has three pubs within a hundred metres (of each other).* 这个村子里有三个酒馆, (相互)距离都在一百米以内. **2** inside the range or limits of (sb/sth) 在(某人[某事物])的范围或限度以内: *We are now within sight of* (ie able to see) *the shore.* 我们现在的距离能看见海岸了. ○ *There is a bell within the patient's reach*, ie which the patient can reach. 在病人伸手可够得着的地方有个电铃. ○ *He finds it hard to live within his income*, ie without spending more than he earns. 他觉得有些入不敷出. ○ *I'd prefer you to keep this information within the family*, ie known only by members of the family. 我希望你只让家人知道这件事. ○ *within the limits of my modest talents* 管窥所及. **3** (*fml* 文) inside (sth) 在(某事物)之内: *within the medieval walls of the city* 在该城中世纪建造的城墙以内 ○ *Interview everyone living within the area shown on the map.* 面见地图所示区内居住的每一个人.

▷ **within** *adv* (*fml* 文) inside 在内部; 到内部: *Shop assistant required. Apply within.* 招聘店员. 请进面洽.

with·out /wɪ'ðaʊt; wɪð'aʊt/ *prep* **1** not having, experiencing or showing (sth) 无、未经历或未显出(某事物): *two days without food* 两天没吃东西 ○ *three nights without sleep* 三夜没睡觉 ○ *You can't leave the country without a passport.* 没有护照就不能离开这个国家. ○ *The letter had been posted without a stamp.* 那封信没贴邮票就寄出去了. ○ *I've come out without any money.* 我没带钱就出来了. ○ *a bedroom without a private bath* 无私用浴室的卧室 ○ *a skirt without pockets* 没有口袋的裙子 ○ *He acted without thought for himself.* 他那样做的时候并没考虑到自己. ○ *She spoke without enthusiasm.* 她讲话时无精打采. **2** in the absence of (sb/sth); not accompanied by (sb/sth) 在无(某人[某事物])的情况下; 无(某人[某事物])相伴: *He said he couldn't live without her.* 他说他没有她就活不了. ○ *I feel very lonely without my dog.* 我的狗不在旁边我就很寂寞. ○ *We can't reach a decision without our chairman.* 主席不在场, 我们无法做出决定. ○ *Don't leave without me.* 别甩下我就走. ○ *They were received without ceremony*, ie informally. 他们受到不拘礼节的欢迎. **3** not using (sth) 不使用(某事物): *How did you open the bottle without a bottle-opener?* 你不用开瓶器是怎么把瓶子打开的? ○ *She can't see to read without her glasses.* 她不戴眼镜就看不见字. **4** (used with the *-ing* form to mean 'not' 与 -ing形式连用, 表示'不、无、没'等): *Try and do it without making any mistakes.* 尽量不要出错. ○ *The party was organized without her knowing anything about it.* 这个聚会已然筹办, 她却一无所知. ○ *He walked past me without speaking.* 他从我身旁走过, 一句话也没说. ○ *I've often cheated in exams without being caught.* 我经常考试作弊, 从来没让人抓住过. ○ *She entered the room without knocking.* 她没敲门就进了房间. **5** (*arch* 古) outside (sth) 在(某物)之外: *without the city walls* 在城墙之外. **6** (idm 习语) **without so much as** ⇨ so[1].

▷ **with·out** *adv part* not having or showing sth 没有或不显示某事物: *We'll have one room with a bathroom and one room without.* 我们要有一间带浴室的屋子, 还要有一间不带浴室的. ○ *If there's no sugar we'll have to manage without.* 要是没有糖, 我们也只好不用糖就凑合了.

with·stand /wɪð'stænd, *also* wɪθ's-; wɪð'stænd, wɪθ's-/ *v* (*pt, pp* **withstood** /-'stʊd; -'stʊd/) [Tn] (*often fml* 常作文雅语) endure (sth) without giving in, collapsing, wearing out, etc; resist 承受住(某事物); 抵住: *withstand attacks, pressure, wind* 禁得住攻击、压力、风吹 ○ *shoes that will withstand hard wear* 耐穿的鞋.

withy /'wɪðɪ; 'wɪðɪ/ *n* tough branch, esp of willow, that bends easily and is used for tying bundles 坚韧的枝条, (尤指)柳条(作捆绑用的).

wit·less ⇨ WIT.

wit·ness /'wɪtnɪs; 'wɪtnɪs/ *n* **1** [C] (**a**) (also '**eye-witness**) person who sees an event take place (and is therefore able to describe it to others) 目击者: *witnesses (at the scene) of the accident* 事故(现场)的目击者 ○ *I was a witness to their quarrel.* 我是他们吵架时的目击者. (**b**) person who gives evidence in a lawcourt after swearing to tell the truth (在法庭上经宣誓的)证人: *a defence/prosecution witness* 被告的[原告的]证人 ○ *a witness for the defence/prosecution* 被告的[原告的]证人 ○ *The witness was cross-examined by the defending counsel.* 证人受到辩护律师的诘问. (**c**) person who is present at an event, esp the signing of a document, in order to testify to the fact that it took place 见证人(尤指见证签署文件的): *Will you act as witness to the agreement between us?* 您作我们协议签署时的见证人行吗? **2** [U, C usu *sing* 作不可数名词或可数名词, 后者通常作单数] (*fml* 文) what is said about an event, etc, esp in a lawcourt; (thing that serves as) testimony or evidence 证词(尤指法庭中的); 证明; 证据: *give witness on behalf of an accused person* 为被告作证 ○ *His ragged clothes were (a) witness to his poverty.* 他的破烂衣物可以证明他很贫穷. **3** (idm 习语) **bear witness** ⇨ BEAR[2].

W

▷ **wit·ness** *v* **1** [Tn] be present at (sth) and see it 当场见到(某事物); 目击: *witness an accident, a murder, a quarrel* 目击一事故、谋杀事件、一场争吵 ○ *We were witnessing the most important scientific development of the century.* 我们亲眼见到本世纪最重要的科学进展. ○ (*fml* 文) *Weather forecasters are not always right: witness* (ie look at the example of) *their recent mistakes.* 天气预报并非一贯正确 —— 就看看他们最近的预报错误吧. **2** [Tn] be a witness to the signing of (a document), esp by also signing the document oneself 为别人签署(文件)时作证(尤指自己也同时签字者): *witness the signing of a contract* 在一份合同签署时作证 ○ *witness a signature, treaty, will* 为一签字、条约、遗嘱签字作证. **3** [Ipr] **~ to sth** (*law or fml* 律或文) give evidence about sth in a lawcourt, etc (在法庭等上)作证: *witness* (ie testify) *to the truth of a statement* 证明某言语属实.

□ '**witness-box** (*Brit*) (*US* '**witness-stand**) *n* enclosure in a lawcourt in which a witness stands when giving evidence 证人席.

wit·ter /'wɪtə(r); 'wɪtɚ/ *v* [I, Ipr, Ip] **~ (on) (about sth)** (*infml usu derog* 口, 通常作贬义) speak in a lengthy and annoying way about sth unimportant 唠叨而讨厌地说琐碎的事: *What are you wittering (on) about?* 你唠叨什么呢?

wit·ti·cism ⇨ WIT.

wit·tingly /'wɪtɪŋlɪ; 'wɪtɪŋlɪ/ *adv* (esp in negative sentences 尤用于否定句中) knowing what one does; intentionally 明知; 有意地: *I would never wittingly offend him.* 我决不会故意得罪他.

witty ⇨ WIT.

wives *pl* of WIFE.

wiz·ard /'wɪzəd; 'wɪzɚd/ *n* **1** male witch (esp in fairy stories); magician 男巫(尤指童话中的); 魔术师. **2** person with extraordinary abilities; genius 有非凡才能的人; 天才: *a financial wizard*, ie sb who is able to make money amazingly easily 财务奇才 ○ *She's a wizard with computers.* 她是计算机天才.

▷ **wiz·ardry** /-drɪ; -drɪ/ *n* [U] (**a**) practice of magic 魔术. (**b**) extraordinary ability 非凡的才能: *financial wizardry* 财务上非凡的才能.

wiz·ened /'wɪznd; 'wɪzṇd/ *adj* having a dried-up wrinkled skin; shrivelled 皮肤干而皱的; 缩小的: *a wizened old woman* 皮肤干而皱的老太婆 ○ *a face wizened with age* 因年老皮肤发皱的脸 ○ *wizened apples* 干瘪的苹果.

wk *abbr* 缩写 = **1** (*pl* **wks**) week. **2** work.

WO /ˌdʌblju: 'əʊ; ˌdʌblju 'o/ *abbr* 缩写 = Warrant Officer 准尉.

woad /wəʊd; wod/ *n* [U] (**a**) blue dye formerly obtained from a plant of the mustard family 菘蓝(旧时取自菘蓝植物的染料). (**b**) this plant 菘蓝(植物).

wobble /'wɒbl; 'wɑbl/ *v* [I, Ipr, Ip, Tn, Tn·pr, Tn·p] **~ (sth) (about/around)** (cause sth to) move from side to side unsteadily (使某物)摆动, 摇动, 震颤: *This table wobbles.* 这张桌子不稳. ○ *I was so terrified my legs were wobbling.* 我吓得腿直打颤. ○ *wobbling along the pavement in high-heeled boots* 穿着高跟靴子在人行道上一摇一摆地走着 ○ (*fig* 比喻) *Her voice sometimes wobbles* (ie quivers, wavers) *on high notes.* 她唱高音时有时发颤. ○ *Please don't wobble the desk (about) when I'm trying to write.* 我写字时请不要摇晃桌子.

▷ **wobble** *n* (usu *sing* 通常作单数) wobbling movement 摆动; 摇动; 震颤.

wob·bly /'wɒblɪ; 'wɑblɪ/ *adj* (*infml* 口) tending to move unsteadily from side to side 摆动的; 摇动的; 震颤的: *a wobbly tooth* 摇晃的牙 ○ *a wobbly line*, ie not drawn straight 弯曲的线 ○ *wobbly jelly* 颤动的果冻 ○ (*fig* 比喻) *He is still a bit wobbly (on his legs) after his illness.* 他病后(腿)仍有点儿发颤. **wob·bli·ness** *n* [U].

wodge /wɒdʒ; wɑdʒ/ *n* **~ (of sth)** (*Brit infml* 口) large piece or amount 大的块或量: *a thick wodge of cake* 一大块蛋糕 ○ *wodges of old newspapers* 大堆的旧报纸.

woe /wəʊ; wo/ *n* (*dated or fml or joc* 旧或文或谑) **1** [U] great sorrow or distress 悲哀; 悲痛; 苦恼: *a cry of woe* 悲鸣 ○ *She needed someone to listen to her tale of woe*, ie the story of her misfortune. 她需要有人听她述说悲惨的遭遇. **2 woes** [pl] things that cause sorrow or distress; troubles or misfortunes 引起悲哀或苦恼的事物; 麻烦事; 不幸的事: *She told him all her woes.* 她把自己的不幸遭遇都告诉他了. **3** (idm 习语) **woe be'tide sb** (*fml or joc* 文或谑) there will be trouble for sb 某人要倒霉: *Woe betide anyone who arrives late!* 谁迟到谁倒霉! ˌ**woe is 'me!** *interj* (*arch or joc* 古或谑) how unhappy I am 我真不痛快!

woe·be·gone /'wəʊbɪgɒn; *US* -gɔ:n; 'wobɪˌgɔn/ *adj* (*fml*

文) looking unhappy 显出悲伤的; 忧愁的; 愁眉苦脸的: *a woebegone child, expression, face* 悲哀的孩子、表情、面孔.

woe·ful /ˈwəʊfl; ˈwofəl/ *adj* (*fml* 文) **1** full of woe; sad 悲哀的; 伤心的: *a woeful cry, look, sight* 悲惨的哭声、神情、情景. **2** [usu attrib 通常作定语] undesirable or regrettable; very bad 不合意的; 令人惋惜的; 糟糕的: *woeful ignorance* 可悲的无知. ▷ **woe·fully** *adv* /-fəlɪ; -fəlɪ/: *The preparations were woefully inadequate.* 准备工作未免太不够了.

wok /wɒk; wɑk/ *n* large pan shaped like a bowl, used for cooking (esp) Chinese food 锅(尤指中国式的). ⇨illus at PAN 见 PAN 插图.

woke *pt* of WAKE[1].

woken *pp* of WAKE[1].

wolf 狼

wolf /wʊlf; wʊlf/ *n* (*pl* **wolves** /wʊlvz; wʊlvz/) **1** fierce wild animal of the dog family, usu hunting in packs 狼. **2** (idm 习语) **cry wolf** ⇨ CRY[1]. **keep the ˈwolf from the door** have enough money to avoid hunger and need 有维持温饱的钱: *Their wages are barely enough to keep the wolf from the door.* 他们的工资勉强够维持生活的. **a lone wolf** ⇨ LONE. **a wolf in ˈsheep's clothing** person who appears friendly or harmless but is really an enemy 披着羊皮的狼. **throw sb to the ˈwolves** leave sb to be roughly treated or criticized without trying to help or defend him 任凭某人遭受粗暴对待或批评而不予协助或辩解.

▷ **wolf** *v* [Tn, Tn·p] **~ sth (down)** (*infml* 口) eat sth quickly and greedily 快而贪婪地吃某物; 狼吞虎咽: *I thought there would be some biscuits left but they've wolfed the lot!* 我还以为能剩下些饼干, 但是他们都给吃光了. ○ *Don't wolf down your food.* 吃东西不要狼吞虎咽.

wolf·ish *adj* of or like a wolf (似)狼的: *a wolfish appetite, grin* 如狼似虎的食欲、狞笑.

□ ˈ**wolf-cub** *n* young wolf 幼狼.

ˈ**wolfhound** *n* any of several types of very large dog originally bred for hunting wolves 猎狼犬: *an Irish wolfhound* 爱尔兰猎狼犬.

ˈ**wolf-whistle** *n* whistling sound made by a man to show that he finds a woman sexually attractive (男子见到动人女子时吹的)口哨声. — *v* [I, Ipr] **~ (at sb)** make this sound 发出此种口哨声.

wolf·ram /ˈwʊlfrəm; ˈwʊlfrəm/ *n* [U] (**a**) = TUNGSTEN. (**b**) tungsten ore 钨矿石.

wo·man /ˈwʊmən; ˈwʊmən/ *n* (*pl* **women** /ˈwɪmɪn; ˈwɪmɪn/) **1** [C] (**a**) adult female human being 成年女子: *men, women and children* 男子、女子和孩子 ○ *a single* (ie unmarried) *woman* 单身女子(未婚的) ○ *It's more than a woman* (ie any woman) *can tolerate.* 任何女子都忍受不了这种情况. ○ [attrib 作定语] (preferred to *lady* which is also used 较 lady 为宜, 但亦可用 lady) *a ˌwoman ˈdriver* 女司机 ○ *ˌwomen ˈdrivers* 女司机们 ○ *I'd prefer a woman doctor to examine me.* 我希望由女医生给我检查. ○ *a ˈwoman friend* 女的朋友 ○ *a ˈFrench woman* 法国女子. (**b**) (as an offensive form of address 用作无礼的称呼): *Shut up, woman!* 住嘴, 你这个娘儿们! **2** [sing] (without *a* or *the* 不用冠词 a 或 the) female human beings in general; the female sex 女的人; 女性: *Woman has been portrayed by artists in many ways.* 艺术家用各种形式塑造了女性的形象. **3 the woman** [sing] the feminine side of a woman's character 女性的特点: *Newborn babies bring out the woman in her.* 新生的婴儿唤起了她女性的特性. **4** (idm 习语) **be twice the man/woman** ⇨ TWICE. **make an honest woman of sb** ⇨ HONEST. **a man/woman of parts** ⇨ PART[1]. **a man/woman of his/her word** ⇨ WORD. **a man/woman of the world** ⇨ WORLD. **wine, women and song** ⇨ WINE. **a woman of easy ˈvirtue** (*euph* 婉) prostitute 妓女.

▷ **-woman** (with *ns* forming compound *ns* 与名词结合构成复合名词) woman concerned with 与某事物有关的女子: *ˈchairwoman* ○ *ˈhorsewoman* ○ *ˈsportswoman*. Cf 参看 -MAN (MAN[1]).

ˈ**wo·man·hood** [U] state of being a woman 成年女子的身分或状态: *grow to/reach womanhood* 长成[成为]成年女子.

wo·man·ish *adj* (*derog* 贬) (of a man) like a woman; suitable for women but not for men (指男子)像女子的, 适合女子的(不适合男子的): *He has a rather womanish manner.* 他太女气了.

wo·man·ize, -ise /-aɪz; ˌnaɪz/ *v* [I] (*usu derog* 通常作贬义) (of a man) have sexual affairs with numerous women (指男子)与许多女子发生性关系. **wo·man·izer, -iser** *n* man who does this 与许多女子发生性关系的男子.

wo·manly *adj* (*approv* 褒) like a woman; feminine 像女子的; 女性的: *a womanly figure* 像女子的外形 ○ *womanly qualities, virtues* 女性的特性、美德. **wo·man·li·ness** *n* [U].

□ ˈ**womankind** *n* [U] (*fml* 文) female human beings in general 女的人; 女性: *the sufferings of womankind* 女性的苦难.

ˌ**Women's Libeˈration** (also *infml* 口语作 ˌ**Women's ˈLib** /lɪb; lɪb/) freedom of women to enjoy the same social and economic rights as men 妇女解放. ˌ**Women's ˈLibber** (*infml* 口) person who campaigns for this ideal; feminist 鼓吹妇女解放的人.

the ˈwomen's movement social and political movement that aims to achieve Women's Liberation by legislation and by changing people's attitudes 妇女解放运动.

womb /wu:m; wum/ *n* (*anatomy* 解) (in women and other female mammals) organ in which offspring is carried and nourished while it develops before birth; uterus 子宫. ⇨illus at FEMALE 见 FEMALE 插图.

wom·bat /ˈwɒmbæt; ˈwɑmbæt/ *n* Australian wild animal similar to a small bear, the female of which carries its young in a pouch 毛鼻袋熊(澳洲产).

wo·men·folk /ˈwɪmɪnfəʊk; ˈwɪmɪnˌfok/ *n* [pl] women, esp the women of a particular group, family, tribe, etc 女子们(尤指某集体、家族、部落等的): *The dead soldiers were mourned by their womenfolk.* 士兵死亡后, 女眷表示沉痛哀悼. Cf 参看 MENFOLK.

won *pt, pp* of WIN.

won·der /ˈwʌndə(r); ˈwʌndɚ/ *n* **1** (**a**) [U] feeling of surprise mixed with admiration, bewilderment or disbelief 惊奇; 惊叹; 惊愕; 惊异: *The children watched the conjuror in silent wonder.* 孩子都一声不响惊奇地看着魔术师. ○ *They were filled with wonder at the sight.* 他们见此情景惊叹不已. (**b**) [C] thing or event that causes this feeling 令人感到惊奇的事物: *the wonders of modern medicine* 现代医学的奇迹 ○ *the seven wonders of the world* 世界七大奇观 ○ [attrib 作定语] *a wonder drug*, ie one that has extremely good, almost miraculous, effects 特效药. **2** (idm 习语) **a chinless wonder** ⇨ CHINLESS (CHIN). **do/work miracles/wonders (for sth)** ⇨ MIRACLE. **it's a wonder (that)...** it's surprising or puzzling (that)... 令人惊奇的是...; 莫名其妙的是...: *It's a wonder (that) he continues to gamble when he always loses!* 令人惊讶的是他一直输还一直赌! **a nine days' wonder** ⇨ DAY. **no/little/small ˈwonder (that...)** it is not/hardly surprising 这并不[不太]出奇: *No wonder you were late!* 难怪你来晚了! ○ *Small wonder (that) he was so tired!* 难怪他这么累! ˌ**wonders will ˌnever ˈcease** (*saying esp ironic* 谚, 尤作反语) (expressing surprise and pleasure at sth, often sth trivial 用以对某事物表示惊喜,常指小事): *'I've washed the car for you.' 'Wonders will never cease!'* '我替你把汽车擦洗了.' '真是无奇不有!'

▷ **won·der** *v* **1** [I, Ipr, It, Tf] **~ (at sth)** (*fml* 文) feel great surprise, admiration, etc; marvel 感到惊奇; 惊叹; 惊讶: *He could do nothing but stand and wonder.* 他只得惊奇地站着不动. ○ *We wondered at the speed with which it arrived.* 我们赞叹其到达速度之快. ○ *I wonder* (ie am amazed) *(at the fact) that you weren't killed.* 你竟未遇难, 令人称奇. ○ *I wondered* (ie was surprised) *to hear her voice in the next room.* 我听到隔壁传出她的声音, 十分惊讶. **2** (**a**) [I, Ipr] **~ (about sth)** feel curious (about sth); ask oneself questions (对某事物)感到好奇; 自问;

自忖: *There has been no news for a week and he is beginning to wonder.* 已经一个星期没有消息了, 他渐渐觉得有些奇怪. ○ *I was just wondering about that myself.* 我就是觉得这件事莫名其妙. (**b**) [Tw] ask oneself 自问; 自忖: *I wonder who he is.* 我不知道他究竟是谁. ○ *I wonder whether they will arrive on time.* 我也不知道他们能不能准时到. ○ *wondered what time it was, where to go, how long it would last, why he had left.* 那时闹不清几点钟了、应该到哪儿去、那件事还要持续多久、他为什么走了. (**c**) [Tw] (used as a polite way of introducing a request 用以提出要求, 为礼貌表达方式): *I wonder if/whether you could...* 请问您是否可以.... **3** (idm 习语) **I ˌshouldn't ˈwonder** (*infml* 口) I should not be surprised (to discover) 我觉得不足为奇: *It's paid for with stolen money, I shouldn't wonder.* 那是用偷来的钱支付的, 我觉得这并不奇怪.

won·der·ful /-fl; -fəl/ *adj* (**a**) causing wonder; very surprising 令人惊奇的; 意想不到的: *It's wonderful that they managed to escape.* 令人惊奇的是他们居然设法逃跑了. ○ *The child's skill is wonderful for his age.* 这个孩子小小年纪, 技巧令人称奇. (**b**) very good or admirable 极好的; 奇妙的; 了不起的: *The weather is wonderful.* 天气好极了. ○ *She is a wonderful mother.* 她是个了不起的母亲. ○ *a wonderful opportunity* 绝妙的机会. **won·der·fully** /-fəlɪ; -fəlɪ/ *adv* (**a**) surprisingly 令人惊奇地: *She is wonderfully active for her age.* 她年纪那么大活跃得不得了. (**b**) extremely; admirably 极度地; 赞叹地: *Their life together has been wonderfully happy.* 他们在一起的生活极为幸福.

won·der·ingly /ˈwʌndrɪŋlɪ; ˈwʌndrɪŋlɪ/ *adv*: *'Where did this come from?' she said wonderingly.* '这是从哪儿来的?'她吃惊地问.

won·der·ment *n* [U] pleasant amazement 惊喜: *She gasped in wonderment at her good luck.* 她运气这样好, 惊奇地倒抽了一口凉气.

won·drous /ˈwʌndrəs; ˈwʌndrəs/ *adj* (*arch or fml* 古或文) wonderful 令人惊奇的; 意想不到的; 极好的; 奇妙的; 了不起的: *a wondrous sight* 奇妙的情景. **won·drously** *adv*.

□ ˈ**wonderland** /-lænd; -ˌlænd/ *n* (usu *sing* 通常作单数) land or place full of marvels or wonderful things 有许多奇妙事物的地方.

wonky /ˈwɒŋkɪ; ˈwɑŋkɪ/ *adj* (**-ier**, **-iest**) (*Brit infml* 口) unsteady or weak; wobbly 不稳的; 弱的; 摆动的; 摇动的; 震颤的: *a wonky chair* 摇摇晃晃的椅子 ○ *She still feels a bit wonky after her accident.* 她出了事故以后仍然觉得有些虚弱.

wont /wəʊnt; *US* wɔːnt; wont/ *adj* [pred 作表语] ~ **to do sth** (*dated or rhet* 旧或修辞) in the habit of doing sth; accustomed to doing sth 惯于或已适应于做某事物: *He was wont to give lengthy speeches.* 他惯于做长篇大论的演说.

▷ **wont** *n* [sing] (*fml or rhet* 文或修辞) custom; habit 习俗; 习惯: *She went for a walk after breakfast, as was her wont.* 她早饭后要散散步已成了习惯.

won't /wəʊnt; wont/ *contracted form of* WILL NOT (WILL[1]) WILL NOT的缩约式(参看 WILL[1]).

W

woo /wuː; wu/ *v* (*pt, pp* **wooed**) [Tn] **1** (**a**) try to obtain the support of (sb) 寻求(某人)的支持: *woo the voters* 拉选票. (**b**) try to achieve or obtain (sth) 想要成就或获得(某事物): *woo fame, fortune, success, etc* 想要获得名声、财富、成功等. **2** (*dated* 旧) try to persuade (a woman) to marry one; court 向(女子)求婚; 求爱.

wood /wʊd; wʊd/ *n* **1** (**a**) [U] hard fibrous substance in the trunk and branches of a tree, enclosed by the bark 木; 木材; 木头: *There are many kinds of wood growing in this forest.* 这片森林出产各种木材. (**b**) this substance, cut and used as building material, fuel, etc 木料; 木柴: *Tables are usually made of wood.* 桌子多为木制的. ○ *Put some more wood on the fire.* 再往火里添点儿柴. ○ [attrib 作定语] *a wood floor*, ie made of wood 木制地板. (**c**) [C] particular type of this 某种木材: *Pine is a soft wood and teak is a hard wood.* 松木是软木, 柚木是硬木. ○ *Oak is a good type of wood for making furniture.* 橡木是制作家具的好材料. **2** [C often *pl* 常作复数] area of land (not as large as a forest) covered with growing trees 树林(不如forest大): *a house in the middle of a wood* 树林中间的一所房子 ○ *go for a walk in the wood(s)* 到林中去散步. **3** [C] (*sport* 体) = BOWL 2. **4** [C] golf-club with a wooden head 顶部为木制的高尔夫球棒. Cf 参看 IRON[1] 4. **5** (idm 习语) **dead wood** ⇨ DEAD. **from the ˈwood** from the cask or wooden barrel 从木桶里: *beer from the wood* 从木桶里取出的啤酒. **neck of the woods** ⇨ NECK. **not see the ˌwood for the ˈtrees** not see or understand the main point, subject, etc because one is paying too much attention to details 见树不见林: *If you add too many notes to the text, the reader won't be able to see the wood for the trees.* 要是给正文加注过多, 读者就觉得喧宾夺主了. **ˌout of the ˈwood(s)** (*infml* 口) (usu with a negative 通常与否定词连用) free from trouble or difficulties 没有麻烦或困难: *She's regained consciousness, but she's not out of the woods* (ie sure to recover) *yet.* 她已恢复了知觉, 但尚未脱险. **touch wood** ⇨ TOUCH[1].

▷ **wooded** *adj* (of land) covered with growing trees (指地)长满树木的: *a wooded valley* 树木茂盛的山谷.

wooden /ˈwʊdn; ˈwʊdn/ *adj* **1** [esp attrib 尤作定语] made of wood 木制的: *wooden furniture, houses, toys* 木制的家具、房子、玩具. **2** stiff and awkward (in one's manner) (举止)僵硬而笨拙的: *She has a rather wooden manner.* 她举止僵硬而笨拙. ○ *a wooden smile, performance* 呆板的笑容、表演. **wood·enly** *adv* stiffly and awkwardly 僵硬而笨拙地. **wood·en·ness** *n* [U]. **ˌwooden ˈspoon** = BOOBY PRIZE (BOOBY).

woody *adj* (**a**) wooded 长满树木的: *a woody hillside* 树木茂盛的山坡. (**b**) of or like growing wood (似)树木的: *a plant with woody stems* 长着木茎的植物 ○ *a woody smell* 像木头的气味.

□ ˈ**woodbine** *n* [U] (**a**) wild honeysuckle 苦壁藤; 野忍冬. (**b**) (*US*) = VIRGINIA CREEPER.

ˈ**wood-block** *n* (**a**) block of wood from which woodcuts are made 木刻板. (**b**) any of many pieces of wood used in making a floor, often arranged in a pattern (铺地板用的)木条, 木块: [attrib 作定语] *a wood-block floor* 木条地板.

ˈ**woodchuck** *n* (*US*) type of N American marmot; groundhog 美洲旱獭.

ˈ**woodcock** *n* (*pl* unchanged 复数不变) (**a**) [C] type of brown game-bird found in woodland with a long, straight bill, short legs and a short tail 丘鹬. (**b**) [U] its flesh eaten as food (食用的)丘鹬肉.

ˈ**woodcraft** *n* [U] knowledge of woodland conditions; skill in finding one's way in woods and forests, esp as used in hunting 森林环境知识, 森林识路技巧(尤指用于打猎的).

ˈ**woodcut** *n* print made from a design, drawing, etc cut in relief on a block of wood 木板画.

ˈ**woodcutter** *n* person who cuts down trees as an occupation 伐木工.

ˈ**woodland** /-lənd; -ˌlənd/ *n* [U] land covered with trees; woods 林地; 树林: [attrib 作定语] *woodland scenery* 林景.

ˈ**wood lot** (*US*) area, eg on a farm, kept for growing trees 林用地(尤指农场中的).

ˈ**wood-louse** *n* (*pl* **-lice**) small wingless insect-like creature that lives in decaying wood, damp soil, etc 潮虫.

ˈ**woodman** /-mən; -mən/ (also *esp US* ˈ**woodsman** /-zmən; -zmən/) *n* (*pl* **-men**) forester; woodcutter 护林人; 在林区居住及工作的人; 伐木工.

ˈ**woodpecker** *n* bird that clings to the bark of trees and taps with its beak to find insects 啄木鸟. ⇨illus at App 1 见附录1插图, page iv.

ˈ**wood-pigeon** *n* type of large wild pigeon 斑尾林鸽.

ˈ**wood-pulp** *n* [U] wood shredded and used for making paper 木浆(造纸用的).

ˈ**wood-shed** *n* shed where wood is stored (esp for fuel) 木料间; (尤指)柴间.

ˈ**woodwind** /-wɪnd; -ˌwɪnd/ *n* [Gp] (players of the) wind instruments of an orchestra, which are (or were formerly) made of wood 木管乐器(的吹奏者): [attrib 作定语] *a woodwind instrument* 木管乐器 ○ *the woodwind section* 木管乐器组. ⇨illus at App 1 见附录1插图, page x.

ˈ**woodwork** *n* [U] **1** things made of wood, esp the wooden parts of a building, eg doors, stairs, etc 木制品, (尤指建筑物的)木结构部分(如门、楼梯等): *The woodwork is painted white.* 这件木制品已漆成白的了. **2** skill or practice of making things from wood; carpentry 木工工艺; 木作.

ˈ**woodworm** *n* (**a**) [C] type of larva that bores through wood and eats it 蛀木虫. (**b**) [U] holes caused by this 蛀木虫钻的孔洞: *This ladder is riddled with woodworm.* 这个梯子已经让蛀虫蛀了很多洞.

woof[1] /wu:f; wuf/ *n* = WEFT.

woof[2] /wʊf; wuf/ *interj, n* (*infml* 口) (used to imitate the sound of the) bark of a dog 狗的叫声; 模仿狗叫声的象声词.

▷ **woof** *v* [I] (*infml* 口) bark 狗叫.

woofer /ˈwʊfə(r); ˈwufɚ/ *n* loudspeaker designed to reproduce low notes accurately 低音扬声器; 低音喇叭. Cf 参看 TWEETER.

wool /wʊl; wul/ *n* **1** (**a**) [U] fine soft hair that forms the coats of sheep, goats and some other animals (eg the llama and alpaca) 羊毛; 其他动物的毛(如亚美利加驼和羊驼的毛): *These goats are specially bred for their wool.* 这些山羊是专为剪取羊毛而饲养的. (**b**) [U] yarn, cloth, clothing, etc made from this 毛线; 毛料; 毛料衣物: *a ball of knitting wool* 一团毛线 ○ *a (type of) fine/heavy wool* (一种)细毛[重脂含杂毛] ○ [attrib 作定语] *the* ˈ*wool trade* 羊毛业 ○ *a wool* (ie woollen) *coat, blanket, etc* 毛料大衣、毛毯. **2** [U] substance that looks and feels like sheep's wool 似羊毛的物质: *cotton wool* 原棉 ○ *wire wool* 金属丝团. **3** (idm 习语) **pull the wool over sb's eyes** ⇨ PULL[2].

▷ **wool·len** (*US* **woolen**) /ˈwʊlən; ˈwulən/ *adj* [usu attrib 通常作定语] (**a**) made wholly or partly of wool 毛纺的; 纯毛的; (含毛)混纺的: *woollen cloth, blankets, socks, etc* 毛料、毛毯、毛袜. (**b**) of woollen fabrics 毛织物的: *woollen manufacturers, merchants, etc* 毛织物制造商、毛织物商人. **wool·lens** (*US* **woolens**) *n* [pl] (esp knitted) woollen garments (尤指针织的)毛织服装: *a special wash programme for woollens* 专为洗涤针织毛料衣物的程序.

woolly (*US* also **wooly**) /ˈwʊlɪ; ˈwulɪ/ *adj* (**-ier, -iest**) **1** (**a**) covered with wool or wool-like hair 长着或覆有羊毛或羊毛状的毛(发)的: *woolly sheep* 毛绒绒的绵羊 ○ *the dog's woolly coat* 狗的羊毛状的毛. (**b**) like or made of wool; woollen 似羊毛的; 羊毛制的; 毛纺的: *a woolly cotton fabric* 棉毛织物 ○ *a woolly hat* 羊毛制的帽子. **2** (also ˌ**woolly-**ˈ**headed**) (of a person or his mind, arguments, ideas, etc) not thinking clearly; not clearly expressed or thought out (指人、人的头脑、论点、思想等)糊涂的, 表达不清楚的, 思路混乱的. — *n* (*infml* 口) woollen garment, esp a sweater 毛料服装; (尤指)套头毛衣: *wear one's winter woollies* 穿着冬季用的毛衣. **wool·li·ness** *n* [U].

□ ˈ**wool-gathering** *n* [U] (*infml* 口) absent-mindedness 心不在焉.

woozy /ˈwu:zɪ; ˈwuzɪ/ *adj* (**-ier, -iest**) (*infml* 口) (**a**) feeling dizzy or sick, eg as a result of drinking too much alcohol 眩晕的, 恶心的(如因喝酒过量所致). (**b**) mentally confused; dazed 糊涂的; 头昏眼花的.

wop /wɒp; wɑp/ *n* (⚠ *sl offensive* 讳, 俚, 蔑) person from southern Europe, esp an Italian 南欧人; (尤指)意大利人.

word /wɜ:d; wɝd/ *n* **1** [C] (**a**) sound or combination of sounds that expresses a meaning and forms an independent unit of the grammar or vocabulary of a language (用声音表达的)词: *The story is told in words and pictures.* 讲这个故事的时候配有图片. ○ *The Latin word for 'table' is 'mensa'.* 'table(桌子)'这个词在拉丁语里叫'*mensa*'. ○ *He couldn't put his feelings into words,* ie express them verbally. 他无法把自己的感情用言语说清楚. ○ *I have no words to* (ie cannot adequately) *express my gratitude.* 我说的话不足以表达我的感激之情. (**b**) this represented as letters or symbols, usu with a space on either side (用书面形式表达的)词: *That word is not spelled correctly.* 那个词拼得不正确. ○ *The words in the dictionary are arranged in alphabetical order.* 词典中的词是按字母顺序排列的. **2** (**a**) [C] anything said; remark or statement (说的)话; 话语; 言语: *He didn't say a word about it.* 他对这件事一句话都没说. ○ *I don't believe a word of his story.* 他说的这件事我一句话都不相信. ○ *a word/a few words of advice, sympathy, warning* 一些劝告、同情、警告的话. (**b**) **words** [pl] things that are said, contrasted with things that are done 说的话(与做的事相对): *You must show your support by deeds, not words.* 你必须用行动支持, 不能空口说白话. **3** [sing] (**a**) (without *a* or *the* 不用冠词 a 或 the) piece of news; message 消息; 信息: *Please send (me)/leave word of your safe arrival/that you have arrived safely.* 请您把平安到达的消息告诉我. ○ *Word came that I was needed at home.* 有信儿来说家里需要我. (**b**) **the word** rumour 谣言; 传闻: *The word is that he's left the country.* 据说他已经离开这个国家了. **4** (usu 通常作 **the word**) [sing] spoken command or signal 口令; 号令: *Stay hidden until I give the word.* 我不下令就藏着别动. ○ *Their word is law,* ie their commands must be obeyed. 他们的命令必须服从. **5 the Word** [sing] (also **the** ˌ**word of** ˈ**God**) (*Bible* 圣经) the Scriptures, esp the Gospels《圣经》; (尤指)福音: *preach the Word* 传福音 ○ *Hear the Word of God.* 听宣讲《圣经》. **6** (idm 习语) **actions speak louder than words** ⇨ ACTION. **at the** ˌ**word of com**ˈ**mand** when the (military) order is given 发(军)令时. **bandy words** ⇨ BANDY[1]. **be as** ˌ**good as one's** ˈ**word** do what one has promised to do 守信: *You'll find that she's as good as her word.* 你能了解到她这个人很讲信用. **be better than one's word** ⇨ BETTER[1]. **be not the** ˈ**word for sth/sb** (*infml* 口) be an inadequate description of sth/sb 不足以形容某事物[某人]: *Unkind isn't the word for it! He treats the animals appallingly!* 岂止是'不好'! 他对待动物是太不成话了! **breathe a word** ⇨ BREATHE. **by** ˌ**word of** ˈ**mouth** in spoken, not written, words 口头上(的): *He received the news by word of mouth.* 他得到的是口头的消息. **a dirty word** ⇨ DIRTY[1]. **eat one's words** ⇨ EAT. **exchange words** ⇨ EXCHANGE[2]. **famous last words** ⇨ FAMOUS. **fighting talk/words** ⇨ FIGHT[1]. **(right) from the word** ˈ**go** (*infml* 口) right from the start 从一开始: *She knew (right) from the word go that it was going to be difficult.* 她从一开始就知道这件事很难办. **(not) get a word in** ˈ**edgeways** (not) be able to interrupt sb who is very talkative (不)能(在某人不断谈话时)插嘴. **give sb one's** ˈ**word (that...)/have sb's** ˈ**word for it (that...)** promise sb/be promised by sb (that...) 许诺某人[得到某人的许诺]: *You have my word for it that the goods will arrive on time.* 我向你保证货物一定准时到达. **go** ˌ**back on one's** ˈ**word** fail to fulfil a promise that one has made 食言. **hang on sb's lips/words/every word** ⇨ HANG[1]. **(not) have a good word to** ˈ**say for sb/sth** (*infml* 口) (not) say anything at all favourable about sb/sth (不)说某人[某事物]的好话: *He doesn't have/seldom has a good word to say for Britain.* 他从不[很少]说英国的好话. **have, etc the last word** ⇨ LAST[1]. **have a word in sb's** ˈ**ear** speak to sb in private/confidentially 和某人说私话[秘密话]. **have a** ˈ**word (with sb) (about sth)** speak (to sb) (about sth), esp privately or confidentially (对某人)说(某事)(尤指私下的或秘密的事): *Could we have a word before you go to the meeting?* 你去开会之前, 咱们能私下说句话吗? **have** ˈ**words (with sb) (about sth)** quarrel (with sb) (about sth) (为某事)(与某人)争吵. **a household name/word** ⇨ HOUSEHOLD. **in a** ˈ**word** briefly 一句话; 简言之: *In a word, I think he's a fool.* 总之, 我认为他是个傻瓜. **in** ˈ**other words** expressed in a different way; that is to say 换句话说; 也就是说. **(not) in so many** ˈ**words** (not) in exactly the same words as are claimed or reported to have been used (并非)一字不差. **in words of** ˈ**one syllable** using very simple language 使用极简单的语言. **keep/break one's word** do/fail to do what one has promised 守信[失信]. **one's last word** ⇨ LAST[1]. **the last word** ⇨ LAST[1]. **a man/woman of his/her** ˈ**word** person that does what he/she has promised to do 守信用的人. **mum's the word!** ⇨ MUM[1]. **(upon) my** ˈ**word!** (*dated or fml* 旧或文) (exclamation expressing surprise or consternation 用作表示惊奇或惊恐的叹词): *My word, you're back early!* 咦, 你回来得真早哇! **not a** ˈ**word (to sb) (about sth)** don't say anything; be silent! (关于某事)(对某人)什么也别说; 别说!: *Not a word (to Mary) (about what I said)!* (我说的话)千万别(对玛丽)说! **not to mince matters/words** ⇨ MINCE. **a play on words** ⇨ PLAY[1]. **put in/say a (good)** ˈ**word for sb** say sth in sb's favour in order to help him 为某人说好话相助. **put** ˈ**words in sb's mouth** suggest that sb has said sth when he has not 硬说某人说过某话: *She accused the journalist of putting words in her mouth.* 她指责该新闻工作者把报道

的事硬说成是她说过的. ˌ**say the** ˈ**word** (*infml* 口) give an order, a signal, etc 发命令、信号等: *If you want me to leave, you only have to say the word.* 你要是想让我走, 尽管说出来就是了. **swallow one's words** ⇨ SWALLOW[2]. **take sb at his** ˈ**word** believe exactly what sb says or promises, without question 完全相信某人的话或承诺而毫不怀疑. **take sb's** ˈ**word for it (that...)** accept sth on sb's authority 认为某人有权威性而相信他的话: *I'll take your word for it that it won't happen again.* 我相信你说的此事下不为例这句话. **take the** ˈ**words (right) out of sb's mouth** say just what sb else was about to say 说出某人要说的话. **too funny, outrageous, sad, shocking, etc for** ˈ**words** so funny, etc that it cannot be expressed in words; extremely funny, etc 有趣、可耻、悲痛、令人震惊...得难以言传; 极为有趣、可耻、悲痛、令人震惊等. **a war of words** ⇨ WAR. **weigh one's words** ⇨ WEIGH. ˌ**without a** ˈ**word** without saying anything 什么也没说: *He left without a word.* 他一句话都没说就走了. ˌ**word for** ˈ**word** in exactly the same or (in translation) exactly equivalent words; verbatim 逐字地; (在翻译方面)一字对一字, 使用对应词: *He repeated what you said word for word.* 他一字不差地复述了您说的话. ○ [attrib 作定语] *a* ˌ*word-for-word ac*ˈ*count, repe*ˈ*tition, trans*ˈ*lation* 逐字的复述、重复、翻译. **sb's** ˌ**word is as** ˌ**good as his** ˈ**bond** sb's promise can be relied upon completely 某人说的话可以绝对相信. **one's** ˌ**word of** ˈ**honour** a solemn promise 庄严的承诺. **a** ˌ**word to the** ˈ**wise** an intelligent person can take a hint, draw his own conclusions, etc without a lot of explanation 对聪明人一点就透(不必详加解释).

▷ **word** *v* [Tn esp passive 尤用于被动语态] express (sth) in particular words; phrase (sth) 用词语表达(某事); 选用(词语): *The advice wasn't very tactfully worded.* 这份通知措辞不太策略. ○ *a carefully worded reminder* 措辞严谨的催促通知 ○ *Be careful how you word your answer.* 回答时要字斟句酌. **word·ing** *n* [sing] words used to express sth; way in which sth is expressed (用以表达某事物的)词语; 说法; 措辞: *A different wording might make the meaning clearer.* 换一种说法意思可能清楚些.

word·less *adj* (*fml* 文) not expressed in words 不用言语表达的: *wordless grief, sympathy* 无言的悲痛、同情.

wordy *adj* (**-ier**, **-iest**) (*derog* 贬) using or expressed in (too) many words; verbose 话(过)多的; 冗长的; 啰嗦的: *a wordy expression of apology* 拖泥带水的道歉. **word·ily** /-ɪlɪ; -ɪlɪ/ *adv*. **wordi·ness** *n* [U].

□ ˈ**word-blindness** *n* [U] = DYSLEXIA.

ˌ**word-**ˈ**perfect** (*US* ˌ**letter-**ˈ**perfect**) *adj* able to say or recite sth from memory without making any mistakes 能靠记忆一字不错说出或背诵出的.

ˈ**word processor** device that records typed words, diagrams, etc and displays them on a visual display unit so that they can be corrected or edited and then automatically printed 文字处理机. Cf 参看 TYPEWRITER (TYPE[2]). ˈ**word processing** (practice of doing) work on a word processor 文字处理: [attrib 作定语] *word-processing skills* 文字处理技巧.

W

wore *pt* of WEAR[2].

work[1] /wɜːk; wɝk/ *n* **1** [U] (**a**) use of bodily or mental power in order to do or make sth (esp as contrasted with rest or play or recreation) 工作; 劳动: *His success was achieved by hard work.* 他靠辛勤劳动而获得成功. ○ *The work of building the bridge took six months.* 建桥工作用了半年的时间. ○ *Years of research work have failed to produce a cure for the disease.* 多年的研究工作未能找到医治这种疾病的疗法. ○ *He never does a stroke of* (ie any) *work.* 他什么活儿都不干. ○ *She was worn out with work.* 她让工作给累坏了. (**b**) use of energy supplied by electricity, steam, etc to do or make sth 使用电、蒸汽等的能量来做某事物: *Work done by machines has replaced manual labour.* 机器生产已经代替了手工劳作. ○ *The work of calculating wages can be done by a computer.* 计算工资的事可以用计算机来做. **2** [U] (**a**) task, etc that is to be done, not necessarily connected with a trade or an occupation 待做的事(不一定与职业有关的): *There is plenty of work to be done in the garden.* 园子里有许多事要做. ○ *I have some work for you to do.* 我有些事要你做. ○ *You've done a good job of work.* 你做了一件很好的事. (**b**) materials needed or used for this 做事时需要的材料或工具: *She took her work* (eg papers or sewing materials) *with her into the garden.* 她把活计带到了园子里(如图纸或缝纫材料). ○ *She often brings work* (eg files, documents) *home with her from the office.* 她常把办公室的工作带回家去做(如文件等). ○ *His work was spread all over the floor.* 地板上到处都是他的工作用品. **3** [U] (**a**) thing or things produced as a result of work 制造物; 制作品; 成品: *an exhibition of the work of young sculptors* 年轻雕刻家的作品展览 ○ *He was very proud of his work.* 他为自己的作品感到自豪. ○ *Is this all your own work?* ie Did you do it without help from others? 这个作品是你独自做的吗? ○ *The craftsmen sell their work to visitors.* 这些手艺人把自己做的工艺品卖给前来参观的人. ○ *She produced an excellent piece of work in the final examination.* 她毕业考试创作成绩优秀. (**b**) result of an action; what is done by sb 行动的结果; 某人做的事: *The damage to the painting is the work of vandals.* 毁坏这幅画的事是恣意破坏公物的人干的. ○ (*ironic* 反语) *I hope you are pleased with your work — you've ruined everything!* 我希望你对自己做的事感到高兴了——你把一切都毁了! **4** [U] (**a**) what a person does as an occupation, esp in order to earn money; employment (作为职业的)工作(尤指为了挣钱的): *It is difficult to find work in the present economic situation.* 在目前的经济情况下很难找到工作. ○ *Many people are looking for work.* 许多人都在找工作. ○ *The accountant described his work to the sales staff.* 那个会计向营业部的职员介绍了自己的工作情况. ○ *unpaid/voluntary work* 无报酬的[义务的]工作 ○ [attrib 作定语] *work experience* 工作经历 ○ *work clothes* 工作服. (**b**) (not used with *the* 不与定冠词 the 连用) place where one does this 工作地点; 工作单位; 工作部门: *He has to leave work early today.* 他今天得早点儿下班. ○ *She goes to/leaves for work at 8 o'clock.* 她8点钟去上班. ○ *What time do you arrive at/get to work in the morning?* 你早晨几点钟上班? ○ *Her friends from work came to see her in hospital.* 她工作部门的朋友到医院来看望她. ⇨Usage 见所附用法. **5** (**a**) [C] piece of literary, musical or artistic composition; artistic creation 文学、音乐或艺术作品; 艺术创作: *Have you read her latest work?* 你读过她最近的作品吗? ○ *a new work on* (ie book about) *Elizabethan poetry* 论述伊丽莎白时代诗歌的新书 ○ *a new work by the composer of 'Cats'* 《猫》的作曲家的新作 ○ *He recognized the painting as an early work by Degas.* 他认出了这幅画是德加的早期作品. (**b**) **works** [pl] all the books written by a writer or the compositions of a composer (一个作家创作的)全部著作; (一个作曲家创作的)全部乐曲: *the collected/complete works of Shakespeare* 莎士比亚选集[全集] ○ *the works of Beethoven* 贝多芬的全部作品. Cf 参看 OPUS 1. **6** [U] (*physics* 物) use of force to produce movement 功; 作功. Cf 参看 JOULE. **7** [U] (in or forming compounds 用以构成复合词) (**a**) things made of or (the skill of) making things in the specified material (用某种材料)制造物品(的技艺)或其制成品: ˈ*wickerwork* ○ ˈ*woodwork* ○ ˈ*metalwork*. (**b**) things made or work done with the specified tool (用某种工具)制作或其制成品: ˈ*needlework* ○ ˈ*brushwork*. (**c**) ornamentation of a specified type 某种类型的装饰: ˈ*latticework* ○ ˈ*paintwork* ○ ˈ*filigree work*. (**d**) structure of the specified type 某种类型的结构: ˈ*framework* ○ ˈ*network* ○ ˈ*bodywork*. **8 the works** [pl] moving parts of a machine, etc; mechanism (机器等的)活动部件; 机械装置: *the works of a clock* 钟的活动部件 ○ *There's something wrong with the works.* 机械装置出故障了. **9 works** [pl] (esp in compounds 尤用以构成复合词) operations involving building or repair 建筑或维修的工程: ˈ*road-works* 道路施工 ○ ˌ*public* ˈ*works* 公共设施工程. **10 works** [sing or pl *v*] (esp in compounds 尤用以构成复合词) place where industrial or manufacturing processes are carried out 工厂: *the engi*ˈ*neering works* 机器制造厂 ○ *a* ˈ*brick-works* 砖厂 ○ *The* ˈ*steel works is/are closed for the holidays.* 这座钢厂假期停工. ○ *There has been an accident at the works.* 这家工厂出了一次事故. ⇨Usage at FACTORY 用法见 FACTORY. **11 the works** [pl] (*infml* 口) everything 所有的事物: *She was wearing a tiara, a diamond necklace and a gold bracelet — the works!* 她戴着个冕状头饰、一条钻石项链还有一个金手镯——全套首饰! **12** (idm 习语) **all in a day's work** ⇨ DAY. **at** ˈ**work**

(**a**) at the place where one works 在工作的地方: *Please don't ring me at work.* 打电话请不要打到我上班的地方. ○ *I've left my bag at work.* 我把提包落在上班的地方了. (**b**) having an effect; operating 在起作用; 在运转: *She suspected that secret influences were at work.* 她怀疑有些势力暗中作祟. **at work (on sth)** busy doing sth 忙着做某事物: *He is still at work on the restoration.* 他仍忙着做维修工作. ○ *They were watching the artist at work.* 他们看着那个艺术家忙个不停. **the devil makes work for idle hands** ⇨ DEVIL[1]. **dirty work** ⇨ DIRTY[1]. **get (down) to/go to/set to 'work (on sth/to do sth)** begin; make a start 开始; 着手干. **give sb/sth the 'works** (*infml* 口) (**a**) give or tell sb everything 把一切都给某人或都告诉某人. (**b**) give sb/sth the full or best possible treatment 全面或周到地对待某人[某事物]: *They gave the car the works and it looks like new.* 他们把这辆汽车彻底维修了一遍, 整旧如新. (**c**) treat sb harshly or violently 粗暴地对待某人. **go/set about one's 'work** do/start to do one's work 做[着手做]自己的工作: *She went cheerfully about her work.* 她高高兴兴地做她的工作. **,good 'works** acts of charity 善行; 善举: *do good works* 做善事. **gum up the works** ⇨ GUM[2]. **have one's 'work cut out (doing sth)** (*infml* 口) have sth difficult to do, esp in the available time 有困难的事要做(尤指在现有的时间内): *You'll have your work cut out getting there by nine o'clock.* 你得在九点钟以前赶到那里. **in 'work/out of 'work** having/not having a paid job 有[没有]工作: *She had been out of work for a year.* 她已失业一年了. ○ *He was looking forward to being in work again.* 他巴不得能再就业. ○ [attrib 作定语] *an ,out-of-work 'actor* 失业的演员. **make hard work of sth** ⇨ HARD[1]. **make light work of sth** ⇨ LIGHT[3]. **make short work of sth/sb** ⇨ SHORT[1]. **many hands make light work** ⇨ HAND[1]. **a nasty piece of work** ⇨ NASTY. **nice work if you can get it** ⇨ NICE. **put/set sb to 'work** make sb start working on sth 使某人开始做某事. **shoot the works** ⇨ SHOOT[1]. **a spanner in the works** ⇨ SPANNER. **the work of a 'moment, 'second, etc** thing that takes the specified (usu short) time to do 某段时间(通常指短时间)可做的事情: *It was the work of a few moments to hide the damage.* 只需一会儿就可以把损坏的地方遮掩起来.

□ **'work-basket** *n* container for sewing materials, needlework, etc 针线筐.

'work-bench *n* table at which a mechanic, carpenter, etc works 工作台.

'workbook *n* book that gives information on a subject and guidance for a student, with practice or exercises that he can do on his own 练习簿; 作业本.

'workday *n* (also **,working 'day**) (**a**) day on which one usu works 工作日: *Saturday is a workday for him.* 星期六是他的工作日. (**b**) day that is not a Sunday or holiday 非星期日或节假日的日子.

'work-force *n* [CGp] total number of workers employed (eg in a factory) or available for work 受雇的(如一工厂中的)或现有的工作人员总数; 劳动人口: *Ten per cent of the work-force will be made redundant.* 有百分之十的劳动力要裁减掉.

'work-horse *n* (**a**) horse that does work, eg pulling heavy loads 使役的马. (**b**) (*fig* 比喻) person who is relied upon by others to do a lot of hard work 大家赖以做重活儿的人: *He's a willing work-horse.* 他是个埋头苦干的老黄牛.

'workhouse (*Brit*) (formerly 旧时) public institution where very poor people were sent to live and given work to do 济贫院.

'work-load *n* amount of work (to be) done by sb 某人(需)做的工作量; 工作负担: *have a heavy work-load* 有很重的工作 ○ *reduce/increase sb's work-load* 减少[增加]某人的工作量.

'workman /-mən; -mən/ *n* (*pl* **-men**) (**a**) man who is employed to do manual or mechanical work (男)工人. (**b**) person who works in the specified way 以某种方式工作的人: *a good, neat, conscientious, etc workman* 工作出色的、仔细的、认真的...人 ○ *skilled/unskilled workmen* 技术熟练的[不熟练的]人 ○ (*saying* 谚) *A bad workman blames his tools.* 技术差的人埋怨工具差.

'workmanlike *adj* of or like a good workman; practical and skilful (似)优秀工人的; 技术娴熟的: *He did a very workmanlike job on it.* 他这件工作做得非常漂亮. ○ *The team produced a very workmanlike performance.* 这个队技巧表现得十分熟练. **'workmanship** *n* [U] (**a**) person's skill in working 手艺; 技艺: *They admired her workmanship.* 他们很钦佩她的手艺. (**b**) quality of this as seen in sth that has been made 工作质量; 工艺: *Our new washing-machine keeps breaking down — it's entirely due to shoddy workmanship.* 我们的新洗衣机老出毛病 —— 完全是因为做的质量太差.

,work of 'art fine picture, poem, building, sculpture, etc 精致的物品(精美的画、诗、建筑物、雕塑等): (*fig* 比喻) *The decoration on the cake was a work of art.* 这个蛋糕的装饰匠心独妙.

'workpeople *n* [pl] people who work in a business, factory, etc without any responsibility for its management; workers (无管理责任的)员工; 工人们.

'workpiece *n* thing (to be) worked on with a tool or machine (用工具或机器制作的)工作物.

'work-room *n* room in which work is done 工作室: *The watchmaker has a work-room at the back of his shop.* 这个钟表匠在他的店铺后面有个工作间.

'worksheet *n* paper on which work that has been done or is in progress is recorded 工作单; 加工单.

'workshop *n* (**a**) room or building in which machines, etc are made or repaired 车间; 工厂; 工场; 修理厂. (**b**) period of discussion and practical work on a particular subject, when a group of people share their knowledge and experience (针对某问题的)研讨与实践, 讲习班: *a poetry workshop* 诗歌研习会 ○ *a theatre workshop* 戏剧研讨班.

'work-shy *adj* (*derog* 贬) not inclined to work (hard); lazy 不愿(努力)工作的; 懒惰的.

'work study system of assessing people's work and working methods, intended to discover whether the work could be done more quickly or efficiently 工效研究.

'work-table *n* table on which work is done, esp one with drawers for eg sewing materials 工作台(尤指有抽屉的, 如盛缝纫材料的).

'work top (also **'work surface**) flat surface in a kitchen, on top of a cupboard, refrigerator, etc, used for preparing food, etc on (厨房的)工作面(柜橱、冰箱等的顶部, 用以制作食物等的).

NOTE ON USAGE 用法: **Job** and **task** are countable nouns indicating a piece of work that a person does. ☆ **job** 和 **task** 均为可数名词, 指人做的工作. **Job** is general and may be hard or easy, pleasant or unpleasant ☆ **job** 用得很广, 所指的工作或难或易, 或喜爱或厌恶均可: *Some people tackle the difficult jobs first.* 有的人爱先做难做的工作. ○ *I've been given the enjoyable job of presenting the prizes.* 要我做的工作是发奖这件美事. It can also refer to a long-term occupation. 这个词还可指长期的职业. A **task** is usually short-term and requires effort. ☆ **task** 通常指短期的且需努力做的工作. It may not be voluntary 这个词指的不一定是自愿做的工作: *The teacher gave the children holiday tasks.* 老师给小学生布置了假期作业. It can also refer to long-term objectives 这个词还可指长期的目标: *the important tasks facing the new government* 新政府面临的重要任务. **Work, labour** and **toil** are uncountable nouns indicating the activity needed to perform a job. ☆ **work**、**labour**、**toil** 均为不可数名词, 指做工作的行为. **Work** is the most general ☆ **work** 用得最广: *This job will require a lot of hard work.* 这项工作要十分努力才能做好. ○ *He's got a lot more work to do on the book.* 这本书他还有许多工作要做. **Labour** suggests physical effort ☆ **labour** 指体力劳动: *He was sentenced to 10 years' hard labour.* 他被判十年劳役. ○ *Manual labour has become unpopular with young people.* 体力劳动年轻人已经不喜欢做了. **Toil** is formal and is used of hard, lengthy work ☆ **toil** 较文, 用以指费力、费时的工作: *workers exhausted by years of toil* 长年辛劳而筋疲力竭的工人.

work[2] /wɜːk; wɝk/ *v* (*pt, pp* **worked** or, in archaic use, esp in sense 7, **wrought** 古语拼作 **wrought**, 尤用于下述第7义 /rɔːt; rɔt/) **1** [I, Ipr, Ip] **~ (away) (at/on sth); ~ (for sb/sth); ~ (under sb)** do work; engage in physical or mental activity 做工作; 从事体力劳动或脑力劳动: *Most people have to work in order to live,* ie to earn a living. 大多数人均须工作以维持生活. ○ *She isn't working now*, eg because she is unemployed or retired. 她现在不工作了(如已失业或退休). ○ *I've been working (away) (at my essay) all day.* 我整天都在(不停地)做着(我的论文). ○ *The miners work (for) 38 hours per week.* 这些矿工每星期工作(达)38小时. ○ *He is working on a new novel.* 他正在写一部新小说. ○ *She works for an engineering company.* 她在一家工程技术公司工作. ○ *I've worked under her* (ie with her as my boss) *for two years.* 我在她手下工作两年了. ○ *This craftsman works in leather*, ie makes leather goods, etc. 这个手艺人是做皮货的. **2** [Ipr, It] **~ against/for sth** make efforts to defeat sth or to achieve sth 努力反对某事物或促成某事物: *work against reform* 竭力反对改革 ○ *a statesman who works for peace* 为争取和平而努力的政治家 ○ *The committee is working to get the prisoners freed.* 委员会正尽力搭救那些遭监禁的人出狱. **3** **(a)** [I] (of a machine, device, etc) function; operate (指机器、设备等)运作, 运转: *a lift, bell, switch that doesn't work* 失灵的电梯、电铃、开关 ○ *The gears work smoothly.* 这个传动装置运转很灵活. ○ *This machine works by electricity.* 这台机器是电动的. **(b)** [I, Ipr] **~ (on sb/sth)** have the desired result or effect (on sb/sth) (对某人[某事物])产生预期的结果或作用: *Did the cleaning fluid work (on that stain)?* ie Did it remove it? 这种洗涤剂(对那块污斑)管用吗? ○ *My plan worked, and I got them to agree.* 我的想法奏效了, 我让他们同意了. ○ *His charm doesn't work on me*, ie doesn't affect or impress me. 他的魅力对我不起作用. **4** [Tn, Tn·pr] cause (oneself/sb/sth) to work; set (sth) in motion 使(自己[某人/某事物])工作; 开动(某物): *She works herself too hard.* 她把自己累坏了. ○ *Do you know how to work a lathe?* 你会开车床吗? ○ *This machine is worked by electricity.* 这台机器是电动的. ○ *Don't work your employees to death.* 别把你的雇员都累死. **5** [Tn] manage or operate (sth) to gain benefit from it 管理或经营(某事物)(以获利): *work a mine, an oil well* 经营一个矿、一个油井 ○ *He works the North Wales area*, eg as a salesman. 他在北威尔士地区做生意(如当推销员). **6** [Tn] produce or obtain (sth) as a result of effort; effect 努力产生或获得(某事物); 使奏效: *work harm, mischief, havoc* 造成伤害、损害、毁坏 ○ *work a cure, change, miracle* 获得痊愈、产生变化、创造奇迹. **7** [Tn, Tn·pr] **~ sth (into sth)** make or shape sth by hammering, kneading, pressing, etc (用锤、揉、压等方法)制作某物或给某物定形: *work gold, iron, etc* 打制金器、铁器等 ○ *work clay*, ie knead it with water 捏黏土 ○ *work dough*, ie when making bread 揉面团 ○ *work the mixture into a paste* 把这种混合物调成糊状 ○ *iron worked into ingots* 铸成锭的铁. Cf 参看 WROUGHT. **8** [Tn, Tn·pr] **~ sth (on sth)** make sth by stitching; embroider sth 缝制或绣制某物: *work (a design on) a cushion-cover* 缝制软垫的套(把图案绣在软垫的套上) ○ *work one's initials on a handkerchief* 把自己名字的首字母绣在手绢儿上. **9** [I] (of yeast) ferment (指酵)发酵. **10** [I] (of sb's features) move violently; twitch (指人的五官)抽动, 扭曲: *His lips worked as he tried to swallow the food.* 他使劲儿把食物咽下去, 嘴唇都扭曲起来. ○ *Her face worked as she stared at him in terror.* 她惊恐地注视着他, 脸也吓得抽动起来. **11** [Ipr, Ip, Tn·pr, Tn·p] (cause sth to) move, pass, etc into a new position, usu gradually or with an effort (使某物)移动到、经过...新的位置(通常指逐渐地或费力地): *Rain has worked in through the roof.* 雨水透过房顶逐渐渗进屋子里. ○ *The back of your shirt has worked out of your trousers.* 你衬衫的后摆已经抻到裤子外边来了. ○ *Work the stick into the hole.* 把棍子慢慢插进洞里. ○ *The story is too serious — can't you work a few jokes in?* 这个故事太正经八百了 —— 你能不能插进几个笑话? **12** [La, Cn·a] (cause sth/sb to) become (free, loose, etc) through pressure, vibration, etc (使某事物[某人])(通过压挤、振动等)变(松脱、松动等): *I was tied up, but managed to work (myself) free.* 我被捆绑起来, 但设法挣脱开了. ○ *The screw worked (itself) loose.* 那个螺丝钉松了. ○ *There's a piece of wood jammed under the door — can you work it clear?* 有块木头挤在门下面了 —— 你能把它弄掉吗? **13** (idm 习语) **work it, things, etc** (*infml* 口) arrange matters 把事情办成: *Can you work it so that we get free tickets?* 你能不能给我们弄几张免费票? ○ *How did you work that?* 你是怎么办成的? (For other idioms containing **work** see entries for *ns*, etc 与 **work** 搭配的其他习语见有关名词等的词条, 如 **work to rule** ⇨ RULE; **work one's way** ⇨ WAY[1].) **14** (phr v) **work around/round to sth/sb** gradually approach (a topic, subject, etc) 逐渐接近(一话题、问题等): *It was a long time before he worked around to what he really wanted to say.* 他说了半天才绕到他真正要说的问题上来.

work sth off get rid of sth by work or activity (通过工作或活动)除去, 消除: *work off a large bank loan* 还清银行大笔贷款 ○ *work off one's anger on sb* 把怒气发泄在某人身上 ○ *work off excess weight by regular exercise* 经常锻炼以减轻不正常的体重.

work out **(a)** develop in a specified way; turn out 按某种方式发展; 结果: *How will things work out?* 事情将成什么样子呢? ○ *Things worked out quite well.* 事情的结果很不错. **(b)** train the body by heavy physical exercise 做大运动量的锻炼: *I work out regulary to keep fit.* 我经常努力锻炼身体以保持健康. **(c)** be capable of being solved 能够解决: *a sum, problem, etc that won't work out* 解决不了的算术题、问题等. **work sb out** understand sb's nature 了解某人的禀性: *I've never been able to work her out.* 我一向无法了解她. **work sth out** **(a)** calculate sth 计算; 算出: *I've worked out your share of the expenses at £10.* 我已经计算出你应分摊的费用是10英镑. **(b)** find the answer to sth; solve sth 找出处理某事物的方法; 解决某事物: *work out a problem, puzzle, coded message, etc* 弄明白一难题、疑问、密码信息等 ○ *Can you work out what these squiggles mean?* 你能辩认出这些潦草的字迹是什么意思吗? **(c)** devise sth; plan sth 设计某事物; 计划某事物: *a well worked-out scheme* 精心设计的方法 ○ *The general worked out a new plan of attack.* 将军制定出了新的进攻方案. **(d)** (usu passive 通常用于被动语态) exhaust (a mine, etc) by taking out the ore, etc 挖尽(矿产等): *a worked-out silver mine* 挖尽了的银矿. **work out at sth** be equal to sth; have sth as a total 等于; 总计为: *The total works out at £10.* 总数为10英镑. ○ *What does your share of the bonus work out at?* 算出你应得的红利是多少?

work sb over (*sl* 俚) beat sb all over, eg to make him give information 痛打某人(如为逼出情报): *He'd been worked over by the gang for giving information to the police.* 他向警方提供情报而遭那群歹徒毒打.

work round to sth/sb ⇨ WORK AROUND/ROUND TO STH/SB.

work to sth follow (a plan, etc) 按(计划等)办事: *Be careful with the money and work to a budget.* 花钱需小心, 要按预算办事. ○ *Journalists have to work to tight deadlines*, ie have little time in which to do their work. 新闻工作者须在极有限的时间内工作.

work towards sth strive to reach or achieve sth 努力达到或完成某事物: *We're working towards common objectives.* 我们正在为达到共同的目标而努力.

work sth up **(a)** develop or improve sth gradually 逐步发展或改进某事物: *work up a business* 逐步发展生意 ○ *working up custom for our products* 逐渐扩展我们产品的用户范围. **(b)** increase sth in numbers or strength 增加某事物的数目或强度: *working up support for the party* 增强对该党的支持力量. **work sb/oneself up (into sth)** rouse sb/oneself to a state of excitement 使某人[自己]激动起来: *work sb into a rage, frenzy, etc* 使某人大怒、发狂等 ○ *Don't work yourself up/get worked up about something so trivial.* 不要为这点小事大动肝火. **work sth up into sth** bring sth to a more complete or more satisfactory state 使某事物达到较全面或满意的状态: *I'm working my notes up into a dissertation.* 我正在把我的笔记修改成论文. **work up to sth** develop to (a climax, etc) 发展到(顶峰等): *The music worked up to a rousing finale.* 该乐曲达到激动人心的高潮而结束.

□ ˈ**work-in** *n* (usu *sing* 通常作单数) form of protest in which workers occupy and run a factory, etc which is due to be closed 工人为反对工厂关闭而接管工厂的抗议形式.

ˌ**working-ˈover** *n* (usu *sing* 通常作单数) (*sl* 俚) physical beating of a person 殴打某人: *give sb a thorough working-over* 把某人痛打一顿.

ˈ**work-out** *n* period of intensive physical training 高强度体育锻炼(期间): *a boxer who has a work-out in the gym every day* 每天都在健身房苦练的拳击手.

ˌ**work-to-ˈrule** *n* form of protest by workers, in which they adhere strictly to the rules made by their employers and refuse to work overtime, etc 按章工作(工作人员严格按照雇主规定的章程办事, 拒不加班等的抗议形式).

work·able /ˈwɜ:kəbl; ˋwɝkəbḷ/ *adj* **1** that will work[2](3); practicable or feasible 行得通的; 切合实际的; 可行的: *a workable compromise, plan, scheme* 行得通的折衷办法、计划、方案. **2** that can be or is worth working (WORK[2] 5) 值得经营的: *The silver mine is no longer workable*, eg because it is flooded or because the ore is exhausted. 这个银矿不值得开采了(如因积水或矿石储量将尽).

work·aday /ˈwɜ:kədeɪ; ˋwɝkəˌde/ *adj* [attrib 作定语] not unusual or especially interesting; ordinary, everyday or practical 平凡的; 不太有趣的; 普通的; 日常的; 实际的: *workaday concerns* 平常的事.

work·aholic /ˌwɜ:kəˈhɒlɪk; ˌwɝkəˈhɔlɪk/ *n* (*derog or approv infml* 贬或褒, 口) person who works obsessively and finds it difficult to stop 拼命工作难以停止的人; 工作狂; 工作迷.

worker /ˈwɜ:kə(r); ˋwɝkɚ/ *n* **1** (**a**) (often in compounds 常用以构成复合词) person who works, esp one who does a particular type of work 工作的人, 工作者(尤指做某类型工作的): *car, factory, office, rescue workers* 汽车行业从业员、工人、职员、救援人员 ○ *The company provides houses for some of its workers.* 这家公司为某些工作人员提供住房. (**b**) person who works in the specified way 以某种方式工作的人: *a good, hard, quick, slow, etc worker* 做事做得好、努力、快、慢...的人. (**c**) (*infml* 口) person who works hard 努力工作的人: *That girl is certainly a worker!* 那个女的真肯干! **2** (**a**) employee, esp one who does manual or non-managerial work 雇员(尤指做体力工作或非管理性工作的); 工人: *The workers in the factory are paid by the hour and the clerical staff are paid a monthly salary.* 这个工厂工人按小时计酬, 职员按月领薪. ○ *Workers are in dispute with management about the redundancies.* 劳方现就裁员问题与资方争论. ○ [attrib 作定语] *worker participation in decision-making* 工人参与决策. (**b**) member of the working class 工人阶级的成员: *a workers' revolution* 工人阶级革命运动. **3** neuter or undeveloped female bee or ant that does the work of the hive or colony but cannot reproduce 工蜂; 工蚁: [attrib 作定语] *a worker bee* 工蜂. Cf 参看 DRONE[1] 1.

work·ing /ˈwɜ:kɪŋ; ˋwɝkɪŋ/ *adj* [attrib 作定语] **1** (**a**) engaged in work, esp manual labour; employed 做工作的; (尤指)从事体力劳动的; 受雇的: *the working man*, ie manual workers in general 工人 ○ *The meeting must be held at a time convenient for working mothers.* 会议召开的时间必须便于有孩子的女工参加. ○ *The working population of the country* (ie The proportion of the population that works or is available for work) *is growing smaller.* 这个国家的劳力正在减少. (**b**) of, for or suitable for work 工作上的; 为工作的; 适于工作的: *My working hours are (from) 9 to 5.* 我的工作时间是(从)9点到5点. ○ *She was still dressed in her working clothes.* 她还穿着工作服呢. ○ *The union has negotiated a 35-hour working week.* 工会经谈判确定为每星期工作35小时. ○ *She had spent all her working life in the factory.* 她一生的工作时间都是在这座工厂里度过的. ○ *Working conditions in the industry have improved greatly.* 这一行业的工作环境已有很大改善. ○ *a working breakfast/lunch*, ie one during which business is discussed 工作早餐[午餐](边就餐边研讨工作) ○ *He has a good working relationship with his boss.* 他和老板工作关系很好. **2** functioning or able to function 起作用的; 能运转的: *a working model of a steam engine* 蒸汽机的工作模型 ○ *The government has a working majority*, ie one that is sufficient to allow it to govern. 这个政府握有稳操胜券的多数票. **3** that is good enough as a basis for work, argument, etc and may be improved later; provisional 有起码的工作、辩论等的基础的; 临时的: *a working definition, hypothesis, theory* 暂定的定义、假设、理论 ○ *She has a working knowledge of French.* 她的法语尚可应付工作. **4** (idm 习语) **in (full) ˈworking order** (esp of a machine) able to function properly; running smoothly (尤指机器)能正常操作的, 灵活运转的.

▷ **work·ing** *n* **1** [C] (part of a) mine or quarry that is being or has been worked (WORK[2] 5) (正在开采的或已开采过的)矿坑, 采石场(的一部分): *The boys went exploring in some disused workings*, eg the shafts of an old tin mine. 那些男孩子到一些废弃的矿坑去探险(如旧锡矿的竖坑中). **2 workings** [pl] **~s (of sth)** (process involved in) the way a machine, an organization, a part of the body, etc operates (机器、组织、身体某部等的)工作方式或过程: *the workings of the human mind* 人的头脑的活动方式 ○ *It was impossible to understand the workings of such a huge bureaucracy.* 要想了解这样庞大的官僚体系的运作情况是不可能的.

□ ˌ**working ˈcapital** capital that is needed and used in running a business, and not invested in its buildings, equipment, etc 营业资本; 周转资本.

the ˈworking class (also **the ˈworking classes**) social class whose members do manual or industrial work for wages 工人阶级: *His duty as a politician was to represent the interests of the working class.* 他身为政治家的责任是代表工人阶级的利益. ○ [attrib 作定语] *working-class attitudes, families, origins* 工人阶级的看法、家庭、出身.

ˌ**working ˈday** (**a**) = WORKDAY (WORK[1]). (**b**) part of the day during which work is done 一天中的工作时间: *The unions are campaigning for a shorter working day.* 工会发起要求减少每日工作时间的运动.

ˈ**working party** group of people appointed (eg by a government department) to investigate sth and report or advise on it 工作组(受委任调查某事并做出报告或建议的小组, 如由政府部门委派的): *set up a working party to look into the matter* 成立一个工作组调查此事.

world /wɜ:ld; wɝld/ *n* **1 the world** [sing] (**a**) everything that exists; the universe 存在的一切事物; 世界; 宇宙: *the creation of the world* 天下万物的创造. (**b**) the earth with all its countries and peoples 地球及其所属的国家和民族; 世界: *a journey round the world* 环球旅行 ○ *travel (all over) the world* 游历(全)世界 ○ *The whole world would be affected by a nuclear war.* 整个世界都会受到核战争的波及. ○ *the rivers and oceans of the world* 地球上的河流和海洋 ○ *Pollution is one of the most important issues in the world today.* 污染问题是当今世界上最重要的问题之一. ○ *Which is the biggest city in the world?* 世界上最大的城市是哪个? ○ [attrib 作定语] *English is now a world language*, ie is used everywhere in the world. 英语现在是一种世界语. (**c**) particular section of the earth 地球上的某部分; 世界: *the eastern/western world* 东方[西方]世界 ○ *the ancient world* 古老的世界 ○ *the Roman world*, ie the part of the earth that the Romans knew 古罗马人的世界 ○ *the New World*, ie America 新世界(美洲) ○ *the Old World*, ie Europe, Asia and Africa 旧世界(欧、亚、非三洲) ○ *the English-speaking world*, ie those parts where English is spoken as the first language 说英语的地区. **2** [C] heavenly body that may be like the earth 近似地球的天体: *other worlds unknown to us beyond the stars* 除已知星体之外, 我们不了解的其他天体. **3** [C] time, state or scene of human existence 人类生存的时间、状况或现象: *this world and the next*, ie life on earth and existence after death 今世及来世 ○ *the world to come*, ie existence after death 来世 ○ *It's a sad world where there is such suffering.* 有这些苦难的地方就是个悲惨的世界. ○ *bring a child into/come into the world*, ie give birth to a child/be born 生孩子[出世]. **4 the world** [sing] (**a**) human affairs; active life 世事; 世情: *He showed no interest in the world around him.* 他对周围的一切都不感兴趣. ○ *know/see the world*, ie have experience of life 洞达世故[见世面] ○ (*rhet* 修辞) *How goes the world with you?* ie How are your affairs going? 你的情况怎样? (**b**) material or similar things and occupations (as contrasted with spiritual ones) 尘世(与精神世界相对): *the temptations of the world* 花花世界的诱惑 ○ *She decided to renounce the world and enter a convent.* 她决定弃绝尘世去当修女. **5 the world** [sing] (**a**) everybody (and everything) 每个人(及一切事物): *He wanted to tell the news to the world.* 他要把这件事告诉每一个人. ○ *The whole world seemed to be at the party.* 聚会上好像每个人都来了. ○ *She felt that the whole world was against her.* 她觉得人人都跟她作对. (**b**) fashionable or respectable society 时髦的或上流的社会: *I don't care what the world thinks.* 我不在乎上流社会怎样看. **6** [C] (often in compounds 常用以构成复合词) people or things belonging to a certain class or sphere of activity, interest, etc 属于某活动、兴趣等范围的人或事物; 范围; 界: *the world of art, politics, sport* 艺术、政治、体育界 ○ *the animal/insect world* 动物[昆虫]世界 ○ *the racing, scientific, theatre world* 赛马、科学、戏剧界 ○ *The medical world is divided on this issue.* 医学界在这个问题上有分歧. **7** (idm 习语) **be ˌall the ˈworld to sb** be very dear or very important to sb 对某人来说, 非常宝贵或非常重要. **be not long for this world** ⇨ LONG[3]. **the best of both worlds** ⇨ BEST[3]. **a brave new world** ⇨ BRAVE. **come/go ˈdown/ˈup in the world** become less/more important in society, successful in one's career, etc or poorer/richer 落魄[发迹]; 变穷[变富]: *They've come up in the world since I last met them.* 自从我上次见到他们以来, 他们已经发迹了. **dead to the world** ⇨ DEAD. **the end of the world** ⇨ END[1]. **for all the world like sb/sth/as if...** (usu expressing surprise 通常表示惊讶) very much or exactly like sb/sth or as if... 就像某人[某事物]; 好像...: *She carried on with her work for all the world as if nothing had happened!* 她继续做她的工作, 就好像什么事都没发生过一样! **(not) for (all) the ˈworld** whatever the inducement is or was 无论诱惑力有多大: *I wouldn't sell that picture for all the world.* 我无论如何也不卖那幅画. **how, what, where, who, etc on earth/in the world** ⇨ EARTH. **in the eyes of the world** ⇨ EYE[1]. **(be/live) in a world of one's ˈown** live a life of fantasy without communicating with other people 生活在自己的小天地之中. **it's a small world** ⇨ SMALL. **the John ˈSmiths, etc of this world** (*infml* 口) people like the person whose name is given 像(说出名字的)这一类人: *'I hear Peter Brown's doing very well.' 'The Peter Browns of this world always do well!'* '我听说彼得·布朗近来很好.' '像彼得·布朗这样的人情况总是很好.' **a man/woman of the ˈworld** person with a lot of experience of life, public affairs, business, etc, esp one who is not easily surprised or shocked 老成练达的人; 老成持重的人. **the next world** ⇨ NEXT[1]. **on top of the world** ⇨ TOP[1]. **ˌout of this ˈworld** (*infml* 口) absolutely wonderful, magnificent, beautiful, etc 好得不得了: *The meal was out of this world.* 这顿饭简直没治了. ○ *The scenery and costumes for the opera are out of this world.* 这个歌剧的布景和戏装顶刮刮. **the ˌoutside ˈworld** people, places, activities, etc that are not those of an enclosed community, group, profession, etc 外部世界(封闭式群体、组织、职业等以外的人、地方、活动等): *working in a remote village cut off from the outside world* 在一个与外界隔绝的偏僻村庄里工作. **set the ˈworld on fire** (*infml* 口) be very successful and cause great excitement 极为成功并引起轰动: *She does the job adequately but she's not going to set the world on fire!* 她工作做得不错, 但也不会有什么惊人之举! **think the world of sb/sth** ⇨ THINK[1]. **watch the world go by** ⇨ WATCH[2]. **the way of the world** ⇨ WAY[1]. **what is the world ˈcoming to?** (used as an expression of disapproving surprise, shock, complaint, etc at changes in attitudes, behaviour, etc 在评论态度、行为等发生变化时, 用以表示不以为然的惊讶、吃惊、抱怨等): *When I read the news these days I sometimes wonder what the world is coming to.* 我阅读近日的新闻报道, 有时觉得事情未免太不像话了. **a window on the world** ⇨ WINDOW. **with the best will in the world** ⇨ BEST[1]. **(all) the ˌworld and his ˈwife** (*infml* 口) large numbers of people, esp when assembled in a place as guests, holiday-makers, etc 许多人(尤指聚在一起的宾客、度假的人等): *The world and his wife were in Brighton that day!* 那天在布赖顿市人山人海! **the ˌworld, the ˌflesh and the ˈdevil** (*fml or rhet* 文或修辞) all that is not holy; all that tempts mankind to wickedness 一切坏事; 诱人作恶的一切事物. **the ˌworld is one's ˈoyster** one is able to enjoy all the pleasures and opportunities that life has to offer 能尽情享受生活中的一切快乐与机遇: *She left school feeling that the world was her oyster.* 她中学毕业了, 感到前途无限美好. **a/the ˈworld of difference, good, meaning, etc** (*infml* 口) a great deal of difference, etc 极大的差别、好处、意义等: *There's a world of difference in the performance of the two cars.* 这两辆汽车的性能有天壤之别. ○ *That holiday did him the world of good.* 这次度假对他大有好处. **the (whole) world ˈover** in any place in the world; everywhere 世界上的任何地方; 各处: *People are basically the same the world over.* 世界各地的人基本上都一样. **(think) the world owes one a ˈliving** (think that) one has a right to be provided for because one deserves it or simply because one exists (认为)生来就得过舒服日子: *It's no use thinking the world owes you a living, you know.* 你要知道, 光想着生来就得舒舒服服的, 那是白想. **(be) ˈworlds apart** completely different 完全不同: *We're worlds apart in our political views.* 我们的政治观点截然不同.

▷ **worldly** *adj* (**-ier**, **-iest**) (**a**) [attrib 作定语] of (the affairs of) the world, esp the pursuit of pleasure or material gain; not spiritual 世事的; (尤指)尘世的, 世俗的: *one's worldly goods*, ie property 个人的财产 ○ *worldly concerns, distractions, preoccupations, etc* 世俗的心思、乐趣、欲念等. (**b**) experienced in the affairs of life; sophisticated; practical 生活经验丰富的; 老成练达的; 实际的: *a worldly person* 老成持重的人 ○ *a few words of worldly wisdom* 人生的经验之谈. **world·li·ness** *n* [U]. **ˌworldly-ˈwise** *adj* [U] having or showing prudence and shrewdness in dealing with worldly matters 善于处世的.

□ **ˈworld-beater** *n* person or thing that is better than all others 举世无匹的人或事物: *She has enough talent as a player to be a world-beater.* 她很有天资, 能成为天下无敌的选手.

ˌworld-ˈclass *adj* as good as the best in the world 世界级的; 世界上一流的: *a ˌworld-class ˈauthor, ˈfootballer* 世界上一流的作家、足球健将 ○ *ˌworld-class ˈtennis* 世界级的网球运动.

ˌworld-ˈfamous *adj* known throughout the world 世界著名的: *a ˌworld-famous ˈfilm star* 世界著名的电影明星.

ˌworld ˈpower *n* country that has major influence in international politics 世界强国.

ˌworld ˈwar war that involves many important countries 世界大战: *a treaty designed to prevent a world war* 防止世界大战的条约 ○ *the First/Second World War* 第一次[第二次]世界大战 ○ *World War One/Two* 第一次[第二次]世界大战.

ˈworld-weary *adj* bored with life or tired of living 厌世的.

ˌworld-ˈwide *adj* found in or affecting the whole world 遍及全世界的; 影响世界的: *world-wide economic trends* 全世界的经济趋势 ○ *a ˌworld-wide ˈmarket* 世界市场. — *adv* all over the world 遍及世界各地: *Our product is sold world-wide.* 我们的产品行销世界各地.

worm 蠕虫

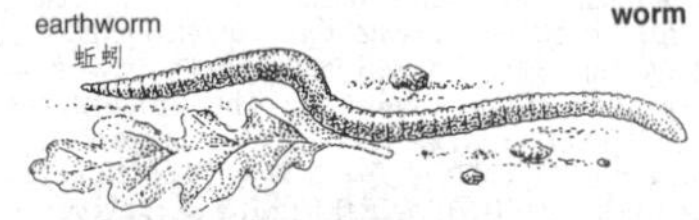

worm /wɜːm; wɝm/ *n* **1** (**a**) [C] small long thin creeping animal with a soft rounded or flattened body and no backbone or limbs 蠕虫: *There are a lot of worms in the soil.* 泥土中有许多蠕虫. ○ *an ˈearthworm* 蚯蚓. (**b**) [pl] worm that causes disease by living as a parasite in the intestines of a person or an animal 肠道寄生虫: *The dog has worms.* 这条狗有肠道寄生虫. (**c**) (esp in compounds 尤用以构成复合词) worm-like larva of an insect, esp in fruit or wood (似蠕虫的)昆虫幼虫(尤指果实或木中的): *The apples are full of worms.* 这些苹果里生了很多虫子. ○ *ˈwoodworm* 蛀木虫 ○ *ˈsilkworm* 蚕. **2** (usu *sing* 通常作单数) (*derog* 贬) person considered weak and insignificant and who is not respected by others 懦弱的、无足轻重的且不受尊重的人. **3** spiral part of a screw (螺钉的)螺旋部分. **4** (idm 习语) **a can of worms** ⇨ CAN[1]. **the early bird catches the worm** ⇨ EARLY. **the ˌworm will ˈturn** even a person who is normally quiet and does not complain will assert himself or rebel in an intolerable situation 老实人忍不住也得反抗.

▷ **worm** *v* **1** [Tn] treat (an animal, usu a cat or a dog) in order to get rid of the worms living in its intestines 为(动物, 通常指猫狗)驱虫: *We'll have to worm the dog*, ie by giving it medicine. 我们得给这条狗打打虫子了. **2** (phr v) **worm one's way/oneself along, through,**

etc move in the specified direction by crawling or wriggling, esp slowly or with difficulty 沿某方向爬行或蠕动(尤指缓慢而艰难地): *They had to worm their way through the narrow tunnel.* 他们得钻过狭窄的隧道. **worm one's way/oneself into sth** (*usu derog* 通常作贬义) establish oneself in sb's affection, confidence, etc, esp in order to deceive 获得某人的好感、信任等(尤指为行骗): *She used flattery to worm her way/herself into his confidence.* 她用阿谀奉承的手段骗取他的信任. **worm sth out (of sb)** obtain information (from sb) slowly and cunningly (从某人处)缓慢而狡诈地获取情报: *Eventually they wormed the truth out of her.* 他们最后从她那里得知了真相.

wormy *adj* **1** containing many worms 有很多蠕虫的: *wormy soil* 有很多蠕虫的土壤. **2** damaged by worms; wormeaten 被蠕虫损坏的; 蠕虫蛀的: *a wormy apple* 生虫的苹果.

□ ˈ**worm-cast** *n* small tubular pile of earth that is pushed up to the surface of the ground by an earthworm 蚯蚓粪.

ˈ**wormeaten** *adj* full of worm-holes 有很多蠕虫蛀的洞的.

ˈ**worm-hole** *n* hole left in wood, fruit, etc by a worm (木材、果实等上面的)由蠕虫蛀成的洞.

worm·wood /ˈwɜːmwʊd; ˈwɝmˌwʊd/ *n* [U] **1** woody plant with a bitter flavour, used in making some alcoholic drinks (eg absinthe) and medicines 蒿, 艾蒿, 洋艾(用以制艾酒和入药). **2** (experience that causes) intense bitterness, humiliation, shame, etc 极大的痛苦、侮辱、羞耻等; 造成这类感觉的经历.

worn[1] *pp of* WEAR[2].

worn[2] /wɔːn; wɔrn/ *adj* **1** damaged by use or wear (经使用或穿戴)破烂的, 损坏的: *These shoes are looking rather worn.* 这双鞋不成样子了. **2** (of a person) looking tired and exhausted (指人)看起来精疲力竭的: *She came back worn and worried.* 她回来时又疲乏又忧虑. **3** (idm 习语) **worn, etc to a frazzle** ⇨ FRAZZLE.

□ ˌ**worn-ˈout** *adj* **1** very worn and therefore no longer usable (过于破旧)不能再使用的: *a ˌworn-out ˈcoat* 破烂不堪的大衣. **2** [usu pred 通常作表语] (of a person) exhausted (指人)筋疲力尽: *You look worn-out after your long journey.* 你走了很长的路, 看上去风尘仆仆.

wor·ri·some /ˈwʌrɪsəm; ˈwɝɪsəm/ *adj* (*dated* 旧) causing worry; troublesome 令人忧虑的; 令人烦恼的.

worry /ˈwʌrɪ; ˈwɝɪ/ *v* (*pt, pp* **worried**) **1** [I, Ipr] ~ **(about sb/sth)** be anxious (about sb, difficulties, the future, etc) (对某人、困难、前途等)担忧, 担心, 发愁: *'Don't worry,' she said, putting an arm round his shoulder.* '别发愁了,' 她边说边用手臂搂住他的肩膀. ○ *Don't worry if you can't finish it.* 你做不完也不必担心. ○ *Your parents are worrying about you: do write to them.* 你父母正担心你呢, 快给他们写封信吧. ○ *There's nothing to worry about.* 没什么可愁的. **2** [Tn, Tn·pr] ~ **sb/oneself (about sb/sth)** make sb/oneself anxious or troubled (about sb/sth) (对某人[某事物])使某人[自己]担忧、担心或发愁: *What worries me is how he will manage now his wife's died.* 他妻子死了, 我担心的是他可怎么办. ○ *I don't want to worry you, but...* 我不想让你担心, 但是... ○ *She worried herself sick/She was worried sick about her missing son.* 她儿子失踪可把她愁坏了. ○ *Many people are worried by the possibility of a nuclear accident.* 许多人都很担心怕可能发生核事故. ○ *It worries me that they haven't answered my letters.* 他们一直没给我回信, 叫人担心. **3** [Tn, Tn·pr] ~ **sb (with sth)** annoy or disturb sb; bother sb 烦扰或打扰某人; 打搅某人: *Don't worry her now; she's busy.* 现在别打扰她, 她正忙着呢. ○ *The noise doesn't seem to worry them.* 这种噪声好像并不影响他们. **4** [Tn] (esp of a dog) seize (sth) with the teeth and shake or pull it about (尤指狗)叼住(某物)甩或拉: *The dog was worrying a rat.* 那条狗撕咬着一只老鼠. **5** (idm 习语) ˌ**not to ˈworry** (*infml* 口) do not worry; let us not worry 别担心; 咱们不必发愁: *We've missed the train, but not to worry, there's another one in ten minutes.* 我们没赶上火车, 但是别着急, 十分钟后还有一趟呢.

▷ **wor·ried** *adj* ~ **(about sb/sth)**; ~ **(that...)** feeling or showing worry about sb/sth; anxious 担忧的; 担心的; 发愁的: *be worried about one's weight, one's job, one's husband* 为自己的体重、工作、丈夫担心 ○ *I was worried that you wouldn't come back.* 我担心你不回来了. ○ *There's no need to look so worried!* 不必那么愁眉苦脸的! ○ *Worried relatives waited at the airport.* 亲属们都焦急地在机场等着. **wor·riedly** *adv.*

wor·rier *n* person who worries a lot 爱担忧的人; 常发愁的人: *Don't be such a worrier!* 别总那么愁眉苦脸的!

worry *n* **1** [U] state of being worried; anxiety 担忧; 担心; 忧愁: *Worry and illness had made him prematurely old.* 他心事重重、疾病缠身, 落得个未老先衰. **2** [C] thing that causes one to worry; cause of anxiety 令人担忧的事物; 忧愁的根源: *He has a lot of financial worries at the moment.* 他现在有很多财务上的烦恼事. ○ *Forget your worries and enjoy yourself!* 不要想那些愁事, 痛快痛快吧! **3** [C usu *sing* 通常作单数] thing that sb is responsible for 某人负责的事情: *Transport? That's your worry!* 交通问题? 那是你负责的事!

wor·ry·ing *adj* **1** causing worry 令人担忧的; 使人发愁的: *worrying problems* 叫人忧虑的问题. **2** full of worry 忧心忡忡的: *It was a very worrying time for them.* 那时他们十分忧虑.

worse /wɜːs; wɝs/ *adj* (*comparative of* BAD[1] ☆ BAD[1]一词的比较级) **1** ~ **(than sth/doing sth)** of a less excellent or desirable kind 更坏的; 更糟的; 更差的: *The weather got worse during the day.* 白天天气更坏了. ○ *The interview was far/much worse than he had expected.* 那次面试比他想的糟得多. ○ *prevent an even worse tragedy* 防止更惨的事 ○ *The economic crisis is getting worse and worse.* 经济危机越来越严重了. ○ *You are only making things worse.* 你反倒把事情弄得更糟了. Cf 参看 WORST. **2** [pred 作表语] in or into worse health 健康恶化; 身体更差: *If he gets any worse, we must phone for an ambulance.* 要是他情况恶化, 我们就得打电话叫救护车了. Cf 参看 BETTER[1]. **3** (idm 习语) **sb's bark is worse than his bite** ⇨ BARK[2]. **be none the ˈworse (for sth)** be unharmed (by sth) (经某遭遇)未受伤害: *The children were none the worse for their adventure.* 孩子们经历这一惊险事倒没受到伤害. **better/worse still** ⇨ STILL[2]. **be the worse for drink** be drunk 喝醉的. **a fate worse than death** ⇨ FATE. **make matters/things ˈworse** worsen a situation or condition that is already difficult or dangerous 使情况更困难或更危险: *To make matters worse, he refused to apologize.* 更糟的是他拒不道歉. **so much the better/worse** ⇨ BETTER[3]. **the ˌworse for ˈwear** (*infml* 口) worn, damaged or tired 破旧的; 损坏的; 疲倦的: *Your copy of the dictionary is looking a bit the worse for wear.* 你这本词典看来有点儿太旧了. ○ *Bill came home from the pub considerably the worse for wear*, ie drunk. 比尔喝得醉醺醺的从酒馆回到家里. ˌ**worse ˈluck!** (*infml* 口) (as a comment on sth that has been mentioned) which is unfortunate or a pity (用以评论所提到的事情)不幸, 可惜: *I shall have to miss the party, worse luck!* 我参加不了这次聚会了, 真可惜!

▷ **worse** *adv* **1** more badly 更坏; 更糟; 更差地: *He is behaving worse than ever.* 他表现得更坏了. Cf 参看 WORST *adv*. **2** more intensely (than before) (比以前)更强烈, 更严重: *It's raining worse than ever.* 雨下得更大了. **3** (idm 习语) **be ˌworse ˈoff** be poorer, unhappier, less healthy, etc than before 比以前更穷、更不愉快、更不健康等: *The increase in taxes means that we'll be £30 a month worse off.* 加税后我们每月收入就要少了30英镑. ○ *I've only broken my arm; other patients are far worse off than me.* 我只是胳膊折了, 其他病人比我严重得多.

worse *n* **1** [U] worse thing(s) 更坏的事物: *I'm afraid there is worse to come.* 我看更糟的还在后头呢. **2** (idm 习语) **can/could do worse than do sth** be correct or sensible in doing sth 做某事是正确的或可取的: *If you want a safe investment, you could do a lot worse than put your money in the building society.* 要想投资而不冒风险, 不如把钱投资到房屋建筑协会. **a change for the better/worse** ⇨ CHANGE[2]. **for better or worse** ⇨ BETTER[3]. **go from ˌbad to ˈworse** (of unsatisfactory conditions, etc) become even worse (指不如意的情况等)越来越坏, 每况愈下: *Under the new management things have gone from bad to worse.* 在新的管理人员领导下, 情况反而更坏了.

worsen /ˈwɜːsn; ˈwɝsn̩/ *v* [I, Tn] (cause sth to) become worse (使某事物)更坏, 恶化: *The patient's condition worsened during the night.* 病人的情况在夜间恶化了. ○

W

the worsening economic situation 每况愈下的经济形势 ○ *The drought had worsened their chances of survival.* 出现干旱后他们就更难活命了.

wor·ship /ˈwɜːʃɪp; ˋwɝʃəp/ *n* **1** [U] (**a**) reverence, respect or love for God or a god (对上帝或神的)崇拜、崇敬或热爱: *an act of worship* 对神的崇拜举动 ○ *a place of worship*, eg a church, mosque or synagogue 拜神的地方(如教堂、清真寺或犹太会堂). (**b**) act or ceremony that shows this 礼拜; 礼拜仪式: *Morning worship begins at 11 o'clock.* 早晨的礼拜从11点开始. ○ *a service of divine worship* 拜神的仪式. **2** [U] admiration, devotion or love felt for sb/sth 对某人[某事物]的崇拜、仰慕、忠心或热爱: *hero-worship* 对英雄的崇拜. **3 his, your, etc Worship** [C] (*esp Brit*) formal and polite form of address or way of referring to a magistrate or a mayor 阁下(对地方法官或市长的尊称): *His Worship the Mayor of Chester* 切斯特市长阁下 ○ *No, your Worship.* 不, 法官阁下.

▷ **wor·ship** *v* (**-pp-**; *US* **-p-**) **1** (**a**) [Tn] give worship to (God) 崇拜、崇敬或热爱(上帝). (**b**) [I] attend a church service 参加礼拜仪式; 做礼拜: *the church where they had worshipped for years* 他们多年做礼拜的教堂. **2** [Tn] feel love and admiration for (sb/sth), esp to such an extent that one cannot see his/its faults; idolize 爱慕, 崇拜(某人[某事物])(尤指达到看不到缺点的地步): *She worshipped him and refused to listen to his critics.* 她很崇拜他, 听不进别人对他的批评. ○ *worship success* 仰望成功 ○ *He worships the ground she walks on*, ie feels intense love for her. 他爱她爱得如醉如痴. **wor·ship·per** (*US* **wor·shiper**) *n* person who worships (对上帝或神)崇拜的人; 做礼拜的人; (对某人[某事物])爱慕的人.

wor·ship·ful /-fl; -fəl/ *adj* **1** [attrib 作定语] showing or feeling reverence, respect and love 崇拜的; 崇敬的; 敬爱的. **2 Worshipful** (*fml* 文 *esp Brit*) title used to address or refer to various distinguished people or bodies用作多种著名的人或团体的称号: *the Worshipful Company of Goldsmiths* (伦敦)金业协会.

worst /wɜːst; wɝst/ *adj* (*superlative of* BAD[1] ☆ BAD[1]一词的最高级) **1** of the least excellent, desirable, suitable, etc kind 最坏的; 最糟的; 最差的: *It was the worst storm for years.* 这场暴风雨是多年来最厉害的. ○ *one of the worst cases of child abuse he'd ever seen* 他见过的虐待儿童最残忍的一例 ○ *This is the worst essay I've read.* 这是我看过的最差的文章. ○ *What you've told me confirms my worst fears*, ie proves they were right. 你说的话证实了我最担心的事(果然属实). Cf 参看 WORSE. **2** (idm 习语) **one's ˌown worst ˈenemy** person whose own faults are worse than the bad things that have happened to him; the cause of one's own misfortunes 自讨苦吃的人; 自己不幸的根源: *With her indecisiveness, she is her own worst enemy.* 她优柔寡断, 自己害了自己.

▷ **worst** *adv* most badly 最坏; 最糟; 最差: *Bill played badly, James played worse, and I played worst of all!* 比尔演奏得很差, 詹姆斯演奏得更差, 我演奏得最差! ○ *Manufacturing industry was worst affected by the fuel shortage.* 由于燃料短缺受到影响, 制造业首当其冲. ○ *He is one of the worst dressed men I know.* 他在我认识的人里穿着最差. Cf 参看 WORSE *adv*.

W

worst *n* **1 the worst** [sing] the most bad part, state, event, possibility, etc 最坏的部分、情况、事情、可能性等: *The worst of the storm is now over.* 暴风雨最厉害的一阵现在已经过去了. ○ *When they did not hear from her, they feared the worst.* 他们那时听不到她的消息, 唯恐发生了最糟的事. ○ *I was prepared for the worst when I saw the wrecked car.* 我见到了出事的汽车, 心里已经想到了最坏的可能性. ○ *She was always optimistic, even when things were at their worst.* 她即使在最糟糕的时候也总是非常乐观. ○ *The worst of it is that I can't even be sure if they received my cheque.* 最糟糕的是我都不清楚他们是否收到了我的支票. **2** (idm 习语) **at (the) ˈworst** if the worst happens 若出现最坏的情况: *At worst we'll have to sell the house so as to settle our debts.* 实在没办法我们就得把房子卖了还债. **bring out the best/worst in sb** ⇨ BEST[3]. **do one's ˈworst** be as difficult, unpleasant, harmful, etc as possible 做出最坏的事: *We'll carry on as arranged and they can do their worst.* 我们还按我们的计划办事, 他们想怎么使坏就随他们便吧. **get the ˈworst of it** be defeated 被打败: *The dog had been fighting and had obviously got the worst of it.* 那条狗打过架而且显然吃了败仗. **if the ˌworst comes to the ˈworst** if circumstances become too difficult or dangerous; if the plan fails 若情况太困难或太危险; 若计划失败: *If the worst comes to the worst, we'll have to cancel our holiday plans.* 要是情况不妙, 我们就只好取消度假计划了.

worst *v* [Tn] defeat (sb) in a fight or competition 在斗争或竞争中打败(某人): *England were worsted in the replay.* 英格兰队在重赛中败北.

wors·ted /ˈwʊstɪd; ˋwʊstɪd/ *n* [U] (**a**) fine twisted woollen yarn or thread 精纺的毛纱或绒线. (**b**) cloth made from this 精纺毛料: [attrib 作定语] *a worsted suit* 一套毛料西装.

worth /wɜːθ; wɝθ/ *adj* [pred 作表语] **1** having a certain value 有某种价值: *Our house is worth about £60 000.* 我们的房子约值60 000英镑. ○ *I paid only £3 000 for this used car but it's worth a lot more.* 我只花了3 000英镑就买下了这辆旧汽车, 其价值远不止这些. ○ *What's the old man worth?* ie What is the value of his possessions? 这个老先生的财产值多少钱? ○ *This contract isn't worth the paper it's written on*, ie It is worthless. 这份合同的价值还比不上写合同的这张纸呢. **2** (sometimes followed by the *-ing* form of a *v* 有时后接动词的 -ing 形式) giving or likely to give a satisfactory or rewarding return for (doing sth) 值得(做某事); 有(做某事)的价值: *The book is worth reading/It's worth reading the book.* 这本书值得一读. ○ *He felt that his life was no longer worth living.* 他觉得他的生命已经没有再活下去的价值了. ○ *It's an idea that's worth considering.* 这是个值得考虑的意见. ○ *It's such a small point that it's hardly worth troubling about.* 这个问题很小, 不值得研究. ○ *It's not worth the effort/the trouble.* 不值得费那个事. ○ *The scheme is well worth a try.* 这个计划倒值得一试. **3** (idm 习语) **a bird in the hand is worth two in the bush** ⇨ BIRD. **for ˌall one is ˈworth** (*infml* 口) with all one's energy and effort 竭尽全力: *The thief ran off down the road, so I chased him for all I was worth.* 那个贼顺着马路逃跑, 我就拼命紧追不舍. **for ˌwhat it's ˈworth** however much or little importance or value sth has 无论某事物价值如何: *And that's my opinion, for what it's worth.* 这就是我的意见, 也别管有用没用吧. **the game is not worth the candle** ⇨ GAME[1]. **not worth a ˈdamn, a ˈstraw, a ˈred cent, a tinker's ˈcuss, etc** (*infml* 口) worthless 毫无价值: *Their promises are not worth a damn.* 他们的承诺分文不值. **ˈworth it** certain or very likely to repay the money, effort or time given 很值得: *The new car cost a lot of money, but it's certainly worth it.* 买这辆新汽车花了很多钱, 但确实物有所值. ○ *I don't bother to iron handkerchiefs — it's not worth it.* 我可不费那个事去熨手绢儿——犯不上. **ˌworth one's ˈsalt** deserving what one earns; doing one's job competently 值得雇用; 称职: *Any teacher worth his salt knows that.* 只要不是混饭吃的教师, 都明白这一点. **ˌworth one's/its ˌweight in ˈgold** extremely helpful, useful, etc; invaluable 非常有用的; 无价的: *A reliable car is worth its weight in gold.* 靠得住的汽车就是无价之宝. **ˌworth sb's ˈwhile** profitable or interesting to sb 对某人有利益或有好处: *It would be (well) worth your while/You would find it (well) worth your while to come to the meeting.* 你要是参加了这个会议就会觉得很有好处. ○ *They promised to make it worth her while* (ie pay or reward her) *if she would take part.* 他们许诺说她要是参加就一定给她报酬.

▷ **worth** *n* [U] **1 ~ of sth** (preceeded by a *n* indicating amount, duration, etc 用于表示数量、持续时间等的名词之后) (**a**) amount of sth that a specified sum of money will buy (某物的)值某金额的量: *The thieves stole £1 million worth of jewellery.* 窃贼偷走了价值100万英镑的珠宝. ○ *ten pounds' worth of petrol* 十英镑的汽油. (**b**) amount of sth that will last for a specified length of time (某物的)能持续某段时间的量: *a day's worth of fuel* 能用一天的燃料 ○ *two weeks' worth of supplies* 能维持两个星期的供应品. **2** value or usefulness 价值; 用处: *items of great, little, not much, etc worth* 很有、简直没有、没什么...用处的物件 ○ *people of worth in the community* 社区里的重要人物. **worth·less** *adj* **1** having no value or usefulness 无价值的; 没用的: *worthless old rubbish* 没用的破烂货 ○ *This contract is now worthless.*

这份合同现在毫无价值了. **2** (of a person) having bad qualities (指人)品质坏的: *a worthless character* 品质坏的人. **worth·less·ness** *n* [U].

□ **worthwhile** /wɜːθˈwaɪl; ˌwɝθˈwaɪl/ *adj* important, interesting or rewarding enough to justify the time, money or effort that is spent 值得的; 值得花时间、钱或精力的: *It's worthwhile taking the trouble to explain a job fully to new employees.* 给新雇员详细解释一下工作要求, 费点事也是值得的. ○ *Nursing is a very worthwhile career.* 护理工作是很值得干的职业.

worthy /ˈwɜːðɪ; ˈwɝðɪ/ *adj* **(-ier, -iest) 1** [pred 作表语] **~ of sth/to do sth** deserving sth or to do sth 应得某事物; 值得做某事: *Their efforts are worthy of your support.* 他们这样努力应得到你的支持. ○ *a statement worthy of contempt* 应该鄙弃的说法 ○ *Her achievements are worthy of the highest praise.* 她的成就值得给予最高赞赏. ○ *She said she was not worthy to accept the honour they had offered her.* 她说她不配接受他们给予的荣誉. **2** [usu attrib 通常作定语] **(a)** (*approv* 褒) deserving respect or consideration 值得尊敬的; 值得考虑的: *a worthy cause* 崇高的事业 ○ *a worthy record of achievements* 以往的突出的成就. **(b)** (*usu joc* 通常作戏谑语) (esp of a person) deserving respect or recognition (尤指人)应受到尊敬或赏识的: *the worthy citizens of the town* 该镇中应受敬重的市民. **3** [pred 作表语] **~ of sb/sth** (*usu approv* 通常作褒义) **(a)** suitable for sth 适合于某事物: *It was difficult to find words worthy of the occasion.* 很难找到适合于那种场合的言词. **(b)** typical of sb/sth 某人[某事物]的典型: *It was a performance worthy of a master.* 那是大师的典型表演.

▷ **wor·thily** /-ɪlɪ; -ɪlɪ/ *adv*.

wor·thi·ness *n* [U].

worthy *n* (*esp joc* 尤作戏谑语) person of importance or distinction 要人; 俊杰: *One of the local worthies has been invited to the ceremony* 本地的一个大人物已被邀请参加典礼.

-worthy (forming compound *adjs* 用以构成复合形容词) deserving of or suitable for the thing specified 值得...的; 应...的; 适于...的: *noteworthy* ○ *roadworthy*.

would[1] /wəd; wəd; *strong form* 强读式 wʊd; wʊd/; *modal v* (*contracted form* 缩约式 **'d** /d; d/; *neg* 否定式 **would not**, *contracted form* 缩约式 **wouldn't** /ˈwʊdnt; ˈwʊdn̩t/) **1 (a)** (used to describe the consequence of an imagined event 用以表示一设想事情的结果): *If he shaved his beard he would look much younger.* 他要是把胡子刮了就少相多了. ○ *If you went to see him, he would be delighted.* 倘若你去看他, 他一定非常高兴. ○ *I would think about it very carefully, if I were you.* 我要是你的话, 我就十分慎重地考虑这件事. **(b)** (used with *have* + a past participle to describe a hypothetical action or event in the past 与 have + 过去分词连用, 表示假想的过去的动作或事情): *If I had seen the advertisement I would have applied for the job.* 我要是看见那个广告了, 我就申请那份工作了. ○ *If she hadn't gone back for the letter, she wouldn't have missed the bus.* 要不是她回去取信, 她就不至于错过那辆公共汽车了. **(c)** (used to describe a hypothetical action or event in the present 用以表示假想的现在的动作或事情): *She'd be a fool to accept*, ie if she accepted. 她要是接受, 她就是个傻瓜. ○ *Don't call her now — it would make us late.* 别现在给她打电话——现在打的话, 我们就迟到了. ○ *It would be difficult to make an accurate forecast.* 预报很难准确. ○ *It would be a pity to miss the main film.* 要是赶不上看这部电影的正片就太可惜了. ○ *I would start from this end.* 要是开始做, 我就从这一头开始. ○ *Would I be able to help?* 我能帮上忙吗? **2 (a)** (used in making polite requests 用以提出客气的请求): *Would you pay me in cash, please?* 请您付给我现金行吗? ○ *You wouldn't have the time to phone him now, would you?* 您现在没有那么多时间给他打电话, 是吧? **(b)** (used with *imagine, say, think*, etc to give tentative opinions 与 imagine、say、think 等连用, 表达试探性的意见): *I would imagine the operation will take about an hour.* 我猜想这个手术大概需要一个小时左右吧. **3 (a)** (used in offers or invitations 用以提出建议或邀请): *Would you like a sandwich?* 您想吃三明治吗? ○ *Would they like to sit down?* 请他们坐下好吗? ○ *Would she like to borrow my bicycle?* 她想借用我的自行车吗? **(b)** (used with *like, love, hate, prefer, be glad/happy*, etc to express preferences 与 like、love、hate、prefer、be glad/happy 等连用, 表达较合意愿的做法): *I'd love a coffee.* 我倒想喝杯咖啡. ○ *I'd hate you to think I was criticizing you.* 我可不愿意让你觉得我是在批评你. ○ *I'd be only too glad to help.* 我非常愿意帮帮忙. **4** (used when commenting on characteristic behaviour 用以评论特有的行为): *That's just what he* ˈ*would say*, ie what he might be expected to say. 他就是爱说这种话. ○ *It* ˈ*would rain* (ie How typical it is of our weather that it should rain) *on the day we chose for a picnic!* 我们哪天去野餐, 它哪天就准下雨! **5** (used after *so that, in order that* to express purpose 用于 so that、in order that 之后, 表示目的): *She burned the letters so that her husband would never read them.* 她把信都烧了, 这样一来她丈夫就绝对看不见了. ⇨Usage 3 at MAY 见 MAY 所附用法第 3 项.

□ ˈ**would-be** *adj* [attrib 作定语] having the hope of becoming (the type of person specified) 有希望成为(所说的那样的人)的: *a would-be artist, model, bride, etc* 即将成为艺术家、模特儿、新娘...的人.

would[2] *pt* of WILL[1].

wound[1] /wuːnd; wund/ *n* **1 (a)** injury caused deliberately to part of the body by cutting, shooting, etc, esp as the result of an attack 伤, 创伤(尤指受攻击造成的): *He died after receiving two bullet wounds in the head.* 他头部中了两颗子弹而死. ○ *The wound was healing slowly.* 伤口慢慢愈合了. **(b)** cut or tear done to the outer surface of a plant or tree (对花草树外皮的)切割或剥离. **2 ~ (to sth)** hurt done to a person's feelings, reputation, etc (对人的感情、名誉等的)伤害: *deep psychological wounds* 很深的心理创伤 ○ *The defeat was a wound to his pride.* 这次失败伤了他的自尊心. **3** (idm 习语) **lick one's wounds** ⇨ LICK. **rub salt into the wound/sb's wounds** ⇨ RUB[2].

▷ **wound** *v* [Tn esp passive 尤用于被动语态] **1** give a wound to (sb) 伤, 伤害(某人): *Ten soldiers were killed and thirty seriously wounded.* 有十名士兵阵亡, 三十名重伤. ○ *The guard was wounded in the leg.* 护卫员腿部受了伤. **2** hurt (sb's feelings, reputation, etc) 伤, 伤害(某人的感情、名誉等): *He was/felt deeply wounded by their disloyalty.* 因为他们不忠, 他十分伤心. ○ *wounding criticism* 伤人感情的批评. **the wounded** *n* [pl *v*] wounded people 受伤的人; 伤员: *The hospital was full of the sick and wounded.* 医院里挤满了伤病员. ○ *Many of the wounded died on their way to hospital.* 许多伤员死在去医院的途中了.

NOTE ON USAGE 用法: **Wound** and **injure** both indicate physical damage to the body. ☆ **wound** 和 **injure** 均指对身体的伤害. A person is **wounded** by a sharp instrument or bullet tearing the flesh. ☆ **wound** 指利器或子弹对肉体造成的伤害. It is a deliberate action, often connected with battles and war. 这种伤害是故意的行为, 常与作战及战争有关. People are usually **injured** in an accident, eg with a machine or in sport. ☆ **injure** 通常指人在意外事故中受到的伤害, 如由机器造成的或在运动中受到的伤害. Compare *In a war there are many more wounded than killed* and *In the coach crash 10 people died and 18 were seriously injured.* 试比较这两个句子: '在一场战争中, 受伤的远比死亡的人多' 和 '在这次旅游车撞车事故中, 有 10 人死亡, 18 人重伤'. **Hurt** may be as serious as **injure** or it may relate to a minor pain ☆ **hurt** 指的伤害可与 **injure** 同样严重, 也可指比较轻的疼痛: *They were badly hurt in the accident.* 他们在事故中受了重伤. ○ *I hurt my back lifting that box.* 我抬那个箱子的时候伤了后背.

wound[2] *pt, pp* of WIND[3].

wove *pt* of WEAVE.

woven *pp* of WEAVE.

wow[1] /waʊ; waʊ/ *interj* (*infml* 口) (used to express astonishment or admiration 用以表示惊奇或钦佩): *Wow! That car certainly goes fast!* 嘿! 那辆汽车开得可真叫快!

▷ **wow** *n* [sing] (*sl* 俚) very great success 极大的成功: *The new play at the National Theatre's a wow.* 国家剧院上演的那出新剧极为轰动.

wow *v* [Tn] (*sl* 俚 *esp US*) fill (sb) with admiration or enthusiasm; impress greatly 激发(某人)仰慕或欣喜

W

之情；使大为赞赏：*The new musical wowed them on Broadway.* 那出新的歌舞喜剧在百老汇众口交赞.

wow[2] /waʊ; waʊ/ *n* [U] variation in the pitch of sounds reproduced from a record or tape, resulting from changes in the speed of the motor 音高失真（发动机速度变化造成的唱片或录音带发出的走音现象）. Cf 参看 FLUTTER *n* 3.

WP /ˌdʌbljuː ˈpiː; ˌdʌbljʊ ˋpi/ *abbr* 缩写 = word processing; word processor: *typing a letter on the WP* 用文字处理机打一封信.

wpb /ˌdʌbljuː piː ˈbiː; ˌdʌbljʊ pi ˋbi/ *abbr* 缩写 = (*Brit infml* 口) waste-paper basket.

WPC /ˌdʌbljuː piː ˈsiː; ˌdʌbljʊ pi ˋsi/ *abbr* 缩写 = (*Brit*) woman police constable 女警察：*WPC (Linda) Green* （琳达·）格林女警察. Cf 参看 PC 1, PW.

wpm /ˌdʌbljuː piː ˈem; ˌdʌbljʊ pi ˋɛm/ *abbr* 缩写 = words per minute 每分钟字数：*60 wpm*, eg typing, taking shorthand, etc 每分钟60个字（如打字、速记等）.

WPS /ˌdʌbljuː piː ˈes; ˌdʌbljʊ pi ˋɛs/ *abbr* 缩写 = (*Brit*) woman police sergeant 女巡佐：*WPS (Jane) Bell* （简·）贝尔女巡佐. Cf 参看 PS 1.

WRAC /ˌdʌbljuː ɑːr eɪ ˈsiː: *or, in informal use,* 俗读作 ræk; ˌdʌbljʊ ɑr e ˋsi, ræk/ *abbr* 缩写 = (*Brit*) Women's Royal Army Corps 皇家陆军妇女队：*join the WRACs* 加入皇家陆军妇女队.

wrack /ræk; ræk/ *n* [U] seaweed that grows on the shore or has been thrown onto it by the waves (and used as manure, etc) （在海岸上长的或冲到海岸上的）海草（用作肥料等）.

WRAF /ˌdʌbljuː ɑːr eɪ ˈef *or, in informal use,* 俗读作 ræf; ˌdʌbljʊ ɑr e ˋɛf, ræf/ *abbr* 缩写 = (*Brit*) Women's Royal Air Force 皇家空军妇女队：*join the WRAF* 加入皇家空军妇女队.

wraith /reɪθ; reθ/ *n* ghostly image of a person seen shortly before or after his death; ghost 活人的灵魂（人临终前后显现的）；鬼魂：*a wraith-like figure*, ie a very thin pale person 瘦骨嶙峋、面色苍白如鬼魂的人.

wrangle /ˈræŋgl; ˋræŋgl/ *n* **~ (with sb) (about/over sth)** noisy or angry argument or dispute (with sb) (about sth) （与某人）（为某事）争吵或争辩：*They were involved in a long legal wrangle (with the company) (over payment).* 他们（与那家公司）（在付款问题上）陷入长期的法律纠纷中.

▷ **wrangle** *v* [I, Ipr] **~ (with sb) (about/over sth)** take part in a wrangle (with sb) (about sth) （与某人）（为某事）争吵或争辩：*The children were wrangling (with each other) over the new toy.* 孩子为新玩具（互相）争吵.

wrap /ræp; ræp/ *v* **(-pp-)** **1** [Tn, Tn·pr, Tn·p] **~ sth (up) (in sth)** cover or enclose sth (in soft or flexible material) （用软的或可弯曲的材料）包或裹某物：*I have wrapped (up) the parcels and they're ready to be posted.* 我把包裹都包好了，可以寄出去了. ○ *The Christmas presents were wrapped (up) in tissue paper.* 圣诞礼物都用薄纸裹起来了. **2 (a)** [Tn·pr] **~ sth round/around sb/sth** wind or fold (a piece of material) round sb/sth as covering or protection 将（一块材料）缠绕或围住某人［某物］（加以遮盖或保护）：*Wrap a scarf round your neck.* 把围巾围在你的脖子上. ○ *He wrapped a clean rag around his ankle.* 他把一小块干净的布缠住脚腕. **(b)** [Tn·pr, Tn·p esp passive 尤用于被动语态] **~ sb/sth in sth** put sb/sth in (a piece of material) as a covering or protection 将某人［某物］置于（一块材料）中（加以遮盖或保护）：*The nurse carried in a baby wrapped (up) in a warm blanket.* 保母抱着个孩子进来，孩子身上裹着暖暖的毯子. **3** (idm 习语) **be wrapped in sth** be thickly covered by sth so that nothing is visible 被遮掩得完全看不见：*The hills were wrapped in mist.* 小山隐没在浓雾之中. ○ (*fig* 比喻) *The events are wrapped in mystery.* 这些事情隐藏在神秘的气氛之中. **be wrapped up in sb/sth** have one's attention deeply occupied by sb/sth; be deeply involved in sb/sth 注意力完全集中于某人［某事物］；与某人［某事物］难解难分：*They are completely wrapped up in their children.* 他们把全部精力都用在孩子身上了. ○ *She was so wrapped up in her work that she didn't realize how late it was.* 她只顾埋头工作，没意识到天已经很晚了. **wrap sb up in cotton wool** (*infml* 口) protect sb too much from dangers or risks 过分保护某人：*She keeps all her children wrapped up in cotton wool.* 她把子女照顾得未免过头了. **4** (phr v) **wrap (it) up** (usu in the imperative 通常用于祈使句) (*sl* 俚) be quiet; shut up 安静；住嘴. **wrap (sb/oneself) up** put warm clothes on (sb/oneself) 给（某人［自己］）穿上暖和的衣物：*Wrap up warm(ly)! It's very cold outside.* 穿暖和点！外面很冷. **wrap sth up** (*infml* 口) complete (a task, a discussion, an agreement, etc) 完成（任务）；进行完（讨论）；签订完（协议）：*The salesman had already wrapped up a couple of deals by lunch-time.* 那个售货员在午饭前已经做完了几笔生意. **wrap sth up (in sth)** obscure (what one is saying) by using difficult or unnecessary words （用晦涩的或多余的词语）使（说的话）费解：*Why does he have to wrap it all up in such complicated language?* 他为什么非得用这么艰深的语言说话呢?

▷ **wrap** *n* **1** outer garment, eg a scarf, shawl or cloak 罩在外面的衣物（如围巾、披肩或斗篷）. **2** (idm 习语) **under ˈwraps** (*infml* 口) secret or hidden 保密；隐藏：*The documents will stay/be kept under wraps for ten more years.* 这些文件要再保密十年.

wrap·per *n* piece of material, usu paper, that covers sth such as a sweet, book, or newspaper that is posted （包装糖果、书籍或邮寄报纸等用的）包装材料（通常指纸）：*Please put all your sweet wrappers in the bin.* 请把你们的糖纸都放进垃圾箱里去.

wrap·ping *n* **(a)** [C] thing used to cover or wrap up sth 用作遮盖或包裹某物的东西：*the wrappings round a mummy* 用以裹木乃伊的东西. **(b)** [U] material used for covering or packing sth 用作盖住或包装某物的材料：*Put plenty of wrapping round the china when you pack it.* 包装瓷器时在周围多放些包装材料. **ˈwrapping paper** strong or decorative paper for wrapping parcels or presents （结实的或装饰性的）包装纸.

wrath /rɒθ; *US* ræθ; ræθ/ *n* [U] (*fml or dated* 文或旧) extreme anger 怒气；怒火：*the wrath of God* 上帝的愤怒 ○ *The children's unruly behaviour incurred the headteacher's wrath.* 小学生不守规矩惹得校长发怒. ▷ **wrath·ful** /-fl; -fəl/ *adj.* **wrath·fully** /-fəlɪ; -fəlɪ/ *adv.*

wreak /riːk; rik/ *v* (*fml* 文) **1** [Tn, Tn·pr] **~ sth (on sb)** carry out (revenge or vengeance) on sb; inflict sth 向某人报（仇）；使（某人）遭受（打击、惩罚等）：*wreak vengeance on one's enemy* 向仇人报仇 ○ *wreak one's fury on sb* 对某人发脾气. **2** (idm 习语) **play/wreak havoc with sth** ⇨ HAVOC.

wreath /riːθ; riθ/ *n* (*pl* **~s** /riːðz; riðz/) **1 (a)** arrangement of flowers and leaves twisted or woven into a circle and placed on a grave, etc as a mark of respect for the dead 花圈：*to lay wreaths at the war memorial* 向阵亡将士纪念碑献花圈. **(b)** circle of flowers or leaves worn as a mark of honour round sb's head or neck; garland 花环；花冠：*a laurel wreath* 桂冠. **2** ring or coil of smoke, cloud, etc （烟、云等的）圈：*wreaths of mist* 薄雾缭绕.

wreathe /riːð; rið/ *v* **1** [usu passive 通常用于被动语态：Tn, Tn·pr] **~ sth (in/with sth)** cover or surround sth (by sth) 遮盖或环绕某事物：*The display was wreathed in/with laurel.* 展品周围环绕着月桂树叶. ○ *The hills were wreathed in mist.* 小山笼罩在薄雾之中. ○ (*fig* 比喻) *Her face was wreathed in smiles*, ie she was smiling a lot. 她笑容可掬. **2** [Tn·pr] **~ oneself/sth round sb/sth** wind oneself, one's arms, etc round sb/sth 将自己、手臂等环绕某人［某物］：*The snake wreathed itself round the branch.* 那条蛇盘绕在树枝上. **3** [Ipr, Ip] (of smoke, mist, etc) move in rings or coils （指烟、雾等）缭绕：*Smoke wreathed slowly upwards.* 烟气袅袅.

wreck /rek; rɛk/ *n* [C] **1 (a)** vehicle, aeroplane, etc that has been badly damaged, esp in an accident 严重损毁的车、飞机等（尤指在事故中）：*The collision reduced the car to a useless wreck.* 那辆汽车在碰撞事故中成了一堆废铁. **(b)** ship that has been destroyed or badly damaged, esp in a storm 破碎或严重损毁的船（尤指在暴风雨中）：*Two wrecks block the entrance to the harbour.* 两艘船的残骸堵塞了通往港口的入口. **2** (usu *sing* 通常作单数) (*infml* 口) person whose physical or mental health has been seriously damaged 身体或精神严重受损伤的人：*The stroke left him a helpless wreck.* 他患中风之后成了不能自理的废人. ○ *Worry about the business has turned her into a nervous wreck.* 她生意上的烦恼事把她愁得不成人样了.

▷ **wreck** *v* [Tn] destroy or ruin (sth) 毁坏或毁灭（某

物): *The road was littered with wrecked cars.* 公路上弃置着撞坏的汽车. ○ *Vandals completely wrecked the train.* 恣意破坏公物的人把那列车完全毁了. ○ *They had been wrecked* (ie shipwrecked) *off the coast of Africa.* 他们的船在非洲沿海遇难损毁. ○ (*fig* 比喻) *The weather wrecked all our plans.* 天气恶劣, 我们的计划全毁了. **wrecker** *n* **1** person who wrecks sth 破坏某事物的人. **2** (*US*) vehicle used to tow away cars, lorries, etc that have broken down, been damaged, etc (拖走出事汽车等的)拖车.

wreck·age /ˈrekɪdʒ; ˋrɛkɪdʒ/ *n* [U] remains of sth that has been wrecked (遭损毁之物的)残骸: *Wreckage of the aircraft was scattered over a wide area.* 那架飞机的残骸散布范围很大. ○ (*fig* 比喻) *attempts to save something from the wreckage of his political career* (他)想从毁掉的政治生涯中再捞一把的各种做法.

wren /ren; rɛn/ *n* type of very small brown songbird with short wings 鹪鹩.

wrench /rentʃ; rɛntʃ/ *v* **1** [Tn·pr, Tn·p, Cn·a] **~ sth off (sth); ~ sb/sth away** twist or pull sb/sth violently away from sth 猛扭或猛拉某人[某物]使之脱离某物: *to wrench a door off its hinges* 把门从合叶处拉脱 ○ *He wrenched his arm away.* 他用力把手臂挣脱开. ○ *He managed to wrench himself free.* 他把身体挣脱出来了. **2** [Tn] injure (one's ankle, shoulder, etc) by twisting 扭伤(踝、肩等): *She must have wrenched her ankle when she fell.* 她准是跌倒时把脚腕子给崴了.

▷ **wrench** *n* **1** [C usu *sing* 通常作单数] sudden and violent twist or pull 猛扭; 猛拉: *He pulled the handle off with a wrench.* 他用力一拉就把把手拉下来了. ○ *She stumbled and gave her ankle a painful wrench*, ie twisted it by accident. 她绊了一交, 把脚崴得很疼. **2** [sing] painful parting or separation 痛苦的离别或分开: *Leaving home was a terrible wrench for him.* 他觉得离开家十分痛苦. **3** [C] (*esp US*) = SPANNER.

wrest /rest; rɛst/ *v* **1** [Tn·pr] **~ sth from sb** take sth away from sb violently 从某人处抢夺某物: *wrest the gun from his grasp* 把枪从他手中夺过来. **2** [Tn·pr] **~ sth from sb/sth** obtain sth from sb/sth by a hard struggle 奋力从某人[某物]处获得某事物: *wrest a confession from sb* 费力取得某人的供词 ○ *Foreign investors are trying to wrest control of the firm from the family.* 外国投资者尽力从这个家族手中夺取对公司的控制权.

wrestle /ˈresl; ˋrɛsl/ *v* **1** (**a**) [I, Ipr] **~ (with sb)** fight (esp as a sport) by grappling with sb and trying to throw him to the ground 摔跤(尤指运动): *Can you wrestle?* 你会摔跤吗? ○ *The guards wrestled with the intruders.* 护卫员同闯入的人扭打起来. (**b**) [Tn·pr] force (sb) to the ground by wrestling 将(某人)摔倒在地上: *He wrestled his opponent to the floor/ground.* 他把对手摔倒在地上. **2** [Ipr] **~ with sth** struggle to deal with or overcome sth 奋力对付或制服某事物: *wrestle with a problem, a difficulty, one's conscience* 努力解决难题、克服困难、与良心搏斗 ○ *The pilot was wrestling with the controls.* 那个飞行员尽力控制住操纵装置.

▷ **wrestle** *n* **1** wrestling match 摔跤比赛. **2 ~ (with sth)** hard struggle 艰苦奋斗; 努力争斗: *a wrestle with one's conscience* 与良心搏斗.

wrest·ler /ˈreslə(r); ˋrɛslɚ/ *n* person who takes part in the sport of wrestling 摔跤运动员.

wrestling 摔跤运动

wrest·ling /ˈreslɪŋ; ˋrɛslɪŋ/ *n* [U] sport in which people wrestle 摔跤运动: *watch (the) wrestling on television* 看电视节目中的摔跤运动.

wretch /retʃ; rɛtʃ/ *n* **1** very unfortunate or miserable person 非常不幸的或痛苦的人: *a poor half-starved wretch* 一个可怜的饿的半死的傢伙. **2** evil or nasty person 坏人; 狠毒的人: *the despicable wretch who stole the old woman's money* 偷了老太婆钱的那个卑鄙的傢伙. **3** (*infml derog esp joc* 口, 贬, 尤用于戏谑语) rogue or rascal 无赖; 流氓: *You wretch! You've taken the book I wanted.* 你这个坏蛋! 你把我想要的书拿走了.

wretched /ˈretʃɪd; ˋrɛtʃɪd/ *adj* **1** (**a**) very unhappy; miserable or pitiable 极不愉快的; 悲惨的; 可怜的: *the wretched survivors of the earthquake* 地震后可怜的幸存者 ○ *His stomach-ache made him feel wretched* (ie ill) *all day.* 他胃疼得整天十分难受. (**b**) causing unhappiness or misery 令人苦恼或难受的: *lead a wretched existence in the slums* 在贫民窟中过着悲惨的日子. **2** of very poor quality; very bad 质量极劣的; 极坏的: *wretched weather* 恶劣的天气 ○ *The hotel food was absolutely wretched.* 这家旅馆的饭菜糟透了. **3** [attrib 作定语] (*infml* 口) (used to express annoyance 用以表示恼怒) damned 该死的: *The wretched car won't start!* 这辆倒霉汽车就是发动不起来! ○ *It's that wretched cat again!* 又是那只该死的猫! ▷ **wretchedly** *adv*. **wretched·ness** *n* [U].

wriggle /ˈrɪgl; ˋrɪgl/ *v* **1** [I, Ip, Tn, Tn·p] (cause sth to) make quick, short, twisting and turning movements (使某物)扭动, 蠕动, 蜿蜒行进: *Stop wriggling (about) and sit still!* 不要扭来扭去, 坐着别动! ○ *I can't brush your hair if you keep wriggling all the time.* 你要是一直扭来扭去, 我就没法给你梳头了. ○ *The baby was wriggling its toes.* 那个小孩扭动着脚趾. **2** [La, Ipr, Ip, Tn·pr, Tn·p, Cn·a] move or make (one's way) in the specified direction with wriggling movements 沿某方向扭动、蠕动或蜿蜒行进: *The thieves left her tied up with rope but she wriggled (herself) free.* 窃贼用绳子把她捆了起来, 但她扭动着(身子)挣脱开了. ○ *The eel wriggled out of my fingers.* 那条白鳝从我指缝中一扭就滑走了. ○ *They managed to wriggle (their way) through the thick hedge.* 他们设法钻过了厚厚的树篱. ○ *He had to wriggle his way out.* 他得扭着身子才钻了出来. **3** (phr v) **wriggle out of sth/doing sth** (*infml* 口) avoid (doing) an unpleasant task by being cunning or by making excuses 靠耍滑或找借口避免(做)(讨厌的工作): *It's your turn to take the dog for a walk — don't try to wriggle out of it.* 轮到你把狗带出去遛一遛了 —— 别想逃避不做. ○ *She managed to wriggle out of answering all the questions.* 她支吾其词避免回答一切问题.

▷ **wriggle** *n* (usu *sing* 通常作单数) wriggling movement 扭动; 蠕动; 蜿蜒行进.

wrig·gly /ˈrɪglɪ; ˋrɪglɪ/ *adj*.

wring /rɪŋ; rɪŋ/ *v* (*pt, pp* **wrung** /rʌŋ; rʌŋ/) **1** (**a**) [Tn, Tn·p] **~ sth (out)** twist and squeeze sth in order to remove liquid from it 拧或绞某物使液体流出: *He wrung the clothes (out) before putting them on the line to dry.* 他把衣服拧干后晾到绳子上. (**b**) [Tn·pr, Tn·p] **~ sth out (of sth)** remove (a liquid) from sth in this way 拧出或绞出(液体): *Wring the water out of your wet bathing costume.* 把你的游泳衣里的水拧出去. **2** [Tn·pr] **~ sth out of/from sb** extract or obtain sth from sb with effort or difficulty 用力或费力从某人处榨出或取得某事物: *wring a confession from sb* 千方百计逼出某人的供词 ○ *They managed to wring a promise out of her.* 他们多方设法挤兑她应允了. **3** [Tn] squeeze (sb's hand) firmly and warmly when shaking hands as a greeting 紧握(某人的手)(热情欢迎时). **4** [Tn] twist (a bird's neck) in order to kill it 拧(鸟的脖子)(为弄死). **5** [Tn] have a deep effect on (sb's heart or soul), causing sb to feel great sadness and pity 在(某人心灵)上产生深刻影响(使之感到伤心或怜悯): *The plight of the refugees really wrung my heart.* 难民处境惨苦真叫我牵肠割肚. **6** (idm 习语) ˌ**wring one's ˈhands** squeeze and twist one's hands together as a sign of anxiety, sadness or despair 搓双手(以示焦急、难过或绝望): *It's no use just wringing our hands — we must do something to help.* 咱们光急得搓手没有用 —— 得想办法帮帮忙. ˌ**wring sb's ˈneck** (*infml* 口) (used as an expression of anger or as a threat 用作气愤或威胁用语) strangle sb 掐死某人: *If I find the person who did this, I'll wring his neck!* 我要是找出这是谁干的, 我非掐死他不可!

▷ **wring** *n* (usu *sing* 通常作单数) act of wringing clothes, etc 拧或绞衣物等: *Give the towels another wring.*

W

把毛巾再拧一拧吧.

wringer /ˈrɪŋə(r); ˋrɪŋɚ/ *n* device with a pair of rollers between which washed clothes, etc are passed so that water is squeezed out 绞衣机(绞干衣物中的水用的). Cf 参看 MANGLE[2].

wring·ing /ˈrɪŋɪŋ; ˋrɪŋɪŋ/ *adj* (also ˌ**wringing ˈwet**) (of clothes, etc) so wet that a lot of water can be wrung out (指衣物等)湿得可拧出许多水来的.

wrinkle /ˈrɪŋkl; ˋrɪŋkl/ *n* **1** (usu *pl* 通常作复数) small fold or line in the skin, esp one of those on the face that are caused by age (皮肤上的)皱纹(尤指老人脸上的): *She's beginning to get wrinkles around her eyes.* 她眼角上开始出现皱纹了. **2** raised fold in a piece of material, eg paper or cloth; small crease (材料上的)皱纹(如纸上或布上的); 小褶: *She pressed her skirt to try to remove all the wrinkles.* 她熨她的裙子, 想把褶儿都熨平. **3** (*infml* 口) useful hint or suggestion; tip 好主意; 好点子.

▷ **wrinkle** *v* **1** [I, Tn] (cause sth to) form wrinkles (使某物)形成皱纹或皱褶: *The paper has wrinkled where it got wet.* 这张纸湿的地方起皱褶了. ○ *Too much sunbathing will wrinkle your skin.* 皮肤晒得过分就能起皱纹. **2** [Tn] draw up (the nose, forehead, etc) into lines or creases by tightening the muscles 皱起(鼻子、前额等): *He wrinkled his brow, confused and worried by the strange events.* 他皱着眉头, 觉得这些怪事莫名其妙又十分担心. **wrinkled** /ˈrɪŋkld; ˋrɪŋkld/ *adj* having or showing wrinkles 有皱纹的; 显出皱纹的: *his old wrinkled face* 他因年老布满皱纹的脸 ○ *wrinkled socks* 有皱褶的短袜. **wrinkly** /ˈrɪŋklɪ; ˋrɪŋklɪ/ *adj* having or forming wrinkles 有皱纹的; 起皱纹的: *an old apple with a wrinkly skin* 一个放陈了而起皱褶的苹果.

wrist /rɪst; rɪst/ *n* (**a**) part of the body between the hand and the forearm; joint on which the hand moves 腕; 腕部; 腕关节. ⇨ illus at HAND 见 HAND 插图. (**b**) part of a garment that covers this (衣服的)腕部.

□ ˈ**wrist-watch** *n* watch attached to a strap or bracelet and worn on the wrist 手表.

wrist·let /ˈrɪstlɪt; ˋrɪstlɪt/ *n* band or bracelet worn round the wrist to strengthen or protect it or as an ornament 护腕; 手镯.

writ /rɪt; rɪt/ *n* formal legal written order to do or not to do sth, issued by a court of law or a person in authority 书面命令; 令状: *serve sb with a writ* (ie deliver a writ to sb officially) *for libel* 向被控犯诽谤罪的某人送交令状.

▷ **writ** **1** (*arch* 古) *pp* of WRITE. **2** (idm 习语) ˌ**writ ˈlarge** (*fml or rhet* 文或修辞) (**a**) easily or clearly recognizable; very obvious 可容易或清楚辨认的; 极明显的: *Disappointment was writ large on the face of the loser.* 输了的那个人脸上显出十分失望的神情. (**b**) in an emphasized form 以突出的或夸大的形式: *This policy is liberalism writ large.* 这项政策是扩大了的自由主义政策.

write /raɪt; raɪt/ *v* (*pt* **wrote** /rəʊt; rot/, *pp* **written** /ˈrɪtn; ˋrɪtn̩/) **1** [I, Ipr] make letters or other symbols on a surface (usu paper), esp with a pen or pencil 写; 写字; 书写: *The children are learning to read and write.* 孩子们正在学习读书写字. ○ *By the age of seven he could write beautifully.* 他七岁时字就写得很漂亮了. ○ *Please write on both sides of the paper, and don't write in the margin.* 请在纸的正反两面书写, 但不要写在四周的边上. ○ *You may write in biro or pencil.* 你用圆珠笔或铅笔书写均可. **2** [Tn, Tn·pr] form (letters, symbols, words, messages, etc), esp on paper 写(字母、符号、字、信息等): *write capitals, Chinese characters, shorthand, etc* 写大写字母、写汉字、做速记 ○ *write one's name* 写自己的名字 ○ *write the answers in a book, on the blackboard, etc* 在本子上、在黑板上…写出答案. **3** [I] (of a pen, pencil, etc) be capable of being used for writing (指钢笔、铅笔等)能用于书写, 能使用: *This pen won't write.* 这枝钢笔写不出字来. ○ *My new pen writes well.* 我的新钢笔很好使. **4** (**a**) [Tn, Dn·n, Dn·pr] **~ sth (for sb/sth)** compose sth in written form (for sb/sth) 写作; 编写; 作曲: *write a book, film script, poem, symphony, etc* 写书、写电影剧本、写诗、创作交响乐曲 ○ *Can you write me a story about your holiday?* 你能不能给我写一篇你度假的见闻? ○ *He writes a weekly column for the local newspaper.* 他为当地报纸每周专栏撰写文章. (**b**) [I, Ipr] **~ (about/on sth)** work as an author or journalist by writing about sth or for a newspaper, etc 当作者或新闻工作者: *He gave up his job in the factory in order to write,* ie earn a living by writing. 他辞去工厂的职务, 专职写作. ○ *She writes (about/on politics) for a weekly journal.* 她为一家周刊写(政治性)文章. (**c**) [Tf, Tw] state in a book or magazine 在书中或杂志中表达: *In his latest book, he writes that the theory has been disproved.* 他在最近写的书里说那种理论已证明不确. **5** (**a**) [I, Ipr, Tf, Tt, Dn·n, Dn·pr] **~ (sth) (to sb)** write and send a letter (to sb) (给某人)写信并寄出: *Please write (to me) often while you're away.* 你走后请常(给我)来信. ○ *He wrote that he would be coming home soon.* 他写信说他很快就要回家了. ○ *They wrote to thank us/he wrote thanking us for the present.* 他们[他]写信表示感谢我们赠送礼物. ○ *She wrote him a long letter/wrote a long letter to him.* 她给他写了一封很长的信. (**b**) [Tn, Dn·f, Dn·w] (*esp US*) write a letter to (sb) 给(某人)写信: *Write me when you get home.* 你到家后给我写封信. ○ *He wrote me that he would be arriving on Wednesday.* 他写信告诉我说他星期三到. **6** [Tn, Tn·p, Dn·n, Dn·pr] **~ sth (out) (for sb)** fill or complete (a sheet of paper, a document, the spaces in a form) with writing 写满(一张纸); 填写(文件、表格): *She usually writes several pages when she makes her report.* 她一写报告往往要写好几页. ○ *He has written (out) 50 job applications.* 他已经写了50份求职申请书了. ○ *I haven't any cash. I'll have to write you (out) a cheque.* 我没有现金. 我得给你开张支票了. ○ *In a day, a doctor may write (out) 30 prescriptions for patients.* 一个医生一天可能要给病人开出30张处方. **7** [Tn] record (data) in or on any computer storage device or medium 将(数据)记录到计算机存储媒体上. **8** (idm 习语) **be written all over sb's ˈface** (usu of a quality or emotion) be very obvious from the expression on sb's face (通常指特质或情绪)形之于色: *Guilt was written all over his face.* 他脸上明显流露着内疚的神情. **have sb written all ˈover it** (*infml* 口) be obviously written, done, etc by the specified person 显然是某人写的、干的等. **nothing (much) to write ˈhome about** (*infml* 口) not outstanding or exceptional; ordinary 不突出的; 不特殊的; 平常的: *The play was nothing (much) to write home about.* 这出戏很一般.

9 (phr v) **write away (to sb/sth) (for sth)** ⇨ WRITE OFF/AWAY (TO SB/STH) (FOR STH).

write back (to sb) write and send a letter in reply to sb (给某人)写回信; 复信: *I wrote back (to him) immediately to thank them for the invitation.* 我立刻(给他)写了回信, 感谢他们盛情邀请.

write sth down (**a**) put sth down in words on paper 将某事写在纸上: *Write down the address before you forget it.* 把地址写下来, 省得忘了. (**b**) (in accounting) reduce the nominal value of (stock, goods, etc) (在记帐时)减低(存货、现货等)的帐面价值: *the written-down value of the unsold stock* 被降低了的存货价格.

write in (to sb/sth) (for sth) write a letter to (an organization, a company, etc) to order sth, state an opinion, etc 给(某组织、公司等)写信订购某物、表示意见等: *Thousands of people have written in to us for a free sample.* 现已有数千人给我们来信索要免费样品.

write sth/sb in (*US politics* 政) add (the name of a candidate) to a ballot paper if this does not include that name; vote for sb in this way 在选票上填写(非原定候选人的姓名); 以这种方式选举. **write sth into sth** include sth as part of (a contract, an agreement, etc) 将某项内容写入(合同、协议等)中: *A penalty clause was written into the contract.* 在合同中写入了一项罚款条款.

write off/away (to sb/sth) (for sth) write to (an organization, a company, etc) to order sth or to ask for information about sth 给(某组织、公司等)写信订购某物或询问情况: *They wrote off (to the BBC) for the special booklet.* 他们(给英国广播公司)写了信索要那种小册子. **write sth off** (**a**) recognize that sth is a loss or failure; cancel (a debt) 确认某事物已损失或无效; 勾销(某债项): *write off a debt, loss, etc* 注销一项债款、损失等 ○ *write off £5 000 for depreciation of machinery* 因机器折旧削减5 000英镑. (**b**) damage sth so badly that it is not worth repairing 严重损坏某物(而不值得修理); 将某物报废: *The driver escaped with minor injuries but the car was completely written off.* 司机只受轻伤幸免于难, 但是汽车完全报废了. Cf 参看 WRITE-OFF. **write sb/**

sth off regard sb/sth as a failure 认为某人[某事物]已经失败: *He lost this match, but don't write him off as a future champion.* 他输了这场比赛, 但不要以为他以后当不了冠军. ○ *It seemed that everyone had written off their marriage even before it had been given a proper chance.* 他们的婚姻出了问题, 还没等认真挽救, 似乎大家都认为已成分钗破镜. **write sb/sth off as sth** regard sb/sth as unimportant, not worth listening to, etc 认为某人[某事物]不重要、不值得听等: *It's easy to write him off as just an eccentric old bore.* 干脆把他看成是个古怪的讨厌傢伙不去理他, 不就完了吗. **write sth out** (**a**) write sth in full or in its final form 将某事全部写出或写出其最后确定的样式: *write out a report, cheque, prescription, etc* 写成报告、开出支票、开出药方. (**b**) copy sth 誊写; 缮写; 抄写: *Write out this word ten times so that you learn how to spell it.* 把这个字抄写十遍就能记住怎么拼写了. **write sb out (of sth)** remove (a character) from a continuing drama series on radio or television (从系列广播剧或电视剧中)除掉(某角色): *After playing the part for over 20 years, she was eventually written out (of the series).* 她扮演了20多年的一个角色, 最后(从连续剧中)去掉了. **write sth up** (**a**) make a full written record of sth 详细写(某事): *write up one's lecture notes, the minutes of a meeting, etc* 详细写出讲稿、会议记录等 ○ *write up one's diary*, ie bring it up to date 记日记记到当日. (**b**) write a review of (a play, etc) or an account of (an event), usu for a newspaper 写(戏剧等)的评论或(事情)的报道(通常指为报纸): *I'm writing up the film for the local paper.* 我现在为本地报纸写影评. Cf 参看 WRITE-UP.

▷ **writ·ten** *adj* (to be) expressed in writing, rather than in speech 书面的(非口头的): *a written examination, request, message* 笔试、书面请求、书面信息 ○ *a written confirmation, agreement, evidence* 书面的确认、协议、证据. **the ˌwritten ˈword** language expressed in writing 书面语言.

□ **ˈwrite-off** *n* thing, esp a vehicle, that is so badly damaged that it is not worth repairing 严重损毁而不值得修理的东西; (尤指)报废的车: *After the accident, the car was a complete write-off.* 出事以后, 那辆汽车完全报废了.

ˈwrite-up *n* written or published account of an event, review of a play, etc 记述; 报道; (戏剧等的)评论: *His latest play got/was given an enthusiastic write-up in the local press.* 他的最新剧本获得当地新闻界的热情赞扬.

writer /ˈraɪtə(r); ˈraɪtər/ *n* **1** (**a**) person who writes or has written sth 书写的人: *the writer of this letter* 写这封信的人. (**b**) (with an *adj* 与形容词连用) person who forms letters in a certain way when writing 以某方式书写的人: *a neat, messy, etc writer* 书写整齐、潦草...的人. **2** person whose job is to write books, stories, etc; author 作者; 作家; 著者: *a short-story writer* 短篇小说家 ○ *a writer of poetry* 诗人.

□ **ˌwriter's ˈcramp** pain or stiffness in the hand, caused by writing for a long time 书写痉挛(因长久书写引起手部的疼痛或强直).

writhe /raɪð; raɪð/ *v* **1** [I, Ip] (of sb or sb's body) twist or roll about, esp because of great pain (指某人或身体)扭动或翻滚(尤指因巨痛): *the writhing coils of a snake* 蛇身体扭动盘绕成的圈 ○ *The patient was writhing (about) on the bed in agony.* 病人疼得在床上直打滚. **2** [I, Ipr] **~ (at/under sth); ~ (with sth)** suffer mental agony (because of sth) (因某事物)遭受精神痛苦: *writhe under sb's insults* 因遭某人侮辱而苦恼 ○ *Her remarks made him writhe with shame.* 她的话羞得他十分难堪.

writ·ing /ˈraɪtɪŋ; ˈraɪtɪŋ/ *n* **1** [U] activity or occupation of writing (esp books) 写; 书写; 写作; 写作的职业: *She doesn't earn much from her writing.* 她写作得到的收入不多. ○ *Writing is a solitary pastime.* 写作是独自一人的消遣. ○ [attrib 作定语] *writing materials*, eg pens, paper, ink 书写用具(如钢笔、纸、墨水). **2** [U] written or printed words 书写的或印刷的文字: *There is some writing on the other side of the page.* 这一页的反面有些字. ○ *The writing on the stone was very faint.* 这块石头上的字迹很模糊. **3** [U] style of written material 文风: *He is admired for the elegance of his writing.* 他文风高雅令人钦佩. **4** [U] way in which a person forms letters when writing; handwriting (个人的)字迹; 笔迹: *I can never read your writing.* 我怎么也看不明白你的笔迹. **5 writings** [pl] works of an author or on a subject 某作家的著作; 某专题的著作: *the writings of Dickens* 狄更斯的作品 ○ *It is frequently mentioned in the poetic writings of the period.* 在那个时期的诗作中经常提到这一点. **6** (idm 习语) **in ˈwriting** in written form, esp in a document or contract 以书面形式(尤指文件或合同的): *You must get his agreement in writing.* 你必须得到他书面的同意. **the ˌwriting (is) on the ˈwall** (there are) clear signs that warn of failure, disaster or defeat (有)失败、灾祸或覆灭的清楚的征兆: *The writing is on the wall for the local football club: bankruptcy seems certain.* 这个本地足球俱乐部厄难临头: 似乎已无法维持下去.

□ **ˈwriting-desk** *n* desk with a flat or sloping surface and with drawers or compartments to keep writing materials in 写字台; 书桌. ⇨illus at App 1 见附录1插图, page xvi.

ˈwriting-paper *n* [U] (usu good-quality) paper cut into sheets of a suitable size for writing letters on 信纸.

writ·ten ⇨ WRITE.

WRNS /ˌdʌblju: ɑ:r en ˈes, *also* renz; ˌdʌbljʊ ɑr ɛn ˈɛs, rɛnz/ *abbr* 缩写 = (*Brit*) Women's Royal Naval Service 皇家海军妇女队: *join the WRNS* 加入皇家海军妇女队.

wrong /rɒŋ; *US* rɔ:ŋ; rɔŋ/ *adj* **1 ~ (to do sth)** not morally right; unjust 不道德的; 不正当的; 不义的: *It is wrong to steal.* 偷窃是不道德的. ○ *You were wrong to take the car without permission.* 你未得许可就把汽车开走是不应该的. ○ *He told me he had done nothing wrong.* 他告诉我说他没做任何不正当的事. Cf 参看 RIGHT[1] 1. **2** (**a**) not true or correct 不确实的; 不正确的; 错误的: *He did the sum but got the wrong answer/got the answer wrong.* 他做了这道算术题, 但答案错了. ○ *Her estimate of the cost was completely wrong.* 她估计的费用完全不正确. (**b**) [pred 作表语] (of a person) mistaken (指人)出错, 有错误: *Am I wrong in thinking* (ie Do you agree) *that it is getting colder?* 天气越来越冷了, 对吧? ○ *Can you prove that I am wrong?* 你能证实我错了吗? ○ *That's where you're wrong.* 在这一点上你错了. ○ *Thousands of satisfied customers can't be wrong, so why don't you try our new washing-powder?* 我们的新型洗衣粉顾客都很满意, 成千上万的人不可能都错了, 您也不妨试一试好吗? **3** [usu attrib 通常作定语] not required, suitable or the most desirable 不合要求的; 不适合的; 并非最合意的: *You're doing it the wrong way.* 你做的方法不当. ○ *We discovered that we were on the wrong train.* 我们发觉上错了火车. ○ *The police arrested the wrong man.* 警方逮错了人. ○ *We came the wrong way/took a wrong turning.* 我们来时走错了路[拐错了弯]. ○ *I'm afraid you've got the wrong number*, ie on the telephone. 很抱歉, 您拨错电话号码了. ○ *You're wearing your jumper the wrong way round*, ie The part that should be at the front is at the back. 你的毛衣前后穿反了. ○ *He's the wrong man for the job.* 他不适合做这项工作. ○ *They live on the wrong side of town*, ie the part that is socially less desirable. 他们住在镇上环境较差的那边(社会地位较低的人住的). ○ *I realized that I had said the wrong thing when I saw her reaction.* 我一看到她的反应就意识到我说话不当. ○ *Their decision proved to be wrong.* 他们的决定证实是错误的. **4** [pred 作表语] **~ (with sb/sth)** (**a**) in a bad condition (and not working properly) 有故障; 有毛病: *What's wrong* (ie What is the problem) *with the engine? It's making an awful noise.* 发动机出什么故障了? 噪音太大了. ○ *There's something wrong with my eyes — I can't see properly.* 我眼睛有毛病了——看不清楚了. (**b**) not as it should be 不正常: *Is anything wrong? You look ill.* 怎么了? 你脸色不好. ○ *What's wrong with you?* 你哪儿不舒服? ○ *What's wrong with telling the truth?* ie How can it be criticized? 说实话有什么不对? **5** (idm 习语) **back the wrong horse** ⇨ BACK[4]. **bark up the wrong tree** ⇨ BARK[2]. **be born on the wrong side of the blanket** ⇨ BORN. **catch sb on the wrong foot** ⇨ CATCH[1]. **do the right/wrong thing** ⇨ THING. **from/on the ˌwrong side of the ˈtracks** (*US*) living in an area (of a town, etc) which is regarded as socially inferior 住在(城镇等中的)社会地位低的人住的地区. **get on the right/wrong side of sb** ⇨ SIDE[1]. **get (hold of) the ˌwrong end of the ˈstick** (*infml* 口) misunderstand completely what has been said (对听到的话)完全误解: *You've got the wrong end of the stick; he doesn't owe me money, I owe him!* 你完全听错了, 他没欠我钱, 是我欠

他的钱! **have got out of bed on the wrong side** ⇨ BED[1]. **hit/strike the right/wrong note** ⇨ NOTE[1]. **not far off/out/wrong** ⇨ FAR[2]. **on the right/wrong side of forty, fifty, etc** ⇨ SIDE[1]. **rub sb up the wrong way** ⇨ RUB[2]. **start off on the right/wrong foot** ⇨ START[2].

ˌwrong side ˈout turned, changed, etc so that the normally inner side is facing outwards 里面被翻转成外面: *You've got your sweater on wrong side out.* 你穿的毛衣里儿冲外了.

▷ **wrong** *adv* (used after *vs* 用于动词之后) **1** in a wrong manner or direction; mistakenly; with incorrect results 方式或方向错误; 错误地; 结果错误: *You guessed wrong.* 你猜错了. ○ *You've spelt my name wrong.* 你把我的名字拼错了. ○ *He played the tune all wrong.* 他演奏的曲调全错了. Cf 参看 WRONGLY. **2** (idm 习语) **get sb ˈwrong** (*infml* 口) misunderstand sb 误会或误解某人: *Please don't get me wrong, I'm not criticizing you.* 请不要误解我, 我并不是批评你. **go ˈwrong** (**a**) make a mistake 犯错误; 做错事: *If you read the instructions, you'll see where you went wrong.* 你要是看一下说明书就知道你错在哪儿了. ○ *You can't go wrong* (ie You will surely succeed) *with our new carpet cleaner.* 使用我们新型的地毯吸尘器绝对不会出错. (**b**) (of a machine) stop working properly (指机器)出故障, 出毛病: *The television has gone wrong again.* 电视机又出毛病了. (**c**) experience trouble 遇到麻烦; 出现问题: *Their marriage started to go wrong when he got a job abroad.* 他找到一份在国外的工作, 他们的婚姻就在那时开始出现问题. ○ *The experiment went disastrously wrong*, ie progressed in an unexpected way with very unpleasant results. 这个试验出了大问题. **put a foot wrong** ⇨ FOOT[1].

wrong *n* **1** [U] what is wrong 坏事; 过失; 罪恶: *He doesn't know the difference between right and wrong.* 他不懂是非. ○ *She could do no wrong* (ie do nothing wrong) *in the opinion of her devoted followers.* 那些忠实于她的人都认为她不会做坏事. **2** [C] (*fml* 文) unjust action; injustice 不义的行为; 不公正的事: *They have done us a great wrong.* 他们对待我们十分不公正. ○ *She complained of the wrongs she had suffered.* 她投诉说她受到委屈. **3** (idm 习语) **in the ˈwrong** in the position of being responsible for a mistake, an offence, a quarrel, etc (在犯错误、犯罪、吵架等方面)负有责任或应受责备: *He admitted that he was in the wrong*, ie that the fault was his. 他承认是他的错. ○ *They tried to put me in the wrong*, ie to make it seem that the fault, error, etc was mine. 他们想把错误栽给我. **the rights and wrongs of sth** ⇨ RIGHT[3]. **ˌtwo ˌwrongs ˌdon't make a ˈright** (*saying* 谚) you cannot justify a wrong action by saying that sb else has done sth similar or that sb has done sth wrong to you 两个错不等于其中一个对(自己做了错事不能说别人也是这样做的来为自己辩护).

wrong *v* (*fml* 文) **1** [Tn usu passive 通常用于被动语态] do wrong to (sb); treat (sb) unjustly or badly 对待(某人)不公正; 使(某人)受到委屈: *a wronged wife* 受委屈的妻子. **2** [Tn] judge (sb) unfairly; attribute a bad motive to (sb) mistakenly 不公正地判断(某人); 冤枉(某人): *You wrong me if you think I only did it for selfish reasons.* 你要是以为我是出于私心, 那你就冤枉我了.

wrong·ful /-fl; -fəl/ *adj* [attrib 作定语] not fair, just or legal 不公正的; 不公平的; 不正当的; 不合法的: *He sued his employer for wrongful dismissal.* 他控告雇主非法解雇他. **wrong·fully** /-fəlɪ; -fəlɪ/ *adv*: *wrongfully arrested* 遭不合法逮捕.

wrongly *adv* (used esp before a past participle or a *v* 尤用于过去分词或动词之前) in a wrong manner; in the wrong way 不正当地; 错误地: *wrongly accused, addressed, informed* 控告错、写错地址、了解错 ○ *He imagines, wrongly, that she loves him.* 他误以为她爱他. ○ *Rightly or wrongly, she refused to accept the offer*, ie I don't know whether she was right or wrong to do so. 不论她做得对不对, 反正她拒绝了那个提议.

□ **wrongdoer** /ˈrɒŋduːə(r); ˈrɔŋˌduɚ/ *n* person who does sth immoral or illegal 做不道德的或不合法的事情的人; 做坏事的人. **wrongdoing** /ˈrɒŋduːɪŋ; ˈrɔŋˌduɪŋ/ *n* [U, C] wrong behaviour; wrong action 不道德的行为; 坏事: *such wrongdoing(s) should be punished* 这种不道德的行为应该受到惩罚.

ˌwrong-ˈfoot *v* [Tn] (esp in sport) catch (sb) unprepared (尤指在体育比赛中)使(某人)措手不及: *Her cleverly disguised lob completely wrong-footed her opponent.* 她做个巧妙的假动作, 一个高球把对手打得乱了阵脚.

ˌwrong-ˈheaded *adj* (of a person) obstinately holding a wrong opinion or taking a wrong course of action (指人)坚持错误意见或错误办法的.

wrote *pt* of WRITE.

wrought /rɔːt; rɔt/ *pt, pp* of WORK[2].

▷ **wrought** *adj* [attrib 作定语] **1** made or manufactured and decorated 制造的; 加工的; 经装饰的: *elaborately wrought carvings* 精制的雕刻品. **2** (of metal) beaten out or shaped by hammering (指金属)锤打成形的, 锻造的.

□ **ˌwrought ˈiron** tough form of iron made by forging or rolling 锻铁; 熟铁: [attrib 作定语] *a ˌwrought-iron ˈbedstead, ˈgate, ˈrailing* 熟铁床架、门、栏杆. Cf 参看 CAST IRON (CAST[1]).

wrung *pt, pp* of WRING.

wry /raɪ; raɪ/ *adj* (**wryer, wryest**) **1** [usu attrib 通常作定语] (of a person's face, features, etc) twisted into an expression of disappointment, disgust or mockery (指人的脸、五官等)扭曲的(表示失望、厌恶或嘲笑): *pull a wry face* 做个鬼脸 ○ *a wry glance, grin, smile, etc* 眯着眼的窥视、讪笑、笑容等. **2** ironically humorous; slightly mocking 用反语表达幽默的; 揶揄的: *She watched their fumbling efforts with wry amusement.* 她看着他们手忙脚乱地瞎使劲, 不觉莞尔. ▷ **wryly** *adv*. **wry·ness** *n* [U].

wt *abbr* 缩写 = weight: *net wt 454 gm*, eg on a jar of jam 净重454克(如果酱罐上的字样).

WWF *abbr* 缩写 = World Wildlife Fund 世界野生动物基金会.

WX /ˌdʌbljuː ˈeks; ˌdʌbljʊ ˈɛks/ *abbr* 缩写 = (esp on clothing) women's extra large (size) (尤作衣物上的标记)女装特大(号).

wych-elm /ˈwɪtʃ elm; ˈwɪtʃˌɛlm/ *n* type of elm tree with broad leaves and spreading branches 无毛榆.

wych-hazel = WITCH-HAZEL (WITCH).

W

X x

X, x /eks; ɛks/ *n* (*pl* **X's**, **x's** /ˈeksɪz; ˋɛksɪz/) the twenty-fourth letter of the English alphabet 英语字母表的第二十四个字母: *'Xylophone' begins with (an) X/'X'.* xylophone一字以x字母开始.

□ ˈ**X chromosome** (*biology* 生) chromosome that occurs as one of an identical pair in female cells to produce a female in the reproductive process, or singly combined with a single Y chromosome in male cells to produce a male X染色体. Cf 参看 Y CHROMOSOME (Y).

X (also **x**) *symb* 符号 **1** Roman numeral for 10 罗马数字的10. **2** (esp in letters, etc, indicating a kiss 尤用于书信等, 表示亲吻的符号): *Love from Cathy XXX* 卡西向你表示爱意, 吻你、吻你、吻你. **3** (indicating a vote on a ballot-paper, etc 选票等上面表示投票的记号): *James Blunt X* 詹姆斯·布伦特X. **4** (indicating an error on corrected written work, etc 在批改书面作业等中, 用作表示错误的符号). **5** (**a**) (*mathematics* 数) unknown quantity 未知数: *4x = x + x + x + x*. (**b**) (*fig* 比喻) unknown or unspecified person, number or influence 未知的或未指明的人、数或影响力: *Mr and Mrs X* X先生及夫人. **6** (indicating a position marked eg on a map 表示标出的某位置(如标于地图上者)): *X marks the spot.* 有X字样者即是该处. **7** (also **Xt**) = Christ (Greek 希腊文之 *Christos*): *Xtian*, 即 Christian ○ *Xmas*, 即 Christmas.

xenon /ˈziːnɒn; ˋzi,nɑn/ *n* [U] chemical element, a colourless and odourless inert gas 氙. ⇨App 10 见附录10.

xe·no·pho·bia /ˌzenəˈfəʊbɪə; ˌzɛnəˋfobɪə/ *n* [U] intense dislike or fear of foreigners or strangers 对外国人或陌生人的憎恶或恐惧: *Excessive patriotism can lead to xenophobia.* 爱国主义过了头即可导致仇视一切外国人.

▷ **xe·no·pho·bic** /-ˈfəʊbɪk; -ˋfobɪk/ *adj*.

Xerox /ˈzɪərɒks; ˋzɪr,ɑks/ *n* (*propr* 专利名) **1** process for producing photocopies without the use of wet materials (干式的)影印, 复印: [attrib 作定语] *a Xerox machine* (干式)影印机. Cf 参看 PHOTOCOPY, PHOTOSTAT. **2** photocopy made using this process (干式影印的)影印件, 复印件: *make/take a couple of Xeroxes of the contract* 复制出合同的影印件.

▷ **xerox** *v* [I, Tn] produce copies of (documents, etc) using the Xerox or a similar process 影印, 复印(文件等): *Could you xerox this letter please, Paula?* 葆拉, 请你把这封信复印一份行吗?

Xhosa /ˈkɔːsə; ˋkɔsə/ *n* **1** [C] member of a Bantu people of Cape Province, S Africa 科萨人(南非开普省班图人的成员). **2** [U] their language 科萨语. ▷ **Xhosa** *adj*.

-xion ⇨ -ION.

XL /ˌeks ˈel; ˌɛks ˋɛl/ *abbr* 缩写 = (esp on clothing) extra large (尤作衣物上的标记)特大号.

Xmas /ˈkrɪsməs, ˈeksməs; ˋkrɪsməs, ˋɛksməs/ *n* [C, U] (*infml* 口) (used as a short form, esp in writing 用作缩略式, 尤用于文字中) = Christmas: *A merry Xmas to all our readers!* 谨向我们所有的读者敬祝圣诞快乐!

X-ray /ˈeks reɪ; ˋɛksˋre/ *n* **1** (usu *pl* except when used attributively 除用作定语外, 通常作复数) type of short-wave electromagnetic radiation that can penetrate solids and make it possible to see into or through them ☆ X射线: *an X-ray machine*, ie one that emits X-rays ☆ X射线机 ○ *an X-ray telescope*, ie one that can examine and measure the X-rays emitted by stars, etc ☆ X射线望远镜 ○ *X-ray therapy*, ie medical treatment using X-rays ☆ X射线疗法. **2** (**a**) (also **radiograph**) photograph made by X-rays, esp one showing bones or organs in the human body ☆ X射线照片(尤指显示人体骨骼或器官者): *a chest X-ray* 胸部X射线照片 ○ *take an X-ray of sb's hand* 拍摄某人手部的X射线照片 ○ *The doctor doesn't think I've broken a bone but he's waiting to see the X-rays.* 医生认为我并未骨折, 但他正等着看X射线照片. (**b**) (*infml* 口) medical examination using X-rays 用X射线作的临床检查.

▷ **X-ray** *v* [Tn] (**a**) examine or photograph (sb/sth) using X-rays 用X射线检查或拍摄(某人[某物]): *When his lungs were X-rayed the disease could be clearly seen.* 对他的肺部进行了X射线检查, 疾病一目了然. (**b**) treat (sb/sth) medically using X-rays 用X射线治疗(某人[某物]).

Xt = X *symb* 符号 7.

xy·lo·phone /ˈzaɪləfəʊn; ˋzaɪlə,fon/ *n* musical instrument consisting of parallel wooden or metal bars mounted on a frame, which are of different lengths and so produce different notes when struck with small wooden hammers 木琴. ⇨illus at App 1 见附录1插图, page xi.

Y y

Y, y /waɪ; waɪ/ *n* (*pl* **Y's, y's** /waɪz; waɪz/) the twenty-fifth letter of the English alphabet 英语字母表的第二十五个字母: *'Yak' begins with (a) Y/'Y'.* yak 一字以 y 字母开始.

□ **'Y chromosome** (*biology* 生) chromosome that occurs singly and only in male cells, and produces a male after combining with an X chromosome during the reproductive process Y 染色体. Cf 参看 X CHROMOSOME (X).

'Y-fronts *n* [pl] (*Brit propr* 专利名) men's underpants, with seams and an opening in the front sewn in the shape of an inverted Y 男用内裤(前有倒Y形开口者): *a pair of Y-fronts* 一条男用内裤(前有倒Y形开口者).

-y[1] (also **-ey**) *suff* 后缀 **1** (with *ns* forming *adjs* 与名词结合构成形容词) full of; having the quality of 充满...的; 多...的; 有...性质的: *dusty* ○ *icy* ○ *clayey*. **2** (with *vs* forming *adjs* 与动词结合构成形容词) tending to 有...倾向的; 易...的: *runny* ○ *sticky*. ▷ **-ily** (forming *advs* 用以构成副词). **-iness** (forming uncountable *ns* 用以构成不可数名词).

-y[2] *suff* 后缀 **1** (with *vs* forming *ns* 与动词结合构成名词) action or process of ...的行动或过程: *inquiry* ○ *expiry*. **2** (also **-ie**) (with *ns* forming diminutives or pet names 与名词结合构成指小词或昵称): *piggy* ○ *doggie* ○ *daddy* ○ *Susie*.

Y *abbr* 缩写 = **1** yen[1]. **2** /waɪ; waɪ/ (*US infml* 口) = YMCA, YWCA.

Y /waɪ; waɪ/ *symb* 符号 (**a**) (also **y**) (*mathematics* 数) unknown quantity 未知数: $x = y + 2$. (**b**) (*fig* 比喻) second unknown or unspecified person, number or influence 第二个未知的或未指明的人、数或影响力: *Mr X met Miss Y.* X先生遇见了Y小姐.

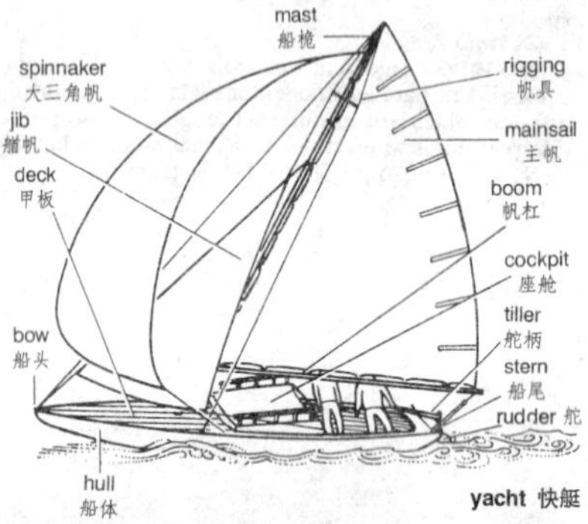

yacht 快艇

yacht /jɒt; jɑt/ *n* **1** light sailing-boat, esp one built specifically for racing 快艇; (尤指专为竞赛用的)帆船: [attrib 作定语] *a yacht race, club, crew* 帆船竞赛、俱乐部、(一组)选手 ○ *a sand yacht*, ie a yacht-like vehicle with wheels for use on sand 沙滩车. **2** large (usu power-driven) vessel used for private pleasure cruising 大型(通常为机动的)游艇. Cf 参看 DINGHY.

▷ **yacht** *v* [I] (usu in the continuous tenses 通常用于进行时态) travel or race in a yacht, especially as a hobby 乘坐快艇、帆船、游艇或进行比赛(尤指作为爱好): *I go yachting most weekends in the summer.* 在夏天, 我大多数周末都乘快艇游玩. **yacht·ing** *n* [U] art, practice or sport of sailing yachts 帆船驾驶(术); 帆船驾驶运动: [attrib 作定语] *yachting equipment* 帆船驾驶设备.

□ **'yachtsman** /-smən; -smən/ *n* (*pl* **-smen** /-smən; -smən/, *fem* 阴性作 **'yachtswoman**) person who has yachting as a hobby 帆船运动爱好者: *a round-the-world yachtsman* 环游世界一周的帆船运动爱好者.

yack /jæk; jæk/ *v* [I, Ipr, Ip] **~ (away/on) (about sb/sth)** (*sl* 俚) talk continuously and often noisily (usu about sth unimportant) 唠唠叨叨, 闲扯(常为高声地): *Joy kept yacking (on) about the wedding.* 乔伊唠唠叨叨地聊着婚礼的事.

▷ **yack** *n* (usu *sing* 通常作单数) (*sl* 俚) persistent or trivial conversation; chatter 絮絮叨叨的谈话; 聊天; 唠叨: *having a good old yack with the neighbours* 与邻居痛快地闲扯往事.

yackety-yack /ˌjækətɪ 'jæk; ˌjækətɪ 'jæk/ *n* [U] (*sl* 俚) persistent chatter 絮絮叨叨的谈话; 唠叨.

ya·hoo /jə'hu:; jə'hu/ *n* (*pl* **~s**) coarse brutish person 粗鲁的人: [attrib 作定语] *a yahoo attitude* 粗鲁的态度.

yak /jæk; jæk/ *n* wild or domesticated ox of Central Asia, with long horns and hair 牦牛(产于中亚、西藏).

Yale /jeɪl; jel/ *n* (also **'Yale lock**) (*propr* 专利名) type of lock with revolving internal parts, commonly used for doors, etc 耶鲁锁, 撞锁(常用作门等的锁): *have a Yale (lock) fitted* 安装耶鲁锁 ○ [attrib 作定语] *a Yale key* 耶鲁锁的钥匙.

yam /jæm; jæm/ *n* **1** (**a**) edible starchy tuber of a tropical climbing plant 薯蓣(通称山药). (**b**) this plant 薯蓣. **2** (*US*) type of sweet potato 甘薯(通称白薯或红薯).

yam·mer /'jæmə(r); 'jæmɚ/ *v* [I, Ipr, Ip] **~ (on) (about sb/sth)** (*infml derog* 口, 贬) talk noisily and continuously; complain or speak in a whining, grumbling manner 高声不停地说; 抱怨; 嘟嘟囔囔地说: *I do wish they'd stop yammering on about the size of the bill.* 我真希望他们别再嘟嘟囔囔地抱怨帐单的价钱了.

yang /jæŋ; jæŋ/ *n* [U] (in Chinese philosophy) the active bright male principle of the universe (中国哲学)阳. Cf 参看 YIN.

Yank /jæŋk; jæŋk/ *n* (*infml* 口) = YANKEE.

yank /jæŋk; jæŋk/ *v* [I, Ipr, Tn, Tn·pr, Tn·p] (*infml* 口) pull (sth) with a sudden sharp tug (often in a specified direction) 猛拉(某物)(常为向某方向): *She yanked (on) the rope and it broke.* 她猛力一拉, 绳子就断了. ○ *yank the bedclothes off one's bed* 把床单从床上拉下来 ○ *yank out a tooth* 拔出一颗牙齿.

▷ **yank** *n* sudden sharp tug 突然的猛拉: *The old chain only needed a couple of yanks before it snapped.* 这条旧链只拉了两下就断了.

Yan·kee /'jæŋkɪ; 'jæŋkɪ/ (also **Yank**) *n* **1** (*Brit infml* 口) inhabitant of the United States of America; American 美国人; 美洲人: [attrib 作定语] *Yankee hospitality* 美国人的好客. **2** (*US*) (**a**) inhabitant of any of the Northern States, esp those of New England 美国北部各州的人; (尤指)新英格兰人. (**b**) Federal soldier in the American Civil War (美国南北战争时的)北军.

yap /jæp; jæp/ *v* (**-pp-**) [I, Ipr] **1 ~ (at sb/sth)** (esp of small dogs) utter short sharp barks (尤指小狗)叫, 吠: *yapping at the postman* 向邮递员狂吠. **2** (*sl* 俚) talk noisily and foolishly 哇啦哇啦地瞎说: *Stop yapping!* 别瞎扯了!

▷ **yap** *n* sound of yapping (小狗的)叫声; 哇啦哇啦的说话声.

yard[1] /jɑ:d; jɑrd/ *n* **1** (**a**) (usu unroofed) enclosed or partly enclosed space near or round a building or group of buildings, often paved 建筑物附近或周围(通常为无顶篷的)围起来的空地(常为经铺设者); 院子. (**b**) (*US*) = BACKYARD (BACK[2]). **2** (usu in compounds 通常用以构成复合词) enclosure for a special purpose or business (为某目的或用途的)场地: *a 'railway yard/'marshalling yard*, ie an area where trains are made up, and where coaches, wagons, etc are stored 铁路站场[调车场] ○ *a 'builder's yard* 建筑场地.

yard[2] /jɑ:d; jɑrd/ *n* **1** (*abbr* 缩写 **yd**) unit of length, equal to 3 feet (36 inches) or 0.9144 metre 码(长度单位, 等于3英尺或0.9144米): *Can you still buy cloth by the yard in Britain?* 在英国买布还论码吗? ⇨App 4, 5

见附录4、5. **2** long pole-like piece of wood fastened to a mast for supporting and spreading a sail 帆桁.

▷ **yard·age** /ˈjɑːdɪdʒ; ˋjɑrdɪdʒ/ *n* [C, U] size measured in yards or square yards 码数; 平方码数: *a considerable yardage of canvas* 有相当大码数的帆布.

□ ˈ**yard-arm** *n* either end of a yard² (2) supporting a sail 帆桁端.

ˌ**yard of** ˈ**ale** (**a**) ale or beer held in a deep slender drinking glass about a yard long (盛于约一码长的细长玻璃杯中的)麦芽酒或啤酒. (**b**) this drinking glass 这种玻璃酒杯.

yard·stick /ˈjɑːdstɪk; ˋjɑrd,stɪk/ *n* ~ **(of sth)** standard of comparison 比较或衡量的标准; 尺度: *Durability is one yardstick of quality.* 耐久性是质量好坏的一个尺度. ○ *We need a yardstick to measure our performance by.* 我们的表现需要一个检验的标准.

yar·mulka /ˈjʌmʊlkə; ˋjɑrməlkə/ *n* skull-cap worn by Jewish men, esp at prayer (犹太男子戴的)无檐小圆帽(尤指祈祷时所戴者).

yarn /jɑːn; jɑrn/ *n* **1** [U] fibres (esp of wool) that have been spun for knitting, weaving, etc 纱; 线; (尤指)毛线. **2** [C] (*infml* 口) story; traveller's tale, esp one that is exaggerated or invented 故事; (旅行者的)奇谈(尤指夸张的或编造的). **3** (idm 习语) **spin a yarn** ⇨ SPIN.

▷ **yarn** *v* [I] (*infml* 口) tell yarns 讲故事; 信口开河: *We stayed up yarning until midnight.* 我们山南海北一直讲到深夜.

yar·row /ˈjærəʊ; ˋjæro/ *n* [C, U] plant with feathery leaves and small strong-smelling white or pinkish flowers in flat clusters 欧蓍草: *hedgerows full of yarrow* 有很多欧蓍草的灌木树篱.

yash·mak /ˈjæʃmæk; ˋjæʃ,mæk/ *n* veil covering most of the face, worn in public by Muslim women in certain countries (某些国家的穆斯林妇女在公众场所戴的)面纱.

yaw /jɔː; jɔ/ *v* [I] (of a ship or aircraft, etc) turn unsteadily off a straight or correct course (指轮船或飞行器等)偏航, 越出航线. Cf 参看 PITCH² 4, ROLL² 6.

▷ **yaw** *n* such a turn 偏航; 越出航线.

yawl /jɔːl; jɔl/ *n* (*nautical* 海) **1** (**a**) sailing-boat with two masts, the second being a short one near the stern (前桅高后桅低的)二桅帆船. (**b**) type of small fishing-boat 小渔船. **2** ship's boat with four or six oars (船载的四桨或六桨的)小艇.

yawn /jɔːn; jɔn/ *v* [I] **1** take (usu involuntarily) a deep breath with the mouth wide open, as when sleepy or bored 打哈欠. **2** (of large holes, etc) be wide open (指大洞穴等)张开, 裂开: *The deep crevasse yawned at their feet.* 他们脚下的冰川有一道深深的裂缝. ○ *a yawning chasm* 地上裂开的大坑 ○ (*fig* 比喻) *a yawning gap between the rich and poor in our society* 我们社会中贫富之间的鸿沟.

▷ **yawn** *n* **1** act of yawning (YAWN *v* 1) 哈欠. **2** (usu *sing* 通常作单数) (*infml derog* 口, 贬) uninteresting or boring thing 乏味的或枯燥的事物: *The meeting was one big yawn from start to finish.* 那会议自始至终十分无聊.

yaws /jɔːz; jɔz/ *n* [sing or pl *v*] tropical skin disease causing raspberry-like swellings 雅司病(热带莓疮).

yd *abbr* 缩写 = (*pl* **yds**) yard (measurement 量度单位): *12 yds of silk* 12码的丝绸. Cf 参看 FT, IN.

ye¹ /jiː; ji/ *pers pron* 人称代词 (*arch* 古) (*pl of thou* ☆ thou 的复数) you 汝等; 君等.

ye² /jiː; ji, *or pronounced as* 或读作 **the**/ *det* (used in the names of pubs, shops, etc as if it were the old-fashioned spelling 用于酒馆、商店等的名称, 作仿古体拼写) = the: *Ye Olde Bull and Bush*, eg on a pub sign 布尔及布什老店(如于酒馆招牌上者).

yea /jeɪ; je/ *adv, n* (*arch* 古) = yes. Cf 参看 NAY.

yeah /jeə; jɛə/ *adv* (*infml* 口) **1** (casual pronunciation of) yes ☆ yes(的俗音). **2** (idm 习语) ˌ**oh** ˈ**yeah?** (used to show that one does not believe what has been said 用以表示对所说的话不相信): *'I'm going to meet the Prime Minister.' 'Oh yeah? Very likely!'* '我要去见首相了.' '噢, 是吗? 那太有可能了!'

year /jɪə(r), *also* jɜː(r); jɪr/ *n* **1** [C] time taken by the earth to make one orbit round the sun, about 365¼ days 年. **2** [C] (also ˈ**calendar year**) period from 1 January to 31 December, ie 365 days (or 366 in a leap year) divided into 12 months 历年: *in the year 1865* 在1865年 ○ *this year* 今年 ○ *the year after next* 后年 ○ *a good year for cheap vegetables*, ie a year in which vegetables are available cheaply 蔬菜便宜的好年成. **3** [C] any period of 365 consecutive days 一年: *It's just a year (today) since I arrived here.* 我来到这里(到今天)整一年了. ○ *I arrived a year ago (today).* 我是一年前(的今天)来的. ○ *She's worked there for ten years.* 她在那里工作十年了. ○ *In a year's time they're getting married.* 一年之后他们就要结婚了. ○ [attrib 作定语] *a five-year forecast* 五年的预测. **4** [C] period of one year associated with sth, such as education or finance 与某事物(如教育或财政)相关的一年的期间: *the ˌacademic ˈyear* 学年 ○ *the fiˌnancial/fiscal/ˌtax ˈyear* 财政[会计/课税]年度 ○ [attrib 作定语] *first year students* 一年级的学生. **5** [C usu *pl* 通常作复数] age; time of life 年纪; 年龄; 年岁: *twenty years old/of age* 二十岁 ○ *a seventy-year-old man* 七十岁的人 ○ *She looks young for her years/for a woman of her years*, ie looks younger than she is. 她看起来比她的岁数年轻. ○ *He died in his sixtieth year*, ie at the age of 59. 他在步入六十岁时去世(即实足年龄59岁). **6 years** [pl] (*infml* 口) a long time 很久: *I've worked for this firm for years (and years).* 我为这家公司工作了很多年(很多年)了. ○ *It's years since we last met.* 我们已经很久没见面了. **7** (idm 习语) **the age/years of discretion** ⇨ DISCRETION.

ˌ**all (the) year** ˈ**round** throughout the year 一年到头: *He swims in the sea all year round.* 他一年到头都在海里游泳. **donkey's years** ⇨ DONKEY. **man, woman, car, etc of the** ˈ**year** person or thing chosen as outstanding in a particular field in a particular year 某年在某领域最杰出的人或事物: *TV personality of the year* 该年度电视圈的名人. **not/never in a hundred, etc** ˈ**years** absolutely not/never 绝对不[决不]. **old beyond one's years** ⇨ OLD. **put** ˈ**years on sb** make sb feel or appear older 使某人觉得或显得老些: *The shock put years on him.* 这一场冲击使他见老. **ring out the old year and ring in the new** ⇨ RING². **take** ˈ**years off sb** make sb feel or appear younger 使某人觉得或显得年轻些: *Giving up smoking has taken years off her.* 她戒烟以后显得年轻了. **the turn of the year/century** ⇨ TURN². **year after** ˈ**year** continuously for many years 年年: *She sent money year after year to help the poor.* 她年年送钱帮助穷人. **year by** ˈ**year** progressively each year 一年一年地: *Year by year their affection for each other grew stronger.* 他们相爱逐年加深. **the year** ˈ**dot** (*infml* 口) a very long time ago 很久以前: *I've been going there every summer since the year dot.* 我从很久以前每年夏天就都到那里去. **year** ˈ**in, year** ˈ**out** every year without exception 年复一年地. ˌ**year of** ˈ**grace**; ˌ**year of our** ˈ**Lord** (*fml* 文) any specified year after the birth of Christ 耶稣纪元某年; 公元某年: *in the year of our Lord 1217*, ie 1217 AD 公元1217年.

▷ **yearly** *adj, adv* (occurring) every year or once a year 每年(的); 一年一次(的): *a yearly conference/a conference held yearly* 一年一度的会议.

□ ˈ**year-book** *n* book issued once a year, giving information (reports, statistics, etc) about a particular subject 年鉴; 年刊; 年报.

ˌ**year-**ˈ**long** *adj* [attrib 作定语] continuing for or throughout a year 持续一年的; 整整一年的: *a ˌyear-long ˈlecture tour* 持续一年的演讲旅行.

year·ling /ˈjɪəlɪŋ; ˋjɪrlɪŋ/ *n* animal, esp a horse, between one and two years old 一岁至两岁的动物(尤指马): *a race for yearlings* 一两岁小马的赛马 ○ [attrib 作定语] *a yearling filly* 一两岁的小雌马.

yearn /jɜːn; jɝn/ *v* [I, Ipr, It] ~ **(for sb/sth)** desire strongly or with compassion or tenderness; be filled with longing 渴望; 怜悯; 思念; 留恋; 盼望: *a yearning desire* 如饥似渴的欲望 ○ *He yearned for his home and family.* 他怀念故国家园. ○ *She yearned to return to her native country.* 她巴不得能回国.

▷ **yearn·ing** *n* [C, U] ~ **(for sb/sth)**; ~ **(to do sth)** strong desire; tender longing 渴望; 热望. **yearn·ingly** *adv*.

yeast /jiːst; jist/ *n* [C, U] (type of) fungous substance used in the making of beer and wine, or to make bread rise²(10) 酵母; 发酵物: *brewer's yeast* 啤酒用酵母 ○ *baker's yeast* 发面用酵母.

▷ **yeasty** *adj* tasting or smelling strongly of yeast; frothy like yeast when it is developing 酵母味的; 发酵的; 起泡的. **yeasti·ness** *n* [U].

yell /jel; jɛl/ *v* **1** [I, Ipr, Ip] **~ (out) (at sb/sth); ~ (out) (in/with sth)** utter a loud sharp cry or cries as of pain, excitement, etc 号叫; 喊叫; 叫喊: *Stop yelling, can't you!* 别嚷了, 行吗? ○ *She yelled (out) at her mischievous child.* 她对她淘气的孩子大喊大叫. ○ *yell out in anguish, terror, pain, etc* 因苦恼、惊恐、疼痛等叫喊起来 ○ *yell with fear, agony, laughter* 害怕、痛苦、笑得喊叫起来. **2** [I, Ipr, Tn, Tn·pr, Tn·p] **~ (at sb) (about/for sth); ~ (out) sth (at sb/sth)** speak or say (sth) in a yelling voice 叫喊着说(某事): *She yelled at him about his constant drunkenness.* 她大嚷大叫说他总是烂醉如泥. ○ *The crowd yelled (out) encouragement at the players.* 人们叫喊着为选手打气. ⇨Usage at SHOUT 用法见 SHOUT.

▷ **yell** *n* **1** loud sharp cry of pain, excitement, etc 叫声; 喊声; 喊叫: *a yell of terror* 恐怖的叫喊声 ○ *let out an ear-splitting yell* 发出震耳欲聋的号叫声. **2** (*US*) particular type of shout or cheer used at a college to encourage a team, etc (学院中拉拉队助威的)喊叫声.

yel·low /ˈjeləʊ; ˋjɛlo/ *adj* **1** (**a**) of the colour of ripe lemons, egg yolks or gold, or of a colour similar to this 黄(色)的. ⇨illus at SPECTRUM 见 SPECTRUM 插图. (**b**) (*often offensive* 常作轻蔑语) having the light brown skin and complexion of certain eastern Asian peoples (某些东亚民族)黄皮肤的. **2** (also ˈ**yellow-bellied**) (*infml derog* 口, 贬) cowardly 胆怯的: *I always suspected he was yellow.* 我总怀疑他很胆小. **3** (idm 习语) **a yellow ˈstreak** cowardice in sb's character 生性怯懦.

▷ **yel·low** *n* (**a**) [C, U] the colour yellow 黄色: *several different yellows* (ie shades of yellow) *in the paintbox* 颜料盒中有几种不同色调的黄色. (**b**) [U] yellow substance, material or covering; yellow clothes 黄色的物质、材料或外层; 黄色的衣服: *wearing yellow* 穿着黄衣服.

yel·low *v* [I, Tn] (cause sth to) become yellow (使某物)变黄或发黄: *yellowing autumn leaves* 变黄的秋叶 ○ *The manuscript had yellowed/was yellowed with age.* 手稿因年久而发黄了.

yel·low·ish, yel·lowy *adjs* rather yellow 微黄的; 发黄的.

yel·low·ness *n* [U].

□ ˌ**yellow ˈcard** (in football, etc) card shown by the referee to a player that he is cautioning (足球等运动中的)黄牌, 黄卡(由裁判员出示, 用以向某运动员提出警告). Cf 参看 RED CARD (RED[1]).

ˌ**yellow ˈfever** [U] infectious tropical disease causing the skin to turn yellow 黄热病.

ˌ**yellow ˈflag** flag coloured yellow, displayed by a ship or hospital which is in quarantine 黄旗, 检疫旗(受隔离检疫的轮船或医院所悬挂的黄色旗子).

ˌ**yellow ˈline** yellow line painted at the side of a road to show restrictions on the parking of vehicles 黄线(路边限制停车者): *You can't park on a double yellow line.* 有双黄线处不准停车.

ˌ**Yellow ˈPages** (*propr* 专利名) telephone directory, or section of one, listing companies according to the goods or services they offer 黄页(用黄色纸印刷的电话簿或其中部分, 按公司类别排列者).

the yellow ˈpress (*infml derog* 口, 贬) newspapers that deliberately include sensational news items, etc in order to attract readers 低级报刊(故作耸人听闻的报道以哗众取宠的报纸).

yel·low·ham·mer /ˈjeləʊhæmə(r); ˋjɛloˌhæmɚ/ *n* type of small bird, the male of which has a yellow head, neck and breast 黄鹀(雄性头颈及胸部均为黄色的小鸟, 亦称黄道眉).

yelp /jelp; jɛlp/ *n* a short sharp cry (of pain, anger, excitement, etc) (因痛苦、气愤、兴奋等的)短而尖的叫声: *The dog gave a yelp when I trod on its paw.* 我踩了那狗的爪子, 它嗥叫了一声.

▷ **yelp** *v* [I] utter such a cry 发出短而尖的叫声.

Y

yen[1] /jen; jɛn/ *n* (*pl* unchanged 复数不变) unit of money in Japan 圆(日本的货币单位).

yen[2] /jen; jɛn/ *n* (usu *sing* 通常作单数) **~ (for sth/to do sth)** (*infml* 口) longing or yearning 渴望; 热望: *I've always had a yen to visit Australia.* 我总想去澳大利亚观光.

yeo·man /ˈjəʊmən; ˋjomən/ *n* (*pl* **-men** /-mən; -mən/) (*Brit*) **1** (*esp arch* 尤为古义) farmer who owns and works his land 自耕农: [attrib 作定语] *yeoman farmers* 自耕农. **2** (formerly) servant in a royal or noble household (旧时)(皇室或贵族的)侍者, 仆人.

▷ **yeo·manry** /-rɪ; -rɪ/ *n* [Gp] (*Brit*) (**a**) country landowners 自耕农. (**b**) (formerly) volunteer cavalry force raised from farmers, etc (旧时)(由农民等组成的)义勇骑兵队.

□ ˌ**Yeoman of the ˈGuard** member of the British sovereign's bodyguard (英国王室的)卫士.

ˌ**yeoman ˈservice** (*esp rhet* 尤作修辞) long and useful service; help, esp at a time of need 长期而有用的服务; 援助(尤指急需时): *retiring after 40 years' yeoman service to the company* 为公司勤勤恳恳工作40年后退休.

yes /jes; jɛs/ *interj* **1** (**a**) (used to answer in the affirmative 用作肯定的答复): *'Is this a painting by Picasso?' 'Yes, it is.'* '这是毕加索的画吗?' '是.' ○ (*emphatic* 强调) *'Don't you want to come with us?' 'Yes, of course I do.'* '你难道不愿意来跟我们在一起吗?' '我当然愿意.' (**b**) (used to show that a statement is correct or that the speaker agrees 用以表示一说法正确或说话人同意): *'English is a difficult language.' 'Yes, but not as difficult as Chinese.'* '英语很难.' '是啊, 但没有汉语那么难.' ○ *'Isn't she sweet?' 'Yes, she is.'* '她很可爱吧?' '对, 她很可爱.' (**c**) (used to agree with a request 用以表示同意一要求): *'Can I borrow this record?' 'Yes, of course.'* '我可以借这张唱片吗?' '当然可以.' **2** (used to accept an invitation or offer 用以表示接受一邀请或提议): *'Coffee?' 'Yes, please.'* '要咖啡吗?' '要, 谢谢.' **3** (used to acknowledge one's presence in a group or to reply when one is called 用以应答呼唤): *'Williams.' 'Yes, sir.'* '威廉.' '到.' ○ *'Waiter!' 'Yes, madam.'* '服务员!' '欸, 小姐.' **4** (used to ask what sb wants 用以询问某人之所需): *'Yes?' 'I'd like 2 tickets, please.'* '要什么?' '请给我来两张票.' Cf 参看 NO *interj*.

yes *n* (*pl* **yeses** /ˈjesɪz; ˋjɛsɪz/) answer that affirms, agrees, accepts, etc 表示肯定、同意、接受等的答复: *Can't you give me a straight* (ie direct) *yes or no?* 你能不能给我一个直截了当的答复, 行还是不行?

□ **yes-man** /ˈjesmæn; ˋjɛsˌmæn/ *n* (*pl* **-men** /-men; -ˌmɛn/) weak person who always agrees with his superior(s) in order to win favour or approval 唯唯诺诺的人.

yes·ter·day /ˈjestədɪ, -deɪ; ˋjɛstɚdɪ, -ˌde/ *adv* on the day just past; on the day before today 在昨天; 在昨日: *He arrived only yesterday.* 他昨天刚到. ○ *It was only yesterday that he arrived.* 昨天他才刚刚到. ○ *I can remember it as if it were yesterday.* 我对此事记忆犹新, 恍如昨日一般. ○ *Where were you yesterday morning/afternoon/evening?* 昨天上午[下午/晚上]你在什么地方?

▷ **yes·ter·day** *n* [U, C often *pl* 作不可数名词或可数名词, 后者常作复数] **1** the day before today 昨天; 昨日: *Yesterday was Sunday.* 昨天星期日. ○ *Where's yesterday's (news)paper?* 昨天的报纸在哪里? **2** the recent past 不久以前; 往昔: *dressed in yesterday's fashions* 穿着不久前流行的服装 ○ *all our yesterdays* 我们的往日. **3** (idm 习语) **be born yesterday** ⇨ BORN. **the day before yesterday** ⇨ DAY.

□ ˌ**yesterday ˈweek** eight days ago 八天以前: *I haven't seen him since yesterday week.* 我有八天没见到他了.

yester-year /ˈjestə jɪə(r), *also* jɜː(r); ˋjɛstɚˌjɪr/ *n* [U] (*arch or rhet* 古或修辞) the recent past 不久以前; 往昔: *recalling holidays of yester-year* 忆往昔之假日.

yet /jet; jɛt/ *adv* **1** (**a**) (used in questions and negative sentences and after *vs* expressing uncertainty, usu in final position; in British English usu with the present or past perfect tense, in US English usu with the simple past 用于疑问句和否定句中及用于表示怀疑的动词之后, 通常位于句末; 在英式英语中通常用于现在或过去完成时态, 在美式英语通常用于简单过去时态) by this or that time; until now/then 到这时; 到那时; 直至现在[当时]; 尚; 还; 仍然: *I haven't received a letter from him yet.* 我至今尚未收到他的信. (Cf 参看 (*US*) *I didn't receive a letter from him yet.*) ○ *'Are you ready?' 'No, not yet.'* '你准备好了吗?' '还没准备好呢.' ○ *She was not yet sure if she could trust him.* 她还没有把握确定是否相信他. ○ *I doubt if he has read it yet.* 我怀疑他是否看过这篇东西. (**b**) now or in the immediate future 现在; 马上; 立刻: *Don't go yet.* 先不要走. ○ *You don't need to start yet.* 你不必立刻就走. ⇨Usage at ALREADY 用法见

ALREADY. **2** (used with a *modal v;* formal if placed immediately after the *modal v* 与情态动词连用; 若紧接情态动词之后则更文雅) at an indefinite time in the future 不久的将来; 迟早; 早晚: *We may win yet.* 我们迟早会获胜的. ○ *She may surprise us all yet.* 她总有一天会让我们大家感到惊奇. ○ (*fml* 文) *We can yet reach our destination.* 我们终究能达到目的. **3** (used after superlatives 用于最高级之后) made, produced, written, etc until and including now/then 直至现在[当时](所制造、生产、书写等): *the most comprehensive study yet of his poetry* 迄今为止对他的诗歌最全面的研究 ○ *the highest building yet constructed* 到现在为止最高的建筑物 ○ *her best novel yet* 她的最好的小说. **4** (used in front of comparatives 用于比较级之前) even 更: *yet one more example of criminal negligence* 另一个过失犯罪之例 ○ *yet another victim of government policy on national health funding* 政府的国民保健拨款政策的另一个受害者 ○ *a recent and yet more improbable theory* 最新的而且也是更加不可信的理论 ○ *advancing yet further* 更进一步的发展. **5** (idm 习语) **as 'yet** until now/then 到现在[当时]为止: *an as yet unpublished document* 现尚未发表的文件 ○ *As yet little is known of the causes of the disease.* 造成这种疾病的原因迄今几乎一无所知. **yet a'gain** (*emphatic* 强调) once more 再; 再一次: *Yet again we can see the results of hasty decision-making.* 我们可以再一次看到仓促作出决定的后果.

▷ **yet** *conj* but at the same time; nevertheless 然而; 而; 但是: *slow yet thorough* 虽然慢但是彻底 ○ *She trained hard all year yet still failed to reach her best form.* 她全年艰苦训练, 然而仍未达到自己的最佳状态.

yeti /ˈjetɪ; ˋjɛtɪ/ *n* (also **A,bominable 'Snowman**) large hairy man-like or bear-like creature reported to live in the highest part of the Himalayas 雪人(据报道生存在喜马拉雅山高处似人或似熊的巨大长毛动物).

yew /juː; ju/ *n* (**a**) (also **'yew-tree**) [C] small evergreen tree with dark-green needle-like leaves and small red berries, often planted for garden hedges and in churchyards 紫杉. ⇨illus at App 1 见附录1插图, page i. (**b**) [U] wood of this tree 紫杉木.

YHA /ˌwaɪ eɪtʃ ˈeɪ; ˏwaɪ etʃ ˋe/ *abbr* 缩写 = (*Brit*) Youth Hostels Association 青年招待所协会.

yid /jɪd; jɪd/ *n* (⚠ *sl offensive* 讳, 俚, 蔑) Jew 犹太人.

Yid·dish /ˈjɪdɪʃ; ˋjɪdɪʃ/ *adj, n* [U] (of the) international Jewish language, a form of old German with words borrowed from Hebrew and several modern languages, used by Jews in or from E or Central Europe 依地语(的); (又译)意第绪语(的): *speak (in) Yiddish* 说依地语 ○ *a Yiddish speaker* 说依地语的人. Cf 参看 HEBREW.

yield /jiːld; jild/ *v* **1** [Tn] bear, produce or provide (a natural product, a result or profit) 生出、产生或提供(自然产物、结果或利润): *trees that no longer yield fruit* 不再结果实的树 ○ *experiments yielding new insights* 得到新的认识的实验 ○ *Building societies' investment accounts yield high interest.* 房屋建筑协会的投资利润获得很高的利息. **2** (**a**) [I, Ipr, Ip] **~ (to sb/sth)** (*fml* 文) allow oneself to be overcome by pressure; cease opposition (to sb/sth) 屈服; 让步; (对某人[某事物])不再反对: *The town was forced to yield after a long siege.* 该城受长期围困而被迫弃守. ○ *The government has not yielded to public opinion.* 政府并未向舆论让步. ○ *She yielded to temptation and had another chocolate.* 她禁不住诱惑, 又吃了一块巧克力. (**b**) [I] be forced out of the usual or natural shape; bend or break under pressure (受外力)变形; (受压力)弯曲或折断: *Despite all our attempts to break it open, the lock would not yield.* 尽管我们想方设法要把锁弄断, 它却仍纹丝不动. ○ *The dam eventually yielded and collapsed under the weight of water.* 水坝在水的压力下终于决口. **3** [Ipr] **~ to sth** be replaced or superseded by sth 被某事物代替或替换: *Increasingly, farm land is yielding to property development.* 地产的发展逐渐占据了农田. ○ *The cinema has largely yielded to the home video.* 电影业在很大程度上已让位给家庭录像电影. **4** [Tn, Tn·pr, Tn·p] **~ sb/sth (up) (to sb)** (*fml* 文) (**a**) reluctantly give control of sth (to sb); deliver sb/sth (to sb) 勉强地将某事物交出(予某人); 将某人[某事物]送交(某人): *The terrorists have yielded two of their hostages (up) to the police.* 恐怖分子已把其中两名人质交给警方. (**b**) reveal sth; disclose sth 泄露、揭露、透露、暴露或露出某事物: *The universe is slowly yielding up its secrets to scientists.* 宇宙慢慢地向科学家展现了自己的秘密. **5** [I, Ipr] **~ (to sb/sth)** (*esp US*) (of traffic) allow other traffic to have right of way (指道路上的来往车辆)让路给有先行权的车辆. **6** [I, Ipr] **~ (to sb/sth)** (*fml* 文) admit that one is inferior (to sb/sth); concede 承认自己比不上(某人[某事物]); 让步; 忍让: *I yield to no one in my admiration for* (ie am one of the greatest admirers of) *her work.* 我比任何人都佩服她的工作.

▷ **yield** *n* [U, C] (amount of) that which is yielded or produced 生产或出产(的量): *a good, high, poor, etc yield of wheat* 小麦的好收成、高产、歉收等 ○ *What is the yield per acre?* 每英亩的产量是多少? ○ *the annual milk yield* 牛奶的年产量.

yield·ing *adj* (**a**) that can bend and give[2](1); pliable rather than stiff 易弯曲的; 有弹性的; 柔软的: *a soft, yielding material* 柔软的、有弹性的材料. (**b**) likely to accept the wishes of others; not obstinate; compliant 顺从的; 不固执的; 依从的: *a gentle, yielding personality* 温柔、和顺的性情 ○ *She is rarely yielding on such an issue.* 在这类问题上她是很少让步的. **yield·ingly** *adv.*

yin /jɪn; jɪn/ *n* [U] (in Chinese philosophy) the passive dark female principle of the universe (中国哲学)阴. Cf 参看 YANG.

yip·pee /ˈjɪpiː; ˋjɪpi/ *interj* (*infml* 口) (used to express pleasure or excitement 用以表示愉快或兴奋).

YMCA /ˌwaɪ em siː ˈeɪ; ˏwaɪ ɛm si ˋe/ (also *US infml* 美式口语作 **Y**) *abbr* 缩写 = Young Men's Christian Association 基督教青年会: *stay at the YMCA (hostel)* 住在基督教青年会(招待所).

yob /jɒb; jɑb/ (also **yobbo** /ˈjɒbəʊ; ˋjɑbo/) *n* (*pl* **~s**) (*dated Brit sl* 旧, 俚) aggressive, ill-tempered and ill-mannered young person; lout 粗俗的青年; 粗人.

yo·del (also **yo·dle**) /ˈjəʊdl; ˋjodḷ/ *v* (**-ll-**; *US* **-l-**) [I, Tn] sing (a song) or utter a musical call, with frequent changes from the normal voice to high falsetto notes, in the traditional Swiss manner 用岳得尔调唱(歌)或呼喊(以瑞士的传统方式用真声和高音假嗓交替).

▷ **yo·del** (also **yo·dle**) *n* yodelling song or call 岳得尔调或呼喊.

yo·del·ler (*US* **yo·deler**) *n.*

yo·ga /ˈjəʊgə; ˋjogə/ *n* [U] (**a**) Hindu philosophy that teaches control over the mind, senses and body in order to produce mystical experience and the union of the individual soul with the universal spirit 瑜伽派(印度哲学的一派). (**b**) system of exercises for the body and the control of breathing for those practising yoga or wanting to become fitter 瑜伽(术); 瑜伽修行法: [attrib 作定语] *yoga classes* 瑜伽学习班.

▷ **yogi** /ˈjəʊgɪ; ˋjogɪ/ *n* (*pl* **~s**) teacher of or expert in yoga 瑜伽论者; 瑜伽(术)的导师或专家.

yog·hurt (also **'yog·urt**, **'yog·hourt**) /ˈjɒgət; *US* ˈjəʊgərt; ˋjogɚt/ *n* [U, C] slightly sour thick liquid food, consisting of milk fermented by added bacteria and often flavoured with fruit, etc 酸乳酪(常以水果等调味): *a breakfast of muesli and yoghurt* 谷物、坚果及酸乳酪的早餐 ○ *a carton of yoghurt* 一纸盒酸乳酪 ○ *Two strawberry yoghurts, please.* 请来两份草莓酸乳酪.

yoke 轭

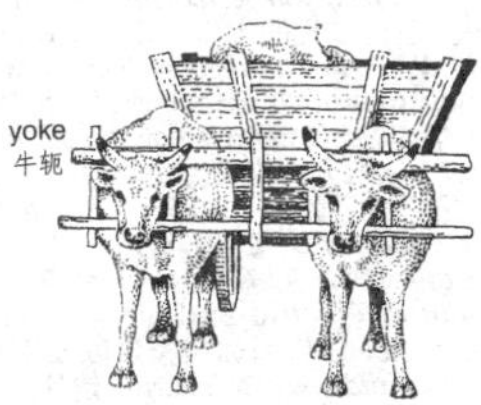

yoke /jəʊk; jok/ *n* **1** [C] (**a**) shaped piece of wood fixed across the necks of two animals (esp oxen) pulling a cart, plough, etc 轭; (尤指)牛轭. (**b**) (*pl* unchanged 复数不变) two oxen working together 共轭牛(共同工作的一对牛): *five yoke of oxen* 五对共轭牛. **2** [C] object like a yoke in form or function, esp a piece of wood shaped to fit across a person's shoulders and support a pail at each end 轭状的或起轭作用的物体; (尤指)轭状

扁担. **3** [C] (in dressmaking) part of a garment fitting round the shoulders or hips and from which the rest hangs (女服制作的)抵肩, (裙等的)腰. **4** [sing] **~ (of sth/sb)** (*fml fig* 文, 比喻) oppressive control; burdensome restraint 束缚; 羁绊: *throw off the yoke of slavery* 摆脱奴隶制的枷锁 ○ *under the yoke of a cruel master* 在残暴的主人的控制之下.

▷ **yoke** *v* [Tn, Tn·pr, Tn·p] **1 ~ sth (to sth); ~ sth and sth (together)** put a yoke on (an animal) 给(动物)上轭: *yoke oxen to a plough* 用轭把牛套在犁上 ○ *yoke oxen together* 用轭把牛套在一起. **2 ~ A (to/with B) (in sth); ~ A and B (together) (in sth)** (*fml* 文) unite or form a bond between (people) 使(人)结合或联合: *yoked to/with an unwilling partner* 与一个不甘心情愿的伙伴结合在一起 ○ *yoked (together) in marriage* 联姻.

yokel /ˈjəʊkl; ˋjokl/ *n* (*joc or derog* 谑或贬) simple-minded country person; bumpkin 乡下佬; 土包子; 土老帽儿.

yolk /jəʊk; jok/ *n* [C, U] round yellow part in the middle of the white of an egg 蛋黄; 卵黄: *Beat up the yolks of three eggs.* 把三个蛋黄搅匀. ⇨ illus at EGG 见 EGG 插图.

Yom Kippur /ˌjɒm ˈkɪpə(r), ˌjɒm kɪˈpʊə(r); ˌjomˋkɪpɚ, ˌjomkɪˋpʊr/ annual Jewish holiday observed with fasting and prayers of penitence 赎罪日(一年一度的犹太人的节日, 于此日禁食及作忏悔祈祷).

yomp /jɒmp; jɑmp/ *v* [I, Ipr, Ip] (*Brit army sl* 英军俚) march with heavy equipment over difficult country 野外负重行军: *yomping across moorland* 穿过荒郊野外负重行军.

yon·der /ˈjɒndə(r); ˋjɑndɚ/ *det, adj, adv* (*arch or dialect* 古或方) (that is or that can be seen) over there (在或可见于)那边(的): *Do you see yonder clump of trees* (ie that clump of trees over there)? 你看见那边的一丛树林了吗? ○ *Whose is that farm (over) yonder?* 那边的农场是谁的?

yore /jɔː(r); jɔr/ *n* (idm 习语) **of yore** (*arch or rhet* 古或修辞) long ago 往昔: *in days of yore* 昔日.

York·shire pud·ding /ˌjɔːkʃə ˈpʊdɪŋ; ˌjɔrkʃɚ ˋpʊdɪŋ/ baked batter[2] often eaten with roast beef 约克郡布丁(常与烤牛肉同食): *a large helping of Yorkshire pudding* 一大块约克郡布丁 ○ *four small Yorkshire puddings* 四小块约克郡布丁.

you /juː; ju/ *pers pron* 人称代词 **1** person or people being addressed 您; 你; 你们. (**a**) (used as the subject or object of a *v* or after a *prep*; also used independently and after *be* 用作动词的主语或宾语或用于介词之后, 也可单独使用及用于be之后): *You said you knew the way.* 你说过你认识路的. ○ *I thought she told you.* 我以为她告诉你了. ○ *This is just between you and me*, ie not to be told to anyone else. 这事只是你知道我知道(不要告诉别人). ○ *I don't think that hair-style is you*, ie It doesn't suit your personality. 我认为那发型不适合你. ○ *Is there anyone among you who is a doctor?* 你们中间有医生吗? (**b**) (used with *ns* and *adjs* to address sb directly 与名词、形容词连用, 作直接称呼): *You girls, stop talking!* 你们这些女孩子, 别说话了! ○ *You silly fool, you've lost us the game.* 你这个傻瓜, 你把我们这一局给输了. ○ *You angel, you've remembered my birthday.* 你这个大好人, 还记得我的生日. **2** everyone; anyone (泛指)任何人: *You learn a language better if you visit the country where it's spoken.* 若到说某种语言的国家去, 就能把该种语言学得好些. ○ *Driving on the left is strange at first but you get used to it.* 沿着路的左侧驾驶刚开始时有些别扭, 可是习惯了就好了. ○ *It's easier to cycle with the wind behind you.* 顺着风骑车省力. ○ *Nobody wants to help you in this town.* 在这座小城市里没有人愿意帮助别人. **3** (idm 习语) **ˌyou and ˈyours** you and your family and close friends 你和你的家属以及密切的朋友: *a souvenir for you and yours to cherish* 请你和你的家人惠存的一件纪念品.

Y

□ **you-all** /ˈjuːɔːl; ˋjuˌɔl/ *pers pron* 人称代词 (*esp southern US* 尤用于美国南部) you (plural) 你们: *Have you-all brought swim-suits?* 你们带游泳衣来了吗?

you'd /juːd; jud/ *contracted form* 缩约式 **1** you had ⇨ HAVE. **2** you would ⇨ WILL[1], WOULD[1].

you'll /juːl; jul/ *contracted form* 缩约式 you will ⇨ WILL[1].

young /jʌŋ; jʌŋ/ *adj* (**-nger** /-ŋgə(r); -ŋgɚ/, **-ngest** /-ŋgɪst; -ŋgɪst/) **1** not far advanced in life, growth, development, etc; of recent birth or origin 年轻的; 幼小的; 新诞生的; 新成立的: *a young woman, animal, tree, nation* 年轻的女人、幼小的动物、幼小的树、新成立的国家. Cf 参看 OLD 2. **2** still near its beginning 仍然接近开始阶段的; 初期的: *The evening is still young.* 晚间刚开始不久. **3 the younger** (*fml* 文) (used before or after a person's name, to distinguish that person from an older person with the same name 用于姓名之前或之后, 以区别于同名之年长者): *the younger Pitt/Pitt the younger* 年纪较轻的那个皮特. Cf 参看 ELDER[1] 2. **4** (*becoming dated* 渐旧) (**a**) (used before a person's name to distinguish esp a son from his father 用于姓名之前, 以区别父子, 指儿子): *Young Jones is just like his father.* 小琼斯真像他的父亲. (**b**) (used as a familiar or condescending form of address 用作亲切的或屈尊俯就的称呼): *Now listen to me, (my) young man/lady!* 听我说, (我的)小伙子[小姐]! **5** for, concerning or characteristic of youth or young people 青年的; 年轻人的: *The young look is in fashion this year.* 今年时兴扮年轻人的样子. ○ *Those clothes she's wearing are much too young for her.* 她穿的那些衣服显得太年轻了. **6** [pred 作表语] **~ in sth** having little practice or experience in sth 对某事物不熟练或无甚经验: *young in crime* 初次犯罪. **7** (idm 习语) **an angry young man** ⇨ ANGRY. **not as/so young as one ˈused to be/(once) ˈwas** old or growing old and losing vigour, good health, etc 年老的; 失去青春活力或健康等的: *I can't play squash twice a week: I'm not as young as I was, you know!* 我不能一星期打两次壁球了, 我的体力大不如前了, 你要知道! **not get any ˈyounger** become older 变老的: *Of course long walks tire you out — you're not getting any younger, you know.* 当然走长路能把你累坏的——青春不再, 你要知道. **an old head on young shoulders** ⇨ OLD. **young and ˈold (aˈlike)** everyone, regardless of age 无论老少: *This is a book for young and old (alike).* 这本书老少咸宜. **ˌyoung at ˈheart** in spite of one's age, still feeling and behaving as one did when one was young 人老心不老. **the ˌyoung iˈdea** (*dated* 旧) young people, esp schoolboys or schoolgirls and students 青少年; (尤指)学生. **one's young ˈlady/young ˈman** (*dated* 旧) one's girl-friend/boy-friend 女朋友; 男朋友: *When's your young man coming to dinner, then?* 你的男朋友什么时候来吃饭呢? **you're only young ˈonce** (*saying* 谚) young people should be allowed to enjoy themselves while they can, because they will have plenty to worry about when they get older 应准予年轻人及时行乐(因为年纪大时要有很多操心事).

▷ **young** *n* [pl] **1** (of animals and birds) offspring; young ones (指鸟兽)雏; 仔; 崽: *The cat fought fiercely to defend its young*, ie its young kittens. 那只猫拼命反抗以保护小猫. **2 the young** young people considered as a group 年轻人(总称): *The young in our society need care and protection.* 我们社会的年轻人需要受到关怀和爱护. **3** (idm 习语) **(be) with ˈyoung** (of animals) pregnant (指动物)怀孕的.

young·ish *adj* fairly young; quite young 相当年轻的; 很幼小的: *a youngish President* 年轻的总统.

young·ster /-stə(r); -stɚ/ *n* child; youth; young person 孩子; 少年; 青年; 年轻人: *How are the youngsters* (ie your children)? 你的孩子怎么样?

NOTE ON USAGE 用法: **Yours faithfully, Yours sincerely,** (*esp US*) **Yours truly** are the commonest ways of ending formal and semi-formal letters. ☆ **Yours faithfully**、**Yours sincerely**、(尤用于美式英语的) **Yours truly** 是信末最常见的敬语, 用于正规的及半正规的书信均可. The correct style is to use **Yours faithfully** to end a letter which begins **Dear Sir/Madam** (ie when the name of the person being addressed is not known to the writer) and **Yours sincerely/truly** after **Dear Mr/Mrs/Miss/Ms Smith** (ie when the name is known but the person is not well known to the writer). 正确的格式是在信的开头用 **Dear Sir/Madam**(即不认识收信人), 则信末用 **Yours faithfully**, 而在信的开头用 **Dear Mr/Mrs/Miss/Ms Smith**(即知其名而不熟悉者)则信末用 **Yours sincerely/truly.** ☆ In US English **Sincerely, Sincerely yours** and **Yours truly** are often used. 在美式英语中常用 **Sincerely**、**Sincerely yours**、**Yours truly.** ☆ If the writer knows the addressee personally, the first name is used and **With best wishes** may be added. 若写信人与收信人相识, 则信的开头用收信人的名字(不用姓), 信末可加 **With best wishes**. ☆ More familiar still is the use of the first name and **Yours (ever).** 关系更密切者, 信的开头用收信人的名字(不用姓), 信末用 **Yours (ever)**.

英文书信头尾格式示例

Dear Madam, ... **Yours faithfully,** Jane Jones	Dear Mrs Brown, ... **Yours sincerely/truly,** Jane Jones
Dear Margaret, ... With best wishes, **Yours sincerely/truly,** Jane (Jones)	Dear Maggie, ... All the best, **Yours,** Jane

For further help with letter writing see Sample Texts 3a and 3b in Appendix 3. 有关书信格式详解见附录 3 中的 3a 和 3b.

your /jɔ:(r); *US* jʊər; jʊr/ *possess det* **1** of or belonging to the person or people being addressed 您的; 你的; 你们的: *Excuse me, is this your seat?* 请问, 这是您的座位吗? ○ *Your hair's going grey.* 你的头发有些灰白了. ○ *You'll see the post office on your right.* 在你的右边能看到那个邮局. ○ *Do you like your new job?* 你喜欢你的新工作吗? **2** (*often derog* 常作贬义) (used to refer to sth that the person being addressed is associated with 用以指与对方有关的事物): *These are your famous Oxford colleges* (ie the ones you talk about). *I suppose.* 我想这些就是你常说的那些著名的牛津学院了. ○ *I don't think much of your English weather.* 我对你们英国的天气可不太欣赏. ○ (*ironic* 反语) *You and your bright ideas!* 你的高见又来了! **3** (also **Your**) (used when addressing royal people, important officials, etc 用以称呼皇室人员、重要官员等): *Your Majesty* 陛下 ○ *Your Excellency* 阁下.
▷ **yours** /jɔ:z; *US* jʊərz; jʊrz/ *possess pron* **1** of or belonging to you 您的; 你的; 你们的: *Is that book yours?* 那本书是您的吗? ○ *Is she a friend of yours?* 她是你的朋友吗? **2** (usu 通常作 **Yours,** *abbr* 缩写 **yrs**) (used in ending a letter 用于信函的结尾): *Yours sincerely* ○ *Yours faithfully* ○ *Yours truly* (相当于中文书信的'谨上、敬上'等). ➪ Usage above 用法见上文.

you're /jʊə(r), *also* jɔ:(r); jʊr, jɔr/ *contracted form* 缩约式 you are ➪ BE.

your·self /jɔ:ˈself; *US* jʊərˈself; jʊrˈsɛlf/ (*pl* **-selves** /-ˈselvz; -ˈsɛlvz/) *reflex, emph pron* 反身、强调代词 (only taking the main stress in sentences when used emphatically 仅用以加强语气时方读重音) **1** (*reflex* 反身) (used when the person or people addressed cause(s) and is/are affected by an action 作第二人称的反身代词): *Have you ˈhurt yourself?* 你把自己弄伤了吗? **2** (*emph* 强调) (used to emphasize the person or people addressed 用以加强第二人称的语气): *You yourself are one of the chief offenders.* 你自己就是其中一个主犯. ○ *You can try it out for yourˈselves.* 你们自己可以试一试. ○ *Do it yourˈself — I haven't got time.* 你自己做——我没有时间. **3** (idm 习语) **by yourˈself/yourˈselves** (**a**) alone 独自; 单独: *How long were you by yourself in the classroom?* 你独自一人在教室里多长时间了? (**b**) without help 独力; 靠自己: *Are you sure you did this exercise by yourself?* 这个练习真是你自己做的吗?

youth /ju:θ; juθ/ *n* (*pl* **~s** /ju:ðz; juðz/) **1** [U] period of being young, esp the time between childhood and maturity 青少年时期: *a wasted* (ie unprofitably spent) *youth* 虚度的青少年时代 ○ *I often went there in my youth.* 我小时候常到那里去. ○ *He painted scenes from his youth,* ie that reminded him of the time when he was young. 他画的是他年轻时的景色. Cf 参看 AGE[1] 2. **2** [U] (*fml* 文) state or quality of being young 青春; 活力; 朝气; 血气: *Her youth gives her an advantage over the other runners.* 她年轻, 这是她比其他赛跑者优越的地方. ○ *She is full of youth and vitality.* 她充满了青春和活力. Cf 参看 AGE[1] 2. **3** [C] (*often derog* 常作贬义) young man (esp one in his teens) 青年男子, 小伙子(尤指十余岁的): *As a youth he showed little promise.* 他这个小伙子, 看不出有什么出息. ○ *The fight was started by some youths who had been drinking.* 这场架是一帮喝醉了的小青年惹起的. **4** (also **the youth**) [sing or pl *v*] young people considered as a group 青年人(总称): *the youth of the country/the country's youth* 全国的青年人 ○ *The youth of today has/have greater opportunities than ever before.* 现在的青年人比以往任何时候都有更多的机会. ○ [attrib 作定语] *youth culture*, ie activities, interests, etc of young people 青年人的文化(活动、兴趣等). **5** (idm 习语) **the first/full flush of youth** ➪ FLUSH[1].
▷ **youth·ful** /-fl; -fəl/ *adj* having qualities typical of youth; young or seeming young 青年人的; 青春的; 有朝气的; 年轻的; 似年轻的: *a youthful managing director* 朝气蓬勃的总经理 ○ *a youthful appearance* 少相 ○ *She's a very youthful sixty-five.* 她已六十五岁却显得很年轻. **youth·fully** /-fəlɪ; -fəlɪ/ *adv*. **youth·ful·ness** *n* [U].
□ ˈ**youth club** club (usu provided by a church, a local authority or a voluntary organization) for young people's leisure and social activities 青年俱乐部.
ˈ**youth hostel** building in which cheap and simple food and accommodation is provided for (esp young) people on walking, riding or cycling holidays 青年招待所.
ˈ**youth hostelling** staying in youth hostels 住在青年招待所里: *go youth hostelling* 到青年招待所里去住.

you've /ju:v; juv/ *contracted form* 缩约式 you have ➪ HAVE.

yowl /jaʊl; jaʊl/ *n* loud wailing cry 哀号; 哭号; 号叫.
▷ **yowl** *v* [I] utter a yowl 哀号; 哭号; 号叫: *kept awake by cats yowling all night* 因整夜的猫叫声而无法入睡.

Yo-Yo /ˈjəʊ jəʊ; ˈjo,jo/ *n* (*pl* **~s**) (*propr* 专利名) toy consisting of two thick discs of wood or plastic with a deep groove between, which can be made to rise and fall on an attached string when this is jerked with a finger 悠悠(玩具, 为木制或塑料制两厚圆盘, 中间有一深沟连接一绳, 用手指抻绳可使之沿绳上下移动): *The price of petrol is going up and down like a Yo-Yo.* 汽油的价格像悠悠一样忽上忽下.

yr *abbr* 缩写 = **1** (*pl* **yrs**) year: *valid for 3 yrs* 3年有效 ○ *a race for 2-yr olds*, ie horses 两岁马的赛事. **2** your.

yrs *abbr* 缩写 = yours: *yrs sincerely*, ie before a signature on a letter (用作书信署名前的敬语, 相当于中文的'谨上、敬上'等).

YTS /ˌwaɪ ti: ˈes; ˌwaɪ ti ˋɛs/ *abbr* 缩写 = (*Brit*) Youth Training Scheme 青年训练计划: *We've got a YTS girl helping us.* 我们获得参加青年训练的一个姑娘的帮助.

yucca /ˈjʌkə; ˋjʌkə/ *n* tall plant with white bell-like flowers and stiff spiky leaves 丝兰(花).

yuck /jʌk; jʌk/ *interj* (*sl* 俚) (used to express disgust, distaste, etc 用以表示厌恶、反感等).
▷ **yucky** *adj* (**-ier, -iest**) (*sl* 俚) nasty; disgusting 讨厌的; 令人厌恶的: *yucky school dinners* 学校里难吃的饭菜.

yule /ju:l; jul/ (also **yule-tide** /ˈju:ltaɪd; ˋjul,taɪd/) *n* (*arch* 古) festival of Christmas 圣诞节: [attrib 作定语] *Yule-tide greetings*, eg on a Christmas card 恭贺圣诞(如于圣诞贺卡上者).
□ ˈ**yule-log** *n* large log of wood traditionally burnt on Christmas Eve 圣诞柴(圣诞节前夕烧的木柴).

yummy /ˈjʌmɪ; ˋjʌmɪ/ *adj* (*infml* 口) (used esp by children in spoken English 尤用作儿童口语) tasty; delicious 味道好的; 好吃的: *Chocolate cake for tea? How yummy!* 有巧克力蛋糕当茶点? 多好吃啊!

yum-yum /ˌjʌm ˈjʌm; ˋjʌmˋjʌm/ *interj* (*infml* 口) (used to express pleasure while eating, or when thinking about eating, pleasant food 用以表示吃好东西时或想到吃好东西时的快乐).

yup·pie /ˈjʌpɪ; ˋjʌpɪ/ *n* (*infml often derog* 口, 常作贬义) young and ambitious professional person, esp one working in a city 雅皮(年轻有为的专业人士, 尤指在城市工作的).

YWCA /ˌwaɪ dʌblju: si: ˈeɪ; ˌwaɪ dʌbljʊ si ˋe/ (also *US infml* 美式口语作 **Y**) *abbr* 缩写 = Young Women's Christian Association 基督教女青年会: *stay at the YWCA (hostel)* 住在基督教女青年会(招待所).

Y

Z z

Z, z /zed; *US* zi:; zi/ *n* (*pl* **Z's, z's** /zedz; *US* zi:z; ziz/) **1** the twenty-sixth and last letter of the English alphabet; zed 英语字母表的第二十六个也是最后一个字母. **2** (idm 习语) **from A to Z** ⇨ A, a[1].

zany /ˈzeɪnɪ; ˋzenɪ/ *adj* (**-ier, -iest**) (*infml* 口) amusingly ridiculous; eccentric 滑稽可笑的; 古怪的: *a zany haircut, lifestyle, personality* 滑稽古怪的发型、生活方式、性格.
▷ **za·nily** *adv*.
za·ni·ness *n*.
zany *n* comical or eccentric person 滑稽的或古怪的人.

zap /zæp; zæp/ *v* (**-pp-**) (*infml* 口) **1** [Tn, Tn·pr] **~ sb (with sth)** (**a**) kill sb, esp with a gun 杀死某人(尤指用枪). (**b**) make sb unconscious with a hit, blow, etc; attack sb 将某人打昏; 攻击某人. **2** [Ipr, Ip] move suddenly or quickly in the specified direction (沿某方向)突然或迅速移动: *Have you seen him zapping around town on his new motor bike?* 你看见没看见他骑着自己的新摩托车在市区飞驰?
▷ **zap** *n* [U] (*infml* 口) feeling of energy, liveliness, etc; vigour 精力; 活力; 元气: *I really admire her — she's so full of zap!* 我真佩服她——精力那么充沛! Cf 参看 ZIP 2. **zappy** *adj* (*infml* 口) lively and energetic; amusing 活泼的; 精力旺盛的; 好笑的.

zeal /zi:l; zil/ *n* [U] (*fml* 文) **~ (for sth)** (usu intense) energy or enthusiasm; keenness (通常为高度的)热忱, 热情; 热心: *show zeal for a cause* 表现出对一事业的热忱 ○ *work with great zeal* 热情洋溢地工作 ○ *revolutionary, religious zeal* 革命的、宗教的热诚.
▷ **zeal·ous** /ˈzeləs; ˋzɛləs/ *adj* full of zeal; eager 热情的; 热心的; 积极的: *zealous for liberty and freedom* 为争取自由而积极的 ○ *zealous to succeed at work* 一心要做好工作. **zeal·ously** *adv*.

zealot /ˈzelət; ˋzɛlət/ *n* (*sometimes derog* 有时作贬义) person who is extremely enthusiastic about sth, esp religion or politics; fanatic (对某事物, 尤指宗教或政治)极热心的人; 狂热者.
▷ **zeal·otry** /-rɪ; -rɪ/ *n* [U] (*fml* 文) zealous attitude or behaviour 极热心的态度或行为.

zebra 斑马

zebra /ˈzebrə, ˈzi:brə; ˋzibrə/ *n* (*pl* unchanged or **~s** 复数或不变或作 **zebras**) African wild animal of the horse family with a body covered by black (or dark brown) and white stripes 斑马.

zebra crossing 斑马线

□ ˌ**zebra ˈcrossing** (*Brit*) part of a road, marked with broad white stripes, where vehicles must stop if pedestrians wish to cross 斑马线(用白色宽条标出的路面部分, 行人欲通过时车辆必须停止). ⇨illus 见插图. Cf 参看 PEDESTRIAN CROSSING (PEDESTRIAN), PELICAN CROSSING (PELICAN).

zed /zed; zɛd/ (*US* **zee** /zi:; zi/) *n* the letter Z Z字母: *There are two zeds in 'puzzle'.* 在puzzle一字中有两个z字母.

Zeit·geist /ˈzaɪtgaɪst; ˋzaɪtˌgaɪst/ *n* (*German* 德) spirit of a particular period of history as shown by the ideas, beliefs, etc of the time 时代精神.

Zen /zen; zɛn/ *n* [U] Japanese form of Buddhism that stresses the importance of meditation more than the reading of religious writings 禅, 禅宗(日本佛教宗派, 注重静坐沉思而并非诵读经文): [attrib 作定语] *Zen Buddhism* 禅宗佛教.

zen·ith /ˈzenɪθ; ˋzinɪθ/ *n* **1** point in the heavens directly above an observer 天顶(观测者正上方的天空). Cf 参看 NADIR. **2** (*fig* 比喻) highest point (of power, prosperity, etc); peak (权力、繁荣等的)最高点; 顶点: *reach the zenith of one's career, power, influence* 达到事业的、权力的、影响力的顶峰 ○ *At its zenith the Roman empire covered almost the whole of Europe.* 罗马帝国在全盛时期几乎占据了整个欧洲.

zephyr /ˈzefə(r); ˋzɛfɚ/ *n* (*dated or fml* 旧或文) soft gentle breeze 和风; 微风.

Zep·pelin /ˈzepəlɪn; ˋzɛpəlɪn/ *n* type of large airship used by the Germans in World War I 齐柏林飞艇(第一次世界大战中德国使用的大型飞艇).

zero /ˈzɪərəʊ; ˋzɪro/ *pron, det* **1** 0; one less than one; nought 0; 零: *Five, four, three, two, one, zero. We have lift-off!* 五、四、三、二、一、零. 我们升空了! **2** lowest point; nothing; nil 最低点; 没有; 无: *Economic growth is at zero,* ie is not increasing. 经济无增长. ○ *Prospects of success in the talks were put at zero.* 会谈没有成功的希望. **3** (**a**) point between plus (+) and minus (–) on a scale, esp on a thermometer (刻度上的)零点, 零位; (尤指温度计的)零度: *The thermometer fell to zero last night.* 昨夜温度计显示气温下降到零度. (**b**) temperature, pressure, etc that corresponds to zero on a scale (相当于零度的)温度、压力等: *It was really cold last night — ten degrees below zero,* ie –10°C, ten degrees below the freezing point of water. 昨夜真冷——零下十度(–10°C). ⇨Usage at NOUGHT 用法见 NOUGHT. **4** (*infml* 口 *esp US*) nothing at all; none 毫无; 没有: *Politics has zero interest for me,* ie I am not at all interested in it. 我对政治丝毫不感兴趣.
▷ **zero** *n* (*pl* **~s**) the number 0 ☆ 0; 零; 零号.
zero *v* (phr v) **zero in on sb/sth** **1** aim guns, etc at or find the range of (a particular target) (将枪炮等)瞄准(某目标)或调整到(某目标的)射程. **2** (*fig* 比喻) fix attention on sb/sth; focus on sb/sth 将注意力集中于某人[某事物]; 将焦点调到某人[某事物]上: *zero in on the key issues for discussion* 把注意力集中到讨论的关键问题上来.
□ **zero ˈgrowth** no increase at all 毫无增长: *zero growth in industrial output, the economy, population* 工业生产、经济、人口毫无增长.
ˈ**zero-hour** *n* time when a military operation, an attack, etc is planned to start (部署的军事行动、攻击等的)开始时刻: *Zero-hour is 3.30 am.* 发动攻击的时刻是凌晨3时30分.
ˈ**zero-rated** *adj* (of goods, services, etc) on which no value added tax is charged (指货物、服务等)免付增值税的.

zest /zest; zɛst/ *n* [U, sing] **1 ~ (for sth)** great enjoyment or excitement; gusto 极大的快乐或兴奋; 热情; 兴趣: *Her zest for life is as great as ever.* 她对生活的极大乐趣一如既往. ○ *He entered into our plans with terrific zest.* 他满腔热情地参加了我们的项目. **2** (quality of) having added interest, flavour, charm, etc 增加的兴

趣、风味、魅力等(的性质): *The element of risk gave (an) added zest to the adventure.* 这种冒险成分更给探险活动平添几分乐趣. **3** outer skin of oranges, lemons, etc when used as a flavouring in cooking (用于烹饪时调味的)橙子、柠檬等的外皮. Cf 参看 PEEL *n*, RIND, SKIN 4. ▷ **zest·ful** /-fʊl; -fəl/ *adj*. **zest·fully** /-fʊlɪ; -fəlɪ/ *adv*.

zig·zag /ˈzɪɡzæɡ; ˋzɪɡzæɡ/ *adj* [attrib 作定语] (of a line, path, etc) turning right and left alternately at sharp angles (指线条、小径等)锯齿形的, 之字形的, Z字形的: *a zigzag road, course, flash of lightning* 弯弯曲曲的道路、路线、闪电.

▷ **zig·zag** *n* line, path, etc forming a zigzag 锯齿形的线条、小径等.

zig·zag *v* (**-gg-**) [I, Ipr, Ip] go in a zigzag 曲折地前进: *The narrow path zigzags up the cliff.* 这条狭窄的小径曲曲折折地向峭壁伸延. ⇨illus at PATTERN 见PATTERN插图.

zil·lion /ˈzɪlɪən; ˋzɪljən/ *n* (*infml* 口 *esp US*) very large but indefinite number 极大而不确定的数目: [attrib 作定语] *She's a zillion times brainier than I am.* 她比我聪明亿万倍.

zinc /zɪŋk; zɪŋk/ *n* [U] chemical element, a bluish-white metal used in alloys and to cover iron sheets, wire, etc as a protection against rust 锌. ⇨App 10 见附录10.

zing /zɪŋ; zɪŋ/ *n* [U] (*infml* 口) liveliness; energy 活力; 精力; 生命力: *You need to put more zing into your playing.* 你在这一活动中需要再增加些干劲.

Zion /ˈzaɪən; ˋzaɪən/ *n* **1** the Jewish religion 犹太教. **2** the Christian Church 基督教会. **3** the kingdom of Heaven 天国; 天堂.

Zi·on·ism /ˈzaɪənɪzəm; ˋzaɪən,ɪzəm/ *n* [U] political movement concerned with the establishment and political and religious development of an independent Jewish state in what is now Israel 犹太复国运动.

▷ **Zi·on·ist** /ˈzaɪənɪst; ˋzaɪənɪst/ *n* person who supports Zionism 犹太复国运动的支持者或拥护者.

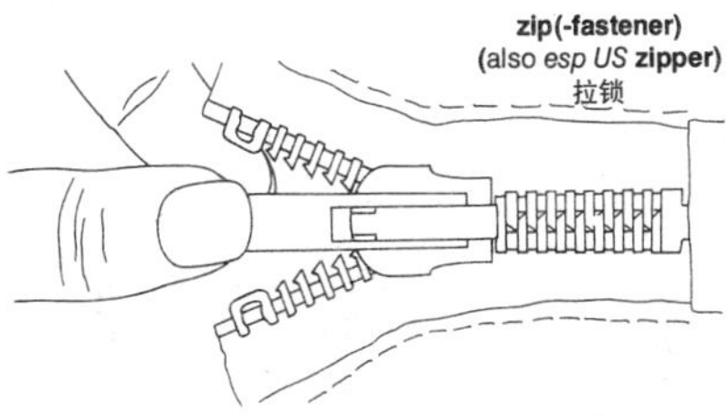

zip /zɪp; zɪp/ *n* **1** (also *esp Brit* ˈ**zip-fastener**, *esp US* **zip·per**) [C] device for bringing together or separating two rows of metal or plastic teeth by means of a sliding tab, used for fastening clothing, baggage, etc 拉链; 拉锁: *The zip on my anorak has got stuck.* 我的皮猴上的拉链卡住了. **2** [U] (*infml* 口) vigour; energy 活力; 精力. Cf 参看 ZAP *n*. **3** [sing] short sharp sound, eg of a bullet going through the air 飕(如子弹穿过空气的尖啸声).

▷ **zip** *v* (**-pp-**) **1** [Tn, Tn·pr, Tn·p, Cn·a] fasten or unfasten (clothes, baggage, etc) with a zip(1) 拉上或拉开(衣物、袋子等)的拉链: *She zipped her bag open.* 她拉开了袋子的拉链. **2** (phr v) **zip across, along, through, etc** move vigorously or quickly in the specified direction 活跃地或迅速地沿某方向运动: *She's just zipped into town to buy some food.* 她像一阵风似的进城去买些食物. ○ *After a slow beginning, the play fairly zips along in the second act.* 这出戏开场演得很慢, 到第二幕时进行得就很快了. ⇨Usage at WHIZ 用法见WHIZ. **zip (sb/sth) up** fasten with a zip 拉上拉链: *Will you zip me up, please?* 请给我拉上拉链行吗? ○ *The dress zips up at the back.* 这件连衣裙是用拉链在后面拉上的.

zippy *adj* (**-ier, -iest**) (*infml* 口) full of zip; lively and energetic 充满活力的; 活泼的; 精力充沛的.

Zip code /ˈzɪp kəʊd; ˋzɪp,kod/ (*US*) = POSTCODE (POST[3]).

zir·con /ˈzɜːkɒn; ˋzɝ,kɑn/ *n* (**a**) [C] translucent bluish-white gem 锆石. (**b**) [U] mineral from which this is cut 锆英石.

zither /ˈzɪðə(r); ˋzɪθɚ/ *n* musical instrument with many strings on a box-like body, played by plucking with a plectrum and the fingers 齐特琴(琴体呈匣形, 上有很多弦, 用拨子及手指拨奏).

zo·diac /ˈzəʊdɪæk; ˋzodɪ,æk/ *n* (**a**) **the zodiac** [sing] imaginary band of the sky containing the positions of the sun, the moon and the main planets, divided into 12 equal parts (the **signs of the zodiac**), named after 12 groups of stars 黄道带(天球上的假想带, 日、月、行星在其中分成12等分, 即黄道12宫 **signs of the zodiac**, 依12星群命名). ⇨illus 见插图. (**b**) [C] (usu circular) diagram of these signs used in astrology to predict the future (通常为圆形的)黄道12宫图(用于占星术中预测未来). Cf 参看 HOROSCOPE. ▷ **zo·di·acal** /zəʊˈdaɪəkl; zoˋdaɪəkḷ/ *adj*.

NOTE ON USAGE 用法: The **signs of the zodiac** are used in astrology and horoscopes (often called 'The Stars') in newspapers and magazines. ☆ **signs of the zodiac** (黄道12宫)用于占星术及报刊中的天宫图(常称为The Stars). ☆ People often refer to the signs and to the influence they are supposed to have on somebody's personality and fate 人们常提到星座及其所谓对人的性格及命运的主宰: *She was born under Gemini.* 她属双子座. ○ *His birthday's on 19 October. He's (a) Libra/a Libran.* 他的生日是10月19日. 他属天秤座. ○ *She is a typical Taurus/Taurean/has a typical Taurean personality.* 她有典型的金牛座性格.

zombie /ˈzɒmbɪ; ˋzɑmbɪ/ *n* **1** (in various African and Caribbean religions) dead body that has been brought to life again by witchcraft (非洲及加勒比人诸宗教中)靠巫术起死回生的僵尸. **2** (*infml* 口) dull lifeless person who seems to act without thinking or not to be aware of what is happening around him; automaton 迟钝无生气的人(举动似不经思考或对周围事物麻木不仁者); 动作呆板而不动脑筋的人.

zone /zəʊn; zon/ *n* **1** area, band or stripe that is different from its surroundings in colour, texture, appearance, etc (颜色、质地、外观等与周围不同的)区域、环带或条. **2** area or region with a particular feature or use (有某特点或用途的)区域或范围: *the erogenous zones of the body* 身体的性感带 ○ *a nuclear-free, parking, war, time* *zone* 无核区、停车场、战区、时区 ○ *industrial, residential, etc zones* 工业、住宅…区 ○ *smokeless zones*, ie urban areas in which only smokeless fuels may be used in houses, factories, etc 无烟区(房屋、工厂等中只准使用无烟燃料的市区) ○ *Danger zone — keep out!* 危险区——不可靠近! **3** one of five parts (the ˈ**torrid zone, North** and **South** ˈ**temperate zones** and **North** and **South** ˈ**frigid zones**) that the earth's surface is divided into by imaginary lines parallel to the equator 地球表面与赤道平行的五条设想的气温带(热带、北温带、南温带、北寒带、南寒带)之一. **4** (*esp US*) area within which certain railway, postal, telephone, etc charges apply (为铁路、邮政、电话等计算费用的)铁路段, 邮区, 电话分区.

▷ **zonal** /ˈzəʊnl; ˋzonl/ *adj* relating to or arranged in zones (ZONE 2) 区域的; 分成区的; 划成范围的.

zone *v* [Tn] **1** divide or mark (sth or a place) into zones (ZONE 2) 将(某物或某处)分成或划成区域或范围. **2** assign (sth) to a particular area 将(某事物)划归某区域. **zon·ing** *n* [U].

zonked /zɒŋkt; zɑŋkt/ *adj* [pred 作表语] **~ (out)** (*sl* 俚) **1** drugged or drunk 麻醉了; 喝醉了. **2** very tired; exhausted 极疲倦; 筋疲力尽: *I feel utterly zonked.* 我感到精疲力竭了.

zoo /zuː; zu/ *n* (*pl* **~s**) (also *fml* 正规作 **zoological gardens**) place (eg a garden, park, etc) where living (esp wild) animals are kept for exhibition, study and breeding 动物园: *The children enjoy going to the zoo.* 儿童喜欢到动物园去.

□ ˈ**zoo-keeper** *n* person employed in a zoo to take care of the animals 动物园管理员.

zoo- *comb form* 构词成分 of or relating to animals or animal life 动物的; 动物生活的: *zoology*.

zo·ology /zəʊˈɒlədʒɪ; zoˈɑlədʒɪ/ *n* [U] scientific study of the structure, form and distribution of animals 动物学.

▷ **zo·olo·gical** /ˌzəʊəˈlɒdʒɪkl; ˌzoəˋlɑdʒɪkl/ *adj* of or relating to zoology 动物学的. **zo·olo·gically** /-klɪ; -klɪ/ *adv*. ˌ**zoological** ˈ**gardens** (*fml* 文) = zoo.

zo·olo·gist /zəʊˈɒlədʒɪst; zoˈɑlədʒɪst/ *n* expert in or student of zoology 动物学家; 动物学研究者. Cf 参看 BIOLOGY, BOTANY.

zoom /zuːm; zum/ *v* **1** [I, Ipr, Ip] (of aircraft, cars, etc) move very quickly, esp with a buzzing or humming noise (指飞行器、汽车等)急速移动(尤指发出嗡嗡声或轰轰声): *zooming along the motorway* 沿高速公路嗡的一声疾驶而去 ○ *The jet zoomed low over our heads.* 喷气式飞机在我们头顶上空轰的一声低飞而过. ⇨Usage at WHIZ 用法见WHIZ. **2** [I, Ip] (*fig infml* 比喻, 口) (of prices, costs, etc) rise sharply; soar (指价格、费用等)急升, 猛涨: *Overnight trading caused share prices to zoom (up).* 一夜的交投使股票价格直线上升. **3** (phr v) **zoom in (on sb/sth)/out** (of cameras) make the size of the object being photographed appear bigger/smaller by using a zoom lens (指照相机等)用变焦距镜头使景物放大[缩小].

▷ **zoom** *n* [sing] sound or act of zooming (ZOOM 1) (指飞行器或汽车等)急速的移动, 急速移动时发出的声音.

□ ˈ**zoom lens** camera lens that can be adjusted to make the object being photographed appear gradually bigger or smaller so that it seems to be getting steadily closer or more distant 变焦距镜头.

zo·ophyte /ˈzəʊəfaɪt; ˋzoəˌfaɪt/ *n* plant-like sea-animal, eg a sea anemone, coral, etc 似植物的海洋动物(如海葵、珊瑚虫等).

zuc·chini /zʊˈkiːnɪ; zuˋkinɪ/ *n* (*pl* unchanged or **~s** 复数或不变或作 **zucchinis**) (*esp US*) = COURGETTE.

Zulu /ˈzuːluː; ˋzulu/ *n* **1** [C] member of a Bantu people of S Africa 祖鲁人(南非班图人的成员). **2** [U] their language 祖鲁语.

▷ **Zulu** *adj* of the Zulu people or their language 祖鲁人的; 祖鲁语的.

Z

APPENDICES
附录
&
A DETAILED GUIDE TO THE ENTRIES
词条使用详细说明

APPENDICES CONTENTS 附录目录

APPENDIX 1 附录 1
ILLUSTRATIONS 插图

TREES COMMON IN BRITAIN 英国常见的树

All the drawings are to scale and represent the average size reached. 例图均符合比例, 为可长到的一般大小.

Deciduous trees 落叶树

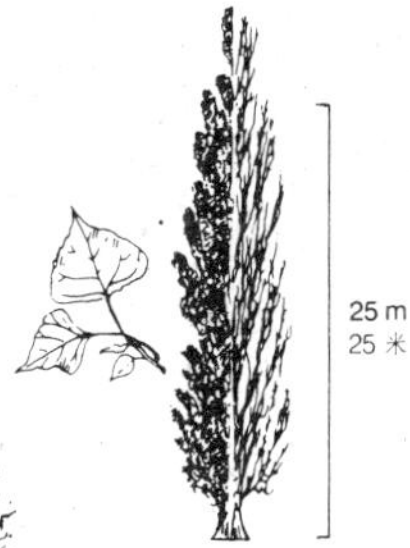

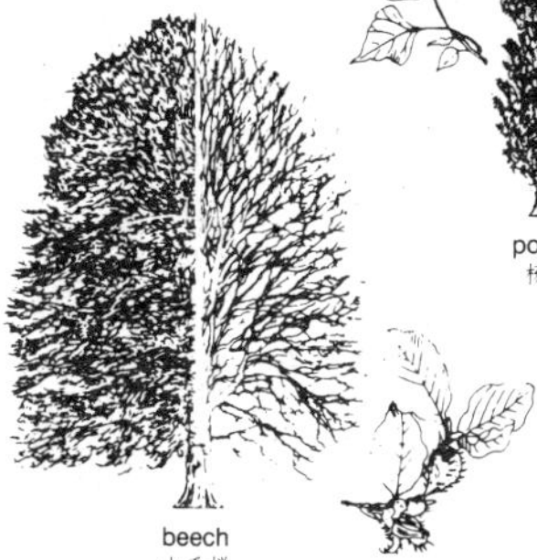

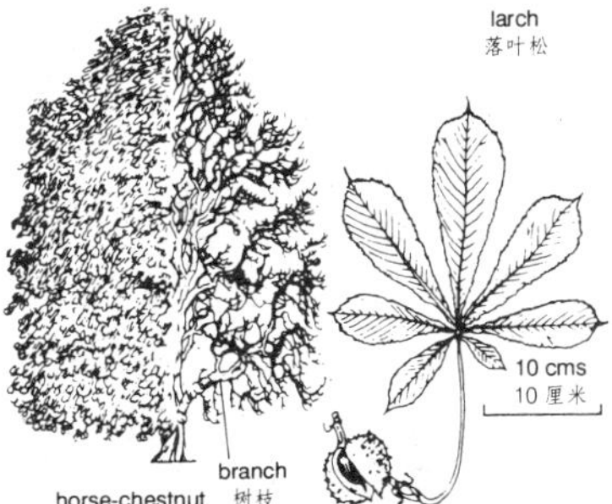

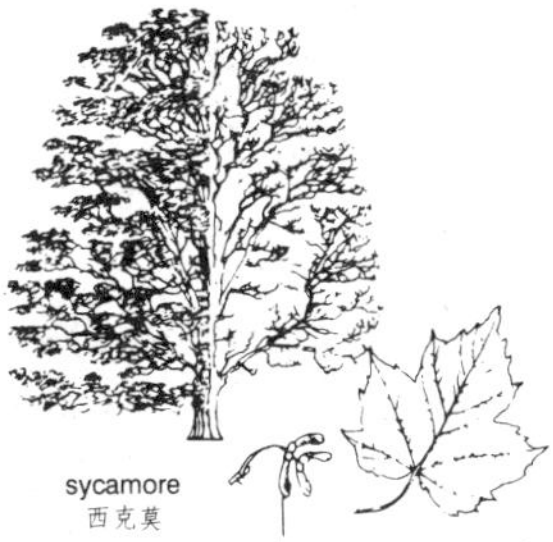

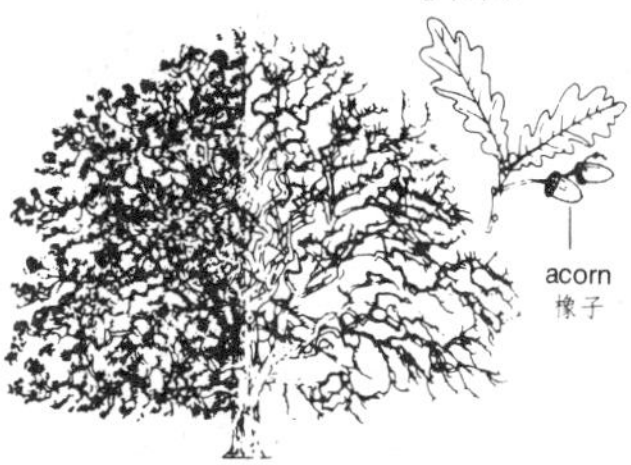

Evergreen trees 常绿树

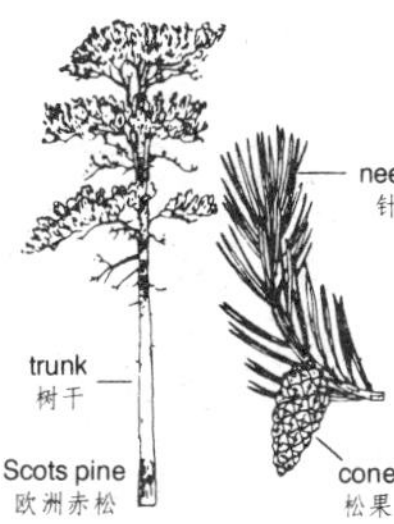

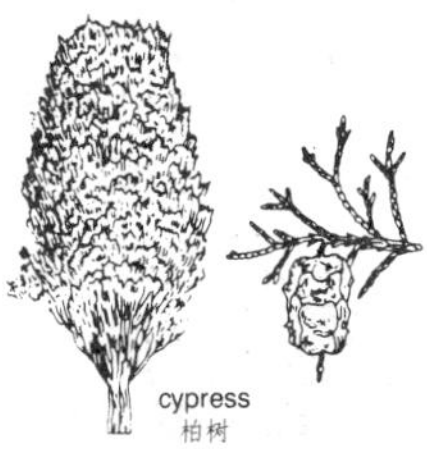

FLOWERING PLANTS COMMON IN BRITAIN
英国常见的开花植物

All the drawings are to scale and represent the average height reached. 例图均符合比例, 为可长到的一般高度.

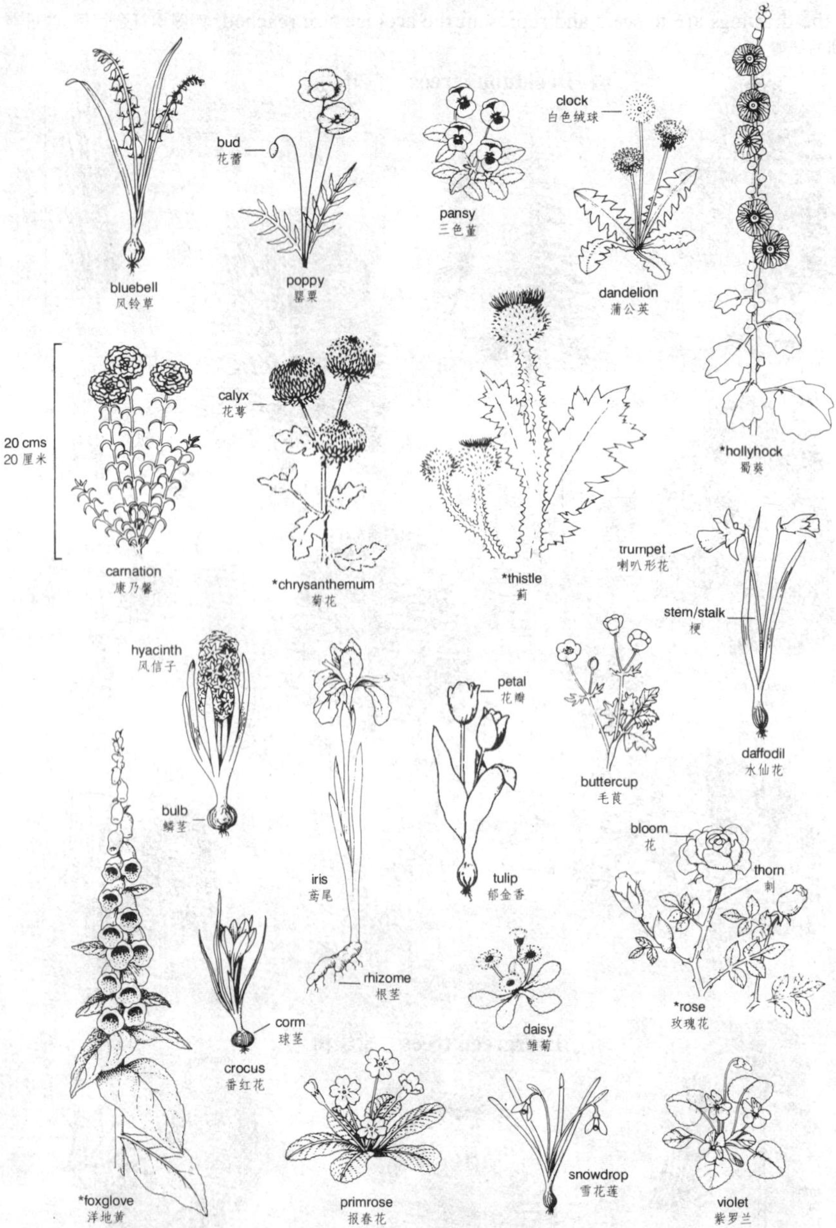

*The illustration shows the top third of the whole plant. 所示为植株上端三分之一的部分.

WILD ANIMALS COMMON IN BRITAIN
英国常见的野生动物

All the drawings are to scale and represent the average size reached. 例图均符合比例，为可长到的一般大小.

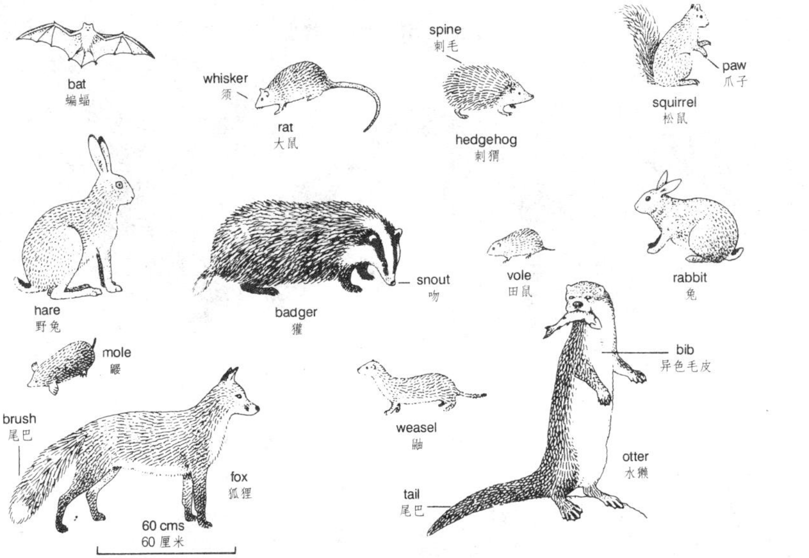

BREEDS OF DOG
狗的品种

All the drawings are to scale and represent the average size reached. 例图均符合比例，为可长到的一般大小.

BIRDS COMMON IN BRITAIN
英国常见的鸟

All the drawings are to scale. 例图均符合比例.
With the exception of hen, male birds are shown throughout. 除母鸡外, 所示均为雄性.

Birds of prey 猛禽

Garden and woodland birds 园林中的鸟

Water-birds and sea-birds 水鸟

Game birds 可捕猎的鸟

Farmyard birds 家禽

SOME TYPICAL BRITISH HOMES
典型的英国房屋

Row of terraced houses/Terrace 排房

1 lintel 过梁
2 lamp-post 路灯柱
3 knocker 门环
4 doorbell 门铃
5 door 门
6 doorstep 门阶
7 drain-pipe 排水管
8 drain 下水道
9 letter-box 投信口
10 sash-window 上下推拉窗
11 window-sill or -ledge 窗台
12 brick 砖
13 slate 石板瓦
14 window-pane 窗玻璃

Semi-detached houses 半独立式住宅

1 skylight 天窗
2 roof 屋顶
3 pane 窗玻璃
4 wall 墙壁
5 porch 门廊
6 hanging basket 悬篮
7 path 小路
8 fence 栅栏
9 bay window 凸窗
10 garden gate 花园门
11 casement window 门式窗

Detached house 独立式住宅

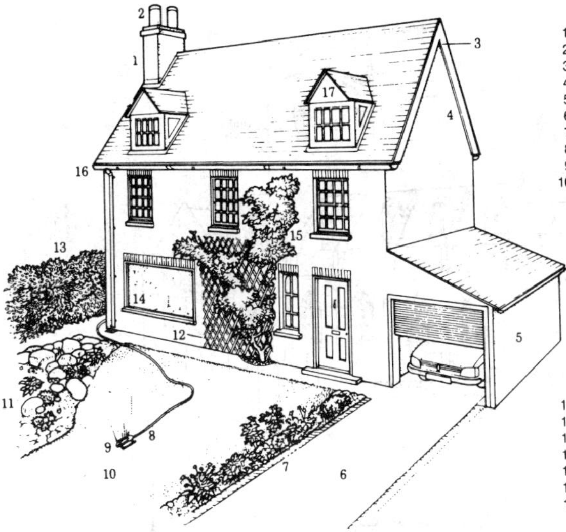

1 chimney 烟囱
2 chimney-pot 烟囱管帽
3 eaves 屋檐
4 gable 山墙
5 garage 汽车房
6 drive 私人车道
7 border 花坛
8 hose 软管
9 sprinkler 洒水装置
10 lawn 草坪
11 rockery 岩石庭园
12 trellis 格子棚架
13 hedge 树篱
14 picture window 观景窗
15 climber 攀缘植物
16 gutter 排水檐沟
17 dormer window 天窗

Bungalow 平房

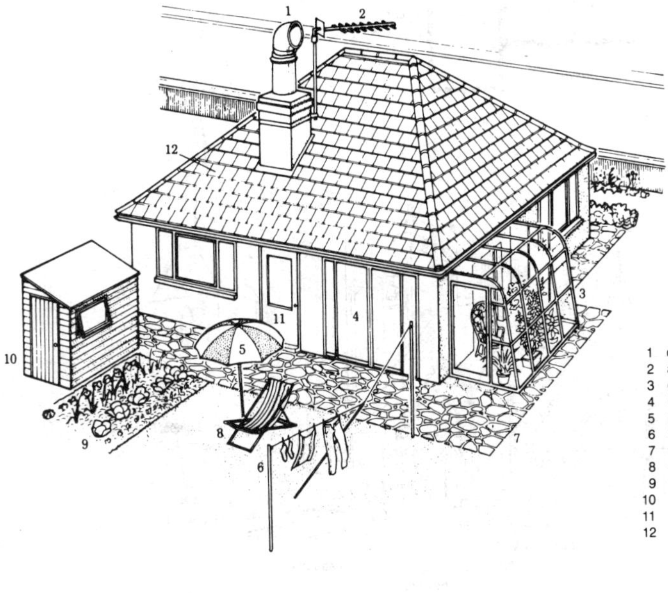

1 cowl 烟囱罩
2 aerial 天线
3 conservatory 温室
4 French window 落地窗
5 parasol 阳伞
6 clothes-line 晾衣绳
7 crazy paving 碎纹石路
8 deck-chair 折叠帆布躺椅
9 vegetable garden 菜园
10 garden shed 花园小房
11 back door 后门
12 tiles 瓦

A CHURCH
教堂

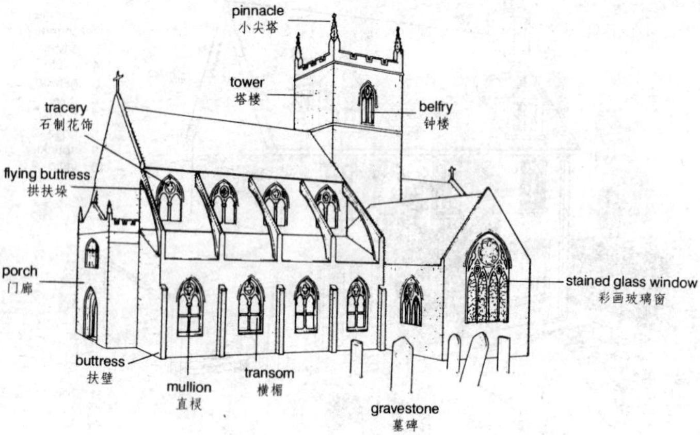
pinnacle
小尖塔
tower
塔楼
belfry
钟楼
tracery
石制花饰
flying buttress
拱扶垛
porch
门廊
stained glass window
彩画玻璃窗
buttress
扶壁
mullion
直棂
transom
横楣
gravestone
墓碑

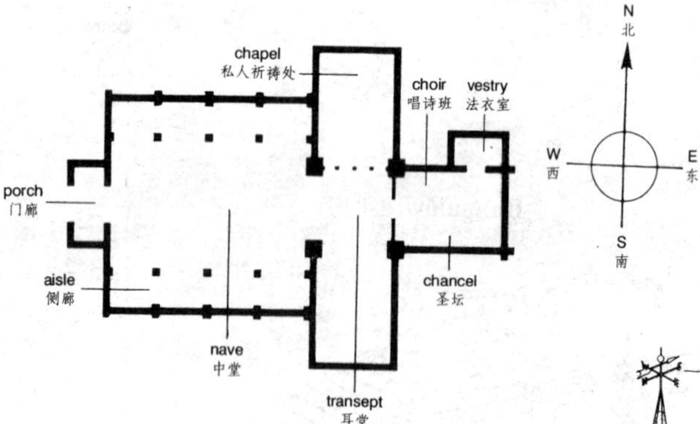
chapel
私人祈祷处
choir
唱诗班
vestry
法衣室
porch
门廊
aisle
侧廊
chancel
圣坛
nave
中堂
transept
耳堂
N
北
W
西
E
东
S
南

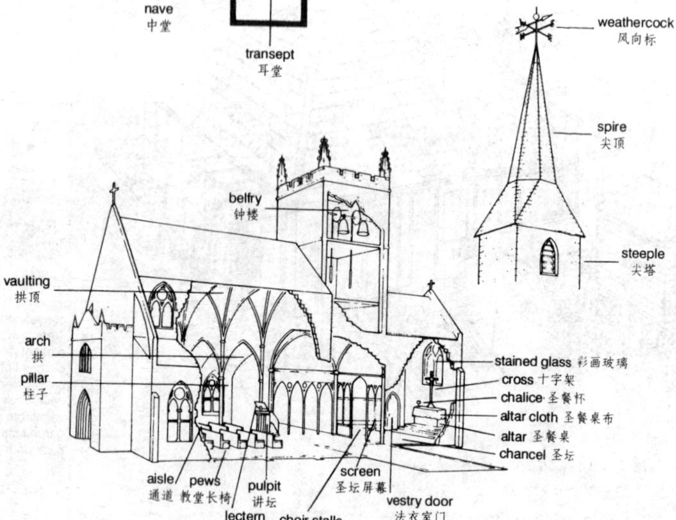
weathercock
风向标
spire
尖顶
steeple
尖塔
belfry
钟楼
vaulting
拱顶
arch
拱
pillar
柱子
stained glass 彩画玻璃
cross 十字架
chalice 圣餐杯
altar cloth 圣餐桌布
altar 圣餐桌
chancel 圣坛
aisle
通道
pews
教堂长椅
pulpit
讲坛
lectern
读经台
choir stalls
唱诗班席位
screen
圣坛屏幕
vestry door
法衣室门

A THEATRE
剧院

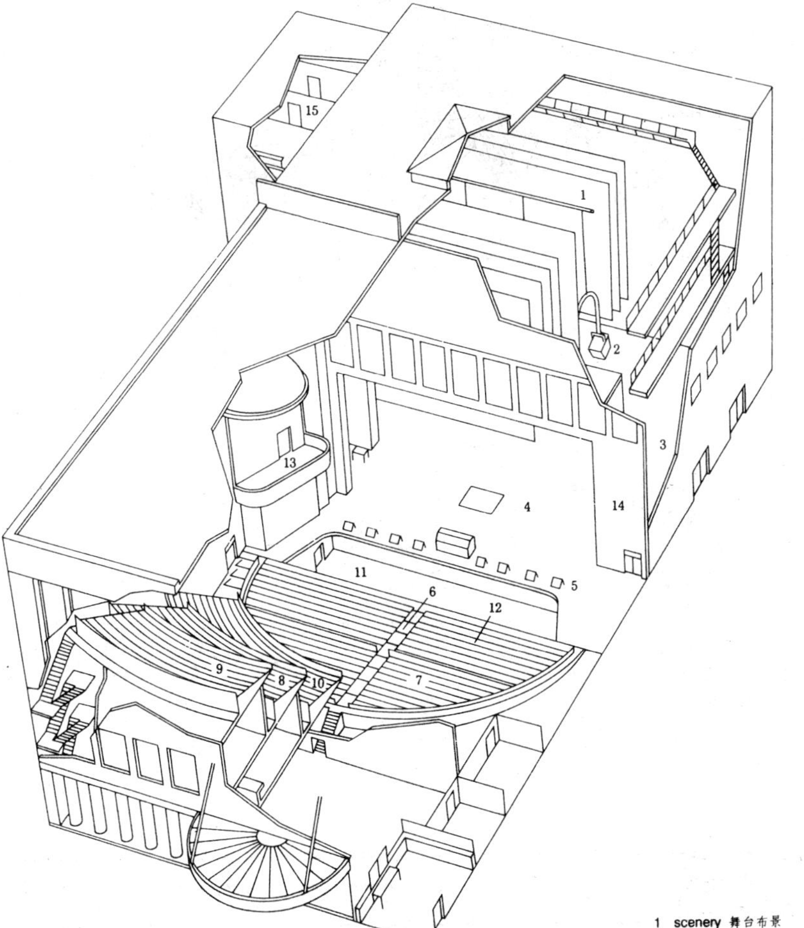

1 scenery 舞台布景
2 spotlight 聚光灯
3 wings 舞台侧面
4 stage 舞台
5 footlights 脚灯
6 aisle 通道
7 stalls 正厅座位
8 upper circle 上层楼厅
9 balcony 楼厅包厢
10 dress circle 下层楼厅
11 pit 乐池
12 front stalls 正厅前座
13 box 包厢
14 proscenium 幕前部分
15 dressing-rooms 化妆室

MUSICAL INSTRUMENTS 乐器

Brass & woodwind 铜管乐器和木管乐器

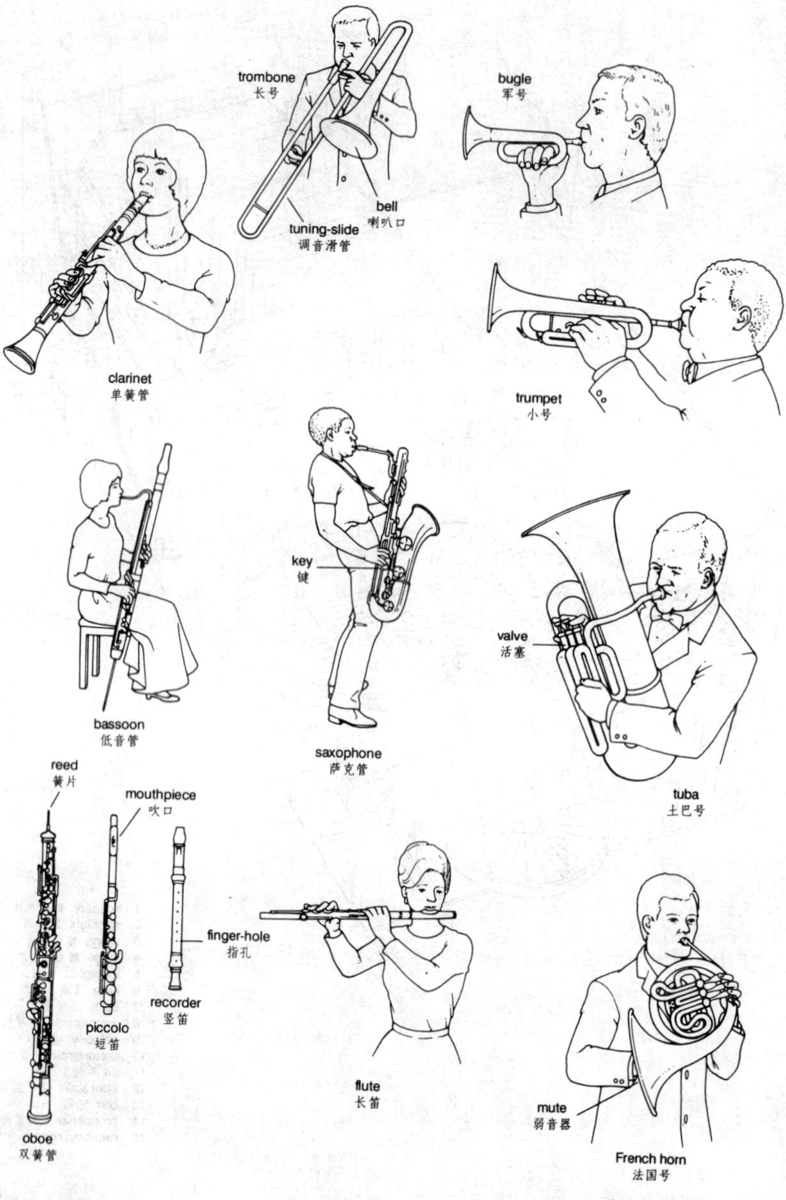

Strings 弦乐器

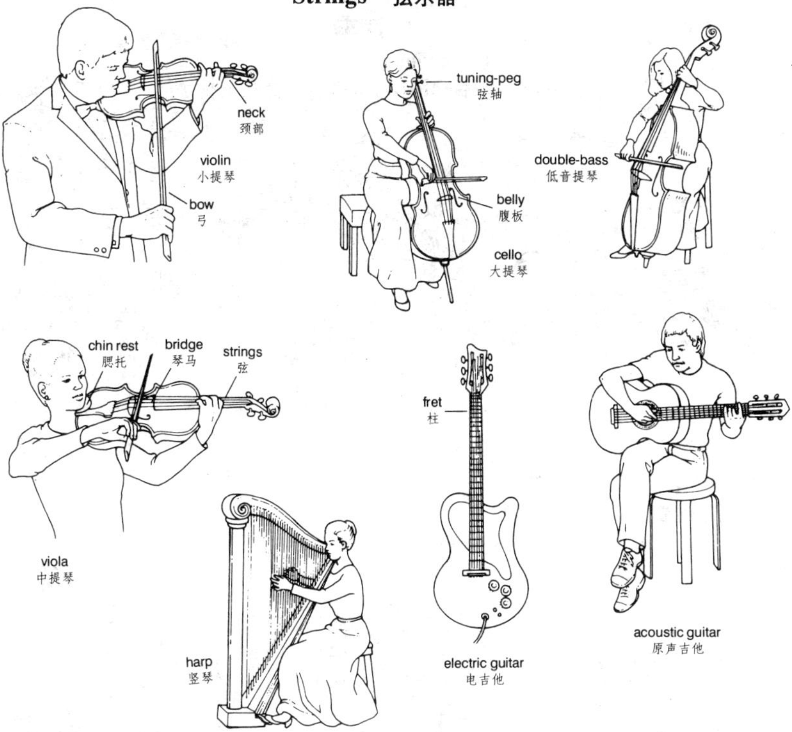

Percussion 打击乐器

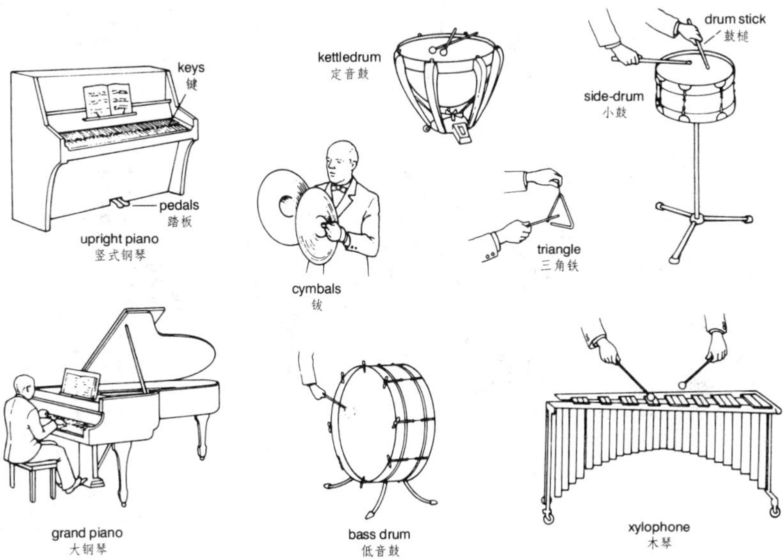

A CAR
汽车

Front view
前视图

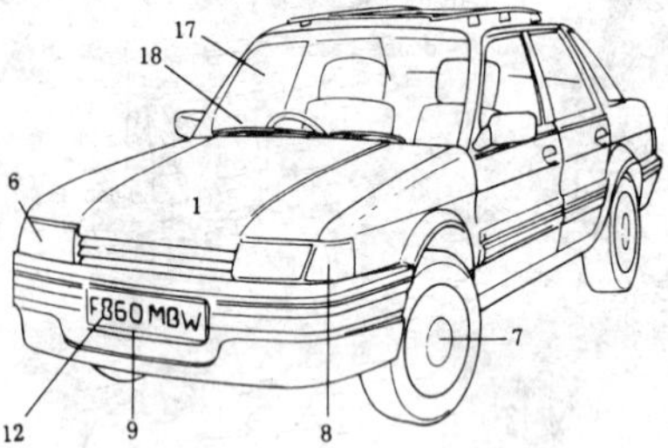

Back view
后视图

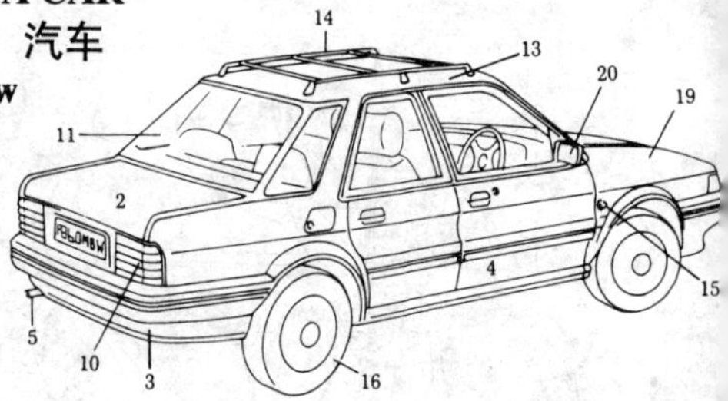

1 bonnet 发动机罩盖
(*US* 美式英语作 hood)
2 boot 行李厢
(*US* 美式英语作 trunk)
3 bumper 保险杠
4 door 门
5 exhaust-pipe 排气管
6 headlight 头灯
7 hubcap 毂盖
8 indicator light 转向灯
(*US* 美式英语作 turn signal)
9 number-plate 牌照
(*US* 美式英语作 license plate)
10 rear light 尾灯
(*US* 美式英语作 taillight)
11 rear window 后窗
12 registration number 牌照号码
13 roof 车顶
14 roof-rack 车顶架
15 sidelight 边灯
(*US* 美式英语作 parking light)
16 tyre 轮胎
(*US* 美式英语作 tire)
17 windscreen 挡风玻璃窗
(*US* 美式英语作 windshield)
18 windscreen wiper 刮水器
19 wing 翼子板
(*US* 美式英语作 fender)
20 wing mirror 后视镜
(*US* 美式英语作 side mirror)

The interior
内部装置

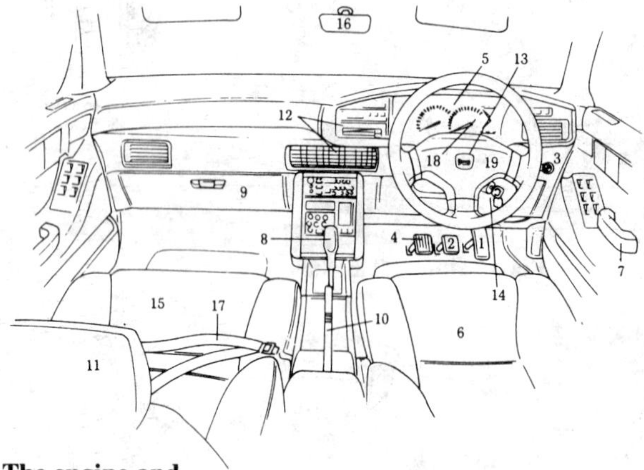

1 accelerator pedal 油门踏板
(*US* 美式英语作 gas pedal)
2 brake pedal 制动器踏板
3 choke 阻风门钮
4 clutch pedal 离合器踏板
5 dashboard/fascia 仪表板
6 driver's seat 司机座
7 door handle 门把儿
8 gear-lever 变速杆
(*US* 美式英语作 gearshift)
9 glove compartment 贮物箱
10 handbrake 手刹车
11 head-rest 头垫
12 heater 暖气设备
13 horn 喇叭
14 ignition switch 点火开关
15 passenger seat 客座
16 rear-view mirror 后视镜
17 seat-belt 安全带
18 speedometer 速度计
19 steering wheel 方向盘

The engine and the chassis
发动机和底盘

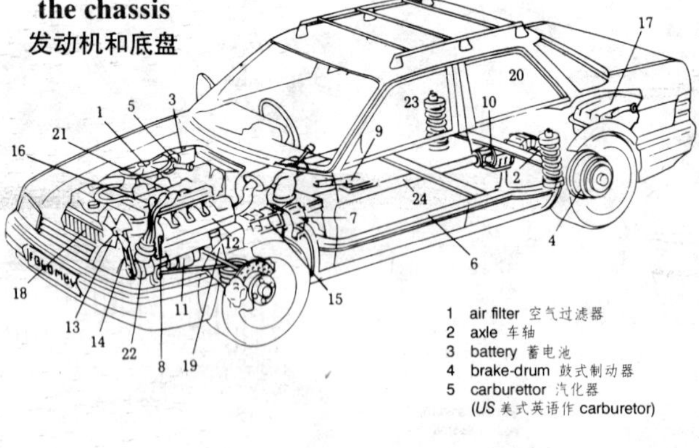

1 air filter 空气过滤器
2 axle 车轴
3 battery 蓄电池
4 brake-drum 鼓式制动器
5 carburettor 汽化器
(*US* 美式英语作 carburetor)
6 chassis 底盘
7 clutch 离合器
8 dip-stick 量油尺
9 handbrake 手刹车
10 differential gear 差速器
11 dynamo 发电机
12 exhaust manifold 排气歧管
13 fan 风扇
14 fan belt 风扇皮带
15 gearbox 变速箱
16 leads 导线
17 petrol tank 汽油箱
(*US* 美式英语作 gas tank)
18 radiator 冷却器
19 shock absorber 避震器
20 silencer 消声器
(*US* 美式英语作 muffler)
21 sparking-plug 火花塞
(*US* 美式英语作 spark plug)
22 starter motor 起动发动机
23 suspension 悬挂装置
24 transmission shaft 传动轴
(*US* 美式英语作 drive shaft)

A BICYCLE
自行车

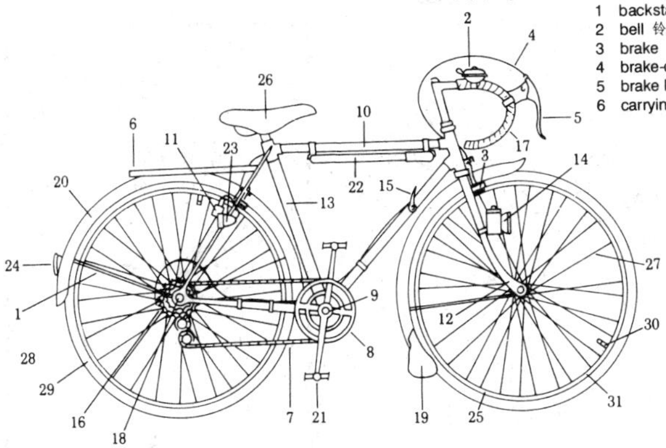

1 backstays 挡泥板支条
2 bell 铃
3 brake 刹车
4 brake-cable 制动钢索
5 brake lever 制动手柄
6 carrying rack 载物架
7 chain 链条
8 chain-wheel 链轮
9 crank 曲柄
10 crossbar 横梁
11 dynamo 发电机
12 forks 前叉
13 frame 车架
14 front light 前灯
15 gear-lever 变速杆
16 gears 传动装置
17 handlebars 把手
18 hub 轮毂
19 mud-flap 挡带
20 mudguard 挡泥板
21 pedal 踏板
22 pump 打气筒
23 rear light 尾灯
24 reflector 反光镜
25 rim 辋圈
26 saddle 鞍座
27 spoke 辐条
28 sprocket 链轮
29 tyre 轮胎
30 valve 气嘴
31 wheel 车轮

A MOTORWAY INTERSECTION
高速公路交叉点

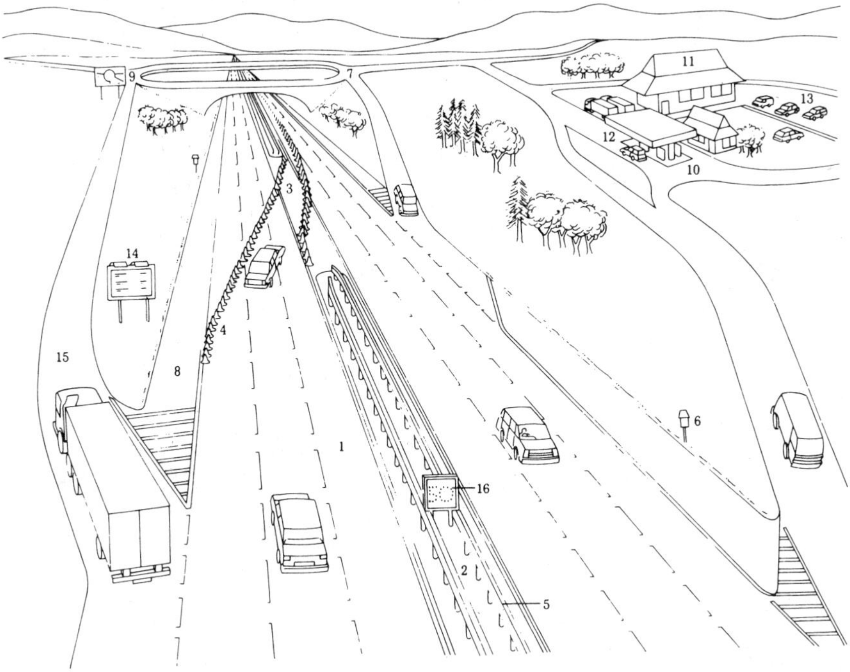

1 acceleration lane 加速车道 (*infml* 俗称 fast lane)
2 central reservation 中央分车带
3 contraflow 逆道行驶
4 cone 锥形警告路标
5 crash barrier 防撞护栏
6 emergency telephone 应急电话
7 flyover 立交桥 (*US* 美式英语作 overpass)
8 hard shoulder 硬质路肩
9 roundabout 环状交叉路 (*US* 美式英语作 rotary)
10 service area 服务区
11 restaurant 餐馆
12 filling-station 汽车加油站
13 car-park 汽车停车场
14 road sign 道路标志牌
15 slip-road 岔道
16 warning light 示警灯

MAPS OF THE UNITED KINGDOM
英国地图

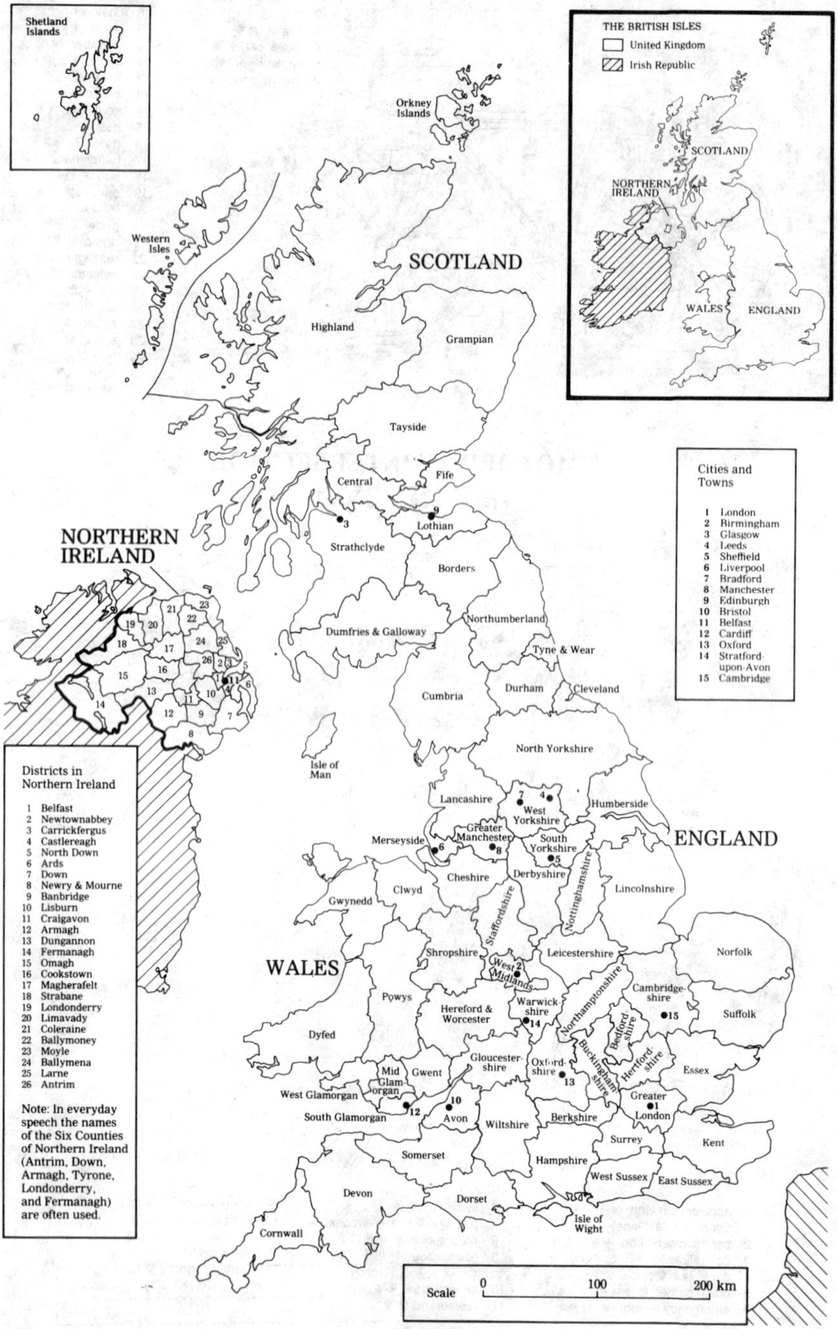

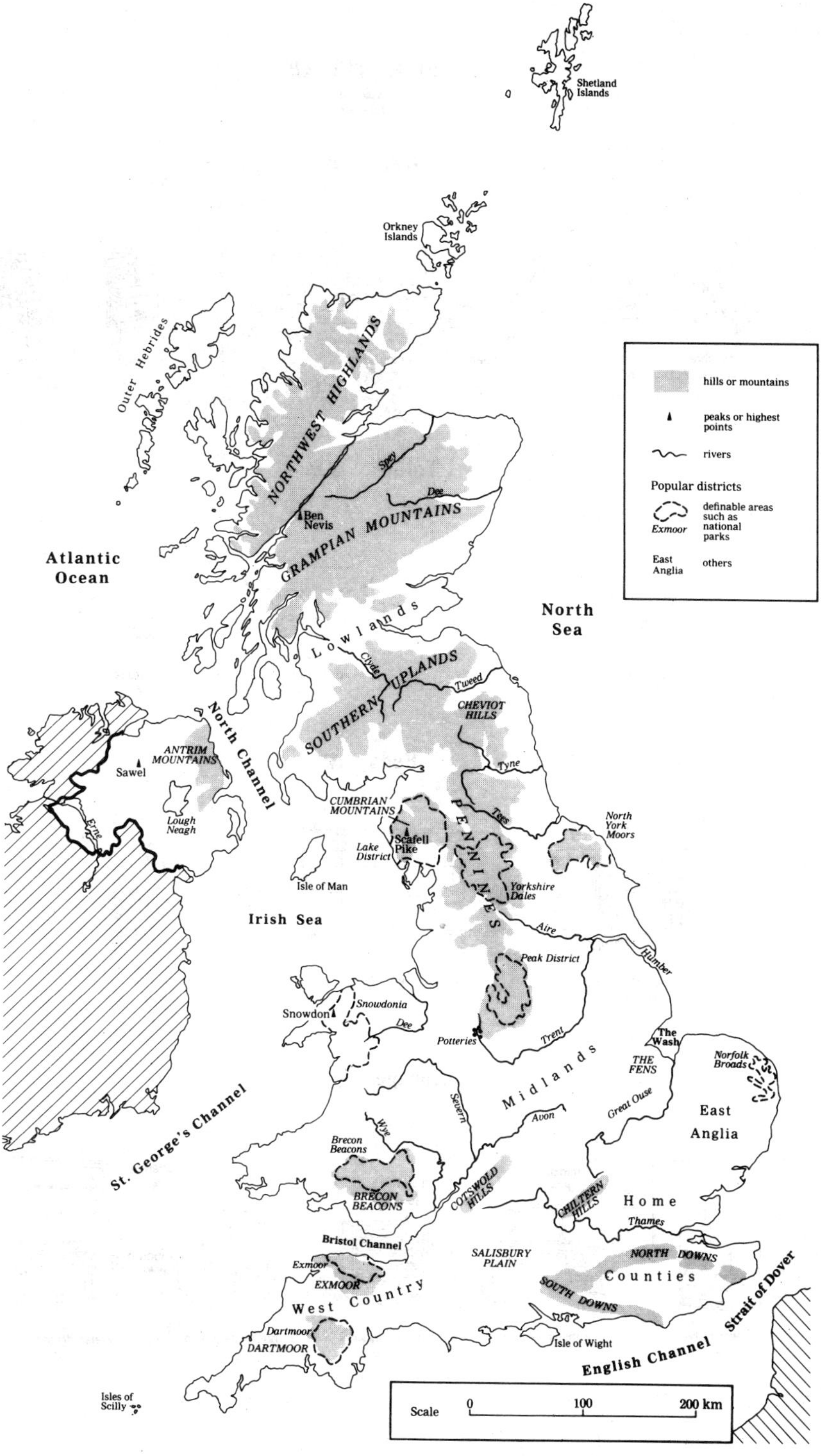

Shetland Islands
Orkney Islands
Outer Hebrides
NORTHWEST HIGHLANDS
Spey
Dee
Ben Nevis
GRAMPIAN MOUNTAINS
Atlantic Ocean
North Sea
Lowlands
Clyde
SOUTHERN UPLANDS
Tweed
CHEVIOT HILLS
North Channel
ANTRIM MOUNTAINS
Sawel
Lough Neagh
Erne
Tyne
CUMBRIAN MOUNTAINS
PENNINES
Tees
North York Moors
Scafell Pike
Lake District
Isle of Man
Yorkshire Dales
Irish Sea
Aire
Humber
Peak District
Snowdonia
Snowdon
Dee
Potteries
Trent
The Wash
THE FENS
Norfolk Broads
Midlands
Severn
Great Ouse
Avon
East Anglia
St. George's Channel
Wye
Brecon Beacons
BRECON BEACONS
COTSWOLD HILLS
CHILTERN HILLS
Home
Thames
Bristol Channel
SALISBURY PLAIN
Exmoor
EXMOOR
NORTH DOWNS
Counties
SOUTH DOWNS
West Country
Strait of Dover
Dartmoor
DARTMOOR
Isle of Wight
English Channel
Isles of Scilly
Scale 0 100 200 km
hills or mountains
peaks or highest points
rivers
Popular districts
definable areas such as national parks
Exmoor
East Anglia
others

FURNITURE
家具

Seats 坐具

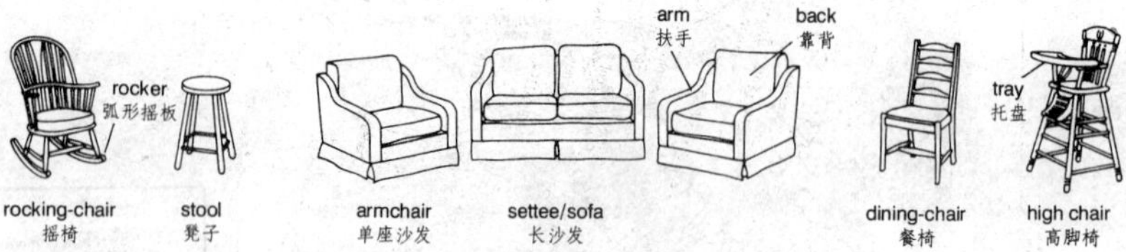

Tables 桌类

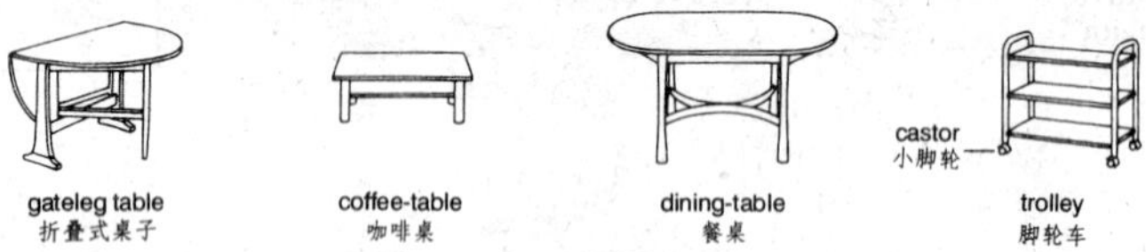

Beds 床

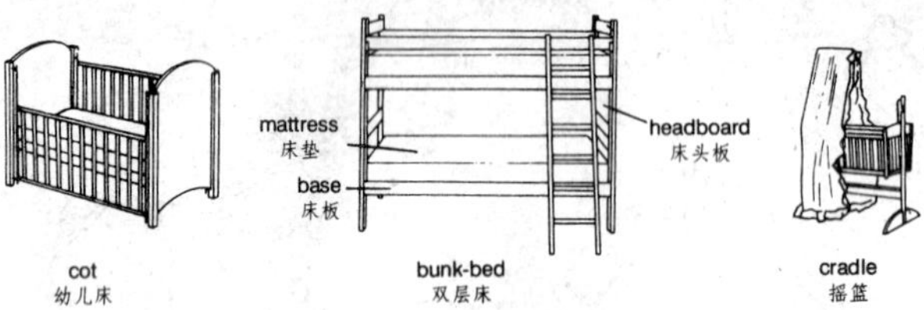

Storage 柜橱

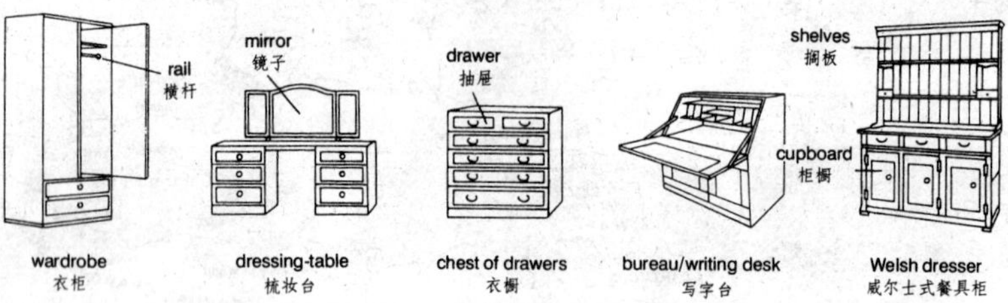

MAP OF THE UNITED STATES
美国地图

DINING ROOM
餐厅

1 dining table
餐桌
2 table leg
桌腿
3 table top
桌面
4 place mat
餐具垫
5 place (place setting, cover)
（每人一份的）全套餐具
6 soup plate (deep plate)
汤盘（深盘）
7 dinner plate
餐盘
8 soup tureen
有盖汤碗（盖碗）
9 wineglass
酒杯
10 dining chair
餐椅
11 seat
（椅子的）座部，椅座
12 lamp (pendant lamp)
灯（吊灯）
13 curtains
窗帘
14 net curtain
网眼帘布
15 curtain rail
窗帘横杆
16 carpet
地毯
17 wall unit
墙壁挂橱
18 glass door
玻璃门
19 shelf
搁架
20 sideboard
餐具柜
21 cutlery drawer
餐具抽屉
22 linen drawer
餐巾/桌巾抽屉
23 base
柜子底座；基座
24 round tray
圆托盘
25 pot plant
盆栽植物
26 china cabinet (display cabinet)
瓷器柜（陈列柜）
27 coffee set (coffee service)
整套咖啡用具
28 coffee pot
咖啡壶
29 coffee cup
咖啡杯
30 saucer
茶杯碟
31 milk jug
牛奶罐
32 sugar bowl
糖钵
33 dinner set (dinner service)
成套餐具

BEDROOM
卧室

1 wardrobe
衣柜
2 linen shelf
放置日用织品的搁板
3 cane chair
藤椅
4 foot of the bed
床脚板
5 bed frame
床架（框）
6 headboard
床头板
7 bedspread
床罩
8 duvet, a quilted duvet
羽绒被；棉被
9 sheet, a linen sheet
被单，用亚麻制成的被单
10 mattress, a foam mattress with drill tick
床垫，一种斜纹布包面的泡沫床垫
11 [wedge-shaped] bolster
楔形长垫枕
12 pillowcase (pillowslip)
枕套
13 tick
褥套
14 bookshelf [attached to the headboard]
床头板上的书架
15 reading lamp
阅读灯
16 electric alarm clock
电子闹钟
17 bedside cabinet
床头柜
18 drawer
抽屉
19 bedroom lamp
卧室灯
20 picture
画
21 picture frame
画框
22 bedside rug
床边小地毯
23 fitted carpet
地毯
24 dressing stool
梳妆凳子
25 dressing table
梳妆台
26 perfume spray
香水喷雾器
27 perfume bottle
香水瓶
28 powder box
粉盒
29 dressing-table mirror (mirror)
梳妆台镜

KITCHEN
厨房

1 housewife 家庭主妇
2 refrigerator (fridge, *US* 美式英语作 icebox) 冰箱
3 refrigerator shelf 冰箱搁板（架）
4 salad drawer 蔬菜抽屉
5 frozen food compartment 食品冷冻室
6 bottle rack (in storage door) 瓶架（在储藏门内）
7 upright freezer 立式冰柜
8 wall cupboard, a kitchen cupboard 壁式橱柜；厨房橱柜
9 base unit 底层设备
10 cutlery drawer 餐具抽屉
11 work top (work surface) 工作面
12 electric cooker (gas cooker) 电炉（煤气炉）
13 oven 烤箱
14 oven window 烤箱窗
15 hotplate (automatic high-speed plate) 加热板（自动高速加热板）
16 kettle (whistling kettle) 水壶（鸣笛壶）
17 cooker hood 排油烟机
18 pot holder 罐、锅、壶等的托垫
19 pot holder rack 托垫挂架
20 kitchen clock 厨房钟
21 timer 记时器
22 hand mixer 手动搅拌器
23 whisk （搅打蛋、奶油的）搅拌器
24 electric coffee grinder (with rotating blades) 电动磨咖啡机（带旋转刀片）
25 lead 导线
26 wall socket 墙上插座
27 corner unit 角落装置
28 revolving shelf 旋转架
29 pot (cooking pot) 锅
30 jug （有柄有嘴的）水壶
31 spice rack 调味品架
32 spice jar 调味品瓶
33 dish drainer 盘碟滴水架
34 tea plate 茶盘
35 sink 洗涤槽
36 water tap (*US* 美式英语作 faucet) (mixer tap, *US* 美式英语作 mixing faucet) 自来水龙头（混合水龙头）
37 pot plant 盆栽植物
38 coffee maker 咖啡（煮）壶
39 kitchen lamp 厨房灯
40 dishwasher (dishwashing machine) 洗碟机
41 dish rack 盘碟架
42 dinner plate 餐盘
43 kitchen chair 厨房椅子（靠背椅）
44 kitchen table 厨房桌

BATHROOM AND TOILET
浴室和洗手间

1 bath 澡盆；浴缸
2 mixer tap for hot and cold water
冷热水混合的水龙头
3 foam bath (bubble bath)
泡沫澡水
4 toy duck 玩具鸭
5 bath salts 浴盐
6 bath sponge (sponge)
洗澡海绵
7 bidet 坐浴盆
8 towel rail 毛巾架
9 terry towel 毛巾
10 toilet roll holder
卫生纸卷架
11 toilet paper, a roll of crepe paper
卫生纸，一种绉纹纸卷
12 toilet (lavatory, W.C., loo)
厕所；卫生间
13 toilet pan (toilet bowl)
抽水马桶
14 toilet lid with terry cover
铺绒布的马桶盖
15 toilet seat 马桶座
16 cistern 水箱
17 flushing lever 冲水杆
18 pedestal mat
基座垫（脚垫）
19 tile 瓷砖
20 ventilator (extraction vent) 通风设备；通风口（抽气孔）
21 soap dish 肥皂碟
22 soap 肥皂
23 hand towel 手巾；毛巾
24 washbasin 洗脸盆
25 overflow 溢流口（孔）
26 hot and cold water tap
冷热水龙头
27 washbasin pedestal with trap (anti-syphon trap)
装有防臭U型管的洗脸盆基座
28 tooth glass (tooth mug)
漱口杯
29 electric toothbrush
电动牙刷
30 detachable brush heads
可拆卸的牙刷头
31 mirrored bathroom cabinet 洗手间的小镜橱
32 fluorescent lamp
荧光灯；日光灯
33 mirror 镜子
34 drawer 抽屉
35 powder box 粉盒
36 mouthwash 漱口药
37 electric shaver 电动剃刀
38 aftershave lotion
剃须后搽的润肤液
39 shower cubicle
淋浴室（间）
40 shower curtain
淋浴（间）门帘
41 adjustable shower head
可调整的淋浴喷头
42 shower nozzle 淋浴喷嘴
43 shower adjustment rail
淋浴调节杆
44 shower base
淋浴间的地板
45 waste pipe (overflow)
废水管（溢流管）
46 bathroom mule 浴室拖鞋
47 bathroom scales
浴室磅秤
48 bath mat 浴室防滑垫子
49 medicine cabinet 药柜

APPENDIX 2 附录 2

IRREGULAR VERBS 不规则动词

This appendix lists all the verbs with irregular forms that are included in the dictionary, except for those formed with a hyphenated prefix (eg *pre-set*, *re-lay*) and the modal verbs (eg *can*, *must*). 本附录列出的是本词典的全部不规则动词, 但不包括以带连接号的前缀构成的动词(如 pre-set、re-lay)和情态动词(如 can、must). Verbs shown in ordinary type (eg mishear) are 'derivative' verbs, with the same irregular forms as the 'base' verb which is shown in dark type (eg **hear**). 用普通字体印刷的动词(如 mishear)是派生词, 其不规则变化形式与基本动词(即用黑体字印刷的动词, 如 **hear**)是一样的. Irregular forms that are only used in certain senses are marked with an asterisk, eg *abode. 仅在某些词义才使用的不规则形式, 以星号为记(如 *abode). Full information on usage, pronunciation, etc will be found at the main entry. 这类动词的用法、读音等的详细说明需查阅各词条.

Infinitive 不定式	Past Tense 过去时态	Past Participle 过去分词
abide	abided, *abode	abided, *abode
arise	arose	arisen
awake	awoke	awoken
backbite	backbitten	backbitten
backslide	backslid	backslid
be	was/were	been
bear	bore	borne
beat	beat	beaten
become	became	become
befall	befell	befallen
beget	begot, (*arch* 古) begat	begotten
begin	began	begun
behold	beheld	beheld
bend	bent	bent
beseech	besought, beseeched	besought, beseeched
beset	beset	beset
bespeak	bespoke	bespoke, bespoken
bestride	bestrode	bestridden
bet	bet, betted	bet, betted
bid	bade, *bid	bidden, *bid
bind	bound	bound
bite	bit	bitten
bleed	bled	bled
bless	blessed	blessed, blest
blow	blew	blown, *blowed
break	broke	broken
breed	bred	bred
bring	brought	brought
broadcast	broadcast	broadcast
browbeat	browbeat	browbeaten
build	built	built
burn	burnt, burned	burnt, burned
burst	burst	burst
bust	bust, busted	bust, busted
buy	bought	bought
cast	cast	cast

catch	caught	caught
chide	chided, chid	chided, chid, chidden
choose	chose	chosen
cleave[1]	cleaved, clove, cleft	cleaved, cloven, cleft
cleave[2]	cleaved, clave	cleaved
cling	clung	clung
come	came	come
cost	cost	cost
countersink	countersank	countersunk
creep	crept	crept
crow	crowed, (*arch* 古) crew	crowed
cut	cut	cut
deal	dealt	dealt
dig	dug	dug
dive	dived; (*US* 美式英语) dove	dived
do[1, 2]	did	done
draw	drew	drawn
dream	dreamt, dreamed	dreamt, dreamed
drink	drank	drunk
drive	drove	driven
dwell	dwelt	dwelt
eat	ate	eaten
fall	fell	fallen
feed	fed	fed
feel	felt	felt
fight	fought	fought
find	found	found
flee	fled	fled
fling	flung	flung
floodlight	floodlighted, floodlit	floodlighted, floodlit
fly	flew	flown
forbear	forbore	forborne
forbid	forbade, forbad	forbidden
forecast	forecast, forecasted	forecast, forecasted
foresee	foresaw	foreseen
foretell	foretold	foretold
forget	forgot	forgotten
forgive	forgave	forgiven
forsake	forsook	forsaken
forswear	forswore	forsworn
freeze	froze	frozen
gainsay	gainsaid	gainsaid
get	got	got; (*US* 美式英语) gotten
gild	gilded, (*arch* 古) gilt	gilded, (*arch* 古) gilt
gird	girded, girt	girded, girt
give	gave	given
go	went	gone
grind	ground	ground
grow	grew	grown
hamstring	hamstringed, hamstrung	hamstringed, hamstrung
hang	hung, *hanged	hung, *hanged
have	had	had
hear	heard	heard

heave	heaved, hove	heaved, hove
hew	hewed	hewed, hewn
hide	hid	hidden
hit	hit	hit
hold	held	held
hurt	hurt	hurt
inlay	inlaid	inlaid
input	input, inputted	input, inputted
inset	inset	inset
interweave	interwove	interwoven
keep	kept	kept
ken	kenned, kent	kenned
kneel	knelt; (*esp US* 尤用于美国) kneeled	knelt; (*esp US* 尤用于美国) kneeled
knit	knitted, *knit	knitted, *knit
know	knew	known
lay	laid	laid
lead	led	led
lean	leant, leaned	leant, leaned
leap	leapt, leaped	leapt, leaped
learn	learnt, learned	learnt, learned
leave	left	left
lend	lent	lent
let	let	let
lie[2]	lay	lain
light	lighted, lit	lighted, lit
lose	lost	lost
make	made	made
mean	meant	meant
meet	met	met
miscast	miscast	miscast
misdeal	misdealt	misdealt
mishear	misheard	misheard
mishit	mishit	mishit
mislay	mislaid	mislaid
mislead	misled	misled
misread /ˌmɪsˈri:d; mɪsˋrid/	misread /mɪsˈred; mɪsˋrɛd/	misread /mɪsˈred; mɪsˋrɛd/
misspell	misspelt, misspelled	misspelt, misspelled
misspend	misspent	misspent
mistake	mistook	mistaken
misunderstand	misunderstood	misunderstood
mow	mowed	mown, mowed
outbid	outbid	outbid
outdo	outdid	outdone
outfight	outfought	outfought
outgrow	outgrew	outgrown
output	output, outputted	output, outputted
outrun	outran	outrun
outsell	outsold	outsold
outshine	outshone	outshone
overbid	overbid	overbid
overcome	overcame	overcome
overdo	overdid	overdone

overdraw	overdrew	overdrawn
overeat	overate	overeaten
overfly	overflew	overflown
overhang	overhung	overhung
overhear	overheard	overheard
overlay	overlaid	overlaid
overpay	overpaid	overpaid
override	overrode	overridden
overrun	overran	overrun
oversee	oversaw	overseen
overshoot	overshot	overshot
oversleep	overslept	overslept
overtake	overtook	overtaken
overthrow	overthrew	overthrown
partake	partook	partaken
pay	paid	paid
plead	pleaded; (*US* 美式英语) pled	pleaded; (*US* 美式英语) pled
prepay	prepaid	prepaid
prove	proved	proved; (*US* 美式英语) proven
put	put	put
quit	quit, quitted	quit, quitted
read /ri:d; rid/	read /red; rɛd/	read /red; rɛd/
rebind	rebound	rebound
rebuild	rebuilt	rebuilt
recast	recast	recast
redo	redid	redone
rehear	reheard	reheard
remake	remade	remade
rend	rent	rent
repay	repaid	repaid
rerun	reran	rerun
resell	resold	resold
reset	reset	reset
resit	resat	resat
retake	retook	retaken
retell	retold	retold
rewrite	rewrote	rewritten
rid	rid	rid
ride	rode	ridden
ring	rang	rung
rise	rose	risen
run	ran	run
saw	sawed	sawn; (*US* 美式英语) sawed
say	said	said
see	saw	seen
seek	sought	sought
sell	sold	sold
send	sent	sent
set	set	set
sew	sewed	sewn, sewed
shake	shook	shaken
shear	sheared	shorn, sheared
shed	shed	shed

shine	shone, *shined	shone, *shined
shit	shitted, shat	shitted, shat
shoe	shod	shod
shoot	shot	shot
show	showed	shown, showed
shrink	shrank, shrunk	shrunk
shrive	shrived, shrove	shrived, shriven
shut	shut	shut
sing	sang	sung
sink	sank	sunk
sit	sat	sat
slay	slew	slain
sleep	slept	slept
slide	slid	slid
sling	slung	slung
slink	slunk	slunk
slit	slit	slit
smell	smelt, smelled	smelt, smelled
smite	smote	smitten
sow	sowed	sown, sowed
speak	spoke	spoken
speed	sped, *speeded	sped, *speeded
spell	spelt, spelled	spelt, spelled
spend	spent	spent
spill	spilt, spilled	spilt, spilled
spin	spun, (*arch* 古) span	spun
spit	spat; (*esp US* 尤用于美国) spit	spat; (*esp US* 尤用于美国) spit
split	split	split
spoil	spoilt, spoiled	spoilt, spoiled
spotlight	spotlit, *spotlighted	spotlit, *spotlighted
spread	spread	spread
spring	sprang	sprung
stand	stood	stood
stave	staved, *stove	staved, *stove
steal	stole	stolen
stick	stuck	stuck
sting	stung	stung
stink	stank, stunk	stunk
strew	strewed	strewed, strewn
stride	strode	stridden
strike	struck	struck
string	strung	strung
strive	strove	striven
sublet	sublet	sublet
swear	swore	sworn
sweep	swept	swept
swell	swelled	swollen, swelled
swim	swam	swum
swing	swung	swung
take	took	taken
teach	taught	taught
tear	tore	torn
tell	told	told

think	thought	thought
thrive	thrived, throve	thrived, (*arch* 古) thriven
throw	threw	thrown
thrust	thrust	thrust
tread	trod	trodden, trod
unbend	unbent	unbent
underbid	underbid	underbid
undercut	undercut	undercut
undergo	underwent	undergone
underlie	underlay	underlain
underpay	underpaid	underpaid
undersell	undersold	undersold
understand	understood	understood
undertake	undertook	undertaken
underwrite	underwrote	underwritten
undo	undid	undone
unfreeze	unfroze	unfrozen
unsay	unsaid	unsaid
unwind	unwound	unwound
uphold	upheld	upheld
upset	upset	upset
wake	woke, (*arch* 古) waked	woken, (*arch* 古) waked
waylay	waylaid	waylaid
wear	wore	worn
weave	wove, *weaved	woven, *weaved
wed	wedded, wed	wedded, wed
weep	wept	wept
wet	wet, wetted	wet, wetted
win	won	won
wind[3] /waɪnd; waɪnd/	wound /waʊnd; waʊnd/	wound /waʊnd; waʊnd/
withdraw	withdrew	withdrawn
withhold	withheld	withheld
withstand	withstood	withstood
work	worked, *wrought	worked, *wrought
wring	wrung	wrung
write	wrote	written

APPENDIX 3 附录 3

PUNCTUATION 标点符号用法

(译者说明: 英文标点符号用法与中文标点符号用法不尽相同, 请留意两者差异.)

Apostrophe

撇号, 省字号, 名词所有格符号 (')

1 Used with 's' to indicate the possessive 与 s 连用表示所有格:

the dog's /dɒgz; dɔgz/ *bone* (singular noun) 狗的骨头(单数名词)

the princess's /prɪnˈsesɪz; ˋprɪnsɪsɪz/ *smile* (singular noun ending in 's') 公主的微笑(以 s 结尾的单数名词)

King Charles's /ˈtʃɑ:lzɪz; ˋtʃɑrlzɪz/ *crown* OR *King Charles'* /ˈtʃɑ:lzɪz; ˋtʃɑrlzɪz/ *crown* (proper noun ending in 's') 查理国王的王冠(以 s 结尾的专有名词)

all the students' /ˈstju:dnts; ˋstudn̩tz/ *books* (plural noun) 学生所有的书(复数名词)

the men's /menz; mɛnz/ *jackets* (irregular plural) 男子的外衣(不规则的复数)

2 Used in contracted forms to indicate that letters or figures have been omitted 用于缩约式表示省略了字母或数字:

I'm (= I am)
he's (= he is/has)
they'd (= they had/would)
the summer of '68 (= 1968)

(Note that apostrophes are not used with possessive determiners 注意: 省字号不可与物主代词连用: *It's lost its top.*)

3 Sometimes used with 's' to form the plural of a letter, a figure or an abbreviation 有时与 s 连用构成字母、数字或缩略语的复数形式:

pronounce the r's more clearly 把 r 音发清楚些
during the 1960's 在 20 世纪 60 年代
all the MP's 国会的所有议员

Colon 冒号 (:)

1 Used after a term describing a group or class or a linking phrase (eg *as follows*, *in the following manner*) to introduce a list of items 用于表示一些或一类事物的用语之后或用于有关系的词义(如 as follows、in the following manner)之后, 用来提起下文各项:

His library consists of two books: the Bible and Shakespeare. 他藏书两部:《圣经》和莎士比亚的著作.

Proceed as follows: switch on the computer, insert a disk and press any key. 操作步骤如下: 打开计算机的开关、插入软盘, 然后按任何一个键.

2 (*fml*) Used before a clause or phrase that illustrates or explains the main clause (郑重文体)用于说明或解释主句的从句或词组之前:

The garden had been neglected for a long time: it was overgrown and full of weeds. 那个花园长期无人照料, 里面长满了杂草.

(A semicolon or a full stop, but *not* a comma, may be used instead of a colon. 英语中可用分号或句号代替冒号, 但不可用逗号.)

3 ⇨ **Quotations** 2

Comma 逗号 (,)

1 Used to separate the items in lists of words, phrases or clauses 用来隔开行文中的词、词组或从句:

If you keep calm, take your time, concentrate and think ahead, you'll pass your driving test. 假若保持镇定、不慌不忙、集中精神注意前方, 驾驶考试就能及格.

(Usually not used before *and* 通常在 and 之前不用逗号: *a bouquet of red, pink, yellow and white roses* 一束红的、粉红的、黄的、白的玫瑰花.)

2 Often used between an adverbial clause or long phrase and the main clause 常用于主句与状语从句或较长的词组之间:

When the sun is shining and the birds are singing, the world seems a happier place. 在阳光普照、百鸟齐鸣的时候, 这个世界也显得更加美好.

In the gales this autumn, many trees were blown down. 在今年秋季强风吹袭下, 很多树都刮倒了.

3 Used after a non-finite or verbless clause at the beginning of a sentence 用于在句首的非限定的或无动词的从句之后:

To be sure of getting there on time, she

left an hour early. 她为了一定准时到达那里,提前一个小时就离开了.
Worn out by their experiences, the children soon fell asleep. 孩子们经过这些事疲惫不堪,很快就睡着了.

4 Used to separate an introductory or a transitional word or phrase (eg *therefore*, *however*, *by the way*, *for instance*, *on the contrary*) from the rest of the sentence 用以将引导性或转折性词语(如 therefore、however、by the way、for instance、on the contrary)与句子的其余部分隔开:
Oh, so that's where it was! 噢,它原来在那里!
As it happens, however, I never saw her again. 但是事情就是这样,我再也没见到她.
He is unreliable and should, for this reason alone, be dismissed. 他这个人靠不住,光凭这一点就应该开除.

5 Used before a dependent clause, etc that interrupts the sentence 用于插入句中的从句等成分之前:
The fire, although it had been burning for several days, was still blazing fiercely. 这场大火,虽然已烧了几天,但火势仍然很猛.
You should, indeed you must, report this matter to the police. 你应该报警,按说你必须报警.

6 Used before and after a non-defining relative clause or a phrase in apposition, giving additional information about the noun it follows 用于非限定性关系从句或同位短语前后,进一步说明前面的名词:
The Pennine Hills, which are very popular with hikers, are situated between Lancashire and Yorkshire. 奔宁山脉,那是远足的人都很熟悉的,位于兰开夏郡和约克郡之间.
Mount Everest, the world's highest mountain, was first climbed in 1953. 埃佛勒斯峰(即珠穆朗玛峰),这座世界最高的山峰,首次有人攀登是在1953年.

(No commas are used around a clause that defines the noun it follows 限定性的从句前后不用逗号: *The hills that separate Lancashire from Yorkshire are called the Pennines*. 兰开夏郡和约克郡之间的山脉叫奔宁山脉.)

7 Sometimes used to separate (especially long) main clauses linked by a conjunction (eg *and*, *as*, *but*, *for*, *or*) 有时用以分隔并列复合句(尤指较长的),用于连词(如 and、as、but、for、or)之前:
He had been looking forward to our camping holiday all year, but unfortunately it rained every day. 他全年都一直盼着我们能去野营度假,可惜天不作美,日日下雨.

8 Used to separate a question tag or similar word or phrase from the rest of the sentence 用以将附加疑问句或类似词语与句中其余部分隔开:
It's quite expensive, isn't it? 这东西很贵,是吧?
You live in Bristol, right? 您住在布里斯托尔,对吧?

9 ⇨ **Conversation** 3, 4

10 ⇨ **Quotations** 1

Conversation 对话

1 Normally a new paragraph is begun with each new speaker 一般来说,换一个人说话要另起一个段落:
'You're sure of this?' I asked. "这一点你肯定吗?"我问道.
He nodded grimly. 他坚决地点了点头.
'I'm certain.' "我有把握."

2 Quotation marks enclose all words and punctuation (but see 3, below) 引语中所有的字和标点符号均置于引号内(但注意下面第3点):
'We must hope,' he replied wearily, 'that things will improve.' 他有气无力地回答:"咱们总得有个盼头,事情是能够改善的."

(In British usage quotation marks are usually single 英式英语通常使用单引号: *'Help!'*; in US usage they are usually double 美式英语通常用双引号: *"Help!"*. When dividing a long speech by one speaker into paragraphs, quotation marks are placed at the beginning of each paragraph and at the end of the speech, but not at the end of the intermediate paragraphs. 引用连续的几个段落时,每段开头用前引号,段落的末尾不用后引号,只在最后一段的结尾处用后引号.)

3 Discourse markers (eg *he said*, *she told me*, *they complained*) are separated from the words spoken by commas unless a question mark or exclamation mark is used 作者提示"某某说"之类的词语(如 he said, she told me, they complained)用逗号与引用语分开，但引用语原用问号或叹号时则保留原用符号:

'That's all I know,' said Nick. "我就知道这些," 尼克说.

'That,' said Nick, 'is all I know.' 尼克说: "我就知道这些."

Nick said, 'That's all I know.' 尼克说: "我就知道这些."

'Why?' asked Nick. "为什么呢?" 尼克问.

4 Speech within speech is introduced by a comma and enclosed by 引语里面的引语用逗号隔开，注意 (**a**) double quotation marks where single quotation marks are otherwise in use 外面一层用单引号时，里面一层用双引号:

'When the judge said, "Not guilty", I could have hugged him.'

(**b**) single quotation marks where double quotation marks are otherwise in use 外面一层用双引号时，里面一层用单引号:

"When the judge said, 'Not guilty', I could have hugged him."

5 Hesitant or interrupted speech is indicated by a dash or by three dots 引用犹豫的或被打断的话，英语中用破折号或用三个点的省略号:

'Pass me – I mean, would you mind passing me the salt, please?' "递给我——我是说，劳您驾请把盐递给我行吗?"

His dying words were, 'The murderer was ...' 他临终说的是: "杀人的是……"

Dash 破折号 (–)

(Cf 参看 **Hyphen**)

1 (*infml*) Used instead of a colon or semicolon to mark off a summary or conclusion of what has gone before (通俗用法)用以代替冒号或分号，表示对前面的话的总结或结论:

Men were shouting, women were screaming, children were crying – it was chaos. 男的喊、女的叫、孩子哭——混成一片.

You've admitted that you lied to me – how can I trust you again? 你已经承认对我撒了谎——我怎么能再信任你呢?

2 (*infml*) Used singly or in pairs to separate extra information, an afterthought or a comment from the rest of the sentence (通俗用法)单个使用或成对使用，以隔开插入句中的附加信息、补充说明或评语:

He knew nothing at all about it – or so he said. 他对此事一无所知——反正他是这样说的.

Winters in the Mediterranean – contrary to what many people think – can be very cold. 地中海的冬天——与许多人想像的相反——有时候非常冷.

3 ⇨ **Conversation** 5

(In formal use, parentheses or commas replace dashes. 郑重的用法，使用括号或逗号而不用破折号.)

Dots 英式省略号 (...)

(also *esp US* 尤用于美式英语称作 **Ellipsis**)

1 ⇨ **Conversation** 5

2 ⇨ **Quotations** 3

Exclamation mark 叹号 (!)

(*US* also 美式英语亦称 **Exclamation point**)

Used at the end of a sentence or remark expressing great anger, surprise, joy or other strong emotion 用以表示大怒、惊讶、欣喜或其他強烈感情，置于句子或话语的末尾:

What wonderful news! 多么好的消息呀!

'Never!' she cried. "绝对不行!" 她喊道.

(In informal and especially in jocular use, more than one exclamation mark, or an exclamation mark and a question mark, are sometimes used 在不规范的用法中，尤其是诙谐用法中，有时用不止一个叹号或一个叹号加一个问号:

'Your wife's just given birth to triplets.' 'Triplets!?' "您妻子刚生了三胞胎." "三胞胎!?")

Footnotes 脚注

Footnotes are indicated in the text by superscript numbers placed after the reference or quotation; the footnotes themselves appear either at the bottom of the page or at the end of the chapter or book 行文中的脚注用数字标于所注的或引语的

右上角，脚注本身置于该页的底部或该章节的末尾或该书的后部:

For a more extended treatment of dialects, see the recent study by Frick[1], *which one reviewer called 'a masterly analysis of this complex subject'*[2]. 关于方言问题详见弗里克(注 1)近著，一位书评家称该书为"对这一复杂问题的精辟分析"(注 2)

………………

[1]Marjorie Frick, *English Dialects (London: Faber and Faber, 1985).*
注 1: 马乔里·弗里克著《英语方言》(伦敦费伯与费伯出版社 1985 年)

[2]Peter Benson, 'Speaking in Tongues,' *Times Literary Supplement*, 11 April 1986.
注 2: 彼得·本森著《用不同方言说话》载于 1986 年 4 月 11 日《泰晤士报文学增刊》.

Full stop 句号 (.)

(*US* 美式英语称 **Period**)

1 Used to mark the end of a sentence that is not a direct question or an exclamation 用于一般句子的末尾，不用于直接问句或感叹句:
I knocked at the door. There was no reply. 我敲了敲门. 没人应门.

2 Sometimes used, though not in this dictionary, in abbreviations 有时用于缩略语之后(但本词典中不用):
Jan.; *e.g.*; *a.m.*

Hyphen 连接号 (-)

(Cf 参看 **Dash**)

1 Used in compounds 用于复合词:
(a) Sometimes used to form a compound word from two other words 有时用以将两个词组成复合词:
hard-hearted; *radio-telescope*; *fork-lift truck*
(b) Used to form a compound from a prefix and a proper name 用以将前缀和专有名词组成复合词:
pre-Raphaelite; *pro-Soviet*; *anti-Nazi*
(c) Used to form a compound from two other words that are separated by a preposition 用以将两个词及夹在中间的介词组成复合词:
mother-in-law; *mother-to-be*; *mother-of-pearl*
(d) Used to vary the first element of a hyphenated compound 用以变换有连接号的复合词的第一部分:
common to both pre- and post-war Europe
(e) Used when forming attributive compounds from two or more proper names 用以连接至少两个专有名词组成修饰性复合词:
the Clinton-Yeltsin summit; services on the London-Bahrain-Hong Kong route
(f) Used when writing out compound numbers between 21 and 99 用于写出从 21 至 99 的两位数字中:
seventy-three; four hundred and thirty-one

2 (*esp Brit*) Sometimes used to separate a prefix ending in a vowel from a word beginning with the same vowel (尤用于英式英语)有时用以隔开某些带前缀的词，这些前缀的尾字母与后面连接的词的首字母为同一元音:
co-ordination; re-elect; pre-eminent

3 Used after the first section of a word that is divided between one line and the next 用于在一行位置的词的前半部之后:
... in order to avoid future mis-
takes of this kind.

4 Used between two numbers or dates to include everything that comes between these numbers or dates 用于两个数字或日期之间，意为包括其中的所有数字或日期:
pp106-131
a study of the British economy, 1947-63

Italics 斜体字

(In handwritten or typed text, and in the examples that follow, italics are indicated by underlining. 在书写或打字机打的文本中以及在下面的示例中，用字下划横线的方式表示斜体字.)

1 Used to indicate stress or emphasis 用以表示着重或加强语气:

I'm not going to do it – you are. 我不去做这件事 —— 你得做.
... proposals which we cannot accept under any circumstances whatsoever. …… 在任何情况下我们都不可能接受的建议.

2 Used for the titles of books, magazines, newspapers, plays, operas, films, paintings, etc 用以表示书籍、报刊、戏剧、电影、绘画作品等的名称:
Joyce's Ulysses 乔伊斯著的《尤利西斯》
a letter in The Times/in today's Times 《泰晤士报》上[今天《泰晤士报》上]的一封信
She has often sung the title-role in Tosca. 她经常在歌剧《托斯卡》中扮演剧名角色.

3 Used for foreign words or phrases that have not been naturalized into English and for the Latin names of plants and animals 用以表示英语中尚未普遍采用的外来词语及动植物的拉丁语名称:
I had to renew my permesso di soggiorno, or residence permit. 我的居留许可证得续期了.
'Tempus fugit,' (ie 'Time flies') as they say. 语云:"光阴似箭."
the English oak (Quercus robur) 英国栎树

Letters 书信

⇨ **Sample Texts** 3a, 3b

Parentheses 括号 ( )

(*Brit* also 英式英语亦作 **Brackets**)

1 Used to separate extra information or an afterthought or a comment from the rest of the sentence 用以隔开句中附加信息、补充说明或评语:
Mount Robson (12 972 feet) is the highest mountain in the Canadian Rockies. 罗布森山(高 12 972 英尺)是加拿大境内的落基山脉最高峰.
He thinks that modern music (ie anything written after 1900) is rubbish. 他认为现代音乐(即 1900 年后创作的音乐)都不堪入耳.

2 Used to enclose cross-references 用以标明相互参照的注释:
This moral ambiguity is a feature of Shakespeare's later works (see Chapter Eight). 揭示道德观的模棱两可, 是莎士比亚后期著作的特征(见第八章).

3 Used to enclose numbers or letters in the text 用以标明号码和字母编号:
Our objectives are (1) to increase output, (2) to improve quality and (3) to maximize profits. 我们的目标是 (1) 增加产量 (2) 提高质量 (3) 最大限度地提高利润.
What you say is (a) untrue and (b) irrelevant. 你所说的一来不真实, 二来与问题无关.

4 ⇨ **Square Brackets**

Question mark 问号 (?)

1 Used at the end of a direct question 用于直接问句末尾:
Where's the car? 汽车在什么地方?
You're leaving? 你就要走了吗?
(Not used at the end of an indirect question 问号不用于间接问句末尾: *He asked if I was leaving.* 他问我是否要走.)

2 Used in parentheses to express doubt 用于括号内表示存疑:
John Marston (?1575-1634) 约翰·马斯顿(?1575-1634)

Quotation marks 引号 (' ' " ")

(*Brit* also 英式英语亦称 **Inverted commas**)

In British usage quotation marks are usually single 在英式英语中, 引号通常用单引号: *'Help!'*. In US usage they are usually double 在美式英语中通常用双引号: *"Help!"*.

1 Used to enclose all words and punctuation in direct speech 用以标明直接引语中的所有词语和标点符号:
'What on earth did you do that for?' he asked. "你这样做到底是为了什么?" 他问道.
'I won't go,' she replied. "我不去," 她回答说.
'Nonsense!' "胡说!"

2 Used to draw attention to a term that is unusual in the context (eg a technical or slang expression) or one that is being used for special effect (eg irony) 用以引起对文中某特殊词语的注意(如术语或俚语或为某种效果而使用的词语(如反语)):
Next the dough is 'proved' to allow the yeast to start working. 然后, 面团"发起"使酵母产生作用.
He told me in no uncertain terms to 'get lost'. 他对我说的确实是"滚开".
Thousands were imprisoned in the name of 'national security'. 成千上万的人在"国家安全"的名义下遭监禁.

3 Used to enclose the titles of articles, short poems, radio and television programmes, etc 用以标明文章、短诗歌、广播及电视节目等的名称:

Keats's 'Ode to Autumn' 济慈的《秋颂》

I was watching 'Match of the Day'. 我正在看"每日赛事".

4 Used to enclose short quotations or sayings 用以标明短小的引语或谚语:

'Do you know the origin of the saying "A little learning is a dangerous thing"?' "你是否知道'A little learning is a dangerous thing'这句谚语的出处?"

5 ⇨ **Conversation, Quotations**

Quotations 引语

1 A short quotation is separated from its introduction by a comma and is enclosed in quotation-marks 短小的引语与作者提示"某某说"之类的词语之间用逗号隔开,置于引号内:

It was Disraeli who said, 'Little things affect little minds'. 迪斯累里说过: "琐事扰庸人."

2 A longer quotation is separated from its introduction by a colon and marked off from the rest of the text by indentation or spacing 较长的引语与作者提示"某某说"之类的词语之间用冒号隔开, 并以缩格或隔行的方式与文中其余部分隔开:

As Kenneth Morgan writes:

The truth was, perhaps, that Britain in the years from 1914 to 1983 had not changed all that fundamentally.

Others, however, have challenged this view ...

肯尼思·摩根写道:

"事实也许是英国自 1914 年至 1983 年并没有多么大的根本变化."

但是,有人对这一看法提出异议……

3 A word or phrase omitted from a quotation is indicated by three dots; a word or phrase inserted into the quotation (eg to make the text grammatically correct) is enclosed in square brackets 引语中省略的词语用三个点的省略号表示;加在引语中的词语(如为使省略后合乎语法)置于方括号内:

challenging Morgan's view that 'Britain in [these] years ... had not changed ...' 针对摩根认为"英国(这么)多年……并未改变……"的看法提出异议.

Semicolon 分号 (;)

1 Used instead of a comma to separate from each other parts of a sentence that already contain commas 用以代替逗号, 隔开句中已含逗号的部分:

She wanted to be successful, whatever it might cost; to achieve her goal, whoever might suffer as a result. 她决意求成, 不惜一切代价; 为达到目的, 不管谁遭殃.

2 (*fml*) Used to separate main clauses, especially those not joined by a conjunction (郑重用法)用以隔开并列从句, 尤用于无连词的句中:

The sun was already low in the sky; it would soon be dark. 太阳落山了, 天快黑了.

He had never been to China; however, it had always been one of his ambitions. 他从未去过中国; 到中国去是他的夙愿.

Slash 斜线号 (/)

(*Brit* also 英式英语亦称 **Oblique**) (*US* 美式英语作 **Virgule**)

1 Used to separate alternative words or terms 用以隔开可供选择的词语:

Take a mackintosh and/or an umbrella. 带着雨衣和[或]雨伞.

I certify that I am married/single/divorced (delete whichever does not apply). 我声明我已婚[未婚/已离婚](删掉不适用者)

2 Used to indicate the end of each line of poetry where several lines are run on 在诗歌中几行连写时, 用以标明每行的末尾:

Wordsworth's famous lines, 'I wandered lonely as a cloud/That floats on high o'er vales and hills...'

Square brackets 方括号 [ ]

(*US* 美式英语称 **Brackets**)

1 Used to enclose editorial comments 用以标明编者按语:

a notice reading 'Everything to be put away in it's [sic] place after use' 一项通知

称: "一切物品用后放回其的(原文如此)原处"
constant references in her diary to 'Mr G[ladstone]'s visits' 在她日记中时常提到"格(Gladstone)先生之到访"

2 ⇨ **Quotations** 3

Sample Texts 示例

1

Serious and cultured speech and writing in America does not greatly differ from that used in Britain. However, during the 300 years in which American English has been developing, many new words or meanings have been added. There are also other differences: spelling (e.g. *color* = colour) and pronunciation, for instance. But these are of slight importance in comparison with the use of words and phrases which give American English its distinctive character. 在美国使用的郑重而文雅的言语与文字同英国的差别不大. 但是 300 年来逐渐发展成的美式英语, 增加了许多新词语或新词义. 还有其他差别, 例如拼法(如 color = colour)和读音. 然而这些与词语用法相比倒不太重要, 词和词组的用法不同体现了美式英语的特色.

This is only part of the picture, however. America is a vast country, and as Robert Burchfield has written, 'American English, as taught to foreigners, is ... not spoken by the majority of Americans.' 但是这仅仅是问题的一个侧面. 美国幅员广大, 正如罗伯特·伯奇菲尔德所述: "美式英语, 教外国人是这么教, 大多数美国人却并不这么说."

2

'But you said you loved me! "I'll never leave you, Sue, as long as I live." That's what you said, isn't it?' "可是你说过你爱我! '休, 只要我活着, 我就决不离开你.' 你是这么说的, 是不是?"

Dave shrugged awkwardly. 戴夫尴尬地耸了耸肩.

'I don't remember exactly what I said,' he began, 'but ...' "我记不清我说的原话了," 他说道, "但是 ......"

'You liar!' Sue screamed, slapping his face. 'Lies, excuses, evasions – that's all I get from you. Well, I've had enough. You understand?' "你这个骗子!" 休尖叫着, 狠狠打了他一个耳光. "撒谎、借口、托词 —— 你跟我说的都是这些. 行了, 我受够了. 你明白吗?"

'Look, I said I was sorry.' "你听我说, 我说过对不起你, 我很后悔."

Fixing him with a withering glare, Sue muttered, 'You *will* be sorry, Dave. I promise you that.' 休直勾勾地瞪着他, 咕哝了一句: "你后悔在后头呢, 戴夫, 我事先告诉你."

3a

3 Willow Street,
Frambleton,
Suffolk
SF5 9PK

6th June, 1989

The Director,
Leisureland Hotels PLC,
409 Piccadilly,
London
WC2 4WW

Dear Sir,

While staying in your hotel in Brighton recently, I mislaid a necklace which, although of little intrinsic value, was a great loss to me, as it belonged to my late mother. I mentioned the matter to the manager of the hotel concerned (Mr Perron), asking him to make enquiries. Several weeks later, I received a letter from him stating that the necklace had been found and asking me to 'call in at my convenience' to collect it.
Since then, I have written no fewer than four times to Mr Perron, explaining that it is not at all convenient for me to travel two hundred miles in order to collect the necklace in person, and asking him to post it to me. I have received no reply to any of these letters. May I ask you to contact Mr Perron and persuade him to send me my necklace as soon as possible?

Yours faithfully,

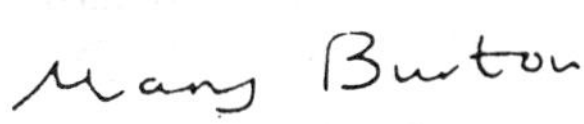

Mary Burton (Mrs)

敬启者:

近日曾于布赖顿市下榻贵旅店，不知将一项链错放何处. 项链本身无甚价值，但于我是莫大损失，因是先母遗物. 此事曾与贵旅店经理(佩龙先生)提及，请代为查询. 几星期后接他一信，称项链已找到，嘱我“于方便的时候前来”领取.

此后，曾去函佩龙先生不下四次，说明为亲自领取项链行程需二百英里十分不方便，请代为邮寄舍下. 这些信件均无回音. 可否请您与佩龙先生联系，请其尽速将项链寄来? 即颂

近安

玛丽·伯顿
1989 年 6 月 6 日

译者注：英文书信中发信人的地址和发信日期写在信瓤的右上角；收信人的姓名或职衔和地址写在下面左侧. 中文书信不这样处理.

3b

Willow St,
Frambleton

Friday

Dear Peter,

Sorry to trouble you, but I've got a bit of a problem with that necklace I lost. They've found it but don't want to send it back – they expect me to come and pick it up, if you please! I've written to their head office in London, but do you think there would be any chance of your picking it up for me next time you're in Brighton on business? If you can do it, phone me in advance so that I can authorize them to give it to you. You'd think it was the Crown Jewels, the way they're carrying on!

Best wishes,

Mary

彼得:

麻烦你一件事，我遗失的那个项链出了个小问题. 他们已找到但不愿寄给我 —— 让我前往领取，竟有这事! 我已去函伦敦总店，但不知你是否有可能下次出差至布赖顿时代我取回? 如可行，事先给我个电话，我好授权让他们交给你. 他们煞有介事，你准以为是凤冠霞帔呢! 顺候

安好

玛丽
星期五

APPENDIX 4 附录 4

NUMERICAL EXPRESSIONS 数字表达法

The following section will give you help in the reading, speaking and writing of numbers and expressions which commonly contain numbers. 下列为数字及常见含有数字的用语, 对使用数字的读、说、写方面有所帮助.

Numbers 数字

CARDINAL 基数词

1 one /wʌn; wʌn/ 一
2 two /tuː; tu/ 二
3 three /θriː; θri/ 三
4 four /fɔː(r); fɔr/ 四
5 five /faɪv; faɪv/ 五
6 six /sɪks; sɪks/ 六
7 seven /ˈsevn; ˋsɛvən/ 七
8 eight /eɪt; et/ 八
9 nine /naɪn; naɪn/ 九
10 ten /ten; tɛn/ 十
11 eleven /ɪˈlevn; ɪˋlɛvən/ 十一
12 twelve /twelv; twɛlv/ 十二
13 thirteen /ˌθɜːˈtiːn; θɝˋtin/ 十三
14 fourteen /ˌfɔːˈtiːn; fɔrˋtin/ 十四
15 fifteen /ˌfɪfˈtiːn; fɪfˋtin/ 十五
16 sixteen /ˌsɪkˈstiːn; sɪksˋtin/ 十六
17 seventeen /ˌsevnˈtiːn; ˌsɛvənˋtin/ 十七
18 eighteen /ˌeɪˈtiːn; eˋtin/ 十八
19 nineteen /ˌnaɪnˈtiːn; naɪnˋtin/ 十九
20 twenty /ˈtwentɪ; ˋtwɛntɪ/ 二十
21 twenty-one /ˌtwentɪˈwʌn; ˋtwɛntɪˋwʌn/ 二十一
22 twenty-two /ˌtwentɪˈtuː; ˋtwɛntɪˋtu/ 二十二
23 twenty-three /ˌtwentɪˈθriː; ˋtwɛntɪˋθri/ 二十三
30 thirty /ˈθɜːtɪ; ˋθɝtɪ/ 三十
40 forty /ˈfɔːtɪ; ˋfɔrtɪ/ 四十
50 fifty /ˈfɪftɪ; ˋfɪftɪ/ 五十
60 sixty /ˈsɪkstɪ; ˋsɪkstɪ/ 六十
70 seventy /ˈsevntɪ; ˋsɛvəntɪ/ 七十
80 eighty /ˈeɪtɪ; ˋetɪ/ 八十
90 ninety /ˈnaɪntɪ; ˋnaɪntɪ/ 九十
100 one hundred /wʌn ˈhʌndrəd; wʌn ˋhʌndrəd/ 一百
200 two hundred /ˌtuː ˈhʌndrəd; ˋtu ˋhʌndrəd/ 二百
1 000 one thousand /wʌn ˈθaʊznd; wʌn ˋθaʊzn̩d/ 一千

ORDINAL 序数词

1st first /fɜːst; fɝst/ 第一
2nd second /ˈsekənd; ˋsɛkənd/ 第二
3rd third /θɜːd; θɝd/ 第三
4th fourth /fɔːθ; fɔrθ/ 第四
5th fifth /fɪfθ; fɪfθ/ 第五
6th sixth /sɪksθ; sɪksθ/ 第六
7th seventh /ˈsevənθ; ˋsɛvənθ/ 第七
8th eighth /eɪtθ; etθ/ 第八
9th ninth /naɪnθ; naɪnθ/ 第九
10th tenth /tenθ; tɛnθ/ 第十
11th eleventh /ɪˈlevnθ; ɪˋlɛvənθ/ 第十一
12th twelfth /twelfθ; twɛlfθ/ 第十二
13th thirteenth /ˌθɜːˈtiːnθ; θɝˋtinθ/ 第十三
14th fourteenth /ˌfɔːˈtiːnθ; fɔrˋtinθ/ 第十四
15th fifteenth /ˌfɪfˈtiːnθ; fɪfˋtinθ/ 第十五
16th sixteenth /ˌsɪkˈstiːnθ; sɪksˋtinθ/ 第十六
17th seventeenth /ˌsevnˈtiːnθ; ˌsɛvənˋtinθ/ 第十七
18th eighteenth /ˌeɪˈtiːnθ; eˋtinθ/ 第十八
19th nineteenth /ˌnaɪnˈtiːnθ; naɪnˋtinθ/ 第十九
20th twentieth /ˈtwentɪəθ; ˋtwɛntɪɪθ/ 第二十
21st twenty-first /ˌtwentɪˈfɜːst; ˋtwɛntɪˋfɝst/ 第二十一
22nd twenty-second /ˌtwentɪˈsekənd; ˋtwɛntɪˋsɛkənd/ 第二十二
23rd twenty-third /ˌtwentɪˈθɜːd; ˋtwɛntɪˋθɝd/ 第二十三
30th thirtieth /ˈθɜːtɪəθ; ˋθɝtɪɪθ/ 第三十
40th fortieth /ˈfɔːtɪəθ; ˋfɔrtɪɪθ/ 第四十
50th fiftieth /ˈfɪftɪəθ; ˋfɪftɪɪθ/ 第五十
60th sixtieth /ˈsɪkstɪəθ; ˋsɪkstɪɪθ/ 第六十
70th seventieth /ˈsevntɪəθ; ˋsɛvəntɪɪθ/ 第七十
80th eightieth /ˈeɪtɪəθ; ˋetɪɪθ/ 第八十
90th ninetieth /ˈnaɪntɪəθ; ˋnaɪntɪɪθ/ 第九十
100th one hundredth /wʌn ˈhʌndrədθ; wʌn ˋhʌndrədθ/ 第一百
200th two hundredth /ˌtuː ˈhʌndrədθ; ˋtu ˋhʌndrədθ/ 第二百
1 000th one thousandth /wʌn ˈθaʊznθ; wʌn ˋθaʊzn̩θ/ 第一千

10 000 ten thousand /ˌten ˈθaʊznd; ˋtɛn ˋθaʊzn̩d/ 一万

100 000 one hundred thousand /wʌn ˌhʌndrəd ˈθaʊznd; wʌn ˋhʌndrəd ˋθaʊzn̩d/ 十万

1 000 000 one million /wʌn ˈmɪlɪən; wʌn ˋmɪljən/ 一百万

10 000th ten thousandth /ˌten ˈθaʊznθ; ˋtɛn ˋθaʊzn̩θ/ 第一万

100 000th one hundred thousandth /wʌn ˌhʌndrəd ˈθaʊznθ; wʌn ˋhʌndrəd ˋθaʊzn̩θ/ 第十万

1 000 000th one millionth /wʌn ˈmɪlɪənθ; wʌn ˋmɪljənθ/ 第一百万

1 000 000 000 one thousand million(s) /wʌn ˌθaʊznd ˈmɪlɪən(z); wʌn ˋθaʊzn̩d ˋmɪljən(z)/ (*US*) one billion /wʌn ˈbɪlɪən; wʌn ˋbɪljən/ 十亿; 一千兆

1 000 000 000 000 one billion /wʌn ˈbɪlɪən; wʌn ˋbɪljən/ (*US*) one trillion /wʌn ˈtrɪlɪən; wʌn ˋtrɪljən/ 一万亿; 一兆兆

1 000 000 000 000 000 one thousand billion(s) /wʌn ˌθaʊznd ˈbɪlɪən(z), wʌn ˋθaʊzn̩d ˋbɪljən(z)/ (*US*) one quadrillion /wʌn kwɒˈdrɪlɪən; wʌn kwɑˋdrɪljən/ 一千万亿; 一千兆兆

1 000 000 000 000 000 000 one trillion /wʌn ˈtrɪlɪən; wʌn ˋtrɪljən/ (*US*) one quintillion /wʌn kwɪnˈtɪlɪən; wʌn kwɪnˋtɪljən/ 一百亿亿; 一兆兆兆

EXAMPLES OF MORE COMPLEX NUMBERS 较复杂数字示例

101 one hundred and one /ˌwʌn ˌhʌndrəd n ˈwʌn; wʌn ˋhʌndrəd n̩ ˋwʌn/ 一百零一

101st one hundred and first /wʌn ˌhʌndrəd n ˈfɜ:st; wʌn ˋhʌndrəd n̩ ˋfɝst/ 第一百零一

334 three hundred and thirty-four /ˌθri: ˌhʌndrəd n ˌθɜ:tɪ ˈfɔ:(r); ˋθri ˋhʌndrəd n̩ ˋθɝtɪˋfɔr/ 三百三十四

542nd five hundred and forty-second /ˌfaɪv ˌhʌndrəd n ˌfɔ:tɪ ˈsekənd; ˋfaɪv ˋhʌndrəd n̩ ˋfɔrtɪˋsɛkənd/ 第五百四十二

1 101 one thousand, one hundred and one /ˌwʌn ˈθaʊznd ˌwʌn ˈhʌndrəd n ˈwʌn; wʌn ˋθaʊzn̩d wʌn ˋhʌndrəd n̩ ˋwʌn/ 一千一百零一

1 234 753 one million, two hundred and thirty-four thousand, seven hundred and fifty-three /ˌwʌn ˈmɪlɪən ˌtu: ˌhʌndrəd n ˌθɜ:tɪ ˌfɔ: ˈθaʊznd ˌsevn ˌhʌndrəd n fɪftɪ ˈθri:; wʌn ˋmɪljən ˋtu ˋhʌndrəd n̩ ˋθɝtɪˋfɔr ˋθaʊzn̩d ˋsɛvən ˋhʌndrəd n̩ ˋfɪftɪ ˋθri/ 一百二十三万四千七百五十三

VULGAR FRACTIONS 分数

$\frac{1}{8}$ an/one eighth /ən, wʌn ˈeɪtθ; ən, wʌn ˋetθ/ 八分之一

$\frac{1}{4}$ a/one quarter /ə, wʌn ˈkwɔ:tə(r); ə, wʌn ˋkwɔrtɚ/ 四分之一

$\frac{1}{3}$ a/one third /ə, wʌn ˈθɜ:d; ə, wʌn ˋθɝd/ 三分之一

$\frac{1}{2}$ a/one half /ə, wʌn ˈhɑ:f; *US* ˈhæf; ə, wʌn ˋhæf/ 二分之一

$\frac{3}{4}$ three quarters /ˌθri: ˈkwɔ:təz; ˋθri ˋkwɔrtɚz/ 四分之三

$5\frac{1}{2}$ five and a half /ˌfaɪv ən ə ˈhɑ:f; *US* ˈhæf; ˋfaɪv ən əˋhæf/ 五又二分之一

$13\frac{3}{4}$ thirteen and three quarters /ˌθɜ:ti:n ən θri: ˈkwɔ:təz; ˋθɝtin ən θri ˋkwɔrtɚz/ 十三又四分之三

DECIMAL FRACTIONS 小数

0.125 (nought) point one two five /(ˌnɔ:t) pɔɪnt ˌwʌn tu: ˈfaɪv; (ˌnɔt) pɔɪnt ˌwʌn tu ˋfaɪv/ (零)点一二五

0.25 (nought) point two five /(ˌnɔ:t) pɔɪnt ˌtu: ˈfaɪv; (ˌnɔt) pɔɪnt ˌtu ˋfaɪv/ (零)点二五

0.33 (nought) point three three /(ˌnɔ: t) pɔɪnt θri: ˈθri:; (ˌnɔt) pɔɪnt θri ˋθri/ (零)点三三

0.5 (nought) point five /(ˌnɔ:t) pɔɪnt ˈfaɪv; (ˌnɔt) pɔɪnt ˋfaɪv/ (零)点五

0.75 (nought) point seven five /(ˌnɔ:t) pɔɪnt ˌsevn ˈfaɪv; (ˌnɔt) pɔɪnt ˌsɛvən ˋfaɪv/ (零)点七五

5.5 five point five /ˌfaɪv pɔɪnt ˈfaɪv; ˌfaɪv pɔɪnt ˋfaɪv/ 五点五

13.75 thirteen point seven five /ˌθɜ:ti:n pɔɪnt ˌsevn ˈfaɪv; ˌθɝtin pɔɪnt ˌsɛvən ˋfaɪv/ 十三点七五

COLLECTIVE NUMBERS 集合数字

6 a half dozen/half a dozen 半打
12 a/one dozen (24 is two *dozen* not two *dozens*) 一打(24 为 two dozen, 不作 two dozens)
20 a/one score 廿; 念
144 a/one gross /grəʊs; gros/ 罗(等于 12 打, 或 144 件)

ROMAN 罗马		ARABIC 阿拉伯	ROMAN 罗马		ARABIC 阿拉伯	ROMAN 罗马	ARABIC 阿拉伯	ROMAN 罗马	ARABIC 阿拉伯
I	i	1	XIV	xiv	14	LX	60	CM	900
II	ii	2	XV	xv	15	LXX	70	M	1000
III	iii	3	XVI	xvi	16	LXXX	80	MC	1100
IV	iv	4	XVII	xvii	17	XC	90	MCD	1400
V	v	5	XVIII	xviii	18	IC	99	MDC	1600
VI	vi	6	XIX	xix	19	C	100	MDCLXVI	1666
VII	vii	7	XX	xx	20	CC	200	MDCCLXXXVIII	1788
VIII	viii	8	XXI	xxi	21	CCC	300	MDCCCXCIV	1894
IX	ix	9	XXV	xxv	25	CD	400	MCM	1900
X	x	10	XXIX	xxix	29	D	500	MCMLXXVI	1976
XI	xi	11	XXX	xxx	30	DC	600	MCMLXXXIX	1989
XII	xii	12	XL	xl	40	DCC	700	MM	2000
XIII	xiii	13	L	l	50	DCCC	800		

A letter placed after another letter of greater value adds, eg VI = 5 + 1 = 6. A letter placed before a letter of greater value subtracts, eg IV = 5 − 1 = 4. A dash placed over a letter multiplies the value by 1 000; thus $\overline{\text{X}}$ = 10 000 and $\overline{\text{M}}$ = 1 000 000. 字母数值左大右小者为加, 如 VI = 5 + 1 = 6. 左小右大者为减, 如 IV = 5 − 1 = 4. 字母上方的横线表示乘以 1 000, 即 $\overline{\text{X}}$ = 10 000, $\overline{\text{M}}$ = 1 000 000.

Notes 注意:

1 In large numbers starting with *'one'* the indefinite article may be substituted in less formal use or when the number is not intended to be exact 以 one 开始的较大数字, 通俗用法或表示概数时可用不定冠词 a 代替 one: *He's got over a thousand records.* 他有上千张唱片.

2 When saying ordinary numbers we can use *'zero', 'nought'* or *'o'*/əʊ; o/ for the number 0; *'zero'* is the most common US usage and the most technical or precise form; *'o'* is the least technical or precise. 说普通数字时, 0 可读作 zero、nought 或字母 O 的读音 /əʊ; o/; zero 为最常见的美式用法, 也是最常用于科技方面或最精确的形式; O /əʊ; o/ 极少用于科技方面, 是最不精确的形式. ⇨Usage at NOUGHT 用法见 NOUGHT.

3 A comma is sometimes used instead of a space to separate the thousands in numbers greater than 999 大于 999 的数字, 采用三位分节法, 节与节之间有时用逗号隔开, 而不用空半个阿拉伯数字的位置的方法: 1 000/1,000; 10 000/10,000; 7 586 954/7,586,954.

4 Thousands may be spoken as hundreds, especially in informal use "千"有时可转换成以"百"为单位的方式表达, 尤见于通俗用法: *eleven hundred* (ie 1 100) 一千一百.

5 Long numbers (eg bank accounts, credit card numbers, etc) are spoken as separate digits grouped rhythmically in twos or threes 大的数字(如银行帐户号码、信用卡编号等), 可以两个或三个数字为一组按节奏读出:
o five four / eight six three / nine double six (ie 054863966).

6 Names for numbers above *trillion* are rarely used. When larger numbers need

to be expressed, eg in astronomy, this is usually done in terms of powers of ten, ie the number of zeros following the 10 大于"一百亿亿"的数字, 很少用其名称. 需要表达时, 如在天文学中, 通常采用 10 的若干次幂的方式, 即 10 后若干个零:
ten to the power fifteen/to the fifteenth (power) 10 的 15 次幂 (ie 10 000 000 000 000 000).

7 In the spoken forms of vulgar fractions, the versions *'and a half/quarter/third'* are preferred to *'and one half/quarter/third'* whether the measurement is approximate or precise. With more obviously precise fractions like $\frac{1}{8}$, $\frac{1}{16}$, *'and one eighth/sixteenth'* is normal. Complex fractions like $\frac{3}{462}$, $\frac{20}{83}$ are spoken as *'three over four-six-two; twenty over eighty-three'*, especially in mathematical expressions, eg *'twenty-two over seven'* for $\frac{22}{7}$. 用口语表达普通的分数, 无论是近似的还是精确的, 宜用 and a half/quarter/third 而不用 one half/quarter/third. 明显的精确分数, 如 $\frac{1}{8}$、$\frac{1}{16}$, 一般用 and one eighth/sixteenth 的说法. 复杂的分数, 如 $\frac{3}{462}$、$\frac{20}{83}$, 分别读作 three over four-six-two、twenty over eighty-three, 尤用于数学方面, 如 $\frac{22}{7}$ 读作 twenty-two over seven.

8 A point is used in writing decimal fractions (rather than a comma, as in continental Europe). The digits after the point are read by saying *'point'* and then each digit separately 小数, 书写时要用小数点(欧洲大陆用逗号作小数点). 小数点后的数字, 读时先说 point 然后逐个读出:
two hundred and seventy-three point two nine six 二百七十三点二九六 (ie 273.296).
In decimal fractions less than one, the 'nought' (or 'zero') before the decimal point may be omitted 小数点前的数字小于 1 时, nought(或 zero)可略去不读:
point seven five 点七五 (ie 0.75).

Mathematical Expressions 数学用语

Where alternative ways of saying the expressions are given, the first is generally more formal or technical. 有不止一种说法时, 列在首位的一般较正规或多用于科技方面.

+	plus / and 加(上)
−	minus / take away 减(去)
±	plus or minus 正负
×	(is) multiplied by/times (*or, when giving dimensions, by*) 乘以; (在表示面积、体积时说)乘
÷	(is) divided by 除以
=	is equal to/equals 等于
≠	is not equal to/does not equal 不等于
≃	is approximately equal to 约等于
≡	is equivalent to/is identical with 全等于
<	is less than 小于
≮	is not less than 不小于
⩽	is less than or equal to 小于或等于
>	is more than 大于
≯	is not more than 不大于
⩾	is more than or equal to 大于或等于
%	per cent 百分之
∞	infinity 无限大
∝	varies as/is proportional to 随……而变化
3:9: :4:12	three is to nine as four is to twelve 3 比 9 等于 4 比 12
$\log_e$	natural logarithm *or* logarithm to the base e /iː; i/ 自然对数或以 e 为底数的对数
√	(square) root 平方根
∛	cube root 立方根
x^2	x /eks; ɛks/ squared x 平方
x^3	x /eks; ɛks/ cubed x 立方
x^4	x /eks; ɛks/ to the power of four/to the fourth x 的四次方(或四次幂)
p	pi /paɪ; paɪ/ 圆周率
r	/ɑː(r); ɑr/ = radius of a circle 半径
∫	the integral of ……的积分
°	degree 度
′	minute (of an arc); foot *or* feet (unit of length) 分; 英尺
″	second (of an arc); inch *or* inches (unit of length) 秒; 英寸

Numbers in Measurements 计量单位名称与数字用法

A: LINEAR MEASUREMENT 长度单位

symb 符号	*abbr* 缩略式	*full word* 全称	*abbr* 缩略式	*full word* 全称
″	in	inch(es) 英寸	mm	millimetre(s) 毫米
′	ft	foot/feet 英尺	cm	centimetre(s) 厘米
	yd	yard 码	m	metre(s) 米
	ml (*US* mi)	mile(s) 英里	km	kilometre(s) 公里

Typical measurements 典型量度示例

(i) Building 建筑
a piece of wood $\frac{1}{8}$″ thick $\frac{1}{8}$英寸厚的木板
a piece of glass 7 mm thick 7 毫米厚的玻璃

(ii) Rainfall 降雨量
$1\frac{1}{2}$″ of rain in 24 hours 24 小时内 $1\frac{1}{2}$ 英寸的降雨量
less than 600 mm of rain a year 年降雨量不足 600 毫米

(iii) Vital statistics 三围
She's 36-24-38 (ie the circumference of her bust, waist and hips is 36, 24 and 38 inches respectively). 她三围是 36-24-38（即胸部、腰部、臀部分别是 36 英寸、24 英寸、38 英寸）.

(iv) Clothing 衣物
He takes a $16\frac{1}{2}$ collar (ie his neck is $16\frac{1}{2}$ inches in circumference). 他的领子的周长是 $16\frac{1}{2}$ 英寸.

(v) Height of people 身高
She's about 5 ft 6 in (tall). 她身高5英尺6英寸.
The average height of the tribe is less than 1 m 20 cm. 这个部落的人平均身高不足 1.2 米.
Note 注意: When referring to people, *'tall'* is used, not *'high'*, and measurements are given in feet and inches (but *not* yards) or metres and centimetres. 指人时, 身高用 tall, 不用 high; 量度用英尺和英寸, 或米和厘米(不用码).

(vi) Height of objects 物体高度
Maximum headroom 7′$2\frac{1}{2}$″ or 2.2 m (ie passage is limited to vehicles of less than this height). 最大净空高度为 7 英尺 $2\frac{1}{2}$ 英寸或 2.2 米（即低于此高度的车辆方可通过）.
Ben Nevis is 4 406 ft high. 本尼维斯山的高度为 4 406 英尺.
The road rises to 2 288 m above sea-level. 这条路达海拔 2 288 米.

(vii) Dimensions 面积; 容积; 体积
a baking dish measuring 9″ × 8″ 9 × 8 英寸的烘盘
A4 paper is 297 × 210 mm. A4 型纸张为 297 × 210 毫米.
a room 16 feet (wide) by 25 feet (long) 16 英尺宽 25 英尺长的房间

(viii) Distance 距离
about 100 yds down the road 沿路大约 100 码处
a bridge 695 metres long 695 米长的桥
New York is 22 915 miles from Los Angeles by road. 纽约至洛杉矶走公路距离为 22 915 英里.
The Amazon is more than 6 450 km long. 亚马逊河长度为 6 450 多公里.

(ix) Speed 速度
a speed limit of 30 mph 限速每小时 30 英里
Sound travels at 331.7 metres per second. 声速为每秒 331.7 米.
Light travels 186 300 miles in a second. 光速为每秒 186 300 英里.

B: AREA MEASUREMENT 面积单位

abbr 缩略式	*full word* 全称	*symb* 符号	*abbr* 缩略式	*full word* 全称
sq in	square inch(es) 平方英寸	mm^2	sq mm	square millimetre(s) 平方毫米
sq ft	square foot/feet 平方英尺	cm^2	sq cm	square centimetre(s) 平方厘米
sq yd	square yard 平方码	m^2	sq m	square metre(s) 平方米
sq ml	square mile(s) 平方英里	km^2	sq km	square kilometre(s) 平方公里
	acre 英亩		ha	hectare(s) 公顷

Typical measurements 典型量度示例

We require 5 000 sq ft of office space. 我们需要 5 000 平方英尺面积的办公处.
Light industrial lot (600 m²) for lease. 轻工业场地（600 平方米）出租.
Dartmoor covers an area of more than 350 square miles in SW England. 达特穆尔高地面积超过 350 平方英里, 位于英格兰西南部.
Greater London is an administrative area of 1 610 sq km(s). 大伦敦是面积为 1 610 平方公里的行政区.
a house for sale with 10 acres of grounds 10 英亩庄园宅第出售
more than 500 hectares of orchard 500 多公顷的果园

C: VOLUME MEASUREMENT 容积和体积单位

abbr 缩略式	*full word* 全称	*symb* 符号	*full word* 全称
cu in	cubic inch(es) 立方英寸	mm^3	cubic millimetre(s) 立方毫米
cu ft	cubic foot/feet 立方英尺	cc, cm^3	cubic centimetre(s) 立方厘米
cu yd	cubic yard 立方码	m^3	cubic metre(s) 立方米

Typical measurements 典型量度示例

a 1300 cc engine (ie the total capacity of the cylinders is 1 300 cubic centimetres) 1 300 立方厘米的发动机（即汽缸总容量为 1 300 立方厘米）
You'll need 30 cubic feet of sand to mix with the cement. 你需要 30 立方英尺的沙子与水泥混合.
a tunnelling machine capable of removing 400 m³ of earth an hour 每小时能挖土 400 立方米的隧道挖掘机

D: LIQUID MEASUREMENT 液量单位

abbr 缩略式	*full name* 全称	*abbr* 缩略式	*full name* 全称
fl oz	fluid ounce(s) 液盎司	ml	millilitre(s) 毫升
pt	pint 品脱	cl	centilitre(s) 厘升
qt	quart(s) 夸脱	l	litre(s) 升
gall	gallon(s) 加仑		

Typical measurements 典型量度示例

Add 8 fl oz stock and bring to the boil. 加入 8 液盎司的原汤并煮沸.
The standard wine bottle contains 75 cl. 标准酒瓶的容量为 75 厘升.
Three pints of bitter and half (a pint) of lager, please. 请给我来三品脱苦啤酒和半品脱贮藏啤酒.
You'll need about five litres of paint for this room. 粉刷这个房间需要五升的漆.
a car averaging 33 miles per gallon (ie that requires approximately 1 gallon of petrol to drive 33 miles) 平均每加仑汽油能行驶 33 英里的汽车

E: WEIGHT MEASUREMENT 重量单位

abbr 缩略式	*full name* 全称	*abbr* 缩略式	*full name* 全称
oz	ounce(s) 盎司	g/gm	gram(s) 克
lb	pound(s) 磅	kg	kilo(gram)(s) 千克; 公斤
st	stone 呫		metric ton (tonne) 公吨
	quarter 夸特		
cwt	hundredweight 英担		
	ton 吨		

Typical measurements 典型量度示例

Add 4 oz (100 gms) finely chopped ham. 加入 4 盎司（100 克）剁碎的火腿.
Four pounds of potatoes and a pound of carrots, please. 给我四磅土豆、一磅胡萝卜.
(Brit) My brother weighs 12 stone eleven (pounds).（英）我弟弟体重为 12 呖 11 磅.
(US) My brother weighs 183 pounds.（美）我弟弟体重为 183 磅.
Note 注意: People's weight is usually measured in stone and pounds in Britain and in pounds only in the US. 在英国量体重通常以呖和磅计算, 在美国只用磅.
Maximum baggage allowance: 32 kg 携带行李限量: 32 公斤
half a hundredweight of gravel 半英担沙砾
a 10-ton lorry (ie a lorry that can carry a maximum load of ten tons) 10 吨的卡车（即可载重十吨的）

Measurement of Temperature 温度的量度

Temperatures in Britain were traditionally measured by the Fahrenheit scale (°F). Although the Celsius or centigrade system (°C) is now officially in use, many people continue to refer informally to degrees Fahrenheit. The Fahrenheit scale is still used in the US for non-scientific purposes. 英国传统上用华氏温标（°F）测量温度. 虽然现在官方使用摄氏温标（°C）, 但是老百姓仍然喜欢使用华氏温标. 华氏温标在美国仍用于非科技方面.
The temperature will fall to minus five tonight. (–5°C) 今天夜间气温将下降到零下五度（–5°C）.
They say we're going to have nine degrees of frost tonight. (23°F) 据说今天夜间气温将从冰点下降九华氏度（23°F）.
It must be ninety-five this afternoon. (95°F) 今天下午气温有九十五华氏度（95°F）.
The normal temperature of the human body is 37°C. 人体正常体温为 37°C.
She's ill in bed with a temperature of a hundred and two. (102°F) 她卧病在床, 体温一百零二华氏度（102°F）.

Numbers in Measuring Time 用于计算时间的数字

A: AGE 年龄

He's 33 (years old). 他 33 岁.
The suspect is believed to be aged about twenty-seven. 疑犯年龄在二十七岁左右.
a man in his thirties (ie between 30 and 39 years old) 三十多岁的男子
He looks fortyish (ie about 40 years old). 他看样子四十岁左右.
She's in her early/middle/late teens (ie 13–15/15–17/17–19 years old). 她十三四岁［十五六岁/近二十岁］.
'How old's your youngest child?' "你最小的孩子几岁了?"
'She's one year and three months/fifteen months (old).' "她一岁零三个月了［十五个月了］."
a two-week-old baby 出生两个星期的婴儿

B: TIME OF DAY 一天的时间

The twelve hour system is most widely used 一昼夜分为十二小时制用得最广:

- 7.00 *seven o'clock; seven am/pm* 七点; 上午［下午］七点
- 8.15 *eight fifteen; a quarter past eight* (*US* also 美式英语亦作 *a quarter after eight*) 八点十五分; 八点一刻
- 9.45 *nine forty-five; a quarter to ten* (*US* also 美式英语亦作 *a quarter of ten*) 九点四十五分: 差一刻十点; 九点三刻
- 4.30 *four thirty; (esp Brit* 尤用于英式英语*) half past four; (infml* 口语*) half four* 四点三十分; 四点半
- 5.10 *five ten; ten (minutes) past five*; (*US* also 美式英语亦作 *ten after five*) 五点十分
- 6.35 *six thirty-five; twenty-five (minutes) to seven* 六点三十五分
- 8.03 *eight o three; three minutes past eight* 八点零三分
- 9.55 *nine fifty-five; five (minutes) to ten*; (*US* also 美式英语亦作 *five of ten*) 九点五十五分; 差五分十点

The twenty-four hour clock is used in travel timetables, official communiqués, military communications, etc 一昼夜分为二十四小时制用于旅行时刻表、官方公报、军事通讯等:

0700/07.00	*(ˌo) ˌseven ˈhundred (hours)*	(7.00 am) 7 点(上午 7 点)
1030/10.30	*ˌten ˈthirty*	(10.30 am) 10 点 30 分(上午 10 点 30 分)
1200/12.00	*ˌtwelve ˈhundred (hours)*	(midday/noon) 12 点(中午)
1345/13.45	*ˌthirteen ˌforty-ˈfive*	(1.45 pm) 13 点 45 分(下午 1 点 45 分)
1515/15.15	*ˌfifteen ˌfifˈteen*	(3.15 pm) 15 点 15 分(下午 3 点 15 分)
1900/19.00	*ˌnineteen ˈhundred (hours)*	(7.00 pm) 19 点(晚上 7 点)
2250/22.50	*ˌtwenty-ˌtwo ˈfifty*	(10.50 pm) 22 点 50 分(晚上 10 点 50 分)
2305/23.05	*ˌtwenty-ˌthree ˌo ˈfive*	(11.05 pm) 23 点 5 分(晚上 11 点 5 分)
2400/24.00	*ˌtwenty-ˌfour ˈhundred (hours)*	(midnight) 24 点; 0 点(午夜)
0000/00.00	*ˌo ˌo ˈdouble o*	

C: DURATION 持续的时间

symb 符号	*abbr* 缩略式	*full word* 全称
″	sec	second 秒
′	min	minute 分
	hr	hour 时

The car does 0 to 60 in 4.5 secs (ie it will accelerate from a stop to 60 miles per hour in four and a half seconds). 这辆汽车从静止状态加速至每小时 60 英里需要 4.5 秒.
The winning runner completed the course in 2 mins 15 secs. 比赛优胜者用 2 分 15 秒跑完全程.

D: DATES 日期

2000 BC/two thousand BC 公元前 2000 年
AD 55/AD fifty-five 公元 55 年
Queen Elizabeth I 1558–1603
Queen Elizabeth the First reigned from fifteen (hundred and) fifty-eight to sixteen (hundred and) three/sixteen o three. 伊丽莎白女王一世从 1558 年到 1603 年在位.
(*Brit* 英式) *3rd/3 January 1989: the third of January/January the third, nineteen eighty-nine.* 1989 年 1 月 3 日
(*US* 美式) *January 3, 1989: January third, nineteen eighty-nine.* 1989 年 1 月 3 日
(*Brit* 英式) 21.3.47; 21/3/47; (*US* 美式) 3.21.47 = 21 March 1947 1947 年 3 月 21 日

Numbers in Sport 体育运动使用的数字

A: SPORTS USING LINEAR MEASURE 使用长度单位的运动项目

(i) Athletics 田径

He holds the world record for the fifteen hundred metres/the metric mile. (1 500 m) 他保持 1 500 米的世界记录.
She ran for her country in the women's two hundred metre hurdles. (200 m) 她代表国家参加 200 米女子跨栏赛跑.
Our team was narrowly beaten in the four by four hundred metres relay. (4 × 400 m) 我队在 4 × 400 米接力赛中略微落后而失败.
He won a bronze medal in the high jump, clearing a height of two point o five metres. (2.05 m) 他越过二米零五的高度而获得跳高铜牌.

(ii) Swimming 游泳

I swam for my school in the eight hundred metres free-style. (800 m) 我代表学校参加 800 米自由泳比赛.
She came second in the women's hundred metres backstroke. (100 m) 她在女子一百米仰泳比赛中获得第二名.

(iii) Horse-racing 赛马

The Derby is run over a distance of twelve furlongs/one mile four furlongs/one and a half miles/a mile and a half. (8 furlongs = 1 mile) 德比马赛全程为十二浪[一英里四浪/一英里半]. (8 浪 = 1 英里)
The winner of the 3.30 at Cheltenham was 'Never Say Die', a fourteen to one outsider; the favourite, 'Moonshine', was second at five to two; eleven ran (ie the race that started at 3.30 pm at Cheltenham race-track was won by a horse called 'Never Say Die', on which the odds were 14–1 against; the horse most favoured by

betters, 'Moonshine', came second, at odds of 5–2 on; a total of eleven horses ran in the race). 在切尔滕纳姆下午三点三十分举行的马赛中获胜的马是"不言败", 赔率为十四比一; 大热门"月光"获第二名, 赔率为五比二; 共十一匹马参赛.

B: SPORTS USING OTHER SCORING METHODS 以其他方式记分的运动项目

(i) Tennis 网球

Miss Smith won the first set six four/by six games to four (6-4). She dropped the second set seven six (7-6) after a tie-break, but won the deciding set six three (6-3). The scoring in the final game was fifteen love (15-0), fifteen all (15-15), fifteen thirty (15-30), thirty all (30-30), forty thirty (40-30), deuce (40-40), advantage Miss Smith, game to Miss Smith. Miss Smith won by two sets to one (2-1), six four, six seven, six three. 史密斯小姐以六比四赢了第一盘. 她第二盘打成了平局后以七比六的比分输掉一盘, 但决定性的一盘以六比三获胜. 最后一局的得分为十五比零(15:0)、十五比十五(15:15)、十五比三十(15:30)、三十平(30:30)、四十比三十(40:30)、四十平(40:40), 史密斯小姐获优势分, 史密斯小姐赢得此局. 史密斯小姐以两盘赢一盘输(2:1)(六比四、六比七、六比三)赢得此次比赛.

(ii) (Association) Football; Soccer 英式足球

In the second half Watford scored twice to equalize (2-2), but five minutes from time (ie after 85 minutes of play), *Bryant scored from a penalty to give Arsenal a three two victory/victory by three goals to two (3-2). Tottenham, at home to Chelsea, were held to a goalless draw/drew nil nil (0-0).* 在下半场比赛中, 沃特福德队两次射门得分, 把比分扳平(2:2), 但终场前五分钟(即开球后 85 分钟), 布赖恩特罚球得分, 结果阿森纳尔队以三比二(3:2)获胜. 托特纳姆队在主方赛场与切尔西队比赛, 以零比零(0:0)踢成平局.

(iii) Rugby (football) 英式橄榄球

Wales beat Scotland sixteen six/by sixteen points to six (16-6). For Wales, Owen scored two tries (4 points each = 8 points). *Price converted the second try* (2 points) *and kicked two penalty goals* (3 points each = 6 points). *Scotland's score came from a penalty and a dropped goal* (3 points), *both kicked by Frazer.* 威尔士队以十六比六(16:6)击败苏格兰队. 威尔士队中, 欧文两次触地球得分(每次 4 分 = 8 分). 普赖斯第二次触地得分后再射踢中球门获附加分两分, 踢罚球两次获六分(每次 3 分 = 6 分). 苏格兰队得分为一次罚球和一次踢落地反弹球(得三分), 两次都是弗雷泽踢的.

(iv) American football 美式足球

In the third quarter, the Dallas quarterback threw a 67-yard pass for a touchdown (6 points). *The conversion* (1 point made by kicking a goal after a touchdown) *was good, giving them a seven point lead. In the final quarter, Miami ran the ball in from the six yard line to even the score (7-7), but ten seconds from the end Dallas kicked a 49-yard field goal* (3 points) *to win by ten points to seven.* 第三个四分之一场, 达拉斯队四分卫一个 67 码长传, 底线得分(6 分). 然后触地射门得分(1 分), 以七分领先. 在最后的四分之一场, 迈阿密队从六码线持球跑进对方球门线内触地得分, 把比分扳平(7:7), 但终场前 10 秒钟, 达拉斯队从 49 码处踢球越过球门横木得分(3 分), 以十比七获胜.

(v) Basketball 篮球

Our team was leading (by) twenty-seven (points) to twenty-two (27-22) at half-time but we gave away too many penalties in the second half, and our opponents won fifty-eight fifty-six (58-56). 我队上半场以二十七(分)比二十二(27:22)领先, 但下半场犯规被罚球失分过多, 我们的对手以五十八比五十六(58:56)获胜.

(vi) Baseball 棒球

The Yankees scored in the third inning on a base hit to left field. A home run by the Red Sox at the bottom (ie second half) *of the fifth (inning) tied the game, until an error by Boston's third baseman gave New York a winning run late in the game.*
Final score: New York two, Boston one. 纽约 Yankees 队在第三回合把球打到左边场地得分. 在第五回合的后半部分, 波士顿 Red Sox 队一个本垒打把比分扳平. 后来比赛近尾声时, 波士顿队第三守垒员失误, 使纽约队获得决定胜负的一分. 最后的比分是: 纽约队二分, 波士顿队一分.

(vii) Golf 高尔夫球

Palmer and Jackson share the lead on 75 at the end of the first round. Palmer was trailing until he birdied the 14th hole (ie completed it in one stroke less than par), *and then sank a 22-foot putt at the 16th. Jackson then failed to hole from 5 feet at the 18th.* 在第一回合结束时, 帕尔默和杰克逊领先, 均获 75 分. 帕尔默开始时落在后面, 后来打入第 14 穴时他比标准少用一杆, 又在 22 英尺远处把球打入 16 穴, 这才改变了局面. 杰克逊在 5 英尺远处未能把球打入 18 穴.

(viii) Cricket 板球

England are 187 for three at tea (ie the team have scored 187 runs and three batsmen have been dismissed), *210 behind the New Zealand first innings total of 397 all out* (ie a score of 397 runs after 10 batsmen were dismissed). *Gatting is not out 42* (ie he has scored 42 runs and his innings will continue). *Broad was caught at the wicket four runs short of a century* (ie he scored 96 runs before being dismissed). *Hadlee finished the session with figures of 2 for 26* (ie this New Zealand bowler dismissed two England batsmen while 26 runs were scored from the balls he bowled). 英格兰队到下午茶点时间有三个击球员出局获 187 分, 与新西兰队第一回合全部十个击球员出局获 397 分相比, 落后 210 分. 加廷获 42 分而仍未出局. 布罗德击球后跑动时对方的守门员把球接住, 差四分不足一百分(96 分). 新西兰队的哈德利投球结束的成绩是 2 人 26 分(即该新西兰队投球员将英格兰队击球员二人杀出局. 英格兰队击球员二人被杀出局时获得 26 分).

Numbers in Using Money 使用货币方面的数字

A: BRITAIN 英国

100 pence (100p) = 1 pound (£1) 100 便士 = 1 镑

symb 符号	*full name* 全称	*infml name* 口语名称	*coin/note* 硬币或纸币
1p	a/one penny	one p	a penny 一便士(硬币)
2p	two pence twopence /ˈtʌpəns; ˋtʌpəns/	two p	a twopenny piece 二便士(硬币)
5p	five pence	five p	a fivepenny piece 五便士(硬币)
10p	ten pence	ten p	a tenpenny piece 十便士(硬币)
20p	twenty pence	twenty p	a twenty pence piece 二十便士(硬币)
50p	fifty pence	fifty p	a fifty pence piece 五十便士(硬币)
£1	a pound	a quid	a pound coin 一镑(硬币)
£5	five pounds	five quid a fiver	a five pound note 五镑(纸币)
£10	ten pounds	ten quid a tenner	a ten pound note 十镑(纸币)

I paid ten pence each for them. 我每件付了 10 便士.
Coffee's 35p a cup. 咖啡 35 便士一杯.
Admission: £2 (adults), 50p (children) 门票: 两镑(成人), 50 便士(儿童)
It costs a couple of quid to get in, but only fifty p for the kids. 入场券要两镑, 儿童 50 便士.
We'll have to charge you a ten pound refundable deposit. 我们须收你 10 镑押金.
A meal for two will set you back a good thirty pounds/thirty pounds odd/somewhere in the region of thirty pounds. 两个人吃一顿饭要足足花上 30 镑 [30 多镑/30 镑左右].

Notes 注意:

1) The penny symbol (*p* /piː; pi/) is never used when writing a sum of money which begins with the pound sign 在英镑符号后写出货币数目时不可使用便士符号 p: *£6.25; £106.00; £0.75*.
2) In informal use, the words *pound(s)* and *pence* are often omitted 在口语中常常省略 pound 和 pence: *He charged me three fifty (£3.50).* 他要我支付三英镑五十便士. *They're reduced from a hundred and fifteen ninety-five to ninety-nine ninety-five* (from £115.95 to £99.95). 这些东西的价钱从 115 英镑 95 便士降到 99 英镑 95 便士.

3) In informal use, sums between £1 100 and £1 900 may be spoken as hundreds 在口语中从 1 100 英镑到 1 900 英镑的数目可以百为单位说出: *This car's only twelve hundred quid* (ie £1 200). 这辆汽车仅仅 1 200 英镑.

B: US AND CANADA 美国及加拿大

100 cents (¢)= 1 dollar ($) 100 分 = 1 元

symb 符号	*full name* 全称	*coin/note* 硬币或纸币
$0.01/1¢	one cent	a penny 一分(硬币)
$0.05/5¢	five cents	a nickel 五分(硬币)
$0.10/10¢	ten cents	a dime 一角(硬币)
$0.25/25¢	twenty-five cents	a quarter 二角五分(硬币)
$0.50/50¢	fifty cents	a half-dollar
		a fifty-cent piece 五角(硬币)
$1/$1.00	one dollar	a dollar bill
	(*infml* 俗称) a buck	a one 一元(纸币)
$5	five dollars	a five (dollar bill) 五元(纸币)
$10	ten dollars	a ten (dollar bill) 十元(纸币)
$20	twenty dollars	a twenty (dollar bill) 二十元(纸币)
$50	fifty dollars	a fifty (dollar bill) 五十元(纸币)
$100	a/one hundred dollars	a hundred (dollar bill) 一百元(纸币)

I bought it for a nickel. 我花了五分钱买的这个东西.
You'll need a couple of quarters for the phone. 打电话需要两个二角五分的硬币.
Coffee's eighty cents a cup. 咖啡八角一杯.
They cost me a couple of bucks each. 这些东西每件花了我两块钱.
Can you change this ten for a five and five ones? 您能不能把这张十块钱的钞票换成五块五块的?
I enclose a check for fifty dollars. 随信附上一张五十元的支票.

Notes 注意:

1) The cents symbol(¢) is never used when writing a sum of money which begins with the dollar sign 在"元"的符号($)后写出货币数目时不可使用"分"(¢)的符号: *$6.25; $106.00; $0.75.*
2) In informal use, the words *dollar(s)* and *cent(s)* are often omitted 在口语中常常省略 dollar(s) 和 cent(s): *He charged me three fifty* ($3.50). 他要我支付三元五角. *It's reduced from a hundred and fifteen ninety-five to ninety-nine ninety-five* (ie from $115.95 to $99.95). 这件东西的价钱从 115 元 9 角 5 分降到 99 元 9 角 5 分.
3) Especially in informal use, sums between $1 100 and $1 900 may be spoken as hundreds 尤用于口语时, 从 1 100 元到 1 900 元的数目可以百为单位读出: *He earns less than sixteen hundred (dollars) a month.* 他每月挣的不到一千六百元.
4) In informal and esp dated use, ˌ*two* ˈ*bits* = $0.25, *four* ˈ*bits* = $0.50 and ˌ*six* ˈ*bits* = $0.75. These expressions are not used in combinations 在口语中, 尤用于旧时, two bits = $0.25, four bits = $0.50, six bits = $0.75. 这些说法不与其他钱数混合使用: *I left two bits as a tip* but *I lent him a dollar twenty-five/one dollar and a quarter.* 我留下了二角五分作小费[我借给他一元二角五分/一块二毛五].

Numbers in Telephoning 电话号码

A: BRITAIN 英国

Telephone numbers consist of a four-digit *national code* and/or the name of the *(telephone) exchange* followed by a three- to seven-digit number 电话号码包含一个四位数的国内代号和[或](电话)交换台名称再加上三至七位数字的号码: *Oxford (0865) 56767.* The national code (also known as the *STD code*) is used when making a call outside the local area. 国内代号(又称 STD 代码)用于

打到外地的电话. Telephones in some large cities, eg London, have a two or three-digit national code followed by a seven-digit number 有些大城市(如伦敦)的电话号码是由两位或三位数的国内代号再加上七位的号码组成: *071-246 8022*.

Both codes and numbers are spoken as a series of separate digits, 0 being pronounced /əʊ; o/ 代号与号码均需按一系列单个数字说出, 0 的发音为 /əʊ/: *ˌo ˌeight ˌsix ˈfive, five ˌsix ˌseven ˌsix ˈseven; ˌo ˌseven ˈone, ˌtwo four ˈsix, ˌeight ˌo ˌdouble ˈtwo*. When giving a telephone number on the phone, the exchange rather than the code is used 在通话时需说出交换台的名称而不说国内代号: *Oxford five six seven six seven*.

B: US AND CANADA 美国及加拿大

Telephone numbers consist of a three-digit *area code* followed by a seven-digit number. 电话号码包含一个三位数的地区代号再加上七位数字的号码.

The area code is only used when dialling from one region to another (ie when *calling long distance/making a long-distance call*) and is often omitted when the number is spoken or written. 地区代号仅用于从一地区打到另一地区(即打长途电话)时使用, 说出或写出电话号码时往往省略地区代号. If included, it is written in parentheses before the individual number, the first three digits of which are separated from the last four by a hyphen 要是写的话, 地区代号要置于括号中, 电话号码前三个数字与后四个数字中间加一个连接号: *(202) 234-5678*. Both the area code and the prefix are spoken as a series of three separate numbers, 0 being pronounced /əʊ; o/, or said as *zero* or *nought* 地区代号和前三个数字均按单个数字说出, 0 的发音为 /əʊ/、zero 或 nought: *ˌtwo ˌo ˈtwo, ˌtwo ˌthree ˈfour*. The last four digits may be spoken either as separate numbers (*five ˈsix ˌseven ˈeight*) or as two sets of tens (*fifty-ˈsix ˌseventy-ˈeight*). 后四位数字可按单个数字说出(five six seven eight)也可按两个两位数字说出(fifty-six seventy-eight). If the last four digits end in 00 or 000, they are usually treated as hundreds or thousands 若后四位数字的末尾为 00 或 000 时, 通常说成"百"或"千": *five ˌo ˈtwo, five ˌsix ˈhundred* (502-5600); *four ˌnine ˈnine, five ˈthousand* (499-5000).

Note: Business firms, etc often have a single telephone number from which callers may be connected to a three- or four-digit internal *extension (number)*: *Oxford 56767 Ext 429*; (202) 234-5678 (x301). 注意: 公司或机关单位等常常只有一个电话号码, 接通后再转接一个三位或四位数字的分机号码: Oxford 56767 转 429; (202)234-5678(转 301).

APPENDIX 5 附录 5

WEIGHTS AND MEASURES 度量衡表

The Metric System 公制

METRIC 公制		length 长度		GB & US 英制及美制
10 millimetres (mm) 毫米	=	1 centimetre (cm) 厘米	=	0.394 inch (in) 英寸
100 centimetres 厘米	=	1 metre (m) 米	=	39.4 inches or 1.094 yards (yd) 39.4 英寸或 1.094 码
1000 metres 米	=	1 kilometre (km) 公里	=	0.6214 mile or about $\frac{5}{8}$ mile 0.6214 英里或约 $\frac{5}{8}$ 英里
		surface 面积		
100 square metres (m^2) 平方米	=	1 are (a) 公亩	=	0.025 acre 英亩
100 ares 公亩	=	1 hectare (ha) 公顷	=	2.471 acres 英亩
100 hectares 公顷	=	1 square kilometre (km^2) 平方公里	=	0.386 square mile 平方英里
		weight 重量		
10 milligrams (mg) 毫克	=	1 centigram (cg) 厘克	=	0.154 grain 格令
100 centigrams 厘克	=	1 gram (g) 克	=	15.43 grains 格令
1000 grams 克	=	1 kilogram (kg) 公斤	=	2.205 pounds 磅
1000 kilograms 公斤	=	1 tonne 公吨	=	19.688 hundredweight 英担
		capacity 容量		
1000 millilitres (ml) 毫升	=	1 litre (l) 升	=	1.76 pints 品脱 (2.1 US pints 美国品脱)
10 litres 升	=	1 decalitre (dl) 十升	=	2.2 gallons 加仑 (2.63 US gallons 美国加仑)

Avoirdupois Weight 常衡

GB & US 英制及美制				METRIC 公制
		1 grain (gr) 格令	=	0.065 gram (g) 克
437$\frac{1}{2}$grains 格令	=	1 ounce (oz) 盎司	=	28.35 grams 克
16 drams (dr) 打兰	=	1 ounce 盎司	=	28.35 grams 克
16 ounces 盎司	=	1 pound (lb) 磅	=	0.454 kilogram (kg) 千克; 公斤
14 pounds 磅	=	1 stone (st) 呫	=	6.356 kilograms 千克; 公斤
2 stone 呫	=	1 quarter 夸特	=	12.7 kilograms 千克; 公斤
4 quarters 夸特	=	1 hundredweight (cwt) 英担	=	50.8 kilograms 千克; 公斤
112 pounds 磅	=	1 hundredweight 英担	=	50.8 kilograms 千克; 公斤
100 pounds 磅	=	1 short hundredweight (US) 短担	=	45.4 kilograms 千克; 公斤
20 hundredweight 英担	=	1 ton 吨	=	1016.04 kilograms 千克; 公斤
2000 pounds 磅	=	1 short ton 短吨	=	0.907 tonne 公吨
2240 pounds 磅	=	1 long ton 长吨	=	1.016 tonnes 公吨

Linear Measure 长度单位

GB & US 英制及美制				METRIC 公制
		1 inch (in) 英寸	=	25.4 millimetres (mm) 毫米
12 inches 英寸	=	1 foot (ft) 英尺	=	30.48 centimetres (cm) 厘米
3 feet 英尺	=	1 yard (yd) 码	=	0.914 metre (m) 米
5½ yards 码	=	1 rod, pole or perch 杆	=	5.029 metres 米
22 yards 码	=	1 chain (ch) 测链	=	20.17 metres 米
220 yards 码	=	1 furlong (fur) 浪	=	201.17 metres 米
8 furlongs 浪	=	1 mile 英里	=	1.609 kilometres (km) 千米; 公里
1760 yards 码	=	1 mile 英里	=	1.609 kilometres 千米; 公里
3 miles 英里	=	1 league 里格	=	4.828 kilometres 千米; 公里

Square Measure 面积单位

GB & US 英制及美制				METRIC 公制
		1 square (sq) inch 平方英寸	=	6.452 sq centimetres 平方厘米
144 sq inches 平方英寸	=	1 sq foot 平方英尺	=	929.03 sq centimetres 平方厘米
9 sq feet 平方英尺	=	1 sq yard 平方码	=	0.836 sq metre 平方米
484 sq yards 平方码	=	1 sq chain 平方测链	=	404.62 sq metres 平方米
4840 sq yards 平方码	=	1 acre 英亩	=	0.405 hectare 公顷
40 sq rods 平方杆	=	1 rood 路得	=	10.1168 ares 公亩
4 roods 路得	=	1 acre 英亩	=	0.405 hectare 公顷
640 acres 英亩	=	1 sq mile 平方英里	=	2.59 sq kilometres or 259 hectares 2.59 平方公里或 259 公顷

Cubic Measure 体积单位

GB & US 英制及美制				METRIC 公制
		1 cubic inch 立方英寸	=	16.39 cu centimetres 立方厘米
1728 cu inches 立方英寸	=	1 cu foot 立方英尺	=	0.028 cu metre 立方米
27 cu feet 立方英尺	=	1 cu yard 立方码	=	0.765 cu metre 立方米

Nautical Measure 海程单位

used for measuring the depth and surface distance of seas, rivers, etc
用于测量海洋、河流的深度和水面距离

GB & US 英制及美制				METRIC 公制
6 feet 英尺	=	1 fathom 英寻	=	1.829 metres 米
608 feet (in the British Navy) 英尺(英国皇家海军)	=	1 cable 链	=	185.31 metres 米
720 feet (in the US Navy) 英尺(美国海军)	=	1 cable 链	=	219.46 metres 米
6080 feet 英尺	=	nautical (or sea) mile 海里 (1.151 statute miles 法定英里)	=	1.852 kilometres 千米; 公里
3 sea miles 海里	=	1 sea league 海里格	=	5.55 kilometres 千米; 公里
60 sea miles 海里	=	1 degree 度 (69.047 statute miles 法定英里)		
360 degrees 度	=	1 circle 圆周		

The speed of one sea mile per hour is called a *knot*. 速度每小时一海里称作"一节".

Measure of Capacity 容量单位

		GB 英制		US 美制		METRIC 公制
4 gills 及耳	=	1 pint (pt) 品脱	=	1.201 pints 品脱	=	0.568 litre 升
2 pints 品脱	=	1 quart (qt) 夸脱	=	1.201 quarts 夸脱	=	1.136 litres 升
4 quarts 夸脱	=	1 gallon (gal) 加仑	=	1.201 gallons 加仑	=	4.546 litres 升

Circular or Angular Measure 圆弧或角度单位

60 seconds (″) 秒	=	1 minute (′) 分	90 degrees 度	=	1 quadrant or right angle (∟) 象限或直角
60 minutes 分	=	1 degree (°) 度	360 degrees 度	=	1 circle or circumference 圆周

the diameter of a circle 圆的直径	=	the straight line passing through its centre 通过圆心的直线
the radius of a circle 圆的半径	=	$\frac{1}{2}$ × the diameter $\frac{1}{2}$ × 直径
the circumference of a circle 圆周长	=	22/7 × the diameter 22/7 × 直径

Temperature Equivalents 温度等值

	FAHRENHEIT (F) 华氏	CELSIUS OR CENTIGRADE (C) 摄氏
Boiling-point 沸点	212°	100°
	194°	90°
	176°	80°
	158°	70°
	140°	60°
	122°	50°
	104°	40°
	86°	30°
	68°	20°
	50°	10°
Freezing-point 冰点	32°	0°
	14°	−10°
	0°	−17.8°
Absolute Zero 绝对零度	−459.67°	−273.15°

To convert Fahrenheit temperature into Celsius or centigrade:
subtract 32 and multiply by 5/9 (five-ninths) 华氏温度换算成摄氏温度: 减去 32 再乘以 5/9.
To convert Celsius or centigrade temperature into Fahrenheit:
multiply by 9/5 (nine-fifths) and add 32 摄氏温度换算成华氏温度: 乘以 9/5 再加上 32.

Time 时间

60 seconds 秒	=	1 minute (min) 分	52 weeks, 1 day; or 13 lunar months, 1 day 52 个星期又 1 日或 13 个太阴月又 1 日	=	1 year (yr) 年
60 minutes 分	=	1 hour (hr) 小时			
24 hours 小时	=	1 day 日			
7 days 日	=	1 week (wk) 星期			
4 weeks, or 28 days 4 个星期或 28 日	=	1 lunar month (mth) 太阴月	365 days, 6 hours 365 日又 6 小时	=	1 (Julian 儒略历) year 年

APPENDIX 6 附录 6

GEOGRAPHICAL NAMES 地区名称

Notes 说明

1 Some countries have different words for the *adjective* and the *person*; in these cases both are given, eg *Swedish*; *Swede*. 英语中用作某些地区名称的形容词和用作这些地区的人的名词的词形不同, 本附录将两种词形的词一并列出, 如 Swedish 瑞典的; Swede 瑞典人.

Adjective 形容词: I admire *Swedish* architecture. 我觉得瑞典的建筑很了不起.
Person 人: My mother is a *Swede*. 我母亲是瑞典人.

2 Words for the *person* ending in '*-ese*', and *Swiss*, remain unchanged in the plural 以 -ese 结尾的指人的词和 Swiss(瑞士人)这个词, 其复数形式不变:

I know many *Japanese*. 我认识许多日本人.
The *Swiss* have arrived. 那些瑞士人已经到了.

3 In some cases, the *adjective* is also the word for the country's language 在有些情况下, 指国家名称的形容词亦是指这些国家语言的词:

I am learning to speak *Chinese*. 我正在学习说汉语.

(译者注: 附录中用斜方括号表示括号中的词与其前面的词可互换, 如 Chinese 中国的[人], 意为: 中国的; 中国人.)

NOUN 名词	ADJECTIVE; PERSON 形容词; 人
Afghanistan /æf'gænɪstɑ:n; *US* 美式英语读作 -stæn; æf'gænə,stæn/ 阿富汗	Afghan /'æfgæn; 'æf,gæn/; Afghani /æf'gænɪ; æf'gænɪ/; Afghanistani /æf'gænɪstɑ:nɪ; *US* 美式英语读作 -stænɪ; æf'gænə,stænɪ/ 阿富汗的[人]
Africa /'æfrɪkə; 'æfrɪkə/ 非洲	African /'æfrɪkən; 'æfrɪkən/ 非洲的[人]
Albania /æl'beɪnɪə; æl'benɪə/ 阿尔巴尼亚	Albanian /æl'beɪnɪən; æl'benɪən/ 阿尔巴尼亚的[人]
Algeria /æl'dʒɪərɪə; æl'dʒɪrɪə/ 阿尔及利亚	Algerian /æl'dʒɪərɪən; æl'dʒɪrɪən/ 阿尔及利亚的[人]
America ⇨ (the) United States (of America)	
Andorra /æn'dɔ:rə; æn'dɔrə / 安道尔	Andorrann /æn'dɔ:rən; æn'dɔrən/ 安道尔的[人]
Angola /æŋ'gəʊlə; æŋ'golə/ 安哥拉	Angolan /æŋ'gəʊlən; æŋ'golən/ 安哥拉的[人]
Anguilla /æŋ'gwɪlə; æŋ'gwɪlə/ 安圭拉岛	Anguillan /æŋ'gwɪlən; æŋ'gwɪlən/ 安圭拉岛的[人]
(the) Antarctic /æn'tɑ:ktɪk; ænt'ɑrktɪk/ 南极地区	Antarctic 南极地区的
Antigua /æn'ti:gə; æn'tigə/ 安提瓜岛	Antiguan /æn'ti:gən; æn'tigən/ 安提瓜岛的[人]
(the) Arctic /'ɑ:ktɪk; 'ɑrktɪk/ 北极地区	Arctic 北极地区的
Argentina /ˌɑ:dʒən'ti:nə; ˌɑrdʒən'tinə/, the Argentine /'ɑ:dʒəntaɪn; 'ɑrdʒən,taɪn/ 阿根廷	Argentinian /ˌɑ:dʒən'tɪnɪən; ˌɑrdʒən'tɪnɪən/; Argentine 阿根廷的[人]
Asia /'eɪʃə; 'eʃə/ 亚洲	Asian /'eɪʃn; 'eʃən/ 亚洲的[人]
Australasia /ˌɒstrə'leɪʃə; ˌɔstrəl'eʃə/ 澳大拉西亚	Australasian /ˌɒstrə'leɪʃn; ˌɔstrəl'eʃən/ 澳大拉西亚的[人]

NOUN 名词	ADJECTIVE; PERSON 形容词; 人
Australia /ɒˈstreɪlɪə; *US* 美式英语读作 ɔ:ˈs-; ɔˋstreljə/ 澳大利亚	Australian /ɒˈstreɪlɪən; *US* 美式英语读作 ɔ:ˈs-; ɔˋstreljən/ 澳大利亚的[人]
Austria /ˈɒstrɪə; *US* 美式英语读作 ˈɔ:s-; ˋɔstrɪə/ 奥地利	Austrian /ˈɒstrɪən; *US* 美式英语读作 ˈɔ:s-; ˋɔstrɪən/ 奥地利的[人]
(the) Bahamas /bəˈhɑ:məz; *US* 美式英语读作 -ˈheɪm-; bəˋheməz/ 巴哈马	Bahamian /bəˈheɪmɪən; bəˋhemɪən/ 巴哈马的[人]
Bahrain, Bahrein /bɑ:ˈreɪn; bɑˋren/ 巴林	Bahraini, Bahreini /bɑ:ˈreɪnɪ; bɑˋrenɪ/ 巴林的[人]
(the) Baltic /ˈbɔ:ltɪk; ˋbɔltɪk/ 波罗的海地区	Baltic 波罗的海地区的
Bangladesh /ˌbæŋgləˈdeʃ; ˌbæŋgləˋdɛʃ/ 孟加拉国	Bangladeshi /ˌbæŋgləˈdeʃɪ; ˌbæŋgləˋdɛʃɪ/ 孟加拉的[人]
Barbados /bɑ:ˈbeɪdɒs; bɑrˋbedəs/ 巴巴多斯	Barbadian /bɑ:ˈbeɪdɪən; bɑrˋbedɪən/ 巴巴多斯的[人]
Belgium /ˈbeldʒəm; ˋbɛldʒəm/ 比利时	Belgian /ˈbeldʒən; ˋbɛldʒən/ 比利时的[人]
Belize /beˈli:z; bɛˋliz/ 伯利兹	Belizean /beˈli:zɪən; bɛˋlizɪən/ 伯利兹的[人]
Benin /beˈni:n; bəˋnɪn/ 贝宁	Beninese /ˌbenɪˈni:z; bəˌnɪnˋiz/ 贝宁的[人]
Bermuda /bəˈmju:də; bɚˋmjudə/ 百慕大	Bermudan /bəˈmju:dən; bɚˋmjudən/ 百慕大的[人]
Bhutan /bu:ˈtɑ:n; buˋtæn/ 不丹	Bhutani /bu:ˈtɑ:nɪ; buˋtænɪ/; Bhutanese /ˌbu:tɑ:ˈni:z; ˌbutəˋniz/ 不丹的[人]
Bolivia /bəˈlɪvɪə; bəˋlɪvɪə/ 玻利维亚	Bolivian /bəˈlɪvɪən; bəˋlɪvɪən/ 玻利维亚的[人]
Botswana /bɒtˈswɑ:nə; bɑtˋswɑnə/ 博茨瓦纳	Botswanan /bɒˈtswɑ:nən; bɑtˋswɑnən/; *also* 亦作 the Tswanan /ˈswɑ:nən; ˋswɑnən/ 博茨瓦纳的[人]
Brazil /brəˈzɪl; brəˋzɪl/ 巴西	Brazilian /brəˈzɪlɪən; brəˋzɪljən/ 巴西的[人]
Britain ⇨ Great Britain	
Brunei /ˈbru:naɪ; ˋbruˌnaɪ/ 文莱	Brunei, Bruneian /bru:ˈnaɪən; bruˋnaɪən/ 文莱的[人]
Bulgaria /bʌlˈgeərɪə; bʌlˋgɛrɪə/ 保加利亚	Bulgarian /bʌlˈgeərɪən; bʌlˋgɛrɪən/ 保加利亚的[人]
Burkina Faso /bɜ:ˌki:nə ˈfæsəʊ; burˋkinəˋfɑso/ 布基纳法索	Burkinese /bɜ:kɪˈni:z; burkɪnˋiz/ 布基纳法索的[人]
Burma /ˈbɜ:mə; ˋbɝmə/ 缅甸	Burmese /ˌbɜ:ˈmi:z; bɝˋmiz/ 缅甸的[人]
Burundi /bʊˈrʊndɪ; buˋrʊndɪ/ 布隆迪	Burundian /bʊˈrʊndɪən; buˋrʊndɪən/ 布隆迪的[人]
Cambodia /kæmˈbəʊdɪə; kæmˋbodɪə/ (*formerly* 旧作 Kampuchea) 柬埔寨	Cambodian /kæmˈbəʊdɪən; kæmˋbodɪən/ 柬埔寨的[人]
Cameroon /ˌkæməˈru:n; ˌkæməˋrun/ 喀麦隆	Cameroonian /ˌkæməˈru:nɪən; ˌkæməˋrunɪən/ 喀麦隆的[人]
Canada /ˈkænədə; ˋkænədə/ 加拿大	Canadian /kəˈneɪdɪən; kəˋnedɪən/ 加拿大的[人]
(the) Caribbean /ˌkærɪˈbi:ən; ˌkærəˋbiən/ 加勒比	Caribbean 加勒比的[人]
Central African Republic /ˌsentrəl ˌæfrɪkən rɪˈpʌblɪk; ˌsɛntrəlˌæfrɪkənrɪˋpʌblɪk/ 中非共和国	
Ceylon /sɪˈlɒn; sɪˋlɑn/ ⇨ Sri Lanka	
Chad /tʃæd; tʃæd/ 乍得	Chadian /ˈtʃædɪən; ˋtʃædɪən/ 乍得的[人]
Chile /ˈtʃɪlɪ; ˋtʃɪlɪ/ 智利	Chilean /ˈtʃɪlɪən; ˋtʃɪlɪən/ 智利的[人]
(the People's Republic of) China /(ˈpi:plz rɪˌpʌblɪk əv) ˈtʃaɪnə; (ˋpiplzrɪˌpʌblɪkəv) ˋtʃaɪnə/ 中国; 中华人民共和国	Chinese /ˌtʃaɪˈni:z; tʃaɪˋniz/ 中国的[人]

NOUN 名词	ADJECTIVE; PERSON 形容词; 人
Colombia /kəˈlɒmbɪə; kəˋlʌmbɪə/ 哥伦比亚	Colombian /kəˈlɒmbɪən; kəˋlʌmbɪən/ 哥伦比亚的[人]
Congo /ˈkɒŋgəʊ; ˋkɑŋgo/ 刚果	Congolese /ˌkɒŋgəˈli:z; ˏkɑŋgəˋliz/ 刚果的[人]
Costa Rica /ˌkɒstə ˈri:kə; ˏkɑstəˋrikə/ 哥斯达黎加	Costa Rican /ˌkɒstə ˈri:kən; ˏkɑstəˋrikən/ 哥斯达黎加的[人]
Cuba /ˈkju:bə; ˋkjubə/ 古巴	Cuban /ˈkju:bən; ˋkjubən/ 古巴的[人]
Cyprus /ˈsaɪprəs; ˋsaɪprəs/ 塞浦路斯	Cypriot /ˈsɪprɪət; ˋsɪprɪət/ 塞浦路斯的[人]
(the) Czech Republic /tʃek rɪˈpʌblɪk; tʃɛkrɪˋpʌblɪk/ 捷克	Czech /tʃek; tʃɛk/ 捷克的[人]
Denmark /ˈdenmɑ:k; ˋdɛnˏmɑrk/ 丹麦	Danish /ˈdeɪnɪʃ; ˋdenɪʃ/ 丹麦的; Dane /deɪn; den/ 丹麦人
Djibouti /dʒɪˈbu:tɪ; dʒəˋbutɪ/ 吉布提	Djiboutian /dʒɪˈbu:tɪən; dʒəˋbuʃən/ 吉布提的[人]
Dominica /dəˈmɪnɪkə, ˌdɒmɪˈni:kə; dəˋmɪnɪkə, ˏdɑməˋnikə/ 多米尼加	Dominican /dəˈmɪnɪkən; dəˋmɪnɪkən/ 多米尼加的[人]
(the) Dominican Republic /dəˌmɪnɪkən rɪˈpʌblɪk; dəˏmɪnɪkənrɪˋpʌblɪk/ 多米尼加共和国	Dominican /dəˈmɪnɪkən; dəˋmɪnɪkən/ 多米尼加的[人]
Ecuador /ˈekwədɔ:(r); ˋɛkwəˏdɔr/ 厄瓜多尔	Ecuadorian /ˌekwəˈdɔ:rɪən; ˏɛkwəˋdɔrɪən/ 厄瓜多尔的[人]
Egypt /ˈi:dʒɪpt; ˋidʒɪpt/ 埃及	Egyptian /ɪˈdʒɪpʃn; ɪˋdʒɪpʃən/ 埃及的[人]
El Salvador /el ˈsælvədɔ:(r); ɛlˋsælvəˏdɔr/ 萨尔瓦多	Salvadorean /ˌsælvəˈdɔ:rɪən; ˏsælvəˋdɔrɪən/ 萨尔瓦多的[人]
England /ˈɪŋglənd; ˋɪŋglənd/ 英格兰	English /ˈɪŋglɪʃ; ˋɪŋglɪʃ/ 英格兰的; Englishman /ˈɪŋglɪʃmən; ˋɪŋglɪʃmən/, Englishwoman /ˈɪŋglɪʃwʊmən; ˋɪŋglɪʃˏwʊmən/ 英格兰人
Equatorial Guinea /ˌekwəˌtɔ:rɪəl ˈgɪnɪ; ˏɛkwəˏtɔrɪəlˋgɪnɪ/ 赤道几内亚	Equatorial Guinean /ˌekwəˌtɔ:rɪəl ˈgɪnɪən; ˏɛkwəˏtɔrɪəlˋgɪnɪən/ 赤道几内亚的[人]
Ethiopia /ˌi:θɪˈəʊpɪə; ˏiθɪˋopɪə/ 埃塞俄比亚	Ethiopian /ˌi:θɪˈəʊpɪən; ˏiθɪˋopɪən/ 埃塞俄比亚的[人]
Europe /ˈjʊərəp; ˋjʊrəp/ 欧洲	European /ˌjʊərəˈpɪən; ˏjʊrəˋpɪən/ 欧洲的[人]
(the) Far East /ˌfɑ:r ˈi:st; ˏfɑrˋist/ 远东	Far Eastern /ˌfɑ:r ˈi:stən; ˏfɑrˋistɚn/ 远东的
Fiji /ˌfi:ˈdʒi: *US* 美式英语读作 ˈfi:dʒi:; ˋfidʒi/ 斐济	Fijian /ˌfi:ˈdʒi:ən; *US* 美式英语读作 ˈfi:dʒɪən; ˋfidʒɪən/ 斐济的[人]
Finland /ˈfɪnlənd; ˋfɪnlənd/ 芬兰	Finnish /ˈfɪnɪʃ; ˋfɪnɪʃ/ 芬兰的; Finn /fɪn; fɪn/ 芬兰人
France /frɑ:ns; *US* 美式英语读作 fræns; fræns/ 法国	French /frentʃ; frɛntʃ/ 法国的; Frenchman /ˈfrentʃmən; ˋfrɛntʃmən/, Frenchwoman /ˈfrentʃwʊmən; ˋfrɛntʃˏwʊmən/ 法国人
Gabon /gæˈbɒn; gæˋbon/ 加蓬	Gabonese /ˌgæbəˈni:z; ˏgæbəˋniz/ 加蓬的[人]
Gambia /ˈgæmbɪə; ˋgæmbɪə/ 冈比亚	Gambian /ˈgæmbɪən; ˋgæmbɪən/ 冈比亚的[人]
(Federal Republic of) Germany /(ˌfedərəl rɪˌpʌblɪk əv) ˈdʒɜ:mənɪ; (ˏfɛdərəlrɪˏpʌblɪkəv)ˋdʒɝmənɪ/ 德意志联邦共和国	German /ˈdʒɜ:mən; ˋdʒɝmən/ 德国的[人]

NOUN 名词	ADJECTIVE; PERSON 形容词; 人
Ghana /ˈgɑːnə; ˋgɑnə/ 加纳	Ghanaian /gɑːˈneɪən; gɑˋneən/ 加纳的[人]
Gibraltar /dʒɪˈbrɔːltə(r); dʒəˋbrɔltɚ/ 直布罗陀	Gibraltarian /ˌdʒɪbrɔːlˈteərɪən; dʒə,brɔlˋtɛrɪən/ 直布罗陀的[人]
Great Britain /ˌgreɪt ˈbrɪtn; ,gretˋbrɪtn̩/; *also* 亦作 (the) United Kingdom (of Great Britain and Northern Ireland) 英国; 大不列颠及北爱尔兰联合王国	British /ˈbrɪtɪʃ; ˋbrɪtɪʃ/ 英国的; Briton /ˈbrɪtn; ˋbrɪtn̩/, *US* 美式英语作 Britisher /ˈbrɪtɪʃə(r); brɪtɪʃɚ/ 英国人
Greece /griːs; gris/ 希腊	Greek /griːk; grik/ 希腊的[人]
Grenada /grɪˈneɪdə; grɪˋnedə/ 格林纳达	Grenadian /grɪˈneɪdɪən; grəˋnedɪən/ 格林纳达的[人]
Guatemala /ˌgwɑːtəˈmɑːlə; ,gwɑtəˋmɑlə/ 危地马拉	Guatemalan /ˌgwɑːtəˈmɑːlən; ,gwɑtəˋmɑlən/ 危地马拉的[人]
Guiana /gɪˈɑːnə, gɪˈænɑ; gɪˋɑnə, gɪˋænə/ 圭亚那地区	Guianan /gɪˈɑːnən, gɪˈænən; gɪˋɑnən, gɪˋænən/ 圭亚那地区的[人]
Guinea /ˈgɪnɪ; ˋgɪnɪ/ 几内亚	Guinean /ˈgɪnɪən; ˋgɪnɪən/ 几内亚的[人]
Guyana /gaɪˈænə; gaɪˋænə/ 圭亚那	Guyanese /ˌgaɪəˈniːz; ,gaɪəˋniz/ 圭亚那的[人]
Haiti /ˈheɪtɪ; ˋhetɪ/ 海地	Haitian /ˈheɪʃn; ˋheʃən/ 海地的[人]
Holland /ˈhɒlənd; ˋhɑlənd/ (*also* 亦作 the Netherlands /ˈneðələndz; ˋnɛðɚləndz/) 荷兰	Dutch /dʌtʃ; dʌtʃ/ 荷兰的; Dutchman /ˈdʌtʃmən; ˋdʌtʃmən/, Dutchwoman /ˈdʌtʃwʊmən; ˋdʌtʃ,wʊmən/ 荷兰人
Honduras /hɒnˈdjʊərəs; *US* 美式英语读作 -ˈdʊə-; hɑnˋdurəs/ 洪都拉斯	Honduran /hɒnˈdjʊərən; *US* 美式英语读作 -ˈdʊə-; hɑnˋdurən/ 洪都拉斯的[人]
Hungary /ˈhʌŋgərɪ; ˋhʌŋgərɪ/ 匈牙利	Hungarian /hʌŋˈgeərɪən; hʌŋˋgɛrɪən/ 匈牙利的[人]
Iceland /ˈaɪslənd; ˋaɪslənd/ 冰岛	Icelandic /aɪsˈlændɪk; aɪsˋlændɪk/ 冰岛的; Icelander /ˈaɪsləndə(r); ˋaɪ,sləndɚ/ 冰岛人
India /ˈɪndɪə; ˋɪndɪə/ 印度	Indian /ˈɪndɪən; ˋɪndɪən/ 印度的[人]
Indonesia /ˌɪndəˈniːzɪə; *US* 美式英语读作 -ˈniːʒə; ,ɪndəˋniʒə/ 印度尼西亚	Indonesian /ˌɪndəˈniːzɪən; *US* 美式英语读作 -ʒn; ,ɪndəˋniʒən/ 印度尼西亚的[人]
Iran /ɪˈrɑːn; ɪˋræn/ (*formerly* 旧作 Persia) 伊朗	Iranian /ɪˈreɪnɪən; ɪˋrenɪən/ 伊朗的[人]
Iraq /ɪˈrɑːk; ɪˋrɑk/ 伊拉克	Iraqi /ɪˈrɑːkɪ; ɪˋrɑkɪ/ 伊拉克的[人]
(the Republic of) Ireland /ˈaɪələnd; ˋaɪrlənd/ (*also* 亦作 Eire /ˈeərə; ˋɛrə/) 爱尔兰(共和国)	Irish /ˈaɪərɪʃ; ˋaɪrɪʃ/ 爱尔兰的; Irishman /ˈaɪərɪʃmən; ˋaɪrɪʃmən/, Irishwoman /ˈaɪərɪʃwʊmən; ˋaɪrɪʃ,wʊmən/ 爱尔兰人
Israel /ˈɪzreɪl; ˋɪzreəl/ 以色列	Israeli /ɪzˈreɪlɪ; ɪzˋrelɪ/ 以色列的[人]
Italy /ˈɪtəlɪ; ˋɪtl̩ɪ/ 意大利	Italian /ɪˈtælɪən; ɪˋtæljən/ 意大利的[人]
Ivory Coast /ˌaɪvərɪ ˈkəʊst; ,aɪvərɪˋkost/ 象牙海岸	Ivorian /ˌaɪˈvɔːrɪən; ,aɪˋvɔrɪən/ 象牙海岸的[人]
Jamaica /dʒəˈmeɪkə; dʒəˋmekə/ 牙买加	Jamaican /dʒəˈmeɪkən; dʒəˋmekən/ 牙买加的[人]
Japan /dʒəˈpæn; dʒəˋpæn/ 日本	Japanese /ˌdʒæpəˈniːz; ,dʒæpəˋniz/ 日本的[人]
Java /ˈdʒɑːvə; ˋdʒɑvə/ 爪哇	Javanese /ˌdʒɑːvəˈniːz; ,dʒævəˋniz/ 爪哇的[人]
Jordan /ˈdʒɔːdn; ˋdʒɔrdn̩/ 约旦	Jordanian /dʒɔːˈdeɪnɪən; dʒɔrˋdenɪən/ 约旦的[人]
Kampuchea /ˌkæmpʊˈtʃɪə; ,kæmpəˋtʃɪə/ ⇨ Cambodia	Kampuchean /ˌkæmpʊˈtʃɪən; ,kæmpəˋtʃɪən/ 柬埔寨的[人]

NOUN 名词	ADJECTIVE; PERSON 形容词; 人
Kashmir /ˌkæʃˈmɪə(r); *US* 美式英语读作 ˈkæʃmɪər; ˋkæʃmɪr/ 克什米尔	Kashmiri /kæʃˈmɪərɪ; kæʃˋmɪrɪ/ 克什米尔的[人]
Katar ⇨ Qatar	
Kenya /ˈkenjə; *US* 美式英语读作 ˈki:njə; ˋkinjə/ 肯尼亚	Kenyan /ˈkenjən; *US* 美式英语读作 ˈki:njən; ˋkinjən/ 肯尼亚的[人]
Korea /kəˈrɪə; kəˋrɪə/ 朝鲜; 韩国: The Democratic People's Republic of Korea 朝鲜民主主义人民共和国 The Republic of Korea 大韩民国	Korean /kəˋrɪən; kəˋrɪən/ 朝鲜的[人]
Kuwait /kʊˈweɪt; *US* 美式英语读作 -ˈwaɪt; kʊˋwaɪt/ 科威特	Kuwaiti /kʊˈweɪtɪ; *US* 美式英语读作 kʊˈwaɪtɪ; kʊˋwaɪtɪ/ 科威特的[人]
Laos /ˈlɑ:ɒs; ˋlɑos/ 老挝	Laotian /ˈlɑ:ɒʃn; *US* 美式英语读作 leɪˈəʊʃn; leˋoʃən/ 老挝的[人]
Lebanon /ˈlebənən; *US* 美式英语读作 -nɒn; ˋlɛbənɑn/ 黎巴嫩	Lebanese /ˌlebəˈni:z; ˌlɛbəˋniz/ 黎巴嫩的[人]
Lesotho /ləˈsu:tu:; ləˋsoto/ 莱索托	Sotho /ˈsu:tu:; ˋsoto/ (person 人: Mosotho /məˈsu:tu:; məˋsoto/; people 民族: Basotho /bəˈsu:tu:; bəˋsoto/) 莱索托的[人]
Liberia /laɪˈbɪərɪə; laɪˋbɪrɪə/ 利比里亚	Liberian /laɪˈbɪərɪən; laɪˋbɪrɪən/ 利比里亚的[人]
Libya /ˈlɪbɪə; ˋlɪbɪə/ 利比亚	Libyan /ˈlɪbɪən; ˋlɪbɪən/ 利比亚的[人]
Liechtenstein /ˈlɪktənstaɪn; ˋlɪktənˌstaɪn/ 列支敦士登	Liechtenstein 列支敦士登的; Liechtensteiner /ˈlɪktənstaɪnə(r); ˋlɪktənˌstaɪnɚ/ 列支敦士登人
Luxemburg /ˈlʌksəmbɜ:g; ˋlʌksəmˌbɝg/ 卢森堡	Luxemburg 卢森堡的; Luxemburger /ˈlʌksəmbɜ:gə(r); ˋlʌksəmˌbɝgɚ/ 卢森堡人
Madagascar /ˌmædəˈgæskə(r); ˌmædəˋgæskɚ/ 马达加斯加	Madagascan /ˌmædəˈgæskən; ˌmædəˋgæskən/; Malagasy /ˌmæləˈgæsɪ; ˌmæləˋgæsɪ/ 马达加斯加的[人]
Malawi /məˈlɑ:wɪ; məˋlɑwɪ/ 马拉维	Malawian /məˈlɑ:wɪən; məˋlɑwɪən/ 马拉维的[人]
Malaysia /məˈleɪzɪə; *US* 美式英语读作 -ˈleɪʒə; məˋleʒə/ 马来西亚	Malaysian /məˈleɪzɪən; *US* 美式英语读作 -ˈleɪʒn; məˋleʒən/ 马来西亚的[人]
Mali /ˈmɑ:lɪ; ˋmɑlɪ/ 马里	Malian /ˈmɑ:lɪən; ˋmɑlɪən/ 马里的[人]
Malta /ˈmɔ:ltə; ˋmɔltə/ 马尔他	Maltese /mɔ:lˈti:z; mɔlˋtiz/ 马尔他的[人]
Mauritania /ˌmɒrɪˈteɪnɪə; *US* 美式英语读作 ˌmɔ:r-; ˌmɔrɪˋtenɪə/ 毛里塔尼亚	Mauritanian /ˌmɒrɪˈteɪnɪən; *US* 美式英语读作 ˌmɔ:r-; ˌmɔrəˋtenɪən/ 毛里塔尼亚的[人]
Mauritius /məˈrɪʃəs; *US* 美式英语读作 mɔ:-; mɔˋrɪʃəs/ 毛里求斯	Mauritian /məˈrɪʃn; *US* 美式英语读作 mɔ:-; mɔˋrɪʃən/ 毛里求斯的[人]
Mediterranean /ˌmedɪtəˈreɪnɪən; ˌmɛdətəˋrenɪən/ 地中海地区	Mediterranean 地中海地区的
Melanesia /ˌmeləˈni:zɪə; *US* 美式英语读作 -ˈni:ʒə; ˌmɛləˋniʒə/ 美拉尼西亚	Melanesian /ˌmeləˈni:zɪən; *US* 美式英语读作 -ˈni:ʒn; ˌmɛləˋniʒən/ 美拉尼西亚的[人]
Mexico /ˈmeksɪkəʊ; ˋmɛksɪˌko/ 墨西哥	Mexican /ˈmeksɪkən; ˋmɛksɪkən/ 墨西哥的[人]
Micronesia /ˌmaɪkrəʊˈni:zɪə; *US* 美式英语读作 -ˈni:ʒə; ˌmaɪkroˋniʒə/ 密克罗尼西亚	Micronesian /ˌmaɪkrəʊˈni:zɪən; *US* 美式英语读作 -ˈni:ʒən; ˌmaɪkroˋniʒən/ 密克罗尼西亚的[人]
(the) Middle East /ˌmɪdl ˈi:st; ˌmɪdlˋist/ 中东地区	Middle Eastern /ˌmɪdl ˈi:stən; ˌmɪdlˋistɚn/ 中东地区的

NOUN 名词	ADJECTIVE; PERSON 形容词; 人
Monaco /ˈmɒnəkəʊ; ˋmɑnə,ko/ 摩纳哥	Monegasque /ˌmɒnəˈgæsk; ,mɑnɪˋgæsk/ 摩纳哥的[人]
Mongolia /mɒŋˈgəʊlɪə; mɑŋˋgolɪə/ 蒙古	Mongolian /mɒŋˈgəʊlɪən; mɑŋˋgolɪən/ 蒙古的; Mongol /ˈmɒŋgl; ˋmɑŋgəl/ 蒙古的[人]
Montserrat /ˌmɒntsəˈræt; ,mɑntsəˋræt/ 蒙塞拉特	Montserratian /ˌmɒntsəˈræʃn; ,mɑntsəˋræʃən/ 蒙塞拉特的[人]
Morocco /məˈrɒkəʊ; məˋrɑko/ 摩洛哥	Moroccan /məˈrɒkən; məˋrɑkən/ 摩洛哥的[人]
Mozambique /ˌməʊzæmˈbi:k; ,mozəmˋbik/ 莫桑比克	Mozambiquean /ˌməʊzæmˈbi:kən; ,mozəmˋbikən/ 莫桑比克的[人]
Namibia /nəˈmɪbɪə; nəˋmɪbɪə/ 纳米比亚	Namibian /nəˈmɪbɪən; nəˋmɪbɪən/ 纳米比亚的[人]
Nauru /ˈnaʊru:; nɑˋuru/ 瑙鲁	Nauruan /naʊˈru:ən; nɑˋrəwən/ 瑙鲁的[人]
Nepal /nɪˈpɔ:l; nəˋpɔl/ 尼泊尔	Nepalese /ˌnepəˈli:z; ,nɛpəˋliz/ 尼泊尔的[人]
(the) Netherlands ⇨ Holland	
New Zealand /ˌnju: ˈzi:lənd; *US* 美式英语读作 ˌnu:-; nuˋzilənd/ 新西兰	New Zealand 新西兰的; New Zealander /ˌnju: ˈzi:ləndə(r); *US* 美式英语读作 ˌnu:-; nuˋziləndɚ/ 新西兰人
Nicaragua /ˌnɪkəˈrægjʊə; *US* 美式英语读作 -ˈrɑ:gwə; ,nɪkəˋrɑgwə/ 尼加拉瓜	Nicaraguan /ˌnɪkəˈrægjʊən; *US* 美式英语读作 -ˈrɑ:gwən; ,nɪkəˋrɑgwən/ 尼加拉瓜的[人]
Niger /ni:ˈʒeə(r); ˋnaɪdʒɚ/ 尼日尔	Nigerien /ni:ˈʒeərɪən; naɪˋdʒɛrɪən/ 尼日尔的[人]
Nigeria /naɪˈdʒɪərɪə; naɪˋdʒɪrɪə/ 尼日利亚	Nigerian /naɪˈdʒɪərɪən; naɪˋdʒɪrɪən/ 尼日利亚的[人]
North Korea ⇨ Korea	
North Yemen ⇨ Yemen	
Northern Ireland /ˌnɔ:ðən ˈaɪələnd; ,nɔrðɚnˋaɪrlənd/ 北爱尔兰	Northern Irish /ˌnɔ:ðən ˈaɪərɪʃ; ,nɔrðɚnˋaɪrɪʃ/ 北爱尔兰的[人]
Norway /ˈnɔ:weɪ; ˋnɔr,we/ 挪威	Norwegian /nɔ:ˈwi:dʒən; nɔrˋwidʒən/ 挪威的[人]
Oman /əʊˈmɑ:n; oˋmɑn/ 阿曼	Omani /əʊˈmɑ:nɪ; oˋmɑnɪ/ 阿曼的[人]
(the) Pacific /pəˈsɪfɪk; pəˋsɪfɪk/ 太平洋地区	Pacific 太平洋地区的
Pakistan /ˌpɑ:kɪˈstɑ:n; ,pækɪˋstæn/ 巴基斯坦	Pakistani /ˌpɑ:kɪˈstɑ:nɪ; *US* 美式英语读作 ˌpækɪˈstænɪ; ,pækɪˋstænɪ/ 巴基斯坦的[人]
Palestine /ˈpæləstaɪn; ˋpælə,staɪn/ 巴勒斯坦	Palestinian /ˌpæləˈstɪnɪən; ,pæləˋstɪnɪən/ 巴勒斯坦的[人]
Panama /ˈpænəmɑ:; ˋpænə,mɑ/ 巴拿马	Panamanian /ˌpænəˈmeɪnɪən; ,pænəˋmenɪən/ 巴拿马的[人]
Papua New Guinea /ˌpæpʊə ˌnju: ˈgɪnɪ; *US* 美式英语读作 -ˌnu:-; ,pæpjʊə,nuˋgɪnɪ/ 巴布亚新几内亚	Papuan /ˈpæpʊən; ˋpæpjʊən/ 巴布亚新几内亚的[人]
Paraguay /ˈpærəgwaɪ; *US* 美式英语读作 -gweɪ; ˋpærə,gwe/ 巴拉圭	Paraguayan /ˌpærəˈgwaɪən; *US* 美式英语读作 -ˈgweɪən; ,pærəˋgweən/ 巴拉圭的[人]
Persia /ˈpɜ:ʃə; ˋpɝʃə/ ⇨ Iran	
Peru /pəˈru:; pəˋru/ 秘鲁	Peruvian /pəˈru:vɪən; pəˋruvɪən/ 秘鲁的[人]
(the) Philippines /ˈfɪlɪpi:nz; ˋfɪlə,pinz/ 菲律宾	Philippine /ˈfɪlɪpi:n; ˋfɪlə,pin/ 菲律宾的; Filipino /ˌfɪlɪˈpi:nəʊ; ,fɪləˋpino/ 菲律宾人
Poland /ˈpəʊlənd; ˋpolənd/ 波兰	Polish /ˈpəʊlɪʃ; ˋpolɪʃ/ 波兰的; Pole /pəʊl; pol/ 波兰人
Polynesia /ˌpɒlɪˈni:zɪə; *US* 美式英语读作 -ˈni:ʒə; ,pɑləˋniʒə/ 波利尼西亚	Polynesian /ˌpɒlɪˈni:zɪən; *US* 美式英语读作 -ˈni:ʒn; ,pɑləˋniʒən/ 波利尼西亚的[人]

NOUN 名词	ADJECTIVE; PERSON 形容词; 人
Portugal /ˈpɔ:tʃʊgl; ˋpɔrtʃəgl̩/ 葡萄牙	Portuguese /ˌpɔ:tʃʊˈgi:z; ˋpɔrtʃə,giz/ 葡萄牙的［人］
Puerto Rico /ˌpwɜ:təʊ ˈri:kəʊ; ,pwɛrtəˋriko/ 波多黎各	Puerto Rican /ˌpwɜ:təʊ ˈri:kən; ,pwɛrtəˋrikən/ 波多黎各的［人］
Qatar (*also* 亦作 Katar) /ˈkʌtɑ:(r); ˋkɑtɚ/ 卡塔尔	Qatari (*also* 亦作 Katari) /kʌˈtɑ:rɪ; ˋkɑtərɪ/ 卡塔尔的［人］
Romania /ru:ˈmeɪnɪə; roˋmenɪə/ 罗马尼亚	Romanian /ru:ˈmeɪnɪən; roˋmenɪən/ 罗马尼亚的［人］
Russia /ˈrʌʃə; ˋrʌʃə/ 俄罗斯	Russian /ˈrʌʃn; ˋrʌʃən/ 俄罗斯的［人］
Rwanda /rʊˈændə; rʊˋɑndə/ 卢旺达	Rwandan /rʊˈændən; rʊˋɑndən/ 卢旺达的［人］
Samoa ⇨ Western Samoa	
San Marino /ˌsæn məˈri:nəʊ; ,sænməˋrino/ 圣马力诺	San Marinese /ˌsæn ˌmærɪˈni:z; ,sæn,mærəˋniz/ 圣马力诺的［人］
Saudi Arabia /ˌsaʊdɪ əˈreɪbɪə; ,saʊdɪəˋrebɪə/ 沙特阿拉伯	Saudi /ˈsaʊdɪ; ˋsaʊdɪ/; Saudi Arabian /ˌsaʊdɪ əˈreɪbɪən; ,saʊdɪəˋrebɪən/ 沙特阿拉伯的［人］
Scotland /ˈskɒtlənd; ˋskɑtlənd/ 苏格兰	Scottish /ˈskɒtɪʃ; ˋskɑtɪʃ/, Scotch /skɒtʃ; skɑtʃ/ 苏格兰的; Scot /skɒt; skɑt/, Scotsman /ˈskɒtsmən; ˋskɑtsmən/, Scotswoman /ˈskɒtswʊmən; ˋskɑts,wʊmən/ 苏格兰人
Senegal /ˌsenɪˈgɔ:l; ,sɛnɪˋgɔl/ 塞内加尔	Senegalese /ˌsenɪgəˈli:z; ,sɛnɪgəˋliz/ 塞内加尔的［人］
(the) Seychelles /seɪˈʃelz; seˋʃɛl(z)/ 塞舌尔	Seychellois /seɪˈʃelwɑ:; ,seʃəlˋwɑ/ 塞舌尔的［人］
Siam /saɪˈæm; saɪˋæm/ ⇨ Thailand	
Sierra Leone /sɪˌerə lɪˈəʊn; sɪ,ɛrəlɪˋon/ 塞拉利昂	Sierra Leonean /sɪˌerə lɪˈəʊnɪən; sɪ,ɛrəlɪˋonɪən/ 塞拉利昂的［人］
Singapore /ˌsɪŋəˈpɔ:(r); ˋsɪŋə,pɔr/ 新加坡	Singaporean /ˌsɪŋəˈpɔ:rɪən; ,sɪŋəˋpɔrɪən/ 新加坡的［人］
Slovakia /sləʊˈvækɪə; sloˋvækɪə/ 斯洛伐克	Slovakian /sləʊˋvækɪən; sloˋvækɪən/; Slovak /ˈsləʊvæk; ˋslovæk/ 斯洛伐克的［人］
Somalia /səˈmɑ:lɪə; səˋmɑlɪə/ 索马里	Somali /səˈmɑ:lɪ; səˋmɑlɪ/ 索马里的［人］
South Africa /ˌsaʊθ ˈæfrɪkə; ,saʊθˋæfrɪkə/ 南非	South African /ˌsaʊθ ˈæfrɪkən; ,saʊθˋæfrɪkən/ 南非的［人］
South Korea ⇨ Korea	
South Yemen ⇨ Yemen	
Spain /speɪn; spen/ 西班牙	Spanish /ˈspænɪʃ; ˋspænɪʃ/ 西班牙的; Spaniard /ˈspænɪəd; ˋspænjɚd/ 西班牙人
Sri Lanka /ˌsri:ˈlæŋkə; srɪˋlɑŋkə/ (*formerly* 旧作 Ceylon) 斯里兰卡	Sri Lankan /ˌsri:ˈlæŋkən; srɪˋlɑŋkən/ 斯里兰卡的［人］
Sudan /su:ˈdɑ:n; suˋdæn/ 苏丹	Sudanese /ˌsu:dəˈni:z; ,sudəˋniz/ 苏丹的［人］
Sumatra /sʊˈmɑ:trə; sʊˋmɑtrə/ 苏门答腊	Sumatran /sʊˈmɑ:trən; sʊˋmɑtrən/ 苏门答腊的［人］
Surinam /ˌsʊərɪˈnæm; ,sʊrɪˋnæm/ 苏里南	Surinamese /ˌsʊərɪnæˈmi:z; ,sʊrɪnæˋmiz/ 苏里南的［人］
Swaziland /ˈswɑ:zɪlænd; ˋswɑzɪ,lænd/ 斯威士兰	Swazi /ˈswɑ:zɪ; ˋswɑzɪ/ 斯威士兰的［人］
Sweden /ˈswi:dn; ˋswidn̩/ 瑞典	Swedish /ˈswi:dɪʃ; ˋswidɪʃ/ 瑞典的; Swede /swi:d; swid/ 瑞典人
Switzerland /ˈswɪtsələnd; ˋswɪtsɚlənd/ 瑞士	Swiss /swɪs; swɪs/ 瑞士的［人］

NOUN 名词	ADJECTIVE; PERSON 形容词; 人
Syria /ˈsɪrɪə; ˋsɪrɪə/ 叙利亚	Syrian /ˈsɪrɪən; ˋsɪrɪən/ 叙利亚的[人]
Tahiti /tɑːˈhiːtɪ; tɑˋhitɪ/ 塔希提岛	Tahitian /tɑːˈhiːʃn; tɑˋhitɪən/ 塔希提岛的[人]
Tanzania /ˌtænzəˈnɪə; ˌtænzəˋnɪə/ 坦桑尼亚	Tanzanian /ˌtænzəˈnɪən; ˌtænzəˋnɪən/ 坦桑尼亚的[人]
Thailand /ˈtaɪlænd; ˋtaɪˌlænd/ (*formerly* 旧作 Siam) 泰国	Thai /taɪ; taɪ/ 泰国的[人]
Timor, East /ˌiːst ˈtiːmɔː(r); ˌist ˋtimɔr/ 东帝汶	Timorese /ˌtiːmɔːˈriːz; ˌtimɔˋriz/ 帝汶的[人]
Togo /ˈtəʊgəʊ; ˋtogo/ 多哥	Togolese /ˌtəʊgəˈliːz; ˌtogəˋliz/ 多哥的[人]
Tonga /ˈtɒŋə, *also* 亦作 ˈtɒŋgə; ˋtɑŋə, ˋtɑŋgə/ 汤加	Tongan /ˈtɒŋən, *also* 亦作 ˈtɒŋgən; ˋtɑŋən, ˋtɑŋgən/ 汤加的[人]
Trinidad /ˈtrɪnɪdæd; ˋtrɪnəˌdæd/ and Tobago /təˈbeɪgəʊ; təˋbego/ 特立尼达和多巴哥	Trinidadian /ˌtrɪnɪˈdædɪən; ˌtrɪnəˋdædɪən/ 特立尼达的[人]; Tobagan /təˈbeɪgən; təˋbegən/; Tobagonian /ˌtəʊbəˈgəʊnɪən; ˌtobəˋgonɪən/ 多巴哥的[人]
Tunisia /tjuːˈnɪzɪə; *US* 美式英语读作 tuːˈnɪʒə; tuˋnɪʒə/ 突尼斯	Tunisian /tjuːˈnɪzɪən; *US* 美式英语读作 tuːˈnɪʒən; tuˋnɪʒən/ 突尼斯的[人]
Turkey /ˈtɜːkɪ; ˋtɝkɪ/ 土耳其	Turkish /ˈtɜːkɪʃ; ˋtɝkɪʃ/ 土耳其的; Turk /tɜːk; tɝk/ 土耳其人
Uganda /juːˈgændə; juˋgændə/ 乌干达	Ugandan /juːˈgændən; juˋgændən/ 乌干达的[人]
(the) United Kingdom ⇨ Great Britain	
(the) United States of America /juːˌnaɪtɪd ˌsteɪts əv əˈmerɪkə; juˌnaɪtɪdˌstetsəvəˋmɛrɪkə/ 美利坚合众国	American /əˈmerɪkən; əˋmɛrɪkən/ 美国的[人]
Uruguay /ˈjʊərəgwaɪ; *US* 美式英语读作 -gweɪ; ˋjʊrəˌgwe/ 乌拉圭	Uruguayan /ˌjʊərəˈgwaɪən; *US* 美式英语读作 -ˈgweɪən; ˌjʊrəˋgweən/ 乌拉圭的[人]
Venezuela /ˌvenɪˈzweɪlə; ˌvɛnəˋzwelə/ 委内瑞拉	Venezuelan /ˌvenɪˈzweɪlən; ˌvɛnəˋzwelən/ 委内瑞拉的[人]
Vietnam /ˌvjetˈnæm; *US* 美式英语读作 -ˈnɑːm; vjɛtˋnɑm/ 越南	Vietnamese /ˌvjetnəˈmiːz; vjɛtnəˋmiz/ 越南的[人]
Wales /weɪlz; welz/ 威尔士	Welsh /welʃ; wɛlʃ/ 威尔士的; Welshman /ˈwelʃmən; ˋwɛlʃmən/, Welshwoman /ˈwelʃwʊmən; ˋwɛlʃˌwʊmən/ 威尔士人
(the) West Indies /ˌwest ˈɪndɪz; ˌwɛstˋɪndɪz/ 西印度群岛	West Indian /ˌwest ˈɪndɪən; ˌwɛstˋɪndɪən/ 西印度群岛的[人]
Western Samoa /ˌwestən səˈməʊə; ˌwɛstɚnsəˋmoə/ 西萨摩亚	Samoan /səˈməʊən; səˋmoən/ 萨摩亚的[人]
(the Republic of) Yemen /ˈjemən; ˋjɛmən/ 也门(共和国)	Yemeni /ˈjemənɪ; ˋjɛmənɪ/ 也门的[人]
Yugoslavia(旧称) /ˌjuːgəʊˈslɑːvɪə; ˌjugoˋslɑvɪə/ 南斯拉夫	Yugoslavian(旧称) /ˌjuːgəʊˈslɑːvɪən; ˌjugoˋslɑvɪən/ 南斯拉夫的[人]; Yugoslav /ˈjuːgəʊslɑːv; ˋjugoˌslɑv/ 南斯拉夫人
Zaire /zɑːˈɪə(r); zɑˋɪr/ 扎伊尔	Zairean /zɑːˈɪərɪən; zɑˋɪrɪən/ 扎伊尔的[人]
Zambia /ˈzæmbɪə; ˋzæmbɪə/ 赞比亚	Zambian /ˈzæmbɪən; ˋzæmbɪən/ 赞比亚的[人]
Zimbabwe /zɪmˈbɑːbwɪ; zɪmˋbɑbwɪ/ 津巴布韦	Zimbabwean /zɪmˈbɑːbwɪən; zɪmˋbɑbwɪən/ 津巴布韦的[人]

APPENDIX 7 附录 7

COMMON FORENAMES 普通人名表

Note 说明: Pet names and short forms (which may sometimes be used as names in their own right) follow the name from which they are formed. 昵称和简称(其本身有时可作名字)列于其正式名字之后.

Female Names 女子名

Abigail /ˈæbɪgeɪl; ˋæbɪˌgel/ 阿比盖尔
Ada /ˈeɪdə; ˋedə/ 埃达
Agatha /ˈægəθə; ˋægəθə/ 阿加莎; Aggie /ˈægɪ; ˋægɪ/ 阿吉
Agnes /ˈægnɪs; ˋægnɪs/ 阿格尼丝; Aggie /ˈægɪ; ˋægɪ/ 阿吉
Aileen ⇨ Eileen
Alexandra /ˌælɪgˈzɑ:ndrə; *US* 美式英语读作 -ˈzæn-; ˌælɪgˋzændrə/ 亚历山德拉; Alex /ˈælɪks; ˋælɪks/ 亚历克斯
Alexis /əˈleksɪs; əˋlɛksɪs/ 亚历克西斯
Alice /ˈælɪs; ˋælɪs/ 艾丽斯
Alison /ˈælɪsn; ˋæləsn̩/ 艾莉森
Amanda /əˈmændə; əˋmændə/ 阿曼达; Mandy /ˈmændɪ; ˋmændɪ/ 曼迪
Amy /ˈeɪmɪ; ˋemɪ/ 埃米
Angela /ˈændʒələ; ˋændʒələ/ 安杰拉; Angie /ˈændʒɪ; ˋændʒɪ/ 安吉
Anita /əˈni:tə; əˋnitə/ 阿妮塔
Ann, Anne /æn; æn/ 安; Annie /ˈænɪ; ˋænɪ/ 安妮
Anna /ˈænə; ˋænə/ 安娜
Annabel, Annabelle /ˈænəbel; ˋænəˌbɛl/ 安纳贝尔
Anne, Annie ⇨ Ann
Annette /æˈnet; æˋnɛt/ 安妮特
Anthea /ˈænθɪə; ænˋθiə/ 安西娅
Antonia /ænˈtəʊnɪə; ænˋtonɪə/ 安东尼娅
Audrey /ˈɔ:drɪ; ˋɔdrɪ/ 奥德丽
Ava /ˈeɪvə; ˋevə/ 埃娃
Barbara, Barbra /ˈbɑ:brə; ˋbɑrbrə/ 巴巴拉; Babs /bæbz; bæbz/ 巴布斯
Beatrice /ˈbɪətrɪs; ˋbiətrɪs/ 比阿特丽斯
Becky ⇨ Rebecca
Belinda /bəˈlɪndə; bəˋlɪndə/ 比琳达
Bernadette /ˌbɜ:nəˈdet; ˌbɝnəˋdɛt/ 伯纳黛特
Beryl /ˈberəl; ˋbɛrəl/ 贝里尔
Bess, Bessie, Beth, Betsy, Bett, Betty ⇨ Elizabeth
Brenda /ˈbrendə; ˋbrɛndə/ 布伦达
Bridget, Bridgit, Brigid /ˈbrɪdʒɪt; ˋbrɪdʒɪt/ 布里奇特; Bid /bɪd; bɪd/ 比德
Candice /ˈkændɪs; ˋkændɪs/ 坎迪斯
Carla /ˈkɑ:lə; ˋkɑrlə/ 卡拉
Carol, Carole /ˈkærəl; ˋkærəl/ 卡罗尔
Caroline /ˈkærəlaɪn; ˋkærəˌlaɪn/; Carolyn /ˈkærəlɪn; ˋkærəlɪn/ 卡罗琳; Carrie /ˈkærɪ; ˋkærɪ/ 卡丽
Catherine, Cathy ⇨ Katherine
Cecilia /sɪˈsi:lɪə; sɪˋsɪlɪə/ 塞西莉亚
Cecily /ˈsesəlɪ; ˋsɛsl̩ɪ/; Cicely /ˈsɪsəlɪ; ˋsɪsl̩ɪ/ 塞西莉
Celia /ˈsi:lɪə; ˋsiljə/ 西莉亚
Charlene /ˈʃɑ:li:n; ˋʃɑrlin/ 查伦
Charlotte /ˈʃɑ:lət; ˋʃɑrlət/ 夏洛特
Cheryl /ˈtʃerəl; ˋtʃɛrəl/ 谢里尔
Chloe /ˈkləʊɪ; ˋklo·ɪ/ 克洛伊
Christina /krɪˈsti:nə; krɪsˋtinə/ 克里斯蒂娜; Tina /ˈti:nə; ˋtinə/ 蒂娜
Christine /ˈkrɪsti:n; krɪsˋtin/ 克里斯廷; Chris /krɪs; krɪs/ 克里斯; Chrissie /ˈkrɪsɪ; ˋkrɪsɪ/ 克里西
Cindy ⇨ Cynthia, Lucinda
Clare, Claire /kleə(r); klɛr/ 克莱尔
Claudia /ˈklɔ:dɪə; ˋklɔdɪə/ 克劳迪娅
Cleo, Clio /ˈkli:əʊ; ˋklio/ 克利奥
Constance /ˈkɒnstəns; ˋkɑnstəns/ 康斯坦斯; Connie /ˈkɒnɪ; ˋkɑnɪ/ 康尼
Cynthia /ˈsɪnθɪə; ˋsɪnθɪə/ 辛西娅; Cindy /ˈsɪndɪ; ˋsɪndɪ/ 辛迪
Daisy /ˈdeɪzɪ; ˋdezɪ/ 戴西
Daphne /ˈdæfnɪ; ˋdæfnɪ/ 达夫妮
Dawn /dɔ:n; dɔn/ 唐
Deborah /ˈdebərə; ˋdɛbərə/ 德博拉; Debbie, Debby /ˈdebɪ; ˋdɛbɪ/ 戴比; Deb /deb; dɛb/ 黛布
Deirdre /ˈdɪədrɪ; ˋdɪrdrɪ/ 迪尔德丽
Delia /ˈdi:lɪə; ˋdilɪə/ 迪莉娅
Della /ˈdelə; ˋdɛlə/ 黛拉
Denise /dəˈni:z; dəˋniz/ 丹尼斯
Diana /daɪˈænə; daɪˋænə/ 黛安娜; Diane /daɪˈæn; daɪˋæn/ 黛安; Di /daɪ; daɪ/ 黛
Dolly /ˈdɒlɪ; ˋdɑlɪ/ 多利
Dora /ˈdɔ:rə; ˋdɔrə/ 多拉

Doreen, Dorene /ˈdɔːriːn; ˋdɔrin/ 多琳
Doris /ˈdɒrɪs; ˋdɔrɪs/ 多丽丝
Dorothy /ˈdɒrəθɪ; ˋdɑrəθɪ/ 多萝西; Dot /dɒt; dɑt/ 多特; Dottie /ˈdɒtɪ; ˋdɑtɪ/ 多蒂
Edith /ˈiːdɪθ; ˋidɪθ/ 伊迪丝
Edna /ˈednə; ˋɛdnə/ 埃德娜
Eileen /ˈaɪliːn; aɪˋlin/; Aileen /ˈeɪliːn; ˋelin/ 艾琳
Elaine /ɪˈleɪn; ɪˋlen/ 伊莱恩
Eleanor /ˈelɪnə(r); ˋɛlɪnɚ/ 埃莉诺; Eleanora /ˌelɪˈnɔːrə; ˌɛləˋnɔrə/ 埃莉诺拉; Ellie /ˈelɪ; ˋɛlɪ/ 埃利
Eliza /ɪˈlaɪzə; ɪˋlaɪzə/ 伊莱扎; Liza /ˈlaɪzə; ˋlaɪzə/ 莉莎; Lisa /ˈliːsə; ˋlisə/ 莉萨
Elizabeth, Elisabeth /ɪˈlɪzəbəθ; ɪˋlɪzəbəθ/ 伊丽莎白; Liz /lɪz; lɪz/ 利兹; Lizzie, Lizzy /ˈlɪzɪ; ˋlɪzɪ/ 利齐; Libby /ˈlɪbɪ; ˋlɪbɪ/ 利比; Beth /beθ; bɛθ/ 贝思; Betsy /ˈbetsɪ; ˋbɛtsɪ/ 贝齐; Bett /bet; bɛt/ 贝特; Betty /ˈbetɪ; ˋbɛtɪ/ 贝蒂; Bess /bes; bɛs/ 贝丝; Bessie /ˈbesɪ; ˋbɛsɪ/ 贝西
Ella /ˈelə; ˋɛlə/ 埃拉
Ellen /ˈelən; ˋɛlən/ 埃伦
Ellie ⇨ Eleanor
Elsie /ˈelsɪ; ˋɛlsɪ/ 埃尔西
Elspeth /ˈelspəθ; ˋɛlspəθ/ 埃尔斯佩思 (*Scot* 用于苏格兰)
Emily /ˈemәlɪ; ˋɛmḷɪ/ 埃米莉
Emma /ˈemə; ˋɛmə/ 埃玛
Erica /ˈerɪkə; ˋɛrɪkə/ 埃里卡
Ethel /ˈeθl; ˋɛθəl/ 埃塞尔
Eunice /ˈjuːnɪs; ˋjunɪs/ 尤妮斯
Eve /iːv; iv/ 伊夫; Eva /ˈiːvə; ˋivə/ 伊娃
Evelyn /ˈiːvlɪn; ˋivlɪn/ 伊夫林
Fay /feɪ; fe/ 费伊
Felicity /fəˈlɪsətɪ; fəˋlɪsətɪ/ 费利西蒂
Fiona /fɪˈəʊnə; fɪˋonə/ 菲奥纳
Flora /ˈflɔːrə; ˋflɔrə/ 弗洛拉
Florence /ˈflɒrəns; *US* 美式英语读作 ˈflɔːr-; ˋflɔrəns/ 弗洛伦斯; Flo /fləʊ; flo/ 弗洛; Florrie /ˈflɒrɪ; ˋflɑrɪ/ 弗洛里
Frances /ˈfrɑːnsɪs; *US* 美式英语读作 ˈfræn-; ˋfrænsɪs / 弗朗西丝; Fran /fræn; fræn/ 弗朗; Frankie /ˈfræŋkɪ; ˋfræŋkɪ/ 弗朗基
Freda /ˈfriːdə; ˋfridə/ 弗雷达
Georgia /ˈdʒɔːdʒɪə; ˋdʒɔrdʒjə/ 乔治亚; Georgie /ˈdʒɔːdʒɪ; ˋdʒɔrdʒɪ/ 乔治; Georgina /dʒɔːˈdʒiːnə; dʒɔrˋdʒinə/ 乔治娜
Geraldine /ˈdʒerəldiːn; ˋdʒɛrəld,in/ 杰拉尔丁
Germaine /dʒɜːˈmeɪn; dʒɝˋmen/ 杰曼
Gertrude /ˈgɜːtruːd; ˋgɝtrud/ 格特鲁德; Gertie /ˈgɜːtɪ; ˋgɝtɪ/ 格蒂
Gillian /ˈdʒɪlɪən; ˋdʒɪlɪən/ 吉利恩; Jill, Gill /dʒɪl; dʒɪl/ 吉尔; Jilly /ˈdʒɪlɪ; ˋdʒɪlɪ/ 吉莉
Ginny ⇨ Virginia
Gladys /ˈglædɪs; ˋglædɪs/ 格拉迪斯
Glenda /ˈglendə; ˋglɛndə/ 格伦达
Gloria /ˈglɔːrɪə; ˋglɔrɪə/ 格洛丽亚
Grace /greɪs; gres/ 格雷斯; Gracie /ˈgreɪsɪ; ˋgresɪ/ 格雷西
Gwendoline /ˈgwendəlɪn; ˋgwɛndḷɪn/ 格温德林; Gwen /gwen; gwɛn/ 格温
Hannah /ˈhænə; ˋhænə/ 汉纳
Harriet /ˈhærɪət; ˋhærɪət/ 哈丽雅特
Hazel /ˈheɪzl; ˋhezḷ/ 黑兹尔
Heather /ˈheðə(r); ˋhɛðɚ/ 希瑟
Helen /ˈhelɪn; ˋhɛlɪn/ 海伦
Henrietta /ˌhenrɪˈetə; ˌhɛnrɪˋɛtə/ 亨里埃塔
Hilary /ˈhɪlərɪ; ˋhɪlərɪ/ 希拉里
Hilda /ˈhɪldə; ˋhɪldə/ 希尔达
Ida /ˈaɪdə; ˋaɪdə/ 艾达
Ingrid /ˈɪŋgrɪd; ˋɪŋgrɪd/ 英格里德
Irene /aɪˈriːnɪ; aɪˋrin/ 艾琳
Iris /ˈaɪərɪs; ˋaɪrɪs/ 艾里斯
Isabel, (*esp Scot* 尤用于苏格兰) Isobel /ˈɪzəbel; ˋɪzə,bɛl/ 伊莎贝尔
Isabella /ˌɪzəˈbelə; ˌɪzəˋbɛlə/ 伊莎贝拉
Ivy /ˈaɪvɪ; ˋaɪvɪ/ 艾维
Jackie ⇨ Jacqueline
Jan ⇨ Janet, Janice
Jane /dʒeɪn; dʒen/ 简; Janey /ˈdʒeɪnɪ; ˋdʒenɪ/ 珍妮
Janet /ˈdʒænɪt; ˋdʒænɪt/; Janette /dʒəˈnet; dʒəˋnɛt/ 珍妮特; Jan /dʒæn; dʒæn/ 简
Janice, Janis /ˈdʒænɪs; ˋdʒænɪs/ 贾尼丝; Jan /dʒæn; dʒæn/ 简
Jacqueline /ˈdʒækəlɪn; ˋdʒækwəlɪn/ 杰奎琳; Jackie /ˈdʒækɪ; ˋdʒækɪ/ 杰基
Jean /dʒiːn; dʒin/ 琼; Jeanie /ˈdʒiːnɪ; ˋdʒinɪ/ 珍妮
Jennifer /ˈdʒenɪfə(r); ˋdʒɛnɪfɚ/ 珍妮弗; Jenny, Jennie /ˈdʒenɪ; ˋdʒɛnɪ/ 珍妮
Jessica /ˈdʒesɪkə; ˋdʒɛsɪkə/ 杰西卡; Jess /dʒes; dʒɛs/ 杰斯; Jessie /ˈdʒesɪ; ˋdʒɛsɪ/ 杰西
Jill, Jilly ⇨ Gillian
Jo ⇨ Joanna, Josephine
Joan /dʒəʊn; dʒon/ 琼
Joanna /dʒəʊˈænə; dʒoˋænə/ 乔安娜; Joanne /dʒəʊˈæn; dʒoˋæn/ 乔安妮; Jo /dʒəʊ; dʒo/ 乔
Jocelyn /ˈdʒɒslɪn; ˋdʒɑslɪn/ 乔斯林
Josephine /ˈdʒəʊzəfiːn; ˋdʒozə,fin/ 约瑟芬; Jo /dʒəʊ; dʒo/ 乔; Josie /ˈdʒəʊsɪ; ˋdʒosɪ/ 乔西

Jody /ˈdʒəʊdɪ; ˋdʒodɪ/ 乔迪
Joyce /dʒɔɪs; dʒɔɪs/ 乔伊斯
Judith /ˈdʒu:dɪθ; ˋdʒudɪθ/ 朱迪思; Judy /ˈdʒu:dɪ; ˋdʒudɪ/ 朱迪
Julia /ˈdʒu:lɪə; ˋdʒuljə/ 朱莉娅; Julie /ˈdʒu:lɪ; ˋdʒulɪ/ 朱莉
Juliet /ˈdʒu:lɪət; ˋdʒulɪət/ 朱丽叶
June /dʒu:n; dʒun/ 琼
Karen, Karin /ˈkærən; ˋkærən/ 卡林
Katherine, Catherine, (*esp US* 尤用于美国) -arine /ˈkæθrɪn; ˋkæθrɪn/ 凯瑟琳; Kathy, Cathy /ˈkæθɪ; ˋkæθɪ/ 凯西; Kate /keɪt; ket/ 凯特; Katie, Katy /ˈkeɪtɪ; ˋketɪ/ 凯蒂; Kay /keɪ; ke/ 凯; Kitty /ˈkɪtɪ; ˋkɪtɪ/ 基蒂
Kim /kɪm; kɪm/ 金
Kirsten /ˈkɜ:stɪn; ˋkɝstɪn/ 柯尔斯滕
Kitty ⇨ Katherine
Laura /ˈlɔ:rə; ˋlɔrə/ 劳拉
Lauretta, Loretta /ləˈretə; ləˋrɛtə/ 洛雷塔
Lesley /ˈlezlɪ; ˋlɛslɪ/ 莱斯利
Libby ⇨ Elizabeth
Lilian, Lillian /ˈlɪlɪən; ˋlɪlɪən/ 莉莲
Lily /ˈlɪlɪ; ˋlɪlɪ/ 莉莉
Linda /ˈlɪndə; ˋlɪndə/ 琳达
Lisa, Liza ⇨ Eliza
Livia /ˈlɪvɪə; ˋlɪvɪə/ 利维亚
Liz, Lizzie, Lizzy ⇨ Elizabeth
Lois /ˈləʊɪs; ˋlo·ɪs/ 洛伊丝
Lorna /ˈlɔ:nə; ˋlɔrnə/ 洛娜
Louise /lu:ˈi:z; luˋiz/ 路易丝; Louisa /lu:ˈi:zə; luˋizə/ 路易莎
Lucia /ˈlu:sɪə, *also* 亦读作 ˈlu:ʃə; ˋluʃə/ 露西亚
Lucinda /lu:ˈsɪndə; luˋsɪndə/ 露辛达; Cindy /ˈsɪndɪ; ˋsɪndɪ/ 辛迪
Lucy /ˈlu:sɪ; ˋlusɪ/ 露西
Lydia /ˈlɪdɪə; ˋlɪdɪə/ 莉迪亚
Lyn(n) /lɪn; lɪn/ 林恩
Mabel /ˈmeɪbl; ˋmebl̩/ 梅布尔
Madeleine /ˈmædəlɪn; ˋmædl̩ɪn/ 马德琳
Madge, Maggie ⇨ Margaret
Maisie /ˈmeɪzɪ; ˋmezɪ/ 梅西
Mandy ⇨ Amanda
Marcia /ˈmɑ:sɪə, *also* 亦读作 ˈmɑ:ʃə; ˋmɑrʃə/ 马西娅; Marcie /ˈmɑ:sɪ; ˋmɑrsɪ/ 马西
Margaret /ˈmɑ:grɪt; ˋmɑrgrɪt/ 玛格丽特; Madge /mædʒ; mædʒ/ 马奇; Maggie /ˈmægɪ; ˋmægɪ/ 玛吉; (*esp Scot* 尤用于苏格兰) Meg /meg; mɛg/ 梅格; Peg /peg; pɛg/ 佩格; Peggie, Peggy /ˈpegɪ; ˋpɛgɪ/ 佩吉
Margery, Marjorie /ˈmɑ:dʒərɪ; ˋmɑrdʒərɪ/ 马杰里; Margie /ˈmɑ:dʒɪ; ˋmɑrdʒɪ/ 玛吉
Maria /məˈrɪə, *also* 亦读作 məˈraɪə; məˋriə, məˋraɪə/ 玛丽亚
Marian, Marion /ˈmærɪən; ˋmærɪən/ 玛丽安（马里恩）
Marie /məˈri:, *also* 亦读作 ˈmɑ:rɪ; məˋri, ˋmɑrɪ/ 玛丽
Marilyn /ˈmærəlɪn; ˋmærəlɪn/ 玛里琳
Marion ⇨ Marian
Marjorie ⇨ Margery
Marlene /ˈmɑ:li:n; ˋmɑrlin/ 马林
Martha /ˈmɑ:θə; ˋmɑrθə/ 马莎
Martina /mɑ:ˈti:nə; mɑrˋtinə/ 马丁娜
Mary /ˈmeərɪ; ˋmɛrɪ/ 玛丽
Maud /mɔ:d; mɔd/ 莫德
Maureen /ˈmɔ:ri:n; mɔˋrin/ 莫林
Mavis /ˈmeɪvɪs; ˋmevɪs/ 梅维斯
Meg ⇨ Margaret
Melanie /ˈmelənɪ; ˋmɛlənɪ/ 梅拉尼
Melinda /məˈlɪndə; məˋlɪndə/ 梅林达
Michelle /mɪˈʃel; mɪˋʃɛl/ 米歇尔
Mildred /ˈmɪldrɪd; ˋmɪldrɪd/ 米尔德里德
Millicent /ˈmɪlɪsnt; ˋmɪləsn̩t/ 米利森特; Millie, Milly /ˈmɪlɪ; ˋmɪlɪ/ 米利
Miranda /mɪˈrændə; məˋrændə/ 米兰达
Miriam /ˈmɪrɪəm; ˋmɪrɪəm/ 米里亚姆
Moira /ˈmɔɪrə; ˋmɔɪrə/ 莫伊拉
Molly /ˈmɒlɪ; ˋmɑlɪ/ 莫利
Monica /ˈmɒnɪkə; ˋmɑnɪkə/ 莫妮卡
Muriel /ˈmjʊərɪəl; ˋmjurɪəl/ 缪里尔
Nadia /ˈnɑ:dɪə; ˋnɑdɪə/ 纳迪亚
Nancy /ˈnænsɪ; ˋnænsɪ/ 南希; Nan /næn; næn/ 南
Naomi /ˈneɪəmɪ; ˋneə,mɪ/ 内奥米
Natalie /ˈnætəlɪ; ˋnætl̩ɪ/ 纳塔利
Natasha /nəˈtæʃə; nəˋtæʃə/ 纳塔莎
Nell /nel; nɛl/ 内尔; Nellie, Nelly /ˈnelɪ; ˋnɛlɪ/ 内利
Nicola /ˈnɪkələ; ˋnɪkl̩ə/ 尼古拉; Nicky /ˈnɪkɪ; ˋnɪkɪ/ 尼基
Nora /ˈnɔ:rə; ˋnɔrə/ 诺拉
Norma /ˈnɔ:mə; ˋnɔrmə/ 诺尔马
Olive /ˈɒlɪv; ˋɑlɪv/ 奥利夫
Olivia /əˈlɪvɪə; oˋlɪvɪə/ 奥利维亚
Pamela /ˈpæmələ; ˋpæmələ/ 帕梅拉; Pam /pæm; pæm/ 帕姆
Pat ⇨ Patricia
Patience /ˈpeɪʃns; ˋpeʃəns/ 佩兴斯
Patricia /pəˈtrɪʃə; pəˋtrɪʃə/ 帕特里夏; Pat /pæt; pæt/ 帕特; Patti, Pattie, Patty /ˈpætɪ; ˋpætɪ/ 帕蒂; Tricia /ˈtrɪʃə; ˋtrɪʃə/ 特里西娅
Paula /ˈpɔ:lə; ˋpɔlə/ 葆拉
Pauline /ˈpɔ:li:n; pɔˋlin/ 波林
Peg, Peggie, Peggy ⇨ Margaret

Penelope /pəˈneləpɪ; pəˋnɛləpɪ/ 佩内洛普; Penny /ˈpenɪ; ˋpɛnɪ/ 彭尼
Philippa /ˈfɪlɪpə; ˋfɪlɪpə/ 菲利帕
Phoebe /ˈfi:bɪ; ˋfibɪ/ 菲比
Phyllis /ˈfɪlɪs; ˋfɪlɪs/ 菲利斯
Polly /ˈpɒlɪ; ˋpɑlɪ/ 波利; Poll /pɒl; pɑl/ 波尔
Priscilla /prɪˈsɪlə; prɪˋsɪlə/ 普里西拉; Cilla /ˈsɪlə; ˋsɪlə/ 西拉
Prudence /ˈpru:dns; ˋprudṇs/ 普鲁登斯; Pru, Prue /pru:; pru/ 普鲁
Rachel /ˈreɪtʃl; ˋretʃəl/ 雷切尔
Rebecca /rɪˈbekə; rɪˋbɛkə/ 丽贝卡; Becky /ˈbekɪ; ˋbɛkɪ/ 贝基
Rhoda /ˈrəʊdə; ˋrodə/ 罗达
Rita /ˈri:tə; ˋritə/ 丽塔
Roberta /rəˈbɜ:tə; roˋbɝtə/ 罗伯塔
Robin /ˈrɒbɪn; ˋrɑbɪn/ 罗宾
Rosalie /ˈrəʊzəlɪ, *also* 亦读作 ˈrɒzəlɪ; ˋrozəlɪ/ 罗莎莉
Rosalind /ˈrɒzəlɪnd; ˋrɑzlɪnd/ 罗莎琳德; Rosalyn /ˈrɒzəlɪn; ˋrɑzlɪn/ 罗莎琳
Rose /rəʊz; roz/; Rosie /ˈrəʊzɪ; ˋrozɪ/ 罗斯
Rosemary /ˈrəʊzmərɪ; ˋroz,mɛrɪ/ 罗斯玛丽; Rosie /ˈrəʊzɪ; ˋrozɪ/ 罗斯
Ruth /ru:θ; ruθ/ 鲁思
Sadie ⇨ Sarah
Sally /ˈsælɪ; ˋsælɪ/ 萨莉; Sal /sæl; sæl/ 萨尔
Samantha /səˈmænθə; səˋmænθə/ 萨曼莎; Sam /sæm; sæm/ 萨姆
Sandra /ˈsɑ:ndrə; *US* 美式英语读作 ˈsæn-; ˋsændrə/ 桑德拉; Sandy /ˈsændɪ; ˋsændɪ/ 桑迪
Sandy ⇨ Alexandra, Sandra
Sarah, Sara /ˈseərə; ˋsɛrə/ 萨拉; Sadie /ˈseɪdɪ; ˋsedɪ/ 塞迪
Sharon /ˈʃærən; ˋʃærən/ 沙伦
Sheila, Shelagh /ˈʃi:lə; ˋʃilə/ 希拉
Shirley /ˈʃɜ:lɪ; ˋʃɝlɪ/ 雪莉
Sibyl ⇨ Sybil
Silvia, Sylvia /ˈsɪlvɪə; ˋsɪlvɪə/ 西尔维亚; Sylvie /ˈsɪlvɪ; ˋsɪlvɪ/ 西尔维
Sonia /ˈsɒnɪə, *also* 亦读作 ˈsəʊnɪə; ˋsonɪə/ 索尼亚
Sophia /səˈfaɪə; səˋfaɪə/ 索菲娅
Sophie, Sophy /ˈsəʊfɪ; ˋsofɪ/ 索菲
Stella /ˈstelə; ˋstɛlə/ 斯特拉
Stephanie /ˈstefənɪ; ˋstɛfənɪ/ 斯蒂法妮
Susan /ˈsu:zn; ˋsuzṇ/ 苏珊; Sue /su:; su/ 休; Susie, Suzy /ˈsu:zɪ; ˋsuzɪ/ 苏西
Susanna, Susannah /su:ˈzænə; suˋzænə/ 苏珊娜; Suzanne /su:ˈzæn; suˋzæn/ 苏珊; Susie, Suzy /ˈsu:zɪ; ˋsuzɪ/ 苏西
Sybil, Sibyl /ˈsɪbəl; ˋsɪbḷ/ 西比尔
Sylvia, Sylvie ⇨ Silvia
Teresa, Theresa /təˈri:zə; təˋrisə/ 特里萨; Tess /tes; tɛs/ 特斯; Tessa /ˈtesə; ˋtɛsə/ 特萨; (*US* 用于美国) Terri /ˈterɪ; ˋtɛrɪ/ 特里
Thelma /ˈθelmə; ˋθɛlmə/ 塞尔马
Tina ⇨ Christina
Toni /ˈtəʊnɪ; ˋtonɪ/ 托妮 (*esp US* 尤用于美国)
Tracy, Tracey /ˈtreɪsɪ; ˋtresɪ/ 特蕾西
Tricia ⇨ Patricia
Trudie, Trudy /ˈtru:dɪ; ˋtrudɪ/ 特鲁迪
Ursula /ˈɜ:sjʊlə; ˋɝsjʊlə/ 厄休拉
Valerie /ˈvælərɪ; ˋvælərɪ/ 瓦莱丽; Val /væl; væl/ 瓦尔
Vanessa /vəˈnesə; vəˋnɛsə/ 瓦内萨
Vera /ˈvɪərə; ˋvɪrə/ 薇拉
Veronica /vəˈrɒnɪkə; vəˋrɑnɪkə/ 维朗妮卡
Victoria /vɪkˈtɔ:rɪə; vɪkˋtɔrɪə/ 维多利亚; Vicki, Vickie, Vicky, Vikki /ˈvɪkɪ; ˋvɪkɪ/ 维基
Viola /ˈvaɪələ; ˋvaɪələ/ 维奥拉
Violet /ˈvaɪələt; ˋvaɪəlɪt/ 瓦奥莱特
Virginia /vəˈdʒɪnɪə; vɚˋdʒɪnjə/ 弗吉尼亚; Ginny /ˈdʒɪnɪ; ˋdʒɪnɪ/ 吉尼
Vivien, Vivienne /ˈvɪvɪən; ˋvɪvɪən/ 维维恩; Viv /vɪv; vɪv/ 维维
Wendy /ˈwendɪ; ˋwɛndɪ/ 温迪
Winifred /ˈwɪnɪfrɪd; ˋwɪnəfrɪd/ 威尼弗雷德; Winnie /ˈwɪnɪ; ˋwɪnɪ/ 威尼
Yvonne /ɪˈvɒn; ɪˋvɑn/ 伊冯娜
Zoe /ˈzəʊɪ; ˋzo·ɪ/ 佐伊

Male Names 男子名

Abraham /ˈeɪbrəhæm; ˋebrə,hæm/ 亚伯拉罕; Abe /eɪb; eb/ 阿贝
Adam /ˈædəm; ˋædəm/ 亚当
Adrian /ˈeɪdrɪən; ˋedrɪən/ 阿德里安
Alan, Allan, Allen /ˈælən; ˋælən/ 艾伦; Al /æl; æl/ 阿尔
Albert /ˈælbət; ˋælbɚt/ 艾伯特; Al /æl; æl/ 阿尔; Bert /bɜ:t; bɝt/ 伯特
Alexander /ˌælɪgˈzɑ:ndə(r); *US* 美式英语读作 -ˈzæn-; ,ælɪgˋzændɚ/ 亚历山大; Alec /ˈælɪk; ˋælɪk/ 亚历克; Alex /ˈælɪks; ˋælɪks/ 亚历克斯; Sandy /ˈsændɪ; ˋsændɪ/ 桑迪
Alfred /ˈælfrɪd; ˋælfrɪd/ 艾尔弗雷德; Alf /ælf; ælf/ 阿尔夫; Alfie /ˈælfɪ; ˋælfɪ/ 阿尔菲
Alistair, Alisdair, Alas- /ˈælɪstə(r); ˋælɪstɚ/ 阿利斯泰尔 (*Scot* 用于苏格兰)

Allan, Allen ⇨ Alan
Alvin /ˈælvɪn; ˋælvɪn/ 阿尔文
Andrew /ˈændruː; ˋændru/ 安德鲁; Andy /ˈændɪ; ˋændɪ/ 安迪
Angus /ˈæŋgəs; ˋæŋgəs/ 安格斯 (*Scot* 用于苏格兰)
Anthony, Antony /ˈæntənɪ; ˋæntənɪ/ 安东尼; Tony /ˈtəʊnɪ; ˋtonɪ/ 托尼
Archibald /ˈɑːtʃɪbɔːld; ˋɑrtʃə,bɔld/ 阿奇博尔德; Archie, Archy /ˈɑːtʃɪ; ˋɑrtʃɪ/ 阿奇
Arnold /ˈɑːnəld; ˋɑrnḷd/ 阿诺德
Arthur /ˈɑːθə(r); ˋɑrθɚ/ 阿瑟
Auberon /ˈɔːbərɒn; ˋɔbə,rɑn/ 奥伯伦
Aubrey /ˈɔːbrɪ; ˋɔbrɪ/ 奥布里
Barnaby /ˈbɑːnəbɪ; ˋbɑrnəbɪ/ 巴纳比
Barry /ˈbærɪ; ˋbærɪ/ 巴里
Bartholomew /bɑːˈθɒləmjuː; bɑrˋθɑlə,mju/ 巴塞洛缪
Basil /ˈbæzl; ˋbæzḷ/ 巴兹尔
Benjamin /ˈbendʒəmɪn; ˋbɛndʒəmən/ 本杰明; Ben /ben; bɛn/ 本
Bernard /ˈbɜːnəd; ˋbɝnɚd/ 伯纳德; Bernie /ˈbɜːnɪ; ˋbɝnɪ/ 伯尼
Bert ⇨ Albert, Gilbert, Herbert, Hubert
Bill, Billy ⇨ William
Bob, Bobby ⇨ Robert
Boris /ˈbɒrɪs; ˋbɔrɪs/ 鲍里斯
Bradford /ˈbrædfəd; ˋbrædfɚd/ 布拉德福德; Brad /bræd; bræd/ 布拉德 (*esp US* 尤用于美国)
Brendan /ˈbrendən; ˋbrɛndən/ 布伦丹 (*Irish* 用于爱尔兰)
Brian, Bryan /ˈbraɪən; ˋbraɪən/ 布赖恩
Bruce /bruːs; brus/ 布鲁斯
Bud /bʌd; bʌd/ 巴德 (*US* 用于美国)
Carl /kɑːl; kɑrl/ 卡尔
Cecil /ˈsesl; *US* 美式英语读作 ˈsiːsl; ˋsisḷ/ 塞西尔
Cedric /ˈsedrɪk; ˋsɛdrɪk/ 锡德里克
Charles /tʃɑːlz; tʃɑrlz/ 查尔斯; Charlie /ˈtʃɑːlɪ; ˋtʃɑrlɪ/ 查利; Chas /tʃæz; tʃæz/ 查斯; Chuck /tʃʌk; tʃʌk/ 查克 (*US* 用于美国)
Christopher /ˈkrɪstəfə(r); ˋkrɪstəfɚ/ 克里斯托弗; Chris /krɪs; krɪs/ 克里斯; Kit /kɪt; kɪt/ 基特
Chuck ⇨ Charles
Clarence /ˈklærəns; ˋklærəns/ 克拉伦斯
Clark /klɑːk; klɑrk/ 克拉克 (*esp US* 尤用于美国)
Claude, Claud /klɔːd; klɔd/ 克劳德
Clement /ˈklemənt; ˋklɛmənt/ 克莱门特
Clifford /ˈklɪfəd; ˋklɪfɚd/ 克利福德; Cliff /klɪf; klɪf/ 克利夫
Clint /klɪnt; klɪnt/ 克林特 (*esp US* 尤用于美国)
Clive /klaɪv; klaɪv/ 克莱夫
Clyde /klaɪd; klaɪd/ 克莱德 (*esp US* 尤用于美国)
Colin /ˈkɒlɪn; ˋkɑlɪn/ 科林
Craig /kreɪg; kreg/ 克雷格
Curt /kɜːt; kɝt/ 柯特
Cyril /ˈsɪrəl; ˋsɪrəl/ 西里尔
Dale /deɪl; del/ 戴尔 (*esp US* 尤用于美国)
Daniel /ˈdænɪəl; ˋdænjəl/ 丹尼尔; Dan /dæn; dæn/ 丹; Danny /ˈdænɪ; ˋdænɪ/ 丹尼
Darrell /ˈdærəl; ˋdærəl/ 达雷尔
Darren /ˈdærən; ˋdærən/ 达伦 (*esp US* 尤用于美国)
David /ˈdeɪvɪd; ˋdevɪd/ 戴维; Dave /deɪv; dev/ 戴夫
Dean /diːn; din/ 迪安
Dennis, Denis /ˈdenɪs; ˋdɛnɪs/ 丹尼斯
Derek /ˈderɪk; ˋdɛrɪk/ 德里克
Dermot /ˈdɜːmɒt; ˋdɝmɑt/ 德莫特 (*Irish* 用于爱尔兰)
Desmond /ˈdezmənd; ˋdɛzmənd/ 德斯蒙德; Des /dez; dɛz/ 德斯
Dick, Dickie, Dicky ⇨ Richard
Dirk /dɜːk; dɝk/ 德克
Dominic /ˈdɒmɪnɪk; ˋdɑmənɪk/ 多米尼克
Donald /ˈdɒnəld; ˋdɑnḷd/ 唐纳德; Don /dɒn; dɑn/ 唐
Douglas /ˈdʌgləs; ˋdʌgləs/ 道格拉斯; Doug /dʌg; dʌg/ 道格
Duane /duːˈeɪn; duˋen/; Dwane /dweɪn; dwen/ 杜安 (*esp US* 尤用于美国)
Dudley /ˈdʌdlɪ; ˋdʌdlɪ/ 达德利; Dud /dʌd; dʌd/ 达德
Duncan /ˈdʌŋkən; ˋdʌŋkən/ 邓肯
Dustin /ˈdʌstɪn; ˋdʌstɪn/ 达斯廷
Dwight /dwaɪt; dwaɪt/ 德怀特 (*esp US* 尤用于美国)
Eamonn, Eamon /ˈeɪmən; ˋɪəmən/ 埃蒙 (*Irish* 用于爱尔兰)
Ed, Eddie, Eddy ⇨ Edward
Edgar /ˈedgə(r); ˋɛdgɚ/ 埃德加
Edmund, Edmond /ˈedmənd; ˋɛdmənd/ 埃德蒙
Edward /ˈedwəd; ˋɛdwɚd/ 爱德华; Ed /ed; ɛd/ 埃德; Eddie, Eddy /ˈedɪ; ˋɛdɪ/ 埃迪; Ted /ted; tɛd/ 特德; Teddy /ˈtedɪ; ˋtɛdɪ/ 特迪; Ned /ned; nɛd/ 内德; Neddy /ˈnedɪ; ˋnɛdɪ/ 内迪
Edwin /ˈedwɪn; ˋɛdwɪn/ 埃德温
Elmer /ˈelmə(r); ˋɛlmɚ/ 埃尔默 (*US* 用于美国)
Elroy /ˈelrɔɪ; ˋɛlrɔɪ / 埃尔罗伊 (*US* 用于美国)

Emlyn /ˈemlɪn; ˋɛmlɪn/ 埃姆林 (*Welsh* 用于威尔士)
Enoch /ˈi:nɒk; ˋinək/ 伊诺克
Eric /ˈerɪk; ˋɛrɪk/ 埃里克
Ernest /ˈɜ:nɪst; ˋɝnɪst/ 欧内斯特
Errol /ˈerəl; ˋɛrəl/ 埃罗尔
Eugene /ju:ˈdʒi:n; juˋdʒin/ 尤金; Gene /dʒi:n; dʒin/ 吉恩 (*US* 用于美国)
Felix /ˈfi:lɪks; ˋfilɪks/ 费利克斯
Ferdinand /ˈfɜ:dɪnænd; ˋfɝdn̩ˌænd/ 费迪南德
Fergus /ˈfɜ:gəs; ˋfɝgəs/ 弗格斯 (*Scot or Irish* 用于苏格兰或爱尔兰)
Floyd /flɔɪd; flɔɪd/ 弗洛伊德
Francis /ˈfrɑ:nsɪs; *US* 美式英语读作 ˈfræn-; ˋfrænsɪs/ 弗朗西斯; Frank /fræŋk; fræŋk/ 弗兰克
Frank /fræŋk; fræŋk/ 弗兰克; Frankie /ˈfræŋkɪ; ˋfræŋkɪ/ 弗兰基
Frederick /ˈfredrɪk; ˋfrɛdrɪk/ 弗雷德里克; Fred /fred; frɛd/ 弗雷德; Freddie, Freddy /ˈfredɪ; ˋfrɛdɪ/ 弗雷迪
Gabriel /ˈgeɪbrɪəl; ˋgebrɪəl/ 加布里埃尔
Gareth /ˈgærəθ; ˋgærəθ/ 加雷思 (*esp Welsh* 尤用于威尔士)
Gary /ˈgærɪ; ˋgærɪ/ 加里
Gavin /ˈgævɪn; ˋgævɪn/ 加文
Gene ⇨ Eugene
Geoffrey, Jeffrey /ˈdʒefrɪ; ˋdʒɛfrɪ/ 杰弗里; Geoff, Jeff /dʒef; dʒɛf/ 杰夫
George /dʒɔ:dʒ; dʒɔrdʒ/ 乔治
Geraint /ˈgeraɪnt; dʒəˋrent/ 杰伦特 (*Welsh* 用于威尔士)
Gerald /ˈdʒerəld; ˋdʒɛrəld/ 杰拉尔德; Gerry, Jerry /ˈdʒerɪ; ˋdʒɛrɪ/ 格里; 杰里
Gerard /ˈdʒerɑ:d; dʒəˋrɑrd/ 杰勒德
Gilbert /ˈgɪlbət; ˋgɪlbɚt/ 吉尔伯特; Bert /bɜ:t; bɝt/ 伯特
Giles /dʒaɪlz; dʒaɪlz/ 贾尔斯
Glen /glen; glɛn/ 格伦
Godfrey /ˈgɒdfrɪ; ˋgɑdfrɪ/ 戈弗雷
Gordon /ˈgɔ:dn; ˋgɔrdn̩/ 戈登
Graham, Grahame, Graeme /ˈgreɪəm; ˋgreəm/ 格雷厄姆; 格雷姆
Gregory /ˈgregərɪ; ˋgrɛgərɪ/ 格雷戈里; Greg /greg; grɛg/ 格雷格
Guy /gaɪ; gaɪ/ 盖伊
Hal, Hank ⇨ Henry
Harold /ˈhærəld; ˋhærəld/ 哈罗德
Henry /ˈhenrɪ; ˋhɛnrɪ/ 亨利; Harry /ˈhærɪ; ˋhærɪ/ 哈里; Hal /hæl; hæl/ 哈尔; Hank /hæŋk; hæŋk/ 汉克 (*US* 用于美国)
Herbert /ˈhɜ:bət; ˋhɝbɚt/ 赫伯特; Bert /bɜ:t; bɝt/ 伯特; Herb /hɜ:b; hɝb/ 赫布
Horace /ˈhɒrɪs; *US* 美式英语读作 ˈhɔ:rəs; ˋhɔrəs/ 霍勒斯
Howard /ˈhaʊəd; ˋhaʊɚd/ 霍华德
Hubert /ˈhju:bət; ˋhjubɚt/ 休伯特; Bert /bɜ:t; bɝt/ 伯特
Hugh /hju:; hju/ 休
Hugo /ˈhju:gəʊ; ˋhjugo/ 雨果
Humphrey /ˈhʌmfrɪ; ˋhʌmfrɪ/ 汉弗莱
Ian /ˈi:ən; ˋiən/ 伊恩
Isaac /ˈaɪzək; ˋaɪzək/ 艾萨克
Ivan /ˈaɪvən; ˋaɪvən/ 伊凡
Ivor /ˈaɪvə(r); ˋaɪvɚ/ 艾弗
Jack ⇨ John
Jacob /ˈdʒeɪkəb; ˋdʒekəb/ 雅各布; Jake /dʒeɪk; dʒek/ 杰克
Jake ⇨ Jacob, John
James /dʒeɪmz; dʒemz/ 詹姆斯; Jim /dʒɪm; dʒɪm/ 吉姆; Jimmy /ˈdʒɪmɪ; ˋdʒɪmɪ/ 吉米; Jamie /ˈdʒeɪmɪ; ˋdʒemɪ/ 杰米 (*Scot* 用于苏格兰)
Jason /ˈdʒeɪsn; ˋdʒesn̩/ 贾森
Jasper /ˈdʒæspə(r); ˋdʒæspɚ/ 贾斯珀
Jed /dʒed; dʒɛd/ 杰德 (*esp US* 尤用于美国)
Jeff, Jeffrey ⇨ Geoffrey
Jeremy /ˈdʒerəmɪ; ˋdʒɛrəmɪ/ 杰里米; Jerry /ˈdʒerɪ; ˋdʒɛrɪ/ 杰里
Jerome /dʒəˈrəʊm; dʒəˋrom/ 杰罗姆
Jerry ⇨ Gerald, Jeremy
Jesse /ˈdʒesɪ; ˋdʒɛsɪ/ 杰西 (*esp US* 尤用于美国)
Jim, Jimmy ⇨ James
Jock ⇨ John
Joe ⇨ Joseph
John /dʒɒn; dʒɑn/ 约翰; Johnny /ˈdʒɒnɪ; ˋdʒɑnɪ/ 约翰尼; Jack /dʒæk; dʒæk/ 杰克; Jake /dʒeɪk; dʒek/ 杰克; Jock /dʒɒk; dʒɑk/ 乔克 (*Scot* 用于苏格兰)
Jonathan /ˈdʒɒnəθən; ˋdʒɑnəθən/ 乔纳森; Jon /dʒɒn; dʒɑn/ 乔恩
Joseph /ˈdʒəʊzɪf; ˋdʒozəf/ 约瑟夫; Joe /dʒəʊ; dʒo/ 乔
Julian /ˈdʒu:lɪən; ˋdʒuljən/ 朱利安
Justin /ˈdʒʌstɪn; ˋdʒʌstɪn/ 贾斯廷
Keith /ki:θ; kiθ/ 基思
Kenneth /ˈkenɪθ; ˋkɛnɪθ/ 肯尼思; Ken /ken; kɛn/ 肯; Kenny /ˈkenɪ; ˋkɛnɪ/ 肯尼
Kevin /ˈkevɪn; ˋkɛvɪn/ 凯文; Kev /kev; kɛv/ 凯夫
Kirk /kɜ:k; kɝk/ 柯克
Kit ⇨ Christopher
Lance /lɑ:ns; *US* 美式英语读作 læns; læns/ 兰斯

Laurence, Lawrence /ˈlɒrəns; *US* 美式英语读作 ˈlɔ:r-; ˋlɔrəns/ 劳伦斯; Larry /ˈlærɪ; ˋlærɪ/ 拉里; Laurie /ˈlɒrɪ; *US* 美式英语读作 ˈlɔ:rɪ; lɔrɪ/ 劳里
Len, Lenny ⇨ Leonard
Leo /ˈli:əʊ; ˋlio/ 利奥
Leonard /ˈlenəd; ˋlɛnɚd/ 伦纳德; Len /len; lɛn/ 莱恩; Lenny /ˈlenɪ; ˋlɛnɪ/ 伦尼
Leslie /ˈlezlɪ; ˋlɛslɪ/ 莱斯利; Les /lez; lɛs/ 莱斯
Lester /ˈlestə(r); ˋlɛstɚ/ 莱斯特
Lewis /ˈlu:ɪs; ˋluɪs/ 刘易斯; Lew /lu:; lu/ 卢
Liam /ˈli:əm; ˋliəm/ 利亚姆 (*Irish* 用于爱尔兰)
Lionel /ˈlaɪənl; ˋlaɪənl̩/ 莱昂内尔
Louis /ˈlu:ɪ; *US* 美式英语读作 ˈlu:ɪs; ˋluɪs/ 路易斯; Lou /lu:; lu/ 卢 (*esp US* 尤用于美国)
Luke /lu:k; luk/ 卢克
Malcolm /ˈmælkəm; ˋmælkəm/ 马尔科姆
Mark /mɑ:k; mɑrk/ 马克
Martin /ˈmɑ:tɪn; *US* 美式英语读作 ˈmɑ:rtn; ˋmɑrtn/ 马丁; Marty /ˈmɑ:tɪ; ˋmɑrtɪ/ 马蒂
Matthew /ˈmæθju:; ˋ mæθju/ 马修; Matt /mæt; mæt/ 马特
Maurice, Morris /ˈmɒrɪs; *US* 美式英语读作 ˈmɔ:r-; ˋmɔrɪs/ 莫里斯
Max /mæks; mæks/ 马克斯
Mervyn /ˈmɜ:vɪn; ˋmɝvɪn/ 默文
Michael /ˈmaɪkl; ˋmaɪkl̩/ 迈克尔; Mike /maɪk; maɪk/ 迈克; Mick /mɪk; mɪk/ 米克; Micky, Mickey /ˈmɪkɪ; ˋmɪkɪ/ 米基
Miles, Myles /maɪlz; maɪlz/ 迈尔斯
Mitchell /ˈmɪtʃl; ˋmɪtʃəl/ 米切尔; Mitch /mɪtʃ; mɪtʃ/ 米奇
Morris ⇨ Maurice
Mort /mɔ:t; mɔrt/ 莫特 (*US* 用于美国)
Murray /ˈmʌrɪ; ˋmʌrɪ/ 默里 (*esp Scot* 尤用于苏格兰)
Myles ⇨ Miles
Nathan /ˈneɪθən; ˋneθən/ 内森; Nat /næt; næt/ 纳特
Nathaniel /nəˈθænɪəl; nəˋθænjəl/ 纳撒尼尔; Nat /næt; næt/ 纳特
Neal ⇨ Neil
Ned, Neddy ⇨ Edward
Neil, Neal /ni:l; nil/ 尼尔
Nicholas, Nicolas /ˈnɪkələs; *US* 美式英语读作 ˈnɪkləs; ˋnɪkləs/ 尼古拉斯; Nick /nɪk; nɪk/ 尼克; Nicky /ˈnɪkɪ; ˋnɪkɪ/ 尼基
Nigel /ˈnaɪdʒl; ˋnaɪdʒəl/ 奈杰尔
Noel /ˈnəʊəl; ˋnoəl/ 诺埃尔
Norman /ˈnɔ:mən; ˋnɔrmən/ 诺曼; Norm /nɔ:m; nɔrm/ 诺姆
Oliver /ˈɒlɪvə(r); ˋɑləvɚ/ 奥利弗; Ollie /ˈɒlɪ; ˋɑlɪ/ 奥利
Oscar /ˈɒskə(r); ˋɔskɚ/ 奥斯卡
Oswald /ˈɒzwəld; ˋɑzwəld/ 奥斯瓦尔德; Oz /ɒz; ɑz/ 奥兹; Ozzie /ˈɒzɪ; ˋɑzɪ/ 奥齐
Owen /ˈəʊɪn; ˋo·ɪn/ 欧文 (*Welsh* 用于威尔士)
Oz, Ozzie ⇨ Oswald
Patrick /ˈpætrɪk; ˋpætrɪk/ 帕特里克 (*esp Irish* 尤用于爱尔兰); Pat /pæt; pæt/ 帕特; Paddy /ˈpædɪ; ˋpædɪ/ 帕迪
Paul /pɔ:l; pɔl/ 保罗
Percy /ˈpɜ:sɪ; ˋpɝsɪ/ 珀西
Peter /ˈpi:tə(r); ˋpitɚ/ 彼得; Pete /pi:t; pit/ 皮特
Philip /ˈfɪlɪp; ˋfɪləp/ 菲利普; Phil /fɪl; fɪl/ 菲尔
Quentin /ˈkwentɪn; *US* 美式英语读作 -tn; ˋkwɛntn̩/; Quintin /ˈkwɪntɪn; *US* 美式英语读作 -tn; ˋkwɪntn/ 昆廷
Ralph /rælf; *also, in British use,* 英式英语亦读作 reɪf; rælf/ 拉尔夫
Randolph, Randolf /ˈrændɒlf; ˋrændɑlf/ 伦道夫; Randy /ˈrændɪ; ˋrændɪ/ 兰迪 (*esp US* 尤用于美国)
Raphael /ˈræfeɪl; ˋræfɪəl/ 拉斐尔
Raymond /ˈreɪmənd; ˋremənd/ 雷蒙德; Ray /reɪ; re/ 雷
Reginald /ˈredʒɪnəld; ˋrɛdʒɪnl̩d/ 雷金纳德; Reg /redʒ; rɛdʒ/; Reggie /ˈredʒɪ; ˋrɛdʒɪ/ 雷吉
Rex /reks; rɛks/ 雷克斯
Richard /ˈrɪtʃəd; ˋrɪtʃɚd/ 理查德; Dick /dɪk; dɪk/ 迪克; Dickie, Dicky /ˈdɪkɪ; ˋdɪkɪ/ 迪基; Rick /rɪk; rɪk/ 里克; Ricky /ˈrɪkɪ; ˋrɪkɪ/ 里基; Richie, Ritchie /ˈrɪtʃɪ; ˋrɪtʃɪ/ 里奇
Robert /ˈrɒbət; ˋrɑbɚt/ 罗伯特; Rob /rɒb; rɑb/ 罗布; Robbie /ˈrɒbɪ; ˋrɑbɪ/ 罗比; Bob /bɒb; bɑb/ 鲍勃; Bobby /ˈbɒbɪ; ˋbɑbɪ/ 博比
Robin /ˈrɒbɪn; ˋrɑbɪn/ 罗宾
Roderick /ˈrɒdrɪk; ˋrɑdrɪk/ 罗德里克; Rod /rɒd; rɑd/ 罗德
Rodge ⇨ Roger
Rodney /ˈrɒdnɪ; ˋrɑdnɪ/ 罗德尼; Rod /rɒd; rɑd/ 罗德
Roger /ˈrɒdʒə(r); ˋrɑdʒɚ/ 罗杰; Rodge /rɒdʒ; rɑdʒ/ 罗吉
Ronald /ˈrɒnəld; ˋrɑnl̩d/ 罗纳德; Ron /rɒn; rɑn/ 罗恩; Ronnie /ˈrɒnɪ; ˋrɑnɪ/ 龙尼
Rory /ˈrɔ:rɪ; ˋrɔrɪ/ 罗里 (*Scot or Irish* 用于苏格兰或爱尔兰)
Roy /rɔɪ; rɔɪ/ 罗伊
Rudolph, Rudolf /ˈru:dɒlf; ˋrudɑlf/ 鲁道夫
Rufus /ˈru:fəs; ˋrufəs/ 鲁弗斯
Rupert /ˈru:pət; ˋrupɚt/ 鲁珀特

Russell /ˈrʌsl; ˋrʌsl̩/ 拉塞尔; Russ /rʌs; rʌs/ 拉斯
Samuel /ˈsæmjʊəl; ˋsæmjuəl/ 塞缪尔; Sam /sæm; sæm/ 萨姆; Sammy /ˈsæmɪ; ˋsæmɪ/ 萨米
Sandy ⇨ Alexander
Scott /skɒt; skɑt/ 斯科特
Seamas, Seamus /ˈʃeɪməs; ˋʃeməs/ 谢默斯 (*Irish* 用于爱尔兰)
Sean /ʃɔ:n; ʃɔn/ 肖恩 (*Irish or Scot* 用于爱尔兰或苏格兰)
Sebastian /sɪˈbæstɪən; sɪˋbæstʃən/ 塞巴斯蒂安; Seb /seb; sɛb/ 塞布
Sidney, Sydney /ˈsɪdnɪ; ˋsɪdnɪ/ 悉尼; Sid /sɪd; sɪd/ 锡德
Simon /ˈsaɪmən; ˋsaɪmən/ 西蒙
Stanley /ˈstænlɪ; ˋstænlɪ/ 斯坦利; Stan /stæn; stæn/ 斯坦
Stephen, Steven /ˈsti:vn; ˋstivən/ 斯蒂芬; Steve /sti:v; stiv/ 史蒂夫
Stewart, Stuart /ˈstju:ət; *US* 美式英语读作 ˈstu:ərt; ˋstuɚt/ 斯图尔特
Ted, Teddy ⇨ Edward
Terence /ˈterəns; ˋtɛrəns/ 特伦斯; Terry /ˈterɪ; ˋtɛrɪ/ 特里; Tel /tel; tɛl/ 特尔
Theodore /ˈθi:ədɔ:(r); ˋθiə,dɔr/ 西奥多; Theo /ˈθi:əʊ; ˋθio/ 西奥
Thomas /ˈtɒməs; ˋtɑməs/ 托马斯; Tom /tɒm; tɑm/ 汤姆; Tommy /ˈtɒmɪ; ˋtɑmɪ/ 汤米
Timothy /ˈtɪməθɪ; ˋtɪməθɪ/ 蒂莫西; Tim /tɪm; tɪm/ 蒂姆; Timmy /ˈtɪmɪ; ˋtɪmɪ/ 蒂米
Toby /ˈtəʊbɪ; ˋtobɪ/ 托比
Tom, Tommy ⇨ Thomas
Tony ⇨ Anthony
Trevor /ˈtrevə(r); ˋtrɛvɚ/ 特雷弗
Troy /trɔɪ; trɔɪ/ 特洛伊
Victor /ˈvɪktə(r); ˋvɪktɚ/ 维克托; Vic /vɪk; vɪk/ 维克
Vincent /ˈvɪnsnt; ˋvɪnsn̩t/ 文森特; Vince /vɪns; vɪns/ 文斯
Vivian /ˈvɪvɪən; ˋvɪvɪən/ 维维安; Viv /vɪv; vɪv/ 维夫
Walter /ˈwɔ:ltə(r), *also* 亦读作 ˈwɒltə(r); ˋwɔltɚ/ 沃尔特; Wally /ˈwɒlɪ; ˋwɑlɪ/ 沃利
Warren /ˈwɒrən; ˋwɑrən/ 沃伦
Wayne /weɪn; wen/ 韦恩
Wilbur /ˈwɪlbə(r); ˋwɪlbɚ/ 威尔伯 (*esp US* 尤用于美国)
Wilfrid, Wilfred /ˈwɪlfrɪd; ˋwɪlfrɪd/ 威尔弗里德
William /ˈwɪlɪəm; ˋwɪljəm/ 威廉; Bill /bɪl; bɪl/ 比尔; Billy /ˈbɪlɪ; ˋbɪlɪ/ 比利; Will /wɪl; wɪl/ 威尔; Willy /ˈwɪlɪ; ˋwɪlɪ/ 威利

APPENDIX 8 附录 8

FAMILY RELATIONSHIPS 亲属关系

Jane's Family 简的家族

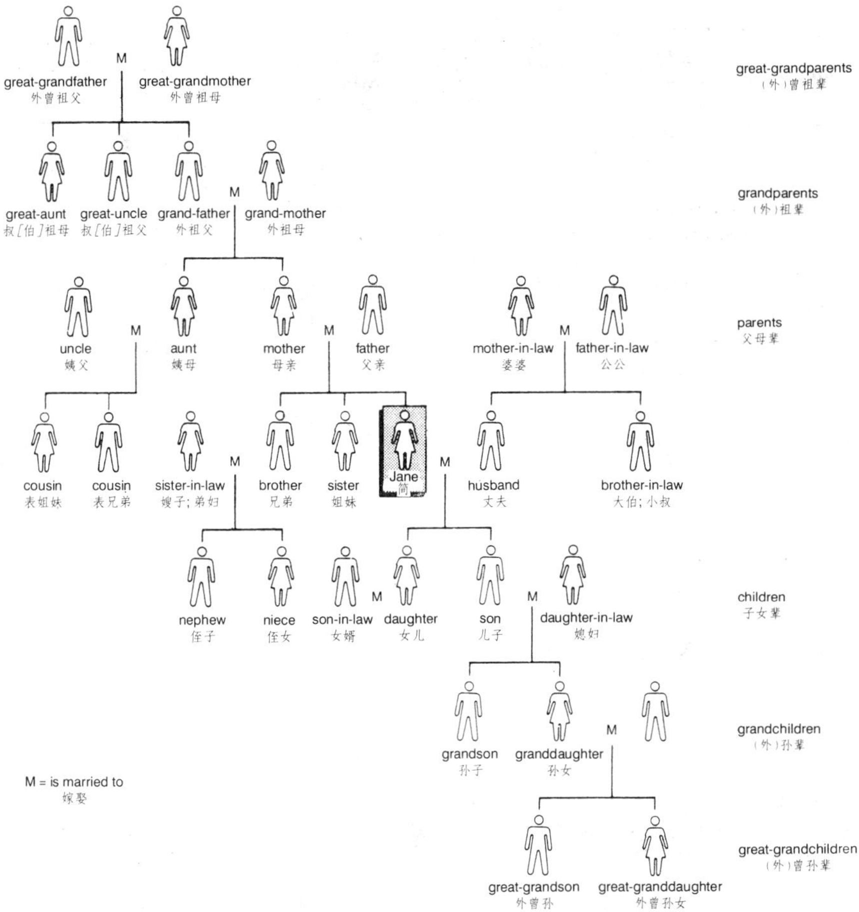

APPENDIX 9 附录 9

MILITARY RANKS 军衔

Royal Navy (RN) 英国皇家海军	United States Navy (USN) 美国海军
Admiral of the Fleet 元帅	* Fleet Admiral 元帅
Admiral (Adm) 上将	Admiral (ADM) 上将
Vice-Admiral (V-Adm) 中将	Vice Admiral (VADM) 中将
Rear-Admiral (Rear-Adm) 少将	Rear Admiral (RADM) 少将
Commodore (Cdre) 准将	Commodore (CDRE) 准将
Captain (Capt) 上校	Captain (CAPT) 上校
Commander (Cdr) 中校	Commander (CDR) 中校
Lieutenant-Commander (Lt-Cdr) 少校	Lieutenant Commander (LCDR) 少校
Lieutenant (Lt) /lef'tenənt; lɛf'tɛnənt/ 上尉	Lieutenant (LT) /lu:'tenənt; lu'tɛnənt/ 上尉
Sub-Lieutenant (Sub-Lt) 中尉	Lieutenant Junior Grade (LTJG) 中尉
Acting Sub-Lieutenant (Act Sub-Lt) 少尉	Ensign (ENS) 少尉
	Chief Warrant Officer (CWO)
Midshipman 准少尉	Midshipman 准尉 (Chief Warrant Officer, Midshipman, Warrant Officer)
Fleet Chief Petty Officer (FCPO) 舰队上士	** Warrant Officer (WO 1)
	Master Chief Petty Officer (MCPO) 一级军士长
	Senior Chief Petty Officer (SCPO) 二级军士长
Chief Petty Officer (CPO) 上士	Chief Petty Officer (CPO) 三级军士长
	Petty Officer 1st Class (PO1) 上士
	Petty Officer 2nd Class (PO2) 中士
Petty Officer (PO) 下士	Petty Officer 3rd Class (PO3) 下士
Leading Seaman (LS) 上等水兵	Seaman (SN) 一等兵
Able Seaman (AB) 一等水兵	
Ordinary Seaman (OD) 二等水兵	
Junior Seaman (JS) 新兵	Seaman Apprentice (SA) 二等兵
	Seaman Recruit (SR) 三等兵

* Wartime rank only 战时军衔

** Rank discontinued 1976 1976 年停止使用的军衔

British Army 英国陆军	United States Army 美国陆军
Field Marshal (FM) 元帅	General of the Army (GEN) 五星上将
General (Gen) 上将	General (GEN) 上将
Lieutenant-General (Lt-Gen) 中将	Lieutenant General (LTG) 中将
Major-General (Maj-Gen) 少将	Major General (MG) 少将
Brigadier (Brig) 准将	Brigadier General (BG) 准将
Colonel (Col) 上校	Colonel (COL) 上校
Lieutenant-Colonel (Lt-Col) 中校	Lieutenant Colonel (LTC) 中校
Major (Maj) 少校	Major (MAJ) 少校
Captain (Capt) 上尉	Captain (CAPT) 上尉

Lieutenant (Lieut) 中尉	First Lieutenant (1 LT) 中尉	
Second Lieutenant (2nd Lt) 少尉	Second Lieutenant (2 LT) 少尉	
	Chief Warrant Officer (CWO) 一级准尉	
	Warrant Officer (WO) 二级准尉	
Warrant Officer 1st Class (WO 1) 一级准尉	Command Sergeant Major (CSM)	军士长
	Staff Sergeant Major (SSM)	军士长
Warrant Officer 2nd Class (WO 2) 二级准尉	1st Sergeant (1 SG)	军士长
	Master Sergeant (MSG)	军士长
	Sergeant 1st Class (SFC)	军士长
Staff Sergeant (S/Sgt) or Colour Sergeant (C/Sgt) 上士	Staff Sergeant (SSG) 上士	
Sergeant (Sgt) 中士	Sergeant (SGT) 中士	
Corporal (Cpl) 下士	Corporal (CPL) 下士	
Lance-Corporal (L-Cpl) 一等兵	Private First Class (P1C) 一等兵	
Private (Pte) 二等兵	Private (PVT) 二等兵	

Note 说明: Warrant Officers in the US Army are the equivalent of Commissioned Officers in the British Army, ie Second Lieutenant and above. 美国陆军中的 Warrant Officers 相当于英国陆军的 Commissioned Officers, 即少尉及其以上的军官.
In the British and US Army the ranks of Corporal and above, to the rank of Second Lieutenant, are referred to as Non-Commissioned Officers (NCOs). 英美陆军中, 从下士到少尉称为无委任状军官.

Royal Air Force (RAF) 英国皇家空军	United States Air Force (USAF) 美国空军	
Marshal of the Royal Air Force 元帅	General of the Air Force 五星上将	
Air Chief Marshal (ACM) 上将	General (GEN) 上将	
Air Marshal (AM) 中将	Lieutenant General (LTG) 中将	
Air Vice Marshal (AVM) 少将	Major General (MG) 少将	
Air Commodore (Air Cdre) 准将	Brigadier General (BG) 准将	
Group Captain (Gp Capt) 上校	Colonel (COL) 上校	
Wing Commander (Wing Cdr) 中校	Lieutenant Colonel (LTC) 中校	
Squadron Leader (Sqn Ldr) 少校	Major (MAJ) 少校	
Flight Lieutenant (Flt Lt) 上尉	Captain (CAPT) 上尉	
Flying Officer (FO) 中尉	First Lieutenant (1 LT) 中尉	
Pilot Officer (PO) 少尉	Second Lieutenant (2 LT) 少尉	
	Chief Warrant Officer (CW-3 and CW-4)	准尉
Warrant Officer (WO) 准尉	Warrant Officer (W-1 and W-2)	准尉
Flight Sergeant (FS) 上士	Chief Master Sergeant (CMSGT)	军士长
	Senior Master Sergeant (SMSGT)	军士长
	Master Sergeant (MSGT)	军士长
Chief Technician (Chf Tech) 总技术军士	Technical Sergeant (TSGT) 上士	
Sergeant (Sgt) 中士	Staff Sergeant (SSGT) 中士	
Corporal (Cpl) 下士	Sergeant (SGT) 下士	
Junior Technician (Jnr Tech) 初级技术军士		
Senior Aircraftman (SAC) 一等兵		
Leading Aircraftman (LAC) 二等兵	Airman First Class (A1C) 一等兵	
Aircraftman 新兵	Airman Basic (AB) 三等兵	

Note 说明: USAF Warrant Officer ranks will be discontinued when those currrently on active duty are retired. 美国空军准尉现役军官退役后, 这一军衔将停止使用.

Royal Marines (RM) 英国皇家海军陆战队

General (Gen) 上将
Lieutenant-General (Lt-Gen) 中将
Major-General (Maj-Gen) 少将
Brigadier (Brig) 准将
Colonel (Col) 上校
Lieutenant-Colonel (Lt-Col) 中校
Major (Maj) 少校
Captain (Capt) 上尉
Lieutenant (Lieut) 中尉
Acting-Lieutenant (Act-Lt) 代理中尉
Second Lieutenant (2nd Lt) 少尉

Warrant Officer 1st Class (WO 1) 一级准尉
Warrant Officer 2nd Class (WO 2) 二级准尉
Colour Sergeant (C/Sgt) 上士

Sergeant (Sgt) 中士

Corporal (Cpl) 下士

Lance-Corporal (L-Cpl) 一等兵
Marine (Mne) 二等兵
Junior Marine (J Mne) 三等兵

United States Marine Corps (USMC) 美国海军陆战队

General (GEN) 上将
Lieutenant General (LTG) 中将
Major General (MG) 少将
Brigadier General (BG) 准将
Colonel (COL) 上校
Lieutenant Colonel (LTC) 中校
Major (MAJ) 少校
Captain (CPT) 上尉
First Lieutenant (1 LT) 中尉

Second Lieutenant (2 LT) 少尉

Sergeant Major (SGM)
Master Gunnery Sergeant (MGSGT)
First Sergeant (1 SGT)
Master Sergeant (MSGT)
Gunnery Sergeant (GSGT)
} 军士长
Staff Sergeant (SSGT) 上士
Sergeant (SGT) 中士
Corporal (CPL) 下士
Lance-Corporal (L-CPL) 一等兵
Private First Class (P1C) 二等兵
Private (PVT) 三等兵

APPENDIX 10 附录 10

THE CHEMICAL ELEMENTS 化学元素

ELEMENT 元素	SYMBOL 符号	ATOMIC NUMBER 原子序数
actinium 锕	Ac	89
aluminium 铝	Al	13
americium 镅	Am	95
antimony 锑	Sb	51
argon 氩	Ar	18
arsenic 砷	As	33
astatine 砹	At	85
barium 钡	Ba	56
berkelium 锫	Bk	97
beryllium 铍	Be	4
bismuth 铋	Bi	83
boron 硼	B	5
bromine 溴	Br	35
cadmium 镉	Cd	48
caesium 铯	Cs	55
calcium 钙	Ca	20
californium 锎	Cf	98
carbon 碳	C	6
cerium 铈	Ce	58
chlorine 氯	Cl	17
chromium 铬	Cr	24
cobalt 钴	Co	27
copper 铜	Cu	29
curium 锔	Cm	96
dysprosium 镝	Dy	66
einsteinium 锿	Es	99
erbium 铒	Er	68
europium 铕	Eu	63
fermium 镄	Fm	100
fluorine 氟	F	9
francium 钫	Fr	87
gadolinium 钆	Gd	64
gallium 镓	Ga	31
germanium 锗	Ge	32
gold 金	Au	79
hafnium 铪	Hf	72
hahnium 铧	Ha	105
helium 氦	He	2
holmium 钬	Ho	67
hydrogen 氢	H	1
indium 铟	In	49
iodine 碘	I	53
iridium 铱	Ir	77
iron 铁	Fe	26
krypton 氪	Kr	36

ELEMENT 元素	SYMBOL 符号	ATOMIC NUMBER 原子序数
lanthanum 镧	La	57
lawrencium 铹	Lr	103
lead 铅	Pb	82
lithium 锂	Li	3
lutetium 镥	Lu	71
magnesium 镁	Mg	12
manganese 锰	Mn	25
mendelevium 钔	Md	101
mercury 汞	Hg	80
molybdenum 钼	Mo	42
neodymium 钕	Nd	60
neon 氖	Ne	10
neptunium 镎	Np	93
nickel 镍	Ni	28
niobium 铌	Nb	41
nitrogen 氮	N	7
nobelium 锘	No	102
osmium 锇	Os	76
oxygen 氧	O	8
palladium 钯	Pd	46
phosphorus 磷	P	15
platinum 铂	Pt	78
plutonium 钚	Pu	94
polonium 钋	Po	84
potassium 钾	K	19
praseodymium 镨	Pr	59
promethium 钷	Pm	61
protactinium 镤	Pa	91
radium 镭	Ra	88
radon 氡	Rn	86
rhenium 铼	Re	75
rhodium 铑	Rh	45
rubidium 铷	Rb	37
ruthenium 钌	Ru	44
rutherfordium 𬬻	Rf	104
samarium 钐	Sm	62
scandium 钪	Sc	21
selenium 硒	Se	34
silicon 硅	Si	14
silver 银	Ag	47
sodium 钠	Na	11
strontium 锶	Sr	38
sulphur 硫	S	16
tantalum 钽	Ta	73
technetium 锝	Tc	43

ELEMENT 元素	SYMBOL 符号	ATOMIC NUMBER 原子序数
tellurium 碲	Te	52
terbium 铽	Tb	65
thallium 铊	Tl	81
thorium 钍	Th	90
thulium 铥	Tm	69
tin 锡	Sn	50
titanium 钛	Ti	22
tungsten 钨	W	74
uranium 铀	U	92
vanadium 钒	V	23
xenon 氙	Xe	54
ytterbium 镱	Yb	70
yttrium 钇	Y	39
zinc 锌	Zn	30
zirconium 锆	Zr	40

APPENDIX 11 附录 11

THE SI UNITS 国际单位制

The International System of Units (Système International d'Unités—SI) is an internationally agreed system of measurement that uses seven base units, with two supplementary units.
All other SI units are derived from the seven base units. In addition, multiples and sub-multiples (= fractions) of units are expressed by the use of approved affixes.
国际单位制(SI)是国际公认的量度制，该制度使用七种基本单位，两种辅助单位. 所有其他国际单位制均由此七种基本单位导出. 此外，单位的倍数与分数用词冠表示.

Base units 基本单位

PHYSICAL QUANTITY 物理量	NAME 名称	SYMBOL 符号
length 长度	metre 米	m
mass 质量	kilogram 千克	kg
time 时间	second 秒	s
electric current 电流	ampere 安培	A
thermodynamic temperature 热力学温度	kelvin 开尔文	K
luminous intensity 照明强度	candela 坎德拉	cd
amount of substance 物质的量	mole 摩尔	mol

Supplementary units 辅助单位

PHYSICAL QUANTITY 物理量	NAME 名称	SYMBOL 符号
plane angle 平面角	radian 弧度	rad
solid angle 立体角	steradian 球面度	sr

Affixes 词冠

MULTIPLE 倍数	AFFIX 词冠	SYMBOL 符号	SUB-MULTIPLE 分数	AFFIX 词冠	SYMBOL 符号
10	deca- 十	da	10^{-1}	deci 分	d
10^2	hecto- 百	h	10^{-2}	centi- 厘	c
10^3	kilo- 千	k	10^{-3}	milli- 毫	m
10^6	mega- 兆	M	10^{-6}	micro- 微	μ
10^9	giga- 京	G	10^{-9}	nano- 纤	n
10^{12}	tera- 垓	T	10^{-12}	pico- 沙	p
10^{15}	peta- 秭	P	10^{-15}	femto- 尘	f
10^{18}	exa- 穰	E	10^{-18}	atto- 渺	a

USING THE DICTIONARY – A DETAILED GUIDE TO THE ENTRIES
本词典用法 —— 词条使用详细说明

The Practical Guide provided at the front of the dictionary is a simple introduction designed to give practice in developing basic reference skills. 本词典前面提供的实用说明是个简单介绍, 目的在于训练查词典的基本技能. The following pages are intended for the more advanced student and the teacher. 此处的详细说明是供程度高的学生和教师参考的. They describe in detail all the major categories of information that the dictionary contains, by identifying problems that the dictionary is designed to solve and explaining how it deals with them. 这里介绍的是本词典包含的主要方面的详细资料, 提出本词典力求解决的问题并说明解决的方法.

ENTRIES AND HEADWORDS 词条和首词

The basic organizational unit of the dictionary is the entry. 本词典的基本组成单位是词条. Each entry is a block of information introduced by a headword, which is made prominent by bold print and set out slightly from the printed column 每个词条是一项独立的资料, 开头是首词, 用较醒目的黑体印刷, 排列稍向左侧突出:

> **dic·tion·ary** /ˈdɪkʃənrɪ; *US* -nerɪ; ˈdɪkʃən,ɛrɪ/ *n* (**a**) book that lists and explains the words of a language, or gives translations of them into one or more other languages, ...

One of the aims of this dictionary is to help the learner understand how longer words (ie derivatives and compounds) are formed from shorter words (or parts of words). 编纂本词典的目的之一是帮助学习者了解较长的词(即派生词和复合词)由较短小的词(或词的组成部分)构成的方法. The various smaller elements involved are themselves listed as headwords, and the first section below explains the different types of headword and, where appropriate, how they can be combined. 各较短小的成分本身亦列为首词, 下面第一部分即是说明首词的类型, 必要时还介绍些构成复合词的方法.

1 TYPES OF HEADWORD 首词类型

1.1 Simple words 单纯词. Most headwords in this dictionary are simple words, or 'roots'. 本词典中大部分首词为单纯词或"词根". A root is the smallest vocabulary item that can occur independently with a meaning of its own, so that *lady*, *child*, *thank* and *happy* are all roots. 词根是词汇中的最小单位, 有本身的词义, 可独立存在. 因此 lady、child、thank、happy 都是词根. Roots can be contrasted with derivatives (eg *thankful*, *happiness*), formed by adding affixes (*-ful, -ness*) to roots, and with compounds (eg *childbirth*) in which two roots are joined together. 词根可与派生词(如 thankful、happiness)相对, 派生词是由词缀(-ful、-ness)加在词根上构成的; 词根也可与复合词(如 childbirth)相对, 复合词是由两个词根结合而成的. As a rule, derivatives and compounds are not placed in entries of their own in this dictionary (⇨ 17, 18). 本词典一般不将派生词和复合词单独列为词条(见 17、18).

1.2 Homographs 同形异义词. Homographs are separate roots which happen to share the same spelling. 同形异义词是拼法相同的独立词根. They differ completely in meaning, and they may differ in grammatical use as well. 它们意义完全不同, 语法上的用法也可能不同. Examples of homographs are *bow* (a type of weapon) and *bow* (to bend the head or body), which apart from the differences of meaning and grammar are also pronounced differently. 同形异义词的示例, 如 bow(用作武器的弓)和 bow(低头或躬身), 两者不仅意义和语法上用法不同, 而且读音也不同. Homographs are given separate numbered entries, as follows 同形异义词分别列为独立词条, 用数字标明区别, 如:

> **bow**[1] /bəʊ; bo/ *n* ...
> **bow**[2] /baʊ; baʊ/ *v* ...

1.3 Affixes 词缀. Meaningful elements such as *-ish*, *-ment* and *-ly* cannot be used independently. 有些有意义的成分如 -ish、-ment、-ly 并不能独立使用. These are affixes, used to form derivatives such as *clownish*, *astonishment* and *bravely*. 这些成分是词缀, 用以构成派生词, 如 clownish、astonishment、bravely 等. To help students understand how affixes (ie prefixes and suffixes) in their various meanings are used to form derivatives, the dictionary lists them as headwords, indicates the classes of words they can be attached to, supplies definitions, and gives examples of the derivatives formed 为帮助学习者了解词缀(即前缀和后缀)各种意义构成派生词的方法, 本词典将词缀列为首词, 表明可与哪类词结合, 再提供定义, 并举出构成派生词的示例:

> **-ship** *suff* (with *ns* forming *ns*) **1** state of being; status; office: *friendship* ○ *ownership* ...
> **-ish** *suff* **1** (with *ns* forming *adjs* and *ns*) (language or people) of the specified nationality: *Danish* ○ *Irish* ...

1.4 Combining forms 构词成分. These are very important elements in the creation of technical or scientific words. 这些是构成科技词语的重要成分. They may occur at the beginning of a word (as *bio-* does in *biodegradable*) or at the end (as *-cide* does in *suicide*). 构词成分可出现在词的开头(如 biodegradable 中的 bio-), 也可出现在词的末尾(如 suicide 中的 -cide). Like a root (a simple word), a combining form can be made into a larger word by adding an affix (eg *neur-* + *-al*), or by joining it to another combining form (eg *biblio-* + *-phile*); but unlike a root, a combining form cannot occur alone. 构词成分和词根(单纯词)一样可以加上词缀(如 neur- + -al)或连接到另一构词成分上(如 biblio- + -phile)构成较大的词; 但构词成分又不同于词根, 它不能单独存在. Entries for combining forms contain definitions and illustrate the types of word that can be formed 构词成分的词条包含有定义并说明可构成的词类:

> **electr(o)-** *comb form* of electricity: *electrocardiogram* ○ *electrolysis*.
> **-mania** *comb form* (forming *ns*) madness or abnormal behaviour of a particular type: *kleptomania* ○ *nymphomania*.

1.5 Abbreviations 缩略式. The dictionary contains many common abbreviations of simple words (Cf *pint, pt; captain, capt*), compounds (Cf *tuberculin-tested, TT*) and phrases (Cf *World Wildlife Fund, WWF*). 本词典包含了许多常见的缩略式, 有单纯词(参看 pint, pt; captain, capt)、复合词(参看 tuberculin-tested, TT)、词组(参看 World Wildlife Fund, WWF)等缩略式. All abbreviations are entered as headwords in the dictionary, with alternative forms, pronunciations and examples as appropriate 全部缩略式都作为首词编入词典, 并附有关的异体、读音及示例:

> **t** (*US* **tn**) *abbr* ton(s); tonne(s): *5t* (ie tonnes) *of wheat per acre.*
> **PA** /ˌpiː ˈeɪ; ˌpi ˈe/ *abbr* **1** (*infml*) personal assistant: *She works as PA to the managing director.* ...

As well as being headwords in their own right, abbreviations appear in the entries for the full words which they represent, after the part of speech label and any accompanying grammatical information 缩略式本身列为首词, 而且还列入其代表的词条中, 置于词类及其他语法资料之后:

volt ... *n* (*abbr* **v**) unit of electrical force, ...
post·script ... *n* ~ **(to sth) 1** (*abbr* **PS**) ...

1.6 Dummy entries 假位词条. When an irregular past tense, plural, etc is so different from the headword to which it relates that the dictionary user may not connect the two, a 'dummy' entry is provided for the irregular form. 有些不规则的动词过去式、名词复数形式等与首词迥异, 恐本词典使用者未必均可联想到原词, 因而将不规则形式列为"假位词条". A dummy entry is one which contains no definitions or examples but is intended simply to refer the user to a normal main entry, thus 假位词条无定义或示例, 仅指示其出自的原词条, 如:

took *pt* of TAKE.
mice *pl* of MOUSE.

(For other uses of the dummy entry ⇨ 3.1, 4. 关于假位词条的其他用法, 见 3.1、3.4.)

2 HEADWORD DIVISION 首词断字

When writing, it is sometimes necessary to divide a word at the end of a line because there is not enough space for the complete word. 在书写时, 有时在一行末尾写不下一个完整的字而需要断字移行. Recommended places of division are shown in the dictionary by means of a raised dot (·). 本词典在适宜移行处用居中的黑点(·)标出. The dot is used in all headwords which can be divided (eg **ches·ter·field, dia·lec·tic**) and in many alternative forms also (⇨ 3.1). 这种黑点标于所有可移行的首词(如 **ches·ter·field**、**dia·lec·tic**)及其异体形式中(见 3.1). Derivatives include the dots at their point of entry (eg **con·tor·tion**, a derivative of **con·tort**), but not compounds, since the places where compounds divide can be checked by referring to the entries for their component words. 若派生词作词条(如 **con·tort** 的派生词 **con·tor·tion**)也在断字处用黑点标出, 但不标于复合词中, 因复合词断字处可见于各构词成分中.

3 ALTERNATIVE FORMS AND SYNONYMS OF THE HEADWORD 首词的异体形式及同义词

3.1 Alternative written forms 首词的异体书写形式. When a word can be spelt in two or more different ways (eg **facia, fascia**) and there are no differences of pronunciation or grammar, the most usual spelling is given as the headword, and the alternative form (or forms) are given immediately after the headword, thus 若一个字有不止一种拼法(如 **facia**、**fascia**)而读音或语法上并无区别时, 则将最通用的拼法列为首词, 其异体形式置于其后, 例如:

fa·cia (also **fas·cia**) /ˈfeɪʃə; ˋfeʃə/ *n* ...

However, if the form chosen as the headword and its alternative(s) are so different in spelling that the user is unlikely to trace the one from the other(s), dummy entries (⇨ 1.6), are given for the alternatives 但是有的首词形式与其异体形式在拼法上差别很大, 不易找到其异体字, 则用假位词条方式(见 1.6)一并列出:

bo'sn, bos'n = BOATSWAIN.
bo'sun = BOATSWAIN.

3.2 US equivalents 美式英语对等词. Differences between British and American equivalents present special problems for the foreign learner. 英美对等词之间的差异给外国学习者造成特殊困难. Sometimes the difference is one of spelling alone. 有时仅为拼法不同. In such cases, the US form follows the British one (given as the headword) but precedes the pronunciation 本词典的处理方法是将美式拼法列于英式拼法(作为首词)之后, 但在读音之前:

hu·mour (*US* **hu·mor**) /ˈhjuːmə(r); ˋhjumɚ/...

If the difference is one of pronunciation as well as spelling, each written form is followed by the appropriate phonetic spelling 若拼法、读音均不同，则分别于每一书写形式后列出其音标：

alu·mi·nium /ˌæljʊˈmɪnɪəm; ˌæljəˈmɪnɪəm/ (*US* **alu·mi·num** /əˈlu:mɪnəm; əˈlumɪnəm/) ...

3.3 US synonyms of British words 英式英语的美式英语同义词. A particular word (eg *nappy*) which is limited to British English may have a synonym (in this case *diaper*) which is restricted to US English. 英式英语的某个词(如 nappy)可能有美式英语的同义词(此例为 diaper). In such cases, the British word will be treated in a full entry, with the US word placed near the beginning in brackets 这类英式英语词列为词条，美式同义词置于括号中列于近首词处：

nappy ... (*US* **diaper**) piece of towelling cloth or similar ...

A dummy entry for the US word directs the dictionary user back to this entry 美式英语同义词另立假位词条，指示查阅英式英语词条：

di·aper ... **2** [C] (*US*) = NAPPY.

If a word is used in both British and US English, but has a synonym which is only British or only US, the former is treated in a full entry, and the synonym is labelled '(*Brit* also ...)' or '(*US* also ...)' 若英式美式英语虽用同一词，但仅于英式或美式英语中另有一同义词，则前者列为词条，其同义词标明(*Brit* also ...)或(*US* also ...)等类似字样：

par·cel /ˈpɑ:sl; ˈpɑrsḷ/ *n* **1** (*US* also **package**) ...

If a word is British only, but its US equivalent can be used by British as well as US speakers, both words are given a special label 若仅用于英式英语的词，其美式英语同义词不仅说美式英语的人使用，而且说英式英语的人也使用，则这两个词均特别标明：

rubber[1] /ˈrʌbə(r); ˈrʌbɚ/ *n* **1** [U] ... **2** [C] (*Brit*) (also *esp US* **eraser**) ...

3.4 Other synonyms 其他同义词. A number of words, especially the names of substances, animals, plants and trees, have quite widely used synonyms. 有些词，尤其是物质、动物、花草、树木名称有广泛使用的同义词. (In some cases the synonym may be a compound. 有的同义词或为复合词.) One word is treated in a full entry and the equivalents are entered prominently after the phonetic spelling 其中一个词列为词条，而对等词均以黑体列出置于音标之后：

bil·berry /ˈbɪlbrɪ; *US* -berɪ; ˈbɪlˌbɛrɪ/ (also **blaeberry, whortleberry**) *n* ...

If the synonyms are more than four entries away alphabetically from the headword (as in both cases here), they are given dummy entries (⇨ 1.6) at their own alphabetical places, and the user is referred to the entry where the definition is to be found 若同义词按字母顺序排列与首词相隔四个词条以上(如本处二例)，则这类同义词均于各自位置另立假位词条(参看 1.6)指示定义所在词条供查阅：

blae·berry /ˈbleɪbrɪ; *US* -berɪ; ˈbleˌbɛrɪ/ *n* = BILBERRY.
whor·tle·berry /ˈwɜ:tlberɪ; *US* ˈhwɜ:rtlberɪ; ˈhwɝtḷˌbɛrɪ/ *n* = BILBERRY.

3.5 Compounds which include an equivalent word 包括一个对等词的复合词. Sometimes a simple word is also the first part of a compound with the same meaning as that simple word: cf *wellington, wellington boot; bowler, bowler hat.* 有时一个单纯词也是一个复合词的第一部分，且与该复合词同义：参看 wellington, wellington boot; bowler, bowler hat. Pairs such as these are treated in the entry for the simple word, thus 这类成对的词归入单纯词词条中处理，如：

wel·ling·ton /ˈwelɪŋtən; ˈwɛlɪŋtən/ *n* (also ˌ**wellington** ˈ**boot**, ...) ...
bowler[2] /ˈbəʊlə(r); ˈbolɚ/ *n* (also ˌ**bowler** ˈ**hat**, ...) ...

PRONUNCIATION 读音

4 SOUNDS AND SPELLING 读音与拼法

4.1 Phonetic alphabet 音标. Any single letter of the English alphabet can often be pronounced in different ways. 英语字母表中的任何一个字母都常有几种读法. For example, the letter *a* is pronounced differently in *hat*, *pass*, *came*, *water*, *dare*, *ago*. 例如 a 这个字母在 hat、pass、came、water、dare、ago 各字中的读音各不相同. Phonetic spelling is a way of writing a word so that one symbol always represents only one sound. 用音标拼写的字, 每个符号永远只代表同一个音. Two words may be spelt differently in ordinary spelling; but if they sound the same then the phonetic spelling is the same. 普通拼法写出的两个字, 尽管拼法不同但若读音相同则音标拼法也相同. For example, **key** and **quay** have the same phonetic spelling /ki:/. 例如, **key** 和 **quay** 的音标拼法相同 /ki:/. Each headword is followed by a phonetic spelling separated from the rest of the text by / /. 每个首词后面列有音标, 两端有斜线号 / /. Inside the cover of the dictionary there is a list of all the letters (phonetic symbols) used in the phonetic spelling. 本词典封里有一音标符号一览表. Phonetic symbols are given at other places within the entry (⇨ 4.4, 7.1) where the user needs to know there is a change in pronunciation. 在同一词条内若有读音变化的地方也另用音标注明(见 4.4、7.1).

4.2 Models of pronunciation 读音模式. A British English pronunciation is given for each word and, in those cases where there is a marked difference, the American version is also shown (⇨ 6.5). 每个字都标有英式英语的读音, 若与美式读音明显不同时, 也标出美式读音(见 6.5). The British English form is that which has been called Received Pronunciation (RP) or General British. 英式英语的读音一向称为标准读音(RP)或通用英语读音. Where there is a choice between several acceptable forms, that form is selected which is likely to be easiest for learners. 有的字有几种公认的读音, 本词典选用最容易为学习者掌握的一种. The user is referred to *An English Pronunciation Companion* (OUP 1982) for further discussion of this and other points concerning pronunciation. 若要进一步探讨读音问题, 可参考《An English Pronunciation Companion》(牛津大学出版社, 1982 年).

4.3 Linking 'r' 连接音 r. In spoken British English an *r* at the end of a written word (either as the final letter or in an *-re* ending as in *fire*) is not sounded unless another word that begins with a vowel sound immediately follows. 在英式英语的口语中, 一个字若写出时字尾是 r (不论是最后的字母还是如 fire 中的 -re 词尾), 除非后面紧跟着一个元音开头的字, 否则不发音. For example, the *r* is not heard in *His car was sold* but it is heard in *His car isn't old*. 例如在 His car was sold 一句中, r 不发音, 但是在 His car isn't old 一句中发出 /r/ 音. To show this, words which end in *r* or *re* have /(r)/ at the end of the phonetic spelling in the dictionary, for example **car** /kɑ:(r)/ (Cf 6.5.3). 为表明这一点, 本词典中以 r 或 re 结尾的字在音标的末尾标出 /(r)/ 音, 例如 **car** /kɑ:(r)/ (参看 6.5.3).

4.4 How an inflection is pronounced 屈折变化的读音方法. An inflection is the suffix added to the end of a word when it is used in a particular grammatical form, for example in the plural (*cups, skies*), in the past tense (*pointed, smiled*), in the comparative (*finer, wilder*). 屈折变化是指一个词在某一语法形式中加在词尾的后缀, 如复数形式(cups、skies)、过去时态(pointed、smiled)、比较级(finer、wilder)等语法形式中的变化. The pronunciation of these inflections follows a set of rules described below. 这些屈折变化的读音有下列一套规则. Phonetic spelling is only given in the entry for inflected forms if they do not follow these rules, eg the plural of *basis*: *bases* /ˈbeɪsi:z/ or the comparative of *young*: *younger* /ˈjʌŋgə(r)/. 只有不符合这些规则的屈折变化, 其读音才在词条中用音标注明, 如 basis 的复数形式: bases /ˈbeɪsi:z/; young 的比较级形式: younger /ˈjʌŋgə(r)/.

4.4.1 -s and -es -s 和 -es. The plural of nouns, and the third person singular present tense of verbs 名词的复数和动词现在时态的单数第三人称:

• If the final sound of the noun's singular or the verb's root form is a *vowel* or /b, d, g, v, ð, m, n, ŋ, l/, the ending is formed by adding the sound /-z/. 若名词单数或动词词根最后的音是元音或 /b, d, g, v, ð, m, n, ŋ, l/, 就在词尾加上 /-z/ 音. For example, *city* /ˈsɪtɪ/, *cities* /ˈsɪtɪz/; *ring* /rɪŋ/, *rings* /rɪŋz/. 例如 city /ˈsɪtɪ/, cities /ˈsɪtɪz/; ring /rɪŋ/, rings /rɪŋz/.

• If the final sound of the noun's singular or the verb's root form is /p, t, k, f, θ/, the ending is formed by the addition of /-s/. 若名词单数或动词词根最后的音是 /p, t, k, f, θ/, 就在词尾加上 /-s/ 音. For example, *work* /wɜ:k/, *works* /wɜ:ks/. 例如 work /wɜ:k/, works /wɜ:ks/.

• If the final sound of the noun's singular or the verb's root form is /s, z, ʃ, ʒ, tʃ, dʒ/, the ending is formed by the addition of /-ɪz/. 若名词单数或动词词根最后的音是 /s, z, ʃ, ʒ, tʃ, dʒ/, 就在词尾加上 /-ɪz/ 音. For example, *match* /mætʃ/, *matches* /ˈmætʃɪz/. 例如 match /mætʃ/, matches /ˈmætʃɪz/.

4.4.2 -d and -ed -d 和 -ed. The past tense and past participle of verbs 动词的过去式和过去分词形式:

• If the final sound of the verb's root form is a *vowel* or /b, g, v, ð, z, ʒ, dʒ, m, n, ŋ, l/, the past tense and the past participle are formed by the addition of /-d/. 若动词词根最后的音是元音或 /b, g, v, ð, z, ʒ, dʒ, m, n, ŋ, l/, 该动词的过去式和过去分词的构成方法是加 /-d/ 音. For example *hurry* /ˈhʌrɪ/, *hurried* /ˈhʌrɪd/; *judge* /dʒʌdʒ/, *judged* /dʒʌdʒd/. 例如 hurry /ˈhʌrɪ/, hurried /ˈhʌrɪd/; judge /dʒʌdʒ/, judged /dʒʌdʒd/.

• If the final sound of the verb's root form is /p, k, f, θ, s, ʃ, tʃ/, the past tense and the past participle are formed by the addition of /-t/. 若动词词根最后的音是 /p, k, f, θ, s, ʃ, tʃ/, 该动词的过去式和过去分词的构成方法是加 /-t/ 音. For example *stop* /stɒp/, *stopped* /stɒpt/. 例如 stop /stɒp/, stopped /stɒpt/.

• If the final sound of the verb's root form is /t, d/, the past tense and the past participle are formed by the addition of /-ɪd/. 若动词词根最后的音是 /t, d/, 该动词的过去式和过去分词的构成方法是加 /-ɪd/ 音. For example *paint* /peɪnt/, *painted* /ˈpeɪntɪd/. 例如 paint /peɪnt/, painted /ˈpeɪntɪd/.

4.4.3 -r and -er -r 和 -er. The comparative and superlative of adjectives and adverbs 形容词和副词比较级和最高级形式:

• The comparative of adjectives or adverbs with only one syllable is formed by the addition of /-ə(r)/ to the final sound of the root word. 单音节的形容词或副词的比较级形式是在原词根后加上 /-ə(r)/. For example *high* /haɪ/, *higher* /ˈhaɪə(r)/; *wild* /waɪld/, *wilder* /ˈwaɪldə(r)/. 例如 high /haɪ/, higher /ˈhaɪə(r)/; wild /waɪld/, wilder /ˈwaɪldə(r)/.

• The superlative of these adjectives and adverbs is formed by the addition of /-ɪst/ to the final sound of the root word. 单音节的形容词或副词的最高级形式是在原词根后加上 /-ɪst/. For example *green* /gri:n/, *greenest* /ˈgri:nɪst/; *fast* /fɑ:st/, *fastest* /ˈfɑ:stɪst/. 例如 green /gri:n/, greenest /ˈgri:nɪst/; fast /fɑ:st/, fastest /ˈfɑ:stɪst/.

4.5 A note on the pronunciation of combining forms 构词成分的读音说明. It often happens, especially in the case of initial combining forms (⇨ 1.4), that more than one pronunciation occurs according to the sound of the remainder of the word. 一个构词成分的读音方法往往不止一种, 特别是在词首的位置(见 1.4)时要看后面部分的读音而定. For instance **bio-, bi-** may have the following different forms: in *biochemistry* /ˌbaɪəʊˈkemɪstrɪ/, *biology* /ˌbaɪˈɒlədʒɪ/, *biopsy* /ˈbaɪɒpsɪ/, *bioscope* /ˈbaɪəskəʊp/. 例如 **bio-, bi-** 可能有下列不同的读音: biochemistry /ˌbaɪəʊˈkemɪstrɪ/, biology /ˌbaɪˈɒlədʒɪ/, biopsy /ˈbaɪɒpsɪ/, bioscope /ˈbaɪəskəʊp/. For this reason, each combining form given in the dictionary has examples, and the user should refer to the entries for these examples for information about the pronunciation in each individual case. 为此, 本词典内每个构词成分都有示例, 应查阅这些词条以便了解每个具体示例的读音方法.

5 STRESS 重音

5.1 Stress-marks 重音符号. When a word has more than one syllable, one of them is spoken with more force than the rest. 一个字的音节若不止一个，其中一个音节说时要比其余音节更加用力. This force is called stress, and the syllable which is stressed is shown with the stress mark /ˈ/ before it in the dictionary. 用力之处叫作重音，在本词典中有重音的音节之前标有重音符号 /ˈ/. For example, *any* /ˈenɪ/ has a stress on the first syllable; *depend* /dɪˈpend/ has a stress on the second syllable. 例如 any /ˈenɪ/ 的第一个音节有重音，depend /dɪˈpend/ 的第二个音节有重音.

In some words, usually long ones, other syllables may also be spoken with more force than the rest, but with a stress that is not as strong as for those syllables marked /ˈ/. 有些字，通常是较长的字，其他音节说时也比其余音节更加用力，但不像标有重音符号 /ˈ/ 的音节用力那么大. The stress mark /ˌ/ is used to show this. 表示这种重音的符号是 /ˌ/. So, /ˈ/ is used to show the strongest or *primary* stress, and /ˌ/ is used to show the *secondary* stress (which is less strong), as in *pronunciation* /prəˌnʌnsɪˈeɪʃn/. 我们用 /ˈ/ 表示最强的重音，又叫主重音，用 /ˌ/ 表示次重音(用力轻些)，如 pronunciation /prəˌnʌnsɪˈeɪʃn/.

5.2 How context affects stress patterns 上下文影响重音模式. English tends to space strong stresses at intervals in speech, particularly avoiding the occurrence of two strong stresses in adjacent syllables. 说英语时重音与重音之间宜间隔开，特别要避免两个重音连在一起. So, for example, the second syllable of *fourteen* is stressed in *There are fourteen* /ˌfɔːˈtiːn/ but in the phrase *fourteen years* the stressing is /ˌfɔːtiːn ˈjɪəz/. 因此，例如 fourteen 一字的第二个音节在 There are fourteen /ˌfɔːˈtiːn/ 一句中有重音，而在 fourteen years 词组中的重音则是 /ˌfɔːtiːn ˈjɪəz/. This type of 'stress shift' applies to all classes of full words (ie noun, verb, adjective or adverb). 这种"重音转移"适用于各类实词(即名词、动词、形容词或副词). Another example would be *ˌrecomˈmend* but *ˌrecommend ˈseveral*. 又如 ˌrecomˈmend 的重音转移见于 ˌrecommend ˈseveral. It should be understood that any word which is shown in the dictionary as having a secondary stress before a later primary stress, may lose the primary stress when the following word begins with a strongly stressed syllable. 须知本词典中任何字若前部有次重音，后部有主重音，碰到下一个字以重音开头，前面的字可失去主重音. This applies to phrasal verbs (as *ˌcome ˈround* but *he'll ˌcome round ˈsoon*) and also to compounds (⇨ 7.2.2), eg *ˌshort-ˈlived*, where the stress shift in *a ˌshort-lived ˈtriumph* is not shown explicitly in the example in the dictionary. 这一规则适用于短语动词(如 ˌcome ˈround 在 he'll ˌcome round ˈsoon 中失去主重音)，也适合用于复合词(见 7.2.2)，如 ˌshort-ˈlived 在 a ˌshort-lived ˈtriumph 中失去主重音，这种失去主重音的现象本词典的示例中不详细注明.

The learner will hear similar shifting in some words which have a single stress, for example *chamˈpagne* but *ˌchampagne ˈcocktail*, *iˈdea* but *the ˌidea ˈpleases me*, and the adjective *comˈpact* /kəmˈpækt/ but *compact disc* /ˌkɒmpækt ˈdɪsk/. 有些字只有一个重音，学英语的人也可听出其中类似的重音转移，如 chamˈpagne 在 ˌchampagne ˈcocktail 中，iˈdea 在 the ˌidea ˈpleases me 中及形容词 comˈpact /kəmˈpækt/ 在 compact disc /ˌkɒmpækt ˈdɪsk/ 中都有重音转移现象.

5.3 Stress in examples 示例有重音. It is a feature of this dictionary that stress is marked on many examples where it is felt that this might be useful information for the learner. 本词典的一个特色是很多示例标有重音，认为对学英语的人或许有所裨益. For example, under **hang**[1], the phrasal verbs **hang aˈbout/aˈround** and **hang ˈon** are shown with primary stress on the particles *about*, *around* and *on*. 例如在 **hang**[1] 词条中，短语动词 **hang aˈbout/aˈround** 和 **hang ˈon** 中的小词 about、around 和 on 上都标明主重音. When an example follows in which the stressing would usually alter in normal speech, the changed stress is explicitly marked, as in *unemployed people hanging about (the ˈstreets)* and *ˌHang on ˈtight*. 在其后的示例中的重音，一般说话时往往改变，因而特地标出，如 unemployed people hanging about (the ˈstreets) 和 ˌHang on ˈtight.

6 VARIANT PRONUNCIATIONS 异读

6.1 British variants 英式异读. Different speakers may choose different pronunciations of the same word, for example *again* /əˈgen/ or /əˈgeɪn/; *exquisite* /ˈekskwɪzɪt/ or /ɪkˈskwɪzɪt/; *telegraph* /ˈtelɪgrɑ:f/ or /ˈtelɪgræf/. 说话的人对同一个字彼此可能有不同的读法，如 again /əˈgen/ 或 /əˈgeɪn/; exquisite /ˈekskwɪzɪt/ 或 /ɪkˈskwɪzɪt/; telegraph /ˈtelɪgrɑ:f/ 或 /ˈtelɪgræf/. This edition of the dictionary now shows variant pronunciations in cases where two acceptable versions of a word are used by speakers of RP English. 若一个字有两个符合规范的读音, 都是说标准英语的人使用的, 本词典本版均标示出这种异读. The dictionary indicates the different status of variants as follows 本词典对异读字的不同类别标示如下:

1 separation by a comma, eg **again** /əˈgen, əˈgeɪn/ (where the variants are almost equal in frequency) 用逗号分开, 如 **again** /əˈgen, əˈgeɪn/ (指两种读音使用频率几乎相等);

2 with the gloss *also*, eg **amenity** /əˈmi:nətɪ, *also* əˈmenətɪ/ (where the second form is common but not equal to the first) 标示 *also* 字样, 如 **amenity** /əˈmi:nətɪ, *also* əˈmenətɪ/ (第二种读音很普通, 但不如第一种读音常用);

3 with the gloss *or, rarely*, eg **despicable** /dɪˈspɪkəbl *or, rarely*, ˈdespɪkəbl/ (where the second form is old-fashioned or otherwise restricted in usage) 标示 *or, rarely* 字样, 如 **despicable** /dɪˈspɪkəbl *or, rarely*, ˈdespɪkəbl/ (第二种为旧式读音, 或使用范围较窄).

In each case the first form listed is the one which the learner is advised to use. 学习英语的人宜使用各项中的第一种读音. The first variant is always a version that is common and acceptable wherever RP is spoken. 第一种均为普通而规范的读音, 说标准英语的任何地方到处通行. Sometimes a rarer RP version is the common US version, as in the case of *poor*. 有时标准读音中不甚普通的读音却是美式英语中的普通读音, 如 poor 即是. Although /pʊə(r)/ may be heard in Britain, /pɔ:(r)/ is the most common RP pronunciation. 虽然 /pʊə(r)/ 的读音在英国也可听到, 但是 /pɔ:(r)/ 是标准读音中最普通的. Accordingly, the entry under **poor** reads /pɔ:(r); *US* pʊər/. 因此, **poor** 词条中标作 /pɔ:(r); *US* pʊər/.

6.2 Strong and weak forms 强读与弱读. The words listed below all have two or more different pronunciations: a *strong* form and one or more *weak* forms. 下列各字都有至少两种读音: 一种强读式和至少一种弱读式. It is the weak forms that occur most frequently in connected speech. 在连贯的话语中弱读式用得最多. For example, *from* is /frəm/ in *He ˌcomes from ˈSpain*. 例如在 He ˌcomes from ˈSpain 一句中 from 的发音是 /frəm/.

The strong form occurs when a word is said in isolation or when it is given special emphasis in connected speech. 孤立地说出一个字时, 或是在连贯的话语中特别强调时, 用强读式. For example *from* is /frɒm/ in *This ˌpresent's not ˈfrom John; it's ˈfor him*. 例如在 This ˌpresent's not ˈfrom John; it's ˈfor him 一句中的 from 即为 /frɒm/. In addition, when prepositions and auxiliary verbs come at the end of a phrase or clause they generally take their strong form, whether or not they are stressed. 此外, 介词和助动词在词组或从句末尾时, 无论是否重读, 一般都用强读式. For example, *ˌWhere do you ˈcome from?* has /frɒm/ (not /frəm/). 例如, ˌWhere do you ˈcome from? 一句中 from 为 /frɒm/ (而不作 /frəm/).

Since in ordinary speech weak forms account for 95% of the occurrences of a grammatical word (ie one which is *not* a noun, an adjective, an adverb or a main verb), the dictionary lists the weak before the strong form which, for some words, may have a special meaning. 在普通说话时, 虚词(即非名词、形容词、副词或主要动词) 95% 为弱读式, 因此本词典将弱读式列在强读式之前, 因为有些虚词的强读式可能有特殊含义. For example, under **and** the more common forms /ən, ənd/ are listed before the less frequent /ænd/. 例如在 **and** 词条中, 常用的 /ən, ənd/ 列在前面, 不常用的 /ænd/ 列在后面. When an additional weak form exists that occurs in a limited context (for example /n/ for **and**), the dictionary user is referred to the list below where that form is given with appropriate comment. 只在某些情况下使用的其他弱读式(如 **and** 的另一弱读式 /n/), 需参看下表的有关说明.

		Weak Forms 弱读式	Strong Form 强读式	Notes on the weak form 弱读注释
Determiner 限定词				
	a	/ə/	/eɪ/	
	an	/ən/	/æn/	
	some	/səm/	/sʌm/	/səm/ is used only when *some* means 'an unspecified amount or number of'. /səm/ 只用于 some 指不定的数量时.
	the	/ðə, ðɪ/	/ði:/	/ðə/ before consonants; /ðɪ/ before vowels. /ðə/ 用于辅音前; /ðɪ/ 用于元音前.
Conjunction 连词				
	and	/ən, ənd, n/	/ænd/	/n/ may be used after /t, d, f, v, θ, ð, s, z, ʃ, ʒ/. /n/ 可用于 /t, d, f, v, θ, ð, s, z, ʃ, ʒ/ 之后.
	as	/əz/	/æz/	
	but	/bət/	/bʌt/	
	than	/ðən/	/ðæn/	
	that	/ðət/	/ðæt/	Also used when *that* is a relative pronoun. that 作关系代词时也用弱读式.
Preposition 介词				
	at	/ət/	/æt/	
	for	/fə(r), fr/	/fɔ:(r)/	/fr/ is optional before vowels. /fr/ 在元音前也可用.
	from	/frəm/	/frɒm/	
	of	/əv/	/ɒv/	
	to	/tə, tʊ/	/tu:/	/tə/ is not used before vowels. /tə/ 不用于元音前.
Pronoun 代词				
	he	/hɪ, i:, ɪ/	/hi:/	These are optional; /i:, ɪ/ are not used to begin a sentence. 弱读式均可选用; /i:, ɪ/ 不用于句首.
	her	/hə, ɜ(r), ə(r)/	/hɜ(r)/	These are optional; /ɜ(r), ə(r)/ are not used to begin a sentence. 弱读式均可选用; /ɜ(r), ə(r)/ 不用于句首.
	him	/ɪm/	/hɪm/	/ɪm/ is optional. /ɪm/ 为可选用者.
	his	/ɪz/	/hɪz/	/ɪz/ is not used to begin a sentence and is optional elsewhere. /ɪz/ 不用于句首, 其他地方可以选用.
	me	/mɪ/	/mi:/	/mɪ/ is optional. /mɪ/ 为可选用者.
	she	/ʃɪ/	/ʃi:/	/ʃɪ/ is optional. /ʃɪ/ 为可选用者.
	them	/ðəm/	/ðem/	
	us	/əs/	/ʌs/	
	we	/wɪ/	/wi:/	/wɪ/ is optional. /wɪ/ 为可选用者.
	you	/jʊ/	/ju:/	/jʊ/ is optional. /jʊ/ 为可选用者.

		Weak Forms 弱读式	Strong Form 强读式	Notes on the weak form 弱读注释
Verb 动词				
	am	/m, əm/	/æm/	
	are	/ə(r)/	/ɑ:(r)/	
	be	/bɪ/	/bi:/	/bɪ/ is optional. /bɪ/ 为可选用者.
	can	/kən/	/kæn/	
	could	/kəd/	/kʊd/	
	do	/də, dʊ/	/du:/	/də/ is not used before vowels. /də/ 不用于元音前.
	does	/dəz/	/dʌz/	
	had	/həd, əd, d/	/hæd/	Auxiliary use only; /həd/ is used to begin a sentence; /d/ is an optional form after vowels. 弱读式只作助动词时用; /həd/ 用于句首; 在元音后可选用 /d/.
	has	/həz, əz, z, s/	/hæz/	Auxiliary use only; /həz/ is used to begin a sentence; /əz/ after /s, z, ʃ, ʒ, tʃ, dʒ/; /s/ after /p, t, k, f, θ/; /z/ elsewhere. 弱读式只作助动词时用; /həz/ 用于句首; /əz/ 用于 /s, z, ʃ, ʒ, tʃ, dʒ/ 之后; /s/ 用于 /p, t, k, f, θ/ 之后; /z/ 用于其他地方.
	have	/həv, əv, v/	/hæv/	Auxiliary use only; /həv/ is used to begin a sentence; /v/ is an optional form after vowels. 弱读式只作助动词时用; /həv/ 用于句首; 在元音后可选用 /v/.
	is	/z, s/	/ɪz/	/z, s/ are not used to begin or end a sentence or after /s, z, ʃ, ʒ, tʃ, dʒ/; /s/ is used after /p, t, k, f, θ/; /z/ elsewhere. /z, s/ 不用于句首或句末或 /s, z, ʃ, ʒ, tʃ, dʒ/ 之后; /s/ 用于 /p, t, k, f, θ/ 之后; /z/ 用于其他地方.
	must	/məst/	/mʌst/	
	shall	/ʃəl/	/ʃæl/	
	should	/ʃəd/	/ʃʊd/	
	was	/wəz/	/wɒz/	
	were	/wə(r)/	/wɜ:(r)/	
	will	/əl, l/	/wɪl/	/əl, l/ are not used to begin or end a sentence. /əl, l/ 不用于句首或句末.
	would	/wəd, əd/	/wʊd/	/əd/ is not used to begin or end a sentence. /əd/ 不用于句首或句末.

6.3 Contractions 缩约式. A contraction is a shortened form used either in speech or in writing. 缩约式是口语或书面语中使用的缩短的词语. In speech some words combine together to form contractions. 说话时有些词结合在一起可构成缩约形式. These are represented in writing that reproduces spoken language (eg drama, personal letters, direct speech in novels and short stories), by omitting one or two letters and replacing the letters that are omitted by an apostrophe ('). 这些形式反映于书面语(如戏剧、私人信件、小说中的直接引语)时，省略其中一两个字母代之以省字号(').

Written contractions are used to represent the weak forms of spoken *has*, *is*, *will* and *would*, for example: *the train's come* (= *train has*), *what's that* (= *what is*), *John'll come* (= *John will*), *that'd help* (= *that would*). 书面语的缩约式用以反映口语中的弱读式 has、is、will、would, 如 the train's come (= train has)、what's that (= what is)、John'll come (= John will)、that'd help (= that would).

In speech there is an area of overlap between weak forms and contractions. 说话时弱读式和缩约式有相互重叠之处. Weak forms (eg the weak forms of *be* and *have*) are used throughout connected speech in close proximity to a wide range of vocabulary. 弱读式(如 be 和 have 的弱读式)用于连贯的话语中可与大多词语连在一起. When personal pronouns are combined with the auxiliary verbs *be* and *have*, the auxiliaries take their weak forms. 人称代词与助动词 be 和 have 相连时, 助动词用弱读式. These are spoken as weak forms and may be written as contractions. 这些口语中的弱读式在书面语中可写成缩约式.

However, strict speech contractions involve the loss of a syllable whilst the remaining syllable contains some vowel other than /ə/. 但是严格的口语缩约式应失去一个音节, 余下的音节应包含除 /ə/ 音外的元音. This applies to certain auxiliary verbs which have special pronunciations when they are combined with *not*. 这也适用于某些发音特殊的助动词与 not 结合而成的缩约式. For example, *can* /kæn/ but *can't* /kɑ:nt/; *do* /du:/ but *don't* /dəʊnt/. 例如 can /kæn/ 与 can't /kɑ:nt/; do /du:/ 与 don't /dəʊnt/. These are not weak forms and may be stressed. 这些并非弱读式, 是可以重读的. When unstressed they retain the vowel of the form listed. 不重读时仍保持下表列出之形式的元音.

For the convenience of the dictionary user, the list below gives examples of some weak forms as well as contractions. 为本词典使用者方便起见,下表将一些弱读式与缩约式一并列出.

Verb 动词 + not

aren't	/ɑ:nt/	are not	*mayn't*	/ˈmeɪənt/	may not
can't	/kɑ:nt/	cannot	*mightn't*	/ˈmaɪtnt/	might not
couldn't	/ˈkʊdnt/	could not	*mustn't*	/ˈmʌsnt/	must not
daren't	/deənt/	dare not	*needn't*	/ˈni:dnt/	need not
didn't	/ˈdɪdnt/	did not	*oughtn't*	/ˈɔ:tnt/	ought not
doesn't	/ˈdʌznt/	does not	*shan't*	/ʃɑ:nt/	shall not
don't	/dəʊnt/	do not	*shouldn't*	/ˈʃʊdnt/	should not
hasn't	/ˈhæznt/	has not	*wasn't*	/ˈwɒznt/	was not
haven't	/ˈhævnt/	have not	*weren't*	/wɜ:nt/	were not
hadn't	/ˈhædnt/	had not	*won't*	/wəʊnt/	will not
isn't	/ˈɪznt/	is not	*wouldn't*	/ˈwʊdnt/	would not

Personal pronoun 人称代词 + Verb 动词

I'm	/aɪm/	I am	*she'll*	/ʃi:l/	she will
I've	/aɪv/	I have	*she'd*	/ʃi:d/	she would; she had
I'll	/aɪl/	I shall/will	*it's*	/ɪts/	it is; it has
I'd	/aɪd/	I would; I had	*it'll*	/ˈɪtl/	it will
you're	/jʊə(r)/	you are	*we're*	/wɪə(r)/	we are
you've	/ju:v/	you have	*we've*	/wi:v/	we have
you'll	/ju:l/	you will	*we'll*	/wi:l/	we shall/will
you'd	/ju:d/	you would; you had	*we'd*	/wi:d/	we would; we had
he's	/hi:z/	he is; he has	*they're*	/ðeə(r)/	they are
he'll	/hi:l/	he will	*they've*	/ðeɪv/	they have
he'd	/hi:d/	he would; he had	*they'll*	/ðeɪl/	they will
she's	/ʃi:z/	she is; she has	*they'd*	/ðeɪd/	they would; they had

6.4 How foreign words are pronounced in English 外来词语的读音方法. There are very many words of foreign origin in English. 英语中有许多外来词语. Nearly all of these have been completely assimilated into the language, with purely English sounds and stress patterns, eg *mutton* /ˈmʌtn/ or more recently *café* /ˈkæfeɪ/. 这些外来词语几乎已全部同化融合于英语中，具备纯英语读音和重音模式，如 mutton /ˈmʌtn/ 或是年代较近的 café /ˈkæfeɪ/. However, some foreign words and phrases commonly used by English speakers and included in the dictionary are still felt to be foreign. 但是有些外来词语，说英语的人普遍使用且已收入词典中，却仍然觉得是外国货. They are nevertheless pronounced with English sounds, eg *à la carte* /ˌɑ: lɑ: ˈkɑ:t/, *table d'hôte* /ˌtɑ:bl ˈdəʊt/. 不过这些词语已采用英语发音，如 à la carte /ˌɑ: lɑ: ˈkɑ:t/、table d'hôte /ˌtɑ:bl ˈdəʊt/. Most of these are borrowings from French, where a difficulty arises in anglicizing the pronunciation of the French nasalized vowels (unknown in English), as in *salon, en route*. 英语中的外来词语大多来自法语，法语的鼻元音很难转化为英语的元音(英语中无这类元音)，如 salon、en route. Native speakers of English use different pronunciations in such cases, ranging from totally anglicized forms to a more or less successful imitation of the French. 因而以英语为母语的人发音不尽相同，有人完全按英语发音，有人模仿法语发音却也差强人意. This dictionary gives completely anglicized forms, eg /ˈsælɒn/, /ˌɒn ˈru:t/. 本词典完全按英语读音标示，如 /ˈsælɒn/、/ˌɒn ˈru:t/.

Similarly, in the case of the relatively few words borrowed from other languages, eg (from Germanic languages) *angst*, *sauerkraut*, *smorgasbord*; (other Romance languages) *adagio*, *ballerina*, *hacienda*, *patio*; (Middle and Far Eastern languages) *harem*, *sheikh*, *guru*, *kimono*, the most commonly used anglicized pronunciation is given in the dictionary. 同样情况，从其他语言中借用为数较少的词语，本词典按使用最普遍的英语读音标示，如(源自日耳曼语的)angst、sauerkraut、smorgasbord, (源自其他罗曼语的)adagio、ballerina、hacienda、patio, (源自中东和远东语言的)harem、sheikh、guru、kimono.

6.5 The pronunciation of American English 美式英语的读音.

6.5.1 American variations 美式英语异读. The model for American English pronunciation is one which is widely acceptable in the US and has been called General American. 美式英语的标准读音就是在美国广为认同的读音，称作通用美式英语读音. Whenever Americans pronounce a word in a very different way from British speakers the dictionary gives the phonetic spelling of the American pronunciation after the British one, for example 若一个字的读音英美差别很大，本词典将美式读音置于英式读音之后，如:

half /hɑ:f; *US* hæf/ ...
ad·dress[1] /əˈdres; *US* ˈædres/ ...

If only part of the pronunciation changes, only that part is given for the American pronunciation, in order to save space, for example 若两者只有部分读音不同，为节省篇幅只标示美式读音有差别的部分，如:

at·ti·tude /ˈætɪtju:d; *US* -tu:d/.

6.5.2 Use of phonetic symbols 音标的使用. American English forms are shown with the same phonetic symbols as are used for British English. 美式读音与英式读音采用同一标音系统. However, particularly in the case of vowels, the same symbol will often mean somewhat different qualities in the British and American varieties. 但是同一音标，特别是元音音标，在英美读音中常表示略微不同的读音. For example, in American English the /ɒ/ in *hot* is similar to the British English /ɑ:/ sound, and the /ʌ/ of *cut* is similar to a stressed /ə/ sound. 例如，美式英语 hot 中的 /ɒ/ 读音近于英式英语的 /ɑ:/ 音，cut 中的 /ʌ/ 音近于重读的 /ə/ 音.

6.5.3 American /r/ 美式英语中的 /r/ 音. An important difference between British and American pronunciation, which is not shown in the dictionary, is the use of the /r/ sound in American English in words where British English does not use it, for example in the words *arm* and *star*. 英美读音有一个重要区别本词典不作标示，就是在有些字里美式读音用 /r/ 音，英式读音不用此音，如 arm 和 star 这两个字. The British pronunciations of these words are /ɑ:m/ and /stɑ:(r)/ (⇨ 4.3); the American pronunciations are /ɑ:rm/ and /stɑ:r/. 英式读音是 /ɑ:m/ 和 /stɑ:(r)/ (参看 4.3); 美式英语读音是 /ɑ:rm/ 和 /stɑ:r/. The rule to follow in the case of the /r/ sound in American English is to sound the /r/ whenever it occurs in the spelling of a word. 按照美式读音规则，只要字中拼法上有 r 的字就读出 /r/ 音来.

One common vowel variant that is not shown in the dictionary is the unstressed vowel of the second syllable of a word such as *happy* /ˈhæpɪ/. 有个普通的元音异读现象本词典未做标示，就是如 happy /ˈhæpɪ/ 等字中第二个音节的非重读元音. This vowel is regularly shown as /ɪ/. 这个元音一般标作 /ɪ/. For most American and some British speakers, the quality of this short vowel is somewhat closer to /i:/, particularly before a following vowel, as in *happier*. 大多数美国人和一些英国人把这个短元音发得有些近于 /i:/, 特别是其后紧接着一个元音时，如 happier 一字中者. Since in such contexts either quality is acceptable and the length is always short, the dictionary always shows /ɪ/ in such words. 这两种读音都符合规范，而且音的长度总是发得很短，本词典将这类字的音一律标作 /ɪ/.

7 PRONUNCIATION OF DERIVATIVES AND COMPOUNDS 派生词和复合词的读音

7.1 Derivatives 派生词. Many derivatives are formed by adding a suffix to the end of a word (⇨ 17). 许多派生词是由词尾加后缀构成的 (见 17). These derivatives are pronounced by simply saying the suffix after the word. 这些派生词的读音就是在词根的读音后面加上后缀的读音. For example, the adverb *slowly* /ˈsləʊlɪ/ is pronounced by joining the suffix *-ly* /lɪ/ to the word *slow* /sləʊ/. 例如，副词 slowly /ˈsləʊlɪ/ 的读音就是将 -ly /lɪ/ 加在 slow /sləʊ/ 之后而成.

However, whenever there may be doubt about how a suffix or a derivative is pronounced, the phonetic spelling is given. 但是在后缀或派生词读音可能有疑问处，均用音标注明. For example *mouthful* /-fʊl/, *regretful* /-fl/. 例如 mouthful /-fʊl/、regretful /-fl/. Also, if a change of stress is caused by adding a suffix to a word, then the pronunciation of the derivative is given in full, eg *arithmetic* /əˈrɪθmətɪk/, *arithmetical* /ˌærɪθˈmetɪkl/, *arithmetician* /əˌrɪθməˈtɪʃn/. 再者，若一个字加上后缀产生重音变化，这种派生词的读音全部用音标注明，如 arithmetic /əˈrɪθmətɪk/, arithmetical /ˌærɪθˈmetɪkl/, arithmetician /əˌrɪθməˈtɪʃn/.

7.2 Compounds 复合词.

7.2.1 Assimilation 音的同化. The pronunciation of a compound is not shown after the compound itself. 复合词其后不标示读音. This is because the pronunciation of the two parts appears elsewhere in the dictionary. 因复合词两部分的读音在本词典中已分别标出. However, the user should note that in speech adjacent sounds influence each other and the pronunciation of the root word may change slightly in one of two different ways 但是应注意到说话时相邻的音可互相影响，词根的读音按下述两种不同情况可产生其中一种轻微音变:

1. It may result in the replacement of a particular sound by a different one. 复合词中的某一个音被其他音取代. Note that within a compound these alterations commonly occur. 注意在复合词中这种变化很普遍. For example, /t/ at the end of *boat* may be replaced by /p/ before /m/ as in *boatman* /ˈbəʊpmən/ (cf *slot-machine* /ˈslɒpməʃi:n/), or /d/ by /g/ before /k/ as in *headquarters* /hegˈkwɔ:təz/. 例如，boat 词尾的 /t/ 在 /m/ 音前可被 /p/ 取代，如在 boatman /ˈbəʊpmən/ 中 (参看 slot-machine /ˈslɒpməʃi:n/)，或是 /d/ 音在 /k/ 音前可被 /g/ 音取代，如在 headquarters /hegˈkwɔ:təz/ 中. Although these are not shown in the dictionary, they follow the same regular pattern. 虽然本词典并未特别为此注明，但其中都有共同规律可循.

2. Instead of being replaced, some sounds are often omitted entirely. 有些音不是被取代而是常常完全省掉. This applies especially to /t/ and /d/ when surrounded by other consonants, eg *postmark* /ˈpəʊstmɑːk/ is often /ˈpəʊsmɑːk/, *windscreen* /ˈwɪndskriːn/ may be pronounced /ˈwɪnskriːn/. 这种情形尤见诸 /t/ 和 /d/ 这两个音前后都有其他辅音时, 如 postmark /ˈpəʊstmɑːk/ 时常作 /ˈpəʊsmɑːk/、windscreen /ˈwɪndskriːn/ 可读作 /ˈwɪnskriːn/.

Such changes in pronunciation may occur whenever these sounds are adjacent in speech. 在说话时只要这些音相邻就可能产生这种读音变化. In the case of a headword eg *landscape* the sound /d/ is often omitted although the fuller version is always shown in the dictionary. 以一个首词为例, 如 landscape, 其中 /d/ 音常常省略, 但是本词典标示的都是全部的音.

Variations of types 1 and 2 occur within the speech of any native speaker of English. 以英语为母语的人说话时都有上述 1 和 2 两种类型的音变. It is not possible to predict exactly when they will be encountered, but these variant forms tend to be used more frequently as the speed or the informality of speech increases. 要想事先准确指出这种音变之处是不可能的, 但是这种变化形式在说话速度加快或说话越随便时发生的也越频繁.

7.2.2 Stress in compounds 复合词的重音. Compounds have their own stress patterns which may be different from the normal pattern of the two separate parts. 复合词有本身的重音模式, 与其两部分各自的正常读音不尽相同. When an adjective modifies a noun, the noun usually has the primary stress, for example *ˌsilver ˈfish*. 若形容词修饰名词, 名词通常有主重音, 如 ˌsilver ˈfish. When an adjective and noun combine to form a compound noun, the compound may be spoken with the strong stress on the first word, for example *ˈsilver-fish* (an insect). 若形容词与名词结合构成复合名词, 说时这个复合词重音可能放在第一个词上, 如 ˈsilver-fish(蠹鱼). This second stress pattern is also especially common when two nouns form a two-word or hyphenated compound, for example: *ˈghost-writer, ˈbus-stop, ˈfield sports*. 这类第二种重音模式在两个名词构成双字复合词或带连接号的复合词时尤其常见, 如 ˈghost-writer、ˈbus-stop、ˈfield sports. To help the dictionary user, the stress is explicitly marked on all compounds. 为方便本词典使用者, 所有复合词均标示重音.

7.3 Idioms 习语. Idioms, like compounds, have their own special stress patterns. 习语像复合词一样有其特殊的重音模式. One of the words in any idiom is always spoken with more force than in other words. 英语习语中总有一个字比其他的字说时更加用力. This stressed word is often the last full word (⇨ 5.2), for example: *rain cats and ˈdogs*. 这个重读的字往往是一习语中最后的一个实词(见 5.2), 如 rain cats and ˈdogs. In some idioms, however, a grammatical word (⇨ 6.2) carries the main stress, for example: *There's nothing ˈfor it*. 但是有些习语主重音却在虚词上(见 6.2), 如 There's nothing ˈfor it. For the sake of clarity, the main stress is marked in each idiom printed in bold type under the heading '(idm)' in the dictionary, except for those few idioms that fall into two categories, namely those where the placing of the main stress can vary (like *to cap it all*) and those which are grammatically incomplete without variable additions (like *be a good thing that*). 为表明此点, 本词典在标有"(idm)"的黑体印刷的习语词条项下都标示主重音, 只两种少数情形例外: 一是主重音可改变的(如 to cap it all), 另一是不加上一些可变成分在语法上就不完整的(如 be a good thing that).

GRAMMAR 语法

8 PARTS OF SPEECH 词类

8.1 Part of speech labels 词类标志. A number of standard abbreviations indicating the appropriate part of speech (ie grammatical class) are used throughout the dictionary. 本词典一律使用标准缩略式标示词类(即词在语法上的分类). The labels, with the parts of speech they represent, are 这些标志及其代表的词类是:

adj (adjective 形容词), *adv* (adverb 副词), *aux v* (auxiliary verb 助动词), *conj* (conjunction 连词), *det* (determiner 限定词), *interj* (interjection 叹词), *n* (noun 名词), *prep* (preposition 介词), *pron* (pronoun 代词), *v* (verb 动词).

More complex labels are produced by adding such modifiers as *rel* (relative) and *possess* (possessive), thus: *rel pron, rel adv, possess det, possess pron,* etc. 比较复杂的标志是增加修饰成分, 如 rel(relative 关系的)和 possess(possessive 属有的)等, 从而组成: rel pron、rel adv、possess det、possess pron 等. (For a full list of the abbreviations used in the dictionary see the list on the front endpapers. 详见本词典前衬页的注解.) All these additional parts of speech labels are defined at their point of entry in the appropriate place in the dictionary. 这些附加的词类标志在本词典各有关词条中均分别注明.

8.2 Position 位置. A part of speech label is provided for each headword and derivative, and for every compound that is written as one word or hyphenated. 每个首词和派生词以及每个合成一个词的或带连接号的复合词都标有词类标志. It is placed immediately after the pronunciation, if this is given, or next to the derivative or compound if not 词类标志置于音标之后, 或置于没有音标的派生词或复合词之后:

ir·regu·lar /ɪˈregjʊlə(r); ɪˋrɛgjələ˞/ *adj* ...
▷ **ir·regu·lar** *n* ...
ir·regu·lar·ity /ɪˌregjʊˈlærətɪ; ɪˌrɛgjəˋlærətɪ/ *n* ...
ir·regu·larly *adv*.

race[1] ... *n* ...
□ ˈ**racecard** *n* ...
ˈ**racecourse** *n* ...

Additional labels are provided when the headword or derivative is used in different ways with no change of meaning 首词或派生词的词义不变但可作不同词类使用时, 用附加标志注明:

chau·vin·ist /ˈʃəʊvɪnɪst; ˋʃovɪnɪst/ *n, adj* ...

9 IRREGULAR WRITTEN FORMS 不规则的书面语形式

9.1 Past tense and past participle forms of verbs 动词的过去时态形式及过去分词形式.

• If a final consonant is doubled when forming the past tense and past participle, the doubling is shown in **bold** print 动词构成过去时态形式和过去分词时, 若最后一个辅音字母需双写, 其双写部分用黑体标示:

bob[1] /bɒb; bɑb/ *v* (-**bb**-) ...

• If a verb has one or two irregular forms, the form or forms are given in full 一个动词若有一两个不规则形式, 其不规则形式全部列出:

catch[1] /kætʃ; kætʃ/ *v* (*pt, pp* **caught** /kɔ:t; kɔt/) ...
see[1] /si:; si/ *v* (*pt* **saw** /sɔ:; sɔ/, *pp* **seen** / si:n; sin/) ...

• If both the past tense and past participle are irregular, but a final consonant is doubled in forming the present participle (*-ing* form), that doubling is shown, thus 一个动词的过去时态形式及过去分词若均为不规则变化, 且构成现在分词(-ing形式)时最后一个辅音字母需双写, 其双写部分这样标示:

be·gin /bɪˈgɪn; bɪˋgɪn/ *v* (-**nn**-; *pt* **began** /bɪˈgæn; bɪˋgæn/, *pp* **begun** /bɪˈgʌn; bɪˋgʌn/) ...

9.2 Plural forms of nouns 名词的复数形式. These are indicated wherever necessary, either because simple addition of *-s* or *-es* is not correct, or where there may be some doubt. 在有需要处标示, 或因不可用加 -s 或 -es 的简单方式构成, 或因学习者对其构成复数方式可能无把握.

• The plural forms of nouns ending in *-o* (whether *-s*, *-es* or both) are always shown 以 -o 结尾的名词复数形式(不论是需加 -s、-es 或两者皆可)一律标示:

mango /ˈmæŋɡəʊ; ˋmæŋgo/ *n* (*pl* **~es** or **~s**) . . .

• When the form of a countable noun is unchanged in the plural, this is indicated as follows 可数名词复数无变化时, 标示如下:

grouse /ɡraʊs; graus/ *n* (*pl* unchanged) . . .

• When the formation of the plural affects the spelling or pronunciation of the headword, the plural spelling and pronunciation are given in full 首词复数形式改变拼法或读音时, 全部标示:

child /tʃaɪld; tʃaɪld/ *n* (*pl* **children** /ˈtʃɪldrən; ˋtʃɪldrən/) . . .

• Other irregular forms are either represented by the last two syllables, preceded by a hyphen 其他不规则形式, 或在最后两个音节前加连接号标示:

syn·thesis /ˈsɪnθəsɪs; ˋsɪnθəsɪs/ *n* (*pl* **-theses** /-si:z; -siz/) . . .

or are given in full, with alternatives where appropriate 或全部标示, 包括变体:

ba·sis /ˈbeɪsɪs; ˋbesɪs/ *n* (*pl* **bases** /ˈbeɪsi:z; ˋbesiz/) . . .

9.3 Comparative and superlative forms of adjectives and adverbs 形容词和副词的比较级和最高级形式. Whenever an adjective (or an adverb) forms its comparative and superlative by adding *-er* and *-est*, or *-r* and *-st*, those endings are shown, as follows 形容词(或副词)构成比较级和最高级时词尾加 -er 和 -est、或 -r 和 -st, 这些词尾标示如下:

cheap /tʃi:p; tʃip/ *adj* (**-er, -est**) . . .
safe /seɪf; sef/ *adj* (**-r, -st**) . . .

If a final consonant is doubled before the comparative or superlative ending, this doubling is shown in the entry 在比较级或最高级词形结尾前, 最后一个辅音字母若需双写, 双写的字母在词条中这样标示:

hot /hɒt; hɑt/ *adj* (**-tter, -ttest**) . . .

Irregular forms of an adjective are given in full at the entry for that adjective (though their special meanings, idioms, etc may be given in separate entries, eg at **worse**, **worst**, etc) 形容词的不规则形式在词条中全部列出(有特殊意义的、构成习语等的另立词条, 如 **worse**、**worst** 等):

bad /bæd; bæd/ *adj* (**worse** /wɜ:s; wɝs/, **worst** /wɜ:st; wɝst/) . . .

10 GRAMMATICAL PATTERNS AND CODES 语法模式及其代码

10.1 Verbs 动词.

10.1.1 Verb patterns and codes 动词模式及其代码. Foreign learners often have great difficulty in deciding which sentence constructions, or patterns, a verb can be used in. 学习英语的外国人往往难以确定某动词可用于何种句子结构或模式中. (They may know that *I liked to help him* and *I liked helping him* are both correct, but be unaware that with the verb *dislike* only the second pattern is possible. 尽管知道 I liked to help him 和 I liked helping him 两句都正确, 但不一定察觉到 dislike 这个动词却只可用于第二种模式.) In this dictionary much help in dealing with this problem is provided in the form of example sentences. 本词典采用例句形式处理这一问题颇有助益. At the first meaning for the verb *bear*, for instance, the pattern 'transitive verb + direct object noun' is illustrated by *The document bore his signature*. 例如在 bear 这一动词的第一项定义之后, 用例句 The document bore his signature 说明"及物动词 + 作直接宾语的名词"这一模式. But the **bear**[2] entry (like other verb entries) also contains a reference to the pattern itself – in the form of a code. 但在 **bear**² 词条(如同其他动词词条)里, 也含有这一模式本身的参考资料 —— 以代码形式标示. The code for the pattern just given is [Tn], in which T = transitive verb and n = noun. 上一示例的模式代码为 [Tn], 其中 T = 及物动词, n = 名词.

10.1.2 The positions of codes 代码的位置. If a verb has only one meaning, or several meanings all with the same pattern(s), the pattern or patterns are placed after the part of speech label 若动词只有一项词义或有几项词义都用于同类模式, 其模式代码置于词类标志之后:

> **re-echo** ... *v* [I] echo again and again ...
> **be·queath** ... *v* [Tn, Dn·n, Dn·pr] ... **1** ... **2** ...

But if the various meanings of a verb correspond to different patterns (or sets of patterns), the codes are placed after the sense numbers, as follows 但若动词有几项词义而语法模式不同, 其模式代码置于义项号码之后, 说明如下:

> **sell** ... *v* ... **1** [I, Ipr, Tn, Tn·pr, Dn·n, Dn·pr] ... **2** [Tn] ... **3** [Tn] ... **4** [I, Ipr, In/pr] ...

The verb pattern scheme described below (⇨ 10.1.4) shows that certain verb patterns (eg [Tn], [Tn·pr], [Tni], etc) regularly have corresponding passive constructions. 下列动词模式表(见 10.1.4)说明某些动词模式(如 [Tn]、[Tn·pr]、[Tni] 等)一般可用作被动结构. Users can assume that when any of those patterns are referred to in an entry *without any further label* a passive is possible. 在词条中有这类模式而没有其他标志者, 意为可用于被动结构. However, if an individual verb or meaning is an exception to the rule for a pattern (eg because it is usually or especially used in the passive, or not used in the passive at all), additional labels are used, as follows 但若某一动词或词义在所标示的模式中有例外用法(如该动词通常或尤其用于被动语态, 或完全不用于被动语态), 则有附加标志, 说明如下:

> **shape**² ... *v* ... **4** [Tn esp passive] ...

When all the patterns to which a verb or meaning belongs are restricted in one of these ways, the label precedes the patterns 若某动词或词义所标示的所有模式均受上述某一种限制, 则这种附加标志置于这些模式之前:

> **breed** ... *v* ... **3** [esp passive: Tn, Tn·pr, Cn·n/a, Cn·t] ...

10.1.3 The meanings of codes 代码的意义. Thirty-two patterns (with matching codes) are used in the dictionary to account for the various ways in which verbs can be used 本词典采用三十二个模式(及相应的代码)说明动词的各种用法. Teachers especially should note that the codes can be read by the dictionary user on two levels 教师尤应注意, 使用本词典的人可在两个层次上理解代码:

• The SIMPLE level 简单层次. A code such as [Dn·pr] (as in *He gave the book to John*) is designed to suggest to the learner 'double-transitive verb + noun + prepositional phrase', ie the parts of speech (or phrase or clause types) of which the pattern is composed. 使用一种代码, 如 [Dn·pr] (如用于 He gave the book to John 句中)目的在于告诉学习英语的人"双及物动词 + 名词 + 介词短语"这一模式, 即构成这一模式的词类(或短语或从句类型). These indications will be sufficient for many learners. 这些资料可满足大多数学习者的需要. Moreover, the meanings of the letters (n = noun, a = adjective, etc) can be easily learnt, so that within a short time the learner should be able to recall patterns simply by looking at their codes. 况且, 字母代表的意思(n = noun 名词、a = adjective 形容词等)容易记住, 在很短的时间内可做到一看代码就能想起是哪个模式. (Learners who wish to be reminded of the meaning of a code at this basic level should refer to the chart inside the back cover. 书后封里的代码一览表可供这一层次学习者随时参考.)

• The STRUCTURAL level 结构层次. But the codes are also designed to indicate the structural elements which the patterns contain (ie whether they have one or more objects, a complement, an adjunct, etc). 这些代码还用以表示一模式包含的结构成分(即是否有一个或不止一个宾语、补语、修饰成分等). The 'D' in the code [Dn·pr], for example, means that the verb is followed by a direct object and an indirect object. 例如 [Dn·pr] 中的 D 指动词后有一个直接宾语和一个间接宾语. The dot in the code shows the division between these elements. 代码中的点号指这些成分之间的分界. (In the example *He gave the book to John, 'the book'* is the direct object and *'to John'* the indirect object. 在 He gave the book to John 一句中, the book 是直接宾语, to John 是间接宾语.) The structural level is important for teachers and more advanced learners because it enables them to distinguish between sentences which are superficially the same. 结构层次对教师和程度高的学习者很重要, 便于区分貌似相同的句子. (*She liked him to play the piano* is [Tnt], *She inspired him to play the piano* is [Cn·t], *She told him to play the piano* is [Dn·t] ☆ She liked him to play the piano 的模式是 [Tnt], She inspired him to play the piano 的模式是 [Cn·t], She told him to play the piano 的模式是 [Dn·t]).

The following table shows what elements are indicated at the structural level by the capital letters L, I, T, C and D 下面的表中大写字母 L、I、T、C、D 表示在结构层次中代表的成分:

L = LINKING verb (followed by a COMPLEMENT, an element which provides more information about the subject of the sentence). 系动词(后面接补语, 即进一步说明句子的主语的成分).

I = INTRANSITIVE verb (NOT followed by a COMPLEMENT or an OBJECT, though it may be followed by an ADJUNCT, an element which tells us about the time, place, manner, etc of the action of the verb). 不及物动词(后面不接补语或宾语, 但可接修饰成分, 即说明动词之动作的时间、地点、方式等的状语).

T = TRANSITIVE verb (followed by a DIRECT OBJECT, an element which often refers to the person or thing affected by the action of the verb). 及物动词(后面接直接宾语, 即受动词动作影响的人或事物).

C = COMPLEX-TRANSITIVE verb (followed by a DIRECT OBJECT and a COMPLEMENT, an element which provides more information about the direct object). 复合及物动词(后面接直接宾语和宾语补语, 即进一步说明直接宾语的成分). Note 说明: in the code, a dot divides the direct object from the complement. 在代码中, 直接宾语和宾语补语之间用点号隔开.

D = DOUBLE-TRANSITIVE verb (followed by a DIRECT OBJECT and an INDIRECT OBJECT, an element which refers to a person who receives something or benefits from an action). 双及物动词(后面接直接宾语和间接宾语, 即因动词之动作而得到某事物的人). Note 说明: in the code, a dot divides the direct from the indirect object. 在代码中, 直接宾语和间接宾语之间用点号隔开.

10.1.4 Verb pattern scheme 动词模式表. At the top of each of the following tables, a full explanation of the pattern is given, thus 在下列各表的上部列出的是动词模式的详细说明, 例如:

[Tt]

subject 主语	transitive verb 及物动词	direct object: non-finite clause (*to*-infinitive) 直接宾语: 非限定式短语(带 to 的不定式)

These explanations are followed by examples and notes. 在这些说明之后有示例和注释. Reference is made in the notes to the possibility or otherwise of a passive construction for that pattern. 在注释里注明某模式是否能用于被动结构.

[La]

subject 主语	linking verb 系动词	subject complement: adjective (phrase) 主语补语: 形容词(短语)
1 The lesson	**was**	interesting.
2 The damage	**appears** (to be)	serious.
3 The soup	**tasted**	delicious.
4 The beach	**looked**	deserted.
5 The game	**became**	more exciting.
6 The actors	**got**	ready.
7 The milk	**went**	sour.
8 The cinemas	**remained**	open all week.
9 To go further	**was**	impossible.
10 To give time to the project	**became**	more difficult.

1 那一课很有意思.
2 看来损失很严重.
3 汤的味道很美.
4 海滩像是遭遗弃的样子.
5 比赛越来越激烈了.
6 演员都准备好了.
7 牛奶酸了.
8 电影院整星期都开放.
9 再走下去是不可能的.
10 给这个项目安排时间更加困难了.

(a) The complement is an adjective or adjective phrase which describes some quality or feature of the subject (Cf Cn·a). 此处的补语是描述主语的性质或特征的形容词或形容词短语(参看 Cn·a).

(b) The verbs *appear*, *seem* and *prove* may be followed by *to be*. 动词 appear、seem、prove 后面可接 to be.

(c) When the subject is a *that*-clause or a *to*-infinitive clause, and the verb is *be*, *appear* or *become*, *it* can be introduced at the beginning and the subject moved to the end. 若主语是 that 从句或带 to 的不定式短语, 而动词是 be、appear 或 become, 可在句首用引导词 it 并将主语移至句尾. This pattern is preferred when the subject is relatively long compared with the complement 这一模式宜用于主语较长补语较短的情形:

- To go further **was** impossible.
- It **was** impossible to go further.

- To give time to the project **became** more difficult.
- It **became** more difficult to give time to the project.

[Ln]

subject 主语	linking verb 系动词	subject complement: noun (phrase) 主语补语: 名词(短语)
1 David	**is**	my younger brother.
2 That	**appears** (to be)	the best answer.
3 Jeffries	**sounds**	just the man we're looking for.
4 Frank	**became**	a teacher.
5 This	**proved** (to be)	a good investment.
6 The boys	**remained**	the best of friends.
7 To stay out of sight	**seemed** (to be)	the wisest thing to do.

1 大卫是我弟弟.
2 这算是最恰当的答案.
3 杰弗里斯的情况听起来正是我们要找的人.
4 弗兰克当上教师了.
5 这项投资果然不错.
6 那些男孩儿一直是最要好的朋友.
7 不出头露面似乎是上策.

(a) The complement is a noun or noun phrase, and it refers to the role, occupation, etc of the subject (Cf Cn·n). 此处的补语是名词或名词短语, 指主语的身分、职业等(参看 Cn·n).

(b) The verbs *appear*, *seem* and *prove* may be followed by *to be*. 动词 appear、seem、prove 后面可接 to be.

(c) When the subject is a *to*-infinitive clause and the verb is *be*, *seem* (*to be*), *appear* (*to be*) or *become*, *it* can be introduced at the beginning and the subject moved to the end. 若主语是带 to 不定式从句而动词是 be、seem(to be)、appear(to be) 或 become, 可在句首用引导词 it 并将主语移至句尾. This pattern is preferred when the subject is relatively long compared with the complement 这一模式宜用于主语较长补语较短的情况:

- To stay out of sight **seemed** (to be) the wisest thing to do.
- It **seemed** the wisest thing to do to stay well out of sight.

[I]

subject 主语	intransitive verb 不及物动词	adjunct: (adverb (phrase) of time, manner, etc) 修饰成分: 表示时间、方式等的副词(短语)
1 The moon	**rose**	early.
2 The clothes-line	**sagged**.	
3 Veronica	is **reading**.	
4 John and Jane	are **arguing**	again.
5 The door	**opened**.	
6 Oil and water	don't **mix**.	

1 月亮升起得很早.
2 晾衣绳下垂了.
3 维朗妮卡正在阅读.
4 约翰和简又争论起来了.
5 门开了.
6 油和水不能混合在一起.

(a) In this pattern, the verb is not followed by an object, a complement or a closely linked adjunct (Cf Ipr). 在这一模式里，动词后面不可接宾语、补语或与之紧密相连的修饰成分(参看 Ipr). Optional adverbs of time, manner, result, etc *can* be used (eg *early*). 表示时间、方式、结果等的副词(如 early)可用于这一模式.

(b) Some verbs can be used in this pattern and the [Tn] pattern without a change of subject (or of verb meaning) 有些动词可用于这一模式和[Tn] 模式而不改变主语(或动词的意思):

- Veronica is **reading**. [I]
- Veronica is **reading** a fairy story. [Tn]

(c) Some verbs can be used in this pattern (with *and* linking two nouns as the subject) and in a corresponding [Ipr] pattern (with *with* following the verb) 有些动词(在 and 连接两个名词作主语时)可用于这一模式，也可(在同类动词后接 with)用于与这一模式相对应的 [Ipr] 模式:

- Oil and water don't **mix**. [I]
- Oil doesn't **mix with** water. [Ipr]

[Ipr]

subject 主语	intransitive verb 不及物动词	adjunct: prepositional phrase 修饰成分: 介词短语
1 Helen	is **coming**	**to** dinner.
2 The minister	**referred**	**to** the importance of exports.
3 Mother	can't **cope**	**with** the extra visitors.
4 People	are **complaining**	**about** the traffic.
5 You	can't **rely**	**on** Martin.
6 Oil	doesn't **mix**	**with** water.

1 海伦要来吃晚饭.
2 那个部长谈到了出口货物的重要性.
3 母亲无法应酬那些额外增加的客人.
4 大家都埋怨交通的现状.
5 你可不能依靠马丁.
6 油不能与水混合在一起.

(a) Here, the verb is closely linked in grammar and meaning to a prepositional phrase. 此处动词在语法上和意义上都与介词短语紧密相连. The exact choice of preposition is shown in **bold print** in the above table and in dictionary entries (Cf Tn·pr). 可使用的介词用**黑体**印出列于上表及本词典词条中(参看 Tn·pr).

(b) After some verbs, the prepositional phrase cannot be removed without producing nonsense (*) or changing the meaning of the verb 在某些动词之后，介词短语不可去掉否则语句不通(*)或动词的意思改变:

- The minister **referred to** the importance of exports.
- *The minister **referred**.

Prepositional phrases which are fixed in this way are shown in entries in **bold print** 不可去掉的介词短语在词条里用**黑体**标示:

refer ... [Ipr ...] **~to sb/sth** ...

(c) After other verbs, the prepositional phrase can be removed freely 在其他动词之后, 介词短语可随意去掉:

- Mother can't **cope with** the extra visitors.
- Mother can't **cope**.

In those cases, the prepositional phrase is shown like this 在这种情形下, 介词短语这样标示:

cope ... [I, Ipr] ~ **(with sb/sth)** ...

(d) After some verbs, a *to*-infinitive or *-ing* form can be added to the prepositional phrase 在某些动词之后, 可在介词短语之后加上带 to 的不定式或动词的 -ing 形式:

- You can't **rely on** Martin.
- You can't **rely on** Martin to help.

This addition to the pattern is shown thus 这一模式的扩展这样标示:

rely ... [Ipr ...] ~ **on/upon sb/sth (to do sth)** ...

(e) Some verbs used in this pattern can be made passive. 用于这一模式的某些动词可用于被动结构. The noun or noun phrase following the preposition in the active pattern becomes the subject of the passive one 在主动模式里介词后面的名词或名词短语变成被动模式中的主语:

- The minister **referred to** the importance of exports.
- The importance of exports was **referred to** (by the minister).

This possibility is illustrated in the entries by examples. 主动被动可转换者, 在词条里用示例说明.

[Ip]

subject 主语	intransitive verb 不及物动词	adjunct: adverbial particle 修饰成分: 副词小词
1 A tiger	has **got**	**out**.
2 A visitor	**came**	**in**.
3 The noise	**faded**	**away**.
4 The house	has **warmed**	**up**.
5 The train	**whistled**	**past**.
6 We'll have to	**toss**	**up**.

1 有只老虎出来了. 2 有个来访者进来了.
3 嘈杂声渐渐消失了. 4 房子里暖和起来了.
5 火车呼啸着飞快驶过. 6 我们得掷硬币来决定了.

(a) Here, the verb is closely linked to an adverbial particle. 此处动词和副词小词紧密相连. The exact choice of particle is shown in **bold print** in the above table and in dictionary entries (Cf Tn·p). 可使用的副词小词用**黑体**印出列于上表及本词典词条中(参看 Tn·p).

(b) After some verbs, the particle cannot be removed without changing the meaning of the verb or producing nonsense (*) 在某些动词之后, 副词小词不可去掉否则动词的意思改变或语句不通(*):

- A tiger has **got out**.
- *A tiger has **got**.

(c) After other verbs, the particle can be deleted freely 在其他动词之后, 副词小词可随意去掉:

- The noise **faded away**. [Ip]
- The noise **faded**. [I]

In such cases the particle is shown thus 在这种情形下, 副词小词这样标示:

fade ... [I, Ip] ~ **(away)** ...

(d) Idiomatic combinations such as **dry up** (= become unable to speak), **blaze away** (= fire continuously), which also fit this pattern, are treated separately in this dictionary (⇨ 16 PHRASAL VERBS). 惯用搭配如 **dry up** (= become unable to speak 说不出话)、**blaze away** (= fire continuously 连续射击)也符合这一模式, 但在本词典里另做处理(见 16 PHRASAL VERBS).

[In/pr]

subject 主语	intransitive verb 不及物动词	adjunct: noun (phrase)/ prepositional phrase 修饰成分: 名词(短语)[介词短语]
1 The book	**cost** (me)	ten dollars.
2 The room	**measures**	10 metres across.
3 The meeting	**lasted**	**(for)** three hours.
4 The sea front	**extends**	**(for)** three miles.

1 那本书花了(我)十块钱. 2 这个房间宽 10 米.
3 会议开了三个小时. 4 滨海区有 3 英里长.

(a) Here, the verb is closely linked to a noun (phrase) or prepositional phrase which indicates 'extent' (eg how much the subject costs, what it measures, how long it lasts). 此处动词与表示"程度"的名词(短语)或介词短语紧密相连(如主语所指的物值多少钱、量度是多少、持续多久).

(b) The correct choice of preposition is *for* or *by*. 可使用的介词是 for 或 by. This is shown in the dictionary as follows 在本词典里这样标示:

last ... [In/pr] ~ **(for) sth** ...

[It]

subject 主语	intransitive verb 不及物动词	adjunct: non-finite clause (*to*-infinitive) 修饰成分: 非限定式短语(带 to 的不定式)
1 Jane	**hesitated**	to phone the office.
2 We all	**longed**	to get away for a family holiday.
3 I	wouldn't **care**	to have a fight with him.
4 They	wouldn't **condescend**	to speak to ordinary mortals.

1 简迟迟不愿给办公室打电话. 2 我们都巴不得全家外出度假.
3 我可不想跟他打架. 4 他们不愿屈尊同老百姓说话.

(a) Here, an intransitive verb is closely linked to a *to*-infinitive clause. 此处不及物动词与带 to 的不定式短语紧密相连.

(b) Verbs in this pattern cannot be made passive. 这一模式的动词不可用于被动结构.

[Tn]

subject 主语	transitive verb 及物动词	direct object: noun (phrase)/pronoun 直接宾语: 名词(短语)[代词]
1 George	was **watching**	television.
2 Veronica	is **reading**	a fairy story.
3 The company	**paid**	a colossal sum.
4 Peter	doesn't **owe**	anything.
5 A small boy	**opened**	the door.

1 乔治正在看电视. 2 维朗妮卡正在阅读童话故事.
3 公司付了一笔巨款. 4 彼得什么也不欠.
5 有个小男孩儿把门打开了.

(a) The direct object is a noun (eg *television*), noun phrase (eg *the door*) or pronoun (eg *anything*) (Cf Dn·n). 直接宾语是名词(如 television)、名词短语(如 the door)或代词(如 anything)(参看 Dn·n).

(b) For verbs used in this pattern and the [I] pattern without a change of subject or meaning, see [I], note (b). 关于可用于这一模式和 [I] 模式的动词(而不改变主语或意思), 见 [I] 模式中的注释(b).

(c) Most verbs in this pattern can be made passive, with the object of the active pattern becoming the subject of the passive one 这一模式的大多数动词均可用于被动结构, 将主动结构中的宾语变成被动结构中的主语:

- A small boy **opened** the door.
- The door was **opened** (by a small boy).

Exceptions are shown in dictionary entries thus 例外情形在本词典的词条里这样标示: [Tn no passive].

[Tn·pr]

subject 主语	transitive verb 及物动词	direct object 直接宾语	adjunct: prepositional phrase 修饰成分: 介词短语
1 The teacher	**referred**	the class	**to** a passage in the textbook.
2 The waiter	**served**	Sarah	**with** a double helping.
3 The Council	have **cleared**	the pavements	**of** rubbish.
4 The lecturer	**confused**	your name	**with** mine.
5 The visiting speaker	**thanked**	the Chairman	**for** his kind remarks.

1 教师让班上同学看课本里的一个段落.
2 服务员给萨拉端来了双份菜.
3 市议会清除了人行道上的垃圾.
4 那个讲师把你的名字和我的名字弄混了.
5 来访的演讲人感谢主席对他的称赞.

(a) In this pattern, the verb is closely linked in grammar and meaning to a prepositional phrase. 在这一模式里，动词在语法上和意义上均与介词短语紧密相连. The exact choice of preposition is shown in **bold print** in the above table and in dictionary entries (Cf Ipr). 可使用的介词在上表及本词典的词条里均用**黑体**标示(参看 Ipr).

(b) After some verbs, the prepositional phrase cannot be removed without producing nonsense (*) or changing the meaning of the verb 在某些动词之后，介词短语不可去掉否则语句不通(*)或动词的意思改变:

- The teacher **referred** the class **to** a passage in the textbook.
- *The teacher **referred** the class.

Prepositional phrases which are fixed in this way are shown in the dictionary in **bold print** 不可去掉的介词短语在词条里用**黑体**标示:

refer ... [Tn·pr ...] ~ **sb/sth to sb/sth**

(c) After other verbs, the prepositional phrase can be removed without changing the meaning of the verb 在其他动词之后，介词短语可去掉而不改变动词的意思:

- The visiting speaker **thanked** the Chairman **for** his kind remarks. [Tn·pr]
- The visiting speaker **thanked** the Chairman. [Tn]

In those cases, the prepositional phrase is shown thus 在这种情形下，介词短语这样标示:

thank ... [Tn, Tn·pr] ~ **sb (for sth)** ...

(d) Most verbs in this pattern can be made passive. 这一模式的大多数动词均可用于被动结构. The direct object of an active verb becomes the subject of the same verb in the passive 主动动词的直接宾语在被动结构中变为该动词的主语:

- The Council have **cleared** the pavements **of** rubbish.
- The pavements have been **cleared of** rubbish (by the Council).

Exceptions are shown in dictionary entries thus 例外情形在本词典的词条里这样标示: [Tn·pr no passive].

[Tn·p]

subject 主语	transitive verb 及物动词	direct object 直接宾语	adjunct: adverbial particle 修饰成分: 副词小词
1 Bill	**has**	a blue shirt	**on**.
2 The frost	has **killed**	the buds	**off**.
3 The nurse	**shook**	the medicine	**up**.
4 Sally	is **tidying**	her room	**up**.

1 比尔穿着蓝色衬衫.
2 寒霜把嫩芽冻死了.
3 护士把药摇匀了.
4 萨莉正在收拾自己的房间.

(a) In this pattern, the verb is closely linked to an adverbial particle. 在这一模式里, 动词与副词小词紧密相连. The exact choice of particle is shown in **bold print** in the above table and in dictionary entries (Cf Ip). 可使用的副词小词在上表及本词典的词条里均用**黑体**标示(参看 Ip).

(b) After some verbs, the particle cannot be removed without changing the meaning of the verb or producing nonsense (*) 在某些动词之后, 副词小词不可去掉否则动词的意思改变或语句不通(*):

- Bill **has** a blue shirt **on**.
- Bill **has** a blue shirt.

(c) After other verbs, the particle can be deleted freely 在其他动词之后, 副词小词可随意去掉:

- Sally is **tidying** her room **up**. [Tn·p]
- Sally is **tidying** her room. [Tn]

In those cases the particle is shown thus 在这种情形下, 副词小词这样标示:

tidy ... [Tn, Tn·p ...] ~ **sth (up)** ...

(d) Idiomatic combinations such as **blow sth up** (= explode sth), **whip sb up** (= excite sb), which also fit this pattern, are treated separately in this dictionary (⇨ 16 PHRASAL VERBS). 惯用搭配如 **blow sth up**(= explode sth 炸掉某物)、**whip sb up** (= excite sb 使某人兴奋)也符合这一模式, 但在本词典里另做处理(见 16 PHRASAL VERBS).

(e) When the direct object is a pronoun, it precedes the particle 直接宾语若是代词, 置于副词小词之前:

- The nurse **shook it up**.

When it is a short noun phrase or a noun (see examples in the table), it can usually either precede or follow the particle 直接宾语若是短的名词短语或一个名词(见表中示例), 通常置于副词小词之前后均可:

- The frost has **killed** the buds **off**.
- The frost has **killed off** the buds.

When the direct object is a long noun phrase, it usually follows the particle 直接宾语若是长的名词短语, 通常置于副词小词之后:

- Bill **has on** a blue shirt and a pair of jeans.

(f) Most verbs in this pattern can be made passive. 这一模式的大多数动词均可用于被动结构. The direct object of an active verb becomes the subject of the same verb in the passive 主动动词的直接宾语在被动结构中变为该动词的主语:

- The frost has **killed** the buds **off**.
- The buds have been **killed off** (by the frost).

Exceptions are shown in dictionary entries thus 例外情形在本词典的词条里这样标示: [Tn·p no passive].

[Tf]

subject 主语	transitive verb 及物动词	direct object: *that*-clause 直接宾语: that 从句
1 The employers	**announced**	that the dispute had been settled.
2 The department	**proposed**	that new salary scales should be introduced.
3 Doctors	had **noted**	that the disease was spreading.
4 Officials	**believe**	that a settlement is possible.
5 We	**consider**	that Frank has been badly treated.
6 The weathermen	**forecast**	that more snow is on the way.

1 雇主宣布纠纷已获解决. 2 这个部门建议采用新的工资级别制. 3 医生均已注意到疾病正在蔓延. 4 官员均认为有可能解决. 5 我们觉得弗兰克受到了虐待. 6 气象台预报还要下雪.

(a) In this pattern, the direct object is a *that*-clause (Cf Dn·f, Dpr·f). 在这一模式里, 直接宾语是 that 从句(参看 Dn·f, Dpr·f).

(b) The conjunction *that* can sometimes be omitted. 连词 that 有时可省略. When it can, *that* is usually shown in brackets in the first (or only) example sentence in entries 可省略时, that 通常置于括号中放在词条的第一个(或唯一的)例句中:

consider ... *We consider (that) Frank has been badly treated.*

(c) Some verbs used in this pattern can be made passive. 这一模式的某些动词可用于被动结构. (Note the construction with *it* 注意带 it 的结构).

- Officials **believe** that a settlement is possible.
- It is **believed** (by officials) that a settlement is possible.

Exceptions are shown in dictionary entries thus 例外情形在本词典的词条里这样标示: [Tf no passive].

[Tw]

subject 主语	transitive verb 及物动词	direct object: finite clause/non-finite clause 直接宾语: 限定从句或短语［非限定从句或短语］
1 The class	doesn't **know**	what time it has to be in school/what time to be in school.
2 The students	haven't **learnt**	which tutors they can rely on/which tutors to rely on.
3 Bill	**discovered**	who he had to give the money to/who to give the money to.
4 We	hadn't **decided**	what we ought to do next/what to do next.

1 全班同学都不知道什么时候上课. 2 这些学生都不知道应该听哪些导师的.
3 比尔知道得把钱给谁了. 4 我们还没决定下一步该做什么.

(a) In this pattern, the direct object is a finite or non-finite clause beginning with 在这一模式里, 直接宾语是限定或非限定从句或短语, 从句或短语的开头

EITHER 或是 (i) A '*wh*-element', which can be a pronoun (*who(m)*, *whose*, *which*, *what*), a determiner + noun (*what time*, *which tutors*, etc) or an adverb (*why* (finite clauses only), *when*, *where*, *how*) 一个"wh-成分", 可为代词(who(m)、whose、which、what)、限定词 + 名词(what time、which tutors 等)或副词(why(仅用于限定从句或短语)、when、where、how);

OR 或是 (ii) One of the conjunctions *if* (finite clauses only) or *whether* (Cf Dn·w, Dpr·w) 连词 if(仅用于限定从句或短语)或 whether(参看 Dn·w, Dpr·w).

(b) Some verbs used in this pattern can be made passive. 这一模式的某些动词可用于被动结构. (Note the construction with *it* 注意带 it 的结构).

- We hadn't **decided** what we ought to do next/what to do next.
- It hadn't been **decided** (by us) what we ought to do next/what to do next.

Exceptions are shown in dictionary entries thus 例外情形在本词典的词条里这样标示: [Tw no passive].

[Tt]

subject 主语	transitive verb 及物动词	direct object: non-finite clause (*to*-infinitive) 直接宾语: 非限定短语(带 to 的不定式)
1 Tom	**loves**	to do the household chores.
2 Bill	**liked**	to arrive early for meetings.
3 Mary	**hates**	to drive in the rush-hour.
4 The laboratories	**failed**	to produce useful results.
5 Jane	**wants**	to finish the job by tomorrow.
6 Peter	**expects**	to be promoted soon.
7 I	**remembered**	to post your letters.
8 The children	will still **need**	to be looked after.

1 汤姆爱做家务事. 2 比尔喜欢开会时提前到.
3 玛丽不喜欢在交通高峰时间开车. 4 实验室没有得出有用的结果.
5 简想明天把工作做完. 6 彼得料想不久就能晋升.
7 我记得要把你的信都发出去. 8 这些孩子仍需要照看.

(a) In this pattern, the direct object is a non-finite clause consisting of or containing a *to*-infinitive (Cf Dn·t, Dpr·t). 在这一模式里，直接宾语是带 to 的不定式构成的非限定短语(参看 Dn·t, Dpr·t).

(b) After *remember* and *forget*, the contrast between the *to*-infinitive and the *-ing* form corresponds to a difference of meaning 在 remember 和 forget 之后，带 to 的不定式与 -ing 形式所表达的意思不同:

- I **remembered** to post your letters. [Tt]
  (= 'I didn't forget to post them.' 我记得要把你的信都发出去.)
- I **remembered** posting your letters. [Tg]
  (= 'I recalled having posted them.' 我记得把你的信都发出去了.)

(c) For *need*, *require*, *want* see [Tg], note (c). 关于 need、require、want, 见 [Tg] 模式中的注释(c).

(d) Verbs in this pattern cannot be made passive. 这一模式的动词不可用于被动结构.

[Tnt]

subject 主语	transitive verb 及物动词	direct object: non-finite clause (noun (phrase)/pronoun + *to*-infinitive) 直接宾语: 非限定短语(名词(短语)[代词] + 带 to 的不定式)
1 Tony	**prefers**	his wife/her to do the housework.
2 The boss	**liked**	the staff/them to arrive early for work.
3 Julia	**hates**	her husband/him to lose his temper.
4 The teacher	**wants**	her class/them to finish the job by Wednesday.
5 I	**expect**	the parcel/it to arrive tomorrow.

1 托尼愿意让他妻子[她]做家务事.
2 这个老板喜欢职员[他们]上班提前到.
3 朱莉娅讨厌她丈夫[他]发脾气.
4 这个女教师要求学生[他们]星期三以前做完这项工作.
5 我料想包裹[它]明天能到.

(a) In this pattern, the direct object is a non-finite clause consisting of a *to*-infinitive introduced by a noun or noun phrase (eg *his wife*, *the staff*) or a pronoun (eg *her*, *them*). 在这一模式里, 直接宾语是非限定短语, 由名词或名词短语(如 his wife、the staff)或代词(如 her、them)后接带 to 的不定式构成. The noun (phrase) or pronoun is the subject of the whole non-finite clause. 名词(短语)或代词是整个非限定短语的主语.

(b) Occasionally, verbs in this pattern can be made passive. 这一模式的动词有时可用于被动结构. The subject of the non-finite clause becomes the subject of the whole passive sentence 非限定短语的主语变为整个被动句的主语:

- I **expect** the parcel to arrive tomorrow.
- The parcel is **expected** to arrive tomorrow.

Exceptions are shown in dictionary entries thus 例外情形在本词典的词条里这样标示: [Tnt no passive].

[Tg]

subject 主语	transitive verb 及物动词	direct object: non-finite clause (*-ing* form) 直接宾语: 非限定短语(-ing 形式)
1 Peter	**enjoys**	playing football.
2 John	**prefers**	walking to the office.
3 Jill	**hates**	working in the garden.
4 Fred	**started**	arguing.
5 This airline	will **finish**	operating next year.
6 The laboratories	**ceased**	producing useful results.
7 I	**remembered**	posting your letters.
8 The children	will still **need**	looking after.

1 彼得爱踢足球.
2 约翰喜欢走着去上班.
3 吉尔不喜欢在园子里干活儿.
4 弗雷德争辩起来了.
5 这家航空公司明年停止营运.
6 试验室得不出有用的结果了.
7 我记得把你的信都发出去了.
8 这些孩子仍需要照看.

(a) In this pattern, the direct object is a non-finite clause consisting of, or containing, an *-ing* form. 在这一模式里, 直接宾语是由 -ing 形式构成的非限定短语.

(b) For *remember* and *forget*, see [Tt], note (b). 关于 remember 和 forget 的说明, 见 [Tt] 模式中的注释(b).

(c) After *need*, *require* and *want* (as in *This shirt wants washing*), the *-ing* form of the verb can be replaced by the passive *to*-infinitive 在 need、require、want(如在 This shirt wants washing 句中)之后, 动词 -ing 形式可由带 to 的不定式的被动结构代替:

- The children will still **need** looking after. [Tg]
- The children will still **need** to be looked after. [Tt]

(d) This pattern has no corresponding passive construction. 这一模式无相应的被动结构.

[Tsg]

subject 主语	transitive verb 及物动词	direct object: non-finite clause (personal pronoun/noun (phrase)/possessive + *-ing* form) 直接宾语: 非限定短语(人称代词[名词(短语)]属有格 + -ing 形式)
1 I	don't **like**	him/John interrupting all the time.
2 Jill	**hates**	him/her husband coming home late.
3 We	**anticipated**	her/Mary('s) taking over the business.
4 Our parents	**dislike**	us/our working late at night.
5 The employers	**resented**	the staff('s)/their being consulted.

1 我不喜欢他[约翰]总是打岔. 2 吉尔讨厌他[她丈夫]回家晚.
3 我们预料到她[玛丽]接管生意而有所准备. 4 我们的父母不愿意我们深夜工作.
5 这些雇主不愿意有人向职员打听事情.

(a) In this pattern, the direct object is a non-finite clause consisting of a *-ing* form of a verb introduced EITHER by a personal pronoun or noun (phrase) (eg *him*, *her*, *us*; *John*, *the staff*) OR by a possessive form (eg *his*, *her our*; *John's*, *the staff's*). 在这一模式里, 直接宾语是含有动词 -ing 形式的非限定短语, 短语的开头或为人称代词或名词(短语)(如 him、her、us、John、the staff)或为属有格形式(如 his、her、our、John's、the staff's). The introductory pronoun, noun, etc is the subject of the whole non-finite clause. 这个开头的代词、名词等是整个非限定短语的主语.

(b) The possessive form at the beginning of the direct object is more formal than a noun (phrase) or pronoun. 直接宾语开头的属有格形式比名词(短语)或代词来得较文些. It is not likely to be used when the verb itself is fairly informal 动词本身若是多用于口语的, 则不宜用这一模式:

- (*)I don't **like** John's interrupting all the time.

(c) The verbs in this pattern cannot normally be made passive. 这一模式的动词一般不能用于被动结构.

[Tng]

subject 主语	transitive verb 及物动词	direct object: non-finite clause (noun (phrase)/pronoun + *-ing* form) 直接宾语：非限定短语（名词（短语）［代词］+ -ing 形式）
1 We	**watched**	the men destroying the furniture.
2 The porter	**heard**	someone slamming the door.
3 The children	**saw**	the cat stealing the meat.
4 The rescuers	**felt**	John losing his grip of the rope.
5 He	**noticed**	a child entering the courtyard.

1 我们看到那些男的正在毁坏家具. 2 搬运工听见有人用力关门的声音. 3 孩子们看见猫正在偷肉. 4 救援人员感觉到约翰渐渐抓不住绳子了. 5 他注意到有个孩子走进院子里.

(a) In this pattern, the direct object is a non-finite clause, in which a noun (eg *John*), noun phrase (eg *the cat*) or pronoun (eg *someone*) introduces the *-ing* form of the verb. 在这一模式里，直接宾语是非限定短语，短语的开头或为名词（如 John）、名词短语（如 the cat）或为代词（如 someone）后接 -ing 形式. Neither the noun nor the pronoun can be in the possessive form (as they can in the [Tsg] pattern). 无论是名词或代词，均不可用属有格形式（在 [Tsg] 模式里则可以）.

Compare 试比较:

- We **watched** the men/*men's destroying the furniture. [Tng]
- We **resented** the men/men's destroying the furniture. [Tsg]

(b) Most verbs in this pattern are 'perception' verbs. 这一模式的大多数动词都是"感知"动词. Of these, *see*, *hear*, *feel*, *watch*, *notice*, *overhear* and *observe* are also used in the [Tni] pattern 在这些动词中，see、hear、feel、watch、notice、overhear、observe 还可用于 [Tni] 这一模式:

- The rescuers **felt** John losing his grip of the rope. [Tng]
- The rescuers **felt** John lose his grip of the rope. [Tni]

Using the 'bare' infinitive here [Tni] implies that John fully lost his hold of the rope while the rescuers were in contact with him. 此处使用不带 to 的不定式 [Tni] 模式，意为救援人员抢救时，约翰完全抓不住绳子了. The *-ing* form [Tng] does not imply this. [Tng] 模式中的 -ing 形式则没有这层含义.

(c) Verbs in this pattern can be made passive. 这一模式的动词可用于被动结构. The noun (phrase) or pronoun introducing the *-ing* form becomes the subject of the whole passive sentence 引导 -ing 形式的名词（短语）或代词变为整个被动句的主语:

- The children **saw** the cat stealing the meat.
- The cat was **seen** stealing the meat (by the children).

Exceptions are shown in dictionary entries thus 例外情形在本词典的词条里这样标示: [Tng no passive].

[Tni]

subject 主语	transitive verb 及物动词	direct object: non-finite clause (noun (phrase)/pronoun + 'bare' infinitive) 直接宾语: 非限定短语(名词(短语)[代词] + 不带 to 的不定式)
1 We	**watched**	the men destroy the furniture.
2 The porter	**heard**	someone slam the door.
3 The children	**saw**	the cat steal the meat.
4 The rescuers	**felt**	John lose his grip of the rope.
5 He	**noticed**	a child enter the courtyard.

1 我们看到那些男的把家具毁坏了. 2 搬运工听见有人用力关门的声音. 3 孩子们看见猫偷肉了. 4 救援人员感觉到约翰抓不住绳子了. 5 他注意到有个孩子走进院子里了.

(a) In this pattern, the direct object is a non-finite clause, in which a noun (eg *John*), noun phrase (eg *the cat*) or pronoun (eg *someone*) introduces a 'bare' infinitive (the infinitive without *to*). 在这一模式里, 直接宾语是非限定短语, 短语的开头或为名词(如 John)、名词短语(如 the cat)或为代词(如 someone)后接不带 to 的不定式.

(b) All the verbs used in this pattern are verbs of perception. 用于这一模式的全部动词都是感知动词. They are *watch*, *hear*, *see*, *feel*, *notice*, *overhear* and *observe*. 这些动词是 watch、hear、see、feel、notice、overhear、observe. All are used in the [Tng] pattern also (see [Tng], note (b)). 这些动词还可用于[Tng]模式(见[Tng]模式中的注释(b)).

(c) Except for *watch* and *notice*, verbs in this pattern can be made passive. 这一模式的动词除 watch 和 notice 以外, 均可用于被动结构. The noun (phrase) or pronoun introducing the bare infinitive becomes the subject of the whole passive sentence, while the bare infinitive itself (eg *slam*, *steal*) becomes the *to*-infinitive (eg *to slam*, *to steal*) 引导不带 to 的不定式的名词(短语)或代词变为整个被动句的主语, 而不带 to 的不定式(如 slam、steal)则变为带 to 的不定式(如 to slam、to steal):

- The porter **heard** someone slam the door.
- Someone was **heard** to slam the door (by the porter).

Exceptions are shown in dictionary entries thus 例外情形在本词典的词条里这样标示: [Tni no passive].

[Cn·a]

subject 主语	complex-transitive verb 复合及物动词	direct object 直接宾语	object complement: adjective (phrase) 宾语补语: 形容词(短语)
1 I	**imagined**	him	much taller than that.
2 Jane	**prefers**	her coffee	black.
3 Peter	**has**	a tooth	loose.
4 The experts	**confessed**	themselves	baffled.
5 The fridge	**keeps**	the beer	cool.
6 The teacher	**made**	the lesson	interesting.
7 The mayor	**declared**	the meeting	open.

1 我原来想像他比那高得多.
2 简爱喝不加奶的咖啡.
3 彼得有颗牙齿松动了.
4 专家们承认这下子给难住了.
5 冰箱把啤酒冻得很凉.
6 那个教师把课讲得很有趣.
7 市长已宣布开会.

(a) In this pattern, the object complement is an adjective or adjective phrase which describes a feature or quality of the direct object (Cf La). 在这一模式里, 宾语补语是形容词或形容词短语, 这类形容词或形容词短语描述的是直接宾语所代表的人或事物的特征或特性(参看 La).

(b) Many verbs in this pattern can be made passive. 这一模式的许多动词均可用于被动结构. The direct object of an active verb becomes the subject of the same verb in the passive 主动动词的直接宾语在被动结构中变为该动词的主语:

- The teacher **made** the lesson interesting.
- The lesson was **made** interesting (by the teacher).

Exceptions are shown in dictionary entries thus 例外情形在本词典的词条里这样标示: [Cn·a no passive].

[Cn·n]

subject 主语	complex-transitive verb 复合及物动词	direct object 直接宾语	object complement: noun (phrase) 宾语补语: 名词(短语)
1 We	**made**	Frank	chairman.
2 The club	**elected**	Mr Jones	membership secretary.
3 We	**declare**	Holroyd	the winner.
4 The court	**considered**	Smith	a trustworthy witness.
5 The rebels	are **holding**	her	prisoner.

1 我们已经让弗兰克当主席了.
2 那个俱乐部已选举琼斯先生为负责成员资格的干事.
3 我们已宣布霍尔罗伊德获胜.
4 法庭认为史密斯是可信的证人.
5 反叛者正扣押着她.

(a) In this pattern, the object complement is a noun or noun phrase which indicates the role, name, status, etc of the direct object (Cf Ln). 在这一模式里, 宾语补语是名词或名词短语, 表示直接宾语所代表的人或事物的角色、名字、地位等(参看 Ln).

(b) Many verbs used in this pattern can be made passive. 这一模式的许多动词均可用于被动结构. The direct object of an active verb becomes the subject of the same verb in the passive 主动动词的直接宾语在被动结构中变为该动词的主语:

- The court **considered** Smith a trustworthy witness.
- Smith was **considered** a trustworthy witness (by the court).

Exceptions are shown in dictionary entries thus 例外情形在本词典的词条里这样标示 [Cn·n no passive].

[Cn·n/a]

subject 主语	complex-transitive verb 复合及物动词	direct object 直接宾语	object complement: *as* + noun (phrase)/ adjective (phrase) 宾语补语: as + 名词(短语 /形容词(短语)]
1 Fellow-sportsmen	**regard**	him	**as** a world-class player.
2 Doctors	**recognize**	Johnson	**as** a leading authority.
3 The police	didn't **accept**	the story	**as** genuine.
4 The club	won't **appoint**	a teenager	**as** the committee treasurer.

1 体育界的人都把他看成是有世界水平的健将.
2 医生都认为约翰逊是主要权威.
3 警方认为那种说法不实.
4 那个俱乐部不会委任十几岁的小青年当委员会的财务主管.

(a) In this pattern, the object complement tells us how the direct object is regarded judged, etc, or what he, she or it is chosen to act or serve as. 在这一模式里, 宾语补语表明直接宾语所代表的人或事物受到何种看待、评论或充当什么角色.

(b) The first word in the complement is always *as*. 此处补语的第一个词一定是 as. It is shown in dictionary entries like this 在本词典的词条里这样标示:

regard ... [Cn·n/a] ~ **sb/sth as sth** ...

(c) A passive construction is possible for all verbs in this pattern except *have*. 这一模式的动词除 have 外均可用于被动结构. The direct object of an active verb becomes the subject of the same verb in the passive 主动动词的直接宾语在被动结构中变为该动词的主语:

- The police didn't **accept** the story **as** genuine.
- The story wasn't **accepted as** genuine (by the police).

[Cn·t]

subject 主语	complex-transitive verb 复合及物动词	direct object 直接宾语	object complement: non-finite clause (*to*-infinitive) 宾语补语: 非限定短语(带 to 的不定式)
1 The reporter	**pressed**	her	to answer his questions.
2 The thief	**forced**	Jane	to hand over the money.
3 The extra money	**helped**	John	to be independent.
4 An official	**declared**	the place	to be free of infection.

1 记者硬要她回答他的问题.
2 窃贼逼迫简把钱交出来.
3 那笔额外的钱有助于约翰自立.
4 一位官员宣布该地无传染病.

(a) In this pattern, the object complement is a *to*-infinitive, either alone or as part of a larger clause. 在这一模式里，宾语补语是带 to 的不定式，这个不定式既可单用也可作为较大短语的一部分. It tells us what the object is made or helped to do or be. 这类宾语补语表明宾语所代表的人或事物被迫或被促使做什么或成为什么.

(b) The verbs in this pattern can be made passive. 这一模式的动词可用于被动结构. The direct object of an active verb becomes the subject of the same verb in the passive 主动动词的直接宾语在被动结构中变为该动词的主语:

- An official **declared** the place to be free of infection.
- The place was **declared** to be free of infection (by an official).

Exceptions are shown in dictionary entries thus 例外情形在本词典的词条里这样标示: [Cn·t no passive].

[Cn·g]

subject 主语	complex-transitive verb 复合及物动词	direct object 直接宾语	object complement: non-finite clause (*-ing* form) 宾语补语: 非限定短语(-ing 形式)
1 This remark	**set**	everyone	thinking.
2 The look on Bill's face	**had**	me	trembling with fear.
3 The policeman	**got**	the traffic	moving.
4 The smoke	**started**	her	coughing.
5 We	**left**	the children	playing in the garden.
6 The driver	**kept**	his engine	running.

1 这番话引起大家深思.
2 比尔的脸色吓得我直发抖.
3 那个警察把来往车辆指挥得动了起来.
4 烟呛得她直咳嗽.
5 我们把孩子们留在花园里玩耍.
6 那个司机一直让发动机转动着.

(a) In this pattern, the object complement is the *-ing* form of a verb, either alone (eg *thinking*) or as part of a larger clause (eg *playing in the garden*). 在这一模式里，宾语补语是动词的 -ing 形式，这个 -ing 形式既可单用(如 thinking)也可作为较大短语(如 playing in the garden)的一部分. It tells us what the object is made to do or is kept doing. 这类宾语补语表明宾语所代表的人或事物被迫做什么或做着什么.

(b) Only the verbs shown in the table are used in this pattern. 只有这个表里的动词才可用于这一模式. Of these, *set*, *have*, *get* and *start* are 'causative' verbs (ie verbs meaning 'cause something to happen'). 在这些动词中, set、have、get、start 是"使役"动词(即意为"使某事发生"的动词).

(c) Except for *have* and *start*, the verbs can be made passive. 这些动词除 have 和 start 外均可用于被动结构. The direct object of an active verb becomes the subject of the same verb in the passive 主动动词的直接宾语在被动结构中变为该动词的主语:

- The policeman **got** the traffic moving.
- The traffic was **got** moving (by the policeman).

[Cn·i]

subject 主语	complex-transitive verb 复合及物动词	direct object 直接宾语	object complement: non-finite clause ('bare' infinitive) 宾语补语: 非限定短语(不带 to 的不定式)
1 His tutor	**made**	him	work.
2 We	**had**	Jane	run through the procedure again.
3 Mother	won't **let**	the children	play in the road.
4 Stephen	**helped**	us	organize the party.

1 他的导师让他用功. 2 我们让简把那个程序又检查了一遍.
3 母亲不让孩子们在马路当中玩耍. 4 斯蒂芬帮助我们组织了那次聚会.

(a) In this pattern, the object complement is the 'bare' infinitive (the infinitive without *to*), either alone (eg *work*) or as part of a larger clause (eg *play in the road*). 在这一模式里, 宾语补语是不带 to 的不定式, 这个不定式既可单用(如 work)也可作为较大短语的一部分(如 play in the road). It tells us what the object is made or allowed to do. 这类宾语补语表明迫使或允许宾语所代表的人或事物做什么.

(b) Only the verbs shown in the table are used in this pattern. 只有这个表里的动词才可用于这一模式.

(c) The verbs *make* and *help* can be made passive, but when they are, they are followed by a *to*-infinitive as in pattern [Cn·t] 动词 make 和 help 可用于被动结构, 但用于被动结构时, 后接带 to 的不定式, 与 [Cn·t] 模式中者相同:

- He was **made** to work (by his tutor).
- We were **helped** to organize the party (by Stephen).

The other verbs shown here cannot be made passive. 此处列出的其他动词不可用于被动结构. This restriction is shown in dictionary entries thus 这种限定在本词典中这样标示: [Cn·i no passive].

[Dn·n]

subject 主语	double-transitive verb 双及物动词	indirect object 间接宾语	direct object: noun (phrase) 直接宾语: 名词(短语)
1 The Queen	**awarded**	the pilot	a gallantry medal.
2 The waiter	**poured**	Sarah	a glass of water.
3 Henri	**taught**	the children	French.
4 Christina	will **lend**	us	her flat.
5 The department	has **offered**	Mary	a job.
6 I	will **make**	everyone	some fresh coffee.
7 Father	**bought**	Emma	a white cat.

1 女王授予那名飞行员一枚英勇勋章. 2 服务员给萨拉倒了杯水.
3 亨利教孩子们法语. 4 克里斯蒂娜将把她那套公寓房借给我们.
5 这个部门已提供给玛丽一份工作. 6 我来给大家新煮些咖啡.
7 父亲给埃玛买了只白猫.

(a) This pattern has an indirect object (without a preposition) followed by a direct object. 这一模式中有个(不带介词的)间接宾语, 后接一直接宾语. Both can consist of a noun or noun phrase. 两者均可由名词或名词短语构成. The indirect but not the direct object can also be a personal pronoun (Cf Tn). 间接宾语(而不是直接宾语)也可为人称代词(参看 Tn).

(b) When the indirect object refers to someone who *receives* something, this pattern can usually be changed to the [Dn·pr] pattern with *to* 若间接宾语指某人接受某事物, 这一模式通常可转换成带 to 的 [Dn·pr] 模式:

- Henri **taught** the children French. [Dn·n]
- Henri **taught** French **to** the children. [Dn·pr]

In dictionary entries, this possibility is shown thus 在本词典的词条里, 这种可转换的情形这样标示:

teach ... [... Dn·n, Dn·pr ...] **~ sth (to sb)** ...

(c) When the indirect object refers to someone who is expected to *benefit* from the action of the verb, the [Dn·n] pattern can be changed to the [Dn·pr] pattern with *for* 若间接宾语指某人可望从动词行动受益时, 这一 [Dn·n] 模式可转换成带 for 的 [Dn·pr] 模式:

- I will **make** everyone some fresh coffee. [Dn·n]
- I will **make** fresh coffee **for** everyone. [Dn·pr]

In dictionary entries, this possibility is shown thus 在本词典的词条里, 这种可转换的情形这样标示:

make ... [... Dn·n, Dn·pr ...] **~sth (for sb)** ...

(d) For reasons why the [Dn·pr] pattern (with *to* or *for*) may be preferred to the [Dn·n] pattern, see [Dn·pr], note (c). 宜用 [Dn·pr] 模式(带 to 或 for)而不宜用 [Dn·n] 模式, 原因见 [Dn·pr] 模式中的注释(c).

(e) Most verbs in this pattern can be made passive, with the *indirect* object becoming the subject 这一模式的大多数动词均可用于被动结构, 其间接宾语变为主语:

- The Queen **awarded** the pilot a gallantry medal.
- The pilot was **awarded** a gallantry medal (by the Queen).

Exceptions are shown in dictionary entries thus 例外情形在本词典的词条里这样标示: [Dn·n no passive].
A passive in which the *direct* object becomes subject is rare 此处的直接宾语转换成主语的被动句很罕见:

- A gallantry medal was **awarded** the pilot (by the Queen).

[Dn·pr]

subject 主语	double-transitive verb 双及物动词	direct object 直接宾语	indirect object: *to*/*for* + noun (phrase)/ pronoun 间接宾语: to/for + 名词(短语)*[代词]*
1 The Queen	**awarded**	the medal	**to** a helicopter pilot.
2 The waiter	**poured**	a glass of water	**for** Sarah.
3 Henri	**taught**	French	**to** the children.
4 Christina	will **lend**	the flat	**to** us.
5 The department	has **offered**	the job	**to** Mary.
6 I	will **make**	fresh coffee	**for** everyone.
7 Father	**bought**	the white cat	**for** Emma.

1 女王将勋章授予一直升飞机驾驶员.
2 服务员给萨拉倒了杯水.
3 亨利教孩子们法语.
4 克里斯蒂娜将把那套公寓房借给我们.
5 这个部门已给玛丽提供了那份工作.
6 我来给大家新煮些咖啡.
7 父亲给埃玛买了只白猫.

(a) In this pattern, the indirect object is placed at the end. 在这一模式里, 间接宾语置于句尾. It consists of *to* or *for* and a noun (eg *Sarah*), noun phrase (eg *the children*) or pronoun (eg *us*, *everyone*). 这类间接宾语是由 to 或 for 与名词(如 Sarah)、名词短语(如 the children)或代词(如 us、everyone)构成.

(b) When introduced by *to*, the indirect object refers to a person or people *receiving* something (see [Dn·n], note (b)). 由 to 开头的间接宾语指接受某事物的人(见 [Dn·n] 模式中的注释(b)). When introduced by *for*, it refers to a person or people intended to *benefit* (see [Dn·n], note (c)). 由 for 开头的间接宾语指从动词行动受益的人(见 [Dn·n] 模式中的注释(c)). The correct choice of preposition is shown in entries like this 可使用的介词在词条里这样标示:

award ... [... Dn·n, Dn·pr ...] **~sth (to sb)** ...
buy ... [... Dn·n, Dn·pr ...] **~sth (for sb)** ...

(c) When the *indirect* object provides new information (eg in answer to a question), this pattern is preferred to [Dn·n], and the main stress falls on the last noun or pronoun. 间接宾语提供新信息时(如回答一问题), 用这一模式比 [Dn·n] 模式为宜, 主重音在最后的那个名词或代词上.

Who did Henri **teach** French **to**?

• Henri **taught** French **to** the 'children. [Dn·pr]

But when the *direct* object refers to information that is new, [Dn·n] is preferred 但若直接宾语指新信息时, 宜用 [Dn·n] 模式:

What did Henri **teach** the children?

• Henri **taught** the children 'French. [Dn·n]

(d) Most verbs in this pattern can be made passive, with the *direct* object of the active pattern becoming the subject of the passive one 这一模式的大多数动词均可用于被动结构. 主动模式中的直接宾语转换为被动模式中的主语:

• Father **bought** the white cat **for** Emma.
• The white cat was **bought for** Emma (by Father).

Exceptions are shown in dictionary entries thus 例外情形在本词典的词条里这样标示: [Dn·pr no passive].

[Dn·f]

subject 主语	double-transitive verb 双及物动词	indirect object 间接宾语	direct object: *that*-clause 直接宾语: that 从句
1 Colleagues	**told**	Paul	that the job wouldn't be easy.
2 The manager	**informed**	the audience	that the show had been cancelled.
3 Police	**warned**	drivers	that the roads were icy.
4 We	**persuaded**	the survivors	that they weren't in any danger.

1 同事们告诉保罗那个工作可不容易. 2 经理通知观众表演已经取消了.
3 警方提醒司机路面已结了冰. 4 我们已让获救者相信他们脱险了.

(a) This pattern has an indirect object without *to* and a direct object consisting of a *that*-clause (Cf Tf). 这一模式中有个不带 to 的间接宾语和一个由 that 从句构成的直接宾语(参看 Tf). The indirect object refers to the person or people addressed by the subject. 间接宾语指主语所代表的人发出信息的对象.

(b) Some verbs in this pattern can be made passive, with the *indirect* object of the active pattern becoming the subject of the passive one 这一模式的某些动词可用于被动结构, 主动模式中的间接宾语转换为被动模式中的主语:

- Colleagues **told** Paul that the job wouldn't be easy.
- Paul was **told** (by colleagues) that the job wouldn't be easy.

Exceptions are shown in dictionary entries thus 例外情形在本词典的词条里这样标示: [Dn·f no passive].

[Dpr·f]

subject 主语	double-transitive verb 双及物动词	indirect object: *to* + noun (phrase) 间接宾语: to + 名词(短语)	direct object: *that*-clause 直接宾语: that 从句
1 The employers	**announced**	**to** journalists	that the dispute had been settled.
2 The consultant	**recommended**	**to** the employers	that new salary scales should be introduced.
3 The garage	**explained**	**to** customers	that the spare parts had not been delivered.

1 雇主们向新闻工作者宣布纠纷已获解决. 2 顾问向雇主们建议采用新的工资级别制.
3 汽车维修站的人向顾客解释说零件尚未运到.

(a) This pattern has an indirect object with *to* and a direct object consisting of a *that*-clause (Cf Tf). 这一模式中有个带 to 的间接宾语和一个由 that 从句构成的直接宾语(参看 Tf). The indirect object refers to the person or people addressed by the subject. 间接宾语指主语所代表的人发出信息的对象.

(b) Some verbs in this pattern can be made passive. 这一模式的某些动词可用于被动结构. (Note the construction with *it* 注意带 it 的结构).

- The garage **explained** to customers that the spare parts had not been delivered.
- It was **explained** to customers (by the garage) that the spare parts had not been delivered.

Exceptions are shown in dictionary entries thus 例外情形在本词典的词条里这样标示: [Dpr·f no passive].

[Dn·w]

subject 主语	double-transitive verb 双及物动词	indirect object 间接宾语	direct object: finite clause/ non-finite clause 直接宾语: 限定从句或短语 [非限定从句或短语]
1 A friendly guard	**showed**	the prisoner	how he could escape/how to escape.
2 Experience	hasn't **taught**	Martha	whom she can trust/whom to trust.
3 The organizers	didn't **tell**	the children	whether they should bring a picnic lunch/whether to bring a picnic lunch.
4 The porter	**reminded**	guests	where they should leave their luggage/where to leave their luggage.

1 有个好心的看守告诉那个囚犯逃跑的方法. 2 马莎没有从经历中学会什么人可以信任.
3 组织者没有告诉孩子们带不带野餐. 4 搬运工人提醒客人应该把行李放在哪里.

(a) In this pattern, the direct object is a finite or non-finite clause beginning with 在这一模式里, 直接宾语是限定或非限定从句或短语, 二者的开头

EITHER 或是 (i) A '*wh*-element', which can be a pronoun (*who(m)*, *whose*, *which*, *what*), or a determiner + noun (*which roads*, *what time*), or an adverb (*why* (finite clauses only), *when*, *where*, *how*) 一个 "wh- 成分", 可为代词(who(m)、whose、which、what)或限定词 + 名词(which roads、what time)或副词(why(仅用于限定从句或短语)、when、where、how);

OR 或是 (ii) One of the conjunctions *if* (finite clauses only) *or whether* (Cf Tw). 连词 if(仅用于限定从句)或 whether(参看 Tw).

(b) Some verbs used in this pattern can be made passive, with the *indirect* object of the active pattern becoming the subject of the passive one 这一模式的某些动词可用于被动结构, 主动模式中的间接宾语转换为被动模式中的主语:

- A friendly guard **showed** the prisoner how he could escape/how to escape.
- The prisoner was **shown** how he could escape/how to escape (by a friendly guard).

Exceptions are shown in dictionary entries thus 例外情形在本词典的词条里这样标示: [Dn·w no passive].

[Dpr·w]

subject 主语	double-transitive verb 双及物动词	indirect object: *to* + noun (phrase)/ pronoun 间接宾语: to + 名词(短语)[代词]	direct object: finite clause/ non-finite clause 直接宾语: 限定从句或短语[非限定从句或短语]
1 We	**explained**	**to** the staff	how they should handle complaints/how to handle complaints.
2 You	should **indicate**	**to** the team	where they are to assemble/where to assemble.

1 我们向职员解释处理投诉的方法.　　2 你应该向全队指明集合地点.

(a) This pattern has an indirect object with *to* and a direct object consisting of a finite or non-finite *wh*-clause (Cf Tw). 这一模式中有个带 to 的间接宾语和一个由限定或非限定 wh- 从句构成的直接宾语(参看 Tw). The indirect object refers to the person or people addressed by the subject. 间接宾语指主语所代表的人发出信息的对象.

(b) Some verbs in this pattern can be made passive. 这一模式的某些动词可用于被动结构. (Note the construction with *it* 注意带 it 的结构).

- It was **explained to** the staff how they should handle complaints/how to handle complaints.

Exceptions are shown in dictionary entries thus 例外情形在本词典的词条里这样标示: [Dpr·w no passive].

[Dn·t]

subject 主语	double-transitive verb 双及物动词	indirect object 间接宾语	direct object: non-finite clause (*to*-infinitive) 直接宾语: 非限定短语(带 to 的不定式)
1 We	**told**	Peter	to see a doctor.
2 His teacher	**advised**	him	to take up the piano.
3 The court	**forbade**	the father	to see his children.
4 John and Mary	**encouraged**	Simon	to stay.

1 我们让彼得去看病.　　2 他的老师建议他学钢琴.
3 法庭禁止那个男的去见他的孩子.　　4 约翰和玛丽劝西蒙留下.

(a) In this pattern, the direct object is a non-finite clause, consisting of or containing a *to*-infinitive (Cf Tt). 在这一模式里，直接宾语是非限定短语，由带 to 的不定式构成(参看 Tt).

(b) Some verbs used in this pattern can be made passive, with the *indirect* object of the active pattern becoming the subject of the passive one 这一模式的某些动词可用于被动结构，主动模式中的间接宾语转换为被动模式中的主语:

- John and Mary **encouraged** Simon to stay.
- Simon was **encouraged** to stay (by John and Mary).

Exceptions are shown in dictionary entries thus 例外情形在本词典的词条里这样标示: [Dn·t no passive].

[Dpr·t]

subject 主语	double-transitive verb 双及物动词	indirect object: *to* + noun (phrase)/ pronoun 间接宾语: to + 名词(短语)〔代词〕	direct object: non-finite clause (*to*-infinitive) 直接宾语: 非限定短语(带 to 的不定式)
1 She	**gestured**	**to** the children	to stand up.
2 Fred	**signalled**	**to** the waiter	to bring another chair.
3 Stephen	**shouted**	**to** the chairman	to let someone else speak.
4 A policeman	**motioned**	**to** us	to move to the side of the road.

1 她向孩子打手势叫他们站起来. 2 弗雷德示意让那个服务员再拿把椅子来.
3 斯蒂芬向主席大声喊，得让别人讲话. 4 警察示意让我们把车开到路边.

(a) This pattern has an indirect object with *to* and a direct object consisting of or containing a *to*-infinitive (Cf Tt). 这一模式中有个带 to 的间接宾语和一个直接宾语，直接宾语由带 to 的不定式构成(参看 Tt). The indirect object refers to the person or people to whom the subject is calling or signalling. 间接宾语指主语招呼或示意的对象.

(b) The verbs in this pattern cannot usually be made passive. 这一模式的动词通常不可用于被动结构.

10.2 Nouns 名词

10.2.1 Noun classes 名词的分类. Foreign learners often have difficulty in using nouns correctly. This may be because of the agreement between noun and verb (Cf *The furniture is old/The news is unreliable*), or because of the rules which govern the proper choice of determiners (Cf *not much furniture, not much news, not many tables*). 学习英语的外国人往往感到在使用名词方面有困难. 困难可能在于名词与动词的一致关系(参看 The furniture is old/The news is unreliable)，或是在于选用适当限定词的规则(参看 not much furniture、not much news、not many tables). To help with these problems, a scheme of noun classes (represented in the entries by codes) has been devised for this dictionary, which reflects the grammatical differences. 为协助解决这些困难，本词典将拟定名词分类法(在词条中以代码标示)，表示语法上的差异.

10.2.2 Codes and their positions 代码及其位置. Each class in the scheme is represented in the dictionary entries by an easily understood code in square brackets, eg [C] (= 'countable noun'). 名词分类中的每一类在本词典的词条中用容易理解的代码标示，代码置于方括号中，如 [C](= countable noun 可数名词). If a noun has only one meaning, or several meanings all of which belong to the same noun class, the code or codes are placed after the part of speech label 若一名词只有一个词义, 或有几个词义而均属同一名词分类, 代码则置于词类标志之后:

con·tinu·ity ... *n* [U] **1** ... **2** ... **3** ... **4** ...

But if a noun in its various senses may belong to more than one class, the labels are placed after the sense numbers, as appropriate 但若一名词有几个不同的义项属于不止一类, 这些标志则置于有关义项顺序号之后:

check[3] ... *n* (**a**) [C] pattern of crossed lines (often in different colours) forming squares ... (**b**) [U] cloth with this pattern ...

A particular noun or meaning of a noun may require more than one class. 某一名词或一名词的某一词义可能需要归入不止一类. In such cases the labels are placed within the same set of brackets, separated by a comma 这些标志置于同一方括号中, 用逗号隔开:

re·cur·rence [C, U] (instance of) recurring; repetition.

No code is given if a noun (in all its various meanings) belongs to the countable ([C]) class 若一名词(包括各义项)属于可数名词([C]), 则不用代码标出.

10.2.3 Noun class scheme 名词分类法. Details of the various classes, with their codes, are given below. 名词各种类别及其代码详细用法如下. (For a quick guide, users should refer to the list on the back endpapers of the dictionary. 本词典后衬页备简表, 一目了然.)

• [C] Countable nouns 可数名词. These are used in the singular and plural forms with *is/are*, etc 这类名词的单数和复数形式分别与 is/are 等连用: *The picture is dusty/The pictures are dusty*. They can be used with *a/an* in the singular and *many/few* in the plural 单数名词可与 a/an 连用, 复数名词可与 many/few 连用: *A complaint was made.* ○ *There were many/few complaints*.

• [U] Uncountable (or mass) nouns 不可数名词(或称物质名词). These are used in the singular form only, with *is*, etc 这类名词只用于单数形式, 与 is 等连用: *The heat is unbearable*. They can be used without a determiner, as in *Butter is cheap*, and can also be preceded by *much/little* 使用不可数名词时可不带限定词, 如 Butter is cheap, 前面还可用 much/little: *Can we expect much support?* ○ *There was very little support for the plan*.

• [CGp] Countable group nouns 可数集合名词. These nouns can be used in both the singular and plural forms, with matching verbs 这类名词既可用于单数形式也可用于复数形式, 各与相应的动词搭配: *The committee has met/The committees have met*. But when used in the singular form, a CGp noun can agree with a plural verb as well, thus suggesting the individuals that make up a group rather than the group itself. 但可数集合名词其单数形式也可与复数动词连用构成一致关系, 意思指集合名词中的所有个体而不将之视为一个整体. Cf 参看 *The committee have not yet chosen their chairman/The committee has not yet chosen its chairman*.

• [Gp] Group nouns 集合名词. These are mostly place names such as *Whitehall*, *the Kremlin*, etc, used to refer to groups of people who govern, manage, etc in those places. 这类名词多为地名, 如 Whitehall、the Kremlin 等, 用以指该处的统治者、管理者之类的集团. They are used in the singular form only, but they can agree with a singular or a plural verb 这类集合名词只用单数形式, 但与单数或复数动词均可搭配形成一致关系: *The Kremlin are studying the President's letter*. ○ *Whitehall was quick to react*.

• [sing *v*] Plural nouns with singular verbs 复数名词与单数动词连用. Nouns such as *measles*, *mumps*; *billiards*, *bowls*; *physics*, *linguistics* have no singular form but take a singular verb 有些名词如 measles、mumps、billiards、bowls、physics、linguistics 没有单数形式, 但却与单数动词连用: *Measles is contagious*. ○ *Physics is a compulsory subject*. *Measles*, *mumps*, etc can be used with *the* or with *a lot of/much/less* ☆ measles、mumps 这类名词可与 the 或 a lot of/much/less 连用: *She's caught (the) mumps.* ○ *There's a lot of measles about.*

• [pl *v*] Singular nouns with plural verb 单数名词与复数动词连用. Nouns such as *police*, *clergy*, etc have no plural form but take a plural verb 有些名词如 police、clergy 没有复数形式, 但却与复数动词连用: *The police have not arrested anyone.* ○ *The clergy have all signed the petition.* Such nouns can be used with *many/few/several* 这类名词可与 many/few/several 连用: *Many police were on duty that night.* ○ *Several staff have resigned.* Also in this class are nouns formed from adjectives, eg *the wounded, the injured, the sick.* 在这一类里还包括由形容词构成的名词, 如 the wounded、the injured、the sick.

• [sing or pl *v*] Plural nouns with singular or plural verb 复数名词与单数或复数动词连用. These have a plural form but may agree with either a singular or a plural verb 这类名词的形式是复数, 但既可与单数动词连用也可与复数动词连用构成一致关系: *The barracks was/were badly damaged in the explosion.* ○ *The firm's headquarters is/are in Manchester.*

• [pl] Plural nouns 复数名词. Nouns in this class are plural in form and agree with a plural verb 这类名词呈复数形式, 与复数动词连用构成一致关系: *Your trousers are torn.* ○ *These premises are vacant.* ○ *Earnings have risen sharply.* Some (like *shorts, braces; pliers, scissors*) can be used with *a pair of/pairs of* 这类复数名词中有些(如 shorts、braces、pliers、scissors)可与 a pair of/pairs of 连用: *I've laddered my new (pair of) tights.* ○ *Fetch some pliers/a pair of pliers.*

• [sing] Singular nouns 单数名词. Nouns in this class are singular in form and agree with a singular verb. 这类名词呈单数形式, 与单数动词连用构成一致关系. They are normally used with *a/an* 单数名词一般可与 a/an 连用: *We'll have to have a quick think.* ○ *There was an abundance of fruit and vegetables.*

10.2.4 Fixed forms of nouns 形式固定的名词. Sometimes a noun in a particular sense can occur only with the definite or indefinite article. 有时一个名词在某义项中只能与定冠词或不定冠词连用. If it is used with the definite article it will be in either the singular or plural form–not both. 这类形式固定的名词若与定冠词连用时, 其形式不是单数就是复数 —— 只居其一. In addition to the article (sometimes instead of it), the noun can have a capital letter. 不仅冠词(有时不用冠词), 这类名词的首字母也可大写. These are fixed forms of nouns, and to help the learner recognize them, they are shown in **bold** print after the sense number and before any grammatical code and/or stylistic label 这些是形式固定的名词, 为便于识别起见, 均用**黑体**标示置于义项编号之后而在语法代码和[或]辞格标志之前:

scene ... *n* ... **7 the scene** [sing] ... (*infml*) the current situation in a particular area of activity or way of life ...
shame ... *n* ... **4 a shame** [sing] (*derog infml*) ...

10.3 Attributive and predicative uses of adjectives 形容词的定语和表语用法. Most adjectives can be used either before a noun or after the verb *to be*, as in *a serious affair/The affair was serious.* 多数形容词既可用于名词之前又可用于动词 to be 之后, 如 a serious affair/The affair was serious. The terms 'attributive' and 'predicative' are used to refer to these functions, abbreviated in this dictionary to [attrib] and [pred]. attributive (定语)和 predicative(表语)这两个术语用以指这两种功能, 在本词典中缩略作 [attrib] 和 [pred]. These labels are not used in entries in which the adjective in its various senses can occur in both positions. 有的形容词含有各义项均可适用于这两个位置上, 这类形容词的词条不用以上标志. When, however, it is restricted in one or more of its meanings to attributive or predicative position, the appropriate label is given 但若有的义项只限用于定语或表语位置, 则有标志注明:

bare[1] ... *adj* ... **3** [attrib] only just sufficient; basic: *the bare necessities of life* ...
ablaze ... *adj* [pred] **1** ... *The whole building was soon ablaze.* **2** ... *The palace was ablaze with lights.*

Nouns are sometimes used in attributive position, as in *a stone wall, a marble column*. All such uses are labelled [attrib] 有时名词可用在定语的位置上, 如 a stone wall、a marble column. 凡是这种用法都在前面加上 [attrib] 这一标志:

iron ... *n* **1** ... *as hard as iron* ○ [attrib] *iron ore* ...

11 COMPLEMENTATION 补语

11.1 Fixed or optional 固定的或可有可无的. Many nouns, adjectives and verbs (⇨ 10.1) are incomplete and ungrammatical without a following prepositional phrase or non-finite construction. 许多名词、形容词、动词(见 10.1)后面若没有介词短语或非限定结构就不完整也不合语法. These fixed elements are called the 'complementation' of the noun, adjective, etc. 这些固定的成分叫做名词、形容词、动词等的"补语". In other cases, the complementation is optional (but highly predictable). 在其他情况下, 补语可有可无(可省略的补语不言而喻). The obligatory type can be seen in *That's tantamount to treason* and *The idea never occurred to me*, and the optional type in *He can't cope (with the extra work)* and *They've already protested (to the authorities)*. 必须有补语的类型可见之于 That's tantamount to treason 和 The idea never occurred to me, 补语可有可无的类型如下: He can't cope (with the extra work) 和 They've already protested (to the authorities). In this dictionary, complementation is shown by means of a pattern in **bold** print after the grammatical code(s) 在本词典中, 补语用**黑体**印刷的模式标示, 置于语法代码之后:

tanta·mount /ˈtæntəmaʊnt; ˋtæntəˌmaʊnt/ *adj* [pred] ~ **to sth** ...

11.2 Brackets and obliques 括号及斜线号. The absence of brackets shows that complementation is fixed; the use of brackets indicates that it is optional 没有括号之处表示补语是必不可少的, 使用括号处指补语可有可无:

oc·cur /əˈkɜ:(r); əˋkɝ/ *v* ... **2** [Ipr] ~ **to sb** ...
cope /kəʊp; kop/ *v* [I, Ipr] ~ **(with sb/sth)** ...

A choice between alternatives is shown by means of an oblique stroke, as here between two non-finite clauses 有两个可供选择的补语用斜线号表示, 如下面两个非限定从句之间者:

happy /ˈhæpɪ; ˋhæpɪ/ *adj* ~ **(doing sth/to do sth)** ...

In this part of an entry, as elsewhere, **sb** = somebody and **sth** = something. 在词条的这个部分, 和其他部分一样, **sb** = somebody 某人, **sth** = something 某事物. The use of '**...**' after a preposition shows that a noun must be used there, but one which refers to a place 在介词之后的"..."表示此处必须用名词, 而这个名词指某个地方:

de·part /dɪˈpɑ:t; dɪˋpɑrt/ *v* [I, Ipr] ~ **(from ...)** ...

11.3 A and B A 和 B. Sometimes a verb or noun can be followed by alternative phrases which are related in structure and meaning. 有时一个动词或一个名词后面可接两个可供选择的短语, 这两个短语在结构和意义上相关联. For example, *supply books to the students* is closely related to *supply the students with books*. 例如 supply books to the students 和 supply the students with books 密切相关. These connected patterns are shown thus 这些相关的模式这样标示:

sup·ply /səˈplaɪ; səˋplaɪ/ *v* ... [Tn, Tn·pr] ~ **sth (to sb)**; ~ **sb (with sth)** ...

However, when two things (or two people) are referred to in BOTH of the alternative phrases (as in the example *sprinkle pepper on one's food/sprinkle one's food with pepper*), **A** and **B** are used to prevent confusion 但若两个可供选择的短语所指的是两个事物(或两个人)(如 sprinkle pepper on one's food/sprinkle one's food with pepper), 就用 **A** 和 **B** 标示以免造成混淆:

sprinkle /ˈsprɪŋkl; ˋsprɪŋkl̩/ *v* [Tn, Tn·pr] ~ **A (on/onto/over B)**; ~ B (with A) ...

MEANING AND USAGE 意义和用法

12 STYLE AND FIELD 辞格和辞域

12.1 The problems of the learner 学习英语者的困难. It is often as difficult for foreign learners to decide how to use words appropriately as it is to be sure about their meanings. 学习英语的外国人很难掌握词语的词义，也往往很难掌握词语的恰当用法. They may not be aware, for instance, that *wireless* is an old-fashioned (and chiefly British) word, now almost entirely replaced by *radio*, or that to call a woman *petite* or *slender* implies an approving attitude towards her–in contrast with *skinny*, which suggests criticism or dislike. 例如可能不察 wireless 这个词是个旧式的词(且主要用于英式英语)，现几乎完全用 radio 代替，又如称女子 petite 或 slender 含褒意 —— 与 skinny 相反，skinny 含贬意或厌恶感. To help learners with these difficulties, a number of labels are used in the dictionary to denote the stylistic values of words or the technical fields in which they are used. 为协助学习者解决这类困难，本词典采用一些标志表明词语的修辞格或所使用的专门领域. Style and field labels are of six major types, described below in sections 12.3–12.8. 辞格和辞域标志有六个主要类型，在下面 12.3–12.8 各节详述.

12.2 Position of labels 标志的位置. Style and field labels are printed in *italics* and placed in round brackets after the grammatical codes and/or complementation 辞格和辞域的标志用斜体印刷，置于圆括号内列于语法代码和[或]补语之后:

> **bags**[1] ... *n* [pl] (*infml*) trousers: *Oxford bags*.

When different stylistic values are attached to different meanings of a word, idiom, etc, the appropriate labels are positioned as follows 一个词、习语等，若不同义项有不同的修辞格，其标志的位置如下:

> **fab·ulous** ... *adj* ... **2** (*infml*) wonderful ... **3** [attrib] (*fml*) appearing in fables ...

Two or more labels may be combined, usually in the order of the major types 'currency', 'region', etc as arranged below. 这类标志若不止一个时可联合使用，其主要先后顺序通常为"流行时期"、"使用地域" 等，见下述排列顺序. Whether used singly or in combination, labels may be modified by *esp* ('especially'), *usu* ('usually'), *sometimes*, etc 无论单独使用或是联合使用，这些标志均可能有限定成分 esp (especially)、usu (usually)、sometimes 等:

> **bally** ... *adj, adv* (*dated Brit sl*) ... *It's a bally nuisance!*
> **bag·gage** ... *n* ... **3** [C] (*dated infml joc*) lively or mischievous girl ...
> ˈ**cheer-leader** *n* (*esp US*) person who leads the cheering by a crowd ...

12.3 Currency 流行时期. Not all words and meanings treated in this dictionary are in general present-day use. 本词典所收的词语及其义项并非均为目前普遍使用的. Certain words (eg *court* (verb), *gramophone*) are still used by some older speakers but not by the majority of younger ones. 有些词(如 court(动词)、gramophone)一些年长者仍使用，但年轻人大多已不再使用. These are words passing out of use, and they are labelled (*dated*). 这些词已逐渐废旧，均有标志(*dated*)标明. Other words (eg *thou* for 'you' or *knave* in the sense of 'dishonest man'), though found in books written in the first half of this century or earlier, have now passed out of use altogether. 还有些词(如作 you 解的 thou 或作 dishonest man 解的 knave)虽然见于本世纪前半叶或更早些时期的书籍中，现在已经完全不再使用了. These are labelled *arch* (= 'archaic'). 这些词标示为 *arch* (= archaic).

Note that when the object, institution, etc being referred to is out of date, rather than the word used to refer to it, this is shown by including 'formerly' in the definition 注意：若某词所指的物体、机构等已过时，而并非该词本身已不再使用，则在定义中用 formerly(旧时)标示:

> ˈ**battering-ram** *n* large heavy log with an iron head formerly used in war for breaking down walls, etc.

12.4 Region 使用地域. A number of words and senses are restricted to (or especially restricted to) one country or area. 有些词语及其义项的使用范围仅限于(或尤其限于)一国或一地区. The largest regionally-restricted groups of words are represented below, with the appropriate labels. 词语使用上最大的地域限制范围列举如下, 均附有标志. Other abbreviations used to denote place of origin are (*S African*) for 'South African', (*Austral*) for 'Australian' and (*NZ*) for 'New Zealand'. 其他表示词语来源的缩略式有(*S African*)指 South African(南非)、(*Austral*)指 Australian(澳大利亚)、(*NZ*)指 New Zealand(新西兰). All other regional labels are spelt out in full. 其他的地域标志均完全拼写出来.

- (*Brit*) denotes specifically British words and senses, eg *banger* ('sausage'), *suspender* ('device for supporting stockings'), *vest* ('garment worn under a shirt, etc'). (*Brit*)指专为英式英语使用的词语及词义, 如 banger (sausage 香肠)、suspender(device for supporting stockings 吊带)、vest(garment worn under a shirt, etc 汗衫).

- (*US*) indicates words and senses used specifically in the United States, eg *suspenders* ('braces'), *vest* ('waistcoat'). (*US*)指专用于美国的词语及词义, 如 suspenders (braces 吊带)、vest(waistcoat西装背心).

- (*Scot*) denotes Scottish words and meanings, eg *bairn* ('child'), *ben* ('mountain peak'), *loch* ('lake'). (*Scot*)指苏格兰词语及词义, 如 bairn(child 小孩儿)、ben(mountain peak 山峰)、loch(lake 湖).

- (*dialect*) refers to words and senses that are restricted to particular regions of the British Isles not including Scotland and Ireland, eg *beck* ('stream'), *parky* ('cold'). (*dialect*) 指限于不列颠群岛(不包括苏格兰和爱尔兰)某些地区使用的词语及词义, 如 beck(stream 山涧)、parky(cold 寒冷的).

12.5 Register 辞域. Certain words must be used with particular care because they reflect a special relationship between speakers (which could vary from very distant to very close) or a special occasion or setting (which could vary from an official ceremony to a relaxed meeting between friends). 某些词使用时必须特别留心, 因为这些词反映说话人之间的某种关系(从极疏远到极亲密之间的种种关系)或反映某种场合或环境(从官方仪式到朋友相会的种种情形). Labels used to indicate such factors are described below in an order which goes from least formal to most formal. 用以表示这类因素的标志按最随便到最郑重的顺序说明如下.

- (⚠) denotes words or senses likely to be thought offensive or shocking or indecent (though not necessarily by everyone or on every occasion), eg *wop*, *nigger*, *Christ!*; *fuck*, *prick*, *shit*, *piss*. (⚠)指可认为是冒犯的或不雅的或下流的词语或词义(但不见得每个人的看法或每个场合均如此), 如 wop 南欧的家伙、nigger 黑(人)家伙、Christ! 天哪! fuck 肏、prick 屌、shit 屎、piss 撒尿. Foreign learners should exercise great care in using these words. 学习英语的外国人使用这些词时应极为小心. They should also note that words such as *wop* and *nigger* are generally used with the deliberate aim of giving offence (Cf (*offensive*) at 12.6). 也应注意到像 wop 和 nigger 之类的词使用时一般含故意冲撞对方的目的(参看 12.6(*offensive*)).

- (*sl*) indicates 'slang' words and senses, ie inventive and often colourful items generally used in a very informal spoken context. (*sl*)指"俚俗(slang)"词语及词义, 即创新的而常为俏皮的词义, 一般用于极随便的口语场合. Such items usually belong to, or originate in, the language of a particular social or occupational group (eg soldiers, nurses, prisoners). 这类词语通常属于或源于某社会的或职业的团体(如士兵、护士、囚犯)使用的语言. Examples include: *the nick* ('prison'), *the fuzz* ('police'), *scarper* ('go away'). 这类词语的示例有: the nick(prison 监狱)、the fuzz(police 警方)、scarper(go away逃跑).

- (*infml*) denotes 'informal' words and senses, ie those indicating a close personal relationship and an unofficial occasion or setting, eg *pinch* ('steal'), *brolly* ('umbrella'), *dad*, *granny*. (*infml*)指"口语的(informal)"词语和词义, 即用于亲密的私人关系和随便的场合或环境的词语, 如 pinch(steal 偷窃)、brolly(umbrella 雨伞)、dad 爹、granny 奶奶(或姥姥).

• (*fml*) denotes 'formal' words and meanings, ie those chosen when speaking or writing in a serious or an official context to someone who is not a close friend or relation, eg *warrant* ('deserve'), *countenance* ('support or approve'), *acquiesce in* ('accept without protest'). (*fml*)指"文的(formal)"词语和词义, 即用于说或写郑重的或公事方面的内容, 对象不是关系密切的亲友, 如 warrant(deserve 应该得到)、countenance(support or approve 支持或赞成)、acquiesce in(accept without protest 默认).

• (*rhet*) 'Rhetorical' items are associated with writing or speech on serious or elevated themes, especially on very formal occasions (eg public meetings, state ceremonies). (*rhet*)指"修辞格的(rhetorical)"词语, 用于郑重文雅内容的言语文字, 尤指于极庄重的场合(如公众集会、国家典礼). The use of such words elsewhere suggests a self-consciously pompous speaker or writer. 在其他场合的语言文字中使用这类词语有华而不实、过甚其辞之嫌. Examples include *tribulation* ('event that causes suffering'), *alas* ('expression of sorrow'). 这类词语的示例有 tribulation(event that causes suffering 疾苦)、alas(expression of sorrow 表示悲哀的词语).

12.6 Evaluation 臧否人物. The use of certain words or phrases implies a particular attitude (disapproving, approving, ironic, etc) towards the person, thing or action referred to. 某些词语使用时含有对所指的人、事物或行为持有某种态度(褒、贬、含反义等). The following categories are recognized in this dictionary 本词典对臧否人物的词语分类如下:

• (*derog*) 'Derogatory' words, etc imply that one disapproves of or scorns the person or thing referred to or described by those words, eg *puerile*, *skulk*, *swagger*. (*derog*)指"贬义词(derogatory)", 使用这类词语的人蔑视或不赞同这类词语所指的或所描述的人或事物, 如 puerile 幼稚愚蠢、skulk 鬼鬼祟祟、swagger 趾高气扬.

• (*approv*) 'Approving' words, etc imply the opposite of derogatory ones; they suggest approval of or admiration for the thing or person referred to or described, eg *petite*, *slender*, *bonny*. (*approv*)指"褒义词(approving)", 与上述贬义词相反, 含有对所指的或所描述的人或事物赞同或钦慕之意, 如 petite 身材娇小的、slender 苗条的、bonny 漂亮的.

• (*offensive*) This label denotes words used to address or refer to people, usually with the deliberate intention of offending them, especially on account of their race or religion. (*offensive*)指"轻蔑语", 这一标志指称呼人或用以指人的词语, 通常含故意冲撞的目的, 尤其是在种族或宗教信仰方面. Words such as *dago*, *wop*, *nigger* are almost always used offensively in this way; words such as *arsehole* and *prick* are often found shocking, but they need not be used as terms of abuse (Cf (⚠) at 12.5). 有些词如 dago 黑不溜秋的外国人、wop 南欧的家伙、nigger 黑(人)家伙, 几乎一定用做轻蔑词语; 有些词如 arsehole 屁眼儿、prick 屌, 很不文雅但不见得用做咒骂词语(参看 12.5(⚠)).

• (*euph*) 'Euphemistic' words, etc are ones chosen to refer to something unpleasant or painful in a pleasant (because more indirect) way, eg *pass away* ('die'), *senior citizen* ('old age pensioner'). (*euph*)指"委婉语(euphemistic)", 用以婉转地(因为较间接)指不悦的或令人痛苦的事物, 如 pass away (die 故去)、senior citizen(old age pensioner 退休老人).

• (*ironic*) This label denotes words, often used within a longer phrase, that are intended to convey a sense opposite to the apparent sense, eg *fine* (as in *a fine mess*), *lovely* (as in *a lovely black eye*). (*ironic*)指"反语", 这一标志常用于较长的词组中, 表达与字面意思相反的含义, 如 fine 好(如 a fine mess 好混乱)、lovely 漂亮的(如 a lovely black eye 被打出个漂亮的黑眼圈儿).

• (*fig*) A 'figurative' sense of a word is a non-literal (often metaphorical) sense which can still be related by native speakers to an original literal one. (*fig*)指"比喻(figurative)", 用于非本义的(常为隐喻的)词义, 说本族语的人仍能联想到原义. (Where there has been such a link in the past, but it is no longer perceived, the label is not used. 有些词过去使用时需要这种联想, 但现已察觉不出需要联想; 这类词均不用此标志.) An example sentence which shows the connection (at **cheer**[1]) is 下面用一例句表明比喻义与原词义的联系(见 **cheer**[1]): (*fig*)

Flowers always cheer a room up. 房间里一有花就满室生辉了. This can be related to a previous literal example 此例句中该词的比喻义可与含原先本义的例句相联系: *Bring her a present – that'll cheer her up.* 给她带一份礼物——让她高兴一下.

• (*joc*) 'Jocular' words and phrases are intended to be funny, whether grim or innocent humour is meant, eg *push up the daisies*, *Alma Mater*, *nothing daunted*, *put one's foot in it*. (*joc*)指"戏谑的(jocular)"词语, 含诙谐意, 可为挖苦的或为单纯的幽默, 如 push up the daisies 进坟墓、Alma Mater 母校、nothing daunted 毫不气馁、put one's foot in it 说的话或做的事使人难堪.

• (*sexist*) This label denotes words and phrases that express a (sometimes unconscious) discriminatory or patronizing attitude towards someone of the opposite sex. (*sexist*)指"含性别偏见的"词语, 这一标志指对异性使用的某些词语, 表示(有时是无意识的)歧视的或屈尊俯就的态度. They are almost always words, etc used by men about or to women, and can be used to express approval in a 'man-to-man' context, eg *chick*, *the weaker sex*, *a bit of skirt/crumpet/stuff*, *an easy lay*. 这些词语几乎都是男性论及女性或对于女性使用的, 在男性与男性之间使用时则可用以表示赞许, 如 chick 黄毛丫头、the weaker sex 女性、a bit of skirt/crumpet/stuff 漂亮的女子、an easy lay 性关系随便的人.

12.7 Technical fields 专门领域. This dictionary contains a large number of words and senses which are normally confined to technical use. 本词典收入大量的一般只作专门用语的词语和义项. Our policy has been to limit coverage to those words which, though they would be used as technical terms by the specialists concerned, are nevertheless known to the educated layman. 我们一向的做法是将收这类词语的范围限于虽为专家使用, 但受过教育的外行也了解. The labels used here are mostly self-explanatory. 此处使用的标志大多一望而知, 毋需解释. The following examples show only a small part of the range 下面仅举其中数例:

basilica (*architecture*)
bastardy (*law*)
chiaroscuro (*art*)
continuity (*cinema or TV*)
cursor (*computing*)
subjunctive (*grammar*)

12.8 Sayings and catchphrases 谚语和警语. These labels denote a variety of longer phrases and sentences, which often have meanings quite different from those of their parts and are used to perform various functions. 这两个标志指多种比词语稍长的词句, 其含义往往与其各组成部分的含义出入很大, 且有多种功能.

• (*saying*) 'Sayings' are fixed phrases or sentences used to make comments, give advice, issue warnings, etc. (*saying*)"谚语(sayings)"是固定词句, 可用作评语、用以提供意见、提出警告等. They often reflect traditional values and rules, eg *too many cooks spoil the broth*; *a stitch in time saves nine*. 这类词句往往反映出传统的价值观和规律, 如 too many cooks spoil the broth 厨子多了做坏了汤、a stitch in time saves nine 及时缝一针省却事后缝九针.

• (*catchphrase*) 'Catchphrases' often originate with public figures, popular entertainers, etc and help to identify them. (*catchphrase*)"警语(catchphrases)"往往源自知名人士、演艺界红星等, 又反过来用以联想到他们. Later, they may pass into general use, and acquire other meanings and functions, eg *the buck stops here*; *if you can't beat them, join them*. 久而久之, 这类警语广为使用, 又增加了其他意义和功能, 如 the buck stops here 责无旁贷、if you can't beat them, join them 若竞争对手占了上风, 那就最好站到他们一边亦从中获益.

12.9 Proprietary names 专利名称. Some words in common use in speech and writing are registered trademarks belonging to manufacturing companies. 在口语及书面语中, 有些常用词语是属于厂商的注册商标. Such words, eg *Jacuzzi*, *Aqualung*, are given the label (*propr*) ('proprietary term') in the dictionary. 这类词语, 如 Jacuzzi 按摩浴缸、Aqualung 水肺, 在本词典中用(*propr* 专利)标示(即 proprietary term 专利名称).

13 DEFINITIONS 定义

13.1 Definitions: phrase and single word 定义: 词组和单词. Definitions usually consist of a phrase which is equivalent in meaning to the headword (and is sometimes substitutable for it in a particular context) 定义通常为与首词意思相若的词组(且有时在某上下文中可代替首词):

> **rep·res·ent·at·ive** ... *adj* **1** ... **(a)** serving to show or portray a class or group ...
> **sack**[3] ... *v* [Tn] steal or destroy property in (a captured town, etc).

If a one-word definition (ie a synonym) exists for a headword in a particular sense, this is placed immediately after the phrase definition, thus 若首词某义项的定义是单词式定义(即同义词), 这个同义词定义紧接在词组式定义之后:

> **safe**[1] ... *adj* ... **1** ... protected from danger and harm; secure ... **4 (a)** [usu attrib] (of a person) unlikely to do dangerous things; cautious ...

Sometimes, such words can replace the headword in a given context (Cf *safe from attack*, *secure from attack*; *a safe driver*, *a cautious driver*). 有时定义中的同义词可代替首词用于某上下文中(参看 safe from attack, secure from attack; a safe driver, a cautious driver). But learners should beware of substituting a word given as a one-word definition without first checking the entry for the word itself. 但是将定义中的同义词替换首词使用时, 应留意不可不先查阅该同义词词条本身. They will often find that words closely related in meaning may differ in grammar (*This driver is safe* is less normal than *This driver is cautious*) or in style (*secure* is more formal than *safe* in sense **1**). 往往有这种情形, 意思上紧密相关的词在语法上可能不同(This driver is safe 不如 This driver is cautious 规范), 或在修辞格上可能不同(secure 比 safe 的第一义项来得较文).

13.2 Sense divisions 义项的划分. In entries with more than one meaning, the meanings are usually arranged in sections introduced by numbers or letters. 有的词条不止有一个词义, 这些词义通常用号码或字母区分开. The use of numbers normally indicates that the senses are fairly distant in relation to each other; this is often further reflected in differences of grammar and/or style 这里的号码一般表示相互间词义差距较大, 常常进一步反映在语法和[或]修辞格上:

> **pack**[1] ... *n* ... **4** [CGp] ... (*derog*) number of people or things ...: *a pack of fools/thieves* ○ *a pack of lies*. **5** [C] ... complete set of 52 playing cards. **6** [C] (only in compounds) thing placed on the body for a period of time ...: *a 'face-pack* ○ *an 'ice-pack*.

The use of letters suggests a closer relationship, as for example when a noun such as *ham*, *beer* or *wine* denotes (a) the food or drink itself, (b) a particular type or brand and (c) a measured quantity 这里的字母表示词义间关系较紧密, 如名词 ham、beer 或 wine 词条中的(a)食物或饮料本身, (b)某种类型或牌子的食物或饮料, (c)某种数量的食物或饮料:

> **beer** ... *n* **1 (a)** [U] alcoholic drink made from malt and flavoured with hops, etc: *a barrel, bottle, glass of beer* ... **(b)** [C] type of beer: *beers brewed in Germany*. **(c)** [C] glass of beer: *Two beers, please*.

Sometimes, two closely related meanings are combined in one definition, for example when referring to a process or action and an individual instance of that process or action 有时两个紧密相关的词义结合在一个定义中, 如指一过程或行动及这类过程或行动的实例:

> **em·bez·zle·ment** ... *n* [C, U] (instance of) embezzling ...

13.3 Indicating subjects and objects in definitions 表明定义中的主语和宾语. Especially when there are no examples, it is important to show the learner whether the *object* of a verb can be a person or a thing or both. 尤其是在定义中没有示例的情形下, 表明动词的宾语可为人或事物或两者均可, 这对学习英语的人颇为重要. Dictionary entries show this by the use of '(sb)', '(sth)', and occasionally '(oneself)', '(itself)' in the definitions 本词典在词条的词义中一一标明(sb 某人)、(sth 某事物[某事/某物]),偶尔用(oneself 自己)、(itself 它本身)标示:

> **chauf·feur** ... *v* [Tn] drive (sb) as a chauffeur.
> **cheapen** ... *v* ... **2** [Tn] make (oneself/sth) less worthy of respect ...

When it is necessary to show whether the *subject* is a person or type of thing, the convention is this 在必要时表明主语是人或某类事物,一般这样表示:

> **drop**² ... **3** [I, Ipr] (of people and animals) collapse from exhaustion ...
> **drive**¹ ... **3** [Tn, Tn·pr, Tn·p] (of wind or water) carry (sth) along ...

13.4 Types of subject or object 主语或宾语的类型. Sometimes the choice of subject or object is limited to one specific noun. 有时主语或宾语仅限于使用某一名词. This too will be placed in brackets 该名词也置于括号中:

> **come in (a)** (of the tide) move towards the land.

In other cases, the user can choose from a range of subject or object nouns: for example, one can *bait* (in the sense of 'torment') a variety of animals. 在其他情形下,可从一定范围内的名词中选用作主语或宾语,如 bait(in the sense of 'torment' 取"撕咬折磨"义)可从多种动物中选用作宾语. In cases like this, the general type of person, animal or thing may be indicated in brackets 在这种情形下,括号中的标记可表明一般的人、动物或事物:

> **bait** *v* ... **2** ... **(a)** torment (a chained animal) by making dogs attack it ...

(For ways of indicating, in example phrases, the *specific* nouns, adjectives, etc which the user can choose when writing or speaking ⇨ 14.3 在语言文字中怎样像示例所示选用具体的名词、形容词等,见 14.3).

13.5 Glosses 注释. Sometimes the meaning of an example may differ in some special way from the definition which it illustrates. 有时一个示例的意思可能与其说明的定义中的意思不尽相同. This special sense may be a figurative extension (⇨ 12.6) of the meaning that has been given in the definition and illustrated by an earlier example. 这种特殊的词义可为定义和前面示例中所解释的意思引申的比喻义(见 12.6). In these cases, a gloss is provided either within or at the end of the example which has the special meaning 在这种情形下,在示例中或示例后加注其特殊词义:

> **come** ... **2** ... travel (a specified distance): *We've come fifty miles since lunch.* ○ *(fig) This company has come a long way* (ie made a lot of progress) *in the last five years.*

Sometimes the definition is a very general one, so that a number of distinct glosses are needed to explain individual examples 有时定义很笼统,因此需要些加以区别的注释来解释各个例子:

> **bal·anced** *adj* ... keeping or showing a balance: *a balanced state of mind*, ie a stable one in which no single emotion is too strong ○ *a balanced decision*, ie one reached after comparing all the arguments ...

14 EXAMPLES 示例

14.1 The learner's needs 学习者的需要. Examples in this dictionary are designed to meet several learning needs. 本词典的示例旨在满足学习上的几种需要. They help learners to understand the meanings of words, they provide models for them to imitate when writing or speaking and they illustrate the grammatical patterns in which words are used. 这些是帮助学习者理解词义,提供在口语或书面语中可供模仿的范例以及说明词语使用的语法模式. Examples are of two main types: sentence examples and phrase examples. 示例分为两大类:句子示例和词组示例.

14.2 Sentence examples 句子示例. Examples which are complete sentences are chiefly helpful in giving the user a clearer impression of a word's meaning and use than a definition is able to do. 完整的例句主要是可供给使用词典的人在某词的意思和用法上更为清晰的印象,这比单纯定义更有帮助. For example 例如:

come out ... **(f)** ... *The full story came out at the trial.*

Here light is thrown on the meaning of *come out* ('be revealed') by its context *at the trial*. 此处由于有上下文 at the trial(在法庭上), come out(be revealed 已揭示出)的意思就很清楚了. In another example, the meaning of *come off* is made clear by its contrast with *fixed on permanently* 在另一示例中, come off(掉下)的意思因有了 fixed on permanently(固定住)相对照, 就十分清楚了:

come off (a) ... *'Does this knob come off?' 'No, it's fixed on permanently.'*

Sentence examples are also an important way of indicating grammatical patterns, and as far as possible each verb pattern is exemplified (⇨ 10.1). 句子示例还是表明语法模式的重要方法, 在可能的情形下, 动词模式均一一举例说明(见 10.1). Sometimes examples are divided by an oblique stroke, or have a part in round brackets, to show alternative patterns in a single sentence 有时示例中有斜线号分隔开, 或某部分置于圆括号中, 表示一句中可供选用的动词模式:

bake ... *v* ... [... Dn·n, Dn·pr] ... *I'm baking Alex a birthday cake/baking a birthday cake for Alex.*

con·tract[2] ... *v* ... [Ipr, It] ... *Having contracted (with them) to do the repairs, we cannot withdraw now.*

14.3 Phrase examples with collocations 短语搭配示例. Phrase examples also help to clarify meaning, but they are chiefly helpful in showing, or suggesting, the kinds of words that regularly combine (or 'collocate') with the headword. 短语示例也有助于澄清词义, 但主要是有助于表明一般可与首词结合(或称搭配)的那一类型的词. (This information is of particular value to the writer or translator. 这种资料对从事写作或翻译的人尤其有用.) Three conventions are used in phrases to show which words collocate with the headword, and how wide the range of choice is 在短语示例中使用了三种方法, 表明哪些词语可与首词搭配, 以及可与之搭配的词语范围有多大:

• A phrase example may show a list of words separated by commas (but without *etc*) 短语示例中可有一系列词, 彼此用逗号隔开(末尾无 etc 字样):

come forward present oneself: *come forward with help, information, money.*

Here the nouns *help*, etc are not closely related in meaning; the list is 'open-ended' and so can suggest other choices, eg *assistance*, *proposals*, *cash*. 此处 help 这一系列名词彼此之间在意思上并无密切关系, 这个系列是"敞开的", 表示还可选用其他词, 如 assistance、proposals、cash.

• Other phrase examples have a list ending in *etc* 另一些短语示例中有一系列词, 末尾有 etc 字样:

cheap ... *adj* ... **5** ... *a cheap gibe, joke, remark, retort, etc.*

Here the choice is again fairly open but the words are more closely related, showing that, for instance, *cheap crack* and *cheap insult* are possible collocations. 此处可选用的词的范围也是较为敞开的, 但是这一系列例词之间关系较密切, 表明如 cheap crack 和 cheap insult 之类均可搭配使用.

• Other examples show a few words divided by an oblique stroke. 还有些短语示例中有斜线号将例词隔开. Here the words may be related or not, but the choice is limited, and foreign learners would be wise to restrict themselves to the collocations shown 此处的例词

彼此之间或有关系或无关系，但可选用的词的范围却是有限的，学习英语的外国人最好仅仅使用所列出的搭配词语:

> **be·set·ting** *adj ... a besetting difficulty/fear/sin.*
> **bet** *n ... place/put a bet on a horse.*
> **ˈcheck-up** *n ... go for/have a check-up.*

SPECIAL TYPES OF WORDS AND PHRASES 特殊类型的词语

15 IDIOMS 习语

15.1 Problems of meaning and form 意义和形式的问题. An idiom is a phrase whose meaning is difficult (often impossible) to recognize from the familiar meanings of the words it contains. 习语是一种短语，其意义很难(往往不可能)从其组成的各部分的普通意思中悟出. For example, the phrase *get sth off one's chest* means 'say something that one has wanted to say for a long time'. 例如 get sth off one's chest 这一短语意为"说出久欲说出的事". Of equal difficulty for foreign learners, though, is the fact that idioms either have a fixed form, or are changeable in quite unpredictable ways. 对学习英语的外国人来说，另一类似的困难是习语或是形式固定或是有些变化却无预知的规律可循. In *show one's teeth*, for instance, nothing can be substituted for *show* or *teeth*. 例如在 show one's teeth 这一习语中, show 或 teeth 不可用任何其他词替换. In the quite separate idiom *draw sb's/sth's teeth*, however, *fangs* can be used in place of *teeth* (though *draw* is unchangeable). 但是在另一习语 draw sb's/sth's teeth 中, teeth 这个词却可用 fangs 来替换(但 draw 不可换). It is important to show possible variation clearly; and in this dictionary an oblique stroke is used to mark alternatives, while brackets are used to show when a word or phrase can be omitted altogether 把能够变换的部分清楚地表示出来是十分重要的; 本词典用斜线号标示出可替换的词, 用括号标示出可完全省略的词语:

> **make one's/sb's ˈflesh crawl/creep**
> **make/pull ˈfaces/a ˈface (at sb)**

15.2 Choice of 'key' word 选出"关键"词. Idioms are listed and defined at the entry for the first 'full' word (noun, verb, adjective or adverb) which they contain. 习语所在的词条根据习语中的实词(名词、动词、形容词或副词)排列并附其定义. Thus *a big cheese* is defined at **big** (not **cheese**), and *(as) different as chalk and/from cheese* at **different** (not **chalk** or **cheese**). 因此, a big cheese 的定义在 **big**(而不在 **cheese**)词条中, (as) different as chalk and/from cheese 的定义在 **different**(而不在 **chalk** 或 **cheese**)词条中. Idioms appear in the last or, with some verbs, next to last numbered section of the entry for their key word (**big**, **different**, etc), headed by the abbreviation '(idm)'. 习语在其关键词(**big**、**different** 等)的词条中的位置, 是在最后一个号码的义项内, 在某些动词词条中则在倒数第二个号码的义项内, 习语前有(idm)这一标志.

15.3 Commonly used words 常用词. The words *bad*, *be*, *break*, *bring*, *come*, *cut*, *do*, *fall*, *get*, *give*, *go*, *good*, *have*, *hold*, *keep*, *lay*, *let*, *look*, *make*, *play*, *put*, *run*, *see*, *set*, *stand*, *take*, *throw*, *turn* and *work* are used in so many idioms that to include them as key words would result in long lists of idioms at **bad**, **break**, **bring**, etc and make individual idioms difficult to find. 许多习语中包含下列常用词: bad、be、break、bring、come、cut、do、fall、get、give、go、good、have、hold、keep、lay、let、look、make、play、put、run、see、set、stand、take、throw、turn、work. 若把这些词作为关键词势必使 **bad**、**break**、**bring** 等词后拖着一长串习语, 难以找到要查阅的习语. Instead, a few specimen idioms are given in each 'heavy-duty' entry and the user is referred to the entries for the nouns and adjectives, etc that occur in the idioms containing these words. 有个变通的办法, 是在每个"负担重的"词条中列出几个"样品"习语, 并指出查找这类习语中含名词和形容词等的词条.

15.4 Idioms consisting of grammatical words 由虚词构成的习语. Idioms which consist entirely of such 'grammatical' words (Cf 'full' words ⇨ 15.2) as *be*, *may*, *it*, *oneself*, etc are normally treated in the entry for the first of these words that occurs in the idiom. 有些习语完全由"虚词"(参看"实词", 见 15.2)构成, 如 be、may、it、oneself 等, 一般列在这类习语中的第一个虚词所在的词条中. Thus, **be oneself** and **be that as it may** both appear in the entry for **be**[1], and nowhere else. 因此, **be oneself** 和 **be that as it may** 均列入 **be**[1] 词条中, 不在他处.

15.5 Alphabetical arrangement 按字母顺序排列. In each entry in which they appear, idioms are arranged in strict alphabetical order, ignoring only *a*/*an*, *the*; *sb*, *sth* and possessive forms (*one's*, *sb's*, *his*, etc); and words in brackets or after obliques. 在每一词条中的习语严格按字母顺序排列, 惟不包括 a/an、the、sb、sth 和属有格形式(one's、sb's、his 等)以及括号中的或斜线号后的词.

15.6 Cross-reference 相互参照. To help any user who may have difficulty in identifying the first full word in an idiom, every idiom containing two (or more) such words has a cross-reference at the entry for each full word other than the first one. 有的习语含有不止一个实词. 使用本词典的人或许有人难于辨识出习语中的第一个实词, 为此在这类习语的每个实词所在的词条内各设一相互参照注. At each cross-reference the user is directed to the entry where the idiom is fully treated. 在每一相互参照注中均指出该习语实际所在的词条. Thus, in the case of **laugh in sb's face**, the user will find the idiom listed alphabetically at **face**[1], but with a cross-reference to the entry for **laugh** 因此, 以 **laugh in sb's face** 为例, 使用本词典的人可在 **face**[1] 词条中按字母顺序找到该习语, 但见到相互参照注指示该习语在 **laugh** 词条中:

> **face**[1] ... (idm) ... **laugh in sb's face** ⇨ LAUGH.

16 PHRASAL VERBS 短语动词

16.1 Verbs with prepositions and particles 带介词和小词的动词. Verbs of many types combine freely with prepositions (*go into the garden*, *hang one's coat on a peg*, *make a figure out of clay*) and adverbial particles (*run away*, *send the goods back*, *beat the eggs up*). 许多类型的动词可与介词自由组合(go into the garden、hang one's coat on a peg、make a figure out of clay)也可与副词小词自由组合(run away、send the goods back、beat the eggs up). Combinations such as these represent 'literal' meanings of the verbs and of the prepositions and particles, and they are illustrated in the numbered sections of the verbs, prepositions, etc concerned, as, for example, at **come** 这类组合表达的是动词和介词及小词的"字面的"意思, 在有关动词、介词等有号码的义项内均有说明, 如在 **come**词条中:

> **come** /kʌm; kʌm/ *v* ... **1 (a)** ... *She comes to work by bus.* ○ *Are you coming out for a walk?*

Many apparently similar combinations, though, have meanings which are more difficult to relate to those of their component words. 但是许多貌似上述这类的组合, 其意思与其各组成部分较难联系. In *He came at me with a knife*, *come at* means 'attack', not 'advance towards'; in *Long hair for men came in while I was at school*, *come in* means 'become fashionable', not 'enter'. 在 He came at me with a knife 句中, come at 意为 attack(攻击), 而并非 advance towards(向……前进); 在 Long hair for men came in while I was at school 句中, come in 意为 become fashionable (流行起来), 而并非 enter (进入). In these examples, *come at* and *come in* are idiomatic combinations (or 'phrasal verbs'), and they are treated in this dictionary in a special way. 在这两个例句中, come at 和 come in 是习语性的组合(或称短语动词), 在本词典中以特殊方法处理.

16.2 Arrangement 排列. Phrasal verbs are listed in bold print in a numbered section headed '(phr v)' and positioned immediately after the idioms section (if there is one). 短语动词用黑体印刷列于有号码的义项中, 前有(phr v)标志, (若有习语时)置于紧接习语部分之后. They are listed alphabetically according to the preposition(s) or particle(s) they contain, thus 短语动词的位置是按照其中的介词或小词的字母顺序排列的, 例如:

check[1] ... **6** (phr v) **check in (at ...); check into ... check sth in ... check sth off ... check (up) on sb ... check (up) on sth ... check out** (of ...) ... **check sth out ...**

16.3 The grammar of phrasal verbs 短语动词的语法. The forms in bold print in which phrasal verbs are presented in the dictionary (eg **come by sth, take sth in**) are designed to show the grammatical patterns in which they are used. 本词典中短语动词用黑体印刷的形式,旨在表明所使用的语法模式. There are six types of phrasal verb. 短语动词共有六种类型. These can be further divided into those *without* a direct object (Group A) and those *with* a direct object (Group B) 这六种类型还可再细分成两组,一组是不带直接宾语的(A 组),一组是带直接宾语的(B 组):

A Group WITHOUT a direct object (**sb** or **sth** is ABSENT altogether from the bold form, as in 1, or it appears at the END, as in 2 and 3). 不带直接宾语的一组(没有黑体字的 **sb** 或 **sth**, 如 1 中者,或置于末尾,如 2 和 3 中者).

1 Type with an adverbial particle, eg **come down** collapse 带副词小词类型, 如 **come down** collapse 倒塌: *The ceiling came down*.

2 Type with a preposition, eg **come by sth** receive sth by chance 带介词类型, 如 **come by sth** receive sth by chance 偶然得到某事物: *How did you come by that scratch?* (NOT 不作 *How did you come that scratch by?*)

3 Type with an adverbial particle and a preposition, eg **come down on sb** criticize sb severely 带副词小词和介词类型, 如 **come down on sb** criticize sb severely 严厉斥责某人: *Don't come down on her too hard*.

B Group WITH a direct object (**sb** or **sth** is in the MIDDLE of the bold form, as in 1, 2 and 3, and possibly *also* at the END, as in 2 and 3). 带直接宾语的一组(**sb** 或 **sth** 置于黑体字的中间, 如于 1、2、3 中者, 且可能也在末尾, 如于 2 和 3 中者).

1 Type with an adverbial particle, **take sth in** understand sth 带副词小词类型, 如 **take sth in** understand sth 理解: *I can't take this information in*. (ALSO 亦作 *I can't take in this information*.)

2 Type with a preposition, eg **take sth off sth** deduct (an amount of money) from sth 带介词类型, 如 **take sth off sth** deduct (an amount of money) from sth: 从某事物中减去(一笔钱): *They've taken 50 pence off the price*.

3 Type with an adverbial particle and a preposition, eg **take sth out on sb** make sb suffer for sth for which he is not responsible 带副词小词和介词类型, 如 **take sth out on sb** make sb suffer for sth for which he is not responsible 因某事拿某人撒气; 使某人因某事受冤枉: *Don't take your frustrations out on me*. (ALSO 亦作 *Don't take out your frustrations on me*.)

(For a full description of these types, see the *Oxford Dictionary of Current Idiomatic English*, Vol. I, pp xxxiv–lvii. 关于这些类型的详细说明, 见《Oxford Dictionary of Current Idiomatic English》第一卷 xxxiv-lvii 页.)

17 DERIVATIVES 派生词

17.1 Position 位置. A derivative is formed from a simple word (root) by the addition of a prefix (eg *assign*: *reassign*) or suffix (eg *resign*: *resignation*). 派生词是由单纯词(词根)加上前缀(如 assign: reassign)或后缀(如 resign: resignation)构成的. Sometimes a word moves from one grammatical class to another without any such addition (eg **head** (*n*): **head** (*v*); **welcome** (*adj*): **welcome** (*n*)). 有时一个词从一个词类变成另一词类并不加词缀(如 **head**(*n*): **head**(*v*); **welcome** (*adj*): **welcome**(*n*)). Derivatives formed with a suffix or with a change of grammatical class only – the latter are called 'zero-derivatives' – are usually set out following the numbered sub-sections of the headword and preceded by the symbol ▷. 通

过加后缀或只改变词类而形成的派生词——后者称作“零位派生词”——通常列于首词有号码的小项之后，其前面标有▷符号.

cheap ... *adj* ...
▷ **cheap** *adv* ...
cheaply *adv* ...
cheap·ness *n* ...

17.2 Derivatives as headwords 作为首词的派生词. When there is no connection of meaning between a simple word and a more complex one similar to it in form, the latter is treated as a separate entry 若一个单纯词与一个词形相似但较复杂的词在词义上没有联系，后者另立词条：

scarce ... *adj* ... not available in sufficient quantities ...
scarcely ... *adv* barely; not quite ...

In cases, too, where the difference in spelling between a simple word and its derivative is such that the dictionary user may not connect the two, the derivative is entered as a separate headword 再者，若一个单纯词与其派生词在拼法上差别较大，使用本词典的人未必均能将二者相联系，该派生词亦另立词条：

sat·isfy ... *v* ... **ex·ample** ... *n* ...
sat·is·fac·tion ... *n* ... **ex·em·plary** ... *adj* ...

17.3 Derivatives of derivatives 派生词的派生词. Often, derivatives are formed not from the headword itself but from one or other of its derivatives. 有的派生词往往并非从其首词本身构成，而是由首词的派生词构成的. *Maniacal*, for instance, is formed from *maniac* (not *mania*), and *maniacally* from *maniacal*. 例如 maniacal 是由 maniac(不是 mania)构成的，maniacally 是由 maniacal 构成的. In cases like these, the derivatives are ‘run on’ (ie not placed at the beginning of a new line in the dictionary) 在这种情形下，这类的派生词则“接排”（即在本词典中不列于新起一行的开头处）：

mania ... *n* ...
▷ **ma·niac** ... *n* ... **ma·ni·acal** ... *adj* ... **ma·ni·ac·ally** ... *adv*.

17.4 Defining derivatives 派生词的定义. When the meaning of a derivative is not straightforwardly related to that of its root (or of another derivative), the various meanings are all given 若一个派生词的词义与其词根(或另一派生词)的词义并非直接相关，则各项词义均予列出：

con·tort ... *v* ... (cause sth to) twist out of its natural shape ...
▷ **con·tor·tion** ... *n* ... contorting or being contorted (esp of the face or body) ...
con·tor·tion·ist ... person who is skilled in contorting his body.

In the many cases where the connection is straightforward, however, the derivatives are not defined. 但是在许多情形下，派生词的词义与其词根的词义明显相关，这类派生词项下不再提供定义. (Thus, at the entry for **chauvinism**, **chauvinist** is defined, but not **chauvinistic** or **chauvinistically**. 因此，在 **chauvinism** 词条中，**chauvinist** 项下有定义，而 **chauvinistic** 或 **chauvinistically** 项下则无定义.) Note, though, that the part of speech and other grammatical information are always given. 注意，为派生词提供词类及其他语法信息则始终如一.

17.5 Zero-derivatives 零位派生词. When a zero-derivative (⇨ 17.1) is formed from a headword, it is shown in full and listed alphabetically in the derivative section of the entry (⇨ **cheap** *adv* at 17.1). 由首词派生的零位派生词(见 17.1)完整列出，按字母顺序置于词条的派生词部分中(见 17.1 **cheap** *adv*). Consider, though, **alcoholic** *adj* and **alcoholic** *n*. 但是出现了这种情形：**alcoholic** *adj* 和 **alcoholic** *n*. Here the zero-derivative noun is identical in form to a word that is itself a derivative (the adjective). 此处的零位派生词名词的词形与另一个词完全相同，而这个词(形容词)本身也是派生词. In such a case, the noun is not shown in full, but represented by a run-on dash, followed by a new part of speech label and a definition 在这种情形下, 这个名词词形不列出, 而是接排一个破折号, 其后列出词类标志和定义:

> **al·co·hol** ... *n* ...
> ▷ **al·co·hol·ic** ... *adj* of or containing alcohol ... — *n* person who drinks too much alcohol ...

18 COMPOUNDS 复合词

18.1 Position 位置. A compound is made up of two or more simple words functioning as a single unit (ie it cannot be interrupted by another word). 复合词是由至少两个单纯词构成的, 起着一个独立单位的作用(即中间不可插入其他词). It may be written as one piece (eg *fireman*, *rattlesnake*) or with a hyphen (eg *check-out*, *king-size*). 有的复合词可以连写在一起(如 fireman、rattlesnake), 有的中间有连接号(如 check-out、king-size). But some compounds appear as separate words (eg *barley sugar*, *traffic warden*). 但是有些复合词却是各自分开而成独立的词(如 barley sugar、traffic warden). In this dictionary, compounds do not normally appear as separate entries but are included in the entry for the first element in each case (thus, **checklist** appears at **check** and **doorknob** at **door**). 在本词典中, 复合词一般不列作单独词条而是置于其第一个成分所在的词条中(因此, **checklist** 在 **check** 词条中, **doorknob** 在 **door** 词条中). This is helpful because it brings close together items which are often related in meaning. 这样排列的好处是把词义相关的词语都放在一起. At the same time, reference to individual compounds is made easier by grouping them in a section at the end of the entry (indicated by the symbol □), with each compound starting a new line at the left-hand margin 同时, 要查找复合词也比较容易, 因为复合词都是一词条最后的部分(标有 □ 符号, 每个复合词自成一行沿左侧排列:

> **cut**[1] ... *v* ...
> □ ˈ**cutaway** *n* ...
> ˈ**cut-back** *n* ...
> ˌ**cut** ˈ**glass** ...
> ˈ**cut-off** *n* ...

18.2 Compounds as headwords 作为首词的复合词. Some compounds are treated in entries of their own. These include items such as *hocus-pocus* and *hurly-burly* (whose first elements do not occur as separate words); technical terms (eg *Bailey bridge*) whose first parts are not listed as headwords in the dictionary; and some loan-words (eg *fait accompli*, *faux pas*). 有些复合词作为独立词条处理. 这类复合词包括 hocus-pocus 和 hurly-burly(这两例中的第一个成分均不作独立的单词); 某些术语, 其中第一个成分在本词典中不作首词(如 Bailey bridge); 某些借词(如 fait accompli、faux pas). A larger group consists of compounds which cannot be understood from the meanings of their parts (eg *barnstorm*, meaning 'travel quickly through rural areas making political speeches, etc'). 为数更多的一类复合词是无法从其组成部分的意思一望而知其含义的(如 barnstorm 意为"下乡作巡回政治演说等").

18.3 Derivatives of compounds 复合词的派生词. Sometimes derivatives are formed from compounds, either by the addition of a suffix or simply by a change of class (⇨ 17.5). 有时派生词是由复合词构成的, 其构成方法或是加上后缀或是改变词类(见 17.5). In such cases, the derivatives are run on, with a dash in place of any zero-derivative 在这种情形下, 这类复合词接排, 若是零位派生词则用破折号表示:

> □ ˈ**baby carriage** (*US*) = PRAM ...
> ˈ**baby-sit** *v* ... be a baby-sitter: *She regularly baby-sits for us.* ˈ**baby-sitter** *n* (*infml*) ... person who looks after a child for a short time while the parents are out.
> □ ˈ**press-gang** *n* ... (**b**) group who force others to do sth — *v* [Tn] force (sb) into service ...

EXTRA INFORMATION 补充资料

19 INFORMATION OUTSIDE THE MAIN ENTRIES 词条以外的资料

19.1 Usage notes and text illustrations 用法说明和插图. For further information of a contrastive or non-lexical type the user is referred from the entry to the usage notes after certain entries or to the illustrations within the main body of the text. 为进一步理解对比性质的或非词汇性质的有关资料，在一些词条中指示本词典使用者参看某些词条所附的用法说明或词典正文中的插图.

19.2 Appendices 附录. For general information about punctuation, weights and measures, etc and for collections of illustrations or tables of similar items the user should consult the Appendices. 本词典后部附英语标点符号用法、度量衡单位等一般资料和综合插图、人名、地名等资料仅供参考.

NEW WORDS SUPPLEMENT

新词补编

编者　：Catherine Nancarrow
译者　：李荫华
　　　　汪庆华
英语顾问：Dianne Maguire
汉语顾问：李德凤
　　　　金绍基

Preface by the editor

If, as most scholars agree, it is a sign of vigour for a language to show change, then English is in excellent health. Such change in any language is seen in grammar and pronunciation but perhaps most clearly of all in the vocabulary.

In the five years since the publication of the fourth edition of *Oxford Advanced Learner's English-Chinese Dictionary* (*OALECD*), thousands of words have moved into the mainstream of current English. Many have come from special areas; the field of computers is a prime example. Others are words which have grown respectable and are no longer regarded as shocking or taboo. A minority are outright inventions.

Many words and longer expressions in this *New Words Supplement* have been selected from sources already made available by Oxford University Press such as *The Oxford Dictionary of New Words* and *Oxford Advanced Learner's Dictionary*, fifth edition. Many others have come from the written and spoken language of newspapers, magazines and broadcasting. Of necessity, excluded words are as numerous as those which are listed here. The overriding criterion applied by the editorial team in making the *Supplement* has been its usefulness to the Chinese learner of English who wants help with current popular writing and speech.

The style, arrangement and format of entries made familiar in *OALECD* have been followed, and once again there are pronunciation guidance and copious illustrations whereas special notes on origins and usage give the *Supplement* a peculiar feature. The *Supplement* does not stand alone; it is recognised that most new words and expressions are relatives of ones that already exist, and readers are guided to other entries in the main dictionary and elsewhere in the *Supplement* through cross-referencing links.

The *Supplement* is the outcome of teamwork and effort by the Dictionaries team of Oxford University Press (China) Ltd, the translator Professor Li Yinhua from Fudan University and myself. We hope that readers find it as useful and relevant as we intend it to be.

One thing is certain: in about five years, the English language will have added enough new words to warrant another supplement.

Catherine Nancarrow
Department of Linguistics
University of Hong Kong

编者序

大多数学者都同意，一种语言发生可见的转变时，就是它有活力的表现。如果这是真的话，那英语可谓精力充沛。这种转变，在任何语言中都可体现于语法和读音，但最明显的则见于词汇中。

自五年前《牛津高阶英汉双解词典》第四版出版以来，日用英语已吸纳数以千计的新词，其中有不少本来是专业用语，电脑词汇便是个最好的例子。有些词以前夸张犯忌，如今已无伤大雅。还有一小部分则纯粹是新创的。

在《新词补编》中，许多单词和词组皆取自牛津大学出版社已出版的其他词典，如《The Oxford Dictionary of New Words》和《Oxford Advanced Learner's Dictionary》第五版等。除此之外，也有不少来自报章杂志和电视电台广播时使用的书面语、口语。然而新词繁多，未能尽收，编辑选取的标准，主要看新词是否有助于以汉语为母语者了解及运用日常英语。

《补编》的编纂与体例以《牛津高阶英汉双解词典》第四版为蓝本，因此亦提供音标和丰富的示例；至于"NOTE 注"一项则是《补编》的特色，说明词的起源和用法。《补编》并不独自成书，因为大部分新词语都是从原有的词语演变出来的；为此，《补编》和第四版正文之间，甚至《补编》本身都有互相参照的内容。

《新词补编》是牛津大学出版社（中国）有限公司词典出版组、来自复旦大学的译者李荫华教授、安徽大学的译者汪庆华女士和本人通力合作的成果。我们期望读者能亲身体会它的参考价值，从中得益。

无庸置疑的是：大约五年后，英语里出现的新词将肯定足够收录成新的补编。

Catherine Nancarrow
香港大学语言学系

Catherine Nancarrow 在英国伦敦附近地区出生和接受教育，为雷丁大学英国文学及哲学学士；及后于 University College London 修毕图书馆管理学，并在伦敦市的 Guildhall Library 任职。她后来举家迁居罗得西亚（今津巴布韦），在当地大学教授英语。

1976年 Nancarrow 女士来港后曾任教于香港大学校外进修部及英国文化协会，1979年加入香港大学英国语文及比较文学系任助教，并于1983年取得语言研究 (Language Studies) 硕士学位。

Nancarrow 女士为香港中小学构思、撰写及审订英语教材逾二十年，目前乃香港大学语言学系导师，教授句法、语音、会话分析等学科。

Aa

abled /'eɪbld; 'ebḷd/ *adj* (usu after adv 通常用于副词后) not disabled; unlike a disabled person in the respect specified 体格健全的；健康的；非残疾的：*hearing-abled* 听觉正常的 ○ *fully abled* 健壮的 Cf 参看 OTHERLY ABLED

ableism /'eɪblɪzəm; 'ebḷɪzəm/ *n* [U] discrimination in favour of the able-bodied or against the disabled 体格歧视；残疾歧视

absolute /'æbsəlu:t; 'æbsəlut/ *n* idea or principle that is always valid 绝对真理；绝对准则：*There are few absolutes in this changing world.* 在这不断变化的世界上几乎不存在什么绝对真理。

academia /ˌækə'di:mɪə; ækə'dimɪə/ *n* [U] world of university teaching and research 学术界：*a career in academia* 学术生涯

access /'ækses; 'æksɛs/ *v* [Tn] get in touch with and thus be better able to deal with one's inner feelings and desires; experience at a deep level 触及内心深处（以缓解心中的情绪和欲望）：*People who have lost someone close to them are helped to access their feelings of grief and anger.* 失去亲人的人得到帮助缓解其内心深处的悲伤及愤怒情绪。

accreditation /əˌkredɪ'teɪʃn; əˌkrɛdɪ'teʃən/ *n* [U] recognition of an institute, esp of education, by a body with monitoring and regulatory powers（尤指监管机构对教育机构的）认可，水平鉴定：*Accreditation is the only guarantee of quality.* 水平鉴定是质量的唯一保证。

ace /eɪs; es/ *interj* (*infml* 口) (used to express strong approval 用以表示大力赞成)：*'Let's meet in the bar after dinner!' 'Ace! See you there.'* '晚饭后我们在酒吧见！''太棒了！到那儿见。'

▷ **ace** *adj* (*infml* 口) very good; the best 最好的；一流的：*their ace player* 他们最好的运动员 ○ *The film was ace.* 这部电影绝对一流。

acid cloud /æsɪd 'klaʊd; æsɪd 'klaʊd/ *n* [U,C] mist or cloud containing a high concentration of acids, eg those formed from sulphur dioxides, nitrogen oxides, etc, caused by traffic and industrial emissions 酸云（含有高浓度的酸的雾或云，如由车辆和工厂排放的二氧化硫、氧化氮等形成）：*Acid cloud is adding to the pollution levels in Mexico City, with terrible effects on the health of the citizens.* 酸云加重了墨西哥城的污染程度，严重危害了居民的健康。

acid house /'æsɪd haʊs; 'æsɪd haus/ *n* [U] type of electronic dance music with a powerful beat, often associated with the drug culture 迷幻狂舞曲（一种节奏强劲的电子舞蹈音乐，常与毒品文化有关）

□ **acid house party** *n* large gathering where acid house is played 迷幻狂舞会

acquired immune deficiency syndrome *n* (*medical* 医) = AIDS[A-Z]

act /ækt; ækt/ *n* [U] (idm 习语) **get one's act together** (*infml* 口) get properly organized so as to work, study, etc more efficiently 组织得当（以求工作、学习有较高效率）：*If you want to keep your job, you'd better get your act together.* 你要想保住饭碗，就得抓紧工作了。

actioner /'ækʃnə(r); 'ækʃənɚ/ *n* film with lots of action and thrills; THRILLER (THRILL[A-Z]) 动作片；惊险片

action fossil /'ækʃn fɒsl; 'ækʃən fɑsḷ/ *n* fossilized (FOSSIL 1[A-Z]) remains which are evidence of some activity that took place in the distant past 动作化石（证明远古时代曾发生过某种活动的化石）：*The trail of dinosaur footprints provided an exciting action fossil, proving that these animals sometimes moved about in packs.* 这块动作化石上留下的一串恐龙脚印令人兴奋，它证明了恐龙有时会成群活动。

action-packed /'ækʃnpækt; 'ækʃənpækt/ *adj* full of excitement and activity 充满刺激的；充满活动的：*an action-packed film* 动作片

active citizenship /ˌæktɪv 'sɪtɪznʃɪp; ˌæktɪv 'sɪtəzṇʃɪp/ *n* [U] positive and responsible participation in the support of the norms, laws and well-being of a community 积极市民精神（积极认真地维护社会原则、奉公守法和努力造福大众）：*What the inner cities need is more active citizenship to reclaim our streets from crime and decay.* 内城区的居民需要进一步发扬积极市民精神以使我们的大街小巷摆脱犯罪与衰落。

activism /'æktɪvɪzəm; 'æktɪvɪzəm/ *n* [U] belief in the use of vigorous action to achieve social or political change 行动主义（主张以激进手段实现社会或政治变革的信念）

activity holiday /æk'tɪvətɪ ˌhɒlədeɪ; æk'tɪvətɪ ˌhɑlədе/ *n* holiday based on a particular activity or interest, esp a sport, a performance, etc 活动假日（为了某种兴趣或参加某种活动，尤其是运动或表演等而放的假）

add-in /'ædɪn; 'ædɪn/ *n, adj* (sth) that is added to a computer to improve its power or efficiency, esp an additional card bearing electronic circuits（可增强计算机功能的）增容附件（的）；（尤指）扩充卡（的）：*A good sound-card add-in makes game-playing much more enjoyable.* 配置好的声卡能使游戏更加有趣。○ *an add-in display card* 内插式显卡

add-on /'ædɒn; 'ædɑn/ *n* something added or included 附加物；附属物：*add-ons to one's basic pay* 某人基本工资外的附加收入 ○ *an add-on figure* 附图

admin /'ædmɪn; 'ædmɪn/ *n* [U] (*infml* 口) administration 管理；行政：*a few admin problems* 一些管理上的问题 ○ *working in admin* 从事行政工作

adoptive immunotherapy /əˌdɒptɪv ɪmju:nəʊ'θerəpɪ; əˌdɑptɪv ɪmjuno'θɛrəpɪ/ *n* [U] (*medical* 医) treatment for cancer in which white blood cells taken from the patient are used to attack cancerous cells in his or her own system 采纳性免疫疗法（用病人自身的白细胞破坏其体内癌细胞的疗法）

adrenalin rush /ə'drenəlɪn rʌʃ; ə'drɛnəlɪn rʌʃ/ *n* feeling of excitement and heightened sensation caused by the release of ADRENALIN[A-Z] esp during exercise（尤指运动时因肾上腺素分泌而引起的）一阵兴奋

advanced technology bomber *n* = ATB[1]

adventure /əd'ventʃə(r); əd'vɛntʃɚ/ *n* type of relatively non-violent computer game in which a player plays a role in a story and explores an imaginary world 电脑探险游戏（一种较少暴力的电脑游戏，游戏者可扮演某个角色在幻想世界中探险）：*My favourite adventure is Riven.* '瑞文'是我最喜欢的探险游戏。

▷ **adventuring** (also **adventure gaming**) *n* [U] act of playing an adventure 玩电脑探险游戏

adversarial /ˌædvə'seərɪəl; ˌædvɚ'sɛrɪəl/ *adj* based upon opposition; involving conflict or confrontation 对立的；敌对的：*an adversarial system of political parties* 不同政党对峙的体制 ○ *an adversarial relationship* 对立关系

aero /'eərəʊ; 'ɛro/ *abbr* 缩写 = aerodynamic (streamlined; reducing drag of air and allowing faster speeds in cars, bicycles, etc) 减低空气阻力以增加汽车、自行车等速度的；流线型的

□ **aero bar** attachment to or replacement for the handlebars of a racing cycle, allowing the rider to adopt a more aerodynamic, forward-sitting posture 流线型把手（自行车的把手，可让赛车者采取较为前倾的、减少空气阻力的姿势）

aero-braking /'eərəʊˌbreɪkɪŋ; 'ɛroˌbrekɪŋ/ *n* [U] way to slow down a spacecraft by using the natural braking effect of an atmosphere 大气制动法（利用大气固有的制动效应使太空船减速的方法）：*Aero-braking will slow the craft as the friction of the atmosphere around* *the planet takes effect.* 地球大气层的摩擦力制动效应将使飞船减速。

affirmative action /əˌfɜ:mətɪv 'ækʃn; əˌfɝmətɪv 'ækʃən/ (also **positive discrimination**) *n* [U] (*esp US*) policy and practice of favouring people in employment, education, etc who might otherwise be unfairly treated because of their race, disability, sex, etc（在就业、受教育等方面照顾可能因种族、残疾或性别等原因而被歧视的人的）积极措施

aftermarket /'ɑ:ftəˌmɑ:kɪt, *US* 'æf-; 'æftɚˌmɑrkɪt/ *n* **1** market in spare parts and components 零部件市场 **2** (*finance* 财) market in shares at a time after their original issue 股票发行后的市场；后继市场

agenda /ə'dʒendə; ə'dʒɛndə/ *n* (*fig* 比喻) **1** (**a**) list of things to be done 日程表；工作日程：*The environment is high on the political agenda at the moment.* 目前环境问题已成为政府亟待解决的问题。(**b**) one's goals or motives for doing sth 目的；动机 **2** (idm 习语) **hidden agenda** one's goals or motives when they are not apparent 隐藏的目的或动机：*We suspected a hidden agenda when the management declared a policy of early retirement for the staff.* 当管理层宣布员工退休年龄提前的新政策时，我们怀疑这背后有什么把戏。

agitpop /'ædʒɪtˌpɒp; 'ædʒɪtˌpɑp/ *n* [U] pop music with a deliberate political message 政治流行乐（含政治信息的流行音乐）Cf 参看 AGITPROP[A-Z]

agony uncle /'ægənɪ ʌŋkl; 'ægənɪ ʌŋkl/ *n* man who answers letters written to an AGONY COLUMN (AGONY[A-Z]) in a magazine, etc or takes part in radio phone-ins and gives advice on personal problems, esp on those which men have 解困大叔（报刊专栏或电台节目中的男性主持人，对涉及尤其男性私事的来信或来电给予意见）Cf 参看 AGONY AUNT (AGONY[A-Z])

agroforestry /ˌægrəʊ'fɒrɪstrɪ, *US* 'fɔ:r-; ˌægro'fɔrɪstrɪ/ *n* [U] agriculture which focuses on the cultivation and conservation of trees 农业林学，林业（专注种植和保育树木的农业）

AIDS awareness /ˌeɪdz ə'weənɪs; ˌedz ə'wɛrnɪs/ *n* [U] campaign to make people aware of AIDS and its victims and to keep the issue in the public eye 关注艾滋病及其患者的运动：*Nearly everyone at the concert was wearing a red ribbon to show they supported the AIDS awareness campaign.* 音乐会上几乎所有人都佩戴红丝带，表示他们对关注艾滋病运动的支持。

air bag /'eə bæg; 'ɛr bæg/ *n* safety device fitted in vehicles which is designed to inflate if a crash occurs, thus protecting the driver and passengers from injuries caused by impact with the internal frame and fittings 安全气袋（汽车内的一种安全装置，汽车碰撞时会自动充气以保护驾驶员和乘车人不被车内装置碰伤）

air bridge /'eə brɪdʒ; 'ɛr brɪdʒ/ *n* (*Brit*) portable bridge or walkway put against an aircraft door for the use of passengers when they board or leave the plane（机场的）旅客登机桥

airdrop /'eədrɒp; 'ɛrdrɑp/ *n* dropping of supplies, etc by parachute（用降落伞）空投（供应品等）

▷ **airdrop** *v*

airhead /'eəhed; 'ɛrhɛd/ *n* (*derog* 贬) person who is considered to be brainless; stupid person 没头脑的人；笨蛋：*She's glamorous but she's a complete airhead.* 她虽漂亮，但却毫无头脑。

NOTE 注： used mainly of women 主要用于女性

airmail letter *n* = AIR LETTER (AIR[1(A-Z)])

Air Miles /'eə maɪlz; 'ɛr maɪlz/ *n* (*propr* 专利名) scheme to encourage people to fly more often by giving them credits for free air-travel as part of certain commercial transactions. This is a marketing strategy to increase consumer spending 飞行里程计分法（为鼓励人们多乘飞机而采取的一种营销手段，即以飞行里程换到一定积分后可享受免费乘机）：*Every credit-card holder can now get Air Miles every time they use their card.* 现在信用卡持有人每次用卡都可得到飞行里程分。

airport fiction /'eəpɔ:t fɪkʃn; 'ɛrpɔrt fɪkʃən/ *n* [U] kind of light, popular fiction published in paperback which people typically buy at airports to read during their flight 航空小说（一种平装本通俗小说，在机场售卖，供乘客在飞行途中阅读）

air quotes /'eə kwəʊts; 'ɛr kwots/ *n* [pl] quotation mark signs made by a speaker's fingers as he or she says something, to convey that this is meant with irony or is not to be taken seriously 手势引号（说话者用手划的引号，表示所说的话是反话或仅仅是玩笑）Cf 参看 QUOTE (... UNQUOTE) (QUOTE *n* 3 [A-Z])

airway /'eəweɪ; 'ɛrwe/ *n* passage for air into a person's body from the mouth to the lungs via the TRACHEA[A-Z] 气道（空气由口吸入肺的管道）：*Make sure the patient's airways are clear before you attempt mouth-to-mouth resuscitation.* 做口对口人工呼吸前，首先要保证病人的气道畅通。

alcohol abuse /'ælkəhɒl əˌbju:s, *US* -hɔ:l; 'ælkəhɔl əˌbjus/ *n* overuse of alcohol that threatens health and a normal life 酗酒

alcopop /'ælkəʊpɒp; 'ælkopɑp/ *n* traditional soft drink, eg lemonade, which is produced with an alcoholic content 含酒精饮料，含酒汽水（如柠檬汽水）：*The packaging and marketing of alcopops is clearly aimed at young people, and this should cause concern.* 含酒精饮料的包装和销售都明显地是针对年轻人的，对此我们应当关注。

NOTE 注： a blend formed from *alcohol* and *pop* 由 alcohol（酒精）和 pop（汽水）二词合成

alien abduction /ˌeɪlɪən əb'dʌkʃn; 'elɪən əbˌdʌkʃən/ *n* supposed capture by aliens, who want to examine and experiment on human beings 外星人绑架（据称是为了对地球人的身体进行研究和做实验）：*The number of people who claim to have undergone alien abduction grows every year.* 自称被外星人绑架过的人逐年增多。

A-list /'eɪlɪst; 'elɪst/ *n* (usu *sing* 通常作单数) the best or most prestigious group, esp of celebrities（尤指名流中的）顶尖层，佼佼者：*Jacky Chan has made it to the A-list of Hollywood celebrities largely because of his hard work and persistence.* 成龙得以跻身于好莱坞上流社会贤达之列，主要靠的是他的努力和执着精神。

alkaloid /'ælkəlɔɪd; 'ælkəlɔɪd/ *n* (*botany or medical* 植或医) poisonous substance found in certain plants, some of which are used as the basis of medicinal drugs 生物硷（某些植物所含的有毒物质，其中有些被用作药物的主要成分）

all-embracing /ˌɔ:lɪm'breɪsɪŋ; ˌɔlɪm'bresɪŋ/ *adj* including everything 包罗万象的：*His powers are all-embracing, covering the government, the judiciary and the military.* 他独揽军、政和司法大权。

all-fired /'ɔ:lfaɪəd; 'ɔlfaɪrd/ *adj* (*US infml* 口) incredible, extreme 难以置信的；极度的：*He had the all-fired nerve to complain.* 他竟敢抱怨，真是胆大包天。

all-seater /ɔ:l'si:tə(r); ɔl'sitɚ/ *adj* (of a sports stadium) providing seats for all the spectators（指体育场）只设坐席的，观众均有座位的：*All-seater stadiums have become the rule in the UK since the tragic overcrowding accident at Hillsborough.* 自从在希尔斯勃罗发生那起因过度拥挤造成的悲剧性事件后，英国的体育场一律改成只设坐席。

all-singing, all-dancing /ɔ:lˌsɪŋɪŋ ɔ:l'dɑ:nsɪŋ, *US* dæns-; ɔlˌsɪŋɪŋ ɔl'dænsɪŋ/ *adj* [attrib 作定语] having many attractive but perhaps not truly valuable characteristics 花哨的；华而不实的：*The all-singing, all-dancing Tory party campaign team has hit town and seems intent on promising everything to everyone.* 保守

党的竞选队伍吹吹打打地到城里来了，他们似乎立意要讨好每一个人。

all terrain bike (also **mountain bike**) *n* = ATB[2]

aloe vera /ˌæləʊ ˈveərə; ˌælo ˈvɛrə/ *n* plant of the ALOE[A-Z] genus found in the Caribbean which contains an oily substance used esp in cosmetics as a moisturiser 芦荟（一种产于加勒比海地区的芦荟属植物，含有油性物质，尤用于润肤品）: *The skin cream contains aloe vera and five other moisturisers for a soft, smooth skin.* 这种润肤乳霜里含有芦荟和其他五种润肤剂，可使皮肤柔嫩光滑。

alternate /ˈɔ:ltənət; ˈɔltɚnɪt/ *n* (*US*) person who takes over position, work, authority, etc while sb is absent 接替者，代行职权者（某人不在时接替其工作或代为行使权力的人）: *Speak to my alternate. I'll be away.* 跟替代我的人说吧，我将要离开。

alternative energy /ɔ:lˌtɜ:nətɪv ˈenədʒɪ; ɔlˌtɝnətɪv ˈɛnɚdʒɪ/ *n* [U] energy obtained from natural and renewable sources, eg from the sun, the wind, the water, etc 替代能，另类能（从太阳、风或水等可再生的自然资源中获得的能量）

alternative fuel /ɔ:lˈtɜ:nətɪv ˌfju:əl, ɔ:lˌtɜ:nətɪv ˈfju:əl; ɔlˌtɝnətɪv ˈfjuəl/ *n* any substance other than petrol that is used to power a motor vehicle 另类燃料，替代燃料（汽油以外的机动车燃料）: *Ethanol and methanol are possible alternative fuels for the car of the future.* 将来乙醇和甲醇有可能成为汽车的替代燃料。

alternative medicine /ɔ:lˌtɜ:nətɪv ˈmedsɪn, *US* ˈmedɪsn; ɔlˌtɝnətɪv ˈmɛdɪsn̩/ (also **complementary medicine**) *n* [U,C] treatment for illness which does not make use of artificial drugs 另类疗法，替代疗法（不使用人造药物的疗法）: *Traditional Chinese herbal medicine is becoming more and more popular as an alternative medicine in the West.* 传统中草药疗法作为一种替代疗法在西方正日益受到欢迎。 Cf 参看 AROMATHERAPY, HOMOEOPATHY[A-Z]

Alzheimer's disease /ˈæltshaɪməz dɪzi:z; ˈæltshaɪmɚz dɪziz/ *n* [U] (*medical* 医) disease causing degeneration of the brain usu, but not only, in elderly people, leading to loss of memory, loss of language, etc 阿尔茨海默氏症，早老性痴呆症（可导致年长者大脑早衰，丧失记忆、语言等能力的疾病，但不只见于长者之中）

NOTE 注: the medical term has become more widely used and the disease has aroused greater concern as the number of elderly people increases 随着老年人口增加，此医学名词日益普及，这种病也引起了更广泛的关注

ambulance chaser /ˈæmbjələns tʃeɪsə(r); ˈæmbjələns tʃesɚ/ *n* (*derog* 贬) (**a**) (*esp US*) lawyer who presses his or her services on people while they are in shock due to a death, accident, etc 趁事故受害者悲痛之际争取提供服务的律师 (**b**) (*fig* 比喻) person who takes advantage of sb who suffers from a disaster 乘人之危谋利者；趁火打劫者

Amerasian /æməˈreɪʃn, *US* -eɪʒn; æməˈreʒən/ *n* person with mixed parentage, ie American and Asian, esp sb born during or soon after the war in Vietnam who has an American serviceman father and a Vietnamese mother 美亚混血儿（尤指越战中或之后不久出生的人，父为美国军人母为越南人）: [attrib 作定语] *Many Amerasian children are still hoping to be acknowledged by their American fathers and be allowed to leave Vietnam to settle in the US.* 越南许多美亚混血儿还在希望获得他们美国父亲的承认，以获准离开越南定居美国。

American Standard Code for Information Interchange /əˌmerɪkən ˌstændəd ˈkəʊd fər ˌɪnfəmeɪʃn ˌɪntətʃeɪndʒ; əˌmɛrɪkən ˌstændɚd ˈkod fɚ ˌɪnfɚmeʃən ˌɪntɚtʃendʒ/ *n* [U] (*abbr* 缩写 **ASCII**) (*computing* 计) set of 128 symbols that allows information transfer between computers or between computers and other data-processors 美国信息交换标准码（满足计算机之间或计算机与其他数据处理器间进行信息交换所需的128个符号）

Amnesty International /ˌæmnəstɪ ɪntəˈnæʃnəl; ˌæmnəstɪ ɪntɚˈnæʃənl̩/ *n* [sing] organization that monitors human rights world-wide, esp those of prisoners of conscience (PRISONER 2[A-Z]) 大赦国际（监察世界各地人权，尤其是政治犯的人权保障的组织）

amniocentesis /ˌæmnɪəʊsenˈti:sɪs; ˌæmnɪosɛnˈtisɪs/ *n* [U,C] (*medical* 医) process during which a small amount of fluid is drawn from the uterus of a pregnant woman in order to check on the condition of the unborn baby, esp for abnormalities leading to DOWN'S SYNDROME 羊膜穿刺术（从孕妇子宫内抽取少量液体用以检查胎儿发育状况，尤指借以发现唐氏综合征先兆的技术）

NOTE 注: from *amnion* (CAUL[A-Z]) 源自 amnion（羊膜）一词

anabolic steroid /ˌænəbɒlɪk ˈsterɔɪd, stɪə-; ˌænəbɑlɪk ˈstɛrɔɪd/ *n* drug that allows more intense exercise and hence greater muscle growth; athletes are banned for its use in competitive sports 促蛋白合成类固醇，代谢性类固醇（服用后可增加运动量，从而使肌肉异常发达的药物，竞技比赛的运动员禁用）

anaesthetic awareness /ænɪsˌθetɪk əˈweənɪs; ænesˌθɛtɪk əˈwɛrnɪs/ *n* [U] state of being conscious though paralyzed while under an ANAESTHETIC (ANAESTHESIA[A-Z]), and able to hear and perhaps even feel pain, etc 麻醉状态中的知觉（处于被麻醉状态中仍有听觉甚至痛感等）: *Reports of anaesthetic awareness are too frequent to be ignored and operating surgeons should be careful to take this into account when they comment on the progress of an operation.* 有关麻醉状态中仍有知觉的报告已多到不容忽视的地步，做手术的外科医生在评估手术进展情况时，应注意将这点考虑在内。

anchorperson /ˈæŋkəpˈɜ:sn; ˈæŋkɚpɝsn̩/ *n* (*pl* ~ **s** or **-people**) ANCHOR MAN (ANCHOR[A-Z]) or anchor woman 电台或电视节目主持人

android /ˈændrɔɪd; ˈændrɔɪd/ *n* ROBOT[A-Z] that looks like a human 人形机器人

angel dust /ˈeɪndʒl dʌst; ˈendʒəl dʌst/ *n* [U] (*sl* 俚) the hallucinogenic drug phencyclidine hydrochloride 天使粉（一种迷幻药）

animal companion /ˌænɪml kəmˈpænjən; ˌænəml̩ kəmˈpænjən/ *n* animal kept as a pet 动物伴侣: *the importance of animal companions especially for elderly or lonely people* 动物伴侣对于人，尤其是老年人或孤独的人的重要性

NOTE 注: the new term stresses the respect and proper status such animals are felt to deserve and which the word *pet* fails to convey 此新词强调这些动物应得的尊敬和地位，而 pet（宠物）一词则无法表达此义

animatronics /ˌænɪməˈtrɒnɪks; ˌænəməˈtrɑnɪks/ *n* [sing v] technique of making and operating lifelike robots, eg for exhibitions or films（如用于展览或电影制作的）机器人技术

NOTE 注: blend of *animated* and *electronics* 由 animated（活动的）和 electronics（电子学）二词合成

anklebiter /ˈæŋkl ˌbaɪtə(r); ˈæŋkl̩ ˌbaɪtɚ/ *n* (*infml joc* 口，谑) child 小家伙；小不点儿 Cf 参看 RUG RAT

Annual Percentage Rate /ˌænjʊəl pəˈsentɪdʒ reɪt; ˌænjuəl pɚˈsɛntɪdʒ ret/ *n* (*abbr* 缩写 **APR**) (*finance* 财) rate of interest return on a loan of money calculated on a yearly basis 年度成本百分率（按年度计算的贷款利率）

anorak /ˈænəræk; ˈænəræk/ *n* (*Brit derog* 贬) conventional, unstylish person, esp one who enjoys what others regard as a boring or pointless hobby 墨守成规者，老派人物（尤指其嗜好被他人视为乏味无聊的人）: *As* *the train pulled out, I saw the usual cluster of anoraks at the end of the platform busily writing down the number.* 火车一开出，我看见月台尽头的那帮老古董又正忙着抄号码。

NOTE 注： the word comes from the type of jacket (ANORAK A-Z) typically worn by such people 此词原意为'带风帽的厚夹克'，是此类人的典型穿着

answering machine *n* = ANSWERPHONE A-Z

antibody-positive /ˌæntɪbɒdɪˈpɒzɪtɪv; ˌæntɪbɑdɪˈpɑzətɪv/ (also **HIV-positive**) *adj* (*medical* 医) having antibodies to HIV in the blood and thus be at risk of developing AIDS A-Z 艾滋病病毒抗体血验呈阳性的（即存在患艾滋病危险的）: *When Chris learnt he was antibody-positive, he was horrified.* 当克里斯得知自己艾滋病抗体血验呈阳性时，他吓呆了。

antibody-resistant bacterium /ˌæntɪbɒdɪ rɪzɪstənt bækˈtɪərɪəm; ˌæntɪbɑdɪ rɪzɪstənt bækˈtɪrɪəm/ *n* (*pl* **bacteria**) (*medical* 医) new strain of a known bacterium, such as the one which causes TB, which cannot be cured by previously effective drugs 耐药菌株（由已知菌系如结核菌演变出的带有抗药性的新菌株）

Antipodean /ˌæntɪpəˈdiːən; ˌæntɪpəˈdiən/ *adj* coming from or related to the ANTIPODES 2 A-Z, ie Australia and New Zealand 澳大利亚和新西兰的；澳新地区的

anti-viral /æntɪ ˈvaɪrəl; æntɪ ˈvaɪrəl/ *adj* (*computing* 计) (of software) designed to detect and protect data on a hard disk against known computer viruses (VIRUS)（指软件）抗电脑病毒的：*The latest anti-viral software ensures that your hard disk is protected against attack from any known virus.* 最新的抗病毒软件能确保你的硬盘不受任何已知病毒的侵害。

antsy /ˈæntsɪ; ˈæntsɪ/ *adj* (*esp US infml* 口) irritable and difficult to please; tired of controlling one's expression of emotions or thoughts 易怒的；难讨好的；暴躁的：*It was terribly hot in the waiting room and the passengers were feeling rather antsy by the time the flight was announced.* 候机室内酷热难当，等到宣布登机的时候，旅客们一个个已焦躁难耐。

Apex /ˈeɪpeks; ˈepɛks/ (also **APEX**) *abbr* 缩写 = Advance Purchase Excursion (system of air travel ticketing that offers cheaper fares if the tickets are reserved a certain time in advance) 预订机票优惠制（以优惠价出售预订机票的航空售票制度）

apparatchik /ˌæpəˈrɑːtʃɪk, *US* -rætʃɪk; ˌæpəˈrætʃɪk/ *n* (*derog joc* 贬，谑) official working for a large organization, eg a political party, who is eager to follow orders and procedures 驯服工具（为大型组织，如政党，效力并唯命是从的工作人员）: *party apparatchiks* 政党的驯服工具

NOTE 注： from a Russian word *apparat* which originates from German meaning 'apparatus' 源自俄语apparat一词，原在德语里意为'器具'

applet /ˈæplet, -ət; ˈæplɛt/ *n* (*computing* 计) small computer program, often one executing a single sub-task 小应用程序（常指执行单项子任务的）: *The printer applet is efficient and makes any basic printing task straightforward.* 这个打印机程序十分有效，使得各项基本的打印任务简捷易行。

application /ˌæplɪˈkeɪʃn; ˌæpləˈkeʃən/ *n* (*computing* 计) program designed to perform a particular task for the user 应用程序

APR *abbr* 缩写 = ANNUAL PERCENTAGE RATE

aquacise /ˈækwəsaɪz; ˈækwəsaɪz/ *n* [U] exercise carried out in shallow water 浅水锻炼：*Aquacise is great for people who are anxious to avoid strained muscles.* 对于那些担心肌肉劳损的人来说，浅水锻炼真是再理想不过了。

▷ **aquacise** *v* do aquacise 进行浅水锻炼

NOTE 注： a blend formed from *aqua* (water) and *exercise* 由aqua（水）和exercise（锻炼）二词合成

arms inspector /ˈɑːmz ɪnspektə(r); ˈɑrmz ɪnspɛktə˞/ *n* expert appointed, esp by the United Nations, to check for illegal production and storage of weapons 武器核查员（尤指联合国指派负责检查非法生产和贮存武器的专家）

aromatherapy /əˌrəʊməˈθerəpɪ; əˌroməˈθɛrəpɪ/ *n* [U] use of sweet-smelling oils and plant extracts for healing or rubbing on during massage 芳香疗法（用含芳香物质的油和植物提取物进行治疗或按摩时涂擦皮肤的做法）

arriviste /ˌæriːˈviːst; ˌæriˈvist/ *adj* [attrib 作定语] (*slightly derog* 略带贬义) new on the scene, PUSHY A-Z and rather BRASH A-Z 抢眼但俗气地亮相的：*an arriviste little restaurant* 一家新开的俗气的小餐馆 ○ *arriviste celebrities* 暴发的新贵

art-house /ˈɑːt haʊs; ˈɑrthaʊs/ *adj* [attrib 作定语] (of a film) made with conscious aesthetic values and meant for the discerning and well-informed audience（指电影）富于艺术性的，供有鉴赏力和见闻广博的观众观赏的：*Cannes is the most important festival where recent art-house films are brought to the attention of a wider audience.* 戛纳电影节是将最新的艺术电影呈现给更多观众的最重要的电影节。

ASCII /ˈæskiː; ˈæski/ *abbr* 缩写 = AMERICAN STANDARD CODE FOR INFORMATION INTERCHANGE

Asian values /ˌeɪʃn ˈvæljuːz, *US* eɪʒn; ˌeʒən ˈvæljuz/ *n* [pl] set of principles considered to be important to Asian peoples, esp in South East Asia, and which include a strong work ethic, family loyalty, respect for authority, etc 亚洲价值观（尤指东南亚人的行为准则，包括很强的职业道德、孝悌、尊重权威等）

assistant professor /əˌsɪstənt prəˈfesə(r); əˌsɪstənt prəˈfɛsə˞/ *n* (*US*) college or university teacher one rank below an ASSOCIATE PROFESSOR 助理教授（比副教授低一级）

assistantship /əˈsɪstəntʃɪp; əˈsɪstəntʃɪp/ *n* (*US*) payment awarded to a college or university student who assists a professor in research or teaching while studying for a higher degree 助研金，助教金（研究生协助教授进行研究或教学所得的报酬）

assisted suicide *n* = DOCTOR-ASSISTED SUICIDE

associate professor /əˈsəʊʃɪət prəˈfesə(r); əˌsoʃɪət prəˈfɛsə˞/ *n* (*US*) college or university teacher one rank below a professor 副教授（比教授低一级）

asylum seeker /əˈsaɪləm siːkə(r); əˈsaɪləm sikə˞/ *n* person who asks for political asylum (ASYLUM 1a A-Z) 寻求政治庇护者

ATB[1] /eɪ tiːˈbiː; e ti ˈbi/ *abbr* 缩写 = (*military* 军) (*US*) advanced technology bomber (esp a bomber aircraft using STEALTH technology) 高级技术轰炸机（尤指利用隐形技术制造的轰炸机）

ATB[2] /eɪ tiːˈbiː; e ti ˈbi/ *abbr* 缩写 = (*sport* 体) all terrain bike (strong bicycle designed for rough surfaces off the roads) 全地形自行车，山地车（适于在崎岖的路面上行驶的自行车）

ATM *abbr* 缩写 = automated teller machine = HOLE-IN-THE-WALL

attack ad /əˈtæk æd; əˈtæk æd/ *n* (*infml* 口) advertisement for a product or a political party which openly criticizes rivals（公开抨击对手的）攻击性商业广告，攻击性政治宣传

attention deficit disorder /əˌtenʃn ˈdefɪsɪt dɪsɔːdə(r); əˌtɛnʃən ˈdɛfəsɪt dɪsɔrdə˞/ *n* (*abbr* 缩写 **ADD**) (*psychology* 心) any of a number of behavioural disorders, esp in children, with such symptoms as poor concentration, hyperactivity and learning difficulties 注意力缺乏症（尤为儿童所患的一种行为失常，表现为注意力不集中、过度活跃和有学习障碍等）

attitude /ˈætɪtjuːd, *US* -tuːd; ˈætətud/ *n* (idm 习语) **with attitude** in an aggressive and confrontational manner 具

有进取性；具有反叛性：*The new band are like the Beatles, but with attitude.* 这支新乐队很像披头士，但更具反叛性。

Aum Shinrikyo /əʊm ʃɪn'rɪkjəʊ; om ʃɪn'rɪkjo/ *n* [sing] name of a Japanese religious cult, now illegal 奥姆真理教（一个现已属非法的日本宗教）

NOTE 注： the name means 'Supreme Truth' 此名称意为'至高无上的真理'

aura /'ɔ:rə; 'ɔrə/ *n* outline of changing colours surrounding sb's physical body which some people claim to be able to see and which indicates the state of the health and emotions（人体）光环（有人自称能看到笼罩人体的光环，其颜色变化可显示人体的健康及情绪状况）：*What's the matter? Your aura's dark red.* 怎么了？你的光环成了暗红色。

NOTE 注： the extended meaning comes from the general term AURA first made by followers of OCCULT[A-Z] religions, esp SPIRITUALISM[A-Z] ☆ aura 一词的引申义，由神秘宗教尤指唯灵论信徒首创

authoring /'ɔ:θərɪŋ; 'ɔθərɪŋ/ *n* (*computing* 计) creation of programs, databases, etc for computer applications（计算机程序、数据库等的）编制，编写

authorized biography /ˌɔ:θəraɪzd baɪ'ɒgrəfɪ; ˌɔθəraɪzd baɪ'ɑgrəfɪ/ *n* biography in which the subject gives permission for or co-operates with the writer 授权传记（作者获被立传者授权撰写或与其合写的传记）Cf 参看 UNAUTHORIZED BIOGRAPHY

auto bra *n* = CAR BRA

automated teller machine *n* (*abbr* 缩写 **ATM**) = HOLE-IN-THE-WALL

automatic pilot /ˌɔ:təmætɪk 'paɪlət; ˌɔtəmætɪk 'paɪlət/ *n* (idm 习语) **on automatic pilot** (*fig* 比喻) carrying out tasks automatically, without conscious thought（做事像自动驾驶仪般）机械地，不假思索地：*After the shock of her death, he carried on with his job entirely on automatic pilot.* 他经历了她去世带来的巨大打击后，完全像机器一样地工作。

autostereogram /ˌɔ:təʊ'sterɪəgræm; ˌɔto'stɛrɪəgræm/ (also **stereogram**) *n* pattern of lines and dots generated by a computer actually hiding a 3-dimensional image which can only be seen by focusing the eyes slightly in front of or behind the surface of the hidden image 立体图，体视图（计算机用线条和点构成的图案，实际上藏有立体图像，但只有把视线对焦于潜藏图像表面的前后位置才能发现）：*When I stared at the autostereogram long enough, I suddenly saw the image of a leaping whale.* 我盯着那幅体视图良久，才突然看见了一幅跃起的鲸鱼的图像。

awesome /'ɔ:səm, *US* 'ɑ:səm; 'ɑsəm/ *interj* (*joc* 谑) (expressing amazement 表示惊异)：*The Great Wall of China? Awesome!* 中国的长城？棒极了！

AZT /eɪ zed 'ti:, *US* eɪ zi: 'ti:; e zi 'ti/ *abbr* 缩写 = (*medical* 医) azidothymidine (drug used in the treatment of AIDS[A-Z]) 迭氮胸苷（一种抗艾滋病药）

Bb

babe /beɪb; beb/ *n* (*sl* 俚) sexually-attractive young woman 性感女郎；性感小猫

NOTE 注： a term usu used by men and which many people now find offensive 此称呼通常为男性使用，现被许多人视为蔑称

baby boom /'beɪbɪ bu:m; 'bebɪ bum/ *n* sharp rise in the birth rate, esp after a war 生育高峰，婴儿潮（尤指战争后的）

▷ **baby boomer** *n* person born in the years immediately after World War II, when the birth rate increased sharply（二次大战结束后头几年内）婴儿潮时期出生的人

baby buggy *n* (*US*) = PRAM[A-Z]

baby-buster *n* = GENERATION X

baby wipe /'beɪbɪ waɪp; 'bebɪ waɪp/ *n* small paper towel moistened with a disinfectant used to wipe a baby's face or to clean a baby's bottom after taking off a dirty nappy 婴儿用消毒湿纸巾（用以抹面或抹屁股）

back-door /ˌbæk'dɔ:(r); ˌbæk'dɔr/ *adj* using indirect or secret means to achieve an end 走后门的，秘密进行的（通过迂回的或秘密的渠道以达到目的的）：*The back-door negotiations achieved an agreement where open meetings had failed.* 公开会议上没有达成的协议，通过秘密谈判办到了。

back-end /bæk'end; bæk'ɛnd/ *adj* [attrib 作定语] (of costs) relating to those that have to be met in the winding-up of a business or as a project nears completion（指费用）工作结束阶段的，工程后期的：*back-end costs/expenses/outgoings* 后期成本 *[费用 / 开支]*

backslapping /'bækslæpɪŋ; 'bækslæpɪŋ/ *n* [U] **1** loud congratulations with physical contact, esp slapping of backs（互有身体接触的）高声祝贺（尤指同时拍背的）**2** (*fig* 比喻) congratulations in the form of words of praise and compliments, esp when this is mutual and reciprocal 以言辞祝贺（尤指相互之间）：*The award ceremony became simply a show of backslapping as each recipient lavished praise on the film board.* 颁奖典礼简直成了各位获奖者极力恭维电影评奖委员会的表演。

backstreet /'bækstri:t; 'bækstrit/ *n* **1** street away from the busy main centre of a town 偏僻街道；后街 **2** [attrib 作定语] secretive, perhaps illegal 偷偷摸摸的，秘密的，（或为）非法的：*a backstreet abortionist* 非法为人堕胎者 ○ *a backstreet money-changer* 黑市钱币兑换商

backswing /'bækswɪŋ; 'bækswɪŋ/ *n* (*sport* 体) (in ball-games) movement backwards of the arm or arms holding a bat, racket, etc before hitting the ball 向后挥臂动作（球类运动中击球前向后挥动握着球拍、球棒等的手臂的动作）：*The champion's short backswing meant she met the ball early, surprising her opponent again and again.* 那位冠军短促地向后挥臂，还以为她迎球过早，这一招再三使对方措手不及。

back to basics /bæk tə 'beɪsɪks; bæk tə 'besɪks/ *n* call made by politicians, esp the Conservative Party in Britain, for a return to fundamental principles of decent living, such as showing self-respect, honesty and accepting responsibility 回复本原（政治家，尤指英国的保守党提出的回复到理想生活的基本原则的主张，例如抱持自尊、为人诚实和富有责任感）

bad hair day /bæd 'heə deɪ; bæd 'hɛr de/ *n* day when you feel bad about your appearance, etc and when everything seems to go wrong 感觉糟糕的一天，不顺心的日子（如对自己的打扮不满等）

bagger /'bægə(r); 'bægɚ/ *n* person whose job is to pack customers' bags at a supermarket check-out counter 装袋工（在超级市场付款台替顾客将所买商品装袋的人）

baguette *n* = FRENCH LOAF（FRENCH[A-Z]）

bail bandit /'beɪl bændɪt; 'bel bændɪt/ *n* person who commits a crime while OUT ON BAIL（BAIL[1] 3[A-Z]）保释期内犯罪者

bailout /'beɪlaʊt; 'belaʊt/ *n* financial assistance given to a failing business, often by government, to prevent its collapse（通常指政府为防止企业倒闭提供的）紧急财政援助：*a five-million-dollar bailout* 五百万美元的紧急援助金

balancing act /'bælənsɪŋ ækt; 'bælənsɪŋ ækt/ *n* (*fig* 比喻) skilled way to avoid offending or neglecting two or more opposing groups or interests 协调；平衡；避免冲突：*Many working women achieve a delicate balancing* *act between the demands of work and family.* 很多职业妇女把工作和家庭照顾得两全其美。

balsamic vinegar /bɔːlˌsæmɪk ˈvɪnɪɡə(r); bɔlˌsæmɪk ˈvɪnɪɡɚ/ *n* [U] dark, sweet Italian vinegar matured in wooden barrels（木桶中酿熟的）意大利香黑醋

Balti /ˈbɔːltɪ, ˈbæltɪ; ˈbɔltɪ, ˈbæltɪ/ *n* Pakistani curry which is usu cooked and served in a dish like a shallow wok 巴尔第咖喱菜（一种通常盛在浅镬中烹调及端上桌的巴基斯坦咖喱菜）

bancassurance /ˈbæŋkəʃɔːrəns, bæŋkəˈʃɔːrəns, *US* -ʃʊərəns; ˈbæŋkəʃuərəns, bæŋkəˈʃuərəns/ (also **bankassurance**) *n* [U] (*finance* 财) direct sale of insurance, esp life assurance, by banks 银行保险（银行直接卖出的保险，尤指人寿保险）

bankable asset /ˌbæŋkəbl ˈæset; ˌbæŋkəbl ˈæsɛt/ *n* skills or talent that can earn sb a good living（使人能过上好日子的）技能或天赋：*Her beauty wasn't her only bankable asset.* 美貌不是她生活富裕的唯一资本。

bankroll /ˈbæŋkrəʊl; ˈbæŋkrol/ *v* [Tn] meet the total expenses of an individual or of a business venture 为个人或企业提供全部资金；全额资助：*With Murdoch bankrolling the new TV station, it's likely to succeed.* 这家新电视台有默多克的全额资助，看来能成功。

banoffi pie /bəˌnɒfɪ ˈpaɪ; bəˌnɑfɪ ˈpaɪ/ *n* dessert consisting of cream, bananas and toffee on a pastry base 香蕉太妃排（用奶油、香蕉、太妃糖和油酥面团制成的甜点）

NOTE 注： blend formed from the words *banana* and *toffee* 由 banana（香蕉）和 toffee（太妃糖）二词合成

barbi /ˈbɑːbɪ; ˈbɑrbɪ/ *n* (*Austral infml* 澳，口) **1** BARBECUE[A-Z] 烧烤野餐 **2** food cooked in a barbecue 烤的食物

Barbie /ˈbɑːbɪ; ˈbɑrbɪ/ (*US propr* 专利名) very popular brand of doll like a glamorous model whose beauty strikes many people as bland or stereotyped 芭比娃娃（十分畅销的一种玩具，形如一个艳丽的模特儿，但此种女性美已被许多人视为老套和乏味）

▷ **barbify** *v* (*derog* 贬) make oneself or sb else look as like a Barbie doll as possible 使芭比化：*The modelling school barbifies women and turns out an endless stream of look-alikes.* 这所模特儿学校把女郎打扮成千人一面的芭比娃娃。

barfly /ˈbɑːflaɪ; ˈbɑrflaɪ/ *n* sb who spends most of his/her time in a bar 吧虫（大部分时间泡在酒吧里的人）

□ **barfly jumping** *n* pastime of throwing oneself at a wall covered with VELCRO[A-Z] with the aim of sticking to it, usu practised in bars 吧蝇跳（一种通常在酒吧中进行的娱乐活动，参与者扑向铺上尼龙刺黏片的墙并黏在其上）

-based /beɪst; best/ *suff* 后缀 (usu with ns and advs 通常与名词和副词连用) at a certain place or in a certain way 在…地方；以…方式：*a London-based company* 总部设在伦敦的公司 ○ *a broadly-based curriculum* 内容广泛的课程

basehead /ˈbeɪshed; ˈbeshɛd/ *n* (*US sl* 俚) person who regularly takes either of the two drugs FREEBASE or CRACK 经常服用精炼可卡因或强效纯可卡因的人；吸毒成瘾的人

NOTE 注： formed from *freebase* (purified cocaine) and *head* (drug addict) 由 freebase（精炼可卡因）和 head（瘾君子）二词构成

BASE jump /ˈbeɪs dʒʌmp; ˈbes dʒʌmp/ *n* (*sport* 体) parachute jump from a high building or natural feature rather than from an aircraft（从高层建筑或地势高处进行的）跳伞

▷ **BASE jump** *v*

NOTE 注： an acronym from *Building, Antenna-tower, Span* (bridge), *Earth* (natural feature, eg a cliff) which denote the high points usu used 由 Building（建筑物）、Antenna-tower（天线塔）、Span（桥面）及 Earth（自然地貌如悬崖）四词的首字母合成，均表示跳伞通常使用的高处

base metal /ˌbeɪs ˈmetl; ˌbes ˈmɛtl/ *n* any metal, eg copper, lead, tin as distinct from the precious metals, eg gold or platinum 普通金属（铜、铅、锡等金属，有别于金、铂等贵金属）

bash /bæʃ; bæʃ/ *n* (*infml* 口) big party or celebration 大型宴会；大型庆祝活动：*There was a terrific bash for the party workers on the night of the election victory.* 选举获胜的当晚该党的工作人员举行了盛大的庆祝活动。Cf 参看 DO[3] 1[A-Z]

basket /ˈbɑːskɪt, *US* ˈbæs-; ˈbæskɪt/ *n* [U] range; quantity 范围；量；组：*The agreement included a whole basket of concessions to the terrorists.* 这一协议对恐怖分子作了一揽子的让步。○ *a basket of currencies* 一批货币

beam me up /biːm miː ˈʌp; bim mi ˈʌp/ (also **beam me up, Scotty**) *interj* (*joc* 谑) (said when one wants to escape an embarrassing or difficult situation, meaning 'get me out of here' 用于某人想逃离尴尬或危险的处境之时，意为'带我离开这儿'): *Oh no, here comes my old girl-friend. Beam me up, Scotty!* 不得了，我以前的女朋友正向我走过来了。让我消失吧！

NOTE 注： from the Star Trek series in which the heroes frequently escape danger, etc by being decomposed into a beam of molecules and transported back aboard their space ship by the Chief Engineer, nicknamed Scotty 源自《星球旅行》连续剧中的情节，主人公们逃离险境时，常由绰号 Scotty 的总工程师将他们化作一道分子束，然后将他们传送回太空船

bean curd *n* = TOFU

beat box /ˈbiːt bɒks; ˈbit bɑks/ *n* (*infml* 口) powerful portable cassette player 手提大功率盒式录音机 Cf 参看 GHETTO BLASTER (GHETTO[A-Z])

bedhead /ˈbedhed; ˈbɛdhɛd/ (*US* **headboard**) *n* (*Brit*) end part of the framework of a bed, behind the head of the person sleeping in it 床架的头部

beefcake /ˈbiːfkeɪk; ˈbifkek/ *n* [U] (*sl* 俚) well-muscled men displayed esp in ads or sex-magazines or appearing in floorshows（尤指广告或性杂志中出现的或夜总会里参加表演的）健美男子

been there, done that /ˈbiːn ðeə ˌdʌn ðæt; ˈbɪn ðɛr ˌdʌn ðæt/ *interj* (*joc* 谑) (claim that the speaker has already visited a place or experienced sth and is probably not interested in hearing any more about it. Short for 'I've been there and I've done that' 表示说话者已去过某处或经历过某事，没有兴趣再听，为 I've been there and I've done that 的简略形式): *When I mentioned my experiences in Lagos, she shouted 'Been there, done that!'* 我说起自己在拉各斯的经历时，她就喊'知道了，知道了！'

bell pepper *n* (*US*) = CAPSICUM[A-Z]

bells and whistles /belz ənd ˈwɪslz, *US* ˈhwɪ-; bɛlz ənd ˈhwɪslz/ *n* (*esp computing* 尤作计算机术语) lots of additional features, attractive but unnecessary, included with software applications（软件应用程序中许多花哨而不实用的）附属功能：*The new application has its own bells and whistles but is really no advance on earlier versions.* 新的应用程序多了些新花样，但与以前的版本相比并无改进。

beltway /ˈbeltweɪ; ˈbɛltwe/ *n* (*US*) RING ROAD (RING[1(A-Z)]), esp the one around Washington 环行公路（尤指环绕华盛顿市那条）

□ **beltway bandit** (also **Beltway bandit**) *n* (*sl* 俚) company or individual, often one formerly employed by a US government agency, hired by a corporation to assist in obtaining government contracts 环路剪径大盗，环路强盗（指受聘协助公司争夺政府合同的公司或个人，他们通常原先受雇于美国政府机构）

bentwood /'bentwʊd; 'bɛntwud/ *n* [U] wood that is artificially shaped and used for making furniture 弯木（人工定型用以制作家具的木头）

beta-test /'bi:tətest, *US* 'beɪtə-; 'betətɛst/ *v* [Tn] test a product made by a different organization before it goes into mass production 进行 β 因素测试（对另一公司在大量生产前的新产品进行测试）

be there for /bi: 'ðeə fɔ:(r); bi 'ðɛr fɔr/ *v* [Ln] be available and prepared to help and support sb whenever the need arises 愿随时（给某人）提供帮助和支援：*Remember, I'll always be there for you.* 记住，无论何时何地，我都是你坚强的后盾。

NOTE 注： an expression that is used to convey sb's promise to be supportive and concerned 用以表达对他人的支持和关心

betting /'betɪŋ; 'bɛtɪŋ/ *n* [U] **1** action of placing money on sth risky and uncertain 赌博；打赌 **2** (idm 习语) **What's the betting** said when sb thinks sth, usu unpleasant, is very likely to happen 你打赌吗（用于当某人认为某事，通常指不愉快的事，极有可能发生时）：*What's the betting that the plane will be late?* 我说飞机要晚点了，你敢打赌吗？

bhaji /'bɑ:dʒɪ; 'bɑdʒɪ/ *n* (*pl* ~ **s**) **1** Indian dish of fried vegetables 印度炒素 **2** small flat cake or ball of vegetables fried in batter（蘸面糊炸的）小菜饼，蔬菜丸子：*Have another onion bhaji.* 再吃一个洋葱饼。Cf 参看 PAKORA

Bhangra /'bæŋgrə, 'bɑ:ŋgrə; 'bæŋgrə/ *n* [U] pop music style developed by British Asians, ie people whose origins are in the Indian subcontinent, combining Punjabi traditional tunes with aspects of Western rock 班格拉流行乐（祖籍印度次大陆的亚裔英国人的一种流行音乐，它糅合了旁遮普的传统曲调和西方摇滚乐的成分）

bible belt /'baɪbl belt; 'baɪbl̩ bɛlt/ *n* [U] (*US*) area chiefly in the southern US and in the prairie region of Canada where fundamental Christian beliefs predominate 圣经地带（基督教原教旨主义派分布地区，主要在美国南部和加拿大大草原地区）：*The town is in the heart of the bible belt.* 这个小镇位于圣经地带的中心。

bicycle path /'baɪsɪkl pɑ:θ, *US* pæθ; 'baɪsɪkl̩ pæθ/ (also **cycle path**) *n* portion of road set aside for cyclists to use 自行车道

big bang /ˌbɪg 'bæŋ; bɪg 'bæŋ/ *n* (usu *sing* 通常作单数) complete and basic change or bundle of changes introduced suddenly rather than gradually 大爆炸式变革；剧变：*Russia's market reformers believe in the big bang, not in the slow evolution of a demand-driven economy.* 俄罗斯的市场改革者们相信剧变论，而不相信受需求引导的经济渐进演变论。

big hair /bɪg 'heə; bɪg 'hɛr/ *n* [U] (*esp US slightly derog* 略带贬义) lot of hair on the head, usu long and thick 长而密的一大堆头发：*Every day there seems to be another story in the papers about a woman with big hair and a sexual adventure to tell.* 每天报上似乎都会有关于长发女郎的风流韵事的报道。

NOTE 注： associated with a type of female personal appearance which some consider showy and rather vulgar 与一种一些人视为俗丽的女子形象有关

bike /baɪk; baɪk/ *n* (idm 习语) **on your bike!** (*Brit*) Off you go! Off with you! 滚开！滚蛋！：*Come on Jones. On your bike! You can't sit around waiting for a job to come to you.* 快，琼斯，动起来吧！你不能坐等工作来找你啊。

biker /'baɪkə(r); 'baɪkɚ/ *n* person who rides a powerful motorcycle, esp a Harley Davidson, for pleasure and usu dresses in black leather to do so 摩托车骑士，（摩托车）飞车族（常穿黑皮衣骑大马力摩托车，尤指哈利·戴维森牌摩托车兜风的人）

□ **biker gang** *n* large number of bikers who habitually meet and ride around together 摩托车帮，（摩托车）飞车党（常聚在一起骑摩托车四处游荡的人）：*Rival biker gangs have become a major problem in some Danish towns.* 在丹麦的一些城镇里，敌对的飞车帮闹事已成为一个严重的问题。

billionaire /ˌbɪljə'neə(r); ˌbɪljə'nɛr/ *n* very rich person; literally sb who has a thousand million dollars, pounds, etc 巨富；亿万富翁

bimbo /'bɪmbəʊ; 'bɪmbo/ *n* **1** (*Brit derog* 贬) sexually attractive but stupid young woman, sometimes one who has an affair with a prominent person 性感但愚蠢的女郎（有时指与名人有染者）**2** (*US derog* 贬) idiot 傻子；白痴：*This department is run by a bunch of bimbos.* 这个部门被一群笨蛋掌管着。

bi-media /baɪ'mi:dɪə; baɪ'midɪə/ *adj* involved with or working in both radio and television 双媒体的；涉及广播和电视的；从事广播和电视工作的：*The Director General of the BBC expects all senior staff to be bi-media professionals.* 英国广播公司总裁期望所有的高级职员都是精通广播和电视的专业人员。

bin /bɪn; bɪn/ *v* [Tn] throw sth away in a wastepaper basket or rubbish bin（把某物当作垃圾）扔进废纸篓或垃圾箱：*I bin most of the mail that lands on my desk every morning.* 我每天早上将派送到桌上的大部分邮件扔进废纸篓。

binge-purge cycle /ˌbɪndʒ'pɜ:dʒ saɪkl; ˌbɪndʒ'pɝdʒ saɪkl̩/ *n* repeated behaviour of overeating and then inducing vomiting to get rid of the food taken in. Often associated with eating disorders such as BULIMIA 暴食—呕吐循环（暴食后再设法诱发自己呕吐出吃进的食物的重复行为，常与食欲亢进症等饮食失调情况有关）

bin-liner /'bɪnlaɪnə (r); 'bɪnlaɪnɚ/ *n* large plastic bag used to line rubbish bin（衬在垃圾箱里的）大塑料袋

biocide /'baɪəˌsaɪd; 'baɪəsaɪd/ *n* [U] **1** poisonous substance, esp a pesticide 对生物有害的物质；（尤指）杀虫剂 **2** destruction of living things 毁灭生命

NOTE 注： formed on analogy with *suicide* 由 suicide（自杀）一词类推构成

biodiversity /ˌbaɪəʊdaɪ'vɜ:sɪtɪ; ˌbaɪodaɪ'vɝsətɪ/ *n* [U] variety of plant and animal life, seen as a desirable goal as opposed to the loss of species and the reliance on too few plants 生物多样性（相对于物种减少及依赖过少种类的粮食植物，一个被视为理想的生物多样化的目标）

biogas /'baɪəʊˌgæs; 'baɪoˌgæs/ *n* gas, eg methane, given off by the decay of organic matter and which can be used as fuel（有机物腐烂后散发出的）生物气（可用作燃料，如沼气）

biohazard /'baɪəʊˌhæzəd; 'baɪoˌhæzɚd/ *n* danger to human life or to the environment posed by scientific investigation and experimental work with micro-organisms 生物危害（以微生物来做科学研究与实验而对人类或自然环境造成的危害）：*The labs experimenting with deadly viruses are treated as a biohazard, so strict safety regulations are followed at all times.* 研究致命病毒的实验室被列为危险场所，因此一直实施严格的安全规定。

biological clock /ˌbaɪəˌlɒdʒɪkl 'klɒk; ˌbaɪəˌlɑdʒɪkl̩ 'klɑk/ *n* (**a**) natural timing mechanism in living creatures which controls their regular physical activities, eg eating, sleeping 生物钟（生物体内天然的周期性节律，可有规律地控制进食、睡眠等活动）(**b**) (in women) natural timing mechanism which hints at the limited number of years appropriate for becoming pregnant 受孕生理钟（妇女体内显示其受孕年限的生理机制）：*My biological clock is ticking. I can't put off starting a family much longer.* 我的生物钟显示，我现在得开始要孩子，不能再拖了。

biological mother *n* = GENETIC MOTHER

biological weapon /ˌbaɪəˌlɒdʒɪkl ˈwepən; ˌbaɪəˌlɑdʒɪkl ˈwɛpən/ *n* weapon which releases bacteria or virus and causes lethal diseases 生物武器（释放细菌或病毒而引起致命疾病的武器）

biomass /ˈbaɪəʊmæs; ˈbaɪomæs/ *n* [U] total quantity or weight of living creatures in a given area or volume（一定面积或体积内的）生物量 : *the biomass of a forest* 森林生物量

biomechanics /baɪəʊməˈkænɪks; ˌbaɪoməˈkænɪks/ *n* [sing v] study of human movement and of the interaction between the human body and equipment in athletics and speed sports in order to maximise efficiency and enhance performance 生物力学（研究人体运动和人体与运动器械之间的互动关系，以求在体育运动及速度运动中取得最高效率和最佳表现）: *Biomechanics in the field of athletics has advanced greatly with the increasing use of powerful computers.* 随着高效用计算机的日益广泛应用，体育运动生物力学的研究取得了很大进展。

biometric /ˌbaɪəʊˈmetrɪk; ˌbaɪoˈmɛtrɪk/ *adj* based on or relating to measurements of human physiology, eg heart rate, fingerprint patterns, etc 基于人体生理测量的（如心率、指纹等）；与人体生理测定有关的 : *New biometric security devices will only admit individuals with recognized speech characteristics.* 新的生理测量安全装置只有在识别出某人的言语特征后，方准许其进入。

biopic /ˈbaɪəʊˌpɪk; ˈbaɪoˌpɪk/ *n* (*infml* 口) film which tells sb's life story 传记片

NOTE 注： a blend of *biography* and *picture* 由 biography（传记）和 picture（电影）二词合成

biosphere /ˈbaɪəʊˌsfɪə(r); ˈbaɪoˌsfɪr/ *n* **1** [U] part of the earth's surface and atmosphere where life is possible 生物圈（地球表面和大气层等适于生物生存的区域）**2** [C] artificially-created living environment, sealed off from the outside and supposedly self-sustaining, built for scientific and experimental purposes 人造生物圈（供科学实验用的封闭式生存环境，里面的生物应可自给自足）: *Biosphere 1, built to sustain life for five years, raised more questions than it answered.* ☆ 1 号生物圈按设计可维持生命五年，但引发了不少问题，弊多于利。

bird flu /ˈbɜːd fluː; ˈbɝd flu/ *n* [U] infection caused by the virus H5N1, thought previously to be contracted only by birds, esp chickens, but which has caused several deaths in the human community (eg Hong Kong in early 1998) 禽流感（由 H5N1 病毒引起的传染病，原先以为只有禽类尤其是鸡才会感染，但此病已引致数人死亡，如 1998 年初在香港就发生这种情况）

bird-strike /ˈbɜːdstraɪk; ˈbɝdstraɪk/ *n* collision between a bird or flock of birds and an aircraft 飞机与鸟（群）相撞 : *The crash was caused by a bird-strike when several wild geese were sucked into the jets of the plane as it took off.* 空难是飞机与鸟相撞造成的，飞机起飞时把几只野雁吸进了喷气发动机。

birthing pool /ˈbɜːθɪŋ puːl; ˈbɝθɪŋ pul/ *n* small pool of warm water at a hospital in which a woman may choose to give birth 分娩池（医院里供产妇分娩的小型温水池）: *Fears have been expressed about the possible risk to new-born babies from bacteria in birthing pools.* 有人担心分娩池中的细菌可能危害新生儿的健康。

birth mother /ˈbɜːθ mʌðə(r); ˈbɝθ mʌðɚ/ *n* woman who carries a foetus to TERM 2A-Z and delivers it. She may be a different woman from the BIOLOGICAL MOTHER who can conceive but not carry a baby to full term 生母（怀胎足月生产的母亲，与基因母亲不一定为同一人，后者只能怀孕，却不能怀胎至足月生产）: *The birth mother carried the baby and delivered it for her sister who was the biological mother.* 这位母亲为其姐姐怀孕生子，她的姐姐是孩子的基因母亲。

bite-sized /ˈbaɪtsaɪzd; ˈbaɪtsaɪzd/ *adj* [usu attrib 通常作定语] **1** having been cut into small pieces which can be put into the mouth whole（小到能）一口（咬）的 **2** (*fig* 比喻) (pieces of information) easily taken in and understood（信息）易于接受和理解的

Black American English *n* = BLACK ENGLISH

black belt /ˌblæk ˈbelt; blæk ˈbɛlt/ *n* person who has reached the highest rank in JUDOA-Z, KARATEA-Z, etc and is thus entitled to wear a black belt（柔道、空手道等）黑带级选手

black-box program /blækˈbɒks ˌprəʊgræm; blækˈbɑks ˌprogrəm/ *n* (*computing* 计) piece of software that cannot be accessed by the user to examine its operating system 黑匣子程序，未知框（用户无法查看其操作程序的软件）

Black English /ˌblæk ˈɪŋglɪʃ; ˌblæk ˈɪŋglɪʃ/ (also **Black American English**) *n* [U] form of English spoken by many black people in US towns and cities and recognized by modern linguists as a dialect in its own right（美国）黑人英语

black information /ˌblæk ɪnfəˈmeɪʃn; ˌblæk ɪnfɚˈmeʃən/ *n* [U] information held by a bank or credit agency about an individual considered to be a bad credit risk 黑资料（银行或信用调查机构掌握的关于某人信用不佳的资料）

black knight /blæk ˈnaɪt; blæk ˈnaɪt/ *n* (*infml* 口) person or company that makes a hostile and unwanted take-over bid for another company 黑骑士（恶意投标竞购某公司的人或公司）Cf 参看 WHITE KNIGHT

black-tie solution /ˌblæktaɪ səˈluːʃn; ˌblæktaɪ səˈluʃən/ *n* civilized and diplomatic solution, avoiding military action 外交谈判解决；非武力解决；和平解决 : *The UN Secretary favoured a black-tie solution to the crisis.* 联合国秘书长倾向赞成以外交谈判方式解决这场危机。

blades /bleɪdz; bledz/ *n* [pl] rollerblades (ROLLERBLADE) 刀刃式旱冰鞋

Blairism /ˈbleərɪzəm; ˈblɛrɪzəm/ *n* [U,C] (*Brit*) policies of the British Prime Minister, Tony Blair, who came to power at the General Election in 1997 布莱尔政策（1997 年大选后上台的英国首相托尼·布莱尔推行的政策）Cf 参看 STAKEHOLDER ECONOMY (STAKEHOLDER)

blankety-blank /ˌblæŋkətɪˈblæŋk; ˌblæŋkətɪˈblæŋk/ *adj* (*infml euph* 口，婉) (used in place of a rude or offensive word, such as) damn, bloody, etc（代替粗鲁无礼言词如 damn、bloody 等的委婉语）该死的 : *The blankety-blank idiot's broken the computer again.* 这个该死的笨蛋又把计算机弄坏了。

blazing /ˈbleɪzɪŋ; ˈblezɪŋ/ *adj* (*fig* 比喻) emotionally strong and violent, like a BLAZE 1A-Z（情感像火焰般）炽烈的，激烈的 : *a blazing row* 剧烈的争吵

blinding /ˈblaɪndɪŋ; ˈblaɪndɪŋ/ *adj* (esp of light or pain) very intense（尤指光线）特强的；（尤指疼痛）剧烈的 : *a blinding light* 刺眼的光线 ○ *a blinding headache* 剧烈的头痛

blini /ˈbliːnɪ; ˈblinɪ/ *n* (*pl* **blinis**) pancake made from BUCKWHEAT FLOUR (BUCKWHEATA-Z), a typical Russian dish 俄国荞麦薄煎饼

blinker /ˈblɪŋkə(r); ˈblɪŋkɚ/ *n* device for flashing a light signal, eg the INDICATOR 3A-Z on a car 闪光信号灯（如汽车的转弯指示灯等）

blitzkrieg /ˈblɪtskriːg; ˈblɪtskrig/ *n* intense military campaign intended to achieve a quick victory 闪电战 : *In 1939, Germany launched its blitzkrieg against Poland.* ☆ 1939 年，德国向波兰发动了闪电战。

NOTE 注： from the German words *blitz* (lightning) and

krieg (war) 源自德语 blitz（闪电）和 krieg（战争）二词

bloodied /'blʌdɪd; 'blʌdɪd/ *adj* **1** (**a**) partly covered with blood 血淋淋的 (**b**) damaged; hurt 受伤的；毁坏的 **2** (idm 习语) **bloodied but unbowed/not bowed** hurt but not ready to submit or to admit defeat 虽受伤但不屈服或不认输；宁死不屈

bluegrass /'blu:grɑ:s, *US* -græs; 'blugræs/ *n* [U] (*US*) country music played on unamplified stringed instruments, eg banjo, guitar 蓝草音乐（用班卓琴、吉他等弦乐器演奏的乡村音乐，不用扩音器）

NOTE 注： from *the Bluegrass state,* nickname of Kentucky 源自肯塔基州的别名 Bluegrass（六月禾州）

blue pencil /ˌblu: 'pensl; ˌblu 'pɛnsḷ/ *n* (*Brit*) **1** pencil traditionally used by censors to cross out offensive parts of a play, book, etc before showing or publication（在戏剧上演或书籍出版之前，审查员删除犯忌的内容所用的）蓝心铅笔 **2** (*fig* 比喻) whatever means are used to effect such censorship（泛指各种形式的）审查，删改：*The Board of Censors has been through the script with a blue pencil.* 审查委员会已对文字稿作了审查。

blue skies research /ˌblu: skaɪz rɪ'sɜ:tʃ; ˌblu skaɪz rɪ'sɝtʃ/ *n* [U] research undertaken by universities, research institutes, etc, with the support of industry but with no limiting restrictions or demands placed upon them 蓝天研究（大学或研究所等进行的研究项目，有企业提供资助但不附加任何限制或提出任何要求）

B-movie /bi: 'mu:vɪ, 'bi: ˌmu:vɪ; bi 'muvɪ/ *n* low-budget film with poor quality special effects 二流电影（特技效果差的低成本电影）：*He's a well-known director of B-movies.* 他是以执导二流电影闻名的导演。

boatyard /'bəʊtjɑ:d; 'botjɑrd/ *n* place where boats are kept, repaired, hired out, etc 船坞

bobbing and peering /bɒbɪŋ ənd 'pɪərɪŋ; bɑbɪŋ ənd 'pɪrɪŋ/ *n* [U] (*infml* 口) (of prostitutes) repeated action of bending down and looking into the windows of cars, which are KERB-CRAWLING（KERB^A-Z^）, for potential customers（指妓女）弯腰寻客（为拉嫖客不断地俯身朝沿路边缓慢开动的车内看）

bobs ⇨ BITS AND BOBS（BIT[1] 4^A-Z^）

bodice ripper /'bɒdɪs rɪpə(r); 'bɑdɪs rɪpɚ/ *n* film or novel which features lots of romance and seduction scenes, often with an historical setting 浪漫情欲电影，浪漫情欲小说（常以某段历史为背景，以大量的浪漫及调情场面为特征的电影或小说）

NOTE 注： in the seduction scenes the heroine's BODICE^A-Z^ is frequently ripped, hence the name 因在调情戏中女主角的紧身胸衣 (bodice) 常被撕破而得名

body bag /'bɒdɪ bæg; 'bɑdɪ bæg/ *n* large usu black plastic sack with zipper, designed to contain a dead body for transportation 运尸袋（通常用黑色塑料制成，装有拉链，用以运送尸体的袋）

body count /'bɒdɪ kaʊnt; 'bɑdɪ kaʊnt/ *n* [U,C] number of fatalities in an accident, military action, etc（意外事故或战争中的）死亡人数：*The body count keeps on rising.* 死亡人数仍在上升。

body double /'bɒdɪ dʌbl; 'bɑdɪ dʌbḷ/ *n* kind of STAND IN（STAND[2] 16^A-Z^）who substitutes for a film actor, esp in nude scenes or when the character needs to display special skills, eg playing a musical instrument or dancing 替身演员（电影演员的替身，尤其在裸戏里或当角色需要表演某种特殊技能如演奏乐器或跳舞时使用）

bodyism /'bɒdɪɪzm; 'bɑdɪɪzəm/ *n* [U] practice of assessing a person's value by his or her physical appearance and/or size 外貌歧视；体形歧视；以貌取人：*Advertisements that insist on 'a pleasant appearance' could almost be accused of bodyism.* 强调'面貌端正'的广告可被指责为外貌歧视。

body piercing /'bɒdɪ pɪəsɪŋ; 'bɑdɪ pɪrsɪŋ/ *n* [U] piercing of body parts other than the ear, eg navel, lips, to accommodate rings or studs for decorative purposes 身体穿刺装饰（为了配戴环或钉以装饰，如在肚脐、嘴唇等耳朵以外的部位穿洞）

bog-standard /'bɒgstændəd; 'bɑgstændɚd/ *adj* (*Brit infml derog* 口，贬) basic; unexceptional; dull 低水平的；普通的；乏味的：*The bog-standard decor of the new restaurant is a disappointment.* 新饭馆毫无新意的装潢令人大失所望。

NOTE 注： from *bog*, the British slang word for *bathroom* or *toilet* 来自英式俚语 bog 一词，意谓浴室或厕所

bonesetter /'bəʊnˌsetə(r); 'bonˌsɛtɚ/ *n* **1** person who sets broken or dislocated bones without any medical qualification to do so（无行医执照的）民间正骨师 **2** (*infml derog* 口，贬) OSTEOPATH^A-Z^ or CHIROPRACTOR^A-Z^ 正骨专家；按摩治疗师

bonk /bɒŋk; baŋk/ *v* [Tn, I] **1** (*sl joc* 俚，谑) have sex with sb 与某人性交 **2** (*infml* 口) hit sb, esp on the head, without hurting them badly 打（尤指某人的头部，但不甚重）

▷ **bonk** *n* : *He only suffered a slight bonk on the head.* 他只是头上被轻打了一下。

□ **bonk journalism** *n* [U] (*sl derog* 俚，贬) journalism that focuses completely on exposing the sexual affairs of celebrities 桃色新闻（专门报道名人的风流韵事的新闻工作）：*You might call it a gossip magazine, but I think it's bonk journalism.* 你可以称它为漫话式杂志，但我认为它是桃色报刊。

bonsai /'bɒnsaɪ; 'bɑnsaɪ/ *n* (*pl* unchanged 复数不变）(**a**) [C] plant, esp a small tree, which is grown in a pot and is prevented from reaching its normal size by systematic trimming of its roots, branches, etc 盆景：*The bonsai were particularly attractive.* 这些盆景特别吸引人。(**b**) [U] art of growing such plants, originally developed in Japan 盆栽艺术（源自日本）：*Her hobby was bonsai.* 她的业余爱好是盆栽艺术。

boohoo /'bu:hu:, ˌbu:'hu:; 'buhu, ˌbu'hu/ *interj* (used in written English to represent the sound of noisy weeping. If spoken, the speaker means he or she is upset about something or is feeling sorry for himself or herself 用于书面语表示哭声，用于口语中表示说话者为某事烦恼或自怜）: *I've got to go to the dentist tomorrow. Boohoo! Poor me.* 我明天得去看牙了，呜，多可怜哪。

boombox /'bu:mbɒks; 'bumbɑks/ *n* (*sl* 俚) (**a**) loudspeaker 扬声器 (**b**) stereo system which projects sound through loudspeakers 立体声音响器材 Cf 参看 BEAT BOX, GHETTO BLASTER（GHETTO^A-Z^）

boondocks /'bu:ndɒks; 'bundɑks/ *n* **the boondocks** [pl] (*US sl derog* 俚，贬) country areas far from cities and perhaps lacking sophistication and variety 穷乡僻壤 Cf 参看 THE STICKS（STICK[1] 9^A-Z^）, THE BACK OF BEYOND（BACK[1] 6^A-Z^）

boot camp /'bu:t kæmp; 'but kæmp/ *n* (esp in the US) institution for young criminals which offers an alternative to prison and which enforces a tough regime of physical exercise and discipline 年轻罪犯训练营（尤指在美国用以代替监狱的机构，营内的犯人要进行艰苦的体能训练并有严格的纪律）

boot sale *n* = CAR-BOOT SALE（CAR^A-Z^）

bordello /bɔ:'deləʊ; bɔr'dɛlo/ *n* (*pl* **-os**) (*US*) BROTHEL^A-Z^ 妓院

bovine spongiform encephalopathy /bəʊvaɪn ˌspʌndʒɪfɔ:m enkefə'lɒpəθɪ, ense-; bovaɪn ˌspʌndʒɪfɔrm ɛnsɛfə'lɑpəθɪ/ (also **mad cow disease**) *n* (*abbr* 缩写 **BSE**) incurable brain condition in cattle which causes neurological disorders and is fatal 疯牛病（导致牛的脑神经紊乱并引致死亡的疾病）

NOTE 注： discovered in the early 90s to be the probable source of the human equivalent of BSE, CREUTZFELDT-JAKOB DISEASE 疯牛病于 90 年代初被发现可能导致人类所患的对等疾病克—雅二氏病

bozo /ˈbəʊzəʊ; ˈbozo/ *n* (*esp US sl* 俚) idiot; stupid or worthless person 白痴；蠢货

brain death /ˈbreɪn deθ; ˈbren dɛθ/ *n* [U] (*medical* 医) final cessation of brain function, but not of the heartbeat, widely accepted as a legal definition of death 脑死亡（心脏虽仍跳动但脑功能已停止的状态，普遍认为应属法定死亡）

▷ **brain dead** *adj* **1** having suffered brain death 脑死亡的 **2** (*fig* 比喻) being very stupid 十分愚蠢的：*All the people I speak to in that company seem to be brain dead.* 在那家公司里我与之说过话的人，全都笨得像没脑子一样。

brain scan /ˈbreɪn skæn; ˈbren skæn/ *n* (*infml* 口) process or result of an electronic examination of the living brain; MAGNETIC RESONANCE IMAGING 脑部电子扫描；磁共振成像

brain spa /ˈbreɪn spɑː; ˈbren spɑ/ *n* establishment that offers rooms where people can relax and enjoy calming images and soft music in order to seek relief from stress 健脑中心（提供让人们欣赏后心里平和的图像和轻柔的音乐以缓解压力的场所）Cf 参看 TRANQUILLITY ROOM

breadbasket /ˈbredbɑːskɪt, *US* -bæs-; ˈbrɛdbæskɪt/ *n* area that provides a large amount of food, esp grain, to the rest of the region or country 产粮区（尤指盛产谷物的）：*The droughts of the 1930s reduced the mid-west from the breadbasket of the US to a dust bowl.* ☆ 20 世纪 30 年代的旱灾将美国中西部由粮仓变成了土坑。

break /breɪk; brek/ *v* [Tn] (*esp US*) change a banknote for coins or for a mixture of coins and banknotes of smaller value 整票兑零，兑开（将钞票兑成硬币或硬币与小面额钞票）：*Can you break a $100 bill?* 你能将这张 100 美元钞票兑成零钱吗？

breakfast television /brekfəst ˈtelɪvɪʒn; brɛkfəst ˈtɛləvɪʒən/ *n* [U] television programmes broadcast early in the morning 早间电视节目：*a star of breakfast television* 早间电视节目的明星 Cf 参看 DAYTIME TELEVISION

bridge-building /ˈbrɪdʒbɪldɪŋ; ˈbrɪdʒbɪldɪŋ/ *n* (*fig* 比喻) promotion of friendly relations between two factions, groups or countries 增进（两派、两团体或两国之间的）友好关系：*We viewed the President's recent visit as an essential bridge-building exercise.* 我们将总统最近的访问视为重要的亲善之举。

bright-eyed /ˌbraɪtˈaɪd; braɪtˈaɪd/ *adj* **1** with bright eyes; lively and eager 眼睛闪亮的；活泼热心的 **2** (idm 习语) **bright-eyed and bushy-tailed** eager, enthusiastic and ready for any challenge 活泼热切的；兴高采烈的；跃跃欲试的：*We're all bright-eyed and bushy-tailed — ready for anything.* 我们都准备就绪，跃跃欲试。

NOTE 注： from the conventional description of a squirrel 来自惯常对松鼠的描述

brill /brɪl; brɪl/ *adj* (*Brit*) wonderful; great 绝妙的；极好的：*He's coming tomorrow! That's brill.* 他明天来！真是太棒了。○ *I've just had a brill idea.* 我有了个绝妙的主意。

NOTE 注： a short form of *brilliant* ☆ brilliant（极妙的）一词的缩写形式

brio /ˈbriːəʊ; ˈbrio/ *n* [U] individual style and energy 个人风格；活力

Britpop /ˈbrɪtpɒp; ˈbrɪtpɑp/ *n* [U] (*infml* 口) British pop music that draws on British rather than American musical styles 英国（而非美国风格的）流行音乐

NOTE 注： blend formed from the words *British* and *pop* 由 British 和 pop（流行音乐）二词合成

brittle-bone disease *n* = OSTEOPOROSIS

broadband /ˈbrɔːdbænd; ˈbrɔdbænd/ *adj* [attrib 作定语] relating to or using signals over a wide range of frequencies, esp in high-capacity telecommunications 宽波段的，宽（频）带的（尤用于高容量电信）

broad-based /ˌbrɔːdˈbeɪst; brɔdˈbest/ (also **broadly-based**) *adj* drawing in many things as a basis; not narrowly limited 基础广泛的：*He pursued a broad-based policy in economic affairs.* 他在经济事务中推行具有广泛基础的政策。

broadleaf /ˈbrɔːdliːf; ˈbrɔdlif/ (also **broad-leaved**) *adj* (of a kind of tree) losing its leaves in winter and having broad leaves rather than needles （指树）阔叶的（而不是针叶的）Cf 参看 DECIDUOUS[A-Z]

brooding /ˈbruːdɪŋ; ˈbrudɪŋ/ *adj* gloomy and dark or threatening 阴郁而黑暗的；恐怖的：*a dark and brooding atmosphere* 阴沉忧郁的气氛

Brownie point /ˈbraʊnɪ pɔɪnt; ˈbraunɪ pɔɪnt/ *n* (*joc* 谑) credit gained for doing well, esp with one's superiors 因表现好而赢得的称赞，分数（尤指博得上司的信任）：*You've remembered the boss's favourite drink. That'll get you some Brownie points.* 你记住了老板最爱喝的饮料，他会给你加上几分的。

NOTE 注： in Britain, little girls join the Brownies (BROWNIE 2[A-Z]) and get points and badges for passing various practical tests in First Aid, cooking, etc 在英国，女孩参加幼年女童子军 (Brownies)，在通过急救、烹饪等各种实际考验后，可以得分并获得奖章

brown land /braʊn ˈlænd; braun ˈlænd/ *n* [U] land previously used for industrial or other purposes that have left it damaged or changed, as compared to land that has not been disturbed 棕色土地，弃用工业地（因曾作为工业用地或其他用处而受到破坏或发生了变化的土地，相对于未受影响的土地而言）：*They argued that the proposed site for the new supermarket was brown land and so nothing of great environmental value was being lost.* 他们辩解说新超级市场拟定的地点是已弃用的工业土地，因此没有怎样损害环境。

brown out /ˈbraʊn aʊt; ˈbraun aut/ *n* period of reduced electricity supply to homes, offices, etc, as opposed to a total loss of power 供电减少期，部分灯火管制期（相对于完全停电）：*People in Manila have become used to frequent brown outs, but are not willing to put up with them for ever.* 马尼拉的居民对不时供电减少已习以为常，但不愿意永远这样忍受下去。Cf 参看 BLACKOUT（BLACK[1(A-Z)]）

browse /braʊz; brauz/ *v* [Tn] (*computing* 计) read or glance through information carried on computer networks, esp on the World Wide Web 浏览（尤指在万维网上）：*the new teenage pastime — browsing the Internet* 青少年的新娱乐——浏览互联网

Brussels /ˈbrʌslz; ˈbrʌslz/ *n* [sing] informal way of referring to the European Commission and Parliament which make decisions for all member states 欧洲委员会和欧洲议会的俗称

bubble bath /ˈbʌbl bɑːθ, *US* bæθ; ˈbʌbl bæθ/ *n* bath of water with perfumed liquid, crystals or powder added to it to make it foam and smell pleasant 泡沫浴（加入香液、晶体或粉末的浴盆水，有泡沫且芳香）

bubble wrap /ˈbʌbl ræp; ˈbʌbl ræp/ *n* [U] packing material made of plastic and with regularly spaced air-bubbles for protecting delicate objects 泡沫塑料包装；泡沫塑料保护层

bud /bʌd; bʌd/ *n* (*US infml* 口) (used as a form of address 用作称呼语) friend 朋友；哥们儿：*Come on, bud; get a move on. I haven't got all day.* 快点儿，哥们儿，我可没那么多时间。

NOTE 注： not always friendly, since it can be used to

address people whose names are not known 并不都表示亲热，因可用以称呼不知其名的人

buddy /'bʌdɪ; 'bʌdɪ/ *n* volunteer who acts as close companion and support to someone with AIDS[A-Z] 艾滋病患者之友（自愿经常陪伴并支持艾滋病患者的人）

▷ **buddy** *v* [Tn] act as a buddy 充当艾滋病患者之友：*I buddied Jason for the last year of his life.* 我陪伴贾森度过了他生命的最后一个年头。

NOTE 注： from the American sense of the word *buddy* meaning 'friend' 源自 buddy 一词作为美式英语时 '朋友' 的意思

bug-eyed monster /ˌbʌgaɪd 'mɒnstə(r); ˌbʌgaɪd 'mɑnstɚ/ *n* (*joc* 谑) ugly alien with bulging eyes（天外来的）暴眼怪物 Cf 参看 LITTLE GREEN MEN FROM MARS

building block /'bɪldɪŋ blɒk; 'bɪldɪŋ blɑk/ *n* basic component of sth 基本成分；基础材料：*Words are the building blocks of any language.* 词是任何语言的基本单位。

bulimia /bjuː'lɪmɪə; bu'lɪmɪə/ *n* [U] (*medical* 医) emotional disorder characterized by compulsive eating followed by deliberate vomiting 食欲亢进 Cf 参看 BINGE-PURGE CYCLE

▷ **bulimic** *n* person suffering from bulimia 患食欲亢进症的人

bull bar /'bʊl bɑː; 'bʊl bɑr/ *n* metal bar or framework on the front of a vehicle intended to protect it from damage in the event of a collision with a large animal（防止一旦与大动物相撞时造成车身损坏的）车头金属挡板

bullet train /'bʊlɪt treɪn; 'bʊlɪt tren/ *n* high-speed passenger train using magnetism technology, esp one of those that runs in Japan（尤指日本的）高速火车，子弹列车

bullish /'bʊlɪʃ; 'bʊlɪʃ/ *adj* optimistic and confident 乐观的；充满信心的：*I'm feeling bullish about this. Let's do it.* 我对此充满信心。让我们干吧。○ *a bullish attitude/atmosphere* 乐观的态度 *[*气氛*]*

NOTE 注： an extension from the original description of rising stock market conditions 原指证券交易行情看涨，今延伸为此义

bum-bag /'bʌmbæg; 'bʌmbæg/ (*US* **fanny pack**) *n* (*Brit infml* 口) small bag for money and other small valuables, eg passport, credit cards, fastened to a belt which is worn around the waist 腰包，腰袋（系于腰带上，放钱和护照、信用卡等小件贵重物品的小包）

bummer /'bʌmə(r); 'bʌmɚ/ *n* [C usu sing 通常作单数] (*infml* 口) event, duty or task which sb regards as very unpleasant and which they would rather not do 不愉快的事；不愿做的工作：*There's a meeting at 6. What a bummer!* ☆ 6 点钟有个会。真讨厌！

bundle /'bʌndl; 'bʌndl/ *v* (*computing* 计) supply various selections of computer software and hardware together at an attractive price 捆绑销售（将各种计算机软硬件放在一起以诱人的价格出售）：*The company caught public interest when they bundled the latest word processing and spreadsheet software with their new PC's.* 这家公司将最新的文字处理软件和电子表格软件与他们新的个人计算机组成套装销售，吸引了公众的关注。

▷ **bundle** *n* bundled package 捆绑出售的软硬件：*The bundle includes a CPU, a monitor and a large selection of useful software.* 这一套包括一个中央处理器、一台显示器和一大批实用软件。

bungee jumping /'bʌndʒɪ ˌdʒʌmpɪŋ; 'bʌndʒɪ ˌdʒʌmpɪŋ/ *n* (*sport* 体) sport of diving from a height while secured by elasticated ropes attached to the ankles 蹦极跳（跳者脚踝上系上弹性绳从高处跃下的运动）

bunker mentality /'bʌŋkə menˌtælɪtɪ; 'bʌŋkɚ mɛnˌtælətɪ/ (also **siege mentality**) (*n*) [U] strongly self-defensive attitude arising from the suspicion that one is threatened or likely to come under attack in some way 地堡心态，围困心态（因怀疑遭恐吓或有遇袭之虞而形成的极强的自我保护心态）：*The remaining white people shared the bunker mentality typical of small minorities.* 剩下的白人都有那种少数民族特有的地堡心态。

bunk-house /'bʌŋkhaʊs; 'bʌŋkhaus/ *n* rough building for ranch hands, campers, etc to sleep in（牧场雇工、野营者等住的）简易住所，工棚

NOTE 注： these houses are typically furnished with *bunk beds* 这些营房一般都设置了 bunk beds（双层床）

bunny hugger /'bʌnɪ hʌgə(r); 'bʌnɪ hʌgɚ/ *n* (*infml derog* 口，贬) person who works for a HUMANITARIAN[A-Z] organization 慈善机构工作者

NOTE 注： the name implies sb with too much sentimental concern for people who perhaps do not even deserve it 此名称暗示此人可能对那些不该同情的人也滥施同情

bunny slope /'bʌnɪ sləʊp; 'bʌnɪ slop/ *n* (*infml slightly derog* 口，略带贬义) easy, gentle ski slope, suitable for beginners; NURSERY SLOPE（NURSERY[A-Z]）（坡度和缓的）适合初学者滑雪的坡地

buppie /'bʌpɪ; 'bʌpɪ/ *n* (*sl* 俚) black YUPPIE[A-Z] 黑人雅皮士

burb /bɜːb; bɝb/ *n* (usu *pl* 通常作复数) (*esp US derog* 贬) SUBURB[A-Z]; suburban area 郊区

NOTE 注： the word often implies that the area so labelled is conventional, dull and boring 这个词常暗示所述地区因循守旧、单调、乏味

burglar bars /'bɜːglə bɑːz; 'bɝglɚ bɑrz/ *n* [pl] decorative or plain steel framework fitted over windows or doors to prevent burglars from breaking in（门窗的）钢质防盗护栏，防盗栅

burn /bɜːn; bɝn/ *n* (*sport* 体) sense of physical well-being reached by intense exercise（通过剧烈运动达到的）舒适感，尽兴：*Go for the burn!* 尽情去玩吧！

burn-out /'bɜːnaʊt; 'bɝnaʊt/ *n* [U,C] **1** time when a rocket or jet has used up all its fuel and has no more power（火箭或喷射机的）燃料耗尽时刻 **2** state of physical and/or mental exhaustion as a result of stress or overwork（因有压力和 *[*或*]* 过度劳累而导致的）精疲力竭：*If you push young athletes too hard, you risk them suffering early burn-out.* 如果逼着年轻运动员训练过度，你小心他们会过早地耗尽精力。

burro /'bʊrəʊ, *US* 'bɜːrəʊ; 'bɝo/ *n* (*pl* **-os**) (*US*) (from Spanish 源自西班牙语) small donkey used to carry heavy loads（用以负重的）小驴

business park /'bɪznəs pɑːk; 'bɪznɪs pɑrk/ *n* industrial estate on or near a research centre, in which high-technology firms are located to encourage scientific discoveries and their commercial applications 高科技工业园区（位于或靠近研究中心的工业园区，设有鼓励科学发明及其产业化应用的高科技公司）

business process re-engineering /bɪznɪs ˌprəʊses riːendʒɪ'nɪərɪŋ, *US* -prɑːses-; bɪznɪs ˌprɑsɛs riɛndʒə'nɪrɪŋ/ *n* [U] process of analysing and then redesigning the way operations are carried out in a business in order to increase efficiency and lower costs 企业运作的重新设计（对企业的运作方式所进行的分析和重新设计，以提高效率、降低成本）

butterfly effect /'bʌtəflaɪ ɪˌfekt; 'bʌtɚflaɪ ɪˌfɛkt/ *n* (in CHAOS THEORY) ever greater and more far-reaching consequences flowing from what seems to be a very slight cause 蝴蝶效应（出自混沌学说，指一件似乎微不足道的小事逐渐产生越来越巨大和深远的影响）

NOTE 注： an image derived possibly from the story by Rudyard Kipling called *The Butterfly that Stamped*

此比喻可能源自拉迪亚得·吉卜林的小说《跺脚的蝴蝶》

butthead /'bʌthed; 'bʌthɛd/ *n* (*US sl derog* 俚，贬) idiot; sb who behaves in a stupid, selfish and anti-social way 白痴；愚蠢、自私且与社会格格不入的家伙

butty /'bʌtɪ; 'bʌtɪ/ *n* (*Brit infml* 口) sandwich 三明治：*She missed the jam butties her mother used to make.* 她非常怀念母亲过去常做的果酱三明治。○ *chip butties* (ie 2 slices of bread with potato chips in the middle) 土豆条三明治

buy into /ˌbaɪ 'ɪntu:; ˌbaɪ 'ɪntu/ *v* [Tn] get involved with 被卷入；参与：*You shouldn't buy into the pro-abortion argument with these people. It's a waste of time.* 你不应参与这帮家伙支持堕胎合法化的辩论。那是在浪费时间。

buy-out /'baɪaʊt; 'baɪaʊt/ *n* act of gaining control of a public company by buying all or the majority of its shares（对全部或大部分股权的）购买（为获得对上市公司的控制权而采取的行动）：*The company was threatened by a buy-out.* 这家公司面临被人买断股权的危机。

buy the farm ⇨ FARM

BYOB /bi: waɪ əʊ 'bi:; bi waɪ o 'bi/ *abbr* 缩写 = **1** (instruction seen inside supermarkets 见于超市内) bring your own bag (to a shop) 请自带购物袋 **2** (instruction seen on party invitations 见于聚会的请柬上) bring your own bottle (or booze, ie wine, beer, etc) to a barbecue or party 请自带饮料（如葡萄酒、啤酒等来赴烤肉野餐会或聚会）

Cc

cable-ready /'keɪblˌredɪ; 'keblˌrɛdɪ/ *adj* designed to be plugged into a cable television network; able to receive cable television 可接入有线电视网的；可接收有线电视的：*The new TVs are all cable-ready. No modification required.* 这些新电视机都可收看有线电视节目，无须改装。

cable up /keɪbl 'ʌp; ˌkebl 'ʌp/ *v* [I] become or cause to become linked to a cable television system（使）与有线电视系统相接：*Our area hasn't been cabled up yet.* 我们这个地区还没有和有线电视系统联网。○ *Cable up and you'll soon see the benefits.* 接上有线电视，你很快就会看到它的好处。

CAD /kæd, ˌsi: eɪ 'di:; kæd, si e 'di/ *abbr* 缩写 = computer-aided design (using computers to design manufactured goods) 计算机辅助设计（利用计算机设计产品）

cafetiére /kæf'tjeə(r); kæf'tjɛr/ *n* (*Brit*) (from French) coffee pot, usu made of heat resistant glass, with a plunger that pushes the coffee grounds to the bottom once hot water has been poured over them, thus separating them from the coffee 法式咖啡壶（通常用耐热玻璃制的咖啡壶，内有活塞，倒进热水时把咖啡渣推至壶底使之与咖啡隔开）：*a one-person cafetiére* 一人用的法式咖啡壶

caff /kæf; kæf/ *n* (*Brit infml* 口) café, esp a cheap and basic one 小餐馆（尤指收费低廉而简陋的）：*a caff used mostly by lorry-drivers* 主要由卡车司机光顾的小餐馆

caffeinated /'kæfɪneɪtɪd; 'kæfənetɪd/ *adj* **1** with a caffeine content; having had caffeine added 含咖啡因的；加咖啡因的 **2** (*fig* 比喻) boosted; made more vigorous 增强的；受振奋的；更具活力的：*He is caffeinated by the applause of the audience and performs with even greater energy.* 他为观众的掌声所鼓舞，表演得更卖力了。

NOTE 注：formed from *decaffeinated* by taking off the prefix *de-* 由 decaffeinated 去掉前缀 de- 逆构而成

call-and-recall /kɔ:lənd'ri:kɔ:l; kɔlənd'rikɔl/ *n* [U] method of sending reminders from a medical practice to patients to ensure that they come for regular check-ups and standard health monitoring procedures, eg cholesterol level checks, smear tests, etc 不断提醒法（医疗机构叮咛嘱咐病人进行定期检查和常规健康检测，如胆固醇含量检查、早期癌变涂片检查等）

calvados /'kælvədɒs; 'kælvədɑs/ *n* apple brandy distilled in Normandy in northern France; apple LIQUEUR[A-Z]（法国北部诺曼底产的）苹果白兰地，苹果甜酒

camera-ready /kæmərə'redɪ; kæmərə'rɛdɪ/ *adj* (of copy to be printed) presented in a form which makes it ready for immediate photographic reproduction with no further processing（指付印原版）无须再处理便可立即拍照制版的：*The manuscript must be camera-ready, with all the maps and diagrams in place.* 手稿必须可拍照制版，所有的地图和图表都应放在适当的位置。

can-do /kæn'du:; kæn'du/ *adj* [attrib 作定语] positive and confident of success 信心十足的；积极乐观的：*managers with a can-do attitude/outlook* 持积极进取态度[看法]的经理们

canker sore /'kæŋkə sɔ:(r); 'kæŋkɚ sɔr/ *n* (*US medical* 医) painful spot inside the mouth 口腔溃疡

canteen culture /kænti:n 'kʌltʃə(r); kæntin 'kʌltʃɚ/ *n* [U] views and actions of the lower ranks of an organization as an influential force quite apart from that of those who are officially in charge 食堂文化（下层人员的观点和行为，与上层领导有很大不同且具有影响力）：*Top management took a strong line, but canteen culture decided otherwise, and it was the decision of lower level workers not to reduce the lunch hour provision that prevailed.* 最高管理层采取了强硬措施，但下层人员却不这样想，他们坚决要求不得缩减午餐时间，最终争取奏效。

cantina /kæn'ti:nə; kæn'tinə/ *n* (*Spanish Italian* 西，意) bar or wine shop 酒吧；酒店

canyoning /'kænjənɪŋ; 'kænjənɪŋ/ *n* [U] sport in which a person, wearing protective clothing, jumps into a mountain stream and hurtles down with the water through narrow gorges and over falls 峡谷漂流（参与者身穿防护服跳入山涧，任由水流将其冲过峡谷和瀑布的一种运动）：*The new sport of canyoning is less risky than it might appear.* 峡谷漂流这项新运动并不那么危险。

capital flight /ˌkæpɪtl 'flaɪt; ˌkæpətl 'flaɪt/ *n* [U] withdrawal of capital previously invested in a country which is now perceived as a poor risk 资本外逃，资金抽离（考虑到现行风险极大而将原先投资在某国的资金撤回的做法）：*Capital flight from the country following the economic woes of the last months has only worsened the situation.* 近几个月经济困难之后随之而来的资本外逃使情况更加恶化。

car bra /'kɑ: brɑ:; 'kɑr brɑ/ (also **auto bra**) *n* (*US*) close-fitting cover which protects the front end of a car from paintwork damage caused by insects, flying stones, the weather, etc 汽车前罩（紧套住车头保护漆面以免被昆虫、飞石、恶劣天气等损坏的罩子）Cf 参看 STEALTH BRA

NOTE 注：thought to resemble the form and function of a woman's bra 因其形状和功能与女性的胸罩相似

carbuncle /'kɑ:bʌŋkl; 'kɑrbʌŋkl/ *n* (*Brit derog* 贬) offensively ugly building, usu modern in style 外观新潮但却丑陋不堪的建筑

card /kɑ:d; kɑrd/ *n* (*computing* 计) board with electronic circuits which may be inserted into a central processing unit to add facilities or to enhance performance, speed, etc 插件卡（一种电路板，可插入中央处理器以增加

功能或提高性能、速度等）: *a sound expansion card* 扩音卡

cardboard city /ˈkɑːdbɔːd ˈsɪtɪ; ˈkɑrbɔrd ˈsɪtɪ/ *n* area of makeshift shelters made of cardboard boxes, etc, set up by homeless people usu in city streets 纸板城（无家可归者在城市街道上用纸板箱等搭起临时住所的区域）

cardholder /ˈkɑːdhəʊldə(r); ˈkɑrdholdɚ/ *n* person who is entitled to use a plastic card issued by a bank, etc when he or she buys sth or wants to draw money 信用卡持有人: *special offer for American Express cardholders* 为美国运通卡持有人提供的特别优惠

care in the community *n* = COMMUNITY CARE

carer /ˈkeərə(r); ˈkɛrɚ/ *n* person who looks after sb who is ill, very old or disabled in their home rather than in a medical institution 私人看护（家庭而非医疗机构雇用的照顾老弱病残者的人）: *carers provided and paid for by the local authority* 由地方当局提供并支付报酬的私人看护

carjacking /ˈkɑːdʒækɪŋ; ˈkɑrdʒækɪŋ/ *n* (*esp US*) (**a**) forcible taking over of a car and sometimes its driver as well 汽车劫持（有时连同司机一并劫持）(**b**) violent theft from a driver in the course of carjacking（劫持汽车时）抢劫司机财物: *Women drivers in urban areas are especially vulnerable to carjackings.* 在城区开车的女性特别容易成为汽车抢劫的目标。

NOTE 注: a blend formed from *car* and *hijacking* 由 car 与 hijacking（劫持）二词合成

carload /ˈkɑːləʊd; ˈkɑrlod/ *n* number of passengers or amount of baggage, shopping, etc that a car can carry 汽车载量；一汽车的量: *a carload of shopping* 满满一汽车采购之物

carob /ˈkærəb; ˈkærəb/ *n* [U] seeds of the carob tree, a southern European plant, ground into powder to be used as a more healthy substitute for chocolate 角豆（产于南欧的角豆树种子，磨成粉后可替代巧克力且更有益健康）

car phone /ˈkɑː fəʊn; ˈkɑr fon/ *n* radio telephone fitted in a car or other vehicle 汽车无线电话

cash /kæʃ; kæʃ/ *v* (idm 习语) **cash in hand** payment in cash rather than by cheque or credit card thus allowing the receiver to avoid paying tax or service charges 现金支付（用现金而不用支票或信用卡付款，收受者可因此而逃税或免付服务费）

cash-back /ˈkæʃbæk; ˈkæʃbæk/ *n* (**a**) cash made available to customers by some larger retail outlets whenever a credit or debit card is used in payment. The amount requested is then added to the bill as part of a single transaction 购物支钱（顾客在一些大型零售店使用信用卡或借记卡购物时可顺便支取的现金，其金额一并记入帐单）: *The limit on cash-backs has been raised to £750 recently.* 购物支钱的上限近来已提高到 750 英镑。(**b**) free facility offering the cash-back service 免费购物支钱服务: *Does that store have cash-back?* 该店有购物支钱服务吗？(**c**) offer of cash rebate on expensive purchases, eg cars, furniture, etc 买贵重物品（如车、家具等）时返还的现金

cashless /ˈkæʃlɪs; ˈkæʃlɪs/ *adj* not requiring the use of actual cash but accepting credit cards, debit cards etc for financial transactions 不用现金的；使用信用卡、借记卡等结算的: *Are we seeing the beginning of a truly cashless society?* 一个真正不用现金的社会正渐显端倪了吗？

caver /ˈkeɪvə(r); ˈkevɚ/ *n* (*sport* 体) person who explores caves as a sport 洞穴探险运动员

CD *abbr* 缩写 = COMPACT DISC (COMPACT[1 (A-Z)])

CD-ROM /siː diː ˈrɒm; si di ˈrɑm/ (*pl* **CD-ROMs**) *abbr* 缩写 = compact disc read-only memory (disc carrying electronically stored information for display on a computer screen) 高容量只读存储器；光盘

CE /siː ˈiː; si ˈi/ *abbr* 缩写 = Current Era (alternative designation to AD for the year in the western calendar) 公历中 AD（公元）的代用词

celebrity novel /sɪˌlebrətɪ ˈnɒvl; səˌlɛbrətɪ ˈnɑvl̩/ *n* novel with a well-known person, not a professional writer, as the author. Such novels are often suspected of being ghosted (GHOST *v* [A-Z]) 名人（非职业作家）撰写的小说（常有由他人代笔之嫌）: *Celebrity novels certainly have a lot of publicity value.* 名人写的小说无疑很有宣传价值。

cell phone *n* = MOBILE

cellular phone *n* = MOBILE

cellulite /ˈseljuːlaɪt; ˈsɛljəlaɪt/ *n* [U] fatty deposits in the human body which cause dimpling and unevenness of the skin, esp in the thighs and buttocks（人体中形成表皮凹凸不平的）脂肪团（尤指位于大腿和臀部的）: *Many products claim to get rid of cellulite, but only diet and exercise really help.* 很多产品声称能消除脂肪团，但其实只有节食和锻炼才真正有效。

cement-mixer *n* = CONCRETE MIXER (CONCRETE[2(A-Z)])

centrefold /ˈsentəfəʊld; ˈsɛntɚfold/ *n* photograph of a nude or semi-nude person appearing on the CENTRE-FOLD (CENTRE[A-Z]) of a magazine 书刊中间折页刊登的裸体或半裸体照

centre-stage /ˌsentəˈsteɪdʒ; ˌsɛntɚˈstedʒ/ (*US* **center-stage**) *n* [U] important or the most important position 重要的或最重要的位置: *The conflict soon took centre-stage in world politics.* 这次冲突很快成为国际政治方面的中心议题。

-centric /ˈsentrɪk; ˈsɛntrɪk/ *suff* 后缀 (forming *adjs* 用以构成形容词) centred on 以…为中心的: *Eurocentric* 以欧洲为中心的 ○ *user-centric banking facilities* 以用户为中心的银行服务设施

CFC *abbr* 缩写 = CHLOROFLUOROCARBON: *Fridges are CFC-free nowadays.* 如今的冰箱都是无氯氟碳化合物的。

chalice ⇨ POISONED CHALICE

chalkface /ˈtʃɔːkfeɪs; ˈtʃɔkfes/ *n* [sing] place of interaction between a teacher and his or her pupils, ie the classroom 教室: *We've put a lot of money into modern equipment, but let's not forget the teacher at the chalkface.* 我们在现代化设备上投入了很多钱，但我们别忘了教室里授课的老师。

NOTE 注: formed on analogy with *coalface* (exposed coal-seam where coal is being cut) and conveying the same idea of active involvement 由 coalface（煤层中的采掘面）一词类推构成，表达同样的积极投入其中的意思

challenged /ˈtʃælɪndʒd; ˈtʃælɪndʒd/ *adj* lacking; deficient 缺乏的；不足的: (*euph* 婉) *vertically challenged* (ie short) 不够高的（即矮的）○ (*joc* 谑) *follicly challenged* (ie bald) 不长毛的（即秃头的）○ *mentally challenged* 心智有障碍的

champagne socialist /ˌʃæmpeɪn ˈsəʊʃəlɪst; ˌʃæmpen ˈsoʃəlɪst/ *n* (*derog* 贬) person who claims to have socialist beliefs but lives in a luxurious style which completely contradicts them 香槟社会主义者（宣称信仰社会主义，但过着的豪华生活方式却完全与之背道而驰的人）

channel-surf /ˈtʃænlsɜːf; ˈtʃænl̩sɝf/ *v* [I] switch rapidly between television channels with a remote control to see what is available（用遥控器）快速转换频道（以搜寻节目）

Channel Tunnel /ˌtʃænl ˈtʌnl; ˌtʃænl̩ ˈtʌnl̩/ *n* **the Channel Tunnel** [sing] the tunnel that runs underneath the CHANNEL 3(b)[A-Z] and carries road and rail traffic between England and France 海峡隧道（横跨英吉利海峡的海底隧道，连结英国和法国的公路和铁路运输）

NOTE 注： the term is sometimes blended as *Chunnel* 此词有时缩合为 Chunnel

chaos theory /ˈkeɪɒs θɪərɪ; ˈkeɑs θiərɪ/ *n* [U] (*physics* 物) theory about dynamic systems in which there is unpredictable and seemingly random behaviour. In these systems a very small initial difference may lead to an enormous change 混沌学说（认为动力系统中存在无法预测的和似乎无规则的运行方式，在这些系统中，发生十分细微的偏差就可能导致巨变）Cf 参看 BUTTERFLY EFFECT

characterful /ˈkærəktəfʊl; ˈkærɪktɚfʊl/ *adj* having a lot of charm or interest, esp of an historical or traditional kind 极具魅力或趣味的（尤指历史或传统方面）: *characterful old cottages* 古色古香的乡村小屋

charbroil /ˈtʃɑːbrɔɪl; ˈtʃɑrbrɔɪl/ *v* grill meat, fish, etc over red-hot charcoal（用木炭）烧烤（肉、鱼等）

NOTE 注： a blend of *charcoal* and *broil* 由 charcoal（木炭）和 broil（烧烤）二词合成

charge-cap /ˈtʃɑːdʒkæp; ˈtʃɑrdʒkæp/ *v* [Tn] (*Brit*) set an upper limit on how much local authorities can charge for the public services they provide, eg education, social services（对地方政府收取的公共服务费，如教育费、社会服务费）定上限

▷ **charge-capping** *n* [U]

charge card /ˈtʃɑːdʒ kɑːd; ˈtʃɑrdʒ kɑrd/ *n* plastic card provided by a particular shop to which purchases can be charged（商店提供的）赊购卡，赊帐卡

NOTE 注： different from a CREDIT CARD (CREDIT[1(A-Z)]) because the full amount has to be paid on demand 付款时所有款项必须付清，与信用卡不同

charge-hand /ˈtʃɑːdʒhænd; ˈtʃɑrdʒhænd/ *n* (*Brit*) worker in charge of others on a particular job 工头；领班

charge-nurse /ˈtʃɑːdʒnɜːs; ˈtʃɑrdʒnɝs/ *n* (*Brit*) nurse who is in charge of a hospital ward 护士长

charm offensive /ˈtʃɑːm əˌfensɪv; ˈtʃɑrm əˌfɛnsɪv/ *n* attempt by individuals or a group, esp political, to achieve a goal by apparent warmth, friendliness and sincerity 魅力攻势（个人或团体，尤指政治方面，表现热情、友好、真诚以达到某种目的的手段）: *the Minister's charm offensive* 部长的魅力攻势 ○ *The military have gone on a charm offensive to improve their image.* 军方为改善形象而发动了一场魅力攻势。

chatline /ˈtʃætlaɪn; ˈtʃætlaɪn/ *n* open telephone line that allows several people to speak to each other at once; esp such a line used to enable callers to take part in phone-in programmes on the radio 聊天热线（可供多人同时对话的电话线，尤指供听众通过电话参与电台直播节目的电话线）: *If you have any opinion or comment you would like to share on this topic, call our chatline.* 如果你对此话题有什么意见或想法，请拨打我们的聊天热线。

chat room /ˈtʃæt ruːm; ˈtʃæt rum/ *n* SITE on the INTERNET or USENET in CYBERSPACE which users can visit in order to exchange information, comment and conversation with other users 聊天室（计算机网络空间中的互联网站或用户网站，用户可进入以便与其他用户交换信息、交流意见或聊天）: *Some parents are becoming concerned about just who their children could be meeting in these chat rooms.* 一些父母开始关心他们的孩子在这些网站聊天室里会遇上些什么人。

chattering classes /ˌtʃætərɪŋ ˈklɑːsɪz, *US* ˈklæ-; ˌtʃætərɪŋ ˈklæsɪz/ *n* [pl] (*esp Brit derog* 贬) educated and well-informed people, esp those in the media, who enjoy commenting on public affairs but whose opinions are not influential 爱品头论足的饶舌族（有学识且见闻广博、乐于评论公共事务但其观点不具影响力的人，尤指媒界人士）: *The consensus amongst the chattering classes was that the whole affair had gone too far.* 饶舌族一致认为整个事情做过了头。

chemical abuse /ˌkemɪkl əˈbjuːs; ˌkɛmɪkl̩ əˈbjus/ *n* [U,C] irresponsible production and disposal of chemicals with consequent harm to the environment 滥用化学产品（恣意生产和弃置会危害自然环境的化学品）

chemical ecology /ˌkemɪkl iːˈkɒlədʒɪ; ˌkɛmɪkl̩ iˈkɑlədʒɪ/ *n* [U] study of how chemicals in the environment or in an organism affect life 化学生态学（对环境或有机体中的化学物质如何影响生命的研究）

chemical weapon /ˌkemɪkl ˈwepən; ˌkɛmɪkl ˈwɛpən/ *n* weapon which uses a chemical or a combination of chemicals deadly to human life or to all forms of life 化学武器 Cf 参看 CHEMICAL WARFARE（CHEMICAL[A-Z]）

chemoprevention /kiːməʊprɪˈvenʃn, keməʊ-; kəmoprɪˈvɛnʃən/ *n* [U] (*medical* 医) use of medication to prevent cancer developing 防癌药疗（预防癌变使用的药物疗法）: *High-risk patients are offered chemoprevention.* 对濒危病人施用防癌药疗。

cherry-pick /ˈtʃerɪpɪk; ˈtʃɛrɪpɪk/ *v* [Tn] pick out from products, personnel, ideas, etc whatever best suits one's purposes and needs 选取心目中的最佳产品、人员、意见等；择优而取: *The early applicants were able to cherry-pick the best holidays on offer.* 先申请的人可以挑选所提供的最佳假期。

chicken /ˈtʃɪkɪ; ˈtʃɪkɪ/ *n* (idm 习语) **chicken-and-egg situation** situation in which it is impossible to say exactly which one of the two things was the cause and which was the effect 鸡与蛋的情况；因果难分的局面

NOTE 注： from the traditional problem *Which came first? The chicken or the egg?* 源自老问题：是先有鸡还是先有蛋？

child-abuse /ˈtʃaɪldəbjuːs; ˈtʃaɪldəbjus/ *n* [U] physical or sexual ABUSE[2] 1(a)[A-Z] of a child 对儿童（身体或性方面）的虐待

child care /ˈtʃaɪld keə(r); ˈtʃaɪld kɛr/ *n* [U] care of children provided by an individual or an institution 儿童托管；儿童照管: *The cost of providing child care for working mothers has become too high.* 为上班母亲提供照看孩子服务的费用现已太高。

chill out /tʃɪl ˈaʊt; tʃɪl ˈaʊt/ *v* [I] (*esp US infml* 口) relax and calm down after a stressful or exciting activity, esp after dancing and perhaps after taking drugs at a RAVE（紧张或兴奋的活动后，尤指在狂舞会上跳舞或者吸毒后）放松下来，平静下来: *The wedding and the party afterwards were great, but I really needed to chill out the next day.* 婚礼及其后的聚会真叫人兴奋，但我第二天确实需要平静下来休息一下。

▷ **chill-out** *adj*: *chill-out rooms at the club* 俱乐部里的休憩室

Chinese restaurant syndrome /ˌtʃaɪniːz ˈrestrɒnt ˌsɪndrəʊm; ˌtʃaɪniz ˈrɛstərənt ˌsɪndrom/ *n* [U] symptoms such as dizziness and rapid heartbeat thought to be caused in some people by eating large amounts of MONOSODIUM GLUTAMATE[A-Z] 中国餐馆综合征（据信因吃进大量含谷氨酸钠的味精而导致的头晕、心跳加速等症状）

chintzy /ˈtʃɪntsɪ; ˈtʃɪntsɪ/ *adj* (*derog* 贬) (**a**) slightly old-fashioned and TWEE[A-Z] 有些过时和过于艳丽的 (**b**) slightly too bright and BUSY 4[A-Z] 过于亮丽的；图案繁杂的: *a taste for chintzy fabrics and furniture* 对俗气艳丽的织品和家具的喜爱

chip shop /ˈtʃɪp ʃɒp; ˈtʃɪp ʃɑp/ (also **chippy, chippie**) *n* (*Brit infml* 口) shop that cooks and sells deep fried foods, esp fish and chips（尤指卖炸鱼和炸土豆条的）油炸食品店

chlorofluorocarbon /ˌklɒrəʊflɔːrəʊˈkɑːbən; ˌkloroflʊəroˈkɑrbən/ *n* (*abbr* 缩写 **CFC**) any of a number of chemical compounds of carbon, chlorine and fluorine, used as refrigerants, aerosol propellants, solvents, etc, which are known to cause harm to the ozone layer when released into the atmosphere 氯氟碳化合物（任何由

碳、氯和氟组成的化合物，用作致冷剂、喷雾器中的压缩气体、溶剂等，据认为释放到大气中会破坏臭氧层）

chopsocky /tʃɒp'sɒkɪ; tʃɑp'sɑkɪ/ *n* film or video, esp against a background of Oriental martial arts, in which a lot of bloodshed and killing are shown（尤指东方的充满血腥暴力镜头的）武打片：*Hong Kong's chopsockies have found new popularity in India.* 香港武打片近来在印度大受欢迎。

chromosome map /'krəʊməsəʊm mæp; 'kroməsom mæp/ *n* (*biology* 生) diagram showing the location of each gene along the length of a CHROMOSOME^A-Z 染色体图（可显示基因在染色体上的位置的图）

Chunnel *n* = CHANNEL TUNNEL

ciabatta /tʃə'bɑ:tə; tʃə'bætə/ *n* [U] type of light Italian bread made with olive oil 意大利鞋形面包（质松软，用橄榄油制成的面包）

NOTE 注： from Italian dialect word meaning 'slipper', from the shape of the loaf 源自意大利方言，意为'拖鞋'，喻面包之形状

cinder block *n* (*US*) = BREEZE-BLOCK^A-Z

cineplex /'sɪnɪpleks; 'sɪnɪplɛks/ *n* (*pl* ~ **es**) building containing several cinema auditoriums, usu showing different films 多厅影院（由多个通常放映不同电影的放映厅组成的影院）

circuit board /'sɜ:kɪt bɔ:d; 'sɝkɪt bɔrd/ *n* board which holds electric circuits (CIRCUIT 2b^A-Z) and is used inside electrical equipment 电路板

circuitry /'sɜ:kɪtrɪ; 'sɝkɪtrɪ/ *n* [U] system of electric circuits or the equipment forming this 电路系统；电路元件

CIS /si: aɪ 'es; si aɪ 'ɛs/ *abbr* 缩写 = Commonwealth of Independent States (a loose organization consisting of Russia and a number of other former members of the Soviet Union) 独立国家联合体，独联体（包括俄罗斯和其他一些前苏联国家在内的松散的组织）

city break /ˌsɪtɪ 'breɪk, 'sɪtɪ ˌbreɪk; ˌsɪtɪ 'brek, 'sɪtɪ ˌbrek/ *n* (in Britain) an offer of cheaper room-rates by certain hotels for guests who stay for a short period, eg a weekend（英国）短期旅客优惠房价（一些旅馆为短期旅客如度周末的人提供的优惠房价）：*exciting city breaks for the autumn* 令人惊喜的秋季短期旅客优惠房价

city hall /ˌsɪtɪ 'hɔ:l; ˌsɪtɪ 'hɔl/ *n* [C,U] (*esp US*) (**a**) building where the local authority is located and, by extension, the authority itself 市政厅；市政府：*open meetings of the council at (the) City Hall* 市政委员会在市政厅举行的公开会议 (**b**) (*fig* 比喻) authority in the abstract, against which individuals may be helpless（个人无力抗拒的）政府权力，权威：*You can't fight city hall.* 你斗不过政府的。

CJD *abbr* 缩写 = CREUTZFELDT-JAKOB DISEASE

clamper /'klæmpə(r); 'klæmpɚ/ *n* person who clamps the wheels of a car and subsequently removes it because the vehicle has been parked illegally 卡轮员（用轮夹锁住违章停放的汽车后将其移走的停车管理员）：*Clampers are increasingly employed by local authorities to help solve the city's parking problems.* 地方当局雇用越来越多的卡轮员来协助解决该市的汽车停放问题。

clay court /'kleɪ kɔ:t; 'kle kɔrt/ *n* (*sport* 体) hard tennis court with a clay surface 黏土硬网球场：*a clay court specialist* 擅长在黏土硬网球场比赛的运动员

cleansing *n* [U] = ETHNIC CLEANSING

clear blue water /klɪə blu: 'wɔ:tə(r); klɪr blu 'wɔtɚ/ *n* [U] (*fig esp politics* 比喻，尤用于政治) obvious difference between the principles, aims and ideologies, etc of two opposing political parties（两对立党派之间的原则、目标和意识形态等方面的）明显分歧，鸿沟

clergyperson /'klɜ:dʒɪˌpɜ:sən; 'klɝdʒɪˌpɝsn̩/ *n* (*pl* **clergypersons**) man or woman who is a fully-qualified and ordained priest（合格并获委任的）牧师，司铎，神职人员

NOTE 注： only applicable to those churches which allow women to become priests; formed on analogy with *chairperson* and *spokesperson* 只适用于允许妇女任牧师的教会，由 chairperson 和 spokesperson 等词类推构成

clichéd /'kli:ʃeɪd, *US* kli:'ʃeɪd; kli'ʃed/ *adj* full of clichés (CLICHÉ^A-Z); CORNY (CORN^1(A-Z)) 陈词滥调的；陈腐的：*a film with a clichéd story-line* 故事情节老掉牙的电影

client-server /klaɪənt'sɜ:və(r); klaɪənt'sɝvɚ/ *n* (*computing* 计) type of NETWORK COMPUTER system linking personal computers (the clients) with a central computer (the server) 用户—服务器系统（将个人计算机即用户与中央计算机即服务器连接起来的网络系统）

climbing /'klaɪmɪŋ; 'klaɪmɪŋ/ *n* [U] (*sport* 体) activity of climbing rocks or mountains as a sport 登山运动：*He loves to go climbing.* 他很爱登山。

clonk /klɒŋk; klɑŋk/ *n* (*infml* 口) short, loud sound of heavy things hitting each other（重物互相撞击时发出的）短而响的声音，当啷声：*From every building-site comes the clonk of heavy machinery.* 每个建筑工地都传来重机器的当啷声。

▷ **clonk** *v* (*infml* 口) [I, Ipr] cause a clonk 发出当啷声：*The heavy pipes clonked against each other as they were lowered into place.* 沉重的管子被放进要放的位置时互相碰撞砰砰作响。

closing date /'kləʊzɪŋ deɪt; 'klozɪŋ det/ *n* last date by which sth must be done, esp getting a job application in, submitting an entry to a competition, etc 截止日期（尤指申请职位、参赛的最后日期）：*Send your entry now or you'll miss the closing date.* 现在就将参赛品送来，不然就过期了。Cf 参看 DEADLINE^A-Z

closure /'kləʊʒə(r); 'kloʒɚ/ *n* [U] (*fig* 比喻) final coming to terms with a demanding or unhappy event in the past which gives one a sense of release and the ability to move on in life 解脱感，了结（终能接受沉重的或不愉快的生活经历，从而获得解脱并继续正常生活下去）：*After her mother's funeral, she felt a profound sense of relief and closure.* 母亲下葬后，她深感宽慰与解脱。

clubland /'klʌblænd; 'klʌblænd/ *n* [U] (*Brit*) part of a town (esp London) where many clubs are located, esp nightclubs where people can have a drink, listen to music and dance（城市中的，尤指伦敦的）俱乐部（尤指夜总会）密集的地区

clumpy /'klʌmpɪ; 'klʌmpɪ/ *adj* (esp of shoes) heavy, clumsy and awkward（尤指鞋）笨重的，粗笨的：*Take off those clumpy shoes in the house!* 在屋子里把笨重的鞋脱下来！

clunker /'klʌŋkə(r); 'klʌŋkɚ/ *n* (in North America) old car in need of repair（北美）破旧汽车，老爷车

coal-fired /ˌkəʊl'faɪəd; ˌkol'faɪrd/ *adj* driven, heated or made to work by burning coal 用煤作燃料的；烧煤的：*a coal-fired locomotive* 燃煤机车 ○ *a coal-fired power station* 燃煤的发电站

Coca cola imperialism /kəʊkə ˌkəʊlə ɪm'pɪərɪəlɪzəm; kokə ˌkolə ɪm'pɪrɪəlɪzəm/ *n* [U] powerful influence of the USA over other countries, esp through the setting up of commercial enterprises closely associated with the national identity 可口可乐帝国主义（美国对其他国家施加的巨大影响力，尤其通过建立带有美国特色的庞大商业机构而行）

cocktail dress /'kɒkteɪl dres; 'kɑktel drɛs/ *n* smart dress, not usu full-length, suitable for cocktail parties and other formal occasions 常礼服（适合鸡尾酒会和其他

庄重场合穿用的女装，长度适中而大方得体）Cf 参看 EVENING DRESS（EVENING^A-Z）

cocktail stick /'kɒkteɪl stɪk; 'kɑktel stɪk/ *n* small sharp piece of wood on which small bits of food, eg cheese, cold meats, are stuck for serving at cocktail parties, etc 鸡尾酒会等场合中用来插小块食品的小木签：*She had made hundreds of cocktail sticks threaded with all kinds of good things to eat.* 她已经用小木签插好了一串串好吃的东西了。

code name /'kəʊd neɪm; 'kod nem/ *n* secret name given to sb or sth to keep the real identity secret（为掩饰真实身分而用的）代号：*a military operation, code name Tiger* 代号为'老虎'的军事行动 ○ *Agents were given code names which changed at irregular intervals.* 间谍的代号不定期地更换。

codependency /kəʊdɪ'pendənsɪ; kodɪ'pɛndənsɪ/ *n* [U] (*US psychology* 心) emotional dependency on supporting or caring for someone else, esp an alcoholic parent, referring esp to the loss of self-confidence and sense of worth experienced by such carers（因供养或照顾他人尤其是酗酒的父母而产生的）情感依赖（尤指本人自信与自我价值感的丧失）

coffee-break *n* = TEA-BREAK（TEA^A-Z）

cold-calling /kəʊld'kɔːlɪŋ; kold'kɔlɪŋ/ *n* [U] practice of telephoning or visiting potential customers, who have not requested this contact, with a view to selling a product or service, esp a financial service, eg insurance or investments 不请自来的推销（事先未经联系径自给潜在顾客打电话或上门推销产品或服务，尤指推销保险或投资等金融服务）Cf 参看 WARM CALL, COLD-FAXING

cold dark matter /kəʊld dɑːk 'mætə(r); kold dɑrk 'mætɚ/ *n* [U] (*physics* 物) invisible matter consisting of low-energy particles which some scientists believe to exist but which have not yet been directly observed 冷暗物质（由低能量粒子组成的无法见到的物质，某些科学家认为存在，但尚未直接观测到）

cold-faxing /kəʊld'fæksɪŋ; kold'fæksɪŋ/ *n* [U] practice of sending material by fax to potential customers who have not asked for it, in the hope of selling them a product or service 不请自来的传真推销（主动给潜在顾客发传真推销产品或服务）Cf 参看 COLD-CALLING

cold fusion /kəʊld 'fjuːʒn; kold 'fjuʒən/ *n* [U] (*chemistry or physics* 化或物) FUSION 2^A-Z of atomic nuclei at around room temperature with the production of energy as the result 冷核聚变（室温条件下发生的以产生能量的核聚变）：*There were for a time great hopes that cold fusion would be the answer to the world's energy needs.* 对于利用冷核聚变解决地球能源需求问题，人们一度寄予厚望。

collateral damage /kəˌlætərəl 'dæmɪdʒ; kəˌlætərəl 'dæmɪdʒ/ *n* [U] (*military euph* 军，婉) unintended civilian casualties caused by the bombing of a military target 意外伤亡，鱼池之殃（因轰炸军事目标而无意造成的平民伤亡）：*The military claimed that collateral damage had been kept to a minimum during the bombing raid.* 军方称突袭轰炸行动中的意外伤亡已被控制到最低限度。

colour supplement /'kʌlə sʌplɪmənt; 'kʌlɚ sʌpləmənt/ *n* magazine with lots of coloured pictures issued with a newspaper, usu on one particular day of the week（报纸的）彩色增刊：*the Daily Telegraph colour supplement*《每日电讯报》的彩色增刊

combo /'kɒmbəʊ; 'kɑmbo/ *n* (*pl* **-os**) (*infml* 口) **1** small band that plays jazz or dance music（演奏爵士乐或舞曲的）小乐队 **2** pre-grouped food items making up a dish on a menu（菜单上的）什锦拼盆

NOTE 注： probably from *combination* 可能源自 combination（组合）一词

come from /'kʌm frɒm, -frəm; 'kʌm frɑm/ *v* [I] (*US*) (usu in continuous form 通常用进行时态) have as one's opinion or as the basis for any action or decision 持有某种观点；以…作为行动或决定的基础：*I see where you're coming from. You think charity should be a private matter.* 我明白你的出发点。你认为行善但求己知。

command economy *n* = PLANNED ECONOMY

community care /kə'mjuːnətɪ 'keə(r); kəˌmjunətɪ 'kɛr/ *n* [U] policy and practice of releasing mental patients from institutions to their own homes or lodgings and thus monitoring them in a less restrictive way 社会监护（将精神病患者放回家中，以较为宽松的方式对其监护的政策和做法）

compact disc read-only memory *n* = CD-ROM

compactor /kəm'pæktə(r); kəm'pæktɚ/ *n* machine which squashes rubbish, including old cars, into small dense blocks 垃圾压碎处理机（垃圾包括废弃的汽车）

compassion fatigue /kəm'pæʃn fətiːg; kəm'pæʃən fətig/ *n* [U] (**a**) loss of desire to give money to charities, usu because one feels that too many pleas for help have already been made or that however much one helps it is never enough 捐赠厌倦感（通常因感到要求捐助的请求过多或无论怎样捐助都不能满足需要，从而失去向慈善机构捐钱的兴趣）(**b**) growing indifference towards those one previously had sympathy for and was willing to help 怜悯疲劳（对自己曾经同情和愿意施以援助的人渐感麻木）：*Too much publicity for the victims of the earthquake could lead to compassion fatigue.* 对地震受害者过多地宣传，有可能导致人们对事件麻木。

complementary medicine *n* = ALTERNATIVE MEDICINE

compote /'kɒmpɒt, *US* 'kɑːmpəʊt; 'kɑmpot/ *n* [C,U] stewed fruit sweetened with sugar 加糖煮的水果：*I'll have the apricot compote, please.* 请给我来一份甜煮杏。

computer abuse /kəm'pjuːtə əˌbjuːs; kəm'pjutɚ əˌbjus/ *n* [U] irresponsible use of a computer, esp to alter and falsify data 滥用计算机（恣意使用计算机，尤指篡改和伪造数据）

computer fiction /kəmˌpjuːtə 'fɪkʃn; kəmˌpjutɚ 'fɪkʃən/ (also **interactive fiction**) *n* [U] narrative stored on a CD-ROM and played on a computer in which different plot lines may be chosen by the player leading to different outcomes 计算机小说，交互式小说（存储在计算机光盘上的故事，读者可选择不同的情节线索得到不同的故事结局）

computer literate /kəmˌpjuːtə 'lɪtərət; kəmˌpjutɚ 'lɪtərɪt/ *adj* being well-informed about or proficient in using computers 很熟悉计算机的；会熟练使用计算机的：*Today's schoolchildren must be computer literate if they are to have any chance of getting work in the future.* 如今学童要想将来能找到工作的话，就必须很熟悉计算机。○ *computer-literate teachers* 通晓计算机的教师们

computer nerd /kəm'pjuːtə nɜːd; kəm'pjutɚ nɝd/ *n* sb, usu male, who is socially unsuccessful and spends all of his time at his computer 不善交际而整天泡在计算机前的人（通常为男子）

Con *abbr* 缩写 = CONS^A-Z

con brio /kɒn 'briːəʊ; kɑn 'brio/ *adj, adv* (*Italian* 意) (**a**) (*music* 音) (of instruction for music performance) played energetically and with vigour（指演奏说明）充满活力的，有力地 (**b**) (of behaviour, actions) done with energy and style（指行为、动作）精神饱满地，充满活力的：*He carries out his public duties con brio.* 他履行公共义务时显得神采飞扬。

conceptualize, -ise /kən'septʃʊəlaɪz; kən'sɛptʃʊəlaɪz/ *v* form an idea of sth in one's mind 构想；构思：*It's hard to conceptualize the finished building.* 很难想像大楼竣工后会是什么样。

conciliator /kən'sɪlɪeɪtə(r); kən'sɪlɪetɚ/ *n* person who tries to mediate and bring two or more parties in an angry dispute into agreement 调解人；斡旋者：*The United Nations Secretary General often finds himself taking on the role of a conciliator.* 联合国秘书长常充当调解人的角色。

condensed milk /kənˌdenst 'mɪlk; kənˌdɛnst 'mɪlk/ *n* [U] milk that has been thickened by being evaporated and then sweetened, usu sold in tins 炼乳 Cf 参看 EVAPORATED MILK (EVAPORATE[A-Z])

conditioning /kən'dɪʃənɪŋ; kən'dɪʃənɪŋ/ *n* [U] training or experience that causes a person or an animal to behave in a certain way or to become used to certain circumstances 调教；（对动物的）训练：*The horses received conditioning so that they would not panic at the sound of gunfire.* 那些马受过训练，听到枪炮声也不惊慌。

conducted tour /kənˌdʌktɪd 'tʊə(r); kənˌdʌktɪd 'tʊr/ (also **guided tour**) *n* tour in which a guide takes visitors around an historic or modern building, town, etc during which information is given about the place 有导游带领的旅游：*a conducted tour of the Sellafield nuclear power plant* 由导游带领参观塞拉菲尔德核电站

connectivity /kənek'tɪvətɪ; kənɛk'tɪvətɪ/ *n* [U] capacity for mutual interchange of information and facilities between different, esp old and new types of computers and computer systems 连通性，互连性（不同的，尤指新旧计算机和计算机系统之间可相互交换信息和设备的能力）

conscience investment *n* = ETHICAL INVESTMENT

consciousness-raising /'kɒnʃəsnɪsreɪzɪŋ; 'kɑnʃəsnɪsˌrezɪŋ/ *adj* causing people to be more aware of sth, esp a moral, social or environmental issue 提高觉悟的（尤指在道德、社会或环境等方面）：*a successful consciousness-raising campaign* 有成效的提高觉悟的运动

Consent Scheme /kən'sent ski:m; kən'sɛnt skim/ *n* system under which money paid in advance for a flat, etc under construction is held in trust by a solicitor and only released to the developer in stages as construction progresses 期房分期预付款方案（将购买正在施工的公寓等房产的预付款交律师保管，而后视工程进展情况分批付给发展商的制度）

conspicuous consumption /kənˌspɪkjʊəs kən'sʌmpʃn; kənˌspɪkjuəs kən'sʌmpʃən/ *n* [U] buying and displaying expensive goods chiefly in order to impress other people and improve one's social status 炫耀性消费：*conspicuous consumption in the form of three Mercedes parked in the driveway* 在自家车道上停上三辆奔驰牌汽车的炫耀性消费行为

conspiracy theory /kən'spɪrəsɪ θɪərɪ; kən'spɪrəsɪ θɪərɪ/ *n* belief that many events, esp those involving important or influential people, as well as the withholding of information are the result of active plotting by a group or even by the government 阴谋论（认为许多事件，尤其那些与要人有关的事件以及消息封锁等，都是某集团或者甚至是政府密谋的结果）：*Conspiracy theories about the assassination of President Kennedy still have a lot of support.* 有人认为肯尼迪总统被暗杀是某些人密谋策划的结果，这一说法仍有很多支持者。

▷ **conspiracy theorist** *n*：*Conspiracy theorists believe that the US government has covered up contacts with alien spaceships for many years.* 阴谋论者认为美国政府多年来一直掩盖与外星人太空船接触的真相。

constructive dismissal /kənˌstrʌktɪv dɪs'mɪsl; kənˌstrʌktɪv dɪs'mɪsl̩/ *n* changing of an employee's working conditions or duties with the aim of forcing him or her to resign 变更雇员的工作环境或职务以逼其辞职

consultancy /kən'sʌltənsɪ; kən'sʌltənsɪ/ *n* company that gives professional advice on business, engineering projects, design, etc 咨询机构；顾问公司：*a management consultancy* 管理顾问公司 ○ *the consultancy making a feasibility study* 进行可行性研究的咨询机构

consumer terrorism /kənˌsju:mə 'terərɪzm, *US* -su:; kənˌsumɚ 'tɛrərɪzəm/ *n* [U] threat of or actual carrying out of tampering with consumer products so that they become dangerous, usu with the aim of blackmailing either the company that makes the product or the retailers who sell it 消费恐怖主义（在商品中掺入危险物质或以此做法相威胁，通常是为了向生产商或零售商敲诈）

▷ **consumer terrorist** *n*：*A consumer terrorist claims to have put poison into the most popular headache pills in stores across the city.* 一个消费恐怖主义者称已在市内所有商店里的最畅销的头痛药片里下了毒。

continental shelf /ˌkɒntɪnentl 'ʃelf; ˌkɑntɪnɛntl̩ 'ʃɛlf/ *n* [sing] area under the sea where the water is comparatively shallow, extending from the shore of a land mass to the deeper ocean 大陆架（大陆从海岸向外延伸渐入深海，其中坡度较缓的部分）

continuous assessment /kənˌtɪnjʊəs ə'sesmənt; kənˌtɪnjuəs ə'sɛsmənt/ *n* [U] system of assessing a student's progress throughout a course by evaluating his or her performance on an ongoing basis as well as or instead of using an examination 持续性评估（通过不断考核学生的学习情况，或连同考试来评估其学业进展的方法）Cf 参看 COURSE-WORK

contoured /'kɒntʊəd; 'kɑnturd/ *adj* having clean-cut, well-defined lines, usu as the result of careful design 轮廓鲜明的，线条优美的（通常因精心设计所得）：*The look of winter fashion is one of well-defined contoured lines.* 冬季时装的流行式样线条明快优美。

convenience store /kən'vi:nɪəns stɔ:(r); kən'vinjəns stɔr/ *n* (*US*) store with limited stock comprising mostly everyday items and which has very long opening hours, sometimes 24 hours 便民店，便利店（经营日用小百货，营业时间可长达 24 小时的小商店）

conventional wisdom /kənˌvenʃənəl 'wɪzdəm; kənˌvɛnʃənl̩ 'wɪzdəm/ *n* [U] opinion of the majority of well-informed people about an issue, person in the news, etc 大众观点，流行的看法，集体共识（大部分有识之士对事件、新闻人物等的看法）：*Conventional wisdom has it that the Oscar for Best Film will go to another British production this year.* 大家普遍认为今年的奥斯卡最佳影片奖会颁给另一部英国影片。

cook-chill /kʊk'tʃɪl, 'kʊktʃɪl; 'kʊktʃɪl/ *adj* (of foods) previously cooked and then chilled, for consumption after re-heating（指食品）经烹调速冻的（食用时需重新加热）：*Cook-chill foods must be heated very thoroughly so as to kill any bacteria.* 食用经烹调速冻的食品，必须充分加热杀菌。

coppery /'kɒpərɪ; 'kɑpərɪ/ *adj* similar to or having the colour of copper 似铜的；铜色的：*coppery leaves* 古铜色的树叶 ○ *coppery hair* 红棕色的头发

cor /kɔ:(r); kɔr/ (also **cor blimey**) *interj* (*Brit infml* 口) (used to express surprise, astonishment, admiration, pleasure, etc 表示惊奇、惊愕、羡慕、高兴等): *Cor! What a view!* 天哪！多美的风景啊！

NOTE 注：*cor blimey* comes from *God blind me!*, ie 'May God strike me blind (if what I am saying is not true)' — a kind of oath 赌咒发誓语， cor blimey 源自 God blind me! 即 'May God strike me blind'（让我变瞎吧！（要是我说谎的话））

cordless /'kɔ:dləs; 'kɔrdləs/ *adj* (of an electric tool or telephone) having its own internal power supply and not needing to be plugged into a main supply（指电动工具或电话）无绳的，无线的，用电池的：*a cordless telephone/drill* 无绳电话 [钻]

corn circle *n* = CROP CIRCLE

coronary heart disease /ˌkɒrənrɪ 'hɑ:t dɪzi:z, *US* ˌkɒrənerɪ; ˌkɔrənɛrɪ 'hɑrt dɪziz/ *n* [U] (*medical* 医)

disease resulting from damage to the coronary arteries 冠心病

corporate welfare /ˌkɔːpərət ˈwelfeə(r); ˌkɔrpərɪt ˈwɛlfɛr/ *n* [U] (*US*) funding of public welfare by commercial companies and organizations that is required by law 公司义务福利制（商业公司和机构依法资助公共福利）

corpus linguistics /ˈkɔːpəs lɪŋˌgwɪstɪks; ˈkɔrpəs lɪŋˌgwɪstɪks/ [sing v] (*linguistics* 语言) investigation of large bodies of spoken and written data in a particular language using the processing power of the computer in order to find statistical backing for claims, generalizations, etc about that language's structures and vocabulary 语料库语言学（一种素材语言学，利用计算机对大量口头和书面语言材料进行分析处理，旨在搜集统计资料以判断、归纳该语言的语言结构和词汇等）

cosmic string /ˌkɒzmɪk ˈstrɪŋ; ˌkɑzmɪk ˈstrɪŋ/ *n* (*physics* 物) hypothetical entity that is the focus of STRING THEORY 宇宙细脉（一种假设的存在物，为细脉学说的核心）

cost-cutting /ˈkɒstkʌtɪŋ, *US* kɔːst-; ˈkɔstkʌtɪŋ/ *n* [U] reduction in expenses on a special project or in a business in order to keep it going, although at a reduced level 降低成本（以完成项目或维持生意）: *Without some cost-cutting, staff will have to be laid off.* 不降低些成本，就得裁员。○ *Cost-cutting threatens to ruin the redevelopment project.* 降低成本使再建工程面临被毁的威胁。

couch potato /ˌkaʊtʃ pəˈteɪtəʊ, ˈkaʊtʃ pəˌteɪtəʊ; ˈkaʊtʃ pəˌteto/ *n* (*joc or derog* 谑或贬) person who spends many hours sitting on a couch, etc watching television rather than doing anything more active or productive 老泡在沙发上看电视的人

coulis /ˈkuːlɪ; ˈkulɪ/ *n* (pl unchanged 复数不变) PURÉE^A-Z made from fruit but thin enough to pour, usu served with a dessert such as ice-cream, cheese-cake, etc 水果酱（稀薄易倒出，常与冰淇淋、干酪饼等甜食一起食用的酱）

NOTE 注： from the French word *couler* meaning 'to flow' 源自法语 couler 一词，意为'流动'

count /kaʊnt; kaunt/ *v* (idm 习语) **count sheep** count imaginary sheep as they jump over a fence in order to help oneself get to sleep 数羊（助眠法）: *I've tried counting sheep but I still can't get to sleep.* 我也数过羊，可还是睡不着。

counterperson /ˈkaʊntəˌpɜːsn; ˈkauntɚˌpɝsn̩/ *n* (*pl* **-persons**) (*US*) shop assistant either male or female 售货员；店员

country-wide /ˌkʌntrɪˈwaɪd; ˌkʌntrɪˈwaɪd/ *adj, adv* over the whole of a country 全国范围的 *[地]*: *The film will be released country-wide next month.* 这部影片将于下月在全国公映。○ *country-wide resistance to the new tax* 对新税收的全国性抵制

course-work /ˈkɔːswɜːk; ˈkɔrswɝk/ *n* [U] essays, projects, etc completed by a student and assessed by the instructor during a COURSE[1] 3(a)^A-Z at school, college or university 课程作业: *Course-work counts for 40% of the total mark.* 作业评分占总成绩的 40%。Cf 参看 CONTINUOUS ASSESSMENT

courtesy car /ˈkɜːtəsɪ kɑː(r); ˈkɝtəsɪ kɑr/ (also **courtesy coach**) *n* transport provided free by a hotel to meet guests at an airport, railway station, etc 迎宾车（由旅馆提供，到机场、火车站等的免费接客车）

courtesy light /ˈkɜːtəsɪ laɪt; ˈkɝtəsɪ laɪt/ *n* small light inside a car that comes on automatically when the car door is opened（门控）车室照明灯（车门打开后自动亮的灯）

court of appeal /ˌkɔːt əv əˈpiːl; ˌkɔrt əv əˈpil/ (also **appeal court**) *n* (*pl* **courts of appeal**) (*law* 律) court to which one can APPEAL *v* 3^A-Z against a judgement one disagrees with 上诉法院

court of inquiry /ˌkɔːt əv ɪnˈkwaɪərɪ, *US* ˈɪnkwərɪ; ˌkɔrt əv ˈɪnkwərɪ/ *n* (*pl* **courts of inquiry**) (*law* 律) special court that is set up to investigate a particular matter（为某案件而专设的）调查法庭

courtroom drama /ˌkɔːtruːm ˈdrɑːmə; ˌkɔrtrum ˈdrɑmə/ *n* television drama series centring on the professional and private lives of a group of fictitious lawyers, esp on their conduct of legal cases in the courtroom 法庭剧（反映一群虚构的律师的工作和生活，尤其是他们在法庭上如何处理案件的电视连续剧）: *LA Law has been one of the most successful courtroom dramas in television history.* 《洛杉矶律师》已成为电视史上最成功的法庭剧之一。

cover story /ˈkʌvə stɔːrɪ; ˈkʌvɚ stɔrɪ/ *n* **1** main article in a magazine, usu advertised on the front cover 封面故事（杂志封面所介绍的该期主要文章）: *Cover stories about any member of the Royal Family boosted sales by up to 5%.* 有关皇室成员的封面故事使销售量剧增了将近 5%。**2** story invented to conceal the truth about sb, esp identities or reasons for doing sth（为掩饰真相，尤指某人的身分或行为动机而编造的）掩饰说辞: *You need a good cover story in case anyone asks you what you're doing here.* 你得编好一套话，以防万一有人问你在这儿干吗。

crack /kræk; kræk/ *n* [U] a highly addictive drug derived from COCAINE^A-Z in the form of pellets（小丸状）强效纯可卡因，强效纯古柯碱

NOTE 注： the name arises from the fact that the pellets are formed by being cracked off from a bigger piece as well as the cracking sound they make when smoked 由大块可卡因敲碎且吸用时发出劈啪声而得名

crackerjack /ˈkækədʒæk; ˈkrækɚdʒæk/ *n* (*US sl* 俚) exceptionally fine or smart person or thing 顶尖人物；极出色的人或物: *When it comes to math, Joe is a real crackerjack.* 要论数学，乔可真是个天才。

crawl space /ˈkrɔːl speɪs; ˈkrɔl spes/ *n* space under the floors of a house, etc which gives access to pipes, electrical ducts, etc（位于房屋地板下，供人进去维修管道、电线等之用的）爬行空隙

CRC /ˌsiː ɑːr ˈsiː; ˌsi ɑr ˈsi/ *abbr* 缩写 = CAMERA-READY copy 照相原版（可立即拍照制版的版本）

creationist /kriːˈeɪʃnɪst; krɪˈeʃənɪst/ *n* person who believes that God created the world and mankind as described in the Bible, and who objects strongly to the teaching in schools of the theory of Darwinian evolution as the only true account of how current life forms have evolved 神创论者（相信《圣经》上所说是上帝创造了世界和人类的人，他们强烈反对学校将达尔文的进化论学说作为生命如何进化至今的唯一说法）

creative accounting /kriːˌeɪtɪv əˈkaʊntɪŋ; krɪˌetɪv əˈkauntɪŋ/ *n* [U] (*derog* 贬) application of professional accountancy skills to the financial affairs of an individual or company so as to create the impression of financial soundness if that is required by the client or to conceal any weaknesses, even if this may border on illegal actions 创造性做帐（在处理私人或公司财务中应客户要求利用专业会计技术做帐，以制造财务状况良好的假象或掩盖问题，而不顾此种做法已近乎犯法）

credit crunch *n* = CRUNCH

Creutzfeldt-Jakob disease /krɔɪtsfeltˈjækɒb dɪˌziːz; krɔɪtsfɛltˈjækəb dɪˌziz/ *n* [U] fatal disease caused by prions（PRION）and resulting in degeneration of the nerve cells in the brain 克罗伊茨费尔特—雅各布症；克—雅二氏病（由朊病毒导致脑神经细胞衰退的致命疾病）Cf 参看 NEW VARIANT CJD

criminality /ˌkrɪmɪˈnælətɪ; ˌkrɪmɪˈnælətɪ/ *n* [U] criminal acts; the state of being involved in crime 罪行；犯罪的

处境：*increased criminality amongst the children of criminals* 不断增加的罪犯子女犯罪行为

criminalize, -ise /ˈkrɪmɪnəlaɪz; ˈkrɪmɪnəlaɪz/ *v* [Tn] **1** make sth illegal by passing a new law（通过立法）将（某事物）定为非法：*moves to criminalize abortion again* 旨在再次将堕胎定为非法的行动 **2** treat sb as a criminal, perhaps unjustly（可能不公正地）把（某人）当罪犯：*Protesters were criminalized in press reports.* 在新闻报道中那些抗议者被视为罪犯。

crinkly /ˈkrɪŋklɪ; ˈkrɪŋklɪ/ (also **wrinkly, crumbly**) *n* (*sl* 俚) old person 老人

crisis management /ˈkraɪsɪs ˌmænɪdʒmənt; ˈkraɪsɪs ˌmænɪdʒmənt/ *n* [U] practical steps taken by the management of a company, political party, etc to minimize damage or restore public confidence after a crisis has arisen 危机处理（公司或政党的管理层在危机发生后为减少损失或重新赢得公众信任而采取的行动）Cf 参看 DAMAGE CONTROL

crispbread /ˈkrɪspbred; ˈkrɪspbrɛd/ *n* [C,U] thin, crisp, savoury biscuit, usu made from RYE[A-Z] and eaten with cheese（通常为用黑麦做的就奶酪吃的）薄脆饼干：*a lunch of crispbreads and cheese* 薄脆饼干加奶酪的一顿午餐

crony capitalism /ˌkrəʊnɪ ˈkæpɪtəlɪzm; ˌkronɪ ˈkæpətl̩ɪzəm/ *n* [U] giving of business opportunities and industrial and development contracts to one's relatives and close friends 唯亲资本主义（将商业机会和工业开发合同留给自己的亲友的做法）

crop circle /ˈkrɒp sɜːkl; ˈkrɑp sɝkl̩/ (also **corn circle**) *n* flattened, usu circular area that occurs every summer in Britain without apparent cause in a field of crops, esp corn or wheat, though various causes have been suggested 作物怪圈（每年夏天英国庄稼地里作物无故呈环状倒伏的区域，人们对它的解释众说纷纭）

cross-cultural /ˌkrɒsˈkʌltʃərəl, *US* ˌkrɔːs-; ˌkrɔsˈkʌltʃərəl/ *adj* involving, or containing ideas or elements from, two or more different cultures 跨文化的；多文化的：*cross-cultural exchanges/studies* 跨文化交流 *[研究]*

cross-dressing /ˌkrɒsˈdresɪŋ, *US* ˌkrɔːs-; ˌkrɔsˈdrɛsɪŋ/ *n* [U] practice of wearing the clothes usu worn by people of the opposite sex; TRANSVESTISM[A-Z] 异性装扮癖

▷ **cross-dresser** *n* sb who practises cross-dressing 有异性装扮癖的人

crossfader /krɒsˈfeɪdə(r), *US* krɔːs-; krɔsˈfedɚ/ *n* device used by a disc jockey which allows for the smooth transition from one tape to another by gradually reducing the volume of one at the same time as the other becomes louder 磁带平稳转换装置（流行音乐节目主持人使用的一种装置，能在降低一盘磁带音量的同时提高另一盘的音量，藉此实现磁带之间的平稳转换）

crossover /ˈkrɒsəʊvə(r), *US* ˈkrɔːs-; ˈkrɔsovɚ/ *n* **1** [C] bridge or other structure which crosses a river, a main road, etc 桥；跨路线桥 **2** [U] process of developing or changing from one type of culture, music, political party, etc to another（文化、音乐、党派等由一种向另一种的）发展或转变的过程：*the crossover from the Democrats to the Republicans amongst urban blacks* 城市黑人由民主党转向共和党

cross-subsidize, -ise /ˌkrɒsˈsʌbsɪdaɪz, *US* ˌkrɔːs-; ˌkrɔsˈsʌbsədaɪz/ *v* (*finance* 财) support an unprofitable business or venture from the profits of another 交叉资助（用某一公司或企业的利润来资助另一不营利的公司或企业）

▷ **cross-subsidy** *n*

cruelty-free /ˌkrʊəltɪˈfriː; ˌkruəltɪˈfri/ *adj* produced without the exploitation of animals, esp without the testing of products on them, eg shampoo and make up（洗发液、化妆品等产品因避免残酷虐待动物而）未经动物试验的：*Her most successful insight was that consumers prefer products that are cruelty-free.* 她最成功之处在于洞察到顾客更愿使用未经动物试验的产品。

cruise control /ˈkruːz kəntrəʊl; ˈkruz kəntrol/ *n* [U] device in a motor vehicle that allows it to maintain the speed that the driver has chosen 定速装置（使机动车保持以司机选择的速度行驶的装置）：*The new model has cruise control.* 这种新型机动车配有定速装置。

crumbly *n* = CRINKLY

crunch /krʌntʃ; krʌntʃ/ *n* (usu *sing* 通常作单数) strict restriction on the availability or free operation of sth, esp loan credit（尤指信贷等）紧缩：*The crunch on credit seems unlikely to be short term.* 信贷紧缩看来不会是短时间的事。Cf 参看 SQUEEZE *n* 5[A-Z]

crusty /ˈkrʌstɪ; ˈkrʌstɪ/ *n* (*Brit*) member of a group of young people in the UK who choose to wear old clothes and live outside regular society, often travelling from place to place 硬壳族（生活在常规社会之外，身穿旧衣服到处游逛的英国青年）Cf 参看 NEW AGE TRAVELLER (NEW AGE)

cryonics /kraɪˈɒnɪks; kraɪˈɑnɪks/ *n* [sing v] application of deep-freezing techniques to sb who has just died of an incurable disease, in the hope that future medical advances might make revival and cure possible 人体冷冻（将刚死于绝症的人体速冻保存，以待日后医学更发达时能使死者复活并将其治愈）

▷ **cryonic** *adj* : *cryonic techniques* 人体冷冻技术

cultbuster /ˈkʌltbʌstə(r); ˈkʌltbʌstɚ/ *n* person who is an expert in removing sb from the influence of a CULT 1[A-Z] and then helping him or her to recover and readjust 宗教崇拜者克星（为宗教崇拜者解除信仰上的影响并帮助他们复原和重寻方向的专家）

NOTE 注： formed on analogy with GHOSTBUSTER 由 ghostbuster（驱鬼人）一词类推构成

Current Era *n* = CE

curve /kɜːv; kɝv/ *n* (idm 习语) **throw sb a curve** (*infml* 口) present sb with a tricky situation to deal with or a difficult task to perform without warning 出其不意给人出难题；令人猝不及防：*He really threw me a curve when he suddenly withdrew from the conference, leaving us with no keynote speaker.* 他突然退出会议，使我们没有了主讲者，真是让我措手不及。

cut /kʌt; kʌt/ *n* one song from a long-playing tape; TRACK 6(a)[A-Z]（密纹唱片中的）一首曲子；唱片的一段录音

cut and paste /ˈkʌt ənd peɪst, kʌt ənd ˈpeɪst; kʌt ənd ˈpest/ *v* [Tn] (*computing* 计) delete text from one document in a computer application and transfer it to a different location in or outside the same document 剪贴（将文字从计算机显示的文件中删除并移至他处）

▷ **cut and paste** *n* : [attrib 作定语] *This icon allows you to access the cut and paste facility.* 此图标显示可进行剪贴处理。

cutesy /ˈkjuːtsɪ; ˈkjutsɪ/ *adj* (*infml* 口) rather too sweet or consciously appealing in appearance, behaviour , etc 矫揉造作的：*I found the latest cartoon rather too cutesy, but the kids loved it.* 我觉得那部新的卡通片太做作了，但孩子喜欢它。

cutting edge /ˌkʌtɪŋ ˈedʒ; ˌkʌtɪŋ ˈɛdʒ/ *n* (usu *sing* 通常作单数) **1** ~ **(of sth)** latest; most advanced stage in the development of sth, eg technology（某事物如科技发展的）前沿，尖端：*working at the cutting edge of fibre-optic technology* 从事尖端光纤技术工作 **2** advantage over sb（对某人的）优势：*With him on the team, we'll have a cutting edge over any opponents.* 有他在队里，我们比任何对手都占优势。

cyber- /ˈsaɪbə(r); ˈsaɪbɚ/ *comb form* 构词成分 (*computing* 计) relating to communications made possible by computer applications 与计算机通讯有关的：*cybernaut* ○ *cyberspace*

cyber crime /'saɪbə kraɪm; 'saɪbɚ kraɪm/ *n* [C,U] act of gaining unauthorized access to the files on an individual's or on an organization's computers esp to obtain confidential information, or to steal money by transferring it from accounts 计算机犯罪，网络犯罪（未经许可私自进入私人或机构的计算机，以窃取机密资料或通过转帐盗取金钱）

▷ **cyber criminal** *n* person who commits cyber crime; HACKER (HACK[2(A-Z)]) 计算机罪犯；黑客

cybernaut /'saɪbənɔ:t; 'saɪbɚnɔt/ *n* person who navigates CYBERSPACE in order to communicate globally, esp an expert at doing this 计算机网络漫游者，网络游侠（通过计算机网络进行全球通讯者，尤指这方面的专家）

NOTE 注： formed on analogy with *astronaut, cosmonaut* etc 由 astronaut（太空人）、cosmonaut（宇航员）等词类推构成

cyberphobic /saɪbə'fəʊbɪk; saɪbɚ'fobɪk/ *n, adj* (being a) person who has a fear or dislike of computers 畏惧计算机的（人）；厌恶计算机的（人）Cf 参看 TECHNOPHOBE

cyber pirate /saɪbə 'paɪrət; saɪbɚ 'paɪrət/ (also **cyber terrorist**) *n* person who breaks copyright law by putting software and music on the Internet without permission for others to download 计算机侵犯版权者（未经许可将拥有版权的软件和乐曲置于互联网上供他人下载的人）Cf 参看 WAREZ SITE

cyberspace /'saɪbəˌspeɪs; 'saɪbɚˌspes/ *n* [U] space within which electronic communication or experience takes place, esp during a VIRTUAL REALITY (VIRTUAL) experience or when using the INTERNET 计算机网络空间（尤指通过体验虚拟现实或运用互联网络进行电子通讯的空间）

cyclo /'saɪkləʊ; 'saɪklo/ *n* (*pl* **-os/-oes**) three-wheeled, pedal-powered vehicle designed to carry one passenger, esp one found in Vietnam（尤指越南的）三轮人力车

czar *n* = DRUG CZAR

Dd

daggy /'dægɪ; 'dægɪ/ *adj* (*US sl* 俚) boring, dull 令人厌烦的；乏味的：*What a daggy party. They all wanted to talk about work!* 这个聚会真闷死人，他们都只想谈工作！

damage control /'dæmɪdʒ kənˌtrəʊl; 'dæmɪdʒ kənˌtrol/ (also **damage limitation**) *n* [U] act of minimizing the effects of a bad situation or harmful event 损失控制（将有害事件的影响减少到最低限度）：*The bishop's angry outburst led to immediate and intense damage control from the leaders of the Church.* 主教大发雷霆后，教会的领袖们立即加紧采取措施将坏影响减少到最低限度。

dangerous dog /ˌdeɪndʒərəs 'dɒg; ˌdendʒərəs 'dɑg/ *n* dog bred for strength and aggression, esp one defined as dangerous in the UK Dangerous Dogs Act of 1991 危险犬，恶犬（指强壮、具有攻击性的狗，尤指 1991 年英国《危险犬条例》中定为危险类的狗）

dataglove /'deɪtəglʌv; 'detəglʌv/ *n* (*computing* 计) single glove which contains sensors to detect the position and movement of the hand and fingers of the wearer and in turn control and manipulate computer-generated images, used esp to experience VIRTUAL REALITY (VIRTUAL) environments 数据手套（装有传感器的单只手套，可测出使用者手与指的位置及活动状况，并据此控制和操纵计算机中的图像，尤用于体验虚拟现实环境）

data warehouse /'deɪtə ˌweəhaʊs; 'detə ˌwɛrhaʊs/ *n* (*computing* 计) (of an organization) collection of data brought from many different sources and processed so that the organization's decision makers can make effective use of it 数据仓（机构经集成、处理后供决策者使用的数据）

date rape /'deɪt reɪp; 'det rep/ *n* rape of a woman by a man with whom she is on a date 约会强奸（男子约会女子而把她强奸的行为）

dawn raid /dɔ:n 'reɪd; dɔn 'red/ *n* (*Brit finance* 财) sudden purchase by an individual or a company of a large proportion of the shares issued by a public company, usu at the start of the day's trading on the Stock Exchange 晨袭（个人或公司突然买下某上市公司的大量股票，通常在一天交易开市时如此做）

daytime soap /deɪtaɪm 'səʊp; detaɪm 'sop/ *n* SOAP OPERA (SOAP[A-Z]) broadcast during daytime hours, ie outside prime viewing time 日间肥皂剧（非黄金时间，即白天播放的肥皂剧）

daytime television /ˌdeɪtaɪm 'telɪvɪʒn; ˌdetaɪm 'tɛləvɪʒən/ *n* [U] programmes broadcast from early morning to early evening, outside prime viewing time 日间电视节目（非黄金时间，即白天播放的电视节目）

dazzle gun /'dæzl gʌn; 'dæzḷ gʌn/ *n* weapon which uses a laser beam to blind an attacker temporarily and to prevent detection from optical sensors 眩目枪（利用激光束使攻击者暂时丧失视力并能使光学传感器失灵的武器）

DCC *abbr* 缩写 = DIGITAL COMPACT CASSETTE

dead cat bounce /ded kæt 'baʊns; dɛd kæt 'baʊns/ *n* (*infml finance* 口，财) (usu *sing* 通常作单数) upward movement in the prices of shares after a fall or a period of low prices but which is not the beginning of a real recovery 死猫式反弹（股票价格在下跌或持续走低后反弹，但并不意味着真正开始回升）

NOTE 注： from the fact that even a dead cat may bounce upwards when it hits the ground after a fall, but this does not mean that it is still alive 死猫从高处落地后也会弹起，但这并不意味着它还活着，此义由此而来

death futures /deθ 'fju:tʃəz; dɛθ 'fjutʃɚz/ *n* [pl] (*US sl* 俚) life insurance policies sold by their holders for immediate cash but for much less than their full redeemable value, esp by younger people who know that they are dying 寿险期货（寿险持有人，尤指自知将死的年纪较轻者，为获得现金而卖掉保险，但所得远低于全额赔偿金）：*Death futures give the insured person the benefit of ready money while they still need it.* 寿险期货的好处在于，保户有需要时可以随时用以换取现金。

death star /'deθ stɑ:; 'dɛθ stɑr/ (also **throwing star**) *n* small disc made of metal in the shape of a star with sharp points which is used as a throwing weapon, esp in martial arts movies 星状飞镖（金属片制成、呈星状、尖端锋利的小型投掷武器，尤见于武打影片）

decaf /'di:kæf; 'dikæf/ *abbr* 缩写 = decaffeinated coffee 不含咖啡因的咖啡

decommission /ˌdi:kə'mɪʃn; ˌdikə'mɪʃn̩/ *v* [Tn] withdraw sth from regular use; close sth down 废弃；关闭：*decommission a nuclear power station* 关闭一家核电站

decommunization /di:ˌkɒmjʊnaɪ'zeɪʃn; diˌkɑmjunaɪ'zeʃən/ *n* [U] process of removing the communist structures within a country's political system, economy, etc 非共产主义化：*East Germany had to undergo a painful process of decommunization in the early nineties.* 九十年代初东德不得不经历了一场非共产主义化的痛苦过程。

deconstruct /ˌdi:kən'strʌkt; ˌdikən'strʌkt/ *v* [Tn] (*technical* 术语) analyze the language of literature and philosophy, esp so as to show that parts of it may not be consistent with each other 解构（对文学或哲学语言进行分析，尤指为显示其中自相矛盾的部分）

▷ **deconstruction** *n* [U] **deconstructionism** *n* [U] theory and practice of deconstructing 解构主义

deconstructionist *n* : *The new lecturer was a deconstructionist.* 那位新讲师以前是个解构主义者。

decryption /diːˈkrɪpʃn; diˈkrɪpʃən/ *n* [U] (*computing* 计) process of decoding data stored in a computer that has previously been encrypted (ENCRYPTION) 解密；解码

deep-set /ˌdiːpˈset; ˌdipˈsɛt/ *adj* (esp of eyes) set deeply back in the face （尤指眼睛）深陷于脸的 : *deep-set eyes under bushy, overhanging brows* 突出的浓眉下一双深陷的眼睛

defence breed /dɪˈfens briːd; dɪˈfɛns brid/ *n* any one of several types of dog especially bred for their aggression and kept as guard dogs, eg rottweiler, doberman 防卫种犬，看门犬（因其性情凶猛而特别配种饲养的狗，如罗特韦尔狗、多波曼狗等）: *Defence breeds are all included in the terms of the new licensing laws.* 新的特许法将所有看门犬都包括在内。

defensive medicine /dɪˌfensɪv ˈmedsn, *US* ˈmedɪsn; dɪˌfɛnsɪv ˈmɛdɪsn̩/ *n* [U] use by medical professionals, esp doctors, of an extremely cautious and conservative approach to the treatment of their patients in order to avoid being sued if sth goes wrong 防御性诊治（医生为避免万一出事而被起诉，对病人采取极其谨慎保守的治疗方法）

demonize /ˈdiːmənaɪz; ˈdimənaɪz/ *v* [Tn] to exaggerate the evil power and threat of sb or sth out of all proportion 把（某人或某事）说成魔鬼；过分夸大（某人或某事）的祸害和威胁 : *Don't demonize Sadam Hussein. We need to keep a firm grasp on reality.* 别把萨达姆·侯赛因说成魔鬼。我们需要深刻地体会现实。

denial /dɪˈnaɪəl; dɪˈnaɪəl/ *n* (idm 习语) **in denial** (of a psychological state) unable to admit the truth of sth to oneself because it is too terrible （因某事太可怕而在心理上）无法承认事实 : *At the moment she is in denial, but she will soon have to face the fact that her husband is not coming back.* 此刻她无法接受，但不久她就得面对她丈夫不会再回来这一现实。

dependency culture /dɪˈpendənsɪ ˌkʌltʃə(r); dɪˈpɛndənsɪ ˌkʌltʃɚ/ *n* [U] way of life which accepts that it is normal and inevitable to rely for one's income on welfare rather than on paid employment 依赖风气（理所当然地依赖政府的福利救济过活而不依靠工资的生活方式）: *We fear that we may be creating a dependency culture through the easy availability of generous social benefits.* 我们担心如此轻而易举地就能得到大量社会救济，我们会助长了一种依赖风气。

desert fever *n* = GULF WAR SYNDROME

desertification /dɪˌzɜːtɪfɪˈkeɪʃn; dɪˌzɝtɪfəˈkeʃən/ *n* [U] process of becoming or making sth a desert 沙漠化 : *Over-grazing and poor rainfall both contribute to the process of desertification.* 过度放牧以及降雨过少造成了土壤沙漠化。

desert storm syndrome *n* = GULF WAR SYNDROME

designer drug /dɪˈzaɪnə drʌg; dɪˈzaɪnɚ drʌg/ *n* drug, eg crack cocaine, ecstasy, etc either made from a mixture of chemicals rather than from natural substances or produced by modifying an already existing drug 化合毒品，改装毒品（如强效可卡因、迷幻药等，由多种化学物质而非天然物质混合制成或将已有毒品改造而成）

des res /dez ˈrez; dɛz ˈrɛz/ *abbr* 缩写 = (*Brit joc* 谑) desirable residence (attractive house, flat, etc) 理想居所（有吸引力的房屋、公寓等）

NOTE 注： an abbreviation often seen in classified ads but also used in speech, from the full form first made popular by estate agents when they described a property 起初为房地产经纪人描述房屋的常用语，后来其缩写形式常见于分类广告及口语中

destablize, -ise /ˌdiːˈsteɪbəlaɪz; ˌdiˈstebl̩aɪz/ *v* [Tn] make a system, group, country, etc become less stable and more likely to break up 使（制度、团体、国家等）不稳定 : *Big currency speculators have been accused of trying to destabilize the money market.* 大量地投机买卖货币的人被指责意图破坏货币市场的稳定。

detailing /ˈdiːteɪlɪŋ, *US* dɪˈteɪl-; dɪˈtelɪŋ/ *n* small additional details put on a building, garment, etc for decoration rather than for any essential structural purpose （建筑物、衣服等的）小件装饰 : *The fashion house is famous for the attractive detailing on its garments.* 这家时装店以其服装上诱人的小装饰而闻名。

detectorist /dɪˈtektərɪst; dɪˈtɛktərɪst/ *n* person who spends a lot of time hunting for buried metallic objects such as coins, etc, using a metal detector 探测器使用者（用仪器搜寻掩盖着的硬币等金属制品的人）: *Every evening the detectorists would scour the beach for dropped coins and even watches.* 每晚那些拿着探测器的人都在海滩上四处搜寻别人遗落的硬币甚至手表。

detox /diːˈtɒks; diˈtɑks/ *abbr* 缩写 = (*infml* 口) detoxification (process of ridding the body of harmful or toxic substances, esp alcohol and drugs) 戒毒；戒酒 : *Addicts may go through detox many times and some never get out of their drug habit.* 吸毒者也许要经过多次戒毒，有一些人则永远戒不了毒瘾。

dialogue box /ˈdaɪəlɒg bɒks, *US* -lɔːg; ˈdaɪəlɔg bɑks/ (*US* **dialog box**) *n* (*computing* 计) small area on the screen which offers the user a choice of actions and gives information about the current set up 对话框（计算机屏幕上显示的一个小框，作操作选择和报告屏幕现况之用）

dickhead /ˈdɪkhed; ˈdɪkhɛd/ *n* (*sl* ⚠ 俚，讳) idiot, contemptible person 白痴；可鄙的家伙

NOTE 注： used mainly of males since *dick* is a taboo word for *penis* 主要用于男性，因 dick 一词乃‘阴茎’的禁忌语

differently abled *adj* = OTHERLY ABLED

diffuser /dɪˈfjuːzə(r); dɪˈfjuzɚ/ *n* funnel-shaped device which can be fitted onto the nozzle of a hair-drier to spread the hot air and allow a gentler flow 吹风嘴（吹风机上的漏斗形装置，用以均匀散热，柔和送风）

digital /ˈdɪdʒɪtl; ˈdɪdʒətl̩/ *adj* of or using computers, esp as a means of improving one's technical or professional skills 计算机的，使用计算机的（尤指将其作为改进专业技术的手段）: *Writers, linguists, designers of all kinds, even poets have all found the benefits of going digital.* 作家、语言学家、各类设计师甚至诗人都已发现了使用计算机的好处。

NOTE 注： most often used with the verb *go* 常与动词 go 连用

Digital Compact Cassette /dɪdʒɪtl kəmˌpækt kəˈset; dɪdʒətl̩ kəmˌpækt kəˈsɛt/ *n* type of tape cassette which makes digital rather than analogue recordings 数字卡式磁带（采用数字而非模拟记录法录制的磁带）

Digital Versatile Disc /dɪdʒɪtl ˌvɜːsətaɪl ˈdɪsk, *US* ˈvɜːrsətl; dɪdʒətl̩ ˌvɝsətl̩ ˈdɪsk/ (also **Digital Video Disc**) *n* (*abbr* 缩写 **DVD**) type of digital recording medium storing much more data, including video data, than is possible on a compact disc 数字式多功能光盘，数码影碟（一种采用数字记录技术储存信息（包括影像）的光盘，其储存量远多于激光唱片）

dinar /ˈdiːnɑː(r); ˈdinɑr/ *n* unit of money, eg in countries of the Middle East and of N Africa 第纳尔（中东、北非等国的货币单位）

Dinky /ˈdɪŋkɪ; ˈdɪŋkɪ/ *abbr* 缩写 = double/dual income, no kids yet (member of a couple in good jobs and with no children) 丁克族（收入高且无子女的夫妇的其中一方）

directory enquiries /dəˌrektərɪ ɪn'kwaɪərɪz, *US* 'ɪnkwərɪz; dəˌrɛktərɪ 'ɪnkwərɪz/ *n* [pl] (*Brit*) telephone service that one can use to find out sb's telephone number 电话（号码）查询台：*I'll ring directory enquiries.* 我要给电话查询台打电话。

dirty dancing /ˌdɜːtɪ 'dɑːnsɪŋ, *US* 'dæn-; ˌdɝtɪ 'dænsɪŋ/ (also **touch dancing**) *n* [U] (*esp US*) dancing usu to pop music which involves close bodily contact 贴身舞；接触舞

dirty trick /ˌdɜːtɪ 'trɪk; ˌdɝtɪ 'trɪk/ *n* **1** unkind or dishonest act 卑鄙的行为：*What a dirty trick! Why did she write to the papers about our decision?* 多卑鄙呀！她为什么将我们的决定投书报社呢？ **2** (usu *pl* 通常作复数) dishonest or secret political activity, esp one aimed at discrediting one's opponent or destroying his or her reputation（骗人的或秘密的）政治伎俩（尤指为诋毁对手或败坏其名声的）：*a dirty tricks campaign* 骗人的政治伎俩的攻势

disbar /dɪs'bɑː(r); dɪs'bɑr/ *v* (**-rr-**) (esp passive 尤用于被动语态) take away the right of a BARRISTER^A-Z to practise 取消（某人的）讼务律师资格

disc drive *n* = DISK DRIVE (DISK^A-Z)

disempower /ˌdɪsɪm'paʊə(r); ˌdɪsɪm'paʊɚ/ *v* take away the power of choice and action from an individual or group 剥夺（个人或团体的）选择与行动权：*Single parents have been disempowered by the latest government measures.* 最新颁布的政府法令剥夺了单亲父母的权利。 Cf 参看 EMPOWER

Disneyfication /ˌdɪznɪfɪ'keɪʃn; ˌdɪznɪfə'kɔʃən/ *n* [U] (**a**) process and end result of making an event, story or place bland and cute, which is regarded by some as ignoring ambiguity or any negative aspect, usu for commercial purposes 迪斯尼化（淡化对某事件、故事或地方的描绘，着意讨俏，有些人认为这是为了迁就商业目的而避免讯息含糊或带有负面意义）：*the Disneyfication of an essentially tragic story* 将本质为悲剧的故事加以迪斯尼动画式的改造 (**b**) introduction of American culture, lifestyles and values into a place with what is considered by some to be a harmful effect 美国化（将美国文化、生活方式和价值观等介绍到某处，这种做法有些人认为具有危害性）：*Some French saw the opening of a Disneyland theme park outside Paris as just a further step in the Disneyfication of Europe.* 一些法国人将在巴黎城外开设迪斯尼主题乐园视为欧洲进一步美国化的象征。

NOTE 注： from the style and ethos behind the entertainment company, Disney, which was started by the founder Walt Disney as a producer of cartoon films in the late 1920s 源自 20 世纪 20 年代末动画制片人沃尔特·迪斯尼创办的迪斯尼娱乐公司的风格及企业精神

dispatcher /dɪ'spætʃə(r); dɪ'spætʃɚ/ *n* (*US*) person whose job is to supervise the departure of trains, planes, buses, etc（火车、飞机、公共汽车等的）调度员

diss /dɪs; dɪs/ *v* [I, Tn] (*US sl* 俚) show disrespect by words or behaviour（言语或行为上）不尊敬，侮辱：*The teacher got dissed in front of the class.* 老师在全班学生面前受辱了。

▷ **diss** *n* (*US sl* 俚) instance of dissing 不尊敬；侮辱

NOTE 注： abbreviation using first syllable of *disrespect*, originating in black American culture 由 disrespect（不尊敬）一词的首音节缩略构成，源自美国黑人用语

distance learning /'dɪstəns lɜːnɪŋ; 'dɪstəns lɝnɪŋ/ *n* [U] education by means other than attendance at a school or college, eg by correspondence, televised courses or through electronic communication systems such as the Internet 远程教育（通过函授、电视课程或互联网之类的电子通讯系统进行的教育）

divided highway *n* (*US*) = DUAL CARRIAGEWAY (DUAL^A-Z)

dividing line /dɪ'vaɪdɪŋ laɪn; dɪ'vaɪdɪŋ laɪn/ *n* distinction made between two things that appear or actually are similar（相似物之间的）区别，分界线：*the dividing line between kindness and over-indulgence* 仁慈与纵容之间的分界线

DNA fingerprinting *n* = GENETIC FINGERPRINTING

DNA profiling *n* = GENETIC FINGERPRINTING

docking station /'dɒkɪŋ steɪʃn; 'dɑkɪŋ steʃən/ *n* (*computing* 计) device which may be added on to a computer which has built-in networking and CONNECTIVITY features, and provides extra disc-drive bays, better sound, etc 坞站（一种可装到具有可联网络及可连通性的计算机上的装置，能提供额外的磁盘驱动器的机架以及更好的音响效果等）

Doc Martens /dɒk 'mɑːtɪnz; dɑk 'mɑrtɪnz/ *n* [pl] (*propr* 专利名) type of heavy boot with laces and a thick sole, usu worn by young people 马登鞋（一种系带厚底靴，通常为年轻人穿用）

NOTE 注： the boots are called after Doctor Klaus Maertens, the German inventor of the sole 此鞋以靴底发明者，德国人 Doctor Klaus Maertens 命名

doctor-assisted suicide /dɒktəəˌsɪstɪd 'suːɪsaɪd; dɑktɚəˌsɪstɪd 'suəsaɪd/ (also **assisted suicide**) *n* suicide committed with the help and advice of a doctor 医助自杀（由医生协助或建议的自杀）

docutainment *n* = INFOTAINMENT

doggy bag /'dɒgɪ bæg, *US* 'dɔːgɪ; 'dɔgɪ bæg/ *n* bag that is given to a customer in a restaurant to take home food he or she has paid for but not been able to finish 狗食袋（饭馆供顾客将吃剩食物打包的袋子）：*Could I have a doggy bag for the rest of the dumplings, please?* 请给我一个袋子将剩下的饺子打包行吗？

NOTE 注： the original idea was that the food would be given to the dog at home 原意为将食物带回家喂狗

dollar diplomacy /ˌdɒlə dɪ'pləʊməsɪ; ˌdɑlɚ dɪ'ploməsɪ/ *n* [U] government policy aimed at promoting a country's business interests abroad 金元外交（为在外国谋取更大经济利益的外交政策）

dollarization /ˌdɒləraɪ'zeɪʃn; ˌdɑləraɪ'zeʃən/ *n* [U] (*finance* 财) process and result of allowing conversion of any currency into US dollars at a fixed and invariable rate; pegging (PEG² 2^A-Z) of a currency to the US dollar 以固定汇率将货币兑换成美元；固定货币与美元的汇率；与美元挂钩

doomsday cult /'duːmzdeɪ kʌlt; 'dumzde kʌlt/ *n* group of people who believe that the world will soon end and that they need to take protective measures to ensure their own survival either here or in the next life 世界末日教（相信世界末日即将到来，需想方设法确保自己今生或来世能得以存活的群体）：*members of the Aum Shinrikyo doomsday cult* 日本奥姆真理世界末日教教徒 ○ *Doomsday cult members were disappointed when the world failed to end on Friday as their leader had predicted.* 当世界并未如他们的领袖预言的那样于星期五毁灭时，世界末日教的教徒大为失望。 Cf 参看 DOOMSDAY^A-Z, MILLENNIUM CULT

doorstep /'dɔːstep; 'dɔrstɛp/ *v* [Tn] (*derog* 贬) (of reporters) go to the home of sb who is in the news and persistently try to get a photo or comment even if he or she does not want this publicity（指记者）登门采访，穷追不舍（不管受访者愿意公开与否也力图拍得照片或打探其看法）：*As soon as the news of the engagement was out, the poor girl was doorstepped mercilessly by hordes of reporters.* 订婚的消息一经公开，那可怜的女孩的家就被蜂拥而至穷追不舍的记者包围住了。

dork /dɔ:k; dɔrk/ *n* (*sl* 俚 *esp US*) **1** stupid or contemptible person 蠢货；坏蛋 **2** penis 阴茎

DOTS /dɒts, di: əʊ ti: 'es; dɑts, di o ti 'ɛs/ *abbr* 缩写 = directly-observed treatment strategy/short-course (system of monitoring patients on medication to ensure that they complete their course of treatment, esp for patients suffering from TB) 直接观察疗法，直接观察短期疗程（监督接受药物治疗的病人以保证他们完成疗程的制度，尤用于肺结核病人）: *DOTS has reduced drastically the number of TB patients suffering relapses.* 直接观察疗法使肺结核病复发的人数大大减少。

double bedroom /dʌbl 'bedru:m; dʌbl̩ 'bɛdrum/ *n* bedroom in a flat, house, etc large enough to put a double bed in and for two people to share 双人卧室（公寓、住房等中能放一张双人床的卧室） Cf 参看 DOUBLE ROOM, TWIN BEDROOM

double life /ˌdʌbl 'laɪf; ˌdʌbl̩ 'laɪf/ *n* life lived by sb who appears to be respectable and normal but who is secretly doing things that are entirely the opposite 双重（人格和身分的）生活: *Spies have always had to live a double life.* 间谍总得过双重生活。○ *By day she was a respected teacher, by night a stripper. Few knew of her extraordinary double life.* 白天她是受人尊敬的教师，晚上却成了脱衣舞女。很少人知道她奇特的双重生活。

double room /dʌbl 'ru:m; dʌbl̩ 'rum/ *n* bedroom in a hotel, boarding house, etc with a double bed or two single beds, intended for use by two people 双人房间（旅馆、宿舍等中放一张双人床或两张单人床的房间） Cf 参看 DOUBLE BEDROOM, TWIN BEDROOM

double whammy /ˌdʌbl 'wæmɪ; ˌdʌbl̩ 'wæmɪ/ *n* blow or setback which is received twice, thus doubling the effect 双重厄运；雪上加霜: *Rising rents and falling retail sales have dealt a double whammy to the smaller local shops.* 本地的小商店遭受了房租上涨和销售额下降的双重打击。

doughnutting /'dəʊnʌtɪŋ; 'donʌtɪŋ/ *n* [U] action of sitting on all sides of sb who is speaking in parliament when a session is being televised in order to give the impression that the debate is an important one and that the chamber is full （电视转播时）围坐在议会发言者周围（以给人留下辩论很重要以及会议室坐满了人的印象）

down /daʊn; daʊn/ *adj* [pred 作表语] **1** (*infml* 口) sad; depressed 难过: *She's feeling a bit down at the moment.* 她这会儿情绪有点低落。 **2** (of a computer, etc) not working （指计算机等）坏了: *I'm sorry we can't process your account at the moment. The computer's down.* 很抱歉现在不能处理您的帐。计算机坏了。

□ **down time** *n* [U] **1** time during which a computer is not operating （因计算机无法运行造成的）停工期 **2** period of time when employees are not working, esp during a labour dispute 停工期（尤指雇员因劳资纠纷而停工的时间）

down at heel /ˌdaʊn ət 'hi:l; ˌdaʊn ət 'hil/ *adj* shabby, rather worn out, usu because of lack of money 破烂的；褴褛的: *a down at heel hotel* 破破烂烂的旅店 ○ *down at heel appearance* 寒酸的外表

NOTE 注： probably from the worn down heels of a pair of old shoes 可能源自旧鞋上穿坏了的鞋跟 (worn down heel) 这个意思

downmarketing /ˌdaʊn'mɑ:kɪtɪŋ; ˌdaʊn'mɑrkɪtɪŋ/ *n* [U] (*commerce* 商) strategy of targeting lower income groups in marketing and advertising campaigns 低层次营销（面向低收入阶层的营销及广告策略）

downplay /ˌdaʊn'pleɪ; ˌdaʊn'ple/ *v* [Tn] make sth appear less important or serious than it actually is 对（某事）轻描淡写: *Although the authorities tried to downplay the situation, it was clear that a serious error had been made.* 尽管当局尽量对局势作轻描淡写的处理，但很显然大错已铸成。 Cf 参看 PLAY STH DOWN (PLAY² 16A-Z)

downshifter /'daʊnʃɪftə(r); 'daʊnʃɪftɚ/ *n* person who opts for a change of career and/or lifestyle from a more to a less demanding one 选择较以前轻松的工作和 *[或]* 生活方式的人；降低要求的人

▷ **downshifting** *n* action of a downshifter and the result 选择较以前轻松的工作和 *[或]* 生活方式及其后果

downside /'daʊnsaɪd; 'daʊnsaɪd/ *n* (usu *sing* 通常作单数) negative aspect; disadvantage or set of disadvantages 消极面；负面效应: *The downside to rising wages is inflation.* 工资上涨的负面效应是通货膨胀。○ *Everything has its downside.* 任何事都有其消极的一面。

downspin /'daʊnspɪn; 'daʊnspɪn/ *n* (*usu derog* 通常作贬义) steep and accelerating fall in house prices, productivity rates, etc （房价、生产率等的）急剧下跌

downturn /'daʊntɜ:n; 'daʊntɝn/ *n* ~ **(in sth)** reduction in economic or business activity （经济或商业活动的）衰退，下降: *a drastic downturn in tourism* 旅游业的急剧滑坡

dowse /daʊz, *US* daʊs; daʊs/ *v* [Ipr] (*medical* 医) diagnose an illness or condition by means of a pendulum suspended over the patient. The pendulum is thought to detect radiation given off by the human body 摆锤探诊（在病人上方悬挂摆锤用以诊病，据认为摆锤可以探测人体辐射）

NOTE 注： derived from the practice of dowsing (DOWSE2(A-Z)) for underground water or minerals by similar means 由 dowse 一词的本义引申而来，即通过类似方法探测地下水源或矿产

drafter /'drɑ:ftə(r), *US* dræft-; 'dræftɚ/ *n* person who drafts a law, document, etc （法律、文件等的）起草人

dragon /'drægən; 'drægən/ *n* any of the four Asian countries or regions, ie South Korea, Taiwan, Singapore and Hong Kong, which developed booming economies in the 1980s and 90s 小龙（20 世纪 80 和 90 年代经济腾飞的亚洲四小龙（即韩国、台湾、新加坡和香港）之一）

dragon boat /'drægən bəʊt; 'drægən bot/ *n* long rowing boat of traditional Chinese design with a carved wooden dragon's head at the prow, used for racing 龙舟

dream team /'dri:m ti:m; 'drim tim/ *n* group of the best possible people for the task, sporting event, political administration, etc 由最佳人选组成的班子；梦之队；梦幻组合: *Britain's World Cup dream team* 英国参加世界杯足球赛的梦之队 ○ *a dream team for the forthcoming elections* 角逐下届竞选的梦幻组合 Cf 参看 DREAM TICKET

dream ticket /dri:m 'tɪkɪt; drim 'tɪkɪt/ *n* (*US*) ideal pair of candidates standing together for election, esp for the positions of President and Vice-President （尤指一起竞选总统和副总统职位的）黄金搭档，完美组合，梦幻组合: *Clinton and Gore gave the Democrats a dream ticket in 1992.* 克林顿和戈尔是 1992 年民主党竞选的黄金搭档。 Cf 参看 DREAM TEAM

dress-down Friday /dresdaʊn 'fraɪdeɪ; drɛsdaʊn 'fraɪde/ *n* (*US*) day, usu a Friday, on which people dress more casually in the office than they do on the other days of the week. The practice is beginning to spread into the rest of the week 便装星期五（穿着较为随便的衣服上班的日子，通常为星期五，此惯例现渐延伸到其他工作日）

drink-driver /ˌdrɪŋk'draɪvə(r); ˌdrɪŋk'draɪvɚ/ (*US* **drunk driver**) *n* (*Brit*) person who drives a vehicle after having drunk more than the legal limit of alcohol （违章）酒后驾车者

drive *n* (*computing* 计) = DISK DRIVE (DISKA-Z)

drive-by /'draɪvbaɪ; 'draɪvbaɪ/ *adj* [usu attrib 通常作定语] **1** (of a crime, usu a shooting) carried out from a moving vehicle （指作案，通常指开枪）从行驶的汽车中进

行的 : *drive-by killings* 从行驶的汽车中开枪杀人 **2** (of any activity) done in passing from a car（指任何活动）驶过的汽车所造成的 : *We suffered frequent drive-by musical attacks from the loud stereos of passing cars.* 我们经常被驶过的汽车上喧闹的立体声音乐吵得不得安宁。 **3** (*fig* 比喻) displaying a careless and unprofessional approach 轻率而外行的 : *drive-by journalism* 蹩脚的新闻报道 ○ *a drive-by documentary* 粗制滥造的纪录片

drongo /ˈdrɒŋɡəʊ; ˈdrɑŋgo/ *n* (*pl* **-os/oes**) (*Austral derog* 澳，贬) idiot; useless person 笨蛋；没用的人

drop-dead /drɒpˈded; drɑpˈdɛd/ *adv* (*sl* 俚) (esp of someone's appearance) extremely, stunningly（尤指人的外貌）极其，惊人地 : *She looks drop-dead gorgeous.* 她真是美艳绝伦。

drophead /ˈdrɒphed; ˈdrɑphɛd/ *n* (*Brit*) adjustable, fabric roof of some cars（某些汽车上可调节的、用织物制成的）活动顶篷

drug czar /ˈdrʌg zɑ:(r), *US* tsɑ:r; ˈdrʌg tsɑr/ (also **drug supremo**) *n* (*infml* 口) person put in charge of the anti-drug efforts of a state or country with wide powers and the best resources available 缉毒总头儿；缉毒总指挥 : *The new drug czar met the press for the first time today.* 新的缉毒总指挥今天首次在媒体前亮相。

druggie /ˈdrʌgɪ; ˈdrʌgɪ/ *n* (*infml* 口) habitual user of drugs, eg a NARCOTIC^A-Z; drug addict 吸毒上瘾者；瘾君子

drug mule *n* = MULE

drug supremo *n* = DRUG CZAR

dry-eyed /ˌdraɪˈaɪd; draɪˈaɪd/ *adj* not crying even though the situation or experience is emotional 无泪的；不哭的 : *He remained dry-eyed all through the funeral service.* 整个葬礼他一直没哭。

dry humour /draɪ ˈhju:mə(r); draɪ ˈhjumɚ/ *n* very subtle sense of humour 冷面幽默；十分微妙的幽默

dry law /ˈdraɪ lɔ:; ˈdraɪ lɔ/ *n* (*US*) law that forbids the selling of alcoholic drinks 禁止售酒法

dry slope /draɪ ˈsləʊp; draɪ ˈslop/ *n* (*sport* 体) artificial ski slope, usu indoors, covered with a plastic material which substitutes for snow 人造滑雪坡（通常设在室内，上覆塑料雪来代替真雪的滑雪坡）: *Spend some time on the dry slopes before you get out onto the real mountainside.* 先在人造滑雪坡上练习一段时间，然后再到真正的山坡上去滑。

dualism /ˈdju:əlɪzəm, *US* du:-; ˈduəlɪzəm/ *n* [U] (*philosophy* 哲) theory based on the existence of two opposite principles, eg physical and spiritual, good and evil, in all things 二元论（基于所有事物都有两个相反的原则的理论，如物质和精神、善和恶）

dude /du:d, *US* dju:d; djud/ *n* (*sl* 俚) **1** man; guy 男人；家伙 **2** (used as a form of address) friend; buddy（用作称呼语）朋友，老兄

NOTE 注 : can have admiring overtones 有时含赞美意 : *He's a real dude.* 他真够哥们儿。

dumb /dʌm; dʌm/ *v* (phr v) **dumb down** reduce the content, language, etc of a film, news report or television programme to the lowest intellectual level because it is felt that otherwise the audience will not be able to understand it 简化（为免观众无法理解而将电影、新闻报道或电视节目的内容、语言等简化到最浅白的程度）: *Is there really any need to dumb down the documentary to that extent?* 真有必要将这部纪录片剪裁简化到那种程度吗？

dumb animals /ˌdʌm ˈænɪmlz; ˌdʌm ˈænəml̩z/ *n* [pl] animals, esp as regarded as helpless or deserving pity（尤指无助或可怜的）哑巴动物 : *the poor dumb animals in the circus* 马戏团里那些可怜的哑巴动物

dumping /ˈdʌmpɪŋ; ˈdʌmpɪŋ/ *n* [U] practice of discarding dangerous, poisonous substances, etc as rubbish（危险、有毒物质等的）倾倒 : *illegal dumping* 有毒废料的非法倾倒 ○ *dumping of nuclear waste at sea* 核废物的倾倒入海

▷ **dumping ground** *n* (usu *sing* 通常作单数) place where sth that is not wanted is dumped 垃圾场；废物倾倒处 : *Get these old newspapers out of my room! This isn't dumping ground for your rubbish.* 把这些旧报纸从我的房间拿出去！这儿可不是你堆垃圾的地方。

(phr v) **dump on** (*US infml* 口) criticize harshly; blame 严厉批评；责备 : *Don't dump on your teachers. You've got some responsibility as well.* 别责备你的老师了。你也有责任。

Dumpster /ˈdʌmpstə(r); ˈdʌmpstɚ/ *n* (*US propr* 专利名) large container put in a public place into which people can dump rubbish or items for recycling 大垃圾箱（置于公共场所供人抛弃垃圾或扔下物件用以循环再造的大型容器）Cf 参看 SKIP^2(A-Z)

dune buggy *n* = BEACH BUGGY (BEACH^A-Z)

dunno /dəˈnəʊ; dəˈno/ *v* (*sl* 俚) (I) don't know（我）不知道 : *I asked him where the post office was but all he said was 'Dunno'.* 我问他邮局在哪里，他只说了个'不知道'。

duopoly /dju:ˈɒpəlɪ, *US* du:-; duˈɑpəlɪ/ *n* (*commerce* 商) right to trade in a particular product or provide a particular service which is limited to only two companies or organizations 两强垄断（由两家机构垄断的专卖权或专营权）: *a powerful duopoly in the supply of domestic electricity* 垄断国内电力供应的两巨头 Cf 参看 MONOPOLY^A-Z

DVD *abbr* 缩写 = DIGITAL VERSATILE DISC

dweeb /dwi:b; dwib/ *n* (*US sl* 俚) contemptible, unfashionable or boring person 讨厌鬼；不合潮流的人；乏味的人

DWEM /dwem; dwɛm/ *abbr* 缩写 = (*derog* 贬) Dead White European Male (any famous male writer, thinker, etc with a European background) 具有欧洲背景的著名的已故男性作家、思想家等 : *African-American students criticized the history course for focusing too narrowly on DWEMs.* 美国黑人学生批评历史课过于偏重欧洲男性名人。

dysergy /ˈdɪsɜ:dʒɪ; ˈdɪsɝdʒɪ/ *n* [U] possible or actual bad effects of the joining together of two companies in terms of lower efficiency or productivity, etc（两公司合并后可能产生或实际产生的）降效作用，降低生产力作用 Cf 参看 SYNERGY

dysfunctional /dɪsˈfʌŋkʃnəl; dɪsˈfʌŋkʃənl̩/ *adj* (*fml* 文) (of human relationships) not operating in a normal or beneficial way（指人际关系）不正常的，不良的 : *a dysfunctional family* 不和睦的家庭

dyspnoea /dɪsˈpni:ə; dɪsˈpniə/ *n* (*medical* 医) difficulty in breathing, esp when this causes some people to stop breathing for periods while they are asleep（尤指导致某些人睡眠中呼吸间歇性停止的）呼吸困难

dyspraxia /dɪsˈpræksɪə; dɪsˈpræksɪə/ *n* [U] (*medical* 医) disorder, esp in children, resulting in poor co-ordination of motor movements and often associated with difficulties in learning to read and spell 运用障碍，运用功能不全（肌肉运动不协调，常伴以读写学习困难，尤指儿童）

Ee

e- /i:; i/ *comb form* 构词成分 (used to form words relating to the publication or exchange of information in an electronic format 用以构成与以电子文本公布或交流信息有关的词) electronic 电子信息的 : *e-mail* ○ *e-text*

E (also **e**) *abbr* 缩写 = ECSTASY

each way /ˌi:tʃ ˈweɪ; ˌitʃ ˈwe/ *adv* (of a bet) placed so that one wins if the horse, greyhound, etc comes first, second or third in a race（指赌博下注方式）赛马、赛狗等进入前三名（下注者）就胜出，独赢位置：*I've got £20 each way on the favourite.* 我在那匹热门马上买了独赢位置，结果赢了 20 英镑。

earner /ˈɜːnə(r); ˈɝnɚ/ *n* (**a**) person who earns a wage 挣工薪者 (**b**) activity or business that makes a profit 赢利的活动或企业：*Tourism is the country's biggest foreign currency earner.* 旅游业是该国最大的外汇收入来源。○ (*infml* 口) *Their shop is a nice little earner.* 他们的小店能赚不少钱。

earthbound /ˈɜːθbaʊnd; ˈɝθbaʊnd/ *adj* **1** attached or limited to the earth 附着于地面的；局限于陆地上的：*earthbound forms of life* (ie unable to fly) 地上的（即不能飞的）生物 ○ (*fig* 比喻) *an earthbound imagination* 平淡无奇的想像 **2** moving or directed towards the earth 向地球移动的；向地球的：*an earthbound meteorite* 撞向地球的陨石

earth-shattering /ˈɜːθʃætərɪŋ; ˈɝθʃætərɪŋ/ *adj* having a profound, powerful and often shocking effect 惊天动地的；影响深远的：*earth-shattering news* 有震撼力的新闻 ○ *The announcement was hardly earth-shattering. We'd been expecting it for days.* 这个声明并非什么惊天动地之举。我们早就预料到了。

eatery /ˈiːtərɪ; ˈitərɪ/ *n* (*esp US infml* 口) restaurant or place that serves food 饭店；餐馆：*one of the little eateries on Main Street* 大街上众多小餐馆中的一间

eating disorder /ˌiːtɪŋ dɪsˈɔːdə(r), ˈiːtɪŋ dɪsˌɔːdə(r); ˈitɪŋ dɪsˌɔrdɚ/ *n* any of a number of psychological disorders resulting in abnormal eating habits, eg BULIMIA and ANOREXIA[A-Z] 进食障碍（由心理障碍造成的反常饮食习惯，如食欲亢进和厌食）

ecocide /ˈiːkəʊˌsaɪd; ˈikoˌsaɪd/ *n* [U] destruction of the natural environment 生态灭绝；破坏自然环境

NOTE 注： formed on analogy with *suicide*, *genocide*, etc 由 suicide（自杀）、genocide（种族灭绝）等词类推构成

eco-friendly /ˌiːkəʊˈfrendlɪ; ˈikoˈfrɛndlɪ/ *adj* not harmful to the environment 不破坏环境的；对环境无害的：*an eco-friendly packaging material* 不破坏环境的包装材料 ○ *eco-friendly chemicals* 对环境无害的化学物质 ○ *eco-friendly products* 环保产品

eco-label /ˈiːkəʊˌleɪbl; ˈikoˌlebl/ *n* label on goods which sets out the manufacturer's or producer's claims that the product meets certain environmentally desirable or required criteria 生态标签（制造商用来贴在产品上，标明其符合某些环保标准的标签）：*Look for the eco-label. I won't buy fruit that's been sprayed with pesticides.* 看看有没有生态标签。我可不买那些喷了农药的水果。

ecological footprint /iːkəˌlɒdʒɪkl ˈfʊtprɪnt; ikəˌlɑdʒɪkl̩ ˈfʊtprɪnt/ *n* (usu *sing* 通常作单数) visible and often harmful effect of sth on the surrounding environment 生态（疤）痕（对周围环境造成可见的、常为有害的影响）：*Heavy tourism is leaving an irreversible ecological footprint on the mountain.* 过多的旅游活动对这座山的生态环境造成不可弥补的损失。

NOTE 注： most often applied to damage caused by people through carelessness or by weight of numbers 常指因疏忽或人多对环境造成的损害

econometric /iːkɒnəʊˈmetrɪk; ikɑnoˈmɛtrɪk/ *adj* (*fml* 文) applying statistical data to the study of economic phenomena and problems 计量经济学的（将统计学数据用于研究经济现象及问题的）：*We hope that an econometric approach to the problem of inner city decay will reveal more about its cause.* 我们希望用计量经济学的方法来研究旧城区的衰败情况可以更好地看清导致问题的原因。

economical /ˌiːkəˈnɒmɪkl, ˌekə-; ˌikəˈnɑmɪkl̩, ɛkə-/ *adj* (idm 习语) **economical with the truth** (**a**) not saying more than is strictly necessary 吝于言辞的；出言谨慎的 (**b**) (*euph* 婉) lying 隐瞒真相的；撒谎的：*Diplomats are often accused of being economical with the truth, but they sometimes have little choice.* 外交官常被指责为对事实真相避重就轻，但他们有时不得不如此。

Economic and Monetary Union /iːkənˌɒmɪk ənd ˌmʌnɪtrɪ ˈjuːnɪən, *US* ˌmʌnɪterɪ; ikənɑmɪk ənd ˌmʌnɪtɛrɪ ˈjunjən/ *n* (*abbr* 缩写 **EMU**) (of the European Union) programme to achieve full economic unity in the EU, including use of the EURO as the common currency（指欧洲联盟）经济和货币联盟（充分实现经济一体化的计划，包括使用欧元作为统一货币）：*make progress towards EMU* 向实现经济和货币联盟迈进 Cf 参看 EUROPEAN MONETARY SYSTEM

Economy Class Syndrome /iːˌkɒnəmɪ klɑːs ˈsɪndrəʊm, *US* klæs; iˌkɑnəmɪ klæs ˈsɪndrom/ *n* [U] (*infml* 口) tendency to form blood clots in the veins which has been observed in air passengers in the more cramped section of the aircraft who have little leg-room or chance to move around during a long flight 经济舱综合征（长途飞行中二等舱乘客因空间狭窄无法活动而导致血栓形成的倾向）

ecotourism /ˌiːkəʊˈtʊərɪzm; ˌikoˈtʊrɪzəm/ *n* [U] tourism focusing on wilderness and unspoilt areas, esp tourism intended to support conservation efforts by bringing in financial resources 生态旅游（到旷野和未受破坏的自然环境去的旅游，尤指旨在为环保筹措资金）：*Ecotourism to the home of the last great gorillas brings in the money needed to conserve their habitat.* 探访濒临绝种的大猩猩栖息地这种生态旅游可为保护它们的生活环境提供了经济来源。

▷ **ecotourist** *n*

ecstasy /ˈekstəsɪ; ˈɛkstəsɪ/ (also **Ecstasy**) *n* [U] (*infml* 口) illegal drug used esp by young people at raves (RAVE) to give energy and a sense of well-being 极乐迷幻药（尤指年轻人在电子乐狂舞会上吸服的迷幻药）

edutainment /ˌedjʊˈteɪnmənt; ˌɛdʒʊˈtenmənt/ *n* [U] printed or otherwise publicly available material intended to entertain as well as to educate and inform, esp applied to MULTIMEDIA materials（集娱乐、教育与提供信息于一体的公开发行的）教育娱乐资料（尤指多媒体资料）

effing and blinding /ˌefɪŋ ənd ˈblaɪndɪŋ; ˌɛfɪŋ ənd ˈblaɪndɪŋ/ *n* [U] (*infml* 口) using very rude words; swearing 使用不堪入耳的字眼；咒骂：*There he stood effing and blinding on live television.* 他在电视直播节目中站着大骂粗言秽语。

NOTE 注： *effing* means saying the 'f' word ie *fuck* ☆ effing 指说 fuck（他妈的）这个词

E-fit /ˈiːfɪt; ˈifɪt/ *abbr* 缩写 = Electronic Facial Identification Technique (method of building up a picture of sb, esp a SUSPECT *n*[A-Z], on the computer screen using stored images of facial parts) 面部特征电子鉴别术（利用储存于计算机的面部特征在荧屏上合成头像，尤其是嫌疑犯的头像的技术）Cf 参看 VIDEOFIT

egg donation /eg dəʊˈneɪʃn; ɛg doˈneʃən/ *n* [U] (in fertility treatment) process by which a human egg from a donor is fertilized and implanted into another woman's uterus 卵捐赠（使捐赠者的卵子受精后植入另一位妇女的子宫的过程）：*Egg donation now allows women to bear a child even after the menopause.* 卵捐赠这技术现在容许妇女在绝经后才生孩子。

egg freezing /eg ˈfriːzɪŋ; ɛg ˈfrizɪŋ/ *n* [U] experimental technique by which human eggs are extracted and frozen for later implantation into the uterus of the donor 卵冷冻（将人类卵子取出冷冻保存，供日后植入捐赠者的子宫的试验性技术）：*The doctors advised her to try egg freezing when she had to undergo radiation treatment which could leave her sterile.* 医生建议她进

行卵冷冻，因为她不得不进行放射性治疗，而这可能会导致不育。

EKG *abbr* 缩写 (*US*) = ECG[A-Z]

elder abuse /ˈeldə əˌbju:s; ˈɛldɚ əˌbjus/ *n* [U] maltreatment of an elderly person, esp such a person in one's care 虐待老人（尤指对其照料的老人）

electrics /ɪˈlektrɪks; ɪˈlɛktrɪks/ *n* [pl] (*infml* 口) system of electrical wires and components in a machine, car, house, etc（机器、汽车、房屋等内的）电线系统及组件：*Don't mess with the electrics unless you really know what you are doing.* 别瞎弄那些电线玩意儿，除非你确实知道该怎么做。

electrifying /ɪˈlektrɪfaɪɪŋ; ɪˈlɛktrɪfaɪɪŋ/ *adj* (*fig* 比喻) very exciting 让人激动的；使人兴奋不已的：*She gave an electrifying performance.* 她的表演慑人心魄。

electronic banking /ɪlekˌtrɒnɪk ˈbæŋkɪŋ(r); ɪlɛkˌtrɑnɪk ˈbæŋkɪŋ/ *n* [U] (*finance* 财) provision of banking and financial services, esp running a bank account, through computer and other communications links 电子银行业务（尤指通过计算机和其他通讯渠道提供的银行和金融服务）

Electronic Facial Identification Technique *n* = E-FIT

electronic publishing /ɪlekˌtrɒnɪk ˈpʌblɪʃɪŋ; ɪlɛkˌtrɑnɪk ˈpʌblɪʃɪŋ/ *n* [U] publishing of a text in a form which can only be read by a machine (ie a computer) and is displayed on a screen, not printed on paper 电子出版（只可用机器（如计算机）阅读的出版方式）

▷ **electronic publication** *n* [U,C]

electronic road pricing /ɪlekˌtrɒnɪk ˈrəʊd praɪsɪŋ; ɪlɛkˌtrɑnɪk ˈrod praɪsɪŋ/ *n* [U] similar to ELECTRONIC TOLLING but with the specific aim of reducing traffic on certain roads at certain times 电子道路收费（与electronic tolling（道路通行电子收费）相似，但其目的是为缓解某些道路在某些时间的交通阻塞现象）

electronic shopping /ɪlekˌtrɒnɪk ˈʃɒpɪŋ; ɪlɛkˌtrɑnɪk ˈʃɑpɪŋ/ *n* [U] making of purchases through services provided by the electronic media, esp cable television and the Internet 电子购物（通过电子媒体尤指有线电视和互联网服务购物）Cf 参看 HOME SHOPPING

electronic tagging /ɪlekˌtrɒnɪk ˈtægɪŋ; ɪlɛkˌtrɑnɪk ˈtægɪŋ/ *n* [U] action or process of attaching an electronic tag to a person or thing for the purpose of monitoring or SURVEILLANCE[A-Z] 电子标签监控（将电子标签附着于某人或某物处用以监控或监视）

electronic text /ɪlekˌtrɒnɪk ˈtekst; ɪlɛkˌtrɑnɪk ˈtɛkst/ *n* (*abbr* 缩写 **e-text**) machine-readable version of a text previously written or printed, usu tagged（TAG[2]）with formatting instructions for display or printing 电子文本（将书写或印刷文本换成的计算机可读文本，通常标有格式指令供显示或打印）

electronic tolling /ɪlekˌtrɒnɪk ˈtɒlɪŋ; ɪlɛkˌtrɑnɪk ˈtɑlɪŋ/ *n* [U] system of charging for road use by installing electronic devices at certain points on roads which detect and identify a vehicle 道路通行电子收费（在道路上安装电子装置来探测和识别车辆以收取通行费的系统）Cf 参看 ELECTRONIC ROAD PRICING

electronic transfer /ɪlekˌtrɒnɪk ˈtrænsfɜ:(r); ɪlɛkˌtrɑnɪk ˈtrænsfɝ/ *n* (*finance* 财) direct transfer of funds from one bank account to another by means of computers and communications links 电子转帐（通过计算机及其通讯途径将资金从一帐户直接转入另一帐户）

elementary school /ˌelɪˈmentrɪ sku:l; ˌɛləˈmɛntərɪ skul/ *n* (*US*) school where elementary subjects, eg reading and writing, are taught to pupils between the ages of six and eleven 小学（教授基础课程如读、写等，学生年龄在六至十一岁之间）Cf 参看 PRIMARY SCHOOL（PRIMARY[A-Z]）

El Nino /el ˈni:njəʊ; el ˈninjo/ (also **El Ni, El Nino Current**) *n* [sing] phenomenon in which there is a reversal of certain winds and ocean currents in the eastern part of the South Pacific ocean which results in the upwelling of abnormally warm water. The phenomenon occurs at irregular intervals and causes unusual and often destructive weather patterns around the world, eg heavier or lighter rainfall, more hurricanes, etc 厄尔尼诺现象（南太平洋东部海域风向和海流逆转导致异常暖和的海水上涌。这种现象不定期发生，导致全球出现常具破坏性的异常气候，如降雨量增加或减少、飓风更加频繁等）

NOTE 注： the name comes from Spanish and means 'the child', since the phenomenon is usually first detected at Christmas time, when the birth of Christ is celebrated 其名称源自西班牙语，意为'圣婴'，因为每每早在圣诞节时就发生此现象 Cf 参看 LA NINA

e-mail /ˈi:meɪl; ˈimel/ (also **email**) *n* [U,C] message sent from one computer user to another via an electronic network; messages of this kind 电邮；电子邮件：*I've already had three long e-mails from her.* 我已经收到她三封长长的电子邮件。

▷ **e-mail** (also **email**) *v* send e-mail to (sb) 给（某人）发电子邮件：*E-mail me as soon as possible.* 尽快给我发电子邮件。

embryo adoption /ˌembrɪəʊ əˈdɒpʃn; ˌɛmbrɪo əˈdɑpʃən/ *n* [U, C] process by which a non-genetically related embryo is implanted in the uterus of a woman who intends to become the adoptive mother of the child when it is born 胚胎收养（妇女在其子宫内植入与自己无遗传关系的胚胎，分娩后收养婴儿）

Emerald Isle /ˌemərəld ˈaɪl; ˌɛmərəld ˈaɪl/ *n* **the Emerald Isle** [sing] (*rhet* 修辞) Ireland 翡翠岛；爱尔兰：*He comes from the Emerald Isle.* 他来自翡翠岛。

NOTE 注： the name has been used because of the greenness of the countryside owing to the plentiful rainfall 爱尔兰乡村因雨水充足而一片翠绿，故名

emotional abuse /ɪˌməʊʃənl əˈbju:s; ɪˌmoʃənl̩ əˈbjus/ *n* [U] mistreatment by means of pressure on a person's emotions rather than on their physical state 精神虐待；精神折磨：*Her old mother's constant appeal to her daughter's sense of gratitude amounted to emotional abuse.* 她年迈的母亲不断提醒她要感激养育之恩，这简直是对她的精神折磨。

Emotional Quotient /ɪˌməʊʃənl ˈkwəʊʃənt; ɪˌmoʃənl̩ ˈkwoʃənt/ *n* [sing] (*abbr* 缩写 **EQ**) measure of sb's social and emotional capability as established by standard tests 情商，情绪智商（通过标准测试测出某人的交际及处理情感方面的能力）：*A person's Emotional Quotient is considered to be as important as their IQ by many employers.* 很多雇主认为一个人的情商和他的智商一样重要。Cf 参看 IQ[A-Z]

empathize, -ise /ˈempəθaɪz; ˈɛmpəθaɪz/ *v* [Ipr] ~ **(with sb/sth)** imagine accurately and share the feelings or experience of another person（对他人的情感或经历）产生同感，产生共鸣：*It's clear that the writer has empathized with his subject using all his fertile imagination.* 显然，作者发挥了自己全部丰富的想像力，对其笔下的人物产生了共鸣。Cf 参看 SYMPATHIZE, -ISE（SYMPATHY[A-Z]）

empower /ɪmˈpaʊə(r), emˈpaʊə(r); ɪmˈpaʊɚ/ *v* [Tn] give a previously subordinated or powerless group or individual the means to assert and help themselves 授权；给予力量：*The regulation requiring all government buildings to provide access for wheelchair users certainly helps to empower this group of people.* 要求所有政府大楼提供轮椅通道的规定无疑提高了坐轮椅者的活动能力。

▷ **empowerment** *n*

empty nest syndrome /emptɪ 'nest ˌsɪndrəʊm; ɛmptɪ 'nɛst ˌsɪndrom/ *n* [U] emotional and psychological state of a couple after their children have grown up and left home, esp feelings of uselessness, difficulty in passing time, or failure to adapt to the changed circumstances 空巢综合征（子女长大离家后父母的心境，尤指感到窝囊、无从打发时间或不适应新环境）: *She lived for her children and now she's suffering badly from empty nest syndrome.* 她一直为她的孩子们而活，现在她备受空巢综合徵的折磨。

EMS *abbr* 缩写 = EUROPEAN MONETARY SYSTEM

EMU *abbr* 缩写 = ECONOMIC AND MONETARY UNION

encash /ɪn'kæʃ; ɪn'kæʃ/ *v* (*fml finance* 文，财) obtain money in return for a cheque, credit note, etc 兑现（支票、贷方票据等）: *Banks may make a small charge for encashing cheques drawn on other banks.* 兑现其他银行的支票，银行可能收取小额费用。

encephalopathy /enˌsefə'lɒpəθɪ, enˌkef-; ɛnˌsɛfə-'lɑpəθɪ/ *n* disease of the brain 脑病

encryption /en'krɪpʃn; ɛn'krɪpʃən/ *n* [U] (*computing* 计) process of encoding data stored in a computer's memory, usu by means of an ALGORITHM[A-Z], so that a DECRYPTION program is required to make it readable again 加编密码，加密（通常通过加密算法将储存在计算机记忆体中的数据加密，以至需运行解密程序才能再读数据）

endowment mortgage /ɪn'daʊmənt mɔ:gɪdʒ; ɪn'daumənt mɔrgɪdʒ/ *n* (*finance* 财) type of MORTGAGE[A-Z] which demands regular payments into an ENDOWMENT POLICY (ENDOW[A-Z]) from which the loan is paid back on a specified date using the money that has accumulated 储蓄保险抵押贷款（定期缴纳保险金，在规定日期用所积累的钱偿还借款的一种抵押贷款）

end result /ˌend rɪ'zʌlt; ˌɛnd rɪ'zʌlt/ *n* [sing] final outcome 最终结果: *We missed the last bus and we hadn't got enough money to get a taxi, so the end result was that we walked home.* 我们没赶上最后一班公共汽车，带的钱又不够坐出租汽车，所以最后只能走回家了。

NOTE 注： a slightly more emphatic way of expressing *the result* 比 the result（结果）一词的语气略微强调些

energy audit /'enədʒɪ ˌɔ:dɪt; 'ɛnədʒɪ ˌɔdɪt/ *n* systematic review of the energy use and needs of a building with a view to improving efficiency 能源使用审计（对建筑物使用和需求能源的情况作全面审核，以提高使用效率）

NOTE 注： a compound formed with *audit* (a review of financial transactions) 由 audit（审查帐目）一词构成的复合词

-engined /'endʒɪnd; 'ɛndʒɪnd/ *comb form* 构词成分 with the specified type or number of engines 使用某类型发动机的；有特定数量的发动机的: *a twin-engined speedboat* 一艘双引擎快艇 ○ *a diesel-engined lorry* 一辆柴油机卡车

entry level /'entrɪ levl; 'ɛntrɪ lɛvl/ *n* [usu attrib 通常作定语] (esp of computers) level of difficulty which is suitable for beginners（尤指计算机）入门水平，初级: *entry-level software/systems* 初级软件 *[系统]* ○ *the need for more hardware at the entry level* 对更多初级硬件的需求

environmental psychology /ɪnˌvaɪərənˌmentl saɪ'kɒlədʒɪ; ɪnˌvaɪrənˌmɛntl saɪ'kɑlədʒɪ/ *n* [U] study of how sb's environment affects him or her mentally and of the mental image he or she has constructed of the environment 环境心理学（研究环境如何影响人的心理以及环境在人的心理上构成的形象）

epigraph /'epɪgrɑ:f, *US* -græf; 'ɛpɪgræf/ *n* (**a**) line or lines of writing, esp inscribed, on a statue, building, etc（尤指塑像、建筑物等上的）刻文，铭文 (**b**) short phrase at the beginning of a book or part of a book（卷首或章节前的）短语

EPROM /'i:prɒm; 'iprɑm/ *abbr* 缩写 = (*computing* 计) erasable programmable ROM (read only memory whose contents can be erased and replaced by a special process) 可擦除可编程序只读存储器

EQ *abbr* 缩写 = EMOTIONAL QUOTIENT

equal opportunities legislation /i:kwəl ɒpə'tju:nətiːz ledʒɪsˌleɪʃn, *US* -tu:-; ikwəl ɑpɚ'tunətɪz lɛdʒɪsˌleʃən/ *n* [U] laws establishing the equal rights of all people to employment, to education, etc irrespective of race, gender, religion, sexual orientation, etc 均等机会法规（规定不分种族、性别、宗教、性取向等，所有的人在就业、受教育等方面均享有均等机会的法例）

er /ɜ:(r); ɝ/ *interj* (in writing, used to express the sound made when one hesitates during a conversation 在书面语中用来表达谈话中犹豫、沉吟的声音): *'Are you going?' 'Er, yes, I suppose I'll have to.'* '你要走了吗？' '嗯，是的，我想我得走了。'

ERM *abbr* 缩写 = EXCHANGE RATE MECHANISM

erstwhile /'ɜ:stwaɪl, *US* -hw-; 'ɝstˌhwaɪl/ *adj* [attrib 作定语] (*fml* 文) former 以前的；原先的: *His erstwhile friends turned against him.* 他原先的朋友与他反目了。

escape key /ɪ'skeɪp ki:; ɪ'skep ki/ *n* (*computing* 计) the key on the computer keyboard which allows the user to cancel and so escape from the current operation（计算机键盘上的）退出键，换码键，转义键: *Hit the escape key to quit the game and return to the main menu.* 按退出键结束游戏，回到主菜单。

Estuary English /ˌestjʊərɪ 'ɪŋglɪʃ, *US* ˌestʃʊerɪ; ˌɛstʃʊɛrɪ 'ɪŋglɪʃ/ *n* [U] kind of British English accent typical of South London and the south-east of England, esp the area of the Thames estuary 河口英语腔（伦敦南部和英格兰东南部，尤指泰晤士河河口地区的英语口音）

NOTE 注： an accent popular with younger people in the area because it avoids sounding too upper class or working class 该地区的年轻人爱操此口音，因可避免上层社会人士的矫揉腔调，亦不过于像工人阶级

e-text *abbr* 缩写 = ELECTRONIC TEXT

ethanol /'eθənɒl; 'ɛθənɑl/ (also **ethyl alcohol**) *n* [U] chemical used as the base of alcoholic drinks, and also as a fuel or solvent 乙醇（用以制含酒精饮料的化学品，也用作燃料或溶剂）

ethical investment /ˌeθɪkl ɪn'vestmənt; ˌɛθɪkl ɪn'vɛstmənt/ *n* [U,C] (*finance* 财) investment made only in companies which meet the moral standards and conscience of the investor 合乎道德的投资（投资者仅对符合其道德和良心准则的公司作出的投资）: *Some people wouldn't consider tobacco shares an ethical investment.* 一些人不认为购买烟草公司的股票是合乎道德的投资。

ethnic cleansing /ˌeθnɪk 'klenzɪŋ; ˌɛθnɪk 'klɛnzɪŋ/ *n* [U] removal of a particular ethnic or religious group by means of forced migration or murder 族群清洗（以强迫迁移或杀害来清除某一种族或宗教集团）: *Ethnic cleansing during the fighting in the former Yugoslavia shocked the world.* 前南斯拉夫在冲突中发生的种族清洗行为震惊了整个世界。

ethnocentric /ˌeθnəʊ'sentrɪk; ɛθno'sɛntrɪk/ *adj* using the standards and norms in one's own culture and ethnic group when making judgements about another 种族中心主义的（用自己的文化和种族的标准及常规来衡量别的文化和种族）

▷ **ethnocentricity** *n*: *The comments of the reporter showed an ignorant ethnocentricity.* 该记者的评论显示出愚昧的种族中心主义。

EU *abbr* 缩写 = EUROPEAN UNION

euro /ˈjʊərəʊ; ˈjʊro/ (also **Euro**) *n* (*symb* 符号为 €) name agreed on by members of the EUROPEAN UNION for the European common currency unit which will replace the national currencies of all participating countries as soon as MONETARY UNION is complete 欧元（欧盟各成员国一致通过，俟欧洲货币联盟运行后即取代各成员国货币的统一货币的名称）

Euro-election /ˈjʊərəʊɪˌlekʃn; ˈjʊroɪˌlɛkʃən/ *n* election of Members of the European Parliament 欧洲议会选举

Euro-MP /ˈjʊərəʊempi:; ˈjʊroɛmpi/ (also **MEP**) *abbr* 缩写 = Member of the European Parliament 欧洲议会议员

Europe /ˈjʊərəp; ˈjʊrəp/ *n* [U] **1** continent bounded by Asia in the east, the Atlantic ocean in the west and the Mediterranean sea in the south 欧洲 **2** (*Brit*) all Europe except Britain（除英国之外的）欧洲大陆：*British holidaymakers in Europe* 到欧洲大陆度假的英国人 **3** the European Union 欧洲联盟

European Monetary System /ˌjʊərəpɪən ˈmʌnɪtrɪ sɪstəm, *US* ˈmʌnəterɪ; ˌjʊrəpɪən ˈmʌnətɛrɪ sɪstəm/ *n* (*abbr* 缩写 **EMS**) (*finance* 财) financial arrangement by which the currencies of some EU countries are linked to the ECU 欧洲货币体系（旨在使某些欧盟成员国的货币与欧洲货币单位挂钩的金融体系）

European Union /jʊərəˌpɪən ˈju:njən; jʊrəˌpɪən ˈjunjən/ *n* [U] federation of European states established in 1992, all of whose members also comprise the EUROPEAN ECONOMIC COMMUNITY (EUROPEAN[A-Z]) 欧洲联盟（1992 年成立的欧洲国家联盟，所有成员亦是欧洲经济共同体的成员国）

Europhile /ˈjʊərəʊfaɪl, ˈjʊərə-; ˈjʊrofaɪl/ *n* (**a**) person who is in favour of Europe and everything European 亲欧洲的人 (**b**) person who supports closer political, financial and economic links between his or her own country and the rest of Europe; supporter of a federal Europe 支持其国家与欧洲其他各国建立更紧密的政治、金融和经济联系的人；欧洲联盟支持者

Europhobe /ˈjʊərəʊfəʊb, ˈjʊərə-; ˈjʊrofob/ *n* (esp in Britain) person who is against closer links between Britain and the rest of Europe, esp the formation of a federal Europe, considering that this threatens British sovereignty（尤指在英国）反对欧洲联合者，欧洲联盟反对者（反对英国与欧洲其他国家建立更紧密的联系，尤其反对建立欧洲联盟，认为这会危及英国主权的人）

Euro-sceptic /ˈjʊərəʊˌskeptɪk, ˌjʊərəʊˈskeptɪk; ˈjʊroˌskɛptɪk/ *n* (*Brit*) person who doubts the benefits, esp to Britain, of Britain's closer integration with Europe, particularly if this means a large increase in the power of the European Union 欧洲统一怀疑论者（在英国与欧洲大陆更紧密的联系中，尤指对英国，能否获益持怀疑论者，尤为怀疑欧盟势力因而扩大）：*Although a well-known Euro-sceptic, the Minister gave public backing to his party's pro-Europe policy.* 虽然众所周知部长是欧洲统一怀疑论者，但他却公开拥护党内欧洲联合的政策。Cf 参看 EUROPHOBE

Eurostar /ˈjʊərəʊstɑ:(r); ˈjʊrostɑr/ *n* [sing] (*propr* 专利名) name of the rail service and the trains that run between Paris, London and Brussels via the CHANNEL TUNNEL 欧洲之星（通过海峡隧道连接巴黎、伦敦和布鲁塞尔的铁路运轮系统及火车名）Cf 参看 LE SHUTTLE

evening class /ˈi:vnɪŋ klɑ:s, *US* klæs; ˈivnɪŋ klæs/ *n* lesson for adults held at a school, college, etc in the evening（供成人就读的）夜校课程：*I'm going to evening classes in legal English.* 我将去夜校学习法律英语。Cf 参看 NIGHT-SCHOOL (NIGHT[A-Z])

evening primrose oil /ˌi:vnɪŋ ˈprɪmrəʊz ɔɪl; ˌivnɪŋ ˈprɪmroz ɔɪl/ *n* [U] oil extracted from a plant with yellow flowers which open in the evening, and is used for both medicinal and cosmetic purposes 月见草油（从月见草中提取的油，可作药用和化妆用）：*evening primrose oil capsules* 月见草油胶囊

evenings /ˈi:vnɪŋz; ˈivnɪŋz/ *adv* (*esp US*) in the evenings; every evening 在晚上；每晚：*She works evenings.* 她上夜班。

Exchange-Rate Mechanism /ɪksˌtʃeɪndʒ reɪt ˈmekənɪzəm; ɪksˌtʃendʒ ret ˈmɛkənɪzəm/ *n* (*abbr* 缩写 **ERM**) (*finance* 财) means by which the currency of a member country in the EU can be linked to the European Currency Unit 汇率机制（使欧盟成员国的货币与欧洲货币单位挂钩的方法）Cf 参看 EUROPEAN MONETARY SYSTEM

exclude /ɪkˈsklu:d; ɪkˈsklud/ *v* [Tn] expel a child from school for bad behaviour 开除（行为不端的学生）：*The number of children being excluded in the area is getting out of hand.* 该地区学生被开除的现象已到了无法控制的地步。

▷ **exclusion** *n* : *Exclusion is really no answer to the problem of children with behaviour problems.* 迫令行为不端的儿童离校并不能解决问题。

executive /ɪgˈzekjətɪv; ɪgˈzɛkjutɪv/ *adj* [attrib 作定语] of the highest quality; the most luxurious 最高级的；最豪华的：*executive suite* 特级豪华套房 ○ *executive town houses* 最豪华的城市住宅

executive flu *n* = MYALGIC ENCEPHALOMYELITIS

exemplar /ɪgˈzemplɑ:(r), *US* -plər; ɪgˈzɛmplɚ/ *n* (*fml* 文) person or thing that serves as a typical or good example; model 榜样；楷模；典型：*an exemplar of how a film can reflect social concerns* 一部展现电影如何反映社会关注的问题的典范作品

exodus /ˈeksədəs; ˈɛksədəs/ *n* (*fig* 比喻) (in finance) sudden and widespread selling of a currency or stock in favour of some other investment（金融）急速而广泛地抛售某一货币或股票（以便投资他处）：*The exodus from the yen continues.* 抛售日元的行动还在继续。

exotica /ɪgˈzɒtɪkə; ɪgˈzɑtɪkə/ *n* [pl] strange or rare objects 新奇事物；稀罕物：*a shop selling exotica from around the world* 出售世界各地奇珍异宝、特色产品的商店

expansion slot /ɪkˈspænʃn slɒt, ek-; ɪkˈspænʃən slɑt/ (also **slot**) *n* (*computing* 计) socket in a personal computer or WORKSTATION into which an additional electronic circuit board may be plugged to add to the capabilities of the system 扩展槽（微机或工作站上的插槽，可插入另一电路板以增强系统的性能）

expert system /ˌekspɜ:t ˈsɪstəm; ˌɛkspɝt ˈsɪstəm/ *n* (*computing* 计) software which supplies very extensive information and responds to questions on a particular subject area 专家系统（就某一特定领域提供十分详尽的信息并回答问题的软件）：*a medical expert system* 医学专家系统

extension lead /ɪksˈtenʃn li:d; ɪksˈtɛnʃən lid/ (also **power bar**) *n* electrical cable with a plug at one end that fits into the wall and a socket or set of sockets at the other into which appliances can be connected if their cables are too short to reach to the wall socket 延长电线，接线板（一端有一插头另一端有一个或一组插座的电线）

extraordinaire /ɪkˌstrɔ:dɪˈneə(r); ɪkˌstrɔrdɪnɛr/ *adj* (*French often joc* 法，常作戏谑语) (after ns 用于名词后) outstanding; remarkable 了不得的；非凡的：*a pianist extraordinaire* 技艺非凡的钢琴家 ○ *the hotel's chef extraordinaire, Monsieur De Bercy* 酒店了不起的大厨，德贝尔西先生

extreme /ɪkˈstri:m; ɪkˈstrim/ *adj* (of sports, eg BUNGEE JUMPING and SNOWBOARDING) risky, demanding more than usual physical strength and nerve（指如蹦极跳、滑板滑雪等运动）危险的、需要超乎寻常的体力与胆量的；极限的：*He is an extreme skier.* 他是个极限滑雪运动员。○ *extreme sports* 极限运动

eyeball /'aɪbɔːl; 'aɪbɔl/ *v* [Tn] (*infml* 口) have visual contact with sth/sb; observe 与（某物 *[某人]*）目光相接触；观察；仔细打量：*Pilots prefer to eyeball the peaks and valleys rather than watch the altimeter.* 飞行员宁可注视山峰和峡谷也不愿留意高度计。

eyephone /'aɪfəʊn; 'aɪfon/ *n* (usu *sing* 通常作单数) headset consisting of two small television screens used to experience the full effects of a VIRTUAL REALITY (VIRTUAL) environment and which provides stereoscopic visual images and synchronized sound 视像耳机（头戴式的有一对微型电视屏幕的耳机，可充分感受虚拟现实环境的效果，并提供立体影像和同步音响）

NOTE 注： formed on analogy with *earphone* 由 earphone（耳机）一词类推构成

eyeprint /'aɪprɪnt; 'aɪprɪnt/ *n* measurement and record of the unique pattern of blood veins in sb's RETINA A-Z, used for identification purposes 眼印（检测和记录人的视网膜内独特的静脉分布构图，用作身分鉴定）：*Entry to the laboratory was gained if one's eyeprint was recognized by the computer.* 能被计算机认得眼印的人就能进入实验室。

NOTE 注： formed on analogy with *fingerprint* and *voiceprint* 由 fingerprint（指纹）和 voiceprint（声纹；声印）等词类推构成

Ff

face-off /'feɪsɒf, *US* -ɔːf; 'fesɔf/ *n* direct challenge, confrontation or debate 对抗；正面交锋：*It's a face-off between the two top clubs for football's most coveted prize.* 这是两家顶级足球队为争夺足球界最令人垂涎的奖项而展开的激烈对抗。

facilitator /fə'sɪlɪteɪtə(r); fə'sɪlətetə/ *n* person or thing that allows sth to happen more easily and efficiently 使某事顺利进行的人或物；提高效率的人或物：*The teacher acts as a facilitator of learning.* 教师的作用是帮助学生学习。

factory shop /'fæktərɪ ʃɒp; 'fæktrɪ ʃɑp/ (also **factory outlet**) *n* shop on or near the factory premises where the public may buy goods directly from the manufacturers at discounted prices 工厂直销店（在工厂内或附近开设的商店，顾客可以折扣价直接从制造商手中购买商品）

fact-sheet /'fæktʃiːt; 'fæktʃit/ *n* piece of paper giving information about a topic, esp one which has been discussed on a television or radio programme 专题介绍单，单张资料（有关某话题，尤其是已在电视或广播节目中讨论过的话题的单张）：*Send for the fact-sheet for further details.* 欲知详情，有专题介绍单供来函备索。

fagged /fægd; fægd/ (also **fagged out**) *adj* (*Brit infml* 口) very tired 精疲力尽的；疲惫不堪的：*The children went to bed early. They were fagged (out) after the birthday party.* 孩子们很早就睡了，生日宴会使他们累极了。○ *I can't be fagged to go to the shops again,* ie too tired to go. 我累坏了，不能再去购物了。

fairy cake /'feərɪ keɪk; 'fɛrɪ kek/ *n* (*Brit*) small soft light cake for one person, usu iced (ICE² 2A-Z) 小精灵蛋糕（小而松软、通常有糖衣的蛋糕，供一人食用）

false colour /fɔːls 'kʌlə(r), fɒls; fɔls 'kʌlə/ *n* colour used during the production of an image to make it clearer and to aid interpretation, but which is not actually present in the viewed object, eg a brain, which has been photographed or scanned electronically 伪色（实际并不存在的颜色，但在成像时可使图像更为清晰、更便于诠释，如拍摄或扫瞄的脑电图）：*False colour makes the picture clear; for example, blue is used to allow us to pick out the areas in the brain which are cooler.* 伪色使图像清晰明了，比如蓝色可以让我们分辨出大脑中温度较低的区域。

false memory syndrome /fɔːls 'memərɪ ˌsɪndrəʊm; fɔls 'mɛmərɪ ˌsɪndrom/ *n* [U] (*psychology* 心) apparent memory, recovered under psychological therapy, of childhood sexual abuse, esp by a close relative, which in fact did not take place 虚妄记忆综合征（心理治疗过程中恢复的虚妄记忆，尤指关于童年受到亲人性虐待却并不真有其事的记忆）：*The accusations she made against her father were an instance of false memory syndrome, and she blamed her therapist for encouraging her to think they were true.* 她对其父多次提出指控，这表明她患有虚妄记忆综合征，而她却指责心理治疗师促使她认为这些指控的内容都是事实。Cf 参看 RECOVERED MEMORY

familial /fə'mɪlɪəl; fə'mɪljəl/ *adj* [attrib 作定语] (*fml* 文) occurring in or characteristic of a family 家庭的；家庭特有的：*familial problems* 家庭问题 ○ *a secure familial setting* 无忧无虑的家庭环境

family credit /ˌfæməlɪ 'kredɪt; ˌfæmlɪ 'krɛdɪt/ *n* [U] (in Britain) regular payment made by the government to a family with an income below an established level（英国）家庭津贴（政府定期付给收入低于一定水平的家庭的款项）

famously /'feɪməslɪ; 'feməslɪ/ *adv* in a way that is known to many people; notably 公开地；引人注目地：*Oscar Wilde once famously said that he could resist anything except temptation.* 奥斯卡·王尔德曾语出惊人地说道，他能抗拒任何事物，唯独无法抗拒诱惑。

fandom /'fændəm; 'fændəm/ *n* [U] world of fans and enthusiasts, esp of fans of science fiction magazines and films（尤指科幻小说杂志和电影的）狂热爱好者（总称）；科幻迷（总称）：*Fandom will flock to the great Star Trek Convention to be held at Atlanta this year.* 星球旅行大会将于今年在亚特兰大举行，届时大批科幻爱好者将蜂拥而至。

fantasy football /fæntəsɪ 'fʊtbɔːl; ˌfæntəsɪ 'fʊtbɔl/ *n* [U] competition in which participants pick imaginary teams from among the players in a league, etc and then score points according to the actual performance of the players they have chosen 虚拟足球（一种想像的足球赛，参与者从参加联赛的球队中挑选球员组成想像中的球队，根据所选球员的实际表现计分）

NOTE 注： also *fantasy cricket* etc 也有 fantasy cricket（虚拟板球赛）等

fanzine /'fænziːn; 'fænzin/ *n* magazine devoted to the interests of a group of fans (FAN3(A-Z)) 爱好者杂志：*a fanzine for basketball enthusiasts* 为篮球迷办的杂志 ○ *a pop music fanzine* 流行音乐爱好者杂志

farm /fɑːm; fɑrm/ *n* (idm 习语) **buy the farm** (*US euph* 婉) die 去世：*I haven't bought the farm yet. I'm still here.* 我还没死，我还在这里来着。

fartlek /'fɑːtlek; 'fɑrtlɛk/ *n* (*sport* 体) method of training for middle- and long-distance running, in which the athlete runs over country, mixing fast work with slow work 中长跑训练法，法特莱克训练法（快慢跑交替的越野训练）

NOTE 注： from a Swedish word blending *fart* (speed) and *lek* (play) 源自瑞典语，由 fart（速度）与 lek（运动）二词合成

fashion-conscious /'fæʃnkɒnʃəs; 'fæʃənkɑnʃəs/ *adj* aware of the latest styles in clothes, hair and accessories and keen to follow them 讲究时髦的；赶时髦的：*my fashion-conscious teenage daughters* 我的十多岁的讲究时髦的女儿们

fashion victim /'fæʃn vɪktɪm; 'fæʃən vɪktɪm/ *n* (*derog* 贬) person who is desperate to keep up with fashion and has to be seen in the latest styles, however expensive or uncomfortable these are 不惜代价赶时髦者；为时尚所累者；潮流受害者

fast breeder /ˌfɑːst ˈbriːdə(r), *US* fæst; ˌfæst ˈbridɚ/ (also **fast breeder reactor**) *n* (*physics* 物) nuclear REACTOR I A-Z which can produce its own fuel automatically when reaction is started 快中子增殖反应堆（反应开始后能自动制造燃料的核子反应堆）

fast track /ˈfɑːst træk, *US* fæst; ˈfæst træk/ (also **fast-track**) *n* the quickest route to one's goals, esp in one's career 快速成功之道；捷径：*He's on the fast track to a directorship.* 他平步青云当了董事。○ [attrib 作定语] *the pressures of fast track promotions* 快速提升的压力

Father's Day /ˈfɑːðəz deɪ; ˈfɑðɚz de/ *n* day when by tradition fathers receive gifts and cards from their children. It is usu the third Sunday in June 父亲节（按惯例孩子们送礼物和贺卡给父亲的节日，通常在六月的第三个星期日）

fat transfer /ˈfæt trænsfɜː(r); ˈfæt trænsfɝ/ *n* surgical process done for cosmetic reasons that removes fat from some parts of the body, eg thighs, using suction techniques and injects it into some other parts of the body, eg face, to restore smoothness and get rid of wrinkles 脂肪移植（利用真空抽吸法从大腿等处吸出脂肪，然后注射入脸部等其他部位以使其表面恢复光滑、去除皱纹的整容外科手术）Cf 参看 LIPOSUCTION

fattyism /ˈfætɪˌɪzəm; ˈfætɪˌɪzəm/ *n* [U] discrimination against people whom one considers fat 对胖人的歧视：*She accused the interviewers of fattyism when she didn't get the job.* 她因未能得到工作而指责面试者歧视胖人。Cf 参看 SIZIST

fatwa /ˈfætwɑː, ˈfɑːtwɑː; ˈfætwɑ/ *n* legal ruling given by an Islamic religious leader（伊斯兰宗教领袖颁布的）法令，裁决：*The fatwa issued against the writer is no longer in force.* 伊斯兰宗教领袖对该作家的裁决已无效。

NOTE 注： best known outside Islamic countries for the 1989 fatwa issued by Ayatollah Khomeini, now withdrawn, which pronounced death against the British writer, Salman Rushdie, for material in a novel he had written 此词为伊斯兰国家之外的人所熟知，乃由于 1989 年伊朗宗教领袖霍梅尼 (Ayatolah Khomeini) 因英国作家拉什迪 (Salman Rushdie) 的一本小说的内容而判他死刑，此判刑现已废除

faux /fəʊ; fo/ *adj* (*esp US*) imitation, not genuine 仿造的；假的：*faux leather* 人造革 ○ *a faux oriental carpet* 假冒的东方地毯

NOTE 注： from the French word meaning 'false' 源自法语，意为'假的'

fax-on-demand /ˌfæksɒndɪˈmɑːnd, *US* -mænd; ˌfæksɑndɪˈmænd/ *n* [U] system allowing callers to dial a communications network and use telephone TONE DIALLING signals to transmit faxes to their own fax machine 即时传真（让用户可拨通通讯网络并使用电话的音频拨号信号通过自己的传真机收到资料的系统）

feasibility study /ˌfiːzəˈbɪlɪtɪ ˌstʌdɪ; fizəˈbɪlətɪ ˌstʌdɪ/ *n* preliminary investigation undertaken by experts in order to determine if a project, proposal, etc would be successful if carried out 可行性研究（专家对工程、提案等所作的先期的研究调查，以判断计划能否实现）：*The government ordered a feasibility study into the proposed new traffic regulations.* 政府下令对新的交通法规的提案进行可行性研究。○ *Feasibility studies suggested that it would be better to site the airport elsewhere.* 可行性研究显示机场最好能重新选址。

feeding frenzy /ˈfiːdɪŋ ˌfrenzɪ; ˈfidɪŋ frɛnzɪ/ *n* **1** greedy and hungry intake of food by a large number of sharks each aggressively trying to get the most（大群鲨鱼）贪婪而饥饿地攫取食物 **2** (*fig* 比喻) fierce competition among would-be purchasers or consumers for a limited supply of objects 抢购：*The January sales spark off a feeding frenzy amongst shoppers.* 一月份的大减价掀起了抢购风潮。

feel-bad /ˈfiːlbæd; ˈfilbæd/ *adj* creating a feeling of gloom and depression, esp in relation to financial and material security 令人灰心的，教人沮丧的（尤指经济和物质保障方面）：*Avian flu and a spate of building fires brought a feel-bad start to the new year.* 禽流感和连串火灾给新的一年带来了一个不快的开端。Cf 参看 FEEL-GOOD

feel-good /ˈfiːlgʊd; ˈfilgʊd/ *adj* creating a feeling of optimism and well-being in people, esp regarding their financial and material security 令人感到乐观和幸福的（尤指经济和物质保障方面）Cf 参看 FEEL-BAD

□ **feel good factor** *n* condition or event, eg national sporting success, a healthy economy and even fine weather which makes people more contented and hence more likely to support the government in power in any local or national election（使人们更乐于在当地或全国选举中支持现政府的）有利的条件或事件（如国家运动队获胜、经济健康发展乃至好的天气等）

feminazi /ˈfemɪnɑːtsɪ, femɪˈnɑːtsɪ; fɛmɪˈnɑtsɪ/ *n* (*US derog* 贬) contemptuous name for an extreme feminist（蔑称）极端女权主义者

NOTE 注： a blend of *feminist* and *Nazi* 由 feminist（女权主义者）和 Nazi（纳粹党）二词合成

fender-bender /ˈfendəbendə(r); ˈfɛndɚbɛndɚ/ *n* (*infml* 口) minor traffic accident in which no one is hurt but one or more of the vehicles involved is slightly damaged, eg a fender is bent（无人受伤的）小车祸，轻微交通事故

feng shui /ˈfeŋ ʃuːɪ, ˈfʌŋ ʃuːɪ; ˈfɛŋ ʃuɪ/ *n* [U] ancient Chinese practice concerned with the siting, orientation and landscaping of buildings and graves, based upon the belief that there are good and bad spiritual influences in natural features 风水

fenland /ˈfenlænd, -lənd; ˈfɛnlænd/ *n* [U] (in Britain) area of flat wet land where few trees grow（英国）沼泽地

feta /ˈfetə; ˈfɛtə/ (also **fetta**) *n* [U] soft white salty cheese made from sheep's milk, esp in Greece（尤指希腊的）羊奶干酪：*a feta salad* 羊奶酪色拉 ○ *slices of feta with ripe tomatoes* 成熟西红柿拌羊奶酪片

field trip /ˈfiːld trɪp; ˈfild trɪp/ *n* visit to a place made by a group of people, usu for an educational or research purpose, or in order to study sth in a practical way 实地考察旅行（出于教学或研究等目的的团体旅行）：*a geology field-trip* 地质考察旅行

filing cabinet /ˈfaɪlɪŋ kæbɪnət; ˈfaɪlɪŋ kæbənɪt/ (*US* **file cabinet**) *n* (*Brit*) piece of office furniture, usu made of metal, with deep drawers for storing files（通常用金属制的）文件柜

filler cap /ˈfɪlə kæp; ˈfɪlɚ kæp/ *n* cap used to cover the pipe through which petrol flows into a motor vehicle（汽车输油管的）管盖

film-maker /ˈfɪlmmeɪkə(r); ˈfɪlmmekɚ/ *n* (*esp Brit*) person who makes films for the cinema and for television 电影制作人；电视制作人

film-on-demand /ˌfɪlmɒndɪˈmɑːnd, *US* -mænd; ˌfɪlmɑndɪˈmænd/ *n* service for cable subscribers by which a film of their choice is transmitted from a network centre and shown in their own home as soon as they ask for it 电影点播，自选影院（有线电视的一种服务，经用户提出要求所选择的电影就会通过网络中心传送到家中播放）Cf 参看 VIDEO-ON-DEMAND

Filofax /ˈfaɪləʊfæks; ˈfaɪlofæks/ *n* (*propr* 专利名) loose-leaf diary, for recording appointments, addresses, etc 活页日记簿（用以记下约会、地址等的日记簿）：*She takes her Filofax with her wherever she goes.* 她到哪儿都随身带着日记本。

filter down /fɪltə ˈdaʊn; ˌfɪltɚ ˈdaʊn/ (also **trickle down**) *v* [I, Ipr] (of the effect of sth) spread gradually and have an increasing influence（指某事的影响）渐渐扩散并

越来越大，渗入：*The law still needs to filter down and change people's attitudes towards drunk driving.* 这项法律仍需慢慢地被人们接受，逐渐改变他们对酒后驾车的态度。

□ **filter down effect** *n* (esp in economics) theory that if the richer section of a society is doing well, their prosperity will spread downwards to the poorer section and everyone will become better off without government intervention, eg by raising taxes 渗入效应，滴入效应（尤指经济学的一种理论，认为社会富裕阶层之财富会逐渐渗入贫困阶层，因此政府毋须采取提高税收等干预措施，全社会都会逐渐富裕起来）

fine-tune /ˌfaɪn'tjuːn, *US* -tuːn; ˌfaɪn'tun/ *v* [Tn] make small adjustments until sth, esp a scheme, process, etc, is as perfect as possible 微调（计划、程序等以臻完美）：*We still need to fine-tune the arrangements for the evening reception.* 我们仍需对晚上招待会的安排作些细微的调整。

finishing line /'fɪnɪʃɪŋ laɪn; 'fɪnɪʃɪŋ laɪn/ (also *esp US* **finish line**) *n* (*Brit*) line across a sports track which marks the end of a race（跑道的）终点线：*Photos revealed that the Kenyan had just crossed the finishing line first.* 多张照片显示那名肯尼亚运动员在冲过终点线时仅稍微领先。

fire door /'faɪə dɔː(r); 'faɪr dɔr/ *n* door made of a material which can withstand heat and resist burning, as well as prevent the rapid spread of fire 防火安全门；防火门：*Make sure that the fire doors are closed and clear of any obstruction at all times.* 要确保在任何时候防火安全门都全部关闭并且周围畅通无阻。

fire-practice *n* [C, U] = FIRE DRILL (FIRE[1(A-Z)])

fire service *n* = FIRE-BRIGADE (FIRE[1(A-Z)])

first-ever /'fɜːstevə(r); 'fɝstɛvɚ/ *adj* [attrib 作定语] never having happened or been experienced before 破天荒头一次的；史无前例的：*Britain's first-ever woman Prime Minister* 英国有史以来第一位女首相

flake /fleɪk; flek/ *n* (*US derog* 贬) unreliable person 不可靠的人

▷ **flaky** (also **flakey**) *adj* : *She has always proved a bit flaky when she plays the really crucial points in the match.* 她在比赛中打真正关键的位置时总有点不让人放心。

flame /fleɪm; flem/ *v* [Tn] send an electronic message to someone over the communications network which contains destructive criticism, abuse or provocative statements（以电子邮件）抨击、辱骂或激怒（他人），开火，发炮：*His ideas were flamed from every corner of the World Wide Web.* 万维网网民从各地发来电子邮件，猛烈抨击他的意见。

▷ **flamer** *n* person who flames sb 以电子邮件抨击他人的人 **flaming** *n*

flashback /'flæʃbæk; 'flæʃbæk/ *n* sudden and very vivid memory or even re-living of a past, usu terrible, experience 往事突然重现，回忆闪现（通常指可怕的往事）：*Flashbacks still experienced by Vietnam war veterans.* 越战老兵仍会感到往事又闪现眼前。○ *Flashbacks are a common symptom of stress amongst survivors of events such as plane crashes.* 回忆闪现是飞机失事等事件的幸存者常见的精神紧张症状。

flash-bang *n* (*infml* 口) = STUN GRENADE

flashing /'flæʃɪŋ; 'flæʃɪŋ/ *n* strip of metal put on a roof where it joins a wall, etc to prevent water getting through 防雨板（置于屋顶与墙等相接处的防水金属板）

flatline /'flætlaɪn; 'flætlaɪn/ *v* [I] **1** die 死亡 **2** (*fig* 比喻) become useless or fail completely 完全失效或失败

NOTE 注： from the *flat line* seen on a heart monitor when a patient dies 由心脏监护仪上显示病人死亡时的flat line（平直线）一词引申而来

flatmate /'flætmeɪt; 'flætmet/ *n* person who shares a flat or apartment with one or more people 合住公寓者；同寓室友：*Needed: flatmate for large, sunny flat near university.* 征求：室友合租宽敞公寓，邻近大学，阳光充足。○ *My flatmate is away for a few days.* 我的室友离开几天。

flesh /fleʃ; flɛʃ/ *n* (idm 习语) **press the flesh** (esp of politicians seeking support) move amongst people shaking hands（尤指寻求支持的政治家）在人群中一一握手：*The Vice-President seems to be comfortable pressing the flesh.* 副总统与人们握手致意，显得很轻松。

flesh-eating bacterium *n* = NECROTIZING FASCIITIS

flesh-eating disease *n* = NECROTIZING FASCIITIS

flight crew /'flaɪt kruː; 'flaɪt kru/ *n* [CGp] people who work on an aircraft, including those operating it 机组；空勤人员

flip chart /'flɪp tʃɑːt; 'flɪp tʃɑrt/ *n* pad consisting of large sheets of paper fixed to a stand and used at conferences, etc to display information to an audience 活动挂图，翻示挂图（举行会议等时固定于架上供展示资料的大型拍纸簿）

flip-flop /'flɪpflɒp; 'flɪpflɑp/ *v* [I] (*US*) change direction completely in one's viewpoint 完全改变观点；彻底改变看法：*The Chairman flip-flopped and reversed his position entirely.* 主席一百八十度推翻了自己的看法。Cf 参看 DO A U-TURN (U[1(A-Z)])

floret /'flɒrət, *US* 'flɔːr-; 'flɔrət/ *n* each of the edible stems of certain vegetables, esp cauliflower and broccoli（尤指花椰菜和花茎甘蓝的）小花，菜茎：*Break the cauliflower into separate florets.* 把这棵花椰菜掰成小块。

flume ride /'fluːm raɪd; 'flum raɪd/ *n* (*US*) ride in a fairground which consists of a long open tube of water along which small boats are pulled and which has one or more sudden drops 激流冲舟，滑浪飞船（在露天游乐场供游人乘小船沿有陡坡的水槽突然下滑的游乐项目）

fluoxetine *n* = PROZAC

fly-drive /'flaɪdraɪv; 'flaɪdraɪv/ *adj* [attrib 作定语] (of a holiday) combining the cost of a return flight and the hire of a car in one package（指假期）空陆联游的，包括来回机票和租车费用的：*We're thinking of a fly-drive holiday in Ireland this summer.* 我们正考虑今年夏天到爱尔兰度一个空陆联游的假期。

foetal reduction /fiːtl rɪ'dʌkʃn; fitl rɪ'dʌkʃən/ (also **selective reduction**) *n* [U] abortion of one or more of the foetuses present in the uterus of a pregnant woman, esp when her condition is the result of using fertility drugs, in order to ensure the survival of the remaining foetus or foetuses 选择性堕胎，减胎（对多胎妊娠尤其是服用怀胎药后的妊娠的一个或多个胎儿进行的流产，旨在保证剩余胎儿的存活）：*She would not agree to foetal reduction and finally lost all the five foetuses she was carrying.* 她不答应减胎，结果她所怀的五个胎儿都没有保住。

folk hero /'fəʊk hɪərəʊ; 'fok hɪro/ *n* man or woman whose past actions or achievements have made him or her a hero to the people of a particular ethnic group or nation 民族英雄：*Robin Hood is one of the folk heroes of the English because he took from the rich, corrupt nobles and churchmen and gave to the poor peasants.* 罗宾汉是英国人的民族英雄，因为他打劫富裕、腐败的贵族和教士，救济贫农。

folk memory /ˌfəʊk 'meməri; ˌfok 'mɛmərɪ/ *n* memory of sth in the past which is very significant to the people of a community or country and which they never forget 民间记忆（民众对过去重大事件的从未忘却的记忆）：*To the Mongols, the victories of Genghis Khan are their most enduring folk memory.* 对蒙古人来说，成吉思汗曾取得的胜利是他们永恒的记忆。Cf 参看 FOLK HERO

folk-singer /'fəʊksɪŋə(r); 'foksɪŋə/ *n* person who sings folk-songs (FOLK[A-Z]) 民歌手

follicle /'fɒlɪkl; 'fɑlɪkḷ/ *n* cluster of cells in any of the tiny holes in the skin, etc from which a cell or structure, eg hair, grows 小囊，滤泡（如毛囊）

foodie /'fu:dɪ; 'fudɪ/ *n* (*infml* 口) person who is very keen on eating, reading about and preparing food; someone who is knowledgeable and choosy about food 讲究饮食的人；美食家：*The Festival of Food attracted foodies from all over the country.* 美食节吸引来了全国各地的美食家。

▷ **foodie-ism** *n* (*derog* 贬) state of being too interested in and focused on food 美食主义；美食至上

food stamp /'fu:d stæmp; 'fud stæmp/ *n* (*US*) paper tokens that can be used to buy food which are given by the government to poor people（政府发给贫民用来买食物的）食品券

fool /fu:l; ful/ *v* (phr v) **fool around** (*esp US infml* 口) have casual sexual relationships, esp when married or with a married person（尤指已婚者或与已婚者）搞不正当性关系：*He accused her of fooling around.* 他指责她乱搞男女关系。

Force /fɔ:s; fɔrs/ *n* (idm 习语) **the Force be with you** (*joc* 谑) may you stay on the side of right and prosper 愿你站在正确和成功的一边

NOTE 注： from the *Star War* movies directed by George Lucas 出自乔治·卢卡斯导演的《星球大战》系列片

for-profit /fɔ:'prɒfɪt; fɔr'prɑfɪt/ *adj* (esp of an organization) concerned with providing public services, intended to make a profit and run as a business（尤指提供公共服务的机构）营利性的，牟利的

NOTE 注： in contrast with NOT-FOR-PROFIT 与 not-for-profit（非营利的）一词相对

forty winks /ˌfɔ:tɪ 'wɪŋks; ˌfɔrtɪ 'wɪŋks/ *n* [pl] (*infml* 口) short sleep or NAP[1(A-Z)], esp during the day（尤指在日间的）盹，小睡：*I was just enjoying forty winks at my desk when the boss walked in.* 我刚靠在桌上打盹，老板就走了进来。

fractal /'fræktl; 'fræktəl/ *n* (*mathematics* 数) irregular or symmetrical shape produced by applying a mathematical formula which is made up of many smaller shapes identical to each other and to the whole shape 不规则碎片形（运用数学公式用许多形状相同的不规则小碎片组成的大图形，其形状跟小碎片的形状相同）

freebase /'fri:beɪs; 'fribes/ *n* (*sl* 俚) COCAINE[A-Z] purified by heating with ether, and inhaled or smoked 精炼可卡因（与乙醚一同加热提炼的可卡因，供吸用）

free lunch /fri:'lʌntʃ; fri'lʌntʃ/ *n* gift or benefit which does not have to be paid for in any way 免费得到的好处；免费午餐：*I don't believe in free lunches. He only bought you the flowers so that you would finish his letters for him.* 我不相信有免费的好事。他买花给你只是想你帮他把信写完。

NOTE 注： a common expression is *There's no such thing as a free lunch* , often attributed to Margaret Thatcher, former British prime-minister 通常说法为 There's no such thing as a free lunch（世上哪有不付钱的午餐），一般认为出自前英国首相撒切尔夫人之口

freeride /'fri:raɪd; 'friraɪd/ *v* [I, Ipr] (*sport* 体) ride on a snowboard (SNOWBOARDING) designed for all-round use without the discipline of racing or performing tricks 自由式滑雪（使用多功能滑雪板进行的滑雪，无一定比赛或花样表演规则）

▷ **freeride** *n* **freeriding** *n* [U]

freeze-frame /'fri:zfreɪm; 'frizfrem/ *n* facility of stopping a running video or film in order to view the still image 定格；定帧

▷ **freeze-frame** *v* use freeze-frame on an image（将图像）定格：*Freeze-frame that image of the man getting out of the car. I think I recognize him.* 将正下车的那男子的图像定格。我想我认出他来了。

French kiss /ˌfrentʃ 'kɪs; ˌfrɛntʃ 'kɪs/ *n* kiss during which one person puts his or her tongue into the other's mouth 法式接吻（将舌头伸入对方口中的接吻方式）

Friday Wear *n* = DRESS-DOWN FRIDAY

friendly fire /ˌfrendlɪ 'faɪə(r); ˌfrɛndlɪ 'faɪr/ *n* [U] bullets, bombs, etc which accidentally kill men who are fighting on the same side, usu because of misidentification（因误认而）向自己人开火；误杀：*They came under friendly fire and three men were killed.* 他们因误会而遭到自己人的火力袭击，三人被打死。

Friesian /'fri:ʒn; 'friʒən/ *n* type of black and white dairy cattle which produces a lot of milk 黑白花奶牛，荷兰乳牛（一种产奶量高的乳牛）

froing *n* (idm 习语) **toing and froing** ⇨ TOING[A-Z]

front office /frʌnt 'ɒfɪs, *US* ɔ:fɪs; frʌnt 'ɔfɪs/ *n* (usu *sing* 通常作单数) room or rooms in a stock exchange where dealers and traders buy and sell shares（股票交易所里进行买卖的）交易室

frozen embryo /ˌfrəʊzn 'embrɪəʊ; ˌfrozṇ 'ɛmbrɪo/ *n* (*medical* 医) human embryo which has been deep-frozen for storage and perhaps for later implantation in a woman's uterus and birth 冷冻胚胎（极低温冷藏的人类胚胎，可供日后植入妇女子宫作生育用）

fruitarian /fru:'teərɪən; fru'tɛrɪən/ *n* person who eats only fruit 只食水果者

fubaritic /fu:bə'rɪtɪk; fubə'rɪtɪk/ *abbr* 缩写 = (*geology sl joc* 地质，俚，谑) fouled up beyond all recognition (term used by geologists to describe rock that cannot be identified because of its unclear structure) 无法辨认，无法鉴定（地质学家描述构造模糊无法辨认的岩石所用之术语）

fugue /fju:g; fjug/ *n* (*psychology* 心) period of time in which a person suffers from loss of memory, and leaves his or her surroundings, wanders aimlessly or starts a new life elsewhere 神游（某人在一段时期内丧失了记忆，离开其生活的环境，漫无目的地游荡或在别处开始新的生活）

full /fʊl; ful/ *adj* (idm 习语) **the full monty** (*sl* 俚) everything; the lot; the whole way 所有；全部；整个儿：*I'm getting married in the full monty — white dress, veil, the lot.* 我准备穿上全套行头结婚——白色婚礼服、面纱等，一应俱全。

full-blown AIDS /ˌfʊlbləʊn 'eɪdz; ˌfulblon 'edz/ *n* final phase of AIDS[A-Z], when the immune system has irrevocably broken down 晚期艾滋病（这时免疫系统已完全损坏）

full-frills /fʊl'frɪlz; fʊl'frɪlz/ *adj* having all the optional extras; luxurious 所有额外设施一应俱全的；豪华的：*I'm staying at one of those full-frills hotels that has everything you can imagine and more.* 我住在一所极其奢华的饭店里，那里不仅设施一应俱全，还有种种你意想不到的东西。

full frontal /fʊl 'frʌntl; ful 'frʌntḷ/ *n* showing the whole of a nude body from the front 正面全裸像：*We need a few full frontals to make the paper more interesting.* 我们需要一些正面全裸像来使报纸更有趣些。○ [attrib 作定语] *full-frontal photos* 正面全裸照

funboard /'fʌnbɔ:d; 'fʌnbɔrd/ *n* (*sport* 体) type of windsurfing board which is less stable but faster than a standard board 快速风帆冲浪板，快速帆板（没有普通帆板那么稳定但较之快速的帆板）

functional food /'fʌŋkʃnəl fu:d; 'fʌŋkʃənḷ fud/ *n* [U] food which includes healthy additives, eg added fibre, enzymes to aid digestion 功能食品；保健食品；健康食品

fundholder /'fʌndhəʊldə(r); 'fʌndholdə/ *n* (in the UK) family doctor (or general practitioner) who works for the government-controlled and funded National Health Service but who has control of his or her own budget 财务自主医生（在英国为政府管辖和资助的国家保健中心工作，但自行掌握财务预算的家庭医生，即全科医生）

fundie /'fʌndɪ; 'fʌndɪ/ *n* FUNDAMENTALIST (FUNDAMENTALISM[A-Z]); person with strong religious, political, environmental, etc convictions 原教旨主义者；具有强烈的宗教、政治或环保等信念的人

fundraiser /'fʌndreɪzə(r); 'fʌndrezɚ/ *n* person whose job is to raise money for charity or a non-profit organization（为慈善或非营利机构）募集资金者

funny money *n* = SILLY MONEY

futon /'fu:tɒn, 'fju:-; 'futɑn/ *n* Japanese mattress on a low wooden frame which can be used as a seat or extended and used as a bed 蒲团；日本床垫

fuzzy logic /fʌzɪ 'lɒdʒɪk; ˌfʌzɪ 'lɑdʒɪk/ *n* [U] (*computing* 计) kind of reasoning applied in the programming and design of computer systems to make computers more like the human brain in the way they deal with inexact data and in being flexible when circumstances change rather than following a fixed set of procedures 模糊逻辑，快思逻辑（用于计算机系统程序编制和设计的一种推理方法，使计算机能像人脑那样处理模糊数据，当情况发生变化时能灵活处理而不是墨守成规）Cf 参看 NEURAL NETWORK

fuzzy matching /fʌzɪ 'mætʃɪŋ; ˌfʌzɪ 'mætʃɪŋ/ *n* [U] (*computing* 计) technique which enables computers to match shapes that are similar but not identical, just as the human brain does 模糊配对（使计算机能像人脑那样配对相似而非相同的形状的技术）

FX *abbr* 缩写 = SPECIAL EFFECTS

Gg

G7 /dʒi: 'sevn; dʒi 'sɛvən/ *n* group of seven leading industrialized nations: Canada, France, Germany, Italy, Japan, the UK, and the US 七大工业国（加拿大、法国、德国、意大利、日本、英国和美国）: *a summit of the G7 nations* 七国首脑会议

gabfest /'gæbfest; 'gæbfɛst/ *n* (*infml* 口) gathering, eg conference, meeting, etc where a lot of talking and exchanging of views is done 长时间的聚谈；长时间的会议

gagging order /'gægɪŋ ɔ:də(r); 'gægɪŋ ɔrdɚ/ *n* (*fml* 正规作 **Public Interest Immunity Certificates**) (*infml* 口) official order in the UK which forbids public discussion of a particular subject either in print or by broadcasting 缄口令（英国关于禁止以书面或广播形式公开讨论某一话题的官方命令）

gain sharing /'geɪn ʃeərɪŋ; 'gen 'ʃɛrɪŋ/ *n* [U] type of profit sharing which pays bonuses to employees in direct proportion to any economies or profits achieved by their company 利润分享（雇员获分与公司所取得的经济效益或利润成正比的红利）

game plan /'geɪm plæn; 'gem plæn/ *n* plan for success worked out in advance, esp in competitive sport, politics or business（尤指体育比赛、政治或商业活动中事先制订以求取胜的）行动方案，计划，策略: *His game plan was totally upset when his opponent began coming to the net on every serve.* 他的对手开始在每一次发球后上网截击，这一来把他的战略全给打乱了。

game show /'geɪm ʃəʊ; 'gem ʃo/ *n* television show in which well-known people or members of the public compete in games or a QUIZ[A-Z], often for prizes（电视上请名人或公众人士参加的）有奖游戏节目，比赛节目: *The game show involved teams of people dressing up in ridiculous costumes and making complete fools of themselves.* 在这个游戏节目中，几组参赛者穿着滑稽可笑的服装出足洋相。

gamete intra-fallopian transfer /ˌgæmi:t ɪntrəfæˌləʊpɪən 'trænsfɜ:(r); ˌgæmit ɪntrəfəˌlopɪən 'trænsfɝ/ *n* (*abbr* 缩写 **GIFT**) technique for helping infertile couples to conceive by which gametes, ie eggs and sperm, are inserted into one of the woman's fallopian tubes (FALLOPIAN TUBE[A-Z]) where fertilization takes place 配子移入输卵管技术（协助不育夫妇怀孕的技术，即将卵子和精子输入女方输卵管受精）Cf 参看 IN VITRO[A-Z]

gang-bang /'gæŋbæŋ; 'gæŋbæŋ/ *n* (*sl* 俚) rape of a woman carried out on one particular occasion by several men 轮奸（妇女）

gang-banger /'gæŋbæŋə(r); 'gæŋbæŋɚ/ *n* (*US sl* 俚) member of a gang of young criminals 少年犯罪团伙成员

▷ **gang-banging** *n* (*US sl* 俚) actions typical of a gang-banger 少年犯罪活动

gang-buster /'gæŋbʌstə(r); 'gæŋbʌstɚ/ *n* law officer who is very successful at breaking up criminal gangs and arresting their members 成功地破获犯罪团伙的司法官员；经常侦破犯罪集团的警察

gap year /'gæp jɪə; 'gæp jɪr/ *n* period of one academic year taken off by a student between leaving school and taking up a place at a university or college 空档年，间隔年（中学生在毕业后与进大学前空出的一学年时间）: *We've decided to travel in South-east Asia during our gap year.* 我们决定在中学毕业后与上大学前的一年空档时间到东南亚旅行。

garbology /gɑ:'bɒlədʒɪ; gɑr'bɑlədʒɪ/ *n* [U] study of garbage, esp domestic, from a sociological viewpoint 垃圾学研究，垃圾处理学（从社会学角度进行的，尤指对家居垃圾的研究）

▷ **garbologist** *n*

gas-cooled /ˌgæs'ku:ld; ˌgæs'kuld/ *adj* using gas to cool sth 气冷的；用气体冷却的: *a gas-cooled nuclear reactor* 气冷核反应堆

gas field /'gæs fi:ld; 'gæs fild/ *n* area with deposits of natural gas for tapping 天然气田

gatherer /'gæðərə(r); 'gæðərɚ/ *n* person who collects plants, nuts, fruits, etc for food instead of growing their own 采集植物、果实等裹腹者；采集者: *early hunters and gatherers in the Stone Age* 石器时代早期的狩猎者和采集者

Gawd /gɔ:d; gɔd/ *n, interj* (*infml* 口) God 上帝: *For Gawd's sake, what do you want now?* 天哪，你现在想要什么？

NOTE 注: used in written English to indicate a special pronunciation expressing surprise, anger, annoyance, etc 用于书面语中，表示说话者在惊奇、愤怒、烦恼等时异常的发音

gay bashing /'geɪ bæʃɪŋ; 'ge bæʃɪŋ/ *n* [U] attacking and beating up people who are thought to be homosexuals 殴打涉嫌同性恋者: *figures for gay bashing in the area* 该地区殴打涉嫌同性恋者的统计数字

gay gene /'geɪ dʒi:n; 'ge dʒin/ *n* (*infml* 口) popular name given to the sequence of DNA which some researchers have speculated could possibly make sb predisposed towards homosexuality 同性恋基因（某些研究人员观察到可能使人有同性恋倾向的基因）

geek /gi:k; gik/ *n* (*sl* 俚) unfashionable, boring and socially inept person, esp one with an obsession about a particular hobby 呆子（不合潮流、乏味、不善交际的人，尤指沉迷某种嗜好的）: *Tony is becoming a complete computer geek.* 托尼快成一个十足的计算机迷了。Cf 参看 NERD, ANORAK

gee-string *n* = G-STRING[A-Z]

gender gap /'dʒendə gæp; 'dʒɛndɚ gæp/ *n* [sing] difference between how women and men judge the importance of varying social, political, cultural or economic issues, which may cause the two sexes to vote differently 性差别（男女在判断社会、政治、文化或经济问题的重要性上的差别，由此可能导致两者投票上的差异）：*The candidate was well aware of the possible gender gap, and emphasized different issues when he spoke to women's groups.* 这位候选人清楚地意识到可能存在的性差别，因此在对妇女组织发言时强调了不同的问题。

gender identity /ˌdʒendə aɪˈdentətɪ; ˌdʒɛndɚ aɪˈdɛntətɪ/ *n* (usu *sing* 通常作单数) person's inner sense of himself or herself as male or female, which may or may not be the same as his or her biological sex 性身分，心理性别（某人内在的性别感觉，有可能不同于自己的生理性别）

gender specific /ˌdʒendə spəˈsɪfɪk; ˌdʒɛndɚ spɪˈsɪfɪk/ *adj* (of job advertisements) openly stating that the post is open only to either male or female applicants（指招聘启事）指定性别的：*Gender specific advertising for employees is now against the law.* 如今指定性别的招聘启事是触犯法律的。

generalist /ˈdʒenrəlɪst; ˈdʒɛnərəlɪst/ *n* person who is competent in several different fields or activities 多面手，通才（精通多方面知识和技能的人）Cf 参看 SPECIALIST[A-Z]

Generation X /dʒenəˌreɪʃn ˈeks; dʒɛnəˌreʃən'ɛks/ *n* [U] label applied to the younger generation regarded as lacking a sense of direction in life and not being involved with the society around them or with the important issues of the day ☆ X 一代（被视为无生活目标、对周围社会及重大时事漠不关心的年轻一代）：*Rapid social change, insecure employment and the loss of religious and moral certainties have all contributed to the creation of our Generation X.* 社会急速变化、就业缺乏保障以及宗教与道德观念丧失，这一切孕育了我们的 X 一代。

genetic engineering /dʒɪˌnetɪk endʒɪˈnɪərɪŋ; dʒəˌnɛtɪk ɛndʒəˈnɪrɪŋ/ *n* [U] modification of a living thing, ie plant, animal or microbe, by making changes at the level of its genetic structure 基因工程，遗传工程（通过改变遗传结构来改造生物的做法）：*Genetic engineering has given us the frost-resistant potato and, more importantly, mass-produced human insulin.* 我们通过遗传工程有了防霜冻马铃薯，更重要的是，得到了批量生产的人体胰岛素。

genetic fingerprinting /dʒɪˌnetɪk ˈfɪŋɡəprɪntɪŋ; dʒəˌnɛtɪk ˈfɪŋɡɚprɪntɪŋ/ (also **DNA profiling, DNA fingerprinting**) *n* [U] FORENSIC[A-Z] technique for finding out the identity of sb through an analysis of genetic information from a small sample of blood, semen, skin, etc 遗传特征鉴别，基因纹印术（凭血液、精液、皮肤等人体组织中的遗传资料确认某人身分的技术）

genetic mother /dʒənetɪk ˈmʌðə(r); dʒənɛtɪk ˈmʌðɚ/ *n* woman whose egg has developed into a particular baby, even if the baby has been carried to term in another woman's uterus; biological mother 基因母亲，生物母亲（拥有孩子的母亲，孩子由自己的卵子长成，可以由自己分娩，或将受精卵植入他人的子宫而足月分娩）：*It's perfectly possible nowadays for the woman who gives birth to a child to be quite different from the genetic mother.* 如今分娩的母亲与基因母亲为不同的人是完全可能的。

gesture politics /ˈdʒestʃə ˌpɒlɪtɪks; ˈdʒɛstʃɚ ˌpɑlətɪks/ *n* [pl] political action which seems to be effective, but which is only for show and publicity value 花架子政治（貌似有效，但实际上只是为了摆样子、作宣传的政治活动）：*The Senator's dedication to the cause of the poorest members of society was widely seen as gesture politics, directed solely towards securing his own re-election.* 大家普遍认为这位参议员致力于为社会最底层的人们谋福利只不过是在摆摆样子，其真实目的是为了自己能再度当选。

get /get; gɛt/ *v* (idm 习语) **get a life** (*infml* 口) (piece of advice to) start living a fuller and more interesting life 过更充实、更有趣的生活（的建议）：*You never leave work until after eight o'clock and you work every weekend. Take things easier, get a life.* 你不过八点钟从不下班，周末也不休息。放松一点儿，过过有意思的生活吧。

getaway /ˈgetəweɪ; ˈgɛtəwe/ *n* house, cottage, etc one can escape to for a holiday and for a complete break from one's usual routine 度假屋；隐居处（供摆脱日常工作度假休憩的住所）：*a little getaway in the Welsh hills* 在威尔士山区的一间小小的度假屋

get down and dirty /ˌget daʊn ənd ˈdɜːtɪ; ˌgɛt daun ənd ˈdɝtɪ/ *v* [I, Ipr] (*infml* 口) deal frankly with the more shocking or scandalous aspects of an event, situation, affair, etc 不加掩饰地揭露某事的阴暗面：*Perhaps the director of the film was afraid to get down and dirty with the life of this notorious man in case he attracted too much criticism.* 该影片的导演可能不敢揭那个臭名昭著的人的疮疤，生怕害他露底会惹太多事。

ghostbuster /ˈgəʊstbʌstə(r); ˈgostbʌstɚ/ *n* (*infml* 口) person who claims to be able to get rid of ghosts and other spirits from buildings, etc 驱鬼人

NOTE 注：the term became widely popular after the release of the films *Ghostbusters* and *Ghostbusters II* in the 1980s 此词在 20 世纪 80 年代随着电影 Ghostbusters 及其续集上映后广为流行

giant-killer /ˈdʒaɪəntkɪlə(r); ˈdʒaɪəntkɪlɚ/ *n* person who defeats an apparently much more powerful opponent in sports, a dispute, etc（在体育比赛或辩论等中）击败看来比自己强的对手的人，以小胜大者：*The fast food chain fell to the giant-killers when they lost the case brought against them by two environmentalists.* 两名环保主义者击败了强大的快餐连锁店，在官司中获得胜诉。

GIF /dʒiː aɪ ˈef; dʒi aɪ ˈɛf/ *abbr* 缩写 = (*computing* 计) graphic image format (popular format for image files, with built-in data compression) 图形图像格式（图像文件的通用格式，具有数据压缩功能）

GIFT *abbr* 缩写 = GAMETE INTRA-FALLOPIAN TRANSFER

gigabyte /ˈdʒaɪgəbaɪt, ˈdʒɪgə-; ˈdʒaɪgəbaɪt, ˈdʒɪgə-/ *n* (*computing* 计) unit of computer memory equal to a thousand megabytes (MEGABYTE) 千兆字节（计算机存储量单位）

gizmo /ˈgɪzməʊ; ˈgɪzmo/ *n* (*pl* **-os**) device or gadget, esp one that is useful and ingenious（尤指实用的、制作精巧的）装置，小玩意儿：*a new gizmo for getting cat's hairs off the furniture* 一种新发明的小玩意儿，可以从家具上除去猫毛

glass ceiling /glɑːs ˈsiːlɪŋ, *US* glæs; ˈglæs ˈsilɪŋ/ *n* (*fig* 比喻) invisible barrier to advancement, esp in one's career（尤指事业上的）无形的晋升障碍，玻璃天花板：*In spite of equal opportunities legislation, many women still find that glass ceiling blocking their way to the higher levels in their chosen careers.* 尽管法律规定男女机会均等，但许多妇女仍发觉在晋升上存在着无形的障碍。

glitterati /glɪˈtrɑːtɪ, glɪtəˈrɑːtɪ; ˌglɪˈtrɑtɪ/ *n* [pl] (*infml* 口) celebrities, esp glamorous people like film stars and models 名流，知名人士（尤指富有魅力者，如影星、模特儿等）：*All the glitterati were there for the launch of the new chain of restaurants.* 所有的名流都参加了新连锁饭店的开张庆典。

NOTE 注：a term used mainly by journalists to describe the people they often photograph and write about, formed on analogy with LITERATI 主要为记者用

来形容他们经常报道并为之拍照的人，由 literati（文人学士）一词类推构成

global village /ˌɡləʊbl 'vɪlɪdʒ; ˌɡlobl̩ 'vɪlɪdʒ/ *n* [sing] the world considered as a single community linked by telecommunications 地球村（由于电信联系，地球被视作单一社区的世界观）

gobsmacked /'ɡɒbsmækt; 'ɡɑbsmækt/ *adj* [usu pred 通常作表语] (*Brit sl* 俚) utterly amazed, made speechless by astonishment 大为吃惊；惊讶得目瞪口呆：*The news left us completely gobsmacked.* 这消息让我们大吃一惊。

NOTE 注： from *gob* meaning 'mouth' in British slang 源自英式俚语 gob，意指嘴巴

God-given /'ɡɒdɡɪvn; 'ɡɑdɡɪvən/ *adj* [attrib 作定语] given or as if given, created or sent by God 天赋的；天赐的：*a God-given opportunity* 天赐良机

gofer /'ɡəʊfə(r); 'ɡofɚ/ *n* (*infml* 口) person whose job is to do minor administrative tasks for others（为别人办杂事的）办事员

NOTE 注： probably from the phrase *go for (sth)* 可能源自 go for (sth)（去拿某物；去买某物）Cf 参看 DOGSBODY[A-Z]

gold card /'ɡəʊld kɑːd; 'ɡold kɑrd/ *n* type of charge or credit card issued by banks only to people considered sufficiently wealthy. It entitles them to a greater range of benefits and services than are offered to holders of a standard charge card 金卡（银行发给他们认为较富有者的一种赊帐卡或信用卡，持金卡者比持标准卡者可享有更多的优惠和服务）

golden goal /ɡəʊldən 'ɡəʊl; ɡoldn̩ 'ɡol/ *n* (*sport* 体) first goal scored in a soccer match during extra time which thus decides the result 金球，黄金入球（足球比赛加时赛中射入的决定胜负的第一球）：*The golden goal came after nearly 28 minutes of extra time.* 决定性的一球是在加时赛开始将近 28 分钟后射入的。

golden goodbye *n* = GOLDEN HANDSHAKE（GOLDEN 3[A-Z]）

golden handcuffs /ɡəʊldən 'hændkʌfs; ɡoldn̩ 'hændkʌfs/ *n* [pl] (*infml* 口) promise of future benefits, eg pensions or share options, to employees who will stay with a company throughout their working lives 金手铐（为使雇员终生为公司效力而给予退休金、股票期权等未来福利的承诺）

golden parachute /ɡəʊldən 'pærəʃuːt; ɡoldn̩ 'pærəʃut/ *n* (*infml* 口) financial compensation guaranteed to executives dismissed as a result of a MERGER（MERGE[A-Z]）or take-over 金降落伞（行政人员因公司合并或被收购而遭解雇，获保证可领取的赔偿金）

gold-plated /ˌɡəʊld'pleɪtɪd; ˌɡold'pletɪd/ *adj* having a thin covering of gold 镀金的：*gold-plated earrings* 镀金耳环

gold standard /'ɡəʊld stændəd; 'ɡold stændɚd/ *n* (*fig* 比喻) (usu *sing* 通常作单数) standard of excellence which should be aspired to in education, technology, etc（教育、技术等方面的）优质标准：*The system is sure to become the new gold standard for video recorders.* 这个系统必将成为录像机新的优质标准。

NOTE 注： from the GOLD STANDARD by which currencies were once evaluated 为作 '金本位（制）' 解的 gold standard 词组的引申义

gomer /'ɡəʊmə(r); 'ɡomɚ/ *n* (*medical sl* 医，俚) hospital patient who is seen as unlikely to respond to treatment because of age or ill-health and who is likely, therefore, to be a waste of time, effort and resources（因年老或体弱）医治无望的住院病人（故可能仅在浪费时间、精力和资源）

NOTE 注： an acronym from the initial letters of *get out of my emergency room* 由 get out of my emergency room（滚出我的急疹病房）首字母缩略构成

goodfella /'ɡʊdfelə; 'ɡʊdfɛlə/ *n* member of the MAFIA 1[A-Z]; a mobster 黑手党成员；歹徒

NOTE 注： from the title of the film *Goodfellas*, 1990 which showed the lives of the lesser members of the Mafia; the word is a variant of *good fellow*, and implies that sb is a reliable member of the gang 源自 1990 年一部反映黑手党喽罗生活的电影的片名 Goodfellas，此词为 good fellow 的变体，暗示某人为犯罪集团的铁杆成员

gopher /'ɡəʊfə(r); 'ɡofɚ/ *n* system for searching for information on the INTERNET（供在互联网上查找信息的）检索工具，信息浏览服务系统：*As the Internet grows ever bigger, an efficient gopher is becoming essential.* 随着互联网不断扩大，高效的信息搜寻系统日趋重要。

NOTE 注： a pun on GOFER (person who does minor administrative work) and GOPHER (a burrowing animal) 为双关语，包含 gofer（做行政琐事的人）和 gopher（囊地鼠）双重意思

gorillagram /ɡə'rɪləɡræm; ɡə'rɪləɡræm/ *n* congratulatory message sent to sb who is celebrating a birthday, STAG-PARTY (STAG), etc which is delivered by a person dressed in a gorilla suit 大猩猩贺信（由装扮成大猩猩的人送给正在庆祝生日或举行雄鹿会的人）Cf 参看 GRAM

goth /ɡɒθ; ɡɑθ/ *n* (pop musician who plays a) type of serious, moody rock music 哥特式庄严低沉的摇滚乐；演奏哥特式摇滚乐的流行音乐乐师

gradualism /'ɡrædʒʊəlɪzəm; 'ɡrædʒʊəlɪzəm/ *n* [U] policy of gradual change rather than sudden change or revolution 渐进主义（反对急剧变革的方针）

graduate school /'ɡrædʒʊət skuːl; 'ɡrædʒʊɪt skul/ *n* (*esp US*) department of a college or university for advanced work by graduates 研究生院；研究院：*a graduate school of business* 商学研究生院

gram /ɡræm; ɡræm/ *n* messenger sent to greet sb on a special social occasion, eg at a STAG-PARTY（STAG[A-Z]）or at a HEN-PARTY（HEN[A-Z]）, usu meant to cause embarrassment（被派去向参加特殊社交聚会如雄鹿会或女性聚会的人表示祝贺，通常旨在使人尴尬的）信使 Cf 参看 GORILLAGRAM, STRIPPERGRAM

grandpa bandit /'ɡrænpɑː bændɪt; 'ɡrænpɑ bændɪt/ *n* (*Austral* 澳) elderly man who is a robber 老强盗

granite-washed *adj* = STONEWASHED

grannexe /'ɡræneks; 'ɡrænɛks/ *n* extra part built on to a house for an elderly relative to live in 老奶奶屋（在住宅旁扩建的供年老的亲戚居住的厢房）Cf 参看 GRANNY FLAT（GRANNY[A-Z]）

NOTE 注： from *granny* and *annexe* 由 granny（老奶奶）和 annexe（增建部分）二词合成

granny creche /'ɡrænɪ kreɪʃ, -kreʃ; 'ɡrænɪ krɛʃ/ *n* facility set up by some large employers to provide recreation and relaxation for the elderly parents of workers and for retired employees 老人休憩所（一些大公司为职工的父母和退休职工提供的休息娱乐场所）：*One of the facilities in the new granny creche is a tranquillity room, filled with soft light and relaxing music.* 新的老人休憩所设置了一间休憩室，里面有柔和的灯光和轻松的音乐。

granny dumping /'ɡrænɪ ˌdʌmpɪŋ; 'ɡrænɪ ˌdʌmpɪŋ/ *n* [U] deliberate abandonment of an elderly person at a hospital, etc in order to get rid of him or her 抛弃老人；遗弃老人：*As young families emigrate, the problem of granny dumping has arisen.* 年轻夫妇不断移民国外，出现了遗弃老人的问题。

grant-in-aid /ˌɡrɑːntɪn'eɪd, *US* ɡrænt-; ˌɡræntɪn'ed/ *n* (*pl* **grants-in-aid**) amount of money given by the central government to a local authority or an institution as a subsidy（中央政府拨给地方政府或机构的）补助款，拨款

grant-maintained /ˌgrɑːntmeɪnˈteɪnd, *US* grænt-; ˌgræntmenˈtend/ *adj* (of a school) receiving financial support from the central government rather than the local authority（指学校）由中央政府资助的，由中央政府拨款的

graze[1] /greɪz; grez/ *v* eat snacks all day rather than have proper meals at the normal times 成天吃点心（而不是定时进餐）

graze[2] /greɪz; grez/ *v* watch short extracts from many different television programmes while switching randomly between channels 不停变换频道观看不同电视节目的片断 Cf 参看 CHANNEL SURF

greasy spoon /ˌgriːsɪ ˈspuːn, ˌgriːzɪ-; ˌgrisɪ ˈspun, ˌgrizɪ-/ *n* (*US infml derog* 口，贬) cheap restaurant which is not very clean 不太卫生的廉价饭馆；邋遢的低级小饭馆：*eat at the greasy spoon (restaurant) off the highway* 在脏兮兮的公路旁的廉价饭馆里吃饭

Great Dane /ˌgreɪt ˈdeɪn; gret ˈden/ *n* very large powerful breed of dog with short hair 丹麦大狗（一种力大、短毛的狗）

green audit /ˌgriːn ˈɔdɪt; ˌgrin ˈɔdɪt/ *n* examination of claims made by producers, manufacturers, etc that they are meeting ecological standards 绿色审核，环保审核（对生产商、制造商自称合乎环保标准的产品进行的检查）：*The vegetables claim to be organically farmed, but a green audit has established strong traces of chemical fertilizers.* 这些蔬菜自称是用有机肥栽培的，但环保审核证实菜上有明显的使用化肥的痕迹。

greenfield /ˈgriːnfiːld; ˈgrinfild/ *adj* [attrib 作定语] (of land) having no previous building on it and therefore having potential for development（指土地）因没有建筑物而可开发的：*a greenfield site* 可开发的地皮

greenhouse gas /ˌgriːnhaʊs ˈgæs; ˌgrinhaus ˈgæs/ *n* any of the gases, esp carbon dioxide, that are thought to contribute to the GREENHOUSE EFFECT（GREEN[1(A-Z)]）温室气体（据认为造成温室效应的气体，尤指二氧化碳）

greening /ˈgriːnɪŋ; ˈgrinɪŋ/ *n* [U] **1** planting of trees, etc in urban or desert areas 绿化（在城市或沙漠等地区种植树木的做法）**2** process of becoming or making aware of or sensitive to ecological issues 环保意识（开始逐渐了解生态问题，并表示关心）：*The greening of America's urban population took a big step forward with the installation of bottle-banks at all major supermarkets and malls.* 在各大超市和购物中心设置废瓶回收箱，大大增强了美国城市居民的环保意识。

green label *n* = ECO-LABEL

green manure /ˌgriːn məˈnjʊə(r); ˌgrin məˈnjur/ *n* [U] growing plants ploughed into the soil to make it more fertile 绿肥（作肥料用的植物）

green pepper (*US* **bell pepper**) *n* = CAPSICUM[A-Z]

green shoots /griːn ˈʃuːts; grin ˈʃuts/ *n* [pl] (*fig* 比喻) signs of growth or renewal, esp of economic recovery 发展或更新的迹象；经济复苏的苗头：*The Chancellor hailed the green shoots of recovery a bit prematurely.* 财政大臣过早地为经济即将复苏大唱颂歌。

greenwashing /ˈgriːnwɒʃɪŋ; ˈgrinwɔʃɪŋ/ *n* attempt to cover up the fact that a certain product causes harm to the environment and to deceive buyers into thinking that is harmless 绿色粉饰，刷绿（试图掩盖某产品对环境有害的真相，让消费者误以为其无害）：*No amount of greenwashing will make me change to that detergent.* 无论怎样文过饰非，说它对环境无害，我也不会改买那种洗涤剂。

NOTE 注：formed on analogy with WHITEWASH *n* 2（WHITE[1(A-Z)]）由 whitewash（粉饰）一词类推构成

grey (also *esp US* **gray**) /greɪ; gre/ *v* [I] (of a population) have an increasingly large number of elderly people in proportion to the rest of the population（指人口）老龄化

▷ **greying** *n* process in which a population greys 人口老龄化：*the greying of Europe* 欧洲人口的老化

grey economy /greɪ ɪˈkɒnəmɪ; gre ɪˈkɑnəmɪ/ (*US* **gray economy**) *n* [U] that part of a country's economy relating to commercial activity which is not accounted for in official statistics 灰市经济，灰色经济（国家经济有关商业活动的部分，但不纳入官方统计中）Cf 参看 MOONLIGHTING（MOON[1(A-Z)]）

grey market /ˌgreɪ ˈmɑːkɪt; gre ˈmɑrkɪt/ *n* (*finance* 财) trading in a company's shares that takes place before those shares have been quoted on a stock exchange and thus made available for public buying 灰市，暗盘市场（在证券交易所上市前，即未作公开买卖前对某公司股票进行的交易）

gridlock /ˈgrɪdlɒk; ˈgrɪdlɑk/ *n* [U] **1** traffic jam that blocks a whole grid or interconnecting network of streets 交通大堵塞（纵横交叉的街道完全被堵塞）**2** (*fig* 比喻) situation where no progress can be made; deadlock; stalemate 停滞状况；僵持；僵局：*We need new ideas to clear the mental gridlock.* 我们需要新观念来突破僵化思想。

grout /graʊt; graʊt/ *n* [U] substance like MORTAR[1] for filling the gaps between tiles on walls, esp in bathrooms, kitchens, etc 薄胶泥（一种像砂浆的物质，用于填塞浴室、厨房等墙面瓷砖之间的缝隙）

▷ **grout** *v* fill sth with grout 用薄胶泥填塞

growbag /ˈgrəʊbæg; ˈgrobæg/ *n* bag containing a growing medium, eg potting COMPOST[A-Z], and often seeds, in which plants such as tomatoes, etc can be grown as an alternative to growing them in a garden 植物生长袋（内有植物生长所需介质如盆栽混合肥料的袋，通常装有种子，让番茄等植物生长以代替在园中种植）

grunge /grʌndʒ; grʌndʒ/ *n* style of rock music distinguished by its raucous guitar sound and by the dress of its devotees which typically features a layered, non-matching, second-hand look and heavy boots 咕隆摇滚（以粗犷的吉他声为特征的摇滚乐，其爱好者服装独特，衣服内外多层、不相称、样子旧，靴子笨重）

guanxi /gwɑːnˈsiː; gwɑnˈsi/ *n* [sing] (in China) network of contacts which an individual can call upon when sth needs to be done and through which he or she can exert an influence 关系（在中国指个人的关系网，凭藉笼络对方让自己好办事，也可以通过它施加影响）

NOTE 注：Pinyin romanization of 关系, used when people realized that the word 'connections' cannot sufficiently reflect its cultural implications 汉语'关系'的拼音。使用此词是因为人们觉得 connections（熟人网络）这个词不足以表达其文化内涵

guest beer /ˈgest bɪə(r); ˈgɛst bɪr/ *n* [U, C] (*Brit*) beer which is not usually available in a particular pub, but which is served there for a limited period, often at a specially reduced price 特选啤酒（在某酒馆中并不经常供应，但在限定的时期内常以低价出售的啤酒）

guest worker /ˈgest wɜːkə(r); ˈgɛst wɝkɚ/ *n* person who lives in a foreign country in order to work there 作客他乡工作的人；外籍工人；外籍雇员：*Turkish guest workers in Germany* 旅居德国的土耳其籍工人

guff /gʌf; gʌf/ *n* [U] (*infml* 口) worthless talk or ideas 毫无价值的话或意见；废话：*politicians talking the usual guff* 说老套废话的政客们

GUI /ˈguːɪ; ˈguɪ/ *abbr* 缩写 = (*computing* 计) graphical user interface (connection by means of a screen with its icons, menus, etc through which a user gains access to the functions of a computer, esp one with a high degree of pictorial representation rather than one requiring combinations of keystrokes) 图形用户界面，图形用户接口（使用户可以通过屏幕上的图标、菜单等而不是凭按键输入方式来运行计算机的接口）

gulag /'gu:læg, -lɑ:g; 'gulæg/ *n* (*Russian* 俄) (in Russia and the former Soviet Union) any one of a network of prison camps used to hold criminals and political prisoners in harsh conditions（俄罗斯和前苏联的）关押罪犯和政治犯的条件极恶劣的集中营，古拉格集中营：*He spent fifteen years in a gulag in a remote part of Siberia.* 他在西伯利亚一处偏远的集中营里呆了十五年。

Gulf War syndrome /gʌlf 'wɔ: sɪndrəʊm; gʌlf 'wɔr ˌsɪndrom/ *n* disorder of the nervous system suffered by many veterans of the Gulf War of 1991, possibly resulting from anti-nerve-gas medication and exposure to harmful chemicals used by the enemy, eg delousing powder 海湾战争综合征（许多经历了 1991 年海湾战争的退伍军人所患的神经系统紊乱征，病因是服用抗神经性毒气药物及接触敌方使用的有害化学物质如除虱粉等）：*Symptoms of Gulf War syndrome include skin rash, headaches and breathing difficulties.* 海湾战争综合症的症状为皮疹、头痛及呼吸困难。

gun club /'gʌn klʌb; 'gʌn klʌb/ *n* (**a**) group of people who meet together to practise the sport of shooting 一群一起练习射击运动的人 (**b**) place where a gun club has its activities 射击俱乐部

gung-ho /ˌgʌŋ'həʊ; gʌŋ'ho/ *adj* enthusiastic and eager, but not taking a situation very seriously or considering the consequences 狂热的：*gung-ho soldiers* 亢奋的士兵 ○ *a gung-ho attitude/spirit* 狂热的态度 *[心态]*

gun lobby /'gʌn lɒbɪ; 'gʌn lɑbɪ/ *n* [CGp] (esp in US) powerful and influential group of people who shoot for sport and thus defend the constitutional right of the American people to bear arms by resisting any greater state or federal control over the buying and ownership of guns（尤指在美国）游说议员反对管制枪支买卖者（一些从事射击运动的有权势者，他们因而抵制州政府或联邦政府对购买和持有枪支进行更严格的控制，以保卫宪法赋予民众携带武器的权利）Cf 参看 LOBBY 3A-Z

gunship /'gʌnʃɪp; 'gʌnʃɪp/ *n* heavily-armoured helicopter or other aircraft 装甲直升机；装甲飞机

gutted /'gʌtɪd; 'gʌtɪd/ *adj* [pred 作表语] (*Brit infml* 口) (**a**) exhausted; shattered; KNACKERED（KNACKER2(A-Z)）精疲力尽；累坏了：*At the end of a twelve-hour day with only half an hour for lunch, I feel gutted.* 十二小时的工作只有半小时吃午饭，一天下来，我累垮了。(**b**) badly shocked and disappointed 极其震惊和失望：*The news left us feeling gutted.* 这消息让我们感到万分震惊和失望。

Hh

hacker /'hækə(r); 'hækɚ/ *n* **1** person who enjoys using computers and writing programs for them 计算机迷（喜爱使用计算机及编写程序的人）**2** person who tries to gain unauthorized access to computer files or networks 黑客（竭力非法存取计算机文件或使用网络的人）：*Hackers have several times broken into files at the Defence Ministry that were thought to be secure.* 黑客已数度侵入国防部的电脑网络，接触已安全存放的文件。

hackette /hæ'ket; hæ'kɛt/ *n* (*infml usu derog* 口，通常作贬义) female reporter 女记者 Cf 参看 HACK3 2A-Z

hair-extension /'heərɪkˌstenʃn; 'hɛrɪkˌstɛnʃən/ *n* piece of false hair which is woven into the hair on sb's head to produce an appearance of greater thickness or length（编入真发使其看上去更厚或更长的）假发；织发 Cf 参看 HAIR-PIECE（HAIRA-Z）

hairspray /'heəspreɪ; 'hɛrspre/ *n* [U] sticky substance sprayed onto the hair to keep it in place 喷发定型剂；发胶

half-care /'hɑ:fkeə(r), *US* hæf-; 'hæfkɛr/ *n* [U] type of care provided in SHELTERED ACCOMODATION for elderly people who are able to look after themselves most of the time but which ensures that they are given help from trained staff if they need it 半自立护理（老年公寓提供的一种护理，老人们大多数时间生活自理，但需要时可得到训练有素的工作人员的帮助）：*If your mother doesn't want to go into a residential home, perhaps she would consider half-care.* 要是你母亲不愿去养老院，也许她会考虑接受半自立护理的。

halon /'heɪlɒn; 'helɑn/ *n* (*chemistry* 化) gaseous compounds consisting of carbon and halogens（HALOGENA-Z）, widely used in fire extinguishers 含碳和卤素的气体化合物（广泛用于灭火器中）

Hamas /hæ'mæs; hæ'mæs/ *n* Palestinian Islamic Fundamentalist (FUNDAMENTALISMA-Z) movement which supports the creation of a Palestinian state and is opposed to the peace negotiations with Israel 哈马斯（巴勒斯坦伊斯兰原教旨主义运动，目的为支持建立巴勒斯坦国家，反对与以色列进行和平谈判）Cf 参看 INTIFADA

handling /'hændlɪŋ; 'hændlɪŋ/ *n* [U] **1** action of touching, holding or moving sth with the hand(s)（用手）触摸，握，移动（某物）：*Constant handling had worn out the book's cover.* 书的封皮因经常翻阅而破损了。○ *rough handling* 粗暴对待 **2** process of dealing with an order or exchange of goods, tickets, etc（对订单、货物及票据更换等的）处理：*a small handling charge/fee* 一小笔手续费 **3** action of dealing with a situation, etc（对事态等的）处理，应付：*I was impressed by your handling of the whole affair.* 你对整个事件的处理令我十分佩服。**4** way in which a motor vehicle responds when driven 机动车开动时的性能：*The handling of the new model is light and quick.* 这部新型号的车开起来轻快灵便。

handset /'hændset; 'hændsɛt/ *n* part of a telephone that one holds to one's ear and also speaks into 电话听筒 Cf 参看 RECEIVER 3A-Z

hands-off /ˌhændz'ɒf, *US* -ɔ:f; hændz'ɔf/ *adj* [attrib 作定语] not interfering with or taking any part in sth 不干涉的：*the government's hands-off approach to industrial disputes* 政府对劳资纠纷的不干涉态度 Cf 参看 HANDS-ON（HAND1(A-Z)）

happening /'hæpənɪŋ; 'hæpənɪŋ/ *adj* (*sl* 俚) trendy; up-to-the-minute 时髦的；最新的：*a happening place* 时髦场所 ○ *Look happening — wear ruffs this summer.* 要新潮——这个夏天穿飞边。

happy hour /'hæpɪ aʊə(r); 'hæpɪ aʊr/ *n* (usu *sing* 通常作单数) (*infml* 口) period of time during a day in a bar when one can buy alcoholic drinks more cheaply than usual or have free snack food 快乐时光，优惠时间（一天中可在酒吧以优惠价买到酒类饮料或享用免费小吃的一段时间）：*Happy hour — 5 to 6 every evening!* 快乐时光——每晚 5 点到 6 点！

harassed /'hærəst, *US* hə'ræst; hə'ræst/ *adj* feeling or showing strain, eg because there are too many demands on one's time or energy（由于时间或精力不够等原因）精疲力尽的，有压力的：*a harassed-looking shop assistant* 一个显得精疲力尽的售货员 ○ *She felt harassed by the demands of family and work and by the strain of moving home.* 她被家庭、工作和搬家的重负压得喘不过气来。

harassment /'hærəsmənt, *US* hə'ræsmənt; hə'ræsmənt/ *n* [U] subjection of sb to pressure or threats, esp through unwanted sexual advances and indirect suggestions（性）骚扰：*Not only women suffer from harassment in* *the workplace; men do as well.* 不仅妇女在工作场所受到性骚扰，男人也不例外。

hardass /'hɑ:dæs, 'hɑ:dɑ:s; 'hɑrdæs, 'hɑrdɑs/ *adj* [attrib 作定语] (*US sl* 俚) difficult; tough; uncompromising 难对付的；强硬的；不妥协的

▷ **hardass** *n* person who has these qualities 难对付的家伙：*The General had the well-earned reputation of being a real hardass.* 那位将军是个名不虚传的硬汉。

NOTE 注： from *hard* and *ass* (Brit arse) 由 hard 和 ass（屁股，英式英语为 arse）二词合成

hardball /'hɑ:dbɔ:l; 'hɑrdbɔl/ *n* [U] (*US infml* 口) **1** baseball, as distinguished from softball 棒球（与垒球相区别）**2** (idm 习语) **play hardball** act aggressively or ruthlessly in business or politics（商业或政治上）出手狠，办事不手软：*Successful politicians learn to play hardball very early on in their careers.* 成功的政治家在他们的政治生涯之初即学会办事决不手软。

hard disk drive /hɑ:d 'dɪsk draɪv; hɑrd 'dɪsk draɪv/ (also **hard drive**) *n* (*computing* 计) part of the central processing unit of a computer that contains the hard disk which allows the user to store and retrieve data from it 硬盘驱动器（计算机中央处理机的一部分，内有供用户存取数据的硬盘）

hard-earned /ˌhɑ:d'ɜ:nd; hɑrd'ɝnd/ *adj* acquired with a lot of effort 来之不易的；经努力才得到的：*hard earned cash/success/victory* 来之不易的钱 *[成功/胜利]*

hard-faced /ˌhɑ:d'feɪst; hɑrd'fest/ *adj* showing no sympathy or feeling 铁石心肠的；冷酷无情的：*hard-faced officials* 铁石心肠的官员

hard-fought /ˌhɑ:d'fɔ:t; hɑrd'fɔt/ *adj* acquired or won by competing or fighting very hard 历尽艰辛获得的；好不容易赢得的：*a hard-fought battle/contest* 赢得艰苦的战斗 *[比赛]* Cf 参看 HARD-WON

NOTE 注： It is possible to lose a hard-fought battle. 艰苦战斗亦可能无法获胜。

hard hat /ˌhɑ:d 'hæt; hɑrd 'hæt/ (also **safety helmet**) *n* (*esp US*) special HELMET[A-Z] designed to protect the head, eg as worn by workers on a construction site 头盔，安全帽（如建筑工人所戴的）：*Hard hats must be worn at all times on the site.* 在工地上任何时候都必须戴头盔。

hard left /ˌhɑ:d 'left; hɑrd 'lɛft/ *n* **the hard left** [Gp] members of a left-wing (LEFT[2(A-Z)]) political group or party who hold the most extreme views 极左派分子 Cf 参看 HARD RIGHT

NOTE 注： the terms *left* and *right* originate from the positions occupied by the two main political parties in the British parliament on the left and right of the SPEAKER 4 (SPEAK[A-Z]) ☆ left（左派）与 right（右派）的名称来源于英国议会中两大党派分坐于下议院议长的左右两侧

hard-luck story /ˌhɑ:d'lʌk stɔ:rɪ; ˌhɑrd'lʌk stɔrɪ/ *n* (*often derog* 常作贬义) account of one's problems told in order to get sb's help, sympathy or money（为博得他人的同情、帮助、金钱等而说的）不幸故事，倒霉故事：*She told me some hard-luck story about losing her job.* 她向我倒苦水，诉说她丢饭碗的事。

NOTE 注： the implication often is that the story is not very believable or has been exaggerated 常暗示其内容不十分可信或是夸大其词 Cf 参看 SOB STORY (SOB[A-Z])

hard right /ˌhɑ:d 'raɪt; hɑrd 'raɪt/ *n* **the hard right** [Gp] members of a right-wing (RIGHT[5(A-Z)]) political group or party who hold the most extreme views 极右派分子 Cf 参看 HARD LEFT

hard rock /ˌhɑ:d 'rɒk; hɑrd 'rɑk/ *n* [U] rock music with a very driving beat and amplified sound 硬摇滚乐（一种节奏迫人的、喧闹的摇滚乐）

hard sell /ˌhɑ:d 'sel; hɑrd 'sɛl/ *n* [U sing] aggressive, pushy method of making a sale 强行推销；硬性推销：*the hard sell tactics of insurance salesmen* 保险公司推销员的强行推销手段 ○ *There was too much of the hard sell about his approach.* 他的推销方法太强硬。

hard up /ˌhɑ:d 'ʌp; hɑrd 'ʌp/ *adj* short of money 穷困的；窘迫的：*They've always been hard up.* 他们一直生活在窘迫之中。○ *hard up students* 穷学生

hard-wired /hɑ:d'waɪəd; hɑrd'waɪrd/ *adj* [usu pred 通常作表语] (of physical and mental abilities) built into the structure, eg of the brain; being part of the physical make up of a person or an animal（指生理和心理特征）固有的，根深蒂固的：*Is our gender identity hard-wired into our brains from the moment of conception?* 心理性别是生命伊始就深深地根植在我们的脑海里了吗？

▷ **hard-wiring** *n*

hard-won /ˌhɑ:d'wʌn; hɑrd'wʌn/ *adj* gained after a hard struggle 来之不易的；艰苦赢得的：*their hard-won political freedom* 他们得来不易的政治自由 ○ *hard-won concessions* 经过艰苦斗争赢得的让步 Cf 参看 HARD-FOUGHT

harvest /'hɑ:vɪst; 'hɑrvɪst/ *v* [Tn] take internal organs, corneas, etc from the bodies of people who have just died in order to transplant them into living patients 取器官（从刚去世的死者身上取出内脏、角膜等器官供移植到活人身上）：*Seventy people have died from receiving infected brain linings harvested from elderly patients.* 有七十人因为植入了从老年人身上取下已受感染的脑膜而死亡。○ *Many children's lives were saved when organs were harvested for transplant from victims of car crashes.* 从车祸死者身上取下器官来移植到病人身上，挽救了许多孩子的生命。

hate mail /'heɪt meɪl; 'het mel/ *n* [U] letters, usu anonymous, expressing hatred and hostility towards the recipient（通常匿名的，对收信人表示敌意的）攻击性信件：*After the trial, she found herself the target of hate mail.* 审判过后，她成为书信攻击的对象。

have nots /ˌhæv 'nɒts; hæv 'nɑts/ *n* **the have nots** [pl] people who have little money and few possessions 穷人 Cf 参看 HAVES

haves /hævz; hævz/ *n* **the haves** [pl] people who have a lot of money and possessions 富人

NOTE 注： often in the expression *the haves and the have nots* 常用于短语 the haves and the have nots（富人与穷人）中

HDTV /ˌeɪtʃ di: ti:'vi:; ˌetʃ di ti 'vi/ *abbr* 缩写 = high-definition television 高清晰度电视

head /hed; hɛd/ *n* (*US sl* 俚) drug addict 吸毒成瘾者；瘾君子 Cf 参看 BASEHEAD

head-butt /'hedbʌt; 'hɛdbʌt/ *n* act of hitting sb's chin or body violently and deliberately with the top of one's head 用头猛撞（某人的下巴或身体）：*He was expelled from the school for hurting a boy with a head-butt.* 他因为用头撞伤了一个男孩而被学校开除了。

▷ **head-butt** *v* [Tn] hit sb with a head-butt 用头猛撞

headcase /'hedkeɪs; 'hɛdkes/ *n* (*Brit sl* 俚) person who behaves violently and without thinking and may be a danger to himself or herself and to others 暴戾的人；疯子

NOTE 注： very similar in meaning to NUT-CASE (NUT[A-Z]) 与 nut-case 一词词义极为相似

headcount /'hedkaʊnt; 'hɛdkaunt/ *n* (act of counting the) total number of people, eg those employed by an organization 人数统计，人数（如机构雇员的）：*do a headcount* 统计人数 ○ *the latest headcount* 最近的人数

headed /'hedɪd; 'hɛdɪd/ *adj* having a LETTERHEAD (a) (LETTER[A-Z]) 印有信笺抬头的；印有姓名或公司名称及地址的：*headed note-paper/stationery* 印有信头的信纸 *[信笺信封]*

head-hunt /'hedhʌnt; 'hɛdhʌnt/ *v* [Tn] find and RECRUIT *v* 1[A-Z] suitable people for senior positions, esp by persuading them to leave their present positions 猎头物色（人才）（找寻并聘用合适人选担任高级职

务，尤指说服其跳槽）: *Did you apply for the job or were you head-hunted?* 你是自己申请来的还是被猎头物色来的？

heads-up /ˈhedzʌp; ˈhɛdzʌp/ *adj* [attrib 作定语] (*US*) showing confidence and achieving one's best and highest standard; alert 信心十足且处于最佳状态的；自信又神气活现的；机敏的 : *a heads-up team of researchers* 充满信心的尖子研究组

head-to-head /ˌhedtəˈhed; ˌhɛdtəˈhɛd/ *adj* facing sb/sth directly and in person in a dispute, contest, debate, etc（争论、竞争、辩论等中）面对面的 : *a head-to-head confrontation with his old rival* 与他的老对手的一次面对面的交锋

▷ **head-to-head** *adv* doing sth in a head-to-head way 面对面地 : *The two presidential candidates went head-to-head in the televised debate.* 两位总统候选人在电视上进行了一场面对面的辩论。

health tourism /ˈhelθ ˌtʊərɪzəm; ˈhɛlθ ˌtʊrɪzəm/ *n* [U] tourism that offers holidays with plenty of healthy activities（提供大量健身活动的）健身旅游（业）Cf 参看 ACTIVITY HOLIDAY

hearing dog /ˈhɪərɪŋ dɒg; ˈhɪrɪŋ dɑg/ *n* dog trained to guide and help the deaf（受训引导和帮助聋人的）助听狗 : *Hearing dogs are trained to draw the attention of their owner to such sounds as a doorbell or a smoke alarm.* 助听狗经过训练，能让主人注意到门铃、烟雾报警器之类的声音。

heft /heft; hɛft/ *n* (*infml* 口) influence and WEIGHT[1] 7 影响；分量 : *not an agreement that will have any real heft* 不是一个真正具有影响力的条约

heli-skiing /ˈhelɪˌskiːɪŋ; ˈhɛlɪˌskiɪŋ/ *n* (*sport* 体) skiing down from a point on a mountain side that has to be reached by helicopter 直升机高山滑雪（须用直升机才可到达山上起点的滑雪活动）

NOTE 注： a blend of *helicopter* and *skiing* 由 helicopter（直升机）和 skiing（滑雪）二词合成

hell /hel; hɛl/ *n* (idm 习语) **from hell** (*joc* 谑) awful; horrible; the worst one can imagine 从地狱来的；极讨厌的；糟糕透顶的 : *We've just endured the holiday from hell.* 我们刚捱过了一个鬼假期。○ *the flat-mate from hell* 同屋住的死鬼

NOTE 注： a joking exaggeration 一种带玩笑的夸张用法

helpdesk /ˈhelpdesk; ˈhɛlpdɛsk/ (also **help desk**) *n* team of specialists within an organization which is trained to help customers or users who have problems with computer equipment or software（计算机）维修处，维修组（机构内部的专业人员小组，经过训练可帮助顾客或用户解决计算机设备或软件的问题）

heptathlon /hepˈtæθlɒn; hɛpˈtæθlɑn/ *n* athletic contest consisting of seven different track-and-field events, officially introduced for women athletes in 1981 七项全能（田径）运动（于 1981 年正式成为女子运动项目）Cf 参看 PENTATHLON[A-Z], TRIATHLON

heritage /ˈherɪtɪdʒ; ˈhɛrətɪdʒ/ *adj* [attrib 作定语] relating to the shared past of a group of people and looked back upon with nostalgia 历史遗留的；怀旧的 : *It's an important heritage site.* 这是个重要的历史遗址。○ *Follow the heritage trail and rediscover ancient York.* 追随历史的足迹，你会重新发现古老的约克郡。Cf 参看 HERITAGE[A-Z]

□ **heritage tourism** *n* [U] tourism that offers holidays focusing on historical and cultural sites and interests 历史文化名胜旅游（业）: *Ireland has greatly benefited from the heritage tourism that brings so many Americans to the land of their ancestors.* 爱尔兰的历史遗迹和文化名胜旅游业将众多的美国人吸引到他们祖先的国度来，为该地区带来了丰厚的收益。

HGH *abbr* 缩写 = HUMAN GROWTH HORMONE

Hib /hɪb; hɪb/ *n* (*medical* 医) bacterium causing MENINGITIS[A-Z] in babies 婴儿脑脊膜炎菌

high /haɪ; haɪ/ *n* (idm 习语) **on a high** at the peak of a feeling of great well-being, satisfaction, etc; experiencing a drug-induced sense of well-being 感觉极好；似吸毒后飘飘欲仙般 : *She's been on a high ever since she got that promotion.* 自从提升后，她一直飘飘然。Cf 参看 HIGH[1] 8[A-Z]

high-end /ˈhaɪend; ˈhaɪɛnd/ *adj* [attrib 作定语] (usu of a technological product) expensive, advanced and aimed at the wealthier customer（常指技术产品）昂贵的，先进的，面向较富有的消费者的，高档的 : *high-end monitors/videos* 先进而昂贵的显示器［录像机］Cf 参看 LOW-END

high-five /haɪˈfaɪv; haɪˈfaɪv/ *n* (*US sl* 俚) gesture in which two people slap their right hands together high over their heads as a sign of celebrating success 击掌相庆（两人高举右手击掌以示庆贺）: *High-fives were exchanged all round when the winning point was scored.* 赢得决定性的一分时，大家高举右手相互击掌庆贺。

high-top /ˈhaɪtɒp; ˈhaɪtɑp/ *n* (*US*) sports-shoe with a high laced upper part reaching above the ankle, used mainly for baseball and basketball but also worn as a fashion item 高帮运动鞋（主要为打棒球和篮球时穿用，但亦为时新式样）

▷ **high-top** *adj* [attrib 作定语] (of a sports shoe) having the style of a high-top（指运动鞋）高帮的

highway *n* = SUPERHIGHWAY

himbo /ˈhɪmbəʊ; ˈhɪmbo/ *n* (*sl* 俚) man whose main asset is his good looks 好看但无特长的男子；帅哥 Cf 参看 BIMBO

NOTE 注： formed on analogy with *bimbo* (beautiful but stupid woman) but without the implication of lacking intelligence and sense 由 bimbo（没脑袋的美女）一词类推构成，但无缺乏聪明才智的含义

hip-hop /hɪpˈhɒp; hɪpˈhɑp/ *n* [U] (*US*) street subculture of urban teenagers which combines RAP music, GRAFFITI[A-Z] art and BREAK-DANCING (BREAK[1(A-Z)]) with ways of dressing and talking which are peculiar to them 嬉蹦族文化（一种街头亚文化，体现于服装及言谈独特的都市年轻人，喜爱唱快板歌、跳霹雳舞、沿街涂鸦）

▷ **hip-hop** *v* [I] dance to hip-hop music 跳嬉蹦舞 **hip-hop** *adj*

NOTE 注： *hip* has the meaning 'cool' and *hop* refers to 'dancing' ☆ hip 意为时髦，hop 意为跳舞

history /ˈhɪstrɪ; ˈhɪstrɪ/ *n* (*esp US infml* 口) done with; no longer of interest 完结；不再让人感兴趣 : *Don't worry about him. As far as I'm concerned, he's history.* 别担心他。据我所知，他已成为历史。○ *If you get on the wrong side of the boss, you're history.* 你要是惹恼了老板的话，你就完了。

hit[1] /hɪt; hɪt/ *n* (*computing* 计) single visit made by a user and recorded at a Web site on the Internet（互联网站记录下的用户的一次）访问 : *This page has recorded 380 hits since February 12.* 该网页自二月十二日以来已记录下 380 次用户的访问。

hit[2] /hɪt; hɪt/ *v* (idm 习语) **hit the ground running** start a new job, political administration, etc with great energy and with a lot of activity 充满干劲地开始（新的工作等）；新官上任三把火 : *The new team promise to hit the ground running. We've got a lot to do and we're determined to get on with it right away.* 新班子保证要大干一场。我们的任务很重，已下定决心马上就干起来。

HIV *abbr* 缩写 = HUMAN IMMUNODEFICIENCY VIRUS

holding operation /ˈhəʊldɪŋ ɒpəˌreɪʃn; ˈholdɪŋ ɑpəˌreʃən/ *n* action taken to control an existing situation which threatens bad consequences or to prevent it becoming any worse 控制局势的做法，维持现状的措

施（以防事态进一步恶化）: *All we can hope for is a holding operation to prevent any run on the bank leading to its collapse.* 我们只有希望有办法控制局面以防发生挤兑导致银行倒闭。

hole in one /həʊl ɪn 'wʌn; hol ɪn 'wʌn/ *n* (*sport* 体) occasion in golf when the ball is hit from the TEE 1(a)[A-Z] and falls into the hole with a single stroke（高尔夫球运动中）从发球区一击入穴: *He got a hole in one at the twelfth.* 他在第十二洞一击入穴。

hole-in-the-wall /'həʊlɪnðəˌwɔːl; 'holɪnðə'wɔl/ *n* (*pl* **holes-in-the-wall**) (*Brit infml* 口) automatic cash machine installed in an outside wall of a bank; automated teller machine (ATM)（银行外墙上的）自动提款机

holiday centre /'hɒlədeɪ sentə(r); 'hɑləde ˌsɛntɚ/ *n* (*Brit*) place with many facilities for tourists and popular with holiday-makers 度假中心；度假村: *Newquay is one of the best holiday centres on the north coast of Cornwall.* 纽基是康沃尔北岸的一个度假胜地。

holiday home /ˌhɒlədeɪ 'həʊm; ˌhɑləde 'hom/ *n* house, villa, flat, etc owned as a second home usu in an attractive area and used only for holidays（通常位于景色宜人地区的）度假屋，度假别墅: *They've bought a holiday home on the Cote d'Azur.* 他们在科达祖尔买下一栋度假别墅。 Cf 参看 SECOND HOME

holistic /həʊ'lɪstɪk; ho'lɪstɪk/ *adj* (**a**) relating to and taking into account the whole of sth rather than just parts of it 整体的；全面的: *a holistic approach to life* 一种全面的人生态度 (**b**) (*medical* 医) treating the whole person, eg their emotional condition, relationships, etc, rather than just the symptoms of a disease 全面医治的（对病人的身心各方面，包括情感、人际关系等进行治疗的，而非仅仅治疗病症的）: *holistic medicine* 全面治疗

home alone /həʊm ə'ləʊn; hom ə'lon/ *adj* (of a child) left at home unattended while the parents are out or away（指儿童）独自在家的，无人照看的: *A home alone child nearly died yesterday when she accidentally started a fire.* 昨天有个小女孩儿一个人在家不小心引起火灾，几乎被烧死。

NOTE 注: the expression became widely used following the release of the 1990 film *Home Alone* and its later sequels 此词组在 1990 年电影 Home Alone 及其续集上映后广为流行

home cinema /həʊm 'sɪnɪmə; hom 'sɪnəmə/ (*US* **home theater**) *n* [U, C] system for showing films at home under conditions very similar to those found in a cinema and making greater possible use of the television set and the video recorder, etc 家庭影院

home loan *n* (*infml* 口) = MORTGAGE[A-Z]

home page /'həʊm peɪdʒ; 'hom pedʒ/ *n* (*computing* 计) site on the Internet set up and maintained by a person or organization which users can visit for interest or to obtain information 主页，网页（私人或机构在互联网上所设的供用户访问的网站）: *I've got my own home page now. Why don't you try accessing it?* 我现在有了自己的主页了。你来看看好吗？

home parole /həʊm pə'rəʊl; hom pə'rol/ *n* [U] (in the US) system of PAROLE[A-Z] that makes use of ELECTRONIC TAGGING so that any unapproved movement away from home can be detected（美国的）家庭保外假释（使用电子监控的假释做法，旨在监视假释者有否违章离家）

home shopping /həʊm 'ʃɒpɪŋ; hom 'ʃɑpɪŋ/ *n* [U] buying goods from home, esp through the medium of cable television 电视购物 Cf 参看 INTERACTIVE SERVICES

NOTE 注: In the UK this term is more strictly limited to the use of mail-order catalogues 在英国此词限指使用邮购目录购物

homesitter /'həʊmsɪtə(r); 'homsɪtɚ/ *n* person who lives in sb's home and looks after it, while the owners are away, usu for a fee but sometimes simply rent-free（房主外出时住在其家中代为）照看房屋者（通常有酬劳）: *My homesitter will look after the cat and the plants while we are away.* 我们外出的时候，代我照看房子的人来照顾猫和花草。

home theater *n* = HOME CINEMA

homophobia /həʊmə'fəʊbɪə, hɒməʊ'fəʊbɪə; homə'fobɪə/ *n* [U] fear or dislike of homosexuals and homosexuality 恐同性恋症；对同性恋（者）的厌恶: *Some people have accused the administration of homophobia.* 有人指责政府厌恶同性恋者。

honcho /'hɒntʃəʊ; 'hɑntʃo/ *n* (*pl* **-os/oes**) (*infml* 口) boss; person in charge; a leader 老板；头儿: *Brown's (the) top honcho at Rover these days.* 布朗近来在罗弗当总头头。

honest broker /ˌɒnɪst 'brəʊkə(r); ˌɑnɪst 'brokɚ/ *n* person, often sb with nothing to gain personally, who tries to get other people to reach an agreement, esp in industrial or international disputes（尤指劳资或国际纠纷中的）中间人，调解人: *The United States has tried for years to play the part of an honest broker in the Israeli-Palestinian peace process.* 在以色列与巴勒斯坦的和平进程中，美国多年来一直努力充当调解人的角色。

'hood /hʊd; hud/ *abbr* 缩写 = (*esp US*) neighbourhood 邻居；邻里: *the kids in the 'hood* 邻里的孩子们

horlicks /'hɔːlɪks; 'hɔrlɪks/ (also **Horlicks**) *n* (*sl propr* 俚，专利名) muddle, mess, balls-up 混乱；一团糟

NOTE 注: the word which is the name of a brand of malted-milk powder is probably used because of its resemblance in sound to the word *bollocks* (BALLOCKS 2[A-Z]), esp in US pronunciation 原为一麦乳精品牌，转为此义可能因其读音，特别是美式读音类似 bollocks（胡言乱语）

hormone abuse /'hɔːməʊn əˌbjuːs; 'hɔrmon əˌbjus/ *n* [U] overuse of hormones, esp steroids, in order to build muscle and increase force and energy 滥用激素（过多服用激素，尤指类固醇，以使肌肉发达，增强体力和活力）: *Hormone abuse by athletes and their trainers is becoming harder and harder to detect.* 运动员及其教练使用激素的事越来越难查出了。

hormone replacement therapy /hɔːməʊn rɪ'pleɪsmənt ˌθerəpɪ; hɔrmon rɪ'plesmənt ˌθɛrəpɪ/ *n* [U] (*abbr* 缩写 **HRT**) (*medical* 医) taking of artificial female hormones under medical supervision, usu to counteract the effects of the MENOPAUSE[A-Z] and prevent OSTEOPOROSIS 荷尔蒙替代疗法（在医生指导下服用人造雌激素，通常旨在减轻绝经带来的影响，以及防止骨质疏松症）

horsiculture /'hɔːsɪˌkʌltʃə(r); 'hɔrsɪˌkʌltʃɚ/ *n* [U] (*Brit derog* 贬) commercial development of farmland and open countryside for horse owners who want grazing land 养马业开发（将农田与旷野供养马者开发成牧场）: *The spread of horsiculture will mean the destruction of the last habitats of Britain's wildflowers.* 养马业不断开发意味着英国仅余的野花生长环境亦将遭摧毁。

hospital drama /ˌhɒspɪtl 'drɑːmə; ˌhɑspɪtl 'drɑmə/ *n* television drama series which focuses on the professional and private lives of a group of doctors, esp their work with patients in a hospital 医院剧（描写一群医生的工作和生活，尤其是他们在医院医治病人的情形的电视系列剧）: *ER is the latest of a long line of successful hospital dramas.* 《急诊室》是一系列成功的医院剧中最新的一部。

hot-desking /hɒt'deskɪŋ; hɑt'dɛskɪŋ/ n [U] sharing of desks between workers rather than allocating one desk to each individual, done in the interests of saving office space and resources（为了节省办公室空间和开支而

实行的）共用办公桌制度：*Hot-desking works quite well when a lot of the workers are often out of the office.* 许多工作人员经常不在办公室，共用办公桌的做法是行得通的。

hot flush /ˌhɒt ˈflʌʃ; hɑt ˈflʌʃ/ *n* sudden sensation of being hot, caused by fear or embarrassment, or experienced by women during the MENOPAUSE^A-Z 潮热（由于害怕、尴尬或妇女更年期产生的一阵突然发热的感觉）

hot housing /ˈhɒt haʊzɪŋ; ˈhɑt hauzɪŋ/ *n* [U] special intensive education and training for children to develop into exceptionally intelligent and able adults 强化培养（对孩子进行特殊的强化教育和培训，使其成为智力和能力超群的人）Cf 参看 HOTHOUSE（HOT^A-Z）

hotting /ˈhɒtɪŋ; ˈhɑtɪŋ/ *n* [U] (*sl* 俚) practice of driving recklessly in a stolen car 驾驶偷来的汽车横冲直撞

▷ **hotter** *n* person who practises hotting 驾驶偷来的汽车横冲直撞者 Cf 参看 JOY-RIDE (JOY^A-Z)

hot tub /hɒt ˈtʌb; hɑt ˈtʌb/ *n* bath of hot aerated water used for pleasure or physical therapy（供娱乐或治疗用的）充气热水浴缸 Cf 参看 JACUZZI^A-Z

hot-wire /ˈhɒtwaɪə(r); ˈhɑtwaɪr/ *v* [Tn] (*sl* 俚 *esp US*) start the engine of a car, etc by bypassing the ignition switch 搭线（不使用点火开关将汽车等发动）：*They hot-wired the car and drove it thirty kilometres before they were stopped.* 他们搭线起动汽车，开了三十公里后被人拦住了。

house /haʊs; haus/ (also **house music**) *n* style of popular music intended for dancing to and featuring synthesized sounds and a repetitive beat 豪斯音乐（以合成音和重复节拍为特色的流行舞曲）

NOTE 注： from the *Warehouse*, a nightclub in Chicago where such music was first created in the mid-1980s and became popular 来自 Warehouse 一词，即芝加哥的韦尔豪斯夜总会，20 世纪 80 年代中期首创豪斯音乐并逐渐流行

house-husband /ˈhaʊshʌzbənd; ˈhaushʌzbənd/ *n* married man who performs the duties around the house traditionally carried out by a woman 家庭主夫；持家男人：*Since my wife was earning so well, we decided that she should go back to work after the birth of our first child and that I should stay home and be a house-husband.* 因为妻子收入很高，所以我们决定在第一个孩子出生后，她回去上班，而我则留在家中，当一名家庭主夫。

NOTE 注： formed on analogy with *housewife* 由 housewife（家庭主妇）一词类推构成

house-plant /ˈhaʊsplɑːnt, *US* -plænt; ˈhausplænt/ *n* plant that is grown indoors and used for decoration or to give pleasure 室内栽培植物

house-sit /ˈhaʊssɪt; ˈhaussɪt/ *v* [I, Ipr] (*esp US*) live in sb else's house without paying rent, sometimes in return for payment, while the owner is away（房主外出时）住在房主家中代为照看房屋（有时有酬劳）：*They asked me to house-sit and look after their plants and pets while they were on holiday.* 他们要我在他们度假时住在他们家中照看房子，并照料花草和宠物。Cf 参看 HOMESITTER

house-sitter *n* = HOMESITTER

housing benefit /ˈhaʊzɪŋ benɪfɪt; ˈhauzɪŋ bɛnəfɪt/ *n* [U] (in Britain) money given to certain people, eg the unemployed, single mothers, etc, by local councils to help them pay for their accommodation（英国地方议会发给失业者、单身母亲等的）住房补贴：*They were worried about cuts in their housing benefits.* 他们担心住房补贴会减少。

HRT *abbr* 缩写 = HORMONE REPLACEMENT THERAPY

hub and spoke /hʌb ənd ˈspəʊk; hʌb ənd ˈspok/ *n* pattern of air routing which is like a series of wheels, with a particular major important airport at each centre, like a HUB^A-Z, from which routes to all other airports radiate out like the spokes（SPOKE[1]）轮毂和车辐式空运系统（一种类似一系列轮子的空运系统，在每个中心，即‘轮毂’有一个指定的重要机场，从它到其他机场的航线则像‘车辐’一样向外辐射）

human growth hormone /hjuːmən ˈgrəʊθ ˌhɔːməʊn; hjumən ˈgroθ ˌhɔrmon/ *n* [U] (*abbr* 缩写 **HGH**) manufactured hormone developed to help AIDS^A-Z patients with skin-wasting conditions, but now sought as an anti-ageing treatment 人体生长激素（一种人造激素，原用于帮助出现皮肤消蚀状况的爱滋病病人，现被用于抗衰老）

human immunodeficiency virus /ˌhjuːmən ɪmjuːnəʊdɪˈfɪʃnsɪ vaɪərəs; ˌhjumən ɪmjunodɪˈfɪʃənsɪ vaɪrəs/ *n* [sing] (*abbr* 缩写 **HIV**) (*medical* 医) the virus responsible for the disease AIDS^A-Z 人体免疫缺损病毒；爱滋病病毒

humanoid /ˈhjuːmənɔɪd; ˈhjumənɔɪd/ *adj* resembling a human being 类人的；形状或特性似人的：*a strange humanoid creature* 一只奇怪的类人生物

NOTE 注： the implication usu is that sth *humanoid* is not actually human 通常指某物类似人但并非人类

▷ **humanoid** *n* humanoid thing 类人动物

human resources /hjuːmən rɪˈsɔːsɪz; hjumən rɪˈsɔrsɪz/ *n* [pl] department in an organization which deals with the administration, management and training of employees 人力资源部（机构内对雇员进行管理培训的部门）：*a post in human resources* 人力资源部门的一个职位

NOTE 注： very similar in function to a personnel department（PERSONNEL 2^A-Z）其职能相当于 personnel department（人事部门）

humongous /hjuːˈmʌŋgəs; hjuˈmʌŋgəs/ (also **humungous**) *adj* (*joc sl* 谑，俚) huge, enormous 巨大的；极大的：*There was a humongous row when she found out what he was really doing in London.* 她发现了他在伦敦干的好事，便大吵了一场。

hump *n* = SPEED BUMP

hunt saboteur /hʌnt sæbəˈtɜː(r); ˌhʌnt sæbəˈtɝ/ *n* (in Britain) person who opposes the hunting and killing of wild animals, esp foxes, by groups of men and women on horseback with hounds, and who tries by various means to prevent the hunt taking place or to make sure that it is unsuccessful（英国的）破坏狩猎者（反对狩猎者成群结队骑马带着猎狗捕杀野生动物，尤其是狐狸，并想方设法进行阻挠破坏的人）：*There is a small group of hunt saboteurs who do not stop short at violence, but they are not typical.* 有一小群不惜以暴力破坏狩猎的人，但这并不反映多数破坏者的行径。

hurt /hɜːt; hɝt/ *v* [I] (usu in continuous form 通常用进行时态) suffer damage caused by sb/sth 受损害的：*Shoppers are staying away this Christmas, and retailers are hurting.* 这个圣诞节顾客都不来了，零售商可惨了。

hydrospeeding /ˈhaɪdrəˌspiːdɪŋ; ˈhaɪdrəˌspidɪŋ/ *n* [U] (*sport* 体) sport in which participants wearing helmet, flippers and padded clothing throw themselves down rapids holding on to a float 急流漂流运动（参加者戴头盔、穿脚蹼和护身服，抱着浮板顺急流而下的一种运动）

NOTE 注： very similar to CANYONING 与 canyoning（峡谷漂流）极为相似

hyper- /ˈhaɪpə(r); ˈhaɪpɚ/ *prefix* 前缀 (*computing* 计) involving the arrangement of text and other machine-readable material so that a mixture of media, eg non-linear text, video, graphics and sound can be made and accessed by the user 超（将文字或其他机器可读资料排列，使非线性文字、影像、图表和音响效果能集于一体供用户使用的综合载体的）

NOTE 注： from the Greek prefix *huper-* meaning above, beyond which implies that the resource goes beyond a simple presentation of text in a linear order 源自希腊语前缀 huper- ，表示‘超出、高于’，此处指超出简单的线性文字排列

hyperinflation /ˌhaɪpərɪnˈfleɪʃn; ˌhaɪpɚɪnˈfleʃən/ *n* [U] situation in which very large and rapid price increases occur 恶性通货膨胀；极度通货膨胀

hyperkinetic syndrome *n* = ATTENTION DEFICIT DISORDER

hypermedia /ˈhaɪpəˌmiːdɪə; ˈhaɪpɚˌmiːdɪə/ *n* [U] (*computing* 计) method of presenting information through a mixture of media, eg text, video, graphics and sound so that related items of information are connected together 超媒体（将文字、影像、图表和声音等资料混合呈现的方法，使相关信息互相连通）: *Video-conferencing is one of the business resources made possible by the development of hypermedia.* 电视会议技术是随着超媒体的发展而实现的一种商业资源。 Cf 参看 MULTIMEDIA

hyperspace /ˈhaɪpəspeɪs; ˈhaɪpɚspes/ *n* [U] space of more than three dimensions, esp (in science fiction) an imaginary space-time CONTINUUM^A-Z which allows travel and communication at speeds greater than the speed of light 超空间，多维空间（尤指在科幻小说中假想的时空连续体，在其中游历和通讯，速度可超过光速）

hypo-allergenic /ˌhaɪpəʊæləˈdʒenɪk; ˌhaɪpoælɚˈdʒɛnɪk/ *adj* unlikely to cause any allergic reaction 不会导致过敏反应的: *a hypo-allergenic shampoo/sun cream* 不刺激皮肤的洗发液 *[防晒霜]*

Ii

IA *abbr* 缩写 = INFORMATION ANXIETY

ibuprofen /ˌaɪbjuːˈprəʊfn; ˌaɪbjuˈprofn̩/ *n* [U] (*medicine* 药) drug that reduces pain and inflammation, trade name Brufen 异丁苯丙酸（一种镇痛消炎药，商品名布洛芬）

icon /ˈaɪkɒn; ˈaɪkɑn/ *n* **1** person or object of particular admiration, esp one seen as a representative symbol of sth 偶像；具代表性的人或物: *that icon of the old West, the cowboy* 牛仔，昔日西部的代表 ○ *Diana came to be treated as an icon as people identified with her problems.* 人们对黛安娜的遭遇产生共鸣，她就逐渐被当作了偶像。

NOTE 注： a transferral of the original meaning of an image, esp of Christ or Mary, painted on wood and respected as a holy object in the Eastern Church 原指画在木头上被尊为东正教圣物的神像，尤指基督或圣母马利亚的像

2 (*computing* 计) image usu present on the start-up screen representing a facility or program on a computer system which is activated when clicked 图标（计算机中常出现于启动屏幕上，代表某一功能或程序的图形，可用鼠标击活）

ICQ /ˌaɪ siː ˈkjuː; ˌaɪ si ˈkju/ *n* computer software for downloading through the INTERNET, which enables account users to seek one another and chat instantly onscreen as well as send messages, Web sites (SITE), etc 网际呼叫器（一种计算机软件，经国际互联网下载后用户可搜寻对方并即时在屏幕上交谈和发送信息、网页等）

NOTE 注： the term is a homophonic representation of *I seek you* , with a linking sound between the consonant ‘k’ and ‘you’ 此词是 I seek you（我找你）的谐音写法，发音时把辅音 k 和 you 连接快读

ideas man /aɪˈdɪəz mæn; aɪˈdiəz mæn/ *n* person who has good ideas about, eg projects, designs, promotion campaigns, etc which other people then put into effect 出谋划策者；谋士: *He's our ideas man. He's always coming up with ways to make the exhibitions interesting.* 他是我们的谋士。他总能想出点子来让展览会办得有声有色。

iffy /ˈɪfɪ; ˈɪfi/ *adj* (*infml* 口) doubtful, dubious; uncertain 可疑的；不确定的: *‘Are you going to Australia again this year?’ ‘Well, at the moment it's all a bit iffy.’* ‘你今年还要去澳大利亚吗？’‘嗯，目前还说不准。’ ○ *She's had a rather iffy relationship with some architect.* 她与某建筑师关系暧昧。

IKBS *abbr* 缩写 = intelligent knowledge-based system = EXPERT SYSTEM

ill-concealed /ˌɪlkənˈsiːld; ˌɪlkənˈsild/ *adj* badly hidden, esp of emotions（尤指情绪）无意掩饰的，掩饰得不好的: *ill-concealed contempt/anger/mirth* 无意掩饰的轻蔑 *[愤怒 / 高兴]*

NOTE 注： the use of this word often implies that there has not been much attempt to conceal the emotion in question and in fact it is clear to see 这个词一般暗指并未努力掩饰感情，而且实际上让人明显看得出来

ill-conceived /ˌɪlkənˈsiːvd; ˌɪlkənˈsivd/ *adj* badly designed or planned; not well thought-out beforehand 考虑欠周的；不明智的: *an ill-conceived attempt to prevent the truth from coming out* 意欲阻止披露真相的不明智行动 ○ *ill-conceived plans* 考虑欠周的计划

ill-equipped /ˌɪlɪˈkwɪpt; ˌɪlɪˈkwɪpt/ *adj* ~ **(to do sth)** without the proper equipment, ability or qualifications 装备不足的；能力或资历不足的: *ill-equipped for the job* 不足以胜任工作 ○ *ill-equipped to deal with the present crisis* 无力应付目前危机 ○ *ill-equipped to meet the terrible weather conditions* 装备不足而无法抗御恶劣天气

ill-prepared /ˌɪlprɪˈpeəd; ˌɪlprɪˈpɛrd/ *adj* (**a**) not ready (for a situation, etc)（对情况等）未准备好的: *ill-prepared for the emergency* 对紧急情况未作充分准备 (**b**) badly planned or organized 计划不周的；组织混乱的: *an ill-prepared speech/expedition* 准备欠周的演讲、组织混乱的探险之旅

ill-tempered /ˌɪlˈtempəd; ˌɪlˈtɛmpɚd/ *adj* showing the effects of a bad mood; rude; IRRITABLE^A-Z 脾气坏的；易怒的: *an ill-tempered waiter/match* 脾气不好的侍者 *[对手]*

image processing /ˈɪmɪdʒ ˌprəʊsesɪŋ, *US* prɒses-; ˈɪmɪdʒ ˌprɑsɛsɪŋ/ *n* [U] (*computing* 计) analysis and manipulation of an image, eg to enhance and clarify it or for artistic effects 图像处理（分析和操纵图像，如为了艺术效果而将其放大和作清晰处理）

immune system /ɪˈmjuːn sɪstəm; ɪˈmjun sɪstəm/ *n* system in the body which produces substances to fight off disease 免疫系统: *In the later stages of AIDS, the immune system of the patient almost ceases to operate.* 在艾滋病晚期，病人的免疫系统几乎完全停止工作。

impaired /ɪmˈpeəd; ɪmˈpɛrd/ *adj* (as the second element of a compound 用以构成复合词的后半部分) having reduced capacity 能力衰减的: *hearing impaired* 听力衰退的

NOTE 注： to date this is the most frequently found formation but some extension into the area of computing has led to forms such as UNIX impaired, describing users who find this particular piece of software impossible to master 目前这是最常见的组合，但已延伸到计算机领域，构成如 UNIX impaired 等词，用以形容使用某软件有困难的用户

import /ɪmˈpɔːt; ɪmˈpɔrt/ *v* [Tn] (*computing* 计) transfer data into a computer from a distant one, or introduce data into one computer application from another（将数据从其他计算机或应用程序中）输入

impro /ˈɪmprəʊ; ˈɪmpro/ (also **improv**) *n* [U] form of live entertainment in which actors improvise their material and interact with the audience 即兴表演（演员作现场发挥，并有观众参与的直播娱乐节目）: *Impro shows usually have comic themes.* 即兴演出的主题通常是喜剧性的。

income support /'ɪnkʌm səpɔ:t; 'ɪnkʌm səpɔrt/ *n* [U] (in Britain) government financial aid given to people with a low income from public funds 收入补助（英国政府从公共基金中发给低收入者的财政资助）: *He's been on income support ever since he was made redundant.* 他被裁后就一直靠收入补助生活。○ *single parent families on income support* 依赖收入补助的单亲家庭

inconvenienced *adj* = CHALLENGED

independent financial adviser /ˌɪndɪpendənt faɪˌnænʃl əd'vaɪzə(r); ˌɪndɪpɛndənt faɪˌnænʃəl əd'vaɪzɚ/ *n* (*abbr* 缩写 **IFA**) professional adviser on personal finances, eg life insurance, investment, etc who is not employed by any company that sells financial services, eg a bank or insurance company 独立财务顾问（不受雇于任何银行或保险公司等金融机构而对私人理财提供专业意见的人士）

in-depth /'ɪndepθ; 'ɪndɛpθ/ *adj* [attrib 作定语] very thorough and detailed 深入的；彻底的；透彻的: *an in-depth analysis/article/discussion/interview* 深入的分析[文章/讨论/采访]

indie /'ɪndɪ; 'ɪndɪ/ *n* (*infml* 口) independent record company or band 独立唱片公司；独立乐队: *an indie label* 独立唱片公司商标 ○ *the indie scene* 独立乐队的现况

induction loop /ɪn'dʌkʃn lu:p; ɪn'dʌkʃən lup/ *n* loop of wire around an area in a building, eg a theatre, that produces an electromagnetic signal, eg sound, which can be picked up by hearing aids worn by partially deaf people 电磁感应圈（环绕建筑物如剧院内某一区域的金属线圈，所发出的电磁信号如声音等可被部分失聪者所戴的助听器接收）

industrial archaeology /ɪnˌdʌstrɪəl ɑ:kɪ'ɒlədʒɪ; ɪnˌdʌstrɪəl ɑrkɪ'ɑlədʒɪ/ *n* [U] study of old machines, factories, bridges, etc used in early industrial times 工业考古学（对工业发展初期的机器、工厂及桥梁等进行的研究）: *Industrial archaeology reveals a lot about how modern society has changed and developed.* 工业考古学大大地揭示了现代社会曾如何变化与发展。

industrial arts /ɪnˌdʌstrɪəl 'ɑ:ts; ɪnˌdʌstrɪəl 'ɑrts/ *n* [sing v] (*US*) training given to students about how to use tools and machines for career purposes 工业技艺（教学生如何使用工具和机器以便为将来谋职作准备的训练课程）

industrial tourism /ɪnˌdʌstrɪəl 'tʊrɪzəm; ɪnˌdʌstrɪəl 'tʊrɪzəm/ *n* [U] organization and experience of holidays in which tourists visit workplaces to see other people at work 工业旅游（到他人的工作场所去参观的旅游）

industrial tribunal /ɪnˌdʌstrɪəl traɪ'bju:nl; ɪnˌdʌstrɪəl traɪ'bjunl/ *n* group of officials authorized to hear and to settle disputes between employees and employers 工业法庭，劳资法庭（被授权负责解决劳资纠纷的裁判团体）: *The case was brought before an industrial tribunal.* 该案件被送交工业法庭裁决。

industry-wide /ˌɪndəstrɪ'waɪd; ˌɪndəstrɪ'waɪd/ *adj* [attrib 作定语] affecting or relating to the whole situation of a particular industry 行业性的；全行业的: *engineering unions battling for an industry-wide cut in working hours* 为全行业争取缩短工作时间的各工程业工会

info /'ɪnfəʊ; 'ɪnfo/ *n* [U] (*infml* 口) information 信息；资料: *For further info visit our web site.* 欲知详情，请看看我们的网页。

infomercial /ˌɪnfə'mɜ:ʃl; ˌɪnfə'mɝʃəl/ (also **informercial**) *n* (*esp US*) advertising film, esp on television, which presents information in an apparently objective way（尤指电视上貌似客观的）商品资讯节目，资讯广告节目: *The travel film was clearly an infomercial for the hotel chain that sponsored it.* 这部旅游片显然是在为那家赞助它的连锁酒店做广告。

information anxiety /ɪnfəˌmeɪʃn æŋ'zaɪətɪ; ɪnfɚˌmeʃən æŋ'zaɪətɪ/ *n* [U] (*abbr* 缩写 **IA**) feeling of anxiety caused by the fear that one will not be able to deal with the very large amount of information that is available through modern means of communication and data storage 信息焦虑感（因担心无力应付现代通讯和数据存储手段所提供的大量信息而产生的焦虑感）

information crime /ɪnfəˌmeɪʃn 'kraɪm; ɪnfɚˌmeʃən 'kraɪm/ *n* [U,C] action of gaining confidential information by hacking (HACK[2(A-Z)]) into computer files that were thought to be secure 信息犯罪（私自打开他人的计算机文件，盗取机密资料）: *Information crime rates are rising fast, and today's police need to be specially trained in this area.* 信息犯罪率正迅速上升，现代警察需要在这方面接受特别训练。Cf 参看 CYBER CRIME

information highway *n* = SUPERHIGHWAY

information overload /ɪnfəˌmeɪʃn 'əʊvələʊd; ɪnfɚˌmeʃən 'ovɚlod/ *n* [U] state of having so much information available, esp as a result of modern means of communication and retrieval, that one is no longer able to process it or use it properly 信息超载（现代通讯和检索手段带来大量的信息，以致人们已无法恰当地处理或使用）

information superhighway *n* = SUPERHIGHWAY

infotainment /ˌɪnfə'teɪnmənt; ˌɪnfə'tenmənt/ *n* [U] broadcast material that is intended both to entertain and to inform 资讯娱乐资料（同时提供资讯和娱乐的广播资料）: *The new multi-media on-line encyclopedia is a superb example of infotainment.* 新的多媒体网上百科全书是资讯娱乐资料的典范。

in-house /ˌɪn'haʊs; ɪn'haʊs/ *adj* [attrib 作定语] produced or happening within a company or an organization 公司内部的；机构内部进行的: *an in-house library/magazine* 公司内部图书馆[杂志] ○ *in-house training* 机构内部培训

in-joke /'ɪndʒəʊk; 'ɪndʒok/ *n* joke shared by a small group of people 内部笑话（某圈子里的人才能领会的笑话）: *'Sorry, it's a bit of an in-joke. You would only get it if you'd been at the party.'* '对不起，这是个外人不得而知的笑话。你只有参加过那个晚会才能领会。'

ink-jet printer /'ɪŋkdʒet ˌprɪntə(r); 'ɪŋkdʒɛt ˌprɪntɚ/ *n* printer linked to a computer in which the characters are formed through the action of minute jets of ink 喷墨打印机

inner child /ɪnə 'tʃaɪld; ɪnɚ 'tʃaɪld/ *n* [sing] original or true self of a person, esp when regarded as damaged or suppressed by bad experiences during childhood（尤指因童年痛苦经历而受伤害或被压抑的）内心自我: *Getting in touch with your inner child will start the healing process.* 正视你的内心自我，你会逐渐康复的。

installation /ˌɪnstə'leɪʃn; ˌɪnstə'leʃən/ (also **installation art**) *n* collection of objects, which may be familiar things in unusual settings and arrangements or very strange things, presented in a gallery or museum as a work of art 奇特展品，装置作品展（在艺术馆或博物馆作为艺术品展出的作品，可能是寻常的东西配以特殊背景，或将之以特殊的方式陈设，又或者本身是十分奇特的东西）: *Some of the installations were amusing and some even allowed viewers to interact with them.* 有些装置展品很有趣，有些甚至可以根据参观者的意图而作相应变化。

intellectual property /ˌɪntəˌlektʃʊəl 'prɒpətɪ; ˌɪntəˌlɛktʃuəl 'prɑpɚtɪ/ *n* [U,C] (*law* 律) books, formulas, designs, etc which only the writer or the inventor has the legal right to reproduce and use freely 知识财产: *uphold* *intellectual property rights* 保护知识产权 ○ *It's becoming more and more difficult to protect intellectual property rights in this era of instant communication and publication.* 在这瞬时通讯和出版的时代，保护知识产权变得越来越困难了。

intelligent knowledge-based system *n* = EXPERT SYSTEM

interactive fiction *n* = COMPUTER FICTION

interactive services /ˌɪntərˌæktɪv ˈsɜːvɪsɪz; ɪntɚˌæktɪv ˈsɝvɪsɪz/ *n* [pl] facility offering such services as HOME SHOPPING, home banking, etc, using the television and telephone lines（通过电视、电话提供电视购物、家庭银行等服务的）交互服务

interactive television service *n* = ITV

interest-free /ˌɪntrəstˈfriː; ˌɪntərɪstˈfri/ *adj* (on borrowed money) having no interest charged（指贷款）无息的：*an interest-free loan* 一笔无息贷款 ○ *interest-free credit* 无息信贷

intergovernmental /ˌɪntəˌɡʌvənˈmentl; ˌɪntɚˌɡʌvɚnˈmɛntl̩/ *adj* concerning or happening between two or more governments 政府间的：*an intergovernmental conference* 一次政府间的会议

intermediate technology /ˌɪntəˌmiːdɪət tekˈnɒlɪdʒɪ; ˌɪntɚˌmidɪət tɛkˈnɑlədʒɪ/ *n* technology suitable for use in developing countries（适用于发展中国家的）中级技术

Internet /ˈɪntəˌnet; ˈɪntɚˌnɛt/ (also **the Net**) *n* [sing] international computer network which consists of a large number of individual computers and computer systems connected by telecommunications circuits 国际互联网；因特网：*The Internet grants access to rich sources of information, but must be used wisely.* 互联网虽可提供丰富的信息资料，但须善加利用才是。

NOTE 注： the word comes from *inter-* plus *network* 由 inter-（互相的）与 network（网络）二词合成

□ **Internet cafe** *n* cafe which provides a number of computer terminals so that customers can log on to the Internet, send and receive e-mail, etc as well as have a cup of coffee 互联网咖啡屋，网吧（备有数台计算机终端的咖啡屋，顾客可登录上网，边收发电子邮件等，边喝咖啡）

interwar /ˌɪntəˈwɔː(r); ˌɪntɚˈwɔr/ *adj* existing or happening between the end of one war and the start of another, esp the First and Second World Wars 两次战争之间的（尤指两次世界大战之间的）：*the interwar period* 两次战争之间的时期

intifada /ɪntɪˈfɑːdə, ɪntəˈfɑːdə; ɪntɪˈfɑdə, ɪntəˈfɑdə/ (also **intifadah**) *n* [sing] Arab uprising, specifically the Palestinian uprising and unrest in the Israeli-occupied area of the West Bank and Gaza Strip, beginning in late 1987 and continuing until the mid-90s 因塔法德暴动（阿拉伯人暴动，尤指自 1987 年末直至 90 年代中期，以色列占领的约旦河西岸及加沙地带的巴勒斯坦人的起义）：*The intifida involved children as young as three and four.* 年仅三四岁的儿童也卷入了因塔法德暴动。○ *The intifida generation has grown up.* 因塔法德暴动时出生的一代已长大成人。

NOTE 注： the word *intifaḍa* in the original Arabic implies a shaking-off of the yoke of an oppressor 在阿拉伯文中 intifaḍa 一词含有摆脱压迫的意思

intranet /ˈɪntrənet; ˈɪntrənɛt/ *n* (*computing* 计) communications network, private to an organization, which uses the same technology as the INTERNET 内联网（在机构内运用 Internet（互联网）技术构建的内部网络）

invisibles /ɪnˈvɪzəblz; ɪnˈvɪzəbl̩z/ *n* [pl] (*commerce* 商) INVISIBLE 2 exports and imports 无形输出与输入

invitational /ˌɪnvɪˈteɪʃənl; ˌɪnvɪˈteʃənl̩/ *adj, n* (*esp US sport* 体) (sports event) in which only invited competitors may take part 只限于被邀请者参加的（体育比赛）：*the invitational Rugby Sevens* 七人橄榄球邀请赛 ○ *the last invitational event of the football season* 足球赛季的最后一场邀请赛

in vitro fertilization (*abbr* 缩写 **IVF**) ⇨ IN VITRO[A-Z]

inward investment /ˌɪnwəd ɪnˈvestmənt; ˌɪnwɚd ɪnˈvɛstmənt/ *n* [U] (*commerce* 商) investment by foreign companies and organizations in a country 内向性投资（外国公司或组织所作的投资）

in your face /ɪn jɔː ˈfeɪs; ɪn jʊr ˈfes/ *interj* (*infml* 口) (used as an exclamation of scorn or derision 用以表示轻蔑或嘲弄)：*Young criminals are plainly saying 'In your face!' to the police.* 现在年轻罪犯干脆直接对警察说'去你的！'

▷ **in your face** (also **in-your-face**) *adj* (*infml* 口) aggressive; provocative 攻击性的；挑衅的：*an in-your-face attitude* 挑衅的态度

ion exchange /ˈaɪən ɪkˌstʃeɪndʒ, *US* also ˈaɪɒn; ˈaɪən ɪksˈtʃendʒ, ˈaɪɑn/ *n* (*physics* 物) exchange of ions (ION[A-Z]) of the same charge between a solution, usu water, and a solid, used esp in the process of water softening 离子交换（在溶液（通常为水）和固体之间作等电荷的离子交换，尤用于软化水质）

ionizer /ˈaɪənaɪzə(r); ˈaɪənaɪzɚ/ *n* device which improves the quality of air in a room by producing negative ions 离子发生器（产生负离子以改善室内空气质量的装置）：*The ionizer might help with your asthma.* 离子发生器可助你治疗哮喘。

IPR /aɪ piː ˈɑː(r); aɪ pi ˈɑr/ *abbr* 缩写 = intellectual property rights (legal rights sb has to his or her INTELLECTUAL PROPERTY) 知识产权

Islamist /ɪzˈlɑːmɪst; ɪsˈlɑmɪst/ *n* follower of Islam who is also a strong supporter of the cause of the Islamic religion and people wherever there is a conflict 伊斯兰教信徒；伊斯兰教事业的坚定支持者

item /ˈaɪtəm; ˈaɪtəm/ *n* [sing] (*infml* 口) couple in a romantic or sexual relationship 情侣；性伴侣：*the latest hot Hollywood item* 最新一对家喻户晓的好莱坞情侣

iTV /ˈaɪ tiː viː; ˈaɪ ti vi/ *abbr* 缩写 = interactive television service (service which offers video-on-demand, shopping-on-demand, etc) 交互式电视服务；互动电视服务（可提供即时点播节目、电视购物等的服务）

IVF (also **in vitro fertilization**) ⇨ IN VITRO[A-Z]

Jj

jacks /dʒæks; dʒæks/ *n* [pl] (*esp US*) (**a**) game in which small metal objects must be picked up while a small ball is bounced and then caught by a player before it touches the ground again 抛接子游戏（游戏者将小球弹起，并在其落地之前将其接住，在此期间要捡起一些小金属物件）(**b**) objects used in the game of jacks 用来玩抛接子游戏的物件

jailbait /ˈdʒeɪlbeɪt; ˈdʒelbet/ *n* (pl unchanged 复数不变) (*sl* 俚) girl or girls under the AGE OF CONSENT (AGE[1(A-Z)]) 未成年女子；牢狱囮子

NOTE 注： such young girls may tempt customers, ie act as *bait*, but anyone who yields to the temptation risks going to *jail* 这类年轻女子或会像诱饵 (bait) 一样诱惑顾客，然而受其诱惑者却有可能入狱 (go to jail)

jam /dʒæm; dʒæm/ *n* (idm 习语) **jam tomorrow** good or pleasant thing which is always promised or expected in the future, but usu never obtained 许而不给的好东西；可望而不可即的事物：*In this job, it's jam tomorrow but never jam today.* 做这份工作，好的回报始终是可望而不可即。Cf 参看 JAM[1] 1[A-Z]

Japanimation /dʒəpænɪˈmeɪʃn; dʒəpænɪˈmeʃən/ *n* [U] animated cartoons produced in Japan 日本卡通片

NOTE 注： a blend of *Japan* and *animation* 由 Japan 和 animation（卡通片）二词合成

Japglais /ˈdʒæpgleɪ; ˈdʒæpgle/ *n* [U] mainly meaningless words and expressions, based on English, made up by Japanese manufacturers and placed on their products（日本制造商标于其产品上，按英语创造但大多无意义的）日式英语：*This T-shirt says 'Let's cuddly our happiful.' What on earth does that Japglais mean?* 这件 T 恤衫上写着 Let's cuddly our happiful 。这日式英语究竟是什么意思？

Java /ˈdʒɑːvə; ˈdʒɑvə/ *n* [U] (*propr computing* 专利名，计) programming language used to create networking applications, esp interactive elements within WORLD WIDE WEB pages ☆ Java 语言（一种用以设计网络应用程序的语言，尤指万维网页上的交互单元编程语言）: *new Java software* 新的 Java 软件

jelly shoes /ˈdʒelɪ ʃuːz; ˈdʒɛlɪ ʃuz/ *n* [pl] brightly coloured sandals made of moulded plastic 果冻鞋（由塑料模压成的色彩鲜艳的凉鞋）

NOTE 注：the name comes from the fact that the material of which the shoes are made has the bright colours and transparency of jelly 制造此种鞋的原材料具有果冻 (jelly) 的亮丽颜色及透明感，故名

Jerusalem artichoke *n* = ARTICHOKE 2^A-Z^

jetfoil /ˈdʒetfɔɪl; ˈdʒɛtfɔɪl/ *n* fast passenger boat which moves on the same principle as the HYDROFOIL^A-Z^ 喷射水翼船

jet ski /ˈdʒet skiː; ˈdʒɛt ski/ *n* (*pl* ~ **s**) (*sport* 体) jet-propelled vehicle rather like a motor-bike, used for riding at speed across water 喷射式滑水橇（以喷射驱动类似摩托车的运载器，可在水上快速行驶）

▷ **jet-ski** *v* ride on a jet ski 驾驶喷射式滑水橇

Jiffy bag /ˈdʒɪfɪ bæg; ˈdʒɪfɪ bæg/ *n* (*Brit propr* 专利名) thick protective envelope used for posting delicate or breakable items（用于邮寄易受损或易碎物品的）厚保护层信封

job-hunt /ˈdʒɒbhʌnt; ˈdʒɑbhʌnt/ *v* [I] (usu in the continuous tenses 通常用进行时态) look for a job 找工作；谋职：*They've been job-hunting ever since they left school.* 他们自离开学校后就一直在找工作。

Joe Sixpack /dʒəʊ ˈsɪkspæk; dʒo ˈsɪkspæk/ *n* (*US slightly derog* 略带贬义) average, blue-collar worker 普通男子；蓝领工人：*Ask any Joe Sixpack.* 随便问谁吧。

NOTE 注：the average working men's favourite drink comes in a sixpack which is a pack of six cans of beer fastened by a plastic collar ☆ sixpack 为用塑料箍扎在一起的六听啤酒，很受一般工人喜爱

Joint Chiefs of Staff /ˌdʒɔɪnt ˌtʃiːfs əv ˈstɑːf, *US* ˈstæf; ˌdʒɔɪnt ˌtʃifs əv ˈstæf/ *n* [pl] military advisers to the US President 参谋长联席会议（美国总统的军事顾问团）

jokesmith /ˈdʒəʊksmɪθ; ˈdʒoksmɪθ/ *n* person who is a professional writer of jokes; comedian 笑话作家；喜剧艺人

NOTE 注：formed on analogy with *blacksmith* 由 blacksmith（铁匠）一词类推构成

judgemental /dʒʌdʒˈmentl; dʒʌdʒˈmɛntḷ/ *adj* **1** very critical 苛刻的；挑剔的：*I dislike her judgemental attitude.* 我不喜欢她吹毛求疵的态度。 **2** of or concerning judgement 判断的：*judgemental errors* 判断上的错误

juice box /ˈdʒuːs bɒks; ˈdʒus bɑks/ *n* small paper carton with an attached plastic straw containing a single portion of fruit juice 盒装果汁（附塑料吸管的小纸盒，内装供一次饮用的果汁）

jumping /ˈdʒʌmpɪŋ; ˈdʒʌmpɪŋ/ *adj* [pred 作表语] (*infml* 口) (esp of places and events) lively, interesting, exciting（尤指地方和事件）充满生气，有趣，令人激动：*London is the place to be this summer; the town is really jumping.* 今夏伦敦是个好去处，整个城市充满生气。 Cf 参看 KICKING

jump-rope /ˈdʒʌmprəʊp; ˈdʒʌmprop/ *n* (*US*) (**a**) children's jumping game in which a SKIPPING-ROPE (SKIP^1(A-Z)^) is used 跳绳游戏 (**b**) SKIPPING-ROPE (SKIP^1(A-Z)^) 跳绳

jungle fever /dʒʌŋgl ˈfiːvə(r); dʒʌŋgḷ ˈfivɚ/ *n* [U] (*joc or derog* 谑或贬) strong desire to have an interracial sexual relationship 丛林热（与异族人发生性关系的强烈欲望）

junior college /ˌdʒuːnɪə ˈkɒlɪdʒ; ˈdʒunjɚ ˈkɑlɪdʒ/ *n* (*US*) type of college offering students courses for two years before they go on to complete their studies in a senior college 初级学院（两年制学院，学生毕业后可进大学继续攻读大学课程）

junior school /ˈdʒuːnɪə skuːl; ˈdʒunjɚ skul/ *n* (*Brit*) school attended by children between 7 and 11（英国 7 到 11 岁儿童上的）小学

junk bond /ˈdʒʌŋk bɒnd; ˈdʒʌŋk bɑnd/ *n* (*commerce* 商) BOND 2^A-Z^ with a high yield but also involving high risk. Junk bonds are often issued by the new owners of a company to raise money quickly so as to pay the loans resulting from the buying process 垃圾债券，低值债券（获利高但也风险大的债券，通常由某公司的新购买者发行以迅速募集资金偿还购买时所借贷款）：*The yield on junk bonds does not compensate for the risks.* 低值债券的利润并不足以抵消它的风险。

junk fax /ˈdʒʌŋk fæks; ˈdʒʌŋk fæks/ *n* material sent to you by fax which you have not asked for, eg advertisements 垃圾传真（不曾索取却自动发来的传真，如广告等）：*The machine won't accept any numbers that you haven't recorded, so you won't be troubled by junk faxes.* 这台传真机只接收你已登录其号码的传真机发来的传真，因此你不会受到垃圾传真的困扰。

junkmail /ˈdʒʌŋkmeɪl; ˈdʒʌŋkmel/ *n* [U] material sent to sb by post which is not asked for, eg advertisements, requests for donations to charity, etc 垃圾邮件（不曾索取却自动寄来的邮件，如广告、慈善募捐信函等）

just-in-time /dʒʌstɪnˈtaɪm; dʒʌstɪnˈtaɪm/ *adj* (*commerce* 商) relating to a manufacturing system in which components are delivered at the time required for assembly rather than taking up storage space and thus adding to the costs 按需及时发送的（在生产制度中为减低成本，产品部件在需要时才运送以避免占用储存空间）

▷ **just-in-time** *n* (*commerce* 商) just-in-time system 产品部件按需及时发送制度：*The advantage of just-in-time is that the manufacturer doesn't have to keep a large inventory of parts on hand.* 按需及时发送产品部件的好处在于制造商手上无须积压大批零件。

Kk

kaizen /ˈkaɪzen; ˈkaɪzɛn/ *n* [U] (*Japanese* 日语) Japanese business philosophy of continuous improvement in working practices and personal efficiency, leading to better performance and productivity 改进式企业经营原则（不断改进工作方法和提高员工效率的日本式经营原则，旨在取得更佳工作表现和生产力）

NOTE 注：from Japanese, literally meaning 'improvement' 源自日语，意谓 '改善'

karaoke /kærəˈəʊkɪ, kærɪˈəʊkɪ; kærɪˈokɪ/ *n* [U] **1** sound system which allows people to sing popular songs as soloists against a pre-recorded backing and also to record their performance on tape or video if they wish 卡拉 OK **2** pastime of singing to the karaoke system 唱卡拉 OK 消遣：[attrib 作定语] *karaoke bars or boxes as they are called in Hong Kong* 卡拉 OK 酒吧或者按香港叫法称做卡拉 OK 房间

NOTE 注：from a Japanese phrase meaning 'empty (ie absent) orchestra' 源自日语，意为 '无人的乐队'

karoshi /kæ'rəʊʃɪ; kæ'roʃɪ/ *n* [U] sudden death caused by overwork or job-related exhaustion（工作劳累过度引起的）猝死：*a victim of karoshi* 因工作过度劳累而猝死者

NOTE 注： a Japanese word containing elements meaning 'excess', 'labour' and 'death' 为日语词，包含'过量'、'劳动'、'死亡'之意

keratotomy /ˌkerə'tɒtəmɪ; ˌkɛrə'tɑtəmɪ/ *n* [sing] (*medical* 医) surgical operation involving cutting into the cornea of the eye, esp to correct short-sightedness（尤为矫正近视所做的）角膜切开术

Kevlar /'kevlɑ:(r); 'kɛvlɑr/ *n* [U] (*US propr* 专利名) very strong synthetic fibre used to make bullet-proof vests for policemen, military personnel, etc 凯夫拉（制作防弹衣的质地牢固的合成纤维）

keyhole surgery /ˌki:həʊl 'sɜ:dʒərɪ; ˌkihol 'sɝdʒərɪ/ *n* [U] (*infml* 口) surgery carried out through a very small incision, using imagery supplied by fibre-optic devices to guide the surgeon 小孔手术，内窥镜手术（根据光纤设备提供的图像，通过一个极细小的切口所做的外科手术）：*keyhole surgery on the knee* 膝关节小孔手术 ○ *Much quicker recovery times are claimed for those who have undergone keyhole surgery.* 据称那些做了小孔手术的病人恢复起来要快得多。

NOTE 注： known more technically as *minimally invasive surgery* 专业名称为 minimally invasive surgery（微创手术）

keylock /'ki:lɒk; 'kilɑk/ *n* remote locking device 遥控锁栓装置：*The keylock allows you to open or close the car doors from a short distance away.* 用这种遥控锁可在离汽车不远处打开或关上车门。

kick ass /kɪk 'ɑ:s, *US* æs; kɪk 'æs/ *v* [I] (*US sl* 俚) get people moving and make things happen in an energetic and forceful way 鞭策；推动；搞活：*When I get over there I'm going to kick ass. Just watch me.* 我到那儿后要把一切搞活，等着瞧好了。

kick-down /'kɪkdaʊn; 'kɪkdaʊn/ *n* (*Brit*) device for changing gear in a motor vehicle by full depression of the accelerator（机动车的）换低挡装置

kicking /'kɪkɪŋ; 'kɪkɪŋ/ *adj* (*sl* 俚) exciting, lively; great, excellent 激动人心的；活泼热烈的；极棒的：*Once the music got going and there were hundreds of people waving their arms and dancing, the place was really kicking.* 音乐一响，群众挥臂起舞，十分热闹。Cf 参看 JUMPING, ALIVE AND KICKING (ALIVE 4A-Z)

kick-start /'kɪkstɑ:t; 'kɪkstɑrt/ *n* (*fig* 比喻) forceful impetus given to get a process or thing started or restarted（促使事物开始或重新开始的）强劲起动力，推动力

▷ **kick-start** *v* [Tn] (*fig* 比喻) give a kick start to something 使（某事物）开始或重新开始：*kick-start the economy/your career* 重振经济 *[你的事业]*

kid /kɪd; kɪd/ *n* (idm 习语) **new kid on the block** (*infml* 口) new person or product on the scene 新来者；新产品：*Compared with the Rolling Stones, popstars for thirty years, this group from the States are very much the new kids on the block.* 与享誉流行乐坛三十载的滚石乐队相比，这个美国演唱组可说是新人了。

killer application /ˌkɪlə æplɪ'keɪʃn; ˌkɪlɚ æplɪ'keʃən/ *n* **1** (also **killer app**) (*computing* 计) piece of software which is so good in terms of being advanced and innovatory that users will feel they have to buy it and often the hardware which runs it as well '爱煞人'应用程序（极先进创新的、用户不能不买的软件，常附带购其硬件）：*Windows 95 wasn't quite the killer application we had all expected.* 视窗 95 软件并未如预料般出尽风头。 **2** any kind of innovative technological product that is irresistible to potential purchasers（极吸引众人购买的）革新技术产品

NOTE 注： from the figurative use of *killer* to mean something that is impressive or excellent 源自 killer 一词的比喻义，即'给人以深刻印象的或完美的事物'

killer cell /'kɪlə sel; 'kɪlɚ sɛl/ *n* (*infml medical* 口，医) white blood cell which detects and destroys infected or cancerous cells 杀伤细胞（发现并杀死受感染或发生癌变的细胞的白细胞）

killing field /'kɪlɪŋ fi:ld; 'kɪlɪŋ fild/ *n* place where mass slaughter has taken place 杀戮场：*Revenge killings have turned the village into a killing field.* 报复性屠杀把这个村庄变成了杀戮场。

NOTE 注： first gained currency with the 1984 film *The Killing Fields* which showed the slaughter carried out by the Khmer Rouge in Cambodia between 1975 and 1979 此词从 1984 年电影 The Killing Fields 放映时开始流行，该电影反映了 1975 年到 1979 年间柬埔寨红色高棉军进行的大屠杀

kiss and tell /kɪs ənd 'tel; kɪs ənd 'tɛl/ (also **kiss-and-tell**) *adj* [attrib 作定语] (of memoirs in the press or other publications) revealing details of a love affair, usu with a well-known person（指报刊或其他出版物的记载）详细披露某人的私情的（通常为涉及名人的）：*She certainly made a lot of money from her kiss-and-tell story about the Lord Chancellor.* 她那本披露她与大法官的私情的书肯定让她大捞了一笔。

kiss-off /'kɪsɒf; 'kɪsɑf/ *n* (*US sl* 俚) abrupt or rude dismissal from a job or official position（突然的）解雇：*The accounts manager was given the kiss-off.* 会计部经理被突然解雇。

knife /naɪf; naɪf/ *n* (idm 习语) **at knife point** being threatened with a knife; threatening sb with a knife 在刀子的威胁下；以刀相逼：*Two men were robbed at knife point in the park last night.* 昨晚两名男子在公园被人持刀抢劫。

Ll

labour force /'leɪbə fɔ:s; 'lebɚ fɔrs/ *n* [U] all the people who could work in a country, company, etc（国家）劳动力；（公司）全体劳工：*the need for a skilled labour force* 对熟练工人的需求 ○ *One in ten of the labour force is now unemployed.* 十分之一的劳动人口现已失业。

laddish /'lædɪʃ; 'lædɪʃ/ *adj* (*Brit derog* 贬) (of men) behaving in a rather MACHOA-Z, loud and inconsiderate way（指男子）粗鲁的，大大咧咧的

▷ **laddishness** *n*：*the new laddishness that today's young men display* 当今青年男子表现出的粗鲁放任新作风 Cf 参看 NEW LAD, NEW MAN

lager lout /'lɑ:gə laʊt; 'lɑgɚ laʊt/ *n* (*Brit infml* 口) young person, esp a young man, who gets drunk and then behaves in a noisy and unpleasant way 酗酒闹事者（尤指年轻男子）：*The holiday resort was spoilt by the large numbers of lager louts who came into the small town every evening.* 这个度假胜地被大群每晚来小城酗酒闹事的人给糟蹋了。

NOTE 注： LAGERA-Z is a type of light beer ☆ lager 是一种淡啤酒

lakeside /'leɪksaɪd; 'leksaɪd/ *n* [sing] area of land around the edge of a lake 湖畔；湖滨；湖岸：*lovely walks along the lakeside* 湖边的宜人小径 ○ [attrib 作定语] *Austrian lakeside resorts* 奥地利湖滨度假胜地

lamping /'læmpɪŋ; 'læmpɪŋ/ *n* [U] form of hunting, practised at night, which uses bright lamps to illuminate and dazzle the hunted animal 强光狩猎（夜晚用强光将猎物照得眼晕以进行狩猎的方式）

▷ **lamper** *n* person who practises lamping 强光狩猎者：*The lampers cornered a badger which was then brought* *down by the dogs.* 这些用强光狩猎的人将一只獾堵住，然后猎狗上去将它扑倒。

LAN *abbr* 缩写 = LOCAL AREA NETWORK

landfill /'lændfɪl; 'lændfɪl/ *n* (**a**) [C] site where refuse is disposed of by being buried under layers of earth（以土埋方式处理垃圾的）垃圾场 (**b**) [U] action of disposal of refuse by burial at a landfill（以土埋方式）处理垃圾 (**c**) [C] material disposed of at a landfill（以土埋方式处理的）垃圾

▷ **landfill** *v* [Tn] (**a**) dispose of refuse by burial at a landfill 用土埋方式处理垃圾：*millions of tons of rubbish being landfilled every year* 每年被土埋处理的几百万吨的垃圾 (**b**) fill a site with landfill 用垃圾填：*to landfill 10.6 acres with sludge* 用淤泥填满 10.6 英亩地

□ **landfill gas** *n* gas produced by the breaking down of rubbish in a landfill (a) , eg methane and carbon dioxide 土埋垃圾废气（土埋的垃圾产生的废气，如甲烷和二氧化碳）

La Nina /læ 'ni:njə; læ 'ninjə/ *n* [sing] reverse weather phenomenon to EL NINO which shows itself as a cooling of the waters of the eastern Pacific bringing more rain to the region 拉尼娜现象（与厄尔尼诺现象相反的天气现象，其表现为太平洋东部海水变冷，为该地区带来更多的雨水）

laptop computer /'læptɒp kəm,pju:tə(r); 'læptɑp kəm,pjutɚ/ (also **laptop**) *n* portable computer small enough to be easily positioned on top of sb's lap 便携式计算机；膝上型计算机 Cf 参看 NOTEBOOK COMPUTER

laser card /'leɪzə kɑ:d; 'lezɚ kɑrd/ *n* card looking like a credit card but with data recorded on it which can be read only by a laser beam, used for providing cardholders with financial or medical services or access to high security areas 激光卡（形似信用卡，其数据只能由激光读取的卡，持卡人凭卡可得到财务或医疗服务，或进入高度戒备区域）

laserdisc /'leɪzə,dɪsk; 'lezɚ,dɪsk/ *n* disc on which signals and data, eg films and music videos, are recorded and can be reproduced by directing a laser beam onto the surface（激光）视盘；光碟；光盘

laser pointer /'leɪzə pɔɪntə(r); 'lezɚ pɔɪntɚ/ *n* small, torch-like device which directs a laser beam at a screen or other visual display so that a speaker or lecturer can point things out to his or her audience 激光指示棒，激光教鞭（类似手电筒的一种小装置，可将激光投射到屏幕或其他显示器上，演讲者藉此可向观众指明所讲内容）

laser printer /'leɪzə prɪntə(r); 'lezɚ prɪntɚ/ *n* printer linked to a computer in which a laser is used to form a pattern of dots on a photosensitive drum corresponding to the pattern of print required 激光打印机

latte /'lɑ:teɪ,'læteɪ; 'læte/ *n* hot drink of steamed milk with a dash of strong coffee 咖啡奶（在蒸的奶中加入少量浓咖啡制成的热饮）：*Two lattes, please.* 请来两杯咖啡奶。

NOTE 注： from the Italian *café latte* meaning 'coffee with milk' or 'milky coffee' 源自意大利语 café latte，意为加奶的咖啡

launcher /'lɔ:ntʃə(r); 'lɔntʃɚ/ *n* (usu in compounds 通常用以构成复合词) (esp in military use) device used to launch a missile, etc（尤指军事用的）导弹等的发射器，发射装置：*a rocket/grenade launcher* 火箭 *[*榴弹*]* 发射装置

laurel wreath /'lɒrəl ri:θ, *US* 'lɔ:r-; 'lɔrəl riθ/ *n* ring of LAUREL[A-Z] leaves worn on the head as a sign of victory or honour 桂冠（月桂树叶编成的花冠，作为胜利或荣誉的象征）

leader board /'li:də bɔ:d; 'lidɚ bɔrd/ *n* (*sport* 体) scoreboard, esp at a golf course, showing the names of the leading competitors in order（尤指高尔夫球场上的）领先选手记分牌：*His name is rarely off the leader boards at the major events in the professional golf tour.* 在职业高尔夫球巡回赛的主要赛事中，他总是名列领先选手记分牌。

lead-free /,led'fri:; lɛd'fri/ (also **unleaded**) *adj* (of petrol) without lead added（指汽油）无铅的

leading edge /,li:dɪŋ 'edʒ; ,lidɪŋ 'ɛdʒ/ *n* (usu *sing* 通常作单数) place where new advances are being made, esp in technology（尤指技术的）前沿，尖端：*The research team operates at the leading edge of molecular biology.* 该研究小组从事分子生物学的前沿研究。○ [attrib 作定语] *leading edge instrument design* 先进的仪器设计 Cf 参看 CUTTING EDGE

league table /'li:g teɪbl; 'lig tebl/ *n* (in Britain) listing of schools, hospitals, etc which ranks them according to defined measures of performance（英国）等级表（根据既定标准，将学校、医院等按表现优劣排列的表）：*School league tables increasingly influence parents in their choice.* 家长在选择学校时越来越受等级表的影响。

NOTE 注： league table originally applied to the ranking of professional football teams based on their performance through the playing season 原指赛季各职业足球队按表现来评定等级名次的表

lean /li:n; lin/ *adj* (*commerce* 商) (of a business or a sector of the economy) made more efficient or competitive through the reduction of unnecessary costs or expenditure（指公司或经济部门通过削减不必要的成本开支而）更高效的，更具竞争力的：*to make the company leaner* 紧缩开支以提高公司效益

lean-burn /'li:nbɜ:n; 'linbɝn/ *adj* (of a motor engine, etc) designed to run on a mixture of fuel and air to reduce pollution（指汽车发动机等为减少污染而）使用稀混合气的：*lean-burn engine* 稀混合气发动机

learner-centred /'lɜ:nə,sentəd; 'lɝnɚ,sɛntɚd/ (also **student-centred**) *adj* (*education* 教) focused on the needs and interests of the learner 按学生的需要和兴趣的；以学习者为中心的：*learner-centred courses/curricula/materials* 以学习者为中心的教程 *[*课程 / 教材*]*

learning curve /'lɜ:nɪŋ kɜ:v; 'lɝnɪŋ kɝv/ *n* process by which sb masters a new skill or set of duties while on the job and through learning from his or her mistakes 学习曲线（在工作岗位上逐步掌握新技能、承担新任务并从错误中学习的过程）：*New government ministers all know that it's a steep learning curve during the first six months in office.* 新上任的部长都知道在任职的头半年里要很快地熟悉新职责。

leaseback /'li:sbæk; 'lisbæk/ (*US* **reversion**) *n* [U] (*Brit*) practice of selling an ASSET 2[A-Z], esp a property, and immediately renting it back from the new owner, in order to obtain cash for use 回租（为获得流动资金而出售房地产，随后又从买主手中租回的做法）

least-worst /li:st'wɜ:st; list'wɝst/ *adj* [attrib 作定语] not desirable or satisfactory, but the best out of several possible options 不算理想但在可供选择的事物中最好的；次中求好的：*the least-worst scenario* 不理想但尽力求得的境况

-led /led; lɛd/ *suff* 后缀 (forming *adjs* 用以构成形容词) influenced (mainly by the things specified)（主要）受…影响的，由…引导的：*a consumer-led campaign* 消费者发起的运动 ○ *a market-led economy* 由市场主导的经济

left-hand drive /,lefthænd 'draɪv; ,lɛfthænd 'draɪv/ *adj* (of a vehicle) with the steering wheel on the left hand side（指车辆）方向盘在左边的，左舵的 Cf 参看 RIGHT-HAND DRIVE

left-of-centre /,leftəv'sentə(r); ,lɛftəv'sɛntɚ/ (*US* **center**) *adj* (*politics* 政) holding more liberal or radical views than the majority in a political party or in a state; LEFT-

WING (LEFT2(A-Z)) 中间偏左的；左翼的：*a left-of-centre Conservative* 中间偏左的保守党党员

Lego /ˈlegəʊ; ˈlɛgo/ *n* [U] (*propr* 专利名) small toy blocks of coloured plastic that can be pressed together to form model houses, bridges, trains, etc 莱阁彩色塑料积木

□ **Legoland** *n* [sing] amusement park built and run by the makers of Lego where everything is made out of the toy blocks 莱阁乐园（所有东西皆由莱阁积木搭成的游乐场）

le Shuttle /lə ˈʃʌtl; lə ˈʃʌtl/ (also **Le Shuttle**) *n* [sing] **1** shuttle service which transports motor vehicles through the Channel Tunnel by train（运送机动车辆穿越海峡隧道的）火车穿梭运输服务 **2** one of the trains used for the le Shuttle service（运送机动车辆穿越海峡隧道的）穿梭火车：*We drove across on le Shuttle.* 我们开车乘穿梭火车穿越海峡隧道。 Cf 参看 EUROSTAR

NOTE 注： from *le* which is the definite article in French and *shuttle* which has the same meaning in both French and English of a form of transport that goes continuously backwards and forwards over a short route between two points 由法语定冠词 le 和在英语、法语中均表示'短程穿梭运输工具'的 shuttle 二词构成

let-out /ˈletaʊt; ˈlɛtaʊt/ *n* (*Brit*) event, statement, etc which allows sb to avoid a responsibility or duty 托辞；故意制造的漏洞：*a convenient let-out for the Minister of Education* 教育部长现成的托辞 ○ *a let-out clause in the contract* 合同中故意制造的漏洞

level playing field /levl ˈpleɪɪŋ fiːld; lɛvl ˈpleɪŋ fild/ *n* (usu *sing* 通常作单数) (*fig* 比喻) situation which offers no advantage to any of the participants; fair state of affairs 公平竞争环境：*Women still complain that there is no level playing field when it comes to employment opportunities.* 说到工作机会，妇女们仍抱怨没有公平竞争的环境。

leveraged buyout /ˌliːvərɪdʒd ˈbaɪaʊt, *US* lev-; ˌlɛvrɪdʒd ˈbaɪaʊt/ *n* (*esp US finance* 财) way of buying a company in which a small company borrows money on its own assets (ASSET 2A-Z) and those of the larger company it wants to buy in order to finance the deal 杠杆购股，借款买股（小公司以自身及其欲收购的大公司的资产作抵押的借款收购方法）

Lib Dem /ˌlɪb ˈdem; lɪb ˈdɛm/ *abbr* 缩写 = (*Brit politics* 政) Liberal Democrat (member or supporter of THE LIBERAL DEMOCRATS (LIBERALA-Z)) 自由民主党党员；自由民主党的支持者：*Being virtually a Lib Dem, he left the Labour Party to join the Liberal Democrats.* 他实际上倾向自由民主党，因此离开工党加入了自由民主党。

liberation priest /lɪbəˌreɪʃn ˈpriːst; lɪbəˌreʃən ˈprist/ *n* minister of the Roman Catholic church, esp in Latin America, who supports LIBERATION THEOLOGY 解放神学神职人员（尤指拉丁美洲的天主教会的）

liberation theology /ˌlɪbəreɪʃn θiːˈɒlədʒɪ; ˌlɪbəreʃən θiˈɑlədʒɪ/ *n* [U] belief esp among Roman Catholic priests that Christian ministers should take up political issues and work to improve the lives of the poorer people in their community, not limiting themselves to a purely spiritual role 解放神学（尤见于天主教的思想，认为神职人员的工作不应仅限于灵性方面，还应关心政治并帮助社区的穷人改善生活）

life imprisonment /ˌlaɪf ɪmˈprɪznmənt; ˌlaɪf ɪmˈprɪzn̩mənt/ *n* [U] spending the rest of one's life or a very long time in prison 终身监禁；长期监禁：*sentenced to life imprisonment* 被判终身监禁

life sentence /ˈlaɪf sentəns; ˈlaɪf sɛntəns/ (also **life**) *n* legal punishment by which sb spends the rest of his/her life or a very long time in prison, usu from 12 to 20 years except in a few unusual cases 无期徒刑；（12至20年的）长期徒刑：*serve a life sentence* 服无期徒刑

▷ **lifer** *n* person serving a life sentence 无期徒刑犯

lifestyle /ˈlaɪfstaɪl; ˈlaɪfstaɪl/ (also **life-style**) *n* (*commerce* 商) (**a**) sum total of the likes and dislikes of particular customers or a section of the market, esp as this is expressed in the products they would buy to fit their self-image and way of life 生活方式（对产品的）信息反馈（某些顾客或某部分消费者对产品的态度，尤指对其购买的符合其形象与生活方式的产品的总体态度） (**b**) marketing strategy based on and aimed at fulfilling a certain lifestyle 生活方式营销策略（基于或旨在满足某种生活方式的营销策略）：*Lifestyle cannot be ignored when planning market strategy.* 制订营销策略不能忽视消费者的生活方式。

▷ **lifestyle** *adj* (*commerce* 商) (**a**) using or belonging to the lifestyle marketing strategy 运用或属于生活方式营销策略的 (**b**) (of a product) fitting into such a strategy, appealing to a customer's sense of lifestyle（指产品）符合顾客生活方式的营销策略的，迎合顾客生活品位的：*lifestyle choices* 符合顾客生活方式的选择

life-threatening /ˈlaɪfθretnɪŋ; ˈlaɪfθrɛtnɪŋ/ *adj* (of diseases or situations) that can cause death（指疾病或情况）致命的，有生命危险的：*a life-threatening drought* 危及生灵的旱灾 ○ *a resurgence of life-threatening viral illnesses* 致命病毒性疾病的死灰复燃

light pollution /ˈlaɪt pəˌluːʃn; ˈlaɪt pəˌluʃən/ *n* [U] brightening of the night sky and the consequent dimming and reduction of visible stars as a result of strong street lighting, etc 光污染（城市强烈灯光导致夜空光亮、星光暗淡的现象）：*Light pollution around our cities means that we rarely see the skies as our grandparents saw them.* 城市的光污染使我们很少能像祖辈那样清楚地看到夜晚的天空。

liming /ˈlaɪmɪŋ; ˈlaɪmɪŋ/ *n* [U] application of a lime paste to the surface of wood, esp for furniture, kitchen fittings, etc, which is allowed to dry and then brushed off to produce a silvery gloss 石灰浆涂抹（将石灰浆涂于木材表面，待干燥后刷去，从而使木材表面带银色光泽，尤用于家具、厨柜等）

▷ **limed** *adj*：*limed oak/beech cabinets in the kitchen* 经过石灰浆涂抹处理的橡木 *[榉木]* 厨柜

limo *n* (*infml* 口) = LIMOUSINEA-Z

line /laɪn; laɪn/ *n* (*sl* 俚) straight narrow row of cocaine arranged on a flat surface, esp a mirror, ready to be snorted (SNORT 3A-Z)（置于平面，尤指镜面上供吸服的）细长条可卡因

line manager /ˈlaɪn ˌmænɪdʒə(r); ˈlaɪn ˌmænɪdʒɚ/ *n* manager to whom an employee is directly responsible 部门经理；部门管理人

lipblock /ˈlɪpblɒk; ˈlɪpblɑk/ *n* [U, C] strong SUNBLOCK, usu in the form of a stick like a lipstick, which is designed esp to protect the lips from sunburn 防晒唇膏（保护嘴唇的唇膏状强力防晒霜）：*Don't forget to put on more lipblock after you've been swimming.* 游泳后别忘了多涂些防晒唇膏。 ○ *lipblocks in many different colours* 五彩缤纷的防晒唇膏

liposuction /ˈlɪpəʊsʌkʃn,ˈlaɪpəʊ-; ˈlaɪposʌkʃən/ *n* [U] (*medical* 医) surgical process of drawing off fat deposits from the thighs, buttocks, etc by means of solvent chemicals and a suction tube, usu done for cosmetic rather than medical reasons 脂肪抽吸术（使用有溶解作用的化学品和吸管去除大腿、臀部等处过多的脂肪的手术）

lip-sync /ˈlɪpsɪŋk; ˈlɪpsɪŋk/ (also **-synch**) *n* (in film acting, etc) movement of a performer's lips in SYNCHRONIZATION (SYNCHRONIZEA-Z) with a pre-recorded sound-track, eg in producing a music video（电影等中）对口型：*It was disappointing because the group used lip-sync instead of giving a live performance of their* *best known songs.* 这个演唱组只是放录音对口型，而不是现场演唱他们的名曲，真让人失望。

listeria /lɪˈstɪərɪə; lɪˈstɪrɪə/ *n* [U] any of various types of bacteria which cause food poisoning 李司忒氏菌（一种导致食物中毒的细菌）: *People were warned not to eat soft cheese following the discovery of listeria in one batch.* 自从在一批软奶酪中发现了李司忒氏菌，人们就被警告不可再食用这些奶酪。

listing /ˈlɪstɪŋ; ˈlɪstɪŋ/ *n* (**a**) list or CATALOGUE 1A-Z 目录；单子: *a complete listing of all our models* 我们所有型号的完整目录 (**b**) place or position on a list（单子上的）位置: *a listing at number 3 among the top ten billionaires* 在最富有的十位亿万富翁中位居第三 ○ (*commerce* 商) *a stock exchange listing* (ie for the trading of shares) 股票在证券交易所的上市（以进行交易）

little dragon *n* = DRAGON

little green men from Mars /ˌlɪtl griːn ˌmen frəm ˈmɑːz; ˌlɪtl grin ˌmɛn frəm ˈmɑrz/ *n* [pl] (*joc* 谑) aliens 外星人

NOTE 注： description based on pictures of aliens from Mars and other planets in popular science fiction books and comics 此语乃从流行科幻小说和连环画中火星人和其他外星人的图画而来

little tiger *n* = DRAGON

living will /ˈlɪvɪŋ wɪl, lɪvɪŋ ˈwɪl; lɪvɪŋ ˈwɪl/ *n* document drawn up by sb while in good health and legally fit to do so, requesting that no artifical means should be used to keep him or her alive should such a decision have to be made in the future as the result of illness or an accident 生存遗嘱（某人在健康时合法签署的书面声明，表示将来如患病或发生事故，可任其自然死亡，不必用人工方法延续其生命）: *A living will gives some assurance that over-zealous attempts to keep one alive will not be made.* 有了生存遗嘱可避免对病人采取不必要的临终挽救措施。

local area network /ˌləʊkl eərɪə ˈnetwɜːk; ˌlokḷ ɛrɪə ˈnɛtwɝk/ *n* (*abbr* 缩写 **LAN**) (*computing* 计) system of linking together computers, usu in the same office or building, so that their users can communicate and share resources 局域网（将各计算机联接起来，通常于同一办公室或大楼里，使用户能交流并共用资源的系统）

logic bomb /ˈlɒdʒɪk bɒm; ˈlɑdʒɪk bɑm/ *n* (*computing* 计) set of instructions secretly put into a program so that if a particular logical condition is satisfied they will be carried out, usu with harmful effects 逻辑炸弹（暗中编入程序，以特定逻辑条件引发的一套指令，通常有破坏性）

lone parent *n* = SINGLE PARENT (SINGLEA-Z)

long-haul /ˈlɒŋ hɔːl; ˈlɔŋ hɔl/ *adj* [attrib 作定语] of or involving the transport of goods or passengers over relatively long distances esp by air 长途运输的（尤指空运）Cf 参看 SHORT-HAUL

long vacation /ˌlɒŋ vəˈkeɪʃn, *US* lɔːŋ; ˌlɔŋ veˈkeʃən/ (also **long vac**) *n* [C usu sing 通常作单数] (*Brit*) period of time during the summer when universities, schools, etc are closed 暑假

loony left /luːnɪ ˈleft; lunɪ ˈlɛft/ *n* **the loony left** [Gp] (*Brit infml derog* 口，贬) extreme left wing of the Labour Party, considered to be too radical by the more moderate members 工党中的极左派: *We can't let the loony left get control of the council. They'll spend all the money on social services.* 我们不能让工党极左派控制议会。他们会把所有的钱用在有关社会公益的事情上。

loop /luːp; lup/ *n* (idm 习语) **out of the loop** (*US infml* 口) not one of those in the know in relation to an issue; lacking the influence or information which is available only to a select few 圈外的；不知情的: *I can't comment on recent policy. I've been out of the loop on Middle Eastern affairs since the summer.* 我无法对最近的政策作评论，从夏天起我就对中东事件一无所知了。

loose cannon /luːs ˈkænən; lus ˈkænən/ *n* (*US fig derog* 比喻，贬) person who behaves in an unpredictable way, cannot be easily controlled and whose actions or words may cause damage to a political party, a cause, etc 变化无常不易控制的人（其言行可能对政党、事业等造成危害）: *They certainly feared the Chancellor becoming a loose cannon once he left office.* 他们无疑担心这位大臣离职后会变得不易控制。

NOTE 注： from the comparison to warfare at sea, when a cannon which became loose on the decks could cause terrible damage 源于海战中甲板上的大炮一旦失去控制会造成极大破坏的比喻

loose end /ˌluːs ˈend; lus ˈɛnd/ *n* (usu *pl* 通常作复数) part of sth that has not been properly finished or explained 未完结的部分；未了的事；未说清楚的事: *tie up a few loose ends* 结束一些未了之事 ○ *The plot has too many loose ends.* 情节里未能解释的地方太多了。

love-rat /ˈlʌvræt; ˈlʌvræt/ *n* (*US sl* 俚) lover who turns out to be worthless, selfish and unfaithful 最后显出其无用、自私又不忠的情人；爱情老鼠: *In this episode, the heroine finds her love-rat in bed with her sister.* 在这一集中，女主角发现她那不忠的情人与她妹妹睡在一起。

low-cal /ləʊˈkæl; loˈkæl/ *adj* low in calories; lower in calories than other foods of a similar kind 低卡路里的；低热量的: *Weight watchers do excellent low-cal frozen meals.* 注重体重的人能做可口的低热量冷冻餐。○ *low-cal yoghurt/cheese* 低热量酸奶 *[奶酪]*

low-end /ləʊˈend; loˈɛnd/ *adj* [attrib 作定语] (usu of technological products) not so expensive or advanced; aimed at the less well off customer（常指技术产品）面向不很富裕的消费者的，低档的: *low-end notebook computers/cell phones* 廉价笔记本型电脑 *[移动电话]* Cf 参看 HIGH-END

lowest common denominator /ˌləʊɪst ˌkɒmən dɪˈnɒmɪneɪtə(r); ˌloɪst ˌkɑmən dɪˈnɑmɪnetɚ/ *n* (*fig often derog* 比喻，常作贬义) thing or level of intellectual content, etc, that appeals to or is understood by the largest number of people in a particular group 迎合公众口味的事物；通俗水平；低级趣味: *pandering to the lowest common denominator of public taste* 迎合公众口味的低级趣味 ○ *The soap opera was criticized as appealing to the lowest common denominator of the television audience.* 这出肥皂剧被批评为迎合电视观众的低级趣味。Cf 参看 DUMB DOWN (DUMB)

Loyalist /ˈlɔɪəlɪst; ˈlɔɪəlɪst/ *n* (in Britain) person who supports the continuing political union between Great Britain and Northern Ireland（英国）忠诚分子（支持大不列颠与北爱尔兰继续保持政治联合的人）: *Loyalists were reassured by the protection of their rights under the new proposals.* 新的提案保证维护忠诚分子的权利。

loyalty card /ˈlɔɪəltɪ kɑːd; ˈlɔɪəltɪ kɑrd/ *n* identity card issued by a retailer to its customers so that each individual transaction can be recorded in order to build up credits for future discounts or other benefits and thus encourage the customer's loyalty to the store 惠顾卡，购物卡（零售店为吸引顾客而发的一种记分卡，每次购物的分数累积到一定数额，便可享受折扣或其他优惠）: *loyalty cards issued by all major supermarkets* 各大超市发出的惠顾卡 ○ *A thousand points on your loyalty card makes you eligible for valuable gifts.* 惠顾卡上积满一千分，您就有资格获得贵重礼品。

lunch /lʌntʃ; lʌntʃ/ *n* (idm 习语) **out to lunch** (*infml derog* 口，贬) mad; crazy; confused 疯的；神志不清的: *I tried to talk to her but she was obviously out to* *lunch and it was a complete waste of time.* 我试图和她说话，但她显然神志不清，因此纯粹是在浪费时间。

Lurex /ˈlʊəreks; ˈlʊrɛks/ *n* [U] (*propr* 专利名) material made with a type of thread which contains thin shiny metal strands 卢勒克斯（一种含有细小闪光金属丝的布料）: *a Lurex evening jacket* 卢勒克斯晚装短上衣

luv /lʌv; lʌv/ *n* (*Brit infml* 口) (esp as a form of address or as a farewell in writing) love（尤作称呼语或作书面告别语）亲爱的，宝贝儿：*Bye for now, luv.* 再见了，亲爱的。○ *Ta very much, luv.* 非常感谢，宝贝儿。

luvvy /ˈlʌvɪ; ˈlʌvɪ/ (also **luvvie**) *n* (*Brit infml* 口) actor or actress, esp one who is particularly gushing (GUSH 2^A-Z^) and affected（尤指口若悬河、矫揉造作的）演员

Lycra /ˈlaɪkrə; ˈlaɪkrə/ *n* [U] (*propr* 专利名) fabric which is elastic and stretches to give a tight fit, used to make swimming costumes, tights, etc 莱卡（一种用于制游泳衣、紧身衣等的弹性纤维）

Mm

machine translation /məˌʃiːn trænzˈleɪʃn; məˌʃin trænzˈleʃən/ *n* [U] translation carried out by a computer using suitable programming 机器翻译；计算机翻译

macroeconomics /ˌmækrəʊˌiːkəˈnɒmɪks, -ˌekə-; ˌmækroˌikəˈnɑmɪks, -ˌɛkə-/ *n* [sing v] study of economic facts on a large scale, eg national economies 宏观经济学

▷ **macroeconomic** *adj* [esp attrib 尤作定语]: *macroeconomic policy* 宏观经济政策

mad /mæd; mæd/ *adj* (*sl* 俚) (used esp by people in the RAVE culture of the 1990s) unusual, remarkable, exciting（尤为 20 世纪 90 年代参加电子乐狂舞会者的用语）不同寻常，非同凡响，刺激的：*It was more than cool. It was a mad house party.* 这个家中聚会不只是棒，它简直令人疯狂。

MAD /mæd; mæd/ *abbr* 缩写 = mutual assured destruction (knowledge that any first use of nuclear weapons will meet with an equally destructive reply and which it is hoped, will prevent any country with nuclear weapons from ever using one) 互相保证摧毁（即明白任何首先使用核武器者将受到同样的回击，希望因此可防止拥有核武器的国家使用核武器）

mad cow disease *n* = BOVINE SPONGIFORM ENCEPHALOPATHY

Mademoiselle /ˌmædəmwəˈzel, *US* -məzel; ˌmædəməˈzɛl/ *n* (*abbr* 缩写 **Mlle**) (*pl* **Mesdemoiselles**, *abbr* 缩写 **Mlles**) (*French* 法) (title or form of address used for a woman who is not married, esp a young one, usu used as a title equivalent to 'Miss') 小姐（对未婚女子，尤其年轻未婚女子的称呼，相当于 Miss）

magic bullet /mædʒɪk ˈbʊlɪt; mædʒɪk ˈbʊlɪt/ *n* (*infml* 口) any highly specific and effective medicine or other means of curing a disease or condition 灵丹妙药；神奇疗法：*There's no magic bullet for skin cancer.* 治疗皮肤癌没有什么灵丹妙药。

Magic Eye *n* (*propr* 专利名) = AUTOSTEREOGRAM

magic realism /mædʒɪk ˈriːəlɪzəm; mædʒɪk ˈriəlɪzəm/ *n* [U] (*literature* 文学) literary style which combines realism, eg recognizable characters and places, with surreal or dreamlike elements 魔幻现实主义（将真实的，如可辨认的人物、地点等，与超现实的或梦幻般的事物相结合的文学形式）

▷ **magic realist** *n* writer in the style of magic realism 魔幻现实主义作家

magnetic resonance imaging /mægˌnetɪk ˌrezənəns ˈɪmədʒɪŋ; mægˌnɛtɪk ˌrɛzənəns ˈɪmədʒɪŋ/ *n* [U] (*abbr* 缩写 **MRI**) (*medical* 医) diagnostic technique which provides sectional images of the internal structure of the patient's body, making use of the nuclear magnetic resonance of the atoms in the body 核磁共振成像（利用病人体内原子的核磁共振形成体内结构的剖面图的诊断技术）

MailMerge /ˈmeɪlmɜːdʒ; ˈmelmɝdʒ/ (also **mail-merge, mail merge**) *n* [U] (*propr computing* 专利名，计) program that draws on both a data file (containing names, addresses, etc) and a text file to produce multiple copies of a letter, each addressed to a different recipient 函件合并（一种计算机程序，利用含有姓名、地址等的数据文件和一份文本文件制成多份相同内容的信件，分送给各收件人）：*If you need to send the same letter to a lot of people, use the mail merge function.* 给很多人发送同样的信件，可使用函件合并功能。

▷ **MailMerge** *v* (*propr computing* 专利名，计)

mailout /ˈmeɪlaʊt; ˈmelaʊt/ (also **mailshot**) *n* CIRCULAR^A-Z^ usu containing promotional material（邮寄的）广告传单

major suit /ˌmeɪdʒə ˈsuːt; ˌmedʒɚ ˈsut/ *n* (in card games) spades or hearts（纸牌戏中）高花色牌（黑桃或红心）

NOTE 注： thus named because games won using the major suits score more highly in bridge, whist, etc 在桥牌、惠斯特牌等纸牌游戏中，以高花色牌取胜的得分较高，故名

mam /mæm; mæm/ *n* (*Brit infml* 口) (often as a form of address) mother（常作称呼语）妈妈

manga /ˈmæŋgə; ˈmæŋgə/ *n* (*Japanese* 日语) type of comic book popular with adults and teenagers, usu featuring heroes and heroines with superhuman powers, and characterized by violence and sexual fantasy（成人和青少年常看，主人公常具有超人能力，书中充满暴力和性幻想的）连环画册，（日本）漫画书

NOTE 注： formed from Japanese *man* (INDISCRIMINATE^A-Z^) and *ga* (picture) 由日语 man（不区分读者对象的）和 ga（图画）二词构成

mantra /ˈmæntrə; ˈmæntrə/ *n* (**a**) word, phrase or sound which is constantly repeated to help concentration, etc, esp during MEDITATION (MEDITATE^A-Z^) 曼特罗，祷文（尤指默念时不断诵念以提高专注力等的词语或声音）：*We heard the devotees repeating over and over the Buddhist mantra 'Om mani pad me om'.* 我们听到虔诚的信徒们一遍又一遍的诵读佛教祷文'唵嘛呢叭咪唵'。(**b**) expression of a currently fashionable concept as if it had some special power in itself（仿佛拥有特殊力量的）流行口号：*the politicians that are currently chanting the mantra of 'welfare to work'* 眼下不断喊着'劳保福利'的政客们

marginalize, -ise /ˈmɑːdʒɪnəlaɪz; ˈmɑrdʒɪnəlaɪz/ *v* [Tn] treat a person or group as unimportant and thus make them feel less influential, powerful, etc 歧视；排斥：*Western society has marginalized elderly people to a considerable extent.* 西方社会在很大程度上歧视老年人。

marketeer /mɑːkɪˈtɪə(r); mɑrkɪˈtɪr/ *n* (*commerce* 商) specialist in marketing, esp in the business of promoting and selling products, including market research and advertising 营销专家（尤指在产品的宣传与销售，包括市场调研和广告方面的专家）

market leader /ˌmɑːkɪt ˈliːdə(r); ˌmɑrkɪt ˈlidɚ/ *n* (**a**) company that has the largest market share for a particular product or service in an area or country 市场领导者（某种产品或服务在某地区或国家拥有最高市场占有率的公司）：*emerge as the market leader* 晋身成为市场领导者 (**b**) product that sells more than any other in competition with it 市场占有率最高的产品：*This drug is the market leader in the treatment of thyroid deficiency.* 此药在市场上是治疗甲状腺病的首选药。

marzipan layer /'mɑ:zɪpæn ˌleɪə(r); 'mɑrzɪpæn ˌleɚ/ *n* [sing] **1** (*Brit infml commerce* 口，商) stockbroking executives ranked immediately below the partners in a firm（职位仅次于公司合伙人的）证券经纪高级主管 **2** people in any community considered to be just below the top stratum of individuals（团体中）仅次于最高层人物的人：*bright young members of the marzipan layer who are sure to make partner one day* 将来必定会成为合伙人的年轻有为的高级管理人员

NOTE 注： a figurative use of *marzipan layer*, the layer of almond paste that comes between the cake and the icing 比喻用法，原指夹在蛋糕与糖衣之间的一层杏仁蛋白糊

masculinism /'mæskju:lɪnˌɪzəm; 'mæskjəlɪnˌɪzəm/ *n* [U] support of a dominant role for men in society and praise of traditional male qualities 男权主义；大男子主义

NOTE 注： formed as an antonym of FEMINISM[A-Z] 与 feminism（女权主义）相对

▷ **masculinist** *n, adj*

massage /'mæsɑ:ʒ, *US* mə'sɑ:ʒ; mə'sɑʒ/ *v* [Tn] **1** pay flattering attention to sb, often with a view to obtaining sth from him or her（常为取得好处而对某人）阿谀奉承，恭维 **2** (idm 习语) **massage sb's ego** praise and flatter sb so as to reinforce the good opinion they have of themselves 为了增强某人自信心而对其赞美、恭维之：*In spite of his huge success, we need to massage his ego for hours before every performance.* 尽管他非常成功，每次演出前我们还需要花上几小时给他打气。

massage-parlour /'mæsɑ:ʒ pɑ:lə(r), *US* mə'sɑ:ʒ; mə'sɑʒ pɑrlɚ/ (*US* **parlor**) *n* (*euph* 婉) establishment where men pay for a massage which may include sex with prostitutes（可提供色情服务的）按摩院

master-plan /'mɑ:stəplæn, *US* 'mæs-; 'mæstɚplæn/ *n* (*often joc* 常作戏谑语) plan for success in a complex operation, giving overall guidance（指挥整个复杂的运作以赢取成就的）总体设计，大计：*It was all part of my master-plan to take control of the company.* 这就是我接管该公司的大计的一部分。

maternity leave /mə'tɜ:nətɪ li:v; mə'tɝnətɪ liv/ *n* [U] period of time off work to have a baby which is allowed to a woman by law（法定）分娩假期，产假：*nine weeks' maternity leave* 九个礼拜的产假 Cf 参看 PATERNITY LEAVE

maternity pay /mə'tɜ:nətɪ peɪ; mə'tɝnətɪ pe/ *n* [U] money paid by an employer to a woman who has temporarily left her job on MATERNITY LEAVE 产假工资（雇主付给因产假暂停工作的女性的钱）

mature student /məˌtʃʊə 'stju:dnt, *US* -tʊər stu:-; məˌtʊr 'studn̩t/ *n* student who studies at a university or college at a later age than normal 大龄学生（迟于正常年龄上大学者）

matzo /'mætsəʊ; 'mætso/ *n* [U,C] (*pl* **-os**) UNLEAVENED[A-Z] bread in the form of large thin biscuits, eaten esp by Jews to commemorate the Passover 无酵饼（犹太人逾越节时吃的一种大而薄的硬面饼）

max /mæks; mæks/ *n* (idm 习语) **to the max** (*US sl* 俚) totally, completely, to the highest degree 完全地；彻底地；最高程度地：*'Do you like it?' 'To the max.'* '你喜欢它吗？' '绝对喜欢。'

NOTE 注： from an abbreviated form of *maximum* 为 maximum（最大的）一词的缩略形式

maxi-series /'mæksɪˌsɪəri:z; 'mæksɪˌsɪrɪz/ *n* [sing] drama series on television which is broadcast in a large number of parts shown on successive days or over a number of weeks 长篇电视连续剧 Cf 参看 MINISERIES

Mb *n* = MEG

Mbyte *n* = MEG

ME *abbr* 缩写 = MYALGIC ENCEPHALOMYELITIS

meat and potatoes /ˌmi:t ənd pə'teɪtəʊz; ˌmit ənd pə'tetoz/ *n* (*infml* 口) basic and most important aspect of sth 基本的部分；最重要的部分：*We mustn't overlook the meat and potatoes of inner urban needs in our enthusiasm for glamorous projects like the Millennium Fair.* 我们在热衷于千禧年博览会这类亮丽生辉的项目时，不能忽视城市贫民区的基本需要。○ [attrib 作定语] *a meat-and-potatoes problem/question* 主要的困难[问题]

mechanically-recovered meat /mɪˌkænɪklɪrɪˌkʌvəd 'mi:t; məˌkænɪklɪrɪˌkʌvɚd 'mit/ *n* [U] (*abbr* 缩写 **MRM**) meat stripped from a CARCASS 1[A-Z] by mechanical means, eg a high-power water jet, and used for making sausages, pet food, etc after the better cuts have already been removed 机械切割肉（动物屠宰后上品的肉被切除后，用机械方法如用水强力喷射取下的肉，用于制香肠、宠物食品等）

Med /med; mɛd/ *n* **the Med** [sing] (*infml* 口) the Mediterranean Sea 地中海

mediagenic /mi:dɪə'dʒenɪk; midɪə'dʒɛnɪk/ *adj* able to look convincing and make a good impression when appearing in the media, esp on television 传媒形象佳的（尤指在电视上）：*It's not enough for politicians to be sincere and principled nowadays; they need to be mediagenic as well.* 如今政治家们光靠真诚和有原则已经不够了，他们还需要具有良好的传媒形象。Cf 参看 TELEGENIC

NOTE 注： formed on analogy with *photogenic* (looking attractive in photographs) 由 photogenic（上照的）一词类推构成

meg /meg; mɛg/ *n* (*infml computing* 口，计) one megabyte (1,048,576 bytes) of computer memory or storage 兆字节（计算机存储容量单位，相等于 1,048,576 字节）Cf 参看 GIGABYTE

mega /'megə; 'mɛgə/ *adj* (*infml* 口) very large or important; on a grand scale; great; excellent 巨大的；重大的；盛大的；极好的：*a mega sale* 大甩卖 ○ *mega bucks* 一大笔钱 ○ *The new shopping centre is mega.* 新的购物中心规模极大。

☐ **megachange** *n* (*infml* 口) violent, sudden and extensive change 剧变；巨变：*These primitive people have been forced to go through a megachange as their forest home has been destroyed and their previous way of life made impossible.* 这些原始人被迫经历一场巨变，他们的森林家园被破坏殆尽，要回到原来的生活方式已不可能。

megaevent *n* large sporting event or spectacle 大型运动会；体坛盛事

megafirm *n* large business, esp one formed by the combination of other firms 大公司；（尤指由其他公司合并组成的）集团公司

megastore *n* very large retail store with its own parking facilities, usu on the outskirts of a town（设有停车场的）大型商场（通常位于城郊）Cf 参看 HYPERMARKET[A-Z]

megatrend *n* sweeping and irresistible changes in circumstances, fashions, opinions, etc 大潮流，大趋势（环境、时尚、观念等广泛而又不可遏止的改变）

megabyte /'megəbaɪt; 'mɛgəbaɪt/ *n* (*computing* 计) 1,048,576 bytes (BYTE[A-Z]) 兆字节（计算机储存容量单位）

megaplex /'megəpleks; 'mɛgəplɛks/ (also **multiplex**) *n* (*pl* ~ **es**) range of cinemas within one building with more auditoriums than is usual in a CINEPLEX（比多厅影院拥有更多放映厅的）大型电影城：*The new megaplex is a 12 screen, 3 thousand-seat movie mall.* 新的大型电影城有十二个银幕，三千个座位。

megathon /'megəθɒn; 'mɛgəθɑn/ *n* event which goes on for a very long time or is on a very large scale, esp a television broadcast 马拉松式的活动（尤指马拉松式

电视节目）: *The charity megathon on TV last night went on until 3.00 in the morning.* 昨晚电视上的马拉松式慈善募捐节目一直播放到凌晨3点。

NOTE 注: formed on analogy with *marathon* 由 marathon（马拉松赛跑）一词类推构成

melamine /ˈmeləmiːn; ˈmɛləmin/ *n* [U] type of plastic used as a covering for other materials, etc 密胺树脂塑料（用以覆盖其他材料）: *a melamine tray/table-top* 密胺树脂盘 *[*桌面*]*

melanoma /ˌmeləˈnəʊmə; ˌmɛləˈnomə/ *n* (*medical* 医) MALIGNANT 2(a)A-Z tumour, ie cancer cells, occuring usu in the skin 黑素瘤（即恶性肿瘤或癌细胞，通常见于皮肤）

meld /meld; mɛld/ *v* ~ **(sth) (into sth)** combine or mix one thing with another so that clear distinctions are lost 融合；合并；混合: *dreams in which past and present meld into each other* 过去与现在混在一起的梦 ○ *The festival melds together Christian and pagan traditions.* 节日融合了基督徒与异教徒的传统。

meltdown /ˈmeltdaʊn; ˈmɛltdaun/ *n* (*fig* 比喻) total loss of order in a system leading to chaos（系统的）完全崩溃（因而导致混乱）: *London Underground faces complete meltdown today as rush-hour crowds struggle to get to work on the few trains running on this second day of the drivers' strike.* 今天是伦敦地铁司机罢工的第二天，上班高峰时间人们争先恐后去挤仅有的几班车，伦敦地铁陷入一片混乱。○ *financial meltdown* 经济崩溃

memorabilia /ˌmeməræˈbɪlɪə; ˌmɛmərəˈbɪlɪə/ *n* [pl] items that are collected or displayed, eg because of their association with a famous person or a past event 搜集在一起的纪念品，纪念展品（如因其与某一名人或过去某事件有关）: *Graceland, the house that belonged to Elvis Presley, is full of memorabilia of the singer.* 格雷斯兰，这座曾属于埃尔维斯·普雷斯利的房子里到处是纪念这位歌手的物品。

men's lib *n* (*infml* 口) = MEN'S MOVEMENT

men's movement /ˈmenz muːvmənt; ˈmɛnz muvmənt/ *n* [U] movement aimed at freeing men from traditional views of the male character and of the proper role of men in society 男性解放运动（旨在改变对男性的传统看法及其在社会中扮演的传统角色的运动）

NOTE 注: probably stimulated by the earlier movement to re-define the role and position of women in society 可能是由早先的妇女解放运动激发出的想法

men's room /ˈmenz ruːm; ˈmɛnz rum/ *n* (*US*) public toilet for men; toilet provided for the use of male staff as one of the facilities in an office, factory, etc 男厕所；男盥洗室

mentally challenged /ˌmentəlɪ ˈtʃælɪndʒd; ˌmɛntl̩ɪ ˈtʃælɪndʒd/ *adj* having some mental disability 精神或智力有问题的；有心智障碍的 Cf 参看 OTHERLY ABLED

NOTE 注: the term gained currency as offering a more positive image than *mentally disabled* or *mentally handicapped* 因比 mentally disabled 或 mentally handicapped（心智伤残）富有较正面的含义而广为使用

menu /ˈmenjuː; ˈmɛnju/ *n* (*computing* 计) list of options within a computer program which can be called up by the user or permanently displayed on the screen and which offers a range of possible commands and facilities 菜单: *pop-up menus* 弹出式菜单 ○ *drop-down menus offering a wide range of options* 提供多种选择的下拉式菜单

NOTE 注: based on the *menu* in a restaurant which offers a list of possible choices 源自餐馆里供顾客点菜的菜单

metal detectorist *n* = DETECTORIST

Michelangelo /ˌmaɪklˈændʒələʊ, *US also* ˌmɪk-; ˌmaɪkl̩ˈændʒəlo, ˌmɪk-/ *n* one of the best-known computer viruses（VIRUS）which acts to destroy any data on the hard disk every 6 March, the birthday of Michelangelo 米开朗琪罗病毒（能破坏硬盘中所有数据的著名计算机病毒，每年3月6日米开朗琪罗生日时发作）

microrobot /ˈmaɪkrəʊˌrəʊbɒt; ˈmaɪkroˌrobɑt/ (also **nanobot**) *n* tiny experimental mechanical device which is intended to enter narrow parts of the body, eg the arteries, to carry out essential medical procedures 微型机械人（一种实验性微型机械装置，用以必要时进入动脉等人体狭窄部位进行治疗）

microwaveable /ˈmaɪkrəʊˌweɪvəbl; ˈmaɪkroˌwevəbl̩/ *adj* (of food products, esp frozen) suitable for cooking or heating through in a microwave oven（指食品，尤指冷冻食品）适于用微波炉烹调或加热的

Middle America /ˌmɪdl əˈmerɪkə; ˌmɪdl̩ əˈmɛrəkə/ *n* [U] the middle class in the USA, esp considered as conservative in religion and politics 美国中产阶级（尤被认为在宗教和政治上持保守态度）: *The populist President knew well how to appeal to Middle America.* 这位信奉平民主义的总统很懂得如何赢得美国中产阶级的好感。

Middle England /ˌmɪdl ˈɪŋglənd; ˌmɪdl̩ ˈɪŋglənd/ *n* [U] middle classes in England outside London, esp as representative of conservative political views（伦敦以外地区的）英国中产阶级（尤指政治保守派的代表）Cf 参看 MIDDLE AMERICA

▷ **Middle Englander** *n* person who shares Middle England's beliefs and values 英国中产阶级人士

middle ground /ˈmɪdl graʊnd; ˈmɪdl̩ graund/ *n* [U] (usu 通常作 **the middle ground**) **1** way of thinking, stance, or choice of action tending to moderation and compromise 中间立场；中庸之道: *Surely we can reach the middle ground on this if we start with the willingness to be flexible.* 我们如果愿意变通的话，当然可以在这个问题上达成妥协。 **2** people regarded as holding moderate views 中间派；温和派: *The middle ground have yet to be convinced of his intentions, in spite of his conciliatory words.* 虽然他已好言好语极力安抚，但他的意见尚未被中间派采纳。

middle management /ˌmɪdl ˈmænɪdʒmənt; ˌmɪdl̩ ˈmænɪdʒmənt/ *n* [U with sing or pl v 用单数或复数动词] (*commerce* 商) people who head departments within a business organization but who do not make major policy or financial decisions 中层管理人员: *increasing job insecurity amongst middle management* 中层管理人员的就业情况日益不稳定

MIDI /ˈmɪdɪ; ˈmɪdɪ/ (also **Midi, midi**) *abbr* 缩写 = (*music or computing* 音或计) Musical Instrument Digital Interface (ie an interface which allows electronic musical instruments, sequencers and synthesizers to be interconnected and controlled by a computer) 乐器数字接口（即将电子乐器、定序器、音响合成器与计算机相联，使其由计算机控制的接口）

▷ **MIDI** (also **Midi, midi**) *adj* making use of this kind of interface 使用乐器数字接口的

mid-life /ˈmɪdlaɪf; ˈmɪdlaɪf/ *adj* [usu attrib 通常作定语] occurring during one's middle age 中年的: *mid-life restlessness/doubts* 中年的焦虑不安 *[*困惑*]*

□ **mid-life crisis** *n* (usu *sing* 通常作单数) time, esp around middle age, when a person stops feeling secure, confident, etc about health, attractiveness or achievements 中年危机（人到中年时在健康、吸引力和成就方面皆失去安全感和信心等）: *going through a mid-life crisis* 经历中年危机

mid-range /ˌmɪdˈreɪndʒ; mɪdˈrendʒ/ *adj* [attrib 作定语] average; neither the best nor the worst that is available and so neither expensive nor cheap 普通水平的；中档的: *accommodation at a mid-range hotel* 在一家普通旅馆住宿 ○ *a mid-range car/computer* 中档汽车 *[*计算机*]*

mid-term /ˌmɪdˈtɜːm; mɪdˈtɝm/ *adj, n* **1** (*politics* 政) (in the) middle of the period that a government, council, president, etc is elected for（政府、议会、总统等任期的）中期（的）: *a mid-term by-election victory* 中期补缺选举胜利 **2** (**a**) (in the) middle of a school or university term（学期的）期中（的）: *mid-term holidays/exams* 期中假期 *[考试]* (**b**) examination given at MID-TERM 2(a) 期中考试

military service /ˌmɪlətrɪ ˈsɜːvɪs, *US* -terɪ; ˌmɪlətɛrɪ ˈsɝvɪs/ *n* [U] period, required by the state, in which one trains or serves as a soldier 兵役: *Women, as well as men, still do military service in Israel.* 在以色列，不单男子要服兵役，妇女也要。

milk round /ˈmɪlk raʊnd; ˈmɪlk raʊnd/ *n* **the milk round** (usu *sing* 通常作单数) (*Brit fig* 比喻) recruiting drive during which representatives of large companies visit universities with talks and exhibitions to attract students who are about to take their final degree exams 巡回招聘（一种招聘方式，大公司的代表到各大学举办讲座和展览以吸引即将毕业的学生）: *The milk round is starting early at Durham this year.* 今年以达勒姆大学为首站的巡回招聘活动开始得早。

millennium bug /mɪˈlenɪəm bʌɡ; mɪˈlɛnɪəm ˌbʌɡ/ (also **Y2K bug**) *n* [sing] (*infml computing* 口，计) coding of dates in software which allows only two digits to the year and which many computers will misread when the year 2000 starts, turning all dates back to 1900 instead 千年虫（将年份定为两位数的软件中的日期编码，当 2000 年开始时，许多计算机将会将日期误读回 1900 年）

millennium cult /mɪˌlenɪəm ˈkʌlt; mɪˌlɛnɪəm ˈkʌlt/ *n* **1** group of believers, usu with one leader, who look forward to the coming of an earthly paradise in which the faithful will be rewarded 千禧教，人间天堂教（相信及期待着人间天堂的来临的群体，通常以一人为首。这些人认为届时虔诚的信徒会得好报） **2** = DOOMSDAY CULT

mind /maɪnd; maɪnd/ *n* (idm 习语) **get one's mind around sth** GRASP 2A-Z; understand fully 领会 *[理解]* 某事物: *I just can't get my mind around the concept of a black hole.* 我就是没法理解黑洞这个概念。

mind-set /ˈmaɪndset; ˈmaɪndsɛt/ *n* set of attitudes or views formed by earlier events, usu firmly held and unlikely to change 思想倾向；既定看法；心态: *You have to understand the mind-set of these people before you introduce changes.* 你在引入变革前，必须了解这些人的心态。

minibar /ˈmɪnɪbɑː(r); ˈmɪnɪbɑr/ *n* selection of mainly alcoholic drinks placed, usu in a refrigerated cabinet, in a hotel room for the use of guests, and charged on the bill if used 小酒柜（旅馆房间内通常放在冰箱里的饮料，客人享用后，费用记入帐单）: *There was a good selection of wines and spirits in the minibar.* 小酒柜里有多种葡萄酒和烈酒可供选择。

minibreak /ˈmɪnɪbreɪk; ˈmɪnɪbrek/ *n* (**a**) brief pause for rest 小休 (**b**) short holiday, eg for a weekend 短假（如周末假期） Cf 参看 CITY BREAK

MiniDisc /ˈmɪnɪdɪsk; ˈmɪnɪdɪsk/ *n* (*propr* 专利名) recordable, small CD, two inches in diameter which can hold about one hour's recorded music 迷你唱片（直径为二英寸，能录约一小时音乐的微型激光唱片）

minimally invasive surgery *n* = KEYHOLE SURGERY

miniseries /ˈmɪnɪˌsɪəriːz; ˈmɪnɪˌsɪriz/ *n* (*esp US*) (pl unchanged 复数不变) drama shown on television in several parts which are broadcast within a few days of each other 小型电视连续剧: *It was said to be the most expensive miniseries ever produced.* 据说这是有史以来制作费最昂贵的小型电视连续剧。○ *starring in several miniseries* 主演若干部小型电视连续剧

misconceived /ˌmɪskənˈsiːvd; ˌmɪskənˈsivd/ *adj* badly planned or judged from the very beginning; not appropriate（从开始便）设计有误的，判断不当的；不合适的: *a misconceived project/policy* 构思错误的工程、不合适的政策

misery index /ˈmɪzərɪ ˌɪndeks; ˈmɪzərɪ ˌɪndɛks/ *n* (usu *sing* 通常作单数) (*infml* 口) measure expressed in statistical terms of the economic hardship endured by a group or a whole society based on the levels of inflation and unemployment 痛苦指数，经济失调指数（基于通货膨胀率和失业率所作的统计，表示某个社群或整个社会遭受的经济困难程度）

misper /ˈmɪspə(r), ˈmɪspɜː(r); ˈmɪspɚ/ *n* (*sl* 俚) (used by the police) missing person（警察用语）失踪者

mission statement /ˈmɪʃn steɪtmənt; ˈmɪʃən stetmənt/ *n* (*commerce* 商) declaration made by a company of its general objectives and principles of operation 宗旨声明（公司对其经营宗旨及运作原则的声明）: *a mission statement full of promises and high-sounding avowals* 满纸承诺和吹嘘的宗旨声明

mixed media *n* = MULTIMEDIA

mixer /ˈmɪksə(r); ˈmɪksɚ/ *n* skilful disc jockey who is able to make use of all possible techniques to make his or her presentation of the music exciting and unusual, eg blending the sound and lyrics of one song into another 音乐播放能手（能灵活运用各种技术使自己播放的音乐独特而刺激的流行音乐节目主持人，如能将一首歌的词曲融入另一首歌）

mobile /ˈməʊbaɪl, *US* ˈməʊbl; ˈmobl̩/ *n* mobile phone 手机；移动电话；手提电话: *Call me on my mobile.* 请打我手机。○ *The insurance doesn't cover mobiles left in cars.* 该保险不包括在汽车上遗失的手提电话。

mole /məʊl; mol/ *n* large piece of burrowing and earth-moving equipment used in constructing modern tunnels（用于建造现代隧道的）大型挖掘机: *The huge mole at last fell silent and the thin remaining wall of earth still separating the two teams of tunnelers was carefully removed by hand.* 巨大的挖掘机终于沉寂了下来，两边的掘隧道工人小心翼翼地用手将他们中间的薄薄的土墙挖走。

molecular archaeology /məˌlekjuːlə ɑːkɪˈɒlədʒɪ; məˌlɛkjələ ɑrkɪˈɑlədʒɪ/ *n* [U] technique of tracing the ancestry of a group of people or of an individual through an examination of their genes 分子考古学（通过研究基因查考群体或个人的祖先的技术）: *Molecular archaeology has confirmed that the Basque people of northern Spain carry unique genes which show that they are not directly related to the other peoples of Europe.* 分子考古研究证实了西班牙北部的巴斯克人所带基因独特，表明他们与欧洲其他民族并无直接关系。

Monetary Union /ˌmʌnɪtrɪ ˈjuːnɪən, *US* -terɪ; ˈmʌnəˌtɛrɪ ˈjunjən/ *n* [sing] achievement of a single currency and a united financial policy amongst the members of the European Union 货币联盟（在欧洲联盟成员国间实现单一货币和统一的金融政策）

monetize, -ise /ˈmʌnɪtaɪz; ˈmʌnətaɪz/ *v* [Tn] **1** turn an asset, a property, etc into money 把（资产、房地产等）换成金钱 **2** realize the cash value of sth 将某物兑成现金: *Once you have a flat in central Berlin, you can always monetize it when the prices rise.* 如果在柏林市中心有一套公寓，价格上涨时就可以随时把它变现。

moneyman /ˈmʌnɪˌmæn; ˈmʌnɪˌmæn/ *n* (*infml* 口) person who deals with money professionally; financier 专业理财人士；金融家

monty ⇨ THE FULL MONTY (FULL)

moonball /ˈmuːnbɔːl; ˈmunbɔl/ *n* (*slightly derog* 略带贬义) (in tennis) ball hit in a high looping arc towards the back of the court（网球）月亮球，高吊弧线球: *The crowd got impatient with the frequent moonballs played by the defending champion as he tired.* 当卫冕球员体力不支，不停地打出高吊弧线球时，观众开始不耐烦起来。Cf 参看 LOBA-Z

Moonie /'mu:nɪ; 'munɪ/ *n* member of the world wide religious sect which follows a charismatic leader from Korea. They wear distinctive robes and often try to recruit new members in streets and at airports, esp in the US 文鲜明统一教团信徒（一世界性宗教派别成员，教主为一位富有号召力的韩国人。他们身着独特的长袍，通常在街头或机场，尤其在美国吸收新成员）

NOTE 注： from the name of its founder, Sun Myung Moon, and with a pun on *moony* (dreamy) 源自其创始人 Sun Myung Moon（文鲜明）的名字，亦为 moony（神思恍惚的）一词的双关语

moonwalk /'mu:nwɔ:k; 'munwɔk/ *v* [I] (of dancing) move backwards with a gliding motion by sliding the feet and placing them toe to heel one after the other 走登月式舞步（一种向后滑行的舞步，舞者双脚交替地将脚尖向脚跟的位置滑动）

▷ **moonwalking** *n* dance movement in which one moonwalks, made popular by American pop star Michael Jackson 登月式舞步（此舞步因美国歌星迈克尔·杰克逊而流行）

moral majority /ˌmɒrəl mə'dʒɒrətɪ, *US* mɔ:rəl; ˌmɔrəl mə'dʒɔrətɪ/ *n* **the moral majority** [Gp] presumed majority of people in a country, regarded as favouring strong moral standards 道德多数派（着重传统道德标准的大多数民众）

morphing /'mɔ:fɪŋ; 'mɔrfɪŋ/ [U] *n* computing technique used to produce the special effect of smoothly transforming one film image into another, eg so that a car becomes an animal 图像变形技术（将某一影视图像顺畅地转换成另一图像以取得特殊效果的计算机技术，如可将一辆汽车变成一只动物）: *Morphing can turn an alien into a human and back again in seconds.* 图像变形技术可在几秒钟内将一个外星人变成地球人，然后又变回去。

mosh /mɒʃ; mɔʃ/ *v* [I] dance in a violent and reckless manner at a rock concert, often jumping up and down, falling on the floor and crashing into other dancers and the walls（在摇滚音乐会上）狂舞（常跳上跳下、跌在地上、碰撞其他舞者和墙）

▷ **mosher** *n* person who moshes 狂舞者

Mossad /'mɒsæd; 'mɔsæd/ *n* [sing] the Israeli secret police 莫萨德（以色列秘密警察）

mother /'mʌðə(r); 'mʌðɚ/ *n* (idm 习语) **the mother of all ...** biggest and most terrible (of sth)（某事物之中）最大的，最严重的 : *Then there was the mother of all rows.* 然后就发生了最大的争吵。

NOTE 注： became more common after Saddam Hussein's use of the expression *the mother of all battles* during the Gulf War 萨达姆·侯赛因在海湾战争时使用短语 the mother of all battles（最大的战争）后此习语更加流行

motion capture /ˌməʊʃn 'kæptʃə(r); ˌmoʃən 'kæptʃɚ/ *n* [U] technique used to make modern animated cartoons. Human actors wearing lights at points on their bodies are photographed performing an action; the photos are then processed by a computer to produce a graphic representation of the movement which is very life-like 动态捕捉（一种现代动画制作技术，在演员身体的某些部位戴上点状的发光物，把其动作拍摄下来然后经计算机处理成非常逼真的动态图像）

motormouth /'məʊtəmaʊθ; 'motɚmaυθ/ *n* (*infml derog* 口，贬) person who talks all the time, esp loudly and rapidly 大声说个没完的人；喋喋不休的人；马达嘴

mouse /maʊs; maυs/ *v* [Tn, Ipr] (*computing* 计) carry out an operation on a computer using a MOUSE 3^{A-Z} 用鼠标操作 : *Mouse your way over to the icon and click on it.* 用鼠标将箭头移至图标处，然后轻击一下。

mouse potato /maʊs pə'teɪtəʊ; maυs pə'teto/ *n* (*sl* 俚) person who spends too much time in front of a computer, esp in order to surf the NET 1(b) 老泡在计算机前的人（尤指浏览网页者）；网虫

NOTE 注： formed on analogy with COUCH POTATO 由 couch potato（老泡在沙发上的人）一词类推构成

movable feast /ˌmu:vəbl 'fi:st; ˌmuvəbl̩ 'fist/ *n* religious festival, of which the date of celebration may change from year to year 节期因年而异的宗教节日 : *Easter is celebrated on a different date every year. It's a movable feast.* 人们每年在不同的时间庆祝复活节，它是一个节期因年而异的节日。○ (*fig* 比喻) *It doesn't matter when we have our meeting — it's a movable feast.* 我们何时开会都没关系 —— 日期可以变动。

movers and shakers /ˌmu:vəz ənd 'ʃeɪkəz; ˌmuvɚz ənd 'ʃekɚz/ *n* [pl] (*esp US*) people with power and who have a lot of influence 有权有势者

movie mall *n* = MEGAPLEX

mozzarella /mɒtsə'relə; mɔtsə'rɛlə/ *n* [U] (*Italian* 意) soft white cheese used in pizzas and salads 软白干酪；莫泽雷勒干酪（用于意大利饼和色拉中的）: *a mozzarella and tomato salad* 一份莫泽雷勒干酪加西红柿色拉

MRI *abbr* = MAGNETIC RESONANCE IMAGING : *MRI has the advantage of showing soft tissue clearly.* 核磁共振成像可以清楚地显现人体的软组织。

MRM *abbr* 缩写 = MECHANICALLY-RECOVERED MEAT

Mufti /'mʌftɪ; 'mʌftɪ/ *n* title of Muslim legal experts or religious leaders 穆夫提（伊斯兰教教法专家或宗教领袖）

mug shot /'mʌg ʃɒt; 'mʌg ʃɑt/ *n* (*sl* 俚) photograph showing sb's face for official use, eg a photograph of a suspected criminal kept by the police as a record（公事使用的）脸部照片（如警方用以存档的嫌疑犯照片）Cf 参看 MUG[1] 2^{A-Z}

mujahedin /ˌmu:dʒəhə'di:n; ˌmudʒəhə'din/ (also **muja-heddin**) *n* [pl] (in certain Muslim countries) GUERILLA^{A-Z} fighters who support the cause of Muslim FUNDAMENTALISM^{A-Z}（某些伊斯兰教国家中支持穆斯林原教旨主义的）穆斯林游击队员

mule /mju:l; mjul/ *n* **1** (also **drug mule**) person acting as a courier for illegal drugs, usu across international boundaries 偷运毒品者（通常指过境者）: *The mules are often caught, but rarely the traffickers who employ them.* 经常能逮到偷运毒品的人，但很少能抓到雇用他们的毒贩。 **2** person who opens a bank account in order to receive money deposited by a CYBER CRIMINAL (CYBER CRIME) who has illegally transferred the money from another bank（计算机罪犯的）帮凶，二传手（在银行开户头接收他人利用计算机非法从其他银行转来的钱的人）

multicultural /ˌmʌltɪ'kʌltʃərəl; ˌmʌltɪ'kʌltʃərəl/ *adj* for or including people of several different races, religions or national traditions 多文化的；融合多种文化的 : *a multicultural society* 融合多种文化的社会 ○ *multicultural education* 多文化教育

▷ **multiculturalism** *n* [U]

multi-gym /'mʌltɪdʒɪm; 'mʌltɪdʒɪm/ (also **multi gym, multigym**) *n* **1** versatile piece of exercise equipment which can be used to exercise most of the muscles in the body 多功能健身器；组合健身器 **2** room containing several pieces of exercise equipment（有多种健身器材的）健身房

multimedia /'mʌltɪmi:dɪə, mʌltɪ'mi:dɪə; ˌmʌltɪ'midɪə/ (also **multi-media**) *n* [U] **1** type of computer system that combines text with audio, video and still images to create an interactive application（计算机系统的）多媒体 : *a multimedia encyclopedia — available on CD-ROM* 一部多媒体百科全书 —— 光盘现已上市 **2** any communications technique that involves more than one medium of expression 运用多种媒介的通信技术

multiparty /ˌmʌltɪˈpɑːtɪ; ˌmʌltɪˈpɑrtɪ/ *adj* [attrib 作定语] allowing the co-existence of several different political parties 多党的；多党并存的：*a multiparty state/democracy* 多党制国家 *[*民主政体*]* Cf 参看 ONE PARTY STATE

multiple-personality disorder /ˌmʌltɪplˌpɜːsəˈnælɪtɪ dɪsˌɔːdə(r); ˌmʌltəpl pɝsnˈælətɪ dɪsˌɔrdɚ/ *n* [U] (*psychology* 心) psychiatric disorder which is characterized by the apparent existence of several quite separate and conflicting personalities within one individual 多重人格障碍（一种精神病症，患者似乎具有多种完全不同的、互相矛盾的人格）：*'The three faces of Eve' recounts the story of a young woman who suffered from multiple-personality disorder.* 《三面人夏娃》讲述了一位深受多重人格困扰的年轻女子的故事。

multiplex *n* = MEGAPLEX

multitasking /ˌmʌltɪˈtɑːskɪŋ, *US* -ˈtæsk-; ˌmʌltɪˈtæskɪŋ/ *n* (*computing* 计) carrying out of a number of tasks at the same time 多任务处理（同时执行多项任务）

musicality /ˌmjuːzɪˈkælətɪ; ˌmjuzɪˈkælətɪ/ *n* [U] state or property of being MUSICAL 2^A-Z 喜爱音乐；精于音乐：*the admirable musicality of the performers* 各表演者令人神往的音乐才华

must- /mʌst; mʌst/ *comb form* 构词成分 essential; very much desired 必不可少的；令人向往的：*a must-visit restaurant* 不能不去的餐馆 ○ *a must-have accessory for the beach this summer* 今夏去海滩必要的装备

mute button /ˈmjuːt bʌtn; ˈmjut bʌtn̩/ *n* (**a**) device on a telephone for temporarily preventing the caller from hearing what is being said in the room of the receiver 静音键（电话上使打电话者暂时听不见接收方声音的装置）(**b**) button on a remote control for instantly cutting out the sound on a television or video-cassette recorder, etc 静音按钮（遥控器上用于即时关掉电视机或录像机的声音的键）

mutual assured destruction *n* = MAD

myalgic encephalomyelitis /maɪˌældʒɪk enˌkefələʊmaɪəˈlaɪtɪs, *US* enˌsef-; maɪˌældʒɪk ɛnˌsɛfəlomaɪəˈlaɪtɪs/ *n* [U] (*abbr* 缩写 **ME**) viral disease with symptoms of fatigue and lack of coordination. People who complain of the illness are often not taken very seriously because it seems to strike only the well-off in society and also because some doctors think it is a psychological rather than a physical condition; YUPPIE FLU 肌痛性脑脊髓炎，雅皮士流感（一种病毒性疾病，症状为易疲劳和协调不良。称病的人一般不获认真对待，因为似乎只有富人才生这种病，而且一些医生认为它是一种心理而非生理问题）

Nn

nail-biting /ˈneɪlbaɪtɪŋ; ˈnelbaɪtɪŋ/ *adj* causing great tension or anxiety 使人万分紧张的；令人焦虑不安的；让人如坐针毡的：*a nail-biting end to the race/match* 赛跑 *[*比赛*]* 的令人万分紧张的最后时刻

nanny state /nænɪ ˈsteɪt; nænɪ ˈstet/ *n* (*derog* 贬) state seen as exercising unnecessary control over individuals, limiting their choices and not allowing them full responsibility over their own lives 保姆式国家（过于干预和控制人民生活的国家）：*The nanny state robs people of initiative and encourages a culture of dependency.* 这个保姆式国家将人们的进取精神消磨殆尽，并助长了一种依赖习气。

nano- /ˈnænəʊ; ˈnæno/ *comb form* 构词成分 **1** (used in names of units of measurement to denote a factor of 10^{-9}（用作测量单位）毫微 (= 10^{-9}): *nanometre* ○ *nanosecond* **2** very small; relating to molecular proportions 极小的；分子般小的

NOTE 注： from the Greek word *nanos* which means 'dwarf' 源于希腊语 nanos，意为'矮子'

nanometre /ˈnænəʊˌmiːtə(r); ˈnænoˌmitɚ/ *n* thousand millionth part of a metre 纳米（十亿分之一米）

nanosecond /ˈnænəʊˌsekənd; ˈnænoˌsɛkənd/ *n* (*physics or electronics* 物或电子) thousand millionth part of a second 纳秒（十亿分之一秒）

nanotechnology /ˌnænəʊtekˈnɒlədʒɪ; ˌnænotɛkˈnɑlədʒɪ/ *n* [U] (*electronics or computing* 电子或计) development and use of devices that have a size of only a few nanometres 纳米技术（用于制造和使用仅几纳米大小的装置的技术）

narcodollars /ˈnɑːkəʊdɒləz; ˈnɑrkodɑlɚz/ *n* [pl] US dollars earned from the export of illegal drugs 毒品美元（通过出口非法毒品赚取的美元）：*Narcodollars are now calculated to represent around 8% of the value of world trade.* 据统计毒品美元现约占世界贸易总额的 8%。

NOTE 注： from *narcotics* and *dollars* 由 narcotics（毒品）和 dollars（美元）二词构成

narrowcast /ˈnærəʊkɑːst, *US* -kæst; ˈnærokæst/ *v* [Tn] (*pt, pp* **-cast** or **-casted**) (*esp US*) transmit (a television programme, etc), esp by cable, to an audience targeted by interests or location（尤指通过电缆为特定观众）小范围播送（电视节目等）：*We're narrowcasting Cajun Comment to the French dialect speakers of Louisiana.* 我们现在向路易斯安那州说法语方言的听众播送'阿卡迪亚人（法裔路易斯安那州人）评论'。

national convention /ˌnæʃnəl kənˈvenʃn; ˌnæʃənl̩ kənˈvɛnʃən/ *n* (*US*) assembly of the officers and members of a major political party, esp to nominate a candidate for the Presidency（尤指政党为提名总统候选人而召开的）全国代表大会：*At the national convention, the Republicans showed overwhelming support for the front runner.* 在全国代表大会上，共和党人对那个最有希望的候选人表示狂热的支持。

national curriculum /ˌnæʃnəl kəˈrɪkjələm; ˌnæʃənl̩ kəˈrɪkjələm/ *n* (*pl* **curricula** or **curriculums**)(usu *sing* 通常作单数) (in Britain) programme of study specifying all major subjects to be followed by all pupils in state schools（英国）全国课程（公立学校学生主修课程）：*the introduction of the national curriculum for England, Wales and Northern Ireland* 在英格兰、威尔士和北爱尔兰开展全国课程

nation-state /ˌneɪʃnˈsteɪt; ˌneʃənˈstet/ *n* nation of people, which is defined by uniting factors such as language, common descent, etc, forming an independent state 单一民族的独立国家：*Some Scottish people support the formation of a separate nation-state.* 一些苏格兰人支持建立一个单一民族的独立国家。

Native /ˈneɪtɪv; ˈnetɪv/ *adj* (forming compounds 用以构成复合词) labelling a specified group of indigenous people in contrast to more recently arrived immigrants or colonizers 当地的；土生土长的：*Native Canadian* 土生土长的加拿大人 ○ *Native Australian* 澳大利亚土著

□ **Native American** (also **American Indian**) *n* (*dated* 旧作 **Amerindian**) original inhabitant of North America 北美土著居民；北美印第安人：*Native Americans are now more aware of the value of preserving their cultural and linguistic heritage.* 北美土著居民如今越发意识到保存他们的文化和语言遗产的价值。Cf 参看 RED INDIAN (RED^1(A-Z))

NOTE 注： the term *Native American* is currently preferred to the older term *American Indian* 现常用 Native American 一词取代旧称呼 American Indian（美洲印第安人）

natural science /ˌnætʃrəl ˈsaɪəns, *US* ˌnætʃərəl; ˌnætʃərəl ˈsaɪəns/ *n* (**a**) [U] group of sciences used in the study of the physical world, eg chemistry, physics, biology, etc 自然科学（总称）(**b**) [C usu pl 通常作复数] any one of these sciences （一门）自然科学：*He studied one of the natural sciences. I can't remember which one.* 他研究的是自然科学，具体哪一门我忘了。Cf 参看 LIFE SCIENCES (LIFE[A-Z])

nature reserve /ˈneɪtʃə rɪzɜːv; ˈnetʃɚ rɪzɝv/ *n* area of land protected from development for the benefit of its animals, plants, physical features, etc 自然保护区：*Britain has a lot of nature reserves considering its small size and dense population.* 就其狭小的面积和密集的人口来说，英国的自然保护区算是很多了。Cf 参看 GAME RESERVE (GAME[1(A-Z)]), SAFARI PARK (SAFARI[A-Z])

nature tourism /ˈneɪtʃə ˌtʊərɪzəm; ˌnetʃɚ ˈtʊrɪzəm/ *n* [U] organization of tours for people interested in wildlife and the countryside 自然风光旅游，自然生态旅游（以观赏野生动物和大自然为主的旅游）：*Whale-watching is one of the best examples of nature tourism.* 观鲸是最典型的自然生态旅游。

NC *abbr* 缩写 = NETWORK COMPUTER

near-abroad /nɪərəˈbrɔːd; nɪrəˈbrɔd/ *n* [sing] (a collective term for the independent republics which were part of the former Soviet Union) 准外国（对现已独立的各前苏联共和国的总称）

NOTE 注： from the Russian phrase which conveys the idea of an area which is both close at hand and distant and which is within Russia's sphere of influence and interest 源自俄语，指属于俄罗斯影响与利益范围以内，虽近在咫尺却又显得疏远的地区

near-death experience /nɪədeθ ɪkˈspɪərɪəns; nɪrdɛθ ɪkˈspɪrɪəns/ *n* sensations reported by people who nearly died usu including seeing a bright light at the end of a tunnel 濒死经历（曾经濒临死亡者所描述的经历，通常包括看见一条隧道尽头的亮光）Cf 参看 OUT-OF-BODY EXPERIENCE

necrotizing fasciitis /ˈnekrətaɪzɪŋ fæsɪˌaɪtɪs; ˈnɛkrətaɪzɪŋ fæsɪˌaɪtɪs/ *n* [U] (*medical* 医) bacterial infection which causes rapid tissue destruction through inflammation of the sheath of fibrous tissue enclosing a muscle or other organ 坏死性筋膜炎

NOTE 注： commonly known as the *flesh-eating disease*; the disease became well-known and feared in the UK in 1994 when twenty people died of it 通常被称作 flesh-eating disease（噬肉病）。此病 1994 年在英国导致二十人死亡而知名并引起恐慌

nega- /ˈnegə; ˈnɛgə/ *comb form* 构词成分 reduction or absence of 缩减；缺少；无：*negamile* ○ *negawatt*

negamile /ˈnegəmaɪl; ˈnɛgəmaɪl/ *n* one mile's journey that is saved, with the consequent economy in terms of energy and reduction of traffic, if a driver drives less 少开车而节省下的一英里路程（由此可节约能源以及减少交通量）

negative equity /ˌnegətɪv ˈekwɪtɪ; ˌnɛgətɪv ˈɛkwətɪ/ *n* [U] debt situation of a house owner when the market value of his or her property falls below the mortgage still owed on it 负衡平抵押（当房产价跌至低于未偿还的抵押贷款时房主负债的情况）：*Many people who were encouraged to take out mortages and buy their own homes later found themselves burdened with negative equity as property prices fell steeply.* 当房地产价格急剧下跌时，许多当初被鼓动以抵押贷款方式购买私房的人背上了负衡平抵押的重担。

negativity /negəˈtɪvɪtɪ; nɛgəˈtɪvɪtɪ/ *n* [U] negative attitude; fact or quality of being negative 消极态度；消极性：*I'm tired of battling the negativity of the other committee members.* 我对抵抗其他委员的消极态度感到厌烦。

negawatt /ˈnegəwɒt; ˈnɛgəwɑt/ *n* one megawatt of electricity that is saved, expressing the concept that a reduction in demand of one megawatt is equivalent to the generation of one megawatt 节省下的一兆瓦电（用来表示节省了一兆瓦电等于生产了一兆瓦电这个概念）

neighbourhood watch /ˌneɪbəhʊd ˈwɒtʃ; ˌnebɚhʊd ˈwɑtʃ/ *n* [sing] (mostly used to form compound nouns 多用以构成复合名词) voluntary scheme in which a group of people living in an area watch each other's houses regularly to discourage burglars 邻里联防（邻里间自愿相互协作照看房屋以防窃贼）：*Warning! This is a neighbourhood watch area.* 警告！这里是邻里联防区。 ○ *We consider that our neighbourhood watch is working well.* 我们认为我们的邻里联防运作得非常好。

neonatal /ˌniːəˈneɪtəl; nioˈnetl̩/ *adj* (*medical* 医) of or relating to a NEWBORN child 新生儿的；新生期的：*a neonatal intensive care unit* 新生儿特别看护室 ○ *neonatal mortality rates* 新生儿死亡率

▷ **neonate** *n* NEWBORN baby 新生儿

neo-poverty /niːəʊˈpɒvətɪ; nioˈpɑvɚtɪ/ *n* [U] poverty experienced by people who were previously financially secure, which is caused by a change of personal or social circumstances, eg job loss, divorce, changes in welfare allowances, etc 新贫困（原先经济有保障者因个人或社会环境发生变化，如失业、离婚、福利津贴改变等而体验到的贫困）

Neoprene /ˈniːəʊpriːn; ˈnioprin/ *n* [U] (*propr* 专利名) waterproof material used esp for making wet suits (WET[A-Z]) 氯丁（二烯）橡胶（防水材料，尤用于制潜水服）

nerd /nɜːd; nɝd/ *n* (*infml* 口) conventional, unstylish and boring person 落伍者；乏味的人

nerve gas /ˈnɜːv gæs; ˈnɝv gæs/ *n* [U] poisonous gas which affects the nervous system, used as a weapon in war 神经性毒气（用作战争武器）：*The production of nerve gas should be outlawed by the international community.* 国际社会应禁止生产神经性毒气。

net /net; nɛt/ *n* (*computing* 计) **1** (**a**) computer network 计算机网络 (**b**) **the Net** [sing] (*infml* 口) the INTERNET 国际互联网 **2** (in compounds 用以构成复合词) of computer networking 计算机网络的

▷ **netter, nettie** *ns* regular user of USENET, perhaps one who spends too much time in this occupation 经常使用用户网的人；网民；网虫

□ **nethead** *n* person who is deeply involved with the net, perhaps excessively so 网痴；网迷

netnews *n* [sing] messages posted electronically by users of USENET（使用用户网的人发送的）网络消息

netsurfer *n* INTERNET user 互联网用户；网上冲浪者

netizen /ˈnetɪzn; ˈnɛtəzn̩/ *n* (*computing* 计) person belonging to the community of network users, esp an INTERNET user 网民（尤指互联网用户）

NOTE 注： a blend formed from *net* and *citizen* 由 net（计算机网络）和 citizen（市民）二词合成

network /ˈnetwɜːk; ˈnɛtwɝk/ *v* [I, Ipr] (**a**) set up and foster a set of useful contacts for the benefit of one's business or professional career（为自己的生意或事业等）建立关系网 (**b**) make use of an informal gathering to renew old acquaintances and make new ones, esp insofar as these are beneficial to one professionally（利用非正式聚会）加强与新朋旧友的联系，交际（尤指对自己的事业有助的）：*Look at Tom, busy networking. He never misses a chance.* 瞧汤姆，正在忙着交际呢。他从不放过任何一个机会。

▷ **networker** *n*

network computer /ˈnetwɜːk kəmˌpjuːtə(r); ˈnɛtwɝk kəmˌpjutɚ/ *n* (*abbr* 缩写 **NC**) low-cost personal computer without local disk storage designed to be connected to the INTERNET, a LOCAL AREA NETWORK or similar network from which it would access applications and data 网络电脑（无磁盘存储器的低成本个人

电脑，可依赖互联网、局域网等获取应用程序和数据）

neural network /ˌnjʊərəl ˈnetwɜ:k, *US* nʊ-; ˈnʊrəl ˈnɛtwɝk/ (also **neural net**) *n* (*computing* 计) function which allows a computer to process a number of bits of unrelated information at the same time instead of one after the other, thus functioning in a way that is similar to the human brain 神经网络（计算机同时地而非一个接一个地处理许多不相关信息的功能，其处理方式类似人脑）Cf 参看 FUZZY LOGIC

neurocomputer /ˈnjʊərəʊkəmˌpju:tə(r), *US* nʊ-; ˈnʊrokəmˌpjutɚ/ *n* (*computing* 计) computer which uses a NEURAL NETWORK 神经计算机（使用神经网络的计算机）

New Age /nju: ˈeɪdʒ, *US* nu:; nu ˈedʒ/ (also **New Age Movement**) *n* diverse and wide-ranging cultural movement chiefly characterized by a rejection of modern Western values and the promotion of a more HOLISTIC, spiritual or even mystic approach to medicine, philosophy and the environment 新时代（运动）（一种广泛多样的文化运动，其主要特征为：摒弃现代西方价值观，宣扬以更全面的、通过心灵去感知的甚至是以神秘的态度对待医学、哲学和大自然）

▷ **New Age** *adj* belonging to, characteristic of, or influenced by the beliefs and activities of the New Age movement 新时代的：*a New Age bookshop* 新时代书店 ○ *His philosophy is more New Age than classical.* 他的哲学观点是新时代的而非传统的。

□ **New Age traveller** *n* member of a group of mainly young people who have rejected the values of modern society and who travel in groups from place to place usu in vans, living on state benefits or from casual jobs. Such people often show a strong concern for the environment 新时代旅行者（反对现代社会价值观念的年轻人，通常成群结队乘坐货车四处旅行，靠政府救济或打零工生活，对环境问题深表关注）

newborn /ˈnju:bɔ:n, *US* nu:-; ˈnubɔrn/ *adj* [attrib 作定语] recently born 新生的：*newborn babies* 新生婴儿 Cf 参看 NEONATAL

new kid on the block ⇨ KID

New Labour /nju: ˈleɪbə(r), *US* nu:; nu ˈlebɚ/ *n* [U] (*Brit*) that section of the Labour Party which accepts and identifies with the modernizing approach of the current leader, Tony Blair, who became Prime Minister in 1997 新工党（工党派别，接受与认同自 1997 年起担任首相的托尼·布莱尔的现代化路线）

▷ **New Labour** *adj* (*Brit*) of or belonging to New Labour 新工党的

New Lad /nju: ˈlæd, *US* nu:; nu ˈlæd/ *n* man, usu young, who shows sexist attitudes and behaviour and seeks to fulfil all the male stereotypes as a reaction against the perceived effeminacy of the NEW MAN 新派小子（以大男子主义者自居的年轻男子，认为 New Man（新派男人）过于女人气，为与之对抗而寻求恢复传统男人形象）

newly-industrializing country *n* = NIC

newly-industrializing economy *n* = NIC

New Man /nju: ˈmæn, *US* nu:; nu ˈmæn/ *n* man who rejects sexist attitudes and aims to be caring, sensitive and non-aggressive as well as taking a substantial role in such domestic areas as housekeeping and child-rearing 新派男人（反对以大男子主义者自居的男人，主张对别人关怀、体贴，不好争斗，并参与料理家务、照顾孩子等）Cf 参看 NEW LAD

NOTE 注： the term has become slightly derogatory since the late 1980s implying that a man like that is too effeminate and somehow not a proper man 此词自 20 世纪 80 年代后期始稍含贬义，即这样的人太女性化，不大像正常的男人

New Romantic /nju: rəʊˈmæntɪk, *US* nu:; nu roˈmæntɪk/ *n* follower of a British youth cult and fashion of the early 1980s which had elements of PUNK 1A-Z but encouraged both sexes to wear flamboyant clothes and often make-up 新浪漫主义者（20 世纪 80 年代初英国一种青年人时尚的追随者，带有'蓬克'的成分，但不论男女多服装艳丽，涂脂抹粉）

▷ **New Romantic** *adj* belonging to or associated with the New Romantics 新浪漫主义者的

news-gatherer /ˈnju:zˌgæðərə(r), *US* nu:z-; ˈnuzˌgæðərɚ/ *n* person who researches news items, esp for broadcast or publication（尤指为广播或出版）采访新闻者

▷ **news-gathering** *n* activity and product of a news-gatherer 新闻采访；采访后制成的新闻作品

newsgroup /ˈnju:zgru:p, *US* nu:z-; ˈnuzgrup/ *n* one of a number of online discussion forums which together make up USENET, an informal communications system now mainly carried on the INTERNET but separate from it 新闻组，新闻讨论群组（用户网上的联机论坛。用户网是设在互联网上但又相对独立的非正式通信系统）

new variant CJD /nju: ˌveəriənt si: dʒeɪ ˈdi:, *US* nu:; nu ˌvɛrɪənt si dʒe ˈdi/ *n* [U] version of the CJD (CREUTZFELDT-JAKOB DISEASE) virus which has been found in younger adults, esp in Britain, and is thought most likely to have been contracted from eating meat or meat products from animals infected with the BSE (BOVINE SPONGIFORM ENCEPHALOPATHY) virus 新变体克一雅二氏病病毒（青年身上发现的一种克一雅二氏症病毒，一般认为有可能因食用感染了疯牛病毒的动物的肉或肉制品而染得，尤见于英国）

new wave /ˌnju: ˈweɪv, *US* nu:; nu ˈwev/ (also **New Wave**) *n* [U sing] (**a**) movement in music, art, etc introducing new styles or fashions 新浪潮运动（音乐、艺术等领域中为引入新的风格或时尚而开展的运动）：*new wave films/designs* 新浪潮电影 *[设计]* (**b**) style of rock music popular in the 1970s 新浪潮音乐（流行于 20 世纪 70 年代的一种摇滚乐）

NFL /ˌen ef ˈel; ˌɛn ɛf ˈɛl/ *abbr* 缩写 = (in the US) National Football League（美国）全国橄榄球联盟：*NFL highlights/game of the week* 全国橄榄球联盟精选赛事 *[本周赛事]*

NIC /ˌen aɪ ˈsi:; ˌɛn aɪ ˈsi/ (also **NIE, newly-industrializing economy**) *abbr* 缩写 = newly-industrializing country (any one of the countries which has transformed its economy during the last thirty years from one that is largely agricultural to one that is largely industrial, esp in hi-tech areas, eg South Korea) 新工业化国家（近三十年里从以农业经济为主发展至以工业经济，尤指高科技领域为主的国家，如南韩）

NICAM /ˈnaɪkæm; ˈnaɪkæm/ *abbr* 缩写 = near instantaneously companded audio multiplex (a digital system used in television transmissions to provide high-quality stereo sound with the video signals. NICAM can be used to transmit at the same time two mono sound channels in different languages) 瞬时缩扩音频多路广播，丽音广播（在播放电视时随视频信号提供高质量立体声的数字系统，可用于同时播放不同语言的两个单声道）：*a NICAM facility* 瞬时缩扩音频多路广播装置

NOTE 注： *compand* is a blend of *compressor* and *expander* ☆ compand 由 compressor（压缩器）和 expander（扩展器）二词合成

niche /ni:ʃ, nɪtʃ; nɪtʃ/ *n* (*commerce* 商) position from which an entrepreneur is able to exploit a gap in the market; profitable section of the market（企业家利用市场供求缺口的）有利的地位，有利可图的那部分市场：*niche market* 缺口产品市场 ○ *niche product* 抓住市场缺口的产品

nicotine replacement therapy /ˌnɪkətiːn rɪˈpleɪsmənt ˌθerəpɪ; ˌnɪkətin rɪˈplesmənt ˌθɛrəpɪ/ *n* [U] (*medical* 医) use of a small and reducing dosage of nicotine through a medicated PATCH, gum or inhalers to help people to stop smoking by relieving the discomfort caused by the withdrawal of nicotine and giving their bodies time to start manufacturing their own nicotine again 尼古丁替代疗法（通过膏药、口香糖、吸入器等将少量并逐渐减量的尼古丁施于戒烟者以帮助其减轻戒烟的不适，并让其体内有时间重新自行制造尼古丁）

NIE *n* = NIC

nigga /ˈnɪgə; ˈnɪgə/ *n* (*pl* **niggaz**) black man 黑人

NOTE 注： a term which can only be used without offence between members of the black community. The word represents the pronunciation of the word *nigger* in an American Black English accent rather than in a Standard American accent which would pronounce the *r* sound 仅在黑人之间使用时方无贬义，按 nigger（黑人）一词的美国黑人英语发音而来，而 r 不发音

nightclothes /ˈnaɪtkləʊðz; ˈnaɪtkloðz/ *n* [pl] clothes worn in bed, eg PYJAMAS 1A-Z ; NIGHT-DRESS（NIGHTA-Z）睡衣；睡袍

night vision glasses /ˌnaɪt ˈvɪʒn glɑːsɪz, *US* glæs-; ˌnaɪt ˈvɪʒən glæsɪz/ *n* [pl] BINOCULARSA-Z which allow the wearer to see clearly even in conditions of almost total darkness 夜视镜（即使在几乎全黑的环境下也能看得清楚的双筒望远镜）

nilk /nɪlk; nɪlk/ *abbr* 缩写 = no income lots of kids (informal way of referring to the lower socio-economic class) 无收入多子女者；尼尔克族（对社会和经济下层阶级的俗称）Cf 参看 DINKY

nip and tuck /nɪp ənd ˈtʌk; nɪp ənd ˈtʌk/ *n* (*infml* 口) cosmetic operation, eg a face lift or LIPOSUCTION 整容手术（如脸部拉皮或抽脂肪）

▷ **nip and tuck** *adv* (*US*) NECK AND NECK（NECK 4A-Z）并驾齐驱；成平局：*The two candidates are running nip and tuck in the race for state governor.* 这两名州长候选人的竞逐目前正旗鼓相当不分上下。

Noddynomics /ˈnɒdɪnɒmɪks; ˈnɑdɪnɑmɪks/ *n* [sing v] (*infml derog* 口，贬) term used of the South-east Asian business scene, implying a lack of professionalism or soundness in the dealings and financial infrastructures 笨蛋经济（形容东南亚商界的词，暗指其贸易和金融基础设施缺乏专业性或不健全）

NOTE 注： probably from *Noddy*, a character in stories for children by Enid Blyton 可能源自伊妮德·布莱顿的儿童故事里的人物 Noddy

no-fault /ˌnəʊˈfɔːlt; noˈfɔlt/ *adj* [attrib 作定语] (*US*) of a type of car insurance that pays for damage after an accident regardless of whether or not it was the policy-holder's fault（指汽车保险）不追究过失责任的（保险公司不论是否投保人的过失而对事故造成的车辆损失均予以赔偿）：*No-fault insurance is always worth the extra cost.* 多花一笔钱买不追究过失责任的保险总是合算的。

no-fly zone /nəʊˈflaɪ zəʊn; noˈflaɪ zon/ *n* zone in which aircraft, usu of a particular country or countries, are forbidden to fly 禁飞区

no-frills /nəʊˈfrɪlz; noˈfrɪlz/ *adj* [attrib 作定语] plain and simple, with no additional features 简朴的；无装饰的；只提供基本服务的：*The airline introduced a no-frills route which served only soft drinks, and this allowed them to bring ticket prices down substantially.* 航空公司增辟了一条只供应软饮料的经济航线，这使他们得以将票价大幅降低。

no-hoper /ˌnəʊˈhəʊpə(r); ˌnoˈhopɚ/ *n* (*infml derog* 口，贬) person who is considered useless or doomed to failure 无用的人；注定要失败的人：*a bunch of no-hopers running the country* 管理这个国家的一群无能之辈

noir /nwɑː; nwɑr/ *adj* (*French* 法) (of artistic works, esp films) dark, MORBIDA-Z and cynical in emotion, tone and content（指艺术作品，尤指电影在感情、格调和内容上）黑色的，病态的，愤世嫉俗的：*a film noir* 一部黑色影片 ○ *a noir detective comic* 黑色侦探连环画

NOTE 注： from the French word meaning 'black'. In the first example, the adjective comes after the noun, following the most common order in French 源自法语，意为'黑色的'。在第 1 示例中，按法语的习惯次序将形容词置于名词之后

-nomics /ˈnɒmɪks; ˈnɑmɪks/ *suff* 后缀 economic policies and principles of 经济政策：*Thatchernomics* 撒切尔经济政策 ○ *Reaganomics* 里根经济政策

non-alcoholic /ˌnɒnælkəˈhɒlɪk, *US* -hɔːlɪk; ˌnɑnælkəˈhɔlɪk/ *adj* (of a drink) containing no alcohol（指饮料）不含酒精的：*non-alcoholic beer/lager* 不含酒精的啤酒 *[淡啤酒]*

non-appearance /ˌnɒnəˈpɪərəns; ˌnɑnəˈpɪrəns/ *n* (*fml* 文) failure to appear or be present, esp when legally required to do so 未到场（尤指未按法律要求到场）；未到法庭：*the non-appearance of the defendant in court for the second time* 被告的第二次未到庭 ○ *Her constant non-appearances got her into trouble.* 她因屡次不出庭而陷入了麻烦。

non-attendance /ˌnɒnəˈtendəns; ˌnɑnəˈtɛndəns/ *n* [U] failure to be present in a place as expected 不出席；不到：*The chairman received three apologies for non-attendance at the meeting.* 主席收到三份不出席会议的致歉书。

non-cooperation /ˌnɒnkəʊˌɒpəˈreɪʃn; ˌnɑnkoˌɑpəˈreʃən/ *n* [U] refusal to cooperate, esp as a form of protest 不合作（尤指作为一种抗议手段）：*An all-out strike is unlikely, but some forms of non-cooperation are being considered.* 全面罢工不大可能，但正在酝酿某种形式的不合作行动。

non-lethal /ˌnɒnˈliːθl; ˌnɑnˈliθəl/ *adj* (*US*) (of foreign aid such as food, medical supplies, books, etc or the money to buy them) not military; humanitarian（指食物、医疗品、书或钱等外国援助）非军事性的，人道主义的：*America has continued non-lethal aid to the state but no longer allows the export of arms or military equipment.* 美国继续向该国提供人道主义援助，但不再允许向其出口武器军备。

no no /ˈnəʊ nəʊ; ˈno no/ *n* [sing] (*infml* 口) something that is considered unacceptable and that should be avoided, esp some action or type of behaviour 不许做的事；应避免的东西：*Smoking in the office is an absolute no no since the new boss took over the department.* 自从新上司接手管理了这个部门，办公室里就严禁抽烟。

no-nonsense /ˌnəʊˈnɒnsns; ˌnoˈnɑnsɛns/ *adj* [attrib 作定语] without fuss; simple and direct 实事求是的；直截了当的：*a no-nonsense approach/attitude/manner* 直截了当的处理方法 *[态度 / 方式]*

non-prescription /ˌnɒnprɪˈskrɪpʃn; ˌnɑnprɪˈskrɪpʃən/ *adj* [attrib 作定语] (esp of drugs) that can be bought directly by a customer without a PRESCRIPTION 1A-Z from a doctor, etc（尤指药物）无需医生处方可以买到的，非处方的：*Aspirin is one of the most frequently taken non-prescription drugs* . 阿司匹林是一种最常用的非处方药物。Cf 参看 OVER THE COUNTER（COUNTER[1] 2A-Z）

non-profit-making /ˌnɒnˈprɒfɪtmeɪkɪŋ; ˌnɑnˈprɑfɪtmekɪŋ/ (*US* **non-profit**) *adj* (of an enterprise, etc) that does not aim to make a profit（指企业）非营利的，不以赢利为目的的，非牟利的：*a non-profit-making organization* 非营利性组织 ○ *a children's charity that is non-profit-making* 不以赢利为目的的儿童慈善机构 Cf 参看 NOT-FOR-PROFIT

non-slip /ˌnɒnˈslɪp; nɑnˈslɪp/ *adj* not slipping easily; preventing sb slipping 不滑的；防滑的：*a non-slip mat/surface* 防滑垫 *[表面]*

non-standard /ˌnɒnˈstændəd; ˌnɑnˈstændɚd/ *adj* (*linguistics* 语言) (esp of language) not standard（尤指语言）不标准的，不规范的：*non-standard dialects/forms/varieties* 不标准的方言 *[词形 / 变体]* ○ *non-standard English* 不规范的英语

notebook computer /ˌnəʊtbʊk kəmˈpjuːtə(r); ˌnotbʊk kəmˈpjutɚ/ *n* (*computing* 计) very small computer that is easy to carry around, smaller than a LAPTOP COMPUTER 笔记本型计算机

not-for-profit /nɒtfəˈprɒfɪt; nɑtfɚˈprɑfɪt/ *adj* (*commerce* 商) not intended to make a profit; non-profit-making 非营利的；非牟利的：*a not-for-profit organization* 非营利组织 Cf 参看 FOR-PROFIT

nouvelle cuisine /ˌnuːvel kwɪˈziːn; ˌnuvɛl kwɪˈzin/ *n* [U] (*French* 法) modern style of cooking that avoids heavy, rich foods and emphasizes the way dishes are presented 新式烹饪（少用油腻和太丰富的食物的烹调方法，并强调菜式的展示方式）：*Airlines have taken a lesson from nouvelle cuisine and now present lighter and more attractive meals.* 航空公司借鉴新式烹饪法，如今提供较清淡而吸引人的饭食。

novella /nəˈvelə; nɑˈvɛlə/ *n* (*pl* **novellas**) (*Italian* 意) short novel 短篇小说

nuclear autumn *n* = NUCLEAR WINTER (NUCLEAR[A-Z])

nuisance call /ˈnjuːsns kɔːl, *US* ˈnuː-; ˈnusn̩s kɔl/ *n* telephone call from sb, often a stranger, who wants to harass or cause trouble for the receiver 骚扰电话：*Customer complaints about the increasing number of nuisance calls has led to our company developing several remedies including the Caller Identity facility.* 顾客抱怨骚扰电话越来越多，因此我们公司采取了几种相应措施，包括增设来电识别装置。

nuke /njuːk, *US* nuːk; nuk/ *v* [Tn] (*infml* 口) destroy utterly 彻底摧毁：*Banners reading 'Nuke Saddam' showed the strong feelings of some members of the crowd.* 写着'彻底消灭萨达姆'的横幅显示出一些老百姓的强烈情感。○ (*fig* 比喻) *The whole scheme was nuked by the administration.* 整个阴谋被政府彻底粉碎。

numbing /ˈnʌmɪŋ; ˈnʌmɪŋ/ *adj* emotionally shocking or depressing, causing sb to lose the ability to think or act 使人呆若木鸡的；令人麻木的：*the numbing monotony of the factory routine* 单调呆板得令人麻木的工厂日常工作 ○ *the numbing effect of the air crash on relatives of the victims* 空难对遇难者家属的沉重打击

numerati /njuːməˈrɑːtɪ, nuː-; numəˈrɑtɪ/ *n* [pl] (*infml* 口) financial geniuses 金融奇才：*Not even the numerati saw the dramatic market fall coming.* 甚至连那些金融奇才也没有料到行情会突然暴跌。

NOTE 注： formed on analogy with *literati* 由 literati（文人学士）一词类推构成

nutraceutical /njuːtrəˈsjuːtɪkl, *US* nuːtrəˈsuː-; nutrəˈsutɪkl̩/ *n* food containing health-promoting additives 营养药膳

▷ **nutraceutical** *adj* of, relating to, or designating nutraceuticals 营养药膳的 Cf 参看 FUNCTIONAL FOOD

NOTE 注： a blend of *nutrition* (food) and *pharmaceutical* (of drugs) 由 nutrition（营养）与 pharmaceutical（成药的）二词合成

Oo

obscurantism /ˌɒbskjʊˈræntɪzəm, *US* əbˈskjʊr-; əbˈskjʊrəntɪzəm/ *n* [U] (*fml* 文) practice of deliberately preventing sb from understanding or discovering sth 蒙昧主义；愚民政策：*the struggle of science against religious obscurantism* 科学对宗教蒙昧主义的斗争

▷ **obscurantist** *n, adj* (*derog* 贬)：*obscurantist religions/myths* 蒙昧主义宗教 *[神话]*

oceanarium /ˌəʊʃəˈneərɪəm; ˌoʃəˈnɛrɪəm/ *n* (*pl* ~**s** or **-ria**) large sea-water aquarium for keeping sea animals and displaying them to the public 大型海洋水族馆

offender profiling *n* = PROFILING

offending /əˈfendɪŋ; əˈfɛndɪŋ/ *adj* [attrib 作定语] causing annoyance or difficulty 令人不快的；引起麻烦的：*There were complaints, so the offending products were recalled to the factory and destroyed.* 有顾客投诉，因此有问题的产品被收回工厂销毁。○ *The offending paragraph was deleted.* 令人不快的段落被删掉了。

off-limits /ɒfˈlɪmɪts; ɔfˈlɪmɪts/ *adj* [pred 作表语] = OUT OF BOUNDS (TO SB) (BOUNDS 2[A-Z])：*The town was off-limits to the soldiers.* 该镇禁止士兵进入。Cf 参看 NO-GO AREA (NO[A-Z])

offshore account /ˌɒfʃɔː əˈkaʊnt; ˌɔfʃɔr əˈkaʊnt/ *n* (*finance* 财) account held in a bank located in a territory, often an island, which has no taxes or lower taxes than one's country of residence 海外帐户（在国外，常指在某岛屿的银行里所开的帐户，开户人无需纳税或所缴税低于国内）：*Good returns are still offered on offshore accounts.* 开设海外帐户仍然有利。

oi /ɔɪ; ɔɪ/ *interj* (*Brit*) (used to call attention, esp in an angry way 用以引起注意，尤指以怒气冲冲的方式)：*Oi, you! What d'you think you're doing?* 哎，你！你在干吗？

old age abuse /əʊld ˌeɪdʒ əˈbjuːs; old ˌedʒ əˈbjus/ *n* [U] **1** mistreatment of an elderly person, esp by sb who is looking after him or her 虐待老人（尤指受照料者施加的虐待） **2** mistreatment by an elderly person of the person who is caring for him or her 老人（对照料老人者的）虐待：*Her treatment of her poor son is nothing less than old age abuse.* 她对待她那可怜的儿子简直是虐待。

NOTE 注： the former meaning is more common 上述第 1 义较常用

old-established /ˌəʊldɪˈstæblɪʃt; ˌoldɪˈstæblɪʃt/ *adj* [attrib 作定语] having been in existence for a long time 早已存在的；早已确立的：*old-established customs/beliefs/companies* 悠久的传统、早已确立的信念、老牌子公司

old-style /ˈəʊldstaɪl; ˈoldstaɪl/ *adj* [attrib 作定语] as in the past; old-fashioned 老一套的；老派的；老式的：*an old-style Conservative politician/preacher/family doctor* 老派的保守党政治家 *[传教士 / 家庭医生]*

omega-3 fatty acids /ˌəʊmɪgəˌθriː fætɪ ˈæsɪdz, *US* əʊˌmegə-; oˌmɛgəˌθri fætɪ ˈæsɪdz/ *n* (usu *pl* 通常作复数) substances found in oily fish, eg herring, salmon, etc, which are thought to give protection against heart disease ☆ Ω3 脂肪酸（鲱鱼、鲑鱼等多油脂鱼类体内的物质，据认为能防止心脏病）

OMOV /əʊˈmɒv; oˈmɑv/ (also **Omov**) *abbr* 缩写 = one member one vote (a slogan used by supporters of universal voting rights within an organization) 一人一票（支持组织内部人人享有选举权的口号）

NOTE 注： formerly 'one man one vote' but changed to be more in keeping with modern ideas of gender equality 原为 one man one vote，后将 man 改为 member，以符合现代男女平等的观念

-on-demand /ɒndɪˈmɑːnd, *US* -mænd; ɑndɪˈmænd/ *comb form* 构词成分 concerning telecommunications services which are made available when the subscriber requests them 一经用户要求即刻提供的电信服务 Cf 参看 FAX-ON-DEMAND, VIDEO-ON-DEMAND

One Nation /wʌn ˈneɪʃn; wʌn ˈneʃən/ (also **one nation**) *n* [usu attrib 通常作定语] **1** nation which is not divided by social inequalities 民族一体（未因社会不平等而分裂的民族）: *one nation theories/practices/policies* 民族一体理论 *[惯例 / 政策]*

NOTE 注: mainly a political principle voiced esp by the British Conservative Party 主要为英国保守党提出的一种政治原则

2 right-wing political party in Australia 民族一体党（澳大利亚右翼政党）

one-parent family /ˌwʌnpeərənt ˈfæməlɪ; ˌwʌnpɛrənt ˈfæməlɪ/ (also **single parent family**) *n* family where children live with only one of their parents, eg after a divorce, death, or separation 单亲家庭: *It's wrong to generalize about one-parent families.* 对单亲家庭一概而论是错误的。

one-party state /ˌwʌnpɑːtɪ ˈsteɪt; ˌwʌnpɑrtɪ ˈstet/ *n* state with only one political party and where opposition parties are illegal 一党制国家；一党专政国家

one-stop /ˈwʌnstɒp; ˈwʌnstɑp/ *adj* [attrib 作定语] able to supply a large variety of goods or services under one roof 同一地点能提供各种商品或服务的: *Visit our one-stop shop — for all your driving needs.* 请光顾我们的商店——一条龙式服务保管满足您在驾驶上的所有需要。○ *a one-stop shopping mall* 货品一应俱全的购物中心

on-track earnings /ˌɒntræk ˈɜːnɪŋz; ˌɑntræk ˈɝnɪŋz/ (also **on-target earnings**) *n* [pl] (*abbr* 缩写 **OTE**) level of pay which includes basic salary plus a commission representing best performance 目标薪金，指标薪金（包括基本工资和按个人最佳表现所定的佣金）

open-door /ˌəʊpənˈdɔː(r); ˌopənˈdɔr/ *adj* [attrib 作定语] (of a policy, system, etc) not restricted; allowing people free access to information, free admission, etc（指政策、制度等）门户开放的: *The government are rethinking their open-door policy towards immigrants.* 政府正重新考虑对入境移民的门户开放政策。

open house /ˌəʊpən ˈhaʊs; ˌopən ˈhaʊs/ *n* [U] place or event at which all comers are welcome 公开场所；公开场合: *It's open house — anyone can come.* 这是公开活动，任何人都可以参加。

opening hours /ˈəʊpənɪŋ aʊəz; ˈopənɪŋ aʊrz/ *n* [pl] period of times during which a shop, bank, library, pub, etc is open for business 营业时间；开放时间: *Opening hours are from 10 am to 12:30 pm on Saturdays.* 星期六的营业时间是从上午 10 点到下午 12 点 30 分。

open market /ˌəʊpən ˈmɑːkɪt; ˌopən ˈmɑrkɪt/ *n* [sing] unrestricted market in which prices are determined by supply and demand; free market 公开市场，开放市场，自由市场（价格由供求情况决定、可自由进行买卖的市场）: *available on the open market* 在公开市场可买得到 ○ *It would cost far more on the open market.* 在公开市场上要贵得多。

open-necked /ˌəʊpənˈnekt; ˌopənˈnɛkt/ *adj* [U] (of a man's shirt) designed to be worn, or actually worn, without a tie（指男子衬衫）开领的

open system /ˈəʊpən sɪstəm; ˈopen sɪstəm/ *n* (*computing* 计) system allowing computer software and hardware from different manufacturers to be used together 开放系统（兼容不同厂家生产的软硬件的计算机系统）: *Open system computing remains more of an ideal than a reality.* 计算机开放系统仍只是个理想，并未实现。○ *the future of open systems* 开放系统的将来

optimize /ˈɒptɪmaɪz; ˈɑptəmaɪz/ *v* [Tn] (*fml* 文) make sth the best possible 使（某事）尽可能完美: *seeking to optimize standards of health and safety at work* 寻求最高的工作卫生及安全标准

opto /ˈɒptəʊ; ˈɑpto/ *adj* of or relating to optoelectronics, the branch of technology concerned with the combined use of electronics and light 光电子的；光电子学的: *An opto isolator isolates electrical circuits from one another by transferring signals into optical form and back again.* 光电子隔离器将信号转化为光学形式然后再转成信号，以使各电路相互隔离。

opt out /ɒpt ˈaʊt; ɑpt ˈaʊt/ *v* [I, Ipr] (in the UK, of a school or hospital) withdraw from local authority control. Such schools or hospitals apply for funding directly from the central government and have control over their own budgets（用于英国，指学校或医院）脱离地方政府控制（即直接向中央政府申请经费并自主预算）

▷ **opt out** *n* act of opting out 脱离地方政府控制的做法

opt-out /ˈɒptaʊt; ˈɑptaʊt/ *n* instance of choosing not to take part in sth 决定不参加；选择不参加: *His mother's visit gave him an opt-out from the department meeting.* 母亲来访使他决定不参加系里的会议。

oregano /ˌɒrɪˈgɑːnəʊ, *US* əˈregənəʊ; əˈrɛgəno/ *n* [U] plant used fresh or dried to give flavour in cooking. It is a type of MARJORAM^A-Z 牛至（属墨角兰的一种植物，新鲜时或制干后用作调味品）

organic farming ⇨ ORGANIC 3^A-Z

organic salmon /ɔːˌgænɪk ˈsæmən; ɔrˌgænɪk ˈsæmən/ *n* [U, C] salmon produced by fish farming methods in contrast to wild salmon 人工养殖的鲑鱼（与野生鲑鱼相对而言）

orgasmic /ɔːˈgæzmɪk; ɔrˈgæzmɪk/ *adj* of or like an ORGASM^A-Z 性高潮的；极度兴奋的: *the almost orgasmic pleasure of winning* 胜利的狂喜

ornery /ˈɔːnərɪ; ˈɔrnərɪ/ *adj* (*US infml* 口) bad-tempered, uncooperative 脾气坏的；不合作的: *'Get moving you ornery beast,' the old man shouted at his stubborn mule.* '往前走，你这只别扭的家伙。'老人向他的顽驴呼喝着。

NOTE 注: variant of *ordinary*, representing a dialect pronunciation ☆ ordinary 一词的变体，表示一种方言发音

osteoporosis /ˌɒstɪəʊpəˈrəʊsɪs; ˌɑstɪopəˈrosɪs/ *n* [U] (*medical* 医) condition in which the bones become brittle and break easily, eg because of a lack of calcium 骨质疏松症

OTE *abbr* 缩写 = ON-TRACK EARNINGS

otherly abled /ˌʌðəlɪ ˈeɪbld; ˌʌðɚlɪ ˈebḷd/ *adj* disabled, having some physical or mental handicap 有某些生理或心理障碍的 Cf 参看 PHYSICALLY CHALLENGED, MENTALLY CHALLENGED

NOTE 注: a rather euphemistic expression preferred by some users because it seems less negative than *handicapped* or *disabled* ☆ handicapped 或 disabled（有缺陷的）的委婉说法，因贬义较弱

otherness /ˈʌðənəs; ˈʌðɚnəs/ *n* [U] (*fml* 文) quality of being different or strange 奇异的特质；不同性: *Westerners have always been fascinated by the otherness of Oriental civilization.* 西方人一直被东方文化的奇异之处所吸引。

other woman /ˌʌðə ˈwʊmən; ˌʌðɚ ˈwʊmən/ *n* (usu *sing* 通常作单数) woman with whom a married man is carrying on an affair outside his marriage 另一位女士；情妇: *She was named as the other woman in the divorce proceedings.* 她在这起离婚诉讼中被称作另一位女士。

OTT /ˌəʊ tiː ˈtiː; ˌo ti ˈti/ *abbr* 缩写 = (*esp Brit infml* 口) over the top (ie excessive) 太过分；过火: *His behaviour was definitely OTT.* 他的行为实在太过分了。

out /aʊt; aʊt/ *adj* [pred 作表语] (*infml* 口) having openly stated that one is homosexual 公开表明了自己为同性恋: *The pressure was off once he was out.* 他公开表明了自己为同性恋者后，压力也随之消失了。

▷ **out** *v* [Tn] (*infml* 口) make public the fact that sb, esp a well-known person, is a homosexual even though he or she would prefer this not to happen 公开某人（尤其是名流）系同性恋者的事实: *When the star was outed,* *her popularity seemed quite unaffected.* 这位明星是同性恋者的事实曝光后，她的受欢迎程度似乎并未受影响。

outing *n* : *Some disagree with the outing of gay people and think that it is often harmful.* 有人反对公开说出谁是同性恋者，认为这往往有害无益。

outboard /ˈaʊtbɔːd; ˈautbɔrd/ *adj, adv* (*technical* 术语) portable and situated on the outside or away from the centre of a boat or an aircraft（船、飞机等的）在外侧（的），在舷外（的）: *outboard wing panels* 外侧翼板

▷ **outboard** *n* = OUTBOARD MOTOR[A-Z]

outbound /ˈaʊtbaʊnd; ˈautbaund/ *adj* (*fml* 文) travelling to a destination away from, rather than returning to, one's home 向外开的；向外去的: *outbound flights/passengers* 离境的飞机 *[乘客]*

outgun /ˌaʊtˈɡʌn; autˈɡʌn/ *v* [Tn] (**-nn-**) have greater military strength and more powerful weapons than sb 比（对手）有更强的军事力量；火力超过（对方）: (*fig* 比喻) *The England team was completely outgunned by the South Africans.* 英格兰队实力远远不及南非队。○ *surrounded and outgunned* 被火力更强的敌人包围

out-of-body experience /ˌaʊtəvbɒdɪ ɪkˈspɪərɪəns; ˌautəvbɑdɪ ɪkˈspɪrɪəns/ *n* sensation of having left one's body, esp of floating and being able to observe oneself from a distance 离体体验（游离于体外并能从远处观察自己的感觉）: *She claimed to have had an out-of-body experience during the operation.* 她声称在动手术时有过一次离体体验。 Cf 参看 NEAR-DEATH EXPERIENCE

out-of-date /ˌaʊtəvˈdeɪt; ˌautəvˈdet/ *adj* [attrib 作定语] **1** old-fashioned and no longer useful or in favour 过时的；老式的；废弃的: *an out-of-date newspaper/dictionary/teaching method* 旧报纸、内容陈旧的字典、过时的教学方法 **2** no longer valid 过期的；无效的: *an out-of-date driving licence/library ticket* 过期的驾驶执照 *[图书馆借书证]* Cf 参看 OUT OF DATE (DATE[1] 4[A-Z]), UP-TO-DATE[A-Z]

outpace /ˌaʊtˈpeɪs; autˈpes/ *v* go faster than sb/sth; be more than sth; surpass 比某人 *[某物]* 跑得快；胜过；超过: *He easily outpaced the other runners.* 他轻而易举地超越了其他赛跑者。○ *Demand is outpacing production.* 供不应求。 Cf 参看 KEEP PACE (WITH SB/STH) (PACE[1] 3[A-Z])

outperform /ˌaʊtpəˈfɔːm; ˌautpɚˈfɔrm/ *v* [Tn] do better than sb/sth 比某人 *[某物]* 做得好；胜过: *The strong economy has helped some smaller banks to outperform their larger rivals.* 强势经济使一些小银行业绩超过了比它们强的竞争对手。

▷ **outperformance** *n* [U]

outplacement /ˈaʊtpleɪsmənt; ˈautplesmənt/ *n* [U] (*commerce* 商) action or process of finding new employment for workers, esp executives, who have been dismissed or made redundant（为被裁职员）谋新职: *Promises of outplacement were not kept.* 为被裁员工安排新工作的承诺没有兑现。

outreach /ˈaʊtriːtʃ; ˈautritʃ/ *n* [U] activity of an organization in providing extended community services, ie outside its usual centres 社区延伸服务，外展服务（在机构以外的地方提供社区服务）: *outreach youth workers in remote rural areas* 在偏远乡村地区以青少年为服务对象的社区延伸服务工作人员

outsource /aʊtˈsɔːs; autˈsɔrs/ *v* [I, Tn] (*commerce* 商) **1** obtain goods, esp component parts, by contract from a source outside an organization or area 外购（商品，尤指零件）: *We can outsource the valve caps to that factory in Shenzhen.* 我们可外购阀盖，送到那家深圳的工厂去。 **2** contract work out（以立约方式）将工作包出去: *It was decided to outsource the editing of the new journal since no one in the company had the necessary expertise.* 已经决定把新刊物的编辑工作包出去做，因为公司里没有专才。

out-take /ˈaʊtteɪk; ˈauttek/ *n* segment of film or tape, etc edited out before it is released because it contains a mistake 剪余片，剪掉的片段（电影胶片或磁带等中因有错而被剪掉的部分）

ovenproof /ˈʌvnpruːf; ˈʌvənpruf/ *adj* suitable for use in a hot oven; heatproof 适用于烤箱的；耐热的: *an ovenproof dish* 耐热盘

overcapacity /ˌəʊvəkəˈpæsətɪ; ˌovɚkəˈpæsətɪ/ *n* [U sing] (*commerce* 商) situation in which an industry or factory cannot sell as much as its plant is designed to produce 生产能力过剩: *problems of overcapacity in the car industry/hotel business* 汽车工业生产能力 *[旅馆客房]* 过剩问题

overcook /ˌəʊvəˈkʊk; ˌovɚˈkuk/ *v* [Tn] cook food for longer than is necessary or desirable 烹调过度: *Don't overcook the pasta. It only needs 12 minutes.* 那些意大利面食不要煮得过久，仅需 12 分钟就够了。○ *Overcooked vegetables lose all their nutritional value.* 蔬菜烹调过度会失去所有的营养价值。

overemphasis /ˌəʊvəˈemfəsɪs; ˌovɚˈɛmfəsɪs/ *n* [U sing] ~ **(on sth)** too much emphasis or importance 过分强调；过分着重: *an overemphasis on arts subjects* 对文科科目的过分重视

▷ **overemphasize, -ise** *v* : *The importance of adequate preparation cannot be overemphasized.* 充分准备的重要性再怎么强调也不过分。

overfishing /ˌəʊvəˈfɪʃɪŋ; ˌovɚˈfɪʃɪŋ/ *n* [U] process of taking so many fish from a river, the sea, etc that the number of fish is reduced to dangerously low levels（对鱼）捕捞过度（以致鱼的数量降至危险水平）: *Overfishing is threatening the fish stocks of the North Sea.* 由于捕捞过度，北海的鱼类供应量正在减少。

overhead projector /ˌəʊvəhed prəˈdʒektə(r); ˌovɚhɛd prəˈdʒɛktɚ/ *n* (*abbr* 缩写 **OHP**) device which projects images onto a wall or screen above and behind the person operating it（高射）投影仪: *I need an overhead projector for my talk.* 我发言时需要一个投影仪。

oversized /ˈəʊvəsaɪzd; ˈovɚsaɪzd/ (also **oversize**) *adj* of larger than usual or necessary size 过大的；极大的: *an oversized helmet/class* 过大的头盔、人数过多的一班

overspend /ˌəʊvəˈspend; ˌovɚˈspɛnd/ *v* [Tn] (*pt, pp* **overspent**) ~ **(on sth)** spend too much money or more than necessary 超支；花销太大: *The company overspent on labour.* 公司在工资上支出太大。○ *The council has overspent its budget again.* 委员会开支再次超过预算。

▷ **overspend** *n* [sing]

overstayer /ˌəʊvəˈsteɪə(r); ˌovɚˈsteɚ/ *n* person who stays beyond a time limit, eg remains in a country of which they are not a national, after their work, tourist or student visa has expired 逾期居留者；逗留期超过签证规定期限者: *France is anxious about the number of overstayers there may be among the many visitors coming for the finals of the World Cup.* 法国担心众多来观看世界杯决赛的外国人中可能有不少会逾期不归。

overstretch /ˌəʊvəˈstretʃ; ˌovɚˈstrɛtʃ/ *v* ~ **oneself/sb/sth** make demands on available resources which cannot be met 要求过高: *an overstretched prison service* 过长的刑期 ○ *They had overstretched themselves to buy their dream house.* 他们全然不顾自己的能力购买那座他们梦寐以求的房子。

overuse /ˌəʊvəˈjuːz; ˌovɚˈjuz/ *v* [Tn] use sth in too great a quantity or too frequently 滥用；过度使用: *one of the most overused words in politics* 一个政治上被滥用的词汇

▷ **overuse** *n* [U sing] : *prevent the overuse of fertilizer* 禁止滥用化肥

overwrite /ˌəʊvəˈraɪt; ˌovɚˈraɪt/ *v* (*pt* **overwrote** , *pp* **overwritten**) (*computing* 计) write and save data over existing data on a file, thus destroying the original 重写（在原已存有数据的文件中再记录数据，原先的数据会被消除）

own goal /ˌəʊn ˈɡəʊl; on ˈɡol/ *n* (*fig* 比喻) action by which a person unintentionally causes harm to himself or herself 无意中伤害自己的行为 : *She scored an own goal by suggesting that the department was overstaffed, since she was one of the first to go.* 她指出部门里人满为患，这真是搬起石头砸自己的脚，因为她属于第一批被裁退的员工。

NOTE 注： from scoring an OWN GOAL (OWN[1(A-Z)]) in soccer ☆ own goal 一词的引申义，原意为足球赛中把球踢入己方球门的意思

oxygen bar /ˈɒksɪdʒən bɑː; ˈɑksədʒən bɑr/ *n* establishment which offers pure oxygen, sometimes scented, for refreshment and relaxation in a quiet setting 氧吧（提供纯氧气，有时还添加香味以提神的休憩场所）

oxygen facial /ˌɒksɪdʒən ˈfeɪʃl; ˌɑksədʒən ˈfeʃəl/ *n* service offered in an OXYGEN BAR which uses pure oxygen to massage and relax the facial muscles 氧气面部按摩（氧吧中提供的用纯氧气进行面部按摩的服务）

oxygen of publicity /ˌɒksɪdʒən əv pəˈblɪsɪtɪ; ˌɑksədʒən əv pəˈblɪsɪtɪ/ *n* [U] revitalizing force of publicity which boosts the causes (CAUSE 3[A-Z]) of groups with extreme views, political, ethical, etc 宣传的激活作用（对政治、伦理等持极端看法的团体进行报道时所起到的推波助澜的作用）: *For many years the terrorist attacks of the extremist group were not reported in the media, in order to deny their cause the oxygen of publicity.* 多年来传媒对极端主义组织的恐怖活动未作报道，是为了不让宣传助长其气焰以示反对其行径。

ozone /ˈəʊzəʊn; ˈozon/ *n* blue gas present in the earth's atmosphere but also produced in harmful amounts in urban environments by the interaction of hydrocarbons (eg in petrol), oxides of nitrogen and sunlight 臭氧（地球大气中的蓝色气体，亦会因汽油等中的烃、氧化氮和阳光之间发生反应而在市区产生，达至有害分量）

□ **ozone depleter** *n* any chemical compound, eg CFC, which is known to break down into chlorine atoms which in turn attack the OZONE LAYER (OZONE[A-Z]) 臭氧损耗物（可分解成氯原子进而损害臭氧层的化合物，如氯氟碳化合物）

ozone-friendly *adj* not containing any substance, eg CFC, which causes damage to the OZONE LAYER (OZONE[A-Z]) surrounding the earth 不含对地球臭氧层有害的物质的；对地球臭氧层无害的 : *The latest models of refrigerators and air-conditioners all claim to be ozone-friendly.* 最近推出的冰箱和空调器都有对地球臭氧层无害的声明。 Cf 参看 OZONE DEPLETER (OZONE)

ozone level *n* (usu *pl* 通常作复数) measured amount of OZONE in the atmosphere（大气中的）臭氧含量 Cf 参看 PHOTOCHEMICAL SMOG

Pp

Pacific Rim /pəˌsɪfɪk ˈrɪm; pəˌsɪfɪk ˈrɪm/ *n* [sing] (usu 通常作 **the Pacific Rim**) countries and regions bordering the Pacific Ocean, esp the small countries of eastern Asia 太平洋沿岸国家及地区（尤指东亚诸小国）

packet switching /ˈpækɪt ˌswɪtʃɪŋ; ˈpækɪt ˌswɪtʃɪŋ/ *n* [U] method of data transmission in which parts of a message are sent independently by the most efficient route for each part and then reunited 分组交换，包交换（数据传输的方法，即将信息分组选择最佳路径发送出去，到达后重新组合复原）

pacy /ˈpeɪsɪ; ˈpesɪ/ *adj* moving or progressing quickly 快速移动的；快速进行的 : *a pacy thriller/film* 节奏快的惊险小说 *[电影]*

paedophile /ˈpiːdəʊfaɪl; ˈpidəfaɪl/ (*US* **pedo-**) *n* person who is sexually attracted to children（在性方面）恋童者，恋童癖者

pager /ˈpeɪdʒə(r); ˈpedʒɚ/ *n* small device operated by radio signals used for receiving messages 传呼机 : *Please turn off all pagers and mobile phones before the concert starts.* 音乐会开始前，请将所有传呼机和手提电话关掉。

paintball /ˈpeɪntbɔːl; ˈpentbɔl/ *n* [sing] game in which participants simulate military combat using airguns to shoot capsules of paint at each other to score 'kills' 彩弹战争游戏（一种模拟作战游戏，参与者用气枪互相发射装了颜料的胶囊，射中则算'杀死'了敌人）

pakora /pəˈkɔːrə; pəˈkɔrə/ *n* piece of cauliflower, carrot or other suitable vegetable, coated in seasoned batter and deep-fried 油炸蔬菜（蘸上加了调料的面糊然后油炸的花椰菜、胡萝卜等蔬菜） Cf 参看 BHAJI

paleo-conservative /ˌpælɪəʊkənˈsɜːvətɪv, *US* ˌpeɪ-; ˌpelɪokənˈsɝvətɪv/ (also **palaeo-conservative**) *n* (*US*) person supporting old or traditional forms of conservatism; extreme right-wing conservative 极右翼保守分子

NOTE 注： from the combining form *paleo-* meaning 'ancient, prehistoric' and the noun *conservative* 由构词成分 paleo-（古老的、史前的）与名词 conservative（保守者）合成

palimony /ˈpælɪmənɪ; ˈpælɪmənɪ/ *n* [U] money which sb is ordered to pay to a person with whom he or she has cohabited (COHABIT[A-Z]) over a long period that has now come to an end 友伴供养费（长期非婚同居者分居后一方按规定付给另一方的赡养费） Cf 参看 ALIMONY[A-Z]

NOTE 注： a blend of *pal* (friend) and *alimony* (money paid to a separated wife) 由 pal（朋友）和 alimony（付给分居后的妻子的赡养费）二词合成

palmtop /ˈpɑːmtɒp; ˈpɑmtɑp/ *n* (*computing* 计) computer that is light and small enough to be held in one hand 掌上型计算机

PALplus /pælˈplʌs; pælˈplʌs/ *n* [sing] enhanced version of the existing PAL (Phase Alternate Line) television system, capable of transmitting pictures in the 16:9 wide-screenformat now commonly used for films 相位逐行交变制加强版，PAL 制加强版（可用于播放现时电影常用的 16 比 9 宽屏幕形式）

paparazzo /ˌpæpəˈrɑːtsəʊ, *US* -ræt-; ˌpæpəˈrætso/ *n* (*pl* **paparazzi**) (usu *pl* 通常作复数) journalist or photographer who follows famous people around in order to get interesting stories and revealing photographs, usu regarded as a nuisance 跟踪名人采访、拍照的记者或摄影师（通常令人厌恶）；狗仔队 : *The paparazzi were out in force when the popstar left for his murdered brother's funeral.* 这位流行歌星去参加他那被谋杀的兄弟的葬礼时，大批狗仔队闻风出动。

NOTE 注： from an Italian word for an irritating type of insect 源自意大利语，指一种讨厌的虫子

paper-pusher *n* (*US*) = PEN PUSHER (PEN[1(A-Z)])

paper round /ˈpeɪpə raʊnd; ˈpepɚ raʊnd/ *n* **1** job of delivering newspapers, usu done by young boys or girls on bikes, to houses usu early in the morning 送报工作（通常由男童或女童清晨骑车挨家挨户去送） **2** route taken in order to do a paper round 送报路线 : *He earned a little money doing a paper round during the school holidays.* 他在学校假期靠送报挣一点钱。

paper-thin /ˌpeɪpə'θɪn; ˌpepɚ'θɪn/ *adj* (of objects) very thin and delicate（指物）薄如纸的，脆弱的：*a soft, light wrap of paper-thin silk* 一条薄如蝉翼的轻柔丝绸披肩 ○ (*fig* 比喻) *a paper-thin line between success and disaster* 成败之间仅一线之隔

para /'pærə; 'pærə/ *n* (*infml* 口) PARATROOPER（PARATROOPS^A-Z）伞兵

paramedic /ˌpærə'medɪk; ˌpærə'mɛdɪk/ *n* person with basic medical training whose job is to assist doctors, etc 医务辅助人员；医疗助手

parapsychology /ˌpærəsaɪ'kɒlədʒɪ; ˌpærəsaɪ'kɑlədʒɪ/ *n* [U] study of mental powers which apparently exist but cannot be explained by current scientific knowledge 通灵学，心理玄学（对一些似乎存在但目前科学尚无法解释的心灵感应能力的研究）Cf 参看 TELEPATHY^A-Z, TELEKINESIS

parenting /'pærəntɪŋ; 'pɛrəntɪŋ/ *n* [U] taking care of a child or children as a parent usually does 父母对子女的抚养；尽父母之责：*Parenting took up much of her time and energy.* 抚育孩子耗费了她大部分的时间和精力。○ [attrib 作定语] *a course in parenting skills* 指导父母教养子女的课程

park-and-ride /ˌpɑːkənd'raɪd; 'pɑrkəndraɪd/ (also **park-n-ride**) *n* system designed to reduce traffic in towns by providing regular, usu free, public transport between the town centre and large car parks on the edge of the town 停车换乘公共交通工具的制度（为减轻市内交通拥挤，在市郊的大型停车场和市中心之间行驶定时的，通常为免费的班车服务）：*Use the new park-and-ride service.* 请使用新的停车换乘公交车服务。○ *park-and-ride system* 停车换乘公共交通工具系统

park home /'pɑːk həʊm; 'pɑrk hom/ (also **trailer, trailer home**) *n* large CARAVAN^A-Z permanently fixed on a site and used as a home 活动住房，拖车屋（永久固定于某处作为居所的大拖车）

particle accelerator /ˌpɑːtɪkl ək'seləreɪtə(r); ˌpɑrtɪkḷ ək'sɛləretɚ/ *n* (*physics* 物) machine which makes sub-atomic particles move at very fast speeds, used for research or generation of high-energy X-rays, etc 粒子加速器（使亚原子粒子高速运动的仪器，用于研究或产生高能 X 射线等）

party animal /'pɑːtɪ ˌænɪml; 'pɑrtɪ ˌænəmḷ/ *n* (*infml* 口) person who very frequently goes to parties and enjoys them very much 热衷于社交聚会的人：*I'm not much of a party animal, but even I went to Tracy's 21st.* 我并不怎么热衷于社交聚会，但也参加了特蕾西的 21 岁生日聚会。Cf 参看 PARTY-GOER

party-goer /'pɑːtɪgəʊə(r); 'pɑrtɪgoɚ/ *n* person who attends a party or frequently goes to parties（经常）参加社交聚会的人

party piece /'pɑːtɪ piːs; 'pɑrtɪ pis/ *n* (*Brit esp joc* 尤作戏谑语) performance at a party in order to entertain or amuse others, eg singing a song, giving a poetry recital or performing a conjuring trick 聚会娱宾节目（如唱歌、朗诵诗歌或表演魔术）：*Have you all got your party pieces ready?* 你们都准备好晚会的表演节目了吗？

party-poop /'pɑːtɪpuːp; 'pɑrtɪpup/ (also **party-pooper**) *n* (*esp US sl* 俚) person who spoils the mood of an otherwise enjoyable social occasion by introducing a serious topic or reminding people there of some unpleasant fact（聚会上）扫兴的人，煞风景的人：*What a party-poop! There we were all enjoying ourselves when Leonard asked how many of us were likely to lose our jobs in the downsizing.* 真扫兴！我们大家正玩得高兴时候，伦纳德却问我们当中多少人会在裁员中被裁掉。

party popper /ˌpɑːtɪ 'pɒpə(r); ˌpɑrtɪ 'pɑpɚ/ *n* small device that throws out paper streamers, used as an amusement at parties and other celebrations 纸带喷射器（能喷出纸带的小装置，供聚会和其他庆典上助兴之用）

passionless /'pæʃnləs; 'pæʃənləs/ *adj* without emotion or enthusiasm, esp where these would be expected and appropriate（尤指该有激情时）无激情的，无热情的，冷漠的：*a passionless performance* 毫无激情的演出

pasting /'peɪstɪŋ; 'pestɪŋ/ *n* [sing] **1** severe beating 痛打 **2** heavy defeat 溃败：*The home team suffered a real pasting at the hands of their opponents.* 主队被对手打得一败涂地。

patch /pætʃ; pætʃ/ *n* (*medicine* 药) adhesive patch of material that is filled with a drug and which is worn on the skin so that the drug is absorbed gradually over a period of time 膏药：*nicotine/angina patch* 戒烟 [心绞痛] 膏药

paternity leave /pə'tɜːnətɪ liːv; pə'tɝnətɪ liv/ *n* [U] legal right of a man to have a period of paid leave from his employment when his wife, or in some countries his partner, has a baby 父假（新生儿的父亲依法享有的带薪假期）Cf 参看 MATERNITY LEAVE

pathogen /'pæθədʒən; 'pæθədʒən/ *n* AGENT 2(b)^A-Z that causes disease 病原体；病原菌：*pathogens in the food/water* 食物 [水] 中的病原体
▷ **pathogenic** *adj*

patterning /'pætənɪŋ; 'pætɚnɪŋ/ *n* [U] **1** design and arrangement of shapes, events, elements, etc in a pattern（把形状、事件、组成部分等按某种形式）设计和安排 **2** (*fml* 文) formation of fixed ways of behaviour by copying or repeating sth（通过模仿或重复而达成的）行为模式的形成：*the patterning of child-parent relationships* 子女与父母关系模式的形成

pax /pæks; pæks/ *n* [sing] (in airline usage) number of passengers booking a specific flight or flights（民航用语）（某航班的）预订旅客数：*BA 206, pax 375* 英国航空公司 206 航班，预订旅客数 375 人

payback period /'peɪbæk ˌpɪərɪəd; 'pebæk ˌpɪrɪəd/ *n* length of time required for an investment to pay for itself in terms of profits or savings 回收期（一项投资能以利润或节约所得作为营运成本的时间）

payout /'peɪaʊt; 'peaʊt/ *n* usu large payment of money（通常指大笔的）付款，支出：*an insurance payout* 一笔保险赔偿金 ○ *the payout on the lottery* 彩票奖金

pay spine *n* = SPINE

PC *n, adj* = POLITICAL CORRECTNESS, POLITICALLY CORRECT

PDA *abbr* 缩写 = PERSONAL DIGITAL ASSISTANT

peace dividend /'piːs dɪvɪdend; 'pis dɪvədɛnd/ *n* (usu *sing* 通常作单数) money which does not need to be spent on a country's defences due to DISARMAMENT (DISARM^A-Z), etc 和平红利（因裁军而省下的费用）：*a peace dividend amounting to well over $20 billion* 远远超过二百亿美元的和平红利

peace process /'piːs prəʊses, *US* prɑːses; 'pis prɑsɛs/ *n* [sing] negotiations towards the settlement of a conflict that has been going on for some time 和平进程；和平谈判：*the peace process in the Middle East* 中东和平进程 ○ *The warring parties have agreed to start a peace process.* 交战各方同意开始和平谈判。

NOTE 注：the term has been closely associated with the negotiations between the Israeli government and the Palestinian leadership and with the ongoing talks between successive British governments and representatives of the various political groups in Northern Ireland 常用于指以色列政府与巴勒斯坦领导人之间的谈判以及历届英国政府与北爱尔兰不同政治团体代表的持续对话

pear-shaped /'peəʃeɪpt; 'pɛrʃept/ *adj* **go ~** (*infml* 口) go completely wrong and get entirely out of control 一团糟的；失去控制的：*The meeting was going well and* *then those demonstrators started throwing rotten vegetables and everything went pear-shaped.* 会议进行得好端端的，忽然那些示威者扔起烂蔬菜来，于是一切变得一团糟。

pedalo /ˈpedələʊ; ˈpɛdəlo/ *n* (*pl* **-os**) small pleasure boat operated by pedals 脚踏式小游船

pedestrianize, -ise /pɪˈdestrɪənaɪz; pəˈdɛstrɪənaɪz/ *v* [Tn] make a street or part of a town an area for pedestrians only（将街道或部分城区）改为行人区：*The local council has pedestrianized the town centre.* 当地议会已将市中心改为行人区。

peer-to-peer /ˈpɪətəpɪə(r); ˈpɪrtəpɪr/ *adj* (*computing* 计) (two or more computers) being connected as equal partners to share processing and control, and each being able to access the files and peripheral equipment of all the others 对等网络的，同位网络的（至少两个计算机之间对等连接，可共同处理数据和控制程序，并可相互存取文件和其他外围设备）

NOTE 注： *peer* has the meaning of equal, as in *peer group* ☆ peer 意为‘同等的’，如 peer group（同辈的人）

pen /pen; pɛn/ *n* (*computing* 计) hand-held device used as a writing tool to input commands and data into a computer via a screen 手写笔（作为书写工具通过屏幕向计算机输入指令和数据的手动装置）

penny arcade *n* (*US*) = AMUSEMENT ARCADE (AMUSE^A-Z)

people carrier /ˈpi:pl kærɪə(r); ˈpipl̩ kærɪɚ/ *n* motor vehicle like a small minibus but with approximately eight seats which may be arranged flexibly, turned around or removed（约有八个可调节座椅的）小客车：*Lower all the back seats of the people carrier to create a comfortable sleeping area at night.* 晚上把小客车的后座放低就可以舒舒服服在上面睡觉了。

people power /ˈpi:pl paʊə(r); ˈpipl̩ paʊɚ/ *n* [U] overwhelming force of popular opinion, esp as this brings about political change 民众的力量（尤指由引起政治变革的民意所产生的压倒性力量）

Pepsification /ˌpepsɪfɪˈkeɪʃn; ˌpɛpsɪfɪˈkeʃən/ *n* [U] spreading of American cultural influence through commercial enterprises and products 百事可乐化（通过企业及产品扩大美国文化的影响）Cf 参看 COCA COLA IMPERIALISM

NOTE 注： from the name of *Pepsi* , a popular American soft drink 源自 Pepsi（百事可乐，一种广受欢迎的美国软饮料）这一名字

performance art /pəˈfɔ:məns ɑ:t; pɚˈfɔrməns ɑrt/ *n* [U,C] kind of visual art in which the activity of the artist forms a central feature 表演视觉艺术（以艺术家的表演为主的视觉艺术）：*The artist lay apparently asleep in a glass case. As an example of performance art it was ridiculous, but it did bring in the public.* 表演者在玻璃罩里睡着似的躺着。作为一种表演视觉艺术这实在是很荒谬的，可是它确实吸引了观众。

perfume dynamics /ˈpɜ:fju:m daɪˌnæmɪks; ˈpɝfjum daɪˌnæmɪks/ *n* [sing v] use of pleasant smells in a building, eg an office, a department store, a supermarket, etc in order to create a particular effect or just to make a comfortable environment 芳香动力学（在建筑物如办公室、百货公司、超市等中运用香味制造特殊效果或舒适氛围）：*The artful use of fresh bread smells just inside the doors of a supermarket is just one way in which perfume dynamics influences your shopping habits.* 在超市入口处放置新鲜面包是巧妙运用芳香动力学影响购物习惯的一个方法。

permaculture /ˈpɜ:məˌkʌltʃə(r); ˈpɝməˌkʌltʃɚ/ *n* [U] development of agricultural ecosystems (ECOSYSTEM^A-Z) intended to be complete and self-sustaining 永久生态农业（一种农业生态系统的发展，旨在使其完整及自给自足）

perp /pɜ:p; pɝp/ *abbr* 缩写 = PERPETRATOR (PERPETRATE^A-Z)：*The perp was seen driving off in a green van which was later found abandoned.* 有人看见罪犯驾一辆绿色客货车逃走，该车后来被发现时已遭遗弃了。

NOTE 注： mainly in police usage 主要为警方用语

Persian war syndrome *n* = GULF WAR SYNDROME

persistent vegetative state /pəˌsɪstənt ˌvedʒɪtətɪv ˈsteɪt; pɚˌsɪstənt ˌvɛdʒɪtətɪv ˈstet/ *n* [U] state of being in a deep coma from which one is unlikely to recover, according to medical opinion 持续植物人状态（医学观点认为不可能康复的昏迷状态）：*Some patients diagnosed as being in a persistent vegetative state have later actually recovered.* 一些被诊断为处于持续植物人状态的病人后来竟然苏醒了。

-person /ˈpɜ:sn; ˈpɝsn̩/ *suff* 后缀 (forming compounds ns 用以构成复合名词) person concerned with (the corresponding role or activity) 与…（的作用或活动）相关的人：*a salesperson* 推销员 ○ *a spokesperson* 发言人

personal communicator /ˌpɜ:sənl kəˈmju:nɪkeɪtə(r); ˌpɝsn̩l kəˈmjunəketɚ/ *n* small device which operates as mobile phone (MOBILE), pager, fax machine, etc 个人通讯装置（具有移动电话、传呼机、传真机等功能的装置）

personal computer /ˌpɜ:sənl kəmˈpju:tə(r); ˌpɝsn̩l kəmˈpjutɚ/ *n* (*abbr* 缩写 **PC**) small computer designed for use at home or in an office 个人计算机；个人电脑

personal digital assistant /ˈpɜ:snl dɪdʒɪtl əˌsɪstnt; ˈpɝsn̩l dɪdʒɪtl̩ əˌsɪstənt/ *n* (*abbr* 缩写 **PDA**) (*computing* 计) small personal computer using PEN technology 个人电脑助理（可使用手写笔输入指令和数据的小型个人电脑）

NOTE 注： in this expression *digital* means *computer* 此处 digital 指计算机

personal organizer, -iser *n* = FILOFAX

personal stereo *n* = WALKMAN (WALK^1(A-Z))

pH /ˌpi: ˈeɪtʃ; ˌpi ˈetʃ/ *n* [sing] (*chemistry* 化) measure of the ACIDITY (ACID^2(A-Z)) of a solution or a substance. A reading of below 7 indicates that the solution is acidic, and above 7 that it is ALKALINE (ALKALI^A-Z) ☆ pH 值，酸碱值（溶液或物质酸碱性的量度，pH 值小于 7 表示酸性，大于 7 表示碱性）：*a pH of 7.5* ☆ pH 值为 7.5 ○ *the pH level of the soil* 土壤的酸碱值

Pharisee /ˈfærɪsi:; ˈfærəsi/ *n* **1** member of an ancient Jewish religious group, known for their strict obedience to the traditional and written law, and commonly held to regard themselves as better or holier than others 法利赛人（古代一以恪守习惯和成文的法律而闻名的犹太宗教的信徒，自认为比他人优越或神圣）**2** (*derog* 贬) person who makes a show of having high religious or moral standards, but is not good or religious in a genuine way; hypocrite 伪善者；伪君子

pharm /fɑ:m; fɑrm/ *n* place where genetically modified plants and animals are grown and reared in order to produce products used as medicinal drugs 药用动植物养殖场

NOTE 注： formed from the first syllable of *pharmaceutical* (of drugs) and punning on the word *farm* 此词为双关语，来自 pharmaceutical（制药的）一词的首音节，及 farm（农场）的意思和发音

pharmafood *n* = NUTRACEUTICAL

phat /fæt; fæt/ *adj* (*sl* 俚) excellent, great, ‘hot’ in the sense of sexy, stylish and cool 绝妙的；性感的；时髦的；帅的：*The group may be unpopular with the authorities but they're phat to the fans.* 这个演唱组可能不受当局青睐，但却能激起拥护者的狂热。

NOTE 注： perhaps formed from the initial letters of *pussy* (female genitals), *hips* , *arse* and *tits* 可能由 pussy（女阴）、hips（臀部）、arse（屁股）和 tits（乳房）的首字母拼合构成

phenomenology /fɪˌnɒmɪˈnɒlədʒɪ; fəˌnɑməˈnɑlədʒɪ/ *n* [U] branch of philosophy that concentrates on what is perceived by the senses in contrast to what is independently real or true about the world 现象学（哲学一分支，摆脱接受既定真理的态度而着重研究感觉到或经验到的现象世界）

pheromone /ˈferəməʊn; ˈfɛrəmon/ *n* chemical substance produced by an animal as a signal to attract another animal of the same species, usu for mating 外激素，信息素（动物通常为求交配而吸引同类所释放的一种化学物质）

phone tapping *n* = TELEPHONE TAPPING

phoney war /ˌfəʊnɪ ˈwɔː(r); ˌfonɪ ˈwɔr/ *n* period of time during which opponents are officially at war but do not actually fight 假战（交战各方并不实际作战的时期）：(*fig* 比喻) *The meeting marked the end of the phoney war and the beginning of an intense campaign for votes.* 会议标志着假战的结束和激烈的选票争夺战的开始。

photo booth /ˈfəʊtəʊ buːð, *US* buːθ; ˈfoto buθ/ *n* small enclosed structure, at a railway station, shopping centre, post office, etc, where one can put money in a machine and thus activate a camera and a developing process which delivers a number of photographs of oneself in a few minutes 快照屋；快照亭

photo-call /ˈfəʊtəʊkɔːl; ˈfotokɔl/ *n* time arranged in advance when photographers or television camera crews are officially invited to take pictures of a famous person（媒体应邀为名人）照相的时间

photochemical smog /fəʊtəʊˌkemɪkl ˈsmɒg; foto,kɛmɪkḷ ˈsmɑg/ *n* [U] condition of the atmosphere caused by the action of sunlight on pollutants, eg exhaust gases from vehicles, resulting in haze and high levels of ozone and nitrogen oxide 光化烟雾（阳光照在车辆废气之类污染物质上产生的烟雾及大量臭氧和氧化氮的情况）Cf 参看 OZONE LEVEL（OZONE）

photodegradable /ˌfəʊtəʊdɪˈgreɪdəbl; ˌfotodɪˈgredəbḷ/ *adj* able to be broken down by the action of light, esp sunlight 可被光降解的；可被光（尤指阳光）分解的：*These chemicals don't pollute the soil because they are photodegradable.* 这些化学物质不会对土壤造成污染，因为它们可以被光降解。

photofit /ˈfəʊtəʊfɪt; ˈfotofɪt/ *n* picture of a person, esp sb wanted by the police, which is made by putting together photographs of different features of the face until a witness to or victim of a crime considers the result a good match with the face of the person he or she saw 照片拼图（根据证人或受害人提供的资料，警方将多幅有不同面部特征的照片拼合而成，尤指通缉犯的图像）：*A photofit of the man the police want to interview is shown on nationwide television.* 全国电视网播放了警方想要会见的男子的拼图。

photo opportunity /ˈfəʊtəʊ ɒpəˌtjuːnətɪ, *US* -tuːn-; ˈfoto ɑpɚˌtunətɪ/ *n* (often *abbr* 常缩写作 **photo op**) favourable occasion, which may be deliberately staged or simply taken advantage of, when a famous person, esp a politician, allows photos and film to be taken which show himself or herself to advantage 拍照时机（名人，尤指政客，经过筹划或乘势让媒体拍下对其有利的镜头的时机）：*The meeting with the refugees provided the new leader with the perfect photo opportunity.* 与难民会面为新领导人提供了绝佳的上镜机会。

photo session /ˈfəʊtəʊ seʃn; ˈfoto sɛʃən/ *n* session during which a photographer, usu a professional, takes photographs of a person for use in advertising, etc（通常由专业摄影师为某人拍照以作广告用途的）拍照时间

physically challenged /ˌfɪzɪklɪ ˈtʃælɪndʒd; ˌfɪzɪklɪ ˈtʃælɪndʒd/ *adj* disabled physically in some way 有某些生理障碍的 Cf 参看 OTHERLY ABLED

NOTE 注： used by some people as a less negative expression than *disabled* or *handicapped* ☆ disabled 或 handicapped（有缺陷的）的委婉说法，因贬义较弱

pic /pɪk; pɪk/ *n* (*infml* 口) picture, esp a photograph, etc to be used as an illustration in printed material（印刷品中的）插图（尤指照片）：*The pic of Mao should be put in here.* 毛泽东的照片应放在这儿。

picture rail /ˈpɪktʃə reɪl; ˈpɪktʃɚ rel/ *n* narrow strip of wood running around the walls of a room just below the ceiling from which pictures are hung 画镜线；挂镜线

picture window /ˈpɪktʃə wɪndəʊ, pɪktʃə ˈwɪndəʊ; pɪktʃɚ ˈwɪndo/ *n* very large window in which a single piece of glass is fitted, usu intended to display a pleasant or striking view（用一块大玻璃做的）观景窗：*A feature of the house is the large picture windows giving extensive views of the coastline.* 这房子的一大特色是可通过那些巨大的观景窗饱览海岸风光。

pill-popper /ˈpɪlpɒpə(r); ˈpɪlpɑpɚ/ *n* (*infml* 口) **1** person who is always taking pills because of health worries（担心自己健康而）服药上瘾者 **2** drug addict 有毒瘾的人；瘾君子

pin-down /ˈpɪndaʊn; ˈpɪndaʊn/ *n* [U] (*esp Brit*) (of institutional care) action or policy of putting children into solitary confinement for periods of time as a method of punishment and to enforce discipline 关禁闭（社会福利机构将孩子单独关一段时间的惩罚）：*The home's use of pin-down to control difficult and troubled youngsters has been severely criticized.* 儿童院用禁闭来惩罚那些难管和好惹事的孩子，遭到了猛烈的批评。

pink pound /ˈpɪŋk paʊnd, pɪŋk ˈpaʊnd; ˈpɪŋk paʊnd/ (*US* **pink dollar**) *n* perceived buying power of homosexuals as a group of consumers 粉红英镑（同性恋者作为一个消费群体的购买力）：*There is fierce competition for a share of the pink pound.* 商家为获得粉红英镑竞争十分激烈。

NOTE 注： *pink* is part of this expression possibly because of the *pink triangle*, an emblem of the homosexual or gay community originally imposed in the Nazi internment camps of WWII 此词中的 pink 可能源于 pink triangle（粉红三角）一词，原为第二次世界大战期间纳粹拘留营中用于同性恋者的标记

pipework /ˈpaɪpwɜːk; ˈpaɪpwɝk/ *n* [U] network of pipes in a house, under the ground, etc 管道；管道系统

piss-up /ˈpɪsʌp; ˈpɪsʌp/ *n* (⚠ *Brit sl* 讳，俚) occasion when a large amount of alcohol is drunk 狂饮；痛饮

pit stop /ˈpɪt stɒp; ˈpɪt stɑp/ *n* **1** (*sport* 体) (in motor racing) occasion when a car in the race pulls into THE PITS（PIT[1] 8b[A-Z]）for refuelling, repair, etc（赛车时）停车加油或维修 **2** (*US*) brief stop during a journey for rest, food, etc（旅途中）停车休息、用餐等

pixel /ˈpɪksl; ˈpɪksḷ/ *n* (*computing* 计) any one of the individual dots on a computer screen which together make up the whole display 像素，像元（计算机屏幕上构成整个画面的小点）

pizzeria /ˌpiːtsəˈrɪːə; ˌpitsəˈriə/ *n* restaurant which specializes in cooking and serving pizzas（款待客人的）比萨饼店；意大利饼餐厅

placeman /ˈpleɪsmən; ˈplesmən/ *n* (*pl* **placemen**) person appointed to a position chiefly to carry out the political policies of a higher authority or power 主要为执行上级政策而任职的人；唯命是从者；傀儡

placing /ˈpleɪsɪŋ; ˈplesɪŋ/ *n* position of sb/sth in an order or a list 排名：*The hockey club has slipped in the overall placings this season.* 该曲棍球会在这一赛季总的排名中名次有所下降。○ *Chart placings are determined by the number of records sold.* 唱片排行榜是由唱片销售量决定的。

planned economy /plænd ɪˈkɒnəmɪ; plænd ɪˈkɑnəmɪ/ *n* economy in which production, prices, incomes, etc are controlled centrally by government 计划经济（由政府

控制生产、物价、收入等的经济制度） Cf 参看 LAISSER-FAIRE[A-Z]

plasterwork /'plɑ:stəwɜ:k, *US* plæs-; 'plæstɚwɝk/ *n* [U] dry PLASTER 1[A-Z] on ceilings, usu formed into decorative shapes and patterns（通常制成装饰图案的）灰泥天花板：*ornamental plasterwork* 灰泥装饰

plastic /'plæstɪk; 'plæstɪk/ *n* (*infml* 口) credit cards, debit cards and other plastic cards which can be used in place of money to pay for goods and services（塑料制的）信用卡，结算卡，借方卡：*Every shop takes plastic nowadays.* 如今所有商店都接受顾客以卡购物。

plastic arts /ˌplæstɪk 'ɑ:ts; ˌplæstɪk 'ɑrts/ *n* [pl] art forms that involve moulding or making models, in clay, wood, wax, etc, or representing things so that they appear three dimensional 造型艺术：*The plastic arts include sculpture, pottery and realistic painting.* 造型艺术包括雕塑、制陶以及写实绘画。

player /'pleɪə(r); 'pleɚ/ *n* person or organization, etc with an active interest and that plays a recognized part in a type of business（某商业的）活动家，积极参与者，玩家：*The big players are the arms manufacturers.* 大玩家是军火制造商。○ *Hoping to join the players is Luxlite, with the 15% share in the company they recently acquired.* 勒克斯利特公司最近购买了一家公司 15% 的股份，希望加入玩家行列。

plonker /'plɒŋkə(r); 'plɑŋkɚ/ *n* (*Brit sl* 俚) **1** idiot; fool 傻瓜；笨蛋 **2** man's penis 男人的阴茎

plug-and-play /'plʌgəndpleɪ; 'plʌgəndple/ *adj* **1** (*computing* 计) allowing additional pieces of equipment or circuit cards to be added to a computer system easily 即插即用的（可容易地将附加设备或电路卡插入计算机系统的）**2** (*fig* 比喻) simple, easy and uncomplicated 简单的；容易的：*Few video cassette recorders are as plug-and-play as their users would like them to be.* 录像机很少能如用户期望的那样易于操作。

pod /pɒd; pɑd/ *n* group of sea-mammals, esp whales or dolphins 一群海洋哺乳动物（尤指鲸或海豚）

poisoned chalice /pɔɪznd 'tʃælɪs; pɔɪznd 'tʃælɪs/ *n* sth, esp a job opportunity, which seems attractive and desirable but which then proves difficult or even fatal to one's career 毒酒（貌似诱人但其实难应付甚至会摧毁自己事业的东西，尤指工作机会）：*The post of Minister for Northern Ireland has proved a poisoned chalice for many a career politician.* 北爱尔兰大臣的职位对许多职业政客来说证明是杯好看却不好喝的毒酒。

pole position /'pəʊl pəzɪʃn; 'pol pəzɪʃən/ *n* [U,C] leading position at the start of a motor race, gained by obtaining the fastest time in the practice laps（汽车赛中赢了练习赛而取得的）首发位置

political correctness /pəˌlɪtɪkl kə'rektnɪs; pəˌlɪtɪkl kə'rɛktnɪs/ *n* [U] (*abbr* 缩写 **PC**) behaviour or speech in line with the current liberal or even radical opinion of the day esp on social matters and which avoids any language or behaviour considered discriminatory or offensive 政治正确性（对社会事务等的态度及言语与当前普遍的开明甚至激进看法一致，避免任何歧视性的或无礼的言语或行为）：*a use of language that shows a lack of political correctness* 缺乏政治正确性的用语

▷ **politically correct** *adj* (*abbr* 缩写 **PC**)：*University courses have been criticized for not being politically correct.* 大学课程被批评为政治不正确。

polluter /pə'lu:tə(r); pə'lutɚ/ *n* person, group of people, or industry, etc that pollutes the environment 污染源；污染（自然环境）者

pooch /pu:tʃ; putʃ/ *n* (*sl* 俚 *esp US*) dog 狗

pooper scooper /'pu:pə sku:pə(r); 'pupɚ skupɚ/ *n* (*infml* 口) tool for clearing up dog excrement 除狗粪器

Popemobile /'pəʊpməˌbi:l; 'popməˌbil/ *n* (usu 通常作 **the Popemobile**) bullet-proof vehicle with a raised, transparent viewing area, used by the Pope on official visits since the shooting of Pope John Paul II in an assassination attempt 教皇专车（教皇约翰·保罗二世在险遭暗杀后出访所乘的防弹车，设有凸起的透明部分用以观察四周）

popmobility /pɒpməʊ'bɪlɪtɪ; pɑpmo'bɪlɪtɪ/ *n* [U] vigorous rhythmic exercise to pop music（节奏强的）流行音乐体操

poppadam /'pɒpədəm; 'pɑpədəm/ (also **poppadom, popadam**) *n* thin, crispy Indian bread eaten with curry, etc（涂咖喱等吃的）印度薄脆扁豆煎饼

population centre /pɒpjʊ'leɪʃn sentə(r); pɑpjə'leʃən sentɚ/ (*US* **center**) *n* area where a lot of people settle to live and work 人口集中地；人口密集地区：*The problem affects the population centres, not the smaller towns.* 该问题影响的是人口密集地区而不是小城镇。

pop-up menu ⇨ MENU

Portakabin /'pɔ:təkæbɪn; 'pɔrtəkæbɪn/ *n* (*Brit propr* 专利名) room or set of rooms designed to be moved and put together quickly, eg as a temporary office on a building site 活动房屋，可移动房屋（如建筑工地的临时办公室）

Portaloo /'pɔ:təlu:; 'pɔrtəlu/ *n* (*propr* 专利名) portable lavatory, ie LOO[A-Z], which can be set up as a temporary facility on a building site, at a pop festival, etc 流动厕所

positive discrimination *n* = AFFIRMATIVE ACTION

positive vetting /ˌpɒzətɪv 'vetɪŋ; ˌpɑzətɪv 'vɛtɪŋ/ *n* [U] (*Brit*) process of thoroughly checking the background, character and associates of a candidate for a post in the Civil Service that involves access to secret material 彻底审查（对政府机密部门职位的候选人所作的调查，范围包括其背景、性格及同事、亲友）

posse /'pɒsɪ; 'pɑsɪ/ *n* (*US*) **1** gang of black (esp Jamaican) youths involved in organized or violent crime, often related to the traffic in drugs（参与有组织或暴力罪行，常与毒品走私有关的）青少年黑人犯罪团伙（尤指牙买加的）**2** one's particular crowd or group of friends 小圈子；团伙；死党

post-Aids /pəʊst'eɪdz; post'edz/ *adj* referring to the period since the start of the global AIDS[A-Z] epidemic 艾滋病在全球流行之后的 Cf 参看 PRE-AIDS

post-feminist /pəʊst'femɪnɪst; post'fɛmənɪst/ *adj* of or relating to the principles and attitudes regarded as formed in the wake of the feminist ideas of the sixties and the decades immediately following 后女权主义的（在六十年代争取女权运动之后数十年中形成的思潮的）

▷ **post-feminist** *n* person with post-feminist principles and attitudes 后女权主义者 **post-feminism** *n*

postindustrial /ˌpəʊstɪn'dʌstrɪəl; ˌpostɪn'dʌstrɪəl/ *adj* (of a place or community) no longer relying on heavy industry（指某地或社会）后工业化的（即不再依赖重工业）：*a postindustrial city/economy now relying more on the service industries such as tourism* 现在较依靠诸如旅游等服务业的后工业化城市 *[经济]*

Post-it note *n* (*propr* 专利名) = STICKY

post-moshing syndrome /pəʊst'mɒʃɪŋ ˌsɪndrəʊm; post'mɑʃɪŋ ˌsɪndrom/ *n* (*infml* 口) suffering from the bruising and other injuires caused by moshing (MOSH) 狂舞综合征（狂舞后的受伤）

postoperative /ˌpəʊst'ɒpərətɪv, *US* -reɪtɪv; ˌpost-ɑpə'retɪv/ *adj* (*medical* 医) occurring in or relating to the period immediately following a surgical operation 手术后的：*postoperative pain/bleeding* 手术后疼痛 *[出血]*

post-structuralism /pəʊst'strʌktʃərəlɪzm; post-'strʌktʃərəlɪzəm/ *n* [U] movement, esp in literature and the visual arts, which criticizes and challenges the claim of STRUCTURALISM[A-Z] that objectivity is possible and emphasizes instead the plurality of meaning in any text or object that expresses the values of a culture 后结构主义（对结构主义认为可以达到客观性的断言提出批评

和质疑的运动，尤指文学与视觉艺术领域方面强调任何表现文化价值的文字或物品都具有多重意义）

▷ **post-structural** *adj* **post-structuralist** *n, adj* Cf 参看 DECONSTRUCTION（DECONSTRUCT）

post-traumatic stress disorder /pəʊstrɔːˌmætɪk 'stres dɪsɔːdə(r), *US* traʊm-; postraʊˌmætɪk 'strɛs dɪsɔrdɚ/ *n* condition which develops in people who have suffered an extremely stressful event or situation, eg a plane crash, being held as a hostage or a military action. Symptoms include bad dreams, sleep disturbance, flashbacks and depression 创伤后紧张症（遭受飞机失事、被扣为人质或参战等极端痛苦经历者的症状，如做恶梦、睡眠紊乱、记忆在脑中重现及抑郁等）: *Post-traumatic stress disorder is recognized as requiring intense therapy.* 一般认为治理创伤后紧张症需进行强化治疗。

pounding /'paʊndɪŋ; 'paʊndɪŋ/ *n* **1** sound or feeling of sth beating heavily 重击（声）: *a pounding on the door* 砰的敲门声 **2** instance of sb/sth being severely damaged or heavily defeated 重创；惨败: *The team took a terrible pounding, going down 12 love.* 该队以 0 比 12 惨败。

powdered sugar *n* [U] (*US*) = CASTOR SUGAR（CASTOR^A-Z）

power-assisted /'paʊəəˌsɪstɪd; 'paʊɚəˌsɪstɪd/ *adj* (esp of steering and brakes in a motor vehicle) employing an additional source of power from the engine to assist manual operation（尤指机动车的转向装置及制动器）利用机动力帮助手动操作的，助力的: *power-assisted steering and brakes* 动力转向装置和刹车器

power-base /'paʊəbeɪs; 'paʊɚbes/ *n* main support for a politician or political party, or of a faction at the management or executive level of a company 权力基础（支持政治家、政党或公司行政管理层的主要力量）: *His main power-base is in the south.* 他的主要权力基础在南方。

power breakfast /'paʊə ˌbrekfəst, ˌpaʊə 'brekfəst; 'paʊɚ brɛkfəst/ *n* working breakfast at which high-level political or business discussions can be held 巨头工作早餐会（政界或商界要人谈工作时吃的早餐）Cf 参看 POWER LUNCH

power-broker /'paʊəbrəʊkə(r); 'paʊɚbrokɚ/ *n* person who influences how much political power others have（能影响他人权势消长的）权力掮客: *The foreign secretary is said to be the real power-broker in the government.* 据说外交大臣是政府里真正操纵权力者。

power dressing /'paʊə dresɪŋ; 'paʊɚ drɛsɪŋ/ *n* [U] style of dressing in favour of formal, well-cut suits for work and business which is intended to convey an impression of efficiency and confidence 专业化穿着（穿庄重、剪裁考究的套装，意在给人高效而自信的印象）

NOTE 注: most frequently applied to the way women dress in order to compete in the business world and the professions 通常指妇女为在商界及专业中立足而穿着的方式

power line /'paʊə laɪn; 'paʊɚ laɪn/ *n* cable supplying electrical power, esp from the generating station to homes and factories（尤指从发电厂供电到家庭和工厂的）电力线，输电线

power lunch /'paʊə lʌntʃ; 'paʊɚ lʌntʃ/ *n* working lunch at which high-level political or business discussions can be held 巨头工作午餐会（政界或商界要人谈工作时吃的午餐）Cf 参看 POWER BREAKFAST

power nap /'paʊə næp; 'paʊɚ næp/ *n* brief, refreshing sleep usu taken during the day by sb involved in important and demanding work（参与重大工作者的）日间小睡

▷ **power nap** *v* [I, Ipr]

power-sharing /'paʊəʃeərɪŋ; 'paʊɚʃɛrɪŋ/ *n* [U] system or policy in which two or more parties or groups agree to share responsibility for making decisions, taking political actions, etc（政党或团体之间的）权力分享: *Negotiations for power-sharing are still going on.* 有关权力的分配还在协商之中。

power-striding *n* = POWER-WALKING

power user /'paʊə juːzə(r); 'paʊɚ juzɚ/ *n* (*computing* 计) person who is not a professional computer expert and yet who shows considerable skill in using a computer system or software, like exercising power and authority over the computer 计算机高手，超级用户（虽非计算机专业人员却能熟练运用计算机系统或软件的人）

power-walking /'paʊəwɔːkɪŋ; 'paʊɚwɔkɪŋ/ (also **power-striding**) *n* [U] walking vigorously at a fast pace as a means of exercise（作为锻炼方式的）快步行走: *Power-walking may be better for you than jogging.* 对你来说，快步走可能比慢跑更好。

practising /'præktɪsɪŋ; 'præktɪsɪŋ/ (*US* **-ticing**) *adj* [attrib 作定语] currently active or engaged in a religion, profession, etc 积极从事…的；执业的: *a practising Christian/solicitor/doctor* 虔诚的基督徒、执业律师[医师]

pragmatics /præg'mætɪks; præg'mætɪks/ *n* [sing v] (*linguistics* 语言) study of the way in which language is used to express or interpret real intentions in particular situations, esp when the actual words may appear on the surface to mean sth different 语用学（对在特定环境下语言使用的研究，尤指当字面意义与真正意图有分别的时候）

prat /præt; præt/ *n* (*Brit sl* 俚) very foolish or stupid person 笨蛋；蠢货: *Don't be such a prat!* 别那么傻了！

praxis /'præksɪs; 'præksɪs/ *n* [U] (*fml* 文) accepted way of doing sth 惯例；常规: *the contemporary praxis of the church* 目下做礼拜的惯例

praying mantis /ˌpreɪɪŋ 'mæntɪs; ˌpreɪŋ 'mæntɪs/ *n* large carnivorous insect which holds its front legs in a position that looks like sb praying, while waiting to catch another insect, etc 螳螂

pre-Aids /priː'eɪdz; priː'edz/ *adj* referring to the period before the outbreak of AIDS^A-Z 艾滋病流行之前的: *Pre-aids sex life was so much less complicated and threatening.* 艾滋病流行以前的性生活远没有现在这样复杂而可怕。Cf 参看 POST-AIDS

predeterminer /ˌpriːdɪ'tɜːmɪnə(r); ˌpridɪ'tɝmɪnɚ/ *n* (*grammar*) word that can precede a DETERMINER^A-Z in a noun phrase, eg *all* in 'all the students' and *such* in 'such a lot of rain' 前置限定词（置于名词短语中限定词之前的词，如 all the students 中的 all 和 such a lot of rain 中的 such）

pre-embryo /priː'embrɪəʊ; pri'ɛmbrɪo/ *n* (*medical* 医) cell or group of cells which could develop into an embryo, esp a fertilized human egg up to fourteen days after fertilization 胚胎前期（可发育成胚胎的一个或一群细胞，尤指受精后十四天以内的人类受精卵）

NOTE 注: after fourteen days, the word *embryo* is used: a distinction which has validity in the ethical and legal debate about the use of the human embryo in genetic and medical research 受精十四天后即使用 embryo（胚胎）一词，此区别可用以判定将人类胚胎用于遗传学和医学研究是否合乎伦理和法律

pre-loaded /priː'ləʊdɪd; pri'lodɪd/ *adj* (*computing* 计) relating to software which is already installed on a personal computer when it is bought so that it can be used immediately 预加载的，预装的（计算机在出售时已预装了软件，用户购买后即能使用）: *pre-loaded with Windows 98* 预装视窗 98 软件的

prenup /priː'nʌp; pri'nʌp/ *n* (*US infml* 口) agreement signed by both parties before a marriage takes place

which says that one party can make legal claims on the estate of the other when the marriage breaks down 婚前财产协议书（婚前双方签署的协议，说明婚姻破裂时，一方可对另一方的财产提出所有权要求）
NOTE 注： abbr of *prenuptial* (before marriage) ☆ prenuptial（婚前的）一词的缩写

preppy /'prepɪ; 'prɛpɪ/ (also **preppie**) *n* (*US infml* 口) person who attends or looks like attending an expensive private school（收费昂贵的私立学校的）学生；像私立学校学生的人

presale /pri:'seɪl; pri'sel/ *n* preview of goods about to go on sale or to be auctioned which is open only to invited customers 售前展览（即将出售或拍卖的商品的展览，只对受到邀请的顾客开放）

preschooler /ˌpri:'sku:lə(r); ˌpri'skulɚ/ *n* child who has not yet reached the official age for schooling 学龄前儿童：*preschoolers and toddlers* 学龄前儿童和学步小孩

presence /'prezns; 'prɛzn̩s/ *n* [U] (*commerce* 商) position or activity of a business in a particular market（公司在某市场上的）地位，活动：*The newly-merged company has an increasingly dominant presence in South-east Asian telecommunications.* 新合并的公司在东南亚电信市场上的主导地位日益巩固。

presentational /ˌprezn'teɪʃənl, *US* pri:zen-; ˌprizɛn'teʃənl̩/ *adj* of or relating to the presentation of sth, eg of new products or policies, esp making use of modern techniques of display（尤指利用现代技术让新产品或新政策得以）展示的，介绍的：*Presentational skills cannot be ignored in the training of managers or of teachers.* 培训管理人员或教师不能忽略表达技巧这一项。

presenteeism /prezn'ti:ɪzəm; prɛzn̩'tiɪzəm/ *n* [U] (*commerce* 商) practice of being present at one's place of work, and making sure that one is seen to be so, for longer hours than are required 在场主义（通过延长工作时间以求在别人面前表现工作积极的做法）：*Presenteeism is one way that employees can show their commitment and, perhaps, hang on to their jobs.* 在场主义是雇员表现敬业精神的一种方法，此外，也许还可保住饭碗。

press the flesh ⇨ FLESH

pre-teen /pri:'ti:n; pri'tin/ (also **preteenager, preteener**) *n* child between the ages of about 9 to 12 ☆ 9至12岁间的儿童；十岁上下的儿童：*a pop group that appeals mainly to the pre-teens* 一个主要为十岁左右儿童喜爱的流行乐歌唱组 ○ *the purchasing power of the pre-teen market* 十岁左右儿童商品市场的购买力

price-sensitive /'praɪsˌsensɪtɪv; 'praɪsˌsɛnsətɪv/ *adj* **1** (of a product) sales of which are greatly influenced by its price（指产品）销售额易受价格影响的 **2** (of information) which would affect prices if made public（指信息）公诸于世后将影响价格的：*a price-sensitive report on areas of likely ground subsidence* 影响价格的地面下陷报道

primary health care /ˌpraɪmərɪ 'helθ keə(r), *US* -meərɪ; ˌpraɪmɛrɪ 'hɛlθ kɛr/ *n* [U] health care given by a GENERAL PRACTITIONER (GENERAL^A-Z) rather than by doctors in a hospital（由全科医师而非医院里的医师提供的）基本保健

prion /'pri:ɒn; 'priɑn/ *n* (*medical* 医) infectious particle consisting only of protein, which is thought to be the cause of diseases such as CREUTZFELDT-JAKOB DISEASE in humans and BOVINE SPONGIFORM ENCEPHALOPATHY in cattle 朊病毒，蛋白质致病颗粒（纯蛋白质构成的传染性颗粒，据认为是引起人类的克—雅二氏病以及牛的疯牛病等的病因）

private practice /ˌpraɪvət 'præktɪs; ˌpraɪvɪt 'præktɪs/ *n* [U] **1** exercise of one's profession, eg as a solicitor, architect, accountant, etc in a self-employed way rather than being employed in a firm（律师、建筑师、会计师等）私人开业 **2** (*Brit*) (**a**) [U] provision of medical care by doctors, dentists, etc outside the National Health Service, and which has to be paid for by the patient（非国家医疗部门提供、就诊者须付费的）私人医疗 (**b**) [C] place providing private practice 私人诊所：*A new private practice has opened up near us.* 我们附近新开了一家私人诊所。

private school /ˌpraɪvət 'sku:l; ˌpraɪvɪt 'skul/ *n* **1** (*Brit*) school which is entirely privately financed, mainly by the fees paid by the parents of pupils attending the school（主要靠学生家长所缴费用维持的）私立学校 **2** (*US*) school which does not receive its main financial support from the government（非政府资助的）私立学校 Cf 参看 PUBLIC SCHOOL (PUBLIC^A-Z)

private secretary /ˌpraɪvət 'sekrətrɪ, *US* -rəterɪ; ˌpraɪvɪt 'sɛkrətɛrɪ/ *n* secretary dealing with sb's more personal and confidential affairs 私人秘书

private sector /ˌpraɪvət 'sektə(r); ˌpraɪvɪt 'sɛktɚ/ *n* **the private sector** [sing] part of a country's economy which is not under the direct control of the state（国家经济中的）私营部分：*a healthy growth of the private sector* 私营经济的健康发展 ○ *inflation caused by steep pay rises in the private sector* 私营企业工资剧增所导致的通货膨胀 Cf 参看 PUBLIC SECTOR

proactive /prəʊ'æktɪv; pro'æktɪv/ *adj* taking charge of a situation and causing things to happen by intervention, rather than reacting after the event（以干预手段）积极（控制情况）的，主动（引发变动）的：*a proactive policy/leader* 积极的政策 *[领导者]*

pro-am /prəʊ'æm; pro'æm/ *n, adj* (competition) involving both professional and AMATEUR 1^A-Z players 包括职业和业余选手的（比赛）：*a pro-am golf tournament* 包括职业和业余选手的高尔夫球赛

pro-choice /prəʊ'tʃɔɪs; pro'tʃɔɪs/ *adj* favouring the right of a pregnant woman to choose to have an abortion 主张妇女有堕胎权的：*He's well-known for his pro-choice views and so the women's groups support him.* 他以主张妇女有堕胎权而著称，因此妇女团体支持他。Cf 参看 RIGHT TO LIFE

profiling /'prəʊfaɪlɪŋ; 'profaɪlɪŋ/ *n* [U] process of constructing an outline or profile of a person's individual characteristics, used as a basic technique for forensic investigation 个人特征勾画（用于法医鉴证的一种基本技巧）Cf 参看 GENETIC FINGERPRINTING

profit-taker /'prɒfɪtˌteɪkə(r); 'prɑfɪtˌtekɚ/ *n* person who sells shares when the price has risen in order to gain a short-term profit（当股票价格上涨即抛出的）获取短期利润者
▷ **profit-taking** *n*

programmable /'prəʊgræməbl; 'progræməbl̩/ *adj* (*computing* 计) able to be controlled by a computer program 可编程的；可用计算机程式控制的：*a programmable remote control for the video* 录影机的编程遥控器

programming /'prəʊgræmɪŋ; 'progræmɪŋ/ *n* [U] **1** activity of writing computer programs 编程；程式设计：*programming with the end-user in mind* 照顾到最终使用者的程式设计 **2** selection and scheduling of radio or television programmes by broadcasting companies（广播或电视的）节目编排：*programming that allows for minority interests as well as catering for the general taste of viewers* 雅俗共赏的节目编排

proletarian /ˌprəʊlə'teərɪən; ˌprolə'tɛrɪən/ *adj* (*often derog* 常作贬义) about or concerning the PROLETARIAT^A-Z 无产阶级的：*a proletarian novel* 无产阶级小说

promo /'prəʊməʊ; 'promo/ *adj* [attrib 作定语], *n* (*infml* 口) (of or relating to) promotion for a performer or a commercial product（表演者或商品的）宣传

（的），推销（的），广告（的）: *a short promo video* 一部宣传短片

protected building *n* (*US*) = LISTED BUILDING (LIST[1(A-Z)])

Prozac /'prəʊzæk; 'prozæk/ *n* [U] (*propr medical* 专利名，医) drug prescribed for the relief of depression, anxiety etc, esp for elderly people; fluoxetine 普罗扎克，氟苯氧丙胺（用于减缓抑郁、焦虑等的药，尤为老年人所用）

psychedelia /ˌsaɪkə'delɪə; ˌsaɪkə'delɪə/ *n* [U] music, art objects, culture, etc inspired by and based on what sb experienced while under the influence of PSYCHEDELIC 1[A-Z] drugs（灵感来自服用迷幻药后的感觉的）迷幻音乐 *[艺术 / 文化]*

psycho /'saɪkəʊ; 'saɪko/ *n* (*pl* **-os**) (*infml derog* 口，贬) person who behaves in an abnormal, often violent, and uncontrolled way 精神失常者；疯子: *He's a real psycho, especially when he's had a drink or two.* 他真是个神经病，喝了一两杯酒后更加疯狂。

psychological profiling /ˌsaɪkəlɒdʒɪkl 'prəʊfaɪlɪŋ; ˌsaɪkəlɑdʒɪkl̩ 'profaɪlɪŋ/ *n* [U] use of profiling techniques in order to build up an understanding of the motives and likely personality of a suspected criminal, esp sb who is suspected of serious crimes 心理特征勾画（通过对个人特征的勾画来加强对嫌疑犯尤指严重罪行嫌疑犯的动机和个性的了解）

PT boat /ˌpi: 'ti: bəʊt; ˌpi 'ti bot/ *n* (*US*) = TORPEDO-BOAT (TORPEDO[A-Z])

NOTE 注： *PT* stands for *powered torpedo* ☆ PT 即 powered torpedo（鱼雷）

pubescent /pju:'besnt; pju'bɛsn̩t/ *adj* going through the physical and hormonal changes associated with PUBERTY[A-Z] 青春期的；发育期的: *pubescent boys and girls* 少男少女们

Public Interest Immunity Certificate *n* (*Brit fml* 文) = GAGGING ORDER

public sector /ˌpʌblɪk 'sektə(r); ˌpʌblɪk 'sɛktɚ/ *n* **the public sector** [sing] part of a country's economy that is directly controlled by the state（国家经济的）国营部分: *public sector housing/employment* 公家住房 *[职位]* Cf 参看 PRIVATE SECTOR

public works /ˌpʌblɪk 'wɜ:ks; ˌpʌblɪk 'wɝks/ *n* [pl] building work, eg of roads, hospitals, schools, etc which is paid for by the government 公共工程，市政工程（如建公路、医院、学校等）: *an ambitious programme of public works* 一项雄心勃勃的市政工程计划

publishing house /'pʌblɪʃɪŋ haʊs; 'pʌblɪʃɪŋ haʊs/ *n* company that publishes books 出版社；出版公司

pull /pʊl; pʊl/ *v* [Tn] (*infml* 口) **1** withdraw; stop short 撤销；终止: *The scheme was pulled after only a few weeks.* 计划实施仅几个星期即告取消。 **2** arrest 逮捕: *The police are far more likely to pull a black man than a white man in this area.* 在这个地区警察大多数情况下逮捕黑人而非白人。

pull-down menu /ˌpʊldaʊn 'menju:; ˌpʊldaʊn 'mɛnju/ *n* (*computing* 计) list of options relating to possible actions which the user can select and access by clicking with a mouse 下拉式菜单 Cf 参看 MENU

pull quote /'pʊl kwəʊt; 'pʊl kwot/ *n* (*publishing* 出版) quote taken from the middle of an article which is printed in larger type elsewhere on the page to draw attention to the topic 醒目引文（摘自文章的引文，以较大字体印于当页的别处以引人注意）

pulse dialling /'pʌls daɪəlɪŋ; 'pʌls daɪəlɪŋ/ *n* [U] system of telephone dialling in which each digit is transmitted as the same number of electrical pulses the digit represents（电话）脉冲式拨号系统或设备 Cf 参看 TONE DIALLING

pump priming /'pʌmp praɪmɪŋ; 'pʌmp praɪmɪŋ/ *n* [U] (*esp US*) investment, esp by a government, intended to stimulate the growth of a business or an industry（尤指政府所作的）刺激工商业发展的投资: *Government investment in the re-cycling business can be accused of pump priming but is welcomed by environmentalists.* 政府在回收废旧物品上的投资或会为人诟病，指为刺激经济的投资，但却受到了环保分子的欢迎。

Punch and Judy show /ˌpʌntʃ ən 'dʒu:dɪ ʃəʊ; ˌpʌntʃ ən 'dʒudɪ ʃo/ *n* (in Britain) traditional show for children often performed at seaside resorts and put on by one man inside a canvas-covered box working glove puppets. Punch and Judy are man and wife and spend most of their time fighting '庞奇和朱迪' 滑稽戏（一种英国传统的常由一人在海滨度假胜地演出的儿童滑稽布袋木偶戏，庞奇和朱迪是一对夫妇，终日吵架不休）

punchbag /'pʌntʃbæg; 'pʌntʃbæg/ (*US* **punching bag**) *n* (*Brit*) heavy stuffed bag, usu of leather, which hangs from a rope or chain and is punched as part of physical training, esp by boxers（练习拳击用的）吊袋，沙包

punt /pʊnt; pʊnt/ *n* unit of money in the Republic of Ireland 爱尔兰镑（爱尔兰共和国的货币单位）

pursuant /pə'sju:ənt, *US* -su:ənt; pɚ'suənt/ *adj* ~ **to sth** (*law fml* 律，文) (usu following *ns* 通常用于名词后) conforming to sth 符合 *[遵从]* 某事物: *to come into effect pursuant to Article X of the convention* 根据协议的第 X 条生效

push /pʊʃ; pʊʃ/ *v* **1** (idm 习语) **push the envelope** go beyond established limits, do sth new or pioneer, and take risks while doing so 超越极限；冒险尝试新事物或充当先锋: *The new mayor is prepared to push the envelope with his crime control scheme involving ordinary citizens.* 新市长准备大胆尝试其全民控制犯罪方案。

NOTE 注： probably derived from the word *envelope* which is used in the aircraft industry to mean the boundary line on a graph representing an aircraft's capabilities 可能源于航空业词汇 envelope，指飞机性能图表上的极限线

when push comes to shove when there is no other choice; when a problem must be faced 别无选择时；必须面对问题时: *I don't like giving anyone the sack, but when push comes to shove I have to do it.* 我不想解雇任何人，但别无选择时也就只好这样了。 **2** (phr v) **push in** [I] break into a line of people or traffic instead of joining at the back of the queue 插队: *Don't let that taxi push in. Why shouldn't he have to wait like everyone else?* 别让那辆计程车插进来。他为什么不能像其他人一样等着？ **push out** [Tn] (*infml* 口) produce quickly and in large quantities 快速大批生产: *By the second year of the war, every factory was pushing out huge quantities of armaments of all kinds.* 战争进入第二年，各家工厂都在加紧生产大批各种武器。

PVA /ˌpi: vi: 'eɪ; ˌpi vi 'e/ *abbr* 缩写 = polyvinyl acetate (chemical substance used in certain types of paint and glue) 聚醋酸乙烯酯（一种用于某些油漆和胶水的化学物质）

pw /pi:'dʌblju:; pi'dʌblju/ *abbr* 缩写 = per week 每周: *The starting salary was £300 pw.* 起薪为每周 300 英镑。

PYO /ˌpi: waɪ 'əʊ; ˌpi waɪ 'o/ *abbr* 缩写 = pick-your-own (seen eg at the entrance to a farm where people can pick their own strawberries, raspberries, potatoes, etc from the fields and then pay for them by weight) 自己动手，自己采摘（见于如农场的入口处，让人们可以自己从田园里采摘草莓、覆盆子、土豆等，然后按斤两计价钱）

pyro-musical /ˌpaɪrəʊ'mju:zɪkl; ˌpaɪro'mjuzɪkl̩/ *adj* [attrib 作定语] blending fireworks and music in a synchronized (SYNCHRONIZE[A-Z]) display 烟花配合音

乐的；放烟花和音乐表演同时进行的：*The celebrations reached their climax with a huge pyro-musical display over the harbour.* 港口处盛大的烟花配合音乐的同步演出将庆祝活动推向了高潮。

Qq

QC *n* = QUALITY CIRCLE
quad bike /ˈkwɒd baɪk; ˈkwɑd baɪk/ *n* (*sport* 体) off-road, four-wheeled motorcycle used for sport and recreation（体育或娱乐用的）四轮摩托车
NOTE 注：*quad* is an abbreviation for *quadruple* and refers to the four wheels of the motorcycle ☆ quad 为 quadruple 的缩写形式，指摩托车的四轮
quality audit /ˈkwɒlɪtɪ ɔːdɪt; ˈkwɑlətɪ ɔdɪt/ *n* (**a**) review of the quality of a product or service（产品或服务的）质量审查 (**b**) review of the processes for monitoring quality which are in place within a company, organization, service industry, etc（公司、机构、服务行业等内部的）质量监督过程的审查
quality circle /ˈkwɒlɪtɪ sɜːkl; ˈkwɑlətɪ sɝkl̩/ *n* (*commerce* 商) group of employees which meets regularly to consider ways of resolving problems and improving production in an organization. The idea originated in Japan and the emphasis on participation and cooperation is part of the Japanese business philosophy known as KAIZEN 品质攻关小组（为解决问题和改进生产而定期聚会的雇员小组。这种强调参与和合作的做法源自日本，是日本经营哲学 kaizen（不断改善经营法）的一部分）
quality control /ˈkwɒlətɪ kəntrəʊl; ˈkwɑlətɪ kəntrol/ *n* [U] practice of checking a product by testing the whole lot or random samples esp in mass production 品质控制，质量管理（对产品进行全面或抽样的测试，尤在大量生产时）：*strict quality control* 严格的品质控制
quality newspaper /ˌkwɒlətɪ ˈnjuːspeɪpə(r), *US* nuːzp-; ˈkwɑlətɪ ˈnuzpepɚ/ (also **quality**) *n* (usu *pl* 通常作复数) newspaper considered to be read by people with a high educational standard, printed as a BROADSHEET 2^A-Z^ rather than a TABLOID^A-Z^, and containing mainly serious news, reports and analysis 高品质报纸；严肃报纸
quality time /ˈkwɒlɪtɪ taɪm; ˈkwɑlətɪ taɪm/ *n* [U] time spent productively or profitably, esp with reference to time spent by working parents with their children 过得有意义 *[*有价值*]* 的时间（尤指上班的父母陪伴孩子所花的时间）：*I always make sure that I spend quality time with the children every evening and on Sundays.* 每个晚上和星期天我一定和孩子们一起度过美好时光。
NOTE 注：at first the expression had only good connotations, implying that the parent gave his or her full attention to the child, but more recently it has come to be a euphemism for the very small amount of time that a busy parent spares for his or her child 起初此词只含褒义，意指家长全心全意地照顾孩子，但近来演变成一种委婉说法，指忙碌的父母留给孩子少得可怜的时间
queercore /ˈkwɪəkɔː(r); ˈkwɪrkɔr/ *n* [sing] cultural movement amongst young homosexuals which deliberately rebels against and separates itself from the established gay scene, and which has as its primary form of expression an aggressive type of punk-style (PUNK 1a^A-Z^) music 同性恋核心运动（年轻同性恋者的一场文化运动，有意违反及脱离传统的同性恋生活方式，其主要表现形式为一种强劲的蓬克音乐）
questioning /ˈkwestʃənɪŋ; ˈkwɛstʃənɪŋ/ *n* [U] session during which sb is asked questions about sth, eg a crime 审问：*The police took her in for questioning, but she was released after a few hours.* 警察将她带进去审问，但几个小时后就把她放了。
quick fix /kwɪk ˈfɪks; kwɪk ˈfɪks/ *n* (*infml* 口) (usu used with a negative 通常与否定词连用) easy, fast but may be only temporary solution 快速简易但可能只是暂时性的解决办法；权宜之计：*There's no quick fix for the problem of homeless young people on our city streets.* 对于我们城市街道上存在无家可归的年轻人的问题，并无便捷的解决办法。
quite /kwaɪt; kwaɪt/ *adv* (idm 习语) **quite something** impressive; notable; great 了不起；棒：*You crossed the Sahara on foot! Wow, that's quite something!* 你徒步穿过撒哈拉沙漠！哇，真了不起！
NOTE 注：expression of admiration and approval, esp for an unusual achievement 赞赏语，尤指对非同寻常的成就
quota hopping /ˈkwəʊtə hɒpɪŋ; ˈkwotə hɑpɪŋ/ *n* practice of evading the limitations imposed on a European Community member state by the quota system, esp for fishing, by registering as belonging to a different state 逃避配额，（尤指）逃避捕鱼配额（通过登记属于另一国的方式逃避对欧洲共同体成员国规定的配额限制）：*Spanish fishing boats have long been suspected of quota hopping.* 西班牙的渔船久已有逃避配额之嫌。

Rr

rad /ræd; ræd/ *adj* (*US sl* 俚) really good or exciting; cool, hip, AWESOME 顶呱呱的；真够劲儿；帅极了
NOTE 注：abbreviated from *radical*, a term of approval amongst the young Californian surfers in the late 60s 缩略自 radical 一词，系 60 年代末加利福尼亚州的年轻冲浪者使用的赞美语
radiation therapy /reɪdɪˈeɪʃn ˌθerəpɪ; redɪˈeʃən ˌθɛrəpɪ/ *n* [U] (*medical* 医) treatment of diseases, esp cancer, using radiation 放射疗法（尤用于治疗癌症）Cf 参看 CHEMOTHERAPY^A-Z^, RADIO-THERAPY^A-Z^
radicalize, -ise /ˈrædɪkəˌlaɪz; ˈrædɪkl̩ˌaɪz/ *v* make sb/sth more RADICAL 3^A-Z^ 使更激进：*an increasingly radicalized opposition* 越演越烈的对抗 ○ *The imprisonment of their leader radicalized the opposition even further.* 囚禁他们的领袖，使对抗更为激烈。
rage /reɪdʒ; redʒ/ *n* [U] (often in compounds 常用以构成复合词) intense anger expressed in an uncontrolled outburst, esp when this is the result of frustration rather than provocation 狂怒（尤指因沮丧而非被激怒引起的）：*road rage* 车道上引发的狂怒 ○ *cycle rage* 骑自行车触发的怒气 ○ *Rage counselling should be available for aggressive drivers.* 应该为好斗的司机提供心理辅导。Cf 参看 ROAD RAGE
raiding party /ˈreɪdɪŋ pɑːtɪ; ˈredɪŋ pɑrtɪ/ *n* group of people who go out on a RAID 1,3^A-Z^ 突击小组；搜查小组
railcard /ˈreɪlkɑːd; ˈrelkɑrd/ *n* (*Brit*) card that allows sb to travel by train at a reduced rate 火车优惠卡：*a student/senior citizen railcard* 学生 *[*老人*]* 火车优惠卡
rail gun /ˈreɪl gʌn; ˈrel gʌn/ *n* electromagnetic projectile launcher used esp as an anti-missile weapon 电磁推进发射器（尤作为反导弹武器）
rainbow coalition /ˌreɪnbəʊ kəʊəˈlɪʃn; ˌrenbo koəˈlɪʃən/ *n* (*politics* 政) political alliance of minority peoples and other disadvantaged groups, from the idea of a union of all possible colours and political, ethnic, etc groups 彩虹联盟（少数民族与其他低下阶层组成的政治联盟，意在联合各色人种、各政治派系和种族等）

Rainbow Nation /ˌreɪnbəʊ ˈneɪʃn; ˌrenbo ˈneʃən/ *n* [sing] name which the people of South Africa use informally for themselves in recognition of the many races that make up their nation 彩虹民族（南非人对自己的非正式称呼，表示其种族的多样性）

ram-raid /ˈræmreɪd; ˈræmred/ *v* [Tn] break into a shop or other premises in order to commit robbery by ramming (RAM *v* 1a^A-Z) a vehicle at speed through a window or wall 飞车入室抢劫（高速驾车破窗或穿墙闯入商店或建筑物抢劫）: *You could describe ram-raiding as a motorized form of smash-and-grab.* 飞车入室抢劫可以说是一种机动化的破门抢劫。

▷ **ram-raid** *n*

ranching /ˈrɑːntʃɪŋ, *US* ræntʃ-; ˈræntʃɪŋ/ *n* activity of running a RANCH^A-Z 牧场经营: *cattle/sheep ranching* 经营牧牛 *[羊]* 场

random breath test /ˌrændəm ˈbreθ test; ˌrændəm ˈbrɛθ tɛst/ *n* (*abbr* 缩写 **RBT**) BREATH TEST (BREATH^A-Z) done on a driver who has not necessarily committed any kind of driving offence, eg speeding and does not appear to be drunk 随机呼吸测验（对司机进行的随机呼吸抽查以测量其体内酒精含量，不论其是否违章或看上去是否喝醉了酒）: *Random breath tests are an ever-present threat and have had an obvious effect on the numbers of people who are ready to risk drinking and driving.* 由于怕随时会碰上抽样呼吸测验，甘冒风险酒后驾车的人数明显减少了。

▷ **random breath testing** *n*

rangy /ˈreɪndʒɪ; ˈrendʒɪ/ *adj* tall and thin with long arms and legs 身材修长的: *His tall, rangy body looked best in jeans and a T-shirt.* 他身材修长，穿牛仔裤和T恤衫最合适。

NOTE 注: used of men rather than of women 用于形容男子

ranking /ˈræŋkɪŋ; ˈræŋkɪŋ/ *n* position relative to others on a scale, esp in a sport 排名（尤指体育运动方面的）: *the first Chilean to reach number one in the world tennis rankings* 第一位名列世界网球排名榜首的智利人

rap /ræp; ræp/ *n* [U] musical style originating in the street music of urban black people in the US. It has a strong beat and an almost spoken vocal line displaying the verbal dexterity and inventiveness of the rapper 绕舌歌，快板乐（源自美国都市黑人的街头音乐，节奏强劲，采用近乎念白方式，能显示演唱者的口齿伶俐和创造性）

▷ **rap** *v* [I] **rapper** *n*

Rasta *n, adj* (*infml* 口) = RASTAFARIAN^A-Z

ratatouille /ˌrætəˈtwiː, -ˈtuːɪ; ˌrætəˈtwi, -ˈtuɪ/ *n* [U] dish made of a selection of vegetables, esp courgettes, onions, mushrooms and eggplant, cooked together in oil 蔬菜什锦，普罗旺斯杂烩（用多种蔬菜，特别是以小胡瓜、洋葱、蘑菇和茄子等加油烧成的菜）

ratchet up, ratchet down /rætʃɪt ˈʌp, rætʃɪt ˈdaʊn; rætʃɪt ˈʌp, rætʃɪt ˈdaun/ *v* [Ipr] (*infml* 口) move up/down to a higher/lower level of, eg intensity, cost, frequency, etc（强度、费用、频率等）变高 *[变低]*: *The pace of life in Russia hasn't ratcheted up to US levels yet.* 俄罗斯的生活节奏还没有赶上美国的水平。

rate /reɪt; ret/ *v* [Tn] value highly 赞赏；推崇: *People living in depressed areas don't rate open-air art. They'd rather have better street-lighting.* 穷困地区的人并不欣赏露天艺术，他们宁可要更好的路灯照明。

rat-run /ˈrætrʌn; ˈrætrʌn/ *n* (*infml* 口) route along minor roads used by traffic in order to avoid congestion at peak periods（车辆为避开高峰期交通堵塞而走的）小路

rattle /ˈrætl; ˈrætl̩/ *v* (idm 习语) **rattle sb's cage** (*infml* 口) provoke sb and make them angry 激怒某人: *If you mention the new highway, that'll really rattle his cage.* 你要是向他们提起这条新的公路，那可真捅了马蜂窝了。

rave /reɪv; rev/ *n* large gathering with dancing to fast electronic music 热舞会；大型电子乐狂舞会: *a rave in a large barn, far out in the country* 在偏远农村的大谷仓里举行的大型电子乐狂舞会

RBT *abbr* 缩写 = RANDOM BREATH TEST

RE /ˌɑːr ˈiː; ɑr ˈi/ *abbr* 缩写 = religious education 宗教教育

reactive /rɪˈæktɪv; rɪˈæktɪv/ *adj* **1** showing a reaction or response 反应性的: *a reactive rather than a preventive strategy* 反应性的而非预防性的策略 Cf 参看 PROACTIVE **2** (*chemistry* 化) prone to REACT 3^A-Z 易起化学反应的；活性的: *a highly reactive substance* 高活性物质

readmit /ˌriːədˈmɪt; ˌriədˈmɪt/ *v* [Tn] ~ **sb (to sth)** (esp passive 尤用于被动语态) **1** allow sb to become a member of a group or an organization again 再次接纳某人（成为某一团体或机构的成员）: *to be readmitted to the United Nations* 让重返联合国 **2** enter a hospital again as a patient, usu for the same or a related health problem to that which caused the original admission（通常因为与前次住院相同的或相关的健康问题而）再次入院: *She was allowed home after the operation, but was readmitted to hospital three days later with complications.* 手术后，她获准回家，但三天后因为并发症再次住进医院。

▷ **readmission** (also **readmittance**) *n* [U] ~ **(to sth)** process or action of being readmitted 重新接纳；再次入院: *Nigeria sought readmission to the Commonwealth.* 尼日利亚寻求重返英联邦。

reapply /ˌriːəˈplaɪ; ˌriəˈplaɪ/ *v* [I, Ipr] **1** ~ **(for sth)** make another formal request for sth or to do sth 再次申请，重新申请（某事或做某事）: *Previous applicants for the post need not reapply.* 原已申请该职位者无需再次申请。○ *reapply for a visa* 重新申请签证 **2** use sth or make a rule, etc operate again 再次使用；再次应用（规则等）: *The formula was reapplied when privatizing the railways.* 铁路私有化时再次采用了这一方案。 **3** put or spread a substance on a surface once again 重涂；重敷: *She reapplied her lipstick/sunscreen.* 她重涂了口红 *[防晒霜]*。

rear-end /rɪəˈend; rɪrˈɛnd/ *v* [Tn] crash into the back of another vehicle 撞上另一辆车的车尾: *The old man's car was rear-ended as he prepared to drive out of the car park.* 那老人刚想把车开出停车场，车尾就被撞了。

reboot /riːˈbuːt; riˈbut/ *v* [Tn,I] restart a computer by reloading its operating system into working memory 重新引导，重自展（重新引导进入操作系统，使计算机再次启动运行）: *In the circumstances, the only way to safely run Windows is to reboot.* 在这种情况下要想安全运行视窗程式，只有重新引导了。

NOTE 注: the verb *boot* is a shortened form of *bootstrap* 动词 boot 系 bootstrap（引导）的缩略形式 Cf 参看 PULL ONESELF UP BY ONE'S OWN BOOTSTRAPS (PULL² 12^A-Z)

rebounder /rɪˈbaʊndə(r); rɪˈbaundɚ/ *n* small TRAMPOLINE^A-Z which is used for exercise（锻炼用的）小型蹦跳床

▷ **rebound** *v* **rebounding** *n*

recovered memory /rɪˈkʌvəd meməri; rɪˈkʌvɚd mɛməri/ *n* [U] repressed memory, esp of childhood sexual abuse, which is apparently recovered during psychoanalysis 恢复的记忆（精神分析治疗期间表面看来恢复了的受压抑的记忆，尤指关于童年受到性虐待的记忆）Cf 参看 FALSE MEMORY SYNDROME

recreational drug /rekrɪˈeɪʃnəl drʌg; rɛkrɪˈeʃənl̩ drʌg/ *n* drug taken for pleasure and enjoyment during one's leisure time, and not necessarily taken because of an established habit 消遣性毒品，开心药（闲暇时服用取乐，不一定因上瘾才吸的毒品）: *I do recreational drugs at the weekends but I have a good job and I'm* *certainly not an addict.* 我在周末虽吃点开心药，但我有份好工作，当然不是瘾君子。

red alert /ˌred əˈlɜːt; ˌrɛd əˈlɝt/ *n* [U,C] situation in which emergency services have been warned about a likely emergency and are ready to deal with it 戒备状态；红色警戒：*The police and the hospitals have been put on red alert.* 警方和医院都处于紧急待命状态。

NOTE 注： often used with *put on* 常与 put on 连用

red cent /ˌred ˈsent; rɛd ˈsɛnt/ *n* [sing] (*US*) (esp after a negative 尤用于否定词后) very small amount of money 很少的钱，一分钱（原为紫铜辅币）：*After all that work, I didn't get a red cent for it.* 做完了那么多工作，我分文未得。

redecorate /ˌriːˈdekəreɪt; ˌriˈdɛkəret/ *v* [I, Tn] decorate a room, etc again, esp to put new paint or wallpaper on walls 重新装修（房间等，尤指重新油漆或重贴墙纸）：*We'll have to redecorate when we move in.* 我们搬进去前将一定要重新装修。○ *redecorate a house/the living-room/an office* 重新装修房子 *[*起居室 / 办公室*]*

▷ **redecoration** *n* [U]：*The place looked so much better after redecoration.* 这个地方重新装修后看起来好多了。

red-eye /ˈredaɪ; ˈrɛdaɪ/ *n* (*US infml* 口) overnight flight; plane that flies overnight 熬夜航班；通宵航班：*They caught the red-eye to Chicago.* 他们乘夜班飞机去芝加哥。○ [attrib 作定语] *the red-eye flight leaving at 1 am* 凌晨 1 点起飞的熬夜航班

NOTE 注： the passengers on these overnight flights tend not to sleep much and so they look tired and red-eyed in the morning 通宵航班乘客通常睡得很少，因此第二天早上看上去疲惫不堪，眼睛布满血丝

red ribbon /ˌred ˈrɪbən; ˌrɛd ˈrɪbən/ *n* small loop of ribbon worn as a sign of sympathy with sufferers from AIDS^A-Z^ and of support for efforts made to find a cure for the condition 红丝带（表示对爱滋病患者的同情和对治疗爱滋病所作努力的支持而佩戴的环形丝带）：*Nearly everyone at the concert wore a red ribbon.* 音乐会上几乎人人都系上了红丝带。

red tide /red ˈtaɪd; rɛd ˈtaɪd/ *n* discoloration of the sea caused by blooming and rapidly spreading of marine red ALGAE^A-Z^ which is poisonous to fish and is thought to be caused partly by pollution 红潮，赤潮（对鱼类有毒的红色海藻大量繁殖而使海水变红，据认为部分因污染造成）：*Local fish farmers sought compensation for their losses during the recent red tides.* 当地的渔民因最近的赤潮给他们造成损失而寻求补偿。

reduced circumstances /rɪˌdjuːst ˈsɜːkəmstənsɪz; rɪˈdjust ˈsɝkəmstænsɪz/ *n* [pl] (*euph* 婉) state of having become poor after being relatively wealthy（由较富裕沦为）生活清贫：*living in reduced circumstances* 生活变得清贫

re-engineering *n* = BUSINESS PROCESS RE-ENGINEERING

reflected glory /rɪˌflektɪd ˈglɔːrɪ; rɪˌflɛktɪd ˈglɔrɪ/ *n* [U] (*derog* 贬) admiration, praise, etc given to sb, not because of what they have achieved themselves, but what sb they are connected with has done 因他人而得的荣耀；间接得来的荣耀：*basking in reflected glory* 沾人家的光荣 ○ *enjoying the reflected glory* 坐享他人的荣耀

NOTE 注： *basking* (BASK^A-Z^) is the most likely verb to co-occur with reflected glory 最常见的与 reflected glory 搭配的动词是 basking（原指坐着取暖）

reformist /rɪˈfɔːmɪst; rɪˈfɔrmɪst/ *adj* in favour of esp gradual change in political or social matters 温和改革派的，改良主义的（主张政治或社会事务逐步改变）：*a strongly reformist administration* 致力改革的政府 ○ *He is reformist rather than revolutionary.* 他与其说是个革命者，不如说是个改良派。

refusenik /rɪˈfjuːznɪk; rɪˈfjuznɪk/ *n* person who refuses to comply with a regulation, requirement, etc; uncooperative person 拒绝遵守规则、规定等的人；拒绝合作的人

NOTE 注： a name first used for political dissidents in the former USSR 此称呼最初指对前苏联持不同政见者

reinterpret /ˌriːɪnˈtɜːprɪt; ˌriɪnˈtɝprɪt/ *v* [Tn] interpret or perceive sth in a new or different way 重新解释；重新诠释：*Historians are continually reinterpreting the events of the past in the light of new discoveries.* 鉴于有新发现，历史学家正不断地重新诠释历史事件。

▷ **reinterpretation** *n* [U,C]

reintroduce /ˌriːɪntrəˈdjuːs, *US* -ˈduːs; ˌriɪntrəˈdus/ *v* [Tn] **1** bring a former rule, system, etc into force again 使（从前的规则、制度等）再度生效；恢复旧制；重新启用：*reintroduce the death penalty/foreign exchange controls* 恢复死刑 *[*外汇管制*]* **2** put a species of plant or animal back in a region where it used to live 使（动物或植物）重回以前的栖息地：*They have had some success reintroducing the condor to the Andes mountains.* 他们在使大秃鹫重返安第斯山区一事上，取得了一定成就。

▷ **reintroduction** *n* [U,C]

reinvent /ˌriːɪnˈvent; ˌriɪnˈvɛnt/ *v* [Tn] change sth so much that it becomes as if sth completely new 革新；彻底改变：*Rembrandt virtually reinvented the art of painting.* 伦勃朗可真是革新了绘画艺术。

reinvest /ˌriːɪnˈvest; ˌriɪnˈvɛst/ *v* [Tn] ~ **(sth) (in sth)** (*finance* 财) invest money made from one investment in other investments, etc（将投资所得的钱）再投资：*The company's profits are reinvested in new equipment.* 公司将所得利润再投资于新设备之上。

▷ **reinvestment** *n* [U,C]

relational /rɪˈleɪʃənl; rɪˈleʃənl/ *adj* (*fml or computing* 文或计) existing or considered in relation to sth else 相关的；关系的：*Science tells us about the structural and relational properties of objects.* 科学告诉我们物体的结构及相关特性。○ *a relational database* (ie one that can recognize the connection between stored items of information) 关系数据库（可识别其储存信息之间的关系的数据库）

relaunch /ˌriːˈlɔːntʃ; ˌriˈlɔntʃ/ *v* [Tn] present sth or set sth going again, esp in a completely new or different way（尤指以一种全新的或完全不同的方式）重新推出；使重新运作：*relaunch a product/magazine/political party* 重新推出产品、重办杂志、重组政党

▷ **relaunch** *n*：*a party to mark the relaunch of the appeal* 一个标志着再次提出呼吁的聚会

rematch /ˈriːmætʃ; ˈrimætʃ/ *n* (usu *sing* 通常作单数) match or game played again between the same people or teams, usu because the first match ended in a draw（通常因首场打成平局而进行的）重赛

remit /ˈriːmɪt; ˈrimɪt/ *n* [sing] area of control or influence that an official person or group has 势力范围；管理范围：*extend/widen/alter a remit* 扩展 *[*拓宽 / 改变*]* 势力范围 ○ *Staff recruitment is outside our remit.* 招聘不属于我们的职责。

remodel /ˌriːˈmɒdl; ˌriˈmɑdl/ *v* [Tn] change the structure or shape of sth 重塑；重组；改造：*The inside of the old house was completely remodelled.* 这间老屋的内部作了彻底改建。○ *The layout for the exhibition will have to be remodelled.* 这个展览必须重新布局。

remote sensing /rɪˌməʊt ˈsensɪŋ; rɪˌmot ˈsɛnsɪŋ/ *n* [U] scanning of the earth by satellite or high-flying aircraft 遥感（卫星或高空飞机对地球的扫描）

repetitive strain injury /rəˌpetɪtɪv ˈstreɪn ɪndʒərɪ; rɪˌpɛtɪtɪv ˈstren ɪndʒərɪ/ *n* (*abbr* 缩写 **RSI**) injury to muscles or tendons caused by continuous repeated use of particular muscles, esp during typing on a keyboard 重

复劳损（因持续使用某部分肌肉，尤其是持续操作键盘而造成的肌肉或肌腱损伤）: *RSI caused acute pain and even partial disability to some people who used a computer keyboard constantly as part of their daily work.* 对一些日常工作中经常使用计算机键盘的人来说，重复劳损不仅带来剧烈疼痛，甚至可能导致局部残废。

repetitive stress syndrome *n* = REPETITIVE STRAIN INJURY

representational /ˌreprɪzenˈteɪʃənl; ˌrɛprɪzɛnˈteʃənl/ *adj* (esp of art) trying to portray and present things as they really appear（尤指艺术）具象派的 : *representational painting* 具象派绘画

reschedule /ˌriːˈʃedjuːl, *US* ˌriːˈskedʒʊl; ˌriˈskɛdʒʊl/ *v* [Tn] **1** revise a plan, esp so that sth happens later than originally intended 修改计划（尤指为了将原定的事推迟）; 修改时间表 **2** (*finance* 财) arrange for a loan, etc to be paid back later than originally planned（将偿还贷款等的期限）推迟

research and development /rɪˌsɜːtʃ ənd dɪˈveləpmənt; rɪˌsɝtʃ ənd dɪˈvɛləpmənt/ *n* [U] (*abbr* 缩写 **R&D**) (in industry, etc) scientific search for the development of new and improved products and manufacturing processes（工业等的）研究与开发 : *Without adequate provision for research and development, no food manufacturer can expect to survive in today's market.* 没有充足的研究与开发资金，任何一个食品生产商都不可能在如今的市场中立足。

reshape /ˌriːˈʃeɪp; ˌriˈʃep/ *v* [Tn] shape or form sth again or in a different way 重塑; 重整 : *reshape the economy* 重整经济 ○ *reshape one's body/life* 重塑体形、更新生活

residency /ˈrezɪdənsɪ; ˈrɛzədənsɪ/ *n* [U,C] (*fml* 文) **1** = RESIDENCE 2[A-Z] : *to be granted permanent residency in Britain* 获得英国永久居住权 **2** engagement or employment of an artist, musician, etc to work at a particular place for a period of time（约请或雇用艺术家、音乐家等）常驻某地工作或演出一段时期 : *during Mozart's residency at the Court* 在莫扎特任宫廷乐师期间

reskill /riːˈskɪl; riˈskɪl/ *v* [Tn] retrain workers in the skills required by modern business 再培训（给予训练使职工掌握现代企业所需的技能）: *reskilling the unemployed* 再培训失业者

retail park /ˈriːteɪl pɑːk; ˈritel pɑrk/ *n* area with shops and parking for customers set in landscaped gardens（设有停车场的）绿化购物中心

retina identification /ˌretɪnə aɪdentɪfɪˈkeɪʃn; ˌrɛtɪnə aɪdɛntəfəˈkeʃən/ *n* [U] form of BIOMETRIC identification that uses the unique pattern of veins in an individual's RETINA[A-Z] 视网膜鉴定法（利用人的视网膜内独特的静脉分布方式进行的一种人体生理测量鉴定）

retrain /ˌriːˈtreɪn; ˌriˈtren/ *v* [Tn, Tn·pr] undertake training or train sb for a new type of work or to use new equipment 培训（某人）做新工作或使用新设备；（接受）重新培训 : *She retrained as a primary school teacher.* 她接受培训，改行当小学教师。

▷ **retraining** *n* [U] : *the retraining of out-of-work miners* 对失业矿工的再培训 ○ *to go on a retraining course* 开始上一门再培训课程

retro /ˈretrəʊ; ˈrɛtro/ *n* [U] **1** (**a**) style or fashion that draws its inspiration from the past 怀旧款式或时尚 (**b**) movement to revive past styles（款式的）复旧运动 : *the trend towards retro* 怀旧趋势 **2** style of popular music which avoids technical innovations 不采用新技术的流行乐; 怀旧音乐

▷ **retro** *adj* **1** reviving or drawing on the past for design ideas（设计款式）复旧的 **2** looking back to the past with longing 怀旧的 : *She likes the retro look in her clothes.* 她喜欢那衣服的怀旧式样。

□ **retro-chic** *n* fashionably NOSTALGIC (NOSTALGIA[A-Z]) style, esp in dress, reviving fashions of the recent past（尤指衣服款式的）怀旧时尚; 早先流行款式的再度流行

reunify /ˌriːˈjuːnɪfaɪ; ˌriˈjunəfaɪ/ *v* [Tn] join two or more territories into a single political unit again（两片或两片以上领土）重新统一 : *It was the Chancellor's dream to reunify East and West Germany.* 重新统一东德和西德曾是总理的梦想。

▷ **reunification** *n* [U] : *Reunification brought unexpected difficulties and strains to the new nation.* 这个新国家因恢复统一而出现了意料不到的问题及重负。

revelatory /ˌrevəˈleɪtərɪ, *US* ˈrevələtɔːrɪ; ˈrɛvələtorɪ/ *adj* revealing sth that was not known or suspected; giving an INSIGHT 2[A-Z] into sth 揭露的; 揭示的 : *His performance of the piece was competent but scarcely revelatory.* 他的表演还不错，但未能深入揭示作品的内涵。

reverse-engineer /rɪˌvɜːsendʒɪˈnɪə(r); rɪˌvɝsɛndʒəˈnɪr/ *v* [Tn] (*computing* 计) (**a**) examine a product so as to work out how it was made and how it operates with a view to manufacturing a similar product 逆向研制（对成品进行详细研究以制造出类似产品）(**b**) make sth by reverse-engineering a product 逆向制造

rework /ˌriːˈwɜːk; ˌriˈwɝk/ *v* [Tn] make changes in sth to improve it or to make it more accurate, suitable, etc 改进; 修订 : *rework the story so that it appeals to modern readers* 改写故事以吸引现代读者

▷ **reworking** *n* : *a reworking of Shakespeare's 'Hamlet'* 莎士比亚《哈姆雷特》新编

right-hand drive /ˌraɪthænd ˈdraɪv; ˌraɪthænd ˈdraɪv/ *adj* (of a vehicle) with the steering wheel on the right side of the driving compartment（指车辆）方向盘在右的，右座驾驶的 Cf 参看 LEFT-HAND DRIVE

right of abode /ˌraɪt əv əˈbəʊd; ˌraɪt əv əˈbod/ *n* [U] legal right for one to live in a certain place 居留权（在某地的法定居住权）: *After seven years you can claim the right of abode.* 七年后你就可以申请居留权。

right-of-centre /ˌraɪtəvˈsentə(r); ˌraɪtəvˈsɛntɚ/ *adj* having political opinions that tend more towards traditional values than to social reform 中间偏右的（政治主张趋于传统而不是革新社会的）: *a right-of-centre party/candidate* 中间偏右的政党 [候选人]

right-on /ˌraɪtˈɒn; ˌraɪtˈɑn/ *adj* (*infml* 口) aware of and sympathetic to current political and social issues, esp involving groups who are not well represented 思想激进的（留意并支持最新的政治和社会观点的，尤其同情其意见未能得到充分反映的阶层）: *a right-on feminist* 思想激进的女权主义者

right to life /ˌraɪt tə ˈlaɪf; ˌraɪt tə ˈlaɪf/ (also **pro-life**) *n* [usu attrib 通常作定语] opinion that it is morally wrong to abort a human foetus 生之权利，反对堕胎（认为堕胎违反道德的看法）: *the influence of the right to life lobby in the US* 美国反堕胎游说团体的影响力

▷ **right-to-lifer** *n* (*infml* 口) person holding strong anti-abortion views 强烈反对堕胎者

rightward /ˈraɪtwəd; ˈraɪtwɚd/ *adj, adv* on or to the right 在右（的）; 向右（的）; 右倾（的）: *a rightward movement* 右倾运动

ring fence /ˈrɪŋ fens; ˈrɪŋ fɛns/ *v* [Tn] protect or guarantee the safety of funds so that no one can lawfully make use of them for any but one specified purpose 严格保证（基金的专门用途）: *funds that have been ring-fenced from the main budget* 不纳入主要预算而受严格保证的基金

ring of steel /rɪŋ əv ˈstiːl; rɪŋ əv ˈstil/ *n* (*Brit infml* 口) form of protection usu for urban areas which effectively seals off such areas through the use of closed-circuit television, control zones and restricted access 铜墙铁壁般的保护网（通过使用闭路电视、设置控制区以及

限制外人进入等措施，有效地将城市某些地区与外界隔绝以提供保护）

riot gear /ˈraɪət ɡɪə(r); ˈraɪət ɡɪr/ *n* [U] equipment, esp protective clothing, used by the police when dealing with riots（警察的）防暴装备（尤指防护服）: *The police were in full riot gear, with shields and helmets.* 警员们配备盾牌、头盔和全副防暴武装。

riot girl /ˈraɪət ɡɜːl; ˈraɪət ɡɝl/ *n* (*US sl* 俚) young militant feminist who expresses her beliefs through rebellious behaviour, dress and music of the punk rock style 叛逆女孩（以叛逆的举止、服饰及蓬克摇滚乐表达其信仰的年轻激进女权主义者）

rip /rɪp; rɪp/ *v* [Tn] (*US infml* 口) attack verbally; criticize severely 口头攻击；严责: *The boss is going to rip you when he sees these figures.* 老板要是看到这些数字，肯定要把你骂得狗血淋头。

ripstop /ˈrɪpstɒp; ˈrɪpstɑp/ *adj* [attrib 作定语] (of fabric, clothing, etc) woven so that a tear will not spread（指织物、衣物等）织后防破裂的: *ripstop fabric* 防破裂织物

rite of passage /ˌraɪt əv ˈpæsɪdʒ; ˌraɪt əv ˈpæsɪdʒ/ *n* (often *pl* 常作复数) ceremony or event, eg marriage, marking an important stage in one's life 标志着人生进入重要阶段的仪式或事件（如婚姻）；人生庆典: *The scholar studied the fascinating rites of passage of the islanders.* 这位学者研究了该岛居民十分有趣的人生庆典。

ritualize, -ise /ˈrɪtʃʊəlaɪz; ˈrɪtʃʊəlaɪz/ *v* [I,Ipr,Tn] make sth into, or perform sth as, a ritual 使（某事）成惯例；将（某事）仪式化: *The old man's birthday celebrations were ritualized over the years by his many relatives.* 多年以来，这位老人的众多亲戚把他的生日庆典变成了惯例。

river abuse /ˈrɪvə əˌbjuːs; ˈrɪvɚ əˌbjus/ *n* [U] careless pollution of rivers and other waterways through uncontrolled discharge of waste matter（因乱排废物造成的）河道污染

road hump *n* = SPEED BUMP

road kill /ˈrəʊd kɪl; ˈrod kɪl/ *n* (*US infml* 口) **1** (**a**) killing of an animal by a vehicle on a road（车子在车道上）辗死（动物）(**b**) animal killed by a vehicle on a road（车道上）被辗死的动物 **2** (*fig* 比喻) helpless victim 孤立无援的受害者: *The defeated team members lay about looking like road kills on a stormy day.* 比赛败阵的队员横七竖八地躺着，就像暴风雨中死于轮下的受害者一样。

road rage /ˈrəʊd reɪdʒ; ˈrod redʒ/ *n* [U] violent outburst of anger often leading to abusive speech or even physical attack, caused by the frustrations of urban traffic 车道上引发的狂怒（因城市交通堵塞而使人大发其火，常导致叫骂或打架）: *The beating of a lorry driver who refused to move over and allow other vehicles to pass was attributed to road rage.* 那卡车司机拒绝挪动，不让其他车辆通过而挨了一顿揍，这全都是交通堵塞引发的狂怒造成的。

rock-hard /ˌrɒkˈhɑːd; ˌrɑkˈhɑrd/ *adj* extremely hard, strong or tough 极其坚硬的；十分坚强的；非常结实的: *a rock-hard body/bed* 极其强壮的身体、结实的床 ○ *He may look soft, but underneath he's rock-hard.* 他外表也许柔弱，内里却极为刚强。

rogue trader /ˌrəʊɡ ˈtreɪdə(r); ˌroɡ ˈtredɚ/ *n* (*infml* 口) dealer with a bank, finance house, etc, who acts without proper supervision or control and risks incurring huge losses 痞子交易商（在与银行、金融公司等的交易中未受适当监督或控制而可能造成巨大损失的人）

role model /ˈrəʊl mɒdl; ˈrol mɑdl̩/ *n* person who may be taken as an example to follow（指人）典范，楷模，榜样: *None of my teachers were particularly good role models.* 我的老师没有一个堪作楷模。

Rollerblade /ˈrəʊləbleɪd; ˈrolɚbled/ (also **rollerblade**) *n* (usu *pl* 通常作复数) (*propr* 专利名) type of roller-skate with the wheels set in one straight line beneath the boot, giving an appearance and action similar to that of an ice-skate 刀刃式旱冰鞋（轮子成一直线排列，其形状与滑行效果类似冰鞋的旱冰鞋）

▷ **rollerblade** *v* [I] move along on rollerblades 穿刀刃式旱冰鞋滑行

NOTE 注: formed on analogy with *roller-skate* but with the added idea that the wheels form a *blade* 由 roller-skate（旱冰鞋）一词类推构成，增加了轮子的排列类似刀刃 (blade) 的意思

rolling /ˈrəʊlɪŋ; ˈrolɪŋ/ *adj* [attrib 作定语] **1** rising and falling; undulating (UNDULATE[A-Z]) 高低起伏的；不平的；崎岖的: *rolling hills/countryside* 高低起伏的山岭 *[乡间]* **2** done, carried out, etc in regular stages or at regular intervals over a period of time 周而复始的；定期举行的: *a rolling programme/schedule of motorway repairs* 一个定期检修高速公路的方案 *[计划表]*

rolling drunk /ˌrəʊlɪŋ ˈdrʌŋk; ˌrolɪŋ ˈdrʌŋk/ *adj* [pred 作表语] so drunk that one cannot control one's movements 烂醉: *The party has just started but he is already rolling drunk!* 晚会刚开始，他却烂醉如泥了。

rolling news /ˈrəʊlɪŋ njuːz, *US* nuːz; ˈrolɪŋ nuz/ *n* [sing] twenty-four-hour radio news service（二十四小时的）滚动新闻

roll-out /ˈrəʊlaʊt; ˈrolaʊt/ *n* **1** (**a**) official wheeling out of a new aircraft or spacecraft for public viewing（新飞机或太空船的）首次正式公开亮相 (**b**) official launch of a new product（新产品的）正式上市: *Lancome plan the roll-out of their new perfume for May.* 兰金计划让他们的新香水在五月上市。 **2** part of a landing during which an aircraft travels along the runway, losing speed（飞机着陆时在跑道上的）滑行

romaine *n* (*US*) = COS[1(A-Z)]

Romo /ˈrəʊməʊ; ˈromo/ *n* [U,C] **1** 1990s revival of the NEW ROMANTIC movement in pop music, esp of the electronic kind, inspired by that of the early 1980s 新浪漫主义复兴运动（发生于 1990 年代的运动，由 1980 年代初的流行音乐（尤其是电子音乐）新浪漫主义运动所引起） **2** follower of the Romo trend 新浪漫主义复兴运动的追随者

roo bar *n* = BULL BAR

rootsy /ˈruːtsɪ; ˈrutsɪ/ *adj* (*infml* 口) (of music) not commercialized, full-blooded, esp showing traditional origins（指音乐）非商业化的，纯正的，（尤指）体现传统风格的

NOTE 注: from *roots* meaning 'origins' 源自 roots 一词，意指'根源'

Rottweiler /ˈrɒtwaɪlə(r), -vaɪlə(r); ˈrɑtwaɪlɚ, -vaɪlɚ/ *n* breed of large dog that is potentially aggressive and can be trained as a guard dog 罗特韦尔狗（一种高大的、攻击型的狗，可训练来看门）

rough edges /ˌrʌf ˈedʒɪz; ˌrʌf ˈɛdʒɪz/ *n* [pl] aspects of a person's character which are not ready or suitable, or of a thing which are not properly finished（人性格上的或物体表面的）粗糙面，棱角: *It'll take a few months to knock the rough edges off the new trainees.* 得用几个月的时间来磨平这些新学员的棱角。

rough justice /ˌrʌf ˈdʒʌstɪs; ˌrʌf ˈdʒʌstɪs/ *n* [U] punishment that is considered unfair, or is fair but not official or legally allowed 粗暴惩罚（被视作不公正或虽公正但不合法的惩罚）: *The suspected arsonist received rough justice at the hands of the crowd when his own house was burned down.* 纵火嫌疑犯遭到群众的粗暴惩罚，他们把他自己的房子也烧掉了。

rough stuff /ˈrʌf stʌf; ˈrʌf stʌf/ *n* [U] (*infml* 口) violent behaviour 粗野的举止；暴力行为: *We don't want any rough stuff in this pub.* 我们不希望在这个酒吧里有任何暴力行为。

RSI *abbr* 缩写 = REPETITIVE STRAIN INJURY
rubber bullet /ˌrʌbə 'bʊlɪt; ˌrʌbɚ 'bʊlɪt/ *n* bullet which is a small metal ball coated with rubber, used by riot police to break up crowds 橡皮子弹（防暴警察用于驱散人群的、在小金属球外面包有橡皮的子弹）: *Injuries can be caused by rubber bullets and even fatalities sometimes occur.* 橡皮子弹可能造成伤害，有时甚至造成死亡。
rubber chicken circuit /ˌrʌbə 'tʃɪkɪn sɜːkɪt; ˌrʌbɚ 'tʃɪkɪn sɝkɪt/ *n* series of fund-raising functions, esp meals, attended by a politician or a celebrity and which guests have paid for. The money goes to campaign expenses or to a charity supported by the celebrity 巡回老鸡宴（有某政客或名流出席的客人自行付费的一连串募捐聚会，尤指宴会。募得的资金用作竞选费用或捐给该名流资助的慈善机构）
NOTE 注： probably called this because chicken is frequently served and it may be rather tough from having been cooked earlier 取此名称可能因为鸡是每次宴会的常备菜，且因预先煮好变得老而难嚼之故
rug /rʌg; rʌg/ *n* (*infml* 口) partial or complete wig（部分或整个）假发 Cf 参看 HAIR-PIECE (HAIR^A-Z)
rug rat /'rʌg ræt; 'rʌg ræt/ *n* (*US sl* 俚) child 小家伙；小孩
rulebook /'ruːlbʊk; 'rulbʊk/ *n* written set of rules governing a game or other circumstances（书面）游戏规则；规则手册: *There's nothing in the rulebook to say that you can't play in jeans if you want to.* 游戏规则里并没有说不许穿牛仔裤。
rumble strip /'rʌmbl strɪp; 'rʌmbl̩ strɪp/ *n* (*infml* 口) any of a series of rough strips across a road, eg before a ROUNDABOUT *n* 2^A-Z. The noise made when a vehicle goes over them is intended to make a driver drive more slowly 隆隆标志带，响带（如环行交叉路口的凸起的横条，汽车驶过时会发出隆隆声，提醒司机放慢车速）
rumbling /'rʌmblɪŋ; 'rʌmblɪŋ/ *n* **1** deep low continuous sound 隆隆声；辘辘声: *the rumbling of the volcano* 火山发出的隆隆声 **2** (esp *pl* 尤作复数) (**a**) signs that people are not satisfied with sth 不满的表示: *rumblings of discontent/unease amongst the workers* 工人中不满 *[不安]* 的怨言 (**b**) rumour 谣言；谣传: *takeover rumblings* 关于接管的谣言
run /rʌn; rʌn/ *v* [Ipr] (*US*) (usu infinitive 通常用不定式) ~ **with (sth)** take an idea further and see how it works out in practical terms 从实践中检验（某观点）: *Let's give him the chance to run with the concept and see what he is capable of.* 给他个机会，让他照这个想法做，看看他到底能力如何。
running light /'rʌnɪŋ laɪt; 'rʌnɪŋ laɪt/ *n* each of a set of small lights on a motor vehicle that remains lit while the vehicle is running, used to ensure that the vehicle is clearly visible if the driver has to leave it briefly in a risky position 行驶灯（机动车辆行驶时一直亮着的一组小灯之一，用以确保紧急情况下司机离车后车辆仍能被清楚地看见）

Ss

SAD *abbr* 缩写 = SEASONAL AFFECTIVE DISORDER
sad /sæd; sæd/ *adj* (*derog* 贬) causing one to feel contempt and scorn; nerdish and totally uncool 令人鄙夷的；愚蠢又土气的: *They're really sad people. They think that it's fun to go on a coach tour with their parents.* 他们真可笑，竟然觉得和父母一起坐长途公共汽车旅行是件趣事。
saddo /'sædəʊ; 'sædo/ *n* (*infml derog* 口，贬) person regarded as socially inadequate, unfashionable, or otherwise contemptible; NERD 不善交际的人；不合潮流的人；讨厌鬼；蠢货: *Faxing is cooler than phoning, only saddos still use the phone.* 发传真比打电话棒多了，只有老土还用电话。
NOTE 注： from *sad* with the meaning of *socially inadequate, pathetic* with an ending similar to that found in WINO^A-Z and SICKO 由 sad（不善社交的、可怜的）一词与类似 wino（酒鬼）及 sicko（令人讨厌的人）等词的词尾构成
safe haven /seɪf 'heɪvn; sef 'hevən/ *n* protected zone in a country where members of a religious or ethnic minority can be safe from persecution, usu guaranteed by an international monitoring force under the United Nations, etc 安全区，保护区（为使弱势宗教团体或少数民族免受迫害而开辟的区域，通常由联合国等管辖下的国际监督部队提供保护）: *safe havens for the Kurds in Iraq* 在伊拉克为库尔德人开辟的安全区
safe sex /seɪf 'seks; sef 'sɛks/ *n* [U] sexual activity during which partners take measures to protect themselves from infection with sexually transmitted diseases, esp AIDS^A-Z, eg by using a condom 安全性交，安全性行为（如采用避孕套等措施以防止性病，尤其是防止染上爱滋病的性交活动）: *Safe sex is the slogan of the nineties, and few would dispute its advice.* 安全性交是九十年代的口号，很少人会对此持异议。
safety helmet *n* (*esp Brit*) = HARD HAT
saggy /'sægɪ; 'sægɪ/ *adj* tending to SAG^A-Z 下陷的；下垂的: *a saggy mattress* 下陷的床垫 ○ *saggy skin on the face* 脸上松弛的皮肤
sailboard *n* = WINDSURFER 1 (WIND^1(A-Z))
salaryman /'sælərɪmæn, -mən; 'sælərɪmæn/ *n* (in Japan) white-collar worker（日本）白领雇员
sales pitch *n* = PITCH^3 9^A-Z
sales representative /'seɪlz reprɪˌzentətɪv; 'selz rɛprɪˌzɛntətɪv/ (also *infml* 口语作 **sales rep, rep**) *n* salesman employed by a company to sell its goods in a certain area（公司在某一地区的）销售代表，营业代表: *He became a sales representative for a vacuum cleaner company.* 他成了一家吸尘器公司的销售代表。
salsa /'sælsə, *US* 'sɑːlsə; 'sɑlsə/ *n* [U] **1** kind of Latin-American style of music and dance 萨尔萨歌舞（一种拉丁美洲风格的音乐和舞蹈）**2** spicy sauce made from tomatoes, onions, chillies etc. 墨西哥辣酱
sampling /'sɑːmplɪŋ, *US* sæ-; 'sæmplɪŋ/ *n* [U] (in electronic music) technique or process of taking a piece of digitally encoded sound and re-using it, often in a modified form, as part of a composition or recording（电子音乐）采样，取样（对以数字编码的声音进行取样的技术或过程，通常加以改变后重新用于创作或录音）
sand surfing /'sænd sɜːfɪŋ; 'sænd sɝfɪŋ/ *n* [U] sport carried out on beaches or other sandy surfaces in which one sits or stands on a flat board with a mast and sail attached. When the wind fills the sail, the board moves rapidly across the sand 沙地冲浪，冲沙（一种在沙滩或其他沙地上进行的运动。运动者坐在或站在装有桅杆和帆的平板上，当风鼓起帆时，板便会在沙地上快速移动）
sandwich class /'sændwɪdʒ klɑːs, *US* -wɪtʃ klæs; 'sænwɪtʃ 'klæs/ *n* [Gp] group of middle-income earners who are too well-off to qualify for any help from the state but who are not rich 三明治阶层，夹心阶层（既没资格拿国家补助又不太富裕的中等收入阶层）: *Housing loans for the sandwich class have been well-received.* 为三明治阶层提供的住房贷款受到了欢迎。
sarin /'særɪn; 'særɪn/ *n* [U] toxic organic phosphorus compound which attacks the nervous systems of humans and animals, developed in Germany during the Second World War 甲氟膦酸异丙酯，沙林（二次世界大战期

间德国研制出的有毒有机磷化物，能侵害人和动物的神经系统）

satellite dish /ˈsætəlaɪt dɪʃ; ˈsætəlaɪt dɪʃ/ *n* device shaped like a dish, usu set up on the wall or roof of a building, which receives radio or other signals relayed from a SATELLITE 1(b)A-Z 卫星抛物面天线，碟形天线（通常安装在墙上或屋顶上，以接收人造卫星发射的无线电或其他信号的碟形装置）

saturation bombing /sætʃʊəˈreɪʃn ˌbɒmɪŋ; sætʃəˈreʃən ˌbɑmɪŋ/ *n* [U] (*military* 军) intensive bombing of an area using one wave of bombs after another 密集轰炸（对某一地区一次又一次地集中轰炸）: *Vietnam still shows the scars of the saturation bombing by American planes.* 在越南仍可见到美军飞机密集轰炸留下的创伤。

schlock /ʃlɒk; ʃlɑk/ *n* [U] (*US sl* 俚) things that are cheap and of poor quality; TRASH 1A-Z 价廉质次的东西；劣品；次货: *the cheap end of town, where the stores are full of schlock* 镇上贫穷地区的商店里次货充斥

▷ **schlocker** *n* (*US sl* 俚) thing or person that is considered worthless 没用的人或物；废物

schmo /ʃməʊ; ʃmo/ (also **schmuck**) *n* (*US sl derog* 俚，贬) foolish or contemptible person 傻瓜；鼠辈

schmuck *n* = SCHMO

science park /ˈsaɪəns pɑːk; ˈsaɪəns pɑrk/ *n* area in which buildings with facilities for scientific research or for the development of industries based on science are grouped 科技园（科技研究机构集中的地区）

scope out /skəʊp ˈaʊt; skop ˈaʊt/ *v* [Tn] move out into and take over; pioneer 迁移进并占据；开拓: *Some hogs that escaped and now live in the wild may be scoping out more space.* 一些逃走的猪现在生活在野外，它们的活动范围可能越来越大。

scorch /skɔːtʃ; skɔrtʃ/ *v* (*US infml* 口) [Tn] attack verbally very fiercely and critically 严辞苛责；口头攻击: *At a public meeting, the local council were thoroughly scorched by residents for their failure to act over increasing violence on the streets of the borough.* 在一次公开会议上，市民严厉批评地方议会未能采取措施对付该地区日益增多的街头暴力事件。

score draw /ˈskɔː drɔː; ˈskɔr drɔ/ *n* result of a football match in which both teams get an equal number of goals（足球比赛的）平局 Cf 参看 SCORELESS

scoreless /ˈskɔːləs; ˈskɔrləs/ *adj* (eg in football) with neither side making a score（足球比赛等）两队均未得分的

Scouse /skaʊs; skaus/ *n* **1** [U] DIALECTA-Z of Liverpool 利物浦方言: *For a few years, Scouse was the language of pop music, when the Beatles from Liverpool became the best known group in the world.* 有几年利物浦方言成为流行音乐的语言，皆因那时来自利物浦的披头士乐队成为世界最著名的演唱组。**2** (also **Scouser**) [C] native of Liverpool 利物浦人

scratch card /ˈskrætʃ kɑːd; ˈskrætʃ kɑrd/ *n* card partly or wholly covered with a thick waxy coating. When this is scratched away a symbol is revealed indicating whether or not a prize has been won in a competition 刮刮乐，刮刮卡（部分或全部涂上一层厚蜡的卡片，根据刮掉蜡后显露的图案判断是否中奖）: *a winning symbol on the scratch card* 刮刮乐上的中奖图案 ○ *Scratch cards! Win instant prizes!* 快买刮刮乐，即刮即中！

screen saver /ˈskriːn seɪvə(r); ˈskrin sevɚ/ *n* (*computing* 计) **1** program which comes into effect after a set time and replaces an unchanging screen with a moving image or with a blank screen, thus preventing damage to the phosphor on the monitor 屏幕保护程序（当一幅画面在屏幕上显示的时间超出设定的限制时即启动的程序，它将画面变成空白或代之以不断移动的图像，以保护显示器上的磷质）**2** image displayed by a screen saver 屏幕保护图像: *Flying toasters is my favourite screen saver.* 飞舞的烤面包炉是我最喜爱的屏幕保护图像。

screenwriter /ˈskriːnraɪtə(r); ˈskrinraɪtɚ/ *n* person who writes the words to be spoken by actors in films 电影剧本作家 Cf 参看 SCRIPT-WRITER (SCRIPTA-Z), PLAYWRIGHT (PLAY1(A-Z))

scroll bar /ˈskrəʊl bɑː(r); ˈskrol ˌbɑr/ *n* (*computing* 计) narrow bar located at the side or bottom of the display containing the image of a cursor which can be moved by using a mouse, thus allowing the desired part of the display to be visible 滚动条（视窗旁边或底部带滚动按钮的窄条，可用鼠标按住拖动以便浏览）Cf 参看 SCROLL *v*A-Z

scrunch-dry /ˈskrʌntʃdraɪ; ˈskrʌntʃdraɪ/ *v* dry one's hair using a hair dryer while with one hand continuously crunching up and releasing portions of hair 揉搓吹干（边用吹风机吹，边用手揉搓头发）: *If you scrunch-dry your hair, it'll look more natural than if you just blow-dry it using a brush.* 你要是边用吹风机吹，边用手揉搓，头发看上去就比吹时光用刷子梳理要自然得多。

scuzzball /ˈskʌzbɔːl; ˈskʌzbɔl/ *n* (*US sl* 俚) person whom one finds completely disgusting 令人极其讨厌的人

sea change /ˈsiː tʃeɪndʒ; ˈsi tʃendʒ/ *n* (usu *sing* 通常作单数) complete and striking change, esp one where the end result is unexpected and not able to be predicted 巨变（尤指后果难以估计和无法预见的）: *one of those momentous events which cause a sea change in public attitudes* 使公众态度发生一百八十度大转变的重大事件

NOTE 注： first used in *The Tempest* by Shakespeare, where a lament is sung for the hero's supposedly drowned father which includes the words: *Nothing of him that doth fade but doth suffer a sea-change into something rich and strange* 莎士比亚在《暴风雨》中首次使用此词，此剧中有一首为主人公疑遭淹死的父亲唱的挽歌，当中有这样的词句：'他的全身消失后在海中经历剧变，化成瑰宝，富丽而奇幻'

seasonal affective disorder /siːznl əˌfektɪv dɪsˈɔːdə(r); siznl̩ əˈfɛktɪv dɪsˈɔrdɚ/ *n* [U] (*abbr* 缩写 **SAD**) (*medical* 医) depressive state associaed with late autumn and winter and thought to be caused by a lack of light 季节性抑郁症（秋末或冬季出现的精神抑郁，据认为由光照不足而引起）: *People with seasonal affective disorder often overeat to make themselves feel better.* 季节性抑郁症患者常常吃得过量，让自己好受一些。

secessionist /sɪˈseʃənɪst; sɪˈsɛʃənɪst/ *n* (*politics* 政) person who favours the SECESSION (SECEDEA-Z) of one part of a country from the rest, usu for reasons of culture, ethnic origins or religion 分离主义者（通常因文化、种族或宗教等原因主张将国家的一部分领土分离出去的人）: *The Quebecois may soon have a majority of secessionists, and then Canada will be split into English- and French-speaking regions.* 魁北克人中可能不久会以分离主义者占大多数，这样加拿大就会分裂成说英语和说法语的两个地区。

second ballot /ˌsekənd ˈbælət; ˌsɛkənd ˈbælət/ *n* second round of voting, esp for the leader of a political party, when no clear result was obtained in the first round（因第一轮投票未有明确结果而举行的）第二轮投票（尤指选举政党领袖）: *Those who are eligible to stand in a second ballot must have obtained a prescribed proportion of the votes in the first ballot.* 候选人必须在第一轮选举中获得规定比例的选票，方有资格参加第二轮选举。

second home /ˌsekənd ˈhəʊm; ˌsɛkənd ˈhom/ *n* **1** house or flat owned by sb in addition to their main residence, which they use only part of the time, esp for holidays, and which may be let or left empty for the remainder of the time 第二住所（除主要住宅之外的房屋，主要供度假使用，其他时间可能出租或闲置）: *a second home in the Welsh countryside* 在威尔士乡下的第二住所 Cf 参看 HOLIDAY HOME **2** [sing] place, eg a city or a country, that sb knows well, feels comfortable in and has strong personal connections with, but which is not their home 第二故乡 : *I was born in New York and still live there most of the year, but Paris is my second home.* 我生于纽约，大部分时间也住在那里，但巴黎是我的第二故乡。

second name /ˈsekənd neɪm, sekənd ˈneɪm; sɛkənd ˈnem/ *n* (usu *sing* 通常作单数) (**a**) SURNAME[A-Z] 姓 (**b**) second personal name; MIDDLE NAME (MIDDLE[A-Z]) 中间名 : *'Do you have a second name?' 'Yes, it's Angela.'* '你有中间名吗？' '有，叫安杰拉。'

second nature /ˌsekənd ˈneɪtʃə(r); ˌsɛkənd ˈnetʃɚ/ *n* [U] ~ **(to sb) (to do sth)** tendency to behave always in a similar way, so that one does it unconsciously and instinctively 第二天性；根深蒂固的习惯 : *It's second nature to me to check my e-mail as soon as I arrive at work.* 我已经养成了习惯，一上班就去查看我的电子邮件。

secret ballot /ˌsiːkrət ˈbælət; ˌsikrət ˈbælət/ *n* way of voting which allows the voter to conceal his or her choice; occasion on which such a ballot takes place 无记名投票；秘密投票 : *The leader was elected for the first time by secret ballot.* 第一次以无记名投票的方式选出领导。

seeker /ˈsiːkə(r); ˈsikɚ/ *n* (often in compounds 常用以构成复合词) person who seeks the specified thing 追寻者；寻求者；追求者 : *an asylum/sun/fun seeker* 寻求庇护者、喜爱阳光的人、寻欢作乐的人 ○ *seekers after truth* 追求真理的人们

see-through /ˈsiːθruː; ˈsiθru/ *adj* (of material) very thin so that one can see through it; SHEER[1] 2[A-Z]（指布料）透明的，薄得几乎透明的 : *a see-through blouse* 透明的女衬衫

segue /ˈsegweɪ; ˈsɛgwe/ *v* [Ipr] (*esp US*) (esp of a piece of music, a scene in a film, a conversation, etc) change into another piece of music, scene, conversation, etc without interruption（尤指乐曲、电影场面、谈话等）不间断地切换（成另一乐曲、电影场面、谈话等）: *The scene of the battle segued almost imperceptibly into a view of the peaceful village street, now under a terrible threat.* 战争的场面不知不觉地切换成面临严重威胁的宁静乡村街道。

selective reduction *n* = FOETAL REDUCTION

self-access /ˌselfˈækses; ˌsɛlfˈæksɛs/ *n* [U] method of learning which allows a student to choose and use appropriate materials for private study 自行选择资料自修 : *The books are colour-coded for self-access.* 这些以色彩分类的书供读者自学之用。 ○ *self-access materials/centres* 供自行选择的自修资料、自选资料自修中心

self-adhesive /ˌselfədˈhiːsɪv; ˌsɛlfədˈhisɪv/ *adj* covered on one side or on part of one side with a stricky substance, and so able to stick to surfaces without glue, etc being applied 自粘的 : *self-adhesive tiles/envelopes* 自粘瓦 *[信封]*

self-build /selfˈbɪld; sɛlfˈbɪld/ *adj* [often attrib 常作定语] building of homes by their future owners 自盖房屋的 : *a self-build cooperative/housing association* 自盖房屋业主团体 *[协会]*

self-congratulation /ˌselfkənˌgrætʃəˈleɪʃn; sɛlfkənˌgrætʃəˈleʃn̩/ *n* [U] satisfaction with and praise for one's own achievements 自我欣赏；沾沾自喜 : *speeches of self-congratulation* 自我欣赏的演讲

▷ **self-congratulatory** *adj* : *self-congratulatory comments* 自我欣赏的评论

self-contradictory /ˌselfˌkɒntrəˈdɪktərɪ; ˌsɛlfˌkɑntrəˈdɪktərɪ/ *adj* containing or expressing two or more ideas that are not consistent with each other 自相矛盾的 : *Promises both to expand social services and to reduce personal taxation seem at first glance to be self-contradictory.* 乍一看，扩展社会福利和降低个人税收的承诺是自相矛盾的。

self-fulfilling /ˌselffʊlˈfɪlɪŋ; ˌsɛlffulˈfɪlɪŋ/ *adj* (esp of a prophecy) will be proven true because the predicted happenings are actually caused by the prophetic act itself（尤指预言）本身自会实现的（因为预期会发生的事其实是由预言导致的）: *Warnings of a dangerous downturn in the market by someone as influential as the President of the American Stock Exchange are likely to be self-fulfilling.* 关于市场有衰退之虞的警告，既然出自美国证券交易所主席这样有影响的人物之口，自然很有可能成为事实。

self-government /ˌselfˈgʌvənmənt; ˌsɛlfˈgʌvɚnmənt/ *n* [U] government or control of a territory, an organization, etc by its own people or members 自治

▷ **self-governing** *adj* : *a self-governing province/state* 自治省 *[州]*

self-inflicted /ˌselfɪnˈflɪktɪd; ˌsɛlfɪnˈflɪktɪd/ *adj* (of an injury, a wound, etc) being inflicted deliberately on oneself（指损伤、创伤等）加于自身的，自己施加的 : *Some soldiers tried to avoid the fighting by shooting themselves in the foot or giving themselves similar self-inflicted wounds.* 有些士兵为了逃避打仗就开枪击伤自己的脚或作类似的自残。 ○ (*fig* 比喻) *The damage he caused to his career was entirely self-inflicted.* 他事业上遭受的损害完全是咎由自取。

sell-off /ˈselɒf; ˈsɛlɑf/ *n* sale of government shares (SHARE[1] 3[A-Z]) or of state-owned services to individual shareholders or to private companies 出售国家股份或国有服务机构（给个人股东或私人公司）: *the government sell-off of the water-industry to shareholders in the late 80s* 政府在 80 年代末将自来水企业的股份出售给个人股东

semi-skimmed /semɪˈskɪmd; sɛmɪˈskɪmd/ *adj* (of milk) from which some but not all of the fat has been removed by skimming (SKIM 1[A-Z])（指奶）半脱脂的

▷ **semi-skimmed** *n* [U] semi-skimmed milk 半脱脂奶 : *Semi-skimmed has less than half the fat of full-cream milk.* 半脱脂奶所含脂肪不及全脂奶的一半。

Semtex /ˈsemteks; ˈsɛmtɛks/ *n* [U] (*propr* 专利名) explosive used esp to make bombs, which is light and easily moulded into different shapes 塞姆泰克斯炸药（一种质轻且易铸成不同形状的炸药，尤用于制造炸弹）；塑胶炸药 Cf 参看 PLASTIC EXPLOSIVE (PLASTIC[A-Z])

serial killer /sɪərɪəl ˈkɪlə(r), ˈsɪərɪəl kɪlə(r); sɪrɪəl ˈkɪlɚ, ˈsɪrɪəl kɪlɚ/ *n* person who commits a series of similar murders with no apparent motive（无明显动机的）连环杀手，系列杀人狂 : *One of the earliest serial killers on record is Jack the Ripper.* '开膛手' 杰克是记录在案的一个早期系列杀手。 Cf 参看 SPREE KILLER

NOTE 注 : formed on the pattern of *serial killing* 以 serial killing（连环杀手）一词的结构形成

serial monogamy /sɪərɪəl məˈnɒgəmɪ; sɪrɪəl məˈnɑgəmɪ/ *n* [U] mode of life characterized by a sequence of monogamous (MONOGAMY[A-Z]) affairs with different partners 连贯式一夫一妻制（先后与不同人结婚，但始终保持一夫一妻制的生活方式）

serious /ˈsɪərɪəs; ˈsɪrɪəs/ *adj* [attrib 作定语] (*infml* 口) in large or even excessive amounts 大量的；过多的 : *The serious money is going into property with the money-market so uncertain.* 货币市场十分不稳定，以致大量的钱流入房地产市场。 ○ *serious drinkers* 酗酒者

▷ **seriously** *adv* (*infml* 口) very much so; intensely 非常；极其 : *The wedding took place at a seriously* *luxurious hotel.* 婚礼在一家极为豪华的饭店里举行。○ *I intend to have a seriously good time.* 我打算尽情地玩乐。

NOTE 注： different from the established usage of *seriously* which usually precedes sth bad or undesirable, eg *seriously ill/injured/worried,etc* ☆ seriously 一词本习惯置于表示坏的或令人不快的词前，如 seriously ill/injured/worried（病重、重伤、十分担忧）等，此处用法不同

seronegative /ˌsɪərəʊˈnegətɪv; ˌsɪroˈnɛgətɪv/ *adj* (*medical* 医) giving a negative result in a test of blood serum, eg for the presence of a virus 血清反应阴性的 Cf 参看 SEROPOSITIVE

seropositive /ˌsɪərəʊˈpɒzɪtɪv; ˌsɪroˈpɑzɪtɪv/ *adj* (*medical* 医) giving a positive result in a test of blood serum, eg for the presence of a virus 血清反应阳性的 Cf 参看 SERONEGATIVE

server /ˈsɜːvə(r); ˈsɝvɚ/ *n* (*computing* 计) central computer which contains a store of data and to which a number of other computers is linked 服务器（储存数据的中央计算机，与其他计算机连接）Cf 参看 CLIENT-SERVER

set-aside /ˈsetəsaɪd; ˈsɛtəsaɪd/ *n* [sing] policy of taking land out of production in order to reduce crop surpluses（为减少农作物过剩而采取的）农田闲置措施

set-top box /ˈsettɒp bɒks; ˈsɛttɑp bɑks/ *n* digital decoding device used to connect a domestic television set to a source of signals such as a cable-network or communications satellite 数字解码匣，数字解码器（将家用电视机与诸如有线电视网或通信卫星等信号源连接起来的装置）

sex line /ˈseks laɪn; ˈsɛks laɪn/ *n* telephone service offering sexually-explicit conversation during which the caller can indulge his or her sexual fantasies 色情电话线，性热线（提供色情谈话的电话服务，打电话者藉此满足自己的性幻想）

sex-positive /seksˈpɒzɪtɪv; sɛksˈpɑzɪtɪv/ *adj* characterized by a positive attitude towards sexual instincts and desires 性肯定的（对性冲动和性欲持肯定态度）

NOTE 注： opposite is *sex-negative* 其反义词为 sex-negative

sex reassignment /ˌseks riːəˈsaɪnmənt; ˌsɛks riəˈsaɪnmənt/ *n* [U] deliberate choice made by a doctor to assign a baby to either male or female sex, in a case when the baby has been born with malformation of the genitals. This decision is then confirmed by surgery and hormone treatment 性别再指定（婴儿出生后发现生殖器出现畸形时，由医生选定性别并做手术和施以激素治疗的做法）

sex tourism /ˈseks tʊərɪzəm; ˈsɛks tʊrɪzəm/ *n* [U] arrangement and taking of holidays in places where sex is widely available for money with the purpose of having as much sexual intercourse as possible 性旅游（到充满色情场所的地方、以满足性欲为目的的旅游）: *The city is trying to shed its image as one of the world's centres for sex tourism.* 该城市正努力摆脱其作为世界知名的性旅游中心的形象。

▷ **sex tourist** *n*

sexy /ˈseksɪ; ˈsɛksɪ/ *adj* (*infml* 口) (**a**) interesting and attractive 有趣的；迷人的：*The airport terminal has got a sexy new look since the recent renovation.* 机场大楼经最近翻修后，变得面貌一新，引人瞩目。(**b**) trendy, in fashion 时髦的；流行的：*Suddenly it's sexy to talk about your financial planning.* 突然间，个人财务计划成了时髦话题。

Shaker /ˈʃeɪkə(r); ˈʃekɚ/ *n* **1** member of a Christian religious group in the US which now has very few members. Shakers live simple lives, free of many material possessions, and do not have sexual relations 震颤派教徒（属于美国一个成员极少的基督教团体，生活俭朴且禁欲）**2** (also **shaker**) style of furniture, usu made of wood, which is plain, simple and functional 震颤派式家具（一种木制、简单实用的家具）: *Shaker-style kitchens are very popular nowadays.* 如今震颤派式厨房家具非常流行。

NOTE 注： the style was named after the Shakers who became famous for their simple, functional carpentry. 震颤派 (Shakers) 以擅长制造简单、实用的木器而著名

shakers ⇨ MOVERS AND SHAKERS

shaman /ˈʃæmən, ˈʃɑːmən; ˈʃæmən/ *n* (*pl* **shamans**) priest in certain religions who is believed to be able to contact the gods or spirits and to cure people 巫师；巫医

shape /ʃeɪp; ʃep/ *v* (phr v) **shape up** (*infml* 口) improve one's behaviour; meet required standards; work harder 改进行为举止；符合规定的标准；努力：*If you don't shape up, you'll fail your exams.* 你要是不努力，考试就通不过。

shareholding /ˈʃeəhəʊldɪŋ; ˈʃɛrholdɪŋ/ *n* percentage of a public company or business held as a number of shares 持股数；股权：*own a majority shareholding* 持多数股

shareware /ˈʃeəweə(r); ˈʃɛrwɛr/ *n* [U] software which may be freely exchanged and used for a trial period but which must be registered and paid for if it continues to be used 试用软件，共享软件（试用期间可免费交换使用，但其后如继续使用必须登记且付费的软件）

shellfire /ˈʃelfaɪə(r); ˈʃɛlfaɪɚ/ *n* [U] attacks or explosions caused by the firing of shells (SHELL 3A-Z) 炮击：*The town came under heavy shellfire.* 该镇遭到猛烈的炮击。

shell suit /ˈʃel suːt; ˈʃɛl sut/ *n* loose, casual top and matching trousers or single garment worn by men and women. Shell suits are often made of a light, slightly shiny material and are often brightly coloured 贝壳装，贝壳衣（一种宽松的休闲套装或单件休闲服，分男、女装，常以略微闪光的轻质衣料制成，颜色一般较鲜艳）

sheltered accommodation /ˌʃeltəd əkɒməˈdeɪʃn; ˌʃɛltɚd əkɑməˈdeʃən/ *n* [U] (in Britain) housing specially designed for elderly or disabled people who are able to be fairly independent but need medical and social help to be readily available（英国）庇护公寓（特别为那些生活尚能自理，但需要随时能得到医疗和社会帮助的老年人或残疾人设计的住所）

sheltered workshop /ˌʃeltəd ˈwɜːkʃɒp; ˌʃɛltɚd ˈwɝkʃɑp/ *n* place where people with a variety of physical or mental disabilities can work in an environment which is adapted to their particular needs（供残疾人或弱智者工作的）福利工场，庇护工场

shiatsu /ʃiːˈætsuː; ʃiˈætsu/ *n* [U] (*Japanese* 日语) kind of therapy in which pressure is applied to sb's body with the fingers, based on the same principles as Chinese acupuncture 指压按摩疗法（此疗法与中国的针刺疗法原理相同）

shift the goalposts (idm 习语) = MOVE THE GOALPOSTS (MOVE2 11A-Z)

shit scared /ˌʃɪt ˈskeəd; ʃɪt ˈskɛrd/ (also **scared shitless**) *adj* [pred 作表语] (*sl usu* ⚠ 俚，通常作避讳语) very frightened 大受惊吓；极恐惧：*I was shit scared when the bull turned towards me.* 当那头牛掉头冲向我时，我真是吓坏了。

shocking pink /ˌʃɒkɪŋ ˈpɪŋk; ˌʃɑkɪŋ ˈpɪŋk/ *n* very bright pink colour 鲜艳的粉红色

▷ **shocking pink** *adj* : *a shocking pink dress* 鲜粉红色的连衣裙

shock jock /ˈʃɒk dʒɒk; ˈʃɑk dʒɑk/ *n* (*US*) radio disc-jockey who is deliberately offensive or provocative, eg by being abusive to callers 令人震惊的电台音乐节目

主持人（故意冒犯或激怒听众，如对打电话来的听众恶语相加的电台音乐节目主持人）

shoebox /ˈʃu:bɒks; ˈʃubɑks/ *n* **1** box in which a new pair of shoes is packed when sb has bought it 鞋盒 **2** (*fig* 比喻) very small room in which to live or work 斗室；小屋；蜗居：*They put me in a shoebox of an office.* 他们将我安排在一间斗室里办公。

shoehorn /ˈʃu:hɔ:n; ˈʃuhɔrn/ *v* [Tn] fit sth large into a space that is rather too small for it 把（大东西）硬塞进小空间：*The van was shoehorned in somehow, between a huge lorry and a stretch limousine.* 不管怎样，这辆客货车终于挤进了一辆大卡车和一辆长轿车之间。

shoot[1] /ʃu:t; ʃut/ *v* (phr v) **shoot up** [I, Ipr] **1** grow very quickly, esp children, plants and buildings（尤指小孩、植物或建筑物）飞速生长，快速增加：*Your children have shot up since I last saw them.* 自从上次见过以后，你的孩子长得飞快。 **2** rise in price suddenly and by a large amount（价格）大幅猛涨：*The price of houses around here has shot up in the last six months.* 这一带的房子在过去六个月内价格大幅上扬。 **3** (of drugs) inject directly into the bloodstream（把毒品）直接注射进血液：*addicts shooting up heroin* 注射海洛因的吸毒者

shoot[2] /ʃu:t; ʃut/ *n* session during which photographs are taken of fashion models for publication in magazines, etc（为刊登相片于杂志上而安排的）时装模特儿拍照时间

shoot-'em-up /ˈʃu:təmʌp, ʃu:təmˈʌp; ʃutəmˈʌp/ *n* (*infml* 口) **1** film in which lots of gun battles take place; western 枪战片；西部片 **2** (also **shooter game**) computer game in which the player shoots down targets on the screen with a variety of weapons 计算机枪战游戏（游戏者用各种武器对准屏幕上的目标射击）

shooter game *n* = SHOOT-'EM-UP 2

shooting /ˈʃu:tɪŋ; ˈʃutɪŋ/ *n* **1** [C, U] firing at or killing of sb with a gun 枪杀；枪击：*the shooting of unarmed civilians* 枪杀手无寸铁的平民 **2** [U] (*sport* 体) firing at targets (TARGET 1[A-Z]) or killing GAME[1] 6[A-Z] with a gun 打靶；射击（猎物）：*a shooting club* 射击俱乐部 ○ *the shooting season* 狩猎季节 ○ *He enjoys riding, fishing and shooting.* 他喜欢骑马、钓鱼和打猎。

□ **shooting spree** *n* sudden, unexpected and apparently motiveless attack on people made by sb armed with a gun or guns 突发性枪杀（持枪者突然地、似乎无目的地对他人攻击）：*Americans have been shocked by the spate of shooting sprees carried out by young students against their schoolmates and teachers.* 美国人对一连串的年轻学生突如其来地枪杀他们的同学和老师的事件感到震惊。Cf 参看 SPREE KILLER

shopfront /ˈʃɒpfrʌnt; ˈʃɑpfrʌnt/ *n* outside of a shop that faces the street 店面

shoreline /ˈʃɔ:laɪn; ˈʃɔrlaɪn/ *n* (usu *sing* 通常作单数) land along the edge of a sea, lake or other large body of water（海、湖等的）岸，畔：*houses built along the shoreline* 建在岸边的房子

short back and sides /ˌʃɔ:t ˌbæk ənd ˈsaɪdz; ˌʃɔrt ˌbæk ənd ˈsaɪdz/ *n* [sing] haircut in which the hair is cut very short at the sides and at the back 盖式发型（脑后和两侧剪得很短的发型）

shortcrust /ˈʃɔ:tkrʌst; ˈʃɔrtkrʌst/ (also **shortcrust pastry**) *n* [U] type of PASTRY[A-Z] that is relatively rich in fat and that crumbles easily, used for pies, tarts and flans 松脆油酥面团（一种油腻易碎的面团，用来制作各种咸、甜馅饼）

short-haul /ˈʃɔ:thɔ:l; ˈʃɔrthɔl/ *adj* [attrib 作定语] of or involving the transport of goods or passengers over relatively short distances, esp by air 短途运输的（尤指空运）：*short haul flights/routes/aircraft* 短途空运 *[*航线 / 飞机*]* Cf 参看 LONG-HAUL

short-run /ˈʃɔ:trʌn; ˈʃɔrtrʌn/ *adj* [attrib 作定语] relating to or lasting for only a short period 短暂的；短期的：*short-run advantages/costs* 短期的优势 *[*开销*]*

short-stay /ˌʃɔ:tˈsteɪ; ˌʃɔrtˈste/ *adj* [attrib 作定语] in which sb or sth can stay only for a short period 供短暂逗留的；临时的：*a short-stay car park/hostel* 临时停车场、短期住宿招待所

short-termism /ʃɔ:tˈtɜ:mɪzm; ʃɔrtˈtɝmɪzəm/ *n* [U] (*finance* 财) concentration on short-term projects, etc for immediate profit at the expense of long-term security 短期效益主义（着重于短期开发而不惜牺牲长期保障以换取眼前利益）

shoulder-high /ˌʃəʊldəˈhaɪ; ˌʃoldɚˈhaɪ/ *adj* at or to the height of the shoulders 齐肩的：*a shoulder-high wall of water* 齐肩高的水墙 ○ *carried shoulder-high* (ie supported on the shoulders) *by the victorious crowd* 被胜利的人群扛在肩上

shoutline /ˈʃaʊtlaɪn; ˈʃaʊtlaɪn/ *n* (*infml* 口) section at the beginning of a promotional leaflet, advertisement, etc which is set out in larger and darker type than the rest in order to catch the eye of a prospective customer 醒目行，醒目标题（产品推销传单、广告等开头的用深色大号字体印刷的标题，以吸引潜在顾客的注意）

shove ⇨ WHEN PUSH COMES TO SHOVE (PUSH)

shuttle trading /ˈʃʌtl treɪdɪŋ; ˈʃʌtḷ tredɪŋ/ *n* [U] (in Russia) practice of travelling long distances to big cities, usu by train, to buy cheap goods which are then taken back and sold in the trader's home town or village（俄罗斯）穿梭买卖，长途贩运（乘长途火车去大城市购买便宜商品，然后回到家乡出售）

▷ **shuttle trader** *n*

sic /sɪk; sɪk/ *v* (*pt,pp* **sicked, sicced**) (*US infml* 口) ~ **sb/sth on sb** set sb/sth onto sb; encourage sb/sth to attack sb 使或唆使（某人 *[*某物*]*）袭击（某人）：*to sic the dog on him* 放狗咬他 ○ *Somebody must have sicced the tax people onto me.* 肯定有人唆使税务人员来找我的麻烦。

sick building syndrome /sɪk ˈbɪldɪŋ ˌsɪndrəʊm; sɪk ˈbɪldɪŋ ˌsɪndrom/ *n* (*medical* 医) **1** set of adverse environmental conditions found in a building which threatens the health of its occupants, esp because of inadequate ventilation or air-conditioning 病楼环境（楼内因通风不好、空调不当等对健康造成威胁的不良环境）：*a building suffering from sick building syndrome* 环境不利于健康的楼房 **2** set of symptoms (such as headache and dizziness) that vulnerable occupants of a health-threatening building suffer 病楼综合症状（楼房住户因楼内环境不利健康而得的症状如头痛、头晕等）

sicko /ˈsɪkəʊ; ˈsɪko/ *n* (*pl* **-os**) (*US sl* 俚) **1** person whose behaviour is judged to be disgusting and intolerable 行为讨厌的人；让人无法忍受的人：*He eats raw meat! What a sicko!* 他吃生肉！真让人恶心！ **2** mentally disturbed or perverted person 精神病患者；神经错乱者

SIDS *abbr* 缩写 = sudden infant death syndrome = COT DEATH (COT[A-Z])

siege mentality *n* = BUNKER MENTALITY

signature dish /ˈsɪgnətʃə dɪʃ; ˈsɪgnətʃɚ dɪʃ/ *n* (in cooking) speciality dish created by and associated with a particular chef（烹饪）厨师的绝活，拿手菜

significant other /sɪgˌnɪfɪkənt ˈʌðə(r); sɪgˌnɪfəkənt ˈʌðɚ/ *n* (*slightly joc* 略带戏谑) one's married or unmarried partner of either sex 异性或同性伴侣；重要的他 *[*她*]*：*We request the pleasure of the company of you and your significant other at the wedding of our daughter.* 我们恭请您和您的另一半参加小女的婚礼。

NOTE 注： the phrase avoids making a judgement about what kind of relationship sb may have with another person and recognizes that there are a number of possibilities 此词避免对他人之间可能存在的多种关系作出判断并容许多个可能性

signing /ˈsaɪnɪŋ; ˈsaɪnɪŋ/ *n* person engaged, esp as a football player, through signing a contract 签约者（尤指足球运动员）: *their recent signing from the Italian club* 他们最近与意大利球会签约而引进的运动员

silicone implant /ˌsɪlɪkən ˈɪmplɑːnt, *US* -plænt; ˌsɪlɪkən ˈɪmplænt/ *n* moulded piece of SILICON[A-Z] gel which is surgically inserted under the skin, usu to enhance the shape and size of female breasts 硅酮植入物（通过手术植入皮下的成型硅胶，通常用于改进女性乳房的形状和大小）

Silicon Valley /ˌsɪlɪkən ˈvælɪ; ˌsɪlɪkən ˈvælɪ/ *n* [sing] name given to the area around Los Angeles which has become the world centre for the manufacture of silicon chips（SILICON[A-Z]）for use in computers 硅谷，矽谷（洛杉矶附近一个地区的名称，这里已成为全球制造计算机硅片的中心）

silly money /ˈsɪlɪ mʌnɪ; ˈsɪlɪ mʌnɪ/ (also **funny money**) *n* [U] (*infml* 口) vast amounts of money used to buy very expensive items 花在昂贵物品上的大量金钱: *The silly money this year is going on fifty-year old champagne and one-off fashion originals.* 今年大量金钱将花在五十年陈香槟酒和只推出一次的手制时装上。

simple fracture /ˌsɪmpl ˈfræktʃə(r); ˈsɪmpl̩ ˈfræktʃɚ/ *n* (*medical* 医) breakage of a bone in which the bone does not break through the skin 无创骨折，单纯骨折（断骨未刺破皮肤的骨折）

sing-along *n* = SINGSONG *n* 2[A-Z]

single currency /ˌsɪŋgl ˈkʌrənsɪ; ˌsɪŋgl̩ ˈkɝənsɪ, ˈsɪŋgl̩ ˌkɝənsɪ/ *n* [sing] unified currency proposed for the use of all member states after the economic and monetary union of Europe 欧洲统一货币；欧洲单一货币 Cf 参看 EURO

single market /ˌsɪŋgl ˈmɑːkɪt; ˌsɪŋgl̩ ˈmɑrkɪt/ *n* association of countries allowing free trade between its members, with a common currency and few restrictions on the movement of goods, money and people between countries 单一市场（允许成员国之间自由贸易，有统一货币，对商品、货币及人员的流动管制较松的联合体）: *The European Community is becoming a single market with the introduction of a common currency.* 欧洲共同体正启用统一货币而成为单一市场。

sister city /ˈsɪstə sɪtɪ, sɪstə ˈsɪtɪ; sɪstɚ ˈsɪtɪ/ *n* city with which another city is twinned（TWIN *v* b[A-Z]）姐妹城市；友好城市

site /saɪt; saɪt/ (also **Web site**) *n* (*computing* 计) place on the INTERNET which has its own address, ie where an individual or an organization has set up a HOME PAGE（互联网上拥有自己的地址即主页的）站点；网站

sit-up /ˈsɪtʌp; ˈsɪtʌp/ *n* exercise to strengthen the abdominal muscles, in which one lifts one's body from a lying position into a sitting position 仰卧起坐: *I do 50 sit-ups a day.* 我每天做 50 个仰卧起坐。

sizist /ˈsaɪzɪst; ˈsaɪzɪst/ (also **sizeist**) *adj* [usu attrib 通常作定语] discriminating unfairly against people because of their large size 对体形庞大者歧视的；体形歧视的: *They complained that the airline was following a sizist employment policy.* 他们抱怨说航空公司实行体形歧视雇佣政策。○ *sizist remarks* 歧视体形庞大者的言语 ▷ **sizism** (also **sizeism**) *n* Cf 参看 FATTYISM

skeletal /ˈskelətl; ˈskɛlətl̩/ *adj* **1** of the SKELETON 1[A-Z] of a person or an animal 骨架的；骨骼的: *skeletal deformities/diseases* 骨骼变形［疾病］**2** very thin, esp because of hunger or disease（尤指因饥饿或疾病）骨瘦如柴的，瘦骨嶙峋的: *skeletal figures searching through the heaps of rubbish for anything to eat* 骨瘦如柴的人在垃圾堆里找寻一切可吃的东西 **3** existing only in outline or as a framework 框架的；概要的: *a skeletal plan for new legislation* 用以制定新法例的框架

skell /skel; skɛl/ *n* (*US*) homeless person, esp one who sleeps in the subway system（尤指睡在地铁站的）无家可归者，流浪汉

NOTE 注: perhaps formed as a shortening of *skeleton* 可能由 skeleton（骷髅）一词缩略而成

skid lid /ˈskɪd lɪd; ˈskɪd lɪd/ *n* (*Brit infml* 口) CRASH HELMET（CRASH[1(A-Z)]）防撞头盔

skins /skɪnz; skɪnz/ *n* [pl] (*esp US*) baked potatoes with the skins left on, cut open after cooking and stuffed with a variety of fillings 连皮土豆（连皮烘烤后切开填入各种馅的土豆）

NOTE 注: British people call them *jacket potatoes*（JACKET 4[A-Z]）英国人称此种食品为 jacket potato(es)

slacker /ˈslækə(r); ˈslækɚ/ *n* (*infml* 口) person regarded as being one of a large group of people, esp the current generation of young people, who are perceived as lacking a sense of direction in life 懒散的人，无生活目标的人（尤指当代年轻人）Cf 参看 GENERATION X

slam-dunk /ˈslæmdʌŋk; ˈslæmdʌŋk/ *v* (*US infml* 口) (**a**) defeat decisively 彻底击败: *That wasn't just a defeat. They slam-dunked you.* 那不单是一场败仗。他们已把你完全击溃了。(**b**) reject without compromise 断然拒绝: *The voters slam-dunked the proposal for a shorter school day.* 投票者断然否决了缩短学校上课时间的议案。

NOTE 注: from basketball, where it refers to the act of thrusting the ball down into the basket 源自篮球用语，指跳起将球猛力塞入篮内的灌篮动作

slap /slæp; slæp/ *v* (*infml* 口) impose a fine or penalty, usu money, on sb（对某人）处以罚款: *The traffic wardens now have the power to slap a fifty pound fine on illegally-parked cars on the spot.* 交通管理员现在有权对违章停车者当场处以五十英镑的罚款。○ *slapped with a 50 thousand dollar fine for allowing toxic wastes to escape into the river* 因让有毒废物流入河里被处以 5 万美元的罚款

slaphead /ˈslæphed; ˈslæphɛd/ *n* (*sl derog* 俚，贬) person, usu male, with no or very little hair（通常指男性）秃顶者，秃子

NOTE 注: perhaps comes from the noise such a person can make when he slaps his head 可能源自秃顶者拍头时发出的响声

slapper /ˈslæpə(r); ˈslæpɚ/ *n* (*Brit sl offensive* 俚，蔑) PROMISCUOUS 2[A-Z] woman; woman who sleeps around 淫娃；荡妇；性生活随便的女子

slaughter /ˈslɔːtə(r); ˈslɔtɚ/ *v* [Tn] criticize with great severity 猛烈抨击；严厉批评: *The critics absolutely slaughtered the new musical and it closed after only five nights.* 这出新音乐剧遭到剧评家的猛烈抨击，仅演了五夜就停了。

Slav /slɑːv; slɑv/ *n* member of any of the peoples of Central and Eastern Europe, eg Russians, Poles and Czechs, who speak Slavonic languages 斯拉夫人（中欧、东欧说斯拉夫语的人，如俄罗斯人、波兰人、捷克人）

sleazebag /ˈsliːzbæg; ˈslizbæg/ *n* (*infml* 口) sordid or despicable person, whose moral standards deserve criticism 卑鄙下流的人；道德败坏的人: *a total sleazebag* 十足的下流坯

NOTE 注: synonymous with *sleazeball* 与 sleazeball 一词同义

sleaze factor /ˈsliːz fæktə(r); ˈsliz fæktɚ/ *n* [U] sordid or SLEAZY[A-Z] aspect of a situation, esp when this affects the image of a political party（事情的）丑恶面，阴暗面（尤指影响某政治集团的形象的）: *The Tories were partly defeated by the sleaze factor which dogged Major's last two years.* 使梅杰在任期最后两年里深感困扰的丑闻也是保守党失利的部分原因。

sleep mode /ˈsliːp məʊd; ˈslip mod/ *n* (*computing* 计) state of the computer system in which only those parts of it needed to respond to some external stimulus and return the remainder to full operational status (eg the user pressing a key) are supplied with electrical power 休眠状态，休止模式（计算机系统中只向有需要对外界信息作出反应的部分供电的状态，如使用者按一个键时可使系统回到全面操作状态）

slimline /ˈslɪmlaɪn; ˈslɪmlaɪn/ *adj* [attrib 作定语] small or thin in shape or design（外形或款式）瘦小的，细长的：*the new slimline bottle shape* 新的瘦小瓶型 ○ *the currently-fashionable slimline silhouette* 当今流行的细长外形

slo-mo *abbr* 缩写 = SLOW MOTION（SLOW[1(A-Z)]）

slugfest /ˈslʌgfest; ˈslʌgfɛst/ *n* (*infml* 口) (**a**) tough and challenging contest, esp in sports such as boxing and baseball（尤指拳击和棒球等运动中）激烈的争夺 (**b**) (*fig* 比喻) heated argument or discussion, usu involving a large number of people which may even come to blows 激烈的争论（通常涉及很多人，甚至会大打出手）：*What started out as a debate soon degenerated into a violent slugfest.* 辩论很快就沦为大殴斗。

SM *abbr* 缩写 = SADO-MASOCHISM[A-Z]

smallish /ˈsmɔːlɪʃ; ˈsmɔlɪʃ/ *adj* fairly small, quite small 较小的；颇小的：*a smallish man in a black coat* 穿黑大衣的瘦小男人

small screen /ˌsmɔːl ˈskriːn; smɔl ˈskrin/ *n* **the small screen** [sing] television as contrasted with the cinema 电视（与电影相比屏幕较小）：*the film's first showing on the small screen* 这部电影在电视上的首次播映

smart /smɑːt; smɑrt/ *adj* **1** (of a machine) able to respond to different conditions and to changes; computerized, intelligent（指机器）计算机化的，智能的 **2** (of a drug) claimed to be capable of increasing intelligence（指药）益智的，有助于智能的

□ **smart bomb** *n* radio- or laser-guided weapon which is claimed to home in accurately on a target 灵巧炸弹，聪明导弹（据称能准确命中目标的无线或激光制导的武器）

smart card *n* plastic bank card which has personal data or financial information encoded on a microprocessor inside it 智能卡，聪明卡（一种塑料银行卡，将个人或财务资料编码存于其微处理器中）

smart house (also **smart building**) *n* house which is built so that its internal systems, eg lighting, heating, energy use, etc are controlled electronically and can run automatically or be accessed by voice or even by a phone call 智能屋（内部系统如照明、供暖、能源使用等都由电子控制，能自动操作或通过声音甚至电话操作的房子或建筑物）：*The modern smart house automatically adjusts temperature, humidity and lighting levels to meet the changing needs of the occupants throughout the day.* 现代智能屋能根据居住者一天中的不同需要自动调节温度、湿度和照明度。

smart phone *n* phone which provides computerized facilities for automatic dialling, network connections or identification of incoming calls 智能电话（具有计算机化设备的电话，可自动拨号、联网或识别来电号码等）

smoke and mirrors /ˈsməʊk ənd mɪrəz; ˈsmok ənd mɪrəz/ *n* [usu attrib 通常作定语] explanation or demonstration which is essentially deceptive 假象；烟幕弹：*The prosecutor's final submission was dramatic, but in essence a smoke and mirrors performance.* 起诉人动人的结案陈词其实只是故弄玄虚的表演。

NOTE 注： from a stage-magician's use of smoke and mirrors to help in the creation of illusions 源自魔术师在台上利用烟雾和镜子来帮助制造幻觉的情景

smoke-filled room /ˌsməʊkfɪld ˈruːm; ˌsmokfɪld ˈrum/ *n* (*fig* 比喻) private or secret location for decision-making by a group of powerful people, avoiding open discussion or accountability 烟雾弥漫的房间，密谈室（有权势者密谈之处）：*We fear the decisions made in smoke-filled rooms which will affect all our lives.* 我们害怕那些在密谈室里作出的决定，因为会影响我们的生活。

smoke-free /ˈsməʊkfriː; ˈsmokfri/ *adj* free from cigarette smoke; where smoking is not allowed 无人吸烟的；禁止吸烟的：*smoke-free public transport* 禁止吸烟的公共交通工具

smoking gun /ˌsməʊkɪŋ ˈgʌn; ˈsmokɪŋ gʌn/ *n* (*fig* 比喻) clear and indisputable evidence that sb is responsible for sth, often a crime 确凿无疑的证据（常指罪证）：*We all want answers but there is no smoking gun in this case.* 我们都希望找到答案，但此案无确凿证据。

NOTE 注： from the image of a gun that has just been fired 以刚开火仍冒烟的枪作比喻

snag-tooth /ˈsnægtuːθ; ˈsnægtuθ/ (also **snaggle-tooth**) *n* irregular or projecting tooth 歪牙；凸牙

▷ **snag-toothed** (also **snaggle-toothed**) *adj* with unevenly spaced and sized teeth 牙齿参差不齐的：*a snag-toothed dog* 犬牙交错的狗

snail mail /ˈsneɪlmeɪl; ˈsnelmel/ *n* [U] (*sl joc* 俚，谑) **1** ordinary postal system, emphasizing its slowness in comparison with electronic mail（相对电子邮件而言，强调其速度之慢的）蜗牛式邮递，普通邮递 **2** communication sent by conventional post 蜗牛式邮件；普通邮件

▷ **snailmail** *v* [Tn] **snailmailed** *adj*

NOTE 注： invented by Internet users using snail as an image of slowness 互联网用户所创，以蜗牛喻其速度之慢

snakeboard /ˈsneɪkbɔːd; ˈsnekbɔrd/ *n* flexible kind of SKATEBOARD（SKATE[1(A-Z)]）蛇行滑板（一种灵活的滑板）

▷ **snakeboard** *v* ride on a snakeboard 踩蛇行滑板滑行

sneak preview /ˌsniːk ˈpriːvjuː; ˌsnik ˈprivju/ *n* (**a**) special showing of a new film, exhibition, etc to certain people before it is shown to the general public（新电影、展览等在公开上映或展出前向特定观众的）内部预展，预映：*He gave a group of journalists a sneak preview of some of the photographs he will be displaying in his exhibition.* 他让一群记者预先看看他即将展出的一些照片。 (**b**) informal look at sth, eg a piece of writing, a plan, a fashion design, etc before it is more formally presented（正式推出著作、计划、时装设计等之前的）非正式预览

sniffer-dog /ˈsnɪfədɒg; ˈsnɪfɚdɑg/ *n* (*infml* 口) dog trained to find drugs or explosives by smell, often employed at ports and airports 嗅犬（常用于港口和机场，经训练可凭嗅觉寻找毒品或炸药）

sniffy /ˈsnɪfɪ; ˈsnɪfɪ/ *adj* (*infml* 口) showing contempt or disapproval 鄙视的；反对的：*Some people are rather sniffy about fast foods.* 有些人对快餐嗤之以鼻。

NOTE 注： a deliberate sniff conveys contempt in some cultures 在一些文化中，故意抽鼻子有轻蔑之意

snowboarding /ˈsnəʊbɔːdɪŋ; ˈsnobɔrdɪŋ/ *n* [U] (*sport* 体) practice of sliding downhill on snow using a snowboard, ie a board resembling a skateboard without wheels 滑板滑雪（踩在状如滑板但无轮的板上来进行的滑雪）：*Snowboarding is the in sport for the young set this winter season.* 滑板滑雪是今年冬天年轻人的时髦运动。

SNP /es en ˈpiː; ɛs ɛn ˈpi/ *abbr* 缩写 = Scottish National Party (Scottish political party in favour of independence for Scotland from the rest of the United Kingdom) 苏格兰民族党（苏格兰一政党，主张苏格兰应从联合王国中独立出来）

snuck (*esp US*) *pt, pp* of SNEAK 2[A-Z]

snuff movie /ˈsnʌf muːvɪ; ˈsnʌf muvɪ/ *n* (*infml* 口) pornographic film which shows sb actually being killed 有凶杀纪实镜头的色情影片

sobering /ˈsəʊbərɪŋ; ˈsobərɪŋ/ *adj* having the effect of making one serious and thoughtful 使人严肃思考的；

发人深省的：*It's a sobering thought.* 这是个严肃的想法。○ *The news had a sobering effect.* 这条新闻发人深省。

social cleansing /ˌsəʊʃl 'klenzɪŋ; ˌsoʃəl 'klɛnzɪŋ/ *n* [U] removal or forced emigration of a group identified by race, religion or language from amongst the people in a particular area 社群清洗（从某地区清除或迫迁某一种族、宗教或讲某种语言的群体）Cf 参看 ETHNIC CLEANSING

social climber /ˌsəʊʃl 'klaɪmə(r); ˌsoʃəl 'klaɪmɚ/ *n* (*derog* 贬) person who wants to rise in social class and so tries to be friendly with people of a higher social class 趋炎附势者；结交权贵向上爬的人

social conscience /ˌsəʊʃl 'kɒnʃəns; ˌsoʃəl 'kɑnʃəns/ *n* (usu *sing* 通常作单数) awareness of the social problems in a community together with a desire to help solve them 社会良知；社会道德心

social democracy /ˌsəʊʃl dɪ'mɒkrəsɪ; ˌsoʃəl dɪ'mɑkrəsɪ/ *n* [U] (*politics* 政) form of SOCIALISM^A-Z favouring less control by the state and greater individual freedom than socialism 社会民主主义（一种倾向赞成国家放宽管制而个人自由度较大的社会主义）

▷ **social democrat** *n* supporter or member of a political party that believes in social democracy 社会民主主义者；社会民主党党员

social drinker /ˌsəʊʃl 'drɪŋkə(r); ˌsoʃəl 'drɪŋkɚ/ *n* person who drinks alcohol only on social occasions 只在应酬时饮酒的人

soft landing /sɒft 'lændɪŋ; sɔft 'lændɪŋ/ *n* (*fig* 比喻) **1** slowing down of economic growth at a manageable rate relative to inflation and unemployment, possibly followed by an upturn after a time of hardship 软着陆（在保持适度的通货膨胀率和失业率的情况下经济增长速度的放慢，在度过一段困难时期后，经济有可能出现好转）**2** fortunate outcome from a difficult or risky situation（困难或危险之后的）幸运的结局；柳暗花明：*I lost my job in the latest round of downsizing, but there turned out to be a soft landing when I was offered a much better position here.* 我在最近一次裁员中丢了工作，但结果却因祸得福，在这儿得到了一份好得多的差使。

soft-top /'sɒftɒp, *US* sɔ:ft-; 'sɔftɑp/ *n* **1** roof of a motor vehicle that is made of soft material and can be folded back（机动车辆的）可折叠软顶篷 **2** vehicle with a soft top（有可折叠软顶篷的）敞篷车，开篷车 Cf 参看 CONVERTIBLE *n*^A-Z, TARGA

software piracy /sɒftweə 'paɪrəsɪ, *US* sɔ:ft-; sɔftwɛr 'paɪrəsɪ/ *n* [U] systematic illegal copying of computer software for financial gain 侵害软件版权；软件盗版：*Software piracy is widespread and it threatens the good relations between the two countries.* 软件盗版活动猖獗，正危及两国的友好关系。

SoHo /'səʊhəʊ; so'ho, 'soho/ *abbr* 缩写 = (*commerce* 商) small office, home office (concerning small businesses, often involving only one person, operating from an office or from home) 小办公室，家庭办公室（通常只有一个人在办公室或家里办公的小企业）：*SoHo buyers will especially welcome this new PC.* 家庭办公用户会特别欢迎这种新型个人电脑。

NOTE 注：in imitation of the area known as *SoHo* in Greenwich Village, New York, where many home offices have taken over converted industrial premises 仿纽约格林尼治村索霍区的地名而成，那里有许多工业大厦改建为家庭办公室

sommelier /sɒ'melɪeɪ; sɑ'mɛlɪe/ *n* expert in wines who is employed by a restaurant or wine merchant to give informed advice to customers（餐馆或酒商聘请的向顾客提供专业意见的）酒类专家

sonogram /'səʊnəgræm; 'sonəgræm/ *n* **1** graph representing a sound, showing the distribution of energy at different frequencies (FREQUENCY 2^A-Z) 声谱图 **2** (*esp medical* 尤用于医学) visual image produced from an ULTRASOUND^A-Z examination 超声波扫描图

sorted /'sɔ:tɪd; 'sɔrtɪd/ *adj* [pred 作表语] (*sl* 俚) well-organized or controlled; fully-prepared or equipped (esp with illegal drugs) 井然有序；受控制；准备充足，有足够配备（尤指违禁毒品）：*Don't worry about the holiday. I've got it sorted.* 别为度假的事儿担心了，我已把一切都弄妥了。

NOTE 注：a figurative use implying that the important aspects of a person or situation having been sorted out or put into order 比喻用法，意指已整理出来 (be sorted out) 或理顺某人或某种情况的重要之处

sound bite /'saʊnd baɪt; 'saund baɪt/ *n* short, telling extract from a longer recorded interview, speech or discussion, used for maximum effect as part of a news item or a party political broadcast 简要节录，摘要，语录（录音访谈、演讲或讨论的摘要，用于新闻或党派政治性广播中以增强效果）：*We are living in the era of the sound bite.* 我们生活在一个语录满天飞的年代。○ *an effective sound bite* 效果颇佳的录音摘要

▷ **sound bite** *v* [Tn] reduce (opinions, debates etc) to a series of sound bites（将观点、辩论等）剪辑成一系列录音摘要

NOTE 注：the term is often used with a negative connotation implying manipulation of the media and a reduction of the quality and intellectual level of public debate on important issues 通常带有贬义，意指媒体的操纵及对重大问题公开辩论的水准下降 Cf 参看 DUMB DOWN (DUMB)

space /speɪs; spes/ *n* [U] freedom to think, act and be oneself（思想、行动、个人的）自由：*You're in my space.* 你妨碍了我的自由。

space blanket /'speɪs blæŋkɪt; 'spes blæŋkɪt/ *n* light metal-coated sheet designed to retain heat 太空毯（一种带有金属涂层的轻软保暖毯）

spaced out /ˌspeɪst 'aʊt; spest 'aut/ *adj* [pred 作表语] (*infml* 口) not properly conscious or aware of what is going on around one, esp because of drugs; feeling strange（尤因使用毒品而）精神恍惚，感觉怪异：*spaced out on acid* 因服迷幻药而昏昏沉沉 Cf 参看 HIGH[1] 8^A-Z

space heater /'speɪs hi:tə(r); 'spes hitɚ/ *n* (*US*) electric fire with a fan mechanism 电取暖器

space nap *n* = ALIEN ABDUCTION

spade /speɪd; sped/ *n* (idm 习语) **in spades** (*infml* 口) in large amounts or to a great extent 大量地；非常：*Then things began to go wrong — in spades.* 然后情况开始变糟——非常地糟。

sparky /'spɑ:kɪ; 'spɑrkɪ/ *adj* (*Brit infml* 口) full of energy or enthusiasm; lively 充满活力的；热情洋溢的：*a sparky sense of humour* 强烈的幽默感 ○ *I feel quite sparky this morning.* 今天早上我感觉精力充沛。

spazz /spæz; spæz/ *v* (phr v) **spazz out** (*infml* 口) lose physical or emotional control of oneself; be overcome（身体上或情绪上）失去控制；不能自持

NOTE 注：probably derived from *space out* (lose control) and *spastic* or *spasm* (uncontrollable muscle jerk) 可能由 space out（失去控制）和 spastic 或 spasm（痉挛）二词引申而成

special effects /ˌspeʃl ɪ'fekts; ˌspɛʃəl ɪ'fɛkts/ (sometimes 有时作 **special FX**) *n* [pl] special techniques in filming or the images created by them which allow film makers to create the illusion of things that it is not possible to film, eg ghosts, space travel, etc（电影制作中的）特技效果；以特别技术制作的影像效果：*Computer imaging has given special effects a vast range of new possibilities.* 电脑成像为特技制作提供了更广阔的天地。

special envoy /ˌspeʃl ˈenvɔɪ; ˌspɛʃəl ˈɛnvɔɪ/ *n* person sent by the head of a state or of an international organization to a country as their representative and with a particular mission to fulfil 特使（国家元首或国际组织首脑派到某国作为其代表的、肩负特殊使命的人）: *The United Nations special envoy to Israel is meeting with the Palestinian leader again today.* 联合国派往以色列的特使今天将与巴勒斯坦领导人再次会晤。

special interest group *n* = PRESSURE GROUP (PRESSURE[A-Z])

specialism /ˈspeʃəlɪzm; ˈspɛʃəlɪzəm/ *n* specialized area of study or work（学习或工作的）专门领域；专业；专长: *His specialism is oriental languages.* 他的专长是东方语言。

special relationship /ˌspeʃl rɪˈleɪʃnʃɪp; ˌspɛʃəl rɪˈleʃənʃɪp/ *n* **the special relationship** [sing] relationship between the US and Britain which is the outcome of the histories and shared language of the two countries（美国和英国之间由于历史和共同语言形成的）特殊关系

speed bump /ˈspiːd bʌmp; ˈspid bʌmp/ (also **hump, road hump, speed hump**) *n* ridge running across a traffic lane or across an entire road intended to force vehicles to slow down（横过车道或整个路面的）减速路脊: *Speed bumps have slowed traffic approaching the school entrance.* 减速路脊使得学校入口处附近的车流速度减慢了。Cf 参看 TRAFFIC CALMING

speed camera /ˈspiːd kæmərə; ˈspid kæmərə/ *n* roadside camera set up by the police, activated by speeding vehicles, which then films or photographs the offending vehicle and records its speed 超速摄录机，超速摄影机（警察设于路边的摄录机或摄影机，如有车辆超速，则自动将其拍下并录下其速度）: *Be careful to keep within the speed limit. There are speed cameras along this stretch of the motorway.* 注意别超速。这一带高速公路装有超速摄录机。Cf 参看 TRAFFIC CALMING

speed hump *n* = SPEED BUMP

spending /ˈspendɪŋ; ˈspɛndɪŋ/ *n* [U] money spent or available to be spent 花费；开支: *public/defence/welfare spending* 公共 *[*国防 */* 福利*]* 开支 ○ *Consumer spending rose steeply in the last quarter of the current year.* 今年最后一个季度消费剧增。

□ **spending money** *n* [U] money intended for small expenses, eg entertainment, gifts, etc 零花钱；零用钱: *How much spending money did you take with you on holiday?* 你那次度假带了多少零用钱？

sperm bank /ˈspɜːm bæŋk; ˈspɝm bæŋk/ *n* holding facility for donated human sperm from which sperm may be selected for use in the treatment of infertility by means of ARTIFICIAL INSEMINATION (ARTIFICIAL[A-Z]) 精子库（存放捐献的精子供人工授精治疗不育症的设施）

sperm donor /ˈspɜːm dəʊnə(r); ˈspɝm donɚ/ *n* man who donates sperm for storage in a SPERM BANK or for use in the treatment of infertility 捐献精子者

sperm-napping /ˈspɜːmnæpɪŋ; ˈspɝmnæpɪŋ/ *n* [U] (of a woman) becoming pregnant by tricking her partner into thinking that she is using a contraceptive when in fact she is not（指女性）欺骗性怀孕（对男伴谎称已采取避孕措施但其实并没有，从而得以怀孕）

spin /spɪn; spɪn/ *n* [sing] interpretation, bias or slant put on information when it is presented to the public through the media or revealed at a press conference（通过媒体或新闻发布会发表的）带倾向性的解释，定调

□ **spin doctor** *n* senior political spokesperson whose role is to promote a favourable interpretation of events to journalists 新闻发言人，定调者（具政治背景的资深人士，其职能是针对事件向新闻界提出有利于己方的解释）: *The public have grown suspicious of spin doctors.* 公众渐渐对有政治背景的发言人产生怀疑。

spine /spaɪn; spaɪn/ *n* (*commerce* 商) linear pay scale in which each graded job corresponds to a particular point on the scale, but which allows flexibility for local and specific conditions 脊柱型薪酬等级（不同职级有相应薪酬的线性薪酬级别，但可根据当地的和特别的情况作灵活调整）

NOTE 注：the image comes from the human spine, which is flexible rather than rigid 以人的脊柱 (spine) 喻其灵活性

spin meister *n* = SPIN DOCTOR (SPIN)

spinsterish /ˈspɪnstərɪʃ; ˈspɪnstərɪʃ/ *adj* (*often derog* 常作贬义) like, or typical of, a SPINSTER (b)[A-Z] 老处女般的；老处女的: *a sour, spinsterish envy of other people* 对他人酸溜溜的、老处女般的嫉妒 ○ *her solitary, spinsterish life* 她那与世隔绝的、老处女般的生活

spiral /ˈspaɪrəl; ˈspaɪrəl/ *v* [I, Ipr] (of the value of shares, property, etc) move upwards or downwards continuously（指股票、房地产等的价值）持续上涨或下跌: *Property prices in the area have spiralled out of control since the motorway was built.* 自从这条高速公路建成后，该地区的房地产价格持续猛涨，完全失控了。

splat /splæt; splæt/ *n* (*infml* 口) sound of sth wet and squashy hitting a surface and, usu, bursting（湿而软的东西击中物体表面而破裂的）啪嗒声: *The tomato hit the wall with a splat.* 西红柿啪嗒一声打在墙上。

▷ **splat** *adv*: *People threw plastic bags filled with coloured water from the windows that went splat as they hit the pavement.* 人们从窗里扔出装满颜料水的塑料袋，劈哩啪拉地落在人行道上。

splatter /ˈsplætə(r); ˈsplætɚ/ *n* (*cinema* 影) type of film in which many characters die in a violent or frightful manner 暴力凶杀影片: [attrib 作定语] *splatter movie* 暴力凶杀影片 Cf 参看 CHOPSOCKY

□ **splatter game** *n* game played on a computer in which there is lots of violent action and the player uses many different weapons（计算机的）暴力游戏: *the latest splatter game from Nintendo* 任天堂最新出的暴力游戏 Cf 参看 SHOOT-'EM-UP 2

NOTE 注：the image comes from the violent physical disintegration of bodies which appear to be splattered across the screen 源自电影中残暴分尸，肢体四散的情景

split ends /ˌsplɪt ˈendz; splɪt ˈɛndz/ *n* [pl] hair on a person's head that is split at the ends 分叉的发梢: *I'll just trim off the split ends before you have a shampoo.* 在你洗头前，我来把你开叉的发梢剪掉。

-spoken /ˈspəʊkən; ˈspokən/ *comb form* 构词成分 (forming *adjs* 用以构成形容词) speaking in a specified way 以某种方式说话的: *She was a soft-spoken woman and rarely criticized anyone.* 她说话轻柔，很少批评人。○ *a well-spoken young man of obvious education* 一个显然受过良好教育、谈吐高雅的年轻男子

spoken for /ˈspəʊkən fɔː(r); ˈspokən fɔr/ *adj* [pred 作表语] already claimed, owned or reserved 已有所属；已被预订: *Don't go after Mark. He's already spoken for* (ie has a steady relationship or is engaged or married). 别再追马克了，他已经心有所属了（他已有关系稳定的情侣或已订婚或已结婚）。

spoken word /ˌspəʊkən ˈwɜːd; ˌspokən ˈwɝd/ *n* **the spoken word** [sing] language expressed in speech 言语；口语: *I always find the spoken word so much more effective than a letter or a note.* 我总觉得用言语表达比用信函或便条要有效得多。

spokesperson /ˈspəʊkspɜːsn; ˈspokspɝsn̩/ *n* (*pl* **-persons** or **-people**) ~ **(for sb/sth)** person who speaks on behalf of a group or an organization（代表团体或组织的）发言人: *They chose the oldest member of the union as their spokesperson.* 他们推选会社中最年长的人作为他们的发言人。

NOTE 注：the word is often preferred as it offers an

alternative to the gender-marked *spokesman* or *spokeswoman* 因此词不显示性别而较 spokesman 或 spokeswoman 常用

sports bar /'spɔ:ts bɑ:(r); 'spɔrts bɑr/ *n* (*US*) bar where non-stop televised sport is shown 体育酒吧（不停地播放电视体育节目的酒吧）

sports day /'spɔ:ts deɪ; 'spɔrts de/ (*US* **field day**) *n* (*Brit*) day on which pupils of a school compete in sports events, and their parents come to watch （学校的）运动日，运动会

sports science /'spɔ:ts saɪəns; 'spɔrts saɪəns/ *n* course taught at universities and colleges which deals with the whole area of sports training and administration 体育科学（大学里关于体育训练和管理的课程）

sportswear /'spɔ:tsweə(r); 'spɔrtswɛr/ *n* [U] clothes worn for playing sports, or as leisure clothing 运动服；休闲服：*Sportswear has become the daily dress of millions who have never played a sport in their life.* 运动服已成为千百万人的日常衣着，尽管他们一辈子没参加过体育运动。

spousal abuse /'spaʊzl ə,bju:s; 'spaʊzl ə,bjus/ *n* [U] physical or emotional abuse of one's husband or wife 虐待配偶（对丈夫或妻子的身体或心理折磨）

sprawled /sprɔ:ld; sprɔld/ *adj* sitting or lying comfortably and carelessly with one's arms and legs spread out （伸展四肢）懒洋洋地坐着或躺着的：*He lay sprawled on the sand, soaking up the hot sun.* 他四肢伸开，懒洋洋地躺在沙滩上享受日光浴。

spray-on /'spreɪɒn; 'spreɑn/ *adj* [attrib 作定语] (*Brit*) that can be sprayed onto sth/sb from a container 喷雾式的：*spray-on furniture polish/hair lacquer* 喷雾式家具上光剂 *[发胶]*

spreader /'spredə(r); 'sprɛdɚ/ *n* **1** tool used for spreading sth 将某物展平的工具；涂抹工具：*a flexible spreader for glue* 弹性胶水刷 ○ *A garden rake makes a good spreader for topsoil.* 园艺耙可将表层土壤耙得很平整。 **2** person who makes sth more widely known, available, etc 传播者：*a spreader of information/gossip/news* 消息 *[流言 / 新闻]* 的散布者

spree killer /'spri: kɪlə(r); 'spri kɪlɚ/ *n* person who kills in a sudden, random and apparently spontaneous and motiveless manner, esp one who kills a number of people at a single location in such an attack 作乐杀人狂（指突然地、随意地、似乎无动机和兴之所至地杀人的人，尤其是在一地一次杀死多人）：*Port Arthur and Dunblane were both locations for attacks by spree killers in 1996.* ☆ 1996 年阿瑟港和邓布兰两处遭到作乐杀人狂的袭击。 Cf 参看 SERIAL KILLER

sprigged /sprɪgd; sprɪgd/ *adj* (esp of fabrics) decorated with designs or patterns of sprigs (SPRIG^A-Z) or sprays, esp of flowers （尤指织物）带枝叶图案的（尤指花枝）

spring-loaded /,sprɪŋ'ləʊdɪd; ,sprɪŋ'lodɪd/ *adj* (of mechanical devices) containing a SPRING¹ 3^A-Z that presses one part against another so that certain mechanical reactions can be triggered off （指机械装置）装有弹簧（以压力触发机械反应）的：*a spring-loaded shotgun/hinge* 弹簧猎枪 *[铰链]*

spritzer /'sprɪtsə(r); 'sprɪtsɚ/ *n* drink made by mixing usu white wine and soda water 汽酒（通常用白酒和苏打水混合而成的饮料）

squall line /'skwɔ:l laɪn; 'skwɔl laɪn/ *n* narrow band of high winds along a cold FRONT 6^A-Z 飑线

squeeze /skwi:z; skwiz/ *n* (*US sl* 俚) girlfriend, boyfriend, or lover 女友；男友；情人：*her latest squeeze* 她最新的情人

NOTE 注： the word implies a primarily physical relationship which is probably only temporary 此词暗指个中关系主要是肉体上的，且可能是短时期的

SRO /es ɑ:r 'əʊ; es ɑr 'o/ *abbr* 缩写 = standing room only (very crowded because of the popularity of sb at an event or the attraction of the event itself) 只有站位（活动中出场的人物极受欢迎或活动本身极具吸引力，因而非常拥挤）：*It was SRO at the celebrity book-signing.* 名人签名售书处异常拥挤。

NOTE 注： if there were no more seats free in the auditorium of a theatre, a notice-board reading *standing room only* would be placed in the entrance lobby 当剧院的观众坐席已满时，门厅处会挂上 standing room only（只有站位）的告示牌

stagecraft /'steɪdʒkrɑ:ft, *US* -'kræft; 'stedʒkræft/ *n* [U] skills involved in presenting plays on a stage 舞台技巧：*The director showed herself a master of stagecraft.* 导演展示了她精湛的舞台技巧。

stage-diving /'steɪdʒdaɪvɪŋ; 'stedʒdaɪvɪŋ/ *n* [U] practice, among members of the audience at a rock concert, of throwing oneself from the stage to be caught and carried aloft by the crowd below 舞台俯跳（摇滚音乐会上乐迷从台上跳下，由众人在下面接住并高举起来的做法）：*Stage-diving is causing concern amongst producers and performers alike.* 舞台俯跳这种行为正引起制片人和演员的普遍关注。 Cf 参看 MOSH

stag night *n* = STAG-PARTY (STAG^A-Z)

stakeholder /'steɪkhəʊldə(r); 'stekholdɚ/ *n* person, company, etc with shares or a financial interest in a business or an industry （公司或企业的）股东，分享利益者：*The company is a 44% stakeholder in the Emerald oilfield.* 这个公司持有绿晶油田 44% 的股份。

□ **stakeholder economy** *n* economy in which every member of a society has an interest in its success 股东经济（与社会上所有人的利益有关的经济制度）：*The new leader promised a stakeholder economy in which everyone has a share.* 新领导人保证其经济政策会使人人受益。

NOTE 注： the term has gained fresh currency as one of the main themes of the new Labour government in the UK 此词作为英国新一届工党政府的主要执政纲领而流行

stalker /'stɔ:kə(r); 'stɔkɚ/ *n* person who follows or pesters sb, often a public figure, with whom he or she has become obsessed 尾随者，纠缠者（通常对某公众人物着迷而尾随其后或纠缠不休的人）：*Many stars have had to deal with the unwanted attention of stalkers.* 许多明星都不得不应付追星族对他们的过分关注。

stalking horse /'stɔ:kɪŋ hɔ:s; 'stɔkɪŋ hɔrs/ *n* person or thing that is used to divert attention from a person's real plans or intentions, esp in contests for political leadership 掩护者，障眼物（尤指在政治竞选中用来引开对某人的真正计划或意图的注意）：*He is seen as a stalking horse candidate and not as a serious challenger for the leadership.* 他被看作是竞选中的掩护性候选人，并不真正具有威胁性。

stamped addressed envelope /,stæmpt ədrest 'envələʊp; ,stæmpt ədrɛst 'ɛnvəlop/ *n* (*abbr* 缩写 **SAE**) (*Brit*) envelope which has one's own address written on it and carries a stamp 贴了邮票的回邮信封：*For further details, send a stamped addressed envelope to the following address.* 欲知详情，请寄一个贴了邮票的回邮信封到下列地址。 Cf 参看 SELF-ADDRESSED^A-Z

stand-alone /'stændələʊn; 'stændəlon/ *adj* operating and capable of operating independently 独立的；能独立操作的：*a stand-alone insurance policy* 独立保险单 ○ *a stand-alone computer* 独立操作的计算机

stand-off /'stændɒf; 'stændɑf/ *n* (*esp US*) complete failure to reach agreement; a DEADLOCK^A-Z 未能达成任何协议的局面；僵局：*a stand-off between the police and the hijackers* 警察与劫持者之间的僵持局面

stand-to /stænd'tu:; stænd'tu/ *n* (*military* 军) readiness for action or attack 战斗准备 : *The order for stand-to had gone out.* 准备战斗的号令已下。

start-up /'stɑ:tʌp; 'stɑrtʌp/ *n* [often attrib 常作定语] act of starting sth up, esp of establishing a new business, etc 创办（尤指公司等）；开始 : *the start-up costs of a new venture* 新企业的创办成本

stasis /'steɪsɪs; 'stesɪs/ *n* [U,C] (*pl* **stases**) (*fml* 文) condition in which there is no change or development 停滞状态 : *The embryos were maintained in stasis for three years, and then implanted and brought to full term.* 这些胚胎整整三年保持停滞不发育，然后才被移植，并成长至足月。

statehood /'steɪthʊd; 'stethʊd/ *n* [U] fact of being a state and possessing all the appropriate rights and power 国家地位（作为一个国家及拥有一切应有的权利和权力的现实）

statementing /'steɪtməntɪŋ; 'stetməntɪŋ/ *n* [U] (*Brit*) official assessment of a child as having special educational needs（对儿童的特殊教育需求的）官方审核 ▷ **statement** *v* [Tn] carry out the process of statementing（对儿童有无特殊教育需求）进行审核 : *Statementing children with handicaps to the local education authorities doesn't solve the problem of how to provide such children with a suitable education.* 向地方教育当局申报残障儿童的特殊教育需求，并不能解决向他们提供适当教育的问题。

statutory rape /ˌstætʃʊtrɪ 'reɪp, *US* -tɔrɪ; 'stætʃʊtɔrɪ 'rep/ *n* [U] (*US*) act of sex with a person under the age of full legal responsibility, even if he or she is willing 法定强奸（与未达法定承诺年龄者发生的性行为，即使对方出于自愿亦属违法）Cf 参看 AGE OF CONSENT (AGE[1(A-Z)])

stealth /stelθ; stɛlθ/ *n* technology enabling a plane to approach enemy positions without alerting radar warning systems 隐形术（可使飞机避开雷达以接近敌方位置的技术）Cf 参看 ATB[1]

stealth bra /'stelθ brɑ:; 'stɛlθ brɑ/ *n* cover made of a carbon-based material which fits over the front bumper of a car and absorbs the microwaves used in radar equipment 反雷达车罩（以碳为基本材料制成，套在汽车前的保险杠上的罩，用来吸收雷达仪器的微波）Cf 参看 CAR BRA

step aerobics /step eə'rəʊbɪks; stɛp ɛ'robɪks/ *n* [sing v] type of aerobic exercise consisting of stepping up onto and down from a portable block 踏板健身操

sticking-point /'stɪkɪŋpɔɪnt; 'stɪkɪŋpɔɪnt/ *n* issue or difference of opinion that prevents progress in a discussion, negotiation, etc（讨论、谈判等中的）分歧点，阻塞点 : *a major sticking-point in the arms talks* 军备谈判中的主要分歧点

sticky /'stɪkɪ; 'stɪkɪ/ (also **Post-it-note**) *n* small sheet of paper peeled off a pad, with glue along one edge, which can be stuck on sth, eg a document, and peeled off again without causing damage 黏贴便笺

stonewashed /'stəʊnwɒʃt, *US* -wɔ:ʃt; 'stonwɔʃt/ (also **granite-washed**) *adj* (of a garment or fabric, esp DENIM[A-Z]) treated to make it look worn or faded（指衣服或织物，尤指粗斜纹棉布）石磨的 : *stonewashed jeans* 石磨牛仔裤

stonking /'stɒŋkɪŋ; 'stɑŋkɪŋ/ *adj* (*Brit sl* 俚) considerable, very impressive; exciting 有价值的；令人难忘的；激动人心的 : *A stonking good time was had by all.* 大家都玩得非常开心。

stop /stɒp; stɑp/ *v* (phr v) **stop in** (*Brit*) stay indoors at home rather than go out 待在家；留在家 : *I wasn't feeling well on Friday night so I stopped in.* 星期五晚上我不大舒服，所以待在家里。 **stop out** (*Brit*) stay out late at night 待在外面至深夜 : *stop out until three o'clock in the morning* 在外面待到凌晨三点

storytelling /'stɔ:rɪtelɪŋ; 'stɔrɪtɛlɪŋ/ *n* [U] art and practice of telling stories, esp in literature or performing arts（尤指文学或表演艺术中的）讲故事，说书

straightaway /ˌstreɪtə'weɪ; ˌstretə'we/ *adv* immediately; at once 立刻；马上 : *Don't wait — do it straightaway.* 别等了，马上做。

street-fighter /'stri:tfaɪtə(r); 'stritfaɪtɚ/ *n* (*infml* 口) aggressive, tough person 好斗者；斗士 : *He's a real street-fighter and he'll soon be back.* 他是个真正的斗士，他很快会卷土重来的。

street-skating /'stri:tˌskeɪtɪŋ; 'stritˌsketɪŋ/ *n* [U] activity of skating on a ROLLERBLADE, usu in the city streets 街头溜冰（穿着刀刃式旱冰鞋在城市街道上滑行）

street-smart *adj* = STREET-WISE (STREET[A-Z])

street style /'stri:t staɪl; 'strit staɪl/ *n* [U] style of dress and music inspired by contemporary urban culture 街头时尚（当代都市文化影响下形成的服饰及音乐时尚）: *Fashion designers have taken note of the street style of the teens and 20 somethings.* 时装设计师已注意到十几二十来岁的年轻人的街头时尚。

stressed out /strest 'aʊt; strɛst 'aʊt/ *adj* [usu pred 通常作表语] (*sl* 俚) exhausted and tired out as a result of stress 因压力而累垮的 : *stressed out by the noise and the crowds in the shops during the sales* 被大减价时商店里的噪音和人群弄得筋疲力竭

stretch marks /'stretʃ mɑ:ks; 'strɛtʃ mɑrks/ *n* [pl] marks left on a woman's body due to the stretching of the skin, esp on the abdomen, after she has carried a baby to full term and given birth to it 萎缩纹，白纹（曾经怀胎生产的妇女身上，尤其在腹部，因皮肤伸张而留下的纹）: *These products claim to reduce stretch marks, but I didn't find them very effective.* 这些产品据称能减少萎缩纹，但我觉得不大有效。

strike-rate /'straɪkreɪt; 'straɪkret/ *n* (usu *sing* 通常作单数) number of successes sb has in relation to the number of attempts they make 命中率；成功率 : *a salesman/player with a high strike rate* 成功率很高的推销员、命中率很高的运动员

NOTE 注： probably derived from scoring rates in sports like baseball and cricket 可能源于棒球和板球等运动中的得分率

string theory /'strɪŋ θɪərɪ; 'strɪŋ θɪərɪ/ *n* [sing] (*physics* 物) theory that the smallest particle in the universe is in fact a one-dimensional string 细脉学说（认为宇宙中最小的粒子其实为一条一维的细线的学说）Cf 参看 COSMIC STRING

strippergram /'strɪpəgræm; 'strɪpɚgræm/ *n* message sent to sb who is celebrating a special occasion, eg a STAG-PARTY (STAG[A-Z]) , a birthday, etc, which takes the form of a performance by a young female or male STRIPPER (STRIP[A-Z]) 脱衣舞祝贺（一种贺礼，请人用脱衣舞表演形式向正在举办雄鹿会或生日庆典等的人表示祝贺）Cf 参看 GRAM, GORILLAGRAM

strongman /'strɒŋmæn; 'strɔŋmæn/ *n* (*pl* **-men**) leader who rules by threats, force, violence or the suppression of any opposition 铁腕人物；强权统治者；独裁者 : *The country has been run by a succession of military strongmen.* 该国接二连三地被军事独裁者所统治。

student-centred *adj* = LEARNER-CENTRED

studentship /'stju:dntʃɪp, *US* stu:-; 'studn̩tʃɪp/ *n* (*Brit*) opportunity offered to a graduate to do research or to study for a higher degree at a university, usu with a grant or other small payment, esp for a fixed period 研究生资格（通常有助学金）: *Higher degree students holding studentships were expected to do a certain amount of tutoring each term.* 享受助学金的研究生每学期需完成一定的助教工作。

stun grenade /'stʌn grəneɪd; 'stʌn grɪned/ *n* GRENADE[A-Z] which explodes with a loud bang and a bright flash of light, intended to stun and confuse rather than to injure 眩晕手榴弹（爆炸时会产生巨大的响声和闪光，旨在使人眩晕而非伤人的手榴弹）: *Stun grenades and rubber bullets are part of the weaponry of the modern riot police force.* 眩晕手榴弹和橡皮子弹是现代防暴警察武器装备的一部分。

stun gun /'stʌn gʌn; 'stʌn gʌn/ *n* weapon that delivers a powerful electric shock causing temporary paralysis 电击枪（可释放出强大电流引起暂时麻痹的枪）

styrofoam /'staɪrə,fəʊm; 'staɪrə,fom/ *n* [U] (*esp US*) kind of expanded POLYSTYRENE[A-Z] 聚苯乙烯泡沫塑料

sub-aqua /,sʌb'ækwə; ,sʌb'ækə/ *adj* [usu attrib 通常作定语] performed under water 水下的；在水底进行的: *sub-aqua diving/archaeology* 潜水、水底考古学

subjectivism /səb'dʒektɪvɪzəm; səb'dʒɛktɪvɪzəm/ *n* [U] (*philosophy* 哲) theory that knowledge is subjective and that no external or absolute truth exists 主观主义，主观论（主张一切知识均为主观经验，不存在任何外在的或绝对的真理）

sudden infant death syndrome *n* = COT-DEATH (COT[A-Z])

sudden unexplained death syndrome /sʌdn ,ʌnɪkspleɪnd 'deθ ,sɪndrəʊm; sʌdn̩ ,ʌnɪksplend 'dɛθ ,sɪndrom/ *n* [U] (*abbr* 缩写 **SUDS**) sudden death of an apparently healthy young person from no clear cause（看上去很健康的年轻人的）原因不明的猝死

suicide bomber /'su:ɪsaɪd bɒmə(r); 'suəsaɪd bɑmɚ/ *n* man or woman who is willing to be killed while carrying out a bomb attack on a place or a person 自杀投弹者，舍身投弹者（不惜牺牲自己生命进行炸弹袭击的人）: *The suicide bomber had strapped sticks of dynamite around herself which were set off by remote control as soon as she got close enough to the platform where the Prime Minister was standing.* 那个自杀投弹者在身上绑满了一管管炸药，当她一走到离首相站立的讲坛够近的地方时，炸药由遥控器引爆了。

suicide mission /'su:ɪsaɪd mɪʃn; 'suəsaɪd mɪʃən/ *n* MISSION 3[A-Z] which is very dangerous and which those who undertake it are unlikely to survive 自杀性任务（十分危险的任务，执行者不大可能生还）

summiteer /,sʌmɪ'tɪə(r); ,sʌmɪ'tɪr/ *n* **1** participant in a summit meeting 高峰会议［首脑会议］参加者 **2** mountaineer who has completed an ascent to the summit of a mountain 登上山的顶峰者；臻极者

sumo /'su:məʊ; 'sumo/ (also **sumo wrestling**) *n* [U] Japanese style of wrestling in which fighters with massive bodies participate. One fighter must force the other out of a marked circle or make him touch the ground with any part of his body other than his feet 相扑: *a 200-kilo sumo wrestler* 一名体重 200 公斤的相扑运动员

sunbed /'sʌnbed; 'sʌnbɛd/ *n* **1** light, usu folding, chair with a seat long enough to support one's legs, and a back which may be lowered into a reclining or flat position 轻便折叠躺椅；日光浴床 **2** bed for lying on under a sunlamp 太阳灯浴床

sunblock /'sʌnblɒk; 'sʌnblɑk/ (also **sunscreen**) *n* [U,C] substance to put on the skin in order to protect it from sunburn 防晒油；防晒霜: *a sunblock with a factor of 18* 防晒系数为 18 的防晒霜

sun protection factor /,sʌn prə'tekʃn fæktə(r); ,sʌn prə'tɛkʃn̩ fæktɚ/ *n* **1** ratio of the time it takes skin to burn when wearing a sunscreen compared with the time it takes to burn without one 防晒系数（涂了防晒品与未涂防晒品的皮肤晒伤所需时间之比）**2** measure of sunscreen effectiveness 防晒系数（作为防晒效果的衡量标准）: *Children need the protection of a cream with a high sun protection factor.* 孩子需要防晒系数高的防晒霜。

sunscreen *n* = SUNBLOCK

superbug /'su:pəbʌg; 'supɚbʌg/ *n* (*infml* 口) strain of bacteria that has evolved to become resistant to most antibiotic drugs（已对大部分抗菌素产生抗药性的）超级病菌: *A superbug scare has closed some hospital wards.* 一些医院的病房因超级病菌引起的恐慌而关闭。

supercollider *n* = PARTICLE ACCELERATOR

supercomputer /'su:pəkəm,pju:tə(r); 'supɚkəm,pjutɚ/ *n* powerful computer with the capacity to deal with complex tasks at high speed 超级计算机（能快速处理复杂任务的计算机）: *the Cray supercomputer* 克雷超级计算机

supergrass /'su:pəgrɑ:s, *US* -græs; 'supɚgræs/ *n* (*Brit infml* 口) criminal who informs the police about the activities of a large number of other criminals, usu in order to get a lighter sentence for his or her own crimes（通常为减轻刑罚）向警方告发很多其他罪犯活动的罪犯 Cf 参看 GRASS[1] 5[A-Z]

superhighway /su:pə'haɪweɪ; supɚ'haɪwe/ *n* (*computing* 计) one of a number of projected national high-speed, high-capacity telecommunications networks linking homes and offices and permitting the transmission of a variety of electronic media, including video, audio, multimedia and text 信息高速公路（连接家居及办公室，能高速和大量传送影像、声音、多媒体资料及文本的电信网络）

supermodel /'su:pə,mɒdl; 'supɚ,mɑdl̩/ *n* highly-paid model employed in high-profile fashion modelling by the most prestigious fashion houses 超级模特儿；超级名模

superstate /'su:pə,steɪt; 'supɚ,stet/ *n* powerful political state, esp one formed from a federation of nations 超级大国（尤指由多个国家组成的联盟）

superunleaded /su:pəʌn'ledɪd; supɚʌn'lɛdɪd/ *adj* (of petrol) with no added lead, but with the addition of aromatic hydrocarbons which have been seen as pollutants themselves, to enhance performance of motor vehicles（指汽油）超级无铅的（虽不含铅但加入了具有污染性的芳香烃以提高机动车的性能）

▷ **superunleaded** *n* superunleaded petrol 超级无铅汽油 Cf 参看 OCTANE[A-Z]

supply-side /sə'plaɪsaɪd; sə'plaɪsaɪd/ *adj* (*finance* 财) of the policy of reducing unemployment benefits, taxes, government expenditure, etc in order to stimulate economic growth 供应经济学政策的（主张减少失业救济金、税收以及政府开支等以刺激经济增长的）: *supply-side economics* 供应经济学

▷ **supply-sider** *n* supporter of supply-side policy 供应经济学支持者；供应学派: *Supply-siders are less in favour now than they were during the Reagon presidency.* 供应学派现已不如里根执政期间那么受欢迎了。

supremo /su:'pri:məʊ; su'primo/ *n* (*pl* **-os**) (*Brit*) high-ranking leader, manager or director 高层领导人；高级主管；权威: *an interview with fashion supremo Jean-Paul Gaultier* 对时装界巨子让·保罗·戈尔捷的采访 ○ *the newly-appointed drugs control supremo* 新任命的禁毒总负责人

surf /sɜ:f; sɝf/ *v* [Tn] (*computing fig* 计，比喻) (used in a variety of compounds, mainly connected with computing or communications 用以构成与计算机或通讯有关的复合词) travel by riding as if on a surfboard; browse 冲浪；浏览: *surfs the Internet* 在互联网上冲浪 Cf 参看 CHANNEL SURF, NETSURFER

surgeon general /,sɜ:dʒən 'dʒenrəl; ,sɝdʒən 'dʒɛnərəl/ *n* (*pl* **surgeons general**) (*US*) director of a public health service or of a medical service in any of the armed forces 卫生局局长；军医局局长: *Cigarette packets must carry a health warning from the surgeon general.* 香烟盒上必须标有卫生局局长发出的关于吸烟有害健康的警告。

survivalist /sɜːˈvaɪvəlɪst; sɚˈvaɪvəlɪst/ *n* person who makes preparations to survive, eg in an atomic war, by collecting food and weapons, esp guns and knives, and takes part in military-style exercises 活命主义者（收集粮食和刀枪等武器并进行军训式锻炼，准备在核战等中活命的人）

sushi /ˈsuːʃɪ; ˈsuʃɪ/ *n* [U] Japanese food which consists of small cakes of cold rice and pieces of raw fish, etc, eaten with spicy sauces 寿司（一种日本食品，用小团的冷米饭和生鱼片等做成，吃时蘸辛辣调料）: *Sushi has become increasingly popular with Chinese diners in Hong Kong.* 寿司越来越受香港的中国人欢迎。

sussed /sʌst; sʌst/ *adj* (*Brit sl* 俚) (**a**) in the know; well-informed; aware 知情的；见多识广的；明智的：*sussed young people* 见多识广的年轻人 (**b**) found out, understood 被发现的；被了解的：*They've got him sussed. They know he's only pretending to care about them.* 他们看出了他的庐山真面目，知道他只不过在假装关心他们。Cf 参看 SUS^A-Z

sustainable /səˈsteɪnəbl; səˈstenəbl̩/ *adj* (of an activity or the use of a resource) able to be sustained over an indefinite period without damage to the environment; renewable（指活动或资源使用）能持续进行而不损害环境的，能再生的，永续的：*sustainable tourism* 持续性旅游业 ○ *sustainable use of timber resources* 木材资源的可持续使用

swagger portrait /ˈswæɡə pɔːtreɪt, -trɪt; ˈswæɡɚ portret, -trɪt/ *n* (*infml* 口) commissioned portrait, esp a painted one, of an important or wealthy person intended to represent the sitter's role, power, or status 名人画像，名流画像（要人或富翁托人作的画像，旨在表现其重要性、权力或地位）: *an exhibition of swagger portraits from the early 18th century up to the present* 展出从 18 世纪初至今的名人画像

swatch /swɒtʃ; swɑtʃ/ *n* sample of fabric, wool, etc（布料、毛料等的）样品；样布：*swatches of different furnishing fabrics* 各种装饰布料的样品

sweatpants /ˈswetpænts; ˈswɛtpænts/ *n* [pl] loose, thick trousers, usu made of cotton, with an elasticated or drawstring waist, worn for sports or as leisurewear 宽松运动裤（运动或休闲时穿的裤子，通常为棉质的，腰部有松紧带或束带）

swimwear /ˈswɪmweə(r); ˈswɪmwɛr/ *n* [U] clothing worn for swimming 泳装；游泳衣：*the swimwear department on the fourth floor* 五楼泳装部

swingbeat /ˈswɪŋbiːt; ˈswɪŋbit/ *n* [U] form of dance music combining elements of rhythm and blues, soul, HIP-HOP and RAP music 强节奏摇摆舞曲（糅合了节奏布鲁斯、黑人灵歌、嬉蹦乐以及绕舌歌等元素的音乐）

swinging /ˈswɪŋɪŋ; ˈswɪŋɪŋ/ *adj* (*infml* 口) lively and modern in style, attitudes, etc（式样、态度等）赶时髦的，新潮的，活泼的：*when London was really swinging* 当伦敦真个时髦的时候

NOTE 注： frequently used in the expression *the swinging sixties* 常用于词组 the swinging sixties（新潮的六十年代）

swipe /swaɪp; swaɪp/ *n* (*infml* 口) electronic device for reading magnetically encoded information, as on a credit card or an identity card, usu incorporating a slot through which the card is passed（用来识别信用卡、身分证等的）电子识码器，刷卡机：*The door of the hotel room was fitted with an electronic swipe.* 旅馆房间的门上装有电子识码器。

switchgear /ˈswɪtʃɡɪə(r); ˈswɪtʃɡɪr/ *n* [U] electrical apparatus used for opening and closing electric circuits（电路的）开关装置

synergy /ˈsɪnədʒɪ; ˈsɪnɚdʒɪ/ *n* [U] possible or actual good effects of the joining together of two companies in terms of higher efficiency or productivity（两公司合并后可能产生或实际产生的）增效作用，增加生产力作用 Cf 参看 DYSERGY

systems software *n* (*computing* 计) = APPLET

Tt

taco /ˈtɑːkəʊ, ˈtækəʊ; ˈtæko/ *n* (*pl* **-os**) Mexican dish consisting of a folded, often crisp, PANCAKE 1^A-Z filled with meat, vegetables, etc and often flavoured with chillies and other spices 墨西哥薄饼卷（以肉、蔬菜等为馅并常以辣椒和其他香料调味的一种食品，通常是脆的）Cf 参看 TAQUERIA

NOTE 注： from a Spanish word 源自西班牙语

tag[1] /tæɡ; tæɡ/ *n* (in HIP-HOP culture) example of graffiti, usu a decorated nickname, word, or initial, made by a graffiti artist as a personal signature and mark of identity（嬉蹦族文化）签名，留名（街头涂鸦者留下的绰号、单字或姓名首字母，作为个人签名和识别标志）: *Tags proclaimed the playground to be the territory of the Catmeat gang.* 猫肉帮留下签名表明这片运动场是他们的领地。

▷ **tag** *v* [Tn] decorate a place or object with graffiti; leave one's graffito signature in a public place 涂鸦装饰；（在公共场所）留下签名

tag[2] /tæɡ; tæɡ/ *v* [Tn] (*computing* 计) mark any part in a data structure for later retrieval, eg label the words of a text as members of word classes, ie verb, noun, etc automatically 标记（将某组数据中的某部分标上记号以便日后检索，如自动将文字部分的词标上词性等）

tagliatelle /ˌtæljəˈtelɪ; ˌtæljəˈtɛlɪ/ *n* [U] form of PASTA^A-Z rolled out and cut into thin flat strips 意大利扁面条

tag sale *n* (*US*) = CAR-BOOT SALE (CAR^A-Z)

taiga /ˈtaɪɡə; ˈtaɪɡə/ *n* [U] birch and fir-tree covered countryside of Siberia in Russia 泰加森林（俄罗斯西伯利亚为桦树和冷杉所覆盖的野外地区）: *All day we travelled through the seemingly endless taiga.* 我们整日穿行在似乎无边无垠的泰加森林里。

take /teɪk; tek/ *n* (usu *sing* 通常作单数) (*infml* 口) opinion; attitude; interpretation 观点；态度；诠释：*What's your take on the possibility of cloning humans?* 你对于克隆人类的可能性怎么看？

take-back legislation /ˈteɪkbæk ledʒɪsˌleɪʃn; ˈtekbæk lɛdʒɪsˌleʃn̩/ *n* [U] legislation which provides for the producers of household electrical goods to take responsibility for the proper disposal of those goods when they are too old to repair any longer 回收法（规定家用电器生产商在其产品因太旧而无法再修时负责将其回收处理的法律）: *Take-back legislation would go some way towards solving the problem of how to get rid of old refrigerators and washing machines.* 回收法在一定程度上能解决如何处理旧冰箱和旧洗衣机的问题。

take-up /ˈteɪkʌp; ˈtekʌp/ *n* [U sing] extent to which sth is accepted by the people to whom it is offered or made available 接受程度；接受率：*The company reports a 70 per cent take-up of its share offer.* 该公司报告说其百分之七十的股份已被认购。

Taliban /ˈtæləbæn; ˈtæləbæn/ *n* **the Taliban** [sing] movement founded by Islamic fundamentalists (FUNDAMENTALISM^A-Z) which is now in power in Afghanistan 塔利班（伊斯兰原教旨主义者创建的组织，现执掌阿富汗）

tamagotchi /ˈtæməɡɒtʃɪ, tæməˈɡɒtʃɪ; ˈtæməɡɑtʃɪ/ *n* (*pl* ~**s**) (*Japanese* 日语) toy for children which is a small electronic device showing a cartoon image on a screen which the owner interacts with and influences and keeps as a pet 电子宠物（作为儿童玩具的一种小电子

装置，其荧屏上显示出卡通形象，成为主人的宠物并对其操控作出反应）

Tamil tigers /'tæmɪl taɪgəz, tæmɪl 'taɪgəz; 'tæmɪl taɪgɚz/ *n* **the Tamil tigers** [pl] guerrilla army fighting the Sri Lankan government for independence for the Tamil-speaking people and a separate state 泰米尔虎游击队（斯里兰卡反政府游击队，旨在争取泰米尔人独立和成立独立国家）

tamoxifen /tæ'mɒksɪfən; tæ'mɑksɪfən/ *n* (*propr medicine* 专利名，药) drug that may prove to provide effective protection against breast cancer and treatment of infertility in women, according to the results of early research 三苯氧胺，它莫西芬（根据早期研究结果，对治疗妇女乳腺癌和不育症有效的一种药）

tamper-evident /'tæmpəˌevɪdənt; 'tæmpɚˌɛvədənt/ (also **tamper-proof**) *adj* (of packaging) designed to show clearly if the package has been opened in any way and the contents tampered with (TAMPER^A-Z^) (指包装) 防拆封的，拆封后易识别的 : *All of our tablets are now packaged in bottles with tamper-evident tops.* 现在我们所有的药片都是用有防拆封瓶盖的瓶包装的。

tamper-proof *adj* = TAMPER-EVIDENT

tanga /'tæŋgə; 'tæŋgə/ *n* (*Brit*) pair of BRIEFS^A-Z^ consisting of small panels of material connected with strings 镶条内裤

NOTE 注： from a Portuguese word 源自葡萄牙语

tape-record *v* = TAPE *v* 2^A-Z^

taqueria /'tɑ:kəri:ə, tækə'ri:ə; 'tækəriə, tækə'riə/ *n* restaurant specialising in Mexican food, esp tacos (TACO) 墨西哥餐馆（尤指专卖煎玉米卷的快餐店）

NOTE 注： formed on analogy with *pizzeria*, a word of Italian origin meaning a place where pizzas are made and sold 由源自意大利语的 pizzeria（制造和出售 pizza（意大利饼）的店家）一词类推构成

targa /'tɑ:gə; 'tɑrgə/ *n* [often attrib 常作定语] type of convertible sports car with a roof hood or panel which can be removed 可卸式敞篷跑车 Cf 参看 CONVERTIBLE *n*^A-Z^

NOTE 注： from the Italian word meaning 'shield'; originally the name of a model of Porsche 源自意大利语，意为'挡风板'；原为保时捷一种车型的名字

tastemaker /'teɪstmeɪkə(r); 'testmekɚ/ *n* person or group whose opinion on fashion, style and taste is highly respected and followed by those who want to be thought stylish and fashionable themselves 左右时尚者，时尚导向者（对时尚、品味的观点倍受尊崇并为爱好时尚者追随的人）: *He is one of the tastemakers of interior decoration and if he says that striped wallpaper is the thing, then everyone who is anyone will have it.* 他是室内装饰潮流的先导，如果他说带条纹的墙纸最时髦，那么大家都会趋之若鹜。

tasty /'teɪstɪ; 'testɪ/ *adj* (*infml* 口) (usu of a woman) attractive, sexy（通常指女性）迷人的，性感的 : *I like the look of the new personal assistant. Really tasty.* 我喜欢那新来的私人助理的样子，的确迷人。

tax avoidance /'tæks əvɔɪdəns; 'tæks əvɔɪdəns/ *n* [U] arrangement of one's financial affairs so that one pays no more than the minimum amount of tax required by law 避税（用合法的方法将应纳税额减至最低）: *His accountant advised him on tax avoidance, but only insofar as this was perfectly legal.* 他的会计师帮他避税，但只限于绝对合法的范围内。Cf 参看 TAX SHELTER

tax break /'tæks breɪk; 'tæks brek/ *n* provision in the tax laws that allows the payer to receive a financial benefit, either by the exemption of an item from tax altogether or by reducing tax in certain circumstances, eg payments made to a registered charity are exempted from taxation in some countries 税额优惠，减税优惠（税法中规定在某些情况下纳税人可以享受某种免税或减免税额的优惠，如在某些国家慈善捐款可以免税）

tax disc *n* (*Brit*) = ROAD TAX DISC (ROAD^A-Z^)

tax-exempt /ˌtæksɪg'zempt; ˌtæksɪg'zɛmpt/ *adj* not subject to the payment of tax 免税的 : *a tax-exempt savings scheme* 一项免税的储蓄方案

taxiway /'tæksɪweɪ; 'tæksɪwe/ *n* route along which an aircraft taxies (TAXI *v*^A-Z^) to or from a runway（与跑道相连的）飞机滑行道

tax relief /'tæks rɪli:f; 'tæks rɪlif/ *n* [U] reduction in the amount of tax one would normally be required to pay, eg because one is paying for a MORTGAGE^A-Z^ 税额减免（如因要偿还抵押借款而获减税）

tax shelter /'tæks ʃeltə(r); 'tæks ʃɛltɚ/ *n* method of organizing business and financial affairs so as to reduce the payment of tax to a minimum 减免纳税手段；避税手段 : *Up to now, offshore accounts have offered tax shelters for high earners.* 迄今为止，在海外开设帐户是高收入者减免纳税的手段。Cf 参看 OFFSHORE ACCOUNT , TAX AVOIDANCE

T-bar /'ti:bɑ:(r); 'tibɑr/ (also **T-bar lift**) *n* type of ski lift in the form of a series of inverted T-shaped bars for towing skiers uphill（载滑雪者上山的）倒 T 字型吊椅

team player /ti:m 'pleɪə(r); tim 'pleɚ/ *n* person who plays or works well as a member of a team and is not solely concerned with his or her own glory 有合作精神的团队成员；良好的合作伙伴 : *She was brilliant as an individual, but never a good team player.* 她的个人表现极为出色，但她绝不是个好的合作伙伴。

techie /'tekɪ; 'tɛkɪ/ *n* (*infml* 口) expert in or enthusiast for technology, esp computing; technician 技术专家（尤指计算机方面的）；技师

NOTE 注： may be slightly derogatory, implying that the techie has rather narrow technical skills 有时略带贬义，暗指其技术范围较窄

techno- /'teknəʊ; 'tɛkno/ *comb form* 构词成分 (*computing* 计) relating to those industrial techniques which use advanced or specialized methods, esp computing 采用先进或专业方法的工业技术（尤指计算机技术）

technobabble /'teknəʊbæbl; 'tɛknoˌbæbḷ/ *n* [U] incomprehensible jargon of the new technologies, esp computing 难懂的新技术用语（尤指计算机技术的）

NOTE 注： formed from *techno-* and *babble* (speech difficult to understand) 由 techno-（先进技术的）和 babble（难懂的话）二词构成

technology transfer /tek'nɒlədʒɪ ˌtrænsfɜ:(r); tɛk'nɑlədʒɪ ˌtrænsfɚ/ *n* [U] (*commerce* 商) transfer of new technology from the originator to a secondary user, eg the licensing of new techniques or processes which have been developed in universities and research centres to industrial firms for commercial exploitation 技术转让（发明者将新技术转让给用户，如准许公司将在大学和研究中心研究成功的新技术或新工艺流程用于商业性开发）

technophile /'teknəʊfaɪl; 'tɛknofaɪl/ *n* person who is attracted to new technologies and adapts to them readily 新技术爱好者（喜爱并能很快掌握新技术的人）

NOTE 注： formed from *techno-* and *philos* , the Greek word meaning 'loving' 由 techno-（先进技术的）与希腊语 philos（喜爱）二词构成 Cf 参看 TECHNOPHOBE

technophobe /'teknəʊfəʊb; 'tɛknofob/ *n* person who is afraid of the products of modern technology and reluctant to use them 恐惧新技术者（恐惧并不愿使用现代科技产品的人）

NOTE 注： formed from *techno-* and *phobos* , the Greek word meaning 'fearing' 由 techno-（先进技术

的）和希腊语 phobos（恐惧）二词构成 Cf 参看 TECHNOPHILE

technothriller /ˈteknəʊˌθrɪlə(r); ˈtɛknoˌθrɪlɚ/ *n* suspense novel in which advances in technology and in turn the creation of new social and physical environments play a central role 科技惊险小说（以先进技术及由此形成的新的社会和自然环境为主要内容的小说）

NOTE 注： a *thriller* may also be called a *suspense novel* ☆ thriller（惊险小说）亦可称作 suspense novel

teeter-totter *n* (*US*) = SEE-SAW 1A-Z

Teflon /ˈteflɒn; ˈtɛflɑn/ *n* [U] (*propr* 专利名) substance forming a non-stick surface on cooking implements, pans, etc 特氟隆，聚四氟乙烯（制成厨具、锅等的不黏层的物质）

▷ **Teflon** *adj* (*fig* 比喻) (of a politician) able to escape any damage from scandal or criticism（指政治家）免受指责的，免受丑闻困扰的：*Reagan was known as the Teflon President because of his apparent imperviousness to politicial damage.* 里根因拥有不受政治伤害的形象而被称为'特氟隆总统'。

telebanking /ˌtelɪˈbæŋkɪŋ; ˌtɛlɪˈbæŋkɪŋ/ *n* [U] **1** banking service accessed by phone or computer 电话［计算机］银行服务；银行事务远程处理 **2** action of using telebanking 通过电话［计算机］处理银行事务

telecommuter /ˌtelɪkəˈmjuːtə(r); ˌtɛlɪkəˈmjutɚ/ *n* person who works from home while remaining in contact with the office and elsewhere via computers 电信远程上班者（在家通过计算机与办公室及他处保持联系的人）：*the growing band of telecommuters* 不断壮大的电信远程上班族

▷ **telecommuting** *n* practice of a telecommuter 远程上班；远距离工作

telecottage /ˈtelɪˌkɒtɪdʒ; ˈtelɪˌkɑtɪdʒ/ *n* centre fitted with office equipment, eg fax, computers, etc for use by people working freelance or at a distance from an employer 远程办公室（配有传真机、计算机等设备的办公中心，供自由职业者或远离雇主工作者使用）

tele-education /ˌtelɪedʒuːˈkeɪʃn; ˌtɛlɪedʒəˈkeʃən/ *n* [U] distance learning using telecommunications 电信远程教育（用电信设备进行的远距离学习）

telegenic /ˌtelɪˈdʒenɪk; ˌtɛlɪˈdʒɛnɪk/ *adj* able to look attractive and convincing on television 电视形象佳的；适于上电视的：*Nowadays, anyone who aspires to hold office in a government has to be telegenic as well as ambitious.* 如今想在政府供职的人既得有抱负还得有好的电视形象。Cf 参看 MEDIAGENIC

telekinesis /ˌtelɪkaɪˈniːsɪs; ˌtɛlɪkaɪˈnisɪs/ *n* [U] ability to move objects from a distance using only the power of the mind 心灵致动，心灵感应（只凭心灵的力量移动物件的能力）

telemarketing /ˌtelɪˈmɑːkɪtɪŋ; ˌtɛlɪˈmɑrkɪtɪŋ/ *n* [U] marketing of goods or services through unsolicited telephone calls 电话推销（商品或服务）：*Telemarketing may be regarded as a nuisance by many of its victims, but the sales figures show just how successful it can be.* 不少人也许讨厌电话推销，但销售额却显示了其成功之处。

▷ **telemarketer** *n* person who works in telemarketing 电话推销员

telemedicine /ˌtelɪˈmedsn; ˌtɛlɪˈmɛdəsn̩/ *n* [U] system of making medical advice and information, including diagnosis, instantly available over a wide area using the TV cable network 电视医疗（通过有线电视网络即时向广大地区提供医疗意见和信息并进行诊断的系统）：*Telemedicine is especially useful in remote areas where expert advice is not otherwise available.* 电视医疗在原本无法获得专家意见的偏远地区尤为有用。

telemessage *n* (*Brit*) = TELEGRAMA-Z

telephone sex /ˈtelɪfəʊn ˌseks, ˌtelɪfəʊn ˈseks; ˈtɛləfon ˌsɛks/ *n* [U] indulgence of sexual fantasies through talking to sb on the phone, sometimes using a commercial SEX LINE 电话色情，电话性行为（通过与人在电话中交谈满足性幻想，有时使用商业色情电话线）

telephone tapping /ˈtelɪfəʊn tæpɪŋ; ˈtɛləfon tæpɪŋ/ (also **phone tapping**) *n* [U] practice of fitting a hidden device to a telephone in order to listen to people's telephone conversations（安装窃听器进行的）电话窃听：*The police carried out telephone tapping operations for several months before they got the evidence they needed.* 警方进行了电话窃听数月，才得到所需的证据。

telepoint /ˈtelɪˌpɔɪnt; ˈtɛlɪˌpɔɪnt/ *n* **1** place where a cordless telephone may be connected to the telephone network（可将无绳电话接入电话网的）入网点 **2** system providing or using telepoints 无绳电话入网系统

telepresence /ˈtelɪˌprezns; ˈtɛlɪˌprɛzn̩s/ *n* [U] **1** use of virtual reality technology, usu for remote control of machinery or apparent participation in distant events 虚拟临场遥控，远距离出席（常指利用虚拟现实技术对机器进行遥控或藉以参与远方发生的事情） **2** sensation of being in another place which is created by telepresence 远地临场感：*Nowadays executives can enjoy telepresence at video conferences instead of travelling so much.* 如今的行政人员无须疲于奔命了，他们可以通过电视会议享受远地临场技术带来的方便。

telethon /ˈteləθɒn; ˈtɛləθɑn/ *n* very long television programme, broadcast to raise money for charity（为慈善募捐而播放的）长时间的电视节目，马拉松式电视节目：*The telethon raised more than $10 million dollars for charity.* 这个马拉松电视节目为慈善事业募捐了超过一千万美元。

NOTE 注： a blend formed from the words *television* and *marathon* 由 television 与 marathon（马拉松赛跑）二词合成

televangelism /ˌtelɪˈvændʒəlɪzəm; ˌtɛlɪˈvændʒəlɪzəm/ *n* [U] preaching of the Christian gospel, esp from a fundamentalist point of view, through the medium of television, usu by TELEGENIC preachers in a lavish and attractive setting with music, dancing and glamorous presenters 电视福音传道（通常由电视形象佳的传教士在富丽的环境中通过电视传播尤其是原教旨主义的基督教，伴以音乐、舞蹈和有魅力的主持人）：*Televangelism is big business in the States, and evangelical preachers are reaching a bigger audience than ever before.* 电视福音布道在美国影响很大，福音传教士今天拥有大量的观众，史无前例。

▷ **televangelist** *n*

televiewer /ˈtelɪˌvjʊə(r); ˈtɛlɪˌvjuɚ/ *n* person who watches television, esp such a person as the target for marketing or as a member of a social group 电视观众（尤指电视广告的目标或某一社会阶层的成员）：*The commercials are targeted at a particular group of televiewers.* 那些广告是针对某一特定电视观众群的。

▷ **televiewing** *adj* : *the televiewing public* 电视观众

teleworker *n* = TELECOMMUTER

teleworking *n* [U] = TELECOMMUTING (TELECOMMUTER)

tentacles /ˈtentəklz; ˈtɛntəkl̩z/ *n* [pl] (*fig often derog* 比喻，常作贬义) influence and power of a large place, organization, system, etc from which it is hard to escape（难以摆脱的来自大的地方、组织、体制等的）魔爪，束缚：*the spreading tentacles of government bureaucracy* 正在伸展的政府官僚主义的魔爪 Cf 参看 TENTACLEA-Z

terraform /ˈterəfɔːm; ˈtɛrəfɔrm/ *v* [Tn] change the terrain, climate and atmosphere of another planet so that it becomes sufficiently like that of the earth to support human life and allow settlement on it 将（另一行星的）地形、气候和空气改造得跟地球相似至足以供人类居住；改造成地球般：*If you want to terraform another planet, you have to think in terms of thousands rather than hundreds of years.* 如果想将另一颗行星改造得适合人类居住，需要的是几千年而不是几百年的时间。

NOTE 注： formed from the Latin word *terra* (earth) and the English verb *form* 由拉丁语 terra（土地）和英语动词 form（形成）二词构成

terrestrial /tə'restriəl; tə'rɛstriəl/ *adj* (of television signals) given out by land-based stations, not by satellites（指电视信号）来自地面站的（而非来自人造卫星的）：*Most households now have access to satellite television as well as to longer-established terrestrial television.* 现在多数家庭都能收看卫星电视和设立已久的地面电视。

TESOL /'ti:sɒl, 'tesɒl; 'tisɑl, 'tɛsɑl/ *abbr* 缩写 = (*esp US*) teaching of English to speakers of other languages 对操外语者的英语教学 Cf 参看 TEFL[A-Z], TESL[A-Z]

testing /'testɪŋ; 'tɛstɪŋ/ *adj* difficult to deal with and requiring certain qualities and abilities 费力的；棘手的：*testing assignments* 艰难使命 ○ *a testing situation* 棘手的情况

testosterone /te'stɒstərəʊn; tɛ'stɑstəron/ *n* [U] (*biology* 生) most important sex HORMONE (a)[A-Z] produced in the testicles (TESTICLE[A-Z]) that is capable of developing and maintaining male characteristics in the body 睾酮，睾丸素（睾丸产生的最重要的男性激素，能促进身体男性特征的发育并使之得以保持）

test run *n* = TRIAL RUN (TRIAL[A-Z])

theatricality /θɪˌætrɪ'kæləti; θɪˌætrɪ'kælətɪ/ *n* [U] exaggerated, dramatic or artificial style or effect of sth, esp an event or sb's behaviour（尤指事件或行为的）戏剧化、夸张或不自然的风格或效果：*The theatricality of the state funeral was impressive.* 国葬仪式操办得很铺张，令人难忘。

theme /θi:m; θim/ *n* [usu attrib 通常作定语] topic around which a restaurant, park, etc is organized and which decides its decor and design（建造和设计餐馆、公园等的）主题，基调：*Restaurants with a definite theme are all the rage in New York.* 在纽约有明确主题的餐馆风靡一时。○ *a new theme park* 一个新的主题公园

▷ **themed** *adj*：*themed restaurants/leisure parks* 主题餐馆 *[乐园]*

thin-skinned /ˌθɪn'skɪnd; θɪn'skɪnd/ *adj* sensitive to criticism or insults（对批评或羞辱）敏感的；脸皮薄的：*You can't afford to be thin-skinned if you want to be a politician.* 你要想成为一名政客，脸皮薄可不行。Cf 参看 THICK-SKINNED (THICK[A-Z])

third umpire /θɜ:d 'ʌmpaɪə(r); θɝd 'ʌmpaɪɚ/ *n* [sing] (in cricket) playback of a television recording of an incident, eg a run-out, which is taken as decisive（板球赛的）第三裁判（作为裁决依据的录像重放，如击中三柱门的情况）：*an appeal to the third umpire* 要求第三裁判判决

NOTE 注： there are two human umpires for a cricket match so the camera replay counts as a third means of reaching a decision, ie acts as a third umpire 板球赛中有两名裁判人员，因此录像重放成为裁决的第三种方法，即充当第三裁判

thirtysomething /'θɜ:tiˌsʌmθɪŋ; 'θɝtɪˌsʌmθɪŋ/ *adj* [usu attrib 通常作定语] somewhere in age between thirty and forty 三十岁到四十岁之间的：*a thirtysomething professional with a well-paid job* 三十来岁收入丰厚的专业人士

throwing star *n* = DEATH STAR

throw-over /'θrəʊˌəʊvə(r); 'θroˌovɚ/ *adj* [attrib 作定语] (of material) able to be thrown over a bed, sofa, etc, as a decorative cover（指物料）可作为装饰罩于床、沙发等上面的：*Brocade is the ideal throw-over material.* 织锦是制作装饰布罩的理想材料。

thruster /'θrʌstə(r); 'θrʌstɚ/ *n* small engine used to make changes in the flight path or altitude of an aircraft, esp a spacecraft 推进器，助推器（用以改变飞机尤其是宇宙飞船的航线或高度的小型发动机）

tie-back /'taɪbæk; 'taɪbæk/ *n* decorative strip of fabric or cord used for holding a curtain back from a window（用来将帘子收拢到窗的一边的）帘帷装饰扣带：*matching tie-backs* 与帘帷相配的扣带

tie-in /'taɪɪn; 'taɪɪn/ *n* ~ **(with sth) 1** joint promotion of related products, eg a book and a film 搭卖，搭配推销（如把某书和有关电影一起推销）：*a TV tie-in* 电视搭卖推销 ○ *a tie-in with the band's latest album* 该乐队最新唱片的搭卖品 **2** any connection or association 关联；关系：*You haven't shown that there was any tie-in with the company under investigation.* 你并未证明那家被调查的公司是否牵涉在内。

tiger *n* = DRAGON

tiger economy *n* = DRAGON

tight-knit /ˌtaɪt'nɪt; taɪt'nɪt/ *adj* (of a family, community, etc) having a strong sense of belonging and loyalty, with close links between members（指家庭、社区等）紧密团结的，成员间关系密切的：*They're a tight-knit group and give each other lots of support.* 他们是一个紧密团结的团体，互相给予很大的支持。

tile /taɪl; taɪl/ *v* [I, Tn] (*computing* 计) **1** arrange individual application areas in a graphically-based computer display in a rectangular array without overlapping 瓷砖式显示，并列式开窗口（在图像显示的计算机中使各个应用程序窗口在屏幕上呈矩形排列，互不覆盖）**2** cover part or all of a computer display with multiple copies of an image arranged in a rectangular grid 瓷砖式覆盖（将一图像的多份拷贝按格子形排列，覆盖部分或整个屏幕）

time-and-motion /ˌtaɪmənd'məʊʃn; ˌtaɪmənd'moʃən/ *adj* [attrib 作定语] concerned with measuring the efficiency of industrial and other operations, usu through a close observation of the behaviour of workers 时间与动作的（通常凭仔细观察工人的作业程序以衡量生产等的效率的）：*a time-and-motion study* 时间与动作研究

time-based media /ˌtaɪmbeɪsd 'mi:diə; ˌtaɪmbesd 'midɪə/ *n* [pl] subject taught in tertiary education institutions which focuses on the use of the computer in areas such as design and film 现代媒体学（高等院校里开设的课程，集中讲授在设计和电影业领域如何运用计算机）

time bomb /'taɪm bɒm; 'taɪm bɑm/ *n* (*computing* 计) type of VIRUS deliberately included in or introduced into a computer program which does not cause any harm immediately but is timed to operate on a specific date 定时炸弹（一种计算机病毒，放进计算机程序后并不立即造成损害，而是到指定的日期发作）：*The Friday the thirteenth virus is a time bomb set to go off every time that date occurs.* '十三号星期五' 病毒是枚定时炸弹，每到那一天就会爆发。

time capsule /'taɪm kæpsju:l, *US* kæpsl; 'taɪm kæpsl/ *n* container holding objects typical of a particular time, buried for discovery in the future 时代文物密藏器（内存代表某一时代的物品，埋藏起来让后世发现的盛器）：*The time capsule buried in the new shopping centre yesterday will be dug up again in 150 years.* 昨天埋在新购物中心的时代文物密藏器会在 150 年后被挖掘出来。

time frame /'taɪm freɪm; 'taɪm frem/ *n* (usu *sing* 通常作单数) limited period of time used or available for an event, etc to take place 时限（事情发生时用上或能够用的时间）：*We expect to complete the project within a* *fairly short time frame.* 我们希望在很短的时间内完成这项工程。

time-lapse /'taɪmlæps; 'taɪmlæps/ *adj* [attrib 作定语] (of moving picture photography) using individual pictures taken at long intervals to film a slow process, eg the growth of a plant. When these are shown at normal speed, the action or process seems much faster（指动态图像摄影）延时的，定时的（如对植物生长等缓慢过程断续进行定时拍摄，按正常速度连续播放时，该动作或过程会显得快了许多）: *He was best known for his time-lapse photography of the development of storms.* 他以延时摄影暴风雨的形成过程而著称。

time out /ˌtaɪm 'aʊt; taɪm 'aʊt/ *n* (*US*) short period of rest from activity, esp during a competitive game（活动，尤指竞赛中的）暂停，休息时间: *At time out, the Packers were 21 points ahead.* 到暂停休息时，帕克斯队领先 21 分。

time-out /ˌtaɪm'aʊt; taɪm'aʊt/ *n* (*US*) form of discipline in which children are sent to their rooms when they have been naughty or told to sit alone to cool off for a while 隔离处分（对顽皮孩子的一种惩罚方式，即将他们送回自己的房间或令其单独冷坐一会儿）

time signature /'taɪm sɪgnətʃə(r); 'taɪm sɪgnətʃɚ/ *n* (*music* 音) sign at the start of a piece of written music, usu in the form of numbers, showing the number of beats in each BAR[1] 4 (b)[A-Z] 拍号（位于乐曲开头、表示每小节的节拍数目的符号，通常用数字表示）⇨ illus at MUSIC[A-Z]

time-span /'taɪmspæn; 'taɪmspæn/ *n* period of time, usu a long one（通常指长的）一段时间，时段: *Over a time-span of millions of years, the dinosaurs ruled the earth.* 恐龙统治地球的时间长达数百万年。

tin can *n* = TIN 2[A-Z]

titanium /tɪ'teɪmɪəm; taɪ'tenɪəm, tɪ-/ *n* [U] (*symb* 符号为 **Ti**) (*chemistry* 化) chemical element, a grey metal used in making various strong light materials 钛（化学元素，一种用于制作轻而牢固的材料的灰色金属）

toast /təʊst; tost/ *adj* (*infml* 口) finished; in big trouble; done for 完蛋的；陷于困境的: *Once the boss hears about it, he's toast.* 一旦老板听到此事，他就完了。

toasty /'təʊstɪ; 'tostɪ/ *adj* (*US*) warm and comfortable 温暖舒适的: *The wind was howling outside, but we were all toasty in the cosy living room.* 外面虽烈风狂啸，但我们在舒适的起居室中，大伙儿都暖呼呼的。

to die for /tə 'daɪ fɔ:(r); tə 'daɪ fɔr/ *adj* (*infml* 口) extremely good or desirable 极好的；令人十分向往的: *with a chocolate mousse to die for* 加馋死人的巧克力奶油冻

tofu /'təʊfu:; 'tofu/ (also **bean curd**) *n* [U] food that looks like soft white cheese made from soya bean milk and used in cooking, esp Chinese and Japanese cooking 豆腐: *Tofu burgers are getting more and more popular as a healthy alternative to beef.* 越来越多人选择以有益于健康的豆腐汉堡包替代牛肉汉堡包。

toggle /'tɒgl; 'tɑgl/ *v* [Tn] (*esp computing* 尤作计算机术语) click on a single icon or press the same key or key combination on the keyboard of a computer to turn a particular function on or off 按双态键（击同一图标或按相同键以执行或关闭某一功能）: *Toggle the caps lock key for capital or smaller letters.* 反复按大写锁定键，可执行或关闭大写功能。

toilet soap /'tɔɪlɪt səʊp; 'tɔɪlɪt sop/ *n* [U,C] soap, usu scented, used for washing oneself 香皂

tokenism /'təʊkənɪzm; 'tokənɪzəm/ *n* [U] (*derog* 贬) principle or practice of granting some small demands of minority groups, etc simply in order to win the support of such groups or to meet legal requirements 表面主义，门面功夫（满足少数派等的一些小要求，目的只是为了赢得其支持或合乎法律规定）: *Feminist groups saw the appointment of two women to the Cabinet as mere tokenism.* 对于两名女性被选入内阁一事，女权主义团体视作仅仅是装点门面的举动而已。

tollbooth /'təʊlbu:ð; 'tolbuθ/ *n* small building where tolls (TOLL[1] 1[A-Z]) are collected 收费亭；收费站

tone dialling /'təʊn daɪəlɪŋ; 'ton daɪəlɪŋ/ *n* [U] process of using a TOUCH TONE TELEPHONE 音频拨号 Cf 参看 PULSE DIALLING

toner /'təʊnə(r); 'tonɚ/ *n* **1** [C] device for making the body firmer and stronger by improving muscle TONE[1] 7[A-Z] 健身器: *an electrical body toner* 电动健身器 **2** [U,C] liquid or cream used for making the skin firm and smooth 柔肤水 *[霜]*；爽肤水 *[霜]*: *a good toner for oily skin* 适用于油性皮肤的爽肤水 ○ *Apply toner after removing your makeup.* 卸妆后抹上柔肤水。 **3** [U,C] = FOUNDATION 5[A-Z] **4** [U] kind of powdered ink used in computer printers, photocopying machines, etc（打印机、复印机等中使用的）色粉，墨粉

toolbar /'tu:lbɑ:(r); 'tulbɑr/ *n* (*computing* 计) row of graphic buttons available on many computer applications, usu with an ICON 2 on each of them, which call up relevant functions and utilities when clicked on with a mouse 工具条（应用软件视窗中的一长串按钮，每个按钮有图标表示不同的功能，可用鼠标击活）

top-down /tɒp'daʊn; tɑp'daʊn/ *adj* [attrib 作定语] **1** proceeding from the general to the particular, or from the top downwards 从一般到具体的；自上而下的: *a top-down presentation/diagram* 全面描述 *[图解]* **2** HIERARCHICAL (HIERARCHY[A-Z]) 分等级的；等级制的: *The company has a clear top-down structure with each level distinguished.* 该公司有一个自上而下等级分明的架构。

tosh /tɒʃ; tɑʃ/ *n* [U] (*Brit infml* 口) nonsense; rubbish 废话: *He talks a load of tosh sometimes.* 他有时会说一大堆废话。

tosser /'tɒsə(r), *US* tɔ:-; 'tɔsɚ/ *n* (*infml* 口) totally useless, contemptible person 没用的人；废物

Total Quality Management /ˌtəʊtl ˌkwɒlɪtɪ 'mænɪdʒmənt; ˌtotl ˌkwɑlətɪ 'mænɪdʒmənt/ *n* (*abbr* 缩写 **TQM**) (in industry) systematic approach with the goal of achieving perfect quality in all products and customer service, etc while reducing production costs 全面品质管理（保证所有产品和对顾客的服务等方面均无可挑剔，同时能降低生产成本的系统管理方法）

touchdown /'tʌtʃdaʊn; 'tʌtʃdaʊn/ *n* (in American football) act or instance of scoring six points by getting possession of the ball on or behind the opponent's goal line（美式橄榄球中）持球触地（攻入对方端区持球触地得六分）

touch football /ˌtʌtʃ 'fʊtbɔ:l; ˌtʌtʃ 'fʊtbɔl/ *n* [U] (*US*) form of American football in which touching, usu with both hands, is used instead of tackling (TACKLE *v* 3a[A-Z]) and gets a score equivalent to that in a TOUCHDOWN in conventional American football 触身式橄榄球（用双手触碰对方持球队员代替阻截拦抱，得分与美式橄榄球的持球触地相同）

touch screen /'tʌtʃ skri:n; 'tʌtʃ skrin/ *n* (*computing* 计) visual display unit that shows data, esp information to customers, in response to a touch on the appropriate portion of the screen 触摸屏幕（一种视象显示装置，使用者轻触屏幕某一部位即可看到有关数据尤其是资讯）

touchstone /'tʌtʃstəʊn; 'tʌtʃston/ *n* thing providing a standard or test of quality, etc 检验标准；试金石: *a touchstone against which later operas were judged* 衡量日后的歌剧的标准

touch tone telephone /ˌtʌtʃ təʊn 'telɪfəʊn; ˌtʌtʃ ton 'tɛləfon/ *n* telephone which has buttons to press when the user dials a number, each of which gives off a musical note 按键式电话；音频拨号电话: *Enter your library* *card number using a touch tone telephone.* 用按键式电话输入你的借书卡号码。 Cf 参看 TONE DIALLING

touchy-feely /ˈtʌtʃɪfiːlɪ; ˈtʌtʃɪfilɪ/ *adj* (*derog infml* 贬，口) likely to give expression to one's emotions through bodily contact, motivated by emotion rather than intellect; over-sentimental 喜欢以触摸表达情感的；过分多愁善感的：*She's one of those touchy-feely people. I find her really embarrassing.* 她属于那种激动起来就在别人身上碰啊摸啊的人。我觉得她真让人难堪。

tough love /tʌf ˈlʌv; tʌf ˈlʌv/ *n* care and concern which is expressed by encouraging a person to make an effort and to take responsibility for his or her behaviour rather than simply by sympathy and indulgence 严厉的爱（以激励人上进、勇于对自己的行为负责等方式表达的爱与关心，而非仅仅对其怜悯和纵容）

tough-minded /ˌtʌfˈmaɪndɪd; ˌtʌfˈmaɪndɪd/ *adj* realistic and determined in attitude; not sentimental 意志坚定的；不为感情所动的：*a tough-minded though sympathetic social worker* 意志坚定而富有同情心的社会工作者 ○ *You need to be tough-minded to take on the job of dealing with would-be immigrants.* 干处理入境移民申请的工作，必须不感情用事。

townscape /ˈtaʊnskeɪp; ˈtaʊnskep/ *n* view of a town, eg from a distance or in a picture 城市风景（如从远处或画中所见到的）：*an industrial townscape* 工业城市景观

NOTE 注： formed on analogy with *landscape* and *seascape* 由 landscape（风景）和 seascape（海景）二词类推构成

toyboy /ˈtɔɪbɔɪ; ˈtɔɪbɔɪ/ (also **boytoy**) *n* (*Brit infml* 口) attractive young man who is kept as a lover by an older, often wealthy, woman or man（被年长的、通常被有钱的年长女人或男人作为情人供养的）男伴，面首，小白脸

trackball /ˈtrækbɔːl; ˈtrækbɔl/ *n* (*computing* 计) small ball set inside the case of a small portable computer which is rotated by hand in order to control a CURSOR[A-Z] on the screen, and which serves as an alternative to an external control such as a mouse 跟踪球，轨迹球（半嵌在便携式电子计算机台面内的小球，可用手旋转来控制屏幕上光标的移动，以代替鼠标之类的外部操纵器）

trade-weighted /ˈtreɪdˌweɪtɪd; ˈtredˌwetɪd/ *adj* (*finance* 财) (of exchange rates) calculated from index numbers given according to the importance of the trading countries involved（指汇率）按贸易额加权的（按贸易国家的重要性所标示的指数而计算的）

traffic calming /ˈtræfɪk kɑːmɪŋ; ˈtræfɪk kɑmɪŋ/ *n* [U] methods of reducing the speed of vehicles esp in built-up areas, eg the use of speed bumps (SPEED BUMP) or speed cameras (SPEED CAMERA) 车辆减速措施（尤指在建筑物多的地区使用如减速路脊或超速摄像机等）

traffic cop /ˈtræfɪk kɒp; ˈtræfɪk kɑp/ *n* (*US infml* 口) police officer who is assigned to direct traffic, esp at busy road junctions 交通警察 Cf 参看 POINT-DUTY (POINT[1(A-Z)])

trailer (also **trailer home**) *n* = PARK HOME

trailer park /ˈtreɪlə pɑːk; ˈtrelɚ pɑrk/ *n* (*US*) area where lots of people live in park homes or trailer homes (PARK HOME) 活动住房区；拖车屋密集区

trainspotter /ˈtreɪnspɒtə(r); ˈtrenspɑtɚ/ *n* (*Brit infml derog* 口，贬) obsessive follower of any minority interest or specialized hobby, esp insofar as this interest is regarded as unfashionable and SAD 入迷者，有嗜痂之癖者（尤指过时乏味的嗜好） Cf 参看 ANORAK, TRAIN-SPOTTER (TRAIN[1(A-Z)])

train surfing /ˈtreɪn sɜːfɪŋ; ˈtren sɝfɪŋ/ *n* [U] practice of riding on the roof of a moving train or hanging on to the outside for the thrill or to prove one's courage 火车冲浪（为求刺激或证明自己的勇气，乘坐在行驶中的火车车顶上或吊在车外）：*Have young boys really been seen train surfing on the London Underground, or is it only a story?* 是确实有人看见有男孩在伦敦地铁的列车上冲浪呢，还是纯属子虚乌有？

tranche /trɑːnʃ, *US* træ-; trænʃ/ *n* (*Brit finance* 财) portion or instalment of money, such as a loan or payment（贷款或付款等的）部分，份额，一期款项

NOTE 注： from the French word meaning 'slice' 源自法语，意为'部分'

tranquillity room /trænˈkwɪlɪtɪ ruːm; trænˈkwɪlɪtɪ rum/ *n* room which has a soothing atmosphere, calming music and quiet decor, intended to refresh and relax people who spend time in it（有着令人舒畅的氛围、柔和的音乐、素净的装饰，可使人身心轻松愉快的）休憩室 Cf 参看 GRANNY CRECHE

transdermal patch *n* = PATCH

transducer /trænzˈdjuːsə(r), *US* -ˈduːsər; trænzˈdusɚ/ *n* (*technical* 术语) device for producing an electrical impulse from another form of energy, eg pressure, or vice versa. Examples include microphone, photocell and loudspeaker 换能器，变换器（将另一能量形式如压力等转换为电脉冲或相反转换的装置，如扩音器、光电池和扬声器）

transgenic /trænzˈdʒenɪk; trænzˈdʒɛnɪk/ *adj* (*medical* 医) relating to an organism which contains inheritable genetic material which has been artificially introduced from another organism 移植基因的，转移基因的（指某一生物被人工植入了另一生物的遗传基因物质）：*The transgenic pig becomes a living factory for the production of human insulin.* 移植了基因的猪成了生产人体胰岛素的活工厂。

transnational /ˌtrænzˈnæʃnəl; ˌtrænzˈnæʃnl/ *adj* (*esp commerce* 尤用于商业) operating in or between many different countries, without having a principal base in any one country 跨国的；跨国经营的：*transnational organizations/corporations* 跨国组织 *[*公司*]* Cf 参看 MULTINATIONAL[A-Z]

trans-species /trænzˈspiːʃiːz; trænzˈspiʃiz/ *adj* crossing from one species to another 跨物种的；物种转移的：*More trans-species viruses are probably still out there waiting to make themselves known.* 可能有更多的跨物种病毒尚待人们去发现。

traumatize, -ise /ˈtrɔːmətaɪz, *US* traʊ-; ˈtraʊmətaɪz/ *v* [Tn, I] (esp passive 尤用于被动语态) cause great shock or distress to sb 使（某人）极为震惊或痛苦：*The boy was traumatized by the shock of his mother's sudden death.* 那个男孩的母亲突然去世，使他痛苦万分。○ *The team were utterly traumatized by their defeat.* 这支队伍被打败后，无比沮丧。

trawl /trɔːl; trɔl/ *v* [Tn] (*fig* 比喻) make an exhaustive and sometimes random search for a person or thing within a defined area（在特定区域）进行全面的、有时是随机的搜索：*Scientists are trawling through the genetic records of affected families in the hope of finding the cause of the inherited disease.* 科学家们正在全面审阅患有该遗传病的家族的基因资料，希望能发现其病因。○ *trawling the Internet for hours* 在互联网上搜寻几小时

tree hugger /ˈtriː hʌgə(r); ˈtri hʌgɚ/ *n* (*derog* 贬) name applied to an enthusiastic environmental campaigner, just like a person who actually hugs a tree in order to prevent it being cut down 环境保护狂（如抱住树木使其免遭砍伐的人）

trekkie /ˈtrekɪ; ˈtrɛkɪ/ *n* (*infml* 口) keen fan of the Star Trek television and movie series, esp one who attends conferences, collects memorabilia, and dresses up in Star Trek costumes 《星球旅行》迷（《星球旅行》电视连续剧及其电影系列的狂热爱好者，尤指参加有关的大会、搜集纪念品以及模仿其人物的穿着打扮的人）

triage /ˈtraɪɪdʒ; ˈtraɪdʒ/ *n* [U] **1** act of sorting according to quality（按质量）分类 **2** (in the casualty department of a hospital) assignment of degrees of urgency to decide the order of treatment of incoming patients 伤病员分类（医院急救室为了决定救治次序而按紧急程度将伤者分类的做法）

triathlon /traɪˈæθlən, -lɒn; traɪˈæθlɑn/ *n* sports event in which each competitor performs three different sports, eg running, swimming and cycling, often in one continuous race 三项全能运动（在同一比赛中连续参加三项不同运动，如赛跑、游泳、骑车）

trickle down *v* = FILTER DOWN

trimester /traɪˈmestə(r); traɪˈmɛstɚ/ *n* (*US*) **1** period of three months 三个月 **2** each of three terms in an academic year（分为三学期的学年中的）一学期 Cf 参看 SEMESTER A-Z

trolley-dolly /ˈtrɒlɪdɒlɪ; ˈtrɑlɪdɑlɪ/ *n* (*sl* 俚) air stewardess 空中小姐；空姐

NOTE 注： from the fact that for a large part of any flight air-stewardesses have to push trolleys of food, etc up and down the aisles 因在飞行的大部分时间里，空中小姐必须推着食物车在过道上走来走去而得名

troubled /ˈtrʌbld; ˈtrʌbl̩d/ *adj* [usu attrib 通常作定语] in trouble; going through a bad time 陷入困境的；处境艰难的：*The troubled company looks as if it may survive after all.* 这间陷入困境的公司看上去最终会挺过来的。○ *a troubled teenager* 一个苦恼的青少年

trove ⇨ TREASURE TROVE (TREASURE A-Z)

trust territory /ˈtrʌst terətrɪ, *US* -tɔːrɪ; ˈtrʌst tɛrətɔrɪ/ *n* territory governed by, or by a country appointed by, the United Nations Organization usu for a specified period 托管领土，托管地（在特定时期内由联合国管理或委托成员国管理的领土）：*Namibia became fully independent after years of being a trust territory under the control of South Africa.* 在托给南非管理多年后，纳米比亚终于获得了完全的独立。

tummytuck /ˈtʌmɪtʌk; ˈtʌmɪtʌk/ *n* (*euph infml* 婉，口) cosmetic surgery which removes fat and tissue from the abdomen and then stitches up the loose skin 腹部整形术，收腹术（去除腹部脂肪和组织，然后将松弛的皮肤缝拢的整形手术）

turbocharger /ˈtɜːbəʊˌtʃɑːdʒə(r); ˈtɝboˌtʃɑrdʒɚ/ (also **turbo**, *pl* **-os**) *n* apparatus driven by a TURBINE A-Z that is powered by an engine's exhaust gases. The turbine sends a mixture of petrol and air into the engine at high pressure, making it more powerful 涡轮增压器（由涡轮机驱动的装置；涡轮机以高压将汽油与空气的混合物送入引擎以增加其性能，涡轮机则由引擎的废气驱动）

turf war /ˈtɜːf wɔː(r); ˈtɝf wɔr/ *n* (*US fig* 比喻) dispute over territory and spheres of influence amongst rival groups or departments（地盘和势力范围的）争夺战：*Turf wars between local police forces and federal law agencies have led to damaging delays, lack of co-operation and even the withholding of information.* 当地警方与联邦法律部门争权夺利，造成破坏性延误，也导致双方缺乏合作甚至向对方隐瞒情报。

tu-whit, tu-whoo /tʊˌwɪt tʊˈwuː, *US* -hw, -hw; tuˈhwɪt tuˈhwu/ *n* (used in writing and speech to represent the cry of an OWL A-Z 用于书面语及口语中表示猫头鹰的叫声）嘟喂嘟呜 Cf 参看 HOOT 1 A-Z

twenty-first /ˌtwentɪˈfɜːst; ˌtwɛntɪˈfɝst/ *n* [sing] (*infml* 口) one's 21st birthday ☆ 21 岁生日：*I got a CD player for my twenty-first.* 我二十一岁生日时得到一台激光唱机作为礼物。

twin bedroom /ˌtwɪn ˈbedruːm, -rʊm; ˌtwɪn ˈbɛdrum/ (also **twin room**) *n* room, eg in a hotel, having a pair of single beds, ie twin beds（旅馆等中）有一对单人床的房间 Cf 参看 DOUBLE BEDROOM, DOUBLE ROOM

twinkling /ˈtwɪŋklɪŋ; ˈtwɪŋklɪŋ/ *n* [sing] (*infml* 口) very short time 眨眼间；一刹那：*It was all over in a twinkling.* 转眼间一切都结束了。

twin-track /ˈtwɪntræk; ˈtwɪntræk/ *adj* (of negotiations and agreements) involving concessions on both sides（指谈判和协议）双方均作让步的：*Under the twin-track agreement, both sides must surrender their arms before substantial talks start.* 按照这一双方均作了让步的协议，双方在具体谈判开始前必须交出武器。

twisted /ˈtwɪstɪd; ˈtwɪstɪd/ *adj* (of a person's mind or behaviour) abnormal in an unpleasant way; devious; perverted (PERVERT 2 A-Z)（指思想或行为）怪异的，变态的，反常的：*He's got a twisted way of looking at things.* 他以一种扭曲的眼光看世事。

twitcher /ˈtwɪtʃə(r); ˈtwɪtʃɚ/ *n* (*Brit infml* 口) fanatically keen bird-watcher who is willing to travel hundreds of kilometres to see a rare bird 狂热的鸟类观察者，观鸟迷（愿意专程到几百公里之外去看珍稀鸟类的人）

two-way mirror /ˌtuːweɪ ˈmɪrə(r); ˌtuwe ˈmɪrɚ/ *n* big piece of glass that can be seen through on one side and is a mirror on the other 单向透明玻璃镜（一块大玻璃，一面可透视而另一面则为镜子）：*The police officers used a two-way mirror to observe the interview with the suspect.* 警察运用单向透明玻璃镜来观察会见嫌疑犯的过程。

typo (*pl* ~ **s**) *n* = LITERAL *n* A-Z

Uu

UCAS /ˈjuːkæs; ˈjukæs/ *abbr* 缩写 = (*Brit*) Universities and Colleges Admissions Service (an official body that processes applications to study at universities) 大学入学申请办事处

ufology /juːˈfɒlədʒɪ; juˈfɑlədʒɪ/ *n* [U] study of UFOs 不明飞行物学；飞碟学：*Ufology is still not considered a respectable study by most scientists.* 对大多数科学家而言，不明飞行物学尚未算是一门体面的科学。

unambitious /ˌʌnæmˈbɪʃəs; ˌʌnæmˈbɪʃəs/ *adj* **1** without ambitions in life; setting oneself easily-achieved goals 无雄心大志的；无抱负的 **2** not involving anything new, exciting or demanding 不新奇的；无趣味的；要求不高的：*an unambitious itinerary/project/novel* 毫无新意的旅程安排、没有挑战性的项目、平淡无奇的小说

▷ **unambitiously** *adv*: *He rather unambitiously turned down the chance of a new job overseas.* 他回绝了一份海外工作的差使，真没志气。

unauthorized biography /ʌnˌɔːθəraɪzd baɪˈɒgrəfɪ; ʌnˌɔθəraɪzd baɪˈɑgrəfɪ/ *n* biography written without the permission or co-operation of the subject 未经授权的传记（未经被立传者同意或未在其合作下撰写之传记）

unban /ˌʌnˈbæn; ʌnˈbæn/ *v* remove the ban on sth 解除禁令：*Opposition parties have now been unbanned.* 反对党现已成为合法组织。

unblock /ˌʌnˈblɒk; ʌnˈblɑk/ *v* [Tn] remove an obstruction from sth; clean sth, eg a pipe, by removing matter that is blocking it 清除障碍；疏通（管道等）：*You'll have to unblock the lavatory; it won't flush properly.* 你得把抽水马桶疏通一下，它冲水不灵了。○ *unblock the passage by removing the piles of rubbish* 清除过道上一堆堆的垃圾

unbundle /ˌʌnˈbʌndl; ˌʌnˈbʌndl̩/ *v* [I, Tn] (*finance* 财) sell off subsidiary companies belonging to a parent company separately（将同属一家母公司的子公司）分开出售

uncapped /ˌʌnˈkæpt; ʌnˈkæpt/ *adj* (*Brit*) (in sport) not having played, esp never having been selected to play, for a national team（体育运动）未参加过国家队的，

（尤指）从未入选国家队的：*Three previously uncapped players have been selected.* 三名从未入选国家队的队员此次入选了。Cf 参看 CAP *v* 3A-Z

uncaring /ʌn'keərɪŋ; ʌn'kɛrɪŋ/ *adj* (*derog* 贬) having no sympathy for the problems or sufferings of others 不关心他人疾苦的：*uncaring employers* 不顾员工死活的雇主 ○ *be selfish and uncaring* 自私自利

uncivilized, -ised /ʌn'sɪvəlaɪzd; ʌn'sɪvḷaɪzd/ *adj* (*derog* 贬) **1** (of people or places) undeveloped; lacking modern conveniences and institutions; BACKWARD 2A-Z（指人或地方）未开化的，不文明的，落后的：*an uncivilized society/country* 不文明的社会 *[国度]* **2** (of behaviour, etc) not acceptable according to one's moral principles or standards（指行为等）不文明的，野蛮的，不能接受的：*uncivilized treatment of prisoners* 对犯人的粗暴对待

uncool /ˌʌn'ku:l; ʌn'kul/ *adj* (*sl* 俚) not considered acceptable or stylish by fashionable young people 不时髦的；落伍的：*Don't wear a baseball cap. It's so uncool.* 别戴棒球帽啦，老早过时了。

uncoordinated /ˌʌnkəʊ'ɔ:dɪneɪtɪd; ˌʌnko'ɔrdṇetɪd/ *adj* **1** (**a**) (of a person) not able to control one's movements; clumsy（指人）动作不灵活的，手脚笨拙的：*He's too uncoordinated to play tennis well.* 他笨手笨脚的，打不好网球。(**b**) (of movements or parts of the body) not controlled（指动作或身体部分）不协调的：*uncoordinated limbs* 不协调的四肢 **2** not well organized; not working well together 组织得不好的；缺乏合作的：*an uncoordinated campaign/team* 组织涣散的运动、缺乏合作的队伍

undated /ˌʌn'deɪtɪd; ˌʌn'detɪd/ *adj* **1** without a date written on it 未标明日期的：*an undated letter* 未注日期的信 **2** of which the date is not known 日期不明的：*undated archaeological remains* 年代不详的考古遗迹

underclass /'ʌndəklɑ:s, *US* -klæs; 'ʌndəklæs/ *n* social class which is very poor or has very low status 下层社会；社会底层：*Recent immigrants tend to form an underclass in their host country.* 新移民往往会在侨居国内形成下层社会。

unemotional /ˌʌnɪ'məʊʃənl; ˌʌnɪ'moʃənḷ/ *adj* (*sometimes derog* 有时作贬义) not showing strong feelings 不动感情的；冷漠的：*Our boss is sometimes accused of being unemotional.* 我们的老板有时会被指责为冷漠的人。

▷ **unemotionally** *adv*：*She spoke unemotionally about her dreadful experiences.* 她淡淡的说着她那些可怕的经历。

NOTE 注： the word implies a smaller degree of coldness in a person than *emotionless* (EMOTIONA-Z) does, which implies not having emotions 与 emotionless（没有任何感情的）相比，此词所形容之冷漠程度较轻

unemployable /ˌʌnɪm'plɔɪəbl; ˌʌnɪm'plɔɪəbḷ/ *adj* not likely to obtain a job owing to lack of skills or qualifications（因缺乏技能或资历等）不可能找到工作的，不会被雇用的：*Many school-leavers are virtually unemployable and desperately need some kind of training.* 许多中学毕业生其实不可能找到工作，他们极需要接受某种训练。

unfazed /ʌn'feɪzd; ʌn'fezd/ *adj* [pred 作表语] not worried, anxious or upset 不担心；不慌不忙：*She was completely unfazed even when I told her that there would be 50 people coming.* 甚至当我告诉她会来 50 个人的时候，她也毫不着急。

NOTE 注： there is no adjective *fazed* 不存在 fazed 这个形容词

unheeded /ʌn'hi:dɪd; ʌn'hidɪd/ *adj* heard or noticed but not responded to 被忽视的；未受到注意的：*Their warnings went unheeded.* 他们的警告被当作耳边风。○ *His cries for help were unheeded.* 没人理会他的求助。

unheralded /ʌn'herəldɪd; ʌn'hɛrəldɪd/ *adj* (**a**) with no advance information or warning 未预先通知或警告的：*He arrived totally unheralded.* 他完全没有预先通知就来了。(**b**) not taken sufficient notice of 未受充分注意的：*The dawn of the computer age went largely unheralded.* 对于计算机时代的来临，没有许多人注意到。

unitary /'ju:nɪtrɪ, *US* -terɪ; 'junətɛrɪ/ *adj* **1** single; having characteristics of a unit 单一的；单元的：*the unitary family* 作为社会单元的家庭 ○ *present a unitary image* 呈现单一的形象 **2** combining or combined in one group; being brought into an integrated whole 统一的；整体的：*unitary policing* 统一监管 ○ *unitary development plans* 整体开发规划

unleaded *adj* = LEAD-FREE

unmet /ˌʌn'met; ʌn'mɛt/ *adj* (esp of a requirement) not satisfied（尤指要求）未满足的，未达到的：*children whose needs remain unmet* 基本需要仍未得到满足的孩子们 ○ *satisfy unmet demands* 满足未达到的要求

unmissable /ʌn'mɪsəbl; ʌn'mɪsəbḷ/ *adj* that one must not miss because it is so good 不可错过的：*an unmissable film/production/exhibition* 不可错过的电影 *[制作/展览]*

unnamed /ˌʌn'neɪmd; ʌn'nemd/ *adj* (esp of a person) whose name is withheld or not known（尤指人）匿名的，不知其名的：*works by an unnamed artist* 一位匿名的艺术家的作品 ○ *information from an unnamed source* 来源不明的情报

NOTE 注： the word implies a deliberate withholding of the name more than *nameless* or *anonymous* do 与 nameless（无名的）和 anonymous（未具名的）相比，此词更含有'故意隐瞒姓名'的意思

unplugged /ʌn'plʌgd; ʌn'plʌgd/ *adj* (of pop groups) performing without the use of electrically-amplified instruments（指流行乐演唱组）不使用电子乐器的：*Hot Wire performing unplugged was a new experience for most of their fans.* '热金属线'乐队不用电子乐器的表演令大部分乐迷耳目一新。

unrelieved /ˌʌnrɪ'li:vd; ˌʌnrɪ'livd/ *adj* (*derog* 贬) not changing; continuing 无变化的；没完没了的：*an unrelieved diet of potatoes and strong tea* 千篇一律的马铃薯加浓茶餐单 ○ *She sank into a state of unrelieved gloom.* 她陷入了无止境的忧郁之中。

unseeded /ʌn'si:dɪd; ʌn'sidɪd/ *adj* not selected as a SEED 3A-Z in a sports contest, esp tennis 未被列为种子选手的（尤指网球赛中）：*the first unseeded player to reach the final* 首位进入决赛的非种子选手

unseeing /ˌʌn'si:ɪŋ; ʌn'siɪŋ/ *adj* (*rhet* 修辞) with the eyes open, but not noticing anything 视而不见的：*He stared, unseeing, into the distance.* 他茫然盯着远方。

unsuspected /ˌʌnsə'spektɪd; ˌʌnsə'spɛktɪd/ *adj* **1** of which one was not previously aware; not expected or known about 未受到注意的；意料之外的：*Then an unsuspected problem arose.* 接着一个未曾料到的问题发生了。○ *show previously unsuspected talent* 显示出以前不为人所知的才干 **2** not suspected of doing sth wrong 未受怀疑的；无嫌疑的：*The serial killer had lived amongst them for years, entirely unsuspected.* 这个连环杀人狂多年来一直生活在他们中间，没有受到丝毫的怀疑。

untamed /ˌʌn'teɪmd; ʌn'temd/ *adj* **1** (of land) remaining in its original state because no one has changed or cultivated it（指土地）未开发的，未开垦的：*an untamed wilderness* 未开发的荒原 **2** (of animals) wild; not having been trained by humans（指动物）野性的，未经驯服的：*Even after years of contact with humans, the wild cats were still completely untamed.* 虽然与人类接触已经多年，野猫丝毫未脱野性。**3** (of people) not controlled or influenced by others; behaving freely and naturally（指人）不受他人控制或影响的，坦率自然的：*an untamed genius* 才华得到充分发挥的天才

up and running /ˌʌp ənd ˈrʌnɪŋ; ʌp ənd ˈrʌnɪŋ/ *adj* working successfully; already underway 顺利进行的；进行中的：*Insert the first disc in your CD-drive and Multimedia Encyclopaedia will be up and running in no time.* 将第一张光盘插入驱动器内，你立刻就可以使用多媒体百科全书了。○ *an up-and-running scheme/procedure* 进行中的计划 *[程序]*

upcoming /ˈʌpkʌmɪŋ; ˈʌpkʌmɪŋ/ *adj (esp US)* due to happen or take place soon; coming soon 即将发生的；即将到来的：*a review of upcoming events* 对即将发生的事件的评论

upfield /ˌʌpˈfiːld; ʌpˈfild/ *adj, adv (sport* 体) in or towards a position at the opposite team's end of the field, ie towards a possible scoring position 在前场（的），向前场（的）（即处于有利得分的位置（的））：*kick the ball upfield* 将球踢向前场

upfront /ˌʌpˈfrʌnt; ʌpˈfrʌnt/ *adj* **1** honest; open; frank 诚实的；开诚布公的：*be upfront about one's motives/private life* 袒露自己的动机、公开个人的私生活 **2** [usu attrib 通常作定语] (of a payment) in advance（指支付的款项）预付的：*upfront charges* 预付的费用

uplighter /ˈʌplaɪtə(r); ˈʌplaɪtɚ/ *n* lamp, etc placed or designed so that it throws light upwards 向上照的灯

upraised /ˌʌpˈreɪzd; ʌpˈrezd/ *adj* (esp of a part of the body) raised in the air（尤指身体某部分）举起的：*They saluted him with upraised arms.* 他们向他举手致敬。

uprate /ʌpˈreɪt; ʌpˈret/ *v* **1** increase the value of a pension, benefit, etc 提高（养老金、救济金等） **2** upgrade 使升级；提升：*The gas plants are to be expanded and uprated.* 那些煤气厂将会扩充及改良。

upstate /ˌʌpˈsteɪt; ʌpˈstet/ *adj, adv* in or to the part of a state of the US which is far from its main cities, esp the northern part 在（美国的）州的边远地区或北部地区的；向（美国的）州的边远地区或北部地区：*upstate New York* 纽约州的边陲地带 ○ *We go upstate every summer for our vacation.* 我们每年夏天都到州的北部地区度假。

urban legend /ˈɜːbən ledʒənd, ɜːbən ˈledʒənd; ˌɝbən ˈlɛdʒənd/ (also **urban myth**) *n* unproven and usu untrue story about some aspect of modern life, esp in urban areas, which is widely told as if true and has acquired the status of folklore 都市传说，都市神话（关于现代生活，尤其是都市生活面貌的故事，这些故事未经证实且往往不准确，但广为流传并带有民间传说的色彩）：*Are the alligators in the sewers of New York merely an urban legend, or are there such creatures?* 纽约的下水道里有鳄鱼，是传说呢，还是确有其事？

Usenet /ˈjuːznet; ˈjuznɛt/ *n* [sing] system of on-line discussion groups or chat rooms（CHAT ROOM）用户网（网上讨论小组或聊天室系统）

utilitarianism /juːtɪlɪˈteərɪənɪzm; ˌjutɪləˈtɛrɪənɪzəm/ *n* [U] philosophy based on UTILITARIAN 2[A-Z] principles 功利主义

Vv

vaccine /ˈvæksiːn, *US* vækˈsiːn; vækˈsin/ *n (computing* 计) program designed to prevent the working of a VIRUS or to eliminate it 杀病毒程序；疫苗程序

V-actor *abbr* 缩写 = VIRTUAL ACTOR（VIRTUAL）

value-added /ˌvæljuːˈædɪd; ˌvæljuˈædɪd/ *n* amount of extra value that a product gains at each stage of its manufacture or production 增值（产品在制造或生产的每一个过程中增加的价值）：*The value-added on agricultural products has been very low at times in the last 20 years.* 近 20 年里农产品的增值有时非常低。

vanity publisher /ˈvænətɪ ˌpʌblɪʃə(r); ˈvænətɪ ˌpʌblɪʃɚ/ *n* publisher who publishes books only at the author's expense 作者自费出版社（由作者支付出书开支的出版社）：*The only way she could get her book published was to pay a vanity publisher.* 她的书要出版，只有找一家自费出版社。

▷ **vanity publishing** *n* [U]

V-chip /ˈviːtʃɪp; ˈvitʃɪp/ *n* computer chip designed to be included in television receivers to prevent children viewing material which is considered to be violent or sexually explicit ☆ V 芯片（供装入电视机防止孩子观看暴力或色情镜头的电脑芯片）：*The President has lent his support to the V-chip.* 总统支持使用 V 芯片。

NOTE 注： originally from the first letter of *viewer*, but now generally interpreted as standing for *violence* 原由 viewer（观众）一词的首字母而来，但现在普遍认为代表 violence（暴力）

vedge *v* = VEG

veejay /viːˈdʒeɪ, ˈviːdʒeɪ; ˈvidʒe/ (also **VJ**) *n* person who presents a programme of music videos, esp on television 电视音乐节目主持人

NOTE 注： formed on analogy with *deejay (DJ)* 由 deejay（DJ）（电台音乐节目主持人）一词类推构成

veep /viːp; vip/ *n (US infml* 口) vice-president 副总统：*Clinton was clever to choose Gore as his veep.* 克林顿选择戈尔为副总统，实为明智之举。

NOTE 注： coming from the pronunciation of the initials VP 来自 vice-president 一词的缩写字母 VP 的发音

veg /vedʒ; vɛdʒ/ *v* [I] *(infml* 口) **1** vegetate; pass the time idly and mindlessly, not doing anything in particular 过呆板单调的生活；无所事事地生活：*I'm going to just veg at home and catch up on lost sleep.* 我打算闲在家里，睡睡觉，补充失去了的睡眠。 **2** (phr v) **veg out** simply slump in front of the television and watch anything that happens to be on 看电视度日：*All I want to do after a day's work is to veg out.* 一天工作下来，我只想懒懒地看电视。

vegeburger /ˈvedʒɪˌbɜːgə(r); ˈvɛdʒɪˌbɝgɚ/ (also **veggieburger**) *n* burger made only of non-animal ingredients 素馅汉堡包

veggie /ˈvedʒɪ; ˈvɛdʒɪ/ *n (infml* 口) VEGETARIAN[A-Z] 素食主义者；素食者：*So many young women are veggies nowadays.* 如今很多年轻女子是素食主义者。○ [attrib 作定语] *veggie food/restaurants* 素食、素食餐馆

Viagra /vaɪˈægrə, viːˈægrə; vaɪˈægrə/ *n* [U] *(propr medicine* 专利名，药) drug which is used in the treatment of impotence in men 伟哥，万艾可（一种治疗阳痿的药）

video camera /ˈvɪdɪəʊ kæmərə; ˈvɪdɪo kæmərə/ *n* camera for taking video film 摄像机 Cf 参看 CAMCORDER[A-Z]

videoconference /ˌvɪdɪəʊˈkɒnfərəns; ˌvɪdɪoˈkɑnfərəns/ *n* meeting of people in different locations made possible through electronic communication which allows them to see and hear each other 电视会议（通过电子通讯技术使身处不同地方的人能一起开会，能从屏幕看到各方的样貌和听到各方的声音）

▷ **videoconference** *v* [I]

videofit /ˌvɪdɪəʊˈfɪt; vɪdɪoˈfɪt/ *n* reconstructed picture of a person (esp sb wanted by the police) which is built up on a computer screen by selecting and combining facial features according to a witness's description（尤指通缉犯的）电脑拼图（根据证人的描述，通过电脑将某人的面部特征拼合而成的图像） Cf 参看 PHOTOFIT

video jockey *n* = VEEJAY

video-on-demand /ˌvɪdɪəʊɒndɪˈmɑːnd, *US* -mænd; ˌvɪdɪoandɪˈmænd/ *n* (*abbr* 缩写 **VOD**) service which allows cable television subscribers to ask at any time for video programmes, eg films, to be transmitted from a network centre to their home television sets 电视点播（对有线电视用户的一种服务，用户可随时选择播放电影之类的录影节目。一经要求，节目便立刻由网络中心传送到用户家里的电视机上播出）Cf 参看 FILM-ON-DEMAND

videotex /ˌvɪdɪəʊˈteks, ˈvɪdɪəʊˌteks; ˈvɪdɪoˌtɛks/ *n* (term proposed for international use instead of) VIEWDATA 视传（系统），可视图文（此词被提议作为国际通用词取代 viewdata 一词）

vidkid /ˈvɪdkɪd; ˈvɪdkɪd/ *n* (*US*) child who is addicted to watching television or videos 儿童电视迷；儿童录像迷：*Are we bringing up a generation of vidkids? Have our children forgotten how to play?* 我们正在培育一代儿童录像迷吗？我们的孩子已忘了怎样玩耍了吗？

viewdata /ˈvjuːdeɪtə; ˈvjudetə/ *n* [U] information system in which computer data is sent along telephone lines to homes and businesses and displayed on a television screen, now more commonly known as VIDEOTEX 视传（系统），可视数据（通过电话线路将计算机信息输向家居，后来主要输向商业机构的电视屏幕的资料系统。现更常用 videotex 一词名之）：*book a holiday by viewdata* 通过视传系统预先安排度假事宜

virtual /ˈvɜːtʃʊəl; ˈvɝtʃʊəl/ *adj* (*computing* 计) **1** not physically existing but made to appear so from the point of view of the user 虚拟的（实际上不存在但能让用者看得到）**2** involving the replication of a physical object by an electronic equivalent 模拟的（通过电子媒体模拟实物的）

□ **virtual actor** *n* (*abbr* 缩写 **V-actor**) actor who exists only as an image stored in computer memory which has been derived from the process of MOTION CAPTURE 虚拟演员（通过动态捕捉而储存于计算机中，只以影像方式存在的演员）

virtual meeting *n* meeting that takes place using videoconferencing (VIDEOCONFERENCE) or similar techniques where the participants do not have to be physically present in the same location but are linked together by means of electronic communication 虚拟会议（利用电视会议技术或类似技术进行的会议，与会者不必到场，只需通过电子通讯来进行联系）

virtual reality *n* [U] computer-generated visual, and to some extent tactile, environment that a person can move about in and interact with 虚拟现实（利用计算机虚拟的视觉、触觉环境，令人恍如身历其境并可在里面活动）Cf 参看 DATAGLOVE

virus /ˈvaɪərəs; ˈvaɪrəs/ *n* (*computing* 计) piece of program code that attaches itself to computer applications, executes when they are activated, attempts to copy itself and which may cause damage or loss of data（计算机）病毒：*the Friday the Thirteenth virus activates every Friday the thirteenth* 十三号星期五病毒每逢十三号和星期五为同一天时发作 Cf 参看 MICHELANGELO

VJ *n* = VEEJAY

VOD *abbr* 缩写 = VIDEO-ON-DEMAND

voice mail /ˈvɔɪs meɪl; ˈvɔɪs mel/ *n* [U] (*computing* 计) system for electronically storing, processing and reproducing verbal messages left through the conventional telephone network, or transmitted through a digital computer network 语音邮递（对通过电话留下的或通过数码计算机网络传送的语音信息进行电子储存、处理和复制的系统）

voluntary school /ˈvɒləntrɪ skuːl, *US* -terɪ; ˈvɑlənˌtɛrɪ skul/ *n* (in the UK) school which has not been established by the local authority, but is funded mainly or entirely by it, and which encourages a particular set of usu religious beliefs（英国）津贴学校，民办学校（非由地方政府创建，但主要由其资助的学校，此类学校通常鼓励某种宗教信仰）

vote of confidence /ˌvəʊt əv ˈkɒnfɪdəns; ˌvot əv ˈkɑnfɪdəns/ *n* (usu *sing* 通常作单数) vote taken by a committee, political party, etc to show general support for a leader, government, etc 信任票（委员会、政党等对领袖、政府等表示支持而投的票）：*The whole committee passed a unanimous vote of confidence in the Chairman.* 委员会一致对主席投了信任票。Cf 参看 VOTE OF NO CONFIDENCE

vote of no confidence /ˌvəʊt əv ˌnəʊ ˈkɒnfɪdəns; ˌvot əv ˌno ˈkɑnfɪdəns/ *n* (usu *sing* 通常作单数) vote taken to show a general lack of support for a leader, government, etc 不信任票（对领袖、政府等表示不支持而投的票）：*survive a vote of no confidence* 被投不信任票而没有倒台 Cf 参看 VOTE OF CONFIDENCE

Ww

waitperson /ˈweɪtpɜːsn; ˈwetpɝsn̩/ *n* waiter or waitress in a restaurant, etc（餐馆等的）侍应生，侍者

NOTE 注： a term preferred by some people because it is neutral as to gender 此词因其中性化而受一些人喜爱

walk-in /ˈwɔːkɪn; ˈwɔkɪn/ *adj* (of accomodation for rent) empty and available to immediate occupation（指出租屋）即可入住的：*walk-in office space/flats* 即租即可迁入的写字楼、即租即住的公寓

walkthrough /ˈwɔːkθruː; ˈwɔkθru/ *n* detailed guide to an adventure game for the computer, with exact instructions as to what to do and with answers to all the puzzles 计算机历险游戏指南（附答案）：*I downloaded this walkthrough from the Internet.* 我从互联网上下载了这个计算机历险游戏指南。

walling /ˈwɔːlɪŋ; ˈwɔlɪŋ/ *n* [U] **1** material from which a wall is built 砌墙材料：*stone/concrete walling* 石头 *[*混凝土*]* 砌墙料 **2** action or skill of building a wall or walls 砌墙；砌墙技术：*a firm specializing in paving and walling* 专事铺路砌墙的公司

wall-mounted /ˌwɔːlˈmaʊntɪd; ˌwɔlˈmaʊntɪd/ *adj* fixed onto a wall 钉在墙上的；固定于墙上的：*wall-mounted lights/boiler/heaters* 壁灯、壁挂式热水器 *[*取暖器*]*

wallpaper /ˈwɔːlpeɪpə(r); ˈwɔlpepɚ/ *n* (*computing* 计) background design chosen by a user to show on the screen of a computer when there is no application in use 计算机屏幕背景图案；屏幕壁纸

▷ **wallpaper** *v* [Tn·pr]：*I wallpapered the screen with pictures we took on holiday last year.* 我用去年我们度假时拍的照片作为计算机的背景图案。

wannabe /ˈwɒnəbɪ; ˈwɑnəbɪ/ (also **wannabee**) *n* (*sl* 俚) **1** devoted fan or follower who hero-worships and tries to imitate a particular celebrity or star, esp in appearance 崇拜并竭力模仿某名人或明星者（尤指在外表上）；狂热崇拜者：*The Madonna wannabes are in town for the star's concert appearances.* 马多娜的崇拜者赶来城里观看她的演唱会。**2** anyone who wants to be sb else 想成为（某人）的人

▷ **wannabe** *adj* aspiring, would-be 渴望成为…的：*a wannabe chat show host* 想做清谈节目主持人的人 ○ *wannabe models* 渴望当模特儿的人

NOTE 注： from the statement *I want to be* 源自短语 I want to be

-ware /weə(r); wɛr/ *comb form* 构词成分 (*computing* 计) certain kind of software 某种软件

warez site /ˈweəz saɪt; ˈwɛrz saɪt/ (also **Warez site**) *n* SITE on the Internet where copyright software and music is illegally made available and can be located and downloaded 盗版网站（互联网上非法提供可下载的受版权保护的软件和乐曲的网站）

warm call /ˈwɔːm kɔːl, wɔːm ˈkɔːl; ˈwɔrm kɔl/ *n* visit or telephone call made by a salesman to an already known customer or by invitation from a potential new customer（推销员对老主顾或应潜在新顾客之邀进行的）上门推销，打电话推销 Cf 参看 COLD-CALLING

war-torn /ˈwɔːtɔːn; ˈwɔrtɔrn/ *adj* [attrib 作定语] (of a place) suffering destruction, loss of life, etc as a result of war（指某地方）饱受战争摧残的：*a war-torn city* 饱受战争摧残的城市

-watch /wɒtʃ; wɑtʃ/ *n* (usu second element of compound 通常作复合词的第二部分) act or process of observing, usu out of interest or for purposes of self-defence（通常出于兴趣或自卫等目的的）观望，观赏：*The tour includes the chance to experience a whale-watch off the coast of Hawaii.* 这次旅行包括在夏威夷沿海观鲸。

water birth /ˈwɔːtə bɜːθ; ˈwɔtɚ bɝθ/ *n* [U] method of childbirth which uses a BIRTHING POOL 水中分娩法

water-colourist /ˈwɔːtəˌkʌlərɪst; ˈwɔtɚˌkʌlərɪst/ *n* painter who uses water-colour as the working medium 水彩画家

water cooler /ˈwɔːtə kuːlə(r); ˈwɔtɚ kulɚ/ *n* device for cooling and storing water for drinking 水冷却器（冷却和贮存饮用水的装置）

water-resistant /ˈwɔːtərɪˌzɪstənt; ˈwɔtərɪˌzɪstənt/ *adj* that does not let water through easily 防水的；水不易渗透的：*The Pearl Seamaster — the diver's watch: water-resistant to a depth of 20 metres.* 海珠王——潜水员的手表：水深达 20 米仍能防水。○ *water-resistant sun-cream* 抗水的防晒霜

wayport /ˈweɪpɔːt; ˈwepɔrt/ *n* airport which is used mainly by passengers on their way to somewhere else rather than as a final destination 中转机场（主要供旅客中转而非作为目的地的机场）：*Most of the traffic through the wayport was going on to Teheran.* 大多数经该机场中转的飞机是去德黑兰的。

weather station /ˈweðə steɪʃn; ˈwɛðɚ steʃən/ *n* building where instruments are kept for observing and recording weather conditions 气象站

weathervane /ˈweðəveɪn; ˈwɛðɚven/ *n* (*fig* 比喻) (in political elections) CONSTITUENCY (a)A-Z which has proved to be a reliable indicator of what the likely final result in an election will be（政治选举中的）风向标（能可靠地反映选举结果的选区）：*Exit polls from Romford East, one of the best known weathervanes, indicate a huge swing to Labour.* 著名的风向标东罗姆福德投票站民意调查结果显示，大量选民转而支持工党。

Web *n* = WORLD WIDE WEB

Web site (also **web site**) *n* = SITE

weeklong /ˈwiːklɒŋ; ˈwiklɔŋ/ *adj* lasting for a week 为期一周的；持续一周的：*a weeklong course/visit* 为期一周的课程 *[访问]*

weight train /ˈweɪt treɪn; ˈwet tren/ *v* [I] (*sport* 体) exercise using weights 举重锻炼：*The champion has begun to weight train again following her knee injury.* 这名冠军在膝盖受伤之后，又开始了她的举重锻炼。

well /wel; wɛl/ *adv* (*infml* 口) extremely, very; really 极其；非常：*He was well pissed off when he found out.* 他发现后大为光火。

well-cut /ˌwelˈkʌt; wɛlˈkʌt/ *adj* (of clothes) skilfully designed and put together, probably also expensive（指衣服）裁制得很好的（多半也昂贵的）：*a well-cut suit* 做工精细的套装

well-earned /ˌwelˈɜːnd; wɛlˈɝnd/ *adj* much deserved 应有的；应得的：*a well-earned rest* 应有的休息 ○ *well-earned praise/success* 当之无愧的褒扬、应得的成功

well-groomed /ˌwelˈgruːmd; wɛlˈgrumd/ *adj* (of a person) looking clean, tidy and carefully dressed（指人）十分整洁的，穿着考究的：*You can't look well-groomed with dirty nails and unpolished shoes.* 如果你的指甲黑乎乎的，鞋也不擦，看上去怎会整洁呢。

well-thought-out /ˌwelθɔːtˈaʊt; ˌwɛlθɔtˈaʊt/ *adj* carefully planned 精心策划的：*a well-thought-out campaign/holiday* 周密部署的运动、精心安排的假期

well-trodden /ˌwelˈtrɒdn; ˌwɛlˈtrɑdn̩/ *adj* (of a road or path) much used（指路）常有人走的：*the well-trodden path leading to the famous castle* 通向那座著名城堡的被无数人踩过的小径 ○ (*fig* 比喻) *He followed the well-trodden route from public school, to Cambridge, to the Foreign Office and finally to an appointment as ambassador to the United States.* 他走的是常规老路，从公学到剑桥，再到外交部，最后被任命为驻美大使。

Wendy house /ˈwendɪ haʊs; ˈwɛndɪ haus/ *n* (*pl* **houses**) small toy house usu of a strong fabric, made for children to play in 温迪屋（由结实的布料制成的供孩子在里面玩耍的游戏屋）

NOTE 注： from the character Wendy in the play Peter Pan by J.M. Barrie, who kept house for Peter and the Lost Boys 出自 J · M · 巴里所写剧本《彼得 · 潘》中的人物 Wendy（温迪），她为彼得和迷失的男孩们照看屋子

wetback /ˈwetbæk; ˈwɛtbæk/ *n* (*US infml* 口) Mexican person who enters the USA illegally 偷渡者，湿背人（非法进入美国的墨西哥人）

NOTE 注： from the fact that such an illegal immigrant will probably have crossed a river to get past border guards 因此类非法入境者可能为了避开边防士兵而得偷渡一条河方能入境

whack and hack *n* = SPLATTER GAME（SPLATTER）

whale-watch *n* boat trip, often as part of a paid tour, made for the purpose of observing whales in their natural environment 观鲸（乘小船观看自然环境里的鲸鱼，通常作为付费短程旅游项目）

▷ **whale-watch** *v* [I] take part in a whale-watch 参加观鲸活动

whammy /ˈwæmɪ; ˈwæmɪ/ *n* **1** (*US infml* 口) evil or unlucky influence 厄运；晦气 **2** (esp in the phrase DOUBLE WHAMMY 尤用于短语 double whammy) blow or setback 打击；挫折

wheelie-bin /ˈwiːliːbɪn, *US* ˈhwiː-; ˈhwilibɪn/ *n* dustbin on wheels, mechanically emptied by tipping it up 带轮垃圾箱（将其倾斜即可倾倒垃圾的一种垃圾箱）

whinge /wɪndʒ, *US* hw-; hwɪndʒ/ *v* (*pres p* **whingeing** or **whinging**) (*Brit infml derog* 口，贬) complain in an irritating and self-pitying way 哀怨不已；抱怨嘀咕：*The President should stop whingeing and start leading.* 总统应停止抱怨，开始承担其领导职责。○ *She whinged (on) about how miserable she was.* 她哀怨地述说着自己是何等不幸。

whistleblower /ˈwɪslˌbləʊə(r), *US* hw-; ˈhwɪslˌbloɚ/ *n* person who blows the whistle on sb/sth（BLOW[1] 14A-Z）阻止某人 *[某事]* 的人；告发者

whiteboard /ˈwaɪtbɔːd, *US* hw-; ˈhwaɪtbɔrd/ *n* board with a wipeable white surface for classroom use, which is written on with special felt-tip pens 白板（用特别的毡头笔在其上书写，字可擦去，用于教室的板）

white-collar crime /ˌwaɪtkɒlə ˈkraɪm, *US* hw-; ˌhwaɪtkɑlɚ ˈkraɪm/ *n* [U,C] crime committed by people who work in WHITE-COLLAR（WHITE[1](A-Z)）jobs, usu financial crimes 白领犯罪（通常指财务上的犯罪）：*White-collar crime is definitely on the increase.* 白领犯罪率明显在上升。

white goods /ˈwaɪt gʊdz, *US* hw-; ˈhwaɪt gʊdz/ *n* [pl] household products such as refrigerators, cookers and washing-machine which usu have white metal covers 白

色家用电器（冰箱、炉具、洗衣机等外壳通常为白色金属的电器）

white knight /ˌwaɪt ˈnaɪt, *US* hw-; hwaɪt ˈnaɪt/ *n* (**a**) person or organization that saves a company from being bought by another company or person at too low a price 白衣骑士，救星（使公司免于被过低价收购的人或机构）(**b**) person that saves another person from a bad situation 白衣骑士；救星（拯救别人于困境的人）

NOTE 注： in many stories of the Middle Ages, good and brave knights rescue people in danger. White is the colour usu associated with goodness 中世纪许多故事里有善良英勇的骑士拯救人们于危难之中。白色通常为正义和善良的象徵

white-knuckle /ˈwaɪtnʌkl, *US* hw-; ˈhwaɪtnʌkl̩/ *adj* [attrib 作定语] (**a**) (esp of a fairground ride) designed to cause excitement（尤指游乐场的机动装置）令人兴奋的，刺激的 (**b**) causing nervous tension and anxiety 使紧张不安的：*a white-knuckle ride/landing* 惊险的搭乘 *[着陆]*

NOTE 注： from the habit people have of gripping a handrail, seat-back, etc very tightly during such a ride which makes the knuckles of the hand look white 人们在乘坐游乐场的机动装置时往往紧紧抓住扶手、座椅靠背等而使指关节 (knuckle) 发白，此词由此而来

white-out /ˈwaɪtaʊt, *US* hw-; ˈhwaɪtaʊt/ *n* heavy SNOWSTORM (SNOW[1(A-Z)]) in which it is impossible to see anything（使人无法看清东西的）暴风雪：*The white-out made it quite impossible to reach the summit.* 暴风雪使得到达山顶几乎无望。Cf also 另参看 BLIZZARD[A-Z]

white squire *n* = WHITE KNIGHT

white stick /ˌwaɪt ˈstɪk, *US* hw-; hwaɪt ˈstɪk/ *n* long thin white rod, often collapsible, carried by blind people to help them walk around without knocking into things and to warn others that they are blind 白色手杖（盲人用以探路并作为标志的白色手杖，常可收缩）

white supremacist /ˌwaɪt suːˈpreməsɪst, *US* hw-; ˌhwaɪt suˈprɛməsɪst/ *n* (*derog* 贬) person who believes in the natural superiority of the white race and works to achieve it, even if this means the exclusion or suppression of other races 白人至上主义者

white-tie /ˌwaɪtˈtaɪ, *US* hw-; hwaɪtˈtaɪ/ *n* man's white bow-tie（男士的）白领结：*dressed in white-tie and tails* 穿燕尾服，打白领结

▷ **white-tie** *adj* (of social occasions) at which full formal EVENING DRESS (EVENING[A-Z]) is worn（指社交场合）穿正式晚礼服的：*The wedding was a white-tie affair.* 在这场婚礼上，人人衣冠楚楚。

white trash /waɪt ˈtræʃ, *US* hw-; hwaɪt ˈtræʃ/ *n* [U] (*derog* 贬) poor white people who are regarded by others as useless, stupid, ignorant and likely to be criminals 白人中的垃圾；贫苦白人

white water /ˌwaɪt ˈwɔːtə(r), *US* hw-; ˌhwaɪt ˈwɔtɚ/ *n* [U] [usu attrib 通常作定语] fast shallow stretch of water; RAPIDS (RAPID[A-Z]) 湍流；急流：*white-water rafting* 急流乘筏运动

whizz /wɪz, *US* hw-; hwɪz/ (also **whiz**) *n* (*infml* 口) person who is extremely good at sth 奇才；高手：*a computer whizz* 计算机奇才 ○ *She's a whizz at maths.* 她是个数学天才。

□ **whizz-kid** (also **whiz-kid**) *n* (*infml* 口 *esp US*) person who becomes successful at sth very quickly and usu while still young 神童：*a technology whizz-kid* 科技神童 ○ *Bill Gates, from whizz-kid to billionaire* 比尔·盖茨，从神童到亿万富翁

wholegrain /ˈhəʊlgreɪn; ˈholgren/ *n* [U], *adj* (made with or containing) whole grains of cereal, eg wheat（制自或包含）完整的谷粒（如麦粒）；全谷物的；全麦的：*wholegrain mustard* 全籽芥末

wholewheat /ˈhəʊlwiːt, *US* -hwiː-; ˈholhwit/ *n* [U], *adj* whole grains of wheat, including the HUSK 1[A-Z]; made from or containing whole grains 全麦（的）：*wholewheat flour/bread* 全麦面粉 *[面包]*

whoosh /wʊʃ, wuːʃ; wʊʃ, wuʃ/ *n, interj* (*infml* 口) sudden powerful and swift movement which causes a rushing sound（物体飞快移动时发出的）嗖的一声，呼的一声；嗖；呼：*a whoosh of flame* 呼的一声冒出的火焰 ○ *The car sped past us with a whoosh.* 汽车呼的一声从我们身边驶过。○ *I lit the firework and — whoosh! — it shot up into the air.* 我点燃烟火，它嗖的一声直冲云霄。

▷ **whoosh** *v* make a whoosh or move with a whoosh 发出嗖的一声；（嗖的一声）飞快移动

wicked /ˈwɪkɪd; ˈwɪkɪd/ *adj* (*sl* 俚) excellent, great, wonderful 了不起的；极好的；顶呱呱的：*We had a wicked time at the rave.* 在电子乐狂舞会上我们开心极了。○ *That's a wicked haircut you've got.* 你的头发剪得好极了。○ *The new chat show is really wicked.* 新的访谈节目真棒。

wicket-gate /ˈwɪkɪtgeɪt; ˈwɪkɪtget/ *n* small gate, esp at the side of a large one（尤指大门边的）侧门，边门

widget /ˈwɪdʒɪt; ˈwɪdʒɪt/ *n* (*infml* 口) any gadget or device 小装置；小器具

NOTE 注： perhaps an alteration of *gadget* 可能是 gadget（小器具）一词的变体

wimp out /wɪmp ˈaʊt, *US* hw-; hwɪmp ˈaʊt/ *v* [I] (*infml* 口) fail to do sth because of loss of nerve 因胆怯而放弃；畏缩：*He was supposed to propose the toast to the bride and bridegroom, but at the last moment he wimped out.* 他本应向新郎新娘祝酒的，但到最后关头他又退缩了。

wind-blown /ˈwɪndbləʊn; ˈwɪndblon/ *adj* (**a**) carried by the wind 随风飘的；由风传送的：*wind-blown snow/seeds* 随风飘的雪花、风吹来的种子 (**b**) made untidy or moved about by the wind 被风吹乱的；被风吹散的：*wind-blown hair/grass* 被风吹乱的头发、被风吹倒的草

wind chill /ˈwɪnd tʃɪl; ˈwɪnd tʃɪl/ *n* [U] combined chilling effect of low temperature and wind on living things or an object 风寒作用（低温与风对生物或物体的冷却作用）：*take into account the wind chill factor* 将风寒因素考虑在内

wind farm /ˈwɪnd fɑːm; ˈwɪnd fɑrm/ (also **wind park**) *n* group of energy-producing windmills or wind turbines, spaced out over the countryside 风力农场（散布在郊野的一组提供能源的风车或风力涡轮机）：*Some people objected to the wind farm as an eyesore.* 有人对风力农场持反对态度，认为有碍观瞻。

NOTE 注： the word expresses the idea that wind as a resource can be farmed as can certain animals 此词表示风力作为一种资源可像动物一样役使

window of opportunity /ˌwɪndəʊ əv ɒpəˈtjuːnɪtɪ, *US* -tuː-; ˌwɪndo əʌ ɑpɚˈtunɪtɪ/ *n* (usu *sing* 通常作单数) chance to accomplish sth important and which will only be available for a short time（完成某重要事情的）稍纵即逝的好机会：*At the moment the window of opportunity is open for aid agencies in the Sudan.* 眼下是苏丹的援助机构发挥作用的大好机会。

wind park *n* = WIND FARM

wine cooler /ˌwaɪn ˈkuːlə(r), ˈwaɪn kuːlə(r); ˈwaɪn kulɚ/ *n* (*US*) drink made from a mixture of wine, fruit juice and FIZZY[A-Z] water 果汁酒饮料（葡萄酒、果汁和汽水混合制成的饮料）

wine list /ˈwaɪn lɪst; ˈwaɪn lɪst/ *n* printed list of the wines which are available in a restaurant for diners to choose from（餐馆的）酒单，酒类一览表：*an extensive wine list* 酒类众多的酒单 ○ *Waiter, could we have the wine list, please?* 服务员，请将酒单拿来好吗？

winery /'waɪnərɪ; 'waɪnərɪ/ *n* (*esp US*) place where wine is made 酿酒厂；葡萄酒厂 Cf 参看 VINEYARD[A-Z]

wine vinegar /ˌwaɪn 'vɪnɪgə(r); ˌwaɪn 'vɪnɪgɚ/ *n* [U] VINEGAR[A-Z] that is made from wine 酒醋（由葡萄酒酿成的醋）

wired[1] /waɪəd; waɪrd/ *adj* (*sl* 俚) in a state of nervous excitement; tense, anxious, edgy 紧张兴奋的；焦虑的；烦躁的：*We were all wired by the time the show opened in the evening.* 晚上演出开始时，我们都兴奋不已。

wired[2] /waɪəd; waɪrd/ *adj* (*computing sl* 计，俚) making use of computers and information technology to transfer or receive information, esp through the Internet 上网的，利用计算机收发信息的（尤指通过互联网）：*I'm wired. I've got my internet connections working and I'm ready to receive e-mail.* 我已上网了。我已经接上互联网，可以收电子邮件了。

witching hour /'wɪtʃɪŋ aʊə(r); 'wɪtʃɪŋ aʊɚ/ *n* **the witching hour** [sing] (*rhet* 修辞) (said to be the) time when witches are active or sth magical happens, esp midnight（传说中）女巫出没的时刻，施魔法的时刻（尤指半夜）：*Few would want to be in that graveyard at the witching hour.* 很少人愿意在半夜三更鬼神出没的时刻到那片墓地去。

wobbly /'wɒblɪ; 'wɑblɪ/ *n* **1** sudden and uncontrollable fit of rage 突然的一阵狂怒 **2** (idm 习语) **throw a wobbly** have a sudden and uncontrollable fit of rage 突如其来地发怒：*We were just discussing the show when all of a sudden he threw a wobbly and went completely crazy.* 我们正在谈论演出之事，突然他大发雷霆，完全像疯了一样。

wold /wəʊld; wold/ *n* (esp *pl*, in the names of places 作地名时尤作复数) (in Britain) piece of high open land that is not cultivated（英国）未开垦的高地，丘陵地带：*the Lincolnshire wolds* 林肯郡丘陵地带 ○ *the Cotswolds* 科茨沃尔德丘陵

wordplay /'wɜːdpleɪ; 'wɝdple/ *n* [U] clever or amusing use of words, esp when this involves playing with the different meanings of a word or with words which sound the same 文字游戏（高明或有趣味的文字运用，尤指一词多义或把同音字放在一起）：*The wordplay in some kinds of crosswords appeals to a lot of people.* 很多人很喜欢一些纵横填字游戏里的双关语设计。Cf 参看 PUN[A-Z]

wordsearch /'wɜːdsɜːtʃ; 'wɝdsɝtʃ/ *n* grid-shaped puzzle of letters in columns in which words written in any direction are hidden 找词游戏（从排在格子里的字母中找出隐藏于其中的词的游戏）

workfare /'wɜːkfeə(r); 'wɝkfɛr/ *n* [U] welfare system which requires some work from or training of those receiving benefits 工作福利制（享受社会福利者必须参与一些工作或接受培训的制度）

workmate /'wɜːkmeɪt; 'wɝkmet/ *n* (*Brit*) person with whom one works, often taking part in the same job, in an office, a factory, etc 同事，工友（常指同参与一项工作）：*He's one of my workmates.* 他是我的同事。

workplace /'wɜːkpleɪs; 'wɝkples/ *n* [C] (often 常作 **the workplace** [sing]) place where people work, eg an office or a factory 工作场所（如办公室或工厂）：*introduce new technology into the workplace* 将新技术引进工作场所 ○ *People spend a great deal of time in their workplaces.* 人们很多时间都呆在工作场所。

work shadowing /wɜːk 'ʃædəʊɪŋ; wɝk 'ʃædəwɪŋ/ *n* [U] process of accompanying a person at work, for training or research purposes（为受训或研究等目的而）跟随工作：*Work shadowing is catching on as a way to introduce potential recruits to the company.* 用跟随工作的方法使未来雇员熟悉公司，已渐成风尚。

workstation /'wɜːksteɪʃn; 'wɝksteʃən/ *n* place in an office, etc where a person works, esp a working surface with a computer（办公室中尤指设有计算机的）工作台

world order /wɜːld 'ɔːdə(r); wɝld 'ɔrdɚ/ *n* [U] system controlling events in the world, esp an international set of arrangements for preserving global political stability 国际秩序（尤指为维护全球政治稳定所作的一系列国际性安排）

NOTE 注： esp used in the phrase *new world order* 尤用于短语 new world order（国际新秩序）

World Wide Web /ˌwɜːld waɪd 'web; ˌwɝld waɪd 'wɛb/ *n* (*abbr* 缩写 **WWW**) (*computing* 计) visually-based system for accessing information (eg text, graphics, sound and video) by means of the INTERNET, which consists of a large number of 'documents' tagged with cross-referencing links by which a user can move between sources 万维网，环球网（通过互联网存取信息的系统，包含大量文件，用户可通过相互参照链来检索资料）：*The World Wide Web makes it possible for anyone to publish any kind of material and tap in at once to a global audience.* 在万维网上任何人都可以随意发表东西，并可立刻将之传送给全球读者。

wrinkling /'rɪŋklɪŋ; 'rɪŋklɪŋ/ *n* [U] process or result of forming wrinkles 起皱（纹）；皱纹；褶皱：*Overexposure to the sun can cause premature wrinkling.* 在日光下暴晒会使皮肤过早出现皱纹。○ *the deep wrinkling on her face* 她脸上深深的皱纹 ○ *Wrinkling will be minimized if the garment is washed by hand.* 这件衣服用手洗就不易起皱。

wrinkly /'rɪŋklɪ; 'rɪŋklɪ/ *n* (*infml* 口) old person 老人 Cf 参看 CRINKLY (CRINKLE[A-Z])

write-down /'raɪtdaʊn; 'raɪtdaʊn/ *n* (*commerce* 商) reduction in the value of assets (ASSET 2[A-Z]), etc（资产等价值的）降低，划减：*a $100 000 write-down in the value of the property* 房地产价值划减 100 000 美元

WWW *abbr* 缩写 = WORLD WIDE WEB

Xx

x-rated /'eksreɪtɪd; 'ɛksretɪd/ *adj* **1** especially horrible and disgusting 极为可怕的；使人反感的：*The football match turned into an x-rated brawl.* 足球赛变成了一场可怕的打斗。**2 X-rated** (esp of films) thought to be not suitable for children under a certain age（尤指电影）X 级的（儿童不宜的）：*X-rated films/videos* ☆ X 级电影 *[录像]*

Yy

yakuza /jæ'kuːzə; jæ'kuzə/ *n* [sing] (*Japanese* 日语) organized crime network in Japan, equivalent to the MAFIA 1[A-Z] 山口组（相当于黑手党的日本犯罪集团）：*Many Yakuza mobsters attended the funeral of the murdered boss.* 许多山口组成员参加了他们被谋杀的头头的葬礼。

Yardie /'jɑːdɪ; 'jɑrdɪ/ *n* (*Brit infml* 口) member of a secret Jamaican criminal organization operating in the international drug trade 牙弟，亚迪（从事国际毒品交易的牙买加秘密犯罪集团成员）

year-on-year /jɪəɒn'jɪə(r); jɪrɑn'jɪr/ *adj* [attrib 作定语] (esp of figures, prices, etc) in a period of 12 months ending on a particular date（尤指数字、价格等）与上年同期相比的：*a small year-on-year increase in house prices* 房价与去年同期相比的小幅增长

year-round /jɪə'raʊnd; jɪr'raʊnd/ *adj* throughout the whole year 全年的；一年到头的：*an island with year-*

round sunshine 终年有阳光的岛屿 ○ *a year-round sport* 四季皆宜的运动

Y2K *n* = MILLENNIUM BUG

NOTE 注： so written because it stands for 'Year 2000' (*K* means 'kilo', unit for 1000) 这个写法代表 Year 2000（ 2000 年），K 代表 kilo（千）

yoof /ju:f; juf/ *n* [U] (*sl* 俚) youth; young people in general 青年；年轻人

NOTE 注： formed from a non-standard pronunciation of youth 源自 youth 一词的不规范发音

youthocracy /ju:ˈθɒkrəsɪ; juˈθɑkrəsɪ/ *n* [sing] group of young people which is very influential in society, esp because of its purchasing power and prestige as leaders of fashion 年青一族（尤指因其购买力和作为时尚的带头人而极具社会影响力的青年群体）

NOTE 注： from the English word *youth* and Greek *kratos* meaning'power' 来自英语 youth 一词和希腊语 kratos ，意谓'权力'

yuan /jʊˈɑ:n; juˈɑn/ *n* (p1 unchanged 复数不变) main unit of money in the People's Republic of China 元（中国的货币单位）

yuppie flu (also **yuppy flu**) *n* [U] (*infml slightly derog* 口，略带贬义) = MYALGIC ENCEPHALOMYELITIS

yuppify /ˈjʌpɪfaɪ; ˈjʌpɪfaɪ/ *v* make typical of or suitable for yuppies (YUPPIE^A-Z) 使雅皮士化；使适合雅皮士：*to yuppify the rather run-down inner urban areas* 将破旧的内城区改造成适合雅皮士居住的地方

▷ **yuppification** *n* : *The yuppification of the previously unfashionable area led to a steep rise in property prices.* 将原先落伍的地区改造成适合雅皮士居住后，房地产价格直线飙升。

NOTE 注： *yuppie* originated in an acronym for *young urban professional* ☆ yuppie 源于短语 young urban professional（城市年轻专业人士）的首字母缩略

Zz

zap /zæp; zæp/ *v* [Tn, Tn·p] make more powerful, exciting or lively; revitalize; spice or pep up 使更充满力量、刺激或活力；赋予新的活力；使增添趣味；振奋：*Zap those dull hamburgers up with a dash of hot pepper sauce.* 那些汉堡包没味道，加点辣椒酱调调味儿。

zero-emission vehicle /zɪərəʊɪˈmɪʃn ˌvi:ɪkl; zɪroɪˈmɪʃən ˌviɪkl̩/ *n* motor vehicle which does not emit pollutant gases 零排放汽车（不排放污染性气体的机动车）；无废气汽车：*Electricity offers the only viable method to achieve a commercial zero-emission vehicle.* 要想生产无废气商用车辆，唯一可行的方法是利用电驱动。

zero tolerance /ˌzɪərəʊ ˈtɒlərəns; ˌzɪro ˈtɑlərəns/ *n* [U] law enforcement policy of cracking down hard on crime (CRACK² 12^A-Z), even of a minor kind（打击犯罪的）零宽容政策，强硬政策：*The police are enforcing a policy of zero tolerance for traffic violations.* 警方实施强硬政策整治交通违规的情况。

Zift /zɪft; zɪft/ *abbr* 缩写 = zygote intra-fallopian transfer (method of ARTIFICIAL INSEMINATION (ARTIFICIAL^A-Z) in which a human egg is fertilized outside a woman's body and then placed in one of her Fallopian tubes (FALLOPIAN TUBE^A-Z)) 将体外受精卵子植入输卵管的人工授精法 Cf 参看 GIFT

Zimmer frame /ˈzɪmə freɪm; ˈzɪmɚ frem/ *n* (*Brit propr* 专利名) metal frame used by old or weak people who find difficulty in walking 齐默助行架（一种帮助老弱者行走的金属架）

标有 ^A-Z 的大写黑字表示可参照词典正文 A 至 Z 条目，其余大写黑字表示参照新词补编条目。

例： MUG¹ 2^A-Z 即参看词典正文 mug¹ 词条下的第二义项。

STAKEHOLDER ECONOMY (STAKEHOLDER) 即参看补编 stakeholder 词条下的 stakeholder economy 。

图书在版编目(CIP)数据

牛津高阶英汉双解词典:第4版:增补本 /(英)霍恩比著;李北达译.—北京:商务印书馆,2002
ISBN 7-100-03415-9

Ⅰ.牛... Ⅱ.①霍...②李... Ⅲ.①英语-词典②双解词典-英、汉 Ⅳ.H316

中国版本图书馆 CIP 数据核字(2001)第083913号

NIÚJĪN GĀOJIĒ YĪNGHÀN SHUĀNGJIĚ CÍDIǍN
牛津高阶英汉双解词典(第四版增补本)

出版:商务印书馆出版
(北京王府井大街36号 邮政编码 100710)
牛津大学出版社(中国)有限公司
(香港英皇道979号太古坊和域大厦东翼十八楼)
国内总发行:商务印书馆
国外以及香港、澳门、台湾地区总发行:牛津大学出版社(中国)有限公司
印刷:商务印书馆上海印刷股份有限公司印刷
ISBN 7-100-03415-9 / H·869

1997年9月第1版 开本880×1230 1/32
2002年1月第1版(增补本) 印张64 1/4 插页1
2002年1月上海第26次印刷 印数50 000册
定价:95.00元

NOUN AND ADJECTIVE CLASSES 名词及形容词的类别

C (Countable noun 可数名词) Refers to people or things that can be counted; singular form agrees with singular verb and plural form with plural verb 指可数的人或事物; 单数形式与单数动词一致, 复数形式与复数动词一致: *a friend, a problem* ○ *these friends, those problems* ○ *A friend is coming to stay.* ○ *Your problem seems to be the same.* ○ *Not many friends were there.* ○ *Few problems were encountered.*

U (Uncountable noun 不可数名词) Refers to substances, qualities, etc that cannot be counted; not used with *a/an*; used in the singular form only, and with a singular verb 指不可数的物质、特性等, 不与 a/an 连用; 只用单数形式, 与单数动词连用: *butter, sympathy* ○ *much butter, little sympathy* ○ *This butter is expensive.* ○ *Not much sympathy was shown.*

CGp (Countable **group** noun 可数集合名词) Refers to a collection of people or things; noun can be singular or plural; when singular, the noun can agree with a singular or plural verb 指一批人或事物; 这类名词可为单数亦可为复数; 作单数时, 可与单数或复数动词一致: *He is on several committees.* ○ *Two new companies have been set up.* ○ *The Council meets/meet tomorrow.*

Gp (**Group** noun 集合名词) Refers to a collection of people or things (and is usually a proper noun); used in the singular form only, but can agree with a singular or plural verb 指一批人或事物(通常为专有名词); 只用单数形式, 但可与单数或复数动词一致: *Whitehall is/are showing interest.* ○ *The Kremlin has/have not yet reacted to the news.*

sing *v* (plural noun with **sing**ular **v**erb 复数名词与单数动词连用) *Dominoes is a relaxing game.* ○ *Measles is an infectious disease.* ○ *Physics is my best subject.*

pl *v* (singular noun with **pl**ural **v**erb 单数名词与复数动词连用) *More/Fewer police were on duty.* ○ *All the wounded have been treated.*

sing or pl *v* (plural noun with **sing**ular **or pl**ural **v**erb 复数名词与单数或复数动词均可连用) *The barracks has/have been empty for some time.* ○ *The new steel works is/are going to create a lot of employment.*

pl (**pl**ural noun with **pl**ural verb 复数名词与复数动词连用) *These premises are unfurnished.* ○ *Our takings have increased.* Some nouns marked [pl] refer to garments, tools, etc, with two matching parts 标示 [pl] 的某些名词, 指有两个对称部件的服装、工具等: *buy a pair of braces* ○ *another pair of trousers* ○ *I cut the wire with pliers.* ○ *These scissors are blunt.*

sing (**sing**ular noun with **sing**ular verb 单数名词与单数动词连用) Can be used with *a/an* 可与 a/an 连用: *Let me have a think.* ○ *An abundance of food was on display.*

attrib (**attrib**utive use 用作定语) An adjective with this label can only be used before a noun 有这一标记的形容词只可用于名词之前: *sheer nonsense* ○ *a complete waste of time* ○ *an absolute disgrace.* A noun with this label can be used in front of another noun, to describe it 有这一标记的名词可用于另一名词之前, 作修饰成分: *a brick wall* ○ *a pottery jar* ○ *a silk blouse.*

pred (**pred**icative use 用作表语) An adjective with this label can only be used after linking verbs (La) such as *be, seem, appear,* etc 有这一标记的形容词只可用于系动词(如 be、seem、appear 等)之后, 动词模式为 La: *The house was ablaze.* ○ *This is tantamount to saying he is guilty.*
译者注: 这类形容词条目中的定义译文无"的"字.